S0-CUN-930

THE ROSTER OF CONFEDERATE SOLDIERS

1861 – 1865

Volume XV

Sudellert, James D.
– to –
Warn, R. C.

M253-464 — M253-499

EDITED BY
Janet B. Hewett

BROADFOOT PUBLISHING COMPANY
Wilmington, NC
1996

"Fine Books Since 1970."
BROADFOOT PUBLISHING COMPANY
1907 Buena Vista Circle * Wilmington, North Carolina 28405

THIS BOOK IS PRINTED ON ACID-FREE PAPER.

ISBN No. 1-56837-306-6 (Multi-Volume Set)

Sudellert, James D. AL 8th Cav. Co.A
Sudelman, John TX Waul's Legion Co.D
Suden, James LA Mil. 1st Regt. 2nd Brig. 1st Div. Co.B
Suder, A.W. SC Hvy.Arty. 15th (Lucas') Bn. Co.B
Suder, M. AL 57th Inf. Co.F
Sudler, J.E. MD Cav. 2nd Bn. Co.E Capt.
Sudmeyer, Henry TX 17th Inf. Co.H
Sudsberry, George A. AR Cav. Wright's Regt. Co.E
Sudsburg, William VA 2nd Arty. Co.K
Sudsbury, James VA 4th Cav. Co.K
Sudsbury, M.W. VA Lt.Arty. 38th Bn. Co.C
Suduth, Elbert AL 62nd Inf. Co.E
Sue, Alexander NC 3rd Inf. Co.H Sgt.
Suell, T.H. MO St.Guard 5th Sgt.
Suelson, William TN Cav. Welcker's Bn. Co.A
Suer, Joseph LA 21st (Patton's) Inf. Co.D
Suernam, Joseph LA Inf. Pelican Regt. Co.H
Suesberry, John W. VA 17th Cav. Co.E
Suez, Jusa J. NC 17th Inf. (2nd Org.) Co.C
Suffeild, Robert GA Cav. 1st Bn.Res. Co.C
Suffert, Charles LA 1st Cav. Co.G
Suffield, R.A. AR 45th Cav. Co.M
Suffington, I.H. GA Cav. 29th Bn.
Suffit, J. GA 22nd Inf. Co.E
Sufflat, --- TX 5th Field Btty.
Suffo, Barcha MS Inf. 2nd Bn. Co.A
Suffo, Barcha MS 46th Inf. Co.A
Suffold, Albert V. MS Inf. 3rd Bn. Co.D
Suffrage, Elihu NC 64th Inf. Co.G
Suffrage, John W. NC 64th Inf. Co.G
Suffurage, A. TN 50th Inf. Co.I
Sufredge, John NC 64th Inf. Co.G
Sugan, Eugene LA Mil. LaFourche Regt. French's Co.
Sugar, A. VA 54th Mil. Co.E,F
Sugar, Harvey VA 28th Inf. Co.B
Sugar, John MS 2nd Inf. Co.C
Sugar, John 1st Creek Mtd.Vol. Co.B
Sugar, Solomon LA 1st Res. Co.A
Sugar, Wesley 1st Creek Mtd.Vol. 2nd Co.I
Sugard, D.J. NC 51st Inf. Co.F
Sugarrough, John TN 50th Inf. Co.E
Sugarrough, John 4th Conf.Inf. Co.A,E
Sugars, John W. AL 9th Inf. Co.E Sgt.
Sugars, M.J. AL 15th Inf. Co.I
Sugars, Thomas 1st Creek Mtd.Vol. Co.H
Sugart, Eli NC 38th Inf. Co.B
Sugart, S.D. GA 3rd Cav. Co.H
Sugart, Thomas C. TN 25th Inf. Co.E
Sugart, W.C. NC 5th Inf. Co.K,D
Sugden, Samuel H. LA 1st (Nelligan's) Inf. Co.K
Sugdes, R.M. AL 50th Inf. Co.G
Sugg, Abner GA 26th Inf. Co.F
Sugg, Andrew M. MS 15th Inf. Co.F
Sugg, Aquilla NC 50th Inf. Co.D
Sugg, Benjamin F. NC 3rd Arty. (40th St.Troops) Co.B
Sugg, C.A. MS Inf. 3rd Bn. (St.Troops) Co.D
Sugg, C.A. TN 50th Inf. Co.E Col.
Sugg, Calvin A. MO 3rd Regt.St.Guards Co.D
Sugg, Charles L. MO 8th Cav. Co.A Sgt.
Sugg, C.L. MO Inf. 4th Regt.St.Guard Co.A
Sugg, E.D. NC 66th Inf. Co.H Music.
Sugg, Eli C. TN 6th (Wheeler's) Cav.
Sugg, Elijah AR 7th Cav. Co.C
Sugg, Ephraim NC 33rd Inf. Co.K
Sugg, F.C. TN 7th (Duckworth's) Cav. Co.A
Sugg, George W. NC 3rd Arty. (40th St.Troops) Co.F
Sugg, G.L. TN 45th Inf. Co.D Music.
Sugg, G.L.P. TN Inf. 4th Cons.Regt. Co.B
Sugg, G.W. AL 3rd Inf. Co.G Sgt.
Sugg, G.W. NC 44th Inf. Co.E
Sugg, H. GA 26th Inf. Co.A
Sugg, Hardy NC 66th Inf. Co.F Sgt.
Sugg, H.H. TN Lt.Arty. Huggins' Co.
Sugg, Holida GA 26th Inf. Co.F Cpl.
Sugg, H.T. MS 8th Cav. Co.E
Sugg, James AL 27th Inf. Co.G
Sugg, James AR 2nd Cav. Co.C
Sugg, James B. KY 1st Inf. Co.K 2nd Lt.
Sugg, James B. Gen. & Staff Capt.,AQM
Sugg, James F. MO Cav. Jackman's Regt. Capt.
Sugg, James N. NC Inf. 13th Bn. Co.C
Sugg, J.B. TN 50th Inf. Capt.,AQM
Sugg, J.B. TN 50th (Cons.) Inf. Capt.,AQM
Sugg, J.D. MS 2nd St.Cav. Co.H
Sugg, J.D. TN 49th Inf. Co.D Sgt.
Sugg, J.D. Inf. Bailey's Cons.Regt. Co.L Sgt.
Sugg, J.F. AR 1st (Dobbin's) Cav. Co.D
Sugg, J.H. KY 7th Mtd.Inf. Co.H Cpl.
Sugg, J.H. LA 14th Inf. Co.A
Sugg, J.H. Inf. Bailey's Cons.Regt. Co.F
Sugg, J.H.L. TN 11th Inf. Co.C
Sugg, John NC 1st Cav. (9th St.Troops) Co.H
Sugg, John Wheeler's Scouts,CSA
Sugg, John A. Conf.Cav. Wood's Regt. Co.E 1st Lt.
Sugg, John H. MO 8th Cav. Co.A Capt.
Sugg, John H. TN 49th Inf. Co.E Cpl.
Sugg, Joseph B. LA 9th Inf. Co.D
Sugg, Joseph E. NC 3rd Arty. (40th St.Troops) Co.F
Sugg, Joseph N. NC 66th Inf. Co.E
Sugg, Joseph P. NC 15th Inf. Co.I Hosp.Stew.
Sugg, J.R. TN 50th Inf. Co.G
Sugg, J.T. TN 49th Inf. Co.D
Sugg, J.T. Inf. Bailey's Cons.Regt. Co.L
Sugg, J.W. AR Cav. McGehee's Regt. Co.B
Sugg, L.C. MS 12th Cav. Co.C
Sugg, Lemuel B. TN 14th Inf. Co.B
Sugg, Lucius D. LA 1st Cav. Co.K
Sugg, M.C. MO 7th Cav. Co.K
Sugg, M.C. MO Inf. 4th Regt.St.Guard Co.A 3rd Lt.
Sugg, Michael AL 16th Inf. Co.H
Sugg, Michael MS 20th Inf. Co.K
Sugg, Milton C. MO 8th Cav. Co.A,C 1st Sgt.
Sugg, Nathaniel TN Cav. 9th Bn. (Gantt's) Co.D Sgt.
Sugg, Nathaniel TN 11th Inf. Co.H
Sugg, Osborn A. AR 4th Inf. Co.A
Sugg, Patrick NC 33rd Inf. Co.K
Sugg, Quintus TN 14th Inf. Co.B
Sugg, Redding S. NC 15th Inf. Co.I 2nd Lt.
Sugg, Reuben NC 3rd Arty. (40th St.Troops) Co.F
Sugg, Richard H. NC 3rd Inf. Co.A Cpl.
Sugg, Roderick P. NC 8th Bn.Part.Rangers Co.A,E Sgt.
Sugg, Roderick P. NC 3rd Arty. (40th St.Troops) Co.F
Sugg, Roderick P. NC 66th Inf. Co.H Sgt.
Sugg, S.C. NC Loc.Def. Croom's Co.
Sugg, S.W. TN 49th Inf. Co.D
Sugg, T.C. AR Cav. McGehee's Regt. Co.B
Sugg, Thomas TN 6th (Wheeler's) Cav.
Sugg, Thomas D. AL 16th Inf. Co.H
Sugg, Thomas H. NC Loc.Def. Croom's Co. 1st Lt.
Sugg, T.J. TN 1st (Turney's) Inf. Co.K Lt.
Sugg, W.G. AR 5th Inf. Co.B
Sugg, W.H. TN 49th Inf. Co.D 2nd Lt.
Sugg, W.H. Inf. Bailey's Cons.Regt. Co.L 2nd Lt.
Sugg, William AL 16th Inf. Co.H
Sugg, William NC 3rd Arty. (40th St.Troops) Co.F
Sugg, William D. KY 2nd (Duke's) Cav. Co.B
Sugg, William G. AR 1st (Dobbin's) Cav. Co.B Sgt.
Sugg, William H. AL Lt.Arty. Phelan's Co.
Sugg, William H. NC 4th Inf. Co.E
Sugg, William Henry AL 5th Inf. Old Co.H
Sugg, William M. NC 1st Inf. (6 mo. '61) Co.D
Sugg, William M. NC 11th (Bethel Regt.) Inf. Co.G Sgt.
Sugg, William S. TN 47th Inf. Co.E 1st Lt.
Sugg, W.J. MO Robertson's Regt.St.Guard Co.6
Sugg, W.R. MS 4th Cav. Co.D
Suggart, J.Z. MD Cav. 2nd Bn. Co.D
Suggart, William AL 44th Inf. Co.D
Sugge, G.W. AL 11th Inf. Co.A
Suggett, John E. MS Bradford's Co. (Conf. Guards Arty.)
Suggett, Manlius MO Unassign.Conscr.
Suggett, M.C. AR 13th Inf.
Suggett, M.P. KY 9th Cav. Co.A Ord.Sgt.
Suggett, R.B. MO St.Guard
Suggett, Robert B. MO 5th Inf. Co.H
Suggett, Robert B. MO Capt.
Suggett, W.L. AR 32nd Inf. Co.B
Suggle, --- TX Cav. Good's Bn. Co.E
Suggs, A. AR 15th (Johnson's) Inf. Co.C
Suggs, A.C. SC 3rd St.Troops Co.D
Suggs, A.H. NC 8th Inf. Co.F
Suggs, A.J. AR Mtd.Vol. Baker's Co.
Suggs, A.J. MS 7th Cav. Co.B
Suggs, A.J. MS 10th Cav. Co.I
Suggs, A.J. MS 26th Inf. Co.G
Suggs, Albert GA Cav. 29th Bn. Co.F
Suggs, Alexander AL 25th Inf. Co.G
Suggs, Alexander AL Cp. of Instr. Talladega
Suggs, Alfred NC 7th Bn.Jr.Res. Co.B
Suggs, Alfred A. NC 3rd Arty. (40th St.Troops) Co.B
Suggs, Allen GA Smith's Legion Co.C
Suggs, Allen T. SC 8th Inf. Co.F,M
Suggs, Allgood M. AL 46th Inf. Co.H
Suggs, Arthur SC Inf. Hampton Legion Co.A
Suggs, A.T. SC 21st Inf. Co.G
Suggs, B. MS Cav. Ham's Regt. Co.B,D
Suggs, B. MS 26th Inf. Co.K
Suggs, Benajah AL 39th Inf. Co.D
Suggs, Calvin A. MS 14th Inf. Co.A
Suggs, Calvin A. TX 12th Inf. Co.C
Suggs, C.H. AR Inf. Adams' Regt. Moore's Co.

Suggs, Charles NC 6th Sr.Res. Co.K
Suggs, Curtis A. NC 20th Inf. Co.K
Suggs, C.W. SC Cav. Tucker's Co.
Suggs, Daniel SC Arty. Manigault's Bn. 1st Co.B
Suggs, Darby William NC 3rd Inf. Co.A
Suggs, Davis GA Arty. 11th Bn. (Sumter Arty.) New Co.C, Co.D
Suggs, Devroh NC Hvy.Arty. 10th Bn. Co.B
Suggs, Dick NC 3rd Inf. Co.A
Suggs, D.M. AR 27th Inf. Co.G
Suggs, D.M. GA 64th Inf. Co.G
Suggs, Doctor F. NC 51st Inf. Co.G Cpl.
Suggs, D.W. TN 6th Inf. Co.C Sgt.
Suggs, E. AL Cp. of Instr. Talladega
Suggs, E. FL 2nd Cav. Co.F
Suggs, E. MS 5th Inf. (St.Troops) Co.A
Suggs, E.D. NC 8th Bn.Part.Rangers Co.A
Suggs, E.G. MS 8th Cav. Co.G Sgt.
Suggs, E.L. AL 18th Inf. Co.H
Suggs, E.L. GA 18th Inf. Co.H
Suggs, Elias GA Inf. 3rd Bn. Co.B
Suggs, Elias GA 37th Inf. Co.A
Suggs, Elijah AL 25th Inf. Co.C
Suggs, Elijah FL 8th Inf. Co.H
Suggs, Elisha AL 17th Inf. Co.E
Suggs, Elisha AL Cp. of Instr. Talladega
Suggs, Enoch AR 33rd Inf. Co.F
Suggs, Enoch GA 65th Inf. Co.G,K
Suggs, Ezekiel FL 7th Inf. Co.I
Suggs, Gabriel GA 31st Inf. Co.A
Suggs, G.B. GA Cav. 19th Bn. Co.D
Suggs, G.B. 10th Conf.Cav. Co.I
Suggs, George AL 53rd (Part.Rangers) Co.G
Suggs, George GA 6th Inf. Co.F
Suggs, George P. AL 11th Inf. Co.A
Suggs, George P. GA 61st Inf. Co.F
Suggs, George T. VA 61st Inf. Co.C Cpl.
Suggs, G.W. AL 17th Inf. Co.F
Suggs, G.W. GA 52nd Inf. Co.B
Suggs, H. GA 3rd Res. Co.C
Suggs, H. MS Inf. 2nd Bn. Co.K
Suggs, H. MS 48th Inf. Co.K
Suggs, H. 8th (Wade's) Conf.Cav. Co.F
Suggs, Harbard AL 26th (O'Neal's) Inf. Co.H
Suggs, Hardy NC 8th Bn.Part.Rangers Co.A,E
Suggs, Henry J. AL 4th Cav. Co.B
Suggs, H.H. MS 6th Cav. Co.L
Suggs, Hiram M. MS 37th Inf. Co.K
Suggs, H.T. MS 3rd Inf. (St.Troops) Co.E
Suggs, Isaac NC 38th Inf. Co.C
Suggs, J. AL 22nd Inf. Co.E
Suggs, J. AL 53rd (Part.Rangers) Co.I
Suggs, J. GA 19th Inf. Co.D
Suggs, Jackson GA Inf. 5th Bn. (St.Guards) Co.A
Suggs, James FL 11th Inf. Co.I
Suggs, James SC 23rd Inf. Co.B
Suggs, James TN 60th Mtd.Inf. Co.I
Suggs, James TX 12th Inf. Co.C
Suggs, James H. NC 3rd Inf. Co.A
Suggs, James McR. NC 2nd Arty. (36th St.Troops) Co.H
Suggs, J.B. LA 9th Inf. Co.H
Suggs, Jesse GA 22nd Inf. Co.A
Suggs, J.G. MS 2nd Cav. Co.I
Suggs, J.H. GA 18th Inf. Co.K
Suggs, J.N. SC Lt.Arty. 3rd (Palmetto) Bn. Co.E
Suggs, J.O. GA 4th (Clinch's) Cav. Co.E
Suggs, Joel V. FL Cav. 3rd Bn. Co.B
Suggs, John AL 62nd Inf. Co.F
Suggs, John GA 24th Inf. Co.I
Suggs, John GA 31st Inf. Co.C
Suggs, John GA 65th Inf. Co.K 2nd Lt.
Suggs, John GA Smith's Legion Co.K
Suggs, John MS 5th Cav. Co.H
Suggs, John NC 20th Inf. Co.D,K
Suggs, John NC 47th Inf. Co.C
Suggs, John SC 10th Inf. Co.C
Suggs, John A. GA 34th Inf. Co.A
Suggs, John D. AL 39th Inf. Co.H
Suggs, John Green 1st Conf.Eng.Troops Co.F
Suggs, John H. NC 27th Inf. Co.C Music.
Suggs, John T. GA 64th Inf. Co.G
Suggs, John Wm. Gen. & Staff Asst.Surg.
Suggs, Joseph NC 47th Inf. Co.I
Suggs, Joseph J. MS 2nd Inf. Co.B
Suggs, Joshua MS 8th Cav. Co.D
Suggs, Joshua MS 31st Inf. Co.H
Suggs, Joshua F. NC 27th Inf. Co.C
Suggs, Joshua R. NC 61st Inf. Co.E Cpl.
Suggs, Josiah H. NC 5th Cav. (63rd St.Troops) Co.B
Suggs, Josiah L. TX 11th Inf. Co.D
Suggs, J.P. NC 1st Jr.Res. Co.D Music.
Suggs, J.S. MS Inf. 1st Bn.St.Troops (30 days '64) Co.D Sgt.
Suggs, J.S. MS 5th Inf. (St.Troops) Co.A
Suggs, J.S. SC 10th Inf. Co.D
Suggs, J.T. FL 2nd Inf. Co.C 1st Lt.
Suggs, J.W. GA 46th Inf. Co.A
Suggs, J.W. MS 28th Cav. Co.F
Suggs, J.W. MS 32nd Inf. Co.F
Suggs, L. AR Cav. McGehee's Regt. Co.I
Suggs, L.B. TN Cav. 26th Regt. Co.K
Suggs, Lewis O. NC 2nd Bn.Loc.Def.Troops Co.B
Suggs, L.G. TX 28th Cav. Co.G QMSgt.
Suggs, L.J. MS 6th Cav. Co.C
Suggs, L.J. MS 8th Cav. Co.G
Suggs, L.L. NC 28th Inf. Co.B Cpl.
Suggs, Loving GA 34th Inf. Co.A
Suggs, L.S. MS 5th Inf. (St.Troops) Co.I
Suggs, L.S. MS 46th Inf. Co.K
Suggs, L.S. TX 22nd Inf. Co.A
Suggs, L.W. MS Cav. 4th Bn. Co.A
Suggs, L.W. 8th (Wade's) Conf.Cav. Co.C
Suggs, Macon C. NC 2nd Arty. (36th St.Troops) Co.A
Suggs, Mark MS 24th Inf. Co.H
Suggs, Matthew GA Inf. 5th Bn. (St.Guards) Co.A
Suggs, McKinley AL Cav. 5th Bn. Hilliard's Legion Co.C
Suggs, Michael SC 4th St.Troops Co.E
Suggs, M.L. GA 13th Inf. Co.H
Suggs, Nathaniel S. NC 34th Inf. Co.K
Suggs, Oliver P. GA Inf. 10th Bn. Co.C
Suggs, Patrick NC 67th Inf. Co.C
Suggs, Peter NC 14th Inf. Co.K
Suggs, Phesinton 7th Conf.Cav. 2nd Co.I
Suggs, Q. MS 9th Cav. Co.C
Suggs, Q. MS 9th Bn.S.S. Co.C
Suggs, Quilla MS 10th Inf. Co.N, New Co.E
Suggs, Quintus KY 2nd (Woodward's) Cav. Co.C
Suggs, R. GA 3rd Res. Co.C
Suggs, R. MS 2nd (Davidson's) Inf. Co.A
Suggs, Ransom GA Arty. 11th Bn. (Sumter Arty) Co.B
Suggs, R.E. GA Arty. 11th Bn. (Sumter Arty.) Old Co.C
Suggs, R.E. GA Cobb's Legion
Suggs, Reuben GA 12th Cav. Co.H
Suggs, Reuben NC 67th Inf. Co.G Cpl.
Suggs, Reuben R. MS 41st Inf. Co.G
Suggs, R.L. NC 61st Inf. Co.E
Suggs, R.M. Gillum's Regt. Co.G
Suggs, Robert MS 32nd Inf. Co.F
Suggs, Robert R. SC 8th Inf. Co.F,M
Suggs, Rufus AR 27th Inf. Co.G
Suggs, Rufus C. MS 31st Inf. Co.G Cpl.
Suggs, R.V. GA Arty. 11th Bn. (Sumter Arty.) Old Co.C, Co.B
Suggs, Samuel P. NC 2nd Arty. (36th St.Troops) Co.D Sgt.
Suggs, Shepherd GA 31st Inf. Co.C,H
Suggs, T.H. MS 7th Inf. Co.H
Suggs, Thomas NC 15th Inf. Co.D
Suggs, Thos. NC Mallett's Bn. Co.F
Suggs, Thomas H. MS 1st (Johnston's) Inf. Co.H
Suggs, Thomas J. TN 1st (Turney's) Inf. Co.K 1st Lt.
Suggs, W. AL 22nd Inf. Co.K
Suggs, W. 8th (Wade's) Conf.Cav. Co.F
Suggs, Washington NC 18th Inf. Co.B
Suggs, Washington B. NC 24th Inf. Co.F
Suggs, W.G. MS 12th Cav. Co.H
Suggs, W.H. TN 14th (Neely's) Cav. Co.C
Suggs, Wiley NC 14th Inf. Co.F
Suggs, Wiley SC 3rd Res. Co.F
Suggs, Wiley C. MS 43rd Inf. Co.D
Suggs, William AL 21st Inf. Co.F,D
Suggs, William FL 7th Inf. Co.I Cpl.
Suggs, William GA Arty. 11th Bn. (Sumter Arty.) New Co.C
Suggs, William GA 19th Inf. Co.D
Suggs, William MS 15th Bn.S.S. Co.A
Suggs, William MS 32nd Inf. Co.F
Suggs, William NC 1st Arty. (10th St.Troops) Co.F
Suggs, William SC 2nd Inf. Co.G
Suggs, William TN 60th Mtd.Inf. Co.I
Suggs, William A. GA 1st Inf. Co.C,F
Suggs, William B. NC 8th Inf. Co.C
Suggs, William C. MS 1st (Johnston's) Inf. Co.H
Suggs, William J. SC 10th Inf. 2nd Co.G Sgt.
Suggs, William L. SC 7th Cav. Co.A
Suggs, William P. NC 2nd Arty. (36th St.Troops) Co.K
Suggs, W.L. SC Cav. Tucker's Co.
Suggs, W.M. MS 8th Cav. Co.K
Suggs, W.P.B. MS 6th Cav. Co.C
Suggs, W.P.D. MS 8th Cav. Co.G
Suggs, Wright GA 9th Inf. Co.K
Sughi, G. AL 1st Regt. Mobile Vol. Co.E
Sugler, William P. TX 7th Cav. Co.I
Sugnot, Gustave VA 24th Cav. Co.B
Sugrue, John LA 6th Inf. Co.D
Sugrue, John LA 11th Inf. Co.F
Sugs, John W. SC 10th Inf. Co.C

Suhajah, H. 1st Chickasaw Inf. Haynes' Co.
Suhr, Augustus W. FL 3rd Inf. Co.C Sgt.
Suhr, Joachim TX 20th Inf. Co.A
Suhren, A.C. LA Mil. Chalmette Regt. Co.D
Suhren, J.D. LA Mil. Chalmette Regt. Co.D
Suia, M. LA Miles' Legion Co.G
Suierling, John GA 59th Inf. Co.H
Suinson, Jesse A. MS 11th Inf. Co.H
Suir, J. LA 18th Inf. Co.K
Suit, A.B. AR Inf. Cocke's Regt. Co.C
Suit, Daniel VA 72hd Mil.
Suit, James A. NC 23rd Inf. Co.E
Suit, John, Sr. AR Lt.Arty. 5th Btty. Artif.
Suit, John AR 18th Inf. Co.I
Suit, John TX 2nd Inf. Co.E
Suit, John VA 17th Inf. Co.H
Suit, John E. NC 50th Inf. Co.A
Suit, John S. NC 15th Inf. Co.G
Suit, Johnson AL 6th Inf. Co.D
Suit, Johnson VA 72nd Mil.
Suit, John W. AR Lt.Arty. 5th Btty.
Suit, J. Washington GA 3rd Cav. (St.Guards) Co.B Cpl.
Suit, M.H. NC Hvy.Arty. 10th Bn. Co.D
Suit, Ransom TN 19th Inf. Co.F
Suit, Riley VA 37th Inf. Co.C
Suit, Riley VA 72nd Mil. 1st Lt.
Suit, Robert AR 20th Inf. Co.E
Suit, Samuel H. AR 25th Inf. Co.I
Suit, Stephen VA 72nd Mil.
Suit, Steven M. TN 19th Inf. Co.F
Suit, W.A. AR 25th Inf. Co.C
Suit, William AR 36th Inf. Co.C
Suit, William J. NC 3rd Arty. (40th St.Troops) Co.G
Suit, William Riley NC 24th Inf. Co.D
Suite, Norris M. MD Arty. 4th Btty.
Suite, Norris M. VA Arty. Forrest's Co.
Suite, Sidney NC 35th Inf. Co.E
Suiter, A. Conf.Cav. Clarkson's Bn. Ind.Rangers Co.F
Suiter, A. Floyd VA 8th Cav. Co.F
Suiter, Andrew MO Inf. Clark's Regt. Co.E Cpl.
Suiter, Andrew J. AL 9th (Malone's) Cav. Co.I
Suiter, Arthur T. NC 12th Inf. Co.G Sgt.
Suiter, A.T. VA 7th Cav. Co.A
Suiter, Charles M. VA 2nd Inf. Co.D
Suiter, Elam NC 7th Inf. Co.C
Suiter, Elbert H. VA 45th Inf. Co.F Sgt.
Suiter, J.A. Exch.Bn. 3rd Co.B,CSA
Suiter, J.L. NC 12th Inf. Co.G Cpl.
Suiter, John A. MO 4th Inf. Co.B
Suiter, John A. MO 16th Inf. Co.B
Suiter, John W. VA 36th Inf. 2nd Co.G, Co.D
Suiter, J.P.H. MS 7th Cav. Co.G
Suiter, P.A. MO St.Guard
Suiter, P.H. LA 18th Inf. Co.D
Suiter, Samuel S. VA 45th Inf. Co.F Jr.2nd Lt.
Suiter, William G. VA 8th Cav. Co.F
Suitor, G.W. MS 32nd Inf. Co.D
Suitor, J.E. MS 23rd Inf. Co.D
Suitor, J.R. KY 9th Mtd.Inf. Co.D
Suitor, M. MS 32nd Inf. Co.D Sgt.
Suitor, Morman M. TN 32nd Inf. Co.D
Suitor, W.N. MS Cav. Ham's Regt. Co.A
Suits, A.W. GA Inf. 1st Bn. (St.Guards) Co.E
Suits, Daniel VA 72nd Mil.
Suits, F.D. NC 53rd Inf. Co.A
Suits, George W. NC 18th Inf. Co.I
Suits, James NC 58th Inf. Co.G
Suits, J.N. VA Inf. 1st Bn. Co.E
Suits, John GA 52nd Inf. Co.H
Suits, Robert L. NC 2nd Bn.Loc.Def.Troops Co.E Sgt.
Suits, S.M. TN 43rd Inf. Co.A
Suits, Steven VA Cav. Ferguson's Bn. Stevenson's Co.
Suits, William M. NC 45th Inf. Co.F
Suitt, Bently NC 11th (Bethel Regt.) Inf. Co.G
Suitt, Jordan P. NC 33rd Inf. Co.F
Suitt, W.R. NC Mallett's Bn. Co.E
Suitts, John AL Cav. 24th Bn. Co.A
Suitzer, B. VA 3rd Res. Co.K
Suitzer, Beverly P. NC Cav. 5th Bn. Co.D
Suitzer, Samuel W. VA 5th Inf. Co.I
Sujen, C.A. AL Talladega Cty.Res. T.M. McClintick's Co.
Suhatz, Gustave TX Comal Res.
Suker, W.H. TN 4th Inf. Co.D
Sukes, H.A. NC 1st Arty. (10th St.Troops) Co.E
Sul, W.W. VA 42nd Inf. Co.K Cpl.
Sulado, Peter TX Inf. 24th Bn. (St.Troops)
Sulakowski, V. Eng.,CSA A.Ch.Eng.
Sulakowski, Valery LA 14th Inf. Col.
Sulans, William P. VA 37th Inf. Co.H
Sulavan, J.T. AR 36th Inf. Co.I
Sulberry, W.T. TN 17th Inf.
Sulcer, Andrew AL 55th Vol. Co.G
Sulcer, George AL Lt.Arty. Ward's Btty.
Sulcer, George MS Lt.Arty. (Jefferson Arty.) Darden's Co.
Suleau, Hypolite LA Miles' Legion Co.A
Suleier, Larkin VA Inf. 21st Bn. 1st Co.D
Sulenberger, James W. GA 36th (Villepigue's) Inf. Co.B
Sulenberger, John S. GA 36th (Villepigue's) Inf. Co.B
Sulenberger, J.S. GA 64th Inf. Co.E Sgt.
Sulengor, Thomas Jefferson MO Inf. 1st Bn. Co.A
Sulerman, P. GA Lt.Arty. 12th Bn.
Sulert, James D. TN 9th Cav. Co.F
Sulevent, James H. TN 54th Inf. Co.B
Sulforth, Charles TN 61st Mtd.Inf. Co.I
Sulfrage, Banister TN 2nd (Ashby's) Cav. Co.B
Sulfrage, Banister TN Cav. 5th Bn. (McClellan's) Co.C
Sulfredge, Alfred TN 5th (McKenzie's) Cav. Co.A
Sulfridge, Alfred TN 5th (McKenzie's) Cav. Co.A Fifer
Sulian, Joel LA 6th Inf. Co.C
Sulinger, William A. TN 8th Inf. Co.K
Sulins, Josh 3rd Conf.Cav. Co.A
Sulivan, A.L. NC 3rd Jr.Res. Co.A
Sulivan, Albert H. TN 14th (Neely's) Cav. Co.I
Sulivan, A.M. NC 30th Inf. Co.A
Sulivan, Ambrose TX 23rd Cav. Co.C
Sulivan, B. GA 1st Reg. Co.C
Sulivan, Bennet AR 45th Mil. Co.G
Sulivan, B.F. SC 4th Bn.Res. Co.B
Sulivan, C. VA 60th Inf. Co.G
Sulivan, C.D. GA 22nd Inf. Co.I
Sulivan, Charles B. TX 13th Cav. Co.C
Sulivan, C.L. TX 11th Cav. Co.B
Sulivan, Clement T. GA 62nd Cav. Co.A
Sulivan, C.W. TN 14th (Neely's) Cav. Co.F
Sulivan, D. NC 2nd Inf. Co.C
Sulivan, Daniel LA 12th Inf. Co.D
Sulivan, Daniel NC 2nd Arty. (36th St.Troops) Co.B
Sulivan, David M. TX 37th Cav. Co.F
Sulivan, D.H. TX 5th Inf. Co.A Capt.
Sulivan, Edward NC 18th Inf. Co.E
Sulivan, E.J. MS Inf. 2nd St.Troops Co.D
Sulivan, E.J. VA 9th Bn.Res. Co.C
Sulivan, F. KY 3rd Mtd.Inf.
Sulivan, F. MS 3rd (St.Troops) Cav. Co.K Cpl.
Sulivan, G.M. AL 12th Cav. Co.E
Sulivan, Frank VA 34th Inf. Co.D
Sulivan, Franklin M. AL Cav. 5th Bn. Hilliard's Legion Co.D
Sulivan, George GA 13th Inf. Co.A
Sulivan, Harden NC 34th Inf. Co.A
Sulivan, J. LA Mil. Chalmette Regt. Co.K
Sulivan, James MS Cav. Powers' Regt. Co.G
Sulivan, James VA 25th Inf. Co.A
Sulivan, James H. TX 30th Cav. Bugler
Sulivan, James W. MS 11th Inf. Co.C
Sulivan, J.B. AR 15th Mil. Co.E Sgt.
Sulivan, Jesse MS 35th Inf. Co.D
Sulivan, J.G. NC Inf. 10th Bn. Co.C
Sulivan, J.H. AR 24th Inf. Co.H 1st Lt.
Sulivan, John GA Lt.Arty. 14th Bn. Co.B
Sulivan, John GA Lt.Arty. Anderson's Btty.
Sulivan, John SC 22nd Inf. Co.E
Sulivan, John TN 21st Inf. Co.I
Sulivan, John W. AR 4th Inf. Co.H
Sulivan, Joseph MS 3rd (St.Troops) Cav. Co.K
Sulivan, Joseph E. MS 43rd Inf. Co.E
Sulivan, Josiah AR 14th (Powers') Inf. Co.D
Sulivan, J.W. GA Inf. 25th Bn. (Prov.Guard) Co.G
Sulivan, J.W. SC 26th Inf. Co.G
Sulivan, J.W. TN 31st Inf. Co.I
Sulivan, L.A. TX Cav. Wells' Regt. Co.C
Sulivan, Larkin MS Moseley's Regt.
Sulivan, Leaborn O. MS 44th Inf. Co.H Cpl.
Sulivan, Levi LA 9th Inf. Co.G
Sulivan, Louis MS 39th Inf. Co.F
Sulivan, Madison H. NC 21st Inf. Co.K Sgt.
Sulivan, Michael VA Hvy.Arty. 18th Bn. Co.D
Sulivan, Monroe M. VA 30th Inf. 2nd Co.I
Sulivan, Owen GA Lt.Arty. Milledge's Co.
Sulivan, P. MS 48th Inf. Co.I
Sulivan, R. AR Pine Bluff Arty.
Sulivan, Raleigh W. VA 40th Inf. Co.B
Sulivan, Richard S. AL 11th Inf. Co.I
Sulivan, R.S. SC 1st Mtd.Mil. Smith's Co. 3rd Lt.
Sulivan, Stephen SC 8th Inf. Co.B
Sulivan, T.A. MS 39th Inf. Co.F
Sulivan, Thomas GA Ind.Cav. (Res.) Humphrey's Co.
Sulivan, Thomas LA Mil. Borge's Co. (Garnet Rangers)
Sulivan, Thomas, Sr. MS 3rd (St.Troops) Cav. Co.K
Sulivan, Thomas VA 23rd Cav. Co.M
Sulivan, Thomas C. MS 34th Inf. Co.A Cpl.
Sulivan, T.J. MS 3rd (St.Troops) Cav. Co.K

Sulivan, Tolivar B. FL 1st Inf. Co.G
Sulivan, William GA 46th Inf. Co.D
Sulivan, William TN Lt.Arty. Polk's Btty.
Sulivan, William TN 31st Inf. Co.I
Sulivan, William TN 48th (Voorhies') Inf. Co.D
Sulivan, William TN 50th (Cons.) Inf. Co.K
Sulivan, W.L. TN 8th (Smith's) Cav. Co.E 2nd Lt.
Sulivan, W.N. MS 3rd Cav. Co.A
Sulivant, John VA 37th Inf. Co.G 1st Sgt.
Sulivant, J.W. TN 3rd (Forrest's) Cav. Co.E Cpl.
Sulivant, Richard VA Cav. 40th Bn. Co.B
Sulivant, W.H. TN 14th (Neely's) Cav. Co.F
Sulivene, E.F. AR 1st Mtd.Rifles Co.K
Sulivent, F.M. AL 31st Inf. Co.I
Sulivent, Marion AR 11th Inf. Co.G
Sulivent, Owen LA 2nd Cav. Co.E
Sulivon, D. MS 2nd (Quinn's St.Troops) Inf. Co.C
Sull, E.W. MS 2nd Cav. Co.C Cpl.
Sullands, J.E. AL 5th Cav. Co.B
Sullans, J.G. MO 9th Bn.S.S. Co.A
Sullans, Ruben MO 10th Inf. Co.C
Sullans, Thomas H. MO 10th Inf. Co.C
Sullards, A.M. AR Cav. McGehee's Regt. Co.G 1st Lt.
Sullards, A.M. MO 16th Inf. Co.A
Sullards, Joseph A. MO 16th Inf. Co.A
Sul la tee skie 1st Cherokee Mtd.Rifles Co.E
Sullavan, James H. MS 1st (Johnston's) Inf. Co.H
Sullavan, James L. VA 9th Cav. Co.D
Sullavan, J.C. AR Inf. Hardy's Regt. Co.G
Sullavan, John L. VA 9th Cav. Co.D
Sullavan, John W. MS 1st (Johnston's) Inf. Co.H Cpl.
Sullavan, R.W. VA 9th Cav. Co.D
Sullavan, William H. MS 1st (Johnston's) Inf. Co.H Cpl.
Sullavant, Jesse MS 24th Inf. Co.F
Sullavant, Ruffin NC 8th Bn.Part.Rangers Co.D
Sullavant, Russel NC 8th Bn.Part.Rangers Co.D
Sullavant, Silus MS 24th Inf. Co.F
Sullavin, C.L. TN 15th (Stewart's) Cav. Co.F
Sullavin, Reason F. TN 18th Inf. Co.A
Sullavin, Thomas M. TN 2nd (Robison's) Inf. Co.A
Sullavin, William L. TN 18th Inf. Co.A Sgt.
Sullavin, W.S. MS 41st Inf. Co.F
Sullavun, James V. VA 92nd Mil. Co.C Cpl.
Sullen, Ambrose NC 26th Inf. Co.A
Sullen, J.F. AL 12th Cav. Co.C
Sullen, Joseph NC 26th Inf. Co.A
Sullenbarger, David TN 61st Mtd.Inf. Co.I
Sullenbarger, John P. TN 3rd (Lillard's) Mtd.Inf. 1st Co.K
Sullenbarger, John P. TN 63rd Inf. Co.E
Sullenberger, James S. 1st Conf.Inf. Co.B
Sullenberger, John M. 1st Conf.Inf. Co.B
Sullenberger, John S. AR 26th Inf. Co.F
Sullenberger, John S. TX 9th Field Btty.
Sullenberger, Joseph P. AR 3rd Inf. Co.I Cpl.
Sullender, William MS 18th Cav. Co.C
Sullender, William VA 10th Bn.Res. Co.C 2nd Lt.
Sullenger, G.T. TX Cav. Terry's Regt. Co.I Sgt.
Sullenger, J.E. MS 5th Inf. Co.F
Sullenger, J.L. MS 41st Inf. Co.I Cpl.
Sullenger, John E. MS 20th Inf. Co.G
Sullenger, Joseph TN 8th Inf. Co.K
Sullens, A. VA Vol. Binford's Co.
Sullens, A.C. MS 15th Inf. Co.I Sgt.
Sullens, Andrew NC 58th Inf. Co.A
Sullens, Andrew VA 48th Inf. Co.B
Sullens, Augustus VA Inf. 5th Bn.Loc.Def. Co.E
Sullens, David Gen. & Staff, QM Dept. Maj.
Sullens, David C. TX 22nd Cav. Co.K
Sullens, James W. VA 53rd Inf. Co.D
Sullens, Jesse D. MO Cav. Schnabel's Bn. Co.A Sgt.
Sullens, John AL 1st Cav. Co.I
Sullens, John MS Inf. 3rd Bn. (St.Troops) Co.C
Sullens, John TN 16th Inf. Co.D
Sullens, John TN 25th Inf. Co.F,E
Sullens, John L. TN 25th Inf. Co.F
Sullens, Mikajah MO 10th Inf. Co.G
Sullens, R. VA 15th Inf. Co.C
Sullens, William TX 27th Cav. Co.I
Sullers, A. AL 30th Inf. Co.G
Sullers, J.G. TX 1st Inf. Co.C
Sullet, B.P. MS 2nd St.Cav. Co.K
Sullevan, J. AR 21st Mil. Co.A
Sulley, R.S. NC 21st Inf.
Sulliman, John P. NC 4th Sr.Res. Co.B
Sullinds, James AR 32nd Inf. Co.C
Sullinger, Charles D. TN 3rd (Forrest's) Cav. Co.E
Sullinger, G. KY 12th Cav. Co.E
Sullinger, James TN 8th Inf. Co.K
Sullinger, James T. KY 4th Cav. Co.B
Sullinger, J.J. TN 22nd Inf. Co.F Cpl.
Sullinger, J.L. MS Inf. 3rd Bn. Co.I Cpl.
Sullinger, Robert TN 22nd Inf. Co.F
Sullinger, S. KY 12th Cav. Co.E
Sullinger, Thomas J. MO 5th Inf. Co.K
Sullinger, W. KY 12th Cav. Co.E
Sullinger, Wiley MO 4th Cav. Co.A
Sullinger, Wiley MO Cav. Preston's Bn. Co.A
Sullings, Edmund M. GA 64th Inf. Co.K
Sullings, G.L. VA 1st Inf. Co.B
Sullings, Richard VA Lt.Arty. 38th Bn. Co.C
Sullins, Adolphus GA 11th Cav. Co.E
Sullins, A.C. MS 4th Inf. Co.A Sgt.
Sullins, A.M. AL 26th (O'Neal's) Inf. Co.H
Sullins, B.N.S. VA 37th Inf. Co.B,K
Sullins, David TN 19th Inf. Chap.
Sullins, Elisha MO 8th Inf. Co.C
Sullins, Elisha VA 37th Inf. Co.B
Sullins, Granger VA 2nd Arty. Co.G
Sullins, Granger VA 87th Mil. Co.D
Sullins, H. KY 3rd Mtd.Inf. Co.E
Sullins, J. VA 21st Cav. 2nd Co.D
Sullins, James TN 35th Inf. Co.E
Sullins, James R. TN 25th Inf. Co.E Sgt.
Sullins, James T. MO 10th Cav. Co.K
Sullins, Jesse D. AR Cav. Harrell's Bn. Co.C
Sullins, Jessee D. AR 27th Inf. Co.K
Sullins, Jesse W. TN 25th Inf. Co.K
Sullins, John VA 37th Inf. Co.B
Sullins, John L. TN 13th (Gore's) Cav. Co.C
Sullins, Joseph T. VA 37th Inf. Co.B
Sullins, J.W. TN 13th (Gore's) Cav. Co.C
Sullins, Lavender TN 35th Inf. Co.E
Sullins, M.C. TN Cav. 16th Bn. (Neal's) Co.B Sgt.
Sullins, M.C. TN Conscr. (Cp. of Instr.) Co.B
Sullins, M.L. TN Inf. 3rd Cons.Regt. Co.A
Sullins, Nathan A. AL 61st Inf. Co.H QMSgt.
Sullins, Riley MO 3rd Cav. Co.G
Sullins, Riley MO 10th Inf. Co.G
Sullins, Robert TN 23rd Inf. Co.H
Sullins, Robert C. MS 4th Inf. Co.A
Sullins, Russell VA 37th Inf. Co.B
Sullins, Samuel TN 8th (Smith's) Cav. Co.K
Sullins, S.B. Gen. & Staff Asst.Comsy.
Sullins, Stephen B. AL Inf. 1st Regt. Co.G,C Asst.Comsy.
Sullins, Walter TN 8th (Smith's) Cav. Co.K
Sullins, Walter TN 7th Inf. Co.A
Sullins, Walter TN 35th Inf. Co.E
Sullins, W.F. TN 25th Inf. Co.E
Sullins, W.H. TN 16th Inf. Co.F
Sullins, William TX 6th Cav. Co.I
Sullins, William P. VA 48th Inf. Co.B
Sullins, Zachariah TN 25th Inf. Co.E
Sullins, Zachariah TN 35th Inf. Co.E
Sullins, Z.P. TN 27th Inf. Co.A
Sullins, Z.P. TX 18th Inf. Co.F
Sullis, W.H. AL Mor.Conscr. Co.B
Sullivaine, E. Clement VA 21st Inf. Co.B
Sullivan, --- GA 45th Inf. Co.B
Sullivan, --- MS 9th Inf. New Co.D
Sullivan, --- SC 1st (Butler's) Inf.
Sullivan, --- TN 8th (Smith's) Cav. Co.L
Sullivan, --- TX 8th Field Btty.
Sullivan, --- TX Lt.Arty. Dege's Bn.
Sullivan, --- VA 2nd St.Res. Co.C
Sullivan, A. GA 2nd Bn.Troops & Defences (Macon) Co.E
Sullivan, A. GA 5th Res. Co.B
Sullivan, A. GA 6th Inf. Co.C
Sullivan, A. MS St.Cav. 2nd Bn. (Harris') Co.C
Sullivan, A. NC 53rd Inf. Co.F
Sullivan, A. TN 51st Inf. Co.D
Sullivan, A. TN 51st (Cons.) Inf. Co.F
Sullivan, A. 3rd Conf.Cav. Co.G
Sullivan, A.A. AL 56th Part.Rangers Co.K Sgt.
Sullivan, A.A. MS Conscr.
Sullivan, Abel GA Inf. 10th Bn. Co.D
Sullivan, Abner NC 8th Bn.Part.Rangers Co.F
Sullivan, Abner NC 66th Inf. Co.I,F
Sullivan, Abner T. VA 44th Inf. Co.I Cpl.
Sullivan, A.C. AR Inf. Cocke's Regt. Co.I
Sullivan, A.D. AR 1st Mtd.Rifles Co.D
Sullivan, A.D. AR 2nd Mtd.Rifles Co.H
Sullivan, Adam NC 51st Inf. Co.C
Sullivan, Adam NC 55th Inf. Co.G
Sullivan, A.J. AL 10th Cav. Co.B
Sullivan, A.J. MS Cav. 6th Bn. Prince's Co.
Sullivan, A.J. SC 12th Inf. Co.I
Sullivan, A.J. TN 1st (Feild's) Inf. Co.I
Sullivan, A.J. 10th Conf.Cav. Co.D
Sullivan, A.J. 20th Conf.Cav. Co.D
Sullivan, A.L. MS 9th Inf. Old Co.H
Sullivan, A.L. NC 1st Inf. (6 mo. '61) Co.E
Sullivan, A.L. NC 4th Bn.Jr.Res. Co.A Sgt.
Sullivan, Alex 2nd Conf.Eng.Troops Co.A
Sullivan, Alexander LA 12th Inf. Co.L
Sullivan, Alexander NC 8th Inf. Co.F
Sullivan, Alexander VA 34th Mil. Co.D

Sullivan, Alfred M. NC 64th Inf. Co.M
Sullivan, Algernon L. MS 19th Inf. Co.G
Sullivan, Allen AR 45th Mil. Co.C
Sullivan, Allen 1st Conf.Inf. Co.A
Sullivan, Alphonso NC 8th Inf. Co.I
Sullivan, A.M. TN Cav. 16th Bn. (Neal's) Co.F Sgt.
Sullivan, Ambrose AR 2nd Mtd.Rifles Co.G
Sullivan, Ambrose TN 3rd (Clack's) Inf. Co.K
Sullivan, Ambrose TN 25th Inf. Co.D
Sullivan, Ambrose W. TX 6th Cav. Co.B Sgt.
Sullivan, Anderson TN 17th Inf. Co.I
Sullivan, Andrew LA 7th Inf. Co.C Cpl.
Sullivan, Andrew MD Arty. 3rd Btty.
Sullivan, Andrew VA Arty. 18th Bn. Co.E
Sullivan, Andrew VA 33rd Inf. Co.E
Sullivan, Andrew A. AL 9th Inf. Co.C
Sullivan, Andrew J. AL 45th Inf. Co.I
Sullivan, Andrew J. FL Cav. (Marianna Drag.) Smith's Co.
Sullivan, Andrew J. MS 21st Inf. Co.D
Sullivan, Andrew J. 15th Conf.Cav. Co.B
Sullivan, Andrew McI. NC 51st Inf. Co.C Sr.2nd Lt.
Sullivan, Andrew W. NC 12th Inf. Co.C
Sullivan, A.N.P. TN 46th Inf. Co.H
Sullivan, A.P. NC 6th Cav. (65th St.Troops) Co.D,C Sgt.
Sullivan, A.P. TX Cav. 1st Regt.St.Troops Co.F 2nd Lt.
Sullivan, A.P. TX 33rd Cav. Co.F
Sullivan, Arthur TN 10th Inf. Co.A
Sullivan, Arthur O.L. VA 4th Inf. Co.G Cpl.
Sullivan, Arthur T. GA Inf. 3rd Bn. Co.A
Sullivan, Asa A. MS 15th Inf. Co.K
Sullivan, A.T. GA Lt.Arty. Van Den Corput's Co.
Sullivan, Augustine M. VA Loc.Def.
Sullivan, Augustus VA 10th Cav. Co.B
Sullivan, B. AL 41st Inf. Co.A
Sullivan, Barthalomew KY 4th Mtd.Inf. Co.H Sgt.
Sullivan, Benjamin NC 2nd Arty. (36th St.Troops) Co.G
Sullivan, Benjamin NC Lt.Arty. 13th Bn. Co.D,A
Sullivan, Benjamin VA 7th Inf. Co.B
Sullivan, Benjamin VA 97th Mil. Co.L
Sullivan, Benjamin F. AL Lt.Arty. Ward's Btty.
Sullivan, Benjamin F. SC 1st (Orr's) Rifles Co.B
Sullivan, Benjamin F. TN 7th Inf. Co.G
Sullivan, Benjamin F. TN 7th Inf. Co.I
Sullivan, Benjamin H. TN 7th Inf. Co.I
Sullivan, Berry GA 5th Res. Co.B
Sullivan, Berry TN 41st Inf. Co.A
Sullivan, B.H. LA 22nd Inf. Wash. Marks' Co.
Sullivan, B.H. NC 67th Inf. Co.F
Sullivan, B.H. TN 4th (McLemore's) Cav. Co.B
Sullivan, B.J. AL 38th Inf. Co.H
Sullivan, Bryant H. NC 3rd Inf. Co.B
Sullivan, C. AR 19th (Dockery's) Inf. Co.E
Sullivan, C. GA 2nd Inf. Co.B
Sullivan, C. GA 5th Res. Co.B
Sullivan, C. LA 3rd Inf. Co.B
Sullivan, C. MS 10th Inf. Old Co.A
Sullivan, C. TN 84th Inf. Co.C
Sullivan, C.A. MS Inf. 2nd Bn. Co.L
Sullivan, C.A. MS 48th Inf. Co.L
Sullivan, Caloway TN Cav. 4th Bn. (Branner's) Co.C
Sullivan, Calvin AL 15th Inf. Co.A
Sullivan, Calvin AL 31st Inf. Co.I Sgt.
Sullivan, Calvin TN Cav. 4th Bn. (Branner's) Co.C
Sullivan, Caswell AR 8th Cav. Co.E
Sullivan, Caswell MO Cav. Clardy's Bn.
Sullivan, C.B. LA Mil. Leeds' Guards Regt. Co.F
Sullivan, C.B. SC Lt.Arty. Beauregard's Co.
Sullivan, C.B. TN Lt.Arty. Phillips' Co.
Sullivan, C.C. AL 11th Inf. Co.G
Sullivan, C.C. MS Cav. Yerger's Regt. Co.E
Sullivan, C. Coatsworth NC 11th (Bethel Regt.) Inf. Co.I
Sullivan, C.D. 3rd Conf.Cav. Co.I
Sullivan, Chandler VA Lt.Arty. Cooper's Co.
Sullivan, Charles AL 62nd Inf. Co.H
Sullivan, Charles AR Inf. Cocke's Regt. Co.H
Sullivan, Charles GA Cav. 1st Bn.Res. Co.C
Sullivan, Charles TX 8th Cav. Sgt.
Sullivan, Charles A. TX 37th Cav. Co.B
Sullivan, Charles D. AR 2nd Inf. Co.A AQM
Sullivan, Charles D. Gen. & Staff Capt.,AQM
Sullivan, Charles M. GA Lt.Arty. (Jackson Arty.) Massenburg's Btty.
Sullivan, Charles W. VA 4th Inf. Co.G Sgt.
Sullivan, Charles William VA 25th Cav. Co.E 1st Lt.
Sullivan, Christopher LA 14th Inf. Co.C
Sullivan, C.I. TX Cav. Waller's Regt. Co.E
Sullivan, C.J. TX 32nd Cav. Co.B
Sullivan, C.L. TN 12th (Green's) Cav. Co.C Jr.2nd Lt.
Sullivan, Clem C. MS 10th Inf. Co.L, New Co.C
Sullivan, Clement Van Dorn's Staff, Lee's Staff Capt.,AAG
Sullivan, Clement C. MS Cav. Ham's Regt. Co.F
Sullivan, Coleman VA Inf. 26th Bn. Co.G
Sullivan, Con MS 1st (King's) Inf. (St.Troops) Co.E
Sullivan, Conley AR Cav. Poe's Bn. Co.A
Sullivan, Corn LA 4th Inf. Co.B
Sullivan, Cornelius GA 1st (Olmstead's) Inf. Co.A,B
Sullivan, Cornelius GA Inf. 2nd Bn. Co.B
Sullivan, Cornelius, Jr. GA Conscr.
Sullivan, Cornelius LA 5th Cav. Co.K
Sullivan, Cornelius LA 6th Inf. Co.I
Sullivan, Corlenius LA 7th Inf. Co.E
Sullivan, Cornelius LA 10th Inf. Co.B Sgt.
Sullivan, Cornelius LA 21st (Patton's) Inf. Co.F,D
Sullivan, Cornelius LA 22nd (Cons.) Inf. Co.K
Sullivan, Cornelius VA 27th Inf. Co.B Sgt.
Sullivan, C.P. AL 56th Part.Rangers Co.D
Sullivan, C.W. MS 2nd Part.Rangers Co.C
Sullivan, C.W. TN 38th Inf. Co.C
Sullivan, C.W. TX 35th (Likens') Cav. Co.C
Sullivan, C.W. VA 13th Cav. Co.A
Sullivan, D. AL 1st Regt. Mobile Vol. Baas' Co.
Sullivan, D. AL Mil. 4th Vol. Co.I
Sullivan, D. AL 19th Inf. Co.G
Sullivan, D. AL 48th Mil. Co.H 2nd Cpl.
Sullivan, D. AR 8th Inf. New Co.D
Sullivan, D. LA 1st Cav. Co.C,I,G
Sullivan, D. LA 1st Cav. Co.F
Sullivan, D. LA 3rd (Wingfield's) Cav. Co.G
Sullivan, D. LA Mil. 1st Regt. 2nd Brig. 1st Div.
Sullivan, D. LA Mil. Chalmette Regt. Co.E
Sullivan, D. SC Mil. 16th Regt. Lawrence's Co.
Sullivan, D. TN 42nd Inf. 2nd Co.E
Sullivan, D. 3rd Conf.Cav. Co.D
Sullivan, D.A. AL 40th Inf. Co.H
Sullivan, D.A. TX Cav. Baird's Regt. 2nd Lt.
Sullivan, D.A.J. SC Mil.Arty. 1st Regt. Pope's Co. Sgt.
Sullivan, D.A.J. SC Arty. Manigault's Bn. 1st Co.A
Sullivan, Dan 3rd Conf.Inf. Co.D
Sullivan, Dan A. TX Cav. Terry's Regt. Co.E Capt.
Sullivan, Daniel AL 8th Inf. Co.I
Sullivan, Daniel AL 30th Inf. Co.G
Sullivan, Daniel AL 60th Inf. Co.C
Sullivan, Daniel AL 3rd Bn. Hilliard's Legion Vol. Co.D
Sullivan, Daniel AR 8th Cav. Peoples' Co.
Sullivan, Daniel AR 18th (Marmaduke's) Inf. Co.D
Sullivan, Daniel AR 31st Inf. Co.E
Sullivan, Daniel AR Mil. Desha Cty.Bn.
Sullivan, Daniel GA Inf. 1st Loc.Troops (Augusta) Co.I
Sullivan, Daniel GA 1st (Olmstead's) Inf. Co.A,B
Sullivan, Daniel GA 19th Inf. Co.B
Sullivan, Daniel GA Cherokee Legion (St.Guards) Co.A
Sullivan, Daniel LA 1st Hvy.Arty. (Reg.) Co.C
Sullivan, Daniel LA Hvy.Arty. 8th Bn. Co.C
Sullivan, Daniel LA 1st (Nelligan's) Inf. Co.G
Sullivan, Daniel LA 28th (Thomas') Inf. Co.A
Sullivan, Daniel MS 28th Cav. Co.K
Sullivan, Daniel MS 8th Inf. Co.C
Sullivan, Daniel MS 17th Inf. Co.C
Sullivan, Daniel MS 30th Inf. Co.G
Sullivan, Daniel NC 1st Inf. Co.E
Sullivan, Daniel NC 18th Inf. Co.K
Sullivan, Daniel SC 1st (McCreary's) Inf. Co.K,I
Sullivan, Daniel SC 4th St.Troops Co.G
Sullivan, Daniel SC 11th Inf. 1st Co.I, 2nd Co.I
Sullivan, Daniel TN 10th Inf. Co.I
Sullivan, Daniel TN 19th Inf. Co.C
Sullivan, Daniel TN Conscr. (Cp. of Instr.)
Sullivan, Daniel TX 1st Hvy.Arty. Co.D
Sullivan, Daniel VA Hvy.Arty. 20th Bn. Co.E
Sullivan, Daniel VA Hvy.Arty. Wilkinson's Co.
Sullivan, Daniel VA 1st Inf. Co.C
Sullivan, Daniel VA 1st St.Res. Co.C
Sullivan, Daniel VA Inf. 1st Bn. Co.B
Sullivan, Daniel VA 5th Inf. Co.F
Sullivan, Daniel VA 47th Inf. Co.A
Sullivan, Daniel 20th Conf.Cav. Co.F
Sullivan, Daniel Conf.Inf. 8th Bn. Co.B
Sullivan, Daniel A. GA 65th Inf. Co.G Jr.2nd Lt.
Sullivan, Daniel A. TX 1st (McCulloch's) Cav. Co.D Sgt.
Sullivan, Daniel A. TX Cav. Waller's Regt. Menard's Co. 2nd Lt.
Sullivan, Daniel E. LA 1st (Nelligan's) Inf. Co.G QMSgt.

Sullivan, Daniel F. VA 2nd Inf. Co.D
Sullivan, Daniel J. TX 1st (Yager's) Cav. Co.B Cpl.
Sullivan, Daniel J. TX Cav. 3rd (Yager's) Bn. Co.B Cpl.
Sullivan, Daniel P. GA 1st (Olmstead's) Inf. Co.B
Sullivan, Daniel W. TX 8th Inf. Co.F 2nd Lt.
Sullivan, David TN 8th Inf. Co.D 2nd Lt.
Sullivan, David TN 14th Inf. Co.A
Sullivan, David VA 41st Inf. Co.B
Sullivan, David A. MS 15th Inf. Co.H
Sullivan, David B. AL 8th Inf. Co.D 1st Lt.
Sullivan, David C. NC 7th Inf. Co.D
Sullivan, David G. AL Eufaula Lt.Arty.
Sullivan, D.C. AR Mil. Desha Cty.Bn.
Sullivan, D.C. SC 3rd Res. Co.C
Sullivan, D.D. MS 3rd Inf. (St.Troops) Co.B
Sullivan, D.D. MS 30th Inf. Co.C
Sullivan, Dempsy F. LA 16th Inf. Co.I 1st Sgt.
Sullivan, Denis TN 10th Inf. Co.I
Sullivan, Dennis AL 8th Inf. Co.D
Sullivan, Dennis AL 8th Inf. Co.I
Sullivan, Dennis GA Inf. 2nd Bn. (St.Guards) Old Co.D
Sullivan, Dennis LA 14th Inf. Co.H
Sullivan, Dennis LA 15th Inf. Co.K
Sullivan, Dennis MS Inf. 2nd Bn. Co.G
Sullivan, Dennis MS 10th Inf. Co.O, New Co.B
Sullivan, Dennis MS 21st Inf. Co.B
Sullivan, Dennis MS 31st Inf. Co.F
Sullivan, Dennis MS 48th Inf. Co.G
Sullivan, Dennis SC 1st Arty. Co.F
Sullivan, Dennis SC 1st (McCreary's) Inf. Co.K
Sullivan, Dennis TN 10th Inf. Co.A
Sullivan, Dennis TN 10th Inf. Co.F Sgt.
Sullivan, Dennis TN 15th Inf. Co.C
Sullivan, Dennis VA 2nd Cav. Co.B
Sullivan, Dennis VA 46th Inf. 1st Co.C
Sullivan, Dennis VA 60th Inf. Co.B
Sullivan, Dennis VA 60th Inf. Co.F
Sullivan, Dennis 9th Conf.Inf. Co.D
Sullivan, D.F. GA 1st (Symons') Res. Co.C Cpl.
Sullivan, D.H. GA Inf. 14th Bn. (St.Guards) Co.C
Sullivan, D.H. TN 50th Inf. Co.A
Sullivan, D.H. TN 50th (Cons.) Inf. Co.A
Sullivan, D.J. LA Mil. Beauregard Bn.
Sullivan, D.L. TN 4th Inf. Co.H
Sullivan, D.M. MO 5th Cav. Co.H
Sullivan, D.O. MS 2nd St.Cav. Co.F Cpl.
Sullivan, D.O.D. LA Mil. Irish Regt. Maj.
Sullivan, D.S. LA Inf. 7th Bn. Co.C
Sullivan, Dunklin AL Cav. Graves' Co.
Sullivan, Dunklin A. AL Mil. 4th Vol. Co.C
Sullivan, E. AL 17th Inf. Co.A
Sullivan, E. MS 46th Inf.
Sullivan, E. TX 12th Cav. Co.G
Sullivan, E., 3rd TX Cav. Crump's Regt. Co.G Lt.
Sullivan, E.B. AL 18th Inf. Co.D Lt.
Sullivan, E.C. MS 43rd Inf. Co.G
Sullivan, E.C. Gen. & Staff 1st Lt.,ADC
Sullivan, Eclemuel T. TN 7th Inf. Co.I
Sullivan, Eclemwel T. KY 14th Cav. Co.C
Sullivan, Ed. GA 8th Inf. Co.D
Sullivan, Ed Conf.Inf. Tucker's Regt. Co.F
Sullivan, Edmund GA Inf. 18th Bn. Co.A
Sullivan, Edward LA 1st Hvy.Arty. (Reg.) Co.D
Sullivan, Edward VA 18th Inf. Co.B
Sullivan, Edward D. MS 2nd Inf. Co.F Sgt.
Sullivan, Edward P. TN 28th Inf. Co.K
Sullivan, E.F. AL 54th Inf.
Sullivan, E.H. TN 15th (Stewart's) Cav. Co.F
Sullivan, E.J. MS 2nd Inf. (A. of 10,000) Co.G Cpl.
Sullivan, E.L. GA Inf. (Anderson Guards) Anderson's Co.
Sullivan, E.L. TX Cav. Bourland's Regt. Co.F
Sullivan, Eldridge G. TN Inf. 1st Bn. (Colms') Co.B
Sullivan, Eldrige S. AR 25th Inf. Co.H
Sullivan, Elias NC 51st Inf. Co.C
Sullivan, Elias SC Inf. 9th Bn. Co.E
Sullivan, Elias SC 26th Inf. Co.F
Sullivan, Elias E. TN Cav. Newsom's Regt. Co.G
Sullivan, Elias F. TX 35th (Brown's) Cav. Co.G
Sullivan, Elias F. TX 13th Vol. 1st Co.K, 2nd Co.C,B,G,I
Sullivan, Elijah TX 3rd Cav. Co.G
Sullivan, Elisha NC 8th Sr.Res. Broadhurst's Co.
Sullivan, E.M. NC 57th Inf. Co.G
Sullivan, E.M. TN 6th Inf. Co.K
Sullivan, Enos TX 20th Inf. Co.A
Sullivan, E.O. LA Mil. Lewis Guards Sgt.
Sullivan, E.P. TN 46th Inf. Co.H
Sullivan, E.R. AL 2nd Cav. Co.D
Sullivan, E.T. MS 8th Inf. Co.C
Sullivan, E.T. TX 2nd Cav.
Sullivan, Eugene AL 61st Inf. Co.C
Sullivan, Eugene GA 1st (Olmstead's) Inf. Co.A,B Cpl.
Sullivan, Eugene LA 5th Inf. Co.C
Sullivan, Eugene LA Mil. Leeds' Guards Regt. Co.F
Sullivan, Eugene SC Mil. 1st Regt. (Charleston Res.) Co.H
Sullivan, Eugene TN Lt.Arty. Scott's Co.
Sullivan, Eugene TN 10th Inf. Co.D
Sullivan, Eugene TN Inf. 154th Sr.Regt. Co.I
Sullivan, E.W. TN 4th Cav. Co.F
Sullivan, F. AL 15th Bn.Part.Rangers Co.D
Sullivan, F. AR 18th (Marmaduke's) Inf. Co.A
Sullivan, F. LA Mil. 4th Regt. 1st Brig. 1st Div. Co.C
Sullivan, F. TN 50th Inf. Co.K
Sullivan, F. 7th Conf.Cav. Co.G
Sullivan, F.D. FL 10th Inf. Co.A Cpl.
Sullivan, Felix AL 18th Inf. Co.F
Sullivan, Finis E. MS 44th Inf. Co.E
Sullivan, F.J. TN 8th (Smith's) Cav. Co.F
Sullivan, F.J. TN 45th Inf. Co.F
Sullivan, Fletcher AR 1st (Monroe's) Cav. Co.E
Sullivan, Florence GA Hvy.Arty. 22nd Bn. Co.E
Sullivan, Florence GA 1st (Olmstead's) Inf. Guilmartin's Co.
Sullivan, Florence MS Inf. 2nd Bn. Co.A
Sullivan, Florence MS 48th Inf. Co.A
Sullivan, Florence TN 10th Inf. Co.G
Sullivan, Florence TN 10th Inf. Co.H
Sullivan, Florence TX Cav. Baylor's Regt. Co.F
Sullivan, Florence TX Waul's Legion Co.A Sgt.
Sullivan, Florence VA 26th Inf. 1st Co.B
Sullivan, F.M. AL 18th Inf. Co.I
Sullivan, F.M. AL 58th Inf. Co.D
Sullivan, F.M. AR 37th Inf. Co.D
Sullivan, F.M. LA 3rd (Wingfield's) Cav. Co.I
Sullivan, F.M. 10th Conf.Cav. Co.D
Sullivan, Francis MS 2nd Inf. Co.E
Sullivan, Francis MS 21st Inf. Co.E
Sullivan, Francis M. Hill's Div.
Sullivan, Frank AL 56th Part.Rangers Co.D
Sullivan, Frank MD 1st Cav. Co.C
Sullivan, Franklin NC 48th Inf. Co.D
Sullivan, Frank M. GA 36th (Broyles') Inf. Co.B
Sullivan, Frederick NC 2nd Arty. (36th St.Troops) Co.D
Sullivan, Frederick NC 1st Inf. Co.E
Sullivan, Frederick VA 30th Inf. Co.B
Sullivan, F.W. VA 2nd Inf.Loc.Def. Co.H
Sullivan, George AR 1st (Monroe's) Cav. Co.C
Sullivan, George AR Lt.Arty. Thrall's Btty.
Sullivan, George LA 22nd Inf. Wash. Marks' Co.
Sullivan, George SC 11th Inf. 1st Co.I, 2nd Co.I
Sullivan, George TN 4th Cav. Co.L
Sullivan, George 1st Seminole Mtd.Vol.
Sullivan, George Inf. School of Pract. Powell's Detach. Co.B
Sullivan, George A. VA Lt.Arty. 38th Bn. Co.C
Sullivan, George C. MS 15th Inf. Co.D
Sullivan, George C. MS 15th Inf. Co.H
Sullivan, George C. TX 27th Cav. Co.D
Sullivan, George R. AR 1st S.S. Co.I
Sullivan, George R. TX 6th Cav. Co.I
Sullivan, George V. AR 2nd Mtd.Rifles Co.D
Sullivan, George W. AL 32nd Inf. Co.A
Sullivan, George W. AR 1st Cav. Co.C
Sullivan, George W. GA 25th Inf. Co.I
Sullivan, George W. GA 44th Inf. Co.H
Sullivan, George W. MS 2nd (Quinn's St.Troops) Inf. Co.E
Sullivan, Gibson J. AL 32nd Inf. Co.A
Sullivan, Giles MS Conscr.
Sullivan, G.J. AL 56th Part.Rangers Co.K
Sullivan, G.J. Sap. & Min. J.W. Green's Co.,CSA
Sullivan, G.M. MO 16th Inf. Co.G
Sullivan, G.P. TN 12th (Cons.) Inf. Co.H
Sullivan, G.P. TN 22nd Inf. Co.B
Sullivan, Green MO 8th Inf. Co.A Cpl.
Sullivan, Green TN Cav. Newsom's Regt. Co.D
Sullivan, G.W. AR 19th (Dawson's) Inf. Co.C
Sullivan, G.W. GA 47th Inf. Co.G
Sullivan, G.W. LA Mil.Conf.Guards Regt. Co.D
Sullivan, G.W. MS 6th Cav. Co.B
Sullivan, G.W. MS 3rd Inf. Co.D
Sullivan, G.W. TN 8th (Smith's) Cav. Co.F
Sullivan, G.W. TN 12th Inf. Co.A
Sullivan, G.W. TN 12th (Cons.) Inf. Co.A
Sullivan, H. AL 51st (Part.Rangers) Co.I
Sullivan, H. AL 56th Part.Rangers Co.D
Sullivan, H. MS 6th Inf. Co.B
Sullivan, H. TN 20th Inf. Co.E
Sullivan, H.C. AL 18th Inf. Co.E
Sullivan, H.D. TX 8th Cav. Co.I Cpl.
Sullivan, Henderson AL 15th Bn.Part.Rangers Co.D
Sullivan, Henry MS Inf. 2nd St.Troops Co.M

Sullivan, Henry NC 38th Inf. Co.A
Sullivan, Henry NC 50th Inf. Co.C
Sullivan, Henry VA 1st Inf. Co.C Sgt.
Sullivan, Henry L. TN Inf. 154th Sr.Regt. Co.E
Sullivan, Henry W. AL Cp. of Instr. Talladega
Sullivan, Henry W. AR 33rd Inf. Co.K
Sullivan, H.G. GA 1st Cav. Co.B
Sullivan, Hickison B. MS 42nd Inf. Co.B
Sullivan, Hilery FL 11th Inf. Co.C
Sullivan, H.J. GA 2nd Cav. (St.Guards) Co.C
Sullivan, H.L. AL 9th Inf. Co.G
Sullivan, H.M. NC 45th Inf. Co.K
Sullivan, H.N. MS 39th Inf. Co.F
Sullivan, H.R. AR 10th Mil. Co.B
Sullivan, H.R. TN 45th Inf. Co.I Cpl.
Sullivan, Humpry LA 13th Inf. Co.A
Sullivan, I.A. MS Cav. Powers' Regt. Co.G
Sullivan, I.B. Gen. & Staff, A. of TN Capt.
Sullivan, Ira H. VA 46th Inf. 2nd Co.D
Sullivan, Isaac C. MS 4th Inf. Co.E 2nd Lt.
Sullivan, Isaac Clark MS 1st Lt.Arty. Co.A
Sullivan, Isaac M. NC 48th Inf. Co.D
Sullivan, Isaac W. AL 4th Inf. Co.F
Sullivan, Isaac W. MS 15th Inf. Co.D
Sullivan, J. AL 11th Cav. Co.D Cpl.
Sullivan, J. AL 56th Part.Rangers Co.K Sgt.
Sullivan, J. AL 8th Inf. Co.K
Sullivan, J. AL 32nd Inf. Co.C
Sullivan, J. AL 42nd Inf. Co.I
Sullivan, J. FL 1st (Res.) Inf. Co.D
Sullivan, J. GA 1st Inf.
Sullivan, J. GA Inf. 18th Bn. Co.A
Sullivan, J. GA 36th (Villepigue's) Inf. Co.F
Sullivan, J. KY 1st (Helm's) Cav.
Sullivan, J. KY Cav. 2nd Bn. (Dortch's) Co.D
Sullivan, J. KY 3rd Mtd.Inf. Co.B
Sullivan, J. LA 15th Inf. Co.B
Sullivan, J. LA 22nd Inf. Co.E
Sullivan, J. LA Mil. Lewis Guards
Sullivan, J. LA Mil. Orleans Fire Regt. Co.H
Sullivan, J. MD Inf. 2nd Bn. Co.E
Sullivan, J. MS 5th Cav. Co.B
Sullivan, J. MS 12th Cav. Co.K
Sullivan, J. SC 2nd Bn.S.S. Co.B
Sullivan, J. TN 10th Inf. Co.H
Sullivan, J., No.1 TN 21st Inf. Co.F
Sullivan, J. VA 50th Inf. Co.D
Sullivan, J. 1st Conf.Inf. 1st Co.F
Sullivan, J.A. AL 8th Inf. Co.I
Sullivan, J.A. AL 32nd & 58th (Cons.) Inf. Co.K
Sullivan, J.A. MS 2nd St.Cav. Co.H Cpl.
Sullivan, J.A. MS Inf. 3rd Bn. (St.Troops) Co.B
Sullivan, J.A. TN 45th Inf. Co.F
Sullivan, Jack MS Inf. Co.K
Sullivan, Jackson AR 3rd Inf. Co.L,A
Sullivan, Jackson LA 3rd (Wingfield's) Cav Co.H
Sullivan, Jackson LA Inf. 9th Bn. Co.A
Sullivan, Jackson R. AL 32nd Inf. Co.A
Sullivan, Jacob J. MO Cav. 2nd Bn.St.Guard Co.A
Sullivan, Jacob J. MO 12th Inf. Co.E
Sullivan, James AL Inf. 2nd Regt. Co.F
Sullivan, James AL 4th Inf. Co.K Capt.
Sullivan, James AL 5th Bn.Vol. Co.D
Sullivan, James AL 18th Inf. Co.L
Sullivan, James AL 58th Inf. Co.A
Sullivan, James AR 2nd Cav. Co.G
Sullivan, James GA Hvy.Arty. 22nd Bn. Co.C
Sullivan, James GA 1st (Cons.) Inf. Co.I
Sullivan, James GA 1st (Olmstead's) Inf. Co.A,B
Sullivan, James GA Inf. 2nd Bn. Co.A
Sullivan, James GA Inf. 2nd Bn. (St.Guards) Co.B
Sullivan, James GA Inf. 14th Bn. (St.Guards) Co.B
Sullivan, James GA 15th Inf. Co.H
Sullivan, James GA 29th Inf. Co.B
Sullivan, James GA 39th Inf. Co.D
Sullivan, James GA 51st Inf. Co.B
Sullivan, James GA 66th Inf. Co.D
Sullivan, James LA 1st Cav. Co.F
Sullivan, James LA 3rd (Wingfield's) Cav. Co.B
Sullivan, James LA 5th Inf. Co.K
Sullivan, James LA 6th Inf. Co.I
Sullivan, James LA 9th Inf. Co.E
Sullivan, James LA 13th Inf. Co.C Cpl.
Sullivan, James LA 14th Inf. Co.B
Sullivan, James LA 30th Inf. Co.I,D
Sullivan, James LA Mil. Irish Regt. Co.F
Sullivan, James MS 10th Inf. Old Co.D
Sullivan, James MS 16th Inf. Co.D
Sullivan, James MS 19th Inf. Co.C
Sullivan, James MO Cav. 2nd Bn.St.Guard Co.B
Sullivan, James MO 15th Cav. Co.H
Sullivan, James MO 12th Inf. Co.E
Sullivan, James NC 54th Inf. Co.F
Sullivan, James NC 55th Inf.
Sullivan, James SC 1st Arty. Co.A
Sullivan, James SC Arty. Manigault's Bn. 1st Co.B
Sullivan, James SC 4th St.Troops Co.B
Sullivan, James SC 5th Bn.Res. Co.E
Sullivan, James SC Inf. 7th Bn. (Enfield Rifles) Co.F
Sullivan, James SC Mil. Co.A
Sullivan, James TN 3rd (Forrest's) Cav. Co.H
Sullivan, James TN 6th (Wheeler's) Cav. Co.E
Sullivan, James TN Cav. Nixon's Regt. Co.D
Sullivan, James TN Lt.Arty. McClung's Co.
Sullivan, James TN 2nd (Walker's) Inf. Co.A
Sullivan, James TN 2nd (Walker's) Inf. Co.K
Sullivan, James TN 12th Inf. Co.A
Sullivan, James TN 12th (Cons.) Inf. Co.A
Sullivan, James TN 12th (Cons.) Inf. Co.D
Sullivan, James TN 16th Inf. Co.D
Sullivan, James TN 24th Inf. Co.C
Sullivan, James TN Inf. 154th Sr.Regt. Co.C
Sullivan, James TX 26th Cav. Co.K
Sullivan, James VA Inf. 1st Bn. Co.C
Sullivan, James VA 2nd St.Res. Co.L
Sullivan, James VA 25th Inf. Co.C
Sullivan, James VA 30th Inf. Co.A
Sullivan, James VA 30th Inf. Co.B
Sullivan, James VA 33rd Inf. Co.E 1st Sgt.
Sullivan, James Conf.Inf. 1st Bn. Co.I
Sullivan, James Conf.Inf. Tucker's Regt. Co.K
Sullivan, James Sig.Corps,CSA
Sullivan, James A. TN 2nd (Smith's) Cav.
Sullivan, James A. TN 7th Inf. Co.I
Sullivan, James A. VA 13th Inf. Co.C
Sullivan, James B. SC 19th Inf. Co.B AQM
Sullivan, James B. SC 22nd Inf. Co.A
Sullivan, James B. SC Inf.Bn. AQM
Sullivan, James C. NC Hvy.Arty. 10th Bn. Co.A
Sullivan, James E. VA 20th Cav. Co.E
Sullivan, James F. GA 4th Inf. Co.F Capt.
Sullivan, James F. TX 35th (Brown's) Cav. Co.G
Sullivan, James F. TX 13th Vol. 1st Co.K, 2nd Co.C,I,B,G
Sullivan, James G. GA 42nd Inf. Co.K
Sullivan, James H. AL 11th Inf. Co.I 2nd Lt.
Sullivan, James H. KY Kirkpatrick's Bn. Co.D
Sullivan, James H. TN 48th (Nixon's) Inf. Co.G
Sullivan, James H. TN 53rd Inf. Co.E
Sullivan, James H. TX 11th Inf. Co.E Music.
Sullivan, James H. VA 30th Inf. Co.B
Sullivan, James H. VA 37th Inf. Co.I,G Sgt.
Sullivan, James H. VA 47th Inf. 2nd Co.G
Sullivan, James I. SC 6th Cav. Co.A
Sullivan, James K.B. TN 4th Cav. Co.F
Sullivan, James L. MO 12th Cav. Co.I 2nd Lt.
Sullivan, James M. AL 17th Inf. Co.A
Sullivan, James M. AR Inf. Hardy's Regt. Co.F
Sullivan, James M. GA Cav. 8th Bn. (St.Guards) Co.D
Sullivan, James M. KY 2nd Cav. Co.D
Sullivan, James M. MS Inf. 3rd Bn. Co.B
Sullivan, James M. TN 33rd Inf. Co.B
Sullivan, James M. TX 1st (McCulloch's) Cav. Co.B
Sullivan, James M. TX 26th Cav. Co.B
Sullivan, James M. VA 18th Inf. Co.G
Sullivan, James Marshall KY 2nd Mtd.Inf. Co.D
Sullivan, James N. GA Smith's Legion Anderson's Co.
Sullivan, James N. TN 21st Cav.
Sullivan, James N. VA 40th Inf. Co.I
Sullivan, James O. NC 1st Inf. (6 mo. '61) Co.K
Sullivan, James O. SC 5th Cav. Co.E
Sullivan, James O. SC 23rd Inf. Co.D,C,B
Sullivan, James P. MS 2nd Part.Rangers Co.K
Sullivan, James P. MS 17th Inf. Co.D
Sullivan, James R. TN 38th Inf. Co.D
Sullivan, James R. VA 17th Inf. Co.F Cpl.
Sullivan, James S. AL 35th Inf. Co.A Cpl.
Sullivan, James S. GA 1st (Olmstead's) Inf. Co.H
Sullivan, James T. VA Lt.Arty. Moore's Co.
Sullivan, James V. AL 10th Inf. Co.F
Sullivan, James W. GA 1st Inf. Co.D Sgt.
Sullivan, James W. MS 1st (Johnston's) Inf. Co.H
Sullivan, Jared D. SC 6th Cav. Co.A 1st Sgt.
Sullivan, J.B. AR 35th Inf. Co.I Cpl.
Sullivan, J.B. AR 36th Inf. Co.E
Sullivan, J.B. KY 9th Mtd.Inf. Co.H
Sullivan, J.B. MS St.Cav. 2nd Bn. (Harris') Co.C
Sullivan, J.B. MS 2nd Part. Co.A
Sullivan, J.B. MS 18th Cav. Co.F
Sullivan, J.B. TN 6th (Wheeler's) Cav. Co.E
Sullivan, J.B. TN 22nd Inf. Co.K
Sullivan, J.C. AR Lt.Arty. Owen's Btty.
Sullivan, J.C. AR 19th (Dawson's) Inf. Co.C
Sullivan, J.C. LA 2nd Cav. Co.F
Sullivan, J.C. LA 27th Inf. Co.K
Sullivan, J.C. LA Inf.Cons.Crescent Regt. Co.G
Sullivan, J.C. SC 16th Inf. Co.E
Sullivan, J.D. MD Cav. 2nd Bn. Co.B
Sullivan, J.D. MD Arty. 2nd Btty.
Sullivan, J.D. SC 4th Bn.Res. Co.D Sgt.

Sullivan, J.E. TN 12th (Green's) Cav. Co.C 1st Lt.
Sullivan, J.E. TN 16th (Logwood's) Cav. Co.I Capt.
Sullivan, J.E. TN 14th Inf. Co.H
Sullivan, J.E. TN 51st Inf. Co.G Sgt.
Sullivan, J.E. VA Lt.Arty. 38th Bn. Co.C Capt.
Sullivan, Jefferson L. TN 7th Inf. Co.F
Sullivan, Jehu AL 28th Inf. Co.F
Sullivan, Jeremiah GA 1st (Olmstead's) Inf. Co.B
Sullivan, Jeremiah GA 25th Inf. Co.A
Sullivan, Jeremiah LA 5th Inf. Co.K
Sullivan, Jeremiah LA 14th Inf. Co.D
Sullivan, Jeremiah LA Mil. Irish Regt. Co.E
Sullivan, Jeremiah LA Mil. Leeds' Guards Regt. Co.F
Sullivan, Jeremiah MD Arty. 3rd Btty.
Sullivan, Jeremiah NC 32nd Inf. Co.H
Sullivan, Jeremiah SC 1st (Butler's) Inf. Co.F
Sullivan, Jeremiah TN 15th Inf. Co.H
Sullivan, Jeremiah, 2nd TN 15th Inf. Co.H
Sullivan, Jeremiah VA Horse Arty. J.W. Carter's Co.
Sullivan, Jeremiah VA Lt.Arty. Kirkpatrick's Co.
Sullivan, Jeremiah VA 17th Inf. Co.I Cpl.
Sullivan, Jeremiah VA 33rd Inf. Co.E Sgt.
Sullivan, Jeremiah C. NC 2nd Arty. (36th St.Troops) Co.A
Sullivan, Jerry AL Stewart's Detach.Loc.Def.
Sullivan, Jerry AR 5th Inf. Co.B
Sullivan, Jerry FL 4th Inf. Co.B
Sullivan, Jerry FL 6th Inf. Co.E
Sullivan, Jerry MS 16th Inf. Co.D
Sullivan, Jerry SC 1st Arty. Co.E Sgt.
Sullivan, Jerry TN Cav. 12th Bn. (Day's) Co.E
Sullivan, Jerry TN 1st (Feild's) Inf. Co.G
Sullivan, Jerry TN 2nd (Walker's) Inf. Co.G
Sullivan, Jerry TN 10th Inf. Co.I
Sullivan, Jerry VA Cav. 39th Bn. Co.B
Sullivan, Jerry VA Lt.Arty. Garber's Co.
Sullivan, Jerry VA 19th Inf. Co.F
Sullivan, Jerry VA Inf. 25th Bn. Co.A
Sullivan, Jerry 3rd Conf.Eng.Troops Co.D Cpl.
Sullivan, Jesse MS Packer's Co. (Pope Guards)
Sullivan, Jesse NC 2nd Cav. (19th St.Troops) Co.H
Sullivan, Jessee MS 21st Inf. Co.F
Sullivan, Jesse D. NC 26th Inf. Co.K
Sullivan, Jesse P. NC 55th Inf. Co.A
Sullivan, J.F. AR Inf. 1st Bn. Co.I
Sullivan, J.F. VA 8th Inf. Co.D
Sullivan, J.H. AR 23rd Inf. Co.C
Sullivan, J.H. AR Inf. Hardy's Regt. Co.E 1st Lt.
Sullivan, J.H. GA Cav. Gartrell's Co.
Sullivan, J.H. GA 55th Inf. Co.B
Sullivan, J.H. KY 6th Mtd.Inf. Co.B
Sullivan, J.H. MD Arty. 2nd Btty.
Sullivan, J.H. MD Weston's Bn.
Sullivan, J.H. NC 50th Inf. Co.C
Sullivan, J.H. SC 5th St.Troops Co.D
Sullivan, J.H. SC 9th Res. Co.A
Sullivan, J.H. TN 50th Inf. Co.A
Sullivan, J.H. TN 50th Inf. Co.B Sgt.
Sullivan, J.H. VA 2nd St.Res. Co.E
Sullivan, Jiles MS 18th Cav. Co.A
Sullivan, J.J. AL Cav. Co.A
Sullivan, J.J. GA 3rd Res. Co.B
Sullivan, J.J. MS 39th Inf. Co.E
Sullivan, J.J. NC 2nd Jr.Res. Co.C
Sullivan, J.J. TX 10th Inf. Co.E
Sullivan, J.L. TX 29th Cav. Co.B
Sullivan, J.L. 7th Conf.Cav. Co.G
Sullivan, J.M. GA 1st (Fannin's) Res. Co.D
Sullivan, J.M. GA 10th Mil.
Sullivan, J.M. GA 27th Inf. Co.G
Sullivan, J.M. MS 14th Inf. Co.E
Sullivan, J.M. SC 1st (McCreary's) Inf.
Sullivan, J.M. SC 3rd Inf. Co.A
Sullivan, J.M. TN 18th (Newsom's) Cav. Co.K
Sullivan, J.M. TN 24th Cav. Co.K
Sullivan, J.M. TN 5th Inf. 2nd Co.F
Sullivan, J.M. TN 37th Inf. Co.D
Sullivan, J.M. TX 12th Cav. Co.E
Sullivan, J. Mims SC 6th Cav. Co.A 1st Lt.
Sullivan, J. Mims SC 2nd Inf. Co.B
Sullivan, J.O. SC Cav. A.W. Cordes' Co.
Sullivan, J.O. SC Manigault's Bn.Vol. Co.B
Sullivan, John AL 51st (Part.Rangers) Co.K
Sullivan, John AL Lt.Arty. 2nd Bn. Co.D Artif.
Sullivan, John AL Seawell's Btty. (Mohawk Arty.)
Sullivan, John AL St.Arty. Co.C
Sullivan, John AL 1st Regt. Mobile Vol. Co.C
Sullivan, John AL Inf. 2nd Regt. Co.H
Sullivan, John AL Mil. 3rd Vol. Co.B
Sullivan, John AL 5th Bn.Vol. Co.D
Sullivan, John AL 7th Inf. Co.I
Sullivan, John AL 8th Inf. Co.I
Sullivan, John AL 12th Inf. Co.C
Sullivan, John AL 32nd Inf. Co.B
Sullivan, John AL 94th Mil. Co.A
Sullivan, John AR 45th Cav. Co.C
Sullivan, John AR Cav. McGehee's Regt. Co.A
Sullivan, John AR Lt.Arty. Rivers' Btty.
Sullivan, John AR 2nd Inf. Co.B
Sullivan, John AR 18th (Marmaduke's) Inf. Co.D
Sullivan, John FL 11th Inf. Co.C
Sullivan, John GA Cav. 19th Bn. Co.C
Sullivan, John GA Cav. 21st Bn. Co.C
Sullivan, John GA Hvy.Arty. 22nd Bn. Co.E
Sullivan, John GA Siege Arty. 28th Bn. Co.F
Sullivan, John GA Arty. Maxwell's Reg.Lt.Btty.
Sullivan, John GA Lt.Arty. Pritchard's Co. (Washington Arty.)
Sullivan, John GA 1st (Olmstead's) Inf. Co.B
Sullivan, John GA 1st (Olmstead's) Inf. Gordon's Co.
Sullivan, John GA 1st (Olmstead's) Inf. Guilmartin's Co.
Sullivan, John GA 1st (Olmstead's) Inf. Screven's Co.
Sullivan, John, #1 GA 1st (Olmstead's) Inf. Co.A
Sullivan, John, #2 GA 1st (Olmstead's) Inf. Co.A
Sullivan, John GA 2nd Bn.S.S. Co.C
Sullivan, John GA 5th Inf. Co.C
Sullivan, John GA 10th Inf. 1st Co.K
Sullivan, John GA Inf. 18th Bn. (St.Guards) Co.D
Sullivan, John GA Inf. 25th Bn. (Prov.Guard) Co.A
Sullivan, John GA 36th (Broyles') Inf. Co.B
Sullivan, John GA 39th Inf. Co.D
Sullivan, John GA 63rd Inf. Co.B,F
Sullivan, John KY 7th Cav. Co.G
Sullivan, John KY 9th Cav. Co.C,D,E
Sullivan, John KY 10th (Diamond's) Cav. Co.A
Sullivan, John KY 2nd Mtd.Inf. Co.I
Sullivan, John KY 5th Mtd.Inf. Co.D
Sullivan, John LA 1st Hvy.Arty. (Reg.) Co.C Sgt.
Sullivan, John LA 1st Hvy.Arty. (Reg.) Co.E
Sullivan, John LA Hvy.Arty. 8th Bn. 1st Co.D, Co.A
Sullivan, John LA Arty. Kean's Btty. (Orleans Ind.Arty.)
Sullivan, John LA Arty. King's Btty.
Sullivan, John LA 3rd Inf.
Sullivan, John LA Mil. 3rd Regt. 1st Brig. 1st Div. Co.A
Sullivan, John LA Mil. 4th Regt. 1st Brig. 1st Div. Co.B
Sullivan, John LA Mil. 4th Regt. 1st Brig. 1st Div. Co.F
Sullivan, John LA 6th Inf. Co.A
Sullivan, John LA 6th Inf. Co.B
Sullivan, John LA 6th Inf. Co.E
Sullivan, John (No.1) LA 6th Inf. Co.K
Sullivan, John (No.2) LA 6th Inf. Co.K
Sullivan, John LA 7th Inf. Co.G,C
Sullivan, John LA 10th Inf. Co.H
Sullivan, John LA 14th Inf. Co.D
Sullivan, John LA 17th Inf. Co.A
Sullivan, John LA 19th Inf. Co.D
Sullivan, John LA 20th Inf. Co.I
Sullivan, John LA 20th Inf. Co.K
Sullivan, John LA 21st (Kennedy's) Inf. Co.E Bvt.2nd Lt.
Sullivan, John LA 30th Inf. Co.D
Sullivan, John LA O'Hara's Co. (Pelican Guards,Co.B)
Sullivan, John LA C.S. Zouave Bn. Co.B
Sullivan, John MD Cav. 2nd Bn. Sadler's Co.
Sullivan, John, 1st MD Arty. 3rd Btty.
Sullivan, John, 2nd MD Arty. 3rd Btty.
Sullivan, John MS 1st (Percy's) Inf. Co.A
Sullivan, John MS 4th Inf.
Sullivan, John MS 15th (Cons.) Inf. Co.I
Sullivan, John MS 20th Inf. Co.K
Sullivan, John MS 39th Inf. Co.G
Sullivan, John MO 8th Inf. Co.A
Sullivan, John NC 8th Bn.Part.Rangers Co.A
Sullivan, John NC 7th Sr.Res. Johnston's Co.
Sullivan, John NC 57th Inf. Co.D
Sullivan, John NC 66th Inf. Co.F
Sullivan, John SC 1st Arty. Co.A
Sullivan, John, 2nd SC 1st Arty. Co.E
Sullivan, John, 3rd SC 1st Arty. Co.E
Sullivan, John, 4th SC 1st Arty. Co.E
Sullivan, John SC Hvy.Arty. Gilchrist's Co. (Gist Guard)
Sullivan, John SC 1st (Butler's) Inf. Co.E
Sullivan, John SC 1st (McCreary's) Inf. Co.K
Sullivan, John SC 4th St.Troops Co.K
Sullivan, John SC 5th Inf. 2nd Co.A
Sullivan, John SC 5th Res. Co.K Cpl.
Sullivan, John SC 9th Inf. Co.A
Sullivan, John SC 22nd Inf. Co.H
Sullivan, John TN 2nd (Ashby's) Cav. Co.C
Sullivan, John TN 4th Cav. Co.E
Sullivan, John TN 11th (Holman's) Cav. Co.G

Sullivan, John TN Holman's Bn.Part.Rangers Co.B
Sullivan, John TN Lt.Arty. Browne's Co. Artif.
Sullivan, John TN Lt.Arty. Huggins' Co.
Sullivan, John TN Lt.Arty. Kain's Co.
Sullivan, John TN Lt.Arty. Winston's Co.
Sullivan, John TN 1st (Feild's) Inf. Co.K
Sullivan, John TN 2nd (Walker's) Inf. Co.C
Sullivan, John TN 2nd (Walker's) Inf. Co.F
Sullivan, John TN 8th Inf. Co.E
Sullivan, John TN 10th Inf. Co.A
Sullivan, John TN 10th Inf. Co.E
Sullivan, John TN 10th Inf. Co.F
Sullivan, John, 1st TN 10th Inf. Co.F
Sullivan, John TN 10th Inf.
Sullivan, John TN 12th (Cons.) Inf. Co.D
Sullivan, John, No.2 TN 21st Inf. Co.F
Sullivan, John TN 33rd Inf. Co.E
Sullivan, John TX 20th Cav. Co.A
Sullivan, John TX 31st Cav. Co.D Sgt.
Sullivan, John TX 37th Cav. 2nd Co.D
Sullivan, John TX Cav. Baylor's Regt. Co.A Sgt.
Sullivan, John TX Arty. 4th Bn. Co.A Cpl.
Sullivan, John VA 6th Cav. 1st Co.E
Sullivan, John VA 14th Cav. Co.G
Sullivan, John VA Cav. 35th Bn.
Sullivan, John VA Lt.Arty. Brander's Co.
Sullivan, John VA Lt.Arty. Garber's Co.
Sullivan, John VA Lt.Arty. Pollock's Co.
Sullivan, John VA 1st Inf. Co.C 1st Lt.
Sullivan, John VA Inf. 1st Bn. Co.A
Sullivan, John VA Inf. 1st Bn. Co.B
Sullivan, John VA Inf. 1st Bn. Co.C
Sullivan, John VA Inf. 1st Bn. Co.E
Sullivan, John, 2nd VA Inf. 1st Bn. Co.E
Sullivan, John VA 4th Inf. Co.H
Sullivan, John VA 15th Inf. Co.F
Sullivan, John VA 17th Inf. Co.E
Sullivan, John VA 21st Inf. Co.G
Sullivan, John VA 33rd Inf. Co.E
Sullivan, John VA 37th Inf. Co.K
Sullivan, John VA 60th Inf. 1st Co.H
Sullivan, John 10th Conf.Cav. Co.H
Sullivan, John Conf.Inf. 1st Bn. Co.I
Sullivan, John 9th Conf.Inf. Co.B Cpl.
Sullivan, John 9th Conf.Inf. Co.C
Sullivan, John Conf.Inf. Tucker's Regt. Co.C
Sullivan, John 5th Regt.Eng. Co.G,CSA
Sullivan, John A. LA 1st Hvy.Arty. (Reg.) Co.A
Sullivan, John A. LA Inf. 9th Bn. Co.A 1st Sgt.
Sullivan, John A. MS Cav. Jeff Davis Legion Co.F
Sullivan, John A. TN Inf. 1st Bn. (Colms') Co.B
Sullivan, John B. LA 14th (Austin's) Bn.S.S. Co.A
Sullivan, John B. NC Inf. 2nd Bn. Co.A
Sullivan, John B. TN 18th Inf. Co.A
Sullivan, John D. TN 7th Inf. Co.F
Sullivan, John D. VA 48th Inf. Co.G
Sullivan, John D. 14th Conf.Cav. Co.B,I
Sullivan, John E. GA Cav. 1st Bn.Res. Co.A
Sullivan, John E. GA 4th Inf. Co.K Bvt.2nd Lt.
Sullivan, John E. MS 2nd Part.Rangers Co.I Sgt.
Sullivan, John E. MS Conscr.
Sullivan, John E. TN 7th Inf. Co.I Cpl.
Sullivan, John E. VA Lt.Arty. E.J. Anderson's Co. Sgt.
Sullivan, John F. TX 6th Cav. Co.I
Sullivan, John H. LA 16th Inf. Co.I
Sullivan, John H. MD 1st Inf. Co.H 1st Sgt.
Sullivan, John H. TN 18th Btty.
Sullivan, John H. VA 53rd Inf. Co.E
Sullivan, John Hewlett SC Inf. 3rd Bn. Co.C
Sullivan, John J. AL 9th Inf. Co.A 1st Lt.
Sullivan, John J. MS 33rd Inf. Co.G
Sullivan, John J. SC 1st Arty. Co.E
Sullivan, John J. TN Cav. 5th Bn. (McClellan's) Co.D
Sullivan, John L. TX 31st Cav. Co.C
Sullivan, John M. SC 6th Cav. Co.A 2nd Lt.
Sullivan, John M. VA Loc.Def.
Sullivan, John N. TN 8th Inf. Co.K 2nd Lt.
Sullivan, John O. LA 1st Hvy.Arty. (Reg.) Co.F
Sullivan, John O. LA 28th (Thomas') Inf. Co.C
Sullivan, John O. VA 33rd Inf. Co.E Cpl.
Sullivan, John O. VA 52nd Inf. Co.D
Sullivan, John P. SC Palmetto S.S. Co.C Sgt.
Sullivan, John R. AL 5th Bn.Vol. Co.B
Sullivan, John S. KY 6th Mtd.Inf. Co.B Capt.
Sullivan, John S. VA Lt.Arty. J.D. Smith's Co.
Sullivan, John T. LA 1st (Strawbridge's) Inf. Co.B
Sullivan, John W. AL 29th Inf. Co.B
Sullivan, John W. NC 1st Arty. (10th St.Troops) Co.I
Sullivan, John W. NC 2nd Arty. (36th St.Troops) Co.A
Sullivan, John W. TN 7th Inf. Co.I
Sullivan, John W. TX 15th Cav. Co.C
Sullivan, Jonas VA 47th Inf. Co.A
Sullivan, Jonathan AR 10th Inf. Co.K
Sullivan, Jordan MO 8th Inf. Co.B
Sullivan, Jordan VA 50th Inf. Co.D
Sullivan, Joseph AL 2nd Bn. Hilliard's Legion Vol. Co.E
Sullivan, Joseph KY 2nd (Duke's) Cav.
Sullivan, Joseph KY 1st Inf.
Sullivan, Joseph MS 5th Inf. (St.Troops) Co.G
Sullivan, Joseph MS 39th Inf. Co.F
Sullivan, Joseph MO Inf. 8th Bn. Co.F
Sullivan, Joseph SC Hvy.Arty. 15th (Lucas') Bn. Co.C
Sullivan, Joseph TN 2nd (Walker's) Inf. Co.H
Sullivan, Joseph TN 14th Inf. Co.F Sgt.
Sullivan, Joseph TN 44th (Cons.) Inf. Co.C
Sullivan, Joseph TN 51st (Cons.) Inf. Co.H
Sullivan, Joseph TN 55th (McKoin's) Inf. James' Co.
Sullivan, Joseph TX 22nd Inf. Co.B
Sullivan, Joseph VA 1st Cav. Co.E
Sullivan, Joseph VA 13th Inf. Co.G
Sullivan, Joseph E. Eng.,CSA
Sullivan, Joseph F. KY 8th Mtd.Inf. Co.C,E
Sullivan, Joseph G. AR 2nd Mtd.Rifles Co.G
Sullivan, Joseph H. TN Cav. Cox's Bn. Co.B
Sullivan, Joseph L. AR 24th Inf. Co.F
Sullivan, Joseph R. AR 20th Inf. Co.A
Sullivan, Josephus TN 24th Inf. Co.C
Sullivan, Josh. GA 22nd Inf. Co.C
Sullivan, Josiah AR 19th (Dockery's) Inf. Co.E
Sullivan, Josiah MO Cav. Jackman's Regt. Co.G
Sullivan, Josiah TX 20th Inf. Co.A
Sullivan, Josiah E. GA 42nd Inf. Co.K
Sullivan, J.P. AR 1st Cav. Co.G Sgt.
Sullivan, J.P. LA 11th Inf. Co.C Cpl.
Sullivan, J.P. SC 4th Inf. Co.B
Sullivan, J.R. AR 2nd Mtd.Rifles Co.H
Sullivan, J.R. SC 16th Inf. Co.E
Sullivan, J.R. SC 16th & 24th (Cons.) Inf. Co.F
Sullivan, J.R. TN 45th Inf. Co.E 1st Sgt.
Sullivan, J.R. Sap. & Min. J.W. Green's Co.,CSA
Sullivan, J.S. AR 12th Inf. Co.A
Sullivan, J.S. GA 27th Inf. Co.G Cpl.
Sullivan, J.S. KY 7th Cav. Co.B
Sullivan, J.S. MS Morgan's Co. (Morgan Riflemen) 2nd Lt.
Sullivan, J.S. TN 51st Inf. Co.A Sgt.
Sullivan, J.S. Gen. & Staff Capt.,AQM
Sullivan, J. Scally KY 6th Mtd.Inf. Co.B Capt.
Sullivan, Julius B. MS 29th Inf. Co.I
Sullivan, J.W. GA Cav. Young's Co. (Alleghany Troopers)
Sullivan, J.W. GA 5th Inf. Co.H
Sullivan, J.W. MS 12th Cav. Co.H 1st Sgt.
Sullivan, J.W. MS Inf. 3rd Bn. (St.Troops) Co.B
Sullivan, J.W. NC 4th Sr.Res. Co.H
Sullivan, J.W. NC 5th Sr.Res. Co.E
Sullivan, J.W. TN 3rd (Forrest's) Cav. Co.E Cpl.
Sullivan, J.W. TN 8th Inf. Co.D
Sullivan, J.W. Gen. & Staff Hosp.Stew.
Sullivan, K.J. AR Cav. McGehee's Regt. Co.A
Sullivan, L. MS 46th Inf. Co.B
Sullivan, L. MO 1st Inf. 2nd Co.A
Sullivan, L.A. AR Mil. Desha Cty.Bn. 1st Lt.
Sullivan, Larkin MS 3rd Cav. Co.G
Sullivan, Laurence GA 1st (Olmstead's) Inf. Co.D
Sullivan, Lawson GA 5th Res. Co.H
Sullivan, L.B. GA 5th Inf. Co.B
Sullivan, Leak L. AR Cav. Poe's Bn. Co.A
Sullivan, Lemuel L. NC 51st Inf. Co.C
Sullivan, Leonard AL 18th Inf. Co.F
Sullivan, Lewis VA 34th Mil. Co.D
Sullivan, Lewis VA 50th Inf. Co.D
Sullivan, L.L. AR 11th Inf. Co.C
Sullivan, L.L. AR 11th & 17th Cons.Inf. Co.C
Sullivan, L.L. TN 40th Inf. Co.H
Sullivan, L.M. AL 4th Res. Co.C
Sullivan, L.O. TN 3rd (Forrest's) Cav. Co.G
Sullivan, Louis FL 1st Inf. New Co.E Sgt.
Sullivan, L.R. Gen. & Staff Asst.Surg.
Sullivan, L.T. TN 5th Inf. 2nd Co.F
Sullivan, M. AL 40th Inf. Co.H
Sullivan, M. GA 1st (Olmstead's) Inf. Gordon's Co.
Sullivan, M. GA 27th Inf. Co.D Lt.
Sullivan, M. GA Inf. (RR Guards) Preston's Co.
Sullivan, M. LA 1st Cav. Robinson's Co.
Sullivan, M. LA Mil. 1st Regt. 3rd Brig. 1st Div.
Sullivan, M. MO Lt.Arty. 3rd Field Btty.
Sullivan, M. SC 27th Inf. Co.D
Sullivan, M. TN 19th & 20th (Cons.) Cav. Co.C
Sullivan, M. TN Arty. Ramsey's Btty.
Sullivan, M. TX 12th Cav. Co.G
Sullivan, M. TX 33rd Cav. Co.F
Sullivan, M. VA Inf. 4th Bn.Loc.Def. Co.C
Sullivan, M. 2nd Conf.Inf. Co.K

Sullivan, M.A. GA 55th Inf. Co.E
Sullivan, M.A. SC 6th Cav. Co.A Capt.
Sullivan, M.A. SC 3rd Inf. Co.A
Sullivan, Manoah W. MS 29th Inf. Co.I
Sullivan, Marcus GA 27th Inf. Co.B
Sullivan, Marion NC 46th Inf. Co.G
Sullivan, Marion TN 48th (Voorhies') Inf. Co.D
Sullivan, Marion TN Conscr. (Cp. of Instr.)
Sullivan, Mark MS 8th Inf. Co.C
Sullivan, Mark VA 2nd Inf.Loc.Def. Co.E
Sullivan, Mark VA Inf. 6th Bn.Loc.Def. Co.B
Sullivan, Mark R. AL 32nd Inf. Co.A
Sullivan, Martin AL 1st Inf. Co.B
Sullivan, Martin AL Inf. 2nd Regt. Co.H
Sullivan, Martin AL 42nd Inf. Co.E
Sullivan, Martin GA 25th Inf. Co.I
Sullivan, Martin GA 47th Inf. Co.I
Sullivan, Martin SC Inf. 1st (Charleston) Bn. Co.C
Sullivan, Martin SC 27th Inf. Co.H
Sullivan, Martin VA Inf. 1st Bn. Co.E
Sullivan, Martin VA 5th Inf.
Sullivan, Martin Conf.Inf. 1st Bn. 2nd Co.E
Sullivan, Martin L. VA 55th Inf. Co.M
Sullivan, Martin M. MS 26th Inf. Co.I 1st Sgt.
Sullivan, Mat. KY 13th Cav.
Sullivan, Mathew LA 18th Inf. Co.A,I
Sullivan, Mathew TN 2nd (Walker's) Inf. Co.I
Sullivan, M.B. LA 3rd Inf. Co.B
Sullivan, Merrill NC 2nd Inf. Co.C
Sullivan, M.H. KY 13th Cav. Co.D
Sullivan, M.H. VA Cav. 41st Bn. Co.G
Sullivan, Michael AR Inf. 2nd Bn. Co.A
Sullivan, Michael AR 18th (Marmaduke's) Inf. Co.D
Sullivan, Michael GA Inf. 1st Loc.Troops (Augusta) Co.I
Sullivan, Michael GA 1st (Olmstead's) Inf. Gordon's Co.
Sullivan, Michael, No.1 GA 5th Inf. Co.C
Sullivan, Michael, No.2 GA 5th Inf. Co.C
Sullivan, Michael GA 47th Inf. Co.A
Sullivan, Michael GA 63rd Inf. Co.B
Sullivan, Michael LA 1st Hvy.Arty. (Reg.) Co.H
Sullivan, Michael LA Arty. Moody's Co. (Madison Lt.Arty.)
Sullivan, Michael LA 1st (Strawbridge's) Inf. Co.C
Sullivan, Michael LA Inf. 1st Sp.Bn. (Rightor's) Co.E
Sullivan, Michael LA Inf. 1st Sp.Bn. (Wheat's) Co.B
Sullivan, Michael LA Inf. 4th Bn. Co.B
Sullivan, Michael LA 6th Inf. Co.K
Sullivan, Michael LA 10th Inf. Co.A
Sullivan, Michael LA 13th Inf. Co.K 4th Cpl.
Sullivan, Michael LA 20th Inf. Co.G
Sullivan, Michael LA Herrick's Co. (Orleans Blues)
Sullivan, Michael MS 1st Lt.Arty. Co.E
Sullivan, Michael MS 25th Inf. Co.K
Sullivan, Michael MO Lt.Arty. 3rd Btty.
Sullivan, Michael SC 1st Arty. Co.A
Sullivan, Michael SC 1st (McCreary's) Inf. Co.K
Sullivan, Michael TN 7th Inf.
Sullivan, Michael TN 10th Inf. Co.C
Sullivan, Michael TN 10th Inf. Co.D,C
Sullivan, Michael TN 10th Inf. Co.K
Sullivan, Michael TN 15th Inf. Co.H
Sullivan, Michael TX 1st Hvy.Arty. Co.F
Sullivan, Michael VA 5th Cav. 1st Co.F
Sullivan, Michael VA Cav. 39th Bn. Co.C
Sullivan, Michael VA 1st Arty. 2nd Co.C, 3rd Co.C
Sullivan, Michael VA Hvy.Arty. 18th Bn. Co.D
Sullivan, Michael VA 11th Inf. Co.E
Sullivan, Michael VA 15th Inf. Co.F
Sullivan, Michael VA 34th Inf. Norton's Co.
Sullivan, Michael A. VA 5th Cav. Coakley's Co.
Sullivan, Michael M. GA Hvy.Arty. 22nd Bn. Co.E 1st Sgt.
Sullivan, Mike MO 1st Inf. Co.C
Sullivan, Mike (2) TN 10th Inf. Co.K
Sullivan, Mike VA Lt.Arty. 13th Bn. Co.B
Sullivan, Millis NC 45th Inf. Co.K
Sullivan, Milton TX 15th Cav. Co.C
Sullivan, Milton TX 25th Cav. Co.E Cpl.
Sullivan, M.N. TN 18th Inf. Co.E
Sullivan, M.O. SC Inf. 1st (Charleston) Bn. Co.D
Sullivan, M.O. VA 2nd Cav.
Sullivan, Mordecai VA Lt.Arty. 38th Bn. Co.C
Sullivan, Mortimer GA 63rd Inf. Co.B
Sullivan, Moses B. AL 4th (Russell's) Cav. Co.B
Sullivan, M.R. SC 4th Cav. Co.D
Sullivan, Munroe TX 8th Cav. Co.E
Sullivan, Muriel VA Mtd.Riflemen St.Martin's Co.
Sullivan, Murthy AL 21st Inf. Co.B
Sullivan, N. TN 3rd (Forrest's) Cav. Co.H
Sullivan, Nath TN 12th (Green's) Cav. Co.C
Sullivan, Nathan TX 7th Cav. Co.K
Sullivan, Nathaniel GA 23rd Inf. Co.K
Sullivan, N.C. TN 41st Inf. Co.C
Sullivan, N.C. TN 44th (Cons.) Inf. Co.K 1st Lt.
Sullivan, N.D. AR 37th Inf. Co.D
Sullivan, N.D. NC 2nd Home Guards Co.C
Sullivan, Newton FL Cav. 5th Bn.
Sullivan, Newton VA 46th Inf. 1st Co.K
Sullivan, Newton C. TN 44th (Cons.) Inf. Co.F
Sullivan, Nimrod, Jr. SC 1st (Orr's) Rifles Co.C
Sullivan, Nimrod K. SC 1st (Orr's) Rifles Co.C 1st Lt.
Sullivan, N.P. AL Cav. Lewis' Bn. Co.B
Sullivan, O. LA Miles' Legion Co.A
Sullivan, O. TN 1st (Feild's) Inf. Co.L
Sullivan, O. TN Inf. Nashville Bn. Fulcher's Co.
Sullivan, O.D. 14th Conf.Cav. Co.H
Sullivan, Oliver TN Inf. 1st Bn. (Colms') Co.C
Sullivan, Owen AL St.Arty. Co.A
Sullivan, Owen AL Inf. 1st Regt. Co.A
Sullivan, Owen GA Lt.Arty. Hamilton's Co.
Sullivan, Owen GA 1st Reg. Co.A
Sullivan, Owen GA 1st (Olmstead's) Inf. Co.B
Sullivan, Owen GA 59th Inf. Co.K
Sullivan, Owen MS 26th Inf. Co.I
Sullivan, Owen MO 7th Cav.
Sullivan, Owen NC 8th Bn.Part.Rangers Co.A
Sullivan, Owen NC 66th Inf. Co.F
Sullivan, Owen TN Cav. 1st Bn. (McNairy's) Co.B
Sullivan, Owen TN 2nd (Walker's) Inf. Co.C
Sullivan, Owen VA Inf. 1st Bn. Co.C
Sullivan, Owen VA 15th Inf. Co.F
Sullivan, Owen VA 17th Inf. Co.I
Sullivan, Owen Lt.Arty. Dent's Btty.,CSA
Sullivan, P. AL 15th Inf. Co.I
Sullivan, P. FL Cav. 5th Bn.
Sullivan, P. GA Inf. (Loc.Def.) Whiteside's Nav.Bn. Co.B
Sullivan, P. LA 3rd (Wingfield's) Cav. Co.I
Sullivan, P. LA Inf. 7th Bn. Co.B
Sullivan, P. LA Mil. Bonnabel Guards
Sullivan, P. LA Mil. Irish Regt. Co.E
Sullivan, P. MS Inf. 2nd Bn. Co.I
Sullivan, P. SC Mil. 1st Regt. (Charleston Res.) Co.B
Sullivan, P. SC 1st Regt. Charleston Guard Co.D
Sullivan, P. TN Inf. 1st Bn. (Colms') Co.B
Sullivan, P. TN 42nd Inf. 2nd Co.E
Sullivan, P.A. TN 46th Inf. Co.C
Sullivan, Patrick AL 2nd Cav. Co.C
Sullivan, Patrick AL Lt.Arty. 2nd Bn. Co.B
Sullivan, Patrick AL 32nd Inf. Co.B
Sullivan, Patrick AR 2nd Inf. Co.B
Sullivan, Patrick AR Mil. Desha Cty.Bn.
Sullivan, Patrick GA Lt.Arty. Fraser's Btty.
Sullivan, Patrick GA 1st (Olmstead's) Inf. Co.K
Sullivan, Patrick GA 2nd Bn.S.S. Co.E
Sullivan, Patrick GA 10th Inf. 1st Co.K
Sullivan, Patrick KY 1st Inf. Co.D
Sullivan, Patrick KY 7th Mtd.Inf. Co.C
Sullivan, Patrick LA 1st Hvy.Arty. (Reg.) Co.E
Sullivan, Patrick LA Mil. 1st Regt. 3rd Brig. 1st Div. Co.D
Sullivan, Patrick LA Inf. 1st Sp.Bn. (Wheat's) Old Co.D
Sullivan, Patrick LA 7th Inf. Co.C
Sullivan, Patrick LA 7th Inf. Co.I
Sullivan, Patrick LA 15th Inf. Co.D
Sullivan, Patrick LA 15th Inf. Co.I
Sullivan, Patrick LA 18th Inf. Co.H
Sullivan, Patrick LA 20th Inf. Co.G
Sullivan, Patrick LA Herrick's Co. (Orleans Blues)
Sullivan, Patrick LA Mil. Leeds' Guards Regt. Co.F
Sullivan, Patrick MS 1st Lt.Arty. Co.E
Sullivan, Patrick MS Lt.Arty. Stanford's Co.
Sullivan, Patrick MS Inf. 2nd Bn. Co.A
Sullivan, Patrick MS 10th Inf. Old Co.D
Sullivan, Patrick MS 48th Inf. Co.A
Sullivan, Patrick MO Lt.Arty. 1st Btty.
Sullivan, Patrick NC 3rd Arty. (40th St.Troops) Co.H
Sullivan, Patrick NC 2nd Inf. Co.A Cpl.
Sullivan, Patrick NC 6th Inf. Co.A Cpl.
Sullivan, Patrick NC 31st Inf. Co.A
Sullivan, Patrick NC 57th Inf. Co.H
Sullivan, Patrick TN 1st Hvy.Arty. Co.F, 2nd Co.D Sgt.
Sullivan, Patrick TN Lt.Arty. Winston's Co.
Sullivan, Patrick TN 10th Inf. Co.H
Sullivan, Patrick TN 10th Inf. Co.K Cpl.
Sullivan, Patrick TN 34th Inf. Co.F
Sullivan, Pat. TN 34th Inf. Co.E Sgt.
Sullivan, Patrick TX Cav. 2nd Regt.St.Troops Co.D
Sullivan, Patrick TX 1st Hvy.Arty. 2nd Co.F
Sullivan, Patrick TX 2nd Inf. Odlum's Co.

Sullivan, Patrick VA 1st Inf. Co.C
Sullivan, Patrick VA 5th Inf. Co.G
Sullivan, Patrick VA 26th Inf. 1st Co.B
Sullivan, Patrick VA 27th Inf. Co.B
Sullivan, Patrick VA 33rd Inf. Co.E Sgt.
Sullivan, Patrick B. LA Mil. Leeds' Guards Regt. Co.F Sgt.
Sullivan, Patrick J. LA 13th Inf. Co.C,I Sgt.
Sullivan, Patrick O. LA 1st (Nelligan's) Inf. Co.F 1st Lt.
Sullivan, Patt K. MO 1st Inf. 2nd Co.A
Sullivan, Paulding A. TN 26th Inf. Co.C Sgt.
Sullivan, Paul T. MS 29th Inf. Co.I Music.
Sullivan, P.B. LA Mil. Bonnabel Guards
Sullivan, P.B. LA Mil. Irish Regt. Co.E
Sullivan, P.B. LA Mil. Leeds' Guards Regt. Co.F Sgt.
Sullivan, P.C. KY 11th Cav. Co.G
Sullivan, Peter AL 9th Inf. Co.K
Sullivan, Peter MS Inf. 2nd Bn. Co.A
Sullivan, Peter MS 48th Inf. Co.A
Sullivan, Peter VA Lt.Arty. Pollock's Co.
Sullivan, Peter VA 26th Inf. 1st Co.B
Sullivan, Peter L. VA 47th Inf. Co.A
Sullivan, P.F. AL 25th Inf. Co.I 1st Sgt.
Sullivan, P.G. AL 17th Inf. Co.G
Sullivan, P.G. AL 32nd & 58th (Cons.) Inf.
Sullivan, P.G. AL 58th Inf. Co.C
Sullivan, P.H. AR 45th Cav. Co.C
Sullivan, P.H. AR 1st Vol. Co.K 1st Sgt.
Sullivan, P.H. AR 38th Inf. Co.B Sgt.
Sullivan, Philip AL 1st Bn. Hilliard's Legion Vol. Co.A
Sullivan, Philip GA Inf. 1st Loc.Troops (Augusta) Co.I
Sullivan, Philip LA 1st (Strawbridge's) Inf. Co.A
Sullivan, Philip LA 7th Inf. Co.C
Sullivan, Philip TN Arty. Fisher's Co.
Sullivan, Philip TN Lt.Arty. Scott's Co.
Sullivan, Phillip GA Inf. 18th Bn. (St.Guards) Co.D
Sullivan, Phillip TN Arty. Marshall's Co.
Sullivan, P.J. AR 6th Inf. Co.H,B
Sullivan, P.J. TN 55th (Brown's) Inf. Co.H
Sullivan, Pleasant SC 6th Cav. Co.A
Sullivan, Pleasant A. GA 42nd Inf. Co.K
Sullivan, Pleasant L. TN Inf. 1st Bn. (Colms') Co.B Cpl.
Sullivan, P.M. KY 3rd Cav. Grant's Co. Sgt.
Sullivan, P.M. LA Mil. Bragg's Bn. Schwartz's Co. Cpl.
Sullivan, P.M. VA 10th Cav. Co.B
Sullivan, P.O. TX 5th Cav. Co.F
Sullivan, P.O. TX 35th (Brown's) Cav. 2nd Co.B
Sullivan, P.P. TX 2nd Cav. Co.I
Sullivan, Presley J. VA 30th Inf. Co.B
Sullivan, Preston KY 5th Mtd.Inf.
Sullivan, Preston SC 24th Inf. Co.I
Sullivan, Pune O. SC 7th Inf. 1st Co.K
Sullivan, Putnam FL Cav. (Marianna Drag.) Smith's Co.
Sullivan, Putnam 15th Conf.Cav. Co.B
Sullivan, R. KY Morgan's Men Co.C
Sullivan, R. TN 7th Inf.
Sullivan, Ransom B. MO 12th Inf. Co.E
Sullivan, Resen AL 23rd Bn.S.S. Co.F
Sullivan, Reuben L. MS 8th Inf. Co.D
Sullivan, R.F. TN 45th Inf. Co.I
Sullivan, Rice MO 1st N.E. Cav. Co.H
Sullivan, Richard AL Mil. 3rd Vol. Co.B
Sullivan, Richard GA Rowland's Bn.Conscr.
Sullivan, Richard S. AL 14th Inf. Co.D,B
Sullivan, Richard T. NC 2nd Arty. (36th St.Troops) Co.I
Sullivan, Richard W. SC 5th Cav. Co.E
Sullivan, Riley AL 28th Inf. Co.F
Sullivan, Risen AL 1st Bn. Hilliard's Legion Vol. Co.F
Sullivan, R. Lafayette MS 20th Inf. Co.I
Sullivan, R.M. AR 8th Cav. Co.E
Sullivan, R.M. SC 4th Cav. Co.D
Sullivan, Robert AR 2nd Inf. Co.G
Sullivan, Robert KY 2nd (Duke's) Cav. Co.I,A
Sullivan, Robert LA 2nd Inf. Co.A
Sullivan, Robert SC 9th Inf. Co.A
Sullivan, Robert SC 22nd Inf. Co.A
Sullivan, Robert TN 45th Inf. Co.C
Sullivan, Robert VA 21st Cav. Co.A
Sullivan, Robert A. TX 4th Inf. Co.F
Sullivan, Robert E. LA 1st Cav. Co.B
Sullivan, Robert H. MS 19th Inf. Co.G
Sullivan, Robert M. SC 1st (Hagood's) Inf. 2nd Co.D
Sullivan, Roger VA Inf. 1st Bn. Co.B
Sullivan, Rogers GA 4th (Clinch's) Cav. Co.C
Sullivan, Rogers GA Hvy.Arty. 22nd Bn. Co.E
Sullivan, Rogger GA 26th Inf. Atkinson's Co.B
Sullivan, R.P. TN 51st Inf. Co.A Cpl.
Sullivan, R.P. TN 51st (Cons.) Inf. Co.H Cpl.
Sullivan, R.R. 2nd Conf.Eng.Troops Co.A Artif.
Sullivan, Rufus MS 35th Inf.
Sullivan, R.W. SC Manigault's Bn.Vol. Co.A
Sullivan, R.W. VA 30th Inf. Co.D
Sullivan, S. GA Inf. 10th Bn. Co.E
Sullivan, S. GA Inf. 14th Bn. (St.Guards) Co.H
Sullivan, S. MS Inf. 2nd Bn. Co.I
Sullivan, S. MS 48th Inf. Co.I
Sullivan, Sampson SC 1st Inf. Co.C
Sullivan, Sampson W. SC 24th Inf. Co.I
Sullivan, Samuel LA 21st (Kennedy's) Inf. Co.E 2nd Lt.
Sullivan, Samuel SC 1st (Butler's) Inf. Co.A,H
Sullivan, Samuel TN 18th Inf. Co.D
Sullivan, Samuel TX 3rd Cav. Co.I
Sullivan, Samuel D. TX 13th Cav. Co.C Cpl.
Sullivan, Samuel J. KY 3rd Cav. Co.B
Sullivan, Samuel J. KY 3rd Mtd.Inf. Co.B
Sullivan, Samuel L. GA 11th Inf. Co.B Sgt.
Sullivan, Samuel N. AL 20th Inf. Co.I
Sullivan, Samuel N. FL 2nd Cav. Co.E
Sullivan, Samuel W. GA 3rd Inf. Co.E
Sullivan, Samuel W. SC Inf. Hampton Legion Co.C Sgt.
Sullivan, Samuel W. TN 20th Cav. Co.A
Sullivan, Samuel W. TX 22nd Cav. Co.E
Sullivan, S.C. TN 84th Inf. Co.C
Sullivan, Seaburn J. TX 6th Inf. Co.E
Sullivan, S.H. GA 6th Inf. (St.Guards) Co.D
Sullivan, Sidney S. GA 4th Inf. Co.K Sgt.
Sullivan, Silas GA 6th Inf. Co.C
Sullivan, Sim MS Inf. 2nd Bn. (St.Troops) Co.F
Sullivan, Simeon VA 30th Inf. Co.D
Sullivan, Simon MS 21st Inf. Co.L
Sullivan, Simon R. LA Arty. Moody's Co. (Madison Lt.Arty.)
Sullivan, Sol AL 15th Bn.Part.Rangers Co.D
Sullivan, Solomon AL 56th Part.Rangers Co.D
Sullivan, Solomon FL 8th Inf. Co.A Cpl.
Sullivan, Solomon L. GA Lt.Arty. 14th Bn. Co.B
Sullivan, Squire TN 2nd (Ashby's) Cav. Co.D
Sullivan, S.R. MS 8th Inf. Co.C
Sullivan, Stephen LA 1st (Strawbridge's) Inf. Co.B
Sullivan, Stephen, Jr. MS 5th Inf. (St.Troops) Co.G
Sullivan, Stephen, Sr. MS 5th Inf. (St.Troops) Co.G
Sullivan, Stephen B. AL 3rd Cav. Co.G
Sullivan, Stephen F. AR Inf. Hardy's Regt. Co.D
Sullivan, Stephen T. AR 24th Inf. Co.F
Sullivan, S.W. FL 2nd Cav. Co.G
Sullivan, S.W. FL Cav. 5th Bn. Co.A
Sullivan, S.W. GA 8th Cav.
Sullivan, Sylvanus TN 41st Inf. Co.A
Sullivan, Sylvester TN 34th Inf. Co.E
Sullivan, T. GA 5th Res. Co.A
Sullivan, T. GA 8th Inf. Co.C
Sullivan, T. KY 9th Cav. Co.C
Sullivan, T. LA 21st (Kennedy's) Inf. Co.D
Sullivan, T. VA 9th Cav.
Sullivan, T.D. TN 4th (Murray's) Cav. Co.H
Sullivan, T.D. TN 8th (Smith's) Cav. Co.C Cpl.
Sullivan, T.E. GA 46th Inf. Co.A Capt.
Sullivan, Templeton R. GA 30th Inf. Co.D
Sullivan, T.G. MS 8th Inf. Co.C 2nd Lt.
Sullivan, T.G. MS 24th Inf. Co.A
Sullivan, Thad LA 11th Inf. Co.I
Sullivan, Thadeus GA 21st Inf. Co.K
Sullivan, Theo AL 56th Part.Rangers Co.D
Sullivan, Theodore KY 4th Mtd.Inf. Co.K
Sullivan, Theodore D. TX 2nd Inf. Co.H
Sullivan, Thomas AL St.Arty. Co.D
Sullivan, Thomas AL 11th Inf. Co.C
Sullivan, Thomas AL 32nd Inf. Co.A
Sullivan, Thomas AL Rives' Supp.Force 9th Congr.Dist.
Sullivan, Thomas AR 5th Inf.
Sullivan, Thomas AR 18th Inf. Co.D
Sullivan, Thomas AR 18th (Marmaduke's) Inf. Co.E
Sullivan, Thomas GA Cav. 10th Bn. (St.Guards) Co.D
Sullivan, Thomas GA Lt.Arty. Daniell's Btty.
Sullivan, Thomas GA 64th Inf. Co.A
Sullivan, Thomas GA 64th Inf. Co.C,F
Sullivan, Thomas LA 3rd (Wingfield's) Cav. Co.F
Sullivan, Thomas LA Arty. Moody's Co. (Madison Lt.Arty.)
Sullivan, Thomas LA 1st (Strawbridge's) Inf. Co.F
Sullivan, Thomas LA Mil. 3rd Regt. 3rd Brig. 1st Div. Co.F
Sullivan, Thomas LA 4th Inf. Co.A
Sullivan, Thomas LA 4th Inf. Co.D
Sullivan, Thomas LA 7th Inf. Co.C
Sullivan, Thomas LA 8th Inf. Co.D
Sullivan, Thomas LA C.S. Zouave Bn. Co.F
Sullivan, Thomas MS 2nd Cav. Co.D
Sullivan, Thomas MS 7th Cav. Co.D

Sullivan, Thomas MS 9th Inf. New Co.B
Sullivan, Thomas MS 10th Inf. Old Co.K
Sullivan, Thomas MS 44th Inf. Co.B
Sullivan, Thomas MO 6th Cav. Co.I
Sullivan, Thomas MO 1st & 4th Cons.Inf. Co.B
Sullivan, Thomas MO 4th Inf. Co.A
Sullivan, Thomas MO 5th Inf. Co.F Cpl.
Sullivan, Thos. MO St.Guard
Sullivan, Thomas SC 1st (McCreary's) Inf. Co.K
Sullivan, Thomas SC 1st Regt. Charleston Guard Co.F
Sullivan, Thomas SC 8th Inf. Co.B
Sullivan, Thomas SC Inf. 9th Bn. Co.E
Sullivan, Thomas SC 26th Inf. Co.F
Sullivan, Thomas TN 1st Inf. Co.E
Sullivan, Thomas TN 10th Inf. Co.B
Sullivan, Thomas TN 12th (Cons.) Inf. Co.D
Sullivan, Thomas TN 22nd Inf. Co.K
Sullivan, Thomas TN 46th Inf. Co.H
Sullivan, Thomas TN 63rd Inf. Co.A
Sullivan, Thomas TX 1st Hvy.Arty. 2nd Co.F
Sullivan, Thomas TX 2nd Inf. Odlum's Co.
Sullivan, Thomas TX 20th Bn.St.Troops Co.B
Sullivan, Thomas TX 22nd Inf. Co.D
Sullivan, Thomas VA Lt.Arty. Hardwicke's Co.
Sullivan, Thomas VA 6th Inf. 2nd Co.E Music.
Sullivan, Thomas Conf.Inf. Tucker's Regt. Co.K
Sullivan, Thomas A. AR 2nd Inf. Co.B
Sullivan, Thomas A. TX 26th Cav. Co.B, 2nd Co.G Cpl.
Sullivan, Thomas B. KY 1st Inf. Co.B
Sullivan, Thomas D. GA 36th (Villepigue's) Inf. Co.F
Sullivan, Thomas E. GA 6th Inf. (St.Guards) Co.D
Sullivan, Thomas E. TN 4th Cav. Co.E
Sullivan, Thomas F. MS Cav. 3rd Bn. (Ashcraft's) Co.F
Sullivan, Thomas F. VA 7th Inf. Co.H
Sullivan, Thomas G. MS 41st Inf. Co.F
Sullivan, Thomas J. AL 5th Bn.Vol. Co.B
Sullivan, Thomas J. AR 11th Inf. Co.A
Sullivan, Thomas J. MS Artif.
Sullivan, Thomas J. SC Simons' Cav.
Sullivan, Thomas J. TN 7th Inf. Co.G Cpl.
Sullivan, Thomas J. TX 7th Cav. Co.I
Sullivan, Thomas L. MS 9th Inf. New Co.D, Old Co.B
Sullivan, Thomas M. GA 10th Cav. (St.Guards) Co.B Sgt.
Sullivan, Thomas R. TN 7th Inf. Co.F
Sullivan, Tim KY Lt.Arty. Cobb's Co.
Sullivan, Tim LA 4th Inf. Co.B
Sullivan, Tim LA 10th Inf. Co.D
Sullivan, Timothy GA Hvy.Arty. 22nd Bn. Co.E
Sullivan, Timothy GA 1st Inf. Co.F
Sullivan, Timothy GA 1st (Olmstead's) Inf. Guilmartin's Co.
Sullivan, Timothy GA 5th Inf. Co.C
Sullivan, Timothy GA 63rd Inf. Co.H,B
Sullivan, Timothy KY 4th Mtd.Inf. Co.D
Sullivan, Timothy LA 1st Hvy.Arty. (Reg.) Co.E
Sullivan, Timothy LA 1st (Nelligan's) Inf. Co.I
Sullivan, Timothy LA 1st (Strawbridge's) Inf. Co.C
Sullivan, Timothy LA 3rd Inf. Co.E
Sullivan, Timothy LA Inf. 4th Bn. Co.F
Sullivan, Timothy LA 5th Inf. Co.C Sgt.
Sullivan, Timothy LA 6th Inf. Co.D
Sullivan, Timothy LA 9th Inf. Co.E
Sullivan, Timothy LA 21st (Kennedy's) Inf. Co.E
Sullivan, Timothy LA 22nd Inf. Wash. Marks' Co.
Sullivan, Timothy NC 33rd Inf. Co.B
Sullivan, Timothy SC 1st Arty. Co.A
Sullivan, Timothy SC 1st Arty. Co.F
Sullivan, Timothy TN Arty. Fisher's Co.
Sullivan, Timothy TN 10th Inf. Co.E
Sullivan, Timothy TN 11th Inf. Co.G
Sullivan, Timothy VA 1st Arty. 2nd Co.C
Sullivan, Timothy VA 1st St.Res. Co.F
Sullivan, Timothy VA Inf. 1st Bn. Co.B
Sullivan, Timothy VA 27th Inf. Co.B
Sullivan, Timothy VA 41st Inf. Co.B
Sullivan, Timothy G. NC 1st Arty. (10th St.Troops) Co.I
Sullivan, Timothy G. NC 2nd Arty. (36th St.Troops) Co.A
Sullivan, Timothy W. MS 2nd Inf. (A. of 10,000) Co.H Sgt.
Sullivan, T.J.H. MS 46th Inf. Co.B
Sullivan, T.M. TN 18th Inf. Co.H
Sullivan, T.O. GA 5th Res. Co.G
Sullivan, T.R. TN 11th (Holman's) Cav. Co.H 1st Sgt.
Sullivan, T.R. TN Douglass' Bn.Part.Rangers Coffee's Co. 1st Sgt.
Sullivan, T.T. AL 15th Bn.Part.Rangers Co.D
Sullivan, Tyson E. 1st Choctaw & Chickasaw Mtd.Rifles 1st Co.K
Sullivan, Ulysess SC Inf. Holcombe Legion Co.D
Sullivan, Ulysses GA 11th Inf. Co.B 1st Sgt.
Sullivan, Uriah NC 2nd Arty. (36th St.Troops) Co.D Sgt.
Sullivan, Uriah Sig.Corps,CSA Cpl.
Sullivan, V.F. KY 9th Cav. Co.A Cpl.
Sullivan, W. AL 28th Inf. Co.C
Sullivan, W. AL Cp. of Instr. Talladega
Sullivan, W. FL 11th Inf. Co.G
Sullivan, W. GA Inf. 19th Bn. (St.Guards) Co.C
Sullivan, W. KY 4th Cav. Co.A
Sullivan, W. TN 14th (Neely's) Cav. Co.G
Sullivan, W. TN Lt.Arty. Rice's Btty.
Sullivan, W. VA Mtd.Riflemen St.Martin's Co.
Sullivan, W.A. MS St.Cav. 2nd Bn. (Harris') Co.C
Sullivan, W.A. TN 84th Inf. Co.C
Sullivan, Wade TX 22nd Inf. Co.D
Sullivan, Warren M. GA 36th (Broyles') Inf. Co.B Cpl.
Sullivan, W.B. NC 14th Inf. Co.H
Sullivan, W.B. TX 2nd Inf. Co.H
Sullivan, W.C. GA 45th Inf. Co.K
Sullivan, W.D. GA Inf. 1st Loc.Troops (Augusta) Co.E,F 1st Sgt.
Sullivan, W.D. GA 65th Inf. Co.G 2nd Lt.
Sullivan, W.D. SC Inf. Hampton Legion Co.E
Sullivan, W.E. TN 12th (Cons.) Inf. Co.D
Sullivan, W.E. TN 22nd Inf. Co.K
Sullivan, Wesley NC 4th Inf. Co.I
Sullivan, Wesley VA 6th Bn.Res. Co.F
Sullivan, Wesley E. NC 14th Inf. Co.I
Sullivan, W.F. VA Inf. 2nd Bn.Loc.Def. Co.F
Sullivan, W.G. MS Cav. Davenport's Bn. (St.Troops) Co.A
Sullivan, W.G. MS 24th Inf. Co.F
Sullivan, W.H. KY 7th Mtd.Inf. Co.B
Sullivan, W.H. SC Inf. Holcombe Legion Co.C
Sullivan, W.H. TN 5th Inf. 2nd Co.I
Sullivan, W.H. TN 46th Inf. Co.E Sgt.
Sullivan, W.H. TN 84th Inf. Co.C
Sullivan, W.H. TX 13th Vol. 1st Co.K
Sullivan, Wiley MS Inf. 2nd St.Troops Co.M
Sullivan, Wiley NC 50th Inf. Co.C
Sullivan, William AL 24th Inf. Co.I
Sullivan, William FL 8th Inf. Co.A Music.
Sullivan, William GA 62nd Cav. Co.A
Sullivan, William GA Inf. 11th Bn. (St.Guards) Co.C
Sullivan, William GA 36th (Villepigue's) Inf. Co.H
Sullivan, William GA 65th Inf. Co.G Sgt.
Sullivan, William KY 4th Mtd.Inf. Co.B
Sullivan, William LA 3rd (Wingfield's) Cav. Co.G
Sullivan, William LA Ogden's Cav. Co.G Sgt.
Sullivan, William LA Mil. 1st Regt. 3rd Brig. 1st Div. Co.D
Sullivan, William LA 10th Inf. Co.F
Sullivan, William LA 13th Inf. Co.B
Sullivan, William LA Mtd.Rifles Miller's Ind.Co.
Sullivan, William MS Inf. 1st Bn.St.Troops (12 mo. '62-3) Co.E
Sullivan, William MO Cav. Coffee's Regt. Co.K
Sullivan, William MO Cav. Freeman's Regt. Co.L
Sullivan, William MO Cav. Williams' Regt. Co.E
Sullivan, William NC 50th Inf. Co.C
Sullivan, William NC 57th Inf. Co.D
Sullivan, William SC Inf. 9th Bn. Co.E
Sullivan, William SC 11th Inf. 2nd Co.I
Sullivan, William SC 26th Inf. Co.F
Sullivan, William TN 2nd (Ashby's) Cav. Co.C 2nd Lt.
Sullivan, William TN 3rd (Forrest's) Cav. Co.C Sgt.
Sullivan, William TN Cav. 5th Bn. (McClellan's) Co.D 2nd Lt.
Sullivan, William TN Lt.Arty. Baxter's Co.
Sullivan, William (No.1) TN Lt.Arty. Kain's Co.
Sullivan, William (No.2) TN Lt.Arty. Kain's Co.
Sullivan, William TN 1st (Turney's) Inf. Co.H
Sullivan, William TN Inf. 1st Bn. (Colms') Co.C
Sullivan, William TN 2nd (Walker's) Inf. Co.I
Sullivan, William TN 3rd (Lillard's) Mtd.Inf. Co.A
Sullivan, William TN Inf. 22nd Bn. Co.A
Sullivan, William TN 60th Mtd.Inf. Co.F
Sullivan, William VA Cav. 34th Bn. Co.F
Sullivan, William 9th Conf.Inf. Co.D
Sullivan, William A. NC 14th Inf. Co.I
Sullivan, William B. TN 7th Inf. Co.I
Sullivan, William B. VA 44th Inf. Co.F
Sullivan, William D. GA Cav. 7th Bn. (St.Guards) Co.D
Sullivan, William D. GA 1st (Olmstead's) Inf. Stiles' Co.
Sullivan, William D. GA 3rd Inf. Co.C
Sullivan, William D. GA Inf. 18th Bn. Co.B,C
Sullivan, William D. TN 7th Inf. Co.I

Sullivan, William E. TN 4th Cav. Co.E
Sullivan, William G. KY 4th Cav. Co.H
Sullivan, William G. MS 42nd Inf. Co.A
Sullivan, William H. AL Lt.Arty. 2nd Bn. Co.A
Sullivan, William H. AL 3rd Inf. Co.K
Sullivan, William H. MS 2nd Inf. Co.H,D
Sullivan, William H. NC 17th Inf. (2nd Org.) Co.H
Sullivan, William H. TN 7th Inf. Co.G
Sullivan, William H. TX 17th Cav. Co.D
Sullivan, William H. VA 1st Inf. Co.E
Sullivan, William H. VA 49th Inf. Co.A
Sullivan, William J. GA 3rd Inf. Co.E
Sullivan, William J. MS Cav. Buck's Co. Sgt.
Sullivan, William J. VA 3rd Inf. Co.F Sgt.
Sullivan, William M. TN 48th (Voorhies') Inf. Co.K 1st Lt.
Sullivan, William M. TX 4th Inf. Co.K
Sullivan, William O. TN Arty. Bibb's Co.
Sullivan, William P. MS 33rd Inf. Co.G
Sullivan, William P. SC 5th Res. Co.I 1st Sgt.
Sullivan, William R. MS 44th Inf. Co.D
Sullivan, William R. TX 15th Cav. Co.G
Sullivan, William R. TX 9th (Nichols') Inf. Atchison's Co. 1st Lt.
Sullivan, William R. TX Waul's Legion Co.E Capt.
Sullivan, William S. GA 36th (Villepigue's) Inf. Co.C
Sullivan, William S. MO 8th Inf. Co.B
Sullivan, William S. TX 18th Inf. Co.D Cpl.
Sullivan, William S. 1st Conf.Inf. 1st Co.A, 2nd Co.E
Sullivan, William T. AL 13th Inf.
Sullivan, William T. NC 2nd Arty. (36th St.Troops) Co.A
Sullivan, William W. GA 36th (Broyles') Inf. Co.B Cpl.
Sullivan, Willis C. MS 42nd Inf. Co.D
Sullivan, Wilson SC 4th Cav. Co.D
Sullivan, W.J. GA 45th Inf. Co.B
Sullivan, W.J. LA 27th Inf. Co.I
Sullivan, W.J. SC Inf. 1st (Charleston) Bn. Co.B
Sullivan, W.J. SC 27th Inf. Co.B
Sullivan, W.J. SC Inf. Hampton Legion Co.G
Sullivan, W.J. TN 8th (Smith's) Cav. Co.E
Sullivan, W.L. NC 53rd Inf. Co.B
Sullivan, W.M. TN Inf. 2nd Cons.Regt. Co.I
Sullivan, W.N. MS Cav. 3rd Bn.Res. Co.A Sgt.
Sullivan, Woodson J. VA Lt.Arty. 38th Bn. Co.C Cpl.
Sullivan, W.P. AR 10th Inf. Co.K,I
Sullivan, W.P. MS 5th Cav. Co.B
Sullivan, W.P. MS 3rd Inf. (St.Troops) Co.H Sgt.
Sullivan, W.P. MS 46th Inf. Co.B
Sullivan, W.P. SC 3rd Inf. Co.A Cpl.
Sullivan, W.P. TN 45th Inf. Co.F Ord.Sgt.
Sullivan, W.R. LA 1st Cav. Robinson's Co.
Sullivan, W.R. SC Arty. Stuart's Co. (Beaufort Vol.Arty.)
Sullivan, W.R. SC 1st St.Troops Co.G
Sullivan, W.R. SC 3rd Res. Co.C
Sullivan, W.R. SC 16th Inf. Co.E
Sullivan, W.R. TX 26th Cav. 1st Co.G 1st Lt.
Sullivan, W.S. AR 45th Cav. Co.C
Sullivan, W.S. AR 38th Inf. Co.B
Sullivan, W.S. LA Mil. Beauregard Bn. Frobus' Co.
Sullivan, W.S. MS 7th Cav. Co.H
Sullivan, W.S. MS 2nd Inf. (A. of 10,000) Co.G
Sullivan, W.T. GA 21st Inf. Co.B
Sullivan, W.T. GA 51st Inf. Co.B
Sullivan, W.T. 2nd Conf.Eng.Troops Co.A
Sullivan, W.T.J. Gen. & Staff Chap.
Sullivan, W.W. AL 56th Part.Rangers Co.K
Sullivan, Z.B. MS Inf. 3rd Bn. Co.I
Sullivan, Z.M. MS Inf. 1st Bn. Ray's Co. Cpl.
Sullivan, Z.M. MS 43rd Inf. Co.G
Sullivan, Z.R. KY 12th Cav. Co.E
Sullivan, Z.T. AR 30th Inf. Co.A Sgt.
Sullivant, Allen FL 10th Inf. Co.A
Sullivant, Andrew J. AR 9th Inf. Co.C
Sullivant, Asabel FL 10th Inf. Co.A
Sullivant, C. FL 9th Inf. Co.F
Sullivant, Caswell AR 36th Inf. Co.E
Sullivant, E.H. TN 14th (Neely's) Cav. Co.D
Sullivant, Gaston AL 41st Inf. Co.A
Sullivant, G.B. AL Cav. Chisolm's Co.
Sullivant, G.V. FL 10th Inf. Co.A
Sullivant, Henry TN 38th Inf. Co.G
Sullivant, Henry M. FL 10th Inf. Co.A Cpl.
Sullivant, Henry W. AR 33rd Inf. Co.K
Sullivant, H.J. AR 11th & 17th Cons.Inf. Co.G
Sullivant, H.R. AR 26th Inf. Co.H
Sullivant, Isaac NC 23rd Inf. Co.A
Sullivant, James MS 18th Cav. Co.H
Sullivant, James M. AR 4th Inf. Co.K
Sullivant, J.B. TN 31st Inf. Co.F
Sullivant, J.C. AR 19th (Dockery's) Inf. Co.C
Sullivant, Jessee MS 27th Inf. Co.D
Sullivant, Jessee, Jr. MS 27th Inf. Co.D
Sullivant, J.H. AR 6th Inf. Co.B
Sullivant, J.H. TN 14th (Neely's) Cav. Co.D
Sullivant, J.M. GA Conscr.
Sullivant, John AR 21st Inf. Co.E Cpl.
Sullivant, John FL 10th Inf. Co.A
Sullivant, John A. GA 26th Inf. Co.A
Sullivant, Joseph KY 1st (Butler's) Cav. Co.G
Sullivant, J.T. TX 26th Cav. Co.G
Sullivant, J.W. TN 14th (Neely's) Cav. Co.F
Sullivant, Levin R. AR 1st (Colquitt's) Inf. Co.I Sgt.
Sullivant, R.C.W. TX Cav. McCord's Frontier Regt. Co.D
Sullivant, Royal B. FL 10th Inf. Co.A 2nd Lt.
Sullivant, Ruffin NC Bass' Co.
Sullivant, Russel NC Bass' Co.
Sullivant, Silas MS 27th Inf. Co.D
Sullivant, T. GA 63rd Inf. Co.F Ch.Cook
Sullivant, Thomas J. AR Cav. Poe's Bn. Co.A
Sullivant, Tobias AL 3rd Res. Co.G
Sullivant, Tobias TN 38th Inf. Co.G
Sullivant, W. MS 9th Inf. Old Co.H
Sullivant, W. NC Mallett's Bn. Co.A
Sullivant, Wiley MS Inf. 3rd Bn. (St.Troops) Co.E
Sullivant, William MS Lt.Arty. 14th Bn. Co.C
Sullivant, William MS Lt.Arty. Merrin's Btty.
Sullivant, William TN 38th Inf. Co.G
Sulliven, Alx. TN 18th Inf. Co.D
Sulliven, C.T. GA 8th Cav. Co.A
Sulliven, P.H. AR 1st Vol. Co.K
Sulliven, Ransom VA 64th Mtd.Inf. 2nd Co.F
Sulliven, W. GA 8th Cav. Co.A
Sullivent, C.C. AR 37th Inf. Co.E
Sullivent, C.G. AR 37th Inf. Co.E
Sullivent, H.J. AR 11th Inf. Co.G
Sullivent, J.M. AR 37th Inf. Co.E
Sullivent, Marion AL 3rd Inf. Co.F
Sullivent, Thomas J. AR 11th Inf. Co.G
Sullivent, T.J. AR 11th Inf. Co.G
Sullivent, T.J. AR 11th & 17th Cons.Inf. Co.G,A
Sullivent, W.A. AR 37th Inf. Co.E
Sullivin, Willis AL 4th Inf. Co.K
Sullivon, Callaway TN 2nd (Ashby's) Cav. Co.D
Sullivon, Calvin TN 2nd (Ashby's) Cav. Co.D Bugler
Sullock, John H. TX 5th Cav. Co.C
Sulloway, Robert VA 1st Arty. Co.I
Sullows, J.W. AR 45th Cav. Co.M
Sullowski, Louis LA C.S. Zouave Bn. Co.B
Sullus, P.G. AR Cav. Davies' Bn. Co.E
Sully, Charles N. AL 43rd Inf. Co.E
Sully, Edwin VA 4th Cav. Co.H
Sully, Edwin VA Horse Arty. G.W. Brown's Co.
Sully, Edwin 1st Conf.Eng.Troops Co.E Sgt.
Sully, R.M. 1st Conf.Eng.Troops Co.E,D 1st Lt.
Sully, Robert M. VA 17th Inf. Co.A
Sully, T.O. Gen. & Staff Vol.ADC
Sulmond, J.B. AR 36th Inf. Co.G
Sulovant, John AR 17th (Lemoyne's) Inf. Co.G Cpl.
Sulph, W.J. VA 52nd Inf. Conscr.
Sulphin, Elijah VA Mil. Carroll Cty.
Sulphin, James VA Mil. Carroll Cty.
Sulphin, John A. VA Mil. Carroll Cty.
Sulphin, M. VA 54th Inf. Co.G
Sulphin, Wesley VA Mil. Carroll Cty.
Sulpice, F. LA Mil. 4th Regt. French Brig. Co.2
Sulpice, J. LA Mil. 3rd Regt. French Brig. Co.8
Suls, William NC 27th Inf. Co.A
Sulser, Adam VA 25th Inf. 1st Co.H
Sulser, Adam VA 62nd Mtd.Inf. 2nd Co.B
Sulser, Adam VA 77th Mil. Co.A
Sulser, Ambrose T. VA 25th Inf. 1st Co.H Music.
Sulser, Ambrose T. VA 62nd Mtd.Inf. 2nd Co.B Music.
Sulser, Andrew TN 42nd Inf. 1st Co.H
Sulser, Daniel T. LA 4th Inf. Co.D
Sulser, Francis O. VA 11th Cav. Co.B
Sulser, John LA 3rd (Wingfield's) Cav. Co.G 1st Sgt.
Sulser, John VA 25th Inf. 1st Co.H
Sulser, John VA 62nd Mtd.Inf. 2nd Co.B
Sulser, John VA 77th Mil. Co.A
Sulser, John T. VA 11th Cav. Co.B
Sulser, Samuel AL 28th Inf. Co.E
Sulsor, Larkin VA 64th Mtd.Inf. Co.I Cpl.
Sult, Harvey VA 63rd Inf. Co.H
Sult, Harvey VA Mil. Wythe Cty.
Sult, John VA Mil. Wythe Cty.
Sult, Peter VA 51st Inf. Co.F
Sult, Rufus VA 63rd Inf. Co.H
Sult, Rufus VA Mil. Wythe Cty.
Sult, William H. VA 37th Inf. Co.B Sgt.
Sulter, William AL Coosa Cty.Res. W.W. Griffin's Co.
Sul te skie 1st Cherokee Mtd.Rifles Co.E
Sultner, M. LA 14th Inf. Co.F

Sultner, Victor LA 14th Inf. Co.F
Sulton, Frederick E. NC 67th Inf. Co.H
Sulton, Joseph SC 15th Inf. Co.I
Sulton, R.J. SC 3rd Inf. Co.C
Sultz, F. VA 7th Bn.Res. Co.B
Sultzbacher, Sigmond MS 9th Inf. Old Co.B
Suly, J. LA Mil. 2nd Regt. 2nd Brig. 1st Div. Co.G
Suly, J.R. AL Coosa Guards J.W. Suttles' Co.
Sulzbuchor, A. AL Mil. 4th Vol. Co.K
Sulzer, J.L. NC 18th Inf. Co.A
Sulzifer, J. TX 7th Field Btty.
Sumach, James TN 15th (Cons.) Cav. Co.C
Sumack, J.W. KY 4th Mtd.Inf.
Suman, J.S. GA 47th Inf. Co.E
Suman, Patrick GA 23rd Inf. Co.C
Sumate, E.T. MS 5th Inf. (St.Troops) Co.I
Sumate, T.E. MS 5th Inf. (St.Troops) Co.I
Sumberland, David NC 17th Inf. (2nd Org.) Co.I
Sumberland, James T. TX 15th Cav. Co.C
Sumberlin, W.H. AL 42nd Inf. Co.E
Sumbers, W.M. NC 37th Inf. Co.K
Sumblin, Eli NC 17th Inf. (2nd Org.) Co.I
Sumblin, W.W. MO Inf. 3rd Regt.St.Guard Surg.
Sumborlin, William J. LA Hvy.Arty. 2nd Bn. Co.D
Sumbra, W.R. GA 10th Inf. Co.B
Sumer, B.B. GA 49th Inf. Co.F
Sumer, David VA Cav. 37th Bn. Co.D
Sumer, J. FL 10th Inf. Co.E Sgt.
Sumer, J. NC 8th Sr.Res.
Sumer, John VA Prov.Guard Avis' Co.
Sumeral, D.W. GA 54th Inf. Co.B
Sumeral, H. AR Lt.Arty. 5th Btty.
Sumeral, John SC 14th Inf. Co.C
Sumeral, John E. LA Inf. 11th Bn. Co.D
Sumeral, M. TX 3rd (Kirby's) Bn.Vol. Co.C
Sumeral, Moses TX 25th Cav. Co.F
Sumeral, Robert MS 46th Inf. Co.A
Sumerall, Eliphalet F. MS 6th Inf. Co.F
Sumerall, James T. TN Lt.Arty. Tobin's Co.
Sumerall, John M.W. GA 4th (Clinch's) Cav. Co.I
Sumerall, Robert MS Inf. 7th Bn. Co.G
Sumerall, W. 15th Conf.Cav. Co.H
Sumerall, William FL 9th Inf. Co.E,H
Sumerel, William VA 9th Inf. Co.E
Sumerell, Atlas NC 3rd Arty. (40th St.Troops) Co.A
Sumerell, Burton P. NC 55th Inf. Co.E Music.
Sumerell, Enoch H. SC 2nd Rifles Co.H
Sumerell, G.W. SC Lt.Arty. Jeter's Co. (Macbeth Lt.Arty.)
Sumerford, Samuel MS 1st (Johnston's) Inf. Co.H
Sumergill, Thomas GA Inf. 1st City Bn. (Columbus) Co.F 2nd Lt.
Sumerhill, H. GA 64th Inf. Co.E
Sumerlan, M.P. LA Inf. 7th Bn. Co.B
Sumerlin, Adam J. NC 55th Inf. Co.G Sgt.
Sumerlin, B. GA 7th Cav. Co.E
Sumerlin, David GA 61st Inf. Co.D
Sumerlin, D.J. FL 2nd Inf. Co.B
Sumerlin, Ivy GA 61st Inf. Co.D
Sumerlin, Jesse C. NC 52nd Inf. Co.F
Sumerlin, J.J. NC 66th Inf. Co.D
Sumerlin, John NC 55th Inf. Co.G
Sumerlin, L. NC 67th Inf. Co.B
Sumerlin, Lemuel NC 66th Inf. Co.K
Sumerlin, Madison FL 3rd Inf. Co.E
Sumerlin, Mitchell GA 1st (Symons') Res. Co.D
Sumerlin, W.A. GA Cav. 21st Bn. Co.B
Sumerlin, W.H. GA 47th Inf. Co.C 1st Lt.
Sumerlin, Wiley NC Loc.Def. Griswold's Co.
Sumerlin, William NC 3rd Arty. (40th St.Troops) Co.G
Sumerlin, W.N. NC 1st Arty. (10th St.Troops) Co.F
Sumero, Calvin NC 26th Inf. Co.I
Sumeroro, M.E. TX 10th Cav. Co.C
Sumerron, W. TN 14th (Neely's) Cav. Co.K
Sumerrow, G.H. TN 15th (Cons.) Cav. Co.G
Sumerrow, J.M. TN 15th (Cons.) Cav. Co.G
Sumers, A.J. MS 31st Inf. Co.I
Sumers, B.F. TN 22nd (Barteau's) Cav. Co.H
Sumers, D.A. AL Cav. Moreland's Regt. Co.F
Sumers, George VA 19th Cav. Co.F
Sumers, H. LA Mil. Chalmette Regt. Co.G
Sumers, H.L. LA 6th Cav. Co.I Sgt.
Sumers, John VA 24th Bn.Part.Rangers Cropper's Co.
Sumers, N.S. TN Inf. 23rd Bn. Co.B
Sumers, Robert AL 46th Inf. Co.H
Sumers, William N. NC 7th Inf. Co.A
Sumers, William R. NC 7th Inf. Co.A
Sumersall, J.L. GA 47th Inf. Co.H
Sumervill, Henry MS 31st Inf. Co.E
Sumervill, John AL Cav. 24th Bn. Co.A Cpl.
Sumerville, H.C. Gen. & Staff Asst.Surg.
Sumerville, H.P. TN 30th Inf. Co.B
Sumerville, Joseph M. TN 30th Inf. Co.B
Sumerville, Robert B. VA 1st St.Res. Co.F Cpl.
Sumerville, William H. TN 30th Inf. Co.B
Sumet, Eli NC 58th Inf. Co.E
Sumey, A. Franklin TN 4th (McLemore's) Cav. Co.D
Sumiga 1st Seminole Mtd.Vol.
Sumit, P.A. TX Cav. Border's Regt. Co.E
Sumler, William NC 3rd Arty. (40th St.Troops) Co.F
Sumlin, David NC 17th Inf. (2nd Org.) Co.F
Sumlin, E. TN Arty. Marshall's Co.
Sumlin, Eph TN 51st (Cons.) Inf. Co.B
Sumlin, Jesse NC 5th Inf. Co.G
Sumlin, Owen NC 15th Inf. Co.I
Sumlin, Richard MS 4th Inf. Co.C
Sumlin, W. AL Cav. 24th Bn. Co.A
Sumlin, Whitfield AL 53rd (Part.Rangers) Co.E
Summa, Alexander VA Inf. 21st Bn. 2nd Co.E
Summan, H. TN Inf. 3rd Bn. Co.G
Summar, J.B. TX 7th Cav. Co.K
Summar, M.S. TX 7th Cav. Co.K
Summar, T.D. TN Cav. 1st Bn. (McNairy's) Co.E
Summar, T.D. TN 21st & 22nd (Cons.) Cav. Co.A
Summarell, Sanford V. SC 14th Inf. Co.E Sgt.
Summars, J.D. TN 22nd (Barteau's) Cav. Co.C
Summars, Patrick GA Cav. 2nd Bn. Co.F
Summars, T.D. TN 22nd (Barteau's) Cav. Co.C Black.
Summay, William TN 29th Inf. Co.C
Summears, John MO 8th Inf. Co.F
Summeau, Joseph GA Inf. 18th Bn. (St.Guards) Co.C
Summer, A. LA 3rd (Wingfield's) Cav. Co.F
Summer, A. MS 3rd (St.Troops) Cav. Co.K
Summer, A.B. TN 35th Inf. Co.E 2nd Lt.
Summer, Adam G. FL 2nd Inf. Co.E 1st Lt.
Summer, Adam L. SC 13th Inf. Co.H Sgt.
Summer, A.G. Gen. & Staff Maj.,Comsy.
Summer, A.L. MS 3rd (St.Troops) Cav. Co.K
Summer, A.L. TN Inf. 22nd Bn. Co.B Sgt.
Summer, A.L. TN 35th Inf. Co.E
Summer, B.D. AL 8th (Livingston's) Cav. Co.H
Summer, B.H. TN 35th Inf. Co.E Sgt.
Summer, C. LA Mil. 3rd Regt. 1st Brig. 1st Div. Co.G
Summer, E. GA Inf. 1st Loc.Troops (Augusta) Co.I
Summer, E. GA 26th Inf. Co.K
Summer, Everett TN 23rd Inf. Co.H
Summer, F.M. SC 3rd Inf. Co.E
Summer, Frank AL 28th Inf. Co.E
Summer, F.W. MO 4th Cav. Co.K
Summer, G.M. SC 13th Inf. Co.H
Summer, G.W. SC 13th Inf. Co.H Cpl.
Summer, H. GA 1st (Ramsey's) Inf.
Summer, H.C. SC 3rd Inf. Co.H
Summer, Henry LA 21st (Kennedy's) Inf. Co.E
Summer, Henry SC 2nd St.Troops Co.F
Summer, Henry SC 4th Bn.Res. Co.C
Summer, H.L. SC 13th Inf. Co.H Sgt.
Summer, H.M. GA 53rd Inf. Co.D
Summer, Ivory TN 23rd Inf. Co.H 1st Sgt.
Summer, J.A. SC Cav. 19th Bn. Co.B
Summer, J.A. SC 13th Inf. Co.H
Summer, J.A. SC 20th Inf. Co.M
Summer, Jacob SC 3rd Inf. Co.H
Summer, Jacob SC 20th Inf. Co.F Sgt.
Summer, Jacob J. SC 13th Inf. Co.G
Summer, James A. SC 20th Inf. Co.M
Summer, James H. SC 13th Inf. Co.H
Summer, J.B. MS 16th Inf. Co.H Ord.Sgt.
Summer, J.B. MO 16th Inf. Co.C
Summer, J.B. SC 3rd Inf. Co.H
Summer, J.C. GA 53rd Inf. Co.D 2nd Lt.
Summer, J.D. MS 16th Inf. Co.H
Summer, J.G. SC 13th Inf. Co.H
Summer, J.J. GA 14th Inf. Co.F
Summer, J.N. MS 3rd (St.Troops) Cav. Co.K Cpl.
Summer, J.N. TN Cav. 1st Bn. (McNairy's) Co.E Cpl.
Summer, John AL 37th Inf. Co.G
Summer, John LA 20th Inf. Co.A
Summer, John LA C.S. Zouave Bn. Co.C
Summer, John NC 43rd Inf. Co.C
Summer, John A. TN 4th (McLemore's) Cav. Co.E
Summer, John A. VA Conscr. Cp.Lee Co.B
Summer, John C. SC 3rd Inf. Co.H Capt.
Summer, John F. SC 13th Inf. Co.H
Summer, John W. MO 2nd Inf. Co.I
Summer, J.P. AL 26th Inf. Co.A
Summer, J.S. AL 62nd Inf. Co.A
Summer, J.W., Jr. SC 20th Inf. Co.C
Summer, J.W., Sr. SC 20th Inf. Co.C
Summer, M. AL 8th (Livingston's) Cav. Co.H
Summer, M.B. SC 3rd Inf. Co.B 1st Sgt.

Summer, M.B. SC 13th Inf. Hosp.Stew.
Summer, N.W. TN Cav. 1st Bn. (McNairy's) Co.E 1st Lt.
Summer, R.P. SC 3rd Inf. Co.H
Summer, S.H. MD Inf. 2nd Bn. Co.A
Summer, T.J. VA 29th Inf. Co.D
Summer, W.A. SC 2nd St.Troops Co.F
Summer, W.H. GA 19th Inf. Co.D Cpl.
Summer, William T. SC 13th Inf. Co.H
Summer, W.L. SC 13th Inf. Co.H
Summeral, B. SC 14th Inf. Co.F
Summeral, James AL 42nd Inf. Co.E
Summeral, James GA 44th Inf. Co.D
Summeral, James 15th Conf.Cav. Co.H
Summeral, J.H. SC 27th Inf. Co.G
Summeral, William LA 1st (Nelligan's) Inf. Howell's Co.
Summerall, Allen FL 1st Cav. Co.K
Summerall, E. GA Mayer's Co. (Appling Cav.)
Summerall, E.B. FL 9th Inf. Co.F
Summerall, Elhaman GA 50th Inf. Co.B
Summerall, Elhannan GA 26th Inf. Co.A
Summerall, Elhannon GA Inf. (Brunswick Rifles) Harris' Ind.Co.
Summerall, G.W. GA Lt.Arty. Clinch's Btty.
Summerall, Henry FL 10th Inf. Co.D
Summerall, Jacob SC 7th Inf. 2nd Co.K
Summerall, J.H. SC 1st Bn.S.S. Co.C
Summerall, John W. FL 8th Inf. Co.I
Summerall, Richard GA Lt.Arty. Pritchard's Co. (Washington Arty.) 2nd Lt.
Summerall, Richard GA 5th Inf. Co.C Cpl.
Summerall, S.J. FL 2nd Inf. Co.B
Summerall, T. AL Mil. 2nd Regt.Vol. Co.B Cpl.
Summerall, W.H. SC Inf. 1st (Charleston) Bn. Co.B Sgt.
Summerall, W.H. SC 27th Inf. Co.B Sgt.
Summerall, Zachariah FL 1st Cav. Co.B
Summeran, R. 1st Conf.Inf. 1st Co.F
Summerau, H.S. GA Inf. 1st Loc.Troops (Augusta) Co.C
Summeraw, R. GA 36th (Villepigue's) Inf. Co.F
Summereau, H. GA Inf. 1st Loc.Troops (Augusta) Co.K
Summerell, Chancy GA 18th Inf. Co.K
Summerell, Charles F. NC 44th Inf. Co.C Sgt.
Summerell, H.W. SC 4th Bn.Res. Co.D
Summerell, Joshua P. AL 50th Inf. Co.A
Summerell, Marcus SC Inf. 3rd Bn. Co.C Cpl.
Summerell, Martin SC Inf. 3rd Bn. Co.E
Summerell, M.O. GA 18th Inf. Co.K
Summerell, Peter P. NC 3rd Arty. (40th St.Troops) Co.A
Summerell, Pleasant M. SC Lt.Arty. Beauregard's Co.
Summerell, P.M. SC 1st Cav. Co.F
Summerell, P.M. SC 4th Inf. Co.I
Summerell, R.A. AR 26th Inf. Co.K
Summerell, R.S. AL 22nd Inf. Co.I Cpl.
Summerell, T. SC Inf. 3rd Bn. Co.E Cpl.
Summerell, T.J. SC 4th Bn.Res. Co.E
Summerell, W.F. SC Inf. 3rd Bn. Co.C
Summerell, William W. NC 3rd Cav. (41st St.Troops) Co.G
Summerell, W.W. AL 57th Inf. Co.H
Summerell, W.W. SC Inf. 3rd Bn. Co.E Sgt.
Summerfield, Allen T. VA 10th Cav. Co.G
Summerfield, Benjamin VA Cav. Hounshell's Bn. Thurmond's Co.
Summerfield, James VA Hvy.Arty. 19th Bn. 2nd Co.C
Summerfield, John VA 62nd Mtd.Inf. 2nd Co.C
Summerfield, Joseph 1st Cherokee Mtd.Vol. 1st Co.A, 2nd Co.B
Summerfield, West 1st Cherokee Mtd.Vol. 1st Co.A, 2nd Co.F
Summerfield, Wilson A. VA 62nd Mtd.Inf. 2nd Co.C
Summerford, A. GA 8th Cav.
Summerford, Abram MS Cav. 3rd Bn. (Ashcraft's) Co.F
Summerford, Eli MS Cav. 3rd Bn. (Ashcraft's) Co.F
Summerford, George TN 3rd (Forrest's) Cav. Co.C
Summerford, George W. GA 45th Inf. Co.C,H
Summerford, G.W. MS 41st Inf. Co.D
Summerford, H.W. AL 60th Inf. Co.E
Summerford, H.W. AL 3rd Bn. Hilliard's Legion Vol. Co.A
Summerford, J. AL Cav. Stuart's Bn. Co.E
Summerford, Jackson GA 55th Inf. Co.A
Summerford, James AL Conscr.
Summerford, James AR Lt.Arty. Key's Btty.
Summerford, James GA 55th Inf. Co.A
Summerford, James T. SC 17th Inf. Co.K 2nd Lt.
Summerford, Jasper GA 55th Inf. Co.A
Summerford, Jasper N. GA 12th Inf. Co.F
Summerford, J.E. AL 1st Regt.Conscr. Co.D
Summerford, John AL Conscr.
Summerford, John GA 55th Inf. Co.A
Summerford, John SC 3rd St.Troops Co.C
Summerford, John H. GA Inf. 10th Bn. Co.D
Summerford, John J. TN 38th Inf. Co.E
Summerford, J.W. GA 31st Inf. Co.E
Summerford, L. MS Cav. 3rd Bn. (Ashcraft's) Co.F 1st Sgt.
Summerford, N. SC 1st Inf. Co.B
Summerford, Noah SC 18th Inf. Co.I
Summerford, Rufus L. 1st Conf.Inf. 2nd Co.H
Summerford, Thomas GA 55th Inf. Co.A
Summerford, T.M.J. SC 23rd Inf. Co.G Cpl.
Summerford, W. GA 5th Res. Co.H
Summerford, W.C. MS 1st (Johnston's) Inf. Co.H
Summerford, W.F. AL 45th Inf. Co.G
Summerford, W.H.H. GA 12th Inf. Co.F Music.
Summerford, William GA Inf. Cobb Guards Co.B
Summerford, William SC 1st Arty. Co.E
Summerford, William SC 5th Bn.Res. Co.C
Summerford, William SC 21st Inf. Co.L
Summerford, William J. AR 26th Inf. Co.A
Summergill, James GA Inf. 1st City Bn. (Columbus) Co.D Cpl.
Summergill, James GA Inf. 19th Bn. (St.Guards) Co.B
Summergill, Thomas GA Inf. 19th Bn. (St.Guards) Co.A Sgt.
Summerhill, E.B. AL 9th Inf. Co.D
Summerhill, H., Jr. AL 7th Inf. Co.K
Summerhill, Horrace AL 4th (Roddey's) Cav. Co.H 1st Lt.
Summerhill, Jackson GA 64th Inf. Co.E
Summerhill, James VA 38th Inf. 1st Co.I
Summerhill, James J. LA 12th Inf. Co.G
Summerhill, James W. MS Inf. 2nd Bn. Co.B 2nd Lt.
Summerhill, James W. MS 48th Inf. Co.B,I 2nd Lt.
Summerhill, Jason I.F. LA 28th (Gray's) Inf. Co.G
Summerhill, J.L. GA 1st Cav. Co.D
Summerhill, Norvel R. TN Holman's Bn.Part.Rangers Co.B
Summerhill, N.R. TN 11th (Holman's) Cav. Co.G
Summerhill, Thompson A. TN 1st Cav. Co.F
Summerhill, Thompson A. TN 7th Cav. Co.C
Summerhill, T.J. TN 11th (Holman's) Cav. Co.D
Summerhill, William GA Cav. Gartrell's Co.
Summerhill, William R. AL 27th Inf. Co.C Cpl.
Summerhill, W.R. MS Inf. 3rd Bn. Co.H Cpl.
Summeril, E.M. AL 5th Inf. Co.L
Summerlain, M.P. LA 15th Inf. Co.I
Summerland, Crocket LA 12th Inf. Co.H
Summerland, D.J. LA 2nd Inf. Co.C
Summerland, E. AL 7th Cav. Co.A
Summerland, J.T. AL 62nd Inf. Co.G
Summerlatte, Frederick TX Lt.Arty. Hughes' Co.
Summerlatte, Karl TX Lt.Arty. Hughes' Co.
Summerleyn, Randolph GA Siege Arty. 28th Bn. Co.H
Summerlin, --- LA 5th Cav. Co.I
Summerlin, A.J. AL 14th Inf. Co.B
Summerlin, Alexander AL 42nd Inf. Co.E
Summerlin, Allen NC 5th Sr.Res. Co.A
Summerlin, Allen L. NC 53rd Inf. Co.K
Summerlin, B. TN 6th Inf. Co.K
Summerlin, Benjamin GA 47th Inf. Co.D
Summerlin, Benjamin NC 8th Bn.Part.Rangers Co.B,E
Summerlin, Benjamin NC 66th Inf. Co.H
Summerlin, Benjamin F. NC 37th Inf. Co.F
Summerlin, Berrien GA 47th Inf. Co.D
Summerlin, B.I. AL 63rd Inf. Co.F
Summerlin, Calvin T. MS Lt.Arty. (The Hudson Btty.) Hoole's Co.
Summerlin, Charles H. NC 2nd Inf. Co.C
Summerlin, C.L. MS Cav. Jeff Davis Legion Co.D
Summerlin, C.M. AL 5th Inf. New Co.F
Summerlin, Columbus AL 63rd Inf. Co.D
Summerlin, Daniel TN 40th Inf. Co.H
Summerlin, Daniel J. FL 10th Inf. Co.F
Summerlin, David C. NC 51st Inf. Co.C
Summerlin, Dennis J. NC 2nd Inf. Co.C
Summerlin, D.J. MS 5th Inf. (St.Troops) Co.E
Summerlin, Eli GA Inf. 10th Bn. Co.D
Summerlin, Eli GA 47th Inf. Co.D
Summerlin, E.P. FL Inf. 2nd Bn. Co.A
Summerlin, F.N. GA 13th Cav. Co.F
Summerlin, George NC 30th Inf. Co.F
Summerlin, Giles GA 31st Inf. Co.C
Summerlin, H.C. 7th Conf.Cav. Co.L Sgt.
Summerlin, Henry C. GA 30th Inf. Co.K Sgt.
Summerlin, J. FL 2nd Cav. Co.H
Summerlin, James E. AL Inf. 1st Regt. Co.G

Summerlin, James E. GA 57th Inf. Co.F
Summerlin, James L. NC 51st Inf. Co.C
Summerlin, James M. NC 33rd Inf. Co.B
Summerlin, James M. NC 37th Inf. Co.F
Summerlin, J.E. GA 37th Inf. Co.F
Summerlin, Jerry NC 8th Inf. Co.C
Summerlin, Jesse NC 8th Sr.Res. Gardner's Co.
Summerlin, Jesse J. NC 8th Bn.Part.Rangers Co.A,C
Summerlin, J.H. TX 14th Inf. Co.B Cpl.
Summerlin, John AL 6th Inf. Co.E
Summerlin, John GA 26th Inf. Co.K
Summerlin, John NC 13th Inf. Co.G
Summerlin, John NC 66th Inf. Co.K
Summerlin, John A. FL 1st Cav. Co.C Capt.
Summerlin, John C. FL 1st Inf. Old Co.I,E
Summerlin, John C.B. FL 5th Inf. Co.E
Summerlin, John D. NC 51st Inf. Co.C
Summerlin, John F. NC 2nd Inf. Co.C
Summerlin, John H. NC 1st Arty. (10th St.Troops) Co.F
Summerlin, John J. NC 51st Inf. Co.C
Summerlin, John S. LA 12th Inf. Co.F
Summerlin, Joseph MS Lt.Arty. (The Hudson Btty.) Hoole's Co.
Summerlin, Joseph J. FL 4th Inf. Co.H 1st Lt.
Summerlin, Lemuel NC 8th Bn.Part.Rangers Co.B
Summerlin, Leroy F. GA 12th Inf. Co.H
Summerlin, Levi NC 51st Inf. Co.C
Summerlin, Luke FL 4th Inf. Co.H
Summerlin, Luke FL 11th Inf. Co.F
Summerlin, Luke GA 25th Inf. Co.D
Summerlin, Madison P. LA Inf. 1st Sp.Bn. (Wheat's) Old Co.D
Summerlin, Oliver NC 20th Inf. Co.E
Summerlin, Pinkney H. NC 2nd Inf. Co.C
Summerlin, Redding AL Inf. 1st Regt. Co.C
Summerlin, Robert MS 3rd Inf. Co.D Cpl.
Summerlin, Sidney NC 55th Inf. Co.B
Summerlin, Thomas NC 51st Inf. Co.C
Summerlin, T.S. AL 63rd Inf. Co.F
Summerlin, W. NC Mil. Clark's Sp.Bn. Co.D
Summerlin, W.A. GA 7th Cav. Co.E
Summerlin, W.E. AL 59th Inf. Co.H
Summerlin, W.E. AL Arty. 4th Bn. Hilliard's Legion Co.D
Summerlin, William NC 43rd Inf. Co.E
Summerlin, William A. GA 30th Inf. Co.D
Summerlin, William H. TX 18th Inf. Co.B
Summerlin, William T. MS 14th Inf. Co.F
Summerlin, W.R. AL 33rd Inf. Co.E
Summerlin, W.S. GA 16th Inf. Co.I
Summerlin, W.T. GA Inf. 26th Bn. Co.C
Summerline, James C. GA 35th Inf. Co.F
Summerline, Syrenius D. GA 35th Inf. Co.F
Summerling, L.D. NC Inf. 76th Vol. Co.D
Summerling, P.R. AL 20th Inf. Co.A
Summeron, George NC 11th (Bethel Regt.) Inf. Co.H
Summerough, W.H. GA Inf. 25th Bn. (Prov. Guard) Co.A
Summerour, Berry GA 2nd Cav. Co.D
Summerour, F. GA Cav. (St.Guards) Bond's Co.
Summerour, Harrison GA Cherokee Legion (St.Guards) Co.E
Summerour, P.L. GA Arty. Maxwell's Reg. Lt.Btty.
Summerour, P.L. GA 1st Reg. Co.D
Summerow, David F. NC 52nd Inf. Co.H
Summerow, George NC 26th Inf. Co.I
Summerow, Henry M. NC 52nd Inf. Co.H Cpl.
Summerow, Peter NC 26th Inf. Co.I
Summerow, Peter J. NC 11th (Bethel Regt.) Inf. Co.I
Summerow, P.L. GA 12th Cav. Co.E Sgt.
Summerow, William A. NC 1st Inf. (6 mo. '61) Co.K Cpl.
Summerow, William A. NC 52nd Inf. Co.H 1st Lt.
Summerower, J.L. GA Cav. Russell's Co.
Summerrall, Thomas J. FL 9th Inf. Co.K
Summerron, G.W. NC 23rd Inf. Co.B
Summerrow, Frank NC 52nd Inf. Co.H
Summerrow, M.P. TX 10th Cav. Co.C
Summers, --- MO St.Guard Lt.Col.
Summers, A. LA Pointe Coupee Arty.
Summers, A. MO 5th Cav. Co.F
Summers, A.B. TX 3rd Cav. Co.C
Summers, Abraham TX 36th Cav. Co.G
Summers, Achelies M. MS 33rd Inf. Co.C
Summers, Adam AL 57th Inf. Co.C
Summers, Adolphus C. NC 33rd Inf. Co.A
Summers, A.J. AR 2nd Inf. New Co.C
Summers, A.J. GA 66th Inf. Co.C 1st Lt.
Summers, A.J. VA 60th Inf. Co.A
Summers, Albert MO 8th Inf. Co.H
Summers, Alex. NC 3rd Arty. (40th St.Troops) Co.I
Summers, Alexander MO 8th Cav. Co.F,B Jr.2nd Lt.
Summers, Alexander NC 53rd Inf. Co.A
Summers, Alfred L. NC 4th Inf. Co.C
Summers, Alpheus M. AL 20th Inf. Co.I
Summers, Alvan H. GA Phillips' Legion Co.O 1st Sgt.
Summers, A.M. LA Mil.Conf.Guards Regt. Co.H 2nd Lt.
Summers, A.M. LA Mil. Fire Bn. Co.E Capt.
Summers, A.M. MS 22nd Inf. Co.E
Summers, Amos NC 54th Inf. Co.H
Summers, Andrew NC 21st Inf. Co.M 2nd Lt.
Summers, Andrew J. VA 19th Cav. Co.H Cpl.
Summers, Andrew J. VA 52nd Inf. Co.I
Summers, Andrew W. GA Inf. 1st Loc.Troops (Augusta) Dearing's Cav.Co.
Summers, A.P. TX 6th Cav. Co.C
Summers, Augustus F. NC 4th Inf. Co.C
Summers, B. GA Inf. 27th Bn. (NonConscr.) Co.E
Summers, Basil NC 33rd Inf. Co.A
Summers, B.F. NC 4th Sr.Res. Co.D
Summers, B.F. TN 45th Inf. Co.H
Summers, B.F. TX 14th Inf. Co.A
Summers, B.N. MO 16th Inf. Co.I
Summers, C. MO Cav. Schnabel's Bn. Co.A
Summers, C. NC Allen's Co. (Loc.Def.)
Summers, Caley A. AL 5th Inf. New Co.I
Summers, C.B. AL 30th Inf. Co.I
Summers, C.E. MO 2nd Cav. Co.E
Summers, C.G. TX 22nd Inf. Co.G,F
Summers, Charles VA 14th Mil. Co.B
Summers, Charles C. VA 17th Inf. Co.G
Summers, Charles H. MS 28th Cav. Co.C,I Cpl.
Summers, Charles M. MO Cav. 2nd Regt. St.Guard Co.G
Summers, Charles S., Jr. TN 14th Inf. Co.F
Summers, Christopher TX 3rd Inf. Co.I
Summers, C.J. TX 15th Inf. Co.C
Summers, C.L. TX Cav. Giddings' Bn. Carrington's Co.
Summers, Clinton H. SC 1st (McCreary's) Inf. Co.B
Summers, Columbus W. MO 8th Cav. Co.K
Summers, C.P. VA 20th Cav. Co.D Capt.
Summers, C.R. VA 8th Cav. 2nd Co.D Cpl.
Summers, C.S. TN 10th (DeMoss') Cav. Co.F Bvt.2nd Lt.
Summers, C.S. TN Cav. Napier's Bn. Co.C Bvt.2nd Lt.
Summers, Culey TX 4th Cav. Co.F
Summers, C.W. AR 27th Inf. New Co.C
Summers, D.A.F. SC 2nd Arty. Co.I
Summers, Daniel J. FL Milton Lt.Arty. Dunham's Co. 1st Sgt.
Summers, Daniel P. AL 11th Inf. Co.I
Summers, David B. VA 10th Inf. Co.G
Summers, David O. MS 16th Inf. Co.H
Summers, D.C. TX 1st Bn.S.S. Co.A
Summers, D.G. GA 3rd Res. Co.C
Summers, D.L. NC 3rd Jr.Res. Co.F
Summers, D.R. TN 4th (McLemore's) Cav. Co.E
Summers, Draton P. SC 1st (McCreary's) Inf. Co.B Cpl.
Summers, E. TX 24th & 25th Cav. (Cons.)
Summers, Ed AR 36th Inf. Co.K
Summers, Ed. LA 6th Inf.
Summers, E.D. TN 46th Inf. Co.F
Summers, Edmond TX Cav. Martin's Regt. Co.D
Summers, Edward KY 6th Cav. Co.I
Summers, E.J. TN 49th Inf. Co.I Cpl.
Summers, E.J. Inf. Bailey's Cons.Regt. Co.D
Summers, Eli VA 3rd (Chrisman's) Bn.Res. Co.B
Summers, Eli VA 146th Mil. Co.C
Summers, Elias NC 27th Inf. Co.E
Summers, E.M. LA 9th Inf. Co.K
Summers, Ephram AR 2nd Mtd.Rifles Co.I
Summers, E.T. AL Cav. Falkner's Co.
Summers, E.T. 8th (Wade's) Conf.Cav. Co.B
Summers, F. VA Cav. 41st Bn. Co.C
Summers, Felix W. MO 3rd Cav. Co.F Artif.
Summers, F.M. GA 18th Inf. Co.A Music.
Summers, F.M. MO 5th Inf. Co.H
Summers, F.M. TN 45th Inf. Co.H
Summers, F.M. TX 1st Hvy.Arty. Co.B,C
Summers, Fountain E.P. AR 27th Inf. Co.A
Summers, Francis GA 14th Inf. Co.F
Summers, Francis TN 34th Inf. Co.G
Summers, Francis M. MO Cav. Poindexter's Regt.
Summers, Gabriel R. SC 2nd St.Troops Co.G
Summers, G.B. MS 20th Inf. Co.K
Summers, George AL 89th Mil. Co.C Sgt.
Summers, George AL Gorff's Co. (Mobile Pulaski Rifles)
Summers, George GA 8th Inf. Co.H Cpl.
Summers, George SC 6th Cav. Co.F

Summers, George J. KY 2nd Mtd.Inf. Co.B 2nd Lt.
Summers, George J. LA 6th Inf. Co.B Jr.2nd Lt.
Summers, George L. KY 2nd (Duke's) Cav. Co.E
Summers, George L. KY 5th Mtd.Inf. Co.A Cpl.
Summers, George L. VA 17th Inf. Co.E Sgt.
Summers, George N. GA 9th Inf. Co.K
Summers, George N. GA Inf. 10th Bn. Co.E
Summers, George P. TN 35th Inf. 3rd Co.F Cpl.
Summers, George P. VA 52nd Inf. Co.I 1st Sgt.
Summers, George W. GA Cav. 20th Bn. Co.C
Summers, George W. MS 17th Inf. Co.H
Summers, George W. MO Cav. Poindexter's Regt.
Summers, George W. MO 1st Inf. Co.I
Summers, George W. NC 5th Cav. (63rd St.Troops) Co.K
Summers, George W. NC 1st Inf. Co.B
Summers, George W. NC 47th Inf. Co.K
Summers, George W. TN Arty. Marshall's Co.
Summers, George W. TN 9th Inf. Capt.,ACS
Summers, George W. TN 44th Inf. Co.K
Summers, George W. TN 44th (Cons.) Inf. Co.F
Summers, George W. VA 7th Cav. Co.D Capt.
Summers, George W. VA Cav. Mosby's Regt. (Part.Rangers) Co.A
Summers, George W. VA 17th Inf. Co.H
Summers, G.H. MS 18th Inf. Co.C
Summers, G.I. VA 11th Cav. Co.I
Summers, Givin L. MS 33rd Inf. Co.C
Summers, G.P. Gen. & Staff Capt.,ACS
Summers, Green TN Inf. 4th Cons.Regt. Co.F
Summers, Green P. AL 10th Inf. Co.A
Summers, G.T. SC 11th Inf. Co.H
Summers, G.W. AL 41st Inf. Music.
Summers, G.W. MO 1st & 4th Cons.Inf. Co.K
Summers, G.W. NC 4th Inf. Co.H
Summers, G.W. SC 5th Cav. Co.D
Summers, G.W. TN Inf. 4th Cons.Regt. Co.F
Summers, G.W. TN 16th Inf. Co.D
Summers, G.W. TN 41st Inf. Co.A
Summers, G.W. TX 1st Bn.S.S. Co.A
Summers, H. KY 2nd (Duke's) Cav. Co.E
Summers, H. KY 8th Cav. Co.C
Summers, H. SC 1st Inf. Co.L
Summers, Harper NC 21st Inf. Co.M Sgt.
Summers, H.C. NC Allen's Co. (Loc.Def.)
Summers, H.C. VA Loc.Def. Morehead's Co.
Summers, Henry KY 5th Cav. Co.G
Summers, Henry MO 1st Inf. Co.D
Summers, Henry TX Conscr.
Summers, Henry D. LA Washington Arty.Bn. Co.2,3
Summers, Hercules KY 3rd Cav. Co.A
Summers, Hezekiah NC 13th Inf. Co.A
Summers, Hezekiah H. LA 28th (Gray's) Inf. Co.F
Summers, Hiram A. MS 24th Inf. Co.F Sgt.
Summers, Hiram A. MS 27th Inf. Co.D Sgt.
Summers, H.J. GA 3rd Bn. (St.Guards) Co.D
Summers, H.J. GA 66th Inf. Co.H
Summers, H.L. MS 1st Bn.S.S. Co.C
Summers, H.M. FL 8th Inf. Co.A Sgt.
Summers, Hubert AL 62nd Inf. Co.G
Summers, Hugh VA 55th Inf. Co.L
Summers, Humphrey NC 4th Inf. Co.C
Summers, I.D. MS 1st Cav.Res. Co.E Cpl.
Summers, I.N. MS Cav. Yerger's Regt. Co.E
Summers, J. AL 3rd Res. Co.G
Summers, J. AL 40th Inf. Co.K
Summers, J. MS Inf. 1st Bn.St.Troops (30 days '64) Co.C Recruit
Summers, J. NC 7th Sr.Res. Boon's Co.
Summers, J. TN Inf. 2nd Cons.Regt. Co.I
Summers, J. TX Cav. Baird's Regt. Co.H
Summers, Jaazaniah NC 21st Inf. Co.M
Summers, Jacob KY 2nd (Woodward's) Cav. Co.A,B
Summers, Jacob SC Lt.Arty. 3rd (Palmetto) Bn. Co.F
Summers, Jacob SC 9th Res. Co.F
Summers, Jacob A. FL 2nd Cav. Co.A
Summers, Jacob W. Gen. & Staff A.Surg.
Summers, James AL 63rd Inf. Co.B
Summers, James GA 1st Inf. (St.Guards) Co.F
Summers, James KY 8th Cav. Co.G
Summers, James LA 16th Inf. Co.H
Summers, James MS Inf. 1st Bn.St.Troops (30 days '64) Co.C
Summers, James MO 4th Cav. Co.D
Summers, James MO 5th Inf. Co.G
Summers, James TN 1st Cav.
Summers, James TN 50th Inf. Co.F
Summers, James TN 50th (Cons.) Inf. Co.F
Summers, James VA 4th Res. Co.C
Summers, James VA 41st Inf. Co.B
Summers, James VA 136th Mil. Co.D
Summers, James A. GA 4th Res. Co.D
Summers, James A. NC 33rd Inf. Co.A Capt.
Summers, James B. AL Inf. 1st Regt. Co.D,G
Summers, James B. AL 5th Inf. New Co.I
Summers, James C. MS 16th Inf. Co.H
Summers, James C. TN 34th Inf. Co.G
Summers, James E. AL 3rd Inf. Co.F
Summers, James E. NC 4th Inf. Co.C 1st Sgt.
Summers, James H. GA Phillips' Legion Co.D
Summers, James H. KY 2nd Mtd.Inf. Co.H
Summers, James H. TN 7th Inf. Co.G
Summers, James M. AR 3rd Inf. Co.C
Summers, James M. GA 42nd Inf. Co.F Capt.
Summers, James M. MS Lt.Arty. (The Hudson Btty.) Hoole's Co.
Summers, James M. NC 37th Inf. Co.G
Summers, James N. NC 54th Inf. Co.I
Summers, James R. MO 5th Inf. Co.K Cpl.
Summers, James Robert MO Inf. 1st Bn. Co.B 1st Cpl.
Summers, James S. KY 3rd Cav. Co.A
Summers, James S. KY 3rd Mtd.Inf. Co.A
Summers, James W. KY Cav. 1st Bn. Co.B
Summers, James W. KY 4th Cav. Co.B
Summers, J.B. MS 26th Inf. Co.G
Summers, J.B. TX 12th Inf. Co.D
Summers, J.C. VA 59th Inf. 1st Co.B Capt.
Summers, J.D. MO 12th Inf. Co.K
Summers, J.E. AL 5th Inf. Co.I
Summers, Jehu AL 49th Inf. Co.B
Summers, Jerome VA Cav. Mosby's Regt. (Part.Rangers)
Summers, Jerome VA 3rd (Archer's) Bn.Res. Co.A
Summers, Jesse GA Cav. 29th Bn. Co.H
Summers, Jesse MS 33rd Inf. Co.F
Summers, Jesse MO 4th Cav. Co.D
Summers, Jesse M.W. AR 33rd Inf. Co.G 1st Sgt.
Summers, J.F. MO Inf. 4th Regt.St.Guard Co.A
Summers, J.F. TN 30th Inf. Co.K 1st Sgt.
Summers, J.H. MO 16th Inf. Co.I
Summers, J. Hugh AL 31st Inf.
Summers, Jim TN 19th & 20th (Cons.) Cav. Co.E
Summers, J.M. AR 5th Inf. Co.D
Summers, J.M. TN 21st (Wilson's) Cav. Co.F
Summers, J.M. TN 21st & 22nd (Cons.) Cav. Co.E
Summers, J.M. TN 16th Inf. Co.D
Summers, J.M. TN 27th Inf. Co.H
Summers, J.M. TX 7th Cav. Co.F
Summers, J.M.E. NC 2nd Jr.Res. Co.C
Summers, J.N. MS 5th Cav. Co.A
Summers, J.N. MS 1st (Johnston's) Inf. Co.K
Summers, J.N. MS 33rd Inf. Co.F
Summers, J.N. NC 64th Inf. Co.E,A
Summers, J.O. MO Cav. 8th Regt.St.Guard Co.A
Summers, John AL 5th Inf. New Co.B Cpl.
Summers, John AR 1st (Colquitt's) Inf. Co.D
Summers, John AR 9th Inf. Co.H
Summers, John AR Mil. Desha Cty.Bn.
Summers, John MS 21st Inf. Co.I
Summers, John MO 1st N.E. Cav. Co.M Sgt.
Summers, John NC 6th Cav. (65th St.Troops) Co.E,D
Summers, John NC Cav. 7th Bn. Co.E
Summers, John TN 10th Inf. Co.A
Summers, John TX 1st Hvy.Arty. Co.C
Summers, John TX 7th Inf. Co.H Music.
Summers, John TX 9th (Nichols') Inf. Co.F
Summers, John VA 8th Cav. Co.H Cpl.
Summers, John VA 25th Inf. 2nd Co.A
Summers, John VA 30th Inf. Co.B
Summers, John VA 62nd Mtd.Inf. 2nd Co.L
Summers, John Conf.Lt.Arty. 1st Reg.Btty.
Summers, John Inf. School of Pract. Powell's Detach. Co.B
Summers, John Inf. School of Pract. Powell's Detach. Co.D
Summers, John A. TN 38th Inf. Co.B QMSgt.
Summers, John A. TX 19th Inf. Co.D
Summers, John C. MS 26th Inf. Co.H
Summers, John C. VA 21st Cav. Co.H Capt.
Summers, John C. VA 60th Inf. Co.A Lt.Col.
Summers, John D. VA 52nd Inf. Co.I 1st Lt.
Summers, John E. VA 61st Mil. Co.E
Summers, John G. AL 16th Inf. Co.G
Summers, John H.P. NC 47th Inf. Co.K
Summers, John L. MO 10th Inf. Co.I
Summers, John M. AR 13th Inf. Co.F
Summers, John M. TX 18th Cav. Co.C
Summers, John N. NC 49th Inf. Co.C
Summers, John S. NC 7th Inf. Co.A Cpl.
Summers, John S. NC 49th Inf. Co.E 2nd Lt.
Summers, John S. TX 4th Inf. Co.B
Summers, John S. VA Cav. 36th Bn. Co.A
Summers, John T. MO 3rd Inf. Co.I 2nd Lt.
Summers, John W. FL 9th Inf. Co.D

Summers, John W. TN 4th (McLemore's) Cav. Co.E
Summers, Jonathan MS Inf. 1st Bn.St.Troops (12 mo. '62-3) Co.A
Summers, Joseph GA Cav. 29th Bn. Co.H
Summers, Joseph NC 15th Inf. Co.B
Summers, Joseph TN 5th Inf. 2nd Co.C,H
Summers, Joseph B. TN Cav. 7th Bn. (Bennett's) Co.D
Summers, Joseph P. TN 22nd (Barteau's) Cav. Co.F
Summers, Joseph T. MS Cav. 24th Bn. Co.A
Summers, Joseph T. NC 2nd Cav. (19th St.Troops) Co.B Sgt.
Summers, J.P. AR 37th Inf. Co.D Cpl.
Summers, J.P. TN 21st & 22nd (Cons.) Cav. Co.C
Summers, J.S. GA 3rd Cav. Co.F
Summers, J.S. TN 27th Inf. Co.B
Summers, J.T. MO 3rd & 5th Cons.Inf. Co.B 2nd Lt.
Summers, J.T. TX 28th Cav. Co.F Cpl.
Summers, Julius A. NC 4th Inf. Co.H 1st Lt.
Summers, Julius A. NC 22nd Inf. Co.A
Summers, Julius B. NC 47th Inf. Co.K Cpl.
Summers, J.W. FL 2nd Cav. Co.A
Summers, J.W. MO Cav. Schnabel's Bn. Co.A
Summers, J.W. NC Allen's Co. (Loc.Def.)
Summers, J.W. SC 2nd St.Troops Co.F
Summers, J.W. TN 55th (Brown's) Inf. Co.A
Summers, J.W. VA 7th Bn.Res. Co.A
Summers, L. GA 8th Inf. Co.H
Summers, L.A. NC Allen's Co. (Loc.Def.)
Summers, Larkin J. SC 1st (McCreary's) Inf. Co.B
Summers, Lasarus MS 4th Inf.
Summers, Lazarus MS 20th Inf. Co.K
Summers, Leonard F. AL 8th Inf. Co.C Capt.
Summers, Lewis P. VA 60th Inf. Co.A 1st Lt.
Summers, Lewis W. NC 37th Inf. Co.G
Summers, L.F. AL 62nd Inf. Co.D
Summers, Louis GA 8th Inf. Co.H
Summers, L.P. VA 59th Inf. 1st Co.B
Summers, Martin MO 3rd Inf. Co.K
Summers, Martin NC 1st Inf. Co.H
Summers, M.C. TN 35th Inf. Co.E, 1st Co.D
Summers, Michael VA 10th Cav. Co.H Cpl.
Summers, M.M. AL 18th Inf. Co.I 1st Sgt.
Summers, Moses TX 12th Inf. Co.G
Summers, M.P. TN 23rd Inf. Co.H
Summers, N. MS 2nd Cav. Co.G
Summers, N. TX Inf. 1st St.Troops Shields' Co.
Summers, N. TX 3rd (Kirby's) Bn.Vol. Co.A
Summers, N.A. NC 54th Inf. Co.E
Summers, Nancy, Mrs. VA 17th Inf. Co.G Laundress
Summers, Nathan C. NC 4th Inf. Co.C
Summers, Nieh M. AL 6th Cav. Co.H
Summers, N.M. AL 3rd Inf. Co.G
Summers, N.M. NC 1st Inf. Co.A
Summers, Noel F. NC 33rd Inf. Co.A
Summers, N.S. KY 9th Mtd.Inf. Co.F
Summers, N.S. TN 14th (Neely's) Cav. Co.H
Summers, P. LA 27th Inf. Co.B
Summers, P. NC 7th Sr.Res. Bradshaw's Co.A
Summers, Patrick GA 5th Cav. Co.B Far.
Summers, P.B. FL 8th Inf. Co.A
Summers, Perrian L. MO 8th Cav. Co.K
Summers, Perry NC 11th (Bethel Regt.) Inf. Co.D
Summers, Perry C. VA 25th Inf. 2nd Co.B
Summers, Peter NC 45th Inf. Co.C
Summers, Peter H. NC 27th Inf. Co.E
Summers, Pinkney NC 13th Inf. Co.K
Summers, P.M. NC Mallett's Bn. Co.B Sgt.
Summers, P.R. NC 53rd Inf. Co.A
Summers, R.M. GA 1st Res.
Summers, Robert AL 50th Inf. Co.B
Summers, Robert AR 21st Mil. Co.E
Summers, Robert AR 31st Inf. Co.G
Summers, Robert LA 1st Hvy.Arty. (Reg.) Co.A
Summers, Robert MS 36th Inf. Co.F
Summers, Robert C. NC 4th Inf. Co.C
Summers, Robert E. GA 56th Inf. Co.D
Summers, Robert E. NC 15th Inf. Co.B
Summers, Robert M. GA 8th Inf. (St.Guards) Comsy.Sgt.
Summers, R.P. GA Phillips' Legion Co.B
Summers, Rufus MO 12th Inf.
Summers, Rufus W. TN 2nd (Robison's) Inf. Co.F
Summers, R.W. AR 36th Inf. Co.B
Summers, S. AL Talladega Cty.Res. D.B. Brown's Co.
Summers, S. NC 3rd Jr.Res. Co.A
Summers, Sampson NC 3rd Jr.Res. Co.A
Summers, Sampson NC 4th Bn.Jr.Res. Co.A
Summers, Samuel AL 13th Inf. Co.A Capt.
Summers, Samuel NC 47th Inf. Co.K
Summers, Samuel H. NC 4th Inf. Co.C
Summers, Samuel R. TN 34th Inf. Co.G
Summers, Sanders NC 4th Bn.Jr.Res. Co.A
Summers, S. Augustus NC 27th Inf. Co.I
Summers, S.B. TX Cav. Giddings' Bn. Carrington's Co.
Summers, S.H. NC Mallett's Bn. Co.A
Summers, S.H. Gen. & Staff EO
Summers, Simeon MO 8th Inf. Co.F
Summers, Smith, Jr. MS 27th Inf. Co.I
Summers, Solomon TN 51st (Cons.) Inf. Co.A
Summers, Squire C. AL 41st Inf. Co.B
Summers, S.W. GA 4th Inf.
Summers, Sylvester VA 8th Cav. Sgt.
Summers, T.F. GA Cav. 9th Bn. (St.Guards) Co.C
Summers, Thomas AL 42nd Inf. Co.G
Summers, Thomas NC 4th Inf. Co.C
Summers, Thomas B. NC 4th Inf. Co.C
Summers, Thomas B. TN 10th (DeMoss') Cav. Co.F
Summers, Thomas F. VA Cav. 35th Bn. Co.A
Summers, Thomas F. VA 8th Inf. Co.D
Summers, Thomas H. TX 12th Inf. Co.G
Summers, Thomas J. AR 37th Inf. Co.F 1st Sgt.
Summers, Thomas J. TX 18th Cav. Co.B
Summers, Thomas J. TX 1st Bn.S.S. Co.A
Summers, Thomas M. MS 11th Inf. Co.D
Summers, Thomas R. TN 14th Inf. Co.F
Summers, T.J. TX 6th Cav. Co.K 1st Sgt.
Summers, T.M. MS 15th Inf. Co.D
Summers, T.M. NC Cav. McRae's Bn. Co.E
Summers, T.R. TN 24th Bn.S.S. Co.A
Summers, T.W. TX 10th Cav. Co.H Capt.
Summers, W. FL 2nd Inf. Co.H
Summers, W. GA 3rd Res. Co.C
Summers, W. GA Inf. 27th Bn. (NonConscr.) Co.E
Summers, W. GA 45th Inf. Co.C
Summers, W. MS 3rd Inf. (St.Troops) Co.K
Summers, W. VA 18th Cav. Co.G
Summers, Wappells VA 17th Inf. Co.H
Summers, Wash TN 63rd Inf. Co.A
Summers, Washington MO Inf. 4th Regt. St.Guard Co.A
Summers, W.B. AL 26th (O'Neal's) Inf. Co.E
Summers, W.C. AL 32nd Inf. Co.F
Summers, W.C. SC 1st (Hagood's) Inf. 1st Co.K, 2nd Co.A Sgt.
Summers, W.D. FL Lt.Arty. Dyke's Co.
Summers, W.E. TN 14th (Neely's) Cav. Co.H
Summers, W.E. Central Div. KY Sap. & Min.,CSA
Summers, Wesley AR 26th Inf. Co.H
Summers, Wesley GA 49th Inf. Co.F
Summers, Wesley W. Conf.Cav. Wood's Regt. Co.I
Summers, W.F. TX 1st Bn.S.S. Co.A
Summers, W.H. MO 3rd Inf. Co.F
Summers, William AL 8th Inf. Co.I
Summers, William AR 26th Inf. Co.E
Summers, William AR Fagan's Williamson's Co.
Summers, William GA 19th Inf. Co.D
Summers, William GA Phillips' Legion Co.D Sgt.
Summers, William MS 14th Inf. Co.B
Summers, William MO Cav. 2nd Regt.St.Guard Co.F Sgt.
Summers, William MO 5th Cav. Co.F
Summers, William MO 8th Cav. Powell's Co.
Summers, William MO Lt.Arty. H.M. Bledsoe's Co. Artif.
Summers, William MO 1st Inf. Co.D
Summers, William MO 1st Inf. Co.I
Summers, William MO 1st & 4th Cons.Inf. Co.D
Summers, William MO Inf. 6th Regt.St.Guard Co.G
Summers, William NC 7th Sr.Res. Bradshaw's Co.A
Summers, William NC 45th Inf. Co.H
Summers, William SC 2nd St.Troops Co.C
Summers, William SC 11th Res. Co.G
Summers, William TN Cav. Williams' Co.
Summers, William TX 28th Cav. Co.B
Summers, William TX 12th Inf. Co.G
Summers, William VA 8th Cav. Co.I
Summers, William VA Cav. Mosby's Regt. (Part.Rangers) Co.A,C
Summers, William VA Inf. 9th Bn. Co.A
Summers, William VA 14th Mil. Co.B Cpl.
Summers, William VA 25th Inf. 2nd Co.A
Summers, William A. SC 6th (Merriwether's) Bn.St.Res. Co.C
Summers, William A. TN 63rd Inf. Co.A 1st Sgt.
Summers, William B. VA 22nd Inf. Co.D
Summers, William C. VA Patrol Guard 11th Congr.Dist. (Mtd.)
Summers, William D. GA 1st (Ramsey's) Inf. Co.G
Summers, William E. KY 2nd (Woodward's) Cav. Co.D

Summers, William E. KY 4th Mtd.Inf. Co.B Music.
Summers, William E. MS Lt.Arty. (Issaquena Arty.) Graves' Co.
Summers, William E. MS 34th Inf. Co.E
Summers, William E. NC 21st Inf. Co.M
Summers, William F. VA 8th Inf. Co.D
Summers, William G. TN 18th Inf. Co.A Cpl.
Summers, William H. MS 16th Inf. Co.H
Summers, William H. MO Inf. Perkins' Bn. Co.B
Summers, William H. TN 2nd Cav. Co.C
Summers, William H. TN 23rd Inf. Co.H
Summers, William J. GA 20th Inf. Co.C
Summers, William J. VA Hvy.Arty. 18th Bn. Co.E 1st Sgt.
Summers, William M. AR 1st (Colquitt's) Inf. Co.C
Summers, William M. GA 52nd Inf. Co.H
Summers, William M. MS 31st Inf. Co.D
Summers, William M. MO 6th Inf. Co.D
Summers, William M. NC 27th Inf. Co.B
Summers, William M. TX 18th Cav. Co.B
Summers, William M. 14th Conf.Cav. Co.H
Summers, William N. NC 13th Inf. Co.K
Summers, William N. TX 18th Cav. Co.B
Summers, William R. NC 4th Inf. Co.A
Summers, William R. VA Lt.Arty. Moore's Co.
Summers, William R. VA 6th Inf. Vickery's Co.
Summers, William S. VA 22nd Inf. Co.H
Summers, William T. AL 11th Inf. Co.I
Summers, William W. MO 4th Cav. Co.I
Summers, W.L. MS 36th Inf. Co.F 2nd Lt.
Summers, W.M. GA 2nd Inf. Co.E
Summers, W.M. Taylor's Corps Capt.,AIG
Summers, W.P. GA Phillips' Legion Co.B
Summers, W.P. MO Inf. Perkins' Bn. Co.B 2nd Lt.
Summers, W.R. GA 19th Inf. Co.D
Summers, W.S. KY 2nd (Duke's) Cav. Co.K
Summers, W.S. LA 17th Inf. Co.B
Summers, W.S. LA Inf. Jeff Davis Regt. Co.J
Summers, W.T. AL 26th Inf. Co.F
Summers, W.T. TX 10th Cav. Co.E
Summers, W.V. AL 4th Res. Co.F
Summers, W.W. Gen. & Staff Asst.Comsy.
Summers, Xavier LA 5th Inf. Co.C
Summers, Zachariah TN 4th (McLemore's) Cav. Co.E
Summers, Zephaniah J. MS 33rd Inf. Co.C
Summers, Z.T. VA 63rd Inf. 1st Co.I, Co.E
Summersall, G.W. GA Cav. 20th Bn. Co.C
Summersell, John F. AL 24th Inf. Co.A Cpl.
Summersell, John W. AL 8th Inf. Co.E
Summersell, William AL Inf. 2nd Regt. Co.H Cpl.
Summersell, William Exch.Bn. 1st Co.A,CSA
Summerselle, George F. AL 3rd Inf. Co.B
Summerselle, William F. AL 3rd Inf. Co.B
Summerset, D.T. NC 1st Inf.
Summerset, Joseph J. AL 61st Inf. Co.G Sgt.
Summersett, Amos P. AL 39th Inf. Co.A
Summersett, Christopher H. NC 3rd Inf. Co.F 2nd Lt.
Summersett, James M. AL 18th Inf. Co.H
Summersett, John M. NC 51st Inf. Co.G
Summersett, John W. AL 1st Regt.Conscr. Co.H
Summersett, John W. AL 18th Inf. Co.H
Summersett, M. AL 18th Inf. Co.H
Summersett, Simeon AL 18th Inf. Co.H
Summersill, Elijah NC 8th Bn.Part.Rangers Co.F
Summersill, Elijah NC 66th Inf. Co.I
Summerson, Albert VA 15th Cav. Co.E
Summerson, Albert VA Cav. 15th Bn. Co.C
Summerson, Albert VA 25th Mil. Co.A
Summerson, Aurelius VA 26th Inf. 2nd Co.B
Summerson, Charles H. VA Inf. 45th Bn. Co.F Lt.
Summerson, J.E. VA 56th Inf. Co.H
Summerson, N.E. TX Cav. (Dismtd.) Chisum's Regt. Co.F
Summerson, Richard VA 21st Mil. Co.C
Summerson, Richard W. VA 26th Inf. 2nd Co.B
Summerson, Robert W. VA 26th Inf. 2nd Co.B
Summerting, J.T. AL 57th Inf. Co.F
Summerville, A.B. VA 10th Cav. Co.F
Summerville, Alexander VA 14th Mil. Co.E
Summerville, Alfo. GA 17th Inf.
Summerville, Charles MS 24th Inf. Co.A
Summerville, E.F. GA Floyd Legion (St.Guards) Co.H
Summerville, H. AL 40th Inf. Co.G Capt.
Summerville, J. KY 3rd Mtd.Inf. Co.E
Summerville, James TX 4th Inf. Co.F
Summerville, James W. AL 3rd Inf. Co.C
Summerville, J.B. NC 12th Inf. Co.F
Summerville, J.C. GA Inf. 4th Bn. (St.Guards) Co.G Cpl.
Summerville, J.L. KY 1st (Butler's) Cav.
Summerville, J.M. TN 15th Inf. Co.G
Summerville, John C. GA 24th Inf. Co.H
Summerville, John F. GA 1st Cav. Co.A Sgt.
Summerville, John W. NC 1st Arty. (10th St.Troops) Co.C
Summerville, Joseph AR 12th Bn.S.S. Co.A Cpl.
Summerville, Joseph AR 18th Inf. Co.H
Summerville, M.W. TX 26th Cav. Co.C, 2nd Co.G
Summerville, P.D. KY 12th Cav. Co.H
Summerville, R.H. Gen. & Staff Capt.,ACS
Summerville, Robert GA 35th Inf. Co.A
Summerville, Robert J. NC 4th Sr.Res. Co.E
Summerville, Solomon MS 15th Inf. Co.I
Summerville, T.N. SC 6th Inf. 1st Co.D, 2nd Co.G
Summerville, W.D. AL 7th Cav. Co.I,C
Summerville, W.H. GA 32nd Inf. Co.I
Summerville, W.H. 8th (Wade's) Conf.Cav. Co.D Lt.
Summerville, William Conf.Inf. Tucker's Regt. Co.I
Summerville, William F. TN 14th Inf. Co.I
Summerville, William I. GA 35th Inf. Co.A
Summes, E. TX Cav. Mann's Regt. Co.A
Summes, Joseph MD 1st Inf. Co.B
Summett, Daniel TN 59th Mtd.Inf. Co.E
Summey, --- 1st Choctaw & Chickasaw Mtd.Rifles Co.A
Summey, Alexander VA 64th Mtd.Inf. Co.E
Summey, A.T. NC Loc.Def. Lee's Co. (Silver Greys)
Summey, Charles GA 12th Cav. Co.E
Summey, Columbus C. NC 25th Inf. Co.A
Summey, David A. NC 52nd Inf. Co.H
Summey, D.F. NC 16th Inf. QM
Summey, D.F. Gen. & Staff Capt.,QM
Summey, F.C. AL 36th Inf. Co.H Cpl.
Summey, G.C. MS 10th Cav. Co.A Sgt.
Summey, G.C. MS Inf. 3rd Bn. (St.Troops) Co.A
Summey, George A. NC 39th Inf. Co.D
Summey, George C. MS Cav. Ham's Regt. Adj.
Summey, George W. NC 25th Inf. Co.H
Summey, James NC 25th Inf. Co.B
Summey, James SC 20th Inf. Co.A
Summey, J.J. FL 2nd Inf. Co.H
Summey, John GA Inf. 17th Bn. (St.Guards) Stocks' Co.
Summey, John SC 22nd Inf. Co.H
Summey, John S. NC 25th Inf. Co.A
Summey, John S.E. NC 1st Inf. (6 mo. '61) Co.E Comsy.Sgt.
Summey, John S.E. NC 11th (Bethel Regt.) Inf. ACS
Summey, Jonas NC 52nd Inf. Co.H
Summey, J.R. GA 66th Inf. Co.B
Summey, J.S.E. Gen. & Staff Asst.Comsy.
Summey, L.D. NC 57th Inf. Co.G
Summey, Nathan GA Inf. 17th Bn. (St.Guards) Stocks' Co.
Summey, Peter A. GA 3rd Cav. (St.Guards) Co.F
Summey, Peter A. GA 4th Inf. Co.F Sgt.
Summey, Thomas NC 39th Inf. Co.D Sgt.
Summey, William NC 16th Inf. Co.K
Summey, William NC 25th Inf. Co.A
Summit, Daniel TN 2nd (Ashby's) Cav. Co.A
Summit, Daniel F. NC 1st Inf. Co.D
Summit, Frederick AZ Cav. Herbert's Bn. Swope's Co.
Summit, Heglar P. NC 28th Inf. Co.C
Summit, Isaac L. NC 46th Inf. Co.K Cpl.
Summit, Joseph TN 62nd Mtd.Inf. Co.D
Summit, Peter TN 59th Mtd.Inf. Co.G
Summit, Pinkney NC 46th Inf. Co.K
Summit, William NC 25th Inf.
Summitt, Frank KY 2nd Bn.Mtd.Rifles Co.C
Summitt, George VA 23rd Inf.
Summonds, J.K. AL Res. J.G. Rankin's Co.
Summons, A.M. AL Cav. Hardie's Bn.Res. Co.C
Summons, Ben F. GA 3rd Cav. Co.A
Summons, G.C. VA 11th Cav. Co.I
Summons, Henry T. GA 45th Inf. Co.C
Summons, John TN Cav. Napier's Bn. Co.E
Summons, John VA 16th Cav. Co.F
Summons, Louis LA 7th Inf. Co.A Cpl.
Summons, W.D. AL 31st Inf. Co.D
Summs, Charles GA Inf. 1st Loc.Troops (Augusta) Co.E
Summy 1st Choctaw Mtd.Rifles Ward's Co.
Summy, Andrew NC 37th Inf. Co.H
Summy, G.C. TN Cav. 17th Bn. (Sanders') Co.C Sgt.
Summy, George SC 1st Arty. Co.K
Summy, Gilbert TN 29th Inf. Co.C
Summy, H.M. GA 1st Inf. (St.Guards) Co.F
Summy, Jason M. TN 29th Inf. Co.B 2nd Lt.
Summy, J.B. NC 11th (Bethel Regt.) Inf. Co.H
Summy, John TN 29th Inf. Co.C
Summy, Judiah NC 6th Sr.Res. Co.C

Summy, Lewis P. NC 62nd Inf. Co.E
Summy, Moses TN 4th Inf. Co.C
Summy, Moses TX 11th Cav. Co.C Sgt.
Summy, Peter W. SC 4th Inf. Co.J
Summy, P.W. SC Palmetto S.S. Co.L
Summy, William NC 20th Inf.
Summy, William SC 1st Arty. Co.K
Sumner, --- GA 45th Inf. Co.I
Sumner, Aaron VA 42nd Inf. Co.B
Sumner, A.C. GA 12th Mil.
Sumner, A.C. GA 28th Inf. Co.K
Sumner, A.E. TX 12th Cav. Co.B Cpl.
Sumner, A.H. TN Lt.Arty. Rice's Btty.
Sumner, A.H. TN 38th Inf. 1st Co.A
Sumner, Albert AR 1st Mtd.Rifles Co.G Sgt.
Sumner, Allen GA 26th Inf. Co.K
Sumner, Allen A. SC 2nd Arty. Co.D
Sumner, Amos L. VA 7th Inf. Co.D
Sumner, Andrew J. NC 61st Inf. Co.E
Sumner, Annuel VA 4th Res. Co.F
Sumner, Armstead VA 4th Res. Co.H
Sumner, Asa NC 3rd Inf. Co.B
Sumner, Asa NC 14th Inf. Co.B
Sumner, Ashley C. GA 1st (Olmstead's) Inf. Co.C
Sumner, B. NC Townsend's Co. (St.Troops)
Sumner, B.B. GA 49th Inf. Co.F
Sumner, B.D. AL 22nd Inf. Co.A
Sumner, Benjamin F. LA Scouts Ind.Co.
Sumner, Benjamin H. NC 38th Inf. ACS
Sumner, Benj. H. Gen. & Staff Capt.,Comsy.
Sumner, Berrien GA Inf. 10th Bn. Co.B
Sumner, B.L. GA Inf. (Emanuel Troops) Moring's Co.
Sumner, Bright NC 1st Arty. (10th St.Troops) Co.K
Sumner, Charles Conf.Reg.Inf. Brooks' Bn. Co.F
Sumner, Charles E. VA 5th Cav. (12 mo. '61-2) Co.G
Sumner, Charles W. NC 42nd Inf. Co.I Sgt.
Sumner, Daniel AR 23rd Inf. Co.G Cpl.
Sumner, Daniel E. VA 31st Inf. Co.C 1st Sgt.
Sumner, Daniel T. GA 11th Cav. (St.Guards) Folk's Co.
Sumner, David VA 63rd Inf. Co.G
Sumner, D.C. GA 28th Inf. Co.A
Sumner, D.C. VA Mil. Carroll Cty.
Sumner, Dempsey L. VA 5th Cav. (12 mo. '61-2) Co.G
Sumner, D.S. GA 64th Inf. Co.D
Sumner, Duke W. TN 1st (Feilds') Inf. Co.A
Sumner, D.W. TX 1st Inf. Co.F Cpl.
Sumner, Edward B. NC 17th Inf. (2nd Org.) Co.L Sgt.
Sumner, Edward B. TX Cav. Madison's Regt. Co.E
Sumner, Edward E. NC 1st Inf. Co.D 1st Lt.
Sumner, Edward E. NC 1st Inf. (6 mo. '61) Co.K 3rd Lt.
Sumner, Edwin D. SC 6th Inf. 2nd Co.E
Sumner, Edwin D. SC 9th Inf. Co.G
Sumner, Eli VA 22nd Cav. Co.K
Sumner, E.M. TN 15th Cav. Co.K
Sumner, E. McKee NC 38th Inf. Co.A
Sumner, Ephraim GA 40th Inf. Co.B
Sumner, Francis M. VA 4th Res. Co.H,I
Sumner, F.S. SC 15th Inf. Co.B
Sumner, G. GA Inf. Collier's Co.
Sumner, George AR 19th (Dawson's) Inf. Co.B
Sumner, George GA 28th Inf.
Sumner, George J. VA 1st St.Res. Co.I
Sumner, George J. Gen. & Staff Capt.,AQM
Sumner, George S. GA 10th Mil.
Sumner, George W. GA Inf. 10th Bn. Co.B Sgt.
Sumner, Giles AL 18th Inf. Co.B
Sumner, G.M. GA 28th Inf. Co.K
Sumner, G.M. GA 45th Inf. Co.H
Sumner, G.W. AL 15th Inf. Co.G
Sumner, G.W. TN 3rd (Clack's) Inf. Co.K
Sumner, Henry AL Inf. 1st Regt. Co.A
Sumner, Henry T. NC 2nd Cav. (19th St.Troops) Co.H
Sumner, H. Iverson AL 3rd Cav. Co.D
Sumner, H.J. AL 47th Inf. Co.F,C Cpl.
Sumner, H.J. AR 19th (Dawson's) Inf. Co.B
Sumner, I.N. KY 3rd Mtd.Inf. Co.G
Sumner, Isaac AL 3rd Res. Co.G
Sumner, Isaac NC 15th Inf. Co.A
Sumner, Isaac VA 45th Inf. Co.E
Sumner, Isaiah VA 63rd Inf. Co.D Cpl.
Sumner, J. AL 18th Inf. Co.B
Sumner, J. GA 54th Inf. Co.C Cpl.
Sumner, J. TN 51st Inf. Co.D
Sumner, J. VA 21st Cav. 2nd Co.D
Sumner, James GA Inf. 27th Bn. Co.A
Sumner, James KY 13th Cav. Co.B
Sumner, James NC 29th Inf. Co.E
Sumner, James TN 14th (Neely's) Cav. Co.F
Sumner, James TN 51st (Cons.) Inf. Co.F
Sumner, James B. NC 15th Inf. Co.H
Sumner, James C. AL 41st Inf. Co.E Sgt.
Sumner, James C. GA 64th Inf. Co.D
Sumner, James E. AL 5th Cav. Co.H
Sumner, James E. MS 1st Lt.Arty. Co.I Cpl.
Sumner, James E. NC 25th Inf. Co.A
Sumner, James J. AR 10th Cav.
Sumner, James O. VA Cav. 37th Bn. Co.D Sgt.
Sumner, James O. VA 24th Inf. Co.C
Sumner, James T. SC 2nd Arty. Co.D Sgt.
Sumner, James T. SC 9th Inf. Co.G
Sumner, Jathan VA 22nd Cav. Co.K
Sumner, Jathan N. VA 51st Inf. Co.H
Sumner, J.B. AL 22nd Inf. Co.A
Sumner, J.B. GA 4th (Clinch's) Cav. Co.F
Sumner, J.B. SC 1st (Hagood's) Inf. 2nd Co.H
Sumner, J.C. GA 1st (Ramsey's) Inf. Co.A
Sumner, J.D. GA 36th (Broyles') Inf. Co.E
Sumner, J.D. GA 42nd Inf. Co.G
Sumner, J.D. MS Cav.Res. Mitchell's Co.
Sumner, J.E. AL 3rd Cav. Co.H
Sumner, Jesse AR 34th Inf. Co.K
Sumner, Jesse C. GA 49th Inf. Co.F
Sumner, Jethro GA 54th Inf. Co.G Cpl.
Sumner, Jethro NC 17th Inf. (1st Org.) Co.D
Sumner, Jethro NC 17th Inf. (2nd Org.) Co.C
Sumner, J.H. MS 46th Inf. Co.G
Sumner, J.J. GA 14th Inf. Co.F
Sumner, J.L. Conf.Cav. Wood's Regt. 2nd Co.D
Sumner, J.M. GA 63rd Inf. Co.H
Sumner, J.M. KY 3rd Mtd.Inf. Co.G
Sumner, J.M. SC 3rd Inf. Co.D
Sumner, J.M. SC 15th Inf. Co.B
Sumner, J.N. MO 11th Inf. Co.D
Sumner, J.N. SC 1st (Butler's) Inf. Co.F,K
Sumner, John GA 1st (Olmstead's) Inf. Co.G
Sumner, John KY 13th Cav. Co.H
Sumner, John MS Part.Rangers Smyth's Co.
Sumner, John MO 8th Cav. Co.E
Sumner, John SC 5th Cav. Co.K
Sumner, John SC 15th Inf. Co.B
Sumner, John TN 63rd Inf. Co.K
Sumner, John TX 31st Cav. Co.C Cpl.
Sumner, John VA 54th Inf. Co.B
Sumner, John C. GA 64th Inf. Co.D
Sumner, John F. MS 20th Inf. Co.H
Sumner, John J. GA 64th Inf. Co.D
Sumner, John L. MS 10th Inf. Old Co.I
Sumner, John M. AR 10th (Witt's) Cav. Co.F
Sumner, John M. TN 9th Inf. Co.C
Sumner, John M. TX 9th Cav. Co.H
Sumner, John M.M. AR 1st (Colquitt's) Inf. Co.F
Sumner, John R. MS 34th Inf. Co.C Lt.
Sumner, John R. NC 22nd Inf. Co.M
Sumner, John S. GA 57th Inf. Co.I
Sumner, John W. GA 28th Inf. Co.K
Sumner, John W. KY 13th Cav. Co.B
Sumner, John W. MO 6th Inf. Co.I
Sumner, John William MO Lt.Arty. Parsons' Co.
Sumner, Jonathan R. VA 45th Inf. Co.E 1st Lt.
Sumner, Joseph GA 12th Inf. Co.F
Sumner, Joseph J. NC 17th Inf. (1st Org.) Co.D
Sumner, Joseph J. NC 17th Inf. (2nd Org.) Co.C
Sumner, Joseph L. GA 14th Inf. Co.G
Sumner, Joseph L. GA 64th Inf. Co.D Bvt.1st Lt.
Sumner, Joseph M. GA Inf. 10th Bn. Co.B Sgt.
Sumner, Joseph M. GA 14th Inf. Co.F Sgt.
Sumner, Joseph T. GA 48th Inf. Co.H
Sumner, Joseph W. AR 34th Inf. Co.K
Sumner, Joshua GA Cav. 10th Bn. (St.Guards) Co.C
Sumner, Joshua VA 22nd Cav. Co.K
Sumner, Joshua VA Inf. 7th Bn.Loc.Def. Co.C
Sumner, Joshua VA 54th Inf. Co.A
Sumner, Josiah VA 45th Inf. Co.E
Sumner, J.R. GA 49th Inf. Co.F
Sumner, J.T. GA 28th Inf. Co.A
Sumner, Julian E. NC 1st Inf. (6 mo. '61) Co.K
Sumner, Julius GA 26th Inf. Co.K
Sumner, J.W. SC 2nd Inf. Co.C
Sumner, Lewis TX 27th Cav. Co.D
Sumner, Lewis TX 20th Inf. Co.H
Sumner, M. AL 10th Inf. Co.B
Sumner, M. SC 1st (Hagood's) Inf. 2nd Co.H Cpl.
Sumner, Marcus L. NC 25th Inf. Co.H
Sumner, Marion M. SC 5th Cav. Co.K
Sumner, Martin NC 3rd Inf. Co.B
Sumner, Mathew AR 34th Inf. Co.K Cpl.
Sumner, Matthew GA 64th Inf. Co.D
Sumner, M.L. MS 18th Inf. Co.H
Sumner, M.M. SC 15th Inf. Co.B,I
Sumner, Nelson NC 22nd Inf. Co.L
Sumner, Nelson N. NC 1st Bn.Jr.Res. Co.A 2nd Lt.
Sumner, Philip B. VA 24th Inf. Co.C
Sumner, R. GA 2nd Mil. Co.H
Sumner, R.A. NC 14th Inf. Co.C
Sumner, R.B. LA Mil.Cont.Regt. Mitchell's Co.
Sumner, R.B. NC 4th Inf. Co.A

Sumner, R.E. TN Cav. Clark's Ind.Co. 2nd Lt.
Sumner, R.E. Buckner's Staff Lt.
Sumner, Reuben F. AL 28th Inf. Co.E
Sumner, R.H. GA 28th Inf. Co.A
Sumner, Richard R. NC 25th Inf. Co.A
Sumner, Robert GA 3rd Inf. Co.A
Sumner, Robert GA 32nd Inf. Co.C
Sumner, Robert GA Inf. (Emanuel Troops) Moring's Co.
Sumner, Robert VA 30th Bn.S.S. Co.E
Sumner, Robert B. NC 3rd Inf. Co.B
Sumner, Robert E. TN 1st (Feild's) Inf. Co.A 2nd Lt.
Sumner, R.R. NC 1st Cav. (9th St.Troops) Co.G Far.
Sumner, R.Y. GA 43rd Inf. 2nd Lt.
Sumner, S. KY 10th (Johnson's) Cav.
Sumner, S. KY Lt.Arty. Cobb's Co.
Sumner, S. TN 51st Inf. Co.D
Sumner, Samuel NC 25th Inf. Co.A
Sumner, Samuel SC 9th Res. Co.H
Sumner, Samuel VA Mil. Carroll Cty.
Sumner, Sebron GA 26th Inf. Co.K
Sumner, Shelby TN 51st (Cons.) Inf. Co.F
Sumner, Simon P. AR Cav. Wright's Regt. Co.F Cpl.
Sumner, Simon P. AR 3rd Inf. Co.C Music.
Sumner, Solomon GA Cav. 16th Bn. (St.Guards) Co.G
Sumner, Sol. R. GA 42nd Inf. Co.G
Sumner, S.R. GA 36th (Broyles') Inf. Co.E
Sumner, Stephen KY 13th Cav. Co.H
Sumner, Stewart GA 1st (Olmstead's) Inf. Co.C
Sumner, S.W.L. GA 28th Inf. Co.K 1st Sgt.
Sumner, T. VA Horse Arty. D. Shank's Co.
Sumner, Tazewell VA 22nd Cav. Co.K
Sumner, Thomas GA 5th Inf. Co.C
Sumner, Thomas J. GA Inf. 10th Bn. Co.B Sgt.
Sumner, Thomas J. VA Cav. 47th Bn. Co.C
Sumner, Thomas J. VA 45th Inf. Co.E
Sumner, T.R. TN Lt.Arty. Morton's Co.
Sumner, Truman L. AL 62nd Inf. Co.A
Sumner, W. KY Morgan's Men Co.E
Sumner, W.A. MS 28th Cav. Co.E
Sumner, W.A. MS 4th Inf. Co.F Capt.
Sumner, Wesley KY 13th Cav. Co.B
Sumner, Wesley VA 54th Inf. Co.B
Sumner, W.H. GA 32nd Inf. Co.E
Sumner, Wiatt VA 54th Inf. Co.B
Sumner, Wiley TX 14th Cav. Co.I
Sumner, William GA Arty. (Chatham Arty.) Wheaton's Co.
Sumner, William GA 1st (Olmstead's) Inf. Co.C
Sumner, William GA 1st (Olmstead's) Inf. Claghorn's Co.
Sumner, William TN 50th Inf. Co.D,F Cpl.
Sumner, Wm. A. AL 22nd Inf. Co.A
Sumner, William A. MS 2nd Part.Rangers Co.F,D 1st Lt.
Sumner, William A. SC 2nd Arty. Co.D
Sumner, William D. TN Lt.Arty. Huggins' Co.
Sumner, William G. AL 57th Inf. Co.E
Sumner, William H. NC 2nd Cav. (19th St.Troops) Co.H
Sumner, William R. GA Inf. 10th Bn. Co.B
Sumner, William R. GA 36th (Broyles') Inf. Co.G Sgt.
Sumner, William S. VA 1st St.Res. Co.D
Sumner, William T. NC 27th Inf. Co.F Cpl.
Sumner, William W. NC Cav. 12th Bn. Co.C,A
Sumner, William W. NC Lt.Arty. 3rd Bn. Co.C,A
Sumner, Willis T. GA 28th Inf. Co.K
Sumner, W.J. GA Phillips' Legion Co.D
Sumner, W.J. TX 11th Inf. Co.B
Sumner, W.M. SC 3rd Bn.Res. Co.A
Sumner, W.M. SC 4th Bn.Res. Co.A
Sumner, Wright GA 57th Inf. Co.B
Sumner, W.W. NC 1st Cav. (9th St.Troops) Co.B
Sumner, W.W. NC 4th Cav. (59th St.Troops) Co.K
Sumner, W.W. 8th (Dearing's) Conf.Cav. Co.A
Sumners, Abner TN 32nd Inf. Co.I
Sumners, Abraham H. TN 32nd Inf. Co.F
Sumners, Dallas AL 8th (Livingston's) Cav. Co.E
Sumners, Daniel M. TN 32nd Inf. Co.I Sgt.
Sumners, George W. TN 32nd Inf. Co.F
Sumners, George W., Sr. TN 32nd Inf. Co.I,F
Sumners, Isaac N. AL 16th Inf. Co.A
Sumners, James M. AL 41st Inf. Co.F
Sumners, J.J. TX Inf. Griffin's Bn. Co.G
Sumners, John AR 27th Inf. Co.A
Sumners, John NC 20th Inf. Co.D
Sumners, John TN 20th Cav.
Sumners, John D. AL 20th Inf. Co.D
Sumners, John M. TN 32nd Inf. Co.F
Sumners, W.H. MS 8th Inf. Co.A
Sumners, William A. TN 32nd Inf. Co.F
Sumners, William A. TN 32nd Inf. Co.I Capt.
Sumners, William E. MS 23rd Inf. Co.A
Sumners, William N. TN 32nd Inf. Co.F 2nd Lt.
Sumners, Willis B. AR 4th Inf. Co.K
Sumners, Wredoric TN 50th Inf. Co.F
Sumners, W.T. TX Inf. Griffin's Bn. Co.G
Sumnr, John A. GA 28th Inf. Co.K
Sumonis, John KY Horse Arty. Byrne's Co.
Sumons, A. AL 62nd Inf. Co.K Sgt.
Sumpayne, Jules LA 3rd Inf. Co.G
Sumpson, G.A. VA 7th Cav. 2nd Lt.
Sumpster, Benjamin VA 23rd Inf. Co.E
Sumpter, A.J. AR 37th Inf. Co.K
Sumpter, Alexander AR 16th Inf. Co.A
Sumpter, Alex. TN Inf. 2nd Cons.Regt. Co.E
Sumpter, Alexander TN 29th Inf. Co.D
Sumpter, Alexander McC. VA Lt.Arty. 38th Bn. Co.D
Sumpter, Asa VA 54th Inf. Co.A
Sumpter, Benjamin F. TN 29th Inf. Co.C Cpl.
Sumpter, B.F. AR 23rd Inf. Co.I
Sumpter, B.H. AR 19th (Dockery's) Inf. Cons.Co.E,D
Sumpter, Caleb MO 3rd Cav. Co.H
Sumpter, D.B. AR Matlock's 32nd Inf. Co.C
Sumpter, Edward TX 1st Field Btty.
Sumpter, Fielden MO 8th Inf. Co.H
Sumpter, Fielding MO Inf. Perkins' Bn. Co.A
Sumpter, George TN 1st Cav. Co.D,L
Sumpter, George TN 29th Inf. Co.D
Sumpter, George VA 63rd Inf. Co.K
Sumpter, George W. TN 29th Inf. Co.C
Sumpter, Harvey TN 29th Inf. Co.D
Sumpter, Harvy VA 25th Cav. Co.B
Sumpter, Henry TN 29th Inf. Co.D
Sumpter, Henry C. KY 1st Inf. Co.K
Sumpter, J. TX 30th Cav. Co.K
Sumpter, Jacob VA 54th Inf. Co.B
Sumpter, James AR 16th Inf. Co.A
Sumpter, James H. AR 26th Inf. Co.H
Sumpter, James H. MO Inf. Perkins' Bn. Co.A
Sumpter, J.H. GA 11th Cav. Co.D
Sumpter, J.L. GA 11th Cav. Co.D
Sumpter, Joel L. NC 39th Inf. Co.A,F Sgt.
Sumpter, John NC 26th Inf. Co.F
Sumpter, John TN 29th Inf. Co.D
Sumpter, John H. MO Inf. Perkins' Bn. Co.A
Sumpter, John H. VA 11th Inf. Co.G
Sumpter, John J. AR 3rd Cav. Co.F 1st Lt.
Sumpter, John W. NC 39th Inf. Co.F
Sumpter, John W. VA 19th Cav. Co.B,E
Sumpter, Joseph VA 54th Inf. Co.A Cpl.
Sumpter, J.R. AR 32nd Inf. Co.C
Sumpter, Lafayette TN 63rd Inf. Co.A
Sumpter, R.B. TN 2nd (Ashby's) Cav. Co.H
Sumpter, R.B. TN 8th (Smith's) Cav. Co.L
Sumpter, Samuel R. VA 2nd Cav. Co.B
Sumpter, W.H. NC Inf. Thomas Legion Co.H
Sumpter, William AR 3rd Cav. Co.F
Sumpter, William VA 63rd Inf. Co.A
Sumpter, William J. MO 1st N.E. Cav. Co.H
Sumpter, William L. NC 26th Inf. Co.F
Sumpter, W.J. MO 9th Inf. Co.C Sgt.
Sumpter, W.J. MO Inf. Clark's Regt. Co.B Sgt.
Sumptin, John W. VA 31st Mil. Co.E
Sumptiny, William VA 8th Bn.Res. Co.A
Sumption, George W. VA 31st Mil. Co.E
Sumption, John VA 49th Inf. Co.D
Sumption, W. VA 23rd Cav. Co.D
Sumptre, Henry TN 1st (Carter's) Cav. Co.L
Sumral, H. MS Inf. 2nd St.Troops Co.E
Sumral, William MS 1st Lt.Arty. Co.F
Sumrall, A. MS Lt.Arty. Turner's Co.
Sumrall, Allen MS 1st (Percy's) Inf. Co.A
Sumrall, Allen MS 3rd Inf. Co.K
Sumrall, Alvin MS Cav. 17th Bn. Co.F
Sumrall, Bang MS 14th Inf. Co.A
Sumrall, C. MS Lt.Arty. Turner's Co.
Sumrall, Calvin G. AL Lt.Arty. 2nd Bn. Co.C
Sumrall, Carney S. MS 37th Inf. Co.E
Sumrall, Charles R. MS 27th Inf. Co.L
Sumrall, D. MS Lt.Arty. Turner's Co.
Sumrall, Daniel MS 5th Inf. (St.Troops) Co.D
Sumrall, Daniel MS 8th Inf. Co.F
Sumrall, Daniel J. MS 14th Inf. Co.A Cpl.
Sumrall, E.F. MS Cav. Powers' Regt. Co.A
Sumrall, Elijah MS 1st (Percy's) Inf. Co.A Sgt.
Sumrall, Elijah G. MS Lt.Arty. Turner's Co.
Sumrall, Elisha AL 36th Inf. Co.I
Sumrall, Elisha MS 37th Inf. Co.E
Sumrall, E.N. MS 4th Cav. Co.E
Sumrall, E.N. MS 36th Inf. Co.K Sgt.
Sumrall, Frank MS 37th Inf. Co.D Cpl.
Sumrall, G.B. MS Inf. 7th Bn. Co.C
Sumrall, George LA Lt.Arty. Fenner's Btty. QMSgt.
Sumrall, George LA Inf. 1st Sp.Bn. (Rightor's) Co.A QMSgt.
Sumrall, George MS Inf. 7th Bn. Co.F
Sumrall, G.H. MS 13th Inf.
Sumrall, Harrison MS Lt.Arty. Turner's Co.

Sumrall, Henry MS Inf. 7th Bn. Co.C
Sumrall, Henry A. AL Lt.Arty. 2nd Bn. Co.C
Sumrall, Howell W. MS 13th Inf. Co.B
Sumrall, Ira E. MS 14th Inf. Co.B,D
Sumrall, Isaac MS Inf. 7th Bn. Co.B
Sumrall, J.A. TN 24th & 25th Cav. (Cons.) Co.B
Sumrall, J.A. TX 25th Cav. Co.A
Sumrall, James E. MS Cav. Jeff Davis Legion Co.B
Sumrall, James G. MS 13th Inf. Co.B
Sumrall, Jesse L. MS 14th Inf. Co.D
Sumrall, J.F. MS 37th Inf. Co.F
Sumrall, J.J. MS Lt.Arty. Turner's Co. Cpl.
Sumrall, J.K.P. MS 37th Inf. Co.F
Sumrall, John MS 3rd Inf. Co.H
Sumrall, John MS Inf. 7th Bn. Co.C
Sumrall, John MS 8th Inf. Co.G
Sumrall, John T. MS 8th Inf. Co.F
Sumrall, Joseph MS 3rd Inf. Co.K
Sumrall, Joseph Y. MS 3rd Inf. Co.A
Sumrall, J.T. MS 38th Cav. Co.I
Sumrall, J.W. MS 27th Inf. Co.G
Sumrall, Levi MS 8th Inf. Co.F
Sumrall, Levi MS 20th Inf. Co.I
Sumrall, Levi MS 27th Inf. Co.G
Sumrall, Marcus B. MS 8th Inf. Co.F
Sumrall, M.B. AL 56th Part.Rangers Co.C
Sumrall, M.B. MS 10th Cav. Co.F
Sumrall, Nowell R. MS 37th Inf. Co.D 3rd Lt.
Sumrall, S.E. Trans-MS Conf.Cav. 1st Bn. Co.D Cpl.
Sumrall, Simeon MS 36th Inf. Co.E Sgt.
Sumrall, Thomas MS 37th Inf. Co.F 1st Sgt.
Sumrall, Thomas V. MS Inf. 7th Bn. Co.B
Sumrall, T.J. MS Inf. 2nd St.Troops Co.B
Sumrall, T.M. AL 21st Inf.
Sumrall, Wesley W. MS 20th Inf. Co.I
Sumrall, W.I. MS Cav. Powers' Regt. Co.I
Sumrall, William MS Arty. (Seven Stars Arty.) Roberts' Co.
Sumrall, William G. MS 20th Inf. Co.I
Sumrall, W.W., Jr. MS Inf. 7th Bn. Co.F
Sumrall, W.W., Sr. MS Inf. 7th Bn. Co.F
Sumray, Alex VA Mil. Scott Cty.
Sumrell, A.E. NC 32nd Inf. Lenoir Braves 1st Co.K
Sumrell, H.R. AR 12th Inf. Co.F
Sumrell, R.B. 14th Conf.Cav. Co.C
Sumrell, Wilson AR 12th Inf. Co.F
Sumrell, W.J. NC 27th Inf. Co.H
Sumril, J.T. AL 61st Inf. Co.C
Sumro, John F. NC 57th Inf. Co.E
Sumrow, Robert H. NC 2nd Cav. (19th St.Troops) Co.B Cpl.
Sumter, James H. AR 3rd Inf.
Sumter, James M. GA Inf. 3rd Bn. Co.A
Sumter, S. SC 7th Cav. Co.D
Sumter, William L. GA 24th Inf. Co.C Capt.
Sumurd, J.M. TN 9th Cav. Co.G
Sumwalt, A.T. VA Cav. 1st Bn. Co.A
Sun, J.A. NC 13th Inf.
Sunaga, Alejandro TX 33rd Cav. 1st Co.H
Sunatubba, F. 1st Chickasaw Inf. McConnell's Co. Cpl.
Sunday 2nd Cherokee Mtd.Vol. Co.I
Sunday, A.J. FL 1st Inf. New Co.F
Sunday, A.J. FL 1st Inf. New Co.I
Sunday, Frederick LA 14th Inf. Co.K Sgt.
Sunday, J.G. FL Cav. 3rd Bn. Co.C
Sunday, J.G. 1st Conf.Inf. 1st Co.K
Sunday, John FL 5th Inf. Co.C
Sunday, John 15th Conf.Cav. Co.E
Sunday, John L. NC 2nd Bn.Loc.Def.Troops Co.C
Sunday, John R. FL 1st Inf. New Co.F, Co.I
Sunday, J.W. FL Cav. 3rd Bn. Co.C
Sunday, J.W. 15th Conf.Cav. Co.E
Sunday, J.W. 1st Conf.Inf. 1st Co.K
Sunday, Richard FL 1st Inf. New Co.F, Co.E,I
Sunday, Tah ne yee sky 1st Cherokee Mtd.Rifles Co.B
Sunday, Thomas TN 28th Inf. Co.C
Sunday, William 1st Cherokee Mtd.Rifles McDaniel's Co. Sgt.
Sunday Hogtoter 1st Cherokee Mtd.Rifles Co.E
Sundblad, Charles AL 5th Inf. New Co.I Cpl.
Sundberg, John V. VA Cav. 40th Bn. Co.A
Sundburg, John V. VA 24th Cav. Co.A
Sundel Harjo 1st Seminole Mtd.Vol.
Sundelin, J.T. AR 15th (Josey's) Inf. 1st Co.C
Sundemer, Fedric TN 27th Inf. Co.I
Sunderland, E.F. AR 35th Inf. Co.E 1st Sgt.
Sunderland, E.F. AR 58th Mil. Co.E 3rd Lt.
Sunderland, I.T. AR 1st Field Btty.
Sunderland, J.O. LA Inf. 4th Bn. Co.B
Sunderland, John MO 10th Inf. Co.A
Sunderland, John TN 61st Mtd.Inf. Co.G
Sunderland, Patrick VA 16th Cav. Co.D
Sunderland, Patrick VA Cav. Ferguson's Bn. Morris' Co.
Sunderland, Seth TX 22nd Cav. Co.D,I 1st Sgt.
Sunderland, Thomas MD Arty. 1st Btty.
Sunderland, Thomas VA Cav. 32nd Bn. Co.A
Sunderland, Thomas F. GA Arty. Maxwell's Reg.Lt.Btty.
Sunderland, Thomas S. GA 1st Reg. Co.L,D
Sunderland, W.H. LA Inf.Crescent Regt. Co.K
Sunderland, William TN 1st (Turney's) Inf. Co.B
Sunderland, William B. GA 4th Bn.S.S. Co.B
Sundermacher, Charles LA 7th Inf. Co.A
Sundermeyer, H.J. VA 19th Inf. Co.C
Sunders, T.S. AL 33rd Inf. Co.K
Sundlin, Robert NC 8th Bn.Part.Rangers Co.B
Sundlung, G.V. VA Loc.Def. Ezell's Co.
Sundrum, Henry AR 15th (Josey's) Inf. Co.D
Sun dul lah Harjo 1st Seminole Mtd.Vol.
Sundy, John NC 1st Inf. (6 mo. '61) Co.H
Suney, M. 1st Choctaw & Chickasaw Mtd.Rifles Co.D 2nd Lt.
Sunier, --- LA Mil. 1st Regt. French Brig. Co.12
Sunier, --- LA Mil. 3rd Regt.Eur.Brig. (Garde Francaise) Euler's Co. Sgt.
Suniga, Antonio TX 6th Inf. Co.K
Sunk, J.F. TN 12th Cav. Co.H
Sunkel, Charles LA 1st Hvy.Arty. (Reg.) Co.E
Sunkins, G.H. GA 10th Inf. Co.C
Sunksville, John LA Miles' Legion Co.E
Sunlin, Giles AL 57th Inf. Co.I
Sunmerlin, J.A. FL 4th Inf.
Sunmers, E.T. AL Vol. Meador's Co.
Sunnall, William G. MS 15th (Cons.) Inf. Co.I
Sunnapah, G. 1st Chickasaw Inf. Haynes' Co.
Sun ne coo yoh 1st Cherokee Mtd.Rifles Co.H
Sunney 1st Creek Mtd.Vol. Co.F
Sunney 1st Creek Mtd.Vol. Co.M
Sunny 1st Choctaw & Chickasaw Mtd.Rifles 2nd Co.C
Sunny, Morris 1st Choctaw & Chickasaw Mtd.Rifles 2nd Co.D
Sunon, W.R. TN 38th Inf. 2nd Co.H
Sunotts, Charles GA 1st Inf. Co.A
Sunpler, William AL 37th Inf. Co.K
Sunrull, Joseph TN 12th (Cons.) Inf. Co.B
Suns, Jesse NC 2nd Jr.Res.
Sunsall, W.H. MS 4th Cav. Co.I
Sun thappee 1st Creek Mtd.Vol. Co.K
Sunther, S.H. AR 1st (Monroe's) Cav. Co.A Sgt.
Sunton, T.T. MD 1st Cav. Co.F
Sun too le 1st Cherokee Mtd.Rifles Co.E
Sunuckee Yo Hola 1st Seminole Mtd.Vol. Cpl.
Super, --- VA 2nd St.Res. Co.L
Superveill, J. LA Mil. 4th Regt. French Brig. Co.1
Superville, Eug LA 28th (Thomas') Inf. Co.E Jr.2nd Lt.
Superville, Frank TX Inf. 1st St.Troops Co.F
Supinger, George VA Cav. 46th Bn. Co.E
Supinger, J. VA Horse Arty. D. Shank's Co.
Supinger, Jacob VA 1st Cav. Co.C
Supinger, Leonard VA Horse Arty. J.W. Carter's Co.
Supinger, Michael VA Hvy.Arty. 20th Bn. Co.E Cpl.
Supinger, Peter VA 18th Cav. Co.D
Supinger, Peter VA 136th Mil. Co.E
Supinger, Robert VA 1st Cav. Co.C
Supinger, Robert O. VA 136th Mil. Co.E
Supke, Herman LA 18th Inf. Co.G
Suples, Henry AR 1st (Colquitt's) Inf. Co.K
Supley, W.M.C. NC 4th Inf.
Supper, John LA Mil. 4th Regt. 2nd Brig. 1st Div. Co.A
Suppetar 1st Creek Mtd.Vol. Co.K
Suppi chee chee 1st Creek Mtd.Vol. 2nd Co.C
Suppington, H.F. KY 14th Cav. Co.B
Supple, James GA Inf. (St.Armory Guards) Green's Co.
Supple, James S. VA Prov.Guard Avis' Co.
Supple, J.B.B. TX 16th Inf. Co.A
Supple, J.B.B. TX 17th Inf. Co.I
Supple, John B.B. TX 6th Inf. Co.F Sgt.
Supple, R.F. VA 7th Bn.Res. Co.D
Supple, T. MS Inf. Lewis' Co.
Supple, T.A. TX 17th Inf. Co.I 1st Sgt.
Supple, Thomas A. VA 5th Inf. Co.E
Supple, William W. MS 5th Inf. (St.Troops) Co.F
Supplee, Lemuel MS 10th Inf. Old Co.G, New Co.H Sgt.
Supples, George Gen. & Staff Surg.,Medical Director
Suppon, T.J. AR Inf. Hardy's Regt. Torbett's Co.
Suppulper 1st Creek Mtd.Vol. Co.K
Suque yeh NC Inf. Thomas Legion 2nd Co.A
Sur, John LA Mil. 3rd Regt. 1st Brig. 1st Div. Co.E
Suran, H.T. SC Mil. 1st Regt.Rifles Palmer's Co.
Suran, H.T. SC 27th Inf. Co.D

Surand, Joseph LA 1st (Nelligan's) Inf. Co.I
Surand, Joseph SC 1st Inf. Co.O
Surat, Henry AL Cav. Forrest's Regt.
Surat, Henry TN 18th (Newsom's) Cav. Co.F
Surat, James AR 30th Inf. Co.D
Suratt, E. AL 30th Inf. Co.D
Suratt, James A. VA Mil. Carroll Cty.
Suratt, J.E. LA Mil. Chalmette Regt. Co.C
Suratt, J.H. MS 10th Cav. Co.H
Suratt, J.M. MS 2nd (Davidson's) Inf. Potts' Co. 2nd Lt.
Suratt, John A. TN 20th Cav.
Suratt, John J. MS 9th Inf. New Co.F
Suratt, M. Gen. & Staff Capt.,QM
Suratt, Malkijah MS 2nd Inf. Co.A QM
Suratt, S.B. LA 19th Inf. Chap.
Suratt, S.B. Gen. & Staff Chap.
Suratt, Thomas E. MS 2nd Inf. Co.A
Suratt, William P. VA Mil. Carroll Cty.
Suratt, William W. MS Cav. Duncan's Co. (Tishomingo Rangers)
Suratt, W.W. MS 2nd (Davidson's) Inf. Potts' Co. Cpl.
Surau, H.T. SC Inf. 1st (Charleston) Bn. Co.D
Suraw, John SC Hvy.Arty. 15th (Lucas') Bn. Co.C
Suraw, W.F. SC 6th Cav. Co.D
Suraw, W.F. SC 27th Inf. Co.I
Surbaugh, --- VA Inf. 3rd Kanawha Regt. Capt.
Surbaugh, Andrew VA 46th Inf. 1st Co.C
Surbaugh, Andrew VA 60th Inf. Co.B 2nd Lt.
Surbaugh, David R. VA 79th Mil. Co.3
Surbaugh, George VA Inf. 26th Bn. Co.B
Surbaugh, George VA 79th Mil. Co.2
Surbaugh, H.C. MO Robertson's Regt.St.Guard Co.1
Surbaugh, Henry VA 79th Mil. Co.3
Surbaugh, J.A. VA Inf. 26th Bn. Co.B
Surbaugh, Jacob A. VA 79th Mil. Co.2 Sgt.
Surbaugh, John A. VA 60th Inf. Co.B
Surbaugh, John Allen VA 46th Inf. 1st Co.C
Surbaugh, John J. VA Cav. Hounshell's Bn. Co.C
Surbaugh, T.L. VA 79th Mil. Co.2 1st Sgt.
Surbaugh, W. VA Inf. 26th Bn. Co.B
Surbaugh, William VA 79th Mil. Co.2 Capt.
Surbeck, J.J. AL Mil. West's Co.
Surber, --- TX Cav. Good's Bn. Co.B
Surber, A. KY 2nd Mtd.Inf. Co.H
Surber, Alfred KY 6th Cav. Co.B,E 2nd Lt.
Surber, Andrew J. VA 108th Mil. Co.C
Surber, Andy KY 6th Cav. Co.B
Surber, Caleb TN 63rd Inf. Co.A
Surber, Carlton G. MO 1st Cav. Co.E
Surber, James VA 50th Inf. Co.L
Surber, James M. VA 28th Inf. Co.B
Surber, John M. MO 10th Cav. Co.D
Surber, Joseph A. MO 10th Cav. Co.D
Surber, Josiah S. VA 14th Cav. Co.A
Surber, Levi VA 28th Inf. Co.B
Surber, Lilburn VA Inf. 23rd Bn. Co.E Cpl.
Surber, Mathew P. VA 11th Cav. Co.F
Surber, Robert TN 19th & 20th (Cons.) Cav. Co.A
Surber, Thomas C. VA 14th Cav. Co.A
Surber, Tilburn VA 50th Inf. Co.L
Surber, T.O. VA 22nd Inf. Co.H
Surber, William VA Inf. 23rd Bn. Co.A
Surber, William VA 63rd Inf. Co.A
Surber, William H. VA Cav. Hounshell's Bn. Co.A
Surbough, John VA 5th Cav.Arty. & Inf.St.Line Co.I
Surbyfield, John NC 4th Inf. Co.A
Surcey, L.S. FL 2nd Inf. Co.D
Surcouf, Paul LA Mil. 2nd Regt. French Brig. Co.5
Surder, A. AL Coosa Guards J.W. Suttles' Co.
Surder, Benjamin MO 7th Cav. Ward's Co.
Surder, John MO 7th Cav. Ward's Co.
Surder, Shadrick MO 7th Cav. Ward's Co.
Surell, John W. GA 3rd Cav. (St.Guards) Co.H
Sureman, William S. MO Lt.Arty. Farris' Btty. (Clark Arty.) Sgt.
Surentine, Joseph LA Mil. 3rd Regt. 2nd Brig. 1st Div. Co.K Sgt.
Suret, Francis SC 1st Arty. Co.E
Suret, Sanford GA 56th Inf. Co.A
Sureton, Wm. MO St.Guard
Surey, William R. NC 6th Cav. (65th St.Troops) Co.E
Surface, A. VA 36th Inf. Co.G
Surface, Andrew VA 4th Res. Co.D
Surface, Andrew M. VA 60th Inf. 2nd Co.H
Surface, Andrew M. VA 151st Mil. Co.D
Surface, Charles O. VA 54th Inf. Co.K
Surface, George W. VA 63rd Inf. Co.D
Surface, Henry VA 4th Res. Co.D
Surface, Henry VA Wade's Regt.Loc.Def. Co.E
Surface, H.R. VA 14th Inf. Co.I
Surface, Hugh C. VA 54th Inf. Co.K
Surface, Jacob VA 36th Inf. Co.F
Surface, James H. VA 24th Inf. Co.F Sgt.
Surface, John VA 54th Inf. Co.E
Surface, John C. VA 4th Inf. Co.L
Surface, John W. VA Cav. 37th Bn. Co.H
Surface, M.C. VA Cav. 37th Bn. Co.H
Surface, Michael VA 54th Inf. Co.E
Surface, Michael C. VA 24th Inf. Co.F
Surface, Philip VA 11th Inf. Co.F
Surface, Phillip VA 21st Cav. 2nd Co.D Cpl.
Surface, Samuel D. VA 11th Inf. Co.F
Surface, William R. VA 42nd Inf. Co.E
Surface, W.L. VA Inf. 7th Bn.Loc.Def. Co.A
Surg, J.C. GA 32nd Inf. Co.F
Surgener, A.R. VA 2nd Cav. Capt.
Surgener, Benjamin MS 1st Cav.Res. Co.H
Surgener, Stephen S. TN Cav. 5th Bn. (McClellan's) Co.D
Surgener, William AL 15th Bn.Part.Rangers Co.D
Surgener, William H. AL 43rd Inf. Co.B
Surgenson, G.D. MO 8th Inf. Co.E
Surgent, B.B. GA 34th Inf. Co.B
Surgent, George Conf.Inf. Tucker's Regt. Co.H Cpl.
Surgeon, G.M. MO 11th Inf. Co.A
Surgeon, John VA 59th Inf. 1st Co.F
Surgeon, John VA 60th Inf. Co.C Cpl.
Surgeoner, Mason M. TN 29th Inf. Co.K Cpl.
Surgeons, James MO Inf. Clark's Regt. Co.B
Surgery, Thomas VA 50th Inf. Co.A
Surges, James M. AR 24th Inf. Co.B
Surget, E. LA 7th Inf. AAG
Surget, E. Gen. & Staff, Adj.Gen.Dept. Lt.Col.,AAG
Surggart, D.W. TX Cav. Wells' Regt. Asst.Surg.
Surghnor, H.C. TX 16th Inf. Co.B,A 1st Sgt.
Surghnor, John TX 6th Cav. Co.F
Surghnor, Lloyd W. TX 16th Inf. Co.A
Surghnor, L.W. TX 9th (Nichols') Inf. Co.I Sgt.
Surghnor, T. VA 18th Cav. Co.A
Surghnor, Thompson VA 25th Inf. 2nd Co.B Sgt.Maj.
Surghnor, Thompson VA 31st Inf. Co.C
Surgi, Alexander LA C.S. Zouave Bn. Co.B Sgt.
Surgi, E. LA Mil. Surgi's Co. (Sap. & Min.) Capt.
Surgi, H. LA 18th Inf. Co.B
Surgi, H. LA Inf.Crescent Regt. Co.H,C
Surgi, Henry LA Inf.Cons.Crescent Regt. Co.G
Surgi, R.A.L. LA Inf. 7th Bn. Co.A
Surginer, John NC Lt.Arty. 13th Bn. Co.A
Surginer, John VA Lt.Arty. 12th Bn. Co.D
Surginer, John P. AL 50th Inf. Co.E
Surginer, R.W. MS 34th Inf. Co.E
Surginer, Thomas J. MS 34th Inf. Co.E
Surginer, William TN 50th (Cons.) Inf. Co.H
Surginor, J. TX Cav. (Dismtd.) Chisum's Regt. Co.C
Surgion, Andrew VA 79th Mil. Co.5
Surgioner, William TN Inf. 1st Bn. (Colms') Co.E
Surgnier, Jacob MO 16th Inf. Co.E
Surgoner, Isaac MO 16th Inf. Co.E
Surguner, Benjamin MS 5th Inf. (St.Troops) Co.D
Surhen, John D. LA Mil. 4th Regt. 1st Brig. 1st Div. Co.K
Suritt, David NC 1st Bn.Jr.Res. Co.A
Surlan, Frederick TX 6th Inf. Co.A
Surles, Alexander A.D. AL 45th Inf. Co.I
Surles, A.W. GA Inf. City Bn. (Columbus) Co.A
Surles, Bright FL 1st Mil.
Surles, Calvin FL Cav. 3rd Bn. Co.A
Surles, Calvin 15th Conf.Cav. Co.A
Surles, Calvin B. NC 24th Inf. Co.I Sgt.
Surles, Dorrant W. GA Siege Arty. 28th Bn. Co.F
Surles, D.W. GA Inf. City Bn. (Columbus) Co.A
Surles, Edw. SC 1st (Butler's) Inf. Co.B
Surles, E.M. SC Inf. 7th Bn. (Enfield Rifles) Co.F
Surles, E.M. 2nd Conf.Eng.Troops Co.G
Surles, James H. NC 24th Inf. Co.I
Surles, John AR 20th Inf. Co.K
Surles, John Exch.Bn. 3rd Co.B,CSA
Surles, Martin GA 5th Inf. Co.I
Surles, M.L. GA 31st Inf. Co.E
Surles, M.L. GA 55th Inf. Co.H
Surles, Robert FL 1st Inf. Old Co.I, New Co.C Cpl.
Surles, Robert TX 20th Inf. Co.K
Surles, Robert D. AL Cav.Res. Brooks' Co. Sgt.
Surles, Samuel R. NC 1st Inf. (6 mo. '61) Co.F
Surles, William R. GA 17th Inf. Co.K Cpl.
Surley, J.H. MO 2nd Inf. Co.G
Surls, Archibald B. SC 1st (Hagood's) Inf. 2nd Co.I

Surls, D.H. NC 50th Inf. Co.D
Surls, John F. GA Inf. 10th Bn. Co.A Sgt.
Surls, Levi SC Arty. Gregg's Co. (McQueen Lt.Arty.)
Surls, Marcus M. GA 46th Inf. Co.G
Surls, W.M. LA Mil. Beauregard Bn. Frobus' Co.
Surman, Gustave MD 1st Cav. Co.C
Surmann, Caspar VA Inf. 25th Bn. Co.B
Surmann, John LA 21st (Patton's) Inf. Co.I
Surmann, Joseph LA 20th Inf. Co.D
Surmans, Lazarus TX 11th (Spaight's) Bn.Vol. Co.D
Surmaus, J.A. 10th Conf.Cav. Co.G
Surmelie, F. LA Mil. 1st Regt. French Brig. Co.3
Surmens, --- TX Cav. Good's Bn. Co.D
Surmon, F. GA 22nd Inf. Co.K
Surmons, James GA 11th Cav. (St.Guards) Godfrey's Co.
Surmons, J.F.H. 20th Conf.Cav. Co.B
Surmons, J.F.M. TX 11th (Spaight's) Bn.Vol. Co.D
Surmons, John W. GA 57th Inf. Co.C
Surmons, Jordan GA 57th Inf. Co.C
Surmons, L. TX 21st Inf. Co.H
Surner, A.J. AL 27th Inf. Co.D
Surney, William L. MO Cav. 2nd Regt.St.Guard Co.G
Suroroff, G. TX 33rd Cav. Co.A
Surper, M.P. VA 2nd Cav. Co.A
Surprise, John B. MS 19th Inf. Co.E
Surpriss, Joseph Conf.Reg.Inf. Brooks' Bn. Co.C
Surraat, James A. VA 63rd Inf. Co.G, 2nd Co.I
Surran, Thomas J. KY 4th Mtd.Inf. Co.E
Surrat, J. SC Lt.Arty. 3rd (Palmetto) Bn. Co.H,I
Surratt, A.J. SC 5th Inf. 1st Co.F
Surratt, A.J. SC Palmetto S.S. Co.D
Surratt, Allen NC 6th Sr.Res. Co.I
Surratt, B.E. AL 55th Vol. Co.H
Surratt, Beverly A. NC 48th Inf. Co.B
Surratt, Daniel L. NC 7th Inf. Co.F
Surratt, G.B. SC 18th Inf. Co.K
Surratt, George VA 4th Inf. Co.A
Surratt, George W. NC 48th Inf. Co.B Music.
Surratt, Gorrell W. NC 22nd Inf. Co.I
Surratt, Gorrell W. NC 46th Inf. Co.F
Surratt, H.J. NC 6th Cav. (65th St.Troops) Co.A
Surratt, Isaac D. TX 33rd Cav. Co.A Sgt.
Surratt, Isom VA 29th Inf. 2nd Co.F
Surratt, Ivy NC 48th Inf. Co.B
Surratt, Jacob TN 42nd Inf. Co.A
Surratt, Jacob 4th Conf.Inf. Co.G
Surratt, James NC 6th Sr.Res. Co.G
Surratt, James R. TN 54th Inf. Co.H
Surratt, J.H. Conf.Cav. Baxter's Bn. Co.A,C
Surratt, J.L. TN 21st (Wilson's) Cav. Co.A
Surratt, J.M. AL Cav. Forrest's Regt.
Surratt, John SC 5th Inf. 1st Co.F
Surratt, John SC Palmetto S.S. Co.D
Surratt, John E. LA 16th Inf. Co.C
Surratt, John G. NC 7th Inf. Co.F
Surratt, Joseph A. VA 36th Inf. 2nd Co.C
Surratt, Joseph P. TX 1st Inf. Co.H
Surratt, Josiah NC 52nd Inf. Co.B
Surratt, Peter P. VA 4th Inf. Co.F
Surratt, Peyton G. NC 7th Inf. Co.F
Surratt, Richard L. NC 6th Sr.Res. Co.C,F Capt.
Surratt, Travis NC 48th Inf. Co.B
Surratt, Uriah VA 18th Inf. Co.E
Surratt, W. NC 3rd Inf. Co.I
Surratt, W.H. TN 21st (Wilson's) Cav. Co.A
Surratt, Wm. NC 64th Inf. Co.G
Surratt, William P. VA 29th Inf. 2nd Co.F
Surratt, W.L. AR 11th Inf. Co.C
Surratt, W.M. NC 14th Inf. Co.D
Surratts, Patrick VA 29th Inf. Co.E
Surraville, J.B. TX 7th Inf. Co.G
Surrency, Alfred H. GA 61st Inf. Co.B,K
Surrency, Allen H. GA 61st Inf. Co.K
Surrency, Henry C. FL 7th Inf. Co.A,E
Surrency, Henry J. GA 21st Inf. Co.K
Surrency, H.W. GA 61st Inf. Co.B
Surrency, James GA 12th Inf. Co.A
Surrency, John E. FL 7th Inf. Co.A
Surrency, John M. GA 26th Inf. Co.F
Surrency, John M. GA 61st Inf. Co.B,K
Surrency, Samuel GA 61st Inf. Co.B,K
Surrency, W.A.M. GA Cav. 20th Bn. Co.G
Surrency, W.A.M. GA Cav. 21st Bn. Co.D
Surrency, Wiley GA Cav. 20th Bn. Co.G
Surrency, Wiley GA Cav. 21st Bn. Co.D
Surrency, William GA 61st Inf. Co.B,K
Surret, Francis H. NC 25th Inf. Co.A
Surrett, H.A. GA 60th Inf. Co.C
Surrett, Henry F. NC 62nd Inf. Co.E
Surrett, James A. TX 4th Inf. Co.A
Surrett, James B. NC 29th Inf. Co.C
Surrett, John NC 60th Inf. Co.A
Surrett, J.R. TN Cav. Williams' Co.
Surrett, K.D. GA 10th Cav. Co.A
Surrett, W.L. TN Cav. Williams' Co.
Surridge, J. MO Inf. 3rd Regt.St.Guard Co.H 3rd Lt.
Surridge, James MO 3rd Cav. Co.B Maj.
Surriitt, Frank AL Arty. 1st Bn. Co.A
Sursey, W.J. NC 49th Inf. Co.K
Surtain, Richard TN 13th (Gore's) Cav. Co.I
Surten, Ananias SC 1st Arty. Co.K
Surtin, J.F. MO 3rd Inf. Co.K
Survants, W.H. TX 28th Cav. Co.G
Survey, John VA 26th Inf. Co.D
Survick, George W. VA Cav. 35th Bn. Co.A
Survine, M. VA 54th Mil. Co.H
Sur wa kee 2nd Cherokee Mtd.Vol. Co.B
Susan, Joseph TX Cav. Giddings' Bn. Onins' Co.
Sus cooner 1st Creek Mtd.Vol. Co.H 2nd Lt.
Suscord, A.J. GA 11th Cav. (St.Guards) McGriff's Co.
Suser, Miss Y. NC Pris.Guard Howard's Co.
Suski, L. TX Inf. 1st St.Troops Martin's Co.A
Suskind, E. LA Arty. Hutton's Co. (Crescent Arty.,Co.A) Orderly Sgt.
Susong, Alfred TN 39th Mtd.Inf. Co.H
Susong, David TN 60th Mtd.Inf. Co.G
Susong, George NC 64th Inf. Co.F 2nd Lt.
Susong, J. TN 42nd Inf. 2nd Co.E
Susong, John VA 25th Cav. Co.G
Susong, John VA Inf. Mileham's Co.
Susong, Martin TN 29th Inf. Co.F
Susong, Martin TN 31st Inf. Co.H
Susong, William F. VA 25th Cav. Co.I,G
Susonge, John M. TN Conscr. (Cp. of Instr.)
Sussard, J.A. SC 27th Inf. Co.I
Sussdorf, Gussdorf E. NC 21st Inf. Co.D Ens.
Sussen, Martin TX Waul's Legion Co.B
Sussman, David AL 6th Inf. Co.E
Sutberry, D.R. TN 11th (Holman's) Cav. Co.C
Sutberry, Harris KY 1st (Butler's) Cav. Co.G
Sutberry, Harris KY 1st Inf. Co.G
Sut chek lar kar 1st Creek Mtd.Vol. Co.A
Sutcliff, George 1st Conf.Eng.Troops Co.H
Sutcliff, George W. MS 26th Inf. Co.B
Sutcliff, James MO 8th Inf. Co.D Sgt.
Sutcliff, Thomas H. LA 9th Inf. Co.G Sgt.
Sutcliff, William MS 2nd (Quinn's St.Troops) Inf. Co.E
Sutcliffe, A.N. SC Cav. 4th Bn. Co.D
Sutcliffe, Daniel AR 35th Inf. Co.B,I Capt.
Sutcliffe, Henry KY 2nd Mtd.Inf. Co.A
Sutcliffe, J. LA Mil. British Guard Bn. Hamilton's Co.
Sutcliffe, L.W. SC Inf. Hampton Legion Co.H
Sutcliffe, W.H. SC Vol. Simons' Co.
Sutcliffe, W.H. SC Inf. 1st (Charleston) Bn. Co.B
Sutcliffe, W.H. SC 27th Inf. Co.B
Suten, E.V. MS 1st (King's) Inf. (St.Troops) Co.C
Suter, A. AR 58th Mil. Co.D
Suter, Alexander R. LA Arty. Green's Co. (LA Guard Btty.)
Suter, Asa MO 15th Cav.
Suter, A.T. KY 1st (Butler's) Cav. Co.C Sgt.
Suter, Carl LA 21st (Patton's) Inf. Co.I
Suter, David VA 97th Mil. Co.D
Suter, Frank Inf. School of Pract. Powell's Detach. Co.C
Suter, J. AL 7th Cav. Co.F
Suter, J.A. KY 3rd Cav. Co.C 1st Sgt.
Suter, Jacob VA 52nd Inf. Co.F
Suter, James A. KY 1st (Butler's) Cav. Co.C Bvt.2nd Lt.
Suter, James M. KY 4th Cav. Co.G
Suter, J.M. KY 3rd Cav. Co.C
Suter, J.N. AR 20th Inf. Co.H
Suter, John AL 22nd Inf. Co.C
Suter, John H. MO Cav. 1st Regt.St.Guard Co.F
Suter, John M. KY 4th Cav. Co.G
Suter, J.T. KY 3rd Cav. Co.C Sgt.
Suter, L. KY 3rd Cav. Grant's Co.
Suter, Lyman KY 1st (Butler's) Cav. Co.C
Suter, Mortimer W. VA 22nd Inf. Co.B Sgt.
Suter, N. KY 3rd Cav. Grant's Co.
Suter, Nathaniel KY 1st (Butler's) Cav. Co.C
Suter, R. TX 14th Field Btty.
Suter, R. TX Inf. 1st St.Troops Sheldon's Co.B
Suter, R.T. KY 6th Cav. Co.I
Suter, Samuel R. KY 4th Mtd.Inf. Co.D
Suter, Thomas C. VA 1st Lt.Arty. Co.B
Suter, Thomas C. VA Lt.Arty. J.S. Brown's Co.
Suter, Thomas H. LA Washington Arty.Bn. Co.2 Cpl.
Suter, William VA Inf. 6th Bn.Loc.Def. Co.A
Suter, William VA Hood's Bn.Res. Tappey's Co.
Suter, William H. AR 26th Inf. Co.H
Suter, William M. VA Cav. 36th Bn. Co.D
Sutfen, John W. VA 21st Cav. 2nd Co.G
Sutfield, J.C. KY 3rd Cav. Co.B
Sutfield, L.C. KY 7th Cav. Co.E

Sutfield, Rich M. Gen. & Staff Surg.
Sutfin, Antny MO 7th Cav. Co.B
Sutfin, Baswell VA 166th Mil. Co.H
Sutfin, C.R. AR 15th (N.W.) Inf. Co.H
Sutfin, David VA 22nd Inf. Co.I
Sutfin, Hendric VA 166th Mil. Co.H
Sutfin, John VA 166th Mil. Co.H
Sutfin, William TN Lt.Arty. Burroughs' Co.
Sutfin, William, Jr. VA 34th Mil. Co.A
Sutfin, William J. AR Cav. Davies' Bn. Co.A,C Cpl.
Suthard, Calvin VA 33rd Inf. Co.H
Suthard, James L. KY 4th Cav. Co.F
Suthard, John VA 3rd (Chrisman's) Bn.Res. Co.B Sgt.
Suthard, John VA 10th Inf. Co.I
Suthard, John F. VA 13th Inf. 2nd Co.E
Suthard, John H. VA 33rd Inf. Co.H
Suthard, R.D. VA 63rd Inf. Co.G
Suthard, William VA 1st Arty. Co.I
Suthard, William VA 13th Inf. 2nd Co.E
Suthards, George W. NC 39th Inf. Co.B
Suthards, John VA 9th Bn.Res. Co.B Sgt.
Suther, A.L. NC 57th Inf. Co.F
Suther, A.M. NC 4th Sr.Res. Co.F
Suther, D.A. AL 3rd Cav. Co.H
Suther, Daniel W. NC 33rd Inf. Co.E,C
Suther, David S. NC 23rd Inf. Co.F
Suther, Greenbury R. NC 52nd Inf. Co.A
Suther, Jack NC 33rd Inf. Co.C
Suther, James W. NC 33rd Inf. Co.C
Suther, J.H. NC 27th Inf.
Suther, John A. NC 23rd Inf. Co.F
Suther, John H. NC 33rd Inf. Co.A
Suther, John P. NC 52nd Inf. Co.A
Suther, J.W. TX 2nd Inf. Co.A
Suther, Richard M. NC 52nd Inf. Co.A
Suther, Robert J. NC 33rd Inf. Co.C Cpl.
Suther, Samuel F. GA 12th Inf. Co.G
Suther, S.W. TX 9th (Young's) Inf. Co.E
Suther, Tobias A. NC 33rd Inf. Co.C
Suther, W.C. AL Cp. of Instr. Talladega
Suther, William C. AL Cav. Holloway's Co.
Suther, William F. NC 33rd Inf. Co.C
Suther, William W. GA 12th Inf. Co.G
Sutherd, Thomas M. VA 8th Bn.Res. Co.B
Sutherfield, John M. TN 1st Cav. Co.G,F
Sutherlain, Francis M. TX Cav. Baylor's Regt. Co.B Sgt.
Sutherlain, James A. TX Cav. Baylor's Regt. Co.B
Sutherlain, William A. TX Cav. Baylor's Regt. Co.B
Sutherlan, Ellis P. MS Griffin's Co. (Madison Guards)
Sutherland, --- KY 3rd Cav. Co.I
Sutherland, A. AR 10th Mil. Co.B
Sutherland, A. GA Inf. 1st City Bn. (Columbus) Co.C 2nd Lt.
Sutherland, A. 2nd Conf.Eng.Troops Co.G
Sutherland, A.J. Gen. & Staff Asst.Surg.
Sutherland, A.L. GA 36th (Broyles') Inf. Co.E
Sutherland, Alexander AL Arty. 1st Bn. Co.A
Sutherland, Alexander MS 16th Inf. Co.E
Sutherland, Alexander TN 4th (Murray's) Cav. Co.K
Sutherland, Alex. TN Inf. 22nd Bn. Co.F
Sutherland, Alexander R. TN 2nd (Robison's) Inf. Co.H 2nd Lt.
Sutherland, Ambrose NC 1st Inf.
Sutherland, Ambrose NC Walker's Bn. Thomas' Legion 2nd Co.D Cpl.
Sutherland, Andrew A. VA 10th Cav. Co.F 1st Sgt.
Sutherland, Andrew J. GA 2nd Cav. Asst.Surg.
Sutherland, Andrew J. VA 24th Inf. Co.C
Sutherland, Archibald VA 17th Inf. Co.D
Sutherland, Arthur V. VA 46th Inf. 1st Co.G 2nd Lt.
Sutherland, B. NC 14th Inf. Co.D
Sutherland, Ben AR 45th Cav. Co.I
Sutherland, Benjamin AR 32nd Inf. Co.H
Sutherland, Benjamin, Jr. MO Robertson's Regt.St.Guard Co.9
Sutherland, B.F. AR 30th Inf. Co.I
Sutherland, B.F. MO Cav. Coleman's Regt. Lenox's Co.
Sutherland, C.H. TX 23rd Cav. Co.B
Sutherland, C.J. TN 17th Inf. Co.I
Sutherland, C.L.B. MS 26th Inf. Co.C Ord.Sgt.
Sutherland, Clement L.B. VA 27th Inf. Co.G
Sutherland, Collins LA Arty. Landry's Co. (Donaldsonville Arty.)
Sutherland, C.R. LA 14th Inf. Co.E
Sutherland, Daniel MS 18th Inf. Co.C
Sutherland, Daniel Forrest's Scouts J.T. Cobb's Co.,CSA
Sutherland, Daniel P. GA 1st Inf. Co.B
Sutherland, D.C. NC 6th Cav. (65th St.Troops) Co.F
Sutherland, Dillon VA 24th Inf. Co.C
Sutherland, Dillon VA 63rd Inf. 2nd Co.I
Sutherland, D.N. AR 30th Inf. Co.O
Sutherland, D.T. VA 21st Cav. 2nd Co.C
Sutherland, D.W. GA Lt.Arty. King's Btty.
Sutherland, E. VA 72nd Mil.
Sutherland, Edgar VA 17th Inf. Co.D
Sutherland, Edward AL Lt.Arty. 2nd Bn. Co.E
Sutherland, Edward VA 46th Inf. 1st Co.G
Sutherland, Edwin VA Lt.Arty. 13th Bn. Co.B
Sutherland, E.J. SC 14th Inf. Co.I
Sutherland, Elbert NC 64th Inf. Co.N
Sutherland, E.P. MS 3rd (St.Troops) Cav. Co.G
Sutherland, Evan NC Inf. Thomas Legion Co.D
Sutherland, Ezekial VA 21st Cav. 1st Co.E
Sutherland, Fernando VA Cav. 37th Bn. Co.A
Sutherland, F.M. SC 14th Inf. Co.I
Sutherland, Frank A. MO Arty. Lowe's Co.
Sutherland, Frederick 2nd Conf.Inf. Co.B
Sutherland, Garrison TN 34th Inf. Co.G
Sutherland, G.B. MS 2nd Cav. Co.A
Sutherland, George W. VA Horse Arty. E. Graham's Co.
Sutherland, G.M. MO 16th Inf. Co.K
Sutherland, G.W. GA 65th Inf. Co.A
Sutherland, G.W. GA Smith's Legion Co.B
Sutherland, G.W. TN 49th Inf. Co.B
Sutherland, H. VA Inf. 25th Bn. Co.G
Sutherland, Harrison VA 21st Cav. 1st Co.E
Sutherland, Hector TX 24th Cav. Co.E Sgt.
Sutherland, Henderson J. AR 35th Inf. Co.B
Sutherland, Henry MS 1st Cav.Res. Co.I Cpl.
Sutherland, Henry NC 35th Inf. Co.E
Sutherland, Henry VA 22nd Cav. Co.G
Sutherland, H.L. MS 3rd (St.Troops) Cav. Co.H
Sutherland, H.R. AL 9th Inf. Co.A 2nd Lt.
Sutherland, Isaac AR Inf. 8th Bn. 1st Co.C
Sutherland, Isaac AR 25th Inf. Co.F
Sutherland, J. AR Inf. Sparks' Co.
Sutherland, J.A. 1st Cherokee Mtd.Vol. 2nd Co.B
Sutherland, Jack TX 4th Inf. Co.F Adj.
Sutherland, Jack TX Inf. Cunningham's Co.
Sutherland, James AR 45th Cav. Co.D
Sutherland, James AR 30th Inf. Co.I
Sutherland, James AR 32nd Inf. Co.I
Sutherland, James AR Inf. Cocke's Regt. Co.C
Sutherland, James MS 2nd Inf. Co.K,B
Sutherland, James TX 9th Cav. Co.B
Sutherland, James VA 9th Cav. Co.E
Sutherland, James VA 22nd Cav. Co.G
Sutherland, James A. VA 19th Inf. Co.D
Sutherland, James C. NC Mallett's Bn. 2nd Lt.
Sutherland, James H. VA Lt.Arty. Taylor's Co.
Sutherland, James J. VA Mil. 179th Regt. QMSgt.
Sutherland, James K. VA Mil. Washington Cty.
Sutherland, James M. GA 10th Inf. Co.F
Sutherland, James T. AR 36th Inf. Co.A
Sutherland, James W. MS 2nd Inf. Co.A
Sutherland, James W. VA 55th Inf. Co.M
Sutherland, Jasper TX Cav. Hardeman's Regt. Co.C
Sutherland, J.B. SC 2nd Cav. Co.F
Sutherland, J.B. SC 3rd Res. Co.H
Sutherland, J.B. VA 1st (Farinholt's) Res. Co.C 1st Sgt.
Sutherland, J.B. VA Inf. 25th Bn. Co.G
Sutherland, J.C. AR 15th (Josey's) Inf. Co.F
Sutherland, Jesse TX Cav. Hardeman's Regt. Co.C
Sutherland, Jesse VA 72nd Mil. 2nd Lt.
Sutherland, J.F. NC 42nd Inf. Co.H
Sutherland, J.F. SC Arty. Fickling's Co. (Brooks Lt.Arty.)
Sutherland, J.J. VA 1st St.Res. Co.D
Sutherland, John GA 12th Cav. Co.I 2nd Lt.
Sutherland, John MS 3rd (St.Troops) Cav. Co.H
Sutherland, John MS 1st (King's) Inf. (St.Troops) Co.F
Sutherland, John MO 16th Inf. Co.H
Sutherland, John TN Cav. Napier's Bn. Co.D
Sutherland, John TN 4th Inf. Co.G Capt.
Sutherland, John TN 49th Inf. Co.B
Sutherland, John, Mrs. VA Hvy.Arty. 18th Bn. Laundress
Sutherland, John VA 17th Inf. Co.A
Sutherland, John VA 47th Mil.
Sutherland, John A. NC 24th Inf. Co.G
Sutherland, John F. VA 30th Inf. Co.D
Sutherland, John H. NC 64th Inf. Co.H
Sutherland, John H. TN 29th Inf. Co.H Chap.
Sutherland, John H. VA 46th Inf. 1st Co.G
Sutherland, John J. TX 10th Cav. Co.G
Sutherland, Johnson VA 21st Cav. 1st Co.E
Sutherland, Johnson O. MS 18th Inf. Co.G
Sutherland, John W. KY 2nd Mtd.Inf. Co.I
Sutherland, John W. VA 17th Inf. Co.D
Sutherland, John W. VA 49th Inf. Co.B
Sutherland, Joseph NC 1st Cav. (9th St.Troops) Co.A
Sutherland, J.W. AR 15th (N.W.) Inf. Co.I

Sutherland, J.W. KY 6th Mtd.Inf. Co.G
Sutherland, J.W. MS Cav. Ham's Regt. Co.B,C 1st Lt.
Sutherland, J.W. TN 7th (Duckworth's) Cav. Co.C Sgt.
Sutherland, Leigh M. VA 17th Inf. Co.H
Sutherland, Leitner N. SC 5th Inf. 1st Co.K
Sutherland, Lev TX Cav. Baylor's Regt. Co.A Capt.
Sutherland, Levi MS 2nd Cav. Co.A
Sutherland, L.M. MD Arty. 1st Btty.
Sutherland, Marcus L. SC 13th Inf. Co.C
Sutherland, M.T. SC 2nd Inf.
Sutherland, M.V. AR 8th Field Btty. Jr.2nd Lt.
Sutherland, Nickolas AR 30th Inf. Co.I
Sutherland, Noah VA 21st Cav. 1st Co.E
Sutherland, N.V. AR Inf. Williamson's Bn. Co.F 3rd Lt.
Sutherland, O.P. TX 3rd Inf. Co.I
Sutherland, P. LA Cav. Greenleaf's Co. (Orleans Lt.Horse)
Sutherland, P. Conf.Cav. Wood's Regt. 2nd Co.D
Sutherland, P.F. LA Mil. Beauregard Bn. Frobus' Co.
Sutherland, P.F. LA Inf.Crescent Regt. Co.G
Sutherland, P.R., Jr. MS 3rd (St.Troops) Cav. Co.H
Sutherland, P.R., Sr. MS 3rd (St.Troops) Cav. Co.H
Sutherland, P.R. MS 1st (King's) Inf. (St.Troops) Co.F
Sutherland, Preston TN 26th Inf. Co.C
Sutherland, R. GA 12th Cav. Co.A
Sutherland, R. MO 5th Cav. Co.B
Sutherland, R.A. TN 49th Inf. Co.B
Sutherland, Ransom GA 12th Cav. Co.I 1st Sgt.
Sutherland, Robert VA Lt.Arty. J.S. Brown's Co.
Sutherland, Robert VA Lt.Arty. Taylor's Co.
Sutherland, Rolla KY 7th Mtd.Inf. Co.C
Sutherland, Rolley KY 11th Cav. Co.C
Sutherland, R.W. SC 5th Cav. Co.B Cpl.
Sutherland, R.W. SC Cav. 17th Bn. Co.C Cpl.
Sutherland, Samp. AR 32nd Inf. Co.I
Sutherland, Sampson AR 2nd Vol. Co.A
Sutherland, Samuel MO Staff 2nd Brig.St.Guard M.MSgt.
Sutherland, Samuel VA 21st Cav. 1st Co.E
Sutherland, Samuel VA Lt.Arty. 13th Bn. Co.B
Sutherland, Samuel VA 1st St.Res. Co.E
Sutherland, Samuel VA 37th Inf. Co.C
Sutherland, Samuel H. MO Inf. 8th Bn. Co.F,A Jr.2nd Lt.
Sutherland, Samuel H. MO 9th Inf. Co.K Jr.2nd Lt.
Sutherland, S.B. Gen. & Staff Chap.
Sutherland, S.F. VA 3rd Inf.Loc.Def. Co.E Capt.
Sutherland, Silas LA 8th Inf. Co.H
Sutherland, S.S. MO 16th Inf. Co.K
Sutherland, T. VA Lt.Arty. Penick's Co.
Sutherland, T.A. MS 8th Inf. Asst.Surg.
Sutherland, T.G. LA Inf.Crescent Regt. Co.E
Sutherland, T.G. Conf.Cav. Powers' Regt. Co.D 2nd Lt.
Sutherland, Th. A. Gen. & Staff Asst.Surg.
Sutherland, Thomas NC 6th Cav. (65th St.Troops) Co.A
Sutherland, Thomas NC 64th Inf. Co.N
Sutherland, Thomas TX Cav. 3rd Regt.St.Troops Co.A
Sutherland, Thomas VA 21st Cav. 2nd Co.C 1st Lt.
Sutherland, Thomas VA Lt.Arty. Taylor's Co.
Sutherland, Thomas A. SC 8th Inf. Co.G
Sutherland, Thomas D. SC 5th Res. Co.G
Sutherland, Thomas R. VA 51st Inf. Co.B
Sutherland, Thomas S. TN 4th (Murray's) Cav. Co.K Bvt.2nd Lt.
Sutherland, T.S. TN Inf. 22nd Bn. Co.F Bvt.2nd Lt.
Sutherland, T.W. AR 2nd Inf.
Sutherland, Van VA 21st Cav. 1st Co.E
Sutherland, W. TX 34th Cav. Co.K
Sutherland, W.A. SC 14th Inf. Co.I
Sutherland, W.C. VA Lt.Arty. 12th Bn. Co.B
Sutherland, W.D. AR 5th Inf. Co.K
Sutherland, W.E. VA Lt.Arty. Penick's Co.
Sutherland, W.F. SC 2nd Inf. Co.E
Sutherland, W.H. TX Cav. Baird's Regt. Co.C
Sutherland, W.H. VA 4th Cav. Co.I
Sutherland, Wiley AR 2nd Vol. Co.A
Sutherland, Wiley NC 21st Inf. Co.H
Sutherland, William KY 6th Cav. Co.D
Sutherland, William KY 14th Cav. Co.B
Sutherland, William KY 1st Inf. Co.F
Sutherland, William LA Inf.Cons.Crescent Regt. Co.H
Sutherland, William NC Walker's Bn. Thomas' Legion 2nd Co.D Cpl.
Sutherland, William TN Cav. 16th Bn. (Neal's) Co.E
Sutherland, William TN 13th Inf. Co.L
Sutherland, William TN 31st Inf. Co.D
Sutherland, William TX 9th (Nichols') Inf. Co.H
Sutherland, William VA Lt.Arty. J.S. Brown's Co.
Sutherland, William VA Lt.Arty. Taylor's Co.
Sutherland, William A. GA 48th Inf. Co.F Lt.
Sutherland, William F. SC 20th Inf. Co.E
Sutherland, William H. AL Cav. Bowie's Co.
Sutherland, William H. MS Part.Rangers Smyth's Co.
Sutherland, William H. NC 2nd Inf. Co.H
Sutherland, William H. TX 15th Cav. Co.C
Sutherland, William H. VA Cav. 1st Bn. Co.A
Sutherland, William H. VA 24th Cav. Co.G
Sutherland, William H. VA 24th Inf. Co.C Capt.
Sutherland, William H. VA 29th Inf. Co.A Sgt.
Sutherland, William H. 8th (Wade's) Conf.Cav. Co.A
Sutherland, William H.H. NC 58th Inf. Co.D
Sutherland, William L. NC 64th Inf. Co.I Cpl.
Sutherland, William N. AL 27th Inf.
Sutherland, William W. MO Cav. Poindexter's Regt.
Sutherland, W.J. MS 10th Cav. Co.H
Sutherland, W.J. Conf.Cav. Baxter's Bn. Co.A
Sutherland, W.M. SC 5th Res. Co.H
Sutherland, W.S. 1st Conf.Cav. 1st Co.D Sgt.
Sutherland, Zachariah MO Inf. Clark's Regt. Co.D
Sutherland, Z.M. KY 6th Mtd.Inf. Co.G
Sutherlin, Bird J. VA 23rd Inf. Co.E
Sutherlin, Carter M. MO 2nd Cav. Co.G 1st Lt.
Sutherlin, Christopher T. VA 23rd Inf. Co.E 1st Sgt.
Sutherlin, Dick TN 7th (Duckworth's) Cav. Co.G
Sutherlin, Edwin J. VA Lt.Arty. 13th Bn. Co.B Cpl.
Sutherlin, Evan NC 1st Inf.
Sutherlin, George H. LA Inf. 11th Bn. Co.D Sgt.
Sutherlin, George H. LA Inf.Cons.Crescent Regt. Co.B,F 2nd Lt.
Sutherlin, George H. VA 38th Inf. Co.E 2nd Lt.
Sutherlin, George P. GA 55th Inf. Co.K
Sutherlin, Jessee M. AR 1st (Colquitt's) Inf. Co.H
Sutherlin, John H. LA 19th Inf. Co.H Capt.
Sutherlin, John V. AL 1st Cav. Co.G
Sutherlin, L. TN 7th (Duckworth's) Cav. Co.G
Sutherlin, M.H. GA Floyd Legion (St.Guards) Co.B
Sutherlin, Nathaniel S. LA 9th Inf. Co.F 2nd Lt.
Sutherlin, P.W. VA Lt.Arty. 13th Bn. Co.B
Sutherlin, Robert H. GA 55th Inf. Co.K
Sutherlin, T.N. TX 5th Inf. Co.I
Sutherlin, W.H.H. MO Robertson's Regt. St.Guard Co.9
Sutherlin, William S. LA 9th Inf. Co.F
Sutherlin, W.T. Gen. & Staff Maj.,QM
Suthern, B.F. TN 15th (Cons.) Cav. Co.K
Suthers, Eph. VA Mil. Wythe Cty.
Suthers, James VA 51st Inf. Co.C
Suthers, James VA Mil. Wythe Cty.
Suthers, J.J. NC 12th Inf. Co.H
Suthers, John VA 51st Inf. Co.C
Suthers, John VA Mil. Wythe Cty.
Suthers, John H. VA 136th Mil. Co.B
Suthers, M. NC 20th Inf. Co.I
Suthin, Henry LA 26th Dismtd.Cav. Co.F
Suthon, Lucius LA Mil. LaFourche Regt.
Suthron, William AL 21st Inf. Co.B
Sutleff, W.G. MS 32nd Inf. Co.K
Sutlemyre, Eli NC 16th Inf. Co.E
Sutler, Asa VA Arty. C.F. Johnston's Co.
Sutler, Asa VA 19th Inf. Co.B
Sutler, Charles K. VA 51st Inf. Co.E
Sutler, George W. VA 52nd Inf. 2nd Co.B
Sutler, James SC 4th Cav. Co.D
Sutler, James SC 10th Inf. 1st Co.G
Sutler, James SC 23rd Inf. Co.D
Sutler, James SC Manigault's Bn.Vol. Co.A
Sutler, James A. VA 51st Inf. Co.E
Sutler, John T. VA 19th Inf. Co.B
Sutler, John T. VA Loc.Def. Mallory's Co.
Sutler, Joseph L. VA 51st Inf. Co.E
Sutler, William C. VA 17th Inf. Co.F
Sutler, William M. VA 19th Inf. Co.B
Sutler, Wilson VA 51st Inf. Co.E
Sutless, Benjamin VA Cav. 36th Bn. Co.C
Sutley, A.H. GA 53rd Inf. Co.D
Sutley, Allen B. GA 61st Inf. Co.F
Sutley, A.R. FL Lt.Arty. Dyke's Co.
Sutley, Benjamin W. GA 61st Inf. Co.F
Sutley, B.W. GA 51st Inf. Co.G
Sutley, E.K. AL 57th Inf. Co.C
Sutley, H. GA 4th Inf. Co.E
Sutley, Harris AL 12th Inf. Co.C
Sutley, James C. AL 31st Inf. Co.C
Sutliff, A. KY 2nd (Duke's) Cav. Co.K

Sutliff, Abraham NC 13th Inf. Co.I
Sutliff, Alexander NC 13th Inf. Co.I
Sutliff, Barnett VA Cav. 37th Bn. Co.G
Sutliff, D. AR 51st Mil. Co.H
Sutliff, James VA 5th Cav. Co.G
Sutliff, Joseph NC 13th Inf. Co.I
Sutliff, Richard MO 1st Cav. Co.G 1st Sgt.
Sutliff, William VA 22nd Cav. Co.K
Sutliffe, James VA 1st Inf. Co.B
Sutlington, John W. VA 62nd Mtd.Inf. 2nd Co.B
Sutlive, John W. GA 9th Inf. Co.D AQM
Sutlive, John W. Anderson's Brig. Capt.,AQM
Sutlon, J. AL 40th Regt.Res. Comsy.Sgt.
Suton, A.J. GA Inf. 11th Bn. (St.Guards) Co.D
Suton, D.C. GA Inf. 11th Bn. (St.Guards) Co.D
Suton, Ely 2nd Cherokee Mtd.Vol. Co.B
Suton, J.L. TX 6th Inf. Co.C 2nd Lt.
Suton, Joshua 2nd Cherokee Mtd.Vol. Co.B
Suton, J.S. VA 37th Mil. 2nd Co.B
Sutphen, A.J. TX 37th Cav. Co.G
Sutphen, Baswell VA 30th Bn.S.S. Co.C,D
Sutphen, David S. TX 4th Cav. Co.H
Sutphen, David S. TX 12th Inf. Co.G
Sutphen, George W. TX 4th Cav. Co.H
Sutphen, Samuel C. TX 4th Cav. Co.H
Sutphen, Samuel C. TX 12th Inf. Co.G
Sutphen, William TX 17th Cav. Co.H
Sutphin, Asa VA 25th Cav. Co.E
Sutphin, Asa L. VA 54th Inf. Co.D
Sutphin, A.W. MS Inf. 2nd Bn. (St.Troops) Co.F
Sutphin, B. VA 5th Cav. Co.C
Sutphin, Bluford VA 54th Inf. Co.G
Sutphin, Charles H. VA 49th Inf. 3rd Co.G
Sutphin, Daniel VA Loc.Def. Neff's Co.
Sutphin, Daniel W. VA 54th Inf. Co.G
Sutphin, David VA 45th Inf. Co.I
Sutphin, Elijah VA 8th Cav.
Sutphin, Elis VA 25th Cav. Co.F
Sutphin, Elkana H. VA 29th Inf. Co.B
Sutphin, Floyd VA 24th Inf. Co.C
Sutphin, Henderson P. VA 54th Inf. Co.D
Sutphin, Hendric VA Inf. 54th Bn. Co.D
Sutphin, Hendrick VA 4th Res. Co.F,K
Sutphin, Hendrick VA 54th Inf. Co.D
Sutphin, Irvin NC 21st Inf. Co.I
Sutphin, J. VA 17th Inf. Co.E
Sutphin, J.A. VA 50th Inf. Co.K
Sutphin, Jacob VA 4th Res. Co.H
Sutphin, James VA 25th Cav. Co.F
Sutphin, James VA Lt.Arty. Jackson's Bn.St.Line Co.B
Sutphin, James D. VA Hvy.Arty. 10th Bn. Co.B
Sutphin, James S. VA 14th Inf. Co.K Capt.
Sutphin, Jno. NC 21st Inf. Co.I
Sutphin, John B. VA 54th Inf. Co.D
Sutphin, John H. VA 54th Inf. Co.D
Sutphin, John W. VA 24th Inf. Co.A
Sutphin, Lafayette VA 54th Inf. Co.D
Sutphin, Leyburn G. VA 24th Inf. Co.C
Sutphin, Leygrand VA 54th Inf. Co.G
Sutphin, Marion VA 4th Res. Co.I
Sutphin, Milton W. VA 4th Res. Co.H
Sutphin, Riley VA 4th Res. Co.H,I
Sutphin, R.L. VA Lt.Arty. Penick's Co. Cpl.
Sutphin, Robert VA 6th Cav. Co.B
Sutphin, Rolen VA 54th Inf. Co.D
Sutphin, Thomas VA 25th Cav. Co.F
Sutphin, Washington VA 4th Res. Co.I
Sutphin, Wesley VA 63rd Inf. Co.G, 2nd Co.I
Sutphin, William VA 24th Inf. Co.A
Sutphin, William VA 1st Cav.St.Line Co.B
Sutpin, Wm. J. AR 13th Inf. Co.B
Sutrell, Thornton Mead's Conf.Cav. Co.L
Sutser, Joseph MO 12th Inf. Co.H
Sutt, John VA 45th Inf. Co.B
Sutt, J.W. TN 4th (McLemore's) Cav. Co.D
Suttah 1st Seminole Mtd.Vol
Suttals, W.F. GA 11th Cav. Co.F
Suttals, W.J. GA 11th Cav. Co.F
Suttan, E.S. AR 1st Cav. Co.B
Suttan, J.H. GA 3rd Inf. Co.D
Suttan, Michael NC 31st Inf. Co.D
Sut tee cah Scontie 1st Cherokee Mtd.Rifles Co.B
Sutten, Harrison TN 46th Inf. Co.G
Sutten, J.E. AL 8th Inf. Co.C
Sutten, J.F. AR 38th Inf. Co.H
Sutten, J.H. Gen. & Staff, Ord.Dept.
Sutten, John GA 17th Inf. Co.C
Sutten, John VA Loc.Def. Tuttle's Bn. Co.A
Sutten, John H. AR 25th Inf. Co.G
Sutten, Julius GA Lt.Arty. Guerard's Btty.
Sutten, Michael W. NC 51st Inf. Co.B
Sutten, Shelby MS Inf. 3rd Bn. (St.Troops) Co.A
Sutten, Valentine MO Cav. 3rd Bn. Co.G
Sutten, W.J. AR 38th Inf. Co.K
Suttenfield, D.M. VA 16th Inf. Co.B
Sutter, Adolph LA Mil. Chalmette Regt. Co.A
Sutter, Adolphe LA Mil. 4th Regt. 1st Brig. 1st Div. Co.I
Sutter, Emanuel MS 3rd Inf. Co.H
Sutter, H.F. Morgan's,CSA
Sutter, J. TN Inf. 3rd Bn. Co.G
Sutter, Jacob AL Res. Belser's Co.
Sutter, James SC 4th Cav. Co.D
Sutter, Joseph AL Lt.Arty. Goldthwaite's Btty.
Sutter, Joshua TX 7th Cav. Co.A
Sutter, Samuel LA 14th Inf. Co.B Cpl.
Sutter, Samuel LA 20th Inf. Co.D Capt.
Sutter, Stephen LA 7th Inf. Co.G
Sutter, W.B. VA 10th Cav. Co.F
Sutter, W.T. LA Arty. Hutton's Co. (Crescent Arty.,Co.A) Artif.
Sutterfield, J.S. AR 16th Inf. Co.F
Sutterfield, Reubin N. 1st Cherokee Mtd.Vol. 1st Co.K Sgt.
Sutterfield, Thomas VA 42nd Inf. Co.A
Sutterfield, U.J. AR 14th (Powers') Inf. Co.D Cpl.
Sutterfield, William AR 14th (Powers') Inf. Co.D
Sutterfield, W.J. AR 16th Inf. Co.K
Suttermyer, William Conf.Cav. Clarkson's Bn. Ind.Rangers Teamster
Sutterny, James MS Hudson's Co. (Noxubee Guards)
Suttin, James AR 8th Cav. Co.L
Suttle, Adam W. VA 64th Mtd.Inf. Co.G
Suttle, Alexander VA Inf. 21st Bn. Co.A Sgt.
Suttle, Alexander VA 64th Mtd.Inf. Co.A 2nd Lt.
Suttle, C. LA 1st Inf. Co.F
Suttle, C.B. NC 2nd Jr.Res. Co.D Sgt.
Suttle, C.N. VA 17th Inf. Co.B
Suttle, David VA 60th Inf. Co.E
Suttle, Drury D. NC 38th Inf. Co.I 2nd Lt.
Suttle, E.B. MS 37th Inf. Co.G Sgt.
Suttle, Edward J. AR 1st Vol. Co.B
Suttle, Elias TN 30th Inf. Co.I
Suttle, Elijah TN 30th Inf. Co.I
Suttle, Ewing Greenberry MO 8th Inf. Co.G Cpl.
Suttle, F.M. TX 13th Vol. Co.H Artif.
Suttle, Friar VA 17th Cav. Co.G
Suttle, George E. TN Cav. 11th Bn. (Gordon's) Co.A
Suttle, George J. AL 62nd Inf. Co.C Sgt.
Suttle, George M. NC 34th Inf. Co.I Sgt.
Suttle, George M. SC 1st Arty. Co.B
Suttle, George W. NC 16th Inf. Co.D
Suttle, G.W. MO 5th Cav. Co.C
Suttle, G.W. NC 1st Bn.Jr.Res. Co.B 1st Lt.
Suttle, Henry F. KY 8th Cav.
Suttle, Isaac T. TX 19th Cav. Co.D
Suttle, J.A. TX 25th Cav. Co.A
Suttle, James MO 8th Inf. Co.G
Suttle, James H. VA 14th Cav. Co.K
Suttle, James H. VA 135th Mil. Co.F
Suttle, James J. GA 36th (Broyles') Inf. Co.C 2nd Lt.
Suttle, James L. GA 36th (Broyles') Inf. Co.A
Suttle, James N. AL 11th Inf. Co.F
Suttle, James N. AL 63rd Inf. Co.H Maj.
Suttle, James V. NC 18th Inf. Co.E
Suttle, James W. NC 16th Inf. Co.D Cpl.
Suttle, Jerry TN 30th Inf. Co.I
Suttle, J. Moore TX Cav. 2nd Regt.St.Troops Co.I
Suttle, J.N. GA 36th (Broyles') Inf. Co.C
Suttle, John MS 3rd Cav. Co.B
Suttle, John MS Cav. Ham's Regt. Co.I
Suttle, John MS Inf. 3rd Bn. Co.C
Suttle, John MS 15th Bn.S.S. Co.A
Suttle, John TN 6th (Wheeler's) Cav. Co.C
Suttle, John TX 24th Cav. Co.G
Suttle, John VA 60th Inf. Co.E
Suttle, John H. NC 50th Inf. Co.G
Suttle, John Joseph VA 14th Cav. Co.K
Suttle, John M. TN 25th Inf. Co.K Sgt.
Suttle, John T. MS Cav. Duncan's Co. (Tishomingo Rangers)
Suttle, John W. TN 2nd (Robison's) Inf. Co.I
Suttle, Jordan VA 5th Inf. Co.F
Suttle, Joseph VA 60th Inf. Co.E
Suttle, Joseph M. GA 23rd Inf. Co.H Sgt.
Suttle, Joseph W. MS 27th Inf. Co.E
Suttle, Josiah TN 30th Inf. Co.F
Suttle, J.W. TN Inf. 4th Cons.Regt. Co.I
Suttle, Lafayette MS Cav. Duncan's Co. (Tishomingo Rangers)
Suttle, Larkin A. MO 10th Cav. Co.D
Suttle, Leroy W. TN 3rd (Clack's) Inf. Co.G
Suttle, M. TX 33rd Cav. Co.B
Suttle, Philip NC 34th Inf. Co.I
Suttle, Robert TN 30th Inf. Co.I
Suttle, Robert G. GA 36th (Broyles') Inf. Co.C
Suttle, Robert V. VA 30th Inf. Co.K
Suttle, Samuel L. MS Cav. Duncan's Co. (Tishomingo Rangers)
Suttle, Sincler M. AL 13th Inf. Co.H 1st Sgt.
Suttle, S.M., Jr. AL 46th Inf. Co.A Lt.
Suttle, S.S. MS 37th Inf. Co.G Cpl.

Suttle, Talmadge MS Cav. Duncan's Co. (Tishomingo Rangers)
Suttle, Tecumseh C. Morgan's Co.A,CSA
Suttle, Thomas GA 36th (Broyles') Inf. Co.A,C
Suttle, V.J. NC 1st Bn.Jr.Res. Co.C
Suttle, W. TX 24th Cav. Co.G
Suttle, W. TX 25th Cav. Co.A
Suttle, W.G. TX Cav. 2nd Regt.St.Troops Co.I
Suttle, W.H.H. MS 13th Inf. Co.A
Suttle, William NC 50th Inf. Co.G
Suttle, William TN 30th Inf. Co.I
Suttle, William VA Cav. Mosby's Regt. (Part.Rangers) Co.C Capt.
Suttle, William VA 60th Inf. Co.E
Suttle, William A. GA 36th (Broyles') Inf. Co.A,C
Suttle, William B. TN 32nd Inf. Co.I Cpl.
Suttle, William D. TN 3rd (Clack's) Inf. Co.G
Suttle, William D. VA 22nd Inf. Taylor's Co.
Suttle, William D. VA 60th Inf. Co.E Sgt.
Suttle, William J. AL 11th Inf. Co.F 2nd Lt.
Suttle, W.J.N. NC 1st Bn.Jr.Res. Co.B
Suttle, W.N. VA 53rd Inf. Co.G
Suttlefield, Allen MO St.Guard
Suttlefield, James MO St.Guard
Suttlemeyer, James W. MS 2nd Inf. Co.L
Suttlemiers, Gabriel M. MS 7th Cav. Co.D
Suttlemiers, J.G. MS 7th Cav. Co.C
Suttlemire, John W. SC 12th Inf. Co.F,D Sgt.
Suttlemires, M.K. MS 7th Cav. Co.C
Suttlemyer, A. NC 26th Inf. Co.F
Suttlemyer, E.K. MS 9th Inf. Old Co.H, New Co.F
Suttlemyer, E.K. MS 9th Bn.S.S. Co.A Sgt.
Suttlemyer, Harrell S. NC Mallett's Bn. (Cp.Guard) Co.B
Suttlemyre, Babel A. AL 4th Inf. Co.A
Suttler, J.B. MS 2nd Part.Rangers Co.D
Suttler, Joseph LA C.S. Zouave Bn. Co.C
Suttlers, Daniel G. GA 56th Inf. Co.A
Suttles, Albert B. VA 15th Cav. Co.E
Suttles, Alfred D.M. GA Lt.Arty. (Jo Thompson Arty.) Hanleiter's Co. Cpl.
Suttles, Alfred G. GA Arty. 9th Bn. Co.A,E
Suttles, Daniel G. GA 26th Inf. Co.A
Suttles, D.B.F. NC 56th Inf. Co.F
Suttles, Franklin G. GA Lt.Arty. (Jo Thompson Arty.) Hanleiter's Co.
Suttles, George MO 9th Inf. Co.B
Suttles, Guilford NC 22nd Inf. Co.K
Suttles, Henry GA 43rd Inf. Co.C
Suttles, H.P. TN 26th Inf. Co.B,H
Suttles, Isaac NC 6th Cav. (65th St.Troops) Co.D,C
Suttles, Isaac NC 6th Inf. Co.E
Suttles, Isaac TX 5th Inf. Co.K
Suttles, Isaac H. MS 36th Inf. Co.I
Suttles, Jackson MO 1st N.E. Cav. Co.M
Suttles, James G. NC 60th Inf. Co.D
Suttles, James M. GA 52nd Inf. Co.B,C
Suttles, John NC 11th (Bethel Regt.) Inf. Co.K
Suttles, John TX 13th Cav. Co.F Cpl.
Suttles, John B. GA 7th Inf. (St.Guards) Co.F 2nd Lt.
Suttles, John H. NC 60th Inf. Co.D
Suttles, John N. NC 60th Inf. Co.D
Suttles, John W. AL 8th Inf. Co.K Cpl.
Suttles, John W. MS 6th Inf. Co.G
Suttles, John W. SC 2nd Rifles Co.D
Suttles, Joseph NC 50th Inf. Co.K
Suttles, J.T. GA 1st Cav. Co.F
Suttles, J.W. AL Coosa Guards J.W. Suttles' Co. Capt.
Suttles, Marion TX 11th Inf. Co.F
Suttles, M.B. AL 8th Inf. Co.K
Suttles, Minor MO 4th Cav. Co.F
Suttles, Richard H. VA 40th Inf. Co.B
Suttles, Robert NC 50th Inf. Co.K
Suttles, Robert S. GA 17th Inf. Co.F
Suttles, Samuel KY 3rd Mtd.Inf. Co.M
Suttles, Samuel F. VA 47th Inf. Co.B
Suttles, Stephen NC 25th Inf. Co.H
Suttles, Thomas D. TX 13th Cav. Co.F
Suttles, W.H. GA 2nd Res. Co.G Cpl.
Suttles, Wiley GA 2nd Res. Co.G
Suttles, William AL 19th Inf. Co.B
Suttles, William NC 50th Inf. Co.K
Suttles, William SC 1st Arty. Co.K
Suttles, William C. AL 13th Inf. Co.C
Suttles, William J. NC 25th Inf. Co.H
Suttles, William M. AL 8th Inf. Co.K
Suttles, William R. TN 63rd Inf. Co.D,I
Suttles, William T. MO Robertson's Regt. St.Guard Co.11
Suttles, W.P. AL 8th Cav. Co.B
Suttles, W.P. AL 8th (Livingston's) Cav. Co.B
Suttles, W.T. MS Inf. 1st Bn.St.Troops (30 days '64) Co.D Cpl.
Suttleton, J. TN 13th (Gore's) Cav. Co.I
Sutton, --- TX Cav. Border's Regt. Co.G
Sutton, --- TX Cav. Mann's Regt. Co.K
Sutton, A.A. FL Kilcrease Lt.Arty.
Sutton, Aaron KY 2nd Cav. Co.D
Sutton, Aaron J. GA 31st Inf. Co.D Sgt.
Sutton, Abraham TN 49th Inf.
Sutton, Abraham TN 59th Mtd.Inf. Co.E
Sutton, A.C. SC 5th St.Troops Co.K
Sutton, A. DeR. LA Washington Arty.Bn. Co.2
Sutton, A. DeR. SC Inf. 1st (Charleston) Bn. Co.E
Sutton, A. DeR. SC 27th Inf. Co.A
Sutton, A.H. FL 1st Inf. New Co.I, Co.C
Sutton, A.J. GA 32nd Inf. Co.H
Sutton, A.J. GA 49th Inf. Co.F
Sutton, A.J. GA 55th Inf. Co.K
Sutton, A.J. GA Cherokee Legion (St.Guards) Co.E Cpl.
Sutton, A.J. TN 16th Inf. Co.F
Sutton, A.L. GA Inf. (Emanuel Troops) Moring's Co.
Sutton, Albert KY 5th Cav. Co.D
Sutton, Alexander NC 2nd Arty. (36th St.Troops) Co.H
Sutton, Alexander NC 27th Inf. Co.C
Sutton, Alfred NC 31st Inf. Co.K
Sutton, Alfred B. AR 14th (McCarver's) Inf. Co.I
Sutton, Alfred B. AR 21st Inf. Co.K
Sutton, Anderson TX 18th Cav. Co.D
Sutton, Andrew NC 54th Inf. Co.F
Sutton, Andrew J. AL Lt.Arty. 2nd Bn. Co.F
Sutton, Andrew J. GA 2nd Inf. Co.H
Sutton, Andrew J. NC 17th Inf. (1st Org.) Co.I
Sutton, Andrew J. NC 68th Inf.
Sutton, Andy TX 6th Inf. Co.F
Sutton, Archibald VA Lt.Arty. Cayce's Co. Bugler
Sutton, Archibald S. VA 9th Cav. Co.B Bugler
Sutton, A.S. VA Lt.Arty. Thornton's Co.
Sutton, Asa H. AR 24th Inf. Co.F
Sutton, Asberry S. AR Inf. Hardy's Regt. Co.D
Sutton, Asel H. AR Inf. Hardy's Regt. Co.D
Sutton, Augustus B. MS 26th Inf. Co.A
Sutton, Augustus B.S. MS 22nd Inf. Co.A
Sutton, Augustus C. AR Inf. Hardy's Regt. Co.D
Sutton, B. GA 24th Inf. Co.K
Sutton, Balam TN 26th Inf. Co.C
Sutton, Benjaman A. AR 1st (Crawford's) Cav. Co.A
Sutton, Benjamin AL 39th Inf. Co.C
Sutton, Benjamin FL 6th Inf. Co.I
Sutton, Benjamin NC 3rd Arty. (40th St.Troops) Co.A
Sutton, Benjamin NC 7th Sr.Res. Bradshaw's Co.B
Sutton, Benjamin NC 8th Inf. Co.I
Sutton, Benjamin NC 17th Inf. (2nd Org.) Co.K
Sutton, Benjamin NC 32nd Inf. Lenoir Braves 1st Co.K
Sutton, Benjamin NC 38th Inf. Co.C
Sutton, Benjamin F. NC 3rd Cav. (41st St.Troops) Co.E 1st Sgt.
Sutton, Benjamin F. NC 27th Inf. Co.C Cpl.
Sutton, Benjamin H. AL 57th Inf. Co.B
Sutton, Benjamin H. MS 28th Cav. Co.D
Sutton, Benjamin L. NC 1st Arty. (10th St.Troops) Co.F
Sutton, Benjamin L. NC 18th Inf. Co.D
Sutton, Benjamin M. GA 31st Inf. Co.D
Sutton, Bennett A. AR 24th Inf. Co.F
Sutton, Berry AR 20th Inf. Co.A
Sutton, B.F. MS 1st (King's) Inf. (St.Troops) Co.I Capt.
Sutton, B.F. MS Inf. 1st Bn.St.Troops (30 days. '64) Co.B Capt.
Sutton, B.F. NC 23rd Inf. Co.A
Sutton, B.F. SC 2nd Inf. Co.H
Sutton, B.J. GA 32nd Inf. Co.H
Sutton, B.L. NC 20th Inf. Co.I Music.
Sutton, Blount GA 2nd Cav. Co.C
Sutton, B.M. FL 10th Inf. Co.K
Sutton, Bryan NC 1st Arty. (10th St.Troops) Co.F
Sutton, Bryant MO 4th Cav. Co.E
Sutton, B.W. GA 48th Inf. Co.H
Sutton, Calab TN 10th (DeMoss') Cav. Co.C
Sutton, Caleb NC 18th Inf. Co.D
Sutton, Caleb, Jr. NC 18th Inf. Co.D
Sutton, Caleb C. TN 6th (Wheeler's) Cav. Co.I
Sutton, Calvin J. NC 38th Inf. Co.C
Sutton, C.C. NC 3rd Cav. (41st St.Troops) Co.E
Sutton, C.D. GA 43rd Inf. Co.D
Sutton, C.G. TX 1st Hvy.Arty. Co.G
Sutton, C.G. TX 13th Vol. 1st Co.B
Sutton, C.H. GA 4th Inf.
Sutton, C.H. GA 40th Inf.
Sutton, Charles NC 31st Inf. Co.K
Sutton, Charles TX 35th (Brown's) Cav. Co.A,F
Sutton, Charles E. TN 32nd Inf. Co.I
Sutton, Charles H. VA 2nd Inf. Co.E
Sutton, Charles H. VA 40th Inf. Co.E

Sutton, Charles J. GA 45th Inf. Co.D
Sutton, Charles W. AL Lt.Arty. Goldthwaite's Btty.
Sutton, Charles W. VA 1st Arty. Co.K
Sutton, Chesley W. NC 13th Inf. Co.E
Sutton, Christopher P. MS 26th Inf. Co.I Cpl.
Sutton, Cincinattus M. TN 2nd (Robison's) Inf. Co.I
Sutton, C.L. GA 31st Inf. Co.D
Sutton, C.L. VA Lt.Arty. Thornton's Co.
Sutton, C.M. TX 27th Cav. Co.K
Sutton, Corry H. VA Horse Arty. Shoemaker's Co.
Sutton, Courtes B. TX 11th Cav. Co.E 1st Lt.
Sutton, Courtes B. TX Cav. Sutton's Co. Capt.
Sutton, C.W. GA Cav. 21st Bn. Co.C
Sutton, C.W. VA Courtney Arty.
Sutton, Dan'l AL Cav. 8th Regt. (Livingston's) Co.C
Sutton, Daniel AR Inf. Cocke's Regt. Co.G
Sutton, Daniel NC 8th Bn.Part.Rangers Co.C
Sutton, Daniel NC 66th Inf. Co.D
Sutton, Daniel M. NC 18th Inf. Co.K Cpl.
Sutton, David AL 12th Inf. Co.G
Sutton, David, Jr. GA 63rd Inf. Co.K
Sutton, David, Sr. GA 63rd Inf. Co.K
Sutton, David NC 8th Bn.Part.Rangers Co.C
Sutton, David NC 2nd Inf. Co.F
Sutton, David NC 8th Inf. Co.G
Sutton, David VA 29th Inf. Co.B
Sutton, David S. MS 22nd Inf. Co.A
Sutton, D.M. NC 2nd Arty. (36th St.Troops) Co.B
Sutton, D.S. FL 11th Inf. Co.E
Sutton, D.W. AR 1st (Monroe's) Cav. Co.B
Sutton, E. SC 2nd Inf. Co.G
Sutton, E. TN 5th Inf. Co.A Lt.
Sutton, E.B. GA Hardwick Mtd.Rifles
Sutton, E.C. SC 5th Inf. Co.F
Sutton, Ed B. NC 17th Inf. (1st Org.) Co.I
Sutton, Edmond GA Cobb's Legion Co.B
Sutton, Edward AL Arty. 1st Bn. Drum.
Sutton, Edward AL St.Arty. Co.A
Sutton, Edward GA Cobb's Legion
Sutton, Edward LA Washington Arty.Bn. Co.4 Driver
Sutton, Edward L. AR 2nd Inf. Co.F
Sutton, E.H. GA 14th Inf. Co.H
Sutton, E.H. GA 24th Inf. Co.K
Sutton, E.L. GA Inf. Grubbs' Co.
Sutton, Elias NC 3rd Inf. Co.B
Sutton, Elias NC 34th Inf. Co.I
Sutton, Elijah F. GA 24th Inf. Porter's Co.
Sutton, Elnathan W. GA 4th Res. Co.H Sgt.
Sutton, E.M. VA 1st Cav. Co.A Sgt.
Sutton, F. AL Conscr.
Sutton, F.B. FL Sp.Cav. 1st Bn. Co.B
Sutton, Felix G. AR 37th Inf. Co.H
Sutton, Felix J. VA Inf. 9th Bn. Duffy's Co.C Sgt.
Sutton, Felix J. VA 25th Inf. 3rd Co.C 2nd Lt.
Sutton, Felix K. VA 9th Cav. Co.B
Sutton, F.L. TN 15th (Cons.) Cav. Co.G
Sutton, F.M. AR 12th Inf. Co.K
Sutton, F.M. KY 3rd Cav. Co.B
Sutton, Francis GA 17th Inf. Co.D
Sutton, Francis LA 1st Hvy.Arty. (Reg.) Co.G
Sutton, Francis M. AL 38th Inf. Co.K
Sutton, Francis M. AR Inf. Hardy's Regt. Co.D
Sutton, Francis M. MS 2nd Inf. Co.K
Sutton, Francis M. MS 21st Inf. Co.C
Sutton, Francis M. NC 27th Inf. Co.C Sgt.
Sutton, Frank KY 9th Cav. Co.F
Sutton, Franklin MS 4th Inf. Co.K
Sutton, Franklin NC 32nd Inf. Co.E,F
Sutton, Franklin J. GA 3rd Inf. Co.I
Sutton, Franklin M. AR 24th Inf. Co.F
Sutton, Frank T. VA Cav. 1st Bn. Co.C
Sutton, Frank T. VA Horse Arty. Shoemaker's Co.
Sutton, Frederick T. VA 111th Mil. Co.5
Sutton, Freeland NC 1st Inf. Co.E
Sutton, Freeland NC 8th Inf. Co.I
Sutton, F.T. VA 5th Cav.
Sutton, F.T. VA 15th Cav. Co.A
Sutton, G.B. FL 2nd Cav. Co.G
Sutton, George AR 20th Inf. Co.G
Sutton, George VA 3rd Cav.
Sutton, George VA 19th Cav. Co.F
Sutton, George VA 20th Cav. Co.E
Sutton, George VA 62nd Mtd.Inf. 2nd Co.D
Sutton, George B. AR 2nd Inf. Co.F
Sutton, George B. NC 18th Inf. Co.A
Sutton, George B. VA 31st Inf. Co.G
Sutton, George B. VA 62nd Mtd.Inf. 2nd Co.A
Sutton, George F. NC 2nd Arty. (36th St.Troops) Co.I
Sutton, George F. NC McDugald's Co.
Sutton, George M. VA 2nd Cav.St.Line McNeel's Co.
Sutton, George R. LA 12th Inf. Co.B
Sutton, George W. AR Inf. 8th Bn. 1st Co.C
Sutton, George W. AR 14th (Powers') Inf. Co.G
Sutton, George W. AR 24th Inf. Co.F
Sutton, George W. AR 25th Inf. Co.F
Sutton, George W. AR Inf. Hardy's Regt. Co.D
Sutton, George W. KY Cav. 2nd Bn. (Dortch's) Co.B,A
Sutton, George W. MS 2nd Inf. Co.K
Sutton, George W. MO Lt.Arty. Barret's Co.
Sutton, George W. NC 47th Inf. Co.K
Sutton, G.M. FL 2nd Cav.
Sutton, Godfrey SC Inf. 7th Bn. (Enfield Rifles) Co.G
Sutton, Green TX 27th Cav. Co.C Cpl.
Sutton, G.W. AR 12th Inf. Co.K
Sutton, G.W. KY 7th Cav. Co.E
Sutton, G.W. KY Morgan's Men Beck's Co.
Sutton, G.W. VA 49th Inf. Co.G
Sutton, H. LA 6th Cav. Co.F
Sutton, H. NC 3rd Cav. (41st St.Troops)
Sutton, Hardry NC Mil. Clark's Sp.Bn. Rountree's Co.
Sutton, Harvey TX 27th Cav. Co.H
Sutton, Hawes R. VA Goochland Lt.Arty.
Sutton, H.C. GA 31st Inf. Co.D
Sutton, Henry AR 7th Inf. Co.F
Sutton, Henry AR 35th Inf. Co.B
Sutton, Henry MO 1st Cav. Co.I Sgt.
Sutton, Henry NC 27th Inf. Co.C
Sutton, Henry NC Inf. Thomas Legion Co.G
Sutton, Henry B. NC 17th Inf. (1st Org.) Co.L
Sutton, Henry C. VA 47th Inf. 2nd Co.K Sgt.
Sutton, Henry D. MO Inf. 8th Bn. Co.A
Sutton, Henry I. AL 41st Inf. Co.K
Sutton, Henry M. FL 3rd Inf. Co.G 2nd Lt.
Sutton, Hiram B. MS 22nd Inf. Co.A 2nd Lt.
Sutton, H.J. TN 24th Inf. 2nd Co.G
Sutton, H.M. LA Cav. Benjamin's Co.
Sutton, H.M. TX Cav. Border's Regt. Co.B
Sutton, H.P. TX 11th Cav. Co.E
Sutton, I.I. GA 50th Inf.
Sutton, I.J. GA 54th Inf. Co.E
Sutton, I.M. MO St.Guard
Sutton, Isaac NC 3rd Inf. Co.G
Sutton, Isham TN 61st Mtd.Inf. Co.H
Sutton, I.T. MO 12th Inf. Co.F
Sutton, I.W. AR 37th Inf. Co.B
Sutton, J. AL 21st Inf.
Sutton, J. GA 44th Inf.
Sutton, J. LA 18th Inf. Co.F
Sutton, J. MS 4th Inf. Co.D
Sutton, J.A. FL Conscr.
Sutton, J.A. MS 22nd Inf. Co.A
Sutton, J.A. NC 66th Inf. Co.C
Sutton, Jackson C. 1st Conf.Inf. 2nd Co.D
Sutton, Jacob TX 17th Field Btty.
Sutton, Jacob B. AL 16th Inf. Co.F
Sutton, Jacob B. GA 51st Inf. Co.E 1st Sgt.
Sutton, James GA Inf. 8th Bn. Co.C
Sutton, James GA 52nd Inf. Co.B
Sutton, James KY 5th Cav. Co.B
Sutton, James MS Cav. 1st Bn. (McNair's) St.Troops Co.C
Sutton, James MS Cav. Gibson's Co. Cpl.
Sutton, James NC 16th Inf. Co.A
Sutton, James NC 39th Inf. Co.K
Sutton, James NC 67th Inf. Co.D
Sutton, James SC 16th Inf. Co.C
Sutton, James TN 21st (Wilson's) Cav. Co.A
Sutton, James TN Inf. 154th Sr.Regt. Co.G
Sutton, James TX Cav. Waller's Regt. Co.A
Sutton, James VA 5th Cav. Co.H
Sutton, James VA 8th Cav. Co.G
Sutton, James VA Cav. 36th Bn. Co.B
Sutton, James VA 4th Res. Co.C
Sutton, James VA Mil. Wythe Cty.
Sutton, James A. VA 40th Inf. Co.A Sgt.
Sutton, James B. AR 16th Inf. Co.B Sgt.
Sutton, James B. MS 21st Inf. Co.F Sgt.
Sutton, James C. AR 6th Inf. New Co.D
Sutton, James C. MO Cav. Poindexter's Regt.
Sutton, James F. LA 12th Inf. Co.E
Sutton, James F. VA 40th Inf. Co.F Cpl.
Sutton, James H. AL 48th Inf. Co.E Cpl.
Sutton, James H. AR 24th Inf. Co.F
Sutton, James H. AR Inf. Hardy's Regt. Co.D
Sutton, James H. GA 31st Inf. Co.D 1st Lt.
Sutton, James H. NC 8th Inf. Co.G
Sutton, James H. NC 16th Inf. Co.D
Sutton, James H. TN 7th Inf. Co.F
Sutton, James L. AR 12th Cav. Co.K
Sutton, James L. GA 57th Inf. Co.G
Sutton, James M. GA 6th Inf. Co.B Sgt.
Sutton, James M. KY 2nd (Duke's) Cav. Co.F
Sutton, James M. MS 20th Inf. Co.G
Sutton, James M. NC 53rd Inf. Co.A Capt.
Sutton, James M. TX 15th Inf. Co.B
Sutton, James N. LA 9th Inf. Co.D
Sutton, James O.L. GA 43rd Inf. Co.K
Sutton, James P. AR 24th Inf. Co.F Cpl.

Sutton, James P. AR Inf. Hardy's Regt. Co.D Cpl.
Sutton, James P. TN 23rd Inf. Co.D
Sutton, James R. NC 67th Inf. Co.E
Sutton, James R. TX 17th Inf. Co.I
Sutton, James S. VA 15th Cav. Co.D
Sutton, James S. VA Cav. 15th Bn. Co.B
Sutton, James T. AL 48th Inf. Co.G 1st Lt.
Sutton, James T. AR 15th (N.W.) Inf. Co.K Ord.Sgt.
Sutton, James T. FL 1st Inf. Co.F
Sutton, James T. FL 11th Inf. Co.E
Sutton, James T., Jr. VA Mil. 33rd Regt.
Sutton, James W. AL 24th Inf. Co.D
Sutton, James W. AR 36th Inf. Co.H
Sutton, Jason A. FL 5th Inf. Co.C
Sutton, Jasper N. GA 1st Bn.S.S. Co.C
Sutton, J.B. AL Lt.Arty. Goldthwaite's Btty.
Sutton, J.B. AL 49th Inf. Co.D
Sutton, J.B. AR Lt.Arty. Key's Btty.
Sutton, J.B. TN 2nd (Ashby's) Cav. Co.A
Sutton, J.B. TN 7th (Duckworth's) Cav. Co.F
Sutton, J.B. TN 7th (Duckworth's) Cav. Co.L
Sutton, J.C. AL 41st Inf. Co.K
Sutton, J.C. AR 12th Inf. Co.K
Sutton, J.C. LA 28th (Gray's) Inf.
Sutton, J.C. VA 50th Inf. Sgt.
Sutton, J.D. AL 8th (Livingston's) Cav. Co.C
Sutton, J.D. AR 32nd Inf. Co.E
Sutton, J.D. SC 6th Inf. 2nd Co.B
Sutton, J.D.N. GA Hvy.Arty. 22nd Bn. Co.B Lt.
Sutton, J.D.N. GA 4th Inf. Co.I
Sutton, J.D.N. GA 25th Inf. 1st Co.K Lt.
Sutton, J.D.W. GA 1st Inf. 2nd Lt.
Sutton, Jefferson KY 5th Mtd.Inf. Co.E
Sutton, Jeremiah GA 1st (Symons') Res. Co.F,H
Sutton, Jeremiah NC Lt.Arty. 13th Bn. Co.F
Sutton, Jeremiah W. NC 3rd Arty. (40th St.Troops) Co.H
Sutton, Jesse MS Inf. 1st Bn.St.Troops (12 mo. '62-3) Co.F
Sutton, Jesse NC 27th Inf. Co.C
Sutton, Jesse TX 17th Cons.Dismtd.Cav. Co.E
Sutton, Jesse TX 6th Inf. Co.F
Sutton, Jesse S. AR 31st Inf. Co.K
Sutton, Jesse S. FL 6th Inf. Co.I Sgt.
Sutton, Jessey R. AR 36th Inf. Co.H
Sutton, J.F. GA 5th Inf. (St.Guards) Russell's Co.
Sutton, J.F. NC 3rd Jr.Res. Co.B
Sutton, J.F. NC 4th Bn.Jr.Res. Co.B
Sutton, J.F. SC Inf. 7th Bn. (Enfield Rifles) Co.F
Sutton, J.F. TN 3rd (Forrest's) Cav. Co.L Bvt.2nd Lt.
Sutton, J.F. TN 42nd Inf. 1st Co.H
Sutton, J.H. AR 1st Vol. Co.K
Sutton, J.H. AR 12th Inf. Co.K
Sutton, J.H. AR 37th Inf. Co.B
Sutton, J.H. FL 2nd Inf. Co.L Sgt.
Sutton, J.H. GA 3rd Res. Co.D
Sutton, J.H. MS 2nd (Quinn's St.Troops) Inf. Co.B
Sutton, J.H. MO 12th Inf. Co.C
Sutton, J.H. TN 17th Inf. Co.I
Sutton, J.H. TN 25th Inf. Co.I
Sutton, J.H. TX 10th Field Btty. Sgt.
Sutton, J.J. AL 47th Inf. Co.C
Sutton, J.J. LA 1st Hvy.Arty. (Reg.) Co.D
Sutton, J.J. SC 5th Inf. 1st Co.I
Sutton, J.J. SC Inf. 7th Bn. (Enfield Rifles) Co.G
Sutton, J.J. TN 21st & 22nd (Cons.) Cav. Co.E
Sutton, J.L. GA 50th Inf. Co.I
Sutton, J.M. MS 6th Cav. Co.G
Sutton, J.M. MS 3rd Inf. (A. of 10,000) Co.C Cpl.
Sutton, J.M. 14th Conf.Cav. Co.A
Sutton, J. Mitchel TN 60th Mtd.Inf. Co.I
Sutton, Joel GA 39th Inf. Co.D 1st Sgt.
Sutton, John GA 12th Cav. Co.B
Sutton, John GA 25th Inf. Co.C Cpl.
Sutton, John GA 59th Inf. Co.C
Sutton, John GA 63rd Inf. Co.K
Sutton, John GA 64th Inf. Co.D
Sutton, John LA 28th (Gray's) Inf. Co.F
Sutton, John NC Inf. 13th Bn. Co.C
Sutton, John NC 16th Inf. Co.A
Sutton, John NC 27th Inf. Co.C
Sutton, John NC 39th Inf. Co.K
Sutton, John NC 66th Inf. Co.E
Sutton, John NC Inf. Thomas Legion 1st Co.A
Sutton, John NC Inf. Thomas Legion Co.G
Sutton, John TN 5th (McKenzie's) Cav. Co.D
Sutton, John TN 11th (Holman's) Cav. Co.I
Sutton, John TN 17th Cav. Co.I
Sutton, John TN 21st (Wilson's) Cav. Co.A
Sutton, John TN 22nd (Barteau's) Cav. Co.A
Sutton, John TN Douglass' Bn.Part.Rangers Perkins' Co.
Sutton, John TN Inf. 1st Cons.Regt. Co.F
Sutton, John TN 1st (Turney's) Inf. Co.I
Sutton, John TN 2nd (Robison's) Inf. Co.D 2nd Lt.
Sutton, John TN 16th Inf. Co.F
Sutton, John TN 29th Inf. Co.C
Sutton, John TN 41st Inf. Co.F
Sutton, John TN 55th (McKoin's) Inf. McEwen, Jr.'s Co.
Sutton, John TX 24th Cav. Co.I
Sutton, John VA Mil. Washington Cty.
Sutton, John 3rd Conf.Cav. Co.G
Sutton, John A. GA 3rd Cav. (St.Guards) Co.C
Sutton, John A. MS 2nd Inf. Co.K
Sutton, John A. NC 8th Bn.Part.Rangers Co.B,C
Sutton, John A. NC Hvy.Arty. 1st Bn. Co.A,D
Sutton, John A. NC Mil. Clark's Sp.Bn. Rountree's Co.
Sutton, John A. NC Loc.Def. Croom's Co.
Sutton, John A. TX 11th Inf. Co.E
Sutton, John B. GA 11th Inf. Co.D
Sutton, John B. KY 9th Cav. Co.F
Sutton, John B. MS 1st Cav. Co.D Sgt.
Sutton, John B. NC 18th Inf. Co.A
Sutton, John B. NC 38th Inf. Co.C
Sutton, John B. NC Giddins' Co. (Detailed & Petitioned Men)
Sutton, John B. TN 2nd (Ashby's) Cav. Co.G
Sutton, John B. TN Cav. 4th Bn. (Branner's) Co.B
Sutton, John C. NC 2nd Arty. (36th St.Troops) Co.G
Sutton, John C. NC 3rd Arty. (40th St.Troops) Co.K,E
Sutton, John C. VA 1st Arty. Co.I Cpl.
Sutton, John C. VA Lt.Arty. 38th Bn. Co.B
Sutton, John E. SC Arty. Gregg's Co. (McQueen Lt.Arty.)
Sutton, John E. SC Arty. Manigault's Bn. 1st Co.C
Sutton, John F. FL Kilcrease Lt.Arty.
Sutton, John F. FL 3rd Inf. Co.G Cpl.
Sutton, John F. NC 8th Inf. Co.I
Sutton, John F. TN 59th Mtd.Inf. Co.B
Sutton, John H. AL 20th Inf. Co.I,H
Sutton, John H. GA 43rd Inf. Co.F
Sutton, John H. NC 5th Cav. (63rd St.Troops) Co.C
Sutton, John H. TN 28th Inf. Co.H Sgt.
Sutton, John J. NC 18th Inf. Co.H Music.
Sutton, John J. NC 30th Inf. Co.A
Sutton, John J. TN Cav. 1st Bn. (McNairy's) Co.B
Sutton, John L. GA 1st Mil. Co.D
Sutton, John M. NC Lt.Arty. 3rd Bn. Co.C Capt.
Sutton, John M. NC 1st Inf. (6 mo. '61) Co.L
Sutton, John M. NC 13th Inf. Co.E
Sutton, John M. NC 16th Inf. Co.D
Sutton, John P. MO 2nd Inf. Co.A
Sutton, John R. NC 5th Cav. (63rd St.Troops) Co.B
Sutton, John T. KY 8th Cav. Co.E
Sutton, John T. KY 10th Cav. Co.E
Sutton, John W. AR 9th Inf. Co.K
Sutton, John W. AR Inf. Hardy's Regt. Co.D
Sutton, John W. KY 14th Cav. Co.B Cpl.
Sutton, John W. TX 24th Cav. Co.C
Sutton, John W. VA Arty. Fleet's Co. Sr.2nd Lt.
Sutton, John W. VA 55th Inf. Co.B 2nd Lt.
Sutton, John Z. MS Inf. 2nd Bn. Co.A Sgt.
Sutton, John Z. MS 12th Inf. Co.C
Sutton, John Z. MS 48th Inf. Co.A Sgt.
Sutton, John Z. VA 26th Inf. 1st Co.B
Sutton, Jonas VA Mil. Wythe Cty.
Sutton, Jonathan GA Cav. Logan's Co. (White Cty. Old Men's Home Guards)
Sutton, Jordan GA 48th Inf. Co.H
Sutton, Joseph GA 40th Inf.
Sutton, Joseph GA 52nd Inf. Co.I
Sutton, Joseph LA 3rd Inf. Co.B
Sutton, Joseph MS 7th Inf. Co.G Sgt.
Sutton, Joseph MO 12th Inf. Co.F 2nd Lt.
Sutton, Joseph NC 2nd Arty. (36th St.Troops) Co.A
Sutton, Joseph NC 3rd Inf. Co.G
Sutton, Joseph NC 20th Inf. Co.I
Sutton, Joseph TN 6th (Wheeler's) Cav. Co.I
Sutton, Joseph TN 11th Inf. Co.D
Sutton, Joseph H. KY 14th Cav. Co.A
Sutton, Joseph M. MS Cav. Garland's Bn. Co.A
Sutton, Joseph M. NC 16th Inf. Co.A Cpl.
Sutton, Joseph M. NC 39th Inf. Co.K Cpl.
Sutton, Joseph M. NC Inf. Thomas Legion 1st Co.A Cpl.
Sutton, Josephus MO 3rd Inf. Co.D
Sutton, Joseph Z. GA 49th Inf. Co.F Cpl.
Sutton, Joshua GA Inf. 4th Bn. (St.Guards) Co.H
Sutton, Joshua MS 40th Inf. Co.D
Sutton, Joshua B. LA Cav. Cole's Co.
Sutton, Joshua J. AR 33rd Inf. Co.E

Sutton, Josiah NC 27th Inf. Co.C Sgt.
Sutton, Josiah P. GA 35th Inf. Co.K
Sutton, J.P. AR 12th Inf. Co.K Drum.
Sutton, J.R. Mead's Conf.Cav. Co.E
Sutton, J. Ross FL 5th Inf. Co.C
Sutton, J.S. KY 10th (Johnson's) Cav. Co.E
Sutton, J.S. MO 12th Inf. Co.C
Sutton, J.S. TX 7th Cav. Lt.Col.
Sutton, J.T. AL 12th Cav. Co.F
Sutton, J.T. FL 2nd Cav. Co.I
Sutton, Julius W. GA 6th Inf. (St.Guards) Co.A
Sutton, Julius W. GA 49th Inf. Co.A
Sutton, J.V. AR 37th Inf. Co.B
Sutton, J.V. TX 8th Cav. Co.D
Sutton, J.W. AR 1st (Monroe's) Cav. Co.L
Sutton, J.W. FL 10th Inf. Co.A
Sutton, J.W. GA 62nd Cav. Co.K
Sutton, J.W. GA Hvy.Arty. 22nd Bn. Co.B
Sutton, J.W. GA Arty. St.Troops Pruden's Btty.
Sutton, J.W. MO 8th Inf. Co.B
Sutton, J.W. VA Cav. 40th Bn. Co.C
Sutton, J.W. Morgan's Co.A,CSA
Sutton, J. West NC 12th Inf. Co.H
Sutton, J.Y. GA Arty. (Macon Lt.Arty.) Slaten's Co.
Sutton, L. VA Lt.Arty. 12th Bn. Co.B
Sutton, Lawson TN 26th Inf. Co.C
Sutton, L.B. AR 27th Inf. Co.I
Sutton, Leander GA Cobb's Legion Co.L
Sutton, Lemuel D. AR 1st Mtd.Rifles Co.I
Sutton, Lemuel H. NC 27th Inf. Co.C
Sutton, Leroy B. AR 1st (Dobbin's) Cav. Co.I
Sutton, Leston J. GA 48th Inf. Co.H
Sutton, Levi NC 8th Bn.Part.Rangers Co.B
Sutton, Levi NC 66th Inf. Co.C
Sutton, Levi TN 53rd Inf. Co.F
Sutton, Levi J. NC 45th Inf. Co.H
Sutton, Levi M. NC 67th Inf. Co.G
Sutton, Lewis NC 38th Inf. Co.C
Sutton, Lewis NC Giddins' Co. (Detailed & Petitioned Men)
Sutton, Lewis B. NC 1st Inf. (6 mo. '61) Co.L
Sutton, Lewis G. NC 8th Inf. Co.I
Sutton, Lewis M. FL 5th Inf. Co.K
Sutton, L.H. GA 23rd Inf. Co.C
Sutton, Lindsey NC 47th Inf. Co.K
Sutton, Linton NC 2nd Arty. (36th St.Troops) Co.A
Sutton, L.M. FL Conscr.
Sutton, L.M. MO 6th Cav. Co.C,H
Sutton, Logan AR 18th (Marmaduke's) Inf. Co.K
Sutton, Logan G. VA 26th Inf. Co.D
Sutton, Louis B. NC 4th Cav. (59th St.Troops) Co.F 2nd Lt.
Sutton, Loyd NC Cumberland Cty.Bn. Detailed Men Co.B
Sutton, L.P. MS Cp.Guard (Cp. of Instr. for Conscr.)
Sutton, M.A. TX 21st Cav. Co.E
Sutton, Madison J. LA 12th Inf. Co.B
Sutton, Malcom H. NC 18th Inf. Co.D
Sutton, Marcus GA 60th Inf. Co.G
Sutton, Martin V.B. NC 18th Inf. Co.K
Sutton, Marvel G. TN 59th Mtd.Inf. Co.E Fifer
Sutton, Maston E. AR 24th Inf. Co.F
Sutton, Maston E. AR Inf. Hardy's Regt. Co.D
Sutton, M.D. MO 6th Cav. Co.C
Sutton, M.G. GA Inf. 9th Bn. Co.E Sgt.
Sutton, Michael NC 20th Inf. Faison's Co.
Sutton, Michael NC 30th Inf. Co.A
Sutton, Miles W. GA Inf. 4th Bn. (St.Guards) Co.H
Sutton, M.L. MS 39th Inf. Co.A
Sutton, Moses NC 38th Inf. Co.D
Sutton, Moses G. GA 15th Inf. Co.A
Sutton, Moses G. GA 29th Inf. Co.H
Sutton, Moses G. GA 37th Inf. Co.H 1st Sgt.
Sutton, Moses H. GA 6th Inf. Co.D
Sutton, Moses L. NC Lt.Arty. 13th Bn. Co.A
Sutton, M.V. AR 33rd Inf. Co.B
Sutton, M.V.B. NC 2nd Arty. (36th St.Troops) Co.B
Sutton, Nathan MS 17th Inf. Co.K
Sutton, Nathan MS 31st Inf. Co.D
Sutton, Nathaniel G. GA 31st Inf. Co.I
Sutton, N.B. MO 4th Cav. Co.E
Sutton, N.E. TX 11th Cav. Co.E 1st Lt.
Sutton, N.F. GA 18th Inf. Co.K
Sutton, N.G. GA 1st Inf. Co.I
Sutton, Nicholas TX Cav. Madison's Regt. Co.F
Sutton, Nickles TX Cav. Madison's Regt. Co.G
Sutton, N.J. GA 26th Inf. Co.H
Sutton, N.J. GA 35th Inf. Co.K
Sutton, N.L. MS 12th Inf. Co.I
Sutton, Noah NC 3rd Cav. (41st St.Troops) Co.E
Sutton, Nors TN 12th (Green's) Cav. Co.I
Sutton, O.A. GA 8th Cav. Co.B
Sutton, O.A. GA 25th Inf. Co.C
Sutton, Oates NC 46th Inf. Co.I Sgt.
Sutton, Oliver A. GA 62nd Cav. Co.B
Sutton, Oscar VA 47th Inf. 2nd Co.K
Sutton, Osco M. TN 42nd Inf. 2nd Co.F Cpl.
Sutton, O.W. NC 1st Arty. (10th St.Troops) Co.F Sgt.
Sutton, O.W. VA 24th Cav. Co.H,G
Sutton, P. GA Arty. Lumpkin's Co.
Sutton, Page T. VA 9th Cav. Co.B
Sutton, Page T. VA 30th Inf. Co.E
Sutton, Park KY Cav. 2nd Bn. (Dortch's) Co.B,A
Sutton, Park K. KY 1st (Butler's) Cav.
Sutton, Patrick H. MO 1st Inf. Co.G
Sutton, P.D. TX 30th Cav. Co.D
Sutton, Peter VA Cav. 46th Bn. Co.D
Sutton, P.F. NC 53rd Inf. Co.A
Sutton, P.H. TN 15th (Cons.) Cav. Co.G 2nd Lt.
Sutton, Philip NC 51st Inf. Co.K
Sutton, Philip T. Gen. & Staff 1st Lt.,ADC
Sutton, P.K. KY 7th Cav. Co.E
Sutton, P.K. KY Morgan's Men Beck's Co.
Sutton, P.L. VA Lt.Arty. Thornton's Co.
Sutton, Pleasant A. AL 11th Inf. Co.H
Sutton, Plummer NC 46th Inf. Dr.M.
Sutton, P.M. GA 43rd Inf. Co.F
Sutton, P.N. AR 12th Inf. Co.K
Sutton, P.S. Gen. & Staff Chap.
Sutton, Pulaski VA 9th Cav. Co.H
Sutton, Pulaski VA 87th Mil. Co.C
Sutton, P.W. KY 1st (Butler's) Cav. Co.A
Sutton, R. GA 7th Inf. Co.I
Sutton, R. VA Cav. 40th Bn. Co.F
Sutton, R.A. AL Gid Nelson Lt.Arty.
Sutton, Randall B. VA 111th Mil. Co.8
Sutton, R.C. MS 28th Cav. Co.D
Sutton, R.E. TN 1st Cav. Co.E
Sutton, R.E. TX 6th Inf. Co.A Capt.
Sutton, R.E. VA 42nd Inf. Co.K
Sutton, R.H.A. GA 3rd Res. Co.D
Sutton, Richard NC Inf. 13th Bn. Co.C
Sutton, Richard NC 27th Inf. Co.C
Sutton, Richard NC Mil. Clark's Sp.Bn. Rountree's Co.
Sutton, Richard A. VA 24th Cav. Co.F
Sutton, Richard A. VA 30th Inf. Co.G
Sutton, Richard C. VA 40th Inf. Co.A
Sutton, Richard M. KY 2nd Mtd.Inf.
Sutton, Richard T. KY 1st (Helm's) Cav. Co.A
Sutton, Richmond R. TX Lt.Arty. Hughes' Co.
Sutton, Richmond S. GA 3rd Inf. Co.I
Sutton, Riley NC 53rd Inf. Co.A
Sutton, R.J. AL 2nd Cav. Co.D
Sutton, R.M. FL Inf. 2nd Bn. Co.D
Sutton, R.M. KY 7th Mtd.Inf. Co.E
Sutton, Robert TN 15th (Stewart's) Cav. Co.A
Sutton, Robert TN 16th Inf. Co.F
Sutton, Robert A. VA 26th Inf. Co.H Capt.
Sutton, Robert B. AL 24th Inf. Co.G
Sutton, Robert E. VA 47th Inf. 2nd Co.K
Sutton, Robert J. 1st Conf.Cav. 2nd Co.E
Sutton, Robert M. GA 26th Inf. Co.C Cpl.
Sutton, Robert M.F. TN 3rd (Forrest's) Cav. Co.A
Sutton, Robert W. TN 1st (Feild's) Inf.
Sutton, Roderick J.P. AL 45th Inf. Co.I
Sutton, R.T. KY Cav. Thompson's Co.
Sutton, Rufus FL 1st Inf. Old Co.F,H
Sutton, Rufus B.I. FL 3rd Inf. Co.G
Sutton, R.W. TN 15th (Cons.) Cav. Co.G,E
Sutton, S. GA Cav. 29th Bn. Co.G
Sutton, S. TX Cav. Baird's Regt. Co.D
Sutton, Sam NC 31st Inf. Co.K
Sutton, Samuel MO 9th Bn.S.S. Co.C
Sutton, Samuel NC 68th Inf. Lt.
Sutton, Samuel 2nd Conf.Eng.Troops Co.A
Sutton, Samuel J. NC Lt.Arty. 13th Bn. Co.A
Sutton, Samuel J. TN 4th (McLemore's) Cav. Co.D
Sutton, Samuel J. VA 31st Inf. Co.G
Sutton, Samuel S. VA 111th Mil. Co.5
Sutton, Sanford NC 8th Inf. Co.I Sgt.
Sutton, S.B. KY 10th (Johnson's) Cav. Co.A
Sutton, S.C. AL 14th Inf. Co.E
Sutton, S.C. VA Arty. C.F. Johnston's Co.
Sutton, S.D. LA 3rd (Wingfield's) Cav. Co.E
Sutton, S.D. LA 4th Inf. Old Co.G
Sutton, Seaborn GA 6th Inf. Co.H Sgt.
Sutton, Seneca KY 2nd Mtd.Inf. Co.F
Sutton, S.H. TX 24th & 25th Cav. (Cons.) Co.B 2nd Lt.
Sutton, S.H. TX 25th Cav. Co.B Jr.2nd Lt.
Sutton, Shelby AL 2nd Cav. Co.D
Sutton, Sidney L. NC 47th Inf. Co.K
Sutton, Silas NC 16th Inf. Co.A
Sutton, Silas NC 39th Inf. Co.K
Sutton, Silvester VA 14th Cav. Co.L
Sutton, Simeon E. GA 48th Inf. Co.H 1st Sgt.
Sutton, S.J. GA 54th Inf. Co.E
Sutton, S.J. VA Lt.Arty. 12th Bn. Co.B
Sutton, S.M. AR 7th Inf. Co.K

Sutton, S.M., Sr. GA 31st Inf. Co.D Band Music.
Sutton, S.M. LA 25th Inf. Co.K Cpl.
Sutton, Solomon NC Inf. Thomas Legion Co.G
Sutton, Solomon A. GA Cav. 29th Bn. Co.H
Sutton, S.P. SC 5th St.Troops Co.K
Sutton, S.P. SC 6th Res. Co.G
Sutton, S.P. VA 55th Inf. Co.E
Sutton, S.S. NC 11th (Bethel Regt.) Inf. Co.F
Sutton, Stanford TN Lt.Arty. Morton's Co.
Sutton, Stark A. NC 1st Inf. (6 mo. '61) Co.L 1st Lt.
Sutton, Stark A. NC 44th Inf. Adj.
Sutton, Stark A. NC 45th Inf. Co.C,F Capt.
Sutton, Stephen NC 31st Inf. Co.K
Sutton, Stephen A. GA 4th Inf. Co.A
Sutton, Stephen M. GA 1st (Ramsey's) Inf. Co.K
Sutton, Stephen M., Jr. GA 31st Inf. Co.D Cpl.
Sutton, Stephen W. NC 1st Arty. (10th St.Troops) Co.F
Sutton, Stephen W. NC 38th Inf. Co.C
Sutton, Sylvester VA 17th Cav. Co.I
Sutton, T. NC 6th Cav. (65th St.Troops) Co.H
Sutton, T. TN 12th (Green's) Cav. Co.H
Sutton, T. Cherokee Regt. Miller's Co. Cpl.
Sutton, T.A. GA 5th Res. Co.A
Sutton, T.C. VA Lt.Arty. 12th Bn. Co.B
Sutton, T.G. SC Inf. 7th Bn. (Enfield Rifles) Co.D,G
Sutton, Theofalus GA 65th Inf. Co.E
Sutton, Theophilus GA Smith's Legion Co.C
Sutton, Thomas AR 31st Inf. Co.D
Sutton, Thomas GA Cav. 12th Bn. (St.Guards) Co.A
Sutton, Thomas GA Cav. Hall's Co.
Sutton, Thomas LA 28th (Gray's) Inf. Co.F
Sutton, Thomas NC 8th Bn.Part.Rangers Co.B,C Cpl.
Sutton, Thomas NC 8th Inf. Co.D Cpl.
Sutton, Thomas NC 66th Inf. Co.D Sgt.
Sutton, Thomas NC 67th Inf. Co.D
Sutton, Thomas NC Mil. Clark's Sp.Bn. Rountree's Co.
Sutton, Thomas TX 12th Inf. Co.C
Sutton, Thomas C. NC Lt.Arty. 13th Bn. Co.A
Sutton, Thomas E. VA 55th Inf. Co.C
Sutton, Thomas E. VA 109th Mil. Co.B
Sutton, Thomas F. FL 3rd Inf. Co.G
Sutton, Thomas H. AR 24th Inf. Co.F
Sutton, Thomas H. AR Inf. Hardy's Regt. Co.D
Sutton, Thomas H. NC 3rd Arty. (40th St.Troops) Co.C
Sutton, Thomas H. NC 18th Inf. Co.I
Sutton, Thomas H. VA 9th Cav. Co.C
Sutton, Thomas J. LA 12th Inf. Co.B
Sutton, Thomas J. MS 28th Cav. Co.D
Sutton, Thomas J. NC 2nd Arty. (36th St.Troops) Co.H
Sutton, Thomas J. NC 18th Inf. Co.D
Sutton, Thomas R. VA 109th Mil. Co.B, 2nd Co.A
Sutton, T.N. 10th Conf.Cav. Co.G 2nd Lt.
Sutton, T.R. MO 7th Cav. Co.F
Sutton, T.W. GA Cav. 19th Bn. Co.B 2nd Lt.
Sutton, T.W. GA 62nd Cav. Co.K
Sutton, T.W. GA Hvy.Arty. 22nd Bn. Co.B
Sutton, U.H. SC 17th Inf. Co.K
Sutton, U.R. TN Cav. 5th Bn. (McClellan's) Co.B
Sutton, Valentine MO 12th Inf. Co.C
Sutton, W. AR 51st Mil. Co.E
Sutton, W. GA 6th Cav. Co.B
Sutton, W. TX 24th Cav. Co.I
Sutton, W. TX 17th Inf. Co.I
Sutton, W. VA Loc.Def. Wood's Co.
Sutton, Wade H. NC 46th Inf. Co.A Sgt.
Sutton, Warren GA 12th Inf. Co.A
Sutton, Wayne MS 6th Inf. Co.I Sgt.
Sutton, Wayne MS 14th (Cons.) Inf. Co.C Sgt.
Sutton, W.B. FL Cav. 5th Bn. Co.G
Sutton, W.B. GA Mil. 12th Regt. Co.B
Sutton, W.B. KY 2nd Mtd.Inf. Co.K
Sutton, W.B. Gen. & Staff QM Agent
Sutton, W.C. MS 1st Cav. Capt.
Sutton, W.C. MS Conscr.
Sutton, W.C. NC 2nd Arty. (36th St.Troops) Co.H
Sutton, W.D. KY 2nd Cav.
Sutton, Wesley TX 5th Cav. Co.I Bugler
Sutton, W.F. TN 8th (Smith's) Cav. Co.A
Sutton, W.F. TN 23rd Inf. Co.E
Sutton, William AL 28th Inf. Co.F
Sutton, William AR 5th Inf. Co.B
Sutton, William AR 7th Inf. Co.D Cpl.
Sutton, William GA Cav. 12th Bn. (St.Guards) Co.A
Sutton, William GA Arty. St.Troops Pruden's Btty.
Sutton, William GA Inf. 26th Bn. Co.C
Sutton, William GA 52nd Inf. Co.C
Sutton, William GA 63rd Inf. Co.K,D
Sutton, William KY 10th (Johnson's) Cav. Co.A
Sutton, William MS 31st Inf. Co.D
Sutton, William NC 2nd Arty. (36th St.Troops) Co.I
Sutton, William NC 3rd Arty. (40th St.Troops) Co.A Capt.
Sutton, William NC 2nd Inf. Co.H
Sutton, William NC 27th Inf. Co.F
Sutton, William NC 29th Inf. Co.A
Sutton, William NC 32nd Inf. 1st Co.K Lenoir Braves Capt.
Sutton, William NC 61st Inf. Co.G
Sutton, William NC 68th Inf.
Sutton, William NC Inf. Thomas Legion Co.I
Sutton, William TX Cav. Border's Regt. Co.H
Sutton, William TX Cav. Crump's Regt. Co.A
Sutton, William TX Cav. Mann's Bn. Cox's Co.
Sutton, William VA Cav. Mosby's Regt. (Part.Rangers) Co.E
Sutton, William VA Lt.Arty. 38th Bn. Co.C Capt.
Sutton, William VA Lt.Arty. E.J. Anderson's Co.
Sutton, William VA 50th Inf. Co.I
Sutton, William 2nd Conf.Eng.Troops Co.G Artif.
Sutton, William A. GA 59th Inf. Co.B
Sutton, William B. NC 18th Inf. Co.D
Sutton, William C. GA 48th Inf. Co.H
Sutton, William C. MO 2nd Inf. Co.A Cpl.
Sutton, William D. AL 19th Inf. Co.A
Sutton, William D. KY 2nd Mtd.Inf. Co.C
Sutton, William D. LA 9th Inf. Co.D
Sutton, William E. AL 42nd Inf. Co.D
Sutton, William E. GA Cobb's Legion Co.D Sgt.Maj.
Sutton, William E. NC 2nd Arty. (36th St.Troops) Co.H
Sutton, William E. SC 5th Inf. Co.F
Sutton, William E. VA 6th Bn.Res. Co.G
Sutton, William F. TX 36th Cav. Co.D
Sutton, William H. MS 2nd Inf. Co.K
Sutton, William H. NC 3rd Arty. (40th St.Troops) Co.A
Sutton, William H. NC 12th Inf. Co.D
Sutton, William H. SC Arty. Gregg's Co. (McQueen Lt.Arty.)
Sutton, William H. SC Arty. Manigault's Bn. 1st Co.C
Sutton, William I. NC 27th Inf. Co.C Sgt.
Sutton, William J. AR 4th Inf. Co.E
Sutton, William J. AR Inf. Hardy's Regt. Co.D
Sutton, William J. FL 3rd Inf. Co.G
Sutton, William J. MS Cav. 24th Bn. Co.B
Sutton, William J. MO Inf. 8th Bn. Co.A Cpl.
Sutton, William J. NC 2nd Arty. (36th St.Troops) Co.B
Sutton, William J. NC 3rd Arty. (40th St.Troops) Co.E
Sutton, William J. NC 2nd Bn.Loc.Def.Troops Co.F Sgt.
Sutton, William J. NC 18th Inf. Co.K
Sutton, Wm. J. Gen. & Staff Lt.,AAQM
Sutton, William L. GA 52nd Inf. Co.I
Sutton, William M. LA 17th Inf. Co.I
Sutton, William M. NC 3rd Inf. Co.G
Sutton, William M. SC 5th St.Troops Co.K
Sutton, William M. SC 6th Res. Co.G
Sutton, Wm. M. VA 2nd St.Res.
Sutton, William M. VA Inf. 25th Bn. Co.D
Sutton, William M. VA 40th Inf. Co.F
Sutton, Wm. M. Gen. & Staff AQM
Sutton, William N. AR 24th Inf. Co.F
Sutton, William N. AR Inf. Hardy's Regt. Co.D Cpl.
Sutton, William P. VA 50th Inf. Co.G Sgt.
Sutton, William R. AL 28th Inf. Co.E
Sutton, William R. NC 38th Inf. Co.C
Sutton, William R. VA 15th Cav. Co.A
Sutton, William R. VA 111th Mil. Co.5 Sgt.
Sutton, William S. AR 3rd Cav. Co.I
Sutton, William S. GA 3rd Inf. Co.I
Sutton, William S. NC 16th Inf. Co.F
Sutton, William T. NC 1st Cav. (9th St.Troops) Co.H
Sutton, William T. NC 2nd Arty. (36th St.Troops) Co.A
Sutton, William T. NC 38th Inf. Co.C Cpl.
Sutton, William T. NC 44th Inf. Surg.
Sutton, William T. TN 7th (Duckworth's) Cav. Co.L
Sutton, Wilson D. MO Inf. 8th Bn. Co.A Sr.2nd Lt.
Sutton, W.J. TN 21st (Wilson's) Cav. Co.A
Sutton, W.L. AL 4th (Russell's) Cav. Co.D
Sutton, W.L. GA Conscr.
Sutton, W.L. Mead's Conf.Cav. Co.F
Sutton, W.M. GA Inf. 8th Bn. Co.C
Sutton, W.M. NC 6th Inf. Co.B
Sutton, W.M. SC 6th Inf. 2nd Co.B

Sutton, W.R. NC Giddins' Co. (Detailed & Petitioned Men)
Sutton, W.R. VA 5th Cav.
Sutton, W.T. NC 8th Sr.Res. Callihan's Co.
Sutton, W.T. NC 21st Inf. Surg.
Sutton, W.T. Gen. & Staff Surg.
Suttrell, P.T. MS 1st Cav. Co.G
Sut tu hah Joe 1st Cherokee Mtd.Rifles Co.D
Sutvan, E. VA 22nd Inf. Co.F
Su Wah tie 1st Cherokee Mtd.Rifles Co.G
Su wa Kee 1st Cherokee Mtd.Rifles Co.K
Su wa Key 1st Squad. Cherokee Mtd.Vol. Co.A
Su wa Kie Dick 1st Cherokee Mtd.Rifles Co.G
Su wa Kie Ezekiel 1st Cherokee Mtd.Rifles Co.I
Su way Kie Wor Sortie 1st Cherokee Mtd.Rifles Co.I
Suydam, J.H. LA Lt.Arty. LeGardeur, Jr.'s Co. (Orleans Guard Btty.) Sgt.
Suzenau, Chs. LA 22nd Inf. Co.E
Suzenaux, C. LA 22nd Inf. Co.B
Suzer, J.S. KY 5th Cav. Co.F
Svaglich, Guiseppe LA Mil. Cazadores Espanoles Regt. Co.2 1st Lt.
Swab, Joseph AR Mil. Desha Cty.Bn.
Swab, William R. TN 4th Cav.
Swabacker, Simon VA 15th Inf. Co.H
Swabb, Christian LA 12th Inf. Co.I
Swabb, Joseph AR 13th Inf. Co.E Sgt.
Swabe, C.A. TN 62nd Mtd.Inf. Co.F Cpl.
Swaby, Ewd. AR 17th (Lemoyne's) Inf. Co.A
Swack, Andrew J. TN Inf. 1st Bn. (Colms') Co.D Cpl.
Swacker, Isaac N. VA 63rd Inf. Co.H
Swackhammer, William MO Lawther's Part. Rangers
Swacord, John FL 8th Inf. Co.B
Swadder, I. TN 40th Inf. Co.K
Swadell, W.D. LA 13th Inf. Co.K
Swader, A. TN Cav. 5th Bn. (McClellan's) Co.C
Swader, Alexander VA 60th Inf. 2nd Co.H
Swader, Andrew J. VA 22nd Cav. Co.F
Swader, Caloway TN 40th Inf. Co.K
Swader, Caloway 3rd Conf.Cav. Co.I
Swader, Calvin TN 2nd (Ashby's) Cav. Co.B
Swader, Calvin 3rd Conf.Cav. Co.K
Swader, David VA 11th Bn.Res. Co.D
Swader, F.M. 3rd Conf.Cav. Co.I
Swader, Francis TN 40th Inf. Co.K
Swader, G. KY Cav. 2nd Bn. (Dortch's) Co.D
Swader, George KY Morgan's Men Beck's Co.
Swader, Greenville VA 60th Inf. 2nd Co.H
Swader, G.W. TN 2nd (Ashby's) Cav. Co.B
Swader, James McHenry VA 60th Inf. 2nd Co.H
Swader, J.H. 3rd Conf.Cav. Co.I
Swader, John 3rd Conf.Cav. Co.I
Swader, John S. VA 60th Inf. Co.H
Swader, Romulus VA 11th Bn.Res. Co.D
Swader, Samuel W. VA 60th Inf. 2nd Co.H
Swader, Thomas AL 9th (Malone's) Cav. Co.I
Swader, Washington 3rd Conf.Cav. Co.K
Swader, William 3rd Conf.Cav. Co.I
Swadley, Adam F. VA 31st Inf. Co.E 2nd Lt.
Swadley, Jacob VA 62nd Mtd.Inf. 2nd Co.K
Swadley, James VA 25th Inf. 2nd Co.I
Swadley, John S. VA 31st Inf. Co.E
Swaexen, J.H. AL 3rd Inf. Co.I
Swafer, George W. TN 43rd Inf. Co.H
Swaffar, B.L. TN 1st (Carter's) Cav. Co.C Ord.Sgt.
Swaffer, James TN 1st (Carter's) Cav. Co.C
Swaffer, John M. TN 40th Inf. Co.K
Swaffer, J.P. MS 28th Cav. Co.E
Swaffer, S. MS 28th Cav. Co.E
Swaffer, Sanders AL 54th Inf. Co.K
Swaffer, Sanders MS 4th Inf. Co.F 2nd Lt.
Swaffer, Sanders TN 40th Inf. Co.K
Swaffield, William C. SC 2nd Cav. Co.A
Swaffoe, Moses GA Arty. 9th Bn. Co.D
Swafford, --- AR Inf. Cocke's Regt. Co.D
Swafford, A. TN 25th Inf. Co.D
Swafford, Abraham TN Cav. 16th Bn. (Neal's) Co.C
Swafford, A.J. GA 23rd Inf. Co.B
Swafford, Alfred MO 9th (Elliott's) Cav.
Swafford, Alfred TN 2nd (Ashby's) Cav. Co.F
Swafford, Alfred, Jr. TN Cav. 4th Bn. (Branner's) Co.F
Swafford, Andrew J. GA 35th Inf. Co.H
Swafford, D.F. TN 22nd Inf. Co.F
Swafford, D.H. GA 56th Inf. Co.C
Swafford, Dread GA 11th Cav. Co.F
Swafford, Ezekiel TN 43rd Inf. Co.H
Swafford, Franklin TN 26th Inf. Co.F
Swafford, George TN Inf. Harman's Regt. Co.K
Swafford, George W. SC Horse Arty. (Washington Arty.) Vol. Hart's Co.
Swafford, G.V. GA 23rd Inf. Co.B
Swafford, G.W. AL 51st (Part.Rangers) Co.A
Swafford, G.W. AL 62nd Inf. Co.B
Swafford, Henry SC 1st (Butler's) Inf. Co.G,I,B
Swafford, I.B. AL 62nd Inf. Co.B
Swafford, Isaac GA 35th Inf. Co.H
Swafford, Jackson AL 55th Vol. Co.E
Swafford, James AL Nitre & Min. Corps Young's Co.
Swafford, James SC 22nd Inf. Co.D
Swafford, James J. GA Smith's Legion Co.K
Swafford, J.B. MS 2nd Cav. Co.B
Swafford, Jessie J. AL 44th Inf. Co.K
Swafford, Joab SC 1st St.Troops Co.E
Swafford, John AL Nitre & Min. Corps Young's Co.
Swafford, John GA 43rd Inf. Co.K Cpl.
Swafford, John NC 22nd Inf. Co.B
Swafford, John SC 1st (Butler's) Inf. Co.G,I
Swafford, John A. AL 55th Vol. Co.I Sgt.
Swafford, John R. NC 6th Inf. Co.A Sgt.
Swafford, Jonas TX Cav. Martin's Regt. Co.D Cpl.
Swafford, J.P. MS 8th Cav. Co.B
Swafford, L.F. TN 43rd Inf. Co.H
Swafford, Maj. P. TN Cav. 4th Bn. (Branner's) Co.F Sgt.
Swafford, Martin NC 22nd Inf. Co.B
Swafford, M.N. Eng.,CSA
Swafford, Moses SC Horse Arty. (Washington Arty.) Vol. Hart's Co.
Swafford, Moses W. GA 35th Inf. Co.H
Swafford, M.P. TN 2nd (Ashby's) Cav. Co.F Sgt.
Swafford, R. TN Inf. Harman's Regt. Co.K
Swafford, Ransom MS 44th Inf. Co.C
Swafford, R.L. GA 23rd Inf. Co.B
Swafford, Robert AL 4th Inf. Co.K
Swafford, Samuel TN Inf. 22nd Bn. Co.C
Swafford, Sanders MS 8th Cav. Co.B
Swafford, Solomon W. GA Cobb's Legion Co.F
Swafford, T.A. TN Inf. 22nd Bn. Co.C
Swafford, T.F. LA Conscr.
Swafford, Thomas GA Lt.Arty. Havis' Btty.
Swafford, Thomas MO 4th Cav. Co.A,C
Swafford, Thomas, Jr. TN 43rd Inf. Co.C
Swafford, Thomas A. TN 2nd (Ashby's) Cav. Co.F
Swafford, Thomas A. TN Cav. 4th Bn. (Branner's) Co.F
Swafford, W.F. TN Inf. 22nd Bn. Co.C Bvt.2nd Lt.
Swafford, Wiley J. AL 4th Cav. Co.B
Swafford, William AL 16th Inf. Co.F
Swafford, William AL 55th Vol. Co.E
Swafford, William AR Inf. Cocke's Regt. Co.D
Swafford, William GA 4th Cav. (St.Guards) Pirkle's Co.
Swafford, William GA 23rd Inf. Co.E
Swafford, William GA 35th Inf. Co.H Sgt.
Swafford, William GA 43rd Inf. Co.E
Swafford, William NC 34th Inf. Co.F
Swafford, William J. GA 1st Reg. Co.A,L,B
Swafford, William W. AL 4th (Russell's) Cav. Co.G
Swaford, Charles TN Cav. 11th Bn. (Gordon's) Co.E
Swaford, F. TN 22nd Inf. Co.F
Swaford, J.L. GA 28th Inf. Co.B
Swaford, M. GA 34th Inf. Co.D
Swaford, Thomas C. MO Cav. Hunter's Regt. Co.A,D
Swaford, T.J. GA 5th Inf. Co.D
Swagar, Charles N. KY 2nd Mtd.Inf. Co.H
Swagar, Hunter B. KY 2nd Cav. Co.H
Swage, F.M. GA 8th Cav. Co.H
Swage, R. AL Cav. Hardie's Bn.Res. Co.G
Swager, Charles Moore Retributors Young's (5th) Co.
Swager, C.M. KY 1st Inf. Co.H,A
Swager, Hunter KY 1st Inf. Co.H,A
Swager, Hunter B. VA Inf. 45th Bn. Co.D
Swagerly, C.A. VA 1st St.Res. Co.B Sgt.
Swagerty, Alexander S. TN 26th Inf. Co.C 2nd Lt.
Swagerty, G.C. TN 63rd Inf. Co.G
Swagerty, George TN 26th Inf. Co.C
Swagerty, G.F. AR 20th Inf. Co.G
Swagerty, James C. TX 13th Cav. Co.F
Swagerty, James C. TX 22nd Inf. Co.D 1st Lt.
Swagerty, Lorenzo N.C. AR 16th Inf. Co.A Maj.
Swagerty, Vance TN 3rd (Lillard's) Mtd.Inf. Co.E
Swagerty, W.A. AR 8th Inf. New Co.D
Swagerty, William TN 63rd Inf. Co.G
Swagerty, William R. TN 26th Inf. Co.C
Swaggard, J. FL 1st (Res.) Inf. Co.H
Swaggart, D.W. MS 38th Cav. Co.D
Swaggart, J. KY 7th Mtd.Inf. Co.A
Swaggart, J.J. AR 13th Inf. Co.F
Swaggert, James MS 8th Inf. Co.C Sgt.
Swaggerty, Hiram W. AR 8th Inf. New Co.D Cpl.
Swaggerty, Jackson TN 43rd Inf. Co.D

Swaggerty, James TN 43rd Inf. Co.D
Swaggerty, John TN 43rd Inf. Co.D
Swails, James P. FL 3rd Inf. Co.K Sgt.
Swails, J.J. FL 1st (Res.) Inf. Co.G
Swails, Morgan SC Lt.Arty. 3rd (Palmetto) Bn. Co.C
Swails, P.J. FL 6th Inf. Co.E
Swails, Pleasant J. FL 8th Inf. Co.E
Swails, Reese GA 49th Inf. Co.A
Swails, Taylor SC Lt.Arty. 3rd (Palmetto) Bn. Co.C
Swails, William A. MS 1st Lt.Arty. Co.E
Swails, William T. FL 8th Inf. Co.E
Swaim, And NC 31st Inf. Co.K
Swaim, B.M. TN 31st Inf. Co.A Cpl.
Swaim, C. NC 31st Inf. Co.K
Swaim, C.F. NC 9th Bn.S.S. Co.B Cpl.
Swaim, Charles F. MS 22nd Inf. Co.K Sgt.
Swaim, Columbus F. NC Inf. 2nd Bn. Co.G 2nd Lt.
Swaim, Columbus H. NC 21st Inf. Co.E
Swaim, Daniel AL 49th Inf. Co.C
Swaim, Eli NC 9th Bn.S.S. Co.B
Swaim, Eli NC 21st Inf. Co.E
Swaim, Elisha MS 22nd Inf. Co.K
Swaim, Embery NC 5th Sr.Res. Co.H
Swaim, E.P. NC 60th Inf. Co.F
Swaim, Felix G. AR 25th Inf. Co.I
Swaim, F.G. AR 1st Mtd.Rifles Co.K
Swaim, George NC 31st Inf. Co.K
Swaim, H.E. NC 60th Inf. Co.F
Swaim, Henry VA 89th Mil. Co.H
Swaim, Hezekiah NC 68th Inf.
Swaim, J. MS 22nd Inf. Co.K
Swaim, Jesse NC 7th Sr.Res. Clinard's Co.
Swaim, J.F. NC 54th Inf. Co.H
Swaim, J.F. NC 60th Inf. Co.F
Swaim, J.J. TN 51st (Cons.) Inf. Co.E
Swaim, John AL 55th Vol. Co.I
Swaim, John, Jr. MS 8th Cav. Co.A
Swaim, John, Sr. MS 8th Cav. Co.A
Swaim, John NC 21st Inf. Co.E
Swaim, John TN 42nd Inf. 1st Co.I
Swaim, Joseph S. NC Inf. 2nd Bn. Co.G 1st Lt.
Swaim, J.P. TN 11th (Holman's) Cav. Co.B 2nd Lt.
Swaim, J.P. TN Holman's Bn.Part.Rangers Co.A 2nd Lt.
Swaim, L. MS 22nd Inf. Co.K Sgt.
Swaim, Lewis VA 29th Inf. Co.D
Swaim, Lewis B. AL 21st Inf. Co.K
Swaim, Lindsey NC 6th Sr.Res. Co.D
Swaim, Little M. NC 28th Inf. Co.I
Swaim, Marmaduke NC 18th Inf. Co.I
Swaim, M.G. NC 44th Inf. Co.G
Swaim, Michael F. NC 54th Inf. Co.H
Swaim, Milas G. NC 28th Inf. Co.I
Swaim, M.M. TN 8th (Smith's) Cav. Co.A Sgt.
Swaim, M.M. TN 11th (Holman's) Cav. Co.B Capt.
Swaim, M.M. TN Holman's Bn.Part.Rangers Co.A Capt.
Swaim, Moses M. TN 4th (McLemore's) Cav. Co.A
Swaim, S.C. AL 55th Vol. Co.F Cpl.
Swaim, S.D. NC 28th Inf. Co.I
Swaim, Silas C. TN 42nd Inf. 1st Co.E
Swaim, Solomon D. NC 44th Inf. Co.G
Swaim, Solomon D. NC 54th Inf. Co.H
Swaim, Thomas W. TN 5th (McKenzie's) Cav. Co.E,C
Swaim, W.G. TN 31st Inf. Co.A 1st Lt.
Swaim, William AR 37th Inf. Co.K
Swaim, William NC 28th Inf. Co.I
Swaim, William VA 89th Mil. Co.D
Swaim, William F. NC 21st Inf. Co.K 2nd Lt.
Swaime, Ashley NC 1st Inf. Co.A
Swaime, Samuel AR 37th Inf. Co.K
Swain, Aaron MO Cav. Davies' Bn. Co.B
Swain, Abijah NC 17th Inf. (1st Org.) Co.H
Swain, Abijah NC 17th Inf. (2nd Org.) Co.E
Swain, Absalom MS 8th Cav. Co.A Capt.
Swain, Adam LA 21st (Patton's) Inf. Co.D
Swain, Adam H. NC 21st Inf. Co.D
Swain, Albert AR Mil. Desha Cty.Bn.
Swain, Alex AL Mil. 2nd Regt.Vol. Co.B
Swain, Alex LA 1st Hvy.Arty. (Reg.) Music.
Swain, Alex LA 22nd (Cons.) Inf. Co.H
Swain, Alexander AL Lt.Arty. 2nd Bn. Co.E
Swain, Alexander AL 1st Regt. Mobile Vol. Co.A
Swain, Alexander M. VA 58th Inf. Co.I Sgt.
Swain, Andrew LA Washington Arty.Bn. Co.5
Swain, A.W. TN 3rd (Lillard's) Mtd.Inf. Co.D
Swain, B.B. TN 45th Inf. Co.E
Swain, Benjamin FL 7th Inf. Co.K
Swain, Benjamin F. NC 17th Inf. (2nd Org.) Co.E
Swain, Benjamin F. NC 30th Inf. Co.C Sgt.
Swain, Benjamin N. TX 21st Cav. Co.D
Swain, B.F. TN 20th Inf. Co.E Cpl.
Swain, C. NC 1st Inf.
Swain, Charles H. MS 18th Inf. Co.I
Swain, Daniel LA 5th Inf. Co.K
Swain, Daniel NC 20th Inf. Co.G
Swain, Darling GA Cav. 19th Bn. Co.B
Swain, Darling GA 10th Inf. Co.H Cpl.
Swain, David AR Mil. Desha Cty.Bn.
Swain, David L. NC 17th Inf. (1st Org.) Co.H
Swain, D.F. TN 45th Inf. Co.E Sgt.
Swain, E. MS 12th Inf. Co.G
Swain, E.C. GA Cav. 2nd Bn. Co.E
Swain, E.C. GA 5th Cav. Co.C
Swain, E.C. GA Inf. (Loc.Def.) Hamlet's Co. Sgt.
Swain, Edward A. LA 7th Inf. Co.H
Swain, E.J. MS 1st Cav. Co.E
Swain, Eldred GA 10th Inf. Co.H
Swain, Elias NC 44th Inf. Co.B
Swain, F.M. LA Lt.Arty. Fenner's Btty.
Swain, F.Mc.C. LA Inf.Crescent Regt. Co.E
Swain, Francis L. KY 4th Cav. Co.F,H
Swain, Francis L. TN 4th Inf. Co.F
Swain, Frank L. KY 9th Cav. Co.F
Swain, Franklin S. NC 17th Inf. (2nd Org.) Co.G
Swain, Frederick C. TX 21st Cav. Co.K
Swain, F.S. AL 20th Inf. Co.I
Swain, G. GA 10th Inf. Co.G
Swain, G.B. LA 3rd Inf. Co.I
Swain, George AR Inf. Ernest's Co. (Loc.Def.)
Swain, George MS Lt.Arty. English's Co.
Swain, George Conf.Inf. 8th Bn. Co.C Sgt.
Swain, George C. MS 7th Cav. Co.E
Swain, George E. VA 46th Inf. 2nd Co.C
Swain, George T. NC 2nd Arty. (36th St.Troops) Co.G
Swain, George T. NC 30th Inf. Co.C Cpl.
Swain, George W. GA Hvy.Arty. 22nd Bn. Co.E
Swain, Harrison VA 122nd Mil. Co.D
Swain, Harvey, Jr. AL 3rd Inf. Co.K
Swain, H.C. AL 51st (Part.Rangers) Co.F
Swain, H.C. LA Inf.Crescent Regt. Co.G Cpl.
Swain, H.C. 14th Conf.Cav. Co.H
Swain, Henderson NC 17th Inf. (2nd Org.) Co.H
Swain, Henry C. FL Lt.Arty. Abell's Co.
Swain, Henry C. FL Milton Lt.Arty. Dunham's Co. Sgt.
Swain, Henry R. NC 17th Inf. (2nd Org.) Co.G
Swain, Hooper C. KY 4th Mtd.Inf. Co.I
Swain, I.D. MS 28th Cav. Co.C
Swain, I.N. KY 7th Cav. Co.K
Swain, I.N. KY 7th Mtd.Inf. Co.K
Swain, Isaac AL 8th Inf. Co.I
Swain, J. MS 22nd Inf. Co.K
Swain, J. TN 45th Inf. Co.B
Swain, J.A. MS 1st (Percy's) Inf. Co.B
Swain, Jack MS Cav. Russell's Co.
Swain, Jacob MS 43rd Inf. Co.F
Swain, James NC 2nd Arty. (36th St.Troops) Co.H Music.
Swain, James NC Lt.Arty. 3rd Bn. Co.B
Swain, James NC 11th (Bethel Regt.) Inf. Co.F
Swain, James TN 25th Inf. Co.K
Swain, James VA 20th Cav. Co.G
Swain, James VA Lt.Arty. Motley's Co.
Swain, James VA 37th Mil. Co.D
Swain, James VA 40th Inf. Co.C
Swain, James 10th Conf.Cav. Co.G
Swain, James A. MS 1st Lt.Arty. Co.D
Swain, James L. GA 10th Inf. Co.H Sgt.
Swain, James M. TN 30th Inf. Co.H
Swain, James N. NC 17th Inf. (2nd Org.) Co.G
Swain, James P. GA 48th Inf. Co.B Sgt.
Swain, James T. GA 1st (Ramsey's) Inf. Co.G
Swain, James T. VA 8th Inf. Co.C
Swain, J.B. TN 38th Inf. 2nd Co.H
Swain, J.D. MS 5th Cav. Co.C
Swain, Jesse GA 1st Inf. (St.Guards) Co.A
Swain, Jesse B. MS 2nd Part.Rangers Co.E
Swain, J.H. MS 18th Inf. Co.F
Swain, J.M. TN 38th Inf. 2nd Co.H
Swain, J.N. KY 12th Cav. Co.K
Swain, Joel AL 53rd (Part.Rangers) Co.G
Swain, Joel C. MS 2nd Part.Rangers Co.E
Swain, John MS Inf. 4th St.Troops Co.F
Swain, John MS 43rd Inf. Co.I
Swain, John NC Coast Guards Galloway's Co.
Swain, John A. NC 47th Inf. Co.K
Swain, John B. LA 9th Inf. Co.C
Swain, John B. NC 60th Inf. Co.G Cpl.
Swain, John C. MS 2nd Part.Rangers Co.E
Swain, John G. AL Lt.Arty. Lee's Btty.
Swain, John G. NC 17th Inf. (1st Org.) Co.H
Swain, John H. MS 9th Inf. Old Co.A, New Co.H
Swain, John H. VA 8th Inf. Co.K
Swain, John K. GA Carlton's Co. (Troup Cty.Arty.) Sgt.
Swain, John L. MS 37th Inf. Co.A
Swain, John L. NC 17th Inf. (2nd Org.) Co.E Capt.

Swain, John R. GA Lt.Arty. Fraser's Btty. Cpl.
Swain, John R. GA 10th Inf. 1st Co.K Cpl.
Swain, John R. GA 17th Inf. Co.D
Swain, John R. GA 59th Inf. Co.A
Swain, John R. NC 30th Inf. Co.C 2nd Lt.
Swain, John W. MS 12th Inf. Co.I
Swain, John W. NC 7th Inf. Co.C Cpl.
Swain, Joseph MS 1st (Patton's) Inf. Co.C
Swain, Joseph MS 43rd Inf. Co.I
Swain, Joseph NC 32nd Inf. Co.A
Swain, Joseph VA Cav. 37th Bn. Co.F
Swain, Joseph VA 37th Mil. Co.D
Swain, Joseph VA 40th Inf. Co.C
Swain, Joseph J. GA 17th Inf. Co.D
Swain, Joseph R. TX 3rd Cav. Co.I
Swain, Joseph S. TX 21st Cav. Co.C
Swain, Joshua L. NC 2nd Cav. (19th St.Troops) Co.G
Swain, J.R. LA Inf.Cons.Crescent Regt. Co.E
Swain, J.S. TN 12th (Green's) Cav. Co.A
Swain, J.T. MS 2nd Cav. Co.C
Swain, J.W. AL 51st (Part.Rangers) Co.F
Swain, J.W. AL 18th Inf. Co.K,E
Swain, J.W. GA 4th (Clinch's) Cav. Co.H
Swain, J.W. GA 40th Inf. Co.H 1st Sgt.
Swain, J.W. GA Inf. 40th Bn. Co.A Ord.Sgt.
Swain, J.W. GA 54th Inf. Co.E 2nd Lt.
Swain, J.W. LA Miles' Legion
Swain, J.W. NC 1st Arty. (10th St.Troops) Co.G
Swain, J.Y. GA 31st Inf. Co.H
Swain, L.B. LA 22nd (Cons.) Inf. Co.H
Swain, L.B. MS Cav. Ham's Regt. Co.A
Swain, L.B. MS 2nd (Davidson's) Inf. Co.G
Swain, L.C. GA Inf. 1st City Bn. (Columbus) Co.F Cpl.
Swain, Leonadis H. AR 14th (Powers') Inf. Co.E
Swain, Levi NC 2nd Arty. (36th St.Troops) Co.G
Swain, L.P. TN 20th Inf. Co.C
Swain, Luther C. GA Inf. 19th Bn. (St.Guards) Co.A
Swain, L.W. GA 10th Inf. Co.H
Swain, M. NC 15th Inf. Co.C
Swain, Mark GA 20th Inf. Co.H Cpl.
Swain, M.J. GA 10th Inf. Co.H
Swain, M.R. TX 10th Cav. Co.B
Swain, M.S. TX 19th Inf. Co.E
Swain, M.W. VA 1st St.Res. Co.B
Swain, Nimrod S. GA 5th Inf. Co.E
Swain, N.R. GA 65th Inf. Co.C
Swain, N.S. GA Inf. 25th Bn. (Prov.Guard) Co.D
Swain, Oscar AR 9th Inf. New Co.I
Swain, Osker 2nd Conf.Inf. Co.G
Swain, Peter NC 17th Inf. (1st Org.) Co.I
Swain, Pleasant P. VA 28th Inf. Co.G
Swain, P.T. GA 11th Cav. (St.Guards) McGriff's Co.
Swain, R.D. MS 13th Inf. Co.F
Swain, Richard LA 5th Inf. Co.E 2nd Lt.
Swain, Richard VA 37th Mil. Co.E
Swain, Richard A. MS 2nd Part.Rangers Co.E
Swain, Richard A. MS 7th Cav. Co.E
Swain, Richard C. NC 39th Inf. Asst.Surg.
Swain, Riley W. MS 9th Inf. New Co.F
Swain, R.J. GA Lt.Arty. 12th Bn. Co.F
Swain, Robert GA Cav. 22nd Bn. (St.Guards) Co.D
Swain, Robert GA 49th Inf. Co.E
Swain, Robert Conf.Inf. Tucker's Regt. Co.B 1st Sgt.
Swain, Robert H. GA 10th Inf. Co.G
Swain, Robert H. TX 15th Cav. Co.F Cpl.
Swain, Robert H. TX Granbury's Cons.Brig. Co.F Cpl.
Swain, Rolando TN 7th Inf. Co.H
Swain, Rowland B. VA 28th Inf. Co.A
Swain, R.R. TX Cav. Morgan's Regt. Co.E 2nd Lt.
Swain, R.T. AL 51st (Part.Rangers) Co.F Cpl.
Swain, R.T. AL 18th Inf. Co.K Cpl.
Swain, R.T. MS 5th Inf. Co.C
Swain, Samuel N. MS 17th Inf. Co.H
Swain, Samuel R. MS 1st Lt.Arty. Co.D
Swain, S.C. AR 1st Cav. Co.B
Swain, S.H. TX Waul's Legion Co.B
Swain, S.M. AL 42nd Inf. Co.I
Swain, S.N. MS Lt.Arty. 14th Bn. Co.B
Swain, Stephen GA 12th Inf. Co.K
Swain, Stephen GA 14th Inf.
Swain, Stephen A. NC Hvy.Arty. 1st Bn. Co.C
Swain, Stephen G. GA Smith's Legion Co.D
Swain, Stephen M. AL Mil. 2nd Regt.Vol. Co.B
Swain, Stephen W. FL Milton Lt.Arty. Dunham's Co.
Swain, Stephen W. GA 1st (Ramsey's) Inf. Co.G
Swain, T. GA Cav. 22nd Bn. (St.Guards) Co.I
Swain, T.E. NC 4th Cav. (59th St.Troops) Co.F
Swain, Thomas AL Arty. 4th Bn. Hilliard's Legion Co.E
Swain, Thomas NC 16th Inf. Co.K
Swain, Thomas TX 19th Inf. Co.I
Swain, Thomas Jackson's Co.,CSA
Swain, Thomas H. VA Lt.Arty. 38th Bn. Co.A
Swain, Thomas J. GA 59th Inf. Co.A
Swain, Thomas W. NC 2nd Arty. (36th St.Troops) Co.G
Swain, T.J. GA 6th Inf. (St.Guards) Sims' Co.
Swain, T.J. MS 13th Inf. Co.F
Swain, V.D.W. NC 66th Inf. Co.G
Swain, W. GA 1st (Olmstead's) Inf. Gordon's Co.
Swain, W.B. TN 45th Inf. Co.B
Swain, W.C. GA 11th Cav. (St.Guards) McGriff's Co.
Swain, W.C. GA Siege Arty. Campbell's Ind.Co.
Swain, W.D. TX Cav. 2nd Bn.St.Troops Hubbard's Co.
Swain, W.H. TN 51st (Cons.) Inf. Co.E
Swain, Whitmell W. NC 1st Inf. (6 mo. '61) Co.L Cpl.
Swain, Wiley F. TX 34th Cav. Co.E
Swain, William GA 63rd Inf. Co.K,D
Swain, William LA 14th Inf. Co.C 2nd Lt.
Swain, William NC 2nd Arty. (36th St.Troops) Co.G 1st Lt.
Swain, William NC 8th Inf. Co.D
Swain, William NC 54th Inf. Co.I
Swain, William SC Inf. Holcombe Legion Co.I
Swain, William VA 37th Mil. Co.E
Swain, William VA 40th Inf. Co.C
Swain, William E. VA 8th Inf. Co.K
Swain, William H. MS 12th Inf. Co.G
Swain, William P. VA Lt.Arty. Thompson's Co.
Swain, William R. MS 12th Inf. Co.I 2nd Lt.
Swain, William W. GA Cav. 7th Bn. (St.Guards) Co.F Capt.
Swain, Willis AR 8th Cav. Peoples' Co.
Swain, Wilson TX 10th Inf. Music.
Swain, Wilson TX 15th Inf. Co.A Music.
Swain, W.J. GA 40th Inf. Co.H 1st Lt.
Swain, W.J. TX 27th Cav. Co.F 1st Lt.
Swain, W.N. NC 3rd Arty. (40th St.Troops) Co.I
Swain, W.R. FL Conscr.
Swaine, Abel W. NC 37th Inf. Co.A
Swaine, Cooper C. KY 4th Cav. Co.I
Swaine, Edward GA Lt.Arty. (Washington Arty.) Pritchard's Co. 1st Lt.
Swaine, J.J. MS 28th Cav. Co.D Cpl.
Swaine, John MS Inf. 5th Bn. Co.A
Swaine, J.R. NC 4th Cav. (59th St.Troops) Co.A
Swaine, M. NC 5th Sr.Res. Co.H
Swaine, Peter NC 1st Inf. Co.A
Swaine, Wilson B. MS 2nd Inf. Co.L
Swaine, W.J. TN 51st (Cons.) Inf. Co.C
Swainey, C. SC 1st (Butler's) Inf. Co.G
Swaingain, William NC 5th Inf. Co.F,B,D
Swaizy, F.M. MS Wilkinson Cty. Minute Men Harris' Co.
Swaizy, S. MS Wilkinson Cty. Minute Men Harris' Co.
Swaker, Peter LA Mil. 4th Regt. 1st Brig. 1st Div. Co.K
Swales, George W. LA 16th Inf. Co.G
Swales, H.C. 20th Conf.Cav. Co.E
Swales, Joseph SC 4th St.Troops Co.E
Swall, Nelson MO 3rd Cav. Co.C
Swall, N.M. MO 15th Cav. Co.A
Swall, Solomon MO 4th Cav. Co.H
Swall, Solomon MO 15th Cav. Co.N
Swallow, Andrew MS 2nd Inf. Co.K
Swallow, A.R. TX Cav. McCord's Frontier Regt. Co.C
Swallow, C. LA Siege Train Bn. Co.D
Swallow, E. LA Siege Train Bn. Co.D
Swallow, Granville TN 25th Inf. Co.D
Swallow, Isaac R. TN 25th Inf. Co.D
Swallow, J. LA 15th Bn.S.S. (Weatherly's) Co.D
Swallow, James TN 13th (Gore's) Cav. Co.A
Swallow, John TN 25th Inf. Co.D
Swallow, L. LA 18th Inf. Co.D
Swallow, M. LA 2nd Cav. Co.A
Swallow, O. LA Siege Train Bn. Co.D
Swallow, Reuben R. TN 25th Inf. Co.D
Swallow, Robert VA 36th Inf. 2nd Co.B Cpl.
Swallows, Ahi TN 25th Inf. Co.D,B
Swallows, Andrew J. TN 13th (Gore's) Cav. Co.E Cpl.
Swallows, J.W. TN 84th Inf. Co.D
Swalm, George VA Cav. 40th Bn. Co.B
Swame, F. NC 60th Inf. Co.F
Swamer, William AL 7th Cav. Co.G
Swamley, F. MD 1st Cav. Co.D
Swammer, G.W. AL 25th Inf. Co.B
Swampe, Jake LA 11th Inf.
Swan, --- AL 22nd Inf. Co.I
Swan, A.G. LA 2nd Cav. Co.C
Swan, A.G. LA 6th Inf. Co.C
Swan, A.J. TX 9th Field Btty.
Swan, Alfred L. LA Res.Corps Scott's Co.
Swan, Andrew J. AR 26th Inf. Co.F
Swan, Augustus GA 42nd Inf. Co.F

Swan, Baptiste H. GA Carlton's Co. (Troup Cty.Arty.)
Swan, Baptiste H. GA 2nd Inf. Stanley's Co.
Swan, Benjamin VA Lt.Arty. Clutter's Co. Sgt.
Swan, Benjamin F. TX Cav. Baylor's Regt. Co.E
Swan, B.M. AL 12th Inf. Co.C
Swan, B.T. GA 53rd Inf. Co.G
Swan, C. AL 51st (Part.Rangers) Co.H
Swan, C. AL 3rd Inf. Co.F
Swan, C. MS 12th Inf.
Swan, C.C. GA Inf. 23rd Bn.Loc.Def. Sims' Co.
Swan, C.H. NC Snead's Co. (Loc.Def.)
Swan, Charles AL 3rd Res. Co.F
Swan, Christopher GA 23rd Inf. Co.A
Swan, Daniel H. FL 8th Inf. Co.G Sgt.
Swan, David AR 32nd Inf. Co.B
Swan, David GA 7th Inf. Co.I
Swan, D.H. TN 10th Cav. Co.K
Swan, Eaton SC 6th Res. Co.E Cpl.
Swan, E.B. TN Cav. Williams' Co.
Swan, Edward LA 15th Inf. Co.A
Swan, Edward TX 11th Inf. Co.H
Swan, Edward B. VA 49th Inf. Co.B
Swan, Elijah GA 35th Inf. Co.B
Swan, Francis M. GA 44th Inf. Co.E
Swan, Franklin NC 1st Cav. (9th St.Troops) Co.G
Swan, F.S. VA 11th Cav. Co.E
Swan, G.B. MS 1st (Johnston's) Inf. Co.D
Swan, George AL 1st Bn. Hilliard's Legion Vol. Co.G
Swan, George W. AL Cav. Lewis' Bn. Co.E Cpl.
Swan, George W. MD 1st Inf. Co.F
Swan, George W. VA 1st St.Res. Co.F
Swan, George Y. TN Lt.Arty. Weller's Co. 1st Sgt.
Swan, G.W. AR 30th Inf. Co.K
Swan, G.W. TN 17th Inf. Co.K
Swan, Harvy R. TX 17th Cav. Co.I Cpl.
Swan, H.C. KY 6th Cav. Co.E
Swan, Henry MO 7th Cav.
Swan, Henry TN 1st Hvy.Arty. Co.L, 3rd Co.B
Swan, Henry VA Cav. Swann's Bn. Carpenter's Co.
Swan, Henry C. MO 8th Cav. Co.K
Swan, Henry J. GA 38th Inf. Co.G
Swan, Henry W. VA 40th Inf. Co.F
Swan, H.J. GA Cobb's Legion Co.L Cpl.
Swan, Hugh LA 21st (Patton's) Inf. Co.D,A
Swan, Hugh B. VA 18th Inf. Co.H Sgt.
Swan, Hy M. LA Inf. 1st Sp.Bn. (Rightor's) Co.F
Swan, Isaac L. AL 10th Inf. Co.G
Swan, J.A. AR Cav. Gordon's Regt. Co.H
Swan, J.A. MO 1st Brig.St.Guard
Swan, J.A. 8th (Wade's) Conf.Cav. Co.K
Swan, Jabez N. GA 38th Inf. Co.G Sgt.
Swan, Jacob LA 5th Inf. Co.D
Swan, Jacob W. AL 1st Cav. Co.K
Swan, James AL 20th Inf. Co.G
Swan, James MD 1st Inf. Co.F
Swan, James MS 23rd Inf. Co.H
Swan, James MO Inf. Perkins' Bn. Co.D
Swan, James TN 1st (Carter's) Cav. Co.K
Swan, James VA 2nd St.Res. Co.B
Swan, James VA 17th Inf. Co.E
Swan, James Conf.Cav. Wood's Regt. 2nd Co.G
Swan, James Gen. & Staff Maj.,CS
Swan, James A. AL 17th Inf. Co.E
Swan, James A. VA Cav. 39th Bn. Co.A
Swan, James B. AL 3rd Res. Co.I
Swan, James B. AL 43rd Inf. Co.H
Swan, James C. GA Cobb's Legion Co.F
Swan, James F. AR 32nd Inf. Co.B
Swan, James H. AL Cav. Holloway's Co.
Swan, James H. TN 19th Inf. Co.E
Swan, James L. LA Mil. Orleans Fire Regt. Hall's Co.
Swan, James M. GA 19th Inf. Co.D,G
Swan, James M. NC Cav. 5th Bn. Co.B
Swan, James S. GA 35th Inf. Co.B
Swan, James W. NC 1st Cav. (9th St.Troops) Co.B
Swan, James Z. TN 37th Inf. Co.I Capt.
Swan, J.D. TX 11th Cav. Co.B
Swan, J.H. MO Cav. Coleman's Regt. Co.F
Swan, J.L. TN Lt.Arty. Barry's Co.
Swan, J.M. NC 6th Cav. (65th St.Troops) Co.K,B
Swan, J.N. NC 2nd Jr.Res. Co.F
Swan, John AL 46th Inf. Co.G
Swan, John AR 1st Mtd.Rifles Co.E
Swan, John AR 2nd Inf. Co.I
Swan, John GA 2nd Res. Co.C
Swan, John MD 1st Inf. Co.I
Swan, John MS 20th Inf. Co.E
Swan, John TN 10th Inf. Co.A
Swan, John TX 4th Cav. Co.A
Swan, John VA 8th Inf. Co.H
Swan, John VA 12th Inf. Co.G
Swan, John A. TN 17th Inf. Co.K
Swan, John C. GA Cobb's Legion Co.F
Swan, John C. Conf.Cav. Wood's Regt. 2nd Co.G
Swan, John H. AR 38th Inf. Co.D
Swan, John N. VA 17th Inf. Co.A
Swan, John R. AR 1st (Dobbin's) Cav. Co.A Capt.
Swan, John T. AL 1st Regt. Mobile Vol. Co.E
Swan, John T. AL Mil. West's Co. 2nd Cpl.
Swan, John T. AL 10th Inf. Co.E
Swan, John T. MO 4th Cav. Co.A
Swan, Joseph NC 35th Inf. Co.B Cpl.
Swan, Joseph TX 17th Cav. 2nd Co.I
Swan, Joseph VA 8th Cav. Co.E
Swan, Joseph N. AL 47th Inf. Co.E 1st Lt.
Swan, Joshua K. GA 38th Inf. Co.I,G
Swan, J.T. GA Phillips' Legion Co.F,P
Swan, J.T. LA Lt.Arty. 2nd Field Btty.
Swan, J.W. TN Inf. 16th Regt. Co.C
Swan, Lemuel GA Inf. Athens Reserved Corps
Swan, Lewis LA 1st (Strawbridge's) Inf. Co.F
Swan, L.M. MO Cav. 1st Regt.St.Guard Co.C 1st Lt.
Swan, L.Y. TX 17th Inf. Co.I
Swan, M.F. GA 18th Inf. Co.B 2nd Lt.
Swan, M.M. TX Cav. 2nd Bn.St.Troops Wilson's Co.
Swan, M.N. GA 12th Cav. Co.B
Swan, M.N. TN 5th (McKenzie's) Cav. Co.E
Swan, M.P. GA Cav. 16th Bn. (St.Guards) Co.E
Swan, M.S. GA 18th Inf. Co.E Sgt.
Swan, M.S. GA Inf. Clemons' Co. Jr.2nd Lt.
Swan, M.V.B. LA 2nd Inf. Co.B 2nd Lt.
Swan, Neil W. GA 4th (Clinch's) Cav.
Swan, N.I. GA 12th Cav. Co.B
Swan, Nicholas AR 18th Inf. Co.H
Swan, N.P. AR 1st Mtd.Rifles Co.G
Swan, Oliver H. VA 48th Inf. Co.H
Swan, Peter VA 18th Cav. Co.D
Swan, P.H. VA 18th Cav. Co.B Lt.
Swan, Philip VA 1st Cav. 1st Co.D
Swan, Phillip T. TN 55th (McKoin's) Inf. Duggan's Co.
Swan, R. AL 4th Res. Co.B
Swan, Richard AL Mil. 2nd Regt.Vol. Co.C
Swan, Richard LA 7th Inf. Co.E
Swan, Robert AL 15th Cav. Co.H
Swan, Robert AL 47th Inf. Co.H
Swan, Robert MS 2nd St.Cav. Co.E
Swan, Robert VA 1st Cav. Maj.
Swan, S.A. TX 11th (Spaight's) Bn.Vol. Co.G
Swan, S.A. TX 21st Inf. Co.K
Swan, Sam E. TN 8th (Smith's) Cav. Co.L
Swan, Samuel MO 10th Cav. Co.I
Swan, Samuel G. TX 14th Cav. Co.D 2nd Lt.
Swan, Samuel H. TN 7th (Duckworth's) Cav. Co.L
Swan, Samuel T. MO Lt.Arty. 3rd Btty.
Swan, S.A.R. TN 3rd (Lillard's) Mtd.Inf. Co.I Music.
Swan, S.B. GA 64th Inf. Co.B Cpl.
Swan, S.C. SC 3rd Bn.Res. Co.B
Swan, S.E. VA 10th Cav. Co.I
Swan, Seaborn H. GA Carlton's Co. (Troup Cty.Arty.)
Swan, S.G. TN 19th Inf. Co.F
Swan, S.G. TX Inf. 2nd St.Troops AQM
Swan, S.G. Gen. & Staff Capt.,AQM
Swan, S.L.G. AL 17th Inf. Co.E
Swan, S.R. Gen. & Staff Surg.
Swan, Stephen NC 60th Inf. Co.A
Swan, T.B. MS 7th Cav. Co.F Cpl.
Swan, T.D. AL 51st (Part.Rangers) Co.K
Swan, Thomas AL 12th Inf. Co.A
Swan, Thomas GA Hvy.Arty. 22nd Bn. Co.D
Swan, Thomas GA Inf. Arsenal Bn. (Columbus) Co.B
Swan, Thomas C. TX 37th Cav. Co.H,G
Swan, Thomas D. AL 51st (Part.Rangers) Co.K Sgt.
Swan, Thomas D. GA 8th Inf. (St.Guards) Co.G 2nd Lt.
Swan, Thomas E. GA 38th Inf. Co.G Sgt.
Swan, Thomas H. AL 17th Inf. Co.E
Swan, Thomas J. AL 3rd Res. Co.D
Swan, Thomas M. GA 1st (Ramsey's) Inf. Co.K
Swan, Thomas W. NC 14th Inf. Co.F
Swan, T.J. AL 3rd Inf. Co.E
Swan, W. TN 30th Inf. Co.K
Swan, W.A. TN 13th Inf. Co.G
Swan, Wade H.K. TN 3rd (Lillard's) Mtd.Inf. Co.E
Swan, W.A.J. AL 14th Inf. Co.K Capt.
Swan, Walter R. TN 1st (Turney's) Inf. Co.C
Swan, W.B. AL 57th Inf. Co.A
Swan, W.C. AL 5th Cav. Co.I
Swan, W.C. AL 12th Cav. Co.C
Swan, W.C. FL Cav. 5th Bn. Co.A
Swan, W.C. VA 8th Cav. Co.G

Swan, W.D. AR 1st (Dobbin's) Cav. Co.D
Swan, W.E. TX 4th Cav. Co.A
Swan, W.H. GA 4th Res. Co.A
Swan, W.H. GA 53rd Inf. Co.G Sgt.
Swan, William AL 9th Inf. Co.E
Swan, William GA 12th (Wright's) Cav. (St.Guards) Stapleton's Co.
Swan, William LA Mil. 3rd Regt. 1st Brig. 1st Div. Co.H 3rd Lt.
Swan, William LA Mil. Chalmette Regt. Co.H
Swan, William Conf.Inf. 8th Bn. Co.A
Swan, William D. VA 52nd Inf. 2nd Co.B Cpl.
Swan, William F. GA 14th Inf. Co.I
Swan, William H. AL Cav. Lewis' Bn. Co.D
Swan, William L. MS 34th Inf. Co.F
Swan, William W. GA 18th Inf. Co.B 2nd Lt.
Swan, W.J. TN Inf. 3rd Cons.Regt. Co.F
Swan, W.M. GA 64th Inf. Co.I
Swan, W.W. GA 2nd Inf. Co.G Sgt.
Swan, W.W. Gen. & Staff Asst.Eng.Off.
Swan, Zebulon Z. GA 35th Inf. Co.B
Swanagan, L.W. KY 2nd Cav. Co.A
Swanagan, L.W. KY 2nd Bn.Mtd.Rifles Co.A
Swanay, William H. TN 29th Inf. Co.I 1st Lt.
Swanback, Henry TN 1st Lt.Arty. Co.B
Swanback, Henry TN Lt.Arty. Weller's Co.
Swanback, Joseph LA 3rd Inf. Co.E
Swancey, John C. GA Inf. 11th Bn. (St.Guards) Co.C
Swancoat, Richard J. VA 13th Inf. Co.G Lt.
Swancoat, R.J. Eng.,CSA 2nd Lt.
Swancoat, R.J. Gen. & Staff Capt.,Vol.ADC
Swancoat, William VA Horse Arty. D. Shank's Co. Sgt.
Swancoat, William VA 13th Inf. Co.G
Swancy, Nathaniel TX 8th Inf. Co.F
Swandel, Charles TN Arty. Marshall's Co.
Swanden, W.W. AL 4th Cav. Co.A
Swanderen, P. SC Mil. 16th Regt. Lawrence's Co.
Swaner, A. AL 17th Inf. Co.K
Swaner, Amon TN 60th Mtd.Inf. Co.F
Swaner, Francis M. AL 17th Inf. Co.B
Swaner, James TX 25th Cav. Co.H
Swaner, John W. NC 17th Inf. (2nd Org.) Co.E
Swaner, Lafayette TN 32nd Inf. Co.I
Swaner, O.B.R. TN 44th (Cons.) Inf. Co.F
Swaner, Thomas F. AL 1st Bn. Hilliard's Legion Vol. Co.B
Swaner, William E. AL 1st Bn. Hilliard's Legion Vol. Co.B
Swaney, Albert M. SC 1st Arty. Co.G
Swaney, Alfred NC 48th Inf. Co.B
Swaney, Alfred Gen. & Staff, QM Dept.
Swaney, A.M. GA 7th Cav. Co.B
Swaney, A.M. GA Cav. 21st Bn. Co.C
Swaney, A.M. GA 9th Inf. Co.I
Swaney, Balie P. TN 2nd (Robison's) Inf. Co.K Sgt.
Swaney, David C. NC Inf. Thomas Legion Co.H
Swaney, Harvey E. SC 1st Arty. Co.G
Swaney, Hiram NC 48th Inf. Co.B
Swaney, Isham H. NC 29th Inf. Co.D
Swaney, James MO Cav. 3rd Bn. Co.B
Swaney, James NC 48th Inf. Co.B
Swaney, James A. MO 2nd Cav. Co.G
Swaney, J.B. TX 14th Inf. 1st Co.K
Swaney, John SC 4th Cav. Co.C
Swaney, John J. NC 39th Inf. Co.F
Swaney, John M. SC 1st Arty. Co.G
Swaney, John W. LA 22nd Inf. Co.A
Swaney, Laborin D. SC 1st Arty. Co.G
Swaney, Merritt R. SC 1st Arty. Co.G
Swaney, Reuben NC 48th Inf. Co.B Cpl.
Swaney, Richard H. SC 1st Arty. Co.G
Swaney, Thos. AL 16th Inf. Co.C
Swanfield, Charles AR 23rd Inf. Co.B Cpl.
Swanford, J.B. AL 22nd Inf. Co.K
Swanger, David F. TN 45th Inf. Co.I
Swanger, Green B. NC 16th Inf. Co.L
Swanger, Green B. NC Inf. Thomas Legion Co.E
Swanger, G.W. NC 32nd Inf. Co.D
Swanger, James NC 16th Inf. Co.L
Swanger, James NC Inf. Thomas Legion Co.E
Swanger, John NC 2nd Cav. (19th St.Troops) Co.A Black.
Swanger, John TN 18th Inf. Co.D
Swanger, Joseph NC 62nd Inf. Co.I
Swanger, William NC 16th Inf. Co.L
Swanger, William NC Inf. Thomas Legion Co.E
Swangim, Thomas AL 3rd Res. Co.D
Swangin, Kinsey F. AL 29th Inf. Co.A
Swangin, Thomas AL 3rd Inf. Co.D
Swanging, S.S. TX 11th (Spaight's) Bn.Vol. Co.C
Swango, David F. KY 5th Mtd.Inf. Co.I 1st Lt.
Swango, D.F. KY 10th (Diamond's) Cav. Co.E Capt.
Swango, G.B. KY 10th (Diamond's) Cav. Co.E Sgt.
Swango, George KY 5th Cav. Co.D
Swango, Green B. KY 5th Mtd.Inf. Co.I Cpl.
Swango, Henry C. KY 2nd Bn.Mtd.Rifles Co.E
Swango, Henry C. KY 5th Mtd.Inf. Co.I Capt.
Swango, Jacob KY 5th Cav. Co.D
Swango, James KY 5th Cav. Co.I,K
Swango, J.C. KY 10th (Diamond's) Cav. Co.E Sgt.
Swango, Martin KY 5th Cav. Co.D
Swango, Samuel KY 5th Cav. Co.D,C
Swango, William H. KY 10th (Diamond's) Cav. Co.E Bvt.2nd Lt.
Swango, William H. KY 5th Mtd.Inf. Co.I Music.
Swangrober, Rudolph MO Cav. Wood's Regt. Co.B
Swangum, Kemsey A. NC 60th Inf. Co.A
Swanigan, George AR 7th Inf. Co.C
Swanigen, L.W. LA 2nd Inf. Co.A
Swank, F. TX Cav. Benavides' Regt. Co.F
Swank, Frank TX Cav. Baylor's Regt. Co.A 3rd Lt.
Swank, James MO 6th Cav. Co.D
Swank, James F. MO 8th Cav. Co.E
Swank, James S. MO 3rd Cav. Co.G
Swank, James W. TX 6th Cav. Co.G
Swank, J.F. TX 12th Inf. Co.K 1st Sgt.
Swank, J.J. MO 6th Inf. Co.D
Swank, L. GA 1st (Ramsey's) Inf. Co.I
Swank, L.S. MS 2nd Cav. Co.D
Swank, Luther L. VA 15th Inf. Co.B Hosp.Stew.
Swank, P. TX Lt.Arty. Hughes' Co.
Swank, T.W. GA 8th Inf. Co.A
Swank, W.A. VA 60th Inf. Capt.
Swank, Walter H. VA Inf. 1st Bn.Loc.Def. Co.E 1st Sgt.
Swank, William A. VA Lt.Arty. Grandy's Co.
Swank, William L. NC 8th Inf. Co.A Music.
Swank, William L. VA 46th Inf. 2nd Co.A Music.
Swank, William P. MO Cav. 1st Regt.St.Guard Co.D 1st Lt.
Swann, --- SC 1st Inf. Co.L
Swann, A.C. AL 6th Inf. Co.F
Swann, A.J. TX 22nd Inf. Co.I
Swann, Alexander S. VA 2nd Cav. Co.H Cpl.
Swann, Alfred AL 3rd Res. Co.A
Swann, A.R. TN 1st (Carter's) Cav. Co.K
Swann, Benjamin AR 17th (Griffith's) Inf. Co.H
Swann, Benjamin R. LA 8th Inf. Co.H
Swann, Benjamin R. VA Cav. Mosby's Regt. (Part.Rangers) Co.F
Swann, B.F. AL 33rd Inf. Co.A
Swann, B.H. MS 3rd Inf. (St.Troops) Co.H
Swann, Charles M. VA 5th Cav. (12 mo. '61-2) Co.A
Swann, Charles W. VA 6th Inf. Co.I
Swann, Christopher VA Arty. Dance's Co.
Swann, Christopher VA 20th Inf. Co.D
Swann, Churchwell A. TN 24th Inf. Co.K
Swann, C.M. VA 5th Cav. Co.A
Swann, Daniel F. TN 39th Mtd.Inf. Co.C
Swann, E.A. TX 17th Field Btty.
Swann, Edward C. VA Arty. Dance's Co. Cpl.
Swann, E.E. SC 5th St.Troops Co.K
Swann, E.E. SC 17th Inf. Co.K
Swann, Erasmus D. GA Inf. Cobb Guards Co.A
Swann, Erasmus D. Sig.Corps,CSA
Swann, F.A. 2nd Conf.Eng.Troops Co.A
Swann, F.L. VA 51st Mil. Co.A Sgt.
Swann, G.A. Gen. & Staff Surg.
Swann, G.B. GA 31st Inf. Co.I Sgt.
Swann, George F. VA 24th Cav. Co.F
Swann, Gustavus A. VA Arty. Dance's Co.
Swann, G.W. VA 23rd Cav. Co.G
Swann, Harvey R. TX 18th Inf. Co.L
Swann, H.C. AL 5th Inf. New Co.F
Swann, Henry M. VA 3rd Cav. Co.G
Swann, H.L. SC 5th Inf. 2nd Co.E
Swann, H.R. TX 14th Inf. 1st Co.K Cpl.
Swann, Isaac TN 16th Inf. Co.C
Swann, Isaac H. MS 12th Cav. Co.A Cpl.
Swann, Isaac W. TN Inf. 16th Regt. Co.C
Swann, J.A. GA 48th Inf. Co.E
Swann, Jacob S. TN 32nd Inf. Co.K
Swann, James AL 28th Inf. Co.G
Swann, James MS 8th Inf. Co.I
Swann, James B. VA 40th Inf. Co.G
Swann, James J. NC 14th Inf. Co.G
Swann, James M. NC 58th Inf. Co.A Cpl.
Swann, James M. VA 14th Inf. Co.E Sgt.
Swann, James N. VA 10th Inf. 1st Co.C Capt.
Swann, James S. LA Inf.Crescent Regt. Co.H
Swann, J.C. AL Cp. of Instr. Talladega
Swann, J.F. TN 35th Inf. Co.G, 1st Co.D
Swann, J.H. GA 55th Inf. Co.A
Swann, J.H. MS 12th Cav. Co.A Cpl.
Swann, J.J. LA Inf.Cons.Crescent Regt. Co.E Sgt.
Swann, John GA 8th Cav. (St.Guards) Co.D

Swann, John LA 11th Inf. Co.L
Swann, John LA 20th Inf. New Co.E
Swann, John Gen. & Staff Asst.Surg.
Swann, John A. GA 2nd Cav. Co.E
Swann, John A. TX 36th Cav. Co.D
Swann, John B. NC 49th Inf. Co.F
Swann, John C. VA Arty. Dance Co.
Swann, John F. MO Cav. Preston's Bn. Co.A
Swann, John G. NC 22nd Inf. Co.B
Swann, John M. NC 3rd Cav. (41st St.Troops) Co.C
Swann, John S. TN 16th Inf. Co.F
Swann, John S. TX 36th Cav. Co.K
Swann, John S. VA 22nd Inf. Swann's Co. Capt.
Swann, John S. VA Inf. 26th Bn. Co.A Capt.
Swann, John S. VA 59th Inf. 2nd Co.K Capt.
Swann, John W. GA 9th Inf. (St.Guards) Co.C 2nd Lt.
Swann, Joseph TX 14th Inf. 1st Co.K
Swann, Joseph TX 18th Inf. Co.L
Swann, Joseph W. VA 47th Inf. 2nd Co.K Sgt.
Swann, J.R. MS 41st Inf.
Swann, J. Ross GA 55th Inf. Co.A
Swann, J.S. GA 6th Inf. Co.K
Swann, Luther VA 23rd Cav. Co.G
Swann, Luther VA Cav. O'Ferrall's Bn. Co.B
Swann, M. MS 1st Cav. Co.F
Swann, M. MS 41st Inf. Co.D
Swann, M. 1st Conf.Cav. 1st Co.C Capt.
Swann, Manvoah 1st Conf.Cav. 1st Co.C
Swann, Minor W. VA Lt.Arty. Arch. Graham's Co.
Swann, Moses NC 7th Sr.Res. Fisher's Co.
Swann, Nathaniel G. AL 17th Inf. Co.E
Swann, Newton MS 11th (Perrin's) Cav. Co.I
Swann, Newton MS St.Cav. Perrin's Bn. Co.B
Swann, Newton MS Inf. 3rd Bn. Co.D
Swann, P.A. AL 47th Inf. Co.C
Swann, P.A. TX 17th Field Btty.
Swann, Philip VA 6th Cav. Co.D
Swann, Porter MS 1st (Foote's) Inf. (St.Troops) Co.B
Swann, Potterfield VA Arty. Dance's Co.
Swann, P.W. NC 4th Inf. Co.C
Swann, R.F. MS 17th Inf. Co.G
Swann, Richard W. VA 11th Inf. Co.H
Swann, R.K. TX Cav. Morgan's Regt. Co.E
Swann, Robert AL Cav. Murphy's Bn. Co.D
Swann, Robert TX 27th Cav. Co.F
Swann, Robert 15th Conf.Cav. Co.K
Swann, Robert B. VA Lt.Arty. 1st Bn. Co.D
Swann, Robert B. VA Lt.Arty. B.H. Smith's Co.
Swann, Robert Bruce VA 1st Arty. Co.D
Swann, Robert L. NC 13th Inf. Co.B Cpl.
Swann, Robert M. TN 1st (Feild's) Inf. Co.C
Swann, Robert R. VA 40th Inf. Co.G
Swann, R.W. VA Lt.Arty. Arch. Graham's Co.
Swann, Samuel MS 39th Inf. Co.D
Swann, Samuel A. VA 9th Cav. Co.B Lt.Col.
Swann, Samuel D. AL 40th Inf. Co.A Cpl.
Swann, Samuel E. VA 30th Inf. Co.G Capt.
Swann, S.C. NC Inf. Thomas Legion Co.A
Swann, S.D. AL 19th Inf. Co.C Sgt.
Swann, S.R. VA Arty. Wise Legion Surg.
Swann, T.B. AR Cav. McGehee's Regt. Co.I
Swann, T.B. AR 30th Inf. Co.B 1st Sgt.
Swann, T.C. TX 14th Inf. Co.C
Swann, Thomas AL 5th Inf. New Co.F
Swann, Thomas B. NC 4th Inf. Co.C
Swann, Thomas B. VA Cav. Swann's Bn. Lt.Col.
Swann, Thomas B. VA 22nd Inf. Co.E Capt.
Swann, Thomas C. VA 30th Inf. Co.E
Swann, Thomas C. VA 47th Inf. 2nd Co.K
Swann, Thomas F. TN 24th Inf. Co.K
Swann, Thomas H. TX 6th Inf. Co.E
Swann, Thomas J. VA 1st Arty. Co.K
Swann, Thomas J. VA Arty. Dance's Co.
Swann, Thomas J. VA Arty. L.F. Jones' Co.
Swann, Thomas M. AL Cav. Holloway's Co.
Swann, Thomas M. GA Arty. 11th Bn. (Sumter Arty.) Co.A
Swann, Thomas R. TX Conscr.
Swann, T.T. FL Adv.Board Member
Swann, T.T. GA Cav. 12th Bn. (St.Guards) Co.C Capt.
Swann, T.T. MS 13th Inf. Co.K
Swann, T.T. MS 33rd Inf. Co.H
Swann, W. TX 14th Inf. Co.C
Swann, W.D. TX Arty. Douglas' Co.
Swann, W.H. FL Conscr. Sgt.
Swann, W.H. 1st Conf.Cav. 1st Co.C Sgt.
Swann, William MO 1st N.E. Cav. White's Co.
Swann, William VA 40th Inf. Co.G Cpl.
Swann, William E. MS 42nd Inf. Co.B
Swann, William J. VA 37th Mil. Co.A
Swann, William L. NC 14th Inf. Co.G
Swann, William M. GA 6th Inf. Surg.
Swann, William M. NC 30th Inf. Co.H Capt.
Swann, Wm. M. Gen. & Staff Surg.
Swann, William T. VA Hvy.Arty. 10th Bn. Co.C
Swann, Willis G. VA 23rd Cav. Co.G
Swann, W.J. AR 30th Inf. Co.G
Swann, W.J. TN 35th Inf. Co.G, 1st Co.D Bvt.2nd Lt.
Swann, W.L. VA 2nd St.Res. Co.E
Swann, W.W. TN 30th Inf. Co.B
Swann, W.W. Gen. & Staff Capt.
Swann, Z.S. MD Inf. 2nd Bn. Co.B
Swanner, Andrew J. NC 43rd Inf. Co.K
Swanner, Asa MS 39th Inf. Co.B Sgt.
Swanner, C. AL 25th Inf. Co.B
Swanner, Daniel AL 25th Inf. Co.B
Swanner, Isaiah NC 43rd Inf. Co.K
Swanner, Isham AL 25th Inf. Co.A
Swanner, James AL 5th Inf. Co.A
Swanner, James A. NC 37th Inf. Co.D
Swanner, J.B. MO 16th Inf. Co.C
Swanner, J.B. MO St.Guard
Swanner, J.B. Exch.Bn. 2nd Co.C,CSA
Swanner, Jesse B. MO 4th Inf. Co.C
Swanner, J.M. NC 4th Sr.Res. Co.I
Swanner, Joseph TN 60th Mtd.Inf. Co.F
Swanner, Joshua AL 25th Inf. Co.B
Swanner, O.B.R. VA Arty. Wise Legion
Swanner, Uriah James T. NC 61st Inf. Co.H
Swanner, Uriah J.T. NC 42nd Inf. Co.B
Swanner, William F. AL 54th Inf. Co.E 2nd Lt.
Swanner, William F. 4th Conf.Inf. Co.D
Swanner, William G. NC 37th Inf. Co.D
Swannes, T.H. AL Cav. Barbiere's Bn. Brown's Co.
Swanney, Hiram H. AR 3rd Cav. Co.K
Swans, John VA 20th Cav. Co.K
Swansan, W. AL 35th Inf. Co.B
Swansey, E.J. GA Cherokee Legion (St.Guards) Co.A Cpl.
Swansey, James R. SC 1st (Orr's) Rifles Co.G Cpl.
Swansey, James V. AL 55th Vol. Co.B
Swansey, J.W. GA 4th Cav. (St.Guards) Pirkle's Co. Sgt.
Swansey, William MS 15th Inf. Co.K
Swanson, A.B. MS 1st (King's) Inf. (St.Troops) Co.C
Swanson, A.B. MS 1st (Percy's) Inf. Co.A
Swanson, A.H. LA Mil. 4th Regt. 1st Brig. 1st Div. Co.B Capt.
Swanson, Anderson C. 1st Conf.Eng.Troops Co.I
Swanson, A.S. GA Smith's Legion Co.C
Swanson, Bartlett W. GA 6th Cav. Co.F
Swanson, C. TN 3rd (Forrest's) Cav. Co.A
Swanson, C.E. TX 14th Inf. Co.B
Swanson, Charles W. AL Inf. 1st Regt. Co.F
Swanson, Charles W. GA 51st Inf. Co.H 1st Lt.
Swanson, C.T. TN 9th Inf. Co.H 1st Lt.
Swanson, Edward TN 4th (McLemore's) Cav. Co.A Surg.
Swanson, Edward Gen. & Staff Surg.
Swanson, Edward T. NC 44th Inf. Co.K
Swanson, E.R. AL 18th Inf. Co.H
Swanson, F.A. VA 21st Inf. Co.I
Swanson, Felix Z. TN Holman's Bn.Part.Rangers Co.B
Swanson, Francis M. FL 1st Inf. Old Co.H, New Co.K
Swanson, Francis M. GA 6th Inf. (St.Guards) Co.C 3rd Lt.
Swanson, F.Z. TN 11th (Holman's) Cav. Co.G
Swanson, George W. NC 42nd Inf. Co.K
Swanson, H.B. Gen. & Staff Capt.,AC
Swanson, Henry C. Gen. & Staff, QM Dept.
Swanson, Ira TN 11th (Holman's) Cav. Co.G Cpl.
Swanson, Isaac B. GA 6th Cav. Co.A
Swanson, Isaac P. GA 39th Inf. Co.F Cpl.
Swanson, J. AL Chas. A. Herts' Co.
Swanson, J.A. GA 55th Inf. Co.B
Swanson, J.A.B. VA 10th Inf. 2nd Co.C
Swanson, J.A.B.C. GA 39th Inf. Co.F
Swanson, James TN 29th Inf. Co.B
Swanson, James TN 36th Inf. Co.F
Swanson, James A. GA 39th Inf. Co.F
Swanson, James M. GA Cherokee Legion (St.Guards) Co.E
Swanson, J.J. GA 1st Inf. (St.Guards) Co.D
Swanson, J.J. TN 11th (Holman's) Cav. Co.G
Swanson, J.M. TX Cav. 1st Regt.St.Troops Co.B 1st Lt.
Swanson, J.M. VA 21st Inf. Co.I
Swanson, John AR 15th (N.W.) Inf. Co.A
Swanson, John GA Murray Cav. Asher's Co.
Swanson, John J. TN Holman's Bn.Part.Rangers Co.B
Swanson, John S. AL 8th (Livingston's) Cav. Co.I
Swanson, John S. AL Cav. Moses' Squad. Co.A
Swanson, John W. AR 11th Inf.
Swanson, Joseph AL 45th Inf. Co.C
Swanson, Joseph VA 10th Inf. 2nd Co.C

Swanson, Joseph J. FL 1st Inf. New Co.K
Swanson, J.T. GA 2nd Cav. (St.Guards) Co.H
Swanson, J.W. AR 1st (Dobbin's) Cav. Co.B
Swanson, J.W. AR 18th Inf. Co.G
Swanson, Lawson NC 58th Inf. Co.H
Swanson, L.T. GA Boddie's Co. (Troup Cty.Ind.Cav.) Sgt.
Swanson, Marcus W. GA 7th Inf. (St.Guards) Co.D
Swanson, M.B. MS 7th Cav. Co.H 2nd Lt.
Swanson, M.B. Gen. & Staff Capt.,Comsy.
Swanson, M.D. AL 8th (Livingston's) Cav. Co.E
Swanson, Mirabean AL 3rd Inf. Co.C
Swanson, Monroe TN 11th (Holman's) Cav. Co.I
Swanson, Monroe TN Douglass' Bn.Part.Rangers Perkins' Co.
Swanson, Mumford NC 44th Inf. Co.K
Swanson, Mumfred E. NC 15th Inf. Co.G
Swanson, N.G. GA Boddie's Co. (Troup Cty.Ind.Cav.) 3rd Lt.
Swanson, P.B. MS 1st Cav. Co.C
Swanson, P.H. AL Auburn Home Guards Vol. Darby's Co.
Swanson, Richard TN 20th Inf. Co.H 1st Lt.
Swanson, Sampson NC 26th Inf. Co.F
Swanson, Samuel A. VA 38th Inf. Co.D 2nd Lt.
Swanson, Samuel F. VA 18th Inf. Co.A Cpl.
Swanson, Samuel F. VA 21st Inf. Co.I Capt.
Swanson, S.F. GA Mil. 37th Regt. Co.A 4th Lt.
Swanson, Simeon NC 44th Inf. Co.K Cpl.
Swanson, Sylvanus B. GA 55th Inf. Co.G
Swanson, T.B. GA 27th Inf. Co.E Sgt.
Swanson, T.B. MS 1st Cav. Co.E
Swanson, Thom. AL Inf. 1st Regt. Co.I Capt.
Swanson, Thos. AL 45th Inf. Co.C 2nd Lt.
Swanson, Thomas GA 6th Cav. Co.L
Swanson, Thomas GA Inf. 2nd Bn. Co.A
Swanson, Thomas LA 1st (Strawbridge's) Inf. Co.G
Swanson, Thomas VA 58th Mil. Co.F
Swanson, T.J. GA Floyd Legion (St.Guards) Co.I Sgt.
Swanson, Vincent W. VA 21st Inf. Co.I 1st Lt.
Swanson, W.C. NC 12th Inf. Co.K
Swanson, W.E.C. GA 12th Cav. Co.K Cpl.
Swanson, W.G. AL 1st Regt.Conscr. Maj.
Swanson, W.G. Gen. & Staff Maj.,AAG
Swanson, William GA Murray Cav. Asher's Co. Striker
Swanson, William VA 7th Cav. Co.B
Swanson, William Dewbartsu GA 39th Inf. Co.A
Swanson, William E.C. GA 36th (Villepigue's) Inf. Co.B
Swanson, William E.C. 1st Conf.Inf. Co.B
Swanson, William G. AL 3rd Inf. Co.C Capt.
Swanson, William G. AL 61st Inf. Col.
Swanson, William H. NC 15th Inf. Co.G
Swanson, William R. GA 2nd (Stapleton's) St.Troops Co.A
Swanson, William S. AL 39th Inf. Co.I 1st Lt.
Swanson, William T. GA 39th Inf. Co.F
Swanston, Robert SC 1st Arty. Co.K Sgt.
Swanton, James Eng.,CSA
Swanton, John LA 1st (Strawbridge's) Inf. Co.F
Swanton, John LA 21st (Kennedy's) Inf. Co.E
Swanton, P.H. TX 8th Cav. Co.I
Swany, David GA Cav. 16th Bn. (St.Guards) Co.E
Swanzey, Samuel A. MS 1st (Patton's) Inf. Co.C
Swanzey, Thomas A. MS 20th Inf. Co.B
Swanzey, William Z. MS 1st (Patton's) Inf. Co.C
Swanzy, J.A. MS Rogers' Co. Jr.2nd Lt.
Swanzy, J.E. MS 20th Inf. Co.B
Swanzy, John A. MS St.Cav. Perrin's Bn. Co.A Sgt.
Swanzy, S.A. MS 43rd Inf. Co.F
Swanzy, T.A. MS 9th Inf. New Co.G
Swanzy, T.N. MS 2nd St.Cav. Co.H Sgt.
Swanzy, T.N. MS Inf. 3rd Bn. (St.Troops) Co.B 1st Lt.
Swanzy, Washington MS 24th Inf. Co.D
Swanzy, William Z. MS 43rd Inf. Co.F
Swar, David J. TX Cav. Ragsdale's Bn. 2nd Co.C
Swaraiger, James AL 50th Inf. Co.D
Swaregame, S.F. NC Mallett's Bn. (Cp.Guard) Co.D
Swarengen, W.B. LA 17th Inf. Co.B Cpl.
Swarengim, Samuel TN 28th (Cons.) Inf. Co.K
Swarengin, James MS 1st (Patton's) Inf. Co.I
Swares, E. TX 25th Cav.
Swarez, Isabel TX Cav. Benavides' Regt.
Swarfend, William R. TN 34th Inf. Co.D
Swarford, T.C. MO 3rd & 5th Cons.Inf. Co.G
Swarford, Thos. MO St.Guard W.H. Taylor's Co.
Swaringan, A. GA 59th Inf. Co.G
Swaringeam, David AL 18th Bn.Vol. Co.B
Swaringeam, James AL 18th Bn.Vol. Co.C,B
Swaringeam, Marion AL 18th Bn.Vol. Co.C,B
Swaringeam, Richard AL 18th Bn.Vol. Co.C,B
Swaringen, G.B. TN 20th (Russell's) Cav. Co.B
Swaringen, George I. NC 27th Inf. Co.I
Swaringen, G.F. GA 5th Res. Co.A,D
Swaringen, Henry C. NC 28th Inf. Co.K
Swaringen, Iva F. NC 4th Inf. Co.G
Swaringen, J. GA 45th Inf. Co.A
Swaringen, J.J. GA 45th Inf. Co.C
Swaringen, John W. AL 1st Regt.Conscr. Co.A
Swaringen, Richard J. AL 1st Regt.Conscr. Co.A
Swaringen, S.T. NC 5th Cav. (63rd St.Troops) Co.H
Swaringen, Thomas MS 7th Inf. Co.K
Swaringen, Wilber F. NC 28th Inf. Co.K
Swaringen, W.T. TN 5th Inf. 2nd Co.F
Swaringer, F.B. MS 1st (Patton's) Inf. Co.E Cpl.
Swaringer, John NC 28th Inf. Co.K
Swaringham, M.M. MS 1st Cav.Res. Co.C
Swaringham, W.B. MS 1st Cav.Res. Co.C 1st Lt.
Swaringin, G.B. TN 19th & 20th (Cons.) Cav. Co.A
Swaringin, John AL 50th Inf. Co.D
Swaringin, Vance TN 28th (Cons.) Inf. Co.F
Swarn, T.C. VA Lt.Arty. W.P. Carter's Co.
Swarner, J. AL 2nd Cav. Co.F
Swarner, J.B. TX 27th Cav. Co.K
Swarner, L.F. TN 14th (Neely's) Cav. Co.K
Swarniger, C. VA 18th Cav. Co.G
Swarrenger, Robert MS 1st (King's) Inf. (St.Troops) Co.E
Swart, Hugh T. Gen. & Staff QM
Swart, H.W. VA Cav. Mosby's Regt. (Part. Rangers) Co.A
Swart, James H. VA 6th Cav. Co.K Sgt.
Swart, William AR 11th & 17th Cons.Inf. Co.H
Swart, William H. VA 15th Cav. Co.G
Swart, William H. VA Cav. 15th Bn. Co.D
Swarting, J.F. TX Inf. 1st St.Troops Sheldon's Co.B
Swarting, William TX 24th Cav. Co.I
Swartley, Valentine VA 15th Inf. Co.D
Swarton, Thomas LA 1st Inf. Co.F,G
Swarts, A. LA 26th Inf.
Swarts, David N. KY 2nd Cav. Co.F
Swarts, F. GA 64th Inf. Co.F
Swarts, Francis M. KY 1st Bn.Mtd.Rifles Co.D
Swarts, Franklin VA 31st Mil. Co.I
Swarts, George W. VA 18th Cav. Co.D
Swarts, Harrison VA 146th Mil. Co.E
Swarts, Henry VA 31st Mil. Co.I
Swarts, J.H. VA 11th Cav. Co.G
Swarts, John VA 21st Cav. 2nd Co.C
Swarts, Joseph G. VA 3rd (Chrisman's) Bn.Res. Co.F
Swarts, Marion M. KY 3rd Bn.Mtd.Rifles Co.F
Swarts, Samuel VA 114th Mil. Co.G
Swarts, William A. KY 5th Mtd.Inf. Co.C
Swartte, A. VA Inf. 44th Bn. Co.B
Swartwout, P. LA Lt.Arty. Barlow's Btty. 1st Sgt.
Swartz, --- VA 3rd (Chrisman's) Bn.Res. Co.B
Swartz, Barney SC 1st (Butler's) Inf. Co.B
Swartz, Benjamin VA 23rd Cav. Co.A
Swartz, Benjamin VA 58th Mil. Co.E
Swartz, C. VA 122nd Mil. Co.B
Swartz, Calvin VA 11th Cav. Co.E
Swartz, Calvin VA 33rd Inf. Co.D
Swartz, Charles TX 26th Cav. 1st Co.G
Swartz, Charles VA Cav. 39th Bn. Co.A
Swartz, Charles VA 2nd Inf. Co.A
Swartz, Charles A. TX 33rd Cav. Co.B
Swartz, D. VA 9th Bn.Res. Co.D Cpl.
Swartz, Dav VA 3rd (Chrisman's) Bn.Res. Co.B
Swartz, David VA 146th Mil. Co.F
Swartz, Ebenezer VA 33rd Inf. Co.I
Swartz, Edward P. VA 11th Cav. Co.D
Swartz, Francis SC 1st Inf. Co.C
Swartz, Frederick TN 1st (Feild's) Inf. Co.E
Swartz, George VA 1st Arty. Co.G
Swartz, George VA Lt.Arty. Page's Co.
Swartz, George VA 32nd Inf. 1st Co.I
Swartz, George W. VA Lt.Arty. J.D. Smith's Co.
Swartz, George W. VA 10th Inf. Co.H
Swartz, H. AL 8th Inf. Co.G
Swartz, H. VA 2nd Inf. Co.C
Swartz, Harrison VA 7th Cav. Co.K
Swartz, H.L. VA 5th Cav. Co.B
Swartz, Isaac VA Inf. Co.K
Swartz, Isaac VA 146th Mil. Co.E
Swartz, J. GA 32nd Inf. Co.E
Swartz, Jacob SC Manigault's Bn.Vol. Co.C
Swartz, Jacob VA 136th Mil. Co.B
Swartz, Jacob F. VA 11th Cav.
Swartz, James VA 23rd Cav. Co.D
Swartz, James VA 146th Mil. Co.K
Swartz, James K. VA 33rd Inf. Co.G
Swartz, Jasper SC 20th Inf. Co.C

Swartz, John TX Cav. Benavides' Regt. Co.H
Swartz, John TX 18th Inf. Co.D
Swartz, John B. VA 8th Inf. Co.C
Swartz, John L. VA 5th Inf. Co.K
Swartz, John R. VA 7th Cav. Co.K
Swartz, John R. VA 97th Mil. Co.B
Swartz, John S. VA 136th Mil. Co.D
Swartz, John T. VA 136th Mil. Co.D
Swartz, John W. VA 33rd Inf. Co.I
Swartz, John William VA 146th Mil. Co.A
Swartz, Joseph VA 136th Mil. Co.E
Swartz, Joseph G. VA Rockbridge Cty.Res. Miller's Co.
Swartz, Lewis TN 1st (Feild's) Inf. Co.E
Swartz, Lewis F. VA Lt.Arty. B.Z. Price's Co.
Swartz, Lewis F. VA Lt.Arty. W.H. Rice's Co.
Swartz, Lorenzo VA 33rd Inf. Co.K
Swartz, Louis NC 4th Cav. (59th St.Troops) Co.C
Swartz, Nathaniel M. VA 62nd Mtd.Inf. 1st Co.A
Swartz, Nathan M. VA Horse Arty. McClanahan's Co.
Swartz, Noah VA 136th Mil. Co.E Capt.
Swartz, Philip W. VA 136th Mil. Co.C
Swartz, Phillip P. VA 97th Mil. Co.G
Swartz, Richard VA Horse Arty. McClanahan's Co.
Swartz, S. VA 11th Cav. Co.E
Swartz, S. VA 12th Cav. Co.F
Swartz, Samuel VA Cav. 40th Bn. Co.A
Swartz, Samuel VA 8th Bn.Res. Co.D
Swartz, Samuel VA 33rd Inf. Co.A
Swartz, Simri VA 136th Mil. Co.E
Swartz, Tunis Q. VA Lt.Arty. W.H. Rice's Co.
Swartz, W. VA Hvy.Arty. 19th Bn. 3rd Co.C
Swartz, William VA 7th Cav. Co.H
Swartz, William VA Hvy.Arty. 18th Bn. Co.E
Swartz, William VA 3rd (Chrisman's) Bn.Res. Co.C
Swartz, William VA 8th Bn.Res. Co.C,D
Swartz, William VA 136th Mil. Co.C Sgt.
Swartz, William VA 136th Mil. Co.E Sgt.
Swartz, William S. VA 5th Inf. Co.K
Swartz, William S. VA 136th Mil. Co.D
Swartze, J.G. VA 1st Cav. Co.C
Swartzel, George VA 5th Inf. Co.K
Swartzel, George A. VA 52nd Inf. Co.H
Swartzel, Harrison S. VA 5th Inf. Co.D
Swartzel, John A. TN 29th Inf. Co.H Sgt.
Swartzel, John W. VA 5th Inf. Co.K
Swartzel, Solom J. TN 29th Inf. Co.H
Swartzell, C.J. KY 8th Mtd.Inf. Co.B
Swartzenberg, John LA Hvy.Arty. 2nd Bn. Co.B
Swartzle, Harrison T. VA 5th Inf. Co.D
Swartzley, Jacob L. VA 5th Inf. Co.A
Swasey, B.Z. LA Hvy.Arty. 2nd Bn. Co.B
Swasey, H.R. LA Mil.Cont.Regt. Mitchell's Co. Cpl.
Swat, Noah AL 18th Inf. Co.L
Swateh, --- NC Inf. Thomas Legion 2nd Co.A Sgt.
Swatezwell, Joseph KY 3rd Mtd.Inf. Co.C
Swats, D. VA 9th Bn.Res. Co.C
Swats, Samuel VA Cav. 41st Bn. Co.E
Swats, Samuel VA 9th Bn.Res. Co.C
Swats, Samuel B. VA 11th Cav. Co.F
Swatsel, Michael TN 61st Mtd.Inf. Co.C
Swatsell, W.L. SC 13th Inf. Co.C
Swatta, Joseph LA 16th Inf. Co.E
Swatts, Augustus VA 5th Inf. Co.K
Swatts, G.B. GA 38th Inf. Co.C
Swatts, Glen B. GA 50th Inf. Co.F
Swatts, John W. VA 5th Inf. Co.K
Swatz, Andrew AL Mil. 3rd Vol. Co.E
Swatz, Henry LA 6th Inf. Co.H
Swatz, Henry TX 17th Inf. Co.B
Swatz, Isaac LA Mil. 1st Regt. 2nd Brig. 1st Div. Co.K
Swatz, L. GA Inf. City Bn. (Columbus) Co.B
Swatz, Lewis VA 11th Cav. Co.F
Swatz, Philip P. VA 8th Bn.Res. Co.C
Swatz, S. VA 23rd Cav. Co.E
Swatz, Samuel VA 24th Cav. Co.A
Swatzel, Charles T. TN Conscr. (Cp. of Instr.)
Swatzel, James H. MS 13th Inf. Co.A
Swatzel, T.T. TN 9th Inf. Co.I
Swatzell, David VA 3rd Bn. Valley Res. Co.D
Swatzell, Jacob VA 3rd Bn. Valley Res. Co.D
Swatzell, T. MS Lt.Arty. Turner's Co.
Swatzhof, S. TX 7th Cav. Co.B 1st Lt.
Swauke, L.S. MD Cav. 2nd Bn. Co.D
Swaw, Samuel TN 49th Inf. Co.K
Swayengame, Alex A. NC Cav. 7th Bn. Co.D,E
Swayengame, John M. NC 6th Cav. (65th St.Troops) Co.D,C
Swayengame, John M. NC Cav. 7th Bn. Co.D,E
Swayengame, William N. NC Cav. 7th Bn. Co.E
Swayengame, W.N. NC 6th Cav. (65th St.Troops) Co.E
Swayine, Jack TN 12th (Green's) Cav. Co.A
Swayne, Darling 10th Conf.Cav. Co.G
Swayne, James GA Cav. 19th Bn. Co.A,B
Swayne, J.N. Blake's Scouts,CSA
Swayne, John TN 11th Inf. Co.K
Swayne, L.B. MS 10th Cav. Co.H
Swayne, S.N. MS Lt.Arty. Yates' Btty.
Swayne, T.B. Conf.Cav. Baxter's Bn. Co.A
Swaynegaim, A.A. NC 6th Cav. (65th St.Troops) Co.E,C,D
Swaynegaim, K.A. NC 6th Cav. (65th St.Troops) Co.C
Swayze, Caldwell C. LA 8th Inf. Co.F 2nd Lt.
Swayze, Caleb MS Wilkinson Cty. Minute Men Co.B
Swayze, C.S. LA 4th Inf. Co.D
Swayze, David C. MS 3rd Inf. Co.C
Swayze, D.N. MS 38th Cav. Co.D
Swayze, Eli A. AR 24th Inf. Co.B
Swayze, Frank B. MS Wilkinson Cty. Minute Men Co.F Capt.
Swayze, Hardy MS 1st Lt.Arty. Co.B Sgt.
Swayze, James MS 3rd Inf. Co.I Cpl.
Swayze, James S. AR 3rd Inf. Co.L,A Cpl.
Swayze, John A. MS 1st Lt.Arty. Co.I Cpl.
Swayze, J.W. MS Cav. Gartley's Co. (Yazoo Rangers)
Swayze, J.W. 1st Conf.Eng.Troops Co.I
Swayze, N.R. MS 10th Inf. Co.O
Swayze, Orange MS 1st Lt.Arty. Co.B
Swayze, Prentiss MS 18th Inf. Co.B 3rd Lt.
Swayze, Prentiss Conf.Cav. Wood's Regt. Co.K, 2nd Co.A 2nd Lt.
Swayze, S.C. LA 4th Inf. Co.D 3rd Lt.
Swayze, Solomon W. MS 18th Inf. Co.B 2nd Lt.
Swayze, Thomas LA 25th Inf. Co.D
Swayze, W.A. MS 3rd Inf. Co.C
Swayze, W.A. 14th Conf.Cav.
Swayze, W.F. LA Mil.Cav. Norwood's Co. (Jeff Davis Rangers)
Swayzee, Jason C. 1st Conf.Eng.Troops Co.H Sgt.
Swayzie, Budd MS Inf. 2nd Bn. (St.Troops) Co.C
Swayzie, C.B. MS Inf. 2nd Bn. (St.Troops) Co.C
Swayzie, D.W. MS 1st Lt.Arty. Co.I
Swazey, Anthony H. AL Lt.Arty. 2nd Bn. Co.E Cpl.
Swazey, L.D. MS 39th Inf. Co.B
Swazey, S. MS 4th Cav. Co.I
Swazey, S.L. LA 31st Inf. Co.D Sgt.
Swazie, Daniel W. MS 7th Inf. Co.A Cpl.
Swazy, Gabriel R. LA Inf. 11th Bn. Co.F
Swazy, William G. TN 2nd (Smith's) Cav. Rankin's Co.
Swazze, Eli A. AR Inf. Hardy's Regt. Co.B
Swazzie, A.C. Conf.Cav. Wood's Regt. 1st Co.A
Swcezy, Jehu B. NC 16th Inf. Co.D Cpl.
Swean, Colin M. AL 39th Inf. Co.C Capt.
Sweaney, A. 1st Conf.Cav. Co.I
Sweaney, James A. MO 11th Inf. Co.D
Sweaney, John NC 3rd Arty. (40th St.Troops) Co.H Cpl.
Sweaney, John NC 2nd Inf. Co.A
Sweaney, John R. MS Lt.Arty. (The Hudson Btty.) Hoole's Co. 1st Lt.
Sweaney, Thomas NC 24th Inf. Co.A
Sweany, James SC 1st Arty. Co.G
Swear, Eli AR 20th Inf. Co.G
Swear, Henry LA 13th Inf. Co.E
Swear, Nat. LA 8th Inf. Co.A
Swearagan, Thomas TX 18th Inf. Co.K
Swearengan, Charles SC 2nd Arty. Co.H
Swearengan, L.G. SC 2nd Arty. Co.H
Swearengen, Benjamin SC 1st Inf. Co.C Cpl.
Swearengen, B.T. SC 14th Inf. Co.D Cpl.
Swearengen, Charles S. MS 29th Inf. Co.E
Swearengen, Claiborne F. MO 6th Inf. Co.C Sgt.
Swearengen, C.R. TX 11th (Spaight's) Bn.Vol. Co.D 1st Lt.
Swearengen, E.A. TX Cav. Waller's Regt. Co.F
Swearengen, Frank B. MS 35th Inf. Co.B
Swearengen, George F. GA 45th Inf. Co.C
Swearengen, G.F. TX 11th (Spaight's) Bn.Vol. Co.G
Swearengen, G.W. MS 3rd Cav. Co.K
Swearengen, James TX 7th Cav. Co.I
Swearengen, James C. MO Searcy's Bn.S.S. Co.E
Swearengen, John SC 1st Inf. Co.C
Swearengen, Lewis TX 20th Inf. Co.A
Swearengen, Newton MO Searcy's Bn.S.S. Co.E
Swearengen, Obed. MO Searcy's Bn.S.S. Co.E
Swearengen, S. MS 3rd Cav. Co.K
Swearengen, Samuel TX 20th Inf. Co.A
Swearengen, T.A. GA Cav. 29th Bn. Co.A
Swearengen, T.F. FL Cav. 5th Bn. Co.C
Swearengen, Thomas GA 12th Inf. Co.F
Swearengen, Thos. A. GA Cav. 29th Bn. Co.A

Swearengen, Thomas F. FL 3rd Inf. Co.H 1st Lt.
Swearengen, W.B. GA 55th Inf. Co.C
Swearengen, W.H. MO 1st & 3rd Cons.Cav. Co.G
Swearengen, William E. GA 31st Inf. Co.I
Swearengen, William N. AL 3rd Inf. Co.C
Swearengen, William T. MS 44th Inf. Co.E
Swearengen, Zack TX 7th Cav. Co.I
Swearengin, A.S. SC 7th Inf. 1st Co.H, Co.A 2nd Lt.
Swearengin, A.W. MS 35th Inf. Co.A
Swearengin, Bryant TN 13th (Gore's) Cav. Co.K Capt.
Swearengin, Daniel T. GA 12th Inf. Co.F
Swearengin, David AL 33rd Inf.
Swearengin, Green AL 12th Inf. Co.G
Swearengin, G.W. MO 11th Inf. Co.G
Swearengin, James TN 28th (Cons.) Inf. Co.K
Swearengin, James M. MS 35th Inf. Co.A
Swearengin, John C. SC 7th Inf. 1st Co.H, Co.A,K Cpl.
Swearengin, J.T. AL 22nd Inf. Co.I
Swearengin, J. Wheeler SC 2nd Cav. Co.I
Swearengin, Lee W. MS 13th Inf. Co.C
Swearengin, Levi S. TN 13th (Gore's) Cav. Co.K
Swearengin, William B. MS 13th Inf. Co.C
Swearigson, S.T. NC 13th Inf. Co.F
Swearingain, Rice GA 3rd Inf. Co.G
Swearingan, Benjamin J. NC 42nd Inf. Co.C
Swearingan, Vance TN 84th Inf. Co.B
Swearingar, W. VA Lt.Arty. Sturdivant's Co.
Swearingen, --- TX Inf. 1st St.Troops Whitehead's Co.
Swearingen, Ab SC 24th Inf. Co.I
Swearingen, Alexander B. FL 9th Inf. Co.F
Swearingen, Andrew Van MO 1st Cav. Co.B Cpl.
Swearingen, Charles SC 22nd Inf. Co.A
Swearingen, Claibourne F. MO Inf. 3rd Bn. Co.A
Swearingen, C.R. TX Inf. 1st St.Troops Wheat's Co.
Swearingen, C.R. TX 21st Inf. Co.K
Swearingen, David MO Cav. Wood's Regt. Co.H
Swearingen, E.A. TX 1st Inf. Co.F
Swearingen, E. Lafayette MS 7th Inf. Co.C
Swearingen, G.F. TX Inf. 1st St.Troops Wheat's Co.A
Swearingen, H.B. TN 40th Inf. Co.H
Swearingen, H.J. FL Lt.Arty. Abell's Co. Cpl.
Swearingen, H.J. GA 11th Cav. (St.Guards) Bruce's Co. 1st Sgt.
Swearingen, H.W. MS 33rd Inf. Co.K
Swearingen, James TN 28th Inf. Co.B
Swearingen, James L.B. NC 14th Inf. Co.H
Swearingen, James M. GA 55th Inf. Co.E
Swearingen, James W. NC 42nd Inf. Co.K,C
Swearingen, J.H. GA Cav. 29th Bn. Co.B
Swearingen, J.H. GA Siege Arty. Campbell's Ind.Co.
Swearingen, J.J. GA 55th Inf. Co.E
Swearingen, John FL 9th Inf. Co.K
Swearingen, John LA 8th Inf. Co.H
Swearingen, John SC 22nd Inf. Co.A
Swearingen, John Edward SC 2nd Cav. Co.I
Swearingen, John J. GA Cav. 29th Bn. Co.G Sgt.
Swearingen, John J. GA 29th Inf.
Swearingen, John T. TX 24th Cav. Co.D Sgt.
Swearingen, J.T. SC 5th Cav. Co.D
Swearingen, J.W. AL 21st Inf. Co.G Sgt.
Swearingen, J. Wheeler SC Cav.Bn. Hampton Legion Co.A
Swearingen, M.B. FL 5th Inf. Co.I 2nd Lt.
Swearingen, Richard SC 7th Inf. 1st Co.H
Swearingen, Richard TN 1st (Carter's) Cav. Co.K Capt.
Swearingen, R.S. AL 1st Cav. 1st Co.K
Swearingen, S. TX 25th Cav. Co.I
Swearingen, Samuel FL Lt.Arty. Perry's Co.
Swearingen, Samuel TN 28th Inf. Co.B Cpl.
Swearingen, Samuel A. FL 9th Inf. Co.K
Swearingen, S.S. TX 21st Inf. Co.K
Swearingen, Thomas MS 7th Inf. Co.K
Swearingen, Thomas MO Cav. 2nd Regt. St.Guard Co.F
Swearingen, Thomas M. LA 6th Cav. Co.C
Swearingen, Thomas M. LA 8th Inf. Co.G
Swearingen, W. GA Cav. Floyd's Co.
Swearingen, W. KY 1st (Butler's) Cav. Co.E Sgt.
Swearingen, W.E. MO Cav. Wood's Regt. Co.H
Swearingen, William MO Cav. Snider's Bn. Co.B
Swearingen, William MO 5th Inf. Co.H Cpl.
Swearingen, William VA 18th Cav. 2nd Co.G
Swearingen, William J. MO 6th Inf. Co.C
Swearingen, William M. MO Cav. Poindexter's Regt.
Swearingen, William P. GA Cav. 29th Bn. Co.G
Swearingen, William W. VA 25th Inf. 1st Co.G
Swearingen, William W. VA 62nd Mtd.Inf. 2nd Co.A
Swearingen, Wilson MS 43rd Inf. Co.K
Swearingen, W.R. TX 11th (Spaight's) Bn.Vol. Co.D
Swearingen, W.R. TX 21st Inf. Co.H,K
Swearinger, A.V. GA 27th Inf. Co.A
Swearinger, Rice GA Inf. 1st Loc.Troops (Augusta) Co.F
Swearinger, R.J. AL Lt.Arty. Clanton's Btty. Lt.
Swearinger, Samuel AR 34th Inf. Co.D
Swearinger, Samuel AR Brooks' Inf. Buchanon's Co.
Swearinger, W. KY 3rd Cav. Co.D Sgt.
Swearingin, B.M. TN 25th Inf. Co.I 2nd Lt.
Swearingin, C. SC 2nd Arty. Co.E
Swearingin, Eli S. NC 52nd Inf. Co.I Sgt.
Swearingin, James N. VA 52nd Inf. Co.K
Swearingin, John FL 11th Inf. Co.L Cpl.
Swearingin, John B. VA 18th Cav. 2nd Co.G
Swearingin, J.W. NC 1st Cav. (9th St.Troops) Co.C
Swearingin, Patrick H. TX 24th Cav. Co.D Lt.Col.
Swearingin, Rice GA 12th Inf. Co.F
Swearingin, William AL 4th (Russell's) Cav. Co.H
Swearingin, William F. TN 25th Inf. Co.F
Swearingin, W.R. TN 21st Inf. Co.C
Swearnegin, Ben TX 12th Cav. Co.G
Swearngan, Lewis KY 5th Mtd.Inf. Co.A
Swearngean, John J. GA 31st Inf. Co.F
Swearngean, William J. GA 31st Inf. Co.F
Swearngin, T.M. LA 13th Bn. (Part.Rangers) Co.F
Sweasey, Chris KY 14th Cav. Co.B Cpl.
Sweasey, E.L. TX 3rd Cav. Co.E
Sweasey, Joseph G. KY 14th Cav. Co.B
Sweasy, Christopher J. KY 2nd (Duke's) Cav. Co.B,A
Sweasy, J. Fisk KY 6th Mtd.Inf. Co.K,A
Sweasy, J.G. KY 6th Mtd.Inf. Co.K,A
Sweasy, Joseph T. KY 6th Mtd.Inf. Co.K,A
Sweat, --- GA Vol.
Sweat, Aaron P. SC 4th St.Troops Co.F
Sweat, A.B. AL Cav. Forrest's Regt.
Sweat, A.B. TN 18th (Newsom's) Cav. Co.E
Sweat, A.B. TN 19th & 20th (Cons.) Cav. Co.E
Sweat, Abner GA 2nd Cav. Co.H
Sweat, Abner B. GA 21st Inf. Co.C
Sweat, Abraham GA 26th Inf. Co.F Cpl.
Sweat, A.D. SC 5th Inf. 2nd Co.E
Sweat, A.D. SC 6th Inf. 1st Co.H
Sweat, Aleck LA 6th Cav. Co.I
Sweat, Alfred FL 10th Inf. Co.D
Sweat, Alfred GA 26th Inf. Co.A
Sweat, Alfred SC 6th Inf. 1st Co.H
Sweat, Alfred J. FL 8th Inf. Co.I
Sweat, Allen FL 9th Inf. Co.E,H
Sweat, Allen A. GA 26th Inf. Co.F
Sweat, Andrew J. GA 21st Inf. Co.C
Sweat, Barney SC 2nd Arty. Co.H
Sweat, Benjamin SC Lt.Arty. 3rd (Palmetto) Bn. Co.F Teamster
Sweat, Brant SC Lt.Arty. 3rd (Palmetto) Bn. Co.F
Sweat, Bryant GA 2nd Inf. 1st Co.B Sgt.
Sweat, Bryant GA 26th Inf. Co.E 1st Sgt.
Sweat, Burrell GA 11th Cav. (St.Guards) Folks' Co. Sgt.
Sweat, B.W. GA 44th Inf. Co.G
Sweat, C.A.J. GA Inf. 18th Bn. Co.C
Sweat, Capers SC 1st (Hagood's) Inf. 1st Co.G, 2nd Co.E
Sweat, Christopher AL 28th Inf. Co.G
Sweat, David SC Lt.Arty. 3rd (Palmetto) Bn. Co.F
Sweat, David SC 2nd Inf. Co.A
Sweat, David SC 10th Inf. Co.K
Sweat, David SC 25th Inf. Co.D
Sweat, David M. SC Lt.Arty. 3rd (Palmetto) Bn. Co.D Cpl.
Sweat, E. AL 31st Inf. Co.D
Sweat, E. LA 6th Cav. Co.I
Sweat, E.B. LA 16th Inf. Co.G,H
Sweat, Edmund FL 7th Inf. Co.I
Sweat, Edward SC 1st (Hagood's) Inf. 2nd Co.D
Sweat, E.H. AL 24th Inf. Co.F Sgt.
Sweat, Elias GA 4th (Clinch's) Cav. Co.G
Sweat, Eph. LA Inf.Crescent Regt. Co.H
Sweat, Evans M. GA 20th Inf. Co.E
Sweat, F. SC 5th Cav. Co.C
Sweat, Farley R. GA Inf. 18th Bn. Co.A,C 1st Sgt.
Sweat, Farley R. GA 26th Inf. Co.K
Sweat, F.R., Jr. GA 1st (Olmstead's) Inf. Screven's Co. Cpl.
Sweat, Fred SC 1st Mtd.Mil. Anderson's Co.

Sweat, Frederick SC Cav. 17th Bn. Co.D
Sweat, Freeman FL 8th Inf. Co.I
Sweat, Gadi SC 4th St.Troops Co.F
Sweat, George SC 1st (Hagood's) Inf. 1st Co.G
Sweat, George SC 10th Inf. Co.K
Sweat, George A. GA Inf. 18th Bn. Co.C
Sweat, George W. GA 55th Inf. Co.I
Sweat, G.W. MS 1st (King's) Inf. (St.Troops) D. Love's Co.
Sweat, H. SC 2nd Bn.S.S. Co.A
Sweat, H. SC 24th Inf. Co.B
Sweat, Henry SC 4th Cav. Co.E
Sweat, Henry SC Cav. 12th Bn. Co.C
Sweat, Henry M. FL 3rd Inf. Co.F Sgt.
Sweat, H.M. SC 1st Mtd.Mil. Anderson's Co.
Sweat, H.M. SC 5th Cav. Co.B
Sweat, H.M. SC Lt.Arty. 3rd (Palmetto) Bn. Co.F
Sweat, Isaac LA 6th Cav. Co.I
Sweat, Isaac L. TN Cav. 12th Bn. (Day's) Co.B
Sweat, J. GA 4th (Clinch's) Cav. Cpl.
Sweat, J. MS Condrey's Co. (Bull Mtn.Invinc.)
Sweat, J. SC 6th Res. Co.C
Sweat, James FL 8th Inf. Co.I
Sweat, James GA 11th Cav. (St.Guards) Folks' Co.
Sweat, James GA Cav. Hendry's Co. (Atlantic & Gulf Guards) 2nd Lt.
Sweat, James GA 1st (Olmstead's) Inf. Co.C
Sweat, James GA 29th Inf. Co.K
Sweat, James SC 2nd St.Troops Co.K
Sweat, James SC Inf. 9th Bn. Co.C
Sweat, James SC 24th Inf. Co.B
Sweat, James A. FL 8th Inf. Co.I
Sweat, James G. FL 5th Inf. Co.I Sgt.
Sweat, James M. FL 9th Inf. Co.E
Sweat, James M. NC 53rd Inf. Co.B
Sweat, James R. SC Lt.Arty. 3rd (Palmetto) Bn. Co.D
Sweat, J.D. GA 6th Res. Co.H
Sweat, J.E. GA 8th Inf. Co.B
Sweat, Jesse GA 1st (Symons') Res. Co.F,H
Sweat, J.F. GA Cav. 2nd Bn. Co.A
Sweat, J.F. GA 5th Cav. Co.I
Sweat, J.F. MS 3rd Inf. (St.Troops) Co.K
Sweat, J.H. TX 1st Inf. Co.M
Sweat, J.J. GA Cav. 24th Bn. Co.A
Sweat, J.N. GA 8th Inf. Co.B
Sweat, Joel GA 4th (Clinch's) Cav. Co.G
Sweat, John FL Inf. 2nd Bn. Co.B
Sweat, John FL 7th Inf. Co.A
Sweat, John FL 10th Inf. Co.G
Sweat, John GA 21st Inf. Co.C
Sweat, John GA 26th Inf. Co.K
Sweat, John MO Lt.Arty. 1st Btty.
Sweat, John MO Lt.Arty. Landis' Co.
Sweat, John SC 4th Cav. Co.B
Sweat, John SC Inf. 9th Bn. Co.C
Sweat, John SC 23rd Inf. Co.F
Sweat, John SC 26th Inf. Co.D
Sweat, John TN 42nd Inf. Co.A Cpl.
Sweat, John A. SC Lt.Arty. Kelly's Co. (Chesterfield Arty.)
Sweat, John B. GA 26th Inf. Co.K Cpl.
Sweat, John J. GA 26th Inf. Co.F
Sweat, John T. SC 1st (Hagood's) Inf. 2nd Co.D
Sweat, John W. FL 1st Inf. New Co.G
Sweat, Joseph AL 19th Inf. Co.I
Sweat, Joseph AL 42nd Inf. Co.K
Sweat, Joseph FL 7th Inf. Co.A
Sweat, Joshua GA 16th Inf. Co.F
Sweat, Joshua SC 17th Inf. Co.D
Sweat, J.W. SC 24th Inf. Co.B
Sweat, L. SC 6th Cav. Co.H
Sweat, Lawrence J. SC 1st (Hagood's) Inf. 1st Co.F, 2nd Co.G Capt.
Sweat, Leonard SC Inf. 9th Bn. Co.C
Sweat, Leonard SC 26th Inf. Co.D
Sweat, Leonard C. LA 27th Inf. Co.C
Sweat, M. GA Mtd.Inf. (Pierce Mtd.Vol.) Hendry's Co. 2nd Lt.
Sweat, Martin GA 4th (Clinch's) Cav. Co.G
Sweat, Mitchell GA 2nd Inf. 1st Co.B
Sweat, Mitchell GA 26th Inf. Co.E
Sweat, N. MS 38th Cav. Co.G
Sweat, N. SC 23rd Inf. Co.E
Sweat, Nathan FL 7th Inf. Co.A
Sweat, Nathan F. GA 50th Inf. Co.B
Sweat, Newton GA 26th Inf. Co.F
Sweat, N.M. MS Inf. 2nd Bn. Co.B
Sweat, N.M. MS 48th Inf. Co.B
Sweat, Noel SC Lt.Arty. 3rd (Palmetto) Bn. Co.F Teamster
Sweat, R. SC Mil. 18th Regt. Co.E
Sweat, Randal M. GA 26th Inf. Co.F Sgt.
Sweat, R.H. AL 33rd Inf. Co.E
Sweat, Robert SC 6th Inf. 1st Co.F, 2nd Co.I
Sweat, Robert S. SC Inf. Hampton Legion Co.A
Sweat, Rowland GA 26th Inf. Co.F
Sweat, Rufus SC 8th Bn.Res. Co.A
Sweat, R.W. AL 42nd Inf. Co.K
Sweat, Samuel SC 10th Inf. Co.K
Sweat, Sanford SC 4th Cav. Co.E
Sweat, Sanford SC Cav. 12th Bn. Co.C
Sweat, S.C. SC 5th Inf. 2nd Co.E Cpl.
Sweat, S.C. SC 6th Inf. 1st Co.H
Sweat, Seaborn TX 21st Cav. Co.D
Sweat, Silas SC 1st Mtd.Mil. Martin's Co.
Sweat, Silas M. SC 3rd Cav. Co.E
Sweat, Simeon SC 2nd Bn.S.S. Co.A
Sweat, Simeon SC 24th Inf. Co.B
Sweat, Solomon GA 13th Inf. Co.F
Sweat, S.T. GA 16th Inf. Co.F
Sweat, Stephen SC 8th Inf. Co.C
Sweat, S.W. GA Lt.Arty. Clinch's Btty.
Sweat, T. GA 4th (Clinch's) Cav. Co.I
Sweat, Thenial TN Inf. 1st Bn. (Colms') Co.B
Sweat, Thomas AR 30th Inf. Co.E
Sweat, Thomas GA 4th (Clinch's) Cav. Co.G
Sweat, Thomas GA 11th Cav. (St.Guards) Folks' Co. 2nd Lt.
Sweat, Thomas GA 26th Inf. Co.K Sgt.
Sweat, Thomas SC Cav. 12th Bn. Co.C
Sweat, Thomas SC 5th Inf. 2nd Co.B
Sweat, Thomas G. SC 8th Inf. Co.C
Sweat, Thomas S. GA 14th Inf. Co.F
Sweat, Thomas W. FL 7th Inf. Co.A 2nd Sgt.
Sweat, Thomas W. FL 10th Inf. Co.F
Sweat, T.S. GA 28th Inf. Co.A
Sweat, Turner H. SC 23rd Inf. Co.F
Sweat, T.W. SC 11th Inf. Co.C
Sweat, W. AL 26th (O'Neal's) Inf. Co.B
Sweat, W. AL 31st Inf. Co.D
Sweat, W. GA Inf. 18th Bn. Co.A
Sweat, W. GA 26th Inf. Co.F
Sweat, W. SC 5th Cav. Co.C
Sweat, W. SC Manigault's Bn.Vol. Co.D
Sweat, Warren SC 1st Arty. Co.I
Sweat, Washt. SC Cav. 17th Bn. Co.D
Sweat, W.B. SC 1st Mtd.Mil. Anderson's Co.
Sweat, W.B. SC Cav. 17th Bn. Co.D
Sweat, W.C. AL 3rd Bn. Hilliard's Legion Vol. Co.D
Sweat, W.H.W. GA 28th Inf. Co.A
Sweat, William GA 4th (Clinch's) Cav. Co.C Cpl.
Sweat, William GA 1st (Olmstead's) Inf. Screven's Co.
Sweat, William GA 21st Inf. Co.C
Sweat, William KY 9th Mtd.Inf. Co.H
Sweat, William SC 4th Cav. Co.B
Sweat, William SC Inf. 9th Bn. Co.C
Sweat, William SC 26th Inf. Co.D
Sweat, William TX Inf. W. Cameron's Co.
Sweat, William D. TN 38th Inf. Co.F
Sweat, William E. AL 19th Inf. Co.F
Sweat, William E. FL 4th Inf. Co.K 2nd Lt.
Sweat, William E. FL 7th Inf. Co.B Capt.
Sweat, William E. SC 1st (Butler's) Inf. Co.A
Sweat, William E. SC 8th Inf. Co.D
Sweat, William F. FL 1st Cav. Co.D
Sweat, William F. GA 4th (Clinch's) Cav. Co.G Sgt.
Sweat, William J. GA 14th Inf. Co.F
Sweat, William S. GA Cav. Hendry's Co. (Atlantic & Gulf Guards)
Sweat, William W. SC 9th Inf. Co.G
Sweat, W.K. SC Cav. 12th Bn. Co.C
Sweat, W.T. GA 4th Inf. Sgt.
Sweater, Jas. T. MS 30th Inf. Co.A 2nd Lt.
Sweatman, --- SC 11th Inf. Co.B
Sweatman, A.G. FL 1st (Res.) Inf. Co.E
Sweatman, C.C. SC Lt.Arty. J.T. Kanapaux's Co. (Lafayette Arty.) Teamster
Sweatman, Cornelius LA 1st (Strawbridge's) Inf. Co.E
Sweatman, Daniel GA 24th Inf. Co.I
Sweatman, Danil GA 4th Cav. (St.Guards) Pirkle's Co.
Sweatman, David NC 1st Inf. Co.F
Sweatman, David NC Inf. Thomas Legion Co.F
Sweatman, David L. MS 15th Inf. Co.D 1st Lt.
Sweatman, Elisha SC Lt.Arty. J.T. Kanapaux's Co. (Lafayette Arty.)
Sweatman, Francis M. FL 2nd Inf. Co.M
Sweatman, Francis M. FL 5th Inf. Co.K Comsy.Sgt.
Sweatman, George FL 6th Inf. Co.A
Sweatman, George GA 4th Cav. (St.Guards) Pirkle's Co.
Sweatman, George W. SC 12th Inf. Co.C
Sweatman, Green FL 10th Inf. Co.E
Sweatman, G.W. AR 19th (Dockery's) Inf. Co.I
Sweatman, Harbin N.C. GA Arty. 9th Bn. Co.A,E
Sweatman, H.H. TX 20th Inf. Co.D
Sweatman, H.N.C. GA Phillips' Legion Co.C
Sweatman, J. GA Cav. Logan's Co. (White Cty. Old Men's Home Guards)
Sweatman, James GA 4th Cav. (St.Guards) Pirkle's Co. Cpl.

Sweatman, James GA 24th Inf. Co.I
Sweatman, James SC Lt.Arty. J.T. Kanapaux's Co. (Lafayette Arty.)
Sweatman, James H. MO 7th Cav. Co.E Cpl.
Sweatman, J.B. AL 27th Inf. Co.G
Sweatman, John GA 36th (Broyles') Inf. Co.A
Sweatman, John GA 52nd Inf. Co.E
Sweatman, John 1st Conf.Eng.Troops Co.I
Sweatman, J.S. MO Searcy's Bn.S.S.
Sweatman, L.P. SC Lt.Arty. 3rd (Palmetto) Bn. Co.D
Sweatman, M.D. MO 1st Brig.St.Guard
Sweatman, M.J. MO Cav. Freeman's Regt. Co.L
Sweatman, P.Y. MO Lt.Arty. H.M. Bledsoe's Co. 1st Sgt.
Sweatman, R.V. SC Lt.Arty. J.T. Kanapaux's Co. (Lafayette Arty.)
Sweatman, S. SC Mil. 18th Regt. Co.D
Sweatman, Samuel GA 1st (Fannin's) Res. Co.A
Sweatman, Sharack W. FL 5th Inf. Co.K
Sweatman, Thomas LA 2nd Inf. Co.A
Sweatman, Thomas J. LA Inf. 11th Bn. Co.G 1st Sgt.
Sweatman, Thomas W. TX 26th Cav. Co.A
Sweatman, William MO Cav. 3rd Bn. Co.E
Sweatman, William MO 4th Inf. Co.G
Sweatman, William M. MO 1st & 4th Cons.Inf. Co.B
Sweatmore, S.W. FL 1st Mil.Inf. Sgt.
Sweatnam, Joseph F. VA Lt.Arty. Pollock's Co.
Sweaton, Francis M. MS 34th Inf. Co.H
Sweatt, A.J. GA 13th Inf. Co.F Cpl.
Sweatt, A.W. TN 5th Inf. Co.A, 2nd Co.G
Sweatt, A.W. TN 46th Inf. Co.F Cpl.
Sweatt, B.W. GA 13th Inf. Co.F
Sweatt, Daniel SC 12th Inf. Co.H
Sweatt, E. AL 30th Inf. Co.D
Sweatt, E.S. GA 13th Inf. Co.F
Sweatt, E.V.B. TX 12th Cav. Co.H Sgt.
Sweatt, George B. TX 12th Cav. Co.H
Sweatt, G.F. MS Inf. 2nd Bn. Co.B
Sweatt, G.F. MS 48th Inf. Co.B
Sweatt, G.H. MS 13th Inf. Co.I
Sweatt, J. AR 30th Inf. Co.E
Sweatt, J.D.B. AR 30th Inf. Co.E
Sweatt, John A. 4th Conf.Inf. Co.G
Sweatt, John D. GA 1st (Symons') Res. Co.G
Sweatt, J.W. GA 13th Inf. Co.F Cpl.
Sweatt, Newton GA 1st (Symons') Res. Co.G
Sweatt, Robbert GA Inf. Dozier's Co. Cpl.
Sweatt, Robert P. Gen. & Staff A.Surg.
Sweatt, W.G. MS 3rd Cav. Co.B
Sweatt, W.H. GA 13th Inf. Co.F
Sweatte, R.P. TX 19th Cav. Co.C
Sweaza, E.L. TX Cav. Terry's Regt. Co.A
Sweaza, Ellie L. TX 37th Cav. Co.F
Sweaza, John AR 15th (N.W.) Inf. Co.C
Sweazea, M. TX 3rd Cav. Co.E
Sweazey, F.M. AR 38th Inf. Co.E
Sweazy, D.S. AR 19th (Dockery's) Inf. Co.B
Sweazy, M. MO Inf. 1st Bn. Co.C
Swebston, Samuel W. VA 21st Cav. Co.B Cpl.
Swecker, Abraham VA 7th Cav. Co.I
Swecker, Abraham VA 58th Mil. Co.E
Swecker, Ambrose VA 162nd Mil. Co.B
Swecker, B.F. VA 51st Inf. Co.B
Swecker, David W. VA 162nd Mil. Co.B
Swecker, Fred VA 5th Cav. Co.G
Swecker, Frederick M. VA 10th Inf. Co.D
Swecker, J.F. VA 51st Inf. Co.F
Swecker, John C. VA 31st Inf. Co.F
Swecker, John M. VA 31st Inf. Co.F
Swecker, Robert VA 51st Inf. Co.B Cpl.
Swecker, Samuel VA 51st Inf. Co.B
Swed, John GA 5th Inf. (St.Guards) Everitt's Co.
Swedan, Robert AR 36th Inf. Co.F
Sweden, F. MS 48th Inf.
Swedenburg, G.W. AL 25th Inf. Co.E
Swedenburg, W.M. AL 3rd Res. Co.I
Swedenburg, W.W. AL 25th Inf. Co.E
Swedenburg, W.W. 3rd Conf.Eng.Troops Co.G
Sweder, John LA 3rd (Wingfield's) Cav. Co.A
Sweede, Ferdinand MS Inf. 2nd Bn. Co.E
Sweede, Ferdinand MS 48th Inf. Co.E
Sweeden, Henry AR Cav. Wright's Regt. Co.H Cpl.
Sweeden, Henry AR 31st Inf. Co.E
Sweeden, James AR 8th Cav. Co.L
Sweeden, John MS 35th Inf. Co.K
Sweeden, L. TX 10th Cav. Co.F
Sweeden, Levi AR 25th Inf. Co.C
Sweeden, Patrick AR 31st Inf. Co.E
Sweeden, P.G. AR 15th (Johson's) Inf. Co.E
Sweeden, Robert AR 15th Mil. Co.H
Sweeden, Thomas AL 4th (Russell's) Cav. Co.D Wag.
Sweeden, Thos. AL 5th Cav. Co.L
Sweeden, William MS 35th Inf. Co.C
Sweedon, B.G. AR 30th Inf. Co.E
Sweegart, George MS 18th Inf. Co.E
Sweeger, Lewis VA 1st St.Res. Co.E
Sweeker, William A. VA 31st Inf. Co.F
Sweem, J.M. TX 6th Inf. Co.G Cpl.
Sweem, John S. TX 14th Cav. Co.F
Sweeney, --- TN 10th Inf. Co.H
Sweeney, Adelbert D.G. 3rd Conf.Eng.Troops Co.B Artif.
Sweeney, Adolphus VA 17th Inf. Co.D
Sweeney, Andrew Nitre & Min. Bureau War Dept.,CSA
Sweeney, Barney VA Hvy.Arty. 18th Bn. Co.E
Sweeney, Bart VA 2nd St.Res Co.L Fifer
Sweeney, Benjamin VA 54th Inf. Co.H
Sweeney, Benjamin F. AR 5th Inf. Lt.Col.
Sweeney, Benton TX Cav. 6th Bn. Co.C Capt.
Sweeney, C. TN 13th Inf. Co.H
Sweeney, C.H. TN 31st Inf. Co.B
Sweeney, Charles LA 13th Inf. Co.H 4th Sgt.
Sweeney, Charles TX 26th Cav. Co.F
Sweeney, Charles TX 1st Hvy.Arty. Co.B
Sweeney, Charles TX 3rd Inf. 1st Co.A, Co.D
Sweeney, Charles H. VA 2nd Cav. Co.H
Sweeney, Charles H. VA Horse Arty. Shoemaker's Co.
Sweeney, Charles H. VA 15th Inf. Co.G Cpl.
Sweeney, Charles W. VA 4th Cav. Co.E Bugler
Sweeney, Christopher C. VA 4th Inf. Co.F
Sweeney, Con TX 8th Inf. Co.D Sgt.
Sweeney, Daniel TX 1st Hvy.Arty. Co.B
Sweeney, David VA 4th Res. Co.E,G
Sweeney, D.C. GA 3rd Cav. Co.A
Sweeney, Dennis VA 2nd St.Res. Co.E
Sweeney, Dennis Central Div. KY Sap. & Min.,CSA
Sweeney, Edward LA 7th Inf. Co.K,G
Sweeney, Edward TN 15th Inf. 2nd Co.F
Sweeney, Edward VA Lt.Arty. 13th Bn. Co.B
Sweeney, Edward VA Inf. 1st Bn.Loc.Def. Co.D
Sweeney, Edward C. NC 34th Inf.
Sweeney, E.J. VA Hvy.Arty. 20th Bn. Co.E
Sweeney, E.L. TX Cav. Madison's Regt. Co.C
Sweeney, F. KY 2nd (Woodward's) Cav. Co.F
Sweeney, Frank KY 1st Inf. Co.B
Sweeney, George W. TN 30th Inf. Co.D
Sweeney, Henry MO St.Guard
Sweeney, Henry TN 12th Inf. Co.A
Sweeney, Henry G. MO Cav. Poindexter's Regt.
Sweeney, Hugh MS 9th Inf. Old Co.H, New Co.A
Sweeney, Hugh MS 16th Inf. Co.D
Sweeney, Hugh W. MS 19th Inf. Co.C
Sweeney, Isaac VA Mil. Grayson Cty.
Sweeney, J. AL 1st Bn.Cadets Co.A
Sweeney, J. KY 5th Mtd.Inf.
Sweeney, J.A. TX 1st Inf. Co.A
Sweeney, Jackson VA 25th Cav. Co.C
Sweeney, James AL 29th Inf. Co.E
Sweeney, James FL 6th Inf. Co.A
Sweeney, James LA 1st (Strawbridge's) Inf. Co.D
Sweeney, James LA Mil. 2nd Regt. 3rd Brig. 1st Div. Co.A
Sweeney, James LA 10th Inf. Co.A,E
Sweeney, James LA 14th Inf. Co.F
Sweeney, James LA 17th Inf. Co.I
Sweeney, James LA 21st (Patton's) Inf. Co.F Cpl.
Sweeney, James LA 21st (Patton's) Inf. Co.G
Sweeney, James LA Mil. Stanley Guards Co.B
Sweeney, James MS 21st Inf. Co.L
Sweeney, James SC Inf. 1st (Charleston) Bn. Co.B
Sweeney, James SC 1st (McCreary's) Inf. Co.K
Sweeney, James SC 27th Inf. Co.B
Sweeney, James TN 10th Inf. Co.C Sgt.
Sweeney, James VA Cav. Mosby's Regt. (Part.Rangers)
Sweeney, James VA Inf. 2nd Bn.Loc.Def. Co.B
Sweeney, James A. AR 3rd Inf. Co.A Cpl.
Sweeney, James C. TN 10th & 11th (Cons.) Cav. Co.I
Sweeney, James P. MO 4th Cav. Co.G
Sweeney, James T. VA Cav. 34th Bn. Co.K Capt.
Sweeney, James T. VA 53rd Inf. Co.G Cpl.
Sweeney, James W. VA Cav. 36th Bn. Lt.Col.
Sweeney, James W. VA 60th Inf. Maj.
Sweeney, Jasper N. VA 4th Inf. Co.F
Sweeney, J.H. MO Cav. 8th Regt.St.Guard Co.A Sgt.
Sweeney, J.H. TX Cav. Ragsdale's Bn. 2nd Co.C
Sweeney, J.J. AR 2nd Cav. Co.B Sgt.
Sweeney, J.J. TX 5th Inf. Co.A
Sweeney, John GA 12th Inf. Co.H
Sweeney, John GA Phillips' Legion Co.F,A
Sweeney, John LA 5th Inf. Co.K
Sweeney, John LA 13th Inf. Co.A
Sweeney, John LA 31st Inf. Co.C
Sweeney, John MS 13th Inf. Co.H

Sweeney, John SC 1st (McCreary's) Inf. Co.K 2nd Lt.
Sweeney, John TN 21st Inf. Co.G Cpl.
Sweeney, John VA Cav. 36th Bn. Co.D
Sweeney, John VA 60th Inf. Co.G
Sweeney, John Inf. School of Pract. Powell's Command Co.A
Sweeney, John A. AL 37th Inf. Co.D
Sweeney, John E. VA 2nd Inf. Co.K
Sweeney, John W. NC 4th Inf. Co.B
Sweeney, John W. VA Inf. 23rd Bn. Co.D Sgt.
Sweeney, Jonathan VA Inf. 1st Bn.Loc.Def. Co.C 1st Lt.
Sweeney, Jonathan H. TN 3rd (Lillard's) Mtd.Inf. Co.C
Sweeney, Joseph MS 12th Inf. Co.E
Sweeney, Joseph SC 1st Inf. Co.K
Sweeney, Joseph M. LA Arty. Moody's Co. (Madison Lt.Arty.) Sgt.
Sweeney, Joseph W. VA 2nd Inf. Co.G
Sweeney, J.T. GA 3rd Cav. Co.A
Sweeney, Lawrence LA 1st (Nelligan's) Inf. Co.K
Sweeney, L.B. TX 2nd Inf. Co.D Cpl.
Sweeney, L.C. AR 30th Inf. Co.B,D
Sweeney, Levi GA Inf. 1st Bn.
Sweeney, M. GA Inf. 1st Loc.Troops (Augusta) Co.I
Sweeney, M. LA Mil. 4th Regt. 1st Brig. 1st Div. Co.E
Sweeney, M. TN Inf. 154th Sr.Regt. Co.A
Sweeney, M. TX 24th & 25th Cav. (Cons.) Co.B
Sweeney, Martin VA 1st St.Res. Co.C
Sweeney, Martin VA Inf. 25th Bn. Co.F,G
Sweeney, Martin VA 59th Inf. Co.E
Sweeney, Mathew MS 12th Inf. Co.E
Sweeney, Mathew C. TX 6th Cav. Co.K
Sweeney, Michael LA 7th Inf. Co.F
Sweeney, Michael LA 9th Inf. Co.E
Sweeney, Michael LA 10th Inf. Co.D Cpl.
Sweeney, Michael LA 13th Inf. Co.K,E 4th Sgt.
Sweeney, Michael TX Cav. Baylor's Regt. Co.A Cpl.
Sweeney, Michael VA 7th Cav. Co.I
Sweeney, Michael VA 17th Inf. Co.C
Sweeney, Michael W. AL Lt.Arty. 2nd Bn. Co.E
Sweeney, Mike TX 26th Cav. Co.F
Sweeney, Miles VA 6th Cav. Co.G
Sweeney, Milton H. VA Lt.Arty. J.D. Smith's Co.
Sweeney, M.M. MO 16th Inf. Co.B
Sweeney, Morgan Inf. School of Pract. Powell's Command Powell's Detach. Cpl.
Sweeney, Morris MO Cav. Green's Regt. Co.H
Sweeney, Owen VA Inf. 1st Bn. Co.E
Sweeney, Pat AL 1st Regt. Mobile Vol. British Guard Co.B
Sweeney, Patrick LA 1st (Strawbridge's) Inf. Co.F,A
Sweeney, Patrick LA 6th Inf. Co.F,G
Sweeney, Patrick LA 13th Inf. Co.B
Sweeney, Patrick LA 15th Inf. Co.I
Sweeney, Patrick LA 21st (Kennedy's) Inf. Co.F
Sweeney, Patrick LA Mil.Cont.Regt. Mitchell's Co.
Sweeney, Patrick LA Inf. McLean's Co.
Sweeney, Patrick MS Inf. 2nd Bn. Co.G
Sweeney, Patrick MS 21st Inf. Co.B
Sweeney, Patrick MS 48th Inf. Co.G
Sweeney, Patrick VA Cav. Young's Co.
Sweeney, Patrick VA Loc.Res.
Sweeney, Patrick 9th Conf.Inf. Co.A
Sweeney, P.B. LA 1st Cav. Co.I
Sweeney, Peter TN 15th Inf. Co.C Bvt.2nd Lt.
Sweeney, P.H. LA 21st (Kennedy's) Inf. Co.A
Sweeney, Philip MS 17th Inf. Co.D 2nd Lt.
Sweeney, R. TN 11th (Holman's) Cav. Co.K
Sweeney, R.E. VA Cav. 36th Bn. Co.D
Sweeney, Reiley KY 5th Mtd.Inf.
Sweeney, Richard VA 3rd Inf. Co.K
Sweeney, Richard L. LA 1st (Nelligan's) Inf. Co.K
Sweeney, R.J. MO 16th Inf. Co.K
Sweeney, Robert TX 1st (Yager's) Cav. Co.G
Sweeney, Robert M. VA 2nd Cav. Co.H Cpl.
Sweeney, S. LA 1st Cav. Chap.
Sweeney, S. VA 4th Res. Co.E,G
Sweeney, Sampson D. VA 2nd Cav. Co.H
Sweeney, S.J. TN 42nd Inf. AAQM
Sweeney, S.T. LA 1st Cav. Co.C
Sweeney, Stephen B. VA 15th Inf. Co.G
Sweeney, Stephen B. VA 53rd Inf. Co.B Cpl.
Sweeney, Stephen B. VA Inf. Tomlin's Bn. Co.A
Sweeney, T. MO 2nd Cav. Co.E
Sweeney, Talbot VA 32nd Inf. Co.C
Sweeney, Thomas AR 2nd Cav. Co.C
Sweeney, Thomas GA 46th Inf. Co.D
Sweeney, Thomas LA Mil. 3rd Regt. 3rd Brig. 1st Div. Co.D
Sweeney, Thomas LA 13th Inf. Co.A
Sweeney, Thomas TX 2nd Cav. Co.I
Sweeney, Thomas P. GA 39th Inf. Co.F
Sweeney, Tim TN 2nd (Walker's) Inf. Co.I
Sweeney, W. VA Inf. 25th Bn. Co.G
Sweeney, Washington AL 32nd Inf.
Sweeney, W.B. TN 16th Inf. Co.A Drum.
Sweeney, W.G. TN 30th Inf. Co.D 2nd Lt.
Sweeney, W.G. VA Lt.Arty. W.P. Carter's Co.
Sweeney, W.H. MD 1st Cav. Co.E
Sweeney, William AL Arty. 1st Bn. Co.F
Sweeney, William LA 3rd Inf. Co.I
Sweeney, William LA Mil. 3rd Regt. 1st Brig. 1st Div. Co.A
Sweeney, William LA 9th Inf. Co.E Cpl.
Sweeney, William MO 2nd Cav. Co.B
Sweeney, William MO 16th Inf. Co.D
Sweeney, William TN 10th Inf. Co.D Capt.
Sweeney, William VA Cav. 32nd Bn. Co.A
Sweeney, William F. VA 1st Inf. Drum.
Sweeney, William J. MS 16th Inf. Co.C Cpl.
Sweeney, William J. TN 42nd Inf. 2nd Co.E Cpl.
Sweeney, William Y. AL 16th Inf. Co.C
Sweeney, Wilson VA 30th Bn.S.S. Co.A
Sweeney, W.J. MO 16th Inf. Co.K
Sweeney, W.J. TN Hvy.Arty. Johnston's Co.
Sweeney, W.J. TN 40th Inf. Co.C Col.'s Orderly
Sweeney, W.J. VA 24th Bn.Part.Rangers Cropper's Co.
Sweenny, Philip MS 16th Inf. Co.C
Sweeny, --- VA 1st Inf. Co.I
Sweeny, A.D.G. TN Inf. 154th Sr.Regt. Co.K
Sweeny, Andrew KY 6th Cav. Co.B
Sweeny, Basil KY 6th Cav. Co.G
Sweeny, C. SC 1st Arty. Co.G
Sweeny, Charles LA 8th Inf. Co.F
Sweeny, Charles K. MS Arty. (Seven Stars Arty.) Roberts' Co.
Sweeny, C.W. VA 1st Cav. Co.B
Sweeny, Dennis TN 10th Inf. Co.C
Sweeny, D.J. MO 2nd Cav. Co.D
Sweeny, Edward NC 32nd Inf. Co.H
Sweeny, Edward TN 14th Inf. Co.D
Sweeny, Francis NC Wallace's Co. (Wilmington RR Guard)
Sweeny, George W. TN 19th Inf. Co.I
Sweeny, Green M. VA Cav. 34th Bn. Co.K Sgt.
Sweeny, Harrison H. MO 3rd Cav. Co.D
Sweeny, Henry GA 1st (Olmstead's) Inf. Co.F
Sweeny, Hiram TN 1st (Feild's) Inf. Co.D
Sweeny, J. LA Mil. Fire Bn. Co.B
Sweeny, Jackson VA 48th Inf. Co.C
Sweeny, Jacob TN 4th (McLemore's) Cav. Co.F Black.
Sweeny, James KY 6th Mtd.Inf. Co.H
Sweeny, James LA Arty. Moody's Co. (Madison Lt.Arty.)
Sweeny, James H. TN 1st (Feild's) Inf. Co.D Cpl.
Sweeny, James Q. AL Inf. 2nd Regt. Co.F Cpl.
Sweeny, J.C. TN 24th Bn.S.S. Co.A Cpl.
Sweeny, J.D. AL Inf. 2nd Regt. Co.E
Sweeny, J.D. Conf.Inf. 1st Bn. 2nd Co.C
Sweeny, Jerome P. TX 18th Inf. Co.L
Sweeny, J.J. AR 5th Inf. Co.E
Sweeny, J.M. VA Cav. 35th Bn. Co.D
Sweeny, John GA 1st (Olmstead's) Inf. Co.A
Sweeny, John KY 14th Cav. Co.D,C
Sweeny, John LA 1st Hvy.Arty. (Reg.) Co.I
Sweeny, John LA 10th Inf. Co.B
Sweeny, John SC Mil. 1st Regt. (Charleston Res.) Co.A
Sweeny, John VA 24th Inf. Co.A
Sweeny, John VA 27th Inf. Co.G
Sweeny, John 9th Conf.Inf. Co.A
Sweeny, John Conf.Reg.Inf. Brooks' Bn. Co.D
Sweeny, John C. VA 27th Inf. Co.G
Sweeny, Joseph VA 53rd Inf. Co.E
Sweeny, Joseph A. MO Cav. 12th Cav.St.Guard Co.A 3rd Lt.
Sweeny, Josephus L. TN Lt.Arty. Baxter's Co. Cpl.
Sweeny, J.R. SC Inf. 1st (Charleston) Bn. Co.D
Sweeny, J.R. SC 27th Inf. Co.D
Sweeny, Levi TN 38th Inf. Co.D
Sweeny, Luke GA Hvy.Arty. 22nd Bn. Co.C
Sweeny, M. KY 1st (Helm's) Cav.
Sweeny, Mathew TN Inf. 154th Sr.Regt. Co.C
Sweeny, Michael LA 14th Inf. Co.G Cpl.
Sweeny, P. LA 13th Inf. Co.K
Sweeny, Patrick AL 21st Inf. Co.D
Sweeny, Patrick TN Arty. Fisher's Co.
Sweeny, Patrick TN 2nd (Walker's) Inf. Co.K
Sweeny, Patrick VA 59th Inf. 2nd Co.A, Co.C
Sweeny, Phillip LA 21st (Kennedy's) Inf. Co.B Sgt.
Sweeny, Phillip LA 21st (Kennedy's) Inf. Co.E
Sweeny, T.C. LA Pointe Coupee Arty. Artif.
Sweeny, Thomas AL 8th Cav. Co.E
Sweeny, Thomas FL Inf. 2nd Bn. Co.C

Sweeny, Thomas LA 9th Inf. Co.E Cpl.
Sweeny, Thos. J. TX Cav. 3rd Regt.St.Troops 1st Lt.
Sweeny, Thomas P. GA 37th Inf. Co.F
Sweeny, Timothy AL 21st Inf. Co.D
Sweeny, Timothy AL 24th Inf. Co.B
Sweeny, W.B. MS 14th Inf. Co.E
Sweeny, William AR 51st Mil. Co.B 1st Sgt.
Sweeny, William SC 1st Cav. Co.D
Sweeny, William VA 24th Cav. Co.G
Sweeny, William H. AL 8th Inf. Co.D
Sweeny, W.J. Conf.Cav. 6th Bn. Co.C Lt.
Sweeny, W.R. TX 26th Cav. Co.K Sgt.
Sweesey, Alfred H. NC 55th Inf. Co.C
Sweesy, Francis M. AR Inf. Ballard's Co.
Sweet, A.A. GA 45th Inf. Co.B
Sweet, Albertus TX 17th Inf. Co.D Sgt.
Sweet, Alexander TX 33rd Cav. Co.A
Sweet, Benjamin F. NC 55th Inf. Co.H
Sweet, B.S. FL Cav. 5th Bn. Co.B 1st Sgt.
Sweet, Charles LA 15th Inf.
Sweet, Charles B. FL Milton Lt.Arty. Dunham's Co.
Sweet, C.L. LA Mil. Orleans Fire Regt. Hall's Co.
Sweet, C.P. TN 27th Inf. Co.E
Sweet, David B. TN 7th Inf. Co.E
Sweet, E. AL 31st Inf. Co.D
Sweet, E.L. SC 21st Inf. Co.L Lt.
Sweet, E.L. SC 21st Inf. Co.L
Sweet, Ennis TX 17th Inf. Co.I Music.
Sweet, Fennan P. VA Tuttle's Bn.Loc.Def. Co.A
Sweet, George H. TX 15th Cav. Co.A Col.
Sweet, George H. TX 4th Inf. Co.F
Sweet, George W. MS 28th Cav. Co.C
Sweet, G.W. MS 12th Inf. Co.E
Sweet, G.W. TX Inf. Townsend's Co. (Robertson Five S.)
Sweet, Henderson TN 34th Inf. Co.A
Sweet, Henry AR 7th Inf. Co.I
Sweet, Henry MO Cav. Fristoe's Regt. Co.D Cpl.
Sweet, Henry TN 21st Inf. Co.D
Sweet, Henry C. TX 18th Cav. Co.F 3rd Lt.
Sweet, Henry I. VA Tuttle's Bn.Loc.Def. Co.A
Sweet, H.Y. TN 21st Inf. Co.D
Sweet, Isaac TN Lt.Arty. Barry's Co.
Sweet, Jacob VA 5th Inf. Co.H
Sweet, Jacob VA 10th Bn.Res. Co.B
Sweet, Jacob VA Rockbridge Cty.Res. Hutcheson's Co.
Sweet, James GA 4th (Clinch's) Cav.
Sweet, James GA 6th Inf. (St.Guards) Sims' Co.
Sweet, James C. AR 14th (Powers') Inf. Co.I
Sweet, James H. TN 32nd Inf. Co.D
Sweet, James L. FL 6th Inf. Co.D
Sweet, James R. TX 33rd Cav. Co.A,B Lt.Col.
Sweet, J.H. TN 9th Inf. Co.C Sgt.
Sweet, John M. AL 16th Inf. Co.G
Sweet, John P. VA 27th Inf. Co.G
Sweet, John W. VA 25th Inf. 2nd Co.H
Sweet, Joseph VA 27th Inf. Co.B
Sweet, J.S. AL 11th Inf. Co.F
Sweet, J.S. TX 1st Hvy.Arty. Co.I
Sweet, J.T. AL 14th Inf. Co.F
Sweet, Marion N. MS 2nd Inf. Co.D
Sweet, N.H. GA 21st Inf. Co.C
Sweet, Patrick H. VA 53rd Inf. Co.D
Sweet, R. James TX 33rd Cav. Co.A,B Lt.Col.
Sweet, Samuel TX 4th Cav. Co.F
Sweet, S.E. TN 9th Inf. Co.C
Sweet, S.H. MO Cav. 11th Regt.St.Guard Co.D 1st Lt.
Sweet, Sidney J. TX 11th (Spaight's) Bn.Vol. Co.B 1st Lt.
Sweet, S.J. TX 21st Inf. Co.H
Sweet, T.C. VA Lt.Arty. W.P. Carter's Co.
Sweet, Thomas GA 17th Inf. Co.F
Sweet, Thomas A. TX Cav. 6th Bn. Co.E Cpl.
Sweet, W.A. TX 35th (Brown's) Cav. Co.B
Sweet, William SC 7th (Ward's) Bn.St.Res. Co.F
Sweet, William A. VA 87th Mil. Co.D
Sweet, William B.A. GA 50th Inf. Co.F
Sweet, William C. GA 3rd Res. Co.I
Sweet, W.P. SC 10th Inf. Co.L
Sweet, W.W. AL 14th Inf. Co.F
Sweet Airs FL McBride's Co. (Indians)
Sweet Cow 1st Cherokee Mtd.Rifles Co.D Sgt.
Sweete, A. MS Arty. (Wesson Arty.) Kittrell's Co.
Sweete, E. LA 27th Inf. Co.B
Sweete, John GA 27th Inf. Co.G
Sweeten, Isaac N. AR 1st (Colquitt's) Inf. Co.E Cpl.
Sweeten, James E. TN 34th Inf. Co.A
Sweeten, John L. AR 2nd Mtd.Rifles Co.B
Sweeten, Lewis TX 14th Cav. Co.C
Sweeten, Moses TN 34th Inf. Co.A
Sweeten, Robert F. AR 1st (Colquitt's) Inf. Co.E
Sweeten, Samuel M. AR 1st (Crawford's) Cav. Co.B Ord.Sgt.
Sweeten, Samuel M. AR 1st (Colquitt's) Inf. Co.E 2nd Lt.
Sweeten, William AR 5th Inf. Co.E
Sweetenburg, J.A. SC 3rd Inf. Co.H
Sweeting, Benjamin F. MD 1st Inf. Co.F
Sweeting, Henry LA 18th Inf. Co.F
Sweetland, William A. VA 16th Cav. Co.K 1st Lt.
Sweetland, William A. VA Cav. Ferguson's Bn. Nounnan's Co. 2nd Lt.
Sweetman, Edward D. VA Loc.Res.
Sweetman, Henry L. TX 32nd Cav. Co.G
Sweetman, James MO 1st N.E. Cav. Co.K
Sweetman, L.P. SC Res. Co.B
Sweetman, N. VA 2nd St.Res. Co.A Sgt.
Sweetman, R.L. Gen. & Staff, Arty. 2nd Lt.
Sweeton, Jesse AR Inf. Cocke's Regt. Co.D
Sweeton, J.M. MS 34th Inf. Co.H
Sweetser, George W. MO 16th Inf. Co.B
Sweet Water 1st Cherokee Mtd.Rifles Co.C
Sweetwind, R.L. Eng.,CSA Capt.
Sweetzer, Henry C. AL 12th Inf. Co.I Music.
Sweetzer, William A. NC 1st Arty. (10th St.Troops) Co.H
Sweeza, Richard AR 8th Inf. New Co.C
Sweezer, L.D. MS 39th Inf. Co.B
Sweezie, Marion MO 6th Inf. Co.K
Sweezy, E.W. NC 1st Bn.Jr.Res. Co.B
Sweezy, George J. NC 34th Inf. Co.B
Sweezy, Henry A.L. NC 16th Inf. Co.D Sgt.
Sweezy, Henry Allen Lawson NC 56th Inf. Co.I 1st Lt.
Sweezy, James Henry NC 56th Inf. Co.I 1st Lt.
Sweezy, J.M. NC 56th Inf. Co.I
Sweezy, John G. MO 3rd Cav. Co.C
Sweezy, J.W., Jr. NC 56th Inf. Co.I
Sweezy, J.W., Sr. NC 56th Inf. Co.I
Sweezy, Thomas Jefferson NC 56th Inf. Co.I
Sweezy, Wm. MO 1st Inf. 2nd Co.A
Sweezy, William A. NC 56th Inf. Co.I
Sweezy, William G. TN 4th (McLemore's) Cav. Co.H
Sweiney, J.F. SC Cav. 12th Bn. Co.A
Sweitman, E. VA 3rd Inf.Loc.Def. Co.K Sgt.
Sweitzer, Charles L. TX 2nd Cav. Co.C
Sweitzer, John W. VA 62nd Mtd.Inf. 2nd Co.A
Sweitzer, William A. KY 4th Cav. Co.A
Swekey, F. TX 24th & 25th Cav. (Cons.) Co.I
Swell, J.F. GA 30th Inf. Co.H
Swell, L.B. AR 36th Inf. Co.K Cpl.
Swemley, Charles AL 43rd Inf. Co.A
Sweneger, John LA 14th Inf. Co.K
Sweney, --- Deneale's Regt. Choctaw Warriors Co.B
Sweney, Bryant TN 35th Inf. 2nd Co.I
Sweney, Daniel AR Cav. Gordon's Regt. Co.A
Sweney, Dennis KY 4th Cav. Co.E
Sweney, Edward LA 21st (Patton's) Inf. Co.G
Sweney, J.C. MS 1st (King's) Inf.St.Troops Co.H
Sweney, J.W. TN 55th (Brown's) Inf. Co.G Sgt.
Sweney, Melton MS 2nd Inf. Co.B
Sweney, Moses MO Lt.Arty. 4th (Harris) Field Btty.
Sweney, Reuben TN Holman's Bn.Part.Rangers Co.D
Sweney, Robert C. LA Lt.Arty. 3rd Btty. (Benton's)
Sweney, William AR 6th Inf. Co.C
Swenney, D.H. AL 15th Inf. Co.B
Swenney, J.P. AL 15th Inf. Co.B
Swenny, F. TN Lt.Arty. Barry's Co.
Swenny, Morgan Conf.Lt.Arty. 1st Reg.Btty. Cpl.
Swenson, A. Conf.Inf. 8th Bn. Co.D
Swenson, August SC 2nd Inf. Co.D
Swenson, Charles C. LA Mil. Chalmette Regt. Co.A
Swenson, E.B. TX 30th Cav. Co.C
Swenson, N.B. TX 30th Cav. Co.C Bugler
Swenson, O.B. TX Cav. McCord's Frontier Regt. Co.E Cpl.
Sweny, Daniel Conf.Inf. 1st Bn. 2nd Co.B 1st Sgt.
Sweny, John T. TN 29th Inf. Co.H
Sweny, M.N. VA Cav. Swann's Bn. Sweny's Co.
Sweny, Patrick AR Mil. Desha Cty.Bn.
Sweny, William NC 53rd Inf. Co.C
Sweny, William J. VA Cav. Swann's Bn. Sweny's Co. Capt.
Swepston, Samuel W. VA 4th Cav. & Inf.St.Line 1st Co.I Cpl.
Swerengen, S.T. AR 25th Inf. Co.C 2nd Lt.
Swerengen, W. GA 4th (Clinch's) Cav. Co.H
Sweringen, J.J. GA 1st Troops & Defences (Macon) Co.G
Sweringen, Jo L. TX 20th Cav. Co.I
Sweringen, John W. AL Conscr. Echols' Co. Sgt.

Sweringen, Richard J. AL Conscr. Echols' Co.
Sweringen, Robert E. AR 35th Inf. Co.G
Sweringim, Smith TN 28th (Cons.) Inf. Co.F
Sweringin, Warren H. MO Cav. 3rd Bn. Co.A
Swerlerting, G.W. AL 5th Inf. Co.B
Sweten, John AR 31st Inf. Co.C
Sweten, T.B. TN Inf. 22nd Bn. Co.E
Swetman, Benjamin MO Conscr.
Swetman, G.H. MO St.Guard
Swetman, James H. MO 4th Cav. Co.G
Swetman, William SC 1st (Butler's) Inf. Co.D
Swetnam, George H. MO 3rd Inf. Co.F
Swetnam, G.H. MO Inf. 1st Regt.St.Guard Co.G
Swetnam, J.D. MO 6th Inf. Co.H
Swetnam, J.D. MO 8th Inf. Co.H
Swetnam, Joseph F. VA 9th Cav. Co.A Cpl.
Swetnam, Joseph S. MO 3rd Inf. Co.F,K
Swetnam, J.W. MO 8th Inf. Co.H
Swetnam, Robert MO 8th Inf. Co.H
Swetnam, Tobias S. KY 1st Bn.Mtd.Rifles Co.B
Sweton, John TN 6th Inf. Co.C
Swets, D. Conf.Cav. Wood's Regt. Co.F
Swett, A.J. AR 6th Inf. Co.E
Swett, A.J. AR 30th Inf. Co.K 1st Sgt.
Swett, Charles AL Cav. Hardie's Bn.Res. Co.C
Swett, Charles M. Lt.Arty. (Warren Lt.Arty.) Swett's Co. Capt.
Swett, Daniel, Jr. MS 21st Inf. Co.A
Swett, David SC 2nd Bn.S.S. Co.C
Swett, E.M. GA Inf. City Bn. (Columbus) Co.B
Swett, George TN 28th Inf. Co.A
Swett, H.H. MS Part.Rangers Armistead's Co. Sgt.
Swett, James H. LA 5th Inf. Co.B 1st Lt.
Swett, James M. VA 62nd Mtd.Inf. 2nd Co.L Cpl.
Swett, Jesse L. VA 16th Inf. Co.A
Swett, J.L. SC 7th Inf. Co.C Teamster
Swett, J.L. VA 13th Cav. Co.B
Swett, John MS 3rd Cav. Co.E
Swett, John W. SC 1st Arty. Co.D
Swett, Joseph L. SC 17th Inf. Co.A
Swett, J.W. SC 1st (Butler's) Inf. Co.B Cpl.
Swett, Robert SC 1st (Butler's) Inf. Co.B
Swett, Rufus LA Arty. Kean's Btty. (Orleans Ind.Arty.)
Swett, Rufus M. AL Recruits
Swett, Rufus M. LA 5th Inf. Co.B
Swett, Rufus M. LA C.S. Zouave Bn. Co.B
Swett, Thomas S. SC 17th Inf. Co.A
Swett, W.G. MS Part.Rangers Armistead's Co.
Swett, William SC 8th Inf. Co.B
Swett, W.T. MS Part.Rangers Armistead's Co.
Swettman, Crawford GA 64th Inf. Co.C
Swettman, James SC 1st Arty. Co.D
Swettman, William D. SC 1st Arty. Co.D
Swetzen, John A. VA 1st Cav. Co.I
Sweyer, Edward T. AR 15th (Josey's) Inf. Co.H
Swezley, John Conf.Inf. 8th Bn. Co.E
Swezy, J.M. SC 17th Inf. Co.F
Swezy, W.B. TN 3rd (Forrest's) Cav. Co.D
Swiant, Charles KY 9th Cav. Co.B
Swiant, Humphreys KY 9th Cav. Co.B
Swiber, L.W. VA 3rd Res. Co.K
Swicegood, Adam AL 5th Inf. New Co.B Sgt.
Swicegood, Alfred NC 48th Inf. Co.B
Swicegood, D.J. NC 1st Inf. Co.C
Swicegood, D.J. NC 1st Jr.Res. Co.C
Swicegood, D.L. NC Allen's Co. (Loc.Def.)
Swicegood, George NC 6th Sr.Res. Co.C
Swicegood, George W. NC 14th Inf. Co.I Cpl.
Swicegood, H. NC 48th Inf. Co.D
Swicegood, Henry H. NC 15th Inf. Co.K
Swicegood, J.A. NC 57th Inf. Co.K
Swicegood, James A. NC 14th Inf. Co.I
Swicegood, James H. NC 42nd Inf. Co.A
Swicegood, John H. NC 54th Inf. Co.A
Swicegood, John L. TN Cav. Welcker's Bn. Kincaid's Co. Sgt.
Swicegood, John L. TN 43rd Inf. Co.F
Swicegood, Romulus S. NC 42nd Inf. Co.A
Swich, G.W. AR 30th Inf. Co.K
Swicher, Alexander C. NC 6th Inf. Co.G
Swicher, Claudius W. NC 6th Inf. Co.G
Swick, H.M. GA 12th Cav. Co.E Cpl.
Swick, Micajah T. TN 35th Inf. 3rd Co.F
Swick, M.T. Conscr. (Cp. of Instr.)
Swicord, Allen J. GA 3rd Res. Co.I Bvt.2nd Lt.
Swicord, David GA 2nd Cav. Co.K
Swicord, James M. FL Lt.Arty. Abell's Co.
Swicord, James S. GA 17th Inf. Co.D
Swicord, M. FL Cav. 5th Bn. Co.B
Swicord, M. GA Lt.Arty. Barnwell's Btty.
Swicord, Mathas GA Brooke's Co. (Terrell Lt.Arty.)
Swicord, Michael GA 2nd Cav. Co.K Bvt.2nd Lt.
Swicord, Thomas GA Cav. 29th Bn. Co.B Sgt.
Swicord, William GA 17th Inf. Co.D
Swicord, W.S. GA Cav. 29th Bn. Co.A Cpl.
Swien, M.D. LA Conscr.
Swift, --- FL Harrison's Co. (Santa Rosa Guards)
Swift, Adoniram J. VA Cav. 15th Bn. Co.B
Swift, A.J. VA 37th Mil. Co.A
Swift, A.M. TX 2nd Cav. Co.H
Swift, A.M. TX 2nd Inf. Co.G
Swift, Benton VA 10th Cav. Co.B
Swift, Berton TN 8th Inf. Co.F
Swift, Charles E. LA Inf.Crescent Regt. Co.I
Swift, Charles T. GA Lt.Arty. 14th Bn. Co.A
Swift, Charles T. GA Lt.Arty. Havis' Btty.
Swift, Charles T. GA 1st (Ramsey's) Inf. Co.C
Swift, Charles W. VA Cav. 39th Bn. Co.C
Swift, Chester A. AR 16th Inf. Co.A
Swift, C.M. VA 1st Bn.Res. Co.C
Swift, C.T. Conf.Arty. Palmer's Bn. Capt.
Swift, C.V. SC 1st Mtd.Mil. Christopher's Co.
Swift, Daniel LA 1st (Strawbridge's) Inf. Co.H
Swift, Dudley NC 37th Inf. Co.E
Swift, E. GA 1st (Symons') Res. Co.B
Swift, E. LA 1st Hvy.Arty. (Reg.) Co.C
Swift, E. NC McLean's Bn.Lt.Duty Men Co.A
Swift, Ecknard LA 1st (Strawbridge's) Inf. Co.A,C
Swift, E.D. KY 7th Cav. Co.A
Swift, E.D. TN 55th (Brown's) Inf. Co.G
Swift, Edward GA 34th Inf. Co.A Cpl.
Swift, Edward GA 43rd Inf. Co.I
Swift, Edward TN 20th Inf. Co.A
Swift, E.J. VA 2nd St.Res. Co.I
Swift, E.M. TN 46th Inf. Co.E
Swift, F.M. TX Cav. St.Troops Doughty's Co.
Swift, G.B. GA 3rd Res. Co.B
Swift, G.B. Inf. Bailey's Cons.Regt. Co.C
Swift, George TX 11th (Spaight's) Bn.Vol. Co.C
Swift, George B. TN 49th Inf. Co.F
Swift, George B. VA 15th Inf. Co.C Capt.
Swift, George C. AL 24th Inf. Sgt.Maj.
Swift, George C. AL 28th Inf. Co.H,J Music.
Swift, George L. VA 15th Inf. Co.E
Swift, George W. AR 26th Inf. Co.B
Swift, George W. NC 12th Inf. Co.D
Swift, George W. NC 43rd Inf. Co.B
Swift, Glocus E. TX 8th Inf. Co.K
Swift, G.R. NC 2nd Inf. Co.G
Swift, H.D. MO 7th Cav. Co.B
Swift, Henry MS Cav. 2nd Bn.Res. Co.I
Swift, Henry MS 1st Bn.S.S. Co.D
Swift, Henry MS 25th Inf. Co.H
Swift, H.L. TN 13th (Gore's) Cav. Co.G
Swift, H.L. TN 25th Inf. Co.I
Swift, Houston B. AL 4th Inf. Co.H
Swift, J. AR 10th Mil.
Swift, J. FL 1st Cav. Co.E
Swift, J. LA Mil. Chalmette Regt. Co.B
Swift, J.A. GA 60th Inf. Co.C
Swift, Jackson AR 16th Inf. Co.A Cpl.
Swift, Jacob LA Red River S.S.
Swift, James AR 27th Inf. Co.B,E Cpl.
Swift, James TN 13th (Gore's) Cav. Co.H
Swift, James TX 37th Cav. Co.G
Swift, James H. TX 17th Cav. Co.A
Swift, James H. VA 2nd Bn.Res.
Swift, James P. AR 16th Inf. Co.A
Swift, J.J.J. FL 1st (Res.) Inf. Co.D
Swift, J.M. TN 12th Inf. Co.B
Swift, J.M. TN 12th (Cons.) Inf. Co.A
Swift, John GA 5th Inf. Co.K
Swift, John LA 15th Inf. Co.C
Swift, John MO 8th Cav.
Swift, John SC 1st (Butler's) Inf. Co.F,H
Swift, John SC Inf. 1st (Charleston) Bn. Co.F
Swift, John TN 2nd (Walker's) Inf. Co.H
Swift, John VA Res.Forces Clark's Co.
Swift, John A. GA 36th (Villepigue's) Inf. Co.D Sgt.
Swift, John A. 1st Conf.Inf. 1st Co.D, 2nd Co.C 1st Sgt.
Swift, John D. MS Cav. Jeff Davis Legion Co.C
Swift, John D. MS Hudson's Co. (Noxubee Guards)
Swift, John H. VA 9th Cav. Co.E
Swift, John R. AR 1st (Colquitt's) Inf. Co.I
Swift, John S. VA 4th Cav. Co.F Sgt.
Swift, John T. GA 3rd Cav. (St.Guards) Co.E
Swift, John W. LA 16th Inf. Co.E Sgt.
Swift, John W. TN 27th Inf. Co.F Cpl.
Swift, Jonathan S. GA 46th Inf. Co.G
Swift, Joseph J.B.H. FL 1st Cav. Co.C Cpl.
Swift, Joseph S. KY 11th Cav.
Swift, J.P.B. TN 18th Inf. Co.B
Swift, J.S. KY 1st Inf. Co.F
Swift, J.T. GA 11th Cav. Co.D
Swift, J.T. TN 50th Inf. Co.A
Swift, J.W. NC 21st Inf. Co.C
Swift, J.W. TN 1st (Feild's) & 27th Inf. (Cons.) Co.I
Swift, Luther R. VA 56th Inf. Co.F
Swift, M. AR 10th Mil. Co.H
Swift, Marion AR 1st Mtd.Rifles Co.C
Swift, Mark W. TN 14th Inf. Co.K

Swift, Matthew M. TN 14th Inf. Co.K
Swift, M.D. AR 2nd Inf. Co.A 2nd Lt.
Swift, M.J. NC 6th Sr.Res. Co.D Sgt.
Swift, M.M. AR Cav. Gordon's Regt. Co.D
Swift, Nathan MO Cav. 3rd Bn. Co.A
Swift, Nathan MO 2nd Inf. Co.D
Swift, N.S. LA 17th Inf. Co.E
Swift, Oswald J. VA 15th Inf. Co.E Sgt.
Swift, Phillip VA 40th Inf. Co.G
Swift, R. Sap. & Min. G.W. Maxson's Co.,CSA
Swift, R.F. VA Hvy.Arty. 20th Bn. Co.C
Swift, Richard LA 8th Inf. Co.E
Swift, Richard VA 21st Cav. 2nd Co.E
Swift, Richard G. VA 9th Cav. Co.E
Swift, R.J. MS 1st Inf.
Swift, R.J. TN Cav. Napier's Bn. Co.B
Swift, Robert KY 2nd (Woodward's) Cav. Co.G,C
Swift, Robert B. MS 1st Cav. Co.G
Swift, Robert B. NC 6th Inf. Co.H
Swift, R.T. VA 39th Bn.Res. Co.C
Swift, Rufus TN 25th Inf. Co.A
Swift, S. MS 18th Cav. Co.A
Swift, S. Sap. & Min. G.W. Maxson's Co.,CSA
Swift, S.A. AR 8th Inf. New Co.C
Swift, Samuel LA Mil.Cont.Regt. Kirk's Co.
Swift, Samuel NC 1st Cav. (9th St.Troops) Co.D
Swift, Samuel NC 37th Inf. Co.E Music.
Swift, S.D. VA 37th Mil. 2nd Co.B
Swift, S.G.W. TX 21st Inf. Co.B
Swift, Sherman NC 37th Inf. Co.E
Swift, Silas G.W. TX 11th (Spaight's) Bn.Vol. Co.E
Swift, Simeon D. FL 1st Cav. Co.C
Swift, Simeon F. TN 25th Inf. Co.A
Swift, S.W. TN 27th Inf. Co.F
Swift, T. FL 1st Cav. Co.E
Swift, T. NC 27th Inf. Co.B
Swift, T.B. MS 41st Inf. Co.K
Swift, T.B. MS Shields' Co.
Swift, T.B. TN 46th Inf. Co.E
Swift, T.F. TN 21st (Wilson's) Cav. Co.D,C
Swift, T.F. TN 21st & 22nd (Cons.) Cav. Co.G
Swift, Thaddeus H. TX 21st Cav. Co.K
Swift, Thomas FL Cav. 5th Bn. Co.G
Swift, Thomas NC 11th Bn. Home Guards Co.A
Swift, Thomas VA Lt.Arty. Waters' Co.
Swift, Thomas VA 37th Mil. 2nd Co.B
Swift, Thomas VA 37th Mil. Co.C
Swift, Thomas C. AL 30th Inf. Co.H
Swift, Thomas H. GA Phillips' Legion Co.B
Swift, T.J. TN 10th (DeMoss') Cav. Co.E
Swift, T.J. TN 12th Inf. Co.B
Swift, T.J. TN 12th (Cons.) Inf. Co.A
Swift, V.A. MS 2nd Part.Rangers Co.C
Swift, V.H. TN 15th (Cons.) Cav. Co.K 2nd Lt.
Swift, W.H. GA 12th Mil.
Swift, W.H. TX 18th Cav. Co.K
Swift, Wilburn NC 58th Inf. Co.I
Swift, William GA 57th Inf. Co.A
Swift, William KY Horse Arty. Byrne's Co. QMSgt.
Swift, William MS 41st Inf. Co.K
Swift, William A. LA 9th Inf. Co.A
Swift, William H. TX 17th Cav. Co.A
Swift, William H. VA 6th Inf. Co.D Sgt.
Swift, William J. VA 40th Inf. Co.F
Swift, William M. TX 9th Cav. Co.G
Swift, William N. GA 34th Inf. Co.G 2nd Lt.
Swift, William T. AR 26th Inf. Co.B Cpl.
Swift, William T., Jr. GA 1st (Ramsey's) Inf. Co.C
Swift, William T. VA 9th Cav. Co.E
Swift, William Z. VA 23rd Inf. Co.G
Swift, W.J. MS 18th Cav. Co.A
Swift, W.L. TN Lt.Arty. Phillips' Co. Sgt.Maj.
Swift, Worther T. VA 23rd Inf. Co.G
Swift, W.P. TN 21st (Wilson's) Cav. Co.C
Swift, W.R. TN 27th Inf. Co.F
Swift, W.W. AR 10th Mil. Co.F
Swift, Young NC 37th Inf. Co.E Cpl.
Swigart, Lewis VA 11th Cav. Co.A
Swigart, Lewis VA 67th Mil. Co.E
Swigart, R.J. MS 46th Inf. Co.G
Swiger, C. VA 19th Inf. Co.C,D
Swiger, G.W. TN 1st (Turney's) Inf. Co.I
Swiger, John MS Inf. 2nd Bn. Co.G
Swiger, John MS 48th Inf. Co.G
Swigert, David VA 13th Inf. Co.H
Swigert, George MS 8th Inf. Co.C
Swigert, Jacob MS 3rd (St.Troops) Cav. Co.K
Swigert, J.M. MS 3rd (St.Troops) Cav. Co.K
Swigert, J.M. MS 8th Inf. Co.C Sgt.
Swigert, J.S. MS 8th Inf. Co.C
Swigert, Reubin MS 8th Inf. Co.C
Swiggart, D.W. MO Inf. 8th Bn. Asst.Surg.
Swiggart, J.R. AR Cav. McGehee's Regt. Co.C
Swighart, D.W. TX Cav. Good's Bn. Surg.
Swight, A.J. 20th Conf.Cav. Co.C
Swike, A.J. TN 50th Inf. Co.K
Swiler, Charles LA 7th Inf. Co.H
Swiler, Henry L. LA 7th Inf. Co.H
Swiler, John LA Mil. Fire Bn. Co.G
Swiles, --- AL 4th (Russell's) Cav. Co.I
Swiley, J.M. AL 4th Inf. Co.F
Swilger, M.M. VA Burks' Regt.Loc.Def.
Swilker, John MS 2nd Inf.
Swiller, Richard M. VA 12th Cav. Co.F
Swilley, A.G. MS 39th Inf. Co.G
Swilley, B.F. MS Cav. Powers' Regt. Co.I
Swilley, B.F. MS 39th Inf. Co.E
Swilley, F. MS St.Cav. 3rd Bn. (Cooper's) 1st Co.A
Swilley, G.M. MS St.Cav. 3rd Bn. (Cooper's) Little's Co.
Swilley, J.S. GA 8th Cav. New Co.I
Swilley, L. MS Cav. Hughes' Bn. Co.D
Swilley, Lafayette MS 4th Cav. Co.E
Swilley, Reason E. FL 5th Inf. Co.F
Swilley, R.F. MS 39th Inf. Co.G
Swilley, S. FL Cav. 5th Bn. Co.B
Swilley, Samuel A.J. AL 20th Inf. Co.E,A
Swilley, Samuel E. GA 12th Inf. Co.I
Swilley, S.R. GA 26th Inf. Co.H
Swilley, Steph E. AL 57th Inf. Co.E
Swilley, T. GA 8th Cav. New Co.I
Swilley, W.G. LA 9th Inf. Co.B 1st Sgt.
Swilley, William FL 10th Inf. Co.B
Swilley, W.J. TX 8th Cav. Co.H
Swilley, W.M. GA 11th Cav. (St.Guards) Staten's Co. Sgt.
Swilley, W.S. MS St.Cav. 3rd Bn. (Cooper's) Little's Co.
Swilling, B.F. AR 1st Mtd.Rifles Co.H
Swilling, E.H. AR 35th Inf. Co.I
Swilling, George E. GA 34th Inf. Co.D Sgt.
Swilling, G.S. GA 37th Inf. Co.F
Swilling, G.T. GA Inf. 9th Bn. Co.C
Swilling, G.W. GA Inf. 9th Bn. Co.C
Swilling, Jack W. AZ Cav. Herbert's Bn. Helm's Co. 1st Lt.
Swilling, James M. GA 38th Inf. Co.I
Swilling, J.H. AR 35th Inf. Co.E
Swilling, J.H. AR 62nd Mil. Co.C
Swilling, J.L. GA 8th Inf. Co.H
Swilling, J.M. GA Inf. 25th Bn. (Prov.Guard) Co.G Sgt.
Swilling, John W. GA 35th Inf. Co.I 2nd Lt.
Swilling, J.W. AZ Cav. Herbert's Bn. Helm's Co. 1st Lt.
Swilling, J.Y. GA Inf. 9th Bn. Co.C
Swilling, J.Z.H. SC 7th Inf. 1st Co.D
Swilling, R.Y. GA 11th Cav. Co.I
Swilling, S.A. GA 8th Inf. Co.H
Swilling, S.M. GA Inf. 9th Bn. Co.C
Swilling, S.W. GA 11th Cav. Co.I Cpl.
Swilling, S.Y. GA 11th Cav. Co.I
Swilling, T.A. GA 37th Inf. Co.F
Swilling, T.P. GA Inf. 9th Bn. Co.C
Swilling, W.H. AR 1st Mtd.Rifles Co.H
Swilling, William GA Inf. 9th Bn. Co.C
Swilling, Wm. L. GA 8th Inf. Co.H
Swilly, E.R. GA 11th Cav. (St.Guards) Staten's Co.
Swilly, F. GA Cav. 20th Bn. Co.A
Swilly, Franklin GA 50th Inf. Co.D
Swilly, G.A. GA 17th Inf. Co.G Cpl.
Swilly, I. GA 4th (Clinch's) Cav. Co.H
Swilly, J. GA 50th Inf. Co.D
Swilly, J.A. GA 11th Cav. (St.Guards) Staten's Co.
Swilly, J.S. GA Cav. 20th Bn. Co.A
Swilly, R.F. 14th Conf.Cav. Co.K
Swilly, T. GA Cav. 20th Bn. Co.A
Swilly, W. GA 1st Reg. Co.H
Swily, Hue TN 22nd Inf. Co.D
Swim, A. MO 2nd Cav. Co.D
Swim, A. TX 17th Cons.Dismtd.Cav. Co.F
Swim, A.H. AR 50th Mil. Co.G
Swim, Amos MO 10th Inf. Co.E
Swim, Asa M. KY 2nd Bn.Mtd.Rifles Co.B
Swim, Asa M. KY 5th Mtd.Inf. Co.C 1st Lt.
Swim, B.W. TX 23rd Cav. Co.C
Swim, Daniel F. AR 37th Inf. Co.H
Swim, Daniel F. MO 7th Cav. Co.I
Swim, D.F. TX 11th Cav. Co.E
Swim, George S. MS 21st Inf. Co.D
Swim, H. TX 2nd Legion Co.D
Swim, H.T. KY 2nd Bn.Mtd.Rifles Co.C
Swim, Hugh GA Inf. 11th Bn. (St.Guards) Co.A
Swim, James A. NC 34th Inf. Co.I
Swim, James H. MO 10th Cav. Co.D
Swim, J.F. VA 63rd Inf. Co.G
Swim, John GA Inf. 11th Bn. (St.Guards) Co.A
Swim, John NC 18th Inf. Co.I
Swim, Josephus NC 54th Inf. Co.G
Swim, L.A.J. GA Inf. 11th Bn. (St.Guards) Co.A
Swim, Samuel AR 50th Mil. Co.G
Swim, Samuel E. TX Cav. Sutton's Co. Sgt.
Swim, S.E. TX 11th Cav. Co.E
Swim, Solomon AL 26th (O'Neal's) Inf.

Swim, Theophilus M. GA 6th Cav. Co.F
Swim, Trumbo AR 8th Inf. New Co.E
Swim, Wat MS Cav. Russell's Co.
Swim, William AR 50th Mil. Co.G
Swim, William MS 10th Cav. Co.B
Swim, William N. GA 6th Cav. Co.F
Swim, W.S. LA Hvy.Arty. 2nd Bn. Co.A 1st Sgt.
Swimley, David VA 2nd Inf. Co.D
Swimley, Harrison VA 12th Cav. Co.D
Swimley, Samuel VA 12th Cav. Co.D
Swimm, A.M. KY 9th Mtd.Inf. Co.H Sgt.
Swimm, Harvey L. KY 5th Mtd.Inf. Co.C
Swimmer (Creek) 1st Cherokee Mtd.Rifles Co.E
Swimmer 1st Cherokee Mtd.Rifles Co.F
Swimmer 1st Cherokee Mtd.Rifles Co.H
Swimmer, Alex 1st Cherokee Mtd.Rifles Co.E
Swimmer, Jacob 1st Cherokee Mtd.Vol. 1st Co.B, 2nd Co.D
Swimmer, Jesse 1st Cherokee Mtd.Rifles Co.E
Swimmer, Joe 1st Cherokee Mtd.Rifles Co.F
Swimmer, Joseph 1st Cherokee Mtd.Rifles Co.K
Swimmer, Ool Skewe Ney 1st Cherokee Mtd.Rifles Co.I
Swimmer, Rider 1st Cherokee Mtd.Rifles Co.K
Swimpon, Jacob NC 67th Inf. Co.H
Swims, C. AL 42nd Inf.
Swin, Duncan E. TX 15th Inf. Co.A
Swinaguin, John TN 46th Inf. Co.H Cpl.
Swinborn, A.C. TX Inf.Riflemen Arnold's Co.
Swinborn, Alva C. TX 17th Cav. Co.A
Swinborn, Edwin N. TX Inf. Riflemen Arnold's Co.
Swinburn, Edwin N. TX 17th Cav. Co.A
Swinburn, E.N. TX 17th Cons.Dismtd.Cav. Co.A
Swinck, Frank VA 5th Cav. Co.D Cpl.
Swindal, D.W. AL 8th Inf. Co.B
Swindal, J.G. AL 8th Inf. Co.B Sgt.
Swindal, Samuel L. AL 2nd Cav. Co.G
Swindall, A.W. MS 12th Cav. Co.A
Swindall, Chester NC 18th Inf. Co.K
Swindall, James D. VA 63rd Inf. Co.C
Swindall, Samuel D. NC 1st Arty. (10th St.Troops) Co.E
Swindall, W.C. AL 14th Inf. Co.D
Swindalle, Chester NC 2nd Arty. (36th St.Troops) Co.B
Swindel, Absalom S. AR 33rd Inf. Co.I
Swindel, Christopher 1st Cherokee Mtd.Vol. 2nd Co.K
Swindel, James H. NC 17th Inf. (1st Org.) Co.K Capt.
Swindell, Albin B. NC Part.Rangers Swindell's Co.
Swindell, Alexander B. NC Part.Rangers Swindell's Co.
Swindell, Ananias NC 61st Inf. Co.B
Swindell, Anson W. NC 2nd Inf. Co.I
Swindell, Benjamin F. NC 17th Inf. (1st Org.) Co.B
Swindell, David F. NC 33rd Inf. Co.F
Swindell, Edward J. NC Part.Rangers Swindell's Co.
Swindell, Edward S. NC Part.Rangers Swindell's Co. Capt.
Swindell, Edward S. NC 17th Inf. (1st Org.) Co.B Ord.Sgt.
Swindell, Erasmus NC 33rd Inf. Co.F
Swindell, Francis M. NC Part.Rangers Swindell's Co.
Swindell, Francis M. NC 1st Arty. (10th St.Troops) Co.K
Swindell, F.W. NC 2nd Jr.Res. Co.I
Swindell, George W. MO 9th (Elliott's) Cav. Co.K
Swindell, Hardy NC Part.Rangers Swindell's Co.
Swindell, Isaac S. NC 4th Inf. Co.E
Swindell, James D. NC 17th Inf. (2nd Org.) Co.B
Swindell, John O. NC 17th Inf. (1st Org.) Co.B 1st Lt.
Swindell, John R. TN 38th Inf.
Swindell, Jonathan NC 3rd Arty. (40th St.Troops) Co.D
Swindell, Joseph NC 33rd Inf. Co.F 2nd Lt.
Swindell, Joseph W. NC 4th Inf. Co.I
Swindell, J.W. NC 3rd Inf. Co.I
Swindell, Lewis L. NC 17th Inf. (1st Org.) Co.B
Swindell, Lewis L. NC 33rd Inf. Co.H Sgt.
Swindell, L.L. NC Part.Rangers Swindell's Co. Sgt.
Swindell, Nathaniel G. NC 33rd Inf. Co.I,H
Swindell, R.D. AR 51st Mil. Co.H
Swindell, Samuel G. NC 4th Inf. Co.I
Swindell, Samuel L. NC 33rd Inf. Co.I,H
Swindell, Scott NC 2nd Jr.Res. Co.I Cpl.
Swindell, Solomon F. NC 4th Inf. Co.I
Swindell, Thomas D. NC 3rd Arty. (40th St.Troops) Co.D Cpl.
Swindell, Thomas M. NC 4th Inf. Co.I
Swindell, W.C. MS 3rd Inf. Co.I 2nd Lt.
Swindell, William NC 1st Arty. (10th St.Troops) Co.F
Swindell, William M.B. NC 17th Inf. (1st Org.) Co.B 2nd Lt.
Swindell, William M.B. NC 33rd Inf. Co.I,H Capt.
Swindell, William Red NC Part.Rangers Swindell's Co.
Swindells, D.H. LA Miles' Legion Co.A
Swindells, James H. AR 32nd Inf. Surg.
Swindells, James H. TX 17th Cav. Co.K Asst.Surg.
Swindells, James H. Gen. & Staff Surg.
Swindells, John W. TX 18th Cav. Co.C Comsy.Sgt.
Swindells, J.W. TX Arty. (St.Troops) Good's Co.
Swindle, A.C. GA 66th Inf. Co.I
Swindle, A.E. TN 49th Inf. Co.I 1st Sgt.
Swindle, A.E. Inf. Bailey's Cons.Regt. Co.D
Swindle, Albert AL 43rd Inf. Co.D
Swindle, Asa TN 27th Inf. Co.A
Swindle, Asa M. TN 1st (Feild's) & 27th Inf. (Cons.) Co.B
Swindle, B. AL Cp. of Instr. Talladega
Swindle, Benj. P. GA Cobb's Legion Co.D
Swindle, Benjamin P. TX 11th Inf. Co.C
Swindle, B.P. TX 4th Field Btty.
Swindle, Cason TN 28th Inf. Co.K
Swindle, C.C. TN 35th Inf. 2nd Co.A 2nd Lt.
Swindle, Charles C. LA 9th Inf. Co.F
Swindle, Clark TN Inf. 22nd Bn. Co.A
Swindle, David NC 67th Inf. Co.B
Swindle, David A. NC 1st Arty. (10th St.Troops) Co.B
Swindle, David C. MS 31st Inf. Co.B
Swindle, D.H. TX Cav. Border's Regt. Co.F
Swindle, D.W. NC Gibbs' Co. (Loc.Def.)
Swindle, E.D. AL 8th Inf. Co.D
Swindle, Edward GA 25th Inf. Co.I
Swindle, Eli NC 61st Inf. Co.I
Swindle, Elias D. AL 43rd Inf. Co.K
Swindle, Francis TN 10th Inf. Co.F
Swindle, Francis M. MS 43rd Inf. Co.D
Swindle, G.C. TN 49th Inf. Co.I
Swindle, George AL 3rd Res. Co.G
Swindle, George MS 3rd Inf. Co.C
Swindle, George TN Inf. 22nd Bn. Co.A
Swindle, George C. TN 38th Inf.
Swindle, George D. GA Cav. 1st Bn. Hughes' Co., Brailsford's Co.
Swindle, George D. GA 5th Cav. Co.H
Swindle, George W. GA 2nd Cav. Co.C
Swindle, George W. GA 25th Inf. Co.I
Swindle, George W. MS 1st Cav.Res. Co.K Sgt.
Swindle, G.L. MS 8th Cav. Co.K
Swindle, G.W. AL Cav. Moreland's Regt. Co.E
Swindle, G.W. AL 20th Inf. Co.A
Swindle, G.W. GA 1st Bn.S.S. Co.A
Swindle, G.W. TN 13th (Gore's) Cav. Co.I
Swindle, H. NC Gibbs' Co. (Loc.Def.)
Swindle, H.A. GA Cav. 1st Bn. Hughes' Co.
Swindle, H.C. TN 49th Inf. Co.I 1st Sgt.
Swindle, H.C. Inf. Bailey's Cons.Regt. Co.D 1st Sgt.
Swindle, Henry FL 7th Inf. Co.C
Swindle, Isaac VA Lt.Arty. Carpenter's Co.
Swindle, J. AL Talladega Cty.Res. D.B. Brown's Co.
Swindle, James FL Fernandez's Mtd.Co. (Supply Force)
Swindle, James GA 25th Inf. Co.I
Swindle, James NC 1st Arty. (10th St.Troops) Old Co.I
Swindle, James TN Cav. Newsom's Regt. Co.H
Swindle, James TN Inf. 22nd Bn. Co.B Sgt.
Swindle, James TN 35th Inf. 2nd Co.A
Swindle, James A. AR Inf. 8th Bn. 1st Co.C
Swindle, James A. AR 25th Inf. Co.F
Swindle, James C. AL 16th Inf. Co.E
Swindle, James D. VA Mil. Grayson Cty.
Swindle, James E. TN 49th Inf. Co.I
Swindle, James E. Inf. Bailey's Cons.Regt. Co.D
Swindle, James H. AL 46th Inf. Co.B
Swindle, James M. TX 4th Inf. Co.K
Swindle, J.D. VA Inf. 54th Bn. Co.C
Swindle, J.E. KY 12th Cav. Co.G
Swindle, J.E. TN 49th Inf. Co.I
Swindle, Jeremiah TN 28th Inf. Co.K
Swindle, Jesse F. AL Pris.Guard Freeman's Co.
Swindle, J.H. KY 7th Mtd.Inf. Co.G
Swindle, J.H. TN 27th Inf. Co.A
Swindle, J.H. TN 27th Inf. Co.A 2nd Lt.
Swindle, J.J. LA 6th Cav. Co.C
Swindle, J.J. TX 1st Field Btty.
Swindle, J.M. TN 27th Inf. Co.A
Swindle, Joel MS Inf. 3rd Bn. Co.C
Swindle, John AL 29th Inf. Co.F

Swindle, John AL 50th Inf. Co.G
Swindle, John AL 50th Inf. Co.K
Swindle, John AL 62nd Inf. Co.K
Swindle, John AL Cp. of Instr. Talladega Co.A
Swindle, John TN Cav. Newsom's Regt. Co.H
Swindle, John TN 38th Inf. 1st Co.K
Swindle, John C. GA 4th Inf. Co.B
Swindle, John E. Inf. Bailey's Cons.Regt. Co.D
Swindle, John J. GA 1st Bn.S.S. Co.A
Swindle, John J. GA 25th Inf. Co.I
Swindle, John S. Inf. Bailey's Cons.Regt. Co.D
Swindle, John T. MS 31st Inf. Co.B
Swindle, John T. TN 38th Inf. Co.G 3rd Lt.
Swindle, J.R. TN 16th Inf. Co.G
Swindle, J.S. TN 49th Inf. Co.I Cpl.
Swindle, J.S. TX 11th Inf. Co.C
Swindle, L.C. AR 45th Cav. Co.G
Swindle, Lem FL 6th Inf. Co.K
Swindle, Manley M. AL 46th Inf. Co.B
Swindle, Owen FL 7th Inf. Co.C
Swindle, Owins C. AL 46th Inf. Co.B Sgt.
Swindle, Samuel GA Cav. 1st Bn. Hughes' Co.
Swindle, Samuel GA 4th Inf. Co.B
Swindle, Samuel O. GA Cobbs' Legion Co.D
Swindle, Solomon M. GA 16th Inf. Co.D
Swindle, S.S. GA 5th Cav. Co.D
Swindle, T. AL Cp. of Instr. Talladega Co.D
Swindle, T. TN Inf. 1st Cons.Regt. Co.I
Swindle, Thomas AL Inf. 1st Regt. Co.E
Swindle, Thomas NC 2nd Arty. (36th St.Troops) Co.C
Swindle, Thomas TN 27th Inf. Co.A
Swindle, Thomas TN 49th Inf. Co.I
Swindle, T.J. TX 19th Inf. Co.B
Swindle, W. MS Lt.Arty. Culbertson's Btty. Capt.
Swindle, W.A. AR 1st Vol. Simington's Co. Sgt.
Swindle, W.A. AR 38th Inf. Co.H
Swindle, W.A. GA Cav. 20th Bn. Co.E
Swindle, W.F. AL 50th Inf. Co.K
Swindle, W.F. TN 38th Inf. 1st Co.K
Swindle, William AL 43rd Inf. Co.K Sgt.
Swindle, William GA Cav. 1st Bn. Hughes' Co.
Swindle, William GA 5th Cav. Co.D
Swindle, William T. MS 35th Inf. Co.D
Swindle, Willis FL 7th Inf. Co.H
Swindle, W.J. TN 22nd Inf. Co.B
Swindle, W.M. MS 3rd Cav. Co.B 2nd Lt.
Swindle, W.T. KY 7th Mtd.Inf. Co.G
Swindler, A.C. VA 7th Cav. 1st Lt.
Swindler, Albert C. VA 12th Cav. Co.G Capt.
Swindler, Albert C. VA 7th Inf. Co.B 1st Lt.
Swindler, Benjamin F. VA 36th Inf. Beckett's Co. Cpl.
Swindler, Henry VA 26th Cav. Co.A Wagon M.
Swindler, James E. TX 5th Inf. Co.C
Swindler, J.W. SC 3rd Inf. Co.H Sgt.
Swindler, M.L. KY Cav. 1st Bn. Recruit
Swindler, Thomas VA 12th Cav. Co.G 1st Lt.
Swindler, Wistar SC 2nd Cav. Co.A
Swindol, Thomas W. MS 11th (Perrin's) Cav. Co.I Cpl.
Swindoll, Augustus W. MS 23rd Inf. Co.I
Swindoll, Augustus W. MS 43rd Inf. Co.E
Swindoll, Thomas J. MS 24th Inf. Co.K
Swindoll, Warren M. MS 43rd Inf. Co.E
Swindoll, Wilburn C., Jr. MS 23rd Inf. Co.I Capt.
Swindoll, William C. MS 43rd Inf. Co.E
Swindoll, William M. MS 24th Inf. Co.K Sgt.
Swindt, John F. LA 5th Inf. Co.E
Swine, S. NC 48th Inf. Co.D
Swinea, Bryant TN 3rd (Clack's) Inf. Co.G
Swinea, Henry S. TN 3rd (Clack's) Inf. Co.A
Swinea, John W. AL 16th Inf. Co.C
Swinea, Seldon W. TN 3rd (Clack's) Inf. Co.A
Swinea, William F. TN 3rd (Clack's) Inf. Co.A
Swinebroad, Andrew J. TN 1st (Turney's) Inf. Co.G Cpl.
Swinebroad, G.W. TN Park's Co. (Loc.Def. Troops)
Swinebroad, Henry G. TX 19th Cav. Co.C
Swinefoot, J.G. VA 8th Bn.Res Co.C
Swinenger, G.P. GA 31st Inf. Co.F
Swiney, Adolphus N. TN 4th (McLemore's) Cav. Co.D
Swiney, Alexander T. GA 41st Inf. Co.K
Swiney, Anderson NC 54th Inf. Co.H
Swiney, C. LA Mil. Irish Regt. O'Brien's Co.
Swiney, Edmund VA 24th Inf. Co.A
Swiney, Ephraim MS 29th Inf. Co.K
Swiney, F.M. GA 4th (Clinch's) Cav.
Swiney, F.M. MO Cav. 2nd Regt.St.Guard Co.G
Swiney, H. TN 12th (Cons.) Inf. Co.F
Swiney, Haden GA 34th Inf. Co.A
Swiney, James M. GA 38th Inf. Co.K Cpl.
Swiney, James W. MS 24th Inf. Co.I Sgt.
Swiney, J.B. TX 17th Cav. Co.I
Swiney, John LA 12th Inf. Co.F
Swiney, John TN 1st (Turney's) Inf. Co.H
Swiney, John 7th Conf.Cav. Co.D
Swiney, Lafayette 1st Cherokee Mtd.Vol. 2nd Co.K 2nd Lt.
Swiney, L.E. GA Inf. 40th Bn. Co.D
Swiney, Littlebery J. TN 4th (McLemore's) Cav. Co.D
Swiney, Mick LA Mil. 3rd Regt. 1st Brig. 1st Div. Co.F
Swiney, O.F. GA Inf. 40th Bn. Co.D
Swiney, O.V. GA Inf. 40th Bn. Co.D
Swiney, Richard TN 32nd Inf. Co.I
Swiney, Robert VA Inf. 23rd Bn. Co.E
Swiney, Samuel MO Cav. Slayback's Regt. Co.B
Swiney, S.J.J. GA 38th Inf. Co.K Cpl.
Swiney, Thomas MS 2nd Inf. Co.A
Swiney, W.A. MS Cav. 3rd Bn. (Ashcraft's) Co.C Sgt.
Swiney, Warren L.D. TN 4th (McLemore's) Cav. Co.D
Swiney, W.B. MS 10th Cav. Co.B
Swiney, W.E. GA 13th Cadets
Swiney, William GA 12th Cav. Co.L
Swiney, William VA 50th Inf. Co.B
Swiney, William D. TN 4th (McLemore's) Cav. Co.D
Swinford, A.N. AR 34th Inf. Co.A
Swinford, E. TX 21st Inf. Co.B
Swinford, Eberle TX 11th (Spaight's) Bn.Vol. Co.E Sgt.
Swinford, Elijah MO 1st Regt.St.Guards Co.C
Swinford, Ezekiel AL 4th (Russell's) Cav. Co.E
Swinford, Harmon AR 3rd Cav. Co.C
Swinford, H.F. AR 1st (Monroe's) Cav. Co.H
Swinford, James MO 1st N.E. Cav.
Swinford, John GA 36th (Broyles') Inf. Co.E Jr.2nd Lt.
Swinford, John TN 41st Inf. Co.D
Swinford, R.T. GA 36th (Broyles') Inf. Co.E
Swinford, Thomas MO 2nd Cav. Co.K
Swinford, W. GA 12th Cav. Co.A
Swinfort, A.C. AR 13th Mil. Co.A
Swing, A. AR 47th (Crandall's) Cav. Co.C
Swing, A. AR Pine Bluff Arty.
Swing, Alfred AR 26th Inf. Co.I
Swing, Alfred R. NC 48th Inf. Co.B
Swing, Anderson NC 48th Inf. Co.B
Swing, Daniel NC 42nd Inf. Co.I
Swing, David NC 6th Sr.Res. Co.C
Swing, Franking NC 6th Inf. Co.G
Swing, H.E. NC 3rd Arty. (40th St.Troops) Co.H
Swing, Henry E. NC 53rd Inf. Co.A
Swing, John D. NC 48th Inf. Co.B
Swing, John H. NC 14th Inf. Co.I
Swing, John H.C. NC 38th Inf. Co.G
Swing, Joseph NC 32nd Inf.
Swing, Kimsey NC 1st Inf. Co.E
Swing, M.L. Gen. & Staff Capt.,AQM
Swing, Obediah NC 18th Inf. Co.G
Swing, R. GA Mil.
Swing, Samuel NC 47th Inf. Co.K
Swing, Wiley D. NC 48th Inf. Co.B
Swingle, B.A. LA 5th Inf. Co.B
Swingle, Charles LA C.S. Zouave Bn. Co.D
Swingle, Henry KY Cav. 2nd Bn. (Dortch's) Co.C
Swingle, Henry KY Morgan's Men Co.D
Swingle, H.F. KY 10th (Johnson's) Cav. Co.D
Swingle, L.C. TX 26th Cav. Co.F
Swingler, George TX 20th Inf. Co.D
Swingler, George TX 22nd Inf. Co.B
Swingley, A.L. TN Cav. Newsom's Regt. Lt.Col.
Swingley, Alf T. MO Cav. 9th Regt.St.Guard Co.A 2nd Lt.
Swingley, J.J. TN 4th (McLemore's) Cav. Co.B
Swingraber, J.R. MO 15th Cav. Co.B
Swings, W.W. LA Miles' Legion Co.E
Swink, --- TX Cav. 4th Regt.St.Troops Co.L
Swink, Adam W. NC 42nd Inf. Co.A
Swink, Archibald NC 11th (Bethel Regt.) Inf. Co.B
Swink, Calvin L. VA 1st Cav. Co.E
Swink, Drew AR 18th Inf. Co.G
Swink, Edward NC 7th Inf. Co.F
Swink, Edward NC 66th Inf. Co.G
Swink, Erasmus VA 3rd Bn. Valley Res. Co.B
Swink, Erasmus VA 52nd Inf. Co.H
Swink, G.B. NC 57th Inf. Co.K
Swink, George NC 7th Sr.Res. Clinard's Co.
Swink, George TN 45th Inf. Co.I
Swink, George R. NC 8th Inf. Co.K
Swink, George T. MS 21st Inf. Co.H 1st Lt.
Swink, George W. NC 7th Inf. Co.F
Swink, George W. NC 52nd Inf. Co.E
Swink, George W. TN 6th Inf. Co.C
Swink, George W. VA 8th Inf. Co.G 2nd Lt.
Swink, George W. VA 52nd Inf. Co.C
Swink, Harrison NC 46th Inf. Co.B
Swink, Henry LA 1st (Nelligan's) Inf. Co.A

Swink, Henry NC 16th Inf. Co.E
Swink, Henry NC 57th Inf. Co.K
Swink, H.H. TN 14th (Neely's) Cav. Co.C 2nd Lt.
Swink, H.P. VA Rockbridge Cty.Res. Bacon's Co.
Swink, Jacob VA 5th Inf. Co.F
Swink, James NC 5th Inf. Co.K
Swink, James NC Snead's Co. (Loc.Def.)
Swink, James VA 5th Inf. Co.G
Swink, James A. AR Inf. 1st Bn. Co.A
Swink, James V. VA 8th Cav. Co.B Sgt.
Swink, James W. VA 5th Inf. Co.F
Swink, James W. VA 52nd Inf. Co.H
Swink, J.G. VA 3rd Bn. Valley Res. Co.B
Swink, Jo MO Cav. Coleman's Regt. Co.F
Swink, John MO 5th Cav. Co.I Sgt.
Swink, John NC 55th Inf. Co.F
Swink, John H. VA 52nd Inf. Co.C Cpl.
Swink, John W. VA 7th Bn.Res. Co.D
Swink, Jonas L. SC 1st Inf. Co.E
Swink, Jonas L. SC 18th Inf. Co.A
Swink, Joseph AL 2nd Cav. Co.I
Swink, Joseph C. VA 8th Inf. Co.G
Swink, J.P. NC 68th Inf. Co.C
Swink, J.R. NC 57th Inf. Co.K
Swink, Leander D. AR 1st (Colquitt's) Inf. Co.B
Swink, Leland L. AL 50th Inf. Co.A
Swink, Leonard AR 8th Cav. Co.L
Swink, Leslie D. NC 8th Inf. Co.K
Swink, Martin V.B. VA 52nd Inf. Co.C
Swink, Mathew VA 52nd Inf. Co.H
Swink, M.H. VA 3rd (Chrisman's) Bn.Res. Co.F
Swink, Milton VA Rockbridge Cty.Res. Bacon's Co.
Swink, P. NC 3rd Jr.Res. Co.G
Swink, Peter NC 8th Bn.Jr.Res. Co.C
Swink, Peter NC 42nd Inf. Co.B
Swink, Peter VA 6th Bn.Res. Co.C
Swink, Peter J. NC 8th Inf. Co.K
Swink, Peter J. NC 66th Inf. Co.G
Swink, Peter R. NC 8th Inf. Co.K
Swink, P.L. TX 20th Cav. Co.I
Swink, P.M. AR 38th Inf. Co.A 2nd Sgt.
Swink, Thomas NC 43rd Inf. Co.K
Swink, Turner NC 43rd Inf. Co.H
Swink, William AL 3rd Inf. Co.I
Swink, William NC 55th Inf. Co.F
Swink, William M. VA 25th Inf. 2nd Co.D
Swink, William S. VA 52nd Inf. Co.H
Swink, William W. AR Inf. 1st Bn. Co.G
Swink, W.W. AR 38th Inf. Co.A
Swink, Zachariah VA 31st Inf. Co.G
Swink, Zachariah VA 62nd Mtd.Inf. 2nd Co.D,A
Swinks, George VA 3rd Res. Co.G
Swinn, George S. MS 2nd Inf.
Swinn, James F. TX 33rd Cav. Co.K
Swinnay, H.H. AR 15th Mil. Co.I
Swinner, John LA 27th Inf. Co.K
Swinnermon, J.O. TN Inf. 154th Sr.Regt. Co.K
Swinney, A.J. GA 10th Mil. Maj.
Swinney, A.W. MS 26th Inf. Co.I
Swinney, Bazil B. LA 12th Inf. Co.H
Swinney, Charles K. MS 36th Inf. Co.E
Swinney, C.W. NC 1st Arty. (10th St.Troops) Co.A
Swinney, D. MO 9th (Elliott's) Cav. Co.H
Swinney, David TN 43rd Inf. Co.F
Swinney, Deany VA 166th Mil. Co.H Wag.
Swinney, D.J. MO 10th Inf. Co.A
Swinney, D.M. AL 15th Bn.Part.Rangers Co.E
Swinney, D.M. AL 56th Part.Rangers Co.E
Swinney, E.B. AL 15th Inf. Co.B
Swinney, Edmond TN 32nd Inf. Co.B
Swinney, Edward TN Lt.Arty. Scott's Co.
Swinney, Eli KY 5th Mtd.Inf. Co.G
Swinney, F. GA Cav. 8th Bn. (St.Guards) Co.A
Swinney, Francis M. GA 34th Inf. Co.A
Swinney, Francis M. MO 2nd Regt.St.Guards Co.C
Swinney, Green M. VA 151st Mil. Co.F
Swinney, G.W. AR 8th Cav. Co.L
Swinney, G.W. KY 8th Cav. Co.E
Swinney, H. TN 22nd Inf. Co.D
Swinney, Hilliard J. MS 26th Inf. Co.G
Swinney, Isaac F. SC 4th St.Troops Co.K
Swinney, Isaac M. VA 63rd Inf. Co.C
Swinney, James MO 3rd Cav. Co.C
Swinney, James VA 166th Mil. W. Lively's Co. Lt.
Swinney, James H. NC 25th Inf. Co.D
Swinney, James P. MO 1st N.E. Cav. Co.M
Swinney, James T. VA 60th Inf. Co.I Sgt.
Swinney, James W. MS 32nd Inf. Co.C Capt.
Swinney, Jasper MO 3rd Cav. Co.C
Swinney, Jasper D. MO Cav. 2nd Regt.St.Guard Co.G
Swinney, J.D. MO 3rd Cav. Co.C
Swinney, J.F. SC 23rd Inf. Co.A
Swinney, J.J. MS 26th Inf. Co.G
Swinney, J.J.H. MS 26th Inf. Co.F
Swinney, Joel 1st Conf.Inf. 2nd Co.G
Swinney, Joel P. NC 24th Inf. Co.A
Swinney, John GA 2nd Cav. (St.Guards) Co.G
Swinney, John GA 10th Cav. Co.D
Swinney, John SC 3rd Res. Co.I
Swinney, John TN 43rd Inf. Co.A
Swinney, John W. MS 38th Cav. Co.A
Swinney, J.W. MS 2nd (Davidson's) Inf. Co.K Sgt.
Swinney, J.W. TX Waul's Legion Co.F
Swinney, M. TX 25th Cav. Co.B
Swinney, Martin N. VA 17th Cav. Co.D
Swinney, M.E. GA 10th Inf. Asst.Surg.
Swinney, M.E. GA 48th Inf. Surg.
Swinney, M.E. Gen. & Staff Surg.
Swinney, M.P. GA 44th Inf. Co.E
Swinney, M.T. VA Second Class Mil. Hobson's Co.
Swinney, O.F. GA 41st Inf. Co.K
Swinney, Olander V. GA 41st Inf. Co.K
Swinney, Ransom TX 5th Inf. Co.F
Swinney, Richard H. TN 35th Inf. 2nd Co.F
Swinney, Richard W. 1st Conf.Inf. 2nd Co.G
Swinney, Robert TX Cav. 8th (Taylor's) Bn. Co.A
Swinney, Robert W. MO 2nd Regt.St.Guards Co.F Capt.
Swinney, Robert William MO 4th Cav. Col.
Swinney, Sampson J.J. GA Cobb's Legion Co.C
Swinney, Thomas FL 3rd Inf.
Swinney, Thomas FL 10th Inf. Co.F,H
Swinney, Thomas MS 32nd Inf. Co.C 1st Sgt.
Swinney, Thomas J. MO 3rd Cav. Co.C
Swinney, T.T. LA 13th Bn. (Part.Rangers) Co.A
Swinney, W. AR Lt.Arty. 5th Btty.
Swinney, Wiley J. MS 2nd Inf. Co.A
Swinney, William AL Lt.Arty. 2nd Bn. Co.C
Swinney, William MS 6th Cav. Co.D
Swinney, William MS Cav. Davenport's Bn. (St.Troops) Co.C
Swinney, William J. VA 17th Cav. Co.D 1st Sgt.
Swinney, William R. VA Inf. 23rd Bn. Co.E
Swinney, William T. MS Cav. Davenport's Bn. (St.Troops) Co.C Cpl.
Swinney, W.J. MS 6th Cav. Co.D Sgt.
Swinney, W.J. MS Cav. Davenport's Bn. (St.Troops) Co.C Sgt.
Swinney, W.J. TN 40th Inf. Co.G Bvt.Lt.
Swinney, W.M. LA 13th Bn. (Part.Rangers) Co.A
Swinney, W.T. MS 6th Cav. Co.D Cpl.
Swinney, W.T. MS 2nd (Davidson's) Inf. Co.K
Swinny, F.M. MO 2nd Cav. Co.E
Swinny, H. TN 12th (Cons.) Inf. Co.A
Swinny, I.W. MS 1st (Percy's) Inf. Co.B
Swinny, Levi MS 29th Inf. Co.I
Swinny, Preston NC 22nd Inf. Co.F
Swinny, Robert AR 2nd Cav. Co.I
Swinny, R.W. GA 3rd Cav. Co.H
Swinny, Taliaferro M. AL Arty.1st Bn. Co.D
Swinny, William A. MS 2nd Inf. Co.E,B
Swinson, A. MS 11th (Perrin's) Cav. Co.H
Swinson, Abram D. NC Loc.Def. Griswold's Co. 2nd Lt.
Swinson, A.J. MS 2nd St.Cav. Co.L
Swinson, A.J. MS 35th Inf. Co.G
Swinson, Albert NC 38th Inf. Co.A
Swinson, Alfred A. MS 11th Inf. Co.H
Swinson, Andrew J. NC 38th Inf. Co.A
Swinson, Anthony NC 32nd Inf. Co.G Cpl.
Swinson, Austin NC 8th Sr.Res. Broadhurst's Co.
Swinson, B. Frank NC 20th Inf. Co.E
Swinson, Buck NC 8th Bn.Part.Rangers Co.E
Swinson, Buck NC 66th Inf. Co.H
Swinson, Daniel NC 31st Inf. Co.C
Swinson, Erasmus NC 10th Inf. Co.E
Swinson, Gabriel G. GA 57th Inf. Co.I
Swinson, George L. NC 27th Inf. Co.D
Swinson, Henry NC 55th Inf. Co.H
Swinson, H.J. MS 24th Inf. Co.B
Swinson, J. NC 61st Inf. Co.H
Swinson, James NC 3rd Inf. Co.G
Swinson, James W. NC 1st Cav. (9th St.Troops) Co.I
Swinson, J.B. MS 44th Inf. Co.F
Swinson, Jeremiah NC 1st Inf. Co.G
Swinson, Jesse NC 8th Bn.Part.Rangers Co.B,E,F
Swinson, Jesse NC 66th Inf. Co.H,I
Swinson, Jesse W. NC 55th Inf. Co.H Sgt.
Swinson, J.H. MS 2nd St.Cav. Co.G
Swinson, J.H. MS 35th Inf. Co.G
Swinson, J.L. NC 61st Inf. Co.H
Swinson, John NC 1st Cav. (9th St.Troops) Co.I
Swinson, John A. GA 11th Inf. Co.G
Swinson, John A. NC 20th Inf. Co.E 1st Sgt.
Swinson, John E. NC 51st Inf. Co.B 1st Lt.
Swinson, Joseph NC 26th Inf. Co.D Music.

Swinson, Joseph NC 31st Inf. Co.I Music.
Swinson, Joseph 2nd Conf.Eng.Troops Co.G
Swinson, L.A. MS Inf. 3rd Bn. (St.Troops) Co.E
Swinson, M. NC 4th Cav. (59th St.Troops) Co.C
Swinson, Major NC 8th Bn.Part.Rangers Co.F
Swinson, Major NC 66th Inf. Co.I,G
Swinson, Nathaniel M. NC 2nd Inf. Co.C
Swinson, Robert J. NC 8th Bn.Part.Rangers Co.B,E 2nd Lt.
Swinson, Robert J. NC 66th Inf. Co.H Lt.
Swinson, Robert W. NC 8th Bn.Part.Rangers Co.B
Swinson, R.W. NC 66th Inf. Co.C
Swinson, Starkey W. GA 57th Inf. Co.I Cpl.
Swinson, T.E. GA Arty. (Macon Lt.Arty.) Slaten's Co.
Swinson, Thomas TX Cav. Ragsdale's Bn. Co.B
Swinson, T.J. TX Cav. Ragsdale's Bn. Co.B 2nd Lt.
Swinson, William P. GA 57th Inf. Co.I
Swinson, William P. MS 11th Inf. Co.H
Swinson, Young W. GA 20th Inf. Co.B
Swint, Andrew J. GA 21st Inf. Co.F
Swint, Bryant B. GA 44th Inf. Co.F
Swint, Daniel GA Lt.Arty. 12th Bn. 2nd Co.A Cpl.
Swint, Daniel GA 1st (Ramsey's) Inf. Co.A Sgt.
Swint, Daniel D. GA 48th Inf. Co.A
Swint, David D. AL Lt.Arty. Clanton's Btty.
Swint, Edmond GA 60th Inf. 1st Co.A
Swint, Edmund GA Hvy.Arty. 22nd Bn. Co.A
Swint, Edmund GA 15th Inf. Co.E Cpl.
Swint, G.W. AL 46th Inf.
Swint, G.W. GA Hvy.Arty. 22nd Bn. Co.A
Swint, G.W. GA 60th Inf. 1st Co.A
Swint, J. AL 4th Res. Co.E
Swint, J.G. AL 14th Inf. Co.C
Swint, John GA 21st Inf. Co.F
Swint, John B. GA 48th Inf. Co.A Cpl.
Swint, John G. AL 61st Inf. Co.F Cpl.
Swint, John T. GA 59th Inf. Co.I
Swint, Joseph AL 8th Inf. Co.F
Swint, J.S. GA 48th Inf. Co.A
Swint, Lee AL 61st Inf. Co.B
Swint, Moses T. GA 49th Inf. Co.C 2nd Lt.
Swint, Patrick H. GA 49th Inf. Co.C
Swint, Thomas GA 1st (Ramsey's) Inf. Co.A 1st Lt.
Swint, Thomas GA 7th Inf. (St.Guards) Co.H 1st Lt.
Swint, William AL 4th Res. Co.E
Swint, William TN 50th Inf. Co.C Cpl.
Swinter, W.A. GA 1st Inf. Co.E
Swintfield, Eidson NC 64th Inf. Co.M 2nd Lt.
Swintner, Joseph LA 21st (Patton's) Inf. Co.B
Swinton, --- SC 1st (Hagood's) Inf. Band (Col'd)
Swinton, E.C. SC 3rd Cav. Co.I
Swinton, Ed. S. SC 23rd Inf. Co.B Sgt.
Swinton, H.R. SC Mil. 1st Regt.Rifles Palmer's Co.
Swinton, James AL Mil. 4th Vol. Co.K
Swinton, R.H. SC Inf. 1st (Charleston) Bn. Co.E
Swinton, R.H. SC 27th Inf. Co.A
Swinton, Thomas L. SC 23rd Inf. Co.B Capt.
Swinton, T.L. SC 10th Inf. 1st Co.G Cpl.
Swinton, T.L. Gen. & Staff Capt.,AQM
Swipton, G.M. TX 1st Hvy.Arty. Co.I
Swire, P. TX 1st Hvy.Arty. Co.B 1st Sgt.
Swisher, A. MS 1st Lt.Arty. Co.I
Swisher, A. MO Robertson's Regt.St.Guard Co.3
Swisher, Abner P. TX Cav. Baylor's Regt. Co.D Capt.
Swisher, A.T. MO 12th Cav. Co.K 1st Sgt.
Swisher, B.B. VA 62nd Mtd.Inf. 1st Co.D
Swisher, Benjamin B. VA 14th Mil. Co.C
Swisher, Benjamin F. VA 114th Mil. Co.E
Swisher, Benjamin R. VA Lt.Arty. Arch. Graham's Co.
Swisher, B.F. VA 18th Cav. Co.C
Swisher, Daniel VA 14th Cav. Co.B
Swisher, Daniel VA 14th Cav. Co.H
Swisher, D.Z. VA 3rd Lt.Arty. (Loc.Def.) Co.D
Swisher, Elbert W. TN 43rd Inf. Co.K Sgt.
Swisher, George VA 18th Cav. Co.I
Swisher, George VA 62nd Mtd.Inf. 1st Co.D
Swisher, George W. VA Lt.Arty. Arch. Graham's Co.
Swisher, Greer F. TX 2nd Cav. Co.I
Swisher, Henry VA 10th Bn.Res. Co.B Cpl.
Swisher, Henry VA 27th Inf. Co.D
Swisher, Henry VA Rockbridge Cty.Res. Hutcheson's Co.
Swisher, Henry C. VA 114th Mil. Co.K
Swisher, James C. NC 6th Inf. Co.G
Swisher, James H. TN 43rd Inf. Co.K Sgt.
Swisher, J.H. VA 18th Cav. Co.E
Swisher, John VA 52nd Inf. Co.F
Swisher, John VA 114th Mil. Co.B
Swisher, John D. VA 37th Mil. Co.E
Swisher, John F. KY 3rd Cav. Co.F
Swisher, John F. KY 5th Cav. Co.F
Swisher, John H. TX 18th Cav. Co.B Sgt.
Swisher, Joseph VA 11th Cav. Co.E
Swisher, Joseph VA 18th Cav. Co.C,K
Swisher, Joseph VA 62nd Mtd.Inf. 1st Co.H
Swisher, Joseph H. VA 146th Mil. Co.G Cpl.
Swisher, Joseph J. VA 114th Mil. Co.G Cpl.
Swisher, M.A. NC Snead's Co. (Loc.Def.)
Swisher, M.S. MO 12th Cav.Co.K
Swisher, Samuel VA 114th Mil. Co.A
Swisher, Samuel S. VA Lt.Arty. Arch. Graham's Co.
Swisher, Simon W. VA 18th Cav. Co.K Cpl.
Swisher, Simon W. VA 114th Mil. Co.G Capt.
Swisher, Stephen VA 13th Inf. Co.I
Swisher, V.B. MO 12th Cav. Co.K Sgt.
Swisher, William F. VA 1st Cav. Co.A
Swisher, William F. VA 33rd Inf. Co.A
Swisher, William S. VA 5th Inf. Co.H Cpl.
Swisi, D. NC 29th Inf. Co.H
Swison, Jackson MO St.Guard
Swissher, Benjamin VA 18th Cav. Co.I
Switcher, F. MS 4th Inf. Co.G
Switcher, M.A.F. AL 12th Inf. Co.G
Swither, P.M. NC 5th Inf. Co.G
Switser, E. AL 31st Inf. Co.D
Switser, J.C. VA Inf. 26th Bn. Co.F
Swittenberg, A.M. MS 16th Inf. Co.H Color Cpl.
Swittenberg, John C. MS 16th Inf. Co.H Capt.
Swittenburg, D.R. SC 3rd Inf. Co.H
Swittenbury, A.J. SC 13th Inf. Co.H
Switzer, --- SC Inf. Hampton Legion Co.E
Switzer, A.A. MS 6th Inf. Co.D Ord.Sgt.
Switzer, A.A. MS 14th (Cons.) Inf. Co.A 1st Sgt.
Switzer, A.M. KY 3rd Mtd.Inf. Co.B
Switzer, Andrew VA 2nd Inf. Co.A
Switzer, Andrew VA 97th Mil. Co.D
Switzer, A.T. GA 17th Inf. Co.G
Switzer, A.T. GA Inf. 25th Bn. (Prov.Guard) Co.G
Switzer, Barnes H. AL Arty. 1st Bn. Co.C
Switzer, Benjamin W. MS 27th Inf. Co.C
Switzer, Bev. P. NC 1st Cav. (9th St.Troops) Co.A Saddler
Switzer, Beverly P. NC 6th Cav. (65th St.Troops) Co.D,B
Switzer, B.W. TN 4th Inf. Co.C
Switzer, C. VA 33rd Inf. Co.I
Switzer, C.A. AR 4th Inf. Co.F
Switzer, Cary A. VA 57th Inf. Co.K
Switzer, Christian VA 52nd Inf. Co.F
Switzer, C.P. VA 2nd Cav. Co.C
Switzer, C.P. VA Burks' Regt.Loc.Def. Price's Co.
Switzer, D. FL Lt.Arty. Dyke's Co.
Switzer, Daniel KY 9th Mtd.Inf. Co.I
Switzer, Daniel VA 58th Mil. Co.E
Switzer, David S. MS 27th Inf. Co.C 1st Sgt.
Switzer, D.M. VA 146th Mil. Co.F
Switzer, D.S. TN 4th Inf. Co.C
Switzer, E.A. LA Red River S.S.
Switzer, Edward G. GA Cobb's Legion Co.A
Switzer, F.R. MO 2nd Cav. Co.D
Switzer, F.R. MO 10th Inf. Co.A
Switzer, Frederick A. AR Cav. Wright's Regt. Co.H
Switzer, Frederick A. AR 37th Inf. Co.G 2nd Lt.
Switzer, George M. VA 24th Inf. Co.A
Switzer, H.C. TX Cav. Waller's Regt. Co.C Sgt.
Switzer, H.S. AR 37th Inf. Co.A Jr.2nd Lt.
Switzer, J. LA Mil. Fire Bn. Co.B
Switzer, J. VA Cav. Hounshell's Bn. Co.A
Switzer, Jacob VA 2nd Inf. Co.G
Switzer, Jacob D. VA 7th Bn.Res. Co.D
Switzer, James KY 9th Mtd.Inf. Co.I
Switzer, James MS 5th Cav. Co.D
Switzer, James R. AR 4th Inf. Co.F 2nd Bvt.Lt.
Switzer, John AR 9th Inf. Co.K
Switzer, John KY 9th Mtd.Inf. Co.I
Switzer, John LA Inf. 1st Sp.Bn. (Wheat's) Co.A
Switzer, John A. MD 1st Cav. Co.I
Switzer, John A. VA 58th Mil. Co.D 2nd Lt.
Switzer, John C. AL 37th Inf. Co.D
Switzer, John D. SC Inf. Holcombe Legion Co.A
Switzer, John G. GA 1st (Olmstead's) Inf. Co.I
Switzer, J.R. SC 5th St.Troops Co.I
Switzer, J.R. SC 9th Res. Co.C
Switzer, J.T. MS 28th Cav. Co.D
Switzer, J.T. MS 28th Cav. Co.I
Switzer, Leonard P. MS 14th Inf. Co.I
Switzer, L.O. SC Inf. 3rd Bn. Co.E
Switzer, L.O. SC 27th Inf. Co.D
Switzer, L.P. MS 14th (Cons.) Inf. Co.D
Switzer, Nathan VA 60th Inf. Co.K
Switzer, Newton VA Burks' Regt.Loc.Def. Beckner's Co.
Switzer, N.W. VA 97th Mil. Co.D

Switzer, P. LA Mil. Fire Bn. Co.B
Switzer, Phillip VA 62nd Mtd.Inf. 2nd Co.A
Switzer, S. VA Burks' Regt.Loc.Def. McCues' Co.
Switzer, Samuel C. VA 33rd Inf. Co.I Sgt.
Switzer, Samuel C. VA 97th Mil. Co.D 1st Sgt.
Switzer, Samuel H. VA 52nd Inf. Co.A
Switzer, Taylor KY 9th Mtd.Inf. Co.I
Switzer, Valentine C. VA 33rd Inf. Co.I
Switzer, V.C. VA 97th Mil. Co.D
Switzer, W.A. KY 5th Cav. Co.I 1st Sgt.
Switzer, W.A. KY 9th Cav. Co.A
Switzer, W.C. MS Scouts Morphis' Ind.Co. Cpl.
Switzer, William KY 5th Mtd.Inf. Co.F
Switzer, William MO 1st N.E. Cav. Co.E 1st Sgt.
Switzer, William B. VA 4th Inf. Co.E
Switzer, William I. VA 33rd Inf. Co.I
Switzer, William T. VA 30th Bn.S.S. Co.A
Switzer, W.M. MS Grace's Co. (St.Troops)
Switzer, W.O. VA 25th Cav. Co.E
Swizer, J.W. LA Red River S.S.
Swoap, George C. TN 18th Inf. Co.A Sgt.
Swoard, J.F. VA Inf. 26th Bn. Co.C
Swob, Joseph KY 7th Mtd.Inf. 1st Co.K Sgt.
Swocker, James VA 51st Inf. Co.B
Swoffield, W.C. FL 2nd Cav.
Swofford, Allen TN 43rd Inf. Co.C
Swofford, A.T. TN 43rd Inf. Co.I
Swofford, B.F. TN 43rd Inf. Co.H
Swofford, Caswell TN 27th Inf. Co.I
Swofford, D.F. TN 27th Inf. Co.F Cpl.
Swofford, D.H. GA 39th Inf. Co.C
Swofford, E.Z. TN 43rd Inf. Co.I
Swofford, George TN 35th Inf. Co.L
Swofford, George TN 36th Inf. Co.L
Swofford, George Conf.Inf. 1st Bn. Co.F
Swofford, George W. GA 11th Inf. Co.A Bvt.2nd Lt.
Swofford, G.W. TX Cav. Benavides' Regt. Co.C
Swofford, Henry TN 5th (McKenzie's) Cav. Co.E
Swofford, Jackson TN 42nd Inf. 1st Co.K
Swofford, James SC 13th Inf. Co.E
Swofford, James TN 43rd Inf. Co.C
Swofford, James B. MO 9th (Elliott's) Cav. Co.A
Swofford, James B. TN 43rd Inf. Co.B
Swofford, James J. GA 65th Inf. Co.K
Swofford, J.B. MS 22nd Inf.
Swofford, J.L.M. TN 43rd Inf. Co.H
Swofford, John TN 36th Inf. Co.F
Swofford, John TN 36th Inf. Co.G
Swofford, John TN 42nd Inf. 1st Co.K
Swofford, John W. TN 43rd Inf. Co.H
Swofford, J.R. MS 8th Cav. Co.B
Swofford, J.W. TN 43rd Inf. Co.H Cpl.
Swofford, Martin V. TN 43rd Inf. Co.C
Swofford, Miles GA 43rd Inf. Co.L,C
Swofford, M.N. TN 43rd Inf. Co.H
Swofford, P.B. TN 43rd Inf. Co.I
Swofford, R. TN 36th Inf. Co.G
Swofford, Reuben TN 36th Inf. Co.F
Swofford, Robert NC 55th Inf. Co.F
Swofford, Samuel TN 43rd Inf. Co.C
Swofford, Thomas AL 4th Cav.
Swofford, Thomas GA Lt.Arty. 14th Bn. Co.D
Swofford, Thomas GA Lt.Arty. King's Btty.
Swofford, William TN 42nd Inf. 1st Co.K
Swofford, Thomas TN 43rd Inf. Co.C
Swofford, Thomas TN 43rd Inf. Co.H
Swofford, William N. GA 43rd Inf. Co.C Sgt.
Swofford, William R. LA Inf. 4th Bn. Co.F Sgt.
Swofford, W.J. AL 4th Inf. Co.I
Swoft, Charles T. Gen. & Staff ACS
Swon, H.C. MO Cav. 1st Regt.St.Guard Co.C
Swon, N.P. AR Inf. 4th Bn. Co.E
Swoop, Sebastian LA Mil.Cont.Regt. Mitchell's Co.
Swoope, Bowling VA Horse Arty. Lurty's Co.
Swoope, B.R. VA 19th Cav.
Swoope, B.R. VA 5th Inf. Co.L
Swoope, Charles VA 5th Inf. Co.L
Swoope, Francis M. VA Lt.Arty. Carrington's Co. 2nd Lt.
Swoope, George W. VA 5th Inf. Co.L 1st Lt.
Swoope, George W. VA 21st Inf. Co.E 1st Lt.
Swoope, J.K. AL 5th Cav. Co.K Capt.
Swoope, J.K. MS 2nd Part. Co.A
Swoope, L. VA 9th Cav. Co.H
Swoope, LaFayette AL 16th Inf. Co.I Capt.
Swoope, Samuel J. AL 16th Inf. Co.C
Swoot, B.S. AL Talladega Cty.Res. W.Y. Hendrick's Co.
Swope, --- VA 7th Bn.Res. Co.D
Swope, B.A. TX 34th Cav. Co.I
Swope, C.C. AL 5th Cav. AQM
Swope, C.C. Gen. & Staff Capt.,AQM
Swope, D. GA Inf. Ezzard's Co.
Swope, David GA 2nd Res. Co.A
Swope, D.M. KY 10th (Johnson's) Cav. Co.A 1st Lt.
Swope, Felix F. KY 3rd Cav. Co.I
Swope, Felix H. KY 6th Cav. Co.A
Swope, F.F. KY 7th Cav. Co.I
Swope, Frederick VA Hvy.Arty. 18th Bn. Co.E
Swope, G.A. AL Inf. 1st Regt. Co.D
Swope, G.H. TN 13th (Gore's) Cav. Co.E Capt.
Swope, Grandison H. TN 25th Inf. Co.H Capt.
Swope, Henry VA 27th Inf. Co.D
Swope, J.F. GA Lt.Arty. (Arsenal Btty.) Hudson's Co.
Swope, J.J. AL Cav. Hardie's Bn.Res. Co.F
Swope, J.J. AL 30th Inf. Co.G
Swope, John VA 9th Bn.Res. Co.C
Swope, John F. GA 36th (Villepigue's) Inf. Co.B
Swope, John H. VA 20th Cav. Co.E
Swope, John R. VA 58th Mil. Co.G
Swope, John S. TX 2nd Cav. Co.I
Swope, Peter VA 9th Bn.Res. Co.A
Swope, R.E. AL 5th Inf. Co.B
Swope, Robert L. AZ Cav. Herbert's Bn. Swope's Co. Capt.
Swope, S.A. TN 84th Inf. Co.C
Swope, W. AL 63rd Inf. Co.K
Swope, William L. VA Lt.Arty. G.B. Chapman's Co.
Swope, William L VA 166th Mil. Ballard's Co. Cpl.
Swopes, Robert MO 11th Inf. Co.K
Swopshire, Joseph TN 62nd Mtd.Inf. Co.C
Swor, Albert G. MS 27th Inf. Co.F Sgt.
Swor, Claudius TN 46th Inf. Co.A
Swor, G.W.L. TN 5th Inf. Co.A Sgt.
Swor, P.G. TN 5th Inf. 2nd Co.C Capt.
Swor, William C. TN 5th Inf. Lt.Col.
Swor, William H. MS 2nd Inf. (A. of 10,000) Co.A
Swor, W.R. TN 5th Inf. Co.A
Sword, Eli VA 22nd Inf. Co.E
Sword, Henry TN 2nd (Ashby's) Cav. Co.B
Sword, Henry TN Cav. 5th Bn. (McClellan's) Co.C
Sword, James W. KY 5th Mtd.Inf. Co.G Sgt.
Sword, John LA 15th Inf. Co.D
Sword, Joshua F. VA 108th Mil. McNeer's Co.
Sword, J.T. VA 22nd Inf. Co.E
Sword, Michael VA Inf. 21st Bn. Co.B
Sword, Nathan VA 19th Cav. Co.F,G Sgt.
Sword, Nathan H. TN Cav. 5th Bn. (McClellan's) Co.C
Sword, N.H. TN 2nd (Ashby's) Cav. Co.B
Sword, Richard VA 37th Inf. Co.G
Sword, Thomas J. VA 22nd Inf. Co.E
Sword, Washington KY 5th Mtd.Inf. Co.G
Sword, William KY 5th Mtd.Inf. Co.G
Swords, A.J. GA 2nd Cav. Co.D Sgt.
Swords, A.J. MS 41st Inf. Co.F
Swords, A.J. Horse Arty. White's Btty.
Swords, A.J.T. AL 31st Inf. Co.B Cpl.
Swords, Alonzo MS 12th Inf. Co.E
Swords, Andrew J. GA 1st Reg. Co.F
Swords, Benj. A. AL 4th (Russell's) Cav.
Swords, Benj. A. TN 3rd (Forrest's) Cav. Co.G
Swords, Cornelius A. SC 7th Inf. 2nd Co.H
Swords, Harvey Z. SC Arty. Bachman's Co. (German Lt.Arty.)
Swords, Henry GA Cav. 24th Bn. Co.A
Swords, Henry GA 1st Bn.S.S. Co.A
Swords, H.H. GA 56th Inf. Co.H
Swords, H.Z. SC 4th Cav. Co.C
Swords, H.Z. SC Cav. 10th Bn. Co.B
Swords, Irvin AL Cav. Lewis' Bn. Co.C
Swords, J. GA Lt.Arty. Barnwell's Btty.
Swords, James AL 24th Inf.
Swords, James B. AL 4th (Russell's) Cav. Co.I,F 1st Sgt.
Swords, Jasper SC 20th Inf. Co.C
Swords, J.H. GA 2nd Cav. Co.D
Swords, J.I. GA Lt.Arty. Barnwell's Btty
Swords, J.K. TX 7th Inf. Co.B
Swords, John GA Cav. Roswell Bn. Co.C
Swords, John TN Inf. Nashville Bn. Fulcher's Co.
Swords, John J. GA Arty. Maxwell's Reg. Lt.Btty.
Swords, John W. GA 51st Inf. Co.H
Swords, J.P. VA 3rd Inf.Loc.Def. Co.C
Swords, J.W. KY 4th Cav. Co.D
Swords, Lewis GA 35th Inf. Co.G
Swords, Marion F. GA 1st Regt.St.Troops Cowan's Co.
Swords, Matthew LA Mil. British Guard Bn. Kurczyn's Co.
Swords, Owen AR 15th (Josey's) Inf. Co.G Cpl.
Swords, Pat GA 10th Inf. Co.A
Swords, Robert D. VA 1st Inf. Co.H
Swords, Shelton AL 4th Cav. Co.I
Swords, Shelton AL 4th (Russell's) Cav. Co.I
Swords, S.J. AL 31st Inf. Co.C Ord.Sgt.
Swords, S.P. AL 31st Inf. Co.B
Swords, T.H. GA 2nd Cav. Co.D

Swords, Thomas AL 57th Inf.
Swords, Thomas LA Mil. British Guard Bn. Kurczyn's Co.
Swords, Thomas TN 1st Hvy.Arty. 2nd Co.C
Swords, Thomas F. AL 4th (Russell's) Cav. Co.I
Swords, Thomas W. TN 1st (Feild's) Inf.
Swords, William MS 11th (Cons.) Cav. Co.E
Swords, William MS 12th Inf. Co.E
Swords, William MS 41st Inf. Co.B
Swords, William S. SC 7th Inf. 2nd Co.H
Swords, W.J. GA 51st Inf. Co.H
Sworford, Howard TN 13th (Gore's) Cav. Co.I
Sworford, James NC 1st Bn.Jr.Res. Co.A
Sworford, J.M. TN 13th (Gore's) Cav. Co.I
Sworford, J.P. TN 13th (Gore's) Cav. Co.I
Sworich, Gilford NC 1st Arty. (10th St.Troops) Co.F
Swortzel, Henry S. VA Hvy.Arty. 19th Bn. Co.D
Swortzel, J.A. TN Inf. 2nd Cons.Regt. Co.E
Swortzel, Jacob L. VA 5th Inf. Co.A
Swortzel, Lorenzo N. VA 5th Bn.Res. Co.D
Swortzel, Lorenzo N. VA 7th Bn.Res. Co.D
Sworzel, David VA 8th Bn.Res. Co.D
Swrader, David VA 151st Mil. Co.D
Swrader, Robert VA 151st Mil. Co.D
Swronce, George NC 12th Inf. Co.E
Swunok Yohola 1st Seminole Mtd.Vol.
Swycord, Mathew GA Lt.Arty. Daniell's Btty.
Swygart, E.Z. SC 15th Inf. Co.C 1st Lt.
Swygart, Henry A. SC 5th Cav. Co.F
Swygart, Henry A. SC Cav. 14th Bn. Co.C
Swygart, Jesse SC 5th Cav. Co.F
Swygart, J.J. SC 5th Cav. Co.F
Swygart, Job SC Cav. 14th Bn. Co.C
Swygart, Job A. SC 5th Cav. Co.F
Swygart, J.W. SC Cav. 19th Bn. Co.B
Swygart, L.C. SC 5th Cav. Co.F
Swygart, M.S. SC 5th Cav. Co.F
Swygert, George S. SC 3rd Inf. Co.H Capt.
Swygert, Joseph H. SC 1st (McCreary's) Inf. Co.C
Swygert, J.W. SC 20th Inf. Co.C,M
Swygert, M.G. GA Inf. 40th Bn. Co.F
Swygert, Morgan G. GA 41st Inf. Co.A
Swygover, Thomas J. GA Cav. 1st Bn. Lamar's Co., Brailsford's Co.
Swymer, J.M. GA Hvy.Arty. 22nd Bn. Co.E
Swytcer, William AR 4th Inf. Co.B
Swytcer, W.L. AR 1st Mtd.Rifles Co.E
Syberg, Arnold Conf.Eng.,CSA Capt.,Ch.Eng.
Sybert, Robert J. AL 7th Cav. Co.K
Sybert, Sol Lt.Arty. Dent's Btty.,CSA
Sybert, William VA 48th Inf. Co.G
Sybley, James A. GA 28th Inf. Co.E
Sydam, J.W. NC Loc.Def. Croom's Co.
Sydell, I.E. TX Inf. Timmons' Regt. Co.K
Sydensticker, Jacob H. VA 59th Inf. 1st Co.F
Sydenstricher, H. VA Inf. 26th Bn.
Sydenstricker, Charles A. VA 59th Inf. 1st Co.G
Sydenstricker, Charles L. VA 14th Cav. Co.D
Sydenstricker, Charles L. VA 59th Inf. 2nd Co.B
Sydenstricker, Christopher VA 26th Cav. Co.D
Sydenstricker, David VA 22nd Inf. Taylor's Co.
Sydenstricker, David VA 60th Inf. Co.E
Sydenstricker, Isaac C. VA Inf. 26th Bn. Co.D 1st Sgt.
Sydenstricker, Isaac C. VA 135th Mil. Co.D
Sydenstricker, James VA 14th Cav. Co.D
Sydenstricker, James VA 59th Inf. 2nd Co.B
Sydenstricker, James H. VA 60th Inf. Co.E
Sydenstricker, Jehu VA Lt.Arty. Turner's Co. 1st Lt.
Sydenstricker, Jehu VA Arty. Wise Legion 1st Sgt.
Sydenstricker, John F. VA Cav. Hounshell's Bn. Co.A
Sydenstricker, John H. VA Inf. 26th Bn. Co.D Cpl.
Sydenstricker, John M. VA Inf. 26th Bn. Co.D Ord.Sgt.
Sydenstricker, John M. VA 60th Inf. Co.E
Sydenstricker, John N. VA 22nd Inf. Taylor's Co.
Sydenstricker, J.T. VA 135th Mil. Co.I
Sydenstricker, Oliver P. VA 60th Inf. Co.E 1st Lt.,Adj.
Sydenstricker, O.P. Gen. & Staff 1st Lt.,Adj.
Sydenstricker, Washington M. VA 46th Inf. Co.C
Sydenstricker, W.M. VA 60th Inf. Co.B
Sydenstriker, Charles A. VA 60th Inf. Co.C
Sydenstriker, Jacob H. VA 60th Inf. Co.C
Sydenstriker, John VA Cav. Hounshell's Bn. Co.A
Syder, L.W. VA 33rd Inf. Co.D
Sydner, J.B. TX Cav. Border's Bn. Co.D Capt.
Sydner, John LA Inf. 4th Bn. Co.A
Sydner, Robert VA Cav. 15th Bn. Co.D
Sydner, Walter VA 1st (Farinholt's) Res. Co.F Sgt.Maj.
Sydney, John LA Inf. 1st Sp.Bn. (Wheat's) Co.C
Sydnor, A. VA 14th Inf. Co.H
Sydnor, Addison VA Cav. 15th Bn. Co.D
Sydnor, Addison VA 40th Inf. Co.E
Sydnor, Addison VA 41st Mil. Co.C
Sydnor, A. Judson VA 40th Inf. Co.B Capt.
Sydnor, Alex VA Lt.Arty. 13th Bn. Co.B
Sydnor, Anthony T. VA 14th Inf. Co.K
Sydnor, Charles W. VA Horse Arty. E. Graham's Co.
Sydnor, C.W. 2nd Corps A. of N.VA Hosp.Stew.
Sydnor, Dandridge VA 40th Inf. Co.E
Sydnor, E. Garland VA 18th Inf. Co.G
Sydnor, Eppa VA 14th Inf. Co.H 2nd Lt.
Sydnor, Fauntleroy VA 51st Mil. Co.D
Sydnor, Fortunatus VA Cav. 15th Bn. Co.D
Sydnor, Fortunatus VA 40th Inf.
Sydnor, Fortunatus VA 41st Mil. Co.C
Sydnor, George B. VA 4th Cav. Co.G Sgt.
Sydnor, George F. VA 12th Cav. Co.C
Sydnor, George W. VA 41st Mil. Co.B
Sydnor, Giles VA 14th Inf. Co.H
Sydnor, Giles VA 38th Inf. Co.H
Sydnor, G.R. VA Cav. Mosby's Regt. (Part. Rangers)
Sydnor, James VA Cav. 15th Bn. Co.D
Sydnor, James B. VA 37th Mil. Co.E
Sydnor, J.B. TX Cav. Border' Regt. Co.D Capt.
Sydnor, J.L. VA 4th Cav. Co.G
Sydnor, John VA Cav. 15th Bn. Co.D
Sydnor, John VA 40th Inf. Co.E
Sydnor, John VA 41st Mil. Co.C
Sydnor, Jno. B. Gen. & Staff Capt.,ACS
Sydnor, John T. VA Inf. 5th Bn. Co.B Sgt.
Sydnor, J.T. VA 53rd Inf. Co.G
Sydnor, Louis R. VA 3rd Cav. 2nd Co.I
Sydnor, Napoleon B. VA 9th Cav. Co.K
Sydnor, P.T. VA 13th Cav. Co.F
Sydnor, R.B.D. VA 40th Inf. Co.B 3rd Lt.
Sydnor, Richard H. VA 12th Cav. Co.C 3rd Lt.
Sydnor, Richard H. VA 51st Mil. Co.D 1st Lt.
Sydnor, R.L. VA Lt.Arty. Penick's Co.
Sydnor, R.L. Conf.Lt.Arty. Richardson's Bn. Co.A
Sydnor, Robert VA 15th Cav. Co.G
Sydnor, Robert T. VA 1st Arty. Co.D
Sydnor, Robert T. VA Lt.Arty. 1st Bn. Co.D
Sydnor, Roger J. VA Arty. B.H. Smith's Co.
Sydnor, R.W. VA 1st (Farinholt's) Res. Co.F Capt.
Sydnor, R.W. VA Averett's Bn.Res. 1st Lt.
Sydnor, Samuel VA 40th Inf. Co.E
Sydnor, S.H. VA 3rd Inf.Loc.Def. Co.C
Sydnor, S.H. VA 14th Inf. Co.H
Sydnor, Silas H. VA 51st Mil. Co.D
Sydnor, Stephen C. VA Lt.Arty. Kirkpatrick's Co.
Sydnor, Stephen C. VA Lt.Arty. Nelson's Co.
Sydnor, Stephen C. VA 56th Inf. Co.K
Sydnor, S.W. TX 26th Cav. Co.C 1st Lt.
Sydnor, Thomas VA 9th Cav. Co.K
Sydnor, Thomas VA 41st Mil. Co.C
Sydnor, Thomas W. VA 4th Cav. Co.G 1st Lt.
Sydnor, W.A. AR 2nd Cav. 1st Co.A
Sydnor, W.A. AR 3rd Cav. 3rd Co.E
Sydnor, Washington F. VA 41st Inf. Co.C, 2nd Co.G Capt.
Sydnor, W.H. VA 3rd Cav. Co.A
Sydnor, William VA 9th Cav. Co.K
Sydnor, William VA 26th Cav. Co.B
Sydnor, William B. VA 41st Mil. Co.C
Sydnor, William I. VA Lt.Arty. 1st Bn. Co.D QMSgt.
Sydnor, William J. VA 1st Arty. Co.D QMSgt.
Sydnor, William J. VA Arty. B.H. Smith's Co. QMSgt.
Sydnor, William P. VA 9th Cav. Co.D
Sydon, J. TX Waul's Legion Co.C
Sydow, Jul TX Inf. Timmons' Regt. Co.K
Syer, Charles S. VA 6th Inf. 1st Co.E Sgt.
Syer, Charles S. VA 61st Inf. Co.D Sgt.
Syer, William LA Mil. 2nd Regt. 3rd Brig. 1st Div. Co.K 3rd Lt.
Syfan, Charles E. SC 20th Inf. Co.G
Syfret, D. FL 1st (Res.) Inf. Co.E
Syfret, D. FL Conscr.
Syfret, William SC 24th Inf. Co.C
Syfrett, A.J. SC 1st (Hagood's) Inf. 1st Co.C
Syfrett, Alfred FL 11th Inf. Co.K
Syfrett, C.W. SC 1st (Hagood's) Inf. 1st Co.C
Syfrett, Francis FL 11th Inf. Co.K
Syfrett, Silas FL Inf. 2nd Bn. Co.E
Syfrett, Thomas A. FL 11th Inf. Co.K
Syfritt, A.J. SC 2nd Arty. Co.F
Syfritt, C.W. SC 2nd Arty. Co.F
Sykes, --- TX Cav. 4th Regt.St.Troops Co.C
Sykes, A. Exch.Bn. 2nd Co.C, 3rd Co.B,CSA
Sykes, Abner C. MS 24th Inf. Co.C
Sykes, Abner D. MS 20th Inf. Co.B

Sykes, A.D. FL 9th Inf. Co.B,F
Sykes, A. Epps GA 15th Inf. Co.E
Sykes, A.F. NC 2nd Jr.Res. Co.B Cpl.
Sykes, A.J. AL 56th Part.Rangers Adj.
Sykes, A.J. AL Cav. Murphy's Bn. Co.B
Sykes, A.J. GA Conscr.
Sykes, A.J. Gen. & Staff 1st Lt.,Adj.
Sykes, Alexander AL 6th Inf. Co.B
Sykes, Alexander F. VA 41st Inf. Co.F
Sykes, Andrew J. MS 48th Inf. Co.L
Sykes, Andrew J. Gen. & Staff Surg.
Sykes, Archelaus C. MS 30th Inf. Co.C
Sykes, Aug. J. AL 15th Bn.Part.Rangers Co.B Adj.
Sykes, Bartlett VA 61st Inf. Co.E
Sykes, Bedford FL 1st (Res.) Inf. Co.G
Sykes, Benjamin F. NC 56th Inf. Co.E
Sykes, Benjamin S. NC 12th Inf. Co.N
Sykes, Benjamin S. NC 32nd Inf. Co.B,C Sgt.
Sykes, Bennett D. NC 56th Inf. Co.E
Sykes, Caleb NC 4th Cav. (59th St.Troops) Co.G
Sykes, Caleb NC Hvy.Arty. 10th Bn. Co.D Music.
Sykes, Calvin L. NC 44th Inf. Co.G
Sykes, Charles SC 4th Bn.Res. Co.D
Sykes, Charles SC 5th St.Troops Co.D
Sykes, Charles SC 9th Res. Co.B
Sykes, Clinton 7th Conf.Cav. Co.F
Sykes, Clinton 8th (Dearing's) Conf.Cav. Co.G
Sykes, C.M. NC 51st Inf. Co.C
Sykes, Columbus MS 43rd Inf. Co.A Lt.Col.
Sykes, Cornelius VA Cav. 14th Bn. Co.A
Sykes, C.W. NC 44th Inf. Co.G
Sykes, Cyrus TN 51st Inf. Co.H Bvt.2nd Lt.
Sykes, Cyrus TN 51st (Cons.) Inf. Co.D 2nd Lt.
Sykes, David G. NC 33rd Inf. Co.F
Sykes, David M. NC 44th Inf. Co.G Sgt.
Sykes, E.A. GA 59th Inf. Co.I
Sykes, Edgar MS Lt.Arty. Stanford's Co.
Sykes, Edgar MS 15th Inf. Co.E Capt.
Sykes, Edward S. MS 30th Inf. Co.I Sgt.
Sykes, Edward T. MS 10th Inf. Old Co.E, New Co.K Capt.
Sykes, Edwin TN 10th Inf.
Sykes, E.F. AL 11th Inf. Co.I
Sykes, E.H. AL 57th Inf. Co.F
Sykes, E.L. MS 6th Cav. Morgan's Co. Sgt.
Sykes, E.L. MS 12th Cav. Co.C Sgt.
Sykes, E.P. GA 59th Inf. Music.
Sykes, E.T. Gen. & Staff Capt.,AAG
Sykes, Eugene O. MS 14th Inf. Co.I Capt.
Sykes, Eugene O. Gen. & Staff, Inf. 2nd Lt.
Sykes, Francis M. MS 30th Inf. Co.C
Sykes, Francis T. NC 44th Inf. Co.K
Sykes, Frederick R. VA 32nd Inf. Co.C
Sykes, G.A. AL 34th Inf. Co.C
Sykes, George FL 9th Inf. Co.C
Sykes, George LA 5th Inf. Co.C
Sykes, George A. LA 30th Inf. Co.F,G
Sykes, George A. VA 61st Inf. Co.B
Sykes, George M. TN 6th Inf. Co.H Cpl.
Sykes, George T. GA 20th Inf. Co.B
Sykes, Harper VA 16th Inf. Co.G
Sykes, Henry A. TX 24th Cav. Co.D
Sykes, Henry C. NC 28th Inf. Co.G
Sykes, Henry C. VA 61st Inf. Co.A
Sykes, Horatio R.E. NC Lt.Arty. 3rd Bn. Co.A
Sykes, H.P. NC Cav. 15th Bn. Co.C
Sykes, H.P. NC 15th Inf. Co.C
Sykes, Hugh A. VA 41st Inf. 2nd Co.E
Sykes, Isaac GA Phillips' Legion Co.E Music.
Sykes, Isaac P. FL 2nd Inf. Co.H
Sykes, Isaiah FL 9th Inf. Co.B
Sykes, J. GA Cav. 1st Bn. Walthour's Co.
Sykes, J. MS 6th Inf. Co.G
Sykes, J. MS 24th Inf. Co.E
Sykes, J.A. AL Inf. 2nd Regt. Co.A
Sykes, J.A. NC Lt.Arty. 13th Bn. Co.C
Sykes, Jacob GA 4th (Clinch's) Cav. Co.D
Sykes, Jacob GA 19th Inf. Co.G
Sykes, Jacob F. GA 26th Inf. Co.A Cpl.
Sykes, James FL 9th Inf. Co.F
Sykes, James GA 5th Res. Co.G,I
Sykes, James GA 16th Inf. Co.G
Sykes, James MS Inf. 1st St.Troops Co.D
Sykes, James TN 19th & 20th (Cons.) Cav. Co.B
Sykes, James B. NC Hvy.Arty. 10th Bn. Co.B
Sykes, James D. MS 41st Inf. Co.G
Sykes, James H. NC 47th Inf. Co.E
Sykes, James M. TN 18th (Newsom's) Cav. Co.B,G
Sykes, James M.D. NC Cav. (Loc.Def.) Howard's Co.
Sykes, James T. NC 15th Inf. Co.A
Sykes, James T. NC 23rd Inf. Co.A
Sykes, James W. GA Carlton's Co. (Troup Cty.Arty.)
Sykes, James W. MS Cav. 4th Bn. Sykes' Co. Capt.
Sykes, James W. VA 41st Inf. Co.F
Sykes, James Wesley NC 47th Inf. Co.E
Sykes, Jasper J. NC 28th Inf. Co.G
Sykes, J.B. 2nd Conf.Eng.Troops Co.A
Sykes, Jesse VA 54th Mil. Co.C,D
Sykes, Jesse F. VA Hvy.Arty. 20th Bn. Co.B
Sykes, Jesse F. VA 38th Inf. 2nd Co.I
Sykes, Jesse W. TN Cav. 1st Bn. (McNairy's) Co.A
Sykes, J.H. NC 16th Inf. Co.G
Sykes, J.H.M. Gen. & Staff Asst.Surg.
Sykes, J.J. AR Lt.Arty. (Helena Arty.) Clarkson's Btty.
Sykes, J.J. MS 1st Cav.Res. Co.K
Sykes, J.N. NC 16th Inf. Co.B
Sykes, J.O. MS 32nd Inf. Co.B
Sykes, John AL 20th Inf. Co.I
Sykes, John AL 26th Inf. Co.I
Sykes, John AL 34th Inf. Co.D
Sykes, John GA 3rd Cav. (St.Guards) Co.K
Sykes, John KY 7th Mtd.Inf. Co.K
Sykes, John NC 1st Arty. (10th St.Troops) Co.F
Sykes, John NC 6th Inf. Co.F
Sykes, John NC 66th Inf. Co.I
Sykes, John TN 22nd Inf. Looney's Co.
Sykes, John TN 38th Inf. Co.L
Sykes, John VA Arty. C.F. Johnston's Co.
Sykes, John VA 9th Inf. Co.E
Sykes, John VA 37th Inf. Co.G
Sykes, John 7th Conf.Cav. Co.F
Sykes, John 8th (Dearing's) Conf.Cav. Co.G
Sykes, John A. NC 28th Inf. Co.G
Sykes, John A. NC 47th Inf. Co.E
Sykes, John C. VA 5th Cav. (12 mo. '61-2) Co.H
Sykes, John C. VA 3rd Inf. Co.G
Sykes, John C.C. VA 61st Inf. Co.A
Sykes, John F. GA 44th Inf. Co.D
Sykes, John H. AL 8th (Hatch's) Cav. Co.K
Sykes, John Henry MS Inf. 1st St.Troops Co.D
Sykes, John J. AR 2nd Mtd.Rifles Co.A
Sykes, John J. VA 6th Inf. Co.F
Sykes, John R. AL 39th Inf. Co.B Cpl.
Sykes, Johnson C. NC 28th Inf. Co.G
Sykes, John T. NC Inf. 13th Bn. Co.D 2nd Lt.
Sykes, John T. NC 18th Inf. Co.I Cpl.
Sykes, John T. NC 66th Inf. Co.K Capt.
Sykes, John V. GA 26th Inf. Co.A
Sykes, John W. AL Lt.Arty. 2nd Bn. Co.F
Sykes, John W. GA 59th Inf. Co.F
Sykes, John W. NC 14th Inf. Co.K
Sykes, Joseph FL 9th Inf. Co.B
Sykes, Joseph FL 10th Inf. Co.D
Sykes, Joseph TN Cav. 16th Bn. (Neal's) Co.C Bugler
Sykes, Joseph VA 61st Inf. Co.A
Sykes, Joseph A. MS 17th Inf. Co.A Adj.
Sykes, Jos. A. Gen. & Staff 1st Lt.,Adj.
Sykes, Joseph A.J. VA Lt.Arty. Pegram's Co.
Sykes, Joseph B. TN 6th Inf. Co.H
Sykes, Joseph H.M. VA 3rd Inf. Co.G Asst.Surg.
Sykes, Joseph P. AL Lt.Arty. 2nd Bn. Co.F Cadet
Sykes, Joseph P. TN Inf. Nashville Bn. Fulcher's Co. Cadet
Sykes, Joseph S. GA Cav. 7th Bn. (St.Guards) Co.E
Sykes, Joseph S. GA 59th Inf. Co.I 2nd Lt.
Sykes, Josephus VA 61st Inf. Co.A
Sykes, Josiah GA 4th (Clinch's) Cav. Co.D,I
Sykes, Josiah J. VA 61st Inf. Co.I,K
Sykes, Josiah J. VA Inf. Cohoon's Bn. Co.C
Sykes, J.P. VA 5th Bn.Res. Co.E Capt.
Sykes, J.P. Gen. & Staff Cadet,AAIG
Sykes, J.T. MS 43rd Inf. Co.L
Sykes, J. Thomas KY Warren Cty. Suspected Spy
Sykes, J.W. MS 6th Inf. Co.K Sgt.
Sykes, J.W. MS 41st Inf. Co.F
Sykes, J.W. NC 1st Jr.Res. Co.I
Sykes, J.W. TN 6th Inf. Co.H
Sykes, J.W. TN 38th Inf. Co.E Sgt.
Sykes, J.W. TX 3rd Cav. Co.B
Sykes, Lawson MS 1st (Patton's) Inf. Co.B
Sykes, Lawson W. MS 43rd Inf. Co.A
Sykes, Levander AR 26th Inf. Co.H
Sykes, Levi VA 72nd Mil.
Sykes, Lewis M. AL 21st Inf. Co.C
Sykes, L.J. AL Gid Nelson Lt.Arty.
Sykes, L.M. MS Cav. 1st Bn. (Miller's) Co.A
Sykes, L.M. Gen. & Staff Prov.Marsh.
Sykes, L.S. TN Cav. 16th Bn. (Neal's) Co.C
Sykes, Lum MS 41st Inf. Co.L
Sykes, Mabon NC 44th Inf. Co.K
Sykes, Marcus NC 26th Inf. Co.B
Sykes, Matthew P. NC 2nd Arty. (36th St.Troops) Co.B
Sykes, M.D. VA Inf. Cohoon's Bn. Co.A
Sykes, Milton MS Inf. 1st Bn.St.Troops (12 mo. '62-3) Co.F
Sykes, Milton 7th Conf.Cav. Co.F

Sykes, Milton 8th (Dearing's) Conf.Cav. Co.G
Sykes, M.J. GA 32nd Inf. Co.K
Sykes, M.M. NC 3rd Cav. (41st St.Troops) Co.A Cpl.
Sykes, Napoleon B. AL 22nd Inf. Co.C Cpl.
Sykes, Napoleon B. TX 18th Inf. Co.E
Sykes, Nathaniel VA 15th Cav. Co.F
Sykes, Newbern VA 37th Inf. Co.G
Sykes, N.M. VA 5th Cav. Co.G
Sykes, Noah Conf.Cav. 7th Bn.
Sykes, Oscar FL 9th Inf. Co.F
Sykes, Patrick H. NC Cav. 12th Bn. Co.C Cpl.
Sykes, P.H. NC Cav. 16th Bn. Co.G Cpl.
Sykes, P.H. 8th (Dearing's) Conf.Cav. Co.C Cpl.
Sykes, Phillip A. GA 11th (St.Troops) Co.E
Sykes, P.M. AL 18th Inf. Co.D
Sykes, R. MS Inf. 3rd Bn. (St.Troops) Co.E
Sykes, Raleigh M. MS 24th Inf. Co.C
Sykes, Ransom AL 38th Inf. Co.K
Sykes, Richard MS 3rd Inf. Co.K
Sykes, Richard A. NC 44th Inf. Co.G
Sykes, Richard L. Gen. & Staff Hosp.Stew.
Sykes, Richard W. MS 48th Inf. Co.L
Sykes, R.L. MS 44th Inf. Co.A Cpl.
Sykes, R.M. 8th Bn.Conf.Inf. Co.D Sgt.
Sykes, Robert AL Cp. of Instr. Talladega
Sykes, Robert NC 3rd Bn.Sr.Res. Durham's Co.
Sykes, Robert TN 11th Inf. Co.D Sgt.
Sykes, Robert TN 55th (Brown's) Inf. Co.B
Sykes, Robert H. GA Inf. 1st Loc.Troops (Augusta) Co.B
Sykes, R.S. FL 2nd Cav. Co.C
Sykes, Samuel Y. NC 44th Inf. Co.G
Sykes, S.M. TN 18th (Newsom's) Cav. Co.I
Sykes, Smith MS 1st Cav. Co.F Cpl.
Sykes, Solon M. MS 15th Inf. Co.E Ord.Sgt.
Sykes, Solon M. Lowry's Brig. Clerk
Sykes, S.P. NC 1st Jr.Res. Co.I
Sykes, S.S. Gen. & Staff Chap.
Sykes, S.T. MS 6th Cav. Co.E
Sykes, S.T. MS 12th Cav. Co.C
Sykes, S.T. MS 43rd Inf. Co.F
Sykes, S. Turner MS 11th Inf. Co.I
Sykes, S. Turner Gen. & Staff, Arty. 1st Lt.,Ord.Off.
Sykes, Sydney A. NC 44th Inf. Co.G Cpl.
Sykes, Syms TN 21st & 22nd (Cons.) Cav. Co.I
Sykes, Syrus TN 21st (Wilson's) Cav. Co.I
Sykes, T. GA Hvy.Arty. 22nd Bn. Co.F
Sykes, Taylor AL Cav. Stuart's Bn. Co.E
Sykes, T.H. MS Lt.Arty. 14th Bn. Co.C
Sykes, Thomas AR Cav. Gordon's Regt. Co.I
Sykes, Thomas NC 31st Inf. Co.E
Sykes, Thomas TN 60th Mtd.Inf. Co.L
Sykes, Thomas 7th Conf.Cav. Co.F
Sykes, Thomas 8th (Dearing's) Conf.Cav. Co.G
Sykes, Thomas A. AL 22nd Inf. Co.E
Sykes, Thomas A. TN 32nd Inf. Co.G Cpl.
Sykes, Thomas B. MS 20th Inf. Co.B Capt.
Sykes, Thos. B. Gen. & Staff Capt.,AIG
Sykes, Thomas H. VA 61st Inf. Co.A Sgt.
Sykes, Thomas J. NC Lt.Arty. 3rd Bn. Co.A Sgt.
Sykes, Troiville LA 1st Cav. Co.D
Sykes, Twilivillo E. LA 1st Cav. Co.D
Sykes, V. AL Res. L.W. Shepard's Co.
Sykes, W. FL 1st (Res.) Inf. Co.D Sgt.
Sykes, W.A. MS 6th Cav. Co.I
Sykes, W.A. MS Cav. 6th Bn. Prince's Co.
Sykes, W.E. MS Cav. 4th Bn. Co.C
Sykes, W.E. 8th (Wade's) Conf.Cav. Co.E
Sykes, Wesley W. FL 4th Inf. Co.A
Sykes, W.G. MS 31st Inf. Adj.
Sykes, W.G. MS 43rd Inf. Co.F 1st Sgt.
Sykes, W.H. AR Cav. Gordon's Regt. Co.I
Sykes, W.H. MS 6th Cav. Co.I
Sykes, W.H. 1st Conf.Inf. 1st Co.F
Sykes, Wiley GA 36th (Villepigue's) Inf. Co.A,B
Sykes, Wiley 1st Conf.Inf. Co.B
Sykes, Wilkie G. FL 7th Inf. Co.C
Sykes, William MS 3rd Inf. (St.Troops) Co.B
Sykes, William MS Inf. 3rd Bn. (St.Troops) Co.E
Sykes, William NC 8th Inf. Co.B
Sykes, William VA 1st Arty. Co.A
Sykes, William VA 32nd Inf. 1st Co.K
Sykes, William VA 54th Mil. Co.H
Sykes, William VA 61st Inf. Co.B
Sykes, William VA 72nd Mil.
Sykes, William A. NC 6th Inf. Co.F
Sykes, William A. VA 6th Inf. Co.H
Sykes, William D. NC 32nd Inf. Co.B
Sykes, William E. GA Inf. 1st Loc.Troops (Augusta) Co.C
Sykes, William E. MS 43rd Inf. 1st Lt.Adj.
Sykes, William E. TN 55th (McKoin's) Inf. James' Co.
Sykes, Wm. E. Gen. & Staff 1st Lt.,Adj.
Sykes, William F. MS 20th Inf. Co.B
Sykes, William F. MS 24th Inf. Co.C
Sykes, William F. NC 44th Inf. Co.K
Sykes, William G. NC 15th Inf. Co.L
Sykes, William G. NC 32nd Inf. Co.K
Sykes, Wm. G. Gen. & Staff Vol.ADC
Sykes, William H. GA Arty. (Chatham Arty.) Wheaton's Co.
Sykes, William H. GA 1st (Olmstead's) Inf. Claghorn's Co.
Sykes, William H. GA 36th (Villepigue's) Inf. Co.F
Sykes, William H. MS 15th Inf. Co.G
Sykes, William H. VA 9th Inf. Co.E
Sykes, William H. Forrest's Scouts T. Henderson's Co.,CSA
Sykes, William H.T. VA 12th Inf. Co.A
Sykes, William J. NC 27th Inf. Co.G
Sykes, William J. NC 30th Inf. Co.I
Sykes, William J. Campbell's Brig. Maj.,CS
Sykes, William L. TX 4th Cav. Co.F
Sykes, William M. NC 47th Inf. Co.E
Sykes, William O. VA 61st Inf. Co.A Cpl.
Sykes, William P. NC 44th Inf. Co.G
Sykes, William S. MS 43rd Inf. Co.B Sgt.
Sykes, William T. MD Arty. 3rd Btty. Cpl.
Sykes, William T. NC 44th Inf. Co.K
Sykes, William W. VA Hvy.Arty. 20th Bn. Co.B
Sykes, William W. VA 16th Inf. Co.G
Sykes, William W. VA 38th Inf. 2nd Co.I
Sykes, Willis AL 12th Cav. Co.G
Sykes, W.J. GA Cav. 8th Bn. (St.Guards) Co.C Cpl.
Sykes, W.J. GA 5th Res. Co.A,D
Sykes, W.L. GA 22nd Inf. Co.K
Sykes, W.L. MS 5th Inf. Co.A Lt.Col.
Sykes, W.L. MS 14th Inf. Co.E Sgt.Maj.
Sykes, W.P. AR 32nd Inf. Co.F
Sykes, W.R.A. MS 8th Cav. Co.G
Sykes, W. Scott VA 41st Inf. Co.F Capt.
Sykes, W.T. GA Lt.Arty. Ritter's Co. Cpl.
Sykes, W.T. GA 16th Inf. Co.B
Sykes, W.W. MS 29th Inf. Co.C
Sykes, Wyatt MS 3rd Inf. Co.K
Sykes, Zachariah VA Cav. 14th Bn. Co.C
Sykes, Zachariah VA 15th Cav. Co.C
Sykey, Stepen P. 1st Chickasaw Inf. Milam's Co. 3rd Lt.
Syland, M. MS 7th Cav. Co.F Cpl.
Sylar, Andrew L. AR 4th Cav. Co.B Sgt.
Sylcox, Burton TN 36th Inf. Co.C
Syler, --- AL Calhoun Cty.Res. Meharge's Co.
Syler, A.L. AR 32nd Inf. Co.B Cpl.
Syler, Fred MO Arty.Regt.St.Guard Co.A
Syler, George W. TN 41st Inf. Co.G 1st Sgt.
Syler, H.H. 1st Conf.Cav. 2nd Co.K Sgt.
Syler, J.F. TN Inf. 23rd Bn. Co.D
Syler, Joseph GA Cobb's Legion Co.I
Syler, J.W. LA Inf. 9th Bn. Co.B
Syler, M.L. GA 12th Cav. Co.K
Syler, Robert W. TN 1st (Turney's) Inf. Co.F
Syler, Thomas TX 1st (Yager's) Cav. Co.F
Syles, J.R. KY 7th Cav. Co.H Sgt.
Syllavan, R. AL Cp. of Instr. Talladega
Syllender, J.H. KY 2nd (Woodward's) Cav. Co.D Cpl.
Sylman, Anderson B. LA 12th Inf. Co.H
Sylman, Joshua T. LA 12th Inf. Co.H Cpl.
Sylow, Manuel TX Conscr.
Sylovant, Andrew J. AL 19th Inf. Co.H
Sylva, A. Conf.Lt.Arty. Richardson's Bn. Co.B
Sylva, Chs. LA Lt.Arty. Bridges' Btty.
Sylva, Charles SC Lt.Arty. 3rd (Palmetto) Bn. Co.E
Sylva, Charles SC Arty. Manigault's Bn. Co.D
Sylva, G. LA Arty. Landry's Co. (Donaldsonville Arty.)
Sylva, Gaetano LA 18th Inf. Co.A
Sylva, James M. VA 47th Inf. Co.E
Sylva, Joseph FL 1st Cav.Co.F
Sylva, Joseph LA Mil. Lartigue's Co. (Bienville Guards)
Sylve, Antoine LA Mil. Lartigue's Co. (Bienville Guards)
Sylve, Augustin LA Mil. Lartigue's Co. (Bienville Guards)
Sylverburge, Edward Gen. & Staff Medical Purveyor
Sylvest, Emanuel LA 3rd (Wingfield's) Cav. Co.A
Sylvester, A. MS 9th Inf. Co.D
Sylvester, A.A. SC 12th Inf. Co.D
Sylvester, Charles W. TX 1st (Yager's) Cav. Co.A
Sylvester, Charles W. TX Cav. 3rd (Yager's) Bn. Co.A
Sylvester, David TN 3rd (Lillard's) Mtd.Inf. Co.F
Sylvester, E. GA 4th (Clinch's) Cav. Co.A
Sylvester, Eli FL 10th Inf. Co.E
Sylvester, Eli M. MO 5th Inf. Co.A
Sylvester, E.M. MO 16th Inf. Co.E

Sylvester, George MS 1st Lt.Arty. Co.E
Sylvester, Henry FL 9th Inf. Co.I
Sylvester, J.A. TX 23rd Cav. Co.A
Sylvester, James FL 1st Inf. Old Co.G
Sylvester, James FL 2nd Cav. Co.D Cpl.
Sylvester, Jas. E. AL 15th Inf. Co.K Sgt.
Sylvester, J.H. AL 23rd Inf. Co.I 1st Lt.
Sylvester, J.H. FL 8th Inf. Co.B
Sylvester, J.H. 15th Conf.Cav. Co.F
Sylvester, J.J. LA Mil.Conf.Guards Regt. Co.K
Sylvester, John AL 22nd Inf. Co.B
Sylvester, John FL Inf. 2nd Bn. Co.A
Sylvester, John FL 10th Inf. Co.I
Sylvester, John GA 26th Inf. Co.D
Sylvester, John A. TX Cav. 6th Bn. Co.A
Sylvester, John A. TX 4th Field Btty.
Sylvester, John P. FL 1st Cav. Co.C 2nd Lt.
Sylvester, John W. TX 13th Vol. 2nd Co.B 1st Lt.
Sylvester, Joseph NC 27th Inf. Co.F
Sylvester, Joseph A. AL 43rd Inf. Co.I Capt.
Sylvester, J.W. TX 35th (Likens') Cav. Co.A
Sylvester, Louis GA 5th Inf. Co.E Sgt.
Sylvester, Nathan B. AL 3rd Res. Co.I
Sylvester, R. LA 6th Inf. Co.K 1st Sgt.
Sylvester, Raymond H. FL 7th Inf. Co.F
Sylvester, Rollin FL 7th Inf. Co.F
Sylvester, Samuel L. TN 19th Inf. Co.B
Sylvester, T.A. TX Cav. 6th Bn. Co.A
Sylvester, T.A. TX 7th Cav. Co.E
Sylvester, Thomas M. TN 3rd (Clack's) Inf. Co.A
Sylvester, W. GA 4th (Clinch's) Cav. Co.A
Sylvester, William FL 9th Inf. Co.B
Sylvester, William GA Cav. Hendry's Co. (Atlantic & Gulf Guards)
Sylvester, William LA 16th Inf. Co.D
Sylvester, William N. FL 6th Inf. Co.C N.C.S. Sgt.Maj.
Sylvester, W.O. AL 63rd Inf. Co.E Sgt.
Sylvester, W.W. TX 1st Inf. Co.M
Sylvestre, Elysee LA Mil. 1st Native Guards
Sylvestre, P. LA 2nd Res.Corps Co.A
Sylvia, F. SC Mil. 16th Regt. Bancroft, Jr.'s Co.
Sylvious, Martin VA 33rd Inf. Co.G
Sylviss, William MS 28th Cav. Co.C
Sylvus, L. VA 12th Cav. Co.H
Sylvy, L. LA Mil. St.James Regt. Gaudet's Co.
Sym, James William MO Maj.
Syman, E. LA 1st Inf. Co.B
Symbal, H. GA 2nd Bn.Troops & Defences (Macon) Co.E
Symcox, Henry FL 7th Inf. Co.B
Syme, Chapman J. VA 14th Cav. Co.K
Syme, Chapman T. VA 19th Cav. Co.C
Syme, C.J. VA 19th Cav. Co.G
Syme, E.J. Sig.Corps,CSA
Syme, John C. NC 14th Inf. Co.K
Syme, John C. NC 47th Inf. Co.C Sgt.
Syme, Richard J. VA 27th Inf. Co.E
Syme, R.J. VA Cav. 36th Bn. Asst.Surg.
Syme, William LA 7th Inf. Co.H
Symer, E. TX 26th Cav. Co.K
Symes, --- Conf.Cav. Clarkson's Bn. Ind.Rangers Co.E
Symes, Benjamin G. GA 22nd Inf. Co.A Sgt.
Symes, B.F. GA 1st (Olmstead's) Inf. Bonaud's Co.
Symes, Charles TX 13th Vol. 1st Co.H
Symes, James TN 10th Inf. Co.D 2nd Lt.
Symes, J.T. MS 3rd Inf. Co.D
Symes, William TX 20th Inf. Co.K
Symington, H. LA Mil. British Guard Bn. Hamilton's Co.
Symington, Hugh LA 7th Inf. Co.C
Symington, J. VA 2nd St.Res. Co.N
Symington, James MS 18th Inf. Co.C Ord.Sgt.
Symington, John VA Lt.Arty. 38th Bn. Co.A
Symington, John Gen. & Staff Rec. for 1st Lt.,ADC
Symington, John B. VA 12th Inf. Co.G
Symington, Thomas VA 10th Cav. 2nd Co.E
Symington, Thomas H. VA Lt.Arty. 38th Bn. Co.D
Symington, W.H. VA 10th Cav. 2nd Co.E Sgt.
Symington, Wm. H. MD Weston's Bn. Co.B
Symington, William H. VA Lt.Arty. 38th Bn. Co.D
Symington, William H. VA 17th Inf. Co.K
Symington, William H. VA 21st Inf. Co.B
Symington, William H. Longstreet's Div. Ord.Sgt.
Symington, W.S. Pickett's Staff Capt.,ADC
Symington, W. Stuart MD Weston's Bn. Co.B 2nd Lt.
Symington, W. Stuart VA 21st Inf. Co.B 2nd Lt.
Symintone, Joel GA 46th Inf. Co.I
Symires, Da TX Cav. Giddings' Bn. Pickerell's Co.
Symires, H.V. TX Cav. Giddings' Bn. Pickerell's Co.
Symires, John TX Cav. Giddings' Bn. Pickerell's Co.
Symmers, George SC Mil.Arty. 1st Regt. Walter's Co.
Symmes, Charles FL 8th Inf. Co.F
Symmes, D.C. TN 35th Inf. Co.A
Symmes, Edwin SC Cav. 10th Bn. Co.B Secretary
Symmes, George W. SC Inf. 1st (Charleston) Bn. Co.B
Symmes, Gustavus Henry SC 4th Inf. Co.K 1st Sgt.
Symmes, G.W. SC 1st St.Troops Co.E
Symmes, G.W. SC 27th Inf. Co.B
Symmes, J.H. SC Rhett's Co.
Symmes, John H. SC Inf. 1st (Charleston) Bn. Co.B 1st Sgt.
Symmes, J.W. SC 7th Cav. Co.B
Symmes, T.B. SC 1st Mtd.Mil. Anderson's Co.
Symmes, Whitner SC 6th Cav. Co.I
Symmington, Hugh AL 1st Regt. Mobile Vol. British Guard Co.A
Symmington, Theo. A. Pickett's Staff Capt.,ADC
Symmons, Henry AL Mil. 3rd Vol. Co.B
Symmons, Thomas M. GA 1st (Symon's) Res. Co.K
Symms, Andrew SC 1st (Orr's) Rifles Co.A
Symms, D.C. TN 32nd Inf. Dr.M.
Symms, George TX 25th Cav. Co.E
Symms, Robert LA 7th Inf. Co.D
Symms, Thomas L. GA 27th Inf. Co.B Cpl.
Symns, J.A. VA Lt.Arty. Lowry's Co. Sgt.
Symns, Lewis C. VA 166th Mil. Co.H Lt.
Symns, Samuel Y. VA Lt.Arty. Lowry's Co.
Symns, William P. VA Lt.Arty. Lowry's Co.
Symon, R.T. AL 11th Inf. Co.C
Symon, W. GA 5th Res. Co.A
Symonds, Alphonso KY 9th Cav. Co.G
Symonds, J. Edward Conf.Lt.Arty. Davis' Co.
Symons, Charles P. AR 2nd Inf. Co.K
Symons, Henry GA 1st (Olmstead's) Inf. Davis' Co.
Symons, Henry Gen. & Staff 1st Lt.,Adj.
Symons, Henry R. GA Hvy.Arty. 22nd Bn. Adj.
Symons, H.R. GA Inf. 18th Bn. Co.C
Symons, Jacob N. VA 6th Cav. Co.H
Symons, James GA 1st (Symons') Res. Co.A
Symons, James K. GA Hvy.Arty. 22nd Bn. Co.C
Symons, James V. NC 6th Sr.Res. Co.C Lt.Col.
Symons, James W. VA 6th Cav. Co.H
Symons, John SC Sea Fencibles Symons' Co. Capt.
Symons, John J. GA Hvy.Arty. 22nd Bn. Co.E Adj.
Symons, John J. GA 1st (Olmstead's) Inf. Davis' Co. Sgt.Maj.
Symons, John J. GA 1st (Olmstead's) Inf. Guilmartin's Co. 1st Lt.
Symons, John J. Gen. & Staff 1st Lt.,Adj.
Symons, John M. MS 35th Inf. Co.H
Symons, Robert MS 21st Inf. Co.L
Symons, Thomas GA 1st (Symons') Res. Co.D
Symons, William GA Hvy.Arty. 22nd Bn. Co.C Cpl.
Symons, William F. GA 1st (Olmstead's) Inf. Stiles' Co.
Symons, William F. GA Inf. 18th Bn. Co.B,C
Symons, Wm. R. GA 1st (Symons') Res. Col.
Symonton, S.R. SC 3rd Bn.Res. Co.B
Symproville, Hymel LA 30th Inf. Locoul's Co.
Sympson, E.W. AR 18th Inf. Co.C 1st Sgt.
Sympton, George W. TX 26th Cav. Co.F
Syms, --- TX Cav. Good's Bn. Co.C
Syms, A.J. VA 8th Cav. ACS
Syms, A.J. Gen. & Staff Asst.Comsy.
Syms, Benjamin F. GA Hvy.Arty. 22nd Bn. Co.F
Syms, B.F. GA 25th Inf. Co.C
Syms, Cicero R.J. FL 8th Inf. Co.K
Syms, Gilbert L. GA 2nd Inf. Co.D
Syms, J. GA 39th Inf. Co.E
Syms, James SC 22nd Inf. Co.D
Syms, James 1st Conf.Cav. 1st Co.K
Syms, James W. AL 12th Inf. Co.K
Syms, J.C. LA Mil. British Guard Bn. West's Co.
Syms, John GA 1st (Olmstead's) Inf. Co.I
Syms, John SC 22nd Inf. Co.D
Syms, John VA Inf. 26th Bn. Co.C
Syms, John J. GA 1st (Olmstead's) Inf. Co.I
Syms, Merrit MS 5th Inf. (St.Troops) Co.H
Syms, Richard NC 37th Inf. Co.D
Syms, Robert FL 2nd Inf. Co.G
Syms, S.R.J. FL 8th Inf. Co.K 1st Sgt.
Syms, T.H. GA Lt.Arty. 12th Bn. 2nd Co.B
Syms, William MS 5th Inf. (St.Troops) Co.H
Syms, William B. VA 14th Inf. Co.B
Syms, William C. FL 4th Inf.
Synan, Edward H. VA 13th Inf. Co.D

Synan, James M. VA 13th Inf. Co.D
Synan, William N. VA 2nd Inf.Loc.Def. Co.C
Synan, William N. VA Inf. 2nd Bn.Loc.Def. Co.E
Synard, H. GA Floyd Legion (St.Guards) Co.K
Synard, Ranson GA 40th Inf. Co.A
Synco, E. VA 2nd St.Res. Co.D
Synco, Edward P. VA Hvy.Arty. 10th Bn. Co.A
Synco, Jackson S. MS 34th Inf. Co.D
Synco, J.B. MS 3rd Inf. (A. of 10,000) Co.C
Synco, Joseph B. MS 34th Inf. Co.D
Synco, T.J. TX 10th Inf. Co.A
Syncoe, T.G. MS 3rd Cav. Co.E,G,D
Synet, Patrick GA 2nd Inf. Co.A
Syniard, Houston GA 65th Inf. Co.B
Synnamon, James MO 6th Inf. Co.G Capt.
Synnolt, Lawrence MS Adair's Co. (Lodi Co.) Cpl.
Synnott, Lawrence MS 15th Inf. Co.D
Synnott, P. MS 15th Inf. Co.D
Synnott, Patrick MS Adair's Co. (Lodi Co.)
Synnott, Stephen LA 8th Inf. Co.K
Synom, William L. NC 55th Inf. Co.I
Synot, F.M. MS 1st Cav.Res. Co.K
Synott, Oliver T. MS 33rd Inf. Co.G
Synott, William D. MS 24th Inf. Co.K
Synther, M. MO Inf. Winston's Regt. Co.A Cpl.
Synther, N. MO 4th Cav. Co.I Cpl.
Syntis, S. GA Inf. 18th Bn. Co.A
Synyard, Andrew J. GA 11th Inf. Co.F
Synyard, Henry GA 6th Inf. Co.D
Sype, R.G. VA Loc.Def. Tayloe's Co.
Sype, W.T. TN 5th (McKenzie's) Cav. Co.A
Sypers, J.W GA 2nd Res. Co.I
Sypert, A.A. TX 7th Inf. Co.H Sgt.
Sypert, B.P. TX 7th Inf. Co.H Ens.
Sypert, Joseph M. TX 21st Cav. Co.D
Sypert, Joseph R. TX 27th Cav. Co.A Cpl.
Sypert, J.R. AR 2nd Mtd.Rifles Hawkins' Co.
Sypert, J.W. TX 7th Inf. Co.H
Sypert, L.A. KY 2nd (Woodward's) Cav. Co.A
Sypert, Lee A. KY 12th Cav. Lt.Col.
Sypert, Lee A. KY Cav. Sypert's Regt. Lt.Col.
Sypert, Leonidas A. KY Cav. Sypert's Regt. Lt.Col.
Sypert, M.W. TN 4th (Murray's) Cav. Co.H 1st Sgt.
Sypert, M.W. TN 8th (Smith's) Cav. Co.C
Sypert, S.G. TX 8th Cav. Co.A
Sypert, T.J. TX 8th Cav. Co.K
Sypert, William R. TX 2nd Inf. Co.E
Sypes, Alexander VA 9th Cav. Co.D
Sypes, G.W. TN 51st (Cons.) Inf. Co.C
Sypher, W.N. LA 21st (Patton's) Inf. Co.C
Syphreet, John W. SC 2nd Bn.S.S. Co.A
Syphreet, J.W.W. SC 26th Inf. Co.G
Syphres, Henry VA Lt.Arty. Douthat's Co.
Syphret, A.H. FL Conscr.
Syphret, John SC Hvy.Arty. Gilchrist's Co. (Gist Guard)
Syphret, John T. AL 8th Inf. Co.H
Syphret, John W.W. SC 11th Inf. Co.H
Syphret, O.J. SC 25th Inf. Co.G
Syphrett, J.W.W. SC Arty. Manigault's Bn. 1st Co.C
Syphrett, R.A. SC 1st Cav. Co.E
Syphyrt, Charles D. AL 38th Inf. Co.A
Syples, George TX Inf. 1st St.Troops Sheldon's Co.B
Sypret, Samuel MO Cav. Fristoe's Regt. Co.I
Syprit, S.S. AR 38th Inf. Co.C
Syrcle, John J. VA 52nd Inf. Co.G
Syre, W.H. LA Pointe Coupee Arty.
Syrears, E.A. AL 15th Inf. Co.D
Syrie, Patrick LA Miles' Legion Co.F
Syrille, Jex LA 28th (Thomas') Inf. Co.G
Syring, F.P. GA Cav. Gartrell's Co.
Syrles, James E. NC 4th Inf. Co.E
Syrock, Milton MO Cav. Snider's Bn. Co.B
Syron, Albert H. AL Lt.Arty. Hurt's Btty.
Syron, J.M. VA 10th Bn.Res. Co.D
Syron, Simon VA 52nd Inf. Co.E
Sysian, G. AR 30th Inf. Co.B
Sysk, A.K. AR 27th Inf. Co.F
Sysk, Miles GA 6th Cav. Co.D
Sysk, S.J.A. AR 27th Inf. Co.F
Sysk, W.J. 3rd Conf.Cav. Co.C
Sysler, Edward MO Inf. 5th Regt.St.Guard Co.C
Sysnne, A. LA 18th Inf.
Sytes, Leonard TX 15th Inf. Co.F
Sythemno, A. AL 22nd Inf. Co.F
Syxe, Frank TX 2nd Inf. Co.D
Syxe, Frank TX 5th Inf. Co.A
Syzemore, Benjamin SC 1st Arty. Co.F
Szar, A. LA Washington Arty.Bn. Co.1 Driver
Szcarbinowsky, Charles A. VA Lt.Arty. Brander's Co.
Szymanski, J. Gen. & Staff, Adj.Gen.Dept. Maj.
Szymauski, Ig. LA Mil. Chalmette Regt. Col.

T

T., A.W. AR 34th Inf. Co.G 1st Sgt.
T., D.T. MS 44th Inf. Co.I
T-chert, --- LA Mil. Orleans Guards Regt. Co.I
T--lt, W.W. VA 10th Bn.Res.
Taaffe, George AR 1st (Monroe's) Cav. Co.D
Taaffe, James LA 21st (Patton's) Inf. Co.C
Taaffe, William TX Lt.Arty. Hughes' Co.
Taalfrank, John TN 1st Hvy.Arty. Co.K, 2nd Co.C Sgt.
Tab, T.S. KY 2nd Cav. Co.F
Tabary, L.E. LA Mil. Chalmette Regt. Co.H
Tabary, Louis E. LA Mil. 3rd Regt. 1st Brig. 1st Div. Co.D Capt.
Tabary, P.A. LA Dreux's Cav. Co.A
Tabb, A. FL 6th Inf.
Tabb, A.C. VA 32nd Inf. 2nd Co.I
Tabb, Ber AL Gid Nelson Lt.Arty. Sgt.
Tabb, Charles Sig.Corps,CSA
Tabb, Charles W. VA 2nd Inf. Co.G
Tabb, Daniel MS 6th Cav. Co.L
Tabb, Daniel MS 8th Cav. Co.E
Tabb, D.B. GA 2nd Inf. Co.D Cpl.
Tabb, Edward TX Cav. 3rd Bn.St.Troops Co.D 3rd Lt.
Tabb, E.J. GA 32nd Inf. Co.D
Tabb, E.R.W. VA 67th Mil. Co.B
Tabb, E.W. VA 1st Cav. Co.B
Tabb, George E., Jr. VA 34th Inf. Co.A Sgt.
Tabb, George E. Conf.Hvy.Arty. Montague's Bn. Co.A Sgt.
Tabb, George E. Sig.Corps,CSA 2nd Lt.
Tabb, G.H.P. TX Cav. Morgan's Regt. Co.F
Tabb, Harlan P. VA Cav. McNeill's Co.
Tabb, H.C. VA Lt.Arty. Pollock's Co.
Tabb, H.C. Gen. & Staff Hosp.Stew.
Tabb, H. Cabell VA 13th Cav. Co.F,K
Tabb, H. Cabell Hosp.Stew.
Tabb, Henry A. VA 3rd Inf. Co.H
Tabb, Henry C. VA 5th Cav. (12 mo. '61-2) Co.F
Tabb, James A. TX 18th Inf. Co.F Jr.2nd Lt.
Tabb, James H. VA 32nd Inf. Co.A
Tabb, James V. GA 55th Inf. Co.E
Tabb, James W. VA 1st Inf. Co.I Capt.
Tabb, J.B. GA 32nd Inf. Co.D
Tabb, J.E. GA 17th Inf. Co.G Cpl.
Tabb, J.F.R. MS 43rd Inf. Co.B Sgt.
Tabb, J.H. MS 8th Cav. Co.E 1st Sgt.
Tabb, J.H. MS St.Cav. Perrin's Bn. Co.H Cpl.
Tabb, J.H. VA 5th Cav. Co.A
Tabb, J. Henry MS 13th Inf. Co.H
Tabb, J.L. KY 6th Mtd.Inf. Co.H
Tabb, John MS 31st Inf. Co.H
Tabb, John B. CSA War Prisoner
Tabb, John E. GA Siege Arty. 28th Bn. Co.A Cpl.
Tabb, John H. TN 19th (Biffle's) Cav. Co.E Sgt.
Tabb, John L. VA 32nd Inf. 2nd Co.H
Tabb, John P. VA 10th Cav. Co.A
Tabb, John P. VA Cav. Young's Co.
Tabb, John P. VA 1st St.Res. Co.F
Tabb, John P. VA 2nd St.Res. Co.C
Tabb, Johnson M. VA 3rd Inf. Co.H Music.
Tabb, John Y. VA 59th Inf. 3rd Co.B
Tabb, Joseph N. MS 44th Inf. Co.C
Tabb, J.P. Gen. & Staff AASurg.
Tabb, J.V. GA 32nd Inf. Co.D
Tabb, Lewis MS 14th Inf. Co.G
Tabb, Lewis 1st Cherokee Mtd.Rifles Co.F
Tabb, Lewis P. VA 32nd Inf. 2nd Co.H Cpl.
Tabb, Mose 1st Cherokee Mtd.Vol. 1st Co.F
Tabb, P., Sr. VA 3rd Inf.Loc.Def. Co.B
Tabb, Phil VA 3rd Inf.Loc.Def. Co.B
Tabb, Philip M., Jr. VA 3rd Lt.Arty. (Loc.Def.) Co.H
Tabb, R.B. VA Loc.Def. Jordan's Co.
Tabb, Robert GA 48th Inf. Co.D
Tabb, Robert B. VA 5th Cav. (12 mo. '61-2) Co.B
Tabb, Robert B. VA Cav. 14th Bn. Co.A
Tabb, Robert B. VA 15th Cav. Co.F
Tabb, Robert L. VA 1st Inf. Co.I
Tabb, Robert M. VA 21st Inf. Co.F Sgt.
Tabb, Ross MS 6th Cav. Co.K Sgt.
Tabb, R.P. VA Cav. McNeill's Co.
Tabb, R.T. GA 32nd Inf. Co.D
Tabb, Samuel G. MS Patton's Co. (St.Troops)
Tabb, Samuel Leroy GA 20th Inf. Co.K
Tabb, Thomas VA 1st Arty. Co.A 2nd Lt.
Tabb, Thomas VA 32nd Inf. 1st Co.K 2nd Lt.
Tabb, Thomas Gen. & Staff Capt.,AQM
Tabb, Thomas A. MS 14th Inf. Co.G
Tabb, Thomas E. GA 51st Inf. Co.I
Tabb, Thomas H. VA 3rd Inf. Co.H
Tabb, Thomas J. GA Cobb's Legion Co.I
Tabb, Thomas S. TX 13th Vol. 1st Co.I
Tabb, Thomas T.T. TN Cav. 7th Bn. (Bennett's) Co.A
Tabb, Thomas T.T. VA 1st St.Res. Co.F
Tabb, W. VA 23rd Cav. Co.D
Tabb, W.A. FL Cav. 5th Bn. Co.F Cpl.
Tabb, W.B. Gen. & Staff, Adj.Gen.Dept. Capt.
Tabb, William GA 2nd Inf. Co.D
Tabb, William LA 2nd Cav. Co.C
Tabb, William VA 9th Inf. Co.K Sgt.
Tabb, William A. FL 2nd Cav. Co.I
Tabb, William B. VA 59th Inf. Col.
Tabb, William H. MS 14th Inf. Co.G Capt.
Tabb, William T. MS 31st Inf. Co.C
Tabb, W. Kemp Gen. & Staff Capt.,A.Adj.
Tabb, W.S. VA Lt.Arty. 13th Bn. Co.A
Tabb, W.V. GA 2nd Inf. Co.E
Tabbe, William 1st Choctaw & Chickasaw Mtd.Rifles 2nd Co.B
Tabben, --- KY 2nd (Duke's) Cav. Co.D
Tabben, John KY 1st Inf. Co.I
Tabben, John LA 1st (Nelligan's) Inf. Co.H
Tabbs, Jackson KY 6th Mtd.Inf. Co.A
Tabbs, Jackson TN 41st Inf.
Tabbs, J.H. LA Inf.Cons.Crescent Regt. Co.N
Tabbs, Thomas S. TX 35th (Brown's) Cav. Co.D Cpl.
Taben, John KY 9th Cav.
Taber, A. AL 1st Regt. Mobile Vol. Baas' Co.
Taber, Adkinson GA 4th Res. Co.C
Taber, A.G. MO Cav. Schnabel's Bn. Co.C
Taber, A.H. LA 2nd Inf. Co.A
Taber, A.J. AL Cav. Hardie's Bn.Res. Co.C
Taber, Albert R. SC 1st Cav. Co.E 2nd Lt.
Taber, Albert R. Gen. & Staff Asst.Surg.
Taber, Alexander H. NC 56th Inf. Co.G Sgt.
Taber, Asbury VA 57th Inf. Co.D
Taber, B.K. AL 18th Inf. Co.G
Taber, Calvin C. NC 5th Inf. Co.G
Taber, C.H. SC Inf. 7th Bn. (Enfield Rifles) Asst.Surg.
Taber, Chas. H. Gen. & Staff Asst.Surg.
Taber, C.R. Gen. & Staff Surg.
Taber, Daniel TN 49th Inf. Co.B
Taber, Daniel Inf. Bailey's Cons.Regt. Co.D
Taber, Elias L. NC 16th Inf. Co.K
Taber, Elzaphan NC 16th Inf. Co.K
Taber, Elzaphan NC 64th Inf. Co.E Sgt.
Taber, E.N. Sig.Corps,CSA Courier
Taber, Fairman F. Gen. & Staff Asst.Surg.
Taber, Ferdinand D. LA 1st (Nelligan's) Inf. Co.A
Taber, Francis 3rd Conf.Cav. Co.I
Taber, Fred R. LA 18th Inf. Co.A
Taber, George W. LA 12th Inf. Co.E
Taber, G.W. TX 2nd Inf. Co.C
Taber, Henry H. VA Cav. Mosby's Regt. (Part.Rangers) Co.B
Taber, Henry H. VA 45th Inf. Co.H Cpl.
Taber, H.H. VA Cav. Mosby's Regt. (Part. Rangers) Co.B
Taber, H.M. KY 4th Mtd.Inf. Co.K
Taber, Hugh J. VA 8th Cav. Co.H
Taber, James KY 1st (Butler's) Cav. Co.A
Taber, James F. 3rd Conf.Cav. Co.I
Taber, J.B. MS 1st Cav.Res. Co.A
Taber, Jeff TX 13th Vol. 2nd Co.H
Taber, John AL Cav. Hardie's Bn.Res. Co.C
Taber, John LA Mil. LaFourche Regt.
Taber, John A. VA 86th Mil. Co.B
Taber, J.R. SC 1st Cav. Co.E Lt.
Taber, N.J. AL Res. J.G. Rankin's Co.
Taber, Robert TX 30th Cav. Co.G
Taber, Robert W. NC 64th Inf. Co.E Cpl.
Taber, S.B. TX 11th Cav. Co.G
Taber, S.T. TN 23rd Inf. Co.E Ch.Music.
Taber, Thomas VA 24th Cav. Co.D
Taber, Thomas VA Cav. 40th Bn. Co.D

Taber, T.M. Gen. & Staff,PACS Maj.,Ord.Off.
Taber, T.T. GA 3rd Bn. (St.Guards) Co.E Sgt.
Taber, Warren A. AR Cav. Poe's Bn. Co.A
Taber, Wiley W. TX 27th Cav. Co.H
Taber, William MS 11th (Cons.) Cav. Co.D
Taber, William TN Cav. 16th Bn. (Neal's) Co.A
Taber, William K. NC 64th Inf. Co.E 1st Lt.
Taber, W.J. TX 2nd Inf. Co.C
Taber, W.R. TX 9th (Nichols') Inf. Co.C
Taber, W.R. TX Waul's Legion Co.C
Taber, W.S. TX 15th Inf. Co.K
Taber, W.T. TX 15th Inf. Co.K
Taber, W.W. KY 4th Mtd.Inf. Co.K
Tabereaux, J.S. GA 23rd Inf. Co.E
Tabin, John J. Gen. & Staff Asst.Surg.
Table, J.W. GA 55th Inf. Co.E
Table, Thomas Gen. & Staff Capt.
Tabler, A.A. VA 67th Mil. Co.B
Tabler, Adam M. VA 2nd Inf. Co.E
Tabler, A.R. MS 10th Cav. Co.B,D Cpl.
Tabler, Charles SC 10th Inf. Co.L
Tabler, Ephraim G. VA 2nd Inf. Co.D Music.
Tabler, George F. AR 8th Cav.
Tabler, George F. VA Lt.Arty. Cutshaw's Co.
Tabler, George F. VA 51st Mil. Co.A
Tabler, Jasper N. VA Arty. Bryan's Co.
Tabler, Jesse NC 12th Inf. Co.K
Tabler, J.F. MS 22nd Inf. Co.F
Tabler, J.F. MS 32nd Inf. Co.F
Tabler, J.N. VA Cav. Swann's Bn. Vaughan's Co. 2nd Lt.
Tabler, John H. VA Cav. 37th Bn. Co.H 1st Lt.
Tabler, John N. VA Cav. 37th Bn. Co.H Sgt.
Tabler, John N. VA 67th Mil. Co.C
Tabler, John R. TN 42nd Inf. Co.A 1st Sgt.
Tabler, John W. VA Cav. 35th Bn. Co.B
Tabler, John W.H. MS 2nd Inf. Co.C
Tabler, Jonas VA Mil. Wythe Cty.
Tabler, J.R. 4th Conf.Inf. Co.G 1st Sgt.
Tabler, M. VA Arty. Bryan's Co. 2nd Lt.
Tabler, Moshier VA Cav. Swann's Bn. Vaughan's Co. 1st Lt.
Tabler, O.E. VA 45th Inf. Co.G Sgt.
Tablert, J.B. GA 12th Mil. Cpl.
Tablock, James AL 29th Inf. Co.C
Tabner, John T. MS 1st (Johnston's) Inf. Co.G
Tabner, Nathaniel TX 9th (Young's) Inf. Co.G
Tabner, William MS 11th Inf. Co.A
Tabo, George VA 16th Cav. Co.I
Tabonney, Anatole LA Mil. Chalmette Regt. Co.H
Tabony, Joseph H. LA 30th Inf. Co.E,B Sgt.
Tabor, --- LA 1st Cav. Co.C
Tabor, --- TX Cav. Mann's Regt. Co.I Sgt.
Tabor, A.A. VA Cav. Caldwell's Bn. Taylor's Co.
Tabor, Abram VA 6th Bn.Res. Co.B
Tabor, A.J. VA Cav. Caldwell's Bn. Taylor's Co.
Tabor, Albert Gen. & Staff Asst.Surg.
Tabor, Alexander W. VA 16th Cav. Co.I
Tabor, Amos H. VA 45th Inf. Co.L Sgt.
Tabor, Anderson G. TX 9th Cav. Co.H
Tabor, Andrew J. GA 14th Inf. Co.G
Tabor, Andrew J. KY 7th Cav. Co.E
Tabor, Andrew J. VA 16th Cav. Co.F Sgt.
Tabor, Aquilla GA Inf. (Madison Cty. Home Guard) Milner's Co.
Tabor, Atkison GA 3rd Cav. (St.Guards) Co.G
Tabor, Augustus VA 17th Cav. Co.E
Tabor, Augustus VA 29th Inf. Co.I
Tabor, Benjamin K. MS 3rd (St.Troops) Cav. Co.B Cpl.
Tabor, Bethel AL 10th Inf. Co.I
Tabor, Beverly K. LA 25th Inf. Co.A
Tabor, Calvin NC 14th Inf. Co.F
Tabor, C.C. MS 2nd Part.Rangers Co.D
Tabor, Charles C. NC 56th Inf. Co.G
Tabor, Charles C. TX 1st Inf. Co.C
Tabor, C.N. TN 25th Inf. Co.K
Tabor, D. AR 2nd Cav. Co.F
Tabor, Daniel T. VA 45th Inf. Co.L
Tabor, David AR Cav. Wright's Regt.
Tabor, E.A. VA 16th Cav. Co.F
Tabor, Elijah MO Cav. Schnabel's Bn.
Tabor, E.W. LA 25th Inf. Co.A
Tabor, F.A. LA 3rd (Harrison's) Cav. Co.D
Tabor, Francis H. LA 28th (Gray's) Inf. Co.I
Tabor, F.W. NC 1st Arty. (10th St.Troops) Co.B
Tabor, George AR 19th (Dawson's) Inf. Co.F
Tabor, George VA Cav. Caldwell's Bn. Graham's Co.
Tabor, George O. VA 17th Cav. Co.E
Tabor, George O. VA Inf. 23rd Bn. Co.B
Tabor, George O. VA 59th Inf. 2nd Co.I
Tabor, George W. TX 10th Inf. Co.G
Tabor, George W. VA 29th Inf. Co.I 1st Sgt.
Tabor, George W. VA 45th Inf. Co.H
Tabor, George W. VA 151st Mil. Co.D
Tabor, Green LA 30th Inf. Co.H
Tabor, H. LA Mil. LaFourche Regt. Co.G 2nd Lt.
Tabor, H.A. MS 1st Cav. Co.C
Tabor, Harrison VA Cav. Caldwell's Bn. Taylor's Co.
Tabor, Henry A. MS 4th Cav. Co.C
Tabor, Henry A. MS 15th Inf. Co.F
Tabor, Henry J. VA 16th Cav. Co.I
Tabor, Henry John TX 10th Inf. Co.I
Tabor, Hezekiah AL 50th Inf. Co.C
Tabor, H.H. LA Inf. 1st Sp.Bn. (Wheat's) Co.C
Tabor, H.J. VA Cav. Caldwell's Bn. Graham's Co.
Tabor, J.A. MS 8th Inf. Co.B
Tabor, Jacob VA 14th Cav. 2nd Co.F Cpl.
Tabor, James AR 16th Inf. Co.K
Tabor, James VA 16th Cav. Co.F
Tabor, James VA 151st Mil. Co.D
Tabor, James C. MO 3rd Inf. Co.H
Tabor, James H. VA 6th Bn.Res. Co.B
Tabor, James P. TN 53rd Inf. Co.A
Tabor, James R. VA 16th Cav. Co.I
Tabor, James R. VA Cav. Caldwell's Bn. Graham's Co.
Tabor, Jefferson VA 36th Inf. 2nd Co.H
Tabor, Jefferson VA 86th Mil. Co.B
Tabor, John AR Cav. Harrell's Bn. Co.A
Tabor, John LA Cav. 18th Bn. Co.C
Tabor, John MS Moseley's Regt.
Tabor, John MO 10th Cav. Co.E
Tabor, John TN 28th Inf. Co.A
Tabor, John TX Cav. (Dismtd.) Chisum's Regt. Co.E
Tabor, John VA 16th Cav. Co.I
Tabor, John VA 4th Inf. Co.C
Tabor, John VA 36th Inf. 2nd Co.H
Tabor, John VA 151st Mil. Co.D
Tabor, John A. VA 50th Inf. Co.C
Tabor, John F. LA 8th Inf. Co.A Cpl.
Tabor, John H. MS 25th Inf. Co.D
Tabor, John L. LA 12th Inf. Co.E
Tabor, John W. AL Lt.Arty. Kolb's Btty.
Tabor, John W. MO 8th Inf. Co.D Cpl.
Tabor, John W. TX 17th Inf. Co.K Maj.
Tabor, Jonathan GA 39th Inf. Co.G
Tabor, J.P.H. MS 2nd St.Cav. Co.K
Tabor, J.P.H. MS Cav. Ham's Regt. Co.K
Tabor, J.S. MS 3rd Inf. (A. of 10,000) Co.C
Tabor, J.S. MS 9th Inf. New Co.I
Tabor, Napoleon B. GA 14th Inf. Co.G Cpl.
Tabor, Nathan J. TX Cav. Hardeman's Regt. Co.E Cpl.
Tabor, Nathan S. TX 36th Cav. Co.K
Tabor, N.C. MS 13th Inf. Co.A
Tabor, Nimrod AR Cav. Harrell's Bn. Co.C
Tabor, Nimrod AR 14th (Powers') Inf. Co.C
Tabor, Nimrod AR 27th Inf. Co.K
Tabor, N.T. GA 11th Cav. Co.G
Tabor, N.T. GA 11th Cav. Co.K Capt.
Tabor, Odel G. KY 2nd Mtd.Inf. Co.H Music.
Tabor, O.H.P. TX Cav. McDowell's Co.
Tabor, Oliver H.P. TX 36th Cav. Co.A Far.
Tabor, R.A. GA Inf. 9th Bn. Co.C
Tabor, R.B. VA Cav. Caldwell's Bn. Graham's Co.
Tabor, Robert F. AL 10th Inf. Co.I
Tabor, Robert J. LA 12th Inf. Co.E Capt.
Tabor, Robert J. NC 35th Inf. Co.G
Tabor, Samuel F. VA 16th Cav. Co.I
Tabor, Samuel F. VA Cav. Caldwell's Bn. Graham's Co.
Tabor, Seborn S. AR 27th Inf. Co.K
Tabor, S.H. VA Cav. Caldwell's Bn. Graham's Co.
Tabor, S.S. AR 14th (Powers') Inf. Co.C
Tabor, S.T. TN Inf. Nashville Bn. Fulcher's Co. Music.
Tabor, Stephen H. VA 16th Cav. Co.I
Tabor, S.W. VA 16th Cav. Co.B
Tabor, Theophile LA Mil. LaFourche Regt.
Tabor, Thomas MS Cav. Ham's Regt. Co.K
Tabor, Thomas MO 16th Inf. Co.D
Tabor, Thomas VA 32nd Inf. Co.F
Tabor, Thomas VA 55th Inf. Co.C
Tabor, Thomas VA 61st Mil. Co.E
Tabor, Thomas A. MS 2nd Inf. Co.E
Tabor, Thomas E. VA 29th Inf. Co.I Sgt.
Tabor, Thomas H. MS 21st Inf. Co.D
Tabor, Thomas W. GA 39th Inf. Co.G Sgt.
Tabor, Thomas Z. LA 12th Inf. Co.B
Tabor, T.W. GA 11th Cav. Co.K 2nd Lt.
Tabor, U.B. MS 13th Inf. Co.A
Tabor, Warren A. AR 11th Inf. Co.A
Tabor, Warren A. AR 11th & 17th Cons.Inf. Co.A
Tabor, W.H. MS 5th Inf. (St.Troops) Co.F
Tabor, Whitley J. VA 36th Inf. 2nd Co.H
Tabor, Whitley J. VA 86th Mil. Co.B,D
Tabor, William C. MS Inf. 3rd Bn. Co.B
Tabor, William F. MS 17th Inf. Co.D 2nd Lt.

Tabor, William H. TN 28th Inf. Co.A
Tabor, William H. TX 17th Inf. Co.K
Tabor, William J. VA 16th Cav. Co.I
Tabor, William J. VA Cav. Caldwell's Bn. Graham's Co.
Tabor, William J. VA 36th Inf. 2nd Co.G
Tabor, William K. NC Cav. 7th Bn. Co.D
Tabor, Wm. W. VA 45th Inf. Co.E
Tabor, W.T. TX 9th (Nichols') Inf. Co.K
Tabors, Jonathan D. TN 25th Inf. Co.K
Tabot, Emile LA Mil. LaFourche Regt.
Tabot, Eugene Conf.Inf. Tucker's Regt. Co.K
Tabot, James Conf.Inf. Tucker's Regt. Co.C
Tabot, John AR 1st Field Btty.
Tabour, Phillip VA 4th Inf. Co.L
Tabour, W.B. MS 5th Cav. Co.C
Tabozi, Peter LA 25th Inf. Co.A
Tabrest, A. TN 32nd Inf. Co.A
Tabscot, Johnathan AL 5th Cav. Co.D
Tabscott, A.B. TN 9th Inf. Co.B
Tabscott, James T. AL 5th Cav. Co.D
Tabscott, J.D. AL 5th Cav. Co.D
Tabsott, A.B. TN 15th (Stewart's) Cav. Co.B
Tacey, H. VA 24th Bn.Part.Rangers Co.B
Tacey, Henry VA 7th Inf. Co.H
Tacey, Hillary MD 1st Cav. Co.G
Tacey, John VA 14th Cav. Co.D
Tacguard, H. 4th Conf.Eng.Troops
Ta cha year 1st Choctaw & Chickasaw Mtd.Rifles 1st Co.E
Tachett, John AL 12th Inf. Co.E
Tachoir, Alphonse AL 12th Inf. Co.I
Tachoir, Michael AL St.Arty. Co.A
Tacosar Harjo, No.1 1st Seminole Mtd.Vol.
Tacosar Harjo, No.2 1st Seminole Mtd.Vol.
Tackaberry, R.F. MS 9th Inf. Old Co.F Cpl.
Tackaberry, S.B. TX 20th Inf. Co.E 1st Sgt.
Tackel, James H. AR 15th (Johnson's) Inf. Co.F
Tacker, A.J. TN Lt.Arty. Phillips' Co.
Tacker, D.L. AR 36th Inf. Co.D
Tacker, John B. MS Cav. 4th Bn. Roddey's Co.
Tacker, John B. TX 10th Inf. Co.D Sr.2nd Lt.
Tacker, John R. TX 10th Inf. Co.D
Tacker, Joshua TN 1st (Feild's) Inf. Co.K
Tacker, Joshua TN 16th Inf. Huggin's Co.
Tacker, Joshua A. AL 4th Cav. Co.F
Tacker, Joshua E. TX 10th Inf. Co.D
Tacker, Robert J. TX 12th Inf. Co.L
Tacker, S.M. AR 27th Inf. New Co.C
Tacker, S.M. AR Inf. Adam's Regt. Co.G
Tacker, Wesley S. TX 10th Inf. Co.D
Tacker, William B. AR 2nd Mtd.Rifles Co.K
Tackerry, T.J. TX Cav. Wells' Regt. Co.K
Tacket, Abner KY 13th Cav. Co.B
Tacket, D.T. AR 36th Inf. Co.E
Tacket, Ezekiel GA 41st Inf. Co.K
Tacket, George KY 13th Cav. Co.B
Tacket, George NC 1st Bn.Jr.Res. Co.E
Tacket, Greenbury B. TX 35th (Brown's) Cav. Co.D,F
Tacket, H. MO 3rd Inf. Co.A
Tacket, Henry 10th Conf.Cav. Co.B
Tacket, Henry F. AR 1st (Colquitt's) Inf. Co.I
Tacket, Henry T. AL Cav. 5th Bn. Hilliard's Legion Co.B
Tacket, Hijah H. MS 31st Inf. Co.E
Tacket, J. NC 5th Cav. (63rd St.Troops) Co.H
Tacket, James GA 7th Inf. (St.Guards) Co.B
Tacket, J.D. TN 63rd Inf. Co.K
Tacket, J.T. AL 43rd Inf. Co.K
Tacket, J.W. KY 14th Regt.
Tacket, J.W. TN 40th Inf. Co.D
Tacket, L.L. AL Inf. 16th Bn. (Conf.Guards Resp.Bn.) Co.B
Tacket, Mathew KY 13th Cav. Co.E
Tacket, M.C. MS 7th Cav. 2nd Co.G
Tacket, M.C. TN Lt.Arty. Polk's Btty.
Tacket, P.C. TN 40th Inf. Co.D
Tacket, William KY 5th Mtd.Inf. Co.C
Tacket, William KY 5th Mtd.Inf. Co.F
Tacket, William A. AL 7th Cav. Co.D Cpl.
Tacket, William C. AL Lt.Arty. 2nd Bn. Co.F
Tacket, William G. GA 2nd Cav. (St.Guards) Co.D
Tacket, William M. KY 5th Mtd.Inf. Co.F
Tackett, Abner MS 12th Cav. Co.I
Tackett, Alex TN 4th (Murray's) Cav. Co.G
Tackett, Alex TN Inf. 22nd Bn. Co.G
Tackett, Alexander KY 5th Cav. Co.B
Tackett, A.W. AL 42nd Inf. Co.F
Tackett, B.F. NC 28th Inf. Co.F
Tackett, David M. VA Inf. Mileham's Co.
Tackett, Dennis VA 64th Mtd.Inf. 2nd Co.F
Tackett, Elija VA 8th Cav. Co.K
Tackett, Elijah T. KY 5th Mtd.Inf. Co.D
Tackett, Elisha T. KY 5th Mtd.Inf. Co.D
Tackett, Enoch B. AL Cav. Moreland's Regt. Co.D
Tackett, E.P.G. AR Inf. Cocke's Regt. Co.A
Tackett, Ezekiel L. GA 60th Inf. Co.K
Tackett, George AL 11th Cav. Co.B
Tackett, George C. GA 21st Inf. Co.A
Tackett, Greenberry B. TX 13th Vol. 1st Co.I
Tackett, G.W. MS 6th Inf. Co.K
Tackett, G.W. MS 15th Inf. Co.I
Tackett, Henry T. GA 35th Inf. Co.E
Tackett, J. AL Cav. Moreland's Regt. Co.D
Tackett, J. MS Adams' Co. (Holmes Cty.Ind.)
Tackett, J. MO 5th Cav. Co.C
Tackett, James AR Cav. Wright's Regt. Co.G
Tackett, James W. AR 2nd Cav. Co.G
Tackett, James W. AR 7th Inf. Co.C
Tackett, James W. NC 28th Inf. Co.F
Tackett, J.B. AL Cav. Moreland's Regt. Co.D
Tackett, Jesse TX 14th Inf. Co.G Cpl.
Tackett, Jessee AR Cav. Gordon's Regt. Co.E
Tackett, J.L. MS 3rd Inf. Co.B
Tackett, John KY 5th Mtd.Inf. Co.G,C
Tackett, John Gen. & Staff Surg.
Tackett, John C. MO St.Guards Sgt.
Tackett, John G.S. AL 30th Inf. Co.I Sgt.
Tackett, John L. GA 60th Inf. Co.K
Tackett, John W. NC 28th Inf. Co.F
Tackett, Joseph M. MO 16th Inf. Co.D
Tackett, Joseph W. MS 20th Inf. Co.C
Tackett, J.P. MS S.W. Red's Co. (St.Troops)
Tackett, J.P. TX 5th Cav. Co.C
Tackett, J.T. VA VMI
Tackett, L. AL 42nd Inf. Co.F
Tackett, L.A. MS 6th Inf. Co.K
Tackett, L.C. MO Cav. 3rd Bn. Co.H
Tackett, Lewis B. AR 15th (N.W.) Inf. Co.E
Tackett, Marion MS 1st Cav. Co.G
Tackett, Marion F. KY 5th Mtd.Inf. Co.H
Tackett, M.C. TN 14th (Neely's) Cav. Co.A
Tackett, N.L. MS 6th Cav. Morgan's Co.
Tackett, N.L. MS 12th Cav. Co.C
Tackett, O.H.P. MS Adams' Co. (Holmes Cty.Ind.)
Tackett, Oldman KY Cav. 1st Bn.
Tackett, Pope MS 12th Cav. Co.E,C
Tackett, Pope MS S.W. Red's Co. (St.Troops)
Tackett, Sevier TX 34th Cav. Maj.
Tackett, Thomas AL 11th Cav. Co.B
Tackett, Thomas A. MO 2nd Inf. Co.E,H
Tackett, Thomas A. NC 48th Inf. Co.H
Tackett, Thomas E. NC 28th Inf. Co.F
Tackett, W.B. GA Inf. 5th Bn. (St.Guards) Co.C
Tackett, Wiley P. GA 21st Inf. Co.A Jr.2nd Lt.
Tackett, William KY 5th Mtd.Inf. Co.K
Tackett, William H. MO 9th (Elliott's) Cav. Co.G
Tackett, William J. AL 12th Inf. Co.E
Tackett, W.M. AL 42nd Inf. Co.F
Tackette, George W. KY 5th Mtd.Inf. Co.G
Tackette, Harvey KY 5th Mtd.Inf. Co.G
Tackette, Solomon KY 5th Mtd.Inf. Co.G
Tackette, William KY 5th Mtd.Inf. Co.G,E
Tackit, --- TX Cav. Border's Regt. Co.K
Tackit, William KY 5th Mtd.Inf. Co.C
Tackitt, David R. TN Inf. Tackitt's Co.
Tackitt, G.W. TX Cav. McCord's Frontier Regt. Co.G
Tackitt, Jesse AR 15th (N.W.) Inf. Co.E
Tackitt, John L. AL 9th Inf. Co.E
Tackitt, John M. AL 42nd Inf. Co.F
Tackitt, Joseph W. TN Inf. Tackitt's Co. Capt.
Tackitt, Lancaster C. AR 15th (N.W.) Inf. Co.E
Tackitt, L.L. TX Cav. McCord's Frontier Regt. Co.G
Tackitt, Louis L. TX 33rd Cav. Co.B
Tackitt, Phillip TN Inf. Tackitt's Co.
Tackitt, Phillip U.J.W. TN Inf. Tackitt's Co.
Tackitt, W.H. TX 34th Cav. Co.B
Tackitt, Wiley B. TN Inf. Tackitt's Co.
Tackitte, J.G. TX Cav. McCord's Frontier Regt. Co.G 1st Sgt.
Tacneau, A. LA 4th Inf. Co.F
Tacon, H. LA Mil. 1st Regt. French Brig. Co.1
Tacon, H. LA Mil. 3rd Regt.Eur.Brig. (Garde Francaise) Co.1
Tacon, Juan LA 10th Inf. Co.G
Taconi, Franco LA Mil. 5th Regt.Eur.Brig. (Spanish Regt.) Co.9
Taconi, Jose LA Mil. 5th Regt.Eur.Brig. (Spanish Regt.) Co.9
Ta cubbee 1st Choctaw & Chickasaw Mtd.Rifles Co.G Cpl.
Tacy, James VA 31st Inf. Co.G
Tacy, John A. VA 19th Cav. Co.I Sgt.
Tadd, John C. TN 5th Cav. Co.E
Tadder, Benjamin FL Inf. 2nd Bn. Co.F
Tadder, George W. FL Inf. 2nd Bn. Co.F
Tade, John TX 32nd Cav. Co.A
Tadei, Massimiliano LA Mil. Cazadores Espanoles Regt. Co.F
Tadlies, W. VA 6th Cav. Co.G
Tadlock, Albert I. AL 41st Inf. Co.E
Tadlock, Alexander NC 37th Inf. Co.D Sgt.
Tadlock, Berton MO Cav. Freeman's Regt. Co.D
Tadlock, B.F. AL 53rd (Part.Rangers) Co.H

Tadlock, C. TX 1st Inf. Co.A
Tadlock, James F. NC 37th Inf. Co.D
Tadlock, James H. AL 11th Inf. Co.K
Tadlock, James W. MO 1st Cav. Co.A
Tadlock, J.C. AL 53rd (Part.Rangers) Co.H
Tadlock, J.C. AR 1st Vol. Kelsey's Co.
Tadlock, J.C. MO Inf. 1st Bn. Co.C
Tadlock, J.C. MO 12th Inf. Co.G
Tadlock, Jo NC 3rd Jr.Res. Co.C
Tadlock, John LA Bickham's Co. (Caddo Mil.) Sgt.
Tadlock, John NC 35th Inf. Co.E
Tadlock, John NC 52nd Inf. Co.B
Tadlock, John TN 61st Mtd.Inf. Co.A
Tadlock, John H. MO 1st N.E. Cav. Co.E
Tadlock, John R. MS 20th Inf. Co.F
Tadlock, John S. TX 36th Cav. Co.A
Tadlock, John W. AL 11th Inf. Co.K
Tadlock, Joseph AL 39th Inf. Co.E
Tadlock, Joseph C. NC 52nd Inf. Co.B
Tadlock, Joshua NC 8th Sr.Res. Gardner's Co.
Tadlock, J.R. AR 8th Inf.
Tadlock, J.T. GA Lt.Arty. Croft's Btty. (Columbus Arty.)
Tadlock, J. Thomas AL 6th Inf. Co.F
Tadlock, J.W. NC Mil. Clark's Sp.Bn. A.R. Davis' Co., Co.B
Tadlock, Malcolmb D.C. AL 11th Inf. Co.K
Tadlock, Piert TN 61st Mtd.Inf. Co.A
Tadlock, Robert J. MS 11th (Perrin's) Cav. Co.K
Tadlock, S.D. NC 30th Inf. Co.E
Tadlock, Severo MO 1st N.E. Cav. Co.E
Tadlock, Sevier TX Cav. McCord's Frontier Regt. 2nd Co.A Bugler
Tadlock, Stephen A. NC 35th Inf. Co.E
Tadlock, Thomas KY 6th Cav. Co.A
Tadlock, Thomas C. NC 46th Inf. Co.F
Tadlock, Thomas W. NC 1st Jr.Res. Co.K
Tadlock, Uriah NC 53rd Inf. Co.I
Tadlock, W. MS Cav. Knox's Co. (Stonewall Rangers) Sgt.
Tadlock, W. MS St.Cav. Perrin's Bn. Co.E Cpl.
Tadlock, W. SC 8th Inf. Co.B
Tadlock, Wiley MS 1st Cav.Res. Co.D Sgt.
Tadlock, Wiley W. AR 14th (McCarver's) Inf. Co.I
Tadlock, William NC 27th Inf. Co.A
Tadlock, William NC 48th Inf. Co.E
Tadlock, William TN 7th (Duckworth's) Cav. Co.L
Tadlock, William C. TN 5th (McKenzie's) Cav. Co.H
Tadlock, William C. TN 61st Mtd.Inf. Co.A
Tadlock, William D. AL 11th Inf. Co.K
Tadlock, William J. NC 2nd Cav. (19th St.Troops) Co.H Cpl.
Tadlock, William N.B. AL 11th Inf. Co.K
Tadlock, William S. NC 46th Inf. Co.I
Tadpole, David 1st Cherokee Mtd.Rifles Co.I
Tadpole, Ely 1st Cherokee Mtd.Rifles Co.I Sgt.
Tadpole, John 1st Cherokee Mtd.Rifles Co.I
Tadpole, Joshua 1st Cherokee Mtd.Rifles Co.I Sgt.
Taeff, Joseph D. TX Cav. Baird's Regt. Co.B 1st Lt.
Tae lus kie, Daniel 1st Cherokee Mtd.Rifles Co.H
Ta fa matubbee 1st Choctaw & Chickasaw Mtd.Rifles Co.G
Tafel, Lewis H. VA 49th Inf. Co.H Sgt.
Taff, Albert G. TN 5th (McKenzie's) Cav. Co.I
Taff, Addison VA 92nd Mil. Co.C
Taff, David A. GA 63rd Inf. Co.I
Taff, E.A. AL 1st Cav. 2nd Co.B
Taff, E.A. AR Lt.Arty. Wiggins' Btty.
Taff, F. AR 18th (Marmaduke's) Inf. Co.B
Taff, F. 3rd Conf.Inf. Co.B
Taff, George W. AL 13th Inf. Co.H
Taff, George W. AR 5th Inf. Co.D
Taff, George W. GA 20th Inf. Co.I
Taff, G.W. MO 7th Cav. Co.H
Taff, Henry C. AL 13th Inf. Co.H
Taff, James AL 13th Inf. Co.H
Taff, James GA 43rd Inf. Co.B Sgt.
Taff, James M. GA 31st Inf. Co.B
Taff, Jasper GA 50th Inf. Co.C
Taff, John AL 5th Inf. Co.H
Taff, John AL 15th Inf. Co.A
Taff, John W. TN 5th (McKenzie's) Cav. Co.I Sgt.
Taff, Joseph D. FL 5th Inf. Co.H
Taff, Joseph Martin MO 8th Inf. Co.E
Taff, L. NC Allen's Co. (Loc.Def.)
Taff, Lawrence AL Pris.Guard Freeman's Co.
Taff, Martin Vanburen MO 8th Inf. Co.E
Taff, Oliver P. AR 14th (Powers') Inf. Co.B
Taff, Patrick AL 20th Inf. Co.K
Taff, Richard GA 20th Inf. Co.I
Taff, Robert GA 31st Inf. Co.B
Taff, Robert GA 50th Inf. Co.C
Taff, Thomas W. GA 31st Inf. Co.B
Taff, William J. AR 14th (Powers') Inf. Co.B
Taff, William L. GA 1st Cav. Co.A
Taff, W.T. FL 10th Inf. Co.D
Taffe, J.H. TN 7th (Duckworth's) Cav. White's Co.
Taffel, Bernhard TX 17th Inf. Co.H
Taffell, John LA 5th Inf. Co.H
Taffer, Iredell NC 29th Inf. Co.B
Taffer, John S. NC 29th Inf. Co.B,K Cpl.
Taffer, W.S. NC 22nd Inf. Co.F
Taffey, Lawrence LA 7th Inf. Co.E
Taffition, C.A. GA 5th Res. Co.G Cpl.
Taffy MS 14th Inf. Co.I Cook
Taflinger, John VA 12th Cav. Co.H
Taflinger, John VA 58th Mil. Co.K
Tafolla, James TX 33rd Cav. Co.B Music.
Taft, Allen H. NC 55th Inf. Co.E Music.
Taft, A.W. SC 25th Inf. Co.B
Taft, A.W. Sig.Corps,CSA Sgt.
Taft, G.E. NC 17th Inf. (1st Org.) Co.C
Taft, Godfrey E. NC 55th Inf. Co.E 2nd Lt.
Taft, James TN 17th Inf. Co.E Sgt.
Taft, J.B. Gen. & Staff Surg.
Taft, J.K.P. GA 12th Cav. Co.G Cpl.
Taft, John AL 2nd Cav. Co.G Cpl.
Taft, John Edward TN 17th Inf. Co.E
Taft, Joseph A. TN 17th Inf. Co.E
Taft, M. AL 41st Inf. Co.G
Taft, Robert M. SC 25th Inf. Co.B Sr.2nd Lt.
Taft, William MS 6th Cav. Co.L
Tafts, A.W. LA 18th Inf. Co.F
Tafts, James G. TN 44th Inf. Co.G
Tafts, James G. TN 44th (Cons.) Inf. Co.F
Tafts, Mathew K. TN 44th (Cons.) Inf. Co.F
Tafts, Matthew H. TN 44th Inf. Co.G
Tagart, A.J. TX 12th Cav. Co.F
Tagart, I.A. TX 27th Cav. Co.M
Tagart, Jas. A. MO 2nd Inf. Co.C Cpl.
Tagart, J.H. TX 3rd Cav. Co.A
Tagart, Leo MO Cav. Poindexter's Regt. Co.I
Tagart, W.R. TX Cav. 1st Bn.St.Troops Co.D
Tage, Tillman Gen. & Staff Chap.
Tagenseh NC Inf. Thomas Legion Co.B
Tager, Anderson SC 1st (Butler's) Inf. Co.E
Tager, John Adam SC 1st (Butler's) Inf. Co.E
Tager, L. NC 2nd Inf. Co.G
Tagert, D.F. TX 21st Cav. Co.G
Tagert, E.C. AL Mil. T. Hunt's Co.
Tagert, J.A. NC Lt.Arty. 3rd Bn. Co.C
Tagert, James S. NC 37th Inf. Co.I
Taget, T.W. AL 48th Mil. Co.A
Taggart, Alfred KY 13th Cav. Co.D
Taggart, A.S. AL 41st Inf. Co.I
Taggart, David C. AL 41st Inf. Co.I
Taggart, George A. MS 15th Inf. Co.C
Taggart, James, Jr. SC 6th Cav. Co.G 1st Lt.
Taggart, J.H. Bradford's Corps Scouts & Guards Co.B
Taggart, J.J. VA 54th Mil. Co.H
Taggart, J.L. MS Cav. Jeff Davis Legion Co.C Sgt.
Taggart, John LA 22nd Inf. Wash. Marks' Co.
Taggart, John MO 1st Inf. Co.F
Taggart, Joseph AR 50th Mil. Co.I
Taggart, Lee MO 7th Cav. Co.E
Taggart, M.A. MS Cav. 4th Bn. Co.B
Taggart, M.A. 8th (Wade's) Conf.Cav. Co.D
Taggart, M.C. SC 1st (Butler's) Inf. Surg.
Taggart, M.C. SC 14th Inf. Co.G Capt.
Taggart, Moses W. AL 11th Inf. Co.H 1st Sgt.
Taggart, M.W. AR 6th Inf. Co.E
Taggart, N.M. MS Cav. Jeff Davis Legion Co.C
Taggart, Oliver C. AL 41st Inf. Co.F
Taggart, Patrick SC 15th Inf. Co.K
Taggart, R.A. VA Inf. 6th Bn.Loc.Def. Co.C
Taggart, R.L. MS Cav. Jeff Davis Legion Co.C Sgt.
Taggart, Robert A. VA 44th Inf. Co.C
Taggart, Robert L. MS 42nd Inf. Surg.
Taggart, Robert L. Gen. & Staff Surg.
Taggart, W.A. AL 8th Inf. Co.D
Taggart, W.A. MS Cav. 4th Bn. Co.B
Taggart, W.A. MS 28th Cav. Co.G
Taggart, W.A. 8th (Wade's) Conf.Cav. Co.D
Taggart, W.H. SC 1st St.Troops Co.I
Taggart, William SC 1st Cav. Co.G,A
Taggart, William H. SC 15th Inf. Co.K 1st Lt.
Taggart, William M. SC 1st Cav.
Taggart, William S. MS Cav. 4th Bn. Sykes' Co.
Taggart, William S. 8th (Wade's) Conf.Cav. Co.G
Taggart, W.M. GA 32nd Inf. Asst.Surg.
Taggart, W.M. Gen. & Staff Asst.Surg.
Taggert, Alexander SC 1st Arty. Co.B
Taggert, George W. AL 3rd Inf. Co.E
Taggert, Jacob A. AL 24th Inf. Co.I
Taggert, J.C. NC 11th (Bethel Regt.) Inf. Co.H
Taggert, John W. AL 42nd Inf. Co.I
Taggert, Philip S. AL Cav. Moreland's Regt.
Taggett, James L. SC 1st Arty. Co.B

Taggett, L. TX Cav. Giddings' Bn. Pickerell's Co.
Taggle, George TN Inf. 2nd Cons.Regt. Co.G
Taggle, Preston TX Cav. Frontier Bn. Co.A
Tagles, M. AR 27th Inf. Co.A
Tagmert, H. TX Inf. 1st St.Troops Biehler's Co.A
Tagne, John N. KY 4th Cav. Co.E 1st Lt.
Tagni, Churubino TN 15th Inf. Co.K Cpl.
Tagott, A. LA Lt.Arty. Bridges' Btty.
Tagt, M.B. NC 7th Inf. Co.E
Tague, A. KY Corbin's Men
Tague, Alonzo KY Jessee's Bn.Mtd.Riflemen Co.A
Tague, George W. KY Jessee's Bn.Mtd.Riflemen Co.A Sgt.
Tague, J. 2nd Conf.Eng.Troops Co.B
Tague, J.A. KY 9th Cav. Co.G
Tague, John GA 1st (Olmstead's) Inf. Co.C
Tague, John LA 7th Inf. Co.C
Tague, John LA 14th Inf. Co.K
Tague, Moses A. NC Inf. Thomas Legion Co.G
Tague, Smith NC Inf. Thomas Legion Co.G
Tague, Thomas J. KY Jessee's Bn.Mtd.Riflemen Co.A
Tague, William TN 2nd (Ashby's) Cav. Co.H Cpl.
Taha 1st Choctaw & Chickasaw Mtd.Rifles 2nd Co.C
Tahaun, Edmund LA Miles' Legion Co.F
Tahbrought, Aug. LA 15th Inf. Co.B
Tah cah Soh Kah Tee Ke chee 1st Cherokee Mtd.Rifles Co.B
Tah chur See Jack 1st Cherokee Mtd.Rifles Co.G
Tah chur see Tah lah 1st Cherokee Mtd.Rifles Co.G
Tah co Sah Harjo 1st Seminole Mtd.Vol.
Tahekobbee 1st Choctaw & Chickasaw Mtd.Rifles 3rd Co.D 1st Lt.
Tahen, Joseph TN 2nd (Walker's) Inf. Co.A
Tahey, James TN 1st Lt.Arty. Co.G 1st Lt.
Tah gah che gee sy 1st Cherokee Mtd.Rifles McDaniel's Co.
Tahgenseh NC Inf. Thomas Legion Co.B
Tahishtubee Thompson 1st Choctaw Mtd.Rifles Co.F Sgt.
Tah ke 1st Creek Mtd.Vol. Co.A
Tahkehyeh NC Inf. Thomas Legion 2nd Co.A
Tah Ker yer oo cha looty 1st Cherokee Mtd.Rifles Co.D
Tah ker yer Wolf 1st Cherokee Mtd.Rifles Co.D Sgt.
Tah lawse Redbird 1st Cherokee Mtd.Rifles Co.H
Tahlee (of Deep Creek) NC Inf. Thomas Legion Co.B
Tahlee Catalstas son NC Inf. Thomas Legion Co.B,D
Tah le eus Ky Scraper 1st Cherokee Mtd.Rifles Co.E
Tahler, J.M. MS 11th (Cons.) Cav. Co.I
Tahlor, Henry A. FL 1st Inf. Old Co.H, New Co.B Sgt.
Tahneenteh NC Inf. Thomas Legion Co.B
Tahnehubbee 1st Choctaw & Chickasaw Mtd.Rifles 2nd Co.H
Tah ne nah la 1st Cherokee Mtd.Rifles Co.E
Tah ne noli, David 1st Cherokee Mtd.Rifles Co.G
Tah ne noli skin tah ee 1st Cherokee Mtd.Rifles Co.G
Tah ner ees ky 1st Cherokee Mtd.Vol. 1st Co.C
Tah ner yes ky 1st Cherokee Mtd.Rifles Co.A Cpl.
Tah ne yes Kie 1st Cherokee Mtd.Rifles Co.C
Tahnie Walkingstick 1st Cherokee Mtd.Rifles Co.E 1st Sgt.
Tahnohlee NC Inf. Thomas Legion 2nd Co.A
Tah Nowie Squirrel 1st Cherokee Mtd.Rifles Co.G
Tahnuwer, Wm. 1st Cherokee Mtd.Vol. Co.H
Ta hobbi 1st Choctaw Mtd.Rifles Co.K
Ta ho ta 1st Choctaw & Chickasaw Mtd.Rifles 1st Co.E
Tahsekeyahgee Arquitage NC Inf. Thomas Legion 2nd Co.A
Tahsekeyahgee Stoogatogeh NC Inf. Thomas Legion 2nd Co.A
Tah skee ge tekee 1st Cherokee Mtd.Vol. 1st Co.A, 2nd Co.E
Tahskeeketehee NC Inf. Thomas Legion 2nd Co.A
Tah ske gat eehe 1st Cherokee Mtd.Vol. 2nd Co.B
Tah ske ke te hee 1st Cherokee Mtd.Vol. 1st Co.C
Ta huk ni che 1st Creek Mtd.Vol. 2nd Co.C
Tahun, Paul C. VA Inf. 22nd Bn. Co.B
Tahunee, Ben 1st Cherokee Mtd.Vol. 2nd Co.H
Tahuwee Henry 1st Cherokee Mtd.Vol. 2nd Co.H
Tah yes Ky 1st Cherokee Mtd.Rifles Co.A Cpl.
Tah yool Sin ee 1st Cherokee Mtd.Rifles Co.D
Taif, Edward TX 3rd Inf. Co.I
Taiff, E. TX 8th Cav. Co.C
Taik ke 1st Creek Mtd.Vol. Co.A
Tailer, E. LA Mil.Cont.Cadets
Tailer, Thomas MO 15th Cav. Co.D
Tailleur, Robert LA 10th Inf. Co.F
Taillot, Laurentine LA Mil. 1st Native Guards
Tailor, A.F. AR Cav. McGehee's Regt. Co.C
Tailor, Allen VA 11th Bn.Res. Co.E
Tailor, Anderson TN Cav. 12th Bn. (Day's) Co.F
Tailor, Harve MO Cav. Clardy's Bn. Co.B
Tailor, J.A. AL 56th Part.Rangers Co.G
Tailor, W.T. TN Lt.Arty. Morton's Co.
Taines, --- GA 16th Inf. Co.E
Tains 1st Choctaw & Chickasaw Mtd.Rifles 1st Co.H
Tainsh, John LA Mil. Irish Regt. O'Brien's Co.
Taintblanc, F. LA Mil. 3rd Regt. French Brig. Co.4
Tainter, Robert LA 1st Cav. Co.B
Taintor, G.M. LA 28th (Gray's) Inf. Co.K
Taiomey, George W. VA 86th Mil. Co.D
Tait, Brantley GA Cav. 1st Bn. Brailsford's Co.
Tait, Brantley GA 5th Cav. Co.H
Tait, Charles H. 1st Conf.Eng.Troops Co.D Music.
Tait, Charles M. GA 2nd Cav. Co.K
Tait, Edmund B., Jr. GA 15th Inf. Co.C 1st Sgt.
Tait, Enos R. GA 15th Inf. Co.C
Tait, Felix AL 3rd Cav. Co.D 1st Sgt.
Tait, Felix AL 23rd Inf. Maj.
Tait, George NC 3rd Arty. (40th St.Troops) Co.K Lt.Col.
Tait, George NC 18th Inf. Co.K Maj.
Tait, James AL 1st Regt. Mobile Vol. Co.E Sgt.
Tait, James TN Cav. 1st Bn. (McNairy's) Co.B
Tait, James VA Inf. 2nd Bn.Loc.Def. Co.E Cpl.
Tait, James E. AR 18th Inf. Co.F
Tait, James M. LA 28th (Gray's) Inf. Co.D
Tait, Jasper S. GA 15th Inf. Co.C Cpl.
Tait, J.H. MS 27th Inf. Co.D
Tait, John H. TN Cav. 9th Bn. (Gantt's) Co.F
Tait, Joseph A. LA Mil. Beauregard Bn. Frobus' Co.
Tait, R.E. LA 17th Inf. Co.H
Tait, Richard Mtd.Spies & Guides Madison's Co.
Tait, Robert NC 18th Inf. Co.B ACS
Tait, Robert Gen. & Staff Capt.,Comsy.
Tait, Robert F. GA 3rd Cav. (St.Guards) Co.H
Tait, R.W. NC 48th Inf. Co.C
Tait, S.T. AL 38th Inf. Co.I
Tait, T.B.C. AL 5th Inf. New Co.I
Tait, Thos. B.C. AL 38th Inf. Co.A
Tait, Walter VA 34th Inf. Norton's Co.
Tait, William AR Sander's Cav. Co.A
Tait, William GA 16th Inf. Co.G
Tait, William MS 9th Cav. Co.B
Tait, William NC 8th Sr.Res. Broadhurst's Co.
Tait, William TN Cav. 17th Bn. (Sanders') Co.A
Tait, William H. GA 16th Inf. Co.B
Tait, William J. TN 54th Inf. Co.E
Tait, William P. AL City Guards Lockett's Co.
Tait, W.J. TN 48th (Nixon's) Inf. Co.K
Taite, G.A. GA 4th (Clinch's) Cav. Co.A,F
Taite, James VA 2nd Inf.Loc.Def. Co.C Cpl.
Taite, Jeremiah M. NC 17th Inf. (1st Org.) Co.B
Taite, Jeremiah M. NC 17th Inf. (2nd Org.) Co.B
Taite, Lewis LA 1st Hvy.Arty. (Reg.) Co.C
Taite, Robert AL Mil. 4th Vol. Co.A
Taite, Wilson L. AR 19th (Dawson's) Inf. Co.A
Taitt, Robert FL 2nd Inf. Co.G
Takaska NC Inf. Thomas Legion
Take, J.W. NC Inf. Thomas Legion
Take, W. TX Inf. Timmons' Regt. Co.K
Tak eesomo 1st Seminole Mtd.Vol.
Ta Ker Na Se nee 1st Cherokee Mtd.Rifles Co.A
Takes tas ker 1st Cherokee Mtd.Vol. 1st Co.C
Takewee, William R. LA Watkins' Bn.Res.Corps Co.C
Takewell, David H. LA 31st Inf. Co.K
Takewell, W.R. LA 31st Inf. Co.K
Taklantubbee 1st Choctaw Mtd.Rifles Co.F
Tak lombi, Lewis 1st Choctaw Mtd.Rifles Co.K Sgt.
Takstas kee, George 1st Cherokee Mtd.Vol. 1st Co.C
Talageeskih NC Inf. Thomas Legion 2nd Co.A Sgt.
Talaggs, Robert AL Res. J.G. Rankin's Co.
Talamante, Eulajio TX Cav. Ragsdale's Bn. 1st Co.C
Talamas, Leon LA Mil. 3rd Regt. French Brig. Co.1
Talamente, Usabio TX Cav. Ragsdale's Bn. 1st Co.A Cpl.
Talamentes, Jose Maria TX 3rd Inf. Co.F
Taland, ---, 1st TX Cav. McCord's Frontier Regt. Co.I
Talanosteh Tagenteh NC Inf. Thomas Legion 2nd Co.A

Talant, Benjamin C. GA 2nd (Stapleton's) St.Troops 3rd Lt.
Talant, R.M. AR 19th (Dawson's) Inf. Co.C
Talant, Thomas GA 2nd (Stapleton's) St.Troops Co.A
Talapoose, John 1st Choctaw & Chickasaw Mtd.Rifles 1st Co.E
Talapoose, John Choctaw Inf. Wilkins' Co.
Talapoose, Washington 1st Choctaw & Chickasaw Mtd.Rifles 2nd Co.H Cpl.
Talaskaskee NC Inf. Thomas Legion 2nd Co.A
Talazac, F. LA Mil. 4th Regt. French Brig. Co.6
Talazac, L. LA Mil. 4th Regt. French Brig. Co.3
Talbatt, E.M. MO Robertson's Regt.St.Guard Co.5
Talberry, J.B. MS Lt.Arty. (Jefferson Arty.) Darden's Co.
Talbert, A. SC 21st Inf. Co.E
Talbert, A.J. MS Cav. Jeff Davis Legion Co.E Cpl.
Talbert, A.J. SC 21st Inf. Co.D
Talbert, A.J. VA 30th Bn.S.S. Co.B
Talbert, Alex. AL 3rd Cav. Co.C
Talbert, Alexander NC 26th Inf. Co.I
Talbert, Austin VA 48th Inf. Co.F
Talbert, B. SC 7th Res. Co.I
Talbert, Barthy M. SC 5th Res. Co.F
Talbert, Bartlet M. SC 1st St.Troops Co.D
Talbert, Basil T. AR 15th (Josey's) Inf. Co.D
Talbert, B.C. AR 34th Inf. Co.G
Talbert, B.M. SC 7th Inf. 1st Co.K Capt.
Talbert, Calvin R. NC 34th Inf. Co.K
Talbert, Chap L. SC Inf. 9th Bn. Co.E
Talbert, Clark C. GA 56th Inf. Co.A
Talbert, Cornelius LA 28th (Gray's) Inf. Co.A
Talbert, Cylus LA 28th (Gray's) Inf. Co.B
Talbert, Davis NC 1st Jr.Res. Co.E
Talbert, D.M. FL 2nd Cav. Co.I Sgt.
Talbert, D.W. TN 8th (Smith's) Cav. Co.G
Talbert, Edmund MS 29th Inf. Co.E
Talbert, E.G. AL Mil. 4th Vol. Co.G
Talbert, E.G. AL 43rd Inf. Co.F
Talbert, Elziran NC 22nd Inf. Co.L
Talbert, F. MD Cav. 2nd Bn. Co.F
Talbert, Francis M. AR 23rd Inf. Co.D
Talbert, Frank AL 38th Inf. Co.H
Talbert, Frank T. AL Mil. 4th Vol. Co.A
Talbert, G.B. NC 5th Sr.Res. Co.D
Talbert, George W. SC 24th Inf. Co.K 2nd Lt.
Talbert, George W. VA 166th Mil. Taylor's Co.
Talbert, Giles NC 26th Inf. Co.I
Talbert, Green AL 55th Vol. Co.H
Talbert, G.W. AL 17th Inf. Co.H
Talbert, G.W. GA 3rd Cav. Co.H,K Cpl.
Talbert, Henry MO Cav. Fristoe's Regt. Co.A
Talbert, H.G. MS 29th Inf. Co.E
Talbert, H.S. MO Cav. Fristoe's Regt. Co.A
Talbert, Isaiah AL 45th Inf. Co.K
Talbert, J. AL Inf. 1st Regt. Co.G Cpl.
Talbert, J. SC Prov.Guard Hamilton's Co.
Talbert, James AL 17th Inf. Co.H
Talbert, James AR 36th Inf. Co.K
Talbert, James B. MS 29th Inf. Co.E Cpl.
Talbert, James C. NC 34th Inf. Co.K
Talbert, James K.P. MS 44th Inf. Co.K
Talbert, James L. LA 1st (Nelligan's) Inf. Co.A
Talbert, J.C. MS Gully's Co.
Talbert, J.D. MS 1st Bn.S.S. Co.D 2nd Lt.
Talbert, J.D. MS 24th Inf. Co.A Capt.
Talbert, J.D. MS 25th Inf. Co.H 2nd Lt.
Talbert, J.D. Conf.Arty. Courtney's Bn. Adj.
Talbert, J.D. 2nd Conf.Inf. Co.H 2nd Lt.
Talbert, Jerry T. MS 15th Inf. Co.H
Talbert, J.H. AL 5th Inf. New Co.I
Talbert, J.H. AR 14th (Powers') Inf. Co.F
Talbert, J.M. AL 21st Inf. Co.C
Talbert, J.M. AR 14th (Powers') Inf. Co.F
Talbert, J.M. GA 13th Cav. Co.I
Talbert, John AR 24th Inf. Co.E
Talbert, John AR 38th Inf. Co.D
Talbert, John MO 10th Cav. Co.I
Talbert, John NC 26th Inf. Co.I
Talbert, John SC Cav.Bn. Hampton Legion Co.A
Talbert, John TX Cav. Hardeman's Regt. Co.B Cpl.
Talbert, John D. MS 29th Inf. Co.G 1st Lt.
Talbert, John F. SC 5th Res. Co.F Capt.
Talbert, John F. SC 7th Inf. 1st Co.K
Talbert, John L. MS Cav. Jeff Davis Legion Co.E
Talbert, John W. AL 36th Inf. Co.F
Talbert, Joseph L. SC 7th Inf. 1st Co.K, 2nd Co.K 1st Lt.
Talbert, Josiah T. GA 1st Cav. Co.E
Talbert, Josiah T. GA Arty. 9th Bn. Co.A
Talbert, J.R. MS 29th Inf. Co.E 1st Lt.
Talbert, Julius NC 1st Jr.Res. Co.E
Talbert, J.W. SC 4th Bn.Res. Co.B
Talbert, Levi NC 6th Sr.Res. Co.A
Talbert, Levi J. GA Phillips' Legion Co.B,H
Talbert, L.P. LA 27th Inf. Co.A Capt.
Talbert, Mark T. NC 34th Inf. Co.K
Talbert, Michael S. SC Inf. 7th Bn. (Enfield Rifles) Co.H
Talbert, Miles NC 34th Inf. Co.K
Talbert, Nathaniel LA 12th Inf. Co.L
Talbert, O.W. SC 8th Inf. Co.D
Talbert, Perry M. VA 31st Inf. Co.H
Talbert, P.W. TN 15th Inf. Co.A
Talbert, Ransom GA Arty. 9th Bn. Co.A
Talbert, S. AL Inf. 1st Regt. Co.C
Talbert, Samuel N. MS 2nd Inf. Co.B,L
Talbert, Samuel N. SC 14th Inf. Co.G
Talbert, S.C. GA Inf. 27th Bn. Co.E
Talbert, Simeon MO Cav. Fristoe's Regt. Co.A,H
Talbert, Simeon MO Cav. Preston's Bn. Co.A
Talbert, T. GA 23rd Inf. Co.G
Talbert, T.B. MO Cav. Fristoe's Regt. Co.A
Talbert, Thomas B. SC 14th Inf. Co.G Sgt.
Talbert, Thomas C. MO 9th (Elliott's) Cav. Co.A
Talbert, Thomas H. TX 22nd Cav. Co.H
Talbert, Thomas N. SC Cav.Bn. Hampton Legion Co.A
Talbert, Thomas W. LA 27th Inf. Co.A Cpl.
Talbert, T.J. LA 2nd Inf. Co.A
Talbert, T.S. MO Cav. Fristoe's Regt. Co.A
Talbert, Walter MO Cav. Fristoe's Regt. Co.A
Talbert, W.H. SC Hvy.Arty. 15th (Lucas') Bn. Co.C
Talbert, Wiley MS 44th Inf. Co.K
Talbert, Wiley L. VA 37th Inf. Co.K
Talbert, William MO Cav. Fristoe's Regt. Co.A
Talbert, William SC 5th Bn.Res. Co.B
Talbert, William A. AL 5th Cav. Co.C
Talbert, William B. MO Cav. Poindexter's Regt.
Talbert, William J. SC Inf. Hampton Legion Co.B
Talbert, William Jasper SC 5th Res. Co.F
Talbert, William L. SC Inf. Hampton Legion Co.B
Talbert, William M. AR 14th (Powers') Inf. Co.F
Talbert, William M. GA 34th Inf. Co.E
Talbert, William T. NC 1st Inf. (6 mo. '61) Co.I
Talbert, William T. SC Inf. 9th Bn. Co.E
Talbert, William W. TX 36th Cav. Co.E
Talbert, W.L. SC 7th Inf. 1st Co.K, 2nd Co.K Sgt.
Talbert, W.T. SC 1st Arty. Co.D
Talbert, W.T. SC 8th Inf. Co.D
Talbert, W.W. GA Cobb's Legion Co.D
Talbird, Franklin SC 11th Inf. Co.A
Talbird, Henry AL 11th Inf. Co.K Capt.
Talbird, Henry AL 41st Inf. Col.
Talbird, John E. SC Arty. Stuart's Co. (Beaufort Vol.Arty.) Artif.
Talbird, John E. SC 11th Inf. Co.A Org.Sgt.
Talbird, John H. AL 12th Inf. Co.K
Talbird, John H. AL 29th Inf. Co.I 1st Lt.
Talbird, Marion B. GA 1st Reg. Co.I 1st Sgt.
Talbird, Marion B. GA Phillips' Legion Co.A,G
Talbird, William H. SC Cav.Bn. Hampton Legion Co.B
Talbirt, C.L. SC 26th Inf. Co.F
Talbirt, W.T. SC 26th Inf. Co.F
Talbort, James R. GA Phillips' Legion Co.D,K
Talbot, A.J. AL 39th Inf. Co.A 1st Sgt.
Talbot, A.J. GA 50th Inf. Co.C
Talbot, Albert F. GA Cobb's Legion Co.D
Talbot, Alex KY 2nd (Duke's) Cav. Co.E
Talbot, Alexander KY 2nd Mtd.Inf. Co.F
Talbot, A.S. TX Inf. Townsend's Co. (Robertson Five S.)
Talbot, Asa F. AR Cav. Harrell's Bn. Co.C
Talbot, Augustin LA 1st Cav. Co.A,I
Talbot, Bailey M. AL 57th Inf. Co.H Capt.
Talbot, Baily M. AL 18th Inf. Co.H 2nd Lt.
Talbot, Benjamin AL 39th Inf. Co.A Cpl.
Talbot, B.M. KY 2nd Mtd.Inf. Co.H
Talbot, Cadwallader R. AL Eufaula Lt.Arty.
Talbot, Calvin GA Cobb's Legion Co.D
Talbot, Charles W. VA 12th Cav. Co.I
Talbot, Clovis LA 1st Hvy.Arty. (Reg.) Co.B
Talbot, D. KY 1st Bn.Mtd.Rifles Co.D
Talbot, David M. VA 6th Bn.Res. Co.E
Talbot, E.B. LA 27th Inf. Co.D
Talbot, Edward LA 2nd Cav. Co.I
Talbot, Edward VA Second Class Mil. Hobson's Co.
Talbot, Edwin GA 3rd Res. Co.K
Talbot, Edwin Ruthvin VA 2nd Cav. Co.G Cpl.
Talbot, E.M. MS 6th Inf. Co.E Cpl.
Talbot, Emile LA 2nd Cav. Co.H
Talbot, Ernest LA 2nd Cav. Co.H
Talbot, Ernest LA Mil. Assumption Regt.
Talbot, Garrett KY 10th Cav. Co.C
Talbot, Gayle TX 35th (Brown's) Cav. Co.D
Talbot, George B. AL 3rd Inf. Co.E
Talbot, George T. LA Inf.Cons.Crescent Regt. Co.B
Talbot, George W. NC 23rd Inf. Co.D

Talbot, George W. VA 14th Inf. Co.H
Talbot, G.O. KY Horse Arty. Byrne's Co. Sgt.
Talbot, H.D. KY 2nd Bn.Mtd.Rifles Co.D
Talbot, Hesekiah AL 18th Inf. Co.B
Talbot, Hugh AL Rives' Supp.Force 9th Congr.Dist.
Talbot, Isaiah T. AL 61st Inf. Co.F
Talbot, Isham KY 1st Inf. Co.H
Talbot, Isham Gen. & Staff AASurg.
Talbot, J. AR 1st Vol. Co.K
Talbot, J. AR 13th Mil. Co.G
Talbot, J.A. AL 4th Res. Co.E 1st Lt.
Talbot, James GA 1st (Olmstead's) Inf. Co.E Cpl.
Talbot, James LA 28th (Thomas') Inf. Gunner
Talbot, James TX 35th (Likens') Cav. Co.E
Talbot, James A. AL 37th Inf. Co.I Capt.
Talbot, James C. MO 3rd Cav. Co.C
Talbot, James M. GA 2nd Bn.S.S. Co.C
Talbot, James W. MO 2nd Cav. 3rd Co.K
Talbot, James W. MO 3rd Cav. Co.D
Talbot, James W. MO Cav. 3rd Bn. Co.D
Talbot, Jason H. AL 39th Inf. Co.F Sgt.
Talbot, J.B. GA 63rd Inf. Co.I
Talbot, J.B. TX Inf. Townsend's Co. (Robertson Five S.)
Talbot, J.B., Sr. TX Inf. Townsend's Co. (Robertson Five S.)
Talbot, J.M. AL 39th Inf. Co.A
Talbot, John TX 20th Inf. Co.D
Talbot, John VA 2nd Inf. Co.D
Talbot, John B. TN 7th Inf. Co.H 2nd Lt.
Talbot, John C. AL Cav. Falkner's Co.
Talbot, John D. VA 6th Inf. Co.C
Talbot, John F. NC 43rd Inf. Co.E
Talbot, John F. TX 35th (Brown's) Cav. Co.G
Talbot, John H. KY 4th Cav. Co.E
Talbot, Johnson VA Lt.Arty. Penick's Co.
Talbot, John T. TX Terry's Mtd.Inf. (St.Troops)
Talbot, J.R. GA 2nd Cav. (St.Guards) Co.C 2nd Lt.
Talbot, J.S. AL Vol. Meador's Co.
Talbot, Julius LA 1st Hvy.Arty. (Reg.) Co.B
Talbot, L. TN 3rd (Forrest's) Cav. Co.D
Talbot, Leslie C. VA Hvy.Arty. 10th Bn. Co.B Jr.2nd Lt.
Talbot, Leslie C. VA Lt.Arty. J.D. Smith's Co. Sgt.
Talbot, Leslie C. Conf.Arty. Lewis' Bn. Co.A Sgt.
Talbot, Levi GA Inf. (Madison Cty. Home Guard) Milner's Co.
Talbot, Levi O. GA Cobb's Legion Co.D
Talbot, Lewis F. MD Arty. 2nd Btty. Cpl.
Talbot, Luke AL 6th Cav. Co.C
Talbot, Luke T. AL 37th Inf. Co.I
Talbot, L.W. AR 7th Inf. Co.I
Talbot, Martin LA 11th Inf. Co.A
Talbot, Mat TX 8th Cav. Co.B
Talbot, Matt, Jr. TX Part.Rangers Peareson's Co. Sgt.
Talbot, Matthew TX 19th Cav. Co.H
Talbot, Melville S. VA 11th Inf. Co.A
Talbot, M. Henry GA 9th Inf. Co.I Capt.
Talbot, Michael VA 14th Inf. Co.H
Talbot, Milton KY Recruit Bourbon Cty.
Talbot, M.T. KY Recruit Bourbon Cty.
Talbot, N. LA 28th (Gray's) Inf. Co.A Cpl.
Talbot, Peter LA 21st (Patton's) Inf. Co.A
Talbot, Pinkney W. TN 17th Inf. Co.B
Talbot, R. TX Cav. Morgan's Regt. Co.E
Talbot, R.C. TX Inf. Timmons' Regt. Co.G
Talbot, Robert S. MO 4th Cav. Co.I
Talbot, Roe TX Inf. Townsend's Co. (Robertson Five S.)
Talbot, Samuel H. MO 3rd Cav. Co.K
Talbot, Sanders W. AL 37th Inf. Co.I
Talbot, Sanford J. MO Cav. 11th Regt.St.Guard Co.A Col.
Talbot, Simon H. AR Cav. Harrell's Bn. Co.C
Talbot, Spencer M. VA Hvy.Arty. Patteson's Co.
Talbot, Theo LA 2nd Cav. Co.G
Talbot, Thomas MO 1st Inf. Co.H
Talbot, Thomas VA 6th Bn.Res. Co.I
Talbot, Valmond LA Inf.Cons.Crescent Regt. Co.H
Talbot, Wallace P. LA 7th Inf. Co.E 2nd Lt.
Talbot, Walter AR Cav. Harrell's Bn. Co.C
Talbot, W.B. MS Hall's Co. Cpl.
Talbot, W.C. GA 20th Inf. Co.I
Talbot, W.H. AL 22nd Inf. Co.F
Talbot, W.H. LA 18th Inf. Co.F
Talbot, William GA Phillips' Legion Co.M
Talbot, William VA 11th Bn.Res. Co.C
Talbot, William A. LA Arty. Kean's Btty. (Orleans Ind.Arty.)
Talbot, William B. MO Mtd.Inf. Boone's Regt.
Talbot, William H. MS 2nd Inf. Co.B
Talbot, William H. SC Lt.Arty. Garden's Co. (Palmetto Lt.Btty.)
Talbot, William H. VA 54th Mil. Co.B
Talbot, William M. 3rd Conf.Cav. Co.I
Talbot, William T. AR 4th Inf. Co.D
Talbot, W.M. TX 20th Inf. Co.D
Talbot, Young TX Inf. Townsend's Co. (Robertson Five S.)
Talbott, --- 1st Choctaw & Chickasaw Mtd.Rifles 2nd Co.B
Talbott, A. KY 3rd Cav. Co.E 1st Lt.
Talbott, A.L. KY 2nd (Duke's) Cav. Co.K
Talbott, Alexander KY 8th Cav. Co.E 1st Lt.
Talbott, Allan VA Inf. 4th Bn.Loc.Def. Lt.,Adj.
Talbott, Allan Gen. & Staff 1st Lt.,Adj.
Talbott, Allen MS 2nd Inf. Co.B
Talbott, Andrew J. VA Lt.Arty. Jeffress' Co.
Talbott, A.S. TX 4th Inf. Co.C
Talbott, Basile LA Arty. 1st Field Btty.
Talbott, B.E. LA 2nd Cav. Co.I
Talbott, Benjamin AR 7th Inf. Co.C 1st Lt.
Talbott, Benjamin MO 1st Cav. Co.I
Talbott, Benjamin A. MO Inf. 8th Bn. Co.E Cpl.
Talbott, C.H. VA 4th Cav. Co.I
Talbott, C.H. VA Cav. 1st Bn.St.Line Co.D 1st Lt.
Talbott, Charles AR 11th & 17th Cons.Inf. Co.I
Talbott, Charles KY 11th Cav. Co.G
Talbott, Charles H. VA 3rd Cav. Co.F
Talbott, Daniel VA 62nd Mtd.Inf. 2nd Co.E
Talbott, David VA 20th Cav. Co.D
Talbott, David VA 53rd Inf. Co.F
Talbott, E.C. AL 15th Inf. Co.C
Talbott, E.L. TX 32nd Cav. Co.F
Talbott, G.E. GA 36th (Villepigue's) Inf. Co.H
Talbott, George E. Lt.Arty. Dent's Btty.,CSA
Talbott, George H. VA Inf. 22nd Bn. Co.A
Talbott, G.H. VA Lt.Arty. Penick's Co.
Talbott, G.O. KY 6th Mtd.Inf. Co.D
Talbott, Hiram P. MO 12th Inf. Co.D
Talbott, Irvin B. VA 62nd Mtd.Inf. 2nd Co.E Sgt.
Talbott, Irvin F. VA 62nd Mtd.Inf. 2nd Co.E
Talbott, James AR 19th (Dawson's) Inf.
Talbott, James KY 4th Mtd.Inf. Co.E
Talbott, James KY 5th Mtd.Inf. Co.E
Talbott, James LA 15th Inf. Co.F Ord.Sgt.
Talbott, James B. AL 4th Inf. Co.H
Talbott, James C. MO 12th Inf. Co.D
Talbott, James F. KY 2nd Mtd.Inf. Co.C Sgt.
Talbott, Jeremiah VA Hvy.Arty. 20th Bn. Co.D
Talbott, Jesse VA Inf. 4th Bn.Loc.Def. Co.C
Talbott, J.H. Conf.Lt.Arty. Richardson's Bn. Co.A
Talbott, J.M., Jr. VA Lt.Arty. 13th Bn. Co.A
Talbott, J.N. NC Cumberland Cty.Bn. Detailed Men Co.B
Talbott, John GA 17th Inf. Co.G 1st Lt.
Talbott, John KY 9th Cav. Co.E
Talbott, John Gen. & Staff, QM Dept.
Talbott, John Gen. & Staff Surg.
Talbott, John B. VA Hvy.Arty. Wright's Co.
Talbott, John H. KY 4th Mtd.Inf. Co.E
Talbott, John P. KY 1st Bn.Mtd.Rifles Co.D
Talbott, John P. KY 3rd Bn.Mtd.Rifles Asst.Surg.
Talbott, Jno. P. Gen. & Staff Asst.Surg.
Talbott, Johnson VA 38th Inf. Co.F
Talbott, John W. VA 12th Inf. Co.D,C
Talbott, John W. Gen. & Staff Asst.Surg.
Talbott, Joseph TX 32nd Cav. Co.F
Talbott, J.T. MS 22nd Inf. Co.A
Talbott, J.W. MO St.Guard 2nd Lt.
Talbott, Lawrence Morgan's,CSA AAG
Talbott, Louis C. VA 62nd Mtd.Inf. 2nd Co.E
Talbott, L.S. Hébert's Staff Capt.,Ord.Off.
Talbott, M.B. KY 8th Cav. Co.D
Talbott, M.S. KY Cav. 1st Bn.
Talbott, Nathan 1st Choctaw & Chickasaw Mtd.Rifles Co.A
Talbott, N.M. MO 16th Inf. Chap.
Talbott, N.M. Gen. & Staff Chap.
Talbott, P.W. TN 15th Inf. Co.A
Talbott, R. TX Waul's Legion Co.A
Talbott, R.L. AR Cav. Gordon's Regt. Surg.
Talbott, R.L. Gen. & Staff Surg.
Talbott, Romulus TX 11th Inf. Co.D
Talbott, Salathiel VA 62nd Mtd.Inf. 2nd Co.E
Talbott, Samuel G. VA Lt.Arty. 13th Bn. Co.A
Talbott, Samuel T. KY 1st Bn.Mtd.Rifles Co.C
Talbott, Spencer M. VA Hvy.Arty. 20th Bn. Co.D
Talbott, S.T. KY 3rd Bn.Mtd.Rifles Sgt.
Talbott, Thomas A. AR 1st Mtd.Rifles Co.A
Talbott, Thomas J. VA Lt.Arty. Jeffress' Co.
Talbott, William LA 14th Inf. Co.G
Talbott, William TX 11th Inf. Co.D
Talbott, William E. VA 31st Inf. Co.I
Talbott, William F. VA 8th Cav. Co.F Black.
Talbott, William H. KY 3rd Bn.Mtd.Rifles Co.D 1st Lt.
Talbott, William H. MO 12th Inf. Co.D Capt.
Talbott, W.O. MO 1st Brig.St.Guard

Talbott, W.R. TN 2nd Cav. Co.A
Talbott, W.S. KY 1st Bn.Mtd.Rifles Co.C
Talbott, W.S. KY 3rd Bn.Mtd.Rifles Co.D
Talbott, W.T. AL 8th Inf. Co.E
Talbott, Y.O. TX 4th Inf. Co.C
Talbox, H.W. SC 5th Bn.Res. Co.C
Talburt, Henry S. AR 8th Cav. Co.G
Talburt, S.H. AR 8th Cav. Co.G Sgt.
Talburt, T.S. AR 8th Cav. Co.G Cpl.
Talbutt, Charles B. AL 56th Part.Rangers Surg.
Talbutt, Charles B. MS 28th Cav. Co.D
Talbutt, Chas. B. Gen. & Staff Surg.
Talbutt, J.B. KY 5th Cav. Co.C 2nd Lt.
Talby, George MD 1st Cav. Co.A
Talby, William VA Cav. 39th Bn. Co.B
Talcott, Andrew VA Eng. Lt.
Talcott, Charles G. VA Inf. 4th Bn.Loc.Def. Co.F Capt.
Talcott, T.M.R. 1st Conf.Eng.Troops Col.
Talcott, T.M.R. Gen. & Staff Maj.
Tale, K.J. NC Cav. 16th Bn. Co.H Sgt.
Taleferro, James L. VA Inf. 6th Bn.Loc.Def. Co.C 2nd Lt.
Talene, John AL Res. J.G. Rankin's Co.
Talenferro, Zach. Jackson's Co.,CSA
Talent, Henry TN 43rd Inf. Co.B Cpl.
Talent, James D. NC 43rd Inf. Co.K
Talent, Joel MO Robertson's Regt.St.Guard Co.6
Talent, John NC Walker's Bn. Thomas' Legion Co.A
Talent, John L.G. AL 18th Bn.Vol. Co.C
Talent, Richard T. NC 43rd Inf. Co.K
Talent, Solomon MS 31st Inf. Co.D
Talent, S.T. TN 28th Inf. Co.K
Talent, Thomas A. TN 25th Inf. Co.E Cpl.
Talent, Thomas A. 3rd Conf.Cav. Co.E
Talents, D. GA 12th Cav. Co.G
Taler, Tobias NC 8th Bn.Part.Rangers Co.D
Tales, L. AL 17th Inf. Co.C
Tales, S. TN 16th Cav. Co.H
Taley, William M. AR 14th (Powers') Inf. Co.F Cpl.
Talgout, George LA Mil. LaFourche Regt.
Talgout, Louis LA Mil. LaFourche Regt.
Taliafaro, F.O. LA 2nd Inf. Co.E
Taliafaro, H.W. Pickett's Div. Capt.,ACS
Taliafaro, W.C. LA 2nd Inf. Co.E
Taliafero, Alexander H. NC 22nd Inf. Co.F
Taliafero, F. VA 4th Cav. Co.C
Taliafero, J.D. 2nd Conf.Inf. Co.B Sgt.
Taliafero, Lesley S. TX 12th Inf. Co.H
Taliafero, Melvin B. NC 22nd Inf. Co.F Cpl.
Taliafero, William B. Taliaferro's Staff Maj.Gen.
Taliaferro, --- TX Cav. Mann's Regt. Co.F
Taliaferro, A.B. VA 2nd Cav.
Taliaferro, A.C. TN 47th Inf. Co.F
Taliaferro, Addison GA 14th Inf. Co.I Adj.
Taliaferro, Adison Gen. & Staff 1st Lt.,Adj.
Taliaferro, A.F. VA Arty. B.H. Smith's Co.
Taliaferro, A.G. VA 23rd Inf. Col.
Taliaferro, Alexander B. VA 49th Inf. Co.I
Taliaferro, Alexander G. VA 13th Inf. Co.G Capt.
Taliaferro, Alfred F. VA 1st Arty. Co.D
Taliaferro, Alfred F. VA Lt.Arty. 1st Bn. Co.D
Taliaferro, Andrew J. LA 19th Inf. Co.A
Taliaferro, Andrew J. TX 3rd Cav. Co.I
Taliaferro, B.B. VA 5th Inf. Co.M
Taliaferro, B.C. VA 9th Cav. 1st Lt.,Adj.
Taliaferro, B.D. TN 7th (Duckworth's) Cav. Co.D
Taliaferro, Benjamin VA 5th Inf. Co.A
Taliaferro, Benjamin B. AR 2nd Inf. Co.I Capt.
Taliaferro, B.L. VA 2nd Cav. Co.E
Taliaferro, C.C. TX 15th Inf. Co.K
Taliaferro, C.C. Gen. & Staff A.Surg.
Taliaferro, C.F. 7th Conf.Cav. Co.A
Taliaferro, Charles GA 14th Inf. Co.I
Taliaferro, Charles MO Inf. 3rd Bn. Co.C
Taliaferro, Charles TN 1st Cav. Co.B
Taliaferro, Charles TN 43rd Inf. Co.A 2nd Lt.
Taliaferro, Charles A. MS 12th Inf. Co.D
Taliaferro, Charles C. VA 4th Cav. Co.H
Taliaferro, Charles C. VA 6th Cav. Co.F Sgt.
Taliaferro, Charles C. VA 1st Inf. Co.G
Taliaferro, Charles F. GA Inf. 2nd Bn. Co.A
Taliaferro, Charles H. VA Lt.Arty. Kirkpatrick's Co.
Taliaferro, Charles M. VA 2nd Cav. Co.E
Taliaferro, Charles S. TN 7th (Ducksorth's) Cav. Co.L 1st Lt.
Taliaferro, Charles T. AL 4th Inf. Co.E Asst.Surg.
Taliaferro, Charles W. MS 3rd Inf. Co.K 3rd Lt.
Taliaferro, Charles W. MS 30th Inf. Co.K 2nd Lt.
Taliaferro, C.J. TN 7th (Duckworth's) Cav. Co.L
Taliaferro, Conway C. VA Cav. 39th Bn. Co.C
Taliaferro, C.S. Gen. & Staff Asst.Surg.
Taliaferro, C.W. TN Inf. Crews' Bn. Surg.
Taliaferro, C.W. Gen. & Staff Surg.
Taliaferro, D. GA 60th Inf. Co.D Capt.
Taliaferro, Daniel A. VA Lt.Arty. 12th Bn. 2nd Co.A
Taliaferro, Daniel A. VA Lt.Arty. Sturdivant's Co.
Taliaferro, D.M. AL 11th Inf. Co.D
Taliaferro, Edward H. VA 30th Inf. Co.C
Taliaferro, Edward T. VA 17th Inf. Co.A
Taliaferro, Edwin VA 1st Inf. Co.I
Taliaferro, Eilbeck H. VA 9th Cav. Co.A Music.
Taliaferro, E.T. TN 26th Inf. Surg.
Taliaferro, E.T. TN 46th Inf. Asst.Surg.
Taliaferro, E.T. Gen. & Staff Surg.
Taliaferro, F.C. TN 7th (Duckworth's) Cav. Co.L
Taliaferro, Felix MS 35th Inf. Co.H
Taliaferro, F.F. MD Cav. 2nd Bn. Co.D Sgt.
Taliaferro, Fitzhugh VA Cav. 39th Bn. Co.C
Taliaferro, Francis W. VA 4th Cav. Co.H
Taliaferro, Garnett H. VA Lt.Arty. Pollock's Co. Cpl.
Taliaferro, Garvin C. VA 9th Cav. Co.C
Taliaferro, George D. VA 9th Cav. Co.F
Taliaferro, G.S. VA 3rd Inf.Loc.Def. Co.C
Taliaferro, Hay B. VA 17th Inf. Co.A
Taliaferro, H.B. Gen. & Staff Asst.Comsy.
Taliaferro, H.B. Gen. & Staff Surg.
Taliaferro, H.D. Gen. & Staff Surg.
Taliaferro, Henry P. VA 34th Inf. Co.A
Taliaferro, H.G. VA Lt.Arty. Pollock's Co.
Taliaferro, Horace G. VA Cav. 39th Bn. Co.C
Taliaferro, H.P. VA Inf. 6th Bn.Loc.Def. Co.C
Taliaferro, J. GA 48th Inf. Co.E
Taliaferro, J. VA 3rd Inf.Loc.Def. 2nd Co.G
Taliaferro, James MO 1st Cav. Co.G 1st Lt.
Taliaferro, James A. MO 16th Inf. Sutter
Taliaferro, James B. VA 12th Inf. Co.B N.C.S. Comsy.Sgt.
Taliaferro, James C. VA 42nd Inf. Co.K 2nd Lt.
Taliaferro, James E. TN 43rd Inf. Co.A
Taliaferro, James E. VA Lt.Arty. Taylor's Co. 2nd Lt.
Taliaferro, James E. VA 19th Inf. Co.I 2nd Lt.
Taliaferro, James E. VA 42nd Inf. Co.K
Taliaferro, James G. VA 9th Cav. Co.K
Taliaferro, James H. AR 2nd Inf. Co.G
Taliaferro, James L. VA 15th Inf. Co.A
Taliaferro, James M. TX 3rd Cav. Co.I
Taliaferro, James T. AR 18th Inf. Co.F 1st Lt.
Taliaferro, J.C. AL Cav. Forrest's Regt.
Taliaferro, J.C. TN 18th (Newsom's) Cav. Co.F
Taliaferro, J.C. TN 13th Inf. Co.F
Taliaferro, Jesse B. GA 1st Reg. Co.E Sgt.
Taliaferro, J.K. VA 4th Cav. Co.H
Taliaferro, J.N. GA 1st (Ramsey's) Inf. Co.I 2nd Lt.
Taliaferro, John GA Floyd Legion (St.Guards) Co.F Capt.
Taliaferro, John MS 6th Cav. Co.H Sgt.
Taliaferro, Jno. VA Cav. Mosby's Regt. (Part.Rangers) Co.D
Taliaferro, John Gen. & Staff, Inf. 2nd Lt.,ADC
Taliaferro, John A. VA 29th Inf. Co.H
Taliaferro, John C. VA 1st Arty. Co.K
Taliaferro, John C. VA Arty. L.F. Jones' Co.
Taliaferro, John M. VA 4th Cav. Co.H
Taliaferro, John M. VA 52nd Inf. Co.H
Taliaferro, John N. AR 9th Inf. Co.C Sgt.
Taliaferro, John N. VA 19th Inf. Co.I 1st Lt.
Taliaferro, John P. VA 21st Mil. Co.D Capt.
Taliaferro, John R. AR 3rd Inf. Co.H 1st Lt.
Taliaferro, John R. MD 1st Inf. Co.D
Taliaferro, John R. TN 3rd (Forrest's) Cav.
Taliaferro, John S. VA 47th Inf. Co.B Cpl.
Taliaferro, John T. VA 111th Mil. Co.2
Taliaferro, John W. MS 42nd Inf. Co.A Ord.Sgt.
Taliaferro, Joseph N. GA Lt.Arty. 12th Bn. 2nd Co.D Capt.
Taliaferro, J.P. VA 5th Cav. Co.A
Taliaferro, J.Q.A. LA 17th Inf. Co.K 1st Lt.
Taliaferro, J.W. GA Lt.Arty. 12th Bn. 2nd Co.D
Taliaferro, Lawrence VA Lt.Arty. Pollock's Co.
Taliaferro, Lawrence VA 47th Inf. Co.B 1st Lt.
Taliaferro, L.C. VA Lt.Arty. King's Co.
Taliaferro, Louis B. TX 3rd Cav. Co.I
Taliaferro, L.S. TX 20th Cav. Co.H
Taliaferro, L.W. TN 7th (Duckworth's) Cav. Co.D Capt.
Taliaferro, M.J. MO St.Guard
Taliaferro, Norborn R. TX 16th Inf. Co.B
Taliaferro, Peachy R. VA 1st Cav. Co.C
Taliaferro, Philip MO 3rd Inf. Co.C
Taliaferro, Philip VA 30th Inf. Co.E
Taliaferro, Philip A. Gen. & Staff 1st Lt.,ADC
Taliaferro, P.R. GA 1st (Ramsey's) Inf. Co.E Sgt.
Taliaferro, P.R. GA 32nd Inf. Co.E Capt.

Taliaferro, P.R. GA 32nd Inf. Co.E Capt.
Taliaferro, R.B. Gen. & Staff AQM
Taliaferro, R.E. TN 7th (Duckworth's) Cav. Co.L Sgt.
Taliaferro, R.H. MS Cav. Hughes' Bn. Co.A
Taliaferro, R.H. TX 16th Inf. Chap.
Taliaferro, Richard D. TN 2nd (Ashby's) Cav. Co.G
Taliaferro, Richard E. VA 12th Inf. Co.B
Taliaferro, Richard H. MS 12th Inf. Co.D
Taliaferro, Richard M. VA 19th Inf. Co.I Capt.
Taliaferro, Richard T. MS 42nd Inf. Co.A
Taliaferro, R.M. VA 2nd Cav. Co.E
Taliaferro, Robert B. VA 5th Cav. Co.A
Taliaferro, Robert L. VA 4th Cav. Co.H
Taliaferro, Robert L. VA 6th Cav. Co.F
Taliaferro, Robert P. Gen. & Staff A.Surg.
Taliaferro, Robert T. AL Inf. 2nd Regt. Co.F
Taliaferro, Roderick VA Hvy.Arty. 19th Bn. Co.D Cpl.
Taliaferro, Rodrick VA 11th Inf. Co.A
Taliaferro, R.T. MS 35th Inf. Co.H
Taliaferro, R.W. KY 9th Cav. Co.G
Taliaferro, Samuel KY 2nd (Woodward's) Cav.
Taliaferro, Samuel L. TN 2nd (Ashby's) Cav. Co.G
Taliaferro, T. AL Lt.Arty. Goldthwaite's Btty.
Taliaferro, T.D. TX 20th Cav. Lt.Col.
Taliaferro, Thomas VA 2nd Bn.Res. Co.C 2nd Lt.
Taliaferro, Thomas S. VA 21st Mil. Maj.
Taliaferro, Thos. S. Gen. & Staff Capt.
Taliaferro, T.J. VA Conscr. Cp.Lee Co.B
Taliaferro, T.J. Gen. & Staff Surg.
Taliaferro, V. TN 38th Inf. 2nd Co.A
Taliaferro, Van VA 11th Inf. Co.G
Taliaferro, Vernon TN 7th (Duckworth's) Cav. Co.L
Taliaferro, V.H. GA 10th Cav. Col.
Taliaferro, V.H. 7th Conf.Cav. Col.
Taliaferro, Voltaire H. GA Inf. 2nd Bn. Surg.
Taliaferro, Warren MO 1st Cav. Co.G
Taliaferro, W.F. GA 60th Inf. Co.D
Taliaferro, W.H. MO 16th Inf. Co.E 1st Sgt.
Taliaferro, Wm. TX 12th Inf. Co.K
Taliaferro, William B. VA 5th Inf. Co.H
Taliaferro, William C., Jr. VA 1st Inf. Co.I
Taliaferro, William C. VA 2nd Bn.Res. Co.D 1st Lt.
Taliaferro, William George VA 30th Inf. Co.H Lt.
Taliaferro, William H. TN 1st Cav. Co.B
Taliaferro, William H. VA 44th Inf. Co.F
Taliaferro, William M. VA 2nd Cav. Co.E Cpl.
Taliaferro, William M. VA 11th Inf. Co.E 1st Lt.
Taliaferro, William P. VA Lt.Arty. 38th Bn. Co.D Sgt.
Taliaferro, William R. VA 13th Inf. Co.A
Taliaferro, William T. VA 24th Inf. Co.B Adj.
Taliaferro, Wm. T. Gen. & Staff Capt.,AAG
Taliaferro, William W. VA 52nd Mil. Co.B 2nd Lt.
Taliaferro, W.R. LA Inf.Cons. 18th Regt. & Yellow Jacket Bn. Co.B
Taliaferro, W.R. Gen. & Staff, Ord.Dept. Ord.Sgt.
Taliaferro, W.T. VA Lt.Arty. R.M. Anderson's Co.
Taliaferro, W.T. VA 40th Inf. Maj.
Taliaferro, Zachariah AR 2nd Inf. Co.G
Talieferro, James R. MO Inf. 3rd Regt.St.Guard Co.B Capt.
Talifarro, George M. AL 16th Inf. Co.C
Talifero, R. AL 11th Cav. Co.K
Talifero, Richard TN Cav. 4th Bn. (Branner's) Co.B
Talifero, Samuel TN Cav. 4th Bn. (Branner's) Co.B
Taliferro, Dardis TN 1st Cav. Co.B
Taliferro, William AL 11th Cav. Co.A
Taliferro, William Conf.Cav. Baxter's Bn. 2nd Co.B
Taliferro, W.J. TN 62nd Mtd.Inf. Co.F
Taling, M. VA 4th Cav. Co.I
Talioferro, Dickerson GA 11th Inf. Co.C
Talioferro, John 1st Conf.Inf. 1st Co.F
Talioffero, William W. Sig.Corps,CSA
Talivast, J.A. SC 6th Inf. 2nd Co.K
Talker, Joseph VA Inf. 4th Bn.Loc.Def. Co.C
Talkington, D. AR 11th & 17th Cons.Inf. Co.I
Talkington, Henry F. AR 36th Inf. Co.A,B
Talkington, Jasper AR 35th Inf. Co.B
Talkington, J.D. AR 17th (Griffith's) Inf. Co.C
Talkington, J.D. AR 35th Inf. Co.A
Talkington, John P. AR 2nd Mtd.Rifles Co.B
Talkington, John W. AR 35th Inf. Co.B
Talkington, Joseph AR 35th Inf. Co.B
Talkington, J.W. AR 15th Mil. Co.D
Talkington, Lee M. TX Cav. Martin's Regt. Co.K
Talkington, M.C. TX Inf. 3rd St.Troops Co.B
Talkington, S.M. TX 18th Inf. Co.H
Talkington, T.M. TX Inf. 3rd St.Troops Co.B
Tall, A.T. AL 62nd Inf. Co.F,E
Tall, G.M. KY 1st Bn.Mtd.Rifles Co.C
Tall, William LA 6th Inf. Co.E
Tall, W.W. VA 42nd Inf. Co.K
Talla, Simon Deneale's Regt. Choctaw Warriors Co.D
Tallaferro, E. Gen. & Staff, Ord.Dept. Arty. Maj.,Ord.Off.
Tallahassa 1st Seminole Mtd.Vol.
Tallalay, George MO Cav. Worder's Bn.
Tallaluk, J. 1st Chickasaw Inf. Haynes' Co.
Tallan, E. GA 56th Inf. Co.F
Talland, O. TN Cav. 12th Bn. (Day's) Co.C
Tallant, Aaron A. NC 11th (Bethel Regt.) Inf. Co.I
Tallant, B.O. MS 3rd Cav. Co.C
Tallant, B.O. MS Inf. 4th St.Troops Co.F
Tallant, C.H. TN 2nd (Ashby's) Cav. Co.A
Tallant, C.H. TN Cav. 5th Bn. (McClellan's) Co.A
Tallant, Daniel NC 1st Arty. (10th St.Troops) Co.C
Tallant, David NC 6th Inf. Co.K
Tallant, J.A. MS 10th Inf. New Co.G
Tallant, Jackson TX 18th Cav. Co.C
Tallant, James 1st Conf.Cav. 2nd Co.K
Tallant, J.C. MS 41st Inf. Co.H Cpl.
Tallant, Jesse NC 1st Arty. (10th St.Troops) Co.C
Tallant, Jesse NC 55th Inf. Co.F
Tallant, J.G. MS 8th Cav. Co.A
Tallant, Joseph TX 12th Cav. Co.E
Tallant, Patrick A. SC 1st (McCreary's) Inf. Co.C
Tallant, Q.O. TN 4th Cav. Co.C
Tallant, R. KY Cav.
Tallant, Ransom C. NC 16th Inf. Co.K
Tallant, Richard AR Cav. Witherspoon's Bn. Co.B 3rd Lt.
Tallant, Richard AR 4th Inf. Co.C
Tallant, Richard 1st Conf.Cav. 2nd Co.K
Tallant, R.M. AR Inf. Hardy's Regt. Co.G 1st Sgt.
Tallant, S. TN 84th Inf. Co.B
Tallant, Samuel H. AL 45th Inf. Co.I
Tallant, Sidney TN 60th Mtd.Inf. Co.A
Tallant, T.A. Horse Arty. White's Btty.
Tallant, T.H. MS 2nd St.Cav. Co.B
Tallant, W.A. AL 15th Bn.Part.Rangers Co.E
Tallant, William TN 7th Inf. Co.C
Tallant, W.R. TN 2nd (Ashby's) Cav. Co.A
Tallant, W.R. TN Cav. 5th Bn. (McClellan's) Co.A
Tallao, George R. MO 1st Cav. Co.A Sgt.
Tallapoose, Sampson 1st Choctaw & Chickasaw Mtd.Rifles 2nd Co.H
Tallar, J.H. TN 4th (McLemore's) Cav. Co.B
Tallar, J.N. TN 4th (McLemore's) Cav. Co.B
Tallard, Charles F. VA 1st Inf. Co.I
Tallart, John L. AL 55th Vol. Co.H
Tallas, M. TX Cav. Hardeman's Regt. Co.G
Tallavast, H.P. SC 8th Inf. Co.F,M Sgt.
Tallawah Fixico 1st Seminole Mtd.Vol.
Tallawah Fixico 1st Seminole Mtd.Vol. Cpl.
Tallawah Harjo 1st Seminole Mtd.Vol.
Tallawah Micco 1st Seminole Mtd.Vol. 1st Sgt.
Tallbott, William VA 3rd (Archer's) Bn.Res. Co.E 1st Sgt.
Talleferro, John D. MS 25th Inf. Co.B Cpl.
Tallen, J.B. AL 8th Inf. Co.C
Tallent, Aaron NC 55th Inf. Co.F
Tallent, David TN 43rd Inf. Co.K
Tallent, Eli NC 39th Inf. Co.B
Tallent, Ephraim NC Cav. 7th Bn. Co.C
Tallent, Ephraim NC 39th Inf. Co.B
Tallent, Ephraim NC Walker's Bn. Thomas' Legion Co.B
Tallent, George W.C. VA 9th Cav. Co.K
Tallent, Isaac James GA 34th Inf. Co.D
Tallent, James GA 42nd Inf. Co.B
Tallent, James TN Inf. 22nd Bn. Co.A
Tallent, James TN 62nd Mtd.Inf. Co.K
Tallent, James E. VA 40th Inf. Co.E 1st Sgt.
Tallent, J.C. TN 19th Inf. Co.H
Tallent, Jeptha TN 36th Inf. Co.D
Tallent, Jeptha TN 37th Inf. Co.G
Tallent, Leroy J. TN 59th Mtd.Inf. Co.H Cpl.
Tallent, M. LA Inf. Pelican Regt. Co.B Sgt.
Tallent, Michael LA 25th Inf. Co.B Sgt.
Tallent, Moses K. TN 42nd Inf. 1st Co.F
Tallent, Patrick VA 27th Inf. Co.B
Tallent, Robert L. VA 9th Cav. Co.C
Tallent, Samuel NC 34th Inf. Co.E
Tallent, Samuel NC 58th Inf. Co.A
Tallent, Samuel TN 37th Inf. Co.G
Tallent, Samuel TN 62nd Mtd.Inf. Co.K
Tallent, S.T. TN 28th (Cons.) Inf. Co.C

Tallent, Thomas VA 40th Inf. Co.B
Tallent, T.J. SC 22nd Inf. Co.H
Tallent, William TN Cav. 16th Bn. (Neal's) Co.E
Tallent, William TN 16th Inf. Co.H
Tallequah, M. 1st Chickasaw Inf. Hansell's Co.
Taller, J. TX 30th Cav. Co.F
Tallery, --- VA Inf. 23rd Bn. Co.C
Tallesen, W.J. AR Inf. Hardy's Regt. Co.G
Tallesson, W.B. AL Cav. Hardie's Bn.Res. Co.C
Tallet, John TN 4th (Murray's) Cav. Co.A
Talley, A.D. AR 8th Cav. Co.L
Talley, A.H. GA 4th Res. Co.I Cpl.
Talley, A.H. TN 9th Inf. Co.F
Talley, Algernon S. GA Arty. 9th Bn. Co.A,C 1st Lt.
Talley, Allen TX 36th Cav. Co.D
Talley, Almond D. VA Hvy.Arty. Wright's Co.
Talley, A.N. Gen. & Staff, Medical Dept. Surg.
Talley, Armstead VA Inf. 5th Bn. Co.B
Talley, A.S. AL 13th Bn.Part.Rangers Co.D Ch.Bugler
Talley, A.S. AL 56th Part.Rangers Co.H
Talley, A.S. 1st Conf.Cav. Co.I
Talley, B.B. GA 60th Inf. Co.F
Talley, B.B. VA 59th Inf. 3rd Co.G
Talley, Benjamin VA 14th Inf. Co.K
Talley, Benjamin D. NC Walker's Bn. Thomas' Legion Co.G
Talley, Benjamin D. TN 1st (Carter's) Cav. Co.H
Talley, Benjamin T. NC 30th Inf. Co.B
Talley, Billey W. VA 1st (Farinholt's) Res. QMSgt.
Talley, Billey W. VA 15th Inf. Co.I Capt.
Talley, B.J. TN 20th Inf. Co.K Bvt.2nd Lt.
Talley, Buckner J. AR 9th Inf. Co.G
Talley, C. TN 19th (Biffle's) Cav. Co.L
Talley, C. TN 22nd Inf. Co.E
Talley, C. VA 3rd (Archer's) Bn.Res. Co.F
Talley, C.A. TN 8th (Smith's) Cav. Co.L
Talley, Carey F. VA 23rd Inf. Co.G
Talley, C.C. TN 20th Inf. Co.G
Talley, C.E. TN 19th & 20th (Cons.) Cav. Co.C
Talley, C.E. Inf. Bailey's Cons.Regt. Co.B 1st Lt.
Talley, Charles TN 60th Mtd.Inf. Co.I
Talley, Charles A. VA 15th Inf. Co.I
Talley, Charles E. TX 7th Inf. Co.D Capt.
Talley, Charles N. GA 29th Inf. Co.G
Talley, Chastine H. VA 18th Inf. Co.C
Talley, Columbus TN Cav. Newsom's Regt. Co.B
Talley, Columbus H. AR 24th Inf. Co.B
Talley, Columbus H. AR Inf. Hardy's Regt. Co.B
Talley, Crawford VA 4th Inf. Co.C
Talley, C.T. TN 19th Inf. Co.K
Talley, D. GA Inf. 8th Bn. Co.C
Talley, D. VA Hvy.Arty. Wright's Co.
Talley, Daniel D. VA 21st Inf. Co.F
Talley, David AL 33rd Inf. Co.E
Talley, David E. TN 8th Inf. Co.I 1st Lt.
Talley, D.C. TN 1st (Carter's) Cav. Co.H 2nd Lt.
Talley, Delaney H. TN 18th Inf. Co.A
Talley, D.H. GA 1st Cav. Co.H Sgt.
Talley, D.N. AL 8th Cav. Co.D
Talley, Dock GA 36th (Broyles') Inf. Co.B
Talley, Dyer SC 20th Inf. Co.A 1st Lt.
Talley, Edward B. VA 15th Inf. Co.C
Talley, Edward B. VA 23rd Inf. Co.A
Talley, Edward P. VA 16th Inf. Co.F Music.
Talley, Edward Peyton VA 12th Inf. Co.B
Talley, E.L. AR 6th Inf. Co.G
Talley, Elijah W. GA 35th Inf. Co.D
Talley, Elisha TN 42nd Inf. 2nd Co.F
Talley, Ephraim M. TX 6th Cav. Co.G
Talley, Ezekiel S. VA 15th Inf. Co.I
Talley, F. VA 3rd Bn. Valley Res. Co.D
Talley, F.D. TN 7th (Duckworth's) Cav. Co.A
Talley, F.H. TN 7th (Duckworth's) Cav. Co.A
Talley, Floyd TN 5th (McKenzie's) Cav. Co.A
Talley, F.M. AR 45th Cav. Co.L
Talley, Gatewood VA 1st St.Res. Co.F
Talley, George VA 46th Inf. Co.F
Talley, George A. VA 12th Inf. Co.B
Talley, George F. VA 56th Inf. Co.F
Talley, George Riley FL 6th Inf. Chap.
Talley, George Riley Gen. & Staff Chap.
Talley, George T. VA 15th Inf. Co.I
Talley, George W. AL 60th Inf. Co.E
Talley, George W. AR 24th Inf. Co.B
Talley, George W. MO 16th Inf. Co.D
Talley, George W. TN 3rd (Lillard's) Mtd.Inf. Co.D
Talley, G.F. KY 2nd (Woodward's) Cav. Co.C
Talley, G.H. AL 45th Inf. Lt.
Talley, Gid L. TN 16th Inf. Co.A Capt.
Talley, Goode W. VA 12th Inf. Co.K
Talley, Greenbery G. AR 21st Inf. Co.D Sgt.
Talley, G.W. TN 47th Inf. Co.D 2nd Lt.
Talley, Hanswood VA 56th Inf. Co.K
Talley, Harley TN 25th Inf. Co.H
Talley, H.B. AL 45th Inf. Co.G
Talley, H.C. GA Inf. 8th Bn. Co.C
Talley, H.C. GA 23rd Inf. Co.D
Talley, H.C. GA 40th Inf. Co.A
Talley, Henry AL 4th Inf. Co.E
Talley, Henry B. TN 4th (McLemore's) Cav. Co.K Sgt.
Talley, Henry B. TN 1st (Turney's) Inf. Co.G Cpl.
Talley, Henry E. VA 12th Inf. 2nd Co.I
Talley, Henry H. TN 2nd (Robison's) Inf. Co.C
Talley, Henry M. VA 14th Inf. 2nd Co.G 2nd Lt.
Talley, Henry W. VA 23rd Inf. Co.G
Talley, H.K. AL 51st (Part.Rangers) Co.H
Talley, H.M. GA 54th Inf. Co.E,D Capt.
Talley, H.M. VA 38th Inf. 1st Co.I Cpl.
Talley, Horace AL 21st Inf. Co.I 1st Lt.
Talley, H.T. GA Inf. 8th Bn. Co.C Cpl.
Talley, Hubbard G. VA Hvy.Arty. Wright's Co.
Talley, I.E. TN 19th & 20th (Cons.) Cav. Co.F
Talley, I.K. VA 59th Inf. Co.G
Talley, Isaac VA 27th Inf. 1st Co.H
Talley, Isaac VA 122nd Mil. Co.A
Talley, Ivin AR 31st Inf. Co.A
Talley, J. AL 17th Inf. Co.C
Talley, J. AL 33rd Inf. Co.E
Talley, J.A. AR 26th Inf. Co.K Sgt.
Talley, J.A. SC Lt.Arty. 3rd (Palmetto) Bn. Co.K,I
Talley, J.A. TN Cav. 12th Bn. (Day's) Co.D
Talley, J.A. VA Cav. 37th Bn. Co.B
Talley, Jacob C. TX 16th Inf. Co.C
Talley, James TN Inf. 3rd Cons.Regt. Co.F
Talley, James TX 15th Inf. 2nd Co.E 1st Lt.
Talley, James VA 2nd Inf. Co.I
Talley, James VA 23rd Inf. Co.A
Talley, James A. TN 11th Inf. Co.F
Talley, James A. TN 44th (Cons.) Inf. Co.B
Talley, James A. VA 5th Inf. Co.E,H
Talley, James B. AR 1st (Crawford's) Cav. Co.E
Talley, James B. VA Lt.Arty. Huckstep's Co.
Talley, James B. VA Lt.Arty. Lamkin's Co.
Talley, James B. VA Lt.Arty. Snead's Co.
Talley, James B. VA 23rd Inf. Co.G
Talley, James F. AL 60th Inf. Co.E
Talley, James H. AR 45th Mil. Co.E
Talley, James H. NC 23rd Inf. Co.I
Talley, James Henderson TN 35th Inf. 1st Co.D, Co.B
Talley, James J. AR Inf. Hardy's Regt. Co.B
Talley, James L. TX 7th Inf. Co.D Sgt.
Talley, James M. GA 9th Inf. Co.G
Talley, James M. NC 21st Inf. Co.K
Talley, James M. TN 53rd Inf. Co.E
Talley, James M. VA 9th Cav. Co.E
Talley, James M. VA 23rd Inf. Co.G
Talley, James P. TN 14th Inf. Co.L
Talley, James T. GA 21st Inf. Co.F
Talley, James T. TN 8th Inf. Co.I
Talley, James W. TN 2nd (Robison's) Inf. Co.I
Talley, J.C. AL 6th Inf. Co.M
Talley, J.C. TN 8th Inf. Co.I
Talley, J.C. TX 4th Inf. Co.H
Talley, J.D. SC Lt.Arty. 3rd (Palmetto) Bn. Co.H,I
Talley, J.E. MS 4th Cav. Co.A Cpl.
Talley, J.E. MS Cav. Stockdale's Bn. Co.A
Talley, J.E. MS 46th Inf. Co.B Cpl.
Talley, J.E. TN 20th (Russell's) Cav. Co.A
Talley, J.E. TN 9th Inf. Co.K
Talley, J.E. TN 47th Inf. Co.G
Talley, Jeptha GA Cav. Russell's Co.
Talley, J.F. TX Cav. (Dismtd.) Chisum's Regt. Co.C
Talley, J.G. TN 62nd Mtd.Inf. Co.E
Talley, J.H. AR 32nd Inf. Co.F
Talley, J.H. NC 4th Bn.Jr.Res. Co.C
Talley, J.I. TN 37th Inf. Co.C 3rd Lt.
Talley, J.K. VA 1st (Farinholt's) Res. Co.A
Talley, J.M. TN Inf. 4th Cons.Regt. Co.G
Talley, J.M. TN 49th Inf. Co.D 2nd Lt.
Talley, J.M. Inf. Bailey's Cons.Regt. Co.L
Talley, J.M.J. AL 24th Inf. Co.K,C 2nd Lt.
Talley, J.M.J. MS 44th Inf. Co.I,G 1st Sgt.
Talley, John GA 65th Inf. Co.D,G
Talley, John GA Smith's Legion Co.F
Talley, John LA Conscr.
Talley, John MO Cav. Fristoe's Regt. Co.F
Talley, John NC 6th Inf. Co.C
Talley, John NC Walker's Bn. Thomas' Legion Co.C
Talley, John VA 12th Cav. Co.I
Talley, John VA Hvy.Arty. Wright's Co.
Talley, John VA 2nd Inf.Loc.Def. Co.C
Talley, John VA Inf. 2nd Bn.Loc.Def. Co.E
Talley, John VA 5th Inf. Co.D
Talley, John, Jr. VA 92nd Mil. Co.B

Talley, John, Sr. VA 92nd Mil. Co.B
Talley, John A. LA 1st Cav. Co.G
Talley, John A. VA 9th Cav. Co.E
Talley, John A.J. VA 15th Inf. Co.I
Talley, John C. TN 2nd (Smith's) Cav.
Talley, John D. VA 4th Cav. Co.F
Talley, John E. MS Graves' Co. (Copiah Horse Guards)
Talley, John H. NC Inf. 2nd Bn. Co.C 1st Sgt.
Talley, John H. VA Hvy.Arty. 10th Bn. Co.C
Talley, John H. VA 1st St.Res. Co.F
Talley, John J. GA 2nd Cav. (St.Guards) Co.H Cpl.
Talley, John J. TN 8th Inf. Co.I Sgt.
Talley, John L. VA 4th Cav. Co.G
Talley, John M. AL 33rd Inf. Co.C
Talley, John S. TN 18th Inf. Co.A
Talley, John T. AL 17th Inf. Co.E Sgt.
Talley, John T. TX 7th Cav. Co.I
Talley, John T. VA 23rd Inf. Co.G
Talley, John W. AR 36th Inf. Co.F Cpl.
Talley, John W. GA 2nd Inf. Co.H
Talley, John W. VA 3rd Cav. Co.G
Talley, John W. VA Goochland Lt.Arty.
Talley, Jonas NC Inf. Thomas Legion Co.D,F
Talley, Jonathan VA Goochland Lt.Arty. Capt.
Talley, Joseph VA 9th Inf. Co.D
Talley, Joseph D. VA Hvy.Arty. Wright's Co.
Talley, Joshua N. TN 8th Inf. Co.I Cpl.
Talley, J.P. MO 16th Inf. Co.B
Talley, J.S. GA 1st (Fannin's) Res. Co.A
Talley, J.S. GA 11th Inf. Co.K Cpl.
Talley, J.T. GA 13th Cav. Co.K
Talley, J.T. MS 35th Inf. Co.E
Talley, J.W. TN 62nd Mtd.Inf. Co.E
Talley, Leander AR 30th Inf. Co.H
Talley, Leonard TX 15th Cav. Co.I
Talley, Leonidas F. GA 60th Inf. Co.B
Talley, Leroy AR 8th Cav. Co.L
Talley, Leroy AR 31st Inf. Co.A
Talley, Leroy TN 53rd Inf. Co.E Cpl.
Talley, Levi NC 43rd Inf. Co.G
Talley, Levi TN Inf. Tackitt's Co.
Talley, Linsey AL 1st Bn. Hilliard's Legion Vol. Co.C
Talley, Littleton H. AR 19th (Dockery's) Inf. Co.B
Talley, M. VA 34th Inf. Co.B
Talley, Madison H. TX 36th Cav. Co.D
Talley, M.A.G. MS 8th Inf. Co.I,H
Talley, Marion AL Inf. 1st Regt. Co.C Sgt.
Talley, Martin H. AL 6th Inf. Co.K
Talley, Martin V.B. NC 2nd Bn.Loc.Def.Troops Co.E Capt.
Talley, M.H. MO Cav. Slayback's Regt. Co.A
Talley, Miles VA Hvy.Arty. Coffin's Co.
Talley, Milton M. TN 53rd Inf. Co.E
Talley, M.J. MS 10th Cav. Co.G
Talley, Monroe M. GA 56th Inf. Co.I
Talley, M.V. GA 23rd Inf. Co.D
Talley, N.A. TN 1st (Carter's) Cav. Co.H
Talley, N.A. TN 37th Inf. Co.C Sgt.
Talley, Nat H. VA 74th Mil. Co.E Sgt.
Talley, Nathaniel, Jr. VA 14th Inf. Co.E Bvt.2nd Lt.
Talley, Nathaniel VA 59th Inf. 3rd Co.G 1st Lt.
Talley, Nathaniel G. GA 9th Inf. Co.G
Talley, N.D. AL 43rd Inf. Co.G
Talley, Nelson F. VA 21st Inf. Co.D
Talley, O.A. GA 19th Inf. Co.E Sgt.
Talley, Obediah J. GA Siege Arty. 28th Bn. Co.A
Talley, Pane AL 1st Bn. Hilliard's Legion Vol. Co.C
Talley, Patrick H. TN 8th Inf. Co.A Sgt.
Talley, Peyton R. NC Inf. 2nd Bn. Co.C
Talley, Peyton R. VA 59th Inf. 3rd Co.G Sgt.
Talley, P.H. TX 9th Bn.Res.Corps Co.B
Talley, Pleasant TN Inf. Tackitt's Co.
Talley, R. TN Cav. 1st Bn. (McNairy's) Co.E
Talley, R. TN 22nd (Barteau's) Cav. Co.C
Talley, R. Brush Bn.
Talley, R.A. GA Inf. 17th Bn. (St.Guards) Fay's Co.
Talley, R.A. GA Inf. (Loc.Def.) Whiteside's Nav.Bn. Co.A
Talley, Ratliff P. GA 23rd Inf. Co.D Adj.
Talley, R.B. NC 12th Inf. Co.K
Talley, Reuben SC 1st St.Troops Co.H
Talley, Reuben TX 4th Inf. Co.H
Talley, R.H. GA 31st Inf. Co.H
Talley, R.H. TN 38th Inf. Co.D 1st Sgt.
Talley, Richard A. VA Arty. C.F. Johnston's Co.
Talley, Richard C. VA 9th Cav. Co.E
Talley, Richard F. VA Goochland Lt.Arty.
Talley, Richard F. VA 23rd Inf. Co.G
Talley, Richard H. GA Siege Arty. 28th Bn. Co.A
Talley, Richard W. VA 3rd Cav. Co.F
Talley, Richard W. VA 23rd Inf. Co.G
Talley, Riley TX 37th Cav. Co.K
Talley, R.J. TN 26th (Cons.) Inf. Co.B 1st Sgt.
Talley, Robert TX 35th (Brown's) Cav. Co.I
Talley, Robert A. NC 2nd Bn.Loc.Def.Troops Co.A 2nd Lt.
Talley, Robert A. TX 36th Cav. Co.D 1st Lt.
Talley, Robert A. VA 1st Arty. Co.I
Talley, Robt. A. Gen. & Staff, Inf. 2nd Lt.
Talley, Robert B. VA 56th Inf. Co.F Cpl.
Talley, Robert H. VA 20th Inf. Co.A Sgt.
Talley, Robert J. TN 28th Inf. Co.F Sgt.
Talley, Robertson AR 45th Mil. Co.E
Talley, R.P. Gen. & Staff Hosp.Stew.
Talley, R.T. SC 16th Inf. Co.H Bvt.2nd Lt.
Talley, R.W. VA 4th Cav. Co.G
Talley, S. TX 7th Inf. Co.B
Talley, Samuel AR Inf. Hardy's Regt. Torbitt's Co.
Talley, Samuel GA 43rd Inf. Co.C Sgt.
Talley, Samuel LA Miles' Legion Co.C Sgt.
Talley, Samuel TN 25th Inf. Co.H
Talley, Samuel C. GA 11th Inf. Co.G
Talley, Samuel C. VA 23rd Inf. Co.G
Talley, S.C. TN 22nd (Barteau's) Cav. Co.G Chap.
Talley, Simeon G. GA 2nd Cav. (St.Guards) Co.K 3rd Lt.
Talley, S.J.R. GA Inf. 8th Bn. Co.C
Talley, S.L. GA Inf. 8th Bn. Co.C
Talley, S. Olin Gen. & Staff 1st Lt.,Dr.M.
Talley, Spencer B. TN 28th Inf. Co.F 1st Lt.
Talley, Spencer B. TN 28th (Cons.) Inf. Co.B 1st Lt.
Talley, S.S. KY 2nd (Woodward's) Cav. Co.C
Talley, Stephen C. TN Cav. 7th Bn. (Bennett's) Co.F
Talley, T.E. MS 35th Inf. Co.E
Talley, Thomas TN 9th (Ward's) Cav. Co.F
Talley, Thomas TN 20th Inf. Co.H
Talley, Thomas VA 6th Bn.Res. Co.E
Talley, Thomas D. AL 14th Inf. Co.E
Talley, Thomas D. AL 17th Inf. Co.E
Talley, Thomas G. VA Hoods' Bn.Res. Co.B
Talley, Thomas J. TN 34th Inf. Co.B
Talley, Thomas J. TN 60th Mtd.Inf. Co.I
Talley, Thomas J. VA 52nd Inf. Co.G
Talley, Thomas W. VA 15th Inf. Co.I
Talley, T.K. VA 37th Mil. 2nd Co.B
Talley, W.A. MS 18th Cav. Co.C
Talley, W.A. VA 53rd Inf.
Talley, Walter SC Hvy.Arty. 15th (Lucas') Bn. Co.A
Talley, Walter R. VA 15th Inf. Co.I
Talley, W.B. MO Cav. Fristoe's Regt. Co.A Cpl.
Talley, W.D. SC Lt.Arty. 3rd (Palmetto) Bn. Co.H,A,I
Talley, W.D.K. GA 5th Inf. Co.K
Talley, W.H. AR 14th (McCarver's) Inf. Co.K
Talley, W.H. AR 21st Inf. Co.A
Talley, W.H. AR Inf. Hardy's Regt. Co.B
Talley, W.H. TN 22nd Inf. Looney's Co.
Talley, W.H. TN 38th Inf. Co.L
Talley, William AR 45th Cav. Co.L
Talley, William GA 13th Inf. Co.D
Talley, William KY 2nd (Woodward's) Cav. Co.E
Talley, William MS 35th Inf. Co.E
Talley, William NC 6th Inf. Co.E
Talley, William VA Arty. J.W. Drewry's Co.
Talley, William VA 12th Inf. Co.F
Talley, William A. VA Inf. 5th Bn. Co.B
Talley, Wm. A. VA Inf. 5th Bn. Co.E
Talley, Wm. A. VA Inf. 44th Bn. Co.C
Talley, William E. VA Lt.Arty. Cooper's Co.
Talley, William E. VA 15th Inf. Co.I
Talley, William E. VA Inf. 25th Bn. Co.F
Talley, William E. VA 56th Inf. Co.K 2nd Lt.
Talley, William F. AR 37th Inf. Co.G
Talley, William G. NC 12th Inf. Co.I
Talley, William G. VA 12th Inf. 2nd Co.I
Talley, William H. GA Inf. 8th Bn. Co.F
Talley, William H. NC 39th Inf. Chap.
Talley, William H. SC 12th Inf. Co.D 1st Lt.
Talley, William H. TX 7th Cav. Co.F
Talley, William H. TX 17th Cav. Co.F
Talley, William H. TX 17th Cons.Dismtd.Cav. Co.F
Talley, William H. VA Cav. Mosby's Regt. (Part.Rangers) Co.L
Talley, William H. VA 2nd Arty. Co.G
Talley, William H. VA Inf. 22nd Bn. Co.G
Talley, William H. VA 56th Inf. Co.F 1st Lt.
Talley, Wm. H. VA 74th Mil. Capt.
Talley, Wm. H. Gen. & Staff, Cav. Capt.
Talley, Wm. H. Gen. & Staff Chap.
Talley, William H., Jr. VA 5th Inf. Co.D
Talley, William H.T. VA Hvy.Arty. Epes' Co.
Talley, William J. GA 9th Inf. Co.G Band Music.
Talley, William J. VA 21st Inf. Co.D

Talley, William L. VA 21st Cav. Co.F
Talley, William N. GA 13th Inf. Co.H,K Sgt.
Talley, William N. VA 23rd Inf. Co.A Cpl.
Talley, William O. VA 23rd Inf. Co.G
Talley, William P. TN 1st (Turney's) Inf. Co.E Capt.
Talley, William R. AL 13th Inf. Co.H
Talley, William R. GA Lt.Arty. 14th Bn. Co.A
Talley, William R. GA Lt.Arty. Havis' Btty.
Talley, William R. TN 42nd Inf. 2nd Co.F
Talley, William T. TN 4th (McLemore's) Cav. Co.K
Talley, William T. TX 14th Inf. Co.F
Talley, William T. VA 12th Inf. 2nd Co.I
Talley, W.J. NC 6th Sr.Res. Co.I
Talley, W.P. NC 7th Sr.Res. Fisher's Co.
Talley, W.R. AL 34th Inf. Co.B
Talley, W.S. VA 1st (Farinholt's) Res. Co.K
Talliafario, C.B. GA Cav. Pemberton's Co.
Talliafero, George GA 34th Inf. Co.A
Talliafero, William TX 3rd Cav. Co.E
Talliaferro, B.D. TN 4th Inf. Co.F
Talliaferro, Charles GA Cav. 29th Bn. Co.G Sgt.
Talliaferro, E Gen. & Staff Capt.
Talliaferro, George W. TN 1st (Carter's) Cav. Co.B
Talliaferro, H.P. VA 2nd Inf.Loc.Def. Co.F
Talliaferro, James M. MO 1st Cav. Co.B
Talliaferro, J.C. TN 4th Inf. Co.F
Talliaferro, John GA 36th (Villepigue's) Inf. Co.F
Talliaferro, John TX 4th Inf. Co.H
Talliaferro, John B. LA 1st Hvy.Arty. (Reg.) Co.H
Talliaferro, J.W. VA 146th Mil. Co.F
Talliaferro, L. TX 4th Inf. Co.F
Talliaferro, L.W. TN 4th Inf. Co.F
Talliaferro, Morgan O. LA 1st (Nelligan's) Inf. Co.A
Talliaferro, R.H. Gen. & Staff Capt.,QM
Talliaferro, R.J. TN 1st (Carter's) Cav. Co.B Bugler
Talliaferro, Samuel TN 26th Inf. Co.I
Talliaferro, T.J. MS 32nd Inf. Surg.
Talliaferro, T.J. VA 4th Cav. Co.G
Talliaferro, W.G. VA Horse Arty. D. Shank's Co.
Talliafferro, James L. VA 2nd Inf.Loc.Def. Co.F 2nd Lt.
Talliafferro, T.H. VA 1st St.Res. Co.B
Tallialf, J. TN 43rd Inf. Co.K
Tallieu, Emile LA 26th Inf. Co.C 2nd Lt.
Tallifaro, Samuel M. GA 2nd Res. Co.D
Tallifero, W.R. LA 18th Inf. Co.C
Talliford, James E. TN 21st (Wilson's) Cav. Co.I Cpl.
Tallings, Samuel FL 7th Inf. Co.I
Tallington, J. TX Cav. Wells' Regt. Co.F
Tallion, L. TX Lt.Arty. Huhges' Co.
Tallis, C.F. MO Lt.Arty. Walsh's Co.
Tallis, C.F. MO 1st Inf.
Tallis, Henry GA Mtd.Inf. (Pierce Mtd.Vol.) Hendry's Co.
Tallivast, A. SC 21st Inf. Co.B
Tallman, James M. TN 35th Inf. 1st Co.A, 2nd Co.D
Tallman, William Henry VA 24th Cav. Co.G
Tallmon, M. NC 34th Inf. Co.K
Tallon, Elisha VA 59th Mil. Riddick's Co.
Tallon, Jack TN 3rd (Forrest's) Cav. Co.I
Tallon, James TN 14th Inf. Co.D
Tallon, James VA Hvy.Arty. 20th Bn. Co.D
Tallon, J.E. LA Mil. Chalmette Regt. Co.D 1st Sgt.
Tallon, John MS 16th Inf. Co.A
Tallon, J.R. LA 6th Inf.
Tallon, Richard F. MS 15th Inf. Co.H
Tallon, William AL 24th Inf. Co.D,A
Tallor, Harrison NC 12th Inf. Co.O
Tallor, Harrison NC 32nd Inf. Co.C,D
Tallot, J.H. AL 22nd Inf. Co.F
Tallow, Jim 1st Cherokee Mtd.Rifles McDaniel's Co.
Tallow, Mays 1st Cherokee Mtd.Rifles Co.H
Tallowacubbee Deneale's Regt. Choctaw Warriors Co.A
Talls, R.E. MS 19th Inf. Co.A
Tally, --- GA 16th Inf. Co.K
Tally, --- Hosp.Stew.
Tally, A. AR 45th Cav. Co.D
Tally, A. LA Miles' Legion Co.A
Tally, A.A.D. MS 1st (Patton's) Inf. Co.E
Tally, A.A.D. MS 37th Inf. Co.I Sgt.
Tally, A.D. AR 38th Inf. Co.A
Tally, A.D. MS 2nd Cav. Co.H Cpl.
Tally, A.H. GA 40th Inf. Co.A
Tally, A.J. TN 13th Inf. Co.H
Tally, Andrew J. NC 45th Inf. Co.F Cpl.
Tally, Asberry TN 5th (McKenzie's) Cav. Co.B
Tally, A.W. KY 10th (Johnson's) Cav. New Co.C
Tally, B. MO St.Guard W.H. Taylor's Co.
Tally, B.B. GA 36th (Broyles') Inf. Co.B
Tally, Berry W. NC 26th Inf. Co.E
Tally, Beverly TN 13th (Gore's) Cav. Co.K
Tally, Bird T. TX 34th Cav. Co.E
Tally, Bradley TN 39th Mtd.Inf. Co.I
Tally, B.W. AR 45th Cav. Co.I
Tally, B.W. AR 14th (Powers') Inf. Co.F
Tally, B.W. TN 62nd Mtd.Inf. Co.I 1st Sgt.
Tally, C. TN 18th (Newsom's) Cav. Co.K
Tally, C. TN 84th Inf. Co.B
Tally, C.A. NC 28th Inf. Co.F
Tally, Caleb MS 14th Inf. Co.B
Tally, Carlin VA 10th Bn.Res. Co.E
Tally, Carter TN 62nd Mtd.Inf. Co.I
Tally, C.F. VA 2nd Arty. Co.H
Tally, C.H. VA 9th Inf. 2nd Co.A Cpl.
Tally, Charles F. VA Inf. 22nd Bn. Co.H
Tally, Crawford A. AL Cav. Shockley's Co.
Tally, C.S. 10th Conf.Cav. Co.A
Tally, C.W.L. LA 6th Cav. Co.A
Tally, D. LA 3rd (Wingfield's) Cav. Co.A
Tally, Daniel D. NC 38th Inf. Co.B
Tally, Daniel F. NC Walker's Bn. Thomas' Legion Co.G
Tally, Daniel F. TN 1st Cav. Co.H
Tally, Daniel F. TN 1st (Carter's) Cav. Co.H
Tally, Daniel Y. NC 4th Cav. (59th St.Troops) Co.B
Tally, David NC 45th Inf. Co.H
Tally, David B. TN Lt.Arty. Baxter's Co.
Tally, D.C. TN Lt.Arty. Scott's Co.
Tally, D.L. LA 3rd (Wingfield's) Cav. Co.G 1st Lt.
Tally, Dudly C. NC Walker's Bn. Thomas' Legion Co.G
Tally, Dudly C. TN 1st (Carter's) Cav. Co.H
Tally, E. AL 7th Cav. Co.G
Tally, E. MO 16th Inf. Co.D
Tally, Edward AL 33rd Inf. Co.C
Tally, Edward VA 6th Bn.Res. Co.I
Tally, E. Green NC 44th Inf. Co.E
Tally, Elijah AL 58th (Part.Rangers) Co.K
Tally, Evan AR 2nd Vol. Co.A
Tally, Evan SC 20th Inf. Co.A Sgt.
Tally, F.E. AL 11th Inf. Co.A
Tally, F.M. AR 27th Inf. Co.E
Tally, Francis W. NC 28th Inf. Co.D Sgt.
Tally, Franklin AL 33rd Inf. Co.E
Tally, Frederick TX 4th Cav. Co.B
Tally, Frederick H. TX 36th Cav. Co.K
Tally, Geo. F. Gen. & Staff Chap.
Tally, George M.D. NC 2nd Bn.Loc.Def.Troops Co.B
Tally, George W. AL 3rd Bn. Hilliard's Legion Vol. Co.A
Tally, George W. TX Cav. Hardeman's Regt. Co.E
Tally, George W. VA 1st Cav. 1st Co.K
Tally, George W. VA 15th Cav. Co.D
Tally, G.H. AL 34th Inf. Black's Co. Cpl.
Tally, Gileas W. VA 5th Inf. Co.F
Tally, Green B. AR 17th (Lemoyne's) Inf. Co.B Sgt.
Tally, G.W. VA 6th Cav. Co.C
Tally, H.C. GA Cav. 9th Bn. (St.Guards) Co.D
Tally, Henry C. NC 13th Inf. Co.C
Tally, Henry N. AL 18th Bn.Vol. Co.C
Tally, Hiram MO 4th Cav. Co.I
Tally, H.M. Gen. & Staff Asst.Surg.
Tally, Horace AL 1st Regt. Mobile Vol. Co.E
Tally, H.P. TX 10th Cav. Co.D
Tally, Hugh L. TX 8th Cav. Co.G
Tally, J. KY Lt.Arty. Cobb's Co.
Tally, J. KY 3rd Mtd.Inf. 1st Co.F
Tally, J. NC 3rd Jr.Res. Co.C
Tally, J. VA 29th Inf. Co.D
Tally, Jacob TX Cav. McDowell's Co.
Tally, Jacob R. TX 4th Cav. Co.B
Tally, James KY 7th Mtd.Inf. Co.K
Tally, James NC 1st Bn.Jr.Res. Co.E
Tally, James TN 50th Inf. Co.H
Tally, James TX 26th Cav. Co.K
Tally, James A. TN 44th Inf. Co.E
Tally, James B. NC 45th Inf. Co.F,A,L
Tally, James F. AL 3rd Bn. Hilliard's Legion Vol. Co.A
Tally, James J. AR 24th Inf. Co.B
Tally, James K. NC 44th Inf. Co.E
Tally, James M. TX 31st Cav. Co.B
Tally, James T. TX 26th Cav. Co.A
Tally, J. Arnold AL 4th Inf. Co.B
Tally, J.E. TN 7th (Duckworth's) Cav. Co.H
Tally, Jesse A. TX 29th Cav. Co.A
Tally, J.H. MS Res.Corps Withers' Co.
Tally, J.H. TX Cav. Giddings' Bn. Carr's Co.
Tally, J.L. LA 17th Inf. Co.H
Tally, John AL 3rd Bn. Hilliard's Legion Vol. Co.A

Tally, John GA Cav. 9th Bn. (St.Guards) Co.D
Tally, John LA 3rd (Wingfield's) Cav. Co.A
Tally, John MO 1st N.E. Cav. Co.B
Tally, John NC 5th Cav. (63rd St.Troops) Co.E
Tally, John NC 7th Sr.Res. Williams' Co.
Tally, John NC 37th Inf. Co.I 1st Sgt.
Tally, John NC 61st Inf. Co.D
Tally, John VA 5th Inf. Co.G
Tally, John VA 40th Inf. Co.A
Tally, John C. TN 20th Cav.
Tally, John D. LA Miles' Legion Co.B
Tally, John F. MS 2nd Inf. Co.C
Tally, John M. AL 18th Bn.Vol. Co.C
Tally, John M.P. AL 33rd Inf. Co.G Cpl.
Tally, John W. AL 45th Inf. Co.E
Tally, John W. NC 13th Inf. Co.C
Tally, John W. TN 43rd Inf. Co.F Sgt.
Tally, John W.R. AL Arty. 1st Bn. Co.E
Tally, John W.R. MS 10th Cav. Co.G
Tally, John W.R. MS 43rd Inf. Co.H
Tally, Joseph SC 1st (Butler's) Inf. Co.D,C
Tally, Joseph C. TN 2nd (Smith's) Cav.
Tally, Josiah MS 6th Inf. Co.B
Tally, J.P. TN 17th Inf. Co.H 1st Lt.
Tally, J.R. NC 26th Inf. Co.E
Tally, J.W. TX Cav. Hardeman's Regt. Co.E
Tally, J.W. TX 20th Inf. Co.D
Tally, Lee AR 45th Cav. Co.D
Tally, Littleton AL 17th Inf. Co.C
Tally, L.P. VA 40th Inf.
Tally, Lucius H. VA 40th Inf. Co.H
Tally, M. AR 15th Inf. Co.C
Tally, M. TX 33rd Cav. Co.E
Tally, Martin B. GA Inf. 8th Bn. Co.C
Tally, Martin V. NC 28th Inf. Co.D
Tally, Merriwether VA 23rd Inf. Co.G
Tally, Michael NC 37th Inf. Co.I
Tally, Milton V. NC 26th Inf. Co.E
Tally, M.J. LA 17th Inf. Co.H Sgt.
Tally, M.V. NC 44th Inf. Co.E Sgt.
Tally, M.W. TX 14th Inf. Co.F
Tally, N. VA 40th Inf. Co.B
Tally, Nathan MS 11th Inf. Co.D
Tally, P. TX 4th Cav. Co.C
Tally, Pinkney F. NC 45th Inf. Co.H
Tally, R. TN 14th (Neely's) Cav. Co.A
Tally, Reuben J. TX 36th Cav. Co.D
Tally, Richard A. VA Hvy.Arty. Epes' Co.
Tally, Robert TX 13th Vol. 3rd Co.I
Tally, Robert D. NC 26th Inf. Co.E
Tally, Robert W. VA 13th Cav. Co.E
Tally, Sanford KY 3rd Mtd.Inf. Co.F
Tally, S.B. SC 1st St.Troops Co.H
Tally, S.B. SC 3rd Res. Co.G
Tally, S.C. VA Cav. Mosby's Regt. (Part. Rangers) Co.F
Tally, S.C. Gen. & Staff Chap.
Tally, S.G. GA Mil. 37th Regt. Co.C 1st Lt.
Tally, Sidney J. NC 26th Inf. Co.E 1st Sgt.
Tally, Sidney J. NC 44th Inf. Co.E 2nd Lt.
Tally, Silas 1st Choctaw Mtd.Rifles Co.E
Tally, S.L. GA 8th Cav. Co.C
Tally, S.P. NC 6th Sr.Res. Co.B Cpl.
Tally, Stephen T. TN 17th Inf. Co.H
Tally, T.A. AL 45th Inf. Co.D
Tally, Tandy J. TN 2nd (Robison's) Inf. Co.H
Tally, Thomas AL 33rd Inf. Co.E
Tally, Thomas GA Hvy.Arty. 22nd Bn.
Tally, Thomas MS 14th Inf. Co.B
Tally, Thomas TN 62nd Mtd.Inf. Co.I
Tally, Thomas A. AL 34th Inf. Black's Co.
Tally, Thomas K. VA 40th Inf. Co.A
Tally, Thornton GA Cav. 1st Gordon Squad. (St.Guards) Reeves' Co.
Tally, Timothy A. AL Arty. 1st Bn. Co.E
Tally, T.J. TX Cav. Barnes' Regt. Upchurch's Co.
Tally, T.J. VA Hood's Bn.Res. Co.B Cpl.
Tally, W.A. AR 35th Inf. Co.G Cpl.
Tally, W.A. TX Cav. (Dismtd.) Chisum's Regt. Co.H
Tally, Walter SC 1st Cav. Co.F
Tally, W.B. TN 1st (Carter's) Cav. Co.B
Tally, W.D.K. GA 13th Inf. Co.D
Tally, Wesley TN 35th Inf. Co.C
Tally, Wiley M. NC 44th Inf. Co.E Sgt.
Tally, William MS 7th Cav. Co.B
Tally, Wm. MO St.Guard W.H. Taylor's Co.
Tally, William MO St.Guard
Tally, William NC 45th Inf. Co.I
Tally, William TN 2nd (Smith's) Cav.
Tally, William TN 13th (Gore's) Cav. Co.A
Tally, William F. NC 45th Inf. Co.F
Tally, William Frank MS 2nd Part.Rangers Co.C
Tally, William H. TX 31st Cav. Co.B Cpl.
Tally, William J. VA 56th Inf. Co.B
Tally, William M. AL 29th Inf. Co.B
Tally, William M. NC 44th Inf. Co.E Sgt.
Tally, William R.P. AL 43rd Inf. Co.A
Tally, William W. TN 2nd (Smith's) Cav.
Tally, W.J. TX 10th Cav. Co.C
Tally, W.R. AL 24th Inf. Co.B
Tally, W.R.P. AL Mil. 4th Vol. Modawell's Co. Sgt.
Tally, W.T. KY 3rd Mtd.Inf. Co.F
Tally, W.T. SC 1st Cav. Co.F
Talma, J. Baptiste LA Mil. 1st Native Guards
Talmachus Harjo 1st Seminole Mtd.Vol.
Talmadge, C.G. GA 11th Cav. Co.D
Talmadge, S. 1st Chickasaw Inf. Wallace's Co.
Talmadge, W.A. GA Inf. 23rd Bn.Loc.Def. Sims' Co.
Talmadge, William P. GA 3rd Cav. (St.Guards) Co.F
Talmage, C.G. GA Arty. Lumpkin's Co. Sgt.
Talmage, Edward GA Arty. Moore's Btty. Can.
Talmage, J.W. MS 6th Inf. Co.E
Talmage, William P. GA Arty. Moore's Btty. Can.
Talman, Albert G. VA Hvy.Arty. 10th Bn. Co.E Cpl.
Talman, H. Clay VA Inf. 25th Bn. Co.E Sgt.
Talman, Henry F. VA 45th Inf. Co.C
Talman, J.L. TX 25th Cav.
Talman, John, Jr. VA 3rd Inf.Loc.Def. Co.F
Talman, John S. VA 3rd Cav. Co.D
Talman, W.A. VA 46th Inf. Co.L
Talman, William VA 3rd Inf.Loc.Def. Co.F
Talman, William A. VA 28th Inf. Co.A
Talman, William A. VA 59th Inf. 3rd Co.F
Talman, William A. VA 60th Inf. 1st Co.H
Talman, William H. VA 3rd Cav. Co.D Cpl.
Talman, William H. VA 1st Arty. Co.K
Talmon, D. TX 8th Inf. Co.G
Talmon, James W. VA 45th Inf. Co.C Cpl.
Talmon, John L. TX Cav. Waller's Regt. Menard's Co.
Talmond, David TX 21st Cav. Co.K
Talom, W.H. TX Cav. Giddings' Bn. Carr's Co.
Ta looke Sam 1st Cherokee Mtd.Rifles Co.C
Talor, Alven TN 59th Mtd.Inf. Co.C
Talor, C.M. KY 11th Cav. Co.H 3rd Lt.
Talor, David NC McMillan's Co.
Talor, E.P. AL Cav. Stuart's Bn. Lt.
Talor, Latson L. FL 1st Inf. New Co.D
Talor, R. VA 46th Inf. Co.F
Talor, Skelly KY 11th Cav. Co.H
Talor, Wiley FL 11th Inf. Co.C
Talse Micco 1st Seminole Mtd.Vol.
Talse Mico 1st Seminole Mtd.Vol.
Talser, W.G. AR 8th Inf. Co.H
Talson, J.A. AL 12th Cav. Co.I
Taltavill, Anto. LA Mil. 5th Regt.Eur.Brig. (Spanish Regt.) Co.9
Talton, A.J. SC 21st Inf. Co.E
Talton, C.M. SC Lt.Arty. Garden's Co. (Palmetto Lt.Btty.)
Talton, Cullen C. LA 9th Inf. Co.C
Talton, Davis L. NC 4th Cav. (59th St.Troops) Co.A
Talton, Dennis D. NC 43rd Inf. Co.I
Talton, Drury NC 43rd Inf. Co.I
Talton, H.W. LA 8th Inf. Co.G
Talton, Iredell NC 2nd Inf. Co.H
Talton, J. NC 6th Inf. Co.B
Talton, James GA 13th Inf. Co.H
Talton, James MS Inf. 2nd Bn. Co.B
Talton, James D. NC 8th Sr.Res. Daniel's Co.
Talton, James D. NC 35th Inf. Co.H
Talton, James D. NC 50th Inf. Co.C
Talton, James H. NC 4th Inf. Co.D
Talton, James T. MS 48th Inf. Co.B Sgt.
Talton, James T. NC 50th Inf. Co.C
Talton, Jesse NC 43rd Inf. Co.I
Talton, J.H. GA 11th Inf. Co.K
Talton, John H. GA Lt.Arty. 14th Bn. Co.A
Talton, John H. GA Lt.Arty. Havis' Btty.
Talton, John W. NC 53rd Inf. Co.C
Talton, Joseph J. AL 47th Inf. Co.B Sgt.
Talton, Lewis, Jr. NC 50th Inf. Co.C Cpl.
Talton, M. NC 20th Inf. Co.H
Talton, Mack NC 2nd Inf. Co.H
Talton, Martin P. GA Lt.Arty. Ritter's Co.
Talton, Martin T. GA 42nd Inf. Co.D
Talton, Newton B. AL 47th Inf. Co.B
Talton, R. NC 6th Inf. Co.B
Talton, R. NC 55th Inf. Co.A
Talton, Randsom GA 62nd Cav. Co.I
Talton, Ruffin GA 48th Inf. Co.I
Talton, Samuel W. NC 42nd Inf. Co.K Cpl.
Talton, Thomas GA Lt.Arty. Ritter's Co.
Talton, Thomas NC 23rd Inf. Co.A
Talton, Thomas E. GA 36th (Broyles') Inf. Co.F
Talton, Turner R. NC 35th Inf. Co.I
Talton, W.A. NC Loc.Def. Croom's Co.
Talton, William MO 2nd Cav. Co.D
Talton, William R. NC 43rd Inf. Co.I
Talton, W.J. AR Inf. Cocke's Regt. 2nd Lt.
Talton, W.J. NC 50th Inf. Co.C
Taltum, D.E. AL Gid Nelson Lt.Arty.
Talty, George TN Lt.Arty. Scott's Co.

Talty, John LA Inf. 1st Sp.Bn. (Wheat's) Co.A
Talty, John LA 28th (Thomas') Inf. Co.C
Talty, John TN Lt.Arty. Scott's Co.
Talty, John (2) TN Lt.Arty. Scott's Co.
Talty, Patrick TN Lt.Arty. Scott's Co. Cpl.
Talty, Peter SC 1st (Butler's) Inf. Co.A
Talty, Samuel TN Lt.Arty. Scott's Co.
Ta lum poo 1st Creek Mtd.Vol. Co.A
Talunatubba, M. 1st Chickasaw Inf. Wallace's Co.
Talunosteh Nickojack NC Inf. Thomas Legion 2nd Co.A
Talupa, H. 1st Chickasaw Inf. Wallace's Co.
Talver, P.S. AR 8th Inf.
Talwahe Fixico 1st Seminole Mtd.Vol.
Talweder, B. LA Mil. 1st Chasseurs a pied Co.8
Talweder, F. LA Mil. 1st Chasseurs a pied Co.8
Talyaferro, C.S. TX 20th Inf. Co.I
Tam, James TX 18th Cav. Co.H
Tamahim lubbee 1st Choctaw Mtd.Rifles Co.G
Tamalacha Sowell 1st Choctaw & Chickasaw Mtd.Rifles 2nd Co.K
Tambbee Greenwood 1st Choctaw Mtd.Rifles Co.G
Tamberlin, A. TX Cav. McCord's Frontier Regt. Co.B
Tamberty, B. TN 5th Cav.
Tamblin, Calvin TN Inf. 4th Cons.Regt. Co.F
Tambourg, A. LA Mil. Orleans Guards Regt. Co.H
Tambourgson, J.B. VA Hvy.Arty. 18th Bn. Co.C
Tamby 1st Choctaw Mtd.Rifles Co.B
Tamby Theoth Deneale's Regt. Choctaw Warriors Co.A
Tameged, Joseph GA 22nd Inf. Co.F
Tamendens, J.M. AL Res. Cpl.
Tamer, G.W. MO Inf. 5th Regt.St.Guard Co.C Sgt.
Tamer, John GA Cav. 19th Bn. Co.D
Tamer, William H.H. MO Inf. 5th Regt.St.Guard Co.C Cpl.
Tames, R. GA Lt.Arty. Clinch's Btty.
Tamez, L. LA Mil. 1st Chasseurs a pied Co.8
Tamez, Leonardo TX Cav. Ragsdale's Bn. 1st Co.C
Tami, --- LA Mil. 3rd Regt.Eur.Brig. (Garde Francaise) Euler's Co.
Tamkins, John VA 11th Cav. Co.C Sgt.
Tamler, G.M. AL 34th Inf. Co.H
Tamlin, Cato FL 10th Inf. Co.F
Tamlins, M.R. AL 2nd Cav. Co.I
Tamlyn, William F. TX 35th (Brown's) Cav. Co.D
Tamlyn, William F. TX 13th Vol. 1st Co.I
Tamm, John H. GA 1st (Olmstead's) Inf. Co.I Cpl.
Tamma, D.C. AR 1st Mtd.Rifles Co.F
Tammerlin, John W. TN 53rd Inf. Co.C
Tamnan, Philip TN 15th Inf. Co.K 2nd Lt.
Tamoni, Philip NC 12th Inf. Co.B,D
Tampke, --- TX 8th Field Btty.
Tampke, --- TX Lt.Arty. Dege's Bn.
Tampke, Charles A. TX 8th Inf. Co.D
Tampke, Ludolph TX 8th Inf. Co.D Cpl.
Tampkin, J. TN 7th (Duckworth's) Cav. Co.C
Tamplin, B.F. TX 11th Inf. Co.E
Tamplin, Edward NC 56th Inf. Co.C
Tamplin, Henry H. TX 28th Cav. Co.A
Tamplin, H.H. TX Cav. 2nd Bn.St.Troops Nelson's Co.
Tamplin, James LA 28th (Gray's) Inf. Co.H
Tamplin, J.H. AL 1st Inf. Co.H Sgt.
Tamplin, J.L. AL Auburn Home Guards Vol. Darby's Co.
Tamplin, T.H. NC 56th Inf. Co.B
Tamplin, Thomas H. NC 17th Inf. (1st Org.) Co.A Sgt.
Tamplin, Thomas H. NC 32nd Inf. Co.B 1st Sgt.
Tamplin, W.H. TX 11th Inf. Co.E Drum.
Tamplin, William H. GA 2nd Inf. Co.I
Tamplin, William H.H. AL Inf. 1st Regt. Co.F
Tamplin, William L. TX 28th Cav. Co.A
Tampson, A. MO Cav. Ford's Bn. Co.D
Tamry, W.R. GA Inf. 23rd Bn.Loc.Def. Cooks' Co.
Tams, W. Gen. & Staff Capt.,AMSK
Tamure, Rodger LA 13th & 20th Inf. N.C.S. Color Sgt.
Tamure, Roger LA 13th Inf. Co.I,E 2nd Lt.
Tanahill, Carleton J. MO 1st Cav. Co.B
Tanampishtobbee 1st Choctaw Mtd.Rifles Co.F
Tanampishtubbee, Thomas 1st Choctaw Mtd.Rifles Co.F
Tananee, John W. GA 2nd Cav. Co.I
Tanant, Ira G. AL 4th Inf. Co.G Cpl.
Tanapaya, Jacob 1st Choctaw & Chickasaw Mtd.Rifles 2nd Co.C Sgt.
Tanar, Joseph TN 9th Inf. Co.A
Tana shay 1st Creek Mtd.Vol. Co.E
Tanatubbe, Adam 1st Choctaw & Chickasaw Mtd.Rifles Maytubby's Co.
Tanay,William P. AL 36th Inf. Co.E
Tanbush, James GA Inf. 27th Inf. Co.A
Tanby, M.L. AL 19th Inf. Co.I
Tancey, Samuel AR 5th (St.Troops) Inf. Dowd's Co.
Tan chu lae Ner 1st Cherokee Mtd.Rifles Co.H
Tancill, John W. MO 2nd Cav. 3rd Co.K
Tancill, John W. MO Cav. Wood's Regt. Co.C Ord.Sgt.
Tancott, A.J. TN 19th (Biffle's) Cav. Co.E
Tand, William P. MO 15th Cav. Co.K
Tandell, W.M. MO St.Guard
Tanden, W.W. AR 19th Inf. Co.H
Tander, Richard AL Cav. Forrest's Regt.
Tandiver, M.L. AL 43rd Inf. Co.G
Tandy 1st Choctaw & Chickasaw Mtd.Rifles 2nd Co.H
Tandy, C.W. TN 7th (Duckworth's) Cav. Co.G
Tandy, D.A. KY 1st (Helm's) Cav. Co.G
Tandy, G.A. KY 1st (Helm's) Cav. New Co.G
Tandy, George KY 13th Cav. Co.H
Tandy, George SC Ord.Guards Loc.Def.Troops
Tandy, George L. KY 1st (Helm's) Cav. Co.A
Tandy, George L. KY Cav. 1st Bn. Co.A
Tandy, J. TX Cav. Sutton's Co.
Tandy, James P. KY 4th Cav. Co.F
Tandy, John A. KY 4th Cav. Co.A
Tandy, Lewis KY 5th Mtd.Inf. Co.I
Tandy, Lewis KY 9th Mtd.Inf. Co.I
Tandy, Moses AR 16th Inf. Co.G
Tandy, Thomas MO 1st N.E. Cav. Co.F
Tandy, T.S. MO 9th Inf. Co.C
Tandy, T.S. MO Inf. Clark's Regt. Co.B
Tandy, T.Z. KY 2nd (Woodward's) Cav. Co.D
Tandy, W. KY 1st (Helm's) Cav. New Co.G
Tandy, William L. TX Cav. 2nd Regt.St.Troops Co.H
Tandy, William L. TX 9th Cav. Co.A
Tane, P.B. AL St.Res.
Taneel, Warren MO St.Guards
Tanehill, B.F. MO 1st Cav. Co.B 1st Lt.
Tanehill, George J. AR 23rd Inf. Co.I Sgt.
Taneman, A. TX 13th Vol. Co.B
Tanentine, J.F. AR 12th Inf. Co.G
Taner, Franklin M. TX 13th Vol. 3rd Co.A
Taner, J.J. NC 2nd Cav. (19th St.Troops) Co.F
Taner, Pablo LA Mil. 5th Regt.Eur.Brig. (Spanish Regt.) Co.9
Taner, William GA Cav. Young's Co. (Alleghany Troopers)
Taney 1st Choctaw & Chickasaw Mtd.Rifles 1st Co.E
Taney, C.C. TN 41st Inf. Co.C
Taney, C.H. LA Mil. Orleans Guards Regt. Co.A
Taney, E.C. AR 2nd Mtd.Rifles Co.H
Taney, F.L. Gen. & Staff, Medical Dept. Surg.
Taney, Frank L. LA 10th Inf. Surg.
Taney, G.H. MO Cav. Fristoe's Regt. Co.A
Taney, Gustave R. LA 10th Inf. Co.F Jr.2nd Lt.
Taney, L.M. LA Inf.Crescent Regt. Co.B
Taney, L.M. Gen. & Staff Maj.,ACS
Taney, Robert J. LA Lt.Arty. LeGardeur, Jr.'s Co. (Orleans Guard Btty.)
Taney, W. AR 38th Inf. Co.B
Taney, William MO 1st Cav. Co.E
Taney, William B. 1st Choctaw Mtd.Rifles Co.I
Taney, W.P. AL Gid Nelson Lt.Arty.
Tanfield, Anthony MS 9th Inf. New Co.F
Tanfor, F. AR 21st Mil. Co.A
Tangipaho, E. 1st Chickasaw Inf. Haynes' Co.
Tangipaho, G. 1st Chickasaw Inf. Hansell's Co.
Tangleson, George 1st Cherokee Mtd.Vol. 2nd Co.G
Tangue, W.J. TN 26th Cav. Co.C
Tanhuser, C. TX 2nd Inf. Co.C
Tanihubbee 1st Choctaw & Chickasaw Mtd.Rifles 2nd Co.H
Tank, Charles N. GA 7th Inf. Co.K
Tank, Charles N. GA Cobb's Legion Co.B
Tank, Louis MS 21st Inf. Co.L
Tankard, John R. VA 39th Inf. Co.D Cpl.
Tankard, Thaddeus J. NC 3rd Arty. (40th St.Troops) Co.B Cpl.
Tanke, Aug TX Waul's Legion Co.B
Tankely, William MO Inf. 4th Regt.St.Guard Co.E
Tankerley, J.C. MS 5th Inf. Co.D
Tankerley, S.V. MS 5th Inf. Co.D
Tankersby, Robert VA 1st Cav. Co.F
Tankersley, A.B. GA 7th Inf. (St.Guards) Co.F
Tankersley, Alexander VA 38th Inf. Co.C
Tankersley, Alucius VA 37th Mil. 2nd Co.B
Tankersley, Benjamin AL 60th Inf. Co.K
Tankersley, B.F. MS 5th Inf. Co.F
Tankersley, B.T. MS 23rd Inf. Co.A
Tankersley, Charles GA Siege Arty. 28th Bn. Co.F
Tankersley, Charles GA 16th Inf. Co.E

Tankersley, C.W. VA Lt.Arty. Ellett's Co.
Tankersley, David S. MS 30th Inf. Co.B
Tankersley, Edwin GA Inf. 1st Loc.Troops (Augusta) Co.C
Tankersley, F.A. AL 1st Regt. Mobile Vol. Co.A
Tankersley, F.A. AL Mil. 2nd Regt.Vol. Co.D
Tankersley, F.A. AL Conscription Bureau
Tankersley, Felix AL 5th Inf. New Co.G
Tankersley, Felix NC 37th Inf. Co.F 1st Lt.
Tankersley, G. 10th Conf.Cav. Co.D
Tankersley, George AL Vol. Goldsmith's Ind.Co. 3rd Lt.
Tankersley, George G. TX Terry's Mtd.Co. (St.Troops)
Tankersley, George W. KY Cav. Bolen's Ind.Co.
Tankersley, George W. TX 7th Field Btty.
Tankersley, George W. TX 13th Vol. Co.E
Tankersley, George W. Conf.Cav. Wood's Regt. 2nd Co.M
Tankersley, G.J. MS 28th Cav. Co.K
Tankersley, G.N. MO 4th Inf. Co.D Sgt.
Tankersley, G.P. GA Inf. 9th Bn. Co.E
Tankersley, Greef J. MS 8th Cav. Co.C
Tankersley, Grief J. MS 2nd Part.Rangers Co.F Cpl.
Tankersley, Griffin GA Inf. 1st Loc.Troops (Augusta) Co.B
Tankersley, Griffin GA 10th Inf. Co.D
Tankersley, G.W. MS 10th Inf. Old Co.K
Tankersley, Harrison TX 8th Cav. Co.H
Tankersley, Isaac MS 2nd Part.Rangers Co.F
Tankersley, J. GA 3rd Res. Co.A
Tankersley, J. MS 3rd Cav. Co.I,B
Tankersley, James TX 7th Field Btty.
Tankersley, James A. TX 13th Vol. Co.E
Tankersley, James E. GA 4th Inf. Co.E
Tankersley, James H. MS 2nd Inf. Co.A
Tankersley, James H. MS 32nd Inf. Co.H Capt.
Tankersley, James M. VA 60th Inf. Co.B
Tankersley, J.D.W. AR Cav. 1st Bn. (Stirman's) Co.D
Tankersley, Jesse E. TX 13th Vol. Co.E
Tankersley, J.H. MS 18th Inf. Co.C
Tankersley, J.M. GA 37th Inf. Co.H
Tankersley, John AL 6th Inf. Co.F
Tankersley, John AL 2nd Bn. Hilliard's Legion Vol. Co.C
Tankersley, John TN 62nd Mtd.Inf. Co.C
Tankersley, John TX 7th Cav. Co.G Sgt.
Tankersley, Joseph B. TN 53rd Inf. Co.G
Tankersley, Joseph B. VA 4th Res. Co.H
Tankersley, Joseph F. VA 54th Inf. Co.E
Tankersley, J.P. MS 6th Cav. Co.B
Tankersley, J.P. MS Cav. Davenport's Bn. (St.Troops) Co.A
Tankersley, J.R. AL 17th Inf. Co.F
Tankersley, Lucius VA 40th Inf. Co.A
Tankersley, M. MS Mil. 4th Cav. Co.L Jr.2nd Lt.
Tankersley, M. MS 29th Inf. Co.D
Tankersley, M. TN 8th (Smith's) Cav. Co.A Cpl.
Tankersley, Martin P. MO 4th Cav. Co.B
Tankersley, Martin P. MO Cav. Preston's Bn. Co.B
Tankersley, Merrill MS 2nd Part.Rangers Co.F
Tankersley, P. AL Cav. Moreland's Regt. Co.C Cpl.
Tankersley, R.A.B. GA 48th Inf. Co.K
Tankersley, Richard TN 53rd Inf. Co.G
Tankersley, Richard C. TX 15th Cav. Co.I
Tankersley, R.J. AL 46th Inf. Co.E
Tankersley, Robert VA 1st (Farinholt's) Res. Co.F
Tankersley, Robert VA 9th Inf. 1st Co.H
Tankersley, Rowland W. MS 42nd Inf. Co.F Sgt.
Tankersley, S. MS Inf. 2nd Bn. (St.Troops) Co.A
Tankersley, S.A. VA Rockbridge Cty.Res. Donald's Co.
Tankersley, Samuel TX 7th Field Btty.
Tankersley, Samuel H. TN 12th Cav. Co.B
Tankersley, Samuel H. TN 53rd Inf. Co.G
Tankersley, Thomas H. GA 45th Inf. Co.A
Tankersley, Thomas Jefferson MS 8th Cav. Co.A
Tankersley, Thomas R. TX 17th Cav. Co.B
Tankersley, W.H. TX Cav. McCord's Frontier Regt. Co.H
Tankersley, William A. MS 32nd Inf. Co.H
Tankersley, William H. TX 15th Cav. Co.D
Tankersley, William T. GA 48th Inf. Co.K
Tankersley, William Z. MS 8th Cav. Co.C
Tankersley, W.N. GA 65th Inf. Co.K
Tankersley, W.T. GA 16th Inf. Co.K
Tankersley, W.Z. MS 28th Cav. Co.K
Tankersly, Daniel B. TX 15th Cav. Co.D
Tankersly, David F. GA Cav. 16th Bn. (St.Guards) Co.F
Tankersly, F. VA 4th Cav. & Inf.St.Line 1st Co.I
Tankersly, G. GA 1st (Symons') Res. Co.I
Tankersly, George MS 1st Cav. Co.M
Tankersly, George P. MS 17th Inf. Co.K
Tankersly, G.W. TX 22nd Inf. Co.A
Tankersly, Henry S. MS 15th Inf.
Tankersly, H.W. GA 27th Inf. Co.B
Tankersly, Jack MO 1st Inf. Co.I
Tankersly, James TX 15th Cav. Co.D
Tankersly, James M. VA 16th Inf. Co.B
Tankersly, J.M. GA Inf. 9th Bn. Co.E
Tankersly, John AL 10th Inf. Co.D
Tankersly, John VA 23rd Cav. Co.H
Tankersly, John W. TX 15th Cav. Co.D
Tankersly, Larkin TX 15th Cav. Co.D
Tankersly, Lemuel GA Cav. 16th Bn. (St.Guards) Co.F
Tankersly, Leonard AR 16th Inf. Co.G
Tankersly, R. VA 2nd Cav. Co.G
Tankersly, Robert VA Inf. 28th Bn. Co.C
Tankersly, Sherwood R. MS 42nd Inf. Co.F
Tankersly, W.B. MS 7th Cav. Co.H
Tankersly, W.B. TN Cav. Napier's Bn. Co.C
Tankersly, W.H. GA 5th Res. Co.D
Tankersly, William MO 1st Inf. Co.I
Tankersly, William VA 10th Bn.Res. Co.E
Tankersly, William B. GA 3rd Inf. Co.G Sgt.
Tankerster, J. MS 10th Cav. Co.D
Tankesley, A.W. GA 39th Inf. Co.I
Tankesley, Barksdel AL 19th Inf. Co.A
Tankesley, Carrol M. TN 34th Inf. 2nd Co.C
Tankesley, F.M. GA 39th Inf. Co.D
Tankesley, George AL 46th Inf. Co.E
Tankesley, George W. VA 9th Inf. 1st Co.A
Tankesley, Henry GA 52nd Inf. Co.C Music.
Tankesley, James E. VA Horse Arty.Lurty's Co. Sgt.
Tankesley, John TN Inf. 23rd Bn. Co.D
Tankesley, John J. TN 34th Inf. 2nd Co.C
Tankesley, R.M. TN 37th Inf. Co.D Maj.
Tankesley, William MO 4th Cav. Co.A
Tankesley, William J. TN 2nd (Robison's) Inf. Co.F
Tankesley, William M. TN 84th Inf. 2nd Co.C
Tankesley, William M. VA 5th Inf. Co.G
Tankesley, Willis TN 34th Inf. 2nd Co.C
Tankesley, W.M. MS 3rd Inf. (St.Troops) Co.A
Tankesly, B.F. MO 2nd Cav. Co.F
Tankesly, Jesse GA 9th Inf. Co.B
Tankesly, T.M. AL 8th (Hatch's) Cav. Co.F
Tankesly, W.B. TN 10th (DeMoss') Cav. Co.F
Tankisley, Edwin SC 5th Res. Co.D
Tankisly, E. SC 2nd St.Troops Co.I
Tankler, James L. TX 12th Cav. Co.H,I
Tankley, H.K. GA Inf. 4th Bn. (St.Guards) Co.F
Tankserly, W.J. TN 4th (McLemore's) Cav. Co.I
Tanksley, Ed. SC 22nd Inf. Co.I
Tanksley, George VA 64th Mtd.Inf. Co.F
Tanksley, George W. TX Cav. Ragsdale's Bn. 2nd Co.C
Tanksley, G.L. MS 1st (Johnston's) Inf. Co.I Sgt.
Tanksley, G.W. AR 23rd Inf. Co.G Sgt.
Tanksley, J.A. TN Inf. Nashville Bn. Cattles' Co.
Tanksley, James M. GA 36th (Broyles') Inf. Co.A Sgt.
Tanksley, J.E. VA 14th Cav. Co.D
Tanksley, J.M. AR 23rd Inf. Co.G
Tanksley, J.M. GA 38th Inf. Co.A
Tanksley, John SC 22nd Inf. Co.H
Tanksley, Marion SC 22nd Inf. Co.H
Tanksley, Martin V. VA 5th Inf. Co.G
Tanksley, William GA 43rd Inf. Co.C
Tanksley, Williams VA 64th Mtd.Inf. Co.F
Tanksley, Wriley AL 55th Vol. Co.I
Tanksley, Wrily TN 42nd Inf. 1st Co.I
Tanksly, A.J. MS 38th Cav. Co.B
Tanksly, John M. TX Cav. Mann's Regt. Co.A
Tanksly, S.A. VA VA 10th Bn.Res. Co.B
Tanlon, J.H. SC 26th Inf. Co.I
Tanlunsen, A. SC Mil.Cav. Theo. Cordes' Co.
Tanman, H.E. VA 61st Mil. Co.I
Tann, Alfred SC 23rd Inf. Co.D
Tann, M.W. TX 5th Inf. Co.B
Tann, O.J. SC Cav. 14th Bn. Co.B
Tann, Oliver J. SC 5th Cav. Co.A
Tann, T.A. AR 2nd Inf. Co.I Sgt.
Tann, William SC Lt.Arty. 3rd (Palmetto) Bn. Co.F
Tann, William SC 23rd Inf. Co.D
Tannahill, E.D. Gen. & Staff, A. of N.VA Capt.,ACS
Tannahill, Edmund D. VA 12th Inf. Co.E
Tannahill, H.H.H. AL 12th Cav. Co.D
Tannahill, J.G. AR 37th Inf. Co.B
Tannahill, Robert VA 5th Cav. (12 mo. '61-2) Co.D
Tannahill, Robert Gen. & Staff, A. of N.VA Maj.,Ch.CS

Tannahill, William A. KY Cav. 2nd Bn. (Dortch's) Co.B
Tannahill, William J. TX 9th Cav. Co.A
Tannahill, William T. VA 12th Inf. Co.E
Tannbald, Charles VA 15th Inf. Co.K
Tanneheiser, A. TX 15th Field Btty.
Tannehill, Benjamin W. MO 1st Cav. Co.B 1st Lt.
Tannehill, Charles O. AR Cav. 1st Bn. (Stirman's) Co.H Cpl.
Tannehill, Charles O. TX 27th Cav. Co.B
Tannehill, F.A. TN Inf. 3rd Bn. Co.A
Tannehill, John AR 30th Inf. Co.I 2nd Lt.
Tannehill, John T. AL 53rd (Part.Rangers) Co.A Adj.
Tannehill, Ninnian W. AL 6th Inf. Co.L
Tannehill, R.D. TX 16th Inf. Co.G
Tannehill, R.P. KY 7th Cav. Co.A
Tannehill, R.P. TX Cav. Gano's Squad. Co.A
Tannehill, William TX Cav. 2nd Regt.St.Troops Co.H
Tannehill, William J. TX 4th Inf. Co.B
Tannehill, W.J. KY 7th Cav. Co.A
Tannehill, W.J. TX Cav. Gano's Squad. Co.A
Tannehill, W.J. TX Inf. Carter's Co.
Tannen, William J. GA 14th Inf. Co.D Sgt.
Tannenbaum, Adolphus MS 14th Inf. Co.B
Tannequin, P. LA Mil. 3rd Regt. French Brig. Surg.
Tanner 1st Cherokee Mtd.Rifles Co.D Far.
Tanner, A. LA Siege Train Bn. Co.E
Tanner, Aaron 1st Cherokee Mtd.Rifles Co.D
Tanner, Abraham VA Lt.Arty. J.S. Brown's Co.
Tanner, Abraham VA Lt.Arty. Taylor's Co.
Tanner, Abraham VA Mil. Greene Cty.
Tanner, A.C. FL 2nd Cav. Co.K
Tanner, A.C. GA 1st Bn.S.S. Co.A
Tanner, A.J. GA 10th Cav. Co.B
Tanner, A.J. GA 12th Inf. Co.E
Tanner, A.K. MS 7th Cav. Co.F Sgt.
Tanner, Alfred GA 36th (Broyles') Inf. Co.A
Tanner, Allain GA Lt.Arty. 14th Bn. Co.D,F
Tanner, Allen GA Lt.Arty. Havis' Btty.
Tanner, Allen GA Lt.Arty. King's Btty.
Tanner, Alonzo SC 13th Inf. Co.C
Tanner, A.M. AR 11th Inf. Co.D
Tanner, A.M. AR 11th & 17th Cons.Inf. Co.D Sgt.
Tanner, Andra J. 7th Conf.Cav. Co.B
Tanner, Andrew SC 5th St.Troops Co.G
Tanner, Andrew J. LA 31st Inf. Co.K
Tanner, Andrew J. VA 14th Inf. Co.F
Tanner, Archabold S. GA 14th Inf. Co.D
Tanner, Ard. GA 16th Inf. Co.F
Tanner, Asa R. GA 49th Inf. Co.F
Tanner, Asberry C. GA 47th Inf. Co.F
Tanner, A.T. AL 9th Inf. Co.K
Tanner, A.W. GA Inf. (Jasper & Butts Cty. Guards) Lane's Co. Cpl.
Tanner, B.A. LA 31st Inf. Co.K
Tanner, Belton O. NC 34th Inf. Co.C
Tanner, Benjamin VA Hvy.Arty. 20th Bn. Co.D Sgt.
Tanner, Benjamin A. MO 1st N.E. Cav. Co.C
Tanner, Benjamin F. MS 1st Lt.Arty. Co.C
Tanner, Benjamin F. TN Cav. 9th Bn. (Gantt's) Co.D
Tanner, Benjamin H. FL 1st Cav. Co.B
Tanner, B.F. LA Mil. Terrebonne Regt.
Tanner, Branch LA Conscr.
Tanner, Branch B. GA 30th Inf. Co.B,E
Tanner, C. NC 6th Inf. Co.I
Tanner, Calton NC 20th Inf. Co.I
Tanner, Calvin B. TX Inf. Griffin's Bn. Co.D Sgt.
Tanner, Carter SC 1st St.Troops Co.K
Tanner, Carter SC 3rd Res. Co.B
Tanner, C.B. TX 5th Inf. Co.B
Tanner, Charles AL 13th Inf. Co.F
Tanner, Charles H. VA Inf. 25th Bn. Co.E
Tanner, Charles Henry AL 49th Inf. Co.C
Tanner, Charles W. MS 15th Inf. Co.I
Tanner, C.L. AL 15th Cav. Co.B
Tanner, C.L. 15th Conf.Cav. Co.B
Tanner, Clem L. MS 1st Lt.Arty. Co.C
Tanner, Columbus P. NC 56th Inf. Co.I
Tanner, Cornelius FL 1st Cav. Co.B
Tanner, C.P. NC 16th Inf. Co.G
Tanner, Daniel F. GA Cobb's Legion Co.I
Tanner, Darius AL Arty. 1st Bn. Co.C
Tanner, David LA 2nd Inf. Co.K Cpl.
Tanner, David NC 26th Inf. Co.F
Tanner, David B. VA 48th Inf. Ch.Music.
Tanner, David F. GA 49th Inf. Co.C Sgt.
Tanner, David S. GA 52nd Inf. Co.I
Tanner, David W. GA 34th Inf. Co.F
Tanner, D.B. GA Lt.Arty. Howell's Co.
Tanner, D.B. GA 55th Inf. Co.D 2nd Lt.
Tanner, D.H. FL 2nd Cav. Co.K
Tanner, Dick TN 19th & 20th (Cons.) Cav. Co.D
Tanner, D.R. TN 35th Inf. 2nd Co.A
Tanner, Duncan NC 20th Inf. Co.F
Tanner, E.D. AL 62nd Inf. Co.F
Tanner, E.D. SC 1st Bn.S.S. Co.B
Tanner, E.D. SC Inf. 6th Bn. Co.A
Tanner, E.D. SC 27th Inf. Co.F
Tanner, E.D. SC Manigault's Bn.Vol. Co.D
Tanner, Edward AR 24th Inf. Co.E
Tanner, E.E. TN 10th (DeMoss') Cav. Co.A
Tanner, E.H. TX 9th Cav. Co.H Sgt.
Tanner, E.H. TX 9th (Young's) Inf. Co.A
Tanner, Elias W. MS Arty. (Seven Stars Arty.) Roberts' Co.
Tanner, Eli H. GA 43rd Inf. Co.K
Tanner, Elijah VA 19th Cav. Co.H
Tanner, E.M. TX Inf. 1st St.Troops Wheat's Co.A
Tanner, E.S. GA 10th Inf. Co.A
Tanner, E.W. MS Cav. 3rd Bn.Res. Co.D Cpl.
Tanner, F.A. TX 13th Vol. 3rd Co.A
Tanner, Fielding A. TX Inf. Griffin's Bn. Co.D
Tanner, Floyd TN 35th Inf. Co.L
Tanner, F.M. SC 13th Inf. Co.I
Tanner, Francis D. GA Cobb's Legion Co.I
Tanner, Francis M. AL 43rd Inf. Co.K
Tanner, Frank AR 18th (Marmaduke's) Inf. Co.B
Tanner, Franklin TX Inf. Griffin's Bn. Co.D
Tanner, Franklin H. MS 1st Lt.Arty. Co.C
Tanner, Frederick VA 30th Bn.S.S. Co.B
Tanner, George VA 52nd Inf. Co.F
Tanner, George C. GA Cobb's Legion Co.I Bugler
Tanner, George G. GA 1st (Ramsey's) Inf. Co.I
Tanner, George M. GA Arty. 9th Bn. Co.A
Tanner, George M. VA 82nd Mil. Co.A Teamster
Tanner, George W. GA 30th Inf. Co.E Sgt.
Tanner, George W. TX 4th Cav. Co.F
Tanner, George W. TX 12th Cav. Co.A
Tanner, Gid GA Inf. 14th Bn. (St.Guards) Co.A
Tanner, G.K. GA 52nd Inf. Co.H
Tanner, G.L. AL 36th Inf. Co.D
Tanner, G.M. MO 1st & 4th Cons.Inf. Co.E
Tanner, Green GA 1st Bn.S.S. Co.A
Tanner, Green GA 47th Inf. Co.F
Tanner, Green M. MO 4th Inf. Co.H
Tanner, G.W. AR 1st (Monroe's) Cav. Co.B
Tanner, G.W. GA 43rd Inf. Co.F
Tanner, G.W. MS Cav. Powers' Regt. Co.A
Tanner, G.W. MS Lt.Arty. (Warren Lt.Arty.) Swett's Co.
Tanner, G. Whitfield VA 6th Cav. Co.I
Tanner, H. KY 8th Mtd.Inf.
Tanner, H. NC 4th Sr.Res. Co.D
Tanner, Hays NC 20th Inf. Co.I
Tanner, Henry LA 9th Inf. Co.B Band
Tanner, Henry C. LA 12th Inf. 1st Co.M, Co.C
Tanner, Henry C. MO 2nd Inf. Co.C
Tanner, H.J. FL 3rd Inf. Co.E
Tanner, H.J. TN 3rd (Clack's) Inf. Co.K
Tanner, Hugh M. GA 18th Inf. Co.B
Tanner, I. GA Lt.Arty. 12th Bn. 3rd Co.B
Tanner, I.S. Hoke's Div. Maj.,Ch.Surg.
Tanner, Isaac MS 9th Cav. Co.A
Tanner, Isaac MS Cav. 17th Bn. Co.A
Tanner, Isaac NC 21st Inf. Surg.
Tanner, Isaac TX 36th Cav. Co.I
Tanner, Isaac 15th Conf.Cav. Co.H
Tanner, Isaac E. TX 11th (Spaight's) Bn.Vol. Co.C
Tanner, Isaac L. TX 35th (Likens') Cav. Co.F
Tanner, Isaac S. GA 49th Inf. Co.C Sgt.
Tanner, Isaac S. Gen. & Staff Asst.Surg.
Tanner, Isaiah GA 1st Bn.S.S. Co.A
Tanner, Isaiah GA 47th Inf. Co.F
Tanner, J. AL Cav. Moreland's Regt. Co.F
Tanner, J. GA 5th Res. Co.K
Tanner, J. MS 37th Inf. Co.G
Tanner, J. VA 13th Inf. Co.K
Tanner, J.A. MS 15th (Cons.) Inf. Co.E
Tanner, J.A. MS Grace's Co. (St.Troops)
Tanner, J.A. TX Cav. 4th Regt.St.Troops Co.D
Tanner, Jack 1st Cherokee Mtd.Rifles Co.D
Tanner, Jacob AR 2nd Inf. Old Co.C, Co.B
Tanner, Jacob F. MO 1st N.E. Cav. Co.C
Tanner, Jacob F. MO 4th Cav. Co.G
Tanner, James GA 2nd Cav.
Tanner, James GA Lt.Arty. King's Btty.
Tanner, James GA 28th Inf. Co.B
Tanner, James SC 1st Bn.S.S. Co.B
Tanner, James SC 27th Inf. Co.F
Tanner, James TN 19th & 20th (Cons.) Cav. Co.E
Tanner, James TX Cav. Frontier Bn. Co.B
Tanner, James VA 14th Cav. Co.E
Tanner, James VA 46th Inf. 2nd Co.B,H
Tanner, James E. AR 1st Mtd.Rifles Co.B
Tanner, James H. AL 13th Inf. Co.F
Tanner, James H. VA 28th Inf. Co.F Sgt.
Tanner, James L. NC Lt.Arty. 3rd Bn. Co.A

Tanner, James M. AL Cav. 5th Bn. Hilliard's Legion Co.D
Tanner, James M. 10th Conf.Cav. Co.D
Tanner, James P. GA 11th Cav. Co.I
Tanner, James P. GA 52nd Inf. Co.I
Tanner, James R. GA Cherokee Legion (St.Guards) Co.D
Tanner, James T. MS 15th Inf. Co.I
Tanner, James W. AL Cav. Forrest's Regt.
Tanner, J.B. GA 1st (Ramsey's) Inf. Co.F
Tanner, J.B. MS Lt.Arty. (Warren Lt.Arty.) Swett's Co.
Tanner, J.B. SC 25th Inf. Co.K
Tanner, J.C. AR 2nd Mtd.Rifles Co.A
Tanner, J.C. MS Lt.Arty. (Warren Lt.Arty.) Swett's Co.
Tanner, J.E. TX 5th Cav. Co.A
Tanner, J.E. TX 21st Inf. Co.E
Tanner, Jesse TN 42nd Inf. 2nd Co.K
Tanner, Jesse VA 30th Bn.S.S. Co.F
Tanner, J.G. TN 11th (Holman's) Cav. Co.B
Tanner, J.G. TN Holman's Bn.Part.Rangers Co.A
Tanner, J.H. GA 5th Cav. Co.F
Tanner, J.H. GA 16th Inf. Co.F
Tanner, J.H. VA Inf. 6th Bn.Loc.Def. Co.A QMSgt.
Tanner, J.J. GA Lt.Arty. 14th Bn. Co.D,F
Tanner, J.J. GA Lt.Arty. King's Btty.
Tanner, J.L. SC Inf. 6th Bn. Co.A
Tanner, J.L. SC 26th Inf. Co.C
Tanner, J.L. SC Manigault's Bn.Vol. Co.D
Tanner, J.L. TN 16th Inf. Co.E
Tanner, J.M. AR Inf. Cocke's Regt. Co.D
Tanner, J.M. GA 18th Inf. Co.A
Tanner, John FL 11th Inf. Co.F Capt.
Tanner, John, Jr. FL 11th Inf. Co.F
Tanner, John GA Cav. 2nd Bn. Co.B
Tanner, John GA Cav. 9th Bn. (St.Guards) Co.E
Tanner, John GA 50th Inf. Co.C
Tanner, John GA Inf. (Mell Scouts) Wyly's Co.
Tanner, John KY 2nd Cav. Co.C
Tanner, John KY 2nd Bn.Mtd.Rifles Co.C
Tanner, John SC 1st Arty. Co.H
Tanner, John SC 10th Inf. Co.I
Tanner, John TX 6th Inf. Co.H
Tanner, John VA 17th Cav. Co.I
Tanner, John A. AR Mil. Desha Cty.Bn.
Tanner, John A. MO 1st N.E. Cav. Co.C
Tanner, John A. MO 4th Cav. Co.G
Tanner, John A. VA 5th Cav.Arty. & Inf.St.Line Co.I
Tanner, John D. VA 28th Inf. Co.F Cpl.
Tanner, John E. TN 42nd Inf. Co.G
Tanner, John E. VA 2nd Inf.Loc.Def. Co.D 2nd Lt.
Tanner, John E. VA Inf. 6th Bn.Loc.Def. Co.A 1st Sgt.
Tanner, John E. VA 56th Inf. Co.B Cpl.
Tanner, John L. GA 29th Inf. Co.D
Tanner, John M. FL 9th Inf. Co.G
Tanner, John M. VA 21st Inf. Co.A
Tanner, John N. MS 11th (Perrin's) Cav. Co.I
Tanner, John N. VA Hvy.Arty. 20th Bn. Co.A
Tanner, John O. AL 12th Inf. Co.I
Tanner, John Q. GA 18th Inf. Co.A
Tanner, John R. GA 43rd Inf. Co.K
Tanner, John R. TX 9th (Nichols') Inf. Co.D
Tanner, John S. GA 6th Cav. Co.A
Tanner, John T. GA 2nd Cav. Co.D
Tanner, John W. FL 1st Cav. Co.K Black.
Tanner, John W. FL 4th Inf. Co.H Music.
Tanner, John W. FL 11th Inf. Co.K
Tanner, John W. VA 7th Inf. Co.E
Tanner, Jno. Y. GA 2nd Inf. Co.D
Tanner, Joseph AL 10th Inf. Co.E Cpl.
Tanner, Joseph TX Inf. 1st St.Troops Wheat's Co.
Tanner, Joseph TX 9th (Nichols') Inf. Co.D
Tanner, Joseph B. GA Arty. 9th Bn. Co.A,E
Tanner, Joseph H. GA 27th Inf. Co.D
Tanner, Joseph J.M. GA 10th Cav. (St.Guards) Co.A
Tanner, Joseph J.M. GA 30th Inf. Co.E
Tanner, Joseph N. LA 28th (Gray's) Inf. Co.I
Tanner, Joseph T. TX 1st (McCulloch's) Cav. Co.E
Tanner, Joshua FL 1st Cav. Co.B
Tanner, Joshua VA 19th Cav. Co.B
Tanner, Joshua VA 3rd Cav. & Inf.St.Line Co.A
Tanner, Josiah G. GA 22nd Inf. Co.K
Tanner, J.R. GA Cherokee Legion (St.Guards) Co.K
Tanner, J.R. TN 35th Inf. 2nd Co.A
Tanner, J.R. TX 25th Cav. Co.G
Tanner, J.S. MO 2nd Inf. Co.C 1st Lt.
Tanner, J.S. VA 1st Cav. Co.F 2nd Lt.
Tanner, J.T. SC Manigault's Bn.Vol. Co.D
Tanner, J.W. MS 3rd Cav. Co.D
Tanner, J.W. MS 12th Cav. Co.D
Tanner, J.W. TN 18th (Newsom's) Cav. Co.E
Tanner, L. AL 47th Inf.
Tanner, L. LA Siege Train Bn. Co.E Bugler
Tanner, L. LA Mil. 3rd Regt. 2nd Brig. 1st Div. Co.H
Tanner, L. MS 5th Inf. Co.B
Tanner, L. MS 15th (Cons.) Inf. Co.G
Tanner, L. SC 10th Inf. Co.I
Tanner, L. TN 7th (Duckworth's) Cav. Co.L
Tanner, L. TX 11th (Spaight's) Bn.Vol. Co.G
Tanner, Lawson VA 30th Bn.S.S. Co.F
Tanner, Lawson VA 60th Inf. Co.G
Tanner, Lee GA 18th Inf. Co.A 1st Lt.
Tanner, Lee NC Unassign.Conscr.
Tanner, Lemuel W. NC 2nd Cav. (19th St.Troops) Co.H
Tanner, Levi AR 19th (Dockery's) Inf. Co.F Ord.Sgt.
Tanner, L.H. AL 3rd Inf. Co.L
Tanner, Linn LA Lt.Arty. 2nd Field Btty. Bugler
Tanner, Lorenzo D. VA 3rd Cav. & Inf.St.Line Co.A
Tanner, Madison AL Mobile City Troop
Tanner, Madison MS Cav. 3rd Bn.Res. Co.E
Tanner, Marlow B. TN 10th Inf. Co.D
Tanner, Mart A. AR Cav. Poe's Bn. Co.A
Tanner, Mathew GA 59th Inf. Co.D
Tanner, Matthew FL 8th Inf. Co.G
Tanner, Matthew NC 20th Inf. Co.I
Tanner, Mayo T. TX 3rd Cav. Co.G Cpl.
Tanner, M.D. GA 1st Cav. Co.H
Tanner, Melvill W. VA 2nd Arty. Co.D
Tanner, Melville W. VA Inf. 22nd Bn. Co.D Cpl.
Tanner, Merrell AL Res. J.G. Rankin's Co.
Tanner, Micajah AL Cav. Falkner's Co.
Tanner, Miles GA 2nd Inf. Co.H
Tanner, Mitchel GA 59th Inf. Co.D
Tanner, Mitchell GA 28th Inf. Co.H
Tanner, Mitchell GA 50th Inf. Co.C
Tanner, M.L. MS Mil. 4th Cav. Co.E Jr.2nd Lt.
Tanner, Morgan J. FL 1st (Res.) Inf. Co.F Sgt.
Tanner, Moses NC 47th Inf. Co.F
Tanner, M.T. TX 32nd Cav. Co.E 1st Sgt.
Tanner, M.W. VA 3rd Cav. 2nd Co.I
Tanner, N. GA 2nd Cav. Co.D
Tanner, N. GA 48th Inf.
Tanner, Nathan FL 7th Inf. Co.B
Tanner, Nathan VA 46th Inf. 2nd Co.B
Tanner, Nathan I. TX 11th (Spaight's) Bn.Vol. Co.C
Tanner, Nathaniel M. VA 5th Cav. (12 mo. '61-2) Co.D
Tanner, N.B. MO 16th Inf. Co.F
Tanner, N.J. TX 21st Inf. Co.E
Tanner, N.M. Grime's Div. Maj.,QM
Tanner, N.O. NC Allen's Co. (Loc.Def.)
Tanner, Noah TN 8th (Smith's) Cav. Co.A
Tanner, N.S. VA 3rd Inf.Loc.Def. Co.B
Tanner, O.B. GA 1st Bn.S.S. Co.A
Tanner, P. VA 3rd Res. Co.G
Tanner, P.D. MS 7th Cav. Co.F Cpl.
Tanner, Peter G. GA 9th Inf. Co.C
Tanner, Philip H. VA 21st Inf. Co.A
Tanner, Pleasant T. TX 11th (Spaight's) Bn.Vol. Co.C
Tanner, P.R. AL 35th Inf. Co.G 2nd Lt.
Tanner, Price VA 13th Inf. Co.K
Tanner, P.T. TX 21st Inf. Co.E
Tanner, R. TN 11th (Holman's) Cav. Co.C
Tanner, R.A. GA 52nd Inf. Co.H
Tanner, Ransum MO 10th Cav. Co.B
Tanner, R.C. TX 9th (Young's) Inf. Co.A
Tanner, Reuben VA 28th Inf. Co.F
Tanner, Reuben T. VA 28th Inf. Co.F
Tanner, R.F. TN Inf. 154th Sr.Regt. Co.I
Tanner, Richard AL City Troop (Mobile) Arrington's Co.A
Tanner, Richard GA 59th Inf. Co.D
Tanner, Richard, Jr. GA 59th Inf. Co.D
Tanner, Richard TN 18th (Newsom's) Cav. Co.F
Tanner, Richard 15th Conf.Cav. Co.H
Tanner, Richard M. TN 32nd Inf. Co.D
Tanner, Richard M. TX 11th (Spaight's) Bn.Vol. Co.C
Tanner, Riley VA 17th Cav. Co.G
Tanner, R.L. LA 8th Cav. Co.K 2nd Lt.
Tanner, R.L. LA 19th Inf. Co.B
Tanner, Robert AL 3rd Res. Co.A
Tanner, Robert LA Lt.Arty. 2nd Field Btty. Sgt.
Tanner, Robert TN 24th Inf. Co.A
Tanner, Robert VA 1st Bn.Res. Co.H
Tanner, Robert A. SC 1st Arty. Co.H
Tanner, Robert E. AL Gid Nelson Lt.Arty.
Tanner, Robert H. TN Cav. 9th Bn. (Gantt's) Co.D
Tanner, Robert H.J. FL 4th Inf. Co.H
Tanner, Robert K. VA 7th Inf. Co.E
Tanner, Robert L., Jr. LA Cav. 2nd Bn. (St.Guards) Ord.Sgt.
Tanner, Robert L. LA 9th Inf. Co.C

Tanner, Robert W. MO Cav. Poindexter's Regt. Co.I
Tanner, R.T. VA 21st Cav. 2nd Co.C Cpl.
Tanner, Rufus AL Lt.Arty. Phelan's Co.
Tanner, R.W. MO St.Guard
Tanner, R.W. TN Inf. 154th Sr.Regt. Co.I
Tanner, S. LA 2nd Cav. Co.G
Tanner, Samuel AR 1st Mtd.Rifles Co.I
Tanner, Samuel AR 7th Inf. Co.H
Tanner, Samuel TN 26th Inf. 1st Co.H
Tanner, Samuel VA 17th Cav. Co.G
Tanner, Samuel B. VA Lt.Arty. Montgomery's Co.
Tanner, Samuel H. VA 21st Inf. Co.G
Tanner, Samuel T. TX Cav. McCord's Frontier Regt. 2nd Co.A
Tanner, Sebran J. GA 41st Inf. Co.C
Tanner, Sequoyah 1st Cherokee Mtd.Rifles Co.D
Tanner, Solomon GA 28th Inf. Co.B
Tanner, Solomon TX 3rd Inf. Co.I
Tanner, S.T. GA 42nd Inf. Co.D
Tanner, Stanly LA Lt.Arty. 2nd Field Btty. Sgt.
Tanner, Steven J. TX 9th (Young's) Inf. Co.A 2nd Lt.
Tanner, T. MS 37th Inf. Co.G
Tanner, Theodric T. MS 1st Lt.Arty. Co.C
Tanner, Theopholis MS Cav. 17th Bn. Co.E,A
Tanner, Thofalus MS 9th Cav. Co.A
Tanner, Thomas AL Lt.Arty. Phelan's Co.
Tanner, Thomas AR 47th (Crandall's) Cav. Co.A
Tanner, Thomas GA 25th Inf. Co.H Music.
Tanner, Thomas MS Cav. 17th Bn. Co.A
Tanner, Thomas NC 9th Bn.S.S. Co.A
Tanner, Thomas TX 1st Inf. Co.A
Tanner, Thomas TX Inf. 1st St.Troops Wheat's Co.A
Tanner, Thomas VA 19th Cav. Co.A
Tanner, Thomas VA 3rd Cav. & Inf.St.Line Co.A
Tanner, Thomas A. TN 4th (McLemore's) Cav. Co.F
Tanner, Thomas A. TN 20th Inf. Co.H
Tanner, Thomas L. GA 12th Cav. Co.F
Tanner, Thomas M. LA 12th Inf. 1st Co.M, Co.C
Tanner, Thomas R. FL 9th Inf. Co.G
Tanner, Thomas W. SC 4th Cav. Co.F
Tanner, T.J. AL 4th (Russell's) Cav. Co.K
Tanner, T.J. TN 3rd (Forrest's) Cav. 1st Co.F
Tanner, T.L. TX Cav. Ragsdale's Bn. Co.A Cpl.
Tanner, T.M. SC Arty. 18th Regt. Co.H
Tanner, T.R. SC 15th Inf. Co.G
Tanner, T.W. SC Cav. 12th Bn. Co.D
Tanner, Vincent FL 7th Inf. Co.B
Tanner, Vinson FL 1st (Res.) Inf. Co.F
Tanner, W. GA 1st Bn.S.S. Co.A
Tanner, W. GA 24th Inf. Co.H
Tanner, W. GA 28th Inf. Co.A
Tanner, W. LA Mil. Terrebonne Regt.
Tanner, W. 1st Chickasaw Inf. McConnell's Co.
Tanner, W.A. GA 39th Inf. Co.F Sgt.
Tanner, W.B. MS Cav. 24th Bn. Co.D
Tanner, W.F. GA 16th Inf. Co.F
Tanner, W.H. VA Hvy.Arty. Coleman's Co.
Tanner, William FL 3rd Inf. Co.E
Tanner, William GA Lt.Arty. 14th Bn. Co.D,F
Tanner, William GA Lt.Arty. King's Btty.
Tanner, William GA 5th Inf. Co.K
Tanner, William GA 5th Res. Co.A
Tanner, William GA 63rd Inf. Co.I
Tanner, William MS 36th Inf. Co.F
Tanner, William NC Lt.Arty. 3rd Bn. Co.C
Tanner, William NC Moseley's Co. (Sampson Arty.)
Tanner, William TN Inf. 22nd Bn. Co.B
Tanner, William VA 21st Inf. Co.A
Tanner, William VA 7th Bn.Res. Co.D
Tanner, William VA 60th Inf. Co.G
Tanner, William A. GA 56th Inf. Co.A Sgt.
Tanner, William A. GA Cobb's Legion Co.A Bugler
Tanner, William A. TN 12th (Green's) Cav. Co.I
Tanner, William A. TN 16th (Logwood's) Cav. Co.I
Tanner, William A. TX Cav. Baylor's Regt. Co.G
Tanner, William A. VA Hvy.Arty. 20th Bn. Co.A
Tanner, William A. VA Courtney Arty. Capt.
Tanner, William B. MS Arty. (Seven Stars Arty.) Roberts' Co.
Tanner, William E. VA Lt.Arty. Brander's Co. 2nd Lt.
Tanner, William E. VA Inf. 6th Bn.Loc.Def. Co.A Maj.
Tanner, William F. GA 39th Inf. Co.E
Tanner, William F. GA 55th Inf. Co.D
Tanner, William H. GA 57th Inf. Co.G
Tanner, William H. GA Inf. (Jasper & Butts Cty.Guards) Lane's Co. Sgt.
Tanner, William H. LA 28th (Gray's) Inf. Co.I
Tanner, William J. GA Arty. 9th Bn. Co.A,E
Tanner, William J. NC 2nd Arty. (36th St.Troops) Co.F
Tanner, William James NC 13th Inf. Co.G
Tanner, William M. GA 26th Inf. Co.F
Tanner, William M. VA 28th Inf. Co.F
Tanner, William N. SC 10th Inf. Co.I
Tanner, William R. SC 13th Inf. Co.C
Tanner, William T. GA 30th Inf.
Tanner, William V. GA Lt.Arty. 12th Bn. 3rd Co.E
Tanner, William W. MO 10th Inf. Co.F 1st Lt.
Tanner, Willis R. VA 28th Inf. Co.F
Tanner, W.J. AL 51st (Part.Rangers) Co.F
Tanner, W.J. GA 1st (Ramsey's) Inf. Co.F
Tanner, W.J. GA 18th Inf. Co.A
Tanner, W.L. NC 24th Inf. Co.C
Tanner, W.N. MS Inf. 1st Bn.St.Troops (30 days '64) Co.H Recruit
Tanner, W.N. MS 5th Inf. (St.Troops) Co.G
Tanner, W.T. SC Lt.Arty. 3rd (Palmetto) Bn. Co.A
Tanner, W.W. MS Cav. 3rd (St.Troops) Co.K
Tanner, W.W. MS Cav. 17th Bn. Co.A
Tanner, W.W. TX 12th Inf. Co.K
Tanner Clow yer Kee 1st Cherokee Mtd.Rifles Co.D
Tannery, A.W. SC 7th Cav. Co.G
Tannery, John A. SC 1st (Orr's) Rifles Co.F
Tannery, S.P. SC 7th Cav. Co.G
Tannery, S.P. SC 1st (Orr's) Rifles Co.F 2nd Lt.
Tannery, W.R. GA 23rd Inf. Co.C
Tanneur, V.H. LA Mil. Orleans Guards Regt. Co.H
Tanney, H. TX 25th Cav. Co.H
Tanney, W. TX 25th Cav. Co.H
Tanneyhill, Frank R. TX 16th Inf. Co.G
Tannihill, C.J. MO 1st & 3rd Cons.Cav.
Tannihill, D.M. LA 3rd Inf. Co.C
Tannihill, Jesse J. TX 13th Vol. 2nd Co.C
Tanning, M. MS 19th Inf. Co.C
Tannis, John H. AL Lt.Arty. 2nd Bn. Co.E
Tannoner, S. LA 13th & 20th Inf. Co.F Lt.
Tannor, Saml. VA 21st Inf. Co.G
Tanns, John SC Lt.Arty. 3rd (Palmetto) Bn. Co.D
Tanns, W. AL 17th Inf. Co.H
Tanny, J.R. TN 35th Inf. Co.A
Tanny, W. LA Mil. 3rd Regt. 1st Brig. 1st Div. Co.D
Tannyhill, Joseph H. VA 5th Inf. Co.L
Tanquary, A.H. VA 12th Cav. Co.C
Tanquary, Alfred B. VA 5th Inf. Co.B
Tanquary, Alfred B. VA 27th Inf. 2nd Co.H
Tanquary, John M. TX 8th Cav. Co.G 1st Sgt.
Tanquary, J.W. VA 122nd Mil. Co.A,B Cpl.
Tansell, W.H. GA 16th Inf. Co.I
Tansell, W.N. VA Cav. Mosby's Regt. (Part.Rangers) Co.H
Tansey, James GA Inf. 1st Bn. (St.Guards) Co.A
Tansey, Job TX 36th Cav. Co.A
Tansey, John AL 21st Inf. Co.B
Tansey, John LA 3rd (Wingfield's) Cav. Co.I
Tansey, L.J. LA 4th Inf. Co.D
Tansey, Timothy TN 10th Inf. Co.H
Tansey, W.A. AR Inf. Cocke's Regt. Co.I
Tansey, William AR Inf. Cocke's Regt. Co.I
Tansey, William TN 15th Inf. Co.C
Tansie, F.M. TN 9th Inf. Co.G
Tansil, Egbert E. TN 31st Inf. Co.A Col.
Tansil, John B. TN 13th Inf. Co.K
Tansil, Samuel T. Conf.Cav. Wood's Regt. 2nd Co.G
Tansill, Barney VA 49th Inf. Co.B
Tansill, George S. VA 7th Inf. Co.A,H Sgt.Maj.
Tansill, James G. VA 7th Inf. Co.H,E Capt.
Tansill, John VA 2nd Inf. Co.C
Tansill, John W. VA 4th Cav. Co.A
Tansill, Robert Gen. & Staff Col.,Insp.Gen.
Tansill, Thomas W. VA 49th Inf. Co.A Sgt.
Tansill, T.W. Gen. & Staff Capt.,Comsy.
Tansill, Wallace VA 15th Cav. Co.H
Tansill, William VA 2nd Inf. Co.C
Tanson, S. AL 46th Inf. Co.B
Tansua, Joseph VA Cav. Young's Co.
Tansy, J.R. AL 3rd Inf. Co.A
Tansy, Patrick LA 10th Inf. Co.A
Tant, Cord AR 5th Inf. Co.G
Tant, Cordy NC 35th Inf. Co.B
Tant, Cordy NC 47th Inf. Co.B
Tant, Davis NC 47th Inf. Co.B
Tant, D.K. GA 10th Inf. Co.B
Tant, Edwin S. GA 48th Inf. Co.C
Tant, Frederick TN 30th Inf. Co.D
Tant, H.H. SC 3rd Cav. Co.B
Tant, H.J. SC 5th Cav. Co.I
Tant, H.L. AR 15th (Josey's) Inf. Co.H
Tant, Isaac S. GA 48th Inf. Co.C
Tant, Jackson MO 8th Cav. Co.D

Tant, James E. GA 48th Inf. Co.C Cpl.
Tant, James W. NC 37th Inf. Co.I
Tant, J.C. SC 5th Cav. Co.I
Tant, J.H. GA 40th Inf. Co.A
Tant, J.J. AL 51st (Part.Rangers) Co.C Sgt.
Tant, J.M. NC 31st Inf. Co.H
Tant, John GA 40th Inf. Co.A
Tant, John NC 3rd Arty. (40th St.Troops) Co.I
Tant, John NC 47th Inf. Co.B
Tant, John B. TN 30th Inf. Co.D
Tant, John G. GA Lt.Arty. 12th Bn. Co.F
Tant, John G. GA Lt.Arty. Milledge's Co.
Tant, John G. GA 3rd Inf. 1st Co.I
Tant, John T. GA Hvy.Arty. 22nd Bn. Co.C
Tant, Joseph GA 40th Inf. Co.A
Tant, Lee W. NC 47th Inf. Co.B
Tant, L.O. SC 11th Inf. Bellinger's 2nd Co.I
Tant, N.J.N. SC 1st (Hagood's) Inf. 1st Co.K
Tant, P.G. TN 30th Inf. Co.D 1st Sgt.
Tant, S.G. SC 11th Inf. 1st Co.I, 2nd Co.I
Tant, Thomas NC 47th Inf. Co.B
Tant, Thomas C. GA Inf. 1st Loc.Troops (Augusta) Co.H
Tant, Thomas J. GA Lt.Arty. Milledge's Co.
Tant, Thomas J. GA 3rd Inf. 1st Co.I
Tant, William H. AL 62nd Inf. Co.G
Tant, William R. GA Inf. 1st Loc.Troops (Augusta) Dearing's Cav.Co.
Tant, W.T. TN 30th Inf. Co.D
Tantarsly, J.M. MS 3rd Cav. Co.I
Tantaum, W. AL 1st Inf. Co.H
Tantbald, John VA Lt.Arty. Garber's Co.
Tante 1st Creek Mtd.Vol. Co.A
Tanting, N. GA 5th Inf. Co.K
Tantno, William LA 1st Inf. 3rd Co.D
Tanton, Andrew J. AL 47th Inf. Co.C Cpl.
Tanton, Asa GA 2nd St.Line Co.A
Tanton, C.B. AL 45th Inf. Co.G
Tanton, Charles AL 60th Inf. Co.A
Tanton, Charles AL 3rd Bn. Hilliard's Legion Vol. Co.B
Tanton, Edmund GA 59th Inf. Co.B
Tanton, Franklin, Dr. AL 47th Inf. Co.C Cpl.
Tanton, G. TX 21st Inf. Co.H
Tanton, Gibson TX 11th (Spaight's) Bn.Vol. Co.D
Tanton, H. GA 2nd Inf. Co.H
Tanton, H.J.D. AL 47th Inf. Co.C
Tanton, Irvin TX 14th Inf. Co.F
Tanton, J.W. AR 24th Inf. Co.K
Tanton, Marion AL 22nd Inf. Co.A
Tanton, M.C. AL 45th Inf. Co.G
Tanton, Morgan C. AL 34th Inf. Breedlove's Co.
Tanton, Nathan TX 10th Cav. Co.C
Tanton, Tillman AL 59th Inf. Co.E
Tantum, H.D. AL 45th Inf. Co.G
Tantze, A. TX Inf. Timmons' Regt. Co.K
Tanubbee 1st Choctaw & Chickasaw Mtd.Rifles 3rd Co.D
Tanubbee, Jackson 1st Choctaw & Chickasaw Mtd.Rifles 3rd Co.D
Tan u hah be 1st Choctaw Mtd.Rifles Co.K
Tan up no ubbee 1st Choctaw & Chickasaw Mtd.Rifles 2nd Co.C
Tanvarter, Basha AL 5th Cav. Co.H
Tany, W.W. VA 4th Res. Co.D
Tanyes, J. KY Lt.Arty. Green's Btty.
Tanzas, Frank LA 8th Inf. Co.D
Tanzie, N.P. AL 10th Inf. Co.K
Tap, C. MS 8th Cav. Co.C
Tapan, Anderson TN 12th (Green's) Cav. Co.G
Tapauller, William GA 12th Cav. Co.A
Tape, Benjamin AR Brown's Regt.
Tape, G.W. AL St.Res. Co.A
Tapel, J. MO 3rd Cav. Co.E Cpl.
Taper, S. AL 40th Inf. Co.K
Taphano, C. 1st Chickasaw Inf. McCord's Co.
Tapia, Antonia TX Cav. Benavides' Regt. Co.I
Tapie, Pierre LA 10th Inf. Co.F
Tapin, J. TX 25th Cav. Co.H
Tapio, --- TX 8th Inf. Co.G
Tapis, B. LA Mil. 4th Regt. French Brig. Co.5
Tapis, Bernard LA C.S. Zouave Bn. Co.B
Tapisan, B. AL 26th (O'Neal's) Inf. Co.I
Taplar, R.O. AL Res. Cook's Co.
Tapley, --- GA 32nd Inf. Co.E Sgt.
Tapley, C.P. MS 39th Inf. Co.I Cpl.
Tapley, Eli AL First & Second Class Mil. Fayette Co.
Tapley, Francis M. GA 48th Inf. Co.F Cpl.
Tapley, Franklin GA 14th Inf. Co.F
Tapley, George W. MS 31st Inf. Co.K
Tapley, G.L. MS 43rd Inf. Co.F
Tapley, Goldman AL 47th Inf. Co.F
Tapley, H.C. MS 39th Inf. Co.I
Tapley, James M. GA 48th Inf. Co.F
Tapley, J.J. MS Lt.Arty. 14th Bn. Co.C
Tapley, J.L. GA 44th Inf. Co.A
Tapley, J.O. MS 39th Inf. Co.I
Tapley, John AL 3rd Cav. Co.E
Tapley, John GA 4th (Clinch's) Cav. Co.F
Tapley, John GA 14th Inf. Co.F Cpl.
Tapley, John KY 10th (Johnson's) Cav. Co.K
Tapley, John MS 1st (King's) Inf. (St.Troops) Co.G Sgt.
Tapley, John TN 35th Inf. 1st Co.I
Tapley, John Conf.Cav. Wood's Regt. 1st Co.D
Tapley, John C. GA 14th Inf. Co.F Cpl.
Tapley, John C. GA 32nd Inf. Co.G
Tapley, John C. GA 48th Inf. Co.F
Tapley, M.L. GA Inf. (Emanuel Troops) Moring's Co. Cpl.
Tapley, Oliver MS 31st Inf. Co.C
Tapley, S.B. MS Cav. Abbott's Co.
Tapley, Southey GA 21st Inf. Co.F Cpl.
Tapley, Thomas L. MS 8th Cav. Co.E
Tapley, Thomas L. MS 1st (Patton's) Inf. Co.C
Tapley, W.C. MS 5th Cav. Co.B
Tapley, W.E. MS 3rd Inf. (St.Troops) Co.H
Tapp, Alexander GA 36th (Broyles') Inf. Co.A
Tapp, B.F. KY 8th Mtd.Inf. Co.A
Tapp, B.F. TN Cav. 16th Bn. (Neal's) Co.A Far.
Tapp, C.J. KY 8th Mtd.Inf. Co.A Lt.
Tapp, C.S. GA 60th Inf. Co.I
Tapp, Curtis MS 2nd Inf. Co.I
Tapp, C.W. GA Cav. 6th Bn. (St.Guards) Co.A
Tapp, E. GA 18th Inf. Co.G
Tapp, E.D. AL 2nd Cav.
Tapp, Elijah VA 6th Cav. Co.B
Tapp, Elijah VA 34th Mil. Co.A Cpl.
Tapp, E.S. GA 23rd Inf. Co.E
Tapp, Henry J. VA 17th Inf. Co.K
Tapp, Henry J. VA 18th Inf. Co.B
Tapp, Hugh GA 36th (Broyles') Inf. Co.A
Tapp, J.A. KY 5th Cav. Co.I
Tapp, J.A. VA 2nd Cav. Co.I
Tapp, James GA 43rd Inf. Co.B Ord.Sgt.
Tapp, James B. VA 7th Inf. Co.C
Tapp, James E. KY 5th Mtd.Inf. Co.H
Tapp, James Madison TX 20th Cav. Co.D 1st Sgt.
Tapp, James R. VA 13th Inf. 1st Co.B
Tapp, J.E. NC Allen's Co. (Loc.Def.)
Tapp, Jesse A. KY 10th (Johnson's) Cav. New Co.I Cpl.
Tapp, J.L. GA Cav. Gartrell's Co.
Tapp, John GA 36th (Broyles') Inf. Co.A
Tapp, John C. KY 10th (Johnson's) Cav. Co.C,B
Tapp, John Pinckney SC 7th Res. Co.M
Tapp, Joseph 1st Cherokee Mtd.Vol. 1st Co.C
Tapp, Joseph V. AR 3rd Cav. Co.I
Tapp, J.R. SC Inf. Holcombe Legion Co.I Sgt.
Tapp, J.W. MO 6th Cav. Co.C
Tapp, Lemuel GA 34th Inf. Co.D Cpl.
Tapp, Leonard GA 36th (Broyles') Inf. Co.A
Tapp, Levi MS 32nd Inf. Co.B Cpl.
Tapp, Lewis E. TN 29th Inf. Co.C
Tapp, L.W. MO 12th Cav. Co.B
Tapp, P.F. GA Phillips' Legion Co.M Sgt.
Tapp, P.H. TN Inf. 3rd Bn. Co.A
Tapp, Pinkney MS 23rd Inf. Co.C Bvt.2nd Lt.
Tapp, Robert L. AR 27th Inf. Co.I
Tapp, S.P. MO St.Guard W.H. Taylor's Co.
Tapp, Thadeus TN 60th Mtd.Inf. Co.K
Tapp, Thomas J. GA 23rd Inf. Co.F
Tapp, T.J. GA 28th Inf. Co.D Cpl.
Tapp, T.L. GA Cav. Gartrell's Co.
Tapp, T.L. GA 60th Inf. Co.I
Tapp, V. TN 3rd (Forrest's) Cav. Co.H
Tapp, Vincent TN 60th Mtd.Inf. Co.K
Tapp, Vincent Jackson TX 20th Cav. Co.D
Tapp, V.J. MS 23rd Inf. Co.C
Tapp, V.T. MS Scouts Morphis' Ind. Co.
Tapp, William NC 64th Inf. Co.K
Tapp, William TN 29th Inf. Co.C
Tapp, William B. VA Horse Arty. G.W. Brown's Co.
Tapp, William C. AR 14th (McCarver's) Inf. Co.A 2nd Lt.
Tapp, William L. NC 24th Inf. Co.A Cpl.
Tapp, W.J. Gen. & Staff Adj.,AAQM
Tapp, W.L. AR 17th (Lemoyne's) Inf. Co.A
Tapp, W.L. AR 21st Inf. Co.D
Tappan, A.B. GA 9th Inf. (St.Guards) Co.C
Tappan, Albert AL 12th Inf. Co.E
Tappan, Amos AR Inf. Hardy's Regt. AAG
Tappan, Amos MS 21st Inf. Co.A Cpl.
Tappan, Amos Tappan's Brig. Capt.,AAG
Tappan, Andrew G. AR 1st (Colquitt's) Inf. Co.H
Tappan, B.S. LA 2nd Cav. Co.H Capt.
Tappan, B.S. LA Mil. 1st Regt. 3rd Brig. 1st Div. Lt.Col.
Tappan, Charles FL Inf. 2nd Bn. Co.A
Tappan, Charles FL 10th Inf. Co.I 1st Sgt.
Tappan, I.A. TN 6th Inf. Co.D
Tappan, James C. Gen. & Staff Brig.Gen.
Tappan, J.C. AR 13th Inf. Col.
Tappan, John C. Tappan's Brig. Brig.Gen.
Tappan, Price MS 21st Inf. Co.A 2nd Lt.

Tappan, S.W. TN 6th Inf. Co.D Sgt.
Tappan, William W. MO 1st Cav. Co.D
Tappe, Charles VA 56th Inf. Co.H
Tappe, W.D. Gen. & Staff Capt.,QM
Tappenbeck, Fred TX 1st Hvy.Arty. Co.C
Tapper, Ed. GA Inf. (Loc.Def.) Whiteside's Nav.Bn. Co.A
Tapper, J. MS 22nd Inf. Co.G
Tapper, James GA 47th Inf. Co.E
Tapper, Joseph MS 33rd Inf. Co.I
Tapper, William MS 33rd Inf. Co.I
Tapperman, William LA C.S. Zouave Bn. Co.B
Tappey, F.J. Gen. & Staff 2nd Lt.,Dr.M.
Tappey, William H. VA 5th Cav. (12 mo. '61-2) Co.D
Tappey, William H. VA Hood's Bn.Res. Tappey's Co. Capt.
Tappin, Joseph 1st Cherokee Mtd.Vol. 2nd Co.E
Tapping, T.H. Hosp.Stew.
Tappley, J.J. MS Lt.Arty. Merrin's Btty.
Tapps, A.J. SC 3rd Inf. Co.A
Tapps, David E. TN 48th (Nixon's) Inf. Co.H Cpl.
Tappscott, A.B. TN 15th (Cons.) Cav. Surg.
Tappscott, J.M. NC 1st Cav. (9th St.Troops) Co.H
Tappscott, T.J. NC 1st Cav. (9th St.Troops) Co.H
Tappy, John VA 3rd (Chrisman's) Bn.Res. Co.C
Tappy, John VA 8th Bn.Res. Co.C
Tappy, Simon VA 2nd Inf. Co.B
Tappy, Simon VA 97th Mil. Co.B
Tappy, William H. VA 9th Inf. 2nd Co.A
Tapscot, A. AL 5th Cav. Co.D
Tapscott, Adair Byron Gen. & Staff Contr.Surg.
Tapscott, Add M. TN 15th (Stewart's) Cav. Surg.
Tapscott, Aulbin D. VA 9th Cav. Co.D 2nd Lt.
Tapscott, B. TN 15th Cons.Cav. Surg.
Tapscott, Benjamin VA Hvy.Arty. 19th Bn. Co.B
Tapscott, Benjamin G. VA Inf. 25th Bn. Co.C
Tapscott, Charles F. VA 55th Inf. Co.F
Tapscott, George N. VA 56th Inf. Co.D
Tapscott, G.W. TN 40th Inf. Co.E
Tapscott, Henry LA 1st (Strawbridge's) Inf. Co.F
Tapscott, Henry C. VA 9th Cav. Co.D
Tapscott, H.K. TN 40th Inf. Co.E
Tapscott, J.A. KY 2nd (Duke's) Cav. Co.C
Tapscott, J.E. MO 12th Cav. Co.I
Tapscott, J.F. VA 46th Inf. 2nd Co.E Jr.2nd Lt.
Tapscott, J.N. VA 4th Cav. Co.K
Tapscott, J.N. VA 20th Inf. Co.E
Tapscott, John B. Eng.,CSA 1st Lt.
Tapscott, John Marion NC 13th Inf. Co.E
Tapscott, Joseph VA 40th Inf. Co.H
Tapscott, Joseph B. VA 2nd Inf. Co.I
Tapscott, J.R. TX Cav. Waller's Regt. Co.C
Tapscott, L.L. MS 2nd (Davidson's) Inf. Co.G
Tapscott, Lycurgus L. MS 2nd Inf. Co.A,I
Tapscott, Napoleon B. VA 1st St.Res. Co.E
Tapscott, Pinckney TN 40th Inf. Co.E
Tapscott, R.C. TX 20th Inf. Co.B
Tapscott, R.L. AL 5th Cav. Co.D
Tapscott, Robert H. AL 4th (Russell's) Cav. Co.D
Tapscott, Samuel B. VA 2nd Inf. Co.B
Tapscott, Thomas MO 16th Inf. Co.D
Tapscott, Vincent A. VA 56th Inf. Co.D 2nd Lt.
Tapscott, W. VA Cav. 37th Bn. Co.I
Tapscott, W. VA 46th Inf. Co.E
Tapscott, W.A. TN 40th Inf. Co.E
Tapscott, William VA 10th Cav. Co.D
Tapscott, William A. AL 54th Inf. Co.I
Tapscott, William C. VA 9th Cav. Co.D
Tapscott, William C. Rives VA 19th Inf. Co.C
Tapsley, B. AL 1st Regt.Conscr. Co.C
Taptscott, W.C.R. VA Cav. 37th Bn. Co.C Capt.
Tapy, John LA 18th Inf. Co.B
Tapy, John VA 12th Cav. Co.K
Taquino, A. LA 27th Inf. Co.A
Taquino, A.A. AL 60th Inf. Co.D
Taquino, A.A. GA Inf. 1st Bn. (St.Guards) Co.B 3rd Lt.
Taquino, F. LA 22nd (Cons.) Inf. Co.H
Taquino, Frank LA 3rd Inf. Co.K
Taquino, T. LA Mil. 1st Chasseurs a pied Co.3 3rd Lt.
Taquino, Thomas LA Pointe Coupee Arty.
Tar, P. SC 22nd Inf. Co.I
Tarance, F.M. GA 40th Inf. Co.K
Tarance, J.M. GA 40th Inf. Co.K
Tarance, Luther NC 2nd Jr.Res. Co.D
Tarango, Julio TX Cav. Benavides' Regt. Co.C
Tarant, J.K. AL 29th Inf. Co.F
Taranto, Carmelo LA Mil. 6th Regt.Eur.Brig. (Italian Guards Bn.) Co.4 Cpl.
Taranto, Felice LA Mil. 6th Regt.Eur.Brig. (Italian Guards Bn.) Co.2
Taranto, Gaetano LA Mil. 6th Regt.Eur.Brig. (Italian Guards Bn.) Co.2
Tarau, J. LA Mil. 4th Regt. French Brig. Co.3
Tarbell, John F. VA 9th Inf. Co.G Cpl.
Tarber, J.F. KY 7th Mtd.Inf. Co.A
Tarber, John B. MS 29th Inf. Co.G
Tarber, J.W. GA 10th Mil.
Tarber, T.A. AL 60th Inf. Co.K
Tarbet, S.A. AR 4th Inf. Co.E
Tarbett, James MO 6th Cav. Co.F
Tarbett, S.A. AR 1st Mtd.Rifles Co.E
Tarbin 1st Choctaw Mtd.Rifles Ward's Co.
Tarbor, H. LA Inf.Cons.Crescent Regt. Co.A
Tarborough, D.B. NC 6th Sr.Res. Co.A
Tarbox, Augustus MO Inf. 8th Bn. Co.A
Tarbox, Augustus MO 9th Inf. Co.A
Tarbox, John W. SC 10th Inf. Co.A Ord.Sgt.
Tarbox, John W. SC Inf.Bn. Ord.Sgt.
Tarbox, R.W. SC Hvy.Arty. 15th (Lucas') Bn. Co.A
Tarbox, R.W. SC Lt.Arty. (Waccamaw Lt.Arty.) M. Ward's Co.
Tarbox, R.W. SC 1st Bn.S.S. Co.C
Tarburton, M. GA 43rd Inf. Co.C
Tarbutton, Alexander J. MS 16th Inf. Co.E
Tarbutton, Elisha W. TX 14th Cav. Co.B
Tarbutton, G.A. GA 1st (Ramsey's) Inf. Co.E
Tarbutton, George A. AL 60th Inf. Co.H Capt.
Tarbutton, George A. AL 1st Bn. Hilliard's Legion Vol. Co.B 1st Lt.
Tarbutton, G.F.M. GA 42nd Inf. Co.B
Tarbutton, James H. TX 14th Cav. Co.B Cpl.
Tarbutton, James M. AL 13th Inf. Co.G Sgt.
Tarbutton, J.M. AL 1st Bn. Hilliard's Legion Vol. Co.B Capt.
Tarbutton, John C. TX 11th Inf. Co.C 1st Lt.
Tarbutton, J.W. AL 60th Inf. Co.H Capt.
Tar Button, Marion GA Inf. (Newton Factory Employees) Russell's Co.
Tarbutton, R.S. GA Inf. 8th Bn. Co.G
Tarbutton, W.B. TN 6th Inf. Co.L
Tarbutton, William MD Arty. 4th Btty.
Tarbutton, William E. AL 61st Inf. Co.I
Tarbutton, William E. GA 42nd Inf. Co.K
Tarby, Henry F. NC 2nd Arty. (36th St.Troops) Co.H
Tar che che Nick 1st Cherokee Mtd.Rifles Co.G Cpl.
Tar co fun na 1st Creek Mtd.Vol. Co.E
Tarcroft, S.F. NC 4th Inf. Co.K
Tardey, A.H. AL Mobile Fire Bn. Mullany's Co.
Tardos, J. LA Mil. 3rd Regt.Eur.Brig. (Garde Francaise) Co.7
Tardrew, Thomas LA Inf.Crescent Regt. Co.I
Tardy, --- VA VMI Co.B
Tardy, A. AL Mil. 3rd Vol. Co.G Sgt.
Tardy, A.B. MS 5th Inf. (St.Troops) Co.D
Tardy, Alexis J. MS 7th Cav. Co.I Sgt.
Tardy, B.A. MS 27th Inf. Co.C 1st Lt.
Tardy, Benjamin F. VA 2nd Cav. Co.I 2nd Lt.
Tardy, Benjamin F. VA 3rd Res. Co.B Capt.
Tardy, Charles A. VA 3rd Res. Co.B
Tardy, C.P. AL Gid Nelson Lt.Arty.
Tardy, E. LA Mil. Orleans Guards Regt. Co.H
Tardy, Edwin AL 1st Regt. Mobile Vol. Co.E
Tardy, George H. LA 22nd Inf. Co.E,C,G 2nd Lt.
Tardy, George H. LA 22nd (Cons.) Inf. Co.C 2nd Lt.
Tardy, H.C. TN 50th (Cons.) Inf. Co.C
Tardy, Henry Clay TN 50th Inf. Co.C
Tardy, J.A. TX Cav. Baird's Regt. Co.F
Tardy, J.A. TX Cav. Coopwood's Spy Co.
Tardy, J.E.A. TX Cav. Madison's Regt. Co.F
Tardy, John A. TX Cav. Baylor's Regt. Co.B Cpl.
Tardy, John A. TX Cav. Madison's Regt. Co.F
Tardy, John B. LA 8th Inf. Co.A
Tardy, Munley F. LA 14th Inf. Co.D Sgt.
Tardy, Nathan C. VA Hvy.Arty. 20th Bn. Co.D
Tardy, Samuel C. VA 1st St.Res. Co.F 2nd Lt.
Tardy, S.E. LA 22nd Inf. Co.E
Tardy, S.E. LA 22nd (Cons.) Inf. Co.E
Tardy, T.H. MS 11th (Cons.) Cav. Co.E
Tardy, Thomas H. MS 27th Inf. Co.C
Tardy, William H. VA Hvy.Arty. Patteson's Co.
Tardy, William J. VA Rockbridge Cty.Res. Miller's Co.
Tare, Abraham V. VA 5th Inf. Co.C 1st Lt.
Tare, Abraham V. VA 28th Inf. Co.A
Tarean, A.L. SC 21st Inf. Co.A
Tarefield, Thomas TN 13th Inf.
Tareid, V. LA Mil. McPherson's Btty. (Orleans Howitzers)
Tarelle, Joseph GA 22nd Inf. Co.A
Tarent, M.R. SC 1st Mtd.Mil. Evans' Co.
Tarewater, Bisho W. AL 16th Inf. Co.K
Targarona, P. LA Red River S.S. Co.A
Targason, Thomas TX 11th Inf. Co.I Cpl.
Targerson, Gregory TX 11th Inf. Co.I
Target, James A. MO 2nd Inf. Co.C Cpl.
Targinton, J.P. AR 32nd Inf. Co.H

Tarhar 1st Choctaw & Chickasaw Mtd.Rifles 2nd Co.C
Tar hok ni che 1st Creek Mtd.Vol. Co.M
Tarican, R.W. MO Cav. Fristoe's Regt. Co.A
Tarido, F. LA Mil. 1st Regt. French Brig. Co.1
Tarieux, B. LA Mil. 4th Regt. French Brig. Co.6
Tariot, O. LA Inf.Cons. 18th Regt. & Yellow Jacket Bn. Co.E
Taris, H.L. TN 12th Inf. Co.C
Tarish, R.S. NC 2nd Jr.Res. Co.E
Tarkenton, Cornelius NC Lt.Arty. 3rd Bn. Co.B Sgt.
Tarkenton, John NC Lt.Arty. 3rd Bn. Co.B
Tarkenton, John W. NC Lt.Arty. 3rd Bn. Co.B
Tarkenton, Joseph TN 10th (DeMoss') Cav. Co.D
Tarkenton, Joseph L. NC 17th Inf. (2nd Org.) Co.H Cpl.
Tarkenton, Josephus NC Lt.Arty. 3rd Bn. Co.B
Tarkenton, Joseph W. NC 2nd Cav. (19th St.Troops) Co.G
Tarkenton, L. LA 2nd Cav. Co.F
Tarkenton, Lawrence S. NC 17th Inf. (2nd Org.) Co.G
Tarkenton, R.B. NC 17th Inf. (2nd Org.) Co.G
Tarkenton, Samuel NC 17th Inf. (2nd Org.) Co.G
Tarkenton, S.M. TX Inf. 2nd St.Troops Co.H
Tarkenton, William B. NC Lt.Arty. 3rd Bn. Co.B
Tarkenton, W.J. TN Inf. Nashville Bn. Fulcher's Co.
Tarker, F. TN 12th Cav. Co.B
Tarkersly, M.M. MS Cav. Yerger's Regt. Co.E 2nd Lt.
Tarkey, J.H. AL 35th Inf. Co.G
Tarkington, A. AR 8th Cav. Co.A
Tarkington, A.T. AR 10th Inf. Co.E Sgt.
Tarkington, Booker C. TX 3rd Cav. Co.H Sgt.
Tarkington, Edward TX 2nd Cav. Co.D
Tarkington, Felix J. TN 34th Inf. Co.B,K 2nd Lt.
Tarkington, G.D. AR 25th Inf. Co.C
Tarkington, George W. TN 11th Inf. Co.H
Tarkington, G.W. TN 10th & 11th (Cons.) Cav. Co.F
Tarkington, Henry A. NC 17th Inf. (1st Org.) Co.A
Tarkington, Henry A. NC 32nd Inf. Co.B
Tarkington, J. TN Cav. Napier's Bn. Co.A
Tarkington, J. TX 25th Cav. Co.I
Tarkington, J.A. AR 31st Inf. Co.G Sgt.
Tarkington, J.C. TN 47th Inf. Co.D
Tarkington, Jeff O. TN 34th Inf. Co.B Capt.
Tarkington, J.H.C. TN Inf. 2nd Cons.Regt. Co.K
Tarkington, J.H.C. TN 11th Inf. Co.H
Tarkington, J.H.C. 3rd Conf.Eng.Troops
Tarkington, Jo C. AR 1st Mtd.Rifles Co.B
Tarkington, John TX 5th Inf. Co.H
Tarkington, John T. AR 9th Inf. Co.G
Tarkington, J.T. AR 1st Mtd.Rifles Co.I
Tarkington, J.W. AR 47th (Crandall's) Cav. Co.E
Tarkington, J.W. AR 32nd Inf. Co.G 1st Sgt.
Tarkington, Lawrence NC 17th Inf. (1st Org.) Co.H
Tarkington, Thomas B. LA 9th Inf. Co.C
Tarkington, W. LA 2nd Cav. Co.F
Tarkington, William MO 1st & 4th Cons.Inf. Co.F
Tarkington, William E. KY 12th Cav. Co.D
Tarkington, William L. TN 34th Inf. Co.B
Tarkington, William T. AR 9th Inf. Co.G
Tarkington, William W. MO 1st Inf. Co.I Cpl.
Tarkington, Wilson TX 21st Cav. Co.E Cpl.
Tarkinton, Andrew J. LA 16th Inf. Co.I Sgt.
Tarkinton, Benjamin F. NC 12th Inf. Co.L
Tarkinton, Benjamin F. NC 32nd Inf. Co.F,A
Tarkinton, Edward NC 17th Inf. (2nd Org.) Co.G
Tarkinton, Henry Z. NC 12th Inf. Co.L
Tarkinton, Henry Z. NC 32nd Inf. Co.F,A
Tarkinton, Leonidas LA 16th Inf. Co.I
Tarkinton, R.P. MO 5th Cav. Co.G
Tarkinton, Samuel NC 1st Arty. (10th St.Troops) Co.G
Tarkinton, W.B. NC 1st Arty. (10th St.Troops) Co.G
Tarkinton, William B. NC 17th Inf. (2nd Org.) Co.G
Tarkinton, William B. NC 61st Inf. Co.H
Tar ko har 1st Creek Mtd.Vol. Co.E
Tar le chee 1st Creek Mtd.Vol. 2nd Co.I Sgt.
Tarleton, A.G. AL 32nd Inf. Co.G
Tarleton, Clemmon SC 1st (Butler's) Inf. Co.D
Tarleton, E. AR 15th (Johnson's) Inf. Co.E
Tarleton, Eneas TN 40th Inf. Co.F
Tarleton, Frank MS 35th Inf. Co.F
Tarleton, George H. AL Mil. 2nd Regt.Vol. Co.C
Tarleton, G.H. AL St.Arty. Co.C
Tarleton, Henry VA 30th Inf. Co.B
Tarleton, J.A. Gen. & Staff Adj.
Tarleton, James J. LA Mil.Conf.Guards Regt. Co.K,I Capt.
Tarleton, James J. VA 3rd Inf.Loc.Def. Co.D
Tarleton, Jasper W. AR Inf. Cocke's Regt. Co.C
Tarleton, John A. LA Washington Arty.Bn. Co.1
Tarleton, John G. AL Inf. 1st Regt. Co.H
Tarleton, Joseph AL 1st Inf. Co.K
Tarleton, Joseph AL Mil. 4th Vol. Co.E
Tarleton, Leo LA 4th Cav. Co.A
Tarleton, M.A. LA Inf.Crescent Regt. Co.E Capt.
Tarleton, Moses T. AL Inf. 1st Regt. Co.K
Tarleton, P.G. AL 4th Res. Co.F
Tarleton, Robert AL Arty. 1st Bn. Co.E 2nd Lt.
Tarleton, Robert AL 3rd Inf. Co.C,A
Tarleton, Robert MS Lt.Arty. Turner's Co.
Tarleton, William E. GA 7th Inf. Co.E
Tarleton, William W. AL 3rd Inf. Co.B
Tarleton, W.R. LA 1st Hvy.Arty. (Reg.) Co.A
Tarling, James AL 1st Bn. Co.F Cpl.
Tarling, James MS 19th Inf. Co.C
Tarling, James MS 22nd Inf. Gaines' Co.
Tarling, M.C. TX 25th Cav. Co.B
Tarlington, S.C. AL 37th Inf. Co.I
Tar loaf Harjo 1st Creek Mtd.Vol. Co.H
Tar los se 1st Cherokee Mtd.Rifles Co.C
Tarlot, M.C. AR 19th (Dawson's) Inf. Co.G
Tarlton, A. NC Wallace's Co. (Wilmington RR Guard)
Tarlton, Adam J. TX 9th (Young's) Inf. Co.B
Tarlton, A.J. TN 9th Inf. Co.C
Tarlton, Benjamin NC 23rd Inf. Co.A
Tarlton, Charles F. AR 1st (Colquitt's) Inf. Co.K
Tarlton, Clemuel M. NC 26th Inf. Co.B
Tarlton, E. NC 2nd Jr.Res. Co.F
Tarlton, Frederick L. AL 10th Inf. Co.I Cpl.
Tarlton, G.H. AL 1st Regt. Mobile Vol. Baas' Co.
Tarlton, H.A. TX 9th (Young's) Inf. Co.B
Tarlton, Jacob B. TX 9th (Young's) Inf. Co.B
Tarlton, James B. NC 43rd Inf. Co.K
Tarlton, James B. TX 9th (Young's) Inf. Co.B
Tarlton, James M. NC Hvy.Arty. 10th Bn. Co.C
Tarlton, J.B. AR 2nd Inf.
Tarlton, J.B. TN 9th Inf. Co.E
Tarlton, J.B. TN 51st Inf. Co.C
Tarlton, J.B. TN 51st (Cons.) Inf. Co.I
Tarlton, J.J. TN 9th Inf. Co.E
Tarlton, John B. LA Arty. 1st Field Btty. 1st Lt.
Tarlton, John Jefferson TN 12th (Cons.) Inf. Co.H Sgt.
Tarlton, John W. NC 3rd Arty. (40th St.Troops) Co.C
Tarlton, John W. TN 2nd (Smith's) Cav. Thomasin's Co.
Tarlton, Josephus AL Cav. Lewis' Bn. Co.B Cpl.
Tarlton, Marshall SC 1st (Butler's) Inf. Co.D
Tarlton, P. NC 2nd Jr.Res. Co.F
Tarlton, Richard P. NC Hvy.Arty. 10th Bn. Co.C
Tarlton, Robert F. TX 22nd Cav. Co.K Cpl.
Tarlton, Robert P. TX 9th Cav. Co.B 1st Lt.
Tarlton, R.S. LA Washington Arty.Bn. Co.6 Can.
Tarlton, R.S. MS 1st Lt.Arty. Co.H
Tarlton, Samuel LA 2nd Cav. Co.C
Tarlton, T.N. AR 7th Inf. Co.A
Tarlton, W.A. TX 28th Cav. Co.F
Tarlton, William MO 7th Cav. Co.B
Tarlton, William A. NC 2nd Jr.Res. Co.F
Tarlton, William J. AR 15th (Josey's) Inf. Co.F Sgt.
Tarlton, Wilson NC Hvy.Arty. 10th Bn. Co.C
Tarlton, W.R. TN 2nd (Smith's) Cav. Thomasin's Co.
Tarman, Joseph VA 8th Inf. Co.C
Tarmer, Joel SC Inf. Hampton Legion Co.I
Tarmer, Paschal Brush Bn.
Tarmer, William AR 15th (N.W.) Inf. Co.A
Tarmike, F. TX Inf. Houston Bn. Co.B Sgt.
Tarn, J.C. TX Cav. Bourland's Regt. Co.H
Tarne, J.W. TN 17th Inf. Co.C
Tarner, T.C. TX Cav. Giddings' Bn. Onins' Co.
Tarney, J. MS Inf. 1st St.Troops Co.I
Tarney, M.G. VA 10th Cav. Co.G
Tarney, P. LA 1st Inf. Co.G
Tarney, Patrick GA 1st Bn.S.S. Co.B
Tarnke, Fred TX 9th (Nichols') Inf. Co.B QMSgt.
Tarnlee, J.A. AR Inf. Hardy's Regt. Co.K
Tarnt, C.M. LA Arty. Guyol's Co. (Orleans Arty.)
Tarnt, William W. GA 42nd Inf. Co.I,F Sgt.
Tar nun po 1st Creek Mtd.Vol. Co.L 1st Lt.
Tar nupse 1st Creek Mtd.Vol. Co.L
Tarper Luna 1st Chickasaw Inf. Hansell's Co.
Tarpley, A.A. GA 66th Inf. Co.K

Tarpley, A.B. GA 10th Inf. Co.I
Tarpley, A.B. GA 44th Inf. Co.G
Tarpley, Abram TN 35th Inf. 2nd Co.F
Tarpley, A.L. AR 1st (Dobbin's) Cav. Co.B Sgt.
Tarpley, A.L. AR 13th Inf. Co.D
Tarpley, A.N. TN Lt.Arty. Huggins' Co.
Tarpley, Asburry MS 12th Inf. Co.K
Tarpley, Augustus W. MS 12th Inf. Co.K
Tarpley, B. TX 24th Cav. Co.B
Tarpley, Barber TX 17th Cons.Dismtd.Cav. Co.B Cpl.
Tarpley, Coleman GA 2nd Res. Co.B
Tarpley, Colin S. TX Cav. Martin's Regt. Co.D
Tarpley, C.S. GA Hvy.Arty. 22nd Bn. Co.A
Tarpley, D.D. TN 1st (Feild's) Inf. Co.K
Tarpley, D.T. GA 5th Res. Co.A Cpl.
Tarpley, Edward TN Arty. Fisher's Co.
Tarpley, Edward A. GA 3rd Inf. Co.F
Tarpley, Franklin W. GA 53rd Inf. Co.F 1st Sgt.
Tarpley, George W.L. VA 38th Inf. Co.D
Tarpley, G.W. TN 23rd Inf. 2nd Co.F
Tarpley, Henry TN Jackson's Cav.
Tarpley, Henry TN 20th Inf. Co.K Sgt.
Tarpley, Henry C. GA 44th Inf. Co.A
Tarpley, Henry L. TN 2nd (Smith's) Cav.
Tarpley, Irwin W. TN 1st (Feild's) Inf. Co.K
Tarpley, James L. TN 1st (Feild's) Inf. Co.K
Tarpley, James M. TN 1st (Turney's) Inf. Co.B
Tarpley, James S. NC 47th Inf. Co.K
Tarpley, James W. TN 7th Inf. Co.H
Tarpley, J.B. MS Stewart's Co. (Yalobusha Rangers)
Tarpley, J.B. TN 11th (Holman's) Cav. Co.K
Tarpley, J.B. TN Cav. Allison's Squad. Co.B
Tarpley, J.B. TN Holman's Bn.Part.Rangers Co.D
Tarpley, J. Hugh B. TN 2nd (Smith's) Cav.
Tarpley, J.L. MS 8th Cav. Co.E
Tarpley, Joel F. GA 44th Inf. Co.A
Tarpley, John MS 18th Inf. Co.K
Tarpley, John E. MS 38th Cav. Co.H 2nd Lt.
Tarpley, John H. NC 47th Inf. Co.K Sgt.
Tarpley, John R. GA 19th Inf. Co.D
Tarpley, Joseph E. VA 6th Cav. 2nd Co.E
Tarpley, Josiah MS 2nd Cav. Co.I
Tarpley, J.R. GA 2nd Cav. Co.F
Tarpley, Kinston M. AR 6th Inf. New Co.D
Tarpley, K.M. AR 12th Inf. Co.B Sgt.
Tarpley, L. GA 44th Inf. Co.A
Tarpley, Lorenzo D. GA 53rd Inf. Co.F Sgt.
Tarpley, Luke P.H. VA 38th Inf. Co.D Color Sgt.
Tarpley, M. NC 57th Inf. Co.I
Tarpley, Mathew C. GA 3rd Inf. Co.H
Tarpley, Matthew C. GA 63rd Inf. Co.G 2nd Lt.
Tarpley, Newton F. AR 25th Inf. Co.D
Tarpley, N.F. AR 1st Mtd.Rifles Co.K
Tarpley, N.F. AR Cav. Crabtree's (46th) Regt. Co.I
Tarpley, P.M. AR 5th Inf. Co.D
Tarpley, R.B. TN 1st Hvy.Arty. Co.L, 3rd Co.B 1st Sgt.
Tarpley, R.B. TN 1st Lt.Arty. Co.G Ord.Sgt.
Tarpley, R.B. TN Arty. Fisher's Co. Ord.Sgt.
Tarpley, R.F. MS 2nd St.Cav. Co.B
Tarpley, Robert P. MS Lt.Arty. Stanford's Co.
Tarpley, S.M. LA 1st Cav. Co.C
Tarpley, Sterling S. MS Hamer's Co. (Salem Cav.) 2nd Lt.
Tarpley, Sterling S. MS 11th Inf. Co.A
Tarpley, Thomas GA 6th Inf. (St.Guards) Co.A
Tarpley, Thomas NC 47th Inf. Co.K
Tarpley, Thomas TN 2nd (Smith's) Cav.
Tarpley, Thomas J. TN 6th Inf. Co.E
Tarpley, Thomas M. GA Lt.Arty. Guerard's Btty.
Tarpley, Thomas W. TN 44th Inf. Co.H 2nd Lt.
Tarpley, Thomas W. TN 44th (Cons.) Inf. Co.A Capt.
Tarpley, T.I. TN Inf. 1st Cons.Regt. Co.A
Tarpley, T.L. MS St.Cav. Perrin's Bn. Co.H
Tarpley, W.A. AR 12th Inf. Co.B
Tarpley, W.F. TN Inf. 1st Cons.Regt. Co.B
Tarpley, W.H. AR 5th Inf. Co.D
Tarpley, W.H. GA Inf. 25th Bn. (Prov.Guard) Co.G Sgt.
Tarpley, William A. AR 6th Inf. New Co.D
Tarpley, William A. NC 6th Inf. Co.K 1st Sgt.
Tarpley, William A. TN 53rd Inf. Co.G
Tarpley, William F. TN 1st (Feild's) Inf. Co.K
Tarpley, William G. GA 10th Inf. Co.I
Tarpley, William H. GA 44th Inf. Co.A
Tarpley, William J. MS 2nd Inf. Co.I
Tarpley, William M. TX Cav. Martin's Regt. Co.I
Tarpley, William W. NC 6th Inf. Co.A Sgt.
Tarpley, W.J. MS Cav. Ham's Regt. Co.A
Tarpley, W.L. MS 2nd Part.Rangers Co.I
Tarplin, John TN 14th Inf. Co.A
Tarply, B.M. TN 51st (Cons.) Inf. Co.C
Tarply, David J. AR 3rd Inf. Co.B
Tarply, G.W. AR 24th Inf. Co.K
Tarply, H.C. GA 44th Inf. Co.A
Tarply, Jason L. AR 33rd Inf. Co.H
Tarply, L.B. TN 30th Inf. Co.K
Tarply, M.W. GA 10th Inf. Co.I
Tarply, R.F. MS Inf. 3rd Bn. (St.Troops) Co.F
Tarply, Robert W. AR 33rd Inf. Co.H
Tarply, Seth M. LA 7th Inf. Co.H
Tarr, Francis B. AL 11th Inf. Co.C
Tarr, J.H. AR 13th Mil. Co.F
Tarr, J.W. SC 12th Inf. Co.F
Tarr, Marcus D. VA Inf. 25th Bn. Co.C
Tarr, Marcus D. VA 55th Inf. Co.H 2nd Lt.
Tarr, T.C. AR 13th Mil. Co.F
Tarr, Washington VA 26th Inf. Co.K
Tarr, William MD Arty. 2nd Btty.
Tarr, William H. MO Lt.Arty. Farris' Btty. (Clark Arty.)
Tarr, William J. KY 2nd Mtd.Inf. Co.K Cpl.
Tarrah, W. SC 5th Bn.Res. Co.A Cpl.
Tarralle, Jacob SC Inf. Holcombe Legion Co.D
Tarrance, Benjamon FL 1st Inf. New Co.D Sgt.
Tarrance, C.C. AR 14th (Powers') Inf. Co.F
Tarrance, D.B. AR 8th Cav. Co.G Cpl.
Tarrance, George W. GA 30th Inf. Co.H
Tarrance, J.C. SC 3rd Cav. Co.D
Tarrance, M.J. AL 4th (Russell's) Cav. Co.G
Tarrance, W.J. AR 14th (Powers') Inf. Co.F
Tarrant, --- AL 22nd Inf. Co.D
Tarrant, A. MO Lt.Arty. 3rd Field Btty.
Tarrant, Andrew J. AL 20th Inf. Co.C Lt.
Tarrant, Archilles, Jr. TN 1st (Turney's) Inf. Co.F
Tarrant, B.F. SC Cav. 4th Bn. Co.A
Tarrant, C.B. SC Inf. Hampton Legion Co.F
Tarrant, Edward AL Lt.Arty. 2nd Bn. Co.F 2nd Lt.
Tarrant, Edward AL Lt.Arty. Tarrant's Btty. Capt.
Tarrant, Edward W. AL Lt.Arty. 2nd Bn. Co.F Cpl.
Tarrant, Edward Williams AL 5th Inf. Co.H
Tarrant, Eleozer O. VA 6th Inf. Co.C
Tarrant, E.W. AL Lt.Arty. Phelan's Co.
Tarrant, E.W. AL Lt.Arty. Tarrant's Btty. 2nd Lt.
Tarrant, Frank KY 9th Cav. Co.E
Tarrant, F.W. MS 19th Inf. Co.A
Tarrant, George W. MS 11th Inf. Co.G
Tarrant, Ira G. AL 41st Inf. Sgt.Maj.
Tarrant, J. MS 8th Cav. Co.K
Tarrant, J.A. SC Inf. Hampton Legion Co.F
Tarrant, James AL Cp. of Instr. Talladega
Tarrant, James SC Inf. Hampton Legion Co.E
Tarrant, James A. TN 4th Inf. Co.K 1st Sgt.
Tarrant, James C. AL 4th Inf. Co.G
Tarrant, James C. AL 41st Inf. Co.E,I Bvt.2nd Lt.
Tarrant, James F. MS 11th Inf. Co.F Cpl.
Tarrant, James H. VA 53rd Inf. Co.D 2nd Lt.
Tarrant, J.B. AL Lt.Arty. Tarrant's Btty.
Tarrant, J.F. MS Cav. Ham's Regt. Co.G,A
Tarrant, J.H. TN 19th (Biffle's) Cav. Co.H
Tarrant, Jno. A. VA Mtd.Res. Rappahannock Dist. Sale's Co.
Tarrant, John F. AL Lt.Arty. 2nd Bn. Co.F
Tarrant, John H. TN 15th (Stewart's) Cav. Co.A
Tarrant, John H. TN 4th Inf. Co.K Sgt.
Tarrant, John T. VA Lt.Arty. Thornton's Co.
Tarrant, John T. VA 59th Inf. 3rd Co.F
Tarrant, John T. VA 60th Inf. 1st Co.H
Tarrant, Lewis C. VA 11th Inf. Co.I
Tarrant, M.M. SC 6th Cav. Co.C
Tarrant, M.M. SC 1st (Orr's) Rifles Co.B
Tarrant, P.H. MS 23rd Inf. Co.D
Tarrant, Richard L. TN 1st (Turney's) Inf. Co.F
Tarrant, S.A. Gen. & Staff Capt.,Asst.Comsy.
Tarrant, Samuel AL 12th Cav. Co.F
Tarrant, Samuel A. AL 28th Inf. Co.H Capt.
Tarrant, Samuel A. MS 11th Inf. Co.F 2nd Lt.
Tarrant, Samuel L. TN 3rd (Clack's) Inf. Co.H Capt.
Tarrant, S.L. AL 29th Inf. Co.F
Tarrant, Sumter W. SC 5th Inf. 1st Co.K
Tarrant, Thomas W. MS 11th Inf. Co.F
Tarrant, T.W. AL 9th Inf. N.C.S. Hosp.Stew.
Tarrant, W.C. VA 54th Mil. Co.E,F
Tarrant, W.F. SC 13th Inf. Co.A
Tarrant, William MS 21st Inf. Co.C
Tarrant, William A. AL 28th Inf. Co.K
Tarrant, William B. GA 20th Inf. Co.H Comsy.Sgt.
Tarrant, William C. VA Inf. Cohoon's Bn. Co.A
Tarrant, William J. AL 28th Inf. Co.G
Tarrant, William W. SC Inf. Hampton Legion Co.F Cpl.
Tarrant, W.T. SC 3rd Inf. Co.E
Tarrants, H.A. AR 27th Inf. Co.D

Tarrants, L.B. TN 1st Hvy.Arty. Co.K, 2nd Co.C 2nd Lt.
Tarrapin Striker 1st Cherokee Mtd.Rifles Co.F Sgt.
Tarrar, J.F. VA 1st St.Res. Co.D
Tarrar, J.T. SC 4th St.Troops Co.A
Tarraro, Bernardo LA Mil. 5th Regt.Eur.Brig. (Spanish Regt.) Co.4
Tarrell, A. SC Mil. 16th Regt. Sigwald's Co.
Tarrell, H. AL Arty. 1st Bn. Co.B
Tarrell, Janes TN 7th (Duckworth's) Cav. Co.I
Tarrell, Thomas TN 21st Inf. Co.F
Tarrels, M.J. AL 15th Inf. Co.G
Tarrence, Robert H. VA 6th Inf. Co.I
Tarrent, G.S. TX 13th Vol. Co.G
Tarrentine, James L. AL Cav. Holloway's Co.
Tarrenton, John W. VA 32nd Inf. Co.F
Tarrents, E.S. TX Cav. 1st Regt.St.Troops Co.D
Tarrer, Henry F. GA Hvy.Arty. 22nd Bn. Co.B 2nd Lt.
Tarrer, Henry F. GA 25th Inf. 1st Co.K
Tarrer, J. Frank SC Cav.Bn. Hampton Legion Co.D
Tarrer, J.H. LA 12th Inf. Co.M
Tarrer, John J. SC Cav.Bn. Hampton Legion Co.D
Tarrer, Joseph S. GA Inf. 10th Bn. Co.A
Tarrey, G.R. AL Cav. Hardie's Bn.Res. Co.L
Tarrey, J. MS 2nd St.Cav. Co.G
Tarrh, Francis M. NC 8th Inf. Co.K
Tarrh, M.G. SC 21st Inf. Co.D Capt.
Tarrid, A. LA Mil. 4th Regt. French Brig. Co.6
Tarrigan, Dennis TN 10th Inf. Co.E
Tarris, T.H. LA 2nd Inf. Co.A
Tarris, William TN 50th Inf. Co.B
Tarron, Jordan LA 2nd Cav. Co.B
Tarrou, Alexander LA 13th Inf. Co.D,I
Tarry, Edward MS Lt.Arty. (Madison Lt.Arty.) Richards' Co.
Tarry, Edward C. AL 62nd Inf. Co.D
Tarry, George VA 3rd Cav. Co.E
Tarry, George P. VA Inf. 25th Bn. Co.A
Tarry, George W. VA 9th Cav. Co.G
Tarry, G.P. VA 3rd Cav. Co.A
Tarry, J. VA Inf. 25th Bn. Co.D
Tarry, James MO 10th Cav. Co.C Sgt.
Tarry, James F. MS 1st Lt.Arty. Co.A
Tarry, J.B. KY 12th Cav. Co.G
Tarry, Joseph H. VA 34th Inf. Co.K
Tarry, J.W. KY 1st Inf. Co.F
Tarry, Samuel VA 34th Inf. Co.K
Tarry, Thomas L. VA 34th Inf. Co.K
Tarry, Thomas L. VA 56th Inf. Co.G
Tarry, T.P. KY 1st Inf. Co.F
Tarsdy, Moses AL 32nd Inf. Co.A
Tars hoh che 1st Creek Mtd.Vol. Co.H
Tarskee 1st Creek Mtd.Vol. 2nd Co.C
Tars yie che 1st Creek Mtd.Vol. Co.M Lt.
Tart, Enos NC 18th Inf. Co.C
Tart, F.M. MS 4th Inf. Co.D
Tart, Frank GA Brooks' Co. (Terrell Lt.Arty.)
Tart, Gadi SC 25th Inf. Co.D
Tart, George W. VA 41st Inf. Co.F Sgt.
Tart, G.W. MS 8th Cav. Co.C
Tart, Henry NC 30th Inf. Co.K
Tart, Henry H. SC Arty. Gregg's Co. (McQueen Lt.Arty.)
Tart, Henry H. SC Arty. Manigault's Bn. 1st Co.C
Tart, H.J. GA Brooks' Co. (Terrell Lt.Arty.) Cpl.
Tart, James NC 20th Inf. Co.H
Tart, James NC 24th Inf. Co.E
Tart, James H. SC Arty. Gregg's Co. (McQueen Lt.Arty.)
Tart, James H. SC Arty. Manigault's Bn. 1st Co.C
Tart, J.C. MS Inf. 3rd Bn. (St.Troops) Co.A
Tart, J.E. NC 5th Inf. Co.D
Tart, J.H. SC Inf. 6th Bn. Co.A
Tart, J.H. SC 26th Inf. Co.C
Tart, J.H. SC Manigault's Bn.Vol. Co.D
Tart, John LA 16th Inf. Co.K
Tart, John LA Mil. Chalmette Regt. Co.F
Tart, John NC 8th Sr.Res. Daniel's Co.
Tart, John NC 56th Inf. Co.B
Tart, John A. NC 46th Inf. Co.I
Tart, John M. SC Arty. Gregg's Co. (McQueen Lt.Arty.)
Tart, John M. SC Arty. Manigault's Bn. 1st Co.C
Tart, John Q. VA 16th Inf. Co.C
Tart, John W. SC Arty. Gregg's Co. (McQueen Lt.Arty.)
Tart, John W. SC Arty. Manigault's Bn. 1st Co.C
Tart, J.S. NC 1st Bn. Home Guards
Tart, J.W. SC 23rd Inf. Co.E Cpl.
Tart, Lee Sylvester NC 56th Inf. Co.B
Tart, Nathan NC 24th Inf. Co.E
Tart, Nathan SC 25th Inf. Co.D
Tart, N.B. SC Lt.Arty. (Waccamaw Lt.Arty.) M. Ward's Co.
Tart, R.M. AL 7th Cav. Co.H
Tart, Samuel A. AL 6th Inf. Co.C
Tart, Saunders P.M. NC Moseley's Co. (Sampson Arty.)
Tart, Thomas NC Hvy.Arty. 10th Bn. Co.B
Tart, Thomas C. MS 11th (Perrin's) Cav. Co.B
Tart, T.S. NC 2nd Jr.Res. Co.H
Tart, Uriah J. NC 20th Inf. Co.H
Tart, Vernon H. AL 6th Inf. Co.I
Tart, West Brook NC Hvy.Arty. 10th Bn. Co.B
Tart, Whitfield NC 24th Inf. Co.E
Tart, Whitfield NC Giddins' Co. (Detailed & Petitioned Men)
Tart, William NC 8th Sr.Res. Daniel's Co.
Tart, William B. NC 24th Inf. Co.E
Tart, William J. SC 21st Inf. Co.F
Tart, William L. NC 17th Inf. (1st Org.) Co.F
Tart, William T. NC 50th Inf. Co.H
Tart, Young F. NC Hvy.Arty. 10th Bn. Co.B
Tar ta ka 1st Creek Mtd.Vol. Co.E
Tartar, Nicholas TN Cav. 16th Bn. (Neal's) Co.F
Tartar, Rush VA 50th Inf. Co.E
Tartell, William AL 7th Inf. Co.A
Tarter, Ephraim VA 51st Inf. Co.C
Tarter, Harvey TN 5th (McKenzie's) Cav. Co.G
Tarter, James H. VA 63rd Inf. Co.H
Tarter, J.W. VA Mil. Wythe Cty.
Tarter, Michael KY 10th Cav. Co.A
Tarter, Randal VA 22nd Cav. Co.G
Tarter, Robert TN 29th Inf. Co.E Cpl.
Tarter, Robert T. VA 6th Bn.Res. Co.A Cpl.
Tarter, W.M. TX 1st Hvy.Arty. 2nd Co.A Sgt.
Tarter, W.M. TX 15th Inf. Co.C, 1st Co.E Sgt.
Tartt, E. B. AL 36th Inf. Co.A
Tartt, J. TX 13th Vol. 2nd Co.H
Tartt, James E. TX Waul's Legion Co.B
Tartt, J.C. TX Inf. Houston Bn. Co.E 1st Sgt.
Tartt, J.W. AL 36th Inf. Co.A
Tartt, L.L. TX 10th Cav. Co.K 2nd Lt.
Tartt, L.M. TX 10th Cav. Co.K Capt.
Tartum, L.D. TN Cav. Napier's Bn. Co.B
Taruplett, C.G. LA Ogden's Cav. Co.I
Tarut, Charles M. LA Lt.Arty. (Orleans Guard Btty.) LeGardeur, Jr.'s Co.
Tarvar, W.L. AL 15th Inf. Co.B,D
Tarver, --- TX Cav. Mann's Regt. Co.C
Tarver, --- TX Inf. 1st St.Troops Whitehead's Co.
Tarver, A.J. TX 19th Inf. Co.C Sgt.
Tarver, Albert G. MS 2nd Cav. Co.F
Tarver, Alfred L. MS 22nd Inf. Co.E
Tarver, Allen MS Cav. Garland's Bn. Co.B
Tarver, Allen MS 40th Inf. Co.B
Tarver, Allen 14th Conf.Cav. Co.B,I
Tarver, Andrew S. AL 6th Cav. Co.H,F 1st Lt.
Tarver, Andrew S. GA Cav. Nelson's Ind.Co.
Tarver, B.C. AL 1st Cav. 1st Co.K Capt.
Tarver, B.C. AL 7th Cav. Co.G Capt.
Tarver, Benjamin AL Cav. Barbiere's Bn. Goldsby's Co.
Tarver, Benjamin E. TX 36th Cav. Co.G
Tarver, Benjamin F. MS 40th Inf. Co.B
Tarver, Benjamin F. MO 2nd Cav. 3rd Co.K
Tarver, Benjamin J. AL 4th Inf. Co.C
Tarver, Benjamin J. TN 7th Inf. Co.K Bvt.2nd Lt.
Tarver, Benjamin L. MS 2nd Inf. Co.F
Tarver, Benjamin Lafayette MS Inf. 1st Bn. Co.D
Tarver, Benjamin T. MO 9th Inf. Co.G
Tarver, B.L. TX 12th Cav. Co.K
Tarver, B.M. GA Phillips' Legion Co.E
Tarver, Byrd TN 18th Inf. Co.G
Tarver, Byrd G. GA 12th (Wright's) Cav. (St.Guards) Wright's Co.
Tarver, Calvin AL Cp. of Instr. Talladega
Tarver, C.B. TX 20th Inf. Co.C
Tarver, C.C. TX 24th & 25th Cav. (Cons.) Co.B
Tarver, C.C. TX 25th Cav. Co.F
Tarver, C.F. MS 39th Inf. Co.K
Tarver, C.H. AL 1st Bn. Hilliard's Legion Vol. Co.E
Tarver, Charles LA 8th Inf. Co.E
Tarver, Dempsey MS 7th Inf. Co.E
Tarver, E. GA 2nd Inf. Co.D
Tarver, E. TX Cav. Morgan's Regt. Co.E
Tarver, E.C. GA Cav. Allen's Co.
Tarver, Edward R. TX 8th Cav. Co.G Cpl.
Tarver, Edward R. Gen. & Staff 1st Lt.
Tarver, E.J. GA 1st Inf. (St.Guards) Co.H
Tarver, E.J. GA Phillips' Legion Co.B
Tarver, E.L. LA 31st Inf. Co.D
Tarver, Elisha L. MS 7th Inf. Co.C
Tarver, Ely MS 37th Inf. Co.A
Tarver, Enoch AR 2nd Mtd.Rifles Co.E
Tarver, E.R. Gen. & Staff Maj.,AAAIG
Tarver, F.B. GA 8th Inf. Co.B
Tarver, F.M. TX 2nd Inf. Co.C

Tarver, F.R. GA 1st (Ramsey's) Inf. Co.E
Tarver, Francis B. GA 1st (Olmstead's) Inf. Co.D
Tarver, Francis R. GA 12th (Wright's) Cav. (St.Guards) Wright's Co.
Tarver, George W. TX 25th Cav. Co.F
Tarver, G.Y. TX 12th Inf. Co.K
Tarver, H. GA Lt.Arty. Anderson's Btty.
Tarver, H.A. KY 2nd Mtd.Inf. Co.A
Tarver, Hamilton AL 17th Inf. Co.F
Tarver, Hamilton AL 61st Inf. Co.A
Tarver, H.B. AL 1st Cav. 2nd Co.E
Tarver, Henry AR Cav. Wright's Regt. Co.C
Tarver, Henry LA Inf. 16th Bn. (Conf.Guards Resp.Bn.) Co.B
Tarver, Hezekiah GA Lt.Arty. 14th Bn. Co.C,G
Tarver, Hezekiah GA Lt.Arty. Ferrell's Btty.
Tarver, H.S. TX 5th Inf. Co.I 1st Sgt.
Tarver, Ira B. MS Cav. Garland's Bn. Co.A
Tarver, Isaac LA Ogden's Cav. Co.D
Tarver, Isaac H. MS 33rd Inf. Co.D
Tarver, J. AL Coosa Guards J.W. Suttles' Co.
Tarver, J. LA 27th Inf. Co.K
Tarver, J.A. AL 15th Inf. Co.B
Tarver, Jacob A. AL 39th Inf. Co.K
Tarver, James AL 46th Inf. Co.A
Tarver, James AR 2nd Mtd.Rifles Co.E
Tarver, James LA 2nd Inf. Co.K
Tarver, James MS 7th Inf. Co.E
Tarver, James MS 33rd Inf. Co.D
Tarver, James TX 12th Cav. Co.A
Tarver, James H. LA 2nd Inf. Co.K,F
Tarver, James W. GA Cav. Nelson's Ind.Co.
Tarver, J.A.S. TX 25th Cav. Co.F
Tarver, Jasper GA 48th Inf. Co.E
Tarver, J.B. MS 36th Inf. Co.A
Tarver, J.F. KY 2nd Mtd.Inf. Co.A
Tarver, J.H. LA Lt.Arty. 3rd Btty. (Benton's)
Tarver, J.J. MO St.Guard Cornet Band
Tarver, J.K. MS 36th Inf. Co.A
Tarver, J.L. TX 14th Inf. Co.I Cpl.
Tarver, J.L. TX 18th Inf. Co.H
Tarver, John AL 46th Inf. Co.A
Tarver, John GA Lt.Arty. 14th Bn. Co.C,G
Tarver, John GA Lt.Arty. Anderson's Btty.
Tarver, John GA Lt.Arty. Ferrell's Btty.
Tarver, John LA Cav. 18th Bn. Co.F
Tarver, John MS 18th Cav. Co.C
Tarver, John MS Cav. 24th Bn. Co.B
Tarver, John MS 2nd (Quinn's St.Troops) Inf. Co.B
Tarver, John MS 3rd Inf. (St.Troops) Co.A
Tarver, John TX 7th Cav. Co.A
Tarver, John 10th Conf.Cav. Co.I
Tarver, John A. MS 16th Inf. Co.E
Tarver, John A. TX 14th Field Btty. 1st Lt.
Tarver, John E.J. MS 16th Inf. Co.E
Tarver, John H. TX 25th Cav. Co.F
Tarver, John M. AL 3rd Inf. Co.C
Tarver, John R. GA 36th (Broyles') Inf. Co.H Sgt.
Tarver, John W. TX 12th Inf. Co.K Cpl.
Tarver, J.R. GA 42nd Inf. Co.I Sgt.
Tarver, J.R. LA 3rd (Wingfield's) Cav. Co.F
Tarver, J.S. GA 10th Inf. Co.C
Tarver, J.S. LA 8th Cav. Co.B
Tarver, Julius MS 7th Cav. Co.H
Tarver, L.B. GA 48th Inf. Co.E
Tarver, Lewis MS Lt.Arty. 14th Bn. Co.C
Tarver, Lewis MS Lt.Arty. Merrin's Btty.
Tarver, L.G. MS 39th Inf. Co.K
Tarver, Lott MS 33rd Inf. Co.B Sgt.
Tarver, Lunsford W. LA 31st Inf. Co.C
Tarver, M. FL Lt.Arty. Dyke's Co.
Tarver, M. 8th (Wade's) Conf.Cav. Co.B
Tarver, Marcellus C. AL 3rd Inf. Co.C
Tarver, Marcellus C. AL Vol. Lee, Jr.'s Co.
Tarver, Marcus C. GA 20th Inf. Co.C
Tarver, Mark E. TX Cav. Ragsdale's Bn. Co.B
Tarver, Martin GA Lt.Arty. 14th Bn. Co.C,G
Tarver, Martin GA Lt.Arty. Anderson's Btty.
Tarver, Martin GA Lt.Arty. Ferrell's Btty.
Tarver, M.C. GA 48th Inf. Co.E
Tarver, M.C. TN 1st Regt. Sap. & Min. Co.A
Tarver, Micajah FL Lt.Arty. Dyke's Co.
Tarver, Michael MS 7th Inf. Co.C
Tarver, Michael MS 22nd Inf. Co.E
Tarver, M.P. TN 6th Inf. Co.K
Tarver, O.G. GA Inf. (Jones Hussars) Jones' Co.
Tarver, Peter AL Cav. 5th Bn. Hilliard's Legion Co.A
Tarver, Peter 10th Conf.Cav. Co.A
Tarver, R. GA 1st Reg. Co.F
Tarver, R. MS 2nd Inf.
Tarver, R. MS Condrey's Co. (Bull Mtn.Invinc.)
Tarver, Reason E. MS 7th Inf. Co.E
Tarver, R.H. AL 42nd Inf. Co.K Cpl.
Tarver, R.H. LA 2nd Inf. Co.F Sgt.
Tarver, Robert MS 3rd Inf. (St.Troops) Co.A
Tarver, Robert B. GA 20th Inf. Co.C
Tarver, Robert M. GA Phillips' Legion Co.B
Tarver, Romain A. AL 53rd (Part.Rangers) Co.K
Tarver, S. TX 3rd (Kirby's) Bn.Vol. Co.C Cpl.
Tarver, S. Otis GA Cobb's Legion Co.E 1st Lt.
Tarver, S.T. GA 1st (Symons') Res. Co.H
Tarver, Stephen AL 36th Inf. Co.G
Tarver, Sterling TX 25th Cav. Co.F
Tarver, T.W. MS 2nd (Quinn's St.Troops) Inf. Co.C
Tarver, T.D. TN 14th (Neely's) Cav. Co.F Cpl.
Tarver, T.D. TN 6th Inf. Co.K
Tarver, T.G. TX 12th Inf. Co.K
Tarver, Thomas GA Inf. 1st Loc.Troops (Augusta) Co.I
Tarver, Thomas MS Cav. 3rd Bn.Res. Co.B
Tarver, Thomas TN Lt.Arty. Palmer's Co.
Tarver, Thomas B. MS 7th Inf. Co.B
Tarver, Thomas I. MS 22nd Inf. Co.E
Tarver, Thomas M. MS 36th Inf. Co.A
Tarver, Thomas M. TX 9th (Young's) Inf. Co.E
Tarver, Thomas P. MS 33rd Inf. Co.B
Tarver, T.I. AR 28th Mil. Co.D 1st Lt.
Tarver, T.W. MS Cav. 3rd Bn. (Ashcraft's) Co.F
Tarver, Uriah LA Res.Corps
Tarver, W. LA 4th Cav. Co.H
Tarver, W.B. GA Cav. 22nd Bn. (St.Guards) Co.C
Tarver, W.B. GA Phillips' Legion Co.E
Tarver, W.D. AL St.Res.
Tarver, Wells MS 23rd Inf. Co.B
Tarver, W.H. GA 1st (Symons') Res. Co.K
Tarver, W.H. TX 5th Inf. Co.G
Tarver, W.H. Gen. & Staff Hosp.Stew.
Tarver, William MS 7th Cav. Co.H
Tarver, William MS 33rd Inf. Co.D
Tarver, William A. MS 22nd Inf. Co.E Sgt.
Tarver, William A. 8th (Wade's) Conf.Cav. Co.B
Tarver, William B. TX 12th Inf. Co.K 1st Sgt.
Tarver, Wm. L. MS 11th (Ashcraft's) Cav. Co.K
Tarver, William W. TX 25th Cav. Co.F
Tarver, W.W. TX 24th & 25th Cav. (Cons.) Co.B
Tarver, John N. GA 19th Inf. Co.D
Tarvin, A.A. GA 39th Inf. Co.K
Tarvin, Aaron GA 39th Inf. Co.K
Tarvin, A.B. 3rd Conf.Cav. Co.E
Tarvin, A.J. KY 3rd Bn.Mtd.Rifles Co.C 1st Sgt.
Tarvin, Alfred L. GA 39th Inf. Co.H
Tarvin, Alvin GA 23rd Inf. Co.H Sgt.
Tarvin, E.J. AL 40th Inf. Co.E
Tarvin, G.C. KY 2nd (Duke's) Cav. Co.B
Tarvin, G.J. GA 54th Inf. Co.G
Tarvin, John J. AR Cav. Wright's Regt. Co.E
Tarvin, John J. AR 24th Inf. Co.G
Tarvin, John J. AR Inf. Hardy's Regt. Co.F
Tarvin, M.E. AL 40th Inf. Co.E 2nd Lt.
Tarvin, Miller T. AL 3rd Cav. Co.A 3rd Cpl.
Tarvin, Miller T. Conf.Cav. Wood's Regt. Co.C
Tarvin, R.P. AR 2nd.Cav. Co.G
Tarvin, Solomon GA 54th Inf. Co.H
Tarvin, T.J. AR 2nd Cav. Co.G
Tarvin, William GA 54th Inf. Co.H
Tarvin, W.T. AR 2nd Cav. Co.G
Tarwater, Alexander TN Lt.Arty. Burroughs' Co.
Tarwater, B.A. TN 31st Inf. Co.A
Tarwater, C. TN 17th Inf. Co.E
Tarwater, E.A. TN 14th Inf. Co.H
Tarwater, H. MO 1st Cav. Co.D
Tarwater, Henry MO 1st Cav. Co.D
Tarwater, Henry MO Cav. 3rd Bn. Co.A
Tarwater, Henry MO 10th Cav. Co.K
Tarwater, Isaac O. MO 11th Inf. Co.I
Tarwater, James GA 64th Inf. Co.I
Tarwater, James N. AR 27th Inf. Co.E
Tarwater, John TN 31st Inf. Co.A
Tarwater, John C. MO 1st Cav. Co.D
Tarwater, J.P. AL Cav. 24th Bn. Co.B
Tarwater, L. AL 42nd Inf. Co.F
Tarwater, M.H. TN 31st Inf. Co.A
Tarwater, Thomas MO 1st Cav. Co.D
Tarwater, Thomas MO Cav. Schnabel's Bn. Co.B
Tarwater, T.J. AL Cav. 5th Bn. Hilliard's Legion Co.E
Tarwater, T.J. 10th Conf.Cav. Co.E
Tarwater, William TN 37th Inf. Co.D
Tarwaters, Charles TN Inf. 23rd Bn. Co.D
Tarwaters, James TN 37th Inf. Co.D
Tarwaters, James P. AL 6th Cav. Co.C
Tarwaters, John W. AL 30th Inf. Co.D
Tarwaters, Polk AL Inf. 1st Regt. Co.D
Tarwaters, Thomas AL 5th Inf. New Co.B
Tar weh 1st Creek Mtd.Vol. Co.H
Tary, James TN Conscr. (Cp. of Instr.)
Tary, S.M. AL 25th Inf. Co.H
Tary, William KY 13th Cav. Co.C
Tasch, Lewis TX Cav. Giddings' Bn. Carr's Co.
Taschner, John LA Mil. 4th Regt.Eur.Brig. Co.D
Taseur, G.W. AL 43rd Inf. Co.K
Tash, Isaac AL 20th Cav. Lee's Co.

Tash, Peter AL Mobile City Troop Sgt.
Tasha, P. LA Miles' Legion Co.H
Tashkabi, William 1st Choctaw & Chickasaw Mtd.Rifles 2nd Co.K
Tasho chee 1st Creek Mtd.Vol. 2nd Co.D
Tas keek Mikko 1st Creek Mtd.Vol. 2nd Co.C
Tasker, Jacob VA 97th Mil. Co.L
Tasker, James VA 25th Inf. 2nd Co.E
Tasker, James VA 46th Mil. Co.A
Tasker, Washington VA 42nd Inf. Co.E
Taskett, S.H. TX 12th Inf. Co.E
Taskett, Wm. AR 34th Inf. Co.K
Taskry, Henry KY 7th Cav. Co.B
Tason, P. KY 5th Cav.
Tass, William H. VA Cav. 37th Bn. Co.H
Tassain, A. LA 15th Bn.S.S. (Weatherly's) Co.C
Tassan, Lucien LA Ogden's Cav. Co.E
Tassant, J.A. LA 25th Inf. Co.F
Tassaro, Benjamin SC 1st Arty. Co.H
Tassaro, F. SC Lt.Arty. Wagener's Co. (Co.A, German Arty.)
Tassarro, Francisco SC Conscr.
Tassel 1st Cherokee Mtd.Rifles Co.C
Tassel 2nd Cherokee Mtd.Vol. Co.I
Tassel, Charles 1st Cherokee Mtd.Vol. 2nd Co.G
Tassel, N. 1st Cherokee Mtd.Vol. Co.J
Tassel Ah hur mah 1st Cherokee Mtd.Rifles Co.B
Tassell, J.B. TN Inf. 3rd Cons.Regt. Co.G
Tassell, J.B. TN 31st Inf. Co.F
Tassen, John VA 16th Cav. Co.K Sgt.
Tassenger, D.F. GA 5th Inf. Co.H
Tasset, Ernest Sap. & Min. Gallimard's Co.,CSA Sgt.Maj.
Tasset, Joseph Sap. & Min. Gallimard's Co.,CSA Cpl.
Tassey, D.F. TN 35th Inf. Co.E
Tassin, A. LA Ogden's Cav. Co.G
Tassin, A. LA 2nd Inf. Co.E
Tassin, A. LA 18th Inf. Co.A
Tassin, B. LA Mil. St.James Regt. Gaudet's Co.
Tassin, Edmond LA Inf.Crescent Regt. Co.D
Tassin, Eugene LA Lt.Arty. 2nd Field Btty.
Tassin, Felix LA 18th Inf. Co.E
Tassin, Felix LA Inf.Cons. 18th Regt. & Yellow Jacket Bn. Co.B
Tassin, Florian LA 18th Inf. Co.E
Tassin, Florian LA Inf.Cons. 18th Regt. & Yellow Jacket Bn. Co.B
Tassin, J.A. LA 25th Inf. Co.F
Tassin, John B. LA 1st Cav. Co.G
Tassin, Joseph LA Mil. 1st Native Guards Cpl.
Tassin, Levi LA Lt.Arty. 2nd Field Btty.
Tassin, Ludger LA Lt.Arty. 2nd Field Btty.
Tassin, Meril LA 1st Cav. Co.G
Tassin, N. LA 18th Inf. Co.C
Tassin, P. LA 18th Inf. Co.C
Tassin, Valere LA 1st Cav. Co.G
Tassing, G.P. VA 2nd Inf. Co.G
Tasso, Francesco LA Mil. 6th Regt.Eur.Brig. (Italian Guards Bn.) Co.1,3,4
Tassor, H.H. LA Mil. Orleans Guards Regt. Co.C
Tatam, J.O. MS 11th (Cons.) Cav. Co.I
Tatam, John FL 2nd Cav. Co.H
Tatam, Jos. F. VA 39th Inf. Co.H
Tatam, Thomas C. AR Inf. 2nd Bn. Co.C Comsy.Sgt.
Tatam, Timothy P. AR Inf. 2nd Bn. Co.C
Tatam, W.A. TN 22nd Inf. Co.I
Tate, --- TX Cav. 4th Regt.St.Troops Co.L
Tate, ---, 1st TX Cav. Mann's Regt. Co.D
Tate, --- VA Arty.Detach. VMI
Tate, A. MS 6th Cav. Co.G
Tate, A. MS Lt.Arty. 1st Regt. Co.D
Tate, A. MS 5th Inf. (St.Troops) Co.I
Tate, A. Sap. & Min. G.W. Maxson's Co.,CSA
Tate, A.B. NC 5th Cav. (63rd St.Troops) Co.I
Tate, Abner MS 41st Inf. Co.K Sgt.
Tate, Abner C. AL 4th Inf. Co.I
Tate, Abner H. NC 1st Inf. (6 mo. '61) Co.B
Tate, Abraham GA Cav. 1st Gordon Squad. (St.Guards) Co.A
Tate, Abraham GA 3rd Cav. Co.G
Tate, Absolom M. NC 4th Cav. (59th St.Troops) Co.E
Tate, A.C. AL Cav. Barbiere's Bn. Goldsby's Co.
Tate, A.C. GA 60th Inf. Co.D Cpl.
Tate, A.D. TN 17th Inf. Co.D
Tate, Adam LA 8th Inf. Co.F
Tate, Adam LA Inf.Crescent Regt. Co.K
Tate, Adam VA 18th Inf. Co.B
Tate, A.H. AL 44th Inf. Co.I
Tate, A.J. AR 6th Inf. New Co.F
Tate, A.J. AR 12th Inf. Co.D
Tate, A.J. TN 45th Inf. Co.F 2nd Lt.
Tate, Albert NC Mallett's Bn. (Cp.Guard) Co.B
Tate, Albert A. NC Inf. 13th Bn. Co.A
Tate, Albert A. NC 66th Inf. Co.A
Tate, Alfred O. NC 38th Inf. Co.B
Tate, Allen TX 11th Inf. Co.E Fifer
Tate, A.M. MS 35th Inf. Co.K
Tate, A.M. SC 16th Inf. Co.C Sgt.
Tate, Andrew VA 22nd Cav. Co.K
Tate, Andrew F. VA 13th Inf. Co.D
Tate, Andrew J. AR 7th Cav. Co.M
Tate, Andrew J. NC 13th Inf. Co.K
Tate, Andrew J. SC 1st Arty. Co.I
Tate, Andrew Jackson AR 4th Cav.
Tate, Armsted J. VA 29th Inf. Co.E
Tate, Armstrong NC 6th Inf. Co.F 1st Sgt.
Tate, Asa NC 4th Sr.Res. Co.H
Tate, Austin B. VA 37th Inf. Co.B
Tate, Austin B. VA 63rd Inf. Co.A Sgt.
Tate, B. VA Inf. 1st Bn.Loc.Def. Co.E
Tate, Bazil L. MS 21st Inf. Co.I
Tate, Benjamin MO 1st N.E. Cav. Co.I
Tate, Benjamin MO 10th Cav. Co.B
Tate, Benjamin MO Mtd.Inf. Boone's Regt.
Tate, Benjamin TN 24th Bn.S.S. Co.B
Tate, Benjamin VA 16th Cav. Co.I
Tate, Benjamin VA 6th Bn.Res. Co.B
Tate, Bethel MS 10th Cav. Co.A
Tate, Branch GA 6th Inf. Co.A
Tate, B.T. AR 27th Inf. Co.A
Tate, B.T. AR Inf. Adams Regt. Co.C Sgt.
Tate, C. VA 2nd Cav. Co.G
Tate, Calaway AR 19th (Dockery's) Inf. Cons.Co.
Tate, Calvin NC 7th Sr.Res. Bradshaw's Co.
Tate, Calvin O. VA 56th Inf. Co.F
Tate, Cary M. TX 29th Cav. Co.A,K Sgt.
Tate, C.B. AL Randolph Cty.Res. Shepherd's Co.
Tate, C.C. MS 41st Inf. Co.K 2nd Lt.
Tate, C.C. TN 59th Mtd.Inf. Co.K
Tate, C.G.S. TN 35th Inf. 1st Co.A, Co.H Cpl.
Tate, Charles LA Arty. Hutton's Co. (Crescent Arty.,Co.A) Cpl.
Tate, Charles LA Mil. Chalmette Regt. Co.F
Tate, Charles C. VA 22nd Cav. Co.K
Tate, Charles C. VA 51st Inf. Co.B
Tate, Charles G. VA Hvy.Arty. 10th Bn. Co.B
Tate, Charles N. TN 1st (Feild's) Inf. Co.H Lt.
Tate, Charles T. VA 23rd Inf. Co.A
Tate, Clarence W. AL 3rd Inf. Co.C
Tate, Clinton GA 6th Inf. Co.A
Tate, C.M. AR 8th Cav. Co.F
Tate, C.Mc. MS 1st Cav. Co.G
Tate, Columbus H. NC 58th Inf. Co.F
Tate, Columbus M. AR 1st Vol. Co.C
Tate, D. AL 39th Inf. Co.K
Tate, D. AL St.Res. Co.A Sgt.
Tate, D. GA 39th Inf. Co.K
Tate, D. VA Mil. Washington Cty.
Tate, Daniel MS 34th Inf. Co.I
Tate, David MS 42nd Inf. Co.F,K
Tate, David 1st Creek Mtd.Vol. Co.M
Tate, David B. KY 6th Mtd.Inf. Co.B
Tate, David C. TX 27th Cav. Co.D Sgt.
Tate, David G. GA 23rd Inf. Co.H
Tate, David L. VA Inf. 54th Bn. Co.F 2nd Lt.
Tate, David L. VA 63rd Inf. Co.A Sgt.
Tate, David W. GA 35th Inf. Co.I
Tate, D.F. TX Cav. 2nd Regt.St.Troops Co.A
Tate, D.G. GA 24th Inf. Co.C Cpl.
Tate, D.L. NC 2nd Cav. (19th St.Troops) Co.H
Tate, D.M. 3rd Conf.Cav. Co.K
Tate, Doc. W. SC 5th Inf. 1st Co.G, 2nd Co.C Sgt.
Tate, Drury VA 6th Bn.Res. Co.E
Tate, Dudley W. TX 18th Cav. Co.K
Tate, E. GA 12th Cav. Co.A
Tate, E. GA 39th Inf. Co.K
Tate, E. VA Inf. 1st Bn.Loc.Def. Co.C Cpl.
Tate, E.A. AL 50th Inf. Co.H
Tate, E.A. AR 1st (Monroe's) Cav. Co.A
Tate, E.A. AR 50th Mil. Co.C Cpl.
Tate, E.A. GA Inf. 9th Bn. Co.D
Tate, E.D. GA 23rd Inf. Co.C
Tate, E.E. TN 21st (Wilson's) Cav. Co.K
Tate, Elias NC 1st Bn.Jr.Res. Co.B
Tate, Elias NC 66th Inf. Co.I
Tate, Elias A. GA 21st Inf. Co.B
Tate, Elick MS 2nd (Quinn's St.Troops) Inf. Co.C
Tate, Elisha AL 18th Inf. Co.B
Tate, Elisha TN 35th Inf. Co.L
Tate, Elisha TN 36th Inf. Co.I 1st Lt.
Tate, Elisha VA 29th Inf. 1st Co.F
Tate, Elisha VA 51st Inf. Co.A Sgt.
Tate, E.M. TN 31st Inf. Co.G
Tate, E.M. TX 9th (Young's) Inf. Co.E Sgt.Maj.
Tate, Enoch MS 38th Cav. Co.A
Tate, Enoch MS 3rd Inf. (St.Troops) Co.G
Tate, E.O. VA 36th Inf. Co.F
Tate, E.R. GA 17th Inf. Co.B
Tate, E.R. MS 38th Cav. Co.I
Tate, Erostus SC 18th Inf. Co.F
Tate, Evans C. GA 40th Inf. Co.D Sgt.

Tate, Ezra M. TX 1st Bn.S.S. Sgt.Maj.
Tate, F.A. NC 5th Cav. (63rd St.Troops) Co.F
Tate, F.A. TN 35th Inf. 2nd Co.D
Tate, F.C. GA 18th Inf. Co.G 1st Lt.
Tate, Fleming D. VA 56th Inf. Co.F
Tate, F.M. GA 18th Inf. Co.K
Tate, F.M. GA 27th Inf. Co.E
Tate, F.M. LA Mil. Chalmette Regt. Co.C
Tate, F.M. TN 35th Inf. 1st Co.A
Tate, Francis AL 17th Bn.S.S. Co.B 2nd Lt.
Tate, Francis C. LA Arty. Moody's Co. (Madison Lt.Arty.)
Tate, Francis M. TN 2nd (Robison's) Inf. Co.G
Tate, Frank AL 39th Inf. Co.E 1st Sgt.
Tate, Frank SC 5th Inf. Co.C
Tate, Frank VA Hvy.Arty. 19th Bn. Co.D
Tate, Fred TX 9th (Nichols') Inf. Co.A Maj.
Tate, Fred Van Dorn's Staff Col.,SSAGen.
Tate, Freeman MO 5th Inf. Co.B
Tate, F.W. MO Cav. Woodson's Co.
Tate, Gabriel TN 39th Mtd.Inf. Co.D
Tate, Gamewell NC 34th Inf. Co.I
Tate, George KY 6th Cav. Co.G
Tate, George LA 10th Inf. Co.D Cpl.
Tate, George MS 46th Inf. Co.E
Tate, George MO Cav. Wood's Regt. Co.E
Tate, George F. VA 56th Inf. Co.F
Tate, George M. MS 9th Inf. Old Co.E
Tate, George S. TN 6th (Wheeler's) Cav. Co.F Ord.Sgt.
Tate, George W. AL 21st Inf. Co.H
Tate, George W. AL 24th Inf. Co.I,B Cpl.
Tate, George W. VA Lt.Arty. 12th Bn. Co.C
Tate, George W. VA Lt.Arty. Taylor's Co.
Tate, G.F.H. LA 9th Inf. Co.K
Tate, G.M. MS 10th Inf. New Co.A,H
Tate, Green FL Mil.
Tate, Greif SC 1st St.Troops Co.C
Tate, Grief SC 2nd Rifles Co.F
Tate, G.W. AL Mil. 4th Vol. Co.K
Tate, G.W. AL Cp. of Instr. Talladega Co.B
Tate, H. LA Inf.Cons. 18th Regt. & Yellow Jacket Bn. Co.E
Tate, H. TX Cav. Morgan's Regt. Lt.
Tate, H.A. AL 4th (Russell's) Cav. Co.F
Tate, H.A. AL 7th Inf. Co.D
Tate, H.A. LA 1st Cav. Co.I
Tate, H.A. NC 1st Inf. (6 mo. '61) Co.C
Tate, H.A. NC 11th (Bethel Regt.) Inf. Co.D Sgt.
Tate, H.A. SC 5th Inf. 2nd Co.C
Tate, Hampton H. AL 31st Inf. Co.E Sgt.
Tate, Hardin L. 1st Chickasaw Inf. Hansell's Co. 1st Sgt.
Tate, H.B. MS St.Cav. 2nd Bn. (Harris') Co.C Sgt.
Tate, H.B. MS 11th (Cons.) Cav. Co.I
Tate, H.C. GA 5th Res. Co.E
Tate, H.C. TN 16th Inf. Co.A
Tate, H.C. TX 22nd Inf. Co.I
Tate, H.C. 8th (Wade's) Conf.Cav. Co.C
Tate, Henry SC 18th Inf. Co.F
Tate, Henry TN Inf. 16th Regt.
Tate, Henry VA Cav. 40th Bn. Co.B
Tate, Henry VA Hvy.Arty. 19th Bn. Co.E
Tate, Henry VA Lt.Arty. W.P. Carter's Co.
Tate, Henry VA 56th Inf. Co.K
Tate, Henry G. VA 23rd Inf. Co.A
Tate, Henry M. MS Cav. Ham's Regt. Co.I
Tate, Henry M. MO 1st Cav. Co.K
Tate, Henry M. MO Cav. Wood's Regt. Co.E
Tate, Henry N. MS 23rd Inf. Co.B
Tate, H.H. MS 1st Bn.S.S. Co.A
Tate, H.H. NC 1st Inf. (6 mo. '61) Co.B
Tate, Hickman TX Cav. Madison's Regt. Co.D
Tate, Hiram G. NC 34th Inf. Co.I
Tate, Hiram Warren TX 20th Cav. Co.G 1stSgt.
Tate, H.J. TN 42nd Inf. 2nd Co.I 2nd Lt.
Tate, H.J. 4th Conf.Inf. Co.A Sgt.
Tate, H.L. TX 13th Vol. 2nd Co.D 1st Sgt.
Tate, H.M. MS 41st Inf. Co.B
Tate, Horatio L. TX 35th (Brown's) Cav. Co.E
Tate, Hosea B. MS 1st (Johnston's) Inf. Co.C Cpl.
Tate, Howard AL 1st Bn. Hilliard's Legion Vol. Co.E
Tate, H.P. MO 9th (Elliott's) Cav.
Tate, Hugh C. NC Cav. 5th Bn. Co.C 1st Sgt.
Tate, Hugh C. NC 6th Cav. (65th St.Troops) Co.H,C 1st Sgt.
Tate, Hugh W. NC 3rd Cav. (41st St.Troops) Co.F
Tate, Hugh W. Gen. & Staff Surg.
Tate, H.W. NC 54th Inf. Asst.Surg.
Tate, I.C. MO 10th Inf. Co.I
Tate, I.F. MS 1st Cav.Res. Co.E
Tate, Isaac AL 34th Inf. Co.K
Tate, Isaac H. AL 15th Inf. Co.A
Tate, J. AL Talladega Cty.Res. D.M. Reid's Co.
Tate, J. NC 1st Bn.Jr.Res. Co.B
Tate, J.A. AL 21st Inf. Co.C,H
Tate, J.A. GA 9th Inf. Co.B
Tate, J.A. LA 3rd (Wingfield's) Cav. Co.D Sgt.
Tate, J.A. MO 1st & 4th Cons.Inf. Co.I
Tate, J.A. MO 4th Inf. Co.I
Tate, J.A. VA 4th Cav. Co.C
Tate, Jack VA 56th Inf. Co.F
Tate, Jackson TN 44th Inf. Co.B
Tate, Jackson TN 44th (Cons.) Inf. Co.K
Tate, Jacob GA Cav. 6th Bn. (St.Guards) Co.C
Tate, Jacob L. GA 24th Inf. Co.C Sgt.
Tate, James KY 5th Cav. Co.C
Tate, James KY 11th Cav. Co.G
Tate, James LA 1st Cav. Co.G
Tate, James MS 5th Cav. Co.D
Tate, James MS 28th Cav. Co.F
Tate, James NC 28th Inf. Co.A
Tate, James SC Palmetto S.S. Co.M
Tate, James TN 7th (Duckworth's) Cav. Co.C
Tate, James TN 7th Inf. Co.K
Tate, James TX Cav. Madison's Regt. Co.D Bugler
Tate, James VA 15th Cav. Co.E
Tate, James VA Cav. 15th Bn. Co.C
Tate, James VA 1st Inf. Co.B
Tate, James A. VA 29th Inf. Co.E
Tate, James Alexander MO 8th Inf. Co.C
Tate, James B. SC 18th Inf. Co.H Sgt.
Tate, James B. TN 35th Inf. 1st Co.A, Co.H
Tate, James B. VA 58th Inf. Co.H
Tate, James Bond English MS 7th Cav. Co.E
Tate, James C. GA 21st Inf. Co.K
Tate, James C. TN 29th Inf. Co.G
Tate, James D. TN 35th Inf. Co.B
Tate, James F. VA Lt.Arty. Arch. Graham's Co.
Tate, James G. GA 1st (Ramsey's) Inf. Co.K
Tate, James G. GA 53rd Inf. Co.K
Tate, James G. NC 2nd Home Guards Co.D
Tate, James G. VA 4th Inf. Co.A Sgt.
Tate, James G. VA Inf. 21st Bn. 2nd Co.D
Tate, James G. VA 64th Mtd.Inf. Co.D
Tate, James H. GA 4th (Clinch's) Cav. Co.F Sgt.
Tate, James H. VA Inf. 22nd Bn. Co.H
Tate, James H.B. VA 56th Inf. Co.F
Tate, James K.P. NC 16th Inf. Co.E Sgt.
Tate, James L. VA 56th Inf. Co.F
Tate, James M. AL 3rd Inf. Co.C 1stLt.
Tate, James M. AL 15th Inf. Co.A
Tate, James M. AL 44th Inf. Co.B
Tate, James M. AL 46th Inf. Co.A
Tate, James M. NC 13th Inf. Co.I
Tate, James M. NC 13th Inf. Co.K
Tate, James R. NC 16th Inf. Co.D Lt.
Tate, James S. GA 21st Inf. Co.D
Tate, James S. TN 1st (Turney's) Inf. Co.A
Tate, James T. AR Inf. 4th Bn. Co.B Sgt.
Tate, James T. NC 13th Inf. Co.E
Tate, James W. AL 28th Inf. Co.G
Tate, James W. LA Inf. 9th Bn. Co.D
Tate, James W. MO 8th Inf. Co.B
Tate, Jasper AL 13th Inf. Co.K Cpl.
Tate, Jasper GA 1st Reg. Co.E Cpl.
Tate, J.B. AL 50th Inf. Co.H
Tate, J.B. TN 16th Inf. Co.A
Tate, J.B. TN 51st Inf. Co.D Capt.
Tate, J.B. TN 51st (Cons.) Inf. Co.F Bvt.2nd Lt.
Tate, J.C. AR 19th (Dawson's) Inf. Co.H
Tate, J.D. GA Inf. 11th Bn. (St.Guards) Co.D Cpl.
Tate, J.D. GA 24th Inf. Co.C
Tate, J.D. TN 63rd Inf. Co.K
Tate, Jefferson AL 4th (Russell's) Cav. Co.G
Tate, Jeremiah GA 45th Inf. Co.D
Tate, Jesse AL 5th Inf. New Co.H
Tate, Jesse NC 66th Inf. Co.I
Tate, Jesse TX 9th (Young's) Inf. Co.G Cpl.
Tate, Jesse M. TN 21st Inf. Co.I 1st Lt.
Tate, Jesse M. VA 25th Cav. Co.G Cpl.
Tate, Jesse N. LA 16th Inf. Co.F
Tate, Jesse O. AL 50th Inf. Co.H
Tate, J.F. AL 15th Inf. Co.K
Tate, J.F. LA 28th (Gray's) Inf. Co.C
Tate, J.F. SC 3rd Bn.Res. Co.A
Tate, J.G. VA Mil. Scott Cty.
Tate, J.H. AR Inf. Adams' Regt. Moore's Co. Cpl.
Tate, J.H. MS Cav. 4th Bn. Co.A
Tate, J.H. TX 12th Cav. Co.G Sgt.
Tate, J.H. VA 2nd Arty. Co.H
Tate, J.H. 8th (Wade's) Conf.Cav. Co.C
Tate, J.H.S. MS 7th Inf. Co.D Sgt.
Tate, J.J. LA 3rd (Wingfield's) Cav. Co.E
Tate, J.J. LA 4th Inf. Old Co.G
Tate, J.J. TN 35th Inf. 1st Co.A
Tate, J.K. TN 33rd Inf. Co.I Sgt.
Tate, J.K. TX 17th Inf. Co.E
Tate, J.K.P. MO 11th Inf. Co.G
Tate, J.L. AR Cav. McGehee's Regt. Co.C
Tate, J.L. AR 6th Inf. New Co.F

Tate, J.L. AR 12th Inf. Co.D
Tate, J.L. AR 38th Inf. New Co.I
Tate, J.L. TN 50th Inf. Co.E
Tate, J.L. 8th (Wade's) Conf.Cav. Co.I
Tate, J.M. AL Cav. (St.Res.) Young's Co.
Tate, J.M. AL 4th Inf. Co.A Cpl.
Tate, J.M. AL 5th Inf. New Co.H
Tate, J.M. AR 8th Cav. Co.F
Tate, J.M. AR 24th Inf. Co.A
Tate, J.M. AR Inf. Cocke's Regt. Co.F
Tate, J.M. GA 1st St.Line 1st Lt.
Tate, J.M. LA Miles' Legion Co.E Sgt.
Tate, J.M. MS Blythe's Bn. (St.Troops) Capt.,AQM
Tate, J.M. TN 12th (Cons.) Inf. Co.G
Tate, J.M. TN 19th Inf. Co.K
Tate, J.M. VA 62nd Mtd.Inf. Co.C
Tate, J.M. VA 72nd Mil. Sgt.
Tate, J.N. GA 23rd Inf. Co.C
Tate, J.N. TN 22nd Inf. Co.G
Tate, J.O. SC 2nd Inf. Co.C
Tate, Jo TN 2nd (Ashby's) Cav. Co.F
Tate, Joel C. VA 10th Cav. Co.C
Tate, John AL 9th (Malone's) Cav. Co.B
Tate, John AL 12th Cav. Co.A
Tate, John AL 32nd Inf. Co.B
Tate, John AR 1st (Monroe's) Cav. Co.H
Tate, John GA Cav. Logan's Co. (White Cty. Old Men's Home Guards)
Tate, John KY 8th Cav. Co.E
Tate, John KY 11th Cav. Co.C
Tate, John MS 10th Cav. Co.I
Tate, John MO 4th Inf. Co.K
Tate, John MO 16th Inf. Co.C
Tate, John TN 2nd (Ashby's) Cav. Co.G
Tate, John TN Cav. 4th Bn. (Branner's) Co.B
Tate, John TN 16th Inf. Co.D
Tate, John TN 24th Bn.S.S. Co.B
Tate, John TX 11th Inf. Co.E
Tate, John VA 16th Cav. Co.C
Tate, John VA Inf. 1st Bn.Loc.Def. Co.B
Tate, John, Jr. VA Inf. 1st Bn.Loc.Def. Co.A
Tate, John 3rd Conf.Eng.Troops Co.G
Tate, John A. GA 39th Inf. Co.B Sgt.
Tate, John A. NC Cav. 5th Bn. Co.C Sgt.
Tate, John A. NC 6th Cav. (65th St.Troops) Co.C Sgt.
Tate, John A. NC 53rd Inf. Co.A Sgt.
Tate, John A. VA 29th Inf. Co.E
Tate, John Bell TN 7th Inf. Co.H
Tate, John C. GA 1st Reg. Co.I
Tate, John C. GA 32nd Inf. Co.H
Tate, John C. NC 4th Cav. (59th St.Troops) Co.B
Tate, John E. AL 37th Inf. Co.H
Tate, John E. GA Phillips' Legion Co.C
Tate, John E. MO Staff St.Guard Capt.,Asst.Div.Com.
Tate, John F. AL 17th Inf. Co.G Lt.Col.
Tate, John G. NC 24th Inf. Co.H
Tate, John H. SC 1st Arty. Co.I
Tate, John H. TN Cav. 9th Bn. (Gantt's) Co.D
Tate, John H. VA Hvy.Arty. A.J. Jones' Co.
Tate, John Harvey Steen MS 7th Cav. Co.E Sgt.
Tate, John J. MS Applewhite's Co. (Vaiden Guards)
Tate, John K. TN 59th Mtd.Inf. Co.K
Tate, John M. AR 26th Inf. Co.E Jr.2nd Lt.
Tate, John M. GA Inf. 19th Bn. (St.Guards) Co.B
Tate, John M. GA 23rd Inf. Co.H
Tate, John M. NC 11th (Bethel Regt.) Inf. Co.D QM
Tate, John M. NC 29th Inf. Co.E
Tate, John M. VA 19th Inf. Co.C
Tate, John M. VA Inf. 21st Bn. 1st Co.D
Tate, John M. Wilcox's Staff Capt.,AQM
Tate, John O. SC 18th Inf. Co.F
Tate, John P. MS 27th Inf. Co.E
Tate, John P. NC 62nd Inf. Co.C
Tate, John P. TX 31st Cav. Co.E
Tate, John R. AR 1st (Crawford's) Cav. Co.G
Tate, John S. GA 1st (Fannin's) Res. Co.D
Tate, John S. MO Inf. Perkins' Bn.
Tate, John S. VA Inf. 9th Bn. Co.A Sgt.
Tate, John S. VA 25th Inf. 2nd Co.A 2nd Lt.
Tate, John S. VA 56th Inf. Co.F
Tate, John W. MO Cav. Wood's Regt. Co.E
Tate, John W. MO 1st & 4th Cons.Inf. Co.H
Tate, John W. TX 22nd Cav. Co.B
Tate, John W. VA Cav. Caldwell's Bn. Hankins' Co.
Tate, John W. VA 45th Inf. Co.A
Tate, John William Steen MS 7th Cav. Co.E Cpl.
Tate, Jonathan GA 1st Inf. (St.Guards) Co.A
Tate, Jos. GA 23rd Inf. Co.C
Tate, Joseph AR 19th (Dawson's) Inf. Co.B
Tate, Joseph GA Inf. (Mell Scouts) Wyly's Co. Orderly Sgt.
Tate, Joseph LA 15th Bn.S.S. (Weatherly's) Co.D
Tate, Joseph NC 7th Sr.Res. Bradshaw's Co.
Tate, Joseph TN Cav. 4th Bn. (Branner's) Co.F
Tate, Joseph TN 11th Cav. Co.D
Tate, Joseph TN 63rd Inf. Co.K
Tate, Joseph VA 34th Inf. Co.H
Tate, Joseph D. TN 29th Inf. Co.G
Tate, Joseph E. VA 48th Inf. Co.H Sgt.
Tate, Joseph L. GA 57th Inf. Co.A Sgt.
Tate, Joseph M. NC 62nd Inf. Co.C 1st Lt.
Tate, Joseph M.C. VA 51st Inf. Co.A
Tate, Joseph P. TX 2nd Cav. Co.D
Tate, Joseph W. NC 33rd Inf. Co.F 2nd Lt.
Tate, Josiah MS 4th Inf. Co.K
Tate, J.P. TX Cav. 2nd Regt. Co.D
Tate, J.R. MS St.Cav. 2nd Bn. (Harris') Co.C
Tate, J.R. MS 11th (Cons.) Cav. Co.I
Tate, J.S. TN 11th (Holman's) Cav. Co.L
Tate, J.T. AL Inf. 2nd Regt. Co.K
Tate, J.T. AR 1st (Monroe's) Cav. Co.H
Tate, J.T. AR 5th Inf. Co.G
Tate, Junius C. NC 3rd Cav. (41st St.Troops) Co.F 1st Lt.
Tate, Junius C. NC Cav. 5th Bn. Co.C Capt.
Tate, Junius C. NC 6th Cav. (65th St.Troops) Co.H,C Capt.
Tate, Junius W. NC 6th Cav. (65th St.Troops) Co.H
Tate, J.W. AR Inf. Cocke's Regt. Co.F
Tate, J.W. MS 7th Cav. Co.F
Tate, J.W. MS 23rd Inf. Co.E
Tate, J.W. TN 4th Inf. Co.B 1st Lt.
Tate, J.W. TN 50th Inf. Co.E
Tate, J.W. TX 8th Inf. Co.K
Tate, J.W. VA 53rd Inf. Co.B
Tate, J.W. Brush Bn.
Tate, J. Yancey TX 17th Inf. Co.D
Tate, Kinchen T. NC 15th Inf. Co.C
Tate, Kinchen T. NC 28th Inf. Co.H
Tate, K.K. MO Cav. Freeman's Regt. Co.E
Tate, Knox P. NC 54th Inf. Co.B Sgt.
Tate, L.A. AL 19th Inf. Co.A
Tate, Lance L. TX 18th Inf. Co.F
Tate, Larkin C. SC 1st St.Troops Co.H
Tate, Lastee LA 2nd Cav. Co.A
Tate, Lawrence VA Mtd.Res. Rappahannock Dist. Sale's Co.
Tate, L.C. SC 3rd Res. Co.C
Tate, L.D. AL 18th Bn.Vol. Co.C
Tate, Lemuel A. AL 31st Inf. Co.E
Tate, Levi VA 29th Inf. Co.E
Tate, Lewis LA Miles' Legion Co.F
Tate, Lewis F. NC 28th Inf. Co.I
Tate, L.F. TN 3rd (Forrest's) Cav. 1st Co.B
Tate, L.O. 8th (Wade's) Conf.Cav. Co.I
Tate, L.R. NC 57th Inf. Co.B
Tate, M. MS 3rd Cav. Co.A
Tate, Madison FL 2nd Cav. Co.A
Tate, Madison GA 29th Inf. Co.C
Tate, Martin V. TX 15th Cav. Co.C 2nd Lt.
Tate, Martin V. TX Granbury's Cons.Brig. Co.F 2nd Lt.
Tate, Mathew W. VA 13th Cav. Co.E
Tate, M.B. VA 51st Inf. QM
Tate, M.D. AR Cav. Gordon's Regt. Co.D
Tate, Menasseh M. SC 5th Inf. 2nd Co.C
Tate, Mitchell B. Gen. & Staff Capt.,QM
Tate, M.J. AR Inf. Hardy's Regt. Torbett's Co.
Tate, M.L. GA 23rd Inf. Co.C Sgt.
Tate, M.L. LA 3rd (Wingfield's) Cav. Co.C
Tate, M.L. LA 16th Inf. Co.C
Tate, M.L. MS 4th Inf. Co.C
Tate, M.M. AR Mtd.Vol. (St.Troops) Abraham's Co.
Tate, M.M. SC 6th Inf. 1st Co.I
Tate, Moses J. AR 19th (Dawson's) Inf. Co.A
Tate, M.V. TX 12th Cav. Co.G
Tate, Nathan MS Lt.Arty. 14th Bn. Co.B
Tate, Nathan TN 7th (Duckworth's) Cav. Co.E
Tate, Nathan G. VA 56th Inf. Co.F
Tate, Nathaniel TN 48th (Voorhies') Inf. Co.E
Tate, Nelson N. VA 23rd Inf. Co.G
Tate, Newton W. GA Inf. 8th Bn. Co.B
Tate, Nicholas B. MS 22nd Inf. Co.E 1st Sgt.
Tate, Norvell F.H. AL 21st Inf. Co.H
Tate, N.W. LA 4th Inf. Co.A
Tate, Obed MS 2nd (Quinn's St.Troops) Inf. Co.C
Tate, O.E. SC 5th Inf. 2nd Co.C
Tate, Onez LA 2nd Cav. Co.A Cpl.
Tate, P. LA 16th Inf. Co.F
Tate, P. NC 7th Sr.Res. Bradshaw's Co.
Tate, P.C. VA 15th Inf. Co.C
Tate, Perryman GA Cav. 10th Bn. (St.Guards) Co.B
Tate, Perryman M. TN Lt.Arty. Barry's Co.
Tate, Peter LA Mil. 1st Regt. 3rd Brig. 1st Div. Co.G
Tate, Philip VA 9th Mil. Co.A
Tate, Phillip VA 2nd Arty. Co.G

Tate, Phocion TX 8th Cav. Co.F 1st Lt.
Tate, Pickens GA Cav. 9th Bn. (St.Guards) Co.C
Tate, Pinckney J. SC 2nd Cav. Co.A
Tate, P.J. SC 4th Cav. Co.K
Tate, Polk TN 62nd Mtd.Inf. Co.H
Tate, R. LA 15th Bn.S.S. (Weatherly's) Co.D
Tate, R.A. TN 17th Inf. Co.D
Tate, R.A. TX 17th Inf. Co.E
Tate, R.B. GA Lt.Arty. 12th Bn. 3rd Co.C
Tate, R.B. MS 1st (Johnston's) Inf. Co.B 1st Lt.
Tate, R.C. AL Cav. Goldsby's Scouts
Tate, R.C. TN 30th Inf. Co.K Cpl.
Tate, R.C. VA 51st Inf. Co.B
Tate, Reuben TX 22nd Inf. Co.E
Tate, Reuben N. VA 56th Inf. Co.F
Tate, R.H. AR Cav. Gordon's Regt. Co.D
Tate, R.H. Brush Bn.
Tate, Richard MO Cav. Wood's Regt. Co.E
Tate, Richard VA 56th Inf. Co.F
Tate, Richard A. VA 38th Inf. Co.C
Tate, Riley J. GA 23rd Inf. Co.H
Tate, R.J. TN 84th Inf. Co.A
Tate, R.L. AR 34th Inf. Co.G
Tate, R.M. NC 6th Cav. (65th St.Troops) Co.H
Tate, Robbert W. AR 27th Inf. Co.K
Tate, Robert AR 5th (St.Troops) Inf. Dowd's Co.
Tate, Robert KY 8th Cav. Co.E
Tate, Robert LA 2nd Cav. Co.A 2nd Lt.
Tate, Robert MS 1st Bn.S.S. Co.B Comsy.Sgt.
Tate, Robert MS 4th Inf. Co.G
Tate, Robert MS 25th Inf. Co.A
Tate, Robert MS 29th Inf. Co.K
Tate, Robert MS 31st Inf. Co.G
Tate, Robert MS Inf. (Red Rebels) D.J. Red's Co.
Tate, Robert NC 13th Inf. Co.A
Tate, Robert NC 33rd Inf. Co.I
Tate, Robert TN 2nd (Walker's) Inf. Co.A
Tate, Robert Sap. & Min. G.W. Maxson's Co.,CSA
Tate, Robert A. NC 6th Cav. (65th St.Troops) Co.H,C
Tate, Robert A. NC 16th Inf. Co.E
Tate, Robert A. NC 22nd Inf. Co.B 1st Lt.
Tate, Robt. B. AL 21st Inf. Co.C
Tate, Robert B. NC 27th Inf. Co.B
Tate, Robert B. VA 51st Inf. Co.A
Tate, Robert F. MS 17th Inf. Co.K
Tate, Robert H. FL 2nd Inf. Co.E Cpl.
Tate, Robert H. VA 1st Arty. Co.D
Tate, Robert H. VA Lt.Arty. 1st Bn. Co.D
Tate, Robert J. VA 1st Lt.Arty. Co.B Cpl.
Tate, Robert J. VA Lt.Arty. J.S. Brown's Co. Sgt.
Tate, Robert J. VA Lt.Arty. Taylor's Co. Sgt.
Tate, Robert McD. NC 16th Inf. Co.E 1stSgt.
Tate, Robert W.E. NC 46th Inf. Co.C
Tate, R.P.H. TN 8th (Smith's) Cav. Co.F
Tate, R.T. AL 3rd Bn. Hilliard's Legion Vol. Co.E
Tate, Russill GA 24th Inf. Co.D
Tate, R.W. AR 16th Inf. Co.K
Tate, S. MS 2nd St.Cav. Co.B
Tate, Samuel GA 23rd Inf. Co.E Capt.
Tate, Samuel MS 31st Inf. Co.H
Tate, Samuel MO 1st N.E. Cav. Co.D
Tate, Samuel MO Cav. Preston's Bn. Co.C
Tate, Samuel MO 2nd Inf.
Tate, Samuel TN 4th Cav. Co.D
Tate, Samuel TN 15th Inf. Co.D
Tate, Samuel 10th Conf.Cav. Co.B
Tate, Samuel Gen. & Staff Col.,Vol.ADC
Tate, Samuel C. AL Cav. 5th Bn. Hilliard's Legion Co.B
Tate, Samuel Ephraim MS 7th Cav. Co.E
Tate, Samuel L. AL 4th (Russell's) Cav. Co.D Cpl.
Tate, Samuel M. VA Courtney Arty.
Tate, Samuel McDowell NC 6th Inf. Co.D Lt.Col.
Tate, Samuel P. NC 22nd Inf. Co.B 1st Lt.
Tate, S.B. VA 37th Inf. Co.A
Tate, S.C.W. NC 1st Inf. (6 mo. '61) Co.G
Tate, S.G. SC 16th & 24th (Cons.) Inf. Co.F
Tate, Silas FL 2nd Cav. Co.A
Tate, S.M. AL 45th Inf. Co.E
Tate, Solon R. AL 63rd Inf. Co.A Cpl.
Tate, S.P. AR 13th Mil. Co.G Capt.
Tate, S.P. MS Cav. 1st Bn. (Montgomery's) St.Troops Hammond's Co.
Tate, Spartan G. SC 16th Inf. Co.K
Tate, Spencer MO 8th Inf. Co.F
Tate, S.S. MS 4th Inf. Co.G
Tate, S.S. MS 19th Inf. Co.A
Tate, Stephen TN 16th Inf. Co.E
Tate, Step T. VA Lt.Arty. King's Co.
Tate, S.W. GA 45th Inf. Co.I
Tate, T. GA 3rd Res. Co.D
Tate, T. MS Inf. 2nd Bn. (St.Troops) Co.D
Tate, T.A. NC 1st Inf. (6 mo. '61) Co.B
Tate, Talifaro S. KY 2nd (Duke's) Cav. Co.F
Tate, T.G. TN 7th (Duckworth's) Cav. Co.A
Tate, T.G. Forrest's Scouts T. Henderson's Co.,CSA
Tate, T.H.B. VA 3rd Cav. Co.E
Tate, Theodore C. GA 21st Inf. Co.G Sgt.
Tate, Thomas AL 23rd Inf. Co.A
Tate, Thomas GA 4th Cav. (St.Guards) Robertson's Co.
Tate, Thomas LA 27th Inf. Co.H
Tate, Thomas MS 5th Cav. Co.I
Tate, Thomas MS 28th Cav. Co.F
Tate, Thomas MS 38th Cav. Co.I
Tate, Thomas NC 16th Inf. Co.D
Tate, Thomas NC 33rd Inf. Co.I
Tate, Thomas TN 7th (Duckworth's) Cav. Co.A Cpl.
Tate, Thomas VA 9th Cav. Sandford's Co.
Tate, Thomas VA 15th Cav. Co.A
Tate, Thomas VA Cav. 15th Bn. Co.A
Tate, Thomas VA 111th Mil. Co.5
Tate, Thomas B. TX Cav. Madison's Regt. Co.F
Tate, Thomas D. SC 6th Inf. 1st Co.I Sgt.
Tate, Thomas G. MS 1st (Johnston's) Inf. Co.D 2nd Lt.
Tate, Thomas J. AL 34th Inf. Breedlove's Co.
Tate, Thomas J. AL 44th Inf. Co.I Sgt.
Tate, Thomas J. MS 3rd Inf. (St.Troops) Co.G
Tate, Thomas Jefferson MS 34th Inf. Co.A
Tate, Thomas L. VA 4th Res. Co.E,G Capt.
Tate, Thomas M. FL 1st Inf. Old Co.C Cpl.
Tate, Thomas M. MS 35th Inf. Co.D
Tate, Thomas R. SC 1st (McCreary's) Inf. Co.G
Tate, Thomas S. TN 4th Inf. Co.A
Tate, Tilman SC 1st St.Troops Co.C
Tate, T.J. MS 3rd Cav. Co.A
Tate, T.N. TN 49th Inf. Co.D
Tate, T. Rudolph SC 1st Inf. Co.H
Tate, T.S., Jr. KY 12th Cav. Maj.
Tate, T.S., Jr. MS 5th Cav. Co.A
Tate, T.S. TN 7th (Duckworth's) Cav. Co.A
Tate, T.Z. MS 40th Inf. Co.H
Tate, T.Z. 8th (Wade's) Conf.Cav. Co.I
Tate, Uriah MS 38th Cav. Co.A
Tate, Uriah VA 29th Inf. Co.E
Tate, Van GA 23rd Inf. Co.H
Tate, Van B. AR 27th Inf. Co.K Capt.
Tate, Vincent S. AR 5th Inf. Co.B 2nd Lt.
Tate, Vincent S. VA Cav. 39th Bn. Co.D
Tate, W. AR 35th Inf. Co.D
Tate, W. MS Inf. 2nd Bn. (St.Troops) Co.C
Tate, Waddy T. GA 11th Inf. Co.A
Tate, Walter AL 3rd Cav. Co.D
Tate, Walter TN 50th Inf. Co.E
Tate, Warren A. VA 2nd Bn.Res. Co.B
Tate, W.B. MS 35th Inf. Co.D
Tate, W.B. NC 3rd Arty. (40th St.Troops) Co.G
Tate, W.C. MS Cav. Part.Rangers Rhodes' Co.
Tate, W.C. 14th Conf.Cav. Co.F
Tate, W.D. GA 12th Cav. Co.C Cpl.
Tate, W.D. GA 9th Inf. Co.B
Tate, W.D. GA 23rd Inf. Co.C
Tate, W.E. TN 3rd (Forrest's) Cav. Co.C
Tate, W.F.M. MS 35th Inf. Co.D
Tate, W.H. FL 2nd Cav.
Tate, W.H. MS Cav. Ham's Regt. Co.I Cpl.
Tate, W.H. TN 21st (Wilson's) Cav. Co.G
Tate, W.H. TN 50th Inf. Co.E
Tate, William AL 16th Inf. Co.K
Tate, William AL 40th Inf. Co.A
Tate, Wm. AL Cp. of Instr. Talladega
Tate, William AR Inf. Cocke's Regt. Co.K
Tate, William GA Cav. 9th Bn. (St.Guards) Co.C
Tate, Wm. GA 1st St.Line Maj.
Tate, William KY 11th Cav. Co.C
Tate, William MS 1st Cav. Co.G
Tate, William MS 1st (Patton's) Inf. Halfacre's Co. Cpl.
Tate, William MO 6th Cav. Co.G
Tate, William MO Cav. Freeman's Regt. Co.E
Tate, William MO Cav. Fristoe's Regt. Co.B Sgt.
Tate, William NC 6th Inf. Co.F
Tate, William NC 8th Inf. Co.I
Tate, William NC 13th Inf. Co.I
Tate, William TN 1st (Turney's) Inf. Co.A
Tate, William TN 19th Inf. Co.K
Tate, William TN 22nd Inf. Looney's Co.
Tate, William TN 38th Inf. Co.L
Tate, William TN 59th Mtd.Inf. Co.B
Tate, William TX 8th Cav. Co.F 2nd Lt.
Tate, William TX Cav. Cater's Bn. Co.I Capt.
Tate, William VA 9th Cav. Sandford's Co.
Tate, William VA 15th Cav. Co.E
Tate, William VA Cav. 15th Bn. Co.C
Tate, William VA 29th Inf. Co.E
Tate, William VA 111th Mil. Co.5
Tate, William VA Mil. Carroll Cty.
Tate, William A. MS 28th Cav. Co.H
Tate, William B. NC 15th Inf. Co.C
Tate, William B. SC 1st (Orr's) Rifles Co.D Cpl.

Tate, William B. TN Cav. 4th Bn. (Branner's) Co.E
Tate, William C. AL 3rd Inf. Co.C
Tate, William C. TX 24th Cav. Co.K Sgt.
Tate, William D. AL Vol. Rabby's Coast Guard Co., No.1
Tate, William D. 1st Conf.Inf. 2nd Co.H
Tate, William F. SC 3rd Res. Co.F
Tate, William G. NC 13th Inf. Co.K
Tate, William H. AL 33rd Inf. Co.H
Tate, William H. AR 1st Vol. Co.C
Tate, William H. GA 4th (Clinch's) Cav. Co.A,F
Tate, William H. MS 11th Inf. Co.F Sgt.
Tate, William H. NC 16th Inf. Co.L Sgt.
Tate, William H. TN 1st (Turney's) Inf. Co.A
Tate, William H. TN 35th Inf. 1st Co.A, Co.H
Tate, William H. TN 48th (Voorhies') Inf. Co.E
Tate, William H. VA 11th Inf. Co.I
Tate, William H. VA 51st Inf. Co.B Capt.
Tate, William I. LA Hvy.Arty. 8th Bn. Co.3
Tate, William J. AL Cp. of Instr. Talladega
Tate, William J. GA 8th Cav. Old Co.D Sgt.
Tate, William J. GA 12th Cav. Co.D
Tate, William J. GA 12th Cav. Co.I
Tate, William J. GA 62nd Cav. Co.D Sgt.
Tate, William J. GA Lt.Arty. Scogin's Btty. (Griffin Lt.Arty.)
Tate, William J. GA 1st Reg. Co.I
Tate, William J. GA 1st (Ramsey's) Inf. Co.K
Tate, William J. GA 6th Inf. Co.A
Tate, William J. GA 32nd Inf. Co.H Cpl.
Tate, William J. GA 36th (Broyles') Inf. Co.B
Tate, William J. TN 19th Inf. Co.I
Tate, William J. VA 4th Inf. Co.A
Tate, William L. NC 6th Cav. (65th St.Troops) Co.C Sgt.Maj.
Tate, William L. NC 1st Inf. (6 mo. '61) Co.E
Tate, William L. VA 10th Cav. Co.F
Tate, William M. MS 2nd Inf. Co.B,L Cpl.
Tate, William M. SC 5th Res. Co.G
Tate, William M. TN 3rd (Lillard's) Mtd.Inf. Co.B,E
Tate, William N. NC 3rd Arty. (40th St.Troops) Co.C
Tate, William N. TN 7th Inf. Co.H Capt.
Tate, William P. AL 18th Inf. Co.C
Tate, William R. AL 3rd Cav. Co.D Sgt.
Tate, William R. MS 37th Inf. Co.C
Tate, William R. NC 6th Inf. Co.F
Tate, William R. TN Lt.Arty. Tobin's Co. Cpl.
Tate, William T. VA Lt.Arty. Kirkpatrick's Co.
Tate, William W. AL Cav. Barbiere's Bn. Brown's Co. Sgt.
Tate, Willis G. SC 16th Inf. Co.C
Tate, Wilson LA 3rd (Wingfield's) Cav. Co.F Capt.
Tate, W.J. GA 60th Inf. Co.D
Tate, W.J. LA Siege Train Bn. Co.D Cpl.
Tate, W.J. LA 25th Inf. Co.G
Tate, W.J. TN 7th (Duckworth's) Cav. Co.E Capt.
Tate, W.K. AL 5th Cav. Co.D
Tate, W.M. GA 12th Cav. Co.I
Tate, W.M. Gen. & Staff Maj.,Comsy.
Tate, W.N. GA 18th Inf. Co.H
Tate, W.P. GA 12th Cav. Co.A 1st Sgt.
Tate, W.P. MO 9th (Elliott's) Cav.
Tate, W.P. NC 6th Inf. Co.K
Tate, W.P. TN 2nd (Ashby's) Cav. Co.I
Tate, W.P. TX 9th Cav. Co.B
Tate, W.R. TN 60th Mtd.Inf. Co.G
Tate, W.S. GA 1st Inf. (St.Guards) Co.B
Tate, W.S. NC 6th Inf. Co.K
Tate, W.T. GA 15th Inf. Co.C
Tate, W.W. AL 54th Inf.
Tate, W.W. AR 1st Mtd.Rifles Co.C Sgt.
Tate, W.W. GA 39th Inf. Co.K
Tate, W.W. GA 60th Inf. Co.D
Tate, W.W. VA Inf. 2nd Bn.Loc.Def. Co.A
Tate, W.Y. AR 50th Mil. Co.C Cpl.
Tate, W.Z. AR 1st (Monroe's) Cav. Co.H
Tate, W.Z. AR 2nd Vol. Co.B
Tate, Z. AR 15th Mil. Co.C
Tate, Z. TN 22nd (Barteau's) Cav. Co.A
Tate, Z. TX 35th (Likens') Cav. Co.H
Tate, Zachariah AL 31st Inf. Co.A
Tate, Zachariah KY 4th Cav. Co.I
Tate, Zachariah KY 9th Cav. Co.I
Tate, Zachariah MS 43rd Inf. Co.L
Tate, Zachariah B. GA 11th Inf. Co.A Cpl.
Tate, Zack TN Cav. 1st Bn. (McNairy's) Co.A
Tate, Z.T. GA 1st Cav.
Tatem, Arthur H. VA 41st Inf. Co.F Cpl.
Tatem, Barry VA 16th Inf. Co.C
Tatem, Benjamin T. VA 41st Inf. Co.F
Tatem, Benjamin T. VA 61st Inf. Co.E QMSgt.
Tatem, B.F. TN 13th Inf. Co.B Sgt.
Tatem, Camillus E. VA 41st Inf. Co.F
Tatem, Camillus E. VA 61st Inf. Co.E Sgt.
Tatem, C.J. AR 15th Inf. Co.I
Tatem, David T. NC 4th Cav. (59th St.Troops) Co.G
Tatem, E.A. VA 5th Cav. Co.K
Tatem, Elijah A. VA 41st Inf. Co.F
Tatem, George W. VA 61st Inf. Co.I,K Sgt.
Tatem, George W. VA Inf. Cohoon's Bn. Co.C Sgt.
Tatem, G.W. LA 25th Inf. Co.I Cpl.
Tatem, Holowell NC 4th Cav. (59th St.Troops) Co.G
Tatem, Jackson AR 19th (Dockery's) Inf. Co.A
Tatem, J.N. AL Inf. 1st Regt. Co.G Sgt.
Tatem, John F. FL 5th Inf. Co.D
Tatem, John J. NC 4th Cav. (59th St.Troops) Co.G
Tatem, John W. VA 41st Inf. Co.F Cpl.
Tatem, Moses H. NC 60th Inf. Co.A
Tatem, Nathaniel C. VA 41st Inf. Co.F
Tatem, Samuel VA 61st Inf. Co.D Cook
Tatem, Thaddeus C. NC 4th Cav. (59th St.Troops) Co.G
Tatem, William TN 14th (Neely's) Cav. Co.H
Tatem, William B. NC 4th Cav. (59th St.Troops) Co.G
Tatem, William B. VA 32nd Inf. Co.E
Tatem, William H. VA 39th Inf. Co.B
Tater, Nicholas VA Mil. Scott Cty.
Tates, W. VA 3rd Cav. Co.B
Tates, William TX Cav. Ragsdale's Bn. Co.C
Tatham, Benton NC Walker's Bn. Thomas' Legion Co.E Sgt.
Tatham, Bernard GA 17th Inf. Co.B
Tatham, David NC 62nd Inf. Co.H
Tatham, George VA 39th Inf. Co.D
Tatham, James NC 62nd Inf. Co.H
Tatham, Jasper N. NC 25th Inf. Co.D Sgt.
Tatham, J.C. AL 49th Inf. Co.B 1st Lt.
Tatham, Jesse VA 39th Inf. Co.G
Tatham, J.F. TN 19th Inf. Co.F 2nd Lt.
Tatham, John NC 16th Inf. Co.A
Tatham, John NC 39th Inf. Co.K
Tatham, John G. NC 25th Inf. Co.D
Tatham, J.R. AL 3rd Inf. Co.C
Tatham, Julius M. NC 25th Inf. Co.D
Tatham, Leander B. NC 25th Inf. Co.D Capt.
Tatham, Pinkney B. NC Walker's Bn. Thomas' Legion Co.E Sgt.
Tatham, Thomas N. NC 16th Inf. Co.A
Tatham, Thomas N. NC 39th Inf. Co.K
Tatham, Thomas N. NC Inf. Thomas Legion 1st Co.A
Tatham, William C. NC Walker's Bn. Thomas' Legion Co.E 2nd Lt.
Tatherly, M.W. NC 17th Inf. (1st Org.) Co.A 3rd Lt.
Tathum, T.A. AL 35th Inf. Co.C
Tatier, B.K. LA 18th Inf.
Tatier, B.K. LA Inf.Cons. 18th Regt. & Yellow Jacket Bn.
Tatliff, W.B. AL Cav. W. Graves' Co. Sgt.
Tatman, Augustus VA 55th Inf. Co.L
Tatman, B.T. TX 15th Inf. Co.A Sgt.,Music.
Tatman, Cyrus LA 16th Inf. Co.H
Tatman, J.N. TN Arty. Bibb's Co.
Tatner, D.E. KY 1st (Butler's) Cav. Co.A
Tatom, --- TX 1st (Yager's) Cav. Co.F
Tatom, A.C. MS 11th (Cons.) Cav. Co.H 2nd Lt.
Tatom, Abner C. MS Cav. Ham's Regt. Co.F 3rd Lt.
Tatom, Abner C. MS 43rd Inf. Co.H
Tatom, Abner L. AL 37th Inf. Co.H
Tatom, Alexander J. NC 2nd Arty. (36th St.Troops) Co.H
Tatom, Daniel S. NC 2nd Arty. (36th St.Troops) Co.I
Tatom, E.G. TN 45th Inf. Co.F
Tatom, Felix G. TX 22nd Cav. Co.A Cpl.
Tatom, George W. LA Inf. Jeff Davis Regt. Co.J
Tatom, George W. TX 1st Hvy.Arty. Co.D
Tatom, G.F. TN 22nd Inf. Co.H
Tatom, G.M. TN 48th (Nixon's) Inf. Co.D
Tatom, Hamilton NC 4th Bn.Jr.Res. Co.A Sgt.
Tatom, Hansom NC 18th Inf. Co.A
Tatom, Hugh McF. AL 32nd Inf. Co.C,B Capt.
Tatom, Ira A. AL 61st Inf. Co.G
Tatom, Ithamar AL 3rd Bn. Hilliard's Legion Vol. Co.B
Tatom, Jacob O. MS 43rd Inf. Co.H
Tatom, James AR 19th (Dockery's) Inf. Co.A
Tatom, James B. MS 43rd Inf. Co.H Sgt.
Tatom, J.F. GA 4th Res. Co.B
Tatom, J.F. MS Cav. 3rd (St.Troops) Co.C
Tatom, J.F. MS 1st Lt.Arty. Co.I
Tatom, J.M. GA 19th Inf. Co.C
Tatom, John MS 35th Inf. Co.D
Tatom, John H. GA 30th Inf. Co.H 1st Sgt.
Tatom, John H. NC 18th Inf. Co.K
Tatom, John R. GA 25th Inf. Cpl.
Tatom, John T. MS 3rd Inf. Co.C Color Cpl.
Tatom, Jordan R. GA 63rd Inf. Co.F

Tatom, Joseph W. GA Inf. 27th Bn. Co.B Cpl.
Tatom, J.P. TN 11th Inf. Co.K
Tatom, J.S. MS 36th Inf. Co.D Capt.
Tatom, J.S. TN 45th Inf. Co.F
Tatom, J.T. AL Hilliard's Legion Vol.
Tatom, L.D. TN 10th (DeMoss') Cav. Co.E
Tatom, Lennon A. NC 2nd Arty. (36th St.Troops) Co.I Cpl.
Tatom, Love A. NC 20th Inf. Co.F
Tatom, Love A. NC 30th Inf. Co.A
Tatom, Marshall N. NC 18th Inf. Co.A Sgt.
Tatom, M.S. GA 1st (Fannin's) Res. Co.C
Tatom, O. TN 15th (Cons.) Cav. Co.B
Tatom, Ollen C. NC 53rd Inf. Co.D
Tatom, Richard AR 24th Inf. Co.C
Tatom, Richard AR Inf. Hardy's Regt. Co.F
Tatom, Richard W. NC 2nd Arty. (36th St.Troops) Co.I 2nd Lt.
Tatom, Robert W. NC 2nd Arty. (36th St.Troops) Co.I
Tatom, Robert W. NC 18th Inf. Co.A
Tatom, S.G. AR 26th Inf. Co.G
Tatom, Simeon S. NC 18th Inf. Co.A
Tatom, S.W. AR 26th Inf. Co.G
Tatom, T.H. TN Arty. Marshall's Co.
Tatom, Thomas B. GA 41st Inf. Co.E
Tatom, Thomas C. AR 1st (Colquitt's) Inf. Co.H
Tatom, T.R. Inf. Bailey's Cons.Regt. Co.D
Tatom, Warren MS 1st Lt.Arty. Co.A
Tatom, W.B. TN 12th (Cons.) Inf. Co.G
Tatom, W.B. TN 22nd Inf. Co.G
Tatom, W.G. MS 4th Cav. Co.C
Tatom, William A. MS Cav. Ham's Regt. Co.F Sgt.
Tatom, William G. GA Inf. 27th Bn. Co.B
Tatom, William L.M. AR 9th Inf. Co.G
Tatom, William P. GA 15th Inf. Co.G
Tatom, William T. SC 1st (Butler's) Inf. Co.E,D,I Capt.
Taton, John A. MS 1st Inf. Co.H
Taton, N.B. Gen. & Staff AASurg.
Tator, Abner V. VA Mil. Grayson Cty.
Tatout, Felix F. LA Inf.Cons. 18th Regt. & Yellow Jacket Bn. Co.D 3rd Sgt.
Tatrell, James L. KY 7th Cav. Co.D Sgt.
Tats, J.E. TX Cav. Terry's Regt. Co.E
Tatsapaugh, William H. VA 17th Inf. Co.H
Tatsch, J. TX 33rd Cav. Co.E Bugler
Tatsch, Peter TX 6th Field Btty.
Tattan, Michael NC 2nd Inf. Co.A
Tatten, Michael NC 3rd Arty. (40th St.Troops) Co.H
Tattersall, William LA 20th Inf. Co.K
Tattman, Cyrus LA 3rd (Harrison's) Cav. Co.K
Tattnall, J.R.T. AL 29th Inf. Col.
Tatton, R. GA 8th Cav. Old Co.I
Tattum, J.H.D. AR 23rd Inf. Co.K
Tattum, Joseph H. VA Lt.Arty. J.S. Brown's Co.
Tatty, F.L. TN 10th (DeMoss') Cav. Co.G
Tatu, A.H. VA 22nd Cav. Co.G
Tatum, A. VA Inf. 44th Bn. Co.A
Tatum, Aaron AR 37th Inf. Co.A
Tatum, A.F. AL 6th Cav. Co.C
Tatum, A.F. MS 35th Inf. Co.A
Tatum, Albert AL 53rd (Part.Rangers) Co.K
Tatum, Alexander VA Hvy.Arty. 18th Bn. Co.C
Tatum, Allen VA Inf. 44th Bn. Co.A
Tatum, Alpha M.C. AL 53rd (Part.Rangers) Co.B
Tatum, A.M.C. AL 15th Inf. Co.F
Tatum, Andrew K. AL 61st Inf. Co.H Cpl.
Tatum, Ansylum AL 45th Inf. Co.C
Tatum, Augustus NC 24th Inf. Co.F
Tatum, Augustus R. VA 21st Inf. Co.F
Tatum, A.V. TN 48th (Voorhies') Inf. Co.D
Tatum, Bart F. TN 3rd (Forrest's) Cav. Co.B Capt.
Tatum, Benjamin AL 24th Inf. Co.H Sgt.
Tatum, Berry W. VA 59th Inf. 3rd Co.E
Tatum, B.F. MS 5th Inf. Co.E
Tatum, B.F. TN 3rd (Forrest's) Cav. Co.E,C
Tatum, B.F. TN 14th (Neely's) Cav. Co.H 1st Lt.
Tatum, B.F. TN 17th (Marshall's) Cav. Lt.
Tatum, B. Franklin AR 30th Inf. Co.B
Tatum, Caleb R. LA 27th Inf. Co.C
Tatum, Carter B. AL 10th Inf. Co.G
Tatum, Casper M. GA 34th Inf. Co.F
Tatum, C.C. LA Hvy.Arty. 2nd Bn. Co.D
Tatum, Charles E. VA Inf. 5th Bn. Co.C
Tatum, Charles J. AR 3rd Inf. Co.E
Tatum, Charles S. AR 23rd Inf. Co.G Cpl.
Tatum, Charles T. MO Cav. 3rd Bn. Co.C
Tatum, Charles William MS 8th Inf. Co.G
Tatum, C.M. GA 42nd Inf. Co.K
Tatum, Columbus M. MO Cav. 3rd Bn. Co.C
Tatum, Columbus N. MO 3rd Cav. Co.A
Tatum, C.T. AL 18th Inf. Co.K,E
Tatum, C.W. MS 10th Cav. Co.F
Tatum, Daniel GA 38th Inf. Co.I Cpl.
Tatum, Daniel MS Inf. 1st St.Troops Co.D
Tatum, Dave MO 5th Cav. Co.E
Tatum, David S. MO 16th Inf. Co.H
Tatum, David T. MO 4th Cav. Co.D
Tatum, D.F. MO 12th Cav. Co.D Cpl.
Tatum, E.A. AL 24th Inf. Co.K
Tatum, E.A. MS 44th Inf. Co.G,I
Tatum, E.A. VA 15th Cav. Co.I
Tatum, E.C. TX 8th Cav. Co.C
Tatum, Edmund P. AR 1st (Colquitt's) Inf. Co.A
Tatum, Edward VA 7th Inf. Co.A
Tatum, Edwin J. AL 45th Inf. Co.E
Tatum, E.J. AL 15th Bn.Part.Rangers Co.A
Tatum, E.L. TN 6th (Wheeler's) Cav. Co.A
Tatum, Elisha GA 38th Inf. Co.G,N
Tatum, Elja P. TN 4th Inf. Co.E
Tatum, E.W. NC 4th Sr.Res. Co.A
Tatum, Floyd GA Phillips' Legion Co.C
Tatum, F.M. GA Inf. 1st Conf.Bn. Co.A
Tatum, F.M. TN 8th (Smith's) Cav. Co.F Cpl.
Tatum, F.P. SC 24th Inf. Co.B 3rd Lt.
Tatum, Francis A. GA 18th Inf. Co.I
Tatum, Francis M. GA 36th (Villepigue's) Inf. Co.B
Tatum, Francis M. 1st Conf.Inf. Co.B
Tatum, Frank M. TN 7th Inf. Co.D Jr.2nd Lt.
Tatum, George GA 21st Inf. Co.H
Tatum, George NC 46th Inf. Co.I
Tatum, George H. GA 39th Inf. Co.D Sgt.
Tatum, George M. NC 5th Cav. (63rd St.Troops) Co.C
Tatum, George W. NC 54th Inf. Co.F 1st Sgt.
Tatum, G.F. TN 12th (Cons.) Inf. Co.D
Tatum, G.J. GA 4th (Clinch's) Cav. Co.F,H
Tatum, G.M. TN 48th (Voorhies') Inf. Co.D
Tatum, Grandison J. NC 17th Inf. (2nd Org.) Co.F
Tatum, G.W. GA 56th Inf. Co.F
Tatum, G.W. TN 12th (Green's) Cav. Co.F
Tatum, G.W. 3rd Conf.Cav. Co.I
Tatum, H. MS 2nd Part. Co.A
Tatum, H. NC 3rd Jr.Res. Co.A Sgt.
Tatum, H.A. TX 5th Inf. Co.B
Tatum, H.A. 1st Conf.Cav. Co.I
Tatum, Hamilton NC 3rd Cav. (41st St.Troops) Co.C
Tatum, Hamlin AL 4th Res. Co.H
Tatum, Hardy L. AR Inf. 2nd Bn. Co.B
Tatum, Hardy L. AR 3rd Inf. Co.I
Tatum, Hardy L. GA 34th Inf. Co.F
Tatum, Henry AL 53rd (Part.Rangers) Co.C
Tatum, Henry AL 21st Inf. Co.I
Tatum, Henry NC 2nd Inf. Co.B
Tatum, Henry TN 19th (Biffle's) Cav. Co.H
Tatum, Henry A. Gen. & Staff Contr.Surg.
Tatum, Henry J. GA 4th (Clinch's) Cav. Co.G,C
Tatum, Hillory S. NC 3rd Inf. Co.G
Tatum, H.McF. AL 32nd & 58th (Cons.) Inf. Capt.
Tatum, H.O. LA 13th Bn. (Part.Rangers) Co.A
Tatum, Hop 1st Conf.Cav. Co.G
Tatum, Horace GA Arty. 11th Bn. (Sumter Arty.) Co.A
Tatum, Horatio GA 38th Inf. Co.N Sgt.
Tatum, Howell VA 12th Inf. Co.K
Tatum, H.S. TN 21st (Wilson's) Cav. Co.A
Tatum, H.T. GA 5th Res. Co.D
Tatum, H.T. VA VA 13th Cav. Co.B
Tatum, Hugh GA 43rd Inf. Co.A,L,C
Tatum, H.W. NC Currituck Guard J.W.F. Banks' Co.
Tatum, I. GA 3rd Res. Co.G
Tatum, Ira GA Inf. 25th Bn. (Prov.Guard) Co.E
Tatum, Isaac TN 19th (Biffle's) Cav. Co.H
Tatum, Isaac L. TN 4th Inf. Co.E
Tatum, J. TN Inf. 4th Cons.Regt. Co.K
Tatum, Jackson AL 24th Inf. Co.H
Tatum, James AR 37th Inf. Co.G
Tatum, James GA 22nd Inf. Co.I Sgt.
Tatum, James LA Mil.Conf.Guards Regt. Co.I
Tatum, James LA Mil. Irish Regt. Enright's Co.
Tatum, James MS Inf. 1st St.Troops Co.D
Tatum, James MS 36th Inf. Co.A
Tatum, James VA 13th Cav. Co.E
Tatum, James VA 12th Inf. Co.D
Tatum, James VA 23rd Inf. Co.K
Tatum, James A. AL 11th Cav. Co.K
Tatum, James A. LA 25th Inf. Co.I 1st Lt.
Tatum, James A. VA 2nd Arty. Co.E
Tatum, James B. MS 7th Inf. Co.F,D
Tatum, James F. MO Cav. 3rd Bn. Co.C
Tatum, James H. VA 38th Inf. Co.B
Tatum, James J. GA Inf. 4th Bn. (St.Guards) Co.H
Tatum, James J. GA 18th Inf. Co.I
Tatum, James M. AL 3rd Inf. Co.C
Tatum, James M. AR 24th Inf. Co.I Sgt.
Tatum, James M. TX 29th Cav. Co.B Orderly Sgt.
Tatum, James Mark TX 20th Cav. Co.F
Tatum, James M.D. VA 12th Inf. Co.C Cpl.

Tatum, James N. VA Lt.Arty. B.Z. Price's Co. Cpl.
Tatum, James R. NC 5th Cav. (63rd St.Troops) Co.C
Tatum, James S. LA 4th Cav. Co.D
Tatum, J.B. TN 49th Inf. Co.E
Tatum, J.C. VA 82nd Mil. Co.C 1st Sgt.
Tatum, J.D. GA Cobb's Legion Co.K
Tatum, J.D. TN 19th (Biffle's) Cav. Co.A
Tatum, J.D. VA 1st (Farinholt's) Res. Co.E,I
Tatum, Jesse C. GA 25th Inf. Co.I Sgt.
Tatum, Jesse C. TX 36th Cav. Co.E
Tatum, Jesse M. MO 4th Inf. Co.F
Tatum, Jesse R. GA 34th Inf. Co.F
Tatum, J.H. AL 2nd Cav. Co.H
Tatum, J.H. AL 27th Inf. Co.H
Tatum, J.H. MO St.Guard
Tatum, J.H. VA 3rd (Archer's) Bn.Res. Co.A
Tatum, J.H. VA 28th Inf. Co.I
Tatum, J.J. GA 11th Cav. Co.H
Tatum, J.J. GA 31st Inf. Co.G
Tatum, J.J. MS Cav. Hughes' Bn. Co.A
Tatum, J.L. KY 7th Mtd.Inf. Co.D 1st Sgt.
Tatum, J.L. MS 29th Inf. Co.E
Tatum, J.M. AR 7th Cav. Co.D
Tatum, J.M. MS 38th Cav. Co.D
Tatum, J.M. TX Cav. Benavides' Regt. Co.K
Tatum, J.M.W. MS Inf. (Res.) Berry's Co.
Tatum, J.N. AL 45th Inf. Co.C Cpl.
Tatum, J.O. MO 6th Cav. Co.F
Tatum, John AL 24th Inf. Co.H
Tatum, John AR 1st (Colquitt's) Inf. Co.A Capt.,AQM
Tatum, John FL 7th Inf. Co.A Cpl.
Tatum, John KY Arty. McEnnis' Detach.
Tatum, John MS 1st Cav. Co.C Cpl.
Tatum, John MS 7th Cav. Co.C Cpl.
Tatum, John MS 18th Cav. Co.C
Tatum, John MS 28th Cav. Co.K
Tatum, John MS Inf. 2nd St.Troops Co.C
Tatum, John MS 3rd Inf. (St.Troops) Co.A
Tatum, John MS 9th Bn.S.S. Co.C
Tatum, John MS 23rd Inf. Co.G
Tatum, John Gen. & Staff Capt.,AQM
Tatum, John A. MO Lt.Arty. 3rd Field Btty. Sgt.
Tatum, John A. VA 42nd Inf. Co.H 1st Lt.
Tatum, Johnathan TN 48th (Voorhies') Inf. Co.B
Tatum, John B. KY 10th (Diamond's) Cav. Co.C
Tatum, John C. VA Lt.Arty. R.M. Anderson's Co.
Tatum, John F. FL 2nd Cav. Co.I
Tatum, John F. GA 47th Inf. Co.G
Tatum, John Hawkins NC 2nd Inf. Co.E
Tatum, John J. GA 4th (Clinch's) Cav. Co.C
Tatum, John M. TN 1st (Feild's) Inf. Co.D
Tatum, John M. TX 4th Inf. Co.B
Tatum, John P. TN 22nd Inf. Co.H
Tatum, John R. VA 12th Inf. Co.C
Tatum, John S. VA 23rd Inf. Co.K
Tatum, John S.C. SC 25th Inf. Co.G
Tatum, John T. VA 38th Inf. Co.B
Tatum, John W. GA Cherokee Legion (St.Guards) Co.I
Tatum, John W. MS 29th Inf. Co.B
Tatum, John W. MO 12th Cav. Co.D Bvt.2nd Lt.
Tatum, John W. VA 10th Inf. Co.L Sgt.
Tatum, John W. VA 82nd Mil. Co.C
Tatum, Joseph MS 8th Cav. Co.C Cpl.
Tatum, Joseph TN 9th Cav. Co.H
Tatum, Joseph F. AR 1st (Colquitt's) Inf. Co.E
Tatum, Joseph H. TX Cav. Martin's Regt. Co.B
Tatum, Joseph H. VA Lt.Arty. Taylor's Co.
Tatum, Josh MS 10th Cav. Co.F Sgt.
Tatum, Joshua AL 15th Bn.Part.Rangers Co.C Sgt.
Tatum, Joshua AL 56th Part.Rangers Co.C Sgt.
Tatum, Joshua MS 3rd Inf. Co.D Sgt.
Tatum, Joshua P. LA 2nd Inf. Co.F
Tatum, J.P. TN 12th (Cons.) Inf. Co.D
Tatum, J.P. VA 24th Cav. Co.H
Tatum, J.R. TX 9th Cav. Co.H
Tatum, J.R. TX Cav. McCord's Frontier Regt. Co.F
Tatum, J.S. LA 17th Inf. Co.H
Tatum, J.S. MS 3rd Inf. (St.Troops) Co.A
Tatum, J.S.C. SC 1st (Hagood's) Inf. 1st Co.A
Tatum, J.T. Trans-MS Conf.Cav. 1st Bn. Co.B
Tatum, J.W. TX 9th (Nichols') Inf. Co.B
Tatum, J.W. TX 18th Inf. Co.K Sgt.
Tatum, J.W. VA 9th Cav. Co.E
Tatum, J. Warren MS 3rd Inf. Co.C
Tatum, L.B. VA 3rd Inf.Loc.Def. Co.E
Tatum, L.C. TX Cav. Wells' Regt. Co.A
Tatum, L.C. TX Cav. Wells' Bn. Co.A
Tatum, Leroy R. VA Lt.Arty. Pegram's Co.
Tatum, Leroy R. VA Inf. 5th Bn. Co.C
Tatum, Littleberry VA 12th Inf. Co.B
Tatum, Lucien B. VA 1st Arty. Co.K
Tatum, Lucien B. VA Arty. L.F. Jones' Co.
Tatum, Luke AL 4th Inf. Co.K
Tatum, M. Brush Bn.
Tatum, Manly VA 8th Cav. Co.I Cpl.
Tatum, Marion A.B. GA 39th Inf. Co.D,K 1st Sgt.
Tatum, Mark D.L. AR 23rd Inf. Co.K
Tatum, Mark T. AR 35th Inf. Co.D Maj.
Tatum, Mark T. AR 51st Mil. Co.E Capt.
Tatum, M.C. TN Cav. Nixon's Regt. Co.D
Tatum, M.D. GA 3rd Res. Co.F
Tatum, M.J. NC 7th Sr.Res. Fisher's Co.
Tatum, Montgomery B. TN 11th Inf. Co.K
Tatum, Moses GA Lt.Arty. Croft's Btty. (Columbus Arty.)
Tatum, Moses GA 38th Inf. Co.N
Tatum, Nathaniel TX 17th Inf. Co.D
Tatum, Nathaniel E. MS 23rd Inf. Co.G
Tatum, N.C. VA Lt.Arty. Pegram's Co.
Tatum, N.E. MS 7th Cav. Co.G
Tatum, Nicholas G. NC 53rd Inf. Co.D
Tatum, N.J. GA 44th Inf. Co.H
Tatum, Organ AR 19th (Dockery's) Inf. Co.G Ord.Sgt.
Tatum, Owen NC 24th Inf. Co.G
Tatum, P.A. AL 45th Inf. Co.C
Tatum, Paul LA 6th Cav. Co.A
Tatum, Paul C. VA Inf. 22nd Bn. Co.B
Tatum, P.B. TN 7th (Duckworth's) Cav. Co.E Adj.
Tatum, P.B. TN 6th Inf. Co.D Cpl.
Tatum, Peter AL Cav. 24th Bn. Co.C
Tatum, Peter LA 9th Inf. Co.E
Tatum, Peter MS 5th Inf. Co.F
Tatum, Peter L. LA 28th (Gray's) Inf. Co.I Sgt.
Tatum, Pinkney A. NC 2nd Cav. (19th St.Troops) Co.F Capt.
Tatum, P.M. GA 60th Inf. Co.F
Tatum, R. AL 12th Inf. Co.G
Tatum, R. TX 18th Inf. Co.K
Tatum, R.E. TN 16th (Logwood's) Cav. Co.I
Tatum, R.F. AL 14th Inf. Co.E
Tatum, R.F. TN 18th Inf. Co.A
Tatum, R.F. Gen. & Staff AASurg.
Tatum, R.G. TN 7th (Duckworth's) Cav. Co.E
Tatum, R.G. TN 6th Inf. Co.D
Tatum, R.H. AR 15th (Johnson's) Inf. Co.E
Tatum, R. Herbert Gen. & Staff Surg.
Tatum, Richard TN Holman's Bn.Part.Rangers Co.B
Tatum, Richard TN 32nd Inf. Co.D
Tatum, Richard J. SC 8th Inf. Co.G Cpl.
Tatum, Robert AL 53rd (Part.Rangers) Co.C
Tatum, Robert B. MS 10th Inf. Old Co.B, New Co.C Cpl.
Tatum, Robert F. VA Cav. 39th Bn. Co.D
Tatum, Robert W. FL 5th Inf. Co.B Sgt.
Tatum, R.P. AL Mil. 4th Vol. Gantt's Co.
Tatum, R.P. AL 40th Inf. Co.I Sgt.
Tatum, R.P. GA 19th Inf. Co.C
Tatum, Samuel GA 43rd Inf. Co.L,C Cpl.
Tatum, Samuel NC 3rd Arty. (40th St.Troops) Co.C
Tatum, Samuel NC 8th Inf. Co.B
Tatum, Seth GA Inf. 40th Bn. Ord.Sgt.
Tatum, Seth GA 41st Inf. Co.E Ord.Sgt.
Tatum, S.G. AL 6th Inf. Co.K
Tatum, S.G. TN 7th (Duckworth's) Cav. Co.M
Tatum, Shelton G. GA Fowler's Cav.
Tatum, Silas E. GA 38th Inf. Co.N
Tatum, Sion F. 1st Conf.Cav. 2nd Co.G
Tatum, S.M. MS Cav. 2nd Bn.Res. Co.B
Tatum, S.O. TX 16th Inf. Co.H Sgt.
Tatum, S.S. LA 2nd Cav. Co.I
Tatum, Sublet A. TN 24th Inf. Co.I
Tatum, T.C. LA 13th Bn. (Part.Rangers) Co.A
Tatum, T.E. MS 27th Inf. Co.G
Tatum, T.E. TN 1st (Feild's) & 27th Inf. (Cons.) Co.I
Tatum, T.E. TN 27th Inf. Co.G 1st Sgt.
Tatum, T.H. TN 38th Inf. Co.I Cpl.
Tatum, Thadious C. NC Currituck Guard J.W.F. Banks' Co.
Tatum, Thomas B. VA 3rd (Archer's) Bn.Res. Co.C
Tatum, Thomas B. VA 41st Inf. Co.C
Tatum, Thomas M. MO Cav. 3rd Bn. Co.C
Tatum, Thomas M. MO Inf. 5th Regt.St.Guard Co.D 3rd Lt.
Tatum, Thomas S. GA 44th Inf. Co.D 2nd Lt.
Tatum, Thomas S. MS 17th Inf. Co.F
Tatum, Thomas T. LA 12th Inf. Co.H Music.
Tatum, T.H.R. GA 65th Inf. Co.H
Tatum, T.H.R. GA Smith's Legion Co.A
Tatum, Timothy P. AR 3rd Inf. Co.E
Tatum, T.J. Trans-MS Conf.Cav. 1st Bn. Co.B
Tatum, T.P. FL 2nd Cav. Co.D
Tatum, T.P. FL Cav. 5th Bn. Co.C
Tatum, T.R. TN 49th Inf. Co.B
Tatum, V.B. GA 38th Inf. Co.I
Tatum, Vivian H. VA 21st Inf. Co.F

Tatum, W. MS Lt.Arty. (Warren Lt.Arty.) Swett's Co.
Tatum, W. TN Lt.Arty. Scott's Co.
Tatum, W.A. MS 20th Inf. Co.I
Tatum, W.A. TN 15th (Cons.) Cav. Co.I
Tatum, W.A. TN 12th (Cons.) Inf. Co.F
Tatum, Walter TX 17th Inf. Co.D
Tatum, Warren MS 18th Inf. Co.K
Tatum, W.B. FL 5th Inf.
Tatum, W.C. TN 31st Inf. Co.C
Tatum, W.D. GA 19th Inf. Co.C Sgt.
Tatum, W.E. MS 2nd Cav. Co.I
Tatum, W.E. VA 4th Cav. Co.K
Tatum, W.E. Gen. & Staff Hosp.Stew.
Tatum, Wesley TX 3rd Cav. Co.B
Tatum, W.F. KY 9th Mtd.Inf. Co.C
Tatum, W.H. AL 2nd Cav. Co.A
Tatum, W.H. AL Cav. 24th Bn. Co.C 1st Sgt.
Tatum, W.H. AL 53rd (Part.Rangers) Co.C
Tatum, W.H. AL Mil. 4th Vol. Co.D
Tatum, W.H. GA 13th Inf. Co.K
Tatum, W.H. TN 15th (Cons.) Cav. Co.K Cpl.
Tatum, William AL 11th Cav. Co.K
Tatum, William AR Unassign.
Tatum, William GA Cav. 16th Bn. (St.Guards) Co.E Cpl.
Tatum, William GA 43rd Inf. Co.L,C
Tatum, William KY 7th Cav. Co.C
Tatum, William LA 9th Inf. Co.E
Tatum, William MS 7th Cav. Co.C
Tatum, William MS 32nd Inf. Co.E
Tatum, William TN 16th (Logwood's) Cav. Co.D
Tatum, William TN 16th (Logwood's) Cav. Co.F
Tatum, William TN 16th (Logwood's) Cav. Co.I
Tatum, William TX Cav. Wells' Regt. Co.A
Tatum, William TX Cav. Wells' Bn. Co.A
Tatum, William VA 5th Inf. Co.E
Tatum, William A. AL 8th Inf. Co.K Cpl.
Tatum, William A. VA 5th Cav. Co.K
Tatum, William B. NC Currituck Guard J.W.F. Banks' Co.
Tatum, William B. TN 11th Inf. Co.K
Tatum, William B. VA 21st Inf. Co.G
Tatum, William C. AR 14th (Powers') Inf. Co.H
Tatum, William E. GA 31st Inf. Co.G Hosp.Stew.
Tatum, William E. VA 3rd Cav. Co.K
Tatum, William E. VA 2nd Arty. Co.I
Tatum, William F. VA 42nd Inf. Co.H Sgt.
Tatum, William H. AL 24th Inf. Co.C Sgt.
Tatum, William H. AR 1st (Crawford's) Cav. Co.F 2nd Lt.
Tatum, William H. VA Lt.Arty. R.M. Anderson's Co.
Tatum, William J. MO 7th Cav. Haislip's Co.
Tatum, William L.M. AR 1st (Crawford's) Cav. Co.A Sgt.
Tatum, William M. MS 9th Inf. Old Co.C Cpl.
Tatum, William M. MS 42nd Inf. Co.F Sgt.
Tatum, William M. TN 23rd Inf. Co.G
Tatum, William R. GA 24th Inf. Co.K
Tatum, William R. VA Inf. 5th Bn. Co.C
Tatum, William R. VA 53rd Inf. Co.C
Tatum, William T. VA 16th Inf. Co.E
Tatum, William V. NC 2nd Cav. (19th St.Troops) Co.F
Tatum, William W. NC 8th Inf. Co.B
Tatum, Williford NC 43rd Inf. Co.D
Tatum, W.J. AL Lt.Arty. Goldthwaite's Btty.
Tatum, W.L. AL 15th Bn.Part.Rangers Co.A
Tatum, W.L. MS Inf. 2nd St.Troops Co.C
Tatum, W.M. TN 12th (Cons.) Inf. Co.D Sgt.
Tatum, W.M. TN 22nd Inf. Co.H Sgt.
Tatum, W.P. KY 12th Cav. Co.G
Tatum, W.T. AL 53rd (Part.Rangers) Co.C
Tatum, W.W. VA 5th Cav. Co.K
Taub, John LA 14th Inf. Co.C
Tauch, --- LA Mil. 3rd Regt.Eur.Brig. (Garde Francaise) Euler's Co.
Tauge, Michael TN 15th Inf. Co.C
Taughnut, --- GA 3rd Inf. Co.G
Taugue, T. VA Loc.Def. Wood's Co.
Taukesley, William MO Cav. Preston's Bn. Co.A
Taul, A.T. AL 3rd Res. Co.A
Taul, Decius KY 1st Bn.Mtd.Rifles Co.C
Taul, H.C. AL 30th Inf. Co.F
Taul, John AL Randolph Cty.Res. D.A. Self's Co.
Taul, John J. KY 1st Bn.Mtd.Rifles Co.C
Taul, Micah AL Cav. Bowie's Co. 2nd Lt.
Taulbee, Howard M. TX 13th Cav. Co.H Black.
Taulbee, James P. KY 5th Mtd.Inf. Co.D
Taulbee, Jefferson KY 5th Mtd.Inf. Co.D
Taulbee, William H. KY 5th Mtd.Inf. Co.A 2nd Lt.
Taulbee, William W. KY 5th Mtd.Inf. Co.D Sgt.
Taulman, F.A. SC Lt.Arty. 3rd (Palmetto) Bn. Culpeper's Co.
Taulman, Franklin A. TX 32nd Cav. Co.G
Taumahill, William M. LA 3rd Inf. Co.C
Tauman, Henry E. VA 5th Cav. 3rd Co.F
Taunair, Jacques LA Arty. 8th Bn. Co.3
Tauney, Gustave VA Cav. Mosby's Regt. (Part.Rangers) Co.B
Taunt, Davis NC 3rd Bn.Sr.Res. Co.A
Taunt, James TN 14th Inf. Co.G
Taunt, Joseph A. GA 14th Inf. Co.K
Taunt, Kennel NC 47th Inf. Co.D
Taunt, W.E. GA Inf. Doxier's Co.
Taunt, William GA 14th Inf. Co.K
Taunton, C.E. AL 14th Inf. Co.H
Taunton, Doctor F. AL 3rd Inf.
Taunton, F.M. AL 14th Inf. Co.H
Taunton, George W. GA Hvy.Arty. 22nd Bn. Co.B
Taunton, George W. GA Inf. 13th Bn. (St.Guards) Douglass' Co. Cpl.
Taunton, George W. GA 25th Inf. 1st Co.K
Taunton, G.W. GA 2nd Cav. Co.A
Taunton, H.G. GA 59th Inf. Co.C
Taunton, I.C. AL 14th Inf. Co.H
Taunton, Isaiah LA Inf. 11th Bn. Co.F
Taunton, John TX 27th Cav. Co.I,N
Taunton, N. GA 5th Res. Co.K
Taunton, Nathan W. AL Inf. 1st Regt. Co.H
Taunton, Neusom AL 3rd Bn.Res. Flemming's Co.
Taunton, Newsom AL 57th Inf. Co.K Capt.
Taunton, N.J. AL 18th Inf. Co.B
Taunton, Samuel C. AL 6th Inf. Co.L
Taunton, T. GA 5th Res. Co.K
Taunton, Temley AL 63rd Inf. Co.C
Taunton, Thomas J. GA 57th Inf. Co.E
Taunton, Thomas J. LA Inf. 11th Bn. Co.F
Taunton, Tillman AL Arty. 4th Bn. Hilliard's Legion Co.E
Taunton, V.C. AL 13th Inf. Co.F
Taunton, W.M. TX 10th Cav. Co.C
Taurance, Samuel AL 12th Cav. Co.F
Taurman, William VA 4th Cav. Co.F
Tausend, G.H. TX Cav. (Dismtd.) Chisum's Regt. Co.A
Tausey, W.A. AR 2nd Mtd.Rifles Co.E
Tausin, Justilien LA 26th Inf. Co.D
Taussel, R.B. GA Inf. Arsenal Bn. (Columbus) Co.A
Taust, William M. KY 4th Mtd.Inf. Co.K
Tauster, Syrumn VA Cav. 35th Bn. Co.C
Taut, Alexander GA 2nd Bn.S.S. Co.C
Taut, David E. GA 10th Inf. Co.D
Taut, Harrison GA Inf. 40th Bn. Co.F
Taut, Henry GA Inf. 1st Loc.Troops (Augusta) Co.H
Taut, John J. AL Cav. Hardie's Bn.Res. Co.A 2nd Lt.
Taut, M. AR 23rd Inf.
Tautah, Joseph Deneale's Regt. Choctaw Warriors Co.A
Tauteman, H. TX 4th Field Btty.
Tauzin, A.M. LA 27th Inf. Co.K 2nd Lt.
Tauzin, H.L. LA 3rd Inf. Co.G Cpl.
Tauzin, J.E. LA Inf.Cons.Crescent Regt. Co.G
Tauzin, Joseph M. LA 3rd Inf. Co.G Sgt.
Tauzin, Justilien LA 30th Inf. Co.G
Tauzin, Louis LA 30th Inf. Co.H,G
Tauzin, Ulysse LA 30th Inf. Co.H,G,F Sgt.
Tauzine, Ulysse LA 30th Inf. Co.H
Tavares, Benjamin LA Mil. Orleans Fire Regt. Hall's Co.
Tavares, W. LA Mil.Conf.Guards Regt. Co.K
Taveau, Augustine L. SC 5th Res. Co.G
Taveaux, A.L. SC Cav. 19th Bn. Co.B
Tavel, B.B. SC 23rd Inf. Co.C Cpl.
Tavel, Ed SC Mil.Arty. 1st Regt. Co.C
Tavel, Ed SC 27th Inf. Co.B
Tavel, I.L. AL Conscr.
Tavel, Sampson FL 1st Cav. Co.E Cpl.
Tavender, J.R. KY 8th Mtd.Inf. Co.D
Tavender, J.W. KY 8th Inf. Co.D
Tavener, A.M. MO 5th Cav. Co.H
Tavener, James H. VA 49th Inf. Co.B
Tavener, Jonah VA Cav. 35th Bn. Co.C
Tavenner, Adolphus VA 1st Cav. Co.H
Tavenner, A.O. VA 8th Inf. Co.E Sgt.
Tavenner, Benjamin VA 8th Inf. Co.E
Tavenner, Edgar H. VA Cav. 35th Bn. Co.A Cpl.
Tavenner, Isaac B. VA 1st Cav. Co.H Cpl.
Tavenner, James E. VA 1st Cav. Co.H
Tavenner, John W. VA 8th Inf. Co.D
Tavenner, John W. VA 8th Inf. Co.E Sgt.
Tavenner, Jonah, Jr. VA 1st Cav. Co.H
Tavenner, Joseph A. VA 8th Inf. Co.E 1st Lt.
Tavenner, Thomas E. VA 8th Inf. Co.F Cpl.
Tavenner, William C. LA 1st (Nelligan's) Inf. Co.F 2nd Lt.
Tavenner, William C. VA 17th Cav. Co.C Lt.Col.
Tavenon, J. LA Inf. 9th Bn. Chinns' Co.
Taver, M.D. TN 7th Cav. Co.L

Taver, Thomas AL Randolph Cty.Res. D.A. Self's Co.
Taverner, J.H. SC 25th Inf. Co.A
Taverner, Pat AR 1st Colquitt's Inf.
Taverra, --- LA Mil. 2nd Regt. French Brig.
Tavis, J. AL 30th Inf. Co.F
Tavlin, William LA 1st (Strawbridge's) Inf. Co.D
Tavner, John MO 11th Inf. Co.E
Tavnon, Peter TN 2nd (Robison's) Inf. Co.C
Tawadske, --- SC Mil.Cav. Theo. Cordes' Co.
Ta wa skilles NC Inf. Thomas Legion Co.B
Tawby, A. GA 32nd Inf. Co.E
Ta we i thle 1st Creek Mtd.Vol. 2nd Co.C
Tawery, William KY 11th Cav. Co.D
Tawes, George R. VA 61st Mil. Co.E
Tawes, Patrick H. VA 39th Inf. Co.H
Tawler, J.F. TN 7th Cav. Co.C Cpl.
Tawn, Jno. AL 9th Inf. Co.B
Tawney, George W. VA 36th Inf. 2nd Co.H
Tawney, William H. VA 36th Inf. 2nd Co.H
Tawsets, J.B. TN 61st Mtd.Inf. Co.G
Tawwater, R. AR 10th Inf. Co.E
Taxon, W.B. TN 20th Inf. Co.G 2nd Lt.
Tay, James MO 11th Inf. Co.B
Tay, J.L. MD Cav. 2nd Bn. Co.A
Ta yar tah nay 1st Creek Mtd.Vol. Co.E
Taybler, G.F. VA Lt.Arty. Carpenter's Co.
Taybor, --- AL 26th (O'Neal's) Inf. Co.C
Taycumath Cocker 1st Seminole Mtd.Vol.
Tayes, J.P. TN 3rd (Clack's) Inf. Co.K
Tayler, --- MS Scouts Montgomery's Co. Cpl.
Tayler, A. KY 8th Mtd.Inf. Co.A
Tayler, C. AR Cav. Davies' Bn. Co.C
Tayler, E.D. AL Randolph Cty.Res. D.A. Self's Co.
Tayler, Evan FL 3rd Inf. Co.E
Tayler, Francis M. AL 18th Bn.Vol. Co.A
Tayler, H.T.B. AR 11th & 17th Cons.Inf. Co.D 1st Sgt.
Tayler, I.D. LA Maddox's Regt.Res.Corps Co.B
Tayler, Jackson TN 19th & 20th (Cons.) Cav. Co.E
Tayler, James VA Inf. 25th Bn.
Tayler, James N. AR 1st Inf. Co.D
Tayler, James N. AR 11th & 17th Inf. Co.D
Tayler, J.B. AR 6th Inf. Co.A
Tayler, J.F. AL Res. J.G. Rankin's Co. Sgt.
Tayler, J.M. SC 4th Cav. Co.H
Tayler, John GA 3rd Res. Co.K
Tayler, John G. AL 25th Inf. Co.K
Tayler, Joseph VA Second Class Mil. Wolff's Co.
Tayler, L.W. AR Cav. Harrell's Bn. Co.D
Tayler, Samuel L. AR 11th & 17th Cons.Inf. Co.D
Tayler, S.H. MS Taylor's Co. (Boomerangs) Capt.
Tayler, Thomas N. TX Cav. Morgan's Regt. Co.E
Tayler, T.J. TX 32nd Cav. Co.I
Tayler, Tobias NC 5th Sr.Res. Co.B
Tayler, Toliver SC 1st St.Troops Co.C
Tayler, W.A. AL 11th Cav. Co.B
Tayler, William NC Bass' Co.
Tayler, William VA 11th Cav. Capt.
Tayler, William C. AR 27th Inf. Co.E
Tayler, William H. VA Inf. 4th Bn.Loc.Def. Co.C
Tayler, William Hillary AL 17th Inf. Co.B
Tayler, W.J. AR 11th & 17th Cons.Inf. Co.D,G
Tayleure, William W. VA 12th Inf. Co.E Sgt.
Tayley, L.E. AL 24th Inf. Co.I
Taylo, J. NC 5th Inf. Co.C
Taylock, J.W. Wickham's Cav. AAG
Tayloe, Bladen T. VA 30th Inf. Co.K Capt.
Tayloe, David T. NC 61st Inf. Surg.
Tayloe, E. Poinsett VA 47th Inf. Co.B Maj.
Tayloe, E. Thornton MS Cav. Jeff Davis Legion Co.E 2nd Lt.
Tayloe, Francis M. NC 1st Inf. (6 mo. '61) Co.L
Tayloe, Francis M. NC 32nd Inf. Co.G 3rd Lt.
Tayloe, George NC 4th Cav. (59th St.Troops) Co.F
Tayloe, George E. AL 11th Inf. Co.D Col.
Tayloe, H.A. VA 10th Cav. Co.G
Tayloe, Henry NC 4th Cav. (59th St.Troops) Co.F
Tayloe, Henry A. VA 40th Inf. Co.B
Tayloe, James NC 4th Cav. (59th St.Troops) Co.F
Tayloe, James NC 1st Inf. Co.F
Tayloe, John NC 1st Inf. Co.F
Tayloe, John VA 9th Cav. Co.I
Tayloe, John VA 9th Cav. Co.I Capt.
Tayloe, John, Jr. VA 9th Cav. Co.I 2nd Lt.
Tayloe, John, Jr. VA Cav. Mosby's Regt. (Part.Rangers)
Tayloe, Jno. VA 42nd Inf. Sgt.Maj.
Tayloe, John Gen. & Staff AQM
Tayloe, J.W. MS Cav. Jeff Davis Legion Co.E Capt.
Tayloe, J.W. VA 2nd Cav. Adj.
Tayloe, J.W. Gen. & Staff Maj.,AAG
Tayloe, Lomax VA 2nd Cav. Adj.
Tayloe, Lomax Gen. & Staff 1st Lt.,Adj.
Tayloe, Thomas H. TN 18th (Newsom's) Cav. Co.D Capt.
Tayloe, T.O. VA Loc.Def. Tayloe's Co. Capt.
Tayloe, T.O. Gen. & Staff Hosp.Stew.
Tayloe, T.P. TN 15th (Stewart's) Cav. Co.B
Tayloe, William VA 30th Inf. Co.K Sgt.
Tayloe, W.M. AL Arty. 1st Bn.
Taylor 1st Creek Mtd.Vol. 2nd Co.C
Taylor 1st Creek Mtd.Vol. 2nd Co.I
Taylor 1st Creek Mtd.Vol. Co.M
Taylor 1st Seminole Mtd.Vol.
Taylor 2nd Cherokee Mtd.Vol. Co.I
Taylor, --- AL Arty. 1st Bn.
Taylor, --- 1st AL 22nd Inf. Co.E
Taylor, --- 2nd AL 22nd Inf. Co.C
Taylor, --- AR 3rd St.Inf. Co.B 3rd Lt.
Taylor, --- FL 4th Inf. Co.H
Taylor, --- GA 5th Inf. Co.L
Taylor, --- KY 1st Inf. Co.D
Taylor, --- LA 5th Cav. Co.I
Taylor, --- LA 1st Hvy.Arty. (Reg.) Co.I
Taylor, --- MO Cav. Snider's Bn. Co.A
Taylor, --- SC Mil. 16th Regt. Steinmeyer, Jr.'s Co.
Taylor, --- TN 12th (Green's) Cav. Co.D
Taylor, --- TX Cav. 3rd Regt.St.Troops Co.B
Taylor, --- TX Cav. 4th Regt.St.Troops Co.I
Taylor, --- TX 25th Cav. Co.E
Taylor, --- TX Cav. Good's Bn. Co.E
Taylor, --- TX Cav. Mann's Regt. Co.C
Taylor, --- TX Cav. Mann's Regt. Co.K
Taylor, --- TX Cav. McCord's Frontier Regt. Co.A
Taylor, --- TX Cav. McCord's Frontier Regt. Co.K
Taylor, --- TX 1st Hvy.Arty. Co.K
Taylor, --- TX 11th (Spaight's) Bn.Vol. Co.B
Taylor, --- TX 21st Inf. Co.D
Taylor, --- VA 49th Inf. Co.B
Taylor, --- VA Mil. 195th Regt. Maj.
Taylor, --- VA Arty.Detach. VMI
Taylor, A. AL 8th Inf.
Taylor, A. AL 9th Inf. Co.A
Taylor, A. AL 46th Inf. Co.C
Taylor, A. AR 10th (Witt's) Cav. Co.C
Taylor, A. AR Cav. McGehee's Regt. Co.I
Taylor, A. AR 51st Mil. Co.E
Taylor, A. FL 9th Inf.
Taylor, A. GA 4th Inf. Co.I
Taylor, A. GA 26th Inf. Sgt.
Taylor, A. GA 32nd Inf. Co.D
Taylor, A. LA 6th Cav. Co.D
Taylor, A. LA 25th Inf. Co.K
Taylor, A. MS Inf. 1st Bn.St.Troops (30 days '64) Co.A
Taylor, A. MS 35th Inf. Co.I
Taylor, A. MS 46th Inf. Co.F
Taylor, A. MS Rogers' Co.
Taylor, A. MS Conscr.
Taylor, A. SC 2nd St.Troops Co.A
Taylor, A. TN 4th (McLemore's) Cav. Co.F
Taylor, A. TN 16th (Logwood's) Cav. Co.D
Taylor, A. TN Lt.Arty. Phillips' Co.
Taylor, A. VA 3rd (Chrisman's) Bn.Res. Co.B Capt.
Taylor, A. VA 30th Inf. Co.H
Taylor, A. VA 46th Inf. Co.F
Taylor, A. Conf.Cav. Wood's Regt. 2nd Co.M
Taylor, A.A. LA Mil.Conf.Guards Regt. Co.C
Taylor, A.A. MS 27th Inf. Co.E
Taylor, A.A. MS Shields' Co.
Taylor, A.A. TN 16th (Logwood's) Cav. Co.I
Taylor, Aaron GA 48th Inf. Co.B
Taylor, Aaron LA 7th Inf. Co.B 1st Lt.
Taylor, Aaron SC 13th Inf. Co.K
Taylor, Aaron E. MS 14th Inf. Co.I
Taylor, Aaron E. MS 24th Inf. Co.L 1st Sgt.
Taylor, Aaron H. AL 16th Inf. Co.A
Taylor, Aaron V. AL 33rd Inf. Co.G
Taylor, A.B. AL 17th Inf. Co.F
Taylor, A.B. AL 58th Inf. Co.C Sgt.
Taylor, A.B. FL Milton Lt.Arty. Dunham's Co.
Taylor, A.B. GA 23rd Inf. Co.E
Taylor, A.B. MS 1st Cav.Res. Co.H
Taylor, A.B. TN 8th (Smith's) Cav. Co.G Sgt.
Taylor, A.B. TN 13th (Gore's) Cav. Co.D
Taylor, A.B. TN 18th Inf. Co.H
Taylor, Abel NC 2nd Inf. Co.F
Taylor, Abigah NC Walker's Bn. Thomas' Legion Co.H
Taylor, Able 3rd Conf.Cav. Co.F
Taylor, Abner B. AL 49th Inf. Co.E
Taylor, Abner C. TN 27th Inf. Co.K Cpl.
Taylor, Abner F. AL 19th Inf. Co.B

Taylor, Abner P. TN 55th (McKoin's) Inf. Dillehay's Co.
Taylor, Abner R. AL Arty. 1st Bn. Co.D
Taylor, Abner T. AL 13th Inf. Co.K
Taylor, Abraham AL 43rd Inf. Co.H
Taylor, Abraham VA 4th Cav. Co.G
Taylor, Abraham VA Lt.Arty. 12th Bn. Co.C
Taylor, Abraham B. TN 4th Inf. Co.D Bvt.2nd Lt.
Taylor, Abram J. NC 51st Inf. Co.I
Taylor, Absalom AR 1st Inf.
Taylor, Absalom MS Inf. 7th Bn. Co.D
Taylor, Absalom NC 33rd Inf. Co.K Cpl.
Taylor, Absalom H. TX 17th Cav. Co.E
Taylor, Absolom AL 10th Inf. Co.E
Taylor, A.C. AL 9th Inf. Co.A
Taylor, A.C. AR 15th (Josey's) Inf. Co.E
Taylor, A.C. MS 14th (Cons.) Inf. Co.D
Taylor, A.C. TN 3rd (Forrest's) Cav. Co.I
Taylor, A.C. TN 12th (Green's) Cav. Co.H
Taylor, A.C. TN 16th Inf. Co.A
Taylor, A.C. TX 7th Cav. Co.C
Taylor, A.C. VA Inf. 25th Bn. Co.B
Taylor, A.C.M. TX 5th Inf. Co.A
Taylor, A.D. GA 52nd Inf. Co.K
Taylor, A.D. GA 63rd Inf. Co.B
Taylor, Ad. LA 2nd Res.Corps Co.B
Taylor, A.D. NC 3rd Arty. (40th St.Troops) Co.F
Taylor, A.D. SC 2nd Inf. Co.B
Taylor, A.D. TN 19th Inf. AQM
Taylor, A.D. TN 46th Inf. Co.D
Taylor, A.D. VA Hvy.Arty. 20th Bn. Co.C
Taylor, Adam VA 37th Inf. Co.A
Taylor, Addison VA Cav. Young's Co.
Taylor, Adolphus GA Inf. 8th Bn. Co.D
Taylor, Adolphus TX 6th Inf. Co.A
Taylor, A.E. MO 15th Cav. Co.B
Taylor, A.E. NC 2nd Bn.Loc.Def.Troops Co.E
Taylor, A.F. AL 48th Inf. Co.A
Taylor, A.F. AR 30th Inf. Co.I
Taylor, A.F. AR 37th Inf. Co.E
Taylor, A.F. KY 1st Bn.Mtd.Rifles Co.A Capt.
Taylor, A.F. TN 11th (Holman's) Cav. Co.E
Taylor, A.F. TN 2nd (Robison's) Inf. Co.G
Taylor, A.F. TX Vol. Rainey's Co.
Taylor, A.G. AL 39th Inf. Co.F
Taylor, A.G. AR Cav. McGehee's Regt. Co.F
Taylor, A.G. NC 3rd Cav. (41st St.Troops) Co.B
Taylor, A.G. NC Lt.Arty. 13th Bn. Co.C
Taylor, A.G. SC 6th Cav. Co.B 2nd Lt.
Taylor, A.G. VA 1st Cav. Co.G
Taylor, A.G. Gen. & Staff 2nd Lt.,Dr.M.
Taylor, A.H. AL Cav. Hardie's Bn.Res. Co.B
Taylor, A.H. AL 39th Inf. Co.G
Taylor, A.H. AR 5th Inf.
Taylor, A.H. MS 14th (Cons.) Inf. Co.F
Taylor, A.H. MS 21st Inf.
Taylor, A.H. NC 2nd Inf. Co.B
Taylor, A.H. TN 21st Inf. Co.H Adj.
Taylor, A.H. TN 47th Inf. Co.K
Taylor, A.H. VA 34th Inf. Co.G
Taylor, A.H. VA 82nd Mil. Co.B Sgt.
Taylor, A.H. 3rd Conf.Inf. Co.E
Taylor, A.I. TX Waul's Legion Co.B
Taylor, A.J. AL 5th Cav. Co.E
Taylor, A.J. AL 7th Cav. Co.G,B
Taylor, A.J. AL 8th (Livingston's) Cav. Co.D
Taylor, A.J. AL 44th Inf. Co.K
Taylor, A.J. AL 62nd Inf. Co.C
Taylor, A.J. AL 3rd Bn. Hilliard's Legion Vol. Co.C
Taylor, A.J. AR 38th Inf. Co.A
Taylor, A.J. GA 12th Cav. Co.G
Taylor, A.J. GA Inf. 11th Bn. (St.Guards) Co.C
Taylor, A.J. GA 16th Inf. Co.K
Taylor, A.J. GA 18th Inf. Co.D Cpl.
Taylor, A.J. KY 9th Cav. Co.B Sgt.
Taylor, A.J. KY 5th Mtd.Inf. Co.I
Taylor, A.J. LA 13th Bn. (Part.Rangers) Co.F
Taylor, A.J. MS Cav. Jeff Davis Legion Co.B
Taylor, A.J. MS Cav. Ham's Regt. Co.I
Taylor, A.J. MS 6th Inf. Co.I
Taylor, A.J. MS 10th Inf. Old Co.E
Taylor, A.J. MS 32nd Inf. Co.B 2nd Lt.
Taylor, A.J. MS Cp.Guard (Cp. of Instr. for Conscr.)
Taylor, A.J. NC 3rd Arty. (40th St.Troops) Co.K
Taylor, A.J. NC 26th Inf. Co.F
Taylor, A.J., Jr. NC 46th Inf. Co.B
Taylor, A.J. NC 49th Inf. Co.K
Taylor, A.J. SC Lt.Arty. 3rd (Palmetto) Bn. Co.G
Taylor, A.J. SC 8th Res.
Taylor, A.J. TN 18th (Newsom's) Cav. Co.D
Taylor, A.J. TN 19th & 20th (Cons.) Cav. Co.C
Taylor, A.J. TN 1st (Turney's) Inf. Co.A Cpl.
Taylor, A.J. TN 5th Inf. 2nd Co.K
Taylor, A.J. TN 15th Inf. Co.A
Taylor, A.J. TN 35th Inf. 2nd Co.D Sgt.
Taylor, A.J. TX 16th Cav. Co.I
Taylor, A.J. TX 37th Cav. 2nd Co.I
Taylor, A.J. VA 2nd Cav. Co.K Sgt.
Taylor, A.J. VA 4th Cav.
Taylor, A.J. VA 18th Cav. Co.A
Taylor, A.J. VA 14th Inf. Co.I
Taylor, A.J. Trans-MS Conf.Cav. 1st Bn. Co.D
Taylor, A.J. Mead's Conf.Cav. Co.B
Taylor, A.L. AR 19th (Dawson's) Inf. Co.E
Taylor, A.L. TN 18th Inf. Co.D Sgt.
Taylor, A.L. TX 22nd Inf. Co.E
Taylor, A.L. VA 5th Cav. Co.I
Taylor, A.L. 2nd Conf.Eng.Troops
Taylor, Alamander A.J. NC Lt.Arty. 13th Bn. Co.A
Taylor, Alamander A.J. VA Lt.Arty. 12th Bn. Co.D
Taylor, Alanson TX 13th Vol. 2nd Co.B 1st Lt.
Taylor, Albert AL 21st Inf. Co.A Sgt.
Taylor, Albert AR 5th Inf.
Taylor, Albert GA 64th Inf. Co.A Sgt.
Taylor, Albert MS 10th Inf. New Co.C
Taylor, Albert MS 26th Inf. Co.H
Taylor, Albert NC Walker's Bn. Thomas' Legion Co.H
Taylor, Albert SC 1st Hvy.Arty. Co.C
Taylor, Albert VA 33rd Inf. Co.I
Taylor, Albert 1st Choctaw Mtd.Rifles Co.H
Taylor, Albert A. MS 29th Inf. Co.E
Taylor, Albert A. NC 32nd Inf. Co.B,C
Taylor, Albert B. GA 4th Inf. Co.F
Taylor, Albert B. NC 22nd Inf. Co.B
Taylor, Albert F. AR 23rd Inf. Co.I Sgt.
Taylor, Albert G. TN 39th Mtd.Inf.
Taylor, Albert G. VA 19th Inf. Co.E 1st Sgt.
Taylor, Albert H. VA 42nd Inf. Co.C
Taylor, Albert J. AR 27th Inf. Old Co.C, Co.D
Taylor, Albert L. VA 1st Cav. Co.H
Taylor, Alen AL 5th Cav. Co.H
Taylor, Alex TN 20th Cav.
Taylor, Alex TX 4th Inf. Co.H
Taylor, Alexander AL 61st Inf. Co.D
Taylor, Alexander FL 2nd Cav. Co.H
Taylor, Alexander FL 5th Inf. Co.F
Taylor, Alexander LA 7th Inf. Co.A
Taylor, Alexander MS 3rd Inf. (St.Troops) Co.I
Taylor, Alexander MS 37th Inf. Co.K
Taylor, Alexander MO 12th Inf. Co.A,B Cpl.
Taylor, Alexander NC 34th Inf. Co.A
Taylor, Alexander SC 1st Hagood's Inf. Co.D
Taylor, Alexander TN 28th Inf. Co.A
Taylor, Alexander TN 29th Inf. Co.H
Taylor, Alexander TX 12th Inf. Co.F
Taylor, Alexander VA 20th Inf. Co.E
Taylor, Alexander VA 40th Inf. Co.I
Taylor, Alexander 1st Choctaw Mtd.Rifles Co.E
Taylor, Alexander B. TN 2nd (Robsions') Inf. Co.D
Taylor, Alexander E. AR Inf. Ballard's Co.
Taylor, Alexander M. VA 60th Inf. Co.F 1st Sgt.
Taylor, Alexander N. VA 5th Inf. Co.I 2nd Lt.
Taylor, Alexander R. SC Cav.Bn. Holcombe Legion Co.B Capt.
Taylor, Alexander W. VA 39th Inf. Co.G Drum.
Taylor, Alexandra VA Inf. 45th Bn. Co.E
Taylor, Alex M. LA 4th Inf. Old Co.G Music.
Taylor, Alex S. VA Loc.Def. Mallory's Co.
Taylor, Alford LA 9th Inf. Co.H
Taylor, Alfred MS 36th Inf. Co.I
Taylor, Alfred SC 2nd Rifles Music.
Taylor, Alfred TN 3rd (Lillard's) Mtd.Inf. 1st Co.K
Taylor, Alfred TN 10th Inf.
Taylor, Alfred TN 63rd Inf. Co.E
Taylor, Alfred VA Cav. Mosby's Regt. (Part. Rangers) Co.C
Taylor, Alfred A. NC 3rd Inf. Co.K
Taylor, Alfred D. Gen. & Staff Capt.,AQM
Taylor, Alfred H. AR 18th (Marmaduke's) Inf. Co.E
Taylor, Alfred J. AR 27th Inf. Old Co.C, Co.D
Taylor, Alfred J. VA 39th Inf. Co.G Sgt.
Taylor, Alfred L. TN 4th Inf. Co.I
Taylor, Alfred M. MS 13th Inf. Co.D
Taylor, Alfred M. VA 42nd Inf. Co.C
Taylor, Alfred S. TN Inf. 1st Bn. (Colms') Co.B
Taylor, Alfred W. GA Inf. 8th Bn. Co.D Cpl.
Taylor, Alison LA 2nd Inf. Co.D
Taylor, Allen NC 2nd Jr.Res. Co.I
Taylor, Allen TN 63rd Inf. Co.B
Taylor, Allen VA 54th Inf. Co.C
Taylor, Allen C. NC 17th Inf. (2nd Org.) Co.I
Taylor, Allen F. NC 15th Inf. Co.I
Taylor, Allen J. AL Cav. Holloway's Co.
Taylor, Allen J. TN 44th Inf. Co.C Cpl.
Taylor, Allen W. AL 16th Inf. Co.A
Taylor, Alonzo TX 6th Cav. Co.F
Taylor, Alonzo P. NC 21st Inf. Co.G Cpl.
Taylor, Alsey Jackson NC 7th Inf. Co.E Capt.
Taylor, Alston J. TN 32nd Inf. Co.D

Taylor, Alx. MS 11th (Perrin's) Cav. Co.C
Taylor, A.M. AR Inf. Hardy's Regt. Co.H
Taylor, A.M. LA 3rd (Wingfield's) Cav. Co.E
Taylor, A.M. MS 4th Cav. Co.D
Taylor, A.M. MS Cav. Yerger's Regt. Co.A
Taylor, A.M. MS Inf. 2nd Bn. (St.Troops) Co.C Cpl.
Taylor, A.M. MS 36th Inf. Co.F
Taylor, A.M. Conf.Cav. Wood's Regt. Co.K, 2nd Co.A
Taylor, A.M. 1st Seminole Mtd.Vol. 2nd Lt.
Taylor, Ambrose VA 5th Cav. Coakley's Co.
Taylor, Ambrose C. MO Cav. Freeman's Regt. Co.A
Taylor, Americus V. VA Goochland Lt.Arty.
Taylor, Ames TX 9th (Nichols') Inf. Co.K
Taylor, Amos NC 27th Inf. Co.D
Taylor, Amos NC 51st Inf. Co.E
Taylor, Amos SC 13th Inf. Co.K
Taylor, Amos TN 2nd Cav. Co.G
Taylor, Amos K. TX 13th Cav. Co.G Cpl.
Taylor, Amos R. KY 12th Cav. Capt.
Taylor, Ampriah L. NC 61st Inf. Co.C
Taylor, Amsterdam L. MS 6th Inf. Co.I
Taylor, Anderson NC 3rdd Arty. (40th St.Troops) Co.H
Taylor, Anderson VA 2nd Arty. Co.K
Taylor, Anderson VA Inf. 45th Bn. Co.I
Taylor, Anderson F. TN 41st Inf.
Taylor, Andrew AL 31st Inf. Co.H
Taylor, Andrew AR 2nd Cav. 1st Co.A
Taylor, Andrew AR Cav. 6th Bn. Co.C
Taylor, Andrew MS 4th Inf. Co.H
Taylor, Andrew MS 8th Inf. Co.D
Taylor, Andrew MS 24th Inf. Co.B
Taylor, Andrew MS 40th Inf. Co.G
Taylor, Andrew NC 2nd Inf. Co.E
Taylor, Andrew NC 3rd Inf. Co.I
Taylor, Andrew NC Inf. Thomas Legion Co.B
Taylor, Andrew TN 14th Inf. Co.D
Taylor, Andrew TX 6th Cav. Co.F Sgt.
Taylor, Andrew TX Arty. (St.Troops) Good's Co.
Taylor, Andrew VA 20th Cav. Co.C
Taylor, Andrew VA 27th Inf. Co.D
Taylor, Andrew 1st Chickasaw Inf. McCord's Co. Sgt.
Taylor, Andrew C. AR 17th (Lemoyne's) Inf. Co.C
Taylor, Andrew C. AR 21st Inf. Co.C,D
Taylor, Andrew D. SC 20th Inf. Co.H
Taylor, Andrew J. AL 10th Inf. Co.K
Taylor, Andrew J. AL 50th Inf. Co.E
Taylor, Andrew J. FL 4th Inf. Co.H
Taylor, Andrew J. GA 6th Cav. Co.A
Taylor, Andrew J. GA 11th Cav. Co.D
Taylor, Andrew J. GA 17th Inf. Co.H
Taylor, Andrew J. LA 5th Cav. Co.E
Taylor, Andrew J. MS 5th Inf. Co.D
Taylor, Andrew J. MS 30th Inf. Co.D
Taylor, Andrew J. NC 2nd Cav. (19th St.Troops) Co.E
Taylor, Andrew J. NC 2nd Inf. Co.F Ord.Sgt.
Taylor, Andrew J. NC 26th Inf. Co.I Cpl.
Taylor, Andrew J. NC 39th Inf. Co.A
Taylor, Andrew J. NC 46th Inf. Co.B
Taylor, Andrew J. NC 58th Inf. Co.H
Taylor, Andrew J. NC Walker's Bn. Thomas' Legion Co.C
Taylor, Andrew J. SC 1st (Hagood's) Inf. 2nd Co.D
Taylor, Andrew J. VA 6th Cav. Co.A
Taylor, Andrew J. VA 6th Bn.Res. Co.I
Taylor, Andrew J. VA 36th Inf. Co.F
Taylor, Andrew J. VA 44th Inf. Co.F
Taylor, Andrew M. TN 59th Mtd.Inf. Co.C Cpl.
Taylor, Andrew M. VA 14th Cav. Co.H
Taylor, Angus MS 46th Inf. Co.A Capt.
Taylor, Angus D. TX 27th Cav. Co.I 1st Sgt.
Taylor, Anias NC 51st Inf.
Taylor, Anthony AR 10th Inf. Co.G
Taylor, Anthony TN 18th (Newsom's) Cav. Co.I
Taylor, A.O. MS Lt.Arty. (Brookhaven Lt.Arty.) Hoskins' Btty.
Taylor, A.O. MO 2nd Cav. Co.D
Taylor, A.P. NC 14th Inf. Co.G
Taylor, A.P. SC 4th Cav. Co.D
Taylor, A.P. SC Manigault's Bn.Vol. Co.A
Taylor, A.P. TX Cav. McCord's Frontier Regt. Co.F
Taylor, A.P. VA 8th Cav. Co.H
Taylor, A.P. VA 1st St.Res. Co.K
Taylor, A.P. VA 46th Inf. 2nd Co.K
Taylor, A.R. GA Mayer's Co. (Appling Cav.)
Taylor, A.R. GA 26th Inf. Asst.Surg.
Taylor, A.R. GA 35th Inf. Co.I
Taylor, A.R. KY 1st (Butler's) Cav. Co.A
Taylor, A.R. SC 4th Cav. Co.K
Taylor, A.R. SC 7th Cav. Co.D Capt.
Taylor, A.R. TN 1st (Feild's) Inf. Co.G
Taylor, A.R. VA 8th Cav. Co.G
Taylor, Arch LA 25th Inf. Co.H
Taylor, Arch NC 1st Bn.Jr.Res. Co.E
Taylor, Archbald VA 146th Mil. Co.A Capt.
Taylor, Archibald NC 32nd Inf. Co.B,A
Taylor, Archibald NC 47th Inf. Co.A
Taylor, Archibald TN 2nd (Walker's) Inf. Co.C
Taylor, Archibald TX 1st Inf. Surg.
Taylor, Archibald VA 3rd Cav. Co.D 2nd Lt.
Taylor, Archibald VA Lt.Arty. Thornton's Co.
Taylor, Archibald VA 9th Bn.Res. Co.B Maj.
Taylor, Archibald VA 25th Inf. Surg.
Taylor, Archibald Gen. & Staff Surg.
Taylor, Archibald A. NC 13th Inf. Co.B Music.
Taylor, Archibald B. LA 12th Inf. Co.H
Taylor, Archibald S. MS 7th Inf. Co.A
Taylor, Archy KY 2nd Mtd.Inf. Co.C
Taylor, Arington AL Cav. 5th Bn. Hilliard's Legion Co.E
Taylor, Aris C. KY 9th Mtd.Inf. Co.D
Taylor, Arthur TN 35th Inf. 2nd Co.D
Taylor, Arthur VA 10th Inf. Co.L
Taylor, Arthur VA 55th Inf. Co.D
Taylor, Arthur K. LA 16th Inf. Co.E
Taylor, Arthur R. SC 13th Inf. Co.K
Taylor, A.S. MS 7th Cav. Co.C
Taylor, A.S. SC 1st Bn.S.S. Co.C
Taylor, A.S. SC Inf. 3rd Bn. Co.D
Taylor, A.S. SC 9th Res. Co.D Cpl.
Taylor, A.S. SC 20th Inf. Co.B
Taylor, A.S. SC 27th Inf. Co.G
Taylor, A.S. TN 44th (Cons.) Inf. Co.G Sgt.
Taylor, A.S. TN 55th (McKoin's) Inf. Bounds' Co. Sgt.
Taylor, A.S. TX 14th Inf. Co.B
Taylor, A.S. VA Hvy.Arty. 19th Bn. 3rd Co.C
Taylor, A.S. Gen. & Staff Maj.
Taylor, Asa FL 6th Inf. Co.G
Taylor, Asa FL 11th Inf. Co.H Sgt.
Taylor, Asa FL Campbellton Boys
Taylor, Asa GA 4th Inf. Co.F
Taylor, Asa NC 22nd Inf. Co.K
Taylor, A.S.B. VA 51st Inf. Co.I
Taylor, Asberry TN Cav. 16th Bn. (Neal's) Co.E
Taylor, Asberry TN Lt.Arty. Winston's Co.
Taylor, Asberry D. GA 47th Inf. Co.F
Taylor, Asbury VA Lt.Arty. Brander's Co.
Taylor, Asbury L. GA 17th Inf. Co.I
Taylor, Ashley MO Cav. Coleman's Regt. Sgt.
Taylor, Asmel F. TX 1st Inf. Co.H Cpl.
Taylor, A.T. VA 4th Cav. Co.K
Taylor, A.T. 15th Conf.Cav. Co.A
Taylor, Atlas S. NC 4th Cav. (59th St.Troops) Co.D Sgt.
Taylor, Augh Gen. & Staff,PACS Surg.
Taylor, Augustus GA 44th Inf. Surg.
Taylor, Augustus SC Lt.Arty. 3rd (Palmetto) Bn. Co.D
Taylor, Augustus VA 7th Cav.
Taylor, Augustus C. GA 43rd Inf. Co.L Sgt.
Taylor, Augustus H. MS 14th Inf. Co.K
Taylor, Augustus H. MS 17th Inf. Co.H Cpl.
Taylor, Augustus R. GA Inf. 10th Bn. Co.C,E Cpl.
Taylor, Augustus R. Gen. & Staff Asst.Surg.
Taylor, Augustus W. VA 1st St.Res. Co.C
Taylor, Ausborn VA Cav. 37th Bn. Co.H
Taylor, Austin SC 5th St.Troops Co.G
Taylor, Austin TN 14th Inf. Co.L
Taylor, Austin J. TN 10th & 11th (Cons.) Cav. Co.B
Taylor, A.V. MO 8th Cav. Reed's Co.
Taylor, A.W. GA 11th Cav. Co.H
Taylor, A.W. GA Inf. 4th Bn. (St.Guards) Co.G 1st Sgt.
Taylor, A.W. NC 1st Cav. (9th St.Troops) Co.C
Taylor, A.W. NC 8th Bn.Part.Rangers Co.B
Taylor, A.W. NC 66th Inf. Co.C Cpl.
Taylor, A.W. SC 1st Mtd.Mil. Anderson's Co.
Taylor, A.W. SC 5th Cav. Co.G
Taylor, A.W. SC Cav. 17th Bn. Co.B
Taylor, A.W. SC Mil. 18th Regt. Co.E
Taylor, A.W. TN Detailed Conscr. Co.A
Taylor, A.W. VA 62nd Mtd.Inf. Co.A
Taylor, A.W. Conf.Inf. Tucker's Regt. Co.F Sgt.
Taylor, B. AL 3rd Inf. Co.H
Taylor, B. AL Cp. of Instr. Talladega
Taylor, B. GA 8th Inf. ASurg.
Taylor, B. GA 30th Inf. Co.A
Taylor, B. GA 51st Inf.
Taylor, B. KY Cav. 2nd Bn. (Dortch's) Co.D
Taylor, B. MS Cav. 1st Bn. (McNair's) St.Troops Co.B
Taylor, B. MS 6th Cav. Co.D
Taylor, B. MS Cav. Davenport's Bn. (St.Troops) Co.C
Taylor, B. MS 27th Inf. Co.F
Taylor, B. NC 5th Sr.Res. Co.C
Taylor, B. TN 3rd (Forrest's) Cav. Co.L
Taylor, B. TN 27th Inf. Co.B
Taylor, B. VA VMI Co.C

Taylor, B. Gen. & Staff Lt.,ADC
Taylor, B.A. KY 1st Inf. Co.C
Taylor, B.A. LA 16th Inf. Co.G
Taylor, B.A. MS 7th Cav. Co.C
Taylor, B.A. TN 17th Inf. Co.K
Taylor, Bailey MO 2nd Cav. Co.F
Taylor, Baldwin H. NC Walker's Bn. Thomas' Legion Co.A
Taylor, Baraseal TN 28th (Cons.) Inf. Co.I
Taylor, Bard MS 2nd St.Cav. Co.L
Taylor, Barker VA 14th Inf. Co.E
Taylor, Barnabas TN 35th Inf. 1st Co.I, Co.G
Taylor, Barnabas B. AR 14th (Powers') Inf. Co.K
Taylor, Bartley AL 4th Res. Co.G
Taylor, Bayley MO 2nd Inf. Co.F
Taylor, Bazel AR 19th (Dockery's) Inf. Cons.Co.E,D
Taylor, Bazel W. GA 41st Inf. Co.C
Taylor, Bazil G. VA 7th Inf. Co.C Sgt.
Taylor, B.B. MS 2nd Cav. 2nd Co.G
Taylor, B.B. MS 5th Cav. Co.B Cpl.
Taylor, B.B. MS 3rd Inf. (St.Troops) Co.B Sgt.
Taylor, B.B. SC 6th Cav. Co.I
Taylor, B.B. TN 1st (Turney's) Inf. Co.A Sgt.
Taylor, B.C. GA 36th (Villepigue's) Inf. Co.F
Taylor, B.C. VA Cav. 35th Bn. Co.C
Taylor, B.C. 1st Conf.Inf. 1st Co.F
Taylor, B.D. MS Cav.Part.Rangers Rhodes' Co.
Taylor, B.D. MS 12th Inf. Co.A
Taylor, B.D. 14th Conf.Cav. Co.F
Taylor, B.D. Eng.,CSA
Taylor, B.E. GA Lt.Arty. Pritchard's Co. (Washington Arty.)
Taylor, B.E. MS Lt.Arty. Stanford's Co.
Taylor, Ben TX 15th Inf. Co.B
Taylor, Benajah NC Snead's Co. (Loc.Def.)
Taylor, Benjamin AL 12th Inf. Co.G
Taylor, Benjamin AR 27th Inf. Co.E
Taylor, Benjamin AR 33rd Inf. Co.F
Taylor, Benjamin GA Hvy.Arty. 22nd Bn. Co.C Lt.
Taylor, Benjamin GA 47th Inf. Co.F
Taylor, Benjamin KY 4th Cav. Co.G
Taylor, Benjamin KY 9th Cav. Co.G
Taylor, Benjamin KY 9th Cav. Co.H Cpl.
Taylor, Benjamin KY 12th Cav.
Taylor, Benjamin LA 17th Inf. Co.C
Taylor, Benjamin NC Cav. 12th Bn. Co.C
Taylor, Benjamin NC 7th Bn.Jr.Res. Co.A
Taylor, Benjamin NC 26th Inf. Co.F
Taylor, Benjamin NC 47th Inf. Co.E
Taylor, Benjamin NC 51st Inf. Co.E
Taylor, Benjamin TN 3rd (Forrest's) Cav. Thompson's Co.
Taylor, Benjamin TN 17th Inf. Co.B
Taylor, Benjamin TN 23rd Inf. Chap.
Taylor, Benjamin TN 36th Inf. Co.D
Taylor, Benjamin TN 44th Inf. Co.H
Taylor, Benjamin TN 62nd Mtd.Inf. Co.A
Taylor, Benjamin TN 63rd Inf. Co.H
Taylor, Benjamin VA 14th Inf. Co.D
Taylor, Benjamin VA 51st Inf. Co.K
Taylor, Benjamin 15th Conf.Cav. Co.K
Taylor, Benjamin A. KY 1st Bn.Mtd.Rifles Co.A
Taylor, Benjamin B. SC 23rd Inf. Co.H
Taylor, Benjamin B. VA 6th Bn.Res. Co.H
Taylor, Benjamin C. AL 6th Inf. Co.G
Taylor, Benjamin C. MS 11th Inf. Co.A
Taylor, Benjamin D. NC 54th Inf. Co.D
Taylor, Benjamin E. GA 5th Inf. Co.C
Taylor, Benjamin F. AL Arty. 1st Bn. Co.D
Taylor, Benjamin F. AL 1st Regt.Conscr. Co.H
Taylor, Benjamin F. AL 9th Inf. Co.I 1st Lt.
Taylor, Benjamin F. AL 21st Inf. Co.G
Taylor, Benj. F. AL 25th Inf. Co.H
Taylor, Benjamin F. AL Conscr. Echols' Co.
Taylor, Benjamin F. AR 14th (McCarver's) Inf. Co.D
Taylor, Benjamin F. AR 21st Inf. Co.K
Taylor, Benjamin F. GA 30th Inf. Co.C
Taylor, Benjamin F. KY 1st Bn.Mtd.Rifles Co.A
Taylor, Benjamin F. KY 2nd Mtd.Inf. Co.I Cpl.
Taylor, Benjamin F. KY 2nd Mtd.Inf. Co.I
Taylor, Benjamin F. NC 14th Inf. Co.G
Taylor, Benjamin F. NC 61st Inf. Co.E
Taylor, Benjamin F. SC 7th Inf. 1st Co.F
Taylor, Benjamin F. TN 3rd (Lillard's) Mtd.Inf. Co.I 2nd Lt.
Taylor, Benjamin F. TX 4th Cav. Co.D
Taylor, Benjamin F. TX 15th Cav. Co.E
Taylor, Benjamin F. TX 11th Inf. Co.C
Taylor, Benjamin F. VA 50th Inf. Cav.Co.B
Taylor, Benjamin J. SC 20th Inf. Co.H
Taylor, Benjamin L. AR 8th Inf. New Co.C
Taylor, Benjamin M. AL 6th Inf. Co.C
Taylor, Benjamin M. NC 35th Inf. Co.G
Taylor, Benjamin N. VA 33rd Inf. Co.H
Taylor, Benjamin P. GA Carlton's Co. (Troup Cty.Arty.)
Taylor, Benjamin P. GA 2nd Inf. Stanley's Co.
Taylor, Benjamin R. NC 1st Inf. (6 mo. '61) Co.I
Taylor, Benjamin W. AL 13th Inf. Co.F QMSgt.
Taylor, Benjamin W. KY 9th Cav. Co.C Cpl.
Taylor, Benjamin W. NC 68th Inf. Co.C
Taylor, Benjamin W. VA 2nd Cav. Co.K
Taylor, Benjamin W. VA Lt.Arty. Pegram's Co.
Taylor, Benj. Walter Gen. & Staff Surg.
Taylor, Benjamin Walters SC 2nd Cav. Asst.Surg.
Taylor, Benjamin W.L. VA 9th Inf. 2nd Co.H
Taylor, Bennett VA 19th Inf. Co.F Maj.
Taylor, Bennett J. TN 23rd Inf. 2nd Co.A
Taylor, Benoni VA 1st Res. Co.I
Taylor, Benoni B. TX 9th Field Btty. Cpl.
Taylor, Bernard Conf.Reg.Inf. Brooks' Bn. Co.D
Taylor, Bernard M. VA Lt.Arty. Pollock's Co. Sgt.
Taylor, Bernard M. VA Inf. Hutter's Co.
Taylor, Berry GA 10th Cav. (St.Guards) Co.D,I
Taylor, Berry K. MO Cav. Freeman's Regt. Co.A
Taylor, Berryman SC Inf. 3rd Bn. Co.C
Taylor, Berryman SC 9th Res. Co.A
Taylor, Berry S. GA 47th Inf. Co.F
Taylor, Beverly K. VA Hvy.Arty. 18th Bn. Co.B 2nd Lt.
Taylor, Beverly K. VA 6th Inf. 1st Co.B 2nd Lt.
Taylor, B.F. AL Lt.Arty. Goldthwaite's Btty.
Taylor, B.F. AR 1st (Dobbin's) Cav. Co.D
Taylor, B.F. AR 12th Bn.S.S. Co.B
Taylor, B.F. GA 5th Res. Co.A,D
Taylor, B.F. GA Cobb's Legion Co.A
Taylor, B.F. KY Morgan's Men Co.H
Taylor, B.F. LA 7th Inf. Co.H 1st Lt.
Taylor, B.F. MS 28th Cav. Co.D
Taylor, B.F. TN 10th & 11th (Cons.) Cav. Co.B
Taylor, B.F. TN 11th (Holman's) Cav. Co.H
Taylor, B.F. TN 5th Inf. 1st Co.F, 2nd Co.E, Co.A Sgt.
Taylor, B.F. TN 55th (McKoin's) Inf. Bounds' Co.
Taylor, B.F. TN 63rd Inf.
Taylor, B.F. TX 3rd Cav. Co.A
Taylor, B.F. TX 2nd Inf.
Taylor, B.F. TX 14th Inf. Co.H 1st Lt.
Taylor, B.F. TX Waul's Legion Co.H
Taylor, B.F. VA 40th Inf. Co.A
Taylor, B.F. Conf.Cav. Wood's Regt. Co.I
Taylor, B.F. 4th Conf.Inf. Co.F Cpl.
Taylor, B.F. Exch.Bn. 1st Co.C,CSA
Taylor, B.G. KY 1st (Butler's) Cav. Co.F
Taylor, B.H. AL 38th Inf. Co.E
Taylor, B.H. AR 1st (Dobbin's) Cav.
Taylor, B.H. AR 32nd Inf. Co.I
Taylor, B.H. TN 23rd Inf. 1st Co.F
Taylor, B.H. TX 20th Inf. Co.F
Taylor, B.H.N. AL 41st Inf. Co.A
Taylor, Bill 1st Cherokee Mtd.Rifles McDaniel's Co.
Taylor, B.J. GA Lt.Arty. Guerard's Btty. Artif.
Taylor, B.J. NC 3rd Arty. (40th St.Troops) Co.A
Taylor, B.J. NC 32nd Inf. Lenoir Braves 1st Co.K
Taylor, B.J. SC Lt.Arty. 3rd (Palmetto) Bn. Co.B
Taylor, B.J. VA Hvy.Arty. Allen's Co.
Taylor, B.J. VA 20th Inf. Co.C
Taylor, B.K. AR 8th Inf. New Co.F
Taylor, B.K. AR 14th (McCarver's) Inf. Co.E
Taylor, B.L. MS 18th Cav. Co.E
Taylor, B.L. MS Adams' Co. (Holmes Cty.Ind.)
Taylor, B.L. TX Cav. Crump's Regt. Co.M
Taylor, Blount NC 3rd Inf. Co.A
Taylor, B.M. GA Lt.Arty. Ferrell's Btty.
Taylor, B.M. GA 6th Inf. (St.Guards) Co.E
Taylor, B.M. Gen. & Staff Chap.
Taylor, B.N. GA Inf. Arsenal Bn. (Columbus) Co.B
Taylor, Bollen NC 30th Inf. Co.I
Taylor, Boswell VA 51st Inf. Co.K
Taylor, Bowling KY 2nd (Duke's) Cav. Co.F
Taylor, B.R. NC 7th Bn.Jr.Res. Ord.Sgt.
Taylor, Brant W. KY 11th Cav. Asst.Surg.
Taylor, Brazelia TN 35th Inf. 1st Co.I,G
Taylor, Bryan NC 2nd Inf. Co.F
Taylor, Bryant NC 24th Inf. Co.E
Taylor, B.S. AL 11th Cav. Co.F
Taylor, B.S. AR Lt.Arty. Zimmerman's Btty.
Taylor, B.S. AR 37th Inf. Co.E
Taylor, B.T. AR 12th Bn.S.S. Co.C
Taylor, B.T. Gen. & Staff, Ord.Dept.
Taylor, Burell GA 47th Inf. Co.F
Taylor, Burket NC 14th Inf. Co.C
Taylor, Burley VA 11th Inf. Co.E
Taylor, Burrell GA Inf. Cobb Guards Co.A 2nd Lt.
Taylor, Burrell NC 4th Inf. Co.F
Taylor, Burt MS Cav. 4th Bn. Sykes' Co.
Taylor, Burt 8th (Wade's) Conf.Cav. Co.G

Taylor, Burton H. NC 33rd Inf. Co.B
Taylor, Bushard Gen. & Staff Surg.
Taylor, Bushrod W. FL 11th Inf. Co.F
Taylor, B.W. AL 39th Inf. Co.D
Taylor, B.W. KY 7th Cav. Asst.Surg.
Taylor, B.W. KY 10th (Johnson's) Cav. Co.E Cpl.
Taylor, B.W. KY Morgan's Men Co.D Cpl.
Taylor, B.W. MS Inf. 1st Bn.St.Troops (30 days '64) Co.A
Taylor, B.W. NC 8th Bn.Part.Rangers Co.D Cpl.
Taylor, B.W. NC 69th Regt. Co.C
Taylor, B.W. NC Bass' Co. Cpl.
Taylor, B.W. SC 2nd Cav. Surg.
Taylor, B.W. Gen. & Staff Capt.,AQM
Taylor, B. Walter SC Inf. Hampton Legion Capt.,Asst.Surg.
Taylor, Byron L. TX 4th Cav. Co.F 1st Lt.
Taylor, Bythel NC 17th Inf. (2nd Org.) Co.E
Taylor, C. AL 7th Cav. Co.G 1st Sgt.
Taylor, C. AR 1st Vol. Co.K
Taylor, C. AR 26th Inf. Co.K
Taylor, C. MS 2nd Part.Rangers Co.K
Taylor, C. MS 2nd (Quinn's St.Troops) Inf. Co.C
Taylor, C. MS 21st Inf.
Taylor, C. TN 11th (Holman's) Cav. Co.L
Taylor, C. TX 12th Inf. Co.E
Taylor, C. VA 13th Cav. Co.E
Taylor, C. VA VMI Co.C
Taylor, C.A. AL 26th (O'Neal's) Inf. Co.D
Taylor, C.A. GA 5th Res. Co.B 2nd Lt.
Taylor, C.A. MS 10th Cav. Co.K
Taylor, C.A. MS 32nd Inf. Co.D
Taylor, C.A. MS 36th Inf. Co.H
Taylor, C.A. VA 4th Cav. Co.G,I
Taylor, Cain L. VA 46th Inf. 2nd Co.K
Taylor, Cal TX Arty. (St.Troops) Good's Co.
Taylor, Caleb NC 4th Cav. (59th St.Troops) Co.D
Taylor, Caleb NC 14th Inf. Co.B
Taylor, Caleb NC 14th Inf. Co.D
Taylor, Caleb SC 20th Inf. Co.C
Taylor, Caleb L. NC 60th Inf. Co.D Sgt.
Taylor, Calhoun C. AL 3rd Bn. Hilliard's Legion Vol. Co.B
Taylor, Callaway NC 26th Inf. Co.A
Taylor, Calvin NC 16th Inf. Co.E
Taylor, Calvin NC 17th Inf. (2nd Org.) Co.I
Taylor, Calvin NC 30th Inf. Co.I
Taylor, Calvin NC 42nd Inf. Co.K
Taylor, Calvin NC 37th Inf. Co.A
Taylor, Calvin C. GA Cobb's Legion Co.H
Taylor, Calvin G. NC 2nd Cav. (19th St.Troops) Co.F
Taylor, Calvin M. TX 22nd Cav. Co.C
Taylor, Calvin S. SC 1st (McCreary's) Inf. Co.B 1st Sgt.
Taylor, Calvin W. VA Loc.Def. Chappell's Co.
Taylor, Cambyous VA 18th Cav. 1st Co.G
Taylor, Campbell H. NC Inf. Thomas Legion Co.B Capt.
Taylor, Cantey McN. AL 3rd Inf. Co.F
Taylor, Carl LA 4th Inf. New Co.G
Taylor, Carrol TX Inf. Griffin's Bn. Co.E
Taylor, Carroll AR 35th Inf. Co.D
Taylor, Carter TX 22nd Cav. Co.C
Taylor, Carter TX Cav. Martin's Regt. Co.D
Taylor, Cary FL 1st (Res.) Inf. Jones' Co.
Taylor, Cassius M. KY 11th Cav. Co.H 2nd Lt.
Taylor, Caswell MS 18th Inf. Co.K
Taylor, Caswell NC 42nd Inf. Co.A
Taylor, C.B. AL 22nd Inf. Co.E 1st Lt.
Taylor, C.B. GA 56th Inf. Co.I Sgt.
Taylor, C.C. AL Cp. of Instr. Talladega Co.C
Taylor, C.C. AR Cav. McGehee's Regt. Co.A
Taylor, C.C. MO 12th Inf. Co.C
Taylor, C.C. TN 19th (Biffle's) Cav. Co.I
Taylor, C.C. TN 21st (Wilson's) Cav. Co.F,C
Taylor, C.C. TN 21st & 22nd (Cons.) Cav. Co.G
Taylor, C.C. TX Inf. Rutherford's Co. Cpl.
Taylor, C.C. VA 4th Cav.
Taylor, C.C.R. AL 4th (Russell's) Cav. Co.E 2nd Lt.
Taylor, C.D. MS Cav.Part.Rangers Rhodes' Co.
Taylor, C.D. VA 4th Cav. Co.G
Taylor, C.D. 14th Conf.Cav. Co.F
Taylor, C.E. MS 7th Cav. Co.K
Taylor, C.E. VA 23rd Cav. Co.C Sgt.
Taylor, C.E. VA Cav. 41st Bn. 2nd Co.H Sgt.
Taylor, C.F. VA 3rd Cav. Co.G
Taylor, C.F. VA 3rd Inf.Loc.Def. 2nd Co.G
Taylor, C.G. SC Mil. 17th Regt. Buist's Co.
Taylor, C.G. SC Shiver's Co.
Taylor, C.H. GA Lt.Arty. Pritchard's Co. (Washington Arty.)
Taylor, C.H. GA 52nd Inf. Co.B
Taylor, C.H. MO 12th Inf. Co.C
Taylor, C.H. VA 15th Inf. Co.E
Taylor, C.H. 1st Conf.Inf. 1st Co.F
Taylor, Charles AR 2nd Cav. Co.C
Taylor, Charles AR 27th Inf. Co.G
Taylor, Charles FL 8th Inf. Co.E
Taylor, Charles GA Lt.Arty. Guerard's Btty.
Taylor, Charles LA Mil. 1st Native Guards
Taylor, Charles LA 5th Inf. Co.E Sgt.
Taylor, Charles MS 8th Cav. Co.C
Taylor, Charles MS 2nd Inf. Co.B
Taylor, Charles MO 1st Inf. Co.I
Taylor, Charles NC 1st Inf.
Taylor, Charles NC 1st Jr.Res. Co.A
Taylor, Charles NC 7th Inf. Co.H
Taylor, Charles NC 11th (Bethel Regt.) Inf. Co.D
Taylor, Charles NC 17th Inf. (1st Org.) Co.K
Taylor, Charles NC 66th Inf. Co.F
Taylor, Charles NC 67th Inf.
Taylor, Charles SC 1st Arty. Co.C
Taylor, Charles TN 25th Inf. Co.B
Taylor, Charles TN 30th Inf. Co.G
Taylor, Charles TN 46th Inf. Co.D
Taylor, Charles TN 60th Mtd.Inf. Co.F
Taylor, Charles TN Inf. 154th Sr.Regt. Co.A
Taylor, Charles VA 17th Cav. Co.I
Taylor, Charles VA 19th Cav. Co.G Cpl.
Taylor, Charles VA Cav. 46th Bn. Co.B
Taylor, Charles VA Cav. 46th Bn. Co.C
Taylor, Charles VA Hvy.Arty. 19th Bn. Co.D
Taylor, Charles VA Lt.Arty. Cayce's Co.
Taylor, Charles VA 2nd Inf.Loc.Def. Co.E Cpl.
Taylor, Charles VA Inf. 6th Bn.Loc.Def. Co.B Cpl.
Taylor, Charles VA Inf. 9th Bn. Duffy's Co.C
Taylor, Charles VA 17th Inf. Co.H
Taylor, Charles VA 25th Inf. 2nd Co.C Cpl.
Taylor, Charles VA 25th Mil. Co.C
Taylor, Charles VA 26th Inf. 2nd Co.B
Taylor, Charles VA 39th Inf. Co.D
Taylor, Charles VA 39th Inf. Co.F
Taylor, Charles VA 45th Inf. Co.H
Taylor, Charles VA 51st Inf. Co.A
Taylor, Charles VA 63rd Inf. Co.F
Taylor, Charles Conf.Cav. Wood's Regt. Co.D,B
Taylor, Charles A. AL 11th Inf. Co.I
Taylor, Charles A. GA 4th Inf. Co.I
Taylor, Charles A. LA 1st (Strawbridge's) Inf. Co.K Capt.
Taylor, Charles A. MO Inf. 8th Bn. Co.C
Taylor, Charles A. NC 2nd Arty. (36th St.Troops) Co.F
Taylor, Charles A. VA Lt.Arty. 38th Bn. Co.D 1st Sgt.
Taylor, Charles B. TX 24th Cav. Co.D
Taylor, Charles C. AR 1st Vol. Co.C
Taylor, Charles C. VA 15th Inf. Co.E 2nd Lt.
Taylor, Charles D. AR 11th Inf. Co.F
Taylor, Charles D. AR 17th (Lemoyne's) Inf. Co.H Sgt.
Taylor, Charles D. AR 21st Inf. Co.H 1st Lt.
Taylor, Charles D. GA 4th Inf. Co.G
Taylor, Charles E. MS 20th Inf. Co.E Jr.2nd Lt.
Taylor, Charles E. MS 29th Inf. Co.C
Taylor, Charles E. VA 10th Cav. Co.F
Taylor, Charles E. VA 8th Inf. Co.I Sgt.
Taylor, Charles E. VA 21st Inf. Co.F
Taylor, Charles E. Sig.Corps,CSA
Taylor, Charles F. MS 15th Inf. Co.H Sgt.
Taylor, Charles F. TN 21st Inf. Co.F
Taylor, Charles F. Conf.Cav. Clarkson's Bn. Ind.Rangers Co.H
Taylor, Charles G. SC Arty. Manigault's Bn. 1st Co.A
Taylor, Charles G. SC 5th Bn.Res. Co.C Cpl.
Taylor, Charles G. TN 44th (Cons.) Inf. Co.A
Taylor, Charles H. GA 36th (Villepigue's) Inf. Co.E,F
Taylor, Charles H. GA 46th Inf. Co.D
Taylor, Charles H. GA 49th Inf. Co.D
Taylor, Charles H. VA 2nd Cav. Co.K Bugler
Taylor, Charles H. VA 18th Cav. Co.D
Taylor, Charles H. VA 18th Cav. 1st Co.G
Taylor, Charles H. VA 25th Cav. Co.A Cpl.
Taylor, Charles H. VA Cav. 41st Bn. Co.A
Taylor, Charles H. VA Inf. 21st Bn. 1st Co.D
Taylor, Charles Harvey VA 33rd Inf. Co.I
Taylor, Charles I. TX 2nd Cav. Co.A
Taylor, Charles J. MD 1st Cav. Co.D
Taylor, Charles J. MS 17th Inf. Co.A
Taylor, Charles J. VA 64th Mtd.Inf. 2nd Co.F
Taylor, Charles L. TX 5th Cav. Co.C
Taylor, Charles L. TX Inf. Whaley's Co.
Taylor, Charles M. AR 19th (Dawson's) Inf. Co.F
Taylor, Charles M. NC 18th Inf. Co.E
Taylor, Charles M. TX 17th Cav. Co.K
Taylor, Charles M. 8th (Wade's) Conf.Cav. Co.D
Taylor, Chas. M. Gen. & Staff Surg.
Taylor, Charles P. AL 17th Inf. Co.A
Taylor, Charles P. TN 44th Inf. Co.D Sgt.
Taylor, Charles R. GA 1st Reg. Co.F

Taylor, Charles R. GA 43rd Inf. Co.I
Taylor, Charles S. MD 1st Inf.
Taylor, Charles S. NC 15th Inf. Co.H Sgt.
Taylor, Charles S. VA 26th Cav. Co.C
Taylor, Charles S. VA Lt.Arty. Arch. Graham's Co.
Taylor, Charles S. VA 29th Inf. Co.G
Taylor, Charles S. VA 50th Inf. Co.F
Taylor, Charles S. Gen. & Staff Capt., Asst.Comsy.
Taylor, Charles T. FL 1st Inf.
Taylor, Chs. V. MS 1st Lt.Arty. Co.H
Taylor, Charles W. AL 6th Inf. Co.B
Taylor, Charles W. NC 37th Inf. Co.I
Taylor, Charles W. NC 53rd Inf. Co.E Cpl.
Taylor, Charles W. TX 17th Cav. Co.B
Taylor, Charles W. VA 3rd Cav. Co.D Sgt.
Taylor, Charles W. VA 37th Inf. Co.A Capt.
Taylor, Charles W. VA 63rd Inf. Co.K
Taylor, Charles W. VA Mil. Carroll Cty.
Taylor, Charnic GA 4th Inf. Co.C
Taylor, Chastain H. VA 15th Inf. Co.E 1st Lt.
Taylor, Chesley TN 28th (Cons.) Inf. Co.I
Taylor, Chester TN 84th Inf. Co.E
Taylor, Chester VA Inf. 45th Bn. Co.F
Taylor, Chester VA 50th Inf. Co.C
Taylor, Chris VA 72nd Mil.
Taylor, Chrisman VA 6th Bn.Res. Co.G
Taylor, Christian C. NC 48th Inf. Co.B Cpl.
Taylor, Christian N. GA Hvy.Arty. 22nd Bn. Co.B Cpl.
Taylor, Christian N. GA 25th Inf. 1st Co.K Cpl.
Taylor, Christopher VA 2nd Arty. Co.G
Taylor, Christopher VA 9th Mil. Co.A
Taylor, Christopher VA Inf. 22nd Bn. Co.G
Taylor, Christopher C. GA 20th Inf. Co.E Cpl.
Taylor, Christopher C. NC 1st Arty. (10th St.Troops) Co.H
Taylor, Cicero C NC 8th Bn.Part.Rangers Co.C,F Sgt.
Taylor, Cicero C. NC 66th Inf. Co.I Sgt.
Taylor, Cicero M. TN 41st Inf. Co.G
Taylor, C.J. VA 1st Res. Co.A
Taylor, C.J. VA 3rd Res. Co.A
Taylor, C.K. VA Wade's Regt.Loc.Def. Co.D Capt.
Taylor, C.L. GA 24th Inf. Co.E
Taylor, C.L. GA 39th Inf. Co.I
Taylor, C.L. TX 12th Cav. Co.B
Taylor, C.L. TX Cav. Mann's Regt. Co.A
Taylor, C.L. TX 4th Inf. Co.H
Taylor, C.L. TX 12th Inf. Co.I
Taylor, C.L. TX Waul's Legion Co.B Cpl.
Taylor, Claborn 10th Conf.Cav. Co.G
Taylor, Clarence E. VA 21st Inf. Co.F
Taylor, Clay MO 7th Cav. Co.D
Taylor, Clay MO Inf. 2nd Regt.St.Guard Co.A 3rd Lt.
Taylor, Clay VA 13th Inf. Co.A Music.
Taylor, Clay Price's Div. Lt.Col.,Ord.Ch.
Taylor, Clay Gen. & Staff Lt.Col.
Taylor, Clayborn GA Cav. 19th Bn. Co.B
Taylor, Clenn MO Arty.Regt.St.Guard Co.C 2nd Lt.
Taylor, Cleve NC 26th Inf. Co.A
Taylor, Cleveland GA 39th Inf. Co.B
Taylor, Cleveland TN 59th Mtd.Inf. Co.D
Taylor, C.M. AL 4th Cav.
Taylor, C.M. AL 24th Inf. Co.C
Taylor, C.M. AR Mil. Desha Cty.Bn.
Taylor, C.M. KY 5th Cav. Co.H 3rd Lt.
Taylor, C.M. MS Cav. 4th Bn. Co.B
Taylor, C.M. MS Cav. Jeff Davis Legion Co.C
Taylor, C.M. SC 2nd Inf. Co.K
Taylor, C.M. SC 4th Inf. Co.H
Taylor, C.M. TN 17th Inf. Co.E
Taylor, C.M. Morgan's Co.D,CSA
Taylor, C. Monroe SC Arty. Fickling's Co. (Brooks Lt.Arty.)
Taylor, Columbus TX 14th Cav. Co.H
Taylor, Columbus C. GA 3rd Inf. Co.D
Taylor, Columbus C. GA 47th Inf. Co.B
Taylor, Columbus J. GA Inf. Cobb Guards Co.A Sgt.
Taylor, Columbus W. GA 15th Inf. Co.D
Taylor, Cornelius AL 45th Inf. Co.F
Taylor, Cornelius VA Hvy.Arty. 19th Bn. Co.D Drum.
Taylor, Cornelius C. VA Lt.Arty. Ancell's Co.
Taylor, Cornelius C. VA Lt.Arty. Snead's Co.
Taylor, Cornelius W. VA 1st Arty. Co.B Sgt.
Taylor, Cornelius W. VA 32nd Inf. 1st Co.H Sgt.
Taylor, C.P. AL 5th Cav. Co.B
Taylor, C.P. AL 10th Cav. Co.A
Taylor, C.P. AL 26th (O'Neal's) Inf. Co.C Sgt.
Taylor, C.P. GA 38th Inf. Co.N
Taylor, C.P. LA Inf. 9th Bn. Co.B
Taylor, C.P. MS Cav. Jeff Davis Legion Co.B
Taylor, C.P. TN 17th Inf. Co.D
Taylor, C.P. TN 24th Inf. Co.A
Taylor, C.P. TN 45th Inf. Co.A
Taylor, C.P. TX 3rd Cav. Co.D
Taylor, C.P. VA 19th Inf. Co.H
Taylor, C.P.D. AL 23rd Inf. Co.B
Taylor, C.R. VA Cav. 1st Bn. Co.C
Taylor, C.R. VA 1st St.Res. Co.C Cpl.
Taylor, Creed TN 32nd Inf. Co.F
Taylor, Creed TN 35th Inf. 2nd Co.F
Taylor, Creed Conf.Cav. Clarkson's Bn. Ind. Rangers Co.A
Taylor, Creed 1st Cherokee Mtd.Vol. 1st Co.I Sgt.
Taylor, C. Rhodes TX Cav. Martin's Regt. Co.B
Taylor, Crosby TX 36th Cav. Co.H
Taylor, C.S. SC 1st Inf. Co.L
Taylor, C.S. VA 3rd Inf.Loc.Def. Co.C
Taylor, C.T. NC 48th Inf. Co.D
Taylor, Curtis F. VA 14th Cav. Co.A
Taylor, C.W., Jr. GA 60th Inf. Co.C Cpl.
Taylor, C.W., Sr. GA 60th Inf. Co.C
Taylor, C.W. MS 41st Inf. Co.F
Taylor, C.W. NC 3rd Jr.Res. Co.C Sgt.
Taylor, C.W. NC 4th Bn.Jr.Res. Co.C Sgt.
Taylor, C.W. TX 12th Cav. Co.A
Taylor, C.W. TX 30th Cav. Co.H
Taylor, C.W. TX 14th Inf. Co.H Sgt.
Taylor, C.W. VA Lt.Arty. 1st Bn. Co.B
Taylor, C.W. VA Arty. Richardson's Co.
Taylor, D. GA 5th Res. Co.G
Taylor, D. GA 63rd Inf. Co.F
Taylor, D. LA 10th Inf. Co.E
Taylor, D. SC 7th Inf. Co.H
Taylor, D. SC 15th Inf. Co.C
Taylor, D. TN 8th (Smith's) Cav. Co.G
Taylor, D. VA 88th Mil.
Taylor, D.A. AL 45th Inf. Co.C
Taylor, D.A. SC 5th Inf. 2nd Co.A
Taylor, D.A. TN 12th (Green's) Cav. Co.H Sgt.
Taylor, D.A. VA 8th Cav. Co.C
Taylor, Dallas TN 45th Inf. Co.C
Taylor, Daniel AL Cav. Murphy's Bn. Co.D
Taylor, Daniel GA Arty. 11th Bn. (Sumter Arty.) Co.A
Taylor, Daniel GA 1st Inf. (St.Guards) Co.F
Taylor, Daniel GA 11th Inf. Co.C
Taylor, Daniel GA 43rd Inf. Co.C
Taylor, Daniel GA 60th Inf. Co.G
Taylor, Daniel KY 9th Cav. Co.F
Taylor, Daniel KY 3rd Bn.Mtd.Rifles Co.E
Taylor, Daniel KY 1st Inf. Co.C
Taylor, Daniel LA Cav. Webb's Co.
Taylor, Daniel MS 2nd Cav. Co.E
Taylor, Daniel NC Inf. 13th Bn. Co.B
Taylor, Daniel NC 54th Inf. Co.D
Taylor, Daniel TN 1st Hvy.Arty. Co.F
Taylor, Daniel TX Granbury's Cons.Brig. Co.A
Taylor, Daniel TX 6th Inf. Co.C
Taylor, Daniel VA 4th Cav. Co.D
Taylor, Daniel VA 97th Mil. Co.M
Taylor, Daniel 3rd Conf.Cav. Co.F
Taylor, Daniel 15th Conf.Cav. Co.K
Taylor, Daniel A. MO Inf. 1st Bn. Co.B
Taylor, Daniel A. MO 5th Inf. Co.K
Taylor, Daniel A. NC 1st Jr.Res. Co.A
Taylor, Daniel A. NC 12th Inf. Co.H
Taylor, Daniel A. NC 60th Inf. Co.D
Taylor, Daniel A. NC Walker's Bn. Thomas' Legion Co.F Sgt.
Taylor, Daniel D. TX 14th Cav. Co.G
Taylor, Daniel F. MS 13th Inf. Co.B
Taylor, Daniel G. NC 27th Inf. Co.D
Taylor, Daniel H. VA 22nd Inf. Co.D
Taylor, Daniel J. AL 3rd Inf. Co.K
Taylor, Daniel J. GA 11th Cav. (St.Guards) Folks' Co.
Taylor, Daniel J. TN 60th Mtd.Inf. Co.H
Taylor, Daniel R. MS 29th Inf. Co.E
Taylor, Daniel R. NC Walker's Bn. Thomas' Legion Co.C
Taylor, Daniel S. TN 54th Inf. Co.G
Taylor, David AL 3rd Bn.Res. Co.C
Taylor, David AL 30th Inf. Co.G
Taylor, David AL 60th Inf. Co.E
Taylor, David AL 89th Mil. Co.D
Taylor, David AL 3rd Bn. Hilliard's Legion Vol. Co.A
Taylor, David AR 1st Vol. Co.F
Taylor, David AR 9th Inf. Old Co.I
Taylor, David AR 32nd Inf. Co.F
Taylor, David AR 45th Mil. Co.C
Taylor, David FL 4th Inf. Co.H
Taylor, David GA 10th Inf. Co.K
Taylor, David GA 22nd Inf. Co.K
Taylor, David GA 49th Inf. Co.F
Taylor, David GA Inf. (Richmond Factory Guards) Barney's Co.
Taylor, David KY Cav. 2nd Bn. (Dortch's) Co.C
Taylor, David LA Inf.Crescent Regt. Co.F
Taylor, David LA Inf.Cons.Crescent Regt. Co.G
Taylor, David MS 21st Inf. Co.D

Taylor, David NC Cav. McRae's Bn. Co.C
Taylor, David NC 8th Inf. Co.K
Taylor, David SC 1st (McCreary's) Inf. Co.E Cpl.
Taylor, David TN Cav. Cox's Bn. Co.C
Taylor, David TN Arty. Marshall's Co.
Taylor, David VA 1st Arty. Co.H
Taylor, David VA 51st Inf. Co.K Cpl.
Taylor, David VA Mil. Scott Cty.
Taylor, David Mead's Conf.Cav. Co.B
Taylor, David Mead's Conf.Cav. Co.D
Taylor, David A. SC 9th Inf. Co.A
Taylor, David B. MS 24th Inf. Co.L Cpl.
Taylor, David B. VA Cav. 14th Bn. Co.B
Taylor, David B. VA 15th Cav. Co.I
Taylor, David B. VA 40th Inf. Co.K
Taylor, David C. GA 3rd Inf. Co.I
Taylor, David C. NC Hvy.Arty. 1st Bn. Co.C
Taylor, David C. TN 28th (Cons.) Inf. Co.I 2nd Lt.
Taylor, David C. VA 12th Inf. Co.A
Taylor, David D. AL 3rd Inf. Co.D
Taylor, David D. NC 51st Inf. Co.F
Taylor, David D. TN 3rd (Lillard's) Mtd.Inf. Co.F
Taylor, David E. VA 5th Cav. (12 mo. '61-2) Co.I
Taylor, David F. AR 20th Inf. Co.A
Taylor, David F. 1st Choctaw & Chickasaw Mtd.Inf. 2nd Co.H
Taylor, David H. KY 1st (Butler's) Cav.
Taylor, David H. SC 13th Inf. Co.G
Taylor, David H. TN 48th (Voorhies') Inf. Co.B
Taylor, David H. TX 5th Cav. Co.A
Taylor, David I. Sap. & Min. G.W. Maxson's Co.,CSA
Taylor, David J. AL 12th Inf. Co.A Sgt.
Taylor, David J. AL 16th Inf. Co.A
Taylor, David J. NC 2nd Arty. (36th St.Troops) Co.A
Taylor, David J. TN 1st (Feild's) Inf. Co.D
Taylor, David J. TX 21st Cav. Co.D
Taylor, David J. 3rd Conf.Eng.Troops Co.F
Taylor, David L. FL 8th Inf. Co.F
Taylor, David L. GA 12th Inf. Co.G
Taylor, David L. TX 27th Cav. Co.C
Taylor, David M. MS 9th Inf. New Co.K
Taylor, David M. NC 34th Inf. Co.E 1st Sgt.
Taylor, David M. NC 62nd Inf. Co.F
Taylor, David M. TX 14th Cav. Co.C
Taylor, David P. MO 6th Cav.
Taylor, David R. VA 6th Inf. Co.D
Taylor, David S. AL 3rd Inf. Co.K Cpl.
Taylor, David S. GA 56th Inf. Co.A Cpl.
Taylor, David S. SC 16th Inf. Co.I Sgt.
Taylor, Davidson C. TN 2nd (Robison's) Inf. Co.D
Taylor, David T. MS 1st Bn.S.S. Co.C
Taylor, David W. GA 5th Inf. Co.H,E Sgt.
Taylor, David W. KY 9th Mtd.Inf. Co.D
Taylor, David W. NC 1st Arty. (10th St.Troops) Co.H
Taylor, Davis K. VA 13th Inf. Co.K Drum.
Taylor, D.B. AL 9th Inf. Co.G Sgt.
Taylor, D.B. AR 38th Inf. Co.A Sgt.
Taylor, D.B. FL 2nd Inf. Co.A Sgt.
Taylor, D.B. KY 1st (Butler's) Cav. Co.F Capt.
Taylor, D.B. KY Cav. Thompson's Co.
Taylor, D.B. NC 4th Cav. (59th St.Troops) Co.E
Taylor, D.B. NC 1st Inf. (6 mo. '61) Co.B
Taylor, D.B. TN 21st Cav. Co.H
Taylor, D.B. TN Cav. Cox's Bn.
Taylor, D.B. TX 3rd Inf. Co.E
Taylor, D.B. VA 5th Cav. Co.K
Taylor, D.B. VA 6th Inf. Vickery's Co.
Taylor, D.B. Perrin's Staff 1st Lt.,ADC
Taylor, D. Belt NC 5th Cav. (63rd St.Troops) Co.F
Taylor, D.C. AR Inf. Cocke's Regt. Co.G
Taylor, D.C. FL 1st (Res.) Inf. Co.L
Taylor, D.C. LA Cav. 18th Bn. Co.B Cpl.
Taylor, D.C. TN 46th Inf. Co.D
Taylor, D.C. TN 84th Inf. Co.E 2nd Lt.
Taylor, D.C. VA 17th Cav. Co.G
Taylor, D.D. AL 9th (Malone's) Cav. Co.B
Taylor, D.E. VA Inf. 5th Bn.Loc.Def. Co.B 1st Lt.
Taylor, Dempsey GA 51st Inf. Co.E
Taylor, Dempsey NC 5th Inf. Co.H
Taylor, Dempsey R. VA 12th Inf. Co.F
Taylor, Dempsy Conf.Cav. Wood's Regt. 1st Co.A
Taylor, Dennis L. AL 16th Inf. Co.A
Taylor, Dennis M. GA 49th Inf. Co.E
Taylor, Derrell C. MS 16th Inf. Co.A Music.
Taylor, D.F. TN 30th Inf. Co.B
Taylor, D.F. TX Cav. Bourland's Regt. Co.I
Taylor, D.G. AL 5th Inf. Co.B
Taylor, D.G. SC 4th Bn.Res. Co.D
Taylor, D.G. TN 28th Cav. Co.A Sgt.
Taylor, D.G. TX 19th Inf. Co.E
Taylor, D.H. KY 10th (Johnson's) Cav. New Co.B
Taylor, D.H. KY Morgan's Men Co.G
Taylor, D.H. KY 4th Mtd.Inf. Co.C
Taylor, D.H. MS 1st Inf.
Taylor, D.H. NC 8th Bn.Part.Rangers Co.C
Taylor, D.H. NC Bass' Co.
Taylor, Dillon MO 10th Inf. Co.A Sgt.
Taylor, Dixon L. AL 17th Inf. Co.A
Taylor, D.J. AL Auburn Home Guards Vol. Darby's Co.
Taylor, D.J. GA 4th (Clinch's) Cav. Co.K
Taylor, D.L. GA Lt.Arty. 12th Bn. Co.F
Taylor, D.M., Sr. LA Inf. 10th Bn. Co.G
Taylor, D.M. TX Cav. 2nd Bn.St.Troops Wilson's Co.
Taylor, D.M. VA 56th Inf. Co.H
Taylor, Doctor L. TX 27th Cav. Co.C
Taylor, Doctor W. NC 14th Inf. Co.G
Taylor, Donson T. VA Cav. Thurmond's Co.
Taylor, Dorwin TX 14th Cav. Co.E
Taylor, Dossey NC 17th Inf. (2nd Org.) Co.D 1st Lt.
Taylor, D.P. AR 8th Inf. New Co.F
Taylor, D.P. AR 18th (Marmaduke's) Inf. Co.A Sgt.
Taylor, D.P. GA 17th Inf. Co.G Cpl.
Taylor, D.P. 3rd Conf.Inf. Co.A Sgt.
Taylor, D.R. MS 36th Inf. Co.F Cpl.
Taylor, D.R. TX 17th Inf. Co.B
Taylor, Drayton T. SC 13th Inf. Co.G
Taylor, D.S. SC Bn.St.Cadets Co.B
Taylor, D.S. TN 48th (Nixon's) Inf. Co.K
Taylor, D.S. VA 17th Cav. Co.G
Taylor, D.T. AR 30th Inf. Co.E
Taylor, D.T. TX 11th Cav. Co.D
Taylor, Duncan NC 3rd Bn.Sr.Res. Durham's Co.
Taylor, Duncan NC 6th Inf. Co.B
Taylor, Duncan D. GA 24th Inf. Co.E
Taylor, Duncan G.C. AL 10th Inf. Co.I
Taylor, Dunklin B. FL 2nd Inf. Co.A Sgt.
Taylor, Durant NC 66th Inf. Co.D
Taylor, D.W. AR 32nd Inf. Co.K
Taylor, D.W. MS 22nd Inf.
Taylor, D.W. NC 48th Inf. Co.D
Taylor, D.W. TX 9th Cav. Co.E
Taylor, D.W. VA 11th Bn.Res. Co.B
Taylor, D.Y. AL 32nd Inf. Co.I
Taylor, E. AL 23rd Inf. Co.D
Taylor, E. AL 62nd Inf. Co.F,H
Taylor, E. AL Cp. of Instr. Talladega
Taylor, E. AR 38th Inf. Co.G
Taylor, E. FL 11th Inf. Co.C
Taylor, E. LA Mil. 1st Chasseurs a pied Co.5
Taylor, E. MS 1st (King's) Inf. (St.Troops) Co.G
Taylor, E. SC 1st Inf. Co.N
Taylor, E. TN 19th & 20th (Cons.) Cav. Co.D
Taylor, E. VA 3rd Inf.Loc.Def. 1st Co.G
Taylor, E. VA 10th Bn.Res. Co.D
Taylor, E. 1st Corps Maj.,QM
Taylor, E.A. AL 9th Inf.
Taylor, E.A. AL 10th Inf. Co.K
Taylor, E.A. AL 2nd Bn. Hilliard's Legion Vol. Co.B
Taylor, E.A. MS Lt.Arty. 14th Bn. Co.B
Taylor, E.A. TX 2nd Inf. Co.A
Taylor, E.A. VA 8th Inf. Co.E
Taylor, Ealbius E. TX 31st Cav. Co.D
Taylor, Earles J. NC 29th Inf. Co.A
Taylor, Eaton GA 26th Inf. Co.G
Taylor, Eaton GA 50th Inf. Co.B
Taylor, E.B. GA 8th Inf. (St.Guards) Co.D 1st Lt.
Taylor, E.B. SC 19th Inf. Co.G
Taylor, E.B. SC Post Guard Senn's Co.
Taylor, E.B. TN 28th (Cons.) Inf. Co.E Sgt.
Taylor, E.B. TN 84th Inf. Co.A Sgt.
Taylor, E.B. TX 3rd Cav. Co.A
Taylor, E.B. VA 18th Cav. Co.A Lt.
Taylor, Eben VA 8th Inf. Co.A Cpl.
Taylor, E.C. AL 29th Inf. Co.A
Taylor, E.C. AL Cp. of Instr. Talladega
Taylor, E.C. TN 28th Inf. Co.A
Taylor, Ed. AL 4th Res. Co.F
Taylor, E.D. AL 22nd Inf. Co.E 1st Lt.
Taylor, Ed AR Mil. Desha Cty.Bn.
Taylor, Ed AR Pickett's Regt. Co.E
Taylor, E.D. GA 2nd Regt.St.Line Co.I
Taylor, E.D. GA 39th Inf. Co.D
Taylor, Ed. LA Hvy.Arty. 8th Bn. Co.C
Taylor, Ed MS 11th (Perrin's) Cav. Co.H
Taylor, E.D. SC 12th Inf. Co.D
Taylor, Ed. TN 40th Inf. Co.B
Taylor, E.D. VA Hvy.Arty. Coffin's Co.
Taylor, Eden GA 8th Inf. (St.Guards) Co.D
Taylor, Edmon TN 10th (DeMoss') Cav. Co.F
Taylor, Edmond TN Cav. Napier's Bn. Co.C
Taylor, Edmond VA 2nd Arty. Co.G Cpl.
Taylor, Edmond VA Lt.Arty. Kirkpatrick's Co.

Taylor, Edmond VA Lt.Arty. Nelson's Co. Cpl.
Taylor, Edmond VA 21st Inf. Co.E
Taylor, Edmond VA 87th Mil. Co.C
Taylor, Edmond G. NC 43rd Inf. Co.K
Taylor, Edmond H. KY 8th Cav. Co.E Sgt.
Taylor, Edmond R. AL 38th Inf. Co.B
Taylor, Edmund GA Lt.Arty. Hamilton's Co. 1st Lt.
Taylor, Edmund GA 5th Inf. Co.H,E
Taylor, Edmund VA Res.Forces Clark's Co. 2nd Lt.
Taylor, Edmund Gen. & Staff, Inf. 1st Lt.
Taylor, Edmund D. TN 11th Inf. Co.A
Taylor, Edmund P. VA 9th Cav. Co.A
Taylor, Edward GA 39th Inf. Co.A
Taylor, Edward KY 9th Cav. Co.C 1st Lt.
Taylor, Edward LA 1st Hvy.Arty. (Reg.) Co.C
Taylor, Edward LA 20th Inf. Co.A
Taylor, Edward MS Cav. 1st Bn. (Mcnair's) St.Troops Co.C
Taylor, Edward MS 8th Inf. Co.I
Taylor, Edward MO 1st Inf. Co.D Cpl.
Taylor, Edward MO 10th Inf. Co.E
Taylor, Edward NC 2nd Inf. Co.E Cpl.
Taylor, Edward SC 1st St.Troops Co.I
Taylor, Edward SC 6th Inf. 2nd Co.G
Taylor, Edward SC 6th Res. Co.F
Taylor, Edward TX 2nd Cav. Co.G
Taylor, Edward A. VA Lt.Arty. Donald's Co.
Taylor, Edward B. SC 4th Bn.Res. Co.B
Taylor, Edward B. VA Arty. Dance's Co.
Taylor, Edward B. VA 21st Inf. Co.F
Taylor, Edward C. VA 49th Inf. Co.A
Taylor, Edward E. TN 24th Inf. Co.D
Taylor, Edward G. GA 66th Inf. Co.D
Taylor, Edward H. VA Hvy.Arty. A.J. Jones' Co.
Taylor, Edward K. TX Cav. 8th (Taylor's) Bn. Co.E Sgt.Maj.
Taylor, Edward L. AL 3rd Inf. Co.H 1st Lt.
Taylor, Edward L. VA 20th Inf. Co.C
Taylor, Edward M. VA Hvy.Arty. 20th Bn. Co.A
Taylor, Edward M. VA 44th Inf. Co.A
Taylor, Edward P. VA Inf. 22nd Bn. Lt.Col.
Taylor, Edward R. VA 51st Inf. Co.C Hosp.Stew.
Taylor, Edward S. NC 49th Inf. Co.F
Taylor, Edward V. VA 9th Cav. Co.A
Taylor, Edwin MO 16th Inf. Co.A
Taylor, Edwin NC 29th Inf. Co.G
Taylor, Edwin NC 42nd Inf. Co.H
Taylor, Edwin TX 15th Inf. Co.K
Taylor, Edwin VA 7th Cav. Co.B Cpl.
Taylor, Edwin J. GA Inf. 10th Bn. Co.A Cpl.
Taylor, Edwin M. TX 1st Inf. Co.H
Taylor, E.E. AL 7th Cav. Co.A Sgt.
Taylor, E.F. AL Lt.Arty. Goldthwaite's Btty. Cpl.
Taylor, E.G. AR 7th Inf. Co.G
Taylor, E.G. SC Inf. 1st (Charleston) Bn. Co.D
Taylor, E.G. SC 27th Inf. Co.D
Taylor, Egbert H. NC 30th Inf. Co.I
Taylor, E.H. GA 11th Cav. (St.Guards) Smith's Co.
Taylor, E.H.L. AL 63rd Inf. Co.D
Taylor, Eiven P. GA 65th Inf. Co.K
Taylor, E.J. SC 1st Cav. Co.G
Taylor, E.J. SC 5th Res. Co.I
Taylor, E.J. VA 17th Cav. Co.C
Taylor, E.L. AR 18th Inf. Co.F Sgt.
Taylor, E.L. GA 44th Inf. Co.H
Taylor, E.L. VA Hvy.Arty. Allen's Co.
Taylor, E.L. Gen. & Staff Hosp.Stew.
Taylor, Elam SC 5th Mil. Beat Co.3
Taylor, Elam 4th Conf.Inf. Co.D
Taylor, Elam B. VA 17th Cav. Co.C
Taylor, Elam B. VA 62nd Mtd.Inf. 2nd Co.H Sgt.
Taylor, Elbert J. SC 20th Inf. Co.K
Taylor, Eleazar GA 46th Inf. Co.H Capt.
Taylor, Elem B VA Cav. 36th Bn. Co.B
Taylor, Eli GA 47th Inf. Co.F
Taylor, Eli LA 26th Inf. Music.
Taylor, Eli MS 2nd Inf. Co.F
Taylor, Eli MS 4th Inf. Co.F
Taylor, Eli VA 17th Cav. Co.C
Taylor, Eli VA 18th Cav. Co.A
Taylor, Eli VA Cav. 36th Bn. Co.B
Taylor, Eli VA 22nd Inf. Co.E
Taylor, Elias AL 1st Bn. Hilliard's Legion Vol. Co.F
Taylor, Elias GA Inf. 8th Bn. Co.A Cpl.
Taylor, Elias LA 5th Cav. Co.I
Taylor, Elias LA 19th Inf. Co.E
Taylor, Elias MS 30th Inf. Co.D
Taylor, Elias NC 37th Inf. Co.I Music.
Taylor, Elias SC Inf. Hampton Legion Co.G
Taylor, Eli C. MS Inf. 3rd Bn. Co.B
Taylor, Elihu VA 6th Bn.Res. Co.G
Taylor, Elijah AR 38th Inf. Co.D
Taylor, Elijah GA 47th Inf. Co.F
Taylor, Elijah KY 5th Cav. Co.E
Taylor, Elijah MO 4th Cav. Co.A
Taylor, Elijah MO 12th Inf. Co.B
Taylor, Elijah A. MO 3rd Inf. Co.B
Taylor, Elijah N. AL 17th Inf. Co.E
Taylor, Elijah S. MO Cav. Preston's Bn. Co.A
Taylor, Elisha GA 47th Inf. Co.F
Taylor, Ellis VA Lt.Arty. Thornton's Co.
Taylor, Ely VA 14th Cav. Co.M Sgt.
Taylor, Elza NC 8th Bn.Part.Rangers Co.B,E
Taylor, Elza NC 66th Inf. Co.H
Taylor, E.M. AL 3rd Cav. Co.C
Taylor, E.M. AR 10th Mil.
Taylor, E.M. LA 17th Inf. Co.C
Taylor, E.M. MS 37th Inf. Co.F
Taylor, Em. TX 16th Inf. Co.D Capt.
Taylor, E.M. TX Vol. Rainey's Co.
Taylor, E.M. VA 5th Cav. Co.G
Taylor, Emanuel LA Miles' Legion Co.C
Taylor, Emanuel NC 17th Inf. (1st Org.) Co.K
Taylor, Emanuel SC 20th Inf. Co.K
Taylor, Emanuel VA 31st Inf. 2nd Co.B,E
Taylor, Emanuel VA 62nd Mtd.Inf. 2nd Co.C
Taylor, E.M.B. SC 7th Inf. 1st Co.D, 2nd Co.D
Taylor, Embey VA Cav. 34th Bn. Co.G
Taylor, Embry VA 72nd Mil.
Taylor, E.McI.P. LA 27th Inf. Co.A
Taylor, Emmet D. AL 43rd Inf. Co.C
Taylor, Emzy TX 4th Inf. Co.E
Taylor, E.N. TN Inf. 1st Cons.Regt. Co.F
Taylor, E.N. TN 16th Inf. Co.G
Taylor, E.N. TN Inf. 22nd Bn. Co.B
Taylor, E.N. TN 46th Inf. Co.D
Taylor, Enoch MS 22nd Inf. Co.A
Taylor, Enoch NC 1st Arty. (10th St.Troops) Co.I
Taylor, Enos VA 9th Inf. Co.E
Taylor, Enos W. VA 11th Cav. Co.D
Taylor, Enos W. VA 77th Mil. Co.A Cpl.
Taylor, E.P. GA 8th Inf. Co.C 2nd Lt.
Taylor, E.P. TN 26th Inf. Co.C
Taylor, E.P. TX 7th Cav. Co.K
Taylor, Ephraim FL 2nd Inf. Co.K
Taylor, Ephraim NC Loc.Def. Croom's Co.
Taylor, Ephraim SC 1st (Hagood's) Inf. 2nd Co.I
Taylor, Ephraim T. LA 16th Inf. Co.D
Taylor, Ephram R. GA Inf. 10th Bn. Co.B
Taylor, E.R. AL Cp. of Instr. Talladega
Taylor, E.R. MO 7th Cav. Co.I
Taylor, E.R. TX Waul's Legion Co.D
Taylor, Erasmus VA 18th Cav. Co.D
Taylor, Erastus H. VA 63rd Inf. Co.D 3rd Lt.
Taylor, Ervin SC Lt.Arty. Kelly's Co. (Chesterfield Arty.)
Taylor, E.S. AL Cav. Barlow's Co.
Taylor, E.S. MO 8th Cav. Reed's Co. 3rd Lt.
Taylor, E.S. 15th Conf.Cav. Co.C
Taylor, E. Sumpter LA 8th Inf. Co.F Capt.
Taylor, Eugene LA 1st Cav. Co.H
Taylor, Eugene G. VA 19th Inf. Co.B Sgt.
Taylor, Eugene L. VA Arty. Dance's Co.
Taylor, Evan AL 17th Inf. Co.D
Taylor, Evan FL 1st Inf. Old Co.A, New Co.B
Taylor, Evan G.T. AL 57th Inf. Co.K Cpl.
Taylor, Evan T. VA Mil. Greene Cty.
Taylor, Everette TX 19th Inf. Co.E
Taylor, E.W. NC 2nd Jr.Res. Co.I
Taylor, E.W. NC 14th Inf. Co.D
Taylor, E.W., Jr. TN 28th (Cons.) Inf. Co.I
Taylor, E.W., Sr. TN 28th (Cons.) Inf. Co.I
Taylor, E.W., Jr. TN 84th Inf. Co.E
Taylor, E.W., Sr. TN 84th Inf. Co.E
Taylor, E.W. TX 19th Inf. Co.A Col.
Taylor, E.W. TX Inf. Houston Bn. Capt.
Taylor, E.W. VA Inf. 4th Bn.Loc.Def. Co.B
Taylor, E.W. Gen. & Staff,PACS Maj.
Taylor, E.W. Gen. & Staff Capt.,AQM
Taylor, E.Z. TN 7th (Duckworth's) Cav. Co.A
Taylor, Ezekiel AR 15th (N.W.) Inf. Emergency Co.I
Taylor, Ezekiel GA 2nd Cav. Co.G
Taylor, Ezekiel MO Lt.Arty. 1st Btty.
Taylor, Ezekiel TN Cav. 12th Bn. (Day's) Co.E
Taylor, Ezekiel TN Inf. 1st Bn. (Colms') Co.A
Taylor, Ezekiel VA Cav. Young's Co. Cpl.
Taylor, Ezekiel 8th (Wade's) Conf.Cav. Co.H Cpl.
Taylor, Ezekiel 1st Cherokee Mtd.Vol. 2nd Co.H
Taylor, Ezekiel 1st Squad. Cherokee Mtd.Vol. Co.A
Taylor, Ezekiel B. GA 45th Inf. Co.D
Taylor, F. GA Siege Arty. 28th Bn. Co.I
Taylor, F. GA Lt.Arty. Fraser's Btty.
Taylor, F. LA 7th Inf. Co.A
Taylor, F. MS 2nd St.Cav. Co.K
Taylor, F. SC Manigault's Bn.Vol. Co.A
Taylor, F. TN 21st Cav. Co.H
Taylor, F. VA 18th Cav. 2nd Co.E
Taylor, F. VA 44th Inf. Co.I

Taylor, F.A. MO 2nd Inf. Co.D
Taylor, F.A. VA 44th Inf. Co.H
Taylor, Farley B. VA Lt.Arty. Woolfolk's Co.
Taylor, F.B. NC 4th Bn.Jr.Res. Co.A
Taylor, F.B. TN Inf. 1st Cons.Regt. Co.E
Taylor, F.B. TN 9th Inf. Co.H
Taylor, F.B. TX 7th Cav. Co.I
Taylor, F.B. VA 8th Inf. Co.E
Taylor, F.B. 15th Conf.Cav. Co.A 2nd Lt.
Taylor, F.C. MO 16th Inf. Co.K Sgt.
Taylor, F. Cicero SC Arty. Fickling's Co. (Brooks Lt.Arty.)
Taylor, Felix G. TX 12th Inf. Co.D
Taylor, Felix W. NC Hvy.Arty. 1st Bn. Co.B
Taylor, Fenton J. GA 42nd Inf. Co.E
Taylor, Fetton AL 42nd Inf. Co.E
Taylor, F.F. AR 1st Cav. Co.A
Taylor, F.G. AL 7th Cav. Co.C,G
Taylor, F.G. AL 8th Inf. Co.D
Taylor, F.G. NC Loc.Def. Croom's Co. Cpl.
Taylor, F.G.H. LA Mil.Conf.Guards Regt. Co.C
Taylor, F.H. AL 31st Inf. Co.A
Taylor, F.H. KY 3rd Cav. Co.F
Taylor, F.H. KY 3rd Bn.Mtd.Rifles Co.F
Taylor, Fielding L. VA 12th Inf. Lt.Col.
Taylor, Filmore AL Talladega Cty.Res. B.H. Ford's Co.
Taylor, FitzWilliam B. FL Cav. 3rd Bn. Co.A 1st Sgt.
Taylor, F.J. TX 9th Field Btty.
Taylor, F.J. TX 12th Inf. Co.I Sgt.
Taylor, F.K. GA 13th Inf. Co.H 2nd Lt.
Taylor, F.L. GA 25th Inf. Co.C
Taylor, F.L. NC 1st Bn.Jr.Res. Co.C
Taylor, Fleuisted MO 10th Cav. Co.D
Taylor, F.M. AL 4th (Russell's) Cav. Maj.
Taylor, F.M. AL 4th Inf. Co.C Capt.
Taylor, F.M. AL 34th Inf. Co.B
Taylor, F.M. AL 55th Vol. Co.G Capt.
Taylor, F.M. AR 10th Inf. Co.A
Taylor, F.M. GA 11th Cav. Co.H
Taylor, F.M. GA 32nd Inf. Co.E
Taylor, F.M. LA 3rd (Harrison's) Cav. Co.D
Taylor, F.M. MS 6th Inf. Co.I Music.
Taylor, F.M. MS 25th Inf. Co.D 1st Lt.
Taylor, F.M. MO 10th Inf. Co.E
Taylor, F.M. NC 8th Sr.Res. Co.C
Taylor, F.M. TN 7th (Duckworth's) Cav. Co.D
Taylor, F.M. TN 10th & 11th (Cons.) Cav. Co.E
Taylor, F.M. TX 30th Cav. Co.C
Taylor, F.M. TX Cav. Crump's Regt.
Taylor, F.M. VA 18th Cav. Co.A
Taylor, F.M. VA 44th Inf. Co.K
Taylor, F.M. 2nd Conf.Inf. Co.D Capt.
Taylor, F.M. Gen. & Staff, Medical Dept. Surg.
Taylor, F.N. TN 49th Inf. Co.F
Taylor, Fountain E. Wheeler's Scouts,CSA
Taylor, F.R. GA 8th Inf. Co.B
Taylor, Frances A. SC 2nd Arty. Co.D
Taylor, Francis AR 19th (Dockery's) Inf. Co.H
Taylor, Francis KY 2nd Mtd.Inf. Co.K
Taylor, Francis MO 7th Cav. Co.H
Taylor, Francis NC 28th Inf. Co.F
Taylor, Francis VA Cav. 35th Bn. Co.D Sgt.
Taylor, Francis B. MS 24th Inf. Co.F Music.
Taylor, Francis B. MS 27th Inf. Co.E Music.
Taylor, Francis H. VA Cav. 41st Bn. Trayhern's Co.
Taylor, Francis L. GA 1st Bn.S.S. Co.A
Taylor, Francis M. AL 37th Inf. Co.B
Taylor, Francis M. AL 61st Inf. Co.H
Taylor, Francis M. NC 2nd Cav. (19th St.Troops) Co.A
Taylor, Francis M. TN 1st (Turney's) Inf. Co.A
Taylor, Francis M. TX Cav. Madison's Regt. Co.F
Taylor, Francis M. VA Lt.Arty. Ancell's Co.
Taylor, Francis M. VA 62nd Mtd.Inf. 2nd Co.H
Taylor, Francis R. GA 1st (Olmstead's) Inf. Co.D Cpl.
Taylor, Francis W. NC 5th Inf. Co.G 1st Lt.
Taylor, Francis W. VA Lt.Arty. Woolfolk's Co.
Taylor, Francois LA Inf. 10th Bn. Co.B
Taylor, Frank AR 2nd Cav. Co.C
Taylor, Frank GA 1st Inf. Co.F
Taylor, Frank GA 1st Reg. Co.F Drum.
Taylor, Frank GA 49th Inf. Co.E
Taylor, Frank GA 63rd Inf. Co.F
Taylor, Frank KY 4th Cav. Co.D,B
Taylor, Frank LA 2nd Cav. Co.A
Taylor, Frank LA Mtd.Rifles Miller's Ind.Co.
Taylor, Frank MS Inf. 3rd Bn. Co.B
Taylor, Frank NC 6th Cav. (65th St.Troops) Co.E
Taylor, Frank SC 2nd Inf. Co.A
Taylor, Frank TN 7th (Duckworth's) Cav. Co.L
Taylor, Frank VA 10th Cav. 1st Co.E
Taylor, Frank E. SC Inf. Hampton Legion Co.A Cpl.
Taylor, Franklin AL 36th Inf. Co.F
Taylor, Franklin MO Cav. 11th Regt.St.Guard Co.A 1st Lt.
Taylor, Franklin NC Cav. 7th Bn. Co.E
Taylor, Franklin NC 38th Inf. Co.H
Taylor, Franklin NC 48th Inf. Co.B
Taylor, Franklin NC 64th Inf. Co.E Sgt.
Taylor, Franklin SC 2nd Rifles Co.B
Taylor, Franklin VA 7th Cav. Co.B
Taylor, Franklin VA 10th Inf. Co.L
Taylor, Franklin VA 29th Inf. Co.A
Taylor, Franklin A. AR 27th Inf. Co.K
Taylor, Franklin C. GA 6th Inf. Co.E
Taylor, Franklin S. VA 55th Inf. Co.D
Taylor, Frank M. FL 11th Inf. Co.L
Taylor, Frank M. GA 48th Inf. Co.I
Taylor, Frank M. TX 3rd Cav. Co.C Capt.
Taylor, Frank S. TX 3rd Inf. Co.D
Taylor, Frank W. MS Cav. Jeff Davis Legion Co.E
Taylor, Frank W. MO 1st Cav. Co.I
Taylor, Frank W. NC Vol. Lawrence's Co.
Taylor, Frank W. 7th Conf.Cav. 1st Co.I,H Music.
Taylor, Fred A. AL 58th Inf. Co.A
Taylor, Fred C. LA Inf. 4th Bn. Co.E
Taylor, Frederick AL 60th Inf. Co.E
Taylor, Frederick AR Inf. 2nd Bn. Co.B
Taylor, Frederick LA 21st (Patton's) Inf. Co.A
Taylor, Frederick NC 2nd Inf. Co.B
Taylor, Frederick SC 4th Cav. Co.D
Taylor, Frederick TX 2nd Cav. Co.D
Taylor, Frederick VA 44th Inf. Co.G
Taylor, Frederick B. AL 13th Inf. Co.F
Taylor, Frederick M. AL 41st Inf. Co.C
Taylor, Fred P. AR 3rd Inf. Co.I
Taylor, Fredrick AL 3rd Bn. Hilliard's Legion Vol. Co.A
Taylor, Fred S. VA 5th Cav. Capt.
Taylor, F.T. MS 18th Inf. Co.I
Taylor, Fullen VA 72nd Mil.
Taylor, Fullen H. VA Cav. Caldwell's Bn. Gent's Co.
Taylor, F.W. KY 4th Cav. Co.I
Taylor, F.W. MS 1st Lt.Arty. Co.L
Taylor, F.W. MO 6th Cav. Co.B 2nd Sgt.
Taylor, G. GA 54th Inf. Co.F
Taylor, G. MS Cav. 3rd Bn. (Ashcraft's) Co.C
Taylor, G. MS Inf. 1st St.Troops Co.I
Taylor, G. TX Cav. Wells' Regt. Co.A
Taylor, G. TX 5th Inf. Martindale's Co.
Taylor, G. VA 21st Cav. Co.D
Taylor, G. VA 166th Mil. Ballard's Co.
Taylor, G. Exch.Bn. 3rd Co.B,CSA
Taylor, G.A. MS 1st Cav.Res. Co.C
Taylor, G.A. SC 22nd Inf. Co.D 1st Lt.
Taylor, G.A. TN 16th (Logwood's) Cav. Co.I
Taylor, G.A. TN 19th & 20th (Cons.) Cav. Co.K
Taylor, G.A. TN 20th (Russell's) Cav. Co.F
Taylor, G.A. TN 5th Inf. Co.A Cpl.
Taylor, G.A. VA 22nd Inf. Co.C
Taylor, Gabriel NC 21st Inf. Co.I
Taylor, Garrett TN 2nd (Ashby's) Cav. Co.G
Taylor, Garrett TN 62nd Mtd.Inf. Co.D
Taylor, Garrison TN 16th Inf. Co.A
Taylor, G.B. GA 17th Inf. Co.B
Taylor, G.B. MS Inf. 3rd Bn. (St.Troops) Co.D
Taylor, G.B. TX 13th Vol. 3rd Co.A
Taylor, G.D. AL 25th Inf. Co.E
Taylor, G.D. MS 4th Inf. Co.H 4th Sgt.
Taylor, George AL 5th Cav. Co.B
Taylor, George AL Cav. Barbiere's Bn. Truss' Co.
Taylor, George AL 19th Inf. Co.E Music.
Taylor, George AL 32nd Inf. Co.I
Taylor, George AR 17th (Griffith's) Inf. Co.H 1st Lt.
Taylor, George AR 18th Inf. Co.E
Taylor, George AR 27th Inf. New Co.C
Taylor, George AR Carroll's Prov.Guard Morris' Co.
Taylor, George GA 1st Inf. (St.Guards) Co.F
Taylor, George GA 5th Res. Co.B
Taylor, George GA Inf. 10th Bn. Co.D
Taylor, George LA 1st (Nelligan's) Inf. Co.A
Taylor, George LA 13th Inf. Co.I Cpl.
Taylor, George LA 25th Inf. Co.I
Taylor, George MD 1st Inf. Co.I
Taylor, George MS 10th Inf. New Co.I
Taylor, George MS 19th Inf. Co.E
Taylor, George MO Lt.Arty. 3rd Btty. Sgt.
Taylor, George MO 1st Inf. Co.B Sgt.
Taylor, George MO 12th Inf. Co.F
Taylor, George NC 3rd Inf. Co.I
Taylor, George NC 13th Inf. Co.K
Taylor, George NC 26th Inf. Co.F
Taylor, George NC 31st Inf. Co.E
Taylor, George NC 31st Inf. Co.K
Taylor, George SC 2nd Cav. Co.G
Taylor, George SC Lt.Arty. 3rd (Palmetto) Bn. Co.E

Taylor, George SC 1st (Orr's) Rifles Co.H
Taylor, George SC 4th St.Troops Co.K
Taylor, George SC 5th Bn.Res. Co.C
Taylor, George SC Inf. 7th Bn. (Enfield Rifles) Co.C
Taylor, George SC 14th Inf. Co.K
Taylor, George TN 12th (Cons.) Inf. 2nd Lt.
Taylor, George TN 26th Inf. Co.D Cpl.
Taylor, George TX Cav. Hardeman's Regt. Co.E
Taylor, George TX Cav. Waller's Regt. Dunn's Co.
Taylor, George VA 1st Cav. Co.G
Taylor, George VA 5th Cav. Co.G
Taylor, George VA 19th Cav. Co.F
Taylor, George VA 25th Cav. Co.D
Taylor, George VA Lt.Arty. 12th Bn. Co.D
Taylor, George VA Hvy.Arty. 19th Bn. 3rd Co.C
Taylor, George VA 14th Inf. Co.I
Taylor, George VA Inf. 25th Bn. Co.B
Taylor, George VA Mil. Scott Cty.
Taylor, George VA Res.Forces Thurston's Co.
Taylor, George Trans-MS Conf.Cav. 1st Bn. Co.A
Taylor, George Mead's Conf.Cav. Co.B
Taylor, George Gen. & Staff Capt.,AQM
Taylor, George A. AR 3rd Cav. Co.G 2nd Lt.
Taylor, George A. AR 3rd Inf. Co.A
Taylor, George A. GA 32nd Inf. Co.A
Taylor, George A. MS 1st Bn.S.S. Co.D
Taylor, George A. MS 25th Inf. Co.H
Taylor, George A. VA 12th Inf. Co.B Sgt.
Taylor, George A. VA 46th Inf. 2nd Co.K Cpl.
Taylor, George B. KY 8th Cav. Co.E
Taylor, George B. MS 14th Inf. Co.K
Taylor, George B. MS 48th Inf. Co.C
Taylor, George B. NC 1st Cav. (9th St.Troops) Co.H
Taylor, George B. SC Inf. Hampton Legion Co.A
Taylor, Geo. B. Gen. & Staff Chap.
Taylor, George Booker MS Inf. 2nd Bn. Co.C
Taylor, George C. TN 48th (Voorhies') Inf.
Taylor, George D. AL 25th Inf. Co.F
Taylor, Geo. D. AL Cp. of Instr. Talladega
Taylor, George D. NC 6th Cav. (65th St.Troops) Co.F,A QMSgt.
Taylor, George D. NC 43rd Inf. Co.H
Taylor, George D. TN 60th Mtd.Inf. Co.K
Taylor, George E. MS 46th Inf. Co.I
Taylor, George E. SC Lt.Arty. Walter's Co. (Washington Arty.)
Taylor, George E. Gen. & Staff Capt.,AQM
Taylor, George F. AL 14th Inf. Asst.Surg.
Taylor, George F. GA Lt.Arty. 12th Bn. Co.F
Taylor, George F. GA 1st (Ramsey's) Inf. Co.B Cpl.
Taylor, George F. 7th Conf.Cav. Co.A
Taylor, George G. NC 2nd Arty. (36th St.Troops) Co.I
Taylor, George G. NC 3rd Arty. (40th St.Troops) Co.G
Taylor, George G. SC 1st Arty. Co.C
Taylor, George H. KY 2nd Mtd.Inf. Co.I Sgt.
Taylor, George H. NC 35th Inf. Co.E
Taylor, George H. VA 23rd Inf. Co.C
Taylor, George H. VA 55th Inf. Co.D 1st Sgt.
Taylor, George H.P. TX 37th Cav. Co.K
Taylor, George J. MS 20th Inf. Co.H Sgt.
Taylor, Geo. K. LA 4th Inf. Co.D
Taylor, George K.P. NC 61st Inf. Co.E
Taylor, George L. AL 3rd Inf. Co.G
Taylor, George L. LA 1st Cav. Co.D
Taylor, George L. MD Inf. 2nd Bn. Co.A
Taylor, George L. MS 20th Inf. Co.B
Taylor, George L. VA 34th Inf. Co.I
Taylor, George M. VA Cav. McNeill's Co.
Taylor, George M. VA 54th Inf. Co.C 1st Lt.
Taylor, George O. TX 13th Cav. Co.K
Taylor, George P. NC 34th Inf. Co.E
Taylor, George P. NC 37th Inf. Co.A
Taylor, George P. VA 11th Inf. Co.F
Taylor, George R. GA Inf. 4th Bn. (St.Guards) Co.D
Taylor, George R. TX Cav. Martin's Regt. Co.K
Taylor, George S. LA 5th Inf. Co.C
Taylor, George S. MS 46th Inf. Co.I
Taylor, George S. VA 24th Inf. Co.I
Taylor, George S. Gen. & Staff Asst.Surg.
Taylor, George T. AL Arty. 1st Bn. Co.C Cpl.
Taylor, George T. FL 11th Inf. Co.K
Taylor, George T. GA 38th Inf. Co.N
Taylor, George T. VA Lt.Arty. Kirkpatrick's Co.
Taylor, George W. AL 11th Inf. Co.F
Taylor, George W. AL 14th Inf. Co.K Maj.
Taylor, George W. AL 17th Inf. Co.D Cpl.
Taylor, George W. AL 22nd Inf. Co.B
Taylor, George W. AL 22nd Inf. Co.D
Taylor, George W. AL 24th Inf. Co.E
Taylor, Geo. W. AL 25th Inf. Co.A
Taylor, Geo. W. AL Cp. of Instr. Talladega
Taylor, George W. AR 6th Inf. Co.I
Taylor, George W. AR 9th Inf. Co.A
Taylor, George W. AR 16th Inf. Co.E
Taylor, George W. GA 19th Inf. Co.K
Taylor, George W. GA 22nd Inf. Co.D
Taylor, George W. GA 49th Inf. Co.E
Taylor, George W. LA 4th Inf. Co.C
Taylor, George W. LA 31st Inf. Co.K Sgt.
Taylor, George W. MS 14th Inf. Co.I
Taylor, George W. MS 15th Inf. Co.E
Taylor, George W. MS 34th Inf. Co.B
Taylor, George W. MO 4th Cav. Co.H Capt.
Taylor, George W. MO Staff St.Guard Lt.Col.,Surg.
Taylor, George W. NC Lt.Arty. 13th Bn. Co.A
Taylor, George W. NC 7th Inf. Co.E
Taylor, George W. NC 11th (Bethel Regt.) Inf. Co.D
Taylor, George W. NC 14th Inf. Co.G
Taylor, George W. NC 44th Inf. Co.D
Taylor, George W. NC 58th Inf. Co.H
Taylor, George W. SC 20th Inf. Co.K
Taylor, George W. TN 2nd (Ashby's) Cav. Co.F
Taylor, George W. TN Cav. 4th Bn. (Branner's) Co.F Bugler
Taylor, George W. TN 22nd Inf. Co.A 2nd Lt.
Taylor, George W. TN 23rd Inf. Co.C
Taylor, George W. TN 32nd Inf. Co.K
Taylor, George W. TX 2nd Cav. Co.G,C 1st Sgt.
Taylor, George W. TX 12th Cav. Co.A
Taylor, George W. TX 24th Cav. Co.C
Taylor, George W. VA 1st Cav. Co.H
Taylor, George W. VA 4th Cav. Co.H
Taylor, George W. VA 16th Cav. Co.F
Taylor, George W. VA Cav. 39th Bn. Co.A
Taylor, George W. VA Cav. Mosby's Regt. (Part.Rangers) Co.C
Taylor, George W. VA 1st Arty. Co.H
Taylor, George W. VA 2nd Arty. Co.A
Taylor, George W. VA 3rd Lt.Arty. Co.C
Taylor, George W. VA Hvy.Arty. 18th Bn. Co.D
Taylor, George W. VA Hvy.Arty. 19th Bn. Co.B
Taylor, George W. VA Arty. Dance's Co.
Taylor, George W. VA Lt.Arty. Donald's Co.
Taylor, George W. VA Hvy.Arty. Patteson's Co.
Taylor, George W. VA 1st Inf. Co.E
Taylor, George W. VA Inf. 1st Bn.Loc.Def. Co.C
Taylor, George W. VA 5th Inf. Co.A
Taylor, George W. VA 10th Inf. Co.D
Taylor, George W. VA 17th Inf. Co.H
Taylor, George W. VA Inf. 22nd Bn. Co.A
Taylor, George W. VA 23rd Inf. Co.A
Taylor, George W. VA 31st Mil. Co.A 2nd Lt.
Taylor, George W. VA 31st Mil. Co.B
Taylor, George W. VA 31st Mil. Co.F
Taylor, George W. VA 39th Inf. Co.E
Taylor, George W. VA 45th Inf. Co.L
Taylor, George W. VA 47th Mil.
Taylor, George W. VA 52nd Inf. Co.H
Taylor, George W. VA 55th Inf. Co.A
Taylor, George W. VA 56th Inf. Co.B
Taylor, George W. VA 57th Inf. Co.A
Taylor, George W. VA 60th Inf. Co.E
Taylor, George W. 1st Choctaw & Chickasaw Mtd.Rifles 1st Co.K
Taylor, Geo. W. Gen. & Staff, Ord.Depot
Taylor, George W. Gen. & Staff Surg.
Taylor, George Washington TN 3rd (Clack's) Inf. Co.H Sgt.
Taylor, George Washington TN 6th Inf. Co.H 2nd Lt.
Taylor, George W.F. AR 2nd Mtd.Rifles Co.G
Taylor, Gerald VA Lt.Arty. Jeffress' Co.
Taylor, Gerdon VA Lt.Arty. Thornton's Co.
Taylor, Gerome LA Conscr.
Taylor, Gerome MS 18th Inf. Co.K
Taylor, G.F. GA 10th Cav. Co.A Sgt.
Taylor, G.F. GA Cav. 29th Bn. Co.A
Taylor, G.H. Conf.Inf. 8th Bn. Co.B
Taylor, Gid LA 9th Inf. Co.G
Taylor, Gilbert GA 9th Inf. Co.F Cpl.
Taylor, Gilbert MS 8th Inf. Co.G
Taylor, Gilbert C. NC Hvy.Arty. 1st Bn. Co.A Cpl.
Taylor, Gilbert D. LA 31st Inf. Co.H Sgt.
Taylor, Giles AR Inf. 2nd Bn. Co.B
Taylor, Giles AR 3rd Inf. Co.I
Taylor, Giles NC 42nd Inf. Co.F
Taylor, Giles H. MS 15th Inf. Co.E
Taylor, Giles H. TN 7th (Duckworth's) Cav. Co.E
Taylor, G.J. GA 25th Inf. Co.C
Taylor, G.K. AR 31st Inf. Co.H
Taylor, G.L. AL 7th Inf. Co.D
Taylor, G.L. KY 6th Mtd.Inf. Co.I
Taylor, G.L. MO 7th Cav. Co.F
Taylor, G.M. GA 61st Inf. Co.C Cpl.
Taylor, G.M. NC 57th Inf. Co.H

Taylor, G.M. TN 50th Inf. Co.G
Taylor, G.M. TX 4th Inf. Co.E
Taylor, G.M. VA Inf. 1st Bn.Loc.Def. Co.F
Taylor, G.N. GA 11th Cav. Co.D
Taylor, G.N. GA 52nd Inf. Co.B
Taylor, G.N. TN 12th (Green's) Cav. Co.H
Taylor, G.N. TN 5th Inf. 2nd Co.K
Taylor, G.N. TX 7th Cav. Co.H Bugler
Taylor, Gordon S. GA 26th Inf. Co.F Sgt.
Taylor, G.P.K. NC Loc.Def. Croom's Co.
Taylor, G.R. FL 1st Inf. Co.G
Taylor, G.R. GA Inf. (Loc.Def.) Whiteside's Nav.Bn. Co.B
Taylor, G.R. KY 12th Cav. Co.B
Taylor, G.R. MS 4th Inf. Co.H
Taylor, G.R. TN 1st Cav. Co.G
Taylor, Grant AL 40th Inf. Co.G
Taylor, Grant TN 34th Inf. Co.B
Taylor, Grant R. LA 27th Inf. Co.H
Taylor, Gray NC 5th Inf. Co.G
Taylor, Great J. AR 5th Inf. Co.K
Taylor, Green SC 2nd Rifles Co.L
Taylor, Green VA 36th Inf. 1st Co.H 2nd Lt.
Taylor, Green B. FL 2nd Inf. Co.M
Taylor, Green B. FL 8th Inf. Co.B
Taylor, Green B. GA 1st (Ramsey's) Inf. Co.G
Taylor, Green B. SC Inf. 3rd Bn. Co.A
Taylor, Green B. TX 16th Cav. Co.F Sgt.
Taylor, Green B. TX Inf. Griffin's Bn. Co.D
Taylor, Greenfield Gen. & Staff Chap.
Taylor, Green T. KY 4th Mtd.Inf. Co.G,D
Taylor, Green W. VA Inf. 45th Bn. Co.E 1st Lt.
Taylor, G.S. VA 23rd Inf. Co.C
Taylor, G.T. AL 17th Inf. Co.A
Taylor, Guilford W. NC 5th Cav. (63rd St.Troops) Co.B
Taylor, G.V. MS 37th Inf. Co.F
Taylor, G.W. AL 6th Cav. Co.C
Taylor, G.W. AL Arty. 1st Bn. Co.F
Taylor, G.W. AL Lt.Arty. Kolb's Btty.
Taylor, G.W. AL 5th Inf. Co.H
Taylor, G.W. AL 9th Inf. Co.B
Taylor, G.W. AL 10th Inf. Co.K
Taylor, G.W. AL 17th Inf. Co.E
Taylor, G.W. AL 34th Inf. Co.B
Taylor, G.W. AL 42nd Inf. Co.B
Taylor, G.W. AL 47th Inf. Co.F
Taylor, G.W. AL 59th Inf. Co.E
Taylor, G.W. AL Arty. 4th Bn. Hilliard's Legion Co.B,E
Taylor, G.W. AR 1st (Monroe's) Cav. Co.F
Taylor, G.W. AR 35th Inf. Co.I
Taylor, G.W. AR Cav. Davies' Bn. Co.D
Taylor, G.W. AR 5th Inf. Co.H
Taylor, G.W. AR 11th Inf. Co.G
Taylor, G.W. AR 15th Mil. Co.E Cpl.
Taylor, G.W. AR 19th (Dawson's) Inf. Co.G,F
Taylor, G.W. AR 24th Inf. Co.K,A
Taylor, G.W. AR Inf. Hardy's Regt. Co.I
Taylor, G.W. GA 1st Inf. Co.G
Taylor, G.W. GA Inf. 1st Loc.Troops (Augusta) Dearing's Cav.Co.
Taylor, G.W. GA 3rd Res. Co.B
Taylor, G.W. GA Inf. 4th Bn. (St.Guards) Co.B
Taylor, G.W. GA 5th Inf. Co.A
Taylor, G.W. GA 27th Inf. Co.H
Taylor, G.W. GA 34th Inf. Co.C
Taylor, G.W. KY 12th Cav. Co.D
Taylor, G.W. KY 11th Cav.
Taylor, G.W. KY 3rd Mtd.Inf. Co.A 2nd Lt.
Taylor, G.W. LA 4th Inf. Co.I
Taylor, G.W. LA 17th Inf. Co.D
Taylor, G.W. MS 1st Cav. Co.E Cpl.
Taylor, G.W. MS Cav. 24th Bn. Co.D
Taylor, G.W. MS 23rd Inf. Co.G
Taylor, G.W. MS Gage's Co.
Taylor, G.W. MO Lt.Arty. Walsh's Co.
Taylor, G.W. MO 12th Inf. Co.H
Taylor, G.W. NC 1st Arty. (10th St.Troops) Co.F
Taylor, G.W. NC Inf. Thomas Legion Co.C
Taylor, G.W. SC 1st Cav. Co.C Sgt.
Taylor, G.W. SC 2nd Rifles Co.E
Taylor, G.W. SC 3rd Res. Co.K
Taylor, G.W. SC 14th Inf. Co.H
Taylor, G.W. TN 15th (Cons.) Cav. Co.A
Taylor, G.W. TN 19th & 20th (Cons.) Cav. Co.E
Taylor, G.W. TN 19th Inf. Co.F
Taylor, G.W. TN 22nd Inf. Co.F 3rd Lt.
Taylor, G.W. TN 24th Bn.S.S. Co.A
Taylor, G.W. TN 31st Inf. Co.H
Taylor, G.W. TN 47th Inf. Co.B
Taylor, G.W. TX 10th Cav. Co.D
Taylor, G.W. TX 17th Cons.Dismtd.Cav. Co.C
Taylor, G.W. TX 32nd Cav. Co.I Cpl.
Taylor, G.W. TX Granbury's Cons.Brig. Co.I
Taylor, G.W. TX 10th Inf. AASurg.
Taylor, G.W. VA Lt.Arty. 13th Bn. Co.A
Taylor, G.W. VA Inf. 1st Bn.Loc.Def. Co.F
Taylor, G.W. VA 3rd Inf.Loc.Def. Co.B
Taylor, G.W. VA Inf. 23rd Bn. Co.C
Taylor, G.W. VA 42nd Inf. Co.A
Taylor, G.W. VA 58th Mil. Co.F
Taylor, G.W. VA 1st Cav.St.Line Co.A Capt.
Taylor, H. GA Cav. Waring's Co.
Taylor, H. GA 5th Inf. Co.N
Taylor, H. GA Inf. 27th Bn. (NonConscr.) Co.E
Taylor, H. GA 55th Inf. Co.B
Taylor, H. LA 13th Inf. Co.D
Taylor, H. LA 14th Inf. Co.D
Taylor, H. MS 6th Cav. Co.D
Taylor, H. MO Cav. Freeman's Regt. Co.E
Taylor, H. NC Walker's Bn. Thomas' Legion Co.G
Taylor, H. SC Inf. 1st (Charleston) Bn. Co.F
Taylor, H. TN 4th (McLemore's) Cav. Co.B
Taylor, H. TN 5th Cav. Co.F
Taylor, H. TX 33rd Cav. Co.E
Taylor, H. VA Cav. 39th Bn. Co.D
Taylor, H. Trans-MS Conf.Cav. 1st Bn. Co.A
Taylor, H.A. GA Mil. Harris' Co.
Taylor, H.A. TX Inf. Whaley's Co.
Taylor, Hails AL 7th Cav. Co.G Sgt.
Taylor, Hails AL Lt.Arty. Goldthwaite's Btty. Cpl.
Taylor, Hails AL 3rd Inf. Co.B
Taylor, Hails AL 3rd Bn. Hilliard's Legion Vol. Sgt.Maj.
Taylor, Hancock Gen. & Staff Lt.,P.Ord.Off.
Taylor, Hanson B. MS 12th Inf. Co.D
Taylor, Hardin H. TN 24th Inf. Co.K
Taylor, Harivren G. MS Graves' Co. (Copiah Horse Guards)
Taylor, Harmand AL 32nd Inf. Co.I
Taylor, Harmon F. SC 1st (McCreary's) Inf. Co.B
Taylor, Harold VA 45th Inf. Co.C
Taylor, Harper S. AR 17th (Lemoyne's) Inf. Co.C
Taylor, Harper S. AR 21st Inf. Co.C Capt.
Taylor, Harrington P. 10th Conf.Cav. Co.E
Taylor, Harris KY 8th Cav. Co.E
Taylor, Harris MS 7th Cav. Co.C
Taylor, Harrison MS 3rd (St.Troops) Cav. Co.C
Taylor, Harrison NC 37th Inf. Co.A
Taylor, Harrison VA Cav. McNeill's Co. 1st Sgt.
Taylor, Harrison VA 25th Inf. 1st Co.K Sgt.
Taylor, Harrison 1st Choctaw & Chickasaw Mtd.Rifles 3rd Co.F
Taylor, Harrison Choctaw Inf. Wilkins' Co.
Taylor, Harvey TN 34th Inf. 1st Co.C
Taylor, Harvey VA 11th Cav. Co.C
Taylor, Harvey VA 72nd Mil.
Taylor, Harvey S. NC 17th Inf. (1st Org.) Co.F
Taylor, Harvey S. NC 17th Inf. (2nd Org.) Co.A
Taylor, Hayward NC Lt.Arty. 13th Bn. Co.E
Taylor, Haywood FL Inf. 2nd Bn. Co.D
Taylor, Haywood FL 10th Inf. Co.K
Taylor, Haywood NC 3rd Arty. (40th St.Troops) Co.G
Taylor, Haywood NC 2nd Inf. Co.H
Taylor, Haywood L. GA Inf. Cobb Guards Co.A
Taylor, Haywood P. TN 1st (Feild's) Inf. Co.G
Taylor, H.B. AL Arty. 1st Bn.
Taylor, H.B. AR 15th (Josey's) Inf. Co.E Cpl.
Taylor, H.B. KY 1st (Helm's) Cav. Co.G
Taylor, H.C. AL 24th Inf. Co.I
Taylor, H.C. AL 34th Inf. Co.E
Taylor, H.C. GA 12th Cav. Co.E
Taylor, H.C. NC Allen's Co. (Loc.Def.)
Taylor, H.C. TN 22nd Cav. Co.I
Taylor, H.C. TN 3rd (Clack's) Inf. Co.H
Taylor, H.C. TX St.Troops Hampton's Co.
Taylor, H.C. VA 3rd Cav. Co.A
Taylor, H.C. VA Lt.Arty. 1st Bn. Co.B
Taylor, H.C. VA Arty. Richardson's Co.
Taylor, H. Clay Gen. & Staff Lt.Col.,Arty.Ch.
Taylor, H.E. LA 1st Hvy.Arty. (Reg.) Co.D
Taylor, H.E. NC 2nd Cav. (19th St.Troops) Co.H
Taylor, Helair LA 26th Inf. Co.A Music.
Taylor, Henderson NC 3rd Bn.Sr.Res. Durham's Co.
Taylor, Henderson B. LA 8th Inf. Co.F
Taylor, Henry AR 2nd Mtd.Rifles Co.K
Taylor, Henry AR 7th Inf. Co.H 1st Sgt.
Taylor, Henry AR 10th Inf. Co.A
Taylor, Henry AR 18th Inf. Co.K
Taylor, Henry AR 36th Inf. Co.H
Taylor, Henry GA Cav. 2nd Bn. Co.F 1st Lt.
Taylor, Henry GA 5th Cav. Co.B 1st Lt.
Taylor, Henry GA 3rd Res. Co.B
Taylor, Henry GA 3rd Res. Co.K
Taylor, Henry GA 26th Inf. Dent's Co.A
Taylor, Henry GA 57th Inf. Co.B
Taylor, Henry GA 59th Inf. Co.B 1st Lt.
Taylor, Henry GA 63rd Inf. Co.H
Taylor, Henry LA 14th Inf. Co.B
Taylor, Henry LA 16th Inf. Co.A

Taylor, Henry LA 21st (Patton's) Inf. Co.A 1st Sgt.
Taylor, Henry MS Cav. Ham's Regt. Co.B
Taylor, Henry MS 22nd Inf. Co.A
Taylor, Henry MS 37th Inf. Co.D
Taylor, Henry MO Cav. 1st Regt.St.Guard Co.F
Taylor, Henry MO 2nd Cav. Co.B,D
Taylor, Henry MO Cav. Freeman's Regt. Co.A
Taylor, Henry MO 11th Inf. Co.F Sgt.
Taylor, Henry NC 5th Sr.Res. Co.B Sgt.
Taylor, Henry NC 44th Inf. Co.D Cpl.
Taylor, Henry NC 46th Inf. Co.A
Taylor, Henry NC 61st Inf. Co.I
Taylor, Henry NC Walker's Bn. Thomas' Legion Co.G
Taylor, Henry SC 1st Bn.S.S. Co.B
Taylor, Henry SC 27th Inf. Co.F
Taylor, Henry TN 5th (Mckenzie's) Cav. Co.A
Taylor, Henry TN 35th Inf. 1st Co.I,G
Taylor, Henry TN 45th Inf. Co.C
Taylor, Henry TN 61st Mtd.Inf. Co.H
Taylor, Henry VA 9th Cav. Co.I
Taylor, Henry VA 19th Cav. Co.I
Taylor, Henry VA 25th Cav. Co.C
Taylor, Henry VA 11th Bn.Res. Co.C
Taylor, Henry VA Inf. 21st Bn. 2nd Co.C
Taylor, Henry VA 24th Inf. Co.A
Taylor, Henry VA 39th Inf. Co.G
Taylor, Henry VA 47th Inf. 3rd Co.H
Taylor, Henry VA 55th Inf. Co.F
Taylor, Henry VA 135th Mil. Co.C
Taylor, Henry Loring's Staff Capt.,ADC
Taylor, Henry A. MS 26th Inf. Co.H
Taylor, Henry A. VA Murphy's Co. 1st Lt.
Taylor, Henry B. AL 21st Inf. Co.E
Taylor, Henry B. MS 16th Inf. Co.B
Taylor, Henry B. VA 34th Inf. Co.K
Taylor, Henry C. AR 18th Inf. Co.E Cpl.
Taylor, Henry C. GA 4th (Clinch's) Cav. Co.B
Taylor, Henry C. GA 20th Inf. Co.A Sgt.
Taylor, Henry C. GA 39th Inf. Co.H 1st Sgt.
Taylor, Henry C. MS 26th Inf. Co.C
Taylor, Henry C. SC Inf. Hampton Legion Co.A
Taylor, Henry C. TN 25th Inf. Co.A
Taylor, Henry C. TX 35th (Brown's) Cav. Co.F
Taylor, Henry C. VA 1st Arty. Co.B
Taylor, Henry C. VA 52nd Inf. Co.G
Taylor, Henry C. VA 56th Inf. Co.B
Taylor, Henry Clay TN 27th Inf. Co.K
Taylor, Henry D. NC 1st Inf. Co.H
Taylor, Henry E. NC 15th Inf. Co.A
Taylor, Henry F.L. AL 10th Inf. Co.I
Taylor, Henry G. AL 57th Inf. Co.K
Taylor, Henry H. GA 41st Inf. Co.I
Taylor, Henry H. GA 49th Inf. Co.E
Taylor, Henry H. TN 5th (McKenzie's) Cav. Co.C
Taylor, Henry H. TN 5th (McKenzie's) Cav. Co.H 1st Lt.
Taylor, Henry H. VA 25th Inf. 2nd Co.H
Taylor, Henry J. GA 10th Inf. Co.G
Taylor, Henry J. GA Inf. 10th Bn. Co.B
Taylor, Henry J. SC 10th Inf. Co.K
Taylor, Henry J. VA 14th Cav. Co.K
Taylor, Henry J. VA 30th Inf. Co.D
Taylor, Henry L. AL 60th Inf. Co.E 1st Sgt.
Taylor, Henry L. AL 3rd Bn. Hilliard's Legion Vol. Co.A Sgt.
Taylor, Henry L. MS 16th Inf. Co.F
Taylor, Henry M. MO Inf. 1st Bn. Co.B
Taylor, Henry P. VA 9th Cav. Co.C
Taylor, Henry P. VA 40th Inf. Co.K
Taylor, Henry P. VA Murphy's Co. 1st Sgt.
Taylor, Henry S. MO 4th Cav. Co.F 1st Lt.
Taylor, Henry S. NC 33rd Inf. Co.K Sgt.
Taylor, Henry S. SC 14th Inf. Co.F
Taylor, Henry S. VA 20th Cav. Co.C
Taylor, Henry T. LA 11th Inf. Co.F
Taylor, Henry T. VA 2nd Arty. Co.A
Taylor, Henry V. GA 60th Inf. Co.G
Taylor, Henry W. GA Inf. 10th Bn. Co.A
Taylor, Henry W. MS 36th Inf. Co.A
Taylor, Henry W. NC 6th Cav. (65th St.Troops) Co.K
Taylor, Henry W. SC 20th Inf. Co.K
Taylor, Henry W. TN 19th Inf. Co.B Sgt.
Taylor, Henry W. TN 26th Inf. Co.B 2nd Lt.
Taylor, Herman TX 8th Inf. Co.C
Taylor, Hewlett P. SC Inf. 3rd Bn. Co.C
Taylor, Hezkiah AR 17th (Lemoyne's) Inf. Co.E
Taylor, Hezkiah AR 21st Inf. Co.I Sgt.
Taylor, H.F. MS 4th Cav. Co.A
Taylor, H.F. MS Cav. Stockdale's Bn. Co.A
Taylor, H.G. GA Lt.Arty. Barnwell's Btty.
Taylor, H.H. AL 63rd Inf. Co.F
Taylor, H.H. MS 18th Cav. Co.A Cpl.
Taylor, H.H. MS 10th Inf. New Co.G
Taylor, H.H. TN 12th (Green's) Cav. Co.F
Taylor, H.H. TN 16th (Logwood's) Cav. Co.F 1st Sgt.
Taylor, H.H. TN 63rd Inf. Co.H
Taylor, H.H. TX 3rd Cav. Co.A
Taylor, H.H. TX Cav. Border's Regt. Co.F
Taylor, H.H. TX Inf. 2nd St.Troops Co.E 3rd Lt.
Taylor, H.H. TX 15th Inf. Co.C
Taylor, H.H. VA 18th Cav. Co.A
Taylor, Hickman KY 9th Cav. Co.B
Taylor, Hillary L. TX 3rd Cav. Co.G 2nd Lt.
Taylor, Hillery NC Inf. 68th Regt. Capt.
Taylor, Hilliard SC 20th Inf. Co.K
Taylor, Hilliard V. MS 18th Inf. Co.I
Taylor, Hinton MS 1st Lt.Arty. Co.A
Taylor, Hiram AL 5th Cav. Co.H
Taylor, Hiram AL 4th Res. Co.H
Taylor, Hiram AL 45th Inf. Co.C
Taylor, Hiram GA 60th Inf. Co.G
Taylor, Hiram KY 1st Bn.Mtd.Rifles Co.B
Taylor, Hiram LA Inf. 9th Bn. Co.C
Taylor, Hiram SC 27th Inf. Co.C
Taylor, Hiram VA Cav. 34th Bn. Co.A
Taylor, Hiram VA 33rd Inf. Co.I
Taylor, Hiram A. MS 1st Bn.S.S. Co.C
Taylor, H.J. AL 6th Inf. Co.L
Taylor, H.J. AL 34th Inf. Co.G
Taylor, H.J. GA 17th Inf. Co.E
Taylor, H.J. NC 3rd Arty. (40th St.Troops) Co.H
Taylor, H.J. NC 2nd Jr.Res. Co.H
Taylor, H.J. TX 3rd Cav. Co.F 1st Lt.
Taylor, H.J. TX 9th Cav. Co.D
Taylor, H.J. TX 37th Cav. Co.I Capt.
Taylor, H.J. VA 46th Inf. 2nd Co.K
Taylor, H.K. GA Lt.Arty. 12th Bn. 3rd Co.E
Taylor, H.K. KY 6th Mtd.Inf. Co.D
Taylor, H.K. MO 10th Inf. Co.F
Taylor, H.K. MO 12th Inf. Co.C
Taylor, H.L. TX 5th Inf. Co.F
Taylor, H.M. GA Phillips' Legion Co.L
Taylor, H.M. KY 8th Cav. Co.E
Taylor, H.M. SC 13th Inf. Co.K
Taylor, H.M. TX 33rd Cav. Co.I 1st Lt.
Taylor, H.M. TX 5th Inf. Co.B
Taylor, H.O. TN 37th Inf. Co.C
Taylor, Holbrook VA Inf. 25th Bn. Co.E
Taylor, Hor VA 22nd Inf. Co.D
Taylor, Horace MO 11th Inf. Co.I
Taylor, Horace H. VA 77th Mil. Co.A
Taylor, Horace M. KY 8th Cav. Co.E
Taylor, Horace P. AL 39th Inf. Co.E
Taylor, Hosea TN 25th Inf. Co.A
Taylor, Hosey TN 13th (Gore's) Cav. Co.I
Taylor, Houston AR 7th Mil. Co.C
Taylor, Houston AR 15th (N.W.) Inf. Co.I
Taylor, Howard L. AR 3rd Inf. Co.K 1st Lt.
Taylor, H.P. AL Cav. 5th Bn. Hilliard's Legion
Taylor, H.P. GA 7th Cav. Co.E
Taylor, H.P. GA Cav. 21st Bn. Co.B
Taylor, H.P. VA 1st Cav. Co.G
Taylor, H.P. VA 1st (Farinholt's) Res. Co.G
Taylor, H.R. KY 9th Cav. Co.G
Taylor, H.R. TN 84th Inf. Co.E Sgt.
Taylor, H.S. GA 45th Inf. Co.H Cpl.
Taylor, H.S. KY 1st Inf. Co.F
Taylor, H.S. NC 11th (Bethel Regt.) Inf. Co.A
Taylor, H.S. NC 62nd Inf. Co.F
Taylor, H.S. SC 3rd Inf. Co.I
Taylor, H.S. TN 30th Inf. Co.B Sgt.
Taylor, H.S. Gen. & Staff Maj.,ACS
Taylor, H.T.B. AR 11th Inf. Co.D
Taylor, Hudson W. MS 21st Inf. Co.D
Taylor, Huey VA Lt.Arty. Parker's Co.
Taylor, Hugh TN 10th (DeMoss') Cav. Co.F
Taylor, Hugh TN Cav. Napier's Bn. Co.C
Taylor, Hugh B. TN 3rd (Forrest's) Cav.
Taylor, Hugh C. GA 40th Inf. Co.F Cpl.
Taylor, Hugh M. NC Inf. 2nd Bn. Co.H
Taylor, Hugh M. TN 50th Inf. Co.F
Taylor, Hugh N. VA Inf. 23rd Bn. Co.E
Taylor, Hugh N. VA 50th Inf. Co.L
Taylor, Hugh S. NC 7th Inf. Co.H
Taylor, H.V. GA Lt.Arty. Clinch's Btty.
Taylor, H.W. MS 7th Cav. Co.F
Taylor, H.W. SC Arty. Fickling's Co. (Brooks Lt.Arty.)
Taylor, H.W. SC 5th St.Troops Co.I
Taylor, H.W. SC 9th Res. Co.E
Taylor, H.W. SC 27th Inf. Co.F
Taylor, H.W. TN 16th Inf. Co.K
Taylor, H.W. TN 63rd Inf. Co.I Sgt.
Taylor, H.W. TX 2nd Inf. Co.F
Taylor, H.W. VA Lt.Arty. Co.D
Taylor, H.W. VA Inf. 28th Bn. Co.D Sgt.
Taylor, H.W. VA 59th Inf. 3rd Co.I Sgt.
Taylor, I. LA 6th Cav. Co.G
Taylor, I. MS 2nd Cav.Res. Co.C
Taylor, I. TN 38th Inf. Co.D
Taylor, I. Brush Bn.
Taylor, I.A. AL 2nd Cav. Co.D
Taylor, I.A. GA 12th Mil.

Taylor, I.A. GA Inf. Asst.Surg.
Taylor, I.G. SC 13th Inf. Co.K
Taylor, I.H. GA Inf. 14th Bn. (St.Guards) Co.D
Taylor, I.H. MO 7th Cav. Co.F
Taylor, I.M. TX 22nd Inf. Co.A Music.
Taylor, I.M. TX Waul's Legion Co.F
Taylor, I.P. AL 2nd Cav. Co.D
Taylor, Ira AL 5th Cav. Co.H
Taylor, Ira Baker TX 20th Cav. Co.G
Taylor, Ira S. MS 1st Lt.Arty. Co.I
Taylor, Iredell R. TX 5th Cav. Co.A Cpl.
Taylor, Irvin L. AL 61st Inf. Co.D
Taylor, Irvin T. MO Cav. Clardy's Bn. Co.B
Taylor, Isaac AL 9th Inf. Co.E
Taylor, Isaac AL 18th Inf. Co.B
Taylor, Isaac AR 8th Inf. New Co.G
Taylor, Isaac AR 14th (McCarver's) Inf. Co.H
Taylor, Isaac AR 34th Inf. Co.C Cpl.
Taylor, Isaac GA 6th Inf. (St.Guards) Co.A
Taylor, Isaac GA 12th Inf. Co.A
Taylor, Isaac GA 47th Inf. Co.F
Taylor, Isaac MS 35th Inf. Co.D
Taylor, Isaac MO 4th Cav. Co.D,K
Taylor, Isaac MO 9th Bn.S.S. Co.F
Taylor, Isaac NC 2nd Cav. (19th St.Troops) Co.K
Taylor, Isaac NC 1st Jr.Res. Co.A
Taylor, Isaac NC 18th Inf. Co.D
Taylor, Isaac NC 27th Inf. Co.D
Taylor, Isaac NC 31st Inf. Co.K
Taylor, Isaac NC 51st Inf. Co.D
Taylor, Isaac TN Inf. 1st Bn. (Colms') Co.B
Taylor, Isaac TN 37th Inf. Co.I
Taylor, Isaac TX Cav. Martin's Regt. Co.D
Taylor, Isaac VA 11th Cav. Co.C
Taylor, Isaac VA 18th Cav. Co.C,K
Taylor, Isaac VA 13th Inf. Co.K
Taylor, Isaac 4th Conf.Inf. Co.H
Taylor, Isaac Conf.Reg.Inf. Brooks' Bn. Co.B
Taylor, Isaac A. VA 56th Inf. Co.B Cpl.
Taylor, Isaac B. TX 16th Cav. Co.C
Taylor, Isaac D. GA 8th Inf. (St.Guards) Co.A
Taylor, Isaac E. NC 27th Inf. Co.D Cpl.
Taylor, Isaac E. VA 25th Inf. 1st Co.H
Taylor, Isaac E. VA 62nd Mtd.Inf. 2nd Co.B
Taylor, Isaac J. NC 2nd Arty. (36th St.Troops) Co.A
Taylor, Isaac L. NC 17th Inf. (1st Org.) Co.D
Taylor, Isaac L. NC 17th Inf. (2nd Org.) Co.D Jr.2nd Lt.
Taylor, Isaac M. VA 4th Inf. Co.I
Taylor, Isaac N. LA 10th Inf. Co.E Sgt.
Taylor, Isaac P. TX 3rd (Kirby's) Bn.Vol. Co.A
Taylor, Isaac S. TX 31st Cav. Co.G Surg.
Taylor, Isaac S. Gen. & Staff Maj.,Surg.
Taylor, Isaac T. VA Inf. 21st Bn. 1st Co.D, 2nd Co.C Sgt.
Taylor, Isaac T. VA 64th Mtd.Inf. Co.C Sgt.
Taylor, Isaac W. LA 31st Inf. Co.E
Taylor, Isaac W. MS 15th Inf. Co.F
Taylor, Isaiah NC 29th Inf. Co.A
Taylor, Isaiah J. GA Inf. 10th Bn. Co.A
Taylor, Isam A. NC 8th Sr.Res. Gardner's Co.
Taylor, Isham U. NC 24th Inf. Co.E
Taylor, Isham W. SC 20th Inf. Co.E
Taylor, Isolam G. SC 20th Inf. Co.H
Taylor, Isom A. NC 35th Inf. Co.G Music.
Taylor, Israel TN 47th Inf. Co.B
Taylor, Israel S. TX 24th Cav. Co.D
Taylor, Ivey NC 1st Arty. (10th St.Troops) Co.B
Taylor, Ivy NC 3rd Cav. (41st St.Troops) Co.E
Taylor, Ivy A. LA Hvy.Arty. 2nd Bn. Co.F
Taylor, J. AL 8th (Hatch's) Cav. Co.D
Taylor, J. AL 12th Cav. Co.D
Taylor, J. AL Chas. A. Herts' Co.
Taylor, J. AL 12th Inf. Co.D
Taylor, J. AL St.Res.
Taylor, J. AR Inf. Sparks' Co.
Taylor, J. GA 5th Cav.
Taylor, J. GA Cav. 24th Bn. Co.D
Taylor, J. GA Lt.Arty. Clinch's Btty.
Taylor, J. GA 1st Inf. Co.A
Taylor, J. GA Inf. 1st Bn. (St.Guards) Co.C 1st Lt.
Taylor, J. GA 5th Res. Co.D
Taylor, J. GA 21st Inf. Co.H
Taylor, J. GA 43rd Inf. Co.K
Taylor, J. GA 54th Inf. Co.A,D
Taylor, J. GA 63rd Inf. Co.C
Taylor, J. GA Inf. (Columbus) Arsenal Bn. Co.B
Taylor, J. LA 18th Inf. Co.F
Taylor, J. LA Mil. Beauregard Bn. Co.C
Taylor, J. MD Arty. 3rd Btty.
Taylor, J. MS 1st Cav. Co.C
Taylor, J. MS 2nd St.Cav. Co.G
Taylor, J. MS 2nd St.Cav. Co.K
Taylor, J. MS 21st Inf.
Taylor, J. MS Stewart's Co. (Yalobusha Rangers)
Taylor, J. MO 5th Cav. Co.K
Taylor, J. MO 1st & 4th Cons.Inf. Co.H
Taylor, J. NC 2nd Inf. Co.D
Taylor, J. SC 1st (Hagood's) Inf. 2nd Co.H
Taylor, J. SC 5th Bn.Res. Co.E
Taylor, J. SC 16th & 24th (Cons.) Inf. Co.H
Taylor, J. SC 25th Inf. Co.H
Taylor, J. TN Cav. Nixon's Regt. Co.C
Taylor, J. TN Inf. 4th Cons.Regt. Co.B Sgt.
Taylor, J. TN Conscr. (Cp. of Instr.)
Taylor, J. TX 11th Cav. Co.D
Taylor, J. TX 24th & 25th Cav. (Cons.) Co.B
Taylor, J. VA 3rd Cav. Co.B Sgt.
Taylor, J. VA 14th Inf. Co.G
Taylor, J.A. AL 6th Cav. Co.C
Taylor, J.A. AL 8th (Livingston's) Cav. Co.D
Taylor, J.A. AL 13th Bn.Part.Rangers Co.C
Taylor, J.A. AL 53rd (Part.Rangers) Co.A
Taylor, J.A. AL 5th Inf. New Co.H
Taylor, J.A. AL 8th Inf. Co.D
Taylor, J.A. AL 8th Inf. Co.G
Taylor, J.A. AL 18th Bn.Vol. Co.A
Taylor, J.A. AL 47th Inf. Co.D Cpl.
Taylor, J.A. GA Cav. 19th Bn. Co.A
Taylor, J.A. GA 10th Inf. Co.E
Taylor, J.A. KY 9th Cav. Co.B
Taylor, J.A. LA Miles' Legion Co.D 2nd Lt.
Taylor, J.A. MS Inf. 2nd St.Troops Co.K
Taylor, J.A. MS 3rd Inf. (A. of 10,000) Co.C
Taylor, J.A. MS 35th Inf. Co.D
Taylor, J.A. MS 44th Inf. Co.G
Taylor, J.A. MO 7th Cav. Co.B
Taylor, J.A. NC 1st Cav. (9th St.Troops) Co.C
Taylor, J.A. SC 3rd Bn.Res. Co.A
Taylor, J.A. TN 11th (Holman's) Cav. Co.C Cpl.
Taylor, J.A. TN 8th Inf. Co.A
Taylor, J.A. TN 21st Inf. Co.H Bvt.2nd Lt.
Taylor, J.A. TN 44th (Cons.) Inf. Co.K
Taylor, J.A. TN 51st Inf. Co.G
Taylor, J.A. TN 51st (Cons.) Inf. Co.H
Taylor, J.A. TX 17th Field Btty.
Taylor, J.A. Gen. & Staff Lt.,AAAG
Taylor, Jack MS 24th Inf. Co.B
Taylor, Jack TN 55th (Brown's) Inf. Co.E
Taylor, Jack S. AL 41st Inf. Co.F
Taylor, Jackson AL Cav. Forrest's Regt.
Taylor, Jackson AL Cav. Moreland's Regt. Co.C,I
Taylor, Jackson AL 27th Inf. Co.A
Taylor, Jackson AR 7th Inf. Co.G
Taylor, Jackson LA 16th Inf. Co.D
Taylor, Jackson NC 30th Inf. Co.H
Taylor, Jackson NC 42nd Inf. Co.B
Taylor, Jackson TN 18th (Newsom's) Cav. Co.E
Taylor, Jackson VA 129th Mil. Williamson's Co.
Taylor, Jackson VA 1st Cav.St.Line Co.A
Taylor, Jackson W. 4th Conf.Inf. Co.F
Taylor, Jack U. AL 37th Inf. Co.F
Taylor, Jacob AL Cav. Graves' Co.
Taylor, Jacob AR 23rd Inf. Co.C
Taylor, Jacob GA Inf. 27th Bn. Co.D
Taylor, Jacob LA 31st Inf. Co.K
Taylor, Jacob MO 7th Cav. Co.G
Taylor, Jacob NC 5th Inf. Co.H Cpl.
Taylor, Jacob NC 37th Inf. Co.A
Taylor, Jacob NC 58th Inf. Co.E
Taylor, Jacob VA Cav. 36th Bn. Co.A
Taylor, Jacob VA Cav. Caldwell's Bn. Hankins' Co.
Taylor, Jacob VA 11th Bn.Res. Co.B
Taylor, Jacob VA 29th Inf. Co.H
Taylor, Jacob VA 31st Inf. Co.G
Taylor, Jacob VA 37th Inf. Co.G
Taylor, Jacob VA 46th Inf. 2nd Co.K
Taylor, Jacob VA 54th Inf. Co.E
Taylor, Jacob VA 62nd Mtd.Inf. 2nd Co.D,A
Taylor, Jacob Deneale's Regt. Choctaw Warriors Co.A
Taylor, Jacob A. MS 16th Inf. Co.F Sgt.
Taylor, Jacob A. VA 34th Inf. Co.I
Taylor, Jacob H. AR 3rd Cav. Asst.Surg.
Taylor, Jacob H. TX 22nd Cav. Co.A
Taylor, Jacob J. AL 11th Inf. Co.F
Taylor, Jacob L. NC 1st Inf. Co.E
Taylor, Jacob N. VA 22nd Inf. Taylor's Co. Capt.
Taylor, Jacob N. VA 60th Inf. Co.E Maj.
Taylor, Jacob S. AR 9th Inf. Co.A Sgt.
Taylor, Jacob S. VA 28th Inf. 2nd Co.C
Taylor, Jacob W. NC Hvy.Arty. 1st Bn. Co.B 1st Lt.
Taylor, J.A.J. AL 17th Inf. Co.F Cpl.
Taylor, J.A.J. AL 58th Inf. Co.C
Taylor, James AL 5th Cav. Co.H
Taylor, James AL Arty. 1st Bn. Co.A Ord.Sgt.
Taylor, James AL 3rd Bn.Res. Flemming's Co.
Taylor, James AL 4th Inf. Co.B
Taylor, James AL 55th Vol. Co.I Sgt.
Taylor, James AL 59th Inf. Co.A Sgt.
Taylor, James AR Cav. Poe's Bn. Co.A
Taylor, James AR 1st Vol. Co.B
Taylor, James AR 1st Vol. Co.F

Taylor, James AR 8th Inf. New Co.K
Taylor, James AR 13th Inf. Co.K
Taylor, James AR 15th (N.W.) Inf. Emergency Co.I
Taylor, James AR 27th Inf. Co.K
Taylor, James AR 32nd Inf. Co.G
Taylor, James FL Cav. 5th Bn. Co.D
Taylor, James FL Cav. 5th Bn. Co.E
Taylor, James FL 1st Inf. New Co.D
Taylor, James FL Inf. 2nd Bn. Co.F
Taylor, James FL 4th Inf. Co.H
Taylor, James FL 6th Inf. Co.A
Taylor, James FL 8th Inf. Co.A
Taylor, James GA 1st Cav. Co.F
Taylor, James GA 6th Cav. Co.A
Taylor, James GA 10th Cav. (St.Guards) Co.D
Taylor, James GA Mayer's Co. (Appling Cav.)
Taylor, James GA Hvy.Arty. 22nd Bn. Co.B Sgt.
Taylor, James GA 18th Inf. Co.K
Taylor, James GA 25th Inf. 1st Co.K Sgt.
Taylor, James GA 49th Inf. Co.K
Taylor, James GA 57th Inf. Co.F
Taylor, James GA Phillips' Legion Co.E
Taylor, James KY 7th Cav. Co.G
Taylor, James KY 10th (Diamond's) Cav. Co.D
Taylor, James KY Lt.Arty. Cobb's Co.
Taylor, James KY 7th Mtd.Inf. 1st Co.K
Taylor, James LA 1st Hvy.Arty. (Reg.) Co.G
Taylor, James LA 1st (Strawbridge's) Inf. Co.A
Taylor, James LA 1st (Strawbridge's) Inf. Co.D
Taylor, James, 1st LA 1st (Strawbridge's) Inf. Co.A,C
Taylor, James, 2nd LA 1st (Strawbridge's) Inf. Co.A
Taylor, James LA Inf. 1st Sp.Bn. (Wheat's) New Co.D
Taylor, James LA 20th Inf.
Taylor, James MS 3rd Cav. Co.H
Taylor, James MS 8th Cav. Co.K
Taylor, James MS Cav. 24th Bn. Co.D
Taylor, James MS Cav. 24th Bn. Co.E
Taylor, James MS Cav. Jeff Davis Legion Asst.Surg.
Taylor, James MS 2nd (Davidson's) Inf. Co.A
Taylor, James MS Inf. 2nd Bn. Co.K
Taylor, James MS 5th Inf. Co.H
Taylor, James MS 10th Inf. Old Co.E
Taylor, James MS 37th Inf. Co.A
Taylor, James MS 40th Inf. Co.B
Taylor, James MS 48th Inf. Co.K
Taylor, James MO 4th Cav. Co.F
Taylor, James MO 10th Cav. Co.H
Taylor, James MO Douglas' Regt.
Taylor, James NC 1st Cav. (9th St.Troops) Co.G
Taylor, James NC 6th Cav. (65th St.Troops) Co.D
Taylor, James NC 1st Inf. (6 mo. '61) Co.I
Taylor, James NC 2nd Inf. Co.A
Taylor, James NC 17th Inf. (2nd Org.) Co.E
Taylor, James NC 27th Inf. Co.D
Taylor, James NC 34th Inf. Co.I
Taylor, James NC 39th Inf. Co.A
Taylor, James NC 60th Inf. Co.G
Taylor, James NC 67th Inf. Co.D
Taylor, James NC Inf. Thomas Legion Co.B Capt.
Taylor, James SC 5th Cav. Co.E
Taylor, James SC 6th Cav. Co.A
Taylor, James SC Vol. Simons' Co.
Taylor, James SC Lt.Arty. Beauregard's Co.
Taylor, James SC 1st St.Troops Co.F
Taylor, James SC 2nd Res.
Taylor, James SC 2nd Rifles Co.H
Taylor, James SC 3rd St.Troops Co.C
Taylor, James SC 4th Bn.Res. Co.B
Taylor, James SC 5th Res. Co.A
Taylor, James SC 7th Inf. 1st Co.B
Taylor, James SC 9th Res. Co.C Sgt.
Taylor, James SC 14th Inf. Co.K
Taylor, James SC 18th Inf. Co.E
Taylor, James SC 24th Inf. Co.G
Taylor, James SC Manigault's Bn.Vol. Co.A
Taylor, James SC Palmetto S.S. Co.F
Taylor, James TN 1st (Carter's) Cav. Co.M Cpl.
Taylor, James TN 5th (McKenzie's) Cav. Co.A
Taylor, James TN 5th (McKenzie's) Cav. Co.C
Taylor, James TN 9th Cav. Co.G
Taylor, James TN 11th Cav.
Taylor, James TN 12th (Green's) Cav. Co.G
Taylor, James TN 16th (Logwood's) Cav. Co.D
Taylor, James TN 1st (Feild's) Inf. Co.G
Taylor, James TN 11th Inf. Co.G
Taylor, James, Sr. TN 16th Inf. Co.B
Taylor, James TN 17th Inf. Co.H
Taylor, James TN 22nd Inf. Co.B
Taylor, James TN 30th Inf. Co.I
Taylor, James TN 42nd Inf. 1st Co.I
Taylor, James TN 44th Inf. Co.I
Taylor, James TN 44th (Cons.) Inf. Co.A
Taylor, James TN 45th Inf. Co.F
Taylor, James TN 51st (Cons.) Inf. Co.B
Taylor, James TN 61st Mtd.Inf. Co.E
Taylor, James TN 62nd Mtd.Inf. Co.I
Taylor, James TN 63rd Inf. Co.F
Taylor, James TN 63rd Inf. Co.G
Taylor, James TX 17th Cons.Dismtd.Cav. Col.
Taylor, James TX 20th Cav. Co.I
Taylor, James TX 28th Cav. Co.C Cpl.
Taylor, James TX Cav. Benavides' Regt. Co.E
Taylor, James TX Cav. Saufley's Scouting Bn. Co.E
Taylor, James TX 3rd Inf. Co.E
Taylor, James TX 6th Inf. Co.G Sgt.
Taylor, James TX 10th Inf. Co.G
Taylor, James TX 14th Inf. 2nd Co.K
Taylor, James TX 21st Inf. Co.C
Taylor, James TX Inf. Griffin's Bn. Co.C QMSgt.
Taylor, James TX Conscr.
Taylor, James VA 8th Cav. Co.C
Taylor, James VA 9th Cav. Co.I
Taylor, James VA 22nd Cav. Co.F
Taylor, James VA 25th Cav. Co.D
Taylor, James VA 1st Arty. 2nd Co.C
Taylor, James VA Hvy.Arty. 10th Bn. Co.E
Taylor, James VA Lt.Arty. Pollock's Co. 1st Sgt.
Taylor, James VA 1st Inf. Co.B
Taylor, James VA 1st (Farinholt's) Res. Co.C
Taylor, James VA 2nd Inf.Loc.Def. Co.C
Taylor, James VA Inf. 2nd Bn.Loc.Def. Co.E
Taylor, James VA 3rd Inf. Co.G
Taylor, James VA 5th Inf. Co.G
Taylor, James VA 6th Inf. 1st Co.B
Taylor, James VA 6th Bn.Res. Co.B
Taylor, James VA 6th Bn.Res. Co.G
Taylor, James VA 6th Bn.Res. Co.H
Taylor, James VA 19th Inf. Co.F
Taylor, James VA Inf. 21st Bn. 1st Co.E,D
Taylor, James VA Inf. 23rd Bn. Co.B
Taylor, James VA 28th Inf. Co.E
Taylor, James VA 31st Inf. Co.G
Taylor, James (Col'd.) VA 32nd Inf. Co.E Cook
Taylor, James VA 36th Inf. 2nd Co.E
Taylor, James VA 54th Mil. Co.B
Taylor, James VA 55th Inf. Co.L
Taylor, James VA 56th Inf. Co.H
Taylor, James VA 60th Inf. Co.D
Taylor, James VA 60th Inf. 2nd Co.H
Taylor, James VA 64th Mtd.Inf. 2nd Co.F
Taylor, James VA 72nd Mil.
Taylor, James VA 86th Mil. Co.F
Taylor, James VA 92nd Mil. Co.A
Taylor, James VA 92nd Mil. Co.B
Taylor, James VA 136th Mil. Co.C
Taylor, James VA 151st Mil. Co.D
Taylor, James VA Mil. Scott Cty.
Taylor, James 8th (Wade's) Conf.Cav. Co.F
Taylor, James 10th Conf.Cav. Co.F
Taylor, James 20th Conf.Cav. Co.F
Taylor, James Gen. & Staff, Ord.Dept. Ord.Sgt.
Taylor, James Deneale's Regt. Choctaw Warriors Co.A
Taylor, James Gen. & Staff Capt.,QM
Taylor, James A. AR Cav. Harrell's Bn. Co.A
Taylor, James A. FL 9th Inf. Co.E Cpl.
Taylor, James A. GA 3rd Bn. (St.Guards) Co.C Capt.
Taylor, James A. GA 6th Inf. Co.E
Taylor, James A. GA 23rd Inf. Co.E
Taylor, James A. KY Horse Arty. Byrne's Co.
Taylor, James A. MS 28th Cav. Co.G 2nd Lt.
Taylor, James A. MS 29th Inf. Co.G
Taylor, James A. MO 7th Cav. Co.I
Taylor, James A. MO 2nd Inf. Co.A
Taylor, James A. SC 7th Inf. 1st Co.F, 2nd Co.F Cpl.
Taylor, James A. TN 7th (Duckworth's) Cav. Co.L Capt.
Taylor, James A. TN 9th (Ward's) Cav. Co.D
Taylor, James A. TN 15th Cav. Co.E
Taylor, James A. TN 24th Inf. 2nd Co.G
Taylor, James A. TN 60th Mtd.Inf. Co.C Cpl.
Taylor, James A. VA 9th Cav. Co.E
Taylor, James A. VA 6th Bn.Res. Co.H
Taylor, James A. VA 11th Inf. Co.B
Taylor, James A. VA 12th Inf. Co.F
Taylor, James A. VA 22nd Inf. Co.C
Taylor, James A. VA 29th Inf. Co.G
Taylor, James A. VA 55th Inf. Co.A
Taylor, James A. VA Mil. Scott Cty.
Taylor, James A. 10th Conf.Cav. Co.F
Taylor, James A. Morgan's,CSA Recruit
Taylor, James B. AL 3rd Inf. Co.C
Taylor, James B. GA 26th Inf. Co.F,A
Taylor, James B. MS 32nd Inf. Co.E
Taylor, James B. NC 1st Inf. Co.H
Taylor, James B. NC 17th Inf. (2nd Org.) Co.H
Taylor, James B. NC 43rd Inf. Co.D

Taylor, James B., Jr. SC Cav.Bn. Hampton Legion Co.B
Taylor, James B. TN 40th Inf. Co.G
Taylor, James B. TX 35th (Brown's) Cav. Co.C
Taylor, James B. TX Cav. Baylor's Regt. Co.A 1st Lt.
Taylor, James B. VA 5th Cav. 1st Co.F
Taylor, James B. VA 10th Cav. Chap.
Taylor, James B. VA 25th Inf. 2nd Co.H
Taylor, James B. Gen. & Staff Capt.,Comsy.
Taylor, James B. Gen. & Staff Chap.
Taylor, James B., Jr. Gen. & Staff Chap.
Taylor, James C. AR 30th Inf. Co.F
Taylor, James C. GA 34th Inf. Co.F
Taylor, James C. MS 11th Inf. Co.A
Taylor, James C. MS 15th Inf. Co.I 3rd Lt.
Taylor, James C. MO Cav. Jackman's Regt. Co.H
Taylor, James C. SC 2nd Cav. Co.I
Taylor, James C. TN 7th (Duckworth's) Cav. Co.H
Taylor, James C. TN 37th Inf. Co.E
Taylor, James C. TX 15th Cav. Co.C
Taylor, James C. TX Granbury's Cons.Brig. Co.F
Taylor, James C. VA Lt.Arty. B.Z. Price's Co.
Taylor, James C. VA 23rd Inf. Co.C
Taylor, James C. VA 54th Inf. Co.C Maj.
Taylor, James Curtis VA 15th Inf. Co.B Cpl.
Taylor, James D. AL Cav. Lewis' Bn. Co.D
Taylor, James D. AR 1st (Crawford's) Cav. Co.C
Taylor, James D. GA 4th (Clinch's) Cav. Co.C Sgt.
Taylor, James D. GA 26th Inf. Atkinson's Co.B
Taylor, James D. VA 3rd Inf. Co.F Sgt.
Taylor, James D. VA 26th Inf. Co.H 1st Lt.
Taylor, James D. VA Mil. Grayson Cty.
Taylor, James E. AR 14th (Powers') Inf. Co.H
Taylor, James E. KY 9th Cav. Co.B
Taylor, James E. NC Cav. 5th Bn. Co.C
Taylor, James E. NC 6th Cav. (65th St.Troops) Co.C
Taylor, James E. NC 8th Bn.Part.Rangers
Taylor, James E. NC 1st Arty. (10th St.Troops) Co.I
Taylor, James E. NC 58th Inf. Co.E,I,C
Taylor, James E. SC 1st (McCreary's) Inf. Co.G
Taylor, James E. TN Inf. 1st Bn. (Colms') Co.B
Taylor, James E. TN 28th (Cons.) Inf. Co.I
Taylor, James E. TN 84th Inf. Co.E
Taylor, James E. VA 4th Cav. Co.F Sgt.
Taylor, James E. VA Cav. Hounshell's Bn. Huffman's Co.
Taylor, James E. VA Cav. Thurmond's Co.
Taylor, James E. VA 5th Inf. Co.L
Taylor, James E. VA 10th Inf. Co.D
Taylor, James E. VA 11th Inf. Co.I 1st 2nd Lt.
Taylor, James E VA 15th Inf. Co.E
Taylor, James E. VA 21st Inf. Co.G 2nd Lt.
Taylor, James E. VA 45th Inf. Co.D
Taylor, James E. VA 166th Mil. Taylor's Co. Capt.
Taylor, James F. AL 29th Inf. Co.K
Taylor, James F. AL 42nd Inf. Co.F
Taylor, James F. AL 57th Inf. Co.B,H Cpl.
Taylor, James F. SC 20th Inf. Co.H
Taylor, James F. TN Cav. Newsom's Regt. Co.F Cpl.
Taylor, James F. TN Inf. 22nd Bn.
Taylor, James F. TN 27th Inf. Co.F
Taylor, James F. VA Hvy.Arty. A.J. Jones' Co.
Taylor, James F. VA 41st Inf. Co.F
Taylor, James G. KY 12th Cav. Co.B Sgt.
Taylor, James G. NC 22nd Inf. Co.H
Taylor, James G. SC 20th Inf. Co.H
Taylor, James G. TN 5th (McKenzie's) Cav. Co.G
Taylor, James G. VA Mtd.Guard 4th Congr.Dist.
Taylor, James H. AL 14th Inf. Co.G
Taylor, James H. AL 20th Inf. Co.D
Taylor, James H. AL 41st Inf. Co.C
Taylor, Jas. H. AR 19th (Dawson's) Inf. Co.A
Taylor, James H. AR 23rd Inf. Co.C Sgt.
Taylor, James H. GA Cav. 19th Bn. Co.A
Taylor, James H. KY 9th Mtd.Inf. Co.D
Taylor, James H. MS 20th Inf. Co.B 1st Sgt.
Taylor, James H. MO 1st N.E. Cav.
Taylor, James H. NC Cav. 16th Bn. Co.G
Taylor, James H. NC 2nd Arty. (36th St.Troops) Co.B
Taylor, James H. NC 1st Inf. (6 mo. '61) Co.F
Taylor, James H. NC 12th Inf. Co.B,D
Taylor, James H. NC 17th Inf. (1st Org.) Co.K
Taylor, James H. NC 51st Inf. Co.I Adj.
Taylor, James H. NC 53rd Inf. Co.K
Taylor, James H. SC 1st (McCreary's) Inf. Co.C Sgt.
Taylor, James H. SC Mil. 1st Regt. (Charleston Res.) Co.C Capt.
Taylor, James H. SC 1st Inf. Co.A Cpl.
Taylor, James H. SC 2nd Rifles Co.K
Taylor, James H. SC 2nd St.Troops Co.A 1st Lt.
Taylor, James H. SC 16th Inf. Co.F 2nd Lt.
Taylor, James H. TN 23rd Inf. 2nd Co.A
Taylor, James H. TN 28th Inf. Co.F Cpl.
Taylor, James H. TX 13th Cav. Co.A
Taylor, James H. TX 12th Inf. Co.D
Taylor, James H. TX 12th Inf. Co.F
Taylor, James H. VA 7th Cav. Co.F
Taylor, James H. VA 25th Cav. Co.E
Taylor, James H. VA Cav. 40th Bn. Co.C
Taylor, James H. VA 5th Inf. Co.E
Taylor, James H. VA 33rd Inf. Co.I Cpl.
Taylor, James H. VA Res.Forces Thurston's Co.
Taylor, Jas. H. 3rd Conf.Cav. Co.F
Taylor, James H. 8th (Dearing's) Conf.Cav. Co.C
Taylor, James H.C. NC 3rd Inf. Co.A
Taylor, James Henry NC Cav. 12th Bn. Co.C
Taylor, James H.R. TN 15th Inf. Lt.Col.
Taylor, James I. GA 57th Inf. Co.I Sgt.
Taylor, James I. TN 63rd Inf. Co.F
Taylor, James J. GA 11th Cav. Co.H
Taylor, James J. GA 64th Inf. Co.D
Taylor, James J. GA 65th Inf. Co.K
Taylor, James J. GA Smith's Legion Co.K
Taylor, James J. KY 3rd Cav. Co.D
Taylor, James J. LA 7th Inf. Co.E
Taylor, James J. NC 61st Inf. Co.F
Taylor, James J. TX 28th Cav. Co.M
Taylor, James J. TX 4th Field Btty.
Taylor, James J. VA 12th Inf. 2nd Co.I
Taylor, James J. VA 24th Inf. Co.K
Taylor, James J. Sig.Corps,CSA
Taylor, James K. NC 33rd Inf. Co.B Sgt.
Taylor, James K.P. VA 55th Inf. Co.D
Taylor, James L. FL Lt.Arty. Dyke's Co.
Taylor, James L. GA 15th Inf. Co.D
Taylor, James L. MS 46th Inf. Co.A
Taylor, James L. NC Lt.Arty. 3rd Bn. Co.B
Taylor, James L. SC 1st (McCreary's) Inf. Co.G
Taylor, James L. TN 2nd (Robison's) Inf. Co.F
Taylor, James L. TX 7th Inf. Co.D,K
Taylor, James L. VA 3rd Inf.Loc.Def. Co.A
Taylor, James L. VA 24th Inf. Co.I
Taylor, James M. AL 56th Part.Rangers Co.A
Taylor, James M., Jr. AL 5th Inf. New Co.G
Taylor, James M. AL 16th Inf. Co.E
Taylor, James M. AL 22nd Inf. Co.C
Taylor, James M. AL 25th Inf. Co.H
Taylor, James M. AL 32nd Inf. Co.I Cpl.
Taylor, James M. AL 43rd Inf. Co.B
Taylor, James M. AL 44th Inf. Co.C
Taylor, James M. AL 63rd Inf. Co.B
Taylor, Jas. M. AL Cp. of Instr. Talladega
Taylor, James M. AR 1st (Crawford's) Cav. Co.G
Taylor, James M. AR 2nd Mtd.Rifles Co.K
Taylor, James M. AR 5th Inf. Co.B
Taylor, James M. AR 23rd Inf. Co.C Cpl.
Taylor, James M. GA 7th Inf. Co.C Cpl.
Taylor, James M. GA 8th Inf. Co.E
Taylor, James M. GA 15th Inf. Co.F
Taylor, James M. GA 22nd Inf. Co.E Sgt.
Taylor, James M. GA 23rd Inf. Co.E
Taylor, James M. GA 45th Inf. Co.D
Taylor, James M. GA Cherokee Legion (St.Guards) Co.F
Taylor, James M. KY 5th Mtd.Inf. Co.C
Taylor, James M. LA 12th Inf. Co.L
Taylor, James M. MS Cav.Res. Butler's Co.
Taylor, James M. MS 1st Bn.S.S. Co.D
Taylor, James M. MS 15th Inf. Co.H
Taylor, James M. MS 26th Inf. Surg.
Taylor, James M. MS 26th Inf. Co.C
Taylor, James M. MS 26th Inf. Co.H
Taylor, James M. MS 29th Inf. Co.D 2nd Lt.
Taylor, James M. MS 31st Inf. Co.E
Taylor, James M. MO 11th Inf. Co.I
Taylor, James M. NC 34th Inf. Co.C Sgt.
Taylor, James M. NC 62nd Inf. Co.F 1st Lt.
Taylor, James M. SC 12th Inf. Co.I
Taylor, James M. TN 19th (Biffle's) Cav. Co.D
Taylor, James M. TN 12th (Cons.) Inf. Co.H Sgt.
Taylor, James M. TN 44th (Cons.) Inf. Co.E
Taylor, James M. TN 50th Inf. Co.H Sgt.
Taylor, James M. TX 19th Cav. Co.E
Taylor, James M. VA 17th Cav. Co.K
Taylor, James M. VA Cav. Thurmond's Co. Cpl.
Taylor, James M. VA 1st St.Res. Co.I
Taylor, James M. VA Inf. 9th Bn. Co.B
Taylor, James M. VA 21st Inf. Co.E
Taylor, James M. VA 25th Inf. 2nd Co.G
Taylor, James M. VA 29th Inf. Co.G
Taylor, James M. VA 34th Inf. Fray's Co.D
Taylor, James M. VA Mil. Greene Cty.
Taylor, James M. Gen. & Staff Capt.,QM
Taylor, James M. Gen. & Staff 1st Lt.,Adj.

Taylor, James Matchett NC 5th Inf. Co.B Capt.
Taylor, Jas. M.B. AL 22nd Inf. Co.I
Taylor, James M.V. NC 25th Inf. Co.I
Taylor, James N. AL 10th Inf. Co.K
Taylor, James O. SC 1st (McCreary's) Inf. Co.I
Taylor, James O. TN 5th (McKenzie's) Cav. Co.I
Taylor, James P. AL 9th (Malone's) Cav. Co.B
Taylor, James P. AL Lt.Arty. 2nd Bn. Co.C Sgt.
Taylor, James P. AL 17th Inf. Co.A
Taylor, James P. AL Cp. of Instr. Talladega
Taylor, James P. LA 2nd Inf. Co.B
Taylor, James P. MS 11th (Perrin's) Cav. Co.G
Taylor, James P. NC 32nd Inf. Co.I Cpl.
Taylor, James P. NC 33rd Inf. Co.E Cpl.
Taylor, James P. NC 39th Inf. Co.C
Taylor, James P. NC 49th Inf. Co.F
Taylor, James P. TN 5th (McKenzie's) Cav. Co.E
Taylor, James P. TN 28th Inf. Co.C
Taylor, James P. VA Lt.Arty. 12th Bn. Co.D
Taylor, James R. AL 7th Cav. Co.C,G
Taylor, James R. AL 23rd Inf. Co.I
Taylor, James R. AR 1st (Dobbin's) Cav. Co.H 2nd Lt.
Taylor, James R. AR 14th (Powers') Inf. Co.H
Taylor, James R. AR 18th Inf. Co.B Cpl.
Taylor, James R. GA 3rd Inf. Co.H
Taylor, James R. GA 49th Inf. Co.D
Taylor, James R. GA 66th Inf. Co.I
Taylor, Jas. R. GA 2nd St.Line Co.C
Taylor, James R. MS 1st Cav. Co.C Capt.
Taylor, James R. NC 1st Arty. (10th St.Troops) Co.E
Taylor, James R. NC 3rd Arty. (40th St.Troops) Co.A
Taylor, James R. NC 6th Inf. Co.D
Taylor, James R. NC 32nd Inf. Lenoir Braves 1st Co.K
Taylor, James R. NC 54th Inf. Co.I
Taylor, James R. TN 28th Inf. Co.C
Taylor, James R. TX 17th Cav. Co.B Col.
Taylor, James R. VA 11th Inf. Co.G
Taylor, James R. VA 42nd Inf. Co.C
Taylor, James R. VA Inf. Tomlin's Bn. Co.A
Taylor, James S. AR 19th (Dockery's) Inf. Cons.Co.E,D, Co.E
Taylor, James S. GA 38th Inf. Co.N
Taylor, James S. MS 1st (Johnston's) Inf. Co.B 2nd Lt.
Taylor, James S. MS 19th Inf. Co.I Cpl.
Taylor, James S. NC 17th Inf. (2nd Org.) Co.D
Taylor, James S. NC 61st Inf. Co.E
Taylor, James S. VA 2nd Cav. Co.D Cpl.
Taylor, James S. VA 39th Inf. Co.E
Taylor, James S. VA 46th Inf. 4th Co.F
Taylor, James S. Gen. & Staff Surg.
Taylor, James T. AL 57th Inf. Co.B
Taylor, James T. KY 9th Mtd.Inf. Co.C
Taylor, James T. NC 17th Inf. (2nd Org.) Co.G
Taylor, James T. TX Cav. McCord's Frontier Regt. 2nd Co.A
Taylor, James T. VA 1st Cav. Co.F
Taylor, James T. VA Hvy.Arty. Allen's Co.
Taylor, James T. VA Horse Arty. E. Graham's Co.
Taylor, James T. VA 56th Inf. Co.I
Taylor, James T. 1st Choctaw & Chickasaw Mtd.Rifles Co.K
Taylor, Jas. Theus Gen. & Staff Surg.
Taylor, James W. AL 6th Cav. Co.H
Taylor, James W. AL 3rd Inf. Co.C
Taylor, James W. AL 19th Inf. Co.B
Taylor, James W. AR 15th (N.W.) Inf. Co.C 2nd Lt.
Taylor, James W. AR 19th (Dockery's) Inf. Co.G
Taylor, James W. AR 27th Inf. Co.E
Taylor, James W. FL 2nd Inf. Co.I
Taylor, James W. FL 2nd Inf. Co.M
Taylor, James W. FL 3rd Inf. Co.D
Taylor, James W. GA 1st Cav. Co.B 1st Lt.
Taylor, James W. GA 2nd Res. Co.K
Taylor, James W. GA 43rd Inf. Co.I
Taylor, James W. MS 1st Lt.Arty. Co.C
Taylor, James W. MS 14th Inf. Co.K
Taylor, James W. MS 15th Inf.
Taylor, James W. MS 15th Inf. Co.E Cpl.
Taylor, James W. MS 19th Inf. Co.B
Taylor, James W. MO Lt.Arty. 1st Btty.
Taylor, James W. NC 2nd Cav. (19th St.Troops) Co.E
Taylor, James W. NC Hvy.Arty. 1st Bn. Co.C
Taylor, James W. NC 3rd Inf. Co.A
Taylor, James W. NC 64th Inf. Co.D Cpl.
Taylor, James W. SC 20th Inf. Co.K
Taylor, James W. TN 14th Cav. Co.C
Taylor, James W. TX Inf. Whaley's Co.
Taylor, James W. VA 6th Cav. Co.F
Taylor, James W. VA 12th Cav. Co.G
Taylor, James W. VA 18th Cav. Co.B
Taylor, James W. VA 34th Inf. Co.D
Taylor, James W. VA 49th Inf. Co.I
Taylor, James W. VA 50th Inf. Co.F
Taylor, James W. VA 59th Inf. 3rd Co.I
Taylor, James W. VA 61st Inf. Co.G
Taylor, James W. 1st Conf.Inf. 2nd Co.H
Taylor, James W.C. NC 3rd Cav. (41st St.Troops) Co.E
Taylor, James Y. VA 44th Inf. Co.H Sgt.
Taylor, Jason NC 64th Inf. Co.E
Taylor, Jason J. NC 34th Inf. Co.C Cpl.
Taylor, Jasper FL 6th Inf. Co.G
Taylor, Jasper KY 4th Cav. Co.D
Taylor, Jasper KY 1st Bn.Mtd.Rifles Co.A
Taylor, Jasper KY 2nd Mtd.Inf. Co.F
Taylor, Jasper N. MS 24th Inf. Co.K Cpl.
Taylor, Jasper N. TN 1st (Turney's) Inf. Co.E Sgt.
Taylor, J.B. AL 25th Inf. Co.G Lt.
Taylor, J.B. AL 30th Inf. Co.I
Taylor, J.B. AL 31st Inf. Co.H
Taylor, J.B. FL 1st (Res.) Inf. Co.B
Taylor, J.B. FL 9th Inf. Co.D
Taylor, J.B. LA Lt.Arty. Holmes' Btty.
Taylor, J.B. LA Mil. Chalmette Regt.
Taylor, J.B. MS 2nd Cav. Co.H
Taylor, J.B. MS 10th Cav. Co.E Cpl.
Taylor, J.B. SC 20th Inf. Co.H
Taylor, J.B. TN 3rd (Clack's) Inf. Co.H
Taylor, J.B. TN 4th Inf. Co.A
Taylor, J.B. TN 51st (Cons.) Inf. Co.I
Taylor, J.B. TN 84th Inf. Co.D
Taylor, J.B. TX 26th Cav. Co.I Sgt.
Taylor, J.B. TX 28th Cav. Co.H
Taylor, J.B. TX 35th (Brown's) Cav. Co.C Cpl.
Taylor, J.B. TX Cav. Benavides' Regt. Co.G
Taylor, J.B. TX Cav. Morgan's Regt. Co.F
Taylor, J.B. TX 13th Vol. 1st Co.H
Taylor, J.B. TX 22nd Inf. Co.F
Taylor, J.B. TX Vol. Teague's Co. (So.Rights Guards)
Taylor, J.B. VA 14th Cav. Co.G
Taylor, J.B. VA 7th Bn.Res. Co.B
Taylor, J.C. AL 3rd Res. Co.A
Taylor, J.C. AL 10th Inf. Co.E
Taylor, J.C. AL 31st Inf. Co.G
Taylor, J.C. AL 34th Inf. Co.B Bvt.2nd Lt.
Taylor, J.C. AL Cp. of Instr. Talladega
Taylor, J.C. AR 3rd Cav. Co.M
Taylor, J.C. AR Cav. Davies' Bn. Co.D
Taylor, J.C. AR 3rd Inf.
Taylor, J.C. AR 12th Inf. Co.I
Taylor, J.C. AR 30th Inf. Co.B
Taylor, J.C. GA 4th Res. Co.K
Taylor, J.C. GA 5th Res. Co.D
Taylor, J.C. GA 31st Inf. Co.K
Taylor, J.C. KY 3rd Mtd.Inf. Co.M
Taylor, J.C. LA 25th Inf. Co.H
Taylor, J.C. MS 18th Cav. Co.E Sgt.
Taylor, J.C. MS 38th Cav. Co.I Cpl.
Taylor, J.C. MS 1st (Patton's) Inf. Halfacre's Co. Cpl.
Taylor, J.C. MS 35th Inf. Co.D
Taylor, J.C. MS 39th Inf. Co.F
Taylor, J.C. MO 5th Cav. Co.H
Taylor, J.C. MO Inf. 1st Bn. Co.C
Taylor, J.C. NC 1st Cav. (9th St.Troops) Co.C
Taylor, J.C. NC 11th (Bethel Regt.) Inf. Co.A
Taylor, J.C. SC 1st (McCreary's) Inf. Co.E
Taylor, J.C. SC 7th Inf. Co.I
Taylor, J.C. TN 19th & 20th (Cons.) Cav. Co.F
Taylor, J.C. TN 20th (Russell's) Cav. Co.A
Taylor, J.C. TN Inf. 4th Cons.Regt. Co.B
Taylor, J.C. TN 45th Inf. Co.A
Taylor, J.C. TX 7th Cav. Co.G Sgt.Maj.
Taylor, J.C. TX Cav. Ragsdale's Bn. 2nd Co.C
Taylor, J.C. TX Cav. Terry's Regt. Co.F
Taylor, J.C. TX 16th Field Btty.
Taylor, J.C. TX 13th Vol. 2nd Co.H
Taylor, J.C. VA 5th Cav. Co.G
Taylor, J.C. VA 3rd Lt.Arty. Co.D
Taylor, J.C. VA 3rd Res. Co.A
Taylor, J.C. VA Inf. 4th Bn.Loc.Def. Co.F
Taylor, J.C. VA 8th Inf. Co.E
Taylor, J.C. VA Inf. 28th Bn. Co.D
Taylor, J.C. VA 54th Mil. Co.B
Taylor, J.C. Pemberton's Staff Capt.,ADC
Taylor, J.C.R. SC 5th Cav. Co.D
Taylor, J.C.R. SC Cav. 17th Bn. Co.A Cpl.
Taylor, J.C.S. Brush Bn.
Taylor, J.C.T. AL 23rd Inf. Co.I
Taylor, J.D. AL 3rd Cav. Co.I
Taylor, J.D. AL Mil. 4th Vol. Co.K
Taylor, J.D. AL 23rd Inf. Co.I
Taylor, J.D. GA Cav. 29th Bn. Co.B
Taylor, J.D. GA 31st Inf. Music.
Taylor, J.D. GA Inf. (Mitchell Home Guards) Brooks' Co.
Taylor, J.D. KY 2nd Mtd.Inf. Co.F Bugler

Taylor, J.D. MS Cav. Gartley's Co. (Yazoo Rangers)
Taylor, J.D. MS 1st (Johnston's) Inf. Co.D
Taylor, J.D. MS 7th Inf. Co.K
Taylor, J.D. MS 9th Inf. New Co.K
Taylor, J.D. SC 4th Cav. Co.G Cpl.
Taylor, J.D. SC 7th Cav. Co.B
Taylor, J.D. SC 7th Cav. Co.E
Taylor, J.D. SC Cav. 10th Bn. Co.C
Taylor, J.D. SC Inf. Hampton Legion Co.G
Taylor, J.D. SC Cav.Bn. Holcombe Legion Co.C
Taylor, J.D. TN 15th (Cons.) Cav. Co.K
Taylor, J.D. TX 14th Inf. Co.A
Taylor, J.D. TX 14th Inf. Co.G
Taylor, J.D. TX Waul's Legion Co.A
Taylor, J.D. VA 5th Bn.Res. Co.D
Taylor, J. Dallas AL Cav. Lenoir's Ind.Co.
Taylor, J.D.B. TX 9th (Nichols') Inf. Co.F Cpl.
Taylor, J.D.K. AL 22nd Inf. Co.C
Taylor, J.E. AL Inf. 1st (Loomis') Bn. Co.A
Taylor, J.E. AL 25th Inf. Co.A
Taylor, J.E. AR 2nd Vol. Co.C
Taylor, J.E. GA Cav. 22nd Bn. (St.Guards) Co.C
Taylor, J.E. GA Lt.Arty. Havis' Btty.
Taylor, J.E. GA 1st (Symons') Res. Co.K
Taylor, J.E. GA 5th Res. Co.A
Taylor, J.E. GA 8th Inf. Co.C
Taylor, J.E. KY 1st Bn.Mtd.Rifles Co.D,B
Taylor, J.E. MS 10th Cav. Co.D
Taylor, J.E. MS Lt.Arty. 14th Bn. Co.C
Taylor, J.E. NC 11th (Bethel Regt.) Inf. Co.F
Taylor, J.E. SC 5th Cav. Co.F
Taylor, J.E. TX 24th & 25th Cav. (Cons.) Co.E
Taylor, J.E. TX 25th Cav. Co.C
Taylor, J.E. TX Cav. (Dismtd.) Chisum's Regt. Co.I
Taylor, J.E. VA 3rd Cav. 2nd Co.I
Taylor, J.E. VA VMI Co.D
Taylor, J.E. 10th Conf.Cav. Co.G
Taylor, Jedson VA 18th Cav. Co.A
Taylor, Jeff MS St.Cav. 2nd Bn. (Harris') Co.C
Taylor, Jeff TN 16th (Logwood's) Cav. Co.D
Taylor, Jefferson MS 2nd St.Cav. Co.H
Taylor, Jefferson MS 18th Inf. Co.K
Taylor, Jefferson M. GA 45th Inf. Co.D
Taylor, Jefferson M. SC 13th Inf. Co.G
Taylor, Jefferson Monroe VA 15th Inf. Co.G
Taylor, Jefferson R. VA 1st Arty. Co.H Ord.Sgt.
Taylor, Jefferson R. VA Lt.Arty. 1st Bn. Ord.Sgt.
Taylor, Jefferson W. GA 10th Inf. Co.D 2nd Lt.
Taylor, J.E.J. AR Lt.Arty. Zimmerman's Btty.
Taylor, Jeptha W. GA 14th Inf. Co.E
Taylor, Jeremiah AR 1st (Monroe's) Cav.
Taylor, Jeremiah TN 26th Inf. Co.A
Taylor, Jeremiah VA 13th Inf. Co.C
Taylor, Jeremiah B. FL 5th Inf. Co.F
Taylor, Jeremiah M. GA 6th Cav. Co.A
Taylor, Jeremiah M. NC 35th Inf. Co.G
Taylor, Jeremiah V. TN 9th (Ward's) Cav. Co.D
Taylor, Jerold D. VA 7th Bn.Res. Co.D
Taylor, Jerome LA Inf. 10th Bn. Co.G
Taylor, Jerome LA C.S. Zouave Bn. Co.C
Taylor, Jerome B. TN 32nd Inf. Co.B
Taylor, Jerry MO Lt.Arty. Walsh's Co.
Taylor, Jerry MO Arty.Regt.St.Guard Co.A
Taylor, Jesse AL 8th Cav. Co.A
Taylor, Jesse AL 19th Inf. Co.K
Taylor, Jesse AR 1st Inf. Co.F
Taylor, Jesse MS 27th Inf. Co.G
Taylor, Jesse MO 3rd Cav. Co.K Cpl.
Taylor, Jesse NC 8th Bn.Part.Rangers Co.A
Taylor, Jesse NC 17th Inf. (2nd Org.) Co.E
Taylor, Jesse NC 27th Inf. Co.K
Taylor, Jesse NC 38th Inf. Co.A
Taylor, Jesse NC 61st Inf. Co.K
Taylor, Jesse NC Bass' Co.
Taylor, Jesse NC Walker's Bn. Thomas' Legion Co.H
Taylor, Jesse SC Lt.Arty. 3rd (Palmetto) Bn. Co.H
Taylor, Jesse SC 16th Inf. Co.F
Taylor, Jesse TN 5th (McKenzie's) Cav. Co.A
Taylor, Jesse TN Lt.Arty. Weller's Co. Capt.
Taylor, Jesse TN Arty.Corps Co.8 Capt.
Taylor, Jesse TN 29th Inf. Co.G
Taylor, Jesse TN 51st Inf. Co.C
Taylor, Jesse TN 53rd Inf. Co.F
Taylor, Jesse VA 34th Inf. Co.I
Taylor, Jesse Brush Bn.
Taylor, Jesse A. LA 28th (Gray's) Inf. Co.A
Taylor, Jesse B. NC 5th Cav. (63rd St.Troops) Co.B
Taylor, Jessee AR Inf. Cocke's Regt. Co.I
Taylor, Jessee M. AR 6th Inf. Co.I
Taylor, Jessee T. AL Cp. of Instr. Talladega Co.B
Taylor, Jesse F. GA Cav. 19th Bn. Co.B
Taylor, Jesse F. 10th Conf.Cav. Co.G
Taylor, Jesse H. AL 17th Inf. Co.F
Taylor, Jesse H. NC 1st Inf. Co.B
Taylor, Jesse J. NC 17th Inf. (2nd Org.) Co.I
Taylor, Jesse J. NC 24th Inf. Co.E
Taylor, Jesse M. AL 3rd Res. Co.B
Taylor, Jesse M. AL 15th Inf. Co.H
Taylor, Jesse M. GA 12th Inf. Co.A
Taylor, Jesse M. GA 19th Inf. Co.K
Taylor, Jesse M. MO Cav. Fristoe's Regt. Co.I
Taylor, Jesse M. NC 2nd Inf. Co.B 1st Sgt.
Taylor, Jesse M. 7th Conf.Cav. Co.H Music.
Taylor, Jesse N. AL 30th Inf. Co.A
Taylor, Jesse P. AL 20th Inf. Co.H,F
Taylor, Jesse S. AL 15th Bn.Part.Rangers Co.B
Taylor, Jesse S. GA 47th Inf. Co.F
Taylor, Jesse S. NC 37th Inf. Co.I
Taylor, Jesse S. TX 35th (Likens') Cav. Co.B
Taylor, Jesse W. FL Cav. 5th Bn. Co.A
Taylor, Jesse W. GA 24th Inf. Co.K
Taylor, Jesse W. NC Inf. 2nd Bn. Co.H
Taylor, Jesse W. NC 25th Inf. Co.H
Taylor, Jewell J. LA 8th Inf. Co.F
Taylor, J.F. AL 8th (Livingston's) Cav. Co.E
Taylor, J.F. AR 10th Inf. Co.H
Taylor, J.F. GA 1st Bn.S.S. Co.A Cpl.
Taylor, J.F. GA 4th Res. Co.A
Taylor, J.F. GA 23rd Inf. Co.H
Taylor, J.F. LA Inf.Cons.Crescent Regt. Co.I
Taylor, J.F. MO Cav. Fristoe's Regt. Co.B
Taylor, J.F. TN Lt.Arty. Phillips' Co. Sgt.
Taylor, J.F. TN 13th Cav. Co.H
Taylor, J.F. TX Cav. Terry's Regt. Co.F
Taylor, J.F. TX 14th Inf. Co.H Cpl.
Taylor, J.F. TX 19th Inf. Co.A
Taylor, J.F. VA 2nd Cav. Co.D
Taylor, J.F. VA 16th Inf. Co.A
Taylor, J.F. VA Inf. 25th Bn. Co.D
Taylor, J.F. VA Conscr. Cp.Lee
Taylor, J.F. 4th Conf.Eng.Troops Cpl.
Taylor, J.F.M. AR 33rd Inf. Co.G
Taylor, J.G. AL Cav. Hardie's Bn.Res. Co.F
Taylor, J.G. AL 25th Inf. Co.F
Taylor, J.G. FL Lt.Arty. Dyke's Co.
Taylor, J.G. FL Kilcrease Lt.Arty.
Taylor, J.G. KY 1st (Helm's) Cav. Co.D Bvt.2nd Lt.
Taylor, J.G. LA 17th Inf. Co.C Capt.
Taylor, J.G. LA 26th Inf. Co.G
Taylor, J.G. MS Inf. 1st Bn.St.Troops (12 mo. '62-3) Co.D
Taylor, J.G. MS 2nd (Davidson's) Inf. Potts' Co.
Taylor, J.G. MS Inf. 2nd Bn. Lt.Col.
Taylor, J.G. NC 3rd Arty. (40th St.Troops) Co.A
Taylor, J.G. SC 17th Inf. Co.B
Taylor, J.G.L. TX 25th Cav. Co.B
Taylor, J.G.L. TX 11th (Spaight's) Bn.Vol. Co.D
Taylor, J.G.L. TX 21st Inf. Co.H
Taylor, J.H. AL 2nd Cav. Co.C
Taylor, J.H. AL Inf. 2nd Regt. Co.G 1st Sgt.
Taylor, J.H. AL 3rd Inf. Co.A
Taylor, J.H. AL Mil. 4th Vol. Co.I
Taylor, J.H. AL 5th Inf. Lt.
Taylor, J.H. AL 43rd Inf. Co.A
Taylor, J.H. AL Rebels
Taylor, J.H. AR 24th Inf. Co.C
Taylor, J.H. AR Inf. Hardy's Regt. Co.F Cpl.
Taylor, J.H. FL Lt.Arty. Dyke's Co.
Taylor, J.H. GA Cav. Hall's Co.
Taylor, J.H. GA 3rd Bn.S.S. Co.A Sgt.
Taylor, J.H. GA 23rd Inf. Co.H
Taylor, J.H. GA 23rd Inf. Co.I Cpl.
Taylor, J.H. GA 52nd Inf. Co.B
Taylor, J.H. KY 3rd Mtd.Inf. 1st Co.F
Taylor, J.H. KY 7th Mtd.Inf. Co.H Cpl.
Taylor, J.H. LA 9th Inf. Co.G
Taylor, J.H. MD 1st Inf. Co.B
Taylor, J.H. MS 28th Cav. Co.I
Taylor, J.H. MS Cav. Stockdale's Bn. Co.A
Taylor, J.H. MO 3rd Cav. Co.D
Taylor, J.H. MO 7th Cav. Co.D
Taylor, J.H. MO Inf. 2nd Regt.St.Guard Co.A 1st Lt.
Taylor, J.H. NC 1st Cav. (9th St.Troops) Co.E
Taylor, J.H. SC 1st (Hagood's) Inf. 2nd Co.H
Taylor, J.H. SC 1st Regt. Charleston Guard Co.A Capt.
Taylor, J.H. SC 5th Inf. 2nd Co.A
Taylor, J.H. SC 6th Inf. Co.H
Taylor, J.H. SC 12th Inf. Co.H
Taylor, J.H. TN 7th (Duckworth's) Cav. Co.I
Taylor, J.H. TN 37th Inf. Co.D
Taylor, J.H. TN 47th Inf. Co.B
Taylor, J.H. TX 35th (Likens') Cav. Co.A
Taylor, J.H. TX Inf. Rutherford's Co.
Taylor, J.H. VA 63rd Inf. Co.D
Taylor, J.H. VA Conscr. Cp.Lee
Taylor, J.H. Conf.Inf. 1st Bn. 2nd Co.E
Taylor, J.H. 2nd Conf.Eng.Troops Co.A
Taylor, J.H. Gen. & Staff,PACS Asst.Surg.

Taylor, J.H.M. AR 3rd Inf. Co.A
Taylor, J.H.R. MS 18th Cav. Co.F
Taylor, J.H.S. AL 23rd Inf. Co.B
Taylor, J.I. TX Cav. McCord's Frontier Regt. Co.G
Taylor, Jim 1st Cherokee Mtd.Rifles McDaniel's Co.
Taylor, Jino TN 8th (Smith's) Cav. Co.G
Taylor, J.J. AL 4th (Russell's) Cav. Co.F
Taylor, J.J. AL 56th Part.Rangers Co.I
Taylor, J.J. AL 8th Inf. Co.B
Taylor, J.J. AL 18th Bn.Vol. Co.A
Taylor, J.J. AL 15th Inf. Co.H
Taylor, J.J. AR 1st Mtd.Rifles Co.C
Taylor, J.J. AR Cav. Gordon's Regt. Co.D Cpl.
Taylor, J.J. AR 10th Mil. Co.H 3rd Lt.
Taylor, J.J. FL Lt.Arty. Dyke's Co.
Taylor, J.J. GA Arty. Lumpkin's Co.
Taylor, J.J. GA Inf. 5th Bn. (St.Guards) Co.E
Taylor, J.J. GA 7th Inf. Co.G
Taylor, J.J. GA 10th Mil.
Taylor, J.J. GA 13th Inf. Co.D
Taylor, J.J. GA 15th Inf. Co.F
Taylor, J.J. GA 39th Inf. Co.K
Taylor, J.J. GA 55th Inf. Co.C
Taylor, J.J. KY 3rd Bn.Mtd.Rifles Co.C
Taylor, J.J. LA 1st Cav. Scott's Co.
Taylor, J.J. LA 2nd Cav. Co.G
Taylor, J.J. LA 18th Inf. Co.F
Taylor, J.J. LA 28th (Gray's) Inf. Co.C
Taylor, J.J. LA Inf.Crescent Regt. Co.H
Taylor, J.J. LA Inf.Cons.Crescent Regt. Co.H
Taylor, J.J. MS 18th Inf. Co.C
Taylor, J.J. MO 10th Inf. Co.F
Taylor, J.J. MO 12th Inf. Co.C
Taylor, J.J. NC 3rd Cav. (41st St.Troops) Co.H
Taylor, J.J. NC 3rd Arty. (40th St.Troops) Co.F
Taylor, J.J. NC 12th Inf. Co.C
Taylor, J.J. SC 1st Inf. Co.O
Taylor, J.J. SC 13th Inf. Co.K
Taylor, J.J. TN 3rd (Forrest's) Cav. Co.C
Taylor, J.J. TN 7th (Duckworth's) Cav. Co.F
Taylor, J.J. TN 16th (Logwood's) Cav. Co.C
Taylor, J.J. TN Inf. 3rd Cons.Regt. Co.B
Taylor, J.J. TN 38th Inf. 2nd Co.K
Taylor, J.J. TN 41st Inf. Co.H
Taylor, J.J. TN 51st (Cons.) Inf. Co.C
Taylor, J.J. 8th (Wade's) Conf.Cav. Co.B
Taylor, J.J. 4th Conf.Eng.Troops
Taylor, J.K. MS 4th Inf. Co.F Cpl.
Taylor, J.K. SC 1st (Hagood's) Inf. 2nd Co.H
Taylor, J.K. TN Inf. 3rd Bn. Co.B Cpl.
Taylor, J.K. TX 3rd Cav. Co.A
Taylor, J.K. TX 1st Inf. Co.E 1st Lt.
Taylor, J.L. AL Cav. Moreland's Regt. Co.A
Taylor, J.L. AL 5th Inf. New Co.H
Taylor, J.L. AL 12th Inf. Co.D
Taylor, J.L. AR 11th Inf. Co.D
Taylor, J.L. AR 37th Inf. Co.D
Taylor, J.L. GA 4th (Clinch's) Cav. Co.K
Taylor, J.L. GA Cav. 22nd Bn. (St.Guards) Co.F
Taylor, J.L. GA Inf. 8th Bn. Co.A Cpl.
Taylor, J.L. KY 2nd (Duke's) Cav. Co.A
Taylor, J.L. KY 12th Cav. Co.B
Taylor, J.L. KY 1st Inf. Co.E
Taylor, J.L. LA 3rd (Wingfield's) Cav. Co.A,K Cpl.
Taylor, J.L. LA 6th Cav. Co.C
Taylor, J.L. LA 2nd Inf. Co.I
Taylor, J.L. LA 17th Inf. Co.H
Taylor, J.L. LA Inf.Cons.Crescent Regt. Co.E
Taylor, J.L. MS 41st Inf. Co.B Cpl.
Taylor, J.L. MO 1st Brig.St.Guard
Taylor, J.L. MO 10th Inf. Lt.
Taylor, J.L. TN 62nd Mtd.Inf. Co.A
Taylor, J.L. TX 10th Cav. Co.E Capt.
Taylor, J.L. TX Granbury's Cons.Brig. Co.C
Taylor, J.L. TX 4th Inf. Co.E
Taylor, J.L. TX 14th Inf. Co.B
Taylor, J.L. TX 14th Inf. Co.I
Taylor, J.L. TX 19th Inf. Co.A
Taylor, J.L. VA 14th Cav. Co.H
Taylor, J.L. VA 42nd Inf. Co.A
Taylor, J.L. Gen. & Staff Capt.,AQM
Taylor, J. Lawton SC Cav. Walpole's Co.
Taylor, J.L.B. 8th (Wade's) Conf.Cav. Co.B
Taylor, J.M. AL 2nd Cav. Co.K
Taylor, J.M. AL 4th (Russell's) Cav. Co.C
Taylor, J.M. AL 15th Bn.Part.Rangers Co.A
Taylor, J.M. AL Mil. 2nd Regt.Vol. Co.D Cpl.
Taylor, J.M. AL 12th Inf. Co.A
Taylor, J.M. AL 17th Inf. Co.A 1st Lt.
Taylor, J.M. AL 21st Inf. Co.C
Taylor, J.M. AL Cp. of Instr. Talladega
Taylor, J.M. AR 5th Inf. Co.A Sgt.
Taylor, J.M. AR 7th Mil. Co.C
Taylor, J.M. AR 15th (N.W.) Inf. Co.I
Taylor, J.M. FL 8th Inf. Co.B
Taylor, J.M. GA Cav. 1st Bn.Res. McKinney's Co.
Taylor, J.M. GA 11th Cav. Co.H
Taylor, J.M. GA 5th Res. Co.D
Taylor, J.M. GA 5th Res. Co.F
Taylor, J.M. GA 5th Inf. (St.Guards) Miller's Co.
Taylor, J.M. GA 8th Inf. (St.Guards) Co.D
Taylor, J.M. GA 16th Inf. Co.E
Taylor, J.M. GA Inf. 27th Bn. (NonConscr.) Co.D
Taylor, J.M. GA 44th Inf. Co.D
Taylor, J.M. GA 52nd Inf. Co.E
Taylor, J.M. GA 64th Inf. Co.B
Taylor, J.M. KY 1st Inf. Co.A
Taylor, J.M. LA 4th Inf. Co.I
Taylor, J.M. LA 17th Inf. Co.H
Taylor, J.M. MS 11th Inf. Co.E
Taylor, J.M. MS 25th Inf. Co.H
Taylor, J.M. MS 26th Inf. Co.F
Taylor, J.M. MS 41st Inf. Co.E
Taylor, J.M. MS 46th Inf. Co.D
Taylor, J.M. MO 9th Inf. Co.K
Taylor, J.M. NC 1st Cav. (9th St.Troops) Co.C
Taylor, J.M. NC 3rd Cav. (41st St.Troops) Co.H
Taylor, J.M. NC 3rd Arty. (40th St.Troops) Co.F
Taylor, J.M. NC 60th Inf. Co.E
Taylor, J.M. NC 64th Inf. Co.B
Taylor, J.M. SC 4th Cav. Co.H
Taylor, J.M. SC Cav. 10th Bn. Co.D
Taylor, J.M. TN 12th Cav. Co.E Sgt.
Taylor, J.M. TN 14th (Neely's) Cav. Co.D
Taylor, J.M. TN 14th (Neely's) Cav. Co.E,B Sgt.
Taylor, J.M. TN 19th & 20th (Cons.) Cav. Co.D Cpl.
Taylor, J.M. TN 20th (Russell's) Cav. Co.D Cpl.
Taylor, J.M. TN 1st Hvy.Arty. 1st Co.C, 2nd Co.A
Taylor, J.M. TN 6th Inf. Co.K
Taylor, J.M. TN 45th Inf. Co.A
Taylor, J.M. TN 50th (Cons.) Inf. Co.I Sgt.
Taylor, J.M. TX 11th Cav. Co.G
Taylor, J.M. TX 27th Cav. Co.K 2nd Lt.
Taylor, J.M. TX Cav. Durant's Co.
Taylor, J.M. TX Cav. Hardeman's Regt. Co.D
Taylor, J.M. TX Cav. Madison's Regt. Co.B
Taylor, J.M. TX 1st Inf. Co.E
Taylor, J.M. TX 12th Inf. Co.I
Taylor, J.M. TX 20th Bn.St.Troops Co.B
Taylor, J.M. TX 22nd Inf. Co.G
Taylor, J.M. TX Inf. Griffin's Bn. Co.G
Taylor, J.M. VA 2nd Cav. Co.B
Taylor, J.M. VA Hvy.Arty. 18th Bn. Co.E
Taylor, J.M. VA 1st (Farinholt's) Res. Co.G
Taylor, J.M. VA 7th Inf. Co.F
Taylor, J.M. VA 36th Inf. Co.A
Taylor, J.M. Gen. & Staff Surg.
Taylor, J.M.G. MS 9th Inf. Co.I
Taylor, J.M.G. MS 41st Inf. Co.L Sgt.
Taylor, J.M.G. 4th Conf.Inf. Co.E Music.
Taylor, J.N. AL Cav. Barbiere's Bn. Truss' Co.
Taylor, J.N. AL Cav. (St.Res.) Young's Co.
Taylor, J.N. GA 25th Inf. Co.E
Taylor, J.N. GA 39th Inf. Co.K
Taylor, J.N. GA 42nd Inf. Co.K
Taylor, J.N. GA 50th Inf. Co.E
Taylor, J.N. GA Phillips' Legion Co.C
Taylor, J.N. KY 10th (Johnson's) Cav. New Co.G Capt.
Taylor, J.N. MS 1st Cav.Res. Co.D
Taylor, J.N. MS Conscr.
Taylor, J.N. SC Lt.Arty. 3rd (Palmetto) Bn. Co.H
Taylor, J.N. TN 31st Inf. Co.D
Taylor, J.N. TX 26th Cav. Co.A
Taylor, J.N. 2nd Cherokee Mtd.Vol. Co.H,K
Taylor, Jo. A. TN 24th Inf. Co.A 1st Lt.
Taylor, Joab MO Cav. Fristoe's Regt. Co.I
Taylor, Joab VA 24th Inf. Co.C
Taylor, Joal T. AR 14th (Powers') Inf. Co.H
Taylor, Joash TX 1st Hvy.Arty. Co.G Cpl.
Taylor, Job E. GA 8th Inf. (St.Guards) Co.D
Taylor, Joe LA 13th Bn. (Part.Rangers) Co.E Sgt.
Taylor, Joe MS 28th Cav. Co.I
Taylor, Joe SC 10th Inf. Co.K
Taylor, Joe TN Inf. 1st Cons.Regt. Co.B 2nd Lt.
Taylor, Joel GA 27th Inf. Co.B
Taylor, Joel NC 4th Inf. Co.F
Taylor, Joel NC 11th (Bethel Regt.) Inf. Co.D
Taylor, Joel VA 2nd Cav. Co.K
Taylor, Joel A. GA 49th Inf. Co.D
Taylor, Joel A. TX 17th Inf. Co.K
Taylor, Joel A. VA 52nd Inf. Co.I
Taylor, Joel E. VA 1st Loc.Def.Troops Co.G
Taylor, Joel F. VA 19th Inf. Co.D
Taylor, Joel R. GA Inf. 25th Bn. (Prov.Guard) Co.A

Taylor, Joel R. GA 36th (Villepigue's) Inf. Co.D
Taylor, Joel T. KY 1st (Butler's) Cav. Co.F
Taylor, Joel W. GA 22nd Inf. Co.H
Taylor, John AL 1st Cav. Co.H
Taylor, John AL 2nd Cav. Co.K Bugler
Taylor, John AL 7th Cav. Co.G,B
Taylor, John AL 9th Cav. Co.G
Taylor, John AL Cav. Lewis' Bn. Co.A
Taylor, John AL Arty. 1st Bn. Co.A
Taylor, John AL Lt.Arty. Phelan's Co.
Taylor, John AL Seawell's Btty. (Mohawk Arty.)
Taylor, John AL 3rd Inf. Co.F
Taylor, John AL 8th Inf. Co.G 1st Sgt.
Taylor, John AL 12th Inf. Co.E
Taylor, John AL 17th Inf. Co.A
Taylor, John AL 17th Inf. Co.G
Taylor, John AL 18th Inf. Co.B
Taylor, John AL 19th Inf. Co.E
Taylor, John AL 20th Inf. Co.I
Taylor, John AL 24th Inf. Co.K
Taylor, John AL 25th Inf. Co.F
Taylor, John AL 30th Inf. Co.G
Taylor, John AL 32nd Inf. Co.H
Taylor, John AL 34th Inf. Co.H
Taylor, John AL 49th Inf. Co.B
Taylor, John AL 49th Inf. Co.F
Taylor, John AL Mobile Fire Bn. Mullany's Co.
Taylor, John AL Cp. of Instr. Talladega
Taylor, John AZ Cav. Herbert's Bn. Oury's Co.
Taylor, John AR 8th Cav. Peoples' Co.
Taylor, John AR 45th Cav. Co.K
Taylor, John AR Cav. Gordon's Regt. Co.H
Taylor, John AR Cav. Harrell's Bn. Co.A
Taylor, John AR Cav. Wright's Regt. Co.K
Taylor, John AR 1st Vol. Co.F
Taylor, John AR 4th Inf. Co.B
Taylor, John AR 5th Inf. Co.F Sgt.
Taylor, John AR 5th Inf. Co.K
Taylor, John AR 8th Inf. New Co.G
Taylor, John AR 14th (McCarver's) Inf. Co.A
Taylor, John AR 23rd Inf. Co.D
Taylor, John FL 10th Inf. Co.A
Taylor, John FL 11th Inf. Co.K
Taylor, John GA 1st Cav. Co.C
Taylor, John GA Cav. 2nd Bn. Co.F
Taylor, John GA 8th Cav. Co.G
Taylor, John GA 12th Cav.
Taylor, John GA Cav. 29th Bn.
Taylor, John GA 62nd Cav. Co.G
Taylor, John GA 62nd Cav. Co.K
Taylor, John GA Lt.Arty. 14th Bn. Co.A,G
Taylor, John GA Lt.Arty. Havis' Btty.
Taylor, John GA Lt.Arty. Pritchard's Co. (Washington Arty.)
Taylor, John GA 1st Inf. (St.Guards) Co.K
Taylor, John GA 1st (Symons') Res. Co.F
Taylor, John GA 1st (Symons') Res. Co.H
Taylor, John GA 2nd Res. Co.D
Taylor, John GA 2nd Bn.S.S. Co.B
Taylor, John GA 5th Inf. Co.D
Taylor, John GA 5th Res. Co.F
Taylor, John GA 5th Inf. (St.Guards) Russell's Co.
Taylor, John GA Inf. 26th Bn. Co.C
Taylor, John GA 27th Inf. Co.G
Taylor, John GA 27th Inf. Co.H
Taylor, John GA Inf. 27th Bn. (NonConscr.) Co.E
Taylor, John GA 45th Inf. Co.K
Taylor, John GA 50th Inf. Co.C
Taylor, John GA 55th Inf. Co.B
Taylor, John GA 56th Inf. Co.G
Taylor, John GA Inf. (Richmond Factory Guards) Barney's Co. Cpl.
Taylor, John GA Inf. (Mell Scouts) Wyly's Co.
Taylor, John KY 1st (Butler's) Cav. Co.A
Taylor, John KY 2nd Cav. Co.I
Taylor, John KY 2nd (Duke's) Cav. Co.D
Taylor, John KY 2nd (Duke's) Cav. Co.F
Taylor, John KY 2nd (Woodward's) Cav. Co.F
Taylor, John KY 5th Cav. Co.E
Taylor, John KY 5th Cav. Co.H
Taylor, John KY 13th Cav. Co.B
Taylor, John KY 5th Mtd.Inf. Co.A
Taylor, John LA 1st Cav. Co.I
Taylor, John LA 1st Hvy.Arty. (Reg.) Co.D
Taylor, John LA 1st Hvy.Arty. (Reg.) Co.I
Taylor, John LA 1st (Nelligan's) Inf. Co.C Sgt.
Taylor, John LA 1st (Strawbridge's) Inf. Co.D
Taylor, John LA 1st (Strawbridge's) Inf. Co.F
Taylor, John LA 8th Inf. Co.F 1st Lt.
Taylor, John LA 22nd Inf. Jones' Co.
Taylor, John LA Mil. Chalmette Regt. Co.F
Taylor, John LA Inf. McLean's Co.
Taylor, John LA Miles' Legion Co.B Cpl.
Taylor, John LA C.S. Zouave Bn. Co.B
Taylor, John MS 1st Cav. Co.I
Taylor, John MS 2nd Part.Rangers Co.F
Taylor, John MS Cav. Hughes' Bn. Co.C
Taylor, John MS Cav. Powers' Regt. Co.A
Taylor, John MS Arty. (Seven Stars Arty.) Roberts' Co.
Taylor, John MS Lt.Arty. Yates' Btty.
Taylor, John MS 1st (King's) Inf. (St.Troops) Co.G
Taylor, John MS 2nd Inf. Co.C
Taylor, John MS 2nd Inf. (A. of 10,000) Co.A
Taylor, John MS 2nd (Davidson's) Inf. Co.E
Taylor, John MS Inf. 2nd St.Troops Co.I 1st Cpl.
Taylor, John MS Inf. 3rd Bn. Co.D
Taylor, John MS Inf. 3rd Bn. (St.Troops) Co.C
Taylor, John MS Inf. 7th Bn. Co.A
Taylor, John MS 10th Inf. Old Co.B, New Co.C
Taylor, John MS 13th Inf. Co.E
Taylor, John MS 22nd Inf. Co.K
Taylor, John MS 39th Inf. Co.G Cpl.
Taylor, John MO 2nd Cav. Co.D Sgt.
Taylor, John MO 3rd Cav. Co.A
Taylor, John MO Cav. 3rd Bn. Co.C
Taylor, John MO 4th Cav. Co.A
Taylor, John MO 7th Cav. Haislip's Co. Sgt.
Taylor, John MO Cav. Snider's Bn. Co.A
Taylor, John MO Lt.Arty. 13th Btty.
Taylor, John MO Searcy's Bn.S.S. Co.F Sgt.
Taylor, John NC 8th Bn.Part.Rangers Co.C
Taylor, John NC Cav. (Loc.Def.) Howard's Co.
Taylor, John NC 1st Arty. (10th St.Troops) Co.B
Taylor, John NC 2nd Arty. (36th St.Troops) Co.K
Taylor, John NC 1st Inf. Co.C
Taylor, John NC 1st Inf. Co.H Sgt.
Taylor, John NC 3rd Inf. Co.D
Taylor, John NC 4th Inf. Co.E
Taylor, John NC 4th Inf. Co.G
Taylor, John NC 4th Sr.Res. Co.A
Taylor, John NC 5th Inf. Co.E
Taylor, John NC 8th Sr.Res. Jacobs' Co.
Taylor, John NC 17th Inf. (1st Org.) Co.K
Taylor, John NC 32nd Inf. Co.B
Taylor, John NC 37th Inf. Co.A Cpl.
Taylor, John NC 42nd Inf. Co.F
Taylor, John NC 45th Inf. Co.K
Taylor, John NC 46th Inf. Co.A
Taylor, John NC 55th Inf. Co.G
Taylor, John NC 58th Inf. Co.E
Taylor, John NC Nelson's Co. (Loc.Def.)
Taylor, John NC Lt.Arty. Levi's Btty. Thomas' Legion
Taylor, John SC 6th Cav. Co.I
Taylor, John SC 7th Cav. Co.D 1st Lt.
Taylor, John SC 17th Cav. Co.A
Taylor, John SC Arty. Bachman's Co. (German Lt.Arty.)
Taylor, John SC Lt.Arty. Garden's Co. (Palmetto Lt.Btty.)
Taylor, John SC 1st (Butler's) Inf. Co.G
Taylor, John SC 3rd Inf. Co.E
Taylor, John SC 3rd Res. Col'd Music.
Taylor, John SC Inf. 3rd Bn. Co.A
Taylor, John SC 4th St.Troops Co.B
Taylor, John SC 4th St.Troops Co.E
Taylor, John SC 4th St.Troops Co.F
Taylor, John SC 24th Inf. Co.K
Taylor, John SC 27th Inf. Co.F
Taylor, John SC Cav.Bn. Holcombe Legion Co.B 2nd Lt.
Taylor, John SC Cav.Bn. Holcombe Legion Co.D
Taylor, John TN 1st (Carter's) Cav. Co.M 2nd Lt.
Taylor, John TN 3rd (Forrest's) Cav. Co.I Sgt.
Taylor, John TN 5th (McKenzie's) Cav. Co.D
Taylor, John TN Arty. Marshall's Co.
Taylor, John TN 2nd (Walker's) Inf. Co.B
Taylor, John TN 3rd (Clack's) Inf. Co.H
Taylor, John TN 3rd (Clack's) Inf. Co.K
Taylor, John TN 3rd (Lillard's) Mtd.Inf. Co.I Sgt.
Taylor, John TN 4th Inf. Co.D
Taylor, John TN 8th Inf. Co.E
Taylor, John TN 19th Inf. Co.C
Taylor, John TN 25th Inf. Co.G
Taylor, John TN 28th Inf. Co.A
Taylor, John TN 37th Inf. Co.C
Taylor, John TN 44th (Cons.) Inf. Co.G
Taylor, John TN 50th Inf. Co.D,F
Taylor, John TN 63rd Inf. Co.D
Taylor, John TN Inf. Nashville Bn. Fulcher's Co.
Taylor, John TX 9th Cav. Co.H
Taylor, John TX 22nd Cav. Co.C Cpl.
Taylor, John TX 29th Cav. Co.F Sgt.
Taylor, John TX 32nd Cav. Co.D
Taylor, John TX 35th (Brown's) Cav. 2nd Co.B
Taylor, John TX Arty. (St.Troops) Good's Co.
Taylor, John VA 2nd Cav.
Taylor, John VA 6th Cav. Co.A
Taylor, John VA 7th Cav. Co.F
Taylor, John VA 8th Cav. Co.C
Taylor, John VA 9th Cav. Co.H

Taylor, John VA 25th Cav. Co.D
Taylor, John VA Cav. 41st Bn. Co.C
Taylor, John VA Arty. C.F. Johnston's Co.
Taylor, John VA Lt.Arty. Moore's Co.
Taylor, John VA Lt.Arty. Pollock's Co.
Taylor, John VA 2nd Inf. Co.C,F
Taylor, John VA 2nd Inf. Co.F
Taylor, John VA 3rd Inf. Co.A
Taylor, John VA Inf. 4th Bn.Loc.Def. Co.D
Taylor, John VA 6th Inf. 1st Co.B
Taylor, John VA 7th Inf. Co.E Capt.
Taylor, John VA 11th Inf. Co.F
Taylor, John VA 12th Inf. Co.H
Taylor, John VA 14th Mil. Co.E
Taylor, John VA 14th Mil. Co.G Capt.
Taylor, John VA 21st Inf. Co.H
Taylor, John VA 31st Mil. Co.I
Taylor, John VA 48th Inf. Co.H
Taylor, John VA 51st Inf. Co.K
Taylor, John VA 58th Mil. Co.K
Taylor, John VA 59th Inf. Co.A
Taylor, John VA 60th Inf. 2nd Co.H Cpl.
Taylor, John VA 63rd Inf. Co.F
Taylor, John VA 64th Mtd.Inf. Co.F
Taylor, John VA 77th Mil. Co.B
Taylor, John 10th Conf.Cav. Co.F
Taylor, John 15th Conf.Cav. Co.E
Taylor, John 3rd Conf.Eng.Troops Co.D
Taylor, John 1st Cherokee Mtd.Rifles McDaniel's Co.
Taylor, John 1st Choctaw & Chickasaw Mtd. Rifles 3rd Co.D
Taylor, John 1st Creek Mtd.Vol. 2nd Co.D, Co.H
Taylor, John 1st Seminole Mtd.Vol.
Taylor, John Conf.Reg.Inf. Brooks' Bn. Co.D Cpl.
Taylor, John Gillum's Regt. Whitaker's Co.
Taylor, John Gen. & Staff 1st Lt.,ADC
Taylor, John A. AL 8th Cav. Co.I
Taylor, John A. AL 28th Inf. Co.D
Taylor, John A. AR Cav. Harrell's Bn. Co.C
Taylor, John A. GA 10th Cav. Co.E
Taylor, John A. GA 41st Inf. Co.C
Taylor, John A. GA 49th Inf. Co.E
Taylor, John A. KY 12th Cav. Co.H
Taylor, John A. MS 19th Inf. Co.A
Taylor, John A. MS 34th Inf. Co.C
Taylor, John A. NC 5th Inf. Co.D,C
Taylor, John A. NC 8th Sr.Res. Daniel's Co.
Taylor, John A. NC 12th Inf. Co.H
Taylor, John A. NC 27th Inf. Co.K Drum.
Taylor, John A. NC 32nd Inf. Co.H
Taylor, John A. SC 7th Res. Co.H
Taylor, John A. TN Arty. Fisher's Co.
Taylor, John A. TN 23rd Inf. Co.G
Taylor, John A. TN 32nd Inf. Co.A
Taylor, John A. TX Cav. Hardeman's Regt. Co.F
Taylor, John A. VA Lt.Arty. Douthat's Co.
Taylor, John A. VA Lt.Arty. Hardwicke's Co.
Taylor, John A. VA 28th Inf. Co.B
Taylor, John A. VA 34th Inf. Co.D
Taylor, John A. VA 59th Inf. 2nd Co.C
Taylor, John A. 7th Conf.Cav. Co.E
Taylor, John A.C. AL 4th Inf. Co.K
Taylor, John Alexander AR Cav. Harrell's Bn. Co.C
Taylor, John Allen MS 1st Lt.Arty. Co.A
Taylor, John A.R. NC 49th Inf. Co.F
Taylor, John Arthur LA 8th Inf. Co.F
Taylor, John B. AL 22nd Inf. Co.D 2nd Lt.
Taylor, John B. AL 25th Inf. Co.G
Taylor, John B. GA 26th Inf. Co.H
Taylor, John B. GA 42nd Inf. Co.C
Taylor, John B. LA Mil. 2nd Regt. 3rd Brig. 1st Div. Co.H 1st Lt.
Taylor, John B. MD 1st Inf. Co.A
Taylor, John B. MS 11th (Perrin's) Cav. Co.C 1st Lt.
Taylor, John B. MS 10th Inf. Old Co.D, New Co.E
Taylor, John B. MS 30th Inf. Co.D 2nd Lt.
Taylor, John B. NC 8th Bn.Part.Rangers Co.F
Taylor, John B. NC 3rd Arty. (40th St.Troops) Co.F
Taylor, John B. NC 66th Inf. Co.I
Taylor, John B. TN 5th (McKenzie's) Cav. Co.I
Taylor, John B. TX 1st (McCulloch's) Cav. Co.H
Taylor, John B. TX Cav. Morgan's Regt. Co.B
Taylor, John B. VA Cav. 35th Bn. Co.D
Taylor, John B. VA Cav. 40th Bn. Co.A
Taylor, John B. VA 11th Bn.Res. Co.B
Taylor, John B. VA 54th Inf. Surg.
Taylor, John B. VA 57th Inf. Co.K Capt.
Taylor, John B. VA 111th Mil. Co.2 1st Lt.
Taylor, Jno. B. Gen. & Staff Surg.
Taylor, John Bunyan LA 4th Inf. Co.I Capt.
Taylor, John C. AL Mtd.Res. Logan's Co.
Taylor, John C. AR Inf. 2nd Bn. Co.A
Taylor, John C. AR 9th Inf. Co.H
Taylor, John C. AR 13th Inf. Co.C
Taylor, John C. AR 23rd Inf. Co.I
Taylor, John C. LA Inf. 4th Bn. Co.C
Taylor, John C. LA 14th Inf. Co.F
Taylor, John C. MS 15th Inf. Co.F
Taylor, John C. MO Inf. 8th Bn. Co.E Sgt.
Taylor, John C. MO 9th Inf. Co.I Sgt.
Taylor, John C. NC 5th Inf. Co.I Sgt.
Taylor, John C. TN 1st (Turney's) Inf. Co.H
Taylor, John C. TN 28th (Cons.) Inf. Co.I 3rd Lt.
Taylor, John C. TN 84th Inf. Co.E Bvt.2nd Lt.
Taylor, John C. TX 2nd Cav. Co.I
Taylor, John C. TX 13th Vol. 2nd Co.F
Taylor, John C. TX Cav. Benavides' Regt. Co.F
Taylor, John C. VA 8th Cav. Co.L
Taylor, John C. VA 14th Cav. Co.A
Taylor, John C. VA Cav. 14th Bn. Co.B
Taylor, John C. VA 17th Cav. Co.A
Taylor, John C. VA Cav. Hounshell's Bn. Huffman's Co.
Taylor, John C. VA 2nd Bn.Res. Co.G 2nd Lt.
Taylor, John C. VA 4th Inf. Co.B
Taylor, John C. VA 5th Inf. Co.E
Taylor, John C. VA 6th Bn.Res. Co.G
Taylor, John C. VA Inf. 9th Bn. Duffy's Co.
Taylor, John C. VA 30th Inf. Co.H
Taylor, John C. VA 39th Inf. Co.I
Taylor, John C. VA 51st Inf. Co.K
Taylor, John C. VA Inf. Hutter's Co.
Taylor, John C. Gen. & Staff 1st Lt.,ADC
Taylor, John C.F. LA Res.Corps Scott's Co.
Taylor, John C.S. TX 22nd Cav. Co.E
Taylor, John D. AL 2nd Cav. Co.G,D
Taylor, John D. AL Cav. Barbiere's Bn. Brown's Co.
Taylor, John D. AL 48th Inf. Co.E Ord.Sgt.
Taylor, John D. GA Lt.Arty. 12th Bn. 3rd Co.B
Taylor, John D. GA 60th Inf. Co.C N.C.S. Drum Maj.
Taylor, John D. LA 28th (Gray's) Inf. Co.A
Taylor, John D. MO Lt.Arty. 3rd Btty.
Taylor, John D. MO 11th Inf. Co.E,I
Taylor, John D. MO Todd's Co.
Taylor, John D. NC Hvy.Arty. 1st Bn. Co.A
Taylor, John D. NC 2nd Arty. (36th St.Troops) Co.K Capt.
Taylor, John D. NC 35th Inf. Co.G
Taylor, John D. NC 42nd Inf. Co.H
Taylor, John D. NC Inf. Thomas Legion Co.K
Taylor, John D. TN Lt.Arty. Morton's Co. Bugler
Taylor, John D. TN 1st (Turney's) Inf. Co.H
Taylor, John D. TN 6th Inf. Co.C Sgt.
Taylor, John D. TN 11th Inf. Co.E
Taylor, John D. TN 24th Inf. 2nd Co.H, Co.M
Taylor, John D.H. LA Cav. Webb's Co. Cpl.
Taylor, John D.K. AL Inf. 1st Regt. Co.A
Taylor, John D.S. SC Inf. 3rd Bn. Co.A
Taylor, John E. AR 23rd Inf. Co.B
Taylor, John E. AR 27th Inf. Co.K
Taylor, John E. GA 11th Inf. Co.B
Taylor, John E. NC Inf. 13th Bn. Co.C Sgt.
Taylor, John E. NC 66th Inf. Co.E 2nd Lt.
Taylor, John E. NC Mil. Clark's Sp.Bn. Co.C
Taylor, John E. SC Arty. Gregg's Co. (McQueen Lt.Arty.)
Taylor, John E. SC Arty. Manigault's Bn. 1st Co.C
Taylor, John E. VA Lt.Arty. Cayce's Co.
Taylor, John E. VA Arty. Paris' Co.
Taylor, John E. VA Inf. 7th Bn.Loc.Def. Co.C
Taylor, John E. VA 14th Inf. Co.F
Taylor, John E.J. AR 18th Inf. Co.H
Taylor, John F. AL 4th (Roddey's) Cav. Co.E 1st Lt.
Taylor, John F. AL 3rd Inf. Co.F
Taylor, John F. KY 2nd Cav. Co.D
Taylor, John F. KY 2nd Bn.Mtd.Rifles Co.B
Taylor, John F. MS 29th Inf. Co.G Capt.
Taylor, John F. NC Hvy.Arty. 1st Bn. Co.B Cpl.
Taylor, John F. NC 17th Inf. (2nd Org.) Co.I
Taylor, John F. NC 35th Inf. Co.G 2nd Lt.
Taylor, John F. NC 51st Inf. Co.C
Taylor, John F. SC 13th Inf. Co.G
Taylor, John F. VA 11th Cav. Co.D
Taylor, John F. VA 13th Inf. Co.K
Taylor, John F. VA 30th Inf. 2nd Co.I
Taylor, John F. VA 31st Inf. Co.F
Taylor, John F. VA 47th Inf. 3rd Co.H
Taylor, John Frank VA 12th Cav. Co.F Sgt.
Taylor, John G. AL 6th Cav. Co.D
Taylor, John G. AL 28th Inf. Co.E
Taylor, John G. KY 2nd (Duke's) Cav. Co.F
Taylor, John G. KY 2nd Bn.Mtd.Rifles Co.F
Taylor, John G. MS 21st Inf. Maj.
Taylor, John G. MS 48th Inf. Lt.Col.
Taylor, John G. MO 3rd Inf. Co.E,B

Taylor, John G. NC 5th Cav. (63rd St.Troops) Co.E
Taylor, John G. NC 61st Inf. Co.K
Taylor, John G. TN Lt.Arty. Rice's Btty.
Taylor, John G. TN 60th Mtd.Inf. Co.C 2nd Lt.
Taylor, John G. TX Cav. Benavides' Regt. Co.F
Taylor, John G. VA 4th Cav. Co.A
Taylor, John G. VA Hvy.Arty. 18th Bn. Co.B
Taylor, John G. VA Inf. 25th Bn. Co.B Cpl.
Taylor, John G.D. TX 14th Cav. Co.G
Taylor, John H. AL 17th Inf. Co.K Sgt.
Taylor, John H. AL 22nd Inf. Co.B
Taylor, John H. AR Lt.Arty. Rivers' Btty.
Taylor, John H. AR 2nd Inf. Co.D
Taylor, John H. GA 1st (Symons') Res. Co.G Cpl.
Taylor, John H. GA 17th Inf. Co.I
Taylor, John H. GA 18th Inf. Co.B
Taylor, John H. GA 35th Inf. Chap.
Taylor, John H. GA 38th Inf. Co.E
Taylor, Jno. H. LA 31st Inf. Co.I
Taylor, John H. MS 8th Inf. Co.B
Taylor, John H. MO 6th Cav. Co.A
Taylor, John H. NC 31st Inf. Co.E
Taylor, John H. NC 51st Inf. Co.I
Taylor, John H. TN 3rd (Clack's) Inf.
Taylor, John H. TN Inf. 3rd Bn. Co.E
Taylor, John H. TN 4th Inf. Co.I
Taylor, John H. TN 26th Inf. Co.I
Taylor, John H. TN 53rd Inf. Co.C Sgt.
Taylor, John H. TN 55th (McKoin's) Inf. Bound's Co.
Taylor, John H. TN 63rd Inf. Co.B
Taylor, John H. TX 22nd Cav. Co.A
Taylor, John H. TX 22nd Cav. Co.D
Taylor, John H. TX 2nd Inf. Co.D
Taylor, John H. VA 6th Cav. Co.G
Taylor, John H. VA 7th Cav. Co.I
Taylor, John H. VA 45th Inf. Co.D
Taylor, John H., Jr. VA 58th Mil. Co.E
Taylor, John H.C. GA 15th Inf. Co.F,I
Taylor, John I. GA 12th Inf. Co.C
Taylor, John J. AL 13th Bn.Part.Rangers Co.E
Taylor, John J. AL Vol. Lee, Jr.'s Co.
Taylor, John J. AR 2nd Inf. Co.G
Taylor, John J. GA Cav. 2nd Bn. Co.F
Taylor, John J. GA 5th Cav. Co.B
Taylor, John J. GA 25th Inf. Co.K
Taylor, John J. GA 57th Inf. Co.I
Taylor, John J. KY 1st Bn.Mtd.Rifles Co.C
Taylor, John J. MS 14th Inf. Co.H
Taylor, John J. MO 7th Cav. Co.A
Taylor, John J. NC 44th Inf. Co.E
Taylor, John J. NC 53rd Inf. Co.E Sgt.
Taylor, John J. NC 54th Inf. Co.K
Taylor, John J. SC 13th Inf. Co.K
Taylor, John J. TN Cav. 12th Bn. (Day's) Co.B Sgt.
Taylor, John J. VA 22nd Inf. Co.A
Taylor, John J. VA 22nd Inf. Co.D
Taylor, John J. VA 36th Inf. Co.A
Taylor, John J. VA 39th Inf. Co.G
Taylor, John J. VA 157th Mil. Co.A
Taylor, John K. GA 52nd Inf. Co.A
Taylor, John L. AL 43rd Inf. Co.A
Taylor, John L. AR 9th Inf. Co.G
Taylor, John L. FL 2nd Cav. Co.E Sgt.
Taylor, John L. FL 1st Inf. Old Co.A,B Sgt.
Taylor, John L. FL 3rd Inf. Co.D
Taylor, John L. KY 9th Mtd.Inf. Co.C
Taylor, John L. LA 5th Cav. Co.K Cpl.
Taylor, John L. NC 8th Sr.Res. Daniel's Co.
Taylor, John L. NC 27th Inf. Co.D
Taylor, John L. NC 45th Inf. Co.I Music.
Taylor, John L. TN 2nd Cav. Co.A
Taylor, John L. TN Douglass' Bn.Part.Rangers Co.A
Taylor, John L. TN 3rd (Lillard's) Mtd.Inf. Co.G
Taylor, John L. TN Inf. 3rd Bn. Co.D Cpl.
Taylor, John L. TN 13th Inf. Co.A
Taylor, John L. VA 2nd Cav. Co.K
Taylor, John L. VA Lt.Arty. 13th Bn. Co.A
Taylor, John L. VA Hvy.Arty. 18th Bn. Co.B
Taylor, John L. VA 4th Inf. Co.G
Taylor, John L. VA 5th Bn.Res. Co.A
Taylor, John L. VA 19th Inf. Co.C
Taylor, John L. VA 46th Inf. 2nd Co.K
Taylor, John L. VA 63rd Inf. Co.A Sgt.
Taylor, John L. VA Mil. Washington Cty.
Taylor, John L.H. MS 1st Cav. Co.L 1st Lt.
Taylor, John L.H. TN 21st Inf. Co.B 1st Lt.
Taylor, John M. AL Mil. 2rd Regt.Vol. Co.A Capt.
Taylor, John M. AL 9th Inf. Co.K
Taylor, John M. FL 10th Inf. Co.D 2nd Lt.
Taylor, John M. GA 31st Inf. Co.F
Taylor, John M. GA 37th Inf. Co.C
Taylor, John M. GA 38th Inf. Co.N
Taylor, John M. GA 49th Inf. Co.K
Taylor, John M. KY 2nd Bn.Mtd.Rifles Co.B
Taylor, John M. LA 1st Cav. Co.B Maj.
Taylor, John M. LA 5th Cav. Co.K
Taylor, John M. LA Inf. 11th Bn. Co.G
Taylor, John M. LA Inf.Cons.Crescent Regt. Co.D
Taylor, John M. MO 5th Cav. Co.G
Taylor, John M. MO 9th Bn.S.S. Co.F
Taylor, John M. NC 27th Inf. Co.D
Taylor, John M. NC 35th Inf. Co.H
Taylor, John M. TN 24th Inf. Co.K 1st Sgt.
Taylor, John M. TN 27th Inf. Co.K Capt.
Taylor, John M. TX 3rd Cav. Co.G Hosp.Stew.
Taylor, John M. TX 12th Cav. Co.A
Taylor, John M. TX 14th Cav. Co.G
Taylor, John M. TX 36th Cav. Co.G
Taylor, John M. TX Cav. Terry's Regt. Co.A
Taylor, John M. TX Inf. Rutherford's Co.
Taylor, John M. VA 14th Cav. Co.L
Taylor, John M. VA 1st Arty. Co.H
Taylor, John M. VA 17th Inf. Co.C
Taylor, John M. VA 24th Inf. Co.C
Taylor, John M. VA 31st Mil. Co.A
Taylor, John M. VA 49th Inf.
Taylor, John M. 1st Conf.Inf. 2nd Co.F Sgt.
Taylor, John N. AR 1st Mtd.Rifles Co.H
Taylor, John N. GA 28th Inf. Co.E
Taylor, John N. NC 5th Cav. (63rd St.Troops) Co.B
Taylor, John N. SC 23rd Inf. Co.H
Taylor, John N. TN 28th Inf. Co.F Cpl.
Taylor, John O. VA 2nd St.Res. Co.F
Taylor, John O. VA 6th Inf. Co.I
Taylor, John Otey VA 2nd Cav. Co.B
Taylor, John P. AL 17th Inf. Co.A
Taylor, John P. AR Lt.Arty. Key's Btty.
Taylor, John P. AR 1st (Colquitt's) Inf. Co.H
Taylor, John P. MS 23rd Inf. Co.E
Taylor, John P. MO 1st Cav. Co.D 1st Lt.
Taylor, John P. MO 7th Cav. Co.F 1st Lt.
Taylor, John P. MO 10th Cav. Co.G
Taylor, John P. NC 8th Bn.Part.Rangers Co.A,D,F
Taylor, John P. NC 46th Inf. Co.B
Taylor, John P. NC 66th Inf. Co.I
Taylor, John P. TN 21st (Wilson's) Cav. Co.H
Taylor, John P. TN 48th (Voorhies') Inf. Co.A
Taylor, John P. VA 9th Cav. Co.I
Taylor, John P. VA 26th Inf. Co.K
Taylor, John P. VA 28th Inf. 2nd Co.C
Taylor, John R. AL 19th Inf. Co.I
Taylor, John R. AR 26th Inf. Co.F
Taylor, John R. MS 1st Cav. Co.K
Taylor, John R. MS 5th Inf. (St.Troops) Co.F
Taylor, John R. MS 20th Inf. Co.G
Taylor, John R. MS 36th Inf. Co.B
Taylor, John R. NC 6th Sr.Res. Co.K
Taylor, John R. NC 12th Inf. Co.H
Taylor, John R. SC Inf. Hampton Legion Co.D
Taylor, John R. TN 35th Inf. 3rd Co.F
Taylor, John R. TN 61st Mtd.Inf. Co.B
Taylor, John R. TX 25th Cav. Co.C Sgt.
Taylor, John R. TX 9th (Nichols') Inf. Co.B Sgt.
Taylor, John R. VA 3rd Cav. Co.G
Taylor, John R. VA Lt.Arty. King's Co.
Taylor, John R. VA Inf. 1st Bn. Co.D
Taylor, John R. VA 3rd Inf. Co.D
Taylor, John R. VA 19th Inf. Co.E
Taylor, John R. VA Loc.Def. Scott's Co.
Taylor, John S. AR 18th Inf. Co.D Sgt.
Taylor, John S. GA 49th Inf. Co.D Cpl.
Taylor, John S. KY 6th Mtd.Inf. Co.F,E Sgt.
Taylor, John S. MS Lt.Arty. (The Hudson Btty.) Hoole's Co.
Taylor, John S. TN 45th Inf. Co.F
Taylor, John S. TN 47th Inf. Co.G Sgt.
Taylor, John S. TX 21st Cav. Co.F
Taylor, John S. VA 6th Cav. Co.F Cpl.
Taylor, John S. VA 11th Cav. Co.I
Taylor, John S. VA 14th Inf. Co.D 1st Lt.
Taylor, John S. VA 54th Inf. Co.C 2nd Lt.
Taylor, Johnson AR 1st Mtd.Rifles Co.B
Taylor, John T. AL 3rd Cav. Co.F
Taylor, John T. AL 1st Regt. Mobile Vol. Co.E
Taylor, John T. AL 3rd Inf. Co.B
Taylor, John T. AL 22nd Inf. Co.I
Taylor, John T. GA Inf. 3rd Bn. Co.E
Taylor, John T. GA 5th Inf. Co.G
Taylor, John T. GA 12th Inf. Co.F
Taylor, John T. GA 17th Inf. Co.B
Taylor, John T. LA Inf. A.J. Gibbs' Co.
Taylor, John T. LA Mil. Borge's Co. (Garnet Rangers)
Taylor, John T. LA 8th Inf. Co.I
Taylor, John T. LA 19th Inf. Co.E
Taylor, John T. MS 15th Inf. Co.E Cpl.
Taylor, John T. MS 18th Inf. Co.B
Taylor, John T. MS 35th Inf. Co.F
Taylor, John T. NC 6th Inf. Co.I
Taylor, John T. NC 12th Inf. Co.D,B Capt.
Taylor, John T. NC 44th Inf. Co.E

Taylor, John T. SC Inf. 3rd Bn. Co.F
Taylor, John T. TN Arty. Fisher's Co.
Taylor, John T. TX 11th Inf. Co.A
Taylor, John T. TX 20th Inf. Co.F
Taylor, John T. VA 12th Cav. Co.A
Taylor, John T. VA Cav. 14th Bn. Co.B
Taylor, John T. VA 13th Inf. Co.D
Taylor, John T. VA Conscr. Cp.Lee
Taylor, John Thomas NC 62nd Inf. Co.F
Taylor, John W. AL 3rd Cav. Co.A
Taylor, John W. AL 3rd Cav. Co.F
Taylor, John W. AL 4th (Russell's) Cav. Co.I Sgt.
Taylor, John W. AL Cav.Res. Brooks' Co.
Taylor, John W. AL St.Arty. Co.A
Taylor, John W. AL 3rd Res. Co.H
Taylor, John W. AL 4th Inf. Co.A
Taylor, John W. AR 6th Inf. Co.K
Taylor, John W. AR 7th Inf. Co.H
Taylor, John W. FL Kilcrease Lt.Arty.
Taylor, John W. FL 2nd Inf. Co.H
Taylor, John W. GA 4th (Clinch's) Cav. Co.B 1st Sgt.
Taylor, John W. GA 4th (Clinch's) Cav. Co.C Sgt.
Taylor, John W. GA 25th Inf. Co.C
Taylor, John W. GA 26th Inf. Dent's Co.A Sgt.
Taylor, John W. GA 34th Inf. Co.C
Taylor, John W. GA Inf. Cobb Guards Co.A
Taylor, John W. KY 1st Bn.Mtd.Rifles Co.G,A
Taylor, John W. LA 5th Inf. Co.H Capt.
Taylor, John W. MS Cav. 4th Bn. Sykes' Co.
Taylor, John W. MS 1st Bn.S.S. Co.C 2nd Lt.
Taylor, John W. MS 2nd Inf.
Taylor, John W. MS 14th Inf. Co.B
Taylor, John W. MS 26th Inf. Co.H
Taylor, John W. MS 27th Inf. Co.C
Taylor, John W. MS 29th Inf. Co.F
Taylor, John W. MS 30th Inf. Co.D
Taylor, John W. MS 37th Inf. Co.B
Taylor, John W. MO 1st Cav. Co.I
Taylor, John W. NC 2nd Cav. (19th St.Troops) Co.H
Taylor, John W. NC 5th Cav. (63rd St.Troops) Co.D
Taylor, John W. NC Hvy.Arty. 1st Bn. Co.B Capt.
Taylor, John W. NC Hvy.Arty. 1st Bn. Co.B
Taylor, John W. NC 2nd Arty. (36th St.Troops) Co.G
Taylor, John W. NC 3rd Arty. (40th St.Troops) Co.C
Taylor, John W. NC 3rd Inf. Co.A Sgt.
Taylor, John W. NC 15th Inf. Co.M Capt.
Taylor, John W. NC 32nd Inf. Co.I Capt.
Taylor, John W. NC 53rd Inf. Co.B
Taylor, John W. SC 20th Inf. Co.K
Taylor, John W. TN 1st (Carter's) Cav. Co.M
Taylor, John W. TN 12th (Green's) Cav. Co.I
Taylor, John W. TN 3rd (Clack's) Inf. Co.A
Taylor, John W. TN 5th Inf. 1st Co.C, Co.A Sgt.
Taylor, John W. TN 19th Inf. Co.B Cpl.
Taylor, John W. TN 22nd Inf. Co.A
Taylor, John W. TN 37th Inf. Co.E
Taylor, John W. TN 37th Inf. Co.E,F
Taylor, John W. TN 49th Inf. Co.A
Taylor, John W. Inf. Bailey's Cons.Regt. Co.G
Taylor, John W. TX 5th Cav. Co.H
Taylor, John W. TX 7th Cav. Co.I Capt.
Taylor, John W. TX 30th Cav. Co.I
Taylor, John W. TX 7th Inf. Co.D,K
Taylor, John W. TX 10th Inf. Co.I
Taylor, John W. TX 14th Inf. Co.B
Taylor, John W. TX Inf. Currie's Co.
Taylor, John W. VA 9th Cav. Co.A Cpl.
Taylor, John W. VA 14th Cav. Co.A
Taylor, John W. VA 17th Cav. Co.H
Taylor, John W. VA 18th Cav. 1st Co.G
Taylor, John W. VA 23rd Cav. Co.A
Taylor, John W. VA Cav. 41st Bn. Co.A
Taylor, John W. VA Horse Arty. E. Graham's Co.
Taylor, John W. VA 2nd Inf. Co.B Sgt.
Taylor, John W. VA 2nd Inf. Co.F
Taylor, John W. VA Inf. 4th Bn.Loc.Def. Co.C Cpl.
Taylor, John W. VA 10th Inf. Co.K
Taylor, John W. VA 11th Inf. Co.F
Taylor, John W. VA 14th Inf. Co.C Sgt.
Taylor, John W. VA 22nd Inf. Co.F Sgt.
Taylor, John W. VA 29th Inf. Co.G
Taylor, John W. VA 30th Inf. Co.K,G
Taylor, John W. VA 34th Inf. Co.E
Taylor, John W. VA 39th Inf. Co.E
Taylor, John W. VA 39th Inf. Co.G Cpl.
Taylor, John W. VA 54th Inf. Co.E
Taylor, John W. VA 58th Mil. Co.E
Taylor, John W. VA 58th Mil. Co.F
Taylor, John W. VA Inf. Cohoon's Bn. Co.A,B Music.
Taylor, John W. 8th (Wade's) Conf.Cav. Co.G
Taylor, John W. Conf.Hvy.Arty. Montague's Bn. Co.D
Taylor, John W. Conf.Reg.Inf. Brooks' Bn. Co.D Cpl.
Taylor, John W. Gen. & Staff Chap.
Taylor, John Wesley TN Inf. 154th Sr.Regt. Co.G
Taylor, John Wesley N. AL 20th Inf. Co.D
Taylor, John W.S. VA 15th Inf. Co.B
Taylor, John Y. AL 3rd Inf. Co.B
Taylor, John Z. AR Cav. McGehee's Regt. Co.A
Taylor, John Z. FL 6th Inf. Co.I
Taylor, John Z. MS 3rd (St.Troops) Cav. Co.E
Taylor, John Z. MS 1st (King's) Inf. (St.Troops) Co.A
Taylor, Jo L. LA 3rd Inf. Co.B
Taylor, Jolley SC 13th Inf. Co.K
Taylor, Jonah NC 17th Inf. (2nd Org.) Co.D
Taylor, Jonathan AL Rives' Supp.Force 9th Congr.Dist.
Taylor, Jonathan AR 14th (McCarver's) Inf. Co.A Cpl.
Taylor, Jonathan FL 4th Inf. Co.H
Taylor, Jonathan GA Cav. 19th Bn. Co.A
Taylor, Jonathan TN 42nd Inf. 2nd Co.H
Taylor, Jonathan TX 17th Cav. Co.C Cpl.
Taylor, Jonathan TX 17th Cons.Dismtd.Cav. Co.C Cpl.
Taylor, Jonathan VA 7th Inf. Co.I
Taylor, Jonathan VA 29th Inf. Co.C
Taylor, Jonathan VA 48th Inf. Co.B Cpl.
Taylor, Jonathan A. NC 25th Inf. Co.H
Taylor, Jonathan C. NC 34th Inf. Co.C
Taylor, Jonathan F. NC 1st Inf. Co.B
Taylor, Jonathan G. KY 3rd Cav. Co.D
Taylor, Jonathan G. KY 7th Cav. Co.D
Taylor, Jonathan H. LA 19th Inf. Co.A
Taylor, Jonathan J. GA 21st Inf. Co.K Sgt.
Taylor, Jonathan J. NC 31st Inf. Co.E Cpl.
Taylor, Jonathan J. TX 13th Vol. Co.K
Taylor, Jonathan J. TX Inf. Griffin's Bn. Co.F
Taylor, Jo R. MO 1st Cav. Co.F Sgt.
Taylor, Jordan NC 33rd Inf. Co.B
Taylor, Jordan VA Lt.Arty. Thornton's Co.
Taylor, Jordan VA 20th Inf. Co.E
Taylor, Joseph AL 2nd Cav. Co.K
Taylor, Joseph AL 1st Regt.Conscr. Co.I
Taylor, Joseph AL 34th Inf. Co.H
Taylor, Joseph AL 37th Inf. Co.H
Taylor, Joseph AL 42nd Inf. Co.I
Taylor, Joseph AR 1st (Crawford's) Cav. Co.A
Taylor, Joseph AR 45th Cav. Co.H
Taylor, Joseph AR 7th Inf. Co.K
Taylor, Joseph AR 15th (Josey's) Inf. Co.I
Taylor, Joseph GA 4th (Clinch's) Cav. Co.E
Taylor, Joseph GA 6th Cav. 1st Co.K 1st Lt.
Taylor, Joseph GA 26th Inf. Co.D
Taylor, Joseph KY 5th Cav. 1st Lt.
Taylor, Joseph KY 6th Cav. Co.C 1st Lt.
Taylor, Joseph KY 9th Cav. Co.F
Taylor, Joseph KY Jessee's Bn.Mtd.Riflemen Co.C 1st Lt.
Taylor, Joseph KY Part.Rangers Rowan's Co. 1st Lt.
Taylor, Joseph LA 1st (Nelligan's) Inf. Co.I Capt.
Taylor, Joseph LA Mil. 1st Regt. 3rd Brig. 1st Div. Co.D
Taylor, Joseph LA 5th Inf. Co.F
Taylor, Joseph LA 28th (Thomas') Inf. Co.A
Taylor, Joseph LA Mil. Beauregard Bn.
Taylor, Joseph LA Inf.Crescent Regt. Co.C
Taylor, Joseph MS 1st Cav.Res. Co.H
Taylor, Joseph MS Inf. 2nd Bn. Co.G Sgt.
Taylor, Joseph MS 21st Inf. Co.B 3rd Sgt.
Taylor, Joseph MS 48th Inf. Co.G Sgt.
Taylor, Joseph MO 1st N.E. Cav. Co.A
Taylor, Joseph MO 7th Cav. Co.D
Taylor, Joseph NC Cav. (Loc.Def.) Howard's Co.
Taylor, Joseph NC 6th Inf. Co.F
Taylor, Joseph NC 12th Inf. Co.H
Taylor, Joseph NC 21st Inf. Co.I Sgt.
Taylor, Joseph NC 67th Inf. Co.H
Taylor, Joseph SC 23rd Inf. Co.F
Taylor, Joseph TN Atkins' Btty.
Taylor, Joseph TN 1st (Feild's) Inf. Co.F 2nd Lt.
Taylor, Joseph TN 5th Inf. 2nd Co.D
Taylor, Joseph TN 35th Inf. Co.G
Taylor, Joseph TN 49th Inf. Co.B
Taylor, Joseph TN 62nd Mtd.Inf. Co.H
Taylor, Joseph TX 1st (McCulloch's) Cav. Surg.
Taylor, Joseph TX Cav. 8th (Taylor's) Bn. Maj.
Taylor, Joseph TX 17th Cav. Co.E
Taylor, Joseph TX 17th Cons.Dismtd.Cav. Co.K
Taylor, Joseph TX 25th Cav. Co.B
Taylor, Joseph TX 36th Cav. Co.G
Taylor, Joseph TX Cav. 1st Bn.St.Troops Maj.

Taylor, Joseph TX 1st Inf. Co.C
Taylor, Joseph TX 1st Bn.S.S. Co.A
Taylor, Joseph TX 9th (Nichols') Inf. Co.D
Taylor, Joseph VA 2nd Cav. Co.E
Taylor, Joseph VA 5th Cav. Co.G
Taylor, Joseph VA 8th Cav. Co.C
Taylor, Joseph VA 19th Inf. Co.F Cpl.
Taylor, Joseph VA 51st Mil. Co.B
Taylor, Joseph VA 54th Mil. Co.C,D
Taylor, Joseph VA 58th Mil. Co.A Sgt.
Taylor, Joseph VA 59th Inf. 3rd Co.I
Taylor, Joseph Conf.Cav. 6th Bn. Co.C 1st Lt.
Taylor, Joseph Conf.Inf. Tucker's Regt. Co.D
Taylor, Joseph Gen. & Staff, Medical Dept. Surg.
Taylor, Joseph A. MS 34th Inf. Co.C
Taylor, Joseph A. SC 5th Cav. Co.F
Taylor, Joseph B. AR 8th Inf. New Co.C
Taylor, Joseph B. NC 5th Cav. (63rd St.Troops) Co.B Sgt.
Taylor, Joseph B. SC 1st (Butler's) Inf. Co.E Hosp.Stew.
Taylor, Joseph B. VA 10th Inf. Co.D
Taylor, Joseph B. Gen. & Staff Hosp.Stew.
Taylor, Joseph C. AR 5th Inf. Co.B
Taylor, Joseph C. GA 48th Inf. Co.I
Taylor, Joseph C. TN 1st (Turney's) Inf. Co.K
Taylor, Joseph C. VA 55th Inf. Co.K
Taylor, Joseph D. LA Dreux's Cav. Co.A
Taylor, Joseph D. LA Inf. 16th Bn. (Conf. Guards Resp.Bn.) Co.B
Taylor, Joseph D. NC 1st Inf. Co.H Sgt.
Taylor, Joseph D. SC Mil. Trenholm's Co.
Taylor, Joseph D. SC Rutledge Mtd.Riflemen & Horse Arty. Trenholm's Co. Cpl.
Taylor, Joseph D. TN 24th Inf. 2nd Co.H
Taylor, Joseph E. MS 38th Cav. Co.A
Taylor, Joseph F. GA 25th Inf. Co.E
Taylor, Joseph F. KY 4th Cav. Co.D
Taylor, Joseph F. LA 12th Inf. Co.L 1st Sgt.
Taylor, Joseph F. VA 2nd Cav. Co.D
Taylor, Joseph F. VA 2nd Inf. Co.F
Taylor, Joseph F. VA Inf. 5th Bn. Co.D
Taylor, Joseph H. AL 3rd Inf. Co.K
Taylor, Joseph H. GA Inf. 13th Bn. (St.Guards) Douglass' Co.
Taylor, Joseph H. GA 23rd Inf. Co.E Sgt.
Taylor, Joseph H. TN Cav. 1st Bn. (McNairy's) Co.C
Taylor, Joseph H. VA 3rd Cav. Co.A
Taylor, Joseph H. VA 1st Lt.Arty. Co.C
Taylor, Joseph H. VA Lt.Arty. Carpenter's Co.
Taylor, Joseph H. VA Lt.Arty. Cutshaw's Co.
Taylor, Joseph H. VA Lt.Arty. Huckstep's Co.
Taylor, Joseph H. VA Lt.Arty. Snead's Co.
Taylor, Joseph H. VA 62nd Mtd.Inf. 2nd Co.G
Taylor, Joseph H. Conf.Inf. 1st Bn. 2nd Co.C
Taylor, Joseph J. AL 34th Inf. Co.A
Taylor, Joseph J. NC 7th Inf. Co.E Sgt.
Taylor, Joseph K. FL 3rd Inf. Co.I
Taylor, Joseph K. TX 1st (Yager's) Cav. Co.I
Taylor, Joseph L. AR 7th Inf. Co.H Cpl.
Taylor, Joseph L. AR 27th Inf. New Co.B
Taylor, Joseph L. MS 11th Inf. Co.A 1st Lt.
Taylor, Joseph L. TX 26th Cav. Co.I
Taylor, Joseph L.B. AL Cav. Falkner's Co.
Taylor, Joseph M. MS 12th Cav. Co.E Cpl.
Taylor, Joseph M. MS 12th Inf. Co.I Sgt.
Taylor, Joseph M. MS 29th Inf. Co.A
Taylor, Joseph M. MO 2nd Cav. 3rd Co.K
Taylor, Joseph M. VA Lt.Arty. Kirkpatrick's Co.
Taylor, Joseph O. FL 3rd Inf. Co.H Sgt.
Taylor, Joseph R. AR 15th (N.W.) Inf. Co.C 1st Sgt.
Taylor, Joseph R. SC 23rd Inf. Co.E
Taylor, Joseph R. TN 62nd Mtd.Inf. Co.A 2nd Lt.
Taylor, Joseph R. Conf.Inf. 1st Bn. 2nd Co.A Sgt.
Taylor, Joseph S. GA 55th Inf. Co.A
Taylor, Joseph S. NC 1st Arty. (10th St.Troops) Co.H
Taylor, Joseph S. NC 3rd Arty. (40th St.Troops) Co.K
Taylor, Joseph S. VA 23rd Inf. Co.C
Taylor, Josephus 1st Choctaw Mtd.Rifles Co.D 3rd Lt.
Taylor, Joseph W. AL Crawford's Co.
Taylor, Joseph W. NC 3rd Inf. Co.G Sgt.
Taylor, Joseph W. NC 11th (Bethel Regt.) Inf. Co.F
Taylor, Joseph W. NC 53rd Inf. Co.E
Taylor, Joseph W. NC Vol. Lawrence's Co. Sgt.
Taylor, Joseph W. TN 30th Inf. Co.B
Taylor, Joseph W. 7th Conf.Cav. Co.H 2nd Lt.
Taylor, Joshua MO 10th Inf. Co.F
Taylor, Joshua MO 12th Inf. Co.F
Taylor, Joshua NC 54th Inf. Co.C
Taylor, Joshua VA 9th Mil. Co.B
Taylor, Joshua VA 26th Inf. Co.C
Taylor, Joshua VA Burks' Regt.Loc.Def. Allen's Co.
Taylor, Joshua 2nd Cherokee Mtd.Vol. Co.F
Taylor, Joshua A. GA 59th Inf. Co.F Sgt.
Taylor, Joshua C. MS 11th Inf. Co.A
Taylor, Joshua D. MS Inf. 2nd Bn. Co.C
Taylor, Joshua D. MS 48th Inf. Co.C
Taylor, Joshua L. NC 55th Inf. Co.H
Taylor, Joshua M. TN Cav. Newsom's Regt. Co.E Cpl.
Taylor, Joshua R. LA 9th Inf. Co.H
Taylor, Josiah AL 5th Cav. Co.E Cpl.
Taylor, Josiah AL 12th Inf. Co.H
Taylor, Josiah AL 20th Inf. Co.F
Taylor, Josiah GA Lt.Arty. Ritter's Co.
Taylor, Josiah NC 32nd Inf. Co.H
Taylor, Josiah TX 36th Cav. Co.G Capt.
Taylor, Josiah TX Inf. 3rd St.Troops Co.H
Taylor, Josiah TX Inf. Rutherford's Co.
Taylor, Josiah Anderson TX 20th Cav. Co.B
Taylor, Josiah B. AR 17th (Lemoyne's) Inf. Co.C Sgt.
Taylor, Josiah B. AR 21st Inf. Co.C
Taylor, Josiah F. VA 64th Mil. Powell's Co. 1st Sgt.
Taylor, Josiah M. AL 17th Inf. Co.E
Taylor, Josiah R. NC 4th Inf. Co.D
Taylor, Josias B. NC Mil. 66th Bn. J.H. Whitman's Co.
Taylor, Joual TX 24th Cav. Co.K
Taylor, Jourdan MS 18th Inf. Co.K
Taylor, J.P. AL 31st Inf. Co.H
Taylor, J.P. AL 36th Inf. Co.H
Taylor, J.P. AL 43rd Inf. Co.D
Taylor, J.P. GA 7th Inf. (St.Guards) Co.H
Taylor, J.P. LA 17th Inf. Co.H
Taylor, J.P. MS 3rd Cav. Co.D Cpl.
Taylor, J.P. MS 4th Cav. Co.A
Taylor, J.P. MO Inf. 1st Regt.St.Guard Co.F Capt.
Taylor, J.P. SC Inf. Hampton Legion Co.I
Taylor, J.P. TN 6th Inf. Co.L
Taylor, J.P. TN 22nd Inf. Co.B
Taylor, J.P. TN 55th (Brown's) Inf. Ford's Co.
Taylor, J.P. TX 20th Inf. Co.B
Taylor, J.P. VA 21st Cav. 2nd Co.I
Taylor, J.P. VA 59th Inf. 3rd Co.I
Taylor, J.P. VA Loc.Def. Jordan's Co.
Taylor, J.P. Gen. & Staff, Medical Dept. Surg.
Taylor, J.Q. NC 11th (Bethel Regt.) Inf. Co.A
Taylor, J.R. AL Lt.Arty. Tarrant's Btty.
Taylor, J.R. AL 28th Inf. Co.L
Taylor, J.R. AL 30th Inf. Co.E
Taylor, J.R. AL 58th Inf. Co.A
Taylor, J.R. AR 7th Cav. Co.C
Taylor, J.R. AR 27th Inf. Co.D
Taylor, J.R. AR 32nd Inf. Co.K
Taylor, J.R. FL 4th Inf. Co.D Sgt.
Taylor, J.R. GA Lt.Arty. Havis' Btty.
Taylor, J.R. GA 5th Inf. Co.I
Taylor, J.R. GA 5th Res. Co.A
Taylor, J.R. GA 6th Inf. (St.Guards) Co.G
Taylor, J.R. GA 19th Inf. Co.G
Taylor, J.R. GA 42nd Inf. Co.A
Taylor, J.R. GA 53rd Inf. Co.E
Taylor, J.R. MS 2nd Cav. Co.E
Taylor, J.R. MO Inf. 1st Bn.St.Guard Co.B Capt.
Taylor, J.R. NC 26th Inf. Co.A
Taylor, J.R. NC 27th Inf. Co.I
Taylor, J.R. SC Arty. Manigault's Bn. 1st Co.B QMSgt.
Taylor, J.R. SC 13th Inf. Co.K
Taylor, J.R. TN 13th (Gore's) Cav. Co.I
Taylor, J.R. TN 3rd (Clack's) Inf. Co.E Cpl.
Taylor, J.R. TN 5th Inf. 2nd Co.K
Taylor, J.R. TN 16th Inf. Co.B
Taylor, J.R. TX 3rd Cav. Co.C
Taylor, J.R. TX 32nd Cav. Co.D
Taylor, J.R. TX Cav. Baird's Regt. Co.G
Taylor, J.R. TX 15th Inf. Co.B
Taylor, J.R. VA 2nd Cav. Co.K
Taylor, J.S. AL 6th Cav.
Taylor, J.S. AL 56th Part.Rangers Co.B
Taylor, J.S. AL Cav. Moreland's Regt. Co.F
Taylor, J.S. GA 46th Inf. Co.E
Taylor, J.S. MS 6th Inf. Co.F Capt.
Taylor, J.S. MO Cav. Freeman's Regt. Co.B
Taylor, J.S. NC 3rd Cav. (41st St.Troops) Co.E Sgt.
Taylor, J.S. NC 26th Inf. Co.F
Taylor, J.S. SC Lt.Arty. 3rd (Palmetto) Bn. Culpeper's Co.
Taylor, J.S. SC 2nd Inf. Co.B
Taylor, J.S. SC 23rd Inf. Co.G Cpl.
Taylor, J.S. TN 5th (McKenzie's) Cav. Co.D
Taylor, J.S. TN 46th Inf. Co.D
Taylor, J.S. TN 63rd Inf. Co.H
Taylor, J.S. TX Cav. (Dismtd.) Chisum's Regt. Co.I
Taylor, J.S. VA 5th Cav. Co.G AQM

Taylor, J.S. 4th Conf.Inf. Co.B
Taylor, J.T. AL 7th Cav. Co.G
Taylor, J.T. AL 10th Cav. Co.B Sgt.
Taylor, J.T. AL 34th Inf. Co.A Cpl.
Taylor, J.T. GA 4th (Clinch's) Cav. Co.F
Taylor, J.T. GA Inf. 18th Bn. Co.C
Taylor, J.T. GA 37th Inf. Co.C
Taylor, J.T. GA 46th Inf. Co.B
Taylor, J.T. LA 6th Inf. Co.A
Taylor, J.T. MS 1st (Johnston's) Inf. Co.G
Taylor, J.T. MS 7th Inf. Co.H
Taylor, J.T. MS 30th Inf. Co.K
Taylor, J.T. MO 1st & 4th Cons.Inf. Co.H
Taylor, J.T. MO 4th Inf. Co.K
Taylor, J.T. SC Lt.Arty. 3rd (Palmetto) Bn. Co.H
Taylor, J.T. SC 16th Inf. Co.F
Taylor, J.T. SC 18th Inf. Co.E
Taylor, J.T. TN 1st (Carter's) Cav. Co.K
Taylor, J.T. TN 8th (Smith's) Cav. Co.G
Taylor, J.T. TX 7th Inf. Co.C
Taylor, J.T. TX 9th (Young's) Inf. Co.D
Taylor, J.T. TX 14th Inf. Co.D
Taylor, J.T. VA Lt.Arty. Grandy's Co.
Taylor, J.T. VA Inf. 1st Bn.Loc.Def. Co.F
Taylor, J.T. VA 3rd Inf.Loc.Def. Co.B
Taylor, J. Temple VA 9th Cav. Co.B
Taylor, Julius GA 9th Inf. Co.F
Taylor, Julius F. GA 45th Inf. Co.K
Taylor, Julius V. AL 3rd Inf. Co.G
Taylor, Julius W. NC Coast Guards Galloway's Co.
Taylor, Junius L. FL 5th Inf. Co.K 1st Lt.
Taylor, J.V. MS Inf. 3rd Bn. (St.Troops) Co.D
Taylor, J.V. MS 34th Inf.
Taylor, J.V. TN 22nd (Barteau's) Cav. Co.G
Taylor, J. Vincent VA 1st Inf. Co.E
Taylor, J. Vinson TN Cav. 7th Bn. (Bennett's) Co.E Cpl.
Taylor, J.W. AL 2nd Inf. Co.I
Taylor, J.W. AL 3rd Inf. Co.D
Taylor, J.W. AL 9th Inf. Co.B
Taylor, J.W. AL 24th Inf. Chap.
Taylor, J.W. AL 26th (O'Neal's) Inf. Co.G Cpl.
Taylor, J.W. AL Cp. of Instr. Talladega
Taylor, J.W. AR 1st (Monroe's) Cav. Co.B
Taylor, J.W. AR Mtd.Vol. Baker's Co.
Taylor, J.W. AR 11th Inf. Co.E
Taylor, J.W. AR 11th & 17th Cons.Inf. Co.E
Taylor, J.W. AR 15th (Johnson's) Inf. Co.E
Taylor, J.W. AR 19th Inf. Co.B
Taylor, J.W. AR 20th Inf. Co.I
Taylor, J.W. AR 26th Inf. Co.K
Taylor, J.W. AR 32nd Inf. Co.B
Taylor, J.W. AR 37th Inf. Co.H
Taylor, J.W. FL 11th Inf.
Taylor, J.W. GA Lt.Arty. Anderson's Btty.
Taylor, J.W., Jr. GA Lt.Arty. Clinch's Btty.
Taylor, J.W., Sr. GA Lt.Arty. Clinch's Btty.
Taylor, J.W. GA 3rd Res. Co.A
Taylor, J.W. GA 5th Res. Co.F
Taylor, J.W. GA 23rd Inf. Co.D
Taylor, J.W. GA 29th Inf. Co.D
Taylor, J.W. GA 32nd Inf. Co.I
Taylor, J.W. GA 39th Inf. Co.I
Taylor, J.W. GA 43rd Inf. Co.A
Taylor, J.W. GA 50th Inf. Co.D
Taylor, J.W. GA 52nd Inf. Co.B
Taylor, J.W. GA 56th Inf. Co.I
Taylor, J.W. KY 2nd (Duke's) Cav. Co.D
Taylor, J.W. KY 10th (Johnson's) Cav. Co.D
Taylor, J.W. KY 12th Cav. Co.C
Taylor, J.W. KY 2nd Mtd.Inf. Co.F
Taylor, J.W. LA 9th Inf. Co.B
Taylor, J.W. LA 28th (Thomas') Inf.
Taylor, J.W. MS 10th Inf. New Co.K
Taylor, J.W. MS 33rd Inf. Co.B
Taylor, J.W. MS 46th Inf. Co.G
Taylor, J.W. NC Cav. 16th Bn. Music.
Taylor, J.W. NC 1st Inf. (6 mo. '61) Co.B
Taylor, J.W. NC Snead's Co. (Loc.Def.)
Taylor, J.W. SC 4th Bn.Res. Co.D
Taylor, J.W. SC 25th Inf. Co.G
Taylor, J.W. TN 7th (Duckworth's) Cav. Co.K
Taylor, J.W. TN Cav. Jackson's Co.
Taylor, J.W. TN 1st Hvy.Arty. 1st Co.C
Taylor, J.W. TN 20th Inf. Co.G
Taylor, J.W. TN Inf. 22nd Bn. Co.B
Taylor, J.W. TN 42nd Inf. 1st Co.H
Taylor, J.W. TN 63rd Inf. Co.G
Taylor, J.W. TX 7th Inf. Co.F Cpl.
Taylor, J.W. TX 18th Vol. 2nd Co.F
Taylor, J.W. TX Waul's Legion Co.F
Taylor, J.W. VA 2nd Cav. Co.H
Taylor, J.W. VA 1st St.Res. Co.F
Taylor, J.W. VA Inf. 1st Bn.Loc.Def. Co.F
Taylor, J.W. VA 1st Bn.Res. Co.D
Taylor, J.W. VA 2nd Inf.Loc.Def. Co.H
Taylor, J.W. VA Inf. 2nd Bn.Loc.Def. Co.B
Taylor, J.W. VA Inf. 2nd Bn.Loc.Def. Co.F
Taylor, J.W. VA Conscr. Cp.Lee Co.A
Taylor, J.W. Inf. Bailey's Cons.Regt. Co.B Sgt.
Taylor, J.W.B. TN 31st Inf. Co.I
Taylor, J.W.G. GA 5th Inf. Co.I
Taylor, J. William TX 7th Inf. Co.D 2nd Lt.
Taylor, J.W.J. AR 3rd Inf. Co.A
Taylor, J.W.J. GA 8th Inf. (St.Guards) Co.D
Taylor, J.W.N. AL 6th Cav. Co.D
Taylor, J.Y. KY Unassign.Conscr.
Taylor, J.Y. MO Lt.Arty. Farris' Btty. (Clark Arty.)
Taylor, J.Z. TN 45th Inf. Co.H
Taylor, J.Z. VA 4th Cav. Co.I,F
Taylor, K. GA 8th Cav. Co.C
Taylor, K. GA 8th Cav. New Co.D
Taylor, K. GA Cav. 20th Bn. Co.A
Taylor, K. LA 4th Inf. New Co.G
Taylor, K. MS 4th Cav. Co.H
Taylor, K. MS Cav. Hughes' Bn. Co.B
Taylor, K. SC Lt.Arty. Gaillard's Co. (Santee Lt.Arty.) Cpl.
Taylor, K. SC 10th Inf. 1st Co.G
Taylor, K. SC Manigault's Bn.Vol. Co.B
Taylor, K. TN 49th Inf. Co.H
Taylor, Kambias VA Cav. 41st Bn. Co.A
Taylor, Kedar VA 6th Inf. 2nd Co.E
Taylor, Kedar VA 9th Inf. Co.I
Taylor, Kenan NC 51st Inf. Co.C
Taylor, Kenyon B. NC 24th Inf. Co.E
Taylor, Kinchen NC 17th Inf. (2nd Org.) Co.D
Taylor, Kinchen NC 17th Inf. (2nd Org.) Co.H
Taylor, Kinchen TN 33rd Inf. Co.A
Taylor, Kinchen VA Horse Arty. E. Graham's Co.
Taylor, Kinchen R. NC 3rd Inf. Co.A Sgt.Maj.
Taylor, Kinchen W. NC 43rd Inf. Co.C
Taylor, Kinchin GA 62nd Cav. Co.C
Taylor, Kirkbride VA 8th Inf. Co.H,I 1st Lt.
Taylor, Knitchen NC 1st Arty. (10th St.Troops) Co.H
Taylor, K.P.D. LA 8th Cav. Co.C
Taylor, L. AL 53rd (Part.Rangers) Co.I
Taylor, L. AL 25th Inf. Co.K
Taylor, L. AL 28th Inf. Co.B
Taylor, L. AR Cav. Gordon's Regt. Co.D
Taylor, L. AR 10th Mil. Co.A Sgt.
Taylor, L. FL 2nd Cav. Co.L
Taylor, L. GA Lt.Arty. Howell's Co.
Taylor, L. GA 5th Res. Co.G
Taylor, L. KY 4th Mtd.Inf. Co.B
Taylor, L. LA Inf.Crescent Regt. Co.H
Taylor, L. MS 1st Cav. Co.A
Taylor, L. MS 8th Cav. Co.D
Taylor, L. NC 1st Arty. (10th St.Troops) Co.A
Taylor, L. NC 68th Inf. Capt.
Taylor, L. NC Mallett's Co.
Taylor, L. SC 15th Inf. Co.C
Taylor, L. SC 15th Inf. Co.E
Taylor, L. TX Inf. Chambers' Bn.Res.Corps Co.D Sgt.
Taylor, L. VA 14th Cav. Co.H
Taylor, L.A. MS 35th Inf. Co.C
Taylor, L.A. TN 50th Inf. Co.G
Taylor, L.A. TX 26th Cav. Co.G
Taylor, Laban MS Inf. 1st Bn.St.Troops (30 days '64) Co.A Sgt.
Taylor, Laborn G. FL 5th Inf. Co.F
Taylor, Lafayett TN Cav. 12th Bn. (Day's) Co.D Jr.2nd Lt.
Taylor, Lafayette GA 2nd Bn.S.S. Co.B 1st Sgt.
Taylor, Lafayette GA 5th Inf. Co.K,L 1st Sgt.
Taylor, Lafayette TN 35th Inf. 1st Co.I, Co.G
Taylor, Lafayette F. TN Inf. 1st Bn. (Colms') Co.B Sgt.
Taylor, Larkin VA Rockbridge Cty.Res. Donald's Co.
Taylor, Larkin G. AL 25th Inf. Co.F
Taylor, Larkin M. MS 30th Inf. Co.C
Taylor, Lawrence TX Inf.Riflemen Arnold's Co.
Taylor, Lawrence B. VA 4th Cav. Co.E
Taylor, Lawrence B. Lee's Div. Col.
Taylor, Lawrence H. NC 61st Inf. Co.F
Taylor, Lawrence S. TX 17th Cav. Co.A
Taylor, Lawson NC 16th Inf. Co.E
Taylor, Lawson W. TN 5th (McKenzie's) Cav. Co.G
Taylor, L.B. GA Inf. 13th Bn. (St.Guards) Guerry's Co.
Taylor, L.B. LA 21st (Patton's) Inf. AQM
Taylor, L.B. TN 38th Inf. Co.D
Taylor, L.B. Gen. & Staff AQM
Taylor, L.C. AR 9th Inf. Co.K
Taylor, L.C. AR 19th (Dawson's) Inf.
Taylor, L.C. MS 2nd Part. Co.A 1st Lt.
Taylor, L.C. MO 8th Cav. Reed's Co.
Taylor, L.C. TX 23rd Cav. Co.D
Taylor, L.C. TX 26th Cav. Co.K Lt.
Taylor, L.C. TX 32nd Cav. Co.D
Taylor, L.D. AR 30th Inf. Co.A
Taylor, L.D. KY 1st Inf. Co.C
Taylor, L.D. TN 51st (Cons.) Inf. Co.F 2nd Lt.

Taylor, L.D. VA Inf. 25th Bn. Co.B
Taylor, L.E. AL 34th Inf. Co.E
Taylor, L.E. GA 44th Inf. Co.H
Taylor, Leander F. GA 2nd Inf. Co.G
Taylor, Leander F. KY 9th Mtd.Inf. Co.H
Taylor, Leander F. NC 16th Inf. Co.I
Taylor, Leander F. TX Inf. W. Cameron's Co.
Taylor, Leander J. MS 31st Inf. Co.B
Taylor, Lee AR 34th Inf. Co.A 2nd Lt.
Taylor, Lee MS 42nd Inf. Co.A
Taylor, Lee TN Cav. 12th Bn. (Day's) Co.C
Taylor, Lemick AL 27th Inf. Co.G
Taylor, Lemiel GA 2nd Cav.
Taylor, Lemon W. MS 22nd Inf. Co.A
Taylor, Lemuel GA 49th Inf. Co.F
Taylor, Lemuel GA 61st Inf. Co.A
Taylor, Lemuel GA Cobb's Legion Co.D
Taylor, Lemuel D. GA 49th Inf. Co.F Sgt.
Taylor, Lemuel T. AR 9th Inf. Co.A
Taylor, Lemuel T. VA 2nd Inf. Co.B Cpl.
Taylor, Leonard MS 4th Inf. Co.H
Taylor, Leonard VA 32nd Inf. Co.C
Taylor, Leroy AR Cav. Carlton's Regt.
Taylor, Leroy GA Inf. 26th Bn. Co.C
Taylor, Leroy KY 10th Cav. Co.L
Taylor, Leroy MS 7th Cav. Co.F
Taylor, Leroy TN 2nd (Ashby's) Cav. Co.G
Taylor, Leroy, Jr. TN 2nd (Ashby's) Cav. Co.G Cpl.
Taylor, Leroy TN Cav. 4th Bn. (Branner's) Co.B
Taylor, Leroy TN Inf. 1st Cons.Regt. Co.B
Taylor, Leroy TN 1st (Feild's) Inf. Co.F
Taylor, Leroy VA 37th Inf. Co.D
Taylor, Leroy J. AR Cav. 1st Bn. (Stirman's) Co.A
Taylor, Leroy R. VA 55th Inf. Co.D
Taylor, Levi NC 8th Bn.Part.Rangers Co.F
Taylor, Levi NC 66th Inf. Co.K
Taylor, Levi SC 6th Inf. 2nd Co.D
Taylor, Levi VA 20th Cav. Co.H
Taylor, Levi VA Lt.Arty. Thornton's Co.
Taylor, Levi J. TX 17th Cav. Co.B
Taylor, Levi J. VA 3rd Cav. & Inf.St.Line Co.A
Taylor, Levi L. FL Lt.Arty. Dyke's Co.
Taylor, Levi M. TX 6th Cav. Co.D
Taylor, Lewellen NC 56th Inf. Co.D
Taylor, Lewis AL 11th Inf. Co.F
Taylor, Lewis AR 33rd Inf. Co.E Cpl.
Taylor, Lewis LA 18th Inf. Co.D
Taylor, Lewis LA Miles' Legion Co.B
Taylor, Lewis NC 8th Bn.Part.Rangers Co.A
Taylor, Lewis NC Hvy.Arty. 1st Bn. Co.B
Taylor, Lewis NC 3rd Arty. (40th St.Troops) Co.G
Taylor, Lewis NC 1st Inf. (6 mo. '61) Co.A
Taylor, Lewis NC 66th Inf. Co.F
Taylor, Lewis NC Mil. Clark's Sp.Bn. F.G. Simmons' Co.
Taylor, Lewis SC Hvy.Arty. 15th (Lucas') Bn. Co.A
Taylor, Lewis TN Cav. 16th Bn. (Neal's) Co.C
Taylor, Lewis TN Inf. 22nd Bn. Co.C
Taylor, Lewis TN 38th Inf. Co.D
Taylor, Lewis Morgan's,CSA
Taylor, Lewis A. GA 12th Inf. Co.E
Taylor, Lewis A. NC 4th Inf. Co.E
Taylor, Lewis G. NC 2nd Inf. Co.F
Taylor, Lewis G. TN 18th Inf. Co.G
Taylor, Lewis H. NC 61st Inf. Co.E
Taylor, Lewis H. TX 18th Cav. Co.I 1st Sgt.
Taylor, Lewis H. VA Inf. 25th Bn. Co.B
Taylor, Lewis J. TN 35th Inf. 1st Co.I, Co.G
Taylor, Lewis L. FL 1st Cav. Co.E
Taylor, Lewis L. FL 3rd Inf. Co.H
Taylor, Lewis R. MO 11th Inf. Co.I
Taylor, Lewis T. AL 6th Inf. Co.G
Taylor, Lewis T. GA 11th Cav. (St.Guards) Folk's Co.
Taylor, L.F. TN 10th & 11th (Cons.) Cav. Co.E
Taylor, L.F. TN Inf. 22nd Bn. Co.A 1st Sgt.
Taylor, L.G. AR 15th (Johnson's) Inf. Co.F Sgt.
Taylor, L.H. AL 6th Inf. Co.E
Taylor, L.H. GA 12th (Robinson's) Cav. (St.Guards) Co.D
Taylor, L.H. GA Lt.Arty. (Jackson Arty.) Massenburg's Btty.
Taylor, L.H. GA 5th Res. Co.B
Taylor, L.H.P. TX 28th Cav. Co.F
Taylor, Liabb FL 11th Inf. Co.K
Taylor, Lin J. VA 19th Cav. Co.A
Taylor, Linus P. TN 21st Cav.
Taylor, Littleton B. GA 3rd Cav. (St.Guards) Co.D 3rd Lt.
Taylor, Livingston G. KY 10th (Johnson's) Cav. Co.B
Taylor, L.J. MO Inf. 1st Regt.St.Guard Co.C Capt.
Taylor, L.L. MS 3rd (St.Troops) Cav. Co.H
Taylor, L.L. TN 1st Cav. Co.C
Taylor, L.M. AL 3rd Inf. Co.L
Taylor, L.M. AL Pris.Guard Freeman's Co.
Taylor, L.M. AR 45th Cav. Co.M
Taylor, L.M. AR 30th Inf. Co.K
Taylor, L.M. GA 18th Inf. Co.G
Taylor, L.M. SC 4th Cav. Co.C
Taylor, L.M. SC Cav. 10th Bn. Co.B
Taylor, L.M. TX 4th Cav. Sr.Surg.
Taylor, L.M. TX 12th Cav. Co.B
Taylor, L.M. TX 22nd Inf. Co.G
Taylor, L.M. Gen. & Staff, Medical Dept. Asst.Surg.
Taylor, Loftin F. NC Hvy.Arty. 10th Bn. Co.A
Taylor, Lomax VA Inf. Hutter's Co.
Taylor, Lorenzo D. GA 3rd Inf. Co.H
Taylor, Lorenzo D. NC 13th Inf. Co.F
Taylor, Lorenzo H. MS 17th Inf. Co.B
Taylor, Louis VA Inf. 4th Bn.Loc.Def. Co.C,A
Taylor, Louis B. LA 1st Hvy.Arty. (Reg.) Co.A,F 1st Lt.
Taylor, Loyid T. NC 42nd Inf. Co.H
Taylor, L.P. MS Cav. 3rd Bn. (Ashcraft's) Co.E 3rd Lt.
Taylor, L.P. SC 15th Inf. Co.C
Taylor, L.P. VA 3rd Cav. Co.B
Taylor, L.R. AL 25th Inf. Co.F
Taylor, L.R. GA 54th Inf. Co.E
Taylor, L.R. MS 36th Inf. Co.F
Taylor, L.R. SC 6th Cav. Co.I
Taylor, L.R. TN 23rd Inf. Co.C Cpl.
Taylor, L.R. TN 25th Inf. Co.F Sgt.
Taylor, L.S. NC 15th Inf. Co.B
Taylor, L.S. SC 4th Bn.Res. Co.A
Taylor, L.S. TX 17th Cons.Dismtd.Cav. Co.A Adj.
Taylor, L.T. MD QM Dept.
Taylor, L.T. MS 11th (Cons.) Cav. Co.I 2nd Lt.
Taylor, Lucas C. VA 5th Inf. Co.E
Taylor, Lucius C. VA Inf. 25th Bn. Co.E
Taylor, Lucius M. GA 53rd Inf. Co.E
Taylor, Lucius M. KY Cav. Bolen's Ind.Co.
Taylor, Lud AL Cav. Holloway's Co.
Taylor, Luke H. SC 2nd Rifles Co.G
Taylor, Luther C. TX Lt.Arty. Hughes' Co.
Taylor, Luther J. MO Lt.Arty. Farris' Btty. (Clark Arty.)
Taylor, L.W. AL 26th Inf. Co.H
Taylor, L.W. KY 9th Cav. Co.C
Taylor, L.W. KY 3rd Mtd.Inf. Co.A
Taylor, L.W. MS 6th Inf. Co.I Music.
Taylor, Lycurgus W. NC Walker's Bn. Thomas' Legion Co.C
Taylor, M. AL 11th Cav. Co.F
Taylor, M. AL Cav. 24th Bn. Co.A
Taylor, M. AR 10th Mil. Co.E
Taylor, M. GA 1st Reg. Co.F
Taylor, M. GA 3rd Res. Co.E
Taylor, M. GA 22nd Inf. Co.E
Taylor, M. GA 46th Inf. Co.E
Taylor, M. MS 8th Cav. Co.K
Taylor, M. TN 1st (Carter's) Cav. Co.G
Taylor, M. TN 21st & 22nd (Cons.) Cav. Co.C
Taylor, M. TN 51st Inf. Co.D Cpl.
Taylor, M. TN 51st (Cons.) Inf. Co.F
Taylor, M. TX 9th Cav. Co.G
Taylor, M. TX Cav. Wells' Regt. Co.F
Taylor, M. 8th (Wade's) Conf.Cav. Co.B
Taylor, M. 1st Conf.Eng.Troops Co.B
Taylor, Mac SC 2nd Arty. Co.E
Taylor, Madison H. NC 5th Inf. Co.C
Taylor, Mahlon VA 6th Cav. Co.K
Taylor, Major VA 54th Mil. Co.C,D
Taylor, Major O. VA 30th Inf. Co.K
Taylor, Malachi AL 3rd Res. Co.E
Taylor, Malachi C. NC 4th Cav. (59th St.Troops) Co.G
Taylor, Manger J. NC Hvy.Arty. 1st Bn. Co.B
Taylor, Manoah TN 11th Inf. Co.C
Taylor, Manuel W. MO Cav. Wood's Regt. Co.E
Taylor, Marcellus VA 46th Inf. 4th Co.F
Taylor, Marcus A. LA 12th Inf. Co.L Music.
Taylor, Marion SC 14th Inf. Co.H
Taylor, Marion TN 48th (Voorhies') Inf. Co.F
Taylor, Marion TX Inf. Griffin's Bn. Co.E
Taylor, Marion R. AL 19th Inf. Co.I
Taylor, Mark P. NC 33rd Inf. Co.K Cpl.
Taylor, Mark Ruffus NC 7th Inf. Co.E
Taylor, Marland AR 17th (Lemoyne's) Inf. Co.E
Taylor, Marshal B. VA Inf. 21st Bn. 2nd Co.C Music.
Taylor, Marshall NC 37th Inf. Co.A
Taylor, Marshall SC 13th Inf. Co.K
Taylor, Marshall VA 26th Inf. Co.K
Taylor, Martin AL 32nd Inf. Co.I
Taylor, Martin FL 7th Inf. Co.A
Taylor, Martin GA 22nd Inf. Co.E
Taylor, Martin KY 1st Bn.Mtd.Rifles Co.B
Taylor, Martin MO 1st N.E. Cav. Co.I
Taylor, Martin TN 22nd Inf. Co.B
Taylor, Martin TX Inf. Griffin's Bn. Co.F
Taylor, Martin L. SC 20th Inf. Co.K Sgt.
Taylor, Martin S. VA Cav. 40th Bn. Co.A

Taylor, Mason NC 33rd Inf. Co.E
Taylor, Massane N. VA Lt.Arty. Pegram's Co. Cpl.
Taylor, Massilon F. NC 12th Inf. Co.D,B Capt.
Taylor, Mat. AR 8th Cav. Peoples' Co.
Taylor, Mat AR 30th Inf. Co.F
Taylor, Mateland VA Cav. 35th Bn. Co.C
Taylor, Mat. L. MO 9th Inf. Co.H
Taylor, Mathew AR Cav. Wright's Regt. Co.K
Taylor, Mathew TN Cav. 16th Bn. (Neal's) Co.E
Taylor, Mathew Conf.Reg.Inf. Brooks' Bn. Co.E
Taylor, Mathew J. VA 2nd Arty. Co.K
Taylor, Mathew J. VA Inf. 22nd Bn. Co.A
Taylor, Mathew L. MO 5th Inf. Co.C
Taylor, Mathew L. MO Inf. 8th Bn. Co.D
Taylor, Mathew N. MO 8th Cav. Co.B,A
Taylor, Mathew P. VA 1st Arty. Co.I 2nd Lt.
Taylor, Mathew T. TX 15th Cav. Co.C
Taylor, Matthew TN 37th Inf. Co.I
Taylor, Matthew P. Gen. & Staff Capt.,ACS
Taylor, M.B. GA Inf. 4th Bn. (St.Guards) Co.B
Taylor, M.B. GA 66th Inf. Co.I
Taylor, M.B. VA 64th Mtd.Inf. Co.C
Taylor, M.C. AL 55th Vol. Co.I
Taylor, M.C. GA Cav. 1st Bn.Res. McKinney's Co.
Taylor, M.C. GA 32nd Inf. Co.I
Taylor, M.C. NC 21st Inf. Co.L
Taylor, M.C. NC 53rd Inf. Co.G
Taylor, M.C. TN 15th (Cons.) Cav. Co.A
Taylor, M.C. TN 42nd Inf. 1st Co.I Cpl.
Taylor, McDonald AL 47th Inf. Co.B
Taylor, McG. NC 17th Inf. (2nd Org.) Co.I
Taylor, McGilbert NC 1st Inf. Co.H
Taylor, McH. AL Cav. Murphy's Bn. Co.D
Taylor, M.D. AR 16th Inf. Co.G
Taylor, M.D. TN Inf. 4th Cons.Regt. Co.G
Taylor, M.D. TN 49th Inf. Co.C Bvt.2nd Lt.
Taylor, M.D. Inf. Bailey's Cons.Regt. Co.F 3rd Lt.
Taylor, M.D.L. TN 63rd Inf. Co.G Ord.Sgt.
Taylor, Meredith S. AL Cav. 4th Bn. (Love's) Co.A
Taylor, Meriland AR 21st Inf. Co.I
Taylor, M.F. AL 26th (O'Neal's) Inf. Co.C
Taylor, M.F. AR 26th Inf. Co.K
Taylor, M.F. MS 6th Inf. Co.I Music.
Taylor, M.F. VA 3rd Res. Co.D
Taylor, M.F. 3rd Corps 1st Lt.,ADC
Taylor, M.H. AL 23rd Inf. Co.B
Taylor, M.H. GA 12th (Robinson's) Cav. (St.Guards) Co.D
Taylor, M.H. NC Home Guards
Taylor, M.H. 15th Conf.Cav. Co.K
Taylor, Micajah S. SC 1st (Orr's) Rifles Co.L
Taylor, Michael AL 49th Inf. Co.F
Taylor, Michael FL 4th Inf. Co.H
Taylor, Michael GA Inf. 3rd Bn. Co.H
Taylor, Michael SC 14th Inf. Co.I
Taylor, Michael VA Cav. 36th Bn. Co.A
Taylor, Michael VA 13th Inf. Co.K
Taylor, Michael VA 58th Mil. Co.K
Taylor, Michael VA 62nd Mtd.Inf. 2nd Co.M
Taylor, Michael G. GA 48th Inf. Co.I
Taylor, Michael J. GA 49th Inf. Co.D
Taylor, Michael N. VA 46th Inf. 2nd Co.K
Taylor, Michael W. AR Cav. Wright's Regt. Co.G Sgt.
Taylor, Middleton SC 1st (Hagood's) Inf. 1st Co.D
Taylor, Middleton SC 25th Inf. Co.F
Taylor, Milam TX 2nd Cav. Co.A Jr.2nd Lt.
Taylor, Milburn MS 4th Inf.
Taylor, Miledge AR 45th Cav. Co.H Cpl.
Taylor, Miles NC 26th Inf. Co.I
Taylor, Miles VA 54th Mil. Co.G
Taylor, Miles G. TX 22nd Cav. Co.B
Taylor, Miles J. AL 26th (O'Neal's) Inf. Co.H 1st Lt.
Taylor, Miles W. GA Inf. 3rd Bn. Co.H
Taylor, Mills VA 59th Mil. Arnold's Co.
Taylor, Milo VA 25th Cav. Co.C Sgt.
Taylor, Milo VA Inf. 21st Bn. 2nd Co.C, 1st Co.D
Taylor, Milton KY 2nd Mtd.Inf. Co.C
Taylor, Milton 4th Conf.Inf. Co.D
Taylor, Milton J. AL Lt.Arty. 2nd Bn. Co.E
Taylor, Milton J. AL 12th Inf. Co.A
Taylor, Mitchell NC 51st Inf. Co.C
Taylor, Mitchell G. GA 30th Inf. Co.C
Taylor, M.J. AL 7th Inf. Co.E
Taylor, M.J. AL Conscr.
Taylor, M.J. GA Smith's Legion Co.D
Taylor, M.J. NC 1st Bn.Jr.Res. Co.B
Taylor, M.K. TN Inf. 22nd Bn. Co.A
Taylor, M.L. LA 6th Inf. Co.A
Taylor, M.L. MS 15th Inf. Co.F
Taylor, M.L. MO St.Guard
Taylor, M.L. TX Cav. McCord's Frontier Regt. Co.F Cpl.
Taylor, M.M. GA 38th Inf. Co.N
Taylor, Mod SC 9th Res. Co.H
Taylor, Monroe NC 23rd Inf. Co.I
Taylor, Monroe NC Walker's Bn. Thomas' Legion Co.H
Taylor, Montgomery L. VA 18th Inf. Co.A
Taylor, Mordecai SC 18th Inf. Co.E
Taylor, Mordecai VA 47th Inf. 2nd Co.K
Taylor, Mordecai R. TX 30th Cav. Co.I
Taylor, Morgan NC 1st Cav. (9th St.Troops) Co.G Cpl.
Taylor, Morgan SC 1st Arty. Co.F
Taylor, Morris A. NC 18th Inf. Co.E
Taylor, Moses TN 7th (Duckworth's) Cav. Co.E
Taylor, Moses TX Cav. Madison's Regt. Co.D
Taylor, Moses VA Cav. Young's Co.
Taylor, Moses VA 59th Inf. 1st Co.G
Taylor, Moses VA 60th Inf. Co.D
Taylor, Moses C. GA 1st Bn.S.S. Co.C
Taylor, Moses M. GA 14th Inf. Co.E
Taylor, Moulton A. NC 6th Inf. Co.D
Taylor, Mozers 1st Choctaw Mtd.Rifles Co.D
Taylor, M.P. MS 41st Inf. Co.E Sgt.
Taylor, M.P. TN 3rd (Clack's) Inf. Co.F
Taylor, M.R. KY 1st (Butler's) Cav. Co.F Sgt.
Taylor, M.R. KY Cav. Thompson's Co.
Taylor, M.S. AL 46th Inf. Co.C 1st Lt.
Taylor, M.S. GA 11th Inf. Co.K
Taylor, Mumphred G. MO 1st Cav. Co.D 2nd Lt.
Taylor, Murray VA 13th Inf. Cadet
Taylor, M.V. AL 5th Cav. Co.H
Taylor, M.V. AL 19th Inf. Co.F
Taylor, M.V. TN 31st Inf. Co.H
Taylor, M.W. AR Cav. 1st Bn. (Stirman's) Co.C
Taylor, M.W. TN 7th Cav. Co.I
Taylor, M.W. TN 12th (Green's) Cav. Co.C
Taylor, M.W. TN 45th Inf. Co.H
Taylor, M.W. TX 35th (Brown's) Cav. Co.C
Taylor, M.W. VA 1st Res. Co.D
Taylor, N. AL 8th Inf. Co.I
Taylor, N. AR 10th Mil. Co.E
Taylor, N. AR 38th Inf. Co.B Sgt.
Taylor, N. GA 11th Inf. Co.C
Taylor, N. LA 3rd (Wingfield's) Cav. Co.H
Taylor, N. MS 2nd Cav. 2nd Co.G Cpl.
Taylor, N. MS 5th Cav. Co.B
Taylor, N. MS 36th Inf. Co.I
Taylor, N. MO Cav. 11th Regt.St.Guard Co.F 1st Lt.
Taylor, N. NC 7th Sr.Res. Clinard's Co.
Taylor, N. VA Hvy.Arty. 20th Bn. Co.C
Taylor, N. VA 5th Inf.
Taylor, N.A. MS 33rd Inf. Co.B
Taylor, N.A. SC 1st (McCreary's) Inf. Co.E
Taylor, N.A. TX 1st Hvy.Arty. Co.A
Taylor, Napoleon B. NC 26th Inf. Co.H
Taylor, Napoleon B. NC 49th Inf. Co.D
Taylor, Napoleon B. VA Hvy.Arty. Coleman's Co.
Taylor, Nat AR 6th Inf. Co.H
Taylor, Nathan GA 25th Inf. Co.K
Taylor, Nathan GA 54th Inf. Co.D
Taylor, Nathan NC 54th Inf. Co.C
Taylor, Nathanael FL 5th Inf. Co.F
Taylor, Nathan H. GA 26th Inf. Co.H
Taylor, Nathan H. LA 4th Cav. Co.E
Taylor, Nathaniel MS 3rd Inf. (St.Troops) Co.B Cpl.
Taylor, Nathaniel MO 2nd N.E. Cav. (Franklin's Regt.) Co.B
Taylor, Nathaniel NC 32nd Inf. Co.I Jr.2nd Lt.
Taylor, Nathaniel VA 25th Cav. Co.D
Taylor, Nathaniel VA 1st Arty. Co.G Sgt.
Taylor, Nathaniel, Jr. VA 32nd Inf. 1st Co.I Sgt.
Taylor, Nathaniel A. TX 31st Cav. Co.C Adj.
Taylor, Nathaniel S. MO 1st N.E. Cav. Co.B
Taylor, N.B. MS 28th Cav. Co.G
Taylor, N.B. MS 6th Inf. Co.B
Taylor, N.B. TN Inf. 1st Bn. (Colms') Co.A
Taylor, N.B. TN 50th (Cons.) Inf. Co.B
Taylor, N.B. TX Cav. Wells' Regt. Co.E
Taylor, N.C. GA Conscr.
Taylor, N.C. TN 21st Inf. Co.H Capt.
Taylor, N.C.C. VA Inf. 1st Bn.Loc.Def. Co.E
Taylor, Neal AL 8th Inf. Co.G
Taylor, Nedom P. FL 11th Inf. Co.K Sgt.
Taylor, Needham NC 54th Inf. Co.C
Taylor, Needham B. LA Cav. Webb's Co.
Taylor, Nelson VA Mil. Scott Cty.
Taylor, Newell VA 46th Inf. Co.F
Taylor, Newton KY 1st Bn.Mtd.Rifles Co.A
Taylor, Newton KY 2nd Mtd.Inf. Co.F
Taylor, Newton MS 3rd (St.Troops) Cav. Co.I
Taylor, Newton TN 28th Inf. Co.E Serv.
Taylor, Newton TX 6th Cav. Co.F Cpl.
Taylor, Newton VA 57th Inf. Co.I
Taylor, Newton TX Cav. Bone's Co.
Taylor, Newton TX Inf. 3rd St.Troops Co.B

Taylor, Newton VA 33rd Inf. Co.H
Taylor, Newton J. MS 14th Inf. Co.K Chap.
Taylor, N.F. SC Vol. Simons' Co.
Taylor, N. Gray TN 60th Mtd.Inf. Co.H
Taylor, N.H. GA 22nd Inf. Co.E
Taylor, N.H. NC 3rd Cav. (41st St.Troops) Co.H
Taylor, N.H. VA 64th Mtd.Inf. Franklin's Co.
Taylor, N.J., Rev. Gen. & Staff Chap.
Taylor, N.M. AR 10th Mil. Co.E
Taylor, N.M. MS 4th Cav. Co.A
Taylor, N.M. MS 46th Inf. Co.B
Taylor, N.N. AL 42nd Inf.
Taylor, Noah NC 2nd Inf. Co.H
Taylor, Noah TN 47th Inf. Co.B
Taylor, Noah TX 21st Cav. Co.B
Taylor, Noah VA 51st Inf. Co.K
Taylor, Nomonal AL 22nd Inf. Co.C
Taylor, Norborne T. VA Hvy.Arty. Coleman's Co. Cpl.
Taylor, N.P. AR 2nd Inf. Co.D Cpl.
Taylor, N.P. FL Conscr.
Taylor, N.P. GA Cav. 1st Bn. Brailsford's Co.
Taylor, N.R. TN 11th (Holman's) Cav. Co.C Cpl.
Taylor, O. MO Cav. Slayback's Regt. Co.A
Taylor, Obadiah GA Cherokee Legion (St.Guards) Co.F 2nd Lt.
Taylor, Obadiah TX 18th Inf. Co.C
Taylor, Obediah MO 3rd Inf. Co.A Capt.
Taylor, O.C. AL 14th Inf. Co.I
Taylor, O.F. VA 53rd Inf. Co.B
Taylor, O.H. TN 19th Inf. Co.F
Taylor, O.J. VA 13th Cav. Co.E
Taylor, O.L. LA Inf.Cons.Crescent Regt. Co.A
Taylor, Oliver AL 45th Inf. Co.E
Taylor, Oliver MO Cav. Coleman's Regt. Co.F Sgt.
Taylor, Oliver TX 12th Cav. Co.D
Taylor, Oliver C. TX 17th Cav. Co.B Capt.
Taylor, Oliver F. VA Inf. Tomlin's Bn. Co.A
Taylor, Oliver H. NC 33rd Inf. Co.E
Taylor, Oliver J. VA 39th Inf. Co.E
Taylor, Oliver P. NC 34th Inf. Co.C
Taylor, O.N. AL Cp. of Instr. Talladega
Taylor, O.P. NC 23rd Inf. Co.I
Taylor, O.P. TN 30th Inf. Co.B Capt.
Taylor, Orville P. VA 2nd Cav. Co.B
Taylor, O.S. VA 3rd Cav.
Taylor, Osborn B. VA 4th Cav. Co.I Cpl.
Taylor, Osborne S. NC 7th Inf. Co.B
Taylor, Osheabud B. NC 2nd Inf. Co.C
Taylor, Osmond B. VA Lt.Arty. 12th Bn. Co.C Jr.1st Lt.
Taylor, Osmond B. VA Lt.Arty. Taylor's Co. Capt.
Taylor, Overton VA 9th Cav. Co.I
Taylor, Overton VA 25th Mil. Co.A
Taylor, Owen AL 33rd Inf. Co.H
Taylor, Owen VA 57th Inf. Co.B
Taylor, Owen H. AL 36th Inf. Co.A
Taylor, Owen H. AL City Guards Lockett's Co.
Taylor, Owen T. VA 51st Inf. Co.K
Taylor, P. GA Inf. 1st Bn. (St.Guards) Co.D
Taylor, P. GA Inf. Arsenal Bn. (Columbus) Co.B
Taylor, P. LA Inf.Crescent Regt. Co.H
Taylor, P. TN Inf. 4th Cons.Rgt. Co.B
Taylor, P. TN 45th Inf. Co.F
Taylor, P. VA 12th Cav. Co.E
Taylor, P. VA 2nd St.Res. Co.B
Taylor, P.A. TN 3rd (Forrest's) Cav. Co.C
Taylor, Paris VA 4th Res. Co.A
Taylor, Paschal H. GA Inf. 3rd Bn. Co.D Sgt.
Taylor, Paschal H. GA 4th Bn.S.S. Co.B Sgt.
Taylor, Patrick AL 1st Inf. Co.E
Taylor, Patrick MS 36th Inf. Co.A
Taylor, Patrick C. NC 43rd Inf. Co.E
Taylor, Patton TN 39th Mtd.Inf. Co.I
Taylor, Paul NC 51st Inf. Co.C
Taylor, Paul TN 14th (Neely's) Cav. Co.E
Taylor, Payton G. TX 22nd Cav. Co.A
Taylor, P.B. MS 3rd Cav. Co.B
Taylor, P.B. MS 1st (King's) Inf. (St.Troops) Co.G
Taylor, P.B. SC Lt.Arty. Gaillard's Co. (Santee Lt.Arty.)
Taylor, P.B. SC Manigault's Bn.Vol. Co.B
Taylor, P.B. TX 3rd Cav. Co.G
Taylor, P.B. TX 23rd Cav. Co.D
Taylor, P.C. AR 45th Cav. Co.H
Taylor, P.C. SC 4th Cav. Co.G
Taylor, P.D. AL 9th Inf. Co.F
Taylor, P.D. KY 8th Mtd.Inf. Co.G
Taylor, P.D. TN 21st (Wilson's) Cav. Co.H
Taylor, P.E. TN Inf. 1st Cons.Regt. Co.G
Taylor, Perry TX 3rd Cav. Co.D
Taylor, Perry VA 18th Cav. Co.A
Taylor, Perry J. MS 27th Inf. Co.C
Taylor, Perry T. TX 37th Cav. Co.K
Taylor, Peter AL 9th Inf. Co.E
Taylor, Peter AR 3rd Cav. Co.I
Taylor, Peter GA 25th Inf. Co.K
Taylor, Peter MS 46th Inf. Co.A Asst.Surg.
Taylor, Peter MO St.Guard Capt.
Taylor, Peter VA 30th Inf. Co.H
Taylor, Peter C. TX 36th Cav. Co.C
Taylor, Peter E. TN 28th (Cons.) Inf. Co.I
Taylor, Peter E. TN 84th Inf. Co.E
Taylor, Peter G. AR 33rd Inf. Co.C Sgt.
Taylor, Peter H. TN 24th Inf. 2nd Co.H
Taylor, Peterson G. VA 8th Inf. Co.G
Taylor, Peterson J. GA Inf. 27th Bn. Co.C
Taylor, Peyton AL 23rd Inf. Co.I
Taylor, Peyton TX 2nd Inf. Co.E
Taylor, Peyton VA 20th Inf. Co.K
Taylor, Peyton VA 46th Inf. Co.F
Taylor, Peyton VA 59th Inf. 3rd Co.C
Taylor, P.G. AR 12th Inf. Co.I
Taylor, P.G. NC 4th Inf. Co.K Sgt.
Taylor, P.H. AL 31st Inf. Co.H
Taylor, P.H. GA 54th Inf. Co.B
Taylor, P.H. KY 12th Cav. Co.A,C
Taylor, P.H. LA Mil.Conf.Guards Regt. Co.D
Taylor, P.H. SC 25th Inf. Co.F
Taylor, P.H. TN 9th (Ward's) Cav. Co.F
Taylor, Pharington TX 6th Cav. Co.F Cpl.
Taylor, Philip VA 9th Mil. Co.B
Taylor, Philip C. VA 4th Cav. Co.F
Taylor, Philip D. VA 26th Inf. Co.C
Taylor, Philip H. AR Cav. 1st Bn. (Stirman's) Adj.
Taylor, Philip Hancock Stirman's Regt.S.S. 1st Lt.,Adj.
Taylor, Phillip H. AR 15th (Josey's) Inf. Co.C Sgt.Maj.
Taylor, Phillip J. AR 1st Mtd.Rifles Co.K
Taylor, Pinckney SC 1st (Hagood's) Inf. 1st Co.D
Taylor, Pinckney F. TX 28th Cav. Co.K,C
Taylor, Pinkney C. TN 2nd (Robison's) Inf. Co.D
Taylor, Pleasant AL 58th Inf. Co.B
Taylor, Pleasant S. VA 15th Inf. Co.H
Taylor, P.M. AR Cav. Harrell's Bn. Co.D Cpl.
Taylor, Powel TN 23rd Inf. 2nd Co.F
Taylor, Powhatan VA Inf. 22nd Bn. Co.A
Taylor, Powhattan VA 2nd Arty. Co.K
Taylor, P.P. AR Cav. Gordon's Regt. Co.D
Taylor, Presley D. KY 1st Inf. Co.G
Taylor, Preston AR 12th Inf. Co.H
Taylor, Preston SC 1st (Hagood's) Inf. 1st Co.H, 2nd Co.E
Taylor, Priestly MS 46th Inf. Co.I
Taylor, P.S. TN 31st Inf. Co.A Sgt.
Taylor, P.S. TX 6th Cav. Co.F 3rd Lt.
Taylor, Quincy S. TX 31st Cav. Co.G
Taylor, R. AL 12th Inf. Co.C Sgt.
Taylor, R. AL QM Dept. Demopolis Wheelwright
Taylor, R. AR 12th Inf. Co.I
Taylor, R. FL 11th Inf. Co.C
Taylor, R. GA Lt.Arty. Clinch's Btty.
Taylor, R. LA Inf.Cons. 18th Regt. & Yellow Jacket Bn. Co.I
Taylor, R. MO 2nd Cav.
Taylor, R. NC 27th Inf.
Taylor, R. SC 1st (Hagood's) Inf. 2nd Co.H
Taylor, R. SC 1st St.Troops Co.F
Taylor, R. SC 15th Inf. Co.E
Taylor, R. TN 3rd (Forrest's) Cav. Co.K
Taylor, R. TX Cav. Border's Regt. Co.C
Taylor, R. TX Cav. Border's Regt. Co.D
Taylor, R. TX Cav. Durant's Co.
Taylor, R. Gen. & Staff Capt.,AAG
Taylor, R.A. AR 2nd Vol. Co.C Cpl.
Taylor, R.A. GA 39th Inf. Co.I
Taylor, R.A. MS 8th Cav. Co.B
Taylor, R.A. MS 28th Cav. Co.E
Taylor, R.A. SC 2nd Cav. Co.B
Taylor, R.A. TN 49th Inf. Co.H Sgt.
Taylor, R.A. TX Cav. Terry's Regt. Co.I
Taylor, R.A. VA 56th Inf. Co.B
Taylor, Randolph TX 25th Cav. Co.D
Taylor, Randolph C. VA 19th Inf. Co.K
Taylor, Randy NC 22nd Inf. Co.A
Taylor, Ranely V. NC 26th Inf. Co.F
Taylor, Raymond T. VA 39th Inf. Co.F
Taylor, R.B. AL 45th Inf. Co.E
Taylor, R.B. FL 1st (Res.) Inf. Co.B
Taylor, R.B. MS 15th (Cons.) Inf. Co.G Cpl.
Taylor, R.B. SC Arty. Zimmerman's Co. (Pee Dee Arty.)
Taylor, R.B. TX 26th Cav. Co.H Far.
Taylor, R.B. VA 9th Cav. Co.A
Taylor, R.C. TN 9th Cav. Co.G
Taylor, R.C. TN 12th (Green's) Cav. Co.F
Taylor, R.C. TN 21st (Wilson's) Cav. Co.F,C
Taylor, R.C. TN 12th Inf. Co.I
Taylor, R.C. TN 12th (Cons.) Inf. Co.I Cpl.
Taylor, R.C. TN 28th Inf. Co.A

Taylor, R.C. TN 31st Inf. Co.H
Taylor, R.C. TN 55th (Brown's) Inf. Co.A
Taylor, R.C. Gen. & Staff Maj.
Taylor, R.C.C. NC 11th (Bethel Regt.) Inf. Co.A
Taylor, R.E. MS 2nd St.Cav. Co.H
Taylor, R.E. MS St.Cav. 2nd Bn. (Harris') Co.C Cpl.
Taylor, R.E. TN 2nd (Ashby's) Cav. Co.I
Taylor, R.E. VA 5th Cav. Co.H
Taylor, Ready 1st Cherokee Mtd.Vol. 1st Co.D, 2nd Co.G QMSgt.
Taylor, Redden AR 5th Inf. Co.B
Taylor, Redding 1st Conf.Inf. 2nd Co.H
Taylor, Rediford J. SC 1st (Hagood's) Inf. 2nd Co.D
Taylor, Redin D. MS 8th Inf. Co.I
Taylor, Redmund H. NC 5th Cav. (63rd St.Troops) Co.B
Taylor, Renno B. LA 19th Inf. Co.A
Taylor, Reuben AL 21st Inf. Co.K Cpl.
Taylor, Reuben GA Arty. 11th Bn. (Sumter Arty.) Co.A
Taylor, Reuben MS 2nd St.Cav. Co.F
Taylor, Reuben MS 8th Inf. Co.D
Taylor, Reuben SC 15th Inf. Co.C
Taylor, Reuben TX Cav. Hardeman's Regt. Co.E
Taylor, Reuben VA 1st Arty. Co.F
Taylor, Reuben VA Arty. Dance's Co. Artif.
Taylor, Reuben VA Inf. 26th Bn. Co.D,H
Taylor, Reuben A. TX 16th Cav. Co.F 1st Lt.
Taylor, Reuben B. GA 66th Inf. Co.A
Taylor, Reuben R. TN 27th Inf. Co.I
Taylor, Reuben S. MS 39th Inf. Co.G
Taylor, Reuben W. AL Cav. Moreland's Regt.
Taylor, Reubin A. TX Inf. 3rd St.Troops Co.D
Taylor, Revel J. VA 39th Inf. Co.G 3rd Lt.
Taylor, Revil J. VA 61st Inf. Co.K 1st Lt.
Taylor, Revil J. VA Inf. Cohoon's Bn. Co.C 2nd Lt.
Taylor, Reziah TN 55th (McKoin's) Inf. Dillehay's Co.
Taylor, R.F. GA 56th Inf. Co.I
Taylor, R.F. MS Cav. Powers' Regt. Co.A
Taylor, R.F. VA 82nd Mil. Co.D
Taylor, R.F. Gen. & Staff Chap.
Taylor, R.G. LA Mil.Conf.Guards Regt. Co.H
Taylor, R.G. MO Cav. 3rd Bn. QMSgt.
Taylor, R.G. SC Palmetto S.S. Co.M
Taylor, R.H. AL Inf. 2nd Regt. Co.D
Taylor, R.H. AL 4th Res. Co.G
Taylor, R.H. AL 38th Inf. Co.I
Taylor, R.H. AR 2nd Cav. Co.C
Taylor, R.H. AR Cav. Gordon's Regt. Co.B
Taylor, R.H. MS 7th Cav. Co.K Capt.
Taylor, R.H. MS 2nd Part.Rangers Co.K Capt.
Taylor, R.H. MO Cav. Jackman's Regt. Co.E
Taylor, R.H. MO St.Guard
Taylor, R.H. NC 57th Inf. Co.D
Taylor, R.H. NC 62nd Inf. Co.F
Taylor, R.H. TN 5th Inf. 1st Co.F, 2nd Co.E
Taylor, R.H. TN 20th Inf. Co.D
Taylor, R.H. TN 24th Inf. Co.D Cpl.
Taylor, R.H. TN 40th Inf. Co.I
Taylor, R.H. TX 17th Inf. Co.I 1st Lt.
Taylor, R.H. VA Cav. Caldwell's Bn. Taylor's Co. Capt.
Taylor, R.H. VA Hvy.Arty. Allen's Co.
Taylor, R.H. VA Inf. 2nd Bn.Loc.Def. Co.C
Taylor, R.H. Gen. & Staff Surg.
Taylor, R.I. AL 14th Inf. Co.B
Taylor, Richard AL 27th Inf. Co.G
Taylor, Richard AL 61st Inf. Co.K
Taylor, Richard AR 7th Inf. Co.G
Taylor, Richard AR 8th Inf. New Co.D Cpl.
Taylor, Richard GA 25th Inf. Co.E
Taylor, Richard GA 38th Inf. 2nd Co.I
Taylor, Richard GA 42nd Inf. Co.E,A
Taylor, Richard GA 60th Inf. 2nd Co.A
Taylor, Richard KY 10th (Johnson's) Cav. Co.D
Taylor, Richard LA 9th Inf. Col.
Taylor, Richard MO 5th Cav. Co.G
Taylor, Richard MO 8th Cav. Co.C
Taylor, Richard MO Cav. Williams' Regt. Co.I
Taylor, Richard NC 17th Inf. (2nd Org.) Co.F
Taylor, Richard NC 31st Inf. Co.G
Taylor, Richard NC 61st Inf. Co.B
Taylor, Richard NC Mallett's Co.
Taylor, Richard TN 5th (McKenzie's) Cav. Co.C
Taylor, Richard TX 33rd Cav. Co.A Capt.
Taylor, Richard VA 14th Inf. Co.I
Taylor, Richard VA 45th Inf. Co.C
Taylor, Richard Gen. & Staff Lt.Gen.
Taylor, Richard A. GA 26th Inf. Co.I
Taylor, Richard B. AL 19th Inf. Co.D,K Sgt.
Taylor, Richard B. GA 35th Inf. Co.A
Taylor, Richard C. VA 5th Inf. Co.E
Taylor, Richard C. VA 6th Inf. Co.H Capt.
Taylor, Richard C. VA 26th Inf. Co.C
Taylor, Richard D. NC 30th Inf. Co.G
Taylor, Richard D.B. GA 3rd Cav. (St.Guards) Co.F
Taylor, Richard E. VA 3rd Cav. 1st Co.I
Taylor, Richard F. MO 2nd Cav. 3rd Co.K
Taylor, Richard F. MO Cav. 3rd Bn. Co.D
Taylor, Richard F. MO Cav. Wood's Regt. Co.C 1st Sgt.
Taylor, Richard G. GA Arty. Moore's Btty. Can.
Taylor, Richard H. TX 1st Inf. Co.L
Taylor, Richard H. VA 12th Inf. 2nd Co.I
Taylor, Richard H. VA 49th Inf. Co.I
Taylor, Richard H. Gen. & Staff Surg.
Taylor, Richard J. LA 1st Cav. Co.E
Taylor, Richard J. MS 13th Inf. Co.D Cpl.
Taylor, Richard K. FL 6th Inf. Co.E
Taylor, Richard L. GA Cav. Nelson's Ind.Co.
Taylor, Richard L. MS 2nd Part.Rangers Co.F,D
Taylor, Richard M. AL 4th Inf. Co.B
Taylor, Richard M. MS 15th Inf. Co.H
Taylor, Richard M. NC 15th Inf. Co.A
Taylor, Richard P. AR Inf. Cocke's Regt. Co.B
Taylor, Richard P. NC 30th Inf. Co.G Capt.
Taylor, Richard S. GA Inf. Taylor's Co. Capt.
Taylor, Richard S. VA Cav. 39th Bn. Co.D
Taylor, Richard S. VA 6th Inf. Co.C
Taylor, Richardson W. VA 15th Inf. Co.B Ord.Sgt.
Taylor, Richard T. VA 34th Inf. Co.F
Taylor, Richmond P. AR Lt.Arty. Zimmerman's Btty.
Taylor, Rinnes VA 9th Cav. Co.B
Taylor, R.J. AL Mil. Bligh's Co.
Taylor, R.J. AR 7th Inf. Co.F Sgt.
Taylor, R.J. MS 9th Inf. Old Co.K
Taylor, R.J. MS 39th Inf. Co.D
Taylor, R.J. SC 1st (Butler's) Inf. Co.F
Taylor, R.J. VA 15th Inf. Co.G
Taylor, R.K. FL 1st Cav. Co.G 1st Lt.
Taylor, R.K. Gen. & Staff Surg.
Taylor, R.L. GA 4th (Clinch's) Cav.
Taylor, R.L. GA 54th Inf. Co.A
Taylor, R.L. MS 6th Cav. Co.A
Taylor, R.L. MS 4th Inf. Co.I
Taylor, R.L. NC 62nd Inf. Co.F
Taylor, R.L. TN 15th (Cons.) Cav. Co.D,E
Taylor, R.M. KY 5th Cav. Co.F
Taylor, R.N. AR 31st Inf. Co.H Sgt.
Taylor, R.N. TX 19th Inf. Co.B
Taylor, R.O. TN 30th Inf. Co.G Sgt.
Taylor, Robert AL 7th Cav. Co.H
Taylor, Robert AL 1st Inf. Co.D
Taylor, Robert AL 3rd Res. Co.B
Taylor, Robert AL 4th Res. Co.H
Taylor, Robert AL 28th Inf. Co.E,L
Taylor, Robert AL 32nd Inf. Co.K
Taylor, Robert AR Cav. McGehee's Regt. Co.A
Taylor, Robert AR 23rd Inf. Co.C
Taylor, Robert FL 5th Inf. Co.B
Taylor, Robert GA 3rd Cav. (St.Guards) Co.D
Taylor, Robert GA 8th Cav. Co.K
Taylor, Robert GA 62nd Cav. Co.H,K
Taylor, Robert GA 1st Reg. Co.F
Taylor, Robert GA 3rd Inf. Co.E
Taylor, Robert GA 39th Inf. Co.D
Taylor, Robert GA 60th Inf. Co.G
Taylor, Robert KY 7th Cav. Co.G
Taylor, Robert KY 10th (Diamond's) Cav. Co.E
Taylor, Robert KY 5th Mtd.Inf. Co.D Sgt.
Taylor, Robert, Jr. LA 18th Inf. Co.F
Taylor, Robert LA Inf.Cons. 18th Regt. & Yellow Jacket Bn. Co.E
Taylor, Robert LA 19th Inf.
Taylor, Robert MS 9th Cav. Co.A
Taylor, Robert MS Cav. Hughes' Bn. Co.B
Taylor, Robert MS 2nd Inf. (A. of 10,000) Co.A
Taylor, Robert MS 11th Inf. Co.A
Taylor, Robert MS 24th Inf. Co.B
Taylor, Robert MO Cav. Williams' Regt. Co.I
Taylor, Robert MO 12th Inf. Co.B
Taylor, Robert NC 1st Cav. (9th St.Troops) Co.G
Taylor, Robert NC 5th Inf. Co.B
Taylor, Robert NC 26th Inf. Co.F
Taylor, Robert SC 4th St.Troops Co.G
Taylor, Robert SC 7th (Ward's) Bn.St.Res. Co.F
Taylor, Robert SC Sea Fencibles Symons' Co. Music.
Taylor, Robert TN 37th Inf. Co.E
Taylor, Robert TN 55th (Brown's) Inf. Co.D
Taylor, Robert TX 8th Cav. Co.I
Taylor, Robert TX 11th Cav. Co.H
Taylor, Robert TX Cav. Madison's Regt. Co.B
Taylor, Robert VA 8th Cav. Co.C
Taylor, Robert VA Cav. 41st Bn. Co.G
Taylor, Robert VA Cav. Hounshell's Bn. Huffman's Co.
Taylor, Robert VA Hvy.Arty. Wilkinson's Co.
Taylor, Robert VA 5th Inf. Co.E
Taylor, Robert VA 6th Inf. Co.I
Taylor, Robert VA 20th Inf. Co.E
Taylor, Robert VA 21st Inf. Co.E

Taylor, Robert VA Inf. 25th Bn. Co.C
Taylor, Robert VA 46th Inf. Co.A Teamster
Taylor, Robert VA 50th Inf. Co.E
Taylor, Robert VA Mil. Grayson Cty.
Taylor, Robert 7th Conf.Cav. Co.E
Taylor, Robert Cherokee Regt. Miller's Co.
Taylor, Robert A. NC 34th Inf. Co.E
Taylor, Robert A. TX 10th Inf. Co.H
Taylor, Robert A. VA Hvy.Arty. Coleman's Co.
Taylor, Robert A. VA 42nd Inf. Co.C
Taylor, Robert B. GA 2nd Cav. Co.A 1st Sgt.
Taylor, Robert B. MS 20th Inf. Co.B
Taylor, Robert B. NC 2nd Arty. (36th St.Troops) Co.G
Taylor, Robert B. TN 1st (Turney's) Inf. Co.A Sgt.
Taylor, Robert B. VA 6th Inf. Co.C,A Maj.
Taylor, Robert B. Gen. & Staff, QM Dept.
Taylor, Robert C. MO Inf. 4th Regt.St.Guard Co.A 1st Lt.
Taylor, Robert C. NC 50th Inf. Co.I
Taylor, Robert C. VA 4th Inf. Co.G 1st Lt.
Taylor, Robert C. VA 6th Inf. Co.A
Taylor, Robert D. AL 61st Inf. Co.H
Taylor, Robert D. SC 6th Inf. 1st Co.B
Taylor, Robert E. AL Inf. 1st Regt. Co.E
Taylor, Robert E. AR Inf. 1st Bn. Co.F
Taylor, Robert E. VA 5th Cav. (12 mo. '61-2) Co.E
Taylor, Robert E. VA 13th Cav. Co.G Sgt.
Taylor, Robert E. VA 4th Res. Co.C
Taylor, Robert E. VA 6th Inf. 2nd Co.E
Taylor, Robert F. FL 2nd Cav. Co.G
Taylor, Robert F. GA 10th Cav. (St.Guards) Co.D
Taylor, Robert G. MS 30th Inf. Co.D
Taylor, Robert G. SC 5th Inf. 1st Co.G
Taylor, Robert G. TN 59th Mtd.Inf. Co.F
Taylor, Robert G. VA 53rd Inf. Co.D
Taylor, Robert H. GA 4th Inf. Co.F
Taylor, Robert H. LA 22nd Inf. Jones' Co.
Taylor, Robert H. LA 31st Inf. Co.H
Taylor, Robert H. MS 17th Inf. Co.H 1st Lt.
Taylor, Robert H. MO 2nd Inf. Co.I
Taylor, Robert H. TN 30th Inf. Co.F
Taylor, Robert H. TX 22nd Cav. Co.G Col.
Taylor, Robert H. VA 16th Cav. Co.F Capt.
Taylor, Robert H. VA 14th Inf. Co.E Cpl.
Taylor, Robert H. VA 18th Inf. Co.K
Taylor, Robert H. VA 45th Inf. Co.H 1st Lt.
Taylor, Robert H. 1st Conf.Eng.Troops Co.K
Taylor, Robert Henry NC 12th Inf. Co.D,B
Taylor, Robert J. AR 6th Inf. Co.I,K
Taylor, Robert J. FL Cav. 5th Bn. Co.A,E
Taylor, Robert J. VA 9th Inf. Chap.
Taylor, Robert J. VA 17th Inf. Co.H
Taylor, Robert J. VA 56th Inf. Co.B
Taylor, Robert J. Gen. & Staff Chap.
Taylor, Robert K. KY 9th Mtd.Inf. Co.G
Taylor, Robert K. MS 42nd Inf. Co.H Sgt.
Taylor, Robert L. TN 59th Mtd.Inf. Co.I
Taylor, Robert L. VA 30th Inf. Co.H
Taylor, Robert M. NC 22nd Inf. Co.H
Taylor, Robert M. VA 4th Inf. Co.A
Taylor, Robert M. VA 55th Inf. Co.C
Taylor, Robert O. AR 33rd Inf. Co.G
Taylor, Robert O. VA 17th Cav. Co.B
Taylor, Robert P. FL 3rd Inf. Co.D
Taylor, Robert P. GA 1st (Ramsey's) Inf. Co.A
Taylor, Robert P. GA 53rd Inf. Co.G Lt.Col.
Taylor, Robert P. VA 32nd Inf. Co.C 2nd Lt.
Taylor, Robert R. AL 5th Cav. Co.B Sgt.
Taylor, Robert R. TN Cav. Newsom's Regt. Co.G
Taylor, Robert R. TN 7th Inf. Co.H
Taylor, Robert S. AR 3rd Inf. Co.D Lt.Col.
Taylor, Robert S. VA 3rd Cav. Co.F
Taylor, Robert S. VA 3rd Arty. Co.B
Taylor, Robertson VA 6th Inf. Co.G Adj.
Taylor, Robertson Gen. & Staff Capt.,AAG
Taylor, Robert T. GA 17th Inf. Co.B
Taylor, Robert T. VA 17th Inf. Co.D
Taylor, Robert T. VA 21st Inf. Co.F
Taylor, Robert T. VA 22nd Inf. Co.D
Taylor, Robert W. MO 3rd Inf. Co.B
Taylor, Robert W. NC Loc.Def. Griswold's Co. Sgt.
Taylor, Robert W. SC 14th Inf. Co.F
Taylor, Robert W. TN 33rd Inf. Co.B
Taylor, Robert W. TX 16th Cav. Co.F
Taylor, Robert W. VA 2nd Arty. Co.G
Taylor, Robert W. VA Inf. 22nd Bn. Co.G
Taylor, Robinson VA 25th Mil. Co.C
Taylor, Roderick LA 19th Inf. Co.H
Taylor, Roger F. LA 1st Cav. Co.H 1st Lt.
Taylor, Roland S. NC 5th Inf. Co.G
Taylor, Rory TN 3rd (Clack's) Inf. Co.A
Taylor, Ross GA 57th Inf. Co.A
Taylor, R.P. TX 14th Inf. Co.H Cpl.
Taylor, R.R. AL 2nd Cav. Co.C
Taylor, R.R. TN 10th (DeMoss') Cav. Co.B
Taylor, R.R. TN 18th (Newsom's) Cav. Co.D
Taylor, R.R. TN 1st (Feild's) & 27th Inf. (Cons.) Co.I
Taylor, R.R. TN 29th Inf. Co.I
Taylor, R.R. TX 14th Field Btty.
Taylor, R.S. GA 2nd Bn.St.Troops Lt.Col.
Taylor, R.S. GA 4th Res. Col.
Taylor, R.S. MS 1st (King's) Inf. (St.Troops) Co.G 1st Sgt.
Taylor, R.S. MS Inf. 1st Bn.St.Troops (30 days '64) Co.A 2nd Lt.
Taylor, R.S. VA 1st (Farinholt's) Res. Co.H Cpl.
Taylor, R.T. AL 56th Part.Rangers Co.B
Taylor, R.T. KY 3rd & 7th (Cons.) Cav. Co.A 1st Lt.
Taylor, R.T. Thomas Brig. Maj.,QM
Taylor, Rufus TN Cav. 12th Bn. (Day's) Co.E Sgt.
Taylor, Rufus TN 26th Inf.
Taylor, Rufus VA 7th Cav. Co.A Sgt.
Taylor, Rufus VA 7th Cav. Co.F
Taylor, Rufus VA 77th Mil. Co.A
Taylor, Rufus H. MO 3rd Cav. Co.H
Taylor, Rufus M. MS 2nd Part.Rangers Co.D,I
Taylor, Rufus M. MS 9th Inf. Old Co.C
Taylor, R.W. KY 3rd Cav. Surg.
Taylor, R.W. KY 10th (Johnson's) Cav. Co.E 1st Sgt.
Taylor, R.W. MO 3rd Inf. Co.E
Taylor, R.W. NC 60th Inf. Co.C
Taylor, R.W. SC 10th Inf. Co.F
Taylor, R.W. Gen. & Staff AQM
Taylor, R.Z. TN 19th & 20th (Cons.) Cav. Co.F
Taylor, R.Z. TN 20th (Russell's) Cav. Co.A
Taylor, S. AL Inf. 2nd Regt. Co.I
Taylor, S. AR 45th Cav. Co.C 3rd Lt.
Taylor, S. GA 11th Inf. Co.C
Taylor, S. GA 66th Inf. Co.A
Taylor, S. KY Cav. 2nd Bn. (Dortch's) Co.D
Taylor, S. KY Morgan's Men Co.D
Taylor, S. LA Lt.Arty. 6th Field Btty. (Grosse Tete Flying Arty.) Sgt.
Taylor, S. LA Mil. 4th Regt. 1st Brig. 1st Div. Co.E
Taylor, S. LA 11th Inf. Co.K
Taylor, S. LA Mil. British Guard Bn. Coburn's Co.
Taylor, S. MS 5th Cav. Co.H
Taylor, S. MS 8th Cav. Co.D
Taylor, S. MS Cav.Part.Rangers Rhodes' Co.
Taylor, S. MS 41st Inf. Co.I
Taylor, S. MO 1st N.E. Cav. Co.I Sgt.
Taylor, S. NC 2nd Inf. Co.E
Taylor, S. NC 3rd Jr.Res. Co.A
Taylor, S. TN 21st Cav. Co.H
Taylor, S. TN 7th Inf. Co.E
Taylor, S. 1st Conf.Cav. 1st Co.C
Taylor, S. 14th Conf.Cav. Co.F
Taylor, S.A. NC 8th Sr.Res. McNeill's Co.
Taylor, S.A. TN 7th (Duckworth's) Cav. Co.L Sgt.
Taylor, S.A. TN 31st Inf. Co.D
Taylor, S.A. Gen. & Staff Hosp.Stew.
Taylor, Sam Deneale's Regt. Choctaw Warriors Co.A
Taylor, Sam C. TX 4th Inf. Co.B
Taylor, Samuel AL 8th Inf. Co.A
Taylor, Samuel AL 13th Inf. Co.H
Taylor, Samuel AR 1st (Crawford's) Cav. Co.G
Taylor, Samuel AR 1st Vol. Anderson's Co.
Taylor, Samuel AR 31st Inf. Co.A
Taylor, Samuel GA 13th Inf. Co.D
Taylor, Samuel GA 38th Inf. Co.N
Taylor, Samuel GA 43rd Inf. Co.F
Taylor, Samuel GA 60th Inf. Co.G
Taylor, Samuel LA 16th Inf. Co.H
Taylor, Samuel MS 2nd Cav. Co.E
Taylor, Samuel MS Cav. 3rd Bn. (Ashcraft's) Co.A
Taylor, Samuel MS Cav. 24th Bn. Co.C
Taylor, Samuel MO 12th Inf. Co.C
Taylor, Samuel NC 3rd Arty. (40th St.Troops) Co.H
Taylor, Samuel NC Lt.Arty. 13th Bn. Co.F
Taylor, Samuel NC 4th Bn.Jr.Res. Co.A
Taylor, Samuel NC 5th Inf. Co.H
Taylor, Samuel NC 13th Inf. Co.I
Taylor, Samuel NC 25th Inf. Co.I
Taylor, Samuel NC 45th Inf. Co.C
Taylor, Samuel NC Hoskins' Co. (Loc.Def.)
Taylor, Samuel NC Inf. Thomas Legion Co.K
Taylor, Samuel SC Arty. Gregg's Co. (McQueen Lt.Arty.)
Taylor, Samuel SC 4th St.Troops Co.K
Taylor, Samuel SC 5th Bn.Res. Co.C
Taylor, Samuel TN 11th Cav.
Taylor, Samuel TN 16th (Logwood's) Cav. Co.F
Taylor, Samuel TN 2nd (Robison's) Inf. Co.I
Taylor, Samuel TX 1st Hvy.Arty. Co.D

Taylor, Samuel VA 4th Cav. Co.K
Taylor, Samuel VA 8th Cav. Co.G
Taylor, Samuel VA 21st Cav. Co.I
Taylor, Samuel VA 25th Cav. Co.D
Taylor, Samuel VA 25th Cav. Co.G
Taylor, Samuel VA 3rd Lt.Arty. Co.D
Taylor, Samuel VA Lt.Arty. E.J. Anderson's Co.
Taylor, Samuel VA 3rd Inf.Loc.Def. 1st Co.G,B, 2nd Co.G 2nd Lt.
Taylor, Samuel VA 15th Inf. Co.H
Taylor, Samuel VA Inf. 21st Bn. 2nd Co.E
Taylor, Samuel VA 48th Inf. Co.H
Taylor, Samuel VA 54th Mil. Co.A
Taylor, Samuel VA 64th Mtd.Inf. Co.E
Taylor, Samuel VA 64th Mtd.Inf. 2nd Co.F
Taylor, Samuel VA Mil. Scott Cty.
Taylor, Samuel Conf.Cav. Clarkson's Bn. Ind. Rangers Co.H
Taylor, Samuel Conf.Inf. 1st Bn. Co.I
Taylor, Samuel Exch.Bn. 1st Co.A,CSA
Taylor, Samuel 1st Cherokee Mtd.Vol. 1st Co.K
Taylor, Samuel Deneale's Regt. Choctaw Warriors Co.A
Taylor, Samuel A. AR 6th Inf. New Co.D
Taylor, Samuel A. AR 12th Inf. Co.I
Taylor, Samuel A. LA 9th Inf. Co.H
Taylor, Samuel A. TN 4th Inf. Co.A
Taylor, Samuel A. TX 10th Inf. Co.F
Taylor, Samuel A. Conf.Inf. 1st Bn. 2nd Co.B 1st Lt.
Taylor, Samuel B. KY 10th (Johnson's) Cav. Co.E Capt.
Taylor, Samuel C. AR Cav. Wright's Regt. Co.E Capt.
Taylor, Samuel C. GA 4th Res. Co.D
Taylor, Samuel C. KY 3rd Mtd.Inf. Co.D Cpl.
Taylor, Samuel C. MS 3rd Cav. Co.I Ord.Sgt.
Taylor, Samuel C. NC 18th Inf. Co.D
Taylor, Samuel C. VA 39th Inf. Co.G
Taylor, Samuel C. VA 64th Mil. Powell's Co. 1st Lt.
Taylor, Samuel E. GA 38th Inf. Co.N 1st Lt.
Taylor, Samuel F. MO Inf. 2nd Regt.St.Guard Maj.
Taylor, Samuel F. MO Inf. 3rd Bn. Co.C Capt.
Taylor, Samuel F. MO 6th Inf. Co.B Capt.
Taylor, Samuel F. NC Cav. 15th Bn. Co.B
Taylor, Samuel F. VA Hvy.Arty. A.J. Jones' Co.
Taylor, Samuel F. VA 52nd Mil. Co.B
Taylor, Samuel G. VA 40th Inf.
Taylor, Samuel H. MS 2nd Inf. Co.H Capt.
Taylor, Samuel H. NC 17th Inf. (2nd Org.) Co.D
Taylor, Samuel H. VA 46th Inf. 2nd Co.A
Taylor, Samuel H. VA 46th Inf. 2nd Co.K Music.
Taylor, Samuel H. Golden's Staff Capt.
Taylor, Samuel J. NC 3rd Cav. (41st St.Troops) Co.E
Taylor, Samuel J. NC 3rd Arty. (40th St.Troops) Co.K
Taylor, Samuel J. NC 64th Inf. Co.D
Taylor, Samuel J. TN 14th Inf. Co.L Cpl.
Taylor, Samuel James SC 4th Inf. Co.K
Taylor, Samuel K. GA 36th (Villepigue's) Inf. Co.E,F
Taylor, Samuel K. SC 14th Inf. Co.E
Taylor, Samuel L. AR 11th Inf. Co.D
Taylor, Samuel L. TN 7th (Duckworth's) Cav. Co.I
Taylor, Samuel M. TN 2nd (Ashby's) Cav. Co.E Sgt.
Taylor, Samuel M. TN Cav. 4th Bn. (Branner's) Co.D
Taylor, Samuel P. VA 42nd Inf. Co.C
Taylor, Samuel R. NC 33rd Inf. Co.K
Taylor, Samuel R. TN 61st Mtd.Inf. Co.A
Taylor, Samuel R. VA 16th Inf. 2nd Co.H, Co.G
Taylor, Samuel R. VA 39th Inf. Co.A
Taylor, Samuel S. AR 14th (McCarver's) Inf. Co.D Sgt.
Taylor, Samuel S. AR 21st Inf. Co.K
Taylor, Samuel T. TN 7th (Duckworth's) Cav. Co.K Capt.
Taylor, Samuel W. GA 64th Inf. Co.K
Taylor, Samuel W. MS 3rd (St.Troops) Cav. Co.F
Taylor, Samuel W. TN 26th Inf. Co.F Sgt.
Taylor, Sanders TN 44th Inf. Co.I Sgt.
Taylor, Sanders TN 44th (Cons.) Inf. Co.A
Taylor, Sanford AR 10th Mil. Co.B
Taylor, Saunders VA Inf. 23rd Bn. Co.C
Taylor, Saunders VA 45th Inf. Co.L
Taylor, Saunders VA Inf. 45th Bn. Co.F
Taylor, S.B. AL 17th Inf. Co.A Cpl.
Taylor, S.B. AR Barker's Cav.
Taylor, S.B. AR Cav. McGehee's Regt. Co.A
Taylor, S.B. MO 6th Cav. Co.F
Taylor, S.B. NC 22nd Inf. Co.B
Taylor, S.C. GA 4th (Clinch's) Cav. Co.E
Taylor, S.C. VA 3rd Cav. Co.B
Taylor, S.C. VA 16th Inf. Co.A
Taylor, Scott VA 72nd Mil.
Taylor, S.E. GA Cav. Alexander's Co.
Taylor, S.E. GA 10th Inf. Co.A 2nd Lt.
Taylor, S.E. TN 51st Inf. Co.G
Taylor, S.E. TN 51st (Cons.) Inf. Co.H
Taylor, S.E. 10th Conf.Cav. Co.G
Taylor, Seaborn AL 60th Inf. Co.E
Taylor, Seaborn AL 3rd Bn. Hilliard's Legion Vol. Co.A
Taylor, Seaborn GA 48th Inf. Co.G
Taylor, Seaborn J. GA 57th Inf. Co.I
Taylor, Seaborn S. GA Inf. 3rd Bn. Co.E
Taylor, Seaborn S. GA 37th Inf. Co.C Cpl.
Taylor, Septimus J. Gen. & Staff AASurg.
Taylor, Sevin AR 30th Inf. Co.F
Taylor, S.F. GA 24th Inf. Co.F
Taylor, S.F. MS 22nd Inf. Co.K
Taylor, S.F. SC Inf. Hampton Legion Co.D
Taylor, S.G. AL 12th Inf. Co.G
Taylor, S.G. MS 31st Inf. Co.H
Taylor, S.G. MS Grace's Co. (St.Troops)
Taylor, S.H. AL 3rd Inf. Co.E
Taylor, S.H. FL 2nd Cav.
Taylor, S.H. GA 55th Inf. Co.F Cpl.
Taylor, S.H. NC 8th Sr.Res. Jacobs' Co.
Taylor, S.H. SC 2nd Rifles Co.F
Taylor, S.H. SC 22nd Inf. Co.F
Taylor, S.H. SC 24th Inf. Co.F
Taylor, Shadrick MS 37th Inf. Co.D
Taylor, Sidney GA 52nd Inf. Co.F
Taylor, Sidney NC 22nd Inf. Co.A
Taylor, Sidney R. NC 14th Inf. Co.E
Taylor, Sidney S. GA 1st (Ramsey's) Inf. Co.C
Taylor, Silas MO 10th Inf. Co.A
Taylor, Silas VA 52nd Inf. Co.A
Taylor, Silas VA 77th Mil. Co.B
Taylor, Silas F. VA Cav. Thurmond's Co.
Taylor, Silas F. VA 79th Mil. Co.1 Capt.
Taylor, Simeon NC 2nd Cav. (19th St.Troops) Co.E
Taylor, Simeon VA 34th Inf. Co.H Sgt.
Taylor, Simeon J. GA Phillips' Legion Co.L
Taylor, Simeon L. TN 13th (Gore's) Cav. Co.B
Taylor, Simon B. NC 35th Inf. Co.A Lt.Col.
Taylor, Simon D. VA 11th Cav. Co.D Cpl.
Taylor, Simon D. VA 13th Inf. Co.K
Taylor, Simon H. LA 8th Inf. Co.F
Taylor, Simon P. SC 13th Inf. Co.G
Taylor, S.J. GA Phillips' Legion Co.F
Taylor, S.J. KY 2nd Mtd.Inf. Co.F
Taylor, S.J. MO 6th Cav. Co.F Cpl.
Taylor, S.J. SC 6th Inf. 2nd Co.K Sgt.
Taylor, S.J. SC 9th Inf. Co.D
Taylor, S.J. SC Palmetto S.S. Co.L Cpl.
Taylor, S.J. TN 45th Inf. Co.H Sgt.
Taylor, S.K. GA Lt.Arty. Pritchard's Co. (Washington Arty.)
Taylor, S.K. GA Mil. Furlow's Bn.Res. Co.C Capt.
Taylor, S.K. SC 5th St.Troops Co.I 3rd Lt.
Taylor, S.K. SC 9th Res. Co.E Sgt.
Taylor, S.K. Lt.Arty. Dent's Btty.,CSA
Taylor, S.K. 1st Conf.Inf. 1st Co.F
Taylor, Skelton TN 1st (Carter's) Cav. Co.M 2nd Lt.
Taylor, Skelton TN 11th Inf. Co.E Sgt.
Taylor, Skelton TN 60th Mtd.Inf. Co.F
Taylor, Skiler KY 2nd (Duke's) Cav. Co.F
Taylor, S.L. LA 14th Inf. Co.A
Taylor, S.L. TN 7th (Duckworth's) Cav. Co.K Sgt.
Taylor, S.L. TX 13th Vol. Co.C
Taylor, S.L. VA 166th Mil. R.G. Lively's Co.
Taylor, S.M. LA 2nd Inf. Co.I
Taylor, S.M. MS 22nd Inf. Co.K
Taylor, S.M. VA 23rd Cav. Co.B
Taylor, Smith TX Cav. Giddings' Bn. Co.A Lt.
Taylor, Smith VA 22nd Cav. Co.K
Taylor, Smith VA 29th Inf. Co.G
Taylor, Smith VA 72nd Mil.
Taylor, Smith R. TX 31st Cav. Co.C
Taylor, S.N. TN Inf. Harman's Regt. Co.A 2nd Lt.
Taylor, Soloman L. GA 12th Cav. Co.F
Taylor, Solomon AR 1st Inf. Co.H
Taylor, Solomon GA 25th Inf. Co.K
Taylor, Solomon NC 1st Arty. (10th St.Troops) Co.I
Taylor, Solomon SC 5th St.Troops Co.G
Taylor, Solomon SC 7th Res. Co.A
Taylor, Solomon VA 52nd Inf. Co.A
Taylor, Solomon C. VA 22nd Inf. Co.D
Taylor, Solomon S. AL 3rd Res. Co.E
Taylor, Solomon T. TX 35th (Brown's) Cav. Co.D,F
Taylor, Solon Z. TN 18th Inf. Co.A
Taylor, Sol R. AL 38th Inf. Co.A
Taylor, S.P. AL 8th Inf. Co.D
Taylor, S.P. AL 32nd Inf. Co.I 2nd Lt.
Taylor, S.P. TX 12th Cav. Co.A

Taylor, S.P. TX 4th Inf. (St.Troops) Co.D
Taylor, Spence MS 42nd Inf. Co.I Cpl.
Taylor, Spencer MS 9th Inf. Co.H
Taylor, Spencer MS 41st Inf. Co.G
Taylor, Spencer C. GA Inf. 10th Bn. Co.A
Taylor, Spencer R. GA 24th Inf. Co.H Cpl.
Taylor, Sporks LA 31st Inf. Co.A
Taylor, Spotswood B. NC 53rd Inf. Co.H Capt.
Taylor, S.R. GA 3rd Cav. (St.Guards) Co.E Sgt.
Taylor, S.R. GA 29th Inf. Co.F
Taylor, S.R. TN 50th (Cons.) Inf. Co.I
Taylor, S.S. AL 15th Bn.Part.Rangers Co.A
Taylor, S.S. AL 56th Part.Rangers Co.A
Taylor, S.S. AL 21st Inf. Co.I Capt.
Taylor, S.S. AL 30th Inf. Co.E
Taylor, S.S. AR 27th Inf. New Co.C Capt.
Taylor, S.S. GA 8th Cav. Co.G Cpl.
Taylor, S.S. GA 62nd Cav. Co.G Cpl.
Taylor, S.S. GA 3rd Res. Co.K
Taylor, S.S. MO 10th Inf. Co.F
Taylor, S.S. VA Inf. 4th Bn.Loc.Def. Co.B
Taylor, S.T. AL 10th Cav. Co.I
Taylor, S.T. AL 32nd Inf. Co.G Capt.
Taylor, S.T. AL 32nd & 58th (Cons.) Inf. Capt.
Taylor, S.T. KY Scouts Capt.
Taylor, S.T. MO St.Guard
Taylor, S.T. TX 13th Vol. 1st Co.I
Taylor, S.T. VA 11th Cav. Co.D
Taylor, Stacker J. TN 14th Inf. Co.F,E
Taylor, Stanford AR 34th Inf. Co.H
Taylor, Stanton NC 3rd Arty. (40th St.Troops) Co.A
Taylor, Stanton T. MO Inf. 3rd Bn. Co.E
Taylor, St.Clair VA 52nd Inf. Co.A
Taylor, Stephen AL 5th Cav. Co.H
Taylor, Stephen AL Mil. 4th Vol. Modawell's Co.
Taylor, Steph. AL 26th Inf. Co.C
Taylor, Stephen AL 41st Inf. Co.H
Taylor, Stephen AL 43rd Inf. Co.F
Taylor, Stephen GA Cav. 9th Bn. (St.Guards) Co.C
Taylor, Stephen GA 2nd Res. Co.E
Taylor, Stephen NC 3rd Cav. (41st St.Troops) Co.H
Taylor, Stephen NC 51st Inf. Co.F
Taylor, Stephen NC 56th Inf. Co.G
Taylor, Stephen SC 1st Arty. Co.A
Taylor, Stephen TN 51st (Cons.) Inf. Co.C
Taylor, Stephen A. MS 19th Inf. Co.G Cpl.
Taylor, Stephen A. NC 26th Inf. Co.K
Taylor, Stephen A. VA Lt.Arty. King's Co.
Taylor, Stephen A. VA Mil. Washington Cty.
Taylor, Stephen H. AL 27th Inf. Co.B
Taylor, Stephen H. AL 55th Vol. Co.B
Taylor, Stephen L. VA Cav. Hounshell's Bn. Huffman's Co.
Taylor, Stephen L. VA Cav. Thurmond's Co.
Taylor, Stephen M. NC 46th Inf. Co.C
Taylor, Stephen P. TN 31st Inf. Co.E
Taylor, Stephen S. MO 5th Inf. Co.B
Taylor, Stephen V. MO Cav. 3rd Bn. Co.C
Taylor, Steptoe B. VA 40th Inf. Co.E Sgt.
Taylor, Stevens M. VA Lt.Arty. Arch. Graham's Co.
Taylor, Stewart MS 42nd Inf. Co.H
Taylor, Stiles L. GA 45th Inf. Co.K
Taylor, Strong R. TN 50th Inf. Co.H,B
Taylor, Sumner TN 18th Inf. Co.B
Taylor, S.V. MO 1st & 3rd Cons.Cav. Co.I Cpl.
Taylor, S.V. MO 3rd Cav. Co.C
Taylor, S.W. GA Cav. 22nd Bn. (St.Guards) Co.F
Taylor, S.W. GA 8th Inf. Co.G 2nd Lt.
Taylor, S.W. LA 17th Inf. Co.C 2nd Lt.
Taylor, Sweeney 1st Choctaw Mtd.Rifles Co.I
Taylor, Sydney J. AR 26th Inf. Co.F
Taylor, Snydnor W. VA 3rd Inf. Co.E
Taylor, Sylus W. AL Lt.Arty. 2nd Bn.
Taylor, Sylvan S. VA 25th Cav. Co.C
Taylor, Sylvan S. VA Inf. 21st Bn. 1st Co.D
Taylor, Sylvester NC 2nd Inf. Co.I Capt.
Taylor, T. AL 10th Inf. Co.I
Taylor, T. AR Cav. McGehee's Regt. Co.F
Taylor, T. SC 24th Inf. Co.F
Taylor, T. TX 17th Cons.Dismtd.Cav. Co.I
Taylor, T. TX 25th Cav. Smith's Co.
Taylor, T. TX Inf. Chambers' Bn.Res.Corps Co.B
Taylor, T. VA 5th Cav. 2nd Co.F
Taylor, T. VA 11th Cav. Co.I
Taylor, T. VA 2nd St.Res. Co.C,A
Taylor, T. VA 46th Inf. Co.C
Taylor, T.A. KY 1st Inf. Co.C
Taylor, T.A. NC 27th Inf. Co.K
Taylor, T.A. TX 14th Inf. Co.H
Taylor, T.A. Lt.Arty. Dent's Btty.,CSA
Taylor, T.A.H. AL 4th (Russell's) Cav. Co.E
Taylor, T.A.H. AL 17th Inf. Co.G
Taylor, Talver L. TX 4th Field Btty.
Taylor, T.B. AL Cav. Barbiere's Bn. Truss' Co.
Taylor, T.B. AL 17th Inf. Co.F
Taylor, T.B. MO 5th Cav. Co.F
Taylor, T.B. NC 12th Inf. Co.H
Taylor, T.B. TN 7th (Duckworth's) Cav. Co.D Bugler
Taylor, T.C. AL 48th Inf. Co.A
Taylor, T.C. TN 47th Inf. Co.B
Taylor, T.C. VA 2nd Cav. Co.B
Taylor, T.C. VA 20th Cav. Co.C
Taylor, T.C.W. LA 4th Inf. New Co.G
Taylor, T.E. AL Cav. 24th Bn. Co.A
Taylor, T.E. AL 53rd (Part.Rangers) Co.E
Taylor, Teackle W. VA 39th Inf. Co.G
Taylor, Teakle FL 11th Inf. Co.K
Taylor, Telemachus VA 3rd Cav. Co.F Capt.
Taylor, Temple LA Millaudon's Co. (Jefferson Mtd.Guards,Co.B)
Taylor, Temple C. TN 44th Inf. Co.I
Taylor, Temple C. TN 44th (Cons.) Inf. Co.A
Taylor, Temple H. VA 2nd Arty. Co.G
Taylor, Temple W. TN 44th Inf. Co.I
Taylor, Temple W. TN 44th (Cons.) Inf. Co.A
Taylor, T.F. MS 1st (Johnston's) Inf. Co.E
Taylor, T.F. SC Inf. Hampton Legion Co.D
Taylor, T.F. TX 24th & 25th Cav. (Cons.) Co.E
Taylor, T.F. 1st Cherokee Mtd.Vol. 2nd Co.G
Taylor, T.G. AL 43rd Inf. Co.D
Taylor, T.H. AL 5th Cav. Co.B
Taylor, T.H. GA 39th Inf. Co.F,G Sgt.
Taylor, T.H. KY 2nd (Duke's) Cav. Co.E
Taylor, T.H. MS 28th Cav. Co.H
Taylor, T.H. NC 62nd Inf. Co.F
Taylor, T.H. TN 18th (Newsom's) Cav. Co.D Capt.
Taylor, T.H. TN 46th Inf. Co.D
Taylor, T.H. TX 3rd Cav. Co.A
Taylor, T.H. TX 19th Cav. Co.I
Taylor, T.H. VA 10th Cav. Co.A Sgt.
Taylor, T.H. VA 49th Inf. Co.B
Taylor, Thad AR Cav. Gordon's Regt. Co.B Capt.
Taylor, Theodore TN 5th Cav. Co.I
Taylor, Theodore TN 3rd (Clack's) Inf. Co.I
Taylor, Theodoric MS 36th Inf. Co.G,K
Taylor, Theodorick J. VA 2nd Arty. Co.G
Taylor, Theophilus NC 17th Inf. Co.D
Taylor, Theophilus B. NC 44th Inf. Co.D
Taylor, Theophilus E. NC 3rd Inf. Co.A
Taylor, Theo. T. Drayton's Brig. Capt.,AAG
Taylor, Tho NC 62nd Inf. Co.F
Taylor, Thomas AL 7th Cav. Co.G,E,A 1st Lt.
Taylor, Thomas AL Cav. Murphy's Bn. Co.C
Taylor, Thomas AL Inf. 2nd Regt. Co.I 1st Lt.
Taylor, Thomas AL 5th Inf. New Co.A
Taylor, Thomas AL 26th (O'Neal's) Inf. Co.D Capt.
Taylor, Thomas AL 34th Inf. Co.C
Taylor, Thomas AL Arty. 4th Bn. Hilliard's Legion Co.A
Taylor, Thomas AL Rives' Supp.Force 9th Congr.Dist.
Taylor, Thomas AR 6th Inf. Co.F
Taylor, Thomas FL 6th Inf. Co.I
Taylor, Thomas GA 1st (Symons') Res. Co.C
Taylor, Thomas GA Inf. 4th Bn. (St.Guards) Co.A
Taylor, Thomas GA 5th Inf. (St.Guards) Russell's Co.
Taylor, Thomas GA 43rd Inf. Co.C
Taylor, Thomas GA 59th Inf. Co.G,I
Taylor, Thomas KY 7th Cav. Co.C
Taylor, Thomas KY 10th (Johnson's) Cav. New Co.I
Taylor, Thomas KY 1st Bn.Mtd.Rifles Co.A
Taylor, Thomas LA 8th Inf. Co.K Cpl.
Taylor, Thomas MS 8th Cav. Co.I
Taylor, Thomas MS 38th Cav. Co.H Cpl.
Taylor, Thomas MS 1st (Percy's) Inf. Co.D
Taylor, Thomas MS 33rd Inf. Co.H
Taylor, Thomas MO 2nd N.E. Cav. (Franklin's Regt.) Co.B
Taylor, Thomas MO Cav. Fristoe's Regt. Co.I
Taylor, Thomas NC 1st Arty. (10th St.Troops) Co.H
Taylor, Thomas NC 2nd Inf. Co.E
Taylor, Thomas NC 5th Sr.Res. Co.H
Taylor, Thomas NC 6th Inf. Co.H
Taylor, Thomas NC 8th Inf. Sgt.
Taylor, Thomas NC 17th Inf. (2nd Org.) Co.D
Taylor, Thomas NC 47th Inf. Co.K 2nd Lt.
Taylor, Thomas NC 64th Inf. Co.E
Taylor, Thomas SC 4th Cav. Co.K
Taylor, Thomas SC 5th Inf. 1st Co.A
Taylor, Thomas SC 8th Res.
Taylor, Thomas SC 13th Inf. Co.K
Taylor, Thomas SC Palmetto S.S. Co.A
Taylor, Thomas SC Cav.Bn. Hampton Legion Co.D Capt.
Taylor, Thomas TN 3rd (Forrest's) Cav. Co.C

Taylor, Thomas TN 3rd (Forrest's) Cav. Co.K
Taylor, Thomas TN 10th (DeMoss') Cav. Co.B
Taylor, Thomas TN 12th (Green's) Cav. Co.F
Taylor, Thomas TN 44th (Cons.) Inf. Co.B
Taylor, Thomas TN 49th Inf. Co.B
Taylor, Thomas TX 15th Cav. Co.D
Taylor, Thomas TX Cav. Mann's Regt. Co.I
Taylor, Thomas VA Cav. Hounshell's Bn. Thurmond's Co.
Taylor, Thomas VA Mil. 38th Regt. Col.
Taylor, Thomas VA 40th Inf. Co.K
Taylor, Thomas VA 47th Inf. Co.E
Taylor, Thomas VA 48th Inf. Co.B Sgt.
Taylor, Thomas VA 55th Inf. Co.C
Taylor, Thomas VA 60th Inf. Co.A
Taylor, Thomas VA 146th Mil. Co.F
Taylor, Thomas VA Murphy's Co.
Taylor, Thomas 15th Conf.Cav. Co.H
Taylor, Thomas 3rd Conf.Eng.Troops Co.D Sgt.
Taylor, Thomas 1st Choctaw & Chickasaw Mtd.Rifles 2nd Co.C
Taylor, Thomas Gen. & Staff 1st Lt.,ADC
Taylor, Thomas A. AR 37th Inf. Co.C
Taylor, Thomas A. TX 1st (Yager's) Cav. Co.I
Taylor, Thomas A. TX Cav. 8th (Taylor's) Bn. Co.D
Taylor, Thomas A. VA 12th Inf. Co.F
Taylor, Thomas B. MS 46th Inf. Co.A Music.
Taylor, Thomas B. NC 1st Arty. (10th St.Troops) Co.I
Taylor, Thomas B. NC 16th Inf. Co.L
Taylor, Thomas B. NC 17th Inf. (2nd Org.) Co.I
Taylor, Thomas B. NC 32nd Inf. Co.H
Taylor, Thomas B. NC Inf. Thomas Legion Co.E
Taylor, Thomas B. TN 2nd (Smith's) Cav. Sgt.
Taylor, Thomas B. TN 4th (McLemore's) Cav. Co.A Sgt.
Taylor, Thomas B. TN 12th (Green's) Cav. Co.I Sgt.
Taylor, Thomas B. TN Cav. Newsom's Regt.
Taylor, Thomas B.C. VA 19th Cav. Co.I
Taylor, Thomas C. TN 20th Cav. Sgt.
Taylor, Thomas C. VA 22nd Cav. Co.E
Taylor, Thomas D. AL 39th Inf. Co.H
Taylor, Thomas D. GA Inf. 5th Bn. (St.Guards) Co.B
Taylor, Thomas D. NC Walker's Bn. Thomas' Legion Co.C
Taylor, Thomas D. TX 15th Cav. Co.B
Taylor, Thomas D. VA 49th Inf. Co.I
Taylor, Thomas E. TN 16th Inf. Co.K 1st Lt.
Taylor, Thomas E. TN Inf. 22nd Bn. Co.A Capt.
Taylor, Thomas E. TX 34th Cav. Co.E
Taylor, Thomas E. VA 23rd Inf. Co.C 1st Lt.
Taylor, Thomas E. VA 47th Inf. 3rd Co.H
Taylor, Thomas F. VA 4th Cav. Co.G 2nd Lt.
Taylor, Thomas F. 1st Cherokee Mtd.Vol. Lt.Col.
Taylor, Thomas G. AL 8th Inf. Co.D
Taylor, Thomas G. AR 26th Inf. Co.K Cpl.
Taylor, Thomas G. NC 34th Inf. Co.E
Taylor, Thomas G. TN 10th (DeMoss') Cav. Co.B Sgt.
Taylor, Thomas H. KY 1st Inf. Col.
Taylor, Thomas H. MS 34th Inf. Co.A
Taylor, Thomas H. TN 1st (Feild's) Inf. Co.C
Taylor, Thomas H. VA Lt.Arty. 12th Bn. Co.D
Taylor, Thomas H. VA 61st Inf. Co.H
Taylor, Thomas H. Gen. & Staff Brig.Gen.
Taylor, Thomas Henry TX 18th Cav. Co.C
Taylor, Thomas I. VA 32nd Inf. 1st Co.H Sgt.
Taylor, Thomas J. AL Lt.Arty. 2nd Bn.
Taylor, Thomas J. AL Inf. 1st Regt. Co.D Sgt.
Taylor, Thomas J. AL 27th Inf. Co.I 1st Sgt.
Taylor, Thomas J. AL 43rd Inf. Co.B
Taylor, Thomas J. AL 43rd Inf. Co.D
Taylor, Thomas J. AL 49th Inf.
Taylor, Thomas J. AL Cav. 5th Bn. Hilliard's Legion Co.A
Taylor, Thomas J. GA 12th (Robinson's) Cav. (St.Guards) Co.K
Taylor, Thomas J. MS 2nd Inf. Co.K
Taylor, Thomas J. MS 9th Inf. Old Co.I
Taylor, Thomas J. MS 26th Inf. Co.C 1st Lt.
Taylor, Thomas J. MO Cav. Jackman's Regt. Co.F
Taylor, Thomas J. NC 6th Inf. Co.F
Taylor, Thomas J. NC 21st Inf. Co.G
Taylor, Thomas J. NC 56th Inf. Co.D
Taylor, Thomas J. TN 29th Inf. Co.I
Taylor, Thomas J. TX Cav. 6th Bn. Co.E
Taylor, Thomas J. TX 8th Cav. Co.D
Taylor, Thomas J. VA 1st Arty. Co.B 2nd Lt.
Taylor, Thomas J. VA Lt.Arty. 1st Bn. Co.B 2nd Lt.
Taylor, Thomas J. VA Arty. Richardson's Co. 2nd Lt.
Taylor, Thomas J. VA 7th Inf. Co.K
Taylor, Thomas J. VA 56th Inf. Co.E Capt.
Taylor, Thomas Jeff. TX 16th Cav. Co.F 1st Lt.
Taylor, Thomas K. GA 2nd Cav. Co.G
Taylor, Thomas K. GA Cav. 15th Bn. (St.Guards) Wooten's Co.
Taylor, Thomas L. GA Lt.Arty. 14th Bn. Co.B Cpl.
Taylor, Thomas L. GA Lt.Arty. Anderson's Btty. Cpl.
Taylor, Thomas L. TX 15th Cav. Co.E
Taylor, Thomas L. TX 28th Cav. Co.I
Taylor, Thomas L. TX Cav. Mann's Bn. Cox's Co.
Taylor, Thomas L. VA 9th Cav. Co.H Asst.Surg.
Taylor, Thomas L.L. TN 6th (Wheeler's) Cav. Co.C
Taylor, Thomas M. AR Cav. 1st Bn. (Stirman's) Co.D
Taylor, Thomas M. AR 23rd Inf. Co.C Sgt.
Taylor, Thomas M. GA Siege Arty. 28th Bn. Co.A
Taylor, Thomas M. GA 34th Inf. Co.H
Taylor, Thomas M. NC 1st Inf. (6 mo. '61) Co.A
Taylor, Thomas M. NC 61st Inf. Co.H
Taylor, Thomas N. MS 31st Inf. Co.D
Taylor, Thomas N. VA 9th Cav. Co.C
Taylor, Thomas P. AL 34th Inf. Co.G
Taylor, Thomas P. KY Cav. 1st Bn. Co.C
Taylor, Thomas P. KY 1st Bn.Mtd.Rifles Co.B
Taylor, Thomas P. LA Inf. 11th Bn. Co.G
Taylor, Thomas P. LA Inf.Cons.Crescent Regt. Co.D
Taylor, Thomas P. VA 2nd Cav. Co.B
Taylor, Thomas R. AL 11th Inf. Co.H
Taylor, Thomas R. FL 1st Cav. Co.D Sgt.
Taylor, Thomas R. KY 2nd (Duke's) Cav. Co.A 1st Sgt.
Taylor, Thomas R. TX 9th Cav. Co.D
Taylor, Thomas R. TX 22nd Cav. Co.B
Taylor, Thomas S. AL 6th Inf. Co.G 1st Lt.
Taylor, Thomas S. MO 10th Cav. Co.H
Taylor, Thomas S. VA 24th Inf. Co.D Capt.
Taylor, Thomas S.L. VA 7th Inf. Co.D 2nd Lt.
Taylor, Thomas T. AR 8th Inf. New Co.I
Taylor, Thomas T. MS Cav. 1st Bn. (Miller's) Cole's Co.
Taylor, Thomas T. MS 14th Inf. Co.I
Taylor, Thomas W. KY 4th Cav. Co.C Cpl.
Taylor, Thomas W. NC 1st Bn.Jr.Res. Co.B 1st Lt.
Taylor, Thomas W. NC 12th Inf. Co.D,B
Taylor, Thomas W. NC Inf. 13th Bn. Co.C
Taylor, Thomas W. TX Cav. Ragsdale's Bn. Co.B Sgt.
Taylor, Thomas W. VA 1st Arty. Co.B
Taylor, Thomas W. VA 8th Inf. Co.B
Taylor, Thomas W. VA 32nd Inf. 1st Co.H
Taylor, Thomas W. VA 49th Inf. Co.I
Taylor, Thomas W. VA 53rd Inf. Co.F
Taylor, Thompson 1st Choctaw Mtd.Rifles Co.I
Taylor, Thompson Y. SC 14th Inf. Co.E Sgt.
Taylor, Thornton A. VA 97th Mil. Co.F
Taylor, Thurgood VA 1st St.Res. Co.D
Taylor, Thurman T. TX Cav. McCord's Frontier Regt. 2nd Co.A
Taylor, Tillman AL 3rd Res. Co.E
Taylor, Tilman FL Inf. 2nd Bn. Co.I
Taylor, Timothy AL 33rd Inf. Co.A
Taylor, T.J. AL 15th Inf. Co.H
Taylor, T.J. AL 27th Inf. Co.G
Taylor, T.J. AL 49th Inf. Co.K Capt.
Taylor, T.J. AL 59th Inf. Co.H
Taylor, T.J. AL Arty. 4th Bn. Hilliard's Legion Co.D
Taylor, T.J. AR 7th Inf. Co.A
Taylor, T.J. AR 15th Mil. Co.A
Taylor, T.J. AR 27th Inf. Co.D
Taylor, T.J. GA 1st Troops & Defences (Macon) Co.B
Taylor, T.J. KY 12th Cav. Co.B
Taylor, T.J. LA 17th Inf. 2nd Co.D
Taylor, T.J. LA 17th Inf. Co.H
Taylor, T.J. MS 18th Cav. Co.A 1st Sgt.
Taylor, T.J. MS Inf. 2nd St.Troops Co.K
Taylor, T.J. MS 32nd Inf. Co.B Color Cpl.
Taylor, T.J. MS 41st Inf. Co.H Sgt.
Taylor, T.J. MS 46th Inf. Co.D
Taylor, T.J. NC 30th Inf. Co.A
Taylor, T.J. NC 67th Inf. Co.F
Taylor, T.J. SC 5th St.Troops Co.C
Taylor, T.J. SC 9th Res. Co.F
Taylor, T.J. SC Post Guard Senn's Co.
Taylor, T.J. TN Inf. 3rd Bn. Co.B
Taylor, T.J. TN 45th Inf. Co.A
Taylor, T.J. 10th Conf.Cav. Co.A Ord.Sgt.
Taylor, T.J. Brush Bn.
Taylor, T.J. Exch.Bn. Co.E,CSA
Taylor, T. James Gen. & Staff Asst.Surg.
Taylor, T.L. GA 50th Inf.
Taylor, T.L. TN 4th Inf. Co.C Sgt.

Taylor, T.L. TX 8th Inf. Co.K
Taylor, T.L. VA 3rd Res. Co.G
Taylor, T.L. Gen. & Staff, Medical Dept. Asst.Surg.
Taylor, T.L.L. TN 20th Inf. Co.B
Taylor, T.M. AL 34th Inf. Co.A
Taylor, T.M. GA Lt.Arty. Croft's Btty. (Columbus Arty.)
Taylor, T.M. GA 1st Reg. Co.I
Taylor, T.M. GA 5th Inf. (St.Guards) Rucker's Co. Cpl.
Taylor, T.M. KY 4th Cav. Co.F
Taylor, T.N. TX 10th Cav. Co.B
Taylor, T.O. TX 5th Inf. Co.B
Taylor, Tobias VA 51st Inf. Co.K
Taylor, T.P. AL 2nd Cav. Co.C
Taylor, T.P. LA 17th Inf. Co.D
Taylor, T.R. TX Granbury's Cons.Brig. Co.A
Taylor, T.R. TX 6th Inf. Co.C
Taylor, Travis NC 42nd Inf. Co.A
Taylor, Travis W. VA 5th Cav. (12 mo. '61-2) Co.E Capt.
Taylor, T.T. AR 32nd Inf. Co.I
Taylor, T.T. MS 1st Cav. Co.K
Taylor, T.T. TX Cav. McCord's Frontier Regt. Co.H
Taylor, T.T. TX 11th Inf. Co.D
Taylor, T.T. VA Inf. 4th Bn.Loc.Def. Co.D
Taylor, Turner S. NC 2nd Cav. (19th St.Troops) Co.K 1st Sgt.
Taylor, Turner T. MS 18th Inf. Co.I Cpl.
Taylor, T.V. Hosp.Stew.
Taylor, T.W. AL 34th Inf. Co.B
Taylor, T.W. TX 10th Cav. Co.D
Taylor, T.W. TX 5th Inf. Co.F
Taylor, T.W. VA Cav. 41st Bn. Co.F
Taylor, T.W. VA Lt.Arty. 1st Bn. Co.B
Taylor, T.W. VA Arty. Richardson's Co.
Taylor, T.W. Conf.Cav. 6th Bn. Co.G 2nd Lt.
Taylor, U. GA Inf. 25th Bn. (Prov.Guard) Co.D
Taylor, Uel E. GA 2nd Bn.S.S. Co.B
Taylor, Uel Ewell GA 1st Bn.S.S. Co.B
Taylor, Upton B. VA 3rd Inf.Loc.Def. Co.D
Taylor, Uriah GA 5th Inf. Co.I
Taylor, Urias AL 28th Inf. Co.L
Taylor, Valentine D. VA 97th Mil. Co.I
Taylor, Virgil TN 18th Inf. Co.D
Taylor, V.M. AL 28th Inf. Co.K
Taylor, W. AL 7th Cav. Co.D
Taylor, W. AL 7th Inf. Surg.
Taylor, W. AL 18th Inf. Co.C
Taylor, W. AL 22nd Inf. Co.K
Taylor, W. AR 12th Bn.S.S. Co.B
Taylor, W. AR 58th Mil. Co.A Cpl.
Taylor, W. AR Inf. Hardy's Regt. Co.I
Taylor, W. FL 2nd Cav. Co.H
Taylor, W. GA 11th Inf. Co.K
Taylor, W. GA 54th Inf. Co.D
Taylor, W. LA Inf. 7th Bn. Co.C
Taylor, W. LA Mil. British Guard Bn. Hamilton's Co. Sgt.
Taylor, W. MS 2nd St.Cav. Co.D,K
Taylor, W. NC Joyner's Bn. Co.F
Taylor, W. SC Arty. Melchers' Co. (Co.B, German Arty.)
Taylor, W. SC 1st (Hagood's) Inf. 2nd Co.H
Taylor, W. SC 23rd Inf. Co.C
Taylor, W. SC Inf. Hampton Legion Asst.Surg.
Taylor, W. TX 24th & 25th Cav. (Cons.) Co.E
Taylor, W. TX 25th Cav. Co.E
Taylor, W. TX Cav. Terry's Regt. Co.I
Taylor, W. 20th Conf.Cav. 2nd Co.H
Taylor, W. 1st Cherokee Mtd.Vol. 1st Co.B
Taylor, W. 1st Chickasaw Inf. Haynes' Co.
Taylor, W.A. AL 1st Cav. 2nd Co.D,A
Taylor, W.A. AL 10th Cav. Co.B
Taylor, W.A. AL Cav. Graves' Co.
Taylor, W.A. AL Arty. 1st Bn. Co.B
Taylor, W.A. AL 12th Inf. Co.G,E
Taylor, W.A. AL 14th Inf. Co.B
Taylor, W.A. AR 3rd Inf. Co.F
Taylor, W.A. AR 21st Inf. Co.F
Taylor, W.A. GA 4th Res. Co.B
Taylor, W.A. GA 5th Inf. (St.Guards) Miller's Co. Sgt.
Taylor, W.A. GA 6th Inf. (St.Guards) Co.G
Taylor, W.A. GA 54th Inf. Co.D Cpl.
Taylor, W.A. LA 16th Inf. Co.G
Taylor, W.A. MS 1st Cav. Co.C
Taylor, W.A. MS 6th Cav. Co.D
Taylor, W.A. MS Cav. Davenport's Bn. (St.Troops) Co.B
Taylor, W.A. MS St.Cav. Perrin's Bn. Co.E
Taylor, W.A. MS 5th Inf. (St.Troops) Co.A
Taylor, W.A. MS 14th (Cons.) Inf. Co.I Cpl.
Taylor, W.A. MS Wilkinson Cty. Minute Men Co.B
Taylor, W.A. NC 37th Inf. Co.C
Taylor, W.A. TN 7th (Duckworth's) Cav. Co.E
Taylor, W.A. TN 21st (Wilson's) Cav. Co.G Sgt.
Taylor, W.A. TN 21st & 22nd (Cons.) Cav. Co.I Sgt.
Taylor, W.A. TN 62nd Mtd.Inf. Co.B Cpl.
Taylor, W.A. TN 63rd Inf. Co.H Drum.
Taylor, W.A. TX 24th & 25th Cav. (Cons.) Co.E Sgt.
Taylor, W.A. TX 25th Cav. Maj.
Taylor, W.A. TX Cav. Giddings' Bn. Carr's Co.
Taylor, W.A. TX 7th Field Btty.
Taylor, W.A. TX 9th (Nichols') Inf. Co.B
Taylor, W.A. VA 4th Cav. Co.B
Taylor, W.A. VA Lt.Arty. Fry's Co.
Taylor, W.A. VA 5th Bn.Res. Co.A
Taylor, W.A. Trans-MS Conf.Cav. 1st Bn. Co.A
Taylor, Wade C. MS 43rd Inf. Co.H
Taylor, Wallace TX 1st Inf. Co.L
Taylor, Waller MS 29th Inf. Co.D
Taylor, Walter AL 1st Bn.Cadets Co.A
Taylor, Walter GA Inf. (St.Armory Guards) Green's Co. 2nd Lt.
Taylor, Walter MS 27th Inf. Co.D
Taylor, Walter NC 5th Cav. (63rd St.Troops) Co.H
Taylor, Walter NC 62nd Inf.
Taylor, Walter VA 54th Mil. Co.A
Taylor, Walter B. TX 11th (Spaight's) Bn.Vol. Co.A
Taylor, Walter C. MO 3rd Cav. Co.C
Taylor, Walter C. NC 29th Inf. Co.A
Taylor, Walter H. VA 6th Inf. Co.G 2nd Lt.
Taylor, Walter J. AL 13th Inf. Co.C Capt.
Taylor, Walton 1st Choctaw & Chickasaw Mtd.Rifles Co.A
Taylor, Ward, Jr. TX 19th Inf. Co.F
Taylor, Warren GA 23rd Inf. Co.C
Taylor, Warren LA 22nd Inf. Co.C
Taylor, Warren H. NC 61st Inf. Co.C
Taylor, W.A.S. VA 3rd Inf.Loc.Def. Co.A 1st Sgt.
Taylor, W.A.S. Gen. & Staff Hosp.Stew.
Taylor, Washington AL 18th Inf. Co.A
Taylor, Washington FL 4th Inf. Co.H
Taylor, Washington KY 2nd Mtd.Inf. Co.F
Taylor, Washington KY 9th Mtd.Inf. Co.D
Taylor, Washington NC Coast Guards Galloway's Co.
Taylor, Washington H. NC 35th Inf. Co.H
Taylor, Washington M. AL 42nd Inf. Co.E
Taylor, Washington W. GA 52nd Inf. Co.A
Taylor, W.B. AL 2nd Cav. Co.K
Taylor, W.B. AL 53rd (Part.Rangers) Co.I
Taylor, W.B. AL 17th Inf. Co.F
Taylor, W.B. AL 22nd Inf. Co.B
Taylor, W.B. AL 37th Inf. Co.C,D
Taylor, W.B. AL 38th Inf. Co.A
Taylor, W.B. GA 5th Inf. Co.G
Taylor, W.B. KY 5th Mtd.Inf. Co.E
Taylor, W.B. MS Cav. Part.Rangers Rhodes' Co.
Taylor, W.B. MS 7th Inf. Co.K
Taylor, W.B. MS Inf. Cooper's Co.
Taylor, W.B. NC 1st Inf. (6 mo. '61) Co.C Cpl.
Taylor, W.B. NC 27th Inf. Co.I
Taylor, W.B. SC 3rd Inf. Co.D
Taylor, W.B. TN 13th (Gore's) Cav. Co.I Sgt.
Taylor, W.B. TN 20th (Russell's) Cav. Co.A,F
Taylor, W.B. TN 22nd Inf. Co.G
Taylor, W.B. TN 55th (Brown's) Inf. Co.H Cpl.
Taylor, W.B. TX 21st Inf. Co.A
Taylor, W.B. VA Hvy.Arty. 20th Bn. Co.C
Taylor, W.B. 14th Conf.Cav. Co.F
Taylor, W.B.F.P. SC 24th Inf. Co.F
Taylor, W.C. GA 12th (Robinson's) Cav. (St.Guards) Co.H
Taylor, W.C. MS 11th (Cons.) Cav. Co.I
Taylor, W.C. NC 1st Arty. (10th St.Troops) Co.I
Taylor, W.C. TN 11th (Holman's) Cav. Co.C
Taylor, W.C. TN 11th (Holman's) Cav. Co.D
Taylor, W.C. TN 35th Inf. Co.E
Taylor, W.C. TN 55th (Brown's) Inf. Co.G
Taylor, W.C. TX 32nd Cav. Co.D Cpl.
Taylor, W.C. TX 1st Hvy.Arty. Co.F,H
Taylor, W.C. VA 5th Cav. Co.K
Taylor, W.C. VA 6th Inf. Vickery's Co.
Taylor, W.C. VA 60th Inf. Co.F
Taylor, W. Calvin SC 20th Inf. Co.K
Taylor, W.C.P. AL 5th Inf. New Co.H
Taylor, W.D. GA 7th Inf. Co.G
Taylor, W.D. KY 3rd Bn.Mtd.Rifles
Taylor, W.D. LA 17th Inf. Co.C
Taylor, W.D. MO Inf. Clark's Regt. Co.C
Taylor, W.D. TX 5th Cav. Co.H
Taylor, W.D. TX 4th Inf. (St.Troops) Co.D
Taylor, W.D. VA Hvy.Arty. Allen's Co.
Taylor, W.E. AL 7th Inf. Co.D
Taylor, W.E. AL Detailed Conscr.
Taylor, W.E. LA 2nd Cav. Co.G
Taylor, W.E. MS 2nd Part.Rangers Co.K
Taylor, W.E. MS 7th Cav. Co.K
Taylor, W.E. NC 31st Inf. Co.G

Taylor, W.E. SC Lt.Arty. 3rd (Palmetto) Bn. Co.C
Taylor, W.E. TN 20th Inf. Co.H
Taylor, W.E. TN Inf. 22nd Bn. Co.B Sgt.
Taylor, W.E. TN 23rd Inf. Co.C
Taylor, W.E. TX 21st Inf. Co.I
Taylor, W.E. VA Inf. 4th Bn.Loc.Def. Co.F
Taylor, W.E., Jr. VA 54th Mil. Co.C,D
Taylor, Weistell NC 58th Inf. Co.E
Taylor, Wesley GA 54th Inf. Co.F
Taylor, Wesley MS Mtd.Inf. (St.Troops) Maxey's Co.
Taylor, Wesley MS 37th Inf. Co.D
Taylor, Wesley MS 46th Inf. Co.D
Taylor, Wesley MO 3rd Inf. Co.H
Taylor, Wesley NC 29th Inf. Co.G
Taylor, Wesley TX 35th (Brown's) Cav. 2nd Co.B
Taylor, Wesley VA 72nd Mil.
Taylor, Wesley G. VA 39th Inf. Co.D
Taylor, Wesly NC 34th Inf. Co.A
Taylor, Wesly NC 54th Inf. Co.B
Taylor, West MS 6th Cav. Co.H
Taylor, Westley AL Inf. 1st Regt. Co.A
Taylor, Weston NC 8th Inf. Co.F
Taylor, W.F. AL 23rd Inf. Co.D
Taylor, W.F. AL 31st Inf. Co.H
Taylor, W.F. AR 16th Inf. Co.G
Taylor, W.F. GA 11th Cav. Co.D
Taylor, W.F. MS 1st Cav. Co.A
Taylor, W.F. MS 12th Cav. Co.A
Taylor, W.F. MS 1st Lt.Arty. Co.B
Taylor, W.F. NC 1st Cav. (9th St.Troops) Co.C
Taylor, W.F. NC 31st Inf. Co.G
Taylor, W.F. SC Cav. 19th Bn. Co.B
Taylor, W.F. TN 7th (Duckworth's) Cav. Co.A Lt.Col.
Taylor, W.F. TN Douglass' Bn.Part.Rangers Coffee's Co.
Taylor, W.F. TN 59th Mtd.Inf. Co.I
Taylor, W.F. 2nd Conf.Eng.Troops Co.A
Taylor, W.G. AR 1st (Monroe's) Cav. Co.L
Taylor, W.G. AR 7th Cav. Co.B 3rd Lt.
Taylor, W.G. AR 10th Mil. Co.B
Taylor, W.G. GA 10th Inf. Co.A
Taylor, W.G. MS 37th Inf. Co.H
Taylor, W.G. TN 2nd (Ashby's) Cav. Co.I
Taylor, W.G. TN Arty. Fisher's Co.
Taylor, W.H. AL Cav. 4th Bn. (Love's) Co.C
Taylor, W.H. AL 7th Cav. Co.G
Taylor, W.H. AL 53rd (Part.Rangers) Co.C
Taylor, W.H. AL 4th Res. Co.G
Taylor, W.H. AL 14th Inf. Co.B,I
Taylor, W.H. AL 27th Inf. Co.E
Taylor, W.H. AL 30th Inf. Co.C
Taylor, W.H. AL Loc.Def. & Sp.Serv. Toomer's Co.
Taylor, W.H. AR Cav. McGehee's Regt. Co.F
Taylor, W.H. AR 14th (McCarver's) Inf. Co.G
Taylor, W.H. AR 15th Mil. Co.A
Taylor, W.H. AR 21st Inf. Co.I
Taylor, W.H. AR 36th Inf. Co.D
Taylor, W.H. AR 37th Inf. Co.C Cpl.
Taylor, W.H. FL 4th Inf. Co.I
Taylor, W.H. GA 3rd Inf. Co.E
Taylor, W.H. GA 5th Res. Co.D
Taylor, W.H. GA 13th Inf. Co.D
Taylor, W.H. MS 6th Inf. Adj.
Taylor, W.H. MS Cav. Jeff Davis Legion Co.K
Taylor, W.H. NC 2nd Cav. (19th St.Troops) Co.C
Taylor, W.H. NC 3rd Inf. Co.E
Taylor, W.H. NC 7th Sr.Res. Fisher's Co.
Taylor, W.H. NC 38th Inf. Co.K
Taylor, W.H. SC 27th Inf. Co.B
Taylor, W.H. TN 8th (Smith's) Cav. Co.G
Taylor, W.H. TN 19th (Biffle's) Cav. Co.L
Taylor, W.H. TN Inf. 4th Cons.Regt. Co.G
Taylor, W.H. TN 18th Inf. Co.H Cpl.
Taylor, W.H. TN 28th (Cons.) Inf. Co.E
Taylor, W.H. TN 38th Inf. Co.C
Taylor, W.H. TN 44th (Cons.) Inf. Co.K
Taylor, W.H. TN 55th (Brown's) Inf. Co.A
Taylor, W.H. TN 62nd Mtd.Inf. Co.B Cpl.
Taylor, W.H. TN 63rd Inf. Co.G
Taylor, W.H. TN 84th Inf. Co.A
Taylor, W.H. Inf. Bailey's Cons.Regt. Co.D 1st Sgt.
Taylor, W.H. TX 10th Cav. Co.F
Taylor, W.H. TX 23rd Cav. Co.D
Taylor, W.H. TX 1st Inf. Co.D
Taylor, W.H. VA 8th Inf. Co.E
Taylor, W.H. VA 54th Mil. Co.H
Taylor, W.H. VA Inf. Montague's Bn. Co.B
Taylor, W.H. Lowry's Brig. 1st Lt.,ADC
Taylor, W.H. Exch.Bn. Co.E,CSA
Taylor, W.H. Gen. & Staff Chap.
Taylor, W.H. Gen. & Staff, A. of N.VA Lt.Col.,AAG
Taylor, W.H.A. VA 54th Mil. Co.G
Taylor, W.H.B. KY 2nd Bn.Mtd.Rifles Co.B
Taylor, W.H.B. VA 3rd Inf.Loc.Def. Co.E
Taylor, W. Henderson AL 17th Inf. Co.B
Taylor, W. Henderson AL 33rd Inf. Co.H
Taylor, W. Hillary AL 33rd Inf. Co.H
Taylor, Wilbourne NC 25th Inf. Co.H
Taylor, Wilburn TN Inf. 1st Bn. (Colms') Co.B
Taylor, Wiles MS 6th Cav. Co.D
Taylor, Wiley AL 31st Inf. Co.H
Taylor, Wiley AL 32nd Inf. Co.F
Taylor, Wiley MS 5th Inf. (St.Troops) Co.C
Taylor, Wiley NC 34th Inf. Co.A
Taylor, Wiley F. NC 1st Inf. Co.H Cpl.
Taylor, Wiley J. NC 51st Inf. Co.H
Taylor, Wiley J. TN 30th Inf. Co.B
Taylor, Wiley M. 7th Conf.Cav. Co.G,M
Taylor, Wiley O. TX 17th Cav. Co.K
Taylor, Wiley O. TX 7th Inf. Co.D
Taylor, Wiley T. MS 10th Inf. Old Co.E
Taylor, Wiley W. VA 34th Inf. Co.I
Taylor, Wilks MS 8th Inf. Co.D
Taylor, William AL 9th (Malone's) Cav. Co.L
Taylor, William AL Lt.Arty. 2nd Bn. Co.B Far.,Black.
Taylor, William AL Lt.Arty. Phelan's Co.
Taylor, William AL Inf. 2nd Regt. Co.G
Taylor, William AL 3rd Bn.Res. Flemming's Co.
Taylor, William AL 10th Inf. Surg.
Taylor, William AL 12th Inf. Co.E
Taylor, Wm. AL 16th Inf. Co.K
Taylor, William AL 17th Inf. Co.B
Taylor, William AL 17th Inf. Co.E
Taylor, William AL 22nd Regt. Co.C
Taylor, William AL 27th Inf. Co.B
Taylor, William AL 29th Inf. Co.C
Taylor, William AL 36th Inf. Co.H
Taylor, William AL 38th Inf. Co.G
Taylor, William AL 41st Inf. Co.G
Taylor, William AL 49th Inf. Co.F
Taylor, William AL 57th Inf. Co.K
Taylor, William AL 62nd Inf. Co.H
Taylor, William AR 1st Mtd.Rifles Co.E
Taylor, William AR Cav. McGehee's Regt. Co.E 1st Lt.
Taylor, William AR 1st (Colquitt's) Inf. Co.K
Taylor, William AR 8th Inf. New Co.G
Taylor, William AR 10th Mil. Co.B
Taylor, William AR 13th Inf. Co.K
Taylor, William AR 14th (McCarver's) Inf. Co.H 1st Sgt.
Taylor, William AR 19th (Dawson's) Inf. Co.D
Taylor, William AR 19th (Dawson's) Inf. Co.E
Taylor, William AR 19th (Dockery's) Inf. Co.K 1st Sgt.
Taylor, William AR 23rd Inf. Co.A
Taylor, William AR 27th Inf. New Co.C
Taylor, William AR 30th Inf. Co.A
Taylor, William AR 31st Inf. Co.A
Taylor, William AR 35th Inf. Co.F
Taylor, William AR 38th Inf. Co.B
Taylor, William AR 62nd Mil. Co.F Sgt.
Taylor, William AR Inf. Hardy's Regt. Co.K
Taylor, William FL 2nd Inf. Co.F
Taylor, William FL Inf. 2nd Bn. Co.F
Taylor, William FL 9th Inf. Co.E
Taylor, William FL 11th Inf. Co.D
Taylor, William FL Campbellton Boys
Taylor, William GA 3rd Cav. Co.D
Taylor, William GA 4th (Clinch's) Cav. Co.G
Taylor, William GA Cav. 20th Bn. Co.C
Taylor, William GA Cav. Nelson's Ind.Co.
Taylor, William GA Hvy.Arty. 22nd Bn. Co.C
Taylor, William GA Inf. 1st Loc.Troops (Augusta) Co.H
Taylor, William GA 2nd Bn.S.S. Co.A
Taylor, William GA 3rd Res. Co.I
Taylor, William GA 5th Inf.
Taylor, William GA 5th Inf. Co.A,M
Taylor, William GA 5th Inf. Co.D
Taylor, William GA 5th Inf. Co.I
Taylor, William GA Inf. 10th Bn. Co.B
Taylor, William GA 11th Inf. Co.C
Taylor, William GA Inf. 14th Bn. (St.Guards) Co.B 2nd Lt.
Taylor, William GA 25th Inf. Co.K
Taylor, William GA 36th (Broyles') Inf. Co.H
Taylor, William GA 39th Inf. Co.A,H
Taylor, William GA 43rd Inf. Co.A Sgt.
Taylor, William GA 47th Inf. Co.F
Taylor, William GA 50th Inf. Co.C
Taylor, William GA 51st Inf. Co.K
Taylor, William GA 66th Inf. Co.A
Taylor, William KY 2nd (Duke's) Cav. Co.L
Taylor, William KY 11th Cav. Co.C
Taylor, William KY 5th Mtd.Inf. Co.C
Taylor, William KY 9th Mtd.Inf. Co.D
Taylor, William LA Arty. Landry's Co. (Donaldsonville Arty.)
Taylor, William LA 1st (Nelligan's) Inf. Co.C
Taylor, William, 1st LA 1st (Strawbridge's) Inf. Co.A

Taylor, William, 2nd LA 1st (Strawbridge's) Inf. Co.A
Taylor, William LA Inf. 1st Sp.Bn. (Rightor's) New Co.C
Taylor, William LA 2nd Inf. Co.E Cpl.
Taylor, William LA 9th Inf. Co.H
Taylor, William LA 21st (Patton's) Inf. Co.G
Taylor, William LA 30th Inf. Co.B
Taylor, William MS 1st Cav. Co.G
Taylor, William MS 2nd Part.Rangers Co.D,F
Taylor, William MS 8th Cav. Co.C
Taylor, William MS Cav. Ham's Regt. Co.B,D
Taylor, William MS Cav. Powers' Regt. Co.A
Taylor, William MS 1st Lt.Arty. Co.B
Taylor, William MS Inf. 1st Bn.St.Troops (30 days '64) Co.A
Taylor, William MS 2nd Inf. (A. of 10,000) Co.A
Taylor, William MS 6th Inf. Co.F
Taylor, William MS 6th Inf. Co.I
Taylor, William MS 8th Inf. Co.D
Taylor, William MS 8th Inf. Co.F
Taylor, William MS 17th Inf. Co.G
Taylor, William MS 22nd Inf. Co.C
Taylor, William MS 39th Inf. Co.G
Taylor, William MO 1st N.E. Cav. Co.L
Taylor, William MO 7th Cav. Co.D
Taylor, William MO 15th Cav. Co.H
Taylor, William MO Cav. Coleman's Regt. Co.F 3rd Lt.
Taylor, William MO Cav. Ford's Bn. Co.A
Taylor, William MO Cav. Freeman's Regt. Co.G 1st Sgt.
Taylor, William MO Cav. Poindexter's Regt.
Taylor, William MO 1st Inf. Co.K
Taylor, William MO 3rd Inf. Co.B Sgt.
Taylor, William MO 10th Inf. Co.A
Taylor, William MO Inf. Clark's Regt. Co.E
Taylor, William NC 1st Inf.
Taylor, William NC 2nd Inf. Co.G
Taylor, William NC 3rd Inf. Co.A
Taylor, William NC 8th Inf. Co.G
Taylor, William NC 8th Sr.Res. Gardner's Co.
Taylor, William NC 12th Inf. Co.M
Taylor, William NC 17th Inf. (1st Org.) Co.F
Taylor, William NC 17th Inf. (2nd Org.) Co.A
Taylor, William NC 17th Inf. (2nd Org.) Co.E
Taylor, William NC 25th Inf. Co.I
Taylor, William NC 26th Inf. Co.A
Taylor, William NC 27th Inf. Co.A
Taylor, William NC 32nd Inf. Co.B
Taylor, William NC 38th Inf. Co.A
Taylor, William NC 47th Inf. Co.A
Taylor, William NC 58th Inf. Co.G
Taylor, William NC 66th Inf. Co.H
Taylor, William NC 68th Inf.
Taylor, William NC Inf. Thomas Legion Co.K
Taylor, William SC 4th Cav. Co.G
Taylor, William SC Cav. 10th Bn. Co.C
Taylor, William SC Inf. 1st (Charleston) Bn. Co.B
Taylor, William SC 5th St.Troops Co.K
Taylor, William SC Inf. 7th Bn. (Enfield Rifles) Co.H
Taylor, William SC 12th Inf. Co.I
Taylor, William SC 13th Inf. Co.K
Taylor, William SC 18th Inf. Co.E
Taylor, William SC 22nd Inf. Co.E
Taylor, William SC 24th Inf. Co.F
Taylor, William TN 4th (McLemore's) Cav. Co.I
Taylor, William TN 5th (McKenzie's) Cav. Co.C
Taylor, William TN 8th Cav. Co.A
Taylor, William TN 10th & 11th (Cons.) Cav. Co.B
Taylor, William TN 10th & 11th (Cons.) Cav. Co.I
Taylor, William TN 22nd (Barteau's) Cav. Co.D
Taylor, William TN Cav. Newsom's Regt.
Taylor, William TN 1st Hvy.Arty. Co.L, 3rd Co.B
Taylor, William TN 3rd (Clack's) Inf. Co.E
Taylor, William TN 7th Inf. Co.C
Taylor, William TN 8th Inf. Co.H
Taylor, William TN 8th Inf. Co.I
Taylor, William TN 12th Inf. Co.H
Taylor, William TN 16th Inf. Co.C
Taylor, William TN 19th Inf. Co.H
Taylor, William TN 19th Inf. Co.K
Taylor, William TN 20th Inf. Co.B
Taylor, William TN 50th Inf. Co.F
Taylor, William TN 62nd Mtd.Inf. Co.E
Taylor, William TX 2nd Cav. 2nd Co.F,G
Taylor, William TX 5th Cav. Co.C
Taylor, William TX 15th Cav. Co.A
Taylor, William TX 17th Cons.Dismtd.Cav. Co.A
Taylor, William TX 23rd Cav. Co.D
Taylor, William TX 23rd Cav. Co.H
Taylor, William TX 25th Cav. Co.C
Taylor, William TX 35th (Brown's) Cav. 2nd Co.B
Taylor, William TX 1st Hvy.Arty. Co.E
Taylor, William TX 1st Inf. Co.D
Taylor, William TX Inf. 1st St.Troops Whitehead's Co. Sgt.
Taylor, William VA 1st Cav. 1st Co.D, Co.B 1st Lt.
Taylor, William VA 6th Cav. Co.D 1st Lt.
Taylor, William VA 8th Cav. Co.K
Taylor, William VA 11th Cav. Co.D Capt.
Taylor, William VA 14th Cav. Co.C
Taylor, William VA 14th Cav. Co.H
Taylor, William VA 16th Cav. Co.B
Taylor, William VA 19th Cav. Co.F
Taylor, William VA 21st Cav. Co.E
Taylor, William VA 22nd Cav. Co.D
Taylor, William VA 23rd Cav. Co.D Lt.
Taylor, William VA 1st Arty. Co.H
Taylor, William VA Lt.Arty. Brander's Co.
Taylor, William VA Arty. C.F. Johnston's Co.
Taylor, William VA 2nd Inf.Loc.Def. Co.A
Taylor, William VA Inf. 2nd Bn.Loc.Def. Co.C
Taylor, William VA 2nd Inf.Loc.Def. Co.D
Taylor, William VA Inf. 6th Bn.Loc.Def. Co.A
Taylor, William VA 11th Bn.Res. Co.A
Taylor, William VA 22nd Inf. Co.B
Taylor, William VA 37th Inf. Co.I
Taylor, William VA 40th Inf. Co.K
Taylor, William VA 41st Inf. Co.H
Taylor, William VA 60th Inf. 2nd Co.H
Taylor, William VA 77th Mil. Co.A Sgt.
Taylor, William of E. VA 77th Mil. Co.B, Blue's Co.
Taylor, William VA 151st Mil. Co.D
Taylor, William VA Inf. Cohoon's Bn. Co.D
Taylor, William 7th Conf.Cav. Co.C
Taylor, Wm. 8th (Wade's) Conf.Cav. Co.A
Taylor, William, No.1 3rd Conf.Eng.Troops Co.D
Taylor, William 1st Choctaw Mtd.Rifles Co.E
Taylor, William Gen. & Staff Maj.,Comsy.
Taylor, Wm. Gen. & Staff, Medical Dept. Surg.
Taylor, Wm. Hosp.Stew.
Taylor, William A. AL 3rd Inf. Co.F Lt.
Taylor, William A. AL 17th Inf. Co.A
Taylor, William A. AR Inf. 2nd Bn. Co.A
Taylor, William A. GA 52nd Inf. Co.F
Taylor, William A. MS 2nd St.Cav. Co.A
Taylor, William A. MS 10th Inf.
Taylor, William A. MS 43rd Inf. Co.F Cpl.
Taylor, William A. NC 42nd Inf. Co.B
Taylor, William A. NC 61st Inf. Co.H
Taylor, William A. TN 5th (McKenzie's) Cav. Co.C
Taylor, William A. TN 24th Inf. 2nd Co.G
Taylor, William A. TX 24th Cav. Co.C Maj.
Taylor, William A. TX 25th Cav. Co.C
Taylor, William A. TX 36th Cav. Co.G Cpl.
Taylor, William A. VA 2nd Arty. Co.G
Taylor, William A. VA Arty. Dance's Co.
Taylor, William A. VA 12th Inf. Co.D
Taylor, William A. VA Inf. 22nd Bn. Co.G
Taylor, William A. VA Mil. Carroll Cty.
Taylor, William Alfred NC 51st Inf. Co.I
Taylor, William Alfred TX 20th Cav. Co.B
Taylor, William A.S. VA 61st Inf. Adj.
Taylor, William A.S. VA Vol. Taylor's Co. Capt.
Taylor, William Augustus KY 12th Cav. Co.E
Taylor, William B. AL St.Arty. Co.A
Taylor, William B. AL 26th (O'Neal's) Inf. Co.I
Taylor, Wm. B. AL 35th Inf. Co.I Capt.
Taylor, William B. AR 1st Inf. J. Caldwell's Co.
Taylor, William B. AR Lt.Arty. Thrall's Btty.
Taylor, William B. FL 5th Inf. Co.G
Taylor, William B. MS 48th Inf. Co.C
Taylor, William B. MO 1st Inf. Co.I
Taylor, William B. MO Inf. 8th Bn. Co.D
Taylor, William B. NC 11th (Bethel Regt.) Inf. Co.A 2nd Lt.
Taylor, William B. NC 22nd Inf. Co.H
Taylor, William B. NC 55th Inf. Co.E
Taylor, William B. NC Walker's Bn. Thomas' Legion Co.C Cpl.
Taylor, William B. TN 2nd (Smith's) Cav. Lea's Co.
Taylor, William B. TN 44th Inf. Co.I 1st Sgt.
Taylor, William B. TN 44th (Cons.) Inf. Co.A Sgt.
Taylor, William B. TX 16th Cav. Co.K
Taylor, William B. TX 15th Inf. 2nd Co.H
Taylor, William B. VA 5th Cav. (12 mo. '61-2) Co.F Sgt.
Taylor, William B. VA 13th Cav. Co.F
Taylor, William B. VA Hvy.Arty. 20th Bn. Co.A
Taylor, William B. VA 3rd (Archer's) Bn.Res. Co.C
Taylor, William B. VA 9th Inf. Co.I
Taylor, William B. VA 30th Inf. Co.K Sgt.
Taylor, William B. 3rd Conf.Cav. Co.I

Taylor, William B. 2nd Cherokee Mtd.Vol. Co.B,K
Taylor, William Brown MS Inf. 2nd Bn. Co.C
Taylor, William C. AL 32nd Inf. Co.C
Taylor, William C. AR 1st (Colquitt's) Inf. Co.D
Taylor, William C. AR 2nd Cav. Co.D
Taylor, William C. FL 2nd Inf. Co.F Sgt.
Taylor, William C. MS 1st Lt.Arty. Co.C
Taylor, William C. MS 42nd Inf. Co.G Cpl.
Taylor, William C. MO 4th Cav. Co.F
Taylor, William C. NC 5th Inf. Co.B Cpl.
Taylor, William C. NC 28th Inf. Co.F
Taylor, William C. SC 1st Arty. Co.C,A
Taylor, William C. SC 1st (Orr's) Rifles Co.H
Taylor, William C. SC 20th Inf. Co.K
Taylor, William C. TN 2nd (Robison's) Inf. Co.F
Taylor, William C. TN 32nd Inf. Co.F
Taylor, William C. TX 16th Inf. Co.I
Taylor, William C. VA 5th Cav. (12 mo. '61-2) Co.I
Taylor, William C. VA Cav. 14th Bn. Co.B
Taylor, William C. VA 15th Cav. Co.I
Taylor, William C. VA 3rd Inf. Co.B 1st Lt.
Taylor, William C. VA 21st Mil. Co.E
Taylor, William C. VA 26th Inf. 2nd Co.B
Taylor, William C. VA 52nd Inf. Co.I
Taylor, William C.R. GA 15th Inf. Co.D
Taylor, William D. AL 19th Inf. Co.C,K Cpl.
Taylor, William D. AL Cp. of Instr. Talladega
Taylor, William D. GA 31st Inf. Co.I
Taylor, William D. GA 47th Inf. Co.F
Taylor, William D. MO 1st Cav. Co.I Cpl.
Taylor, William D. MO 6th Cav.
Taylor, William D. MO 7th Cav. Haislip's Co.
Taylor, William D. VA Arty. Dance's Co.
Taylor, William D. VA 20th Inf. Co.C
Taylor, William D. VA 21st Inf. Co.A Cpl.
Taylor, William D.K. AR 2nd Mtd.Rifles Co.G
Taylor, William E. AL 3rd Bn.Res. Co.A
Taylor, William E. AL 4th Inf. Co.C
Taylor, William E. AR 27th Inf. Old Co.C
Taylor, William E. KY 2nd Bn.Mtd.Rifles Co.C 1st Sgt.
Taylor, William E. KY 8th Mtd.Inf. Co.D
Taylor, William E. SC 12th Inf. Co.C
Taylor, William E. TN 2nd (Robison's) Inf. Co.B
Taylor, William E. TX Inf. Griffin's Bn. Co.A
Taylor, William E., Jr. VA Lt.Arty. Grandy's Co. Sgt.
Taylor, William E. VA 6th Inf. Co.F
Taylor, William E. VA 6th Inf. Ferguson's Co.
Taylor, William E. VA 12th Inf. Co.H
Taylor, William E. VA 16th Inf. 1st Co.H
Taylor, William E. VA Prov. A. of VA 2nd Lt.
Taylor, William E. Gen. & Staff Hosp.Stew.
Taylor, William E.S. GA Inf. 2nd Bn. Co.C
Taylor, Wm. F. AL 8th Inf. Co.K Cpl.
Taylor, William F. AL 19th Inf. Co.F Sgt.
Taylor, William F. AL 24th Inf. Co.E
Taylor, Wm. F. AL Cp. of Instr. Talladega
Taylor, William F. AR 14th (Power's) Inf. Co.H
Taylor, William F. GA 49th Inf. Co.E
Taylor, William F. MS Cav. 1st Bn. (Miller's) Co.E
Taylor, William F. MS 1st Lt.Arty. Co.L
Taylor, William F. MS 16th Inf. Co.B
Taylor, William F. SC 14th Inf. Co.F
Taylor, William F. TN Cav. Jackson's Co.
Taylor, William F. TN 1st (Turney's) Inf. Co.E 2nd Lt.
Taylor, William F. TX 35th (Brown's) Cav. Co.D
Taylor, William F. TX 13th Vol. 2nd Co.F
Taylor, William F. VA 1st St.Res. Co.F
Taylor, William F. VA 8th Inf. Co.K Cpl.
Taylor, William F. VA 47th Inf. 3rd Co.H
Taylor, Wm. F. VA Inf. Lyneman's Co.
Taylor, William G. FL Inf. 2nd Bn.
Taylor, William G. GA Phillips' Legion Co.O Sgt.
Taylor, William G. MO 2nd Cav. Co.B
Taylor, William G. TN Cav. 4th Bn. (Branner's) Co.E
Taylor, William G. TN 61st Mtd.Inf. Co.E
Taylor, William G. VA Cav. 1st Bn. Co.C
Taylor, William G. VA 2nd Inf. Co.I
Taylor, William G. VA 20th Inf. Co.E
Taylor, William H. AL 4th (Russell's) Cav. Co.D Capt.
Taylor, William H. AL Cav. Lenoir's Ind.Co.
Taylor, William H. AL Lt.Arty. 20th Bn. Co.A,B
Taylor, William H. AL 3rd Inf. Co.F
Taylor, William H. AL 4th Inf. Co.F 1st Lt.
Taylor, William H. AL 6th Inf. Co.B
Taylor, William H. AL 6th Inf. Co.G
Taylor, William H. AR 1st (Colquitt's) Inf. Co.C
Taylor, William H. AR 17th (Lemoyne's) Inf. Co.E
Taylor, William H. AR 33rd Inf. Co.C
Taylor, William H. AR 35th Inf. Co.B
Taylor, William H. AR 35th Inf. Co.H Sgt.
Taylor, William H. AR 37th Inf. Co.G
Taylor, William H. FL 6th Inf. Co.G
Taylor, William H. GA 12th Cav. Co.L
Taylor, William H. GA 38th Inf. Co.N Cpl.
Taylor, William H. GA 42nd Inf. Co.F
Taylor, William H. LA 5th Cav. Co.E
Taylor, William H. MS 12th Inf. Co.A Col.
Taylor, William H. MS 16th Inf. Co.C
Taylor, William H. MO Cav. 7th Regt.St.Guard QM
Taylor, Wm. H. MO St.Guard W.H. Taylor's Co. Capt.
Taylor, Wm. H. NC Alleghany Gray's Doughton's Co.
Taylor, William H. NC 2nd Inf. Co.B
Taylor, William H. NC 2nd Bn.Loc.Def.Troops Co.F
Taylor, William H. NC 11th (Bethel Regt.) Inf. Co.C
Taylor, William H. NC 14th Inf. Co.K
Taylor, William H. NC 26th Inf. Co.A Cpl.
Taylor, William H. SC Cav.Bn. Hampton Legion Co.D 2nd Lt.
Taylor, William H. TN Cav. 7th Bn. (Bennett's) Co.C
Taylor, William H. TN 10th (DeMoss') Cav. Co.B
Taylor, William H. TN 20th Cav.
Taylor, William H. TN 44th Inf. Co.C
Taylor, William H. TN 49th Inf. Co.B 2nd Lt.
Taylor, William H. TX 16th Cav. Co.F Capt.
Taylor, William H. TX 29th Cav. Co.A Black.
Taylor, William H. VA 1st Cav. Co.C
Taylor, William H. VA 18th Cav. Co.A Capt.
Taylor, William H. VA Cav. 39th Bn. Co.C
Taylor, William H. VA Cav. Mosby's Regt. (Part.Rangers)
Taylor, William H. VA Hvy.Arty. 10th Bn. Co.A Sgt.
Taylor, William H. VA Lt.Arty. 13th Bn. Co.C
Taylor, William H. VA Hvy.Arty. 18th Bn. Co.D
Taylor, William H. VA Lt.Arty. Garber's Co.
Taylor, William H. VA Hvy.Arty. Patteson's Co.
Taylor, William H. VA 5th Inf. Co.A Cpl.
Taylor, William H. VA 7th Inf. Co.C
Taylor, William H. VA 11th Inf. Co.A Sgt.
Taylor, William H. VA 11th Inf. Co.E
Taylor, William H. VA 11th Inf. Co.F
Taylor, William H. VA 19th Inf. Surg.
Taylor, William H. VA Inf. 23rd Bn. Co.C
Taylor, William H. VA 24th Inf. Co.A Sgt.
Taylor, William H. VA 45th Inf. Co.D
Taylor, William H. VA 45th Inf. Co.L
Taylor, William H. VA 49th Inf. Co.I
Taylor, William H. VA 53rd Inf. Co.I
Taylor, William H. VA 62nd Mtd.Inf. 2nd Co.H 1st Lt.
Taylor, William H. VA 63rd Inf. Co.K
Taylor, William H. VA 97th Mil. Co.F
Taylor, Wm. H. Gen. & Staff Surg.
Taylor, William H.B. NC Loc.Def. Griswold's Co. 2nd Lt.
Taylor, William H.B. VA 1st Arty. Co.D
Taylor, William H.R. VA 12th Inf. Co.A
Taylor, William J. AR 26th Inf. Co.K Sgt.
Taylor, William J. GA 6th Cav. Co.A
Taylor, William J. GA Siege Arty. 28th Bn. Co.A
Taylor, William J. GA 8th Inf. Co.E
Taylor, William J. GA 20th Inf. Co.D
Taylor, William J. GA 34th Inf. Co.C
Taylor, William J. GA 36th (Villepigue's) Inf. Co.C
Taylor, William J. GA 2nd Bn.S.S. Co.C
Taylor, William J. MS 24th Inf. Co.B
Taylor, William J. MO 11th Inf. Co.I,E
Taylor, William J. NC 8th Bn.Part.Rangers Co.B,E
Taylor, William J. NC 3rd Arty. (40th St.Troops) Co.H
Taylor, William J. NC 2nd Bn.Loc.Def.Troops Co.G
Taylor, William J. NC 13th Inf. Co.B
Taylor, William J. NC 30th Inf. Co.A
Taylor, William J. NC 35th Inf. Co.G
Taylor, William J. NC 66th Inf. Co.H
Taylor, William J. SC Inf. 7th Bn. (Enfield Rifles) Co.C,G 2nd Lt.
Taylor, Wm. J. SC 26th Inf. Co.K Lt.
Taylor, William J. TN 8th Inf. Co.K
Taylor, William J. TN 24th Inf. Co.K
Taylor, William J. VA 5th Cav. (12 mo. '61-2) Co.B
Taylor, William J. VA Horse Arty. E. Graham's Co.
Taylor, William J. VA Lt.Arty. Grandy's Co.
Taylor, William J. VA 6th Inf. Vickery's Co.
Taylor, William J. VA 16th Inf. 1st Co.H

Taylor, William J. VA 22nd Inf. Co.K
Taylor, William J. VA Inf. 22nd Bn. Co.B
Taylor, William J. VA 59th Inf. 3rd Co.E
Taylor, William James NC 51st Inf. Co.I
Taylor, Wm. J.H. AL Cp. of Instr. Talladega
Taylor, William K. NC Cav. 7th Bn. Co.E
Taylor, William K. VA 7th Cav. Preston's Co.
Taylor, William K. VA 14th Cav. Co.G
Taylor, William K. VA 4th Inf. Co.B
Taylor, William L. AL 36th Inf. Co.C
Taylor, William L. AL Cav. 5th Bn. Hilliard's Legion Co.A Far.
Taylor, William L. FL 6th Inf. Co.K
Taylor, William L. GA 53rd Inf. Co.G 2nd Lt.
Taylor, William L. MS 18th Inf. Co.B Cpl.
Taylor, William L. MO 12th Inf. Co.B
Taylor, William L. NC 27th Inf. Co.E
Taylor, William L. TN 5th (McKenzie's) Cav. Co.C,G
Taylor, William L. TX 14th Cav. Co.G
Taylor, William L. TX 10th Inf. Co.D 1st Lt.
Taylor, William L. VA 3rd Cav. 1st Co.I
Taylor, William L. VA Hvy.Arty. Coleman's Co.
Taylor, William L. VA 30th Inf. Co.G
Taylor, William L. VA 47th Inf. 2nd Co.K
Taylor, William M. AL 8th Cav. Co.K
Taylor, William M. AL 44th Inf. Co.I 1st Sgt.
Taylor, William M. AR 6th Inf. Co.I
Taylor, William M. GA 62nd Cav. Co.L
Taylor, William M. LA Inf. 11th Bn. Co.E
Taylor, William M. LA 14th Inf. Co.I Cpl.
Taylor, William M. LA 17th Inf. Co.C
Taylor, William M. MS 11th (Perrin's) Cav. Co.C
Taylor, William M. MS Cav. Drane's Co. (Choctaw Cty.Res.)
Taylor, William M. MS 17th Inf. Co.D
Taylor, William M. MS 22nd Inf. Co.H
Taylor, William M. MS 42nd Inf. Co.H Sgt.
Taylor, William M. MO 10th Inf. Co.C Cpl.
Taylor, William M. NC Hvy.Arty. 10th Bn. Co.C
Taylor, William M. NC 42nd Inf. Co.E Sgt.
Taylor, William M. SC Lt.Arty. Kelly's Co. (Chesterfield Arty.)
Taylor, William M. TN 11th Cav.
Taylor, William M. TX 13th Cav. Co.F Cpl.
Taylor, William M. TX 17th Cav. Co.E
Taylor, William M. TX 5th Inf. Co.F
Taylor, William M. TX 22nd Inf. Co.D
Taylor, William M. VA 5th Cav. Co.H
Taylor, William M. VA 24th Cav. Co.K
Taylor, William M. VA Cav. 35th Bn. Co.A,B
Taylor, William M. VA Lt.Arty. Montgomery's Co.
Taylor, William M. VA Lt.Arty. Wimbish's Co.
Taylor, William M. VA 4th Inf. Co.E
Taylor, William M. VA 6th Inf. Co.I
Taylor, William M. VA 60th Inf. Co.F
Taylor, William M. 8th (Dearing's) Conf.Cav. Co.E
Taylor, William M. 2nd Conf.Eng.Troops Co.H
Taylor, William M. 2nd Cherokee Mtd.Vol. Co.H,A,C 1st Lt.
Taylor, William Mc. TX 12th Inf. Co.F
Taylor, William N. AR 27th Inf. New Co.B
Taylor, William N. FL Lt.Arty. Dyke's Co.
Taylor, William N. MO 4th Cav. Co.B
Taylor, William N. MO Cav. Ford's Bn. Co.A
Taylor, William N. MO Cav. Preston's Bn. Co.B
Taylor, William N. TN 41st Inf. Co.G 1st Lt.
Taylor, William N. VA Hvy.Arty. 10th Bn. Co.C Music.
Taylor, William O. VA 1st Inf. Co.I Capt.
Taylor, William P. MS 17th Inf. Co.A
Taylor, William P. MS 17th Inf. Co.H
Taylor, William P. MO Inf. 8th Bn. Co.F
Taylor, William P. MO 9th Inf. Co.K
Taylor, William P. VA 2nd Cav. Co.E
Taylor, William P. VA 9th Cav. Co.H
Taylor, William P. VA Cav. Hounshell's Bn.
Taylor, William P. VA Cav. Mosby's Regt. (Part.Rangers) Co.G
Taylor, William P. VA Cav. Thurmond's Co.
Taylor, William P. VA 1st Arty. Co.B
Taylor, William P. VA Lt.Arty. Kirkpatrick's Co.
Taylor, William P. VA 9th Inf. 2nd Co.A
Taylor, William P. VA 9th Inf. 2nd Co.H Sgt.
Taylor, William P. VA 12th Inf. 1st Co.I Cpl.
Taylor, William P. VA 32nd Inf. 1st Co.H
Taylor, William P. VA 42nd Inf. Co.E
Taylor, William P. VA 56th Inf. Co.B
Taylor, William P. VA 64th Mtd.Inf. Co.D
Taylor, William P. VA 72nd Mil.
Taylor, William R. AL Lt.Arty. Goldthwaite's Btty.
Taylor, William R. AR 25th Inf. Co.K
Taylor, William R. FL Cav. 3rd Bn. Co.A
Taylor, William R. FL 3rd Inf. Co.F
Taylor, William R. GA 31st Inf. Co.F Cpl.
Taylor, William R. MS 19th Inf. Co.A
Taylor, William R. NC 6th Inf. Co.D Cpl.
Taylor, William R. NC 12th Inf. Co.G
Taylor, William R. NC 60th Inf. Co.D Music.
Taylor, William R. VA 18th Inf. Co.D
Taylor, William R. VA Inf. 26th Bn. Co.F
Taylor, William R. VA 45th Inf.
Taylor, William R. VA 54th Inf. Co.F
Taylor, William R. VA 166th Mil. Taylor's Co.
Taylor, William R.J. GA 10th Inf. Co.K
Taylor, William Robinson VA 9th Cav. Co.C
Taylor, William S. AL Lt.Arty. 2nd Bn.
Taylor, William S. AL 8th Inf. Co.E 1st Sgt.
Taylor, William S. AL 40th Inf. Co.B
Taylor, William S. AL Recruits
Taylor, William S. GA 26th Inf. Co.F
Taylor, William S. MS 10th Cav. Co.G
Taylor, William S. MS 1st (Johnston's) Inf. Co.K
Taylor, William S. NC 3rd Inf. Co.A
Taylor, William S. NC 33rd Inf. Co.K 1st Lt.
Taylor, William S. NC 67th Inf. Co.K 1st Lt.
Taylor, William S. SC 2nd Rifles Co.K
Taylor, William S. TN 27th Inf. Co.I 1st Sgt.
Taylor, William S. VA 19th Cav. Co.F
Taylor, William S. VA 20th Cav. Co.E
Taylor, William S. VA 3rd Res. Co.H
Taylor, William S. VA 11th Bn.Res. Co.B
Taylor, William S. VA 15th Inf. Co.A
Taylor, William S. VA 31st Inf. Co.C
Taylor, William S. VA 108th Mil. McNeer's Co.
Taylor, William S. VA 2nd Cav.St.Line McNeel's Co.
Taylor, Wm. S. Gen. & Staff Surg.
Taylor, Williamson B. VA 9th Inf. Co.I
Taylor, William T. AL 15th Bn.Part.Rangers Co.A Lt.
Taylor, William T. AL 33rd Inf. Co.H
Taylor, William T. AL 37th Inf. Co.E
Taylor, William T. AR 19th (Dawson's) Inf. Co.E
Taylor, William T. FL Cav. 3rd Bn. Co.A
Taylor, William T. GA Inf. 10th Bn. Co.A
Taylor, William T. GA 15th Inf. Co.C,F
Taylor, William T. GA 61st Inf. Co.I
Taylor, William T. KY 2nd (Duke's) Cav. Co.E,H
Taylor, William T. MS 43rd Inf. Co.B
Taylor, William T. NC 1st Inf. (6 mo. '61) Co.F
Taylor, William T. NC Inf. 13th Bn. Co.D
Taylor, William T. NC 56th Inf. Co.B Sgt.Maj.
Taylor, William T. NC Vol. Lawrence's Co. Cpl.
Taylor, William T. SC 20th Inf. Co.E
Taylor, William T. TN Inf. 1st Bn. (Colms') Co.B Sgt.
Taylor, William T. TX 16th Cav. Co.F
Taylor, William T. TX 35th (Brown's) Cav. Co.D,F
Taylor, William T. TX 13th Vol. 1st Co.I
Taylor, William T. VA 1st Cav. Co.H
Taylor, William T. VA Cav. Herrington's Co.
Taylor, William T. VA Hvy.Arty. 18th Bn. Co.C
Taylor, William T., Jr. VA Horse Arty. E. Graham's Co.
Taylor, William T., Sr. VA Horse Arty. E. Graham's Co.
Taylor, William T. VA Lt.Arty. Huckstep's Co.
Taylor, William T. VA Lt.Arty. B.Z. Price's Co.
Taylor, William T. VA Lt.Arty. Snead's Co.
Taylor, William T. VA 22nd Inf. Co.D
Taylor, William T. VA 29th Inf. Co.C
Taylor, William T. VA 47th Inf. 3rd Co.H
Taylor, William T. 7th Conf.Cav. Co.H Cpl.
Taylor, William T.H. GA 45th Inf. Co.D
Taylor, Wm. V. Gen. & Staff Maj.,Ord.Off.
Taylor, William W. AL 21st Inf. Co.A
Taylor, William W. AL 38th Inf. Co.I
Taylor, William W. AL 49th Inf. Co.G
Taylor, William W. GA Inf. 10th Bn. Co.B
Taylor, William W. GA 20th Inf. Co.A
Taylor, William W. GA 52nd Inf. Co.A
Taylor, William W. KY 1st Bn.Mtd.Rifles Co.A
Taylor, William W. MS Cav. Duncan's Co. (Tishomingo Rangers)
Taylor, William W. MS 27th Inf. Co.C
Taylor, William W. MS 30th Inf. Co.C
Taylor, William W. NC 14th Inf. Co.G
Taylor, William W. NC 43rd Inf. Co.K
Taylor, William W. NC 46th Inf. Co.A
Taylor, William W. SC 1st (Hagood's) Inf. 1st Co.A
Taylor, William W. SC 25th Inf. Co.G
Taylor, William W. TN 1st (Feild's) Inf. Co.G
Taylor, William Walker TX 20th Cav. Co.G
Taylor, Willie AR 10th Mil. Co.B
Taylor, Willis MO Cav. 13th Regt.St.Guard Co.B 3rd Lt.
Taylor, Willis NC 51st Inf. Co.E
Taylor, Willis VA 56th Inf. Co.C
Taylor, Willis B. MO 16th Inf. Co.G Lt.

Taylor, Willis F. GA 47th Inf. Co.F
Taylor, Willis J. TN 1st (Turney's) Inf. Co.F
Taylor, Willis J. TN 35th Inf. 2nd Co.D 2nd Lt.
Taylor, Willis W. GA 57th Inf. Co.F
Taylor, Wilson AL 61st Inf. Co.C
Taylor, Wilson MS 8th Cav. Co.A,K
Taylor, Wilson MS 18th Cav. Co.E
Taylor, Wilson NC 34th Inf. Co.K
Taylor, Wilson SC 1st Inf. Co.O
Taylor, Wilson SC 13th Inf. Co.K
Taylor, Wilson TN Inf. 1st Bn. (Colms') Co.C
Taylor, Wilson TX Cav. Durant's Co. Sgt.
Taylor, Wilson TX Cav. Madison's Regt. Co.B Sgt.
Taylor, Wilson VA 6th Inf. 2nd Co.E
Taylor, Wilson VA 6th Bn.Res. Co.D
Taylor, Wilson G. NC 32nd Inf. Co.H
Taylor, Wilson G. NC 43rd Inf. Co.E Sgt.
Taylor, Windal AL 18th Inf. Co.B
Taylor, Winfield S. VA Loc.Def. Chappell's Co.
Taylor, Winston TN 13th (Gore's) Cav. Co.F
Taylor, W.J. AL Inf. 2nd Regt. Co.D
Taylor, W.J. AL 6th Inf. Co.I
Taylor, W.J. AL 17th Inf. Co.E
Taylor, W.J. AL 26th (O'Neal's) Inf. Co.G
Taylor, W.J. AL 34th Inf. Co.F
Taylor, W.J. AL 38th Inf. Co.I
Taylor, W.J. AL 38th Inf. Co.I 1st Sgt.
Taylor, W.J. AL 55th Vol. Co.G
Taylor, W.J. AR 8th Inf. Co.B
Taylor, W.J. AR 11th Inf. Co.D
Taylor, W.J. GA Hvy.Arty. 22nd Bn. Co.B
Taylor, W.J. GA Arty. (Macon Lt.Arty.) Slaten's Co.
Taylor, W.J. GA 1st Reg. Co.I
Taylor, W.J. GA 10th Inf. Co.K
Taylor, W.J. GA 17th Inf. Co.G
Taylor, W.J. GA 49th Inf. Co.D
Taylor, W.J. GA 53rd Inf. Co.H
Taylor, W.J. KY 1st (Butler's) Cav. Co.A Capt.
Taylor, W.J. KY 4th Cav. Co.F
Taylor, W.J. LA Mil.Conf.Guards Regt. Co.C
Taylor, W.J. LA Inf.Cons.Crescent Regt. Co.O
Taylor, W.J. MS 3rd (St.Troops) Cav. Co.H Sgt.
Taylor, W.J. MS 26th Inf. Co.G
Taylor, W.J. MS Cav. Jeff Davis Legion Co.E
Taylor, W.J. MO 2nd Inf. Co.I
Taylor, W.J. NC Lt.Arty. 13th Bn. Co.F
Taylor, W.J. SC Arty. Manigault's Bn. 1st Co.B Ord.Sgt.
Taylor, W.J. SC 1st Inf. Co.A
Taylor, W.J. SC 2nd Bn.S.S. Co.C
Taylor, W.J. SC 3rd Inf. Co.I
Taylor, W.J. SC 4th Bn.Res. Co.E
Taylor, W.J. SC 10th Inf. Co.B
Taylor, W.J. SC 10th Inf. Co.M Capt.
Taylor, W.J. SC 24th Inf. Co.F
Taylor, W.J. SC 26th Inf. Co.K 1st Lt.
Taylor, W.J. TN 11th (Holman's) Cav. Co.H
Taylor, W.J. TN 28th Cav. Co.E 2nd Lt.
Taylor, W.J. TN Inf. 3rd Cons.Regt. Co.F
Taylor, W.J. TX 17th Cav. Co.D
Taylor, W.J. VA 79th Mil. Co.1
Taylor, W.J. Mead's Conf.Cav. Co.D
Taylor, W.J. Conf.Inf. 1st Bn. 2nd Co.E
Taylor, W.J. 2nd Conf.Eng.Troops Co.G
Taylor, W.J.N. AL 21st Inf. Co.I
Taylor, W.K. AL 7th Cav. Co.F,A
Taylor, W.K. TX Waul's Legion Co.B
Taylor, W.L. AR 19th (Dawson's) Inf. Co.G
Taylor, W.L. GA Cav. 7th Bn. (St.Guards) Co.B
Taylor, W.L. GA 6th Inf. (St.Guards) Co.G
Taylor, W.L. MS 6th Inf. Co.I
Taylor, W.L. SC 2nd Inf. Co.G
Taylor, W.L. TN 63rd Inf. Co.H
Taylor, W.L. TX Granbury's Cons.Brig. Co.E 1st Lt.
Taylor, W.L. TX 14th Inf. Co.H Sgt.
Taylor, W.M. AL 7th Cav. Co.I
Taylor, W.M. AL Cav. Moreland's Regt. Co.H
Taylor, W.M. AL 9th Inf.
Taylor, W.M. AL 10th Inf. Co.K
Taylor, W.M. AL 17th Inf. Co.F
Taylor, W.M. AL 38th Inf. Co.F
Taylor, W.M. AL 58th Inf. Co.C Sgt.
Taylor, W.M. AL Cp. of Instr. Talladega
Taylor, W.M. AR 12th Inf. Co.I
Taylor, W.M. AR 13th Inf. Co.C
Taylor, W.M. AR 37th Inf. Co.D
Taylor, W.M. GA 1st Troops & Defences (Macon) Co.B
Taylor, W.M. LA Inf.Cons.Crescent Regt. Co.N
Taylor, W.M. NC 1st Cav. (9th St.Troops) Co.K
Taylor, W.M. SC 4th Cav. Co.G
Taylor, W.M. NC Wallace's Co. (Wilmington RR Guard)
Taylor, W.M. TN 7th (Duckworth's) Cav. Co.I
Taylor, W.M. TN Arty. Fisher's Co.
Taylor, W.M. TN 12th (Cons.) Inf. Co.K
Taylor, W.M. VA 30th Inf. Co.H
Taylor, W.M. Conf.Cav. Clarkson's Bn. Ind. Rangers Co.A
Taylor, W.McD. MS Inf. 3rd Bn. Co.H 1st Sgt.
Taylor, W.N. FL Kilcrease Lt.Arty. Sgt.
Taylor, W.N. MO 9th Inf. Co.H
Taylor, W.N. SC Lt.Arty. 3rd (Palmetto) Bn. Co.I
Taylor, W.N. SC 16th Inf. Co.F
Taylor, W.N. SC 16th & 24th (Cons.) Inf. Co.A
Taylor, W.O. TN 14th (Neely's) Cav. Co.E
Taylor, Woodson NC Walker's Bn. Thomas' Legion Co.H
Taylor, Woody R. TN 1st (Turney's) Inf. Co.E
Taylor, W.P. GA Lt.Arty. Clinch's Btty. Cpl.
Taylor, W.P. GA 3rd Res. Co.K
Taylor, W.P. GA 55th Inf. Co.C
Taylor, W.P. GA 56th Inf. Co.G
Taylor, W.P. GA 56th Inf. Co.I
Taylor, W.P. MS 9th Cav. Co.A
Taylor, W.P. MS Cav. 17th Bn. Co.A
Taylor, W.P. NC 1st Inf.
Taylor, W.P. NC 31st Inf. Co.G Cpl.
Taylor, W.P. SC 5th Cav. Co.K
Taylor, W.P. SC Lt.Arty. 3rd (Palmetto) Bn. Co.H,I
Taylor, W.P. SC 16th Inf. Co.F
Taylor, W.P. SC 17th Inf. Co.B 1st Lt.
Taylor, W.P. SC 17th Inf. Co.B
Taylor, W.P. TX 25th Cav. Co.K
Taylor, W.P. TX 9th (Nichols') Inf. Co.E
Taylor, W.P. VA Lt.Arty. 1st Bn. Co.B
Taylor, W.P. VA Arty. Richardson's Co.
Taylor, W.P. VA Mil. Scott Cty.
Taylor, W.P. 15th Conf.Cav. Co.H
Taylor, W.P.W. VA 1st St.Res. Co.F
Taylor, W.R. AL 15th Cav. Co.H
Taylor, W.R. AL Cav. Moreland's Regt. Co.F
Taylor, W.R. AL 19th Inf. Co.I
Taylor, W.R. AL 35th Inf. Co.F
Taylor, W.R. MS 1st Lt.Arty. Co.F
Taylor, W.R. MS Inf. 1st Bn. Co.A
Taylor, W.R. SC 6th Cav. Co.I
Taylor, W.R. SC 9th Res. Co.E
Taylor, W.R. TN 3rd (Forrest's) Cav. Co.C
Taylor, W.R. TN 11th (Holman's) Cav. Co.C
Taylor, W.R. TN Lt.Arty. Rice's Btty.
Taylor, W.R. TN 5th Inf. 1st Co.F
Taylor, W.R. TX 29th Cav. Co.H Cpl.
Taylor, W.R. VA 14th Cav. Co.G
Taylor, W.R. VA 79th Mil. Co.1
Taylor, W.R. 15th Conf.Cav. Co.A
Taylor, W.R. Conf.Cav. Powers' Regt. Co.A
Taylor, W.R.H. AL 17th Inf. Co.D
Taylor, W.R.H. AL 23rd Inf. Co.B
Taylor, Wright AL 7th Cav. Co.A Cpl.
Taylor, Wright NC Walker's Bn. Thomas' Legion Co.A
Taylor, Wright L. NC 3rd Cav. (41st St.Troops) Co.E
Taylor, W.S. AL 7th Cav. Co.H,A
Taylor, W.S. GA 6th Inf.
Taylor, W.S. GA 11th Inf. Co.K
Taylor, W.S. GA 24th Inf. Co.G
Taylor, W.S. MS 1st Cav. Co.F
Taylor, W.S. MS 4th Cav. Co.A
Taylor, W.S. NC 47th Inf. Co.E
Taylor, W.S. VA 79th Mil. Co.1
Taylor, W.S.H. VA 3rd Inf.Loc.Def. Co.D
Taylor, W.T. AL 4th (Russell's) Cav. Co.F
Taylor, W.T. AL 56th Part.Rangers Co.A 2nd Lt.
Taylor, W.T. AL 34th Inf. Co.H
Taylor, W.T. KY 1st Inf. Co.C
Taylor, W.T. MS 14th (Cons.) Inf. Co.H
Taylor, W.T. NC Cav. 16th Bn. Co.F
Taylor, W.T. TN 7th (Duckworth's) Cav. Co.F
Taylor, W.T. TN 1st (Feild's) Inf. Co.F
Taylor, W.T. TN Inf. 1st Cons.Regt. Co.B
Taylor, W.T. 15th Conf.Cav. Co.A
Taylor, W.V. TN 13th Inf. Co.A,G
Taylor, W.V. TN Inf. 154th Sr.Regt.
Taylor, W.W. AL Mil. 4th Vol. Co.E
Taylor, W.W. AL 18th Inf. Co.B
Taylor, W.W. AR 1st Vol. Co.K Sgt.
Taylor, W.W. AR 7th Mil. Co.C 3rd Lt.
Taylor, W.W. KY 3rd Bn.Mtd.Rifles Co.A Cpl.
Taylor, W.W. KY 1st Inf. Co.C
Taylor, W.W. LA 6th Cav. Co.I 1st Lt.
Taylor, W.W. LA 16th Inf. Co.G Jr.2nd Lt.
Taylor, W.W. LA Mil. British Guard Bn. Kurczyn's Co.
Taylor, W.W. MS Cav. 1st Bn. (Montgomery's) St.Troops Hammond's Co. 1st Lt.
Taylor, W.W. MS 38th Cav. Co.A
Taylor, W.W. MS Lt.Arty. 14th Bn. Co.B
Taylor, W.W. MS 12th Inf. Co.A
Taylor, W.W. MS 20th Inf. Co.G Sgt.
Taylor, W.W. NC 54th Inf. Co.K
Taylor, W.W. SC Arty. Manigault's Bn. Co.A
Taylor, W.W. SC 1st (Hagood's) Inf. 1st Co.K

Taylor, W.W. TN 15th (Cons.) Cav. Co.D,E
Taylor, W.W. TN 30th Inf. Co.B
Taylor, W.W. TN 31st Inf. Co.E Sgt.
Taylor, W.W. TN 31st Inf. Co.G
Taylor, W.W. TN 55th (Brown's) Inf. Co.G
Taylor, W.W. TX 23rd Cav. Co.G
Taylor, W.W. TX 35th (Brown's) Cav. Co.I
Taylor, W.W. TX Cav. Hardeman's Regt. Co.G
Taylor, W.W. TX Cav. Morgan's Regt. Co.F
Taylor, W.W. TX Inf. Chambers' Bn.Res.Corps Co.D
Taylor, W.W. VA 3rd Bn. Valley Res. Co.D
Taylor, W.W. VA 4th Res. Co.A 2nd Lt.
Taylor, W.W. VA 4th Bn.Res. Co.B 2nd Lt.
Taylor, Wyatt AL 42nd Inf. Co.G
Taylor, Wyatt A. AL 51st (Part.Rangers) Co.F
Taylor, Wyatt A. TN 51st Inf. Co.E
Taylor, Wyley N. AL 3rd Bn.Res. Co.A
Taylor, Young AR 2nd Mtd.Rifles Co.E Sgt.
Taylor, Young AR Mtd.Vol. (St.Troops) Abraham's Co.
Taylor, Young TN 41st Inf. Co.A
Taylor, Young A. TN 44th (Cons.) Inf. Co.A
Taylor, Y.P. KY Cav. Buckner Guards
Taylor, Y.P. Mead's Conf.Cav. Co.B 3rd Lt.
Taylor, Z. AR 11th & 17th Cons.Inf. Co.D
Taylor, Z. MS 21st Inf. Co.F
Taylor, Z. NC 2nd Jr.Res. Co.H
Taylor, Z. TN 4th Inf. Co.D
Taylor, Zacaria AL Talladega Cty.Res. B.H. Ford's Co.
Taylor, Zach GA Inf. Cobb Guards Co.A
Taylor, Zachariah AL 33rd Inf. Co.G
Taylor, Zachariah MO Cav. Poindexter's Regt.
Taylor, Zachariah NC 26th Inf. Co.F
Taylor, Zachariah SC 20th Inf. Co.K
Taylor, Zachariah VA 9th Inf. Co.G
Taylor, Zachariah F. AL 13th Inf. Co.D
Taylor, Zachary B. GA 15th Inf. Co.F
Taylor, Zeb AL 32nd Inf. Co.F
Taylor, Zenos NC 3rd Arty. (40th St.Troops) Co.A
Taylor, Zenus NC 32nd Inf. Lenoir Braves 1st Co.K
Taylor, Z.F. GA 3rd Bn.S.S. Co.F
Taylor, Z.F. GA Phillips' Legion Co.C
Taylor, Z.T. TX 12th Cav. Co.B
Taylor, Z.W.F. NC 2nd Jr.Res. Co.E
Taylors, John AR 14th (Powers') Inf. Co.F
Taylors, W.T. Brush Bn.
Tayman, Benjamin TN 19th Inf. Co.F
Tayne, Louis VA 54th Inf. Co.K
Taynes, William T. LA Mil. C.S. Zouave Bn. Co.H
Tayolsey 1st Creek Mtd.Vol. Co.D
Tayroe, S. MS 5th Inf. (St.Troops) Co.F
Tays, H. TX 3rd Inf. Co.B
Tays, James L. AL 9th Inf. Co.I
Tays, James M. MO 3rd Inf. Co.G
Tays, J.T. NC 4th Inf. Co.C
Tays, Logan TN 28th Inf. Co.A Cpl.
Tays, Samuel TN 25th Inf. Co.D
Tays, Samuel L. NC 49th Inf. Co.E Sgt.
Tays, S.M. TN 28th (Cons.) Inf. Co.H
Tays, S.M. TN 84th Inf. Co.D
Tays, Thomas VA Cav. Hounshell's Bn. Co.A
Tayse, R.W. TN 4th (Murray's) Cav. Co.D
Tayse, R.W. 1st Conf.Cav. 2nd Co.C
Taytom, George W. TN 3rd (Forrest's) Cav. Co.K
Tayton, F.M. MS 14th (Cons.) Inf. Co.C
Taytor, C. VA 3rd Res. Co.H
Taytor, F.M. AR 8th Cav. Co.A
Tazr, M. GA 32nd Inf.
Tazton, G.W. AR Inf. Hardy's Regt. Co.I
Tazy, C. GA 1st Inf.
T'Bout, Thomas NC 2nd Arty. (36th St.Troops) Co.I
Tcah wah te ski 1st Cherokee Mtd.Vol. Co.J
Tchappa, R. TX 5th Cav. Co.D
Tchoepe, Louis TX 4th Cav. Co.C
Tea, Giovanni LA Mil. 4th Regt.Eur.Brig. Cognevich's Co.
Tea, Jacob LA 14th Inf. Co.G
Teabo, James W. VA Lt.Arty. Garber's Co.
Teaboe, Philip NC 51st Inf. Co.G
Teaboe, William W. NC 51st Inf. Co.G
Teabout, Elijah NC 5th Inf. Co.F
Teabout, Nicholas NC 33rd Inf. Co.E
Teabout, Thomas SC 25th Inf. Co.I,G
Teacher 1st Cherokee Mtd.Rifles Co.F
Teacher, James 1st Cherokee Mtd.Vol. 1st Co.A, 2nd Co.B
Teacher, T. NC 3rd Inf.
Teacher Smith 1st Cherokee Mtd.Rifles Co.F
Teachey, Atlas NC 30th Inf. Co.E
Teachey, Daniel, Jr. NC 30th Inf. Co.E Jr.2nd Lt.
Teachey, Daniel W. NC 3rd Inf. Co.B
Teachey, Jacob T. NC 30th Inf. Co.E
Teachey, James W. NC 30th Inf. Co.E Sgt.
Teachey, Marshall NC 30th Inf. Co.E Sgt.
Teachey, Owen NC McDugald's Co.
Teachey, Robert NC 3rd Arty. (40th St.Troops) Co.A 1st Sgt.
Teachey, Robert NC 12th Inf. Co.C
Teachey, S.B. NC 2nd Jr.Res. Co.A
Teachey, S.B. NC 57th Inf. Co.B
Teachey, W.B. NC 30th Inf. Co.E Cpl.
Teachey, William NC 51st Inf. Co.G
Teachy, Enoch NC McDugald's Co.
Teachy, Owen J. NC 67th Inf. Co.L
Teachy, Thaddeus NC McDugald's Co.
Teachy, Wiley NC 8th Sr.Res. Broadhurst's Co.
Teacle, William LA Inf. 9th Bn. Co.A
Teadford, James K.P. AR 14th (Powers') Inf. Co.E
Teadmarsh, James VA 52nd Inf. Co.G
Teady, R. NC 2nd Inf. Co.D
Teaff, Henry AR 27th Inf.
Teaff, James M. TX 21st Cav. Co.D Sgt.
Teaff, J.D. TX 26th Cav. Co.E
Teaff, John H. AR 27th Inf. Co.K Sgt.
Teaff, N.F. TX 6th Inf. Co.G Sgt.
Teaff, Oliver P. AR 27th Inf. Co.K
Teaff, William J. AR 27th Inf. Co.K 2nd Lt.
Teaffekiller, Jefferson TN Cav. 5th Bn. (McClellan's) Co.E
Teaford, Daniel VA 14th Cav. Co.C
Teaford, David VA 1st Cav. Co.A
Teaford, David VA 27th Inf. Co.B
Teaford, Elijah VA Rockbridge Cty.Res. Hutcheson's Co.
Teaford, George W. VA 58th Inf. Co.G 1st Lt.
Teaford, Jacob P.S. VA 25th Inf. 2nd Co.H Cpl.
Teaford, Joseph H. VA 14th Cav. Co.I
Teaford, Martin L. VA 2nd Inf. Co.D
Teafs, J.T. VA 2nd Cav. Co.G
Teagan, J.P. LA Mil. 3rd Regt. 1st Brig. 1st Div. Co.C
Teagarden, A.L. TX 6th Cav. Co.H
Teagarden, Thomas TX 6th Cav. Co.H
Teagardner, J.R. KY 3rd Bn.Mtd.Rifles White's Co.
Teage, D.G. MO Cav. Ford's Bn. Co.C
Teage, J. MO Cav. Ford's Bn. Co.C
Teage, Jackson AR Inf. Hardy's Regt. Co.A
Teage, J.P. MS 1st (Percy's) Inf. Co.I
Teage, Robert AR Cav. McGehee's Regt. Co.C
Teage, R.S. MO Cav. Ford's Bn. Co.C
Teager, F.M. AL 6th Cav. Co.E
Teagire, J.B. TN 19th (Biffle's) Cav. Co.G
Teagle, Cornelius VA 26th Inf. Co.A,F Music.
Teagle, Edward W. VA 21st Mil. Co.B Drum.
Teagle, Edward W. VA 26th Inf. Co.A Music.
Teagle, H.T. GA 13th Cav. Co.F,I
Teagle, Isaac GA 13th Cav. Co.I
Teagle, J.G. LA 2nd Cav. Co.F
Teagle, John MD Cav. 2nd Bn. Co.D
Teagle, John TN 38th Inf. Co.F
Teagle, John A. VA 26th Inf. Co.A
Teagle, John G. LA 12th Inf. Co.C
Teagle, John W. LA 3rd Inf. Co.C
Teagle, M. FL 3rd Inf. Co.K
Teagle, Nat GA 1st Cav. Co.B
Teagle, Theodore F. VA 62nd Mtd.Inf. Co.B Sgt.
Teagle, Theodore S. VA Lt.Arty. Garber's Co.
Teagle, T.J. LA 22nd (Cons.) Inf. Co.F
Teagle, T.J. LA 27th Inf. Co.F
Teagle, W.C. LA 27th Inf. Co.F
Teagle, William C. LA 12th Inf. Co.C
Teagle, William E.C. VA 21st Mil. Co.B Capt.
Teagle, William E.C. VA 26th Inf. Co.A
Teagne, Jo. MS 15th (Cons.) Inf. Co.E
Teague, --- TX 1st (McCulloch's) Cav. Co.A Bugler
Teague, --- TX Cav. Bourland's Regt. Co.G
Teague, A.A. AL Res. Brown's Co.
Teague, A.B. AR 15th Mil. Co.A
Teague, Abner A. AL Cav. Barbiere's Bn. Brown's Co.
Teague, Abraham MO 15th Cav. Co.N
Teague, Abram TN 20th Inf. Co.A
Teague, Absalom F. TX 17th Cav. Co.C Cpl.
Teague, A.D. AR 5th Inf. Co.I
Teague, A.D. 3rd Conf.Eng.Troops Co.F Cpl.
Teague, Adam B. MO Inf. 8th Bn. Co.D
Teague, Adolphus H. NC 29th Inf. Co.C
Teague, A.E. MS 20th Inf. Co.A
Teague, A.E. Gen. & Staff A.Surg.
Teague, A.F. NC 57th Inf. Co.D Sgt.
Teague, A.F. TX 17th Cons.Dismtd.Cav. Co.C
Teague, A.F. TX 28th Cav. Co.B,D Cpl.
Teague, A.J. GA 8th Cav. Old Co.D
Teague, A.J. GA 62nd Cav. Co.D
Teague, A.J. NC Cav. 16th Bn. Co.H
Teague, A.J. SC 5th St.Troops Co.C
Teague, A.J. TN 3rd (Forrest's) Cav. Co.F
Teague, Alex GA Cav. Young's Co. (Alleghany Troopers)

Teague, Alpheus A. NC 46th Inf. Co.F Music.
Teague, Amos LA 17th Inf. Co.E
Teague, Andrew J. NC 37th Inf. Co.E
Teague, Andrew J. NC 62nd Inf. Co.A
Teague, Aquilla NC 4th Cav. (59th St.Troops) Co.B
Teague, Augustus TN 43rd Inf. Co.H,E
Teague, A.W. SC 2nd Cav. Co.G Bvt.2nd Lt.
Teague, A.W. SC 3rd Inf. Co.A Sgt.
Teague, Barney Conf.Cav. Wood's Regt. Co.E
Teague, B.F. TN 13th Inf. Co.E
Teague, B. Hammet SC Inf. Hampton Legion Co.B
Teague, B.K. NC 49th Inf. Co.H
Teague, Bloomington NC 58th Inf. Co.E
Teague, C. AL 12th Cav. Co.G
Teague, C. AL 62nd Inf. Co.B
Teague, C. TN 15th (Cons.) Cav. Co.K
Teague, C.B. TX 7th Cav. Co.K
Teague, C.C. SC 2nd St.Troops Co.F Music.
Teague, C.C. SC Cav.Bn. Holcombe Legion Co.C Cpl.
Teague, C.F. AL 11th Inf. Co.K
Teague, Chesley J. AL 18th Inf. Co.L
Teague, C.J. AL 58th Inf. Co.G
Teague, C.J. AL Cp. of Instr. Talladega
Teague, C.M. TN 14th Cav.
Teague, Daniel NC 37th Inf. Co.E
Teague, David AR 33rd Inf. Co.F
Teague, David NC 6th Sr.Res. Co.D Sgt.
Teague, D.G. AR 32nd Inf. Co.C
Teague, D.H. NC 1st Jr.Res. Co.H
Teague, Drayton TX 37th Cav. Co.E Sgt.
Teague, D.S. MO 7th Cav. Co.E
Teague, E.A. AL 17th Inf. Co.E
Teague, E.A. AL Cp. of Instr. Talladega
Teague, E.C. AL 31st Inf. Co.D 1st Lt.
Teague, Edmund NC 33rd Inf. Co.C
Teague, Edward NC Cav. 5th Bn. Co.A
Teague, Edwin NC 6th Cav. (65th St.Troops) Co.A
Teague, E.F. AL Randolph Cty.Res. D.A. Self's Co.
Teague, Elijah AL 44th Inf. Co.K
Teague, Elijah AL Cp. of Instr. Talladega
Teague, Elijah GA 65th Inf. Co.B
Teague, Elijah NC Mil. 66th Bn. J.H. Whitman's Co.
Teague, Eli NC 26th Inf. Co.H
Teague, Elijah W. AL 6th Inf. Co.B 2nd Lt.
Teague, E.M. AR 32nd Inf. Co.D 2nd Lt.
Teague, Emry O. AL 44th Inf. Co.I
Teague, E.T. AL 30th Inf. Co.G
Teague, E.T. AL Cp. of Instr. Talladega
Teague, Eugene MS 1st Lt.Arty. Co.A
Teague, E.W. AL 31st Inf. Co.D
Teague, F. AR 5th Mil. Co.E
Teague, Felix AR 17th (Griffith's) Inf. Co.B
Teague, F.M. GA Cav. 16th Bn. (St.Guards) Co.D
Teague, Francis M. GA 1st Inf. Co.H
Teague, Francis M. NC Mallett's Bn. (Cp.Guard) Co.B Cpl.
Teague, General M. TX 15th Cav. Co.E
Teague, George GA 23rd Inf. Co.B
Teague, George C. MS Cav. 3rd Bn.Res. Co.B
Teague, George W. KY Corbin's Men
Teague, George W. NC 37th Inf. Co.A Cpl.
Teague, George W. NC 29th Inf. Co.E
Teague, George W. TN 36th Inf. Co.B
Teague, George W.L. SC 5th Inf. 1st Co.A
Teague, Gilbrite NC 22nd Inf. Co.A
Teague, G.M. TX 6th Inf. Co.G
Teague, G.W. LA 42nd Inf. Co.A
Teague, G.W.L. SC Palmetto S.S. Co.A Sgt.
Teague, H. AL 56th Part.Rangers Co.K
Teague, Harris AL 63rd Inf. Co.A
Teague, Hardy J. TX 9th (Nichols') Inf. Co.K
Teague, Harrison H. NC 39th Inf. Co.A,E
Teague, Henry MS 22nd Inf. Co.F
Teague, Henry MO 15th Cav. Co.N
Teague, Henry NC 7th Inf. Co.K
Teague, Henry SC 5th Inf. 2nd Co.I
Teague, Henry SC 6th Inf. 1st Co.I
Teague, Heny P. TX 3rd Cav. Co.F 2nd Lt.
Teague, Hez D. NC 6th Sr.Res. Co.B
Teague, H.F. AL 18th Inf. Co.I
Teague, Hillary F. AL 10th Inf. Co.K
Teague, Hiram AR 27th Inf. Co.D
Teague, H.J. TX Waul's Legion Co.C
Teague, H.M. TN 4th Inf. Co.B
Teague, H.M. Eng.,CSA
Teague, Hosea AR 33rd Inf. Co.F
Teague, H.S. TN 14th (Neely's) Cav. Co.E
Teague, Isaac MS 29th Inf. Co.B
Teague, Isaac NC 26th Inf. Co.H
Teague, Isaac SC 20th Inf. Co.A
Teague, Isaac B.H. NC Hvy.Arty. 10th Bn. Co.A,D
Teague, Isaac H. NC 7th Sr.Res. Clinard's Co.
Teague, Isaac M. GA Lt.Arty. (Jo Thompson Arty.) Hanleiter's Co.
Teague, Isaac M. GA 38th Inf. Co.M
Teague, Isaac N. GA 64th Inf. Co.A
Teague, J. AR 32nd Inf. Co.C
Teague, J. AR Nichols' Regt. Co.I
Teague, J. NC 22nd Inf. Co.A
Teague, J. SC 9th Res. Co.F
Teague, J. TN 21st (Wilson's) Cav. Co.G
Teague, J.A. AR 35th Inf. Co.H
Teague, J.A. GA 8th Cav. Old Co.D
Teague, J.A. GA 11th Cav. Co.C
Teague, J.A. GA 62nd Cav. Co.D
Teague, Jacob AR 8th Inf. Old Co.A
Teague, Jacob MO 7th Cav. Co.E
Teague, Jacob NC Inf. 2nd Bn. Co.G
Teague, James GA Cav. 16th Bn. (St.Guards) Co.D
Teague, James MS 2nd Part.Rangers Co.L,D
Teague, James MO Cav. Coffee's Regt. Co.A
Teague, James TN 7th (Duckworth's) Cav. Co.K
Teague, James TN 43rd Inf. Co.A
Teague, James Anderson AL 35th Inf. Co.F
Teague, James A. MS 29th Inf. Co.I
Teague, James A.J. AL 2nd Cav. Co.B
Teague, James E. NC 26th Inf. Co.E
Teague, James F. NC Cav. 5th Bn. Co.A Sgt.
Teague, James F. NC 6th Cav. (65th St.Troops) Co.A,I Sgt.
Teague, James J. NC 58th Inf. Co.E
Teague, James K. AR 14th (Powers') Inf. Co.D
Teague, James L. GA 11th Inf. Co.D
Teague, James M. LA 15th Inf. Co.G Sgt.
Teague, James N. GA 1st Reg. Co.I
Teague, James P. AR 2nd Inf. Co.G
Teague, James R. AL 27th Inf. Co.A
Teague, James R. AL 55th Vol. Co.C
Teague, James R. TN 38th Inf. Co.E Ord.Sgt.
Teague, J.B. TN 22nd Inf. Co.B Sgt.
Teague, J.C. MS 20th Inf. Co.A
Teague, J.E. TN 4th (McLemore's) Cav. Co.H Capt.
Teague, J.E. TX Vol. Teague's Co. (So.Rights Guards) Capt.
Teague, Jeff TN Cav. Nixon's Regt. Co.C
Teague, J.H. MO 1st & 4th Cons.Inf. Co.I
Teague, J.H. MO 4th Inf. Co.I
Teague, J.H. TX 32nd Cav. Co.F Music.
Teague, J.H. TX 19th Inf. Co.K
Teague, J.H. TX Vol. Teague's Co. (So.Rights Guards)
Teague, J.L. TN 3rd (Forrest's) Cav. Co.D
Teague, J.M. GA Inf. 8th Bn. Co.G
Teague, J.M. NC 15th Inf. Co.H
Teague, J.M. TN 14th (Neely's) Cav. Co.H,C
Teague, J.M. TX Cav. 1st Regt.St.Troops Co.C
Teague, J.M. Eng.,CSA Ord.Sgt.
Teague, J.N. MS 12th Inf. Co.I Cpl.
Teague, Jo. B. AL 18th Inf. Co.I
Teague, John AR 15th (Johnson's) Inf. Co.D Cpl.
Teague, John AR 35th Inf. Co.D
Teague, John GA 15th Inf. Co.B
Teague, John MO 15th Cav. Co.N
Teague, John NC 5th Sr.Res. Co.D
Teague, John NC 6th Sr.Res. Co.H
Teague, John, Sr. NC 7th Inf. Co.K Cpl.
Teague, John NC 29th Inf. Co.H
Teague, John SC 1st Arty. Co.C
Teague, John TN 21st & 22nd (Cons.) Cav. Co.I
Teague, John TN 23rd Inf. Co.H Sgt.
Teague, John 1st Conf.Inf. 2nd Co.E
Teague, John A. GA 11th Cav. Co.C Bvt.2nd Lt.
Teague, John A. GA 1st Reg. Co.I
Teague, John A. NC 26th Inf. Co.I
Teague, John A. NC 29th Inf. Co.E Capt.
Teague, John A. NC 37th Inf. Co.G
Teague, John C. AR 14th (Powers') Inf. Co.A Sgt.
Teague, John E. TN 2nd (Smith's) Cav. Rankin's Co. 2nd Lt.
Teague, John F. TX 12th Inf. Co.I
Teague, John M. AL 44th Inf. Co.K Capt.
Teague, John M. NC 7th Inf. Co.K
Teague, John M. TN 6th Inf. Co.C
Teague, John N. MO Inf. 8th Bn. Co.D
Teague, John R. TX 18th Inf. Co.B
Teague, John T. NC 5th Sr.Res. Co.D
Teague, John W. AR 4th Inf. Co.A 1st Lt.
Teague, Joseph NC 48th Inf. Co.K
Teague, Joseph F. NC Inf. 2nd Bn. Co.G
Teague, Joshua AR 14th (Powers') Inf. Co.D 3rd Lt.
Teague, Joshua AR 16th Inf. Co.K
Teague, Joshua AR 18th Inf. Co.H
Teague, Joshua AR 27th Inf. Co.F
Teague, Joshua C. MS 2nd Cav. Co.B
Teague, Joshua F. MS 42nd Inf. Co.C
Teague, J.P. MS 13th Inf. Co.I
Teague, J.S. TX 17th Inf. Co.B

Teague, J.T. AL Cav. Hardie's Bn.Res. Co.F
Teague, J.W. AR 5th Mil. Co.E Sgt.
Teague, J.W. AR 6th Inf. 1st Co.B
Teague, J.W. SC 20th Inf. Co.A
Teague, J.W. TN 21st (Wilson's) Cav. Co.G
Teague, J.W. TN Conscr. (Cp. of Instr.) Co.B
Teague, King D. TX 15th Cav. Co.G
Teague, Latinus L. AL 6th Inf. Co.B
Teague, L.B. AL 55th Vol. Co.C
Teague, L.D. AR 10th Mil. Co.D
Teague, Lewis T. NC 26th Inf. Co.E Sgt.
Teague, L.K. SC 1st Bn.S.S. Co.C
Teague, L.K. SC 27th Inf. Co.G
Teague, Logan NC 22nd Inf. Co.A
Teague, Logan NC 26th Inf. Co.F
Teague, Logan NC 58th Inf. Co.E
Teague, Lorenzo D. TX 8th Inf. Co.D
Teague, Loss L. NC 1st Cav. (9th St.Troops) Co.G
Teague, Ludy K. SC Inf. 3rd Bn. Co.A Cpl.
Teague, M. NC 5th Sr.Res. Co.B
Teague, M. TX 8th Inf. Co.D
Teague, M.A. AR 34th Inf. Co.E
Teague, Magnes AL 19th Inf. Co.G
Teague, Marion MO Cav. Coleman's Regt. Co.G Sgt.
Teague, M.B. GA 13th Inf. Co.K Cpl.
Teague, M.E. GA Cav. Young's Co. (Alleghany Troopers)
Teague, Meredith M. NC 46th Inf. Co.F Capt.
Teague, Merriman E. GA 1st Reg. Co.E Cpl.
Teague, Michael NC Cav. 5th Bn. Co.A
Teague, Michael NC 16th Inf. Co.B
Teague, Mike NC 6th Cav. (65th St.Troops) Co.A,I
Teague, M.M. AL Jeff Davis Arty.
Teague, M.M. AL Cp. of Instr. Talladega
Teague, M.M. SC 2nd Cav. Co.G
Teague, M.M. SC 3rd Inf. Co.A
Teague, M.M. TN 38th Inf. Co.C
Teague, Monroe SC 18th Inf. Co.K
Teague, Moses NC 37th Inf. Co.E
Teague, Moses A. NC 33rd Inf. Co.H
Teague, M.R. NC Inf. 2nd Bn. Co.B
Teague, M.S. MS 15th Inf. Co.A
Teague, Nathan NC 22nd Inf. Co.A
Teague, Nimrod GA 11th Inf. Co.D
Teague, Nimrod KY 3rd Cav. Co.D
Teague, O.F. TX 29th Cav. Co.B Cpl.
Teague, O.S. AL Jeff Davis Arty.
Teague, O.S. AL Cp. of Instr. Talladega
Teague, R.A. AR 36th Inf. Co.D
Teague, R.B. AR Nichols' Regt. Co.I
Teague, R.E. SC 1st (Hagood's) Inf. 2nd Co.H Sgt.
Teague, Richard A. AR 31st Inf. Co.E Sgt.
Teague, Richard M. TN 6th Inf. Co.G
Teague, R.J. AL 31st Inf. Co.D
Teague, R.J. AL 37th Inf. Co.D
Teague, R.L. AR 7th Inf. Co.E
Teague, R.M. GA Lt.Arty. (Arsenal Btty.) Hudson's Co.
Teague, Robert GA 1st Bn.S.S.
Teague, Robert GA 1st Inf. (St.Guards)
Teague, Robert H. GA 42nd Inf. Co.A
Teague, Robert H. NC 7th Inf. Co.K 1st Lt.
Teague, Romulus NC Inf. 2nd Bn. Co.G
Teague, S. AR 5th Mil. Co.E Cpl.
Teague, S. AR 51st Mil. Co.E
Teague, S. TN 15th (Cons.) Cav. Co.K
Teague, Samuel D. MS 3rd Cav.
Teague, Samuel D. MS 12th Inf. Co.I
Teague, Samuel E. NC 26th Inf. Co.G 2nd Lt.
Teague, Samuel M. TN 36th Inf. Co.B
Teague, S.G. AL Cav. Barbiere's Bn. Bowie's Co., Co.F
Teague, Silas AR 35th Inf. Co.D
Teague, Smith NC 60th Inf. Co.H
Teague, S.P. TX 4th Inf. Co.B
Teague, Stephen G. AR 14th (Powers') Inf. Co.D
Teague, T.B. LA 13th Bn. (Part.Rangers) Co.C
Teague, Thomas AR 15th (Johnson's) Inf. Co.D
Teague, Thomas TN 10th Cav. Co.H
Teague, Thomas TN Waterhouse Btty.
Teague, Thomas A. TX 15th Cav. Co.G
Teague, Thomas F. MO Inf. 8th Bn. Co.D
Teague, Thomas J. KY 3rd Cav. Co.A
Teague, Thomas J. Gen. & Staff Asst.Surg.
Teague, T.J. AL 31st Inf. Co.D
Teague, T.J. SC 3rd Inf. Co.A
Teague, T.S. SC 7th Cav. Co.E
Teague, T.S. SC 13th Inf. Co.H
Teague, T.S. SC Cav.Bn. Holcombe Legion Co.C
Teague, Van NC 18th Inf. Co.D
Teague, Vandaver NC 55th Inf. Co.H Capt.
Teague, Vandaver M. NC 58th Inf. Co.I
Teague, Vandever NC 37th Inf. Co.G 1st Sgt.
Teague, Vandiver S. NC 37th Inf. Co.G
Teague, W. SC 18th Inf. Co.H
Teague, W.A. AR 38th Inf. New Co.I
Teague, Warren H. AL 19th Inf. Co.G
Teague, Washington NC 26th Inf. Co.I
Teague, W.B. NC 48th Inf. Co.D
Teague, W.C. NC 6th Cav. (65th St.Troops) Co.A
Teague, W.C. SC 9th Res. Co.K
Teague, W.F. TX Vol. Teague's Co. (So.Rights Guards)
Teague, W.H. TN 29th Inf. Co.A
Teague, Wilbur F. AL 18th Inf. Co.I
Teague, William AL Talladega Cty.Res. J.T. Smith's Co.
Teague, William AR Cav. 1st Bn. (Stirman's) Co.G
Teague, William AR 16th Inf. Co.K
Teague, William GA 38th Inf. Co.F
Teague, William GA 65th Inf. Co.B
Teague, William MO 15th Cav. Co.N
Teague, William NC 26th Inf. Co.H
Teague, William SC 6th Res. Co.G
Teague, William SC 20th Inf. Co.A
Teague, William TN 14th (Neely's) Cav. Co.E
Teague, William TN Cav. 17th Bn. (Sanders') Co.A
Teague, William A. TN 23rd Inf. Co.H Cpl.
Teague, William C. MO Inf. Clark's Regt. Co.G
Teague, William C. SC 6th Cav. Co.E
Teague, William C. TN Cav. 4th Bn. (Branner's) Co.A
Teague, William C. Conf.Cav. Clarkson's Bn. Ind.Rangers Co.E
Teague, William D. GA 6th Cav. Co.F Bvt.2nd Lt.
Teague, William D. GA 1st Reg. Co.B
Teague, William F. TX 3rd Inf. Co.G 1st Sgt.
Teague, William G. NC 7th Inf. Co.K
Teague, William J. AR 9th Inf. Old Co.I, Co.C Cpl.
Teague, William M. AL 3rd Inf. Co.I 1st Sgt.
Teague, William M. MS 12th Inf. Co.I Cpl.
Teague, William M. NC 26th Inf. Co.G
Teague, William O. AR 2nd Inf. Co.D
Teague, William P. NC 42nd Inf. Co.F
Teague, William R. GA 52nd Inf. Co.H
Teague, William S. AR 2nd Inf. Co.G Sgt.
Teague, William S. TX 19th Inf. Co.G,B,K
Teague, William W. NC Unassign.Conscr.
Teague, Willis NC 26th Inf. Co.G
Teague, W.J. AL 1st Cav. 1st Co.C
Teague, W.J. TX 17th Inf. Co.B
Teague, W.L. AR 2nd Cav. Co.F
Teague, W.M. MO Cav. Coffee's Regt. Co.A
Teague, W.N. AR Pine Bluff Arty.
Teague, W.P. NC 66th Inf. Hosp.Stew.
Teague, W.P. TX 28th Cav. Co.D Cpl.
Teague, W.S. TN 14th Cav.
Teague, W.T. LA 31st Inf. Co.E
Teague, W.T. TN 6th Inf. Co.C
Teague, W.W. AR 15th Mil. Co.A
Teague, Z. TX Waul's Legion Co.F
Teah, Abraham TX 12th Inf. Co.G Sgt.Maj.
Teah, Bernard TX 13th Cav. Co.E 1st Lt.
Teahan, B.J. MS 21st Inf. Co.L
Teahan, Joseph 9th Conf.Inf. Co.D
Teahan, W.M. 3rd Conf.Eng.Troops Co.B Sgt.
Teahen, W.M. Eng.Dept. Polk's Corps A. of TN Sap. & Min. Co.,CSA Sgt.
Teairney, Patrick SC Ord.Guards Loc.Def.Troops
Teakeil, James M. AL 2nd Cav. Co.G
Teakell, Josiah AL 2nd Cav. Co.G Sgt.
Teakell, N.A. AL 2nd Cav. Co.G
Teakle, W. LA 1st Cav. Co.B
Teal, A.J. GA 9th Inf. Co.E
Teal, Alexander NC 43rd Inf. Co.I
Teal, Alexander C. AL 39th Inf. Co.H
Teal, Alexander C. NC 14th Inf. Co.C
Teal, Allen GA 9th Inf. Co.B Cpl.
Teal, Allen GA 32nd Inf. Co.F
Teal, Andrew J. AR 1st Vol. Simington's Co.
Teal, Asa GA 9th Inf. Co.E
Teal, B. NC 1st Jr.Res. Co.I
Teal, Benjamin NC 43rd Inf. Co.I
Teal, Benjamin F. SC 4th St.Troops Co.K
Teal, B.K. AL 15th Inf. Co.A
Teal, B.K. AL 46th Inf. Co.E Sgt.
Teal, Bradberry AL 46th Inf. Co.E
Teal, B.T. VA 3rd (Chrisman's) Bn.Res. Co.B
Teal, C. VA 6th Inf. Co.H
Teal, Charles LA 2nd Res.Corps Co.I Sgt.
Teal, Charles MO Cav. Williams' Regt. Co.H
Teal, Chris C. LA 15th Inf. Co.C
Teal, Christopher C. AL 39th Inf. Co.H
Teal, Collins J. VA 1st Bn.Res. Co.A
Teal, Daniel AL 27th Inf. Co.G
Teal, Daniel AL 57th Inf. Co.B
Teal, Daniel MS Cav. 6th Bn. Prince's Co. Cpl.
Teal, Daniel SC Hvy.Arty. 15th (Lucas') Bn. Co.C
Teal, Daniel W. MS 5th Cav. Co.C Sgt.

Teal, David GA Inf. 8th Bn. Co.D
Teal, David R. SC 21st Inf. Co.E
Teal, Duncan SC 6th Cav. Co.K
Teal, Duncan A. GA 21st Inf. Co.G
Teal, D.W. MS 28th Cav. Co.C Sgt.
Teal, Edward GA Lt.Arty. (Jackson Arty.) Massenburg's Btty.
Teal, Elias GA 32nd Inf. Co.B
Teal, Elias GA 46th Inf. Co.E
Teal, Eli J. NC 43rd Inf. Co.I
Teal, Erasmus GA 32nd Inf. Co.F,A
Teal, Felix S. TX 11th (Spaight's) Bn.Vol. Co.A
Teal, F.S. TX 21st Inf. Co.A
Teal, G.B. 8th (Wade's) Conf.Cav. Co.I
Teal, George GA 11th Cav. Co.E
Teal, George GA Inf. 11th Bn. (St.Guards) Co.B
Teal, George W. GA 40th Inf. Co.F
Teal, G.M. GA 66th Inf. Co.K
Teal, G.M. TX 29th Cav. Co.H
Teal, G.M. TX 21st Inf. Co.D
Teal, G.M. TX Inf. Griffin's Bn. Co.E
Teal, G.W. GA Cav. 9th Bn. (St.Guards) Co.A
Teal, Harrison SC Hvy.Arty. 15th (Lucas') Bn. Co.C
Teal, Hiram C. AR 15th (N.W.) Inf. Co.A
Teal, Isaac GA Cav. 9th Bn. (St.Guards) Co.A,F
Teal, J. NC 1st Jr.Res. Co.I
Teal, J. TX 22nd Inf. Co.K
Teal, James GA 40th Inf. Co.F Sgt.
Teal, James A. NC 26th Inf. Co.K
Teal, James C. SC 1st (McCreary's) Inf. Co.L
Teal, James R. GA Cav. 29th Bn. Co.E
Teal, James W. NC 43rd Inf. Co.I
Teal, James W. SC 6th Cav. Co.D
Teal, J.C. TX 2nd Inf. Co.A
Teal, Jesse AL 14th Inf. Co.A
Teal, Jesse GA 3rd Cav. Co.I
Teal, J.J. GA Inf. 1st Bn. (St.Guards) Co.C Cpl.
Teal, Joel G. AL 29th Inf. Co.G
Teal, John GA 10th Cav. (St.Guards) Co.B
Teal, John GA Cav. 19th Bn. Co.B
Teal, John GA 32nd Inf. Co.F
Teal, John LA 2nd Res.Corps Co.I Cpl.
Teal, John SC 21st Inf. Co.D
Teal, John TN 44th Inf. Co.F
Teal, John VA 8th Inf. Co.C
Teal, John A. GA Inf. 8th Bn. Co.D
Teal, John C. NC 23rd Inf. Co.C
Teal, John M. TX 2nd Inf. Co.A
Teal, John R. GA 1st (Fannin's) Res. Co.H
Teal, John W. AL 13th Inf. Co.B
Teal, John W. GA 35th Inf. Co.C
Teal, Joseph GA 3rd Cav. Co.I
Teal, Joseph P. NC 26th Inf. Co.K
Teal, J.K. GA 7th Inf. (St.Guards) Co.B
Teal, Lawson M. AL 13th Inf. Co.B Sgt.
Teal, Lawson M. GA 35th Inf. Co.C
Teal, Levi Lt.Arty. Dent's Btty.,CSA
Teal, Lovett GA 21st Inf. Co.A Sgt.
Teal, Luther GA 66th Inf. Co.B
Teal, Martin GA 40th Inf. Co.F
Teal, Martin 1st Conf.Inf. 2nd Co.C
Teal, Miles W. NC 26th Inf. Co.K
Teal, Nathan GA 40th Inf. Co.F
Teal, Nicholas TX 21st Cav. Co.K
Teal, Noah F. NC 43rd Inf. Co.I
Teal, Paul LA Inf.Crescent Regt. Co.D
Teal, Peter TX 11th (Spaight's) Bn.Vol. Co.B
Teal, R. GA 46th Inf. Co.E
Teal, R. TX 24th & 25th Cav. (Cons.) Co.B
Teal, Richard TX 17th Cons.Dismtd.Cav. Co.B
Teal, Richard 7th Conf.Cav. Co.K
Teal, Robert AR 15th (N.W.) Inf. Co.A
Teal, Robert Lt.Arty. Dent's Btty.,CSA
Teal, Robert W. GA Lt.Arty. Croft's Btty. (Columbus Arty.)
Teal, Samuel H.F. GA 35th Inf. Co.C
Teal, Terry VA 6th Inf. Co.H
Teal, Thomas GA 9th Inf. Co.E
Teal, Thomas GA 21st Inf. Co.A Sgt.
Teal, Thomas TN 21st & 22nd (Cons.) Cav. Co.K
Teal, Thomas B. GA 41st Inf. Co.I
Teal, Thomas F. NC 28th Inf. Co.E
Teal, Thomas H. NC 53rd Inf. Co.I
Teal, Tilman GA 32nd Inf. Co.F
Teal, T.J. SC 8th Inf. Co.B
Teal, T.N. Brush Bn.
Teal, T.R.C. AL 53rd (Part.Rangers) Co.H
Teal, W. NC 1st Jr.Res. Co.I
Teal, W. SC 21st Inf. Co.D
Teal, W.A. 7th Conf.Cav. Co.A
Teal, W.B.T. TX 2nd Inf. Co.G
Teal, W.C. TX 26th Cav. Co.K Bugler
Teal, W.C. TX 11th (Spaight's) Bn.Vol. Co.G,A
Teal, W.D. TX 21st Inf. Co.K
Teal, W.H. GA 40th Inf. Co.F
Teal, W.H. KY 1st (Butler's) Cav. Co.C
Teal, W.H. SC Hvy.Arty. 15th (Lucas') Bn. Co.C
Teal, William AL 29th Inf. Co.G
Teal, William GA 1st Reg. Co.B,D
Teal, William GA 46th Inf. Co.E
Teal, William SC 4th St.Troops Co.K
Teal, William C. TX Cav. Ragsdale's Bn. Co.A
Teal, William D. TX 11th (Spaight's) Bn.Vol. Co.A,G
Teal, William E. NC 3rd Inf. Co.D
Teal, William F. GA 56th Inf. Co.A
Teal, William H. NC 26th Inf. Co.K
Teal, William H. VA 8th Inf. Co.C
Teal, William J. AL 13th Inf. Co.B
Teal, William M. GA 40th Inf. Co.F
Teal, William R. NC 4th Cav. (59th St.Troops) Co.A Cpl.
Teal, William T. NC 26th Inf. Co.K
Teal, W.R. GA 41st Inf. Co.I
Teal, W.T. AL 29th Inf. Co.G
Teal, W.T. GA 41st Inf. Co.I
Teal, W.T. VA 36th Inf. Co.G
Teal, W.W. SC 21st Inf. Co.E
Teale, A.J. SC 7th Cav. Co.K
Teale, Ferdinand TX 4th Cav. Co.A
Teale, Moses O. VA Lt.Arty. 12th Bn. Co.C
Tealy, S.J. GA 8th Inf. Co.C
Team, John W. SC 2nd Inf. Co.E
Team, P. SC 9th Inf. Co.E Cpl.
Team, P.M. SC 7th Cav. Co.H
Team, Powell M. SC Cav.Bn. Holcombe Legion Co.E
Team, William A. NC 6th Inf. Co.D
Teamey, James LA 20th Inf. Co.I
Teammell, H.C. TX 9th (Young's) Inf. Co.D
Teams, George GA Cav. 10th Bn. (St.Guards) Co.A
Teams, John GA 23rd Inf. Co.D
Teams, W.W. SC 7th Cav. Co.K
Teanalt, Joseph VA 146th Mil. Co.D
Teaney, Charles VA 4th Inf. Co.C
Teaney, Charles L. VA 4th Inf. Co.C,D
Teaney, James D. MO 1st Cav. Co.E
Teaney, John TN 37th Inf.
Teaney, John B. VA 4th Inf. Co.C
Teaney, William B. VA 4th Inf. Co.C
Tear, J.M. MS Cav. Hughes' Bn. Co.C
Tear, T.T. MS 4th Inf. Co.B
Tear, William AR 16th Inf. Co.A
Tearce, William KY 10th (Johnson's) Cav. Co.E,F
Tearney, Barney LA 19th Inf. Co.B
Tearney, Daniel TX Inf. 1st St.Troops Stevenson's Co.F
Tearney, James VA 60th Inf. Co.F
Tearney, John GA Arty. (Chatham Arty.) Wheaton's Co.
Tearney, John GA 1st (Olmstead's) Inf. Claghorn's Co.
Tearney, Leonidas VA 12th Cav. Co.B
Tearns, George GA 12th Cav. Co.C
Teary, John H. MS 25th Inf. Co.D
Teas, Charles TN 19th (Biffle's) Cav. Co.H Sgt.
Teas, Edmond TN 24th Bn.S.S. Co.B
Teas, Edwin D. MO 1st N.E. Cav. Co.L
Teas, Jesse T. TX 36th Cav. Co.K
Teas, John H. MS 29th Inf. Co.A Cpl.
Teas, John S. AL Cav. Falkner's Co.
Teas, J.S. 8th (Wade's) Conf.Cav. Co.B
Teas, Thaddeus A. TX 36th Cav. Co.K
Teas, Thomas A. VA 108th Mil. Co.G
Teas, W.B. TX 20th Inf. Co.I
Teasdale, C.R. GA Inf. Arsenal Bn. (Columbus) Co.A
Teasdale, George NC 57th Inf. Co.K
Teasdale, George A. MD 1st Inf. Co.H
Teasdale, George A. MS 44th Inf. Co.A
Teasdale, H.M. Gen. & Staff Hosp.Stew.
Teasdale, Howard M. MS 43rd Inf. Co.B Hosp.Stew.
Teasdale, H.R. Jones' Staff Maj.,Ch.QM
Teasdale, John MO 8th Cav. Co.B
Teasdale, John TX 12th Inf. Co.G
Teasdale, John TX 18th Inf. Co.C
Teasdale, R. SC Ord.Guards Loc.Def.Troops
Teasdale, R.H. SC Mil.Arty. 1st Regt. Walter's Co.
Teasdale, Robert L. MS 10th Inf. Old Co.E ACS
Teasdale, Robert L. MS 43rd Inf. Co.B 1st Lt.
Teasdale, T.A. MS 44th Inf. Co.A Sgt.
Teasdale, Thomas A. Shelley's Staff Lt.,Ord.Off.
Teasdale, William MO 8th Cav. Co.B
Tease, Edmond TN Cav. Napier's Bn. Co.C
Tease, F.M. AL 16th Inf. Co.C
Tease, Henry TN 10th (DeMoss') Cav. Co.F
Tease, Henry TN Cav. Napier's Bn. Co.C
Tease, J.W. GA Phillips' Legion Co.E
Tease, Robert TN 10th (DeMoss') Cav. Co.F
Tease, Robert TN Cav. Napier's Bn. Co.C
Teash, William A. NC 28th Inf. Co.I Cpl.
Teasle, --- FL Cav. 5th Bn. Co.G
Teasley, Alexander KY 13th Cav. Co.D

Teasley, Alferd TN Conscr. (Cp. of Instr.)
Teasley, Alfred J. GA 15th Inf. Co.I 2nd Lt.
Teasley, Algenon NC 2nd Inf. Co.I
Teasley, Algernon NC 46th Inf. Co.E
Teasley, Allen D. GA 34th Inf.
Teasley, Anderson MO 10th Inf. Co.D
Teasley, D.U. GA 59th Inf. Co.F
Teasley, F.M. TN 42nd Inf. Co.C
Teasley, George VA 34th Inf. Fray's Co.
Teasley, George R. VA 7th Inf. Co.A Sgt.
Teasley, George Wash. TN Cav. Shaw's Bn.
Teasley, G.W. TN 1st (Feild's) Inf. Co.L
Teasley, G.W. TN 49th Inf. Co.K
Teasley, G.W. Inf. Bailey's Cons.Regt. Co.E
Teasley, Haywood NC 3rd Arty. (40th St.Troops) Co.H
Teasley, J.A. GA 1st (Fannin's) Res. Co.D
Teasley, J.A. GA Inf. 25th Bn. (Prov.Guard) Co.B
Teasley, James A. TN 49th Inf. Co.K
Teasley, James H. LA 28th (Gray's) Inf. Co.H
Teasley, Jefferson NC 2nd Cav. (19th St.Troops) Co.K
Teasley, J.J. GA 38th Inf. Co.F
Teasley, J.J. TN 49th Inf. Co.K
Teasley, John H.H. GA 38th Inf. Co.F 1st Lt.
Teasley, J.R. Inf. Bailey's Cons.Regt. Co.E
Teasley, J.W. MS 1st (King's) Inf. (St.Troops) Co.I
Teasley, Leander W. TN 49th Inf. Co.K 1st Lt.
Teasley, Leonard F. TN 49th Inf. Co.K Cpl.
Teasley, L.F. Inf. Bailey's Cons.Regt. Co.E Cpl.
Teasley, L.W. Inf. Bailey's Cons.Regt. Co.E 2nd Lt.
Teasley, Nicholas H. NC 6th Inf. Co.B
Teasley, P.H. GA 60th Inf. Co.E 1st Sgt.
Teasley, R.D. AL 1st Cav. 2nd Co.E
Teasley, Robert AL 10th Inf. Co.B
Teasley, S.M. GA 1st (Fannin's) Res. Co.D
Teasley, T.F. AL Cp. of Instr. Talladega
Teasley, Thomas AL 18th Inf. Co.G
Teasley, Thomas GA 51st Inf. Co.F
Teasley, T.W. AL 20th Cav. Lee's Co.
Teasley, W.A. GA 43rd Inf. Co.A ACS
Teasley, W.B. MS 30th Inf. Co.A
Teasley, Wilie NC Inf. 13th Bn. Co.A
Teasley, William GA 3rd Cav. (St.Guards) Co.H
Teasley, William GA 2nd Res. Co.C
Teasley, William NC 46th Inf. Co.E Cpl.
Teasley, William TN 49th Inf. Co.K
Teasley, William Inf. Bailey's Cons.Regt. Co.E
Teasley, William A. GA 3rd Cav. (St.Guards) Co.H
Teasley, William A. GA 37th Inf. Co.A
Teasley, Wm. A. Gen. & Staff, Comsy.Dept. Capt.
Teasley, William H. TN 45th Inf.
Teasley, William J. GA 24th Inf. Co.B Cpl.
Teasley, William W. TX 18th Cav. Co.I
Teasley, William W. VA Lt.Arty. Utterback's Co.
Teasley, Willie NC 66th Inf. Co.A
Teasley, W.W. VA 82nd Mil. Co.D 1st Sgt.
Teasly, Anderson MO Cav. Coleman's Regt.
Teasly, James R. GA 3rd Cav. (St.Guards) Co.H Sgt.
Teasly, Wesley M. 3rd Conf.Cav. Co.F
Teasly, William A. GA Inf. 3rd Bn. Co.B
Teass, Thomas VA 14th Cav. Co.E Cpl.
Teass, Thomas VA Arty. Bryan's Co.
Teass, William H. VA Lt.Arty. G.B. Chapman's Co.
Teaster, C.D. TN 11th Inf. Co.I Sgt.
Teaster, David NC 6th Cav. (65th St.Troops) Co.G
Teaster, J. VA 6th Cav. Co.G
Teaster, J. Harrison NC 37th Inf. Co.E
Teaster, John TN 11th Inf. Co.I
Teaster, Joseph NC 4th Cav. (59th St.Troops) Co.D
Teaster, Samuel NC 37th Inf. Co.E
Teat, --- GA 5th Inf. Co.L
Teat, A.T. FL 5th Inf. Co.H
Teat, David H. GA 4th Res. Co.D
Teat, David S. GA 22nd Inf. Co.G
Teat, G.H. MS 4th Inf. Co.K
Teat, G.K. LA 3rd (Harrison's) Cav. Co.D
Teat, G.K. LA 25th Inf. Co.H
Teat, Harrison G. GA 7th Inf. Co.E 1st Sgt.
Teat, Harvey GA 20th Inf. Co.B
Teat, Harvey M. GA 1st Inf. Co.E,B
Teat, Harvey M. GA 2nd Bn.S.S. Co.B
Teat, Irwin L. GA 7th Inf. Co.E
Teat, Isaac N. GA 22nd Inf. Co.G
Teat, J. FL Conscr.
Teat, James H. AL 47th Inf. Co.A
Teat, James H. MS 15th Inf. Co.A
Teat, James P. AL 41st Inf. Co.D
Teat, J.B. LA 6th Cav. Co.F
Teat, J.H. AL 17th Inf. Co.G
Teat, J.H. GA 9th Inf. (St.Guards) Culp's Co.
Teat, J.H. LA 25th Inf. Co.H
Teat, J.I. GA Floyd Legion (St.Guards) Co.D
Teat, J.L. GA 9th Inf. (St.Guards) Culp's Co.
Teat, John L. GA 22nd Inf. Co.G
Teat, John T. MS 21st Inf. Co.G
Teat, L.B. AL 38th Inf. Co.F
Teat, L.B. AL Cp. of Instr. Talladega
Teat, Littleton B. GA 41st Inf. Co.C
Teat, M.A. MS 1st Cav.Res. Co.F
Teat, M.T. GA 46th Inf. Co.A
Teat, Samuel AL 35th Inf. Co.A
Teat, W.C. GA 9th Inf. (St.Guards) Culp's Co. Cpl.
Teat, W.E. GA 46th Inf. Co.A
Teat, W.H. AL 38th Inf. Co.F
Teat, W.H. AL Cp. of Instr. Talladega
Teat, W.H. GA 1st (Fannin's) Res. Co.A
Teat, W.H. MS 1st (King's) Inf. (St.Troops) D. Love's Co. Sgt.
Teat, W.T. GA 28th Inf. Co.E
Teate, Jasper J. GA Inf. White's Co.
Teate, Jasper R. SC 2nd Rifles Co.K
Teate, John H. GA Inf. White's Co.
Teate, M.L. 20th Conf.Cav. 1st Co.H
Teate, William A.J. GA 27th Inf. Co.A 2nd Lt.
Teaten, H.C. TN 22nd (Barteau's) Cav. Co.I
Teater, Amos J. VA 62nd Mtd.Inf. 2nd Co.F
Teater, B.W. TN 21st & 22nd (Cons.) Cav. Co.C
Teater, Henry H. TX 2nd Field Btty.
Teater, John TN 21st & 22nd (Cons.) Cav. Co.C
Teater, William C. VA 62nd Mtd.Inf. 2nd Co.F
Teaters, M. TN 35th Inf. Co.H
Teates, George VA 11th Cav. Co.B
Teates, Levi VA 11th Cav. Co.B
Teatom, J.D. TN 20th Inf. Co.G
Teats, George W. VA 18th Cav. Co.B
Teats, Noah VA 31st Inf. Co.K
Teaugue, Samuel AR Cav. Gordon's Regt. Co.C
Teavalt, Peter W. VA 11th Cav. Co.H
Teaver, James AR 19th (Dawson's) Inf. Co.K
Teaver, James M. MS 17th Inf. Co.G
Teaver, John C. GA 13th Inf. Co.K
Teaver, W.A. TX 9th (Young's) Inf. Co.D
Teaver, William H. GA 13th Inf. Co.K
Teawalt, Joseph VA 136th Mil. Co.E
Teawalt, William VA 136th Mil. Co.E
Teawalt, William H. VA Horse Arty. J.W. Carter's Co. Cpl.
Teays, Stephen VA 22nd Inf. Co.H
Tebault, Benjamin F. VA 54th Mil. Co.E,F
Tebault, B.F. VA 3rd Inf.Loc.Def. Co.F
Tebault, C.H. SC 10th Inf. Asst.Surg.
Tebault, C.H. Johnson's Corps Asst Surg.
Tebault, Daniel VA Hvy.Arty. 20th Bn. Co.B
Tebault, George TX Cav. 3rd (Yager's) Bn. Co.A Surg.
Tebault, George Gen. & Staff Surg.
Tebbetts, A.G. VA 8th Inf. Co.B
Tebbetts, Robert B. VA 6th Cav. Co.H
Tebbs, --- VA 9th Cav. Co.D
Tebbs, Algernon S. TX 4th Inf. Co.A
Tebbs, A.S. VA 23rd Cav. Co.F
Tebbs, A.S. VA Cav. 41st Bn. Co.F
Tebbs, Charles AL 13th Inf. Co.A
Tebbs, Charles AL 22nd Inf. Co.G
Tebbs, Charles 8th (Wade's) Conf.Cav. Co.K
Tebbs, Charles B. VA 3rd Inf.Loc.Def. Co.E
Tebbs, Charles B. VA 8th Inf. Lt.Col.
Tebbs, Charles B. VA 17th Inf. Co.C Lt.Col.
Tebbs, C.K. TX Cav. Mann's Bn. Cox's Co.
Tebbs, F.C. Gen. & Staff Chap.
Tebbs, Foushee C. VA 4th Inf. Chap.
Tebbs, J.H. SC Arty. Melchers' Co. (Co.B, German Arty.)
Tebbs, John W. VA 1st Arty. Co.H
Tebbs, J.W. SC 7th Cav. Co.A
Tebbs, O.B. AR 2nd Cav. Co.F Capt.
Tebbs, Obediah B. AR 3rd Inf. Co.A
Tebbs, R.T. VA 9th Inf.
Tebbs, Thomas F. Gen. & Staff Asst.Surg.
Tebbs, William H. AR 3rd Inf. Co.A Lt.Col.
Tebbs, Willoughby W. VA 2nd Cav. Co.K Capt.
Tebe, William H. MO 8th Cav. Co.B 1st Sgt.
Tebeau, F.E. GA 63rd Inf. Co.B
Tebeau, John R. CSA Military Eng.
Tebeau, S.W. GA 1st (Symons') Res. Co.B
Tebo, James 1st Choctaw & Chickasaw Mtd.Rifles Co.A
Tebo, John A. VA 52nd Inf. Co.C
Teboe, Adam NC 7th Inf. Co.C
Teboe, William W. NC 1st Arty. (10th St.Troops) Co.E
TeBow, John GA 15th Inf. Co.G
Tebow, John H. MS 22nd Inf. Co.E
Tebow, Leroy AL 37th Inf. Co.I
Tebuche, Hernando TX 12th Inf. Co.K
Te cah noole Cloud 1st Cherokee Mtd.Rifles Co.B
Tecathlee 1st Seminole Mtd.Vol.
Techan, John GA 25th Inf. Co.A

Teche, Daniel 1st Cherokee Mtd.Vol. 2nd Co.H
Techee, George 1st Cherokee Mtd.Vol. 2nd Co.H
Techee, John 1st Cherokee Mtd.Vol. 2nd Co.H
Techner, Isaac Gen. & Staff Chap.
Teclas, Bartolome LA Mil. 5th Regt.Eur.Brig. (Spanish Regt.) Co.2
Tecoa, John GA 25th Inf. Co.A
Te co cha nay 1st Creek Mtd.Vol. Co.E
Te co fon ne 1st Creek Mtd.Vol. Co.E
Te co he ste skee 1st Cherokee Mtd.Vol. 2nd Co.E
Tecolageeskih NC Inf. Thomas Legion 2nd Co.A
Te coo sah 1st Creek Mtd.Vol. 2nd Co.D
Tecora, A. LA Arty. Guyol's Co. (Orleans Arty.) Cpl.
Tecters, G.W. AL 16th Inf. Co.E
Te cul Kee 1st Cherokee Mtd.Rifles Co.C
Te cum see 1st Creek Mtd.Vol. Co.G
Tecumseh 1st Choctaw & Chickasaw Mtd.Rifles 2nd Co.I
Tecumseh 1st Seminole Mtd.Vol.
Tecumseh unah 1st Creek Mtd.Vol. Co.A
Tecumsey 1st Creek Mtd.Vol. Co.M
Tecu we skey 1st Cherokee Mtd.Vol. 1st Co.A, 2nd Co.E
Teddar, Benjamin SC 9th Inf. Co.G
Teddar, B.W. GA 28th Inf. Co.D
Teddar, L. SC Arty. Manigault's Bn. 2nd Co.C
Teddar, L. SC Arty. Zimmerman's Co. (Pee Dee Arty.)
Teddar, L. SC 1st (McCreary's) Inf. Co.D
Teddards, W. SC 6th Cav. Co.C
Teddards, Wiley SC 5th Res. Co.B
Tedder, A. Ben LA 19th Inf. Co.G
Tedder, Alex. SC 18th Inf. Co.I
Tedder, Alfred NC 5th Inf. Co.E
Tedder, Andrew J. FL Inf. 2nd Bn. Co.B
Tedder, Archibald AL 34th Inf. Co.H
Tedder, B. MS 18th Inf. Co.F
Tedder, Benjamin A. FL 1st Cav. Co.H Sgt.
Tedder, Benjamin A. FL 1st Inf. Old Co.H
Tedder, Benjamin W. FL 10th Inf. Co.K
Tedder, D. MS 2nd St.Cav. Co.G
Tedder, Daniel SC 1st (Butler's) Inf. Co.C
Tedder, Daniel W. FL 11th Inf. Co.E 1st Sgt.
Tedder, David C. SC 2nd Arty. Co.D
Tedder, David P. GA Cherokee Legion (St.Guards) Co.D
Tedder, D.M. SC 21st Inf. Co.L
Tedder, D.S. MS 31st Inf. Co.C
Tedder, E. AL 34th Inf. Co.H Cpl.
Tedder, E.E. SC 18th Inf. Co.I
Tedder, Eli FL 6th Inf. Co.G
Tedder, Farrington AR 8th Cav.
Tedder, George NC 5th Inf. Co.E
Tedder, George W. FL 11th Inf. Co.D
Tedder, G.W. MS 3rd Inf. (St.Troops) Co.E
Tedder, Henry GA 43rd Inf. Co.B
Tedder, Hill AL 37th Inf. Co.G
Tedder, Houston NC 52nd Inf. Co.F
Tedder, J. MS Inf. 3rd Bn. (St.Troops) Co.F
Tedder, James MS 3rd Inf. (St.Troops) Co.I
Tedder, James NC 52nd Inf. Co.F
Tedder, James SC 2nd Arty. Co.D
Tedder, James J. NC McDugald's Co.
Tedder, James J. SC 18th Inf. Co.I
Tedder, James M. AL 22nd Inf. Co.E Sgt.
Tedder, James M. GA 23rd Inf. Co.F
Tedder, James S. MS Cav. Ham's Regt. Co.I
Tedder, Joel H. NC 26th Inf. Co.C
Tedder, John NC 2nd Arty. (36th St.Troops) Co.I
Tedder, John TN 5th Inf. 2nd Co.H
Tedder, John H. FL 1st Cav. Co.A
Tedder, John Lane LA 19th Inf. Co.D
Tedder, John W. GA 56th Inf. Co.G
Tedder, John W. NC 18th Inf. Co.H
Tedder, Joseph M. MS 14th Inf. Co.A
Tedder, J.R. MS 5th Inf. Co.D
Tedder, J.S. MS 26th Inf. Co.B
Tedder, L. SC 1st Inf. Co.B
Tedder, Lawrence AL 37th Inf. Co.G,E Sgt.
Tedder, Morgan MS 7th Cav. Co.C
Tedder, Newton J. MS 17th Inf. Co.D
Tedder, Putman GA 43rd Inf. Co.B
Tedder, R.F. GA 23rd Inf. Co.F Cpl.
Tedder, R.G. GA 56th Inf. Co.G
Tedder, Richard F. SC Lt.Arty. 3rd (Palmetto) Bn. Co.C
Tedder, Robert MS 14th Inf. Co.D
Tedder, Robert S. AL 22nd Inf. Co.I
Tedder, Roland NC 1st Jr.Res. Co.E
Tedder, R.W. GA Inf. 17th Bn. (St.Guards) Stocks' Co.
Tedder, S. SC 3rd Inf. Co.G
Tedder, Samuel NC 18th Inf. Co.H
Tedder, Sidney NC 30th Inf. Co.K Sgt.
Tedder, Thomas AR 24th Inf. Co.K
Tedder, Thomas FL 1st Cav. Co.H
Tedder, Thomas TN 2nd (Smith's) Cav.
Tedder, Thomas J. MS 15th Inf. Co.C,F
Tedder, W. AL 22nd Inf. Co.K
Tedder, W. MS 2nd St.Cav. Co.G Cpl.
Tedder, W.B. FL Inf. 2nd Bn.
Tedder, W.B. MS Inf. 1st Bn.St.Troops (30 days '64) Co.F
Tedder, Wilkins AL 34th Inf. Co.H
Tedder, William MS 31st Inf. Co.C
Tedder, William NC 55th Inf. Co.B
Tedder, William SC 4th St.Troops Co.E
Tedder, William B. AL 17th Inf. Co.E
Tedder, Wm. B. AL Cp. of Instr. Talladega
Tedder, William B. FL 10th Inf. Co.K
Tedder, William B. MS 1st (King's) Inf. (St.Troops) Co.C
Tedder, Wiley SC 18th Inf. Co.I
Tedder, W.J. SC 6th Cav. Co.I
Tedder, Wright H.B. MS 17th Inf. Co.D
Tedders, Charles LA 10th Inf. Co.D
Tedders, Charles M. GA 44th Inf. Co.B
Tedders, G.W. GA 1st (Olmstead's) Inf.
Tedders, James TX 9th (Nichols') Inf. Co.E
Tedders, James TX 20th Inf. Co.H
Teddlee, W.J. LA 27th Inf. Co.F
Teddlie, B.F. LA Res.Corps Co.D Lt.
Teddlie, J.B. LA 1st Res. Co.D
Teddlie, Solomon TX Cav. Waller's Regt. Co.E
Teddlie, Theodore F. LA 12th Inf. Co.C Cpl.
Teddlie, Thomas J. LA 12th Inf. Co.C 2nd Lt.
Teddlier, Solomon TX Cav. Waller's Regt. Co.E
Teddux, W.J. LA 3rd Inf. Co.C
Teddor, George AR Inf. 8th Bn. 1st Co.C
Teddor, J.A. MS Grace's Co. (St.Troops)
Teddor, P.F. TN 22nd (Barteau's) Cav. Co.C
Teder, Irvine AL 24th Inf. Co.H Cpl.
Teder, Jessee MS 5th Inf. Co.A
Tedeton, Jesse G. LA Arty. Moody's Co. (Madison Lt.Arty.)
Tedeton, John LA Arty. Moody's Co. (Madison Lt.Arty.)
Tedford, A.F. 4th Conf.Inf. Co.I
Tedford, A.M. TX 24th Cav. Co.C
Tedford, Augustus MO Cav. Freeman's Regt. Co.G
Tedford, A.W. TN 51st (Cons.) Inf. Co.C
Tedford, Elijah VA 10th Bn.Res. Co.B
Tedford, F.N. TX 2nd Inf. Co.I
Tedford, Frank TX 33rd Cav. Co.B
Tedford, George MO Cav. Jackman's Regt. Co.F
Tedford, George TX 17th Inf. Co.G
Tedford, G.W. KY 4th Mtd.Inf. Co.K
Tedford, G.W. TN 51st (Cons.) Inf. Co.C
Tedford, Howard J. NC Walker's Bn. Thomas' Legion Co.C
Tedford, Isaac O. MO 5th Inf. Co.I
Tedford, J. AR Cav. Harrell's Bn. Co.D
Tedford, J. MS 3rd Inf. (St.Troops) Co.K
Tedford, J.A. MO 5th Inf. Co.I
Tedford, J.A. TN 12th (Cons.) Inf. Co.E
Tedford, J.A. TX 22nd Inf. Co.A
Tedford, James M. MO 5th Inf. Co.I
Tedford, James T. TX 4th Cav. Co.A
Tedford, James W. TN 13th Inf. Co.K
Tedford, J.B.F. MO 10th Inf. Co.A
Tedford, J.C. TN 51st (Cons.) Inf. Co.C
Tedford, J.J. TN 14th (Neely's) Cav. Co.A
Tedford, J.J. 1st Conf.Cav. 1st Co.B
Tedford, John AR Cav. Harrell's Bn. Co.D
Tedford, John B.T. MO 10th Inf. Co.A
Tedford, Joseph H. NC Walker's Bn. Thomas' Legion Co.C
Tedford, Joseph H. TN 62nd Mtd.Inf. Co.E Lt.
Tedford, Rich. H. AL 19th Inf. Co.F
Tedford, R.J. TX 4th Inf. Co.H 3rd Lt.
Tedford, R.T. TX Vol. Duke's Co. Sgt.
Tedford, S.H. TN 62nd Mtd.Inf. Co.E
Tedford, W.H. TX 17th Inf. Co.G
Tedford, William TX Inf. 3rd St.Troops Co.C
Tedford, William H. MS 17th Inf. Co.K
Tedford, William H. TX 1st (McCulloch's) Cav. Co.A
Tedford, William P. AR Lt.Arty. Rivers' Btty.
Tedleton, William TN 12th Inf. Co.H
Tedley, T.J. LA 3rd Inf. Co.C
Tedlington, Joseph TN 6th Inf. Co.B
Tedlington, Richard TN 6th Inf. Co.B
Tedlington, William TN 6th Inf. Co.B
Tedmore, H.J. 3rd Conf.Cav. Co.B
Tedmore, J.E. 3rd Conf.Cav. Co.B
Tednell, R. GA Inf. 40th Bn. Co.D
Tedrick, D. MO 4th Cav. Co.G
Tedrick, George MO 4th Cav. Co.A
Tedrick, George MO Cav. Preston's Bn. Co.A
Tedwards, David F. SC 2nd Inf. Co.F
Tedwell, B.J. 3rd Conf.Cav. Co.D
Tedwell, Charles R. MO Inf. Walker's Regt.
Tedwell, James MS 2nd Inf. (A. of 10,000) Co.A
Tedwell, J.J. AL 48th Inf. Co.H
Tedwell, L. TN 21st Cav. Co.H
Tedwell, Levy TN Cav. Wilson's Regt. Wharton's Co.

Tedwell, R.H. TN 51st (Cons.) Inf. Co.C
Tedwell, Samuel M. TX 36th Cav. Co.D
Tedwell, William TN 10th & 11th (Cons.) Cav. Co.A
Tedwill, John LA 31st Inf. Co.G
Tedwill, P. GA 19th Inf. Co.H Cpl.
Tee, John C. VA 3rd Inf. Co.H Cpl.
Tee, William VA 16th Inf. 2nd Co.H, Co.G
Tee cah nee ye skie 1st Cherokee Mtd.Rifles Co.E
Tee ca tos Kee 1st Cherokee Mtd.Rifles Co.D
Teechee Stephen 1st Cherokee Mtd.Vol. 2nd Co.H
Teed, Moses E. VA 27th Inf. 2nd Co.H
Teehare, John AL Inf. 1st Regt. Co.D
Tee hee, Charles 1st Cherokee Mtd.Rifles Co.B
Teehee Ketchee 1st Cherokee Mtd.Vol. 2nd Co.H 2nd Lt.
Teehee Tom 1st Cherokee Mtd.Vol. 2nd Co.H
Tee Ho Tubbee 1st Choctaw Mtd.Rifles Co.H
Tee hurnee skie Tahlie Stayskie 1st Cherokee Mtd.Rifles Co.I
Teek, P.D. LA 3rd Inf. Co.K
Teekel, N. TX Cav. Ragsdale's Bn. Co.D
Teekell, --- TX 5th Field Btty.
Tee Ker n ye sky 1st Cherokee Mtd.Rifles Co.A
Tee Kin ee Mouse 1st Cherokee Mtd.Rifles Co.D
Te eksar 1st Creek Mtd.Vol. Co.H, 2nd Co.D
Teel, Abraham VA 53rd Inf. Co.H
Teel, Alex GA 54th Inf. Co.H Sgt.
Teel, Alvin GA 19th Inf. Co.G
Teel, Andrew J. AR 25th Inf. Co.A
Teel, Andrew J. TX 11th Inf. Co.I
Teel, Benjamin NC 55th Inf. Co.E
Teel, Bernard VA 58th Mil. Co.C
Teel, B.P. VA 9th Bn.Res. Co.A Sgt.
Teel, Bradberry GA 12th Inf. Co.A
Teel, B.V. TX St.Troops Teel's Co. Surg.
Teel, Calvin GA 20th Inf. Co.B
Teel, Daniel W. KY Horse Arty. Byrne's Co. Music.
Teel, Daniel W. KY 4th Mtd.Inf. Co.C Music.
Teel, Druery W. NC 55th Inf. Co.E
Teel, E.B. TX 32nd Cav. Co.F Cpl.
Teel, E.C. KY 7th Cav. Co.A
Teel, E.C. TX Cav. Gano's Squad. Co.A
Teel, Edward 1st Conf.Inf. 2nd Co.E
Teel, Eli C. KY 3rd Cav. Co.A
Teel, Elisha A. TX 29th Cav. Co.A Cpl.
Teel, Erasmus GA 20th Inf. Co.B
Teel, Gashimer AL 60th Inf. Co.B
Teel, G.D. NC 27th Inf. Co.H Cpl.
Teel, George L. VA 7th Inf. Co.F 1st Lt.
Teel, George H. AL 46th Inf. Co.B
Teel, Gersham AL 1st Regt.Conscr. Co.C
Teel, Henry AL 42nd Inf. Co.E
Teel, Henry GA 36th (Villepigue's) Inf. Co.A
Teel, Henry 1st Conf.Inf. Co.A
Teel, Henry 2nd Conf.Eng.Troops Co.C Artif.
Teel, Henry C. AL 13th Inf. Co.H Surg.
Teel, Humphrey M. TX 11th Inf. Co.I
Teel, Isham L. GA 41st Inf. Co.I
Teel, James GA Inf. 1st City Bn. (Columbus) Co.D
Teel, James NC 55th Inf. Co.E
Teel, James SC 21st Inf. Co.G
Teel, James A. TX 11th Inf. Co.I
Teel, James E. MS 17th Inf. Co.F Ens.
Teel, James R. NC 44th Inf. Co.C
Teel, J.L. GA 3rd Cav. Co.I
Teel, Joel H. VA 53rd Inf. Co.H
Teel, John MS 18th Cav. Co.A Sgt.
Teel, John B. AL 57th Inf. Co.I
Teel, John C. AL 60th Inf. Co.B
Teel, John L. AL 54th Inf. Co.A
Teel, John L. NC 8th Inf. Co.G
Teel, John L. VA 54th Inf. Co.A
Teel, John W. AL 15th Inf. Co.A
Teel, Joseph Peter VA 42nd Inf. Co.K
Teel, Josiah VA 12th Inf. Co.G
Teel, Josiah W. VA 24th Inf. Co.B
Teel, J.W. TX 30th Cav. Co.H
Teel, Levi AL Inf. 1st Regt. Co.A
Teel, Lewis VA 2nd Cav. Co.K
Teel, Lewis VA 19th Inf. Co.E
Teel, M. VA 42nd Inf. Co.K
Teel, McG. NC 17th Inf. (1st Org.) Co.C
Teel, McG. NC 27th Inf. Co.H
Teel, McGilbra NC 17th Inf. (2nd Org.) Co.K
Teel, M.O. KY 1st Inf. Co.I Cpl.
Teel, Moses LA 1st (Nelligan's) Inf. Co.K
Teel, Moses M. NC 44th Inf. Co.C
Teel, Nicholas VA 12th Inf. Co.G
Teel, Peter AR 34th Inf. Co.C
Teel, Peter Horny AR Gunter's Inf.
Teel, Preston G.J. AR 25th Inf. Co.A
Teel, R. GA 10th Cav. Co.K
Teel, Richard NC 67th Inf. Co.I
Teel, Richard TX 25th Cav. Co.B
Teel, Richard A. NC 3rd Cav. (41st St.Troops) Co.K
Teel, R.J. TX St.Troops Teel's Co.
Teel, Robert AL Inf. 1st Regt. Co.A
Teel, Robert AR 25th Inf. Co.A
Teel, Robert TN 24th Inf. Co.K
Teel, Robert W. MS 9th Inf. Old Co.G, New Co.A
Teel, Thomas NC 44th Inf. Co.C
Teel, T.M. TX 11th Inf. Co.I
Teel, Trevanion T. TX 2nd Field Btty. Capt.
Teel, Trevanion T. TX St.Troops Teel's Co. Capt.
Teel, T.T. Gen. & Staff Maj.
Teel, W.H. KY 3rd Cav. Co.C
Teel, William AL 42nd Inf. Co.E
Teel, William GA 7th Inf. (St.Guards) Co.G
Teel, William GA 17th Inf. Co.H
Teel, William LA 3rd (Wingfield's) Cav. Co.B
Teel, William SC 23rd Inf. Co.A
Teel, William 7th Conf.Cav. Co.K
Teel, William J. NC 24th Inf. Co.D
Teel, W.J.J. GA Inf. 9th Bn. Co.A
Teel, W.J.J. GA 12th Inf. Co.E
Teel, W.J.J. GA 37th Inf. Co.D
Teel, W.R. AL 8th (Livingston's) Cav. Co.B
Teel, W.S. AL 8th (Livingston's) Cav. Co.B Cpl.
Teel, Wyatt J. TX 27th Cav. Co.C
Tee lah ski ske Stop 1st Cherokee Mtd.Rifles Co.G
Tee lah ski ske Tar che chee 1st Cherokee Mtd.Rifles Co.G
Tee lah ski ske Twister 1st Cherokee Mtd.Rifles Co.G
Teele, --- TX Cav. Ragsdale's Bn. Co.D
Teele, Asa GA 19th Inf. Co.G
Teele, D. SC Hvy.Arty. 15th (Lucas) Bn. Co.C
Teele, H. SC Hvy.Arty. 15th (Lucas) Bn. Co.C
Teele, James GA 54th Inf. Co.A
Teele, Manson GA 46th Inf. Co.K
Teele, Moses O. VA Lt.Arty. Taylor's Co.
Teele, Roderick AL 24th Inf. Co.B
Teele, W. GA 40th Inf. Co.F
Teeler, J.W. MS 26th Inf.
Teeley, W. MO 9th (Elliott's) Cav. Co.H
Teeling, John Gen. & Staff Chap.
Teely, P. NC 45th Inf. Co.E
Teem, G.W. GA Cav. 16th Bn. (St.Guards) Co.E
Teem, Israel GA Cav. 16th Bn. (St.Guards) Co.E Cpl.
Teem, Israel P. NC 58th Inf. Co.E
Teem, Isreal GA 12th Inf. Co.I
Teem, J.M. GA 19th Inf. Co.E
Teem, John W. GA 13th Cav. Co.C
Teem, John W. TN Cav. 16th Bn. Co.C
Teem, J.P. NC 11th (Bethel Regt.) Inf. Co.B
Teem, Leander NC 29th Inf. Co.E
Teem, Martin V. GA 65th Inf. Co.A Sgt.
Teem, M.V. GA Smith's Legion Co.B Sgt.
Teem, Peter A. NC 1st Inf. (6 mo. '61) Co.G
Teem, W.C. NC Cav. McRae's Bn. Co.E
Teem, William GA 11th Cav. Co.K
Teem, William C. NC 11th (Bethel Regt.) Inf. Co.B
Teems, Absalom NC 25th Inf. Co.G
Teems, D. GA 38th Inf. Co.G
Teems, F.V. GA 23rd Inf. Co.D
Teems, Peter M. SC 1st Arty. Co.H
Teems, William MS 1st (Johnston's) Inf. Co.D
Teen, Daniel LA 20th Inf. Co.I
Teen, John LA 13th Inf. Co.B
Teen, William GA 19th Inf. Co.D
Teener, John TX 11th Cav. Co.F
Teenley, William AL 49th Inf. Co.F
Teenor, A.H. TX 27th Cav. Co.F
Teenor, John A. TN 1st (Carter's) Cav. Co.B 1st Lt.
Teenor, J.P. TX 9th (Young's) Inf. Co.B
Teenor, J.W. TX 27th Cav. Co.F Sgt.
Teeple, Clinton VA 1st Cav.
Teeple, Jacob MO 10th Inf. Co.H Sgt.
Teepler, S. MO 10th Inf. Co.C
Teeples, Isaac MO 10th Inf. Co.K
Teeples, John TN 35th Inf. Co.E Cpl.
Teer, A. AR 1st Cav. Co.H
Teer, A. Exch.Bn. 3rd Co.B, 2nd Co.A,CSA
Teer, Albert J. AL 19th Inf. Co.A
Teer, Allen MS 33rd Inf. Co.G
Teer, Amasiah H. AL 19th Inf. Co.A Cpl.
Teer, Asmore MS 11th (Perrin's) Cav. Co.I
Teer, B.F. LA 2nd Cav. Co.F
Teer, Elbert MS Cav. (St.Troops) Gamblin's Co. Sgt.
Teer, Elbert MS 5th Inf. Co.I
Teer, Elbert MS 46th Inf. Co.K
Teer, Eli MS Cav. (St.Troops) Gamblin's Co.
Teer, Haywood NC 6th Cav. (65th St.Troops) Co.B
Teer, Iredell AL 40th Inf. Co.G Sgt.
Teer, J. AL Cp. of Instr. Talladega
Teer, James MS 6th Cav. Co.A
Teer, James MS 40th Inf. Co.I

Teer, James MS 46th Inf. Co.K
Teer, James TX 14th Inf. 1st Co.K Sgt.
Teer, James A. NC 2nd Inf. Co.F Sgt.
Teer, J.M. MS 4th Cav. Co.D,A
Teer, John LA 7th Cav. Co.K
Teer, John LA 6th Inf. Co.C
Teer, John MS Cav. (St.Troops) Gamblin's Co.
Teer, John MS Inf. 2nd St.Troops Co.C
Teer, Joseph MS Cav. (St.Troops) Gamblin's Co.
Teer, Joseph D. TX 11th Inf. Co.K
Teer, Lewis S. TX 11th Inf. Co.K
Teer, Louis TX Cav. (Dismtd.) Chisum's Regt. Co.E
Teer, Rufus A. TX 11th Inf. Co.K
Teer, Silas LA 9th Inf. Co.B
Teer, William MS 46th Inf. Co.K Cpl.
Teer, William NC 1st Arty. (10th St.Troops) Co.I
Teer, William NC 67th Inf. Co.B
Teer, William TX 4th Cav. Co.K
Teer, William VA 59th Inf. 2nd Co.F
Teer, William J. NC 6th Inf. Co.F
Teer, W.J. TX 4th Cav. Co.K
Teerney, --- TX 1st Hvy.Arty. Co.K
Teernon, Thomas J. MS 10th Inf. Old Co.C
Teers, R.S. TX Cav. Hardeman's Regt. Co.D
Tee Sah skie 1st Cherokee Mtd.Rifles Co.F
Tee sah tai skie Musk mellon 1st Cherokee Mtd.Rifles Co.G
Tee Say skie 1st Cherokee Mtd.Rifles Co.B
Tee see yor kee 1st Cherokee Mtd.Rifles McDaniel's Co.
Tee Ser Ne he 1st Cherokee Mtd.Rifles Co.A
Teeslin, L. AL 4th Inf. Co.C
Tee soo yoh que, Bill 1st Cherokee Mtd.Rifles Co.G
Teest, Edmond MS 3rd (St.Troops) Cav. Co.I
Teester, Finley P. NC 58th Inf. Co.D
Teet, James TN Cav. Napier's Bn. Co.A
Teet, Joseph VA Cav. 41st Bn. Co.A
Teet, W.J. AL 23rd Inf. Co.I
Teet, W.L. TN Cav. Napier's Bn. Co.C
Teetah Nur Sue, Allick 1st Cherokee Mtd.Rifles Co.G
Tee te na hee 1st Cherokee Mtd.Vol. 1st Co.C
Teeter, Andrew H. TX 16th Cav. Co.F Sgt.
Teeter, David C. TX 16th Cav. Co.F
Teeter, George T. TX 17th Cav. Co.B 2nd Lt.
Teeter, Giles D. NC 7th Inf. Co.H
Teeter, H. TX Waul's Legion Co.A
Teeter, H.M. MO 3rd Inf. Co.D
Teeter, James J. NC 42nd Inf. Co.C
Teeter, James L. MS 4th Cav. Co.G
Teeter, J.B. NC 57th Inf. Co.F
Teeter, J.E. NC 2nd Jr.Res. Co.B
Teeter, J.L. MS 2nd Cav. 1st Co.G
Teeter, Joseph C. VA 10th Inf. Co.F
Teeter, Levi VA 14th Mil. Co.E
Teeter, Marshall H. NC 7th Inf. Co.H
Teeter, Milus W. MS Bradford's Co. (Conf. Guards Arty.)
Teeter, Monroe NC 7th Inf. Co.H
Teeter, Peter N. AR Cav. 1st Bn. (Stirman's) Co.F
Teeters, A.F. MO 10th Inf. Co.A
Teeters, J.M. AL 38th Inf. Co.I
Teeters, John AL Lt.Arty. 2nd Bn. Co.D
Teeters, John AL Inf. 2nd Regt. Co.K
Teeters, John TN Lt.Arty. Browne's Co.
Teeters, John TN Lt.Arty. Kain's Co.
Teeters, John S. MO Cav. Poindexter's Regt. Co.D
Teeters, Sylvester KY 5th Mtd.Inf. Co.F
Teeters, Wesley KY 5th Mtd.Inf.
Teeters, William GA 6th Cav. 1st Co.K
Teeters, William KY 1st Inf. Co.D
Teeters, William KY 9th Mtd.Inf. Co.H
Teeters, William KY Jessee's Bn.Mtd.Riflemen Co.C
Teeters, William T. KY 4th Cav.
Teetey, William KY Morehead's Regt. (Part. Rangers) Co.A
Teetle, John TX 28th Cav. Co.I
Teets, Joseph VA 18th Cav. 1st Co.G
Teets, Labom W. VA 33rd Inf. Co.F
Teetz, Martin SC 21st Inf. Co.C
Teetz, Martin SC 25th Inf. Co.I
Teevan, George D. AR 1st (Monroe's) Cav. Palmer's Co.
Tefepaugh, H.P. AL 8th Inf. Co.F
Teferteller, J.N. TX 29th Cav. Co.K
Tefertoler, J.W. TN 1st (Carter's) Cav. Co.B
Teffatalar, J.W. Central Div. KY Sap. & Min.,CSA
Teffertaller, E.L. TN Inf. 2nd Cons.Regt. Co.H
Teffertaller, John TN 3rd (Lillard's) Mtd.Inf. Co.G
Tefferteller, Joseph NC Walker's Bn. Thomas' Legion Co.C
Tefferteller, Washington TN 26th Inf. Co.F
Teffertiller, John W. TN 39th Mtd.Inf. Co.B
Teffeteller, Anderson TN 37th Inf. Co.I
Teffeteller, Daniel TN 3rd (Lillard's) Mtd.Inf. Co.E
Teffeteller, E.L. TN 29th Inf. Co.A
Teffeteller, Michael TN 37th Inf. Co.I
Teffeteller, William TN 39th Mtd.Inf. Co.B
Teffeteller, Wilson TN 39th Mtd.Inf. Co.B
Tefft, George VA 36th Inf. Co.A N.C.S. Music.
Tefft, William A. VA Cav. 36th Bn. Co.D
Tefleteller, Jeff. TN 2nd (Ashby's) Cav. Co.K Cpl.
Teft, Edward A. VA 16th Cav. Love's Co.
Teftiller, Thomas C. TX 9th Field Btty. Sgt.
Tegahhoogeeskih NC Inf. Thomas Legion 2nd Co.A
Tegange, J.C. MS Inf. 2nd Bn. Co.C
Tegange, J.C. MS 48th Inf. Co.C
Tegar, Mike M. KY 2nd Bn.Mtd.Rifles Co.B
Tegart, A.B. TN 15th (Cons.) Cav. Co.F
Tegart, E.W. LA 3rd Inf. Co.I
Tegart, John LA 31st Inf. Co.B
Tegder, B.H. LA Mil. 3rd Regt. 1st Brig. 1st Div. Co.C Sgt.
Tegder, G.H. TN Hvy.Arty. Sterling's Co.
Tegder, T.G. LA Mil. 3rd Regt. 1st Brig. 1st Div. Co.K
Tege, Bernard LA Arty. Kean's Btty. (Orleans Ind.Arty.)
Teggal, J.T. TN 19th (Biffle's) Cav. Co.A
Tegge, F. TX Waul's Legion Co.C Cpl.
Teggner, --- TX 5th Inf. Co.B
Teghin, C. LA Mil. 1st Regt. 2nd Brig. 1st Div.
Tegil, S. AL 4th Inf. Co.D
Tegner, Lewis C. AL 20th Inf. Co.K,G
Tegno, L. VA 37th Mil. 2nd Co.B
Tegue, John TN 51st (Cons.) Inf. Co.A
Tegue, William NC 5th Sr.Res. Co.B
Tehan, John Lt.Arty. Dent's Btty.,CSA
Tehan, R.J. NC 55th Inf.
Tehan, W.N. Sap. & Min. Flynn's Co.,CSA
Tehee, Jonny NC Inf. Thomas Legion 2nd Co.A
Tehern, W. VA 45th Inf. Co.H
Tehille, F.D. GA 28th Inf. Co.A
Tehl, W. LA Mil. Chalmette Regt. Co.G
Tehlen, C. LA Mil. Moreau Guards
Tehon, Thomas TN 15th Inf. Co.G
Te ho Sar 1st Creek Mtd.Vol. Co.H, 2nd Co.D
Tehotubbee, Edmund 1st Choctaw & Chickasaw Mtd.Rifles 3rd Co.K
Te ho yah nee 1st Creek Mtd.Vol. Co.K
Te ho yo kine 1st Seminole Mtd.Vol.
Teichmann, J. TX Inf. 1st St.Troops Shields' Co.B Sgt.
Teidimann, E.G. AL Chas. A. Herts' Co.
Teige, Joshua M. TN Cav. Newsom's Regt. Co.H 1st Sgt.
Teige, Thomas TN Cav. Newsom's Regt. Co.H 3rd Lt.
Teige, William P. NC 2nd Jr.Res. Co.C
Teigh, J. LA Mil. 4th Regt. 1st Brig. 1st Div. Co.C
Teigle, William R. MS 9th Inf. Old Co.G, New Co.A
Teigue, A.B. MO Quantrill's Co.
Teigue, J.F. MO Quantrill's Co.
Teigue, John MO Quantrill's Co.
Teil, William TX Conscr.
Teille, H. TX Inf. 1st St.Troops Martin's Co.A
Teiman, Deidrick LA Mil. 3rd Regt. 1st Brig. 1st Div. Co.D
Teimann, Clemens LA Mil. 4th Regt.Eur.Brig. Co.D
Tein, Michael AR Arty. 4th Btty.
Teinert, J. TX 5th Field Btty.
Teiney, Michael SC Sea Fencibles Symons' Co.
Teins, Herman LA 20th Inf. New Co.B
Teir, James P. NC 44th Inf. Co.G
Teir, J.P. NC 44th Inf. Co.G
Teir, Russell NC 44th Inf. Co.G
Teir, William NC 7th Sr.Res. Bradshaw's Co.
Teirney, Edward P. VA 15th Inf. Co.F
Teirney, Patrick LA 13th Inf. Co.A
Teirnia, Thomas LA 16th Inf. Co.G
Teiron, J. NC 12th Inf. Co.F
Teis, John LA Mil. 3rd Regt. 1st Brig. 1st Div. Co.E
Teis, Peter LA 21st (Patton's) Inf. Co.I
Teiser, J.G. Gen. & Staff AQM
Teiss, Jacob William LA 6th Inf. Co.G
Teitenberg, C. LA 22nd Inf. Co.D Cpl.
Teitjen, J.H. SC Mil.Arty. 1st Regt. Co.A
Teitz, John KY 4th Mtd.Inf. Co.K
Teiver, Jacob D. GA 41st Inf. Co.E
Tejada, Emeterio TX 3rd Inf. Co.F
Tejada, Rafael TX Cav. L. Trevinio's Co.
Tejada, Severiano TX Cav. L. Trevinio's Co.
Tejida, --- TX 8th Inf. Co.H
Tejida, G. TX 8th Inf. Co.H
Tejida, Ignacio TX 33rd Cav. Co.B

Te Kah tos Kee, Joseph 1st Cherokee Mtd.Rifles Co.A
Tek bom bi, Silas 1st Choctaw Mtd.Rifles Co.K
Tekbombo, George 1st Choctaw Mtd.Rifles Co.K
Te Ke che Ah hur Nah 1st Cherokee Mtd.Rifles Co.G
Tekel, W. LA 3rd (Wingfield's) Cav. Co.F
Tekell, J.C. AL 2nd Bn. Hilliard's Legion Vol. Co.B
Teklombi Solomon 1st Choctaw Mtd.Rifles Co.K Cpl.
Te kobbi Moses 1st Choctaw Mtd.Rifles Co.K
Tek O bee 1st Choctaw Mtd.Rifles Co.K 3rd Lt.
Tekota, William MO 5th Inf. Co.H
Tekotle, William MO Lt.Arty. 3rd Btty.
Tekotte, Antonio MO 1st Cav. Co.K
Tekotte, William MO Cav. Poindexter's Regt.
Tekotte, William MO Arty. Lowe's Co.
Tela, H.C. GA 20th Inf. Co.B
Telahlah, --- NC Inf. Thomas Legion 2nd Co.A
Telbrunn, H. GA 12th (Wright's) Cav. (St.Guards) Brannen's Co.
Telee, W.H. MO Cav. 2nd Regt.St.Guard Co.A
Telfair, Felix GA 1st (Olmstead's) Inf. Gordon's Co. Music.
Telfair, Felix GA 63rd Inf. Co.B Drum.
Telfer, Charles LA 22nd Inf. Co.B
Telfer, Charles LA 22nd (Cons.) Inf. Co.B
Telford, David W. MS 2nd Part.Rangers Co.E
Telford, Edwin M. SC Palmetto S.S. Co.L
Telford, F.R. AR 11th Inf. Co.F Cpl.
Telford, F.R. AR 11th & 17th Cons.Inf. Co.F 2nd Lt.
Telford, G.B. SC 1st St.Troops Co.C
Telford, James SC 2nd Rifles Co.G
Telford, James W. AL 57th Inf. Co.G
Telford, John C. SC 1st (Orr's) Rifles Co.K
Telford, R. GA 28th Inf. Co.G
Telford, Robert TN 13th Inf. Co.A
Telford, Robert C. SC 1st (Orr's) Rifles Co.K Sgt.
Telford, Samuel S. SC 1st (Orr's) Rifles Co.K
Telford, T.F.M. MO 1st & 4th Cons.Inf. Co.B
Telford, T.F.M. MO 4th Inf. Co.G
Telford, William B. SC 4th Inf. Co.J
Telford, William B. SC Palmetto S.S. Co.L
Telford, William S. TX 13th Vol. 2nd Co.C
Telford, William T. TN 28th Inf. Co.F
Telford, W.J. MS 35th Inf. Co.C,D
Telford, W.J. SC Inf. 7th Bn. (Enfield Rifles) Co.C 1st Sgt.
Telier, John LA Mil. Beauregard Regt. 2nd Lt.
Telina, J. LA 3rd (Harrison's) Cav. Co.C
Teling, P.H. GA 1st (Olmstead's) Inf. Co.G
Telkil, J.J. GA Cav. 29th Bn. Co.F
Telkins, W.W. FL 2nd Cav.
Tell, Charles L. AL 21st Inf. Co.A 1st Lt.
Tell, John TN 18th Inf. Co.D
Tell, Monroe NC 1st Arty. (10th St.Troops) Co.C
Telledge, J.C. VA 14th Inf. Co.I
Tellenborn, Ch TX 6th Field Btty. Bugler
Teller, --- Conf.Cav. Wood's Regt. 1st Co.A
Teller, B.H. MS 15th Cav. Co.G Capt.
Teller, Daniel TN 60th Mtd.Inf. Co.H
Teller, Emanuel NC 18th Inf. Co.A
Teller, Gaynam TN 4th (Murray's) Cav. Co.K
Teller, J.G. AL 8th Inf. Co.E
Teller, John C. VA 3rd Inf.Loc.Def. Co.F
Teller, John C. VA 41st Mil. Co.B
Teller, L.H. TN Park's Co. (Loc.Def.Troops)
Teller, William TX 2nd Cav. Co.I
Teller, William R. VA 1st Inf. Co.A
Teller, William R. VA 3rd Inf.Loc.Def. Co.F 2nd Lt.
Teller, William R. VA 12th Inf. Co.G
Tellery, William H. TN 3rd (Clack's) Inf. Co.A
Tellet, Charles L. LA Ogden's Cav. Co.A
Tellett, J.L. VA 8th Inf. Co.E
Telley, --- LA 13th Inf. Co.H
Telley, Alfred TN Conscr. (Cp. of Instr.)
Telley, T.G. AL 37th Inf. Co.K
Telley, T.G. NC 7th Sr.Res. Fisher's Co.
Tellgmann, Charles TX 5th Cav. Co.D
Tellice, John C. VA 9th Cav.
Tellier, Stanislas LA Mil. 1st Regt. 3rd Brig. 1st Div. Co.G
Tellier, Stanislaus LA Lewis Regt. Co.B
Telling, George AL 36th Inf. Co.D
Tellinghast, E.H. AL Inf. 36th Regt. Co.B
Tellinghast, J.W. AL Inf. 36th Regt. Co.B
Tellis, E.D. MS 2nd Cav. Co.A
Tellkemper, H. MO 2nd Cav. Co.E
Tellman, James AL 24th Inf. Co.B
Tellock, David TN 61st Mtd.Inf. Co.A
Tellon, H.P. TN 9th Inf. Co.K
Tellp, J.T. LA Miles' Legion Co.E
Tells, J.C. AR 1st Cav. Co.I
Telly, Wilkison 1st Choctaw & Chickasaw Mtd.Rifles 2nd Co.I
Telly, William VA 53rd Inf. Co.G
Telott, Charles L. LA 11th Inf. Co.I
Telott, Charles L. 14th Conf.Cav. Co.D
Telotte, J.V. LA 30th Inf. Co.C
Telton, A.E. VA Inf. 25th Bn. Music.
Teltow, Aurelius E. VA 19th Inf. Co.A Ch.Music.
Telyea, John GA Lt.Arty. Ritter's Co.
Telyea, John MD Arty. 3rd Btty.
Temahsee 1st Seminole Mtd.Vol.
Temalicha Wilson 1st Choctaw & Chickasaw Mtd.Rifles 2nd Co.K
Temalth Harjo 1st Seminole Mtd.Vol.
Teman, K. TX 24th & 25th Cav. (Cons.) Co.I
Teman, Thomas AL Mil. 2nd Regt.Vol. Co.B
Temawe lah 1st Seminole Mtd.Vol.
Temberlake, Samuel R. MS 15th Inf. Co.B
Temberton, Z. MO 12th Cav. Co.I
Tembey, J.H. NC 16th Inf. Co.E Lt.
Temblee, John B. NC 7th Sr.Res. Co.C
Tembus, S. LA Mil. Chalmette Regt. Co.E
Temis, Perry AL 33rd Inf. Co.D
Temler, E.A. TN 21st Cav. Co.C
Temlergrass, J.R. MS 7th Cav. Co.F
Temly, John AL 24th Inf. Co.H
Temmons, B.F. TX Cav. Bourland's Regt. Co.C
Temms, J.B. VA Lt.Arty. Jackson's Bn.St.Line Co.A
Te mo car le 1st Creek Mtd.Vol. Co.M
Temon, Alonzo MS Lt.Arty. English's Co.
Temous, Theodore TX 20th Inf. Co.A
Tempel, Charles W. LA 4th Inf. Co.D Cpl.
Tempels, John MO Cav. Fristoe's Regt. Co.D
Tempels, J.S. MS 8th Inf. Co.B
Tempen, A.P. AL 53rd (Part.Rangers) Co.K
Templar, Thomas VA 8th Inf. Co.G
Temple, --- VA Arty.Detach. VMI
Temple, A.B. MS 1st (King's) Inf. (St.Troops) Co.F
Temple, A.L. AR 1st (Monroe's) Cav. Co.B
Temple, Alex Conf.Reg.Inf. Brooks' Bn. Co.D
Temple, Alex. H. VA 2nd Arty. Co.E
Temple, Alexander H. VA Inf. 22nd Bn. Co.E
Temple, Alfred H. NC 26th Inf. Co.D
Temple, Anderson F. MS 20th Inf. Co.K Sgt.
Temple, Andrew J. FL 6th Inf. Co.C
Temple, Andrew J. VA 32nd Inf. Co.E
Temple, Andrew J. VA 41st Inf. 2nd Co.E
Temple, A.W. MO 12th Cav. Co.A
Temple, B. AL 24th Inf. Hosp.Stew.
Temple, Bellville AL 34th Inf. Co.H N.C.S. Hosp.Stew.
Temple, Benjamin B. VA 1st Arty. Co.K
Temple, Benjamin F. AL 2nd Bn. Hilliard's Legion Vol. Co.C
Temple, Benjamin F. MS 7th Inf. Co.A
Temple, Bernard VA 55th Inf. Co.M
Temple, Bernard M. VA Lt.Arty. Cayce's Co.
Temple, B.F. 14th Conf.Cav. Co.I 2nd Lt.
Temple, B.L. AR Inf. Hardy's Regt. Co.C
Temple, B.M. NC 1st Arty. (10th St.Troops) Co.H Ord.Sgt.
Temple, Brooks B. VA 9th Cav.
Temple, Burwell W. NC 24th Inf. Co.E
Temple, B.Z. AL Inf. 1st Regt. Co.D
Temple, B.Z. AL 17th Inf. Co.D
Temple, C. LA Inf. 1st Sp.Bn. (Rightor's) Co.D
Temple, C. TN Inf. 154th Sr.Regt. Co.A Sgt.
Temple, C.A. LA 13th Bn. (Part.Rangers) Co.D
Temple, Caswell NC 50th Inf. Co.D
Temple, Charles AL 1st Cav. Co.K
Temple, Charles LA 3rd Inf. Co.E
Temple, Charles TN 43rd Inf. Co.K
Temple, Charles Echols' Staff Capt.
Temple, Charles A. LA 31st Cav. Co.A
Temple, Charles A. LA 1st (Nelligan's) Inf. Co.C
Temple, Charles K. TN Cav. 11th Bn. (Gordon's) Co.E Cpl.
Temple, Charles R. TN 11th (Holman's) Cav. Co.I
Temple, Charles W. MS 48th Inf. Ch.Bugler
Temple, Charles W. VA 9th Cav.
Temple, Christopher C. MS 10th Inf. Old Co.H Cpl.
Temple, C.M. AL 59th Inf. Co.B
Temple, C.M. MS Inf. 2nd St.Troops Co.H
Temple, Columbus C. MS 3rd Inf. Co.K 2nd Lt.
Temple, C.P. SC 1st Arty. Co.B
Temple, C.R. TN Lt.Arty. Morton's Co.
Temple, Daniel G. LA Res.Corps Williams' Co.
Temple, Drewery H. VA Hvy.Arty. Epes' Co.
Temple, Drewry H. VA Arty. C.F. Johnston's Co.
Temple, Ed. M. MS 44th Inf. Co.D
Temple, Edward W. AR Lt.Arty. 5th Btty.
Temple, Elias C. NC 56th Inf. Co.C
Temple, Elverton E. VA Inf. 5th Bn. Co.C Sgt.
Temple, Elverton E. VA 53rd Inf. Co.C
Temple, Frank LA 1st Cav. Co.C
Temple, Frank G. TN 2nd (Robison's) Inf. Co.C

Temple, George G. MS 11th Inf. Co.C
Temple, George W.B. VA 41st Inf. 2nd Co.E
Temple, Henry NC 56th Inf. Co.C
Temple, H.H. LA 25th Inf. Co.E
Temple, J.A. AL 45th Inf. Co.B
Temple, James AR Mil. Borland's Regt. Pulaski Lancers Sgt.
Temple, James MO 7th Cav. Haislip's Co.
Temple, James VA Cav. McNeill's Co.
Temple, James A. AR 9th Inf. Co.D
Temple, James A. NC 31st Inf. Co.H Sgt.
Temple, James B. AR 16th Inf. Co.C Sgt.
Temple, James F. VA 12th Inf. Co.D
Temple, James H. AR 1st Mtd.Rifles Co.F
Temple, James S. VA 5th Cav. (12 mo. '61-2) Co.F
Temple, James S. VA 13th Cav. Co.F
Temple, James W. VA 2nd Arty. Co.E
Temple, James W. VA Lt.Arty. Pegram's Co.
Temple, James W. VA Inf. 22nd Bn. Co.E
Temple, J.B. MS 28th Cav. Co.E
Temple, J.B. NC 7th Sr.Res. Johnston's Co.
Temple, J.C. AR 13th Mil. Co.F
Temple, J.D. TN 2nd (Ashby's) Cav. Co.K Sgt.
Temple, J.D. TN Cav. 5th Bn. (McClellan's) Co.E Cpl.
Temple, J. Dobson NC Walker's Bn. Thomas' Legion 1st Co.D
Temple, J. Dobson TN 1st (Carter's) Cav. Co.I
Temple, Jesse F. MS 20th Inf. Co.K
Temple, J.H. AR 24th Inf. Co.D
Temple, J.H. AR Inf. Hardy's Regt. Co.C
Temple, J.H. TN Inf. 154th Sr.Regt. Co.L Cpl.
Temple, J.L. AR 10th Mil. Co.B
Temple, J.L. AR 26th Inf. Co.H
Temple, J.M. MS 33rd Inf. Co.D
Temple, J.M. 14th Conf.Cav. Co.I Cpl.
Temple, John LA Mil. Claiborne Regt. Co.A
Temple, John NC 8th Inf. Co.A
Temple, John VA 9th Cav.
Temple, John VA Cav. Young's Co.
Temple, John VA 1st St.Res. Co.I
Temple, John VA 9th Inf. 2nd Co.H
Temple, John VA 12th Inf. 1st Co.I
Temple, John B. VA Inf. 4th Bn.Loc.Def. Co.C
Temple, John F. MS 40th Inf. Co.D
Temple, John H. TX 6th Cav. Co.I Sgt.
Temple, John L. TN 42nd Inf. Co.B Fifer
Temple, John N. VA Mtd.Res. Rappahannock Dist. Sale's Co.
Temple, John T. VA 30th Inf. Co.B 2nd Lt.
Temple, Joseph W. TN 6th Inf. Co.C Cpl.
Temple, Josiah NC 6th Sr.Res. Co.B
Temple, J.R. MS 18th Cav. Co.A
Temple, J.W.F. MS Inf. 2nd St.Troops Co.H
Temple, J.W.F. MS 5th Inf. (St.Troops) Co.C
Temple, L. VA 1st (Farinholt's) Res. Co.H
Temple, Listone McNairy MS 2nd Part.Rangers Co.C Cpl.
Temple, Lloyd A. MS 7th Inf. Co.A
Temple, L.M. TN 3rd (Forrest's) Cav. Co.F Cpl.
Temple, L.M. TN Hvy.Arty. Johnston's Co. Cpl.
Temple, L.M. Gen. & Staff, QM Dept.
Temple, Ludwell VA 9th Cav. Co.B
Temple, L.W. MS Conscr.
Temple, M. MS 10th Cav. Co.G
Temple, Marke H. FL 4th Inf. Co.A Cpl.
Temple, Mathew MS 41st Inf. Co.A
Temple, M.D.C. 7th Conf.Cav. Co.C
Temple, Miles NC 8th Inf. Co.A
Temple, Miles NC 32nd Inf. Co.B
Temple, Milton MS 41st Inf. Co.A Cpl.
Temple, P.E. AL St.Res.
Temple, P.J. AR 10th Mil. Sgt.
Temple, P.J. AR 26th Inf. Co.H Sgt.
Temple, R. VA Inf. 44th Bn. Co.A
Temple, Raymond NC 24th Inf. Co.I
Temple, R.H. NC 47th Inf. Co.H
Temple, R.H. NC Walker's Bn. Thomas' Legion 1st Co.D
Temple, R.H. TN 1st (Carter's) Cav. Co.I
Temple, R.H. TN 17th Inf. Co.H
Temple, R.H. Nitre & Min. Bureau War Dept.,CSA Capt.
Temple, Robert MO Cav. Williams' Regt. Lt.
Temple, Robert VA Hvy.Arty. Coleman's Co.
Temple, Robert G. VA Cav. 39th Bn. Co.D 1st Lt.
Temple, Robert G. VA 20th Inf. Co.G 2nd Lt.
Temple, Robert H. TN 1st Cav. Sgt.
Temple, Rod VA 21st Inf. Co.G Sgt.
Temple, Rowan MS Cav. Garland's Bn. Co.B
Temple, Rowan MS 7th Inf. Co.A
Temple, Rowan 14th Conf.Cav. Co.B
Temple, Roy VA Lt.Arty. W.P. Carter's Co.
Temple, Rufus F. NC 47th Inf. Co.E Comsy.Sgt.
Temple, S. MO 10th Inf. Co.B
Temple, Samuel W. VA 41st Inf. Co.C
Temple, S.E. NC 24th Inf. Co.E
Temple, Simon P. NC 24th Inf. Co.I
Temple, S.J. FL Fernandez's Mtd.Co. (Supply Force) Sgt.
Temple, S.M. AR 20th Inf. Co.I Sgt.
Temple, Solimon TN 17th Inf. Co.D
Temple, S.W. AR 1st Vol. Co.K,E Adj.
Temple, Theodore T. VA Lt.Arty. Pegram's Co.
Temple, Theodore T. VA Inf. 5th Bn. Co.C
Temple, Thomas MS 18th Cav. Co.A
Temple, Thomas D. VA Hvy.Arty. Coleman's Co.
Temple, Thomas P. VA 6th Inf. Surg.
Temple, Thomas P. VA 56th Inf. Co.K 1st Lt.
Temple, Thos. P. Gen. & Staff Surg.
Temple, Timothy B. NC 8th Inf. Co.A
Temple, T.P. VA 53rd Inf. Surg.
Temple, Tracy Turner TX 20th Cav. Co.E Sgt.
Temple, Victorine LA Inf. 16th Bn. (Conf. Guards Resp.Bn.) Co.B
Temple, W. VA 10th Cav. 2nd Co.E
Temple, W.B. LA 15th Inf. Asst.Surg.
Temple, W.B. TX Cav. Terry's Regt. Asst.Surg.
Temple, W.B. TX Inf. Griffin's Bn. Co.G
Temple, W.B. Gen. & Staff, Medical Dept. Surg.
Temple, W.C. FL 1st (Res.) Inf. Co.I
Temple, W.C. FL Fernandez's Mtd.Co. (Supply Force) Cpl.
Temple, W.I. TN 6th (Wheeler's) Cav. Co.A
Temple, William LA Mil. Claiborne Regt. Co.A
Temple, William NC 4th Cav. (59th St.Troops) Co.G
Temple, William VA Inf. 25th Bn. Co.C
Temple, William VA 34th Inf. Co.K Cpl.
Temple, William VA 52nd Inf. Co.D
Temple, William B. TX 6th Cav. Co.I Sgt.
Temple, William C. FL 8th Inf. Co.F
Temple, William D. VA 8th Cav. Co.H
Temple, William H. VA Hvy.Arty. 10th Bn. Co.D
Temple, William M. NC 56th Inf. Co.C
Temple, William M. NC Walker's Bn. Thomas' Legion 1st Co.D
Temple, William M. TN 1st (Carter's) Cav. Co.I
Temple, William P. AL 53rd (Part.Rangers) Co.K
Temple, William P. VA 18th Inf. Co.C 3rd Lt.
Temple, William R. MS 3rd Inf. Co.K
Temple, William S. MO 1st Cav. Co.H
Temple, William S. VA 5th Cav. (12 mo. '61-2) Co.I
Temple, William S. VA 9th Cav.
Temple, William S. VA Cav. 14th Bn. Co.B
Temple, William S. VA 15th Cav. Co.I
Temple, William S. VA Lt.Arty. Pollock's Co. Sgt.
Temple, William T. GA 18th Inf. Co.D
Temple, William T. VA Inf. 5th Bn. Co.C
Temple, William T. VA 53rd Inf. Co.C 2nd Lt.
Temple, Wilson S. NC 8th Inf. Co.A Color Cpl.
Temple, Wilson S. NC 17th Inf. (1st Org.) Co.L
Temple, Wilson S. NC 17th Inf. (2nd Org.) AASurg.
Temple, W.M. AR 15th (Johnson's) Inf. Co.F
Temple, W.R. MS Cav. Powers' Regt. Co.I
Temple, W. Skyren VA Lt.Arty. Cayce's Co. Sgt.
Templelon, John D. TN 11th Cav.
Templeman, Andrew J. VA 26th Inf. Co.E
Templeman, James VA Inf. 1st Bn.Loc.Def. Co.F
Templeman, James A. VA 7th Cav. Co.A
Templeman, James E. VA 12th Cav. Co.I
Templeman, M.M. TX 5th Inf. Co.H
Templeman, Robert B. VA 7th Cav. Co.A
Templeman, Robt. B. Gen. & Staff AAAG
Templeman, W.C. VA 3rd Inf.Loc.Def. 1st Co.G, 2nd Co.G Sgt.
Templeman, William VA 26th Inf. Co.F
Templer, A.L. AR 33rd Inf. Co.F
Temples, Andrew GA 5th Res. Co.H
Temples, B. GA 46th Inf. Co.K
Temples, B.F. GA 16th Inf. Co.C
Temples, Columbus M. AL 2nd Bn. Hilliard's Legion Vol. Co.E
Temples, C.W. GA 10th Cav. Co.C 2nd Lt.
Temples, C.W. GA 16th Inf. Co.C Cpl.
Temples, C.W. 7th Conf.Cav. Co.C 1st Lt.
Temples, E.J. TN 38th Inf. 2nd Co.K
Temples, George W. FL Inf. 2nd Bn. Co.B
Temples, Hudson GA 57th Inf. Co.K
Temples, Irwin N. GA 59th Inf. Co.E
Temples, Isham NC 26th Inf. Co.D
Temples, Isham NC 53rd Inf. Co.C
Temples, J.A. GA 59th Inf. Co.G Cpl.
Temples, J.A. NC 26th Inf. Co.E
Temples, Jacob MS 38th Cav. Co.I
Temples, Jacob MS 7th Inf. Co.D
Temples, James AR Inf. 4th Bn. Co.E
Temples, James AR 36th Inf. Co.B

Temples, James GA 3rd Res. Co.C
Temples, James GA 57th Inf. Co.K
Temples, James F. AR 24th Inf. Co.B
Temples, James S. AR Inf. Hardy's Regt. Co.B
Temples, J.L.F. TN Inf. 3rd Cons.Regt. Co.F
Temples, J.L.F. TN 35th Inf. 1st Co.D, Co.C
Temples, J.M. MO 7th Cav. Co.B
Temples, John GA 57th Inf. Co.I
Temples, John MS 40th Inf. Co.H
Temples, John NC 5th Inf. Co.A
Temples, John TN 7th (Duckworth's) Cav. Co.M
Temples, John G. TN 35th Inf. 1st Co.D
Temples, John M. MO 6th Inf.
Temples, John T.T. AR 5th Inf. Co.C
Temples, Jonas GA Siege Arty. 28th Bn. Co.C
Temples, Jones R. MS 7th Inf. Co.D
Temples, J.Q. NC 1st Jr.Res. Co.H Sgt.
Temples, J.W. AR Inf. 4th Bn. Co.E
Temples, J.W. AR 27th Inf. Co.I
Temples, Lorenzo J. MS 37th Inf. Co.E
Temples, Manuel MS 26th Inf. Co.B
Temples, Michael GA 13th Inf. Co.G
Temples, Michael J. GA 51st Inf. Co.A
Temples, M.V. AR 2nd Mtd.Rifles Co.A 1st Sgt.
Temples, Needham H. MS 37th Inf. Co.E
Temples, N.H. MS Clayton's Co. (Jasper Defend.)
Temples, P.H. GA 23rd Inf. Co.D
Temples, S. SC 2nd St.Troops Co.B
Temples, Samuel AR Inf. 4th Bn. Co.E
Temples, Samuel AR 36th Inf. Co.B
Temples, Samuel FL 10th Inf. Co.A
Temples, Seaborn SC 5th Res. Co.K
Temples, Seaborn SC 6th Inf. Co.D
Temples, S.M. TN 35th Inf. Co.C
Temples, W.H. TX 11th Inf. Co.C
Temples, William GA 23rd Inf. Co.D
Temples, William MS 5th Inf. (St.Troops) Co.H
Temples, William MS 37th Inf. Co.K
Temples, William A. MS 36th Inf. Co.I
Temples, William J. MS 7th Inf. Co.D
Temples, William R. MS 33rd Inf. Co.D
Temples, W.R. MS 22nd Inf. Co.D Music.
Templet, A. LA Ogden's Cav. Co.A
Templet, Adolphe LA 8th Inf. Co.K
Templet, Amadeo LA 4th Inf. Co.H
Templet, Arthur LA 2nd Cav. Co.H
Templet, Camille LA 2nd Cav. Co.H Cpl.
Templet, Camille LA Arty. Landry's Co. (Donaldsonville Arty.)
Templet, Charles LA Conscr.
Templet, Enos LA 1st Hvy.Arty. (Reg.) Co.A
Templet, Eugene LA 1st Hvy.Arty. (Reg.) Co.A
Templet, Hypolite LA Arty. Landry's Co. (Donaldsonville Arty.)
Templet, Jean Baptize LA Ogden's Cav. Co.A
Templet, John B. 14th Conf.Cav. Co.D
Templet, Joseph 14th Conf.Cav. Co.D
Templet, Narcisse LA 2nd Cav. Co.H
Templet, Orillien LA 2nd Cav. Co.H
Templet, Severin LA 28th (Thomas') Inf. Co.H
Templet, Theodule LA 1st Hvy.Arty. (Reg.) Co.A
Templet, Ursin LA 2nd Cav. Co.H
Templet, Victorain 14th Conf.Cav. Co.D
Templet, Victorine LA Inf.Cons.Crescent Regt. Co.A
Templeton, A. AR 6th Inf. New Co.F
Templeton, A. AR 12th Inf. Co.D
Templeton, A. GA Lt.Arty. 12th Bn. 2nd Co.D
Templeton, A. TN Inf. 22nd Bn. Co.E
Templeton, A.A. TN 9th Inf. Co.C
Templeton, A.D. AL Cav. Forrest's Regt.
Templeton, A.D. TN 18th (Newsom's) Cav. Co.H
Templeton, A.D. TN 19th & 20th (Cons.) Cav. Co.D
Templeton, A.F. MO 9th Bn.S.S. Co.A Cpl.
Templeton, A.G. TN Cav. 7th Bn. (Bennett's) Co.F
Templeton, A.G. TN 22nd (Barteau's) Cav. Co.G
Templeton, A.J. GA Cav. Allen's Co.
Templeton, A.J. TX 22nd Inf. Co.F
Templeton, Alx. TN 13th (Gore's) Cav. Co.A
Templeton, A.N. TX 20th Cav. Co.A
Templeton, A.N. TX Cav. Morgan's Regt. Co.F
Templeton, A.N. TX 4th Inf. Co.I
Templeton, Andrew J. GA 3rd Inf. Co.A
Templeton, Andrew J. GA 48th Inf. Co.I Sgt.
Templeton, B.C. SC 3rd Inf. Co.I
Templeton, B.C. SC 5th St.Troops Co.I Sgt.
Templeton, B.C. SC 9th Res. Co.D Sgt.
Templeton, Benjamin P. SC 14th Inf. Co.F
Templeton, Benton B. TN Inf. 23rd Bn. Co.C
Templeton, Burl TN 35th Inf. Co.L
Templeton, Burrel TN Inf. 3rd Cons.Regt. Co.A
Templeton, C. TX 17th Inf. Co.I
Templeton, C.E. GA Inf. (Jones Hussars) Jones' Co.
Templeton, D.C. SC 3rd Inf. Co.G Cpl.
Templeton, D.D. VA 1st Cav. 2nd Co.K
Templeton, D.E. MS Inf. 2nd St.Troops Co.G
Templeton, D.H. SC 4th Inf. Co.I Cpl.
Templeton, D.H. SC Palmetto S.S. Co.I Cpl.
Templeton, D.J.H. AR 1st Vol. Anderson's Co.
Templeton, D. McDuffee SC Inf. Hampton Legion Co.E
Templeton, D.R. TN 5th Inf. 2nd Co.B
Templeton, E. TN 45th Inf.
Templeton, E. VA 64th Mtd.Inf. Co.D
Templeton, Edward MO 1st & 4th Cons.Inf. Co.B
Templeton, Edward MO 4th Inf. Co.F
Templeton, Edward H. MS Inf. 3rd Bn. Co.D
Templeton, Edward J. VA 18th Inf. Co.A
Templeton, E.H. MS 15th Inf. Co.K
Templeton, E.J. TN 24th Inf. Co.E
Templeton, E.M. TN 51st Inf. Co.K
Templeton, E.M. TN 51st (Cons.) Inf. Co.G
Templeton, Eugene SC 2nd Arty. Co.B
Templeton, Ezekiel TN 35th Inf. Co.L
Templeton, Ezekiel TN 36th Inf. Co.L
Templeton, Fielding H. VA 14th Cav. Co.H Sgt.
Templeton, F.M. MS 39th Inf. Co.E
Templeton, Francis TX Cav. Saufley's Scouting Bn. Co.B
Templeton, Frank AL 3rd Cav. Co.F
Templeton, Frank TX 2nd Cav. Co.H
Templeton, George TX Cav. Wells' Regt. Co.A
Templeton, George TX Cav. Wells' Bn. Co.A
Templeton, George G. NC 7th Inf. Co.I
Templeton, G.G. TN 51st Inf. Co.G
Templeton, G.H. TN Inf. 1st Cons.Regt. Co.F
Templeton, G.H. TN 16th Inf. Co.K
Templeton, G.M. SC 14th Inf. Co.F
Templeton, Gus TN 9th Inf. Co.C
Templeton, H. MO 4th Cav. Co.E
Templeton, Harvey VA 8th Cav. 2nd Co.D
Templeton, H.B. SC Mil. 14th Regt. Co.B
Templeton, Henry T. SC 3rd Inf. Co.A,E
Templeton, H.T. SC 3rd Inf. Co.A,E
Templeton, Ira G. SC 15th Inf. Co.A
Templeton, I.W. MS St.Cav. 2nd Bn. (Harris') Co.C
Templeton, I.W. MS 31st Inf. Co.K
Templeton, J.A. SC 3rd Inf. Co.F
Templeton, James AL 23rd Inf. Co.G
Templeton, Jas. AL 31st Inf. Co.D
Templeton, James AL Talladega Cty.Res. D.B. Brown's Co.
Templeton, James TN 16th Inf. Co.D
Templeton, James TN 35th Inf. Co.C
Templeton, James TN 36th Inf. Co.C
Templeton, James TN 62nd Mtd.Inf. Co.A Cpl.
Templeton, James VA 52nd Inf. Co.H
Templeton, James Gen. & Staff A.Surg.
Templeton, James A. VA 4th Res. Surg.
Templeton, James A. VA Inf. 23rd Bn. Surg.
Templeton, James A. VA 36th Inf. Asst.Surg.
Templeton, James E. NC 56th Inf. Co.K
Templeton, James Edward MO 8th Inf. Co.I
Templeton, James L. TN 40th Inf. Co.K
Templeton, James M. NC 42nd Inf. Co.D
Templeton, James M. NC 56th Inf. Co.K
Templeton, James R. VA 21st Inf. Co.H
Templeton, J.D. SC 3rd Inf. Co.I
Templeton, J.D. TX Cav. Morgan's Regt. Co.F
Templeton, J.D. VA 64th Mtd.Inf. Franklin's Co.
Templeton, J.E. SC 2nd Arty. Co.B
Templeton, J.E. TX 11th Cav. Co.G
Templeton, J.F. MS 21st Inf. Co.A
Templeton, J.G. AL 31st Inf. Co.D
Templeton, J.H. SC 3rd Inf. Co.F
Templeton, J.H. 8th (Wade's) Conf.Cav. Co.I
Templeton, J.L. AL 54th Inf. Co.K
Templeton, J.L. SC 3rd Inf. Co.A
Templeton, J.L. VA 8th Cav. 2nd Co.D
Templeton, J.L. Exch.Bn. 1st Co.A,CSA
Templeton, J.M. NC Unassign.Conscr.
Templeton, J.M. VA 8th Cav. 2nd Co.D
Templeton, J.M. VA 10th Bn.Res. Co.B Capt.
Templeton, J.N. MS 35th Inf. Co.C
Templeton, John LA 31st Inf. Co.H
Templeton, John NC 64th Inf. Co.M
Templeton, John SC 2nd Arty. Co.B
Templeton, John TN 35th Inf. Co.B
Templeton, John, Jr. TN 35th Inf. Co.L
Templeton, John TX 24th Cav. Co.H
Templeton, John A. SC 15th Inf. Co.B
Templeton, John A. TN Arty. Bibb's Co.
Templeton, John A. TX 10th Cav. Co.I Sgt.
Templeton, John C. GA Cobb's Legion Co.E
Templeton, John C. TN 19th Inf. Co.A
Templeton, John D. VA Mil. Scott Cty.
Templeton, John Dekalb TX 20th Cav. Co.G
Templeton, John F. MS 1st Lt.Arty. Co.G

Templeton, John Howard MO 8th Inf. Co.I Cpl.
Templeton, John M. VA Inf. 25th Bn. Co.A
Templeton, John M. VA Mil. 144th Regt. Col.
Templeton, John M. VA Rockbridge Cty.Res. Donald's Co. 1st Lt.
Templeton, John P. SC 3rd Inf. Co.G
Templeton, John W. TN 44th (Cons.) Inf. Co.D Hosp.Stew.
Templeton, John Y. NC 7th Inf. Co.I,G 1st Lt.
Templeton, Joseph TN 35th Inf. Co.L
Templeton, Joseph A. NC 7th Inf. Co.I
Templeton, Joseph N. NC 7th Inf. Co.I,B
Templeton, Joseph O. SC 14th Inf. Co.F
Templeton, Joseph W. SC 12th Inf. Co.B
Templeton, J.S. TN 4th Inf. Co.K
Templeton, J.T. SC 4th Bn.Res. Co.E
Templeton, J.T. SC 5th St.Troops Co.I
Templeton, J.T. SC 9th Res. Co.D
Templeton, Julius R. NC 7th Inf. Co.I
Templeton, J.W.T. GA 11th Inf. Co.G
Templeton, L.A.J. TX 22nd Inf. Co.I
Templeton, L.W. 3rd Conf.Cav. Co.K
Templeton, M. MS 39th Inf. Co.E
Templeton, Madison MS 6th Inf. Co.F
Templeton, Madison Gillum's Regt. Whitaker's Co.
Templeton, Martin VA 18th Inf. Co.A
Templeton, M.B. TX Cav. Mann's Regt. Co.G 3rd Lt.
Templeton, M.B. TX 4th Inf. Co.I
Templeton, M.M. MO 6th Cav. Co.F
Templeton, Newton TN Cav. Newsom's Regt. Co.E
Templeton, Newton TN Inf. 23rd Bn. Co.C
Templeton, N.J. MS 2nd St.Cav. Co.E Sgt.
Templeton, P.C. TN 16th Inf. Co.K
Templeton, P.M. MO 4th Cav. Co.E
Templeton, Ransom VA 16th Cav. Co.K Cpl.
Templeton, Ransom VA Cav. Ferguson's Bn. Nounnan's Co.
Templeton, R.D. MS 31st Inf. Co.K 1st Sgt.
Templeton, R.F. MO 6th Cav. Co.F 1st Sgt.
Templeton, Richard D. AL 7th Cav. Co.B
Templeton, Richard S. TN 12th (Green's) Cav. Co.C
Templeton, R.J. SC 1st Bn.S.S. Co.C
Templeton, R.J. SC 9th Res. Co.E
Templeton, R.J. SC 27th Inf. Co.G
Templeton, Robert A. VA 21st Inf. Co.H Sgt.
Templeton, Robert H. TN 44th (Cons.) Inf. Co.B
Templeton, Robert R. AL 19th Inf. Co.F
Templeton, Robert S. NC 56th Inf. Co.K
Templeton, R.W. SC 3rd Inf. Co.C
Templeton, R.W. TX 21st Cav. Co.L
Templeton, S. SC 9th Res. Co.D
Templeton, S.A. MS Inf. 1st Bn. Co.C
Templeton, S.A. MS 35th Inf. Co.C Sgt.
Templeton, S.A. TN 16th Inf. Co.D
Templeton, Samuel GA 54th Inf. Co.F
Templeton, Samuel SC 5th St.Troops Co.I
Templeton, Samuel SC 14th Inf. Co.F
Templeton, Samuel VA 21st Inf. Co.H
Templeton, Samuel F. SC 2nd Rifles Co.E Music.
Templeton, Samuel M. LA 1st (Nelligan's) Inf. Co.F Cpl.
Templeton, Samuel M. VA Mil. 93rd Regt. Maj.
Templeton, Samuel R. LA 31st Inf. Co.I
Templeton, S.B. GA Cav. Allen's Co.
Templeton, S.C. AL 1st Cav. 2nd Co.C
Templeton, Seaborn MS 6th Inf. Co.F
Templeton, S.M. KY 1st Inf. Co.I
Templeton, S.P. SC 2nd St.Troops Co.H
Templeton, S.P. SC 3rd Inf. Co.A,I
Templeton, S.P. SC 8th Bn.Res. Fishburne's Co. Sgt.
Templeton, S.T. TX 16th Inf. Co.H
Templeton, S.W. MS 39th Inf. Co.E
Templeton, T. MS 1st (King's) Inf. (St.Troops) Co.B
Templeton, T.G. MS 10th Inf. Old Co.D
Templeton, Thomas AL St.Arty. Co.C
Templeton, Thomas AR Cav. 1st Bn. (Stirman's) Co.D
Templeton, Thomas MS Cav. 3rd Bn.Res. Co.D
Templeton, Thomas MS 44th Inf. Co.A
Templeton, Thomas TN 16th Inf. Co.K
Templeton, Thomas L. TX 16th Inf. Co.H
Templeton, T.J. TN Inf. 1st Cons.Regt. Co.F
Templeton, T.J. TN 16th Inf. Co.D
Templeton, W. AL 62nd Inf. Co.B
Templeton, W. GA 4th (Clinch's) Cav. Co.D
Templeton, W.A. GA Hvy.Arty. 22nd Bn. Co.F
Templeton, W.A. SC 3rd Inf. Co.A
Templeton, W.A. SC 3rd Inf. Co.C
Templeton, W.A. SC 3rd Inf. Co.I
Templeton, W.A. SC 7th Inf. Co.B
Templeton, W.C. SC 1st Bn.S.S. Co.C
Templeton, W.C. SC 9th Res. Co.D
Templeton, W.C. SC 22nd Inf. Co.F
Templeton, W.C. SC 27th Inf. Co.G
Templeton, Webster LA 6th Inf. Co.H Sgt.
Templeton, W.F. VA Mil. Scott Cty.
Templeton, William NC McLean's Bn.Lt.Duty Men Co.A
Templeton, William TN 16th Inf. Co.D
Templeton, William TN Inf. 22nd Bn. Co.E
Templeton, William TX Cav. Baylor's Regt. Co.D
Templeton, William TX 4th Inf. Co.I
Templeton, William A. GA 18th Inf. Co.F
Templeton, William A. SC 5th Inf. 2nd Co.F
Templeton, William A. SC 12th Inf. Co.B
Templeton, William A. SC 15th Inf. Co.A
Templeton, William C. SC 14th Inf. Co.F
Templeton, William E. VA 21st Inf. Co.H
Templeton, William F. VA 25th Cav. Co.A
Templeton, William H. VA 21st Inf. Co.H
Templeton, William H. VA Horse Arty. Jackson's Co.
Templeton, William J. MS 20th Inf. Co.B
Templeton, William L. SC 15th Inf. Co.A
Templeton, William M. TX 11th Inf. Co.C
Templeton, William N. NC Unassign.Conscr.
Templeton, William N. TN 54th Inf. Co.A
Templeton, William P. VA Lt.Arty. Donald's Co. Sgt.
Templeton, William W. VA Rockbridge Cty.Res. Donald's Co.
Templeton, W.J. MS 9th Inf. New Co.G
Templeton, W.K. 3rd Conf.Cav. Co.K
Templeton, W.W. TN 28th (Cons.) Inf. Co.E
Templeton, W.W. TN 84th Inf. Co.A
Templin, Abraham AL 17th Inf. Co.H
Templin, Adolph LA 2nd Cav. Co.G,H
Templin, B.F. AL 5th Inf. New Co.F
Templin, Charles AL 17th Inf. Co.H Cpl.
Templin, David T. TN 62nd Mtd.Inf. Co.I
Templin, George AL 29th Inf. Co.D
Templin, Henry AL 17th Inf. Co.H
Templin, John LA 18th Inf. Co.K
Templin, O. TX 5th Field Btty.
Templin, R.F. TX 21st Cav. Co.F
Templin, William TN 61st Mtd.Inf. Co.I
Templin, William J. AL Jeff Davis Arty.
Templin, W.W. VA Lt.Arty. 13th Bn. Co.A
Tempy, George AR Mil. Desha Cty.Bn.
Temy, William GA 11th Cav. Co.D Cpl.
Ten, J. LA 4th Cav. Co.C
Tenan, H.S. AL St.Res. Co.L 1st Lt.
Tenan, Thomas AL St.Res. Co.A
Tenant, A.J. AL 4th Res. Co.F
Tenant, A.J. GA 55th Inf. Co.E
Tenant, Charles 10th Conf.Cav. Co.B Cpl.
Tenant, Charles W. AL Cav. 5th Bn. Hilliard's Legion Co.B Cpl.
Tenant, G. MS Lt.Arty. (Warren Lt.Arty.) Swett's Co.
Tenant, James L. SC Cav. 10th Bn. Co.A
Tenant, J.K. SC 4th St.Troops Co.D
Tenant, John VA 2nd St.Res. Co.L
Tenant, L. MS Lt.Arty. (Warren Lt.Arty.) Swett's Co.
Tenant, Lemon VA 31st Inf. Co.A
Tenant, M. VA 30th Inf. Co.K
Tenant, M.G. SC 23rd Inf. Co.F
Tenant, Milton VA Cav. 46th Bn. Co.C
Tenant, Robert LA 14th Inf. Co.A
Tenant, Thomas M. VA 30th Bn.S.S QMSgt.
Tenant, William AL Cav. 5th Bn. Hilliard's Legion Co.B
Tenant, William VA 2nd St.Res. Co.L
Tenant, William 10th Conf.Cav. Co.B
Tenants, J.S. SC Cav.Bn. Hampton Legion Co.K
Tenbrink, William LA Lewis Regt. Co.A Col.
Tenbrock, H.H. VA Inf. 4th Bn.Loc.Def. Co.F
Tenbrook, J. VA 60th Inf. Co.G
Tenbrook, John D. GA Arty. (Chatham Arty.) Wheaton's Co.
Tenbrook, John D. GA 1st (Olmstead's) Inf. Claghorn's Co.
Tenburg, P. TX 20th Inf. Co.A
Tench, Andrew W. GA Inf. 2nd Bn. Co.C
Tench, Charlie VA 41st Inf. 2nd Co.E Music.
Tench, Edward VA Hvy.Arty. 10th Bn. Co.D
Tench, Edwin J. VA 24th Inf. Co.D
Tench, G. GA 16th Inf. Co.E
Tench, George E. VA Hvy.Arty. 10th Bn. Co.D
Tench, Henry G. GA 36th (Villepigue's) Inf. Co.F
Tench, Henry G. 1st Conf.Inf. 1st Co.F
Tench, H.G. AL 23rd Inf. Co.B
Tench, H.G. AL 46th Inf. Co.F
Tench, James A. GA 1st (Ramsey's) Inf. Co.A
Tench, James R. VA Lt.Arty. Pegram's Co.
Tench, James R. VA 12th Inf. Branch's Co.
Tench, James R. VA 16th Inf. Co.K
Tench, James William VA Hvy.Arty. 10th Bn. Co.D
Tench, John D. VA 41st Inf. 2nd Co.E Sgt.
Tench, John W. GA 1st Cav. Co.K Maj.

Tench, John W. GA 1st (Ramsey's) Inf. Co.A
Tench, Otis VA 10th Cav. Co.C
Tench, R.M. GA 1st Cav. Co.K Sgt.
Tench, Robert M. GA 1st (Ramsey's) Inf. Co.A
Tench, R.S. GA 16th Inf. Co.E
Tench, Theophilus VA 12th Inf. Co.E Music.
Tench, W.G. GA 16th Inf. Co.E
Tench, W.H. MS 3rd Inf. Co.A
Tench, William H. VA 12th Inf. Branch's Co.
Tench, William H. VA 16th Inf. Co.K
Tench, Winfield E. VA Hvy.Arty. 10th Bn. Co.D
Tencir, Charles VA 59th Inf. 3rd Co.F
Tendell, W.T. AL 6th Inf. Co.A
Tender, G.W. MO Cav. Stallard's Co.
Tendley, W.C. AL 38th Inf. Co.I Cpl.
Tendsay, Thompson MO 15th Cav. Co.A
Tene, T.R. TN Cav. Nixon's Regt. Co.H 1st Sgt.
Tenebaugh, J.Z. MO Cav. Fristoe's Regt. Co.F
Tenepurgh, W.D. NC 29th Inf.
Tenegeesee NC Inf. Thomas Legion 2nd Co.A
Teneley, Geo. C. Gen. & Staff A.Surg.
Teneller, W. TX Res.Corps Bauvinghauser's Co.
Tenely, Samuel TX 24th Cav. Co.F
Tenerson, Cook AL 30th Inf. Co.G
Tenerson, John P. AL 48th Inf. Co.G,E Cpl.
Teneson, William P. SC 9th Inf. Co.I
Tenett, A.J. GA 22nd Inf. Co.F
Teney, Thomas KY 2nd (Duke's) Cav. Co.L
Teney, W. AL 26th (O'Neal's) Inf. Co.I
Ten Eyck, Alfred TX 21st Cav. Co.B 2nd Lt.
Ten Eyck, E. TX Res.Corps
Tengle, J.T. LA 6th Cav. Co.B
Tenglet, John LA Mil. 4th Regt. 2nd Brig. 1st Div. Co.H 1st Lt.
Tenhet, J.R.N. VA 3rd Inf.Loc.Def. Co.F
Tenhit, Arthur U. MS 43rd Inf. Co.D
Tenhit, Charles T. MS 43rd Inf. Co.D
Tenhit, W.L. MS 3rd Inf. (St.Troops) Co.H
Tenier, John VA Cav. 32nd Bn. Co.A
Tenille, A.A. GA Cav. Ragland's Co.
Tenio, H. MS 21st Inf. Co.A Sgt.
Tenishaw, Lewis TX 1st Hvy.Arty. Co.G
Tenison, Cook M. TN 40th Inf. Co.K
Tenison, Isaac A. TN 4th (McLemore's) Cav. Co.A
Tenison, James GA 55th Inf. Co.A
Tenison, James A. GA Lt.Arty. 12th Bn. 3rd Co.C
Tenison, J.C. AL 7th Inf. Co.G
Tenison, J.D. GA Cav. 12th Bn. (St.Guards) Co.B
Tenison, J.H. MO 6th Cav. Co.B
Tenison, L.C. LA 3rd Cav. Co.I 2nd Lt.
Tenison, Leonard C. LA 25th Inf. Co.C Bvt.2nd Lt.
Tenison, L.H. AR 30th Inf. Co.H
Tenison, William P. NC Inf. Co.I
Tenkle, W.S. TX Inf. 2nd St.Troops Co.A
Tenley, Charles R. TX Inf. 1st Bn. Co.B
Tenley, C.K. TX Inf. Rutherford's Co.
Tenly, W.J. KY 5th Cav. Co.D
Tenn, F. LA Mil. 4th Regt. 2nd Brig. 1st Div. Co.H
Tennant, A.D. TX Lt.Arty. Jones' Co. Sgt.
Tennant, Albert VA 5th Cav. 2nd Co.F
Tennant, Alpheus VA 19th Cav. Co.A
Tennant, Alpheus VA 20th Cav. Co.A
Tennant, Alpheus VA Horse Arty. Lurty's Co.
Tennant, Alpheus VA 3rd Cav. & Inf.St.Line Co.A
Tennant, Andrew VA 20th Cav. Co.B
Tennant, Gilbert Gen. & Staff AASurg.
Tennant, Gilbert C. SC 7th Inf. 1st Co.C, 2nd Co.C
Tennant, James SC 4th Cav. Co.B
Tennant, J.B. SC Post Guard Senn's Co.
Tennant, J.K. SC Arty. Fickling's Co. (Brooks Lt.Arty.)
Tennant, John SC 3rd Bn.Res. Co.E
Tennant, John C. NC 32nd Inf. Chap.
Tennant, Jno. H. AL Cp. of Instr. Talladega
Tennant, Moses SC Shiver's Co.
Tennant, Thomas M. MD Weston's Bn. Co.B
Tennant, William SC 4th Cav. Co.B
Tennant, William SC Inf. Hampton Legion Co.K
Tennant, William W. VA 15th Inf. Co.H
Tennel, Charles KY 1st (Butler's) Cav. New Co.H
Tennel, John M. MO 5th Cav. Co.E
Tennell, Charles L. KY 6th Mtd.Inf.
Tennell, J. AL 1st Inf. Co.K
Tennell, James KY 6th Mtd.Inf. Co.A
Tennell, J.W. VA 42nd Inf. Co.E
Tennell, W.A. GA 47th Inf. Co.H
Tennelle, Albert GA Cav. Nelson's Ind.Co.
Tennelle, G.C. TX 2nd Inf.
Tennelle, James T. VA Courtney Arty.
Tennent, Alexander VA Cav. 15th Bn. Co.C
Tennent, A.W. VA 15th Cav. Co.E Bugler
Tennent, A.W. VA 25th Mil. Co.B Sgt.
Tennent, Charles LA 26th Inf. Co.K 2nd Lt.
Tennent, Charles B. VA Lt.Arty. 38th Bn. Co.C
Tennent, Charles B. VA Lt.Arty. E.J. Anderson's Co.
Tennent, Charles H. VA Lt.Arty. Thornton's Co. Sgt.
Tennent, C.J. SC Inf. 1st (Charleston) Bn. Co.D
Tennent, C.J. Eng.,CSA Asst.Eng.
Tennent, E.S. SC Inf. 1st (Charleston) Bn. Co.C
Tennent, G. GA Cav. 9th Bn. (St.Guards) Co.B
Tennent, G. SC 7th Inf. 2nd Co.I
Tennent, George W. GA 1st (Olmstead's) Inf. Co.H
Tennent, George W. VA 30th Inf. Co.K Cpl.
Tennent, G.V. SC Inf. 1st (Charleston) Bn. Co.E
Tennent, G.V. SC Mil. Charbonnier's Co. Bvt.2nd Lt.
Tennent, Henry A. GA 15th Inf. Co.I
Tennent, J.A. SC 23rd Inf. Adj.
Tennent, J.A. Eng.,CSA Asst.Eng.
Tennent, J.B. SC 1st Cav. Co.I
Tennent, J.B. SC 1st (Butler's) Inf. Co.F
Tennent, J.H. AL 12th Inf. Co.F
Tennent, Jno. C. Gen. & Staff Chap.
Tennent, Jno. H. AL Cp. of Instr. Talladega
Tennent, John J. VA 47th Inf. 2nd Co.G
Tennent, J.S. SC Inf. 1st (Charleston) Bn. Co.E
Tennent, Julian R. VA Lt.Arty. 38th Bn. Co.C Sgt.
Tennent, Julian R. VA Lt.Arty. E.J. Anderson's Co.
Tennent, Orville T. GA 15th Inf. Co.I Sgt.
Tennent, Pat. SC 7th Inf. 1st Co.C
Tennent, Samuel AL Lt.Arty. 2nd Bn. Co.B
Tennent, Samuel LA Mil. 4th Regt. 1st Brig. 1st Div. Co.G
Tennent, Thomas MD 1st Cav. Co.C
Tennent, Thomas M. VA 21st Inf. Co.B
Tennent, W.A. GA Phillips' Legion Co.C
Tennent, William AR 18th Inf. Co.K
Tennent, William LA Inf. 9th Bn. Co.D Sgt.
Tennent, William SC 1st Cav. Co.G
Tennent, William, Jr. SC Inf. 1st (Charleston) Bn. Co.D
Tennent, William C. GA 15th Inf. Co.I
Tenner, C.L. KY 3rd Cav. Co.E
Tennery, E.K.P. TN 3rd (Clack's) Inf. Co.G
Tennery, J.M. TN 11th (Holman's) Cav. Co.K
Tennery, Pleasant H. TN 3rd (Clack's) Inf. Co.G
Tenneson, Wm. A. Gen. & Staff, Hvy.Arty. 1st Lt.
Tenneson, William M. TN 54th Inf. Co.E 1st Lt.
Tenney, Charles B. LA 6th Inf. Co.B Capt.
Tenney, J. AL 31st Inf. Co.G,C
Tenney, J.A. AL 45th Inf. Maj.
Tenney, James AL 20th Inf. Co.H
Tenney, John B. LA 6th Inf. Co.D Cpl.
Tenney, John W. GA 3rd Inf. Co.K
Tenney, Joseph T. LA 4th Inf. Co.D
Tenney, L.M. TX 25th Cav. Co.H
Tenney, Nathaniel B. NC Inf. 11th (Bethel Regt.) Co.G 2nd Lt.
Tenney, O.S. KY 2nd Bn.Mtd.Rifles Maj.
Tenney, Samuel F. GA 3rd Inf. Co.K
Tenney, Thomas 10th Conf.Cav. Co.B 1st Sgt.
Tenney, William C. NC 1st Inf. (6 mo. '61) Co.D
Tenney, William C. Conf.Arty. Marshall's Co.
Tennill, Charles L. KY Cav. Buckner Guards
Tennill, Grafton T. VA 54th Mil. Co.C,D
Tennill, John E. VA 54th Mil. Co.C,D
Tennille, Albert A. GA 9th Inf. Co.D Sgt.
Tennille, Alexander St.C. GA 9th Inf. Co.D ACS
Tennille, A.S. GA 28th Inf. Co.B
Tennille, A.St.C. Gen. & Staff, A. of N.VA Capt.,ACS
Tennille, B.F. VA 54th Mil. Co.B
Tennille, Francis T. GA 9th Inf. Co.D Cpl.
Tennille, James T. VA Lt.Arty. Weisiger's Co.
Tennille, James T. VA 6th Inf. Weisiger's Co.
Tennille, James T. VA 16th Inf. Co.I
Tennille, John C. GA 49th Inf. Co.H
Tennille, J.T. VA Inf. 4th Bn.Loc.Def. Co.B
Tennille, William FL Cav. 5th Bn. Co.I
Tennille, William A. GA 9th Inf. Co.D 1st Lt.
Tennille, William A. GA 49th Inf. Co.H
Tennin, Allen MO Cav. Preston's Bn. Co.C
Tennis, A. TX 13th Vol. 2nd Co.H,B
Tennis, Anthony LA Mil. 1st Regt. 3rd Brig. 1st Div. Co.A
Tennis, Augustus TX Brazoria Cty. Minute Men Stock Raiser
Tennis, Joseph G. VA 32nd Inf. Co.E
Tennis, P.O. GA 4th Res. Co.H Cpl.
Tennis, Richard VA 115th Mil. Co.B Cpl.
Tennis, Sylvanus T. VA 6th Inf. 1st Co.E
Tennis, Theodore S. VA 9th Inf. Co.I Cpl.
Tennis, W. VA 3rd Cav. Co.B

Tennis, William VA 6th Inf. 1st Co.E
Tennis, William VA 115th Mil. Co.B
Tennis, William C. VA 9th Inf. Co.I
Tennison, A.M. AR Inf. 4th Bn. Co.C Adj.
Tennison, Bernard Z. MD Inf. 2nd Bn. Co.B
Tennison, C. Edward MS 7th Inf. Co.G 1st Lt.
Tennison, Edward A. MO 8th Inf. Co.H
Tennison, H.A. MS 26th Inf. Co.A
Tennison, H.F. AR 13th Inf. Co.B Capt.
Tennison, H.F. MS 26th Inf. Co.A
Tennison, H.F., Jr. MS 26th Inf. Co.A,E
Tennison, H.F. MS 32nd Inf. Co.H
Tennison, Hiram TN 4th (McLemore's) Cav. Co.D
Tennison, Hiram F. AR Cav. Davies' Bn. Co.A
Tennison, James GA Lt.Arty. 12th Bn. 3rd Co.C
Tennison, James GA Inf. 1st Loc.Troops (Augusta) Co.E,B
Tennison, James H. MO 16th Inf. Co.E
Tennison, Jessee GA Lt.Arty. 12th Bn. 3rd Co.C
Tennison, J.F. TN 4th (McLemore's) Cav. Co.D
Tennison, J.H. MS 26th Inf. Co.A
Tennison, J.H. MS 32nd Inf. Co.H
Tennison, J.L. AL 34th Inf. Black's Co.
Tennison, Joe T. TX 21st Cav. Co.A
Tennison, John AR 1st (Monroe's) Cav. Palmer's Co.
Tennison, John GA 2nd Inf. Co.D
Tennison, John C. AL 41st Inf. Co.K
Tennison, John Lewis AL 45th Inf. Co.I
Tennison, John W. MS 17th Inf. Co.A
Tennison, J.W. TX 29th Cav. Co.H
Tennison, Lemuel L. AL 4th Inf. Co.B
Tennison, M. TX Inf. 2nd St.Troops Co.D
Tennison, P.R. AL 30th Inf. Co.G
Tennison, Presley Rias AL Love's Regt. Co.B
Tennison, R.C. AL 30th Inf. Co.G
Tennison, R.F. MS 26th Inf. Co.A
Tennison, R.L. TX 12th Inf. Co.E
Tennison, Shelby TN 11th (Holman's) Cav. Co.I
Tennison, Shelby TN Douglass' Bn.Part.Rangers Perkins' Co.
Tennison, T.F. MS 32nd Inf. Co.H
Tennison, Thomas TX Inf. 2nd St.Troops Co.D 1st Lt.
Tennison, Thomas B. MO 10th Inf. Co.E Sgt.
Tennison, W.G. MO 10th Inf. Co.E Sgt.
Tennison, W.H. TX 7th Cav. Co.E
Tennison, Wm. VA 4th Cav. Co.C
Tennison, William C. MS 32nd Inf. Co.H Cpl.
Tennison, William P. SC Palmetto S.S. Co.H
Tennison, W.J. TX 11th Cav. Co.B
Tennison, W.J. VA Hvy.Arty. 20th Bn.
Tennison, W.S. GA 59th Inf. Co.H Ord.Sgt.
Tennisson, Charles E. VA 17th Inf. Co.H
Tennisson, George A. MS 22nd Inf. Co.A 1st Sgt.
Tennisson, L.H. AR 13th Inf. Co.F Lt.
Tennisson, T.F. MS Lt.Arty. 14th Bn. Co.C
Tennisson, Thomas F. MS 26th Inf. Co.A
Tennisson, William C. MS 26th Inf. Co.A
Tennisson, William H. LA Cav. Greenleaf's Co. (Orleans Lt.Horse)
Tennons, J.T. GA 29th Inf. Co.G
Tenns, J.S. AL 51st (Part.Rangers) Co.C
Tenny, Edward LA 1st Hvy.Arty. (Reg.) Co.C
Tenny, John AR Lt.Arty. Auston's Btty.
Tenny, John AR Lt.Arty. Wiggins' Btty.
Tenny, William C. NC 11th (Bethel Regt.) Inf. Co.G
Tennyson, Jesse GA 66th Inf. Co.A
Tenover, Henry AR 2nd Inf. Co.B
Tenpenny, John TN 8th (Smith's) Cav. Co.E
Tenpenny, J.W. AR 27th Inf. Co.I
Tenpeny, David TN 8th (Smith's) Cav. Co.E
Tenpleton, D.J.H. AR 30th Inf. Co.L,A
Tensely, A. Gen. & Staff Surg.
Tenser, Charles VA Lt.Arty. 38th Bn. Co.C
Tenser, Charles VA Lt.Arty. E.J. Anderson's Co.
Tensler, Rudolph AL 12th Inf. Co.C
Tensley, Joshua Y. GA 13th Cav. Co.B
Tensley, Steven VA 59th Inf. Co.E
Tensly, A.J. TN 9th Inf. Co.E
Tensly, W.D. TN 9th Inf. Co.E
Tenson, S. AL 13th Inf. Co.F
Tensor, A.L. VA 2nd St.Res. Co.F
Tent, B. VA 3rd Cav. Co.G
Tent, John F. AR 8th Inf. Old Co.C
Tent, S.W. FL 2nd Cav. Co.E
Tent, W.A. AR Cav. Harrell's Bn. Co.D
Tenthorg, Daniel VA 22nd Inf. Co.B
Tentil, Richard TN Cav. Napier's Bn. Co.B
Tentler, Abram A. NC 18th Inf. Co.I
Tentsch, W. TX Inf. 2nd St.Troops Co.C
Tenwick, S.T. TX 17th Cons.Dismtd.Cav. Co.G
Teny, J.C. AL 30th Inf. Co.F Sgt.
Teny, J.J. AL 30th Inf. Co.F
Teoff, Henry AR 27th Inf.
Teogue, I.P. GA Inf. (Anderson Guards) Anderson's Co.
Teogue, William GA Inf. (Anderson Guards) Anderson's Co.
Teos, Luis TX 33rd Cav. 1st Co.I
Teoulet, --- LA Mil. 2nd Regt. French Brig. Co.2
Teparie, Pierre LA 22nd Inf. Co.D
Tepe, Frank A. MS 9th Inf. Old Co.B
Tepe, William MO 3rd Cav. Co.A Sgt.
Tephabock, Isaac VA Cav. McNeill's Co.
Tepinpaw, A.R. GA Inf. 17th Bn. (St.Guards) McCarty's Co. Cpl.
Tepp, F. SC Mil. 1st Regt. (Charleston Res.) Co.D
Teppate, Wesley MO Robertson's Regt.St.Guard Co.8
Teppe, F. SC Mil. 16th Regt. Bancroft, Jr.'s Co.
Tepper, Hermann F. MO 2nd Inf. Co.G
Tepper, H.F. 2nd Conf.Eng.Troops Co.D
Tepper, J.D. AL 23rd Inf. Co.A
Teppet, W.H. AR Lt.Arty. Hart's Btty.
Teppett, Abner NC 61st Inf. Co.C
Teppie, William, Jr. SC 5th Cav. Co.D
Teppie, William, Jr. SC Cav. 17th Bn. Co.A
Tepps, John A. VA Lt.Arty. 38th Bn. Co.D
Tepssich, Steff LA Mil. 4th Regt.Eur.Brig. Cognevich's Co.
Teque eeskih NC Inf. Thomas Legion 2nd Co.A Sgt.
Teralf, Adam LA Mil. 4th Regt. 1st Brig. 1st Div. Co.I
Terance, J.T. TX 13th Inf.
Terapin Nelson 1st Cherokee Mtd.Rifles Co.G Sgt.
Terbifill, Henry GA 36th (Broyles') Inf. Co.D
Terbine, J.W. MS 1st Lt.Arty. Co.A
Terbit, William F. TN Detailed Conscr. Co.B
Terby, B.F. MS Cav. Semple's Co.
Tercher, L.C. AL 9th (Malone's) Cav. Co.C
Tercis, Joseph LA Mil. 1st Regt. French Brig. Co.6
Terell, A.J. SC Hvy.Arty. 15th (Lucas') Bn.
Terell, J.L. LA Inf.Cons.Crescent Regt. Co.O
Terell, Lindsey E. AR 33rd Inf. Co.A
Terell, T.W. LA 1st Res. Co.E
Terelly, B.F. MD Inf. 2nd Bn. Co.E
Terence, Clement LA Mil. 1st Native Guards
Terentine, James A. AR 5th Inf. Co.K
Terepaugh, William A. NC 49th Inf. Co.F
Terguban, D.W. AL 6th Cav. Co.H
Terguem, David AL 24th Inf. Co.A
Terguson, Henry LA Inf.Cons.Crescent Regt. Co.B
Terhon, E. TX 11th (Spaight's) Bn.Vol. Co.E
Terhone, G.A. LA 22nd (Cons.) Inf. Co.A
Terhoun, James TN Conscr. (Cp. of Instr.)
Terhue, Adaire LA 7th Cav. Co.I
Terhune, A.A. GA Floyd Legion (St.Guards) Co.D Capt.
Terhune, David R. TN Arty. Ramsey's Btty.
Terhune, D.K. KY 6th Cav. Co.D
Terhune, G.A. MO 1st & 3rd Cons.Cav. Co.H
Terhune, George A. MO Cav. 3rd Bn. Co.B
Terhune, H. TX 26th Cav. Co.C Far.
Terhune, J. TX 1st Regt.St.Troops Co.D
Terhune, James TN Art. Ramsey's Btty. QMSgt.
Terhune, James G. KY 6th Cav. Co.A
Terhune, John GA Floyd Legion (St.Guards) Co.D
Terhune, Madison KY 6th Cav. Co.D
Terhune, S.S. KY 6th Cav. Co.D 2nd Lt.
Terhune, W.B. GA Floyd Legion (St.Guards) Co.D
Terhune, William B. GA 29th Inf. Co.D
Tericke, H. TX Waul's Legion Co.C
Teriot, O. LA 18th Inf. Co.H
Teris, Robinson E. KY 7th Cav. Co.B
Terle, William LA 11th Inf. Co.L
Terley, Thomas VA 45th Inf. Co.L 2nd Lt.
Terley, W.O. AR 14th (McCarver's) Inf. Co.K
Terly, John A. AL 48th Inf. Co.G
Terman, C.M. AL 16th Inf. Co.A
Terman, Gibson AL 26th (O'Neal's) Inf. Co.H Cpl.
Terman, G.R. MS 2nd Cav. Co.I
Terman, J.H. MO 15th Cav. Co.E
Ter Nah ee 1st Cherokee Mtd.Rifles Co.D Cpl.
Ternan, Thomas M. AL 38th Inf.
Terner, George H. GA 23rd Inf. Co.E
Terner, James NC Inf. Thomas Legion Co.I
Ternert, August TX 17th Inf. Co.B
Ternert, Ernest TX 17th Inf. Co.B
Terney, J.P. MS Lt.Arty. English's Co.
Ternier, Honore LA Maddox's Regt.Res.Corps Co.B
Ternier, P.N. LA 26th Inf. Co.G 1st Sgt.
Ternoir, Leon LA Mil. 1st Native Guards
Ternot, J.B. LA Mil. 1st Regt. French Brig. Co.4
Terping, J.T. MO 8th Inf. Co.B Capt.
Terquem, D. LA 22nd Inf. Co.B
Terquem, David LA 22nd (Cons.) Inf. Co.B
Terr, Joseph AL 25th Inf. Co.B

Terrade, P. LA Mil. 4th Regt. French Brig. Co.1 Lt.
Terrade, Paul LA Mil.Bn. French Vol. Co.10 1st Lt.
Terrail, J.B. LA Mil. Cazadores Espanoles Regt. Co.D Sgt.
Terral, E.H. MS 1st Cav.Res. Co.B
Terral, James S. MS 9th Cav. Co.G,F Sgt.
Terral, James S. MS 1st (Patton's) Inf. Co.K
Terral, James S., Jr. MS Inf. 7th Bn. Lt.Col.
Terral, J.S. MS Inf. 2nd St.Troops Co.E Sgt.
Terral, J.S. MS Inf. 7th Bn. Co.D
Terral, M.A. AL 34th Inf. Co.C
Terral, Milton MS 1st (Patton's) Inf. Co.K
Terral, Samuel MS 9th Cav. Co.G
Terral, Samuel MS 37th Inf. Co.K
Terral, Thomas M. MS 37th Inf. Co.C 2nd Lt.
Terral, W.F. MS 27th Inf. Co.H
Terrall, Edward Y. MS Lt.Arty. Turner's Co.
Terrall, Edward Y. MS 16th Inf. Co.F
Terrall, Henry A. VA 6th Inf. Co.C Sgt.
Terrall, James E. MS 1st Cav.Res. Co.B
Terrall, James S. MS Lt.Arty. Turner's Co. Capt.
Terrall, Jasper FL Lt.Arty. Perry's Co.
Terrall, Nathan D. MS 11th (Perrin's) Cav. Co.F
Terrall, W.G. NC Mallett's Bn. (Cp.Guard) Co.D
Terrand, Simon LA Mil. 2nd Regt. French Brig. Co.8 Cpl.
Terrapin Shell 1st Cherokee Mtd.Vol. 1st Co.B, 2nd Co.C
Terras, Louis LA Mil. 1st Regt. French Brig. Co.6
Terreberry, John S. LA Inf. 1st Sp.Bn. (Rightor's) New Co.C
Terrebonne, E.D. LA Washington Arty.Bn. Co.4
Terrebonne, E.D. LA Miles' Legion Co.A 1st Lt.
Terrebonne, L. LA Mil. 4th Regt. French Brig. Co.1
Terrebonne, M. LA Inf.Cons.Crescent Regt. Co.C
Terrebonne, O.D. LA 2nd Cav. Co.H Sgt.
Terrebonne, P.D. LA Miles' Legion Co.A Cpl.
Terrebonne, V.D. LA Inf. 1st Sp.Bn. (Rightor's) Co.E
Terree, Richard VA Hvy.Arty. Wright's Co.
Terreice, William J. AL Lt.Arty. 2nd Bn. Co.A
Terrel, --- TX Cav. Mann's Regt. Co.C
Terrel, --- TX Cav. Ragsdale's Bn. Co.D
Terrel, A.J. GA Cav. 29th Bn. Co.C
Terrel, A.J. MS 2nd (Quinn's St.Troops) Inf. Co.G
Terrel, Andrew J. VA 10th Inf. Co.D
Terrel, Edmund GA Cav. 6th Bn. (St.Guards) Co.A Sgt.
Terrel, G.D. 14th Conf.Cav. Co.I
Terrel, G.M. TX 9th Cav. Co.G Cpl.
Terrel, Harris MS Cav. 24th Bn. Co.B
Terrel, Henry P. GA 24th Inf. Co.I
Terrel, James MS 5th Inf. (St.Troops) Co.B
Terrel, James TX Arty. 4th Bn.
Terrel, James VA 3rd Bn. Valley Res. Co.B
Terrel, James E. Gen. & Staff 1st Lt.,Adj.
Terrel, Jesse Exch.Bn. Co.E,CSA
Terrel, L. MS 29th Inf. Co.E
Terrel, S.G. MS Cav. 1st Bn. (McNair's) St.Troops Co.B
Terrel, St.Clair VA 10th Inf. Co.D
Terrel, Thomas VA 38th Inf. 1st Co.I
Terrel, T.L. MS Lt.Arty. Merrin's Btty.
Terrel, Warren M. LA 2nd Cav. Co.F
Terrel, W.B. NC 46th Inf. Co.H
Terrel, William VA 146th Mil. Co.B
Terrel, W.J. LA 31st Inf. Co.E
Terrel, Z.R. TX 23rd Cav. Co.G
Terrell, A. TX 30th Cav. Co.C
Terrell, A.B. AL 45th Inf. Co.B Sgt.
Terrell, A.B. MS 4th Cav. Co.D,B
Terrell, A.B. MS 18th Cav. Co.I
Terrell, A.B. TX 9th (Young's) Inf. Asst.Surg.
Terrell, A.D. GA 13th Inf. Co.A Cpl.
Terrell, A.J. GA 11th Cav. (St.Guards) Smith's Co.
Terrell, A.J. LA 22nd Inf. Co.A
Terrell, A.J. LA 22nd (Cons.) Inf. Co.A
Terrell, Alexander MS 19th Inf. Co.I,B
Terrell, Alexander C. TN Holman's Bn. Part.Rangers Co.B
Terrell, Alexander W. TX 37th Cav. Col.
Terrell, Alex B. MS 36th Inf. Co.K
Terrell, Alfred A. LA 31st Inf. Co.G,I
Terrell, Alfred B. VA 9th Cav. Co.B
Terrell, A.N. SC 6th Res. Co.C Cpl.
Terrell, A.N. SC 17th Inf. Co.D
Terrell, Andrew FL 2nd Cav. Co.B
Terrell, Andrew J. KY 8th Mtd.Inf.
Terrell, Andrew J. VA 52nd Inf. 2nd Co.B
Terrell, Arthur B. AL 20th Inf. Co.B
Terrell, Arthur B. Gen. & Staff Asst.Surg.
Terrell, Asa L. LA 31st Inf. Co.I
Terrell, B.A.W. TN 35th Inf. Co.C
Terrell, B.D. GA Inf. 4th Bn. (St.Guards) Co.G
Terrell, Benjamin H. TN Lt.Arty. Baxter's Co.
Terrell, Benjamin S. TX 4th Inf. Co.A
Terrell, Berry VA Lt.Arty. 38th Bn. Co.C
Terrell, Berry VA Lt.Arty. E.J. Anderson's Co.
Terrell, C. TN 12th (Green's) Cav. Co.K
Terrell, C.D. TX 6th Inf. Co.G
Terrell, C.H. TN 12th Inf. Co.A Cpl.
Terrell, Charles VA 15th Inf. Co.E
Terrell, Charles F. GA 2nd Inf. Co.C
Terrell, Charles J. Gen. & Staff AASurg.
Terrell, Charles M. TX 5th Inf. Co.B
Terrell, Charles T. GA 3rd Cav. Co.G
Terrell, Charles T. GA 23rd Inf. Co.C
Terrell, Cicero W. GA 42nd Inf. Co.G Sgt.
Terrell, C.J. TX 3rd Cav. Co.G
Terrell, C. James VA Lt.Arty. Woolfolk's Co. 2nd Lt.
Terrell, C.L. TX 33rd Cav. Co.K
Terrell, Cleveland A. AL 4th Inf. Co.D Cpl.
Terrell, C.M. VA Cav. 1st Bn. Co.A
Terrell, C.R. TX 25th Cav. Co.E
Terrell, C.W. GA 16th Inf. Co.F
Terrell, D. MD Cav. 2nd Bn. Co.D
Terrell, D. MS 20th Inf. Co.I
Terrell, David NC 4th Cav. (59th St.Troops) Co.B
Terrell, David H. AR 23rd Inf. Co.H Sgt.
Terrell, David R. VA 49th Inf. Co.B Sgt.
Terrell, David W. LA 19th Inf. Co.F Sgt.
Terrell, D.B. VA 51st Inf. N.C.S.
Terrell, Demandra S. VA Inf. 25th Bn. Co.A
Terrell, D.G. MS 12th Cav. Co.C Sgt.
Terrell, D.W. GA 12th Inf. Co.I
Terrell, D.W. NC 57th Inf. Co.B Cpl.
Terrell, E.B. GA 62nd Cav. Co.D
Terrell, Edmond GA 60th Inf. Co.C
Terrell, Edmond D. TX 8th Inf. Co.K
Terrell, Edward L. KY 1st Inf. Co.G
Terrell, Edward T. Gen. & Staff Asst.Surg.
Terrell, E.H. MS 19th Inf. Co.A
Terrell, E.L. KY 7th Cav. Co.K
Terrell, E.R. TX 8th Cav. Co.B
Terrell, E.T. TX 4th Inf. Co.G Asst.Surg.
Terrell, F.B. AL 4th Inf. Co.D
Terrell, F.B. GA 1st (Olmstead's) Inf. Co.D
Terrell, F.B. MS 40th Inf. Co.A 3rd Lt.
Terrell, Fleming B. GA 47th Inf. Co.H Cpl.
Terrell, Foster MS 7th Inf. Co.B
Terrell, Foster MS 9th Bn.S.S. Co.C Cpl.
Terrell, Francis M. AL 46th Inf. Co.A
Terrell, Franklin N. GA 42nd Inf. Co.F
Terrell, G.B. VA 6th Inf. Co.A
Terrell, G.D. 20th Conf.Cav. Co.B
Terrell, George FL 2nd Inf. Co.H
Terrell, George A. VA Hvy.Arty. A.J. Jones' Co.
Terrell, George L. VA 13th Inf. Co.D
Terrell, George P. AR 14th (Powers') Inf. Co.K
Terrell, George R. LA 3rd Inf. Co.A
Terrell, George T. NC 3rd Arty. (40th St.Troops) Co.D
Terrell, George W. GA 21st Inf. Co.G
Terrell, George W. MS 29th Inf. Co.B
Terrell, George W. NC 44th Inf. Co.G
Terrell, George W. VA Lt.Arty. Carrington's Co.
Terrell, George W.P. VA 19th Inf. Co.B
Terrell, G.F. MS 4th Cav. Co.I
Terrell, G.H. GA 13th Inf. Co.A
Terrell, G.J. TN 47th Inf. Co.K
Terrell, G.J. TX 9th (Young's) Inf. Co.K
Terrell, G.L. MS 2nd Cav. Co.A
Terrell, G.W. TN 12th Inf. Co.C
Terrell, H. AR 12th Inf. Co.C
Terrell, H.A. GA 23rd Inf. Co.I
Terrell, Haney MS Cav. Garland's Bn. Co.A
Terrell, H.C. 2nd Conf.Inf. Co.H
Terrell, Henderson NC 45th Inf. Co.I
Terrell, Henry A. GA 3rd Cav. Co.G,K Cpl.
Terrell, Henry C. GA 24th Inf. Co.H
Terrell, Henry C. GA Phillips' Legion Co.C
Terrell, Henry C. VA Hvy.Arty. A.J. Jones' Co.
Terrell, Henry L. KY 2nd Mtd.Inf. Co.C Sgt.
Terrell, Henry L. VA 14th Cav. Co.H
Terrell, H.L. VA Lt.Arty. R.M. Anderson's Co.
Terrell, H.M. GA Phillips' Legion Co.D
Terrell, Hubbard H. Gen. & Staff Asst.Surg.
Terrell, Hunt TX 5th Inf. Co.B
Terrell, H.W. VA 34th Inf. Co.F
Terrell, I.C. AL Cav. Moreland's Regt. Co.B
Terrell, J. AL 9th Inf. Hosp.Stew.
Terrell, J. TN 3rd (Forrest's) Cav. Co.D
Terrell, J.A. MS 2nd Cav. Co.E
Terrell, James AL 1st Regt. Mobile Vol. British Guard Co.A
Terrell, James AL 49th Inf. Co.A
Terrell, James AR 8th Inf. Old Co.I

Terrell, James LA Mil. Irish Regt. Laughlin's Co.
Terrell, James MS 48th Inf. Co.A
Terrell, James NC 4th Cav. (59th St.Troops) Co.B
Terrell, James SC 5th Inf. 2nd Co.B
Terrell, James SC 6th Inf. 1st Co.B
Terrell, James TX 1st (Yager's) Cav. Co.F
Terrell, James VA 52nd Inf. 2nd Co.B
Terrell, James Exch.Bn. Co.E,CSA
Terrell, James A. AL 3rd Bn. Hilliard's Legion Vol. Co.C 1st Sgt.
Terrell, James A. GA 3rd Cav. Co.G Cpl.
Terrell, James A. GA Phillips' Legion Co.C Cpl.
Terrell, James A. MS 23rd Inf. Co.I
Terrell, James C. VA Cav. 35th Bn. Co.F Cpl.
Terrell, James E. TX 19th Cav. Co.G Adj.
Terrell, James F. GA 1st Reg. Co.G
Terrell, James H. AL 16th Inf. Co.G
Terrell, James H. VA 47th Inf. 2nd Co.K 2nd Lt.
Terrell, James J. NC 1st Inf. Co.I 2nd Lt.
Terrell, Jas. Leonidas AL 4th Inf. Co.D
Terrell, James M. NC 12th Inf. Co.F
Terrell, James M. VA 11th Inf. Co.C
Terrell, James M. VA 46th Inf. Co.F
Terrell, James N. MS 18th Cav. Co.K
Terrell, James S. VA 24th Cav. Co.F
Terrell, James S. VA 30th Inf. Co.G
Terrell, James W. NC 8th Inf. Co.I
Terrell, James W. NC Inf. Thomas Legion 2nd Co.A Capt.,AQM
Terrell, James W. TX 15th Cav. Co.E Capt.
Terrell, Jas. W. Gen. & Staff Capt.,AQM
Terrell, Jasper D. MS 7th Inf. Co.I 2nd Lt.
Terrell, J.B. TN 3rd (Clack's) Inf. Co.F
Terrell, J.B. TX Cav. Border's Regt. Co.D
Terrell, J.C. AL 41st Inf. Co.I
Terrell, J.C. GA 6th Inf. (St.Guards) Co.E
Terrell, J.C. TX 4th Cav. Co.B
Terrell, J.C. TX Cav. Waller's Regt. Co.F Capt.
Terrell, J.D. MS 4th Cav. Co.B
Terrell, J.D. VA 4th Cav. Co.G
Terrell, J.E. LA 7th Cav. Co.K
Terrell, J.E. VA 4th Cav. Co.I,F
Terrell, J.E. VA 88th Mil.
Terrell, Jefferson NC 4th Cav. (59th St.Troops) Co.B
Terrell, Jerry TN 20th (Russell's) Cav. Co.D
Terrell, Jerry Forrest's Cav.,CSA Conscr.
Terrell, Jerry P. TN 2nd (Robison's) Inf. Co.C
Terrell, Jesse NC 4th Cav. (59th St.Troops) Co.B
Terrell, J.F. GA 47th Inf. Co.H
Terrell, J.F. MS 41st Inf. Co.K 2nd Lt.
Terrell, J.H. MS 39th Inf. Co.H
Terrell, J.H. TX 3rd Cav. Co.F
Terrell, J.H. 4th Conf.Inf. Co.E
Terrell, J.J. MS 4th Cav. Co.I
Terrell, J.J. TN 16th (Logwood's) Cav. Co.E
Terrell, J.J. TN 12th Inf. Co.C
Terrell, J.J. VA 3rd Inf.Loc.Def. Co.I
Terrell, J.L. LA Inf. 1st Bn. (St.Guards) Co.B
Terrell, J.M. NC 48th Inf. Co.E Sr.2nd Lt.
Terrell, J.N. MS 39th Inf. Co.H
Terrell, Joel L. NC 50th Inf. Co.K
Terrell, Joel Massey NC Hvy.Arty. 10th Bn. Co.C,D Jr.1st Lt.
Terrell, John AL 1st Regt. Mobile Vol. British Guard Co.A
Terrell, John AL 5th Inf. New Co.G
Terrell, John GA 18th Inf. Co.K
Terrell, John NC 4th Cav. (59th St.Troops) Co.B,D
Terrell, John NC 45th Inf. Co.K
Terrell, John NC 49th Inf. Co.C
Terrell, John A. AL 14th Inf. Co.G Capt.
Terrell, John A. VA Lt.Arty. Carrington's Co.
Terrell, John C. GA 7th Inf. (St.Guards) Co.F
Terrell, John D. GA Phillips' Legion Co.C
Terrell, John D. MS 4th Inf. Co.I
Terrell, John E. TX 25th Cav. Co.E
Terrell, John E. VA Lt.Arty. Woolfolk's Co.
Terrell, John E. VA 56th Inf. Co.F
Terrell, John H. TX 12th Inf. Co.D Sgt.
Terrell, John H. VA Lt.Arty. Nelson's Co.
Terrell, John H. VA Lt.Arty. Woolfolk's Co.
Terrell, John H. Conf.Cav. 6th Bn. Co.G
Terrell, John J. MS 19th Inf. Co.F Sgt.
Terrell, John J. Gen. & Staff A.Surg.
Terrell, John L. NC 25th Inf. Co.B,C
Terrell, John M. VA 9th Cav. Co.B
Terrell, John M. VA 30th Inf. Co.H 1st Lt.
Terrell, John O. GA 3rd Cav. (St.Guards) Co.H
Terrell, John T. AL 4th Inf. Co.F
Terrell, John T. GA 34th Inf. Co.G Lt.
Terrell, John T. MD 1st Cav. Co.B
Terrell, John T. MS 14th Inf. Co.I Sgt.
Terrell, John Tyler TX 8th Inf. Co.K
Terrell, John Uriel VA 2nd Inf. Co.G
Terrell, John W. NC 12th Inf. Co.F Cpl.
Terrell, John W. VA 52nd Inf. 2nd Co.B
Terrell, Jonathan NC 13th Inf. Co.D Sgt.
Terrell, J. Oscar LA 3rd Inf. Co.A Sgt.
Terrell, Joseph AL Cav. Moses' Squad. Co.B
Terrell, Joseph KY 7th Mtd.Inf. Co.C
Terrell, Joseph MS 2nd (Quinn's St.Troops) Inf. Co.B
Terrell, Joseph NC 45th Inf. Co.K
Terrell, Joseph VA 1st Arty. Co.K
Terrell, Joseph VA Arty. L.F. Jones' Co.
Terrell, Joseph G. VA Hvy.Arty. A.J. Jones' Co.
Terrell, Joseph R. VA Lt.Arty. Nelson's Co.
Terrell, Joseph R. VA Lt.Arty. Woolfolk's Co.
Terrell, Joseph T. VA 24th Cav. Co.F Sgt.
Terrell, Joseph T. VA 47th Inf. 2nd Co.K 2nd Lt.
Terrell, Joseph Thomas VA Cav. 40th Bn. Co.F Sgt.
Terrell, Joseph W. NC 4th Cav. (59th St.Troops) Co.B
Terrell, Joshua MS 27th Inf. Co.H
Terrell, Josiah J. NC 37th Inf. Co.D
Terrell, Josiah M. VA 30th Inf. Co.G Sgt.
Terrell, J.R. FL 9th Inf. Co.F
Terrell, J.R. SC 1st (Butler's) Inf. Co.C
Terrell, J.S. FL 2nd Cav.
Terrell, J.S. MS 27th Inf. Co.H 3rd Lt.
Terrell, J.T. AL 5th Cav. Co.K
Terrell, J.T. GA Cav. 1st Gordon Squad. (St.Guards) Co.A
Terrell, J.T. GA 66th Inf. Co.C 2nd Lt.
Terrell, Julian F. VA 13th Inf. Co.D 2nd Lt.
Terrell, J.W. TN 15th Inf. Co.A 3rd Lt.
Terrell, J. Wm. AL 49th Inf. Co.G
Terrell, Kenan T. Gen. & Staff Capt.,Comsy.
Terrell, Kennan T. GA 24th Inf. Co.F ACS
Terrell, Larkin VA 72nd Mil.
Terrell, L.C. NC 1st Arty. (10th St.Troops) Co.A
Terrell, Legh R. AL 4th Inf. Co.D 2nd Lt.
Terrell, Lewis F. VA Lt.Arty. Nelson's Co. 1st Lt.
Terrell, Lewis F. Gen. & Staff, Arty. Maj.
Terrell, L.H. GA Inf. 4th Bn. (St.Guards) Co.G 2nd Lt.
Terrell, Louis C. MS 18th Inf. Co.E Sgt.
Terrell, Louis C. NC 3rd Arty. (40th St.Troops) Co.G
Terrell, L.R. AL 47th Inf. Lt.Col.
Terrell, Luke W. KY 5th Cav. Co.A
Terrell, M. SC 6th Res. Co.C
Terrell, Maddrd AL 5th Cav. Co.G
Terrell, Mahlon VA 1st Arty. Co.K Sgt.
Terrell, Martin MS 7th Inf. Co.B
Terrell, Martin VA Hvy.Arty. A.J. Jones' Co.
Terrell, Martin 14th Conf.Cav. Co.A
Terrell, Mich AL 1st Regt. Mobile Vol. British Guard Co.A
Terrell, Moses A. SC 1st (Orr's) Rifles Co.F 1st Sgt.
Terrell, Napoleon VA 72nd Mil.
Terrell, Napoleon B. VA Lt.Arty. Nelson's Co.
Terrell, Nathaniel A. VA Lt.Arty. Carrington's Co. Bugler
Terrell, N.B. VA Lt.Arty. Woolfolk's Co.
Terrell, N.D. MS 6th Cav. Co.E
Terrell, Nichols VA Lt.Arty. Nelson's Co. Sgt.
Terrell, Nicholas VA Lt.Arty. Woolfolk's Co. Sgt.
Terrell, O.H.P. VA Hvy.Arty. 20th Bn. Co.D
Terrell, Oliver H.P. VA 1st Arty. Co.H
Terrell, Oscar VA 72nd Mil.
Terrell, P. LA 31st Inf. Co.F
Terrell, P.A. MS Inf. 1st Bn.St.Troops (12 mo. '62-3) Co.A
Terrell, P.A. MS Hall's Co.
Terrell, Patrick AL 1st Regt. Mobile Vol. British Guard Co.A
Terrell, Patrick MS 22nd Inf. Co.C
Terrell, Peter KY 7th Mtd.Inf. Co.C
Terrell, Philip M. VA 25th Inf. 1st Co.G 1st Lt.
Terrell, P.L. MS Lt.Arty. 14th Bn. Co.C
Terrell, P.O. AL Mil. 4th Vol. Moore's Co. Cpl.
Terrell, P.O. TX 14th Inf. Co.B
Terrell, R. AL 27th Inf. Co.C
Terrell, R. TX 33rd Cav. Co.K
Terrell, R.A. GA Cav. 1st Gordon Squad. (St.Guards) Co.A
Terrell, R.A. TX 12th Cav. Co.G
Terrell, Richmond A. VA Hvy.Arty. A.J. Jones' Co.
Terrell, Richmond H. VA 1st Res. Co.C
Terrell, Richmond L. GA 12th (Wright's) Cav. Stapleton's Co. Sgt.
Terrell, Richmond Q. VA 56th Inf. Co.F Sgt.
Terrell, R.J. TN 47th Inf. Co.K
Terrell, Robert VA 30th Inf. Co.H Sgt.
Terrell, Robt. B. KY 11th Cav. Co.E Capt.

Terrell, Robert C. VA Hvy.Arty. A.J. Jones' Co.
Terrell, Robert H. KY 1st Inf. Co.G
Terrell, Robert H. KY 8th Mtd.Inf. Co.E
Terrell, Robert H. VA Prov.Guard Avis' Co.
Terrell, Robert L. MO 1st N.E. Cav.
Terrell, R.W. FL Cav. 5th Bn.
Terrell, S. GA Cav. 20th Bn. Co.A
Terrell, Samuel AL Conscr.
Terrell, Samuel, Jr. MS 9th Cav. Co.G
Terrell, Samuel TX 5th Cav. Co.A
Terrell, Samuel D. FL 4th Inf. Co.K
Terrell, Samuel H. MS 37th Inf. Co.C Lt.Col.
Terrell, Samuel H. TX 19th Cav. Co.G
Terrell, S.C. MS 1st (King's) Inf. (St.Troops) Co.G
Terrell, S.F. MS 10th Cav. Co.C
Terrell, S.F. TN 2nd Cav. Co.D
Terrell, Sidney M. NC 13th Inf. Co.D
Terrell, Simeon KY 14th Cav. Co.B Sgt.
Terrell, Solomon T. TN 1st Hvy.Arty. Co.B
Terrell, Solomon W. GA 21st Inf. Co.G
Terrell, Spot F. TN 49th Inf. Co.H
Terrell, Stephen LA Miles' Legion Co.H
Terrell, Steven TN 19th Inf. Co.F
Terrell, Steven M. MS 18th Inf. Co.E
Terrell, T.B. GA 47th Inf. Co.H
Terrell, T.C. TN 31st Inf. Co.A
Terrell, T.H. MS Cav. Brown's Co. (Foster Creek Rangers)
Terrell, Thomas AL 2nd Cav. Co.C
Terrell, Thomas AL 11th Inf. Co.K
Terrell, Thomas AL 13th Inf. Co.H
Terrell, Thomas KY 7th Mtd.Inf. Co.C
Terrell, Thomas NC 1st Arty. (10th St.Troops) Co.D
Terrell, Thomas TN Cav. Newsom's Regt. Co.B
Terrell, Thomas Gen. & Staff Contr.Physician
Terrell, Thomas A. AL Lt.Arty. 2nd Bn. Co.D
Terrell, Thomas C. AR 19th (Dockery's) Inf. Co.G
Terrell, Thomas G. NC 14th Inf. Co.E Cpl.
Terrell, Thomas H. MS Cav. 24th Bn. Co.C
Terrell, Thomas H. VA Hvy.Arty. A.J. Jones' Co.
Terrell, Thomas M. GA Cav. 20th Bn. Co.A Sgt.
Terrell, Thomas P. TX 12th Inf. Co.D
Terrell, Thomas T. NC 15th Inf. Co.G Capt.
Terrell, Thomas W. LA Inf. 11th Bn. Co.D Sgt.
Terrell, Timothy GA Philips' Legion Co.C,I
Terrell, T.J. AL Barns' Arty.
Terrell, T.M. GA 8th Cav. New Co.L Sgt.
Terrell, T.W. AR 6th Inf. Co.H
Terrell, T.W. GA 10th Mil.
Terrell, T.W. GA 42nd Inf. Co.G
Terrell, V. TN 20th (Russell's) Cav. Co.I
Terrell, V.L. MS 4th Cav. Co.A,B Capt.
Terrell, V.L. MS Cav. Stockdale's Bn. Co.A,B Capt.
Terrell, V.L. MS Cav. Terrell's Unatt.Co. Capt.
Terrell, W.A. MS Inf. 3rd Bn. Co.E
Terrell, W.B. TN 20th (Russell's) Cav. Co.D
Terrell, W.H. AR 19th Inf. Co.F
Terrell, W.H. LA 8th Cav. Co.D Capt.
Terrell, W.H. LA Inf. 1st Bn. (St.Guards) Co.B Capt.
Terrell, W.H. MS 5th Inf. Co.A
Terrell, W.H. TX 4th Inf. Co.G
Terrell, William AL 13th Inf. Co.H
Terrell, William AL 26th (O'Neal's) Inf. Co.H
Terrell, William MS 12th Cav. Co.C
Terrell, William MS St.Cav. Perrin's Bn. Co.D
Terrell, William TN 7th (Duckworth's) Cav. Co.F
Terrell, William TN 12th Cav.
Terrell, William VA 7th Cav. Co.I
Terrell, William VA 18th Cav. Co.D
Terrell, William VA Hvy.Arty. A.J. Jones' Co.
Terrell, William 1st Chickasaw Inf. Minnis' Co.
Terrell, William A. VA 3rd Cav. Co.F
Terrell, William B. TX 1st (Yager's) Cav. Co.F
Terrell, William D. NC 33rd Inf. Co.F
Terrell, William D. VA Lt.Arty. Woolfolk's Co. Lt.
Terrell, William F. AL 4th Inf. Co.D
Terrell, William G. SC 1st (Orr's) Rifles Co.F Capt.
Terrell, William H. GA 13th Inf. Co.A
Terrell, William H. GA 42nd Inf. Co.G
Terrell, William H. LA 1st Cav. Co.I 2nd Lt.
Terrell, William H. LA 19th Inf. Co.F 2nd Lt.
Terrell, William H. MS 11th (Perrin's) Cav. Co.B 1st Sgt.
Terrell, William H. MS 29th Inf. Co.F
Terrell, William H. MO Inf. 6th Regt.St.Guard Co.B 2nd Lt.
Terrell, William H. VA Lt.Arty. Carrington's Co.
Terrell, William J. AL 13th Inf. Co.G
Terrell, Wm. J. AL 26th Inf. Co.H
Terrell, William J. GA 10th Cav. (St.Guards) Co.K Sgt.
Terrell, William J. MS 34th Inf. Co.F
Terrell, William J. TN Holman's Bn. Part.Rangers Co.B
Terrell, William Jones TX 12th Inf. Co.D Sgt.
Terrell, William L. GA Phillips' Legion Co.C
Terrell, William L. KY 1st Inf. Co.G
Terrell, William M. GA 24th Inf. Co.H Sgt.
Terrell, William M. 1st Conf.Inf. 2nd Co.C
Terrell, William P. NC 45th Inf. Co.G,H
Terrell, William S. NC 25th Inf. Co.C
Terrell, William S. NC Inf. Thomas Legion 2nd Co.A 2nd Lt.
Terrell, William T. AL 26th (O'Neal's) Inf. Co.H
Terrell, Winburn B. AL 13th Inf. Co.H
Terrell, W.J. VA 19th Inf. Co.C
Terrell, W.J. Gen. & Staff Hosp.Stew.
Terrell, W. Joseph TX 12th Inf. Co.D
Terrell, W.R. TN 12th (Cons.) Inf. Co.I
Terrell, W.S. TX Cav. 2nd Regt.St.Troops Co.B
Terrell, W.T. GA 23rd Inf. Co.I
Terrell, W.T. SC 21st Inf. Co.F
Terrell, W.W. MS 5th Cav. Co.H
Terrell, W.W. MS 18th Cav. Co.K
Terrell, W.W. MS Cav. Part.Rangers Rhodes' Co.
Terrell, Zack NC 2nd Jr.Res. Co.K
Terrence, J.T. TN 13th Inf. Co.B
Terrentine, William A.T. AL 10th Inf. Co.I
Terres, James NC 34th Inf. Co.G
Terret, Edward LA 21st (Patton's) Inf. Co.A
Terrett, B.A. AR 8th Inf. New Co.E 2nd Lt.
Terrett, Berry MD Cav. 2nd Bn. Co.D
Terrett, Burdett A. Gen. & Staff Cadet
Terrett, Edward MS 18th Inf. Co.K
Terrett, George H. VA Col.
Terrett, William VA 17th Inf. Co.H
Terrett, Wm. E. MS 18th Inf. Co.K
Terrey, E.C. MS Cav. 24th Bn. Co.H
Terrey, J.B. TN 16th (Logwood's) Cav. Co.K
Terriberry, J.S. VA Horse Arty. D. Shanks' Co.
Terrick, B.F. VA 5th Cav.
Terridoes, Joseph AL 95th Mil. Co.D
Terrie, Hermogine LA 33rd Regt.Vol.
Terrier, J. AL 59th Inf. Co.B
Terrier, John AL Cav. Murphy's Bn. Co.C
Terrier, John 15th Conf.Cav. Co.H Cpl.
Terrier, John E. VA 61st Mil. Co.B Ens.
Terrier, William H. VA 61st Mil. Co.G
Terril, Calvin VA 10th Inf. Co.D
Terril, J.P. GA 1st Inf. (St.Guards) Co.K 3rd Lt.
Terril, W.L. TX 9th (Young's) Inf. Co.A
Terrill, A.C. TN 11th (Holman's) Cav. Co.G
Terrill, A.J. AR 20th Inf. Co.A
Terrill, A.N. SC 4th Cav. Co.H
Terrill, Arch KY 8th Cav. Co.G
Terrill, Arthur KY 5th Cav. Co.G
Terrill, C.J. Gen. & Staff AASurg.
Terrill, C.S. VA Lt.Arty. Utterback's Co.
Terrill, D.C. AL 49th Inf. Co.F
Terrill, D.W. TN 30th Inf. Co.K
Terrill, E.B. GA 8th Cav. Old Co.D
Terrill, Edward KY 9th Mtd.Inf. Co.B
Terrill, Eustace VA Cav. 39th Bn. Co.A
Terrill, Eustace VA 136th Mil.
Terrill, E.J. TX Cav. Morgan's Regt. Co.F
Terrill, F.M. GA 53rd Inf. Co.H
Terrill, Francis M. AR 26th Inf. Co.B
Terrill, Geo. P. Gen. & Staff Contr.Surg.
Terrill, George W. KY 5th Cav. Co.G Capt.
Terrill, G.P. AL 8th Inf. Co.H
Terrill, G.P. AL Cp. of Instr. Talladega
Terrill, H. MS 28th Cav. Co.D
Terrill, Henry TX 8th Cav. Co.F
Terrill, H.M. TX Cav. Border's Regt. Co.A
Terrill, H.M. TX Cav. Border's Regt. Co.C
Terrill, Holmes KY 5th Cav. Co.F
Terrill, James AL 13th Inf.
Terrill, James GA 23rd Inf. Co.I
Terrill, James B. VA 13th Inf. Lt.Col.
Terrill, James B. Gen. & Staff Brig.Gen.
Terrill, James M. VA 20th Inf. Co.K
Terrill, James M. VA 59th Inf. 3rd Co.C
Terrill, James W. TX 6th & 15th (Cons.) Vol. Co.E Capt.
Terrill, J.B. MO St.Guard
Terrill, J.C. KY 5th Cav. Co.G
Terrill, J.C. MS 28th Cav. Co.D
Terrill, J.C. TX 24th & 25th Cav. (Cons.) Co.E
Terrill, J.J. TN 12th (Cons.) Inf. Co.B
Terrill, J.M. LA Inf. 1st Bn. (St.Guards) Co.B
Terrill, John C. KY 5th Cav. Co.G
Terrill, John C. KY 11th Cav. Co.E 2nd Lt.
Terrill, John G. LA 9th Inf. Co.K,F
Terrill, John H. VA Cav. 39th Bn. Co.C
Terrill, John U. VA 12th Cav. Co.B
Terrill, John W. MO 1st Cav. Co.K
Terrill, Joseph C. AL 4th Inf. Co.H Sgt.
Terrill, Joseph H. TN 3rd (Forrest's) Cav.
Terrill, Joseph M. TN 3rd (Forrest's) Cav.

Terrill, Joshua AR 26th Inf. Co.A
Terrill, Lewis F. Stuart Horse Arty.,CSA Maj.
Terrill, L.M. TX Cav. Giddings' Bn. Weisiger's Co. Sgt.
Terrill, Lyman 1st Choctaw & Chickasaw Mtd.Rifles 2nd Co.C
Terrill, Oliver Towles VA 13th Inf. Co.A
Terrill, P.A. AL 9th Inf. Co.D
Terrill, Philip VA 12th Cav. Co.B
Terrill, Philip M. VA 62nd Mtd.Inf. 2nd Co.A 1st Lt.
Terrill, R.A. Gen. & Staff Capt.,AQM
Terrill, R.C. KY 11th Cav. Co.E Capt.
Terrill, Richard KY 8th Cav. Co.G
Terrill, Richmond H. VA Lt.Arty. Ancell's Co.
Terrill, R.M. GA 9th Inf. Surg.
Terrill, Rob KY 2nd (Woodward's) Cav. Co.F
Terrill, Robert A. AL Cav. Barbiere's Bn. Truss' Co. 1st Lt.
Terrill, Robert M. VA 6th Cav. Co.I
Terrill, Robt. M. Gen. & Staff Surg.
Terrill, R.W. MO Cav. Williams' Regt. Co.I
Terrill, Samuel F. MS 2nd Inf. Co.C
Terrill, S.F. KY 5th Cav. Co.G
Terrill, S.F. Inf. Bailey's Cons.Regt. Co.C
Terrill, S.H. TX Cav. Border's Regt. Co.D
Terrill, Simeon F. KY 9th Cav. Co.G
Terrill, S.M. MO 2nd Inf. Co.I
Terrill, S.O. TX 3rd Cav. Co.F 1st Lt.
Terrill, Sylvanus AR 1st Cav. Co.G,D
Terrill, Sylvanus AR Cav. Witherspoon's Bn. Co.D
Terrill, Thomas GA 8th Inf. Co.F
Terrill, Thomas MS 1st Bn.S.S. Co.D
Terrill, Thomas MO 2nd Cav. New Co.H
Terrill, Thomas VA Cav. 39th Bn. Co.A
Terrill, Thomas VA 136th Mil.
Terrill, Thomas J. AR 26th Inf. Co.B
Terrill, Thomas P. VA 30th Inf. Co.B Music.
Terrill, T.J. GA 13th Inf. Co.A
Terrill, T.J. MS 25th Inf. Co.H
Terrill, Towles VA 13th Inf. Co.A
Terrill, W. NC Allen's Co. (Loc.Def.)
Terrill, W.A.D. GA 62nd Cav. Co.F
Terrill, W.C. MS 28th Cav. Co.D
Terrill, W.G. MS Res.Corps Withers' Co.
Terrill, Whitefield P. MO 5th Inf. Co.H Cpl.
Terrill, William TN 11th (Holman's) Cav. Co.G
Terrill, William A. KY 8th Cav. Co.B
Terrill, William H. KY 5th Cav. Co.A
Terrill, William H. MO 5th Inf. Co.B Sgt.
Terrill, William J. VA 14th Inf. Co.D
Terrill, William M. GA 7th Inf. Co.B
Terrill, William T. TX 34th Cav. Co.H
Terrill, W.M. MS 28th Cav. Co.D
Terrill, W.T. TN 30th Inf. Co.K
Terrille, C.S. GA 49th Inf. Co.H
Terrio, Charles LA 18th Inf. Co.D
Terrio, Charles LA Inf.Cons. 18th Regt. & Yellow Jacket Bn. Co.D
Terrio, Edward LA Arty. Landry's Co. (Donaldsonville Arty.) Bugler
Terris, Charles E. NC 5th Cav. (63rd St.Troops) Co.F 2nd Lt.
Terris, H. NC 1st Inf. (6 mo. '61) Co.C Cpl.
Terris, J.B. Gen. & Staff Hosp.Stew.
Territt, B.A. Allen's Cav.Div. Capt.,AAG
Territt, Cornelius AR 25th Inf. Co.D Sgt.
Terrivelle, Frank LA 21st (Kennedy's) Inf. Co.C
Terrol, John MS 3rd Inf. Co.H
Terry, A. TX Cav. Wells' Regt. Co.K
Terry, A. VA Inf. 45th Inf. Co.F 2nd Lt.
Terry, A. 4th Conf.Inf. Co.I
Terry, A.B. VA 30th Bn.S.S. Co.C
Terry, Abner MO 1st Inf. Co.K
Terry, Abner R. NC 13th Inf. Co.C Sgt.
Terry, A.C. TX 11th (Spaight's) Bn.Vol. Co.C
Terry, Addison VA 9th Cav. Co.K
Terry, A.E.C. AL 10th Inf. Co.E
Terry, A.G. MS 5th Cav. Co.A 1st Sgt.
Terry, A.J. VA 4th Res. Co.H
Terry, Albert AL 54th Inf.
Terry, Albert MS Lt.Arty. 14th Bn. Co.B
Terry, Albert G. MS 2nd Inf. (A. of 10,000) Co.H
Terry, Albert G. MS 42nd Inf. Co.A Sgt.
Terry, Alexander VA 25th Inf. 2nd Co.K
Terry, Alexander VA 162nd Mil. Co.C
Terry, Alexander P. NC 2nd Cav. (19th St.Troops) Co.F
Terry, Alfred GA 1st Cav. Co.D
Terry, Alfred H. NC 56th Inf. Co.G
Terry, Alfred H. SC 4th Inf. Co.F
Terry, Alonzo AL Cav. 5th Bn. Hilliard's Legion Co.A Sgt.
Terry, Ambrose E. MS 26th Inf. Co.G,K Jr.2nd Lt.
Terry, Anderson NC Unassign.Conscr.
Terry, Andrew J. GA 7th Inf. Co.E
Terry, Ansolim TX 22nd Cav. Co.C
Terry, A.P. TN 25th Inf. Co.I
Terry, A.R. MS Cav. Powers' Regt. Co.C
Terry, Archibald AL 19th Inf. Co.D
Terry, Augustus J. MS 16th Inf. Co.C
Terry, Aurelius J. TX Terry's Mtd.Co. (St.Troops) Capt.
Terry, B.A. MS 12th Cav. Co.H Sgt.
Terry, B.A. MS 5th Inf. (St.Troops) Co.G
Terry, Bartholomew TX Inf. Griffin's Bn. Co.D
Terry, Bedford M. NC 33rd Inf. Co.F
Terry, Ben D. KY Morgan's Men Co.D Capt.
Terry, Benjamin NC 16th Inf. Co.I
Terry, Benjamin D. KY 1st (Helm's) Cav. Old Co.G Capt.
Terry, Benjamin D. KY 5th Cav. Co.I,K Capt.
Terry, Benjamin F. SC Inf. 3rd Bn. Co.C
Terry, Benjamin W. AL 3rd Res. Co.I Sgt.
Terry, B.F. KY 3rd Bn.Mtd.Rifles Co.D
Terry, B.F. TX 8th Cav. Col.
Terry, B.H. Bradford's Corps Scouts & Guards Co.A
Terry, Bird TN 25th Inf. Co.I
Terry, B.P. Mo 3rd Inf. Co.K
Terry, Britton AR 23rd Inf. Co.G
Terry, B.S. NC 21st Inf. Co.D
Terry, B.T. MS 28th Cav. Co.B
Terry, B.T. MS 35th Inf. Co.C
Terry, B.T. Gen. & Staff Surg.
Terry, C. LA Arty. Hutton's Co. (Crescent Arty.,Co.A)
Terry, C. TX 26th Cav. Co.H
Terry, C. TX Cav. Frontier Bn. Co.A
Terry, C. TX Cav. McCord's Frontier Regt. Co.E
Terry, Calvin MS 29th Inf. Co.F
Terry, Calvin G. TX 1st (McCulloch's) Cav. Co.H
Terry, Calvin G. TX Cav. Morgan's Regt. Co.B
Terry, Calvin S. NC 3rd Inf. Co.F
Terry, Carlisle Gen. & Staff, Medical Dept. Surg.
Terry, C.C. KY 2nd (Duke's) Cav. Co.C
Terry, C.E. AL 4th Inf. Co.C
Terry, C.F. NC 1st Inf. (6 mo. '61) Co.G
Terry, Champ GA 60th Inf. Co.E
Terry, Champ G. NC 52nd Inf. Co.E
Terry, Champ P. SC 21st Inf. Co.D
Terry, Charles VA 24th Cav. Co.E
Terry, Charles VA 25th Cav. Co.E,F
Terry, Charles A. TN 19th Inf. Co.I
Terry, Charles C. MS Hamer's Co. (Salem Cav.) 1st Sgt.
Terry, Charles C. MS 34th Inf. Co.K 1st Sgt.
Terry, Charles H. VA 24th Inf. Co.K
Terry, Charles M.D. MS 19th Inf. Co.I Cpl.
Terry, Charles N. KY 2nd (Duke's) Cav. Co.E
Terry, Charles W. MS 13th Inf. Co.C
Terry, Charles W. VA 11th Inf. Co.G Sgt.
Terry, Christopher G. GA 22nd Inf. Co.C
Terry, Clark AR 34th Inf. Co.E
Terry, Clark SC 23rd Inf. Co.F
Terry, C.M. GA Cav. 19th Bn. Co.A Cpl.
Terry, C.M. MS 4th Inf. Co.F
Terry, C.M. MS 9th Bn.S.S. Co.C
Terry, C.M. MS 29th Inf. Co.F
Terry, C.M. SC Cav. 19th Bn. Co.A Cpl.
Terry, C.M. SC Part.Rangers Kirk's Co. Cpl.
Terry, C.M. SC 24th Inf. Co.D Sgt.
Terry, C.N. GA Inf. City Bn. (Columbus) Williams' Co.
Terry, Cornelius TX 21st Cav. Co.E
Terry, Couch KY 13th Cav. Co.K
Terry, C.R. MS 8th Inf. Co.A
Terry, Curtis MS 42nd Inf. Co.H
Terry, C. Willson SC Inf. Hampton Legion Co.E Cpl.
Terry, Cyrus TX 22nd Cav. Co.C
Terry, Cyrus TX Cav. Baylor's Regt. Co.K
Terry, Cyrus C. SC 2nd Rifles Co.K Sgt.
Terry, D. GA 5th Cav. Co.E
Terry, D. GA Siege Arty. 28th Bn. Co.G
Terry, D. GA 47th Inf. Co.G
Terry, Dabney S. MS Cav. Hughes' Bn. Co.D
Terry, Daniel KY 13th Cav. Co.C
Terry, David AL Mil. 4th Vol. Moore's Co.
Terry, David AL 36th Inf. Co.H
Terry, David GA Cav. 12th Bn. (St.Guards) Co.D
Terry, David NC 46th Inf. Co.B
Terry, David SC 3rd Cav. Co.F
Terry, David C. TX Cav. Martin's Regt. Co.F
Terry, David M. AL 25th Inf. Co.E
Terry, David S. TX 8th Cav. Co.H Cpl.
Terry, Davis E. Conf.Reg.Inf. Brooks' Bn. Co.C
Terry, D.C. TX 31st Cav. Co.A
Terry, D.D. TN 12th (Green's) Cav. Co.K
Terry, D.M. TX 1st Bn.S.S. Co.B
Terry, Doctor F. SC Hvy.Arty. 15th (Lucas') Bn. Co.A
Terry, D.S. TX Cav. Terry's Regt. Col.
Terry, D.S., Jr. Gen. & Staff 1st Lt.,ADC

Terry, D.W. Wheeler's Scouts,CSA
Terry, E. AR 20th Inf. Co.K
Terry, E. MS 1st (King's) Inf. (St.Troops) Co.F
Terry, E. TX 26th Cav. Co.F
Terry, E.C. AR Cav. Crabtree's (46th) Regt. Co.B
Terry, E.C. AR 36th Inf. Co.D Cpl.
Terry, E.C. 20th Conf.Cav. Co.C
Terry, Edmond W. VA 47th Inf. 2nd Co.K
Terry, Edward AL 16th Inf. Co.I
Terry, Edward AR 20th Inf. Co.K
Terry, Edward TN 20th Inf. Co.G
Terry, Edward A. SC Hvy.Arty. 15th (Lucas') Bn. Co.C,B Sgt.
Terry, Edward A. SC Arty. Childs' Co.
Terry, Edward A. SC Arty. Lee's Co.
Terry, Edward G. NC 2nd Arty. (36th St.Troops) Co.G
Terry, Edward W. VA 38th Inf. Co.C
Terry, E.G. NC Lt.Arty. 13th Bn. Co.D
Terry, E.H. VA Inf. 25th Bn. Co.D Sgt.
Terry, E.L. SC Inf. 1st (Charleston) Bn. Co.D
Terry, E.L. SC 27th Inf. Co.D Cpl.
Terry, E.L. 2nd Conf.Eng.Troops Co.G
Terry, Eli SC Inf. 9th Bn. Co.E
Terry, Eli SC 26th Inf. Co.F
Terry, Eli TN 7th (Duckworth's) Cav. Co.E
Terry, Eli TN 42nd Inf. Co.D
Terry, Eli 4th Conf.Inf. Co.K
Terry, Elias AR 34th Inf. Co.E
Terry, Elijah M. GA 38th Inf. Co.F
Terry, Elisha TX 12th Cav. Co.B
Terry, Elisha Gen. & Staff Chap.
Terry, Elisha S.N. TN Inf. 23rd Bn. Co.C
Terry, E.O. SC Mil. 16th Regt. Sigwald's Co.
Terry, Ephraim B. NC 52nd Inf. Co.K Cpl.
Terry, E.S. TN 17th Inf. Co.A
Terry, E.W. TN 13th (Gore's) Cav. Co.K 2nd Lt.
Terry, F.G. KY 8th Mtd.Inf. Co.G Capt.
Terry, F.G. TN 3rd (Forrest's) Cav. Co.B Sgt.
Terry, F.M. AL 40th Inf. Co.H
Terry, F.M. AR Cav. Harrell's Bn. Co.D
Terry, F.M. GA Cav. 1st Bn.Res. McKinney's Co.
Terry, F.M. GA 1st Lt.Duty Men Co.A
Terry, F.M. GA 5th Inf. (St.Guards) Johnston's Co.
Terry, F.M. GA 20th Inf. Co.D
Terry, F.M. TX 24th Cav. Co.G
Terry, F.M. TX 25th Cav. Co.A
Terry, F.M. TX Cav. Hardeman's Regt. Co.C
Terry, Francis A. AL Lt.Arty. Phelan's Co.
Terry, Francis A. AR Inf. 4th Bn. Lt.Col.
Terry, Frank TN 1st (Carter's) Cav. Co.K
Terry, Franklin GA 3rd Cav. Co.I
Terry, Franklin B. TN 17th Inf. Co.A Capt.
Terry, Fredrick M. GA 4th Inf. Co.A
Terry, F.R.J. MS 6th Inf. Co.F
Terry, F.R.J. Conf.Cav. Powers' Regt. Co.A Sgt.
Terry, G.A. MS 8th Cav. Co.H
Terry, G.A. MS 28th Cav. Co.L Sgt.
Terry, G.A. TX 13th Vol. 3rd Co.A
Terry, G.A. TX Inf. Griffin's Bn. Co.D
Terry, G.A. TX Inf. Timmons' Regt. Co.H
Terry, G.A. TX Waul's Legion Co.A
Terry, G.A. VA 1st (Farinholt's) Res. Co.B
Terry, G.D. TX Cav. Baylor's Regt. Co.K
Terry, G.E. AL Lt.Arty. Kolb's Btty.
Terry, George AL 16th Inf. Co.I
Terry, George AL 32nd Inf. Co.C
Terry, George AR 2nd Mtd.Rifles Co.I Cpl.
Terry, George TX Cav. Waller's Regt. Co.A
Terry, George VA 6th Inf. 1st Co.B
Terry, George A. AL 4th (Russell's) Cav. Co.D
Terry, George A. AL 4th Inf. Co.D
Terry, George A. TX Lt.Arty. H. Van Buren's Co.
Terry, George A. VA 30th Bn.S.S. Co.C
Terry, George A. VA 166th Mil. Ballard's Co.H
Terry, George B. AR 24th Inf. Co.F
Terry, George B. AR Inf. Hardy's Regt. Co.D
Terry, George D. GA 57th Inf. Co.H
Terry, George F. SC Inf. Hampton Legion Co.E
Terry, George H. TX 9th (Nichols') Inf. Co.C
Terry, George J. VA 26th Inf. Co.D
Terry, George N. GA 46th Inf. Co.G
Terry, George P. MS 30th Inf. Co.G
Terry, George P. VA 3rd Cav. Co.A
Terry, George R. VA Horse Arty. D. Shanks' Co.
Terry, George W. AR 1st Mtd.Rifles Co.I Cpl.
Terry, George W. AR 9th Inf. Co.G Cpl.
Terry, George W. GA 3rd Bn. (St.Guards) Co.B 1st Lt.
Terry, George W. GA 21st Inf. Co.F Cpl.
Terry, George W. GA 39th Inf. Co.A
Terry, George W. MS 5th Inf. Co.A
Terry, George W. NC 2nd Arty. (36th St.Troops) Co.G
Terry, George W. NC Lt.Arty. 13th Bn. Co.D
Terry, George W. SC 25th Inf. Co.K Cpl.
Terry, George W. TX Cav. 2nd Regt. Co.F
Terry, George W. TX 31st Cav. Co.I
Terry, George W. VA 8th Cav. Co.F
Terry, George W. VA 64th Mil. Campbell's Co.
Terry, George W. 3rd Conf.Cav. Co.F
Terry, G.L. TN 3rd (Forrest's) Cav. 1st Co.F
Terry, G.P. AR 10th Inf. Co.F,C
Terry, G.P. AR 15th Inf. Co.F
Terry, G.T. TX Waul's Legion Co.E Sgt.
Terry, G.W. GA 11th Inf. Co.C
Terry, G.W. SC 3rd Cav. Co.K
Terry, G.W. TN Cav. Nixon's Regt. Co.K
Terry, G.W. TX Cav. 2nd Bn.St.Troops Nelson's Co.
Terry, G.W. TX 11th Cav. Co.B
Terry, G.W. TX 18th Inf. Co.D
Terry, Hampton H. MS 29th Inf. Co.F
Terry, Harris H. AR 13th Inf. Co.K
Terry, Harvey VA Lt.Arty. W.P. Carter's Co.
Terry, H.E. MS Cav. Jeff Davis Legion Co.E
Terry, Henderson AL 5th Cav.
Terry, Henry AR 7th Inf. Co.K
Terry, Henry TX 3rd Cav. Co.B
Terry, Henry C. AL 63rd Inf. Co.D
Terry, Henry C. GA Siege Arty. 28th Bn. Co.F
Terry, Henry C. MS 2nd Inf. Co.K Capt.
Terry, Henry C. VA 51st Inf. Co.H
Terry, Henry E. VA 25th Cav. Co.B
Terry, Henry H. VA 53rd Inf. Co.I
Terry, Henry M. VA 59th Inf. 1st Co.G
Terry, Henry M. VA 60th Inf. Co.D
Terry, H.H. TX 13th Vol. Co.K
Terry, Hilliard J. AL 36th Inf. Co.H
Terry, Hilliard J.T. TX 20th Inf. Co.A
Terry, Hiram TX 22nd Cav. Co.C
Terry, Hiram VA 13th Inf. Co.I
Terry, Hiram VA 50th Inf. Co.A
Terry, H.M. AR 1st Mtd.Rifles Co.I
Terry, Horton AL Arty. 1st Bn. Co.E
Terry, H.R. TN 25th Inf. Co.I Cpl.
Terry, Hugh M. AR 9th Inf. Co.G
Terry, H.W. TN 11th (Holman's) Cav. Co.E
Terry, H.W. TN Holman's Bn.Part.Rangers Co.C
Terry, I.C. TN Inf. 2nd Cons.Regt. Co.G
Terry, Ichabud VA Cav. 34th Bn. Co.A Sgt.
Terry, I.N. TX 15th Cav. Co.C
Terry, I.N. TX 31st Cav. Co.G
Terry, I.N. Conf.Cav. Wood's Regt. Co.K
Terry, Isaac KY 5th Mtd.Inf. Co.K
Terry, Isham AR 16th Inf. Co.I
Terry, Isom AR 27th Inf. Co.H
Terry, J. AL 40th Inf. Co.H
Terry, J. LA 21st (Kennedy's) Inf. Co.D
Terry, J. TX Cav. Bourland's Regt. Co.H
Terry, J. TX Inf. 1st St.Troops Stevenson's Co.F
Terry, Jacob A. VA 63rd Inf. Co.D
Terry, James AL Inf. 1st Regt. Co.D
Terry, James AL 12th Inf. Co.K
Terry, James AL Talladega Cty.Res. J. Henderson's Co.
Terry, James AR 5th Inf. Co.F
Terry, James AR 8th Inf. New Co.D
Terry, James AR 17th (Lemoyne's) Inf. Co.C
Terry, James AR 21st Inf. Co.C
Terry, James GA 48th Inf. Co.B
Terry, James MS Cav. Powers' Regt. Co.C 2nd Lt.
Terry, James MS 9th Inf. Old Co.I
Terry, James MS 36th Inf. Co.B Lt.
Terry, James MS 42nd Inf. Co.B Cpl.
Terry, James NC 6th Inf. Co.C
Terry, James NC 48th Inf. Co.B
Terry, James TX Cav. 2nd Regt.St.Troops Co.D
Terry, James TX 10th Cav. Co.E
Terry, James TX Arty. 4th Bn.
Terry, James TX 8th Inf. Co.A
Terry, James TX 11th Inf. Co.K
Terry, James VA 72nd Mil.
Terry, James VA 166th Mil. R.G. Lively's Co.
Terry, James VA 166th Mil. Taylor's Co.
Terry, James A. NC Conscr.
Terry, James A. SC Inf. Hampton Legion Co.E
Terry, James A. TX Inf. 24th Bn. Sgt.Maj.
Terry, James B. NC 53rd Inf. Co.H
Terry, James B. SC Lt.Arty. Beauregard's Co.
Terry, James C. AL 11th Inf. Co.I
Terry, James D. GA 1st Reg. Co.L
Terry, James D. MO Lt.Arty. 1st Btty. Cpl.
Terry, James D. TN Inf. 1st Bn. (Colms') Co.A
Terry, James D. TN 50th (Cons.) Inf. Co.B
Terry, James D. TX Cav. Mann's Regt. Co.A 1st Sgt.
Terry, James D. TX Cav. Mann's Bn. Co.A Ord.Sgt.
Terry, James D. TX Waul's Legion Co.B 1st Sgt.
Terry, James E. AL 28th Inf. Co.C

Terry, James E. SC 1st (Butler's) Inf. Co.D
Terry, James E. TX Cav. Baylor's Regt. Co.A
Terry, James E. VA 14th Inf. Co.H
Terry, James F. AL 62nd Inf. Co.K
Terry, James F. NC 31st Inf. Co.E
Terry, James F.M. NC 2nd Cav. (19th St.Troops) Co.K
Terry, James H. AR 18th Inf. Co.A
Terry, James H. GA 19th Inf. Co.A
Terry, James H. MS 20th Inf. Co.H
Terry, James H. VA 16th Cav. Co.A
Terry, James H. VA Cav. Ferguson's Bn. Stevenson's Co.
Terry, James J. AL 16th Inf. Co.I
Terry, James J. GA 15th Inf. Co.F
Terry, James K. TX 8th Cav. Co.A
Terry, James K. VA Inf. 45th Bn. Co.F
Terry, James Kib TN Cav. 7th Bn. (Bennett's) Co.F
Terry, James L. MS 2nd St.Cav. Co.D
Terry, James M. AR 6th Inf. New Co.F
Terry, James M. MS Inf. 2nd Bn. Co.D
Terry, James M. MS 48th Inf. Co.D
Terry, James M. NC 6th Cav. (65th St.Troops) Co.D
Terry, James M. SC 5th Inf. 1st Co.K, 2nd Co.K
Terry, James M. VA Lt.Arty. Montgomery's Co.
Terry, James M. VA Lt.Arty. B.Z. Price's Co.
Terry, James M. VA 162nd Mil. Co.C Capt.
Terry, James N. AL 20th Inf. Co.H
Terry, James P. GA 3rd Cav. Co.C
Terry, James R. MS 41st Inf. Co.H
Terry, James S. TN 4th Inf. Co.A Cpl.
Terry, James T. VA Lt.Arty. Nelson's Co.
Terry, James T. VA Lt.Arty. Woolfolk's Co.
Terry, James W. AL 36th Inf. Co.H
Terry, James W. TN 34th Inf. Co.F 2nd Lt.
Terry, James W. TX 16th Inf. Co.I
Terry, James William KY 1st Bn.Mtd.Rifles Co.A
Terry, Jasper AL 20th Inf. Co.A
Terry, Jasper TN 12th Inf. Co.F
Terry, Jasper N. TN 13th (Gore's) Cav. Co.K
Terry, J.B. MS Inf. 3rd Bn. Co.E
Terry, J.B. TN 13th (Gore's) Cav. Co.K 1st Sgt.
Terry, J.B. TN 16th (Logwood's) Cav. Co.H
Terry, J.B. TN 9th Inf. Co.L,D
Terry, J.B. TX Cav. Hardeman's Regt. Co.C
Terry, J.C. AL 20th Inf. Co.E
Terry, J.C. AL Talladega Cty.Res. J. Henderson's Co.
Terry, J.C. GA 38th Inf. Co.F
Terry, J.C. KY 9th Mtd.Inf. Co.F
Terry, J.C. MD Cav. 2nd Bn. Co.B
Terry, J.C. NC 12th Inf. Co.B,D
Terry, J.C. TN 13th (Gore's) Cav. Co.K
Terry, J.C. TN 21st (Wilson's) Cav. Co.D
Terry, J.C. TN 21st & 22nd (Cons.) Cav. Co.H
Terry, J.C. TN Inf. 23rd Bn. Co.B
Terry, J.C. TN 38th Inf. Co.I
Terry, J.C. TX 3rd Cav. Co.D
Terry, J.C. TX 4th Inf. Co.E
Terry, J.D. MO Lt.Arty. Walsh's Co.
Terry, J.D. SC 6th Cav. Co.H
Terry, J.D. TX Cav. 3rd Regt.St.Troops Townsend's Co.
Terry, J.E. VA Lt.Arty. Penick's Co.
Terry, Jefferson J. MO Inf. Perkins' Bn. Co.B
Terry, Jerome LA 1st Cav. Co.I
Terry, Jesse KY 5th Mtd.Inf. Co.B
Terry, Jesse MS 7th Cav. Co.F
Terry, Jesse C. TX 3rd Cav. Co.K
Terry, Jessee MS 28th Cav. Co.H
Terry, J.F. AL 35th Inf. Co.G
Terry, J.F. TN 13th Inf. Co.H
Terry, J.G. GA 8th Cav. New Co.D Cpl.
Terry, J.G. GA Cav. 20th Bn. Co.A,D Cpl.
Terry, J.H. AL Cp. of Instr. Talladega
Terry, J.H. MS 41st Inf. Co.H
Terry, J.H. MO 9th (Elliott's) Cav.
Terry, J.H. MO Quantrill's Co.
Terry, J.H. SC 7th Cav. Co.I 1st Lt.
Terry, J.H. SC 3rd Inf. Co.G
Terry, J.H. SC 7th Inf. 1st Co.I
Terry, J.H. TX 7th Inf. Co.D,H
Terry, J.H. TX 14th Inf. Co.B
Terry, J.H. 2nd Conf.Inf. Co.D
Terry, J.J. AL 20th Inf. Co.A
Terry, J.L. MS 8th Inf. Co.B
Terry, J.L. TN 8th (Smith's) Cav. Co.A
Terry, J.L. TX 4th Cav. Co.B 2nd Lt.
Terry, J.L. TX 12th Inf. Co.C
Terry, J.M. AL 54th Inf. Co.H
Terry, J.M. AR 10th Inf. Co.D
Terry, J.M. GA Lt.Arty. (Arsenal Btty.) Hudson's Co.
Terry, J.M. MS Lt.Arty. 14th Bn. Co.B
Terry, J.M. MS 1st (Johnston's) Inf. Co.D
Terry, J.M. MS 4th Inf. Co.F
Terry, J.M. SC 2nd Cav. Co.B
Terry, J.M. SC 3rd Cav. Co.A
Terry, J.M. SC 4th Cav. Co.D
Terry, J.M. SC 5th St.Troops Co.E
Terry, J.M. SC 7th Res. Co.L
Terry, J.M. TN 7th (Duckworth's) Cav. Co.I
Terry, J.M. VA 46th Inf. 2nd Co.K
Terry, J. Miles SC 11th Res. Co.I Cpl.
Terry, J.N. MS 4th Inf. 3rd Lt.
Terry, J.N. SC 14th Inf. Co.F
Terry, J.N. TN 12th (Cons.) Inf. Co.B
Terry, Jo TN 12th Inf. Co.A
Terry, John AL 9th Inf. Co.F
Terry, John AL 16th Inf. Co.I
Terry, John AL 31st Inf. Co.C
Terry, John AR Cav. Wright's Regt. Co.I
Terry, John AR Lt.Arty. Owen's Btty.
Terry, John AR 24th Inf. Co.E
Terry, John GA 8th Inf. (St.Guards) Co.F
Terry, John GA 21st Inf. Co.F Cpl.
Terry, John GA 46th Inf. Co.G Cpl.
Terry, John GA 56th Inf. Co.G
Terry, John MS 1st Cav.Res. Co.C
Terry, John MS 5th Cav. Co.K
Terry, John MS 1st Lt.Arty.
Terry, John MS 1st (Patton's) Inf. Co.E
Terry, John MS 6th Inf. Co.F
Terry, John MS 40th Inf. Co.I
Terry, John MS 41st Inf. Co.H
Terry, John NC Hvy.Arty. 1st Bn. Co.B Music.
Terry, John NC Walker's Bn. Thomas' Legion Co.E
Terry, John VA 1st Inf. Co.B
Terry, John A. NC 43rd Inf. Co.G
Terry, John A. TN 28th (Cons.) Inf. Co.K
Terry, John A. VA 166th Mil. Co.H
Terry, John B. AL Lt.Arty. Kolb's Btty.
Terry, John B. AL 16th Inf. Co.K
Terry, John C. TN 23rd Inf. Co.H
Terry, John C. VA 17th Cav. Co.E Cpl.
Terry, John D. GA 3rd Cav. Co.C
Terry, John D. NC 13th Inf. Co.H
Terry, John D. TN 13th (Gore's) Cav. Co.K
Terry, John D. VA 14th Inf. Co.K Cpl.
Terry, John F. AR 15th (Josey's) Inf. Co.C Cpl.
Terry, John F. KY 6th Mtd.Inf. Co.F
Terry, John F. VA Lt.Arty. Nelson's Co.
Terry, John F. VA 37th Inf. Co.A Lt.Col.
Terry, John Frank VA Lt.Arty. Woolfolk's Co. Wagon driver
Terry, John G. GA 8th Inf. (St.Guards) Co.B
Terry, John H. AL 20th Inf. Co.H
Terry, John H. AL 44th Inf. Co.F
Terry, John H. AL 55th Vol. Co.A Music.
Terry, John H. GA 41st Inf. Co.C
Terry, John H. GA Phillips' Legion Co.A,G
Terry, John H. LA 12th Inf. Co.L
Terry, John H. MO 10th Cav. Co.A
Terry, John H. SC 6th Cav. Co.B,D
Terry, John H. SC 8th Inf. Co.D
Terry, John H. SC Cav.Bn. Holcombe Legion Co.A 2nd Lt.
Terry, John H. TN 55th (Brown's) Inf. Co.G
Terry, John H. VA 30th Bn.S.S. Co.A
Terry, John H. VA 38th Inf. Co.C
Terry, John H.W. TN 2nd (Robison's) Inf. Co.K
Terry, John J. VA 4th Cav. Co.G
Terry, John J. VA Lt.Arty. W.P. Carter's Co.
Terry, John J. VA Goochland Lt.Arty.
Terry, John J. VA 51st Inf. Co.H
Terry, John K. TX 14th Cav. Co.D
Terry, John L. GA 31st Inf. Co.H
Terry, John M. AR 2nd Inf. Co.H,B
Terry, John M. SC 11th Inf. Co.D
Terry, John M. SC Inf. Hampton Legion Co.E
Terry, John N. SC 18th Inf. Co.E
Terry, John P. GA Cav. 1st Bn.Res. McKinney's Co.
Terry, John R. TX 19th Cav. Co.D
Terry, John R. TX 18th Inf. Co.I
Terry, John R. VA 47th Inf. 2nd Co.K
Terry, John R.L. TX Res.Corps Co.C
Terry, John S. AL 18th Inf. Co.B,E
Terry, John S. AR 1st (Crawford's) Cav. Co.G
Terry, John S. AR 3rd Cav. Co.C
Terry, John S. NC 2nd Cav. (19th St.Troops) Co.K Bugler
Terry, John T. AL 16th Inf. Co.K
Terry, John T. AL 32nd Inf. Co.A
Terry, John T. AL 40th Inf. Co.B 1st Lt.
Terry, John T. GA 3rd Res. Co.F
Terry, John W. AL Cav. Lewis' Bn. Co.A,C 2nd Lt.
Terry, John W. AL 19th Inf. Co.D
Terry, John W. AL 54th Inf. Co.A
Terry, John W. AR Cav. Wright's Regt. Co.H 1st Lt.
Terry, John W. AR 19th (Dockery's) Inf. Co.G
Terry, John W. GA 15th Inf. Co.F
Terry, John W. GA 36th (Broyles') Inf. Co.A
Terry, John W. GA 56th Inf. Co.A 3rd Lt.
Terry, John W. TN 3rd (Forrest's) Cav.

Terry, John W. TX 17th Cav. Co.F Sgt.
Terry, John W. TX 17th Cons.Dismtd.Cav. Co.F Jr.2nd Lt.
Terry, John W. VA 14th Inf. Co.B Cpl.
Terry, John W. VA 42nd Inf. Co.F
Terry, Jonathan A. TX 4th Cav. Co.B
Terry, Joseph AL 5th Cav. Cpl.
Terry, Joseph AL 5th Cav. 1st Lt.
Terry, Joseph AR 19th (Dockery's) Inf. Co.E Sgt.
Terry, Joseph AR 37th Inf. Co.C
Terry, Joseph GA 3rd Cav. Co.I
Terry, Joseph GA Murray Cav. Asher's Co. 1st Sgt.
Terry, Joseph GA 39th Inf.
Terry, Joseph LA 25th Inf. Co.E
Terry, Joseph MS 9th Inf. New Co.K
Terry, Joseph NC 47th Inf. Co.E
Terry, Joseph TN 12th (Cons.) Inf. Co.A
Terry, Joseph TN 22nd Inf. Looney's Co. Sgt.
Terry, Joseph TN 38th Inf. Co.L 1st Sgt.
Terry, Joseph TX 9th Cav. Co.G
Terry, Joseph TX 11th Cav. Co.E
Terry, Joseph TX 19th Cav. Co.D
Terry, Joseph VA 6th Cav. Co.G
Terry, Joseph A. MS 18th Inf. Co.H Hosp.Stew.
Terry, Joseph A. TN 50th Inf. Co.F
Terry, Joseph A. Gen. & Staff Hosp.Stew.
Terry, Joseph C., Jr. VA 26th Inf. Co.K 1st Sgt.
Terry, Joseph D. NC 13th Inf. Co.C Sgt.
Terry, Joseph E. GA 30th Inf. Co.B
Terry, Joseph E. VA Lt.Arty. 13th Bn. Co.B Sgt.
Terry, Joseph M. VA 38th Inf. Co.H Capt.
Terry, Joseph P. SC 14th Inf. Co.G
Terry, Joseph P. VA 22nd Inf. Co.G
Terry, Joseph P. VA 36th Inf. 2nd Co.H
Terry, Joseph P. VA 60th Inf. Co.D
Terry, Joseph R. MS 15th Inf. Co.A 1st Sgt.
Terry, Joseph S. MS Cav. Powers' Regt. Lt.Col.
Terry, Joseph S. MS 16th Inf. Co.C
Terry, Joseph S. MS 18th Inf. Co.H
Terry, Joseph S. Conf.Cav. Powers' Regt. Co.A Capt.
Terry, Joseph W. GA 17th Inf. Co.C
Terry, Joseph W. MS 1st (Patton's) Inf. Co.E Sgt.
Terry, Joseph W. MS 40th Inf. Co.I 2nd Lt.
Terry, Joseph W. NC 22nd Inf. Co.G
Terry, Joseph W. NC 53rd Inf. Co.H
Terry, Joseph W. TX 12th Inf. Co.I
Terry, Joseph W. 3rd Conf.Cav. Co.F
Terry, Josiah AL 51st (Part.Rangers) Co.F
Terry, Josiah MO 10th Inf. Co.A
Terry, J.P. AL 3rd Cav. Co.C
Terry, J.P. GA 5th Inf. (St.Guards) Johnston's Co.
Terry, J.P. SC 22nd Inf. Co.A
Terry, J.P. VA 166th Mil. Co.H
Terry, J.R. SC 4th St.Troops Co.B
Terry, J.S. AL Lt.Arty. 20th Bn. Co.B
Terry, J.S. TN Hvy.Arty. Johnston's Co.
Terry, J.S. TX Cav. Hardeman's Regt. Co.C
Terry, Junius MO 5th Cav. Surg.
Terry, Junius Gen. & Staff Surg.
Terry, J.W. AL 11th Cav. Co.D
Terry, J.W. AL Cav. Moreland's Regt. Co.E
Terry, J.W. AL 16th Inf. Co.I
Terry, J.W. AL 20th Inf. Co.A,I
Terry, J.W. AR Inf. 4th Bn. Co.B
Terry, J.W. AR 9th Inf. Co.G
Terry, J.W. AR 9th Inf. Co.K 2nd Lt.
Terry, J.W. GA 1st Regt.Eng.Troops Cpl.
Terry, J.W. LA 17th Inf. Co.F
Terry, J.W. NC Allen's Co. (Loc.Def.)
Terry, J.W. TN 12th Inf. Co.G
Terry, J.W. TN 40th Inf. Co.H
Terry, J.W. VA 1st (Farinholt's) Res. Co.D
Terry, Kibble AL 9th (Malone's) Cav. Co.I
Terry, Lafayette TN 13th (Gore's) Cav. Co.K
Terry, Lafayette F. TX 7th Inf. Co.K
Terry, Lamkin S. MS 15th Inf. Co.A Maj.
Terry, Larkin NC 3rd Cav. (41st St.Troops) Co.F
Terry, L.B. MS 7th Cav. Co.F
Terry, L.C. VA Inf. 25th Bn. Co.D
Terry, L.D. TN 1st (Feild's) Inf. Co.B
Terry, Lee TN 4th (McLemore's) Cav. Co.A
Terry, Lee A.B. VA 27th Inf. Co.C
Terry, Lewis J. NC 21st Inf. Co.F Cpl.
Terry, Lewis L. MS 30th Inf. Co.G
Terry, Lewis T. GA 46th Inf. Co.G
Terry, L.L. MS 38th Cav. Co.G
Terry, L.L. TX 12th Cav. Co.A
Terry, Louis D. NC 2nd Arty. (36th St.Troops) Co.G
Terry, M. TN 20th (Russell's) Cav. Co.K Cpl.
Terry, Marion TN 4th Cav. Co.A
Terry, Mathew MS 42nd Inf. Co.G
Terry, M.B. TX 3rd Inf. 2nd Co.C
Terry, M.B. TX Conscr.
Terry, M.C. MS 4th Inf. Co.F 4th Sgt.
Terry, M.E. SC 3rd Cav. Co.A
Terry, M.E. SC 11th Res. Co.I Sgt.
Terry, Michael LA Arty. Castellanos' Btty.
Terry, Michael TN 5th Inf. 2nd Co.E
Terry, Miles KY 13th Cav. Co.K
Terry, Miles KY 5th Mtd.Inf. Co.A
Terry, Milton NC 43rd Inf. Co.I
Terry, M.L. TX 12th Inf. Co.C
Terry, M.M. AR 7th Cav. Co.C
Terry, M.M. AR 45th Mil. Co.D Capt.
Terry, M.M. MS 33rd Inf. Co.F
Terry, M.M. 3rd Conf.Inf. Co.I 1st Lt.
Terry, Morgan M. AR 18th (Marmaduke's) Inf. Co.I 1st Lt.
Terry, Moses AR 9th Inf. Co.C
Terry, Moses G. GA 42nd Inf. Co.K
Terry, Moses P. AL 36th Inf. Co.H
Terry, M.T. AL Cav. Lewis' Bn. Co.A
Terry, M.W. TN 10th (DeMoss') Cav. Co.A
Terry, M.Z. AL 53rd (Part.Rangers) Co.D
Terry, N. TX Cav. Mann's Regt. Co.F
Terry, Napoleon F. GA Siege Arty. 28th Bn. Co.F
Terry, Napoleon W. VA Goochland Lt.Arty. Sgt.
Terry, Nat TX 7th Cav. Co.K Sgt.
Terry, Nathanel TN 19th (Biffle's) Cav. Co.A
Terry, Nathaniel SC Inf. 9th Bn. Co.E
Terry, Nathaniel TX Cav. Ragsdale's Bn. Co.D Sgt.
Terry, Nathaniel VA Lt.Arty. J.R. Johnson's Co. 2nd 2nd Lt.
Terry, Nathaniel VA 28th Inf. 1st Co.C
Terry, Nath'l. J. Gen. & Staff AASurg.
Terry, Nathaniel W. TX 11th Cav. Co.C
Terry, N.B. GA 1st Cav. Co.G
Terry, N.B. TX 5th Cav. Co.E Capt.
Terry, N.B. VA 51st Inf. Co.H 1st Lt.
Terry, Newton M. MS 7th Cav. Co.I
Terry, N.G. TN 17th Inf. Co.A
Terry, Nicholas SC 1st (Butler's) Inf. Co.E
Terry, N.J. VA 53rd Inf. Co.I
Terry, N.J. VA Inf. Montague's Bn. Co.B
Terry, N.M. MS 1st (Johnston's) Inf. Co.B
Terry, N.R. VA 10th Cav. Co.C
Terry, N.W. Horse Arty. White's Btty.
Terry, N.W. 1st Conf.Eng.Troops Co.D Sgt.
Terry, Obadiah F. VA 18th Inf. Co.I Cpl.
Terry, Orrin F. LA 7th Inf. Co.K 1st Sgt.
Terry, Oscar AL 59th Inf. Co.I Sgt.
Terry, Oscar AL Arty. 4th Bn. Hilliard's Legion Co.A Sgt.
Terry, Overton T. VA 13th Inf. Co.D
Terry, P. GA 5th Cav. Co.C Sgt.
Terry, P. KY 7th Cav. Co.C
Terry, Parton TN 13th (Gore's) Cav. Co.K Cpl.
Terry, P.E. SC Cav. 19th Bn. Co.A 1st Lt.
Terry, P.E. SC Part.Rangers Kirk's Co. 1st Lt.
Terry, P.E. Morgan's Co.H,CSA
Terry, Peter VA 57th Inf. Co.C Cpl.
Terry, Peyton L. VA 28th Inf. Co.I Ord.Sgt.
Terry, P.H. TX Cav. 3rd (Yager's) Bn. Co.B
Terry, Philip, Jr. GA Cav. 2nd Bn. Co.E Sgt.
Terry, Pickett H. TX 1st (Yager's) Cav. Co.B
Terry, P.J. TN 27th Inf. Co.H
Terry, Pleasant AR 5th Inf. Co.F
Terry, Powell E. KY 6th Cav. Co.E
Terry, P.P. MS Terry's Co. Capt.
Terry, R. MS 19th Inf. Co.D
Terry, R.C. AL 11th Inf. Co.I
Terry, Reuben MS 40th Inf. Co.B
Terry, Reuben C. TN 2nd (Robison's) Inf. Co.H
Terry, Reuben P. VA 12th Inf. Co.D
Terry, R.F. AR 27th Inf. Co.D
Terry, R.G. MS 6th Inf.
Terry, Richard MS 40th Inf. Co.I
Terry, Richard J. NC 4th Cav. (59th St.Troops) Co.D
Terry, Richard S. SC 12th Inf. Co.I
Terry, R.L. MS 4th Inf. Co.F
Terry, R.N. SC 2nd Cav. Co.B Cpl.
Terry, R. Nelson SC Cav.Bn. Hampton Legion Co.C
Terry, Robert AR 11th Cav. Co.H,K
Terry, Robert AR Inf. Cocke's Regt. Co.D
Terry, Robert VA Cav. 35th Bn. Co.C
Terry, Robert A. MS Lt.Arty. (The Hudson Btty.) Hoole's Co.
Terry, Robert A. VA Hvy.Arty. 10th Bn. Co.C
Terry, Robt. E. Gen. & Staff Chap.
Terry, Robert S. VA 34th Inf. Co.C
Terry, Robert W. MS 12th Inf. Co.F
Terry, Robert W. TN Inf. 154th Sr.Regt. 2nd Co.B
Terry, Robert W. VA 4th Cav. Co.F
Terry, Robert Y.H. AR 37th Inf. Co.A 1st Sgt.
Terry, Roland GA 1st (Olmstead's) Inf. Gordon's Co.
Terry, Roland GA 63rd Inf. Co.F

Terry, Roland TN 13th (Gore's) Cav. Co.K
Terry, Roland G. MS 36th Inf. Co.B Cpl.
Terry, R.P. NC Snead's Co. (Loc.Def.)
Terry, R.P. VA 50th Inf. Co.K
Terry, R.W. GA 7th Inf. (St.Guards) Co.B 3rd Lt.
Terry, R.W. TN 12th (Green's) Cav. Co.A
Terry, S. AR 20th Inf. Co.K
Terry, S. VA Cav. Mosby's Regt. (Part.Rangers) Co.E
Terry, Samuel FL 6th Inf. Co.H
Terry, Samuel MS Cav. Yerger's Regt. Co.C
Terry, Samuel TX 17th Cons.Dismtd.Cav. Co.B
Terry, Samuel TX 24th Cav. Co.B
Terry, Samuel VA 25th Cav. Co.H
Terry, Samuel VA 24th Inf. Co.A
Terry, Samuel VA 48th Inf. Co.G
Terry, Samuel VA 166th Mil. Ballard's Co.H
Terry, Samuel B. KY 2nd (Duke's) Cav. Co.C Sgt.
Terry, Samuel B. VA 4th Res. Co.H
Terry, Samuel B. VA 57th Inf. Co.C
Terry, Samuel C. KY 2nd Cav. Co.E
Terry, Samuel D. TX 3rd Cav. Co.B 1st Sgt.
Terry, Samuel M. VA 51st Inf. Co.H
Terry, Samuel P. NC 2nd Cav. (19th St.Troops) Co.K
Terry, Samuel W. TX 11th Inf. Co.K
Terry, Sanford W. VA Hvy.Arty. 10th Bn. Co.B
Terry, S.C. AL 36th Inf. Co.H
Terry, S.D. MS Inf. 1st Bn.St.Troops (12 mo. '62-3) Co.C
Terry, S. Hillsman NC 3rd Inf. Co.D Music.
Terry, S.J. MS 11th (Perrin's) Cav. Co.H
Terry, S.L. GA Murray Cav. Asher's Co. Sgt.
Terry, S.L. GA 27th Inf. Co.A
Terry, S.M. GA 4th Inf. Co.A
Terry, Squire C. AL 5th Cav. 3rd Lt.
Terry, S.T. MS 29th Inf. Co.F
Terry, Stephen GA 2nd Cav. Co.H
Terry, Stephen KY 5th Mtd.Inf. Co.A
Terry, Stephen VA 47th Inf. 2nd Co.K
Terry, Stephen A. GA 35th Inf. Co.K
Terry, Stephen D. NC 12th Inf. Co.B,D
Terry, Stephen F. AL 5th Cav. Cpl.
Terry, Stephen L. NC 1st Inf. Co.E
Terry, Stephen L. NC 24th Inf. Co.H
Terry, Stephen O. NC 2nd Cav. (19th St.Troops) Co.K Sgt.
Terry, Stephen W. LA 14th (Austin's) Bn.S.S. Co.A
Terry, S.W. AR 2nd Inf. Co.K
Terry, S.W. LA 11th Inf. Co.G
Terry, T. GA 3rd Cav. Co.C
Terry, Tandy SC Inf. Hampton Legion Co.E
Terry, Taylor TN 8th Cav. Co.A,E
Terry, T.B. VA 22nd Cav. Co.K Sgt.
Terry, T.C. MS 2nd (Quinn's St.Troops) Inf. Co.G
Terry, T.F. SC Inf. Hampton Legion Co.E Sgt.
Terry, Thadeus AL 25th Inf. Co.A
Terry, Theophilus R. TN 2nd (Robison's) Inf. Co.D
Terry, Thomas AL Cav. Hardie's Bn.Res. Co.A
Terry, Thomas AL 16th Inf. Co.I
Terry, Thomas AL 17th Inf. Co.F
Terry, Thomas AL 20th Inf. Co.I
Terry, Thomas AR 31st Inf. Co.A
Terry, Thomas GA 2nd Cav. Co.H
Terry, Thomas GA Lt.Arty. 14th Bn. Co.C
Terry, Thomas GA Lt.Arty. Ferrell's Btty.
Terry, Thomas KY 13th Cav. Co.F
Terry, Thomas KY 13th Cav. Co.K
Terry, Thomas KY 5th Mtd.Inf. Co.A
Terry, Thomas LA Mil. 3rd Regt. French Brig. Co.4
Terry, Thomas MS 29th Inf. Co.F
Terry, Thomas MS 42nd Inf. Co.K
Terry, Thomas NC 39th Inf. Co.A
Terry, Thomas SC Lt.Arty. Garden's Co. (Palmetto Lt.Btty.)
Terry, Thomas TX 17th Cav. Co.E
Terry, Thomas TX 23rd Cav. Co.G Cpl.
Terry, Thomas VA 7th Cav. Co.A Sgt.
Terry, Thomas A. TX 13th Vol. 1st Co.H, 2nd Co.F
Terry, Thomas B. AL 4th Inf. Co.C
Terry, Thomas B. TX 22nd Cav. Co.C
Terry, Thomas B. TX Inf. Rutherford's Co.
Terry, Thomas C. MS 29th Inf. Co.F
Terry, Thomas D. AL 6th Inf. Co.G Music.
Terry, Thomas F. VA 47th Inf. 2nd Co.K
Terry, Thomas J. TX 18th Cav. Co.G
Terry, Thomas J. VA Lt.Arty. 38th Bn. Co.D
Terry, Thomas J. VA Lt.Arty. J.R. Johnson's Co.
Terry, Thomas J. VA 28th Inf. 1st Co.C
Terry, Thomas L. NC 46th Inf. Co.B
Terry, Thomas M. LA 7th Inf. Co.K Lt.Col.
Terry, Thomas O.P. AR Cav. Wright's Regt. Co.H
Terry, Thomas P. MS Cav. 3rd Bn.Res. Co.B
Terry, Thomas P. MS Cav. Ham's Regt. Co.I
Terry, Thomas S. TX 5th Cav. Co.C
Terry, Thomas S. VA 10th Cav. Co.D Sgt.
Terry, Thomas S. VA Cav. 32nd Bn. Co.A
Terry, Thomas S. VA 74th Mil. Co.E
Terry, Thomas W. GA 59th Inf. Co.G
Terry, T.J. MS 1st Cav.Res. Co.C 3rd Lt.
Terry, T.J. MS 41st Inf. Co.C 2nd Lt.
Terry, T.J. SC 7th Inf. 2nd Co.K
Terry, T.L. GA 3rd Res. Co.E
Terry, T.R. TN 41st Inf. Co.F
Terry, Uriah TN 25th Inf. Co.I
Terry, V.F. VA 30th Bn.S.S. Co.C
Terry, Vincent AL 31st Inf. Co.C
Terry, Vincent A. GA 59th Inf. Co.G Cpl.
Terry, Vitrivius P. LA 7th Inf. Co.K 2nd Lt.
Terry, W. AR 13th Inf. Co.K
Terry, W. TX 24th & 25th Cav. (Cons.) Co.F
Terry, W. TX 33rd Cav. Co.K
Terry, W.A. TN 84th Inf. Co.B
Terry, W.A.J. GA 15th Inf. Co.F
Terry, Walter MS 4th Inf. Co.F
Terry, Walter Q. VA 24th Cav. Co.E
Terry, Warwick VA 162nd Mil. Co.C
Terry, W.B. KY 2nd (Woodward's) Cav. Co.G
Terry, W.B. LA 13th Bn. (Part.Rangers) Co.A
Terry, W.C. AL Lt.Arty. 20th Bn. Co.B
Terry, W.C. MS 3rd Cav. Co.K
Terry, W.C. MS 22nd Inf. Co.F
Terry, W.C. SC Inf. Hampton Legion Co.E
Terry, W.C. TN 25th Inf. Co.I
Terry, W.C.D. TX 3rd Cav. Co.B
Terry, W.D. AL 20th Inf. Co.A
Terry, W.D. SC 4th Cav. Co.I
Terry, W.D. SC Cav. 12th Bn. Co.B
Terry, W.E. GA 32nd Inf. Co.G
Terry, W.E. GA 44th Inf. Co.I
Terry, W.E. MS 2nd Cav. Co.D Cpl.
Terry, W.E. TX Cav. 3rd Regt.St.Troops Townsend's Co.
Terry, W.G. AR Inf. 10th Regt. Co.C
Terry, W.H. AR 36th Inf. Co.I
Terry, W.H. MS 4th Inf. Co.F
Terry, W.H. MS 10th Inf. New Co.I
Terry, W.H. MO 5th Cav. Co.D
Terry, W.H.C. TX 12th Inf. Co.I Sgt.
Terry, William AL Cav. Hardie's Bn.Res. Co.C
Terry, William AL 4th Res. Co.I
Terry, William AR 1st (Dobbin's) Cav. Co.B
Terry, William AR 5th Inf. Co.F
Terry, William AR 36th Inf. Co.H
Terry, William AR Inf. Cocke's Regt. Co.D
Terry, William GA 66th Inf. Co.H
Terry, William GA Floyd Legion (St.Guards) Co.D
Terry, William LA Mil. 3rd Regt. French Brig. Co.4
Terry, William MS 3rd Cav. Co.F
Terry, William MO Cav. Snider's Bn. Co.A
Terry, William NC Lt.Arty. 3rd Bn. Co.C,B
Terry, William NC 26th Inf. Co.G
Terry, William NC 46th Inf. Co.B
Terry, William SC 11th Inf. 2nd Co.F Sgt.
Terry, William TN 7th Inf. Co.A
Terry, William TN 12th Inf. Co.C
Terry, William TN 12th (Cons.) Inf. Co.B
Terry, William TN 25th Inf. Co.I
Terry, William TX Cav. 3rd (Yager's) Bn. Co.A
Terry, William TX 24th Cav. Co.G
Terry, William TX 25th Cav. Co.B
Terry, William TX 27th Cav. Co.F
Terry, William TX Loc.Def.Troops McNeel's Co. (McNeel Coast Guards)
Terry, William VA 24th Cav. Co.E
Terry, William VA Cav. 40th Bn. Co.E
Terry, William VA 4th Inf. Co.A Col.
Terry, William VA 11th Bn.Res. Co.A
Terry, William VA 12th Inf. Co.D
Terry, William VA 50th Inf. Co.F
Terry, William VA 50th Inf. Co.K
Terry, William VA 57th Inf. Co.C
Terry, William VA 63rd Inf. Co.A
Terry, William VA 63rd Inf. Co.K
Terry, William 1st Chickasaw Inf. Hansell's Co. Sgt.
Terry, Wm. Gen. & Staff Brig.Gen.
Terry, William A. KY 6th Mtd.Inf. Co.F,E 2nd Lt.
Terry, William A. TN 28th Inf. Co.B
Terry, William A. TX 1st (Yager's) Cav. Co.A
Terry, William A. VA Lt.Arty. B.Z. Price's Co.
Terry, William A. VA 14th Inf. Co.K
Terry, William A. VA 51st Inf. Co.H
Terry, William B. AL 5th Cav. Co.C
Terry, William B. AL 5th Inf. Co.C
Terry, William B. MO 1st N.E. Cav. Co.H
Terry, William B. MO 11th Inf. Co.F
Terry, William B. MO Inf. Clark's Regt. Co.B
Terry, William B. VA 45th Inf. Co.F

Terry, William C. MS 2nd Inf. Co.L
Terry, William C. MS 42nd Inf. Co.B
Terry, William C. VA 3rd Cav. Co.A
Terry, William D. SC 4th Inf. Co.F
Terry, William E. MS 6th Inf. Co.G
Terry, William F. AL Roddey's/Hardee's Escort Troops Co.H
Terry, William F. TN 44th (Cons.) Inf. Co.C 1st Lt.
Terry, William F. TN 55th (McKoin's) Inf. James' Co.
Terry, William F. VA 1st Inf. Co.I Sgt.
Terry, William G. NC 24th Inf. Co.D
Terry, William G. VA Lt.Arty. Montgomery's Co.
Terry, William H. AR 1st Inf.
Terry, William H. GA 4th Inf. Co.B
Terry, William H. GA 23rd Inf. Co.C Cpl.
Terry, William H. MS 15th Inf. Co.A
Terry, William H. MS 19th Inf. Co.D Sgt.
Terry, William H. MO 10th Cav. Co.A
Terry, William H. NC 47th Inf. Co.E
Terry, William H. SC 14th Inf. Co.C
Terry, William H. TN 4th (McLemore's) Cav. Co.F
Terry, William H. VA Lt.Arty. Nelson's Co.
Terry, William H. VA Lt.Arty. Woolfolk's Co.
Terry, William H. VA 46th Inf. 4th Co.F
Terry, William I. SC Cav.Bn. Hampton Legion Co.C
Terry, William J. GA 38th Inf. Co.F
Terry, William J. GA 39th Inf. Co.A
Terry, William J. SC 1st (Butler's) Inf. Co.A
Terry, William J. SC 9th Inf. Co.F
Terry, William J. TN 8th Cav.
Terry, William J. TX 19th Cav. Co.F
Terry, William J. VA 41st Inf. 2nd Co.E
Terry, William L. AL Talladega Cty.Res. J. Henderson's Co.
Terry, William L. AR 23rd Inf. Co.E
Terry, William L. MS 1st (Patton's) Inf. Co.C
Terry, William L. NC 27th Inf. Co.G
Terry, Wm. L. Gen. & Staff, Medical Dept. Surg.
Terry, William M. AR 14th (McCarver's) Inf. Co.H
Terry, William M. MS 3rd Inf. (St.Troops) Co.A
Terry, William M. MS 16th Inf. Co.C
Terry, William P. SC 24th Inf. Co.D
Terry, William P. TX Cav. Martin's Regt. Co.F Sgt.
Terry, William R. MO Inf. Clark's Regt. Co.H
Terry, William R. VA 2nd Cav. Co.A Capt.
Terry, Wm. R. VA 2nd Cav.
Terry, William R. VA 24th Inf. Col.
Terry, William R. VA 51st Inf. Co.G 2nd Lt.
Terry, Wm. R. Gen. & Staff Brig.Gen.
Terry, William R.A. TX 20th Inf. Co.A 2nd Lt.
Terry, William Robin VA 30th Bn.S.S. Co.A 1st Lt.
Terry, William S. AL 7th Inf. Co.K
Terry, William S. NC 57th Inf. Co.I
Terry, William S. SC 6th Cav. Co.A
Terry, William S. SC 19th Inf. Co.C
Terry, William T. VA 4th Cav. Co.G
Terry, William W. SC Lt.Arty. Kelly's Co. (Chesterfield Arty.)
Terry, William W. SC 12th Inf. Co.I
Terry, William W. VA 9th Inf. 1st Co.H
Terry, Wm. W. Gen. & Staff Asst.Surg.
Terry, Willis H. TN 53rd Inf. Co.F
Terry, W.J. KY 9th Mtd.Inf. Co.F
Terry, W.J. SC 6th Cav. Co.H
Terry, W.J. SC 8th Inf. Co.B
Terry, W.J. TN 25th Inf. Co.I
Terry, W.J. TX 7th Cav. Co.K
Terry, W.J. TX 5th Inf. Co.G 1st Lt.
Terry, W.J. TN 9th (Nichols') Inf. Co.D
Terry, W.L. MS 37th Inf. Co.H
Terry, W.M. MS 28th Cav. Co.B
Terry, W.M. MS Cav. Powers' Regt. Co.C
Terry, W.M. MS 6th Inf. Co.F
Terry, W.P. TN 63rd Inf. Co.K
Terry, W.P. TX Cav. 3rd Regt.St.Troops Townsend's Co.
Terry, W.P. TX 33rd Cav. Co.B
Terry, W.R. MO 9th Inf. Co.E
Terry, W.R. VA 10th Cav. Co.B
Terry, W.S. AL Cav. Hardie's Bn.Res. Co.A
Terry, W.S. AL 57th Inf. Co.A
Terry, W.T. GA 15th Inf. Co.F
Terry, W.T. MS 28th Cav. Co.B
Terry, Young GA 8th Inf. (St.Guards) Co.F
Terry, Zachary T. AL Cav. 8th Regt. (Livingston's) Co.I
Terry, Zachary T. AL Cav. Moses' Squad. Co.A
Terry, Zebulon AL 37th Inf. Co.C Sgt.
Terryeaux, D. LA Inf.Crescent Regt. Co.A
Terrygle, J.F. TN 1st Cav. Co.A
Ter shun a cha 1st Choctaw & Chickasaw Mtd.Rifles 1st Co.E
Tersil, S. LA Mil. 2nd Regt. French Brig. Co.4
Tersiot, V. Conf.Lt.Arty. 1st Reg.Btty.
Terson, H.M. AL 6th Inf. Co.I
Terson, M.A. LA 3rd Inf. Co.E
Terson, T.C. AL 6th Inf. Co.I Sgt.
Tertress, William T. Gen. & Staff,PACS Hosp.Stew.
Tertron, A. LA Mil. Orleans Guards Regt. Co.A
Tertron, Chas. LA Mil. Orleans Guards Regt. Co.D Capt.
Tertrose, A.L. LA Inf.Cons.Crescent Regt. Co.H
Tertrou, A. LA Mil. Orleans Guards Regt. AQM
Tertulien, V. LA Mil. 3rd Regt. French Brig. Co.6
Terult, Pat AR 51st Mil. Co.B
Tervalon, A.F. LA Mil. 1st Native Guards
Terver, Jame LA Mil. Borge's Co. (Garnet Rangers)
Tervis, --- TX 36th Cav. Co.B
Tery, A.B. VA 166th Mil. Co.H
Tery, David SC 1st Mtd.Mil. Smart's Co.
Tery, Jesse VA 24th Cav. Co.H
Tery, John C. TX 22nd Cav. Co.C
Tery, T.B. AL 5th Cav. Co.H
Tery, W.A. TN 28th (Cons.) Inf. Co.F
Terzaghi, Basquale LA Mil. Cazadores Espanoles Regt. Co.F
Te sa chee 1st Creek Mtd.Vol. 2nd Co.C
Te sah we 1st Creek Mtd.Vol. Co.E
Tesaneer, J.G.B. GA 23rd Inf. Co.G
Tesanier, N. GA 23rd Inf. Co.G
Te sar Tah ske 1st Cherokee Mtd.Rifles Co.D
Te sa tees kih NC Inf. Thomas Legion Co.B
Te sa tes kih (Owkson) NC Inf. Thomas Legion Co.B
Teschke, F.R. TX Inf. Timmons' Regt. Co.K
Teschke, F.R. TX Waul's Legion Co.B
Teschke, Robert TX 1st Hvy.Arty. Co.C
Tesdale, Shirly AR 1st Mtd.Rifles Co.K
Tese, J. TX 17th Inf. Co.K
Teseeyogih NC Inf. Thomas Legion 2nd Co.A
Teseneer, Nickolas NC 54th Inf. Co.I
Teseneer, William NC 54th Inf. Co.I
Tesenger, Thomas NC 7th Inf. Co.C
Te ses kee NC Inf. Thomas Legion 2nd Co.A
Te ses kih NC Inf. Thomas Legion 2nd Co.A
Teseteskih NC Inf. Thomas Legion 2nd Co.A
Tesh, George W. NC 15th Inf. Co.H
Tesh, G.W. NC 6th Sr.Res. Co.C
Tesh, Henry T. NC 33rd Inf. Co.C
Tesh, Jacob NC 21st Inf. Co.A
Tesh, James M. NC 53rd Inf. Co.D Cpl.
Tesh, John NC 3rd Home Guards Co.C Cpl.
Tesh, Leven NC 15th Inf. Co.B
Tesh, Levi NC 6th Sr.Res. Co.C
Tesh, Levi NC 48th Inf. Co.K
Tesh, Romulus NC 48th Inf. Co.K
Tesh, Solomon NC 15th Inf. Co.H Cpl.
Teshee, S. AL 47th Inf. Co.C
Tesiah Harjo 1st Seminole Mtd.Vol.
Teske, Ferdinand TX 1st Hvy.Arty. Co.C
Teske, John VA 15th Inf. Co.K
Teskey, R. SC Mil.Arty. 1st Regt. Co.C
Tesnah Deneale's Regt. Choctaw Warriors Co.B
Tesneer, John A. NC 56th Inf. Co.F
Tesney, Charles E. AL 20th Inf. Co.C
Tesseidre, Alexandre LA 18th Inf. Co.B
Tessendore, Louis LA 6th Inf. Co.C
Tessenear, Jackson NC 56th Inf. Co.I
Tessenear, Joseph NC 56th Inf. Co.I
Tesseneer James, Jr. GA 22nd Inf. Co.I
Tessenk, Henry AL Rebels
Tessero, Tom L. TN 22nd Inf. Co.A
Tessier, D.E. Gen. & Staff Prov.Marsh.
Tessier, G. Gen. & Staff, QM Dept.
Tessier, George D. LA 2nd Cav. Co.C
Tessier, H.V. LA Maddox's Regt.Res.Corps Co.B
Tessier, John M. LA Hvy.Arty. 2nd Bn. Co.C
Tessier, M.M. GA Mil. 2nd Div. A.Surg.
Tessier, M.M. GA 32nd Inf. Co.C
Tessier, M.M. Gen. & Staff Sr.Surg.
Tessier, Rush E. GA 2nd St.Troops Co.E
Tessio, Ulgire LA Inf. 10th Bn. Co.C
Tesson, A.A. LA Mil. Orleans Guards Regt. Co.I
Tesson, Jabez MO 10th Inf. Co.I
Test, Conrad AR 3rd Cav. Co.K
Testament, James TN Conscr. Hoffmaster's Co.
Testament, Jesse VA 64th Mtd.Inf. Co.G
Testament, Peter VA 64th Mtd.Inf. 2nd Co.F
Testament, T.M. NC 26th Inf. Co.A
Testament, Wilson J. TN Conscr. Hoffmaster's Co.
Testard, Adolph TX 5th Cav. Co.E 2nd Lt.
Testard, Adolph TX 16th Inf. Co.B 1st Lt.
Tester, B.F. KY 2nd Bn.Mtd.Rifles Co.A
Tester, Columbus TN 19th Inf. Co.B
Tester, Daniel NC 6th Cav. (65th St.Troops) Co.A
Tester, Elcana TN 19th Inf. Co.B

Tester, James NC 6th Cav. (65th St.Troops) Co.F,A
Tester, John W. KY 2nd Bn.Mtd.Rifles Co.A Cpl.
Tester, Ransom NC 58th Inf. Co.D
Tester, Riley TN 19th Inf. Co.B
Tester, W.J. GA 18th Inf. Co.B
Testerd, B. TX 8th Inf. Co.G
Testerman, A.S. VA Mil. Grayson Cty.
Testerman, Calvin NC 37th Inf. Co.A
Testerman, Hugh NC 58th Inf. Co.L
Testerman, James J. NC 37th Inf. Co.A Cpl.
Testerman, Johnson NC 37th Inf. Co.A
Testerman, William P. TN Cav. 16th Bn. (Neal's) Co.F
Testermon, Morgan NC 58th Inf. Co.L
Testmant, Frank M. NC 58th Inf. Co.B
Teston, Benjamin GA 50th Inf. Co.C
Teston, Henry GA 50th Inf. Co.C
Teston, James GA 50th Inf. Co.C
Te tah co we 1st Creek Mtd.Vol. Co.E
Te tal e to gah NC Inf. Thomas Legion Co.B
Te tar co har 1st Creek Mtd.Vol. Co.E
Tete, Aaron H. SC 2nd Rifles Co.L
Tete, Emile LA 1st Hvy.Arty. (Reg.) Co.D
Tete, H. LA 18th Inf. Co.H
Tete, John C. SC 2nd Rifles Co.L
Teter, Amos J. VA 25th Inf. 1st Co.F
Teter, Balaam VA 62nd Mtd.Inf. 2nd Co.C
Teter, Charles NC 5th Sr.Res. Co.D
Teter, Cyrus VA 46th Mil. Co.B
Teter, Cyrus VA 62nd Mtd.Inf. 2nd Co.C
Teter, Daniel W. VA 52nd Inf. Co.A Cpl.
Teter, David VA 46th Mil. Lantz's Co.
Teter, David VA 62nd Mtd.Inf. 1st Co.A
Teter, Eli P. VA 62nd Mtd.Inf. 2nd Co.C
Teter, Isaac VA 62nd Mtd.Inf. Co.F
Teter, James AR 3rd Cav. Co.K
Teter, James W. VA 52nd Inf. Co.A
Teter, John VA 46th Mil. Lantz's Co.
Teter, John A. VA 46th Mil. Lantz's Co. Cpl.
Teter, Laban VA 46th Mil. Lantz's Co.
Teter, P.M. AR 35th Inf. Co.I
Teter, Salem VA 25th Inf. 2nd Co.K
Teter, Salem VA 31st Inf. 1st Co.B
Teter, Salem VA 62nd Mtd.Inf. 2nd Co.C
Teter, Samuel VA 62nd Mtd.Inf. Co.C
Teter, Samuel C. VA 62nd Mtd.Inf. 2nd Co.C
Teter, W.C. VA 18th Cav. Co.A
Teter, Whitson A. NC 42nd Inf. Co.H
Teter, William C. VA 25th Inf. 1st Co.F
Teter, William J. TN 59th Mtd.Inf. Co.G
Teter, W.N. LA 17th Inf. Co.F
Teters, David TX Cav. Baird's Regt. Co.E
Teters, F. AR 24th Inf. Co.A
Teters, George TN 44th Inf. Co.D
Teters, George W. MS 15th Bn.S.S. Co.A
Teters, George W. TN 44th (Cons.) Inf. Co.D
Teters, J.A. TN Inf. 22nd Bn. Co.E
Teters, Jacob NC 22nd Inf. Co.A
Teters, John KY 13th Cav. Co.F
Teters, John TN Inf. 22nd Bn. Co.G
Teters, Moses S. TX 2nd Cav. Co.H Cpl.
Tetherington, R.M. KY 10th (Johnson's) Cav. New Co.C Surg.
Tetlow, William LA 21st (Patton's) Inf. Co.A
Tetram, Lewis GA 8th Inf. Co.K
Tetrau, H. LA Mil. Assumption Regt.
Tetreau, Leon LA 8th Inf. Co.K
Tetrick, Peter AR 34th Inf. Co.B
Tett, J.W. AL 22nd Inf. Co.E
Tettenborn, Ch. TX Lt.Arty. Dege's Bn.
Tettenborn, Charles TX 4th Field Btty.
Tettenborn, Charles TX 3rd Inf. Co.H Fifer
Tetter, A.J. VA 18th Cav. Co.A
Tetter, Green B. AR Lt.Arty. Zimmerman's Btty.
Tetter, William NC 1st Home Guards
Tetterington, A.W. MO 11th Inf. Co.F
Tetterton, Hosea W. NC 61st Inf. Co.B
Tetterton, James H. NC 42nd Inf. Co.B
Tetterton, James H. NC 61st Inf. Co.H
Tetterton, Nathan W. NC 1st Arty. (10th St.Troops) Co.B
Tetterton, N.W. NC 66th Inf. Co.H
Tetterton, Ometa NC 47th Inf. Co.H
Tetterton, Samuel D. NC 17th Inf. (1st Org.) Co.F
Tetterton, Thomas R. NC 4th Inf. Co.E Cpl.
Tetterton, William R. NC 1st Inf. Co.H
Tettle, Adam E.W. TX 29th Cav. Co.E
Tettleton, John W. TN 8th Cav. Co.D
Tettleton, Robert AR 36th Inf. Co.E
Tetus, John NC 1st Bn.Jr.Res. Co.E
Tet yer ner skie 1st Cherokee Mtd.Rifles Co.E
Tetyre, W. NC 46th Inf. Co.K
Teubbee, Jacob 1st Choctaw & Chickasaw Mtd.Rifles 2nd Co.D Cpl.
Teubner, John TX 2nd Inf. Co.F
Teuche, Faustin LA Inf. 10th Bn. Co.C
Teufel, Joseph TN Inf. 3rd Bn. Co.G
Teutsch, Augustus TX 11th Inf. Co.A Sgt.
Teutsch, Fred LA 17th Inf. Co.F
Teutsch, Jacob LA 8th Inf. Co.G
Teutsch, Reuben LA 19th Inf. Co.A
Teutsch, Robert TX 11th Inf. Co.A
Tevalt, Isaac M. VA 51st Mil. Co.E
Tevalt, John H. VA 51st Mil. Co.E Sgt.
Tevebaugh, J.F. KY 3rd Bn.Mtd.Rifles Co.D
Tevebough, Jonathan F. KY 1st Bn.Mtd.Rifles Co.C
Tevelin, Peter LA 25th Inf. Co.C
Tevilley, George AL 3rd Cav. Co.C
Tevilley, R.L. AL 3rd Cav. Co.C Sgt.
Tevis, Benjamin F. TX Cav. Ragsdale's Bn. Co.F
Tevis, Benjamin F. TX 11th (Spaight's) Bn.Vol. Co.E
Tevis, James KY 7th Cav. Co.F 3rd Lt.
Tevis, James H. KY 11th Cav. Co.F 3rd Lt.
Tevis, James H. TX Cav. Saufley's Scouting Bn. Co.E Capt.
Tevis, John D. KY 6th Cav. Co.A Cpl.
Tevis, Jno D. Gen. & Staff, Subs.Dept. Agent
Tevis, John W. TX 16th Cav. Co.D
Tevis, Nathaniel AR 37th Inf. Co.B Cpl.
Tevis, Robert KY 11th Cav. Co.B
Tevis, Robert H. TN 5th Inf. 2nd Co.G
Tevis, Robert M. Gen. & Staff Maj.,Comsy.
Tevis, R.W. TX 26th Cav. Co.K
Tevis, Squire KY 5th Cav. Co.B
Tevis, Squire KY 11th Cav. Co.B Sgt.
Tevis, Squire T. Retributors Young's (5th) Co.
Tevis, T.D. AR 37th Inf. Co.B
Tevis, T.J. AR 37th Inf. Co.B
Tevis, T.N. KY 7th Cav. Co.I
Tevis, T.N. TN 3rd (Forrest's) Cav. 1st Co.G
Tevis, William KY 8th Cav. Co.B
Tevis, William H. KY 6th Cav. Co.A
Tevis, W.J. AR 37th Inf. Co.B
Tevis, W.T. Retributors Young's (5th) Co.
Tevlin, James LA 1st (Nelligan's) Inf. Co.E
Tew, Alex. AL 15th Inf. Co.H
Tew, Alexander NC 51st Inf. Co.I
Tew, Alex. Sig.Corps,CSA
Tew, Allen AL 57th Inf. Co.B
Tew, Alston NC 20th Inf. Co.I
Tew, Archie AR 2nd Cav. 1st Co.A
Tew, Ashley B. NC 20th Inf. Co.E
Tew, Ausbon, Jr. NC 20th Inf. Co.F
Tew, Bedford NC 51st Inf. Co.K
Tew, Blackman AL 1st Bn.Cadets Co.B
Tew, Blackman NC 30th Inf. Co.A
Tew, B.T. NC 2nd Inf. Co.C
Tew, Charles C. NC 2nd Inf. Col.
Tew, Charles H. LA 1st (Strawbridge's) Inf. Co.A,C,F,B,H Capt.
Tew, Daniel MS 37th Inf. Co.F
Tew, Daniel NC 46th Inf. Co.I
Tew, Daniel C. NC 51st Inf. Co.I
Tew, Daniel L. NC 46th Inf. Co.I
Tew, Daniel W. NC 2nd Jr.Res. Co.A
Tew, E.J. MS 3rd (St.Troops) Cav. Co.K 1st Sgt.
Tew, H. NC 53rd Inf. Co.I
Tew, Henry MS 37th Inf. Co.F
Tew, Henry NC 8th Sr.Res. Bryan's Co.
Tew, Henry NC Giddins' Co. (Detailed & Petitioned Men)
Tew, Hesehiah AL 27th Inf. Co.G Cpl.
Tew, Hezekiah AL 1st Regt.Conscr. Co.I
Tew, Hezekiah AL 57th Inf. Co.B
Tew, Hillery AL 40th Inf. Co.E
Tew, Holly NC 2nd Inf. Co.E
Tew, Ira Nelson NC 20th Inf. Co.H
Tew, Jackson NC 51st Inf. Co.I
Tew, James AL Lt.Arty. 2nd Bn. Co.A
Tew, James AL 29th Inf. Co.K
Tew, James GA 31st Inf. Co.I
Tew, James MS Inf. 7th Bn. Co.E
Tew, James A. AL 27th Inf. Co.G
Tew, James Martin NC 51st Inf. Co.I
Tew, Jeremiah AL 32nd Inf. Co.F
Tew, Jeremiah NC 51st Inf. Co.I
Tew, Jesse NC 2nd Jr.Res. Co.A Cpl.
Tew, Joel AL 15th Inf. Co.H
Tew, Joel MS Inf. 7th Bn. Co.E 2nd Lt.
Tew, John AL 9th Inf. Co.A
Tew, John AL 15th Inf. Co.H
Tew, John GA 2nd Bn.S.S. Co.E
Tew, John NC 51st Inf. Co.I
Tew, John A. NC 38th Inf. Co.D
Tew, John C. AL 44th Inf. Co.C
Tew, John J. NC 51st Inf. Co.K 2nd Lt.
Tew, John L. NC 51st Inf. Co.K
Tew, John L.W. NC 20th Inf. Co.E
Tew, John R. NC 51st Inf. Co.I
Tew, Jonathan MS 3rd Cav.Res. Co.A
Tew, J.W. MS 37th Inf. Co.F,H
Tew, L. NC 2nd Inf. Co.F
Tew, Lace M. GA 59th Inf. Co.A
Tew, Lemic J. NC 20th Inf. Co.E

Tew, Lemick J. NC 51st Inf. Co.I
Tew, Lewis NC 46th Inf. Co.I
Tew, L.M. GA 17th Inf. Co.D
Tew, L.M. NC 51st Inf. Co.K Cpl.
Tew, Loudin NC 2nd Bn.Loc.Def.Troops Co.B
Tew, Loudin Blew NC 51st Inf. Co.I
Tew, Martin B. NC 51st Inf. Co.K
Tew, M.M. NC 51st Inf. Co.K
Tew, M.W. NC 25th Inf.
Tew, Nathan AL 3rd Inf. Co.L
Tew, Newbern NC 20th Inf. Co.I
Tew, Osborn NC 2nd Inf. Co.C
Tew, Osborne NC 38th Inf. Co.D
Tew, Osburn MS 37th Inf. Co.F
Tew, Osburn NC 8th Sr.Res. Bryan's Co.
Tew, Peter F. AL 27th Inf. Co.G
Tew, Peter H. AL 57th Inf. Co.B
Tew, Phillip A. NC 2nd Arty. (36th St.Troops) Co.A Sgt.
Tew, Richard NC 46th Inf. Co.I
Tew, Robert NC 20th Inf. Co.I
Tew, Sampson M. NC 20th Inf. Co.H
Tew, Samuel AL 29th Inf. Co.K
Tew, Samuel MS Inf. 7th Bn. Co.D
Tew, Sherwood NC 51st Inf. Co.G
Tew, Silas NC 46th Inf. Co.I
Tew, S.M. GA 20th Inf. Co.H
Tew, Thomas L. NC 2nd Arty. (36th St.Troops) Co.A
Tew, Thomas R. AL 94th Mil. Co.A 1st Lt.
Tew, T.R. AL Conscr.
Tew, Walter A. LA Washington Arty.Bn. Co.3
Tew, Wiley NC 30th Inf. Co.A
Tew, William AL 54th Inf. Co.C
Tew, William MS Cav. (St.Troops) Gamblin's Co.
Tew, William H. NC 51st Inf. Co.I
Tew, William R. NC 20th Inf. Co.E
Tew, William R. NC 38th Inf. Co.C Cpl.
Tew, William Roberson NC 20th Inf. Co.H
Tew, Willie NC 8th Sr.Res. Bryan's Co.
Tew, W.R. NC 2nd Inf. Co.C
Tew, Zachariah AL 29th Inf. Co.K
Tewalt, George VA 136th Mil. Co.C
Tewalt, John H. VA 33rd Inf. Co.D
Te Wayke 1st Seminole Mtd.Vol.
Tewel, Calvin C. VA Inf. 23rd Bn. Co.A
Tewel, James H. VA Inf. 23rd Bn. Co.A
Tewel, Robert X. VA Inf. 23rd Bn. Co.A
Tewell, R.A. AR 13th Mil. Co.F
Tewell, R.A. GA 18th Inf. Co.M Cpl.
Tewes, J. SC Inf. 1st (Charleston) Bn. Co.F
Tewes, John SC 25th Inf. Co.H
Te wi ke 1st Seminole Mtd.Vol. Sgt.
Tewill, Thomas MO 4th Cav. Co.G
Tewis, Edward TX 3rd Inf. Co.I
Tewlis, J.M. MO 3rd Inf. Co.H
Tewox, Peter MS 5th Inf. (St.Troops) Co.H
Tewyeh, Nickojack NC Inf. Thomas Legion 2nd Co.A
Texada, Jerome LA 1st Cav. Co.A
Texada, Jerome LA Inf.Cons.Crescent Regt.
Texada, J.W. LA 8th Cav. Co.A Capt.
Texada, J.W. LA Inf.Crescent Regt. Co.K,G Sgt.
Texada, T. LA 2nd Cav. Co.G
Texas (Slave) VA 32nd Inf. 2nd Co.I Cook
Texas, W. MD Arty. 2nd Btty. Music.
Texier, H. LA Mil. 3rd Regt.Eur.Brig. (Garde Francaise) Co.7
Tex tas kee 1st Cherokee Mtd.Vol. 2nd Co.E Cpl.
Texter, Paul LA 21st (Kennedy's) Inf. Co.F
Teycumcke 1st Seminole Mtd.Vol.
Tey cumse cocker 1st Seminole Mtd.Vol.
Teylor, M. TN 4th Cav. Co.C
Teynac, A. GA 1st (Olmstead's) Inf. Co.F
Teynac, Andrew GA Hvy.Arty. 22nd Bn. Co.C
Teynac, J.F. GA 1st (Olmstead's) Inf. Co.F
Teynac, J.F. GA 25th Inf. Pritchard's Co.
Teynac, John F. GA Hvy.Arty. 22nd Bn. Co.C
Teyuletohhee, Jim NC Inf. Thomas Legion Co.B
Thach, Frank AR 3rd Inf. Co.H Capt.
Thach, W.T. AL 35th Inf. Co.D 1st Lt.
Thacher, Benjamin TN 8th Inf. Co.G
Thacher, Moses 1st Choctaw & Chickasaw Mtd.Rifles 2nd Co.D
Thacher, Thomas MO 1st N.E. Cav. Co.H
Thack, James N. NC 68th Inf.
Thackara, Serrano Eng.,CSA 2nd Lt.
Thacken, T. TX 25th Cav.
Thacker, --- AR Lt.Arty. Key's Btty.
Thacker, A. KY 2nd (Duke's) Cav. Co.B
Thacker, A. KY 5th Cav. Co.F
Thacker, Alexander VA Lt.Arty. Montgomery's Co.
Thacker, Alex. L. VA 22nd Inf. Co.A
Thacker, Alfred F. KY 2nd Cav. Co.B Sgt.
Thacker, And J. VA Lt.Arty. Woolfolk's Co.
Thacker, Andw. J. GA 64th Inf. Co.K
Thacker, Andrew J. VA Lt.Arty. Nelson's Co.
Thacker, Benjamin S. VA Lt.Arty. Montgomery's Co.
Thacker, Bernard M. LA 10th Inf. Co.F
Thacker, Cargal VA Hvy.Arty. Coleman's Co.
Thacker, Carodin VA Hvy.Arty. Wilkinson's Co.
Thacker, Chesley E. NC 45th Inf. Co.A
Thacker, Corridon VA Hvy.Arty. 10th Bn. Co.C
Thacker, Corydon VA 20th Inf. Co.D
Thacker, Daniel VA 46th Inf. 2nd Co.I
Thacker, Daniel M. GA 20th Inf. Co.D
Thacker, Dillard SC 12th Inf. Co.G,K
Thacker, Dilley VA 34th Inf. Co.C
Thacker, D.L. GA 24th Inf. Co.A
Thacker, E. VA 88th Mil.
Thacker, E.A. NC 7th Sr.Res. Williams' Co.
Thacker, Edmond J. KY 5th Cav. Co.F
Thacker, Edward VA 47th Inf. 2nd Co.K
Thacker, Edwin W. VA 19th Inf. Co.G 1st Sgt.
Thacker, Elias VA 46th Inf. 2nd Co.I Sgt.
Thacker, Elias A. VA Lt.Arty. 12th Bn. 2nd Co.A
Thacker, Elias A. VA Lt.Arty. Sturdivant's Co.
Thacker, Elijah VA 47th Inf. 2nd Co.K
Thacker, E. Newton TN 24th Inf. 2nd Co.G
Thacker, E.T. GA Inf. (High Shoals Defend.) Medlin's Ind.Co. Cpl.
Thacker, Evan GA 3rd Cav. Co.B,K Cpl.
Thacker, Ezekiel D. GA Cobb's Legion Co.A
Thacker, F.L. VA 19th Inf. Co.K
Thacker, F.M. AL 7th Cav. Co.K
Thacker, F.M. AL 6th Inf. Co.G
Thacker, F.M. VA 3rd Res. Co.H
Thacker, Francis M. TN 1st (Turney's) Inf. Co.A
Thacker, George KY 10th (Diamond's) Cav. Co.C
Thacker, George VA Inf. 1st Bn.Loc.Def. Co.D
Thacker, George W. AL 38th Inf. Co.L
Thacker, George W. KY 5th Mtd.Inf. Co.G
Thacker, George W. VA Lt.Arty. Rives' Co. Cpl.
Thacker, Granville VA 56th Inf. Co.K
Thacker, Green M. VA 1st Cav. Co.E
Thacker, Greenville KY 10th (Diamond's) Cav. Co.C
Thacker, G.T. GA Inf. (Wright Loc.Guards) Holmes' Co.
Thacker, G.W. TN 38th Inf. Co.L
Thacker, H.A. AL 48th Inf. Co.C
Thacker, Hiram NC 21st Inf. Co.L
Thacker, Hiram TN 61st Mtd.Inf. Co.H Cpl.
Thacker, H.L. VA 15th Cav. Co.B
Thacker, Hugh T. VA Lt.Arty. Montgomery's Co. Cpl.
Thacker, Isaac GA 21st Inf. New Co.E
Thacker, Isaac NC 5th Cav. (63rd St.Troops) Co.D
Thacker, Isaac NC Inf. 2nd Bn. Co.D
Thacker, Isaac G. NC 45th Inf. Co.H
Thacker, J. GA 1st Cav. Co.D
Thacker, J. MS Blythe's Bn. (St.Troops) Co.A
Thacker, J.A. MS Cav. Hughes' Bn. Co.F
Thacker, Jacob S. VA 62nd Mtd.Inf. 2nd Co.H
Thacker, James GA 12th Cav. Co.D
Thacker, James GA 21st Inf. New Co.E
Thacker, James NC Inf. 2nd Bn. Co.D
Thacker, James SC 22nd Inf. Co.D
Thacker, James TN 47th Inf. Co.F
Thacker, James VA 2nd Inf. Co.E
Thacker, James VA 146th Mil. Co.F
Thacker, James A. GA 12th Inf. Co.K 1st Sgt.
Thacker, James A. VA 46th Inf. 2nd Co.I Sgt.
Thacker, James H. KY 5th Cav. Co.F
Thacker, James M. AL 32nd Inf. Co.I
Thacker, James M. VA 15th Inf. Co.E
Thacker, James R. GA 3rd Bn.S.S. Co.E
Thacker, J.B. NC 38th Inf. Co.B
Thacker, J.C. TN 49th Inf. Co.F
Thacker, J.C. Inf. Bailey's Cons.Regt. Co.C
Thacker, Jeremiah VA 41st Inf. Co.B
Thacker, Jesse VA 2nd Inf.Loc.Def. Co.E
Thacker, Jesse VA Inf. 6th Bn.Loc.Def. Co.B
Thacker, J.H. KY 2nd Cav. Co.C
Thacker, J.H. KY 2nd (Duke's) Cav. Co.B
Thacker, J.H. VA Lt.Arty. Lamkin's Co. 2nd Lt.
Thacker, J.J. GA 24th Inf. Co.D
Thacker, J.J. SC Cav. 2nd Bn.Res. Co.H
Thacker, J.M. TN 15th (Cons.) Cav. Co.A
Thacker, J.M. TN 15th (Stewart's) Cav. Co.B
Thacker, J.M. VA 2nd Inf.Loc.Def. Co.F
Thacker, John TN 39th Mtd.Inf. Co.G
Thacker, John TN 61st Mtd.Inf. Co.H
Thacker, John A. TN 37th Inf. Co.B Cpl.
Thacker, John H. NC 22nd Inf. Co.E
Thacker, John J. VA Lt.Arty. Lamkin's Co.
Thacker, John M. VA Inf. 6th Bn.Loc.Def. Co.C
Thacker, Johnson H. VA 3rd Res. Co.H Capt.
Thacker, Joseph KY 5th Mtd.Inf. Co.G,B
Thacker, Joseph VA Lt.Arty. Fry's Co.
Thacker, Joseph G. VA Lt.Arty. Woolfolk's Co.

Thacker, Joseph S. TN 1st (Turney's) Inf. Co.A
Thacker, J.P. SC 22nd Inf. Co.D
Thacker, J.R. AL 7th Cav. Co.K
Thacker, J.R. GA 18th Inf. Co.A
Thacker, J.S. VA 62nd Mtd.Inf. Co.H
Thacker, L. TN 38th Inf. Co.L
Thacker, Lafayette W. VA 19th Inf. Co.G Sgt.
Thacker, Larkin GA 36th (Broyles') Inf. Co.E
Thacker, Lavender NC 38th Inf. Co.B
Thacker, Levi TN 22nd Inf. Looney's Co.
Thacker, Lewis VA 46th Inf. 2nd Co.I
Thacker, Madison NC 45th Inf. Co.E
Thacker, Madison VA 64th Mtd.Inf. Co.D
Thacker, Madison VA Mil. Scott Cty.
Thacker, Michael TN 29th Inf. Co.K Cpl.
Thacker, M.J. TN 28th (Cons.) Inf. Co.F
Thacker, Nathan AR 1st (Colquitt's) Inf. Co.F
Thacker, Nathan AR 10th Inf. Co.F,C
Thacker, Nathan W. GA 64th Inf. Co.K
Thacker, N.W. VA 19th Inf. Co.G
Thacker, Oscar J. NC 13th Inf. Co.K
Thacker, Peter TN 61st Mtd.Inf. Co.H
Thacker, Philip VA 15th Inf. Co.I
Thacker, Philip VA 56th Inf. Co.K
Thacker, R. MS 18th Cav. Co.E
Thacker, Reuben KY 13th Cav. Co.A
Thacker, Robert TN 29th Inf. Co.K
Thacker, Robert VA 64th Mtd.Inf. Co.D
Thacker, Samuel VA 13th Inf. Co.K
Thacker, S.D. VA 15th Cav. Co.B
Thacker, Silas J. VA Lt.Arty. Montgomery's Co.
Thacker, Solomon GA 12th Cav. Co.D
Thacker, S.W. VA 3rd Res. Co.H 1st Sgt.
Thacker, Thomas KY 10th (Diamond's) Cav. Co.C
Thacker, W.A. VA Lt.Arty. Lamkin's Co.
Thacker, William GA 12th Cav. Co.D
Thacker, William VA Hvy.Arty. 10th Bn. Co.A
Thacker, William VA Lt.Arty. Carrington's Co.
Thacker, William VA Lt.Arty. Fry's Co.
Thacker, William VA 23rd Inf. Co.A
Thacker, William VA 64th Mtd.Inf. Co.I
Thacker, William VA 94th Mil. Co.A
Thacker, William VA 2nd St.Res. Co.B
Thacker, William A. VA Lt.Arty. Kirkpatrick's Co.
Thacker, William C. VA 47th Mil. 2nd Lt.
Thacker, William H. GA Inf. (High Shoals Defend.) Medlin's Ind.Co.
Thacker, William H. VA 15th Cav. Co.B
Thacker, William H. VA Lt.Arty. Montgomery's Co.
Thacker, William H. VA Lt.Arty. Nelson's Co.
Thacker, William H. VA Lt.Arty. Woolfolk's Co.
Thacker, William H. VA 74th Mil. Co.C
Thacker, William L. MS 26th Inf. Co.I
Thacker, William M. VA Lt.Arty. Carrington's Co.
Thacker, William S. VA 52nd Inf. Co.G
Thacker, William W. TX 16th Cav. Co.I Cpl.
Thacker, W.J. VA 13th Cav. Co.E
Thacker, W.L. AL 62nd Inf. Co.F
Thacker, W.W. AL 53rd (Part.Rangers) Co.E
Thacker, W.W. GA 64th Inf. Co.K
Thacker, W.W. MS 39th Inf. Co.B Sgt.
Thacker, W.W. VA 19th Inf. Co.G
Thacker, Wyatt N. VA Lt.Arty. Lamkin's Co. Bugler
Thacker, Wyatt N. VA 19th Inf. Co.G
Thackersen, G.W. MS 2nd Cav. Co.A
Thackersen, J.W. AL 30th Inf. Co.E
Thackerson, --- AL Randolph Cty.Res. B.C. Raney's Co.
Thackerson, J.S. AL 3rd Inf. Co.G
Thackerson, J.S. AL 31st Inf. Co.G
Thackerson, R.J. AL 58th Inf. Co.F
Thackerson, R.J. MS 31st Inf. Co.I
Thackerson, Robert J. AL 50th Inf. Co.H
Thackerson, Thomas AL Randolph Cty.Res. B.C. Raney's Co.
Thackerson, V.M. AL 5th Bn.Vol. Co.C Sgt.
Thackerson, W.W. AL 23rd Inf. Co.I
Thackett, James W. AR 2nd Cav. Co.H
Thackleford, Jno. T. Gen. & Staff, Medical Dept. Asst.Surg.
Thackson, A.E. MS 15th Inf. Co.K
Thackson, Charles D. GA 56th Inf. Co.D
Thackson, John SC 16th Inf. Co.C Cpl.
Thackston, Benjamin F. TN 7th Inf. Co.B
Thackston, B.H. VA 3rd Inf.Loc.Def. Co.D
Thackston, Blake B. TN 7th Inf. Co.B Sgt.
Thackston, C.G. SC Inf. Hampton Legion Co.F
Thackston, Christopher G. SC 16th Inf. Co.A Cpl.
Thackston, David B. MO Cav. 3rd Bn. Co.C
Thackston, D.B. VA 18th Inf. Co.F
Thackston, E.R. SC 3rd Inf. Co.G Cpl.
Thackston, F.T. VA Inf. 25th Bn. Co.C
Thackston, George W. MS 11th (Perrin's) Cav. Co.I
Thackston, George W. SC 16th Inf. Co.A
Thackston, G.W. SC 16th & 24th (Cons.) Inf. Co.E 2nd Lt.
Thackston, H.C. TX 10th Field Btty.
Thackston, H.S. SC 1st St.Troops Co.K
Thackston, James H. VA 23rd Inf. Co.I
Thackston, James H. VA Inf. 25th Bn. Co.C Sgt.
Thackston, James H. VA Inf. 25th Bn. Co.H
Thackston, James M. SC 16th Inf. Co.A
Thackston, J.E. VA 3rd Res. Co.D
Thackston, J.G. MS 15th (Cons.) Inf. Co.G
Thackston, J.H. GA 18th Inf. Co.M
Thackston, J.H. GA 28th Inf. Co.F
Thackston, J.M. GA 38th Inf. Co.I
Thackston, J.M. SC Inf. Hampton Legion Co.F
Thackston, Joel E. VA 18th Inf. Co.B
Thackston, John H. MO Cav. 3rd Bn. Co.C
Thackston, J.S. SC 16th Inf. Co.I
Thackston, Nathaniel VA 3rd Cav. Co.K
Thackston, Nathaniel VA 20th Inf. Co.G
Thackston, Newport C. GA 36th (Broyles') Inf. Co.E
Thackston, Richard D. VA 18th Inf. Co.D,F
Thackston, Robert VA Inf. 1st Bn.Loc.Def. Co.F Sgt.
Thackston, R.Y. GA Cav. 9th Bn. (St.Guards) Co.E
Thackston, S.R. SC 3rd Inf. Co.G,D Cpl.
Thackston, Thomas M. SC Inf. Hampton Legion Co.F
Thackston, T.J. SC 16th Inf. Co.F
Thackston, T.M. SC 16th Inf. Co.I
Thackston, W.B. GA 18th Inf. Co.M
Thackston, William B. GA 28th Inf. Co.F
Thackston, William D. VA 44th Inf. Co.G
Thackston, William P. SC Inf. Hampton Legion Co.F
Thackston, William S. SC 16th Inf. Co.I 1st Lt.
Thackston, William S. SC Inf. Hampton Legion Co.F
Thackston, W.W.H. VA 3rd Res. Co.D
Thackston, Z. SC 3rd Inf. Co.I
Thackston, Zadock SC 3rd Inf. Co.I
Thadeaux, James AL 39th Inf. Co.G
Thadford, George VA Inf. 4th Bn.Loc.Def. Co.F
Thadford, G.W.B. TN 49th Inf. Co.D
Thagard, A.J. AL 17th Inf. Co.C
Thagard, Alexander NC 44th Inf. Co.E Cpl.
Thagard, G.W. AL 3rd Bn.Res. Jackson's Co. 1st Lt.
Thagard, John MS 1st Cav.Res. Co.B Sgt.
Thagard, Joseph NC 44th Inf. Co.E
Thagard, Thomas AL 12th Inf. Co.A
Thagard, W.R. AL 17th Inf. Co.C
Thagart, William C. NC 46th Inf. Co.H
Thaggard, Amos J. NC 3rd Arty. (40th St.Troops) Co.K
Thaggard, Isaac NC 2nd Arty. (36th St.Troops) Co.C
Thaggard, James L. MS 9th Cav. Co.G 1st Sgt.
Thaggard, J.B. NC 2nd Arty. (36th St.Troops) Co.C
Thaggard, J.C. NC 2nd Arty. (36th St.Troops) Co.B
Thaggard, John B. GA 12th Inf. Co.K
Thaggard, Joseph G. NC 2nd Arty. (36th St.Troops) Co.I Cpl.
Thaggard, Neill C. NC 24th Inf. Co.F Sgt.
Thaggard, Stephen L. NC 24th Inf. Co.F
Thaggard, Warren R. 1st Conf.Inf. 2nd Co.H
Thaggard, William M. GA 63rd Inf. Co.E
Thaggard, W.M.D. NC 5th Inf. Co.A
Thain, Alexander NC 5th Inf. Co.C Music.
Thain, Henry E. NC 1st Arty. (10th St.Troops) Co.A
Thain, T. AL 4th Inf. Co.H Cpl.
Thaines, W.E. MS 1st Cav.Res. Co.D
Thaipe, Joseph MO 1st Inf. Co.H
Thairhill, Jasper O. LA 22nd Inf. Co.D
Thairson, Thomas KY 1st Inf.
Thalaker, Henry VA 25th Inf. 1st Co.K
Thaler, John AR 20th Inf. Co.C
Thales, J.W. GA 32nd Inf. Co.H
Thalheimer, David TX 2nd Cav. Co.G
Thalheimer, G. VA 3rd Inf.Loc.Def. Co.K
Thalheimer, P. LA Inf. 9th Bn. Co.B 2nd Lt.
Thall, C.W. LA 16th Inf. Co.D
Thally, David J. NC 2nd Arty. (36th St.Troops) Co.G
Thally, D.M.D. GA 10th Inf. Co.E
Thalozan, E. LA Arty. 1st Field Btty.
Thamas, Benjamin F. GA Cav. 16th Bn. (St.Guards) Co.C Cpl.
Thames, A.B. LA 3rd (Wingfield's) Cav. Co.D
Thames, Albert GA 2nd Res. Co.C
Thames, Alexander NC 2nd Arty. (36th St.Troops) Co.C

Thames, Alfred W. SC Cav.Bn. Holcombe Legion Co.E Sgt.
Thames, Andrew SC 5th Bn.Res. Co.F
Thames, A.S. NC 23rd Inf. Co.I
Thames, A.W. SC 7th Cav. Co.H Sgt.
Thames, Calvin AL 5th Inf. New Co.G
Thames, C.C. SC 4th Cav. Co.I
Thames, C.C. SC Cav. 12th Bn. Co.B
Thames, Christian TX 4th Cav. Co.B
Thames, Cornelius AL 38th Inf. Co.E,A Sgt.
Thames, C.P. MS 1st (King's) Inf. (St.Troops) Co.I Sgt.
Thames, C.P. 14th Conf.Cav. Co.K
Thames, D. NC 14th Inf. Co.D
Thames, F. AL 4th Res. Co.F
Thames, F.W. SC 11th Inf. Co.D
Thames, G.W. GA Cav. 8th Bn. (St.Guards) Co.B Sgt.
Thames, Hugh 14th Conf.Cav. Co.K
Thames, J. TX Cav. Terry's Regt. Co.C
Thames, James AL 42nd Inf. Co.A
Thames, James GA 7th Inf. (St.Guards) Co.F
Thames, James MS 13th Inf. Co.D
Thames, James W. AL 30th Inf. Co.D
Thames, J.B. AL 4th Res. Co.D
Thames, J.E. AL 18th Inf. Co.E
Thames, J.E. SC Mil. 1st Regt. (Charleston Res.) Co.D
Thames, J.J. AL 62nd Inf. Co.E
Thames, J.L. MS 12th Cav. Co.L
Thames, J.L. MS Inf. 1st Bn.St.Troops (12 mo. '62-3) Co.E
Thames, J.M. GA Cav. 8th Bn. (St.Guards) Co.B
Thames, John AL 14th Cav.
Thames, John AL 11th Inf. Co.K
Thames, John AL 17th Inf. Co.H
Thames, John AL 41st Inf. Co.E 2nd Lt.
Thames, John MS 5th Inf. Co.I
Thames, John F. AL 30th Inf. Co.D
Thames, John J. AL 6th Inf. Co.B
Thames, John J. AL 33rd Inf. Co.G
Thames, John S. SC 5th Cav. Co.H
Thames, Joseph MS 38th Cav. Co.F
Thames, Joseph NC 18th Inf. Co.E Comsy.Sgt.
Thames, J.P. SC 9th Inf. Co.D
Thames, J.P. SC Palmetto S.S. Co.E
Thames, J.R. SC 4th Cav. Co.D
Thames, J.R. TX 7th Cav. Co.E Sgt.
Thames, J.S. MS 39th Inf. Co.F
Thames, J.S. SC 6th Inf. 2nd Co.K
Thames, J.S. SC 9th Inf. Co.D
Thames, J.T. GA 2nd Cav. Co.F
Thames, J.W. MS 13th Inf. Co.D
Thames, J.W. SC 23rd Inf. Co.I Cpl.
Thames, N.C. AL 17th Inf. Co.H
Thames, N.J. AL 36th Inf. Co.F
Thames, R. 14th Conf.Cav. Co.K
Thames, R.D. SC Rutledge Mtd.Riflemen & Horse Arty. Trenholm's Co.
Thames, R.H. MS 39th Inf. Co.A
Thames, Richard MS 39th Inf. Co.F
Thames, Richard D. SC 5th Cav. Co.H
Thames, R.J. SC 4th Cav. Co.D
Thames, R.J., Jr. SC 23rd Inf. Co.I
Thames, R.J., Sr. SC 23rd Inf. Co.I
Thames, R.M. KY 4th Cav. Co.D
Thames, Robert MS Inf. 1st Bn.St.Troops (30 days '64) Co.B
Thames, R.R. MS 12th Cav. Co.L Cpl.
Thames, R.R. SC 4th Cav. Co.D
Thames, Rufus M., Jr. SC Inf. Hampton Legion Co.C
Thames, S. GA 2nd Res.
Thames, S.A. MS 39th Inf. Co.A
Thames, Samuel AL 32nd Inf. Co.K
Thames, Samuel M. AL 30th Inf. Co.D 2nd Lt.
Thames, S.J. SC 4th Cav. Co.D
Thames, S.J. SC 23rd Inf. Co.I
Thames, S.J. SC Manigault's Bn.Vol. Co.A
Thames, Stephen AL 33rd Inf. Co.A
Thames, S.W. AL 38th Inf. Co.E
Thames, T.D. LA 3rd (Wingfield's) Cav. Co.F
Thames, Thomas MS Cav. Stockdale's Bn. Co.A,B
Thames, Thomas A. AL 30th Inf. Co.D Cpl.
Thames, Thomas J. GA 57th Inf. Co.F
Thames, Thomas J.C. AL 57th Inf. Co.K
Thames, Thomas L. SC Inf. Hampton Legion Co.C
Thames, T.M. MS Cav. 1st Bn. (McNair's) St.Troops Co.A
Thames, T.M. MS 39th Inf. Co.A
Thames, T.M. MS Home Guards Barnes' Co.
Thames, T.T. MS 2nd Cav. Co.B
Thames, T.T., Jr. MS 3rd (St.Troops) Cav. Co.B
Thames, T.T., Sr. MS 3rd (St.Troops) Cav. Co.B
Thames, T.W. SC 23rd Inf. Co.I
Thames, W.C. FL 1st (Res.) Inf. Co.G
Thames, W.E. SC 5th Bn.Res. Co.F
Thames, Wm. AL 22nd Inf. Co.K
Thames, William MS 3rd (St.Troops) Cav. Co.B Capt.
Thames, William MS St.Cav. Perrin's Bn. Co.E
Thames, William MS Inf. 1st Bn.St.Troops (12 mo. '62-3) Co.E
Thames, William MS 27th Inf. Co.F
Thames, William G. AL 33rd Inf. Co.C Sgt.
Thames, William H. MS 39th Inf. Co.A
Thames, William R. GA 57th Inf. Co.F 2nd Lt.
Thames, William T. TX 10th Inf. Co.A
Thames, W.J.B. SC 23rd Inf. Co.I
Thames, W.M. MS Cav. 24th Bn. Co.F
Thames, W.N. MS 1st (King's) Inf. (St.Troops) Co.B
Thames, W.S. SC 9th Inf. Co.D
Thames, W.S. SC Palmetto S.S. Co.E
Thames, W.W. MS 6th Inf. Co.H
Thames, W.W. 14th Conf.Cav. Co.K
Thamm, Arthur TX 1st (McCulloch's) Cav. Co.E
Thamm, Arthur TX 36th Cav. Co.H
Thand, W. MS Cav. Powers' Regt. Co.C
Thands, A.C. TN 2nd (Robison's) Inf. Co.D
Thane, Alexander TN 32nd Inf. Co.E
Thanhousen, G. AL 23rd Inf. Co.A
Thannisch, George W.H. MO 15th Cav. Co.A
Thannisch, William MO 15th Cav. Co.A Lt.
Tharel, William E. NC 43rd Inf. Co.B
Tharian, Xavier LA 20th Inf. New Co.B
Tharin, Alexander W. SC Lt.Arty. Walter's Co. (Washington Arty.)
Tharin, A.W. SC Mil. Arty. 1st Regt. Walter's Co.
Tharin, Daniel C., Jr. AL 6th Inf. Co.M 1st Sgt.
Tharin, E. SC Mil. Charbonnier's Co.
Tharin, E.B. SC 25th Inf. Co.B
Tharin, E.C. SC 1st Regt. Charleston Guard Co.H
Tharin, E.C. SC Mil. 1st Regt. (Charleston Res.) Co.B Cpl.
Tharin, John SC Cav. 17th Bn. Co.A
Tharin, John M. SC 5th Cav. Co.D
Tharin, Manly R. SC 1st (McCreary's) Inf. Co.L 2nd Lt.
Tharin, Theo. C. SC Mil. 1st Regt. (Charleston Res.) Co.G 2nd Lt.
Tharington, A.J. MS Inf. 1st Bn.St.Troops (30 days '64) Co.E
Tharington, A.J. MS 5th Inf. (St.Troops) Co.A
Tharington, David NC 1st Jr.Res. Co.A
Tharington, Pugh H. NC 47th Inf. Co.F
Tharington, T.M. NC 8th Bn.Part.Rangers Co.B
Tharington, T.M. NC 66th Inf. Co.C
Tharington, W.G. GA 31st Inf. Co.C
Tharington, W.H. NC 47th Inf. Co.G
Tharington, W.W. NC 12th Inf. Co.B,D
Tharke to pah 1st Seminole Mtd.Vol.
Tharp, --- SC 27th Inf. Co.I
Tharp, --- TX Cav. Mann's Regt. Co.F
Tharp, --- TX Cav. Mann's Regt. Co.K
Tharp, A. LA 13th Bn. (Part.Rangers) Co.B
Tharp, A. Gen. & Staff A.Surg.
Tharp, Adam VA 18th Cav. Co.I
Tharp, Adam VA 14th Mil. Co.E
Tharp, Adam VA 62nd Mtd.Inf. 1st Co.D
Tharp, A.J. TN 20th Cav. 2nd Lt.
Tharp, Albert GA Lt.Arty. 14th Bn. Co.A Cpl.
Tharp, Albert A. GA 1st (Ramsey's) Inf. Co.C
Tharp, Albert H. GA Lt.Arty. Havis' Btty. Cpl.
Tharp, Alexander GA Phillips' Legion Co.E
Tharp, Allen KY 7th Mtd.Inf. Co.K
Tharp, Allen NC 64th Inf. Co.D
Tharp, Allen R. GA Cav. 29th Bn. Co.F
Tharp, Alonzo J.A. GA Inf. 1st Conf.Bn. Co.D
Tharp, A.M. GA 6th Inf. Co.C
Tharp, Andrew J. TN Cav. 2nd Bn. (Biffle's) Co.B
Tharp, Andrew J. TN 6th (Wheeler's) Cav. Co.G Sgt.
Tharp, Augustus LA 5th Cav. Co.B
Tharp, A.W. LA Maddox's Regt.Res.Corps Co.B
Tharp, Ballard S. TN 54th Inf. Co.A
Tharp, Benjamin VA 64th Mtd.Inf. Co.K
Tharp, Benjamin F. VA Lt.Arty. Arch. Graham's Co.
Tharp, B.S. TN 48th (Nixon's) Inf. Co.F Cpl.
Tharp, Burden A. AL 38th Inf. Co.D
Tharp, C. AR 9th Inf. Co.K
Tharp, C.A. AL 45th Inf. Co.A
Tharp, Calvin AR Cav. Wright's Regt. Co.H
Tharp, Calvin AR 9th Inf. Co.K
Tharp, Calvin MS 1st Lt.Arty. Co.C
Tharp, Campbell VA 94th Mil. Co.A
Tharp, Cary M. TN Cav. 9th Bn. (Gantt's) Co.F
Tharp, C.J. TN Cav. 11th Bn. (Gordon's) Co.A
Tharp, C.P. MS 8th Cav. Co.H
Tharp, C.P. MS 28th Cav. Co.L
Tharp, Daniel LA Watkins' Bn.Res.Corps Co.C
Tharp, Daniel B. MS 31st Inf. Co.B Cpl.

Tharp, David NC 5th Sr.Res. Co.K
Tharp, David NC 26th Inf. Co.C
Tharp, David C. TN Cav. 9th Bn. (Gantt's) Co.D,F
Tharp, D.V. LA Inf. 1st Sp.Bn. (Rightor's) Co.D
Tharp, E. MO St.Guard
Tharp, Eli E. Conf.Cav. Wood's Regt. Co.E,L
Tharp, Elijah VA 34th Mil. Co.B
Tharp, E.M. GA 5th Inf. (St.Guards) Miller's Co. 1st Lt.
Tharp, E.M. GA 46th Inf. Co.C
Tharp, F. KY 7th Cav. Co.K
Tharp, F. KY 7th Mtd.Inf. Co.K
Tharp, F.A. GA 8th Cav. Co.A Ch.Bugler
Tharp, Francis A. GA 62nd Cav. Co.A Music.
Tharp, G. KY 7th Mtd.Inf. Co.K
Tharp, G.A. TX Cav. Baird's Regt. Co.E
Tharp, George MO 7th Cav. Co.F
Tharp, George VA Cav. 41st Bn. 2nd Co.H
Tharp, George A. KY 4th Cav. Co.E
Tharp, George N. MS 43rd Inf. Co.B
Tharp, George W. GA 4th Res. Co.B
Tharp, G.P. MO Cav. 3rd Regt.St.Guard Co.C
Tharp, Harmon FL Conscr.
Tharp, Henry GA 3rd Res. Co.D
Tharp, Henry TN 2nd (Smith's) Cav. Rankins' Co.
Tharp, Henry TN 4th (McLemore's) Cav. Co.H Cpl.
Tharp, Henry B. MS 11th Inf. Co.E 1st Sgt.
Tharp, Idomeius NC 2nd Arty. (36th St.Troops) Co.K
Tharp, Ira TX 19th Cav. Co.B Sgt.
Tharp, Isaac A. GA 13th Inf. Co.K
Tharp, J. KY 4th Cav. Co.F
Tharp, J. VA 62nd Mtd.Inf. 1st Co.D
Tharp, J.A. LA 19th Inf. Co.I 1st Sgt.
Tharp, J.A. SC 4th Bn.Res. Co.B
Tharp, Jackson VA 14th Mil. Co.E Sgt.
Tharp, James AR 9th Inf. Co.K
Tharp, James AR 21st Inf. Co.F
Tharp, James MO 1st Cav. Co.D
Tharp, James NC 2nd Arty. (36th St.Troops) Co.G Cpl.
Tharp, James VA 18th Cav. Co.H
Tharp, James VA 14th Mil. Co.E
Tharp, James VA 62nd Mtd.Inf. 1st Co.D
Tharp, James A. VA 18th Inf. Co.K
Tharp, James C. AL 4th (Russell's) Cav. Co.D
Tharp, James D. GA 1st (Ramsey's) Inf. Co.C
Tharp, James H. NC 54th Inf. Co.F
Tharp, J.B. MS 17th Inf. Co.G
Tharp, J.B. TN Cav. 9th Bn. (Gantt's) Co.D
Tharp, J.C. TN 13th Inf. Co.B
Tharp, J.D. GA 12th (Robinson's) Cav. (St.Guards) Co.D
Tharp, Jesse KY 4th Cav. Co.I
Tharp, Jesse VA 64th Mtd.Inf. Co.G
Tharp, Jesse VA 94th Mil. Co.A
Tharp, J.G. SC 2nd St.Troops Co.I
Tharp, John AR 32nd Inf. Co.I 1st Lt.
Tharp, John KY 2nd (Duke's) Cav. Co.D
Tharp, John LA 27th Inf. Co.E
Tharp, John MO Cav. Jackman's Regt.
Tharp, John SC Cav. 12th Bn. Co.B
Tharp, John TX 10th Inf. Co.B
Tharp, John VA 18th Cav. Co.B Cpl.
Tharp, John VA 33rd Inf. Co.F
Tharp, John VA 114th Mil. Co.B
Tharp, John A. AL 39th Inf. Co.H
Tharp, John A. FL Cav. 5th Bn. Co.B
Tharp, John A. GA Inf. 10th Bn. Co.D
Tharp, John A. GA 35th Inf. Co.D 1st Sgt.
Tharp, John A. TX Cav. Baird's Regt. Co.E
Tharp, John B. TX 21st Cav. Co.H
Tharp, John H. MS 33rd Inf. Co.G
Tharp, John I. GA Cav. 29th Bn. Co.F
Tharp, John L. NC 30th Inf. Co.C
Tharp, John L. TN 5th (McKenzie's) Cav. Co.G
Tharp, John P. AL Inf. 1st Regt. Co.K
Tharp, John S. VA 34th Mil. Co.B
Tharp, John T. MS 43rd Inf. Co.B
Tharp, John T. VA 7th Cav. Co.E
Tharp, John Willet KY 2nd (Duke's) Cav. Co.D
Tharp, Jonathan VA 14th Mil. Co.A
Tharp, Jonathan VA 18th Cav. Co.I
Tharp, Joseph KY 7th Mtd.Inf. Co.K
Tharp, Joshua D.A. GA 41st Inf. Co.E
Tharp, Jourdan KY 4th Cav. Co.I
Tharp, J.T. AR 9th Inf. Co.K
Tharp, J.T. MS 14th (Cons.) Inf. Co.H
Tharp, J.W. KY 8th Mtd.Inf. Co.A
Tharp, J.W. MS 46th Inf. Co.C
Tharp, Leander NC 4th Inf. Co.H
Tharp, Lemuel AL 11th Inf. Co.B
Tharp, Lemuel W. TN 54th Inf. Co.A
Tharp, Levi VA 60th Inf. Co.C
Tharp, Lewis TN 35th Inf. Co.L Sgt.
Tharp, L.W. TN 48th (Nixon's) Inf. Co.F
Tharp, M. MO St.Guard
Tharp, Marcellas A. GA 4th Inf. Co.C Sgt.
Tharp, Marshall KY 4th Cav. Co.I
Tharp, Martin H. MS 1st Bn.S.S. Co.C
Tharp, Matthew GA 11th Inf. Co.K
Tharp, M.H. KY 7th Mtd.Inf. Co.K
Tharp, M.H. MS 7th Cav. Co.H
Tharp, M.J. TX 3rd (Kirby's) Bn.Vol. Co.A
Tharp, Mort GA Lt.Arty. 14th Bn. Co.A QMSgt.
Tharp, Moses AR Cav. 1st Bn. (Stirman's) Co.E Cpl.
Tharp, Peter NC 60th Inf. Co.F
Tharp, Peter NC 64th Inf. Co.G
Tharp, P.J. KY 4th Cav. Co.C
Tharp, P.P. AR 36th Inf. Co.E
Tharp, P.T. LA 27th Inf. Co.E
Tharp, R.G. TX 10th Cav. Co.A
Tharp, Riley N. MS 33rd Inf. Co.G
Tharp, Robert AL 16th Inf. Co.E
Tharp, Robert AR 21st Inf. Co.F
Tharp, Robert D.A. GA 41st Inf. Co.E
Tharp, Robert J.A. GA 56th Inf. Co.K 2nd Lt.
Tharp, R.Z. NC 42nd Inf. Co.B
Tharp, S. AL 15th Inf. Co.D
Tharp, S. 2nd Conf.Eng.Troops Co.C Artif.
Tharp, Samuel VA 18th Cav. Co.B
Tharp, Samuel VA 114th Mil. Co.B
Tharp, Samuel P. NC 30th Inf. Co.C 2nd Lt.
Tharp, Samuel P. NC Coast Guards Galloway's Co.
Tharp, S.B. AR 1st (Dobbin's) Cav.
Tharp, S.B. AR Inf. Cocke's Regt. Co.E Cpl.
Tharp, Simeon GA 4th Inf. Co.C 1st Lt.
Tharp, Simeon V. MS 31st Inf. Co.B
Tharp, S.J. SC 4th Cav. Co.I
Tharp, S.J. SC Cav. 12th Bn. Co.B
Tharp, S.J. SC Arty. Melchers' Co. (Co.B, German Arty.)
Tharp, Solomon AL 29th Inf. Co.K
Tharp, S.T. SC Cav. 19th Bn. Co.D
Tharp, T. KY Cav. 2nd Bn. (Dortch's) Co.C,D 1st Lt.
Tharp, T.A. TN 48th (Nixon's) Inf. Co.F
Tharp, T.G. VA 3rd Res. Co.A
Tharp, Thomas KY Cav. 2nd Bn. (Dortch's) Co.C 1st Lt.
Tharp, Thos. MO St.Guard
Tharp, Thomas A. TN 54th Inf. Co.A
Tharp, Thomas E. TN Cav. 11th Bn. (Gordon's) Co.B Cpl.
Tharp, Thomas G.A. TX Cav. Baird's Regt. Co.E 1st Lt.
Tharp, T.J. SC 5th Res. Co.B
Tharp, V.A. LA 1st (Nelligan's) Inf. Co.H
Tharp, V.D. GA Inf. City Bn. (Columbus) Williams' Co.
Tharp, W. SC Inf.Bn. Co.B
Tharp, W.A. TN 46th Inf. Co.E Capt.
Tharp, W.A. TX Cav. Baird's Regt. Co.E
Tharp, W.D. NC 4th Inf. Co.G
Tharp, W.D. NC 57th Inf. Co.G
Tharp, Wesley SC 10th Inf. Co.M
Tharp, William AL 39th Inf. Co.C
Tharp, William AR 1st Vol. Co.E
Tharp, William GA 25th Inf. Co.E
Tharp, William GA 28th Inf. Co.F
Tharp, William GA Inf. Arsenal Bn. (Columbus) Co.B
Tharp, William VA 33rd Inf. Co.C
Tharp, William VA 33rd Inf. Co.F
Tharp, William VA 64th Mtd.Inf. Co.K
Tharp, William VA 136th Mil. Co.C
Tharp, William VA 146th Mil. Co.K
Tharp, William D. TX 10th Inf. Co.B
Tharp, William H. NC 30th Inf. Co.C
Tharp, William J. AR 9th Inf. Co.F
Tharp, William J. AR 11th Inf. Co.I
Tharp, William J. KY 4th Cav. Co.I
Tharp, William S. VA 34th Inf. Co.B
Tharp, Wingate SC 10th Inf. Co.M
Tharp, W.L. TN 46th Inf. Co.F Cpl.
Tharp, W.P. TX 17th Inf. Co.G
Tharp, W.T. VA 46th Inf. 2nd Co.D
Tharp, Z. VA 26th Cav. Co.A
Tharp, Zachariah VA Cav. 46th Bn. Co.F
Tharp, Zachariah VA Inf. 9th Bn. Co.B
Tharp, Zachariah W. VA 25th Inf. 2nd Co.G
Tharp, Zeph KY 8th Cav. Co.G
Tharpe, Alexander C. GA 6th Inf. Co.I
Tharpe, Alonzo J.A. GA 30th Inf. Co.D
Tharpe, A.R. GA Cav. 19th Bn. Co.E
Tharpe, A.R. 10th Conf.Cav. Co.K
Tharpe, Benjamin AR 30th Inf. Co.E
Tharpe, Benjamin NC 4th Inf. Co.H
Tharpe, Benjamin A. GA 1st Bn.S.S. Co.A
Tharpe, Charnice GA 6th Inf. Co.I
Tharpe, Cicero A. GA 30th Inf. Maj.
Tharpe, George W. VA Lt.Arty. 12th Bn. 1st Co.A
Tharpe, George W. VA Lt.Arty. Utterback's Co.
Tharpe, Hanson H. NC 52nd Inf. Co.F

Tharpe, Henry AL 39th Inf. Co.C
Tharpe, Isaac T. NC 42nd Inf. Co.K
Tharpe, James S. MS 42nd Inf. Co.H
Tharpe, J.D. GA Cav. 22nd Bn. (St.Guards) Co.C
Tharpe, Jefferson GA 30th Inf. Co.D
Tharpe, Jesse W. MS 1st Lt.Arty. Co.I
Tharpe, J.G. GA Hvy.Arty. 22nd Bn. Co.B
Tharpe, J.J. TN 15th (Cons.) Cav. Co.K
Tharpe, John AL 39th Inf. Co.C
Tharpe, John M. NC Moseley's Co. (Sampson Arty.)
Tharpe, John P. NC 48th Inf. Co.C
Tharpe, John W.C.A. GA 30th Inf. Co.D
Tharpe, Joshua TN 15th (Cons.) Cav. Co.K
Tharpe, Joshua C. TN Lt.Arty. Palmer's Co.
Tharpe, J.P. AL 1st Cav. 1st Co.K
Tharpe, J.T. NC 42nd Inf. Co.E
Tharpe, Judson GA 6th Inf. Co.I
Tharpe, Judson GA 48th Inf. Co.G
Tharpe, J.W. NC 4th Inf. Co.H
Tharpe, J.W.C.A. GA 5th Res. Co.A
Tharpe, L.M. TN 20th (Russell's) Cav. Co.K Sgt.
Tharpe, Mortimer GA Lt.Arty. Havis' Btty. QMSgt.
Tharpe, Samuel FL 8th Inf. Co.E
Tharpe, Simeon GA 6th Inf. Co.I Sgt.
Tharpe, T. GA Arty. St.Troops Pruden's Btty.
Tharpe, V.W. GA Cav. 22nd Bn. (St.Guards) Co.A Sgt.
Tharpe, William FL 6th Inf. Co.C
Tharpe, William GA 27th Inf. Co.B
Tharpe, William GA 66th Inf. Co.D
Tharpe, William C. MS 2nd Part.Rangers Co.D,F
Tharpley, C.S. GA Hvy.Arty. 22nd Bn.
Tharran, H. GA 53rd Inf. Co.H
Tharranton, William H. NC 15th Inf. Co.G
Tharrington, Alexander NC 8th Inf. Co.F
Tharrington, A.P. NC 8th Inf. Co.D 1st Sgt.
Tharrington, Herbert NC 47th Inf. Co.G
Tharrington, Madison L. NC 15th Inf. Co.E
Tharrington, M.L. NC 8th Inf. Co.D
Tharrington, Presley NC 15th Inf. Co.E
Tharrington, Robert NC 47th Inf. Co.G
Tharrington, Sylvester NC 15th Inf. Co.E
Tharrington, Willis NC 15th Inf. Co.E
Thart, Zachariah W. VA 19th Cav. Co.K
Thartert, James GA 21st Inf. Co.F
Tharthlo Harjo 1st Seminole Mtd.Vol.
Thary, J.R. NC 5th Cav. (63rd St.Troops) Co.F
Thasher, G.W. AL Gid Nelson Lt.Arty.
Thasher, R. AL 26th Inf. Co.F
Thatch, Andrew J. GA 36th (Broyles') Inf. Co.G
Thatch, David MS 9th Cav. Co.G
Thatch, David MS 9th Inf. Co.G
Thatch, David MS 37th Inf. Co.K
Thatch, George W. AL Lt.Arty. Clanton's Btty.
Thatch, Henry C. NC 11th (Bethel Regt.) Inf. Co.F
Thatch, Jesse TN 35th Inf. Co.L
Thatch, John TN 63rd Inf. Co.H
Thatch, John H. TN 5th (McKenzie's) Cav. Co.C
Thatch, Joseph TN 35th Inf. Co.L
Thatch, Robert H. AL 9th Inf. Co.H,F
Thatch, Samuel H. 3rd Conf.Eng.Troops Co.C
Thatch, S.H. TN 13th Inf. Co.G
Thatch, S.H. TN 26th Inf. Co.G
Thatch, S.H. 1st Conf.Inf. 2nd Co.K
Thatch, Stephen NC 11th (Bethel Regt.) Inf. Co.C
Thatch, Stephen TN 14th Inf. Co.L
Thatch, William TN 35th Inf. Co.L
Thatchcock, J. AR Cav. Gunter's Bn. Co.F 2nd Lt.
Thatcher, Brannon VA 31st Mil. Co.C
Thatcher, Charles MO 1st Cav. Co.D
Thatcher, Charles MO 1st & 3rd Cons.Cav.
Thatcher, David M. VA 1st Cav. Co.B
Thatcher, Evan VA 31st Mil. Co.C
Thatcher, Even H. Gen. & Staff, Comsy.Dept. Comsy. of Subs.
Thatcher, George E. LA 2nd Inf. Co.D
Thatcher, George E. Gen. & Staff, Arty. Capt.
Thatcher, J. AL 50th Inf.
Thatcher, John TN 12th (Green's) Cav. Co.K
Thatcher, John TN 40th Inf. Co.I
Thatcher, John TX Nolan's Mtd.Co. (Loc.Def.) 3rd Lt.
Thatcher, John W. TX 35th (Brown's) Cav. Co.C
Thatcher, Luther T. KY 4th
Thatcher, N. 3rd Conf.Cav. Co.E
Thatcher, Samuel GA 11th Inf. Co.I Capt.
Thatcher, Samuel TN 12th (Green's) Cav. Co.K
Thatcher, Samuel TN 40th Inf. Co.I
Thatcher, Theo. AL 20th Inf. Co.G
Thatcher, Thomas TX Cav. Mann's Regt. Co.B
Thatcher, Thomas T. VA 2nd Inf. Co.I
Thatcher, William AR 45th Mil. Co.G
Thatcher, William Mtd.Spies & Guides Madison's Co.
Thatere, A.T. AL 5th Inf. Co.A Lt.
Thatford, George A. VA 6th Inf. Co.I
Thatford, John H. VA 6th Inf. Co.I
Thatjenhorst, Chs. SC 3rd Cav. Co.G
Thatjenhorst, Charles H. SC Mil.Cav. Theo. Cordes' Co.
Thatjenhorst, Charles H. SC Arty.Bn. Hampton Legion Co.A
Thatt, John C. AL 20th Inf. Co.D
Thau, Corth TX 32nd Cav.
Thauss, F.W. SC Mil. 16th Regt. Steinmeyer, Jr.'s Co.
Thauts, F.W. SC 1st Regt. Charleston Guard Co.F
Thavenell, John TX 1st Hvy.Arty. Co.E
Thavenell, Joseph TX Hvy.Arty. Sgt.
Thaw, William S. VA 1st St.Res. Co.F
Thaxton, A.E. MS 15th Inf. Co.K
Thaxton, A.L. GA Inf. 27th Bn. Co.F
Thaxton, A.L. VA 1st Bn.Res. Co.E
Thaxton, A.M. TX 8th Cav. Co.K
Thaxton, Anthony W. TN 28th Inf. Co.G
Thaxton, Banister GA Cherokee Legion (St.Guards) Co.H Sgt.
Thaxton, B.H. AL 46th Inf. Co.D
Thaxton, C.G. GA 2nd Cav. (St.Guards) Co.G Sgt.
Thaxton, Charles AL 47th Inf. Co.A,D
Thaxton, Charles D. GA Cherokee Legion (St.Guards) Co.H
Thaxton, David VA 9th Inf. Co.B
Thaxton, D.B. VA Inf. 25th Bn. Co.D
Thaxton, Ditron W. NC 24th Inf. Co.H
Thaxton, D.L. AL 17th Inf. Co.D 1st Lt.
Thaxton, F.K. TN 35th Inf. 2nd Co.D
Thaxton, Francis M. AL 49th Inf. Co.E
Thaxton, Frank M. TN 18th Inf. Co.E
Thaxton, George D. VA 1st Arty. Co.D Sgt.
Thaxton, George D. VA Lt.Arty. 1st Bn. Co.D Sgt.
Thaxton, George D. VA Arty. B.H. Smith's Co. Sgt.
Thaxton, G.W. AL 53rd (Part.Rangers) Co.C
Thaxton, Henry GA Tiller's Co. (Echols Lt.Arty.)
Thaxton, Henry TX 17th Inf. Co.G
Thaxton, Henry J.C. GA 14th Inf. Co.I 2nd Lt.
Thaxton, Henry S. NC 4th Cav. (59th St.Troops) Co.B 2nd Lt.
Thaxton, H.J. TN 16th Inf. Co.C
Thaxton, H.N. GA 6th Inf. Co.K
Thaxton, Jacob N. VA Hvy.Arty. 10th Bn. Co.B
Thaxton, James GA 1st Reg. Co.K
Thaxton, James GA 41st Inf. Co.I
Thaxton, James SC 3rd Res. Co.A
Thaxton, James TN 18th Inf. Co.E Cpl.
Thaxton, James VA Hvy.Arty. Wright's Co.
Thaxton, James F.D. GA 14th Inf. Co.I
Thaxton, James J. NC 24th Inf. Co.H
Thaxton, James L. MS 15th Inf. Co.G
Thaxton, James M. GA 14th Inf. Co.I
Thaxton, James M.C. GA 53rd Inf. Co.I Cpl.
Thaxton, J.E. GA 3rd Res. Co.G
Thaxton, J.H. GA 55th Inf. Co.B
Thaxton, J.M. GA 20th Inf. Co.E
Thaxton, John MS 28th Cav. Co.E
Thaxton, John MS Cav. Shelby's Co. (Bolivar Greys)
Thaxton, John MS 20th Inf. Co.A
Thaxton, John A. VA Hvy.Arty. 10th Bn. Co.B
Thaxton, John F. GA 53rd Inf. Co.I Hosp.Stew.
Thaxton, John J. VA 20th Inf. Co.K
Thaxton, John J. VA 59th Inf. 3rd Co.C
Thaxton, John M. NC 24th Inf. Co.H
Thaxton, John S. VA 23rd Inf. Co.I
Thaxton, Jordan J. NC 24th Inf. Co.H
Thaxton, J.S. SC 6th Cav. Co.A
Thaxton, J.T. GA 8th Inf. Co.K
Thaxton, J.W. TN 4th (Murray's) Cav. Co.G
Thaxton, J.W. TN Inf. 22nd Bn. Co.G
Thaxton, M. TX 28th Inf. Co.E
Thaxton, M.D.F. MS 10th Inf. New Co.G
Thaxton, Meredith TN 28th (Cons.) Inf. Co.D
Thaxton, N.G. MO Inf. 3rd Regt.St.Guard Co.F 2nd Lt.
Thaxton, Peter GA 3rd Inf. Co.G
Thaxton, R. VA Cav. 36th Bn. Co.A
Thaxton, Richmond R. GA 53rd Inf. Co.I
Thaxton, Robert B. VA Hvy.Arty. 10th Bn. Co.B
Thaxton, Robert C. VA 23rd Inf. Co.I
Thaxton, Robert L. VA 23rd Inf. Co.I,B
Thaxton, Robert Y. NC 24th Inf. Co.K
Thaxton, Samuel AL Res.
Thaxton, Samuel VA 3rd Res. Co.G
Thaxton, T.B. TX 7th Cav. Co.C
Thaxton, Thomas C. NC 6th Inf. Co.G Cpl.
Thaxton, Thomas J. GA 30th Inf. Co.H Cpl.
Thaxton, Thomas J. TX 16th Inf. Co.G
Thaxton, T.M. GA 14th Inf. Co.I

Thaxton, W. GA 2nd Cav. Co.E
Thaxton, W.C. GA 66th Inf. Co.H
Thaxton, W.H. GA 38th Inf. Co.B
Thaxton, W.H. MO 15th Cav. Co.A
Thaxton, Wiley W. GA 45th Inf. Co.I 1st Sgt.
Thaxton, William Gen. & Staff Capt.,Enrolling Off.
Thaxton, William C. VA Cav. 39th Bn. Co.B
Thaxton, William E. VA 14th Inf. Co.K
Thaxton, William R. GA 14th Inf. Co.I Cpl.
Thaxton, William T. NC 24th Inf. Co.H
Thaxton, William W. VA 2nd Cav. Co.F Cpl.
Thaxton, William W. VA Cav. 46th Bn. Co.E Sgt.
Thaxton, William Wesley GA 6th Inf. (St.Guards) Pittman's Co. Cpl.
Thaxton, W.J. LA Mil.Conf.Guards Rgt. Co.D
Thaxton, W.M. TN 11th (Holman's) Cav. Co.L
Thaxton, W.W. GA 3rd Res. Co.G
Thaxton, Yelventon, Jr. GA 14th Inf. Co.I
Thay, --- MO St.Guard Capt.
Thayer, --- TX 1st Hvy.Arty. Co.B
Thayer, Charles MO 1st N.E. Cav. Co.I
Thayer, Charles L. VA 12th Inf. Co.K
Thayer, C.L. TX 1st Hvy.Arty. Co.B,C
Thayer, Coote GA 6th Inf. Co.H
Thayer, Curtis J. GA Cobb's Legion Co.B
Thayer, F.N. LA Washington Arty.Bn. Co.5 Cpl.,Driver
Thayer, Fred N. LA Res.Corps Allston's Co.
Thayer, George W. AL Lt.Arty. 2nd Bn. Co.E
Thayer, J. LA Mil.Conf.Guards Regt. Co.D
Thayer, Jas. GA 6th Inf. Co.H
Thayer, James VA Lt.Arty. Barr's Co.
Thayer, James VA Loc.Def. Morehead's Co.
Thayer, James M. VA Lt.Arty. 12th Bn. 1st Co.A
Thayer, James M. VA Lt.Arty. Utterback's Co.
Thayer, James M. VA 41st Inf. 2nd Co.G Cpl.
Thayer, James W. VA Lt.Arty. Grandy's Co.
Thayer, James W. VA 6th Inf. Vickery's Co.
Thayer, James W. VA 16th Inf. 1st Co.H
Thayer, J.N. AR 51st Mil. Co.H
Thayer, John NC Inf. Thomas Legion
Thayer, John B. MS 1st Cav. Co.H
Thayer, John R. VA Lt.Arty. 38th Bn. Co.A Cpl.
Thayer, Joseph N. AR 35th Inf. Co.D
Thayer, L. LA Siege Train Bn. Co.D
Thayer, M. LA 25th Inf. Co.H
Thayer, Martin G. VA Inf. 1st Bn.Loc.Def. Co.E Sgt.
Thayer, Martin G. VA 12th Inf. Co.K 1st Sgt.
Thayer, M.G. VA 15th Inf. Co.H
Thayer, Mortimer VA 19th Cav. Co.B
Thayer, Nerlos M. NC 37th Inf. Co.B
Thayer, R. LA 25th Inf. Co.H
Thayer, Robert VA Lt.Arty. 13th Bn. Co.C
Thayer, Seva VA Inf. 44th Bn. Co.B
Thayer, Sheldon TX 12th Cav. Co.C
Thayer, Stephen B. VA Hvy.Arty. 18th Bn. Co.B
Thayer, Stephen B. VA 41st Inf. 1st Co.E
Thayer, T.N. GA 44th Inf. Co.G
Thayer, T.N. Gen. & Staff, Subs.Dept.
Thayer, William H. VA 41st Inf. 2nd Co.G Cpl.
Thayer, William S. VA 11th Inf. Co.H 1st Lt.
Thayer, W.T. TX Cav. 2nd Regt.St.Troops Co.E
Thayher, A.T. VA 46th Inf. Co.C
Thaylor, R. VA 2nd St.Res. Co.B
Thea, John TX 6th Inf. Co.I
Theabold, W.T. LA 22nd Inf. Hosp.Stew.
Thead, C.A. AL 17th Inf. Co.G
Thead, C.A. 4th Conf.Inf. Co.F
Thead, George W. AL Conscr.
Thead, George W. MS 13th Inf. Co.B
Thead, G.W. AL Cp. of Instr. Talladega Co.B
Thead, G.W. 4th Conf.Inf. Co.F
Thead, Hamp L. MS 13th Inf. Co.G
Thead, James J. 4th Conf.Inf. Co.F
Thead, John O. MS 13th Inf. Co.G
Thead, Joseph J. AL 54th Inf. Co.F
Thead, William MS 13th Inf. Co.G
Theadford, T.J. GA 3rd Cav. Co.D Sgt.
Theadgill, W.H. AL 62nd Inf. Co.I
Theain, D.C. SC Charleston Arsenal Bn. Co.B 2nd Lt.
Theall, James H. GA Inf. 2nd Bn. Co.B
Theall, Ruffin B. LA Arty. 1st Field Btty.
Theaman, Benjamin VA Inf. 4th Bn.Loc.Def. Co.C
Theard, A. LA 22nd Inf. Co.E
Theard, Arthur LA 22nd (Cons.) Inf. Co.D
Theard, James C. LA 22nd Inf. Co.D Capt.
Theard, James C. LA 22nd (Cons.) Inf. Co.D Capt.
Theard, N. LA Mil. 1st Chasseurs a pied Co.3
Theard, Numa LA C.S. Zouave Bn. Co.E
Theard, Paul E. LA 22nd Inf. Col.
Theard, Rodolph Lagan LA 15th Inf. Co.H 2nd Lt.
Theard, R.P. AL St.Arty. Co.C
Theard, R.P. LA Mil. Orleans Guards Regt. Co.E,H
Theard, William AL St.Arty. Co.C
Theato, Emanuel AL 24th Inf. Co.B Drum.
Theban, E. LA Mil. Irish Regt. O'Brien's Co.
Theban, Louis LA Inf. 10th Bn. Co.C
Thebideaux, J. LA Miles' Legion
Thebirge, --- LA Mil. 2nd Regt. French Brig. Co.3
Thebo, James 1st Choctaw & Chickasaw Mtd.Rifles Co.A
Thebodeau, Alex LA Inf. 10th Bn. Co.A Capt.
Thebodeaux, P. LA Inf. Crescent Regt. Co.F
Thebold, A. TN Lt.Arty. Polk's Btty. Artif.
Thedford, A.H. TX 15th Inf. 2nd Co.D
Thedford, Andrew J. TX 13th Vol. 1st Co.F Cpl.
Thedford, Andrew J. TX 15th Inf. 2nd Co.D
Thedford, B.C. TX 15th Inf. 2nd Co.D
Thedford, Charles L. GA 20th Inf. Co.B
Thedford, D.A. AR 15th (Johnson's) Inf. Co.E
Thedford, F.A.C. GA 4th Res. Co.H
Thedford, Hiram J. AR 33rd Inf. Co.E
Thedford, H.P. TX Cav. (Dismtd.) Chisum's Regt.
Thedford, I.H. TX 15th Inf. 2nd Co.D
Thedford, J. MS Mil. 4th Cav. Co.H 2nd Lt.
Thedford, J.A. TN 12th Inf. Co.G
Thedford, Jacob TN 14th (Neely's) Cav. Co.B
Thedford, James MS 8th Cav. Co.B Sgt.
Thedford, James A.P. 1st Conf.Inf. 2nd Co.D
Thedford, J.H. MS 28th Cav. Co.E
Thedford, J.H. MS 3rd Inf. (St.Troops) Co.E 2nd Lt.
Thedford, John TN 12th Inf. Co.H
Thedford, John TN 12th (Cons.) Inf. Co.K Cpl.
Thedford, Joseph MS 4th Inf. Co.I Cpl.
Thedford, M.D. TX 15th Inf. 2nd Co.D
Thedford, M.D. TX 22nd Inf. Co.I
Thedford, M.V.B. TX 15th Inf. 2nd Co.D
Thedford, S.B. AR 3rd Cav.
Thedford, Thomas J. AL 3rd Res. Co.D 2nd Lt.
Thedford, T.J. AL 3rd Inf. Co.D 2nd Lt.
Thedford, W.F. GA 46th Inf. Co.E
Thedford, William AR 33rd Inf. Co.E
Thedford, William TN 11th Inf. Co.K Lt.Col.
Thedford, William A. 1st Conf.Inf. 2nd Co.D
Thedford, William T. GA 20th Inf. Co.B
Thedford, Wilson S. TX 13th Vol. 1st Co.F
Thedford, Wilson S. TX 15th Inf. 2nd Co.D
Thedy, Leopold LA Mil. Mech.Guard
Thees, H. SC Mil.Arty. 1st Regt. Werners' Co. Cpl.
Thees, Henry SC 3rd Cav. Co.G
Thefary, L.J. AL 11th Inf. Co.B
Theil, E.A. LA Lt.Arty. 2nd Field Btty.
Theil, P.W. LA Mil. 4th Regt. 2nd Brig. 1st Div. Co.B 1st Lt.
Theile, --- SC 5th Inf. 1st Co.K, 2nd Co.D
Theilemann, George LA 16th Inf. Co.K
Theiler, Henry TX 26th Cav. Co.A
Theiling, F.W. SC 3rd Cav. Co.G
Theiling, Henry SC 3rd Cav. Co.G
Theill, William TX 8th Inf. Co.K
Theim, A. LA Mil. 4th Regt.Eur.Brig. Co.B
Theime, Henry F. TX 2nd Cav. Co.G
Theineman, Charles A. LA 5th Inf. Co.D
Theineman, Fred W.B. LA 5th Inf. Co.D Cpl.
Theirot, C. LA Inf.Cons. 18th Regt. & Yellow Jacket Bn. Co.H
Theirry, Honore TX Waul's Legion Co.A
Theis, Alexander NC Hvy.Arty. 1st Bn. Co.A
Theis, Alexander W. NC 18th Inf. Co.A Cpl.
Theis, Christian VA Lt.Arty. B.Z. Price's Co.
Theis, Christian VA 97th Mil. Co.B Sgt.
Theis, F.H. SC 2nd Arty. Co.C
Theis, Jacob TX 8th Field Btty.
Theis, Phillip TX 25th Cav. Co.A
Theisman, O.F. LA Mil.Cont.Regt. Mitchell's Co.
Theiss, Henry LA 20th Inf. Old Co.B, Co.A
Theiss, Henry TX 4th Field Btty.
Thelan, Nicholas VA 5th Inf. Co.G
Thelb, Joel VA 29th Inf. Co.D
Thelen, F. GA Inf. 1st Loc.Troops (Augusta) Co.K
Thelen, F. GA Inf. 18th Bn. (St.Guards) Co.B
Thelen, Joseph TN 7th (Duckworth's) Cav. Co.C
Thelford, King TX Inf. 2nd St.Troops Co.H
Thelin, William T. MD Inf. 2nd Bn. Co.A
Thelwall, William H. LA 7th Inf. Co.B
Themasen, S.M. AL Talladega Cty.Res. J. Henderson's Co.
Theme, John T. TX 2nd Cav. Co.G
Theme, Otey TX 2nd Cav. Co.G
Themegley, T.F. NC 51st Inf. Co.B
Themes, H.H. NC Townsend's Co. (St.Troops)
Themeska, --- TX Waul's Legion Co.D
Thempson, J.L. MS 5th Inf. Co.G

Thenard, C. LA Mil. 1st Regt. French Brig. Co.3
Thennes, J.R. MS 6th Inf. Co.A
Thennis, J.J. AR 15th (N.W.) Inf. Co.K
Theobald, A. LA 6th Inf. Co.G Sgt.
Theobald, C. TX 11th (Spaight's) Bn.Vol. Co.B Music.
Theobald, C. TX 13th Vol. 4th Co.I
Theobald, G.P. Gen. & Staff Capt.,AQM
Theobald, Nat. B. MO 5th Inf. Co.F Sgt.
Theobald, N.B. MO St.Guard
Theobald, Samuel KY 2nd Cav. Hill's Co.
Theobald, Samuel H. KY 6th Cav. Co.I 1st Sgt.
Theobalds, William T. LA 2nd Inf. Co.C 1st Sgt.
Theobold, Griff P. KY 4th Mtd.Inf. Co.D AQM
Theobold, Samuel A. KY 4th Mtd.Inf. Co.D
Theocatt, C.P. Conf.Cav. Wood's Regt. 2nd Co.D
Theodore, Crescent LA Mil. 1st Native Guards
Theodore, Jeremiah 1st Cherokee Mtd.Rifles Co.G
Theodore, Louis LA Mil. Chalmette Regt. Co.C
Theodore, Oscar L. LA 4th Inf. Co.F
Theral, Thomas B. MS 1st (Johnston's) Inf. Co.A
Theratt, Hiram AL 8th Inf. Co.C
Therber, George TN 34th Inf. Co.H
Therell, W.T. MS Barr's Co. Cpl.
Therenon, Francois LA 13th Inf. Co.E
Therey, J. LA Inf.Crescent Regt. Co.H
Theriaux, J. LA 18th Inf. Co.A
Therides, C.V. LA 4th Zouaves Co.D Cpl.
Therieaux, Etienne LA 1st Hvy.Arty. (Reg.) Co.A
Therin, --- SC Inf. Holcombe Legion Co.C
Therio, Charles LA Inf. 10th Bn. Co.A
Therio, Lucien LA 1st Hvy.Arty. (Reg.) Co.B
Theriot, A.D. LA Inf.Cons.Crescent Regt. Co.H
Theriot, Adam LA Inf. 10th Bn. Co.C
Theriot, Alcide F. LA Arty. 1st Field Btty. Cpl.
Theriot, Aristide LA Inf. 10th Bn. Co.A,C
Theriot, Aristide LA Inf.Cons. 18th Regt. & Yellow Jacket Bn. Co.A,C
Theriot, Arthur LA 18th Inf. Co.A
Theriot, Augustave LA 18th Inf. Co.G
Theriot, Augustave LA Inf.Cons. 18th Regt. & Yellow Jacket Bn. Co.F 4th Cpl.
Theriot, Aurelle LA 26th Inf. Co.H Sgt.
Theriot, Belisaire LA Arty. 1st Field Btty. Sgt.
Theriot, Bidebert LA Inf. 10th Bn. Co.C
Theriot, C. LA 18th Inf. Co.I
Theriot, F. LA Inf.Crescent Regt. Co.H
Theriot, H. LA Inf.Cons. 18th Regt. & Yellow Jacket Bn. Co.H
Theriot, J. LA Inf.Crescent Regt. Co.H
Theriot, J.B. LA 27th Inf. Co.D
Theriot, J.B. LA Inf.Cons.Crescent Regt. Co.H
Theriot, Joseph LA Inf. 10th Bn. Co.C Cpl.
Theriot, Louis LA Mil. LaFourche Regt.
Theriot, Lucien LA Mil. St.James Regt. Gaudet's Co.
Theriot, N. LA Inf.Cons.Crescent Regt. Co.P
Theriot, Oliva LA 26th Inf. Co.H
Theriot, Philogene LA Conscr.
Theriot, Seraphim LA Mil. LaFourche Regt.
Theriot, Z. LA 18th Inf. Co.I
Therist, A. LA Inf.Cons. 18th Regt. & Yellow Jacket Bn. Co.C
Therle, W. LA Mil. Chalmette Regt. Co.G
Therman, A. MS 6th Inf. Co.H
Therman, Charles KY 13th Cav. Co.K
Therman, Franklin A. TN 1st (Turney's) Inf. Co.E
Therman, Henry AR Inf. 4th Bn. Co.B
Therman, H.F. TX 17th Cons.Dismtd.Cav. Co.F
Therman, James TN Cav. 9th Bn. (Gantt's) Co.B
Therman, J.D. MO Inf. Clark's Regt. Co.A
Therman, Jeremiah AL 60th Inf. Co.H
Therman, J.G. MS 10th Inf. Old Co.K
Therman, Joseph W. FL 5th Inf. Co.B
Therman, Linsey VA 2nd Cav. Co.K Cpl.
Therman, N.D. MO Cav. Williams' Regt. Co.C
Therman, R.D. LA 1st Cav. Co.C
Therman, Samuel Conf.Cav. 8th Bn. Co.G
Therman, Thomas J. KY 1st Bn.Mtd.Rifles Co.D
Therman, Thomas J. KY 3rd Bn.Mtd.Rifles Co.F
Therman, William TX Cav. Giddings' Bn. Carr's Co.
Thermon, Elijah MS 6th Inf. Co.H
Thermon, George MS 6th Inf. Co.H
Thermon, J.D. MO 9th Inf. Co.B
Thermon, M.B. SC 8th Inf. Co.B Capt.
Thermond, Benjamin F. TX 35th (Brown's) Cav. Co.E
Thermond, J.C. TX 9th Field Btty.
Thermond, John T. KY 2nd Cav. Co.B
Thermond, Louis G. TX 2nd Inf. Co.K
Thernna, Charles AR Lt.Arty. Marshall's Btty.
Therperan, --- LA Mil. French Co. of St.James
Therral, William M. MS 8th Inf. Co.D
Therrall, Elijah MS 5th Inf. (St.Troops) Co.D
Therrel, James A. LA 31st Inf. Co.B
Therrel, James D. MS 16th Inf. Co.K
Therrel, John B. MS Gordon's Co. (Loc.Guard Wilkinson Cty.) 2nd Lt.
Therrel, John F. MS 16th Inf. Co.K
Therrell, Alexander MS 19th Inf. Co.I,B
Therrell, A.P. TX 1st Inf. Co.D
Therrell, B.F. MS Lt.Arty. Turner's Co.
Therrell, David SC 1st (Butler's) Inf. Co.E
Therrell, Henry SC 8th Inf. Co.B
Therrell, James SC 1st (Butler's) Inf. Co.H
Therrell, James W. MS 44th Inf. Co.C
Therrell, James W. NC 35th Inf. Co.F
Therrell, James W. NC 48th Inf. Co.A
Therrell, John D. MS 44th Inf. Co.C Sgt.
Therrell, Lewis SC 8th Inf. Co.D
Therrell, Thomas MS 8th Cav. Co.B
Therrell, Thomas B. MS 19th Inf. Co.B
Therrell, Wade H. MS 14th Inf. Co.D
Therrell, William MS Lt.Arty. Turner's Co.
Therrell, William A. SC Lt.Arty. Kelly's Co. (Chesterfield Arty.)
Therrell, W.T. MS 8th Cav. Co.B Capt.
Therrill, Elijah L. MS 8th Inf. Co.G
Therrill, Ellick J. MS 1st (Johnston's) Inf. Co.A
Therrill, Lewis SC Lt.Arty. Kelly's Co. (Chesterfield Arty.)
Therrill, Reuben J.W. MS 8th Inf. Co.G
Therrill, W.S. MS 1st Cav. Co.E
Therrill, Willis P. MS 14th Inf. Co.D
Therriot, P.J. LA 7th Cav. Co.C
Ther tho chuper 1st Creek Mtd.Vol. Co.F
Ther wi key 1st Creek Mtd.Vol. Co.F 1st Lt.
Thery, H. LA Arty. Landry's Co. (Donaldsonville Arty.)
Thestis, --- VA 46th Inf. Co.H
Thetford, A.E. AR 10th Inf. Co.H
Thetford, A.I. TX 1st Hvy.Arty. Co.D
Thetford, A.J. TX 7th Inf. Co.D
Thetford, A.W. AR 10th Inf. Co.H Cpl.
Thetford, Benjamin F. MS 44th Inf. Co.C
Thetford, B.F. MS 3rd Cav. Co.F
Thetford, B.F., Jr. MS 3rd Cav. Co.F
Thetford, B.F. MS Morgan's Co. (Morgan Riflemen)
Thetford, D.A. TN 40th Inf. Co.F
Thetford, D.C. AR 31st Inf. Co.H
Thetford, G.W. MS Lt.Arty. 14th Bn. Co.A
Thetford, J. TX Cav. Bourland's Regt. Co.E
Thetford, J.B. AR Pine Bluff Arty.
Thetford, John TN 1st Hvy.Arty. 2nd Co.B
Thetford, John H. AL 40th Inf. Co.A
Thetford, J.W. AR 31st Inf. Co.H
Thetford, Preston MS 7th Inf. Co.E
Thetford, Preston 14th Conf.Cav. Co.C
Thetford, Robert B. MS 12th Inf. Co.H
Thetford, S.B. AR Inf. Cocke's Regt. Co.B
Thetford, T.C. TX 6th Inf. Co.C
Thetford, Walt AR Inf. Cocke's Regt. Co.B
Thetford, William F. AL 11th Inf. Co.B
Thetford, W.T. TX 1st Hvy.Arty. Co.D
Thetfort, Dennis, Jr. TX 7th Cav. Co.A
Thetfort, D.G. TX 7th Cav. Co.A
Thetfort, E. TX 7th Cav. Co.A
Theticks, G.B. GA 35th Inf. Co.E
Theticks, J.J. GA 35th Inf. Co.E
Theulkeld, Francis M. GA 27th Inf. Co.F
Theumann, E.L. TX 4th Inf. (St.Troops) Co.A
Theurer, George AR 51st Mil. Co.B
Theus, A.R. GA 59th Inf. Co.C
Theus, Bailey H. GA 1st (Olmstead's) Inf. Co.C
Theus, Benjamin O. GA 1st (Olmstead's) Inf. Co.C
Theus, Daniel GA 59th Inf. Co.F
Theus, E.P. LA 19th Inf. Co.B Sgt.
Theus, George T. GA 1st (Olmstead's) Inf. Stiles' Co., Screven's Co. Sgt.
Theus, G.T. GA Inf. 18th Bn. Co.B Sgt.
Theus, Hezekiah P. LA 9th Inf. Co.C
Theus, James M. GA 1st (Olmstead's) Inf. Co.C 2nd Lt.
Theus, James T. GA 1st (Symons') Res. Co.G Cpl.
Theus, J.C. LA 13th Bn. (Part.Rangers) Co.F
Theus, J.J. GA 59th Inf. Co.C Cpl.
Theus, John B. GA 59th Inf. Co.C
Theus, John C. GA 59th Inf. Co.F Cpl.
Theus, John C. LA 9th Inf. Co.C 1st Lt.
Theus, John J. GA Hvy.Arty. 22nd Bn. Co.C
Theus, Joshua GA Inf. 10th Bn. Co.B
Theus, Joshua GA 60th Inf. Co.G
Theus, Richard A. GA 59th Inf. Co.C
Theus, S. SC Inf. 1st (Charleston) Bn. Co.D
Theus, Samuel LA 13th Bn. (Part.Rangers) Co.E Sgt.
Theus, Samuel LA 31st Inf. Co.E Sgt.
Theus, S.F. GA 59th Inf. Co.C
Theus, Simeon B. GA 59th Inf. Co.F Sgt.
Theus, Simeon E. GA Inf. 2nd Bn. Co.B Sgt.

Theus, Thomas GA Arty. (Chatham Arty.) Wheaton's Co.
Theus, Thomas GA 59th Inf. Co.C
Theus, Thomas N. GA 1st (Olmstead's) Inf. Co.C, Claghorn's Co. Cpl.
Theus, W.H. GA 59th Inf. Co.C
Theus, William S. AL Inf. 1st Regt. Co.B,K
Theveatt, James R. MS 17th Inf. Co.K
Thevenot, G. LA Mil. 3rd Regt.Eur.Brig. (Garde Francaise) Co.4
Thevenotte, Simon LA Mil. 1st Native Guards
Thewett, Patrick NC 3rd Arty. (40th St.Troops) Co.H
Thewett, Patrick NC 2nd Inf. Co.A
Thewitts, Lewelen GA 51st Inf. Co.H Sgt.
Thews, P. TX 24th & 25th Cav. (Cons.) Co.B
Thexton, J. KY 3rd Cav. Co.E
They, L. LA Mil.Squad. Guides d'Orleans
They, W. MO 5th Inf. Co.F
Theyer, John R. VA 49th Inf. 1st Co.G
Thezau, Theodore LA Mil. 1st Native Guards
Theze, A. LA Mil. 2nd Regt. French Brig. Co.3 3rd Lt.
Theze, B. LA Mil. 2nd Regt. French Brig. Co.4
Theze, Jean LA Mil. 1st Regt. French Brig. Co.7
Theze, Victorien LA Mil. 3rd Regt.Eur.Brig. (Garde Francaise) Frois' Co.
Thian, John TX 8th Inf. Co.F
Thiard, R.L. LA Mil. Orleans Guards Regt. Co.D
Thibadeaux, Alen LA 18th Inf. Co.D
Thibadeaux, Joseph LA Inf.Cons.Crescent Regt. Co.C
Thibadeaux, Peter LA 18th Inf. Co.D
Thibadeaux, Placide LA 18th Inf. Co.D
Thibaud, Florent LA 18th Inf. Co.E
Thibault, J. LA Mil. 2nd Regt. French Brig. Co.4
Thibaut, --- TX Cav. Mann's Regt. Co.C
Thibaut, A. LA Mil. Orleans Guards Regt. Co.F
Thibaut, Dominique LA Mil. 1st Native Guards
Thibaut, John LA Mil. Orleans Guards Regt. Co.F Capt.
Thibaut, Louis LA Arty. Green's Co. (LA Guard Btty.)
Thibaut, Louis LA Mil. 1st Regt. 2nd Brig. 1st Div. Co.K 1st Lt.
Thibbadeu, Lessin LA Inf.Cons.Crescent Regt. Co.P
Thibbodeaux, Place LA 7th Cav. Co.D
Thibeaut, Filbert LA Ogden's Cav. Co.A
Thibedeaux, B. LA Arty. 1st Field Btty.
Thibedeaux, C. LA Inf. 10th Bn. Co.H
Thibedeaux, L. LA Arty. 1st Field Btty.
Thibideaux, Dennis LA Miles' Legion Co.A
Thibideaux, Dorestin LA Miles' Legion Co.A
Thibit, Thomas MO Lt.Arty. Parsons' Co.
Thibit, Thomas MO 6th Inf. Co.I
Thibodaux, Adinar LA 26th Inf. Co.H
Thibodaux, Alfred LA 26th Inf. Co.C
Thibodaux, Andear LA 26th Inf. Co.E
Thibodaux, Augustine LA Mil. LaFourche Regt.
Thibodaux, B. LA Mil. LaFourche Regt.
Thibodaux, C. LA 26th Inf. Co.I
Thibodaux, Clement LA Inf. 10th Bn. Co.A
Thibodaux, Emile P. LA 26th Inf. Co.H Sgt.
Thibodaux, Eugene LA Mil. Assumption Regt.
Thibodaux, Evariste LA 26th Inf. Co.F,H
Thibodaux, H. LA Mil. LaFourche Regt.
Thibodaux, Hilairo LA 26th Inf. Co.F
Thibodaux, J.B. LA Mil. LaFourche Regt.
Thibodaux, Joseph LA 26th Inf. Co.C
Thibodaux, Joseph LA Mil. LaFourche Regt.
Thibodaux, Joseph T. LA Mil. Orleans Guards Regt.
Thibodaux, L.A. LA Mil. LaFourche Regt. Lt.
Thibodaux, Louis LA Mil. Assumption Regt.
Thibodaux, Louis LA Mil. LaFourche Regt.
Thibodaux, M. LA Inf. 10th Bn. Co.A
Thibodaux, N. LA Mil. Assumption Regt.
Thibodaux, N. LA C.S. Zouave Bn. Co.C
Thibodaux, Narcisse LA 26th Inf. Co.C
Thibodaux, Orville LA 26th Inf. Co.F
Thibodaux, P. LA 7th Cav. Co.F
Thibodaux, Paul LA 18th Inf. Co.G
Thibodaux, Simon Conf.Lt.Arty. Richardson's Bn. Co.B
Thibodaux, T. LA Mil. LaFourche Regt.
Thibodeary, S. LA Arty. 1st Field Btty.
Thibodeau, Aphonse LA 26th Inf. Co.I
Thibodeau, Joseph LA 26th Inf. Co.A
Thibodeau, Ls. LA 2nd Res.Corps Co.B
Thibodeau, Martin LA 26th Inf. Co.A
Thibodeau, Oscar LA 18th Inf. Co.F
Thibodeau, Valery LA Inf. 10th Bn. Co.A Capt.
Thibodeaux, A. LA 4th Inf. Co.F
Thibodeaux, A. TX 11th (Spaight's) Bn.Vol. Co.E
Thibodeaux, A. TX 21st Inf. Co.B
Thibodeaux, Achille LA Inf. 1st Sp.Bn. (Rightor's) Co.E
Thibodeaux, Adonis LA 4th Inf. Co.F
Thibodeaux, Alex. LA Inf. 10th Bn. Co.A Capt.
Thibodeaux, Alexandre LA Conscr.
Thibodeaux, Alfred LA Inf. 1st Sp.Bn. (Rightor's) Co.E
Thibodeaux, Alfred LA 4th Inf. Co.F
Thibodeaux, Alfred LA 18th Inf. Co.F
Thibodeaux, Alfred LA Inf.Cons. 18th Regt. & Yellow Jacket Bn. Co.F
Thibodeaux, Alphonse LA 4th Inf. Co.F
Thibodeaux, Auguste LA 1st Hvy.Arty. (Reg.) Co.I
Thibodeaux, C.G. LA 26th Inf. Co.I Sgt.
Thibodeaux, Charles LA 26th Inf. Co.G
Thibodeaux, Charles TX 25th Cav. Co.B,H
Thibodeaux, Cleber LA 1st Hvy.Arty. (Reg.) Co.C
Thibodeaux, E. LA Arty. 5th Field Btty. (Pelican Lt.Arty.)
Thibodeaux, Edgar LA 4th Inf. Co.F
Thibodeaux, Edmond LA 1st Hvy.Arty. (Reg.) Co.I
Thibodeaux, Elysse LA Mil. LaFourche Regt. Co.C
Thibodeaux, Emile LA 2nd Cav. Co.K
Thibodeaux, Emile LA Miles' Legion Co.H
Thibodeaux, Eusebe LA 18th Inf. Co.F
Thibodeaux, Ferdinand LA 1st Hvy.Arty. (Reg.) Co.C
Thibodeaux, Francois LA 26th Inf. Co.D
Thibodeaux, H. LA Mil. St.Martin's Regt. Co.H 2nd Lt.
Thibodeaux, Isaac LA Conscr.
Thibodeaux, Jacques LA Conscr.
Thibodeaux, Jean Baptiste LA 1st Hvy.Arty. (Reg.) Co.I
Thibodeaux, Jean D. TX 11th (Spaight's) Bn.Vol. Co.E
Thibodeaux, J.O. LA Inf. 10th Bn. Co.A 2nd Lt.
Thibodeaux, Joseph LA 1st Hvy.Arty. (Reg.) Co.C
Thibodeaux, Joseph LA 4th Inf. Co.F
Thibodeaux, Joseph LA 26th Inf. Co.D
Thibodeaux, Joseph TX 25th Cav. Co.B,H,A
Thibodeaux, Joseph N. LA Inf.Crescent Regt. Co.E
Thibodeaux, Jules LA 4th Inf. Co.F
Thibodeaux, N. LA 30th Inf. Co.A
Thibodeaux, Nicholas LA Conscr.
Thibodeaux, O. LA Inf.Crescent Regt. Co.G
Thibodeaux, O. Exch.Bn. 1st Co.B,CSA
Thibodeaux, Olymp LA Conscr.
Thibodeaux, Omer LA Conscr.
Thibodeaux, Paul LA Inf.Cons. 18th Regt. & Yellow Jacket Bn. Co.F
Thibodeaux, Paul LA Conscr.
Thibodeaux, Pierre LA 8th Inf. Co.C
Thibodeaux, Pierre A. LA Mil. Orleans Guards Regt. Co.A,C
Thibodeaux, Pierre S. LA 11th Inf. Co.B,K
Thibodeaux, R. LA 30th Inf. Co.A
Thibodeaux, Simon LA Arty. Landry's Co. (Donaldsonville Arty.)
Thibodeaux, Simon LA Inf. 1st Sp.Bn. (Rightor's) Co.E
Thibodeaux, Theodule LA Inf.Cons. 18th Regt. & Yellow Jacket Bn. Co.K
Thibodeaux, Theodule LA Miles' Legion Co.A
Thibodeaux, V. LA 26th Inf. Co.G
Thibodeaux, Valery LA Inf. 10th Bn. Co.A 1st Lt.
Thibodeaux, Zephirin LA 1st Hvy.Arty. (Reg.) Co.I
Thibodeux, Joseph Conf.Cav. Wood's Regt. 2nd Co.F
Thice, Henry GA 12th Cav. Co.L
Thice, Henry VA Lt.Arty. Garber's Co.
Thickstone, J.S. KY 2nd (Duke's) Cav. Co.L
Thidford, G.W. MS Lt.Arty. Yates' Btty.
Thie, Charles F. TX 36th Cav. Co.G Bugler
Thieas, John AL 42nd Inf. Co.K
Thiebauld, Claude LA Mil. 2nd Regt. French Brig. Co.4
Thiebauld, Joseph LA Mil. 2nd Regt. French Brig. Co.4
Thiebes, Wilhelm VA 1st Inf. Co.K
Thiebes, William VA 20th Inf. Co.A
Thiehoff, John H. TX 16th Inf. Co.B
Thiel, A. NC 3rd Cav. (41st St.Troops) Co.A
Thiel, C. TX 25th Cav. Co.I
Thiel, Daniel TX Waul's Legion Co.B
Thiel, Louis TX 1st Hvy.Arty. Co.C
Thiel, R.A. LA Lt.Arty. 2nd Field Btty.
Thiel, T. LA Mil. Chalmette Regt. Co.K
Thiel, Theophanel LA Mil. Lartigue's Co. (Bienville Guards)
Thiel, William TX 1st (McCulloch's) Cav. Co.B
Thiele, Albert LA Mil. Orleans Guards Regt. Co.D

Thiele, F. SC Mil.Arty. 1st Regt. Werner's Co.
Thiele, H. TX 4th Inf. (St.Troops) Co.A
Thiele, J.H. SC Mil.Arty. 1st Regt. Harms' Co.
Thiele, Philip SC Lt.Arty. Wagener's Co. (Co.A,German Arty.)
Thiele, Robert VA 15th Inf. Co.K
Thielin, Charles J. TX 13th Vol. 2nd Co.C
Thieling, F. SC Mil.Arty. 1st Regt. Werner's Co.
Thieling, F.W. SC Mil.Arty. 1st Regt. Harms' Co.
Thieling, F.W. SC Arty. Melchers' Co. (Co.B, German Arty.)
Thieling, W. SC Mil.Arty. 1st Regt. Werner's Co.
Thiell, Charles H. LA 1st (Nelligan's) Inf. Co.K Sgt.
Thiell, Charles O. LA 1st Hvy.Arty. (Reg.) Co.F Cpl.
Thielman, Chr. TX Inf. Timmons' Regt. Co.K
Thielman, Christian TX Waul's Legion Co.B
Thiemann, J. LA Mil. 3rd Regt. 1st Brig. 1st Div. Co.C
Thieme, Christian 4th Conf.Eng.Troops Co.E
Thieme, Christian Kellersberg's Corps Sap. & Min.,CSA
Thieneman, C.A.D. LA Washington Arty.Bn. Co.2
Thieneman, C.A.D. VA 3rd Inf.Loc.Def. Co.D
Thieneman, Theodore F. LA Mil. 4th Regt. 1st Brig. 1st Div. Co.C Capt.
Thienerman, Anthony LA 1st Cav. Co.I
Thierrvat, Jean Baptiste TX 5th Field Btty. Cpl.
Thierry, Ch. LA Mil. 3rd Regt. French Brig. Co.3
Thierry, Edw. LA Mil.Bn. French Vol. Co.5 1st Lt.
Thierry, Honore LA C.S. Zouave Bn. Co.F,A
Thies, A. TX 5th Inf. (St.Troops) Martindale's Co. Cpl.
Thies, John LA Mil. 4th Regt.Eur.Brig. Co.D
Thiesen, --- LA 22nd Inf. Co.C
Thiesfield, Fritz TX 26th Cav. Co.F
Thiess, Jacob GA Cav. 1st Bn. Winn's Co.
Thiess, John MS Cav. 3rd Bn. (Ashcraft's) Co.F
Thietz, Paul LA Mil. 3rd Regt.Eur.Brig. (Garde Francaise) Co.9 Cpl.
Thigben, M. GA 54th Inf. Co.B
Thigben, William B. AL 6th Cav. Co.M,A
Thighpen, Robert MS 5th Inf. (St.Troops) Co.B
Thighpen, T.H. AL 20th Inf. Co.I,D
Thighpen, William H. MS 18th Inf. Co.C
Thigpen, --- TX Cav. Good's Bn. Co.D
Thigpen, A. AL Cp. of Instr. Talladega
Thigpen, A. GA 54th Inf. Co.C
Thigpen, A. SC Lt.Arty. 3rd (Palmetto) Bn. Co.E
Thigpen, Abram H. LA Inf. 11th Bn. Co.A 2nd Lt.
Thigpen, Abram H. LA Inf.Cons.Crescent Regt. Co.B 1st Lt.
Thigpen, Alfred AL 8th (Livingston's) Cav. Co.B,H
Thigpen, Alfred M. NC 1st Inf. (6 mo. '61) Co.A
Thigpen, Alexander M. Gen. & Staff Chap.
Thigpen, Allen NC 1st Cav. (9th St.Troops) Co.I
Thigpen, Allen NC 51st Inf. Co.G
Thigpen, A.M. AL 23rd Cav.
Thigpen, A.M. AL 27th Inf. Co.E
Thigpen, A.M. NC 66th Inf. Co.D 2nd Lt.
Thigpen, A. Marion NC Hvy.Arty. 10th Bn. Co.D
Thigpen, Amaziah N. GA Arty. 11th Bn. (Sumter Arty.) Co.A
Thigpen, Amos NC 3rd Inf. Co.B
Thigpen, Andrew M. NC 44th Inf. Co.C 1st Lt.
Thigpen, Benjamin F. MS 11th (Perrin's) Cav. Co.F
Thigpen, Benjamin F. TX 26th Cav. Co.I
Thigpen, Benton MS 3rd Inf. Co.G
Thigpen, B.J. 4th Conf.Eng.Troops Co.E Sgt.
Thigpen, B.J. Kellersberg's Corps Sap. & Min.,CSA Sgt.
Thigpen, B.J. Gen. & Staff AASurg.
Thigpen, Bryan NC 2nd Inf. Co.F
Thigpen, Bryant NC 3rd Inf. Co.B
Thigpen, Bythel LA 13th Bn. (Part.Rangers) Co.C Sgt.
Thigpen, Bythel NC 3rd Inf. Co.B
Thigpen, Clemon LA 16th Inf. Co.B
Thigpen, David M. AL 17th Inf. Co.A
Thigpen, E. Gen. & Staff Asst.Surg.
Thigpen, E.A. AL 6th Cav.
Thigpen, E.C. SC Lt.Arty. 3rd (Palmetto) Bn. Co.E
Thigpen, Ed TX 27th Cav. Co.A
Thigpen, Elijah LA Inf. 11th Bn. Co.C
Thigpen, Elijah LA Inf.Cons.Crescent Regt. Co.F
Thigpen, E.S. KY Jessee's Bn.Mtd.Riflemen Co.C
Thigpen, E.S. KY Part.Rangers Rowan's Co.
Thigpen, E.S. TX 4th Inf. Co.H
Thigpen, E.T. AL 53rd (Part.Rangers) Co.I
Thigpen, F.B. GA 32nd Inf. Co.H
Thigpen, Francis M. AL 33rd Inf. Co.C Jr.2nd Lt.
Thigpen, Frank A. MS 18th Inf. Co.E
Thigpen, Franklin A. MS 12th Inf. Co.A
Thigpen, Franklin L. NC 3rd Arty. (40th St.Troops) Co.D
Thigpen, F.S. TX Cav. 2nd Bn.St.Troops Co.A
Thigpen, G. 15th Conf.Cav. Co.E
Thigpen, G.A. AL Cav. McJones Cty.
Thigpen, G.B. GA Lt.Arty. 12th Bn. 3rd Co.E
Thigpen, G.C. TX Cav. Benavides' Regt. Co.K
Thigpen, G.C. TX 4th Inf. Co.H
Thigpen, George E. GA 57th Inf. Co.B
Thigpen, George W. AL 17th Inf. Co.K
Thigpen, George W. AL Vol. Goldsmith's Ind.Co. 1st Lt.
Thigpen, George W. NC 43rd Inf. Co.C
Thigpen, George W. NC Loc.Def. Croom's Co.
Thigpen, Gray AL Arty. 1st Bn. Co.B
Thigpen, Gray L. AL 36th Inf. Co.A
Thigpen, G.W. AL 53rd (Part.Rangers) Co.I
Thigpen, G.W. AL 21st Inf. Co.E
Thigpen, G.W. GA 48th Inf. Co.A
Thigpen, Hiram GA 48th Inf. Co.A
Thigpen, Henry LA Res.Corps Scott's Co.
Thigpen, H.H. TX 8th Cav. Co.I
Thigpen, H.J. SC 26th Inf. Co.H
Thigpen, Ira B. AL Williams' Bn. Co.B
Thigpen, J. AL Mil. 4th Vol. Moore's Co.
Thigpen, J.A. AR Inf. Cocke's Regt. Co.E
Thigpen, Jackson SC Hvy.Arty. 15th (Lucas') Bn. Co.A
Thigpen, James LA Miles' Legion Co.C
Thigpen, James MS 6th Inf. Co.K
Thigpen, James NC 8th Bn.Part.Rangers Co.A,C
Thigpen, James NC Inf. 13th Bn. Co.C
Thigpen, James NC 66th Inf. Co.D
Thigpen, James A. 7th Conf.Cav. 2nd Co.I
Thigpen, James B. NC Vol. Lawrence's Co.
Thigpen, James C. FL 8th Inf. Co.F
Thigpen, James K. MS 37th Inf. Co.K,A
Thigpen, James N. AL Cav. 5th Bn. Hilliard's Legion Co.A
Thigpen, James N. 10th Conf.Cav. Co.A
Thigpen, James R. NC 43rd Inf. Co.E Capt.
Thigpen, James T. GA 57th Inf. Co.B
Thigpen, Jason N. AL 20th Inf. Co.I Cpl.
Thigpen, J.E. AL 63rd Inf. Co.F
Thigpen, J.E. GA 10th Mil. Co.H Lt.
Thigpen, J.E. SC 1st (Hagood's) Inf. 1st Co.E
Thigpen, J.E. SC Inf. 6th Bn. Co.C Sgt.
Thigpen, J.E. SC 26th Inf. Co.I 1st Sgt.
Thigpen, J.E. SC Manigault's Bn.Vol. Co.E
Thigpen, Jesse J. NC 3rd Inf. Co.B
Thigpen, Jesse L. NC 27th Inf. Co.H
Thigpen, Jessy FL 5th Inf. Co.E
Thigpen, J.G. MS 3rd (St.Troops) Cav. Co.G
Thigpen, J. Gray MS Cav.Res. Butler's Co. Sgt.
Thigpen, J.J. LA 3rd (Wingfield's) Cav. Co.A
Thigpen, J.J. NC 8th Bn.Part.Rangers Co.B,E
Thigpen, J.J. NC 66th Inf. Co.H
Thigpen, J.J. SC 4th St.Troops Co.I
Thigpen, J.J. SC 5th Bn.Res. Co.B
Thigpen, J.M. GA 5th Res. Co.K Cpl.
Thigpen, Job NC Hvy.Arty. 1st Bn. Co.B
Thigpen, Job NC 8th Sr.Res. Broadhurst's Co.
Thigpen, Job NC 38th Inf. Co.A
Thigpen, Joel J. MS 3rd Inf. Co.C
Thigpen, John FL 9th Inf. Co.I
Thigpen, John GA 10th Inf. Co.G
Thigpen, John GA 32nd Inf. Co.G
Thigpen, John NC 8th Sr.Res. Broadhurst's Co.
Thigpen, John TX 27th Cav. Co.D
Thigpen, John C. MS 18th Inf. Co.H 2nd Lt.
Thigpen, John J. AR 2nd Mtd.Rifles Hawkins' Co. Sgt.
Thigpen, John J. TX 27th Cav. Co.A Sgt.
Thigpen, John Q. NC 4th Cav. (59th St.Troops) Co.H
Thigpen, Joseph AL Inf. Co.I
Thigpen, Joseph C. LA 12th Inf. Co.G
Thigpen, Joseph J. MS 13th Inf. Co.D
Thigpen, Joseph W. NC 38th Inf. Co.A
Thigpen, J.R. GA 1st (Fannin's) Res. Co.K
Thigpen, J.R. GA 25th Inf. Co.C
Thigpen, J.W. NC 66th Inf. Co.C,D
Thigpen, K. TX Cav. Wells' Regt. Co.I
Thigpen, Keenan NC 8th Bn.Part.Rangers Co.E
Thigpen, Keenan NC 66th Inf. Co.H
Thigpen, Kenneth AR 2nd Mtd.Rifles Hawkins' Co.
Thigpen, Kenneth NC 3rd Arty. (40th St.Troops) Co.G 1st Lt.
Thigpen, Kenneth NC 1st Inf. (6 mo. '61) Co.A 1st Sgt.
Thigpen, Kenneth TX 27th Cav. Co.A

Thigpen, Kinsey W. NC 3rd Inf. Co.B
Thigpen, LaFayette NC 4th Cav. (59th St.Troops) Co.H
Thigpen, Lewis AL 41st Inf. Co.E
Thigpen, Lewis MS 38th Cav. Co.C
Thigpen, L.G. AL 21st Inf. Co.E
Thigpen, L.G. AL Vol. Goldsmith's Ind.Co.
Thigpen, Limon LA 3rd (Wingfield's) Cav. Co.A
Thigpen, Lucien B. GA 14th Inf. Co.C Cpl.
Thigpen, Malenthen T. GA 57th Inf. Co.B Cpl.
Thigpen, M. Judson MS 18th Inf. Co.E Sgt.
Thigpen, Nathan MS 3rd Inf. Co.G 1st Cpl.
Thigpen, O.A. FL 2nd Cav. Co.K
Thigpen, R. GA 3rd Inf. Co.G
Thigpen, Redding G. FL 6th Inf. Co.D
Thigpen, R.F.M. AL 27th Inf. Co.E
Thigpen, Richard T. GA 57th Inf. Co.B
Thigpen, R.J. Boyd AL 42nd Inf. Co.C Cpl.
Thigpen, R.S. MS Inf. 2nd St.Troops Co.D
Thigpen, S.C. TX 8th Cav. Co.F
Thigpen, S.J. MS Conscr.
Thigpen, Stafford G. GA 50th Inf. Co.C
Thigpen, T. TX 4th Cav. Co.B
Thigpen, T.H. AL 15th Inf. Co.I
Thigpen, Thomas NC Lt.Arty. 13th Bn. Co.B
Thigpen, Thomas NC 51st Inf. Co.G
Thigpen, Thomas D. NC 1st Inf. (6 mo. '61) Co.A
Thigpen, Thomas J. FL Conscr.
Thigpen, T.T. GA 4th (Clinch's) Cav. Co.E
Thigpen, W. AL Vol. Goldsmith's Ind.Co.
Thigpen, W.H. SC 1st (Hagood's) Inf. 1st Co.E
Thigpen, W.H. SC Inf. 6th Bn. Co.C Cpl.
Thigpen, W.H. SC 26th Inf. Co.I Sgt.
Thigpen, W.H. SC Manigault's Bn.Vol. Co.E
Thigpen, William AL 18th Inf. Co.F
Thigpen, William FL 2nd Cav. Co.I
Thigpen, William FL Cav. 5th Bn. Co.F
Thigpen, William FL 8th Inf. Co.F
Thigpen, William GA 3rd Inf. Co.G
Thigpen, William GA 57th Inf. Co.B
Thigpen, William NC Mil. Clark's Sp.Bn. Co.D
Thigpen, William 1st Conf.Inf. Co.H
Thigpen, William H. FL 3rd Inf. Co.C
Thigpen, William H. NC 38th Inf. Co.A
Thigpen, William J. GA 49th Inf. Co.A
Thigpen, W.J. LA 3rd (Wingfield's) Cav. Co.A
Thigpen, Yale FL 1st (Res.) Inf. Co.A
Thigpen, Zachariah GA 12th Inf. Co.B
Thigpin, A.J. GA 28th Inf. Co.I
Thigpin, Alx. M. GA 6th Inf. Chap.
Thigpin, Amazar N. GA 4th Inf. Co.I
Thigpin, Clinton FL 2nd Cav. Co.A Capt.
Thigpin, Clinton FL 10th Inf. Thigpin's Co. Capt.
Thigpin, F.J. FL 2nd Cav. Co.A
Thigpin, G.A. AL Cav.Res. Brooks' Co.
Thigpin, J.A. AR 23rd Inf. Co.F
Thigpin, John C. FL 7th Inf. Co.C 2nd Lt.
Thigpin, John T. FL 2nd Cav. Co.A Sgt.
Thigpin, John W. NC 8th Bn.Part.Rangers Co.B
Thigpin, William FL 2nd Cav. Co.B
Thigpur, J.N. AL 18th Inf. Co.F
Thilbodeau, L.C. LA 7th Cav. Co.D
Thileman, L. LA Lewis Regt. Co.G
Thill, Nicholas AR Lt.Arty. Owen's Btty.
Thillen, A. LA Mil. Orleans Guards Regt. Co.K
Thilman, D. AR Mil. Desha Cty.Bn.
Thimmons, Charles B. TN 44th (Cons.) Inf. Co.B
Think, D.M. NC 7th Inf.
Thin Legs FL McBride's Co. (Indians)
Thiodore, A. LA Mil. 1st Native Guards
Thiot, Armand LA Mil. 1st Native Guards Cpl.
Thiot, Charles H. GA 12th (Wright's) Cav. (St.Guards) Thiot's Co. Capt.
Thiot, Charles H. GA Arty. (Chatham Arty.) Wheaton's Co.
Thiot, Charles H. GA 1st (Olmstead's) Inf. Claghorn's Co.
Thirdgill, W.H. TN 21st Cav. Co.G
Thirldkeld, Tulley H. GA 16th Inf. Co.D
Thirlhill, George H. GA 30th Inf. Co.E
Thirlkill, John V. GA 20th Inf. Co.E
Thirman, Jeptha MO 1st N.E. Cav. Co.D
Thirny, N. LA 13th Inf. Co.K
Thiroux, A. LA Lt.Arty. LeGardeur, Jr.'s Co. (Orleans Guard Btty.) Cpl.
Thiroux, A. MO Lt.Arty. Barret's Co.
Thiroux, Charles V. LA C.S. Zouave Bn. Co.D
Thiroux, Emile LA C.S. Zouave Bn. Co.D,C Sgt.
Thiroux, V. LA 22nd Inf. Co.E
Thiroux, Victor LA 22nd (Cons.) Inf. Co.E,D
Thirstin, B. VA 46th Inf. Co.H
Thirston, --- VA Cav. 39th Bn. Co.D
Thirston, W. KY 10th (Johnson's) Cav. Co.E Cpl.
Thirsty, George MO Cav. Williams' Regt. Co.K
Thirsty Tyger 1st Cherokee Mtd.Rifles Co.D
Thishotubbi 1st Choctaw & Chickasaw Mtd.Rifles 2nd Co.K
Thisse, C.C. MS 2nd Cav. Co.I
Thistle, G.L. MS Cav. Jeff Davis Legion Co.A
Thistle, Lewis H. MO 10th Cav. Co.G
Thistle, Thomas L. MS Cav. Jeff Davis Legion Co.A
Thiston, K. NC 3rd Inf.
Thitus, W.A. LA Arty. Watson Btty.
Thivett, James H. Wheeler's Scouts,CSA
Thixton, J. KY Cav. 2nd Bn. (Dortch's) Co.D
Thixton, John KY 8th Cav. Co.G
Thixton, John KY Morgan's Men Co.D
Thixton, John S. KY 6th Mtd.Inf. Co.G
Thlanco ka 1st Seminole Mtd.Vol.
Thlar con shun ney 1st Creek Mtd.Vol. Co.E
Thlar fichee 1st Creek Mtd.Vol. Co.K
Thlar ke ter 1st Creek Mtd.Vol. Co.A Capt.
Thlar kin shin a 1st Creek Mtd.Vol. Co.E
Thlar sah ye 1st Creek Mtd.Vol. Co.M
Thlar si ye 1st Creek Mtd.Vol. 2nd Co.I
Thlars le ti ke 1st Creek Mtd.Vol. Co.M
Thlars le ti key 1st Creek Mtd.Vol. 2nd Co.I
Thlars tumka 1st Creek Mtd.Vol. Co.K
Thlarthla Fixico 1st Seminole Mtd.Vol.
Thlarthle Harjo 2nd Creek Mtd.Vol. Co.E
Thlar thlo Fixico 1st Creek Mtd.Vol. Co.G
Thlar thlo Harjo 1st Creek Mtd.Vol. Co.B Cpl.
Thlar thlo ya ho la 1st Creek Mtd.Vol. 2nd Co.C
Thlaruerhee 1st Seminole Mtd.Vol.
Thla Yagh 1st Creek Mtd.Vol. 2nd Co.D
Thle mar heh che 1st Creek Mtd.Vol. Co.H
Thle muhe chee 1st Creek Mtd.Vol. 2nd Co.D
Thle seh me 1st Creek Mtd.Vol. Co.K
Thle wah le 1st Creek Mtd.Vol. Co.G
Thle wa ley 1st Creek Mtd.Vol. Co.A, 2nd Co.D
Thle wallee Fixico 1st Creek Mtd.Vol. Co.B 2nd Lt.
Thlin e Hargo 1st Creek Mtd.Vol. Co.G
Thlors Yicho 1st Creek Mtd.Vol. Co.M Ens.
Thlor Toy harjo 1st Creek Mtd.Vol. 2nd Co.I
Thlo see 1st Creek Mtd.Vol. Co.E Sgt.
Thlos tum kee 1st Creek Mtd.Vol. Co.B
Thlothlo Fixico 1st Seminole Mtd.Vol. 2nd Lt.
Thoburn, James TN Inf. 154th Sr.Regt. Co.H
Thock, William TX Lt.Arty. Jones' Co.
Thockmorton, Charles R. VA 56th Inf. Co.A
Thockmorton, John W. VA 56th Inf. Co.A
Thodberg, Samuel M. TX 11th Inf. Co.I
Thode, H.P. SC 12th Inf. Co.K 1st Lt.
Thoeington, W. TN 19th & 20th (Cons.) Cav. Co.B
Thoele, A. LA Mil. Chalmette Regt. Co.E
Thoele, H. LA Mil. Chalmette Regt. Co.E Cpl.
Thoele, Joseph LA Mil. Chalmette Regt. Co.F
Thof ka, Jimmy 1st Creek Mtd.Vol. Co.G
Tholbert, Ezra 8th (Wade's) Conf.Cav. Co.F
Thole, Theo LA 1st Cav. Co.I
Thom, A.C. Gen. & Staff,PACS Capt.,AAG
Thom, C. AR 1st (Monroe's) Cav. Co.D
Thom, Cameron E. Gen. & Staff Vol.ADC
Thom, David M. NC Snead's Co. (Loc.Def.)
Thom, George LA Mil.Cont.Regt. Roder's Co.
Thom, I. AR 30th Inf. Co.H
Thom, J. VA 3rd Inf.Loc.Def. Co.B
Thom, John TX 35th (Likens') Cav. Co.H
Thom, J.P. VA Inf. 1st Bn. Co.C Capt.
Thom, Ramsey 1st Choctaw Mtd.Rifles Co.G Music.
Thom, Reuben AL 5th Bn.Vol. Co.A
Thom, Reuben AL 11th Inf. Co.H Lt.
Thom, S.D. GA 5th Inf. (St.Guards) Everitt's Co.
Thom, William AR 1st Inf. Co.E
Thom, William Deneale's Regt. Choctaw Warriors Co.C
Thom, Wm. Alex Gen. & Staff Surg.
Thoma, --- AL 3rd Inf.
Thoma, Felix LA 30th Inf. Co.D
Thoma, Lewis LA Mil.Cont.Regt. Lang's Co.
Thomalen, P. LA Mil. 4th Regt. 1st Brig. 1st Div. Co.K
Thomalson, H.H. GA 2nd Bn.S.S. Co.H
Thomalty, Brian LA 21st (Patton's) Inf. Co.D
Thoman, Dennis LA Mil. 3rd Regt. 1st Brig. 1st Div. Co.D Sgt.
Thoman, H.D. LA Mil. 3rd Regt. 1st Brig. 1st Div. Co.C
Thoman, Henry LA Mil. 3rd Regt. 1st Brig. 1st Div. Co.D 3rd Lt.
Thoman, Joseph LA Mil. 3rd Regt. 1st Brig. 1st Div. Co.D Cpl.
Thomarson, Joseph R. VA 2nd Arty. Co.D
Thomas (Col'd) SC Inf. 1st (Charleston) Bn. Co.G Col'd Cook
Thomas (Colored) SC Cav.Bn. Holcombe Legion Co.B Cook
Thomas VA Inf. 25th Bn. Co.G Cook
Thomas (Slave) VA 32nd Inf. Co.F Cook
Thomas 1st Cherokee Mtd.Rifles Co.G
Thomas (Creek) 1st Cherokee Mtd.Rifles Co.K

Thomas 1st Choctaw Mtd.Rifles Co.D
Thomas 1st Choctaw Mtd.Rifles Ward's Co.
Thomas 1st Choctaw & Chickasaw Mtd.Rifles 2nd Co.H
Thomas 1st Choctaw & Chickasaw Mtd.Rifles Maytubby's Co.
Thomas 1st Creek Mtd.Vol. Co.A
Thomas 1st Creek Mtd.Vol. 2nd Co.C
Thomas 1st Creek Mtd.Vol. 2nd Co.C,D
Thomas 1st Creek Mtd.Vol. 2nd Co.I Bugler
Thomas Deneale's Regt. Choctaw Warriors Co.B
Thomas, --- AL 22nd Inf. Co.G
Thomas, --- AL 22nd Inf. Co.H
Thomas, --- AL 22nd Inf. Co.H Sgt.
Thomas, --- AL 25th Inf. Co.A
Thomas, --- AL 25th Inf. Co.B Music.
Thomas, --- AL 25th Inf. Co.H
Thomas, --- AL 29th Inf. Co.B
Thomas, --- AL 44th Inf. Co.I Sgt.
Thomas, --- AL 62nd Inf. Co.I
Thomas, --- SC 11th Inf. Sgt.
Thomas, --- SC Mil. 18th Regt. Music.
Thomas, --- SC Inf. Hampton Legion Chap.
Thomas, --- TN 3rd (Lilliard's) Mtd.Regt.
Thomas, --- TX Cav. Good's Bn. Co.A
Thomas, --- TX Cav. Mann's Regt. Co.B
Thomas, --- TX Cav. Mann's Regt. Co.H
Thomas, --- TX Cav. Mann's Regt. Co.K Sgt.
Thomas, --- TX Cav. McCord's Frontier Regt. Co.A
Thomas, --- TX Cav. Morgan's Regt. Co.K
Thomas, --- TX 1st Inf. Co.G
Thomas, --- VA 46th Inf. Co.C
Thomas, --- VA 46th Inf. Co.D
Thomas, ---, Rev.Mr. Gen. & Staff Chap.
Thomas, A. AL 33rd Inf. Co.A
Thomas, A. AR 18th Inf. Co.F
Thomas, A. AR 30th Inf. Co.A
Thomas, A. FL 1st (Res.) Inf. Co.I
Thomas, A. GA 2nd Res.
Thomas, A. GA 10th Mil.
Thomas, A. GA 35th Inf. Co.E
Thomas, A. GA 59th Inf. Co.H
Thomas, A. GA Inf. (Milledgeville Guards) Caraker's Co.
Thomas, A. KY Morgan's Men Co.E
Thomas, A. MS 4th Cav. Co.D
Thomas, A. MS 19th Inf. Co.K Sgt.
Thomas, A. MS 34th Inf. Co.C
Thomas, A. SC 4th Cav. Co.G
Thomas, A. SC Cav. 10th Bn. Co.C
Thomas, A. TN 6th Inf. Co.L
Thomas, A. TN 55th (Brown's) Inf. Ford's Co.
Thomas, A. TX Cav. 2nd Regt.St.Troops Co.B Sgt.
Thomas, A. TX 23rd Cav. Co.E
Thomas, A.A. LA 25th Inf. Co.E
Thomas, A.A. TX 2nd Cav. Co.B,H 1st Lt.
Thomas, Aaron AL Hardy's Co. (Eufaula Minute Men)
Thomas, Aaron NC 58th Inf. Co.C,D
Thomas, Aaron SC 5th Inf. 1st Co.F, 2nd Co.K
Thomas, A.B. GA 11th Inf. Co.I
Thomas, A.B. VA 1st Bn.Res. Co.D
Thomas, Abe AR 2nd Vol. Co.A
Thomas, Abel NC 17th Inf. (1st Org.) Co.F
Thomas, Abel NC 17th Inf. (2nd Org.) Co.A
Thomas, Abel NC 17th Inf. (2nd Org.) Co.K
Thomas, Abel C. AL 32nd Inf. Co.B
Thomas, Abner TN 19th Inf. Co.F
Thomas, Abraham LA 7th Inf. Co.H Color Sgt.
Thomas, Abraham J. VA 38th Inf. Co.D
Thomas, Abram AL 39th Inf. Co.C
Thomas, Abram MS 44th Inf. Co.A
Thomas, Abram D. MS St.Cav. Perrin's Bn. Co.F
Thomas, Absalom GA Mtd.Inf. (Pierce Mtd.Vol.) Hendry's Co.
Thomas, A.C. TN 5th (McKenzie's) Cav. Co.C
Thomas, A.C. VA 34th Inf. Co.E
Thomas, A.C. 7th Conf.Cav. Co.E
Thomas, A.D. MS 12th Cav. Co.G 1st Lt.
Thomas, A.D. TN 51st Inf. Co.B Capt.
Thomas, A.D. TN 51st (Cons.) Inf. Co.H 1st Sgt.
Thomas, Adam AR 15th (N.W.) Inf. Co.D
Thomas, Adam FL 11th Inf. Co.C
Thomas, Adam TN Lt.Arty. Weller's Co.
Thomas, Adam TN 63rd Inf. Co.E
Thomas, Adam VA 58th Mil. Co.H
Thomas, Adam J. AL 6th Cav. Co.H
Thomas, Admiral NC 4th Cav. (59th St.Troops) Co.I
Thomas, Admiral NC Cav. 12th Bn. Co.B
Thomas, Admiral 8th (Dearing's) Conf.Cav. Co.B
Thomas, A.E. SC 4th Cav. Co.D
Thomas, A.E. SC Manigault's Bn.Vol. Co.A,E
Thomas, A.F. AL 13th Bn.Part.Rangers Co.B
Thomas, A.F. AL 56th Part.Rangers Co.F
Thomas, A.F. AL 1st Inf. 3rd Co.G
Thomas, A.F. AL Inf. 1st (Loomis') Bn. Co.E
Thomas, A.F. AL 45th Inf. Co.C
Thomas, A.F. GA 4th (Clinch's) Cav. Co.F
Thomas, A.F. GA 11th Cav. (St.Guards) Folks' Co. Cpl.
Thomas, A.F. GA 3rd Res. Co.A
Thomas, A.G. KY 9th Cav. Co.D
Thomas, A.G. TX 12th Cav. Co.A
Thomas, A.G. Gen. & Staff Chap.
Thomas, A.G. Gen. & Staff Surg.
Thomas, A.H. GA 27th Inf. Co.I
Thomas, A.H. LA 8th Cav. Co.C Sgt.
Thomas, A.H. LA Inf. 1st Bn. (St.Guards) Co.B 1st Sgt.
Thomas, A.H. NC Walker's Bn. Thomas' Legion Co.A
Thomas, A.H. TN 27th Inf. Co.H
Thomas, A.H. TX 35th (Brown's) Cav.
Thomas, A.H. Gen. & Staff AAQM
Thomas, Ahijah NC 58th Inf. Co.A
Thomas, A.J. AL 6th Inf. Co.I
Thomas, A.J. AL 19th Inf. Co.G
Thomas, A.J. AR 16th Inf. Co.D Sgt.
Thomas, A.J. GA 7th Inf. Chap.
Thomas, A.J. GA 38th Inf. Co.I
Thomas, A.J. GA 46th Inf. Co.E
Thomas, A.J. GA 48th Inf. Co.C Sgt.
Thomas, A.J. KY 1st (Butler's) Cav. New Co.H
Thomas, A.J. LA 3rd Inf. Co.E 2nd Lt.
Thomas, A.J. LA 22nd (Cons.) Inf. Co.H 2nd Lt.
Thomas, A.J. MS 4th Cav. Co.F
Thomas, A.J. MS Cav. Hughes' Bn. Co.E
Thomas, A.J. NC 7th Inf. Co.E
Thomas, A.J. TN 5th (McKenzie's) Cav. Co.A
Thomas, A.J. TN 7th (Duckworth's) Cav. Co.L
Thomas, A.J. TN 21st & 22nd (Cons.) Cav. Co.A
Thomas, A.J. TN 22nd (Barteau's) Cav. Co.C
Thomas, A.J. TN Lt.Arty. Burroughs' Co.
Thomas, A.J. TN 37th Inf. Co.D
Thomas, A.J. TX 24th & 25th Cav. (Cons.) Co.E
Thomas, A.J. TX 25th Cav. Co.G
Thomas, A.J. TX 2nd Inf. Co.C
Thomas, A.J. VA Lt.Arty. Fry's Co.
Thomas, A.J. VA 38th Inf. Co.F
Thomas, A.J. Gen. & Staff Lt.
Thomas, A.K. 20th Conf.Cav. Co.E
Thomas, A.L. AL 50th Inf. Co.E Sgt.
Thomas, A.L. GA 32nd Inf. Co.I
Thomas, A.L. GA 42nd Inf. Co.D
Thomas, A.L. NC 4th Inf. Cpl.
Thomas, A.L. TN 47th Inf. Co.H
Thomas, Albert AL 53rd (Part.Rangers) Co.C
Thomas, Albert AR 18th Inf. Co.F
Thomas, Albert KY 9th Cav.
Thomas, Albert LA 8th Inf. Co.C
Thomas, Albert MS 18th Inf. Co.A
Thomas, Albert SC 6th Inf. 2nd Co.A
Thomas, Albert SC 24th Inf. Co.H
Thomas, Albert C. KY 4th Mtd.Inf. Co.G,I Sgt.
Thomas, Albert G. GA 10th Inf. Co.F
Thomas, Albert G. MS 2nd Inf. Co.A
Thomas, Albert G. TX 16th Cav. Co.G Sgt.
Thomas, Albert R. TX 6th Cav. Co.B 2nd Lt.
Thomas, Alex LA 9th Inf. Co.I
Thomas, Alex MS Cav. Jeff Davis Legion Co.A
Thomas, Alex NC 6th Sr.Res. Co.E
Thomas, Alexander AL 6th Inf. Co.F
Thomas, Alexander AR 18th Inf. Co.F
Thomas, Alexander GA 28th Inf. Co.E
Thomas, Alexander KY 5th Cav. Capt.,CS
Thomas, Alexander LA 31st Inf. Co.B
Thomas, Alexander SC 1st Arty. Co.H Sgt.
Thomas, Alexander TX 8th Inf. Co.D
Thomas, Alexander VA 5th Inf. Co.H
Thomas, Alexander VA 47th Inf. 3rd Co.H
Thomas, Alexander B. VA 13th Inf. Co.A Cpl.
Thomas, Alexander C. GA 11th Inf. Co.E
Thomas, Alexander C. TN 24th Inf. 2nd Co.G
Thomas, Alex. J. AL 34th Inf. Co.K
Thomas, Alexander J. NC 15th Inf. Co.I
Thomas, Alexander R. VA 4th Cav. Co.C
Thomas, Alfred GA 1st (Olmstead's) Inf. Gordon's Co.
Thomas, Alfred GA 63rd Inf. Co.K Music.
Thomas, Alfred GA Brooks' Co. (Terrell Lt.Arty.)
Thomas, Alfred MO Cav. Freeman's Regt. Co.D
Thomas, Alfred NC 4th Inf. Co.F
Thomas, Alfred TN 5th (McKenzie's) Cav. Co.C
Thomas, Alfred VA 24th Cav. Co.A
Thomas, Alfred A. SC 10th Inf. Co.L
Thomas, Alfred C. TN 2nd Cav. Co.D
Thomas, Alfred E. SC 2nd Cav. Co.D Cpl.
Thomas, Alfred N. TN 6th Inf. Co.D Bvt.2nd Lt.
Thomas, Alfred S. AL 19th Inf. Co.G
Thomas, Algernon W. VA Hvy.Arty. 19th Bn. Co.A

Thomas, Alick MS 1st Lt.Arty. Co.H
Thomas, Alison A. FL 1st Inf. Old Co.C
Thomas, Allen GA 36th (Broyles') Inf. Co.D
Thomas, Allen GA 43rd Inf. Co.B
Thomas, Allen LA 28th (Thomas') Inf. Col.
Thomas, Allen NC 45th Inf. Co.K
Thomas, Allen Gen. & Staff Brig.Gen.
Thomas, Allen B. AL 6th Inf. Co.F
Thomas, Allen F. TX 17th Cav. Co.H
Thomas, Allen M. VA 5th Cav. Co.C Sgt.
Thomas, Allen W. LA 31st Inf. Co.I
Thomas, Alvin AL 23rd Bn.S.S. Co.G
Thomas, Alvin AL 1st Bn. Hilliard's Legion Vol. Co.G
Thomas, A.M. GA 63rd Inf. Co.I
Thomas, A.M. TN 17th Inf. Co.I
Thomas, A.M. TX 14th Inf. Co.G
Thomas, A.M. VA 8th Cav. Co.A
Thomas, A.M. VA 37th Inf. Co.E
Thomas, A.M. Morgan's,CSA
Thomas, Ambrose NC 26th Inf. Co.E
Thomas, A.M.C. AR Lt.Arty. Zimmerman's Btty.
Thomas, A.M.C. AR 16th Inf. Co.K
Thomas, Amos NC 43rd Inf. Co.H
Thomas, And GA 48th Inf. Co.G
Thomas, Anderson AL 12th Inf. Co.A
Thomas, Anderson AL 34th Inf. Co.K
Thomas, Anderson LA 31st Inf. Co.B
Thomas, Andrew AL Lt.Arty. Clanton's Btty.
Thomas, Andrew AL 19th Inf. Co.G
Thomas, Andrew FL 7th Inf. Co.A
Thomas, Andrew KY 9th Cav. Co.D
Thomas, Andrew VA 11th Inf. Co.E
Thomas, Andrew VA 29th Inf. Co.H
Thomas, Andrew VA 37th Inf. Co.F
Thomas, Andrew VA 63rd Inf. Co.A
Thomas, Andrew B. GA 5th Inf. Co.H,E
Thomas, Andrew B. MS 18th Inf. Co.E
Thomas, Andrew B. VA 40th Inf. Co.E
Thomas, Andrew C. TX 18th Inf. Co.C
Thomas, Andrew H. GA 47th Inf. Co.F
Thomas, Andrew J. AL 28th Inf. Co.L
Thomas, Andrew J. GA 7th Inf. Co.E Cpl.
Thomas, Andrew J. GA 22nd Inf. Co.G Sgt.
Thomas, Andrew J. GA Cobb's Legion Co.A
Thomas, Andrew J. MS 27th Inf. Co.G Sgt.
Thomas, Andrew J. VA Arty. Wise Legion
Thomas, Andrew J. VA 5th Cav. (12 mo. '61-2) Co.F
Thomas, Andrew J. VA 22nd Cav. Co.B
Thomas, Andrew J. VA 54th Inf. Co.H
Thomas, Andrew J. VA 58th Inf. Co.K
Thomas, Andy TX 3rd Cav. Co.I
Thomas, Anthony KY 1st (Butler's) Cav. Co.C
Thomas, Anthony KY 3rd Cav. Co.C
Thomas, Anthony J. NC 1st Arty. (10th St.Troops) Co.K 1st Lt.
Thomas, Antoine LA Mil. 1st Native Guards
Thomas, A.O. AL 6th Inf. Co.L
Thomas, A.O. GA 1st Cav. Co.K
Thomas, A.P. AL 2nd Cav. Co.H
Thomas, A.P. MS 36th Inf. Co.F
Thomas, A.P. SC Cav. 19th Bn. Co.C
Thomas, A.P. SC Part.Rangers Kirk's Co.
Thomas, A.Q. TN Cav. Woodward's Co.
Thomas, A.R. AL 23rd Inf. Co.B,I
Thomas, A.R. AL Inf. Hooper's Bn. Co.A
Thomas, A.R. NC 57th Inf. Co.I
Thomas, A.R. TN 18th (Newsom's) Cav. Co.B
Thomas, Arch 3rd Conf.Cav. Co.G
Thomas, Archer VA 10th Cav. Co.D
Thomas, Archibald MS 40th Inf. Co.B
Thomas, Archibald TN 1st (Feild's) Inf. Co.G
Thomas, Archibald TN 30th Inf. Co.A 2nd Lt.
Thomas, Archibald VA 15th Cav. Co.A
Thomas, Archibald VA 34th Inf. Co.C
Thomas, Archibald C. MS 37th Inf. Co.K
Thomas, Archibald D. TN Lt.Arty. Barry's Co.
Thomas, Archibald E.L. TN 32nd Inf. Co.D
Thomas, Archibald J. VA 54th Inf. Co.H
Thomas, Archibald W. VA Lt.Arty. B.Z. Price's Co. Cpl.
Thomas, Archy 1st Chickasaw Inf. Milam's Co.
Thomas, Arterberry AR 15th (N.W.) Inf. Co.G
Thomas, A.S. AR 26th Inf. Co.G
Thomas, A.S. TN 14th Cav. Co.A
Thomas, A.S. TX 15th Inf. 2nd Co.F
Thomas, A.S. VA 9th Cav. Co.C Sgt.
Thomas, Asa NC 5th Cav. (63rd St.Troops) Co.G
Thomas, Asa G. NC 56th Inf. Co.E Sgt.
Thomas, A.T. GA Floyd Legion (St.Guards) Co.B
Thomas, A.T. MS 40th Inf. Co.D Sgt.
Thomas, A.V.B. MS 2nd Part.Rangers Co.I
Thomas, A.V.B. MS 7th Cav. Co.F
Thomas, A.W. AR 1st (Monroe's) Cav. Co.A
Thomas, A.W. AR 11th Inf. Co.H
Thomas, A.W. AR 11th & 17th Cons.Inf. Co.C
Thomas, A.W. AR 50th Mil. Co.B
Thomas, A.W. KY 12th Cav. Co.B Sgt.
Thomas, A.W. MS 39th Inf. Co.G
Thomas, A.W. TN 5th Inf. 2nd Co.K
Thomas, B. AL 6th Cav. Co.I
Thomas, B. AR 35th Inf. Co.A
Thomas, B. FL 1st (Res.) Inf. Co.L
Thomas, B. GA 54th Inf. Co.K Cpl.
Thomas, B. MS Inf. 3rd Bn. (St.Troops) Co.E
Thomas, B. SC 2nd St.Troops Co.D
Thomas, B. SC 8th Bn.Res. Fishburne's Co.
Thomas, B. TX 3rd Cav. Co.A
Thomas, B. VA 2nd St.Res. Co.B
Thomas, B. VA 18th Inf.
Thomas, B.A. NC 3rd Inf. Co.C
Thomas, B.A. 1st Conf.Eng.Troops Co.D Artif.
Thomas, Baily VA 42nd Inf. Co.B
Thomas, Balaam GA Inf. 10th Bn. Co.C
Thomas, Banner GA Mtd.Inf. (Pierce Mtd.Vol.) Hendry's Co.
Thomas, Barney MS 32nd Inf. Co.A
Thomas, Batz B. GA 5th Inf. Co.E,L
Thomas, Bazal AR 45th Mil. Co.C
Thomas, B.B. AL 26th (O'Neal's) Inf. Co.K
Thomas, B.B. AR 7th Cav. Co.C
Thomas, B.B. GA Conscr.
Thomas, B.B. LA 3rd (Harrison's) Cav. Co.E
Thomas, B.B. MS 1st Cav. Co.F
Thomas, B.B. MS 4th Cav. Co.D 1st Lt.
Thomas, B.B. MS Cav. Hughes' Bn. Co.C 1st Lt.
Thomas, B.B. MS 1st (Foote's) Inf. (St.Troops) Co.B
Thomas, B.B. MS 35th Inf. Co.H
Thomas, B.D. KY 8th Mtd.Inf. Co.H
Thomas, B.D. VA Lt.Arty. Grandy's Co. QMSgt.
Thomas, Beauchamp B. MS 12th Inf. Co.A 3rd Lt.
Thomas, Ben H. MO Lt.Arty. Barret's Co. Sgt.
Thomas, Ben H. MO Inf. 3rd Regt.St.Guard Comsy.
Thomas, Benina TX 8th Cav. Co.G
Thomas, Benjamin AL 3rd Res. Co.B
Thomas, Benjamin AR Cav. Wright's Regt. Co.G Cpl.
Thomas, Benjamin AR 15th (N.W.) Inf. Co.D Bvt.2nd Lt.
Thomas, Benjamin AR 45th Mil. Co.C 1st Sgt.
Thomas, Benjamin FL 4th Inf. Co.I Music.
Thomas, Benjamin FL 29th Regt. Co.E
Thomas, Benjamin GA 50th Inf. Co.C
Thomas, Benjamin LA 3rd (Wingfield's) Cav. Co.A
Thomas, Benjamin LA 7th Inf. Co.I
Thomas, Benjamin NC 1st Inf. Co.A
Thomas, Benjamin NC 6th Inf. Co.F
Thomas, Benjamin NC 48th Inf. Co.E
Thomas, Benjamin NC 50th Inf. Co.F
Thomas, Benjamin TN 3rd (Lillard's) Mtd.Inf. Co.I
Thomas, Benjamin VA 12th Cav. Co.C
Thomas, Benjamin A. VA Hvy.Arty. A.J. Jones' Co.
Thomas, Benjamin D. AL 12th Inf. Co.B Sgt.
Thomas, Benjamin D. VA 6th Inf. Vickery's Co.
Thomas, Benjamin D. VA 16th Inf. 1st Co.H Cpl.
Thomas, Benjamin F. AL Inf. 1st Regt. Co.B
Thomas, Benjamin F. GA 11th Inf. Co.I Cpl.
Thomas, Benjamin F. GA 49th Inf. Co.G
Thomas, Benjamin F. LA 13th Bn. (Part. Rangers) Co.F
Thomas, Benjamin F. LA Inf. 4th Bn. Co.B Sgt.
Thomas, Benjamin F. NC 47th Inf. Co.G
Thomas, Benjamin F. TN 12th (Cons.) Inf. Co.H
Thomas, Benjamin F. TN 27th Inf. Co.I
Thomas, Benjamin F. VA Lt.Arty. Lamkin's Co.
Thomas, Benjamin F. VA 19th Inf. Co.E
Thomas, Benjamin F. VA 34th Inf. Co.A
Thomas, Benj. Harden Gen. & Staff Asst.Surg.
Thomas, Benjamin J. MS 40th Inf. Co.D
Thomas, Benjamin J. VA 56th Inf. Co.B
Thomas, Benjamin L. VA 189th Mil. Co.C
Thomas, Benjamin M. NC 52nd Inf. Co.E
Thomas, Benjamin S. TN 3rd (Clack's) Inf. Co.E Ord.Sgt.
Thomas, Benjamin W. KY 1st (Butler's) Cav. Co.B 1st Lt.
Thomas, Bennett MO 1st Inf. Co.I
Thomas, Bennett SC 11th Res. Co.G
Thomas, Bennette TX 4th Cav. Co.B
Thomas, Benton D. VA Lt.Arty. Hankins' Co.
Thomas, Ben S. NC 46th Inf. Co.C
Thomas, Berry GA Inf. 25th Bn. (Prov.Guard) Co.A
Thomas, Berry NC 21st Inf. Co.G
Thomas, Berry Conf.Inf. 1st Bn. 2nd Co.A Sgt.
Thomas, Beverly L. TN 47th Inf. Co.E
Thomas, B.F. AL 13th Bn.Part.Rangers Co.C
Thomas, B.F. AL 56th Part.Rangers Co.G

Thomas, Charles H. KY 2nd Mtd.Inf. Co.C 1st Lt.
Thomas, Charles H. LA Pointe Coupee Arty.
Thomas, Charles H. MS 35th Inf. Co.B
Thomas, Charles H. MO 5th Inf. Co.H Capt.
Thomas, Chas. H. MO St.Guard
Thomas, Charles H. NC 15th Inf. Co.L AQM
Thomas, Charles H. NC 32nd Inf. Co.K
Thomas, Charles H. TX 24th Cav. Co.H
Thomas, Chas. H. Gen. & Staff Capt.,QM
Thomas, Charles L. TN 49th Inf. Co.A
Thomas, Charles L. Inf. Bailey's Cons.Regt. Co.G
Thomas, Charles M. MS 11th (Perrin's) Cav. Co.B Capt.
Thomas, Charles M. MS St.Cav. Perrin's Bn. Co.G Capt.
Thomas, Charles M. SC 24th Inf. Co.I
Thomas, Charles R. VA 21st Cav. Co.B
Thomas, Charles S. AL 6th Inf. Co.A,L
Thomas, Charles S. VA Lt.Arty. Huckstep's Co. Sgt.
Thomas, Charles S. VA Lt.Arty. Snead's Co. 2nd Lt.
Thomas, Charles T. VA 57th Inf. Co.C
Thomas, Charles W. NC 4th Cav. (59th St.Troops) Co.E Cpl.
Thomas, Charles W. VA Inf. 9th Bn. Co.B
Thomas, Charles W. VA 25th Inf. 2nd Co.G
Thomas, Charles W. VA 56th Inf. Co.B
Thomas, Charles W. VA 61st Inf. Co.H Music.
Thomas, Charles W. Gen. & Staff, A. of N.VA Capt.,AQM
Thomas, Charles W. Gen. & Staff Chap.
Thomas, Chison MS Inf. 3rd Bn. (St.Troops) Co.B
Thomas, C.H.P. TX 17th Cons.Dismtd.Cav. Co.C
Thomas, Christopher GA 4th (Clinch's) Cav. Co.I
Thomas, Christopher MS 12th Cav. Co.F
Thomas, Christopher Alonzo MS 7th Cav. Co.E
Thomas, Christopher C. NC 1st Arty. (10th St.Troops) Co.K
Thomas, Christopher C. TN 4th (McLemore's) Cav. Co.D
Thomas, C.J. AR 1st (Dobbin's) Cav. Co.A
Thomas, C.J. SC 8th Inf. Co.G
Thomas, C.J. SC Bn.St.Cadets Co.A
Thomas, C. Jasper AL 29th Inf. Co.K
Thomas, C.L. AL Randolph Cty.Res. J. Hightower's Co.
Thomas, Claiborn TX 27th Cav. Co.B
Thomas, Claiborne R. VA 5th Cav. Co.I
Thomas, Clark TX Cav. Martin's Regt. Bugler
Thomas, Clem TX 9th (Nichols') Inf. Co.K
Thomas, Clem TX Waul's Legion Co.E
Thomas, C.M. KY 2nd (Duke's) Cav. Co.L
Thomas, C.M. MS 11th Inf. Co.F Cpl.
Thomas, C.M. MS 19th Inf. Co.A Capt.
Thomas, C.M. TN Cav. Looney's Regt.
Thomas, C.M. TX Inf. Rutherford's Co.
Thomas, Coden H. FL Lt.Arty. Abell's Co.
Thomas, Colin FL 10th Inf. Co.I
Thomas, Colin GA 50th Inf. Co.G
Thomas, Colon FL Inf. 2nd Bn. Co.A
Thomas, Columbus NC 33rd Inf. Co.I
Thomas, Columbus A. NC 2nd Cav. (19th St.Troops) Co.E Capt.
Thomas, Columbus A. NC 56th Inf. Surg.
Thomas, Columbus A. Gen. & Staff Surg.
Thomas, Columbus V. VA Lt.Arty. Ancell's Co.
Thomas, Colvin M. LA 9th Inf. Co.I
Thomas, Corbin VA 39th Inf. Co.E
Thomas, Cornelius AL 61st Inf. Co.C
Thomas, Cornelius FL 1st Cav. Co.C
Thomas, Cornelius MS 8th Inf. Co.E
Thomas, Cornelius VA Inf. 26th Bn. Co.B
Thomas, C.P. AR 45th Mil. Forage M.
Thomas, C.R. GA 12th Inf. Co.F Capt.
Thomas, C.R. TN 6th Inf. Co.D Sgt.
Thomas, C.R. VA 15th Cav. Co.B
Thomas, Craft H. MS 12th Inf. Co.D
Thomas, Craig TX 21st Cav. Co.I
Thomas, Cread AR Cav. Poe's Bn. Dismuks' Co.
Thomas, Cread AR 2nd Vol. Co.B Cpl.
Thomas, Creed AR 23rd Inf. Co.B
Thomas, Creed AR 50th Mil. Co.G
Thomas, Creed T. VA 38th Inf. Co.E
Thomas, Crosby TX 18th Inf. Co.D
Thomas, C.S. GA 13th Cav. Co.K Cpl.
Thomas, Cuddy MS 18th Inf. Co.E 1st Lt.
Thomas, Curry MS 37th Inf. Co.K
Thomas, C.W. FL 9th Inf. Co.D
Thomas, C.W. NC 1st Jr.Res. Co.E
Thomas, C.W. NC 56th Inf. Co.E
Thomas, C.W. TN 15th (Cons.) Cav. Co.K Sgt.
Thomas, C.W. Gen. & Staff, A. of TN Asst.Surg.
Thomas, C. Wayne TX Cav. Martin's Regt. Co.B 2nd Lt.
Thomas, C.W.H. SC 4th Cav. Co.G
Thomas, Cyrus A. AL Cav. Holloway's Co.
Thomas, D. AL 9th Inf. Co.A
Thomas, D. FL 1st Cav. Co.D
Thomas, D. GA 4th (Clinch's) Cav. Co.I
Thomas, D. GA 4th Inf. Co.C
Thomas, D. GA 5th Inf. (St.Guards) Johnston's Co.
Thomas, D. GA 13th Inf. Co.H
Thomas, D. MS Cav. 3rd Bn. (Ashcraft's) Co.C
Thomas, D. MO 1st & 4th Cons.Inf. Co.E
Thomas, D. SC 4th Cav. Co.I Cpl.
Thomas, D. SC Hvy.Arty. Gilchrist's Co. (Gist Guard)
Thomas, D. SC 1st (Hagood's) Inf. 2nd Co.H
Thomas, D. TX Cav. Bourland's Regt. Co.F
Thomas, D. VA Cav. Mosby's Regt. (Part. Rangers) Co.E
Thomas, D.A. GA Lt.Arty. Croft's Btty. (Columbus Arty.)
Thomas, D.A. GA 6th Inf. (St.Guards) Co.I
Thomas, D.A. MS 2nd Inf. Co.L
Thomas, D.A. MS 14th Inf. Co.C
Thomas, D.A., Jr. SC Palmetto S.S. Co.A
Thomas, D.A. TX Inf. Timmons' Regt. Co.I
Thomas, D.A. TX Waul's Legion Co.E
Thomas, D.A. VA 3rd Cav. 2nd Co.I
Thomas, Dan MS 5th Inf. Co.D
Thomas, Daniel AL 17th Inf. Co.B,D
Thomas, Daniel AL 1st Bn. Hilliard's Legion Vol. Co.B
Thomas, Daniel FL 1st Cav. Co.B
Thomas, Daniel GA Cav. 6th Bn. (St.Guards) Co.A
Thomas, Daniel GA 6th Inf. (St.Guards) Co.A
Thomas, Daniel GA 51st Inf. Co.G
Thomas, Daniel GA 60th Inf. Co.C
Thomas, Daniel MS 5th Cav. Co.I
Thomas, Daniel MS 17th Inf. Co.B
Thomas, Daniel MO 4th Cav. Co.I
Thomas, Daniel MO 4th Inf. Co.E
Thomas, Daniel SC Cav. 12th Bn. Co.B Cpl.
Thomas, Daniel VA 1st Cav. 2nd Co.K
Thomas, Daniel A. TN 27th Inf. Co.I
Thomas, Daniel B. AR 2nd Inf.
Thomas, Daniel B. NC 26th Inf. Co.E
Thomas, Daniel D. LA 1st Cav. Co.B
Thomas, Daniel F. NC 12th Inf. Co.C
Thomas, Daniel F. NC 38th Inf. Co.A
Thomas, Daniel J. FL 5th Inf. Co.I
Thomas, Daniel L. MD 1st Cav. Co.K
Thomas, Daniel L. MD 1st Inf. Co.C
Thomas, Daniel L. VA Cav. Mosby's Regt. (Part.Rangers) Co.F
Thomas, Daniel M. NC Hvy.Arty. 10th Bn. Co.A
Thomas, Daniel Martin MO 8th Inf. Co.C
Thomas, Daniel R. AL 33rd Inf. Co.G
Thomas, Daniel R. FL 10th Inf. Co.E 2nd Music.
Thomas, Daniel R. GA 1st (Olmstead's) Inf. Co.G
Thomas, Daniel W. NC 42nd Inf. Co.E
Thomas, Daniel W. NC 45th Inf. Co.E
Thomas, Daniel Y. SC Lt.Arty. 3rd (Palmetto) Bn. Co.F
Thomas, Darius AR 35th Inf. Co.B
Thomas, David AL Inf. 1st Regt. Co.H,K
Thomas, David AL 23rd Inf. Co.D
Thomas, David GA 35th Inf. Co.F
Thomas, David GA 39th Inf. Co.A Sgt.
Thomas, David LA Red River S.S.
Thomas, David MS 18th Cav. Co.A
Thomas, David NC Cav. 5th Bn. Co.A
Thomas, David NC 1st Arty. (10th St.Troops) Co.H
Thomas, David NC 2nd Arty. (36th St.Troops) Co.B
Thomas, David NC Lt.Arty. 13th Bn. Co.B
Thomas, David NC Inf. 2nd Bn. Co.H
Thomas, David NC 64th Inf. Co.C
Thomas, David NC Walker's Bn. Thomas' Legion 1st Co.D
Thomas, David SC Lt.Arty. Jeter's Co. (Macbeth Lt.Arty.)
Thomas, David SC 1st (McCreary's) Inf. Co.E
Thomas, David TN 1st (Carter's) Cav. Co.I
Thomas, David TN 13th Inf. Co.F
Thomas, David TN 32nd Inf. Co.K
Thomas, David TN 40th Inf. Co.C
Thomas, David TN Conscr. (Cp. of Instr.)
Thomas, David TX 14th Cav. Co.C
Thomas, David TX 31st Cav. Co.A
Thomas, David TX 11th Inf. Co.G
Thomas, David VA 11th Cav. Co.F
Thomas, David VA 6th Bn.Res. Co.I
Thomas, David VA 7th Inf. Co.F
Thomas, David VA 16th Regt.Res. Co.A
Thomas, David VA Inf. 25th Bn. Co.B

Thomas, David VA 48th Inf. Co.B
Thomas, David VA 57th Inf. Co.C
Thomas, David VA Tuttle's Bn.Loc.Def. Co.A
Thomas, David A. AL 6th Inf. Co.A
Thomas, David A. GA 28th Inf. Co.G Cpl.
Thomas, David A. NC 50th Inf. Co.F
Thomas, David Anderson SC 1st Inf. Co.E 2nd Lt.
Thomas, David B. VA 3rd Res. Co.C
Thomas, David C. NC 37th Inf. Co.D
Thomas, David C. TN 2nd (Robison's) Inf. Co.D Cpl.
Thomas, David C. VA 29th Inf. Co.E Cpl.
Thomas, David Dyre TN Lt.Arty. Barry's Co. Cpl.
Thomas, David E. AL 24th Inf. Co.E Capt.
Thomas, David E. VA 60th Inf. Co.K
Thomas, David G. AL 22nd Inf. Co.K
Thomas, David G. AL Cp. of Instr. Talladega
Thomas, David G. VA Tuttle's Bn.Loc.Def. Co.A Capt.
Thomas, David J. AL 49th Inf. Co.H
Thomas, David J. AL 1st Bn. Hilliard's Legion Vol. Co.B
Thomas, David L. AR 14th (Powers') Inf. Co.H
Thomas, David R. NC 54th Inf. Co.F 3rd Lt.
Thomas, David S. AL 22nd Inf. Co.H
Thomas, David S. MO 1st Cav. Co.G
Thomas, David S. SC 1st Inf. Co.K
Thomas, David W. AR 3rd Inf. Co.H
Thomas, David W. SC 14th Inf. Co.D
Thomas, Davis GA Cobb's Legion Co.I
Thomas, D.B. AR 34th Inf. Co.A
Thomas, D.B. NC 27th Inf. Co.E
Thomas, D.B. TX 6th Cav. Surg.
Thomas, D.B. TX Arty. (St.Troops) Good's Co.
Thomas, D.B. Gen. & Staff, Medical Dept. Surg.
Thomas, D.C. LA 2nd Cav. Co.F
Thomas, D.C. MS 19th Inf. Co.A
Thomas, D.E. LA 17th Inf. Co.F
Thomas, D.E. MS Cav. 2nd Bn.Res. 1st Lt.
Thomas, D.E. SC 17th Inf. Co.K
Thomas, DeWitt C. TX 1st (McCulloch's) Cav. Co.A 2nd Lt.
Thomas, Dewitt C. TX Waul's Legion Co.A
Thomas, D.F. TN 21st (Wilson's) Cav. Co.B
Thomas, D.G. MS Cav. 3rd Bn. (Ashcraft's) Co.E
Thomas, D.G. MS 11th (Cons.) Cav. Co.I
Thomas, D.H. AL 11th Cav. AQM
Thomas, D.H. AL 15th Inf. Co.H Sgt.
Thomas, D.H. AL 25th Inf. Co.C
Thomas, D.H. AL 29th Inf. Co.B Sgt.Maj.
Thomas, D.H. AR 15th (Josey's) Inf. Co.B
Thomas, D.H. GA 13th Inf. Co.H
Thomas, D.H. MS 1st Cav. Co.F
Thomas, D.H. MS 5th Inf. Co.H 2nd Lt.
Thomas, D.H. NC 5th Inf. Co.G
Thomas, D.H. SC 4th St.Troops Co.E Sgt.
Thomas, D.H. Gen. & Staff Capt.,AQM
Thomas, Dixon FL 1st Cav. Co.B
Thomas, Dixon A. AL 33rd Inf. Co.G
Thomas, D.J. AL 60th Inf. Co.H
Thomas, D.J. AL Talladega Cty.Res. D.M. Reid's Co.
Thomas, D.J. GA Inf. 4th Bn. (St.Guards) Co.B Sgt.
Thomas, D.J. GA 13th Inf. Co.H
Thomas, D.J. SC 5th Cav. Co.I
Thomas, D.J. SC Cav. 14th Bn. Co.D
Thomas, D.J. SC 4th St.Troops Co.G
Thomas, D.J. TN 20th (Russell's) Cav. Co.C,B
Thomas, D.J. TX 30th Cav. Co.H
Thomas, D.J. TX 9th (Nichols') Inf. Co.I
Thomas, D.J.S. TX Waul's Legion Co.E 1st Lt.
Thomas, D.K. TN 20th (Russell's) Cav. Co.C
Thomas, D.K. TX 18th Cav.
Thomas, D.L. FL 1st (Res.) Inf. Co.L
Thomas, D.L. MD Weston's Bn. Co.A
Thomas, D.L. SC Arty. Gregg's Co. (McQueen Lt.Arty.)
Thomas, D.M. TN 12th Inf. Co.C
Thomas, D.M. TX Cav. Waller's Regt. Co.F
Thomas, D.N. AL 48th Inf. Co.H
Thomas, D.P. TN 24th Bn.S.S. Co.C 2nd Lt.
Thomas, D.R. AL 60th Inf. Co.H
Thomas, D.R. GA Cav. 10th Bn. (St.Guards) Co.C
Thomas, D.R. MS 2nd Cav. Co.I
Thomas, D.R. SC 2nd Arty. Co.K
Thomas, D.R. SC 27th Inf. Co.F
Thomas, D.R. TX 26th Cav. Co.I
Thomas, D.R. TX 20th Inf. Co.B
Thomas, D.R. VA Mtd.Riflemen St.Martin's Co.
Thomas, D.R. VA 56th Inf. Co.I
Thomas, Drewry GA 16th Inf. Co.H
Thomas, D.S. SC Lt.Arty. 3rd (Palmetto) Bn. Co.F
Thomas, D.T. KY 8th Mtd.Inf. Co.F Sgt.
Thomas, Dudley TX 20th Inf. Co.A
Thomas, Duncan AL 33rd Inf. Co.A
Thomas, D.W. Gen. & Staff Surg.
Thomas, D.Y. TX Cav. Border's Regt. Co.C Sgt.
Thomas, E. AL 15th Inf. Co.H
Thomas, E. AL 19th Inf. Co.G
Thomas, E. FL Cav. 5th Bn. Co.G
Thomas, E. GA Lt.Arty. 14th Bn. Co.D
Thomas, E. GA Lt.Arty. King's Btty.
Thomas, E. GA 7th Inf. (St.Guards) Co.A
Thomas, E. GA 52nd Inf. Co.C
Thomas, E. MS 1st Cav.Res. Co.A
Thomas, E. MS 2nd St.Cav. Co.C
Thomas, E. MS 6th Cav. Co.D
Thomas, E. MS Inf. 2nd St.Troops Co.B
Thomas, E. MS 4th Inf. Co.H
Thomas, E. MO 6th Inf. Co.B
Thomas, E. NC 39th Inf. Co.G
Thomas, E. SC 1st (Hagood's) Inf. 2nd Co.H
Thomas, E. SC 20th Inf. Co.B
Thomas, E. SC Bn.St.Cadets Co.A Sgt.Maj.
Thomas, E. TX Cav. 1st Regt.St.Troops Co.F
Thomas, E. TX 35th (Brown's) Cav. Co.C
Thomas, E. TX 35th (Brown's) Cav. Co.D
Thomas, E. TX 9th (Nichols') Inf. Co.G Cpl.
Thomas, E.A. VA Inf. Montague's Bn. Co.B
Thomas, E.B. GA 16th Inf. Co.I 1st Lt.
Thomas, E.B. GA 24th Inf. Co.F Capt.
Thomas, E.B. TX 8th Cav. Co.B
Thomas, E.B. VA 53rd Inf. Co.G Cpl.
Thomas, Ebenezer H. GA 11th Inf. Co.F Cpl.
Thomas, E.C. AL 24th Inf. Co.K
Thomas, E.C. GA 41st Inf. Co.I
Thomas, E.C. GA 42nd Inf. Co.K 1st Lt.
Thomas, E.C. GA 56th Inf. Co.K
Thomas, E.C. NC 5th Sr.Res. Co.I
Thomas, E.C. TX 28th Cav. Co.C
Thomas, E.C. VA 54th Mil. Co.G
Thomas, E.D. AL 34th Inf. Co.I
Thomas, E.D. GA 54th Inf. Co.K
Thomas, Ed NC 7th Sr.Res. Fisher's Co.
Thomas, E.D. TN 21st & 22nd (Cons.) Cav. Co.A
Thomas, E.D. TN 22nd (Barteau's) Cav. Co.C
Thomas, Ed, 2nd TX Inf. Timmons' Regt. Co.G 1st Lt.
Thomas, Ed TX Waul's Legion Co.A 1st Lt.
Thomas, E.D. VA 157th Mil. Co.B
Thomas, Edgar LA Mil. 1st Regt. 3rd Brig. 1st Div. Co.E 1st Lt.
Thomas, Edgar VA 17th Inf. Co.D
Thomas, Edmond GA 50th Inf. Co.A Sgt.
Thomas, Edmond MS 10th Cav.
Thomas, Edmond H. GA Inf. 27th Bn. Co.A
Thomas, Edmund NC 8th Inf. Co.D
Thomas, Edmund VA Cav. 35th Bn. Co.B
Thomas, Ed R. KY 2nd Mtd.Inf. Co.H
Thomas, Edwar TX Inf. Timmons' Regt. Co.G 1st Lt.
Thomas, Edward AL 21st Inf. Co.A
Thomas, Edward AL 51st (Part.Rangers) Co.K
Thomas, Edward FL 5th Inf. Co.H
Thomas, Edward GA 47th Inf. Co.F
Thomas, Edward GA 50th Inf. Co.C
Thomas, Edward KY 1st (Butler's) Cav. Co.C
Thomas, Edward KY 3rd Cav. Co.C
Thomas, Edward LA 1st (Strawbridge's) Inf. Co.C
Thomas, Edward LA Inf.Cons. 18th Regt. & Yellow Jacket Bn. Co.A 2nd Sgt.
Thomas, Edward MD Cav. 2nd Bn. Co.B,C
Thomas, Edw. (alias Amos Hill) MD Cav. 2nd Bn.
Thomas, Edward MS 11th Inf. Co.B
Thomas, Edward MO 2nd Cav. Co.G
Thomas, Edward SC 20th Inf. Co.F
Thomas, Edw. SC 25th Inf. Co.K
Thomas, Edward VA 2nd Arty. Co.D
Thomas, Edward VA Inf. 22nd Bn. Co.A
Thomas, Edward VA Inf. 22nd Bn. Co.D
Thomas, Edward A. VA 53rd Inf. Co.I
Thomas, Edward B. VA Inf. 5th Bn. Co.B
Thomas, Edward C. GA Carlton's Co. (Troup Cty.Arty.)
Thomas, Edward C. GA 3rd Inf. Co.K
Thomas, Edward J. FL 6th Inf. Co.C Sgt.
Thomas, Edward L. GA 35th Inf. Col.
Thomas, Edward L. Thomas' Brig. Brig.Gen.
Thomas, Edward S. VA Inf. 4th Bn.Loc.Def. Co.B
Thomas, Edward S. VA 61st Mil. Co.D Ens.
Thomas, Edward W. FL 7th Inf. Co.A Cpl.
Thomas, Edwin GA 51st Inf. Co.G
Thomas, Edwin MD 1st Cav. Co.B
Thomas, Edwin W. VA 37th Inf. Co.F
Thomas, E.E. AR 31st Inf. Co.H
Thomas, E.E. GA 1st (Ramsey's) Inf.
Thomas, E.F. TN 15th (Cons.) Cav. Co.B
Thomas, E. Frank TX 21st Cav. Co.B
Thomas, E.H. AL 3rd Bn.Res. Appling's Co.

Thomas, E.H. GA Cav. 16th Bn. (St.Guards) Co.B
Thomas, E.H.H. MS 43rd Inf. Co.B
Thomas, E.J. GA Cav. 1st Bn. Winn's Co., Walthour's Co. Cpl.
Thomas, E.J. GA 4th (Clinch's) Cav. Co.H
Thomas, E.J. GA 5th Cav. Co.G Cpl.
Thomas, E.J. GA 6th Cav. Co.G
Thomas, E.J. 7th Conf.Cav. Co.G,M Sgt.
Thomas, Elam TN 16th (Logwood's) Cav. Co.K
Thomas, Eldridge TN 38th Inf. Co.G
Thomas, Eldridge VA Hvy.Arty. 10th Bn. Co.B
Thomas, Election T. AL 29th Inf. Co.B
Thomas, Eli AL 50th Inf.
Thomas, Eli FL 1st Cav. Co.B
Thomas, Eli MO 9th Inf. Co.F
Thomas, Eli SC 10th Inf. Co.D
Thomas, Eli VA 37th Mil. Co.A
Thomas, Eli VA 40th Inf.
Thomas, Elias FL Sp.Cav. 1st Bn. Co.B
Thomas, Elias B. VA 54th Inf. Co.K Cpl.
Thomas, Elias D. VA 25th Cav. Co.F
Thomas, Elias M. AL 11th Inf. Co.F
Thomas, Elihu SC 1st Bn.S.S. Co.C
Thomas, Elihu SC 9th Res. Co.I
Thomas, Elihu SC 27th Inf. Co.G
Thomas, Elihu D. TN 2nd (Smith's) Cav.
Thomas, Elijah MS 8th Inf. Co.G
Thomas, Elijah MO 12th Inf. Co.I
Thomas, Elijah TX 8th Cav. Co.B
Thomas, Elijah TX 35th (Brown's) Cav. Co.G
Thomas, Elijah TX 11th Inf. Co.K Cpl.
Thomas, Eliot O. SC 14th Inf. Co.E Sgt.
Thomas, Eliphus SC 1st Bn.S.S. Co.C
Thomas, Eliphus SC 9th Res. Co.I
Thomas, Elisha GA 36th (Broyles') Inf. Co.L,C
Thomas, Elisha NC 3rd Arty. (40th St.Troops) Co.F
Thomas, Elisha TX 8th Cav. Co.B
Thomas, Eli W. TX 13th Cav. Co.D
Thomas, Eli W. TX 1st Inf. Co.H
Thomas, E.M. AL 60th Inf. Co.B Cpl.
Thomas, E.M. MS 5th Inf. Co.E
Thomas, E.M. TN 31st Inf. Co.C
Thomas, Emanuel J. AR 26th Inf. Co.A
Thomas, Emiel SC 15th Inf. Co.F
Thomas, Enoc GA 42nd Inf. Co.E
Thomas, E.P. VA 8th Cav. Co.B
Thomas, Ephraim M.B. LA 8th Inf. Co.G
Thomas, E.R. AL 15th Inf. Co.I
Thomas, E.R. MS 13th Inf. Co.G
Thomas, E.R. SC 6th Cav. Co.I
Thomas, E.R. SC 21st Inf. Co.G
Thomas, E.R. VA 36th Inf. Beckett's Co.
Thomas, Erasmus A. MS 11th Inf. Co.F
Thomas, Erby TN 2nd (Ashby's) Cav. Co.A 2nd Lt.
Thomas, Erby TN Cav. 5th Bn. (McClellan's) Co.A 2nd Lt.
Thomas, E.S. MS 3rd Cav. Co.A
Thomas, E.S. NC 42nd Inf. Co.E
Thomas, E.S. TN 19th Inf. Co.E
Thomas, E.S. VA 1st St.Res. Co.D
Thomas, E.T. GA 10th Inf. Co.D
Thomas, E.T. KY 12th Cav. Co.B
Thomas, Etheldred NC 47th Inf. Co.C
Thomas, Eugene A. SC Inf. Hampton Legion Co.A Capt.
Thomas, Eugene W. AL 37th Inf. Co.I,D
Thomas, E.V. LA Lt.Arty. LeGardeur, Jr.'s Co. (Orleans Guard Btty.)
Thomas, Evan H. MS 12th Inf. Co.A
Thomas, E.W. FL 2nd Cav. Co.F
Thomas, E.W. MS 28th Cav. Co.K
Thomas, E.W. SC 5th Cav. Co.A
Thomas, E.W. TN 7th (Duckworth's) Cav. Co.A
Thomas, E.W. TN Hvy.Arty. Johnston's Co.
Thomas, E.W. TX Vol. Rainey's Co.
Thomas, Ewell VA 40th Inf. Co.E
Thomas, Ezekiel GA 34th Inf. Co.G
Thomas, Ezekiel MS 44th Inf. Co.I
Thomas, Ezekiel TX 36th Cav. Co.E
Thomas, Ezekiel TX Cav. Ragsdale's Bn. Co.F
Thomas, Ezeriah N. AL 3rd Bn. Hilliard's Legion Vol. Co.C
Thomas, F. AL Lt.Arty. Tarrant's Btty.
Thomas, F. LA Mil. 3rd Regt. French Brig. Co.2
Thomas, F. LA Mil. Orleans Fire Regt. Co.H
Thomas, F. MO 1st N.E. Cav. Co.G
Thomas, F. NC 42nd Inf. Co.B
Thomas, F. TX Cav. Giddings' Bn. Weisiger's Co.
Thomas, F. VA 2nd St.Res. Co.K Cpl.
Thomas, F. VA Inf. 2nd Bn.Loc.Def. Co.C
Thomas, F. 2nd Cherokee Mtd.Vol. Co.C
Thomas, F.A. FL 1st (Res.) Inf. Co.L
Thomas, F.B. SC 7th Inf. 1st Co.I
Thomas, F.B. TX 5th Inf. Co.A
Thomas, F.C. GA Inf. 8th Bn. Co.A
Thomas, F.C. SC 18th Inf. Co.G Cpl.
Thomas, Felix MO St.Guard
Thomas, Ferdinand A. TN 28th Inf. Co.G
Thomas, Ferdinand C. AL 22nd Inf. Co.H
Thomas, F.G. MS Cav. 3rd Bn. (Ashcraft's) Co.E 1st Lt.
Thomas, F.G. MS 11th (Cons.) Cav. Co.I 1st Lt.
Thomas, F.J. Gen. & Staff, Ord.Dept. Col.
Thomas, F.K. AL 29th Inf. Co.F Music.
Thomas, F.L. Gen. & Staff 1st Lt.,Adj.
Thomas, Fleming VA 57th Inf. Co.C
Thomas, Floyd, Jr. GA 3rd Inf. Co.G
Thomas, Floyd, Jr. GA 63rd Inf. Co.A
Thomas, Floyd J. AL Lt.Arty. 2nd Bn. Co.A Cpl.
Thomas, F.M. AR 8th Inf. New Co.C
Thomas, F.M. AR 19th (Dawson's) Inf. Co.I
Thomas, F.M. AR 19th (Dockery's) Inf. Co.B
Thomas, F.M. GA 3rd Cav. Co.A
Thomas, F.M. GA Inf. (Loc.Def.) Whiteside's Nav.Bn. Co.C
Thomas, F.M. LA 25th Inf. Co.E
Thomas, F.M. MS 6th Inf. Co.E
Thomas, F.M. MS 36th Inf. Co.F
Thomas, F.M. MS 39th Inf. Co.E 1st Lt.
Thomas, F.M. MO 2nd Inf. Co.D
Thomas, F.M. TN 21st (Wilson's) Cav. Co.H
Thomas, F.M. TN 16th Inf. Co.F
Thomas, Fountain VA Cav. 35th Bn. Co.F
Thomas, Fountain VA 13th Inf. Co.F
Thomas, F.R. TX 32nd Cav. Co.H Music.
Thomas, Frances VA Lt.Arty. E.J. Anderson's Co.
Thomas, Francis AL 51st (Part.Rangers) Co.K
Thomas, Francis KY 3rd Cav. Co.C
Thomas, Francis TX 5th Inf. Co.I
Thomas, Francis M. AL 11th Cav. Co.F Cpl.
Thomas, Francis M. AR 9th Inf. Co.D
Thomas, Francis M. GA 35th Inf. Co.H
Thomas, Francis M. KY 6th Mtd.Inf. Co.B
Thomas, Francis M. MS 10th Inf. Old Co.H 2nd Lt.
Thomas, Francis M. TX 22nd Cav. Co.A 1st Lt.
Thomas, Francis M. Exch.Bn. Co.E,D,CSA 1st Lt.
Thomas, Francis Marion AL 49th Inf. Co.B
Thomas, Frank GA 3rd Res. Co.D
Thomas, Frank KY 1st (Butler's) Cav. Co.C
Thomas, Frank E. NC 1st Jr.Res. Co.C Jr.2nd Lt.
Thomas, Frank G. MS Inf. 11th Regt. Co.C
Thomas, Franklin MO 5th Cav. Co.H
Thomas, Franklin MO 8th Cav. Co.A
Thomas, Franklin VA 10th Inf. Co.E
Thomas, Franklin VA 46th Inf.
Thomas, Franklin 3rd Conf.Cav. Co.A Sgt.
Thomas, Franklin A. MS 22nd Inf. Co.H
Thomas, Franklin C. AR 31st Inf. Co.A 1st Sgt.
Thomas, Franklin G. MS 11th Inf. Co.C
Thomas, Franklin L.D. NC 62nd Inf. Co.E Sgt.
Thomas, Frederic LA Mil. Orleans Guards Regt. Co.C 1st Lt.
Thomas, Frederick MS 3rd Inf. Co.F
Thomas, Freeman H. TN 24th Inf. 2nd Co.C Sgt.
Thomas, French S. VA 14th Cav. Co.D
Thomas, F.R.L. GA 3rd Cav. Co.H
Thomas, F.T. MO 8th Inf. Co.F
Thomas, F.W. AL Lt.Arty. Kolb's Btty.
Thomas, F.W. KY 3rd Mtd.Inf. Co.D Sgt.
Thomas, F.W. LA 27th Inf. Co.E
Thomas, G. AR 3rd Inf. (St.Troops) Co.A
Thomas, G. GA 35th Inf. Co.A
Thomas, G. LA 15th Inf. Co.E
Thomas, G. MS Cav. 3rd Bn. (Ashcraft's) Co.C
Thomas, G. NC 3rd Cav. (41st St.Troops) Co.B
Thomas, G. NC McLean's Bn.Lt.Duty Men Co.B
Thomas, G. TX 2nd Inf. Co.G
Thomas, G.A. KY 12th Cav. Co.E Cpl.
Thomas, G.A. TX 35th (Brown's) Cav. Co.I
Thomas, G.A. VA 2nd Cav. Co.K
Thomas, Gabriel AL Arty. 1st Bn. Co.E Music.
Thomas, Gabriel GA 6th Cav.
Thomas, Gabriel M. SC 1st (Orr's) Rifles Co.A Cpl.
Thomas, G.B. VA 11th Bn.Res. Co.A
Thomas, G.C. MS 28th Cav.
Thomas, G.D. TN Cav. 12th Bn. (Day's) Co.E
Thomas, G.D. TN 15th (Stewart's) Cav. Co.H
Thomas, G.D. TX 34th Cav. Co.I
Thomas, G.E. GA 54th Inf. Co.G,F Capt.
Thomas, G.E., Jr. Gen. & Staff Ord.Sgt.
Thomas, Gehu MS 6th Cav. Co.G
Thomas, George AL 15th Bn.Part.Rangers Co.B
Thomas, George AL 56th Part.Rangers Co.B
Thomas, George AL 1st Inf. Co.A
Thomas, George AL 19th Inf. Co.G
Thomas, George AL 59th Inf. Co.B

Thomas, George AL 2nd Bn. Hilliard's Legion Vol. Co.E
Thomas, George GA Lt.Arty. Howell's Co.
Thomas, George GA 6th Inf. (St.Guards) Co.H
Thomas, George GA 7th Inf. Co.A
Thomas, George GA Inf. 26th Bn. Co.B
Thomas, George LA 12th Inf. 1st Co.M
Thomas, George LA Inf. 16th Bn. (Conf.Guards Resp.Bn.) Co.A
Thomas, George MD Arty. 3rd Btty.
Thomas, George MD 1st Inf. 2nd Co.H 1st Lt.
Thomas, George MD Inf. 2nd Bn. Co.A Capt.
Thomas, George MD Weston's Bn. Co.D 1st Lt.
Thomas, George MS 12th Inf. Co.B
Thomas, George MO 1st Cav. Co.B
Thomas, George MO Cav. Fristoe's Regt. Co.H
Thomas, George MO Inf. 5th Regt.St.Guard Co.B
Thomas, George NC 2nd Inf. Co.D
Thomas, George SC Inf. Holcombe Legion Co.A
Thomas, George TN 1st Cav. Co.A
Thomas, George TN Cav. 1st Bn. (McNairy's) Co.A
Thomas, George TN Cav. 12th Bn. (Day's) Co.A
Thomas, George TN Cav. 12th Bn. (Day's) Co.C
Thomas, George TN Cav. 12th Bn. (Day's) Co.D
Thomas, George TN Corbit's Btty.
Thomas, George TN 6th Inf. Co.A
Thomas, George TN 13th Inf. Co.A
Thomas, George TN 44th Inf. Co.B
Thomas, George TN 62nd Mtd.Inf. Co.I
Thomas, George TX 10th Cav. Co.C
Thomas, George TX 11th Inf. Co.K
Thomas, George TX 22nd Inf. Co.C
Thomas, George VA Cav. 46th Bn. Co.F
Thomas, George VA Inf. 1st Bn.Loc.Def. Co.F
Thomas, George VA 2nd St.Res.
Thomas, George Ind.Scouts & Rangers Lillard's Co.
Thomas, George A. AL 5th Inf. New Co.A 1st Lt.
Thomas, George A. GA 7th Inf. Co.E
Thomas, George A. NC 5th Cav. (63rd St.Troops) Co.G
Thomas, George A. TX 21st Cav. Co.H,A
Thomas, George A. VA 4th Cav. Co.C
Thomas, George A. VA 6th Cav. Co.F Sgt.
Thomas, George C. TN 4th (McLemore's) Cav. Co.D
Thomas, George C. TN 31st Inf. Co.K Capt.
Thomas, George E. LA Arty. 1st Field Btty.
Thomas, George E. VA 61st Mil. Co.H 2nd Lt.
Thomas, George F. VA 17th Inf. Co.G
Thomas, George H. AL 4th (Russell's) Cav. Co.I
Thomas, George H. GA 26th Inf. Co.A
Thomas, George H. GA Inf. (Brunswick Rifles) Harris' Ind.Co.
Thomas, George H. TN 14th Inf. Co.C
Thomas, George H. VA 9th Inf. Co.B
Thomas, George H. VA 39th Inf. Co.C
Thomas, George H. VA 57th Inf. Co.D Sgt.
Thomas, George I., Jr. VA 17th Inf. Co.A
Thomas, George J., Jr. LA Washington Arty.Bn. Co.3,2
Thomas, George J. VA 1st Arty. 1st Co.C
Thomas, George J. VA 1st Inf. Co.F
Thomas, George J. VA 54th Mil. Co.G
Thomas, George K. AL 43rd Inf. Co.I
Thomas, George L. AL 36th Inf. AQM
Thomas, George L. NC 30th Inf. Co.B
Thomas, George L. VA Cav. Ferguson's Bn. Nounnan's Co.
Thomas, George L. VA Lt.Arty. 38th Bn. Co.C 2nd Lt.
Thomas, George L. Gen. & Staff Capt.,AQM
Thomas, George M. AL 59th Inf. Co.C
Thomas, George M. AL 2nd Bn. Hilliard's Legion Vol. Co.F
Thomas, George M. GA 42nd Inf. Co.D Cpl.
Thomas, George M.F. GA 42nd Inf. Co.G
Thomas, George N. MS 14th Inf. Co.H
Thomas, George O. TX 19th Cav. Co.H
Thomas, George P. AR 1st (Colquitt's) Inf. Co.G Sgt.Maj.
Thomas, George P. VA 30th Bn.S.S. Co.B
Thomas, George S. GA 20th Inf. Co.F 1st Lt.
Thomas, George S. GA 64th Inf. Co.C Capt.
Thomas, George S. VA Patrol Guard 11th Congr.Dist. (Mtd.)
Thomas, George S. VA Lt.Arty. Cayce's Co.
Thomas, George S. VA Inf. 21st Bn. Co.A
Thomas, George S. VA 64th Mtd.Inf. Co.A
Thomas, George T. AL 57th Inf. Co.K
Thomas, George W. AL 4th Inf. Co.D Sgt.
Thomas, George W. AL 12th Inf. Co.B Sgt.
Thomas, George W. AL 19th Inf. Co.C
Thomas, George W. AR 9th Inf. Old Co.B, Co.F
Thomas, George W. FL 2nd Inf. Co.E
Thomas, George W. FL 7th Inf.
Thomas, George W. GA 12th Inf. Co.A Asst.Surg.
Thomas, George W. GA 22nd Inf. Co.G Capt.
Thomas, George W. GA 35th Inf. Co.G
Thomas, George W. GA 57th Inf. Co.D
Thomas, George W. KY 1st (Butler's) Cav. Co.C
Thomas, George W. KY 3rd Cav. Co.C
Thomas, George W. MS 12th Cav. Co.B,E Sgt.
Thomas, George W. MS 3rd Inf. Co.B
Thomas, George W. MS 5th Inf. Co.K
Thomas, George W. MS 11th Inf. Co.H
Thomas, George W. MS 14th Inf. Co.K
Thomas, George W. MS 15th Inf. Co.C
Thomas, George W. MS 16th Inf. Co.K 1st Cpl.
Thomas, George W. MO 1st Cav. Co.B
Thomas, George W. MO 9th (Elliott's) Cav. Co.G
Thomas, George W. NC Inf. 2nd Bn. Co.A
Thomas, George W. NC 2nd Bn.Loc.Def.Troops Co.A Laborer
Thomas, George W. NC 15th Inf. Co.K Cpl.
Thomas, George W. NC 42nd Inf. Co.D
Thomas, George W. NC 66th Inf. Co.G
Thomas, George W. NC Pris.Guard Howard's Co.
Thomas, George W. TN 2nd (Ashby's) Cav. Co.G
Thomas, George W. TN 15th (Cons.) Cav. Co.K 1st Lt.
Thomas, George W. TN 16th (Logwood's) Cav. Co.B
Thomas, George W. TN 16th (Logwood's) Cav. Co.G 1st Lt.
Thomas, George W. TN 1st (Turney's) Inf. Co.G
Thomas, George W. TN 3rd (Lillard's) Mtd.Inf. Co.B Cpl.
Thomas, George W. TN 3rd (Lillard's) Mtd.Inf. Co.C
Thomas, George W. TN Inf. 154th Sr.Regt. 2nd Co.B
Thomas, George W. TX 22nd Cav. Co.C
Thomas, George W. VA 25th Cav. Co.F Capt.
Thomas, George W. VA Cav. 46th Bn. Co.E
Thomas, George W. VA 1st Bn.Res. Co.D Sgt.
Thomas, George W. VA 30th Inf. Co.B
Thomas, George W. VA 37th Inf. Co.F
Thomas, George W. VA 42nd Inf. Co.E 1st Lt.
Thomas, George W. VA 48th Inf. Co.B
Thomas, George W. VA 58th Inf. Co.B
Thomas, George W. Conf.Cav. Clarkson's Bn. Ind.Rangers Co.H
Thomas, Geo. W. Gen. & Staff AQM
Thomas, George W. Gen. & Staff Adj.,1st Lt.
Thomas, George W. Gen. & Staff Asst.Surg.
Thomas, George Wa MO Inf. Clark's Regt. Co.D,B
Thomas, George W.J. VA 108th Mil. Co.F
Thomas, G.F. KY Morgan's Men Co.C
Thomas, G.H. AL 5th Inf. New Co.A
Thomas, Gideon B. GA 51st Inf. Co.A
Thomas, Giles VA Mil. Stowers' Co.
Thomas, Giles D. VA 4th Inf. Co.E
Thomas, Gilford C. TN Lt.Arty. Rice's Btty.
Thomas, Gilson AL 20th Inf. Co.E
Thomas, Gilson AL 30th Inf. Co.F Cpl.
Thomas, G.J. GA Hvy.Arty. 22nd Bn. Co.F QMSgt.
Thomas, G.J. GA Inf. 1st Loc.Troops (Augusta) Barnes' Lt.Arty.Co.
Thomas, G.J. MO 5th Cav. Co.H Black.
Thomas, G.J. VA 3rd Inf.Loc.Def. Co.F
Thomas, G.L. NC 3rd Inf.
Thomas, G.M. FL 1st (Res.) Inf. Co.I
Thomas, G.M. LA 9th Inf. Co.C
Thomas, G.M. NC 22nd Inf. Co.G
Thomas, G.N. TX 1st Hvy.Arty. Co.B
Thomas, G.O. TX 2nd Inf.
Thomas, G.P. AL Cp. of Instr. Talladega
Thomas, G.R. GA 5th Inf. Co.F
Thomas, Grandison M. GA 24th Inf. Co.A
Thomas, Granville Smith VA 19th Inf. Co.C
Thomas, Green MS 5th Cav. Co.H,D
Thomas, Green NC 64th Inf. Co.G
Thomas, Green VA 30th Bn.S.S. Co.B
Thomas, Green B. AL 33rd Inf. Co.G
Thomas, Green D. TN 2nd (Robison's) Inf. Co.F
Thomas, Green T. NC 26th Inf. Co.K
Thomas, Greenville MO 5th Cav. Co.A
Thomas, Green W. MS 15th (Cons.) Inf. Co.H
Thomas, Green W. MS 20th Inf. Co.C
Thomas, Grey VA 3rd Cav. Co.D
Thomas, Griffin SC 1st (McCreary's) Inf. Co.B
Thomas, Griffin T. TX 2nd Cav. Co.B
Thomas, Griffin T. Gen. & Staff Hosp.Stew.
Thomas, Grigsby E., Jr. TA Inf. 2nd Bn. Co.A
Thomas, G.S. VA 11th Cav. Co.G
Thomas, G.T. AL 42nd Inf. Co.F
Thomas, Guilford AR 11th & 17th Cons.Inf. Co.I Sgt.
Thomas, Guilford AR 17th (Griffith's) Inf. Co.F Sgt.

Thomas, G.W. AL 1st Inf. Co.I
Thomas, G.W. AL 3rd Bn.Res. Co.H
Thomas, G.W. AL 17th Inf.
Thomas, G.W. AR 13th Inf.
Thomas, G.W. AR 30th Inf. Co.D
Thomas, G.W. AR 38th Inf. Co.E
Thomas, G.W. GA Lt.Arty. Howell's Co.
Thomas, G.W. GA 8th Inf. (St.Guards) Co.C
Thomas, G.W. GA 11th Inf. Co.A
Thomas, G.W. GA 16th Inf. Co.I
Thomas, G.W. GA 20th Inf. Co.A
Thomas, G.W. GA 46th Inf. Co.A
Thomas, G.W. GA 60th Inf. Co.E
Thomas, G.W. GA Floyd Legion (St.Guards) Co.D
Thomas, G.W. KY 3rd Cav. Co.C
Thomas, G.W. KY 10th (Johnson's) Cav. Co.G
Thomas, G.W. KY 3rd Mtd.Inf. Co.E 1st Lt.
Thomas, G.W. KY B.W.
Thomas, G.W. MS 3rd (St.Troops) Cav. Co.H Sgt.
Thomas, G.W. MS 18th Inf. Co.I 1st Sgt.
Thomas, G.W. MO 6th Cav. Co.B Cpl.
Thomas, G.W. MO Cav. Fristoe's Regt. Co.H
Thomas, G.W. MO Cav. Williams' Regt. Co.B
Thomas, G.W. MO 1st & 4th Cons.Inf. Co.I
Thomas, G.W. MO 4th Inf. Co.D
Thomas, G.W. MO 10th Inf. Co.D
Thomas, G.W. NC 6th Sr.Res. Co.H
Thomas, G.W., Jr. NC Inf. 13th Bn. Co.B
Thomas, G.W., Sr. NC Inf. 13th Bn. Co.B
Thomas, G.W., Jr. NC 66th Inf. Co.B
Thomas, G.W., Sr. NC 66th Inf. Co.B
Thomas, G.W. TN 3rd (Lillard's) Mtd.Inf. Co.D
Thomas, G.W. TN 34th Inf. Co.G
Thomas, G.W. TN 51st (Cons.) Inf. Co.A Cpl.
Thomas, G.W. TN 52nd Inf. Co.D Sgt.
Thomas, G.W. TX 32nd Cav. Co.I 2nd Lt.
Thomas, G.W. VA 10th Cav. Co.G
Thomas, G.W. VA Cav. 36th Bn. Co.C
Thomas, G.W. VA Arty. Bryan's Co.
Thomas, G.W. Brush Bn.
Thomas, G. William Gen. & Staff, QM Dept.
Thomas, G.W.J. VA 14th Cav. Co.E
Thomas, G.Y. MS 9th Cav. Co.D
Thomas, G.Y. MS Cav. 17th Bn. Co.F
Thomas, H. AL 36th Inf. Co.F
Thomas, H. AR Lt.Arty. Marshall's Btty.
Thomas, H. AR 12th Inf. Co.E
Thomas, H. FL 9th Inf. Co.F
Thomas, H. GA 11th Cav. (St.Guards) Smith's Co.
Thomas, H. GA 50th Inf. Co.D
Thomas, H., Jr. LA Lt.Arty. Fenner's Btty.
Thomas, H. LA 3rd Inf. Co.K
Thomas, H. MS 4th Cav. Co.D
Thomas, H. MO 1st N.E. Cav. Co.G
Thomas, H. MO 4th Inf. Co.K
Thomas, H. NC 61st Inf. Co.F
Thomas, H. TN 14th (Neely's) Cav. Co.F
Thomas, H. 1st Chickasaw Inf. Milam's Co. Cpl.
Thomas, H. 1st Creek Mtd.Vol. 2nd Co.D
Thomas, H.A. AL Lt.Arty. Kolb's Btty. Sgt.
Thomas, H.A. SC 4th Inf. Co.G
Thomas, H.A. TX 25th Cav. Co.G
Thomas, H.A. VA Lt.Arty. Snead's Co.
Thomas, Hamilton GA 4th (Clinch's) Cav. Co.C
Thomas, Hamilton GA Inf. (Brunswick Rifles) Harris' Ind.Co.
Thomas, Hamilton GA 26th Inf. Co.H,K
Thomas, Hampton TX 14th Cav. Co.K Cpl.
Thomas, Hampton H. NC 26th Inf. Co.B Sgt.
Thomas, Hardin TX 11th Inf. Co.K
Thomas, Hardin T. VA 44th Inf. Co.K
Thomas, Hardy GA 61st Inf. Co.F
Thomas, Harmon GA 39th Inf. Co.D
Thomas, Harril A. AR 15th (Josey's) Inf. Co.B
Thomas, Harrison KY 4th Cav. Co.B,K
Thomas, Harrison TN 13th (Gore's) Cav. Co.C
Thomas, Harrison TN 43rd Inf. Co.G
Thomas, Harry B. AL 36th Inf. Co.B
Thomas, Hartwill J. GA 3rd Inf. Co.L
Thomas, Harvey AL Lt.Arty. Ward's Btty.
Thomas, Harvey LA 17th Inf. Co.C Sgt.
Thomas, H.B. AL 3rd Cav. Co.H
Thomas, H.B. AL 37th Inf. Co.F
Thomas, H.B. KY 12th Cav. Co.D 2nd Lt.
Thomas, H.B. SC Inf. 6th Bn. Co.C
Thomas, H.B. SC 25th Inf. Co.K
Thomas, H.B. TN 5th Inf. 2nd Co.F
Thomas, H.B. TX 15th Cav. Co.B
Thomas, H.B. TX 20th Inf. Co.D
Thomas, H.B. TX Inf. Timmons' Regt. Co.I
Thomas, H.B. VA 22nd Inf. Co.C
Thomas, H.C. AL Cav. 4th Bn. (Love's) Co.C
Thomas, H.C. AL 8th (Hatch's) Cav. Co.D
Thomas, H.C. AL 14th Inf. Co.H,E
Thomas, H.C. KY Morgan's Men Co.C
Thomas, H.C. TN 49th Inf. Co.D Cpl.
Thomas, H.C. Inf. Bailey's Cons.Regt. Co.L Cpl.
Thomas, H.C. TX 8th Cav. Co.E
Thomas, H.C. VA Lt.Arty. Penick's Co.
Thomas, H.C. Conf.Lt.Arty. Richardson's Bn. Co.A
Thomas, H. Clay KY 2nd (Duke's) Cav. Co.C
Thomas, H.E. LA 7th Inf. Co.A
Thomas, Henderson AL 29th Inf. Co.C
Thomas, Henderson GA 35th Inf. Co.E
Thomas, Henderson NC 2nd Cav. (19th St.Troops) Co.I 2nd Lt.
Thomas, Henderson F. VA 30th Bn.S.S. Co.B
Thomas, Henly E. AL 41st Inf. Co.A
Thomas, Henry AL 4th (Russell's) Cav. Co.I
Thomas, Henry AL 49th Inf. Co.H
Thomas, Henry AL Conscr.
Thomas, Henry AR 11th & 17th Cons.Inf. Co.I
Thomas, Henry AR 17th (Griffith's) Inf. Co.F
Thomas, Henry AR 25th Inf. Co.B
Thomas, Henry AR 32nd Inf. Co.I
Thomas, Henry FL 4th Inf. Co.B
Thomas, Henry GA 6th Cav. Co.B
Thomas, Henry GA 15th Inf. Co.B
Thomas, Henry GA 27th Inf. Co.B
Thomas, Henry GA 34th Inf. Co.A
Thomas, Henry GA 51st Inf. Co.G
Thomas, Henry KY 2nd (Duke's) Cav. Co.E
Thomas, Henry LA 16th Inf. Co.I
Thomas, Henry LA Mil. Chalmette Regt. Co.C
Thomas, Henry LA C.S. Zouave Bn. Co.C
Thomas, Henry MS 12th Cav. Co.A
Thomas, Henry MS 34th Inf. Co.E
Thomas, Henry MS Inf. (Res.) Berry's Co.
Thomas, Henry MO 1st Cav. Co.D
Thomas, Henry MO 9th (Elliott's) Cav. Co.B
Thomas, Henry MO 1st & 4th Cons.Inf. Co.H
Thomas, Henry NC 44th Inf. Co.E
Thomas, Henry NC 53rd Inf. Co.B
Thomas, Henry SC 10th Inf. Co.D
Thomas, Henry SC 20th Inf. Co.F
Thomas, Henry SC 21st Inf. Co.H
Thomas, Henry TN 2nd (Smith's) Cav.
Thomas, Henry TN 7th (Duckworth's) Cav. Co.E
Thomas, Henry TN 12th (Green's) Cav. Co.D Cpl.
Thomas, Henry TN 6th Inf. Co.D
Thomas, Henry TN 18th Inf. Co.F
Thomas, Henry TN 35th Inf. 1st Co.D
Thomas, Henry TN 37th Inf. Co.I
Thomas, Henry TX 11th Cav. Co.F
Thomas, Henry TX 30th Cav. Co.H
Thomas, Henry TX 5th Inf. (St.Troops) Co.B
Thomas, Henry TX Waul's Legion Co.E
Thomas, Henry VA Hvy.Arty. 19th Bn. 1st Co.E
Thomas, Henry VA Hvy.Arty. Wright's Co.
Thomas, Henry VA 13th Inf. Co.F
Thomas, Henry VA 45th Inf. Co.E Cpl.
Thomas, Henry Conf.Reg.Inf. Brooks' Bn. Co.C
Thomas, Henry A. AL Inf. 1st Regt. Co.B
Thomas, Henry A. GA 10th Inf. Co.F Sgt.Maj.
Thomas, Henry A. VA Cav. 39th Bn. Co.D
Thomas, Henry A. VA 19th Inf. Co.C
Thomas, Henry A. VA Inf. 54th Bn. Co.A
Thomas, Henry A. VA 63rd Inf. Co.E
Thomas, Henry B. VA Lt.Arty. Penick's Co.
Thomas, Henry C. AL 4th Inf. Co.E
Thomas, Henry C. AL 12th Inf. Co.B Cpl.
Thomas, Henry C. AL 12th Inf. Co.B
Thomas, Henry C. AL 28th Inf. Co.A
Thomas, Henry C. AL Hardy's Co. (Eufaula Minute Men)
Thomas, Henry C. NC Hvy.Arty. 10th Bn. Co.A
Thomas, Henry C. NC 14th Inf. Co.B
Thomas, Henry C. VA Goochland Lt.Arty.
Thomas, Henry C. VA 37th Inf. Co.H
Thomas, Henry Clay TX Cav. Martin's Regt. Co.C
Thomas, Henry F. GA 26th Inf. Co.K
Thomas, Henry F. VA Hvy.Arty. 19th Bn. Co.B
Thomas, Henry F. 1st Conf.Inf. 2nd Co.C
Thomas, Henry H. NC 6th Inf. Co.A
Thomas, Henry J. GA 1st (Fannin's) Res. Co.G
Thomas, Henry J. GA 1st (Symons') Res. Co.K
Thomas, Henry J. GA Cobb's Legion Co.B
Thomas, Henry J. VA 30th Inf. Co.B
Thomas, Henry L. GA 4th (Clinch's) Cav. Co.I
Thomas, Henry L. GA 31st Inf. Co.A
Thomas, Henry M. GA 3rd Inf. Co.G
Thomas, Henry P. GA 16th Inf. Lt.Col.
Thomas, Henry P. GA 45th Inf. Co.G Sgt.
Thomas, Henry P. NC 50th Inf. Co.F
Thomas, Henry R. VA Hvy.Arty. Coleman's Co. Music.
Thomas, Henry S. LA 12th Inf. Co.B
Thomas, Henry S. VA 59th Inf. 3rd Co.E
Thomas, Henry T. NC 23rd Inf. Co.D
Thomas, Henry Tilman NC 30th Inf. Co.H
Thomas, Henry W. GA 12th Inf. Co.G Hosp.Stew.
Thomas, Henry W. GA 35th Inf. Co.F QMSgt.

Thomas, Henry W. NC 15th Inf. Co.L
Thomas, Henry W. TN 14th Cav. Co.A
Thomas, Hezekiah MS 43rd Inf. Co.G
Thomas, Hezekiah NC 58th Inf. Co.D
Thomas, Hezekiah D. FL 6th Inf. Co.C
Thomas, H.F. GA Cav. Nelson's Ind.Co.
Thomas, H.F. LA 25th Inf. Co.K
Thomas, Hillary B. GA 56th Inf. Co.C
Thomas, Hilliard NC 4th Cav. (59th St.Troops) Co.H
Thomas, Hilliard SC 7th Res. Co.A 1st Sgt.
Thomas, Hiram GA 26th Inf. Co.K
Thomas, Hiram B. GA 11th Inf. Co.E
Thomas, H.J. AL 3rd Inf.
Thomas, H.J. GA Inf. 1st Loc.Troops (Augusta) Co.K
Thomas, H.J. MS 6th Inf. Co.B
Thomas, H.J. TN 7th (Duckworth's) Cav. Co.H
Thomas, H.J. VA 4th Cav. Co.K
Thomas, H.K. AL 3rd Cav. Co.C
Thomas, H.L. GA Cav. Pemberton's Co. 3rd Lt.
Thomas, H.L. GA Lt.Arty. Clinch's Btty.
Thomas, H.L. NC 37th Inf.
Thomas, H.L. SC Lt.Arty. Gaillard's Co. (Santee Lt.Arty.) Guidon
Thomas, H.L. SC Arty. Manigault's Bn. 2nd Co.C
Thomas, H.L. SC 11th Inf. Co.H
Thomas, H.L. TX 4th Inf. Surg.
Thomas, H.L. VA 3rd Cav. Co.A
Thomas, H.M. NC 53rd Inf. Co.A
Thomas, H.M. NC Mallett's Bn. Co.A
Thomas, H.M. VA 8th Cav. Co.A
Thomas, Holsford TN 19th (Biffle's) Cav. Co.E
Thomas, Houston 3rd Conf.Cav. Co.G
Thomas, Howell VA 38th Inf. 1st Co.I
Thomas, Howell L. Gen. & Staff, Medical Dept. Surg.
Thomas, H.P. SC 20th Inf. Co.A
Thomas, H.R. AL Inf. Hooper's Bn. Co.A
Thomas, H.R. GA 51st Inf. Co.H Capt.
Thomas, H.R. TN 13th Inf. Co.F Cpl.
Thomas, H.T. KY Horse Arty. Byrne's Co.
Thomas, H.T. Morgan's,CSA Guerrilla
Thomas, H. Taylor MS 4th Inf. Co.I
Thomas, Hugh SC 1st Bn.S.S. Co.B
Thomas, Hugh SC 27th Inf. Co.F
Thomas, Hugh TN 12th Inf. Co.C
Thomas, Hugh TN 37th Inf. Co.I
Thomas, Hugh C. NC 1st Arty. (10th St.Troops) Co.E
Thomas, Hugh P. AL Jeff Davis Arty. 1st Lt.
Thomas, Hugh P. Conf.Arty. R.C.M. Page's Bn. 2nd Lt.
Thomas, Hugh T. TN 5th (McKenzie's) Cav. Co.I
Thomas, Hugh T. TX 6th Cav. Co.B
Thomas, H.W. GA 11th Inf. Co.K
Thomas, H.W. LA 13th Bn. (Part.Rangers) Co.D
Thomas, I. GA 66th Inf. Co.K
Thomas, I. TN Lt.Arty. Winston's Co.
Thomas, I. TN 32nd Inf. Co.B
Thomas, I.A. GA 9th Inf. Co.B
Thomas, I.A. GA 9th Inf. Co.H
Thomas, I.A. TN 21st & 22nd (Cons.) Cav. Co.A
Thomas, I.G. MS Cav. 2nd Bn.Res. Co.B
Thomas, I.H. Gen. & Staff Capt.,AQM
Thomas, I.N. TN 2nd (Ashby's) Cav. Co.F
Thomas, Ira D. AL 17th Inf. Co.I Sgt.
Thomas, Ira I. GA 51st Inf. Co.G
Thomas, Ired TN Conscr. (Cp. of Instr.) Co.B
Thomas, Isaac AL 23rd Inf. Co.A
Thomas, Isaac AR 23rd Inf. Co.F
Thomas, Isaac MS 36th Inf. Co.I
Thomas, Isaac VA 6th Bn.Res. Co.F
Thomas, Isaac VA 37th Inf. Co.H
Thomas, Isaac A. TN 4th (McLemore's) Cav. Co.D
Thomas, Isaac C. LA 17th Inf. Co.I
Thomas, Isaac F. GA Conscr.
Thomas, Isaac F. VA 45th Inf. Co.C
Thomas, Isaac G. TX 13th Cav. Co.E
Thomas, Isaac H. NC 4th Inf. Co.H Ord.Sgt.
Thomas, Isaac L. VA 25th Cav. Co.B Cpl.
Thomas, Isaac N. GA 4th Inf. Co.F
Thomas, Isaac N. TN Cav. 4th Bn. (Branner's) Co.F
Thomas, Isaac W. GA 5th Inf. Co.E
Thomas, Isaac W. TX 4th Inf. Co.G
Thomas, Isaiah FL 9th Inf. Co.C
Thomas, Isaiah NC 4th Cav. (59th St.Troops) Co.I Cpl.
Thomas, Isaiah NC Cav. 12th Bn. Co.B
Thomas, Isaiah NC 17th Inf. (2nd Org.) Co.H
Thomas, Isaiah 8th (Dearing's) Conf.Cav. Co.B
Thomas, Isham FL 2nd Inf. Co.B
Thomas, Isham R. 1st Conf.Cav.
Thomas, Isham W. MS Lt.Arty. Stanford's Co.
Thomas, Isham W. MS 6th Inf. Co.B Cpl.
Thomas, Isma W. GA Cobb's Legion Co.E Sgt.
Thomas, Israel AL 28th Inf. Co.H
Thomas, Iven AR 31st Inf. Co.H
Thomas, Iverson J. KY 6th Mtd.Inf. Co.G
Thomas, Ivery A. FL 1st Inf. Old Co.F,H
Thomas, I.Y. NC 2nd Cav. (19th St.Troops) Co.K
Thomas, J. AL 6th Cav. Co.I
Thomas, J. AL 8th Cav. Co.G Sgt.
Thomas, J. AL 9th (Malone's) Cav. Co.G
Thomas, J. AL 53rd (Part.Rangers) Co.A
Thomas, J. AR 6th Inf. Co.E
Thomas, J. FL 2nd Cav. Co.H
Thomas, J. GA Lt.Arty. Clinch's Btty.
Thomas, J. GA 21st Inf. Co.F
Thomas, J. GA Inf. (Milledgeville Guards) Caraker's Co.
Thomas, J. KY 8th Cav. Co.H
Thomas, J. KY 12th Cav. Co.C
Thomas, J. MS 38th Cav. Co.F
Thomas, J. MS Inf. 1st Bn.St.Troops (12 mo. '62-3) Co.A
Thomas, J. MS 5th Inf. (St.Troops) Co.A
Thomas, J. MS 6th Inf. Co.B
Thomas, J. MS 19th Inf. Co.K
Thomas, J. MO 1st N.E. Cav. Co.G
Thomas, J. MO 5th Cav. Co.K
Thomas, J. MO Cav. Coffee's Regt. Co.F
Thomas, J. NC 7th Sr.Res. Johnston's Co.
Thomas, J. NC 42nd Inf. Co.B
Thomas, J. SC Inf. 9th Bn. Co.A
Thomas, J. SC 11th Inf. 2nd Co.F, Co.D
Thomas, J. SC Mil. 16th Regt. Sigwald's Co.
Thomas, J. TN 1st (Carter's) Cav. Co.G
Thomas, J. TN 12th (Green's) Cav. Co.A
Thomas, J. TX 12th Inf. Co.B
Thomas, J. TX 33rd Cav. Co.H
Thomas, J. TX Cav. Terry's Regt. Co.C
Thomas, J. TX 6th Field Btty.
Thomas, J. TX Lt.Arty. Dege's Bn. Co.D
Thomas, J. TX 4th Inf. (St.Troops) Co.D
Thomas, J. TX 7th Inf. Co.B
Thomas, J. TX Inf. Timmons' Regt. Co.I
Thomas, J. VA 6th Cav. Co.C
Thomas, J. VA 3rd Res. Co.A
Thomas, J. VA 3rd Res. Co.G
Thomas, J. VA 82nd Mil. Co.D
Thomas, J. VA 88th Mil.
Thomas, J. 20th Conf.Cav. Co.E
Thomas, J.A. AL 7th Cav. Co.G,B
Thomas, J.A. AL 13th Bn.Part.Rangers Co.D
Thomas, J.A. AL 56th Part.Rangers Co.K
Thomas, J.A. AL Mil. 4th Vol. Co.I
Thomas, J.A. AL 5th Inf. New Co.H
Thomas, J.A. AL 41st Inf. Co.B
Thomas, J.A. AR 15th (Johnson's) Inf. Co.A
Thomas, J.A. AR 19th Inf. Co.C
Thomas, J.A. AR 33rd Inf. Co.H
Thomas, J.A. FL 5th Inf. Co.D
Thomas, J.A. GA 4th (Clinch's) Cav. Co.I
Thomas, J.A. GA Lt.Arty. 14th Bn. Co.D Sgt.
Thomas, J.A. GA Lt.Arty. Anderson's Btty.
Thomas, J.A. GA Lt.Arty. King's Btty. Sgt.
Thomas, J.A. GA 3rd Res. Co.A
Thomas, J.A. KY 2nd Mtd.Inf. Co.G
Thomas, J.A. MS 2nd Cav. Co.K
Thomas, J.A. MS 5th Inf. Co.K
Thomas, J.A. MS 9th Bn.S.S. Co.C
Thomas, J.A. MS 10th Inf. New Co.K
Thomas, J.A. MS 23rd Inf. Knight's Co. 1st Lt.
Thomas, J.A. MO 5th Cav. Co.A
Thomas, J.A., Jr. NC 1st Arty. (10th St.Troops) Co.K
Thomas, J.A. SC Inf. 1st (Charleston) Bn. Co.F
Thomas, J.A. SC 3rd Inf. Co.K,D Sgt.
Thomas, J.A. SC 7th Res. Co.B 2nd Lt.
Thomas, J.A. SC 13th Inf. Co.I
Thomas, J.A. SC 17th Inf. Co.K
Thomas, J.A. TN 7th (Duckworth's) Cav. Co.B
Thomas, J.A. TN 7th (Duckworth's) Cav. Co.L
Thomas, J.A. TN 14th (Neely's) Cav. Co.D
Thomas, J.A. TN 16th (Logwood's) Cav. Co.I
Thomas, J.A. TN 24th Bn.S.S. Co.A
Thomas, J.A. TN 49th Inf. Co.C
Thomas, J.A. TN 51st (Cons.) Inf. Co.F
Thomas, J.A. TX 30th Cav. Co.B
Thomas, J.A. TX Cav. Terry's Regt. Co.A
Thomas, J.A. TX 15th Inf. Co.C
Thomas, J.A. VA 5th Cav. Co.D
Thomas, J.A. VA Horse Arty. D. Shank's Co.
Thomas, J.A. Gen. & Staff AASurg.
Thomas, Jackson AL Cav. Lewis' Bn. Co.D
Thomas, Jackson GA 50th Inf. Co.A
Thomas, Jackson MS Inf. 1st St.Troops Co.D
Thomas, Jackson TN 5th (McKenzie's) Cav. Co.E
Thomas, Jackson VA 57th Inf. Co.F Cpl.
Thomas, Jackson J. NC 50th Inf. Co.F
Thomas, Jacob GA 36th (Broyles') Inf. Co.E
Thomas, Jacob LA Inf. 11th Bn. Co.B

Thomas, Jacob MS Cav. Garland's Bn. Co.C
Thomas, Jacob NC 6th Inf. Co.E
Thomas, Jacob NC 22nd Inf. Co.L
Thomas, Jacob NC 43rd Inf. Co.H
Thomas, Jacob TN 26th Inf. Co.C
Thomas, Jacob VA Hvy.Arty. 20th Bn. Co.C
Thomas, Jacob VA 1st Cav. Co.B
Thomas, Jacob VA 8th Cav. Co.C
Thomas, Jacob VA 63rd Inf. Co.H
Thomas, Jacob VA Mil. Wythe Cty.
Thomas, Jacob 14th Conf.Cav. Co.C
Thomas, Jacob A. AL 6th Cav. Co.D,E
Thomas, Jacob E. MO 2nd Cav. 3rd Co.K
Thomas, Jacob J. TN 54th Inf. Co.A
Thomas, Jacob N. VA Cav. 35th Bn. Co.B
Thomas, Jacob W. VA 11th Cav. Co.G
Thomas, J.A.L. SC 6th Inf. 1st Co.E
Thomas, J.A.L. VA Inf. 25th Bn. Co.A Cpl.
Thomas, James AL 5th Cav.
Thomas, James AL 6th Cav. Co.H
Thomas, James AL 7th Cav. Co.M
Thomas, James AL 9th (Malone's) Cav. Co.K
Thomas, James AL Cav. Moreland's Regt. Co.B
Thomas, James AL 3rd Res. Co.A
Thomas, James AL 4th Res. Co.D
Thomas, James AL 5th Bn.Vol. Co.D
Thomas, James AL 29th Inf. Co.K
Thomas, James AL 32nd Inf. Co.B
Thomas, James AL 37th Inf. Co.I
Thomas, James AL 49th Inf. Co.A
Thomas, James AR 14th (Powers') Inf. Co.I Sgt.
Thomas, James AR 16th Inf. Co.I
Thomas, James AR 35th Inf. Co.K
Thomas, James FL 4th Inf. Co.B
Thomas, James FL 4th Inf. Co.K
Thomas, James GA 1st Cav. Co.I
Thomas, James GA 6th Cav. Co.F
Thomas, James GA Cav. Gartrell's Co.
Thomas, James GA Lt.Arty. 12th Bn. 3rd Co.E
Thomas, James GA 1st Reg. Co.I
Thomas, James GA 1st (Ramsey's) Inf. Co.D
Thomas, James GA 2nd Bn.S.S. Co.B Cpl.
Thomas, James GA 5th Inf. Co.K.L Cpl.
Thomas, James GA 19th Inf. Co.E
Thomas, James GA 34th Inf. Co.G
Thomas, James GA 35th Inf. Co.A
Thomas, James GA 42nd Inf. Co.G Cpl.
Thomas, James GA 51st Inf. Co.G
Thomas, James GA Cobb's Legion Co.K
Thomas, James GA Phillips' Legion Co.G Cpl.
Thomas, James GA Inf. (Newton Factory Employees) Russell's Co.
Thomas, James GA Smith's Legion Co.C
Thomas, James KY 13th Cav. Co.I
Thomas, James KY 8th Mtd.Inf. Co.G
Thomas, James LA 2nd Cav. Co.F
Thomas, James LA Inf. 11th Bn. Co.G
Thomas, James LA 16th Inf. Co.E
Thomas, James LA 16th Inf. Co.I
Thomas, James LA 25th Inf. Co.A
Thomas, James LA Mil. Bragg's Bn. Schwartz's Co.
Thomas, James MD 1st Cav.
Thomas, James MD Walters' Co. (Zarvona Zouaves)
Thomas, James MS 2nd St.Cav. Co.I
Thomas, James MS 1st (Johnston's) Inf. Co.H
Thomas, James MS Inf. 2nd Bn. Co.A
Thomas, James MS 3rd Inf. Co.A
Thomas, James MS 6th Inf. Co.A
Thomas, James MS 13th Inf. Co.C
Thomas, James MS 36th Inf. Co.E
Thomas, James MS 48th Inf. Co.A
Thomas, James MO 5th Cav. Co.F
Thomas, James MO Cav. Ford's Bn. Co.F
Thomas, James NC Cav. 5th Bn. Co.A
Thomas, James NC 1st Inf. Co.A
Thomas, James NC 6th Inf. Co.K
Thomas, James NC 12th Inf. Co.K
Thomas, James NC 13th Inf. Co.C
Thomas, James NC 25th Inf. Co.E
Thomas, James NC 39th Inf. Co.B
Thomas, James NC 42nd Inf. Co.D
Thomas, James NC 43rd Inf. Co.H
Thomas, James NC 46th Inf. Co.C
Thomas, James NC 49th Inf. Co.C
Thomas, James NC 51st Inf. Co.A
Thomas, James NC 52nd Inf. Co.E
Thomas, James NC 64th Inf. Co.C
Thomas, James SC Cav. 12th Bn. Co.C
Thomas, James SC 2nd Arty. Co.K
Thomas, James SC 1st (McCreary's) Inf. Co.E
Thomas, James SC 11th Inf. Co.D Sgt.
Thomas, James SC 27th Inf. Co.F
Thomas, James TN 8th (Smith's) Cav. Co.A
Thomas, James TN 8th (Smith's) Cav. Co.K Sgt.
Thomas, James TN 21st (Wilson's) Cav. Co.F
Thomas, James, Jr. TN 21st (Wilson's) Cav. Co.F
Thomas, James TN Arty. Ramsey's Btty. Cpl.
Thomas, James TN 9th Inf. Co.H
Thomas, James TN 51st Inf. Co.F 1st Sgt.
Thomas, James TN 51st (Cons.) Inf. Co.F 1st Sgt.
Thomas, James TX 11th Cav. Co.F
Thomas, James TX 19th Cav. Co.K Capt.
Thomas, James TX 37th Cav. Co.F
Thomas, James TX Cav. Wells' Regt. Co.H
Thomas, James TX 5th Inf. Co.I
Thomas, James VA 4th Cav. Co.C
Thomas, James VA 18th Cav. 2nd Co.E
Thomas, James VA Lt.Arty. 13th Bn. Co.B
Thomas, James VA 1st Inf. Co.C
Thomas, James VA 13th Inf. Co.I
Thomas, James VA 21st Mil. Co.A
Thomas, James VA 22nd Inf. Co.A
Thomas, James VA 24th Inf. Co.G
Thomas, James VA 26th Inf. 1st Co.B
Thomas, James VA 30th Bn.S.S. Co.B
Thomas, James VA 46th Inf. 2nd Co.E
Thomas, James VA 122nd Mil. Co.A
Thomas, James VA Inf. Gregory's Co.
Thomas, James VA Lt.Arty. Jackson's Bn. St.Line Co.A
Thomas, James 1st Choctaw & Chickasaw Mtd.Rifles 2nd Co.K
Thomas, James Conf.Inf. Tucker's Regt. Co.I
Thomas, James A. AL 19th Inf. Co.H
Thomas, James A. AR 45th Mil. Co.D
Thomas, James A. FL Inf. 2nd Bn. Co.B Cpl.
Thomas, James A. GA 4th Cav. (St.Guards) Gower's Co.
Thomas, James A. GA 1st (Olmstead's) Inf. 1st Co.A
Thomas, James A. GA 1st Bn.S.S. Co.B
Thomas, James A. GA 9th Inf. (St.Guards) Co.G
Thomas, James A. KY 2nd (Duke's) Cav. Co.B Capt.
Thomas, James A. NC 16th Inf. Co.B
Thomas, James A. NC 50th Inf. Co.H
Thomas, James A. SC 12th Inf. Co.D
Thomas, James A. SC 23rd Inf. Co.F
Thomas, James A. SC 24th Inf. Co.H Capt.
Thomas, James A. TN 2nd (Robison's) Inf. Co.A
Thomas, James A. TN 37th Inf. Co.A
Thomas, James A. TX Cav. 6th Bn. Co.A
Thomas, James A. VA Goochland Lt.Arty. Cpl.
Thomas, James A. VA Lt.Arty. Lamkin's Co. Sgt.
Thomas, James A. VA 10th Cav. Co.D
Thomas, Jas. A. VA Lt.Arty. 13th Bn. Co.B
Thomas, James A. VA 17th Inf. Co.D
Thomas, James A. VA 18th Inf. Co.K
Thomas, James A. VA 30th Bn.S.S. Co.D
Thomas, James A. VA 151st Mil. Co.C
Thomas, James B. GA Lt.Arty. 12th Bn. 2nd Co.A
Thomas, James B. GA 1st (Ramsey's) Inf. Co.G
Thomas, James B. GA 24th Inf. Co.K
Thomas, James B. LA 9th Inf. Co.C
Thomas, James B. TX 1st (McCulloch's) Cav. Co.A 1st Sgt.
Thomas, James B. TX 1st Inf. Co.H
Thomas, James B. TX Waul's Legion Co.A 2nd Lt.
Thomas, James B. VA Lt.Arty. Griffin's Co.
Thomas, James B. VA Lt.Arty. Lowry's Co.
Thomas, James B. VA 9th Inf. 1st Co.A
Thomas, James B. VA 61st Mil. Co.D
Thomas, James C. AL 4th Inf. Co.E
Thomas, James C. AL 40th Inf. Co.A
Thomas, James C. FL Cav. 5th Bn. Co.I,A
Thomas, James C. NC 27th Inf. Co.B
Thomas, James C. TX 9th Cav. Co.A
Thomas, James C. VA Lt.Arty. B.Z. Price's Co.
Thomas, James C. VA 19th Inf. Co.E
Thomas, James D. AL 1st Inf. Co.E
Thomas, James D. AL 19th Inf. Co.K
Thomas, James D. GA Carlton's Co. (Troup Cty.Arty.) Bugler
Thomas, James D. GA 3rd Inf. Co.K
Thomas, James D. SC Horse Arty. (Washington Arty.) Vol. Hart's Co.
Thomas, James D. SC 25th Inf. Co.K
Thomas, James D. TN 11th Inf. Co.K Cpl.
Thomas, James D. TN 37th Inf. Co.B Capt.
Thomas, James D. TN 61st Mtd.Inf. Adj.
Thomas, James D. VA 1st Arty. Co.I
Thomas, James D. VA Hvy.Arty. 19th Bn. Chap.
Thomas, James D. VA Lt.Arty. 38th Bn. Co.B
Thomas, James D. VA 37th Inf. Co.H
Thomas, James D. Eng.,CSA 2nd Lt.
Thomas, Jas. D. Gen. & Staff Maj.,QM
Thomas, James D. Gen. & Staff Chap.
Thomas, James E. AL 26th Inf. Co.E
Thomas, James E. AL 39th Inf. Co.B Jr.2nd Lt.
Thomas, James E. AL Hardy's Co. (Eufaula Minute Men) Cpl.

Thomas, James E. AR 36th Inf. Co.F
Thomas, James E. FL 1st Cav. Co.G
Thomas, James E. GA 63rd Inf. Co.A
Thomas, James E. MO 10th Cav. Co.H
Thomas, James E. MO Cav. Williams' Regt. Co.H
Thomas, James E. TN Cav. Wilson's Regt. Stinnett's Co.
Thomas, James E. TX 3rd Cav. Co.E
Thomas, James E. VA 2nd Arty. Co.K
Thomas, James E. VA 2nd Cav. Co.I
Thomas, James E. VA 7th Cav. Co.G
Thomas, James E. VA 57th Inf. Co.K
Thomas, James F. AL 2nd Bn. Hilliard's Legion Vol. Co.F
Thomas, James F. GA 50th Inf. Co.A
Thomas, James F. MO 12th Cav. Co.G 2nd Lt.
Thomas, James F. NC 13th Inf. Co.H
Thomas, James F. TN 11th Cav. Co.H
Thomas, James F. TN 16th Cav. Co.C
Thomas, James F. TN 32nd Inf. Co.H Cpl.
Thomas, James F. TX 34th Cav. Co.C
Thomas, James G. AL 41st Inf. Co.F
Thomas, James G. LA 12th Inf. Co.B
Thomas, James G. NC 4th Inf. Asst.Surg.
Thomas, James G. NC 43rd Inf. Co.G
Thomas, James G. TX 16th Cav. Co.B 2nd Lt.
Thomas, James G. VA 9th Cav. Co.K
Thomas, James G. VA 37th Mil. Co.A
Thomas, James G. VA 44th Inf. Co.K
Thomas, Jas. G. Gen. & Staff, Medical Dept. Surg.
Thomas, James H. AL 4th Inf. Co.E
Thomas, James H. GA 3rd Cav. Co.A
Thomas, James H. FL 7th Inf. Co.B
Thomas, James H. FL 8th Inf. Co.K
Thomas, James H. KY 3rd Bn.Mtd.Rifles Co.D
Thomas, James H. MS 3rd Inf. Co.D
Thomas, James H. MO 5th Cav. Co.E
Thomas, James H. NC 27th Inf. Co.D
Thomas, James H. NC 29th Inf. Co.I
Thomas, James H. NC 43rd Inf. Co.H Cpl.
Thomas, James H. NC 62nd Inf. Co.F
Thomas, James H. SC 1st Arty. Co.K
Thomas, James H. TN 1st (Feild's) Inf. Co.A
Thomas, James H. TX 4th Cav. Co.H
Thomas, James H. TX 4th Inf. Co.B
Thomas, James H. VA 14th Cav. Co.G
Thomas, James H. VA Cav. 37th Bn. Co.E Wagon M.
Thomas, James H. VA Horse Arty. D. Shanks' Co.
Thomas, James H. VA 2nd Inf. Co.G
Thomas, James I. TN 17th Inf. Co.K
Thomas, James J. FL Lt.Arty. Abell's Co.
Thomas, James J. FL Milton Lt.Arty. Dunham's Co.
Thomas, James J. GA 6th Cav. Asst.Surg.
Thomas, James J. GA 36th (Broyles') Inf. Co.B
Thomas, James J., Jr. NC 47th Inf. Co.F AQM
Thomas, James J. VA 14th Inf. Co.C
Thomas, James J. VA 54th Inf. Co.A
Thomas, James J. VA 63rd Inf. Co.K
Thomas, James J., Jr. Gen. & Staff Capt.,QM
Thomas, James K. GA 55th Inf. Co.H
Thomas, James K. KY 8th Cav. Co.H
Thomas, James K. NC 52nd Inf. Co.E
Thomas, James K.P. NC 1st Inf. Co.H
Thomas, James K.P. NC 15th Inf. Co.H
Thomas, James L. GA 6th Inf. (St.Guards) Co.I
Thomas, James L. GA 49th Inf. Co.I
Thomas, James L. NC 25th Inf. Co.E Music.
Thomas, James L. TX 27th Cav. Co.D,M
Thomas, James Loyde TX 20th Cav. Co.E
Thomas, James M. AL 4th (Russell's) Cav. Co.G
Thomas, James M. AL 17th Inf. Co.B
Thomas, James M. AL 22nd Inf. Co.B
Thomas, James M. AL 41st Inf. Co.K
Thomas, James M. AL 58th Inf. Co.F,E
Thomas, James M. FL 1st Cav. Co.C
Thomas, James M. FL 7th Inf. Co.H
Thomas, James M. GA Cav. 8th Bn. (St.Guards) Co.C Sgt.
Thomas, James M. GA 10th Cav. 1st Lt.
Thomas, James M. GA 11th Cav. Co.D
Thomas, James M. GA 1st Bn.S.S. Co.B
Thomas, James M. GA 8th Inf. Co.G
Thomas, James M. GA 26th Inf. Co.F
Thomas, James M. GA 40th Inf. Co.H Sgt.
Thomas, James M. GA Cobb's Legion Co.L
Thomas, James M. KY 1st Bn.Mtd.Rifles Co.B Capt.
Thomas, James M. LA 1st Cav. Co.I
Thomas, James M. LA 9th Inf. Co.C Sgt.
Thomas, James M. LA 27th Inf. Co.H
Thomas, James M. MS 35th Inf. Co.A Sgt.
Thomas, James M. MO 2nd Inf. Co.F
Thomas, James M. MO 3rd Inf. Co.F
Thomas, James M. TN 12th Inf. Co.C
Thomas, James M. TN 34th Inf. Co.B
Thomas, James M. TX 1st (McCulloch's) Cav. Co.A
Thomas, James M. TX 7th Cav. Co.E
Thomas, James M. TX 13th Cav. Co.D
Thomas, James M. TX Waul's Legion Co.A Sgt.
Thomas, James M. VA 24th Cav. Co.H
Thomas, James M. VA 10th Inf. Co.L
Thomas, James M. VA 22nd Inf. Swann's Co.
Thomas, James M. VA 23rd Inf. Co.F
Thomas, James M. VA Inf. 26th Bn. Co.A 2nd Lt.
Thomas, James M. VA 29th Inf. Co.H
Thomas, James M. VA 37th Inf. Co.A,K
Thomas, James M. VA 37th Inf. Co.H
Thomas, James M. VA 59th Inf. 2nd Co.K Sgt.
Thomas, James M. VA 67th Mil. Co.A
Thomas, James N. TN 12th Inf. Co.C
Thomas, James O. AL Cav. Holloway's Co.
Thomas, James O. Conf.Cav. Wood's Regt. Co.E
Thomas, James P. AR 15th (Johnson's) Inf. Co.F
Thomas, James P. LA 31st Inf. Co.K
Thomas, James P. TX 18th Cav. Co.E 2nd Lt.
Thomas, James P. VA 34th Inf. Co.F
Thomas, James P. VA 37th Inf. Co.A
Thomas, James R. AL 17th Bn.S.S. Co.A
Thomas, James R. AL 19th Inf. Co.G
Thomas, James R. GA Arty. 11th Bn. (Sumter Arty.) Co.B
Thomas, James R. GA 21st Inf. New Co.E
Thomas, James R. GA 50th Inf. Co.A
Thomas, James R. MS 32nd Inf. Co.C,A
Thomas, James R. MO 2nd Cav. 3rd Co.K
Thomas, James R. NC Inf. 2nd Bn. Co.D
Thomas, James R. NC 48th Inf. Co.F
Thomas, James R. TX 5th Inf. Co.I
Thomas, James R. VA Lt.Arty. 38th Bn. Co.C
Thomas, James R. VA Lt.Arty. Lowry's Co. Cpl.
Thomas, James R. VA 55th Inf. Co.K
Thomas, James R. VA 59th Inf. 1st Co.F
Thomas, James R. VA 60th Inf. Co.C Sgt.
Thomas, James S. AR Inf. 4th Bn. Co.B
Thomas, James S. AR Inf. Cocke's Regt. Co.K 3rd Lt.
Thomas, James S. AR Hardy's Regt. Co.B
Thomas, James S. GA 4th (Clinch's) Cav. Co.C,A
Thomas, James S. GA Cav. 29th Bn. Co.A
Thomas, James S. GA Smith's Legion Co.D, Anderson's Co.
Thomas, James S. MO 3rd Cav. Co.D
Thomas, James S. SC Inf. 7th Bn. (Enfield Rifles) Co.H
Thomas, James S. TN 2nd Cav. Co.H
Thomas, James S. VA 5th Inf. Co.B
Thomas, James S. VA 27th Inf. 2nd Co.H Sgt.Maj.
Thomas, James S. VA 28th Inf. Co.A Cpl.
Thomas, James S. VA 64th Mtd.Inf.
Thomas, James S. 8th (Wade's) Conf.Cav. Co.A
Thomas, James T. AL Mt.Res. Logan's Co.
Thomas, James T. AL Res. Co.H
Thomas, James T. LA Mtd.Rifles Miller's Ind.Co.
Thomas, James T. NC 1st Arty. (10th St.Troops) Co.H Cpl.
Thomas, James T. TX Cav. Martin's Regt. Co.C Sgt.
Thomas, James T. VA 34th Inf. Co.H Capt.
Thomas, James T. Conf.Hvy.Arty. Montague's Bn. Co.C 1st Lt.
Thomas, James V. MS 2nd Cav. Co.A 1st Sgt.
Thomas, James V. VA Inf. 23rd Bn. Co.A
Thomas, James W. AL 9th Inf. Co.E
Thomas, James W. AL 32nd & 56th (Cons.) Inf.
Thomas, James W. AR 1st (Colquitt's) Inf. Co.C
Thomas, James W. GA Inf. 2nd Bn. Co.B
Thomas, James W. GA 5th Inf. Co.H,E
Thomas, James W. GA 35th Inf. Co.K
Thomas, James W. GA 42nd Inf. Co.E
Thomas, James W. GA Phillips' Legion Co.D,K
Thomas, James W. GA Smith's Legion Co.C
Thomas, James W. LA Hvy.Arty. 8th Bn. Hart's Co.
Thomas, James W. LA 9th Inf. Co.I
Thomas, James W. MD 1st Inf. 2nd Co.H Sgt.
Thomas, James W. MD Inf. 2nd Bn. Co.A Sgt.
Thomas, James W. MS 1st (Johnston's) Inf. Co.B
Thomas, James W. MO 6th Cav. Co.C Sgt.
Thomas, James W. NC 26th Inf. Co.K
Thomas, James W. SC 5th Cav. Co.A
Thomas, James W. SC 2nd Rifles Co.K
Thomas, James W. SC 5th Res. Co.F
Thomas, James W. TN Cav. 12th Bn. (Day's) Co.D
Thomas, James W. TN 14th Inf. Co.L
Thomas, James W. TN 20th Inf. Co.C Adj.
Thomas, James W. TN 34th Inf. Co.B
Thomas, James W. TX 17th Cav. Co.H
Thomas, James W. TX 22nd Inf. Co.D
Thomas, James W. VA 21st Cav. Co.E

Thomas, James W. VA Hvy.Arty. 20th Bn. Co.A
Thomas, James W. VA 13th Inf. Co.F
Thomas, James W. VA 22nd Inf. Co.B
Thomas, James W. VA 26th Inf. Co.F Cpl.
Thomas, James W. 1st Conf.Eng.Troops Co.H
Thomas, James W. Gen. & Staff 1st Lt.,Adj.
Thomas, James W.B. TN Cav. 9th Bn. (Gantt's) Co.B
Thomas, Jarrett, Jr. GA 31st Inf. Co.D Cpl.
Thomas, Jasper AR 16th Inf. Co.D
Thomas, Jasper MO 7th Cav. Haislip's Co.
Thomas, Jasper MO 12th Inf. Co.I
Thomas, Jasper NC 50th Inf. Co.F
Thomas, Jasper SC Hvy.Arty. 15th (Lucas') Bn. Co.A
Thomas, Jasper TX 19th Inf. Co.B Ord.Sgt.
Thomas, Jasper J. TX Waul's Legion Co.E
Thomas, Jasper N. AR 19th (Dawson's) Inf. Co.A
Thomas, J.A.W. SC 21st Inf. Co.F Capt.
Thomas, J.B. FL Lt.Arty. Dyke's Co.
Thomas, J.B. GA Lt.Arty. Howell's Co.
Thomas, J.B. GA 11th Inf. Co.F
Thomas, J.B. GA Inf. 25th Bn. (Prov.Guard) Co.E
Thomas, J.B. GA 54th Inf.
Thomas, J.B. GA 55th Inf. Co.F
Thomas, J.B. GA 65th Inf. Co.K,B
Thomas, J.B. LA 1st Cav. Robinson's Co.
Thomas, J.B. LA 17th Inf. Co.C,D Sgt.
Thomas, J.B. MS 5th Cav. Co.G 1st Sgt.
Thomas, J.B. MS 30th Inf. Co.C
Thomas, J.B. MS Cp.Guard (Cp. of Instr. for Conscr.)
Thomas, J.B. SC Cav. 19th Bn. Co.E
Thomas, J.B. SC 2nd Arty. Co.I
Thomas, J.B. SC 20th Inf. Co.N
Thomas, J.B. TN 3rd (Forrest's) Cav. Co.E
Thomas, J.B. TN 12th (Green's) Cav. Co.E
Thomas, J.B. TX Cav. (Dismtd.) Chisum's Regt. Co.D
Thomas, J.B. VA 4th Res. Co.D
Thomas, J.B. VA Inf. 26th Bn. Co.I
Thomas, J.B. VA Inf. 26th Bn.
Thomas, J.C. AL 6th Cav. Asst.Surg.
Thomas, J.C. AL 6th Cav. Co.C
Thomas, J.C. AL 7th Cav. Co.B
Thomas, J.C. AL 20th Cav. Lee's Co.
Thomas, J.C. AL 24th Inf. Co.B
Thomas, J.C. AL 28th Inf. Co.A
Thomas, J.C. AR Cav. Davies' Bn. Co.B 1st Lt.
Thomas, J.C. AR 30th Inf. Co.H Cpl.
Thomas, J.C. KY Lt.Arty. Cobb's Co.
Thomas, J.C. LA 3rd (Wingfield's) Cav. Co.A
Thomas, J.C. LA 6th Cav. Co.A
Thomas, J.C. LA Inf.Crescent Regt. Co.K
Thomas, J.C. MS 23rd Inf. Co.F
Thomas, J.C. MS 32nd Inf. Co.A
Thomas, J.C. MO 3rd Cav. Co.F
Thomas, J.C. MO Cav. 3rd Bn. Co.F
Thomas, J.C. MO 7th Cav. Co.K
Thomas, J.C. SC Cav. 19th Bn. Co.D
Thomas, J.C. SC Cav. (St.Troops) Rodgers' Co.
Thomas, J.C. TN 8th (Smith's) Cav. Co.A Ord.Sgt.
Thomas, J.C. TN 14th (Neely's) Cav. Co.C,B
Thomas, J.C. TN Robison's Cav.
Thomas, J.C. TX 26th Cav. Co.D
Thomas, J.C. VA Hvy.Arty. 20th Bn. Co.C
Thomas, J.C. VA 30th Bn.S.S. Co.E
Thomas, J.C.C. LA Inf. 4th Bn. Co.B
Thomas, J.C.C. LA Inf. Pelican Regt. Co.F
Thomas, J.D. AL 56th Part.Rangers Co.B
Thomas, J.D. AL 32nd Inf. Co.H
Thomas, J.D. GA 35th Inf. Co.K
Thomas, J.D. MS Cav. 17th Bn. Co.F Sgt.
Thomas, J.D. NC 31st Inf. Co.I
Thomas, J.D. TX 3rd Cav. Co.E
Thomas, J.D. VA 8th Cav. Co.I
Thomas, J.D. Gen. & Staff Maj.,QM
Thomas, J. Dudley TX 20th Inf. Co.B
Thomas, J.E. AL Cav. 4th Bn. (Love's) Co.C
Thomas, J.E. AL 32nd & 58th (Cons.) Inf.
Thomas, J.E. AL 38th Inf. Co.E
Thomas, J.E. FL 2nd Cav. Co.H
Thomas, J.E. GA Lt.Arty. 12th Bn. 1st Co.A
Thomas, J.E. GA Inf. 4th Bn. (St.Guards) Co.B
Thomas, J.E. KY 1st (Helm's) Cav. Old Co.G
Thomas, J.E. KY 12th Cav. Co.C
Thomas, J.E. LA 25th Inf. Co.G
Thomas, J.E. LA Mil.Conf.Guards Regt. Co.C Cpl.
Thomas, J.E. MS 10th Inf. New Co.C
Thomas, J.E. MO 6th Cav. Co.H
Thomas, J.E. SC Cav. 19th Bn. Co.D
Thomas, J.E. SC Cav. (St.Troops) Rodgers' Co.
Thomas, J.E. SC 11th Inf. Co.K
Thomas, J.E. TN 7th (Duckworth's) Cav. Co.H
Thomas, J.E. TN 3rd (Clack's) Inf. Co.F
Thomas, J.E. TN 6th Inf. Co.A
Thomas, J.E. TX Waul's Legion Co.E
Thomas, J.E. VA 34th Inf. Co.E
Thomas, Jefferson GA Inf. 2nd Bn. (St.Guards) Co.B
Thomas, Jefferson GA 35th Inf. Co.A
Thomas, Jefferson GA Cherokee Legion (St.Guards) Co.C 1st Sgt.
Thomas, Jefferson NC 30th Inf. Co.H
Thomas, Jefferson SC Lt.Arty. J.T. Kanapaux's Co.
Thomas, Jefferson SC Mil. 18th Regt. Co.D
Thomas, Jefferson E. TX 28th Cav. Co.A
Thomas, Jeffrey VA 36th Inf. 2nd Co.B
Thomas, Jeffrey W. VA 17th Cav. Co.E
Thomas, Jeffrey W. VA 24th Inf. Co.G
Thomas, Jeptha G. TN 38th Inf. 1st Co.H
Thomas, Jeremiah NC 8th Bn.Part.Rangers Co.C
Thomas, Jeremiah NC 66th Inf. Co.D
Thomas, Jeremiah VA 19th Inf. Co.E
Thomas, Jerrard B. LA 31st Inf. Co.B
Thomas, Jerry MS 3rd (St.Troops) Cav. Co.I
Thomas, Jerry TX 11th Cav. Co.E
Thomas, Jesse AL Lt.Arty. 2nd Bn. Co.F
Thomas, Jesse AL Conscr. Echols' Co.
Thomas, Jesse GA 4th (Clinch's) Cav. Co.F
Thomas, Jesse GA Inf. (Franklin Cty.Guards) Kay's Co.
Thomas, Jesse MO Cav. Poindexter's Regt.
Thomas, Jesse NC 4th Inf. Co.C
Thomas, Jesse NC 44th Inf. Co.C
Thomas, Jesse NC 49th Inf. Co.D
Thomas, Jesse SC Inf. 6th Bn. Co.C
Thomas, Jesse SC Inf. 7th Bn. (Enfield Rifles) Co.H
Thomas, Jesse SC 26th Inf. Co.I
Thomas, Jesse VA 26th Cav. Co.C
Thomas, Jesse VA Cav. 46th Bn. Co.C Cpl.
Thomas, Jesse VA Inf. 23rd Bn. Co.D
Thomas, Jesse VA 46th Inf. 2nd Co.I
Thomas, Jesse 3rd Conf.Cav. Co.D
Thomas, Jesse A. AL 25th Inf. Co.G Sgt.
Thomas, Jesse A. TN 42nd Inf. 1st Co.H Cpl.
Thomas, Jesse B. KY 2nd Cav. Co.L
Thomas, Jesse D. VA Lt.Arty. Grandy's Co.
Thomas, Jesse D. VA Inf. 4th Bn.Loc.Def. Co.E Capt.
Thomas, Jesse D. VA 6th Inf. Vickery's Co.
Thomas, Jesse D. VA 16th Inf. 1st Co.H
Thomas, Jessee AL Cav. Holloway's Co.
Thomas, Jesse E. NC 33rd Inf. Co.H
Thomas, Jesse E. TX 2nd Inf. Co.G Sgt.
Thomas, Jesse G. NC Hvy.Arty. 10th Bn. Co.C Cpl.
Thomas, Jesse H. AL 1st Regt.Conscr. Co.D
Thomas, Jesse N. VA 19th Inf. Co.C
Thomas, Jesse R. MS 6th Inf. Co.F
Thomas, Jethro GA 5th Cav. Co.C
Thomas, J.F. AL 1st Bn.Cadets Co.A
Thomas, J.F. AL 12th Inf. Co.H
Thomas, J.F. AL 23rd Inf. 1st Lt.,Ens.
Thomas, J.F. AL 29th Inf. Co.G
Thomas, J.F. AL 32nd Inf. Co.H
Thomas, J.F. AL 46th Inf. Co.C
Thomas, J.F. AL Cp. of Instr. Talladega Co.B
Thomas, J.F. AR 3rd Cav.
Thomas, J.F. AR 32nd Inf. Co.E
Thomas, J.F. GA Lt.Arty. Fraser's Btty.
Thomas, J.F. GA Cobb's Legion Co.E
Thomas, J.F. LA Mil. Beauregard Bn. Pay M.
Thomas, J.F. SC Lt.Arty. J.T. Kanapaux's Co. (Lafayette Arty.)
Thomas, J.F. TN 23rd Inf. Co.I
Thomas, J.F. TN 47th Inf. Co.H
Thomas, J.F. VA 7th Inf. Co.F
Thomas, J.G. AL 39th Inf. Surg.
Thomas, J.G. AL 50th Inf. Co.I
Thomas, J.G. AL 59th Inf. Co.H
Thomas, J.G. GA Lt.Arty. Clinch's Btty.
Thomas, J.G. GA 1st (Fannin's) Res. Co.B
Thomas, J.G. MS 3rd Cav. Co.D
Thomas, J.G. NC 2nd Cav. (19th St.Troops) Surg.
Thomas, J.G. NC 49th Inf. Co.H
Thomas, J.G. SC 4th Cav. Co.I
Thomas, J.G. SC Cav. 12th Bn. Co.B
Thomas, J.G. TN 51st (Cons.) Inf. Co.C
Thomas, J.G. TX 34th Cav. Co.B
Thomas, J.G. TX Cav. Giddings' Bn. Co.A
Thomas, J.G. TX Waul's Legion Co.A Capt.
Thomas, J.G. Gen. & Staff Surg.
Thomas, J.H. AL 6th Cav. Co.C
Thomas, J.H. AL 7th Cav. Co.G
Thomas, J.H. AL 25th Inf. Co.B
Thomas, J.H. GA 1st Cav. Co.I
Thomas, J.H. GA 6th Cav. Co.B
Thomas, J.H. GA 40th Inf. Co.D
Thomas, J.H. GA 46th Inf. Co.C
Thomas, J.H. GA 55th Inf. Co.C
Thomas, J.H. GA Smith's Legion Co.D
Thomas, J.H. KY 1st Bn.Mtd.Rifles Co.D
Thomas, J.H. LA Inf. 11th Bn. Co.B

Thomas, J.H. LA 25th Inf. Co.I
Thomas, J.H. LA 25th Inf. Co.K
Thomas, J.H. LA Inf.Cons.Crescent Regt. Co.K
Thomas, J.H. MO 12th Inf. Co.A
Thomas, J.H. NC 4th Bn.Jr.Res. Co.D Cpl.
Thomas, J.H. SC 21st Inf. Co.D
Thomas, J.H. TN Cav. 9th Bn. (Gantt's) Co.B
Thomas, J.H. TN 12th (Green's) Cav. Co.I
Thomas, J.H. TN 14th (Neely's) Cav. Co.I,D 2nd Lt.
Thomas, J.H. TN 16th (Logwood's) Cav. Co.H
Thomas, J.H. TN 21st & 22nd (Cons.) Cav. Co.A
Thomas, J.H. TN 21st & 22nd (Cons.) Cav. Co.E
Thomas, J.H. TN 22nd (Barteau's) Cav. Co.C
Thomas, J.H. TN 9th Inf. Co.L,D 1st Sgt.
Thomas, J.H. TN 12th Inf. Co.G
Thomas, J.H. TN 12th (Cons.) Inf. Co.E
Thomas, J.H. TN 24th Inf. Co.C
Thomas, J.H. TN 24th Bn.S.S. Co.A
Thomas, J.H. TN 40th Inf. Co.B
Thomas, J.H. TN 40th Inf. Co.D
Thomas, J.H. TX 14th Inf. Co.C
Thomas, J.H. TX 20th Inf. Co.I
Thomas, J.H. VA 7th Cav. Co.G
Thomas, J.H. VA 22nd Inf. Co.E
Thomas, J.H. VA 28th Inf. Co.E
Thomas, J.H. 3rd Conf.Cav. Co.A
Thomas, J. Hanson, Jr. MD Weston's Bn. Co.D
Thomas, J. Hanson Loring's Div. 1st Lt.,AAAG
Thomas, J. Hanson Gen. & Staff Lt.,ADC
Thomas, J. Henry VA Horse Arty. D. Shanks' Co. Sgt.
Thomas, J.H.F. TX 22nd Inf. Co.D
Thomas, J.I GA 66th Inf. Co.I
Thomas, J.J. AL Inf. 1st Regt. Co.E
Thomas, J.J. AR 11th & 17th Cons.Inf. Co.H,K 2nd Lt.
Thomas, J.J. FL 3rd Cav.
Thomas, J.J. GA 6th Cav. Co.E
Thomas, J.J. GA Inf. (Newton Factory Employees) Russell's Co.
Thomas, J.J. KY 3rd Cav. Co.C
Thomas, J.J. KY 8th Mtd.Inf. Co.C
Thomas, J.J. LA Mil. 2nd Regt. 2nd Brig. 1st Div. Co.B
Thomas, J.J. MS 46th Inf. Co.D Sgt.
Thomas, J.J. SC 5th St.Troops Co.M
Thomas, J.J. SC 7th Res. Co.K
Thomas, J.J. TX 12th Cav. Co.K
Thomas, J.J. TX 20th Inf. Co.G
Thomas, J.J. VA Lt.Arty. Ellett's Co. Ord.Sgt.
Thomas, J.J. VA 3rd Res. Co.H
Thomas, J.J. VA 46th Inf. Co.L
Thomas, J.J. VA 59th Inf. 3rd Co.F Cpl.
Thomas, J.J. VA Loc.Def. Tayloe's Co.
Thomas, J. Jefferson GA Inf. 1st Loc.Troops (Augusta) Dearing's Cav.Co. 1st Lt.
Thomas, J. Jefferson GA Cobb's Legion Co.A,I Capt.
Thomas, J.K. AL Cp. of Instr. Talladega
Thomas, J.K. TX 17th Cons.Distmd.Cav. Co.E
Thomas, J.K.P. LA Inf.Cons.Crescent Regt. Co.G
Thomas, J.K.P. TN 17th Inf. Co.F
Thomas, J.K.P. TX 29th Cav. Co.D
Thomas, J.L. AL 56th Part.Rangers Co.F
Thomas, J.L. AL Cav. (St.Res.) Young's Co.
Thomas, J.L. AL 4th Res.
Thomas, J.L. AL 6th Inf. Co.C,E
Thomas, J.L. AL 19th Inf. Co.H
Thomas, J.L. AL 31st Inf. Co.G,C
Thomas, J.L. AL 32nd Inf. Co.A
Thomas, J.L. AL 32nd & 58th (Cons.) Inf. Co.K
Thomas, J.L. AL 55th Vol. Co.F
Thomas, J.L. GA 7th Cav. Co.G
Thomas, J.L. GA Cav. 15th Bn. (St.Guards) Allen's Co.
Thomas, J.L. GA Cav. 24th Bn. Co.A
Thomas, J.L. GA 4th Mil.
Thomas, J.L. GA Inf. 4th Bn. (St.Guards) Co.B
Thomas, J.L. GA 66th Inf. Co.I
Thomas, J.L. KY 7th Mtd.Inf. Co.D Cpl.
Thomas, J.L. LA 2nd Cav. Co.F
Thomas, J.L. LA Inf. 11th Bn. Co.B
Thomas, J.L. MS 2nd St.Cav. Co.E
Thomas, J.L. MS Cav. Yerger's Regt. Co.A
Thomas, J.L. MS 6th Inf. Co.A
Thomas, J.L. NC 6th Cav. (65th St.Troops) Co.D,C
Thomas, J.L. SC Lt.Arty. Gaillard's Co. (Santee Lt.Arty.)
Thomas, J.L. TN Cav. 1st Bn. (McNairy's) Co.E
Thomas, J.L. TN 19th & 20th (Cons.) Cav. Co.F
Thomas, J.L. TN 22nd (Barteau's) Cav. Co.C
Thomas, J.L. TN 42nd Inf. 1st Co.E
Thomas, J.L. TX Cav. 2nd Regt.St.Troops Co.G
Thomas, J.L. TX 28th Cav. Co.C
Thomas, J.L. TX 12th Inf. Co.H
Thomas, J.L. TX Waul's Legion Co.C 3rd Lt.
Thomas, J.L. VA 5th Cav. Co.G
Thomas, J.L. VA 8th Cav. Co.A
Thomas, J.L. VA 46th Inf. Co.E
Thomas, J.L.T. SC Inf. 3rd Bn. Co.D Sr.2nd Lt.
Thomas, J.M. AL Arty. 1st Bn. Co.F
Thomas, J.M. AL 5th Inf. New Co.E
Thomas, J.M. AL 34th Inf. Co.K
Thomas, J.M. AL 50th Inf. Co.K
Thomas, J.M. AR 37th Inf. Co.D Sgt.
Thomas, J.M. FL Cav. 5th Bn. Co.H Cpl.
Thomas, J.M. GA 4th (Clinch's) Cav. Co.A,C,D Music.
Thomas, J.M. GA Cav. 6th Bn. (St.Guards) Co.F Sgt.
Thomas, J.M. GA Cav. 19th Bn. Co.C 1st Lt.
Thomas, J.M. GA 11th Inf. Co.E Cpl.
Thomas, J.M. GA 39th Inf. Co.C
Thomas, J.M. GA 56th Inf. Co.F 1st Sgt.
Thomas, J.M. KY 3rd Cav. Co.I Cpl.
Thomas, J.M. KY 7th Cav. Co.I
Thomas, J.M. LA Inf. 7th Bn. Co.A
Thomas, J.M. LA 27th Inf. Co.G Ens.
Thomas, J.M. LA 31st Inf. Co.D Jr.2nd Lt.
Thomas, J.M. NC 18th Inf. Co.A Sgt.
Thomas, J.M. NC 42nd Inf. Co.D
Thomas, J.M. NC 61st Inf. Co.D
Thomas, J.M. SC 3rd Cav. Co.A
Thomas, J.M. SC 5th Inf. 2nd Co.I
Thomas, J.M. SC Inf. 6th Bn. Co.C 1st Sgt.
Thomas, J.M. SC 8th Inf. Co.F,M
Thomas, J.M. SC 11th Inf. Co.K
Thomas, J.M. SC 15th Inf. Co.G
Thomas, J.M. SC 26th Inf. Co.I Sgt.
Thomas, J.M. SC 28th
Thomas, J.M. SC Manigault's Bn.Vol. Co.E
Thomas, J.M. TN 16th (Logwood's) Cav. Co.I
Thomas, J.M. TN 12th (Cons.) Inf. Co.B
Thomas, J.M. TN 18th Inf. Co.F
Thomas, J.M. TN 49th Inf. Co.C
Thomas, J.M. TN 51st Inf. Co.H 1st Sgt.
Thomas, J.M. Inf. Bailey's Cons.Regt. Co.F
Thomas, J.M. TX 1st Inf. Co.D 1st Lt.
Thomas, J.M. TX 2nd Inf. Co.K
Thomas, J.M. TX 10th Inf. Co.E
Thomas, J.M. TX 20th Inf. Co.B
Thomas, J.M. VA 14th Cav. 1st Co.F
Thomas, J.M. VA 23rd Cav. Co.E
Thomas, J.M. VA Cav. 32nd Bn. Co.B
Thomas, J.M. VA Cav. 36th Bn. Co.E
Thomas, J.M. VA Loc.Def. Wood's Co.
Thomas, J.M. 10th Conf.Cav. Co.H 1st Lt.
Thomas, J.M. 20th Conf.Cav. Co.E
Thomas, J.M.C. GA 11th Inf. Co.E Cpl.
Thomas, J.N. AR 8th Inf. New Co.A
Thomas, J.N. GA 1st Inf. (St.Guards) Co.B
Thomas, J.N. GA Cobb's Legion Co.L
Thomas, J.N. KY 10th (Johnson's) Cav. Co.A
Thomas, J.N. KY 8th Mtd.Inf. Co.F
Thomas, J.N. MS 1st (Johnston's) Inf. Co.I
Thomas, J.N. NC 13th Inf. Co.I
Thomas, J.N. SC Cav. (St.Troops) Rodgers' Co. 2nd Lt.
Thomas, J.N. SC 9th Inf. Co.C
Thomas, J.N. SC Inf. Hampton Legion Co.C
Thomas, J.N. SC Inf. Holcombe Legion Co.A
Thomas, J.N. VA Lt.Arty. Fry's Co.
Thomas, J.N. VA 15th Cav. Co.B
Thomas, J.O. TX 30th Cav.
Thomas, J.O. TX 12th Inf. Co.B
Thomas, J.O. VA Loc.Def. Morehead's Co.
Thomas, Jo R. TN 16th Inf. Co.C
Thomas, Job NC 58th Inf. Co.C,D
Thomas, Job VA 82nd Mil. Co.C Cpl.
Thomas, Joe SC Inf. Hampton Legion Co.H
Thomas, Joel GA 6th Cav. Co.K
Thomas, Joel GA 35th Inf. Co.E
Thomas, Joel NC 37th Inf. Co.F
Thomas, Joel NC 47th Inf. Co.G
Thomas, Joel TN 18th Inf. Co.D
Thomas, Joel VA 14th Inf. Co.K
Thomas, Joel VA 26th Inf. Co.F Cpl.
Thomas, Joel A. AL Lowe's Cav.
Thomas, Joel C. VA Lt.Arty. Armistead's Co.
Thomas, Joel C. VA 61st Mil. Co.D
Thomas, Joel C. Conf.Lt.Arty. Stark's Bn.
Thomas, Joel W. AR 2nd Mtd.Rifles Co.H Sgt.
Thomas, John AL 2nd Cav. Co.K Sgt.
Thomas, Jno. AL 9th (Malone's) Cav. Co.E
Thomas, John AL Cav. Murphy's Bn. Co.D
Thomas, John AL Arty. 1st Bn. Co.B
Thomas, John AL Lt.Arty. Goldthwaite's Btty.
Thomas, John AL 16th Inf. Co.F
Thomas, John AL 19th Inf. Co.G
Thomas, John AL 29th Inf. Co.B
Thomas, John AL 29th Inf. Co.F
Thomas, John AL 30th Inf. Co.E
Thomas, John AL 33rd Inf. Co.G
Thomas, John AL 34th Inf. Co.I
Thomas, John AL 42nd Inf. Co.G,F

Thomas, John AL 62nd Inf. Co.G
Thomas, John AR 2nd Cav. 1st Co.A
Thomas, John AR 3rd Cav. Co.F Cpl.
Thomas, John AR 45th Cav. Co.B
Thomas, John AR Lt.Arty. Hart's Btty.
Thomas, John AR 2nd Vol. Co.C
Thomas, John AR 7th Inf. Co.F
Thomas, John AR 12th Inf. Co.K
Thomas, John AR 13th Mil. Co.E
Thomas, John AR 16th Inf. Co.D
Thomas, John AR 16th Inf. Co.I
Thomas, John AR 17th (Griffith's) Inf.
Thomas, John AR 19th Inf. Co.G
Thomas, John AR 27th Inf. Co.H
Thomas, John FL 1st Inf. New Co.H
Thomas, John FL 8th Inf. Co.I Capt.
Thomas, John FL 10th Inf. Co.E
Thomas, John GA 4th (Clinch's) Cav. Co.I
Thomas, John GA 11th Cav. Co.F
Thomas, John GA Lt.Arty. Guerard's Btty.
Thomas, John GA 1st Reg. Co.I
Thomas, John GA 1st Inf. (St.Guards) Co.B
Thomas, John GA 13th Inf. Co.H
Thomas, John GA 23rd Inf. Co.D
Thomas, John GA 29th Inf. Co.H
Thomas, John GA 34th Inf. Co.F Sgt.
Thomas, John GA 36th (Broyles') Inf. Co.B
Thomas, John GA 36th (Broyles') Inf. Co.D
Thomas, John GA 42nd Inf. Co.C
Thomas, John GA 42nd Inf. Co.K
Thomas, John GA 63rd Inf. Co.E
Thomas, John GA 65th Inf. Co.B
Thomas, John GA Smith's Legion Co.C
Thomas, John KY 1st (Butler's) Cav. Co.A
Thomas, John KY 10th Cav. Co.D
Thomas, John LA 1st Hvy.Arty. (Reg.) Co.B
Thomas, John LA 1st Inf. Co.B,F
Thomas, John LA 1st (Nelligan's) Inf. 1st Co.B
Thomas, John LA 6th Inf. Co.A
Thomas, John LA Inf. 11th Bn. Co.B
Thomas, John LA Inf. 11th Bn. Co.D
Thomas, John LA 22nd Inf. Co.C
Thomas, John LA 25th Inf. Co.A
Thomas, John LA 28th (Gray's) Inf. Co.K
Thomas, John LA 30th Inf. Co.A
Thomas, John LA Inf.Cons.Crescent Regt. Co.B
Thomas, John LA Inf.Cons.Crescent Regt. Co.K
Thomas, John LA Mil. Mech.Guard
Thomas, John LA C.S. Zouave Bn. Co.A
Thomas, John MD Inf. 2nd Bn. Co.A Capt.
Thomas, John MS 2nd St.Cav. Co.A
Thomas, John MS 2nd St.Cav. Co.F
Thomas, John MS 6th Cav. Co.G
Thomas, John MS Inf. 2nd St.Troops Co.F
Thomas, John MS Inf. 3rd Bn. Co.D
Thomas, John MS 5th Inf. (St.Troops) Co.B
Thomas, John MS 6th Inf. Co.K
Thomas, John MS 14th Inf. Co.B
Thomas, John MS 14th (Cons.) Inf. Co.D
Thomas, John MO 7th Cav. Co.I
Thomas, John MO Cav. Fristoe's Regt. Co.H
Thomas, John MO Cav. Jackman's Regt. Co.A
Thomas, John MO Cav. Slayback's Regt. Co.D
Thomas, John MO 4th Inf. Co.D
Thomas, John NC Lt.Arty. 3rd Bn. Co.C
Thomas, John NC 1st Inf. (6 mo. '61) Co.L
Thomas, John NC 7th Sr.Res. Williams' Co.
Thomas, John NC 13th Inf. Co.A
Thomas, John NC 13th Inf. Co.H
Thomas, John NC 24th Inf. Co.E
Thomas, John NC 26th Inf. Co.E
Thomas, John NC 34th Inf. Co.K
Thomas, John NC 42nd Inf. Co.D
Thomas, John NC 43rd Inf. Co.H
Thomas, John NC 45th Inf. Co.I
Thomas, John NC 53rd Inf. Co.F
Thomas, John NC 64th Inf. Co.C
Thomas, John NC Walker's Bn. Thomas' Legion Co.E
Thomas, John SC 2nd Cav. Co.C
Thomas, John SC Cav. 4th Bn. Co.B
Thomas, John SC 7th Cav. Co.C
Thomas, John SC 1st Inf. Co.E
Thomas, John SC 1st (Orr's) Rifles Co.C
Thomas, John SC 1st Bn.S.S. Co.C
Thomas, John SC 4th St.Troops Co.E
Thomas, John SC 5th St.Troops Co.H Cpl.
Thomas, John SC 7th Inf. Co.E
Thomas, John SC 9th Res. Co.I Cpl.
Thomas, John SC 9th Res. Co.I
Thomas, John SC 18th Inf. Co.G
Thomas, John SC 21st Inf. Co.D
Thomas, John SC 26th Inf. Co.A Sgt.
Thomas, John SC 27th Inf. Co.G
Thomas, John SC Cav.Bn. Holcombe Legion Co.D
Thomas, John TN 1st Cav. Co.H
Thomas, John TN 2nd (Ashby's) Cav. Co.G
Thomas, John TN 16th (Logwood's) Cav. Co.E 1st Lt.
Thomas, John TN 21st (Wilson's) Cav. Co.G
Thomas, John TN 21st & 22nd (Cons.) Cav. Co.K,I
Thomas, John TN Lt.Arty. Phillips' Co. Cpl.
Thomas, John TN 3rd (Lillard's) Mtd.Inf. Co.I
Thomas, John TN Inf. Harman's Regt. Co.K
Thomas, John TX 6th Cav. Co.B
Thomas, John TX 13th Cav. Co.F Sgt.
Thomas, John TX 14th Cav. Co.I
Thomas, John TX 16th Cav. Co.F
Thomas, John TX 25th Cav. Co.K Jr.2nd Lt.
Thomas, John TX Cav. Benavides' Regt. Co.C
Thomas, John TX Cav. Wells' Regt. Co.D
Thomas, John TX 4th Inf. Co.H
Thomas, John TX 7th Inf. Co.H
Thomas, John TX 8th Inf. Co.D
Thomas, John TX 13th Vol. Co.E
Thomas, John TX 14th Inf. Co.B
Thomas, John VA 11th Cav.
Thomas, John VA 18th Cav. 2nd Co.G
Thomas, John VA 19th Cav. Co.I
Thomas, John VA 25th Cav. Co.H
Thomas, John VA 3rd Lt.Arty. (Loc.Def.) Co.H
Thomas, John VA Arty. Fleet's Co.
Thomas, John VA Arty. Kevill's Co.
Thomas, John VA Arty. (Loc.Def. & Sp.Serv.) Lanier's Co.
Thomas, John VA 1st (Farinholt's) Res. Co.E
Thomas, John VA 4th Res. Co.H 1st Lt.
Thomas, John VA 5th Inf. Co.H
Thomas, John VA 6th Inf. Co.C
Thomas, John VA 6th Bn.Res. Co.B Sgt.
Thomas, John VA 7th Inf. Co.K
Thomas, John VA 10th Inf. Co.L
Thomas, John VA Inf. 21st Bn. Co.B,A
Thomas, John VA 29th Inf. Co.E
Thomas, John VA 33rd Inf. Co.I
Thomas, John VA 48th Inf. Co.B
Thomas, John VA 48th Inf. Co.D
Thomas, John VA 62nd Mtd.Inf. 2nd Co.L
Thomas, John VA 64th Mtd.Inf. Co.A
Thomas, John VA 64th Mtd.Inf. 2nd Co.F
Thomas, John VA 82nd Mil. Co.A
Thomas, John VA 115th Mil. Co.A
Thomas, John VA Mil. 130th Regt. Capt.
Thomas, John VA Mil. Carroll Cty.
Thomas, John VA Mil. Grayson Cty.
Thomas, John VA Mil. Scott Cty.
Thomas, John 15th Conf.Cav. Co.K
Thomas, John Conf.Reg.Inf. Brooks' Bn. Co.B
Thomas, John A. AL Inf. 1st Regt. Co.H Sgt.
Thomas, John A. AL Arty. 4th Bn. Hilliard's Legion Co.A
Thomas, John A. GA 11th Inf. Co.I Cpl.
Thomas, John A. GA 13th Inf. Co.D
Thomas, John A. GA 59th Inf. Co.D
Thomas, John A. KY 2nd Mtd.Inf. Co.G
Thomas, John A. KY 6th Mtd.Inf. Co.K,A,B
Thomas, John A. NC 3rd Arty. (40th St.Troops) Co.B 1st Sgt.
Thomas, John A. NC 13th Inf. Co.I
Thomas, John A. TN 4th Inf.
Thomas, John A. TX 8th Cav. Co.G
Thomas, John A. TX 2nd Inf. Co.H
Thomas, John A. VA Lt.Arty. Cayce's Co.
Thomas, John A. VA 63rd Inf. Co.A
Thomas, John B. AL 20th Inf. Co.K
Thomas, John B. AL 22nd Inf. Co.G
Thomas, John B. AL 34th Inf. Co.K
Thomas, John B. AL 38th Inf. Co.B
Thomas, John B. FL Kilcrease Lt.Arty. Cpl.
Thomas, John B. FL 2nd Inf. Co.I
Thomas, John B. FL 4th Inf. Co.D
Thomas, John B. GA 6th Inf. Co.D
Thomas, John B. GA 52nd Inf. Co.C Music.
Thomas, John B. MS St.Cav. Perrin's Bn. Co.B 1st Sgt.
Thomas, John B. NC 2nd Bn.Loc.Def.Troops Co.B
Thomas, John B. NC 13th Inf. Co.F
Thomas, John B. SC 10th Inf. Co.A
Thomas, John B. TN Lt.Arty. Winston's Co. Jr.2nd Lt.
Thomas, John B. TN 4th Inf. Co.A
Thomas, John B. TN 55th (Brown's) Inf. Co.A
Thomas, John B. TX 36th Cav. Co.B
Thomas, John B. VA 26th Inf. Co.D 1st Sgt.
Thomas, John B. VA 31st Inf. Co.G
Thomas, John C. AL 12th Inf. Co.B
Thomas, John C. AL 29th Inf. Co.F
Thomas, John C. AR 9th Inf. Co.K
Thomas, John C. FL 5th Inf. Co.I
Thomas, John C. MS 8th Inf. Co.K
Thomas, John C. MO 1st Cav. Co.I
Thomas, John C. MO 1st N.E. Cav.
Thomas, John C. MO 6th Cav. Co.A
Thomas, John C. MO 11th Inf. Co.B,D Sgt.
Thomas, John C. NC 49th Inf. Co.D
Thomas, John C. TN 41st Inf. Asst.Surg.
Thomas, John C. VA 5th Cav. 3rd Co.F
Thomas, John C. VA 37th Inf. Co.H

Thomas, John C. VA 52nd Inf. Co.H Cpl.
Thomas, John C. VA 61st Mil. Co.I Sgt.
Thomas, John C. 1st Conf.Cav. 2nd Co.G
Thomas, John Calvin TN 41st Inf. Co.H
Thomas, John D. AR 25th Inf. Co.C Capt.
Thomas, John D. GA 4th (Clinch's) Cav. Co.I
Thomas, John D. MS 9th Cav. Co.D 1st Sgt.
Thomas, John D. MS 2nd Inf. Co.E Cpl.
Thomas, John D. MS 10th Inf. Old Co.B
Thomas, John D. MS 11th Inf. Co.I
Thomas, John D. NC 2nd Arty. (36th St.Troops) Co.K
Thomas, John D. TN 38th Inf. Co.G Sgt.
Thomas, John D. TN 39th Mtd.Inf. Co.C Capt.
Thomas, John E. GA Arty. 11th Bn. (Sumter Arty.) Co.B Cpl.
Thomas, John E. GA 44th Inf. Co.C
Thomas, John E. VA 24th Cav. Co.C
Thomas, John E. MS 9th Inf. New Co.C
Thomas, John E. VA 34th Inf. Co.E
Thomas, John F. AL 1st Inf. Co.F
Thomas, John F. AL 46th Inf. Lt.
Thomas, John F. AL Cp. of Instr. Talladega
Thomas, John F. GA 6th Inf. Co.B
Thomas, John F. GA 7th Inf. Co.H
Thomas, John F. GA Cherokee Legion (St.Guards) Co.A
Thomas, John F. LA 12th Inf. Co.C
Thomas, John F. MS 2nd Inf. Co.L
Thomas, John F. NC 28th Inf. Co.B
Thomas, John F. TN Inf. 3rd Bn. Co.D
Thomas, John F. TN 24th Inf. 2nd Co.H
Thomas, John F. TX 11th (Spaight's) Bn.Vol. Co.F
Thomas, John F. VA 47th Inf. 2nd Co.F
Thomas, John G. FL 1st Inf. Old Co.D
Thomas, John G. GA 26th Inf. Co.F
Thomas, John G. MS 2nd Inf. Co.D
Thomas, John G. MS 34th Inf. Co.K
Thomas, John G. NC 25th Inf. Co.F
Thomas, John G. VA 63rd Inf. Co.F
Thomas, John G. Gen. & Staff 1st Lt.
Thomas, John H. AL 41st Inf. Co.I
Thomas, John H. AR Inf. 2nd Bn. Co.C
Thomas, John H. AR 3rd Inf. Co.G
Thomas, John H. AR 16th Inf. Co.K Cpl.
Thomas, John H. GA Inf. 18th Bn. Co.B
Thomas, John H. GA 42nd Inf. Co.D
Thomas, John H. GA 66th Inf. Co.E
Thomas, John H. KY 4th Cav. Co.A 2nd Lt.
Thomas, John H. LA 28th (Gray's) Inf. Co.B
Thomas, John H. MD 1st Cav. Co.B
Thomas, John H., Jr. MD 1st Inf. 2nd Co.H
Thomas, John H. MS Lt.Arty. (Issaquena Arty.) Graves' Co. Cpl.
Thomas, John H. MO Cav. 2nd Regt.St.Guard Surg.
Thomas, John H. NC 5th Cav. (63rd St.Troops) Co.G
Thomas, John H. NC 1st Inf. (6 mo. '61) Co.E
Thomas, John H. NC 12th Inf. Co.L Cpl.
Thomas, John H. NC 32nd Inf. Co.F,A Capt.
Thomas, John H. SC Inf. 7th Bn. (Enfield Rifles) Co.D
Thomas, John H. TN 21st (Wilson's) Cav. Co.H
Thomas, John H. TN Cav. Newsom's Regt. Co.F
Thomas, John H. TX 15th Cav. Co.D
Thomas, John H. TX 19th Cav. Co.G
Thomas, John H. TX 18th Inf. Co.F
Thomas, John H. VA 4th Cav. Co.G
Thomas, John H. VA Lt.Arty. Rogers' Co. Artif.
Thomas, John H. VA 7th Cav. Co.B
Thomas, John H. VA 9th Cav. Co.C
Thomas, John H. VA Cav. Mosby's Regt. (Part.Rangers) Co.A
Thomas, John H. VA Cav. Mosby's Regt. (Part.Rangers) Co.G
Thomas, John H. VA Inf. 1st Bn. Co.C 2nd Lt.
Thomas, John H. VA 15th Inf. Co.D
Thomas, John H. VA 27th Inf. Co.F
Thomas, John H. VA 30th Bn.S.S. Co.D
Thomas, John H. VA 34th Inf. Co.E
Thomas, John H. VA 38th Inf. 1st Co.I
Thomas, John H. VA 41st Inf. 1st Co.G
Thomas, John H. VA Conscr. Cp.Lee
Thomas, Jno. H. Gen. & Staff AQM
Thomas, John Hawkins AL 2nd Bn. Hilliard's Legion Vol. Co.A
Thomas, John Henry VA Lt.Arty. Rogers' Co.
Thomas, John Huguenin GA 1st (Olmstead's) Inf. Stiles' Co.
Thomas, John J. AL 3rd Bn.Res. Co.A
Thomas, John J. AR 17th (Griffith's) Inf. Co.H
Thomas, John J. FL 1st Cav. Co.B
Thomas, John J. GA 1st Cav. Co.B
Thomas, John J. GA 3rd Cav. (St.Guards) Co.F 3rd Lt.
Thomas, John J. KY 1st (Butler's) Cav. Co.C Cpl.
Thomas, John J. KY 4th Mtd.Inf. Co.I
Thomas, John J. LA 1st Cav. Co.B
Thomas, John J. MS Inf. 2nd Bn. Co.B Sgt.
Thomas, John J. NC 27th Inf. Co.K
Thomas, John J. NC 51st Inf. Co.C Cpl.
Thomas, John J. VA Hvy.Arty. 19th Bn. Co.B
Thomas, John J. VA Lt.Arty. Ancell's Co.
Thomas, John J. VA Lt.Arty. Snead's Co.
Thomas, John J. VA 10th Bn.Res. Co.E
Thomas, John J. VA 52nd Inf. Co.K
Thomas, John K.E. MS 37th Inf. Co.C
Thomas, John L. AL 22nd Inf. Co.H 2nd Lt.
Thomas, John L. AL 63rd Inf. Co.A
Thomas, John L. FL Lt.Arty. Dyke's Co.
Thomas, John L. FL 1st Inf. New Co.I
Thomas, John L. GA 50th Inf. Co.A
Thomas, John L. KY 14th Cav. Co.D
Thomas, John L. MS 7th Cav. Co.E
Thomas, John L. MS 2nd Inf. Co.E
Thomas, John L. NC 50th Inf. Co.F
Thomas, John L. TN 62nd Mtd.Inf. Co.I
Thomas, John L. VA Inf. 4th Bn.Loc.Def. Co.D
Thomas, John M. AL Mobile City Troop
Thomas, John M. AL 24th Inf. Co.H
Thomas, John M. AL 25th Inf. Co.B
Thomas, John M. AL 65th Inf. AAQM
Thomas, John M. AR 2nd Inf. New Co.C 2nd Lt.
Thomas, John M. FL 6th Inf. Co.C 2nd Lt.
Thomas, John M. NC 48th Inf. Co.A Sgt.
Thomas, John M. NC 68th Inf. Co.A Sgt.
Thomas, John M. SC 22nd Inf. Co.C 2nd Lt.
Thomas, John M. SC Inf. Holcombe Legion Co.E
Thomas, John M. TN 17th Inf. Co.C
Thomas, John M. TX 13th Vol. 1st Co.I
Thomas, John M. VA Lt.Arty. Griffin's Co.
Thomas, John M. VA 9th Inf. 1st Co.A
Thomas, John M. VA 13th Inf. Co.D
Thomas, John M. VA 22nd Inf. Co.A
Thomas, John M. VA 26th Inf. Co.F
Thomas, John M. VA 44th Inf. Co.D
Thomas, John M. VA 44th Inf. Co.K,I
Thomas, John M. VA 58th Inf. Co.K
Thomas, John M.B. NC 50th Inf. Co.F
Thomas, John N. TN 12th Inf. Co.C
Thomas, John N. TN 41st Inf. Co.B
Thomas, John Nick TN 14th Inf. Co.H
Thomas, John O. TX 28th Cav. Co.C 2nd Lt.
Thomas, John O. VA 1st Bn.Res. Co.D
Thomas, John O. VA 14th Inf. Co.F
Thomas, John P. AL 8th (Hatch's) Cav. Co.K
Thomas, John P. FL 3rd Inf. Co.H
Thomas, John P. KY 1st (Butler's) Cav.
Thomas, John P. KY 5th Cav. Co.F
Thomas, John P. MS 23rd Inf. Co.E Cpl.
Thomas, John P. MS 33rd Inf. Co.F
Thomas, John P. NC 43rd Inf. Co.H
Thomas, John P. NC 50th Inf. Co.F
Thomas, John P. TN 13th Inf. Co.I Ord.Sgt.
Thomas, John P. TX 13th Vol. 2nd Co.G
Thomas, John P. VA 17th Inf. Co.K
Thomas, John P. VA 24th Inf. Co.G
Thomas, John P. VA 32nd Inf. Co.F
Thomas, John Q. AL 18th Inf. Co.D
Thomas, John Q. NC 17th Inf. (1st Org.) Co.D Sgt.
Thomas, John Q. NC 17th Inf. (2nd Org.) Co.C 1st Lt.
Thomas, John Q. Gen. & Staff Maj.,CS
Thomas, John R. AL 46th Inf. Co.D
Thomas, John R. GA Inf. 2nd Bn. Co.C
Thomas, John R. GA 35th Inf. Co.G
Thomas, John R. GA 41st Inf. Co.H Sgt.
Thomas, John R. LA Arty. Green's Co. (LA Guard Btty.)
Thomas, John R. LA 1st (Nelligan's) Inf. Co.B
Thomas, John R. MD Arty. 1st Btty.
Thomas, John R. NC 33rd Inf. Co.I
Thomas, John R. SC 12th Inf. Co.C Capt.
Thomas, John R. TN 1st (Turney's) Inf. Co.D
Thomas, John R. TX 4th Cav. Co.D
Thomas, John R. TX 18th Cav. Co.E
Thomas, John R. VA 9th Cav. Co.G
Thomas, John R. VA 25th Inf. 1st Co.G
Thomas, John R. VA 60th Inf. 2nd Co.H
Thomas, John R. VA 62nd Mtd.Inf. 2nd Co.A
Thomas, John R. VA 115th Mil. Co.D Capt.
Thomas, John R. VA 151st Mil. Co.F
Thomas, John Riley SC 17th Inf. Co.B
Thomas, John S. AL 30th Inf. Co.B Cpl.
Thomas, John S. AL 34th Inf. Breedlove's Co.
Thomas, John S. FL 11th Inf. Co.E 2nd Lt.
Thomas, John S. VA 9th Inf. 2nd Co.A Cpl.
Thomas, John S. VA 22nd Inf. Co.C
Thomas, John S. VA 57th Inf. Co.C
Thomas, John S. VA 59th Inf. 3rd Co.F
Thomas, John S. 1st Conf.Cav. 2nd Co.E

Thomas, John S. Forrest's Scouts T.N. Kizer's Co.,CSA
Thomas, John S.M. MO 1st N.E. Cav. Co.F
Thomas, John S.M. MO 5th Inf. Co.F
Thomas, Johnson 1st Cherokee Mtd.Vol. 1st Co.F, 2nd Co.G
Thomas, John T. AL 4th Inf. Co.B
Thomas, John T. AR 36th Inf. Co.B
Thomas, John T. GA Siege Arty. Chatham Res.Corps Co.A
Thomas, John T. GA 34th Inf. Co.F
Thomas, John T. MS 2nd Cav. Co.K
Thomas, John T. MS 44th Inf. Co.D
Thomas, John T. TX 6th Cav. Co.C Sgt.
Thomas, John T. TX 19th Cav. Co.K
Thomas, John T. VA 14th Inf. 2nd Co.G
Thomas, John T. VA 20th Inf. Co.F
Thomas, John T. VA 57th Inf. Co.A
Thomas, John V. VA Inf. 23rd Bn. Co.F
Thomas, John W. AL 6th Cav.
Thomas, John W. GA Lt.Arty. Clinch's Btty.
Thomas, John W. GA 5th Inf. Co.F,H 2nd Lt.
Thomas, John W. GA 56th Inf. Co.A
Thomas, John W. GA Cobb's Legion Co.L
Thomas, John W. KY 5th Mtd.Inf. Co.H
Thomas, John W. KY 8th Mtd.Inf. Co.G
Thomas, John W. LA 31st Inf. Co.I Cpl.
Thomas, John W. MS Lt.Arty. Stanford's Co.
Thomas, John W. MS 1st (Johnston's) Inf. Co.H
Thomas, John W. MO 1st Cav. Co.H Sgt.
Thomas, John W. MO Inf. 8th Bn. Co.F
Thomas, John W. NC 16th Inf. Co.B
Thomas, John W. NC 43rd Inf. Co.H
Thomas, John W. NC 47th Inf. Co.I
Thomas, John W. NC 50th Inf. Co.F
Thomas, John W. NC 54th Inf. Co.F
Thomas, John W. SC 1st (Orr's) Rifles Co.A
Thomas, John W. SC 17th Inf. Co.A,C
Thomas, John W. TN 4th (McLemore's) Cav. Co.B
Thomas, John W. TX 15th Cav. Co.B
Thomas, John W. TX Cav. Ragsdale's Bn. Co.F
Thomas, John W. VA Cav. 46th Bn. Co.D
Thomas, John W. VA 1st Bn.Res. Co.D
Thomas, John W. VA 3rd Inf. 2nd Co.K
Thomas, John W. VA 9th Inf. Co.B
Thomas, John W. VA 19th Inf. Co.A
Thomas, John W. VA 26th Inf. Co.D Sgt.
Thomas, John W. VA 44th Inf. Co.I
Thomas, John W. VA 48th Inf. Co.B
Thomas, John W. VA 54th Inf. Co.I
Thomas, John W. VA 61st Mil. Co.D
Thomas, John W. VA 63rd Inf. Co.F
Thomas, John W. 14th Conf.Cav.
Thomas, John W. Gen. & Staff, Comsy.Dept. Capt.
Thomas, John West NC 30th Inf. Co.H
Thomas, John Whit AL 6th Inf. Adj.
Thomas, John Whit GA 5th Inf. Co.F,H 2nd Lt.
Thomas, Jonathan AL Vol. Lee, Jr.'s Co.
Thomas, Jonathan LA 12th Inf. 1st Co.M
Thomas, Jonathan MO 1st & 4th Cons.Inf. Co.I
Thomas, Jonathan MO 4th Inf. Co.I
Thomas, Jonathan NC 50th Inf. Co.E
Thomas, Jonathan C. AL 63rd Inf. Co.D
Thomas, Jonathan W. VA Cav. 35th Bn. Co.A
Thomas, Jordan W. AR 23rd Inf. Co.B Cpl.
Thomas, Joseph, Jr. AL 6th Inf. Co.K
Thomas, Joseph AL 23rd Inf. Co.D
Thomas, Joseph AL 38th Inf. Co.G
Thomas, Joseph AR Lt.Arty. Key's Btty.
Thomas, Joseph AR 11th & 17th Cons.Inf. Co.K
Thomas, Joseph AR 17th (Griffith's) Inf. Co.D
Thomas, Joseph AR 38th Inf. Co.E
Thomas, Joseph FL 10th Inf. Co.F
Thomas, Joseph GA 12th (Robinson's) Cav. (St.Guards) Co.E
Thomas, Joseph GA 1st (Olmstead's) Inf. Co.F
Thomas, Joseph GA 12th Inf. Co.A
Thomas, Joseph GA 52nd Inf. Co.C
Thomas, Joseph GA Cherokee Legion (St.Guards) Co.B,I
Thomas, Joseph LA Mtd.Rifles Miller's Ind.Co.
Thomas, Joseph MS 3rd (St.Troops) Cav. Co.K
Thomas, Joseph MS St.Cav. Perrin's Bn. Co.F
Thomas, Joseph MO Lt.Arty. 3rd Btty.
Thomas, Joseph MO Inf. Perkins' Btty. Co.D
Thomas, Joseph NC 3rd Arty. (40th St.Troops) Co.C
Thomas, Joseph NC 2nd Bn.Loc.Def.Troops Co.A Laborer
Thomas, Joseph NC 6th Sr.Res. Co.H
Thomas, Joseph NC 12th Inf. Co.K
Thomas, Joseph NC 13th Inf. Co.I
Thomas, Joseph NC 18th Inf. Co.E
Thomas, Joseph NC 62nd Inf. Co.K
Thomas, Joseph SC 1st (Orr's) Rifles Co.H
Thomas, Joseph SC 5th St.Troops Co.K
Thomas, Joseph SC 6th Res. Co.G
Thomas, Joseph SC 21st Inf. Co.F
Thomas, Joseph TN Cav. 2nd Bn. (Biffle's)
Thomas, Joseph TN 3rd (Forrest's) Cav. Co.D
Thomas, Joseph TN Cav. 5th Bn. (McClellan's) Co.F
Thomas, Joseph TN 43rd Inf. Co.B
Thomas, Joseph TX 23rd Cav. Co.K
Thomas, Joseph TX 9th (Young's) Inf. Co.E
Thomas, Joseph TX 18th Inf. Co.H
Thomas, Joseph VA 1st Cav. Co.H Sgt.
Thomas, Joseph VA Lt.Arty. 12th Bn. 1st Co.A
Thomas, Joseph VA Lt.Arty. Utterback's Co.
Thomas, Joseph VA 2nd Inf.Loc.Def. Co.I
Thomas, Joseph VA Inf. 2nd Bn.Loc.Def. Co.G
Thomas, Joseph VA 11th Bn.Res. Co.E
Thomas, Joseph VA 54th Inf. Co.I
Thomas, Joseph VA 64th Mtd.Inf. 2nd Co.F
Thomas, Joseph 1st Choctaw & Chickasaw Mtd.Rifles 3rd Co.D Sgt.
Thomas, Joseph 1st Choctaw & Chickasaw Mtd.Rifles 2nd Co.H
Thomas, Joseph A. AL 4th Inf. Co.E Cpl.
Thomas, Joseph A. AR Trader's Regt. Co.A
Thomas, Joseph A. SC 18th Inf. Co.G
Thomas, Joseph B. NC 62nd Inf. Co.K
Thomas, Joseph B. VA 17th Inf. Co.C
Thomas, Joseph B. VA 22nd Inf. Co.I
Thomas, Joseph C. VA 25th Cav. Co.G,I
Thomas, Joseph D. LA 8th Inf. Co.E
Thomas, Joseph E. VA Lt.Arty. E.J. Anderson's Co.
Thomas, Joseph F. MO 4th Cav. Co.I
Thomas, Joseph G. AL 5th Cav. Co.L
Thomas, Joseph G. MO 15th Cav. Co.H
Thomas, Jos. H. AL 7th Cav. Co.G
Thomas, Joseph H. GA 31st Inf. Co.I
Thomas, Joseph H. MS 3rd Inf. Co.I Cpl.
Thomas, Joseph H. NC Cav. (Loc.Def.) Howard's Co. Sgt.
Thomas, Joseph H. NC Hvy.Arty. 1st Btty. Co.B
Thomas, Joseph H. NC 2nd Bn.Loc.Def. Co.F,G
Thomas, Joseph H. NC 50th Inf. Co.F
Thomas, Joseph H. TX 17th Cav. Co.H
Thomas, Joseph H. TX 37th Cav. Co.F
Thomas, Joseph H. VA 5th Inf. Co.E
Thomas, Joseph J. NC 3rd Arty. (40th St.Troops) Co.B
Thomas, Joseph J. VA 44th Inf. Co.K Cpl.
Thomas, Joseph L. MO 2nd Cav. 3rd Co.K
Thomas, Joseph L. NC 55th Inf. Co.K Cpl.
Thomas, Joseph L. Gen. & Staff Capt.,AQM
Thomas, Joseph M. AL 33rd Inf. Co.A Sgt.
Thomas, Joseph M. NC 31st Inf. Co.I
Thomas, Joseph M. SC 8th Inf. Co.G
Thomas, Joseph M. VA 4th Inf. Co.D Capt.
Thomas, Joseph M. VA 47th Inf. Co.D
Thomas, Joseph M. VA 63rd Inf. Co.F
Thomas, Joseph N. LA 17th Inf. Co.K
Thomas, Joseph N.B. VA 5th Cav. (12 mo. '61-2) Co.H
Thomas, Joseph N.B. Sig.Corps,CSA
Thomas, Joseph P. MS 5th Inf. Co.G
Thomas, Joseph P. NC 49th Inf. Co.D
Thomas, Joseph P. VA 15th Inf. Co.E
Thomas, Joseph P. VA 51st Inf. Co.D
Thomas, Joseph R. GA 30th Inf. Co.F
Thomas, Joseph R. VA 25th Cav. Co.G
Thomas, Joseph R. VA Inf. 21st Bn. Co.B Cpl.
Thomas, Joseph R. VA Inf. Mileham's Co.
Thomas, Joseph S. GA 14th Inf. Co.I
Thomas, Joseph S. SC 4th St.Troops Co.F
Thomas, Joseph T. NC 1st Inf. (6 mo. '61) Co.L
Thomas, Jos. V. Gen. & Staff 1st Lt.,ADC
Thomas, Josephus SC 9th Res. Co.F
Thomas, Joseph W. AR 20th Inf. Co.B
Thomas, Joseph W. KY 5th Mtd.Inf. Co.E Sgt.
Thomas, Joseph W. MO 16th Inf. Co.B
Thomas, Joseph W. TN 24th Inf. 2nd Co.G 2nd Lt.
Thomas, Joseph W. VA Hvy.Arty. 19th Bn. Co.B, 3rd Co.E
Thomas, Joseph W. VA 9th Cav. Co.B
Thomas, Joseph W. VA 39th Inf. Co.C
Thomas, Joshua MS 12th Inf. Co.C Cpl.
Thomas, Joshua SC 5th Mil. Beat Co.3
Thomas, Joshua VA Cav. 39th Bn. Co.D
Thomas, Joshua VA 17th Inf. Co.A
Thomas, Joshua M.D. FL 11th Inf. Co.C
Thomas, Joshua P. GA 17th Inf. Co.E
Thomas, Joshua T. TN 3rd (Lillard's) Mtd.Inf. Co.A 2nd Lt.
Thomas, Joshua T. TN 39th Mtd.Inf. Co.C
Thomas, Josiah GA 30th Inf. Co.F
Thomas, Josiah MS Cav. 4th Bn. Sykes' Co.
Thomas, Josiah NC 12th Inf. Co.H
Thomas, Josiah SC 7th Cav. Co.C
Thomas, Josiah SC Cav.Bn. Holcombe Legion Co.D
Thomas, Josiah VA 2nd Inf.Loc.Def. Co.E
Thomas, Josiah VA Inf. 6th Bn.Loc.Def. Co.B
Thomas, Josiah 8th (Wade's) Conf.Cav. Co.G
Thomas, Josiah H. NC 18th Inf. Co.C

Thomas, Josiah S. GA 2nd Bn.S.S. Co.D
Thomas, J.P. AL 48th Inf. Co.A
Thomas, J.P. AR Cav. Gordon's Regt. Co.G
Thomas, J.P. GA Cav. 19th Bn. Co.C Cpl.
Thomas, J.P., Jr. MS Cav. Gartley's Co. (Yazoo Rangers)
Thomas, J.P. SC Lt.Arty. Beauregard's Co.
Thomas, J.P. SC Lt.Arty. M. Ward's Co. (Waccamaw Lt.Arty.)
Thomas, J.P. SC 16th Inf. Co.K
Thomas, J.P. SC Maj.
Thomas, J.P. TN 14th (Neely's) Cav. Co.D
Thomas, J.P. TX 2nd Inf. Co.C
Thomas, J.P. TX Inf. Timmons' Regt. Co.I
Thomas, J. Pinkney GA Cobb's Legion Co.A
Thomas, J. Pinkney TX 17th Cons.Dismtd.Cav. 1st Co.G, Co.E Sr.2nd Lt.
Thomas, J.R. AL 43rd Inf. Co.G 1st Lt.
Thomas, J.R. FL 2nd Cav. Co.H
Thomas, J.R. GA 11th Cav. Co.D
Thomas, J.R. GA 62nd Cav. Co.G,H
Thomas, J.R. GA 1st (Fannin's) Res. Co.B
Thomas, J.R. GA 2nd Res. Co.I
Thomas, J.R. GA 36th (Broyles') Inf. Co.A
Thomas, J.R. GA Cobb's Legion Co.D
Thomas, J.R. KY 2nd Mtd.Inf. Co.H
Thomas, J.R. MS 23rd Inf. Co.L
Thomas, J.R. MS 36th Inf. Chap.
Thomas, J.R. NC 35th Inf. Co.D
Thomas, J.R. TN 17th Inf. Co.A
Thomas, J.R. (Sr.) TX 5th Inf. Co.I
Thomas, J.R. TX 13th Vol. 2nd Co.D 1st Lt.
Thomas, J.R.E. MS 13th Inf. Co.G
Thomas, J.S. AL Cav. Hardie's Bn.Res. Co.C
Thomas, J.S. AR 24th Inf. Co.E
Thomas, J.S. GA Lt.Arty. 14th Bn. Co.B
Thomas, J.S. GA Lt.Arty. Anderson's Btty.
Thomas, J.S. MS 6th Cav. Co.G Sgt.
Thomas, J.S. MS 5th Inf. (St.Troops) Co.E
Thomas, J.S. MS 31st Inf. Co.C
Thomas, J.S. SC 2nd Res.
Thomas, J.S. SC Inf. Holcombe Legion Co.H
Thomas, J.S. TN 20th Cav. Co.A
Thomas, J.S. TN 20th (Russell's) Cav. Co.A
Thomas, J.S. TN 28th Cav. Co.D
Thomas, J.S. TX 19th Cav.
Thomas, J.S. TX 35th (Brown's) Cav. Co.C
Thomas, J.S. VA 46th Inf. Co.L
Thomas, J.S. 10th Conf.Cav. Co.H Sgt.
Thomas, J. Solon MO 3rd Cav. Co.D,I
Thomas, J.T. AL Vol. Goldsmith's Ind.Co.
Thomas, J.T. AL Res. J.G. Rankin's Co.
Thomas, J.T. GA 3rd Cav. (St.Guards) Co.K Cpl.
Thomas, J.T. GA 1st (Symons') Res. Co.A
Thomas, J.T. MS 12th Cav. Co.G
Thomas, J.T. MS 9th Inf. New Co.K
Thomas, J.T. SC 6th Inf. 2nd Co.A Cpl.
Thomas, J.T. SC 18th Inf. Co.G 1st Sgt.
Thomas, J.T. TN 1st (Carter's) Cav. Co.H 1st Lt.
Thomas, J.T. TN Lt.Arty. Scott's Co.
Thomas, J.T. 1st Conf.Cav. 2nd Co.G
Thomas, Judson P. AL 47th Inf. Co.H
Thomas, Julius VA Inf. 1st Bn.Loc.Def. Co.B
Thomas, Julius E. TN 36th Inf. Co.C Fifer
Thomas, Jurdin D. AL 7th Inf. Co.B
Thomas, J.V. KY 12th Cav. Co.C,K
Thomas, J.V. TX 1st Bn.S.S. Co.B
Thomas, J.W. AL 6th Cav. Co.E
Thomas, J.W. AL 9th Cav. Co.C
Thomas, J.W. AL 6th Inf. Co.K
Thomas, J.W. AL 43rd Inf. Co.F
Thomas, J.W. AL 47th Inf. Co.G
Thomas, J.W. AL Mtd.Inf. J. Oden's Co.
Thomas, J.W. AR Lt.Arty. Hart's Btty. 1st Lt.
Thomas, J.W. AR 6th Inf.
Thomas, J.W. AR 20th Inf. Co.G Sgt.
Thomas, J.W. AR 37th Inf. Co.A Sgt.
Thomas, J.W. AR 37th Inf. Co.D
Thomas, J.W. FL 2nd Cav. Co.H
Thomas, J.W. GA 13th Inf. Co.B
Thomas, J.W. GA 31st Inf. Co.G Cpl.
Thomas, J.W. GA 39th Inf. Co.E Sgt.
Thomas, J.W. GA 42nd Inf. Co.H
Thomas, J.W. GA 48th Inf. Co.H
Thomas, J.W. KY 1st Bn.Mtd.Rifles Co.B
Thomas, J.W. LA Mil. 4th Regt. 3rd Brig. 1st Div. Co.A 3rd Lt.
Thomas, J.W. LA 14th Inf. Co.A Cpl.
Thomas, J.W. LA Inf. 16th Bn. (Conf.Guards Resp.Bn.) Co.B
Thomas, J.W. LA 18th Inf. Co.H
Thomas, J.W. LA Inf.Cons. 18th Regt. & Yellow Jacket Bn. Co.H
Thomas, J.W. LA Inf.Cons.Crescent Regt. Co.A
Thomas, J.W. MS Cav. 2nd Bn.Res. Co.G
Thomas, J.W. MS 6th Inf. Co.B Cpl.
Thomas, J.W. MS 32nd Inf. Co.A
Thomas, J.W. MS 32nd Inf. Co.C
Thomas, J.W. MS 37th Inf. Co.H
Thomas, J.W. MS 46th Inf. Co.G
Thomas, J.W. MS Blythe's Bn. (St.Troops)
Thomas, J.W. MO 3rd Cav. Co.H Capt.
Thomas, J.W. NC 7th Sr.Res. Fisher's Co.
Thomas, J.W. NC 23rd Inf. Co.I
Thomas, J.W. NC 27th Inf.
Thomas, J.W. NC 32nd Inf. Co.I
Thomas, J.W., Sr. NC 50th Inf. Co.F
Thomas, J.W. NC 60th Inf. Co.K
Thomas, J.W. SC 3rd Cav. Co.A
Thomas, J.W. SC 3rd Cav. Co.D
Thomas, J.W. SC Cav. 14th Bn. Co.B
Thomas, J.W. SC Arty. Fickling's Co. (Brooks Lt.Arty.)
Thomas, J.W. SC 7th Inf. 2nd Co.K
Thomas, J.W. SC 11th Res. Co.G
Thomas, J.W. SC 20th Inf. Co.B,O
Thomas, J.W. SC 27th Inf. Co.I
Thomas, J.W. TN 2nd (Ashby's) Cav. Co.F
Thomas, J.W. TN 12th (Green's) Cav. Co.E
Thomas, J.W. TN 20th (Russell's) Cav. Co.A
Thomas, J.W. TN 20th Inf. Co.A
Thomas, J.W. TN 26th Inf. Co.G
Thomas, J.W. TX 4th Cav. Co.I
Thomas, J.W. TX 15th Cav. Co.B
Thomas, J.W. TX 29th Cav. Co.H
Thomas, J.W. TX 12th Inf. Co.B 1st Sgt.
Thomas, J.W. TX 20th Inf. Co.D
Thomas, J.W. VA 1st (Farinholt's) Res. Co.F
Thomas, J.W. VA 2nd Inf.Loc.Def. Co.E
Thomas, J.W., Jr. VA 3rd Inf.Loc.Def. Co.E Sgt.
Thomas, J.W. VA 3rd Inf.Loc.Def. Co.F Ord.Sgt.
Thomas, J.W. VA Inf. 6th Bn.Loc.Def. Co.B
Thomas, J.W. VA 8th Inf. Co.E
Thomas, J.W. 1st Conf.Cav. 2nd Co.F 1st Lt.
Thomas, J.W. 1st Conf.Inf. 2nd Co.K Sgt.
Thomas, J.W. Sig.Corps,CSA
Thomas, J. Walt TX 2nd Inf. Co.H Cpl.
Thomas, J.W.B. TN 9th Inf. Co.B
Thomas, J. Wesley AL 12th Inf. Co.I Sgt.
Thomas, J. Whit Gen. & Staff 1st Lt.,Adj.
Thomas, J. William MD Weston's Bn. Co.D
Thomas, J.W.J. TX 22nd Inf. Co.K
Thomas, K. MS 3rd Cav. Co.G
Thomas, Keller KY 5th Cav. Co.C
Thomas, Kimeon GA 35th Inf. Co.A
Thomas, K.J. AL Inf. 1st Regt. Co.I,D
Thomas, K.M. AL 23rd Inf. Co.B
Thomas, Knox GA 55th Inf. Co.H
Thomas, K.T. AL 9th Inf. Co.B
Thomas, L. AL 6th Cav. Co.I
Thomas, L. AL 20th Inf.
Thomas, L. AL 30th Inf. Co.K
Thomas, L. FL 1st (Res.) Inf. Co.D
Thomas, L. MO Dismtd.Cav. Lawther's Temporary Regt.
Thomas, L. NC 8th Sr.Res. Williams' Co.
Thomas, L. SC 16th & 24th (Cons.) Inf. Co.C
Thomas, L. SC 24th Inf. Co.A
Thomas, L. TX 14th Field Btty.
Thomas, L. TX 13th Vol. 4th Co.I Sgt.
Thomas, L. VA Cav. O'Ferrall's Bn. Co.C
Thomas, L.A. MS 6th Inf. Co.K
Thomas, L.A. TN 14th (Neely's) Cav. Co.I,D Capt.
Thomas, L.A. TN 9th Inf. Co.A Bvt.2nd Lt.
Thomas, L.A. VA 46th Inf. 2nd Co.E
Thomas, Lafayette GA 5th Inf. (St.Guards) Brooks' Co.
Thomas, LaFayette GA 31st Inf. Co.B
Thomas, Lafayette GA 54th Inf. Co.H,F
Thomas, Lafayette LA 19th Inf. Co.E
Thomas, Lafayette MO 2nd Cav. Co.G
Thomas, Lafayette MO St.Guard
Thomas, Lafayette SC 5th Inf. 2nd Co.C
Thomas, Lafayett H. VA 37th Inf. Co.A,K
Thomas, L.A.M. FL Sp.Cav. 1st Bn. Co.B
Thomas, Lamkin M. VA 30th Bn.S.S. Co.B
Thomas, Larick P. GA 42nd Inf. Co.A Lt.Col.
Thomas, Larkin A. NC 26th Inf. Co.F
Thomas, Larkin S. LA 28th (Gray's) Inf. Co.E
Thomas, Laughlin LA 7th Inf. Co.A
Thomas, Lawrence R. MD Inf. 2nd Bn. Co.A Cpl.
Thomas, Lawrence Ringgold VA 1st Inf. Co.H
Thomas, L.B. TX 12th Cav. Co.H
Thomas, L.C. KY 6th Mtd.Inf. Co.A
Thomas, L.C. LA 7th Inf. Co.A
Thomas, L.C. TN 19th (Biffle's) Cav. Co.K
Thomas, L.C. TX 19th Inf. Co.K
Thomas, L.D. AL 23rd Inf. Co.B
Thomas, L.D. AR 1st (Dobbin's) Cav. Co.K
Thomas, L.D. AR 16th Inf. Co.I
Thomas, L.D. LA 4th Cav. Co.C Sgt.
Thomas, L.D. SC 3rd St.Troops Co.A
Thomas, L.E. AL 35th Inf. Co.B
Thomas, L.E. TX 4th Cav. Co.B

Thomas, Leander SC 1st (Orr's) Rifles Co.C
Thomas, Leander TN 61st Mtd.Inf. Co.E
Thomas, Leander A. MS 27th Inf. Co.E
Thomas, Lee TN 23rd Inf. Co.E
Thomas, Lemuel SC 1st St.Troops Co.B Cpl.
Thomas, Lemuel SC 3rd Res. Co.I 2nd Lt.
Thomas, Lemuel D. AL 35th Inf. Co.B
Thomas, Lemuel L. MS 1st Lt.Arty. Co.D
Thomas, Lemuel T. NC 2nd Arty. (36th St.Troops) Co.C
Thomas, Leonidas TN 55th (McKoin's) Inf. Dillehay's Co.
Thomas, Leonidas TX 11th (Spaight's) Bn.Vol. Co.B Sgt.
Thomas, Leroy AL 8th Inf. Co.F
Thomas, Leroy MO 1st Brig.St.Guard
Thomas, Leroy L. LA 9th Inf. Co.I Sgt.
Thomas, Leroy S. VA 41st Inf. Co.C
Thomas, Levi NC 6th Inf. Co.K
Thomas, Levi VA 21st Mil. Co.D 1st Sgt.
Thomas, Levi VA 58th Inf. Co.G
Thomas, Levi VA Mil. Carroll Cty.
Thomas, Levi D. VA 29th Inf. 2nd Co.F
Thomas, Levi L. AR 31st Inf. Co.E
Thomas, Levin VA Cav. 35th Bn. Co.B
Thomas, Lewis AL 4th Inf. Co.C
Thomas, Lewis GA Mtd.Inf. (Pierce Mtd.Vol.) Hendry's Co.
Thomas, Lewis GA Lt.Arty. Clinch's Btty.
Thomas, Lewis GA 21st Inf. New Co.E
Thomas, Lewis GA 54th Inf. Co.K
Thomas, Lewis KY 11th Cav. Co.A
Thomas, Lewis MO 4th Cav. Co.A
Thomas, Lewis MO Cav. Preston's Bn. Co.A
Thomas, Lewis NC 4th Cav. (59th St.Troops) Co.F
Thomas, Lewis NC Inf. 2nd Bn. Co.D
Thomas, Lewis NC 12th Inf. Co.C
Thomas, Lewis NC 38th Inf. Co.A Cpl.
Thomas, Lewis NC 43rd Inf. Co.B
Thomas, Lewis TN 16th (Logwood's) Cav. Co.K
Thomas, Lewis TX 5th Cav. Co.F
Thomas, Lewis VA 9th Inf. Co.B
Thomas, Lewis VA Inf. 25th Bn. Co.G
Thomas, Lewis VA 36th Inf. Co.F
Thomas, Lewis Conf.Inf. Tucker's Regt. Co.H Sgt.
Thomas, Lewis A. AL 38th Inf. Co.G
Thomas, Lewis A.M. FL 11th Inf. Co.E
Thomas, Lewis L. NC 6th Sr.Res. Co.C AQM
Thomas, Lewis M. KY 7th Cav. Co.A
Thomas, Lewis O. AL 12th Inf. Co.I
Thomas, Lewis P. GA 4th Inf. Co.F
Thomas, Lewis R. FL 7th Inf. Co.B Sgt.
Thomas, Lewis R. GA 50th Inf. Co.A Sgt.
Thomas, Lewis R. NC 30th Inf. Co.K
Thomas, Lewis R. VA Lt.Arty. Clutter's Co.
Thomas, Lewis R. VA 51st Inf. Co.E
Thomas, Lewis T. VA 51st Inf. Co.D
Thomas, Lewis W. VA 26th Inf. Co.D 2nd Lt.
Thomas, L.G. AR 21st Mil. Co.D
Thomas, L.G. LA 17th Inf. Co.D Sgt.
Thomas, L.G. LA 31st Inf. Co.K
Thomas, L.G. NC 3rd Cav. (41st St.Troops) Co.H
Thomas, L.G. TX 20th Inf. Co.D
Thomas, L.G. VA 46th Inf. 2nd Co.E
Thomas, L.G. VA 51st Inf. Co.I Cpl.
Thomas, L.H. GA 66th Inf. Co.K
Thomas, L.H. TN 12th (Cons.) Inf. Co.F
Thomas, L.H. TN 22nd Inf. Co.I
Thomas, L.H. Gen. & Staff Rec. for 1st Lt.,Adj.
Thomas, Lilburn TN 5th (McKenzie's) Cav. Co.C
Thomas, Lindsay AL 50th Inf. Co.E Sgt.
Thomas, Lindsey AL 28th Inf. Co.G
Thomas, Lindsey AR 3rd Cav. Co.G
Thomas, Lindsey NC 45th Inf. Co.G
Thomas, L.J. AL 8th (Livingston's) Cav. Co.A
Thomas, L.J. FL 5th Inf. Co.H
Thomas, L.J. MO Inf. 5th Regt.St.Guard Co.C
Thomas, L.L. AL 7th Cav. Co.K
Thomas, L.L. Eng.,CSA
Thomas, L.M. AL 25th Inf. Co.C
Thomas, L.M. AR 15th (Johnson's) Inf. Co.A 2nd Lt.
Thomas, L.M. Gen. & Staff Post Adj.,Dr.M.
Thomas, Logan 1st Choctaw & Chickasaw Mtd.Rifles 2nd Co.H Cpl.
Thomas, Lore SC 10th Inf. Co.L
Thomas, Lott AL 47th Inf. Co.I
Thomas, Louis LA Mil. 1st Native Guards
Thomas, Louis LA C.S. Zouave Bn. Co.B Sgt.
Thomas, Louis TX 19th Cav. Co.I
Thomas, Louis A. MS 16th Inf. Co.D 2nd Lt.
Thomas, Louis F. VA 44th Inf. Co.D,I
Thomas, Louis R. FL 8th Inf. Co.K
Thomas, Louis S. FL Cav. 5th Bn. Co.A
Thomas, Louis W. VA 2nd Cav. Co.I
Thomas, Lovic H. GA 12th Inf. Co.G
Thomas, Lovick P. Gen. & Staff Capt.,AQM
Thomas, L.P. GA 35th Inf. AQM
Thomas, L.P. GA Cobb's Legion Co.C
Thomas, L.P. SC 3rd Inf. Co.K
Thomas, L.P. Morgan's Co.C,CSA
Thomas, L.R. VA 46th Inf. 2nd Co.I
Thomas, L.T. NC Lt.Arty. 13th Bn. Co.C
Thomas, L.T. TN 38th Inf. Co.E Music.
Thomas, L.T. TX 35th (Brown's) Cav.
Thomas, Lucius J. TX 15th Inf. 2nd Co.E Sgt.
Thomas, Luther NC 50th Inf. Co.F
Thomas, Luther NC 50th Inf. Co.H
Thomas, Luther J. GA Inf. 10th Bn. Co.D
Thomas, Luther J. GA 27th Inf. Co.B
Thomas, L.W. AL 42nd Inf. Co.I
Thomas, L.W. AR 35th Inf. Co.G
Thomas, L.W. TX 1st Inf. Co.D
Thomas, L.W. VA 11th Cav. Co.A
Thomas, M. AL 7th Cav. Co.K
Thomas, M. AL 63rd Inf. Co.E
Thomas, M. AR 34th Inf. Co.E
Thomas, M. GA 6th Cav. Co.K
Thomas, M. GA 49th Inf. Co.F
Thomas, M. MS Cav. Jeff Davis Legion Co.D
Thomas, M. MS Inf. 2nd Bn. Co.E
Thomas, M. MS 48th Inf. Co.E
Thomas, M. SC 7th Cav. Co.C 1st Lt.
Thomas, M. SC 2nd Bn.S.S. Co.C
Thomas, M. SC Inf. Holcombe Legion Co.D
Thomas, M. TN 2nd Cav. Co.D
Thomas, M. TX 5th Inf. Co.B
Thomas, M. TX Waul's Legion Co.E
Thomas, M. VA 11th Cav. Co.I
Thomas, M. VA 2nd Inf. Co.K
Thomas, M.A. AL 34th Inf. Co.K
Thomas, M.A. GA Lt.Arty. 12th Bn. 3rd Co.C
Thomas, M.A. MS 18th Cav. Co.D
Thomas, M.A. MS 23rd Inf. Co.D
Thomas, M.A. MS 32nd Inf. Co.D
Thomas, M.A. NC 4th Inf. Co.G
Thomas, M.A. SC 4th Cav. Co.G Artif.
Thomas, M.A. SC Cav. 10th Bn. Co.C
Thomas, M.A. Sap. & Min. G.W. Maxson's Co.,CSA
Thomas, Mabery C. NC Walker's Bn. Thomas' Legion Co.G
Thomas, Mabry SC 3rd Bn.Res. Co.A 1st Sgt.
Thomas, Mabry SC Cav.Bn. Holcombe Legion Co.D 1st Lt.
Thomas, Mabry C.G. SC 5th Inf. 1st Co.D
Thomas, Madison MS 10th Inf. Co.C
Thomas, Madison NC 21st Inf. Co.K
Thomas, Madison M. AL 17th Inf.
Thomas, Major VA 55th Inf. Co.K
Thomas, Malachi VA 15th Cav. Co.D
Thomas, Malachi VA Cav. 15th Bn. Co.B
Thomas, Mangum B. NC Hvy.Arty. 10th Bn. Co.A
Thomas, Mangum B. NC 22nd Inf. Co.L
Thomas, Manning GA 48th Inf. Co.F
Thomas, Marcellus A. VA Lt.Arty. 13th Bn. Co.C
Thomas, Marchant AR 7th Mil. Co.D Sgt.
Thomas, Marcus TX 4th Inf. Co.B
Thomas, Marcus VA 10th Cav. Co.H
Thomas, Marcus L. TN 6th Inf. Co.H
Thomas, Marion MO Cav. Ford's Bn. Co.E
Thomas, Marion L. VA 19th Inf. Co.C
Thomas, Marion P. AR 23rd Inf. Co.C
Thomas, Mark MS Lt.Arty. (Jefferson Arty.) Darden's Co.
Thomas, Mark M. VA 10th Inf. Co.L
Thomas, Maro TN 49th Inf. Co.C
Thomas, Marshall VA 36th Inf. 2nd Co.B
Thomas, Marshall G. NC 30th Inf. Co.H
Thomas, Martin GA Murray Cav. Asher's Co.
Thomas, Martin MO 8th Inf. Co.C
Thomas, Martin NC 33rd Inf. Co.D
Thomas, Martin NC 54th Inf. Co.F
Thomas, Martin H. GA 49th Inf. Co.G
Thomas, Martin R. GA 11th Cav. Co.D Cpl.
Thomas, Martin V. NC 20th Inf. Co.F
Thomas, Marville H. TX 9th Cav. Co.H
Thomas, Mason GA 3rd Cav. Co.G
Thomas, Mason 3rd Conf.Cav. Co.G
Thomas, Mason M. MS 35th Inf. Co.H
Thomas, Mathew MS Blythe's Bn. (St.Troops) Co.A
Thomas, Matthew AL 61st Inf. Co.A
Thomas, Matt. FL Lt.Arty. Abell's Co.
Thomas, Matthew H. AL 61st Inf. Co.B
Thomas, Maurice O. VA 10th Cav. Co.A
Thomas, Maurice O. VA Lt.Arty. 13th Bn. Co.C
Thomas, Maurice S. NC 55th Inf. Co.K
Thomas, Maybery C. TN 1st (Carter's) Cav. Co.H
Thomas, M.B. LA 17th Inf. Co.C,D Sgt.
Thomas, M.B. TN 11th (Holman's) Cav. Co.B
Thomas, M.B. TN 16th (Logwood's) Cav. Co.K
Thomas, M.B. TN Holman's Bn.Part.Rangers Co.A

Thomas, M.B. TN 16th Inf. Co.E
Thomas, M.C. AL 12th Inf.
Thomas, M.C. AL 59th Inf. Co.K Sgt.
Thomas, M.C. NC 46th Inf. Co.H
Thomas, McCleary VA 22nd Cav. Co.B
Thomas, M.E. AL 26th (O'Neal's) Inf. Co.K
Thomas, M.E. TX 8th Cav. Co.D
Thomas, M.E. Horse Arty. White's Btty. Sgt.
Thomas, Mel TX 2nd Cav. Co.K
Thomas, Mesley TN 1st Cav.
Thomas, M.G. NC 61st Inf. Co.D
Thomas, M.G. TX 12th Inf. Co.B Capt.
Thomas, M.H. AL Arty. 1st Bn. Co.F
Thomas, M.H. GA 4th Cav. (St.Guards) Cartledge's Co. Ord.Sgt.
Thomas, M.H. TX 8th Cav. Co.D
Thomas, M.H. VA 51st Inf. Co.I
Thomas, Micajah AL Inf. 1st Regt. Co.H
Thomas, Micajah NC 35th Inf. Co.A
Thomas, Micajah TX 8th Inf. Co.G Jr.2nd Lt.
Thomas, Micajah C. AL 3rd Bn. Hilliard's Legion Vol. Co.C
Thomas, Michael VA 7th Cav. Co.I
Thomas, Michael VA 146th Mil. Co.B
Thomas, Milburn VA 1st Arty. Co.I
Thomas, Milburn VA Lt.Arty. 38th Bn. Co.B
Thomas, Miles TN 27th Inf. Co.I
Thomas, Miles VA 46th Inf. 2nd Co.I
Thomas, Miles D. AR 36th Inf. Co.A
Thomas, Miles K. VA Lt.Arty. Armistead's Co.
Thomas, Miles K. VA 61st Mil. Co.G
Thomas, Milledge SC 2nd Arty. Co.G
Thomas, Milton LA Miles' Legion Boone's Btty. Capt.
Thomas, Milton B. KY 5th Cav.
Thomas, Milton B. KY 6th Cav. Co.K
Thomas, Milton H. GA 10th Cav. (St.Guards) Co.G
Thomas, Minor B. TN 11th Inf. Co.K
Thomas, M.J. AL 63rd Inf. Co.E
Thomas, M.J. MS 32nd Inf. Co.A
Thomas, M.J. TN 5th Inf. 2nd Co.K
Thomas, M.K. Conf.Lt.Arty. Stark's Bn. Co.A
Thomas, M.L. GA 2nd Cav. (St.Guards) Co.F
Thomas, M.L. GA 37th Inf. Co.I
Thomas, M.L. GA 54th Inf. Co.E 1st Lt.
Thomas, M.L. SC 13th Inf. Co.C
Thomas, M.L. TN 5th Inf. 2nd Co.F
Thomas, M.M. AL 42nd Inf. Co.F Sgt.
Thomas, M.M. GA 31st Inf. Co.I
Thomas, M.M. TN 1st (Carter's) Cav. Co.K Cpl.
Thomas, M.M. VA 82nd Mil. Co.D
Thomas, M.N. AL Inf. 1st (Loomis') Bn. Co.E Cpl.
Thomas, M.N. AL 25th Inf. Co.E Cpl.
Thomas, M.N. AL Cp. of Instr. Talladega
Thomas, M.N. Gen. & Staff Asst.Surg.
Thomas, Monroe TN 7th Inf. Co.D
Thomas, Montgomery VA 14th Cav. Co.G, 2nd Co.F
Thomas, Montgomery L. GA Lt.Arty. 12th Bn. 2nd Co.A
Thomas, Montgomery L. GA 1st (Ramsey's) Inf. Co.A
Thomas, Moore B. GA Inf. 2nd Bn. Co.B
Thomas, Morris FL Cav. 5th Bn. Co.C
Thomas, Morris S. NC 2nd Cav. (19th St.Troops) Co.C
Thomas, Moses AL 10th Inf. Co.H
Thomas, Moses AL 17th Inf. Co.G
Thomas, Moses AL 58th Inf. Co.C
Thomas, Moses KY 1st (Butler's) Cav. Co.B
Thomas, Moses KY 5th Cav. Co.I
Thomas, Moses KY 3rd Bn.Mtd.Rifles Co.B
Thomas, Moses MO Cav. 3rd Regt.St.Guard Co.A
Thomas, Moses NC 42nd Inf. Co.D
Thomas, Moses VA 37th Inf. Co.F
Thomas, Moses E. VA 63rd Inf. Co.F
Thomas, Moses T. MO 10th Inf. Co.D
Thomas, Moses W. AL 6th Cav. Co.H
Thomas, Moses W. NC 1st Inf. Co.D
Thomas, M.P. KY 12th Cav. Co.D
Thomas, M.P. TN 37th Inf. Co.I
Thomas, M.R. AL 3rd Cav. Co.H
Thomas, M.S. FL 2nd Inf. Surg.
Thomas, M.S. VA 3rd Inf. Surg.
Thomas, M.S. Gen. & Staff, Medical Dept. Surg.
Thomas, M.T. NC 3rd Inf. Co.H
Thomas, M. Thomas GA 26th Inf. Co.A
Thomas, Murphy J. NC 30th Inf. Co.H
Thomas, Murrel H. AR 1st S.S. Co.K
Thomas, M.W. AL Lt.Arty. 20th Bn. Co.A
Thomas, M.W. AL 57th Inf. Co.H
Thomas, M.W. TN 6th Inf. Co.B Cpl.
Thomas, N. AL 29th Inf. Co.E,C
Thomas, N. AR 11th & 17th Cons.Inf. Co.K
Thomas, N. GA 3rd Inf. Co.A
Thomas, N. SC 3rd Cav. Co.D
Thomas, N. TX 27th Cav. Co.K
Thomas, N. TX 8th Inf. Co.G
Thomas, N.A. AL 27th Inf. Co.C
Thomas, N.A. TN Lt.Arty. Rice's Btty.
Thomas, N.A. TN 38th Inf. Co.G
Thomas, N.A. VA 2nd Inf.Loc.Def. Co.F
Thomas, Napoleon B. GA 5th Inf. Co.D
Thomas, Napoleon B. KY 7th Mtd.Inf. Co.A
Thomas, Nathan AL 48th Inf. Co.H
Thomas, Nathan AR 34th Inf. Co.A
Thomas, Nathan AR 36th Inf. Co.F
Thomas, Nathan NC 16th Inf. Co.C
Thomas, Nathan SC 4th Cav. Co.E
Thomas, Nathan SC Cav. 12th Bn. Co.C
Thomas, Nathan TN 19th Inf. Co.G Sgt.
Thomas, Nathan TX 6th Cav. Co.B
Thomas, Nathan TX Cav. Waller's Regt. Co.D
Thomas, Nathan TX 9th (Young's) Inf. Co.B
Thomas, Nathan VA Inf. 4th Bn.Loc.Def. Co.F
Thomas, Nathan G. NC 37th Inf. Co.D
Thomas, Nathan H. KY Cav. Bolen's Ind.Co.
Thomas, Nathaniel GA 27th Inf. Co.I
Thomas, Nathaniel NC 26th Inf. Co.E
Thomas, Nathaniel A. VA 51st Inf. Co.D
Thomas, Nathaniel B. AL 38th Inf. Co.E
Thomas, Nathaniel H. TN 10th Inf. Co.I
Thomas, Nathan J. GA 6th Inf. Co.D
Thomas, Nathan R. VA 28th Inf. Co.B
Thomas, Nathan W. MS 7th Cav. Co.E Jr.2nd Lt.
Thomas, N.B. TX Cav. Waller's Regt. Co.F
Thomas, N.B. VA 15th Cav. Co.B
Thomas, N.C. GA Phillips' Legion Co.C
Thomas, N.D. AR 3rd Cav. Co.A
Thomas, N.E. AL Cav. Lewis' Bn. Co.B
Thomas, N.E. AL 40th Inf. Co.C Jr.2nd Lt.
Thomas, N.E. TN Lt.Arty. Winston's Co.
Thomas, Neil NC 5th Cav. (63rd St.Troops) Co.G
Thomas, Nelson GA 27th Inf. Co.B
Thomas, Nelson SC Hvy.Arty. Gilchrist's Co. (Gist Guard)
Thomas, Nelson SC Arty. Manigault's Bn. 1st Co.C
Thomas, Nelson S. TX 13th Cav. Co.C
Thomas, Newton GA 6th Cav. (St.Guards) Co.A Cpl.
Thomas, Newton SC Inf. Holcombe Legion Co.A
Thomas, Newton A. NC 16th Inf. Co.C Sgt.
Thomas, Newton H. SC 1st Inf. Co.E
Thomas, N.F. AL 13th Bn.Part.Rangers Co.B
Thomas, N.F. GA 11th Cav. Co.D
Thomas, N.G. AR Cav. Chrisman's Bn.
Thomas, N.G. NC 2nd Jr.Res. Co.F
Thomas, N.G. VA 60th Inf. Co.K
Thomas, N.H. AL 3rd Bn. Hilliard's Legion Vol. Co.C
Thomas, N.H. SC Lt.Arty. Jeter's Co. (Macbeth Lt.Arty.)
Thomas, N.H. TN 50th Inf. Co.H
Thomas, Nicholas 1st Cherokee Mtd.Vol. 2nd Co.D
Thomas, N.J. SC Prov.Guard Hamilton's Co.
Thomas, N.J. TX 1st Inf. Co.F
Thomas, N.J. VA 46th Inf. AQM
Thomas, N.J. Wise's Brig. Capt.,AQM
Thomas, N.M. AL 29th Inf. Co.E
Thomas, N.M. VA 3rd Res. Co.H
Thomas, Noah NC 64th Inf. Co.C,G
Thomas, Noah NC Walker's Bn. Thomas' Legion Co.C
Thomas, Noah VA 1st Arty. Co.A
Thomas, Noah VA Lt.Arty. W.P. Carter's Co.
Thomas, Noah VA 32nd Inf. 1st Co.K
Thomas, Noah L. TN 60th Mtd.Inf. Co.B
Thomas, Noel G. TX 3rd Cav. Co.E Cpl.
Thomas, N.T. AL 56th Part.Rangers Co.F
Thomas, N.T. GA 3rd Bn.S.S. Co.A
Thomas, N.T. GA 31st Inf. Co.D
Thomas, N.W. AL 12th Inf. Co.A
Thomas, N.W. GA 31st Inf. Co.I
Thomas, O. LA Mil.Conf.Guards Regt. Co.F
Thomas, O. MO 3rd & 5th Cons.Inf.
Thomas, O. SC Manigault's Bn.Vol. Co.D
Thomas, Obediah AL 39th Inf. Co.C
Thomas, O.E. LA Inf. 4th Bn. Co.E Cpl.
Thomas, O.E. TX 1st Inf. 2nd Co.K
Thomas, O.F. SC 27th Inf.
Thomas, O.G. LA 2nd Cav. Co.F
Thomas, Oliver SC 1st Bn.S.S. Co.B
Thomas, Oliver SC Inf. 6th Bn. Co.A
Thomas, Oliver SC 10th Inf. Co.D
Thomas, Oliver SC 27th Inf. Co.F
Thomas, Oliver TX 9th (Nichols') Inf. Co.K
Thomas, Oliver H. Gen. & Staff 1st Lt.,ADC
Thomas, Oliver H.P. TX 17th Cav. Co.C Sgt.
Thomas, Oliver P. KY 5th Mtd.Inf. Co.C
Thomas, O.P. GA 36th (Broyles') Inf. Co.A
Thomas, O.P. KY 2nd Bn.Mtd.Rifles Co.C
Thomas, O.P. LA 3rd (Wingfield's) Cav. Co.A
Thomas, O. Perry LA 9th Inf. Co.I

Thomas, Orlando P. AL 26th Inf. Co.E,I 1st Lt.
Thomas, Osborne NC 48th Inf. Co.A
Thomas, Oscar TX 2nd Cav. Co.C
Thomas, Oscar E. TX Inf.Riflemen Arnold's Co.
Thomas, O.T. TN 28th (Cons.) Inf. Co.E
Thomas, O.T. TN 84th Inf. Co.A
Thomas, O.V. GA 27th Inf. Co.K
Thomas, Ovando A. MS 11th (Perrin's) Cav. Co.A
Thomas, Overton MO 1st & 4th Cons.Inf. Co.H
Thomas, Overton MO 4th Inf. Co.K
Thomas, P. AL Gid Nelson Lt.Arty.
Thomas, P. SC Manigault's Bn.Vol. Co.A
Thomas, P. TN Cav. 12th Bn. (Day's) Co.E
Thomas, P. VA Inf. 25th Bn. Co.E Sgt.
Thomas, P. Sig.Corps,CSA
Thomas, P.A. AL 14th Inf. Co.G
Thomas, Pall AL 15th Inf. Co.E
Thomas, Parker C. GA 20th Inf. Co.I
Thomas, Pat VA Inf. 2nd Bn.Loc.Def. Co.C
Thomas, Patrick AL 12th Inf. Co.B Capt.
Thomas, Patrick LA 14th Inf. Co.K
Thomas, Patrick LA Miles' Legion Co.F
Thomas, Patrick B. MS 1st Lt.Arty. Co.D
Thomas, Patrick H. VA 28th Inf. Co.D
Thomas, Patrick H. Gen. & Staff AASurg.
Thomas, Patrick K. SC Arty. Manigault's Bn. 1st Co.C
Thomas, Paul Blake's Scouts,CSA
Thomas, P.B. LA 3rd Inf. Co.F
Thomas, P.C. SC 2nd Cav. Co.H
Thomas, P.C. VA 63rd Inf. Co.E
Thomas, Persons S. VA 3rd Inf. Co.G
Thomas, Peter KY 6th Mtd.Inf. Co.B
Thomas, Peter NC 13th Inf. Co.I
Thomas, Peter NC 64th Inf. Co.C,G
Thomas, Peter SC 5th Cav. Co.D
Thomas, Peter SC Cav. 17th Bn. Co.A
Thomas, Peter SC Mil.Arty. 1st Regt. Tupper's Co. Sgt.
Thomas, Peter VA 58th Mil. Co.G
Thomas, Peter 1st Cherokee Mtd.Vol. 2nd Co.D
Thomas, Peter 1st Choctaw & Chickasaw Mtd.Rifles 2nd Co.K,C
Thomas, Peter F. AL 6th Inf. Co.A
Thomas, Peter J. VA 51st Inf. Co.D
Thomas, Peter P. MO 4th Cav. Co.D
Thomas, Peyre SC 6th Res. Co.H
Thomas, P.F. TN 9th (Ward's) Cav. Co.F
Thomas, P.F.M. FL 6th Inf. Co.A
Thomas, P.G. SC Palmetto S.S. Co.A
Thomas, P.H. AL 25th Inf. Co.C
Thomas, P.H. GA Cav. 19th Bn. Co.B
Thomas, P.H. LA Conscr.
Thomas, P.H. TN 14th (Neely's) Cav. Co.D
Thomas, P.H. VA 34th Inf. Co.E
Thomas, P.H. VA 53rd Inf. Co.G
Thomas, Phelps GA 1st (Fannin's) Res. Co.D
Thomas, Phendal VA 52nd Inf. Co.E
Thomas, Philip AL 42nd Inf. Co.G
Thomas, Philip AR 15th (Johnson's) Inf. Co.A
Thomas, Philip NC 45th Inf. Co.C
Thomas, Philip NC 64th Inf. Co.C Cpl.
Thomas, Philip SC 5th Cav. Co.E
Thomas, Philip SC 24th Inf. Co.D Cpl.
Thomas, Philip VA 5th Cav. Co.C 1st Sgt.
Thomas, Phillip SC 23rd Inf. Co.G
Thomas, P. Howard GA 66th Inf. Co.K 1st Sgt.
Thomas, Pierre LA Mil. 1st Native Guards
Thomas, Pinkney GA Cherokee Legion (St.Guards) Co.B
Thomas, P.K. SC Arty. Gregg's Co. (McQueen Lt.Arty.)
Thomas, Pleasant TN 55th (McKoin's) Inf. Dillehay's Co.
Thomas, Pleasant VA 10th Cav. Co.K
Thomas, Pleasant C. AL 24th Inf. Co.D Cpl.
Thomas, Pleasant C. AL 28th Inf. Co.A Cpl.
Thomas, Pleasant C. NC 14th Inf. Co.B 1st Lt.
Thomas, Pleasant F. TN 5th Cav.
Thomas, Pleasant P. VA 64th Mtd.Inf. Co.K,A
Thomas, Pledger P. LA 25th Inf. Co.A Cpl.
Thomas, P.M. SC 3rd Inf. Co.K
Thomas, P.N. TX 13th Cav. Co.D
Thomas, P.N. 2nd Cherokee Mtd.Vol. Co.E
Thomas, P.O.J. VA 8th Cav. Co.C Sgt.
Thomas, Polk TN 20th Cav.
Thomas, Polk F. VA 4th Res. Co.H Sgt.
Thomas, P.P. LA 1st Hvy.Arty. (Reg.) Co.D
Thomas, P.R. MS 2nd St.Cav. Co.E
Thomas, Presley H. KY Cav. 1st Bn.
Thomas, Presley P. VA Lt.Arty. 38th Bn. Co.A
Thomas, Presley P. VA 49th Inf. 1st Co.G
Thomas, Presley S. VA 30th Bn.S.S. Co.A
Thomas, Presly KY 5th Cav. Co.F,A
Thomas, P.T. AL 32nd Inf. Co.F
Thomas, P.W. KY 10th (Johnson's) Cav. New Co.G
Thomas, P.W. SC 4th Cav. Co.G
Thomas, P.W. SC Cav. 10th Bn. Co.C
Thomas, P.Y. MO Cav. 7th Regt.St.Guard Co.A 3rd Lt.
Thomas, Quincy TX 13th Vol. 2nd Co.C
Thomas, R. AL 13th Bn.Part.Rangers Co.B
Thomas, R. AL 56th Part.Rangers Co.F
Thomas, R. AL 14th Inf. Co.H
Thomas, R. AL 37th Inf. Co.F
Thomas, R. GA 5th Res. Co.A
Thomas, R. GA 5th Res. Co.D
Thomas, R. MS 1st (King's) Inf. (St.Troops) Co.I
Thomas, R. MO 1st N.E. Cav. Co.G
Thomas, R. NC 2nd Jr.Res. Co.G
Thomas, R. SC Lt.Arty. Jeter's Co. (Macbeth Lt.Arty.)
Thomas, R. SC 11th Inf. Co.D
Thomas, R. SC 11th Res. Co.G
Thomas, R. SC Manigault's Bn.Vol. Co.D
Thomas, R. TX 7th Cav. Co.A
Thomas, R.A. LA 1st (Strawbridge's) Inf. Co.A Cpl.
Thomas, R.A. LA 21st (Kennedy's) Inf. Co.A
Thomas, R.A. MS 12th Inf.
Thomas, R.A. VA 1st Bn.Res. Co.D
Thomas, R.A. VA 3rd Res. Co.H
Thomas, R.A. VA Inf. 44th Bn. Co.E Sgt.
Thomas, Raleigh AL 28th Inf. Co.G Cpl.
Thomas, Ransom SC 11th Inf. Co.K
Thomas, R.B. FL 2nd Inf. Co.C 1st Lt.,Adj.
Thomas, R.B. MS 6th Cav. Co.I
Thomas, R.B. SC 5th Inf. 2nd Co.E
Thomas, R.B. TX 15th Cav. Co.D
Thomas, R.C. AL Cp. of Instr. Talladega
Thomas, R.C. KY 2nd Mtd.Inf. Asst.Surg.
Thomas, R.C. KY 6th Mtd.Inf. Asst.Surg.
Thomas, R.C. MD 1st Cav. Co.C
Thomas, R.C. Stark's Brig. 1st Lt.,ADC
Thomas, R.C. Gen. & Staff Asst.Surg.
Thomas, R.D. KY 8th Mtd.Inf. Co.H
Thomas, R.D. SC 2nd Res.
Thomas, R.D. SC 5th Bn.Res. Co.D Sgt.
Thomas, R.D. SC 8th Inf. Co.G
Thomas, R. Daniel GA 44th Inf. Co.D Bvt.2nd Lt.
Thomas, R.E. MO Cav. Snider's Bn. Co.E
Thomas, R.E. MO 9th Inf. Co.E
Thomas, R.E. SC 8th Inf. Co.F
Thomas, R.E. TN 50th Inf. Co.B 2nd Lt.
Thomas, Redin W. NC 15th Inf. Co.K 1st Sgt.
Thomas, Renatus SC 2nd Cav. Co.C Cpl.
Thomas, Renatus SC Cav. 4th Bn. Co.B Cpl.
Thomas, Reuben AR 6th Inf. Co.E Cpl.
Thomas, Reuben AR Inf. Cocke's Regt. Co.E Cpl.
Thomas, Reuben NC Inf. 2nd Bn. Co.D
Thomas, Reuben TN 59th Mtd.Inf. Co.E
Thomas, Reuben B. VA Hvy.Arty. 20th Bn. Co.A
Thomas, Reuben C. TX 14th Cav. Co.C
Thomas, Reuben L. VA 2nd Cav. Co.E
Thomas, Reuben M. AL Cav. Holloway's Co.
Thomas, Reuben N. 1st Conf.Eng.Troops Co.A Cpl.
Thomas, Reuben P. VA 1st Cav. Co.A
Thomas, Reuben P. VA 27th Inf. Co.B
Thomas, Reuben S. VA 7th Inf. Co.A
Thomas, Reubin M. GA 26th Inf. Co.F
Thomas, R.F. KY 12th Cav. Co.D Cpl.
Thomas, R.F. MS 10th Inf. New Co.G
Thomas, R.F. VA 8th Inf. Co.G
Thomas, R.G. AR 2nd Vol. Co.C
Thomas, R.G. AR 8th Inf. New Co.K
Thomas, R.G. AR 32nd Inf. Co.H
Thomas, R.G. KY 12th Cav. Co.I
Thomas, R.G. NC 3rd Inf. Co.H
Thomas, R.G. SC Cav.Bn. Holcombe Legion Co.D
Thomas, R. Gilliam SC 7th Cav. Co.C
Thomas, R.H. MD Cav. 2nd Bn. Co.D Sgt.
Thomas, R.H. TN 12th Inf. Co.C
Thomas, R.H. TN 48th (Nixon's) Inf. Co.H
Thomas, R.H. VA 34th Inf. Co.G
Thomas, Richard AL 50th Inf. Co.D
Thomas, Richard AR 3rd Cav. Co.H
Thomas, Richard GA 35th Inf. Co.A
Thomas, Richard MS 2nd St.Cav. Co.I 2nd Lt.
Thomas, Richard MS Lt.Arty. (Brookhaven Lt.Arty.) Hoskins' Btty.
Thomas, Richard MS 31st Inf. Co.C
Thomas, Richard MO 1st N.E. Cav. Co.D
Thomas, Richard NC 17th Inf. (2nd Org.) Co.H
Thomas, Richard SC 1st Mtd.Mil. Smith's Co.
Thomas, Richard SC 11th Inf. Co.C
Thomas, Richard TN 54th Inf. Co.C
Thomas, Richard VA Arty. Bryan's Co.
Thomas, Richard VA 14th Cav. Co.D
Thomas, Richard VA Cav. Moorman's Co.
Thomas, Richard VA Inf. 25th Bn. Co.A
Thomas, Richard VA Forces Col.
Thomas, Richard Inf. School of Pract. Powell's Detach. Co.C Cpl.

Thomas, Richard A. MS 2nd Inf.
Thomas, Richard A. VA 10th Cav. Co.H
Thomas, Richard A. VA 15th Inf. Co.I
Thomas, Richard B. FL 2nd Inf. Co.E,I
Thomas, Richard Coleman AL 22nd Inf. Co.K
Thomas, Richard D. VA 44th Inf. Co.K
Thomas, Richard E. KY 1st Bn.Mtd.Rifles Co.A
Thomas, Richard E. KY 2nd Bn.Mtd.Rifles Co.C 2nd Lt.
Thomas, Richard F. KY 2nd Mtd.Inf. Co.A
Thomas, Richard G. NC 2nd Arty. (36th St.Troops) Co.H
Thomas, Richard H. MO 2nd Cav. 3rd Co.K
Thomas, Richard H. VA 15th Inf. Co.I
Thomas, Richard L. VA 74th Mil. Co.E
Thomas, Richard S. VA 6th Inf. Co.G
Thomas, Ridley B. TX Cav. Baylor's Regt. Co.G 2nd Lt.
Thomas, R.J. GA 13th Inf. Co.H
Thomas, R.J. MS 24th Inf. Co.H
Thomas, R.J. TX Granbury's Cons.Brig. Co.F
Thomas, R. James GA 2nd Res. Co.B
Thomas, R.K. AL 32nd & 58th (Cons.) Inf.
Thomas, R.L. AL 12th Cav. Co.I
Thomas, R.L. GA 2nd Res. Co.E Cpl.
Thomas, R.M. AR 26th Inf. Co.K
Thomas, R.M. FL 1st (Res.) Inf. Co.L
Thomas, R.M. 1st Conf.Eng.Troops Co.D
Thomas, R.O. TX 9th (Young's) Inf. Co.A Sgt.
Thomas, Roan SC 1st Bn.S.S. Co.B
Thomas, Robert AL 7th Inf. Co.B
Thomas, Robert AL 10th Inf. Co.H
Thomas, Robert AL 47th Inf. Co.K
Thomas, Robert AL 48th Inf. Co.K
Thomas, Robert GA Cav. 9th Bn. (St.Guards) Co.C Cpl.
Thomas, Robert GA 2nd Inf. Stanley's Co.
Thomas, Robert GA Inf. 8th Bn. Co.F
Thomas, Robert GA 16th Inf. AQM
Thomas, Robert KY 1st (Butler's) Cav. Co.C
Thomas, Robert KY 3rd Cav. Co.C
Thomas, Robert KY 12th Cav. Co.B
Thomas, Robert KY 8th Mtd.Inf. Co.A Sgt.
Thomas, Robert MO 9th Inf. Co.C
Thomas, Robert NC 2nd Inf. Co.E
Thomas, Robert NC 12th Inf. Co.B,D
Thomas, Robert NC 52nd Inf. Co.E
Thomas, Robert SC 5th Inf. 2nd Co.E
Thomas, Robert SC 6th Inf. 1st Co.E
Thomas, Robert TN 15th (Cons.) Cav. Co.F
Thomas, Robert TN 9th Inf. Co.B 1st Lt.
Thomas, Robert TN 17th Inf. Co.G
Thomas, Robert TN 62nd Mtd.Inf. Co.C
Thomas, Robert TX 13th Cav. Co.F
Thomas, Robert TX 32nd Cav. Co.F
Thomas, Robert TX Cav. Border's Regt. Co.D,I 1st Lt.
Thomas, Robert VA 2nd Inf. Co.B
Thomas, Robert VA Inf. 4th Bn.Loc.Def. Co.E
Thomas, Robert VA 21st Mil. Co.A
Thomas, Robert VA 29th Inf. Co.E
Thomas, Robert VA 46th Inf. 2nd Co.I
Thomas, Robert VA 47th Inf. 3rd Co.H
Thomas, Robert VA 58th Mil. Co.E
Thomas, Robert VA Mil. Carroll Cty.
Thomas, Robert Conf.Cav. Clarkson's Bn. Ind.Rangers Co.H
Thomas, Robert Cobb's Staff Maj.,QM
Thomas, Robert Cherokee Regt. (Sp.Serv.) Miller's Co.
Thomas, Robert A. MS Hamer's Co. (Salem Cav.)
Thomas, Robert A. MS 19th Inf. Co.H 1st Sgt.
Thomas, Robert A. VA 7th Inf. Co.A Cpl.
Thomas, Robert B. KY 5th Mtd.Inf. 1st Lt.
Thomas, Robert B. NC 13th Inf. Co.H
Thomas, Robert B. NC 50th Inf. Co.F
Thomas, Robert B. Gen. & Staff, Arty. 1st Lt.
Thomas, Robert D. NC 23rd Inf. Co.D
Thomas, Robert D. SC 4th St.Troops Co.F
Thomas, Robert E. MO Inf. Clark's Regt. Co.H
Thomas, Robert E. NC 45th Inf. Co.D
Thomas, Robert E. SC 14th Inf. Co.A
Thomas, Robert Elheldred TX 20th Cav. Co.D
Thomas, Robert F. GA Cobb's Legion Co.I
Thomas, Robert F. VA Cav. 35th Bn. Co.C
Thomas, Robert H. NC 21st Inf. Co.M
Thomas, Robert H. NC 27th Inf. Co.E
Thomas, Robert H.B. NC 30th Inf. Co.D Cpl.
Thomas, Robert J. MS 34th Inf. Co.K
Thomas, Robert J. TX 15th Cav. Co.E
Thomas, Robert J. VA 2nd St.Res. Co.F
Thomas, Robert L. TX 35th (Brown's) Cav. Co.I
Thomas, Robert L. TX 13th Vol. 3rd Co.I
Thomas, Robert L. VA Goochland Lt.Arty.
Thomas, Robert M. AL 38th Inf. Co.C
Thomas, Robert M. VA Lt.Arty. Armistead's Co.
Thomas, Robert M. VA Hvy.Arty. Coleman's Co.
Thomas, Robert M. VA 61st Mil. Co.H
Thomas, Robert N. NC 24th Inf. Co.G
Thomas, Robert N. VA 9th Cav. Co.B
Thomas, Robert N. VA 56th Inf. Co.F Capt.
Thomas, Robert R. GA 21st Inf. Co.C
Thomas, Robert S. GA Carlton's Co. (Troup Cty.Arty.)
Thomas, Robert S. VA Mil. 179th Regt.
Thomas, Robert T. GA 3rd Bn. (St.Guards) Co.B
Thomas, Robert W. FL 4th Inf. Co.K
Thomas, Robert W. MO 3rd Cav. Co.D
Thomas, Robert W. NC 15th Inf. Co.K
Thomas, Robert W. NC 55th Inf. Co.K Capt.
Thomas, Robert W. TX 4th Inf. Cpl.
Thomas, Robert W. VA 2nd Arty. Co.K
Thomas, Robert W. VA 38th Inf. Co.G
Thomas, Robert W. VA 40th Inf. Co.G
Thomas, Robert W. VA 56th Inf. Co.B
Thomas, Robert W.C. NC 62nd Inf. Co.E
Thomas, Robert Y.H. FL 7th Inf. Co.H 1st Sgt.
Thomas, Roland AL 2nd Cav. Co.D
Thomas, Roland FL 2nd Cav. Co.F Cpl.
Thomas, Roland FL 3rd Inf. Co.C
Thomas, Roland FL 7th Inf. Co.A Capt.
Thomas, Rol M. SC 18th Inf. Co.E
Thomas, Roman S. MS Cav. Jeff Davis Legion Co.B
Thomas, Romulus NC 17th Inf. (1st Org.) Co.F
Thomas, Romulus NC 17th Inf. (2nd Org.) Co.A
Thomas, Rowan SC Inf. 6th Bn. Co.A
Thomas, R.P. AL 23rd Inf. Co.H
Thomas, R.S. GA Arty. Lumpkin's Co.
Thomas, R.S. MS 1st (Patton's) Inf. Co.H
Thomas, R.S. MS 41st Inf. Co.E 2nd Lt.
Thomas, R.S. VA 1st St.Res. Co.D
Thomas, R.S. VA 59th Inf. Co.D
Thomas, R.T. AL 11th Cav. Co.F
Thomas, R.T. VA Lt.Arty. Fry's Co.
Thomas, Ruben TN 3rd (Lillard's) Mtd.Inf. Co.I
Thomas, Rufus AL 4th Cav.
Thomas, Rufus KY 12th Cav. Co.D 1st Lt.
Thomas, Rufus MO 1st Cav. Co.B
Thomas, Rufus TN 48th (Nixon's) Inf. Co.B Sgt.
Thomas, Rufus TN 48th (Voorhies') Inf. Co.F Sgt.
Thomas, Rufus TN 53rd Inf. Co.I
Thomas, Rufus TX 2nd Inf. Co.C
Thomas, Rufus B. MS St.Cav. Perrin's Bn. Co.F
Thomas, Rufus H. MO 1st Cav. Co.B
Thomas, Rufus H. MO 1st & 3rd Cons.Cav. Co.B
Thomas, Rufus N. VA 2nd Cav. Co.A
Thomas, R.V. Conf.Cav. Wood's Regt. 2nd Co.F
Thomas, R.W. MO Cav. Ford's Bn. Co.C
Thomas, R.W. TN 21st (Wilson's) Cav. Co.D
Thomas, R.W. TX 13th Cav. Co.F
Thomas, R.W. 2nd Corps Hosp.Stew.
Thomas, R.W. Gen. & Staff AASurg.
Thomas, S. AL 59th Inf. Co.E
Thomas, S. AL Arty. 4th Bn. Hilliard's Legion Co.E
Thomas, S. GA 5th Res. Co.A
Thomas, S. MO Lt.Arty. 3rd Field Btty. Cpl.
Thomas, S. MO 11th Inf. Co.G
Thomas, S. SC 4th Cav. Co.I
Thomas, S. TX 20th Inf. Co.I
Thomas, S.A. SC 27th Inf. Co.C
Thomas, S.A. TN 12th Inf. Co.C 2nd Lt.
Thomas, S.A. TN 18th Inf. Co.E
Thomas, Sackfield F. NC 2nd Bn.Loc.Def. Troops Co.B
Thomas, Sam M. MS 1st Lt.Arty. Co.K
Thomas, Sampson TN 18th Inf. Co.F
Thomas, Sampson C. VA Inf. 23rd Bn. Co.A
Thomas, Samuel AL 3rd Cav. Co.E 4th Sgt.
Thomas, Samuel AL 6th Cav. Co.E
Thomas, Samuel AL Inf. 2nd Regt. Co.G
Thomas, Samuel GA 2nd Res. Co.F
Thomas, Samuel GA 21st Inf. New Co.E
Thomas, Samuel GA 23rd Inf. Co.H
Thomas, Samuel GA 26th Inf. 1st Co.G
Thomas, Samuel GA 36th (Broyles') Inf. Co.L
Thomas, Samuel LA 25th Inf. Co.B,C
Thomas, Samuel LA 31st Inf. Co.I
Thomas, Samuel MS Inf. 1st Bn.St.Troops (12 mo. '62-3) Co.F Cpl.
Thomas, Samuel MS 18th Inf. Co.A
Thomas, Samuel MS 36th Inf. Co.K
Thomas, Samuel MS 43rd Inf. Co.G
Thomas, Samuel MO 1st N.E. Cav.
Thomas, Samuel MO 15th Cav. Co.H
Thomas, Samuel MO Cav. Williams' Regt. Co.F
Thomas, Samuel NC 1st Arty. (10th St.Troops) Co.H
Thomas, Samuel NC Inf. 2nd Bn. Co.D
Thomas, Samuel NC 12th Inf. Co.K
Thomas, Samuel NC 26th Inf. Co.E
Thomas, Samuel NC 45th Inf. Co.G
Thomas, Samuel NC 47th Inf. Co.F
Thomas, Samuel NC 53rd Inf. Co.F
Thomas, Samuel NC 61st Inf. Co.D

Thomas, Samuel NC 66th Inf. Co.B
Thomas, Samuel SC Hvy.Arty. 15th (Lucas') Bn. Co.B
Thomas, Samuel SC 22nd Inf. Co.D
Thomas, Samuel TN 11th Cav. Co.A
Thomas, Samuel TN 16th (Logwood's) Cav. Co.E
Thomas, Samuel TN 59th Mtd.Inf. Co.E Cpl.
Thomas, Samuel TN 63rd Inf. Co.E
Thomas, Samuel TX 2nd Inf. Co.D
Thomas, Samuel TX 13th Vol. 2nd Co.G
Thomas, Samuel VA 7th Cav. Co.I
Thomas, Samuel VA 8th Cav. Co.H
Thomas, Samuel VA 11th Cav. Co.F
Thomas, Samuel VA 3rd Inf. Co.H
Thomas, Samuel, Jr. VA 4th Res. Co.F
Thomas, Samuel VA 29th Inf. Co.E Sgt.
Thomas, Samuel VA 146th Mil. Co.B
Thomas, Samuel Conf.Cav. Wood's Regt. Co.E
Thomas, Samuel Conf.Cav. Wood's Regt. 1st Co.D
Thomas, Samuel Conf.Cav. Wood's Regt. Co.M 2nd Lt.
Thomas, Samuel Conf.Cav. Wood's Regt. 2nd Co.M
Thomas, Samuel Conf.Inf. 1st Bn. 2nd Co.E
Thomas, Samuel B. AL 12th Cav. Co.B
Thomas, Samuel B. MS 12th Inf. Co.A Lt.Col.
Thomas, Samuel B. TN 54th Inf. Co.A
Thomas, Samuel B. TX 13th Cav. Co.F Capt.
Thomas, Samuel B. VA 7th Cav.
Thomas, Samuel B. VA 37th Inf. Co.H
Thomas, Samuel C. TN 12th Inf. Co.H
Thomas, Samuel E. AL 32nd Inf. Co.B Sgt.
Thomas, Samuel E. LA 12th Inf. Co.K
Thomas, Samuel F. VA Cav. 35th Bn. Co.B
Thomas, Samuel H. TX 36th Cav. Co.C
Thomas, Samuel H. VA 82nd Mil. Co.A Sgt.
Thomas, Samuel J. NC 24th Inf. Co.K
Thomas, Samuel J. VA Hvy.Arty. 19th Bn. Co.B
Thomas, Samuel L. AL 2nd Bn. Hilliard's Legion Vol. Co.C
Thomas, Samuel L. AR 24th Inf. Co.G
Thomas, Samuel L. AR Inf. Hardy's Regt. Co.F
Thomas, Samuel M. GA 29th Inf. Co.E Sgt.
Thomas, Samuel M. MO 8th Inf. Co.B
Thomas, Samuel M. VA 2nd Cav. Co.A
Thomas, Samuel M. 1st Conf.Cav. 2nd Co.G
Thomas, Samuel N. TN 2nd (Smith's) Cav. 2nd Lt.
Thomas, Samuel P. TX 5th Inf. Co.C
Thomas, Samuel P. TX Inf. Whaley's Co.
Thomas, Samuel P. VA 3rd Lt.Arty. (Loc.Def.) Co.H
Thomas, Samuel P. VA Lt.Arty. Clutter's Co.
Thomas, Samuel R. SC 4th St.Troops Co.F
Thomas, Samuel S. AL 19th Inf. Co.K
Thomas, Samuel S. MD Arty. 1st Btty.
Thomas, Samuel S. VA Burks' Regt.Loc.Def. Beckner's Co.
Thomas, Samuel W. GA 19th Inf. Co.C
Thomas, Samuel W. VA 42nd Inf. Co.E Cpl.
Thomas, Samuel W. VA 57th Inf. Co.A
Thomas, Sargett GA Inf. 10th Bn. Co.D Cpl.
Thomas, Sawney AL 34th Inf. Co.G
Thomas, S.B. AL 53rd (Part.Rangers) Co.C
Thomas, S.B. FL 1st (Res.) Inf. Co.D
Thomas, S.B. LA 31st Inf. Co.D
Thomas, S.B. MO 12th Cav. Co.B
Thomas, S.B. MO 9th Inf. Co.C
Thomas, S.B. MO Inf. Clark's Regt. Co.B
Thomas, S.B. SC Arty. Manigault's Bn. Co.A
Thomas, S.B. SC Arty. Melchers' Co. (Co.B, German Arty.)
Thomas, S.B. SC 20th Inf. Co.L
Thomas, S.B. SC 21st Inf. Co.L
Thomas, S.B. TN 19th (Biffle's) Cav. Co.L
Thomas, S.B. VA Loc.Def. Wood's Co.
Thomas, S.C. AL 59th Inf. Co.A
Thomas, S.C. TN Inf. 2nd Cons.Regt. Co.D
Thomas, S.C. TN 12th (Cons.) Inf. Co.K
Thomas, S.E. SC 2nd Cav. Co.D
Thomas, S.E. SC Cav. 4th Bn. Co.D
Thomas, S.E. SC Lt.Arty. J.T. Kanapaux's Co. (Lafayette Arty.)
Thomas, S.E. TN 47th Inf. Co.G 2nd Lt.
Thomas, S.E. Forrest's Scouts T.N. Kizer's Co., CSA
Thomas, Seaborn E. GA 17th Inf. Co.E
Thomas, Seaborn J. GA 31st Inf. Co.K Sgt.
Thomas, S.E.H. TN 18th Inf. Co.D
Thomas, Seth TN 27th Inf. Co.E
Thomas, S.H. GA 22nd Inf. Co.G
Thomas, S.H. TN 20th (Russell's) Cav. Co.C
Thomas, S.H. TN 18th Inf. Co.F
Thomas, S.H. TX St.Troops Teel's Co.
Thomas, Shadrach T. SC 12th Inf. Co.D
Thomas, S.I. MO 9th (Elliott's) Cav. Co.A Sgt.
Thomas, Sidney MO 1st & 3rd Cons.Cav. Co.H
Thomas, Sidney MO 3rd Cav. Co.B
Thomas, Sidney MO Cav. 3rd Bn. Co.B
Thomas, Silas VA 47th Inf. 2nd Co.K
Thomas, Silas M. GA 14th Inf. Co.I
Thomas, Simeon GA 34th Inf. Co.G
Thomas, Simeon MS Cav. Dunn's Co. (MS Rangers)
Thomas, Simeon Deneale's Regt. Choctaw Warriors Co.E
Thomas, Simeon B. AL 16th Inf. Co.K
Thomas, Simeon F. GA 42nd Inf. Co.G
Thomas, Simon VA 22nd Inf. Co.C
Thomas, Simon J. TX 29th Cav. Co.A
Thomas, Simpson SC Inf. Holcombe Legion Co.A
Thomas, Sinclair M. VA 10th Inf. Co.L
Thomas, S.J. GA 28th Inf. Co.E Cpl.
Thomas, S.J. TN 51st (Cons.) Inf. Co.C
Thomas, S.J. TX Cav. 3rd Regt.St.Troops Kelly's Co.
Thomas, S.J. TX Inf. 2nd St.Troops Co.A
Thomas, S.J. TX 19th Inf. Co.G
Thomas, S.J. VA 54th Mil. Co.G
Thomas, S.L. AL 59th Inf. Co.A
Thomas, S.L. VA 53rd Inf. Co.B
Thomas, S.M. AR 11th Inf. Co.H
Thomas, S.M. GA 66th Inf. Co.A
Thomas, S.M. LA Lt.Arty. 2nd Field Btty. Capt.
Thomas, S.M. MO Cav. Freeman's Regt. Co.L 1st Sgt.
Thomas, S.M. SC Rutledge Mtd.Riflemen & Horse Arty. Trenholm's Co.
Thomas, S.M. TN Cav. 4th Bn. (Branner's) Co.A
Thomas, S.M. TN 42nd Inf. A.Adj.
Thomas, S.M.D. TN 1st (Carter's) Cav. Co.K Sgt.
Thomas, Smith MO 9th Bn.S.S. Co.E
Thomas, Smith TN Lt.Arty. Morton's Co.
Thomas, Smith TN 3rd (Lillard's) Mtd.Inf. Co.F
Thomas, Smith A. NC 26th Inf. Co.F
Thomas, S.N. TN Cav. Shaw's Bn.
Thomas, S. Nelson TN 7th (Duckworth's) Cav. Co.K
Thomas, S.O. LA 25th Inf. Co.G Cpl.
Thomas, S.O. MS 1st (Patton's) Inf. Co.A
Thomas, Solomon AL 27th Inf. Co.K Sgt.
Thomas, Solomon AL 57th Inf. Co.I Sgt.
Thomas, Solomon FL Inf. 2nd Bn. Co.A
Thomas, Solomon FL 3rd Inf. Co.F
Thomas, Solomon NC 1st Arty. (10th St.Troops) Co.G
Thomas, Solomon VA Inf. 26th Bn. Co.B
Thomas, Solomon VA 79th Mil. Co.5
Thomas, S.P. SC Lt.Arty. 3rd (Palmetto) Bn. Co.E
Thomas, S.P. TN 55th (Brown's) Inf. Co.E Bvt.2nd Lt.
Thomas, Spencer AR 23rd Cav. Co.F
Thomas, Spencer KY 1st (Butler's) Cav. Co.C
Thomas, Spencer KY 3rd Cav. Co.C
Thomas, Spencer KY 5th Mtd.Inf. Co.E
Thomas, Spencer LA 27th Inf. Co.G
Thomas, Sprewell TX Cav. Waller's Regt. Co.D Sgt.
Thomas, Sprig AR 11th & 17th Cons.Inf. Co.K
Thomas, Sprig AR 17th (Griffith's) Inf. Co.D
Thomas, S.R. LA 3rd (Wingfield's) Cav. Co.C
Thomas, S.S.M. AL 4th Inf. Co.K
Thomas, Stanhope N. NC 48th Inf. Co.C Ord.Sgt.
Thomas, Stanley O. MS 1st Lt.Arty. Co.H 1st Lt.
Thomas, Starling GA Inf. 3rd Bn. Co.C
Thomas, Stephen GA 61st Inf. Co.H
Thomas, Stephen SC 10th Inf. Co.D
Thomas, Stephen SC 24th Inf. Co.K
Thomas, Stephen VA 58th Inf. Co.B
Thomas, Stephen C. AL 2nd Bn. Hilliard's Legion Vol. Co.C
Thomas, Stephen L. GA 27th Inf. Co.B
Thomas, Stephen L. VA 63rd Inf. Co.C Cpl.
Thomas, Stephen L. VA Mil. Grayson Cty.
Thomas, Stephen M. NC 46th Inf. Co.D 1st Lt.
Thomas, Stephen S. VA 39th Inf. Co.E
Thomas, Stephen S. VA 46th Inf. 4th Co.F
Thomas, Sterling H. GA 37th Inf. Co.I
Thomas, Stevens GA Inf. Athens Reserved Corps
Thomas, Stewart VA Lt.Arty. Utterback's Co.
Thomas, Stokely VA 38th Inf. 1st Co.I
Thomas, Sumner SC 1st Arty. Co.A,D Cpl.
Thomas, S.W. SC 1st (McCreary's) Inf. Co.E
Thomas, S.W. Gen. & Staff 1st Lt.,Adj.
Thomas, T. AL 6th Inf. Co.K
Thomas, T. VA 46th Inf.
Thomas, Tandy R. AL 40th Inf. Co.B Jr.2nd Lt.
Thomas, Taylor VA Lt.Arty. W.P. Carter's Co.
Thomas, Tazewell VA Lt.Arty. Fry's Co.
Thomas, Tazewell P. VA 51st Inf. Co.D Cpl.
Thomas, Tazwell S. VA 19th Inf. Co.E

Thomas, T.C. TN 19th (Biffle's) Cav. Co.K 1st Lt.
Thomas, T.C. TN 12th Inf. Co.H
Thomas, T.C. TN 12th (Cons.) Inf. Co.K
Thomas, T.C. Forrest's Scouts T.N. Kizer's Co.,CSA
Thomas, T.D. AL 9th Inf. Co.B,D
Thomas, T.E. GA 4th (Clinch's) Cav. Co.I
Thomas, T.E. GA 2nd Res. Co.B
Thomas, T.E. Forrest's Scouts T.N. Kizer's Co.,CSA
Thomas, T.F. NC 18th Inf. Co.E
Thomas, Theophelus TX 4th Inf. Co.A Sgt.
Thomas, Theopholous MS 3rd (St.Troops) Cav. Co.K
Thomas, Thomas GA 4th Res. Co.G
Thomas, Thomas GA Cherokee Legion (St.Guards) Co.H Cpl.
Thomas, Thomas MO 1st N.E. Cav. Co.G
Thomas, Thomas MO 5th Cav. Co.A
Thomas, Thomas NC 1st Arty. (10th St.Troops) Co.D
Thomas, Thomas NC 58th Inf. Co.A
Thomas, Thomas TN 45th Inf. Co.I
Thomas, Thomas TX 22nd Cav. Co.A
Thomas, Thomas A. AL 33rd Inf. Co.A
Thomas, Thomas A. AR 1st (Colquitt's) Inf. Co.I
Thomas, Thomas B. GA Phillips' Legion Co.C
Thomas, Thomas C. AL Mil. 4th Vol. Co.H
Thomas, Thomas C. GA 52nd Inf. Co.D
Thomas, Thomas C. NC 62nd Inf. Co.D
Thomas, Thomas C. VA 27th Inf. Co.E
Thomas, Thomas C. 1st Cherokee Mtd.Vol. 1st Co.F, 2nd Co.G Cpl.
Thomas, Thomas E. AL 1st Inf. Co.H Sgt.
Thomas, Thomas H. NC 31st Inf. Co.I Cpl.
Thomas, Thomas J. GA 38th Inf. Co.A
Thomas, Thomas J. GA 38th Inf. Co.A,D
Thomas, Thomas J. NC 35th Inf. Co.B
Thomas, Thomas J. TX 31st Cav. Co.B
Thomas, Thomas J. VA 63rd Inf. Co.F
Thomas, Thomas L. GA Inf. 2nd Bn. (St.Guards) Old Co.D
Thomas, Thomas P. Lt.Arty. Dent's Btty.,CSA Sgt.
Thomas, Thomas S. Gen. & Staff Asst.Surg.
Thomas, Thomas W. AL 20th Inf. Co.E
Thomas, Thomas W. GA 3rd Cav. (St.Guards) Co.H
Thomas, Thomas W. GA 15th Inf. Col.
Thomas, Timothy SC 2nd St.Troops Co.I
Thomas, Timothy SC 5th Res. Co.K
Thomas, T.J. MS 9th Inf. Old Co.H
Thomas, T.J. SC 1st (Butler's) Inf. Co.K
Thomas, T.J. TN 7th (Duckworth's) Cav. Co.A
Thomas, T.J. VA Inf. 26th Bn. Co.A
Thomas, T.L. GA Lt.Arty. (Arsenal Btty.) Hudson's Co.
Thomas, T.M. GA 34th Inf. Co.I
Thomas, T.M. MO 16th Inf. Co.F
Thomas, T.N. GA 11th Cav. Co.D
Thomas, T.P. AL 15th Inf. Co.B
Thomas, T.P. FL 1st Inf. Old Co.G
Thomas, T.P. TN 21st Inf. Co.G
Thomas, T.R. AL 13th Inf. Co.K
Thomas, T.R. MS 2nd St.Cav. Co.F
Thomas, Tristram S. AL 11th Inf. Co.H
Thomas, Troy GA 7th Cav. Co.F
Thomas, Troy GA Cav. 21st Bn. Co.B,E
Thomas, Try W. AL 33rd Inf. Co.A
Thomas, T.S. LA 17th Inf. Co.D Cpl.
Thomas, T.S. MS Cav. 1st Bn. (Montgomery's) St.Troops Hammond's Co.
Thomas, T.S. MS S.W. Red's Co. (St.Troops)
Thomas, T.S. SC 3rd Inf. Co.K
Thomas, T.S. SC 13th Inf. Co.C
Thomas, T.S. 20th Conf.Cav. 1st Co.H
Thomas, T.T. GA 5th Res. Co.E
Thomas, T.T. VA Lt.Arty. Fry's Co.
Thomas, Tullius SC 1st Arty. Co.H
Thomas, T.V. GA 36th (Broyles') Inf. Co.H Cpl.
Thomas, T.W. AR 1st (Dobbin's) Cav. Co.C
Thomas, T.W. MS Cav. Vivion's Co.
Thomas, T.W. VA 13th Inf. Co.I
Thomas, U.M. AR Inf. 8th Bn.
Thomas, U.M. AR 25th Inf. Co.F Cpl.
Thomas, U.M. TN 10th (DeMoss') Cav. Co.I Cpl.
Thomas, U.M.C. GA 52nd Inf. Co.E
Thomas, U.Q. AL 62nd Inf. Co.C Sgt.
Thomas, Urban MO 15th Cav. Co.F
Thomas, Uriah AL 34th Inf. Co.C
Thomas, V.A. AR 6th Inf. Co.G
Thomas, Valentine L. TX 13th Vol. 2nd Co.G,A
Thomas, Van LA 1st Cav. Co.K 1st Lt.,Adj.
Thomas, V.B. TN 15th (Cons.) Cav. Co.I
Thomas, V.D. GA 12th Cav. Co.I
Thomas, V.D. Conf.Cav. Wood's Regt. 2nd Co.F
Thomas, Vernon L. VA 41st Inf. Co.B
Thomas, Vincent NC 45th Inf. Co.C
Thomas, Vincent H. VA 50th Inf. Co.C 1st Lt.
Thomas, Vineyard TN 37th Inf. Co.I
Thomas, Virginius VA Inf. 4th Bn.Loc.Def. Co.E
Thomas, V.J. SC 11th Inf. Co.D
Thomas, Volentine TX 35th (Brown's) Cav. Co.H
Thomas, W. AL 12th Cav. Co.D
Thomas, W. AL 21st Inf. Co.K
Thomas, W. AL 34th Inf. Co.A
Thomas, W. GA Lt.Arty. 12th Bn. 1st Co.A
Thomas, W. GA 5th Res. Co.A
Thomas, W. GA Inf. Pool's Co.
Thomas, W. LA 2nd Inf. Co.H
Thomas, W. LA Inf. Pelican Regt. Co.B
Thomas, W. MS 1st Cav.Res. Co.G
Thomas, W. MS 2nd Part.Rangers Co.C
Thomas, W. MO Cav. Schnabel's Bn. Co.B
Thomas, W. NC 8th Sr.Res. Co.A
Thomas, W. NC 22nd Inf. Cpl.
Thomas, W. NC 47th Inf. Co.G
Thomas, W. SC 1st (McCreary's) Inf. Co.B
Thomas, W. TN 12th (Cons.) Inf. Co.I
Thomas, W. TN 13th Inf. Co.H
Thomas, W. TN 53rd Inf. Co.E
Thomas, W. TX 18th Cav. Co.B
Thomas, W. TX 30th Cav.
Thomas, W. TX Cav. Terry's Regt. Co.K
Thomas, W. TX 4th Inf. (St.Troops) Co.D
Thomas, W. TX Waul's Legion Co.C
Thomas, W. VA Lt.Arty. (Loc.Def.) Otey's Co.
Thomas, W. VA 13th Inf. Co.C
Thomas, W. VA 62nd Mtd.Inf. Co.G
Thomas, W. 1st Conf.Inf. 1st Co.H
Thomas, W. Gen. & Staff Chap.
Thomas, W.A. AL Cav. 24th Bn. Co.B Sgt.
Thomas, W.A. AL 26th Inf. Co.G
Thomas, W.A. AR 11th Inf. Co.G 1st Lt.
Thomas, W.A. MS 1st Cav.Res. Co.C
Thomas, W.A. MS 18th Cav. Co.C Cpl.
Thomas, W.A. MO 1st Brig.St.Guard
Thomas, W.A. TN 31st Inf. Co.K Sgt.
Thomas, W.A. TX 9th Cav. Co.C
Thomas, W.A. VA Inf. 6th Bn.Loc.Def. Co.C
Thomas, W.A. Trans-MS Conf.Cav. 1st Bn. Co.A
Thomas, W.A. 3rd Conf.Cav. Co.D
Thomas, W.A. Brush Bn.
Thomas, Wade AL 5th Inf. New Co.G
Thomas, Wade MS Cav. Jeff Davis Legion Co.E
Thomas, W.A.H. AL 1st Cav. 2nd Co.B
Thomas, Walker VA 10th Cav. Co.I
Thomas, Walter SC 1st Cav. Co.A
Thomas, Walter T.C. GA 14th Inf. Co.A
Thomas, Warren MS 10th Inf. Old Co.G
Thomas, Warren NC 3rd Inf. Co.E
Thomas, Washington NC 5th Cav. (63rd St.Troops) Co.B
Thomas, Washington VA 21st Mil. Co.A
Thomas, Washington VA 135th Mil. Co.I
Thomas, Washington 1st Choctaw Mtd.Rifles Co.K
Thomas, Washington G. NC 39th Inf. Co.B
Thomas, Washington H. NC 55th Inf. Co.K
Thomas, Watkins AL 22nd Inf. Co.H
Thomas, W.B. GA 5th Res. Co.A
Thomas, W.B. GA 5th Res. Co.D
Thomas, W.B. GA 63rd Inf. Co.C
Thomas, W.B. KY 1st (Butler's) Cav. Co.B 2nd Lt.
Thomas, W.B. LA 6th Cav. Co.A
Thomas, W.B. MS 8th Inf. Co.E
Thomas, W.B. SC 7th Inf. Co.A
Thomas, W.C. AL 5th Cav. Co.H
Thomas, W.C. FL Sp.Cav. 1st Bn. Co.A
Thomas, W.C. GA 11th Cav. (St.Guards) Bruce's Co.
Thomas, W.C. GA Lt.Arty. Howell's Co.
Thomas, W.C. GA 9th Inf. Co.C
Thomas, W.C. GA 17th Inf. Co.F
Thomas, W.C. GA 24th Inf. Co.I Cpl.
Thomas, W.C. KY 12th Cav. Co.E
Thomas, W.C. LA Inf. Pelican Regt. Co.F
Thomas, W.C. MS 3rd Inf. (A. of 10,000) Co.C
Thomas, W.C. MS Inf. 3rd Bn. Co.H
Thomas, W.C. MS Inf. 3rd Bn. (St.Troops) Co.B 2nd Lt.
Thomas, W.C. MS 24th Inf. Co.E
Thomas, W.C. MO 10th Inf. Co.F Sgt.
Thomas, W.C. SC 20th Inf. Co.O
Thomas, W.C. TN Anderson's Cav.
Thomas, W.C. TN 8th Inf. Co.E
Thomas, W.C. VA Lt.Arty. Carpenter's Co.
Thomas, W.C. VA Inf. 4th Bn.Loc.Def. Co.B
Thomas, W.D. AL Inf. 1st Regt. Co.C
Thomas, W.D. AL 59th Inf. Co.H
Thomas, W.D. MO 16th Inf. Co.F
Thomas, W.D. TX 36th Cav. Co.K
Thomas, W.E. AL 23rd Inf. Co.K
Thomas, W.E. GA 5th Res. Co.H Sgt.

Thomas, W.E. MS 1st Cav. Co.F
Thomas, W.E. MS 1st Cav.Res. Co.D Sgt.
Thomas, W.E. MS 11th (Cons.) Cav. Co.I 2nd Lt.
Thomas, W.E. MS Inf. 3rd Bn. (St.Troops) Co.C
Thomas, W.E. MS 41st Inf. Co.E
Thomas, W.E. SC Inf. Hampton Legion Co.H
Thomas, Wesley MS 43rd Inf. Co.G
Thomas, Wesley TX Inf. 1st Bn. Co.E
Thomas, Wesley TX Inf. Rutherford's Co.
Thomas, Wesley VA Arty. (Loc.Def. & Sp.Serv.) Lanier's Co.
Thomas, Wesley H. NC 7th Inf. Co.K
Thomas, Wesley W. GA Phillips' Legion Co.D,K
Thomas, Wesley W. GA Phillips' Legion Co.F,P Maj.
Thomas, Western B. GA 10th Inf. Co.K 1st Lt.
Thomas, W.F. AL 7th Cav. Co.G
Thomas, W.F. AL 14th Inf. Co.A
Thomas, W.F. FL Cav. 3rd Bn. Co.C
Thomas, W.F. GA 65th Inf. Co.E Capt.
Thomas, W.F. NC 9th Bn.S.S. Co.B
Thomas, W.F. SC 17th Inf. Co.K Cpl.
Thomas, W.F. TN 9th Inf. Co.B Sgt.
Thomas, W.F. TX 34th Cav. Co.I
Thomas, W.F. VA 23rd Cav. Co.H
Thomas, W.F. 15th Conf.Cav. Co.E
Thomas, W.F. Brush Bn.
Thomas, W.F. Gen. & Staff, A. of N.VA Capt.,QM
Thomas, W.G. GA 23rd Inf. Co.G
Thomas, W.G. LA 2nd Cav. Co.E
Thomas, W.G. MS 28th Cav. Co.A
Thomas, W.G. TX Inf. (St.Serv.) Carter's Co. Sgt.
Thomas, W.H. AL 2nd Cav. Co.G Cpl.
Thomas, W.H. AL Inf. 2nd Regt. Co.G Cpl.
Thomas, W.H. AL 5th Inf. New Co.A
Thomas, W.H. AL 15th Inf. Co.E
Thomas, W.H. AL 25th Inf. Co.C
Thomas, W.H. AL 34th Inf. Co.A,H
Thomas, W.H. AL 44th Inf. Co.A
Thomas, W.H. AL 60th Inf. Co.B
Thomas, W.H. AR 3rd Cav. Co.D Bugler
Thomas, W.H. AR 1st (Colquitt's) Inf. Co.C
Thomas, W.H. AR 36th Inf. Co.D
Thomas, W.H. AR Mil. Borland's Regt. Peyton Rifles
Thomas, W.H. GA Cav. Pemberton's Co.
Thomas, W.H. GA 55th Inf. Co.B
Thomas, W.H. GA Inf. Arsenal Bn. (Columbus) Co.B
Thomas, W.H. KY 2nd Mtd.Inf. Co.F Sgt.
Thomas, W.H. LA 6th Cav. Co.A
Thomas, W.H. LA 25th Inf. Co.A
Thomas, W.H. LA Mil.Conf.Guards Regt. Co.B
Thomas, W.H. MS 18th Cav. Co.C,F Sgt.
Thomas, W.H. MS Cav. Jeff Davis Legion Co.E
Thomas, W.H. MS Cav. Garland's Bn. Co.C Capt.
Thomas, W.H. MS 25th Inf. Co.F
Thomas, W.H. NC 3rd Inf. Co.C
Thomas, W.H. NC 32nd Inf. Co.K
Thomas, W.H. NC 35th Inf. Co.E
Thomas, W.H. SC 3rd St.Troops Co.A
Thomas, W.H. TN Arty. Marshall's Co.
Thomas, W.H. TN 18th Inf. Co.F
Thomas, W.H. TN 24th Inf. Co.F
Thomas, W.H. TN 51st (Cons.) Inf. Co.A
Thomas, W.H. TX 8th Cav. Co.K 2nd Lt.
Thomas, W.H. TX 20th Inf. Co.D
Thomas, W.H. VA 10th Inf. Co.L
Thomas, W.H. VA 22nd Inf. Co.H
Thomas, W.H. 1st Conf.Cav. 2nd Co.F
Thomas, W.H. 14th Conf.Cav. Co.C Capt.
Thomas, W.H. Gen. & Staff, Trans-MS Dept. Maj.,CS
Thomas, W.H.H. AR 1st Cav. 1st Lt.
Thomas, W.H.H. GA 54th Inf. Co.H
Thomas, W.H.H. MO 9th (Elliott's) Cav. 1st Lt.,Adj.
Thomas, W.H.H. MO 12th Inf. Co.B Adj.
Thomas, Whit GA 63rd Inf. Co.A
Thomas, Whitefield TX 30th Cav. Co.I
Thomas, Whitley VA 21st Cav. Jr.2nd Lt.
Thomas, Whitley VA Cav. 37th Bn. Co.K 2nd Lt.
Thomas, Whitley VA 72nd Mil.
Thomas, Wiat L. GA 38th Inf. Co.A
Thomas, Wiley NC 48th Inf. Co.E
Thomas, Wiley NC 49th Inf. Co.D
Thomas, Wiley A. AL 28th Inf. Co.C
Thomas, Wiley B. TN 27th Inf. Co.I Sgt.
Thomas, Wiley J. SC 5th Cav. Co.B
Thomas, Wiley N. AL Cp. of Instr. Talladega
Thomas, William AL 7th Cav. Co.A
Thomas, William AL Inf. 2nd Regt. Co.B
Thomas, William AL Inf. 2nd Regt. Co.E
Thomas, William AL 3rd Res. Co.I
Thomas, William AL 8th Inf. Co.G
Thomas, William AL 14th Inf. Co.G
Thomas, William AL 18th Bn.Vol. Co.A
Thomas, William AL 24th Inf. Co.G
Thomas, William AL 27th Inf. Co.I
Thomas, William AL 33rd Inf. Co.A
Thomas, William AL 34th Inf. Co.H
Thomas, William, Jr. AL 34th Inf. Co.H
Thomas, William, Sr. AL 34th Inf. Co.H
Thomas, William AL 41st Inf. Co.A Sgt.
Thomas, William AL 45th Inf. Co.G Cpl.
Thomas, William AL 49th Inf. Co.A
Thomas, William AL 57th Inf. Co.I
Thomas, William AL 3rd Bn. Hilliard's Legion Vol. Co.C
Thomas, William AR Cav. McGehee's Regt. Co.C
Thomas, William AR 2nd Vol. Co.B
Thomas, William AR 9th Inf. Old Co.B 3rd Lt.
Thomas, William AR 18th (Marmaduke's) Inf. Co.B Cpl.
Thomas, William AR 31st Inf. Co.D
Thomas, William AR 34th Inf. Co.C
Thomas, William AR 37th Inf. Co.K
Thomas, William FL 1st Cav. Co.B
Thomas, William FL 2nd Cav. Co.D
Thomas, William FL Inf. 2nd Bn. Co.B
Thomas, William FL 6th Inf. Co.C
Thomas, William FL 7th Inf. Co.H
Thomas, William FL 8th Inf. Co.B
Thomas, William FL 10th Inf. Co.G
Thomas, William GA 2nd Cav. (St.Guards) Co.F
Thomas, William GA 3rd Cav. Co.K Cpl.
Thomas, William GA 4th (Clinch's) Cav. Co.I
Thomas, William GA Cav. Dorough's Bn.
Thomas, William GA 1st (Olmstead's) Inf. Gordon's Co.
Thomas, William GA 2nd Bn.Troops & Defences (Macon) Co.D
Thomas, William GA 4th Res. Co.K
Thomas, William GA 7th Inf. Co.G
Thomas, William GA 9th Inf. Co.F
Thomas, William GA Inf. 10th Bn. Co.A
Thomas, William GA 11th Inf. Co.E
Thomas, William GA 17th Inf. Co.D
Thomas, William GA 23rd Inf. Co.C
Thomas, William GA 26th Inf. Co.K
Thomas, William GA 35th Inf. Co.A
Thomas, William GA 36th (Villepigue's) Inf. Co.H
Thomas, William GA 49th Inf. Co.A
Thomas, William GA 50th Inf. Co.B
Thomas, William GA 51st Inf. Co.K
Thomas, William GA 54th Inf. Co.H
Thomas, William GA 55th Inf. Co.B
Thomas, William GA 60th Inf. Co.D
Thomas, William GA 63rd Inf. Co.F
Thomas, William GA Inf. Anderson's Co. (Anderson Guards)
Thomas, William GA Inf. Jones' Co. (Jones Hussars)
Thomas, William GA Phillips' Legion Co.D
Thomas, William GA Phillips' Legion Co.M
Thomas, William KY 5th Cav. Sgt.
Thomas, William KY 10th (Diamond's) Cav. Co.L Sgt.
Thomas, William KY 1st Bn.Mtd.Rifles Co.A
Thomas, William KY 4th Mtd.Inf. Co.G,D
Thomas, William KY 5th Mtd.Inf. Co.A
Thomas, William LA 3rd (Harrison's) Cav. Co.K 1st Sgt.
Thomas, William LA 5th Cav. Co.I
Thomas, William LA Pointe Coupee Arty.
Thomas, William LA 11th Inf. Co.E
Thomas, William LA 21st (Patton's) Inf. Co.F
Thomas, William LA 25th Inf. Co.E
Thomas, William MD 1st Cav. Co.D
Thomas, William MS 3rd (St.Troops) Cav. Co.A
Thomas, William MS Cav. Buck's Co.
Thomas, William MS 1st Lt.Arty. Co.L,E
Thomas, William MS 1st (King's) Inf. (St.Troops) Co.I
Thomas, William MS 5th Inf. Co.C
Thomas, William MS 36th Inf. Co.E Sgt.
Thomas, William MS Inf. 56th Regt. Co.A
Thomas, William MS S.W. Red's Co. (St.Troops)
Thomas, William MO 5th Cav. Co.H
Thomas, William MO 1st Inf. 2nd Co.A
Thomas, William MO Robertson's Regt.St.Guard Co.1
Thomas, William NC 7th Sr.Res. Williams' Co.
Thomas, William NC 37th Inf. Co.D
Thomas, William NC 38th Inf. Co.A
Thomas, William NC 42nd Inf. Co.B
Thomas, William NC 48th Inf. Co.G
Thomas, William NC 61st Inf. Co.D
Thomas, William SC 1st (Butler's) Inf. Co.G Sgt.
Thomas, William SC 1st (Butler's) Inf. Co.H
Thomas, William SC 4th St.Troops Co.A
Thomas, William SC 5th St.Troops Co.H

Thomas, William SC Inf. 7th Bn. (Enfield Rifles) Co.C
Thomas, William SC 9th Res. Co.I
Thomas, William SC 11th Inf. Co.D
Thomas, William SC 11th Res. Co.L
Thomas, William SC 12th Inf. Co.D
Thomas, William SC 13th Inf. Co.I
Thomas, William SC Mil. 16th Regt. Steinmeyer, Jr.'s Co. 2nd Lt.
Thomas, William SC 24th Inf. Co.D Cpl.
Thomas, William SC Inf. Hampton Legion Co.C
Thomas, William SC Cav.Bn. Holcombe Legion Co.C
Thomas, William TN 2nd (Smith's) Cav. Lea's Co.
Thomas, William TN 3rd (Forrest's) Cav. Co.D
Thomas, William TN 5th (McKenzie's) Cav. Co.G
Thomas, William TN Lt.Arty. Weller's Co.
Thomas, William TN 4th Inf.
Thomas, William TN 13th Inf. Co.I
Thomas, William TN 18th Inf. Co.D
Thomas, William TN 37th Inf. Co.K
Thomas, William TN 39th Mtd.Inf. Co.G
Thomas, William TN 62nd Mtd.Inf. Co.I
Thomas, William TN Inf. Crews' Bn. Co.B 2nd Lt.
Thomas, William TX 5th Cav. Co.D
Thomas, William TX 5th Cav. Co.F
Thomas, William TX 15th Cav. Co.B
Thomas, William TX 15th Cav. Co.D
Thomas, William TX 15th Cav. Co.E
Thomas, William TX 20th Cav. Co.G
Thomas, William TX Cav. McCord's Frontier Regt. Co.E
Thomas, William TX Cav. Morgan's Regt. Co.F
Thomas, William TX Cav. Morgan's Regt. Co.G
Thomas, William TX 1st Hvy.Arty. Co.B Music.
Thomas, William TX 8th Inf. Co.E
Thomas, William TX 9th (Nichols') Inf. Co.E
Thomas, William TX 9th (Nichols') Inf. Co.K
Thomas, William TX 18th Inf. Co.D
Thomas, William TX 22nd Inf. Co.A Cpl.
Thomas, William VA 4th Cav. Co.C
Thomas, William VA 4th Cav. Co.C Capt.
Thomas, William VA 7th Cav. Preston's Co.
Thomas, William VA 9th Cav. Co.K
Thomas, William VA 25th Cav. Co.I
Thomas, William VA 26th Cav. Co.F
Thomas, William VA Cav. 46th Bn. Co.D
Thomas, William VA Cav. O'Ferrall's Bn. Co.C
Thomas, William VA 1st Arty. Co.G
Thomas, William VA Lt.Arty. 13th Bn. Co.B
Thomas, William VA Lt.Arty. Page's Co.
Thomas, William VA Lt.Arty. J.D. Smith's Co.
Thomas, William VA 1st Bn.Res. Co.H
Thomas, William VA 3rd Inf. Co.B
Thomas, William VA 8th Inf. Co.F Cpl.
Thomas, William VA 19th Inf. Co.B
Thomas, William VA Inf. 23rd Bn. Co.E
Thomas, William VA 32nd Inf. 1st Co.I
Thomas, William VA 32nd Inf. 2nd Co.I
Thomas, William VA 32nd Inf. 2nd Co.K Cpl.
Thomas, William VA 41st Mil. Co.D
Thomas, Wm. VA Inf. 44th Bn. Co.A
Thomas, William VA Inf. 44th Bn. Co.E Capt.
Thomas, William VA 47th Inf. 3rd Co.H
Thomas, William VA 47th Inf. 2nd Co.K
Thomas, William VA 49th Inf. Co.B
Thomas, William VA 54th Mil. Co.G
Thomas, William VA 60th Inf. Co.K
Thomas, William VA 82nd Mil. Co.A Capt.
Thomas, William VA Inf. Gregory's Co.
Thomas, William 3rd Conf.Cav. Co.A 2nd Lt.
Thomas, William 14th Conf.Cav. Co.I
Thomas, William Conf.Inf. 1st Bn. 2nd Co.C
Thomas, William 1st Conf.Eng.Troops Co.C
Thomas, William A. AL 29th Inf. Co.F
Thomas, William A. AL 30th Inf. Co.H
Thomas, William A. AR 9th Inf. Old Co.B
Thomas, William A., Jr. FL 5th Inf. Co.H
Thomas, William A. GA 1st (Olmstead's) Inf. Stiles' Co.
Thomas, William A. GA 8th Inf. Co.F Cpl.
Thomas, William A. GA 15th Inf. Co.K Cpl.
Thomas, William A. GA Inf. 18th Bn. Co.B
Thomas, William A. GA 24th Inf. Co.K
Thomas, William A. KY Horse Arty. Byrne's Co.
Thomas, William A. KY 3rd Bn.Mtd.Rifles Co.D
Thomas, William A. KY 4th Mtd.Inf. Co.H
Thomas, William A. LA 5th Inf. Co.F
Thomas, William A., Jr. LA 8th Inf. Co.E
Thomas, William A. MS 2nd Inf. Co.B,D
Thomas, William A. MS 2nd Inf. Co.D
Thomas, William A. MS 35th Inf. Co.B
Thomas, William A. MS 41st Inf. Co.G
Thomas, William A. MO St.Guard
Thomas, William A. NC 2nd Arty. (36th St.Troops) Co.H
Thomas, William A. NC 16th Inf. Co.B
Thomas, William A. NC 30th Inf. Co.H
Thomas, William A. TN 24th Inf. 2nd Co.H
Thomas, William A. TN 47th Inf. Co.G 2nd Lt.
Thomas, William A. VA Hvy.Arty. 19th Bn. Co.B
Thomas, William A. VA Lt.Arty. Douthat's Co. Cpl.
Thomas, William A. VA 28th Inf. Co.H
Thomas, William A. VA 44th Inf. Co.D
Thomas, Wm. A. VA Inf. 44th Bn. Co.B
Thomas, William A. VA 58th Inf. Co.K Sgt.
Thomas, Wm. A. Conf.Cav. 6th Bn. Co.D Sgt.
Thomas, William B. AR 9th Inf. Co.H
Thomas, William B. GA 25th Inf. Co.F
Thomas, William B. GA 42nd Inf. Co.D
Thomas, William B. MS 12th Inf. Co.A 2nd Lt.
Thomas, William B. NC 30th Inf. Co.K Cpl.
Thomas, William B. TX 7th Field Btty. Cpl.
Thomas, William B. VA Cav. Young's Co.
Thomas, William B. VA 2nd Arty. Co.D
Thomas, William B. VA Inf. 4th Bn.Loc.Def. Co.E
Thomas, William B. VA 22nd Inf. Co.C
Thomas, William B. VA Inf. 22nd Bn. Co.D
Thomas, William B. VA 25th Inf. 2nd Co.H Cpl.
Thomas, William B. VA Loc.Def. Mallory's Co.
Thomas, William B.A. GA 7th Inf. Co.E Cpl.
Thomas, William C. AL 4th (Russell's) Cav. Co.I
Thomas, William C. AL 16th Inf. Co.C
Thomas, William C. AL Nitre & Min.Corps Young's Co.
Thomas, William C. AR 1st (Colquitt's) Inf. Co.A
Thomas, William C. GA 11th Inf. Co.C Sgt.
Thomas, William C. GA Inf. 11th Bn. (St.Guards) Co.B Sgt.
Thomas, William C. GA 20th Inf. Co.I
Thomas, William C. GA 27th Inf. Co.D
Thomas, William C. GA 52nd Inf. Co.C
Thomas, William C. LA Inf. 4th Bn. Co.B
Thomas, William C. MS 34th Inf. Co.E
Thomas, William C. MO 12th Inf. Co.C 1st Sgt.
Thomas, William C. TN 44th (Cons.) Inf. Co.K
Thomas, William C. VA 61st Mil. Co.D Bvt.2nd Lt.
Thomas, William D. AL 19th Inf. Co.G
Thomas, William D. AL Arty. 4th Bn. Hilliard's Legion Co.D
Thomas, William D. GA 6th Inf. Co.D
Thomas, William D. GA 45th Inf. Co.I 1st Lt.
Thomas, William D. MS 40th Inf. Co.D Cpl.
Thomas, William D. TN 20th Cav.
Thomas, William D. TX Part.Rangers Thomas' Co. Capt.
Thomas, William D. VA 28th Inf. Co.D
Thomas, William D. VA 46th Inf. 2nd Co.K
Thomas, William E. AL 39th Inf. Co.H
Thomas, William E. GA 24th Inf. Co.D
Thomas, William E. MS Cav. 3rd Bn. (Ashcraft's) Co.E 2nd Lt.
Thomas, William E. MS 2nd Inf. Co.E
Thomas, William E. MS 3rd Inf. Co.D Capt.
Thomas, Wm. E. TN Forrest's Cav.
Thomas, William E. TN 29th Inf. Co.D Sgt.
Thomas, William E. VA 29th Inf. Co.E
Thomas, William E. VA 41st Inf. 1st Co.G
Thomas, William E. VA 44th Inf. Co.D,I
Thomas, William E. VA 44th Inf. Co.F
Thomas, William E. VA 49th Inf. Co.I
Thomas, William E. VA 56th Inf. Co.H
Thomas, William E. VA 58th Inf. Co.C
Thomas, William F. AL 4th Inf. Co.E Cpl.
Thomas, William F. AL 29th Inf. Co.G
Thomas, William F. GA 1st Inf. Co.C
Thomas, William F. GA Inf. 2nd Bn. Co.D
Thomas, William F. GA 2nd Bn.S.S. Co.B
Thomas, William F. GA 5th Inf. Co.B,L
Thomas, William F. GA 6th Inf. (St.Guards) Co.I Cpl.
Thomas, William F. GA 60th Inf. Co.H
Thomas, William F. NC 66th Inf. Co.G
Thomas, William F. VA 10th Inf. Co.L
Thomas, William F. VA 20th Inf. Co.I
Thomas, William F. VA 26th Inf. Co.F
Thomas, William F. VA 82nd Mil. Co.A
Thomas, William F.M. GA 22nd Inf. Co.G Cpl.
Thomas, William G. GA 47th Inf. Co.A
Thomas, William G. NC 43rd Inf. Co.H
Thomas, William G. NC 48th Inf. Co.F
Thomas, William G. TN 7th Inf. Co.F
Thomas, William G. VA Lt.Arty. Hardwicke's Co.
Thomas, William G. VA 44th Inf. Co.I Cpl.
Thomas, William G. VA 48th Inf. Co.B,F
Thomas, Wm. G. Gen. & Staff Capt.,AQM
Thomas, William H. AL 6th Inf. Co.I

Thomas, William H. AL 13th Inf. Co.H
Thomas, William H. AL 23rd Bn.S.S. Co.E
Thomas, William H. AL 1st Bn. Hilliard's Legion Vol. Co.E
Thomas, William H. AR 1st (Colquitt's) Inf. Co.I
Thomas, William H. AR 7th Inf. Co.A
Thomas, William H. AR 27th Inf. Co.H
Thomas, William H. FL 5th Inf. Co.D
Thomas, William H. GA 11th Cav. Co.E Cpl.
Thomas, William H. GA 7th Inf. Co.C,A
Thomas, William H. GA 13th Cadets
Thomas, William H. GA 36th (Villepigue's) Inf. Co.B
Thomas, William H. MS 43rd Inf. Co.K Cpl.
Thomas, Wm. H. MO 1st Inf. Co.C Cpl.
Thomas, William H. NC 21st Inf. Co.D Cpl.
Thomas, William H. NC 30th Inf. Co.B
Thomas, William H. NC Inf. Thomas Legion 2nd Co.A Col.
Thomas, William H. SC 2nd Arty. Co.D
Thomas, William H. TX 6th Cav. Co.C 2nd Lt.
Thomas, William H. TX Part.Rangers Thomas' Co. Jr.2nd Lt.
Thomas, William H. TX 16th Inf. Co.I Cpl.
Thomas, William H. TX 20th Inf. Co.C Sgt.
Thomas, William H. VA 14th Cav. Co.G
Thomas, William H. VA Lt.Arty. 13th Bn. Co.C
Thomas, William H. VA Hvy.Arty. 19th Bn. Co.B
Thomas, William H. VA 4th Inf. Co.E Cpl.
Thomas, William H. VA 4th Inf. Co.L Lt.
Thomas, William H. VA 17th Inf. Co.C Cpl.
Thomas, William H. VA 19th Inf. Co.D
Thomas, William H. VA 24th Inf. Co.H
Thomas, William H. VA 29th Inf. Co.E
Thomas, William H. VA 29th Inf. 2nd Co.F
Thomas, William H. VA 54th Mil. Co.E,F
Thomas, William H. VA Mil. Carroll Cty.
Thomas, William H. 1st Conf.Inf. Co.B
Thomas, William H.C. LA 3rd Inf. Co.F
Thomas, William Henry VA 28th Inf. Co.K
Thomas, William H.H. SC 1st (Orr's) Rifles Co.A
Thomas, William H.H. SC 12th Inf. Co.G
Thomas, William H.J. VA 3rd Inf. 2nd Co.I
Thomas, William J. AL 29th Inf. Co.F
Thomas, William J. AL 33rd Inf. Co.I
Thomas, William J. AR 16th Inf. Co.K
Thomas, William J. GA Inf. 2nd Bn. Co.C Cpl.
Thomas, William J. GA 30th Inf. Co.A
Thomas, William J. LA 12th Inf. Co.G
Thomas, William J. NC 54th Inf. Co.B Cpl.
Thomas, William J. NC 56th Inf. Co.E 1st Sgt.
Thomas, William J. NC McDugald's Co.
Thomas, William J. SC 5th Cav. Co.E
Thomas, William J. TN 24th Inf. 2nd Co.G
Thomas, William J. TN 51st Inf. Co.H 1st Sgt.
Thomas, William J. VA 2nd Arty. Co.K
Thomas, William J. VA Horse Arty. Jackson's Co.
Thomas, William J. VA Lt.Arty. Rogers' Co. Cpl.
Thomas, William J. VA 2nd St.Res. Co.F
Thomas, William J. VA 21st Inf. Co.I
Thomas, William J. VA Inf. 25th Bn. Co.C
Thomas, William James VA 9th Inf. Co.G
Thomas, William K. MS 18th Inf. Co.E Sgt.
Thomas, William Kelly SC 7th Cav. Co.C Sgt.
Thomas, William Kelly SC Cav.Bn. Holcombe Legion Co.D Sgt.
Thomas, William L. AL 19th Inf. Co.H
Thomas, William L. AL 41st Inf. Co.D
Thomas, William L. GA 30th Inf. Co.E
Thomas, William L. NC Cav. 5th Bn. Co.D,C
Thomas, William L. NC 6th Cav. (65th St.Troops) Co.D,B
Thomas, William L. SC Inf. 7th Bn. (Enfield Rifles) Co.B
Thomas, William L. SC 22nd Inf. Co.C Cpl.
Thomas, William L. TN 34th Inf. Co.G
Thomas, William L. TN 41st Inf. Co.B
Thomas, William M. AL 2nd Cav. Co.B
Thomas, William M. AL Jeff Davis Arty.
Thomas, Wm. M. AL 26th Inf. Co.C
Thomas, William M. AL 2nd Bn. Hilliard's Legion Vol. Co.B
Thomas, Wm. M. AL Cp. of Instr. Talladega
Thomas, William M. AR 30th Inf.
Thomas, William M. AR 33rd Inf. Co.F
Thomas, William M. GA Cav. 1st Bn. Brailsford's Co.
Thomas, William M. GA Inf. 1st Loc.Troops (Augusta) Co.A
Thomas, William M. GA 1st (Symons') Res. Co.K
Thomas, William M. GA 6th Inf. Co.C
Thomas, William M. GA 15th Inf. QM
Thomas, William M. GA 31st Inf. Co.F
Thomas, William M. GA 31st Inf. Co.I Cpl.
Thomas, William M. GA 34th Inf. Co.A
Thomas, William M. MS Lt.Arty. 14th Bn. Co.C
Thomas, William M. MS 4th Inf.
Thomas, William M. MS 24th Inf. Co.D Cpl.
Thomas, William M. MS 43rd Inf. Co.G Sgt.
Thomas, William M. MO 1st Cav. Co.H
Thomas, William M. NC 61st Inf. Co.D
Thomas, William M. SC 4th Cav. Co.G
Thomas, William M. SC Inf. 7th Bn. (Enfield Rifles) Co.H 1st Lt.,Adj.
Thomas, William M. TN Miller's Co. (Loc. Def.Troops)
Thomas, William M. TX 15th Cav. Co.F
Thomas, William M. TX Waul's Legion Co.E
Thomas, William M. VA 44th Inf. Co.K,I
Thomas, William M. VA 45th Inf. Co.A 2nd Lt.
Thomas, William N. AL 59th Inf. Co.K
Thomas, William N. AL 2nd Bn. Hilliard's Legion Vol. Co.B
Thomas, William N. GA 21st Inf. Co.G
Thomas, William N. MS 14th Inf. Co.G
Thomas, William N. MS 48th Inf. Co.L
Thomas, William O. AR 1st Mtd.Rifles Co.K
Thomas, William O. NC 14th Inf. Co.E
Thomas, William O. VA 8th Inf. Co.D Cpl.
Thomas, William O. VA 44th Inf. Co.K
Thomas, William P. KY 11th Cav. Co.B
Thomas, William P. LA 31st Inf. Co.D
Thomas, William P. MD 1st Inf. Co.C 2nd Lt.
Thomas, William P. MD Weston's Bn. Co.A AAQM
Thomas, William P. MO 8th Inf. Co.B 1st Lt.
Thomas, William P. TN 4th (McLemore's) Cav. Co.A
Thomas, William P. TN 19th Inf. Co.D
Thomas, William P. VA Cav. Mosby's Regt. (Part.Rangers) Co.D
Thomas, William P. VA Lt.Arty. J.R. Johnson's Co.
Thomas, William P. VA 28th Inf. 1st Co.C
Thomas, William P. VA 34th Inf. Co.E
Thomas, William P. VA 38th Inf. Co.E
Thomas, William P. VA 58th Inf. Co.K Cpl.
Thomas, William P.C. VA 14th Inf. Co.C
Thomas, William R. AL Cav. Lewis' Bn. Co.D
Thomas, William R. AL 26th (O'Neal's) Inf. Co.E
Thomas, William R. AL 33rd Inf. Co.G
Thomas, William R. AL 33rd Inf. Co.H
Thomas, William R. GA 30th Inf. Co.E
Thomas, William R. MS 22nd Inf. Co.H
Thomas, William R. MS 23rd Inf. Co.E
Thomas, William R. NC 28th Inf. Co.B
Thomas, William R. NC 60th Inf. Co.D
Thomas, William R. SC 1st (Orr's) Rifles Co.A
Thomas, William R. SC 3rd Inf. Co.K 3rd Lt.
Thomas, William R. TX Cav. Martin's Regt. Co.C 1st Lt.
Thomas, William R. VA 9th Cav. Co.G
Thomas, William R. VA Lt.Arty. Lowry's Co.
Thomas, William R. VA 44th Inf. Co.K
Thomas, William R. VA 50th Inf. Co.F
Thomas, William S. AL 16th Inf. Co.H
Thomas, William S. AL 61st Inf. Co.I 2nd Lt.
Thomas, William S. GA 40th Inf. Co.D
Thomas, William S. KY 7th Mtd.Inf. Co.C
Thomas, Williams MS 3rd Inf. (St.Troops) Co.F
Thomas, William S. MS 8th Inf. Co.F
Thomas, William S. TX 2nd Cav. Co.C
Thomas, William S. VA Lt.Arty. 13th Bn. Co.B
Thomas, William S. VA Lt.Arty. 13th Bn. Co.C
Thomas, William S. VA 20th Inf. Co.F
Thomas, William S. VA 59th Inf. 3rd Co.B 2nd Lt.
Thomas, William S. Gen. & Staff Enrolling Off.
Thomas, Williamson C. VA 56th Inf. Co.E
Thomas, William T. AR 1st (Colquitt's) Inf. Co.A
Thomas, William T. MS 46th Inf. Co.G
Thomas, William T. 2nd Cherokee Mtd.Vol. Co.A
Thomas, William W. GA 31st Inf. Co.G
Thomas, William W. KY 14th Cav. Co.I,D
Thomas, William W. LA Watkins' Bn.Res.Corps Co.C
Thomas, William W. MS 23rd Inf. Co.F
Thomas, William W. MS 27th Inf. Co.G
Thomas, William W. TN 55th (McKoin's) Inf. McEwen, Jr.'s Co.
Thomas, William W. VA 9th Cav. Co.B
Thomas, William W. VA Hvy.Arty. 19th Bn. Co.B
Thomas, William W. VA 14th Mil. Co.C
Thomas, William W. VA 39th Inf. Co.C
Thomas, William W.J. GA 59th Inf. Co.D
Thomas, William Y. NC 13th Inf. Co.H
Thomas, Willie F. VA Inf. 5th Bn. Co.A
Thomas, Willis 1st Conf.Cav. 2nd Co.G
Thomas, Willson TN 8th Inf. Co.I
Thomas, Wilson 1st Choctaw & Chickasaw Mtd.Rifles 2nd Co.C

Thomas, Wilson 1st Choctaw & Chickasaw Mtd.Rifles 2nd Co.K
Thomas, Wily TN 14th Inf. Co.E
Thomas, Winton R. VA 4th Inf. Co.C
Thomas, W.J. AL Cav. Moreland's Regt. Co.B
Thomas, W.J. AL 12th Inf. Co.D
Thomas, W.J. AL 38th Inf. Co.D
Thomas, W.J. AL 42nd Inf. Co.H
Thomas, W.J. GA Cav. 8th Bn. (St.Guards) Co.C 3rd Lt.
Thomas, W.J. GA 5th Res. Co.A
Thomas, W.J. GA 36th (Broyles') Inf. Co.L
Thomas, W.J. GA 55th Inf. Co.B
Thomas, W.J. KY 8th Cav. Co.H 2nd Lt.
Thomas, W.J. KY 2nd Mtd.Inf. Co.G
Thomas, W.J. MS Inf. 1st Bn.St.Troops (12 mo. '62-3) Co.D
Thomas, W.J. SC Cav. 17th Bn. Co.C
Thomas, W.J. TN 7th Cav. Co.F
Thomas, W.J. TN 21st (Carter's) Cav. Co.A
Thomas, W.J. TN Cav. Nixon's Regt. Co.I
Thomas, W.J. TN 51st (Cons.) Inf. Co.D Ord.Sgt.
Thomas, W.J. TX 7th Cav. Co.K
Thomas, W.J. TX 20th Inf. Co.E
Thomas, W.J.C. MS 14th (Cons.) Inf. Co.H
Thomas, W.J.C. MS 43rd Inf. Co.B
Thomas, W.J.M. GA Inf. Bard's Co.
Thomas, W.J.R. AL 21st Inf. Co.K
Thomas, W.K. SC 3rd Bn.Res. Co.A
Thomas, W.L. AL 55th Vol. Co.B
Thomas, W.L. AL 59th Inf. Co.H
Thomas, W.L. AL Arty. 4th Bn. Hilliard's Legion CoD
Thomas, W.L. GA 4th (Clinch's) Cav. Co.D
Thomas, W.L. GA 1st Bn.S.S. Co.D
Thomas, W.L. GA 19th Inf. Co.C
Thomas, W.L. MS 18th Cav.
Thomas, W.L. MS Cav. Ham's Regt. Co.B
Thomas, W.L. MS 32nd Inf. Co.C
Thomas, W.L. MO 5th Cav. Co.A
Thomas, W.L. NC 8th Bn.Part.Rangers Co.C
Thomas, W.L. NC 66th Inf. Co.D
Thomas, W.L. SC 1st (Hagood's) Inf. 2nd Co.H
Thomas, W.L. SC 6th Inf. 1st Co.F
Thomas, W.L. TN Cav. Nixon's Regt. Co.K
Thomas, W.L. TN Lt.Arty. Rice's Btty.
Thomas, W.L. TX 7th Cav. Co.A
Thomas, W.L. VA 2nd Cav. Co.I
Thomas, W.L. VA 10th Cav. Co.I
Thomas, W.L. VA 3rd Inf.Loc.Def. Co.B
Thomas, W.L. VA 11th Inf. Co.A
Thomas, W.M. AL Cav. 4th Bn. (Love's) Co.A
Thomas, W.M. AL Lt.Arty. Kolb's Btty.
Thomas, W.M. AL Mil. 4th Vol. Co.D
Thomas, W.M. AL 22nd Inf. Co.B
Thomas, W.M. AL 34th Inf. Co.A
Thomas, W.M. AL 59th Inf. Co.K
Thomas, W.M. GA 42nd Inf. Co.D
Thomas, W.M. GA 55th Inf. Co.E
Thomas, W.M. MS Cav. Jeff Davis Legion Co.H
Thomas, W.M. MS Rogers' Co.
Thomas, W.M. MO Cav. Fristoe's Regt. Co.L
Thomas, W.M. MO 1st Inf. Co.A
Thomas, W.M. NC 7th Inf. Co.F
Thomas, W.M. SC Cav. 10th Bn. Co.C
Thomas, W.M. SC Lt.Arty. 3rd (Palmetto) Bn. Co.K
Thomas, W.M. TN 20th Inf. Co.E
Thomas, W.M. TX 10th Cav. Co.F
Thomas, W.M. TX 29th Cav. Co.K
Thomas, W.M. TX 12th Inf. Co.B
Thomas, W.M. TX Inf. Timmons' Regt. Co.I
Thomas, W.M. Gen. & Staff Capt.,QM
Thomas, W.M. Gen. & Staff Asst.Surg.
Thomas, W.N. MS Inf. 2nd Bn. Co.L
Thomas, W.N. MO 1st Inf. Co.C Cpl.
Thomas, W.O. AL 17th Inf. Co.F
Thomas, W.O. AR 45th Cav. Co.A
Thomas, W.O. MS 2nd (Davidson's) Inf. Co.F
Thomas, W.O. MS 10th Inf. New Co.C
Thomas, Woodard NC 55th Inf. Co.A
Thomas, Woodley AL 30th Inf. Co.E
Thomas, Woodlief Gen. & Staff Chap.
Thomas, Woodliff TX 18th Cav. Chap.
Thomas, Woodson H. VA 60th Inf. Co.C
Thomas, W.P. AR 15th Mil.
Thomas, W.P. AR 15th (Johnson's) Inf. Co.C
Thomas, W.P. LA 4th Cav. Co.F
Thomas, W.P. NC 6th Cav. (65th St.Troops) Co.A,F 2nd Lt.
Thomas, W.P. SC Post Guard Senn's Co.
Thomas, W.P. VA 17th Cav. Co.H
Thomas, W.P.C. VA 18th Inf. Co.E
Thomas, W.Q. AL 31st Inf. Co.K Sgt.
Thomas, W.R. AL 31st Inf. Co.H
Thomas, W.R. AR Cav. Gordon's Regt. Co.D
Thomas, W.R. GA 1st Bn.S.S. Co.D
Thomas, W.R. GA 55th Inf. Co.I
Thomas, W.R. NC 6th Cav. (65th St.Troops) Co.D
Thomas, W.R. TX 29th Cav. Co.D
Thomas, W.R. VA 2nd Cav. Co.A
Thomas, W.R. VA 3rd Arty. Co.F
Thomas, W.R. VA Inf. 1st Bn.Loc.Def. Co.C
Thomas, W.S. AL Cav. Barbiere's Bn. Co.G
Thomas, W.S. AL Cav. Barbiere's Bn. Bowie's Co.
Thomas, W.S. AL Lt.Arty. Goldthwaite's Btty.
Thomas, W.S. GA 11th Inf. Co.G
Thomas, W.S. GA 35th Inf. Adj.
Thomas, W.S. GA 40th Inf. Co.C
Thomas, W.S. KY 3rd Cav. Co.D
Thomas, W.S. SC 1st Arty. Co.A
Thomas, W.S. TX 20th Inf. Co.B
Thomas, W.S. VA 1st (Farinholt's) Res. Co.F
Thomas, W.S. VA 21st Inf. Co.I
Thomas, W. Scott GA 13th Cav. Co.K Capt.
Thomas, W.T. AL 17th Inf. Co.I
Thomas, W.T. AR 6th Inf. Co.H
Thomas, W.T. MS Inf. 2nd Bn. Co.B
Thomas, W.T. MS 48th Inf. Co.B
Thomas, W.T. SC 1st Arty. Co.D
Thomas, W.T. SC 3rd Inf. Co.D
Thomas, W.T. TN 12th Inf. Co.C
Thomas, W.T. TN 50th Inf. Co.I,B 1st Lt.
Thomas, W.T. TX 32nd Cav. Co.C
Thomas, W.T. Gen. & Staff Capt.,AQM
Thomas, W.W. AL 46th Inf. Co.D Sgt.
Thomas, W.W. KY 9th Cav. Co.D
Thomas, W.W. KY Lt.Arty. Cobb's Co.
Thomas, W.W. MS Inf. 1st Bn.St.Troops (12 mo. '62-3) Co.B
Thomas, W.W. TN 27th Inf. Co.A
Thomas, W.W. TN Inf. Nashville Bn. Cattles' Co.
Thomas, W.W. Inf. Bailey's Cons.Regt. Co.F
Thomas, W.W. VA 10th Cav. Co.G
Thomas, W.W. VA 15th Cav. Co.B
Thomas, W.W. VA Inf. 23rd Bn. Co.D
Thomas, W.W. VA 46th Inf. 2nd Co.E
Thomas, W.W. 2nd Conf.Eng.Troops Co.G Cpl.
Thomas, Wyatt AR 1st (Colquitt's) Inf. Adj.
Thomas, Wyatt C. Fagan's Brig. Lt.Col.,AAG
Thomas, Wych GA 3rd Cav. Co.E
Thomas, Wych GA Inf. 13th Bn. (St.Guards) Beall's Co.
Thomas, Xerxes KY 8th Mtd.Inf. Co.H
Thomas, Y.C. MO Robertson's Regt.St.Guard Co.1
Thomas, Y.G. AR 12th Inf. Co.G
Thomas, Young E. MO 1st Inf. Co.E
Thomas, Z. GA 38th Inf. Co.A
Thomas, Zachariah AR 25th Inf. Co.D
Thomas, Zachariah TN 45th Inf. Co.I
Thomas, Zachariah T. AL 63rd Inf. Co.D Sgt.
Thomas, Zechariah GA 3rd Cav. (St.Guards) Co.E Cpl.
Thomas, Zephania GA 3rd Inf. Co.G
Thomas, Zera SC 13th Inf. Co.E
Thomas, Zerah SC 7th Res. Co.C
Thomas, Z.G. LA 2nd Cav. Co.F
Thomas, Z.T. GA 63rd Inf. Co.D
Thomas, Z.T. TX Cav. Mann's Regt. Co.A
Thomasee, C.L. LA 3rd Inf. Co.K
Thomason, A. GA 17th Inf. Co.H Sgt.
Thomason, A. LA 27th Inf. Co.B
Thomason, Adam NC 16th Inf. Co.C
Thomason, A.F. KY 5th Cav. Co.B,A
Thomason, A.H. TN 84th Inf. Co.E
Thomason, A.J. TN Inf. 1st Cons.Regt. Co.G
Thomason, A.J. TN 84th Inf. Co.E
Thomason, A.J.M. TN Greer's Regt.Part. Rangers Co.A
Thomason, A.L. TN Cav. 16th Bn. (Neal's) Co.A
Thomason, Alexander R. GA Inf. 4th Bn. (St.Guards) Co.C
Thomason, Amos 1st Choctaw & Chickasaw Mtd.Rifles 2nd Co.I
Thomason, Andrew NC 42nd Inf. Co.I
Thomason, Andrew VA 56th Inf. Co.B
Thomason, Archy AL 5th Bn.Vol. Co.C
Thomason, Arnold SC Inf. Holcombe Legion Co.G
Thomason, A.T. TN 23rd Inf. 2nd Co.F Sgt.
Thomason, Austin SC Inf. Hampton Legion Co.F
Thomason, B.A. SC 6th Cav. Co.A
Thomason, Bartlet AR 45th Cav. Co.L
Thomason, B.B. KY Jessee's Bn.Mtd.Riflemen Co.C
Thomason, B.B. KY Part.Rangers Rowan's Co.
Thomason, B.B. VA 5th Cav. 1st Co.F
Thomason, Benjamin A. AL 50th Inf. Co.A
Thomason, Benjamin C. GA 42nd Inf. Co.B
Thomason, Bevely J. NC 37th Inf. Co.H
Thomason, B.F. GA 45th Inf. Co.K
Thomason, B.R. TN 44th (Cons.) Inf. Co.G 2nd Lt.
Thomason, B.W. TN 11th Inf. Co.C

Thomason, B. Wesley SC Inf. Hampton Legion Co.F
Thomason, C. KY Jessee's Bn.Mtd.Riflemen Co.C
Thomason, C.E. NC Allen's Co. (Loc.Def.)
Thomason, C.G. NC 54th Inf. Co.K
Thomason, C.G. TX 1st Inf. Co.C
Thomason, C.H. AL 58th Inf. Co.D,H
Thomason, C.H. AR 6th Inf. Co.H, 1st Co.B
Thomason, Charles GA 6th Cav. 1st Co.K
Thomason, Charles J. GA Arty. 9th Bn.
Thomason, Charles M. AL 12th Inf. Co.E 1st Lt.
Thomason, Churchwell SC Inf. Hampton Legion Co.F
Thomason, C.J. GA 40th Inf. Co.E Cpl.
Thomason, C.M. AL 9th (Malone's) Cav. Co.F
Thomason, C.M. Bradford's Corps Scouts & Guards Co.B 1st Sgt.
Thomason, Columbus H. MS 2nd Part.Rangers Co.F
Thomason, Daniel AR 11th & 17th Cons.Inf. Co.K
Thomason, Daniel AR 17th (Griffith's) Inf. Co.E
Thomason, Daniel B. TX 26th Cav. Co.D Sgt.
Thomason, Daniel J. AL 49th Inf. Co.F Cpl.
Thomason, Daniel R. MS 4th Cav. Co.F
Thomason, David SC Inf. Hampton Legion Co.F
Thomason, Davis 1st Choctaw & Chickasaw Mtd.Rifles 2nd Co.I
Thomason, D.C. MS 26th Inf. Co.A
Thomason, D.R. MS 4th Inf. Co.F
Thomason, D.S. GA 12th (Robinson's) Cav. (St.Guards) Co.H
Thomason, E. LA 27th Inf. Co.B
Thomason, Edgar P. KY 5th Cav. Co.A
Thomason, Edwin NC 64th Inf. Co.A
Thomason, Edwin D. AL 19th Inf. Asst.Surg.
Thomason, Elijah D. TN 14th Inf. Co.G
Thomason, Elisha G. TX 11th Inf. Co.D
Thomason, Elisha P. LA 31st Inf. Co.B
Thomason, Ellis 1st Choctaw & Chickasaw Mtd.Rifles 2nd Co.I
Thomason, E.M. AR 11th & 17th Cons.Inf. Co.K
Thomason, E.M. AR 17th (Griffith's) Inf. Co.E
Thomason, Enfield D. VA 36th Inf. 2nd Co.C Lt.
Thomason, Enfield D. VA 36th Inf. 2nd Co.C
Thomason, Enoch T. AR 25th Inf. Co.D Cpl.
Thomason, Ephraim H. MO 16th Inf. Co.H Sgt.
Thomason, E.W. Conf.Arty. Courtney's Bn. Surg.
Thomason, E.W. Lt.Arty. Dent's Btty.,CSA Asst.Surg.
Thomason, Festus NC 44th Inf. Co.K
Thomason, F.M. TX 24th Cav. Co.B
Thomason, F.M. TX 24th & 25th Cav. (Cons.) Co.G
Thomason, Francis M. AL 43rd Inf. Co.B Cpl.
Thomason, Francis M. GA 34th Inf. Co.I
Thomason, Francis M. TX 11th Inf. Co.I
Thomason, Francis Preston VA 5th Inf. Co.E
Thomason, Frank W. NC 6th Inf. Co.G
Thomason, G.B. AR 20th Inf. Co.C
Thomason, G.B. SC 1st St.Troops Co.G 1st Lt.
Thomason, G.C. Gen. & Staff AQM,Capt.
Thomason, George SC 1st St.Troops Co.G
Thomason, George A. TX 18th Inf. Co.A
Thomason, George C. MS 32nd Inf. Co.K Capt.
Thomason, George C. MS 46th Inf. Co.I
Thomason, George L. NC 37th Inf. Co.H Sgt.
Thomason, George S. GA 42nd Inf. Co.C
Thomason, George W. GA 34th Inf. Co.I
Thomason, George W. TN 53rd Inf. Co.E Cpl.
Thomason, George W. TN 59th Mtd.Inf. Co.H Cpl.
Thomason, George W. TX 17th Cav. Co.B
Thomason, George W. TX 18th Inf. Co.C
Thomason, George W. VA 3rd Arty. Co.E
Thomason, Gideon B. GA 42nd Inf. Co.C
Thomason, G.L. GA 18th Inf. Co.M
Thomason, G.L. GA 28th Inf. Co.F
Thomason, G.W. MS 37th Inf. Co.G Cpl.
Thomason, G.W. SC Inf. Hampton Legion Co.E
Thomason, G.W. TN 21st (Wilson's) Cav. Co.K
Thomason, G.W. TN 5th Inf. 2nd Co.F
Thomason, G.W. TN 33rd Inf. Co.C
Thomason, G.W. TN 51st (Cons.) Inf. Co.K 2nd Lt.
Thomason, G.W. VA Cav. 37th Bn. Co.H
Thomason, H. GA 17th Inf. Co.H
Thomason, H. LA Inf. 4th Bn. Co.C
Thomason, H.C. GA 1st Lt.Duty Men Co.A
Thomason, H.C. TX 4th Inf. Co.H
Thomason, H.D. AL 56th Part.Rangers Co.I
Thomason, Henry GA 55th Inf. Co.A
Thomason, Henry NC 1st Jr.Res. Co.B
Thomason, Henry NC 21st Inf. Co.D Cpl.
Thomason, Henry D. AR 27th Inf. Old Co.B
Thomason, H.J. TX 1st Inf. Co.B
Thomason, Hugh AL 13th Inf.
Thomason, Hughey NC 13th Inf. Co.H
Thomason, Hyram M. AR 27th Inf. Old Co.B Cpl.
Thomason, I.B. AL 50th Inf. Co.C
Thomason, Ira G. LA 8th Inf. Co.E
Thomason, Isaac I. TX 4th Cav. Co.F
Thomason, Isaac S. GA 64th Inf. Co.K
Thomason, J. AL 23rd Inf. Co.A
Thomason, J. GA 5th Inf. Co.A
Thomason, J. MS Cav. Ham's Regt. Co.D
Thomason, J. TX 21st Inf. Co.A
Thomason, J.A. AL 51st (Part.Rangers) Co.A
Thomason, Jack TN 48th (Voorhies') Inf. Co.B
Thomason, Jack C. GA 6th Inf. (St.Guards) Co.C Cpl.
Thomason, Jackson AL 49th Inf. Co.F
Thomason, James GA 13th Cav. Co.G
Thomason, James GA 40th Inf. Co.E
Thomason, James KY 2nd (Duke's) Cav. Co.E
Thomason, James TN 26th Inf. Co.I
Thomason, James TN 50th Inf. Co.A
Thomason, James TN 55th (Brown's) Inf. Co.D Music.
Thomason, James TX 20th Cav. Co.C
Thomason, James A. NC 64th Inf. Co.A
Thomason, James B. MS 2nd Inf. Co.H
Thomason, James B. TX 24th Cav. Co.B
Thomason, James B. TX 9th (Nichols') Inf. Co.I Cpl.
Thomason, James C. AR Cav. Wright's Regt. Co.C
Thomason, James D. TN 40th Inf. Co.G
Thomason, James G. NC 47th Inf. Co.G
Thomason, James G. SC 12th Inf. Co.A
Thomason, James H. TX 17th Cav. Co.A
Thomason, James H. TX 17th Cons.Dismtd.Cav. Co.A Cpl.
Thomason, James H. VA Inf. 5th Bn. Co.F
Thomason, James H. VA 53rd Inf. Co.F
Thomason, James I. AL 13th Inf. Co.I
Thomason, James M. MS 2nd Part.Rangers Co.D,F Cpl.
Thomason, James M. TX 18th Cav. Co.A
Thomason, James R. TN 48th (Voorhies') Inf. Co.B
Thomason, James S. AL 1st Inf. 3rd Lt.
Thomason, James S. NC 16th Inf. Co.C 2nd Lt.
Thomason, James W. NC 6th Inf. Co.G
Thomason, J.B. GA 35th Inf. Co.K
Thomason, J.B. MS Cav. Ham's Regt. Co.H
Thomason, J.B. SC Inf. Hampton Legion Co.F
Thomason, J.B.H. KY 5th Cav. Co.B
Thomason, J.C. AR 11th & 17th Cons.Inf. Co.K
Thomason, J.C. AR 17th (Griffith's) Inf. Co.E
Thomason, J.D. AR 2nd Mtd.Rifles Co.E
Thomason, J.D. AR 33rd Inf. Co.H
Thomason, J.D. LA 27th Inf. Co.B
Thomason, J.D. MS Cav. Ham's Regt. Co.H 1st Lt.
Thomason, Jesse M. AL 50th Inf. Co.A
Thomason, Jesse Pinkney NC 6th Inf. Co.G
Thomason, J.F. AL 57th Inf. Co.H
Thomason, J.F. GA 19th Inf. Co.B
Thomason, J.F. MS 2nd Cav. Co.C
Thomason, J.F. SC Inf. Hampton Legion Co.F
Thomason, J.F. TN Cav. 53rd Regt. Co.E
Thomason, J.G. TN 51st (Cons.) Inf. Co.K Capt.
Thomason, J.G. TN 52nd Inf. Co.E Capt.
Thomason, J.H. AL 40th Inf. QMR
Thomason, J.H. LA 27th Inf. Co.B
Thomason, J.H. TN 27th Inf. Co.A
Thomason, J.H.F. TX 37th Cav. Co.G
Thomason, J.J. AL St.Res. Co.A
Thomason, J.J. (1) LA 27th Inf. Co.B
Thomason, J.J. MS 37th Inf. Co.D
Thomason, J. Joshua LA 27th Inf. Co.B
Thomason, J.L. TN 12th (Green's) Cav. Co.C
Thomason, J.L.A. AR 27th Inf. Old Co.B, Co.E
Thomason, J.M. AL 9th Inf. Co.D Capt.
Thomason, J.M. GA 10th Cav. Co.K
Thomason, J.M. MS Cav. Yerger's Regt. Co.E
Thomason, J.M. NC 23rd Inf. Co.G
Thomason, J.M. TN 38th Inf. Co.C
Thomason, J.M. 7th Conf.Cav. Co.K
Thomason, J.M. Gen. & Staff Maj.,QM
Thomason, J.M. Gen. & Staff A.Surg.
Thomason, J.N. AL Cp. of Instr. Talladega
Thomason, Joel D. AR 13th Inf. Co.H Cpl.
Thomason, Joel S. KY 5th Cav. Co.A
Thomason, John GA 2nd Res. Co.C 2nd Lt.
Thomason, John GA 3rd Bn. (St.Guards) Co.G
Thomason, John GA Inf. 25th Bn. (Prov.Guard) Co.E
Thomason, John MO 16th Inf. Co.H
Thomason, John NC 49th Inf. Co.B
Thomason, John SC 11th Inf. Co.C
Thomason, John TN 14th Inf. Co.G

Thomason, John TX Cav. 2nd Regt.St.Troops Co.G
Thomason, John 1st Conf.Inf. 2nd Co.F
Thomason, John A. NC 37th Inf. Co.H
Thomason, John A. TX 11th (Spaight's) Bn.Vol. Co.A
Thomason, John B. VA 52nd Inf. Co.I
Thomason, John C. FL Cav. (Marianna Drag.) Smith's Co.
Thomason, John F. GA 22nd Inf. Co.C 1st Sgt.
Thomason, John F. TN 2nd (Smith's) Cav. Thomason's Co. Capt.
Thomason, John H. AL 41st Inf. Co.B
Thomason, John H. SC 2nd Cav. Co.E
Thomason, John H.F. VA Inf. 5th Bn. Co.F
Thomason, John I. TX 4th Cav. Co.F
Thomason, John J. LA 8th Inf. Co.F
Thomason, John L. GA 19th Inf. Co.H
Thomason, John L. NC 30th Inf. Co.K
Thomason, John M. GA Cherokee Legion (St.Guards) Co.B
Thomason, John M. SC 12th Inf. Co.A
Thomason, John P. GA 21st Inf. Co.A
Thomason, John Pliney NC 6th Inf. Co.G
Thomason, John R. AR 15th (N.W.) Inf. Co.C
Thomason, John S. TN 19th Inf. Co.D Cpl.
Thomason, John T. AR 2nd Mtd.Rifles Co.H
Thomason, John W. GA Arty. 9th Bn. Co.B
Thomason, John W. MS 10th Inf. New Co.C
Thomason, Joseph MS Cav. 2nd Bn.Res. Co.E
Thomason, Joseph 1st Choctaw & Chickasaw Mtd.Rifles 2nd Co.I
Thomason, Joseph A. VA 36th Inf. 2nd Co.C
Thomason, Joseph M. GA 42nd Inf. Co.C
Thomason, Joseph R. VA Hvy.Arty. Coleman's Co.
Thomason, Josephus AL 5th Bn.Vol. Co.C
Thomason, Joshua AL 41st Inf. Co.B
Thomason, Joshua W. LA 12th Inf. Co.L
Thomason, J.P. TN 31st Inf. Co.I 2nd Lt.
Thomason, J.P. TX 12th Cav. Co.K Cpl.
Thomason, J.R. AL Inf. 1st (Loomis') Bn. Co.A
Thomason, J.R. GA 11th Cav. Co.I
Thomason, J.R. KY 14th Cav. Co.C 2nd Lt.
Thomason, J.R. KY 1st Inf. Co.C
Thomason, J.R. SC 6th Cav. Co.A
Thomason, J.S. TN 44th (Cons.) Inf. Co.G Sgt.
Thomason, J.S. TX 21st Cav. 2nd Lt.
Thomason, J.S. TX 24th Cav. Co.B 1st Lt.
Thomason, J.T. GA 43rd Inf. Co.F
Thomason, J.W. LA 19th Inf. Co.C
Thomason, J.W. LA Inf. Pelican Regt. Co.D
Thomason, J.W. SC 9th Res. Co.C
Thomason, J.W. TX 10th Cav. Co.I
Thomason, J.W. VA 8th Cav. Co.H
Thomason, L. AL Cp. of Instr. Talladega
Thomason, Lamus 1st Chocatw & Chickasaw Mtd.Rifles 2nd Co.K
Thomason, L.C. MS 4th Inf. Co.D
Thomason, Leander AL 25th Inf. Co.D
Thomason, Lemuel L. NC Inf. Thomas Legion Co.F
Thomason, Logan NC 16th Inf. Co.C Cpl.
Thomason, Math M. AL 55th Vol. Co.F
Thomason, Math M. TN 42nd Inf. 1st Co.E
Thomason, M.F. AR 8th Cav. Co.C
Thomason, Micajah L. TN Cav. 3rd Bn. (Gantt's) Co.B
Thomason, M.M. AR 11th & 17th Cons.Inf. Co.K
Thomason, M.M. AR 17th (Griffith's) Inf. Co.E
Thomason, M.N. SC Arty. Fickling's Co. (Brooks Lt.Arty.)
Thomason, M.R. SC 6th Cav. Co.A
Thomason, N.N. AL 58th Inf. Co.D
Thomason, O. LA Inf.Cons. 18th Regt. & Yellow Jacket Bn. Co.C
Thomason, O. 7th Conf.Cav. Co.K
Thomason, Orval KY 12th Cav. Co.B
Thomason, Oscar GA 9th Inf. (St.Guards) Co.B
Thomason, P.A. Lt.Arty. Dent's Btty.,CSA
Thomason, Peter LA 15th Inf. Co.E
Thomason, Pleasant A. NC 58th Inf. Co.A,K
Thomason, Presley Y. NC 3rd Inf. Co.I
Thomason, R.F. GA Mil. 37th Regt. Co.B Capt.
Thomason, Richard TN 20th (Russell's) Cav. Co.B
Thomason, Richard TN 19th Inf. Co.D Sgt.
Thomason, Richard F. MS 17th Inf. Co.F
Thomason, R.J. TX Inf. 2nd St.Troops Co.C
Thomason, R.J. TX 11th Inf. Co.A
Thomason, Robert SC Inf. Hampton Legion Co.F 2nd Lt.
Thomason, Robert D. AR 2nd Mtd.Rifles Co.E
Thomason, Rufus NC 57th Inf. Co.K
Thomason, S. GA 2nd Inf. Co.C
Thomason, S. KY 12th Cav. Co.H
Thomason, Samuel E. GA 2nd Res. Co.F
Thomason, Samuel H. MS 26th Inf. Co.I
Thomason, Samuel H. VA 14th Inf. Co.C Cpl.
Thomason, S.B. AL Cav. 8th Regt. (Livingston's) Co.G
Thomason, S.B. GA Hvy.Arty. 22nd Bn. Co.E
Thomason, S.F. TN 55th (Brown's) Inf. Co.D Cpl.
Thomason, S.H. MS Cav. 3rd Bn.Res. Co.C Sgt.
Thomason, Simeon GA Inf. 2nd Bn. Co.C
Thomason, S.J. AL 5th Bn.Vol. Co.C
Thomason, Solomon D. GA Inf. (Franklin Cty. Guards) Kay's Co.
Thomason, S.W. GA 53rd Inf. Co.A
Thomason, T.A. AR 6th Inf. Co.E
Thomason, T.B. AL 5th Bn.Vol. Co.C
Thomason, T.C. TX 10th Cav. Co.I
Thomason, Thomas AL Cav. Lewis' Bn. Co.C Cpl.
Thomason, Thomas GA 2nd St.Line Co.E
Thomason, Thos. MO St.Guard
Thomason, Thomas TX 7th Cav. Co.C Sgt.
Thomason, Thomas E. AL 9th (Malone's) Cav. Co.C
Thomason, Thomas J. NC 16th Inf. Co.C
Thomason, Thomas M. GA 42nd Inf. Co.B Sgt.
Thomason, Thomas S. AR 4th Inf. Co.C
Thomason, T.I. MO 8th Cav. Co.H
Thomason, T.J. AL 14th Inf. Co.K
Thomason, T.J. AR 5th Inf. Co.H
Thomason, T.J. MO 7th Cav. Co.K
Thomason, T.M. NC 23rd Inf. Co.G
Thomason, T.R. AL 25th Inf. Co.A
Thomason, Turner P. NC 2nd Jr.Res. Co.B Jr.2nd Lt.
Thomason, Turner P. NC 49th Inf. Co.C
Thomason, T.W. AR 11th & 17th Cons.Inf. Co.K,H Capt.
Thomason, T.W. AR 17th (Griffith's) Inf. Co.E Capt.
Thomason, Uriah KY 2nd (Duke's) Cav. Co.E
Thomason, W.A. GA 11th Cav. Co.B
Thomason, W.A. MS Cav. Ham's Regt. Co.D
Thomason, W.A. TN 40th Inf. Co.G
Thomason, W.C. AR 2nd Cav. Co.G
Thomason, W.C. MS 5th Cav. Co.D
Thomason, W.C. SC 6th Inf. 2nd Co.C
Thomason, W.D. AL 4th (Roddey's) Cav. AQM
Thomason, W.D. Gen. & Staff Capt.,QM
Thomason, W.D. Gen. & Staff Maj.,QM
Thomason, Wesley J. VA 58th Inf. Co.D 2nd Lt.
Thomason, W.F. SC 3rd Inf. Co.G
Thomason, W.G. GA 37th Inf. Co.G
Thomason, W.G. NC Lt.Arty. 13th Bn. Co.B
Thomason, W.H. AR Cav. Gordon's Regt. Co.G
Thomason, W.H. NC Inf. Thomas Legion Co.F
Thomason, W.H. TX 27th Cav. Co.F
Thomason, William AL Cav. Lewis' Bn. Co.C Sgt.
Thomason, William AL 16th Inf. Co.E
Thomason, William AL 55th Vol. Co.F Cpl.
Thomason, William AL 1st Bn. Hilliard's Legion Vol. Co.B
Thomason, William AR 23rd Inf. Co.I
Thomason, William AR 34th Inf. Co.E Cpl.
Thomason, William GA Arty. 9th Bn. Co.B
Thomason, William GA Siege Arty. 28th Bn. Co.E
Thomason, William GA Inf. 14th Bn. (St.Guards) Co.B
Thomason, William MS 41st Inf. Co.F
Thomason, William TN 42nd Inf. 1st Co.E
Thomason, William VA Lt.Arty. Ellett's Co.
Thomason, William A. AR 23rd Inf. Co.H
Thomason, William A. NC 49th Inf. Co.C
Thomason, William D. AL Cp. of Instr. Talladega
Thomason, William G. GA 38th Inf. Co.F
Thomason, William G. NC 2nd Arty. (36th St.Troops) Co.B
Thomason, William G. NC 51st Inf. Co.I
Thomason, William J. NC 12th Inf. Co.D,B
Thomason, William J. NC 58th Inf. Co.E,K
Thomason, William L. GA 5th Inf. Co.H
Thomason, William O. VA 23rd Inf. Co.D
Thomason, William P. GA 42nd Inf. Co.B Cpl.
Thomason, William P. SC 14th Inf. Co.C Cpl.
Thomason, William R.E. VA Inf. 5th Bn. Co.F
Thomason, William R.E. VA 56th Inf. Co.B,K
Thomason, William S. KY 2nd (Duke's) Cav. Co.F
Thomason, William Va GA 22nd Inf. Co.C
Thomason, Wilson TN 46th Inf. Co.K Cpl.
Thomason, W.J. AL 25th Inf. Co.H
Thomason, W.K. MS 41st Inf. Co.L
Thomason, W.K. MO Inf. Perkins' Bn. Co.I
Thomason, W.L. GA Inf. 25th Bn. (Prov.Guard) Co.B
Thomason, W.L. TN Cav. 16th Bn. (Neal's) Co.A
Thomason, W.P. GA 11th Cav. Co.E

Thomason, W.P. LA 27th Inf. Co.B
Thomason, W.R. AR Cav. Davies' Bn. Co.D
Thomason, W.R. AR 1st Vol. Anderson's Co.
Thomason, W.R. AR 5th Inf. Co.D
Thomason, W.S. TX 9th (Nichols') Inf. Co.A
Thomason, W.S. TX Inf. Timmons' Regt. Co.E
Thomason, W.S. TX Waul's Legion Co.D
Thomason, W.T. AR 5th Inf. Co.D Cpl.
Thomason, W.T. NC 66th Inf. Co.G
Thomason, Z. AL 9th (Malone's) Cav. Lt.Col.
Thomason, Z. 3rd Conf.Cav. Co.C
Thomason, Zachariah GA 24th Inf. Co.G
Thomason, Zachariah TN 2nd (Smith's) Cav. Thomason's Co.
Thomason, Zacharus GA 13th Cav. Co.G
Thomason, Zack TX 15th Inf. Co.C, 1st Co.E
Thomason, Zemri V. GA 64th Inf. Co.K
Thomason, Zimri GA Inf. 25th Bn. (Prov.Guard) Co.E
Thomason, Z.M. TX 1st Hvy.Arty. 2nd Co.A
Thomassee, L. LA 27th Inf. Co.K
Thomassi, Clement LA 2nd Cav. Co.D
Thomassi, Oscar LA 2nd Cav. Co.D
Thomassie, Oge LA 1st Hvy.Arty. (Reg.) Co.D Music.
Thomassie, Oliver LA 1st Hvy.Arty. (Reg.) Co.D
Thomassin, Benjamin LA Mil. 1st Native Guards
Thomasson, A. AL 11th Cav. Co.F
Thomasson, A. GA Inf. 27th Bn. Co.D
Thomasson, A.B. AR 21st Mil. Co.G 1st Lt.
Thomasson, A.H. TN 28th (Cons.) Inf. Co.I Cpl.
Thomasson, A.J. GA Phillips' Legion Co.F
Thomasson, A.J. TN 13th Inf. Co.F Cpl.
Thomasson, A.J. TN 28th (Cons.) Inf. Co.I
Thomasson, B.F. AR Inf. Cocke's Regt. Co.C Cpl.
Thomasson, Calaway TN 35th Inf. Co.C
Thomasson, Charles J. VA 23rd Inf. Co.A
Thomasson, Charles R. NC 46th Inf. Co.E
Thomasson, C.S. AL 6th Inf. Co.E
Thomasson, David NC 42nd Inf. Co.I
Thomasson, D.G. SC 32rd Bn.Res. Co.C
Thomasson, D.J. SC 6th Res. Co.G
Thomasson, D.W. SC 17th Inf. Co.E Sgt.
Thomasson, Edgar F. VA 13th Inf. Co.D
Thomasson, Edwin W. Gen. & Staff Surg.
Thomasson, Ely LA Miles' Legion Co.D
Thomasson, E.S. KY 2nd Mtd.Inf. Co.F
Thomasson, E.W. KY 2nd Mtd.Inf. Co.B
Thomasson, F.B. SC Lt.Arty. J.T. Kanapaux's Co. (Lafayette Arty.)
Thomasson, George Exch.Bn. Co.E,CSA Cpl.
Thomasson, George A. NC 42nd Inf. Co.I Sgt.
Thomasson, George W. GA 40th Inf. Co.E Cpl.
Thomasson, G.H. KY 2nd Mtd.Inf. Co.A
Thomasson, Green KY 11th Cav.
Thomasson, Green TN 21st (Wilson's) Cav. Co.K
Thomasson, G.W. TN 52nd Inf. Co.G 1st Lt.
Thomasson, H. AL 11th Cav. Co.F
Thomasson, H.D. KY 7th Mtd.Inf. Co.C
Thomasson, Henry T. NC 46th Inf. Co.E
Thomasson, H.R. TX 26th Cav. Co.F
Thomasson, J. 1st Conf.Cav. 1st Co.B
Thomasson, J.A. 7th Conf.Cav. Co.K
Thomasson, James GA Inf. 2nd Bn. (St.Guards) Co.A
Thomasson, James MS 3rd Inf. Co.I
Thomasson, James C.T. GA 15th Inf. Co.B
Thomasson, James E. TX Cav. Border's Regt. Co.E
Thomasson, James E. VA 58th Inf. Co.I
Thomasson, James G. SC 17th Inf. Co.E
Thomasson, James H. VA 24th Inf. Co.D
Thomasson, James M. TN Cav. 16th Bn. (Neal's) Co.A
Thomasson, James M. TN 59th Mtd.Inf. Co.A Asst.Surg.
Thomasson, James M. VA 60th Inf. Co.G
Thomasson, James O. VA Hvy.Arty. 10th Bn. Co.B
Thomasson, James O. VA Lt.Arty. J.D. Smith's Co.
Thomasson, James R. VA 24th Inf. Co.H
Thomasson, J.B. NC 11th (Bethel Regt.) Inf. Co.A
Thomasson, J.B. SC 1st Cav. Co.H
Thomasson, J.B. SC 12th Inf. Co.H
Thomasson, J.D. MS 7th Cav. Co.B
Thomasson, Jefferson C. GA 6th Inf. (St.Guards) Pittman's Co. Sgt.
Thomasson, Jesse NC 42nd Inf. Co.I
Thomasson, J.F. SC 18th Inf. Co.H
Thomasson, J.F. VA 24th Cav. Co.H
Thomasson, J.F. VA Cav. 32nd Bn. Co.B
Thomasson, J.J. MS 35th Inf. Co.D
Thomasson, J.M. AL 18th Inf. Capt.
Thomasson, J.M. SC 18th Inf. Co.G
Thomasson, John LA Miles' Legion Co.D
Thomasson, John C. TX 19th Cav. Co.B
Thomasson, John F. GA 15th Inf. Co.B
Thomasson, John F. VA 24th Inf. Co.H
Thomasson, John H. VA 15th Cav. Co.B Sgt.
Thomasson, John N. VA Hvy.Arty. 10th Bn. Co.B
Thomasson, John P. VA 60th Inf. Co.G 2nd Lt.
Thomasson, John S. VA 24th Inf. Co.H
Thomasson, Joseph G. VA 58th Inf. Co.I
Thomasson, Joseph Q. VA 13th Inf. Co.D
Thomasson, J.S. AL 6th Inf. Co.E
Thomasson, Judge L. MS 3rd Inf. Co.I
Thomasson, J.V. AR 13th Inf. Co.C
Thomasson, L.B. TN 1st Arty.
Thomasson, Lee Roy TN 26th Inf. Co.I
Thomasson, Lewis B. MS 4th Inf. Sgt.
Thomasson, M. LA 13th Bn. (Part.Rangers) Co.B
Thomasson, M. VA 24th Cav. Co.H
Thomasson, M. VA Cav. 32nd Bn. Co.B
Thomasson, Mark N. SC 2nd Inf. Co.K
Thomasson, Matthew D. GA 15th Inf. Co.F
Thomasson, M.D. AL 8th Inf. Co.C
Thomasson, Mitchell TN 21st (Wilson's) Cav. Co.K
Thomasson, M.N. SC 24th Inf. Co.A
Thomasson, Monroe L. SC 5th Inf. 1st Co.H, 2nd Co.F Cpl.
Thomasson, Newton B. TX 19th Cav. Co.B
Thomasson, Richard D. NC 42nd Inf. Co.I Cpl.
Thomasson, Robert A. VA 13th Inf. Co.D
Thomasson, Robert W. VA 24th Inf. Co.H
Thomasson, S. GA Lt.Arty. Van Den Corput's Co.
Thomasson, Samuel LA Arty. Moody's Co. (Madison Lt.Arty.)
Thomasson, Samuel NC 46th Inf. Co.E
Thomasson, S.B. AR 9th Inf. Co.B Capt.
Thomasson, S.H. VA Goochland Lt.Arty.
Thomasson, S.P. MS Inf. 1st Bn. Co.A
Thomasson, St.Clair B. LA 16th Inf. Co.K
Thomasson, Stephen G. VA 24th Inf. Co.H
Thomasson, T. MO Cav. Woodson's Co.
Thomasson, T.C. SC 18th Inf. Co.H
Thomasson, T.F. AL Montgomery Guards
Thomasson, Thomas MO 6th Inf. Co.D
Thomasson, Thomas Exch.Bn. Co.E,CSA
Thomasson, Thomas B. MS 17th Inf. Co.E
Thomasson, Thomas E. AL 16th Inf. Co.A
Thomasson, Thomas J. MS 17th Inf. Co.E
Thomasson, T.N. SC Lt.Arty. J.T. Kanapaux's Co. (Lafayette Arty.)
Thomasson, T.R. MO 10th Inf. Co.I
Thomasson, U.S. KY Morgan's Men Co.I
Thomasson, Virgil H. GA 49th Inf. Co.C
Thomasson, W.C. AR 1st (Monroe's) Cav. Co.B
Thomasson, W.H. VA 24th Cav. Co.H Sgt.
Thomasson, W.H. VA Cav. 32nd Bn. Co.B Sgt.
Thomasson, William AL 11th Cav. Co.F
Thomasson, William LA 5th Inf. Co.H
Thomasson, William LA 16th Inf. Co.K
Thomasson, William LA Miles' Legion Co.D
Thomasson, William MO St.Guard
Thomasson, William NC 46th Inf. Co.E
Thomasson, William SC 1st Cav. Co.H
Thomasson, William SC 18th Inf. Co.G
Thomasson, William VA Hvy.Arty. 10th Bn. Co.B
Thomasson, William A. NC 43rd Inf. Co.D
Thomasson, William B. GA 41st Inf. Co.I Capt.
Thomasson, William C. MS 1st Lt.Arty. Co.C
Thomasson, William F. GA 10th Cav. (St.Guards) Co.G
Thomasson, William H. VA 58th Inf. Co.I 1st Sgt.
Thomasson, William J. AL 35th Inf.
Thomasson, William L. TN 26th Inf. Co.I
Thomasson, William P. VA 36th Inf. 2nd Co.E Cpl.
Thomasson, William S. KY 4th Mtd.Inf. Co.E
Thomasson, Wilson O. VA 24th Inf. Co.H
Thomasson, W.J. AL 11th Cav. Co.F,K
Thomasson, W.J. SC 17th Inf. Co.E
Thomasson, W.L. 1st Conf.Cav. 1st Co.B, 2nd Co.A
Thomasson, W.M. TN 9th Inf. Co.G
Thomasson, Zimarah 1st Cherokee Mtd.Vol. 2nd Co.A
Thomassy, Oliver LA 3rd Inf. Co.D
Thomassy, Onora LA 18th Inf. Co.C
Thomaston, F.M. AL 3rd Res. Co.C
Thomaston, Garrison GA 40th Inf. Co.G
Thomaston, Henry C. GA 11th Inf. Co.H
Thomaston, James M. GA 21st Inf. Co.I Cpl.
Thomaston, John C. 15th Conf.Cav. Co.B
Thomaston, John S. GA 20th Inf. Co.G Sgt.
Thomaston, John W. GA 31st Inf. Co.G Cpl.
Thomaston, J.W. GA Lt.Arty. Ferrell's Btty.
Thomaston, Matthew D. GA 15th Inf. Co.F

Thomaston, M.R. AL Cp. of Instr. Talladega
Thomaston, N.W.R. GA Cav. 12th Bn. (St.Guards) Co.D
Thomaston, R.A. GA 5th Res. Co.B
Thomaston, William C. GA 20th Inf. Co.G Cpl.
Thomaston, William T. GA 35th Inf. Co.K
Thomaston, W.M. MS 4th Inf. Co.G
Thomaston, W.R. AL 25th Inf. Co.F
Thomaston, Z.W. TN 35th Inf. Co.L
Thomatisse, Alexander LA Mil. 1st Native Guards
Thomatisse, Leonce LA Mil. 1st Native Guards
Thombley, Edward H. FL 2nd Inf. Co.I
Thombley, John GA Siege Arty. 28th Bn. Co.C
Thomblinson, David VA 19th Cav. Co.H Cpl.
Thombs, George MS 29th Inf. Co.H
Thombs, George W. MS 7th Inf. Co.H
Thombs, G.W. MS 9th Bn.S.S. Co.C
Thombs, John T. VA 41st Inf. Co.B
Thombs, Levi VA 41st Inf. Co.B
Thombs, Lewis Conf.Cav. Powers' Regt. Co.G
Thombs, Louis TX 5th Cav. Co.C
Thombson, Collumbus AL 9th (Malone's) Cav. Co.M
Thomburg, Daniel TN 62nd Mtd.Inf. Co.H
Thombuson, J. NC 49th Inf. Co.B
Thome, Christian VA Inf. 4th Bn.Loc.Def. Co.B
Thomel, J.H.H. AL 46th Inf. Co.B
Thomerson, Benjamin F. GA 35th Inf. Co.G
Thomerson, Benjamin H. NC 3rd Arty. (40th St.Troops) Co.B
Thomerson, Gasper S. VA 34th Inf. Co.D
Thomerson, Guideon A. GA 35th Inf. Co.G
Thomerson, J.H. SC Cav. 4th Bn. Co.C
Thomerson, John P. VA 34th Inf. Co.D
Thomerson, J.W. TN 21st (Wilson's) Cav. Co.B
Thomerson, Louis NC 31st Inf. Co.I
Thomerson, Thomas TN 3rd (Forrest's) Cav. Co.C
Thomes, C.E. Gen. & Staff Maj.,QM
Thomes, John MO Cav. Ford's Bn. Co.F
Thomes, Sam 1st Choctaw & Chickasaw Mtd.Rifles 3rd Co.K
Thomeson, J.S. GA 40th Inf. Co.F
Thomeson, Nathaniel AR 7th Cav. Co.L
Thomeson, T.R. AL Inf. 1st (Loomis') Bn. Co.A
Thomeson, William AR 7th Cav. Co.L
Thomesson, J.K.P. TN 21st (Wilson's) Cav. Co.K
Thomilson, C. LA Mil. 1st Regt. 2nd Brig. 1st Div.
Thomilson, J.L. AL Inf. 1st Regt. Co.B
Thominson, J.M. AL 9th Inf. Co.I
Thomis, John W. MO 3rd Cav. Co.H Sgt.
Thomison, Alexander H. MO 4th Cav. Co.A
Thomison, A.M. TX Cav. Hardeman's Regt. Co.D Music.
Thomison, Augustus GA 59th Inf. Co.D
Thomison, Franklin SC 18th Inf. Co.H
Thomison, G.B. SC 3rd Res. Co.C 2nd Lt.
Thomison, G.C. Gen. & Staff AQM
Thomison, George SC 3rd Res. Co.C
Thomison, George R. AL 49th Inf. Co.F Cpl.
Thomison, Henry TN Inf. 22nd Bn. Co.E
Thomison, James M. TN 16th Inf. Co.I
Thomison, J.D. AR Inf. Cocke's Regt. Co.E Cpl.
Thomison, John B. TN 8th Inf. Co.K
Thomison, John F. MO 16th Inf. Co.B
Thomison, John S. TN Cav. 16th Bn. (Neal's) Co.C
Thomison, John W. MO 7th Cav. Haislip's Co.
Thomison, J.T. AL 41st Inf. Co.C
Thomison, J.W. AR 24th Inf. Co.A
Thomison, J.W. TN 33rd Inf. Co.E
Thomison, Marcus MO 7th Cav. Haislip's Co.
Thomison, Marion TN Inf. 22nd Bn. Co.E
Thomison, Tennessee TN 1st (Feild's) Inf. Co.H
Thomison, W.B. AR Inf. Cocke's Regt. Co.E 1st Sgt.
Thomison, W.B. MO 7th Cav. Co.K
Thomison, William MS Moseley's Regt.
Thomison, William P. TN Cav. 16th Bn. (Neal's) Co.C 2nd Lt.
Thomison, W.P., Jr. TN Cav. 16th Bn. (Neal's) Co.C
Thomison, W.R. AR Inf. Cocke's Regt. Co.E
Thomison, W.S. KY 12th Cav. Co.I Sgt.
Thomkins, D.C. MS 10th Inf. New Co.G
Thomkins, Gus A. TN 14th Inf. Co.A
Thomkins, Pheocian L. VA 50th Inf. Co.D
Thomkins, S.O. MS 12th Cav. Co.A,K
Thomley, Benjamin AL 33rd Inf. Co.B
Thomley, Robert AL 32nd Inf. Co.C
Thomley, William AL 3rd Bn.Res. Co.A
Thomlin, Sherrod AL 50th Inf. Co.A
Thomlinson, F.F. SC 8th Inf. Co.F
Thomlinson, F.M. AR 18th Inf. Co.G Cpl.
Thomlinson, Frederick F. SC 1st (McCreary's) Inf. Co.L
Thomlinson, Gary T. AR 18th Inf. Co.G Sgt.
Thomlinson, J.N. AR 45th Cav. Co.A
Thomlinson, Joseph AR 1st (Dobbin's) Cav. Co.B
Thomlinson, Joseph SC Cav. 19th Bn. Co.E
Thomlinson, Joseph R. SC 23rd Inf. Co.A 1st Lt.
Thomlinson, J.R. MS 24th Inf. Co.B
Thomlinson, L. SC Cav. 19th Bn. Co.E
Thomlinson, L. SC 10th Inf. 1st Co.G
Thomlinson, L.L. TX 30th Cav. Co.D Cpl.
Thomlinson, M.H. SC Mil. 16th Regt. Sigwald's Co.
Thomlinson, Moses AR 21st Inf. Co.D
Thomlinson, R. SC 1st Mtd.Mil. Heyward's Co.
Thomlinson, R. SC 3rd Cav. Co.H
Thomlinson, R.J. SC 6th Cav. Co.D Cpl.
Thomlinson, R.J. SC 23rd Inf. Co.A
Thomlinson, Robert SC Cav. 19th Bn. Co.E
Thomlinson, Robert J. SC Inf. Hampton Legion Co.A
Thomlinson, W.A. TN 9th Inf. Co.G
Thomlinson, W.E. LA 25th Inf. Co.D
Thomlinson, W.G. AR 18th Inf. Co.G Sgt.
Thomlinson, W.H. AR 45th Cav. Co.A
Thomlinson, William VA Tuttle's Bn.Loc.Def. Co.A
Thomlinson, William H. NC Inf. 13th Bn. Co.D
Thomlinson, W.T. AR 18th Inf. Co.G
Thommas, B.B. AR 32nd Inf. Co.F Cpl.
Thommas, Flemen VA 54th Inf. Co.A
Thommas, Howell V. TN 14th (Neely's) Cav. Co.I
Thommas, H.V. TN 15th (Stewart's) Cav. Co.F
Thommas, John TN 15th (Stewart's) Cav. Co.C
Thommas, Marshall TN 15th (Stewart's) Cav. Co.C,B Bvt.2nd Lt.
Thommas, R. AR Cav. McGehee's Regt. Co.G
Thommas, R.G. TN 15th (Stewart's) Cav. Co.C
Thommasson, W.L. AR 26th Inf. Co.A Cpl.
Thomme, Anthony H. GA 13th Inf. Co.B
Thommosson, Z.W. KY Arty. McEnnis' Detach.
Thomoson, George W. AL 47th Inf. Co.C Sgt.
Thompkin, L.T. LA Inf. 4th Bn. Co.B
Thompkin, T. MO St.Guard Capt.,Div.Dr.M.
Thompkins, B.F. LA Inf. 4th Bn. Co.B
Thompkins, C.C. VA 14th Cav. Co.B,I
Thompkins, Charles GA 28th Inf. Co.B
Thompkins, Don FL Conscr.
Thompkins, F. GA 32nd Inf. Co.E
Thompkins, Gabriel SC Arty. Manigault's Bn. 1st Co.B
Thompkins, Giles FL 10th Inf. Co.H
Thompkins, G.W. TX 12th Inf. Co.E Cpl.
Thompkins, H. MS Yerger's Co. (St.Troops)
Thompkins, H.C. VA 4th Cav.
Thompkins, Henry SC 1st (Butler's) Inf. Co.I
Thompkins, H.H. AL 18th Inf. Co.B
Thompkins, H.H. MS Cav. 3rd Bn.Res. Co.D
Thompkins, H.H. MS 1st (King's) Inf. (St.Troops) Co.A
Thompkins, Isaac S. TX 9th Cav. Co.A
Thompkins, I.W. Gen. & Staff AASurg.
Thompkins, James AL 42nd Inf. Co.E
Thompkins, James VA Cav. 1st Bn. (Loc.Def. Troops) Co.C
Thompkins, James J. MO Inf. Perkins' Bn. Co.B
Thompkins, James M. AL 66th Inf. Co.G
Thompkins, James S. GA 57th Inf. Co.G Cpl.
Thompkins, J.J. MO 11th Inf. Co.A
Thompkins, J.L. AL 8th Inf.
Thompkins, John C. MO Inf. Perkins' Bn. Co.B
Thompkins, J.P. AR 17th (Griffith's) Inf. Co.H
Thompkins, J.W. AL 1st Cav. 2nd Co.B
Thompkins, Robert L. VA 50th Inf. Co.D
Thompkins, R.T. TN 45th Inf. Co.C 1st Lt.
Thompkins, Samuel H. VA 60th Inf. Co.G Capt.
Thompkins, S.A.R. GA 28th Inf. Co.I
Thompkins, Solomon GA 57th Inf. Co.G Cpl.
Thompkins, S.R. AL 18th Inf. Co.B
Thompkins, Stephen TN 60th Mtd.Inf. Co.K
Thompkins, Theodocious MO 6th Inf. Co.K
Thompkins, Thomas B. LA 13th Bn. (Part. Rangers) Co.F 1st Lt.
Thompkins, W.F. GA 1st Mil. Co.K Sgt.
Thompkins, W.R. TN 45th Inf. Co.C
Thompkins, W.R. Gen. & Staff Hosp.Stew.
Thompkins, W.T. VA 15th Cav. Co.B
Thomplain, W.B. GA 13th Inf. Co.E
Thomplenson, J.A. TN 33rd Inf. Co.I Sgt.
Thompon, J.F. MS 24th Inf. Co.K
Thompon, J.F. 1st Conf.Cav. 1st Co.D
Thompon, J.L. 1st Conf.Cav. 1st Co.D
Thompon, J.R. AL Cav. 5th Bn. Hilliard's Legion Co.E
Thompon, J.W. AR Cav. Davies' Bn. Co.D
Thomps, A. GA 18th Inf. Co.G
Thomps, R.R. NC 53rd Inf. Co.C
Thompsen, J.H. AL 8th Inf. Co.H
Thompsen, W.H. AL Mtd.Inf. J. Oden's Co.
Thompson 1st Cherokee Mtd.Vol. Co.J

Thompson 1st Choctaw & Chickasaw Mtd.Rifles 3rd Co.F
Thompson 1st Choctaw & Chickasaw Mtd.Rifles 2nd Co.H
Thompson 1st Choctaw & Chickasaw Mtd.Rifles 3rd Co.H
Thompson 1st Choctaw & Chickasaw Mtd.Rifles 2nd Co.I
Thompson 1st Creek Mtd.Vol. Co.A
Thompson Deneale's Regt. Choctaw Warriors Co.A
Thompson, --- AL 22nd Inf. Co.A Sgt.
Thompson, --- AL 22nd Inf. Co.C
Thompson, --- AL 25th Inf. Co.A Sgt.
Thompson, --- AL 60th Inf. Lt.
Thompson, --- AR 8th Cav. Co.E
Thompson, --- KY Lt.Arty. Cobb's Co.
Thompson, --- LA Lewis Regt. Co.E
Thompson, --- MO Quantrill's Co.
Thompson, ---, 2nd SC Inf. 1st (Charleston) Bn. Co.A
Thompson, --- TX 24th Cav. Co.G
Thompson, --- TX 24th & 25th Cav. (Cons.) Co.E
Thompson, --- TX 35th (Likens') Cav. Co.F
Thompson, --- TX Cav. Border's Regt. Co.B
Thompson, --- TX Cav. Border's Regt. Co.K
Thompson, --- TX Cav. Good's Bn. Co.A
Thompson, --- TX Cav. Good's Bn. Co.E
Thompson, --- TX Cav. Mann's Regt. Co.C
Thompson, --- TX Cav. Morgan's Regt. Co.K
Thompson, --- VA 13th Cav. Co.E
Thompson, --- VA Arty. B.H. Smith's Co.
Thompson, --- VA Arty.Detach. VMI
Thompson, --- VA VMI Co.C
Thompson, --- Mtd.Spies & Guides Madison's Co.
Thompson, A. AL 7th Cav. Co.D,E
Thompson, A. AL 26th (O'Neal's) Inf. Co.B 1st Lt.
Thompson, A. AL 31st Inf. Co.E
Thompson, A. AL St.Res.
Thompson, A. AR 7th Cav. Co.M
Thompson, A. AR 18th Inf.
Thompson, A. GA 7th Cav. Co.B
Thompson, A. GA Inf. 5th Bn. (St.Guards) Co.E
Thompson, A. GA 9th Inf. (St.Guards) Co.D Sgt.
Thompson, A. GA 16th Inf. Co.B
Thompson, A. GA 20th Inf. Co.E
Thompson, A. GA Inf. (E. to W. Point Guards) Matthews' Co.
Thompson, A. LA 6th Cav. Co.I
Thompson, A. LA 18th Inf. Co.I
Thompson, A. LA Inf.Crescent Regt. Co.C Bvt.2nd Lt.
Thompson, A. LA Mil. Leeds' Guards Regt. Co.A Capt.
Thompson, A. LA Mil. Mooney's Co. (Saddlers Guards) 1st Lt.
Thompson, A. MS Cav. Ham's Regt. Co.H
Thompson, A. MS Inf. 3rd Bn. Co.I 1st Sgt.
Thompson, A. MS 5th Inf. Co.A
Thompson, A. MO 6th Cav. Co.C
Thompson, A. NC 30th Inf. Co.C
Thompson, A. TN 19th (Biffle's) Cav. Co.I
Thompson, A. TN 19th (Biffle's) Cav. Co.L 1st Sgt.
Thompson, A. SC 25th Inf. Co.H
Thompson, A. TN 38th Inf. Co.E
Thompson, A. TX 32nd Cav. Co.I
Thompson, A. TX 1st Inf. Co.M
Thompson, A. VA Cav. 39th Bn. Co.C
Thompson, A. VA Arty. Wise Legion
Thompson, A. Nitre & Min. Bureau War Dept.,CSA
Thompson, A.A. AL 53rd (Part.Rangers) Co.D 1st Lt.
Thompson, A.A. AL 23rd Inf. Co.B
Thompson, A.A. AL 40th Inf. Co.K,A
Thompson, A.A. AL 45th Inf. Co.G
Thompson, A.A. GA 43rd Inf. Co.K 1st Lt.
Thompson, A.A. LA Res.Corps Hatcher's Co.
Thompson, A.A. MS 28th Cav. Co.C
Thompson, A.A. TX Cav. 1st Regt.St.Troops Co.G Capt.
Thompson, A.A. TX 13th Vol. Co.G Capt.
Thompson, A.A. TX 14th Inf. Co.D Sgt.
Thompson, Aaron GA 4th Res. Co.D
Thompson, Aaron GA 65th Inf. Co.C,G
Thompson, Aaron NC McLean's Bn.Lt.Duty Men Co.A Sgt.
Thompson, Aaron TN 4th (McLemore's) Cav. Co.A Capt.
Thompson, Aaron C. TX 18th Cav. Co.C
Thompson, Aaron P. GA 5th Inf. Co.F
Thompson, A.B. AL 15th Bn.Part.Rangers Co.D
Thompson, A.B. AL 40th Inf. Co.D
Thompson, A.B. AR 8th Inf. Old Co.F
Thompson, A.B. AR 27th Inf. Co.E
Thompson, A.B. AR 36th Inf. Co.B Capt.
Thompson, A.B. TX 20th Inf. Co.B 1st Lt.
Thompson, Abel GA 47th Inf. Co.H
Thompson, Abner AL 29th Inf. Co.F,I Sgt.
Thompson, Abraham AL 12th Inf. Co.I
Thompson, Abraham VA Inf. 1st Bn. Co.C
Thompson, Abraham VA 2nd Inf. Co.D
Thompson, Abram LA 28th (Gray's) Inf. Co.G
Thompson, Abram MS 10th Cav. Co.A
Thompson, Abram J. TX 5th Field Btty.
Thompson, Absalom AL 10th Inf. Co.B
Thompson, Absalom TN Cav. 16th Bn. (Neal's) Co.E
Thompson, Absalom C.C. GA 3rd Inf. Co.I Asst.Surg.
Thompson, A.C. AL 22nd Inf. Co.H
Thompson, A.C. AL 39th Inf. Co.C
Thompson, A.C. AR 18th Inf. Co.A 3rd Lt.
Thompson, A.C. GA Cav. 8th Bn. (St.Guards) Co.A
Thompson, A.C. GA 16th Inf. Co.G Capt.
Thompson, A.C. TN 3rd (Clack's) Inf. Co.B
Thompson, A.C. TN 37th Inf. Co.D
Thompson, Aca C. VA Horse Arty. Jackson's Co.
Thompson, A.C.C. Gen. & Staff Asst.Surg.
Thompson, A.D. TN 19th (Biffle's) Cav. Co.F
Thompson, A.D. TN 45th Inf. Co.D
Thompson, A.D. 8th (Wade's) Conf.Cav. Co.H
Thompson, Adam AL 45th Inf. Co.D
Thompson, Adam TN 45th Inf. Co.D
Thompson, Adam VA 7th Inf. Co.D
Thompson, Adam F. VA 2nd Inf. Co.C
Thompson, Adam T. VA 37th Inf. Co.K Sgt.
Thompson, Addin VA Cav. Hounshell's Bn.
Thompson, Adolphus NC 16th Inf. Co.K Cpl.
Thompson, Adrian TN Inf. 23rd Bn. Co.D
Thompson, A.E. AR Cav. Gordon's Regt. Co.G
Thompson, A.E. TX 9th Field Btty.
Thompson, A.F. KY 2nd Cav. Co.C
Thompson, A.F. TN Cav. 9th Bn. (Gantt's) Co.B
Thompson, A.F. TN Inf. 1st Cons.Regt. Co.F
Thompson, A.F. TN 3rd (Clack's) Inf. Co.E Sgt.
Thompson, A.F. Conf.Inf. 1st Bn. 2nd Co.E
Thompson, A.G. AL 18th Inf. Co.B Sgt.
Thompson, A.G. GA 19th Inf. Co.E
Thompson, A.G. NC 62nd Inf. Co.F
Thompson, A.G. TN Inf. 154th Sr.Regt. Co.G
Thompson, A.G. VA 2nd Cav. Co.G
Thompson, A.G. VA 62nd Mtd.Inf. Co.I
Thompson, A.G. VA Mil. Stowers' Co.
Thompson, A.G.H. SC 3rd Inf. Co.G Cpl.
Thompson, A.G.R. AR 62nd Mil. Co.C
Thompson, A.H. AR Cav. McGehee's Regt. Co.F Sgt.
Thompson, A.H. AR 32nd Inf. Co.B Sgt.
Thompson, A.H. GA 10th Cav. (St.Guards) Co.E
Thompson, A.H. GA 44th Inf. Co.C
Thompson, A.H. NC 38th Inf. Co.H
Thompson, A.H. SC 4th St.Troops Co.D
Thompson, A.H. SC 5th Bn.Res. Co.F
Thompson, A.H. TN Cav. 9th Bn. (Gantt's) Co.B
Thompson, A.H. TN 15th (Cons.) Cav. Co.C
Thompson, A.H. TN 15th (Stewart's) Cav. Co.A
Thompson, A.H. TN 3rd (Clack's) Inf. Co.E
Thompson, A.H. TN 6th Inf. Co.E
Thompson, A.H. TN 47th Inf. Co.C
Thompson, Ahab N. AR 36th Inf. Co.A
Thompson, A. Hayter KY 4th Mtd.Inf. Co.F Cpl.
Thompson, A.J. AL 10th Inf.
Thompson, A.J. AL 29th Inf. Co.A
Thompson, A.J. AR 1st (Dobbin's) Cav. Co.C
Thompson, A.J. AR 1st (Dobbin's) Cav. Co.K 2nd Lt.
Thompson, A.J. AR 21st Mil. Co.E
Thompson, A.J. AR 33rd Inf.
Thompson, A.J. AR 36th Inf. Co.B
Thompson, A.J. AR 37th Inf. Co.E Hosp.Stew.
Thompson, A.J. GA 4th (Clinch's) Cav. Co.E
Thompson, A.J. GA Cav. Russell's Co.
Thompson, A.J. GA Lt.Arty. 12th Bn. 3rd Co.C
Thompson, A.J. GA 2nd Inf. Co.A
Thompson, A.J. GA 47th Inf. Co.C
Thompson, A.J. GA Inf. (GA RR Guards) Porter's Co.
Thompson, A.J. KY 2nd (Duke's) Cav. Co.K
Thompson, A.J. KY 1st Inf. Co.C
Thompson, A.J. KY 9th Mtd.Inf. Co.I
Thompson, A.J. LA 3rd (Wingfield's) Cav. Co.E
Thompson, A.J. LA 2nd Res.Corps Co.A
Thompson, A.J. LA 4th Inf. Old Co.G, Co.A
Thompson, A.J. MS Inf. 7th Bn. Co.G Capt.
Thompson, A.J. TN 1st (Carter's) Cav. Co.C Capt.
Thompson, A.J. TN Cav. 9th Bn. (Gantt's) Co.B
Thompson, A.J. TN 1st (Feild's) Inf. Co.K

Thompson, A.J. TN 12th (Cons.) Inf. Co.G
Thompson, A.J. TN 22nd Inf. Co.E Cpl.
Thompson, A.J. TN 38th Inf. Co.F
Thompson, A.J. TN 48th (Voorhies') Inf. Co.G Cpl.
Thompson, A.J. TX 26th Cav. Co.I
Thompson, A.J. TX 27th Cav. Co.F
Thompson, A.J. TX 31st Cav. Co.G
Thompson, A.J. TX 13th Vol. 2nd Co.H, Co.E
Thompson, A.J. VA 16th Cav. Co.I,C
Thompson, A.J. VA Cav. Caldwell's Bn. Graham's Co.
Thompson, A.J. VA Inf. 26th Bn. Co.F
Thompson, A.J. VA 57th Inf. Co.K
Thompson, A.J. Gen. & Staff A.Surg.
Thompson, A.L. GA 48th Inf. Co.H
Thompson, A.L. LA 27th Inf. Co.F
Thompson, A.L. NC 1st Arty. (10th St.Troops) Co.A
Thompson, A.L. NC 21st Inf.
Thompson, A.L. TN 12th Inf. Co.C
Thompson, A.L. TN 26th Inf.
Thompson, Alanson FL 1st Inf. Old Co.C
Thompson, Albert AL 46th Inf. Co.I,B
Thompson, Albert LA Inf.Cons.Crescent Regt. Co.G Jr.2nd Lt.
Thompson, Albert MO St.Guard
Thompson, Albert NC 12th Inf. Co.N
Thompson, Albert NC 32nd Inf. Co.B,C
Thompson, Albert TX 1st Inf. Co.G
Thompson, Albert VA 2nd Inf. Co.I
Thompson, Albert J. TX 12th Cav. Co.F
Thompson, Albert L. AR 10th Cav. Co.B
Thompson, Albert N. VA 45th Inf. Co.F Sgt.
Thompson, Alburn AR 15th (N.W.) Inf. Co.E Sgt.
Thompson, Alex SC 4th Cav. Co.D
Thompson, Alexander FL 3rd Inf. Co.F
Thompson, Alexander FL 5th Inf. Co.E
Thompson, Alex. GA Lt.Arty. Havis' Btty.
Thompson, Alexander GA 7th Inf. Co.A
Thompson, Alexander GA 10th Inf. Co.I
Thompson, Alexander KY 4th Mtd.Inf. Co.F
Thompson, Alexander LA 1st Hvy.Arty. (Reg.) Co.F Cpl.
Thompson, Alexander MO 1st Inf. Co.A
Thompson, Alexander NC 16th Inf. Co.K
Thompson, Alexander NC 62nd Inf. Co.D
Thompson, Alexander SC Inf. 1st (Charleston) Bn. Co.C
Thompson, Alexander SC 27th Inf. Co.H
Thompson, Alexander TN Conscr. (Cp. of Instr.)
Thompson, Alexander TX 19th Inf. Co.B
Thompson, Alexander VA Lt.Arty. Utterback's Co.
Thompson, Alexander VA 28th Inf. Co.H
Thompson, Alexander VA 45th Inf. Co.F
Thompson, Alexander VA 45th Inf. Co.I
Thompson, Alexander VA 58th Inf. Co.G
Thompson, Alexander A. NC 6th Inf. Co.F Sgt.
Thompson, Alexander G. AR 1st (Colquitt's) Inf. Co.H
Thompson, Alexander N. VA 45th Inf. Co.G Sgt.
Thompson, Alexander S. NC 35th Inf. Co.G Cpl.
Thompson, Alexander W. MS 5th Inf. Co.D 1st Sgt.
Thompson, Alex C. TX Cav. 8th (Taylor's) Bn. Co.B 1st Sgt.
Thompson, Alex H. MO Cav. Preston's Bn. Co.A
Thompson, Alex N.B. NC Walker's Bn. Thomas' Legion 1st Co.D
Thompson, Alex N.B. TN 1st (Carter's) Cav. Co.I
Thompson, Alford GA 11th Inf. Co.E
Thompson, Alfred AR Mil. Desha Cty.Bn.
Thompson, Alfred GA 44th Inf. Co.A
Thompson, Alfred LA Inf. 4th Bn. Co.B Sgt.Maj.
Thompson, Alfred MO 2nd Inf. Co.G 1st Lt.
Thompson, Alfred VA Cav. Mosby's Regt. (Part.Rangers) Co.F
Thompson, Alfred G. GA 42nd Inf. Co.G,C
Thompson, Alfred G. NC 39th Inf. Co.C
Thompson, Alfred R. GA Cobb's Legion Co.C
Thompson, Alfred R. NC 28th Inf. Co.I
Thompson, Alla P. LA 19th Inf. Co.A
Thompson, Allen AL 47th Inf. Co.H
Thompson, Allen FL 5th Inf. Co.K
Thompson, Allen GA Cav. 21st Bn. Co.C
Thompson, Allen GA 2nd Inf. 1st Co.B
Thompson, Allen GA 26th Inf. Co.E
Thompson, Allen KY 2nd Bn.Mtd.Rifles Co.C
Thompson, Allen TX 3rd Cav. Co.F Sgt.
Thompson, Allen TX 11th Inf. Co.I Cpl.
Thompson, Allen VA 8th Cav. 1st Co.D
Thompson, Allen VA Cav. Swann's Bn. Lilly's Co.
Thompson, Allen 8th (Wade's) Conf.Cav. Co.H
Thompson, Allen 1st Choctaw & Chickasaw Mtd.Rifles Co.A
Thompson, Allen C. VA 45th Inf. Co.H
Thompson, Allen J. GA 57th Inf. Co.C
Thompson, Allen R. VA 19th Cav. Co.B Sgt.
Thompson, Allen R. VA 22nd Inf. Swann's Co.
Thompson, Allison W. MS Cav. Hughes' Bn. Co.H
Thompson, Alvin AL 3rd Inf. Co.I
Thompson, Alonzo VA 7th Inf. Co.D
Thompson, A.L.R. AL 5th Inf. New Co.K
Thompson, Alson G. NC 6th Inf. Co.F
Thompson, Alvis TX 25th Cav. Co.K
Thompson, A.M. AR 36th Inf. Co.C
Thompson, A.M. GA 16th Inf. Co.G
Thompson, A.M. NC 35th Inf. Co.B
Thompson, Ambrose M. AR 1st (Colquitt's) Inf. Co.E 2nd Lt.
Thompson, Ambrose W. TN 38th Inf. Co.M Lt.
Thompson, Ammon D. AR Cav. Harrell's Bn. Co.C Cpl.
Thompson, Amon FL 8th Inf. Co.C
Thompson, Amon H. GA 29th Inf. Co.C
Thompson, Amos VA 25th Inf. 2nd Co.K
Thompson, Amos VA 31st Inf. Co.H Sgt.
Thompson, Amos VA Mil. Scott Cty.
Thompson, Amos D. VA 11th Bn.Res. Co.D
Thompson, Amos H. GA 45th Inf. Co.C
Thompson, Amzy C. GA 4th (Clinch's) Cav. Co.B
Thompson, A.N. AL Cav. Lewis' Bn. Co.A,C 2nd Lt.
Thompson, A.N. AR 21st Mil. Dollar's Co.
Thompson, A.N. FL Cav. J.D. Morrison's Co. 2nd Lt.
Thompson, A.N. KY 6th Mtd.Inf. Co.I
Thompson, A.N. TN 49th Inf. Co.D Sgt.
Thompson, A.N. Inf. Bailey's Cons.Regt. Co.L
Thompson, Anderson L. GA 5th Inf. Co.E
Thompson, Anderson L. GA Inf. 25th Bn. (Prov.Guard) Co.C
Thompson, Andrew KY 5th Cav. Sgt.
Thompson, Andrew KY 10th (Diamond's) Cav. Co.E
Thompson, Andrew MO 3rd Cav. Co.D
Thompson, Andrew SC Hvy.Arty. 15th (Lucas') Bn. Co.C
Thompson, Andrew SC Arty. Childs' Co. Sgt.
Thompson, Andrew TX 2nd Cav. Co.A Cpl.
Thompson, Andrew TX 15th Inf. Co.I 2nd Lt.
Thompson, Andrew VA 36th Inf. 1st Co.H
Thompson, Andrew VA 36th Inf. 2nd Co.K
Thompson, Andrew VA 64th Mtd.Inf. Co.C
Thompson, Andrew VA Loc.Def. Earhart's Co.
Thompson, Andrew 10th Conf.Cav. Co.B 1st Lt.
Thompson, Andrew F. GA 43rd Inf. Co.G
Thompson, Andrew G. VA 36th Inf. 2nd Co.G
Thompson, Andrew G. VA 48th Inf. Co.I
Thompson, Andrew H. AR 25th Inf. Co.B 3rd Lt.
Thompson, Andrew H. VA Hvy.Arty. 18th Bn. Co.C Sgt.
Thompson, Andrew J. AL Arty. 1st Bn. Co.E
Thompson, Andrew J. AL Lt.Arty. 2nd Bn. Co.F
Thompson, Andrew J. AL Inf. 1st Regt. Co.K Sgt.
Thompson, Andrew J. AL 28th Inf. Co.F
Thompson, Andrew J. AL 63rd Inf. Co.C
Thompson, Andrew J. AL Cav. 5th Bn. Hilliard's Legion Co.B 2nd Lt.
Thompson, Andrew J. GA 1st Inf. (St.Guards)
Thompson, Andrew J. GA 1st Bn.S.S.
Thompson, Andrew J. GA 38th Inf. Co.C 1st Sgt.
Thompson, Andrew J. GA 57th Inf. Co.C Sgt.
Thompson, Andrew J. GA Cherokee Legion (St.Guards) Co.D Sgt.
Thompson, Andrew J. KY 5th Mtd.Inf. Co.I
Thompson, Andrew J. MO 3rd Cav. Co.E Capt.
Thompson, Andrew J. NC 6th Inf. Co.H Cpl.
Thompson, Andrew J. NC 7th Inf. Co.F
Thompson, Andrew J. NC 18th Inf. Co.D
Thompson, Andrew J. NC 30th Inf. Co.E
Thompson, Andrew J. TN 7th Inf. Co.F
Thompson, Andrew J. TN 20th Inf.
Thompson, Andrew J. TN 32nd Inf. Co.H
Thompson, Andrew J. TN 63rd Inf. Co.I
Thompson, Andrew J. VA 7th Inf. Co.D
Thompson, Andrew J. VA 36th Inf. 2nd Co.C
Thompson, Andrew J. VA 31st Inf. Co.H Sgt.
Thompson, Andrew J. VA 52nd Inf. 2nd Co.B Capt.
Thompson, Andrew J.R. AR 9th Inf. Co.D
Thompson, Andrew L. GA 38th Inf. Co.G
Thompson, Andrew L. KY 2nd Bn.Mtd.Rifles Co.D Sgt.
Thompson, Andrew L. TX 26th Cav. Co.D
Thompson, Andrew L. TX Cav. Baylor's Regt. Co.E

Thompson, Andrew M. MS 14th Inf. Co.C
Thompson, Andrew M. MO 9th (Elliott's) Cav. Co.B
Thompson, Andrew M. MO 10th Cav.
Thompson, Andrew M. MO 3rd Inf. Co.C
Thompson, Andrew R.M. AR 1st (Colquitt's) Inf. Co.F Sgt.
Thompson, Andrew T. VA 129th Mil. Chambers' Co., Avis' Co.
Thompson, Andrew W. TN 11th Cav. Co.B
Thompson, Andrew W. VA 6th Cav. Co.G
Thompson, Ansalom B. AL 32nd Inf. Co.A
Thompson, A.O. TN 10th (DeMoss') Cav. Co.B
Thompson, A.P. GA 9th Inf. (St.Guards) Co.F
Thompson, A.P. GA Inf. 25th Bn. (Prov.Guard) Co.C
Thompson, A.P. KY 3rd Mtd.Inf. Col.
Thompson, A.P. TN 2nd Arty. Co.B Capt.
Thompson, A.P. TN 19th Inf. Co.A 1st Sgt.
Thompson, A.R. AL 6th Cav. Co.D Sgt.
Thompson, A.R. GA 18th Inf. Co.B
Thompson, A.R. MS 9th Cav. Co.B
Thompson, Arch AL Cav. Moreland's Regt. Co.G
Thompson, Arch AR Cav. Gordon's Regt. Co.H
Thompson, Arch VA Loc.Def. Patterson's Co.
Thompson, Archibald AL 3rd Inf. Co.K
Thompson, Archibald AR 16th Inf. Co.I
Thompson, Archibald AR 35th Inf. Co.D
Thompson, Archibald GA 47th Inf. Co.H 2nd Lt.
Thompson, Archibald VA 54th Inf. Co.A
Thompson, Archibald D. NC 3rd Arty. (40th St.Troops) Co.E
Thompson, Archibald H. TX 13th Vol. Co.M Lt.
Thompson, Archibald H. TX 15th Inf. 2nd Co.H 1st Lt.
Thompson, Archibald L.R. AL 6th Inf. Co.M
Thompson, Archibald P. GA 25th Inf. Co.F
Thompson, A.R.M. AR Lt.Arty. Wiggins' Btty. Artif.
Thompson, A.R.M. AR Mil. Borland's Regt. King's Co.
Thompson, Armistead VA 8th Inf. Co.G Sgt.
Thompson, Arthur P. SC 10th Inf. Co.M
Thompson, A.S. GA 10th Inf. Co.I
Thompson, A.S. GA 17th Inf. Co.K
Thompson, A.S. TX 26th Cav. Co.B
Thompson, A.S. VA 2nd Cav. Co.G
Thompson, A.S. VA 13th Inf. Co.I Sgt.
Thompson, A.S. Hosp.Stew.
Thompson, Asa AR Inf. Hardy's Regt. Co.A
Thompson, Asa VA Cav. 37th Bn. Co.K
Thompson, Asa VA 37th Inf. Co.D
Thompson, Asa V. LA 8th Inf. Co.G
Thompson, Asa W. TX 35th (Brown's) Cav. Co.D Sgt.
Thompson, Asa W. Gen. & Staff AAQM
Thompson, A.T. AL Inf. 2nd Regt. Co.G
Thompson, A.T. AR 15th (Johnson's) Inf. Co.B
Thompson, A.T. GA 31st Inf. Co.H Sgt.
Thompson, A.T. LA 27th Inf. Co.B
Thompson, A.T. TN 8th Inf. Co.D
Thompson, Augustus AL 6th Inf. Co.C
Thompson, Augustus F. GA 1st Reg. Co.H
Thompson, Augustus H. AL Arty. 1st Bn. Co.E
Thompson, Augustus L. AL 17th Inf. Co.I
Thompson, Augustus N. AL 36th Inf. Co.F
Thompson, Augustus R. AL 39th Inf. Co.E
Thompson, Austin A. VA 45th Inf. Co.K 1st Lt.
Thompson, A. Vance AL Cp.Preston Maj.
Thompson, A.W. AL 44th Inf. Co.F
Thompson, A.W. AL 50th Inf. Co.G 2nd Lt.
Thompson, A.W. AR 6th Inf. Co.G
Thompson, A.W. FL 4th Inf. Co.D
Thompson, A.W. MS 4th Cav. Co.K
Thompson, A.W. MS 25th Inf. Co.C
Thompson, A.W. TN 5th Inf. 2nd Co.B
Thompson, A.W. VA Lt.Arty. Lamkin's Co.
Thompson, A.W. VA 54th Mil. Co.C,D
Thompson, A.W. Gen. & Staff, Medical Dept. Surg.
Thompson, A.Y. SC 3rd Inf. Co.G,D
Thompson, B. AL Cav. Barlow's Co.
Thompson, B. AL 14th Inf. Co.G
Thompson, B. AL 63rd Inf. Co.B
Thompson, B. AR 15th Inf. Co.E
Thompson, B. GA 4th (Clinch's) Cav. Co.D
Thompson, B. GA 16th Inf. Co.D
Thompson, B. MS 10th Cav. Co.F
Thompson, B. TN 15th Inf. Co.E
Thompson, B. 8th (Wade's) Conf.Cav. Co.B
Thompson, B. 15th Conf.Cav. Co.C
Thompson, B. Conf.Inf. 1st Bn. Co.I
Thompson, Bailis GA 3rd Cav. Co.G
Thompson, Baler VA 122th Mil. Co.E
Thompson, Ballard VA 45th Inf. Co.F
Thompson, Barnabas GA 19th Inf. Co.F
Thompson, Barney GA 47th Inf. Co.H
Thompson, Barthew TN Cav. 16th Bn. (Neal's) Co.E
Thompson, Bartlett Y. NC 62nd Inf. Co.D Sgt.
Thompson, Bart W. TN Cav. 5th Bn. (McClellan's) Co.E 2nd Lt.
Thompson, Baxter AL Cav. Falkner's Co.
Thompson, Bayly LA Arty. Green's Co. (LA Guard Btty.)
Thompson, B.B. GA 5th Res. Co.H
Thompson, B.C. AL Inf. 2nd Regt. Co.K
Thompson, B.C. AR 2nd Inf.
Thompson, B.C. GA 4th (Clinch's) Cav. Co.G
Thompson, B.C. Conf.Cav. Powers' Regt. Co.E
Thompson, B.D. MS 37th Inf. Co.H
Thompson, B.D. TN 2nd (Ashby's) Cav. Co.H
Thompson, Ben AL 15th Bn.Part.Rangers Co.C
Thompson, Benajah S. GA 3rd Inf. Co.L Sgt.
Thompson, BenjaminAL 12th Inf. Co.H
Thompson, Benjamin FL 1st Inf. New Co.E
Thompson, Benjamin LA 28th (Gray's) Inf. Co.G
Thompson, Benjamin MS 1st Lt.Arty.
Thompson, Benjamin MS 14th Inf. Co.F
Thompson, Benjamin MS 37th Inf. Co.K
Thompson, Benjamin NC 3rd Bn.Sr.Res. Williams' Co.
Thompson, Benjamin NC 26th Inf. Co.D
Thompson, Benjamin TN Inf. 1st Bn. (Colms') Co.B
Thompson, Benjamin TN 59th Mtd.Inf. Co.D
Thompson, Benjamin TX 2nd Cav. 2nd Co.F
Thompson, Benjamin TX 2nd Cav. Co.H
Thompson, Benjamin VA 11th Cav. Co.G
Thompson, Benjamin A. GA 5th Inf. Co.D
Thompson, Benjamin B. AL 29th Inf. Co.K
Thompson, Benjamin B. TN 24th Inf. 2nd Co.G Sgt.
Thompson, Benjamin D. TN Cav. 4th Bn. (Branner's) Co.A
Thompson, Benjamin D. VA Inf. 22nd Bn. Co.B
Thompson, Benjamin E. NC 2nd Cav. (19th St.Troops) Co.E
Thompson, Benjamin F. AR 9th Inf. Co.G
Thompson, Benjamin F. AR Inf. Hardy's Regt. Co.F
Thompson, Benjamin F. KY 4th Mtd.Inf. Co.I
Thompson, Benjamin F. LA 31st Inf. Co.G
Thompson, Benjamin F. MS 2nd Inf. Co.B
Thompson, Benjamin F. MS 7th Inf. Co.F Ens.
Thompson, Benjamin F. MS 23rd Inf. Co.A
Thompson, Benjamin F. MO 2nd Cav. Co.C
Thompson, Benjamin F. NC 5th Inf. Co.B
Thompson, Benjamin F. NC 5th Inf. Co.I Sgt.
Thompson, Benjamin F. TX 2nd Cav. Co.I Sgt.
Thompson, Benjamin F. TX 22nd Cav. Co.H
Thompson, Benjamin F. VA 2nd Inf. Co.I
Thompson, Benjamin F. VA 64th Mtd.Inf. Co.G 3rd Lt.
Thompson, Benjamin F. VA 94th Mil. Co.A Sgt.
Thompson, Benjamin Franklin MS 1st Lt.Arty. Co.C
Thompson, Benjamin J. AR Lt.Arty. Thrall's Btty.
Thompson, Benj. L. MS 15th Inf. Co.L 2nd Lt.
Thompson, Benjamin Lafayette TX 20th Cav. Co.E
Thompson, Benjamin P. Conf.Inf. 1st Bn. 2nd Co.A
Thompson, Benj. S. GA 44th Inf. Co.C Sgt.
Thompson, Benj. S. Gen. & Staff Maj.,QM
Thompson, Benjamin T. NC 49th Inf. Co.C
Thompson, Benjamin W. AL Inf. 1st Regt. Co.B
Thompson, Benjamin W. FL 1st Inf. Old Co.K, New Co.A
Thompson, Berlin M. TX 10th Inf. Co.E
Thompson, Berry FL 8th Inf. Co.E
Thompson, Berry GA 38th Inf. Co.C
Thompson, Berry GA 40th Inf. Co.A
Thompson, Berry NC 64th Inf. Co.E 1st Sgt.
Thompson, Berry M. GA 66th Inf. Co.I Cpl.
Thompson, B.F. AL Lt.Arty. Tarrant's Btty.
Thompson, B.F. AR 1st (Dobbin's) Cav. Co.K
Thompson, B.F. AR 1st (Monroe's) Cav. Co.H
Thompson, B.F. AR 8th Inf. New Co.D 2nd Lt.
Thompson, B.F. AR 11th Inf. Co.D
Thompson, B.F. AR 15th (Josey's) Inf. 1st Co.G
Thompson, B.F. AR 24th Inf. Co.C
Thompson, B.F. AR 37th Inf. Co.K 1st Sgt.
Thompson, B.F. AR Inf. Hardy's Regt. Co.G
Thompson, B.F. GA Inf. 8th Bn. Co.B
Thompson, B.F. GA 18th Inf. Co.A
Thompson, B.F. MS 2nd Part. Co.D 2nd Lt.
Thompson, B.F. MS 18th Cav. Co.G 2nd Lt.
Thompson, B.F. MS 4th Inf. Co.A 1st Sgt.
Thompson, B.F. MS Inf. (Res.) Berry's Co.
Thompson, B.F. SC 6th Cav. Co.C
Thompson, B.F. TN 14th (Neely's) Cav. Co.G
Thompson, B.F. TN Lt.Arty. Rice's Btty.
Thompson, B.F. TX 3rd Cav. Co.B
Thompson, B.F. TX 10th Cav. Co.G
Thompson, B.F. VA 36th Inf. AQM

Thompson, B.H. TN 84th Inf. Co.G Sgt.
Thompson, Bin AL 56th Part.Rangers Co.C
Thompson, B.J. GA Conscr.
Thompson, B.J. TN 24th Inf. 2nd Co.G
Thompson, B.L. MS 1st Bn.S.S. Co.C 2nd Lt.
Thompson, B.L. SC 2nd Cav. Co.F
Thompson, B.L. SC Cav. 4th Bn. Co.A
Thompson, B.L. TN 20th (Russell's) Cav. Co.K
Thompson, B.L. TN Inf. 4th Cons.Regt. Co.I
Thompson, B.L. TN 30th Inf. Co.K
Thompson, Blackburn M. MO 15th Cav. Co.A Cpl.
Thompson, Blount J. NC 2nd Cav. (19th St.Troops) Co.E
Thompson, B.M. GA Inf. (Madison Cty.Home Guard) Milner's Co. Cpl.
Thompson, B.N. LA Lt.Arty. 2nd Field Btty.
Thompson, B.O. GA 4th Cav. (St.Guards) Armstrong's Co.
Thompson, B.P. GA Inf. 25th Bn. (Prov.Guard) Co.A
Thompson, B.Q. MS 37th Inf. Co.H
Thompson, B.R. MS 2nd Cav.Res. Co.G
Thompson, Brannon GA 11th Inf. Co.D
Thompson, Bright NC Nelson's Co. (Loc.Def.)
Thompson, Bryant NC 46th Inf. Co.H
Thompson, Bryant NC 47th Inf. Co.D
Thompson, Bryant TN Cav. 16th Bn. (Neal's) Co.B
Thompson, Bryant G. NC 18th Inf. Co.B Cpl.
Thompson, Bryant W. NC 3rd Inf. Co.E
Thompson, B.S. TX 9th (Young's) Inf. Co.F
Thompson, B.T. AR 50th Mil. Co.G
Thompson, Bunyon NC 2nd Arty. (36th St.Troops) Co.I
Thompson, Burrall C. AL 31st Inf. Co.E
Thompson, Burrell LA 17th Inf. Co.E
Thompson, Buse H. VA 166th Mil. Ballard's Co.H Wag.
Thompson, B.V. SC 16th Inf. Co.E 2nd Lt.
Thompson, B.W. AR 2nd Inf.
Thompson, B.W. GA 53rd Inf. Co.F
Thompson, B.W. LA 4th Inf. Co.I
Thompson, B.W. TN 1st (Carter's) Cav. Co.K
Thompson, B.W. TN 2nd (Ashby's) Cav. Co.K
Thompson, B.W. TX 32nd Cav. Co.E
Thompson, B.W. 3rd Conf.Inf. Co.B
Thompson, B.W. Morgan's,CSA
Thompson, C. AL 1st Cav. Co.D
Thompson, C. AL St.Arty. Co.C Jr.1st Lt.
Thompson, C. AL St.Arty. Co.C
Thompson, C. AL 21st Inf. Co.E
Thompson, C. AL Rebels
Thompson, C. AR 35th Inf. Co.A
Thompson, C. GA 27th Inf. Co.B
Thompson, C. MS 2nd St.Cav. Co.L
Thompson, C. MS St.Cav. Perrin's Bn. Co.H
Thompson, C. MO Cav. Freeman's Regt. Co.D
Thompson, C. SC 27th Inf. Co.B
Thompson, C. TN 19th (Biffle's) Cav. Co.L
Thompson, C. TN 21st (Wilson's) Cav. Co.F
Thompson, C. TN 12th (Cons.) Inf. Co.G Cpl.
Thompson, C. TN 34th Inf. Co.K
Thompson, C. TX 5th Cav. Co.G
Thompson, C. VA Inf. 22nd Bn. Co.B
Thompson, C. VA 46th Mil. Lantz's Co.
Thompson, C.A. GA 8th Inf. (St.Guards) Co.A
Thompson, C.A. NC 2nd Arty. (36th St.Troops) Co.A
Thompson, C.A. TN Inf. 1st Cons.Regt. Co.H
Thompson, C.A. TX 10th Cav. Co.I
Thompson, Cal AL 11th Cav. Co.F,K
Thompson, Calloway VA Cav. Ferguson's Bn. Nounnan's Co.
Thompson, Calvin GA 26th Inf. Co.G
Thompson, Calvin GA 50th Inf. Co.B
Thompson, Calvin MO 3rd Cav. Co.H
Thompson, Calvin NC 34th Inf. Co.A
Thompson, Calvin C. NC 28th Inf. Co.K
Thompson, Calvin R. GA 14th Inf. Co.G
Thompson, Cameron VA 22nd Inf. Co.H
Thompson, Campbell FL 6th Inf. Co.K
Thompson, Canady G. VA 45th Inf. Co.F
Thompson, Carrol MS 1st (Patton's) Inf. Co.G Sgt.
Thompson, Carroll AL 6th Inf. Co.D Jr.2nd Lt.
Thompson, Carroll MS 8th Cav. Co.E
Thompson, Carrol M. AL 26th (O'Neal's) Inf. Co.G
Thompson, Carter NC 56th Inf. Co.G
Thompson, C.B. AL Inf. 2nd Regt. Co.H Cpl.
Thompson, C.B. VA Inf. 22nd Bn. Co.D
Thompson, C.B. Conf.Inf. 1st Bn. Co.I Cpl.
Thompson, C.C. AL Inf. 2nd Regt. Co.E
Thompson, C.C. AL 17th Inf. Co.C
Thompson, C.C. AR Cav. Gordon's Regt. Co.C
Thompson, C.C. AR 35th Inf. Co.D
Thompson, C.C. AR 62nd Mil. Co.F Cpl.
Thompson, C.C. GA 4th Cav. (St.Guards) White's Co. 2nd Lt.
Thompson, C.C. GA 18th Inf. Co.E
Thompson, C.C. GA Inf. 27th Bn. (NonConscr.) Co.D
Thompson, C.C. GA 60th Inf. Co.I
Thompson, C.C. LA 4th Inf. Co.I
Thompson, C.C. TN Inf. 3rd Cons.Regt. Co.C
Thompson, C.C. TX 23rd Cav. Co.E Capt.
Thompson, C.C. TX 32nd Cav. Co.I Sgt.
Thompson, C.C. VA 47th Inf. Co.B Cpl.
Thompson, C.C. VA Loc.Def. Tayloe's Co.
Thompson, C.D. MS Cav. 4th Bn. Co.C
Thompson, C.D. MS 15th Bn.S.S. Co.B
Thompson, C.D. 8th (Wade's) Conf.Cav. Co.E
Thompson, C.D. Sap. & Min. G.W. Maxson's Co.,CSA
Thompson, C.E. AL 49th Inf. Co.A
Thompson, C.E. SC Inf. Hampton Legion Co.E
Thompson, C.E. TX 35th (Brown's) Cav. Co.B
Thompson, C.E. TX Cav. Waller's Regt. Menard's Co.
Thompson, C.E. TX 7th Field Btty.
Thompson, Cephas LA 16th Inf. Co.H 1st Lt.
Thompson, Cero. G. MS 11th (Perrin's) Cav. Co.F
Thompson, C.F. LA Lt.Arty. 3rd Btty. (Benton's)
Thompson, C.F. MS 32nd Inf. Co.D
Thompson, C.G. AR 2nd Inf. Co.A
Thompson, C.G. LA 21st (Kennedy's) Inf. Co.D
Thompson, C.G. TN 42nd Inf. Co.H
Thompson, C. Gratiot MD Arty. 1st Btty. Sgt.
Thompson, C. Gratiot Gen. & Staff,PACS 2nd Lt.,Arty.Off.,Ord.Off.
Thompson, C.H. AL 14th Inf. Co.A
Thompson, C.H. AL 33rd Inf. Co.K
Thompson, C.H. AR Cav. Gordon's Regt. Co.C
Thompson, C.H. GA 4th Cav. (St.Guards) Armstrong's Co.
Thompson, C.H. LA 2nd Inf. Co.I
Thompson, C.H. TX 10th Cav. Co.I
Thompson, C.H. VA Lt.Arty. 13th Bn. Co.A
Thompson, C.H. 3rd Conf.Eng.Troops Co.F
Thompson, C.H. Sap. & Min. G.W. Maxson's Co.,CSA
Thompson, Charles AL 32nd Inf. Co.K
Thompson, Charles AR 1st Vol. Co.G
Thompson, Charles AR 4th Inf. Co.D
Thompson, Charles GA 6th Cav. Co.H
Thompson, Charles GA Lt.Arty. 14th Bn. Co.D
Thompson, Charles GA Lt.Arty. King's Btty.
Thompson, Charles GA Arty. Maxwell's Reg.Lt.Btty.
Thompson, Charles GA 1st Reg. Co.L,D
Thompson, Charles LA 2nd Cav. Co.D
Thompson, Charles LA Washington Arty.Bn. Co.2 Driver
Thompson, Charles LA 2nd Res.Corps Co.H
Thompson, Charles LA Mil. 4th Regt. 1st Brig. 1st Div. Co.G
Thompson, Charles LA 11th Inf. Co.H
Thompson, Charles LA 15th Inf. Co.D
Thompson, Charles LA 16th Inf. Co.H
Thompson, Charles MS 1st (King's) Inf. (St.Troops) Co.K
Thompson, Charles MO 12th Inf. Co.B
Thompson, Charles MO 16th Inf. Co.A
Thompson, Charles MO 16th Inf. Co.H
Thompson, Charles NC 1st Inf. (6 mo. '61) Co.H
Thompson, Charles SC 20th Inf. Co.B
Thompson, Charles TN Cav. 17th Bn. (Sanders') Co.A
Thompson, Charles TX Cav. Waller's Regt. Menard's Co.
Thompson, Charles TX 3rd Inf. Co.I
Thompson, Charles VA 11th Cav. Co.G
Thompson, Charles VA 12th Cav. Co.A
Thompson, Charles VA Lt.Arty. Cayce's Co.
Thompson, Charles VA 26th Inf. Co.E
Thompson, Charles VA 27th Inf. Co.C
Thompson, Charles VA 48th Inf. Co.B
Thompson, Charles VA 56th Inf. Co.F Sgt.Maj.
Thompson, Charles VA 79th Mil. Co.3
Thompson, Charles Conf.Cav. Clarkson's Bn. Ind.Rangers Co.A
Thompson, Charles Conf.Inf. Tucker's Regt. Co.H
Thompson, Charles 3rd Conf.Eng.Troops Co.F
Thompson, Charles Sig.Corps,CSA
Thompson, Charles A. GA 40th Inf. Co.I
Thompson, Charles A. GA Inf. White's Co.
Thompson, Charles A. LA Arty. Green's Co. (LA Guard Btty.) Capt.
Thompson, Charles A. LA 1st (Nelligan's) Inf. 1st Co.B Cpl.
Thompson, Charles A. NC 3rd Arty. (40th St.Troops) Co.E
Thompson, Charles A. NC Moseley's Co. (Sampson Arty.) 2nd Lt.
Thompson, Charles A. TN 1st (Feild's) Inf. Co.B
Thompson, Charles B. VA 22nd Inf. Co.G

Thompson, Charles C. NC 22nd Inf. Co.G
Thompson, Charles C. TN 3rd (Clack's) Inf.
Thompson, Charles C. TN 19th Inf. Co.I,C Sgt.
Thompson, Charles C. VA Lt.Arty. 38th Bn. Co.D
Thompson, Charles C.S. VA 3rd Inf.Loc.Def. Co.E
Thompson, Charles C.S. VA 15th Inf. Co.B
Thompson, Charles C.S. VA Inf. 25th Bn. Co.H
Thompson, Charles D. MS 11th Inf. Co.E
Thompson, Charles D. VA 135th Mil. Co.A
Thompson, Charles E. AL Lt.Arty. 2nd Bn. Co.A
Thompson, Chas. E. TX Cav. Terry's Regt. Co.E
Thompson, Charles E. VA 2nd Inf. Co.A
Thompson, Charles E. VA 19th Inf. Co.C
Thompson, Charles F. GA Inf. 27th Bn. Co.F Sgt.
Thompson, Charles F. LA 2nd Inf. Co.F
Thompson, Charles F. MS 44th Inf. Co.K
Thompson, Charles G. MS 18th Inf. Co.D
Thompson, Charles G. VA 1st St.Res. Co.F 1st Sgt.
Thompson, Charles H. AR 36th Inf. Co.H
Thompson, Charles H. VA 6th Cav. Co.I
Thompson, Charles H. VA 14th Cav. Co.K
Thompson, Charles H. VA 5th Inf. Co.A Cpl.
Thompson, Charles H. VA 46th Inf. 2nd Co.A Cpl.
Thompson, Charles L. SC 12th Inf. Co.I
Thompson, Charles L. TX Inf.Riflemen Arnold's Co.
Thompson, Charles M. NC 14th Inf. Co.I
Thompson, Charles O. NC 47th Inf. Co.K
Thompson, Charles P. KY 6th Mtd.Inf. Co.G Cpl.
Thompson, Charles R. MD 1st Cav. Co.E
Thompson, Charles R. VA Lt.Arty. Nelson's Co.
Thompson, Charles R. VA Lt.Arty. Woolfolk's Co.
Thompson, Charles S. MS 39th Inf. Co.C
Thompson, Charles T. NC 28th Inf. Co.A Sgt.
Thompson, Charles T. VA 19th Inf. Co.I
Thompson, Charles V. TN 13th Inf. Co.H Adj.
Thompson, Charles V. AR Cav. Poe's Bn. Dismuks' Co.
Thompson, Chas. Virgil Gen. & Staff Adj.,Lt.
Thompson, Charles W. AR 1st Mtd.Rifles Co.B Bugler
Thompson, Chs. W. GA 1st (Olmstead's) Inf. Gallie's Co.
Thompson, Charles W. GA 24th Inf. Co.F
Thompson, Charles W. MS 3rd Inf. Co.D 3rd Lt.
Thompson, Charles W. TN Cav. 11th Bn. (Gordon's) Co.D
Thompson, Charles W. TX 20th Inf. Co.B Sgt.
Thompson, Charles W. VA 2nd Inf. Co.E
Thompson, Charlton AL 45th Inf. Co.F Cpl.
Thompson, Charlton GA Inf. 2nd Bn. Co.A
Thompson, Charlton VA 54th Inf. Co.A Sgt.
Thompson, Chesley AL 33rd Inf. Co.K
Thompson, Christopher VA 61st Inf. Co.B
Thompson, Cicero AL 5th Cav. Co.D
Thompson, Cicero MS 11th Inf. Co.K
Thompson, Cicero MS 15th Inf. Co.H
Thompson, Cicero B. AL 61st Inf. Co.F
Thompson, Cicero H. GA 6th Inf. (St.Guards) Co.F
Thompson, C.J. LA 2nd Cav. Co.F
Thompson, C.L. GA 52nd Inf. AQM
Thompson, C.L. MS 37th Inf. Co.A
Thompson, C.L. TX 32nd Cav. Co.F
Thompson, C.L. TX Cav. Border's Regt. Co.C,E 1st Lt.
Thompson, C.L. TX Inf. 2nd St.Troops Co.C
Thompson, C.L. VA 88th Mil.
Thompson, C.L. Terry's Brig. Capt.,AQM
Thompson, Clark AL Lt.Arty. Kolb's Btty.
Thompson, Clark GA 22nd Inf. Co.E Sgt.
Thompson, Clark NC 44th Inf. Co.F
Thompson, Clarke H. VA 7th Inf. Co.G 1st Lt.
Thompson, Clay MO 2nd Inf. Co.E
Thompson, Clay MO 5th Inf. Co.G
Thompson, Clay TX Waul's Legion Co.H
Thompson, Clinton AL 3rd Cav. Co.H
Thompson, Clinton AL 53rd (Part.Rangers) Co.K
Thompson, C.M. MS 40th Inf. Co.K
Thompson, C.M. MS Inf. Comfort's Co.
Thompson, C.M. TN Cav. Allison's Squad. Co.C
Thompson, C.M. Gen. & Staff Capt.,QM
Thompson, Columbus TX 22nd Inf. Co.B
Thompson, Columbus VA 25th Cav. Co.C
Thompson, Columbus C. AL 11th Inf. Co.H
Thompson, Columbus M. MS 1st Lt.Arty. Co.L
Thompson, Corban AR 62nd Mil. Co.F
Thompson, Cord. GA 48th Inf. Co.G
Thompson, Corder GA 26th Inf. Co.I
Thompson, Council GA Lt.Arty. Daniell's Btty.
Thompson, C.P. TN 22nd Inf. Co.E
Thompson, C.R. GA Siege Arty. 28th Bn. Co.K
Thompson, C.R. GA 1st (Olmstead's) Inf. Surg.
Thompson, C.R. SC 1st Cav. Co.E
Thompson, Creed F. VA 29th Inf. Co.G
Thompson, Creed T. VA 19th Inf. Co.C
Thompson, C.S. MS 38th Cav. Co.B
Thompson, C.S. NC 39th Inf. Co.C
Thompson, C.S. SC 2nd Cav. Co.E 1st Lt.
Thompson, C.S. SC Cav. 4th Bn. Co.C 2nd Lt.
Thompson, C.S. VA 9th Bn.Res. Co.A Sgt.
Thompson, C.S. 20th Conf.Cav. Co.G
Thompson, C.T. AR 1st (Monroe's) Cav. Co.A
Thompson, C.T. AR Inf. 4th Bn. Co.B
Thompson, C.T. AR 5th Inf. Co.G
Thompson, C.T. AR 50th Mil. Co.G Sgt.
Thompson, C.T. TX 25th Cav. Co.A
Thompson, Cummings VA 22nd Cav. Co.D
Thompson, Cummins VA 37th Inf. Co.G
Thompson, C.V. Gen. & Staff AAQM
Thompson, C.W. AR 1st (Monroe's) Cav. Co.H 1st Lt.
Thompson, C.W. AR 1st Mtd.Rifles Co.B Bugler
Thompson, C.W. AR 6th Inf. New Co.F
Thompson, C.W. GA 16th Inf.
Thompson, C.W. GA 31st Inf. Co.K
Thompson, C.W. GA 60th Inf. Co.H
Thompson, C.W. MS 3rd Inf. Co.D
Thompson, C.W. TN 6th (Wheeler's) Cav. Co.D
Thompson, C.W. TN 47th Inf. Co.D
Thompson, C.W. TX 20th Inf. Co.B
Thompson, Cyrus H. AR 1st Mtd.Rifles Co.C
Thompson, D. AL 23rd Inf. Co.D
Thompson, D. AL 43rd Inf. Co.D
Thompson, D. GA 14th Inf. Co.G
Thompson, D. GA Inf. 26th Bn. Co.B
Thompson, D. GA 56th Inf. Co.K
Thompson, D. GA Inf. Collier's Co.
Thompson, D. GA Inf. (GA RR Guards) Porter's Co.
Thompson, D. NC 1st Inf. Co.C
Thompson, D. NC McIlhenny's Co.
Thompson, D. TN 15th (Cons.) Cav. Co.D,E Sgt.
Thompson, D. TN Cav. Nixon's Regt. Co.C
Thompson, D. 1st Conf.Eng.Troops Co.B
Thompson, D. 1st Choctaw & Chickasaw Mtd.Rifles Co.C 3rd Lt.
Thompson, D.A. AR Cav. Harrell's Bn. Co.D
Thompson, D.A. AR Inf. Cocke's Regt. Co.G
Thompson, D.A. MS Inf. 3rd Bn. (St.Troops) Co.B Capt.
Thompson, Dabua S. KY 2nd (Duke's) Cav. Co.G Cpl.
Thompson, Dallas TX 31st Cav. Co.A
Thompson, Daniel MO 15th Cav. Co.N
Thompson, Daniel NC 35th Inf. Co.A
Thompson, Daniel NC 43rd Inf. Co.G
Thompson, Daniel NC 52nd Inf. Co.G Sgt.
Thompson, Daniel SC Lt.Arty. Gaillard's Co. (Santee Lt.Arty.)
Thompson, Daniel TN 40th Inf. Co.G
Thompson, Daniel VA 64th Mtd.Inf. 2nd Co.F
Thompson, Daniel A. AR 3rd Cav. Co.G
Thompson, Daniel A. AR Cav. Harrell's Bn. Co.C
Thompson, Daniel A. AR 14th (Powers') Inf. Co.G
Thompson, Daniel A. TX Waul's Legion Co.A
Thompson, Daniel G. NC 28th Inf. Co.I
Thompson, Daniel H. NC 67th Inf. Co.H
Thompson, Daniel J. AL 46th Inf. Co.A 1st Lt.
Thompson, Daniel J. KY 14th Cav. Co.B
Thompson, Daniel N. FL Inf. 2nd Bn. Co.B
Thompson, Daniel P. GA 2nd Inf. 1st Co.B
Thompson, Daniel P. GA 26th Inf. Co.E
Thompson, Daniel P. MO 3rd Inf. Co.C
Thompson, Daniel R. GA 62nd Cav. Co.I
Thompson, Daniel R. GA 25th Inf. Co.K
Thompson, Daniel W. GA 10th Inf.
Thompson, Darley A. GA 3rd Inf. Co.G
Thompson, Dave KY 12th Cav. Co.A,H
Thompson, David AL 23rd Inf. Co.H
Thompson, David AL 28th Inf. Co.H
Thompson, David AL Cp. of Instr. Talladega
Thompson, David GA Inf. 27th Bn. Co.B
Thompson, David MS 31st Inf. Co.C Sgt.
Thompson, David MO 3rd Inf. Co.D Capt.
Thompson, David MO St.Guards Capt.
Thompson, David MO St.Guard 3rd Lt.
Thompson, David NC 2nd Cav. (19th St.Troops) Co.F Sgt.
Thompson, David NC 1st Inf. (6 mo. '61) Co.L
Thompson, David NC 11th (Bethel Regt.) Inf. Co.C Sgt.
Thompson, David NC 27th Inf. Co.G Cpl.
Thompson, David NC McIlhenny's Co.
Thompson, David NC Walker's Bn. Thomas' Legion 1st Co.D Sgt.

Thompson, David TN 1st (Carter's) Cav. Co.I Sgt.
Thompson, David TN Cav. 5th Bn. (McClellan's) Co.B
Thompson, David TN 8th Inf. Co.D
Thompson, David TN 12th Inf. Co.B
Thompson, David TN 12th (Cons.) Inf. Co.A
Thompson, David VA 2nd Arty. Co.E
Thompson, David VA 11th Bn.Res. Co.D Cpl.
Thompson, David VA 45th Inf. Co.I
Thompson, David VA 54th Mil. Co.E,F
Thompson, David VA Mil. Carroll Cty.
Thompson, David A. GA 53rd Inf. Co.B Sgt.
Thompson, David A. NC 34th Inf. Co.K
Thompson, David A. NC 56th Inf. Co.H
Thompson, David A. VA Inf. 22nd Bn. Co.E
Thompson, David B. MS 37th Inf. Co.B
Thompson, David B. MO 11th Inf. Co.E Asst.Surg.
Thompson, David C. LA 4th Inf. Co.A Sgt.
Thompson, David C. MS 14th Inf. Co.G
Thompson, David D. AL 1st Regt.Conscr. Co.I
Thompson, David E. VA 2nd Cav. Co.A
Thompson, David F. VA 45th Inf. Co.F
Thompson, David G. Shecoe's Chickasaw Bn. Mtd.Vol. Co.A
Thompson, David J. AL 18th Inf. Co.A
Thompson, David J. NC 2nd Inf. Co.H
Thompson, David J. NC 55th Inf. Co.G
Thompson, David L. TX 10th Inf. Co.I
Thompson, David M. AR 1st Mtd.Rifles Co.E Black.
Thompson, David M. NC 3rd Inf. Co.H
Thompson, David M. NC 60th Inf. Co.G 2nd Lt.
Thompson, David M. NC Inf. 69th Regt. Co.A
Thompson, David S. NC 5th Cav. (63rd St.Troops) Co.K Sgt.
Thompson, David S. NC 15th Inf. Co.H 1st Lt.
Thompson, David S. VA Hvy.Arty. 18th Bn. Co.B
Thompson, David T. VA 14th Cav. Co.K
Thompson, David T. VA Lt.Arty. 1st Bn. Co.C
Thompson, David T. VA 79th Mil. Co.3 Sgt.
Thompson, David V. SC 1st (Hagood's) Inf. 1st Co.D
Thompson, David W. GA 29th Inf. Co.C Cpl.
Thompson, Davis TN 2nd (Robison's) Inf. Co.K
Thompson, Dawson GA 2nd Cav. (St.Guards) Co.A
Thompson, D.B. AL 9th Inf. Co.F
Thompson, D.B. GA 17th Inf. Co.F Capt.
Thompson, D.B. GA Inf. 19th Bn. (St.Guards) Lt.Col.
Thompson, D.B. MS Rogers' Co.
Thompson, D.B. VA 30th Bn.S.S. Capt.,ACS
Thompson, D.B. Wharton's Staff Capt.
Thompson, D. Bouly VA 21st Inf. Co.B 1st Lt.
Thompson, D. Bowly MD Weston's Bn. Co.B 4th Sgt.
Thompson, D.C. AL Cav. Moreland's Regt. Co.G,I Sgt.
Thompson, D.C. AR 1st Mtd.Rifles Co.B
Thompson, D.C. GA Cav. Dorough's Bn.
Thompson, D.C. GA 53rd Inf. Co.B Cpl.
Thompson, D.C. MS 7th Cav. 1st Co.H
Thompson, D.C. TN 15th (Cons.) Cav. Co.E,D
Thompson, D.D. TX Cav. Steele's Command Co.A 2nd Lt.
Thompson, Dempsy D. AR 1st (Crawford's) Cav. Co.C
Thompson, Dempsy D. TX 15th Cav. Co.D
Thompson, Devereaux Daniel 1st Conf.Eng. Troops Co.F Artif.
Thompson, Dewitt Clinton MO 8th Inf. Co.I
Thompson, Dewitte C. MS 6th Cav. Co.K
Thompson, D.G. AR Lt.Arty. Key's Btty.
Thompson, D.G. NC 39th Inf. Co.C
Thompson, D.G. TX 8th Cav. Co.A
Thompson, D.H. AL 50th Inf. Co.G
Thompson, D.H. NC 3rd Cav. (41st St.Troops) Co.B
Thompson, D.H.C. GA 42nd Inf. Co.C
Thompson, D. Henry H. TX 26th Cav. Co.B
Thompson, D.J. AL Cav. Barbiere's Bn. Bowie's Co.
Thompson, D.J. AL Cav. Murphy's Bn. Co.D
Thompson, D.J. AL 23rd Inf. Co.A 1st Lt.
Thompson, D.J. AR 1st (Monroe's) Cav. Co.A
Thompson, D.J. GA 42nd Inf. Co.F
Thompson, D.J. GA 48th Inf. Co.E
Thompson, D.J. MO Cav. Schnabel's Bn. Co.F
Thompson, D.J. Trans-MS Conf.Cav. 1st Bn. Co.E
Thompson, D.J. 15th Conf.Cav. Co.K
Thompson, D.K. NC 6th Sr.Res. Co.G
Thompson, D.L. SC 11th Inf. Co.A
Thompson, D.M. MS 6th Inf. Co.F
Thompson, D.N. FL 10th Inf. Co.G
Thompson, Dock R.M. TX 10th Inf. Music.
Thompson, Doctor F. NC Vol. Lawrence's Co.
Thompson, Doctor F. 7th Conf.Cav. 1st Co.I, Co.H Cpl.
Thompson, Doctor J.H. NC 2nd Arty. (36th St.Troops) Co.A
Thompson, Doctor P. TX 18th Cav. Co.D
Thompson, Dorsey MD 1st Cav. Co.A
Thompson, Dowin AL 45th Inf. Co.F
Thompson, D.R. AL 15th Inf.
Thompson, D.R. GA 8th Cav. Old Co.I
Thompson, D.R. GA Lt.Arty. King's Btty.
Thompson, D.R. LA 6th Inf. Co.A
Thompson, D.R. MO 3rd Inf. Co.K
Thompson, D. Robert GA Lt.Arty. 14th Bn. Co.B,F
Thompson, D. Robert GA Lt.Arty. Anderson's Btty.
Thompson, Drury AL 8th Inf. Co.G 2nd Lt.
Thompson, Drury MS 34th Inf. Co.H
Thompson, Drury NC 12th Inf. Co.K
Thompson, D.S. KY 6th Mtd.Inf. Co.A
Thompson, D.S. MS 5th Cav. Co.E Cpl.
Thompson, D.S. MS 18th Cav. Co.I Cpl.
Thompson, D.S. MS 1st (King's) Inf. (St.Troops) Co.H Cpl.
Thompson, D.S. MS 2nd (Davidson's) Inf. Co.K
Thompson, D.S. VA Cav. Hounshell's Bn. Gwinn's Co.
Thompson, D.S. 1st Conf.Eng.Troops
Thompson, D.S.P. AL 11th Inf. Co.D
Thompson, D.T. AL 15th Bn.Part.Rangers Co.C
Thompson, D.T. AL 56th Part.Rangers Co.C
Thompson, D.T. MS 10th Cav. Co.F
Thompson, D.T. VA 1st Arty. 3rd Co.C
Thompson, Dudly MS 5th Inf. (St.Troops) Co.G
Thompson, Duncan A. NC 35th Inf. Co.C
Thompson, D.V. SC 25th Inf. Co.F
Thompson, D.W. AL 5th Inf. New Co.I
Thompson, D.W. GA 13th Cav. Co.K
Thompson, D.W. KY 12th Cav. Co.H
Thompson, D.W. LA 16th Inf. Co.F Capt.
Thompson, D.W. MS 27th Inf. Co.A
Thompson, D.W. SC 4th Cav. Co.I
Thompson, D.W. TN 6th Inf. Co.I
Thompson, D.W. TN 27th Inf. Co.G Cpl.
Thompson, D.W. 1st Conf.Cav. 2nd Co.B
Thompson, E. AL Cav.
Thompson, E. AL 26th (O'Neal's) Inf. Co.B
Thompson, E. GA Lt.Arty. Havis' Btty.
Thompson, E. GA 2nd Inf.
Thompson, E. GA 10th Inf. Co.I
Thompson, E. GA 27th Inf. Co.E
Thompson, E. LA 6th Cav. Co.I
Thompson, E. LA 22nd Inf.
Thompson, E. MS 2nd Cav. Co.I
Thompson, E. MS 5th Cav. Co.I
Thompson, E. MS Condrey's Co. (Bull Mtn. Invinc.)
Thompson, E. MO 6th Cav. Co.K
Thompson, E. SC 5th Cav. Co.E
Thompson, E. VA Cav. 37th Bn. Co.F Sgt.
Thompson, E. VA Cav. Mosby's Regt. (Part.Rangers) Co.H Lt.
Thompson, E. VA Lt.Arty. Grandy's Co.
Thompson, E.A. AL 53rd (Part.Rangers) Co.D
Thompson, E.A. AR 9th Inf. New Co.B
Thompson, E.A. AR 18th Inf. Co.A
Thompson, E.A. MS 2nd St.Cav. Co.H 1st Sgt.
Thompson, E.A. TN 4th (McLemore's) Cav. Co.C
Thompson, E.A. TN 3rd (Clack's) Inf. Co.B 1st Lt.
Thompson, E.B. AL 4th (Russell's) Cav. Co.K
Thompson, E.B. AL 27th Inf. Co.C Capt.
Thompson, E.B. GA 13th Inf. Co.D 2nd Lt.
Thompson, E.B. MS Cav. 24th Bn. Co.F,B Cpl.
Thompson, E.B. TN Lt.Arty. Sparkman's Co. Lt.
Thompson, E.B. TN Arty.Corps Co.13 Lt.
Thompson, E.B. Conf.Cav. Wood's Regt. 1st Co.A
Thompson, E.C. GA Cav. 29th Bn. Co.H
Thompson, E.C. KY 7th Cav. Co.G
Thompson, E.C. KY Horse Arty. Byrne's Co.
Thompson, E.C. NC Mallett's Bn. Co.E
Thompson, Ed AL Inf. 2nd Regt. Co.K
Thompson, Ed MS 28th Cav. Co.I
Thompson, Ed MS 1st Lt.Arty. Co.C
Thompson, E.D. TN 8th (Smith's) Cav. Co.A
Thompson, Edgar TX 9th (Nichol's) Inf. Co.F 2nd Lt.
Thompson, Edgar Gen. & Staff, Conf.Arty. Surg.
Thompson, Edgar W. TX 24th Cav. Co.H
Thompson, Ed. J. TN 1st Hvy.Arty. 2nd Co.D,B,A Jr.1st Lt.
Thompson, Edmond FL 1st Cav. Co.E
Thompson, Edmond GA 38th Inf. Co.G
Thompson, Edmund FL 10th Inf. Co.B
Thompson, Ed Porter KY 6th Mtd.Inf. Co.F,E AQM

Thompson, Edward AL 9th (Malone's) Cav. Co.B
Thompson, Edward KY 2nd Bn.Mtd.Rifles Co.C
Thompson, Edward LA 1st Hvy.Arty. (Reg.) Co.K
Thompson, Edw. LA Inf. McLean's Co.
Thompson, Edward MD 1st Cav. Co.A
Thompson, Edward MS 4th Inf. Co.A
Thompson, Edward MO 9th Bn.S.S. Co.A
Thompson, Edward NC 2nd Arty. (36th St.Troops) Co.D
Thompson, Edward SC 1st Arty. Co.D,C
Thompson, Edward TX 6th Inf. Co.E 2nd Lt.
Thompson, Edward TX 6th & 15th (Cons.) Vol. Co.E 2nd Lt.
Thompson, Edward VA 59th Inf. 2nd Co.A 1st Sgt.
Thompson, Edward D. NC 3rd Arty. (40th St.Troops) Co.E
Thompson, Edward F. MS Inf. 7th Bn. Co.E
Thompson, Edward F. VA 5th Cav. 2nd Co.F
Thompson, Edward M. MO Cav. 3rd Bn. Co.C
Thompson, Edward P. AL 47th Inf. Co.K
Thompson, Edward P. MS 11th Inf. Co.C
Thompson, Edward T. FL 10th Inf. Co.D Cpl.
Thompson, Edward W. AL 6th Inf. Co.M
Thompson, Edwin B. VA Inf. 5th Bn. Co.B
Thompson, Edwin F. VA Hvy.Arty. 10th Bn. Co.A
Thompson, Edwyn B. VA 53rd Inf. Co.E
Thompson, E.F. AL 32nd Inf. Co.G
Thompson, E.F. TX 10th Cav. Co.F
Thompson, E.F. TX 16th Inf. Co.D
Thompson, E.F. VA Cav. Mosby's Regt. (Part.Rangers) Co.E
Thompson, E.G. TN Inf. 23rd Bn. Co.E
Thompson, Egbert B. GA 10th Inf. Co.D 2nd Lt.
Thompson, Egbert C. KY 3rd Cav. Co.G
Thompson, E.H. AL 50th Inf. Co.I
Thompson, E.H. GA Lt.Arty. Croft's Btty. (Columbus Arty.) Cpl.
Thompson, E.J. GA 32nd Inf. Co.A
Thompson, E.J. MO 1st Inf. Co.C
Thompson, E.J. TN 49th Inf. Co.D
Thompson, E.J. TX 1st Hvy.Arty. Co.B
Thompson, E.J. TX 15th Inf. 2nd Co.F
Thompson, E.J. TX 20th Inf. Co.A
Thompson, E.L. AR 1st (Monroe's) Cav. Co.F
Thompson, E.L. LA 1st Hvy.Arty. (Reg.) Co.D
Thompson, E.L. LA 22nd (Cons.) Inf. Co.G
Thompson, E.L. MS Cav. 3rd Bn.Res. Co.C
Thompson, E.L. MS 1st (King's) Inf. (St.Troops) Co.F
Thompson, E.L. TN 13th (Gore's) Cav. Co.K
Thompson, Elam 1st Choctaw & Chickasaw Mtd.Rifles Co.A
Thompson, Elbert MS 20th Inf. Co.D
Thompson, Elbert C. TX 16th Cav. Co.F
Thompson, Elbert H. MS 11th Inf. Co.E,F
Thompson, Elbridge G. NC 6th Inf. Co.F
Thompson, Elbridge S. NC 44th Inf. Co.G
Thompson, Eli AL 42nd Inf. Co.K
Thompson, Eli GA 9th Inf. Co.I
Thompson, Eli LA 3rd Inf. Co.C
Thompson, Elias AR 2nd Inf. Old Co.C,B
Thompson, Elias GA 29th Inf.
Thompson, Elias LA 5th Inf. Co.D
Thompson, Elias VA 11th Bn.Res. Co.C
Thompson, Elias B. AL 11th Inf. Co.K Sgt.
Thompson, Elias W. MO Cav. Hobbs' Co.
Thompson, Elihu GA Lt.Arty. 14th Bn. Co.B,F
Thompson, Elihu GA Lt.Arty. Anderson's Btty.
Thompson, Elihu LA 15th Inf. Co.G
Thompson, Elihu NC 54th Inf. Co.H
Thompson, Elihu S. GA 14th Inf. Co.G
Thompson, Elija C. AR 33rd Inf. Co.H
Thompson, Elijah GA 3rd Cav. Co.G
Thompson, Elijah GA 1st Reg. Co.H
Thompson, Elijah GA 55th Inf. Co.E
Thompson, Elijah LA 28th (Gray's) Inf. Co.G
Thompson, Elijah MS Inf. (Choctaw Silver Greys) Drane's Co. Sgt.
Thompson, Elijah NC 2nd Arty. (36th St.Troops) Co.E
Thompson, Elijah NC 20th Inf. Co.C
Thompson, Elijah NC 64th Inf. Co.E Sgt.
Thompson, Elijah SC 2nd Bn.S.S. Co.A
Thompson, Elijah SC 13th Inf. Co.I
Thompson, Elijah SC 24th Inf. Co.E
Thompson, Elijah TN 33rd Inf. Co.K
Thompson, Elijah TX 27th Cav. Co.D
Thompson, Elijah E. MO 5th Inf. Co.C
Thompson, Elijah L. AL 28th Inf. Co.C
Thompson, Elijah M. LA 27th Inf. Co.H
Thompson, Elijah S. MS 26th Inf. Co.I
Thompson, Elijah S. NC 47th Inf. Co.E
Thompson, Elijah T. NC 28th Inf. Co.A 1st Lt.
Thompson, Elijah W. TX 2nd Inf. Co.E
Thompson, Elis SC 9th Res. Co.C 3rd Lt.
Thompson, Elisha MS 1st (King's) Inf. (St.Troops) Co.H
Thompson, Elisha MS 2nd (Quinn's St.Troops) Inf. Co.G
Thompson, Elisha NC Walker's Bn. Thomas' Legion Co.A Fifer
Thompson, Elisha TN 39th Mtd.Inf. Co.F
Thompson, Elisha VA 6th Bn.Res. Co.B Sgt.
Thompson, Elisha B. MS 24th Inf. Co.K
Thompson, Elisha G. TN Cav. 2nd Bn. (Biffle's) Co.B 2nd Lt.
Thompson, Elisha G. VA 45th Inf. Co.L
Thompson, Elliott D. VA 17th Inf. Co.B
Thompson, Ellis SC 5th St.Troops Co.I
Thompson, E.M. AL 60th Inf. Co.B Cpl.
Thompson, E.M. FL 11th Inf.
Thompson, E.M. GA 16th Inf. Co.G QMSgt.
Thompson, E.M. LA 22nd (Cons.) Inf. Co.F Sgt.
Thompson, E.M. Gen. & Staff Asst.Surg.
Thompson, Emanuel C. NC 1st Inf. (6 mo. '61) Co.H
Thompson, Emanuel C. NC 33rd Inf. Co.G Cpl.
Thompson, E. Marion LA 27th Inf. Co.H Sgt.
Thompson, Emmett B. TN 3rd (Forrest's) Cav. 1st Co.F
Thompson, Emory AR 4th Inf. Co.C
Thompson, Emsley NC 46th Inf. Co.G
Thompson, Ennis AR 3rd Inf. Co.F
Thompson, Ennis S. VA 11th Inf. Co.F Sgt.
Thompson, Enoch AL 57th Inf. Co.B
Thompson, Enoch AR 4th Inf. Co.I
Thompson, Enoch MO 8th Cav. Co.E,F Sgt.
Thompson, Enoch MO Inf. 4th Regt.St.Guard Co.F
Thompson, Enoch F. MS 3rd Inf. (St.Troops) Co.B
Thompson, Eph KY 8th Cav. Co.A
Thompson, Ephraim GA 63rd Inf. Co.A Cpl.
Thompson, Ephraim W. VA 45th Inf. Co.F
Thompson, Ephraim W. VA 45th Inf. Co.F,K
Thompson, Ephram W. FL 7th Inf. Co.E
Thompson, E. Porter Gen. & Staff Capt.,AQM
Thompson, E.R. NC 28th Inf. Co.K
Thompson, Erasmus L. SC 5th Inf. 1st Co.A
Thompson, Erasmus M. FL 1st Cav. Co.K
Thompson, E.S. AL 2nd Cav. Co.D
Thompson, E.S. GA Cav. 6th Bn. (St.Guards) Co.D
Thompson, E.S. GA Cav. 19th Bn. Co.A
Thompson, E.S. GA Lt.Arty. (Jackson Arty.) Massenburg's Btty.
Thompson, E.S. TX 2nd Cav. Co.D
Thompson, E.S. TX Waul's Legion Co.B
Thompson, E.S. 10th Conf.Cav. Co.F
Thompson, E.T. AL 31st Inf. Co.D Capt.
Thompson, E.T. GA 10th Cav. Co.E
Thompson, E.T. 7th Conf.Cav. Co.E
Thompson, Ethbert C. KY 2nd Cav.
Thompson, Eugene VA Hvy.Arty. 18th Bn. Co.C
Thompson, Eugene A. GA 10th Inf. Co.C Cpl.
Thompson, Eugene L. MO 3rd Cav. Co.G
Thompson, Eugene M. MS Cav. Jeff Davis Legion Co.B
Thompson, Eugene W. NC 43rd Inf. Chap.
Thompson, Eugene W. Gen. & Staff Chap.
Thompson, E.W. AL 5th Inf. Co.K Cpl.
Thompson, E.W. GA Lt.Arty. 12th Bn. 1st Co.A
Thompson, E.W. GA 5th Inf. (St.Guards) Co.E
Thompson, E.W. KY 6th Mtd.Inf. Co.F,E
Thompson, E.W. MS 35th Inf. Co.D Capt.
Thompson, E.W. NC 1st Inf.
Thompson, E.W. TX 9th (Nichols') Inf. Co.F 2nd Lt.
Thompson, Ewing K. MS 30th Inf. Co.H
Thompson, E.Y. NC 1st Inf. Co.C
Thompson, E.Y.H. LA Mil. Claiborne Regt. Co.A
Thompson, E.Y.H. MS 3rd Inf. Co.D
Thompson, E.Z. AL 17th Inf. Co.D
Thompson, Ezekiel A. GA 45th Inf. Co.E
Thompson, Ezekiel H. GA 14th Inf. Co.H
Thompson, F. AL Arty. 1st Bn. Co.F
Thompson, F. AL Inf. 2nd Regt. Co.K
Thompson, F. AR 10th Inf. Co.D Sgt.
Thompson, F. GA Lt.Arty. 14th Bn. Sgt.
Thompson, F. KY 7th Cav. Co.A
Thompson, F. MS 18th Cav. Co.F
Thompson, F. NC 1st Inf. Co.C
Thompson, F. NC 1st Jr.Res. Co.C
Thompson, F. SC 16th & 24th (Cons.) Inf. Co.B
Thompson, F. 1st Conf.Cav. 2nd Co.B
Thompson, F. Gen. & Staff Lt.,AACS
Thompson, F.A. AL Cp. of Instr. Talladega
Thompson, F.A. AR Inf. Cocke's Regt. Co.C Sgt.
Thompson, F.A. KY 9th Mtd.Inf. Co.E
Thompson, F.A. TN Inf. 23rd Bn. Co.A
Thompson, Falcon NC 1st Jr.Res. Co.A

Thompson, Farley AL 4th Cav. Co.C
Thompson, F.B. SC 6th Res. Co.E Cpl.
Thompson, F.C. MO 3rd Inf. Co.K
Thompson, F.C. TN 45th Inf. Co.I
Thompson, F.D. VA Cav. Mosby's Regt. (Part.Rangers) Co.B
Thompson, Fendal VA 14th Inf. Co.F
Thompson, Ferdinand C. MO 5th Inf. Co.B
Thompson, F.G. MS 40th Inf. Co.A
Thompson, F.G. TN 5th Inf. Co.A
Thompson, F.H. GA Inf. 1st Bn. (St.Guards) Co.D
Thompson, F.H. LA 2nd Res.Corps Co.A
Thompson, F.H. VA Cav. 32nd Bn.
Thompson, F.J. TN 23rd Inf. Co.I
Thompson, F.L. MS 3rd Inf. (A. of 10,000) Co.A 1st Sgt.
Thompson, F.L. MS 36th Inf. Co.D Capt.
Thompson, Flandes AL 22nd Inf. Co.G
Thompson, Flem MS 9th Inf. New Co.K
Thompson, Fleming KY 2nd Bn.Mtd.Rifles Co.D Cpl.
Thompson, Fleming MS 9th Bn.S.S. Co.B Sgt.Maj.
Thompson, Fleming MS 44th Inf. Co.D
Thompson, Fleming SC 16th Inf. Co.H
Thompson, Fleming W. AL 11th Inf. Co.B Sgt.
Thompson, F. Leslie TX 1st Inf. Co.L
Thompson, Fletcher GA 40th Inf. Co.K
Thompson, Fletcher NC 4th Inf. Co.K
Thompson, Fletcher J. VA 24th Inf. Co.B Cpl.
Thompson, Floyd VA 4th Res. Co.F Cpl.
Thompson, F.M. AL 9th Inf. Co.E
Thompson, F.M. AL 22nd Inf. Co.B
Thompson, F.M. AL 34th Inf. Co.B
Thompson, F.M. AL 38th Inf. Co.K
Thompson, F.M. AR 23rd Inf. Co.F
Thompson, F.M. AR Mil. Desha Cty.Bn.
Thompson, F.M. GA 2nd Inf. Co.H
Thompson, F.M. GA 31st Inf.
Thompson, F.M. GA Inf. Allen's Dept.
Thompson, F.M. KY 12th Cav. Co.H
Thompson, F.M. KY Fields' Co. (Part.Rangers) Cpl.
Thompson, F.M. LA Washington Arty.Bn. Co.5
Thompson, F.M. LA Mil. 2nd Regt. 2nd Brig. 1st Div. Co.C
Thompson, F.M. MS 35th Inf. Co.C
Thompson, F.M. MO 6th Cav. Co.D Cpl.
Thompson, F.M. MO 16th Inf. Co.B Cpl.
Thompson, F.M. TN Cav. 16th Bn. (Neal's) Co.A
Thompson, F.M. TN 11th Inf. Co.K
Thompson, F.M. TN 14th Inf. Co.G
Thompson, F.M. TX 16th Cav. Co.F Cpl.
Thompson, F.M. TX 14th Inf. Co.C
Thompson, F.M. TX 17th Inf. Co.A
Thompson, F.M. TX 20th Inf. Co.A Sgt.
Thompson, F.M. VA 11th Bn.Res. Co.F
Thompson, F.M. 8th (Wade's) Conf.Cav. Co.H Cpl.
Thompson, Ford MS 15th Inf. Co.B
Thompson, Foster H. GA 5th Inf. Co.D Lance Sgt.
Thompson, Fowler AL 4th (Russell's) Cav. Co.C Sgt.
Thompson, F.P. AL Mil. 4th Vol. Co.F
Thompson, F.P. AL 19th Inf. Co.C
Thompson, F.P. AL 40th Inf. Co.K
Thompson, F.R. LA Mil.Cav.Squad. (Ind. Rangers Iberville)
Thompson, Francis AR Inf. Hutchinson's Co. (4th Vol.)
Thompson, Francis B. VA Lt.Arty. E.J. Anderson's Co.
Thompson, Francis Baker AL 30th Inf. Co.A
Thompson, Francis M. AL Arty. 1st Bn. Co.E
Thompson, Francis M. AL 37th Inf. Co.D
Thompson, Francis M. MO 3rd Cav. Co.E
Thompson, Francis M. MO 5th Cav. Co.C
Thompson, Francis M. NC Inf. 13th Bn. Co.A
Thompson, Francis M. NC 66th Inf. Co.A
Thompson, Francis M. VA 17th Cav. Co.G Cpl.
Thompson, Francis M. VA 86th Mil. Co.C
Thompson, Francis P. VA 64th Mtd.Inf. 2nd Co.F Sgt.
Thompson, Francis T. VA 22nd Inf. Co.H
Thompson, Francis W. NC 28th Inf. Co.B
Thompson, Frank GA 1st (Fannin's) Res. Co.E
Thompson, Frank LA 28th (Gray's) Inf. Co.G
Thompson, Frank MS 18th Cav. Co.A Cpl.
Thompson, Frank MO Inf. 4th Regt.St.Guard Co.B 3rd Lt.
Thompson, Frank TN 4th Inf.
Thompson, Frank TN 16th Inf. Co.I Comsy.Sgt.
Thompson, Frank TN 19th Inf. Co.D
Thompson, Frank TN 45th Inf. Co.I
Thompson, Frank TX Cav. Baylor's Regt. Co.E
Thompson, Frank VA Cav. 35th Bn. Co.A
Thompson, Franklin AR 15th (N.W.) Inf. Co.D
Thompson, Franklin NC 18th Inf. Co.D
Thompson, Franklin SC 1st Arty. Co.A,D
Thompson, Franklin J. AL 41st Inf. Co.F 2nd Lt.
Thompson, Frank M. AR 19th (Dawson's) Inf. Co.G 2nd Lt.
Thompson, Frank P. VA Horse Arty. Lurty's Co.
Thompson, Frank W. VA 3rd Cav. Co.A
Thompson, Fred LA 2nd Cav. Co.I
Thompson, Fred SC 23rd Inf. Co.D
Thompson, Fred C. VA 36th Inf. Co.A
Thompson, Frederick GA Arty. Maxwell's Reg.Lt.Btty.
Thompson, Frederick GA 1st Reg. Co.D
Thompson, Frederick GA 15th Inf. Co.G Sgt.
Thompson, Frederick NC 18th Inf. Co.E Capt.
Thompson, Frederick VA 20th Inf. Co.A
Thompson, Frederick G. GA 29th Inf. Co.C
Thompson, Frederick M. MO 3rd Inf. Co.D,F
Thompson, F.S. SC 1st (Hagood's) Inf. 2nd Co.G
Thompson, F.W. MS 18th Cav. Co.A
Thompson, F.W. SC 7th Inf. Co.K
Thompson, F.W. TN 41st Inf. Co.A
Thompson, F.W. VA 14th Inf. Co.F
Thompson, G. AL 9th (Malone's) Cav. Co.H
Thompson, G. AL 6th Inf. Co.C
Thompson, G. LA Mil. 4th Regt. 1st Brig. 1st Div. Co.E
Thompson, G. LA 28th (Gray's) Inf. Co.A
Thompson, G. MS 38th Cav. Co.G
Thompson, G. MO 11th Inf. Co.G
Thompson, G. TN 38th Inf. Co.E
Thompson, G. VA 34th Inf. Co.B
Thompson, G.A. AL 3rd Inf. Co.B
Thompson, G.A. AL 41st Inf. Co.F Cpl.
Thompson, G.A. GA 8th Cav. Co.K
Thompson, G.A. GA 62nd Cav. Co.K
Thompson, G.A. TN Cav. Allison's Squad. Co.C
Thompson, Gabriel T. VA 46th Inf. 2nd Co.K
Thompson, Gabriel T. VA 57th Inf. Co.E
Thompson, Gaines GA 39th Inf. Co.H
Thompson, Gains GA 65th Inf. Co.D
Thompson, Gardner G. VA Lt.Arty. Cayce's Co. Cpl.
Thompson, Garland 1st Conf.Eng.Troops Co.F
Thompson, Garland N. VA 4th Cav. Co.G Sgt.
Thompson, Garret NC 35th Inf. Co.C
Thompson, Gaston NC 46th Inf. Co.H
Thompson, Gaston 4th Conf.Inf. Co.F
Thompson, Gaston Gen. & Staff AASurg.
Thompson, Gaston M. MS Cav. Jeff Davis Legion Co.B
Thompson, Gaston M. MS 11th Inf. Co.C
Thompson, G.B. MO Cav. Schnabel's Bn. Co.A Capt.
Thompson, G.B. MO 10th Inf. Co.E
Thompson, G.B. TX 1st Inf. Co.A 2nd Lt.
Thompson, G.C. NC Mallett's Bn. (Cp.Guard) Co.A
Thompson, G.E. MS 5th Cav. Co.D 2nd Lt.
Thompson, G.E. MS 28th Cav. Co.F
Thompson, George AL 23rd Bn.S.S. Co.G
Thompson, George AL 43rd Inf. Co.G
Thompson, George AL 48th Inf. Co.F
Thompson, George AL 1st Bn. Hilliard's Legion Vol. Co.G
Thompson, George AR Cav. Gordon's Regt. Co.C
Thompson, George AR 11th & 17th Cons.Inf. Co.I
Thompson, George AR 17th (Griffith's) Inf. Co.F
Thompson, George FL 3rd Inf. Co.D
Thompson, George GA 53rd Inf. Co.F
Thompson, George GA Inf. (Loc.Def.) Whiteside's Nav.Bn. Co.A
Thompson, George KY 1st Bn.Mtd.Rifles Co.E
Thompson, George LA 1st Hvy.Arty. (Reg.) Co.A
Thompson, George LA Inf. 4th Bn. Co.B
Thompson, George LA 7th Inf. Co.E
Thompson, George LA Mil. Chalmette Regt. Co.B
Thompson, George MD Cav. 2nd Bn. Co.F
Thompson, George MS 6th Cav. Co.K
Thompson, George MS 12th Inf. Co.G
Thompson, George MO 15th Cav. Co.N
Thompson, George NC 20th Inf. Co.H
Thompson, George NC 52nd Inf. Co.E
Thompson, George NC 53rd Inf. Co.F
Thompson, George NC 57th Inf. Co.K
Thompson, George SC 2nd Arty. Co.I
Thompson, George SC 1st (Butler's) Inf. Co.C
Thompson, George SC 3rd Res. Co.D
Thompson, George SC 16th Inf. Co.H
Thompson, George TN 4th Inf. Co.H
Thompson, George TN 44th Inf. Co.I
Thompson, George TN 44th (Cons.) Inf. Co.A
Thompson, George TX 5th Cav. Co.B

Thompson, George TX 15th Cav. Co.H
Thompson, George TX 18th Cav. Co.F
Thompson, George TX Cav. Baylor's Regt. Co.A
Thompson, George TX Cav. Madison's Regt. Co.E
Thompson, George TX 22nd Inf. Co.F
Thompson, George VA 11th Cav. Co.K
Thompson, George VA 17th Cav. Co.B
Thompson, George VA Cav. 32nd Bn. Co.A
Thompson, George VA Lt.Arty. Griffin's Co.
Thompson, George VA Arty. Kevill's Co.
Thompson, George VA 9th Inf. 1st Co.A
Thompson, George VA 25th Inf. 2nd Co.B
Thompson, George, 1st VA 41st Inf. 1st Co.E
Thompson, George, 2nd VA 41st Inf. 1st Co.E
Thompson, George VA 51st Mil. Co.C
Thompson, George Conf.Cav. Clarkson's Bn. Ind.Rangers Co.E
Thompson, George 4th Conf.Inf. Co.B
Thompson, George A. NC 5th Cav. (63rd St.Troops) Co.A
Thompson, George A. NC 1st Inf. (6 mo. '61) Co.H
Thompson, George A. NC 6th Inf. Co.F
Thompson, George A. NC 7th Inf. Co.K
Thompson, George A. TN 6th (Wheeler's) Cav. Co.E
Thompson, George A. TN 1st Lt.Arty. Co.B
Thompson, George A. TN 7th Inf. Co.H Cpl.
Thompson, George B. TX 18th Cav. Co.F
Thompson, George B. VA 86th Mil. Co.E,C 1st Sgt.
Thompson, George C. MO 4th Cav. Co.E
Thompson, George C. VA 30th Inf. Co.K
Thompson, George E. VA 9th Inf. Co.K Drum Maj.
Thompson, George F. AR 2nd Cav. Co.C
Thompson, George F. GA Lt.Arty. 14th Bn. Co.A
Thompson, George F. GA Lt.Arty. Havis' Btty.
Thompson, George F. MO Lt.Arty. 4th (Harris') Field Btty.
Thompson, Geo. F. MO St.Guard
Thompson, George F.B. GA 5th Inf. Co.D
Thompson, George G. AL 54th Inf. Co.I
Thompson, George G. VA 13th Inf. 1st Co.E
Thompson, George H. GA 1st (Ramsey's) Inf. Lt.Col.
Thompson, George H. AR 3rd Cav. Co.G
Thompson, George H. KY 4th Mtd.Inf. Co.C
Thompson, George H. KY Recruiting Off. Owen Cty. 2nd Lt.
Thompson, George H. MO 1st & 4th Cons.Inf. Co.H 1st Sgt.
Thompson, George H. VA Arty. Bryan's Co.
Thompson, George H. VA 38th Inf. Co.B
Thompson, George J. TX 18th Cav. Co.H
Thompson, George L. GA Lt.Arty. Croft's Btty. (Columbus Arty.)
Thompson, George M. GA 47th Inf. Co.D Jr.2nd Lt.
Thompson, George M. SC 4th Inf. Co.I
Thompson, George M. TX 18th Cav. Co.F
Thompson, George M. VA 7th Inf. Co.H Cpl.
Thompson, George N. TX 31st Cav. Co.F
Thompson, George P. AL 17th Inf. Co.I
Thompson, George P. GA 48th Inf. Co.I
Thompson, George P. VA 8th Cav. Co.H Sgt.
Thompson, George R. NC 3rd Arty. (40th St.Troops) Co.K
Thompson, George S. NC 28th Inf. QM
Thompson, Geo. S. Gen. & Staff Maj.,QM
Thompson, George T. SC 16th Inf. Co.E
Thompson, George T. VA 31st Inf. Co.H Capt.
Thompson, George V. MO Arty. Lowe's Co.
Thompson, George W. AL 8th Inf. Co.K
Thompson, George W. AL 13th Inf. Co.E
Thompson, George W. AL 30th Inf. Co.F
Thompson, George W. AL 36th Inf. Co.G
Thompson, George W. AR 6th Inf. Co.K Cpl.
Thompson, George W. AR 11th Inf. Co.F 3rd Lt.
Thompson, George W. AR 11th & 17th Cons. Inf. Co.F 3rd Lt.
Thompson, George W. AR 14th (McCarver's) Inf. Co.F
Thompson, George W. AR 37th Inf. Co.K 3rd Lt.
Thompson, George W. GA 3rd Inf. Co.I
Thompson, George W. GA Inf. 8th Bn. Co.B
Thompson, George W. GA 20th Inf. Co.F Cpl.
Thompson, George W. GA 39th Inf. Co.F
Thompson, George W. GA 46th Inf. Co.D
Thompson, George W. GA 64th Inf. Co.C Sgt.
Thompson, George W. GA Cobb's Legion Co.D
Thompson, George W. LA 12th Inf. Co.H
Thompson, George W. MS 1st Lt.Arty. Co.I
Thompson, George W. MS 16th Inf. Co.I,K
Thompson, George W. MO 2nd Cav. Co.K
Thompson, George W. MO 3rd Cav. Co.I
Thompson, George W. MO 15th Cav. Co.A
Thompson, George W. NC Lt.Arty. 3rd Bn. Co.A
Thompson, George W. NC 2nd Bn.Loc.Def. Troops Co.F
Thompson, George W. NC 8th Sr.Res. Gardner's Co.
Thompson, George W. NC 28th Inf. Co.A
Thompson, George W. NC 31st Inf. Co.G,A 2nd Lt.
Thompson, George W. NC 34th Inf. Co.D
Thompson, George W. NC 44th Inf. Co.G
Thompson, George W. NC 64th Inf. Co.M
Thompson, George W., Jr. NC 64th Inf. Co.M
Thompson, Geo. W. NC Inf. 68th Regt. Co.K 1st Lt.
Thompson, George W. SC 5th Inf. 1st Co.B 2nd Lt.
Thompson, George W. TN 4th (McLemore's) Cav. Co.K
Thompson, George W., Jr. TN Cav. 16th Bn. (Neal's) Co.F
Thompson, George W. TN 2nd (Robison's) Inf. Co.K
Thompson, George W. TN 33rd Inf. Co.D Ch.Music.
Thompson, George W. TN 41st Inf. Co.G Sgt.
Thompson, George W. TX 2nd Cav. Co.G
Thompson, George W. TX 10th Cav. Co.I
Thompson, George W. TX 18th Cav. Witt's Co.
Thompson, George W. TX Cav. Wells' Bn. Co.B 1st Sgt.
Thompson, George W. TX 16th Inf. Co.G
Thompson, George W. TX Inf. 25th Regt.
Thompson, George W. VA 4th Cav. Co.G Sgt.
Thompson, George W. VA 6th Cav. Co.A,D
Thompson, George W. VA 6th Cav. Co.G
Thompson, George W. VA 20th Cav. Co.I
Thompson, George W. VA Cav. 37th Bn. Co.F 1st Lt.
Thompson, George W. VA Cav. Mosby's Regt. (Part.Rangers) Co.B
Thompson, George W. VA 2nd Arty. Co.E
Thompson, George W. VA 14th Inf. Co.F
Thompson, George W. VA 15th Inf. Co.C Cpl.
Thompson, George W. VA 18th Inf. Co.G
Thompson, George W. VA 19th Inf. Co.I
Thompson, George W. VA Inf. 21st Bn. 2nd Co.C 1st Lt.
Thompson, George W. VA Inf. 22nd Bn. Co.E
Thompson, George W. VA Inf. 23rd Bn. Co.C Cpl.
Thompson, George W. VA 31st Inf. Co.H Sgt.
Thompson, George W. VA 45th Inf. Co.L
Thompson, George W. VA 57th Inf. Co.A
Thompson, George W. VA 59th Inf. 3rd Co.F
Thompson, George W. VA 136th Mil. Co.E
Thompson, George W. VA Res.Forces Clark's Co.
Thompson, Geo. W. Gen. & Staff Capt.,AQM
Thompson, George Washing MO 10th Inf. Co.D
Thompson, George W.H. AR 1st (Colquitt's) Inf. Co.C
Thompson, George Winlon NC 44th Inf. Co.F
Thompson, G.F. AL 47th Inf. Co.K
Thompson, G.F. GA Lt.Arty. Howell's Co.
Thompson, G.F. KY 5th Cav. Co.A
Thompson, G.F. MS 38th Cav. Co.G
Thompson, G.F. TN 21st Inf. Co.D
Thompson, G.F.M. GA 38th Inf. Co.A
Thompson, G.G. GA 4th Cav. (St.Guards) Dorsey's Co. 1st Lt.
Thompson, G.H. GA Cav. Alexander's Co.
Thompson, G.H. GA 60th Inf. Co.E
Thompson, G.H. GA Inf. (Milledgeville Guards) Caraker's Co.
Thompson, G.H. MS 2nd Cav. Co.A
Thompson, G.H. MO 4th Inf. Co.K 1st Sgt.
Thompson, G.H. TN 3rd (Forrest's) Cav. Co.A
Thompson, G.H. TX 14th Cav. Co.H Sgt.
Thompson, Gibson VA 30th Bn.S.S. Co.A
Thompson, Gideon AR 14th (Powers') Inf. Co.A 2nd Lt.
Thompson, Gideon MO Cav. Schnabel's Bn. Co.F Jr.2nd Lt.
Thompson, Gideon A. AL 3rd Res. Co.B
Thompson, Gideon N. AL Cav. 5th Bn. Hilliard's Legion Co.D
Thompson, Gideon W. MO St.Guard
Thompson, Gilbert NC 35th Inf. Co.C
Thompson, Gilbert VA Cav. Mosby's Regt. (Part.Rangers) Co.G
Thompson, Gilbert VA 17th Inf. Co.B
Thompson, Gilbert T. GA 40th Inf. Co.I
Thompson, Giles W. NC 12th Inf. Co.D
Thompson, Giles W. NC 51st Inf. Co.E 1st Lt.
Thompson, G.J. AL Cav. Falkner's Co.
Thompson, G.J. 8th (Wade's) Conf.Cav. Co.B
Thompson, G.L. MD 1st Cav. Co.A
Thompson, G.M. AL Cav. Forrest's Regt.

Thompson, G.M. MS 38th Cav. Co.D
Thompson, G.M. MS 6th Inf. Co.F
Thompson, G.M. SC Palmetto S.S. Co.I Sgt.
Thompson, G.M. TN 22nd (Barteau's) Cav. Co.A
Thompson, G.M. TN Cav. Newsom's Regt. Hosp.Stew.
Thompson, G.M. TX 4th Cav. Co.I Sgt.
Thompson, G.M. Gen. & Staff Chap.
Thompson, G.N. NC Inf. 2nd Bn. Co.F
Thompson, G.N. 10th Conf.Cav. Co.D
Thompson, Gordon VA 60th Inf. 2nd Co.H Sgt.
Thompson, Gordon C. VA 45th Inf. Co.K
Thompson, Gould B. MO Cav. 3rd Bn. Co.E
Thompson, Govan NC 64th Inf. Co.E
Thompson, G.P. AL 17th Inf. Co.F
Thompson, G.P. AR Inf. Hardy's Regt. Torbett's Co.
Thompson, G.P. TN 4th (McLemore's) Cav. Co.C
Thompson, G.R. GA 27th Inf. Co.H
Thompson, G.R. GA 40th Inf. Co.H
Thompson, G.R. KY 2nd (Woodward's) Cav. Co.D
Thompson, G.R. KY 3rd Mtd.Inf. Co.I
Thompson, G.R. TN 84th Inf. Co.G
Thompson, Green VA 36th Inf. 2nd Co.K
Thompson, Green B. AR Cav. Harrell's Bn. Co.C
Thompson, Green B. GA 2nd Cav. Co.G Sgt.
Thompson, Green F. GA 20th Inf. Co.B
Thompson, Green H. AL 6th Inf. Co.G Capt.
Thompson, Greenville VA 24th Inf. Co.C
Thompson, Green W. 1st Choctaw Mtd.Rifles Co.E Capt.
Thompson, G.R.H. TN 18th Inf. Co.I
Thompson, Grow LA 28th (Gray's) Inf. Co.G
Thompson, G.T. NC 56th Inf. Co.F
Thompson, G.T. SC 16th & 24th (Cons.) Inf. Co.F
Thompson, Gus KY 9th Mtd.Inf. Co.C
Thompson, G.V. MO Lt.Arty. 3rd Btty.
Thompson, G.W. AL 9th (Malone's) Cav. Co.B Sgt.
Thompson, G.W. AL Poss.Cav.
Thompson, G.W. AL 8th Inf.
Thompson, G.W. AL 14th Inf. Co.D
Thompson, G.W. AL 14th Inf. Co.E
Thompson, G.W. AL 35th Inf. Co.A
Thompson, G.W. AL 42nd Inf. Co.A
Thompson, G.W. AR 1st (Dobbin's) Cav. Co.C
Thompson, G.W. AR 2nd Cav. 1st Co.A
Thompson, G.W. AR 3rd Cav. 3rd Co.E
Thompson, G.W. AR 8th Cav. Co.D Black.
Thompson, G.W. AR 2nd Inf. Co.D
Thompson, G.W. AR 2nd Inf. Old Co.E
Thompson, G.W. AR 21st Inf. Co.B
Thompson, G.W. GA Lt.Arty. 12th Bn. 3rd Co.C
Thompson, G.W. KY 3rd Mtd.Inf. Co.L 2nd Lt.
Thompson, G.W. LA Inf. 7th Bn. Co.A
Thompson, G.W. LA 25th Inf. Co.F
Thompson, G.W. MS 1st Cav.Res. Co.E 2nd Lt.
Thompson, G.W. MS 2nd St.Cav. 2nd Co.C
Thompson, G.W. MS 4th Cav. Co.H
Thompson, G.W. MS 5th Cav. Co.I
Thompson, G.W. MS 7th Cav. 2nd Co.G
Thompson, G.W. MS 38th Cav. Co.D
Thompson, G.W. MS 8th Inf. Co.C
Thompson, G.W. MS 11th Inf. Co.H
Thompson, G.W. MO Cav. 2nd Regt.St.Guard Co.E
Thompson, G.W. MO 6th Cav. Col.
Thompson, G.W. MO 10th Cav. Co.A
Thompson, G.W. MO Cav. Schnabel's Bn. Co.E
Thompson, G.W. MO Lt.Arty. Barret's Co. Artif.
Thompson, G.W. NC 2nd Cav. (19th St.Troops) Co.B
Thompson, G.W. NC 3rd Jr.Res.
Thompson, G.W. NC Mallett's Bn. Co.F
Thompson, G.W. SC Lt.Arty. Gaillard's Co. (Santee Lt.Arty.) QMSgt.
Thompson, G.W. SC 5th Inf. 2nd Co.G 2nd Lt.
Thompson, G.W. SC Manigault's Bn.Vol. Co.B Sgt.
Thompson, G.W. TN 1st (Carter's) Cav. Co.C
Thompson, G.W. TN 14th (Neely's) Cav. Co.A
Thompson, G.W. TN Cav. Nixon's Regt. Co.G
Thompson, G.W. TN 12th Inf. Co.E Sgt.
Thompson, G.W. TN 42nd Inf. Co.D
Thompson, G.W. TX 26th Cav. Co.I Sgt.
Thompson, G.W. TX Cav. Wells' Regt. Co.B 2nd Lt.
Thompson, G.W. TX 9th (Young's) Inf. Co.B 1st Lt.
Thompson, G.W. TX 9th (Young's) Inf. Co.K Sgt.
Thompson, G.W. TX 12th Inf. Co.E
Thompson, G.W. TX 15th Inf. Co.A
Thompson, G.W. TX 19th Inf. Co.E 1st Sgt.
Thompson, G.W. VA 4th Cav. Co.C
Thompson, G.W. Conf.Cav. Wood's Regt. Co.K
Thompson, G.W. 4th Conf.Inf. Co.K
Thompson, G. William AL 5th Cav. Co.A
Thompson, H. AL 1st Bn.Cadets Co.B
Thompson, H. AL 12th Inf. Co.G
Thompson, H. AL Chas. A. Herts' Co.
Thompson, H. AL Conscr.
Thompson, H. AR 1st (Dobbin's) Cav. Co.F
Thompson, H. GA 7th Cav. Co.E
Thompson, H. GA Cav. 21st Bn. Co.B
Thompson, H. GA Inf. 27th Bn. Co.F
Thompson, H. KY 3rd Mtd.Inf. Co.G
Thompson, H. LA 6th Cav. Co.K
Thompson, H. LA Lt.Arty. 2nd Field Btty. QMSgt.
Thompson, H. LA 15th Inf. Co.B
Thompson, H. NC 3rd Jr.Res. Co.B
Thompson, H. SC 2nd Res.
Thompson, H. SC 23rd Inf. Co.G
Thompson, H. TN 16th (Logwood's) Cav. Co.E
Thompson, H. TN 84th Inf. Co.G Sgt.
Thompson, H. TX 24th & 25th Cav. (Cons.) Co.G
Thompson, H. VA 2nd Cav. Co.G
Thompson, H. VA 21st Cav. 2nd Co.D
Thompson, H. VA Cav. Swann's Bn. Carpenter's Co.
Thompson, H. VA Hvy.Arty. 19th Bn. Co.D
Thompson, H. VA Burks' Regt.Loc.Def. Price's Co.
Thompson, H. VA Mil. Scott Cty.
Thompson, H. Conf.Reg.Inf. Brooks' Bn. Co.A
Thompson, H.A. AL 15th Inf. Co.I Sgt.
Thompson, H.A. GA 23rd Inf. Co.G
Thompson, H.A. LA 18th Inf. Co.F
Thompson, H.A. LA Inf.Crescent Regt. Co.E N.C.S. Ord.Sgt.
Thompson, H.A. LA Inf.Cons.Crescent Regt. Ord.Sgt.
Thompson, H.A. SC 14th Inf. Co.E
Thompson, H.A. TN 5th Inf. 1st Co.H
Thompson, H.A. TN 42nd Inf. Co.C
Thompson, H.A. Gen. & Staff Lt.,Ord.Off.
Thompson, Haaley TX 27th Cav. Co.A
Thompson, Hal. GA 51st Inf. Co.K
Thompson, Hamilton Trans-MS Conf.Cav. 1st Bn. Co.D
Thompson, Hamilton William NC Walker's Bn. Thomas' Legion Co.C
Thompson, Hampton TN 34th Inf. Co.F
Thompson, Hanes W. NC 4th Inf. Co.D,E
Thompson, Hardee C. GA 47th Inf. Co.D
Thompson, Hardy MO 3rd Inf. Co.A
Thompson, Harris GA 40th Inf. Co.F
Thompson, Harris NC 6th Sr.Res. Co.A
Thompson, Harris SC 16th & 24th (Cons.) Inf. Co.F
Thompson, Harris SC Inf. Hampton Legion Co.E
Thompson, Harrison TX 21st Cav. Co.I
Thompson, Harrison VA 30th Bn.S.S. Co.A
Thompson, Harrison 1st Choctaw Mtd.Rifles Co.G Cpl.
Thompson, Harrison P. VA Lt.Arty. Lowry's Co.
Thompson, Harvey VA 37th Inf. Co.D
Thompson, Harvey G. VA 36th Inf. 2nd Co.G Cpl.
Thompson, Harvy A. TN 59th Mtd.Inf. Co.G
Thompson, Hawkins VA 37th Inf. Co.I
Thompson, Hays F. NC 2nd Inf. Co.H
Thompson, Haywood GA Cav. 22nd Bn. (St.Guards) Co.C
Thompson, H.B. AL 51st (Part.Rangers) Co.B Capt.
Thompson, H.B. AL 14th Inf. Co.A
Thompson, H.B. GA 32nd Inf. Co.A
Thompson, H.B. MS 22nd Inf. Co.A
Thompson, H.B. VA Lt.Arty. Hardwicke's Co.
Thompson, H.C. AL 11th Cav. Co.F
Thompson, H.C. AL Pris.Guard Freeman's Co.
Thompson, H.C. AR 25th Inf. Co.C
Thompson, H.C. GA 1st Mil. Co.G
Thompson, H.C. LA Inf.Crescent Regt. Co.H
Thompson, H.C. TN 20th (Russell's) Cav. Co.A
Thompson, H.C. TN 21st (Wilson's) Cav. Co.D
Thompson, H.C. TX 12th Cav. Co.F
Thompson, H.C. TX 23rd Cav. Co.C
Thompson, H.C. TX 2nd Inf. Co.A
Thompson, H.D. AL 36th Inf. Co.G
Thompson, H.D. MO 1st & 4th Cons.Inf. Co.F 2nd Lt.
Thompson, H.E. LA 20th Inf. New Co.E
Thompson, H.E. MS 28th Cav. Co.I
Thompson, H.E. TX 20th Cav. Co.E
Thompson, Henry AL Arty. 1st Bn. Co.D Cpl.
Thompson, Henry AL 1st Regt. Mobile Vol. Co.E Sgt.
Thompson, Henry AL Inf. 2nd Regt. Co.F

Thompson, Henry AL 9th Inf. Co.H
Thompson, Henry AR 1st (Monroe's) Cav. Co.D
Thompson, Henry AR 34th Inf. Co.A
Thompson, Henry FL 1st Inf. Old Co.I
Thompson, Henry FL 8th Inf. Co.K
Thompson, Henry GA 3rd Inf. Co.E
Thompson, Henry GA 27th Inf. Co.B
Thompson, Henry GA 47th Inf. Co.E
Thompson, Henry GA 47th Inf. Co.H
Thompson, Henry KY 2nd (Duke's) Cav. Co.D
Thompson, Henry KY 5th Cav. Co.B
Thompson, Henry KY 6th Cav. Co.D
Thompson, Henry LA 16th Inf. Co.H
Thompson, Henry MD 1st Cav. Co.C
Thompson, Henry MS 1st Cav.Res. Co.F
Thompson, Henry MS 7th Inf. Co.G
Thompson, Henry MO 12th Inf. Co.D Cpl.
Thompson, Henry NC Lt.Arty. 3rd Bn. Co.A
Thompson, Henry NC 4th Sr.Res. Co.D
Thompson, Henry NC 15th Inf. Co.K
Thompson, Henry NC 44th Inf. Co.F
Thompson, Henry SC 4th St.Troops Co.F
Thompson, Henry TN 15th Inf. 2nd Co.F, Co.E
Thompson, Henry TN 23rd Inf.
Thompson, Henry TX 29th Cav. Co.G
Thompson, Henry VA Hvy.Arty. 18th Bn. Co.B Sgt.
Thompson, Henry VA Lt.Arty. Lowry's Co.
Thompson, Henry VA 11th Cav. Co.F
Thompson, Henry VA Cav. 41st Bn. Co.C Cpl.
Thompson, Henry VA Inf. 21st Bn. Co.B
Thompson, Henry VA 41st Inf. 1st Co.E
Thompson, Henry VA 45th Inf. Co.E Cpl.
Thompson, Henry VA 54th Inf. Co.D
Thompson, Henry VA 64th Mtd.Inf. Co.D
Thompson, Henry VA 64th Mtd.Inf. 2nd Co.F
Thompson, Henry 1st Conf.Inf. 2nd Co.G
Thompson, Henry Conf.Inf. 8th Bn.
Thompson, Henry Conf.Reg.Inf. Brooks' Bn. Co.A
Thompson, Henry 1st Choctaw & Chickasaw Mtd.Rifles 2nd Co.B Cpl.
Thompson, Henry A. NC 3rd Cav. (41st St.Troops) Co.I
Thompson, Henry C. AL 13th Inf. Co.C
Thompson, Henry C. KY 3rd Mtd.Inf.
Thompson, Henry C. KY 6th Mtd.Inf. Co.H
Thompson, Henry C. LA 7th Inf. Co.I 1st Lt.
Thompson, Henry C. NC 13th Inf. Co.A
Thompson, Henry C. NC 47th Inf. Co.E
Thompson, Henry C. TX 15th Cav. Co.A,D 1st Lt.
Thompson, Henry C. TX 2nd Inf. Co.B
Thompson, Henry C. VA Lt.Arty. Pegram's Co.
Thompson, Henry C. VA 12th Inf. Co.D,C
Thompson, Henry C. VA 24th Inf. Co.G
Thompson, Henry D. MO 1st Inf. Co.E,G 2nd Lt.
Thompson, Henry D. TX 14th Cav. Co.K
Thompson, Henry E. GA 9th Inf. (St.Guards) Co.B
Thompson, Henry E. LA 11th Inf. Co.L Sgt.
Thompson, Henry E. Inf. School of Pract. Powell's Detach. Co.A
Thompson, Henry G. AL 37th Inf. Co.G
Thompson, Henry H. AL 39th Inf. Co.C
Thompson, Henry H. AR 45th Mil. Co.D Cpl.
Thompson, Henry H. VA 13th Inf. Co.F
Thompson, Henry J. NC 2nd Cav. (19th St.Troops) Co.K Sgt.
Thompson, Henry Jack TX St.Mil. Capt.
Thompson, Henry L. MS 2nd Inf. Co.D 3rd Lt.
Thompson, Henry L. MS 3rd Inf. Co.C
Thompson, Henry L. MS 23rd Inf. Co.C
Thompson, Henry L. MO 8th Cav. Co.F Cpl.
Thompson, Henry M. NC 56th Inf. Co.G
Thompson, Henry M. NC Loc.Def. Griswold's Co. Cpl.
Thompson, Henry M. TN Lt.Arty. Burroughs' Co.
Thompson, Henry P. MS Arty. (Seven Stars Arty.) Roberts' Co.
Thompson, Henry R. VA Lt.Arty. Motley's Co. Cpl.
Thompson, Henry S. GA Lt.Arty. Howell's Co.
Thompson, Henry T. SC Mil. Trenholm's Co.
Thompson, Henry T. SC Cav. Walpole's Co.
Thompson, Henry T. VA 11th Inf. Co.D Sgt.
Thompson, Henry W. GA 14th Inf. Co.F
Thompson, Henry W. LA 17th Inf. Co.K
Thompson, Henry W. LA 19th Inf. Co.B
Thompson, Henry W. NC 25th Inf. Co.E
Thompson, Henry W. TN 44th (Cons.) Inf. Co.F
Thompson, Heywood GA 6th Inf. Co.I
Thompson, Hezekiah MO 8th Inf. Co.C
Thompson, Hezekiah NC 17th Inf. (1st Org.) Co.G
Thompson, Hezekiah B. VA 24th Inf. Co.K
Thompson, Hezekiah T. AR 1st (Crawford's) Cav. Co.F Sgt.
Thompson, H.F. SC Lt.Arty. Parker's Co.
Thompson, H.G. AR 16th Inf. Co.I Sgt.
Thompson, H.G. TX Cav. 1st Regt.St.Troops Co.F
Thompson, H.G. VA Inf. 7th Bn.Loc.Def. Co.C
Thompson, H.H. AL Lt.Arty. Kolb's Btty.
Thompson, H.H. AL 35th Inf. Co.E
Thompson, H.H. KY 8th Cav. Co.A
Thompson, H.H. KY 8th Mtd.Inf. Co.B
Thompson, H.H. MS Lt.Arty. 14th Bn. Co.B
Thompson, H.H. NC 3rd Cav. (41st St.Troops) Co.B
Thompson, H.H. NC 67th Inf. Co.H
Thompson, H.H. TX 30th Cav. Co.C
Thompson, Hilliard GA 42nd Inf. Co.G
Thompson, Hiram GA Cav. 1st Bn.Res. McKinney's Co., Co.C, Stark's Co.
Thompson, Hiram VA 3rd (Chrisman's) Bn.Res. Co.E
Thompson, Hiram VA 10th Bn.Res. Co.B
Thompson, Hiram A.S. MS 39th Inf. Co.C
Thompson, Hiram F. GA 12th (Robinson's) Cav. (St.Guards) Co.G Sgt.
Thompson, Hiram P. VA 45th Inf. Co.F
Thompson, H.J. AL 34th Inf. Co.E Sgt.
Thompson, H.J. LA 18th Inf. Co.D
Thompson, H.J. LA Inf.Cons. 18th Regt. & Yellow Jacket Bn. Co.E
Thompson, H.J. MS 1st (Percy's) Inf. Co.F
Thompson, H.J. MS 33rd Inf. Co.E
Thompson, H.J. SC 5th Bn.Res. Co.E
Thompson, H.J. SC Inf. 7th Bn. (Enfield Rifles) Co.F
Thompson, H.J. SC Inf. Holcombe Legion Co.B
Thompson, H.J. TX 10th Cav. Co.I
Thompson, H.J. VA Cav. 37th Bn. Co.F
Thompson, H.J.B. GA 12th Inf. Co.F
Thompson, H. Jones GA 42nd Inf. Co.A
Thompson, H.L. AR 18th Inf. Co.A
Thompson, H.L. GA Inf. 27th Bn. Co.F
Thompson, H.L. TN 15th (Cons.) Cav. Co.D,E
Thompson, H.L. TN 3rd (Clack's) Inf. Co.B
Thompson, H.L.W. MO St.Guard
Thompson, H.M. AL Cav. Falkner's Co.
Thompson, H.M. FL 4th Inf. Co.D Sgt.
Thompson, H.M. GA 53rd Inf. Co.F
Thompson, H.M. MS Cav. 1st Bn. (Montgomery's) St.Troops Co.C
Thompson, H.M. MS Cav. Gartley's Co. (Yazoo Rangers) 1st Lt.
Thompson, H.M. MS Cav. Yerger's Regt. Co.F Capt.
Thompson, H.M. TN 1st (Carter's) Cav. Co.C
Thompson, H.M. TN 5th Inf. 2nd Co.B
Thompson, H.M. TN 47th Inf. Co.F
Thompson, H.M. TX 20th Inf. Co.D
Thompson, H.M. 8th (Wade's) Conf.Cav. Co.B
Thompson, Horace KY 4th Mtd.Inf. Co.C
Thompson, Horatio H. VA 14th Cav. Co.H
Thompson, Hosa H. NC 50th Inf. Co.I
Thompson, Hosea B. MS 12th Inf. Co.D
Thompson, Howard M. VA 1st Arty. Co.A
Thompson, H.P. AL 7th Cav. Co.B,C
Thompson, H.P. MS Cav. 24th Bn. Sgt.Maj.
Thompson, H.P. TX 10th Cav. Co.C
Thompson, H.R. AL 3rd Cav. Co.C
Thompson, H.R. VA 32nd Inf. Co.F
Thompson, H.R. VA Loc.Def. Ezell's Co.
Thompson, H.S. MS Cav.Res. Mitchell's Co.
Thompson, H.S. SC Bn.St.Cadets Co.A Capt.
Thompson, H.S. TN 3rd (Clack's) Inf. Co.B
Thompson, H.S. TN 16th Inf. Co.F Cpl.
Thompson, H.T. AL 10th Inf.
Thompson, H.T. MS 5th Inf. (St.Troops) Co.F
Thompson, H.T. VA 48th Inf. Co.D,B
Thompson, Hugh AL Lt.Arty. 2nd Bn. Co.A
Thompson, Hugh AR 13th Inf. Co.G
Thompson, Hugh GA 51st Inf. Co.K
Thompson, Hugh LA Washington Arty.Bn. Co.3 Driver
Thompson, Hugh LA 13th Inf. Co.H
Thompson, Hugh LA 20th Inf. Co.H Cpl.
Thompson, Hugh LA Mil. Irish Regt. Co.F
Thompson, Hugh MS Inf. 1st Bn.St.Troops (30 days '64) Co.H Sgt.
Thompson, Hugh MS Inf. 3rd Bn. Co.E
Thompson, Hugh SC 1st (Orr's) Rifles Co.B
Thompson, Hugh SC 10th Inf. Co.M
Thompson, Hugh G. AL 44th Inf. Co.G
Thompson, Hugh L. GA 43rd Inf. Co.C
Thompson, Hugh L. TN 53rd Inf. Co.I
Thompson, Hugh W. TN Inf. 23rd Bn. Co.A
Thompson, Hugh W. TX 34th Cav. Co.H
Thompson, Hughs 1st Cherokee Mtd.Vol. 1st Co.B, 2nd Co.F
Thompson, Humphrey AR 1st (Colquitt's) Inf. Co.C
Thompson, Hute TN 51st Inf. Co.F Cpl.
Thompson, H.W. AL 22nd Inf. Co.B
Thompson, H.W. AL Cp. of Instr. Talladega
Thompson, H.W. KY 9th Mtd.Inf. Co.E

Thompson, H.W. SC 11th Inf. 1st Co.F, Co.K
Thompson, H.W. 1st Conf.Inf. 2nd Co.K 1st Sgt.
Thompson, I. MS Cav. Yerger's Regt. Co.A
Thompson, I. NC 1st Bn.Jr.Res. Co.D
Thompson, I.A. TN 11th (Holman's) Cav. Co.E
Thompson, I.C. TN 3rd (Forrest's) Cav. Co.D
Thompson, I.H. LA 28th (Gray's) Inf. Co.F
Thompson, I.H. MS Cav. 2nd Bn.Res. Co.B
Thompson, I.H. MS 4th Inf. Co.K
Thompson, I.I. MO Lt.Arty. 1st Btty. Sgt.
Thompson, I.L. LA Inf.Cons.Crescent Regt. Co.O
Thompson, I.M. AL 2nd Cav. Co.D
Thompson, I.M. Conf.Cav. Raum's Co.
Thompson, Inman VA 27th Inf. Co.A Cpl.
Thompson, Inman H. VA Lt.Arty. Carpenter's Co.
Thompson, Irby W. TN 62nd Mtd.Inf. Co.K
Thompson, Irvin AL 47th Inf. Co.A
Thompson, Irvin MS 16th Inf. Co.H
Thompson, Irvin MS 40th Inf. Co.A Cpl.
Thompson, Irvin MS Clayton's Co. (Jasper Defend.)
Thompson, Irzael H. VA 22nd Cav. Co.H
Thompson, I.S. GA 11th Inf.
Thompson, Isaac AR 7th Mil. Co.C
Thompson, Isaac AR 32nd Inf. Co.F
Thompson, Isaac AR 34th Inf. Co.I
Thompson, Isaac MS Wilkinson Cty.Minute Men Co.A
Thompson, Isaac NC Inf. 2nd Bn. Co.B
Thompson, Isaac NC 29th Inf. Co.D
Thompson, Isaac NC 35th Inf. Co.B
Thompson, Isaac NC 46th Inf. Co.H
Thompson, Isaac TN 21st (Wilson's) Cav. Co.H
Thompson, Isaac TN 21st & 22nd (Cons.) Cav. Co.E
Thompson, Isaac TN 6th Inf. Co.E
Thompson, Isaac TN 43rd Inf. Co.K
Thompson, Isaac VA 2nd Inf. Co.A
Thompson, Isaac VA 15th Inf. Co.I
Thompson, Isaac VA Inf. 21st Bn. Co.B
Thompson, Isaac VA Inf. 26th Bn. Co.B
Thompson, Isaac VA 45th Inf. Co.I
Thompson, Isaac VA 64th Mtd.Inf. 2nd Co.F
Thompson, Isaac 1st Choctaw & Chickasaw Mtd.Rifles 2nd Co.B
Thompson, Isaac A. TN 36th Inf. Co.B
Thompson, Isaac B. VA 45th Inf. Co.H
Thompson, Isaac F. 3rd Conf.Cav. Co.D Sgt.
Thompson, Isaac G. VA Cav. 47th Bn. Co.B
Thompson, Isaac L. FL 7th Inf. Co.C
Thompson, Isaac M. SC 5th Inf. 1st Co.H, 2nd Co.B
Thompson, Isaac N. GA 11th Inf. Co.I
Thompson, Isaac N. TN 60th Mtd.Inf. Co.A
Thompson, Isaac P. TN 2nd (Robison's) Inf. Co.K,I Capt.
Thompson, Isaac P. VA 11th Bn.Res. Co.F
Thompson, Isaac V. MO 3rd Cav. Co.B
Thompson, Isac N. AR 32nd Inf. Co.B Sgt.
Thompson, Isaiah TX Inf. 1st Bn. (St.Troops) Co.E
Thompson, Isaiah L. FL 3rd Inf. Co.F
Thompson, Isam 1st Choctaw Mtd.Rifles Co.H
Thompson, Isham AL 34th Inf. Co.I
Thompson, Isham NC 26th Inf. Co.G
Thompson, Isom VA 51st Inf. Co.K
Thompson, Ivy F. GA Phillips' Legion Co.D Sgt.
Thompson, Iyantooga NC Inf. Thomas Legion 2nd Co.A
Thompson, J. AL 6th Cav. Co.A
Thompson, J. AL 1st Inf. Co.A
Thompson, J. AL 10th Inf. Co.E
Thompson, J. AL 26th (O'Neal's) Inf. Co.B
Thompson, J. AL 43rd Inf. Co.K
Thompson, J. AL 50th Inf. Co.F
Thompson, J. AL 1st Bn. Hilliard's Legion Vol. Co.G
Thompson, J. AR 15th (Josey's) Inf. 1st Co.C
Thompson, J. AR 18th (Marmaduke's) Inf. Co.H
Thompson, J. AR Inf. Cocke's Regt. Co.B
Thompson, J. GA 4th (Clinch's) Cav. Co.E
Thompson, J. GA 4th Cav. (St.Guards) Deadwyler's Co.
Thompson, J. GA Cav. 29th Bn. Co.C
Thompson, J. GA Arty. Lumpkin's Co.
Thompson, J. GA Arty. Maxwell's Reg.Lt.Btty.
Thompson, J. GA 5th Res. Co.K
Thompson, J. GA 12th Inf. Co.F
Thompson, J. KY 3rd Cav. Grant's Co.
Thompson, J. KY Huey's Bn.
Thompson, J. LA Arty. 8th Bn. Co.3
Thompson, J. LA Mil. 4th Regt. 1st Brig. 1st Div. Co.A
Thompson, J. LA 25th Inf. Co.F
Thompson, J. LA Miles' Legion Co.A
Thompson, J. MO Cav. Woodson's Co. Cpl.
Thompson, J. MO Inf. 5th Regt.St.Guard Co.G
Thompson, J. NC 3rd Jr.Res. Co.I
Thompson, J. NC 7th Sr.Res. Bradshaw's Co.
Thompson, J. NC 15th Inf. Co.D
Thompson, J. NC 18th Inf. Co.I
Thompson, J. SC Arty. Fickling's Co. (Brooks Lt.Arty.)
Thompson, J. SC 1st Regt.Charleston Guard Co.F
Thompson, J. SC Inf. 9th Bn. Co.A 1st Lt.
Thompson, J. SC 17th Inf. Co.B
Thompson, J. TN 14th (Neely's) Cav. Co.I
Thompson, J. TN 14th (Neely's) Cav. Co.K
Thompson, J. TN 21st (Wilson's) Cav. Co.G
Thompson, J. TN 47th Inf. Co.H Sgt.
Thompson, J. TX Cav. 1st Regt.St.Troops Co.C
Thompson, J. TX 7th Cav. Co.D
Thompson, J. TX Cav. Terry's Regt. Co.F Sgt.
Thompson, J. TX 6th Field Btty.
Thompson, J. TX 13th Vol. 2nd Co.H
Thompson, J. TX Inf. Timmons' Regt. Co.G
Thompson, J. VA 11th Cav. Co.I Sgt.
Thompson, J. VA 22nd Cav. Co.K
Thompson, J. VA Cav. Swann's Bn. Carpenter's Co.
Thompson, J. VA Inf. 2nd Bn.Loc.Def. Co.D
Thompson, J. VA 45th Inf. Co.C
Thompson, J. VA 46th Inf. Co.B
Thompson, J. VA Mil. Wythe Cty.
Thompson, J. Bradford's Corps Scouts & Guards Co.B
Thompson, J.A. AL 11th Cav. Co.F
Thompson, J.A. AL Lowndes Rangers Vol. Fagg's Co.
Thompson, J.A. AL Lt.Arty. Kolb's Btty.
Thompson, J.A. AL Mil. 4th Vol. Co.I
Thompson, J.A. AL 12th Inf. Co.G
Thompson, J.A. AL 19th Inf. Co.E
Thompson, J.A. AL 40th Inf. Co.D
Thompson, J.A. AR Inf. 4th Bn. Co.E
Thompson, J.A. AR 24th Inf. Co.E Sgt.
Thompson, J.A. GA 10th Inf. Co.I
Thompson, J.A. GA 16th Inf. Co.A
Thompson, J.A. GA 16th Inf. Co.D
Thompson, J.A. GA 55th Inf. Co.A
Thompson, J.A. GA Conscr.
Thompson, J.A. KY 12th Cav. Co.H
Thompson, J.A. LA 3rd Inf. Co.B
Thompson, J.A. LA 22nd (Cons.) Inf. Co.H
Thompson, J.A. LA Miles' Legion Co.D
Thompson, J.A. MS 2nd Cav. Co.I
Thompson, J.A. MS 3rd Cav. Co.E Cpl.
Thompson, J.A. MS 4th Cav. Co.I
Thompson, J.A. MS 2nd Inf. Co.E
Thompson, J.A. MS 33rd Inf. Co.K
Thompson, J.A. MO 7th Cav. Co.E,K
Thompson, J.A. MO 16th Inf. Co.I
Thompson, J.A. NC 1st Inf. Co.B
Thompson, J.A. NC 4th Inf. Co.A
Thompson, J.A. SC 1st Cav. Co.D
Thompson, J.A. SC 1st Cav. Co.G Music.
Thompson, J.A. SC 1st Mtd.Mil. Anderson's Co.
Thompson, J.A. SC 5th Cav. Co.G
Thompson, J.A. SC Cav. 10th Bn. Co.A
Thompson, J.A. SC Lt.Arty. Garden's Co. (Palmetto Lt.Btty.)
Thompson, J.A. SC 5th Bn.Res. Co.F
Thompson, J.A. SC Inf. 7th Bn. (Enfield Rifles) Co.E
Thompson, J.A. SC 18th Inf. Co.I Sgt.
Thompson, J.A. TN 1st (Carter's) Cav. Co.A
Thompson, J.A. TN 12th (Green's) Cav. Co.D
Thompson, J.A. TN 14th (Neely's) Cav. Co.F
Thompson, J.A. TN Cav. 16th Bn. (Neal's) Co.A Cpl.
Thompson, J.A. TN 3rd (Clack's) Inf. Co.F
Thompson, J.A. TN 61st Mtd.Inf. Co.A
Thompson, J.A. TX 32nd Cav. Co.E
Thompson, J.A. TX Cav. Border's Regt. Co.B
Thompson, J.A. TX 1st Hvy.Arty. Co.I
Thompson, J.A. VA 38th Inf. 1st Co.I
Thompson, J.A. 3rd Conf.Cav. Co.F
Thompson, J.A. 2nd Conf.Eng.Troops Co.C
Thompson, J.A. Gen. & Staff Contr.Surg.
Thompson, Jabes M. GA 12th (Wright's) Cav. (St.Guards) Stapleton's Co.
Thompson, Jabez M. GA 8th Inf. (St.Guards) Co.B
Thompson, Jack AL 5th Inf. New Co.C
Thompson, Jack GA 17th Inf. Co.H
Thompson, Jack KY Cav. 1st Bn. Co.A
Thompson, Jack P. Deneale's Regt. Choctaw Warriors Co.B
Thompson, Jack S. AR 1st (Crawford's) Cav. Co.I 1st Lt.
Thompson, Jackson AL 48th Inf. Co.K
Thompson, Jackson GA 40th Inf.
Thompson, Jackson TN Cav. 5th Bn. (McClellan's) Co.B
Thompson, Jackson J. SC 9th Inf. Co.G
Thompson, Jackson M. AL 28th Inf. Co.K

Thompson, Jack W. MS 26th Inf. Co.A 1st Lt.
Thompson, Jacob AL Rives' Supp.Force 9th Congr.Dist.
Thompson, Jacob NC 21st Inf. Asst.Surg.
Thompson, Jacob TN 10th (DeMoss') Cav. Co.B
Thompson, Jacob TN 21st (Wilson's) Cav. Co.H
Thompson, Jacob TN 27th Inf. Co.I
Thompson, Jacob TX 15th Inf. Co.A
Thompson, Jacob VA 72nd Mil.
Thompson, Jacob VA 89th Mil. Co.H
Thompson, Jacob Gen. & Staff Maj.
Thompson, Jacob Gen. & Staff Col.,Vol.ADC
Thompson, Jacob A. NC 21st Inf. Asst.Surg.
Thompson, Jacob F. TN 41st Inf. Co.F 2nd Lt.
Thompson, Jacob H. SC 20th Inf. Co.F
Thompson, Jacob M. TN 55th (McKoin's) Inf. Duggan's Co.
Thompson, Jacob T. GA 27th Inf. Co.I
Thompson, Jake TN 12th (Green's) Cav. Co.D
Thompson, Jake Deneale's Regt. Choctaw Warriors Co.A
Thompson, J. Alexander AL 59th Inf. Co.D
Thompson, J. Alexander AL Arty. 4th Bn. Hilliard's Legion Co.B
Thompson, J. Alexander SC 13th Inf. Co.I
Thompson, James AL 9th (Malone's) Cav. Co.E
Thompson, James AL 51st (Part.Rangers) Co.F
Thompson, James AL Inf. 1st Regt. Co.D
Thompson, James AL 1st Regt. Mobile Vol. British Guard Co.B
Thompson, James AL Mil. 2nd Regt.Vol. Co.B
Thompson, James AL 9th Inf. Co.A
Thompson, James AL 17th Inf. Co.G
Thompson, James AL 22nd Inf. Co.B
Thompson, James AL 23rd Bn.S.S. Co.G
Thompson, James AL 27th Inf. Co.E
Thompson, James AL 29th Inf. Co.I
Thompson, James AL 31st Inf. Co.I
Thompson, James AL 40th Inf. Co.I
Thompson, James AL 42nd Inf. Co.I
Thompson, James AL 95th Mil. Co.D
Thompson, James AL Cp. of Instr. Talladega
Thompson, James AR 18th (Marmaduke's) Inf. Co.K
Thompson, James FL Lt.Arty. Perry's Co.
Thompson, James FL 10th Inf. Co.D Music.
Thompson, James GA Lt.Arty. Croft's Btty. (Columbus Arty.)
Thompson, James GA Lt.Arty. Ritter's Co.
Thompson, James GA 1st (Symons') Res. Co.F
Thompson, James GA 6th Inf. Co.G
Thompson, James GA 10th Inf. Co.D
Thompson, James GA 11th Inf. Co.I
Thompson, James GA 13th Inf. Co.F
Thompson, James GA 19th Inf. Co.A
Thompson, James GA 28th Inf. Co.D
Thompson, James GA 63rd Inf. Co.A
Thompson, James KY 10th (Diamond's) Cav. Co.E
Thompson, James KY 10th (Johnson's) Cav. Co.A
Thompson, James KY 1st Bn.Mtd.Rifles Co.D
Thompson, James KY 2nd Mtd.Inf.
Thompson, James LA 1st Hvy.Arty. (Reg.) Co.A
Thompson, James LA 1st Hvy.Arty. (Reg.) Co.C
Thompson, James LA Arty. Kean's Btty. (Orleans Ind.Arty.)
Thompson, James LA 9th Inf. Co.E
Thompson, James LA Mil.Conf.Guards Regt. Co.E
Thompson, James LA Inf.Crescent Regt. Co.C Sgt.
Thompson, James LA Inf.Crescent Regt. Co.G
Thompson, James LA Inf.Cons.Crescent Regt. Co.G
Thompson, James LA C.S. Zouave Bn. Co.D
Thompson, James MS Lt.Arty. (Jefferson Arty.) Darden's Co. Cpl.
Thompson, James MS 1st (Johnston's) Inf. Co.A
Thompson, James MS 2nd Part.Rangers Co.E
Thompson, James MS 21st Inf. Co.E
Thompson, James MO 3rd Cav. Co.E
Thompson, James MO 5th Cav. Co.C
Thompson, James MO Cav. Snider's Bn. Co.C
Thompson, James MO Lt.Arty. H.M. Bledsoe's Co.
Thompson, James MO 2nd Inf. Co.A
Thompson, James MO 16th Inf. Co.D
Thompson, James NC 2nd Arty. (36th St.Troops) Co.B
Thompson, James NC 1st Inf. Co.K
Thompson, James NC 7th Inf. Co.K
Thompson, James NC 7th Bn.Jr.Res. Co.C
Thompson, Jas. NC 28th Inf. Co.E
Thompson, James NC 30th Inf. Co.K
Thompson, James NC 44th Inf. Co.G
Thompson, James NC 46th Inf. Co.F
Thompson, James NC 54th Inf. Co.F
Thompson, James NC 56th Inf. Co.G,A
Thompson, James NC 67th Inf. Co.B
Thompson, James NC Troops
Thompson, James SC 1st Arty. Co.E
Thompson, James SC 6th Inf. 2nd Co.H
Thompson, James SC 11th Inf. Co.B
Thompson, James SC 16th Inf. Co.H
Thompson, James TN 1st (Carter's) Cav. Co.C Cpl.
Thompson, James TN 8th (Smith's) Cav. Co.E
Thompson, James TN 8th (Smith's) Cav. Co.H
Thompson, James TN 11th Cav.
Thompson, James TN 18th (Newsom's) Cav. Co.E
Thompson, James TN Lt.Arty. Phillips' Co.
Thompson, James TN 10th Inf. Co.K
Thompson, James TN 11th Inf. Co.B
Thompson, James TN 16th Inf. Co.B
Thompson, James TN 25th Inf. Co.F Sgt.
Thompson, James TN 28th (Cons.) Inf.
Thompson, James TN 39th Mtd.Inf. Co.F
Thompson, James TN 41st Inf. Co.H
Thompson, James TX 8th Cav. Co.K
Thompson, James TX 10th Cav. Co.I
Thompson, James TX 17th Cons.Dismtd.Cav. Co.K
Thompson, James TX 22nd Cav. Co.E
Thompson, James TX 25th Cav. Co.B
Thompson, James TX 31st Cav. Co.F
Thompson, James TX Cav. (Dismtd.) Chisum's Regt. Co.K
Thompson, James TX Cav. Coopwood's Spy Co.
Thompson, James TX 9th (Nichols') Inf. Co.D
Thompson, James TX 11th Inf. Co.G
Thompson, James TX 14th Inf. 1st Co.K
Thompson, James TX 18th Inf. Co.L
Thompson, James VA 2nd Cav. Co.K
Thompson, James VA 4th Cav. Co.C
Thompson, James VA 9th Cav. Co.I
Thompson, James VA 12th Cav. Co.F
Thompson, James VA 21st Cav. 2nd Co.E
Thompson, James VA 22nd Cav. Co.F
Thompson, James VA 24th Bn.Part.Rangers Co.D
Thompson, James VA 11th Bn.Res. Co.F
Thompson, James VA 17th Inf. Co.G
Thompson, James VA Inf. 23rd Bn. Co.F
Thompson, James VA 88th Mil.
Thompson, James VA 89th Mil. Co.H
Thompson, James VA 129th Mil. Baisden's Co.
Thompson, James VA Loc.Def. Morehead's Co.
Thompson, James VA Mil. Stowers' Co.
Thompson, James VA Loc.Def. Wade's Regt. Co.A Sgt.
Thompson, James Conf.Cav. Wood's Regt. Co.K
Thompson, James Conf.Inf. Tucker's Regt. Co.C
Thompson, James 1st Choctaw Mtd.Rifles Co.G
Thompson, James 1st Choctaw Mtd.Rifles Co.H
Thompson, James 1st Choctaw Mtd.Rifles Co.K
Thompson, James 1st Choctaw & Chickasaw Mtd.Rifles Asst.Comsy.Subs.
Thompson, James 1st Choctaw & Chickasaw Mtd.Rifles 2nd Co.B
Thompson, James 1st Choctaw & Chickasaw Mtd.Rifles 3rd Co.F
Thompson, James 1st Choctaw & Chickasaw Mtd.Rifles 2nd Co.H 1st Lt.
Thompson, James 1st Creek Mtd.Vol. 2nd Co.D Sgt.
Thompson, James A. AL Inf. 1st Regt. Co.C
Thompson, James A. AL 3rd Bn.Res. Co.C
Thompson, James A. AL 17th Inf. Co.C
Thompson, James A. AL 18th Inf. Co.D
Thompson, James A. GA Cav. 20th Bn. Co.A,E,D
Thompson, James A. GA 26th Inf. Co.G
Thompson, James A. GA 61st Inf. Co.I
Thompson, James A. GA Floyd Legion (St.Guards) Co.H
Thompson, James A. LA 17th Inf. Co.B
Thompson, James A. MS 22nd Inf. Co.H
Thompson, James A. MS 43rd Inf. Co.C
Thompson, James A. MO 4th Cav. Co.E
Thompson, James A. NC 18th Inf. Co.B
Thompson, James A. NC 29th Inf. Co.F 1st Lt.
Thompson, James A. NC Inf. Thomas Legion Co.C
Thompson, James A. SC Arty. Manigault's Bn. 1st Co.B 1st Lt.
Thompson, James A. SC 4th Inf. Co.B
Thompson, James A. TN Cav. 9th Bn. (Gantt's) Co.B
Thompson, James A. TN 7th Inf. Co.F Sgt.
Thompson, James A. TX 31st Cav. Co.F Capt.
Thompson, James A. TX 37th Cav. Co.B
Thompson, James A. VA Horse Arty. Jackson's Co.
Thompson, James A. VA 22nd Cav. Co.C Cpl.
Thompson, James A. VA Cav. 46th Bn. Co.F
Thompson, James A. Cav. Murchison's Bn. Co.D,CSA
Thompson, James B. AL 20th Inf. Co.D
Thompson, James B. AR 16th Inf. Co.B

Thompson, James B. MS 8th Inf. Co.E
Thompson, James B. NC 2nd Arty. (36th St.Troops) Co.E,I
Thompson, James B. TN Lt.Arty. Baxter's Co.
Thompson, James B. TN 59th Mtd.Inf. Co.E
Thompson, James B. TX 1st (Yager's) Cav. Co.C 1st Lt.
Thompson, James B. TX Cav. Waller's Regt. Co.E Sgt.
Thompson, James B. VA 6th Cav. Co.I Cpl.
Thompson, James B. VA 51st Inf. Co.E
Thompson, James C. AR 18th Inf. Co.A Capt.
Thompson, James C. FL Lt.Arty. Abell's Co.
Thompson, James C. FL 8th Inf. Co.K 1st Sgt.
Thompson, James C. GA Lt.Arty. 12th Bn. 2nd Co.A Music.
Thompson, James C. GA 57th Inf. Co.C
Thompson, James C. NC 26th Inf. Co.F
Thompson, James C. VA 8th Cav. Co.A
Thompson, James C.S. TX 1st Inf. Co.L 1st Lt.
Thompson, James D. AL 56th Part.Rangers Co.D
Thompson, James D. AL 28th Inf. Co.H
Thompson, James D. AL 50th Inf. Co.E
Thompson, James D. GA 5th Inf. Co.G
Thompson, James D. GA Floyd Legion (St.Guards) Co.G
Thompson, James D. NC 3rd Arty. (40th St.Troops) Co.E
Thompson, James D. TN 38th Inf. Co.E 2nd Lt.
Thompson, James D. TX 2nd Cav. Co.E Sgt.
Thompson, James D. VA 166th Mil. W. Lively's Co.
Thompson, James E. AL 6th Inf. Co.C Cpl.
Thompson, James E. AL 36th Inf. Co.I
Thompson, James E. GA 19th Inf. Co.G
Thompson, James E. MS 37th Inf. Co.B Sgt.
Thompson, James E. TN 2nd (Smith's) Cav.
Thompson, James E. TN 4th (McLemore's) Cav. Co.G Cpl.
Thompson, James E. TX 4th Inf. Co.A
Thompson, James E. TX 9th (Nichols') Inf. Co.D
Thompson, James E. VA 56th Inf. Co.B Sgt.
Thompson, James F. AL 47th Inf. Co.H,K
Thompson, James F. AR Cav. Wright's Regt. Co.B
Thompson, James F. FL 9th Inf. Co.A
Thompson, James F. FL 9th Inf. Co.A 1st Lt.
Thompson, James F. GA Cobb's Legion Co.I
Thompson, James F. MS 36th Inf. Co.A Sgt.
Thompson, James F. TN Cav. 9th Bn. (Gantt's) Co.E
Thompson, James F. VA 25th Cav. Co.B
Thompson, James F. VA 135th Mil. Co.A
Thompson, James G. MS 14th Inf. Co.F
Thompson, James H. AL Inf. 1st Regt. Co.B
Thompson, James H. AL 45th Inf. Co.K
Thompson, James H. AR 8th Inf. New Co.D
Thompson, James H. AR 15th (N.W.) Inf. Co.E
Thompson, James H. GA Cav. Roswell Bn. Co.C
Thompson, James H. GA 6th Inf. (St.Guards) Pittman's Co.
Thompson, James H. GA 21st Inf. Co.D
Thompson, James H. GA 45th Inf. Co.E Sgt.
Thompson, James H. KY 5th Cav. Co.I 1st Lt.
Thompson, James H. KY 1st Inf. Co.G Sgt.
Thompson, James H. LA 4th Cav. Co.D Sgt.
Thompson, James H. LA 9th Inf. Co.D
Thompson, James H. MS 20th Inf. Co.D
Thompson, James H. MS 29th Inf. Co.E Cpl.
Thompson, James H. NC 1st Cav. (9th St.Troops) Co.H
Thompson, James H. NC 35th Inf. Co.I 2nd Lt.
Thompson, James H. TN 1st (Turney's) Inf. Co.F Capt.
Thompson, James H. TN 14th Inf. Co.K
Thompson, James H. VA 6th Cav. Co.D
Thompson, James H. VA Lt.Arty. Carrington's Co.
Thompson, James H. VA Lt.Arty. Garber's Co.
Thompson, James H. VA 4th Inf. Co.E
Thompson, James H. VA 11th Inf. Co.G
Thompson, James H. VA 28th Inf. Co.I
Thompson, James H. VA 136th Mil. Co.C
Thompson, James H. Lt.Arty. Dent's Btty.,CSA
Thompson, James H. 1st Cherokee Mtd.Vol. 1st Co.K Capt.
Thompson, James Henry TN Douglass' Bn. Part.Rangers Co.A 1st Sgt.
Thompson, James J. AL 4th Inf. Co.C
Thompson, James J. AL 18th Inf. Co.I Fifer
Thompson, James J. GA 65th Inf. Co.A Sgt.
Thompson, James J. GA Smith's Legion Co.B Sgt.
Thompson, James J. MS 21st Inf. Co.I
Thompson, James J. NC 11th (Bethel Regt.) Inf. Co.G
Thompson, James J. SC 1st (Butler's) Inf. Co.D
Thompson, James J. VA 51st Inf. Co.B Sgt.
Thompson, James J. VA Prov.Guard Avis' Co.
Thompson, James L. AL 28th Inf. Co.B
Thompson, James L. AL 37th Inf. Co.C
Thompson, James L. GA 50th Inf. Co.H
Thompson, James L. KY 9th Mtd.Inf. Co.E
Thompson, James L. MS 2nd St.Cav. Co.K,L
Thompson, James L. MS Inf. 3rd Bn. Co.A 1st Cpl.
Thompson, James L. TN 23rd Inf. Surg.
Thompson, James L. TN Inf. 23rd Bn. Co.A
Thompson, James L. VA 2nd Arty. Co.E
Thompson, James L. VA Inf. 22nd Bn. Co.E
Thompson, James L. VA 51st Inf. Co.E
Thompson, James L. Gen. & Staff Surg.
Thompson, James M. AL 3rd Bn.Res. Co.A
Thompson, James M. AL 6th Inf. Co.G 1st Sgt.
Thompson, James M. AL 55th Vol. Co.D Capt.
Thompson, James M. AR 17th (Lemoyne's) Inf. Co.C
Thompson, James M. AR 21st Inf. Co.C Sgt.
Thompson, James M. GA Cav. 1st Bn.Res. Co.C
Thompson, James M. GA 14th Inf. Co.E
Thompson, James M. GA 30th Inf. Co.I Sgt.
Thompson, James M. GA 51st Inf. Co.E Cpl.
Thompson, James M. KY 12th Cav. Co.I
Thompson, James M. KY 4th Mtd.Inf. Co.K Sgt.
Thompson, James M. LA 2nd Cav. Co.A Maj.
Thompson, James M. LA 2nd Res.Corps Col.
Thompson, James M. MS 40th Inf. Co.D Sgt.
Thompson, James M. NC 1st Inf. Co.B
Thompson, James M. SC 16th Inf. Co.E
Thompson, James M. SC 20th Inf. Co.M
Thompson, James M. TN 5th (McKenzie's) Cav. Co.D
Thompson, James M. TX 1st (Yager's) Cav. Co.C
Thompson, James M. TX Cav. 3rd (Yager's) Bn. Co.C
Thompson, James M. TX 1st Hvy.Arty. Co.I 2nd Lt.
Thompson, James M. TX 15th Inf. 2nd Co.H
Thompson, James M. VA 2nd Cav. Co.E
Thompson, James M. VA 24th Inf. Co.G
Thompson, James M. 1st Conf.Cav. 2nd Co.E
Thompson, James M. Gen. & Staff Asst.Surg.
Thompson, James M. Gen. & Staff, Arty. 1st Lt.
Thompson, James N. GA Inf. 40th Bn. Co.B Sgt.
Thompson, James N. GA 41st Inf. Co.E
Thompson, James N. MO 1st Inf. Co.B
Thompson, James N. MO Inf. 8th Bn. Co.E 2nd Lt.
Thompson, James N. MO 9th Inf. Co.I 2nd Lt.
Thompson, James N. MO Searcy's Bn.S.S.
Thompson, James N. NC 1st Arty. (10th St.Troops) Co.A Cpl.
Thompson, James N. VA 25th Cav. Co.I 1st Sgt.
Thompson, James N. Gen. & Staff Asst.Surg.
Thompson, James O. NC 28th Inf. Co.G Sgt.
Thompson, James P. AL 3rd Inf. Co.I
Thompson, James P. AL 7th Inf. Co.C
Thompson, James P. AL 13th Inf. Co.E
Thompson, James P. AL 18th Inf. Co.A Cpl.
Thompson, James P. AL 2nd Bn. Hilliard's Legion Vol. Co.C
Thompson, James P. MS 17th Inf. Co.I Sgt.
Thompson, James P. NC 1st Inf. Co.B
Thompson, James P. NC 51st Inf. Co.E Sgt.
Thompson, James P. SC Lt.Arty. Kelly's Co. (Chesterfield Arty.) 1st Lt.
Thompson, James P. TN Lt.Arty. Tobin's Co.
Thompson, James P. TN 41st Inf. Co.B
Thompson, James P. TX 3rd Cav. Co.G
Thompson, James P. TX 21st Cav. Co.L
Thompson, James P. VA 22nd Cav. Co.F
Thompson, James R. AL 19th Inf. Co.D
Thompson, James R. AL 40th Inf. Co.F
Thompson, James R. GA 2nd Cav. Co.A
Thompson, James R. GA 10th Mil. Capt.
Thompson, James R. GA 14th Inf. Co.E Cpl.
Thompson, James R. GA 43rd Inf. Co.F
Thompson, James R. GA Cherokee Legion (St.Guards) Co.K
Thompson, James R. TN 4th (McLemore's) Cav. Co.A
Thompson, James R. TN 16th Inf. Co.A Sgt.
Thompson, James R. TX Part.Rangers (Loc.Def.) Peareson's Co.
Thompson, James R. VA 48th Inf. Co.A Cpl.
Thompson, James R. VA Burks' Regt.Loc.Def.
Thompson, James R. 10th Conf.Cav. Co.E Cpl.
Thompson, James Richard TX 20th Cav. Co.B
Thompson, James S. AL 17th Inf. Co.A
Thompson, James S. AL 60th Inf. Co.B
Thompson, James S. AL 3rd Bn. Hilliard's Legion Vol. Co.E
Thompson, James S. GA 1st Inf. (St.Guards) Co.B 1st Sgt.

Thompson, James S. MS St.Cav. Perrin's Bn. Co.F
Thompson, James S. MS Inf. 5th Bn. Co.B
Thompson, James S. MS 24th Inf. Co.F
Thompson, James S. MS 27th Inf. Co.K
Thompson, James S. MO 1st N.E. Cav.
Thompson, James S. MO 6th Cav. Co.C
Thompson, James S. MO 16th Inf. Co.B
Thompson, James S. NC 28th Inf. Co.G
Thompson, James S. NC 42nd Inf. Co.B
Thompson, James S. VA Cav. 39th Bn. Co.D
Thompson, James S. VA Lt.Arty. Montgomery's Co. Sgt.
Thompson, James T. AL 18th Inf. Co.D Sgt.
Thompson, James T. GA 11th Inf. Co.H
Thompson, James T. MS 8th Inf. Co.E
Thompson, James T. MS 11th Inf. Co.H
Thompson, James T. MS 20th Inf. Co.C
Thompson, James T. SC 21st Inf. Co.D
Thompson, James T. TN 3rd (Forrest's) Cav. Co.A
Thompson, James T. TN Cav. Allison's Squad. Co.C
Thompson, James T. TN Lt.Arty. Palmer's Co.
Thompson, James T. TN Inf. 154th Sr.Regt. 1st Co.B
Thompson, James W. AL 4th Inf. Co.C Cpl.
Thompson, James W. AL 11th Inf. Co.D
Thompson, James W. AL 3rd Bn. Hilliard's Legion Vol. Co.C Sgt.
Thompson, James W. AR 20th Inf. Co.A
Thompson, James W. GA 13th Inf. Co.F
Thompson, James W. GA 56th Inf. Co.F
Thompson, James W. MS 1st Cav.Res. Co.B
Thompson, James W. MS 13th Inf. Co.H Cpl.
Thompson, James W. MO 7th Cav. Co.D Sgt.
Thompson, James W. MO 11th Inf. Co.B
Thompson, James W. NC 25th Inf. Co.E Sgt.
Thompson, James W. NC 57th Inf. Co.A Cpl.
Thompson, James W. TN 21st Cav.
Thompson, James W. TN 24th Inf. Co.B
Thompson, James W. TX 3rd Inf. Co.I
Thompson, James W. TX 13th Vol. Co.M
Thompson, James W. TX 15th Inf. 2nd Co.H
Thompson, James W. VA 7th Cav. 1st Lt.
Thompson, James W. VA 5th Inf. Co.D
Thompson, James W. VA 5th Inf. Co.K
Thompson, James W. VA 36th Inf. 2nd Co.G
Thompson, James W. VA 47th Inf. Co.E Cpl.
Thompson, James W. Conf.Cav. Wood's Regt. Co.E
Thompson, James William VA 16th Cav. Co.I
Thompson, James Z. AL 63rd Inf. Co.C
Thompson, Jarrett AL 10th Inf. Co.E Sgt.
Thompson, Jason A. NC 62nd Inf. Co.I
Thompson, Jason J. TX 18th Inf. Co.D
Thompson, Jasper MS 40th Inf. Co.A
Thompson, Jasper VA 28th Inf. Co.K
Thompson, Jasper M. AL 12th Cav. Co.F
Thompson, Jasper M. TX 1st (Yager's) Cav. Co.K Cpl.
Thompson, Jasper M. TX Cav. 8th (Taylor's) Bn. Co.B
Thompson, Jasper N. AL 3rd Cav. Co.H
Thompson, Jasper N. VA 25th Cav. Co.G
Thompson, J.B. AL 12th Cav.
Thompson, J.B. AL 13th Bn.Part.Rangers Co.C
Thompson, J.B. AL 56th Part.Rangers Co.G
Thompson, J.B. AL 18th Inf. Co.I
Thompson, J.B. AR Cav. Gordon's Regt. Co.C
Thompson, J.B. AR Lt.Arty. Owen's Btty. Cpl.
Thompson, J.B. AR 15th Inf. Co.H
Thompson, J.B. AR 40th Inf. Co.B
Thompson, J.B. AR Inf. Hardy's Regt. Co.C Sgt.
Thompson, J.B. GA Inf. 1st Bn. (St.Guards) Co.E Ord.Sgt.
Thompson, J.B. GA 9th Inf. (St.Guards) Co.F
Thompson, J.B. GA 37th Inf. Co.E
Thompson, J.B. GA 54th Inf. Co.I
Thompson, J.B. GA Inf. City Bn. (Columbus) Co.A
Thompson, J.B. GA Phillips' Legion Co.B,H
Thompson, J.B. KY 6th Mtd.Inf. Co.D
Thompson, J.B. MS Lt.Arty. English's Co.
Thompson, J.B. MS 40th Inf. Co.A
Thompson, J.B. MS Inf. Cooper's Co.
Thompson, J.B. MO St.Guard 3rd Lt.
Thompson, J.B. NC 8th Sr.Res. McNeill's Co.
Thompson, J.B. NC 11th (Bethel Regt.) Inf. Co.A
Thompson, J.B. NC 12th Inf. Co.K
Thompson, J.B. NC 55th Inf. Co.H
Thompson, J.B. TN Cav. 16th Bn. (Neal's) Co.D Cpl.
Thompson, J.B. TN 21st & 22nd (Cons.) Cav. Co.A
Thompson, J.B. TN Cav. Allison's Squad. Co.B
Thompson, J.B. TN 23rd Inf. Co.H
Thompson, J.B. TX Cav. 1st Regt.St.Troops Co.B
Thompson, J.B. TX Cav. Waller's Regt. Co.E Sgt.
Thompson, J.B. TX 15th Field Btty.
Thompson, J.B. TX Inf. 1st St.Troops Wheat's Co.A
Thompson, J.B. TX 13th Vol. 1st Co.K Ord.Sgt.
Thompson, J.B. TX 15th Inf. 2nd Co.F
Thompson, J.B. VA Mil. Stowers' Co.
Thompson, J.B. 2nd Conf.Inf. Co.B
Thompson, J. Berry MS 14th Inf. Co.B
Thompson, J.C. AL 13th Bn.Part.Rangers Co.B
Thompson, J.C. AL 1st Regt. Mobile Vol. Co.E
Thompson, J.C. AR 1st Cav. Co.E
Thompson, J.C. AR 15th (Josey's) Inf. 1st Co.C 3rd Lt.
Thompson, J.C. AR 19th (Dockery's) Inf. Co.C
Thompson, J.C. AR 30th Inf. Co.K
Thompson, J.C. GA Cav. Waring's Co.
Thompson, J.C. GA 1st (Ramsey's) Inf. Co.A Band Music.
Thompson, J.C. GA 8th Inf. Co.B
Thompson, J.C. GA Inf. 18th Bn. Co.A
Thompson, J.C. GA 32nd Inf. Co.I Lt.
Thompson, J.C. MS 6th Cav. Co.I
Thompson, J.C. MS 46th Inf. Co.A
Thompson, J.C. NC 5th Inf. Co.I
Thompson, J.C. NC 6th Inf.
Thompson, J.C. NC 21st Inf. Co.H
Thompson, J.C. NC 39th Inf. Co.C
Thompson, J.C. NC 57th Inf. Co.B
Thompson, J.C. SC Lt.Arty. 3rd (Palmetto) Bn. Co.G
Thompson, J.C. SC 3rd St.Troops Co.C
Thompson, J.C. SC 8th Res.
Thompson, J.C. SC 26th Inf. Co.I
Thompson, J.C. TN 3rd (Forrest's) Cav. Co.I
Thompson, J.C. TN 12th (Green's) Cav. Co.F
Thompson, J.C. TN 9th Inf. Co.A
Thompson, J.C. TN 9th Inf. Co.H
Thompson, J.C. TN 45th Inf. Co.F
Thompson, J.C. TN 61st Mtd.Inf. Co.A
Thompson, J.C. TX 2nd Cav. Co.C
Thompson, J.C. TX 10th Cav. Co.F
Thompson, J.C. TX 33rd Cav. Co.F
Thompson, J.C. TX 12th Field Btty.
Thompson, J.C. TX 9th (Young's) Inf. Co.B Sgt.
Thompson, J.C. TX 20th Inf. Co.I Cpl.
Thompson, J.C. VA 14th Cav. Co.B
Thompson, J.C. VA 21st Inf. Co.C
Thompson, J.C. Forrest's Scouts T. Henderson's Co.,CSA
Thompson, J.C. Gen. & Staff Asst.Surg.
Thompson, J.C.C. SC 1st Cav. Co.F
Thompson, J.D. AR 2nd Cav. Co.E
Thompson, J.D. AR 10th Inf. Co.A
Thompson, J.D. AR 15th (Johnson's) Inf. Co.D
Thompson, J.D. AR 37th Inf. Co.A Sr.2nd Lt.
Thompson, J.D. GA 10th Cav. (St.Guards) Co.E Sgt.
Thompson, J.D. GA 12th (Robinson's) Cav. (St.Guards) Co.D
Thompson, J.D. GA Siege Arty. 28th Bn. Co.K Cpl.
Thompson, J.D. GA Inf. 1st Loc.Troops (Augusta) Barnes' Lt.Arty.Co.
Thompson, J.D. GA 31st Inf. Co.G
Thompson, J.D. GA 60th Inf. Co.I
Thompson, J.D. KY 1st Inf.
Thompson, J.D. MS 4th Inf. Co.I
Thompson, J.D. MO 11th Inf. Co.D
Thompson, J.D. MO 16th Inf. Co.F
Thompson, J.D. SC Cav. 4th Bn. Co.A
Thompson, J.D. SC 10th Inf. Co.M
Thompson, J.D. TN 22nd Inf. Looney's Co.
Thompson, J.D. TN 38th Inf. Co.L
Thompson, J.D. TX 4th Cav. Co.K Cpl.
Thompson, J.D. TX St.Troops Teel's Co.
Thompson, J.D. VA Cav. Mosby's Regt. (Part.Rangers) Co.B
Thompson, J.D. VA 30th Bn.S.S. Co.C
Thompson, J.D. Gen. & Staff Surg.
Thompson, J. Davis Gen. & Staff Surg.
Thompson, J.D.H. GA 46th Inf. Co.A
Thompson, J.E. AL St.Troops
Thompson, J.E. AR 38th Inf. Co.A Asst.Surg.
Thompson, J.E. GA 10th Inf. Co.B
Thompson, J.E. GA 28th Inf. Co.C QMSgt.
Thompson, J.E. GA 48th Inf. Co.I 1st Sgt.
Thompson, J.E. MS Lt.Arty. (Jefferson Arty.) Darden's Co.
Thompson, J.E. SC 3rd Res. Co.G
Thompson, J.E. TN Inf. 1st Cons.Regt. Co.E
Thompson, J.E. TN 9th Inf. Co.A
Thompson, J.E. TX 12th Cav. Co.K
Thompson, J.E. TX 25th Cav. Co.B
Thompson, J.E. TX 11th (Spaight's) Bn.Vol. Co.D
Thompson, J.E. TX 21st Inf. Co.H
Thompson, J.E. VA 3rd Cav. 2nd Co.I

Thompson, Jeff AR 1st Mtd.Rifles Co.D
Thompson, Jeff AR 2nd Mtd.Rifles Co.E
Thompson, Jeff GA 36th (Villepigue's) Inf. Co.K
Thompson, Jeff. LA 8th Inf. Co.G
Thompson, Jefferson FL Cav. 3rd Bn. Co.C
Thompson, Jefferson VA Cav. 34th Bn. Co.D
Thompson, Jefferson VA 129th Mil. Carter's Co.
Thompson, Jefferson 1st Conf.Inf. 1st Co.K
Thompson, Jefferson J. LA Pointe Coupee Arty. 1st Lt.
Thompson, Jehile VA 51st Inf. Co.F
Thompson, Jeptha AL 25th Inf. Co.H
Thompson, Jeptha AL Cp. of Instr. Talladega
Thompson, Jeptha MS 4th Inf. Co.A
Thompson, Jepthy J. GA 53rd Inf. Co.B
Thompson, Jeremiah GA 16th Inf. Co.D
Thompson, Jeremiah MS 27th Inf. Co.A
Thompson, Jesse AL 7th Cav. Co.B
Thompson, Jesse FL 1st Inf. New Co.E
Thompson, Jesse GA 26th Inf. 1st Co.G
Thompson, Jesse GA 29th Inf. Co.E
Thompson, Jesse MS 3rd (St.Troops) Cav. Co.F 2nd Lt.
Thompson, Jesse MS Arty. (Seven Stars Arty.) Roberts' Co.
Thompson, Jesse, Jr. MS 12th Inf. Co.D 2nd Lt.
Thompson, Jesse NC Inf.
Thompson, Jesse SC 1st Inf. Co.I
Thompson, Jesse TX 8th Cav. Co.H Sgt.
Thompson, Jesse TX Cav. Hardeman's Regt. Co.G
Thompson, Jesse VA Inf. 26th Bn. Co.D
Thompson, Jesse Conf.Arty. Nelson's Bn. Co.I 2nd Lt.
Thompson, Jesse B. AL Cav. 5th Bn. Hilliard's Legion Co.D
Thompson, Jessee GA Cav. (St.Guards) Bond's Co.
Thompson, Jessee LA 28th (Gray's) Inf. Co.G
Thompson, Jesse E. Gen. & Staff Asst.Surg.
Thompson, Jessee W. AL 28th Inf. Co.D
Thompson, Jesse F. NC 44th Inf. Co.G
Thompson, Jesse G. MS 27th Inf. Co.L 2nd Lt.
Thompson, Jesse J. NC 18th Inf. Co.D
Thompson, Jesse L. TN 11th Cav.
Thompson, Jesse L. VA Lt.Arty. J.D. Smith's Co. Sgt.
Thompson, Jesse L. VA 28th Inf. 1st Co.C Sgt.
Thompson, Jesse M. AL 22nd Inf. Co.F
Thompson, Jesse M.N. VA 45th Inf. Co.F Cpl.
Thompson, Jesse P. GA 57th Inf. Co.D
Thompson, Jesse R. NC 8th Sr.Res. Daniel's Co.
Thompson, Jesse S. AL 36th Inf. Co.F
Thompson, Jesse S. AL 47th Inf. Co.H Cpl.
Thompson, Jesse S. GA Lt.Arty. Milledge's Co. 2nd Lt.
Thompson, Jesse S. SC 1st Arty. Co.G
Thompson, Jesse W. TN 41st Inf. Co.B Cpl.
Thompson, Jesse W. VA 30th Bn.S.S. Co.C
Thompson, Jethro GA 11th Inf. Co.I
Thompson, Jezrael VA 63rd Inf. Co.H
Thompson, J.F. AL 3rd Bn.Res. Appling's Co.
Thompson, J.F. AR Lt.Arty. Owen's Btty.
Thompson, J.F. AR Lt.Arty. Owen's Btty. Sr.2nd Lt.
Thompson, J.F. FL 3rd Inf. Co.F
Thompson, J.F. GA Cav. 20th Bn. Co.E
Thompson, J.F. KY 4th Mtd.Inf. Co.F 1st Sgt.
Thompson, J.F. LA 6th Cav. Co.A
Thompson, J.F. LA 17th Inf. Co.F
Thompson, J.F. MS 28th Cav. Co.D
Thompson, J.F. MS Cav.Res. 1st Lt.
Thompson, J.F. MS 26th Inf. Co.D
Thompson, J.F. MS 32nd Inf. Co.I
Thompson, J.F. MO 5th Cav. Co.C
Thompson, J.F. MO 2nd Inf. Co.D
Thompson, J.F. NC 1st Inf. Co.B
Thompson, J.F. TN 3rd (Forrest's) Cav. Co.B
Thompson, J.F. TN 5th (McKenzie's) Cav. Co.A
Thompson, J.F. TN 12th (Green's) Cav. Co.D
Thompson, J.F. TN 42nd Inf. Co.C
Thompson, J.F. TX 2nd Inf. Co.H
Thompson, J.F. Horse Arty. White's Btty.
Thompson, J.F. Gen. & Staff Capt.,QM
Thompson, J. Frank AR 9th Inf. Co.K
Thompson, J.G. AL 33rd Inf. Co.D
Thompson, J.G. GA 28th Inf. Co.I
Thompson, J.G. MS Inf. 3rd Bn. (St.Troops) Co.D
Thompson, J.G. NC 2nd Inf. Co.B
Thompson, J.G. NC 15th Inf. Co.H
Thompson, J.G. NC 35th Inf. Co.G
Thompson, J.G. TX 5th Cav. Sgt.
Thompson, J.G. TX 14th Inf. Co.I
Thompson, J.G. TX Inf. Yarbrough's Co. (Smith Cty.Lt.Inf.)
Thompson, J.G. VA 6th Cav. Co.I
Thompson, J.G. VA Mil. Stowers' Co.
Thompson, J.G. Gen. & Staff Maj.,AIG
Thompson, J.H. AL 1st Cav. 2nd Co.E
Thompson, J.H. AL 3rd Cav. Co.G
Thompson, J.H. AL 53rd (Part.Rangers) Co.A
Thompson, J.H. AL 24th Inf. Co.G
Thompson, J.H. AL 40th Inf. Co.D Cpl.
Thompson, J.H. AL 45th Inf. Co.K
Thompson, J.H. AL 63rd Inf. Co.B Sgt.
Thompson, J.H. AR 10th (Witt's) Cav. Co.C
Thompson, J.H. AR Cav. McGehee's Regt. Co.E Sgt.
Thompson, J.H. AR Lt.Arty. 5th Btty.
Thompson, J.H. AR 15th (Josey's) Inf. Co.G
Thompson, J.H. AR 31st Inf. Co.D
Thompson, J.H. GA Arty. Lumpkin's Co.
Thompson, J.H. GA 3rd Res. Co.H
Thompson, J.H. GA 8th Inf. Co.C
Thompson, J.H. GA 40th Inf. Co.A
Thompson, J.H. GA 43rd Inf. Co.F
Thompson, J.H. KY 2nd (Woodward's) Cav. Co.F 1st Sgt.
Thompson, J.H. LA 14th Inf. Co.I
Thompson, J.H. LA Miles' Legion Co.D
Thompson, J.H. MS Cav. 1st Bn. (McNair's) St.Troops Co.A
Thompson, J.H. MS 7th Cav. Co.E
Thompson, J.H. MS 28th Cav. Co.D
Thompson, J.H. MS Cav. Ham's Regt. Co.E
Thompson, J.H. MS 27th Inf. Co.H
Thompson, J.H. MS 33rd Inf. Co.K
Thompson, J.H. MS 37th Inf. Co.I
Thompson, J.H. MO Thompson's Command
Thompson, J.H. NC 62nd Inf. Co.F
Thompson, J.H. NC Lt.Arty. Thomas' Legion Levi's Btty.
Thompson, J.H. SC 1st (Butler's) Inf. Co.B
Thompson, J.H. SC 1st (Hagood's) Inf. Co.E Capt.
Thompson, J.H. SC 1st (Hagood's) Inf. 1st Co.F, 2nd Co.G Sgt.
Thompson, J.H. SC Inf. 1st (Charleston) Bn. Co.A
Thompson, J.H. SC Mil. 16th Regt. Jones' Co.
Thompson, J.H. TN 4th (McLemore's) Cav. Co.C
Thompson, J.H. TN 5th (McKenzie's) Cav. Co.A
Thompson, J.H. TN 14th (Neely's) Cav. Co.I
Thompson, J.H. TN 15th (Cons.) Cav. Co.K
Thompson, J.H. TN 19th (Biffle's) Cav. Co.L
Thompson, J.H. TN 19th & 20th (Cons.) Cav. Co.K
Thompson, J.H. TN 20th Cav.
Thompson, J.H. TN 20th (Russell's) Cav. Co.F
Thompson, J.H. TN 38th Inf. Co.E Ord.Sgt.
Thompson, J.H. TN 44th (Cons.) Inf. Co.G
Thompson, J.H. TN 51st (Cons.) Inf. Co.C Sgt.
Thompson, J.H. TN 55th (McKoin's) Inf. Duggan's Co.
Thompson, J.H. TX 5th Cav. Co.H
Thompson, J.H. TX 11th Cav. Co.G
Thompson, J.H. TX 12th Cav. Co.B
Thompson, J.H. TX Cav. Wells' Regt. Co.E
Thompson, J.H. VA Lt.Arty. Barr's Co.
Thompson, J.H. VA Lt.Arty. Penick's Co.
Thompson, J.H. VA 2nd Inf.Loc.Def. Co.A
Thompson, J.H. VA Inf. 2nd Bn.Loc.Def. Co.C
Thompson, J.H. VA 7th Inf. Co.K
Thompson, J.H. VA Mil. Washington Cty.
Thompson, J.H. 8th (Wade's) Conf.Cav. Co.B
Thompson, J.H. Jones' Staff Surg.
Thompson, J.H. Gen. & Staff Chap.
Thompson, J.H. Gen. & Staff, QM Dept. Capt.,AQM
Thompson, J.H. Gen. & Staff Hosp.Stew.
Thompson, J. Henry LA 8th Inf. Co.D
Thompson, J.H.L. TN 9th Inf. Co.F
Thompson, J.I. TX Cav. Hardeman's Regt. Co.G
Thompson, Jimson 1st Choctaw Mtd.Rifles Co.H
Thompson, Jimson 1st Choctaw & Chickasaw Mtd.Rifles 3rd Co.F Cpl.
Thompson, J.J. AL 2nd Cav. Co.E
Thompson, J.J. AL 5th Cav. Co.D
Thompson, J.J. AL 51st (Part.Rangers) Co.I
Thompson, J.J. AR 30th Inf.
Thompson, J.J. FL 2nd Inf. Co.B Capt.
Thompson, J.J. GA Cav. 16th Bn. (St.Guards) Co.D
Thompson, J.J. GA 3rd Res. Co.E
Thompson, J.J. GA 8th Inf. (St.Guards) Co.I
Thompson, J.J. GA Inf. 25th Bn. (Prov.Guard) Co.B
Thompson, J.J. GA 43rd Inf. Co.L
Thompson, J.J. GA Inf. (Milledgeville Guards) Caraker's Co.
Thompson, J.J. GA 2nd St.Line 1st Lt.
Thompson, J.J. LA 1st Cav. Co.F
Thompson, J.J. LA 2nd Cav. Co.A
Thompson, J.J. LA 1st (Strawbridge's) Inf. Co.B
Thompson, J.J. LA 21st (Kennedy's) Inf. Co.E
Thompson, J.J. MS 5th Cav. Co.B
Thompson, J.J. MS 7th Cav. Co.H Capt.

Thompson, J.J. MS Cav. Dunn's Co. (MS Rangers)
Thompson, J.J. MO Cav. Schnabel's Bn. Co.F
Thompson, J.J. SC 16th Inf. Co.D
Thompson, J.J. SC 23rd Inf. Co.K
Thompson, J.J. SC 24th Inf. Co.B
Thompson, J.J. SC Inf. Holcombe Legion Co.B
Thompson, J.J. TN 10th (DeMoss') Cav. Co.E Cpl.
Thompson, J.J. TN 14th Cav. Co.I
Thompson, J.J. TN Cav. Napier's Bn. Co.B Cpl.
Thompson, J.J. TN 24th Bn.S.S. Co.B
Thompson, J.J. TN 37th Inf. Co.F
Thompson, J.J. TN 55th (Brown's) Inf. Co.F,B
Thompson, J.J. TX 35th (Brown's) Cav. Co.A,F,C
Thompson, J.J. TX 9th (Young's) Inf. Co.I Comsy.Sgt.
Thompson, J.J. TX 13th Vol. 1st Co.B
Thompson, J.J. TX 19th Inf. Co.D
Thompson, J.J. TX 22nd Inf. Co.C
Thompson, J.J. VA Arty. Young's Co.
Thompson, J.J. VA 23rd Cav. Co.D Cpl.
Thompson, J.J. Sig.Corps,CSA
Thompson, J.J.A. TN Conscr. (Cp. of Instr.)
Thompson, J.J.F. AL 9th (Malone's) Cav. Co.B Far.
Thompson, J.J.V. GA 45th Inf. Co.F
Thompson, J.K. AL 53rd (Part.Rangers) Co.D Sgt.
Thompson, J.K. GA 36th (Broyles') Inf. Co.C
Thompson, J.K. MS Inf. 1st Bn.St.Troops (30 days '64) Co.D Recruit
Thompson, J.K. TN 8th (Smith's) Cav. Co.A
Thompson, J.K. TX Cav. Waller's Regt. Co.A
Thompson, J.L. AL 2nd Cav. Co.K
Thompson, J.L. AL 53rd (Part.Rangers) Co.A
Thompson, J.L. AL 53rd (Part.Rangers) Co.F
Thompson, J.L. AL Lt.Arty. Goldthwaite's Btty.
Thompson, J.L. AL 5th Inf. New Co.C
Thompson, J.L. AL 11th Inf. Co.D
Thompson, J.L. GA Arty. Lumpkin's Co.
Thompson, J.L. GA 22nd Inf. Co.C
Thompson, J.L. KY 12th Cav. Co.H
Thompson, J.L. LA 2nd Inf. Co.I
Thompson, J.L. MS 3rd Cav. Co.A
Thompson, J.L. MS 3rd Inf. (St.Troops) Co.I
Thompson, J.L. MS 5th Inf. Co.G
Thompson, J.L. MS 32nd Inf. Co.B
Thompson, J.L. MS 41st Inf. Co.L
Thompson, J.L. NC 57th Inf. Co.K
Thompson, J.L. SC 1st (Hagood's) Inf. 2nd Co.F Cpl.
Thompson, J.L. SC Prov.Guard Hamilton's Co.
Thompson, J.L. TN 19th (Biffle's) Cav. Co.F Cpl.
Thompson, J.L. TN Lt.Arty. Morton's Co.
Thompson, J.L. TN Inf. 1st Cons.Regt. Co.K
Thompson, J.L. TN 3rd (Clack's) Inf. Co.B
Thompson, J.L. TN Inf. 4th Cons.Regt. Co.C
Thompson, J.L. TN 16th Inf. Co.C Capt.
Thompson, J.L. TN 49th Inf. Co.D
Thompson, J.L. Inf. Bailey's Cons.Regt. Co.L
Thompson, J.L. TX 9th (Young's) Inf. Co.K
Thompson, J.L. VA 2nd Cav. Co.K Cpl.
Thompson, J.L. VA 21st Inf. Co.C
Thompson, J.L. VA 74th Mil. Maj.
Thompson, J.L. Conf.Cav. Wood's Regt. Co.H
Thompson, J.M. AL 53rd (Part.Rangers) Co.A
Thompson, J.M. AL 13th Inf. Co.I Sgt.
Thompson, J.M. AL 22nd Inf. Co.G
Thompson, J.M. AL 34th Inf. Co.K
Thompson, J.M. AL 45th Inf. Co.D
Thompson, J.M. AL 46th Inf.
Thompson, J.M. AL 50th Inf. Co.G
Thompson, J.M. AL 62nd Inf. Co.H
Thompson, J.M. AL Cp. of Instr. Talladega
Thompson, J.M. AR 2nd Inf. Co.F
Thompson, J.M. AR 36th Inf. Co.I
Thompson, J.M. GA 1st (Symons') Res. Co.F,E,A
Thompson, J.M. GA 5th Inf. (St.Guards) Rucker's Co. Sgt.
Thompson, J.M. GA 15th Inf.
Thompson, J.M. GA 38th Inf. Co.A
Thompson, J.M. GA 46th Inf. Co.E
Thompson, J.M. GA 53rd Inf. Co.F
Thompson, J.M. GA 63rd Inf. Co.I Sgt.
Thompson, J.M. GA Inf. Clemons' Co.
Thompson, J.M. KY 3rd Mtd.Inf. Co.H Cpl.
Thompson, J.M. LA 4th Inf. Co.B
Thompson, J.M. LA Inf.Crescent Regt. Co.I
Thompson, J.M. MS 8th Cav. Co.A
Thompson, J.M. MS Lt.Arty. Lomax's Co.
Thompson, J.M. MS 25th Inf. Co.B
Thompson, J.M. MO 6th Cav. Co.A,I
Thompson, J.M. NC 57th Inf. Co.I
Thompson, J.M. NC 64th Inf. Co.D
Thompson, J.M. SC 20th Inf. Co.M
Thompson, J.M. TN 14th (Neely's) Cav. Co.A
Thompson, J.M. TN 15th (Cons.) Cav. Co.C
Thompson, J.M. TN Cav. 16th Bn. (Neal's) Co.A
Thompson, J.M. TN 3rd (Clack's) Inf. Co.B 1st Lt.
Thompson, J.M. TN 5th Inf. 2nd Co.B
Thompson, J.M. TN 26th Inf.
Thompson, J.M. TN 44th (Cons.) Inf. Co.G
Thompson, J.M. TN 49th Inf. Co.D
Thompson, J.M. TX Cav. 2nd Bn.St.Troops Co.A Sgt.
Thompson, J.M. TX Cav. Crump's Regt. Co.G Capt.
Thompson, J.M. TX 15th Inf. Co.C
Thompson, J.M. VA 4th Cav. Co.F
Thompson, J.M. VA 8th Cav. Co.H
Thompson, J.M. VA 36th Inf. Co.A
Thompson, J.M. VA Mil. Stowers' Co.
Thompson, J.M. 2nd Conf.Inf. Co.B
Thompson, J.M. 2nd Conf.Eng.Troops
Thompson, J.M. 3rd Conf.Eng.Troops Co.C Sgt.
Thompson, J.M. Gen. & Staff Maj.,QM
Thompson, J.M.J. GA Arty. (Chatham Arty.) Wheaton's Co.
Thompson, J.M.J. GA 1st (Olmstead's) Inf. Claghorn's Co.
Thompson, J. Morgan AL 51st (Part.Rangers) Co.D Sgt.
Thompson, J.N. AL 5th Cav. Co.D
Thompson, J.N. AL 35th Inf. Co.B Cpl.
Thompson, J.N. AR Cav. Gordon's Regt. Co.C
Thompson, J.N. GA 46th Inf. Co.C
Thompson, J.N. KY 12th Cav. Co.H
Thompson, J.N. LA Inf. 4th Bn. Co.B
Thompson, J.N. MS 9th Cav. Co.A
Thompson, J.N. MO Cav. 1st Regt.St.Guard Co.C 1st Sgt.
Thompson, J.N. MO 7th Cav. Co.E
Thompson, J.N. NC 1st Cav. (9th St.Troops) Co.C
Thompson, J.N. TX 29th Cav. Co.C
Thompson, J.N. TX 22nd Inf. Co.D Music.
Thompson, J.O. FL 1st Inf. New Co.G Sgt.
Thompson, J.O. LA Miles' Legion Co.C
Thompson, J.O. MS 8th Inf. Co.A
Thompson, J.O. MS 37th Inf. Co.G
Thompson, J.O. NC 2nd Jr.Res. Co.C
Thompson, Jobery SC 1st St.Troops Co.H
Thompson, Joe AL 26th Inf. Co.F
Thompson, Joe AL 35th Inf. Co.B
Thompson, Joe TX Cav. 1st Bn.St.Troops Co.D
Thompson, Joe TX Cav. Morgan's Regt.
Thompson, Joe TX Inf. 3rd St.Troops Co.A
Thompson, Joe A. TN Inf. 3rd Cons.Regt. Co.E Sgt.
Thompson, Joe C. LA 17th Inf. Co.F
Thompson, Joe C. TX Waul's Legion Co.E
Thompson, Joel GA Inf. 9th Bn. Co.D
Thompson, Joel GA 24th Inf. Co.D
Thompson, Joel TN 2nd (Ashby's) Cav. Co.I
Thompson, Joel B. GA Inf. 9th Bn. Co.B
Thompson, Joel H. AL 43rd Inf. Co.A
Thompson, Joel P. AL 56th Part.Rangers Co.D
Thompson, Joel T. VA 41st Inf. Co.A
Thompson, Joe T. GA 1st (Olmstead's) Inf. Co.K
Thompson, Johile VA 22nd Inf. Co.I
Thompson, John AL 2nd Cav. Co.A
Thompson, John AL 9th (Malone's) Cav. Co.B
Thompson, John AL Inf. 2nd Regt. Co.K
Thompson, John AL 4th Inf. Co.H
Thompson, John AL 6th Inf. Co.D
Thompson, John AL 12th Inf. Co.C
Thompson, John AL 17th Inf. Co.F
Thompson, John AL 31st Inf. Co.D
Thompson, John AL 39th Inf.
Thompson, John AL 55th Vol. Co.D
Thompson, John AL 61st Inf. Co.G
Thompson, John AL 63rd Inf. Co.B
Thompson, John AR 1st (Monroe's) Cav. Co.K
Thompson, John AR Lt.Arty. Rivers' Btty. Sgt.
Thompson, John AR 1st Vol. Anderson's Co.
Thompson, John AR 19th (Dawson's) Inf. Co.H
Thompson, John AR 19th (Dockery's) Inf. Co.C
Thompson, John FL Cav. 5th Bn. Co.H
Thompson, John FL 3rd Inf. Co.D
Thompson, John GA 2nd Cav. Co.K
Thompson, John GA 2nd Cav. (St.Guards) Co.H
Thompson, John GA 11th Cav. Co.C
Thompson, John GA 1st (Symons') Res. Co.F
Thompson, John GA 5th Inf. Co.D Capt.
Thompson, John GA 46th Inf. Co.C
Thompson, John GA 47th Inf. Co.E
Thompson, John GA 52nd Inf. Co.H
Thompson, John GA Phillips' Legion
Thompson, John KY 2nd Cav. Co.C
Thompson, John KY 10th (Johnson's) Cav. Co.D 2nd Lt.
Thompson, John KY Morgan's Men Co.I,E
Thompson, John KY 1st Inf. Co.E
Thompson, John KY 3rd Mtd.Inf. Co.G

Thompson, John LA 1st (Strawbridge's) Inf. Co.E
Thompson, John LA 1st Inf. Co.D
Thompson, John LA Inf. 1st Sp.Bn. (Wheat's) Co.B
Thompson, John LA Mil. 3rd Regt. 1st Brig. 1st Div. Co.F
Thompson, John LA Inf. 4th Bn. Co.B
Thompson, John LA 5th Inf. Co.G
Thompson, John LA 10th Inf. Co.H Sgt.
Thompson, John MD 1st Cav. Co.E
Thompson, John MD Walters' Co. (Zarvona Zouaves)
Thompson, John MS 6th Cav. Co.L
Thompson, John MS 11th (Perrin's) Cav. Co.G
Thompson, John MS Cav. Ham's Regt.
Thompson, John MS 7th Inf. Co.D 2nd Lt.
Thompson, John MS 9th Inf. New Co.G Cpl.
Thompson, John MS 10th Inf. Old Co.C
Thompson, John MS 19th Inf. Co.A
Thompson, John MS 19th Inf. Co.C
Thompson, John MS 25th Inf. Co.B
Thompson, John MS 25th Inf. Co.F
Thompson, John MS 36th Inf. Co.I
Thompson, John MO 1st N.E. Cav. Co.A
Thompson, John MO 3rd Cav. Co.F
Thompson, John MO 5th Cav. Co.B
Thompson, John MO 7th Cav. Co.G
Thompson, John MO 12th Cav. Co.C
Thompson, John MO Cav. Preston's Bn. Co.C 1st Sgt.
Thompson, John MO 1st Inf. Co.C
Thompson, John MO Robertson's Regt.St.Guard Co.3
Thompson, John MO Robertson's Regt.St.Guard Co.4 1st Sgt.
Thompson, John MO St.Guard
Thompson, John NC 2nd Cav. (19th St.Troops) Co.E
Thompson, John NC 1st Inf. Co.K
Thompson, John NC 1st Jr.Res. Co.G
Thompson, John NC 2nd Inf. Co.E
Thompson, John NC 7th Inf. Co.K
Thompson, John NC 8th Inf. Co.K
Thompson, John NC 14th Inf. Co.H
Thompson, John NC 16th Inf. Co.E
Thompson, John NC 18th Inf. Co.H
Thompson, John NC 20th Inf. Co.K
Thompson, John NC 31st Inf. Co.E Sgt.
Thompson, John NC 31st Inf. Co.K
Thompson, John NC 51st Inf. Co.E
Thompson, John NC 52nd Inf. Co.G
Thompson, John NC 57th Inf. Co.I
Thompson, John NC 64th Inf. Co.I
Thompson, John NC Inf. Thomas Legion Co.G
Thompson, John SC 5th Cav. Co.C
Thompson, John SC 7th Cav. Co.H
Thompson, John SC Cav. 17th Bn. Co.D
Thompson, John SC 1st Arty. Co.G
Thompson, John SC Hvy.Arty. Gilchrist's Co. (Gist Guard)
Thompson, John SC Lt.Arty. J.T. Kanapaux's Co. (Lafayette Arty.)
Thompson, John SC 1st (Butler's) Inf. Co.A
Thompson, John SC 3rd Bn.Res. Co.B
Thompson, John SC 4th St.Troops Co.C 2nd Lt.
Thompson, John SC 4th St.Troops Co.H
Thompson, John SC 5th Bn.Res. Co.D Capt.
Thompson, John SC 6th Res. Co.F
Thompson, John SC Inf. Holcombe Legion Co.F
Thompson, John TN 2nd (Smith's) Cav.
Thompson, John TN 12th (Green's) Cav. Co.D
Thompson, John TN 18th (Newsom's) Cav. Co.C
Thompson, John TN 21st (Carter's) Cav. Co.G
Thompson, John TN 21st (Wilson's) Cav. Co.D
Thompson, John TN 21st & 22nd (Cons.) Cav. Co.G
Thompson, John TN Arty. Marshall's Co. Sgt.
Thompson, John TN 2nd (Walker's) Inf. Co.F Cpl.
Thompson, John TN Inf. 3rd Cons.Regt. Co.D
Thompson, John TN Inf. 3rd Cons.Regt. Co.I
Thompson, John TN 5th Inf. Co.D
Thompson, John TN 11th Inf. Co.B
Thompson, John TN 12th (Cons.) Inf. Co.H
Thompson, John TN 19th Inf. Co.F
Thompson, John TN 21st Inf. Co.H Sgt.
Thompson, John TN 22nd Inf. Co.B
Thompson, John TN 23rd Inf. Co.D
Thompson, John TN 33rd Inf. Co.D Ord.Sgt.
Thompson, John TN 34th Inf. Co.E
Thompson, John TN 36th Inf. Co.B
Thompson, John TN 41st Inf. Co.B
Thompson, John TN 43rd Inf. Co.B
Thompson, John TN 48th (Nixon's) Inf. Co.D
Thompson, John TN 48th (Voorhies') Inf. Co.D
Thompson, John TN 51st Inf. Co.K
Thompson, John TX 1st (McCulloch's) Cav. Co.B Far.
Thompson, John TX 1st (Yager's) Cav. Co.F Far.
Thompson, John TX 2nd Cav. Co.I
Thompson, John TX 3rd Cav. Co.F
Thompson, John TX 12th Cav. Co.D
Thompson, John TX 22nd Cav. Co.D,I
Thompson, John TX Cav. Baylor's Regt. Co.D
Thompson, John TX Cav. Morgan's Regt.
Thompson, John TX Cav. Waller's Regt. Co.A
Thompson, John TX Arty. Douglas' Co.
Thompson, John TX 12th Inf. Co.A
Thompson, John TX 12th Inf. Co.B
Thompson, John TX Conscr.
Thompson, John, Jr. VA 2nd Cav. Co.E
Thompson, John VA 6th Cav. Co.K
Thompson, John VA 7th Cav. Preston's Co.
Thompson, John VA 8th Cav. Co.L
Thompson, John VA 14th Cav. Co.A
Thompson, John VA 14th Cav. Co.G, 2nd Co.F
Thompson, John VA 16th Cav. Co.G Cpl.
Thompson, John VA 18th Cav. Co.A
Thompson, John VA 22nd Cav. Co.F Cpl.
Thompson, John VA 24th Cav. Co.C
Thompson, John VA 25th Cav. Co.G 1st Sgt.
Thompson, John VA Cav. 34th Bn. Co.D
Thompson, John VA Cav. 40th Bn. Co.A
Thompson, John VA Cav. Ferguson's Bn. Ferguson's Co., Parks' Co.
Thompson, John VA Cav. Mosby's Regt. (Part.Rangers)
Thompson, John VA Hvy.Arty. 19th Bn. 2nd Co.C
Thompson, John VA Lt.Arty. R.M. Anderson's Co.
Thompson, John VA Lt.Arty. Douthat's Co.
Thompson, John VA Horse Arty. Jackson's Co.
Thompson, John VA 2nd Inf. Co.D
Thompson, John VA 5th Inf. Co.L
Thompson, John, Jr. VA 13th Inf. Co.I
Thompson, John VA Inf. 21st Bn. 1st Co.D
Thompson, John VA Inf. 23rd Bn. Co.C
Thompson, John VA Inf. 26th Bn. Co.D Sgt.
Thompson, John VA 27th Inf. 2nd Co.H
Thompson, John VA 36th Inf. 1st Co.B
Thompson, John VA 36th Inf. 2nd Co.K
Thompson, John VA 38th Inf. Co.B
Thompson, John VA 45th Inf. Co.A Capt.
Thompson, John VA 46th Mil. Co.B
Thompson, John VA 46th Mil. Lantz's Co.
Thompson, John VA 48th Inf. Co.D
Thompson, John VA 59th Inf. 2nd Co.D
Thompson, John VA 64th Mtd.Inf. 2nd Co.F Cpl.
Thompson, John VA 89th Mil. Co.H
Thompson, John VA 135th Mil. Co.D
Thompson, John VA Inf. Mileham's Co.
Thompson, John VA Rockbridge Cty.Res. Miller's Co.
Thompson, John 20th Conf.Cav. 2nd Co.H
Thompson, John Horse Arty. White's Btty.
Thompson, John 2nd Conf.Inf. Co.B
Thompson, John 9th Conf.Inf. Co.D Cpl.
Thompson, John 9th Conf.Inf. Co.E
Thompson, John 9th Conf.Inf. Co.H
Thompson, John Inf. School of Pract. Powell's Detach. Powell's Co.
Thompson, John 1st Choctaw Mtd.Rifles Co.F
Thompson, John 1st Choctaw & Chickasaw Mtd.Rifles 1st Co.E, 2nd Co.K
Thompson, John Deneale's Regt. Choctaw Warriors Co.B
Thompson, John Deneale's Regt. Choctaw Warriors Co.E
Thompson, John 1st Conf.Eng.Troops Co.G
Thompson, John A. AL Jeff Davis Arty.
Thompson, John A. AL Inf. 1st Regt. Co.F,A
Thompson, John A. AL 22nd Inf. Co.F
Thompson, John A. AL 23rd Bn.S.S. Co.F
Thompson, John A. AL 41st Inf. Co.E
Thompson, John A. AL 1st Bn. Hilliard's Legion Vol. Co.F
Thompson, John A. FL 8th Inf. Co.A Sgt.
Thompson, John A. GA 4th (Clinch's) Cav. Co.G 2nd Lt.
Thompson, John A. GA 26th Inf. Co.K Sgt.
Thompson, John A. GA 47th Inf. Co.H,D
Thompson, John A. GA 53rd Inf. Co.B Cpl.
Thompson, John A. MS Cav. 1st Bn. (Miller's) Co.A
Thompson, John A. MS St.Troops (Herndon Rangers) Montgomery's Ind.Co.
Thompson, John A. NC 2nd Arty. (36th St.Troops) Co.B
Thompson, John A. NC 1st Inf. (6 mo. '61) Co.H
Thompson, John A. NC 6th Inf. Co.F
Thompson, John A. NC 23rd Inf. Co.K Sgt.
Thompson, John A. NC 30th Inf. Co.B
Thompson, John A. NC 33rd Inf. Co.F
Thompson, John A. NC 48th Inf. Co.G 1st Lt.

Thompson, John A. TN 3rd (Forrest's) Cav. 1st Co.F
Thompson, John A. VA Lt.Arty. Arch. Graham's Co.
Thompson, John A. VA Cav. 35th Bn. Co.C Sgt.
Thompson, John A. VA 14th Inf. 2nd Co.G
Thompson, John A. VA 72nd Mil.
Thompson, John B. AR 1st (Colquitt's) Inf. Lt.Col.
Thompson, John B. AR 5th Inf. Sgt.
Thompson, John B. GA 2nd Res. Co.F
Thompson, John B. GA 38th Inf. Co.K
Thompson, John B. KY 2nd (Duke's) Cav. Co.E
Thompson, John B. MS Cav. Powers' Regt. Co.B
Thompson, John B. MS 1st (Patton's) Inf. Co.K
Thompson, John B. MS 37th Inf. Co.A
Thompson, John B. NC 8th Sr.Res. McLean's Co. Cpl.
Thompson, John B. NC 33rd Inf. Co.H
Thompson, John B. SC 12th Inf. Co.I
Thompson, John B. TN 42nd Inf. Co.C 1st Lt.
Thompson, John B. TN 59th Mtd.Inf. Co.E
Thompson, John B. VA 25th Cav. Co.A Capt.
Thompson, John B. VA 14th Inf. Co.K
Thompson, John B. VA 28th Inf. Co.I
Thompson, John B. VA 45th Inf. Co.I
Thompson, John B. VA 114th Mil. Co.A
Thompson, John B.W. Conf.Cav. Powers' Regt. Co.G
Thompson, John C. FL 1st Cav. Co.B
Thompson, John C. GA 25th Inf. Co.H
Thompson, John C. GA 49th Inf. Co.K
Thompson, John C. KY 5th Cav. Co.H
Thompson, John C. MS 30th Inf. Co.A Cpl.
Thompson, John C. MS 44th Inf. Co.D Maj.
Thompson, John C. NC 37th Inf.
Thompson, John C. SC 2nd Res.
Thompson, John C. SC 13th Inf. Co.I
Thompson, John C. SC 17th Inf. Co.I
Thompson, John C. TN 20th Inf. Co.C 2nd Lt.
Thompson, John C. TX 36th Cav. Co.D Cpl.
Thompson, John C. VA Lt.Arty. Lowry's Co.
Thompson, John C. VA 11th Inf. Co.F
Thompson, John C. 3rd Conf.Eng.Troops Co.A
Thompson, Jno. C. Gen. & Staff Maj.,AIG
Thompson, John D. AL Inf. 1st Regt. Co.D
Thompson, John D. GA 45th Inf. Co.H
Thompson, John D. GA 45th Inf. Co.I
Thompson, John D. KY 6th Cav. Co.E
Thompson, John D. LA 1st (Nelligan's) Inf.
Thompson, John D. NC 14th Inf. Co.K Sgt.
Thompson, John D. NC 37th Inf. Co.H
Thompson, John D. SC Inf. Hampton Legion Co.C
Thompson, John D. TN 12th (Green's) Cav. Co.C
Thompson, John D. TN 40th Inf. Co.G
Thompson, John D. VA 151st Mil. Co.C
Thompson, John DeLaF. KY 2nd Mtd.Inf. Co.K 2nd Lt.
Thompson, John E. AL 2nd Cav. Co.K
Thompson, John E. AL 3rd Inf.
Thompson, John E. AL 8th Inf. Co.D
Thompson, John E. GA 1st Cav. Co.H,E
Thompson, John E. GA 19th Inf. Co.F
Thompson, John E. MD Inf. 2nd Bn. Co.F,C
Thompson, John E. NC 24th Inf. Co.E
Thompson, John E. TX 31st Cav. Co.E
Thompson, John E. VA 8th Cav. Co.E 2nd Lt.
Thompson, John E. VA 17th Inf. Co.A
Thompson, John E. VA 17th Inf. Co.C
Thompson, John Easy NC 51st Inf. Co.E
Thompson, John F. AL 58th Inf. Co.I
Thompson, John F. AR 9th Inf. Co.E
Thompson, John F. GA 17th Inf. Co.K
Thompson, John F. GA 45th Inf. Co.F Lt.
Thompson, John F. MS 31st Inf. Co.C
Thompson, John F. MS 40th Inf. Co.A 1st Sgt.
Thompson, John F. MS Clayton's Co. (Jasper Defend.)
Thompson, John F. MO Cav. Snider's Bn. Co.C
Thompson, John F. NC 4th Inf. Co.K
Thompson, John F. NC 27th Inf. Co.G Cpl.
Thompson, John F. NC 44th Inf. Co.G
Thompson, John F. NC 54th Inf. Co.A 3rd Lt.
Thompson, John F. NC 62nd Inf. Co.H
Thompson, John F. TX 1st (McCulloch's) Cav. Co.E
Thompson, John F.C. TX 10th Inf. Co.I Cpl.
Thompson, John G. AL 16th Inf. Co.H
Thompson, John G. GA 47th Inf. Co.D Sgt.
Thompson, John G. NC 6th Cav. (65th St.Troops) Co.E,D
Thompson, John G. NC Cav. 7th Bn. Co.D,E
Thompson, John G. TX 31st Cav.
Thompson, John H. AL Cav. Falkner's Co.
Thompson, John H. AL 13th Inf. Co.E
Thompson, John H. AL 13th Inf. Co.F Sgt.
Thompson, John H. AR 35th Inf. Co.C 1st Sgt.
Thompson, John H. FL 8th Inf. Co.C
Thompson, John H. GA 25th Inf. Co.K
Thompson, John H. GA 66th Inf. Co.G
Thompson, John H. KY 4th Cav. Co.D
Thompson, John H. NC 1st Inf. Co.B
Thompson, John H. NC 2nd Inf. Co.D
Thompson, John H. NC 58th Inf. Co.D Sgt.
Thompson, John H. TX 34th Cav. Co.A Cpl.
Thompson, John H. VA Hvy.Arty. A.J. Jones' Co.
Thompson, John H. VA Lt.Arty. Thompson's Co. 1st Lt.
Thompson, John H. VA 8th Cav. Co.A Capt.
Thompson, John H. VA 18th Cav. Co.C
Thompson, John H. VA 18th Inf. Co.K
Thompson, John H. VA 63rd Inf. Co.D
Thompson, John H.W. MO 3rd Cav. Sgt.
Thompson, John I. AR 33rd Inf. Co.G
Thompson, John I. NC 3rd Arty. (40th St.Troops) Co.K
Thompson, John J. AL 17th Inf. Co.C
Thompson, John J. AR Lt.Arty. Rivers' Btty.
Thompson, John J. FL 1st Inf. Old Co.B
Thompson, John J. FL 2nd Inf. Co.F
Thompson, John J. GA 38th Inf. Co.G
Thompson, John J. GA 53rd Inf. Co.B
Thompson, John J. GA 65th Inf. Co.C
Thompson, John J. MS Standefer's Co.
Thompson, John J. MO Lt.Arty. Landis' Co.
Thompson, John J. NC 3rd Inf. Co.B
Thompson, John J. TN 5th Inf. Co.A
Thompson, John J. TX 11th Inf. Co.K
Thompson, John J. VA 1st Arty. 3rd Co.C
Thompson, John J. VA Lt.Arty. 1st Bn. Co.C
Thompson, John J. VA 14th Inf. 1st Co.G
Thompson, John J. VA 19th Inf. Co.I
Thompson, John J. VA 151st Mil. Co.B
Thompson, John K. NC 48th Inf. Co.K Sgt.
Thompson, John K. VA 22nd Inf. Co.A Capt.
Thompson, John L. AL 51st (Part.Rangers) Co.A
Thompson, John L. AL 2nd Inf. Co.A
Thompson, John L. AR 3rd Cav. Co.G
Thompson, John L. AR 8th Cav. Co.E 2nd Lt.
Thompson, John L. FL 3rd Inf. Co.F
Thompson, John L. GA Lt.Arty. Croft's Btty. (Columbus Arty.) Sgt.
Thompson, John L. LA 28th (Gray's) Inf. Co.D Jr.2nd Lt.
Thompson, John L. MO 11th Inf. Co.B
Thompson, John L. NC 31st Inf. Co.A
Thompson, John L. NC 64th Inf. Co.E Cpl.
Thompson, John L. TN 2nd (Smith's) Cav. Thomason's Co.
Thompson, John L. VA Lt.Arty. Nelson's Co.
Thompson, John L. VA Lt.Arty. Woolfolk's Co.
Thompson, John L. VA 8th Inf. Co.D
Thompson, John L. VA 10th Inf. Co.D Cpl.
Thompson, John M. AL 41st Inf. Sgt.
Thompson, John M. AR 3rd Cav.
Thompson, John M. GA 41st Inf. Co.D
Thompson, John M. MS 7th Inf. Co.C
Thompson, John M. MS 21st Inf. Co.F
Thompson, John M. MS 27th Inf. Co.G 3rd Lt.
Thompson, John M. MS 35th Inf. Co.F
Thompson, John M. MO 16th Inf. Co.B
Thompson, John M. NC 6th Inf. Co.D
Thompson, John M. SC Lt.Arty. 3rd (Palmetto) Bn. Co.D 1st Lt.
Thompson, John M. SC Inf. Hampton Legion Co.A
Thompson, John M. TX 10th Cav. Co.G Capt.
Thompson, John M. VA 22nd Inf. Swann's Co.
Thompson, John M. VA 151st Mil. Co.D 1st Lt.
Thompson, John Madison TX 20th Cav. Co.E
Thompson, John McNairy TN 1st (Feild's) Inf. Co.D Cpl.
Thompson, John M.P. AL 14th Inf. Co.D
Thompson, John N. AR 10th Cav. Co.A
Thompson, John N. GA 20th Inf. Co.G,D
Thompson, John N. MS 43rd Inf. Co.D
Thompson, John N., Jr. NC 49th Inf. Co.C
Thompson, John N., Sr. NC 49th Inf. Co.C 2nd Lt.
Thompson, John N. TN 34th Inf. 2nd Co.C
Thompson, John O. SC 24th Inf. Co.C
Thompson, John O. TX 20th Cav. Co.F
Thompson, John O. TX 11th Inf. Co.I
Thompson, John P. AL 61st Inf. Co.D
Thompson, John P. AR Inf. Hardy's Regt. Co.B
Thompson, John P. GA 15th Inf. Co.K
Thompson, John P. GA 47th Inf. Co.B
Thompson, John P. KY 8th Cav. Co.K
Thompson, John P. KY 12th Cav. Maj.
Thompson, John P. KY 1st Inf. Co.G Capt.
Thompson, John P. MS 15th Inf. Co.B
Thompson, John P. MS 42nd Inf. Co.D
Thompson, John P. MO 7th Cav. Ward's Co.
Thompson, John P. NC 4th Inf. Co.B
Thompson, John P. SC Inf. Hampton Legion Co.E Sgt.

Thompson, John P. TX 17th Cons.Dismtd.Cav. Co.C
Thompson, John P. TX 11th Inf. Co.C
Thompson, John P. VA Cav. 37th Bn. Co.A
Thompson, John P. Gen. & Staff Maj.
Thompson, John Q. AR 26th Inf. Co.B
Thompson, John Q. LA 3rd Inf.
Thompson, John R. AR 26th Inf. Co.D
Thompson, John R. GA 9th Inf. (St.Guards) Co.F
Thompson, John R. GA 25th Inf. Co.K
Thompson, John R. GA 46th Inf. Co.E
Thompson, John R. LA 12th Inf. Co.H
Thompson, John R. MO 7th Cav. Co.B
Thompson, John R. MO Green's Regt.St.Guards 2nd Lt.
Thompson, John R. NC 3rd Bn.Sr.Res. Durham's Co.
Thompson, John R. TX 18th Cav. Co.F
Thompson, John R. TX Cav. Baird's Regt. Co.D
Thompson, John R. TX 19th Inf. Co.H
Thompson, John R. VA 1st Cav. Co.A
Thompson, John R. VA 3rd Res. Co.D Capt.
Thompson, John R. VA 27th Inf. Co.C
Thompson, John R. VA 42nd Inf. Co.C
Thompson, John R. VA 60th Inf. Co.D
Thompson, John R. VA 62nd Mtd.Inf. 2nd Co.H 1st Sgt.
Thompson, John R. Conf.Reg.Inf. Brooks' Bn. Co.C
Thompson, John S. AL 4th Inf.
Thompson, John S. MS 14th Inf. Co.D Sgt.
Thompson, John S. MS 21st Inf. Co.H
Thompson, John S. MO 2nd Cav. Co.B Capt.
Thompson, John S. MO St.Guard Capt.,Asst.Div.QM
Thompson, John S. NC 2nd Cav. (19th St.Troops) Co.B
Thompson, John S. NC 51st Inf. Co.E
Thompson, John S. VA 1st St.Res. Co.D
Thompson, Johnson Gen. & Staff Capt.,AQM
Thompson, Johnson 1st Cherokee Mtd.Vol. AQM
Thompson, Johnson R. MS 14th Inf. Co.E 1st Sgt.
Thompson, John T. AR Inf. 4th Bn. Co.C
Thompson, John T. AR 15th (N.W.) Inf. Co.E
Thompson, John T. GA 3rd Inf. Co.L
Thompson, John T. GA Inf. 3rd Bn. Co.C 2nd Lt.
Thompson, John T. GA 37th Inf. Co.I 2nd Lt.
Thompson, John T. GA 53rd Inf. Co.B Sgt.Maj.
Thompson, John T. MS 14th Inf. Co.C
Thompson, John T. NC 23rd Inf. Co.K
Thompson, John T. NC 51st Inf. Co.H
Thompson, John T. SC 5th Inf. 1st Co.H, Co.B Sgt.
Thompson, John T. SC 16th Inf. Co.E
Thompson, John V. Eng.,CSA
Thompson, John W. AL 51st (Part.Rangers) Co.B Cpl.
Thompson, John W. AL 10th Inf. Co.G
Thompson, John W. AL 14th Inf. Co.K
Thompson, John W. AL 22nd Inf. Co.B
Thompson, John W. AR 1st Inf. Co.F
Thompson, John W. AR 36th Inf. Co.A
Thompson, John W. FL 6th Inf. Co.D
Thompson, John W. GA Hvy.Arty. 22nd Bn. Co.B
Thompson, John W. GA 11th Inf. Co.H
Thompson, John W. GA 18th Inf. Co.F
Thompson, John W. GA 23rd Inf. Co.H
Thompson, John W. GA 25th Inf. 1st Co.K
Thompson, John W. GA 26th Inf. Co.F Cpl.
Thompson, John W. GA 65th Inf. Co.A
Thompson, John W. KY 7th Cav. Co.C
Thompson, John W. LA 3rd (Wingfield's) Cav. Co.E
Thompson, John W. MD Inf. 2nd Bn. Co.G
Thompson, John W. MS Inf. 3rd Bn. Co.E Capt.
Thompson, John W. MS Inf. 3rd Bn. Co.F
Thompson, John W. MS 5th Inf. Co.A Jr.2nd Lt.
Thompson, John W. MS 12th Inf. Co.D Sgt.
Thompson, John W. MS 21st Inf. Co.I
Thompson, John W. MS Clayton's Co. (Jasper Defend.)
Thompson, John W. MO 1st Cav. Co.B
Thompson, John W. MO Cav. Poindexter's Regt.
Thompson, John W. MO Cav. Williams' Regt. Co.G
Thompson, Jno. W. MO 2nd & 6th Cons.Inf.
Thompson, John W. MO 3rd Inf. Co.K
Thompson, John W. MO 11th Inf. Co.B 2nd Lt.
Thompson, John W. MO Milton's Bn.St.Guard Co.D
Thompson, John W. MO Thompson's Command
Thompson, John W. NC 2nd Arty. (36th St.Troops) Co.G
Thompson, John W. NC 13th Inf. Co.A
Thompson, John W. NC 22nd Inf. Co.B
Thompson, John W. TX 5th Inf. Co.G,I
Thompson, John W. NC 35th Inf. Co.H
Thompson, John W. NC 58th Inf. Co.E
Thompson, John W. SC 22nd Inf. Co.E
Thompson, John W. TN 44th (Cons.) Inf. Co.E
Thompson, John W. TN 60th Mtd.Inf. Co.A
Thompson, John W. TX 1st (McCulloch's) Cav. Co.K
Thompson, John W. TX 1st (Yager's) Cav. Co.I
Thompson, John W. TX Cav. 8th (Taylor's) Bn. Co.D
Thompson, John W. TX 13th Cav. Co.A
Thompson, John W. TX 17th Cav. Co.C Sgt.
Thompson, John W. TX 18th Cav. Co.H
Thompson, John W. TX 22nd Cav. Co.I Cpl.
Thompson, John W. TX 27th Cav. Co.D
Thompson, John W. TX Waul's Legion Co.E
Thompson, John W. VA Cav. Hounshell's Bn. Co.C 3rd Lt.
Thompson, John W. VA Hvy.Arty. 18th Bn. Co.C
Thompson, John W. VA 4th Inf. Co.E
Thompson, John W. VA Inf. 5th Bn. Co.B
Thompson, John W. VA 9th Inf. Co.D
Thompson, John W. VA 14th Inf. Co.A
Thompson, John W. VA Inf. 23rd Bn. Co.C
Thompson, John W. VA 25th Inf. 2nd Co.H
Thompson, John W. VA 45th Inf. Co.L
Thompson, John W. VA 48th Inf. Co.A Sgt.
Thompson, John W. VA 63rd Inf. Co.G
Thompson, John W. VA 79th Mil. Co.3 Cpl.
Thompson, John W. VA 135th Mil. Co.A
Thompson, John W. Bradford's Corps Scouts & Guards Co.A 1st Sgt.
Thompson, John Wm. MD Walters' Co. (Zarvona Zouaves)
Thompson, Jonas VA 10th Cav. Co.B
Thompson, Jonathan MO Cav. Coleman's Regt.
Thompson, Jonathan SC 12th Inf. Co.I
Thompson, Jonathan F. MO 1st N.E. Cav.
Thompson, Jonathan S. GA 4th (Clinch's) Cav. Co.I
Thompson, Jones B. MO Lt.Arty. 2nd Field Btty.
Thompson, Jordan AL 53rd (Part.Rangers) Co.B
Thompson, Joseph AL 12th Inf. Co.K
Thompson, Joseph AL 24th Inf. Co.H
Thompson, Joseph AR 19th (Dawson's) Inf. Co.B
Thompson, Joseph GA Lt.Arty. Croft's Btty. (Columbus Arty.)
Thompson, Joseph, Jr. GA 1st (Ramsey's) Inf. Co.F Sgt.Maj.
Thompson, Joseph GA 2nd Res. Co.C
Thompson, Joseph GA 40th Inf. Co.A
Thompson, Joseph KY 4th Mtd.Inf. Co.F
Thompson, Joseph LA Mil. 1st Native Guards Cpl.
Thompson, Joseph LA 28th (Gray's) Inf. Co.G
Thompson, Joseph MD 1st Inf. Co.I
Thompson, Joseph MS 9th Cav. Co.A
Thompson, Joseph MO 5th Cav. Co.B
Thompson, Joseph MO 1st Inf. Co.F
Thompson, Joseph MO 3rd Inf. Co.K
Thompson, Joseph MO 10th Inf. Co.D
Thompson, Joseph NC Inf. 2nd Bn. Co.C
Thompson, Joseph NC 12th Inf. Co.B,D
Thompson, Joseph NC 13th Inf. Co.B 1st Lt.
Thompson, Joseph NC 33rd Inf. Co.F
Thompson, Joseph NC 39th Inf. Co.B
Thompson, Joseph SC 26th Inf. Co.A 1st Lt.
Thompson, Joseph TN 5th (McKenzie's) Cav. Co.B
Thompson, Joseph TN 19th Inf. Co.G
Thompson, Joseph TN 19th Inf. Co.I Sgt.
Thompson, Joseph TN 37th Inf. Co.H
Thompson, Joseph TN 48th (Nixon's) Inf. Co.I
Thompson, Joseph TN 54th Inf. Hollis' Co.
Thompson, Joseph TN 59th Mtd.Inf. Co.D
Thompson, Joseph TN 60th Mtd.Inf. Co.K
Thompson, Joseph TX 1st (Yager's) Cav. Co.K
Thompson, Joseph TX Cav. 2nd Bn.St.Troops Hubbard's Co.
Thompson, Joseph TX 17th Cav. Co.E
Thompson, Joseph TX 25th Cav. Co.B
Thompson, Joseph TX Cav. Morgan's Regt. Co.C
Thompson, Joseph TX Arty. 4th Bn.
Thompson, Joseph TX 8th Inf. Cpl.
Thompson, Joseph TX 9th (Nichols') Inf.
Thompson, Joseph TX 12th Inf. Co.A
Thompson, Joseph TX Waul's Legion Co.H
Thompson, Joseph VA 5th Cav. 2nd Co.F Sgt.
Thompson, Joseph VA 6th Cav. Co.K Cpl.
Thompson, Joseph VA 8th Cav. 1st Co.D
Thompson, Joseph VA 17th Cav. Co.D
Thompson, Joseph VA Cav. 41st Bn. Co.G
Thompson, Joseph VA Cav. Caldwell's Bn. Graham's Co.
Thompson, Joseph VA 2nd Inf. Co.D

Thompson, Joseph VA Inf. 23rd Bn. Co.F
Thompson, Joseph 7th Conf.Cav. Co.M
Thompson, Joseph 4th Conf.Eng.Troops Cpl.
Thompson, Joseph, Jr. Gen. & Staff 2nd Lt., Dr.M.
Thompson, Joseph A. GA 6th Inf. Co.H
Thompson, Joseph A. MS Inf. (Res.) Berry's Co. 1st Lt.
Thompson, Joseph A. SC Cav. 17th Bn. Co.B
Thompson, Joseph A. TN 41st Inf. Co.F Sgt.
Thompson, Joseph B. MS 16th Inf. Co.F
Thompson, Joseph B. NC 6th Inf. Co.F
Thompson, Joseph B. TX 36th Cav. Co.A
Thompson, Joseph B. TX 13th Vol. Co.M
Thompson, Joseph B. TX 15th Inf. 2nd Co.H
Thompson, Joseph C. AL 11th Inf. Co.H
Thompson, Joseph C. GA 1st (Olmstead's) Inf. Screven's Co.
Thompson, Joseph C. GA 47th Inf. Co.H,C Capt.
Thompson, Joseph C. TN 1st (Feild's) Inf. Co.H
Thompson, Joseph C. TN 1st (Turney's) Inf. Co.F
Thompson, Joseph E. GA Floyd Legion (St.Guards) Co.C
Thompson, Joseph E. NC 24th Inf. Co.E
Thompson, Joseph E. VA 8th Cav. Co.G 1st Lt.
Thompson, Joseph E. VA 47th Inf. Co.B Sgt.
Thompson, Joseph F. TX 6th Cav. Co.K Cpl.
Thompson, Joseph F. 1st Cherokee Mtd.Vol. 1st Co.E Maj.
Thompson, Joseph G. MS 11th (Perrin's) Cav. Co.G
Thompson, Joseph G. MS 14th Inf. Co.G
Thompson, Joseph G. MS 35th Inf. Co.D
Thompson, Joseph G. TX 3rd Cav. Co.K
Thompson, Joseph H. MS 1st (King's) Inf. (St.Troops) Co.C Sgt.
Thompson, Joseph H. MS 27th Inf. Co.K
Thompson, Joseph H. NC 6th Inf. Co.F Sgt.
Thompson, Joseph Harkins TN 40th Inf. Co.A
Thompson, Joseph L. KY 4th Cav. Co.D
Thompson, Joseph L. MS 15th Inf. Co.K
Thompson, Joseph L. NC 58th Inf. Co.E
Thompson, Joseph L. VA Lt.Arty. 38th Bn. Co.D 1st Lt.
Thompson, Joseph L. 1st Cherokee Mtd.Vol. 2nd Co.K
Thompson, Joseph M. AR 18th Inf. Co.A Sgt.
Thompson, Joseph M. MS 19th Inf. Co.H
Thompson, Joseph M. MO 3rd Cav. Co.I
Thompson, Joseph M. NC 25th Inf. Co.F
Thompson, Joseph M. SC 26th Inf. Co.A
Thompson, Joseph M. VA 23rd Inf. Co.A
Thompson, Joseph N. AR 15th (Josey's) Inf. Co.F
Thompson, Joseph N. AR Inf. Cocke's Regt. Co.C 2nd Lt.
Thompson, Joseph N. MS 44th Inf. Co.E
Thompson, Joseph N. 1st Cherokee Mtd.Vol. 2nd Co.K
Thompson, Joseph P. TN 4th Inf.
Thompson, Joseph P. VA 36th Inf. Beckett's Co. Cpl.
Thompson, Joseph R. AR 3rd Cav. Co.G
Thompson, Joseph R. GA Cav. 2nd Bn. Co.D
Thompson, Joseph R. GA Seige Arty. 28th Bn. Co.E
Thompson, Joseph R. GA 11th Inf. Co.H
Thompson, Joseph R. TX 14th Cav. Co.H
Thompson, Joseph R. VA 15th Cav. Co.E
Thompson, Joseph Roger VA 57th Inf. Co.A
Thompson, Joseph S. MS 23rd Inf. Co.B Capt.,AQM
Thompson, Joseph S. VA 38th Inf. Co.F
Thompson, Joseph S. Gen. & Staff Capt.,AQM
Thompson, Joseph Savier AL 3rd Inf. Co.K
Thompson, Joseph T. NC 4th Inf. Co.K
Thompson, Joseph U. GA 53rd Inf. Co.B
Thompson, Joseph U. MS 27th Inf. Co.L
Thompson, Josephus S. AL 36th Inf. Co.G Sgt.
Thompson, Joseph W. AR Inf. 4th Bn.
Thompson, Joseph W. MS 10th Inf. Old Co.K
Thompson, Jos. W. Gen. & Staff Surg.
Thompson, Joshua VA 42nd Inf. Co.B
Thompson, Joshua F. KY Kirkpatrick's Bn. Co.A
Thompson, Joshua J. GA 1st (Olmstead's) Inf. Co.K
Thompson, Josiah MS 1st Cav.Res. Co.K
Thompson, Josiah MO 1st Cav. Co.A
Thompson, Josiah MO Cav. Poindexter's Regt.
Thompson, Josiah MO St.Guard
Thompson, Josiah NC Hvy.Arty. 10th Bn. Co.D
Thompson, Josiah NC 8th Inf. Co.I
Thompson, Josiah NC 55th Inf. Co.G
Thompson, Josiah NC Mil. Clark's Sp.Bn. D.N. Bridgers' Co.
Thompson, Josiah TX Inf. Rutherford's Co.
Thompson, Josiah VA 7th Cav. Glenn's Co.
Thompson, Josiah 1st Choctaw & Chickasaw Mtd.Rifles Co.A
Thompson, Josiah N. AR 15th (Josey's) Inf. Co.F
Thompson, Jotham Brown MO 8th Inf. Co.H,K Cpl.
Thompson, J.P. AL 8th (Hatch's) Cav. Co.C
Thompson, J.P. AL 15th Bn.Part.Rangers Co.D
Thompson, J.P. AR 24th Inf. Co.A
Thompson, J.P. AR Inf. Hardy's Regt. Co.H
Thompson, J.P. GA 4th Cav. (St.Guards) White's Co. 1st Sgt.
Thompson, J.P. GA 4th Mil. Co.B
Thompson, J.P. GA 63rd Inf. Co.H
Thompson, J.P. MS 2nd Cav. Co.D Sgt.
Thompson, J.P. MS 28th Cav. Co.B
Thompson, J.P. MS Cav. Ham's Regt. Co.H
Thompson, J.P. MS Inf. (Res.) Berry's Co.
Thompson, J.P. NC 4th Bn.Jr.Res. Co.B
Thompson, J.P. SC 4th Cav. Co.I
Thompson, J.P. SC Cav. 12th Bn. Co.B
Thompson, J.P. SC 2nd Arty. Co.I
Thompson, J.P. SC 14th Inf. Co.B
Thompson, J.P. TN 3rd (Forrest's) Cav. Co.C
Thompson, J.P. TN Inf. 4th Cons.Regt. Co.I Capt.
Thompson, J.P. TN 30th Inf. Co.C 1st Lt.
Thompson, J.P. TX 17th Cons.Dismtd.Cav. Co.C
Thompson, J.P. TX 14th Inf. Co.C
Thompson, J.P.S. LA Cav. 18th Bn. Co.G
Thompson, J.P.S. LA 16th Inf. Co.F Sgt.
Thompson, J.R. AL Cav. 5th Bn. Hilliard's Legion Co.E
Thompson, J.R. AR 19th Inf. Co.C
Thompson, J.R. GA 5th Cav. Co.A
Thompson, J.R. GA 3rd Res. Co.H
Thompson, J.R. GA 5th Res. Co.C
Thompson, J.R. GA 10th St.Troops Capt.
Thompson, J.R. GA 27th Inf. Co.E
Thompson, J.R. GA 40th Inf. Co.F
Thompson, J.R. GA 46th Inf. Co.E
Thompson, J.R. GA 53rd Inf. Co.B
Thompson, J.R. LA 17th Inf. Co.C
Thompson, J.R. LA 25th Inf. Co.F
Thompson, J.R. MS 6th Inf. Co.F
Thompson, J.R. MO 9th Inf. Co.B
Thompson, J.R. MO Inf. Clark's Regt. Co.A
Thompson, J.R. NC 1st Inf. Co.C
Thompson, J.R. SC 7th Cav. Co.K
Thompson, J.R. TX Waul's Legion Co.F Cook
Thompson, J.R. VA Hvy.Arty. Coffin's Co.
Thompson, J.R. VA 8th Cav. Co.H
Thompson, J.R. VA 13th Cav. Co.E
Thompson, J.R. VA Inf. 5th Bn.Loc.Def. Co.F
Thompson, J.R. 2nd Conf.Eng.Troops Co.D Artif.
Thompson, J.R. Gen. & Staff Chap.
Thompson, J. Richard MS 30th Inf. Co.K
Thompson, J.R.W. AL Inf. 1st Regt. Co.H
Thompson, J.S. AL 1st Bn.Cadets Co.A
Thompson, J.S. AL 48th Inf. Co.H
Thompson, J.S. GA 1st Troops & Defences (Macon) Co.C
Thompson, J.S. GA 2nd Res. Co.K
Thompson, J.S. GA 5th Res. Co.B
Thompson, J.S. GA 25th Inf. Co.F
Thompson, J.S. GA 51st Inf. Co.H
Thompson, J.S. GA Cobb's Legion Co.A
Thompson, J.S. MS 1st Cav. Co.D
Thompson, J.S. MS 12th Cav. Co.F
Thompson, J.S. MS 3rd Inf. AQM
Thompson, J.S. MS Inf. 3rd Bn. (St.Troops) Co.D
Thompson, J.S. SC 1st Cav.
Thompson, J.S. SC 4th Cav. Co.K
Thompson, J.S. SC 4th St.Troops Co.C
Thompson, J.S. SC Inf. 7th Bn. (Enfield Rifles) Co.E Cpl.
Thompson, J.S. TN 11th Inf. Co.H
Thompson, J.S. TN 28th Inf. Co.G
Thompson, J.S. VA Lt.Arty. 38th Bn. Co.B
Thompson, J. Shockley MS Inf. (Res.) Berry's Co.
Thompson, J.T. AL 1st Cav. Co.G
Thompson, J.T. AL 3rd Inf.
Thompson, J.T. AL 28th Inf. Co.D
Thompson, J.T. AL Cp. of Instr. Talladega
Thompson, J.T. AR 11th Inf. Co.D
Thompson, J.T. GA 10th Cav.
Thompson, J.T. GA 49th Inf. Co.K
Thompson, J.T. KY 3rd Mtd.Inf. Co.E
Thompson, J.T. LA 1st Res. Co.D
Thompson, J.T. MS St.Cav. 2nd Bn. (Harris') Co.C
Thompson, J.T. MS 1st (Patton's) Inf. Co.G
Thompson, J.T. MS Inf. 3rd Bn. (St.Troops) Co.E
Thompson, J.T. MS 9th Inf. Co.I
Thompson, J.T. MS 41st Inf. Co.L Sgt.
Thompson, J.T. MS 46th Inf. Co.B

Thompson, J.T. SC 21st Inf. Co.L
Thompson, J.T. TN 7th (Duckworth's) Cav. Co.H
Thompson, J.T. TN 9th (Ward's) Cav. Co.E
Thompson, J.T. TN 14th (Neely's) Cav. Co.F
Thompson, J.T. TN 15th Cav. Co.A
Thompson, J.T. TN 3rd (Clack's) Inf. Co.E
Thompson, J.T. TN 51st (Cons.) Inf. Co.F
Thompson, J.T. TX 12th Cav. Co.D
Thompson, J.T. TX 1st Hvy.Arty.
Thompson, J.T. TX 14th Inf. Co.D 2nd Lt.
Thompson, J.T. VA 23rd Cav. Co.A
Thompson, J.T.S. TN 3rd (Clack's) Inf. Co.E Asst.Surg.
Thompson, J.T.S. TN 3rd (Clack's) Inf. Co.F
Thompson, J.T.S. Gen. & Staff A.Surg.
Thompson, J.U. MS Cav. 17th Bn. Co.A QMSgt.
Thompson, J.U. MS 43rd Inf. Co.C
Thompson, Julius A. AR 6th Inf. Co.H Sgt.
Thompson, Julius A. SC Inf. Hampton Legion Co.A
Thompson, Julius W. NC 13th Inf. Co.A
Thompson, Junius KY Cav. 1st Bn. Co.A
Thompson, Junius TX 23rd Cav. Co.K
Thompson, J.V. Conf.Reg.Inf. Brooks' Bn. Co.A
Thompson, J.W. AL 8th (Hatch's) Cav. Co.E
Thompson, J.W. AL Cav. Moreland's Regt. Co.I Capt.
Thompson, J.W. AL Arty. 1st Bn. Co.D
Thompson, J.W. AL Mil. 3rd Vol. Co.C
Thompson, J.W. AL 9th Inf. Co.F
Thompson, J.W. AL 18th Inf. Co.I
Thompson, J.W. AL 32nd Inf. Asst.Surg.
Thompson, J.W. AL 34th Inf. Co.E
Thompson, J.W. AL 37th Inf. Co.F
Thompson, J.W. AL 50th Inf. Co.C
Thompson, J.W. AL 60th Inf. Co.B Sgt.
Thompson, J.W. AL 62nd Inf. Co.E Cpl.
Thompson, J.W. AR 1st (Monroe's) Cav. Co.A
Thompson, J.W. AR Cav. 1st Bn. (Stirman's) Co.I
Thompson, J.W. AR 8th Inf. New Co.C
Thompson, J.W. AR 10th Inf. Co.E Cpl.
Thompson, J.W. AR 13th Inf. Co.F
Thompson, J.W. AR 15th (Johnson's) Inf. Co.D Sgt.
Thompson, J.W. AR 32nd Inf. Co.G
Thompson, J.W. AR 37th Inf. Co.K
Thompson, J.W. AR 47th (Crandall's) Cav.
Thompson, J.W. AR 50th Mil. Co.G
Thompson, J.W. FL 1st (Res.) Inf. Co.E
Thompson, J.W. FL 5th Inf. Co.K
Thompson, J.W. GA 11th Cav. Co.G
Thompson, J.W. GA Cav. Arnold's Co.
Thompson, J.W. GA Lt.Arty. Croft's Btty. (Columbus Arty.)
Thompson, J.W. GA 4th Res. Co.A
Thompson, J.W. GA 24th Inf. Co.E
Thompson, J.W. GA 39th Inf.
Thompson, J.W. GA 46th Inf. Co.C
Thompson, J.W. GA 60th Inf. Co.E
Thompson, J.W. GA 65th Inf. Co.D
Thompson, J.W. GA Phillips' Legion Co.C
Thompson, J.W. GA Smith's Legion Co.B
Thompson, J.W. KY 12th Cav. Co.A
Thompson, J.W. KY 3rd Mtd.Inf. Co.B Surg.
Thompson, J.W. KY 8th Mtd.Inf. Co.B
Thompson, J.W. LA 1st Hvy.Arty. (Reg.) Co.E
Thompson, J.W. LA 3rd Inf. Co.K
Thompson, J.W. MS 2nd Cav. Co.E
Thompson, J.W. MS 7th Cav. 1st Co.H
Thompson, J.W. MS 1st (King's) Inf. (St.Troops) Co.B
Thompson, J.W. MS 8th Inf. Co.A
Thompson, J.W. MS 18th Inf. Co.D Hosp.Stew.
Thompson, J.W. MS 19th Inf. Co.A
Thompson, J.W. MS Hosp.Stew.
Thompson, J.W. MO 7th Cav. Co.K
Thompson, J.W. MO Cav. Woodson's Co. Cpl.
Thompson, J.W. MO Lt.Arty. H.M. Bledsoe's Co.
Thompson, J.W. MO 2nd & 6th Cons.Inf.
Thompson, J.W. MO 16th Inf. Co.B
Thompson, J.W. MO St.Guard
Thompson, J.W. NC 1st Inf. Co.C
Thompson, J.W. NC 17th Inf. (2nd Org.) Co.L
Thompson, J.W. NC 42nd Inf. Co.B
Thompson, J.W. NC 62nd Inf. Co.F
Thompson, J.W. NC Alex. Brown's Co.
Thompson, J.W. NC Mallett's Bn. Co.E
Thompson, J.W. NC Wallace's Co. (Wilmington RR Guard)
Thompson, J.W. SC 1st (Hagood's) Inf. 1st Co.F, 2nd Co.G
Thompson, J.W. SC 9th Inf. Co.F
Thompson, J.W. SC 11th Res. Co.G
Thompson, J.W. SC 27th Inf. Co.I
Thompson, J.W. SC Palmetto S.S. Co.E
Thompson, J.W. TN 1st (Carter's) Cav. Co.B
Thompson, J.W. TN 8th (Smith's) Cav. Co.D
Thompson, J.W. TN 14th (Neely's) Cav. Co.I
Thompson, J.W. TN 15th (Stewart's) Cav. Co.F
Thompson, J.W. TN 1st (Feild's) & 27th Inf. (Cons.) Co.I
Thompson, J.W. TN 3rd (Clack's) Inf. Co.E
Thompson, J.W. TN 4th Inf. Co.G
Thompson, J.W. TN 13th Inf. Co.H
Thompson, J.W. TN 27th Inf. Co.G
Thompson, J.W. TN 51st Inf. Co.K
Thompson, J.W. TN 51st (Cons.) Inf. Co.G
Thompson, J.W. TX 4th Cav. Co.I
Thompson, J.W. TX 8th Cav. Co.A
Thompson, J.W. TX 26th Cav. Co.I
Thompson, J.W. TX 33rd Cav. Co.G
Thompson, J.W. TX Cav. Morgan's Regt.
Thompson, J.W. TX 20th Inf. Co.B
Thompson, J.W. TX Inf. Timmons' Regt. Co.I
Thompson, J.W. VA 15th Cav. 2nd Lt.
Thompson, J.W. VA Inf. 1st Bn. Co.B
Thompson, J.W. VA 13th Inf. Co.F
Thompson, J.W. VA Inf. 26th Bn. Co.B
Thompson, J.W. Conf.Inf. 1st Bn. Co.A
Thompson, J.W. Conf.Inf. Tucker's Regt. Co.A
Thompson, J. Waddy SC 5th St.Troops Co.G
Thompson, J. Walker MO 3rd Inf. Co.K
Thompson, J. West MO Lt.Arty. 1st Btty. Sgt.
Thompson, J.W.F. SC 20th Inf. Co.A
Thompson, J.W.F. TX 19th Inf. Co.G
Thompson, J.W.J. TX 22nd Cav. Co.E
Thompson, J.Y. AL 1st Regt. Mobile Vol. Co.E
Thompson, J.Z. AL Inf. 1st Regt. Co.A
Thompson, J.Z. MS Grace's Co. (St.Troops)
Thompson, K. AL 45th Inf. Co.E
Thompson, K. TX 10th Cav.
Thompson, Kibble W. TN 7th Cav. Co.M
Thompson, Kible W. MS 23rd Inf. Co.D Cpl.
Thompson, Kin 3rd Conf.Cav. Co.F
Thompson, Kirk AR 1st (Crawford's) Cav. Co.B
Thompson, Knox VA VMI Co.C
Thompson, K.W. MS 3rd Inf. Co.D
Thompson, K.W. Forrest's Scouts T. Henderson's Co.,CSA
Thompson, L. AL 6th Cav. Co.A
Thompson, L. AL 5th Inf. Co.H
Thompson, L. AL 10th Inf. Co.E
Thompson, L. AL 18th Inf. Co.E
Thompson, L. AL 26th (O'Neal's) Inf. Co.B
Thompson, L. AL 32nd Inf. Co.G
Thompson, L. AL 46th Inf. Co.D
Thompson, L. KY 1st Bn.Mtd.Rifles
Thompson, L. LA 3rd (Harrison's) Cav. Co.G
Thompson, L. LA Lt.Arty. 2nd Field Btty.
Thompson, L. MO 7th Cav. Sgt.
Thompson, L. NC 4th Inf.
Thompson, L. SC 1st Arty. Co.D
Thompson, L. TN 3rd (Forrest's) Cav. Co.G 1st Sgt.
Thompson, L. TN 12th (Green's) Cav. Co.F
Thompson, L. TX 14th Field Btty.
Thompson, L. TX Inf. 1st St.Troops Whitehead's Co. 3rd Lt.
Thompson, L. TX 7th Inf. Co.D
Thompson, L. TX 11th (Spaight's) Bn.Vol. Co.B
Thompson, L. TX 13th Vol. 4th Co.I
Thompson, L. TX 16th Inf. Co.A
Thompson, L. VA Cav. 35th Bn. Co.D
Thompson, L.A. FL 11th Inf. Co.I
Thompson, L.A. Conf.Cav. Wood's Regt. Co.L
Thompson, Laban VA Cav. Ferguson's Bn. Spurlock's Co.
Thompson, Laben VA 16th Cav. Co.E Cpl.
Thompson, Lacy T. GA 57th Inf. Co.D
Thompson, Lafayett LA 12th Inf. 2nd Co.M
Thompson, LaFayette LA 2nd Inf. Co.F
Thompson, Landon VA 9th Cav. Co.I Cpl.
Thompson, Landon VA 25th Mil. Co.A
Thompson, Larkin NC 35th Inf. Co.F
Thompson, Larkin VA 8th Cav. Co.H
Thompson, Lausine MS Stricklin's Co. (St.Troops)
Thompson, Lawrence KY 2nd (Duke's) Cav. Co.A
Thompson, Lawrence KY 8th Cav. Co.A
Thompson, Lawrence LA 13th Inf. Co.F 1st Sgt.
Thompson, Lawrence D. TN 9th (Ward's) Cav. Co.E
Thompson, Lawson GA 48th Inf. Co.A Sgt.
Thompson, Lawson MS Cav. 3rd Bn. (Ashcraft's) Co.E
Thompson, L.B. AR 31st Inf. Co.H Cpl.
Thompson, L.B. MS 32nd Inf. Co.G Cpl.
Thompson, L.C. AL Mil. 4th Vol. Gantt's Co. Sgt.
Thompson, L.C. AL 40th Inf. Co.I Sgt.
Thompson, L.C. AL 59th Inf. Co.C
Thompson, L.C. AR 46th Inf. Co.D
Thompson, L.C. NC Hvy.Arty. 1st Bn. Co.A
Thompson, L.C. SC 7th Cav. Co.K
Thompson, L.C. SC Bn.St.Cadets Co.A
Thompson, L.C. TN 20th (Russell's) Cav. Co.C

Thompson, L.C. TN 12th Inf. Co.C
Thompson, L.D. MS 3rd Cav. Co.D
Thompson, L.D MS 9th Inf. New Co.C
Thompson, L.D. TN 9th (Ward's) Cav. Co.E
Thompson, L.D. TN 19th (Biffle's) Cav. Co.F
Thompson, L.D. TX 18th Inf. Co.G
Thompson, L.D. VA Lt.Arty. Lamkin's Co.
Thompson, L.E. GA 63rd Inf. Co.C
Thompson, Lee LA 12th Inf. 2nd Co.M
Thompson, Lee NC 30th Inf. Co.K
Thompson, Lee TN 14th (Neely's) Cav. Co.E
Thompson, Lee TX 27th Cav. Co.E
Thompson, Lee C. TX 1st (Yager's) Cav. Co.G
Thompson, Lee C. TX Cav. 8th (Taylor's) Bn. Co.A Cpl.
Thompson, Lemuel NC 3rd Arty. (40th St.Troops) Co.E
Thompson, Lemuel B. MS 30th Inf. Co.G
Thompson, Lemuel H. GA 22nd Inf. Co.K Ord.Sgt.
Thompson, Lenmons B. MS 26th Inf. Co.F 2nd Lt.
Thompson, Lenard MO 3rd Cav. Co.H
Thompson, Leonard AR 1st (Crawford's) Cav. Co.B
Thompson, Leonard MO Inf. 8th Bn. Co.E
Thompson, Leonard F. AL 6th Cav. Co.C,E 2nd Lt.
Thompson, Leonard F. AL 13th Inf. Co.D
Thompson, Leonard H. LA 4th Cav. Co.E
Thompson, Leonard J. MO 9th Inf. Co.I
Thompson, Leonidas A. TN 7th Inf. Co.B Sgt.
Thompson, Leonidas L. TX 36th Cav. Co.A
Thompson, Leonidas S. AL 51st (Part.Rangers) Co.B
Thompson, Leslie A. TX 1st Inf.
Thompson, Lesly C. VA Inf. 23rd Bn. Co.A
Thompson, Levi VA 25th Cav. Co.E
Thompson, Levi VA 3rd Res. Co.F
Thompson, Levi VA 45th Inf. Co.F
Thompson, Levin W. NC 1st Inf. Co.B
Thompson, Levi P. MS 48th Inf. Co.B
Thompson, Levi R. GA 11th Cav. (St.Guards) Folks' Co.
Thompson, Levi T. LA 9th Inf. Co.K
Thompson, Levi W. 1st Choctaw & Chickasaw Mtd.Rifles 2nd Co.K
Thompson, Lewellen VA 17th Cav. Co.C,G Cpl.
Thompson, Lewellyn O. TN 1st (Feild's) Inf. Co.H
Thompson, Lewis GA Lt.Arty. Milledge's Co.
Thompson, Lewis GA 3rd Inf. 1st Co.I
Thompson, Lewis GA Cherokee Legion (St.Guards) Co.I
Thompson, Lewis LA 1st Hvy.Arty. Co.I
Thompson, Lewis MS St.Cav. Perrin's Bn. Co.B
Thompson, Lewis MS 43rd Inf. Co.D
Thompson, Lewis NC 1st Arty. (10th St.Troops) Co.I
Thompson, Lewis NC 2nd Arty. (36th St.Troops) Co.A
Thompson, Lewis NC 30th Inf. Co.K
Thompson, Lewis TN 12th (Green's) Cav. Co.D
Thompson, Lewis A. AL 19th Inf. Co.G
Thompson, Lewis B. GA Inf. 2nd Bn.
Thompson, Lewis B. GA Cobb's Legion
Thompson, Lewis E. TN Lt.Arty. Baxter's Co.
Thompson, Lewis F. FL 1st Inf. Old Co.C, New Co.B
Thompson, Lewis L. AL 11th Inf. Co.D
Thompson, Lewis M. GA 29th Inf. Co.C
Thompson, Lewis O. TN 3rd (Forrest's) Cav. Co.B,E, Julian's Co.
Thompson, Lewis R. AR 1st (Colquitt's) Inf.
Thompson, Lewis S. MS 48th Inf. Co.F
Thompson, Lewis S. VA 31st Inf. Co.A 2nd Lt.
Thompson, Lewis W. MS 27th Inf. Co.L
Thompson, L.F. AL Cp. of Instr. Talladega
Thompson, L.F. NC 64th Inf. Co.E
Thompson, L.F. TN Cav. Jackson's Co.
Thompson, L.H. VA 8th Cav. Co.A
Thompson, Lindsey VA 7th Inf. Co.C
Thompson, Linsey KY 2nd Bn.Mtd.Rifles Co.D Sgt.
Thompson, Linsey L. TN 41st Inf. Co.H
Thompson, Littleton NC 8th Inf. Co.F
Thompson, L.J. AL Lt.Arty. Tarrant's Btty.
Thompson, L.J. GA 1st (Olmstead's) Inf. Co.K
Thompson, L.J. GA 47th Inf. Co.H
Thompson, L.J. LA Inf. 9th Bn. Co.C Cpl.
Thompson, L.L. AR Cav. Gordon's Regt. Col.
Thompson, L.L. GA 5th Res.
Thompson, L.M. AL 50th Inf. Co.F
Thompson, L.M. GA 14th Inf. Co.C
Thompson, L.M. GA 34th Inf. Co.I
Thompson, L.O. AL 11th Cav.
Thompson, Lornt D. TN 6th (Wheeler's) Cav. Co.G
Thompson, Lott B. MS 8th Inf. Co.E Cpl.
Thompson, Louis LA Arty. Kean's Btty. (Orleans Ind.Arty.)
Thompson, Louis NC 1st Cav. (9th St.Troops) Co.C
Thompson, Lovett J. AL 32nd Inf. Co.A
Thompson, Loyd VA 54th Inf. Co.I
Thompson, L.P. GA 48th Inf. Co.B
Thompson, L.P. MS 1st (King's) Inf. (St.Troops) Co.F
Thompson, L.P. VA Mil. Stowers' Co.
Thompson, L.P. Lt.Arty. Dent's Btty.,CSA
Thompson, L.Q. GA Floyd Legion (St.Guards)
Thompson, L.R. AL 14th Inf. Co.D
Thompson, L.R. GA 4th (Clinch's) Cav. Co.F
Thompson, L.R. MS 35th Inf. Co.C
Thompson, L.S. AL Lt.Arty. 20th Bn.
Thompson, L.S. AL 5th Inf. New Co.E
Thompson, L.S. MS Inf. 2nd Bn. Co.F
Thompson, L.T. GA Inf. 26th Bn.
Thompson, L.T. LA 12th Inf. Co.H
Thompson, L.T. MS 2nd St.Cav. Co.C
Thompson, L.T. TN 38th Inf. Co.E
Thompson, Lucas P. VA Lt.Arty. Arch. Graham's Co.
Thompson, Luke H. AR 8th Inf. New Co.G
Thompson, Luke H. AR 14th (McCarver's) Inf. Co.H
Thompson, Luke R. VA 6th Cav.
Thompson, L.W. GA Arty. (Chatham Arty.) Wheaton's Co.
Thompson, L.W. GA 1st (Olmstead's) Inf. Claghorn's Co.
Thompson, L.W. GA 13th Inf. Co.G
Thompson, L.W. MS 3rd (St.Troops) Cav. Co.G
Thompson, L.W. NC Walker's Bn. Thomas' Legion 1st Co.D
Thompson, L.W. TN 1st (Carter's) Cav. Co.I
Thompson, L.W. TN 3rd (Forrest's) Cav.
Thompson, L.W. TX 28th Cav. Co.H
Thompson, Lycurgus L. AR 1st Mtd.Rifles Co.I 1st Lt.
Thompson, Lynch MO Cav. 2nd Regt.St.Guard Co.G
Thompson, Lynch MO 4th Cav. Co.H 2nd Lt.
Thompson, M. AL 4th (Russell's) Cav.
Thompson, M. AL 6th Cav. Co.E
Thompson, M. FL 1st (Res.) Inf. Co.E
Thompson, M. GA 6th Inf. (St.Guards) Co.A
Thompson, M. GA Inf. 17th Bn. (St.Guards) McCarty's Co.
Thompson, M. KY 12th Cav. Co.H
Thompson, M. KY 3rd Mtd.Inf. Co.G
Thompson, M. MS 39th Inf. Co.H 2nd Lt.
Thompson, M. MO St.Guard
Thompson, M. SC 6th Cav. Co.C
Thompson, M. SC Cav. 19th Bn. Co.B
Thompson, M. SC Inf. 9th Bn. Co.A
Thompson, M. TN 9th Cav. Co.L
Thompson, M. TN 15th (Cons.) Cav. Co.G
Thompson, M. TN 46th Inf. Co.H
Thompson, M. TX Cav. Bourland's Regt. Co.D
Thompson, M. VA Cav. Swann's Bn. Vincent's Co. Cpl.
Thompson, M.A. AL 18th Bn.Vol. Co.C
Thompson, M.A. LA 17th Inf. Co.B 2nd Lt.
Thompson, M.A Trans-MS Conf.Cav. 1st Bn. Co.C Cpl.
Thompson, Madison KY 9th Mtd.Inf. Co.E
Thompson, Madison TN Inf. 23rd Bn. Co.A
Thompson, Magnus VA Cav. 35th Bn. Co.D,C
Thompson, Magnus S. VA Cav. 41st Bn. Trayhern's Co.
Thompson, Malachi GA 47th Inf. Co.E
Thompson, Malcolm VA Cav. 35th Bn. Co.C
Thompson, Malcomb TX 10th Cav. Co.I Ens.
Thompson, Malcomb Cicero GA 20th Inf. Co.K Sgt.
Thompson, Manasa SC 26th Inf. Co.A Cpl.
Thompson, Marcus A. TX 15th Cav. Co.A
Thompson, Marias F. VA 1st Arty. Co.B
Thompson, Marien TX 16th Cav. Co.F
Thompson, Marion GA 31st Inf. Co.A
Thompson, Marion D. AL Lt.Arty. 2nd Bn. Co.F
Thompson, Mark L. AL 40th Inf. Co.B
Thompson, Marriott LA Lt.Arty. Fenner's Btty.
Thompson, Marriott MS 15th Inf. Co.G
Thompson, Marshal VA 6th Cav. Co.I
Thompson, Marshall H. GA 1st (Ramsey's) Inf. Co.C
Thompson, Marshall J. MS Cav. 24th Bn. Co.E Cpl.
Thompson, Martin NC 2nd Inf. Co.A
Thompson, Martin NC 47th Inf. Co.C
Thompson, Martin TX Cav. Madison's Regt. Co.D
Thompson, Martin J. MS 14th Inf. Co.D
Thompson, Martin L. MS St.Cav. Perrin's Bn. Co.F
Thompson, Martin V. GA 49th Inf. Co.K
Thompson, Martin V. TN 53rd Inf. Co.D

Thompson, Martin V. TX 1st (McCulloch's) Cav. Co.D
Thompson, Martin V. TX 16th Inf. Co.G
Thompson, Marvell G. MS 15th Inf. Co.B
Thompson, Mason VA 11th Cav. Co.G
Thompson, Massellon W. MS 42nd Inf. Co.D 2nd Lt.
Thompson, Maston TN 40th Inf. Co.H
Thompson, Mathew LA 6th Inf. Co.K
Thompson, Mathew SC Inf. Hampton Legion Co.E
Thompson, Mathew TX Cav. Hardeman's Regt. Co.B
Thompson, Mathias VA 89th Mil. Co.H
Thompson, Matthew MO St.Guard Capt.
Thompson, Matthew C. NC 58th Inf. Co.E
Thompson, Matthew H. LA 1st Cav. Co.D
Thompson, Matthews LA 28th (Gray's) Inf. Co.G Cpl.
Thompson, Matthew S. VA 58th Inf. Co.H
Thompson, Maurice TN 6th Inf. Co.D
Thompson, Maurice VA Arty. Dance's Co.
Thompson, M.B. LA 2nd Cav. Co.C
Thompson, M.C. AR 8th Inf. Co.A
Thompson, McD. GA 29th Inf. Co.A
Thompson, M.D. AL 8th Inf. Co.C
Thompson, M.D. AL 15th Inf. Co.A
Thompson, M.D. NC 3rd Jr.Res. Co.I
Thompson, M.D. NC 18th Inf. Co.K
Thompson, M.D. TN 19th Inf. Co.A
Thompson, M.E. TX 7th Cav. Co.G
Thompson, M.E. VA 8th Inf. Co.G
Thompson, Meggs MS Lt.Arty. Stanford's Co.
Thompson, Mehemiah NC Walker's Bn. Thomas' Legion Co.A Drum.
Thompson, Melehezedec FL 1st Cav. Co.F
Thompson, Mellville TN Arty. Ramsey's Btty.
Thompson, Melton AR 4th Inf. Co.E
Thompson, Melvin NC 35th Inf. Co.G
Thompson, Meredith A. TN 1st Cav. Co.B
Thompson, M.F. AL 22nd Inf. Co.I
Thompson, M.F. LA Pointe Coupee Arty.
Thompson, M.F. MS Cav. (St.Troops) Gamblin's Co.
Thompson, M.F. TX 13th Vol. 2nd Co.D
Thompson, M.F. VA Lt.Arty. 1st Bn. Co.B
Thompson, M.F. VA Arty. Richardson's Co.
Thompson, M.G. TN 15th (Cons.) Cav. Co.C
Thompson, M.G. Gen. & Staff AASurg.
Thompson, M.H. AL 11th Cav. Co.I
Thompson, M.H. GA 13th Cav. Co.C
Thompson, M.H. KY 2nd Mtd.Inf. Co.A
Thompson, M.H. NC 18th Inf. Co.K
Thompson, M.H. TN 3rd (Forrest's) Cav.
Thompson, M.H. TN 8th (Smith's) Cav. Co.D
Thompson, Michael SC 13th Inf. Co.I
Thompson, Michael S. NC 14th Inf. Co.E
Thompson, Micheam NC Lt.Arty. 3rd Bn. Co.A
Thompson, Middleton GA 9th Inf. (St.Guards) Co.G
Thompson, Miles GA 4th Cav. (St.Guards) Cannon's Co.
Thompson, Miles MO 7th Cav. Co.I
Thompson, Miller F. TX 15th Inf. 2nd Co.D
Thompson, Milton GA 16th Inf. Co.G
Thompson, Milton F. NC 37th Inf. Co.E
Thompson, Milton L. TN 48th (Nixon's) Inf. Co.G Sgt.
Thompson, Milton L. TN 54th Inf. Co.B
Thompson, Milton M. NC 1st Inf. Co.B
Thompson, Milus GA 11th Cav. Co.F
Thompson, Minor C. VA Cav. Mosby's Regt. (Part.Rangers)
Thompson, Minor L. VA 17th Inf. Co.D
Thompson, Minus E. AR 36th Inf. Co.A
Thompson, Mitchel AR 50th Mil. Co.B
Thompson, Mitchel NC 4th Cav. (59th St.Troops) Co.D
Thompson, Mitchell AR 3rd Inf. Co.A
Thompson, Mitchell H. TN 2nd (Smith's) Cav.
Thompson, M.J. GA 11th Inf.
Thompson, M.J. MS Arty. (Seven Stars Arty.) Roberts' Co.
Thompson, M.J. MS 14th (Cons.) Inf. Co.E
Thompson, M. Jeff. MO Inf. 3rd Regt.St.Guard Lt.Col.
Thompson, M. Jeff. MO St.Guard Staff Brig.Gen.
Thompson, M. Jeff. Gen. & Staff Brig.Gen.
Thompson, M.L. AL 19th Inf. Co.H
Thompson, M.L. LA Lt.Arty. Fenner's Btty.
Thompson, M.L. LA Miles' Legion
Thompson, M.L. MS 12th Cav. Co.G Cpl.
Thompson, M.L. MO 9th (Elliott's) Cav. 2nd Lt.
Thompson, M.L. TN 19th (Biffle's) Cav. Co.F
Thompson, M.M. GA 5th Cav. Co.F
Thompson, M.M. GA 28th Inf. Co.D
Thompson, M.M. TN 5th Inf. 2nd Co.B
Thompson, M.N. Gen. & Staff, QM Dept.
Thompson, Monroe NC 61st Inf. Co.D
Thompson, Monroe SC Horse Arty. (Washington Arty.) Vol. Hart's Co.
Thompson, Montgomery B. LA 28th (Gray's) Inf. Co.G
Thompson, Moses AL 39th Inf. Co.C
Thompson, Moses D. GA 57th Inf. QMSgt.
Thompson, Moses E. NC 58th Inf. Co.E Sgt.
Thompson, Moses F. AL 50th Inf. Co.A
Thompson, Moses J. GA 57th Inf. Co.D
Thompson, Moses M. GA 57th Inf. Co.D
Thompson, Moses S. TN 48th (Voorhies') Inf. Co.A Cpl.
Thompson, Moses W. AL 3rd Inf. Co.D
Thompson, Moses W. SC Inf. Hampton Legion Co.E 2nd Lt.
Thompson, M.R. AL 1st Cav. 2nd Co.C
Thompson, M.R. AL Inf. 1st Regt. Co.D
Thompson, M.S. SC 11th Res. Co.K
Thompson, M.T. AR 15th Inf. Co.C
Thompson, M.V.B. AR 31st Inf. Co.B
Thompson, M.V.B. VA 36th Inf. Co.A
Thompson, M.W. AR 35th Inf. Old Co.F
Thompson, M.W. GA 3rd Res. Co.F
Thompson, M.W. KY Morgan's Regt.
Thompson, M.W. MO 11th Inf. Co.H
Thompson, M. Wirt MS 17th Inf. Co.I Sgt.
Thompson, M.Y. AR 15th (Johnson's) Inf. Co.C
Thompson, M.Y. MS 2nd Cav. Co.A
Thompson, N. AR Mtd.Vol. (St.Troops) Abraham's Co.
Thompson, N. AR 35th Inf. Co.A
Thompson, N. AR 62nd Mil. Co.C
Thompson, N. GA Inf. 1st City Bn. (Columbus) Co.D
Thompson, N. GA Inf. 19th Bn. (St.Guards) Co.B
Thompson, N. MS 31st Inf. Co.K
Thompson, N. MO 3rd & 5th Cons.Inf. Co.D
Thompson, N. NC 1st Jr.Res. Co.E
Thompson, N. SC 4th St.Troops Co.A
Thompson, N. SC 5th Bn.Res. Co.A Bvt.2nd Lt.
Thompson, N. TN 50th (Cons.) Inf. Co.C
Thompson, N. TX 17th Cons.Dismtd.Cav. Co.K
Thompson, N. TX Cav. Border's Regt. Co.E Cpl.
Thompson, N. VA 88th Mil.
Thompson, N.A. GA 27th Inf. Co.K
Thompson, N.A. GA Inf. 27th Bn. (NonConscr.) Co.A
Thompson, N.A. GA Inf. (NonConscr.) Howard's Co.
Thompson, N.A. TN 6th (Wheeler's) Cav. Co.F
Thompson, N.A. TN Lt.Arty. Rice's Btty.
Thompson, N.A. TN 3rd (Clack's) Inf. Co.C
Thompson, N.A. VA 21st Cav. AQM
Thompson, N.A. Gen. & Staff Capt.,AQM,CS
Thompson, Napoleon B. KY 1st (Butler's) Cav. Co.E
Thompson, Napoleon B. KY 3rd Bn.Mtd.Rifles Co.E
Thompson, Napoleon B. MS 1st (Patton's) Inf. Co.K
Thompson, Napoleon B. MS 37th Inf. Co.A Cpl.
Thompson, Nathan AL 44th Inf. Co.B
Thompson, Nathan GA 18th Inf. Co.G
Thompson, Nathan NC 6th Sr.Res. Co.F
Thompson, Nathan NC 52nd Inf. Co.I
Thompson, Nathan TN 30th Inf. Co.G
Thompson, Nathaniel LA 1st Cav. Co.K 1st Sgt.
Thompson, Nathaniel NC 47th Inf. Co.H
Thompson, Nathaniel VA 25th Cav. Co.F
Thompson, Nathaniel VA 54th Inf. Co.G Cpl.
Thompson, Nathaniel A. GA 8th Inf. (St.Guards) Co.G Cpl.
Thompson, Nathaniel B. VA 15th Inf. Co.C
Thompson, Nathaniel W. VA 28th Inf. 1st Co.C
Thompson, Nathan J. NC 20th Inf. Co.C
Thompson, Nathan J. NC 51st Inf. Co.G
Thompson, N.B. KY 3rd Cav. Co.E
Thompson, N.B. KY 5th Cav. Co.H
Thompson, N.B. KY 11th Cav. Co.A
Thompson, N.B. KY 1st Bn.Mtd.Rifles Co.B
Thompson, N.B. KY 6th Mtd.Inf. Co.F,A
Thompson, N.B. MS Cav. Jeff Davis Legion Co.E Sgt.
Thompson, N.B. TX 11th Inf. Co.G
Thompson, N.C. AR 1st Mtd.Rifles Co.C
Thompson, N.E. TX Cav. Bourland's Regt. Co.C
Thompson, Neal TX 26th Cav. Co.H
Thompson, Needham J. NC 18th Inf. Co.D Sgt.
Thompson, Nehemiah M. NC Walker's Bn. Thomas' Legion Co.A Drum.
Thompson, Neil TN 9th Inf.
Thompson, Neill NC 26th Inf. Co.H
Thompson, Neill NC 46th Inf. Co.H

Thompson, Neill TN 38th Inf. Co.E
Thompson, Nelson FL Cav. 5th Bn. Co.E
Thompson, Nelson MO 7th Cav. Co.G
Thompson, Nelson VA Mil. Carroll Cty.
Thompson, Nelson A. NC 4th Inf. Co.K
Thompson, Nelson M. GA 66th Inf. Co.D
Thompson, Nelson M. NC 25th Inf. Co.E Cpl.
Thompson, Nero MO 9th Inf. Co.B
Thompson, Nero MO Inf. Clark's Regt. Co.A
Thompson, Nevils A. AL 4th Inf. Co.K
Thompson, Newton AR 11th & 17th Cons.Inf. Co.I
Thompson, Newton AR 17th (Griffith's) Inf. Co.F
Thompson, Newton KY 9th Mtd.Inf. Co.E
Thompson, Newton TN Inf. 23rd Bn. Co.A
Thompson, Newton B. MS 40th Inf. Co.G
Thompson, Newton H. AL 44th Inf. Co.F Sgt.
Thompson, Newton J. TN Inf. 1st Bn. (Colms') Co.D 1st Lt.
Thompson, Newton J. Gen. & Staff Asst.Surg.
Thompson, N.G. TN 7th Cav. Co.E
Thompson, N.G. TN 14th (Neely's) Cav. Co.E
Thompson, N.G. TN 22nd Inf. Co.C
Thompson, Nicholas TX 14th Inf. 1st Co.K
Thompson, Nicholas TX 18th Inf. Co.L
Thompson, Nicholas VA Cav. 39th Bn. Co.C
Thompson, Nimrod W. AR 9th Inf. Co.G Music.
Thompson, N.J. KY 5th Mtd.Inf. Asst.Surg.
Thompson, N.J. TN 50th (Cons.) Inf. Co.K Capt.
Thompson, N.M. AR 1st Vol. Anderson's Co.
Thompson, N.M. NC 35th Inf.
Thompson, N.M. 20th Conf.Cav. 2nd Co.H
Thompson, N.N. AL 40th Inf. Co.D Sgt.
Thompson, N.O. VA Cav. 37th Bn. Co.F
Thompson, Noah AL 46th Inf. Co.D
Thompson, Noah TN 50th Inf. Co.C
Thompson, Noah H. MS 39th Inf. Co.I 1st Sgt.
Thompson, Noah L. AL 7th Cav. Co.K
Thompson, Noah L. FL 7th Inf.
Thompson, Noah M. NC 51st Inf. Co.H
Thompson, Norborne F. VA Arty. J.W. Drewry's Co.
Thompson, Norman AL 6th Cav. Co.H
Thompson, Norman VA Cav. McFarlane's Co.
Thompson, Norman Conf.Cav. 6th Bn.
Thompson, Norton D. VA Arty. Paris' Co.
Thompson, N.R. GA 42nd Inf. Co.H
Thompson, N.S. 8th (Wade's) Conf.Cav. Co.B
Thompson, N.W. AL 31st Inf. Co.H
Thompson, N.W. AR 1st Mtd.Rifles Co.I
Thompson, N.W. TN 20th (Russell's) Cav. Co.F Sgt.
Thompson, N.W. TN 46th Inf. Co.I Sgt.
Thompson, N.W. VA 1st St.Res. Co.D
Thompson, O. AL Cav. Barlow's Co.
Thompson, O. GA 24th Inf. Co.A
Thompson, O. MS Inf. 2nd St.Troops Co.B
Thompson, O. TN Inf. 4th Cons.Regt. Co.G
Thompson, O. 15th Conf.Cav. Co.C
Thompson, Obadiah F. MS 1st Lt.Arty. Co.L
Thompson, O.C. GA 2nd Cav. Co.F
Thompson, O.C. GA 10th Cav. (St.Guards) Co.F
Thompson, O.C. MS 27th Inf. Co.H Music.
Thompson, O.D. VA 1st (Farinholt's) Res. Co.C
Thompson, O.F. MS Inf. Comfort's Co.
Thompson, O.G. SC 3rd Inf. Co.G
Thompson, O.L. AL Cav. Murphy's Bn. Co.C
Thompson, O.L. KY 2nd (Duke's) Cav. Co.H
Thompson, O.L. KY 1st Inf. Co.A,C
Thompson, O.L. VA Lt.Arty. Jackson's Bn. St.Line Co.A Sgt.
Thompson, Oli VA 8th Cav. 1st Co.D
Thompson, Olin F. GA 55th Inf. Co.G
Thompson, Oliver VA Cav. Hounshell's Bn. Gwinn's Co.
Thompson, Oliver VA 60th Inf. Co.B
Thompson, Oliver VA 108th Mil. Co.C
Thompson, Oliver N. NC 1st Inf. Co.B
Thompson, Oliver T. NC 51st Inf. Co.E Cpl.
Thompson, O.M. TN 7th (Duckworth's) Cav. Co.C
Thompson, Ooliyoih NC Inf. Thomas Legion 2nd Co.A
Thompson, O.P. MO Inf. 3rd Bn. Co.C
Thompson, O.R. SC 6th Res. Co.I Capt.
Thompson, O.R. SC Manigault's Bn.Vol. Co.C 1st Lt.
Thompson, Osborn D. 8th (Wade's) Conf.Cav. Co.H 2nd Lt.
Thompson, Osceola TX 14th Inf. Co.B
Thompson, Otes C. MS Inf. 2nd St.Troops Co.F
Thompson, O.W. MS 2nd (Davidson's) Inf. Co.A
Thompson, O.W. MS 43rd Inf. Co.L
Thompson, O.W. NC 7th Sr.Res. Bradshaw's Co.
Thompson, Owen VA 8th Cav. Co.K
Thompson, P. AL 6th Cav. Co.I
Thompson, P. AL Talladega Cty.Res. G.M. Gamble's Co.
Thompson, P. GA 19th Inf. Co.F
Thompson, P. KY 10th (Johnson's) Cav. Co.A
Thompson, P. KY 9th Mtd.Inf. Co.B
Thompson, P. LA 5th Inf. Co.G
Thompson, P. MS Cav. Powers' Regt. Co.K,B 1st Lt.
Thompson, P. TX 1st Hvy.Arty. Co.H
Thompson, P. TX 16th Inf. Co.G
Thompson, P. VA 8th Cav. Co.E
Thompson, P. VA Cav. 34th Bn. Co.D
Thompson, P. 3rd Conf.Eng.Troops
Thompson, Pallas AL 11th Cav. Co.D
Thompson, Paraham LA 12th Inf. Co.M,C
Thompson, Paschal VA 34th Inf. Co.H
Thompson, Paschal Conf.Hvy.Arty. Montague's Bn. Co.C
Thompson, Paschal W. MS 5th Inf. Co.F Sgt.
Thompson, Paten VA Loc.Def. Patterson's Co.
Thompson, Patrick TN 8th Inf. Co.G
Thompson, Patrick VA 11th Bn.Res. Co.D
Thompson, Patton VA 6th Bn.Res. Co.G
Thompson, Patton VA 72nd Mil.
Thompson, P.B. GA 1st Cav. Co.H
Thompson, P.B. KY 2nd (Duke's) Cav. Co.E
Thompson, P.B. LA 9th Inf. Co.D
Thompson, P.C. AR 2nd Inf. Co.A
Thompson, P.E. TX Cav. Baird's Regt. Co.D
Thompson, Perry TX 4th Inf. Co.A
Thompson, Pet LA 21st (Kennedy's) Inf. Co.F
Thompson, Peter AL St.Arty. Co.D
Thompson, Peter LA 20th Inf. New Co.B
Thompson, Peter LA 20th Inf. Co.K
Thompson, Peter NC Lt.Arty. 3rd Bn. Co.A
Thompson, Peter NC 12th Inf. Co.N
Thompson, Peter NC 32nd Inf. Co.B,C
Thompson, Peter TN 3rd (Forrest's) Cav.
Thompson, Peter TN 3rd (Clack's) Inf. Co.G
Thompson, Peter VA Hvy.Arty. 18th Bn. Co.B
Thompson, Peter VA 20th Cav. Co.B
Thompson, Peter G. LA Inf.Cons.Crescent Regt. Co.D
Thompson, Peter J. GA Hardwick Mtd.Rifles Co.B
Thompson, Peter L. GA Inf. 13th Bn. (St.Guards) Guerry's Co. Cpl.
Thompson, Peter R. GA 55th Inf. Co.A
Thompson, Peyton G. AL 3rd Inf. Co.D
Thompson, P.F. AL 11th Inf. Co.D
Thompson, P.F. AL 3rd Bn. Hilliard's Legion Vol. Co.A 3rd Lt.
Thompson, P.F. AR 27th Inf. New Co.C
Thompson, P.F. MO Cav. Freeman's Regt. Co.F
Thompson, P.G.W. TN 19th (Biffle's) Cav. Co.I Sgt.
Thompson, P.H. LA 1st (Strawbridge's) Inf. Co.F,B Capt.
Thompson, P.H. TN 42nd Inf. Co.D
Thompson, P.H. VA 8th Cav. Co.H
Thompson, P.H. 4th Conf.Inf. Co.K
Thompson, Phil B. Gen. & Staff Col.
Thompson, Philip KY Morgan's Men Co.I
Thompson, Philip TX 7th Field Btty.
Thompson, Philip TX Lt.Arty. Jones' Co.
Thompson, Philip VA 8th Cav. 1st Co.D 1st Lt.
Thompson, Philip A. VA 60th Inf. Co.D 1st Sgt.
Thompson, Phillip LA 2nd Res.Corps Co.A
Thompson, Phillip VA 59th Inf. 1st Co.G
Thompson, Phillip B. LA 1st Cav. Co.C
Thompson, Phillipp S. NC 15th Inf. Co.H
Thompson, Pierre LA Mil. 1st Native Guards
Thompson, Pinkney A. NC 62nd Inf. Co.I
Thompson, P.J. GA 7th Cav. Co.H
Thompson, P.L. GA Cav. 19th Bn. Co.E
Thompson, P.L. 10th Conf.Cav. Co.K
Thompson, Pleasant F. MS 42nd Inf. Co.G Sgt.
Thompson, Pleasant H. AR 3rd Inf. Co.G 1st Lt.
Thompson, Pleasant N. AL 44th Inf. Co.K
Thompson, Pleasant W. TN 2nd (Robison's) Inf. Co.F
Thompson, P.M AL 63rd Inf. Co.F
Thompson, Portlock GA 55th Inf. Co.C
Thompson, Potter TX 15th Inf. Co.A
Thompson, Powell C. AL 41st Inf. Co.C
Thompson, President F. AL 11th Inf. Co.D
Thompson, Presley SC Inf. Holcombe Legion Co.G
Thompson, Presley C. VA 50th Inf. Cav.Co.B
Thompson, Preston S. MO 1st Inf. Co.E,H Sgt.
Thompson, Priam A. LA 9th Inf. Co.C
Thompson, Pryor L. MO 2nd Cav. Co.K
Thompson, Pryor L. MO 3rd Cav. Co.I
Thompson, P.S. GA 1st (Olmstead's) Inf. Co.E
Thompson, P.S. MS 3rd Inf. Co.I
Thompson, P.S. MO 1st & 4th Cons.Inf. Co.F
Thompson, P.T. GA 2nd Bn. Troops & Defences (Macon) Co.D
Thompson, P.T. MS 2nd (Davidson's) Inf. Co.I

Thompson, P.T. MS 32nd Inf. Co.D
Thompson, P.V. TX 27th Cav. Co.I,N Sgt.
Thompson, P.W. KY 9th Mtd.Inf. Co.E
Thompson, P.W. TN Inf. 23rd Bn. Co.A
Thompson, P.W. TN 41st Inf. Co.A
Thompson, Q.A. MO Robertson's Regt.St.Guard Co.5
Thompson, Quarles J. TN 14th Inf. Co.C
Thompson, R. AL Cav. Barbiere's Bn. Bowie's Co.
Thompson, R. AL Cav. Barlow's Co.
Thompson, R. AL 35th Inf. Co.G
Thompson, R. AR 19th Inf. Co.B
Thompson, R. FL 2nd Cav. Co.I Cpl.
Thompson, R. GA 3rd Cav. Co.A Col.
Thompson, R. GA 19th Inf. Co.F,D
Thompson, R. GA Mil. Coast Guard Bn. Co.A 4th Lt.
Thompson, R. MD Cav. 2nd Bn. Co.A
Thompson, R. MS 8th Cav. Co.D 1st Lt.
Thompson, R. SC 4th Cav. Co.B
Thompson, R. SC 1st Arty. Co.I
Thompson, R. SC Simons' Co.
Thompson, R. TN 3rd (Forrest's) Cav. Co.H
Thompson, R. TN 15th (Stewart's) Cav. Co.D
Thompson, R. VA Cav. Swann's Bn. Carpenter's Co.
Thompson, R. VA Inf. 4th Bn.Loc.Def. Co.C
Thompson, R. VA 59th Inf. Co.F
Thompson, R. VA 72nd Mil.
Thompson, R. 4th Conf.Inf. Co.E
Thompson, R.A. NC 1st Bn.Jr.Res. Co.D
Thompson, R.A. TN 9th (Ward's) Cav. Co.A,G
Thompson, Raiford NC 2nd Inf. Co.B
Thompson, Raleigh VA 22nd Cav. Co.H
Thompson, Raleigh VA 6th Bn.Res. Co.D
Thompson, Randolph S. VA 1st Cav. Co.H
Thompson, Ransom AL 3rd Bn.Res. Co.A
Thompson, Ransom AR Mil. Borland's Regt. King's Co. Sgt.
Thompson, Ransom MS Cav. Jeff Davis Legion Co.B
Thompson, Ransom P. NC 16th Inf. Co.K
Thompson, Ransom R. TN 48th (Voorhies') Inf. Co.H
Thompson, Rawson VA 13th Inf. Co.F Cpl.
Thompson, Raymond SC 4th Cav. Co.B
Thompson, Raymond SC Cav. 10th Bn. Co.A
Thompson, Raymond SC 6th Inf. 2nd Co.G Sgt.
Thompson, R.B. AL 25th Inf. Co.A
Thompson, R.B. GA Arty. Lumpkin's Co.
Thompson, R.B. GA 8th Inf. Co.B
Thompson, R.B. KY 2nd Cav. Co.B
Thompson, R.B. MS 37th Inf. Co.B
Thompson, R.B. VA 45th Inf. Co.G
Thompson, R.C. MS 8th Inf. Co.C
Thompson, R.C. MO 3rd Inf. Co.D Sgt.
Thompson, R.C. SC Cav.Bn. Holcombe Legion Co.D
Thompson, R.C. TX 21st Cav. Co.F
Thompson, R.C. VA 3rd Res. Co.H
Thompson, R.D. GA Inf. (Madison Cty. Home Guard) Milner's Co. Cpl.
Thompson, R.D. NC 1st Jr.Res. Co.G
Thompson, R.D. SC 4th Cav. Co.I
Thompson, R.E. LA 2nd Inf. Co.I
Thompson, R.E. SC 1st (Butler's) Inf. Co.I
Thompson, R.E. SC 1st (Orr's) Rifles Co.D
Thompson, Reece NC 28th Inf. Co.F
Thompson, Reg H. AR 13th Inf. Co.E Capt.
Thompson, R.E.J. Gen. & Staff AASurg.
Thompson, Reuben L. VA 6th Cav. Co.I Sgt.
Thompson, Reubin AL 4th Inf. Co.I
Thompson, R.E.W. AL 41st Inf. Co.F Ch.Music.
Thompson, R.F. TX 10th Cav. Co.B
Thompson, R.G. MS 2nd Cav. Co.B
Thompson, R.G. MO 10th Inf. Co.A
Thompson, R.G. NC 1st Cav. (9th St.Troops) Co.C
Thompson, R.G. NC Mallett's Bn. Co.E
Thompson, R.G. SC Lt.Arty. Wagener's Co. (Co.A,German Arty.)
Thompson, R.G. SC 3rd St.Troops Co.A
Thompson, R.G. TN 63rd Inf. Co.H
Thompson, R.G. TX 3rd Cav. Co.C
Thompson, R.G. TX Cav. Crump's Regt. Co.O Cpl.
Thompson, R.G. TX Cav. Saufley's Scouting Bn. Co.B
Thompson, R.H. AL 18th Inf. Co.I
Thompson, R.H. AL 23rd Inf. Co.E
Thompson, R.H. AL 60th Inf. Co.H
Thompson, R.H. AL 1st Bn. Hilliard's Legion Vol. Co.B
Thompson, R.H. AR Cav. Carlton's Regt. Lt.Col.
Thompson, R.H. GA 53rd Inf. Co.B
Thompson, R.H. KY 7th Mtd.Inf. 1st Co.K 1st Lt.
Thompson, R.H. MS Cav. 24th Bn. Co.D,E Cpl.
Thompson, R.H. NC 3rd Jr.Res. Co.G
Thompson, R.H. NC McDugald's Co.
Thompson, R.H. TN 6th (Wheeler's) Cav. Co.A
Thompson, R.H. TX 13th Vol. 3rd Co.D
Thompson, R.H. VA Lt.Arty. 13th Bn. Co.B
Thompson, R.H.F. 2nd Cherokee Mtd.Vol. Co.B
Thompson, R.H. Smith Gen. & Staff A.Ord.Off.
Thompson, Richard AL 23rd Inf. Co.D
Thompson, Richard AL Cp. of Instr. Talladega
Thompson, Richard FL 5th Inf. Co.D,E
Thompson, Richard GA 8th Inf. Co.F
Thompson, Richard GA 26th Inf. Co.G
Thompson, Richard KY 8th Mtd.Inf. Co.K Sgt.
Thompson, Richard LA 15th Inf. Co.E
Thompson, Richard NC 2nd Arty. (36th St.Troops) Co.E
Thompson, Richard NC 1st Inf. Co.K
Thompson, Richard NC 20th Inf. Co.C
Thompson, Richard VA 61st Inf. Co.A
Thompson, Richard A. GA 50th Inf. Co.B
Thompson, Richard C. VA 14th Inf. Co.F
Thompson, Richard E. SC 2nd Rifles Co.G
Thompson, Richard F. VA 4th Res. Co.F
Thompson, Richard G. GA 38th Inf. Co.A
Thompson, Richard G. TN 5th (McKenzie's) Cav. Co.C
Thompson, Richard H. NC 43rd Inf. Co.G
Thompson, Richard H. TX 15th Inf. 2nd Co.D
Thompson, Richard K. MO 9th Bn.S.S. Co.E 1st Sgt.
Thompson, Richard L. KY 8th Cav. Co.K Sgt.
Thompson, Richard M. AL 16th Inf. Co.A
Thompson, Richard R. GA 20th Inf. Co.D 2nd Lt.
Thompson, Richard R. NC 24th Inf. Co.E
Thompson, Richard S. GA 22nd Inf. Co.H
Thompson, Richard S. VA Lt.Arty. J.D. Smith's Co. Sgt.
Thompson, Richard W. GA 61st Inf. Co.B
Thompson, Richard W. Gen. & Staff Chap.
Thompson, Riden M. MS 36th Inf. Co.E
Thompson, Riley AR 1st (Crawford's) Cav. Co.E
Thompson, Riley AR 19th (Dockery's) Inf. Co.C Cpl.
Thompson, Riley LA 17th Inf. Co.K
Thompson, Risden N. NC 52nd Inf. Co.I
Thompson, R.J. GA 4th (Clinch's) Cav. Co.F
Thompson, R.J. GA Siege Arty. 28th Bn. Co.K
Thompson, R.J. GA 31st Inf. Co.G
Thompson, R.J. MS Cav. 1st Bn. (Miller's) Co.E
Thompson, R.J. MS 10th Cav. Co.H
Thompson, R.J. Conf.Cav. Baxter's Bn. Co.A
Thompson, R.K. GA 22nd Inf. Co.E Cpl.
Thompson, R.K. MS 1st Cav.Res. Co.B
Thompson, R.K. MS 2nd (Quinn's St.Troops) Inf. Co.A
Thompson, R.K. TN 10th (DeMoss') Cav. Co.B
Thompson, R.K. VA Burks' Regt.Loc.Def. Price's Co.
Thompson, R.L. GA 19th Inf. Co.E
Thompson, R.L. MS Inf. 3rd Bn. (St.Troops) Co.E
Thompson, R.L. SC 11th Res. Co.G
Thompson, R.L. VA Cav. 36th Bn. Co.I Sgt.
Thompson, R.L.J. SC 2nd Arty. Co.C
Thompson, R.M. AL 56th Part.Rangers Co.G
Thompson, R.M. AL 27th Inf. Co.B
Thompson, R.M. AL 55th Vol. Co.G
Thompson, R.M. AR 3rd Cav. Co.H Far.
Thompson, R.M. AR Inf. Cocke's Regt. Co.E
Thompson, R.M. GA Lt.Arty. 12th Bn. 2nd Co.B
Thompson, R.M. MS 6th Inf. Co.F
Thompson, R.M. MS 41st Inf. Co.D
Thompson, R.M. MO 7th Cav. Co.K Cpl.
Thompson, R.M. TN 10th (DeMoss') Cav. Co.K
Thompson, R.M. TN 29th Inf. Co.C
Thompson, R.M. TX 15th Inf. Co.A Music.
Thompson, R.N. NC 2nd Inf. Co.G
Thompson, R.N.B. VA 8th Cav. Co.G
Thompson, Robbert F. AL 36th Inf. Co.F
Thompson, Roberson NC 22nd Inf. Co.L
Thompson, Robert AL St.Arty. Co.A
Thompson, Robert AL 38th Inf. Co.H
Thompson, Robert AL 39th Inf. Co.C
Thompson, Robert AL 42nd Inf. Co.C
Thompson, Robert AL Pris.Guard Freeman's Co. Music.
Thompson, Robt. AL Cp. of Instr. Talladega
Thompson, Robert AR 1st (Colquitt's) Inf. Co.A
Thompson, Robert AR 33rd Inf. Co.B 1st Sgt.
Thompson, Robert GA Inf. 1st City Bn. (Columbus) Co.D
Thompson, Robert GA 9th Inf. Co.D Sgt.
Thompson, Robert GA Inf. 19th Bn. (St.Guards) Co.B
Thompson, Robert LA 2nd Cav. Co.F
Thompson, Robert LA 16th Inf. Co.H

Thompson, Robert KY 2nd (Woodward's) Cav. Co.D
Thompson, Robert MS 1st Cav. Co.G
Thompson, Robert MS 44th Inf. Co.E
Thompson, Robert MO 1st Cav. Co.A
Thompson, Robert MO 1st N.E. Cav. Co.M
Thompson, Robert MO Cav. Poindexter's Regt. Co.E
Thompson, Robert MO Inf. 5th Regt.St.Guard Co.B Cpl.
Thompson, Robert MO 9th Inf. Co.I
Thompson, Robert MO 10th Inf. Co.B
Thompson, Robert NC 1st Inf. (6 mo. '61) Co.B
Thompson, Robert NC 22nd Inf. Co.I
Thompson, Robert NC 52nd Inf. Co.F
Thompson, Robert SC 1st (Butler's) Inf. Co.D
Thompson, Robert TN 2nd (Ashby's) Cav. Co.K
Thompson, Robert TN Cav. 2nd Bn. (Biffle's) Co.C
Thompson, Robert TN Cav. 5th Bn. (McClellan's) Co.E
Thompson, Robert TN Lt.Arty. Palmer's Co.
Thompson, Robert TN 8th Inf.
Thompson, Robert TN 13th Inf. Co.A
Thompson, Robert TN 34th Inf. Co.E
Thompson, Robert TX Cav. Bourland's Regt. Co.A 2nd Lt.
Thompson, Robert TX 10th Inf. Co.E
Thompson, Robert TX 15th Inf. Co.A
Thompson, Robert VA 7th Cav. Co.K
Thompson, Robert VA 23rd Cav. Co.M
Thompson, Robert VA Cav. 34th Bn. Co.D
Thompson, Robert VA Hvy.Arty. 18th Bn. Co.D
Thompson, Robert VA Hvy.Arty. 19th Bn. Co.D
Thompson, Robert VA 6th Inf. Co.H
Thompson, Robert VA 34th Inf. Norton's Co.
Thompson, Robert VA 45th Inf. Co.H
Thompson, Robert VA 46th Inf. Co.L
Thompson, Robert 3rd Conf.Cav. Co.F
Thompson, Robert Sap. & Min. Flynn's Co.,CSA Cpl.
Thompson, Robert A. GA 5th Inf. Co.B
Thompson, Robert A. KY 4th Mtd.Inf. Co.E 2nd Lt.
Thompson, Robert A. SC 2nd Rifles Co.B Lt.Col.
Thompson, Robert A. TN 7th Inf. Co.B Sgt.
Thompson, Robert B. AR 1st Vol. Co.C Cpl.
Thompson, Robert B. GA 48th Inf. Co.H
Thompson, Robert B. NC 25th Inf. Co.D Sgt.
Thompson, Robert B. VA 61st Mil. Co.B Sgt.
Thompson, Robert C. AL 2nd Cav. Co.E,C
Thompson, Robert C. AR 62nd Mil. Co.C Cpl.
Thompson, Robert C. KY 2nd (Duke's) Cav. Co.E Sgt.
Thompson, Robert C. KY 1st Inf. Co.H Cpl.
Thompson, Robert C. MO 16th Inf. Co.H Jr.2nd Lt.
Thompson, Robert C. TN 41st Inf. Co.H 2nd Lt.
Thompson, Robert C. VA 7th Cav. Co.C
Thompson, Robert C. VA 13th Cav. Co.G
Thompson, Robert C. VA 3rd Inf. 1st Co.I
Thompson, Robert C. VA 23rd Inf. Co.A
Thompson, Robert E. GA 45th Inf. Co.C
Thompson, Robert E. LA Cav. Webb's Co.
Thompson, Robert F. GA 47th Inf. Co.D Sgt.
Thompson, Robert F. MS 15th Inf. Co.H Cpl.
Thompson, Robert G. VA 12th Inf. Co.C
Thompson, Robert H. NC 8th Bn.Jr.Res. Co.C
Thompson, Robert H. TN 24th Inf. Co.B
Thompson, Robert H. VA 2nd Arty. Co.D
Thompson, Robert H. VA 48th Inf. Co.B 2nd Lt.
Thompson, Robert H.W. AL 6th Inf. Co.A
Thompson, Robert J. VA 18th Cav. Co.C
Thompson, Robert J. VA 114th Mil. Co.F, Mtd.Co.
Thompson, Robert K. GA 8th Inf. (St.Guards) Co.F Ens.
Thompson, Robert K. MO 5th Cav. Co.E 1st Lt.
Thompson, Robert K. VA 11th Inf. Co.D Capt.
Thompson, Robert L. AL 16th Inf. Co.G
Thompson, Robert L. KY 9th Cav. Co.F
Thompson, Robert L. NC 47th Inf. Co.E Sgt.
Thompson, Rob. M. AL 21st Inf. Co.E
Thompson, Robert M. SC 2nd Inf. Co.D Sgt.
Thompson, Robert O. TX 29th Cav. Co.E
Thompson, Robert O. 1st Choctaw & Chickasaw Mtd.Rifles 1st Co.I
Thompson, Robert S. TN 18th Inf. Co.A Sgt.
Thompson, Robert S. TX 7th Field Btty.
Thompson, Robert S. TX 13th Vol. 3rd Co.A
Thompson, Robert S. VA 45th Inf. Co.F
Thompson, Robert T. AL 61st Inf. Co.H
Thompson, Robert T. MS 14th Inf. Co.F
Thompson, Robert T. TX 24th Cav. Co.H
Thompson, Robert T. VA Lt.Arty. Armistead's Co. Sgt.
Thompson, Robert T. VA 61st Mil. Co.H Sgt.
Thompson, Robert W. KY O'Neal's Bn. Co.A
Thompson, Robert W. NC Hvy.Arty. 10th Bn. Co.C
Thompson, Robert W. TN 43rd Inf. Co.A
Thompson, Robert W. TX 1st Inf. Co.I
Thompson, Robert W. TX 20th Inf. Co.A
Thompson, Robert W. VA 16th Cav. Co.F 1st Sgt.
Thompson, Robert W. VA Cav. Caldwell's Bn. Taylor's Co. 1st Sgt.
Thompson, Robert W. VA 2nd Inf. Co.H 2nd Lt.
Thompson, Robert W. VA Inf. 22nd Bn. Co.D
Thompson, Robt. W. Gen. & Staff Hosp.Stew.
Thompson, Roden MO Cav. Ford's Bn. Co.A
Thompson, Rodney AR 8th Cav. Co.H
Thompson, Roland B. MS 44th Inf. Co.K
Thompson, Royal MO 4th Cav. Co.D
Thompson, R.P. GA 12th Cav. Co.C
Thompson, R.P. GA 1st (Fannin's) Res. Co.D
Thompson, R.P. MS 2nd Cav. Co.I
Thompson, R.P. MS 3rd Cav. Co.C
Thompson, R.P. MS Inf. 4th St.Troops Co.F Cpl.
Thompson, R.P. MS 46th Inf. Co.F
Thompson, R.P. TN 4th (McLemore's) Cav. Co.C
Thompson, R.R. GA Floyd Legion (St.Guards) Co.H
Thompson, R.S. GA 18th Inf. Co.A
Thompson, R.S. LA 4th Inf. Co.C Cpl.
Thompson, R.S. TN 12th (Green's) Cav. Co.G 1st Sgt.
Thompson, R.S. TX 35th (Brown's) Cav. Co.B
Thompson, R.S. TX Inf. Griffin's Bn. Co.D
Thompson, R.S. VA 3rd (Archer's) Bn.Res. Co.D
Thompson, R.S. VA Second Class Mil. Wolff's Co.
Thompson, R.T. AL 63rd Inf. Co.E
Thompson, R.T. MS 43rd Inf. Co.C
Thompson, R.T. MO 3rd Inf. Co.D,B
Thompson, R.T. SC Lt.Arty. J.T. Kanapaux's Co. (Lafayette Arty.)
Thompson, Ruben P. MS 37th Inf. Co.A
Thompson, Ruffin MS 18th Inf. Co.H
Thompson, Ruffin T. GA 6th Inf. Co.I
Thompson, Rufus NC 35th Inf. Co.C
Thompson, Rufus NC 42nd Inf. Co.E
Thompson, Rufus M. GA Phillips' Legion Co.B
Thompson, Rush TN 10th & 11th (Cons.) Cav. Co.G
Thompson, Russel W. AL 18th Inf. Co.L
Thompson, R.V. TN 5th Inf. 2nd Co.B
Thompson, R.W. AL Cp. of Instr. Talladega
Thompson, R.W. AR 36th Inf. Co.K
Thompson, R.W. AR 50th Mil. Co.I
Thompson, R.W. MS 2nd Part.Rangers Co.L
Thompson, R.W. MS Inf. 3rd Bn. (St.Troops) Co.D
Thompson, R.W. NC 1st Jr.Res. Co.G
Thompson, R.W. TN 10th (DeMoss') Cav. Co.B
Thompson, R.W. TX 7th Cav. Co.D 1st Lt.
Thompson, R.W. TX 27th Cav. Co.F
Thompson, R.W. VA Lt.Arty. 13th Bn. Co.A
Thompson, R.W. VA 1st (Farinholt's) Res. Co.K
Thompson, R.W. VA 3rd Inf.Loc.Def. 1st Co.G, Co.I
Thompson, R.W. Gen. & Staff Chap.
Thompson, R. Wesley TN 59th Mtd.Inf. Co.G Cpl.
Thompson, S. AL Cav. Moreland's Regt. Co.I
Thompson, S. AL Randolph Cty.Res. Shepherd's Co.
Thompson, S. GA 54th Inf. Lt.
Thompson, S. NC 7th Sr.Res. Bradshaw's Co.
Thompson, S. TN 21st & 22nd (Cons.) Cav. Co.C
Thompson, S. TN 22nd (Barteau's) Cav. Co.A
Thompson, S. VA 2nd Cav. Co.A
Thompson, S. VA 15th Cav. Co.B
Thompson, S. VA Cav. 37th Bn. Co.F
Thompson, S.A. AL 8th Cav. Co.F
Thompson, S.A. AR 58th Mil. Co.D
Thompson, S.A. TN Inf. 23rd Bn. Co.A
Thompson, S.A. TN Inf. 154th Sr.Regt. Co.D
Thompson, S.A. TX Arty. Douglas' Co.
Thompson, S.A. TX Waul's Legion Co.B
Thompson, S.A. Bradford's Corps Scouts & Guards Co.B
Thompson, Sabert W. NC 44th Inf. Co.G
Thompson, S.A.H. GA 28th Inf. Co.I
Thompson, Salem VA 18th Cav. Co.A Cpl.
Thompson, Sam M. MO Cav. Schnabel's Bn. Co.G
Thompson, Sampson MS 9th Inf. Old Co.E
Thompson, Samuel AL 8th Inf. Co.A
Thompson, Samuel AL 21st Inf. Co.I Sgt.
Thompson, Samuel AL 28th Inf. Co.K
Thompson, Samuel AL 36th Inf. Co.A

Thompson, Samuel AR 18th (Marmaduke's) Inf. Co.K
Thompson, Samuel AR 19th (Dockery's) Inf. Co.C
Thompson, Samuel GA 8th Inf. (St.Guards) Co.I
Thompson, Samuel GA 16th Inf. Co.A
Thompson, Samuel MD Arty. 1st Btty.
Thompson, Samuel MO 15th Cav. Co.H
Thompson, Samuel NC 3rd Arty. (40th St.Troops) Co.H
Thompson, Samuel NC 25th Inf. Co.E
Thompson, Samuel SC 1st Cav. Co.D Sgt.
Thompson, Samuel SC 5th Inf.
Thompson, Samuel TN 6th (Wheeler's) Cav. Co.H
Thompson, Samuel TN 21st (Wilson's) Cav. Co.H
Thompson, Samuel TN 22nd (Barteau's) Cav. Co.K
Thompson, Samuel TN 27th Inf. Co.I
Thompson, Samuel TN 33rd Inf. Co.G
Thompson, Samuel TN 34th Inf. Co.A
Thompson, Samuel TN 42nd Inf. 2nd Co.H
Thompson, Samuel VA 16th Cav. Co.F
Thompson, Samuel VA 2nd Inf. Co.D
Thompson, Samuel VA 45th Inf. Co.G 2nd Lt.
Thompson, Samuel VA 49th Inf. Co.F
Thompson, Samuel VA 51st Inf. Co.E
Thompson, Samuel VA 59th Inf. 2nd Co.I
Thompson, Samuel VA 89th Mil. Co.H
Thompson, Samuel Allen TX 1st Hvy.Arty.
Thompson, Samuel B. AL 6th Inf. Co.L
Thompson, Samuel C. GA 5th Inf. Co.A
Thompson, Samuel C. GA Inf. 25th Bn. (Prov.Guard) Co.C
Thompson, Samuel C. VA 37th Inf. Co.E
Thompson, Samuel D. AR 3rd Inf. Co.C,D
Thompson, Samuel D. NC 1st Inf. Co.E
Thompson, Samuel D. SC 21st Inf. Co.D
Thompson, Samuel E. MS Inf. 5th Bn. Co.B
Thompson, Samuel E. MS 27th Inf. Co.K
Thompson, Samuel E.M. VA 45th Inf. Co.H
Thompson, Samuel F. TN 2nd (Smith's) Cav.
Thompson, Samuel G. NC 53rd Inf. Co.A
Thompson, Samuel G. VA Lt.Arty. Arch. Graham's Co.
Thompson, Samuel H. AL 19th Inf. Co.D
Thompson, Samuel H. AR 38th Inf. Co.F
Thompson, Samuel H. AR Inf. Cocke's Regt. Co.C Sgt.
Thompson, Samuel H. GA Cobb's Legion Co.A
Thompson, Samuel H. MS Inf. 1st Bn. Co.A
Thompson, Samuel H. TN 59th Mtd.Inf. Co.H 1st Lt.
Thompson, Samuel J. AR 23rd Inf. Co.H 1st Sgt.
Thompson, Samuel J. KY 5th Mtd.Inf. Co.A
Thompson, Samuel J. TX 25th Cav. Co.A
Thompson, Samuel J. VA 38th Inf. Co.C
Thompson, Samuel J. VA 38th Inf. Co.D
Thompson, Samuel M. AL 13th Inf. Co.E,G
Thompson, Samuel M. AR 7th Inf. Surg.
Thompson, Samuel M. GA 22nd Inf. Co.K
Thompson, Samuel M. GA 41st Inf.
Thompson, Samuel M. TN 41st Inf. Co.F Surg.
Thompson, Samuel N. TX 17th Cav. Co.C
Thompson, Samuel P. NC 1st Inf. Co.K Cpl.
Thompson, Samuel P. TN 2nd (Smith's) Cav. Capt.
Thompson, Samuel S. NC 6th Inf. Co.F
Thompson, Samuel S.B. NC 51st Inf. Co.H
Thompson, Samuel T. NC 23rd Inf. Co.K 1st Sgt.
Thompson, Samuel T. NC 28th Inf. Co.I 2nd Lt.
Thompson, Samuel W. AR 35th Inf. Co.C Cpl.
Thompson, Samuel W. GA 23rd Inf. Surg.
Thompson, Samuel W. KY 13th Cav. Co.F,K,D 1st Lt.
Thompson, Samuel W. KY 5th Mtd.Inf. Co.B 2nd Lt.
Thompson, Samuel W. NC 3rd Arty. (40th St.Troops) Co.G
Thompson, Samuel W. VA 16th Cav. Co.I Jr.2nd Lt.
Thompson, Samuel W. 1st Cherokee Mtd.Vol. 2nd Co.K
Thompson, Sam W. TN 5th Inf. Co.A 1st Sgt.
Thompson, Sanders NC 34th Inf. Co.A
Thompson, Sanders VA 21st Cav. 2nd Co.I
Thompson, Sanford H. MO Inf. 1st Regt. St.Guard Co.E 3rd Lt.
Thompson, S.C. LA 4th Cav. Co.H
Thompson, S.C. MS Inf. 3rd Bn. Co.E
Thompson, S.C. NC 1st Inf. Co.B
Thompson, S.C. TN 12th (Green's) Cav. Co.B
Thompson, S.C. TN 11th Inf. Co.A
Thompson, Scipio TN 6th (Wheeler's) Cav. Co.F Sgt.
Thompson, S.D. TN 19th (Biffle's) Cav. Co.C Cpl.
Thompson, S.E. AL 37th Inf. Co.F
Thompson, S.E. MS 10th Inf. New Co.A
Thompson, Seborn GA 26th Inf. Co.K
Thompson, Seth AR 35th Inf. Co.A Cpl.
Thompson, Seth T. AR 17th (Griffith's) Inf. Co.D
Thompson, S.F. GA 3rd Inf. Co.G
Thompson, S.F.R. TX Cav. Hardeman's Regt. Co.A
Thompson, S.G. NC 5th Inf. Co.K
Thompson, S.G. NC 7th Sr.Res. Boon's Co.
Thompson, S.G. NC 62nd Inf. Co.F
Thompson, S.G. TX Cav. McCord's Frontier Regt. Co.C Capt.
Thompson, S.G.W. MO Lt.Arty. Landis' Co.
Thompson, S.H. GA 54th Inf. Co.D
Thompson, S.H. MS Cav. 1st Bn. (Montgomery's) St.Troops Cameron's Co.
Thompson, S.H. MS 28th Cav. Co.I
Thompson, S.H. MS 3rd Inf. Co.B
Thompson, S.H. MS 22nd Inf. Co.F Sgt.
Thompson, S.H. MO Cav. 1st Regt.St.Guard Co.E
Thompson, S.H. NC 2nd Detailed Men Co.F Capt.
Thompson, S.H. SC 26th Inf. Co.K
Thompson, S.H. TN 51st (Cons.) Inf. Co.F
Thompson, S.H. TX 28th Cav. Co.K
Thompson, S.H. 3rd Conf.Eng.Troops Co.G Cpl.
Thompson, S.H. Eng.Dept. Polk's Corps A. of TN Sap. & Min. Co.,CSA
Thompson, Shadrach AL 4th Res. Co.I
Thompson, Shadrack GA 41st Inf. Co.H
Thompson, Shadrack B. NC 3rd Arty. (40th St.Troops) Co.K
Thompson, Shem D. AL 20th Inf. Co.K Sgt.
Thompson, Shia he ka 1st Choctaw Mtd.Rifles Co.K
Thompson, Sidney NC 5th Sr.Res. Co.D
Thompson, Sidney TN 21st (Wilson's) Cav. Co.C Cpl.
Thompson, Sidney A. NC 56th Inf. Co.H Sgt.
Thompson, Sidney J. NC 52nd Inf. Co.H
Thompson, Sidney W. NC 44th Inf. Co.F
Thompson, Silas VA 14th Cav. 1st Co.F 2nd Lt.
Thompson, Silas H. MS 33rd Inf. Co.K Sgt.
Thompson, Silas P. VA Cav. 36th Bn. Co.E 2nd Lt.
Thompson, Simeon AL 18th Inf. Co.B
Thompson, Simeon GA Arty. St.Troops Pruden's Btty.
Thompson, Simeon MS 9th Cav. Co.A
Thompson, Simeon NC 53rd Inf. Co.F
Thompson, Simon MS 27th Inf. Co.L
Thompson, Simon TX 10th Cav. Co.A Sgt.
Thompson, Singleton W. MO 1st N.E. Cav. Co.C
Thompson, Sion A. MO 16th Inf. Co.H
Thompson, S.J. AL Cav. Barbiere's Bn. Bowie's Co.
Thompson, S.J. AL 23rd Inf. Co.H Sgt.
Thompson, S.J. AR Lt.Arty. Owen's Btty.
Thompson, S.J. AR 24th Inf. Co.E
Thompson, S.J. GA 44th Inf. Co.G
Thompson, S.J. GA 63rd Inf. Co.H
Thompson, S.J. SC 2nd St.Troops Co.H
Thompson, S.J. TX Cav. Morgan's Regt. Co.D
Thompson, S.J. VA 18th Inf. Co.I
Thompson, S.J. Cherokee Bn.,CSA
Thompson, S.K. AR 11th Inf. Co.B
Thompson, S.K. AR 11th & 17th Cons.Inf. Co.A
Thompson, S.K. TX 25th Cav. Co.B
Thompson, S.L. GA Inf. 27th Bn. Co.F
Thompson, S.L. GA Inf. (Jasper & Butts Cty. Guards) Lane's Co.
Thompson, S.M. AL 18th Inf. Co.E 1st Sgt.
Thompson, S.M. AL 33rd Inf. Surg.
Thompson, S.M. AR 7th Inf. Surg.
Thompson, S.M. GA Lt.Arty. Howell's Co.
Thompson, S.M. GA 46th Inf. Co.A
Thompson, S.M. MS 1st Cav. Co.B
Thompson, S.M. MO 16th Inf. Co.F
Thompson, S.M. TN 10th Inf. Co.B Lt.Col.
Thompson, S.M. TX 12th Cav. Co.F
Thompson, S.M. Cheatham's Div. Surg.
Thompson, Smith W. VA 2nd Inf. Co.E
Thompson, Smith W. VA 97th Mil. Co.M Cpl.
Thompson, S.M.J. MO Cav. 6th Regt.St.Guard Co.C
Thompson, Solloman T. GA 1st (Olmstead's) Inf. Co.K
Thompson, Solomon AL Mil. Gueringer's Co.
Thompson, Solomon GA 38th Inf. Co.C Sgt.
Thompson, Solomon NC 30th Inf. Co.D
Thompson, Solomon VA 16th Cav. Co.G
Thompson, Solomon VA Cav. Ferguson's Bn. Parks' Co.
Thompson, Solomon J. SC 24th Inf. Co.H
Thompson, Solomon P. GA 57th Inf. Co.D
Thompson, Solon F. KY 8th Cav. Co.K

Thompson, Solon F. KY 8th Mtd.Inf. Co.K
Thompson, S.P. KY 8th Cav. Co.K
Thompson, S.P. SC 16th Inf. Co.H
Thompson, S.P. SC 16th & 24th (Cons.) Inf. Co.B
Thompson, S.P. TN 2nd (Ashby's) Cav. Co.D
Thompson, S.P. TN Cav. 4th Bn. (Branner's) Co.C
Thompson, S.P. VA 24th Cav. Co.B
Thompson, Spencer NC 22nd Inf. Co.M
Thompson, S.P.M. SC 12th Inf. Co.K
Thompson, Squire VA 14th Cav. 1st Co.F, Co.C
Thompson, Squire VA 22nd Cav. Co.D
Thompson, Squire VA Cav. 36th Bn. Co.E
Thompson, Squire VA 36th Inf. 2nd Co.B 2nd Lt.
Thompson, Squire VA 72nd Mil.
Thompson, S.R. GA 12th (Wright's) Cav. (St.Guards) Stapleton's Co.
Thompson, S.R. VA 46th Inf. 2nd Co.E
Thompson, S.S. MS 37th Inf. Co.I
Thompson, S.S.P. VA 4th Res. Co.E
Thompson, S.T. AL Cp. of Instr. Talladega
Thompson, S.T. AR 11th & 17th Cons.Inf. Co.K
Thompson, S.T. NC 4th Sr.Res. Co.I
Thompson, Stephen AL 61st Inf. Co.G
Thompson, Stephen AR 7th Cav. Co.D
Thompson, Stephen AR 15th (N.W.) Inf. Co.D
Thompson, Stephen GA 51st Inf. Co.G
Thompson, Stephen MO 7th Cav. Co.F
Thompson, Stephen MO 9th (Elliott's) Cav. Co.F
Thompson, Stephen NC 52nd Inf. Co.E
Thompson, Stephen TN Arty. Marshall's Co.
Thompson, Stephen TN 29th Inf. Co.D 1st Sgt.
Thompson, Stephen TX Lt.Arty. Jones' Co.
Thompson, Stephen TX 12th Inf. Co.A
Thompson, Stephen TX 19th Inf. Co.E
Thompson, Stephen VA 25th Cav. Co.I Bvt.2nd Lt.
Thompson, Stephen VA 67th Mil. Co.D
Thompson, Stephen A. NC 12th Inf. Co.D Sgt.
Thompson, Stephen A. NC 18th Inf. Co.D Sgt.
Thompson, Stephen B. VA 25th Cav. Co.I
Thompson, Stephen B. VA Inf. Mileham's Co.
Thompson, Stephen C. TX 15th Cav. Co.A Adj.
Thompson, Stephen C. Gen. & Staff 1st Lt.,Adj.
Thompson, Stephen H. AR 12th Bn.S.S. Co.A Jr.2nd Lt.
Thompson, Stephen H. AR 15th (Josey's) Inf. Co.B Sgt.
Thompson, Stephen N. VA 25th Cav. Co.I
Thompson, Stephen R. MS 3rd Inf. Co.A 2nd Lt.
Thompson, Stephen T. TX 15th Cav. Co.A
Thompson, Street FL 4th Inf. Co.F
Thompson, S.W. LA 19th Inf. Co.C
Thompson, S.W. NC 1st Inf. Co.B
Thompson, S.W. TX 24th & 25th Cav. (Cons.) Co.B
Thompson, S.W. TX 25th Cav. Co.B
Thompson, S.W. TX 9th (Nichols') Inf. Co.D
Thompson, S.W. VA Cav. Caldwell's Bn. Graham's Co.
Thompson, S.W. VA 1st (Farinholt's) Res. Co.K
Thompson, Swan TN Cav. 1st Bn. (McNairy's) Co.B
Thompson, S.Y. GA 53rd Inf. Co.B
Thompson, Sydney B. SC 15th Inf. Co.G
Thompson, Sylvester NC 1st Arty. (10th St.Troops) Co.D
Thompson, Sylvester VA 30th Bn.S.S. Co.A
Thompson, Sylvester R. TN 39th Mtd.Inf. Co.F
Thompson, Symon A. MS Cav. 17th Bn. Co.E,A Sgt.
Thompson, Syms VA 59th Inf. 2nd Co.I
Thompson, T. AL St.Arty. Co.C
Thompson, T. AR 2nd Inf. New Co.E 1st Sgt.
Thompson, T. AR 11th Inf. Co.A Sgt.
Thompson, T. AR 11th & 17th Cons.Inf. Co.A 1st Sgt.
Thompson, T. AR 30th Inf. Co.H
Thompson, T. AR Inf. Cocke's Regt. Co.B
Thompson, T. GA 44th Inf. Co.A
Thompson, T. LA 3rd (Wingfield's) Cav. Co.I
Thompson, T. LA Mil. 3rd Regt. 1st Brig. 1st Div. Co.H
Thompson, T. MO Cav. Freeman's Regt. Co.E Sgt.
Thompson, T. TN 15th (Cons.) Cav. Co.B
Thompson, T. TN 21st & 22nd (Cons.) Cav. Co.C
Thompson, T. TN 84th Inf. Co.B Cpl.
Thompson, T. TX 2nd Cav. Co.K
Thompson, T.A. AL Cav. Barbiere's Bn. Co.F
Thompson, T.A. NC Mil. Clark's Sp.Bn. A.R. Davis' Co. 2nd Lt.
Thompson, T.A. SC 4th Bn.Res. Co.A 1st Lt.
Thompson, T.A. TN 12th (Cons.) Inf. Co.B
Thompson, T.A. TX 3rd Cav. Co.F
Thompson, T.A. TX 34th Cav. Co.G
Thompson, Taliaferro VA 49th Inf. Co.I Sgt.
Thompson, Tandy GA Cav. 29th Bn. Co.F
Thompson, Tazewell VA 9th Cav. Co.H
Thompson, Tazewell VA 26th Inf. Co.F
Thompson, Tazewell Gen. & Staff Maj.,CS
Thompson, T.B. AL 19th Inf. Co.F
Thompson, T.B. MS 35th Inf. Co.E
Thompson, T.B. SC 1st St.Troops Co.K
Thompson, T.B. TN 51st Inf. Co.C
Thompson, T.B., Jr. TN 51st (Cons.) Inf. Co.I
Thompson, T.B. 1st Conf.Cav. 1st Co.B
Thompson, T.C. LA 2nd Cav. Asst.Surg.
Thompson, T.C. NC 8th Sr.Res. Callihan's Co.
Thompson, T.C. TN 23rd Inf. Co.D
Thompson, T.C. TX Waul's Legion Asst.Surg.
Thompson, T.C. Gen. & Staff Asst.Surg.
Thompson, T.D. MO Inf. 2nd Regt.St.Guard Co.F 3rd Lt.
Thompson, T.D. TN 11th Inf. Co.H Sgt.Maj.
Thompson, T.E. GA 3rd Res. Co.F
Thompson, T.E. GA Cobb's Legion Co.A
Thompson, T.E. TX Cav. Wells' Regt. Co.E
Thompson, Tecumseh H. VA 13th Cav. Co.G
Thompson, Terrill TN 5th (McKenzie's) Cav. Co.E
Thompson, Terry TN Park's Co. (Loc.Def. Troops)
Thompson, T.F. AL 28th Inf. Co.L
Thompson, T.F. TN 23rd Inf. Co.C
Thompson, T.F. TN 38th Inf. 1st Co.K
Thompson, T.F. TX 5th Cav. Co.G
Thompson, T.F. VA Inf. 4th Bn.Loc.Def. Co.E Cpl.
Thompson, T.G. MS Cav. 1st Bn. (Montgomery's) St.Troops Hammond's Co.
Thompson, T.G. MS Cav. Yerger's Regt. Co.A
Thompson, T.G. MS Inf. (Choctaw Silver Greys) Drane's Co.
Thompson, T.G. SC 16th & 24th (Cons.) Inf. Co.F
Thompson, T.G. TX 17th Inf. Co.C
Thompson, T.H. GA 27th Inf. Co.A
Thompson, T.H. LA 2nd Cav. Co.A
Thompson, T.H. MS 3rd (St.Troops) Cav. Co.B
Thompson, T.H. MS 4th Inf. Co.K
Thompson, T.H. MS 5th Inf. (St.Troops) Co.A
Thompson, T.H. MS 18th Inf. Co.D
Thompson, T.H. MO 3rd Cav.
Thompson, T.H. TN 19th Inf. Co.A
Thompson, T.H. VA 5th Cav. Co.K
Thompson, T.H. VA Lt.Arty. Hankins' Co.
Thompson, Thaddeus VA 8th Cav. Co.E
Thompson, Thaddeus S. VA 15th Inf. Co.C Cpl.
Thompson, Tharon B. 1st Conf.Inf. Co.B Sr.2nd Lt.
Thompson, Theodore KY 5th Cav. Co.H
Thompson, Theodore A. NC 51st Inf. Co.E
Thompson, Theodore B. SC 3rd Res. Co.B Cpl.
Thompson, Theodore B. SC 16th Inf. Co.K
Thompson, Theron B. GA 36th (Villepigue's) Inf. Co.B 2nd Lt.
Thompson, Thomas AL 5th Bn.Vol. Co.D
Thompson, Thomas AL 23rd Inf. Co.H
Thompson, Thomas AL 30th Inf. Co.F
Thompson, Thomas AL 49th Inf. Co.C
Thompson, Thomas AL 59th Inf. Co.D
Thompson, Thomas AR 1st Mtd.Rifles Co.H Cpl.
Thompson, Thomas AR 7th Cav. Co.B
Thompson, Thomas GA 1st Cav. Co.H Cpl.
Thompson, Thomas GA Siege Arty. 28th Bn. Co.H
Thompson, Thomas GA 2nd Res. Co.H
Thompson, Thomas GA Inf. 3rd Bn. Co.F
Thompson, Thomas GA 4th Res. Co.B
Thompson, Thomas GA 6th Inf. Co.I
Thompson, Thomas GA 7th Inf. Co.I
Thompson, Thomas GA 7th Inf. (St.Guards) Co.B
Thompson, Thomas GA 9th Inf. (St.Guards) Co.B
Thompson, Thomas GA 27th Inf. Co.E
Thompson, Thomas GA 37th Inf. Co.B Cpl.
Thompson, Thomas GA 47th Inf. Co.H
Thompson, Thomas KY 3rd Mtd.Inf. Co.I
Thompson, Thomas LA 22nd Inf. Co.I
Thompson, Thomas LA Inf.Cons.Crescent Regt. Co.E
Thompson, Thomas LA Res.Corps
Thompson, Thomas MS 2nd Cav.
Thompson, Thomas MS 5th Inf. Co.H Cpl.
Thompson, Thomas MS 6th Inf. Co.B
Thompson, Thomas MS 19th Inf. Co.A
Thompson, Thomas MS 35th Inf. Co.G
Thompson, Thomas MO 7th Cav. Conyard's Co.
Thompson, Thomas MO 8th Inf. Co.H
Thompson, Thomas MO 9th Bn.S.S. Co.A
Thompson, Thomas MO Inf. Perkins' Bn. Co.A
Thompson, Thomas NC 4th Cav. (59th St.Troops) Capt.,ACS

Thompson, Thomas NC 2nd Arty. (36th St.Troops) Co.A
Thompson, Thomas NC Lt.Arty. 3rd Bn. Co.A
Thompson, Thomas NC 3rd Inf. Co.F
Thompson, Thomas NC 3rd Bn.Sr.Res. Durham's Co.
Thompson, Thomas NC 17th Inf. (2nd Org.) Co.H
Thompson, Thomas NC 27th Inf. Co.A
Thompson, Thomas NC 43rd Inf. Co.I
Thompson, Thomas SC 11th Inf. Co.B
Thompson, Thomas SC 16th Inf. Co.E
Thompson, Thomas SC Mil. 16th Regt. Eason's Co.
Thompson, Thomas TN Cav. 16th Bn. (Neal's) Co.A
Thompson, Thomas TN 22nd (Barteau's) Cav. Co.K
Thompson, Thomas TN 1st (Feild's) Inf. Co.K
Thompson, Thomas TN 3rd (Clack's) Inf. Co.F 1st Lt.
Thompson, Thomas TN 10th Inf.
Thompson, Thomas TN 11th Inf. Co.I
Thompson, Thomas TN 19th Inf. Co.B
Thompson, Thomas TN 29th Inf. Co.F
Thompson, Thomas TN 31st Inf. Co.H
Thompson, Thomas TN 32nd Inf. Co.A Cpl.
Thompson, Thomas TN 41st Inf. Co.F Cpl.
Thompson, Thomas TX 31st Cav. Co.F
Thompson, Thomas TX 9th (Nichols') Inf. Co.D
Thompson, Thomas TX 12th Inf. Co.A
Thompson, Thomas VA 2nd Cav. Co.E
Thompson, Thomas VA 12th Cav. Co.A
Thompson, Thomas VA Cav. 34th Bn. Co.D
Thompson, Thomas VA Cav. Mosby's Regt. (Part.Rangers) Co.C
Thompson, Thomas VA Cav. Swann's Bn. Carpenter's Co.
Thompson, Thomas VA 36th Inf. 1st Co.C, 2nd Co.D
Thompson, Thomas VA 41st Inf. 1st Co.E
Thompson, Thomas VA 49th Inf. Co.I
Thompson, Thomas VA 58th Inf. Co.G
Thompson, Thomas VA 62nd Mtd.Inf. Co.A
Thompson, Thomas VA 77th Mil. Co.A
Thompson, Thomas 1st Conf.Cav. 2nd Co.F
Thompson, Thomas Conf.Inf. Tucker's Regt. Co.K
Thompson, Thomas Gen. & Staff Capt.,Comsy.
Thompson, Thos. A. AL Inf. 36th Regt. Co.B
Thompson, Thomas A. GA 62nd Cav. Co.I
Thompson, Thomas A. NC 5th Cav. (63rd St.Troops) Co.D
Thompson, Thomas A. NC 28th Inf. Co.H Capt.
Thompson, Thomas A. TX 22nd Cav. Co.E
Thompson, Thomas B. AL 7th Inf. Co.A Music.
Thompson, Thomas B. AL 13th Inf. Co.F 1st Sgt.
Thompson, Thomas B. AR 8th Inf. New Co.F
Thompson, Thomas B. AR 14th (McCarver's) Inf. Co.B
Thompson, Thomas B. GA 16th Inf. Co.D
Thompson, Thomas B. MS 43rd Inf. Co.D Capt.
Thompson, Thomas B. NC 52nd Inf. Co.G Sgt.
Thompson, Thomas B. TN 51st Inf. Co.E
Thompson, Thomas B. TX Cav. Martin's Regt. Co.F
Thompson, Thomas B. TX Cav. Ragsdale's Bn. 2nd Co.C
Thompson, Thomas B. TX 4th Field Btty.
Thompson, Thomas B. VA 14th Inf. Co.F
Thompson, Thomas B. VA 45th Inf. Co.G 2nd Lt.
Thompson, Thos. B. Gen. & Staff 1st Lt.,ADC
Thompson, Thomas C. GA 42nd Inf. Co.G,C
Thompson, Thomas C. MS 2nd Part.Rangers Co.C
Thompson, Thomas C. NC 1st Arty. (10th St.Troops) Co.D
Thompson, Thomas C. TN 16th Inf. Co.K
Thompson, Thomas C. TX 27th Cav. Co.G
Thompson, Thomas C. TX 13th Vol. 1st Co.I
Thompson, Thomas C. VA 14th Inf. Co.F
Thompson, Thomas D. AR 33rd Inf. Co.B Lt.Col.
Thompson, Thomas D. NC 8th Inf. Co.B
Thompson, Thomas D. TN 10th Cav. Sgt.Maj.
Thompson, Thomas D. VA 41st Inf. Co.B
Thompson, Thos. D. Gen. & Staff ADC
Thompson, Thomas E. NC 4th Inf. Co.F Capt.
Thompson, Thomas F. AR 5th Inf. Co.C
Thompson, Thomas F. VA 26th Inf. Co.D
Thompson, Thomas G.N MS 2nd Inf. Co.F
Thompson, Thomas H. AL 11th Inf. Co.F
Thompson, Thomas H. AL 36th Inf. Co.B
Thompson, Thomas H. AR Inf. 1st Bn. Co.F
Thompson, Thomas H. MS 24th Inf. Co.K
Thompson, Thomas H. MO 6th Cav. Co.D
Thompson, Thomas H. NC 28th Inf. Co.G
Thompson, Thomas H. VA Lt.Arty. Cayce's Co. Cpl.
Thompson, Thomas H. VA 63rd Inf. Co.D
Thompson, Thomas J. AL 13th Bn.Part.Rangers Co.E
Thompson, Thomas J. AL 56th Part.Rangers Co.I
Thompson, Thomas J. AL Arty. 1st Bn. Co.E
Thompson, Thomas J. AR 1st (Crawford's) Cav. Co.F
Thompson, Thomas J. FL Milton Lt.Arty. Dunham's Co. Sgt.
Thompson, Thomas J. GA 1st (Ramsey's) Inf. Co.G Sgt.
Thompson, Thomas J. GA 44th Inf. Co.C
Thompson, Thomas J. KY 4th Mtd.Inf. Co.C Cpl.
Thompson, Thomas J. LA 19th Inf. Co.C Jr.2nd Lt.
Thompson, Thomas J. LA 28th (Gray's) Inf. Co.G Cpl.
Thompson, Thomas J. MS 13th Inf. Co.H
Thompson, Thomas J. MO 11th Inf.
Thompson, Thomas J. SC 4th St.Troops Co.F
Thompson, Thomas J. TN 1st (Turney's) Inf. Co.F
Thompson, Thomas J. TN 54th Inf. Hollis' Co.
Thompson, Thomas J. VA 19th Inf. Co.I
Thompson, Thomas J. 1st Choctaw & Chickasaw Mtd.Rifles 2nd Co.K 2nd Lt.
Thompson, Thomas Jefferson TX 3rd Cav. Co.G,B,D
Thompson, Thomas L. AL 6th Inf. Co.G
Thompson, Thomas L. AR 3rd Inf. Co.C
Thompson, Thomas L. GA 65th Inf. Co.C
Thompson, Thomas L. NC 49th Inf. Co.C
Thompson, Thomas M. AL 3rd Inf. Co.D
Thompson, Thomas M. AL 9th Inf. Co.H
Thompson, Thomas M. GA 46th Inf.
Thompson, Thomas M. MD 1st Inf. Co.I
Thompson, Thomas M. MS 11th (Perrin's) Cav. Co.K
Thompson, Thomas M. NC Moseley's Co. (Sampson Arty.)
Thompson, Thomas M. TN 6th Inf.
Thompson, Thomas M. TX 3rd Cav. Co.F
Thompson, Thomas M. Trans-MS Conf.Cav. 1st Bn. Co.E
Thompson, Thomas N. AL 19th Inf. Co.H
Thompson, Thomas N. TN Cav. 9th Bn. (Gantt's) Co.B
Thompson, Thomas P. AL 13th Inf. Co.D
Thompson, Thomas P. LA 12th Inf. Co.D 1st Sgt.
Thompson, Thomas P. NC 5th Inf. Co.B Capt.
Thompson, Thomas P. TX 13th Cav. Co.H
Thompson, Thomas R. SC Hvy.Arty. Gilchrist's Co. (Gist Guard)
Thompson, Thomas R. SC 13th Inf. Co.C
Thompson, Thomas R. SC 15th Inf.
Thompson, Thomas R. VA Lt.Arty. 13th Bn. Co.A
Thompson, Thomas S. SC 2nd Res.
Thompson, Thomas S. TX 13th Cav. Co.F
Thompson, Thomas S. TX 18th Inf. Co.C Cpl.
Thompson, Thomas S. TX 22nd Inf. Co.D
Thompson, Thomas S. VA 6th Cav. Co.G
Thompson, Thomas W. AL 33rd Inf. Co.A 2nd Lt.
Thompson, Thomas W. AR 4th Inf. Co.E
Thompson, Thomas W. FL 7th Inf. Co.I
Thompson, Thomas W. GA 14th Inf. Co.C
Thompson, Thomas W. KY 4th Mtd.Inf. Co.I Col.
Thompson, Thomas W. NC 1st Inf. (6 mo. '61) Co.L
Thompson, Thomas W. NC 13th Inf. Co.A
Thompson, Thomas W. VA 1st Cav. Maj.
Thompson, Thomas W. VA 19th Inf. Co.B
Thompson, Thomas W. VA Inf. 26th Bn. Co.C Capt.
Thompson, Thomas W. VA 57th Inf. Co.H 1st Lt.
Thompson, Thomas W. VA 59th Inf. 2nd Co.I Sgt.
Thompson, Thomas W. Bell's,CSA
Thompson, Thompson R. SC 10th Inf.
Thompson, Thompson T. GA 54th Inf. Co.E
Thompson, T.I. MS 28th Cav. Co.B
Thompson, T.I. TN 47th Inf. Co.K
Thompson, Tillman J. VA 4th Inf. Co.C,D
Thompson, Timothy AR 27th Inf. New Co.B
Thompson, T.J. AL 8th Cav.
Thompson, T.J. AL 9th Inf. Co.D
Thompson, T.J. AL 14th Inf. Co.C
Thompson, T.J. AL 24th Inf. Co.D,K
Thompson, T.J. AL 30th Inf. Co.B
Thompson, T.J. AR 2nd Inf. Co.I
Thompson, T.J. AR 11th Inf. Co.A
Thompson, T.J. AR 11th & 17th Cons.Inf. Co.A
Thompson, T.J. AR 19th (Dawson's) Inf. Co.I
Thompson, T.J. GA 24th Inf. Co.A

Thompson, T.J. GA 53rd Inf. Co.F
Thompson, T.J. GA Floyd Legion (St.Guards) Co.K
Thompson, T.J. LA 1st Cav. Co.C
Thompson, T.J. LA 17th Inf. Co.I Sgt.
Thompson, T.J. LA 19th Inf. Co.C
Thompson, T.J. MS Lt.Arty. (Jefferson Arty.) Darden's Co.
Thompson, T.J. MS Inf. 2nd Bn. (St.Troops) Co.E Sgt.
Thompson, T.J. MS 46th Inf. Co.E
Thompson, T.J. MO 3rd Cav.
Thompson, T.J. SC Lt.Arty. M. Ward's Co. (Waccamaw Lt.Arty.) Cpl.
Thompson, T.J. SC 3rd Inf. Co.C
Thompson, T.J. TN 16th (Logwood's) Cav. Co.E
Thompson, T.J. TN 51st Inf. Co.D
Thompson, T.J. 8th (Wade's) Conf.Cav. Co.B
Thompson, T.K. TX 8th Cav. Co.B
Thompson, T.L. AL Cav. Moreland's Regt. Co.I
Thompson, T.L. TN 6th (Wheeler's) Cav. Co.K
Thompson, T.L. TX 7th Cav. Co.I
Thompson, T.M. AL 2nd Cav. Co.D
Thompson, T.M. FL 11th Inf.
Thompson, T.M. GA 27th Inf. Co.H
Thompson, T.M. LA 9th Inf. Co.E
Thompson, T.M. MD Arty. 2nd Btty.
Thompson, T.M. TN Inf. 1st Bn. (Colms') Co.B
Thompson, T.M. TX 10th Cav. Co.G
Thompson, T.N. GA 40th Inf. Co.F
Thompson, T.N. TX 3rd (Kirby's) Bn.Vol. Co.A
Thompson, Tobias FL 6th Inf. Co.A
Thompson, Tobias FL 10th Inf. Davidson's Co.
Thompson, T.P. AL 15th Inf. Co.B
Thompson, T.P. TX 22nd Cav. Co.C Sr.2nd Lt.
Thompson, T.R. GA Cav. 12th Bn. (St.Guards) Co.D
Thompson, T.R. SC Arty. Manigault's Bn. Co.E
Thompson, T.R. SC 3rd Inf. Co.C
Thompson, T.S. AL Cav. Chisolm's Co.
Thompson, T.S. AR 15th (Johnson's) Inf. Co.E
Thompson, T.S. SC 4th Cav. Co.I
Thompson, T.S. SC 5th Cav. Surg.
Thompson, T.S. SC 2nd Inf. Co.I
Thompson, T.S. TN Cav. 1st Bn. (McNairy's) Co.B
Thompson, T.S. Gen. & Staff Surg.
Thompson, T.T. AL 23rd Inf. Co.H
Thompson, T.T. MO 8th Cav. Co.K
Thompson, T.T. TN 14th (Neely's) Cav. Co.F
Thompson, T.T. TN 19th (Biffle's) Cav. Co.L
Thompson, T.T. TN 51st Inf. Co.D Cpl.
Thompson, T.T. TN 51st Inf. Co.D
Thompson, T.T. TN 51st (Cons.) Inf. Co.F
Thompson, T.U. TX 11th Inf. Co.G
Thompson, Tucker GA 6th Inf. Co.I
Thompson, T.W. AR 1st Mtd.Rifles Co.E
Thompson, T.W. AR 18th (Marmaduke's) Inf. Co.B
Thompson, T.W. GA Cav. Dorough's Bn.
Thompson, T.W. VA 8th Cav. Co.H
Thompson, U. NC 1st Arty. (10th St.Troops) Co.B
Thompson, Uriah A. VA Horse Arty. E. Graham's Co.
Thompson, V. AL 21st Inf. Co.F
Thompson, Van Duren TX 25th Cav.
Thompson, V.B. LA 3rd Inf. Co.C
Thompson, V.B. LA 28th (Gray's) Inf. Co.G Sgt.
Thompson, V.D. TN 21st & 22nd (Cons.) Cav. Co.B
Thompson, V.D. TN 22nd (Barteau's) Cav. Co.G
Thompson, V.H. AR 30th Inf. Co.K
Thompson, Victor W. TX Waul's Legion Co.D
Thompson, Vincent D. TN Cav. 7th Bn. (Bennett's) Co.E
Thompson, Virgil LA 14th Inf. Co.I 2nd Lt.
Thompson, V.N. MS 41st Inf. Co.F
Thompson, V.O. Gen. & Staff Asst.Surg.
Thompson, V. Oscar NC 46th Inf. Co.C Asst.Surg.
Thompson, V.P. GA 43rd Inf. Co.F Cpl.
Thompson, V.T. 8th (Wade's) Conf.Cav. Co.H
Thompson, V.W. MS 1st Cav. Co.B
Thompson, W. AL 6th Cav. Co.A
Thompson, W. AL 7th Cav. Co.F,G Capt.
Thompson, W. AL 6th Inf. Co.C
Thompson, W. AL 24th Inf. Co.K
Thompson, W. AL 26th (O'Neal's) Inf. Co.B Cpl.
Thompson, W. AL Cp. of Instr. Talladega
Thompson, W. AR 18th (Marmaduke's) Inf. Co.H
Thompson, W. GA 6th Res. Co.I
Thompson, W. GA 16th Inf. Co.D
Thompson, W. GA 55th Inf. Co.E
Thompson, W. KY 1st (Butler's) Cav.
Thompson, W. LA 1st Cav. Co.F
Thompson, W. LA Mil. 3rd Regt. 1st Brig. 1st Div. Co.C Sgt.
Thompson, W. MS Cav. Yerger's Regt. Co.C Capt.
Thompson, W. NC Cav. 16th Bn.
Thompson, W. SC Lt.Arty. 3rd (Palmetto) Bn. Co.K
Thompson, W. SC Inf. 1st (Charleston) Bn. Co.B
Thompson, W. TN 14th (Neely's) Cav. Co.E
Thompson, W. TX 35th (Brown's) Cav. Co.B
Thompson, W. TX Cav. Terry's Regt. Co.K
Thompson, W. TX 4th Inf. (St.Troops) Co.D
Thompson, W. TX Res.Corps Bauvinghauser's Co.
Thompson, W. VA Cav. Swann's Bn. Carpenter's Co.
Thompson, W. VA 3rd Bn. Valley Res. Co.B
Thompson, W. VA 46th Inf. Co.B
Thompson, W. VA 46th Inf. Co.I
Thompson, W. 8th (Dearing's) Conf.Cav. Co.G Sgt.
Thompson, W. 4th Conf.Inf. Co.C
Thompson, W. Gen. & Staff Surg.
Thompson, W.A. AL Cav. Lewis' Bn. Co.A
Thompson, W.A. AL 4th Inf. Co.C
Thompson, W.A. AL 27th Inf. Co.C 1st Sgt.
Thompson, W.A. AL 29th Inf. Co.C
Thompson, W.A. GA 7th Cav. Co.G
Thompson, W.A. GA 8th Cav. Old Co.E Capt.
Thompson, W.A. GA Cav. 24th Bn. Co.A
Thompson, W.A. GA 62nd Cav. Co.E Capt.
Thompson, W.A. GA 4th Inf. Co.A
Thompson, W.A. GA 50th Inf.
Thompson, W.A. GA Floyd Legion (St.Guards) Co.E
Thompson, W.A. KY 10th (Johnson's) Cav. Co.D
Thompson, W.A. KY 12th Cav. Surg.
Thompson, W.A. KY 1st Inf. Co.E Asst.Surg.
Thompson, W.A. KY 6th Mtd.Inf. Co.K,A
Thompson, W.A. LA 4th Inf. Co.A
Thompson, W.A. MS Inf. 3rd Bn. Co.H 1st Cpl.
Thompson, W.A. NC Cav. 16th Bn. Co.A Capt.
Thompson, W.A. NC Hvy.Arty. 1st Bn. Co.C Sgt.
Thompson, W.A. NC 2nd Arty. (36th St.Troops) Co.C
Thompson, W.A. NC 7th Sr.Res. Bradshaw's Co.
Thompson, W.A. NC 23rd Inf. Co.B 2nd Lt.
Thompson, W.A. NC 27th Inf. Co.A
Thompson, W.A. SC 13th Inf. Co.C Sgt.
Thompson, W.A. SC 16th Inf. Co.D
Thompson, W.A. TN Cav. Jackson's Co.
Thompson, W.A. TN 5th Inf. 1st Co.H, 2nd Co.E Cpl.
Thompson, W.A. TN 8th Inf. Co.D
Thompson, W.A. TN 33rd Inf. Asst.Surg.
Thompson, W.A. TN 44th (Cons.) Inf. Co.G
Thompson, W.A. TN 55th (McKoin's) Inf. Bound's Co.
Thompson, W.A. TN Inf. 154th Sr.Regt. Co.K
Thompson, W.A. TX Cav. Morgan's Regt. Co.E
Thompson, W.A. TX 13th Vol. 1st Co.K
Thompson, W.A. TX 20th Inf. Co.A
Thompson, W.A. VA 3rd (Archer's) Bn.Res. Co.A Cpl.
Thompson, W.A. Wright's Staff Capt.,ACS
Thompson, W.A. Gen. & Staff Surg.
Thompson, Waddy AL 7th Cav. Co.B 2nd Lt.
Thompson, Waddy AL 15th Inf. Co.H Cpl.
Thompson, Waddy SC 3rd Inf. Co.G
Thompson, Waddy SC 6th Inf. Surg.
Thompson, Waddy SC Palmetto S.S. Asst.Surg.
Thompson, Waddy TN 36th Inf. Co.F
Thompson, Waddy TX Cav. Madison's Regt. Co.B
Thompson, Waddy VA Lt.Arty. 12th Bn. Surg.
Thompson, Waddy Gen. & Staff Surg.
Thompson, Waddy T. GA Inf. Taylor's Co.
Thompson, Wade H. VA 8th Cav. Co.K
Thompson, Waitman NC 1st Cav. (9th St.Troops) Co.H
Thompson, Waitmon 7th Conf.Cav. Co.F Sgt.
Thompson, Waldo TX 7th Field Btty.
Thompson, Waldredge C. AL Cav. Callaway's Co.
Thompson, Walker K. MS Lt.Arty. Stanford's Co.
Thompson, Wallace SC Inf. 3rd Bn. Co.E
Thompson, Wallace SC Inf. Holcombe Legion Co.E
Thompson, Waller AL 32nd Inf. Co.I Capt.
Thompson, Wallis 1st Choctaw Mtd.Rifles Ward's Co.
Thompson, Walter AL 1st Bn.Cadets Co.A
Thompson, Walter AL 32nd & 58th (Cons.) Inf. Capt.
Thompson, Walter MS Lt.Arty. Stanford's Co.

Thompson, Walter A. GA 2nd Inf. Co.D Capt.
Thompson, Walter A. NC 27th Inf. Co.G
Thompson, Walter K. MS Lt.Arty. Stanford's Co.
Thompson, Walter S. GA 12th (Wright's) Cav. (St.Guards) Stapleton's Co.
Thompson, Walter S. MO 1st Cav. Co.E
Thompson, Walter W. VA 6th Bn.Res. Co.B
Thompson, Washington MO 15th Cav. Co.A
Thompson, Washington NC 6th Sr.Res. Co.A
Thompson, Washington NC 46th Inf. Co.F
Thompson, Washington 1st Choctaw Mtd.Rifles Co.C 3rd Lt.
Thompson, Washington G. AL 22nd Inf. Co.G
Thompson, Watson W. MS 8th Cav. Co.C
Thompson, W.B. AL 26th (O'Neal's) Inf. Co.F 2nd Lt.
Thompson, W.B. AL 42nd Inf. Co.E
Thompson, W.B. AL 43rd Inf. Co.D
Thompson, W.B. AL 59th Inf. Co.A
Thompson, W.B. AL Pris.Guard Freeman's Co.
Thompson, W.B. GA 1st (Symons') Res. Co.H Cpl.
Thompson, W.B. GA 6th Res. Co.B
Thompson, W.B. GA 36th (Villepigue's) Inf. Co.F
Thompson, W.B. GA 43rd Inf. Co.B
Thompson, W.B. KY 6th Mtd.Inf. Co.E
Thompson, W.B. MS 2nd St.Cav. Co.E
Thompson, W.B. MS 7th Cav. 1st Co.H
Thompson, W.B. MS Cav. Ham's Regt. Co.E
Thompson, W.B. MS 6th Inf. Co.F
Thompson, W.B. MS Cp.Guard (Cp. of Instr. for Conscr.)
Thompson, W.B. MO 1st Cav.
Thompson, W.B. NC 8th Sr.Res. McLean's Co.
Thompson, W.B. SC 6th Cav. Co.D
Thompson, W.B. SC 1st St.Troops Co.H
Thompson, W.B. SC 2nd Inf. Co.B
Thompson, W.B. SC 2nd Inf. Co.D
Thompson, W.B. SC 3rd Res. Co.E Cpl.
Thompson, W.B. SC Inf. 7th Bn. (Enfield Rifles) Co.F
Thompson, W.B. SC 17th Inf. Co.I
Thompson, W.B. TN Lt.Arty. Scott's Co.
Thompson, W.B. TX 9th (Young's) Inf. Co.D
Thompson, W.B. TX 18th Inf. Co.K
Thompson, W.B. VA 3rd Res. Co.H
Thompson, W.B. 1st Conf.Inf. 1st Co.F
Thompson, W.C. AR 19th (Dockery's) Inf. Co.H Capt.
Thompson, W.C. GA 3rd Cav. Co.A
Thompson, W.C. GA 17th Inf. Co.K
Thompson, W.C. LA Lt.Arty. 1st Bn. Co.4
Thompson, W.C. LA Mil. Chalmette Regt. Co.G
Thompson, W.C. MS 2nd St.Cav. Co.K,L
Thompson, W.C. MS 4th Inf. Co.E
Thompson, W.C. MS 6th Inf. Co.H Capt.
Thompson, W.C. NC 6th Sr.Res. Co.I
Thompson, W.C. TN 19th (Biffle's) Cav. Co.I
Thompson, W.C. TN 21st (Wilson's) Cav. Co.H
Thompson, W.C. TN 48th (Voorhies') Inf. Co.G
Thompson, W.C. TN 55th (Brown's) Inf. Co.F,B Sgt.
Thompson, W.C. TX 2nd Cav. Co.D
Thompson, W.C. TX 25th Cav. Co.E
Thompson, W.C. TX Cav. Hardeman's Regt. Co.D
Thompson, W.C. TX 7th Inf. Co.B
Thompson, W.C. TX 16th Inf. Co.B
Thompson, W.C. TX Waul's Legion Co.B
Thompson, W.C.D. AL 18th Inf. Co.B
Thompson, W.D. AL 5th Cav. Co.C
Thompson, W.D. AL 40th Inf. Co.I
Thompson, W.D. AR 18th (Marmaduke's) Inf. Co.C Sgt.
Thompson, W.D. GA Inf. 8th Bn. Co.C
Thompson, W.D. KY 4th Cav. Co.A
Thompson, W.D. MS 18th Cav. Co.A
Thompson, W.D. MS 4th Inf. Co.C
Thompson, W.D., Jr. MS 20th Inf. Co.I
Thompson, W.D., Sr. MS 20th Inf. Co.I
Thompson, W.D. MS 37th Inf. Co.H,A Cpl.
Thompson, W.D. TN 4th (McLemore's) Cav. Co.C
Thompson, W.D. TN 14th (Neely's) Cav. Co.H
Thompson, W.D. TN Cav. Jackson's Regt.
Thompson, W.D. TN Cav. Nixon's Regt. Co.C
Thompson, W.D. TX 33rd Cav. Co.F Cpl.
Thompson, W.D. VA 15th Cav. Co.E
Thompson, W.D. VA 25th Mil. Co.C
Thompson, W. Drayton SC Inf. Hampton Legion Co.E
Thompson, W.E. AL 1st Cav. 2nd Co.E, Co.H
Thompson, W.E. AL Inf. 2nd Regt. Co.3
Thompson, W.E. GA 1st (Fannin's) Res. Co.F,I
Thompson, W.E. GA 25th Inf. Co.D
Thompson, W.E. TN 8th Inf. Co.D
Thompson, W.E. TX Cav. 2nd Bn.St.Troops Wilson's Co.
Thompson, Wells AL Inf. 1st Regt. Co.F
Thompson, Wells AL 36th Inf. Co.I Capt.
Thompson, Wells GA Carlton's Co. (Troup Cty.Arty.)
Thompson, Wesley AR 8th Cav. Co.E Sgt.
Thompson, Wesley NC 3rd Arty. (40th St.Troops) Co.E
Thompson, Wesley NC 52nd Inf. Co.F
Thompson, Wesley VA 16th Cav. Co.G
Thompson, Wesley VA Cav. Ferguson's Bn. Spurlock's Co., Ferguson's Co.
Thompson, W.F. AL 2nd Cav. Co.D
Thompson, W.F. GA Lt.Arty. King's Btty.
Thompson, W.F. GA 13th Inf. Co.D
Thompson, W.F. GA 16th Inf. Co.A
Thompson, W.F. GA 17th Inf. Co.K
Thompson, W.F. SC Cav. A.W. Cordes' Co.
Thompson, W.F. SC Manigault's Bn.Vol. Co.B
Thompson, W.F. TN 8th (Smith's) Cav. Co.A
Thompson, W.F. TN 16th (Logwood's) Cav. Co.H
Thompson, W.F. TN 16th (Logwood's) Cav. Co.K
Thompson, W.F. TN 5th Inf. 2nd Co.H
Thompson, W.F. TN 9th Inf. Co.L,D
Thompson, W.F. TX 17th Cons.Dismtd.Cav. Co.C Capt.
Thompson, W.F. TX 7th Inf. Co.B
Thompson, W.F. TX 18th Inf. Co.H
Thompson, W.F. TX 18th Inf. Co.K
Thompson, W.F. TX 22nd Inf. Co.E
Thompson, W.G. GA 38th Inf. Co.I
Thompson, W.G. MS 9th Cav. Co.A
Thompson, W.G. MS Cav. Jeff Davis Legion Co.G Capt.
Thompson, W.G. MS 32nd Inf. Co.D
Thompson, W.G. SC 2nd Res.
Thompson, W.G. TN 15th (Stewart's) Cav. Co.E
Thompson, W.G. TN 5th Inf. 2nd Co.B
Thompson, W.G. TN 30th Inf. Co.C
Thompson, W.G. TN 45th Inf. Co.F
Thompson, W.G. TX 29th Cav. Co.C
Thompson, W.G. TX 1st Hvy.Arty. Co.I
Thompson, W.G. VA 9th Cav.
Thompson, W.G. VA Inf. 26th Bn. Co.C
Thompson, W.H. AL 3rd Cav. Co.C
Thompson, W.H. AL 51st (Part.Rangers) Co.D
Thompson, W.H. AL 6th Inf. Lynch's Co.
Thompson, W.H. AL 15th Inf. Co.I
Thompson, W.H. AL 18th Inf. Co.K,E
Thompson, W.H. AL 23rd Inf. Co.I
Thompson, W.H. AL Coosa Guards J.W. Suttles' Co.
Thompson, W.H. AR 8th Cav. Co.D
Thompson, W.H. AR 10th (Witt's) Cav. Co.I
Thompson, W.H. AR 1st Vol. Co.F
Thompson, W.H. AR 38th Inf. Co.B
Thompson, W.H. FL 1st (Res.) Inf. Co.G
Thompson, W.H. GA 3rd Cav. Co.I
Thompson, W.H. GA Lt.Arty. 14th Bn. Co.D
Thompson, W.H. GA Lt.Arty. King's Btty.
Thompson, W.H. GA Inf. 1st Bn. (St.Guards) Co.E
Thompson, W.H. GA 1st Bn.S.S. Co.D
Thompson, W.H. GA Inf. 8th Bn. Co.A
Thompson, W.H. GA Inf. 25th Bn. (Prov.Guard) Co.A
Thompson, W.H. GA 31st Inf. Co.B
Thompson, W.H. KY 2nd Cav. Co.A
Thompson, W.H. KY 9th Mtd.Inf. Co.E
Thompson, W.H. LA Inf. Jeff Davis Legion Co.J
Thompson, W.H. MS 2nd Cav. Co.I 1st Sgt.
Thompson, W.H. MO Inf. 3rd Regt.St.Guard Co.I 1st Lt.
Thompson, W.H. MO 16th Inf. Co.F
Thompson, W.H. NC 2nd Jr.Res. Co.C
Thompson, W.H. NC 43rd Inf. Co.D
Thompson, W.H. SC 2nd Cav. Co.H
Thompson, W.H. SC 1st Regt. Charleston Guard Co.H
Thompson, W.H. SC 3rd Inf. Co.E
Thompson, W.H. TN 1st (Carter's) Cav. Co.B
Thompson, W.H. TN 12th (Green's) Cav. Co.D
Thompson, W.H. TN Cav. 16th Bn. (Neal's) Co.A
Thompson, W.H. TN 19th (Biffle's) Cav. Co.L
Thompson, W.H. TN 5th Inf. 2nd Co.I
Thompson, W.H. TN Inf. 23rd Bn. Co.A 2nd Lt.
Thompson, W.H. TN 26th Inf. Co.E Sgt.
Thompson, W.H. TN 41st Inf. Co.A
Thompson, W.H. TN 50th Inf. Co.K
Thompson, W.H. TN 50th (Cons.) Inf. Co.G
Thompson, W.H. TX Cav. Border's Regt. Co.F
Thompson, W.H. TX Cav. Terry's Regt. Co.H
Thompson, W.H. TX 7th Inf. Co.F
Thompson, W.H. VA Lt.Arty. Lamkin's Co.
Thompson, W.H. Conf.Inf. 1st Bn. 2nd Co.A Cpl.
Thompson, W.H. Blake's Scouts,CSA

Thompson, W.H. Gen. & Staff Hosp.Stew.
Thompson, W.H.H. AL 5th Cav. Co.D
Thompson, W.I. AL 3rd Inf. Co.K
Thompson, W.I. MO Cav. Freeman's Regt. Co.E
Thompson, Wilbur GA 56th Inf. Co.G
Thompson, Wilbur GA 59th Inf. Co.G
Thompson, Wildridge P. AL 3rd Inf. Co.D
Thompson, Wiley AR 2nd Inf. Co.A
Thompson, Wiley GA Inf. 9th Bn. Co.C
Thompson, Wiley GA 44th Inf. Co.A
Thompson, Wiley SC 1st (McCreary's) Inf. Co.G
Thompson, Wiley TN 34th Inf. Co.H
Thompson, Wiley D. TX 10th Cav. Co.I
Thompson, Wiley J. TX 4th Cav. Co.K 2nd Lt.
Thompson, Wiley M. MS 36th Inf. Co.E
Thompson, Wiley M. TX 17th Cav. Co.C
Thompson, Wiley V. VA 25th Cav. Co.G
Thompson, Wiley Y. GA 12th Inf. Co.F Lt.
Thompson, Will LA Arty. Castellanos' Btty.
Thompson, Wm. AL 5th Cav. Co.C
Thompson, William AL 5th Cav. Co.F
Thompson, William AL 6th Cav. Co.H
Thompson, William AL 9th (Nelson's) Cav. Co.C
Thompson, William AL 51st (Part.Rangers) Co.F,D
Thompson, William AL City Troop (Mobile) Arrington's Co.A
Thompson, William AL Lt.Arty. 2nd Bn. Co.E
Thompson, William AL Seawell's Btty. (Mohawk Arty.)
Thompson, William AL Inf. 2nd Regt. Co.E
Thompson, William AL Inf. 2nd Regt. Co.H
Thompson, William AL 3rd Inf.
Thompson, William AL 4th Inf. Co.K
Thompson, William AL 13th Inf. Co.C
Thompson, William AL 15th Inf. Co.C
Thompson, William AL 16th Inf. Co.H
Thompson, William AL 18th Bn.Vol. Co.C
Thompson, William AL 21st Inf. Co.H
Thompson, William AL 23rd Bn.S.S. Co.F
Thompson, William AL 26th (O'Neal's) Inf. Co.H
Thompson, William AL 35th Inf. Co.B
Thompson, William AL 45th Inf. Co.I
Thompson, William AL 62nd Inf. Co.H
Thompson, William AL 1st Bn. Hilliard's Legion Vol. Co.F
Thompson, William AL St.Res.
Thompson, William AR 1st (Crawford's) Cav. Surg.
Thompson, William AR 1st Mtd.Rifles Co.C,I Cpl.
Thompson, William AR 2nd Mtd.Rifles Co.B
Thompson, William AR Cav. Harrell's Bn. Co.C 1st Lt.
Thompson, William AR 3rd Inf. Co.F
Thompson, William AR 5th Inf. Co.H
Thompson, William AR 15th (N.W.) Inf. Co.C
Thompson, William AR 15th (N.W.) Inf. Co.F Maj.
Thompson, William AR 34th Inf. Co.I
Thompson, William FL 1st Inf. New Co.E
Thompson, William FL 1st Inf. New Co.H
Thompson, William FL 8th Inf. Co.C
Thompson, William FL 8th Inf. Co.E
Thompson, William FL 9th Inf. Co.I
Thompson, William GA 1st Cav. Co.H
Thompson, William GA Cav. 1st Bn. Hopkins' Co.
Thompson, William GA 2nd Cav. (St.Guards) Co.A Cpl.
Thompson, William GA 3rd Cav. Co.G
Thompson, William GA 5th Cav. Co.K
Thompson, William GA 12th Cav. Co.H Cpl.
Thompson, William GA 1st (Olmstead's) Inf. Co.D
Thompson, William GA 1st (Olmstead's) Inf. Co.E
Thompson, William GA 2nd Inf. Co.L
Thompson, William GA 2nd Bn.S.S. Co.A Cpl.
Thompson, William GA Inf. 3rd Bn. Co.F
Thompson, William GA 5th Inf. Co.H,M Music.
Thompson, William GA 6th Inf. Co.D
Thompson, William GA 8th Inf. (St.Guards) Co.D
Thompson, William GA 13th Inf. Co.F
Thompson, William GA 16th Inf. Co.B
Thompson, William GA 19th Inf. Co.G
Thompson, William GA 22nd Inf. Co.F
Thompson, William GA 34th Inf. Co.A
Thompson, William GA 39th Inf. Co.C
Thompson, William GA 48th Inf. Co.B
Thompson, William GA 53rd Inf. Co.B 1st Lt.
Thompson, William GA 53rd Inf. Co.B
Thompson, William GA 56th Inf. Co.G
Thompson, William GA 57th Inf. Co.D
Thompson, William GA 60th Inf. Co.B
Thompson, William GA 67th Inf. Co.B,D
Thompson, William GA Inf. (Emanuel Troops) Moring's Co.
Thompson, William KY 1st (Butler's) Cav.
Thompson, William, Jr. KY 6th Cav. Co.C
Thompson, William, Sr. KY 6th Cav. Co.C
Thompson, William KY Lt.Arty. Cobb's Co.
Thompson, William KY 8th Mtd.Inf. Co.K
Thompson, William LA 6th Cav. Co.I
Thompson, William LA 1st Hvy.Arty. (Reg.) Co.F Sgt.
Thompson, William LA Arty. Moody's Co. (Madison Lt.Arty.)
Thompson, William LA Pointe Coupee Arty.
Thompson, William LA 1st (Strawbridge's) Inf. Co.F Cpl.
Thompson, William LA Inf. 1st Sp.Bn. (Wheat's) Co.C
Thompson, William LA Mil. 3rd Regt. 1st Brig. 1st Div. Co.D
Thompson, William LA 5th Inf. Co.H
Thompson, William LA 20th Inf. New Co.B
Thompson, William LA 31st Inf. Co.H
Thompson, William LA C.S. Zouave Bn. Co.A Cpl.
Thompson, William MS Cav. 1st Bn. (Montgomery's) St.Troops Hammond's Co.
Thompson, William MS Cav. 2nd Bn.Res. Co.A Capt.
Thompson, William MS 3rd Cav. Co.F
Thompson, William MS 5th Cav. Co.C
Thompson, William MS 11th (Perrin's) Cav. Co.I
Thompson, William MS Cav. 24th Bn. Co.C
Thompson, William MS Cav. Garland's Bn. Co.C
Thompson, William MS St.Cav. Perrin's Bn. Co.F Cpl.
Thompson, William MS Lt.Arty. (Jefferson Arty.) Darden's Co.
Thompson, William MS 1st (Johnston's) Inf. Co.C
Thompson, William MS Inf. 1st St.Troops Co.G
Thompson, William MS Inf. 5th Bn. Co.A
Thompson, William MS 15th Inf. Co.B
Thompson, William MS 15th Inf. Co.I Sgt.
Thompson, William MS 22nd Inf. Co.A
Thompson, William MS 34th Inf. Co.H
Thompson, William MS 43rd Inf. Co.I
Thompson, William MO 1st Cav. Co.D 2nd Lt.
Thompson, William MO 1st Cav. Co.I
Thompson, William MO Cav. 1st Regt.St.Guard Co.A
Thompson, William MO 2nd Cav. Co.C
Thompson, William MO 2nd Cav. Co.D
Thompson, William MO Cav. 4th Regt.St.Guard Co.C Comsy.
Thompson, William MO 12th Cav. Co.C Cpl.
Thompson, William MO Cav. Schnabel's Bn. Co.B 1st Lt.
Thompson, William MO Cav. Wood's Regt. Co.D,B
Thompson, William MO 4th Inf. Co.A
Thompson, William MO 4th Inf. Co.B Cpl.
Thompson, William MO 16th Inf. Co.A
Thompson, William NC 3rd Bn.Sr.Res. Co.C
Thompson, William NC 6th Sr.Res. Co.B
Thompson, William NC 6th Sr.Res. Co.G Lance Cpl.
Thompson, William NC 7th Bn.Jr.Res. Co.C
Thompson, William NC 13th Inf. Co.E
Thompson, William NC 15th Inf. Co.K Cpl.
Thompson, William NC 25th Inf. Co.F
Thompson, William NC 27th Inf. Co.G
Thompson, William NC 29th Inf. Co.F
Thompson, William NC 52nd Inf. Co.E
Thompson, William NC 57th Inf. Co.I
Thompson, William NC Mil. Clark's Sp.Bn. D.N. Bridgers' Co.
Thompson, William SC 2nd Arty. Co.C
Thompson, William SC Hvy.Arty. 15th (Lucas') Bn. Co.B
Thompson, William SC Inf. 3rd Bn. Co.B
Thompson, William SC 5th St.Troops Co.F
Thompson, William SC 9th Res. Co.E
Thompson, William SC 11th Inf. Co.A
Thompson, William SC 16th Inf. Co.E
Thompson, William SC Post Guard Senn's Co.
Thompson, William SC Inf. Hampton Legion Co.E
Thompson, William SC Inf. Holcombe Legion Co.F
Thompson, William SC Inf. Holcombe Legion Co.I
Thompson, William TN 2nd Cav. Co.B,D
Thompson, William TN 13th (Gore's) Cav. Co.C
Thompson, William TN 13th (Gore's) Cav. Co.K
Thompson, William TN 14th (Neely's) Cav. Co.C
Thompson, William TN 19th (Biffle's) Cav. Co.I
Thompson, William TN 19th (Biffle's) Cav. Co.L
Thompson, William TN 1st Hvy.Arty. Co.F, 2nd Co.D

Thompson, William TN Arty. Fisher's Co.
Thompson, William TN Arty. Marshall's Co.
Thompson, William, 1st TN Lt.Arty. Polk's Btty.
Thompson, William, 2nd TN Lt.Arty. Polk's Btty.
Thompson, William TN 1st Cav. Co.I
Thompson, William TN 2nd (Robison's) Inf. Co.E
Thompson, William TN 2nd (Walker's) Inf. Co.G
Thompson, William TN 4th Inf. Co.B Sgt.
Thompson, William TN 6th Inf. Co.G
Thompson, William TN 28th Inf. Co.C
Thompson, William TN 29th Inf. Co.F
Thompson, William TN 30th Inf. Co.C
Thompson, William TN 40th Inf. Co.B
Thompson, William TN 48th (Voorhies') Inf.
Thompson, William TX 1st (McCulloch's) Cav. Co.D
Thompson, William TX 2nd Cav. 2nd Co.F
Thompson, William TX Cav. 2nd Regt.St.Troops Co.D
Thompson, William TX Cav. 2nd Bn.St.Troops Hubbard's Co.
Thompson, William TX 12th Cav. Co.D
Thompson, William TX 22nd Cav. Co.E
Thompson, William TX 36th Cav. Co.I
Thompson, William TX Cav. Baylor's Regt. Co.D
Thompson, William TX Inf. 1st St.Troops White's Co.D
Thompson, William TX 1st Bn.S.S. Co.D
Thompson, William TX 9th (Nichols') Inf. Co.E
Thompson, William TX 15th Inf. Co.C,I
Thompson, William TX 20th Inf. Co.A Cpl.
Thompson, William TX McMinn's Co.
Thompson, William TX Waul's Legion Co.A
Thompson, William VA 5th Cav. Co.G
Thompson, William VA 11th Cav. Co.K Cpl.
Thompson, William VA 16th Cav. Co.G
Thompson, William VA 17th Cav. Co.C
Thompson, William VA 19th Cav. Co.G Sgt.
Thompson, William VA Cav. Ferguson's Bn. Spurlock's Co., Ferguson's Co.
Thompson, William VA Hvy.Arty. 18th Bn. Co.E
Thompson, William VA Goochland's Lt.Arty.
Thompson, William VA 1st St.Res. Co.C,K
Thompson, William VA 11th Bn.Res. Co.C
Thompson, William VA 18th Inf. Co.A
Thompson, William VA 22nd Inf. Co.A Drum.
Thompson, William VA 32nd Inf. Co.C
Thompson, William VA 46th Mil. Co.B
Thompson, William VA 46th Mil. Lantz's Co., Co.A
Thompson, William VA 54th Mil. Co.H
Thompson, William VA 57th Inf. Co.H Capt.
Thompson, William VA 58th Mil. Co.G
Thompson, William VA 59th Inf. 2nd Co.D
Thompson, William VA 60th Inf. Co.A
Thompson, William VA 64th Mtd.Inf. Co.C
Thompson, William VA 72nd Mil.
Thompson, William VA 146th Mil. Co.F
Thompson, William Trans-MS Conf.Cav. 1st Bn. Co.D
Thompson, William 15th Conf.Cav. Co.F
Thompson, William Conf.Inf. 1st Bn. 2nd Co.C
Thompson, William Conf.Inf. 1st Bn. Co.I
Thompson, William 3rd Conf.Inf. Co.E Ord.Sgt.
Thompson, William Brush Bn.
Thompson, William Conf.Inf. Tucker's Regt. Co.C
Thompson, William 1st Cherokee Mtd.Vol. 1st Co.C
Thompson, William 2nd Cherokee Mtd.Vol. Co.E Sgt.
Thompson, William 2nd Cherokee Mtd.Vol. Co.F Cpl.
Thompson, William 1st Choctaw & Chickasaw Mtd.Rifles Co.A
Thompson, William 1st Choctaw & Chickasaw Mtd.Rifles 2nd Co.I
Thompson, William A. AL 43rd Inf. Co.K
Thompson, William A. AR 2nd Mtd.Rifles Co.E
Thompson, William A. GA Cav. 10th Bn. (St.Guards) Co.D
Thompson, William A. GA 2nd Inf. 1st Co.B
Thompson, William A. GA 9th Inf. Co.G
Thompson, William A. GA 16th Inf. Co.A
Thompson, William A. GA 26th Inf. Co.E Sgt.
Thompson, William A. GA 38th Inf. Co.G
Thompson, William A. KY Fields' Co. (Part.Rangers)
Thompson, William A. KY 5th Mtd.Inf. Co.D
Thompson, William A. LA 8th Cav. Co.E
Thompson, William A. NC 1st Arty. (10th St.Troops) Co.A Sgt.
Thompson, William A. NC 2nd Inf. Co.E Sgt.
Thompson, William A. NC Inf. 2nd Bn. Co.C
Thompson, William A. NC 39th Inf. Co.B
Thompson, William A. NC 43rd Inf. Co.D
Thompson, William A. NC 44th Inf. Co.G
Thompson, William A. NC 49th Inf. Co.C
Thompson, William A. NC 51st Inf. Co.E
Thompson, William A. TN 62nd Mtd.Inf. Co.K
Thompson, William A. TX 26th Cav. Co.B
Thompson, William A. TX 2nd Inf. Co.E
Thompson, William A. TX 11th Inf. Co.F
Thompson, William A. VA 8th Inf. Co.E 1st Sgt.
Thompson, William A. VA 13th Inf. 1st Co.B
Thompson, William A. VA 37th Inf. Co.G
Thompson, William A. VA 42nd Inf. Co.B
Thompson, William A. VA 46th Inf. 2nd Co.B
Thompson, William A. VA 49th Inf. Co.C 1st Sgt.
Thompson, William A. VA 79th Mil. Co.2
Thompson, Wm. B. AL 54th Inf. Co.G
Thompson, William B. AR 3rd Cav. Co.A QMSgt.
Thompson, William B. GA Lt.Arty. Pritchard's Co. (Washington Arty.)
Thompson, William B. GA 5th Inf. Co.D
Thompson, William B. GA 42nd Inf. Co.E
Thompson, William B. MD 1st Cav. Co.E
Thompson, William B. NC 1st Arty. (10th St.Troops) Maj.
Thompson, William B. NC Hvy.Arty. 1st Bn. Co.A,D
Thompson, William B. SC Inf. Hampton Legion Co.C
Thompson, William B. TX 2nd Cav. Co.I A.Surg.
Thompson, William B. TX 18th Cav. Co.C
Thompson, William B. TX 18th Cav. Co.F
Thompson, William B. TX Cav. Ragsdale's Bn. Asst.Surg.
Thompson, William B. TX 7th Inf. Co.D
Thompson, William B. VA Lt.Arty. J.D. Smith's Co.
Thompson, William B. VA 18th Inf. Co.B
Thompson, William B. Conf.Arty. Lewis' Bn. Co.A
Thompson, Wm. B. Eng.,CSA Arty.Maj.
Thompson, Wm. B. Gen. & Staff Asst.Surg.
Thompson, William B.B. NC 3rd Arty. (40th St.Troops) Co.E
Thompson, William C. AL 23rd Inf. Co.H
Thompson, William C. AR 30th Inf. Co.F 1st Sgt.
Thompson, William C. GA 12th Inf. Co.F
Thompson, William C. GA 43rd Inf. Co.B
Thompson, William C. MS 16th Inf. Co.F
Thompson, William C. MS Adair's Co. (Lodi Co.) 1st Sgt.
Thompson, William C. NC 60th Inf. Co.G
Thompson, William C. TX 14th Cav. Co.G
Thompson, William C. TX 20th Cav. Co.B
Thompson, William C. TX 21st Cav. Co.C
Thompson, William Crockett VA 8th Cav. Co.F
Thompson, William Crote TN 14th Inf. Co.F,E
Thompson, William D. GA Arty. 9th Bn. Co.D
Thompson, William D. MS Cav. 24th Bn. Co.E
Thompson, William D. MS Arty. (Seven Stars Arty.) Roberts' Co.
Thompson, William D. MS 37th Inf. Co.B
Thompson, William D. NC 52nd Inf. Co.G 1st Sgt.
Thompson, William D. NC 61st Inf. Co.I
Thompson, William D. TN Lt.Arty. Burroughs' Co.
Thompson, William D. TN 29th Inf. Co.C Sgt.
Thompson, William D. TN 46th Inf. Co.I Sgt.
Thompson, William D. TX Cav. Martin's Regt. Co.F
Thompson, William D. TX 11th Inf. Co.G Capt.
Thompson, William D. VA 1st (Farinholt's) Res. Co.C
Thompson, William D. VA Inf. 1st Bn. Co.C
Thompson, William E. AL 9th (Malone's) Cav. Co.G Capt.
Thompson, William E. AL 4th Inf. Co.C
Thompson, William E. AL 50th Inf. Co.B
Thompson, William E. VA 15th Cav. Co.K
Thompson, William E. VA 20th Inf. Co.K
Thompson, William E. VA 59th Inf. 3rd Co.C
Thompson, William F. AL 61st Inf. Co.B
Thompson, Wm. F. AR Inf. 8th Bn. Co.D 2nd Lt.
Thompson, William F. FL 3rd Inf. Co.F
Thompson, William F. KY 1st (Butler's) Cav. Co.A
Thompson, William F. KY 2nd (Woodward's) Cav. Co.D
Thompson, William F. KY 1st Inf. Co.G
Thompson, William F. NC 8th Bn.Jr.Res. Co.A Cpl.
Thompson, William F. SC 5th Cav. Co.E Sgt.
Thompson, William F. SC 21st Inf. Co.B
Thompson, William F. TN 12th (Green's) Cav. Co.I

Thompson, William F. TX 17th Cav. Co.D Capt.
Thompson, William F. VA 122nd Mil. Co.C
Thompson, Wm. G. AL 26th Inf. Co.H
Thompson, William G. AL 30th Inf. Co.D
Thompson, William G. GA 6th Inf. Co.G Cpl.
Thompson, William G. GA 14th Inf. Co.E
Thompson, William G. KY 4th Cav. Co.G
Thompson, William G. KY 2nd Mtd.Inf. Co.F Sgt.
Thompson, William G. LA 25th Inf. Co.C
Thompson, William G. MS Cav. 17th Bn. Co.E,A
Thompson, William G. MS 9th Inf. Old Co.A
Thompson, William G. MO 8th Cav. Co.F,D
Thompson, William G. NC 13th Inf. Co.F 2nd Lt.
Thompson, William G. SC 26th Inf. Co.G
Thompson, William G. TN 29th Inf. Co.C Cpl.
Thompson, William G. TN 44th (Cons.) Inf.
Thompson, William G. VA 1st Arty. Co.D
Thompson, William G. VA Lt.Arty. 1st Bn. Co.D
Thompson, William G. VA 2nd Arty. Co.E
Thompson, William H. AR 2nd Cav. Co.C
Thompson, William H. AR 5th Inf. Co.C
Thompson, William H. AR 8th Inf. New Co.A
Thompson, William H. AR 9th Inf. Co.G Cpl.
Thompson, William H. AR 15th (N.W.) Inf. Co.E
Thompson, William H. AR 18th Inf. Co.H
Thompson, William H. GA Siege Arty. 28th Bn. Co.G Sgt.
Thompson, William H. GA 1st Mil. Co.G Cpl.
Thompson, William H. GA 1st (Ramsey's) Inf. Co.B Sgt.
Thompson, William H. GA 9th Inf. (St.Guards) Co.B
Thompson, William H. GA 35th Inf. Co.D
Thompson, William H. GA Phillips' Legion Co.D Cpl.
Thompson, William H. MS Arty. (Seven Stars Arty.) Roberts' Co. 1st Sgt.
Thompson, William H. MO 8th Cav. Co.D
Thompson, William H. MO 8th Cav. Co.F
Thompson, William H. MO Inf. 1st Bn. Co.C 3rd Lt.
Thompson, William H. MO 6th Inf. Co.K Hosp.Stew.
Thompson, William H. NC 1st Inf. Co.C Capt.
Thompson, William H. NC 3rd Inf. Co.B
Thompson, William H. NC 13th Inf. Co.C Cpl.
Thompson, William H. NC 26th Inf. Co.B
Thompson, William H. NC 49th Inf. Co.C Cpl.
Thompson, William H. NC 76th Mil.
Thompson, William H. SC 2nd Cav. Co.K
Thompson, William H. SC Cav.Bn. Hampton Legion Co.B Cpl.
Thompson, William H. TN 14th Inf. Co.D Sgt.
Thompson, William H. TX Cav. 2nd Regt. St.Troops Co.B
Thompson, William H. TX 13th Cav. Co.H
Thompson, William H. TX 14th Cav. Co.B
Thompson, William H. TX 17th Cav. Co.C
Thompson, William H. VA 8th Cav. Co.A
Thompson, William H. VA 8th Cav. Co.H
Thompson, William H. VA 19th Cav. Co.G
Thompson, William H. VA 25th Cav. Co.G
Thompson, William H. VA Cav. 35th Bn. Co.C
Thompson, William H. VA 2nd Inf. Co.C QMSgt.
Thompson, William H. VA 4th Inf. Co.H Cpl.
Thompson, William H. VA 5th Inf. Co.C
Thompson, William H. VA 5th Inf. Co.D,C
Thompson, William H. VA 17th Inf. Co.E
Thompson, William H. VA 19th Inf. Co.I
Thompson, William H. VA Inf. 21st Bn. 2nd Co.C
Thompson, William H. VA 45th Inf. Co.F
Thompson, William H. VA 48th Inf. Co.D
Thompson, William H. VA 50th Inf. Co.C Sgt.
Thompson, William H. VA 51st Inf. Co.C Cpl.
Thompson, William H. VA 64th Mtd.Inf. Co.C
Thompson, William H. VA 86th Mil. Co.C
Thompson, William H. VA 151st Mil. Co.D Cpl.
Thompson, William Henry KY 2nd (Duke's) Cav.
Thompson, William J. AL 4th (Russell's) Cav. Co.K
Thompson, William J. AL 11th Inf. Co.I
Thompson, William J. AL 59th Inf. Co.D
Thompson, William J. AR 1st Mtd.Rifles Co.F
Thompson, William J. AR 8th Cav. Co.H
Thompson, William J. AR 1st Vol. Co.C
Thompson, William J. AR 1st (Colquitt's) Inf. Co.K
Thompson, William J. AR 5th Inf. Co.G 2nd Lt.
Thompson, William J. FL 8th Inf. Co.I
Thompson, William J. GA 2nd Cav. Co.A Bugler
Thompson, William J. GA 14th Inf. Co.E
Thompson, William J. GA 27th Inf. Co.K Sgt.
Thompson, William J. GA Inf. (High Shoals Defend.) Medlin's Ind.Co.
Thompson, William J. LA 4th Cav. Co.K
Thompson, William J. LA 11th Inf. Co.E
Thompson, William J. LA 12th Inf. 2nd Co.D
Thompson, William J. MS 7th Inf. Co.F
Thompson, William J. MS 36th Inf. Co.A Cpl.
Thompson, William J. MO 5th Cav. Co.C 1st Sgt.
Thompson, William J. MO 5th Cav. Co.D
Thompson, William J. MO 6th Cav. 1st Lt.,Adj.
Thompson, William J. MO 10th Inf. Co.H
Thompson, William J. NC 13th Inf. Co.B Music.
Thompson, William J. TN 3rd (Forrest's) Cav. 1st Co.F
Thompson, William J. TN 39th Mtd.Inf. Co.F
Thompson, William J. VA 4th Inf. Co.I
Thompson, William J. VA 15th Inf. Co.C
Thompson, William J. VA 23rd Inf. Co.A
Thompson, William J. Jackson's Staff Capt.,AAAG
Thompson, William J. Gen. & Staff Asst.Surg.
Thompson, William K. MO Cav. 3rd Bn. Co.B
Thompson, William K. SC Cav.Bn. Holcombe Legion Co.E
Thompson, William K. SC Inf. Holcombe Legion Co.B Cpl.
Thompson, Wm. K. VA Inf. 23rd Bn. Co.C
Thompson, William L. AL 4th Inf. Co.I
Thompson, William L. AL 3rd Bn. Hilliard's Legion Vol. Co.C 3rd Lt.
Thompson, William L. AR 1st (Colquitt's) Inf. Co.A
Thompson, William L. AR Inf. 4th Bn. Co.E
Thompson, William L. FL 9th Inf. Co.G
Thompson, William L. GA 48th Inf. Co.A,E
Thompson, William L. KY 8th Cav. Co.K Cpl.
Thompson, William L. LA 1st (Nelligan's) Inf. Co.G
Thompson, William L. LA 4th Inf. Old Co.G
Thompson, William L. MS 7th Cav. Co.D
Thompson, William L. MS St.Cav. Perrin's Bn. Co.F Cpl.
Thompson, William L. MS Inf. 3rd Bn. (St.Troops) Co.E
Thompson, William L. NC 5th Inf. Co.I Cpl.
Thompson, William L. NC 14th Inf. Co.I Cpl.
Thompson, William L. SC 5th Inf. 1st Co.H, 2nd Co.B 2nd Lt.
Thompson, William L. TN Cav. 7th Bn. (Bennett's) Co.E Trump.
Thompson, William L. VA 5th Inf. Co.G 2nd Lt.
Thompson, William L. VA 27th Inf. Co.D
Thompson, Wm. L. VA 54th Inf. Co.A
Thompson, William L. Lt.Arty. Dent's Btty.,CSA
Thompson, William M. GA 3rd Inf. Co.E
Thompson, William M. LA Mil.Cav.Squad. (Ind.Rangers Iberville) Jr.Capt.
Thompson, William M. LA 3rd Inf. Co.E
Thompson, William M. LA 16th Inf. Co.B
Thompson, William M. MS Lt.Arty. (Issaquena Arty.) Graves' Co.
Thompson, William M. NC 2nd Bn.Loc.Def.Troops Co.B
Thompson, William M. NC 3rd Inf. Co.G
Thompson, William M. NC 13th Inf. Co.E
Thompson, William M. NC 14th Inf. Co.E 1st Lt.
Thompson, William M. NC 47th Inf. Co.E
Thompson, William M. NC 51st Inf. Co.H 2nd Lt.
Thompson, William M. NC 56th Inf. Co.H
Thompson, William M. SC 10th Inf. Co.L
Thompson, William M. TN 41st Inf. Co.F
Thompson, William M. TX 15th Cav. Co.F
Thompson, William M. VA Lt.Arty. Cooper's Co.
Thompson, William M. VA 19th Inf. Co.I 2nd Lt.
Thompson, William M. VA 23rd Inf. Co.G
Thompson, William M. VA 37th Inf. Co.K
Thompson, Wm. M. Gen. & Staff Pvt.Physician
Thompson, William Mc. MS St.Cav. 2nd Bn. (Harris') Co.A
Thompson, William M.C. NC 5th Inf. Co.K
Thompson, William M.T. MS 2nd Inf. Co.H
Thompson, William N. AL 3rd Bn.Res. Co.C
Thompson, William N. AL Mil. 4th Vol. Co.B Sgt.
Thompson, Wm. N. AL Mil. 25th Regt. Col.
Thompson, William N. AR 3rd Cav. Co.G
Thompson, William N. AR 33rd Inf. Co.C
Thompson, William N. FL 7th Inf. Co.C
Thompson, William N. GA 3rd Cav. Co.B
Thompson, William N. VA Mil. Washington Cty.

Thompson, William O. MS 36th Inf. Co.E Sgt.
Thompson, William O. TX 24th Cav. Co.D
Thompson, William P. AL 10th Inf. Co.G
Thompson, Wm. P. AL 45th Inf. Co.K
Thompson, William P. AR 21st Mil. Dollar's Co.
Thompson, William P. AR 36th Inf. Co.A
Thompson, William P. GA 3rd Inf. Co.E
Thompson, William P. GA 65th Inf. Co.F
Thompson, William P. LA 7th Inf. Co.A Capt.
Thompson, William P. MS 3rd (St.Troops) Cav. Co.E
Thompson, William P. MS 1st Lt.Arty. Co.C
Thompson, William P. MS 15th Inf. Co.I
Thompson, William P. NC Lt.Arty. 13th Bn. Co.D
Thompson, William P. NC 1st Inf. Co.B
Thompson, William P. NC 25th Inf. Co.E
Thompson, William P. NC 39th Inf. Co.A
Thompson, William P. NC 44th Inf. Co.G Cpl.
Thompson, William P. NC 51st Inf. Co.H
Thompson, William P. VA 19th Cav. Lt.Col.
Thompson, William P. VA 24th Inf. Co.B 2nd Lt.
Thompson, William P., Jr. VA 24th Inf. Co.B
Thompson, William P. VA 31st Inf. Co.A Capt.
Thompson, William R. AL 59th Inf. Co.D
Thompson, William R. AR 14th (McCarver's) Inf. Co.F
Thompson, William R. AR 21st Inf. Co.B
Thompson, William R. GA 43rd Inf. Co.G
Thompson, William R. GA 49th Inf. Co.A
Thompson, William R. KY 8th Cav. Co.K
Thompson, William R. MS 12th Inf. Co.K
Thompson, Wm. R. MO St.Guard
Thompson, William R. NC 4th Inf. Co.A 1st Sgt.
Thompson, William R. NC 11th (Bethel Regt.) Inf. Co.B
Thompson, William R. NC 18th Inf. Co.B
Thompson, William R. NC 52nd Inf. Co.I
Thompson, William R. VA 57th Inf. Co.E
Thompson, William S. AL 3rd Inf. Co.K
Thompson, William S. AR 1st Mtd.Rifles Co.H
Thompson, William S. AR 9th Inf. Co.F QMSgt.
Thompson, William S. FL 3rd Inf. Co.F
Thompson, William S. GA Cav. 2nd Bn. Co.F Sgt.
Thompson, William S. GA 3rd Cav. Co.A
Thompson, William S. GA 5th Cav. Co.B Sgt.
Thompson, William S. GA 16th Inf. Co.D
Thompson, William S. MS 19th Inf. Co.A
Thompson, William S. MO 10th Inf. Co.H
Thompson, William S. SC 10th Inf. Co.M
Thompson, William S. TX 2nd Cav. 1st Co.F Far.
Thompson, William S. TX 33rd Cav. Co.B
Thompson, William S. TX Cav. Morgan's Regt. Co.I Far.
Thompson, William S. TX 7th Inf. Co.D
Thompson, William S. VA 2nd Inf. Co.G
Thompson, William T. AL Lt.Arty. 2nd Bn.
Thompson, William T. AL 4th Inf. Co.C
Thompson, William T. AR 1st (Colquitt's) Inf. Co.A 1st Lt.
Thompson, William T. AR 30th Inf. Co.A
Thompson, William T. GA Inf. Cobb Guards Co.A Cpl.
Thompson, William T. MO 8th Cav. Co.D Capt.
Thompson, William T. MO Staff St.Guard Lt.Col.,ADC
Thompson, William T. SC 13th Inf. Co.I
Thompson, William T. TN 16th Inf. Co.C
Thompson, William T. VA 5th Cav. (12 mo. '61-2) Co.E
Thompson, William T. VA 13th Cav. Co.G
Thompson, William T. VA Cav. 36th Bn. Co.C
Thompson, William V. AL 47th Inf. Co.A
Thompson, William V. TN Cav. 9th Bn. (Gantt's) Co.A Adj.
Thompson, William W. AL 10th Inf. Co.I
Thompson, William W. AL 30th Inf. Co.B 1st Lt.
Thompson, William W. AR 5th Inf. Co.C
Thompson, William W. AR 25th Inf. Co.B Capt.
Thompson, William W. GA 13th Inf. Co.D
Thompson, William W. KY 5th Cav. Co.D
Thompson, William W. LA Lt.Arty. Fenner's Btty.
Thompson, William W. LA 7th Inf. Co.H
Thompson, William W. TN 14th Inf. Co.A Capt.
Thompson, William W. TN 44th (Cons.) Inf. Co.E Sgt.
Thompson, William W. TN 55th (McKoin's) Inf. Co.H Sgt.
Thompson, William W. VA 2nd Arty. Co.D
Thompson, William W. VA Inf. 22nd Bn. Co.D
Thompson, William W. VA 26th Inf. Co.E
Thompson, William Wirt TX 18th Inf. Co.I Capt.
Thompson, Willie NC 27th Inf. Co.K Sgt.
Thompson, Willis AL 4th Res. Co.D
Thompson, Willis AR 3rd Inf. Co.F
Thompson, Willis TN 12th (Green's) Cav. Co.D
Thompson, Willis VA 3rd Cav. Co.B Sgt.
Thompson, Willis A. GA 44th Inf. Co.G
Thompson, Willis G. KY 4th Mtd.Inf. Co.A
Thompson, Willis R. KY 4th Mtd.Inf. Co.C
Thompson, Willis W. GA Phillips' Legion Co.C Cpl.
Thompson, Wilson KY 5th Cav. Co.A
Thompson, Wilson TN 30th Inf. Co.D
Thompson, Wilson B. AL 2nd Bn. Hilliard's Legion Vol. Co.C
Thompson, Wilson J. VA 5th Cav. (12 mo. '61-2) Co.D
Thompson, Wilson J. VA 13th Cav. Co.B
Thompson, Wilson T. SC Inf. Hampton Legion Co.E
Thompson, Wily V. VA Inf. Mileham's Co.
Thompson, Winton VA 36th Inf. 2nd Co.C 3rd Lt.
Thompson, W.J. AL 35th Inf. Co.K
Thompson, W.J. AL 44th Inf.
Thompson, W.J. AL 11th Cav. Co.D
Thompson, W.J. AL 11th Cav. Co.F
Thompson, W.J. AL 14th Inf. Co.G Sgt.
Thompson, W.J. AR 11th Inf. Co.I
Thompson, W.J. AR 11th & 17th Cons.Inf. Co.C
Thompson, W.J. AR 18th (Marmaduke's) Inf. Co.I
Thompson, W.J. AR 21st Mil. Co.G
Thompson, W.J. AR 30th Inf. Co.A
Thompson, W.J. AR 36th Inf. Co.I
Thompson, W.J. FL 2nd Inf. Co.F
Thompson, W.J. FL 2nd Inf. Co.L
Thompson, W.J. GA 13th Cav. Co.B
Thompson, W.J. GA Cav. 19th Bn. Co.A
Thompson, W.J. GA 1st (Symons') Res. Co.H
Thompson, W.J. GA 3rd Res. Co.E
Thompson, W.J. GA 40th Inf. Co.K
Thompson, W.J. KY 2nd Cav. Co.G
Thompson, W.J. LA 30th Inf. Co.A
Thompson, W.J. LA Inf.Crescent Regt. Co.A
Thompson, W.J. MS 46th Inf. Co.I
Thompson, W.J. SC 4th Cav. Co.I
Thompson, W.J. SC Cav. 12th Bn. Co.B
Thompson, W.J. TN 12th (Green's) Cav. Co.G
Thompson, W.J. TN 5th Inf. 2nd Co.I
Thompson, W.J. TN 17th Inf. Co.H
Thompson, W.J. TN Inf. 23rd Bn. Co.A
Thompson, W.J. TX 3rd Cav. Co.E
Thompson, W.J. TX 10th Cav. Co.I
Thompson, W.J. TX 28th Cav. Co.E 1st Lt.
Thompson, W.J. VA 13th Cav. Co.B
Thompson, W.J. VA 15th Cav. Co.E
Thompson, W.J. VA 19th Cav. Asst.Surg.
Thompson, W.J. VA 46th Inf. 2nd Co.E
Thompson, W.J. 3rd Conf.Cav. Co.B
Thompson, W.J. 8th (Wade's) Conf.Cav. Co.H
Thompson, W.J. 10th Conf.Cav. Co.F Cpl.
Thompson, W.J.F. GA Siege Arty. 28th Bn. Co.G
Thompson, W.J.F. GA 1st Reg. Co.E
Thompson, W.K. GA Inf. 1st Loc.Troops (Augusta) Co.C
Thompson, W.K. SC 7th Cav. Co.H
Thompson, W.K. TN 23rd Inf. Co.E
Thompson, W.L. AL Cav. Falkner's Co.
Thompson, W.L. AL Inf. 2nd Regt. Co.E
Thompson, W.L. AL 32nd Inf. Co.G
Thompson, W.L. AL 63rd Inf. Co.H 1st Sgt.
Thompson, W.L. AR 1st (Monroe's) Cav. Co.A
Thompson, W.L. AR Cav. Gordon's Regt. Co.C
Thompson, W.L. AR 5th Inf. Co.G Sgt.
Thompson, W.L. AR 19th (Dockery's) Inf. Co.F
Thompson, W.L. GA 3rd Cav. Co.H
Thompson, W.L. GA 63rd Inf. Co.C
Thompson, W.L. KY 1st Bn.Mtd.Rifles Co.C
Thompson, W.L. LA 3rd (Wingfield's) Cav. Co.E
Thompson, W.L. LA Dreux's Cav. Co.A
Thompson, W.L. MS 10th Inf. New Co.K
Thompson, W.L. TN 22nd (Barteau's) Cav. Co.G Sgt.
Thompson, W.M. AL 34th Inf. Co.E
Thompson, W.M. AR Lt.Arty. Owen's Btty.
Thompson, W.M. KY 12th Cav. Co.H
Thompson, W.M. LA Res.Corps
Thompson, W.M. MS 39th Inf. Co.H 2nd Lt.
Thompson, W.M. NC 26th Inf. Co.F
Thompson, W.M. NC 66th Inf. Co.B
Thompson, W.M. SC 7th Cav. Co.G
Thompson, W.M. SC Rutledge Mtd. Riflemen & Horse Arty. Trenholm's Co.
Thompson, W.M. TX 12th Cav. Co.K
Thompson, W.M. 20th Conf.Cav. 2nd Co.I
Thompson, W. Marion MS Cav. 24th Bn. Co.C
Thompson, W.N. AL Lt.Arty. Tarrant's Btty.

Thompson, W.N. AL 24th Inf. Co.I
Thompson, W.N. GA 7th Inf. Co.A
Thompson, W.N. MS 35th Inf. Co.C
Thompson, W.N. NC 3rd Cav. (41st St.Troops) Co.F
Thompson, W.N. VA Arty. C.F. Johnston's Co.
Thompson, W.N. VA 48th Inf. Co.B
Thompson, W.O. AR 19th Inf. Co.C
Thompson, W.O. SC Cav. 10th Bn. Co.D
Thompson, W.O. SC 1st (Butler's) Inf. Co.G
Thompson, W.O. SC 1st (Hagood's) Inf. 2nd Co.C
Thompson, W.P. AL 1st Inf. 3rd Co.G
Thompson, W.P. AL 9th Inf.
Thompson, W.P. AL 60th Inf. Co.F
Thompson, W.P. AL Coosa Guards J.W. Suttles' Co.
Thompson, W.P. GA Cav. 15th Bn. (St.Guards) Wooten's Co.
Thompson, W.P. GA 1st (Fannin's) Res. Co.A
Thompson, W.P. MS 1st Cav. Co.A
Thompson, W.P. MS 7th Inf. Co.A
Thompson, W.P. MS 37th Inf. Co.H
Thompson, W.P. MS 44th Inf. Co.F
Thompson, W.P. MO 12th Cav. Co.D Sgt.
Thompson, W.P. NC 7th Sr.Res. Fisher's Co., Bradshaw's Co.
Thompson, W.P. NC 31st Inf. Co.K
Thompson, W.P. VA Inf. 7th Bn.Loc.Def. Co.C
Thompson, W.R. AL Cav. Moreland's Regt. Co.G
Thompson, W.R. AR 34th Inf. Co.F
Thompson, W.R. GA 62nd Cav. Co.F
Thompson, W.R. GA 28th Inf. Co.I
Thompson, W.R. GA 46th Inf. Co.C
Thompson, W.R. GA 48th Inf. Co.E
Thompson, W.R. GA 54th Inf. Co.B
Thompson, W.R. MS 8th Cav. Co.A
Thompson, W.R. MS Scouts Montgomery's Co.
Thompson, W.R. MO 9th (Elliott's) Cav. Co.G
Thompson, W.R. NC 17th Inf. (2nd Org.) Co.B
Thompson, W.R. SC 2nd St.Troops Co.C
Thompson, W.R. SC 12th Inf. Co.I
Thompson, W.R. TN 12th (Green's) Cav. Co.E
Thompson, W.R. TX Cav. 2nd Bn.St.Troops Wilson's Co.
Thompson, W.R. TX 10th Cav. Co.I
Thompson, W.R. TX 29th Cav. Co.D
Thompson, W.R. VA 51st Inf. Co.E
Thompson, W.R.D. NC 64th Inf. Co.E
Thompson, W.R.D. Gen. & Staff AASurg.
Thompson, Wright S. MS 15th Inf. Co.I
Thompson, W.R.T. TX Cav. Baird's Regt. Capt.
Thompson, W.S. AL 1st Cav. 2nd Co.D
Thompson, W.S. AL 3rd Cav. Co.H
Thompson, W.S. AL 18th Inf. Co.E
Thompson, W.S. AL Detailed Conscr.
Thompson, W.S. AR 2nd Inf.
Thompson, W.S. GA 8th Cav. Co.F 3rd Lt.
Thompson, W.S. GA 62nd Cav. Co.F Bvt.2nd Lt.
Thompson, W.S. GA 5th Res. Co.C
Thompson, W.S. GA 12th Mil.
Thompson, W.S. GA 16th Inf. Co.G
Thompson, W.S. GA 40th Inf. Co.K
Thompson, W.S. GA 53rd Inf. Co.E 1st Sgt.
Thompson, W.S. GA Inf. (St.Guards) Hansell's Co.
Thompson, W.S. MS 2nd (Quinn's St.Troops) Inf. Co.D
Thompson, W.S. MS Inf. 2nd St.Troops Co.D
Thompson, W.S. SC 12th Inf. Co.I
Thompson, W.S. TN 16th Inf. Co.C Cpl.
Thompson, W.S. TN 32nd Inf. Co.D
Thompson, W.S. Inf. Bailey's Cons.Regt. Co.B
Thompson, W.S. TX 3rd Cav. Co.A
Thompson, W.S. VA 1st (Farinholt's) Res. Comsy.Sgt.
Thompson, W.S. VA 10th Bn.Res. Co.D
Thompson, W.S. Conf.Cav. Wood's Regt. 1st Co.G
Thompson, W.T. AL 42nd Inf. Co.A
Thompson, W.T. AR Cav. Davies' Bn. Co.E
Thompson, W.T. GA Lt.Arty. 14th Bn. Co.D
Thompson, W.T. MS 2nd St.Cav. Co.B
Thompson, W.T. MS 5th Inf. Co.G Sgt.
Thompson, W.T. NC 3rd Jr.Res. Co.F Cpl.
Thompson, W.T. SC 7th Cav. Co.A
Thompson, W.T. SC Cav. Tucker's Co.
Thompson, W.T. SC 2nd Inf. Co.D
Thompson, W.T. TN Inf. 2nd Cons.Regt. Co.K
Thompson, W.T. TN 11th Inf. Co.K
Thompson, W.T. TN 23rd Inf. 2nd Co.F
Thompson, W.T. TX 7th Cav. Co.C Capt.
Thompson, W.T. VA Lt.Arty. 13th Bn. Co.A
Thompson, W.T. VA 8th Cav. Co.G
Thompson, W.V. AL Lt.Arty. Goldthwaite's Btty.
Thompson, W.V. TN 18th Inf. Co.I
Thompson, W.W. AL Arty. 1st Bn. Co.B
Thompson, W.W. AL Arty. 1st Bn. Co.E
Thompson, W.W. AL 22nd Inf. Co. Sgt.
Thompson, W.W. AL 26th (O'Neal's) Inf. Co.G Music.
Thompson, W.W. AL Cp. of Instr. Talladega
Thompson, W.W. AR 7th Cav.
Thompson, W.W. AR 8th Cav. Co.I Cpl.
Thompson, W.W. AR 7th Inf. Co.F
Thompson, W.W. GA 8th Cav. New Co.I
Thompson, W.W. GA Cav. 20th Bn. Co.A,D Sgt.
Thompson, W.W. GA Lt.Arty. 14th Bn. Co.D
Thompson, W.W. GA Lt.Arty. King's Btty.
Thompson, W.W. KY 2nd (Woodward's) Cav. Co.A,B
Thompson, W.W. LA Mil.Conf.Guards Regt. Co.H
Thompson, W.W. MS 2nd Part.Rangers Co.C
Thompson, W.W. MS 18th Cav. Co.B
Thompson, W.W. MS 28th Cav. Co.K
Thompson, W.W. MS Lt.Arty. 14th Bn. Co.C
Thompson, W.W. MS 8th Inf. Co.C
Thompson, W.W. MO 15th Cav. Co.H Sgt.
Thompson, W.W. MO Inf. Clark's Regt. Co.A
Thompson, W.W. TN 4th (McLemore's) Cav. Co.C Cpl.
Thompson, W.W. TN Inf. 2nd Cons.Regt. Co.I
Thompson, W.W. TN 3rd (Lillard's) Mtd.Inf. Co.E
Thompson, W.W. TN 50th Inf. Co.G Sgt.
Thompson, W.W. TN 50th (Cons.) Inf. Co.G Sgt.
Thompson, W.W. TX 1st Hvy.Arty. Co.I Sgt.
Thompson, W.W. TX 13th Vol. Co.E
Thompson, W.W. VA Cav. 34th Bn. Co.G
Thompson, W.W. Inf. School of Pract. Powell's Detach. Co.C
Thompson, Wyatt AL Cav. Lewis' Bn. Co.A
Thompson, Y.H.J. GA 1st (Ramsey's) Inf. Co.A Ch.Music.
Thompson, Young TN 45th Inf. Co.I
Thompson, Young H.B. GA Lt.Arty. 12th Bn. 2nd Co.A Music.
Thompson, Z. AR Mil. Desha Cty.Bn.
Thompson, Z. LA 25th Inf. Chap.
Thompson, Zacariah AR 31st Inf. Co.D
Thompson, Zach TN 8th (Smith's) Cav. Co.F
Thompson, Zachariah MO 8th Cav. Co.F
Thompson, Zachariah T. TN 7th Inf. Co.H,K
Thompson, Zadock L. 7th Conf.Cav. Co.F
Thompson, Zedekiah D. AL 36th Inf. Co.G
Thompson, Z.L. 8th (Dearing's) Conf.Cav. Co.G
Thompson, Z.S. LA 17th Inf. Co.A Sgt.
Thompson, Z.T. MS 1st Cav.Res. Co.B
Thompson, Z.U. TN Cav. Allison's Squad. Co.C
Thompson, Zuachin LA 28th (Gray's) Inf. Co.G
Thompsons, T.S. AL 3rd Bn.Res. Appling's Co.
Thoms, H.T. MS Gordon's Co. (Wilkinson Cty. Loc.Guard)
Thoms, J.C. LA 11th Inf. Co.I
Thoms, John AL 37th Inf. Co.H
Thoms, John W. VA Horse Arty. Shoemaker's Co.
Thoms, R.J. LA 4th Inf. Co.K
Thoms, Robert MS Wilkinson Cty. Minute Men Co.B
Thoms, Robert J. LA 11th Inf. Co.I
Thoms, Robert W. MS 21st Inf. Co.E
Thoms, Steven LA 4th Inf. Co.D N.C.S. Hosp.Stew.
Thoms, William T. MS 16th Inf. Co.K
Thoms, William T. MS 21st Inf. Co.D
Thomsberry, John B. KY 10th (Diamond's) Cav. Co.A
Thomsbery, O. AR 7th Cav. Co.E
Thomsen, Charles LA Mil. Chalmette Regt. Co.A
Thomser, Benjamin TX 13th Vol. 2nd Co.B Music.
Thomson, A. GA 53rd Inf. Co.G
Thomson, A. TN 9th Inf. Co.I
Thomson, A. Cromwell TX 1st (Yager's) Cav. Co.K 1st Sgt.
Thomson, A.H. VA 13th Inf. Co.A
Thomson, A.H.S. MS Inf. 7th Bn. Co.A
Thomson, A.J. LA 18th Inf. Co.H
Thomson, A.J. TX 17th Inf. Co.D
Thomson, Albert G. NC Mallett's Bn. (Cp.Guard) Co.B
Thomson, A.S. Gen. & Staff Hosp.Stew.
Thomson, A. Spotswood TX 26th Cav. Co.B
Thomson, A.W. SC 1st (Hagood's) Inf. Co.E Cpl.
Thomson, A.W. SC 5th Inf. Surg.
Thomson, A.W. Gen. & Staff Surg.
Thomson, Ben TN 50th (Cons.) Inf. Co.H
Thomson, Benjamin SC 1st Mtd.Mil. Martin's Co. Sgt.
Thomson, Benjamin J. AR 2nd Inf. Co.F
Thomson, B.P. MO St.Guard

Thomson, B.S. SC 7th Cav. Co.A
Thomson, B.S. SC Cav. Tucker's Co.
Thomson, C.C. AL Vol. Goldsmith's Ind.Co.
Thomson, C.E. AL 47th Inf. Co.A
Thomson, Charles SC 12th Inf. Co.I
Thomson, Charles B. AR 2nd Inf. Co.F Sgt.
Thomson, Daniel P. GA 12th Inf. Co.A
Thomson, Daniel S. GA Siege Arty. 28th Bn. Co.D
Thomson, David A. NC 38th Inf. Co.D,A 1st Sgt.
Thomson, David H. KY 1st Inf. Co.C 2nd Lt.
Thomson, David L. Gen. & Staff Asst.Comsy.
Thomson, D.B. MS 5th Inf. (St.Troops) Co.A
Thomson, D.L. SC Arty. Stuart's Co. (Beaufort Vol.Arty.) Gy.Cpl.
Thomson, E.F. VA 11th Cav. Co.I
Thomson, E.J. TX 13th Vol. 1st Co.K
Thomson, E.L. AL 11th Inf. Asst.Medical Off.
Thomson, E.L. Gen. & Staff Asst.Surg.
Thomson, Eli GA Cav. 22nd Bn. (St.Guards) Co.I
Thomson, Elijah S. MS 44th Inf. Co.K
Thomson, E.S. AL 9th Inf. Asst.Surg.
Thomson, Estes H. MS 24th Inf. Co.A Sgt.
Thomson, Ewing L. AL 4th Inf. Co.F
Thomson, Francis VA Loc.Def. Dulany's Co.
Thomson, Francis M. Wheeler's Scouts,CSA
Thomson, Frank TN 5th Inf. 2nd Co.H
Thomson, Franklin TN 13th Inf. Reed's Co.
Thomson, G. GA 24th Inf. Co.A
Thomson, G.B. VA 8th Cav. Co.F 1st Sgt.
Thomson, Geo. A. Gen. & Staff, Inf. 2nd Lt.
Thomson, George W. NC 44th Inf. Co.B
Thomson, G.S. Gen. & Staff Maj.,QM
Thomson, Guy GA 9th Inf. Co.E
Thomson, H. GA 10th Inf. Co.I
Thomson, H. MS 5th Inf. Co.C
Thomson, H.A. 4th Conf.Inf. Co.H
Thomson, H.D. MS 1st Inf. Co.F Cpl.
Thomson, Henry GA Inf. (Ogeechee Minute Men) Garrison's Co. Sgt.
Thomson, Henry H. SC 5th Inf. 1st Co.K 2nd Lt.
Thomson, Henry H. SC Palmetto S.S. Co.K 1st Lt.
Thomson, Henry W. TN 44th Inf. Co.K
Thomson, Ignatius Davis Gen. & Staff Surg.
Thomson, Isaac AR 45th Mil. Co.C
Thomson, Isom D. GA 2nd Res. Co.K
Thomson, I.T. AL 33rd Inf. Co.F
Thomson, J. GA 16th Inf. Co.D
Thomson, J.A. AR 2nd Inf. Co.F
Thomson, J.A. SC 1st Inf. Co.B
Thomson, James AL Cav. Forrest's Regt.
Thomson, James AL 5th Bn.Vol. Co.A
Thomson, James A. SC Palmetto S.S. Co.C Cpl.
Thomson, James F. TX 17th Cav. Co.F Sgt.
Thomson, James H. TN Greer's Regt.Part. Rangers Co.A
Thomson, James J. TN 6th (Wheeler's) Cav. Co.E Sgt.
Thomson, James J. TX 25th Cav. Co.D Jr.2nd Lt.
Thomson, James M. AR 2nd Inf. Co.F Ord.Sgt.
Thomson, James M. NC Inf. 2nd Bn. Co.H
Thomson, James S. SC 2nd Cav. Co.A
Thomson, James T. FL 9th Inf. Co.I
Thomson, James W. MS 24th Inf. Co.A,H
Thomson, James W. VA Horse Arty. J.W. Carter's Co. Capt.
Thomson, J.B. 4th Conf.Inf. Co.H Sgt.
Thomson, J.C. AR 32nd Inf. Chap.
Thomson, J.C. TN Inf. 22nd Bn. Co.C Cpl.
Thomson, J.D. GA 16th Inf. Co.A
Thomson, J.D. TX 2nd Inf. Co.G
Thomson, Jesse L. VA Lt.Arty. J.R. Johnson's Co.
Thomson, J.F. 4th Conf.Inf. Co.H
Thomson, J.H. MS 5th Inf. (St.Troops) Co.A
Thomson, J. Leonidas TX 27th Cav. Co.L
Thomson, J.M. TX 2nd Inf. Co.K
Thomson, J.M. Chalmer's Brig. Maj.,QM
Thomson, John AL 55th Vol. Co.C
Thomson, John GA Inf. Gibson's Bn. Ruley's Co.
Thomson, John LA 1st (Nelligan's) Inf. Co.E 2nd Lt.
Thomson, John SC Mil.Arty. 1st Regt. Co.C Cpl.
Thomson, John SC 2nd Arty. Co.A
Thomson, John VA Mil. 55th Regt. 2nd Lt.
Thomson, John 1st Seminole Mtd.Vol.
Thomson, John A. MS 10th Inf. Old Co.E
Thomson, John A. SC 2nd Rifles Co.A 1st Sgt.
Thomson, John F. TX 17th Inf. Co.A Sr.2nd Lt.
Thomson, John H. SC 1st (Hagood's) Inf. 1st Co.G 2nd Lt.
Thomson, John H. Gen. & Staff Surg.
Thomson, John L. AR 1st (Monroe's) Cav. Co.F
Thomson, John P. VA Burks' Regt.Loc.Def. Miller's Co.
Thomson, John R. Conf.Reg.Inf. Brooks' Bn. Co.C
Thomson, John S. MO St.Guard
Thomson, John S.R. SC 5th Inf. 1st Co.K
Thomson, John S.R. SC Palmetto S.S. Co.K Sgt.
Thomson, John W. SC 1st (Orr's) Rifles Co.G Cpl.
Thomson, Joseph AL 11th Inf. Co.K
Thomson, Joseph M. TN 5th Inf. 2nd Co.F
Thomson, Joseph R. GA Inf. 27th Bn. Co.A
Thomson, J.P. SC Mil.Arty. 1st Regt. Co.C
Thomson, J.R. TX 20th Cav. Co.A 1st Lt.
Thomson, J.S.R. Gen. & Staff 1st Lt.,EO
Thomson, J.W. AL 3rd Bn.Res. Co.A
Thomson, J.W. GA 16th Inf. Co.A
Thomson, J.W. MS 6th Inf. Co.K
Thomson, J.W. TX 25th Cav. Co.B
Thomson, J.W. Gen. & Staff Vol.ADC
Thomson, Lee L. AR Cav. Anderosn's Unatt.Bn. Co.A 1st Lt.
Thomson, Lee L. AR Cav. Gordon's Regt. Lt.Col.
Thomson, L.M. KY 1st Inf. Co.C 2nd Lt.
Thomson, M.D. SC 15th Inf. Co.F
Thomson, M.G. SC 2nd Arty. Co.F
Thomson, M.H. GA 8th Cav. Co.G 1st Lt.
Thomson, M.H. GA 62nd Cav. Co.G Bvt.2nd Lt.
Thomson, Micajah NC 8th Sr.Res. Kelly's Co.
Thomson, Michael A. VA 27th Inf. Co.D
Thomson, M. Jeff. MO St.Guards Brig.Gen.
Thomson, M. King VA 7th Cav. Co.G
Thomson, M.S. SC 3rd Cav. Co.B
Thomson, N. SC 5th Bn.Res. Co.A 2nd Lt.
Thomson, Nathaniel W. VA Lt.Arty. J.R. Johnson's Co. Cpl.
Thomson, Nathan S. NC 42nd Inf. Co.B Sgt.
Thomson, Nathan S. NC 61st Inf. Co.H
Thomson, Neill TN 14th (Neely's) Cav. Co.B
Thomson, Nelson A. TX 26th Cav. Co.B
Thomson, N.W. VA Lt.Arty. Cayce's Co.
Thomson, Peter K. AL 11th Inf. Co.G Sgt.
Thomson, P.H. Gen. & Staff Capt.,AAG
Thomson, Preston KY 5th Cav. Lt.Col.
Thomson, Randolph C. AL 11th Inf. Co.G
Thomson, Ransom M. GA 2nd Res. Co.K
Thomson, Reddick S. MS 44th Inf. Co.K
Thomson, Richard C. SC 7th Cav. Co.C
Thomson, R.J. MS Packer's Co. (Pope Guards)
Thomson, Robert A. GA 2nd Cav. Co.E Capt.
Thomson, Robert M. AL 1st Regt.Conscr. Co.F
Thomson, R.R. VA Hvy.Arty. 20th Bn. Co.C
Thomson, S. TX 1st Inf.
Thomson, Sandy TX 27th Cav. Co.F
Thomson, S.B. GA Cobb's Legion Co.A
Thomson, S.H. AR 1st S.S. Co.A
Thomson, T.D. AR 15th (Johnson's) Inf. Co.C,E
Thomson, Thomas SC 2nd Rifles Co.A Col.
Thomson, Thomas C. TX 2nd Inf. Co.G
Thomson, Thomas L. GA Smith's Legion Co.D
Thomson, Thomas S. Cav. Butler's Div. Maj.
Thomson, Thos. S. Gen. & Staff Surg.
Thomson, T.N. TX 18th Inf. Co.C
Thomson, W. LA 22nd Inf. Co.E
Thomson, W. LA Mil. Chalmette Regt. Kirk's Co. Cpl.
Thomson, W. NC 51st Inf. Co.E
Thomson, W. 9th Conf.Inf. Co.E
Thomson, Walter B. VA 5th Cav. (12 mo. '61-2) Co.I
Thomson, Walter B. VA Cav. 14th Bn. Co.B
Thomson, Warren SC 5th Inf. 1st Co.K Sgt.
Thomson, W.B. SC 7th Cav. Co.A
Thomson, W.B. SC Cav. Tucker's Co.
Thomson, W.E. TX 29th Cav. Co.K
Thomson, W.G. GA Cav. 1st Bn. Winn's Co.
Thomson, William GA 59th Inf.
Thomson, William MO 5th Cav. Co.C
Thomson, William SC Arty. Stuart's Co. (Beaufort Vol.Arty.) Sgt.
Thomson, William TN 2nd (Robison's) Inf. Co.D
Thomson, William E. VA 5th Cav. (12 mo. '61-2) Co.I
Thomson, William E. VA Cav. 14th Bn. Co.B
Thomson, William G. GA Cav. 20th Bn. Co.B Maj.
Thomson, William J. FL 5th Inf. Co.F
Thomson, William J. LA Mil. British Guard Bn. Burrowes' Co.
Thomson, William P. VA 18th Cav. Co.C
Thomson, William P. VA Burks' Regt.Loc.Def. Miller's Co.
Thomson, William S. VA 12th Cav. Co.B
Thomson, William T. SC 5th Inf. Maj.
Thomson, William W. AL 4th Inf. Co.K
Thomson, William W. MS 24th Inf. Co.A Capt.
Thomson, W.J. KY 9th Mtd.Inf. Co.E
Thomson, W.J. SC 7th Cav. Co.A

Thomson, W.J. TX 27th Cav. Co.F
Thomson, W.R. TX 27th Cav. Co.F
Thomson, W.S. VA Horse Arty. J.W. Carter's Co.
Thomsuden, H. LA Mil. 1st Regt. 3rd Brig. 1st Div. Co.A
Thomure, Felix MO Lt.Arty. McDonald's Co.
Thomure, Felix MO 6th Inf. Co.D
Thomure, Leon MO 6th Inf. Co.D
Thomure, Lewis MO Lt.Arty. McDonald's Co.
Thomuson, H.C. GA Cav. 8th Bn. (St.Guards) Co.B
Thomwell, James H. SC 4th St.Troops Co.G 1st Sgt.
Thon, C.H. Gen. & Staff Capt.,Enrolling Off.
Thon, Charles J. GA Cav. 1st Bn. Lamar's Co.
Thonbey, Jacob A. VA 5th Cav.Arty. & Inf. St.Line Co.I Cpl.
Thonburgh, B. MO Cav. 2nd Regt.St.Guard Co.B 1st Lt.
Thone, C.J. FL 2nd Cav. Co.H
Thonet, August LA 30th Inf. Co.D
Thoney, J.R. VA 55th Inf. Sgt.
Thonig, Fr. Aug TX Waul's Legion Co.D
Thonlkill, J.H. AR 47th (Crandall's) Cav. Co.E Sgt.
Thonpon, R. TX Cav. Wells' Regt. Co.K
Thonpson, William TX Cav. Wells' Regt. Co.A
Thonson, George W. NC 2nd Arty. (36th St.Troops) Co.I
Thonton, Frank VA 34th Mil. Co.B
Thonton, M.C. MS 2nd Cav. Co.B
Thonton, R.A. GA 11th Inf.
Thonton, W.E. AR 1st Field Btty.
Thoompson, Bland NC 7th Inf. Co.A
Thoomy, John T. MS 3rd Cav.Res. Co.A
Thopson, G.W. TX 2nd Inf. Co.H
Thopson, P.C. TN 16th (Logwood's) Cav. Co.I
Thoranton, W.T. AL 59th Inf. Co.F
Thorburn, C.E. VA 14th Cav. Col.
Thorburn, C.E. Gen. & Staff Lt.Col.
Thorburn, Charles E. VA 50th Inf. Maj.
Thorburn, H.C. Gen. & Staff, QM Dept. Capt., AQM
Thorburn, Henry C. VA Lt.Arty. Pollock's Co. 2nd Lt.
Thorburn, Samuel H. VA Lt.Arty. Pollock's Co.
Thordalsen, Thomas LA 8th Inf. Co.D
Thore, John H. TN 1st (Turney's) Inf. Co.G 1st Sgt.
Thorgmorton, George NC 3rd Arty. (40th St.Troops) Co.I
Thorhill, Gabriel A. LA 31st Inf. Co.B
Thorington, David C. NC 15th Inf. Co.E
Thorington, J. AL 1st Bn. Hilliard's Legion Vol. Lt.Col.
Thorington, Jack AL 7th Cav. Co.F
Thorington, James AL 33rd Inf. Co.B
Thorington, J.J. AL 53rd (Part.Rangers) Co.C
Thorington, L.H. MS 14th Inf. Co.H
Thorington, R.D. AL 53rd (Part.Rangers) AADC
Thorington, W.H. AL 60th Inf. Co.B
Thorington, W.H. AL 3rd Bn. Hilliard's Legion Vol. Co.C
Thorington, W.S. AL 1st Bn.Cadets 1st Lt.,Adj.
Thoris, W. GA 29th Inf. Co.I
Thormahlen, John TX 17th Inf. Co.H Ch.Music.
Thormahlen, R. LA Mil. 3rd Regt. 1st Brig. 1st Div. Co.K
Thormahler, J. TX Inf. 4th Bn. (Oswald's) Co.A Drum.
Thorn, --- TX Cav. 4th Regt.St.Troops Co.G
Thorn, --- TX Cav. Mann's Regt. Co.C
Thorn, A. AR 20th Inf. Co.I
Thorn, A.G. AR 30th Inf. Co.M,B
Thorn, A.J. GA 1st Inf. (St.Guards) Co.E
Thorn, Albert G. VA 19th Cav. Co.C
Thorn, Allen C. VA Arty. Curtis' Co. 1st Lt.
Thorn, A.N. AL 9th Inf. Co.C
Thorn, A.N. VA 25th Cav. Co.E
Thorn, B.A. AL Lt.Arty. Kolb's Btty.
Thorn, Benjamin F. LA 8th Inf. Co.E
Thorn, Benjamin F. TX 2nd Cav. Co.A
Thorn, Benjamin F. VA 14th Cav. Crawford's Co.
Thorn, Benjamin F. VA 17th Cav. Co.F
Thorn, C. Gillum's Regt. Co.F Sgt.
Thorn, Charles LA Mil.Conf.Guards Regt. Co.G
Thorn, Charles TX 17th Cav. Co.A
Thorn, Charles VA 49th Inf. Co.E
Thorn, Charles A. TX 12th Inf. Co.G
Thorn, Charles A. TX Inf.Riflemen Arnold's Co.
Thorn, Clarence MS 12th Cav. Co.E
Thorn, Clarence MS 15th Inf. Co.C
Thorn, Clarence MS 29th Inf. Co.K
Thorn, David H. TX 22nd Cav. Co.F
Thorn, Dempsey NC 17th Inf. (2nd Org.) Co.I
Thorn, D.W. VA 6th Cav. Co.A
Thorn, E. TN 9th Inf. Co.I
Thorn, Ed. C. TN 3rd (Clack's) Inf. Co.F
Thorn, Ed T. TX 8th Cav. Co.I
Thorn, Edward AL 17th Inf. Co.F
Thorn, Edward GA Inf. 8th Bn. Co.B
Thorn, Enoch B. GA 25th Inf. Co.K Cpl.
Thorn, F. SC 18th Inf. Co.H
Thorn, George P. NC 2nd Arty. (36th St.Troops) Co.C
Thorn, George W.R. GA Inf. 8th Bn. Co.B
Thorn, Henry LA 21st (Patton's) Inf. Co.F
Thorn, Henry SC 4th St.Troops Co.C
Thorn, Henry C. TN 1st Cav. Co.E
Thorn, Hezekiah MS 34th Inf. Co.B
Thorn, H.G.B. GA 3rd Bn.S.S. Co.A Sgt.
Thorn, H.G.B. GA 18th Inf. Co.B
Thorn, H.J. AR 30th Inf. Co.M,B
Thorn, J. LA Mil.Bn. British Fusileers Co.A Cpl.
Thorn, Jackson GA Inf. 8th Bn. Co.B
Thorn, James GA 12th (Wright's) Cav. (St.Guards) Brannen's Co.
Thorn, James TX 7th Inf. Co.F
Thorn, James VA Cav. 46th Bn. Co.D
Thorn, James A. NC 54th Inf. Co.I 1st Lt.
Thorn, James H. MS 6th Inf. Co.D
Thorn, James M. AL 16th Inf. Co.E
Thorn, James M. NC 5th Cav. (63rd St.Troops) Co.I 2nd Lt.
Thorn, James P. VA Inf. 7th Bn.Loc.Def. Co.A 1st Sgt.
Thorn, James P. VA 86th Mil. Co.F,A Sgt.
Thorn, Jasper 1st Cherokee Mtd.Vol. 2nd Co.I
Thorn, J.C. MS 12th Cav. Co.E
Thorn, J.C. SC 5th Inf. 2nd Co.I
Thorn, J. Chinton SC 9th Inf. Co.I
Thorn, J.D. VA Inf. 7th Bn.Loc.Def. Co.A
Thorn, J.E. GA 17th Inf. Co.C
Thorn, Jeramiah D. VA Inf. 7th Bn.Loc.Def. Co.A
Thorn, Jesse M. LA 8th Inf. Co.E
Thorn, J.F. GA 18th Inf. Co.B
Thorn, J.J. NC 8th Sr.Res. Co.C
Thorn, J.M. AL 61st Inf. Co.F
Thorn, J.N. AR Cav. McGehee's Regt. Co.C
Thorn, J.N. AR 30th Inf. Co.M,B
Thorn, Job VA Lt.Arty. Donald's Co.
Thorn, Joel J. NC 27th Inf. Co.B Sgt.
Thorn, John AL Cav. Moreland's Regt. Co.H
Thorn, John AL 57th Inf. Co.B Cpl.
Thorn, John GA 1st Inf. (St.Guards) Co.E
Thorn, John LA Washington Arty.Bn. Co.6 Can.
Thorn, John TN 1st Hvy.Arty. Co.B
Thorn, John TX 37th Cav. Co.C
Thorn, John C. MS 2nd Inf. Co.C
Thorn, John D. NC Vol. Lawrence's Co.
Thorn, John D. 7th Conf.Cav. Co.H
Thorn, John E. GA Arty. Baker's Co. Jr.2nd Lt.
Thorn, John T. MS 2nd Inf. Co.B
Thorn, Joshua MS Cav. Jeff Davis Legion Co.A 2nd Lt.
Thorn, Josiah MO Inf. 8th Bn. Co.B
Thorn, Josiah NC 55th Inf. Co.A
Thorn, J.R. SC Inf. 7th Bn. (Enfield Rifles) Co.D,G
Thorn, J.W. TN 19th (Biffle's) Cav. Co.I
Thorn, L. MS Cav. Yerger's Regt. Co.A
Thorn, L.B. TN 51st (Cons.) Inf. Co.F
Thorn, Lorain VA 36th Inf. 3rd Co.I
Thorn, Lunsford VA 36th Inf. 2nd Co.E Cpl.
Thorn, M.A. VA Horse Arty. Jackson's Co.
Thorn, M.A. VA 51st Inf. Co.F 1st Sgt.
Thorn, Martin R. NC 2nd Inf. Co.B
Thorn, N. MS Inf. 1st Bn.St.Troops (30 days '64) Co.A
Thorn, N.H. MS 6th Inf. Co.D
Thorn, Reuben T. Page's Staff Capt.,AIG
Thorn, Reubin AL 11th Inf. Co.H 2nd Lt.
Thorn, R.M. NC 16th Inf. Co.D
Thorn, Robert GA 1st Inf. (St.Guards) Co.E
Thorn, Robert J. AL 16th Inf. Co.E
Thorn, Samuel TN 54th Inf. Co.C
Thorn, Samuel B. TX 22nd Inf. Co.B
Thorn, S.E. Gen. & Staff Capt.,AAG
Thorn, Stephen Moore LA 8th Inf. Co.E
Thorn, T. Gen. & Staff Hosp.Stew.
Thorn, T.C.H. MS Inf. 3rd Bn. Co.I
Thorn, Thomas LA 7th Inf. Co.E Cpl.
Thorn, Thomas NC 67th Inf. Cpl.
Thorn, Thomas SC 5th Bn.Res. Co.D
Thorn, Thomas A. NC 37th Inf.
Thorn, Thomas J. NC 16th Inf. Co.D 2nd Lt.
Thorn, Thomas J. TX Cav. 6th Bn. Co.D 1st Lt.
Thorn, Thomas S. AR 15th (Josey's) Inf. Co.C
Thorn, T.I. MO Cav. Snider's Bn. Co.B Sgt.
Thorn, T.J. MS 1st (Patton's) Inf. Co.G
Thorn, T.J. MO St.Guard
Thorn, T.J. 7th Conf.Cav. Co.M
Thorn, T.S. SC Inf. 7th Bn. (Enfield Rifles) Co.F
Thorn, T.T. AR 36th Inf. Co.I
Thorn, W.A. Gen. & Staff Surg.

Thorn, W.B. AR 10th Inf. Co.I
Thorn, W.H. AL 9th Inf. Co.C
Thorn, W.H. KY 7th Mtd.Inf. Co.I
Thorn, William AL Cav. Moreland's Regt. Co.F Cpl.
Thorn, William LA Miles' Legion Co.A
Thorn, William MO 7th Cav. Co.K
Thorn, William MO 4th Inf. Co.H
Thorn, William MO Inf. 8th Bn. Co.B
Thorn, William MO Mtd.Inf. Boone's Regt.
Thorn, William VA Inf. 7th Bn.Loc.Def. Co.A
Thorn, William VA 146th Mil. Co.H
Thorn, William A. NC 30th Inf. Co.I
Thorn, William A. TX 16th Cav. Co.E
Thorn, William A. VA 39th Inf. Surg.
Thorn, William A. Gen. & Staff Surg.
Thorn, William F. NC 16th Inf. Co.D 2nd Lt.
Thorn, William H. AL 27th Inf. Co.B
Thorn, William H. AR Inf. Cocke's Regt. Co.K 1st Sgt.
Thorn, William H. TX 36th Cav. Co.B
Thorn, William M. NC Vol. Lawrence's Co.
Thorn, William M. VA Inf. 7th Bn.Loc.Def. Co.A
Thorn, William M. 7th Conf.Cav. Co.H
Thorn, William S. VA 4th Inf. Co.A
Thorn, William S. VA 57th Inf. Co.H
Thorn, William T. SC 13th Inf. Co.E 1st Lt.
Thorn, William T. SC Cav.Bn. Holcombe Legion Co.B 3rd Lt.
Thorn, William W. VA 4th Cav. Co.H
Thorn, W.M.T. AR 5th Inf. Co.G
Thorn, W.R. SC 6th Inf. 1st Co.H, 2nd Co.B
Thorn, W.T. AR 8th Inf. New Co.E
Thorn, W.T. AR 13th Inf. Co.B Cpl.
Thorn, W.T. MO 8th Cav. Co.G
Thorn, W.T. SC 7th Cav. Co.D 2nd Lt.
Thorn, W.T. TN Inf. 4th Cons.Regt. Co.B
Thorn, W.T. TN 45th Inf. Co.E Sgt.
Thorn, W.W. MS 28th Cav. Co.D
Thornal, John H. AL 46th Inf. Co.B
Thornal, S.A. TX 14th Inf. Co.C
Thornall, A.A. FL 1st Inf. Old Co.C,H
Thornall, Asbury A. FL 7th Inf. Co.I
Thornall, W.R. AL 23rd Inf. Co.F
Thornback, S.H.F. MO 2nd & 6th Cons.Inf. Co.I 2nd Lt.
Thornberg, Joseph VA 12th Cav. Co.F
Thornberry, Benjamin L. TN 1st (Turney's) Inf. Co.B
Thornberry, George W. KY 4th Mtd.Inf. Co.E,D
Thornberry, James W. GA Hvy.Arty. 22nd Bn.
Thornberry, Jefferson AR 3rd Inf. Co.H
Thornberry, J.M. TX Inf. Chambers' Bn.Res.Corps Co.C
Thornberry, John F. VA 49th Inf. Co.A
Thornberry, John W. MS 31st Inf. Co.F Music.
Thornberry, Joseph 1st Conf.Eng.Troops Co.A
Thornberry, J.W. GA Cav. 15th Bn. (St.Guards) Jones' Co.
Thornberry, William VA Hvy.Arty. Wilkinson's Co.
Thornberry, William L. MO 16th Cav. Co.C,B
Thornberry, William T. KY 1st Inf. Co.K
Thornberry, W.T. TX 17th Inf. Co.K Chap.
Thornbery, W.J. GA Siege Arty. 28th Bn. Co.K
Thornbrough, Allen W. GA Inf. 8th Bn. Co.C Sgt.Maj.
Thornbrough, Edward SC Lt.Arty. 3rd (Palmetto) Bn. Co.C
Thornbrough, J.B. GA 1st Inf. (St.Guards) Co.A Capt.
Thornbrough, J.B. GA Inf. 8th Bn. Co.C Capt.
Thornbrough, J.H. GA Inf. 8th Bn. Co.C Sgt.
Thornbrough, R.W. AR 10th Inf. Co.A Cpl.
Thornbrough, Samuel B. AR 31st Inf. Co.D Hosp.Stew.
Thornbrough, S.B. AR 47th (Crandall's) Cav. Co.I Hosp.Stew.
Thornburg, A. AL 48th Inf. Co.A
Thornburg, A.L. GA 34th Inf. Co.D
Thornburg, A.M. NC 20th Inf. Co.I
Thornburg, Amos 3rd Conf.Cav. Co.E Maj.
Thornburg, Amos Gen. & Staff A.Surg.
Thornburg, A.W. AL 48th Inf. Co.E
Thornburg, Collins N. VA 27th Inf. 1st Co.H 2nd Lt.
Thornburg, Daniel NC 4th Sr.Res. Co.E
Thornburg, Daniel E. TN Inf. 2nd Cons.Regt. Co.H
Thornburg, Daniel E. TN 29th Inf. Co.G
Thornburg, Ely MO Cav. Ford's Bn. Co.E Sgt.
Thornburg, Felix H. TX 5th Cav. Co.H
Thornburg, Fields B. NC 13th Inf. Co.B
Thornburg, George J. NC 13th Inf. Co.B
Thornburg, Henry M. NC 13th Inf. Co.B
Thornburg, I.W. MO 8th Cav. Co.G
Thornburg, Jacob A. VA 21st Cav. Co.B
Thornburg, Jacob L. NC 28th Inf. Co.B
Thornburg, James W. MO 7th Cav. Co.I
Thornburg, J.M. MO Lt.Arty. Farris' Btty. (Clark Arty.)
Thornburg, J.N. LA 25th Inf. Co.F Cpl.
Thornburg, J.N. LA Inf. Pelican Regt. Co.C Cpl.
Thornburg, John AL 4th (Russell's) Cav. Co.I
Thornburg, John C. NC 22nd Inf. Co.L
Thornburg, John L. NC 43rd Inf. Co.B
Thornburg, John S. VA 8th Cav. Co.E
Thornburg, John S. VA 10th Cav. 1st Lt.
Thornburg, Joseph AR 13th Inf. Co.E
Thornburg, Joseph AR Mil. Desha Cty.Bn.
Thornburg, Joseph KY 7th Mtd.Inf. 1st Co.K
Thornburg, J.P. MS 12th Cav. Co.L
Thornburg, J.R. TN Cav. 12th Bn. (Day's) Co.D
Thornburg, J.S. TX 2nd Inf. Co.C
Thornburg, J.W. SC 2nd Cav. Co.K
Thornburg, L.A. NC 5th Inf. Co.E
Thornburg, Mark M. TN 14th Inf. Co.K
Thornburg, Martin S. NC 3rd Inf. Co.H
Thornburg, Millard VA 27th Inf. 1st Co.H
Thornburg, Newton TN 61st Mtd.Inf. Co.G Cpl.
Thornburg, P.H. TN Cav. 12th Bn. (Day's) Co.D Capt.
Thornburg, S. VA 67th Mil. Co.C
Thornburg, S. Lewis NC 13th Inf. Co.B
Thornburg, S.T. VA 5th Inf. Co.I
Thornburg, W.A. TN 61st Mtd.Inf. Co.C
Thornburg, Wesley TN 1st (Carter's) Cav. Co.M
Thornburg, Wesley P. TN Vol. McLin's Co.
Thornburg, William NC 4th Sr.Res. Co.E
Thornburg, William J. VA 45th Inf. Co.B
Thornburg, William L. NC 38th Inf. Co.H
Thornburgh, Eli AR 1st Mtd.Rifles Co.E Cpl.
Thornburgh, Ellis GA 34th Inf. Co.D
Thornburgh, J.G. AR 38th Inf. Co.C
Thornburgh, Patrick H. TN 39th Mtd.Inf. Co.I 1st Lt.
Thornburgh, Thomas J. AL 16th Inf. Co.B Cpl.
Thornburgh, W.A. MO Lt.Arty. Farris' Btty. (Clark Arty.)
Thornburn, Joseph MO 6th Regt.St.Guards
Thornbury, Chas. W. AL 48th Inf. Co.E
Thornbury, Mark 1st Creek Mtd.Vol. Co.B
Thornbury, R.N. 3rd Conf.Cav. Co.I 1st Sgt.
Thornbury, Robert TN 2nd (Walker's) Inf. Co.C
Thornby, Thomas H. VA 17th Cav. Co.A
Thorndyke, --- MO 1st Inf. 2nd Co.A
Thorne, A.C. MS 1st (King's) Inf. (St.Troops) Co.K
Thorne, Andrew KY 4th Cav. Co.H
Thorne, D. VA Cav. Mosby's Regt. (Part. Rangers) Co.E
Thorne, Edward A. NC 24th Inf. Co.D 2nd Lt.
Thorne, Eli MO 4th Cav. Co.H
Thorne, Ferdinand MO Cav. Snider's Bn. Co.A
Thorne, George A. VA 22nd Inf. Co.D Sgt.
Thorne, Geo. L. Gen. & Staff Capt.,AQM
Thorne, Henry VA 5th Inf. Co.L
Thorne, Hezekiah G.B. GA Inf. 3rd Bn. Co.A
Thorne, J. NC 66th Inf. Co.K
Thorne, James TN 23rd Inf. Co.G
Thorne, James R. VA Inf. 23rd Bn. Co.B,G
Thorne, J.D. NC Cav. 16th Bn. Co.F
Thorne, Jesse A.B. NC 17th Inf. (2nd Org.) Co.I 2nd Lt.
Thorne, J.F. NC 49th Inf. Co.H
Thorne, J.H.H. NC 3rd Jr.Res. Co.F
Thorne, John AL 22nd Inf. Co.I
Thorne, John H.H. NC 8th Bn.Jr.Res. Co.A
Thorne, John W. MS Inf. 2nd St.Troops Co.D
Thorne, Josiah MO 9th Inf. Co.F
Thorne, Josiah MO Mtd.Inf. Boone's Regt. Co.A
Thorne, Josiah SC 9th Inf. Co.G
Thorne, J.T. MS 39th Inf. Co.D 2nd Lt.
Thorne, J.W. Conf.Cav. Baxter's Bn. Co.C
Thorne, Raymond C. NC 4th Cav. (59th St.Troops) Co.H
Thorne, Stephen GA 25th Inf. Co.K
Thorne, Thomas LA Conscr.
Thorne, W.B. NC 2nd Jr.Res. Co.H
Thorne, William MO 9th Inf. Co.F
Thorne, William TX 14th Inf. Co.E
Thorne, William VA Lt.Arty. 12th Bn. Co.B
Thorne, William T. VA 3rd Inf. Co.C
Thorne, W.M. NC Cav. 16th Bn. Co.F
Thorne, W.T. MS 23rd Inf. Co.A
Thorneburg, Leonard L. NC 46th Inf. Co.K
Thornehill, John A. MO Cav. Schnabel's Bn. Co.E
Thornell, A.G. MS 9th Inf. Co.D
Thornell, Amos MS 11th Inf. Co.D
Thornell, Amos TX 20th Inf. Co.E
Thornell, A.R. MS 44th Inf. Co.F
Thornell, Benjamin AL 36th Inf. Co.A
Thornell, B.F. MS 12th Cav. Co.A,H
Thornell, C.M. MS 12th Cav. Co.A,H
Thornell, Henry G. NC 2nd Cav. (19th St.Troops) Co.E
Thornell, Martin V. NC 2nd Inf. Co.B

Thornell, Thomas MS 40th Inf. Co.I Cpl.
Thornell, W.H. NC Cav. (Loc.Def.) Howard's Co.
Thornell, William H. NC 3rd Cav. (41st St.Troops) Co.H
Thornell, William H. NC 2nd Arty. (36th St.Troops) Co.B
Thornell, William R. AL 46th Inf. Co.B
Thornesberry, --- AR 30th Inf. Co.C
Thornewell, Gillespie SC 2nd Cav. Co.H
Thorney, Barnet TN Conscr. (Cp. of Instr.)
Thornhill, A. MS 3rd (St.Troops) Cav. Co.H Sgt.
Thornhill, Alfred VA 7th Inf. Co.G
Thornhill, Armstead VA 7th Inf. Co.G
Thornhill, B.B. SC 1st Bn.S.S. Co.B
Thornhill, B.B. SC Inf. 6th Bn. Co.B
Thornhill, B.B. SC 27th Inf. Co.F
Thornhill, B.B. SC Manigault's Bn.Vol. Co.D
Thornhill, C. VA 18th Cav. Co.A
Thornhill, Champ VA 62nd Mtd.Inf. 2nd Co.H
Thornhill, Champ C. VA 7th Inf. Co.G
Thornhill, Charles VA 7th Inf. Co.G
Thornhill, D.G. VA 82nd Mil. Co.B
Thornhill, E.A. GA 16th Inf. Co.I
Thornhill, Eastham VA 7th Inf. Co.G
Thornhill, Edward C. AL Arty. 1st Bn. Co.E Cpl.
Thornhill, E.E. SC 21st Inf. Co.K
Thornhill, E.W. MS 38th Cav. Co.E
Thornhill, F. LA 21st (Kennedy's) Inf. Co.B
Thornhill, Franklin TX 16th Cav. Co.C Sgt.
Thornhill, George MS 3rd (St.Troops) Cav. Co.H
Thornhill, George VA 4th Cav. Co.C
Thornhill, George M. Conf.Cav. Wood's Regt. 2nd Co.D
Thornhill, George W. VA 11th Inf. Co.B Surg.
Thornhill, G.W. Gen. & Staff Surg.
Thornhill, H. LA Cav. Greenleaf's Co. (Orleans Lt.Horse) Sgt.
Thornhill, H. MS 39th Inf. Co.G
Thornhill, Hamilton MO Inf. Perkins' Bn. Co.E
Thornhill, Harvey J. VA 58th Inf. Co.B
Thornhill, H.C. MS 38th Cav. Co.F
Thornhill, H.E. MS Cav. 1st Bn. (McNair's) St.Troops Co.C
Thornhill, Henry Sig.Corps,CSA
Thornhill, Irwin E. MS 16th Inf. Co.E
Thornhill, James VA 4th Cav. Co.C
Thornhill, James VA 34th Mil. Co.D
Thornhill, James M. MS 7th Inf. Co.E
Thornhill, James R. AL 4th Cav. Co.G
Thornhill, James R. AL 6th Inf. Co.I
Thornhill, James W. GA Inf. 10th Bn. Co.B Cpl.
Thornhill, J.B. AL 23rd Inf. Co.C
Thornhill, J.C. MS 4th Cav. Co.I
Thornhill, J.C. MS 38th Cav. Co.F
Thornhill, Jesse B. AL 6th Inf. Co.I
Thornhill, Jesse T. VA 11th Inf. Co.A
Thornhill, J.H. VA 4th Cav. Co.C
Thornhill, J.J. MS 22nd Inf. Co.E Sgt.
Thornhill, J.L.A. VA Inf. 26th Bn. Co.F
Thornhill, J. Martin MS 7th Inf. Co.H
Thornhill, J. Newton MS 7th Inf. Co.H
Thornhill, John AL 7th Cav. Co.H,D Surg.
Thornhill, John AL 6th Inf. Co.I
Thornhill, John MS 22nd Inf. Co.C
Thornhill, John SC 21st Inf. Co.K
Thornhill, John A. VA 23rd Cav. Co.D Sgt.
Thornhill, John F. AL 3rd Inf. Co.I
Thornhill, John J. MS 33rd Inf. Co.C Sgt.
Thornhill, John O. VA 2nd Cav. Co.B 1st Lt.
Thornhill, Joseph VA 12th Cav. Co.G
Thornhill, Joseph M. MS 7th Inf. Co.H Asst.Surg.
Thornhill, Joshua T. VA 8th Cav. Co.B Cpl.
Thornhill, J.P. TN 21st (Carter's) Cav. Co.G
Thornhill, J.T. AR Cav. Gordon's Regt. Co.F
Thornhill, J.W. MS 38th Cav. Co.F Sgt.
Thornhill, J.W. SC Lt.Arty. 3rd (Palmetto) Bn. Co.C
Thornhill, J.W. SC 9th Inf. Co.C
Thornhill, J.W. SC Palmetto S.S. Co.E
Thornhill, L.C. MS Cav. Garland's Bn. Co.A
Thornhill, L.C. 14th Conf.Cav. Co.A
Thornhill, Mallory VA 12th Cav. Co.G
Thornhill, Mallory VA 34th Mil. Co.C
Thornhill, Martin 20th Conf.Cav. Co.B
Thornhill, Middleton MS Cav. 24th Bn. Co.B
Thornhill, Miles MO 12th Inf. Co.F
Thornhill, Peter W. VA Hvy.Arty. 19th Bn. Co.A
Thornhill, Peter W. VA Hvy.Arty. Kyle's Co.
Thornhill, Philetus VA 12th Cav. Co.I
Thornhill, P.W. VA 3rd Res. Co.I
Thornhill, R. SC 26th Inf. Co.H
Thornhill, R.B. MS 38th Cav. Co.I
Thornhill, Robert MO Cav. Schnabel's Bn. Co.E
Thornhill, Robert H. VA Hvy.Arty. 20th Bn. Co.A
Thornhill, Samuel A. VA 2nd Cav. Co.H
Thornhill, T.E. GA 19th Inf. Co.K
Thornhill, Thomas VA 4th Cav. Co.C
Thornhill, Thomas VA 34th Mil. Co.D
Thornhill, W. VA 13th Cav. Co.K
Thornhill, W.A. AL 55th Vol. Co.H
Thornhill, W.A. VA 2nd Cav. Co.H
Thornhill, Wade H. MS 7th Inf. Co.D
Thornhill, W.E. SC 6th Inf. 2nd Co.K
Thornhill, W.E. SC 9th Inf. Co.C
Thornhill, W.E. SC 26th Inf. Co.H
Thornhill, W.H. AL 23rd Inf. Co.C
Thornhill, William AL Lt.Arty. Goldthwaite's Btty. Artif.,Carp.
Thornhill, William A. TN 42nd Inf. 1st Co.F
Thornhill, William A. VA Hvy.Arty. Kyle's Co. 2nd Lt.
Thornhill, William D. VA Hvy.Arty. 20th Bn. Co.D
Thornhill, William D. VA Hvy.Arty. Patteson's Co.
Thornhill, William J. SC 2nd Arty. Co.D
Thornhill, William W. VA 12th Cav. Co.G
Thornhill, Willis MS 2nd (Quinn's St.Troops) Inf. Co.E
Thornhill, Willis 20th Conf.Cav. Co.B
Thornhill, W.J. VA 82nd Mil. Co.B
Thornhill, W.L. TN 23rd Inf. Co.E Ord.Sgt.
Thornhill, W.L. Gen. & Staff Asst.Surg.
Thornhill, Wyatt MS 7th Inf. Co.H Sgt.
Thorniley, Thomas Hesketh VA 8th Cav. 1st Co.D
Thornley, James VA 1st Arty. Co.H
Thornley, James Gen. & Staff,PACS Asst.Surg.
Thornley, James L. MS 11th (Cons.) Cav. Co.K
Thornley, J.F. AL 56th Part.Rangers Co.C
Thornley, J.M. AL 63rd Inf. Co.E
Thornley, John SC 11th Inf. Co.G
Thornley, John L. SC 2nd Inf. Co.B
Thornley, John T. MS 11th (Cons.) Cav. Co.K
Thornley, John T. MS 14th Inf. Co.E Cpl.
Thornley, Joseph MS 6th Cav. Morgan's Co.
Thornley, Joseph R. SC 5th Cav. Co.E
Thornley, J.R. SC Manigault's Bn.Vol. Co.A
Thornley, Lawrence AL 56th Part.Rangers Co.I
Thornley, Nathaniel AL 13th Inf. Co.A
Thornley, Robert AL 37th Inf. Co.D
Thornley, Samuel W. SC 5th Cav. Co.E
Thornley, S.W. SC Manigault's Bn.Vol. Co.A
Thornley, Thomas B. KY 14th Cav.
Thornley, William, Jr. VA 30th Inf. Co.F 2nd Lt.
Thornley, William L. MS 24th Inf. Co.L
Thornly, G.W. MS 29th Inf. Co.H
Thornly, J.L. AL 13th Bn.Part.Rangers Co.C,E
Thornly, Joseph MS 12th Cav. Co.C
Thornly, T.W. GA Conscr.
Thorns, John F. KY Kirkpatrick's Bn. Co.B
Thornsberry, Enoch KY 13th Cav. Co.E
Thornsberry, Jackson 2nd Cherokee Mtd.Vol. Co.A
Thornsberry, J.J. VA 17th Cav. Co.B
Thornsberry, John KY 13th Cav. Co.B
Thornsberry, John W.T. KY 3rd Bn.Mtd.Rifles Co.E
Thornsberry, Martin V. KY 13th Cav. Co.E
Thornsberry, William KY 10th (Diamond's) Cav. Co.A
Thornsberry, William KY 1st Bn.Mtd.Rifles Co.B
Thornsberry, William KY 3rd Bn.Mtd.Rifles Co.E
Thornsburg, Jacob MS Cav. Buck's Co.
Thornsburg, James M. MO 4th Inf. Co.A
Thornsburg, J.D. MS Inf. 1st Bn.St.Troops (30 days '64) Co.B
Thornsburg, John VA 16th Cav. Co.K
Thornsburg, William M. MO 4th Inf. Co.A
Thornsburgh, E.D. KY 4th Cav. Co.I
Thornsbury, Lewis AL 9th Inf. Co.I
Thornsbury, Samuel G. LA 8th Inf. Co.I
Thornsbury, William LA 8th Inf. Co.I
Thornthwaite, Jonathan TX 19th Cav. Co.B
Thorntin, L. AL 30th Inf. Co.H
Thornton (Boy) TX 23rd Cav. Co.A Laundress
Thornton, --- AL 4th (Russell's) Cav. Co.B Lt.
Thornton, --- AR 30th Inf. Co.C
Thornton, --- MS 33rd Inf. Co.E
Thornton, --- VA Inf. 25th Bn. Co.F Cook
Thornton, A. AL 31st Inf. Co.A
Thornton, A. GA 43rd Inf. Co.F
Thornton, A. MS 18th Cav. Co.C
Thornton, A.B. AR 4th Inf. Co.B
Thornton, A.B. AR Inf. Cocke's Regt. Co.I
Thornton, A.B. FL 6th Inf. Co.A
Thornton, A.B. GA Cav. 1st Bn.Res. Stark's Co.
Thornton, A.B. GA 6th Inf. (St.Guards) Co.G
Thornton, A.B. VA 30th Inf. Co.H
Thornton, Abe AL 22nd Inf. Co.A

Thornton, Abner K. VA 57th Inf. Co.B
Thornton, Abram AL 4th Inf. Co.G
Thornton, Absalom VA 52nd Inf. Co.I Cpl.
Thornton, A.D. MS 46th Inf. Co.H
Thornton, Addison H. VA 57th Inf. Co.B Sgt.
Thornton, Adolph LA 16th Inf. Co.G
Thornton, A.H. AL 18th Inf. Co.K
Thornton, A.J. AL 1st Cav. 1st Co.K Lt.
Thornton, A.J. AL 3rd Inf. Co.I
Thornton, A.J. AL 31st Inf. Co.I
Thornton, A.J. AL Rebels
Thornton, A.J. AR 13th Mil. Co.F
Thornton, A.J. MO Lt.Arty. 3rd Field Btty.
Thornton, A.J. TN 10th & 11th (Cons.) Cav. Co.F
Thornton, Albert J. AL 63rd Inf. Co.B 2nd Lt.
Thornton, Alexander TX Cav. 6th Bn. Co.A
Thornton, Alexander B. GA Conscr.
Thornton, Alexander N. GA 39th Inf. Co.C,D Sgt.
Thornton, Alfred LA 1st Hvy.Arty. (Reg.) Co.K
Thornton, Alfred TN Lt.Arty. Huggins' Co.
Thornton, Allen M. AL 7th Inf. Co.C
Thornton, A.N. AL 22nd Inf. Co.A
Thornton, Andrew J. AL 41st Inf. Co.B
Thornton, Andrew J. MO 9th Bn.S.S. Co.F
Thornton, Andrew J. MO Searcy's Bn.S.S.
Thornton, Andrew J. VA 30th Bn.S.S. Co.B
Thornton, Andrew W. TN 32nd Inf. Co.E
Thornton, A.R. AL 1st Cav. 2nd Co.D
Thornton, A.R. AL Inf. 1st Regt. Co.A
Thornton, A.R. TN Lt.Arty. Morton's Co.
Thornton, Arthur F. AL Lt.Arty. 2nd Bn. Co.F
Thornton, Arthur S. TX 36th Cav. Co.B
Thornton, A.S. AR 30th Inf. Co.F Sgt.
Thornton, A.S. AR Inf. Kuykendall's Co. Sgt.
Thornton, A.S. TX 8th Cav. Co.L Cpl.
Thornton, Asa C. GA 38th Inf. Co.F
Thornton, A.T. TX Inf. 2nd St.Troops Co.F
Thornton, A.T. TX 13th Vol. Co.G
Thornton, A.T. TX 14th Inf. Co.D
Thornton, Atlas M. GA 3rd Inf. Co.K
Thornton, Augustus MS 7th Cav. Co.F Sgt.
Thornton, Augustus S.C. 1st Conf.Inf. 2nd Co.E
Thornton, Austin L. AR 11th Inf. Co.E
Thornton, A.W. AL Mil. 2nd Regt.Vol. Co.E
Thornton, A.Y. GA Inf. 5th Bn. (St.Guards) Co.H
Thornton, A.Y. GA 8th Inf. Co.D
Thornton, A.Y. GA Inf. 25th Bn. (Prov.Guard) Co.D 1st Sgt.
Thornton, B.A. GA Inf. (Muscogee Guards) Thornton's Co. Capt.
Thornton, B.B. AL 3rd Cav.
Thornton, B.C. KY 10th Cav. Sgt.
Thornton, B.C. MS Home Guards Barnes' Co.
Thornton, Benjamin C. GA 3rd Cav. (St.Guards) Co.H
Thornton, Benjamin F. GA 38th Inf. Co.F
Thornton, Benjamin F. GA 45th Inf. Co.D
Thornton, Benjamin F. MS 13th Inf. Co.H
Thornton, Benjamin F. TN 42nd Inf. Co.B
Thornton, Benjamin F. VA 24th Cav. Co.E
Thornton, Benjamin F. VA Cav. 40th Bn. Co.C
Thornton, Benjamin F. VA 109th Mil. 1st Co.A
Thornton, Benjamin L. VA 36th Inf. 2nd Co.B
Thornton, Benjamin W. NC 1st Inf. (6 mo. '61) Co.F
Thornton, Benjamin W. NC 56th Inf. Co.B Jr.2nd Lt.
Thornton, Benjamin W. VA 26th Inf. Co.A
Thornton, Bennett C. GA 55th Inf. Co.G 1st Lt.
Thornton, Beverly A. GA 3rd Cav. Co.B Capt.
Thornton, B.F. LA 2nd Inf. Co.I
Thornton, B.F. MS 44th Inf. Co.F
Thornton, B.F. TN 5th Inf. 2nd Co.H
Thornton, B.F. TX 19th Inf. Co.B
Thornton, B.H. AL 54th Inf. Adj.
Thornton, B.S. GA 3rd Mil. Co.G 1st Lt.
Thornton, B.W. TN 42nd Inf. Co.A
Thornton, B.W. TX Cav. 2nd Regt.St.Troops Co.G
Thornton, B.W. 4th Conf.Inf. Co.G
Thornton, Calvin 2nd Cherokee Mtd.Vol. Co.B
Thornton, Causey L. AL 3rd Inf. Co.D
Thornton, C.C. MS 34th Inf. Co.G
Thornton, C.E. AR 19th (Dockery's) Inf. Cons.Co.E,D, Co.E
Thornton, C.H. GA 3rd Res. Co.G Sgt.
Thornton, C.H. MO Inf. 3rd Regt.St.Guard Surg.
Thornton, Champ B. VA 47th Inf. Co.E Sgt.
Thornton, Charles KY 4th Cav. Co.K
Thornton, Charles MO 1st N.E. Cav. Co.K
Thornton, Charles VA Lt.Arty. Cayce's Co.
Thornton, Charles VA Lt.Arty. Pollock's Co.
Thornton, Charles VA 6th Cav.
Thornton, Charles C. MS 1st Lt.Arty. Co.G Asst.Surg.
Thornton, Chas. C. Gen. & Staff Asst.Surg.
Thornton, Charles F. VA 7th Inf. Co.B
Thornton, Charles H. VA Lt.Arty. E.J. Anderson's Co. 1st Lt.
Thornton, Charles H. VA Cav. 1st Bn. Co.C
Thornton, Chas. H. Gen. & Staff Asst.Comsy.
Thornton, Charles L. KY 5th Mtd.Inf. Co.E
Thornton, Charles P. LA Inf. 1st Sp.Bn. (Rightor's) Co.A
Thornton, Charles R. KY 5th Cav. Co.A
Thornton, Charles R. KY 13th Cav. Co.A
Thornton, Charles S. VA Lt.Arty. Pollock's Co. Cpl.
Thornton, Charles W. AL 31st Inf. Co.C
Thornton, Charles W. KY 2nd Mtd.Inf. Co.B
Thornton, Charles W. MO 1st N.E. Cav. Co.E
Thornton, Charles Whitfield GA 20th Inf. Co.K
Thornton, Christopher L. GA 45th Inf. Co.D Sgt.
Thornton, Cincinnattus F. LA 28th (Gray's) Inf. Co.D
Thornton, C.J. GA 31st Inf. Co.K
Thornton, C.J.H. GA Cav. 29th Bn. Co.E 2nd Lt.
Thornton, C.M. AL Armstead's Cav. Co.H
Thornton, Cornelius A. GA 2nd Cav. (St.Guards) Co.E
Thornton, C.P. VA Inf. 25th Bn. Co.D Sgt.
Thornton, C.R. GA 31st Inf. Co.I
Thornton, C.W. AR Inf. Cocke's Regt. Co.I
Thornton, D. GA 36th (Villepigue's) Inf. Co.F
Thornton, D. MS 46th Inf. Co.G
Thornton, D. 1st Conf.Inf. 1st Co.F
Thornton, D.A. AR 37th Inf. Co.I
Thornton, Daniel MS 46th Inf. Co.G
Thornton, Daniel B. MO Searcy's Bn.S.S.
Thornton, Daniel R. TX 15th Cav. Co.D Sgt.
Thornton, Darovontas D. Conf.Cav. Clarkson's Bn. Ind.Rangers Co.H
Thornton, David GA Lt.Arty. Pritchard's Co. (Washington Arty.)
Thornton, David SC 1st Arty. Co.B
Thornton, David F. AL 43rd Inf. Co.H
Thornton, David L. KY 5th Cav. Co.A
Thornton, David M. TN 42nd Inf. Co.B Sgt.
Thornton, David T. MS 2nd Part.Rangers Co.F
Thornton, David W. VA 41st Inf. 1st Co.G Sgt.
Thornton, David W. VA 61st Inf. Co.I Sgt.
Thornton, Davis GA 4th (Clinch's) Cav. Co.A,K
Thornton, D.B. AL 8th Inf. Co.F 2nd Lt.
Thornton, D.F. MS 10th Inf. New Co.I
Thornton, D.F. VA 3rd Res. Co.B 1st Sgt.
Thornton, D.H. LA 13th Bn. (Part.Rangers) Co.A 1st Lt.
Thornton, D.M.F. VA 3rd Inf.Loc.Def. Co.F
Thornton, Dock MS 8th Cav. Co.F
Thornton, Dozier AL 15th Inf. Co.D 1st Lt.
Thornton, D.T. MS 2nd Inf. (A. of 10,000) Co.G
Thornton, D.W. AL Res. J.G. Rankin's Co.
Thornton, E. GA Lt.Arty. Pritchard's Co. (Washington Arty.)
Thornton, Earnest M. MD Arty. 3rd Btty.
Thornton, E.B. AL 5th Inf. New Co.E
Thornton, E.B. LA Inf.Crescent Regt. Co.K
Thornton, E.B. MS 5th Cav. Co.K
Thornton, E.C. MS 37th Inf. Co.H
Thornton, E.C. TN 38th Inf. Co.C
Thornton, Edmund GA Lt.Arty. Croft's Btty. (Columbus Arty.) Cpl.
Thornton, Edward AL 19th Inf. Co.D Capt.
Thornton, Edward Q. AL Inf. 1st Regt. Co.B
Thornton, Edward Q. AL 39th Inf. Co.K 1st Lt.
Thornton, Edw. Q. Gen. & Staff 1st Lt.,ADC
Thornton, Edward S. MO 2nd Inf. Co.H Sgt.
Thornton, Edward W. TX 34th Cav. Co.E Principal Music.
Thornton, Edwin J. MS 33rd Inf. Co.F
Thornton, Edwin R. GA 56th Inf. Co.A Sgt.
Thornton, E.H. GA Arty. St.Troops Pruden's Btty.
Thornton, E.H. MS 38th Cav. Co.H
Thornton, E.H. MS 35th Inf. Co.G
Thornton, E.H. MS 44th Inf. Co.F
Thornton, E.H. MS 48th Inf. Co.B
Thornton, Elijah C. MS 20th Inf. Co.I
Thornton, Elijah F. AR 33rd Inf. Co.E
Thornton, Eli S. AL 24th Inf. Co.E
Thornton, Elisha GA 1st Inf. Co.H,F
Thornton, Elisha GA 47th Inf. Co.H
Thornton, Elisha GA 48th Inf. Co.H
Thornton, Elisha H. MS Inf. 2nd Bn. Co.B
Thornton, Emmett GA 55th Inf. Co.F
Thornton, Enoch H.C. GA 20th Inf. Co.K
Thornton, E.R. GA 39th Inf. Sgt.Maj.
Thornton, Erastus T. VA 5th Cav. (12 mo. '61-2) Co.C Sgt.
Thornton, Erastus T. VA 13th Cav. Co.H
Thornton, Ethard NC 1st Arty. (10th St.Troops) Co.D
Thornton, E.V.F. AL 11th Inf. Co.I

Thornton, E.W. GA 48th Inf. Co.K
Thornton, E.W. MS Inf. 1st Bn.St.Troops (30 days '64) Co.E
Thornton, F. MS 2nd Cav.Res. Co.F
Thornton, F.C. VA 1st (Farinholt's) Res. Co.B
Thornton, F.D. TX 21st Cav. Co.A Cpl.
Thornton, Felix B. GA 10th Inf. Co.I
Thornton, Felix F. VA 3rd Cav. Co.H
Thornton, Felix F. VA 38th Inf. Co.F Sgt.
Thornton, Felix R. NC 8th Inf. Co.I
Thornton, F.H. VA 4th Cav. Co.K Cpl.
Thornton, Fitzhugh C. VA 30th Inf. Co.F
Thornton, Flavius J. MS 11th Inf. Co.C
Thornton, Fleming P. GA 3rd Cav. (St.Guards) Co.H Cpl.
Thornton, F.M. GA 5th Res. Co.C
Thornton, F.M. MO Inf. 4th Regt.St.Guard Co.B 3rd Lt.
Thornton, F.M. TN 8th Inf. Co.E
Thornton, F.M. TX 10th Cav. Co.G
Thornton, F.N. TX 22nd Inf. Co.F
Thornton, Francis VA 36th Inf. 2nd Co.E
Thornton, Francis VA 36th Inf. Co.F Capt.
Thornton, Francis Gen. & Staff Surg.
Thornton, Francis A. MD Weston's Bn. Co.A
Thornton, Francis C. VA 21st Mil. Co.D Sgt.
Thornton, Francis C. VA 34th Inf. Co.K
Thornton, Francis D. AR 23rd Inf. Co.E 2nd Lt.
Thornton, Francis M. AR 1st (Crawford's) Cav. Co.H
Thornton, Frank MS St.Cav. 2nd Bn. (Harris') Co.A
Thornton, Frank VA Horse Arty. D. Shanks' Co.
Thornton, Frank A. MD 1st Inf. Co.C
Thornton, Frederick R. LA 28th (Gray's) Inf. Co.E
Thornton, F.W. MS 18th Cav. Co.A,F
Thornton, F.W. MS 1st Bn.S.S. Co.A
Thornton, F.W. MS 25th Inf. Co.I
Thornton, G. AL 33rd Cav. Co.K
Thornton, G.A. MS Inf. 1st Bn.St.Troops (12 mo. '62-3) Co.A Sgt.
Thornton, G.B. MS 8th Cav. Co.D
Thornton, G.B. TN Hvy.Arty. Johnston's Co.
Thornton, G.B. Walthall's Div. Maj.,Ch.Surg.
Thornton, General Jesse AL 1st Regt.Conscr. Co.E
Thornton, George MS 16th Inf. Co.K
Thornton, George SC 1st Arty. Co.F
Thornton, George TN 5th Inf. 2nd Co.H Cpl.
Thornton, George A. MS 2nd Cav. Co.K
Thornton, Geo. A. Gen. & Staff Capt.,AAA, Insp.Gen.
Thornton, George D. VA 51st Inf. Co.G
Thornton, George E. TX 20th Inf. Co.A
Thornton, George F. AL 53rd (Part.Rangers) Asst.Surg.
Thornton, Geo. F. Gen. & Staff Asst.Surg.
Thornton, George H. GA Cobb's Legion Co.B
Thornton, George M. NC Hvy.Arty. 1st Bn. Co.A
Thornton, Geo. P. Gen. & Staff Asst.Surg.
Thornton, George W. AL 5th Inf. New Co.E
Thornton, George W. AL 13th Inf. Co.I
Thornton, George W. AL 41st Inf. Co.B
Thornton, George W. AL Cp.Talladega Conscr.
Thornton, Geo. W. AL Cp. of Instr. Talladega Co.B
Thornton, Geo. W. GA Mil. 7th Regt. Co.G
Thornton, George W. GA 44th Inf. Co.G
Thornton, George W. GA 45th Inf. Co.D
Thornton, George W. VA 36th Inf. Co.F 2nd Lt.
Thornton, George Washington AL 49th Inf. Co.C Sgt.
Thornton, G.G. AL 45th Inf. Co.C
Thornton, G.J. AL 24th Inf. Co.F
Thornton, G.P. LA 2nd Inf. Co.I
Thornton, Green MS Inf. 3rd Bn. Co.D
Thornton, Green B. AL 6th Inf. Co.L
Thornton, G.T. Gen. & Staff Surg.
Thornton, Gus B. TN Arty.Corps Asst.Surg.
Thornton, G.W. AL 4th Inf. Co.A
Thornton, G.W. AL Mil. 4th Vol. Co.F
Thornton, G.W. AL 40th Inf. Co.K
Thornton, G.W. AL Cp. of Instr. Talladega Co.B
Thornton, G.W. GA 7th Cav. Co.G
Thornton, G.W. GA Cav. 24th Bn. Co.A
Thornton, G.W. GA 3rd Res. Co.G 1st Lt.
Thornton, G.W. MS Cav. Abbott's Co.
Thornton, G.W. MS Inf. 3rd Bn. (St.Troops) Co.F
Thornton, G.W. TN 51st (Cons.) Inf. Co.A
Thornton, G.W. TN 52nd Inf. Co.A
Thornton, G.W.G. GA 55th Inf. Co.I Cpl.
Thornton, H. GA Inf. 1st City Bn. (Columbus) Co.A
Thornton, H.A. AL 41st Inf. Co.B
Thornton, H.A. MS 28th Cav. Co.G
Thornton, Hampton C. GA 4th Bn.S.S. Co.C
Thornton, Harry I. AL 56th Part.Rangers Co.B
Thornton, Harry J. AL 58th Inf. Maj.
Thornton, Haywood T. GA 2nd Cav. Co.F
Thornton, H.C. AL Cav. 4th Bn. (Love's) Co.C
Thornton, H.C. AL 18th Inf. Co.E
Thornton, H.C. TN 2nd (Robison's) Inf. Co.E
Thornton, H.C. TN 3rd (Forrest's) Cav. Co.E
Thornton, H.C. TX 12th Inf. Co.F
Thornton, H.E. MS 2nd Part.Rangers Co.K
Thornton, H.E. MS 5th Cav. Co.H
Thornton, H.E. MS 18th Cav. Co.K
Thornton, Henry AL 47th Inf. Co.A
Thornton, Henry AL Hardy's Co. (Eufaula Minute Men) Cpl.
Thornton, Henry MS 7th Cav. Co.F
Thornton, Henry TN 5th Inf. 2nd Co.H
Thornton, Henry VA 30th Bn.S.S. Co.B
Thornton, Henry C. MS Cav. Jeff Davis Legion Co.K
Thornton, Henry C. MS 29th Inf. Co.D
Thornton, Henry C. VA 44th Inf. Co.G
Thornton, Henry F. VA 1st Arty. Co.D
Thornton, Henry F. VA Cav. 1st Bn. Co.C
Thornton, Henry F. VA 30th Inf. Co.F
Thornton, Henry H. NC 45th Inf. Co.A
Thornton, Henry J. AL 19th Inf. Co.D 2nd Lt.
Thornton, Henry J. GA 2nd Cav. Co.A
Thornton, Henry J. MS 28th Cav. Co.G
Thornton, Henry M. AL 43rd Inf. Co.H
Thornton, H.F. VA Lt.Arty. Thornton's Co.
Thornton, H.G. VA 6th Cav. Co.F
Thornton, H.H. NC 23rd Inf. Co.F Sgt.
Thornton, H.I. AL Tuscaloosa Cadets
Thornton, H.I. Gen. & Staff 1st Lt.,ADC
Thornton, Hiram H. GA 53rd Inf. Co.C
Thornton, H.J. GA 53rd Inf. Co.H
Thornton, H.J. MS 6th Cav. Co.E
Thornton, H.J. MS 5th Inf. (St.Troops) Co.G
Thornton, H.J. MS 20th Inf. Co.F
Thornton, Horatio M. AL 17th Inf. Co.D
Thornton, Howard G. TX 4th Inf. Co.F
Thornton, Howell J. TN 48th (Voorhies') Inf.
Thornton, I.R. LA 2nd Cav. Co.G
Thornton, Isaac AR 38th Inf. Co.A
Thornton, Isaac LA 27th Inf. Co.C
Thornton, Isaac I. NC 1st Arty. (10th St.Troops) Co.F
Thornton, Isaac L. GA 4th (Clinch's) Cav. Co.K
Thornton, Isaac R. GA 16th Inf. Co.G
Thornton, Isham FL 9th Inf. Co.G,I
Thornton, J. AL 51st (Part.Rangers) Co.E
Thornton, J. GA 13th Inf. Co.D
Thornton, J. GA 54th Inf. Co.K
Thornton, J. KY 1st (Butler's) Cav.
Thornton, J. KY 3rd Bn.Mtd.Rifles Co.C Cpl.
Thornton, J. SC Inf. 7th Bn. (Enfield Rifles) Co.C
Thornton, J. TX 2nd Cav. Co.K
Thornton, J. TX 13th Cav. Co.F
Thornton, J. Conf.Inf. 8th Bn. Co.B
Thornton, J.A. AL 3rd Inf.
Thornton, J.A. AL 8th Inf. Co.F
Thornton, J.A. GA 54th Inf. Co.K
Thornton, J.A. MS 10th Cav. Co.F
Thornton, J.A. MS 38th Cav. Co.B
Thornton, J.A. MO Lt.Arty. Farris' Btty. (Clark Arty.)
Thornton, J.A. TN Cav. 17th Bn. (Sanders') Co.B 3rd Lt.
Thornton, J.A. TX 14th Inf. Co.F
Thornton, J.A. Conf.Cav. Powers' Regt. Co.A Cpl.
Thornton, Jack MS 8th Cav. Co.K
Thornton, Jacob L. NC 2nd Bn.Loc.Def.Troops Co.E
Thornton, Jacob P. VA 2nd Inf. Co.K
Thornton, J.A.J. MS Cav. 2nd Bn.Res. Co.C Cpl.
Thornton, James GA 20th Inf. Co.G
Thornton, James GA 41st Inf. Co.I
Thornton, James GA 53rd Inf. Co.H
Thornton, James KY Cav. 2nd Bn. (Dortch's) Co.A
Thornton, James MS 25th Inf. Co.C
Thornton, James MO Cav. Wood's Regt. Co.H Sgt.
Thornton, James MO 1st Inf. Co.A
Thornton, James MO 1st & 4th Cons.Inf. Co.A
Thornton, James SC Hvy.Arty. 15th (Lucas') Bn. Co.B
Thornton, James TN 3rd (Forrest's) Cav. Co.A
Thornton, James TN 3rd (Forrest's) Cav. Co.B
Thornton, James TX Cav. 6th Bn. Co.A
Thornton, James VA Lt.Arty. Clutter's Co.
Thornton, James VA Arty. Fleet's Co.
Thornton, James VA 55th Inf. Co.B
Thornton, James A. GA 1st Bn.S.S. Co.C Sgt.
Thornton, James A. MS Cav. 4th Bn. Co.A 2nd Lt.
Thornton, James A. VA 30th Bn.S.S. Co.B

Thornton, James B. GA 59th Inf. Co.I
Thornton, James B. LA Inf. 25th Regt. Co.H
Thornton, Jas. B. Gen. & Staff Capt.,AQM
Thornton, James C. AL 49th Inf. Co.C Sgt.
Thornton, James C. GA 38th Inf. Co.F,I
Thornton, James D. VA 46th Inf. 2nd Co.F 3rd Lt.
Thornton, James E. MS 5th Inf. (St.Troops) Co.G
Thornton, James E. VA 6th Inf. 1st Co.E, Co.D Cpl.
Thornton, James F. VA 8th Inf. Co.C
Thornton, James H. AL Inf. 2nd Regt. Co.D
Thornton, James H. AL 38th Inf. Co.H,I Cpl.
Thornton, James H. MS 38th Cav. Co.H Cpl.
Thornton, James H. MS 36th Inf. Co.K
Thornton, James M. AR 33rd Inf. Co.D
Thornton, James M. GA Cobb's Legion Co.B Cpl.
Thornton, James M. LA 28th (Gray's) Inf. Co.E
Thornton, James Madison GA Cobb's Legion Co.B
Thornton, James P. SC 2nd Cav. Co.C
Thornton, James R. VA 7th Inf. Co.B Cpl.
Thornton, James R. VA 38th Inf. Co.K
Thornton, James S. TN Cav. Jackson's Co.
Thornton, James T. AL 63rd Inf. Co.G
Thornton, James T. GA 3rd Cav. Co.E Lt.Col.
Thornton, James T. MO 6th Inf. Co.A
Thornton, James T. NC Giddins' Co. (Detailed & Petitioned Men)
Thornton, James W. AR 19th (Dawson's) Inf. Co.A
Thornton, James W. GA 3rd Cav. (St.Guards) Co.H
Thornton, James W. GA 38th Inf. Co.F
Thornton, James W. NC 22nd Inf. Co.A
Thornton, J.B. AL 15th Inf. Co.K
Thornton, J.B. GA Tiller's Co. (Echols Lt.Arty.)
Thornton, J.B. GA 5th Inf. Co.C
Thornton, J.B. GA 54th Inf. Co.K,F
Thornton, J.B. KY 7th Cav. Co.E
Thornton, J.B. LA 25th Inf. Co.H
Thornton, J.B. NC 2nd Jr.Res. Co.H
Thornton, J.B. Gen. & Staff Surg.
Thornton, J.C. AR 11th & 17th Cons.Inf. Co.C Sgt.
Thornton, J.C. AR 18th Inf. Co.A
Thornton, J.C. GA 7th Cav. Co.C
Thornton, J.C. GA Cav. 24th Bn. Co.B
Thornton, J.C. GA 1st (Fannin's) Res. Co.D Capt.
Thornton, J.C. MS 10th Inf. New Co.I
Thornton, J.C. TX 11th (Spaight's) Bn.Vol. Co.B
Thornton, J.D. KY 8th Cav. Co.C
Thornton, J.D. TN 5th Inf. 2nd Co.L
Thornton, J.E. MS 3rd (St.Troops) Cav. Co.K
Thornton, J.E. MS 5th Inf. Co.K
Thornton, J.E. TX 6th Cav. Co.C Lt.
Thornton, J.E. TX 8th Cav. Co.C
Thornton, J.E. TX 5th Inf. Co.G
Thornton, Jeff MO Lt.Arty. Parsons' Co.
Thornton, Jeptha M. GA 38th Inf. Co.F
Thornton, Jere MO St.Guard
Thornton, Jeremiah VA 50th Inf. Co.I
Thornton, Jes. GA 66th Inf. Co.I Capt.
Thornton, Jesse AL Lt.Arty. 2nd Bn. Co.B
Thornton, Jesse GA 1st (Ramsey's) Inf. Co.F
Thornton, Jesse GA 5th Inf. Co.A
Thornton, Jesse M. GA 38th Inf. Co.F Cpl.
Thornton, Jessie 1st Choctaw & Chickasaw Mtd.Rifles Welch's Co.
Thornton, Jessup G. AL 61st Inf. Co.E
Thornton, J.F. AL 34th Inf. Co.C
Thornton, J.F. GA 3rd Mil. Co.G
Thornton, J.F. GA 8th Inf. Co.I
Thornton, J.F. GA 55th Inf. Co.F
Thornton, J.F. GA Cobb's Legion Co.B
Thornton, J.F. MO 5th Cav. Co.K
Thornton, J.G. MS Lt.Arty. 14th Bn.
Thornton, J.G. MS Lt.Arty. Yates' Btty.
Thornton, J.H. AL 14th Inf. Co.H Sgt.
Thornton, J.H. AL 22nd Inf. Co.I
Thornton, J.H. AL 38th Inf. Co.I
Thornton, J.H. GA 13th Inf.
Thornton, J.H. MS 9th Cav. Co.E 3rd Lt.
Thornton, J.H. MS 40th Inf. Co.K
Thornton, J.J. GA Cobb's Legion Co.B
Thornton, J.J. Gen. & Staff Asst.Surg.
Thornton, J.K. MS 4th Inf. Co.B
Thornton, J.L. AR Inf. Cocke's Regt. Co.I
Thornton, J.L. GA Mayer's Co. (Appling Cav.)
Thornton, J.L. MS 2nd Cav. Co.D
Thornton, J.M. AL Inf. 1st Regt. Co.D Comsy.Sgt.
Thornton, J.M. GA 1st Mil.
Thornton, J.M. GA 39th Inf. Co.F
Thornton, J.M. KY 8th Cav. Co.C
Thornton, J.M. LA 17th Inf. Co.G
Thornton, J.M. MS 3rd Cav. Co.F 1st Sgt.
Thornton, J.M. MS 15th Inf. Co.I
Thornton, J.M. MS 37th Inf. Co.H
Thornton, J.M. TN 9th Inf. Co.D Cpl.
Thornton, J.M. VA 9th Cav. Co.B
Thornton, J.M. Eng.Dept. Polk's Corps A. of TN Sap. & Min. Co.,CSA
Thornton, J.N. AL Inf. 1st Regt. Co.D
Thornton, J.N GA 17th Inf. Co.H Cpl.
Thornton, J.N. GA Cobb's Legion Co.D
Thornton, Joe MS 10th Cav. Co.F
Thornton, Joel R. GA 8th Inf. Co.I Sgt.
Thornton, John AL 17th Inf. Co.B
Thornton, John AL 27th Inf. Co.I
Thornton, John AL 61st Inf. Co.E
Thornton, John AR 37th Inf. Co.F
Thornton, John AR Inf. Hardy's Regt. Co.A
Thornton, John FL Inf. 2nd Bn. Co.C
Thornton, John FL 10th Inf. Co.H
Thornton, John FL Conscr.
Thornton, John GA 1st Reg. Co.G
Thornton, John KY 3rd Cav. Co.C Cpl.
Thornton, John KY 4th Cav. Co.G
Thornton, John LA 14th (Austin's) Bn.S.S. Co.A
Thornton, John, Jr. MS 3rd (St.Troops) Cav. Co.K
Thornton, John MS Inf. 3rd Bn. (St.Troops) Co.F
Thornton, John MS 40th Inf. Co.D Cpl.
Thornton, John MS 46th Inf. Co.G
Thornton, John MS Blythe's Bn. (St.Troops) Co.B Cpl.
Thornton, John NC 8th Inf. Co.A
Thornton, John NC 38th Inf. Co.B
Thornton, John SC 2nd Cav. Co.C
Thornton, John SC Cav. 4th Bn. Co.B
Thornton, John SC 1st Inf. Co.O
Thornton, John SC Inf. Holcombe Legion Co.B
Thornton, John TN 19th (Biffle's) Cav. Co.F
Thornton, John TN 5th Inf. 2nd Co.H
Thornton, John TX 14th Cav. Co.E
Thornton, John TX Inf. 1st St.Troops Lawrence's Co.D Sgt.
Thornton, John TX 20th Inf. Co.H
Thornton, John 1st Cherokee Mtd.Vol. 1st Co.G
Thornton, John B. GA 6th Inf. Co.K
Thornton, John C. AR 11th Inf. Co.C Cpl.
Thornton, John C. GA 38th Inf. Co.F Capt.
Thornton, John C. MO 3rd Cav. Co.E
Thornton, John C. MO 5th Cav. Co.E
Thornton, John C.C. MO St.Guard Lt.Col.
Thornton, John D. GA 43rd Inf. Co.G
Thornton, John E. AL 17th Inf. Co.A
Thornton, John F. TN 10th Cav. Co.A
Thornton, John G. MS 14th Inf. Co.H
Thornton, John H. AL 43rd Inf. Co.F
Thornton, John H. AL Cp. of Instr. Talladega
Thornton, John H. GA 16th Inf. Co.K
Thornton, John H. GA 43rd Inf. Co.F
Thornton, John H. Conf.Cav. Wood's Regt. Co.L
Thornton, John J. GA 43rd Inf. Co.G 2nd Lt.
Thornton, John J. GA 55th Inf. Co.K
Thornton, John J. MS 6th Inf. Co.I Col.
Thornton, John J. MS 7th Inf. Co.H Capt.
Thornton, John J. MS 9th Inf. Old Co.G
Thornton, John J. 2nd Cherokee Mtd.Vol. Co.F
Thornton, John L. LA 11th Inf. Co.E
Thornton, John L. VA 38th Inf. Co.F 2nd Lt.
Thornton, John M. GA Inf. 10th Bn. Co.A
Thornton, John M. MS 46th Inf. Co.G
Thornton, John M. NC 24th Inf. Co.F
Thornton, John M. NC 56th Inf. Co.B
Thornton, John R. AR 5th Inf. Co.C
Thornton, John R. AR 6th Inf. Co.H N.C.S. Sgt.Maj.
Thornton, John R. AR 12th Inf. 1st Lt.
Thornton, John R. VA 34th Mil. Co.B
Thornton, John S. GA 54th Inf. Co.G
Thornton, John S. VA 57th Inf. Co.B Cpl.
Thornton, John T. AL 15th Inf. Co.A
Thornton, John T. AL 27th Inf. Co.F
Thornton, John T. MS 4th Inf. Co.B Cpl.
Thornton, John T. TN 44th Inf. Co.G
Thornton, John T. TN 44th (Cons.) Inf. Co.F
Thornton, John T. VA 3rd Cav. Co.K Lt.Col.
Thornton, John V. MO Cav. Jackman's Regt. Co.G
Thornton, John W. AL 47th Inf. Co.K
Thornton, John W. TN Inf. 154th Sr.Regt. 2nd Co.B Cpl.
Thornton, John W. VA 6th Cav. Co.B
Thornton, John W. VA 3rd Arty. Co.I
Thornton, John W. VA 1st (Farinholt's) Res. Color Sgt.
Thornton, Jonathan GA 1st Bn.S.S. Co.C Cpl.
Thornton, J.O.R. MS 8th Cav. Co.F
Thornton, Joseph MS 9th Cav. Co.E
Thornton, Joseph MO Arty. Jos. Bledsoe's Co.
Thornton, Joseph SC 19th Inf. Co.H
Thornton, Joseph TN 4th (Murray's) Cav. Co.F Black.

Thornton, Joseph TN Cav. 16th Bn. (Neal's) Co.D
Thornton, Joseph TN Cav. 17th Bn. (Sanders') Co.B
Thornton, Joseph TX 15th Inf. 1st Co.E,C
Thornton, Joseph A. VA 57th Inf. Co.B
Thornton, Joseph B. AL 61st Inf. Co.I
Thornton, Joseph P. AL 62nd Inf. Co.F Capt.
Thornton, Joseph T. GA 53rd Inf. Co.H Cpl.
Thornton, Jos. W. AL 48th Inf. Co.C
Thornton, J.P. AL Mil. 2nd Regt.Vol. Co.D
Thornton, J.P. AL 3rd Inf. Co.A
Thornton, J.P. GA Lt.Arty. Croft's Btty. (Columbus Arty.)
Thornton, J.P. MS 12th Cav. Co.L
Thornton, J.P. NC 23rd Inf. Co.A
Thornton, J.P. SC Cav. 4th Bn. Co.B
Thornton, J.R. GA 27th Inf. Co.E
Thornton, J.R. TN 6th Inf. Co.C
Thornton, J.R. VA Horse Arty. J.W. Carter's Co.
Thornton, J.S. GA 11th Inf.
Thornton, J.S. TN 3rd (Forrest's) Cav. Co.D
Thornton, J.S. TN 15th Inf. Co.A Cpl.
Thornton, J.T. AR Lt.Arty. Owen's Btty.
Thornton, J.T. AR 11th Inf. Co.C
Thornton, J.T. AR 11th & 17th Cons.Inf. Co.C
Thornton, J.T. AR Inf. Cocke's Regt. Co.I
Thornton, J.T. GA Cobb's Legion Co.D
Thornton, J.T. MS Inf. 2nd Bn. Co.B
Thornton, J.T. MS 15th Inf. Co.A
Thornton, J.T. MS 48th Inf. Co.B
Thornton, J.T. MO Col.,Pay M.Gen.
Thornton, J.T. VA 10th Cav. Co.I
Thornton, Julius AL 31st Inf. Co.I
Thornton, J.V. MO Cav. Coleman's Regt. Co.F
Thornton, J.W. AL 40th Inf. Co.B Cpl.
Thornton, J.W. AL 47th Inf. Co.A
Thornton, J.W. GA 44th Inf. Co.F
Thornton, J.W. LA 17th Inf. Co.H
Thornton, J.W. MS 38th Cav. Co.B
Thornton, J.W. MS 35th Inf. Co.A
Thornton, J.W. TN 38th Inf. Co.F
Thornton, J.W. TX 24th Cav. Co.F
Thornton, J.W. TX Granbury's Cons.Brig. Co.I
Thornton, K.C. VA 36th Inf. 2nd Co.I
Thornton, K.H. AL 17th Inf. Co.C Cpl.
Thornton, Kinchen D. GA Phillips' Legion Co.D,K Black.
Thornton, L.A. MO 1st Cav. Co.C
Thornton, Lafayette L. MS 35th Inf. Co.G
Thornton, L.B. TX 15th Cav. Co.E
Thornton, L.C. AL 59th Inf. Co.F
Thornton, L.C. AL 2nd Bn. Hilliard's Legion Vol. Co.A
Thornton, L.C. TX 4th Inf. Co.B
Thornton, L.C. TX Inf. Carter's Co.
Thornton, L.D. VA 3rd Inf.Loc.Def. 1st Co.G, Co.F Cpl.
Thornton, Leander A. AL Lt.Arty. 20th Bn. Co.A
Thornton, Lewis AL 5th Inf. New Co.E
Thornton, Lewis N. GA 42nd Inf. Co.D
Thornton, Lewis T. TX 13th Cav. Co.K
Thornton, Lindsey AL 18th Inf. Co.K,E
Thornton, Littleton MS 1st Cav.Res. Co.D
Thornton, Littleton MS 36th Inf. Co.D 1st Lt.
Thornton, L.J. LA 12th Inf. Co.C Cpl.
Thornton, Louis R. Conf.Cav. Clarkson's Bn. Ind.Rangers Co.D
Thornton, Lovett D. TN Cav. 2nd Bn. (Biffle's) Co.B
Thornton, Luke AL 20th Inf. Co.E 1st Sgt.
Thornton, Luke LA 15th Inf. Co.F
Thornton, Luke MS 23rd Inf. Co.L Sgt.
Thornton, Luther J. NC 8th Inf. Co.F 1st Lt.
Thornton, M. AR 18th (Marmaduke's) Inf. Co.A
Thornton, M. AR Mil. Borland's Regt. Peyton Rifles
Thornton, M. AR Inf. Cocke's Regt. Co.I
Thornton, M. GA 54th Inf. Co.F Sgt.
Thornton, M. 3rd Conf.Inf. Co.A
Thornton, M.A. MS 9th Inf. New Co.A
Thornton, M.A. MS Blythe's Bn. (St.Troops) Co.B
Thornton, Mallory J. GA 15th Inf. Co.K Cpl.
Thornton, Marion SC 2nd Cav. Co.C
Thornton, Marion SC Cav. 4th Bn. Co.B
Thornton, Mark MO 8th Inf. Co.C
Thornton, Martin V. Gen. & Staff Asst.Surg.
Thornton, M.B. MS 9th Inf. New Co.E Music.
Thornton, M.B. MS 9th Bn.S.S. Co.C
Thornton, M. Carter VA 6th Cav. Co.I
Thornton, M.D. AL 22nd Inf. Co.I
Thornton, M.D. AL 26th Inf. Co.A
Thornton, M.D. MS 9th Inf. New Co.K
Thornton, M.G.L. TX 9th Cav. Co.G
Thornton, M.G.L. TX 9th (Young's) Inf. Co.F
Thornton, M.H. AL 46th Inf. Co.E
Thornton, Michael GA Cav. 1st Bn.Res. Co.C
Thornton, Mike LA 10th Inf. Co.B
Thornton, Miles D. AR 45th Mil. Co.D Cpl.
Thornton, Miles L. GA 31st Inf. Co.E
Thornton, Milton B. MS 10th Inf. Old Co.G Music.
Thornton, M.L. NC Hvy.Arty. 1st Bn. Co.A
Thornton, M.M. AL 34th Inf. Co.C
Thornton, M.N. AR 11th Inf. Co.C
Thornton, M.N. AR Inf. Cocke's Regt. Co.I
Thornton, Morton V. AL 43rd Inf. Co.H
Thornton, Moses FL 9th Inf. Co.A
Thornton, Moses MS 36th Inf. Co.D
Thornton, Moses T. VA 38th Inf. Co.K
Thornton, Munroe VA 36th Inf. 2nd Co.E
Thornton, M.V. AR 32nd Inf. Co.F
Thornton, N. AL 3rd Inf. Sgt.
Thornton, N.A. AR 11th Inf. Co.C
Thornton, N.A. AR 11th & 17th Cons.Inf. Co.C Cpl.
Thornton, N.A. GA Cav. 19th Bn. Co.E
Thornton, N.A. MS 2nd Cav. Co.H
Thornton, N.A. 10th Conf.Cav. Co.K
Thornton, Nathan LA 9th Inf. Co.H
Thornton, Nathan H. AL Eufaula Lt.Arty. Sgt.
Thornton, Nathaniel H. AL Inf. 1st Regt. Co.A 1st Sgt.
Thornton, Nathaniel M. VA 3rd Cav. Co.A
Thornton, Nathan V. LA 5th Cav. Co.H
Thornton, Newton Sap. & Min.,CSA
Thornton, N.J. LA 25th Inf. Co.G
Thornton, N.J. LA Inf. Pelican Regt. Co.B
Thornton, N.M. GA 46th Inf. Co.G
Thornton, N.M. TX Cav. Giddings' Bn. Maddox's Co. Cpl.
Thornton, N.R. AR 11th Inf. Co.C
Thornton, N.W. LA 13th Bn. (Part.Rangers) Co.F
Thornton, N.W. LA 17th Inf. Co.C Cpl.
Thornton, N.W. LA 22nd (Cons.) Inf. Co.G Cpl.
Thornton, Oceola 1st Cherokee Mtd.Vol. 1st Co.B, 2nd Co.D
Thornton, O.M. AR Inf. Cocke's Regt. Co.I
Thornton, O.S. GA 55th Inf. Co.B
Thornton, Otis S. GA Cav. 7th Bn. (St.Guards) Co.D Cpl.
Thornton, P. AR Inf. Hardy's Regt. Co.I
Thornton, P. MO St.Guard
Thornton, Page J. VA 57th Inf. Co.B
Thornton, Patrick LA 1st Cav. Co.I
Thornton, Patrick LA 1st Hvy.Arty. (Reg.) Co.F Cpl.
Thornton, Patrick H. GA 12th Inf. Co.E Sgt.
Thornton, Paul MO Cav. 3rd Bn. Sgt.Maj.
Thornton, Paul F. MO 2nd Cav. 3rd Co.K
Thornton, Paul F. MO Cav. Wood's Regt. Co.C Capt.
Thornton, Peter SC Inf. 7th Bn. (Enfield Rifles) Co.C Cpl.
Thornton, Peter VA 4th Inf. Co.C
Thornton, Peter VA 30th Inf. Co.F
Thornton, P.H. GA Inf. Arsenal Bn.(Columbus) Co.A Cpl.
Thornton, P.H. Gen. & Staff Asst.Surg.
Thornton, Philip TN 20th Cav.
Thornton, Philip TX 15th Cav. Co.D
Thornton, Philip H. MS 21st Inf. Co.F QMSgt.
Thornton, Pickens S. MS 14th Inf. Co.H
Thornton, Pickens S. MS 37th Inf. Co.K
Thornton, P.L. GA 12th Cav. Co.F
Thornton, P.P. GA 50th Inf.
Thornton, P.P. VA 50th Inf. Co.F
Thornton, Presley L.W. VA 21st Inf. Co.H 1st Lt.
Thornton, Preston W. AL 11th Inf. Co.I
Thornton, Q.C. TN 15th Inf. Co.A,E 2nd Lt.
Thornton, R. VA Inf. 26th Bn. Co.I
Thornton, R.A. AL 31st Inf. Co.I
Thornton, R.A. GA 3rd Res. Co.G
Thornton, R.A. VA Horse Arty. J.W. Carter's Co.
Thornton, Ransom D. TX Cav. 6th Bn. Co.A
Thornton, R.B. AL 14th Inf. Co.K
Thornton, R.B. AL 1st Bn. Hilliard's Legion Vol. Co.E
Thornton, R.B. AR 20th Inf. Co.E
Thornton, R.B. GA 38th Inf. Co.F
Thornton, R.B. GA 53rd Inf. Co.H
Thornton, R.B.F. TX 18th Inf. Co.H
Thornton, R.C. AL Inf. 1st Regt. Co.C
Thornton, R.C. AL 45th Inf. Co.E
Thornton, R.C. MS 5th Inf. (St.Troops) Co.A
Thornton, R.C. Conf.Cav. Baxter's Bn. Co.C
Thornton, R.D. AL 29th Inf. Co.K
Thornton, R.D. AL 39th Inf. Co.H
Thornton, Reuben J. AL Eufaula Lt.Arty.
Thornton, Reuben J. AL Inf. 1st Regt. Co.A
Thornton, Reuben N. TN 15th Cav. Cox's Co.
Thornton, Reuben T. MO 3rd Regt.St.Guard J.H. Britt's Co. Cpl.
Thornton, R.F. GA 10th Cav. Co.A 1st Lt.

Thornton, R.F. NC Lt.Arty. 13th Bn. Co.D
Thornton, R.F. 7th Conf.Cav. Co.A Bvt.2nd Lt.
Thornton, R.H. MS Cav. 1st Bn. (McNair's) St.Troops Co.E
Thornton, Richard AR 6th Inf. New Co.K
Thornton, Richard AR 19th (Dawson's) Inf. Co.B
Thornton, Richard A. AL 44th Inf. Co.A Sgt.
Thornton, Richard A. VA Lt.Arty. Douthat's Co.
Thornton, Richard A. VA 4th Cav. Co.G
Thornton, Richard W. NC 1st Inf. (6 mo. '61) Co.F
Thornton, Richard W. NC 56th Inf. Co.B 1st Lt.
Thornton, Richard W. Conf.Cav. Raum's Co.
Thornton, R.L. TN 19th & 20th (Cons.) Cav. Co.E
Thornton, R.L. TN 20th (Russell's) Cav. Co.C
Thornton, R.M. AR 12th Inf. Co.G
Thornton, R.M. TX 7th Cav. Co.E
Thornton, Robert GA 3rd Cav. Co.B
Thornton, Robert GA 3rd Cav. Co.I Cpl.
Thornton, Robert MS Inf. 3rd Bn. Co.H 1st Cpl.
Thornton, Robert SC 19th Inf. Co.H
Thornton, Robert VA 14th Inf. Co.K
Thornton, Robert VA Inf. 26th Bn. Co.I
Thornton, Robert VA 36th Inf. 2nd Co.B
Thornton, Robert VA 46th Inf. Co.B
Thornton, Robert B. NC 12th Inf. Co.F
Thornton, Robert C. VA Lt.Arty. Thornton's Co. 1st Lt.
Thornton, Robert C. VA 30th Inf. Co.C
Thornton, Robert D. AL Vol. Lee, Jr.'s Co.
Thornton, Robert F. AL 7th Inf. Co.A
Thornton, Robert F. VA Arty. Paris' Co.
Thornton, Robert F. VA 38th Inf. Co.F 2nd Lt.
Thornton, Robert T.J. TX Cav. Mann's Regt. Co.A
Thornton, R.O.J. MS 6th Cav. Co.F,K
Thornton, R.P. VA Inf. 7th Bn.Loc.Def. Co.C
Thornton, R.R. MS 46th Inf. Co.G
Thornton, R.S. GA 3rd Cav. (St.Guards) Co.K
Thornton, R.T. GA 2nd St.Line 2nd Lt.
Thornton, R.T. VA 36th Inf. Co.C
Thornton, Rufus GA 2nd Inf. Co.K
Thornton, S. GA 2nd Cav. (St.Guards) Co.B
Thornton, S. GA 13th Inf. Co.H
Thornton, S. GA 29th Inf. Co.A
Thornton, S.A. TN 3rd (Forrest's) Cav. Co.C
Thornton, Samuel GA 4th (Clinch's) Cav. Co.E
Thornton, Samuel GA 61st Inf. Co.G
Thornton, Samuel MS 5th Cav. Co.G
Thornton, Samuel MS St.Cav. Perrin's Bn. Co.B
Thornton, Samuel TX 5th Inf. Co.K 2nd Lt.
Thornton, Samuel A. GA 38th Inf. Co.E 1st Lt.
Thornton, Samuel Dixon MO 4th Cav. Co.I
Thornton, Samuel R. NC 13th Inf. Co.C 1st Lt.
Thornton, Samuel S. NC 20th Inf. Co.H
Thornton, Samuel S. Cp. of Instr. Co.C
Thornton, Samuel W. VA 57th Inf. Co.B
Thornton, Sanford H. GA 31st Inf. Co.C
Thornton, S.C. GA 8th Cav. Old Co.D 2nd Lt.
Thornton, S.C. GA 62nd Cav. Co.D 2nd Lt.
Thornton, S.C. NC Cav. 16th Bn. Co.H 2nd Lt.
Thornton, Scott S. MS 11th Inf. Co.C
Thornton, Seaborn AL 59th Inf. Co.F
Thornton, Seaborn AL 2nd Bn. Hilliard's Legion Vol. Co.A
Thornton, Seaborn NC Inf. 2nd Bn. Co.E
Thornton, Seaborn B. GA 27th Inf. Co.E
Thornton, Seaborn J. GA 47th Inf. Co.B
Thornton, Seaborn W. GA 31st Inf. Co.K Capt.
Thornton, Seburn GA Inf. 1st Conf.Bn. Co.D
Thornton, S.G. TX 11th Inf. Co.C
Thornton, S.H. GA 11th Inf.
Thornton, Silas GA 54th Inf. Co.K Sr.2nd Lt.
Thornton, Silb KY 3rd Cav. Co.B
Thornton, Simeon Wills GA Cobb's Legion Co.B
Thornton, Singleton A. GA 13th Inf. Co.E Capt.
Thornton, S.J. NC 24th Inf. Co.E
Thornton, Solomon GA 13th Inf. Co.G
Thornton, Solomon M. MS 31st Inf. Co.B Capt.
Thornton, S.R. MS Inf. 3rd Bn. Co.D
Thornton, S.R. TX 20th Bn.St.Troops Co.I
Thornton, S.S. AL 63rd Inf. Co.K Cpl.
Thornton, S.S. GA 2nd Cav. (St.Guards) Co.A
Thornton, S.S. GA Inf. 26th Bn. Co.B
Thornton, Sterling VA Res.Forces Clark's Co. 1st Sgt.
Thornton, Sterling S. VA 53rd Inf. Co.H Sgt.
Thornton, S.W. GA Inf. (Collier Guards) Collier's Co. Sgt.
Thornton, T. GA Inf. 27th Bn. Co.E
Thornton, T. GA 54th Inf. Co.B
Thornton, T. MS 11th (Perrin's) Cav. Co.K
Thornton, T. MS Cav. Yerger's Regt. Co.A
Thornton, T. NC Arty. 10th Regt. Co.D
Thornton, T. Conf.Cav. Wood's Regt. 2nd Co.M
Thornton, T.A. TN 21st (Wilson's) Cav. Co.I
Thornton, T.A. TN 21st & 22nd (Cons.) Cav. Co.K
Thornton, T.A. TN 5th Inf. 2nd Co.H
Thornton, T.A. TN 12th Inf. Co.F
Thornton, T.B. MS 2nd Inf. Co.F
Thornton, T.D. MS 36th Inf. Co.D
Thornton, T.H. AL 14th Inf. Co.K
Thornton, Tho. AL Cav. Callaway's Co.
Thornton, Thomas AL 9th (Malone's) Cav. Co.E
Thornton, Thomas LA 10th Inf. Co.A Sgt.
Thornton, Thomas LA Inf.Cons.Crescent Regt. Co.G,D Sgt.
Thornton, Thomas MS Cav. 1st Bn. (Montgomery's) St.Troops Hammond's Co.
Thornton, Thomas MS 8th Inf. Co.B
Thornton, Thomas MS 15th Inf. Co.C
Thornton, Thomas NC 3rd Arty. (40th St.Troops) Co.B
Thornton, Thomas TX Cav. 2nd Bn.St.Troops Hubbard's Co.
Thornton, Thomas TX 3rd Cav. Co.I
Thornton, Thomas VA 4th Cav. Co.A 1st Sgt.
Thornton, Thomas A. KY 4th Cav. Co.G
Thornton, Thomas A. NC 8th Sr.Res. Bryan's Co.
Thornton, Thomas A.F. AR 4th Inf. Co.A 2nd Lt.
Thornton, Thomas B. MS 22nd Inf. Co.F
Thornton, Thomas C. VA 9th Cav. Co.B
Thornton, Thomas C. VA 30th Inf. Co.F Cpl.
Thornton, Thomas D. GA 38th Inf. Co.F 1st Lt.
Thornton, Thomas F. LA Inf.Crescent Regt. Co.H Cpl.
Thornton, Thomas H. MS 18th Inf. Co.E
Thornton, Thomas J. AL 7th Inf. Co.B
Thornton, Thomas J. NC 51st Inf. Co.B Sgt.
Thornton, Thomas L. TN 32nd Inf. Co.E
Thornton, Thomas P. VA 30th Bn.S.S. Co.B
Thornton, Thomas P. 1st Conf.Inf. 2nd Co.E
Thornton, Thomas R. VA Lt.Arty. Thornton's Co. Capt.
Thornton, Thos. T. GA 17th Inf. Co.G
Thornton, Thomas T. GA 31st Inf. Co.E
Thornton, Thoroughgood SC 12th Inf. Co.D
Thornton, Thurgood SC 1st (McCreary's) Inf. Co.B
Thornton, Timothy GA 1st Bn.S.S. Co.C Sgt.
Thornton, T.J. AL 45th Inf. Co.E Cpl.
Thornton, T.J. MS 2nd Cav. Co.D
Thornton, T.J. MS 5th Cav. Co.K
Thornton, Tom MS 36th Inf. Co.K Sgt.
Thornton, T.S. MS Conscr.
Thornton, T.T. TX 7th Cav. Co.E Cpl.
Thornton, Van B. LA 22nd (Cons.) Inf. Asst.Surg.
Thornton, Van B. Gen. & Staff Asst.Surg.
Thornton, V.B. MS 28th Cav. Co.G
Thornton, V.C.B. MS 6th Inf. Co.I
Thornton, W. AL 11th Cav. Co.E
Thornton, W. AR 1st Inf. Co.B
Thornton, W. FL Conscr.
Thornton, W. GA 4th (Clinch's) Cav. Co.A
Thornton, W. GA 7th Cav. Co.G
Thornton, W. GA Cav. 24th Bn. Co.A
Thornton, W. GA Cav. 24th Bn. Co.A,C Cpl.
Thornton, W. GA 54th Inf. Co.B
Thornton, W. MS 4th Cav. Co.F
Thornton, W. NC 2nd Jr.Res. Co.H
Thornton, W. Bradford's Corps Scouts & Guards Co.B
Thornton, W.A. GA Arty. Lumpkin's Co.
Thornton, W.A. GA 17th Inf. Co.G Cpl.
Thornton, W.A. MS 9th Inf.
Thornton, Wade A. VA 30th Inf. Co.K
Thornton, Walter 1st Cherokee Mtd.Vol. 2nd Co.E
Thornton, Warren AR 3rd Cav. Co.L
Thornton, Warren D. AR 11th Cav. Co.L
Thornton, W.B. AR 10th Inf. Co.D
Thornton, W.C. GA 31st Inf. Co.K Capt.
Thornton, W.C. MS 3rd (St.Troops) Cav. Co.K
Thornton, W.C. MS 7th Cav. Co.D
Thornton, W.C. MS 11th (Perrin's) Cav. Co.K
Thornton, W.C. MS 23rd Inf. Co.B
Thornton, W.D. MS 18th Cav. Co.A
Thornton, W.D. TX 9th (Young's) Inf. Co.H
Thornton, W.E. AR 23rd Inf. Co.H Sgt.
Thornton, W.E. VA 3rd Inf.Loc.Def. Co.D
Thornton, Wells Conf.Cav. Wood's Regt. Co.K
Thornton, W.F. AL 38th Inf. Co.I
Thornton, W.F. KY Cav.
Thornton, W.F. MS 18th Cav. Co.A
Thornton, W.G. GA 31st Inf. Co.C
Thornton, W.H. AL 7th Inf. Co.G
Thornton, W.H. AL 46th Inf. Co.E
Thornton, W.H. AR 26th Inf. Co.D
Thornton, W.H. TX Cav. Morgan's Regt. Co.G
Thornton, Whit LA 17th Inf. Co.C
Thornton, W.I. TX 34th Cav. Co.E Sgt.
Thornton, Wiley AL 2nd Bn. Hilliard's Legion Vol. Co.A Cpl.
Thornton, Wiley MS 20th Inf. Co.I
Thornton, Wiley A. GA 3rd Cav. (St.Guards) Co.F Music.

Thornton, Wiley A. GA 3rd Inf. Co.L
Thornton, Wiley D. MS 8th Cav. Co.C 2nd Lt.
Thornton, Wiley D. MS 15th Inf. Co.F
Thornton, Wiley M. AL 47th Inf. Co.H,K
Thornton, Wiley M. LA 28th (Gray's) Inf. Co.E
Thornton, William AL 3rd Cav. Co.H
Thornton, William AL 3rd Cav. Co.H
Thornton, William AL 4th Res. Capt.
Thornton, William AL 13th Inf. Co.B
Thornton, William AL Talladega Cty.Res. J. Henderson's Co. Sgt.
Thornton, William AR 23rd Inf. Co.G
Thornton, William FL 1st Inf. New Co.E Sgt.
Thornton, William GA 7th Cav. Co.D
Thornton, William GA 1st Bn.S.S. Co.C Cpl.
Thornton, William GA 29th Inf. Co.A
Thornton, William GA 31st Inf. Co.C
Thornton, William GA 66th Inf. Co.H
Thornton, William LA 9th Inf. Co.B
Thornton, William LA 9th Inf. Co.H
Thornton, William LA 13th Inf. Co.K
Thornton, William LA 17th Inf. Co.C
Thornton, William MS 2nd Part.Rangers Co.I
Thornton, William MS 9th Cav. Co.E Sgt.
Thornton, William MS 10th Cav. Co.C
Thornton, William MS 38th Cav. Co.B
Thornton, William MS Cav. Hughes' Bn. Co.E
Thornton, William MS Mtd.Inf. (St.Troops) Maxey's Co. 2nd Lt.
Thornton, William MS 9th Inf. New Co.A
Thornton, William MO 12th Cav. Co.D
Thornton, William NC 5th Inf. Co.I
Thornton, William TN Cav. 9th Bn. (Gantt's) Co.D
Thornton, William TN Cav. 17th Bn. (Sanders') Co.B Sgt.
Thornton, William TX 8th Cav. Co.F
Thornton, William TX Cav. Hardeman's Regt. Co.G
Thornton, William TX 1st Bn.S.S. Co.A,E
Thornton, William TX 19th Inf. Co.G
Thornton, William VA 13th Cav. Co.H
Thornton, William VA Inf. 1st Bn.Loc.Def. Co.F
Thornton, William VA 41st Inf. Co.A
Thornton, William Conf.Cav. Wood's Regt. 1st Co.M
Thornton, William 1st Cherokee Mtd.Vol. 1st Co.G
Thornton, William A. AL 3rd Inf. Co.D
Thornton, William A. AL 12th Inf. Co.D
Thornton, William A. MO 2nd Cav. Co.G Sr.2nd Lt.
Thornton, William A. TN 32nd Inf. Co.E Cpl.
Thornton, William B. GA 31st Inf. Co.E
Thornton, William B. TN 24th Inf. Co.I
Thornton, William C. FL 9th Inf. Co.G
Thornton, William C. GA 14th Inf. Co.E
Thornton, William Craford TX Cav. 2nd Regt. Co.K
Thornton, William Crawford MS Inf. 1st Bn. Co.D
Thornton, William D. AR Cav. Wright's Regt. Co.G
Thornton, William D. AR 37th Inf. Co.G
Thornton, William E. AR 9th Inf. Co.F
Thornton, William E. GA 17th Inf. Co.H
Thornton, William E. GA 20th Inf. Co.B
Thornton, William E. NC 50th Inf. Co.D
Thornton, William G. AR Cav. Harrell's Bn. Co.G
Thornton, William G. AR 14th (Powers') Inf. Co.B Cpl.
Thornton, William H. AL 57th Inf. Co.H Cpl.
Thornton, William H. AL Talladega Cty.Res. J. Henderson's Co.
Thornton, William H. MS 3rd Cav. Co.F 1st Lt.
Thornton, William H. MS 15th Inf. Co.F
Thornton, William H. VA 6th Cav. 1st Lt.
Thornton, William J. AL 22nd Inf. Co.G
Thornton, William J. GA 44th Inf. Co.B
Thornton, William J. TN 6th (Wheeler's) Cav. Co.G
Thornton, William M. GA 6th Inf. Co.K
Thornton, William M. GA 17th Inf. Co.D
Thornton, William M. GA 38th Inf. Co.F Sgt.
Thornton, Wm. M. MS 6th Inf. Sgt.Maj.
Thornton, William M. MS 21st Inf. Co.A
Thornton, William M. MS 22nd Inf. Co.F
Thornton, William M. VA 17th Cav. Co.A Sgt.
Thornton, William Marion VA 8th Cav. 1st Co.D Cpl.
Thornton, William N. 3rd Conf.Eng.Troops Co.D
Thornton, William P. AR 1st Mtd.Rifles Co.B
Thornton, William R. AL 3rd Res. Co.H
Thornton, William R. LA 28th (Gray's) Inf. Co.B
Thornton, William R. NC 1st Cav. (9th St.Troops) Co.E Cpl.
Thornton, William R. VA 60th Inf. 2nd Co.H
Thornton, William Russell VA 8th Cav. 1st Co.D
Thornton, William S. KY 2nd (Woodward's) Cav. Co.D 2nd Lt.
Thornton, William T. GA Inf. 10th Bn. Co.A
Thornton, William T. GA 38th Inf. Co.F Sgt.
Thornton, William T. GA Inf. Athens Reserved Corps
Thornton, William T. MO 2nd Cav. 3rd Co.K
Thornton, William T. TX 14th Cav. Co.D Cpl.
Thornton, William T. VA Lt.Arty. Clutter's Co. Artif.
Thornton, William T. VA Arty. Fleet's Co.
Thornton, William T. VA 1st St.Res. Co.F Sgt.
Thornton, William T. VA 39th Inf. Co.G
Thornton, William T. VA 55th Inf. Co.B
Thornton, William W. VA 4th Cav. Co.A Capt.
Thornton, William W. Early's Div. Maj.,CS
Thornton, Willis D. AL 17th Inf. Co.K
Thornton, Wily MS 8th Inf. Co.B
Thornton, W.J. GA Inf. 27th Bn. Co.E
Thornton, W.J. GA 41st Inf.
Thornton, W.J. GA 53rd Inf. Co.H
Thornton, W.J. MS 38th Cav. Co.H
Thornton, W.J. TN 5th Inf. 2nd Co.C Cpl.
Thornton, W.L. 8th (Wade's) Conf.Cav. Co.F
Thornton, W.M. AR Inf. Cocke's Regt. Co.I
Thornton, W.M. MS 3rd (St.Troops) Cav. Co.I 2nd Lt.
Thornton, W.M. MS 6th Cav. Co.E
Thornton, W.M. TN 22nd (Barteau's) Cav. 1st Co.H
Thornton, W.R. AR Inf. Cocke's Regt. Co.I
Thornton, W.R. LA 2nd Inf. Co.C
Thornton, Wright B. GA 46th Inf. Co.I
Thornton, Wright B. TN 18th (Newsom's) Cav. Co.C,G
Thornton, W.S. GA 7th Cav.
Thornton, W.S. TN Inf. 2nd Cons.Regt. Co.A
Thornton, W.S. TN 13th Inf. Co.G
Thornton, W.T. GA Cav. 1st Bn.Res. Stark's Co. Sgt.
Thornton, W.T. GA 7th Cav.
Thornton, W.T. GA Inf. 5th Bn. (St.Guards) Co.F Cpl.
Thornton, W.T. MS 8th Inf. Co.B
Thornton, W.T.H. GA 53rd Inf. Co.H Cpl.
Thornton, W.W. Conf.Cav. Wood's Regt. Co.K
Thornton, Y. GA 1st Cav. Co.B
Thornton, Yancey AL 53rd (Part.Rangers) Co.K
Thornton, Yancey 8th (Wade's) Conf.Cav. Co.I
Thornton, Yancy A. AL 30th Inf. Co.A
Thornton, Y.E. AL Cav. 24th Bn. Co.A
Thornton, Y.N. NC A. Brown's Co.
Thornton, Young O. NC 56th Inf. Co.B
Thornton, Z.C. AL 4th (Russell's) Cav. Co.B Sgt.
Thornton, Z.C. TN 3rd (Forrest's) Cav. 1st Co.E Cpl.
Thornune, Felix F. MO Inf. 5th Regt.St.Guard Co.C
Thornune, Leon MO Inf. 5th Regt.St.Guard Co.C
Thornwell, Charles A. SC 8th Inf. Co.G
Thornwell, Gillespie SC Cav.Bn. Hampton Legion Co.D
Thornwell, J.H. SC Cav. 19th Bn. Co.E
Thornwell, Peyton L. TN 60th Mtd.Inf.
Thorogood, John F. VA 54th Mil. Co.C,D
Thoron, D.H. AR Cav. McGehee's Regt. Co.C
Thoroughgood, George VA 6th Inf. Co.D
Thoroughman, E. MO 1st N.E. Cav.
Thoroughman, Thomas MO 5th Div.St.Guards Lt.Col.
Thorp, ---, 1st TX Cav. Mann's Regt. Co.I
Thorp, ---, 2nd TX Cav. Mann's Regt. Co.I
Thorp, A. KY Arty. Corbett's Co.
Thorp, Alfred B. AR 1st (Crawford's) Cav. Co.D
Thorp, Arthur VA Cav. Mosby's Regt. (Part. Rangers) Co.B
Thorp, Benjamin GA 25th Inf. Co.E
Thorp, Benjamin NC 3rd Bn.Sr.Res. Co.C
Thorp, Benjamin NC 55th Inf. Co.K
Thorp, C.F.M. TN 3rd (Clack's) Inf. Co.B
Thorp, Charles F. TN 32nd Inf. Co.I
Thorp, Daniel P. MS 17th Inf. Co.H
Thorp, David MO Cav. Clardy's Bn. Co.C
Thorp, Eli W. MO Cav. 1st Regt.St.Guard Co.E 1st Lt.
Thorp, F. MO 9th (Elliott's) Cav. Co.E Sgt.
Thorp, F.T. MO 5th Cav. Co.I
Thorp, George W. VA Courtney Arty.
Thorp, Harris KY Dudley's Ind.Cav.
Thorp, Harris KY 7th Cav. Co.F
Thorp, Harris KY 11th Cav. Co.F
Thorp, H.D. TX 33rd Cav. Co.D
Thorp, Henry R. AL 12th Inf. Co.F
Thorp, I. VA 51st Mil. Co.F
Thorp, James AR 14th (McCarver's) Inf. Co.G
Thorp, James TX Cav. McCord's Frontier Regt. Co.I
Thorp, James H. VA Lt.Arty. 38th Bn. Co.C
Thorp, James T. MO 1st Cav. Co.E
Thorp, James V. VA Courtney Arty.

Thorp, J.C. AL 4th (Russell's) Cav. Co.C 2nd Lt.
Thorp, J.C. TN 7th Cav. Co.D
Thorp, J.E. AL 4th (Roddey's) Cav. Co.G
Thorp, J.E. AL Mil. West's Co. 1st Sgt.
Thorp, Jesse KY Cav. 1st Bn. Co.A
Thorp, J.M. MO 12th Cav. Co.F
Thorp, John FL 11th Inf.
Thorp, John VA 49th Inf. Co.G
Thorp, John C. VA Courtney Arty.
Thorp, John H. NC 47th Inf. Co.A Capt.
Thorp, John L. VA 5th Cav. (12 mo. '61-2) Co.H
Thorp, John N. VA Cav. 1st Bn. (Loc.Def. Troops) Co.B
Thorp, John N. VA 24th Cav. Co.B
Thorp, Joseph LA 7th Inf. Co.F
Thorp, Joseph G. SC 5th Res. Co.D
Thorp, J.P. TN 3rd (Clack's) Inf. Co.B
Thorp, J.T. MO Inf. Clark's Regt. Co.A
Thorp, J.V. TX 22nd Inf. Co.D
Thorp, J.W. TX Waul's Legion Co.A
Thorp, Levi AL 55th Vol.
Thorp, Lewis TN 44th (Cons.) Inf. Co.K
Thorp, L.S. AL 55th Vol. Co.D 2nd Lt.
Thorp, L.S. MS 25th Inf. Co.B Sgt.
Thorp, L.S. 2nd Conf.Inf. Co.B 1st Sgt.
Thorp, Martin F. VA Lt.Arty. 38th Bn. Co.A
Thorp, M.H. KY Hosp.Stew.
Thorp, Patrick A. Morgan's Staff Capt.,ADC
Thorp, Peter H. VA 5th Cav. (12 mo. '61-2) Co.C Jr.2nd Lt.
Thorp, Peter H. VA 13th Cav. Co.H 2nd Lt.
Thorp, Peterson, Jr. NC 12th Inf. Co.B,D
Thorp, Peterson NC 55th Inf. Co.K Hosp.Stew.
Thorp, Richard NC 3rd Bn.Sr.Res. Co.C
Thorp, Robert AR 14th (McCarver's) Inf. Co.G
Thorp, Robert D. VA Courtney Arty.
Thorp, R.S. NC 53rd Inf. Co.C
Thorp, S.A. VA 3rd Res. Co.A
Thorp, Spencer R. KY 2nd Cav. Co.A 2nd Lt.
Thorp, Spencer R. MO 2nd Cav. Co.A 2nd Lt.
Thorp, S.R. MS 16th Inf. Co.A
Thorp, T. AL Mil. 4th Vol. Co.I 1st Lt.
Thorp, Thomas KY 6th Mtd.Inf. Co.G 1st Lt.
Thorp, Thomas MO St.Guard
Thorp, Thomas TN 37th Inf. Co.B
Thorp, W. MO 5th Cav. Co.K
Thorp, W. TX Cav. Border's Regt. Co.D
Thorp, W.A. AL 61st Inf. Co.K
Thorp, W.A. GA 38th Inf. 2nd Co.I
Thorp, Walter C. VA 9th Inf. Co.B
Thorp, W.D. KY 2nd (Duke's) Cav.
Thorp, W.G.H. TX 12th Inf. Co.F
Thorp, William FL 11th Inf. Co.C
Thorp, William KY 2nd (Duke's) Cav. Co.B
Thorp, William LA 6th Inf. Co.C
Thorp, William TX 33rd Cav. Co.D
Thorp, William VA 51st Mil. Co.F
Thorp, William H. NC 7th Inf. Co.C
Thorp, William J. VA Courtney Arty.
Thorp, William M. TN 43rd Inf. Co.B
Thorp, William N. MO Inf. 6th Regt.St.Guard Co.B Capt.
Thorp, William T. MO 1st Cav. Co.E Cpl.
Thorp, W.N. MO 5th Cav. Co.I Capt.
Thorpe, A. KY 14th Cav. Co.E
Thorpe, Albert NC 1st Jr.Res. Co.B 1st Lt.
Thorpe, Benjamin F. VA 11th Cav. Co.B
Thorpe, Charles H.R. GA 1st (Olmstead's) Inf. Co.D
Thorpe, David W. AL City Guards Lockett's Co.
Thorpe, D.W. TN 38th Inf. Co.G
Thorpe, Elias TX 26th Cav. Co.A
Thorpe, F.L. LA 2nd Cav. Co.G
Thorpe, Francis VA 49th Inf. Co.G
Thorpe, George KY 2nd (Woodward's) Cav. Co.F
Thorpe, George J. TX 1st (McCulloch's) Cav. Co.G
Thorpe, George J. TX 1st (Yager's) Cav. Co.G Bugler
Thorpe, George J. TX Cav. 8th (Taylor's) Bn. Co.A
Thorpe, George W. VA Lt.Arty. 38th Bn. Co.C
Thorpe, H.R. Gen. & Staff,PACS Surg.
Thorpe, Isaac MO 8th Inf. Co.H
Thorpe, Isaac VA 1st Cav. Co.A
Thorpe, James TN 34th Inf. Co.D 1st Lt.
Thorpe, James A. VA 1st Inf. Co.C
Thorpe, James W. AL 12th Inf. Co.C Music.
Thorpe, James W. VA 8th Bn.Res. Co.B
Thorpe, J.D. GA Cav. 1st Bn.Res. Tufts' Co.
Thorpe, J.E. SC 5th Res. Co.D
Thorpe, J.H. GA 5th Cav. Co.D Cpl.
Thorpe, John GA Cav. 1st Bn. Hughes' Co. Cpl.
Thorpe, John H. NC 1st Inf. (6 mo. '61) Co.A Cpl.
Thorpe, John N. VA 1st Inf. Co.H
Thorpe, John P. MS 14th Inf. Co.I
Thorpe, Joseph GA Cav. 1st Bn. Hughes' Co.
Thorpe, J.P. MS Cav. Buck's Co.
Thorpe, J.S. LA Inf. 16th Bn. (Conf.Guards Resp.Bn.) Co.A Sgt.
Thorpe, J.S.L. GA 5th Cav. Co.I
Thorpe, O. KY 2nd (Woodward's) Cav. Co.F
Thorpe, P.H. KY 2nd (Duke's) Cav. Co.A
Thorpe, P.H. KY 1st Inf. Co.H Capt.
Thorpe, P.H. MS 16th Inf. Co.A 3rd Lt.
Thorpe, R.H. NC 49th Inf. Asst.Surg.
Thorpe, Samuel GA 5th Cav. Co.D
Thorpe, Samuel J. GA Cav. 1st Bn. Hughes' Co.
Thorpe, Simeon NC 53rd Inf. Co.C
Thorpe, Spencer R. KY 1st Inf. Co.H
Thorpe, S.R. KY 2nd (Duke's) Cav. Co.A
Thorpe, Thomas KY 3rd Cav. 1st Lt.
Thorpe, Thomas LA 7th Inf. Co.G Sgt.
Thorpe, William MS 18th Inf. Co.D
Thorpe, William VA Lt.Arty. Cayce's Co.
Thorpe, William N. MO 3rd Cav. Co.I 2nd Lt.
Thorpe, William N. MO 2nd Regt.St.Guards Co.I Lt.
Thorpe, William T. GA Cav. 1st Bn. Hughes' Co.
Thorpe, W.M. MS 1st Lt.Arty. Co.F
Thorps, Richard VA Inf. 4th Bn.Loc.Def. Co.B
Thorrington, Thomas FL 1st Cav. Co.I
Thorton, B.D. TX 10th Cav. Co.D
Thorton, C.A. MO Lt.Arty. 3rd Btty.
Thorton, George VA 10th Cav. Co.B
Thorton, John A. MS Cav. Powers' Regt. Co.A 3rd Lt.
Thorton, R.S. AL 31st Inf. Co.A
Thosse, Alexander NC 3rd Arty. (40th St.Troops) Co.B
Thouler, S.W. AL 26th (O'Neal's) Inf. Co.C
Thouron, J.E. SC Mil. 16th Regt. Jones' Co. 1st Lt.
Thouron, N.J. SC 6th Cav. Co.D
Thouroughgood, Paul NC 4th Cav. (59th St.Troops) Co.G
Thouvassi, O. LA 26th Inf. Co.D
Thouvenell, L. MO 10th Inf. Co.E
Thraan, R. TX Inf. Timmons' Regt. Co.G
Thraan, R. TX Waul's Legion Co.A
Thradgill, J.E. AR 12th Inf. Co.H 2nd Lt.
Thradkill, Green MS 43rd Inf. Co.F
Thrailkele, John MS 31st Inf. Co.E
Thrailkell, William F. MO 1st N.E. Cav. Co.L
Thrailkill, Clifton SC 17th Inf. Co.A
Thrailkill, G.W. GA 2nd Inf. Co.H
Thrailkill, Henry GA 12th Cav.
Thrailkill, Isaac P. GA 36th (Broyles') Inf. Co.B Sgt.
Thrailkill, James MS Inf. 5th Bn. Co.B
Thrailkill, James MS 27th Inf. Co.K
Thrailkill, J.B. NC 35th Inf. Co.D
Thrailkill, Jesse B. NC 5th Cav. (63rd St.Troops) Co.G
Thrailkill, John MS 38th Cav. Co.H
Thrailkill, John MO 1st Cav. Co.F Capt.
Thrailkill, Joseph M. NC 20th Inf. Faison's Co.
Thrailkill, Joseph M. NC 30th Inf. Co.A Sgt.
Thrailkill, L.W. GA 2nd Inf. Co.H
Thrailkill, M. MS 14th (Cons.) Inf. Co.I
Thrailkill, M. MS 43rd Inf. Co.F
Thrailkill, Neill A. NC 31st Inf. Co.I
Thrailkill, Thomas MO 1st Cav. Co.C
Thrailkill, W.C. MS 1st (King's) Inf. (St.Troops) Co.H
Thrailkill, William AR 2nd Inf. Co.D
Thrailkill, William MS 43rd Inf. Co.F
Thrailkill, William D. MO 1st Cav. Co.C
Thrailkill, William J. NC 35th Inf. Co.D Music.
Thrailkille, James M. AR 17th (Lemoyne's) Inf. Co.K
Thralekill, Green S. TN Cav. Newsom's Regt. Co.F
Thralekill, William H. TN Cav. Newsom's Regt. Co.F Cpl.
Thrall, James C. AR Lt.Arty. Thrall's Btty. Capt.
Thrall, John LA 22nd Inf. Jones' Co. Cpl.
Thrall, Richard P. MO 5th Inf. Co.H
Thralls, J.M. MS 1st Lt.Arty. Co.K
Thrap, Thomas NC 4th Sr.Res. Co.D
Thrash, Augustus B. NC 25th Inf. Co.I Capt.
Thrash, C.C. GA 41st Inf. Co.F
Thrash, D. GA Inf. 26th Bn. Co.B
Thrash, David H. VA 20th Cav. Co.F
Thrash, David L. MS 20th Inf. Co.F
Thrash, D.B. AL Cav. Barbiere's Bn. Goldsby's Co.
Thrash, D.B. AL Mil. 4th Vol. Co.G
Thrash, D.B. AL 21st Inf. Co.C
Thrash, D.B. TN Lt.Arty. Tobin's Co. Cpl.
Thrash, D.L. MS 15th (Cons.) Inf. Co.G Cpl.
Thrash, D.M. GA Inf. 26th Bn. Co.B
Thrash, E.B. AL Cav. Barbiere's Bn. Goldsby's Co.

Thrash, E.C. GA 12th (Robinson's) Cav. (St.Guards) Co.F
Thrash, Elmore C. GA 41st Inf. Co.F 2nd Lt.
Thrash, Fielding GA 2nd Cav. Co.G
Thrash, G.A. GA 2nd Cav. Co.G
Thrash, G.B. AL 5th Inf. New Co.F
Thrash, George GA 2nd Cav. Co.G
Thrash, George A. AL 44th Inf. Co.D
Thrash, George W. GA 60th Inf. Co.B
Thrash, G.H. NC Mil. 109th Regt. Sgt.
Thrash, G.W. AL 40th Inf. Co.D
Thrash, Hillary D. GA 64th Inf. Co.F Sgt.
Thrash, Isaac GA 55th Inf. Co.K
Thrash, Isaac R. GA 28th Inf. Co.E
Thrash, James H. AL 4th Inf. Co.A
Thrash, James H. LA 9th Inf. Co.F
Thrash, James J. GA 41st Inf. Co.E
Thrash, James M. GA 14th Inf. Co.A Sgt.
Thrash, J.J. GA Inf. 26th Bn. Co.B
Thrash, John B. GA 28th Inf. Co.E
Thrash, John D. AL Cp. of Instr. Talladega
Thrash, John M. NC 25th Inf. Co.I Cpl.
Thrash, John S. GA Cobb's Legion Co.D
Thrash, John W. AL 20th Inf. Co.B
Thrash, John W. TX 18th Cav. Co.A
Thrash, J.T. GA Inf. 5th Bn. (St.Guards) Co.F
Thrash, J.W. TX Granbury's Cons.Brig. Co.H
Thrash, Leroy N. GA 14th Inf. Co.A
Thrash, Levi GA 12th (Robinson's) Cav. (St.Guards) Co.F Cpl.
Thrash, Levi GA Arty. Maxwell's Reg.Lt.Btty.
Thrash, L.H. GA Inf. 26th Bn. Co.B
Thrash, Mack R. MS 20th Inf. Co.F
Thrash, McR. MS 36th Inf. Co.F
Thrash, P. GA 1st (Fannin's) Res. Co.H
Thrash, Patrick H. NC 16th Inf. Co.F Capt.
Thrash, Patrick H. Gen. & Staff 1st Lt.,Adj.
Thrash, Peter LA Arty.
Thrash, P.H. NC 62nd Inf. Capt.,ACS
Thrash, P.P. GA Inf. 26th Bn. Co.B
Thrash, Terrell GA 55th Inf. Co.F
Thrash, Thomas E. GA 28th Inf. Co.E
Thrash, W.C. AL 5th Inf.
Thrash, W.D.J. AL 40th Inf. Co.C
Thrash, W.F. MS 15th (Cons.) Inf. Co.G
Thrash, W.H. GA Cav. 10th Bn. (St.Guards) Co.B
Thrash, W.H. GA Inf. 25th Bn. (Prov.Guard) Co.F
Thrash, W.H. 2nd Conf.Eng.Troops Co.D Artif.
Thrash, William GA 55th Inf. Co.K
Thrash, William H. GA Lt.Arty. (Jo Thompson Arty.) Hanleiter's Co. Sgt.
Thrash, William H. GA 38th Inf. Co.M Sgt.
Thrash, William T. MS 1st Cav.Res. Co.I
Thrash, W.J. TN 8th Inf. Co.K Capt.
Thrash, W.L. AL 7th Cav. Co.G,F
Thrash, W.V. AL 63rd Inf. Co.K
Thrashar, W.A. TX Conscr.
Thrasher, A.C. AL 9th Inf. Co.D
Thrasher, Adam TN 8th Inf. Co.B 3rd Lt.
Thrasher, Albert C. GA 66th Inf. Co.C
Thrasher, Albert M. GA 3rd Inf. Co.D 1st Lt.
Thrasher, Albert R. 8th (Wade's) Conf.Cav. Co.G Sgt.Maj.
Thrasher, Alonzo P. VA 59th Inf. 2nd Co.C Sgt.
Thrasher, Andrew J. AL 22nd Inf. Co.F
Thrasher, A.P. TX Inf. 1st Bn. (St.Troops) Co.C
Thrasher, A.R. TN 3rd (Forrest's) Cav. Co.A
Thrasher, A.R. TN 38th Inf. 2nd Co.K
Thrasher, B.A. AL 44th Inf.
Thrasher, Barton H. AL Inf. 1st Regt. Co.G
Thrasher, B.C. GA Inf. Jackson's Co.
Thrasher, B.G. AR 2nd Inf. Co.I
Thrasher, B.H. AL 57th Inf. Adj.
Thrasher, B.H. KY 2nd Cav. Co.A
Thrasher, C. AL 22nd Inf. Co.F
Thrasher, C.B. GA Inf. (Collier Guards) Collier's Co. Cpl.
Thrasher, Conway B. FL Milton Lt.Arty. Dunham's Co.
Thrasher, David B. AL 50th Inf. Co.F
Thrasher, David H. FL Milton Lt.Arty. Dunham's Co.
Thrasher, David O. FL Milton Lt.Arty. Dunham's Co.
Thrasher, D.H. TN 38th Inf. 2nd Co.K Capt.
Thrasher, D.N. AL 41st Inf. Co.K Cpl.
Thrasher, D.O. GA Inf. (Collier Guards) Collier's Co.
Thrasher, D.R. GA 18th Inf. Co.B
Thrasher, E. AL 9th (Malone's) Cav. Co.L Cpl.
Thrasher, F. 20th Conf.Cav. Co.E
Thrasher, F.G. VA 166th Mil. Co.H Capt.
Thrasher, Francis M. AL Cav. Moses' Squad. Co.A
Thrasher, Fredrick G. VA Lt.Arty. G.B. Chapman's Co. Jr.1st Lt.
Thrasher, G. MS 5th Inf. (St.Troops) Co.F
Thrasher, George C. VA Burks' Regt.Loc.Def. Beckner's Co.
Thrasher, Gilbert AL 44th Inf. Co.I
Thrasher, G.W. AL 18th Inf. Co.I
Thrasher, H. GA 15th Inf. Co.H
Thrasher, H. KY 3rd Bn.Mtd.Rifles Co.C
Thrasher, Harrison KY 1st (Butler's) Cav. Co.C,E
Thrasher, H.R. TX 22nd Inf. Co.I
Thrasher, Isaac VA 19th Cav. Co.B Sgt.
Thrasher, Isaac C. GA Inf. Taylor's Co.
Thrasher, Isaiah MS Inf. 1st Bn.St.Troops (12 mo. '62-3) Co.B
Thrasher, J. 20th Conf.Cav. Co.E
Thrasher, Jacob VA Cav. 46th Bn. Co.C
Thrasher, Jacob C. TX 34th Cav. Co.C
Thrasher, James AL 8th (Hatch's) Cav. Co.K
Thrasher, James C. FL Milton Lt.Arty. Dunham's Co.
Thrasher, James C. TN 38th Inf. Co.F Capt.
Thrasher, James F. MS 15th Inf. Co.C
Thrasher, James H. MO 2nd Inf. Co.A
Thrasher, James McD. VA 28th Inf. Co.I Sgt.
Thrasher, J.C. AR 26th Inf. Co.C
Thrasher, J.C. FL 11th Inf. Co.G
Thrasher, J.C. GA 53rd Inf. Co.F
Thrasher, Jesse C. MS 15th Inf. Co.C
Thrasher, Jessee S. GA 64th Inf. Co.A Capt.
Thrasher, Jesse S. GA 7th Inf. Co.K
Thrasher, J.H. AL 27th Inf. Co.E Cpl.
Thrasher, J.H. AL 49th Inf. Co.G Cpl.
Thrasher, J.H. Exch.Bn. Co.D,CSA Cpl.
Thrasher, J.J. GA Inf. (Collier Guards) Collier's Co. QM
Thrasher, J.M. GA 29th Inf. Co.F
Thrasher, Joel MO 1st N.E. Cav.
Thrasher, John AL 8th (Hatch's) Cav. Co.K
Thrasher, John AL 36th Inf. Co.D
Thrasher, John AL 62nd Inf. Co.D
Thrasher, John LA 28th (Gray's) Inf. Co.K Sgt.
Thrasher, John TX 20th Cav. Co.G
Thrasher, John B. TX 15th Cav. Co.C
Thrasher, John C. AL 20th Inf. Co.D
Thrasher, John H. AL 16th Inf. Co.C
Thrasher, John O. GA 3rd Cav. (St.Guards) Co.F 2nd Lt.
Thrasher, John O. GA Inf. Taylor's Co.
Thrasher, John Q.A. VA 2nd Cav. Co.C
Thrasher, John T. AL 44th Inf. Co.G
Thrasher, John W. AL 22nd Inf. Co.E
Thrasher, J.T. AL 50th Inf.
Thrasher, J.T. FL 1st (Res.) Inf. Co.G Sgt.
Thrasher, L.A. SC 1st (Butler's) Inf. Co.I
Thrasher, L.C. VA Inf. 26th Bn. Co.F Capt.
Thrasher, Leroy C. VA 59th Inf. 2nd Co.C Capt.
Thrasher, L.H. GA 15th Inf. Co.H
Thrasher, Marion J. MS 15th Inf. Co.A
Thrasher, M.F. VA 22nd Inf. Co.H
Thrasher, M.J. AL 27th Inf. Co.E
Thrasher, M.J. AL 49th Inf. Co.G,F
Thrasher, M.J. MS 1st (Percy's) Inf. Co.I
Thrasher, M.J. Exch.Bn. Co.D,CSA
Thrasher, M.T. AL 44th Inf. Co.E,G
Thrasher, Nelson W. KY 3rd Bn.Mtd.Rifles Co.C 2nd Lt.
Thrasher, R. AL Cav. Moreland's Regt. Co.C
Thrasher, R.B. AR 6th Inf. Co.C Cpl.
Thrasher, R.B. AR 12th Inf. Co.A 2nd Lt.
Thrasher, Richard MS Inf. 5th Bn. Co.A
Thrasher, Richard MS 43rd Inf. Co.I
Thrasher, Richard VA 33rd Inf. Co.F Cpl.
Thrasher, R.J. VA 50th Inf.
Thrasher, R.M. AR 18th Inf. Co.B Capt.
Thrasher, Robert B. AR 12th Bn.S.S. Co.A Sr.2nd Lt.
Thrasher, Robert J. VA 22nd Inf. Co.I
Thrasher, Samuel MO 1st N.E. Cav. Co.A
Thrasher, Stephen MS 12th Inf. Co.K
Thrasher, T. AL 11th Inf. Co.G
Thrasher, T. KY 3rd Bn.Mtd.Rifles Co.C
Thrasher, Talbott MS 26th Inf. Co.I
Thrasher, Thomas AL 3rd Inf. Co.G
Thrasher, Thomas AL 48th Inf. Co.A
Thrasher, Thomas AL 49th Inf. Co.G
Thrasher, Thomas GA 1st (Fannin's) Res. Co.D
Thrasher, Thomas Exch.Bn. Co.D,CSA
Thrasher, Thomas C. MS 15th Inf. Co.G
Thrasher, Thomas J. AR 3rd Inf. Co.F Capt.
Thrasher, T.J. GA 15th Inf. Co.H
Thrasher, T.L. VA 7th Cav. Co.G 2nd Lt.
Thrasher, Tolbert MS 32nd Inf. Co.K
Thrasher, T.T. GA 18th Inf. Co.B
Thrasher, Tyrrel GA 15th Inf. Co.H
Thrasher, W.F. AL 41st Inf. Co.D
Thrasher, Wm. AL 22nd Inf. Co.F
Thrasher, William AL 29th Inf. Co.F
Thrasher, William AR 32nd Inf. Co.A
Thrasher, William GA 10th Cav. (St.Guards) Co.C Sgt.
Thrasher, William MS 27th Inf. Co.I
Thrasher, William H. GA 3rd Inf. Co.L 1st Sgt.

Thrasher, William H. GA 9th Inf. (St.Guards) Co.G 2nd Lt.
Thrasher, William I. LA 28th (Gray's) Inf. Co.K
Thrasher, William J. GA 36th (Broyles') Inf. Co.F
Thrasher, William L. AR 10th (Witt's) Cav. Co.F
Thrasher, William L. AR 27th Inf. Co.A
Thrasher, William L. GA 3rd Inf. Co.D
Thrasher, William N. MS 13th Inf. Co.A
Thrasher, W.J. GA Inf. 2nd Bn. (St.Guards) Co.C 3rd Lt.
Thrasher, W.L. 7th Conf.Cav. Co.C,A Cpl.
Thrasher, W.W. AL 46th Inf. Co.C
Thrasher, W.W. AL Randolph Cty.Res. D.A. Self's Co.
Thrasher, W.W. Gen. & Staff Hosp.Stew.
Thraves, John VA Inf. 4th Bn.Loc.Def. Co.F
Thraves, John T. VA 44th Inf. Co.H
Thraves, J.T. VA 10th Cav. Co.E
Thravis, John T. VA Conscr. Cp.Lee Co.A
Thrayard, A. LA Mil. 4th Regt. French Brig. Co.7
Threadaway, Isham AR 47th (Crandall's) Cav. Co.E
Threadcraft, Francis M. GA 1st (Olmstead's) Inf. Davis' Co., Co.C
Threader, Robert KY 2nd (Woodward's) Cav. Co.F Sgt.
Threadgill, Benjamin K. NC 14th Inf. Co.C
Threadgill, Charles F. AL 15th Bn.Part.Rangers Co.B
Threadgill, E.J. AR 2nd Inf. Co.K Capt.
Threadgill, George W. AL 6th Inf. Co.I
Threadgill, George W. MS Cav. Jeff Davis Legion Co.E
Threadgill, George Washington NC 43rd Inf. Co.I Sgt.
Threadgill, G.G. MS 28th Cav. Co.C
Threadgill, H. AL 38th Inf. Co.H 1st Sgt.
Threadgill, H.D.A. AL 21st Inf. Co.F
Threadgill, Henry D. MS 19th Inf. Co.I
Threadgill, Hull D. TX 18th Inf. Co.L
Threadgill, J. TX Cav. Border's Regt. Co.E
Threadgill, J.A. TN 21st & 22nd (Cons.) Cav. Co.F,G
Threadgill, James AR 1st (Colquitt's) Inf. Co.C
Threadgill, James NC 6th Sr.Res. Co.G Cpl.
Threadgill, James A. AL Cav. Gachet's Co.
Threadgill, Joe B. TX 32nd Cav. Co.E Sgt.
Threadgill, John AL 3rd Inf. Co.C
Threadgill, John AL 45th Inf. Co.G
Threadgill, John NC 14th Inf. Co.C
Threadgill, John TN 21st (Wilson's) Cav. Co.C
Threadgill, John TX 26th Cav. Co.H
Threadgill, John H. NC 43rd Inf. Co.I 1st Lt.
Threadgill, John N. AL 6th Inf. Co.I
Threadgill, Joshua AL 39th Inf. Co.E
Threadgill, J.T. AL 24th Inf. Co.K
Threadgill, J.W. AL 44th Inf. Co.F
Threadgill, L.N. TN 27th Inf. Co.F
Threadgill, Miles NC 14th Inf. Co.C
Threadgill, Miles NC 43rd Inf. Co.H
Threadgill, N.G. MS 13th Inf. Co.K
Threadgill, Noah AL Lt.Arty. Clanton's Btty.
Threadgill, Patrick R. NC 43rd Inf. Co.I
Threadgill, Peter AL Lt.Arty. Clanton's Btty.
Threadgill, Pinckney AL 45th Inf. Co.G
Threadgill, Samuel AL 3rd Res. Co.I Sgt.
Threadgill, S.G. MS 7th Cav. Co.A
Threadgill, Stephen H. NC 43rd Inf. Co.I Cpl.
Threadgill, Thomas AL 43rd Inf. Co.B
Threadgill, Thomas MS 30th Inf. Co.A
Threadgill, Thomas A. AL 38th Inf. Co.B
Threadgill, Thomas A. AL 43rd Inf. Co.B
Threadgill, T.S. MS 24th Inf. AQM
Threadgill, T.S. MS 30th Inf. Co.A AQM
Threadgill, T.S. Hill's Div. Capt.,QM
Threadgill, W.C. AL 22nd Inf. Co.H
Threadgill, W.H. AL 40th Inf. Co.E
Threadgill, W.H. AR 2nd Cav. Co.D
Threadgill, William TN 51st (Cons.) Inf. Co.D
Threadgill, William A. NC 14th Inf. Co.C 2nd Lt.
Threadgill, William B. NC 4th Cav. (59th St.Troops) Co.A
Threadgill, William C. NC 14th Inf. Co.C Cpl.
Threadgill, William H. AL 47th Inf. Co.B
Threadgill, William T. AL 38th Inf. Co.C 1st Lt.
Threadgill, W.R.J.P. AL 23rd Inf. Co.A 2nd Lt.
Threadgill, W.T. TX 26th Cav. Co.H
Threadwell, J. TX Cav. Border's Regt. Co.E
Threasher, J. AR 8th Cav. Co.C
Threat, A. KY 12th Cav. Co.H
Threat, B.R. SC 1st (Butler's) Inf. Co.D
Threat, Burrell SC 17th Inf. Co.I
Threat, D.H. AL 30th Inf. Co.H 1st Lt.
Threat, Evan SC 4th St.Troops Co.K
Threat, J. KY 12th Cav. Co.H
Threat, James M. TN 25th Inf. Co.H
Threat, Jeremiah SC 1st (Butler's) Inf. Co.A,H
Threat, Jesse AL 11th Inf. Co.I
Threat, Jesse, Jr. TN 25th Inf. Co.H
Threat, Jesse, Sr. TN 25th Inf. Co.H
Threat, J.J. AR 34th Inf. Co.F
Threat, J.M. TN 44th (Cons.) Inf. Co.G
Threat, J.N. MS Lt.Arty. (Warren Lt.Arty.) Swett's Co.
Threat, John GA 2nd Cav. (St.Guards) Co.E
Threat, Joseph AL Pris.Guard Freeman's Co.
Threat, Joseph SC 4th St.Troops Co.K
Threat, Joseph J. TN 19th (Biffle's) Cav. Co.B
Threat, J.P. TN 19th (Biffle's) Cav. Co.B
Threat, J.S. VA 5th Cav. Co.B
Threat, Robert SC 1st (Butler's) Inf. Co.K Cpl.
Threat, W.F. KY 12th Cav. Co.H
Threat, W.F. TN 19th (Biffle's) Cav. Co.B
Threate, J.M. TN 55th (McKoin's) Inf. Bound's Co.
Threaton, John LA Inf. 9th Bn. Co.D
Threats, John 1st Conf.Inf. 2nd Co.C
Threatt, Benjamin SC Lt.Arty. Kelly's Co. (Chesterfield Arty.)
Threatt, Burwell MS 11th Inf. Co.D
Threatt, E. MS 40th Inf. Co.E Cpl.
Threatt, E.J. MS 35th Inf. Co.E
Threatt, E.J. MS Walsh's Co. (Muckalusha Guards)
Threatt, Evan MS 10th Inf. New Co.H
Threatt, H.A. SC 26th Inf. Co.B
Threatt, Hiram SC Inf. 9th Bn. Co.B
Threatt, J. MS Walsh's Co. (Muckalusha Guards)
Threatt, J.A. SC 26th Inf. Co.F
Threatt, James SC Inf. 9th Bn. Co.B
Threatt, James SC 26th Inf. Co.B
Threatt, John A. SC 8th Inf. Co.D
Threatt, John R. SC Inf. 9th Bn. Co.B
Threatt, John W. SC 8th Inf. Co.B
Threatt, John W. SC 26th Inf. Co.F Sgt.
Threatt, Joseph AL Freeman's Bn. Co.A
Threatt, Joseph SC 8th Inf. Co.D
Threatt, Joseph SC Loc.Guard
Threatt, Joshua MS 11th Inf. Co.D Cpl.
Threatt, Joshua MS 35th Inf. Co.E
Threatt, J.R. AL 60th Inf. Co.E
Threatt, J.R. MS 17th Inf. Co.K
Threatt, J.W. SC Inf. 9th Bn. Co.E Sgt.
Threatt, Miles SC 26th Inf. Co.F
Threatt, Peter L. SC 1st (Butler's) Inf. Co.K
Threatt, Robert SC 8th Inf. Co.D
Threatt, Thomas SC 8th Inf. Co.B
Threatt, Thomas SC Inf. 9th Bn. Co.B
Threatt, Thomas SC 26th Inf. Co.B
Threatt, Thomas C. GA Inf. 9th Bn. Co.B
Threatt, Willson SC 8th Inf. Co.B
Threatte, Joseph S. SC 8th Inf. Co.D Cpl.
Threawtt, I.T. Conf.Cav. Raum's Co.
Thredder, Robert KY 1st Inf. Co.A Sgt.
Thredgill, Harvy AL Mil. 4th Vol. Co.A
Thredgill, John H. AL 6th Inf. Co.G
Thredwell, William AR 45th Mil. Co.D
Threece, Henry AR 45th Mil. Co.D
Threefoot, A. MS Conscr.
Threefoot, M. AL Mil. 2nd Regt.Vol. Co.B Sgt.
Threet, Evin B. AR 18th Inf. Co.H
Threet, George W. TN 25th Inf. Co.H
Threet, Hugh AR 18th Inf. Co.H
Threet, Nathan AL 26th (O'Neal's) Inf. Co.A Cpl.
Threet, Thomas AR 11th Inf. Co.A
Threet, Thomas AR 11th & 17th Cons.Inf. Co.A
Threet, William AR 34th Inf. Co.F
Threewits, T.D. GA Inf. 25th Bn. (Prov.Guard) Co.B 2nd Lt.
Threldkill, E.H. GA 6th Inf. (St.Guards) Co.E 1st Sgt.
Threlked, J.J. GA 2nd Inf. Co.B
Threlkeld, A.L. KY 3rd Cav. Co.D
Threlkeld, Alonzo KY 7th Cav. Co.D
Threlkeld, C.W. KY 4th Cav. Co.G 1st Sgt.
Threlkeld, D.T. KY 7th Cav. Co.D 2nd Sgt.
Threlkeld, Elijah KY 5th Cav. Co.B Sgt.
Threlkeld, G. KY 8th Cav. Co.C Sgt.
Threlkeld, George B. KY 4th Cav. Co.C
Threlkeld, George B. KY 9th Cav. Co.C
Threlkeld, I.B. TX 6th Inf. Co.A
Threlkeld, J.A. KY 3rd Mtd.Inf. Co.K Sgt.
Threlkeld, James L. MS 19th Inf. Co.E
Threlkeld, James M. GA 34th Inf. Co.H
Threlkeld, Lewis MS 19th Inf. Co.E
Threlkeld, Madison W. GA 34th Inf. Co.H
Threlkeld, N.H. KY 10th (Johnson's) Cav. Co.D,A
Threlkeld, P. AL 4th (Roddey's) Cav. Co.A Capt.
Threlkeld, R.P. TX Cav. Waller's Regt. Co.F
Threlkeld, Samuel C. MS 2nd Inf. Co.I
Threlkeld, Thomas J. GA 34th Inf. Co.H
Threlkeld, Thomas W. KY 4th Mtd.Inf. Co.C
Threlkeld, Weston KY 5th Cav. Co.B
Threlkeld, William KY 4th Cav. Co.G

Threlkeld, William H.C. GA 46th Inf. Co.B
Threlkeld, William S. MS 19th Inf. Co.E Sgt.
Threlkeld, Willis D. SC 4th Inf. Co.G
Threlkeld, W.W. GA 3rd Mil. Co.B
Threlkell, Uriah H. KY 3rd Cav. Co.I
Threlkild, M.W. GA 39th Inf. Co.B
Thresher, George B. TX 14th Cav.
Thresher, I.M. TN 25th Inf. Co.I Cpl.
Thresher, James F. TX 22nd Cav. Co.F
Thresher, J.W. TN 25th Inf. Co.I
Thresher, Robert TN 25th Inf. Co.I
Thresher, W.F. GA 10th Inf. Co.I
Thresher, W.F. TN 25th Inf. Co.I
Threshie, C. LA Mil.Conf.Guards Regt. Co.K
Threshie, C. LA Mil.Cont.Regt. Mitchell's Co.
Threter, R. VA 2nd St.Res. Co.H
Threwer, J. MS 2nd St.Cav. 2nd Co.C
Threwitts, Thomas D. GA Inf. 2nd Bn. Co.A
Thrielkill, Levi GA 1st Inf. Co.D
Thrift, A.E. VA 9th Inf. 2nd Co.A
Thrift, Alex E. VA Hood's Bn.Res. Tappey's Co.
Thrift, Allen SC 6th Inf. 1st Co.I
Thrift, Allen SC Palmetto S.S. Co.M
Thrift, Allen E. VA 9th Inf. 2nd Co.A
Thrift, A.N. VA Arty. Wise Legion
Thrift, A.T. 1st Conf.Cav. Co.I
Thrift, Augustus VA Hvy.Arty. 19th Bn. 2nd Co.C
Thrift, Benjamin VA Cav. Mosby's Regt. (Part.Rangers) Co.H
Thrift, Benjamin P. VA 26th Inf. Co.A
Thrift, B.L. AR 9th Inf. Co.K
Thrift, C. SC 3rd Inf. Co.B
Thrift, Carver AL 46th Inf. Co.B
Thrift, Charles MS 28th Cav. Co.I
Thrift, Elliott VA 40th Inf. Co.E
Thrift, E.W. VA Arty. Wise Legion
Thrift, E.W. 1st Conf.Cav. Co.I
Thrift, Fleet VA Cav. 15th Bn. Co.B
Thrift, Fleet W. VA 111th Mil. Co.2
Thrift, George VA Cav. 35th Bn. Co.A
Thrift, George VA Murphy's Co.
Thrift, George N. VA 7th Inf. Co.A 2nd Lt.
Thrift, George W. AL 3rd Bn.Res.
Thrift, George W. VA 41st Mil. Co.B
Thrift, G.W. AL 6th Inf. Co.G
Thrift, G.W. SC 3rd Inf. Co.B,A
Thrift, G.W. 8th (Wade's) Conf.Cav. Co.K
Thrift, Henry VA Mtd.Res. Rappahannock Dist. Sale's Co.
Thrift, Henry VA Res.Forces Clark's Co.
Thrift, Henry L. VA 9th Cav. Co.C
Thrift, Hiram D. VA 21st Mil. Co.E
Thrift, Hiram L. VA 34th Inf. Co.A
Thrift, James VA 8th Inf. Co.G Maj.
Thrift, James E. VA Cav. 35th Bn. Co.F
Thrift, James T. VA 5th Cav. Co.A
Thrift, James T. VA 26th Inf. 2nd Co.B
Thrift, James T. VA 55th Inf. Co.H
Thrift, Jeremiah C. VA 111th Mil. Co.2
Thrift, J.H. TN 9th Inf. Co.H
Thrift, J.H. VA Res.Forces Clark's Co.
Thrift, J.L. TX Inf. 2nd St.Troops Co.C
Thrift, J.L. TX 12th Inf. Co.G
Thrift, J.N. KY 3rd Mtd.Inf. Co.H
Thrift, John GA 50th Inf. Co.B
Thrift, John GA 61st Inf. Co.B
Thrift, John SC 1st Arty. Co.I
Thrift, John SC 1st Bn.S.S. Co.H
Thrift, John SC 20th Inf. Co.F
Thrift, John SC 27th Inf. Co.E
Thrift, John B. VA 14th Inf. Co.A
Thrift, John H. TN 15th (Stewart's) Cav. Co.A
Thrift, John W. NC 22nd Inf. Co.L
Thrift, John W. VA 15th Cav. Co.G
Thrift, John W. VA Cav. 15th Bn. Co.D
Thrift, John W. VA 41st Mil. Co.A
Thrift, Joseph B. VA 9th Cav. Co.C
Thrift, L.D. SC Palmetto S.S. Co.I
Thrift, L.J. GA 4th (Clinch's) Cav.
Thrift, Lorenzo Dow SC 4th Inf. Co.I
Thrift, Nathaniel S. VA 9th Inf. 2nd Co.A
Thrift, Peter NC 5th Inf. Co.E
Thrift, Pinkney NC 1st Inf. (6 mo. '61) Co.D
Thrift, Pinkney NC 11th (Bethel Regt.) Inf. Co.G
Thrift, Pleasant SC 5th Inf. 1st Co.G
Thrift, Pleasant SC Palmetto S.S. Co.M
Thrift, R. VA 1st (Farinholt's) Res. Co.I
Thrift, R.H. VA Inf. 44th Bn.
Thrift, Richard A. VA 40th Inf. Co.E
Thrift, Richard C. VA 9th Cav. Co.K
Thrift, Richard O. VA 40th Inf. Co.I
Thrift, Robert SC Inf. 3rd Bn. Co.F
Thrift, Robert C. VA 20th Inf. Co.D
Thrift, R.T. GA Cav. 24th Bn. Co.A,C
Thrift, Sanderson VA 6th Cav. Co.K
Thrift, T.E. SC Inf. Hampton Legion Co.C
Thrift, Theota VA 5th Cav. Co.A
Thrift, Thomas J. VA 5th Cav. Co.A
Thrift, T.J.W. SC 12th Inf. Co.K Sgt.
Thrift, T.M. VA 3rd (Archer's) Bn.Res. Co.B
Thrift, W.H. AL Randolph Cty.Res. A.P. Hunter's Co.
Thrift, W.H. NC 66th Inf. Co.G
Thrift, W.H. VA 40th Inf. Co.B
Thrift, William NC 11th (Bethel Regt.) Inf. Co.G
Thrift, William VA 6th Cav. Co.K 2nd Lt.
Thrift, Wm. H. AL 25th Inf. Co.F,G
Thrift, Wm. H. AL Cp. of Instr. Talladega
Thrift, William H. NC 2nd Cav. (19th St.Troops) Co.F
Thrift, William H. SC 1st (Orr's) Rifles Co.A
Thrift, William J. VA 5th Cav. Co.A
Thrift, William Jackson VA 21st Mil. Co.E
Thrift, William J.J. VA 24th Cav. Co.D
Thrift, William J.J. VA Cav. 40th Bn. Co.D
Thrift, William J.J. VA 21st Mil. Co.E Capt.
Thrift, William T. VA Lt.Arty. Clutter's Co.
Thrift, William T. VA Arty. Fleet's Co.
Thrift, William T. VA 12th Inf. 1st Co.I
Thrift, William T. VA 41st Inf. 2nd Co.E
Thrift, William T. VA 55th Inf. Co.B
Thrift, W.M. VA 3rd Cav. 2nd Lt.
Thrift, Young AL 26th (O'Neal's) Inf. Co.B
Thrift, Young MS 5th Inf. Co.A
Thro, Milton M. MO 2nd Inf. Co.C
Throa, G.W. NC 3rd Jr.Res. Co.C
Throcatt, A.M. GA Inf. 1st Bn. (St.Guards) Co.E
Throckmorton, --- KY 7th Mtd.Inf. Co.B
Throckmorton, --- TX 8th Inf.
Throckmorton, Andrew J. VA 3rd Inf. 2nd Co.K Cpl.
Throckmorton, Branch VA 20th Inf. Co.H
Throckmorton, Branch S. VA 3rd Inf. 2nd Co.K Sgt.
Throckmorton, C.F. AL 11th Cav. Co.I
Throckmorton, Henry S. TN 14th Inf. Co.L 1st Sgt.
Throckmorton, J.A. Gen. & Staff Surg.
Throckmorton, James NC 45th Inf. Co.F
Throckmorton, Jas. C. NC 21st Inf. Co.L
Throckmorton, James W. TX 6th Cav. Co.K Capt.
Throckmorton, J.H. GA Cav. Hawkins' Co.
Throckmorton, J.H. KY 1st (Butler's) Cav. Co.G
Throckmorton, John KY Cav. 2nd Bn. (Dortch's) Co.D
Throckmorton, John A. VA 6th Cav. Co.F Capt.
Throckmorton, John J. VA Hvy.Arty. 10th Bn. Co.C Sgt.
Throckmorton, John W. MS 16th Inf. Co.C Cpl.
Throckmorton, Joseph C. VA 2nd Arty. Co.D
Throckmorton, Joseph G. VA Inf. 22nd Bn. Co.D
Throckmorton, J.W. TX Cav. (Dismtd.) Chisum's Regt. Maj.
Throckmorton, P.S. MS Inf. 2nd Bn. Co.F
Throckmorton, P.S. MS 48th Inf. Co.F
Throckmorton, Robert M. TX 29th Cav. Co.E
Throckmorton, Robert M. 1st Choctaw & Chickasaw Mtd.Rifles 1st Co.I Sgt.
Throckmorton, R.P. MO Cav. Freeman's Regt. Co.C 2nd Lt.
Throckmorton, T.N. VA 24th Cav. Co.B
Throckmorton, T.N. VA Cav. 40th Bn. Co.B
Throckmorton, W.C. TX 8th Inf.
Throckmorton, William VA 28th Inf. Co.E
Throckmorton, William C. VA 21st Inf. Co.K Cpl.
Throckmorton, William E. TX 21st Cav. Co.K
Throckmorton, William E. TX 29th Cav. Co.E
Throckmorton, William E. 1st Choctaw & Chickasaw Mtd.Rifles 1st Co.I
Throckmorton, William W. VA 7th Cav. Co.F
Throer, Edward AR 1st (Crawford's) Cav. Co.D
Throg, William VA Lt.Arty. Clutter's Co.
Throgg, William VA 3rd Lt.Arty. (Loc.Def.) Co.H
Throgmarten, C.N. TN 19th & 20th (Cons.) Cav. Co.K
Throgmartin, C.N. TN 20th (Russell's) Cav. Co.F
Throgmartin, T.E. VA 56th Inf. Co.K
Throgmorten, Us. MO Cav. Freeman's Regt. Co.C
Throgmorton, A. Christian VA 15th Inf. Co.G
Throgmorton, Albert VA Lt.Arty. Rives' Co.
Throgmorton, Atheleus VA 15th Inf. Co.G
Throgmorton, Charles VA Hvy.Arty. 10th Bn. Co.E
Throgmorton, D.S. NC 5th Sr.Res. Co.F
Throgmorton, Henry VA 15th Inf. Co.G
Throgmorton, James A. VA Hvy.Arty. 10th Bn. Co.E
Throgmorton, James C. TN Cav. 9th Bn. (Gantt's) Co.F
Throgmorton, James D. TN 48th (Voorhies') Inf.
Throgmorton, J.C. TN 6th (Wheeler's) Cav. Co.G
Throgmorton, Jesse P. VA 15th Inf. Co.G

Throgmorton, John M. VA Inf. 5th Bn. Co.D
Throgmorton, Joseph VA Inf. 5th Bn. Co.D
Throgmorton, Joseph VA 53rd Inf. Co.A
Throgmorton, L.W. TX Cav. Giddings' Bn. Co.A
Throgmorton, Marshall VA Hvy.Arty. 10th Bn. Co.E
Throgmorton, Robert F. MO Inf. 8th Bn. Co.B
Throgmorton, Robert P. MO 3rd Regt.St.Guards Co.E Sgt.
Throgmorton, Thomas VA 15th Inf. Co.G
Throgmorton, William TN 5th Inf. 2nd Co.C
Throgmorton, William P. TN Cav. 9th Bn. (Gantt's) Co.F Cpl.
Throm, Henry VA 47th Inf. Co.B
Thromer, T. AR Cav. McGehee's Regt. Co.E
Thron, D. LA Mil. Orleans Fire Regt. Co.A
Thronberry, A.J. TN 23rd Inf. Co.D
Thronberry, J.K.P. TN 23rd Inf. Co.D
Throne, R.C. AR 1st Mtd.Rifles Co.I
Throneberry, David R. TN 44th Inf. Co.H
Throneberry, David R. TN 44th (Cons.) Inf. Co.A
Throneberry, James P. TN 44th Inf. Co.H
Throneberry, James P. TN 44th (Cons.) Inf. Co.A
Throneberry, Joseph N. TN 44th Inf. Co.H
Throneberry, Joseph N. TN 44th (Cons.) Inf. Co.A
Throneberry, Levi T. TN 44th Inf. Co.H
Throneburg, Jonathan S. NC 28th Inf. Co.C
Throneburg, Mathias M. NC 28th Inf. Co.C 2nd Lt.
Throneburg, M. Augustus NC 28th Inf. Co.C 1st Lt.
Thronley, J.L. AL 26th (O'Neal's) Inf. Co.K
Throop, Benjamin B. TX Inf. 24th Bn. Surg.
Throop, Hardy O. TX 34th Cav. Co.A Cpl.
Throop, James M. TX 34th Cav. Co.A
Throop, Samuel G. MS 22nd Inf. Co.I
Throop, T.B. TX St.Troops Hampton's Co.
Throop, Tho. VA Cav. Mosby's Regt. (Part. Rangers) Co.C
Throop, T.R. TX 4th Cav. Co.C
Throp, F.W. TN 22nd (Barteau's) Cav. Co.E Ens.
Throp, George F. Burroughs' Bn.Part.Rangers Co.A
Thrope, C.H. TN 8th (Smith's) Cav. Co.C
Thropp, C.H. TN 4th (Murray's) Cav. Co.H
Thropp, Franklin W. TN Cav. 7th Bn. (Bennett's) Co.B
Thropp, George T. VA 6th Inf. Co.F
Throps, W. KY 2nd (Duke's) Cav.
Thropshire, Andrew J. GA 2nd Cav. Co.I
Thropshire, John GA 2nd Cav. Co.I
Throqmartin, Albert VA Hvy.Arty. 19th Bn. 2nd Co.C, 3rd Co.C
Throster, Jacob VA Inf. 4th Bn.Loc.Def. Co.A
Throuz, F. LA Mil.Squad. Guides d'Orleans
Throvoir, D.S. AR 23rd Inf. Co.K
Thrower, Alex NC 11th (Bethel Regt.) Inf. Co.H Cpl.
Thrower, Benjamin AL 60th Inf. Co.A
Thrower, Benjamin AL 61st Inf. Co.C Cpl.
Thrower, Benjamin NC 2nd Arty. (36th St.Troops) Co.F
Thrower, B.F. AL 1st Cav. 1st Co.B
Thrower, C. AR 10th (Witt's) Cav. Lt.,Adj.
Thrower, Charles N. NC 18th Inf. Co.F
Thrower, Choice W. GA 4th Inf. Co.D
Thrower, Christopher AR 1st (Colquitt's) Inf. Co.C
Thrower, Cincinatus R. AR 23rd Inf. Co.K
Thrower, Dallas NC 31st Inf. Co.H
Thrower, Dewitt Clinton 1st Conf.Eng.Troops Co.F Cpl.
Thrower, E. TN Arty. Ramsey's Btty.
Thrower, Eli AL Cav. Moreland's Regt. Co.H
Thrower, Eli AL 50th Inf. Co.C
Thrower, Eli AL 54th Inf. Co.A
Thrower, Eli AR 11th Inf. Co.B
Thrower, Eli LA 1st Cav. Robinson's Co.
Thrower, Eli TN 40th Inf. Co.H
Thrower, F. AL 56th Part.Rangers Co.B
Thrower, Fremont AL 15th Bn.Part.Rangers Co.B
Thrower, G. NC 7th Bn.Jr.Res. Co.C
Thrower, George NC Inf. 2nd Bn. Co.A
Thrower, George W. AL Arty. 4th Bn. Hilliard's Legion Co.A
Thrower, G.W. AL 59th Inf. Co.I
Thrower, G.W. NC 4th Bn.Jr.Res. Co.C
Thrower, H.D. MS 6th Cav. Co.K
Thrower, Henry AL Cav. Murphy's Bn. Co.C
Thrower, Henry MO 4th Cav. Co.A
Thrower, Henry MO Cav. Preston's Bn. Co.A
Thrower, Henry 15th Conf.Cav. Co.H
Thrower, Henry C. AL St.Arty. Co.A Cpl.
Thrower, Henry M. NC 18th Inf. Co.F
Thrower, Hezekiah Dudley MS Inf. 1st St.Troops Co.G
Thrower, Hezikiah S. AL 37th Inf. Co.G,E
Thrower, I.E. MS 6th Cav. Co.K
Thrower, I.N AL 14th Inf. Co.B
Thrower, J. NC 3rd Jr.Res. Co.I
Thrower, James AL 37th Inf. Co.G
Thrower, James M. AL 50th Inf. Co.C
Thrower, J.C. MS 11th (Perrin's) Cav. Co.H
Thrower, J.D. NC 1st Jr.Res. Co.D
Thrower, Jeff T. NC 11th (Bethel Regt.) Inf. Co.H
Thrower, Jesse H. NC 38th Inf. Co.E Cpl.
Thrower, J.K. GA 2nd Cav. (St.Guards) Co.C Cpl.
Thrower, John NC 7th Bn.Jr.Res. Co.C
Thrower, John B. AR 1st (Crawford's) Cav. Co.A
Thrower, John T. AL Lt.Arty. 2nd Bn. Co.F
Thrower, John T. NC 49th Inf. Co.D Sgt.
Thrower, Joseph MO 4th Cav. Co.A
Thrower, Joseph MO Cav. Preston's Bn. Co.A
Thrower, J.R. GA Inf. Exempts Roberts' Co.
Thrower, J.T. AL 30th Inf. Co.G
Thrower, J.W. MS 2nd Cav. Co.I
Thrower, Levi AL 61st Inf. Co.C
Thrower, Lewis AL 37th Inf. Co.G
Thrower, Littleton B NC 24th Inf.
Thrower, Mark GA 25th Inf. Co.C
Thrower, Meredith 8th (Wade's) Conf.Cav. Co.B
Thrower, Meridith AL Cav. Falkner's Co.
Thrower, Miles AL 60th Inf. Co.A
Thrower, Miles AL 3rd Bn. Hilliard's Legion Vol. Co.B
Thrower, Newbern NC Inf. 2nd Bn. Co.A
Thrower, Oliver P. NC 43rd Inf. Co.F
Thrower, R. GA Inf. (E. to W.Point Guards) Matthews' Co.
Thrower, Robert N. GA 7th Inf. Co.K
Thrower, Rufus GA 3rd Res. Co.G
Thrower, Sion AL 20th Inf. Co.K
Thrower, S.J. AL 59th Inf. Co.I 1st Sgt.
Thrower, S.S. AL 59th Inf. Co.I Sgt.
Thrower, Starling J. AL Arty. 4th Bn. Hilliard's Legion Co.A Sgt.
Thrower, Stephen S. AL Arty. 4th Bn. Hilliard's Legion Co.A
Thrower, Sterling AL Mobile City Troop
Thrower, S.W. NC 61st Inf. Co.D
Thrower, Thomas J. AL Cav. Falkner's Co.
Thrower, Thomas J. NC 30th Inf. Co.K
Thrower, Thomas M. AL 3rd Cav.
Thrower, T.J. AL 63rd Inf. Co.F
Thrower, T.L. GA 3rd Bn. (St.Guards) Co.B
Thrower, T.L. 8th (Wade's) Conf.Cav. Co.B
Thrower, T.W. AL 14th Inf. Co.B
Thrower, Wesley P. NC 1st Inf. Co.I
Thrower, Westley AL 61st Inf. Co.C
Thrower, W.H. VA 14th Inf. Co.F
Thrower, Whitfield AL 1st Bn.Cadets Co.A Cpl.
Thrower, William NC 1st Inf. Co.K
Thrower, William NC Inf. 2nd Bn. Co.A
Thrower, William H. NC 52nd Inf. Co.E
Thrower, William M. AL 59th Inf. Co.
Thrower, William M. AL Arty. 4th Bn. Hilliard's Legion
Thrower, William N. NC 8th Inf. Co.E Cpl.
Thrower, William N. NC 54th Inf. Co.C Cpl.
Thrower, William P. NC 47th Inf. Co.E,C
Thrower, W.L. AL 14th Inf. Co.B
Thrower, Young S. TN 37th Inf. Co.H 1st Lt.
Throwers, C.S. AR 10th Mil. Co.F Sgt.
Throws, M.P. NC 1st Inf. Co.I
Throyer, Andrew LA Mil. 4th Regt. 3rd Brig. 1st Div. Co.A
Thrundale, David L. GA 4th (Clinch's) Cav. Co.G
Thrush, John M. VA 2nd Inf. Co.D
Thrush, William VA 18th Cav. Co.K
Thrusher, J. AL 8th Cav. Co.A
Thruston, Edward T. VA 26th Inf. Co.E 1st Lt.
Thruston, E.J. VA 5th Cav. Co.A
Thruston, James R. VA 26th Inf. Co.C Sgt.
Thruston, Jasper AR 34th Inf. Co.F
Thruston, Joseph S. MO 2nd Inf. Co.D
Thruston, Stephen D. NC 3rd Inf. Co.B Col.
Thruston, William R. VA 24th Cav. Co.D
Thruston, William R. VA Cav. 40th Bn. Co.D
Thrut, Bery NC 52nd Inf. Co.D
Thry, W.S. AR 36th Inf. Co.I
Thudgill, F. TN 20th Cav. Co.B
Thuemler, A. TX Inf. 4th Bn. (Oswald's) Co.A
Thuer, John LA Cav. Greenleaf's Co. (Orleans Lt.Horse)
Thuer, John LA Inf.Crescent Regt. Co.H
Thuey, Michael TN 5th Inf. Co.E Cpl.
Thuilier, Theodore Eng.,CSA
Thuing, James SC Arty. Manigault's Bn. 2nd Co.C Sgt.
Thulemeyer, F. TX 5th Inf. Martindale's Co.

Thulemeyer, Simon TX Cav. Benavides' Regt. Co.D
Thullen, Peter TN Arty. Marshall's Co. Cpl.
Thulliet, G. LA Inf. 16th Bn. (Conf.Guards Resp.Bn.) Co.B
Thulliet, John Batiste LA Inf. 16th Bn. (Conf. Guards Resp.Bn.) Co.B
Thum, M. AR 7th Inf. Surg.
Thum, S.G. TN 9th Inf. Co.K Cpl.
Thum, Thomas B. MO 4th Cav. Co.I
Thuma, C. AR Mil. Borland's Regt. Peyton Rifles
Thuma, Charles AR 6th Inf. Co.A
Thuma, C.J. VA Horse Arty. J.W. Carter's Co.
Thuma, Robert VA 52nd Inf. Co.D
Thuma, Thomas VA 10th Inf. Co.D
Thuma, Thomas J. VA 58th Mil. Co.G
Thumb, John TN 1st Hvy.Arty. 2nd Co.B, 3rd Co.B, Co.L
Thumings, Shedrick VA 23rd Cav. Co.A
Thumles, Frederick TX 4th Field Btty.
Thumond, --- AL 1st Bn. Hilliard's Legion Vol. Co.C
Thumond, J.E. TN 16th Cav. Co.E
Thumulson, Joseph H. GA 37th Inf. Co.I
Thun, Lawrence LA Mil. Chalmette Regt. Co.D
Thunat, John A. TN 1st (Feild's) Inf. Co.D
Thundbank, J. AL 11th Inf. Co.H
Thunderberk, J.B. SC 8th Inf. Co.B
Thunder Billy 1st Choctaw & Chickasaw Mtd.Rifles 2nd Co.D
Thune, Daniel A. TN 8th Inf.
Thung, A. GA 21st Inf. Co.I
Thuntry, A. TX Inf. Timmons' Regt. Co.D
Thurber, Amos MO 12th Inf. Co.H
Thurber, Ferdinand H. AL 4th (Russell's) Cav. Co.F
Thurber, H.G. KY 9th Cav. Co.I
Thurber, J.A. LA Mil. British Guard Bn. Burrowes' Co.
Thurber, J.A. LA Mil. Orleans Guards Regt. Co.D
Thurber, John LA Miles' Legion Co.G
Thurber, J.R. AL 5th Inf. Co.D
Thurbish, Thomas MS 7th Cav. Co.C
Thure, Dan TN 1st Hvy.Arty. Co.D
Thuren, Frank LA C.S. Zouave Bn. Co.F
Thurer, George AR 35th Inf. Co.C
Thurer, U. LA Mil. Chalmette Regt. Co.D
Thurin, E. LA Mil. 4th Regt. French Brig. Co.1
Thurin, G. TX 26th Cav. Co.E
Thurlee, B. MS 11th Inf.
Thurlkeld, J.M. AR 21st Inf. Co.G
Thurlkill, George W. AR 9th Inf. Co.K
Thurlkill, James A. AL 48th Inf. Co.G
Thurlkill, J.B. GA 4th Res. Co.C
Thurlkill, John AR 5th Mil. Co.E
Thurlkill, John AR 35th Inf. Co.G
Thurlkill, John W. GA 17th Inf. Co.A,H
Thurlkill, J.T. GA 4th Res. Co.C
Thurlkill, Newton H. SC 20th Inf. Co.E
Thurlkill, Richard 1st Conf.Inf. 2nd Co.C
Thurlkill, T.A. MS Inf. 3rd Bn. (St.Troops) Co.B
Thurlkill, T.D. GA 4th Res. Co.C
Thurlkill, William E. GA 2nd Res. Co.D Cpl.
Thurm, Charles LA Mil. Mooney's Co. (Saddlers Guards)
Thurm, M. AL 5th Inf. Co.A Lt.
Thurman, A.B. AL 30th Inf. Co.F
Thurman, A.D. VA Inf. 1st Bn.Loc.Def. Co.B
Thurman, A.J. KY 7th Cav. Co.I Cpl.
Thurman, A.J. TN 3rd (Forrest's) Cav. 1st Co.G Cpl.
Thurman, A.J. 2nd Cherokee Mtd.Vol. Co.A
Thurman, Alexander VA 2nd Cav. Co.B
Thurman, A.M. GA 18th Inf. Co.C
Thurman, Andrew J. KY 3rd Cav. Co.I Cpl.
Thurman, Ansalem A. GA 1st Cav. Co.A
Thurman, Ben VA 2nd Cav. Co.K
Thurman, Benjamin F. VA Lt.Arty. 12th Bn. 2nd Co.A
Thurman, Benjamin F. VA Lt.Arty. Sturdivant's Co. Artif.
Thurman, Benjamin W. VA 19th Inf. Co.E 2nd Lt.
Thurman, B.F. GA 60th Inf. Co.C
Thurman, B.F. VA 88th Mil. Sgt.
Thurman, B.O. GA 23rd Inf. Co.A
Thurman, B.S. TN 4th Inf. Co.A 2nd Lt.
Thurman, C. VA 42nd Inf. Co.E
Thurman, Charles TN Inf. 22nd Bn. Co.C
Thurman, Clement J. AL 1st Bn. Hilliard's Legion Vol. Co.C Sgt.
Thurman, C.Y. TN 5th (McKenzie's) Cav. Co.D
Thurman, D. MS Cav. Yerger's Regt. Co.B
Thurman, D. VA 46th Inf. Co.D
Thurman, Darling AL 60th Inf. Co.E
Thurman, David GA Cav. 6th Bn. (St.Guards) Co.A
Thurman, David GA Arty. 9th Bn. Co.A,E
Thurman, D.H. VA 1st Res. Co.E
Thurman, D.R. GA 1st (Ramsey's) Inf. Co.F
Thurman, Dudley L. VA Cav. 37th Bn. Co.A
Thurman, Dudley L. VA 58th Inf. Co.E 2nd Lt.
Thurman, E.C. TN 19th Inf. Co.F
Thurman, Elijah MS 39th Inf. Co.A
Thurman, E.M. VA 8th Cav. Co.A Sgt.
Thurman, Emanuel AL 3rd Bn. Hilliard's Legion Vol. Co.A
Thurman, Erasmus S. TN 14th Cav. Co.E 2nd Lt.
Thurman, E.S. TN 3rd (Clack's) Inf. Co.I
Thurman, E.S. TN Inf. 4th Cons.Regt. Co.C
Thurman, E.S. VA 48th Inf. Co.B
Thurman, Evander TN Inf. 22nd Bn. Co.C
Thurman, Evander TN 43rd Inf. Co.B
Thurman, Fendal VA 46th Inf. 2nd Co.D
Thurman, F.M. MS 39th Inf. Co.A
Thurman, Frank AR 11th & 17th Cons.Inf. Co.D 2nd Lt.
Thurman, F.T. GA Arty. Lumpkin's Co.
Thurman, General W. MO 3rd Cav. Co.G
Thurman, George GA Arty. Lumpkin's Co.
Thurman, George TN 9th (Ward's) Cav. Co.G
Thurman, George G. KY 6th Cav. Co.A
Thurman, George M. NC 22nd Inf. Co.G Dr.M.
Thurman, George W. VA 4th Inf. Co.B
Thurman, G.G. 3rd Conf.Cav. Co.A,G
Thurman, Giles VA 42nd Inf. Co.K
Thurman, Grandison W. VA 41st Inf. Co.D Cpl.
Thurman, G.W. MS 39th Inf. Co.A
Thurman, G.W. NC 7th Sr.Res. Johnston's Co.
Thurman, H.C. TN Inf. 22nd Bn. Co.C Sgt.
Thurman, Henry TX 2nd Inf. Co.D Sgt.
Thurman, Henry VA 58th Inf. Co.D
Thurman, H.F. TX 3rd Cav. Co.B
Thurman, Hugh MS Cav. 1st Bn. (McNair's) St.Troops Co.A
Thurman, Hugh MS Home Guards Barnes' Co.
Thurman, I.H. NC Mallett's Bn. (Cp.Guard) Co.E
Thurman, Isaac GA 21st Inf. Co.C
Thurman, J. AL 15th Inf. Co.D
Thurman, J. GA 66th Inf. Co.M
Thurman, J.A. SC 2nd Res.
Thurman, J.A. TN 24th Inf. Co.I Cpl.
Thurman, J.A. VA 3rd Res. Co.H
Thurman, James GA 36th (Broyles') Inf. Co.F Cpl.
Thurman, James VA 22nd Cav. Co.F
Thurman, James C. GA 10th Cav. (St.Guards) Co.A
Thurman, James G. MO Cav. Slayback's Regt. Co.I
Thurman, James M. TN 53rd Inf. Co.K Sgt.
Thurman, James O. VA 11th Inf. Co.A 2nd Lt.
Thurman, James P. TN 3rd (Clack's) Inf. Co.I
Thurman, James S. VA 36th Inf. 2nd Co.B
Thurman, James T. MO 5th Inf. Co.B
Thurman, James W. VA 36th Inf. 2nd Co.B
Thurman, J.B. GA 3rd Res. Co.H 1st Lt.
Thurman, J.C. SC 26th Inf. Co.F
Thurman, Jeramiah AL 3rd Bn. Hilliard's Legion Vol. Co.A
Thurman, Jeremiah F. AL 39th Inf. Co.B
Thurman, Jerome S. TX 14th Cav. Co.K
Thurman, Jerry AL Arty. 4th Bn. Hilliard's Legion Co.E,B
Thurman, Jesse TN 21st & 22nd (Cons.) Cav. Co.B
Thurman, Jesse TN 22nd (Barteau's) Cav. Co.E
Thurman, Jesse M. GA 1st Reg. Co.B
Thurman, J.F. TN 8th Inf. Co.F
Thurman, J.G. MS Lt.Arty. 14th Bn. Co.A
Thurman, J.G. MS Lt.Arty. Yates' Btty.
Thurman, J.G. MS 9th Inf. Old Co.H
Thurman, J.H. AR 38th Inf. Co.G Cpl.
Thurman, J.H. TX 28th Cav. Co.F
Thurman, J.H. TX Inf. Rutherford's Co.
Thurman, J.J.L. TN 37th Inf. Co.D
Thurman, J.K. GA 13th Cav. Co.E
Thurman, J.M. AR Lt.Arty. Rivers' Btty.
Thurman, J.M. KY 9th Cav. Co.E
Thurman, J.M. TN Inf. 4th Cons.Regt. Co.K Sgt.
Thurman, J. Monroe AR 16th Inf. Co.B
Thurman, John GA 12th Cav. Co.D
Thurman, John KY Morgan's Men Co.E
Thurman, John TN 16th (Logwood's) Cav. Co.H 3rd Lt.
Thurman, John TN 59th Mtd.Inf. Co.H
Thurman, John F. GA 3rd Inf. Co.K
Thurman, John F. KY 1st (Butler's) Cav. Co.E Sgt.
Thurman, John H. MO 5th Inf. Co.E Sgt.
Thurman, John L. TN Lt.Arty. Huggins' Co.
Thurman, John M. NC Walker's Bn. Thomas' Legion Co.A
Thurman, John M. GA 41st Inf. Co.H
Thurman, John R. NC 17th Inf. (2nd Org.) Ch.Music.

Thurman, John R. TX 29th Cav. Co.E
Thurman, John R. VA Horse Arty. E. Graham's Co. Bugler
Thurman, John R. VA Lt.Arty. J.D. Smith's Co. 1st Lt.
Thurman, John R. VA 54th Mil. Co.E,F
Thurman, John R. 1st Choctaw & Chickasaw Mtd.Rifles 1st Co.I
Thurman, John W. AR 35th Inf. Co.B
Thurman, John W. GA 8th Inf. (St.Guards) Co.B
Thurman, Joseph KY 8th Cav. Co.C
Thurman, Joseph TX 14th Cav. Co.H Far.
Thurman, Joseph C. GA 12th Inf. Co.E
Thurman, Joseph C. SC 4th Cav. Co.A Sgt.
Thurman, Joseph C. SC Cav. 12th Bn. Co.A Cpl.
Thurman, Joseph W. GA Cobb's Legion Co.A
Thurman, J.P. TN 3rd (Forrest's) Cav. Co.B Sgt.
Thurman, J.T. KY 2nd (Duke's) Cav. Co.K
Thurman, J.T. KY 3rd Cav. Co.D Sgt.
Thurman, J.T. MS Lt.Arty. 14th Bn. Co.A
Thurman, J.T. MS Lt.Arty. Yates' Btty.
Thurman, J.W. AL 45th Inf. Co.A
Thurman, J.W. TX 12th Cav. Co.K
Thurman, Lewis H. VA 14th Cav. Co.G, 2nd Co.F Sgt.
Thurman, Lewis H. VA 42nd Inf. Co.B Sgt.
Thurman, M.B. VA Lt.Arty. Brander's Co.
Thurman, M.B. VA 20th Inf. Co.E
Thurman, M.D. GA 1st Cav. Co.K
Thurman, Miles P. SC 6th Cav. Co.K
Thurman, Miles P. SC 8th Inf. Co.B Cpl.
Thurman, Milton TN 28th Inf. Co.C Sgt.
Thurman, M.P. SC 26th Inf. Co.F
Thurman, M.V. MO 2nd Inf. Co.K
Thurman, Nathaniel VA 4th Cav. Co.F
Thurman, N.S. VA 44th Inf. Co.D
Thurman, Oats AR Cav. Wright's Regt. Co.H
Thurman, P. KY 3rd Mtd.Inf. 1st Co.F
Thurman, Parker N. KY 10th Cav. Co.C
Thurman, Peter TN 43rd Inf. Co.G
Thurman, Philip KY 6th Mtd.Inf. Co.G
Thurman, P.M. KY Lt.Arty. Cobb's Co.
Thurman, Powhatan VA 2nd Cav. Co.B
Thurman, Powhatan VA 11th Inf. Co.A
Thurman, R.C. GA 29th Inf. Co.I
Thurman, R.E. GA 56th Inf. Co.C
Thurman, R.F. TN 8th Inf. Co.B Cpl.
Thurman, R.H. NC Arty. 1st Lt.
Thurman, Richard F. GA 41st Inf. Co.H
Thurman, Richard F. GA Cobb's Legion Co.B
Thurman, Richd. O. GA 44th Inf. Co.C
Thurman, Riley W. AR Inf. 2nd Bn. Co.B
Thurman, R.N. VA 2nd Cav. Music.
Thurman, R.O. GA Inf. 23rd Bn.Loc.Def. Sims' Co.
Thurman, Robert AR 37th Inf. Co.A
Thurman, Robert H. VA 41st Inf. Co.D 1st Sgt.
Thurman, Robert K. VA 58th Inf. Co.E
Thurman, Robert M. VA 14th Cav. Co.G, 2nd Co.F
Thurman, R.S. KY 9th Cav. Co.E
Thurman, R. Sidney TN 9th Cav.
Thurman, Samuel KY 5th Mtd.Inf. Co.C
Thurman, Samuel VA 3rd Res. Co.G Sgt.
Thurman, Samuel R. VA 12th Inf. Co.E Music.
Thurman, Samuel S. AR 35th Inf. Co.B Sgt.
Thurman, S.P. GA Inf. 1st Loc.Troops (Augusta) Co.G
Thurman, Stephen H. GA 39th Inf. Co.E
Thurman, Tazwell VA Cav. 37th Bn. Co.G
Thurman, Tazwell VA 53rd Inf. Co.B
Thurman, T.D. TN 14th (Neely's) Cav. Co.G Cpl.
Thurman, T.H. TX Cav. Saufley's Scouting Bn. Co.C
Thurman, Thomas AL 40th Inf. Co.C
Thurman, Thomas MO St.Guard Lt.Col.
Thurman, Thomas TX 17th Cav. Co.C
Thurman, Thomas N. TN 4th (McLemore's) Cav. Co.K
Thurman, Thomas S. VA Conscr. Cp.Lee
Thurman, Thomas W. MS 13th Inf. Co.D Capt.
Thurman, W. KY 3rd Cav. Co.E
Thurman, W. MO 5th Cav. Co.K
Thurman, W.A. GA 2nd Inf. Co.K
Thurman, W.C. TN 26th Inf. Co.E
Thurman, W.D. 2nd Conf.Eng.Troops Co.A
Thurman, W.H. AR 45th Cav. Co.M
Thurman, W.H.H. AL 40th Inf. Co.H
Thurman, W.H.H. AL 60th Inf. Co.E
Thurman, William AR 25th Inf. Co.C
Thurman, William AR 34th Inf. Co.A
Thurman, William AR 36th Inf. Co.C
Thurman, William KY 1st (Butler's) Cav. Co.D Sgt.
Thurman, William KY 4th Cav. Co.I
Thurman, William TN 14th (Neely's) Cav. Co.E
Thurman, William TN Conscr. (Cp. of Instr.) Co.B
Thurman, William C. MO 3rd Cav. Co.G
Thurman, William D. AL 1st Bn. Hilliard's Legion Vol. Co.C
Thurman, William F. TN 53rd Inf. Co.K
Thurman, William H. TN 43rd Inf. Co.G
Thurman, William H. VA 53rd Inf. Co.G Sgt.
Thurman, William H.H. AL 37th Inf. Co.H
Thurman, William H.H. AL 3rd Bn. Hilliard's Legion Vol. Co.A
Thurman, William J. TX 14th Cav. Co.B,C
Thurman, William M. GA 1st Inf. (St.Guards)
Thurman, William P. AL 6th Inf. Co.B Sgt.
Thurman, William P. VA Lt.Arty. J.D. Smith's Co.
Thurman, William P. VA 34th Inf. Co.G
Thurman, William P. Conf.Arty. Lewis' Bn. Co.A
Thurman, Wm. Pleasant Gen. & Staff Asst.Surg.
Thurman, William R. AR 3rd Inf. Co.I
Thurman, William T. GA 57th Inf. Co.A
Thurman, Willis W. TN 5th Cav.
Thurman, Willis W. TN 5th Inf. Co.I
Thurman, W.J. AR 11th & 17th Cons.Inf. Co.K
Thurman, W.J. AR 17th (Griffith's) Inf. Co.E
Thurman, W.J. AR 24th Inf. Co.C
Thurman, W.P. AL 24th Inf. Asst.Surg.
Thurman, W.R. VA 53rd Inf. Co.G
Thurman, W.T. TN Inf. 22nd Bn. Co.E
Thurman, W.W. TN 3rd (Clack's) Inf. Co.I
Thurman, W.W. TX 12th Cav. Co.K
Thurmand, B. KY 12th Cav. Co.G
Thurmand, D.T. TN 14th (Neely's) Cav. Co.F
Thurmand, F. TN 14th (Neely's) Cav. Co.E Cpl.
Thurmand, J.F. MS 18th Cav. Co.H
Thurmand, Joseph W. TN Cav. 4th Bn. (Branner's) Co.E
Thurmand, R. KY 12th Cav. Co.G
Thurmann, M.J. TX Waul's Legion Co.F
Thurmann, William TX Waul's Legion Sgt.
Thurmon, A.F. GA Cav. 8th Bn. (St.Guards) Co.C
Thurmon, Cicero GA 34th Inf. Co.E
Thurmon, C.J. AL 60th Inf. Co.K Sgt.
Thurmon, E.S. TN 15th (Stewart's) Cav. Co.C 1st Sgt.
Thurmon, G.B. TN 22nd (Barteau's) Cav. Co.G
Thurmon, Henry AR 20th Inf. Co.H
Thurmon, James M. TN Cav. 7th Bn. (Bennett's) Co.F
Thurmon, Jeremiah GA 54th Inf. Co.A Sgt.
Thurmon, J.M. TN 22nd (Barteau's) Cav. Co.G
Thurmon, John MO 2nd Cav. Co.H
Thurmon, John M. GA 19th Inf. Co.G
Thurmon, John M. GA 61st Inf. Band Music.
Thurmon, J.P. AR 1st (Monroe's) Cav. Co.L
Thurmon, P.J. TN 15th (Stewart's) Cav. Co.C Sgt.
Thurmon, R.F. AR 10th Inf. Co.B
Thurmon, Riley W. AR 3rd Inf. Co.I
Thurmon, R.P. AL Mil. 4th Vol. Modawell's Co.
Thurmon, R.V. GA 21st Inf. Co.H Cpl.
Thurmon, Singleton J. TX 17th Cav. Co.B Cpl.
Thurmon, Warren SC 1st Inf. Co.C
Thurmon, W.H. MO Cav. 3rd Regt.St.Guard
Thurmon, Wiley A. GA 2nd Cav. Co.K
Thurmon, William AR 1st (Monroe's) Cav. Co.L
Thurmon, William GA 16th Inf. Co.G Cpl.
Thurmon, William GA 47th Inf. Co.B
Thurmon, William T. TN 16th Inf. Co.I
Thurmon, William W. TN Cav. 7th Bn. (Bennett's) Co.F
Thurmon, W.W. TN 22nd (Barteau's) Cav. Co.G
Thurmond, Alfred S. TX 7th Cav. Co.A Capt.
Thurmond, A.T. GA 6th Inf. (St.Guards) Co.H
Thurmond, Augustus G. FL 2nd Cav. Co.E
Thurmond, B. KY 7th Mtd.Inf. Co.E
Thurmond, B.F. GA Cav. Alexander's Co.
Thurmond, B.F. TX 13th Vol. 2nd Co.F
Thurmond, Bolton GA 34th Inf. Co.E
Thurmond, C. AR 1st (Colquitt's) Inf. Co.I
Thurmond, Charles GA 1st (Fannin's) Res. Co.K
Thurmond, Charles GA Phillips' Legion Co.F
Thurmond, Charles A. LA 31st Inf. Co.E
Thurmond, Christopher C. GA 21st Inf. Co.D
Thurmond, C.M.B. MO 2nd Inf. Co.F Capt.
Thurmond, D. AL 63rd Inf. Co.E Cpl.
Thurmond, D. MS St.Cav. 3rd Bn. (Cooper's) 2nd Co.A
Thurmond, David GA 21st Inf. Co.C
Thurmond, David H. GA 1st (Ramsey's) Inf. Co.A
Thurmond, D.C. TN Inf. 154th Sr.Regt. Co.K Sgt.
Thurmond, Edmund W. VA 22nd Inf. Co.K
Thurmond, Edward MS 17th Inf. Co.B Capt.
Thurmond, Elias M. VA Cav. Thurmond's Co.
Thurmond, Elisha J. GA 65th Inf. Co.C

Thurmond, E.S. TN 15th (Cons.) Cav. Co.F 2nd Lt.
Thurmond, E.S. TN 4th Inf. Co.K
Thurmond, F.D. GA 2nd Res. Co.A
Thurmond, F.M. AL 3rd Inf. Co.D
Thurmond, Frank J. GA 42nd Inf. Co.G
Thurmond, Franklin TX 9th (Young's) Inf. Co.A
Thurmond, George SC 24th Inf. Co.K
Thurmond, George W. SC 2nd St.Troops Co.I Sgt.
Thurmond, George W. SC 5th Res. Co.C Sgt.
Thurmond, G.H.L. GA Inf. (High Shoals Defend.) Medlin's Ind.Co.
Thurmond, G.W. AL 6th Cav. Co.E
Thurmond, G.W. SC 7th Inf. 1st Co.K
Thurmond, G.W. SC 22nd Inf. Co.A Cpl.
Thurmond, G.W. TN 47th Inf. Co.C Cpl.
Thurmond, Harrison GA Carlton's Co. (Troup Cty.Arty.)
Thurmond, Harrison GA 2nd Inf. Stanley's Co.
Thurmond, Harrison TX 9th (Young's) Inf. Co.A
Thurmond, Henry C. VA Hvy.Arty. 19th Bn. Co.D
Thurmond, Henry C. VA Hvy.Arty. Kyle's Co.
Thurmond, H.H. GA 27th Inf. Co.D
Thurmond, H.H. TN 31st Inf. Co.G
Thurmond, J. KY 10th (Johnson's) Cav. New Co.C
Thurmond, J. TN 14th (Neely's) Cav. Co.E
Thurmond, J.A. TN 15th (Cons.) Cav. Co.G
Thurmond, James H. GA 18th Inf. Co.C
Thurmond, James H. GA 41st Inf. Co.D Cpl.
Thurmond, James H. TN Cav. 4th Bn. (Branner's) Co.E
Thurmond, James H. TN 61st Mtd.Inf. Co.G Sgt.
Thurmond, James M. KY 4th Cav. Co.E
Thurmond, James R. GA 13th Cav. Co.H
Thurmond, Jasper J. TX 35th (Brown's) Cav. Co.H
Thurmond, Jasper J. TX 13th Vol. 2nd Co.A
Thurmond, Jeff TN 31st Inf. Co.G
Thurmond, Jesse GA Inf. 11th Bn. (St.Guards) Co.B
Thurmond, J.F. TN 30th Inf. Co.C
Thurmond, J.G. TN 14th (Neely's) Cav. Co.E Maj.
Thurmond, J.G. TN 22nd Inf. Co.C 1st Lt.
Thurmond, J.L. TX 34th Cav. Co.A
Thurmond, J.M GA 5th Res. Co.B Sgt.Maj.
Thurmond, Joel M. GA 1st (Ramsey's) Inf. Co.A
Thurmond, John GA 21st Inf. Co.C Cpl.
Thurmond, John B. AL 6th Inf. Co.A
Thurmond, John C. GA 41st Inf. Co.A
Thurmond, John D. VA Cav. Thurmond's Co. Jr.2nd Lt.
Thurmond, John M. GA 3rd Cav. Co.A,K
Thurmond, John M. GA 37th Inf. Band Music.
Thurmond, John M. GA 54th Inf. Co.K Music.
Thurmond, Joseph TN 2nd (Ashby's) Cav. Co.I
Thurmond, J.P. TN 47th Inf. Co.D Cpl.
Thurmond, J.R. GA 1st (Fannin's) Res. Co.A
Thurmond, J.W. SC 7th Inf. 1st Co.I
Thurmond, J.W.W. TN 2nd Cav.
Thurmond, Marcus GA 2nd Cav. (St.Guards) Co.F
Thurmond, Merideth B. VA 14th Inf. Co.C
Thurmond, Norborne B. VA 11th Inf. Co.B
Thurmond, Phillip GA 13th Cav. Co.E
Thurmond, Phillip M. SC 24th Inf. Co.I
Thurmond, Phillipson GA 1st (Ramsey's) Inf.
Thurmond, P.J. TN 15th (Cons.) Cav. Co.F 1st Lt.
Thurmond, P.J. VA Cav. Thurmond's Co. Capt.
Thurmond, Pleasant TX Cav. Baylor's Regt. Co.D
Thurmond, Pleasant L. VA 11th Inf. Co.B
Thurmond, R. TN 14th (Neely's) Cav. Co.F,E
Thurmond, R.A. VA 15th Cav. Co.B 1st Sgt.
Thurmond, R.D. GA Cav. Alexander's Co.
Thurmond, Reddin TX Cav. 6th Bn. Co.A
Thurmond, R.G. VA 11th Inf. Co.B
Thurmond, Richard AR 1st Mtd.Rifles Co.A
Thurmond, Richard TX 29th Cav. Co.I
Thurmond, Richard C. VA Cav. Hounshell's Bn. Thurmond's Co. 2nd Lt.
Thurmond, Richard C. VA 22nd Inf. Co.K
Thurmond, R.J. MS Cav. 3rd Bn. (Ashcraft's) Co.E Capt.
Thurmond, R.J. MS Stricklin's Co. (St.Troops)
Thurmond, Robert G. VA Cav. Hounshell's Bn. Thurmond's Co. Sgt.
Thurmond, Robert G. VA 22nd Inf. Co.K
Thurmond, Robert P. AL 43rd Inf. Co.A
Thurmond, Samuel P. GA 3rd Cav. (St.Guards) Co.F
Thurmond, Samuel S. VA 19th Inf. Co.D
Thurmond, Thomas GA Lt.Arty. Daniell's Btty.
Thurmond, Thomas SC 19th Inf. Co.B
Thurmond, Thomas J. GA 14th Inf. Co.D
Thurmond, Thomas J. GA 21st Inf. Co.D
Thurmond, Thomas J. SC 24th Inf. Co.I
Thurmond, T.J. TN 31st Inf. Co.G
Thurmond, T.O. SC 7th Inf. 1st Co.I
Thurmond, Tolber D. SC Inf.Bn. Co.C
Thurmond, Vincent H. GA Inf. 27th Bn. Co.B
Thurmond, Wade MS 29th Inf. Co.K
Thurmond, Walker G. VA 11th Inf. Co.B
Thurmond, W.G. VA 2nd Cav. Co.G
Thurmond, W.H. GA Inf. (Collier Guards) Collier's Co.
Thurmond, W.H. VA Loc.Def. Mallory's Co.
Thurmond, William GA Cav. 10th Bn. (St.Guards) Co.E
Thurmond, William GA 13th Cav. Co.G 1st Lt.
Thurmond, William GA 13th Inf. Co.E
Thurmond, William GA Inf. 27th Bn. Co.D
Thurmond, William GA 61st Inf. Co.G
Thurmond, William TN 39th Mtd.Inf. Co.G
Thurmond, William VA 1st Arty. Co.H 1st Lt.
Thurmond, William VA Arty. C.F. Johnston's Co. 1st Lt.
Thurmond, Wm. Gen. & Staff, Arty. 1st Lt., Ord.Off.
Thurmond, William D. VA Cav. Hounshell's Bn. Thurmond's Co. Capt.
Thurmond, William H. KY 7th Mtd.Inf. Co.H
Thurmond, William J. VA 49th Inf. Co.H
Thurmond, William R. KY 10th (Johnson's) Cav. Co.H
Thurmond, William T. GA 16th Inf. Co.G
Thurmond, William T. GA 18th Inf. Co.C
Thurmond, Wilson TX Cav. Baylor's Regt. Co.D
Thurmond, W.M. TN 15th (Cons.) Cav. Co.F
Thurmond, W.T. GA 2nd Cav. (St.Guards) Co.F 1st Sgt.
Thurmond, W.T. GA Phillips' Legion Co.D
Thurmond, W.T. Gen. & Staff Capt.,AQM
Thurmond, W.W. TN Inf. 154th Sr.Regt. Co.G
Thurmond, Z. GA 9th Inf. Co.C
Thurndale, D.L. GA 4th Inf. Co.E
Thurner, R.W. VA 2nd Cav. Music.
Thurp, E.M. GA 6th Inf.
Thurph, Henry AR 1st (Colquitt's) Inf.
Thursby, James KY 9th Mtd.Inf. Co.G Cpl.
Thursby, J.E. GA Cav. 29th Bn. Co.B
Thursby, J.E. GA Siege Arty. Campbell's Ind.Co.
Thursby, John W. GA 31st Inf. Co.I Sgt.
Thursby, Lewis P. FL Mil.
Thursby, W.J. GA 3rd Res. Co.I
Thurston, A.J.D. TN 1st Zouaves Lt.Col.
Thurston, Andrew J. VA 7th Inf. Co.I
Thurston, Bartlet SC 16th Inf. Co.H
Thurston, Benjamin F. VA 26th Inf. Co.G
Thurston, B.L. VA Loc.Def. Mallory's Co.
Thurston, Charles VA 46th Inf. 2nd Co.H
Thurston, Charles H. LA 7th Inf. Co.H
Thurston, Daniel LA 21st (Patton's) Inf. Co.C
Thurston, David AR 23rd Inf. Co.E
Thurston, David LA 14th Inf. Co.D
Thurston, E. VA 2nd Inf.Loc.Def. Co.A
Thurston, E. VA Inf. 2nd Bn.Loc.Def. Co.C
Thurston, E. VA Conscr. Cp.Lee Co.A
Thurston, Ed. TN 62nd Mtd.Inf. Co.C 1st Sgt.
Thurston, Edward TN 26th Inf. Co.I Cpl.
Thurston, Edward VA Goochland Lt.Arty.
Thurston, Edward N. Gen. & Staff, Ord.Dept. Maj.
Thurston, E.N. SC Mil.Arty. 1st Regt. Parker's Co.
Thurston, George H. VA Loc.Def. Mallory's Co.
Thurston, George R. VA 7th Inf. Co.I
Thurston, G.H. VA 56th Inf. Co.H
Thurston, G.H. VA 88th Mil.
Thurston, Henry VA 46th Inf. 2nd Co.H
Thurston, Henry C. MO 4th Cav. Co.I
Thurston, Hesicia VA 9th Mil. Co.B
Thurston, Hezekiah S. AR 35th Inf. Co.B
Thurston, Isaac N. VA Goochland Lt.Arty.
Thurston, J. SC 2nd Inf. Co.A
Thurston, J. TX 4th Inf. (St.Troops) Co.D
Thurston, James MO Cav. Williams' Regt. Co.K
Thurston, James SC 2nd Cav. Co.A Cpl.
Thurston, James B. VA 61st Mil. Co.G 1st Lt.
Thurston, James M. SC 1st Arty. Co.H
Thurston, James R. SC 10th Inf. Co.K Sgt.
Thurston, Jasper N. AR 35th Inf. Co.B
Thurston, J.C. VA Inf. 1st Bn.Loc.Def. Co.E
Thurston, J.F. VA Inf. 6th Bn.Loc.Def. Co.A
Thurston, J.G. SC 4th Cav. Co.K
Thurston, J.H. GA 13th Inf. Co.C
Thurston, J.J. AL 4th Res. Co.I 1st Sgt.
Thurston, J.M. VA 2nd St.Res. Co.B
Thurston, J.N. VA 7th Inf. Co.I
Thurston, John SC Mil.Cav. Rutledge's Co.
Thurston, John VA 9th Mil. Co.B
Thurston, John D. VA Lt.Arty. W.P. Carter's Co.
Thurston, John D. VA Goochland Lt.Arty.
Thurston, John G. SC Mil. Trenholm's Co.

Thurston, John H. VA Res.Forces Thurston's Co. Capt.
Thurston, John L. AL 28th Inf. Co.D
Thurston, John M. VA 5th Cav. Co.A
Thurston, John T. VA 7th Inf. Co.I
Thurston, Josh A. VA 5th Cav. Co.G
Thurston, J.R. GA 45th Inf. Co.I Cpl.
Thurston, J.S. MO 11th Inf. Co.G
Thurston, J.W. SC 4th Cav. Co.D
Thurston, L. VA Cav. 40th Bn. Co.E
Thurston, Lafayette C. MO 4th Cav. Co.I
Thurston, L.B. VA 7th Inf. Co.I
Thurston, M.O. VA 46th Inf. 2nd Co.H
Thurston, Napoleon B. VA 22nd Inf. Swann's Co.
Thurston, Napoleon B. VA 59th Inf. 2nd Co.K
Thurston, N.B. VA Inf. 26th Bn. Co.A
Thurston, N.J. VA 46th Inf. 2nd Co.H
Thurston, Ole LA 9th Inf. Co.A
Thurston, P. VA 46th Inf.
Thurston, Poindexter VA 2nd Bn.Res. Co.A
Thurston, P.R. MS 3rd Inf. (St.Troops) Co.K
Thurston, R. VA 1st Inf. Co.A
Thurston, Reuben J. VA 7th Inf. Co.I
Thurston, Reubin VA 46th Inf. 2nd Co.H
Thurston, R.M. AR 5th Mil. Co.E
Thurston, Robt. Gen. & Staff AASurg.
Thurston, Robert T. SC Cav.Bn. Hampton Legion Co.B
Thurston, R.T. SC 16th Inf. Asst.Surg.
Thurston, R.T. Gen. & Staff Asst.Surg.
Thurston, Samuel VA Cav. 40th Bn. Co.F
Thurston, Samuel VA 9th Mil. Co.B
Thurston, Seth GA 51st Inf. Co.E
Thurston, T.G. LA Dreux's Cav. Co.A
Thurston, T.G. LA 17th Inf. Co.A Music.
Thurston, Thomas H. VA 55th Inf. Co.C
Thurston, Thomas W. AR 35th Inf. Co.B
Thurston, T.J. GA 3rd Res. Co.G
Thurston, T.M. KY 4th Cav. Co.E
Thurston, W.H. TN 7th (Duckworth's) Cav. Co.G
Thurston, William Conf.Inf. Tucker's Regt. Co.E
Thurston, William B. VA Lt.Arty. Clutter's Co.
Thurston, William F. VA 26th Inf. Co.G
Thurston, William J.Y. NC 3rd Inf. Co.D 2nd Lt.
Thurston, William W. AR 2nd Inf. Co.D
Thurston, W.R. GA 51st Inf. Co.E
Thurston, W.S. VA 46th Inf. 2nd Co.A
Thurton, J.M. NC 28th Inf. Co.A
Thusby, W.J. GA 51st Inf. Co.K
Thussel, J.W. GA 51st Inf. Co.D
Thuston, J. MO 2nd Inf. Co.D
Thwaits, James S. TX 1st (Yager's) Cav. Co.A Sgt.
Thweat, Frederick TX Cav. 2nd Regt.St.Troops Co.D
Thweate, J.F. GA Inf. (NonConscr.) Howard's Co. 2nd Lt.
Thweatt, A.F. AR 9th Inf. Co.K
Thweatt, A.F. VA 1st Cav. Co.G
Thweatt, Alfred F. VA 1st Cav. Co.G
Thweatt, A.M. GA Inf. City Bn. (Columbus) Co.B
Thweatt, Archibald, Jr. VA 3rd Cav. 2nd Co.I Sgt.
Thweatt, A.T. Gen. & Staff,PACS 1st Lt.
Thweatt, Charles AL 47th Inf. Co.K
Thweatt, C.P. AR 2nd Cav. Co.B
Thweatt, D.H. AL Cav. Barbiere's Bn. Co.G
Thweatt, D.J. TN 49th Inf. Co.H Sgt.
Thweatt, D.M. AL 18th Inf. Co.K
Thweatt, E.G. MS 1st (King's) Inf. (St.Troops) Co.H
Thweatt, F.G. GA Inf. City Bn. (Columbus) Co.A
Thweatt, Francis F. VA 3rd Cav. 2nd Co.I Cpl.
Thweatt, George C. VA Inf. 44th Bn. Co.A
Thweatt, George C.G. VA 5th Cav. (12 mo. '61-2) Co.F Bvt.2nd Lt.
Thweatt, George C.G. VA 13th Cav. Co.F 2nd Lt.
Thweatt, H. AL 8th (Livingston's) Cav. Co.C
Thweatt, Henry G. VA 34th Inf. Co.K
Thweatt, H.V. LA Arty. Watson Btty.
Thweatt, James GA 13th Inf. Co.D
Thweatt, James MS 2nd Cav. Co.A Sgt.
Thweatt, James TX 14th Inf. Co.E Ord.Sgt.
Thweatt, James E. VA 12th Inf. Co.A
Thweatt, J.H. TN Cav. 17th Bn. (Sanders') Co.A
Thweatt, J.M. AR 13th Inf.
Thweatt, John H.H. TN 44th (Cons.) Inf. Co.I Sgt.
Thweatt, John H.H. TN 55th (McKoin's) Inf. McEwen, Jr.'s Co. Cpl.
Thweatt, Joseph T. TN Cav. 17th Bn. (Sanders') Co.A Lt.
Thweatt, J.T. GA Inf. 27th Bn. (NonConscr.) Co.B Capt.
Thweatt, J.W. TX Cav. Bourland's Regt. Co.K
Thweatt, L.B. AL 18th Inf. Co.I
Thweatt, L.M. GA Inf. City Bn. (Columbus) Co.B 1st Sgt.
Thweatt, M. GA 1st Reg. Co.K
Thweatt, Malajah W. GA Inf. 2nd Bn. Co.A
Thweatt, M.W. GA Lt.Arty. 14th Bn. Co.D 2nd Lt.
Thweatt, M.W. GA Siege Arty. 28th Bn. Co.G
Thweatt, M.W. GA Lt.Arty. King's Btty. 2nd Lt.
Thweatt, O.T. GA 5th Res. Adj.
Thweatt, Owen T. GA 17th Inf. Co.C
Thweatt, P. AL 15th Inf. Co.K
Thweatt, Peter O. AR 1st Mtd.Rifles Co.K
Thweatt, P.S. Gen. & Staff Hosp.Attendant
Thweatt, R.G. MS 27th Inf. Co.E
Thweatt, Richard TN Cav. 17th Bn. (Sanders') Co.A
Thweatt, Robert GA 5th Inf. (St.Guards) Russell's Co.
Thweatt, Robert B. VA Hvy.Arty. Epes' Co.
Thweatt, Roland S. MS 21st Inf. Co.G
Thweatt, R.R. GA Inf. 27th Bn. (NonConscr.) Co.D Capt.
Thweatt, Simon N. TN 44th (Cons.) Inf. Co.I
Thweatt, Sowell W. GA Inf. 2nd Bn. Co.A
Thweatt, Thacker AL 3rd Bn. Hilliard's Legion Vol. Co.F
Thweatt, Thacker H. GA Inf. 2nd Bn. Co.A
Thweatt, Thomas VA 3rd Cav. 2nd Co.I Sgt.
Thweatt, Thomas T. SC 2nd Cav. Co.D
Thweatt, T.T. SC Cav. 4th Bn. Co.D
Thweatt, U.J. TX 35th (Brown's) Cav. 2nd Co.B Asst.Surg.
Thweatt, U.S. Gen. & Staff Asst.Surg.
Thweatt, U.W. MS 1st (King's) Inf. (St.Troops) Co.H 2nd Lt.
Thweatt, W.B. GA 45th Inf. Co.H
Thweatt, W.H. AR 1st Mtd.Rifles Co.K 1st Lt.
Thweatt, William B. AR 5th Inf. Co.K
Thweatt, William H. AR 15th (Josey's) Inf. Co.A Lt.
Thweatt, William H. AR 25th Inf. Co.H 1st Lt.
Thweatt, William H. VA Inf. 5th Bn. Co.B
Thweatt, William J. AR 9th Inf. Co.F Sgt.
Thweatt, W.J. AR 1st Mtd.Rifles Co.H Sgt.
Thweatte, J.R. LA 9th Inf. Co.F
Thweatte, N.W. MS Cav. 3rd Bn.Res. Co.B Sgt.
Thweeatt, Willis MS 21st Inf. Co.G
Thweet, J.R. MS Inf. 3rd Bn. (St.Troops) Co.B
Thweett, Jonathan D. TN Inf. 1st Bn. (Colms') Co.C Sgt.
Thweett, Thomas J. TN Inf. 1st Bn. (Colms') Co.C
Thwiatt, F.G. GA Inf. 1st Bn. (St.Guards) Co.E Lt.
Thwing, J.A. SC 1st Inf. Co.B
Thwing, James SC Arty. Zimmerman's Co. (Pee Dee Arty.) Cpl.
Thwing, James SC 1st (McCreary's) Inf. Co.D Cpl.
Thye, Dominick LA 11th Inf. Co.C
Thye, Dominique LA 13th Inf. Co.A,B
Thye, Guillaume LA Mil. 6th Regt.Eur.Brig. (Italian Guards Bn.) Co.5
Thynne, Bernard FL 3rd Inf. Co.F
Thyrian, Xafer LA 21st (Kennedy's) Inf. Co.C
Thys, Francis NC 1st Arty. (10th St.Troops) Co.E
Thysseus, Francois L.J. Eng.,CSA Capt.
Thytho, Augustus M. NC 31st Inf. 2nd Lt.
Tiarchel Yo Hola 1st Seminole Mtd.Vol.
Tiarks, U. TX 4th Inf. (St.Troops) Co.F
Tiarn, Thomas Conf.Inf. Tucker's Regt. Co.I
Tias, Albertas GA Cav. 1st Bn.Res. Co.C
Tiavi, C. LA Mil. 4th Regt. French Brig. Co.6
Tibb, William H. VA 49th Inf. Co.H
Tibber, --- MS 1st Lt.Arty. Co.B Cpl.
Tibbets, Charles LA Ogden's Cav. Co.A
Tibbets, C.O. LA Inf. 9th Bn. Co.B
Tibbets, Henry C. TX 22nd Cav. Co.D
Tibbets, J. LA Miles' Legion Co.A
Tibbets, John J.B. 3rd Conf.Cav. Co.D
Tibbets, J.T.O. AR 4th Inf. Co.K
Tibbett, G.W. LA Red River S.S.
Tibbett, Jerry TN 51st (Cons.) Inf. Co.H
Tibbetts, Asberry AR 4th Inf. Co.K
Tibbetts, H.W. GA Inf. 1st City Bn. (Columbus) Co.A
Tibbetts, Napoleon B. MO Cav. Schnabel's Bn. Co.H,G
Tibbetts, Silas S. LA 8th Inf. Co.I
Tibbetts, Thomas D. VA 4th Cav. Co.B Cpl.
Tibbetts, U.W. AL 3rd Inf. Co.C
Tibbetts, W.A. AR 6th Inf. Co.H
Tibbit, J.S. TN 51st Inf. Co.A
Tibbits, Eli TX 29th Cav. Co.B Jr.2nd Lt.
Tibbits, Green M. GA 14th Inf. Co.K

Tibbits, James W. GA 14th Inf. Co.K Cpl.
Tibbits, J.T. AR 1st Mtd.Rifles Co.F
Tibbits, J.W. AR 5th Inf. Co.I
Tibbits, Martin V. TX 22nd Cav. Co.K
Tibbits, Thomas J. GA 14th Inf. Co.K Sgt.
Tibbitts, A.P. MO 12th Cav. Co.A
Tibbitts, J.J. TX 29th Cav. Co.B Cpl.
Tibbitts, S.W. TX 29th Cav. Co.B
Tibbles, Francis SC 1st Arty. Co.C
Tibbotts, Alfred G. VA 7th Cav. Co.A
Tibbs, A.A. VA 51st Inf. Co.F Sgt.
Tibbs, Andrew J. AL 50th Inf. Co.F
Tibbs, C.H. TN 2nd (Ashby's) Cav. Co.A 2nd Lt.
Tibbs, C.H. TN Cav. 5th Bn. (McClellan's) Co.A
Tibbs, C.H. TX 1st Inf. Co.A
Tibbs, Columbus AL 4th (Roddey's) Cav. Co.H
Tibbs, David VA Lt.Arty. Leake's Co.
Tibbs, David A. AL 11th Inf. Co.G
Tibbs, D.D. TN 5th (McKenzie's) Cav. Co.D
Tibbs, Eugenius VA 19th Cav. Co.A 1st Sgt.
Tibbs, Eugenius VA 3rd Cav. & Inf.St.Line Co.A 1st Sgt.
Tibbs, F.M. VA 51st Inf. Co.F
Tibbs, F.M. VA 60th Inf. Co.G
Tibbs, Francis M. VA 19th Cav. Co.A
Tibbs, Francis M. VA 3rd Cav. & Inf.St.Line Co.A
Tibbs, George T. VA Lt.Arty. W.P. Carter's Co. Cpl.
Tibbs, G.M. VA Loc.Def. Patterson's Co.
Tibbs, H. LA Mil. 2nd Regt. French Brig. Co.4
Tibbs, Henry VA 50th Inf. Co.E
Tibbs, H. Marsh TN 5th Inf. 2nd Co.D
Tibbs, Isaac M. VA 21st Inf. Co.A
Tibbs, J.A. MS 22nd Inf. Sgt.
Tibbs, J.A. VA Hvy.Arty. 20th Bn. Co.D
Tibbs, James AL 50th Inf.
Tibbs, James A. AL 50th Inf. Co.F
Tibbs, James A. MS 2nd Cav. Co.K 2nd Lt.
Tibbs, James A. MS 1st (Percy's) Inf. Co.K Sgt.
Tibbs, James A. TX 18th Cav. Co.K
Tibbs, James A. VA Inf. 45th Bn. Co.F
Tibbs, James A. VA Loc.Def. Patterson's Co.
Tibbs, James W. VA 3rd Res. Co.F
Tibbs, John AR 6th Inf. 1st Co.B
Tibbs, John VA 4th Inf. Co.D
Tibbs, John VA 11th Bn.Res. Co.A
Tibbs, John VA 51st Inf. Co.F
Tibbs, John VA Loc.Def. Patterson's Co. 2nd Lt.
Tibbs, John A. 1st Conf.Eng.Troops Co.D
Tibbs, John B. VA 6th Inf. Co.I
Tibbs, John J. TN 2nd (Ashby's) Cav. Co.A
Tibbs, John J. VA 3rd Lt.Arty. Co.I 2nd Lt.
Tibbs, John James VA Hvy.Arty. 20th Bn. Co.A
Tibbs, John S. VA Lt.Arty. W.P. Carter's Co.
Tibbs, John W. TN 1st (Carter's) Cav. Co.B
Tibbs, John W. TN Lt.Arty. Barry's Co. Cpl.
Tibbs, John W. VA 50th Inf. Co.E
Tibbs, Joseph AL 50th Inf. Co.F Cpl.
Tibbs, J.S. AL 50th Inf. Co.F
Tibbs, Marcus VA Courtney Arty.
Tibbs, N.J. AR 30th Inf. Co.C
Tibbs, Peter VA 22nd Cav. Co.H
Tibbs, Philip VA Hvy.Arty. 10th Bn. Co.A
Tibbs, Pleasant J. VA 56th Inf. Co.C
Tibbs, R.A. MS 3rd (St.Troops) Cav. Co.I
Tibbs, Robert MS 2nd Cav. Co.K
Tibbs, Robert L. VA Inf. 23rd Bn. Co.E
Tibbs, Robert L. VA 50th Inf. Co.L
Tibbs, Robert T. VA Lt.Arty. W.P. Carter's Co.
Tibbs, S.F. VA 1st Bn.Res. Co.A 2nd Lt.
Tibbs, S.K. AL 50th Inf.
Tibbs, Tarlton H. VA 6th Inf. Co.I
Tibbs, Thomas AL Cp. of Instr. Talladega
Tibbs, Thomas A. VA 2nd Cav. Co.H 1st Lt.
Tibbs, Thomas A. VA 34th Inf. Co.C 1st Lt.
Tibbs, Thomas C. MS 20th Inf. Co.H 2nd Lt.
Tibbs, Thomas J. AL 18th Inf. Co.K
Tibbs, Thomas J. AL Cp. of Instr. Talladega
Tibbs, T.J. AL Cp. of Instr. Talladega
Tibbs, William VA 3rd Res. Co.F
Tibbs, William VA 50th Inf. Co.E
Tibbs, William 1st Choctaw & Chickasaw Mtd.Rifles 2nd Co.B
Tibbs, William A. TN 24th Inf. Co.I
Tibbs, William J. VA 46th Inf. 2nd Co.H
Tiber, Thomas LA 1st Hvy.Arty. (Reg.) Co.G
Tibler, T.B. GA 3rd Inf. Co.K
Tiblier, B. LA Mil. 3rd Regt.Eur.Brig. (Garde Francaise) Co.4
Tiblier, Emile MS 3rd Inf. Co.E
Tiblier, Eugene MS 3rd Inf. Co.E
Tibodeau, Celesten LA 7th Cav. Co.K
Tibodeau, Clemar LA Inf.Cons. 18th Regt. & Yellow Jacket Bn. Co.D
Tibodeau, Desire P. LA Inf.Cons. 18th Regt. & Yellow Jacket Bn. Co.D
Tibodeau, Risner L. LA Inf.Cons. 18th Regt. & Yellow Jacket Bn. Co.D
Tibodeau, Sevigner LA Inf.Cons. 18th Regt. & Yellow Jacket Bn. Co.D
Tibston, William GA Inf. 18th Bn. (St.Guards) Co.B
Tiburnt, Hy. LA Mil. 1st Regt. 2nd Brig. 1st Div.
Ticbamba, Silas Deneale's Regt. Choctaw Warriors Co.B
Ticbuntubbee 1st Choctaw & Chickasaw Mtd.Rifles 3rd Co.K
Tice, Abner N. VA 21st Cav. 2nd Co.G
Tice, A.J. GA 59th Inf. Co.K
Tice, Alexander H. AL 43rd Inf. Co.E
Tice, Alfred T. NC 61st Inf. Co.H
Tice, Andrew W. TN 54th Inf. Co.G
Tice, Asa D. GA 2nd Res. Co.D
Tice, B. VA 42nd Inf. Co.B
Tice, Costen S. NC 42nd Inf. Co.A
Tice, Costum NC Inf. 2nd Bn. Co.G
Tice, Daniel AL 11th Inf. Co.A
Tice, Daniel VA 4th Res. Co.I Sgt.
Tice, E. VA 21st Cav. Co.E Lt.
Tice, Fleming J. VA 21st Cav. 2nd Co.G Cpl.
Tice, F.M. AL 8th Inf. Co.B
Tice, George M. SC Inf. Holcombe Legion Co.I
Tice, George W. AL Arty. 1st Bn. Co.F
Tice, Hamilton NC 42nd Inf. Co.A
Tice, Henry GA 59th Inf. Co.K
Tice, Jacob M. TN 54th Inf. Co.G
Tice, James NC 43rd Inf. Co.K
Tice, James R. VA 42nd Inf. Co.B Sgt.
Tice, James W. VA 1st Cav. Co.F
Tice, Jason, Jr. NC 42nd Inf. Co.B Cpl.
Tice, Jason, Jr. NC 61st Inf. Co.H Cpl.
Tice, John TN 21st Inf. Co.H Sgt.
Tice, John D. GA Lt.Arty. Milledge's Co.
Tice, John D. GA 3rd Inf. 1st Co.I
Tice, John W. VA 54th Inf. Co.B 1st Sgt.
Tice, John W. VA Inf. 54th Bn. Co.B Sgt.
Tice, Jonathan 9th Conf.Inf. Co.C 1st Sgt.
Tice, Joseph TN 23rd Inf. Co.B
Tice, Lafayette MO Cav. Freeman's Regt. Co.L
Tice, Lafayette MO 1st & 4th Cons.Inf. Co.C
Tice, Lafayette MO 4th Inf. Co.C Sgt.
Tice, Marion GA Inf. 1st Loc.Troops (Augusta) Co.D
Tice, M.M. AR Lt.Arty. Hart's Btty.
Tice, M.M. LA 22nd (Cons.) Inf. Co.I
Tice, Peter M. GA 10th Inf. Co.D
Tice, S.W. GA 7th Cav. Co.A
Tice, S.W. GA Cav. 21st Bn. Co.A
Tice, W.B. NC 1st Arty. (10th St.Troops) Co.B
Tice, W.E. GA 16th Inf. Co.E
Tice, W.F. 1st Conf.Eng.Troops Co.K
Tice, W.H. FL Inf. 2nd Bn. Co.C
Tice, W.H. 7th Conf.Cav. Co.D,K
Tice, William TN 48th (Nixon's) Inf. Co.K
Tice, William E. VA 54th Inf. Co.I Sgt.
Tice, William E. VA Inf. 54th Bn. Co.G Sgt.
Tice, William H.T. AL 11th Inf. Co.A
Tice, William J. GA 10th Inf. Co.D
Tice, W.W. GA 19th Inf. Co.I
Ticen, J.F. NC 1st Arty. (10th St.Troops) Co.H
Ticer, G.W. TN 51st Inf. Co.K Cpl.
Ticer, G.W. TN 51st (Cons.) Inf. Co.G
Ticer, H.A. AR 27th Inf. Co.F Sgt.
Ticer, James F. MS 7th Cav. Co.E
Ticer, J.M. TN 10th Inf. Co.I
Ticer, John M. MS Cav. 4th Bn. Roddey's Co.
Ticer, J. Pinkney MS 2nd Inf. Co.B Cpl.
Ticer, J.T. AL 31st Inf. Co.K
Ticer, M.H. MS 2nd St.Cav. Co.E
Ticer, Robert C.S. NC 13th Inf. Co.B
Ticer, W.A. AR 27th Inf. Co.F
Ticer, W.A. AR 45th Mil. Co.A
Ticer, William AR 2nd Cav. 1st Co.A
Ticer, William M. AR 3rd Cav. 3rd Co.E
Ticero, Theodore GA Conscr.
Tichener, G.H. TN 22nd (Barteau's) Cav. 1st Sgt.
Tichenor, Fred W. VA 10th Cav. Co.E 1st Lt.
Tichenor, F.W. VA 10th Cav. Co.A
Tichenor, J.T. AL 17th Inf. Chap.
Tichenor, L.D. TX Cav. 2nd Regt.St.Troops Co.C
Ticher, Richard LA 13th Inf. Co.A
Tichinor, G.H. TN Cav. 1st Bn. (McNairy's) Co.C
Tichner, Gabriel KY 14th Cav. Co.B
Tichnor, L.D. Brush Bn.
Tickaneeskeh, Joe NC Inf. Thomas Legion Co.B
Tick but tubbee 1st Choctaw & Chickasaw Mtd.Rifles Co.A
Tickeah, John MS Cav. 17th Bn. Co.D
Ticke Eater 1st Cherokee Mtd.Rifles Co.I Cpl.
Tickel, Absalom B. NC 47th Inf. Co.K
Tickel, Brooks NC Inf. 2nd Bn. Co.B
Tickel, Jackson N. VA 11th Bn.Res. Co.A
Tickel, Lindsay NC Inf. 2nd Bn. Co.B

Tickel, Solomon D. VA 86th Mil. Co.E,C
Tickel, William G. VA 86th Mil. Co.C
Tickenberg, J. SC Mil. 1st Regt. (Charleston Res.) Co.F
Tickenberg, P. SC Mil. 1st Regt. (Charleston Res.) Co.F
Tickenen, D.D. AL Talladega Cty.Res. R.N. Ware's Cav.Co.
Ticker, James Wood Gen. & Staff Maj.,QM
Ticker, J.H. AL 8th Cav. Co.A
Tickerneeskee, George 2nd Cherokee Mtd.Vol. Co.K
Ticklantubbee Deneale's Regt. Choctaw Warriors Co.E
Tickle, A.J. VA Mil. Stowers' Co.
Tickle, Andrew F. NC 47th Inf. Co.K
Tickle, Andy TX 19th Cav.
Tickle, A.W. VA Horse Arty. Jackson's Co.
Tickle, A.W. VA Loc.Def. Morehead's Co.
Tickle, Brooks NC 53rd Inf. Co.E
Tickle, C. NC 3rd Jr.Res. Co.B
Tickle, Caleb NC 4th Bn.Jr.Res. Co.B
Tickle, Calvin NC 47th Inf. Co.K
Tickle, Charles A. NC 47th Inf. Co.K
Tickle, Daniel L. VA 36th Inf. 2nd Co.G
Tickle, F.C. NC 8th Inf. Co.I Capt.
Tickle, George R. NC 47th Inf. Co.K
Tickle, George S. NC 53rd Inf. Co.A
Tickle, Harvy B. VA 45th Inf. Co.F
Tickle, H.C. VA 45th Inf. Co.F
Tickle, James NC 53rd Inf. Co.E
Tickle, John NC 20th Inf. Co.A
Tickle, John C. NC 8th Inf. Co.I
Tickle, John W. NC 53rd Inf. Co.A
Tickle, Josiah VA 54th Inf. Co.F
Tickle, Julius R. NC 47th Inf. Co.K
Tickle, L.C. VA Horse Arty. Jackson's Co.
Tickle, L.C. VA Loc.Def. Morehead's Co.
Tickle, Levi R. NC 21st Inf. Co.M
Tickle, Levi R. NC 47th Inf. Co.K
Tickle, Lewis C. NC 8th Inf. Co.I
Tickle, Lindsay NC 53rd Inf. Co.E Cpl.
Tickle, Peter TX 26th Cav. Co.D
Tickle, Peter C. VA 36th Inf. 3rd Co.I
Tickle, Rankin S. NC 45th Inf. Co.B Sgt.
Tickle, S. NC 7th Sr.Res. Bradshaw's Co.A
Tickle, Simeon NC 47th Inf. Co.K
Tickle, Solomon D. VA 36th Inf. 3rd Co.I
Tickle, William G. VA 36th Inf. 3rd Co.I
Tickle, William R. NC 21st Inf. Co.M
Tickle, Y. NC 4th Inf. Co.E
Ticklin, --- Deneale's Regt. Choctaw Warriors Co.B
Tickling, W.H. VA 9th Cav. Co.C
Tickner, David A. GA 11th Inf. Co.B
Ticknor, George M. GA 1st (Olmstead's) Inf. Co.G
Ticknor, William O. GA 6th Inf. (St.Guards) Co.H
Ticont, Hugh MS 36th Inf. Co.G
Ticont, L.V. MS 36th Inf. Co.G
Ti coo ka nay 1st Creek Mtd.Vol. Co.E
Ticsher, H. TX 1st Hvy.Arty. Co.F
Tidball, Thomas A. VA Lt.Arty. Arch. Graham's Co.
Tidd, James H. GA 45th Inf. Co.F
Tidd, Mathew M. GA 2nd Inf. Co.I
Tidd, Wiley B. GA 27th Inf. Co.A
Tidd, William J. GA 27th Inf. Co.A
Tidd, W.J. GA 7th Inf. Co.H
Tidder, J.M. AL 22nd Inf. Co.E Cpl.
Tidder, T. TN 84th Inf. Co.C
Tiddle, J.M. MS 7th Inf. Co.F
Tiddler, G.W. VA 23rd Cav. Co.G
Tiddleton, M.J. AL 2nd Inf. Co.D
Tiddy, James NC 34th Inf. Co.E 1st Lt.
Tiddy, J.F. NC 1st Inf. (6 mo. '61) Co.B
Tiddy, John F. NC 33rd Inf. Co.A
Tiddy, R.N. NC 1st Inf. (6 mo. '61) Co.B
Tidebotone, A. TX 17th Inf. Co.C
Tideman, John H. TX 3rd Inf. Co.H Cpl.
Tidford, J.A. TN 19th & 20th (Cons.) Cav. Co.G
Tidgy, D.W. NC 3rd Inf.
Tidings, Charles KY 2nd (Duke's) Cav. Co.A
Tidings, Thomas MO Inf. Perkins' Bn. Co.A
Tidler, George M. VA 97th Mil. Co.B
Tidler, George W. VA Cav. O'Ferrall's Bn. Co.B
Tidler, George W. VA 10th Inf. Co.I
Tidler, John M. VA 97th Mil. Co.B
Tidler, Samuel L. VA Lt.Arty. W.H. Rice's Co.
Tidler, William VA 136th Mil. Co.B
Tidman, A. AL 15th Inf. Co.I
Tidman, J. AL Talladega Cty.Res. D.M. Reid's Co.
Tidmarsh, Charles LA Inf. 1st Sp.Bn. (Wheat's) Co.A
Tidmarsh, Charles VA 51st Inf. Co.H
Tidmarsh, Charles 10th Conf.Cav. Co.D
Tidmarsh, T.N. Gen. & Staff, Ord.Serv. 1st Lt.
Tidmarsh, T.U. TN 1st Hvy.Arty. Co.K
Tidmarsh, T.U. Gen. & Staff 1st Lt.,ACS
Tidmore, --- AL 62nd Inf. Co.F
Tidmore, A. AL Mil. 4th Vol. Co.I
Tidmore, Adam AL 8th Cav. Co.H
Tidmore, A.J. AL 9th (Malone's) Cav. Co.H
Tidmore, Henry AL 36th Inf. Co.H
Tidmore, Henry M. MS 9th Inf. Old Co.C Sgt.
Tidmore, J. AL Pris.Guard Freeman's Co.
Tidmore, James F. AR 19th (Dawson's) Inf. Co.B
Tidmore, J.C. 3rd Conf.Cav. Co.B
Tidmore, Jerry J. AL 8th Cav. Co.C
Tidmore, J.H. 3rd Conf.Cav. Co.B 1st Sgt.
Tidmore, J.M. AL 36th Inf. Co.H
Tidmore, J.M. 3rd Conf.Cav. Co.B
Tidmore, John AL 3rd Res. Co.H
Tidmore, John MS 9th Inf. New Co.C
Tidmore, Maximillion AL 28th Inf. Co.C Capt.
Tidmore, S. AL Talladega Cty.Res. D.M. Reid's Co.
Tidmore, William AL Cp. of Instr. Talladega Co.B
Tidmore, Wm. H. AL 49th Inf. Co.I
Tidmore, William T. AL 62nd Inf. Co.K
Tidrow, John A.C. MO 4th Cav. Co.H,B
Tidrow, John C. MO 1st Regt.St.Guards Co.D
Tidrow, William M. MO 1st Inf. Co.E
Tidwell, A. AR 15th (Johnson's) Inf. Co.D
Tidwell, A.G. SC Hvy.Arty. Gilchrist's Co. (Gist Guard)
Tidwell, A.G. SC Arty. Manigault's Bn. Co.E
Tidwell, A.H.S. AR 8th Inf. New Co.D Sgt.
Tidwell, A.J. AL 48th Inf. Co.D Cpl.
Tidwell, A.J. AR 20th Inf. Co.K
Tidwell, A.J. MS 28th Cav. Co.B
Tidwell, Albert AL 62nd Inf. Co.A
Tidwell, Albert MS 1st Lt.Arty. Co.A
Tidwell, Albert MS 1st (King's) Inf. (St.Troops) Co.K
Tidwell, Alexander AL 34th Inf. Breedlove's Co.
Tidwell, Alexander W. AR 33rd Inf. Co.K
Tidwell, Andersen AL 49th Inf. Co.B
Tidwell, Anderson Exch.Bn. Co.D,CSA
Tidwell, Andrew TN 40th Inf. Co.G Cpl.
Tidwell, Andrew J. MS Cav. Hughes' Bn. Co.H
Tidwell, Aquilla TN Lt.Arty. Baxter's Co.
Tidwell, A.T. KY 3rd Mtd.Inf. Co.L
Tidwell, A.T. TN 12th Inf. Co.E
Tidwell, Benjamin TN 11th Inf. Co.K Cpl.
Tidwell, Benjamin F. FL 8th Inf. Co.F
Tidwell, Benjamin F. GA 30th Inf. Co.D
Tidwell, Benjamin J. GA 55th Inf. Co.F
Tidwell, Benton TX 34th Cav. Co.C
Tidwell, B.J. AL 56th Part.Rangers Co.H
Tidwell, B.L. AL 46th Inf. Co.K
Tidwell, B.M. TN 3rd (Clack's) Inf. Co.D
Tidwell, B.N. SC 4th Cav. Co.B
Tidwell, B.N. SC Cav. 10th Bn. Co.A
Tidwell, B.N. SC 15th Inf. Co.E
Tidwell, Booker S. AL 28th Inf. Co.C
Tidwell, C. GA 34th Inf. Co.I Capt.
Tidwell, C. LA 8th Cav. Co.D
Tidwell, C. TN 14th (Neely's) Cav. Co.K
Tidwell, Callaway H. TN 53rd Inf. Co.G 1st Sgt.
Tidwell, Calvry AL 34th Inf. Breedlove's Co.
Tidwell, C.C. AL 48th Inf. Co.A Cpl.
Tidwell, C.D. AL 45th Inf. Co.C
Tidwell, C.G. TX Cav. Hardeman's Regt. Co.G
Tidwell, Chas. MO St.Guard
Tidwell, Charles K. FL 10th Inf. Co.F
Tidwell, Charles L. SC Inf. 7th Bn. (Enfield Rifles) Co.B
Tidwell, Charles W. TN 3rd (Clack's) Inf. Co.K Sgt.
Tidwell, C.K. MO 3rd & 5th Cons.Inf.
Tidwell, Clayton AL Cp. of Instr. Talladega
Tidwell, Clayton 3rd Conf.Cav. Co.A
Tidwell, C.M. TN 10th (DeMoss') Cav. Co.K
Tidwell, C.M. TN 15th (Cons.) Cav. Co.F
Tidwell, C.M. TX 5th Cav. Co.F
Tidwell, C.N. AL 49th Inf. Co.B
Tidwell, Colbert TX 34th Cav. Co.C
Tidwell, C.R. MO 1st & 4th Cons.Inf. Co.K
Tidwell, C.R. Exch.Bn. 3rd Co.B,CSA
Tidwell, Dan AL Cp. of Instr. Talladega
Tidwell, Daniel AL 19th Inf. Co.C
Tidwell, David AL 1st Cav. Co.F
Tidwell, David AL 12th Cav. Co.B Sgt.
Tidwell, David AL 33rd Inf. Co.F
Tidwell, David W. LA 19th Inf. Co.H
Tidwell, D.H. FL 2nd Inf. Co.B
Tidwell, Dillard H. TX 14th Cav. Co.E
Tidwell, D.M. TN 19th (Biffle's) Cav. Co.D
Tidwell, D.R. AL Cav. Roddey's Escort
Tidwell, D.W. LA Inf. Pelican Regt. Co.E
Tidwell, D.W. SC 2nd Inf. Co.E Cpl.
Tidwell, E. GA 10th Inf. Co.H Cpl.
Tidwell, Edward FL 2nd Inf. Co.F Cpl.
Tidwell, E.J. AR 19th (Dockery's) Inf. Co.C

Tidwell, E.M. TN 11th Inf. Co.K
Tidwell, F. SC Arty. Manigault's Bn. Co.E Sgt.
Tidwell, F.A. SC 4th St.Troops Co.I
Tidwell, F.A. SC 20th Inf. Co.G
Tidwell, F.L. TX 7th Inf. Co.G Lt.
Tidwell, F.L. Inf. Bailey's Cons.Regt. Co.B 2nd Lt.
Tidwell, F.M. AL 34th Inf. Co.C
Tidwell, F.M. GA Cav. 20th Bn. Co.A
Tidwell, F.M. GA 46th Inf. Co.E
Tidwell, F.M. GA 53rd Inf. Co.A
Tidwell, F.M. MO 7th Cav. Co.I Sgt.
Tidwell, F.M. TX 17th Inf. Co.A
Tidwell, F. Marion GA 1st (Olmstead's) Inf. Co.D
Tidwell, F.N. AR 1st (Monroe's) Cav. Co.B
Tidwell, Francis SC 1st Arty. Co.K
Tidwell, Francis G. MS 17th Inf. Co.C
Tidwell, Francis M AR 9th Inf. Co.D
Tidwell, Francis M. GA 2nd Inf. Co.F
Tidwell, Francis M. MO 8th Cav. Co.G 1st Sgt.
Tidwell, Francis M. TX 22nd Inf. Co.C 2nd Lt.
Tidwell, Frank TN 19th & 20th (Cons.) Cav. Co.E
Tidwell, Frank TN 20th (Russell's) Cav. Co.I
Tidwell, Franklin AR 8th Inf. New Co.C
Tidwell, Franklin MO 2nd Cav. Co.F 2nd Sgt.
Tidwell, Franklin MO Cav. 3rd Regt.St.Guard Co.E
Tidwell, Franklin J. TX 10th Inf. Co.F Sgt.
Tidwell, Frank W. AR 1st (Crawford's) Cav. Co.A
Tidwell, Fulton F. TN 11th Inf. Co.K Capt.
Tidwell, G. AR 32nd Inf. Co.H
Tidwell, Garlan AR 8th Inf. Old Co.F
Tidwell, Gasm AL Cp. of Instr. Talladega
Tidwell, Gazzam AL 22nd Inf. Co.K
Tidwell, Geo. M. AL Cp. of Instr. Talladega
Tidwell, George W. AL 34th Inf. Breedlove's Co.
Tidwell, Gideon G. LA 31st Inf. Co.A
Tidwell, G.N.D. AL 12th Cav. Co.B
Tidwell, Green H. AR 15th (Josey's) Inf. Co.G
Tidwell, G.W. AL 53rd (Part.Rangers) Co.I
Tidwell, G.W. MS 22nd Inf. Co.D
Tidwell, G.W. MS 26th Inf. Co.D
Tidwell, G.W. MS 32nd Inf. Co.I
Tidwell, Harrison MS 18th Inf. Co.C
Tidwell, H.C. TN Inf. 2nd Cons.Regt. Co.C 2nd Lt.
Tidwell, Henry GA 43rd Inf. Co.E
Tidwell, Henry TN 19th (Biffle's) Cav. Co.I
Tidwell, H.F. TX 23rd Cav. Co.D
Tidwell, Hickman C. TN 11th Inf. Co.E 2nd Lt.
Tidwell, H.M. TN 49th Inf. Co.D
Tidwell, H.V. TX 12th Cav. Co.K
Tidwell, Isaac AL 34th Inf. Breedlove's Co.
Tidwell, Isaiah AL 49th Inf. Co.I Sgt.
Tidwell, Isaiah Exch.Bn. Co.E,CSA Sgt.
Tidwell, J. GA 54th Inf. Co.A
Tidwell, J.A. AR 1st (Monroe's) Cav. Co.H
Tidwell, Jackson SC 6th Res. Co.H
Tidwell, James AL 49th Inf. Co.B
Tidwell, James AL 49th Inf. Co.D,F
Tidwell, James GA Cherokee Legion (St.Guards) Co.K Sgt.
Tidwell, James MS 14th Inf. Co.B
Tidwell, James A.J. GA 41st Inf. Co.F Ens.,1st Lt.
Tidwell, James C. TX 15th Cav. Co.F
Tidwell, James E. TN 40th Inf. Co.G Sgt.
Tidwell, James F. AR 20th Inf. Co.H
Tidwell, James H. MS 1st Lt.Arty. Co.D
Tidwell, James H. LA 31st Inf. Co.G
Tidwell, James J. AR 33rd Inf. Co.G
Tidwell, James M. AL 28th Inf. Co.C Sgt.
Tidwell, James M. AR 16th Inf. Co.K Sgt.
Tidwell, James M. AR 25th Inf. Co.I
Tidwell, James M. MS 2nd Inf. Co.D,F
Tidwell, James P. TN Holman's Bn.Part.Rangers Co.D
Tidwell, James S. AL Lt.Arty. Ward's Btty.
Tidwell, James W. MO 8th Cav. Co.A
Tidwell, J.B. TN 49th Inf. Co.D
Tidwell, J.B. Inf. Bailey's Cons.Regt. Co.L
Tidwell, J.C. SC Arty. Manigault's Bn. Co.E
Tidwell, Jefferson AL 37th Inf. Co.K
Tidwell, Jefferson T. AL 28th Inf. Co.B
Tidwell, Jesse P. GA 6th Inf. Co.B
Tidwell, J.F. AL 62nd Inf. Co.D
Tidwell, J.F. GA 13th Inf. Co.B
Tidwell, J.F. SC 4th Cav. Co.H
Tidwell, J.F. SC Hvy.Arty. Gilchrist's Co. (Gist Guard)
Tidwell, J.H. AL 5th Cav. Co.B
Tidwell, J.H. TN 15th (Stewart's) Cav. Co.A
Tidwell, J.J. AR 3rd Inf.
Tidwell, J.J. AR 6th Inf. Co.B
Tidwell, J.J. GA Cav. 20th Bn. Co.B
Tidwell, J.J. GA Lt.Arty. Croft's Btty. (Columbus Arty.)
Tidwell, J.J. MS 35th Inf. Co.E
Tidwell, J.L. GA 19th Inf. Co.A
Tidwell, J.L. LA Inf.Cons.Crescent Regt. Co.O
Tidwell, J.L. MO 12th Inf. Co.G
Tidwell, J.M. AR 1st Mtd.Rifles Co.K
Tidwell, J.M. GA Cav. 1st Bn.Res. Stark's Co.
Tidwell, J.M. GA 1st (Fannin's) Res. Co.E Cpl.
Tidwell, J.M. MS 14th (Cons.) Inf. Co.D
Tidwell, J.M. TX 32nd Cav. Co.E
Tidwell, John AL 56th Part.Rangers Co.K
Tidwell, John AL Inf. 1st Regt. Co.D
Tidwell, John AL 24th Inf. Co.C
Tidwell, John AR 8th Inf. New Co.C
Tidwell, John GA 48th Inf. Co.G Cpl.
Tidwell, John KY 9th Mtd.Inf. Co.F Cpl.
Tidwell, John LA 12th Inf. Co.I
Tidwell, John MS Adams' Co. (Holmes Cty.Ind.)
Tidwell, John TN 14th Inf. Co.G
Tidwell, John 8th (Wade's) Conf.Cav. Co.G
Tidwell, John C. AL 34th Inf. Breedlove's Co. Music.
Tidwell, John C. FL Inf. 2nd Bn. Co.E
Tidwell, John C. FL 11th Inf. Co.A
Tidwell, John C. GA Cherokee Legion (St.Guards) Co.K Cpl.
Tidwell, John H. GA 41st Inf. Co.F
Tidwell, John H. TN Lt.Arty. Baxter's Co.
Tidwell, John Henry MS 34th Inf. Co.C
Tidwell, John J. GA 1st (Olmstead's) Inf. Co.D Jr.2nd Lt.
Tidwell, John J. GA 56th Inf. Co.I
Tidwell, John L. LA 31st Inf. Co.G
Tidwell, John L. TN 40th Inf. Co.G Cpl.
Tidwell, John S. SC Inf. 7th Bn. (Enfield Rifles) Co.B 1st Lt.
Tidwell, John W. AL 16th Inf. Co.C
Tidwell, Jonas E. TX 1st (Yager's) Cav. Co.F
Tidwell, Jonathan GA 4th Inf. Co.C
Tidwell, Jones TX 22nd Cav. Co.F
Tidwell, Joseph AL 24th Inf. Co.H
Tidwell, Joseph MO 10th Cav. Co.I
Tidwell, Joseph D. TN 6th Inf. Co.G
Tidwell, Joseph L. AR 4th Inf. Co.E
Tidwell, Joseph L. LA Inf. 11th Bn. Co.D
Tidwell, Josiah TN 11th Inf. Co.K Bvt.2nd Lt.
Tidwell, Josiah J. AR 1st (Colquitt's) Inf. Co.E
Tidwell, Josiah J. AR Inf. 2nd Bn. Co.B
Tidwell, J.P. AL 29th Inf. Co.F,J
Tidwell, J.P. TN 11th (Holman's) Cav. Co.K
Tidwell, J.P. TX 23rd Cav. Co.D
Tidwell, J.R. TX 32nd Cav. Co.H
Tidwell, J.S.C. SC 4th Cav. Co.H
Tidwell, J.S.C. SC Cav. 10th Bn. Co.D
Tidwell, J.S.C. SC Hvy.Arty. Gilchrist's Co. (Gist Guard)
Tidwell, J.W. AR 8th Inf. New Co.K Capt.
Tidwell, J.W. GA 19th Inf. Co.I
Tidwell, J.W. TX 12th Cav. Co.K
Tidwell, L. TN 14th Cav. Co.B
Tidwell, Lafayette MS 1st Lt.Arty. Co.A
Tidwell, L.B. GA 55th Inf. Co.A
Tidwell, Leroy GA 39th Inf. Co.D,K
Tidwell, Levi MS 11th Inf. Co.H
Tidwell, Levi MS 35th Inf. Co.E
Tidwell, Levi MO 4th Cav. Co.B
Tidwell, Levi MO Cav. Preston's Bn. Co.B
Tidwell, Levi TN 3rd (Forrest's) Cav. Co.E
Tidwell, Lewis G. TX 10th Inf. Co.A
Tidwell, L.M. 20th Conf.Cav. Co.F
Tidwell, M. GA 1st (Olmstead's) Inf. Co.F
Tidwell, M. GA 25th Inf. Pritchard's Co.
Tidwell, Mansell GA 1st Cav. Co.D
Tidwell, Mathew AL 33rd Inf. Co.F
Tidwell, Mathew M. GA 22nd Inf. Co.K
Tidwell, Matthew L. GA 20th Inf. Co.E
Tidwell, M.H. AR 1st (Monroe's) Cav. Co.K
Tidwell, M.H. TN Inf. 49th Regt.
Tidwell, M.H. Inf. Bailey's Cons.Regt. Co.L
Tidwell, Mial M. GA 7th Inf. (St.Guards) Co.D Capt.
Tidwell, Mial M. GA 30th Inf. Lt.Col.
Tidwell, M.J. AL 13th Bn.Part.Rangers Co.D
Tidwell, M.J. AL 56th Part.Rangers Co.H
Tidwell, M.J. LA 13th Bn. (Part.Rangers) Co.B
Tidwell, M.J. TX 13th Vol. 1st Co.K Sr.2nd Lt.
Tidwell, M.J. TX 15th Inf. 2nd Co.I
Tidwell, M.M. GA 19th Inf. Co.G
Tidwell, M.N. MS 3rd Inf. (St.Troops) Co.G
Tidwell, Monroe TN 6th (Wheeler's) Cav. Co.E
Tidwell, M.T. SC 4th Cav. Co.H
Tidwell, M.T. SC Cav. 10th Bn. Co.D
Tidwell, M.T. SC Hvy.Arty. Gilchrist's Co. (Gist Guard)
Tidwell, M.T. SC Arty. Manigault's Bn. Co.E
Tidwell, Obediah GA 21st Inf. Co.C Sgt.
Tidwell, P. AR 32nd Inf. Co.H
Tidwell, P.B. AR 19th (Dawson's) Inf. Co.C
Tidwell, P.B. AR 24th Inf. Co.C
Tidwell, Peter AR 8th Inf. Old Co.F
Tidwell, Peter H. AR 24th Inf. Co.G

Tidwell, P.H. AR 12th Bn.S.S. Co.C
Tidwell, P.H. AR 20th Inf. Co.H Cpl.
Tidwell, P.M. GA 7th Inf. (St.Guards) Co.B
Tidwell, Polk GA 28th Inf. Co.E
Tidwell, P.S. TN 22nd (Barteau's) Cav. 1st Co.H
Tidwell, R.A. AL 33rd Inf. Co.F
Tidwell, R.C. AR 36th Inf. Co.A
Tidwell, Reuben AL Inf. 1st Regt. Co.D
Tidwell, Reuben AL 16th Inf. Co.C
Tidwell, Reuben W. GA 30th Inf. Co.H 1st Lt.
Tidwell, R.H. AL 46th Inf.
Tidwell, Richard AL 41st Inf. Co.K,C
Tidwell, Richard M. GA 14th Inf. Co.E
Tidwell, R.L. TX 23rd Cav. Co.D Cpl.
Tidwell, R.L. TX 32nd Cav. Co.H
Tidwell, Robert AR 30th Inf. Co.I
Tidwell, Robert MS 34th Inf. Co.K
Tidwell, Robert A.W. GA 41st Inf. Co.F
Tidwell, Robert M. GA 56th Inf. Co.I
Tidwell, Roland GA 48th Inf. Co.G
Tidwell, Rowan AL 49th Inf. Co.I
Tidwell, Rowland AR 18th Inf. Co.I
Tidwell, Rown Exch.Bn. Co.E,CSA
Tidwell, R.S. TN 31st Inf. Co.F
Tidwell, R.T. TX 24th Cav. Co.I
Tidwell, R.T. TX Granbury's Cons.Brig. Co.I
Tidwell, R.W. NC Inf. Thomas Legion 2nd Co.A, Co.C,I
Tidwell, R.W. Gen. & Staff Capt.,ACS
Tidwell, S. AR 27th Inf. Co.E
Tidwell, S. TN 15th (Cons.) Cav. Co.D,E
Tidwell, S. TN Lt.Arty. Rice's Btty.
Tidwell, S.A. GA Inf. 25th Bn. (Prov.Guard) Co.C
Tidwell, Samuel AL 27th Inf. Co.C
Tidwell, Samuel TN Cav. Nixon's Regt. Co.A
Tidwell, Samuel TX 3rd Inf. Co.I
Tidwell, Seaborn S. TX 10th Inf. Co.B
Tidwell, Silas TN 11th Inf. Co.K
Tidwell, Silas TN 32nd Inf. Co.C
Tidwell, Simeon AL 28th Inf. Co.B
Tidwell, Simeon E. GA 28th Inf. Co.E Teamster
Tidwell, S.K. AL 55th Vol. Co.G
Tidwell, S.K. TN 42nd Inf. 1st Co.H
Tidwell, S.N. TX 32nd Cav. Co.H
Tidwell, Solomon TN Lt.Arty. Baxter's Co.
Tidwell, S.P. AL 13th Bn.Part.Rangers Co.E
Tidwell, S.P. AL 56th Part.Rangers Co.I
Tidwell, S.P. SC 24th Inf. Co.G
Tidwell, S.R. AL 48th Inf. Co.H 1st Lt.
Tidwell, Stephen AL Cav. Lewis' Bn. Co.E
Tidwell, Strother LA 19th Inf. Co.E
Tidwell, T. GA Cav. 9th Bn. (St.Guards) Co.F
Tidwell, T. SC 9th Inf. Co.E
Tidwell, Thomas TN 10th (DeMoss') Cav. Co.I
Tidwell, Thomas 4th Conf.Eng.Troops
Tidwell, Thomas E. AL 12th Cav. Co.B
Tidwell, Thomas J. GA 30th Inf. Co.C Cpl.
Tidwell, Thomas L. MS Cav. Hughes' Bn. Co.H Cpl.
Tidwell, T.J. AL Cp. of Instr. Talladega
Tidwell, T.J. AR 5th Inf. Co.I
Tidwell, T.J. AR 36th Inf. Co.C
Tidwell, T.L. MS 4th Cav. Co.K
Tidwell, T.M. GA 8th Cav. New Co.I
Tidwell, Troy SC Cav. 10th Bn. Co.A
Tidwell, Uriah AL 1st Cav. Co.F Sgt.
Tidwell, Uriah AL 12th Cav. Sgt.
Tidwell, W. AL 6th Inf. Co.K
Tidwell, W. AR 51st Mil. Co.E
Tidwell, W. GA 55th Inf. Co.F
Tidwell, W.A. AR Inf. Hardy's Regt. Co.G
Tidwell, W.A. GA 13th Inf. Co.A
Tidwell, W.C. AR 15th (Johnson's) Inf. Co.D
Tidwell, W.C. TX 24th & 25th Cav. (Cons.) Co.E
Tidwell, W.C. TX 25th Cav. Co.E
Tidwell, W.C. TX 4th Inf. Co.G
Tidwell, W.D. MS 34th Inf. Co.C
Tidwell, W.G. TN 19th (Biffle's) Cav. Co.D
Tidwell, W.G. TN 27th Inf. Co.K
Tidwell, W.H. AR 15th Inf. Co.B
Tidwell, William AL 12th Cav. Co.I
Tidwell, William AL 13th Bn.Part.Rangers Co.B
Tidwell, William AL Cav. Graves' Co.
Tidwell, William AL 34th Inf. Breedlove's Co.
Tidwell, Wm. AL Cp. of Instr. Talladega
Tidwell, William AR 14th (Powers') Inf. Co.D
Tidwell, William GA Lt.Arty. Croft's Btty. (Columbus Arty.)
Tidwell, William TX 23rd Cav. Co.D
Tidwell, William TX 15th Inf. 2nd Co.F
Tidwell, William B. NC 2nd Cav. (19th St.Troops) Co.A 1st Lt.
Tidwell, William G. TN 53rd Inf. Co.G
Tidwell, William H. TX 10th Inf. Co.B
Tidwell, William J. AR 9th Inf. Co.D
Tidwell, William J. GA 40th Inf. Co.F
Tidwell, William J. MS 18th Inf. Co.K
Tidwell, William J. MS Page's Co. (Lexington Guards)
Tidwell, William L. FL Lt.Arty. Perry's Co. 2nd Lt.
Tidwell, William M. AL 45th Inf. Co.H,C
Tidwell, William M. GA 6th Inf. Co.B Capt.
Tidwell, William M. GA 43rd Inf. Co.E
Tidwell, William R. SC 20th Inf. Co.G
Tidwell, William R. TX 23rd Cav. Co.D
Tidwell, William T.A. NC 12th Inf. Co.E
Tidwell, William T.A. NC 49th Inf. Co.F
Tidwell, William W. AL 34th Inf. Breedlove's Co.
Tidwell, W.L. TX 23rd Cav. Co.D
Tidwell, W.M. AL Inf. 1st Regt. Co.C
Tidwell, W.M. AL 46th Inf. Co.E Cpl.
Tidwell, W.M. AR 8th Inf. New Co.K
Tidwell, W.M. AR 36th Inf. Co.C
Tidwell, W.M. TX Inf. 3rd St.Troops Co.G
Tidwell, W.N. MO 7th Cav. Co.I
Tidwell, W.P. GA 53rd Inf. Co.G Cpl.
Tidwell, W.R. GA 10th Inf. Co.I 1st Sgt.
Tidwell, W.R. SC 1st Arty. Co.C,F
Tidwell, W.W. MS 10th Inf. Old Co.A, New Co.D
Tie, Cullen MS Cav. Ham's Regt. Co.B
Tie, Frank FL 6th Inf. Co.E
Tiebout, Henry TX Home Guards Killough's Co.
Tiedemann, Henry LA 20th Inf. Co.F
Tiedemann, O. SC Lt.Arty. Wagener's Co. (Co.A,German Arty.)
Tiefenback, George T. LA 14th Inf. Co.B
Tiefenthal, Adolphus SC Lt.Arty. Walter's Co. (Washington Arty.)
Tiefenthal, Adolphus SC Arty.Bn. Hampton Legion Co.A
Tiefey, Cornelius TN 1st Hvy.Arty. Co.F
Tiege, William NC 4th Sr.Res. Co.E
Tielman, W. TX Waul's Legion Co.A
Tieman, Fritz TX Waul's Legion Co.E
Tieman, H. TN 15th Inf. Co.I
Tieman, Lewis T. MS 21st Inf. Co.D
Tieman, Louis TX 8th Inf. Co.K Sgt.
Tiemann, Gebhardt LA Mil.Cont.Regt. Roder's Co.
Tiemann, H. LA Mil.Cont.Regt. Roder's Co.
Tienchen, C.H. SC Mil.Arty. 1st Regt. Harms' Co.
Tiencken, C.H. SC Arty. Melcher's Co. (Co.B,German Arty.)
Tiencken, D. SC Mil.Arty. 1st Regt. Werner's Co.
Tiencken, D. SC Lt.Arty. Wagener's Co. (Co.A,German Arty.)
Tiencken, H. SC Mil.Cav. Theo. Cordes' Co.
Tiencken, J. SC Mil.Arty. 1st Regt. Werner's Co.
Tiencken, John SC Lt.Arty. Wagener's Co. (Co.A,German Arty.)
Tienken, C.H. SC Arty. Manigault's Bn. Co.A
Tienken, H. SC 3rd Cav. Co.G
Tienmans, R. TX 24th & 25th Cav. (Cons.) Co.H
Tiepence, G.W.C. AL Arty. 1st Bn. Co.A
Tiepence, G.W.C. AL Inf. 2nd Regt.
Tier, James TX 18th Inf. Co.L
Tier, James M. LA 17th Inf. Co.D
Tier, Jb. LA Mil. 3rd Regt. 1st Brig. 1st Div. Co.F
Tier, John MO Todd's Co.
Tier, John NC 44th Inf. Co.G
Tier, William S. MS 15th Inf. Co.I
Tierbout, J. VA Lt.Arty. 12th Bn. Co.B
Tierbout, Jethro NC Lt.Arty. 13th Bn. Co.A
Tierce, B.F. TN 38th Inf. 1st Co.K
Tierce, Constantine AL Lt.Arty. Phelan's Co.
Tierce, Constantine AL 5th Inf. Co.H
Tierce, David S. GA 40th Inf. Co.B
Tierce, D.S. GA 18th Inf. Co.H
Tierce, E.L. TN 38th Inf. 1st Co.K
Tierce, J. TX 7th Inf.
Tierce, James MS 2nd Inf. (A. of 10,000) Co.G
Tierce, James MS 17th Inf. Co.K
Tierce, J.P. TN 20th Inf. Co.H
Tierce, L. AL 32nd Inf. Co.I
Tierce, Lewis MS 16th Inf. Co.K
Tierce, Thadeus TX 9th Cav. Co.D
Tierce, William F. GA 2nd Inf. Co.F
Tierman, Miles SC 1st Arty. Co.E
Tiern, Pedro LA Mil. 5th Regt.Eur.Brig. (Spanish Regt.) Co.4 Cpl.
Tiernan, Auguste, 1st LA 1st (Strawbridge's) Inf. Co.F
Tiernan, Bernard TX 1st Regt.St.Troops Co.A
Tiernan, Edward GA 1st (Olmstead's) Inf. Co.E
Tiernan, Henry MO 10th Inf. Co.I
Tiernan, Henry L. MO Lt.Arty. 1st Btty.
Tiernan, J. AL 32nd & 58th (Cons.) Inf.
Tiernan, James TN 2nd (Walker's) Inf. Co.I
Tiernan, James TX 26th Cav. Co.C

Tiernan, James TX 11th (Spaight's) Bn.Vol. Co.E
Tiernan, Ludwig Q. LA 1st (Strawbridge's) Inf. Co.F
Tiernan, Patrick LA Miles' Legion Co.G
Tiernan, Patrick MS 17th Inf. Co.D
Tiernay, John VA 34th Inf. Norton's Co.
Tiernay, Michael LA 1st (Strawbridge's) Inf. Co.C Cpl.
Tiernay, Nicholas GA Inf. 18th Bn. Co.C
Tiernay, Thomas MS Lt.Arty. Hoskins' Btty. (Brookhaven Lt.Arty.)
Tierney, Daniel LA 10th Inf. Co.B Cpl.
Tierney, Frank AL 17th Inf. Co.K Ord.Sgt.
Tierney, George W. GA 2nd Cav. Co.D
Tierney, James AL Mil. 3rd Vol. Co.B
Tierney, J.O.B. MS 21st Inf. Co.E
Tierney, John GA 11th Inf. Co.B
Tierney, John LA 1st (Nelligan's) Inf. Co.E
Tierney, John LA 9th Inf. Co.B
Tierney, John LA 10th Inf. Co.B
Tierney, John MS 38th Cav. Co.D
Tierney, John MS 9th Inf. New Co.B
Tierney, John TN 10th Inf. Co.G
Tierney, John VA Hvy.Arty. 18th Bn. Co.D
Tierney, John VA 2nd Inf.Loc.Def. Co.G
Tierney, John VA Inf. 2nd.Bn.Loc.Def. Co.A
Tierney, John VA 27th Inf. Co.G
Tierney, Joseph MS 3rd Inf. Co.F
Tierney, M. SC Inf. 1st (Charleston) Bn. Co.F
Tierney, Martin MS 10th Inf. Co.C
Tierney, Martin MS 19th Inf. Co.C Sgt.
Tierney, Michael VA 17th Inf. Co.I Sgt.
Tierney, Michael J. LA 16th Inf. Co.I
Tierney, Nicholas LA Mil. Lafayette Arty.
Tierney, P. SC 1st Inf. Co.M
Tierney, Patrick GA Hvy.Arty. 22nd Bn. Co.E
Tierney, Patrick GA 1st (Olmstead's) Inf. Guilmartin's Co.
Tierney, Patrick LA 1st Hvy.Arty. (Reg.) Co.G
Tierney, Patrick MO Cav. Williams' Regt. Co.I
Tierney, Patrick VA 26th Cav. Co.A
Tierney, Patrick VA Inf. 1st Bn. Co.B
Tierney, Richard AR 1st Mtd.Rifles Co.B
Tierney, Thomas AR 3rd Inf. Co.E,K
Tierney, Thomas AR 17th (Griffith's) Inf. Co.A
Tierney, Thomas MS Conscr.
Tierney, Thomas TN 7th Cav.
Tierney, Timothy LA 1st (Strawbridge's) Inf. Co.B
Tiernoulet, H. LA Arty. Guyol's Co. (Orleans Arty.)
Tierns, John MS 20th Inf. Co.K
Tierny, Martin VA 67th Mil. Co.E
Tierny, Thomas AR 11th & 17th Cons.Inf. Co.I
Tieron, Henry LA Mil. 1st Regt. French Brig. Drum.
Tierrelly, D. SC 2nd Arty. Co.F
Tierselin, Aime LA Inf.Cons.18th Regt. & Yellow Jacket Bn. Co.D
Ties, George NC 43rd Inf. Co.K
Ti e skie 1st Cherokee Mtd.Rifles Co.H
Tiesennier, John GA 38th Inf. Co.I
Tiesing, Gideon P. VA 3rd (Chrisman's) Bn.Res. Co.C
Tiessinger, Lewis KY Lt.Arty. Cobb's Co.
Tiesten, H.T. SC 1st Cav. Co.A
Tietgene, R. LA Mil. 4th Regt.Eur.Brig. Co.A
Tietjen, C. SC Mil.Arty. 1st Regt. Harms' Co.
Tietjen, Claus NC 18th Inf. Co.A
Tietjen, Henry TX 17th Inf. Co.H
Tietjen, J.H. SC Mil.Arty. 1st Regt. Werner's Co.
Tietz, J. KY 4th Mtd.Inf. Co.K
Tietz, John A. SC 3rd Bn.Res. Co.B
Tie ye skie 1st Cherokee Mtd.Rifles Co.D
Tie yes kie 1st Cherokee Mtd.Rifles McDaniel's Co.
Tiff, Jacob GA Inf. Co.I
Tiffa, A.B. AR 32nd Inf. Co.C
Tiffany, A.J. GA 28th Inf. Co.I Sgt.
Tiffany, A.S. GA 28th Inf. Co.I Sgt.
Tiffany, Charles C. VA 27th Inf. Co.D
Tiffany, H. SC 6th Inf.
Tiffany, Henry, Jr. MD Weston's Bn. Co.B
Tiffany, Henry VA 21st Inf. Co.B
Tiffany, Hugh S. VA 27th Inf. Co.D Capt.
Tiffany, J. VA 31st Mil. Co.B
Tiffany, John VA 27th Inf. Co.D 2nd Lt.
Tiffany, Joseph McD. VA 27th Inf. Co.D Sgt.
Tiffany, L.H. TX 17th Inf. Co.F
Tiffany, William VA 27th Inf. Co.D
Tiffany, William S. VA Lt.Arty. Lowry's Co.
Tiffany, William W. VA Lt.Arty. Lowry's Co.
Tiffen, H. MS 41st Inf. Co.I
Tiffen, W. MS 41st Inf. Co.I
Tifferteller, M. TN Inf. 4th Cons.Regt. Co.A
Tiffey, C.C. AR 38th Inf. Co.A
Tiffey, G.W. AR 38th Inf. Co.A
Tiffey, J.B. AR 38th Inf. Co.A
Tiffey, Robert B. VA 5th Cav. Sgt.
Tiffey, Robert B. VA 9th Cav. Sandford's Co.
Tiffey, Robert B. VA 15th Cav. Co.A Sgt.
Tiffey, Robert B. VA Cav. 15th Bn. Co.A Sgt.
Tiffey, Robert B. VA 41st Mil. Co.D Capt.
Tiffin, James T. AR Cav. Wright's Regt. Co.B
Tiffin, J.H. AL 23rd Inf. Co.C
Tiffin, J.J. AR Cav. Wright's Regt. Co.C
Tiffin, John AL 49th Inf. Co.F
Tiffin, John H. AL Cp. of Instr. Talladega
Tiffy, Charles C. AR 2nd Vol. Co.A
Tift, Julius AL 1st Bn.Cadets Co.A Cpl.
Tift, Julius A. AL Arty. 1st Bn.
Tift, N.F. GA Cav. Nelson's Ind.Co.
Tift, N.F. GA Cav. Ragland's Co.
Tift, William VA 62nd Mtd.Inf.
Tigar Thomas 1st Creek Mtd.Vol. 2nd Co.D
Tigar Weley 1st Creek Mtd.Vol. 2nd Co.D
Tigart, D.P. TN 2nd (Robison's) Inf.
Tigart, William MS 37th Inf. Co.B
Tigby, R. GA 56th Inf. Co.E
Tiger 1st Creek Mtd.Vol. Co.E
Tiger Billy 1st Choctaw & Chickasaw Mtd.Rifles 2nd Co.K Cpl.
Tiger Daniel 1st Creek Mtd.Vol. Co.H
Tiger David 1st Creek Mtd.Vol. Co.H
Tiger George 1st Creek Mtd.Vol. Co.A
Tiger Jefferson 1st Creek Mtd.Vol. Co.H
Tiger Robert 1st Creek Mtd.Vol. Co.F Sgt.
Tiger Wilson 1st Creek Mtd.Vol. Co.A
Tigerate, Elisha AR 13th Inf. Co.G Cpl.
Tigert, David P. MS 2nd Inf. Co.L 1st Sgt.
Tigert, James MO 1st Cav. Co.K Sgt.
Tigert, J.M. TX 9th (Young's) Inf. Co.D
Tigert, J.M. TX 18th Inf. Co.F
Tigert, John AL Mil. Campbell's Co.
Tigert, John TX 18th Inf. Co.F
Tigert, T.B. MS 10th Cav. Co.H
Tigert, Thomas KY Owen Co.
Tigert, William H. TX 18th Inf. Co.F
Tiggin, Henry AL 2nd Cav. Co.I
Tiggs, William J. TN Cav. Newsom's Regt. Donnell's Co.
Tigh, Dominick LA 14th Inf. Co.K
Tigh, James MS 20th Inf. Co.K
Tigh, Thomas 9th Conf.Inf. Co.D
Tigha, William KY Cav. 1st Bn. Co.B
Tigha, William KY 4th Cav. Co.B
Tighe, Patrick GA 1st (Olmstead's) Inf. Reed's Co.
Tighe, Patrick GA 47th Inf. Co.A
Tighe, Patrick TX 1st (Yager's) Cav. Co.A
Tighe, Peter MO Cav. Poindexter's Regt.
Tighe, R.H.L. VA 2nd St.Res. Co.E
Tighlford H. TN 7th (Duckworth's) Cav. Co.C
Tighlman, Frank E. MS 16th Inf. Co.C Sgt.
Tighlman, Jackson NC 2nd Inf. Co.H
Tighlmon, Andrew G. TX 27th Cav. Co.G
Tigirina, Juan TX Part.Rangers Thomas' Co. Sgt.
Tiglman, Joseph MS Inf. 7th Bn. Co.B
Tignal, Edmond VA 39th Inf. Co.L
Tigne, Felix AR Inf. Cocke's Regt. Co.E
Tigner, Abram TN 20th Inf. Co.A
Tigner, B.F. GA 2nd Cav. (St.Guards) Co.B
Tigner, Charles T. VA 32nd Inf. 2nd Co.I
Tigner, J.A. GA Inf. 5th Bn. (St.Guards) Co.E
Tigner, James J. GA 27th Inf. Co.K
Tigner, John T. LA 31st Inf. Co.E
Tigner, J.W. AR 15th (Josey's) Inf. 1st Co.C
Tigner, L.H. Gen. & Staff Asst.Surg.
Tigner, Samuel H. LA 12th Inf. Co.E Sgt.Maj.
Tigner, T.B. GA 4th Res. Co.A,F
Tigner, Urban C. GA 46th Inf. Co.I
Tigner, Wesley F. AL 6th Inf. Co.B Ord.Sgt.
Tigner, W.F. LA 9th Inf. Co.D
Tigner, William R. VA 3rd Cav. Co.B
Tignes, L.H. GA 42nd Inf. Asst.Surg.
Tignieres, --- LA Mil. 1st Regt. French Brig. Co.5
Tignor, Albert C. VA 47th Inf. 2nd Co.G
Tignor, C.A. AL 3rd Cav. Co.C
Tignor, Charles W. TX 11th Cav. Co.B
Tignor, D.A. GA Cav. 1st Bn.Res.
Tignor, Elihu H. TN Cav. 16th Bn. (Neal's) Co.F
Tignor, E.W. AL 11th Cav. Co.B
Tignor, Giles VA Lt.Arty. W.P. Carter's Co.
Tignor, James W. AR 13th Inf. Co.B
Tignor, John M. TN 24th Inf. Co.B
Tignor, Leander H. GA 41st Inf. Co.E Asst.Surg.
Tignor, M.B. VA 55th Inf.
Tignor, Milton B. VA 55th Inf. Co.K
Tignor, Patrick VA 16th Cav. Co.A
Tignor, Patrick VA Cav. Ferguson's Bn. Stevenson's Co.
Tignor, Robert VA 47th Inf. 2nd Co.G
Tignor, Robert VA 55th Inf. Co.D
Tignor, Samuel VA Cav. 15th Bn. Co.B
Tignor, Samuel S. VA 15th Cav. Co.D

Tignor, S.D. VA Lt.Arty. W.P. Carter's Co.
Tignor, S.S. VA 37th Mil. 2nd Co.B
Tignor, Thomas VA 13th Cav. Co.F
Tignor, W.C. VA 9th Mil. Co.A
Tignor, William B. VA Res.Forces Clark's Co.
Tignor, William J. VA 40th Inf. Co.A
Tignor, William R. VA 115th Mil. Co.B
Tignor, Woodford C. VA 55th Inf. Co.K
Tignor, W.R. VA Inf. 25th Bn. Co.G
Tigret, James W. VA 30th Bn.S.S. Co.C
Tigret, Levi MO Cav. Poindexter's Regt.
Tigret, Thomas J. SC 13th Inf. Co.A
Tigue, Abraham SC Arty. 1st Regt. Co.F
Tigue, F.C. TX Cav. Hardeman's Regt. Co.A
Tigue, Jacob NC 14th Inf. Co.G
Tigue, Michael LA 7th Inf. Co.D
Tigue, R.L. AR 8th Cav. Co.D
Tigue, William W. AL 19th Inf. Co.G
Tigue, Willis NC 54th Inf. Co.E
Tigus, A.J. GA Cav. 1st Bn.Res. McKinney's Co.
Tigus, J.A. AL 51st (Part.Rangers) Co.I
Tikbattabee 1st Choctaw & Chickasaw Mtd.Rifles 2nd Co.C
Tikbonna 1st Choctaw & Chickasaw Mtd.Rifles 2nd Co.I
Tike, I.C. AL Unassign.Conscr.
Tike, Sam Deneale's Regt. Choctaw Warriors Co.D
Tike, William E. GA 46th Inf. Co.A
Tiket, J.T. AL 49th Inf. Co.B
Tikiah, John MS 9th Cav. Co.B
Tilangin, W.R. AL 12th Cav. Co.A
Tilano, Hampton LA 7th Inf. Co.B
Tilano, Michael LA 11th Inf. Co.H
Tilberd, C.C. VA Cav. 39th Bn. Co.C
Tilbrath, Joseph AR 5th Mil. Co.I
Tilbs, John A. VA Lt.Arty. 38th Bn. Co.D
Tilden, C.B. MO Lt.Arty. 3rd Field Btty. Capt.
Tilden, Robert J. VA 7th Cav. Co.F
Tilden, Robert J. VA 62nd Mtd.Inf. Capt.,AQM
Tilden, Robert J. Gen. & Staff AQM
Tilden, Samuel VA Lt.Arty. Brander's Co.
Tilders, Henry W. MS 42nd Inf. Co.I
Tildes, John FL 5th Inf. Co.B
Tildon, Norwood LA 27th Inf. Co.A Hosp.Stew.
Tildree, James AL 34th Inf. Co.A
Tile, Charles SC Hvy.Arty. 15th (Lucas') Bn. Co.B
Tiler, D. AL 50th Inf.
Tilery, Daniel W. MS 11th Inf. Co.C
Tilery, John W. TN 32nd Inf. Co.E
Tilery, S.T. AL 37th Inf. Co.K
Tilery, William AR 33rd Inf. Co.A
Tiles, John AL 42nd Inf. Co.E
Tileston, W.E.M. GA Inf. 1st Loc.Troops (Augusta) Co.K Music.
Tileston, W.E.M. GA 1st (Symons') Res. Co.K 1st Sgt.
Tiley, William TN 18th Inf. Co.E
Tilford, David M. TN 13th Inf. Co.E
Tilford, Edward LA 14th Inf. Co.E Sgt.
Tilford, George M. KY 5th Cav. Co.B Capt.
Tilford, James S. TN 41st Inf. Co.F
Tilford, James W. TN 7th Inf. Co.I
Tilford, J.H. TN 9th Inf. Co.I 2nd Lt.
Tilford, John VA Inf. 4th Bn.Loc.Def. Co.E Cpl.
Tilford, John C. VA 3rd Cav. Co.B
Tilford, John C. VA 32nd Inf. Co.A
Tilford, M.A. TN 7th (Duckworth's) Cav. White's Co.
Tilford, Robert TN 9th (Ward's) Cav. Co.A,G
Tilford, Samuel TN 23rd Inf. 2nd Co.F
Tilford, S.C. MO 3rd Inf. Co.D
Tilford, Thomas MO 3rd & 5th Cons.Inf.
Tilghman, A. AL Cp. of Instr. Talladega
Tilghman, Albert MS 2nd Part.Rangers Co.C
Tilghman, Alexander NC Inf. 13th Bn. Co.C
Tilghman, C.C. TN 22nd (Barteau's) Cav.
Tilghman, E.R. TN 38th Inf. Co.D Bvt.2nd Lt.
Tilghman, George M. VA 1st Inf. Co.B
Tilghman, James MD 1st Cav. Co.B
Tilghman, James NC 27th Inf. Co.C
Tilghman, J.C. TN 21st & 22nd (Cons.) Cav. Co.C
Tilghman, J.E. MS 3rd Inf. (St.Troops) Co.D
Tilghman, J.H. MS 10th Inf. New Co.I
Tilghman, John MD Cav. 2nd Bn. Co.F
Tilghman, John MS 18th Cav. Co.A
Tilghman, John NC 33rd Inf. Co.K
Tilghman, John L. VA Lt.Arty. Moore's Co. 1st Lt.
Tilghman, John L. Eng.,CSA 1st Lt.
Tilghman, John N. MS 34th Inf. Co.B Cpl.
Tilghman, Joseph AL Lt.Arty. 2nd Bn. Co.E
Tilghman, Joseph NC 27th Inf. Co.D Cpl.
Tilghman, L. FL 2nd Inf. Co.F
Tilghman, Levi W. LA 7th Inf. Co.B
Tilghman, Lloyd KY 3rd Mtd.Inf. Col.
Tilghman, Lloyd 4th Div. Brig.Gen.
Tilghman, Lloyd, Jr. Gen. & Staff Lt.,ADC
Tilghman, M. MS 3rd Inf. (St.Troops) Co.D
Tilghman, M.L. MS 3rd Cav. Co.G,K
Tilghman, N.L. TN Inf. 3rd Bn. Co.A
Tilghman, O. MS 18th Cav. Co.A Sgt.
Tilghman, O. TN 1st Lt.Arty. Co.B 1st Lt.
Tilghman, Oswald TN Lt.Arty. Weller's Co. Sr.2nd Lt.
Tilghman, P.L. TN 47th Inf. Co.H
Tilghman, R.B. MS 10th Inf. New Co.I
Tilghman, Richard C. MD Inf. 2nd Bn. Co.A
Tilghman, S.J. MS 17th Inf. Co.I
Tilghman, S.R. TN 38th Inf. Co.D
Tilghman, S.R. TN 47th Inf. Co.H
Tilghman, W.B. TN 47th Inf. Co.H Cpl.
Tilghman, William AL 21st Inf. Co.I
Tilghman, William MS 17th Inf. Co.I
Tilghman, William J. NC 8th Bn.Part.Rangers Co.A
Tilghman, W.M. TN 38th Inf. Co.D 2nd Lt.
Tilgman, J.M. MS 9th Inf. New Co.G
Till, A.D. AL 1st Bn. Hilliard's Legion Vol. Co.D
Till, Calvin GA 66th Inf. Co.D Sgt.
Till, D. MS Inf. 1st Bn.St.Troops (30 days '64) Co.A
Till, D. MS Hall's Co.
Till, Daniel AL 17th Inf. Co.B
Till, D.G. AL 1st Bn. Hilliard's Legion Vol. Co.D
Till, E. MS Inf. 1st Bn.St.Troops (30 days '64) Co.A
Till, E.R. AL 9th Inf. Co.D Ens.
Till, George W. AR 2nd Mtd.Rifles Co.F
Till, G.W. AR 1st (Monroe's) Cav. Co.F
Till, G.W. MS 6th Inf. Co.A
Till, G.W. TX 29th Cav. Co.I
Till, Henry MS 6th Inf. Co.B
Till, Henry SC 24th Inf. Co.E
Till, Henry F. SC 20th Inf. Co.B
Till, Irvin A. SC 1st (Hagood's) Inf. 1st Co.C Cpl.
Till, Ivy SC 5th Cav. Co.A Sgt.
Till, Ivy SC Cav. 14th Bn. Co.B Cpl.
Till, J.A. SC 2nd Arty. Co.C
Till, James AL 8th Inf. Co.I
Till, James G. MS 6th Inf. Co.B Cpl.
Till, James H. AL Cav. 5th Bn. Hilliard's Legion Co.D
Till, Jeff MS 6th Inf. Co.B
Till, J.H. AL 1st Bn. Hilliard's Legion Vol. Co.D
Till, J.J. SC 20th Inf. Co.B
Till, Joel W. MS 6th Inf. Co.B
Till, John AL 9th Inf. Co.D
Till, John TX 32nd Cav. Co.H
Till, J.W. LA 12th Inf. Co.I
Till, N.W. AL 6th Inf. Co.M
Till, Oliver MS 6th Inf. Co.B
Till, Roland SC 1st (Butler's) Inf. Co.H,K
Till, Samuel W. AL 13th Inf. Co.A
Till, T.M. MS 6th Inf. Co.A
Till, W. SC Lt.Arty. Wagener's Co. (Co.A, German Arty.)
Till, William AR 2nd Mtd.Rifles Co.F
Till, William T. AL 17th Inf. Co.A
Till, W.W. AL 4th (Roddey's) Cav. Co.F
Tillage, Joseph VA 21st Mil. Co.B Sgt.
Tillage, William J. VA 21st Mil. Co.B
Tillar, Drury D. NC 5th Sr.Res. Co.H
Tillar, J. Thomas W. AR 3rd Inf. Co.D 2nd Lt.
Tillar, S.O. VA Lt.Arty. Lowry's Co.
Tillar, Stephen O. VA Lt.Arty. Lowry's Co.
Tillar, Thomas H. VA 53rd Inf. Co.F
Tillary, George W. AL 36th Inf. Co.D
Tillary, Hopkin GA 48th Inf. Co.I
Tillary, John AL 36th Inf. Co.G
Tillary, Thomas AL 36th Inf. Co.G
Tillas, Charles TN 10th Inf. Co.B
Tille, A.T. VA 2nd St.Res. Co.B
Tilled, J.M. TX 12th Cav. Co.I
Tilledge, John C. VA 32nd Inf. Co.C 1st Sgt.
Tilledge, William J. VA 34th Inf. Co.K
Tillen, George VA Inf. 21st Bn. 2nd Co.F
Tillen, Jerry VA 22nd Cav. Co.F
Tillen, Samuel J. VA Inf. 21st Bn. 2nd Co.F
Tiller, Aaron L. AL 4th (Russell's) Cav. Co.C
Tiller, Alen VA Inf. 45th Bn. Co.E
Tiller, Allen S. FL 6th Inf. Co.K Cpl.
Tiller, Anderson VA Inf. 45th Bn. Co.E
Tiller, A.P. TN 12th Cav. Co.F
Tiller, A.P. TN 6th Inf. Co.K Sgt.
Tiller, Benjamin S.L. AL 3rd Bn. Hilliard's Legion Vol. Co.A Cpl.
Tiller, B.S.L. AL 60th Inf. Co.E Sgt.
Tiller, B.W. TX 11th Cav. Co.K
Tiller, Clenny SC Inf. 7th Bn. (Enfield Rifles) Co.A

Tiller, Cornelius 1st Choctaw & Chickasaw Mtd.Rifles 1st Co.K
Tiller, Crayton C. FL 6th Inf. Co.K
Tiller, E.B. FL Conscr.
Tiller, Edmond FL 11th Inf. Co.C,F
Tiller, Evans F. VA 48th Inf. Co.H 1st Sgt.
Tiller, Evans F. VA Inf. French's Bn. Co.D
Tiller, Evans F. Kemper's Staff Capt.,AAG
Tiller, F.C. GA Cobb's Legion Co.D
Tiller, F.T. GA Tiller's Co. (Echols Lt.Arty.)
Tiller, Gainum TN Inf. 22nd Bn. Co.F
Tiller, George W. MS 46th Inf. Co.E 2nd Lt.
Tiller, George W. VA Lt.Arty. Montgomery's Co.
Tiller, Gilmore GA 44th Inf. Co.C
Tiller, G.R. TN 13th Inf. Co.E
Tiller, H.A. SC Inf. 7th Bn. (Enfield Rifles) Co.G,C
Tiller, Harrison VA 45th Inf. Co.H
Tiller, Hartwell F. AL 6th Inf. Co.B Fifer
Tiller, H.D. SC 1st Inf. Co.N
Tiller, H.D. SC Inf. 7th Bn. (Enfield Rifles) Co.A,F 1st Lt.
Tiller, H.F. AL 60th Inf. Co.E Music.
Tiller, H.F. AL 3rd Bn. Hilliard's Legion Vol. Co.A Sgt.
Tiller, Hiram VA 30th Bn.S.S. Co.B
Tiller, Hiram D. VA 30th Bn.S.S. Co.A
Tiller, H.R. GA Tiller's Co. (Echols Lt.Arty.)
Tiller, Ira VA 6th Bn.Res. Co.B
Tiller, James GA 8th Inf. Co.F
Tiller, James GA 64th Inf. Co.A
Tiller, James C. GA 6th Inf. Co.K
Tiller, James M. AL 3rd Bn. Hilliard's Legion Vol. Co.A Cpl.
Tiller, James N. MO 9th (Elliott's) Cav. Co.C 1st Sgt.
Tiller, Jasper M. GA Conscr.
Tiller, Jehu H. VA 15th Inf. Co.C
Tiller, J.H. GA Lt.Arty. 12th Bn. Capt.
Tiller, J.H., Jr. GA Tiller's Co. (Echols Lt.Arty.)
Tiller, J.H. TN 7th Inf. Co.D
Tiller, J.H. TX 11th Cav. Co.K
Tiller, J.H. TX 32nd Cav. Co.E
Tiller, J.J. GA 1st (Fannin's) Res. Co.B
Tiller, J.J. SC Inf. 7th Bn. (Enfield Rifles) Co.F
Tiller, J.L. LA 13th Bn. (Part.Rangers) Co.A
Tiller, J.L. TX Cav. Morgan's Regt. Co.C
Tiller, J.M. GA 4th Res. Co.C
Tiller, J.M. SC Inf. 7th Bn. (Enfield Rifles) Co.A
Tiller, John GA 42nd Inf. Co.I
Tiller, John MS 1st Lt.Arty. Co.B Sgt.
Tiller, John SC Inf. 7th Bn. (Enfield Rifles) Co.A
Tiller, John VA 8th Cav. Co.E Black.
Tiller, John C. GA 6th Inf. Co.K
Tiller, John G. GA 38th Inf. Co.E Cpl.
Tiller, John G. VA 15th Inf. Co.C Cpl.
Tiller, John H. GA Tiller's Co. (Echols Lt.Arty.) Capt.
Tiller, John J. VA Inf. 5th Bn. Co.F Sgt.
Tiller, John P. VA 151st Mil. Co.B
Tiller, J.P. GA Tiller's Co. (Echols Lt.Arty.)
Tiller, J.R. GA Arty. Lumpkin's Co.
Tiller, J.T. GA Tiller's Co. (Echols Lt.Arty.)
Tiller, J.U. GA 4th Res. Co.C
Tiller, J.V. GA 4th Inf. Co.C
Tiller, J.W. GA Tiller's Co. (Echols Lt.Arty.)
Tiller, J.W. TN 38th Inf. Co.C
Tiller, Kenzie VA 151st Mil. Co.F
Tiller, Lemuel S. VA 15th Inf. Co.C
Tiller, L.H. TN 9th Inf. Co.E
Tiller, Marshall GA 6th Inf. Co.K
Tiller, Moses D. VA 36th Inf. 1st Co.B, 2nd Co.D
Tiller, M.T. GA Arty. Lumpkin's Co.
Tiller, N.J. MO Cav. 3rd Bn. Co.F
Tiller, Oscar S. MS 1st Lt.Arty. Co.I
Tiller, P.W.C. SC Lt.Arty. 3rd (Palmetto) Bn. Co.G
Tiller, Richard A. VA 36th Inf. 2nd Co.D
Tiller, R.M. GA Hvy.Arty. 22nd Bn. Co.B
Tiller, Robert E. GA Inf. 27th Bn. Co.D
Tiller, Robert E. VA 15th Inf. Co.C
Tiller, Sanford GA 34th Inf. Co.E
Tiller, Sanford GA 39th Inf. Co.A
Tiller, Seborn FL 6th Inf. Co.K Cpl.
Tiller, S.H. 10th Conf.Cav. Co.A
Tiller, Shimer GA Tiller's Co. (Echols Lt.Arty.)
Tiller, Stephen H. AL Cav. 5th Bn. Hilliard's Legion Co.A
Tiller, T.H. MS 2nd Part.Rangers Co.L,D
Tiller, T.H. TN 13th Inf. Co.E
Tiller, Thomas GA 38th Inf. Co.E
Tiller, Thomas E.H. AL 3rd Bn. Hilliard's Legion Vol. Co.A
Tiller, Thomas J. VA 30th Bn.S.S. Co.B Sgt.
Tiller, Thomas M. VA 15th Inf. Co.A
Tiller, Tim 3rd Conf.Eng.Troops Co.C
Tiller, Timothy TN 43rd Inf. Co.C
Tiller, T.P. GA 4th Res. Co.C Sgt.
Tiller, Wesley Jefferson LA 15th Inf. Co.I Cpl.
Tiller, William AL Eufaula Lt.Arty.
Tiller, William AL 33rd Inf. Co.B
Tiller, William GA 1st (Fannin's) Res. Co.B
Tiller, William LA Mil. 3rd Regt. 1st Brig. 1st Div. Co.I
Tiller, William A. VA 30th Bn.S.S. Co.B Black.
Tiller, William D. VA 60th Inf. 2nd Co.H
Tiller, William D. VA 151st Mil. Co.B
Tiller, William H. AL 6th Inf. Co.B
Tiller, William J. FL 11th Inf. Co.C
Tiller, William J. LA Inf. 1st Sp.Bn. (Wheat's) Old Co.D
Tiller, William T. AR Lt.Arty. Hart's Btty. Ord.Sgt.
Tiller, W.J. LA Inf. 7th Bn. Co.B
Tiller, W.M. GA Tiller's Co. (Echols Lt.Arty.)
Tiller, Wootson GA Tiller's Co. (Echols Lt.Arty.)
Tiller, W.T. TX Lt.Arty. Jones' Co. 2nd Lt.
Tillerry, D.W. MS 4th Cav. Co.I
Tillerry, J.S. AR 10th Inf. Co.C
Tillers, J.M. GA 11th Cav. Co.A
Tillerson, Spencer GA 35th Inf. Co.H
Tillerson, William J. GA 29th Inf. Co.G,D
Tillery, Abraham W. LA 27th Inf. Co.H
Tillery, Andrew J. AL 3rd Cav. Co.G
Tillery, Charles 7th Conf.Cav. Co.F
Tillery, Charles 8th (Dearing's) Conf.Cav. Co.G
Tillery, Coffield 3rd Conf.Cav. Co.H
Tillery, Daniel S. AL 36th Inf. Co.D
Tillery, Elephlet NC 2nd Arty. (36th St.Troops) Co.F
Tillery, Emerson MO Searcy's Bn.S.S. Co.B
Tillery, Epinetas NC 2nd Arty. (36th St.Troops) Co.F
Tillery, Eppey Bynum TN 40th Inf. Co.A
Tillery, Eppy P. NC 5th Inf. Co.I
Tillery, G.L. AL 23rd Inf. Co.I
Tillery, G.T. TN 2nd (Ashby's) Cav. Co.F
Tillery, H.C. AL 60th Inf. Co.I
Tillery, H.C. AL 1st Bn. Hilliard's Legion Vol. Co.D
Tillery, Henry Lee NC 12th Inf. Co.G Cpl.
Tillery, H.T. AR 1st (Monroe's) Cav. Co.H
Tillery, Hugh AR 3rd Inf. Co.F
Tillery, Hugh TN 26th Inf. Co.A
Tillery, Hugh 3rd Conf.Cav. Co.H
Tillery, Hugh T. AR Inf. 2nd Bn. Co.A
Tillery, H.Z. AL 53rd (Part.Rangers) Co.G
Tillery, Isaac NC 64th Inf. Co.D
Tillery, J. AL 34th Inf. Co.F
Tillery, J. GA 63rd Inf. Co.G Cpl.
Tillery, James GA Inf. 19th Bn. (St.Guards) Co.E
Tillery, James M. MS 7th Inf. Co.K
Tillery, James W. AL 1st Bn. Hilliard's Legion Vol. Co.D 2nd Lt.
Tillery, J.B. AL 3rd Inf. Co.L
Tillery, J.B. Inf. Bailey's Cons.Regt. Co.A
Tillery, J.B. TX 7th Inf. Co.H
Tillery, J.C. GA Siege Arty. 28th Bn. Co.B
Tillery, J.C. TX 21st Cav. Co.E
Tillery, J.H. AL 23rd Inf. Co.B
Tillery, J.L. MS 7th Inf. Co.K
Tillery, John AL 5th Bn.Vol. Co.C
Tillery, John SC 20th Inf. Co.I
Tillery, John TN 1st (Carter's) Cav. 2nd Lt.
Tillery, John TN 8th (Smith's) Cav. Co.L 1st Lt.
Tillery, John P. AL 15th Inf. Co.A Cpl.
Tillery, John R. NC 3rd Cav. (41st St.Troops) Co.G
Tillery, J.R. 3rd Conf.Cav. Co.H
Tillery, J.S. AL 60th Inf. Co.I
Tillery, L.B. AR 1st (Monroe's) Cav. Co.H 1st Lt.
Tillery, Llewellyn MO 3rd Inf. Co.D Sgt.
Tillery, L.M. AL 3rd Inf. Co.L Sgt.
Tillery, M. GA 10th Mil.
Tillery, Milton J. TX 2nd Cav. 1st Co.F
Tillery, Milton J. TX Cav. Morgan's Regt.
Tillery, M.N. AL 60th Inf. Co.I
Tillery, M.N. AL 1st Bn. Hilliard's Legion Vol. Co.D
Tillery, M.W. 7th Conf.Cav. Co.F
Tillery, M.W. 8th (Dearing's) Conf.Cav. Co.G
Tillery, N.H. AL 3rd Cav.
Tillery, Presley GA Inf. 3rd Bn. Co.H
Tillery, R. MS Wilkinson Cty.Minute Men Co.B
Tillery, R.C. TN 2nd (Ashby's) Cav. Co.H
Tillery, R.C. TN 26th Inf. Co.F
Tillery, Richard AR 33rd Inf. Co.A
Tillery, Richard C. NC 3rd Arty. (40th St.Troops) Co.F Capt.
Tillery, Richard C. TN Cav. 4th Bn. (Branner's) Co.A
Tillery, R.J. GA Inf. City Bn. (Columbus) Co.A
Tillery, R.M. TN Lt.Arty. Barry's Co.
Tillery, R.S. 20th Conf.Cav. Co.D
Tillery, Sam TN 26th Inf. Co.F
Tillery, Samuel GA 41st Inf. Co.F

Tillery, Samuel NC 2nd Arty. (36th St.Troops) Co.F
Tillery, Samuel TN 5th (McKenzie's) Cav. Co.I
Tillery, Samuel TX 8th Cav. Co.B
Tillery, Samuel TX 15th Cav. Co.G
Tillery, Samuel L. NC 5th Inf. Co.I
Tillery, Thomas AL 60th Inf. Co.F
Tillery, T.J. AR 11th Inf. Co.I
Tillery, T.J. AR 11th & 17th Cons.Inf. Co.C,D
Tillery, V. AL 21st Inf. Co.G
Tillery, V.H. AL 3rd Inf. Co.L Cpl.
Tillery, Virgil A. AL 1st Regt.Conscr. Co.I
Tillery, William AL 25th Inf. Co.G
Tillery, William AL 34th Inf. Co.G
Tillery, William AR 3rd Cav. Co.F
Tillery, William GA Inf. 1st City Bn. (Columbus) Co.C
Tillery, William MS 17th Inf. Co.K
Tillery, William TN 40th Inf. Co.A
Tillery, William TX 36th Cav. Co.D
Tillery, William H. GA 3rd Inf. Co.F
Tillery, William J. MS 21st Inf. Co.E
Tillery, William J. TX 17th Cav. Co.E
Tillery, W.J. AL 15th Inf. Co.F
Tillery, W.L. TN 1st (Carter's) Cav. Co.E
Tilleson, William J. GA 39th Inf. Co.G,D
Tillet, George W. VA 15th Cav. Co.H
Tillet, Henry T. VA 15th Cav. Co.H
Tillet, James VA Cav. Mosby's Regt. (Part. Rangers)
Tillet, James F. VA 17th Inf. Co.F
Tillet, John R. VA 15th Cav. Co.H
Tillett, Edward NC 8th Inf. Co.B
Tillett, Edward VA 8th Inf. Hampton's Co.E
Tillett, George J. FL 3rd Inf. Co.C
Tillett, Isaac TN 29th Inf. Co.I
Tillett, Isaac N. NC 4th Cav. (59th St.Troops) Co.G 2nd Lt.
Tillett, James MO 1st N.E. Cav. Co.D
Tillett, James W. NC 5th Cav. (63rd St.Troops) Co.E,G 1st Sgt.
Tillett, James W. NC 23rd Inf. Co.D.
Tillett, James W. TN 1st Cav. Co.K
Tillett, Jessee KY 5th Cav. Co.B
Tillett, John MO 1st N.E. Cav. Co.D
Tillett, John R. VA Cav. Mosby's Regt. (Part.Rangers) Co.H
Tillett, John W. FL 3rd Inf. Co.C
Tillett, Jonathan NC 68th Inf. Co.B
Tillett, Reubin MO 1st N.E. Cav. Co.D
Tillett, Samuel R. VA 8th Inf. Co.H
Tillett, Thomas TN 32nd Inf. Co.D
Tillett, Tine KY 11th Cav. Co.B
Tillettson, D.W. Exch.Bn. 1st Co.A,CSA
Tilley, Aaron B. NC Inf. 2nd Bn. Co.A
Tilley, A.B. NC 54th Inf. Co.E
Tilley, A.B. VA 42nd Inf. Co.H
Tilley, Abner J. NC 56th Inf. Co.D Sgt.
Tilley, Abner W. TX 2nd Cav. Co.G Cpl.
Tilley, Adams C. LA 28th (Gray's) Inf. Co.H
Tilley, Alex F. Gen. & Staff Capt.,Conscr.Off.
Tilley, Allen NC 6th Inf. Co.B
Tilley, Amos J. NC 22nd Inf. Co.H,K
Tilley, Andrew AR 21st Inf. Co.C
Tilley, Asberry LA 28th (Gray's) Inf. Co.H
Tilley, Benjamin M. GA 52nd Inf. Co.H
Tilley, Brittain S. TX 17th Cav. Co.D Lt.
Tilley, Burley J. NC 22nd Inf. Co.H
Tilley, C.J. LA 3rd (Wingfield's) Cav. Co.C
Tilley, David NC 6th Cav. (65th St.Troops) Co.A,F Sgt.
Tilley, David NC 21st Inf. Co.F
Tilley, DeWitt C. NC 6th Inf. Co.B
Tilley, Edmund NC 22nd Inf. Co.H
Tilley, Elijah TX Cav. McCord's Frontier Regt. Co.B
Tilley, Elisha H. NC 6th Inf. Co.B
Tilley, E.N. LA 9th Inf. Co.I
Tilley, F.J. TN 14th Inf. Co.K
Tilley, Fletcher NC 18th Inf. Co.B Drum.
Tilley, Frank NC 21st Inf. Co.F
Tilley, F.T. NC 4th Bn.Jr.Res. Co.A 2nd Lt.
Tilley, Gaberal M. NC 22nd Inf. Co.H
Tilley, G.D. SC 5th Cav. Co.A
Tilley, George NC 3rd Arty. (40th St.Troops) Co.G
Tilley, George NC Lt.Arty. 13th Bn. Co.E
Tilley, Haywood NC 6th Inf. Co.B Sgt.
Tilley, Henry NC 2nd Cav. (19th St.Troops) Co.K
Tilley, H.H. TN Cav. 1st Bn. (McNairy's) Co.C
Tilley, Hosea H. NC 23rd Inf. Co.A
Tilley, J. NC 4th Bn.Jr.Res. Co.C
Tilley, Jacob G. NC 2nd Cav. (19th St.Troops) Co.K
Tilley, James MO 8th Inf. Co.I
Tilley, James NC 2nd Inf. Co.I
Tilley, James NC 7th Inf. Co.G
Tilley, James NC Walker's Bn. Thomas' Legion Co.A
Tilley, James TN Cav. Nixon's Regt. Co.F
Tilley, James D. NC 6th Inf. Co.B
Tilley, James E. NC 22nd Inf. Co.K
Tilley, James L. NC 28th Inf. Co.A
Tilley, James M. NC 22nd Inf. Co.H
Tilley, James M. NC 37th Inf. Co.K
Tilley, James M. TX 34th Cav. Co.A
Tilley, James W. NC Lt.Arty. 13th Bn. Co.C
Tilley, Jeremiah GA Inf. (St.Guards) Hansell's Co.
Tilley, Jerry TN Cav. Welcker's Bn. Kincaid's Co.
Tilley, J.J. NC 53rd Inf. Co.E
Tilley, J.M. LA 28th (Gray's) Inf. Co.H
Tilley, Joel F. VA 29th Inf. Co.E
Tilley, John MD Arty. 3rd Btty.
Tilley, John MS 20th Inf. Co.D
Tilley, John MO 3rd Cav. Co.B,E
Tilley, John NC 2nd Cav. (19th St.Troops) Co.K
Tilley, John NC 11th (Bethel Regt.) Inf. Co.G
Tilley, John TN 1st (Carter's) Cav. Lt.
Tilley, John B. LA 5th Inf. Co.H
Tilley, John B. NC 3rd Inf. Co.I
Tilley, John C. NC 37th Inf. Co.K
Tilley, Jno. F. NC 22nd Inf. Co.H
Tilley, John F. VA 24th Cav. Co.H Cpl.
Tilley, John G. KY 1st (Butler's) Cav. Co.D
Tilley, John H. AR 15th (N.W.) Inf. Co.H
Tilley, John H. NC 22nd Inf. Co.H
Tilley, John H. NC 22nd Inf. Co.H,K
Tilley, John H. NC 53rd Inf. Co.H
Tilley, John H. VA 42nd Inf. Co.H
Tilley, John M. GA Arty. 9th Bn. Co.C
Tilley, John M. GA 15th Inf. Co.D 1st Lt.
Tilley, John N. GA 20th Inf. Co.I
Tilley, John P. NC Vol. Lawrence's Co.
Tilley, John R. NC 30th Inf. Co.D
Tilley, John W. AL 51st (Part.Rangers) Co.A
Tilley, John W. AL 2nd Inf. Co.A
Tilley, Joseph NC 37th Inf. Co.K
Tilley, Joseph S. AR Inf. Ballard's Co.
Tilley, Joseph S. MO 6th Inf. Co.K
Tilley, J.T. GA Cav. 20th Bn. Co.E
Tilley, J.W. MO Cav. Coffee's Regt. Co.C
Tilley, J.W.F., Jr. GA 10th Cav.
Tilley, J.W.F. GA 10th Cav. (St.Guards) Co.A Cpl.
Tilley, J.W.F., Jr. GA Cav. 20th Bn. Co.E
Tilley, J.W.F., Sr. GA Cav. 20th Bn. Co.E
Tilley, L. GA 49th Inf. Co.D
Tilley, L.D. NC 22nd Inf. Co.A
Tilley, Lewis MO 15th Cav. Co.H
Tilley, Lewis L. GA 61st Inf. Co.F
Tilley, L.M. SC 1st Cav. Co.K
Tilley, Louis AR Lt.Arty. Marshall's Btty.
Tilley, Louis AR 38th Inf. Co.H
Tilley, L.T. GA 48th Inf.
Tilley, Monroe GA Inf. 27th Bn. (NonConscr.) Co.C
Tilley, Osborn P. GA Inf. 8th Bn. Co.E
Tilley, Peter L. NC 2nd Inf. Co.A Fifer
Tilley, Peter M. NC 22nd Inf. Co.H
Tilley, P.J. NC 53rd Inf. Co.G
Tilley, R.A. GA Floyd Legion (St.Guards) Co.B
Tilley, Richard AR 17th (Lemoyne's) Inf. Co.C
Tilley, Richard AR 21st Inf. Co.C
Tilley, Robert C. NC 31st Inf. Co.E
Tilley, Robert J. NC 2nd Cav. (19th St.Troops) Co.K 1st Sgt.
Tilley, Samuel F. LA Mil. British Guard Bn. Kurczyn's Co.
Tilley, Solomon D. NC 14th Inf. Co.K
Tilley, Stephen D. NC 3rd Inf. Co.I
Tilley, Thomas G. TN 26th Inf. Co.D
Tilley, Thomas J. NC 53rd Inf. Co.E
Tilley, T.J. NC 22nd Inf. Co.K,H
Tilley, Valentine GA 48th Inf. Co.D
Tilley, W.B. AR 15th (Josey's) Inf. Co.G
Tilley, W.B. AR 36th Inf. Co.D
Tilley, W.C. KY 8th Mtd.Inf. Co.C
Tilley, W.H. NC 22nd Inf. Co.A
Tilley, Wiley P. NC 2nd Cav. (19th St.Troops) Co.K
Tilley, William AR 38th Inf. Co.H
Tilley, William MO 8th Inf. Co.I
Tilley, William NC 53rd Inf. Co.H
Tilley, William SC Mil. 14th Regt. Co.A,D,I
Tilley, William SC 16th Inf. Co.H
Tilley, William TN 5th (McKenzie's) Cav. Co.B
Tilley, William B. NC 31st Inf. Co.E
Tilley, William C. VA 25th Cav. Co.C
Tilley, William H. NC 6th Inf. Co.B
Tilley, William J. 7th Conf.Cav. Co.A
Tilley, William L. TX 2nd Cav. Co.C
Tilley, William M. LA 28th (Gray's) Inf. Co.H Jr.2nd Lt.
Tilley, William M. NC 22nd Inf. Co.H
Tilley, William M. NC 53rd Inf. Co.G Cpl.
Tilley, W.J. GA 10th Cav. Co.A
Tilling, James Jackson's Co.,CSA
Tillinghast, Edwin L. SC 3rd Cav. Co.C

Tillinghast, E.L. SC 2nd Inf. Co.I
Tillinghast, E.L. Gen. & Staff Asst.Surg.
Tillinghast, Elias H. AL 22nd Inf. Co.H
Tillinghast, Elias H. AL Inf. 36th Regt. Co.B
Tillinghast, E.W. AL Inf. 36th Regt. Co.B
Tillinghast, George W. FL 2nd Inf. Co.F
Tillinghast, Harrison FL 2nd Inf. Co.F Capt.
Tillinghast, Henry A. FL 1st Inf. Old Co.A
Tillinghast, John H. NC 44th Inf. Chap.
Tillinghast, John H. Gen. & Staff Chap.
Tillinghast, Joseph W. AL Lt.Arty. 2nd Bn. Co.E
Tillinghast, J.W. AL 36th Inf. Ens.
Tillinghast, Robert G. SC 3rd Cav. Co.C
Tillinghast, Thomas S. SC 3rd Cav. Co.C
Tillingworth, J.G. GA 51st Inf. Co.I Sgt.
Tillis, A.J. AR 50th Inf. Co.I
Tilles, Dempsey FL 2nd Inf. Co.F
Tillis, H.B. MS 2nd (Quinn's St.Troops) Inf. Co.A
Tillis, James FL 8th Inf. Co.C
Tillis, James L. GA 20th Inf. Co.H
Tillis, J.D. FL 1st (Res.) Inf. Co.B
Tillis, J.D. FL 9th Inf. Co.F
Tillis, Jim 1st Choctaw Mtd.Rifles Co.F
Tillis, John AL 18th Inf. Co.A
Tillis, Joseph FL 7th Inf. Co.I
Tillis, Joseph D. FL 5th Inf. Co.F
Tillis, Richard FL 2nd Cav. Co.I
Tillis, Richard FL 11th Inf. Co.E
Tillis, T. FL 2nd Cav. Co.H
Tillis, Tapley FL 7th Inf. Co.C
Tillis, T.B. FL 2nd Cav. Co.H
Tillis, Temple AL 27th Inf. Co.K
Tillis, T.W. MS Inf. 2nd St.Troops Co.L 1st Cpl.
Tillis, W. FL 2nd Cav. Co.H
Tillis, Wayne FL 9th Inf. Co.I
Tillis, Willoughby FL 4th Inf. Co.E
Tillis, Willoughby FL 8th Inf. Co.C
Tillison, Charles MO Cav. Poindexter's Regt.
Tillison, George W. MO 10th Cav. Co.C
Tillison, Henry NC 3rd Bn.Sr.Res. Co.C
Tillison, James B. VA 6th Bn.Res. Co.C
Tillison, James P. VA 6th Bn.Res. Co.C
Tillison, Lorenzo D. MO Cav. Poindexter's Regt.
Tillison, Martin Van Buren MO 10th Inf. Co.I
Tillison, S.W. MO 10th Cav. Co.C
Tillison, Thomas MO 10th Cav. Co.C
Tillison, W.P. MO Inf. Clark's Regt. Co.C
Tillit, Isaac NC 1st Inf. (6 mo. '61) Co.M
Tillitson, William L. MO 9th Inf. Co.I
Tillitt, George TN 29th Inf. Co.I
Tillman 1st Choctaw Mtd.Rifles Co.H
Tillman, A. MS Yerger's Co. (St.Troops)
Tillman, Aaron E. NC 5th Cav. (63rd St.Troops) Co.E
Tillman, A.E. NC 3rd Cav. (41st St.Troops) Co.E
Tillman, A.J. MS 3rd (St.Troops) Cav. Co.E
Tillman, A.J. MS 1st (King's) Inf. (St.Troops) Co.B 2nd Lt.
Tillman, Alfred AL 45th Inf. Co.A
Tillman, Alfred R. MS 18th Inf. Co.H
Tillman, A.S. VA 3rd Cav. Co.D
Tillman, Bassett S. GA 7th Inf. Co.F
Tillman, Benjamin J. GA 50th Inf. Co.H
Tillman, Bennett TN 21st (Wilson's) Cav. Co.D
Tillman, Bennette TN 21st & 22nd (Cons.) Cav. Co.H
Tillman, B.M. TN 51st (Cons.) Inf. Co.C Sgt.
Tillman, B.S. TN 1st Hvy.Arty. 2nd Co.A, 1st Co.C
Tillman, Calvin MS 7th Cav. 1st Co.H
Tillman, Calvin TN 18th (Newsom's) Cav. Co.B,G
Tillman, Daniel AR 8th Inf. New Co.K 1st Lt.
Tillman, Daniel M. AR 26th Inf. Co.B 1st Sgt.
Tillman, Daniel M. FL 7th Inf. Co.D
Tillman, David AR 7th Cav. Co.D
Tillman, David C. NC 14th Inf. Co.C
Tillman, David S. MS 18th Inf. Co.H
Tillman, D.N. Gen. & Staff, Comsy.Dept. Comsy.Sgt.
Tillman, D.R. TN 13th Inf. Co.I
Tillman, D.T. NC 35th Inf. Co.E
Tillman, Elbert GA 50th Inf. Co.H
Tillman, Eli MS 14th Inf. Co.H
Tillman, Eli MS 14th (Cons.) Inf. Co.E
Tillman, Elijah GA 11th Cav. (St.Guards) Tillman's Co. Capt.
Tillman, Elijah GA 50th Inf. Co.H 2nd Lt.
Tillman, E. Tillman GA 2nd Res. Co.B
Tillman, F.C. GA 46th Inf. Co.C Capt.
Tillman, F.M. MS 1st Lt.Arty. Co.F
Tillman, Frances M. GA 47th Inf. Co.E
Tillman, Francis M. MS 10th Inf. Old Co.H
Tillman, Frank TX Cav. Waller's Regt. Dunn's Co.
Tillman, Frank TX 13th Vol. 2nd Co.A, Co.E
Tillman, G.D. SC 2nd Arty. Co.E
Tillman, George GA 62nd Cav. Co.B
Tillman, George NC 35th Inf. Co.E
Tillman, George D. SC 5th Res. Co.E Bvt.Lt.
Tillman, George D. VA 44th Inf. Co.K
Tillman, Geo. L. AR 2nd Cav. Capt.,Recruiting Off.
Tillman, George W. GA 47th Inf. Co.E
Tillman, George W. MS 6th Inf. Co.F
Tillman, George W. NC 44th Inf. Co.E
Tillman, G.L. AR 9th Inf. New Co.B Capt.
Tillman, G.W. AL 40th Inf. Co.E
Tillman, G.W. GA 8th Cav. Co.B
Tillman, H. GA 4th (Clinch's) Cav. Co.K
Tillman, Hampton S. GA 1st (Olmstead's) Inf. Co.D
Tillman, Harrison GA 50th Inf. Co.H
Tillman, H.C. MS 39th Inf. Co.E
Tillman, H.D. MS 6th Inf. Co.F
Tillman, Henry GA 61st Inf. Co.L Lt.Col.
Tillman, Henry C. MS 1st (Percy's) Inf. Co.A
Tillman, Hezekiah D. GA 10th Cav. (St.Guards) Co.G Sgt.
Tillman, H.P. MS 2nd Cav. Co.K Cpl.
Tillman, H.P. MS 22nd Inf.
Tillman, I.M. MS Cav. Powers' Regt. Co.A
Tillman, Isaac W. SC 9th Inf. Co.A
Tillman, I.Y. MS 22nd Inf. Co.A Sgt.
Tillman, J.A. MS Cav. 1st Bn. (McNair's) St.Troops Co.D
Tillman, J.A. MS Cav. Powers' Regt. Co.A
Tillman, J.A. MS 39th Inf. Co.E
Tillman, J.A. TN 14th (Neely's) Cav. Co.A
Tillman, J.A. TN 1st Hvy.Arty. Co.B
Tillman, J.A. TN 9th Inf. Co.F
Tillman, J.A. TN 12th (Cons.) Inf. Co.D
Tillman, J.A. 15th Conf.Cav. Asst.Surg.
Tillman, James AR 7th Cav. Co.D
Tillman, James AR 62nd Mil. Co.F 2nd Lt.
Tillman, James FL Cav. 5th Bn. Co.A
Tillman, James GA 4th (Clinch's) Cav. Co.K
Tillman, James MS 30th Inf. Co.I
Tillman, James VA 1st Inf. Co.C
Tillman, James A. SC 24th Inf. Co.I 1st Lt.
Tillman, Jas. Augustus Gen. & Staff Asst.Surg.
Tillman, James D. NC 14th Inf. Co.C
Tillman, James D. TN Inf. 3rd Cons.Regt. Col.
Tillman, James D. TN 41st Inf. Co.F Col.
Tillman, James L. AL 6th Cav. Co.A
Tillman, James M. GA 2nd Inf. Co.B
Tillman, James M. TX 1st Inf. Co.H
Tillman, James R. MS 6th Inf. Co.F
Tillman, James S. TN 19th (Biffle's) Cav. Co.H
Tillman, James T. AL 24th Inf. Co.K,F
Tillman, James W. GA 11th Inf. Co.H
Tillman, James W. GA Inf. 27th Bn. Co.C
Tillman, James W. MS 39th Inf. Co.C
Tillman, Jarratt NC 26th Inf. Co.G
Tillman, J.B. FL Cav. 5th Bn. Co.H Sgt.
Tillman, J.C. GA 54th Inf. Co.B
Tillman, J.C. KY 12th Cav. Co.F
Tillman, J.C. TN 5th Inf. 2nd Co.F 1st Lt.
Tillman, J.E. MS Conscr.
Tillman, J.E. TX 10th Inf. Co.A
Tillman, Jeremiah FL 2nd Cav. Co.I Cpl.
Tillman, Jeremiah NC 5th Inf. Co.A
Tillman, Jesse FL 2nd Cav. Co.F
Tillman, J.F. MS 6th Inf. Co.F
Tillman, J.H. AL 4th Cav. Co.I
Tillman, J.H. TN 15th (Cons.) Cav. Co.G Cpl.
Tillman, J.I. 4th Conf.Inf. Co.K
Tillman, J.K.F AL 21st Inf. Co.I Sgt.
Tillman, J.M. GA Inf. (Loc.Def.) Whiteside's Nav.Bn. Co.C Sgt.
Tillman, J.M. MS 39th Inf. Co.E
Tillman, J.M. TX 1st Inf.
Tillman, John AL 45th Inf. Co.A
Tillman, John AR 7th Cav. Co.D
Tillman, John AR 62nd Mil. Co.C 1st Lt.
Tillman, John GA 4th (Clinch's) Cav.
Tillman, John GA Cav. 29th Bn. Co.C Sgt.
Tillman, John GA 26th Inf. Co.C
Tillman, John 8th (Wade's) Conf.Cav. Co.E
Tillman, John A. GA 50th Inf. Co.H Sgt.
Tillman, John B. AL 39th Inf. Co.E
Tillman, John E. FL Lt.Arty. Perry's Co.
Tillman, John E.C. GA 61st Inf. Co.D,K 2nd Lt.
Tillman, John H. GA 37th Inf. Co.C
Tillman, John O.L. VA 25th Inf. 2nd Co.B Sgt.
Tillman, John R. NC 2nd Arty. (36th St.Troops) Co.I
Tillman, John R. 4th Conf.Inf. Co.K
Tillman, John S. GA Inf. 1st City Bn. (Columbus) Co.F
Tillman, John S. GA 31st Inf. Co.K
Tillman, John Y. MS 1st Bn.S.S. Co.D Sgt.
Tillman, John Y. MS 25th Inf. Co.H
Tillman, Jordan J. GA 50th Inf. Co.H 2nd Lt.
Tillman, Joseph AR 1st Mtd.Rifles Co.H
Tillman, Joseph FL 5th Inf. Co.D

Tillman, Joseph GA 4th (Clinch's) Cav.
Tillman, Joseph GA 29th Inf. Co.A 1st Sgt.
Tillman, Joseph TN 44th (Cons.) Inf. Co.D
Tillman, Joseph A. NC 3rd Cav. (41st St.Troops) Co.E
Tillman, Joseph A. SC 16th & 24th (Cons.) Inf. Co.G Capt.
Tillman, Josiah GA 26th Inf. Co.H 2nd Lt.
Tillman, J.P. TN 13th Inf. Co.F 2nd Lt.
Tillman, J.R. MS 6th Inf. Co.F
Tillman, J.W. GA 32nd Inf. Co.I
Tillman, J.W. KY 12th Cav. Co.F
Tillman, J.W. MS 28th Cav. Co.G
Tillman, J.W. SC Cav. 10th Bn. Co.D
Tillman, J.W. SC 4th Cav. Co.H
Tillman, L. AL 46th Inf.
Tillman, Leonidas H. MS 1st (Percy's) Inf. Co.A 1st Lt.
Tillman, Leven MO Inf. Clark's Regt. Co.B
Tillman, L.H. MS 39th Inf. Co.E Capt.
Tillman, L.P. MS 39th Inf. Co.E
Tillman, M. AR 8th Inf. Co.C
Tillman, M. MS 3rd (St.Troops) Cav. Co.E
Tillman, Malichi J. MO 1st Inf. Co.G
Tillman, Mitchell GA 50th Inf. Co.H
Tillman, M.M. FL 2nd Cav. Co.C
Tillman, M.T. TN 17th Inf. Co.H Cpl.
Tillman, Nathan P. MS Cav. 24th Bn. Co.C
Tillman, O. TX 8th Cav. Co.B
Tillman, Polk MS 1st (Percy's) Inf. Co.A
Tillman, R.D. MS Yerger's Co. (St.Troops) 1st Sgt.
Tillman, R.D. MS St.Cav. 3rd Bn. (Cooper's) Little's Co.
Tillman, R.D. MS 1st (King's) Inf. (St.Troops) Co.B
Tillman, R.I. MS Yerger's Co. (St.Troops) 1st Lt.
Tillman, Richard AL 1st Regt. Mobile Vol. Co.E
Tillman, Richard AL 4th Res. Co.C
Tillman, Robert D. MS 1st (Percy's) Inf. Co.A
Tillman, Robert D. MS 3rd Inf. Co.K
Tillman, Rufus MS 37th Inf. Co.D
Tillman, Sam H.J. MO 3rd Cav. Co.G
Tillman, Samuel LA Res.Corps Williams' Co.
Tillman, Samuel C. VA Lt.Arty. Ancell's Co.
Tillman, Samuel C. VA Lt.Arty. Snead's Co.
Tillman, S.D. LA Mil. Caldwell Regt. 11th Brig. Col.
Tillman, S.J. MS 7th Inf. Co.I
Tillman, S.P. AL 15th Inf. Co.F
Tillman, S.S. AR 2nd Inf. Old Co.E
Tillman, S.S. TX 10th Cav. Co.D
Tillman, Stephen VA 12th Inf. Co.H
Tillman, Stephen A. VA 21st Inf. Co.G 2nd Lt.
Tillman, T.B. MS 16th Inf. Co.C
Tillman, Thomas GA 50th Inf. Co.H
Tillman, Thomas MS 1st Inf. Co.E Cpl.
Tillman, Thomas A. VA Lt.Arty. Brander's Co.
Tillman, Thomas B. MS 6th Inf. Co.F Sgt.
Tillman, Thos. R. TN 52nd Inf. Co.C 2nd Lt.
Tillman, Thomas W. VA Cav. 39th Bn. Co.D
Tillman, Timothy T. TN 41st Inf. Co.H
Tillman, T.R. TN 14th (Neely's) Cav. Co.A
Tillman, T.R. TN 9th Inf. Co.F
Tillman, T.R. TN Inf. 154th Sr.Regt. Co.I
Tillman, W.C. GA 13th Inf. Co.G
Tillman, W.D. FL 2nd Cav. Co.F,C
Tillman, W.F. TN 1st Hvy.Arty. 2nd Co.A, 1st Co.C
Tillman, W.G. AR 8th Inf. New Co.K 3rd Lt.
Tillman, William AR 15th (N.W.) Inf. Co.D
Tillman, William GA 19th Inf. Co.K
Tillman, William LA Mil. 4th Regt.Eur.Brig. Co.B
Tillman, William TN 16th (Logwood's) Cav. Co.I
Tillman, William H. LA 12th Inf. Co.L
Tillman, William H.H. AL Lt.Arty. Clanton's Btty.
Tillman, William J. GA 10th Mil.
Tillman, William M. VA Goochland Lt.Arty.
Tillman, William R.F. TN 41st Inf. Co.H
Tillman, William T. NC 44th Inf. Co.E Cpl.
Tillman, Willis AL 21st Inf. Co.I Drum.
Tillman, W.J. GA Cav. 15th Bn. (St.Guards) Allen's Co.
Tillman, W.J. MS 39th Inf. Co.E 2nd Lt.
Tillman, W.L. KY 1st (Helm's) Cav. New Co.G
Tillman, W.R. MS 3rd Inf. (St.Troops) Co.K Cpl.
Tillman, W.W. TX 11th Cav. Co.F
Tillmam, James C. AL 21st Inf. Co.I Sgt.
Tillmon, J.A. MS 7th Cav. 2nd Co.G
Tillmon, J.R. TN 9th Inf. Co.F
Tillmon, T.R. MS 7th Cav. 2nd Co.G
Tillmon, T.T. TN 35th Inf. 2nd Co.I
Tillory, Alm F. AR 9th Inf. New Co.I 3rd Lt.
Tillory, John P. 7th Conf.Cav. 1st Co.I, Co.H
Tillory, Seraney GA 41st Inf. Co.E
Tillory, Virgil AL Conscr. Echols' Co.
Tillory, William T. TN 5th Cav. Co.C
Tilloson, Aaron GA Cherokee Legion (St.Guards) Co.B
Tillot, Charles LA 20th Inf. Co.F
Tillot, John LA 20th Inf. Co.I
Tillotson, Benjamin C. SC Inf. Holcombe Legion Co.I 2nd Lt.
Tillotson, Calvin AR 10th Inf. Co.I
Tillotson, Daniel W. MS 33rd Inf. Co.K
Tillotson, D.H.O. NC 21st Inf. Co.G
Tillotson, Farbury L. SC 13th Inf. Co.B
Tillotson, George MS 28th Cav. Co.E
Tillotson, James W. GA 38th Inf. Co.B
Tillotson, Jeff SC Inf. Holcombe Legion Co.C
Tillotson, J.M. AR 13th Inf.
Tillotson, John J. GA 38th Inf. Co.B Cpl.
Tillotson, John N. MS 41st Inf. Co.G
Tillotson, J.W. SC 1st Cav. Co.B
Tillotson, J.W. SC 5th Inf. 1st Co.F, 2nd Co.I Cpl.
Tillotson, Lycurgus F. AL 2nd Cav. Co.B
Tillotson, M. NC 23rd Inf. Co.I
Tillotson, R. NC 23rd Inf. Co.I
Tillotson, Richard SC Inf. Holcombe Legion Co.C
Tillotson, R.S. MS Inf. 1st Bn.St.Troops (30 days '64) Co.F Recruit
Tillotson, Thomas NC 21st Inf. Co.G
Tillotson, William I. MO Cav. Williams' Regt. Co.I
Tillotson, W.R. NC 23rd Inf. Co.I
Tillottson, E. AR Cav. Gordon's Regt. Co.D
Tills, Joseph S. VA 23rd Inf. Co.H
Tillson, George B. VA 12th Inf. 1st Co.I
Tillson, H.H. VA 2nd Inf.Loc.Def. Co.G
Tillson, H.H. VA Inf. 2nd Bn.Loc.Def. Co.A
Tillson, Jacob GA 65th Inf. Co.B
Tillson, J.H. TN 20th Inf. Co.A
Tillson, W.H.H. TX 32nd Cav. Co.H
Tillson, William GA 65th Inf. Co.B Cpl.
Tillson, Zed TN 16th Cav. Co.C
Tillsworth, D.R. VA Mil. Scott Cty.
Tillsworth, J.P. TN Arty. Marshall's Co. 1st Lt.
Tilly, --- NC 7th Sr.Res. Watts' Co.
Tilly, Andrew AR 17th (Lemoyne's) Inf. Co.C
Tilly, B.M. GA 11th Inf. Co.E
Tilly, B.W. LA 28th (Gray's) Inf. Co.H
Tilly, C.C. TN 14th Inf. Co.H
Tilly, Edmond TX 4th Inf. Co.E Lt.
Tilly, Elijah S. AR 4th Inf. Co.I
Tilly, Elihu TN Lt.Arty. Phillips' Co.
Tilly, E.M. TX Inf. Whaley's Co.
Tilly, F.H. NC 2nd Jr.Res. Co.I
Tilly, Fletcher NC McDugald's Co. 1st Drum.
Tilly, F.T. NC 3rd Jr.Res. Co.A Jr.2nd Lt.
Tilly, George F. NC 18th Inf. Co.H Drum.
Tilly, George W. NC 2nd Cav. (19th St.Troops) Co.K
Tilly, Gibb TX 36th Cav. Co.C
Tilly, G.M. NC 53rd Inf. Co.G
Tilly, G.W. AR 37th Inf. Co.B
Tilly, Haskins NC 44th Inf. Co.A
Tilly, Hosea NC 5th Sr.Res. Co.D
Tilly, James AR 18th (Marmaduke's) Inf. Co.I
Tilly, James NC 37th Inf. Co.K
Tilly, James NC 39th Inf. Co.G
Tilly, James H. NC 2nd Arty. (36th St.Troops) Co.C
Tilly, J.C. AR 45th Mil. Co.A
Tilly, J.G. KY 1st Bn.Mtd.Rifles Co.D
Tilly, John NC 7th Sr.Res. Watts' Co.
Tilly, John C. MO Cav. Fristoe's Regt. Co.F
Tilly, John M. NC 55th Inf. Co.A
Tilly, John W. AR 17th (Lemoyne's) Inf. Co.C
Tilly, John W. AR 21st Inf. Co.C Cpl.
Tilly, John W. Conf.Inf. 1st Bn. 2nd Co.E
Tilly, J.R. MS 35th Inf. Co.F
Tilly, J.R. TN Lt.Arty. Rice's Btty.
Tilly, J.S. MO 15th Cav. Co.L 2nd Lt.
Tilly, J.S. MO Inf. 1st Bn. Co.C
Tilly, L. NC 5th Sr.Res. Co.B
Tilly, Martin NC 53rd Inf. Co.H
Tilly, R. NC 44th Inf. Co.K
Tilly, Robert NC 47th Inf. Co.I
Tilly, R.P. NC 53rd Inf. Co.G Sgt.
Tilly, Samuel AL Lt.Arty. Tarrant's Btty.
Tilly, S.L. TN 21st (Wilson's) Cav. Co.H
Tilly, Sylvestus GA 48th Inf. Co.D Cpl.
Tilly, Thornton VA Mil. Grayson Cty.
Tilly, Walter J. GA 21st Inf. Co.I
Tilly, William NC 44th Inf. Co.A
Tilly, William A. GA 11th Inf. Co.E
Tilly, William A. NC 11th (Bethel Regt.) Inf. Co.G
Tilly, William B. NC 30th Inf. Co.D
Tilly, William H.L. NC 30th Inf. Co.D
Tilly, William L. NC 30th Inf. Co.D
Tilly, Z.D. LA 28th (Gray's) Inf. Co.H
Tillye, Jesse AL 30th Inf. Co.I

Tilman 1st Choctaw & Chickasaw Mtd.Rifles 3rd Co.F
Tilman, Aaron J. NC 44th Inf. Co.E Cpl.
Tilman, A.B. NC 30th Inf. Co.F
Tilman, A.N. GA 19th Inf. Co.F
Tilman, B. AL 8th Inf. Co.H
Tilman, B.D. LA 27th Inf. Co.B
Tilman, B.M. GA 19th Inf. Co.F
Tilman, B.M. TN 52nd Inf. Co.C Capt.
Tilman, Colsien TN 19th & 20th (Cons.) Cav. Co.B
Tilman, Daniel NC 13th Inf. Co.D
Tilman, Daniel NC Mallett's Bn. Co.C
Tilman, D.S. MS 2nd Inf. Co.K
Tilman, F.M. MS 46th Inf. Co.H
Tilman, George M. VA 44th Inf. Co.K Sgt.
Tilman, George W. GA 4th Inf. Co.G
Tilman, Gid AL 21st Inf. Co.I,D
Tilman, G.W. VA 46th Inf. Co.F
Tilman, H. TX Waul's Legion Co.A
Tilman, H.D. MS Cav. Jeff Davis Legion Co.C
Tilman, Henry TN 21st Inf. Lt.Col.
Tilman, Henry M. TX 10th Cav. Co.I
Tilman, Hiram D. MS 35th Inf. Co.B Sgt.
Tilman, Hugh H. VA 46th Inf. 2nd Co.E
Tilman, J.A. TN 22nd Inf. Co.H
Tilman, Jacob M. VA 44th Inf. Co.K 2nd Lt.
Tilman, James A. VA Lt.Arty. Cayce's Co. Cpl.
Tilman, James A. VA Inf. 25th Bn. Co.B Cpl.
Tilman, James P. VA 49th Inf. Co.F
Tilman, James W. VA 44th Inf. Co.K
Tilman, J.B. VA 1st Bn.Res. Co.B 1st Lt.
Tilman, J.C. AL 61st Inf. Co.K
Tilman, J.C. NC 1st Jr.Res. Co.H
Tilman, J.C. TN 19th & 20th (Cons.) Cav. Co.G
Tilman, J.F. GA 3rd Cav. Co.B
Tilman, J.I. TN 42nd Inf. Co.D
Tilman, J.L. AL 34th Inf. Co.F
Tilman, John MS Moseley's Regt.
Tilman, John H. GA Inf. 3rd Bn. Co.E
Tilman, Joseph E. AR 1st Inf. Co.I
Tilman, Joshua J. GA 11th Cav. (St.Guards) Groover's Co.
Tilman, J.W. TN 19th & 20th (Cons.) Cav. Co.G
Tilman, Morris TN 12th Inf. Co.D
Tilman, O.G. VA 49th Inf. Co.D
Tilman, R.C. MS 18th Cav. Co.G
Tilman, Richard GA 44th Inf. Co.B
Tilman, Richard A. GA 4th Inf. Co.D
Tilman, S. LA 27th Inf. Co.B
Tilman, S.A. MO Cav. Coleman's Regt. Co.F
Tilman, Samuel C. VA 44th Inf. Co.K,I
Tilman, Thomas MS 1st Cav. Co.A
Tilman, W. TX Inf. Timmons' Regt. Co.G
Tilman, W.B. VA Loc.Def. Mallory's Co.
Tilman, William B. AR 1st Mtd.Rifles Co.D,A
Tilman, William D. FL 1st (Res.) Inf. Co.A
Tilman, William F. VA 19th Inf. Co.K
Tilman, William M. VA Inf. 25th Bn. Co.B
Tilman, William R. MS 8th Cav. Co.E,A
Tilman, Z.T. VA 15th Cav. Co.B
Tilmon, J.D. GA 32nd Inf. Co.I
Tilmon, John FL 7th Inf. Co.A
Tilmon, John TN 31st Inf. Co.C
Tilmon, John R. TN 42nd Inf. Co.D Sgt.
Tilmon, Moses MO 6th Cav. Co.D
Tilory, J. MO 11th Inf. Co.H
Tilory, James AL 61st Inf. Co.H
Tilory, William A. AL 61st Inf. Co.H
Tilow 1st Creek Mtd.Vol. Co.A
Tilpatt, J. MO 5th Cav. Co.D
Tilsel, A. MO Cav. Coleman's Regt.
Tilson, A.F. MS 8th Inf. Co.A
Tilson, A.F. MS 37th Inf. Co.G
Tilson, E.J. MS 37th Inf. Co.G
Tilson, F.M. MS 46th Inf. Co.H
Tilson, Francis M. VA Inf. 23rd Bn. Co.A
Tilson, Harman H. VA 21st Cav. Co.K
Tilson, Henry C. TN 29th Inf. Co.E 2nd Lt.
Tilson, Henry H. VA 26th Inf. Co.D
Tilson, H.H. VA 198th Mil.
Tilson, Hugh C. TX 9th Cav. Co.K 1st Sgt.
Tilson, Jacob GA Smith's Legion Co.C
Tilson, Jacob TN 29th Inf. Co.E
Tilson, James H. TN 25th Inf. Co.A
Tilson, James H. VA Inf. 23rd Bn. Co.A
Tilson, J.C. TN 29th Inf. Co.E 1st Lt.
Tilson, J.E. NC 64th Inf. Co.K 1st Lt.
Tilson, Jesse A. NC Walker's Bn. Thomas' Legion Co.B Fifer
Tilson, John R. VA Inf. 23rd Bn. Co.A
Tilson, J.W. MS 46th Inf. Co.H
Tilson, J.W. NC 64th Inf. Co.K
Tilson, M.B. VA 45th Inf. Co.B
Tilson, Stephen VA 37th Inf. Co.F
Tilson, Thomas NC 64th Inf. Co.A
Tilson, Thomas D. NC 64th Inf. Co.A
Tilson, Thomas E. NC 64th Inf. Co.K Cpl.
Tilson, Thomas J. VA Inf. 23rd Bn. Co.A
Tilson, William GA Smith's Legion Co.C
Tilson, William TN 29th Inf. Co.E
Tilson, William TN 63rd Inf. Co.B
Tilson, William VA 48th Inf. Co.D
Tilson, William E. NC 64th Inf. Co.K Capt.
Tilson, William K. TN 63rd Inf. Co.C
Tilson, William M. VA Inf. 23rd Bn. Co.A
Tilson, William P. NC 6th Cav. (65th St.Troops) Co.G,C 2nd Lt.
Tilson, William P. TN Cav. 16th Bn. (Neal's) Co.E
Tilson, William V.B. VA 8th Cav. Co.A
Tilson, W. TN 28th Inf. Co.E
Tilton, Benjamin W. TX 11th (Spaight's) Bn.Vol. Co.F
Tilton, B.W. TX 21st Inf. Co.F
Tilton, Daniel C. SC 10th Inf. Co.E
Tilton, David TX 5th Inf. Co.F
Tilton, D.C. SC Inf.Bn. Co.B
Tilton, E.M. GA Inf. 1st City Bn. (Columbus) Co.A
Tilton, E.M. LA 25th Inf. Co.I
Tilton, H.W. SC Mil.Arty. 1st Regt. Co.C
Tilton, James C. LA 28th (Gray's) Inf. Co.A
Tilton, J.M. TX 2nd Inf. Co.C
Tilton, Joshua A. AL 8th Inf. Co.D
Tilton, J.W. AL Cav. Moreland's Regt. Co.C
Tilton, Nathaniel O. GA 1st (Olmstead's) Inf. Way's Co. 1st Lt.
Tilton, Nath. O. GA 25th Inf. Capt.,AQM
Tilton, Nath. O. Gen. & Staff Maj.,Field Insp.
Tilton, N.O. GA 25th Inf. QM
Tilton, R. MO St.Guard
Tilton, R.F. SC Inf. 6th Bn. Co.C
Tilton, R.F. SC 26th Inf. Co.I Cpl.
Tilton, R.F. SC Manigault's Bn.Vol. Co.E
Tilton, Theo SC Mil.Arty. 1st Regt. Walter's Co.C
Tilton, T.W. SC 5th Cav. Co.B
Tilton, T.W. SC Cav. 17th Bn. Co.C
Tilton, W.C. GA 25th Inf. Co.H
Tilton, William SC 3rd St.Troops Co.A
Tilton, William C. SC Arty.Bn. Hampton Legion Co.A QMSgt.
Tilton, William H. MO Staff St.Guard Lt.Col., ADC
Tilton, William J. SC 15th Inf. Co.G
Tilton, W.R. AL Inf. 1st Regt. Co.H 1st Lt.
Tim, J. MS Henley's Co. (Henley's Invinc.)
Tim, Thomas SC 5th Regt.Rifles Co.F
Timanus, Henry Gen. & Staff Capt.,Comsy.
Timbelake, E. TN 21st (Wilson's) Cav. Co.H
Timberlage, Ritchard 2nd Cherokee Mtd.Vol. Co.B
Timberlake, A.A. FL 2nd Cav. Co.F
Timberlake, Albert VA 53rd Inf. Co.B
Timberlake, Albert VA Inf. Tomlin's Bn. Co.A
Timberlake, Alexander W. Sig.Corps,CSA
Timberlake, Alpheus R. VA Cav. 40th Bn. Co.A Sgt.
Timberlake, Alpheus R. VA 56th Inf. Co.K 1st Lt.
Timberlake, A.R. VA 24th Cav. Co.A 2nd Lt.
Timberlake, A.W. 2nd Cherokee Mtd.Vol. QMSgt.
Timberlake, Bartlett VA 6th Inf. 2nd Co.B
Timberlake, B.E. AR 35th Inf. Co.K
Timberlake, Benjamin VA 2nd Inf.Loc.Def. Co.I
Timberlake, Benjamin N. VA 53rd Inf. Co.E Cpl.
Timberlake, Benjamin N. VA Inf. Tomlin's Bn. Co.A
Timberlake, Benjamin P. MS Inf. 5th Bn. Co.A Cpl.
Timberlake, Benjamin T. VA 2nd Inf. Co.G
Timberlake, Beny VA Inf. 2nd Bn.Loc.Def. Co.G
Timberlake, C.G. VA 1st Bn.Res. Co.B 1st Lt.
Timberlake, Chapman VA Lt.Arty. Montgomery's Co.
Timberlake, Charles VA 6th Inf. Weisiger's Co.
Timberlake, Charles VA 13th Inf. Co.D
Timberlake, Charles VA 16th Inf. Co.I
Timberlake, Charles VA 56th Inf. Co.C
Timberlake, Charles M. VA Courtney Arty.
Timberlake, Charles M. VA Lt.Arty. Weisiger's Co.
Timberlake, Christopher GA 1st Reg. Co.L
Timberlake, David VA Hvy.Arty. 18th Bn. Co.B
Timberlake, David VA Lt.Arty. Brander's Co.
Timberlake, David VA 41st Inf. 1st Co.E
Timberlake, David A. AL 4th Inf. Co.F Cpl.
Timberlake, David A. VA 4th Cav. Co.G Capt.
Timberlake, David W. VA 2nd Inf. Co.G
Timberlake, Dick 1st Cherokee Mtd.Vol. 1st Co.D, 2nd Co.B
Timberlake, E.A. AL 4th Inf. Co.F
Timberlake, Edward T. VA Cav. 40th Bn. Co.A
Timberlake, E.M. VA 1st Arty. Co.B
Timberlake, E.M. VA Lt.Arty. 1st Bn. Co.B
Timberlake, E.M. VA Arty. Richardson's Co.
Timberlake, E.T. VA 24th Cav. Co.A

Timberlake, F.H. VA Conscr. Cp. Lee Co.B Cpl.
Timberlake, Fountain P. TN 7th Inf. Co.B
Timberlake, Francis A. TN 7th Inf. Co.B 1st Lt.
Timberlake, Francis H. VA Lt.Arty. Arch. Graham's Co.
Timberlake, Francis H. VA 44th Inf. Co.H
Timberlake, Francis P. NC 24th Inf. Co.A
Timberlake, Frank J. NC 47th Inf. Co.G
Timberlake, Franklin VA 53rd Inf. Co.E
Timberlake, George VA 1st St.Res. Co.B 1st Lt.
Timberlake, George A. VA 12th Cav. Co.B
Timberlake, George A. VA 2nd Inf. Co.G
Timberlake, George A. VA 53rd Inf. Co.B,E 2nd Lt.
Timberlake, George A. VA Inf. Tomlin's Bn. Co.A Cpl.
Timberlake, George W. KY 3rd Mtd.Inf. Co.B 1st Lt.
Timberlake, George W. NC 3rd Inf. Co.A Sgt.
Timberlake, George W. VA 53rd Inf. Co.B
Timberlake, Harman VA 53rd Inf. Co.E
Timberlake, Harry C. VA 53rd Inf. Co.H Sgt.
Timberlake, Henry 1st Conf.Cav. 2nd Co.A
Timberlake, Henry C. MS Enrolled Conscr.
Timberlake, I. MO 11th Inf. Co.H
Timberlake, James VA 2nd Inf.Loc.Def. Co.I
Timberlake, James VA Inf. 2nd Bn.Loc.Def. Co.G
Timberlake, James A. VA Lt.Arty. Sturdivant's Co.
Timberlake, James B. VA 1st St.Res. Co.F
Timberlake, James B. VA 53rd Inf. Co.B Capt.
Timberlake, James B. VA Inf. Tomlin's Bn. Co.A 3rd Lt.
Timberlake, James E. MO 10th Cav. Co.K
Timberlake, James E. MO Inf. 3rd Bn. Co.E
Timberlake, James E. MO 6th Inf. Co.C
Timberlake, James H. VA 12th Cav. Co.B
Timberlake, James H. VA 2nd Inf. Co.G
Timberlake, James L. VA 12th Cav. Co.B Cpl.
Timberlake, James L. VA 15th Inf. Co.H Sgt.
Timberlake, James P. VA 3rd Cav. Co.F
Timberlake, James S. NC 42nd Inf. Co.B Sgt.
Timberlake, James W. VA 53rd Inf. Co.B Cpl.
Timberlake, James W. VA Inf. Tomlin's Bn. Co.A Cpl.
Timberlake, J.C. SC Post Guard Senn's Co.
Timberlake, J.D. AR Inf. Hardy's Regt. Co.G
Timberlake, J.F. TN 24th Inf. Adj.
Timberlake, J.H. VA 4th Cav. Co.G
Timberlake, J.H. Gen. & Staff, QM Dept.
Timberlake, J. Henry VA Lt.Arty. Carrington's Co. 1st Lt.
Timberlake, J. Henry VA 47th Mil. Col.
Timberlake, J.L. NC 35th Inf. Co.E
Timberlake, J.L. VA 4th Cav. Co.G
Timberlake, John LA Mil.Conf.Guards Regt. Co.F
Timberlake, John SC 3rd Bn.Res. Co.C Cpl.
Timberlake, John VA Lt.Arty. W.P. Carter's Co.
Timberlake, John VA 2nd Inf.Loc.Def. Co.I
Timberlake, John VA Inf. 2nd Bn.Loc.Def. Co.G
Timberlake, John C. VA 53rd Inf. Co.E Lt.Col.
Timberlake, John F. VA 53rd Inf. Co.E 2nd Lt.
Timberlake, John F. VA Inf. Tomlin's Bn. Co.A
Timberlake, John H. VA 24th Cav. Co.A
Timberlake, John H. VA Cav. 40th Bn. Co.A
Timberlake, John H. Conf.Arty. Nelson's Bn. Co.E Jr.1st Lt.
Timberlake, John M. VA Inf. 4th Bn.Loc.Def. Co.E
Timberlake, John M. VA 13th Inf. Co.D
Timberlake, John M. VA 53rd Inf. Co.B
Timberlake, John M. VA Inf. Tomlin's Bn. Co.A
Timberlake, John O. VA 19th Inf. Co.D
Timberlake, John W. MO 11th Inf. Co.H 1st Lt.
Timberlake, John W. VA Lt.Arty. Carrington's Co.
Timberlake, John W. VA 13th Inf. Co.D
Timberlake, John W. VA 40th Inf. Co.H
Timberlake, Jno. W. Gen. & Staff Chap.
Timberlake, Joseph VA 2nd Cav. Co.G
Timberlake, Joseph VA Cav. 39th Bn. Co.D
Timberlake, Joseph E. VA 2nd Inf. Co.G
Timberlake, Joseph G. MS 42nd Inf. Co.A Cpl.
Timberlake, J.S. NC 1st Inf. (6 mo. '61) Co.G
Timberlake, Junius A. VA 15th Inf. Co.I
Timberlake, J.W. AR 35th Inf. Old Co.F 2nd Lt.
Timberlake, J.W. FL 2nd Inf. Chap.
Timberlake, J.W. VA 10th Cav. Co.F Capt.
Timberlake, Lebbeus W. VA 1st Arty. Co.K
Timberlake, Lewis VA Lt.Arty. Pollock's Co. Cpl.
Timberlake, L.W. VA 46th Inf. 2nd Co.A
Timberlake, Philip VA Horse Arty. D. Shanks' Co.
Timberlake, Philip VA 56th Inf. Co.C
Timberlake, P.T. GA Cav. 8th Bn. (St.Guards) Co.C 1st Lt.
Timberlake, R. SC 12th Inf. Co.A
Timberlake, R.H. TN 21st (Wilson's) Cav. Co.H
Timberlake, Richard L. VA 12th Cav. Co.B
Timberlake, Richard L. VA 17th Inf. Co.B Sgt.
Timberlake, Richard T. LA 1st (Strawbridge's) Inf. Co.D
Timberlake, Robert VA Inf. 5th Bn. Co.D Cpl.
Timberlake, Robert L. VA 53rd Inf. Co.B Cpl.
Timberlake, Robert L. VA Inf. Tomlin's Bn. Co.A
Timberlake, Robert W. VA 24th Cav. Co.A
Timberlake, Ro W. VA Cav. 40th Bn. Co.A
Timberlake, S. VA 3rd Inf.Loc.Def. 1st Co.G Jr.2nd Lt.
Timberlake, Samuel R. MS 22nd Inf. Co.G
Timberlake, Seth M. VA 12th Cav. Co.B 1st Sgt.
Timberlake, Seth M. VA 2nd Inf. Co.G
Timberlake, Sidney P. NC 3rd Inf. Co.A
Timberlake, S.R. AL Cav. Shockley's Co.
Timberlake, Stephen D. VA 12th Cav. Co.B
Timberlake, S.W. VA 56th Inf. Co.K 1st Sgt.
Timberlake, Thomas W. VA 1st Cav. 1st Co.D
Timberlake, Thomas W. VA 6th Cav. Co.D
Timberlake, Thomas W. VA 12th Cav. Co.B
Timberlake, Thomas W. VA 2nd Inf. Co.G
Timberlake, Thomas W. VA 146th Mil. Co.H Sgt.
Timberlake, T.W.B. VA Lt.Arty. Parker's Co.
Timberlake, Warren W. VA Hvy.Arty. A.J. Jones' Co. Sgt.
Timberlake, W. Burt NC 47th Inf. Co.F
Timberlake, W.C. Ord.Dept. 2nd Corps Ord.Sgt.
Timberlake, W. Clarke VA Lt.Arty. Carrington's Co.
Timberlake, W.F. TX 9th (Young's) Inf. Co.G
Timberlake, W.H. AR 35th Inf. Old Co.F
Timberlake, Wm. VA 3rd Arty. Co.H
Timberlake, William VA 2nd Inf.Loc.Def. Co.I
Timberlake, William VA Inf. 2nd Bn.Loc.Def. Co.G
Timberlake, William VA 6th Inf. 2nd Co.B
Timberlake, William A. VA 24th Cav. Co.A
Timberlake, William A. VA Cav. 40th Bn. Co.A
Timberlake, William D. VA 146th Mil. Co.H
Timberlake, William E. VA 20th Cav. Co.I Sgt.
Timberlake, William H. MO 11th Inf. Co.H Cpl.
Timberlake, William H. VA 19th Inf. Co.D
Timberlake, William M. Gen. & Staff Capt., AQM
Timberlake, William P. TN 27th Inf. Co.D Capt.
Timberlake, William T. VA Lt.Arty. Montgomery's Co.
Timberlake, William W. VA 1st St.Res. Co.A
Timberlake, Wilson H. VA 46th Inf. 2nd Co.A Cpl.
Timberlake, W.M. TN 24th Inf. Co.F AQM
Timberlake, W.P. Forrest's Scouts T. Henderson's Co.,CSA
Timberlick, Francis VA 54th Mil. Co.A
Timberlick, Henry KY 1st (Butler's) Cav. Co.A
Timberlick, James J. NC 1st Jr.Res. Co.A
Timberlin, Moses GA 27th Inf. Co.I
Timberly, D.A. AL 4th Cav. Co.L
Timberville, George R. VA Cav. Mosby's Regt. (Part.Rangers) Co.A
Timbes, Marion GA 36th (Villepigue's) Inf. Co.D
Timble, I.P. TX 32nd Cav. Co.I
Timbrook, Gibson VA 13th Inf. Co.I
Timbrook, Isaac VA 18th Cav. Co.K
Timbrook, Isaac VA 33rd Inf. Co.A
Timbrook, Isaac VA 114th Mil. Co.B
Timbrook, Joseph VA 18th Cav. Co.K
Timbrook, Joseph VA 114th Mil. Co.B
Timbrook, William VA 114th Mil. Co.B
Timbrough, W. MO 5th Cav. Co.H
Timbrough, W.D. VA 15th Inf. Co.C
Timbs, B. AL 31st Inf. Co.D
Timbs, Garrison SC Inf. Hampton Legion Co.D
Timbs, J.E. SC Inf. Hampton Legion Co.F
Timbs, John SC Inf. Hampton Legion Co.D
Timbs, John TN Cav. Newsom's Regt. Co.H
Timbs, John VA 9th Inf. Co.K
Timbs, John H. TN Cav. Newsom's Regt. Co.H
Timbs, J.S. AL Cav. Moreland's Regt. Co.D
Timbs, Noble H. VA 40th Inf. Co.F 1st Lt.
Timbs, R.A. AL 22nd Inf. Co.F
Timbs, Robert D. GA 14th Inf. Co.I
Timbs, William L. VA 40th Inf. Co.F 2nd Lt.
Timbs, Wiseman T. TN Cav. Newsom's Regt. Co.H Cpl.
Timcke, J.H. TX 3rd Inf. Co.B
Times, F. TN 19th (Biffle's) Cav. Co.B
Times, J.H. MS 14th Inf. Co.A
Times, John B. GA 1st Reg. Co.E
Times, J.T. SC Inf. Hampton Legion Co.F
Times, William TX Cav. Benavides' Regt. Co.H

Timiltay, Matthew LA 30th Inf. Co.C
Timins, John B. AL 58th Inf. Co.G
Timison, W.A. TX Inf. Timmons' Regt. Co.C
Tim kar 1st Creek Mtd.Vol. Co.G Cpl.
Timkins, Henry LA Mil. 3rd Regt. 1st Brig. 1st Div. Co.A Sgt.
Timkins, James LA Mil. 3rd Regt. 1st Brig. 1st Div. Co.A
Timlin, Edward H. AR Lt.Arty. Clarkson's Btty. (Helena Arty.)
Timlin, Edward H. AR Lt.Arty. Key's Btty. Cpl.
Timlin, James LA Mil. Leeds' Guards Regt. Co.F
Timm, August TX 13th Vol. 2nd Co.C
Timm, Fridrich W. TX 13th Vol. Co.C
Timmaheka, Thompson 1st Choctaw & Chickasaw Mtd.Rifles Co.C
Timmans, Thomas SC 1st (Butler's) Inf. Co.C
Timmans, William M. SC 1st (Butler's) Inf. Co.C
Timme chi che 1st Creek Mtd.Vol. 1st Co.C
Timmens, J.L. AL 60th Inf. Co.C
Timmens, J.W. AL 8th (Livingston's) Cav. Co.C
Timmer, H. TN Inf. 2nd Cons.Regt. Co.G
Timmer, Henry TN 13th Inf. Co.H
Timmer, W.O. SC 6th Res. Co.A
Timmerer, A.J. GA 64th Inf. Co.B
Timmerman, Andrew J. SC 14th Inf. Co.K Cpl.
Timmerman, Benjamin SC 5th Res. Co.F
Timmerman, Benjamin SC 14th Inf. Co.K
Timmerman, Benjamin SC 24th Inf. Co.K
Timmerman, B.W. SC 14th Inf. Co.K
Timmerman, David SC 19th Inf. Co.K
Timmerman, David SC 24th Inf. Co.K
Timmerman, Edward SC 14th Inf. Co.K
Timmerman, Elijah SC 1st St.Troops Co.D
Timmerman, Felix SC 14th Inf. Co.K
Timmerman, F.L. SC 7th Inf. 1st Co.K
Timmerman, Frank SC 24th Inf. Co.K
Timmerman, Franklin SC 15th Inf. Co.K
Timmerman, George SC 24th Inf. Co.K
Timmerman, G.H. SC 7th Inf. 1st Co.K, 2nd Co.K
Timmerman, Goodey M. SC 14th Inf. Co.K Cpl.
Timmerman, Henry C.G. VA 12th Inf. Co.E Music.
Timmerman, J. GA 47th Inf. Co.C
Timmerman, Jacob B. SC 1st (McCreary's) Inf. Co.H,G
Timmerman, James M. AL 20th Inf. Co.F Far.,Black.
Timmerman, J.L. SC 14th Inf. Co.K
Timmerman, J.M. AL 24th Inf. Co.K
Timmerman, J.N. MS 44th Inf. Co.G,I
Timmerman, John GA 29th Inf. Co.H,K
Timmerman, John MS 20th Inf. Co.D
Timmerman, John SC 19th Inf. Co.C,K 1st Sgt.
Timmerman, Josh AL Mil. 4th Vol. Moore's Co.
Timmerman, Joshua AL 36th Inf. Co.I
Timmerman, J.T. SC 14th Inf. Co.K
Timmerman, J.T. SC 19th Inf. Co.C
Timmerman, M. GA Cav. 15th Bn. (St.Guards) Jones' Co.
Timmerman, N.D. SC 19th Inf. Co.C,K
Timmerman, N. Douglas SC 2nd Cav. Co.I
Timmerman, R.W. SC 14th Inf. Co.K
Timmerman, S. GA 11th Cav. (St.Guards) Johnson's Co.
Timmerman, Samuel W. TX 1st Bn.S.S. Co.D Cpl.
Timmerman, Simeon SC 24th Inf. Co.K
Timmerman, T.H. SC 14th Inf. Co.K
Timmerman, W. SC 16th & 24th (Cons.) Inf. Co.H
Timmerman, W.B. SC 7th Inf. Co.D
Timmerman, W.H. SC 19th Inf. Co.K Capt.
Timmerman, Wiley SC 5th Res. Co.F 1st Lt.
Timmerman, Wiley SC 7th Inf. 1st Co.K Cpl.
Timmerman, William SC 6th Cav. Co.B
Timmerman, William SC 5th Res. Co.F
Timmerman, William SC 24th Inf. Co.K
Timmerman, William E. SC 14th Inf. Co.K
Timmerman, Wily SC 1st St.Troops Co.D Cpl.
Timmerman, W.J. AL Lt.Arty. Goldthwaite's Btty.
Timmerman, W.T. GA Cav. Allen's Co.
Timmermann, F. LA Mil. 4th Regt.Eur.Brig. Co.E
Timmes, Joseph F. TN 1st (Turney's) Inf. Co.D
Timmie, George SC 6th Inf. 2nd Co.I
Timmie, W.O. SC 6th Inf. 2nd Co.I
Timmins, George TN Lt.Arty. Huggins' Co.
Timmins, James G. LA Washington Arty.Bn. Co.1 QMSgt.
Timmins, James G. Sig. Corps,CSA
Timmins, M.V. SC 1st Arty. Co.B Cpl.
Timmins, William MS 1st Lt.Arty.
Timmins, William C. TX 2nd Inf. Co.B Lt.Col.
Timmoche 1st Creek Mtd.Vol. Co.M
Timmon, James 9th Conf.Cav. Co.C
Timmonds, A.B. MS St.Cav. 2nd Bn. (Harris') Co.C
Timmonds, J.H. GA 2nd Res. Co.A
Timmonds, R. LA 27th Inf. Co.I
Timmons, A.A. GA 16th Inf. Co.F Sgt.
Timmons, Abraham SC 4th Inf. Co.G
Timmons, Abr. SC Inf. 13th Bn. Co.B
Timmons, A.J. SC Inf. 1st (Charleston) Bn. Co.B,G
Timmons, A.J. SC Mil. 6th Regt. Triest's Co. Cpl.
Timmons, Alexander NC 21st Inf. Co.C
Timmons, Alexander B. MS 42nd Inf. Co.K
Timmons, Alfred J. SC 27th Inf. Co.K,B
Timmons, A.T. KY 3rd Mtd.Inf. Co.H
Timmons, A.T. VA 8th Inf. Co.K
Timmons, B. LA Mil.Conf.Guards Regt. Co.G
Timmons, B. TX 9th (Nichols') Inf. Co.A Capt.
Timmons, B. TX Inf. Timmons' Regt. Col.
Timmons, B. TX Waul's Legion Co.D Lt.Col.
Timmons, Benson E.L. GA 56th Inf. Co.C
Timmons, Bernard H. AL 51st (Part.Rangers) Co.K
Timmons, Charnel MS 10th Cav. Co.D
Timmons, Charles B. TN 44th Inf. Co.E
Timmons, C.M. VA 47th Inf. Co.B
Timmons, Commadore A. KY 8th Cav.
Timmons, E.H. KY 8th Mtd.Inf. Co.A
Timmons, Eli TX 17th Cav. 1st Co.I
Timmons, Eli TX 28th Cav. Co.B
Timmons, Elija KY 4th Mtd.Inf. Co.G,I
Timmons, Enoch S. VA 9th Cav. Co.A
Timmons, F.E. GA Inf. 1st Loc.Troops (Augusta) Co.E 1st Lt.
Timmons, Felix KY 8th Mtd.Inf. Co.A
Timmons, Finis KY 8th Mtd.Inf. Co.A
Timmons, Frank VA 47th Inf. Co.A
Timmons, Franklin VA 11th Inf. Co.I
Timmons, G.C. SC Arty. Fickling's Co. (Brooks Lt.Arty.)
Timmons, G.C. SC 1st (Butler's) Inf. Co.I,G
Timmons, G.C. SC 22nd Inf. Co.A
Timmons, George VA 25th Inf. 2nd Co.A,D
Timmons, George C. SC 2nd Inf. Co.K
Timmons, G.W. TX 2nd Inf. Co.C
Timmons, H. Gen. & Staff Capt.,ACS
Timmons, Hamil C. GA 56th Inf. Co.C Cpl.
Timmons, Harrison Mead's Conf.Cav. Co.D
Timmons, H.R. SC 23rd Inf. Co.I
Timmons, Hugh LA Inf.Crescent Regt. Co.A
Timmons, Isaac GA 51st Inf. Co.A
Timmons, Isaac NC 21st Inf. Co.C
Timmons, Isaac VA 13th Cav. Co.F
Timmons, Isaac VA 10th Inf. Co.B
Timmons, Isaac John SC 8th Inf. Co.D 1st Lt.
Timmons, Isaac T. SC 6th Cav. Co.K
Timmons, I.T. SC 26th Inf. Co.F
Timmons, J.A. AL 57th Inf. Co.F
Timmons, J.A. SC 21st Inf. Co.C
Timmons, J.A. 2nd Conf.Eng.Troops Co.G
Timmons, Jacob TN 29th Inf. Co.H
Timmons, James GA 5th Res. Co.B
Timmons, James GA 12th Inf. Co.A
Timmons, James TN 44th Inf. Co.B
Timmons, James E. SC 2nd Arty. Co.D
Timmons, James K.P. TN Cav. 9th Bn. (Gantt's) Co.A
Timmons, James M. GA 20th Inf. Co.D
Timmons, James P. GA 23rd Inf. Co.G
Timmons, J.B. KY 7th Mtd.Inf. Co.H
Timmons, J.B. SC Inf. 6th Bn. Co.A
Timmons, J.B. SC 26th Inf. Co.C
Timmons, J.C. GA 7th Inf. (St.Guards) Co.I
Timmons, J.D. GA Inf. 1st Loc.Troops (Augusta) Co.E 1st Sgt.
Timmons, Jesse A. GA 2nd Res. Co.A
Timmons, Jesse H. GA 57th Inf. Co.E
Timmons, Jesse L. AL 3rd Bn. Hilliard's Legion Vol. Co.D
Timmons, J.H. TN 5th Inf. 1st Co.H
Timmons, J.J. AR 32nd Inf. Co.K
Timmons, J.J. KY 1st Inf. Co.F
Timmons, J.J. SC 18th Inf. Co.I
Timmons, J.L. TX 7th Inf. Co.E
Timmons, J. Morgan SC Lt.Arty. 3rd (Palmetto) Bn. Co.C 1st Lt.
Timmons, John AL 61st Inf. Co.B
Timmons, John GA Cherokee Legion (St.Guards) Co.G
Timmons, John SC Cav. 19th Bn. Co.E
Timmons, John SC 1st (Hagood's) Inf. 2nd Co.F
Timmons, John SC 3rd Res. Co.F
Timmons, John TN 2nd (Walker's) Inf. Co.F 1st Sgt.
Timmons, John VA 40th Inf. Co.K
Timmons, John A. GA 51st Inf. Co.A Cpl.
Timmons, John A. NC 21st Inf. Co.C
Timmons, John B. AL 6th Inf. Co.G
Timmons, John B. SC Cav. 12th Bn. Co.D

Timmons, John B 2nd Conf.Eng.Troops Co.H
Timmons, John H. MO 3rd Cav. Co.F,A
Timmons, John M. SC 18th Inf. Co.I
Timmons, John W. GA 51st Inf. Co.E
Timmons, John W. 9th Conf.Inf. Co.D Sgt.
Timmons, Jordan TX 10th Cav. Co.I
Timmons, J.P. Mead's Conf.Cav. Co.D
Timmons, J.T. GA 51st Inf. Co.E
Timmons, J.T. GA 64th Inf. Sgt.
Timmons, J.T. SC 6th Cav. Co.K
Timmons, J.W. SC Lt.Arty. 3rd (Palmetto) Bn. Co.C
Timmons, L. GA Arty. (Macon Lt.Arty.) Slaten's Co.
Timmons, Lester E. FL 1st Inf. Co.C,H Sgt.
Timmons, Lester E. FL 7th Inf. Co.I 1st Sgt.
Timmons, L.R. SC Inf. 6th Bn. Co.A
Timmons, L.R. SC 26th Inf. Co.C
Timmons, L.R. SC Manigault's Bn.Vol. Co.D
Timmons, Martin V. SC 15th Inf. Co.G Bvt.2nd Lt.
Timmons, Michael MS 1st Lt.Arty. Co.D
Timmons, Mike MS 4th Inf. Co.D
Timmons, Moses AL 3rd Bn. Hilliard's Legion Vol. Co.D
Timmons, Moses GA 51st Inf. Co.E
Timmons, Nimrod P. MS 42nd Inf. Co.K
Timmons, Noble H. MS 42nd Inf. Co.K
Timmons, N.S. MS 44th Inf. Co.I
Timmons, Polk KY 10th (Johnson's) Cav. New Co.I
Timmons, R.E. SC Lt.Arty. 3rd (Palmetto) Bn. Co.C
Timmons, R.M. SC 1st Arty. Co.C,F
Timmons, Robert GA 1st Cav. Co.H
Timmons, Robert TX 2nd Cav. Co.A
Timmons, Robert A. AL Cav. 5th Bn. Hilliard's Legion Co.C
Timmons, S. GA Mil. Camden Cty. (Mtd.)
Timmons, Samuel GA Cherokee Legion (St.Guards) Co.B
Timmons, Samuel A. FL 7th Inf. Co.I
Timmons, Samuel B. FL 6th Inf. Co.B Cpl.
Timmons, Samuel C. SC 5th Bn.Res. Co.C 1st Lt.
Timmons, Samuel D. SC 4th St.Troops Co.K Capt.
Timmons, Samuel E. FL Lt.Arty. Perry's Co.
Timmons, S.B. FL 10th Inf. Love's Co.
Timmons, Scott Mead's Conf.Cav. Co.D
Timmons, S.M. GA Cav. Floyd's Co. Ens.
Timmons, S.T. GA 64th Inf. Co.B
Timmons, Stephen M. NC 48th Inf. Co.A
Timmons, T.H. AL 9th Inf. Sgt.
Timmons, Thomas SC Cav. 4th Bn. Co.C
Timmons, Thomas H. GA 56th Inf. Co.C,G 3rd Lt.
Timmons, Thomas Q. TN Cav. 9th Bn. (Gantt's) Co.A
Timmons, Thomas T. SC 2nd Cav. Co.E
Timmons, T.M. GA 20th Inf. Co.B
Timmons, T.M. SC 4th St.Troops Co.D
Timmons, T.T. GA 2nd Res. Co.H
Timmons, T.W. AR 5th Inf. Co.A
Timmons, W.B. SC 8th Inf. Co.E
Timmons, W.B. SC 21st Inf. Co.K
Timmons, W.C. SC Lt.Arty. 3rd (Palmetto) Bn. Co.C
Timmons, W.E. LA 31st Inf. Co.E
Timmons, W.F. SC 18th Inf. Co.I
Timmons, W.H. SC 8th Inf. Co.B
Timmons, William AL 10th Inf.
Timmons, William GA 12th Cav. Co.D
Timmons, William D. GA 23rd Inf. Co.G
Timmons, Wm. E. MD 1st Inf. Co.A
Timmons, William H. SC Lt.Arty. Kelly's Co. (Chesterfield Arty.)
Timmons, William H. TN Cav. 9th Bn. (Gantt's) Co.A Cpl.
Timmons, William J. GA Cherokee Legion (St.Guards) Co.G
Timmons, William M. SC Palmetto S.S. Co.D
Timmons, William S. VA 47th Inf. Co.B
Timmons, William T. KY 7th Cav.
Timmons, Willis NC 64th Inf. Co.H
Timmons, W.J. GA 56th Inf. Co.D
Timmons, W.J. SC 21st Inf. Co.C
Timmons, W.J. SC 25th Inf. Co.I
Timmons, W.M. GA 10th Inf. Co.E
Timmons, W.R.M. TN 31st Inf. Co.G Cpl.
Timmons, W.T. KY 1st Inf. Co.F
Timmony, James LA 14th Inf. Co.A
Timms, Absalom MS 10th Cav. Co.G,K
Timms, A.J.D. AL 22nd Inf. Co.C
Timms, Allen AL 40th Inf. Co.F
Timms, Allen MS 37th Inf. Co.D
Timms, Andrew M. SC 12th Inf. Co.F
Timms, Benjamin NC 49th Inf. Co.K
Timms, Benjamin F. TN 7th (Duckworth's) Cav. Co.B
Timms, Calvin MS 14th Inf. Co.A
Timms, Chas. W. Gen. & Staff Asst.Surg.
Timms, C.W. VA 8th Cav. Asst.Surg.
Timms, David SC 6th Inf. 1st Co.D, 2nd Co.G
Timms, David TN 12th (Green's) Cav. Co.K
Timms, E.W. VA Cav. 37th Bn. Asst.Surg.
Timms, Garrison SC 13th Inf. Co.B
Timms, George TN 12th (Green's) Cav. Co.K
Timms, I.J. SC 2nd Cav. Co.G
Timms, Isaac AR 2nd Inf. Co.E,D
Timms, J.A. GA 8th Inf. (St.Guards) Co.C
Timms, J.A. GA Conscr.
Timms, Jabez TN 12th (Green's) Cav. Co.K
Timms, Jackson MS 37th Inf. Co.D
Timms, James TN 12th (Green's) Cav. Co.K
Timms, James E. SC 2nd Rifles Co.K
Timms, James T. SC 12th Inf. Co.F
Timms, J.E. SC 13th Inf. Co.B
Timms, Jerome F. TX 1st (Yager's) Cav. Co.A,G
Timms, J.F. AR 1st Cav. Co.A
Timms, J.F. TN Arty. Ramsey's Btty.
Timms, J.J. GA 43rd Inf. Co.I
Timms, J.J. MS 10th Cav. Co.G
Timms, J.J. SC 7th Inf. 1st Co.B, 2nd Co.B
Timms, J.K. MS 37th Inf. Co.D
Timms, J.M. SC Inf. 1st (Charleston) Bn. Co.D
Timms, John MS 37th Inf. Co.D
Timms, John NC 49th Inf. Co.K
Timms, John TN 12th (Green's) Cav. Co.K
Timms, John TN 21st & 22nd (Cons.) Cav. Co.G
Timms, John TN 34th Inf. Co.B
Timms, John TN 51st Inf. Co.E
Timms, John TN 51st (Cons.) Inf. Co.I
Timms, John C. AR Inf. 8th Bn. Co.A
Timms, John E. VA 36th Inf. Co.A
Timms, John E. Sig. Corps,CSA
Timms, John H. MS Inf. 7th Bn. Co.E
Timms, John J. NC Inf. 2nd Bn. Co.G
Timms, J.W. GA 8th Inf. (St.Guards) Co.C
Timms, J.W. MS Inf. 7th Bn. Co.E,D
Timms, Lewis LA Red River S.S.
Timms, L.J. LA Red River S.S. Co.A
Timms, L.J. VA 36th Inf. Co.A
Timms, O.H. MS 37th Inf. Co.D
Timms, Rufus G. MO 10th Cav. Co.K
Timms, Sanford AR 1st (Crawford's) Cav. Co.B
Timms, T. MS 8th Inf. Co.A
Timms, Thomas TN 12th (Green's) Cav. Co.K
Timms, Thomas S. AR 1st Cav. Co.B
Timms, W.A.J. AL 40th Inf. Co.F
Timms, William AR Inf. Cocke's Regt. Co.E
Timms, William TN 3rd (Forrest's) Cav. Polk's Co.
Timms, William TN 42nd Inf. Co.G
Timms, William A. GA 4th Inf. Co.F
Timms, Wise TN 22nd Inf. Co.B
Timms, Wiseman TN 13th Cav.
Timms, W.L. GA 43rd Inf. Co.I
Timmy, John TN Cav. Newsom's Regt.
Timns, John AL Cav. Forrest's Regt.
Timns, John TN 18th (Newsom's) Cav. Co.H
Timoding, Henry LA Mil. 2nd Regt. 3rd Brig. 1st Div. Co.G
Timon, Alonzo MS 21st Inf. Co.D
Timon, Dan'l N. AR Lt.Arty. Etter's Btty.
Timon, D.H. TN 5th Cav. Co.I
Timon, Hubert TX 2nd Cav. Co.G 2nd Lt.
Timon, James TN 21st Inf. Co.F
Timon, John MO Cav. 3rd Regt.St.Guard Co.D
Timon, John TX 1st (Yager's) Cav. Co.F
Timon, John H. MS 1st Lt.Arty. Co.F
Timon, Patrick LA Mil. Bonnabel Guards
Timon, Peter TX 2nd Cav. Co.G
Timon, S.N. MS 21st Inf. Co.D
Timons, James GA 1st Cav. Co.C
Tim o se li key 1st Creek Mtd.Vol. 2nd Co.I
Timothy, Cornelius NC 5th Cav. (63rd St.Troops) Co.C
Timothy, H. TX 1st Hvy.Arty. Co.F
Timothy, T. SC Sea Fencibles Symons' Co. Cpl.
Timothy, William AL Seawell's Btty. (Mohawk Arty.)
Timothy, William LA C.S. Zouave Bn. Co.D
Timpson Bear 1st Cherokee Mtd.Vol. 1st Co.E, 2nd Co.C
Timpson Clay 1st Cherokee Mtd.Vol. Co.J
Timpson Clay 1st Squad. Cherokee Mtd.Vol. Co.A
Timpson Ned 1st Cherokee Mtd.Rifles Co.H
Timpson Owalar 1st Cherokee Mtd.Vol. 1st Co.E
Timpson Samuel 1st Cherokee Mtd.Vol. 1st Co.E, 2nd Co.C
Timpson Sunday 1st Cherokee Mtd.Vol. 1st Co.E, 2nd Co.C
Timpson Walker 1st Cherokee Mtd.Vol. 2nd Co.C.
Timpson, W.F. GA 26th Inf. Co.K
Timrod, Henry SC 20th Inf. Co.B
Tims, A. AL 22nd Inf. Co.F Cpl.

Tims, Abert M. LA 4th Cav. Co.E Sgt.
Tims, Absolom TN 1st (Carter's) Cav. Co.B
Tims, Alexander SC 17th Inf. Co.K
Tims, Alfred AL 40th Inf.
Tims, Allan MS Inf. 7th Bn. Co.E
Tims, Anderson MO 1st Cav. Co.H
Tims, Daniel AL 5th Inf. New Co.H
Tims, David GA 5th Res. Co.I Sgt.
Tims, Edward 1st Choctaw Mtd.Rifles Co.G Cpl.
Tims, Elliott M. LA 12th Inf. Co.H
Tims, Frank AL 22nd Inf. Co.A
Tims, George W. AL 16th Inf. Co.A
Tims, George W. GA 21st Inf. Co.G
Tims, Harrison TX 2nd Inf. Co.A
Tims, Harrison 3rd Conf.Cav. Co.I
Tims, H.M. SC 18th Inf. Co.D
Tims, H.P. GA 1st Inf. (St.Guards) Co.C
Tims, I. TN 7th (Duckworth's) Cav. Co.K
Tims, J. GA 55th Inf. Co.I
Tims, James A. SC 12th Inf. Co.H
Tims, James B. TX 3rd Cav. Co.E
Tims, James F. TN 6th Inf. Co.D
Tims, James H. TN 4th Inf. Co.C
Tims, J.B. TN 6th Inf. Co.C
Tims, Jesse E. AL 44th Inf. Co.I
Tims, Jesse S. SC 23rd Inf. Co.F Cpl.
Tims, J.H. TN 3rd (Forrest's) Cav. Co.A
Tims, J.L.P. MS 10th Cav. Co.B
Tims, John AL Cav. Moreland's Regt. Co.H
Tims, John NC Hvy.Arty. 10th Bn. Co.A
Tims, John TN 21st (Wilson's) Cav. Co.B
Tims, John TX 10th Cav. Co.F
Tims, John H. AL 16th Inf. Co.A
Tims, John T. TN 14th (Neely's) Cav. Co.C
Tims, John W. TN 34th Inf. 2nd Co.C
Tims, Joseph S. TX 28th Cav. Co.K
Tims, J.R. LA 2nd Inf. Co.K Cpl.
Tims, J.R. TN 21st (Wilson's) Cav. Co.B
Tims, J.T. SC 3rd Bn.Res. Co.B
Tims, J.T. SC 18th Inf. Co.D
Tims, J.W. GA Inf. 8th Bn. Co.D
Tims, J.W. MS 46th Inf. Co.G
Tims, Nathan C. MS 14th Inf. Co.D
Tims, N.M. GA 4th Cav. (St.Guards) Pirkle's Co. Sgt.
Tims, Oliver H. MS Inf. 7th Bn. Co.E
Tims, P.H. AL Randolph Cty.Res. Shepherd's Co.
Tims, P.W. SC Palmetto S.S. Co.C
Tims, R.G. MO Dismtd.Cav. Lawther's Temporary Regt.
Tims, R.W. AL 34th Inf. Co.G 2nd Lt.
Tims, Samuel AL 29th Inf. Co.B
Tims, Simon LA Arty. Moody's Co. (Madison Lt.Arty.)
Tims, Stephen 3rd Conf.Cav. Co.C
Tims, T.A. AL 22nd Inf. Co.C
Tims, T.C. TN 1st (Carter's) Cav. Co.K
Tims, Volantine TN 18th (Newsom's) Cav. Co.B
Tims, Volantine TN 6th Inf. Co.F
Tims, William TN 21st (Wilson's) Cav. Co.B
Tims, William C. MS 1st Lt.Arty. Co.L
Tims, William C. MS 14th Inf. Co.D
Tinch, A.G. TN 25th Inf. Co.K Cpl.
Tinch, Charles A. AL Cav. Holloway's Co.
Tinch, Henry TN Inf. 22nd Bn. Co.D
Tinch, Jos. W. VA Hvy.Arty. 10th Bn. Co.D
Tinch, J.W. VA Hvy.Arty. 10th Bn. Co.D
Tincher, Albert VA 21st Cav. Co.B
Tincher, Albert VA 5th Cav.Arty. & Inf.St.Line Co.I
Tincher, Alexander A. VA 79th Mil. Co.2
Tincher, Alexis VA 79th Mil. Co.2
Tincher, Andrew VA Inf. 26th Bn. Co.B
Tincher, Andrew M. VA Cav. Hounshell's Bn. Thurmond's Co.
Tincher, Asberry G. VA Cav. Hounshell's Bn. Huffman's Co.
Tincher, Asberry G. VA Cav. Thurmond's Co.
Tincher, Charles VA Inf. 26th Bn. Co.B
Tincher, Charles L. VA Cav. Thurmond's Co.
Tincher, Christopher L. VA 22nd Inf. Co.A
Tincher, C.L. VA 59th Inf. 1st Co.B
Tincher, C.L. VA 60th Inf. Co.A
Tincher, F.M. VA 79th Mil. Co.1
Tincher, F.M. VA 5th Cav.Arty. & Inf.St.Line Co.I
Tincher, James VA Inf. 26th Bn. Co.B
Tincher, James VA 79th Mil. Co.1
Tincher, James VA 5th Cav.Arty. & Inf.St.Line Co.I
Tincher, James G. VA 79th Mil. Co.5 1st Sgt.
Tincher, Jehu L. VA Cav. Thurmond's Co. 1st Lt.
Tincher, Joel VA 22nd Inf. Co.I
Tincher, Joel VA 79th Mil. Co.4
Tincher, Levi, Jr. VA 22nd Inf. Co.K
Tincher, Levi, Sr. VA 22nd Inf. Co.K
Tincher, Levy VA 79th Mil. Co.2
Tincher, Lewis VA 166th Mil. Co.B
Tincher, Nicholas VA 46th Inf. 1st Co.C
Tincher, Nicholas VA 60th Inf. Co.B
Tincher, William VA Inf. 26th Bn. Co.B
Tincher, William VA 79th Mil. Co.2
Tincher, William VA 166th Mil. Co.B
Tincher, William C. VA Lt.Arty. Lowry's Co.
Tincher, Willis VA 22nd Inf. Co.K
Tincher, Willis VA 79th Mil. Co.2
Tincker, William C. TX 31st Cav. Co.D
Tincture, H. TX Cav. 1st Bn.St.Troops Co.F Cpl.
Tincup Jase 1st Cherokee Mtd.Vol. 2nd Co.C
Tincup Jesse 1st Cherokee Mtd.Vol. 1st Co.E, 2nd Co.C
Tindal, A.J. SC 5th Bn.Res. Co.F Sgt.
Tindal, A.J. SC 21st Inf. Co.C
Tindal, A.L. TX 4th Cav. Co.H
Tindal, A.S. TX Cav. (Dismtd.) Chisum's Regt. Co.B
Tindal, Asburry MO 10th Cav. Co.I
Tindal, Benjamin M. SC Inf. Hampton Legion Co.C
Tindal, Charles W. 4th Conf.Inf. Co.D
Tindal, Costin NC 38th Inf. Co.D
Tindal, David D. GA 57th Inf. Co.F
Tindal, E. AL 22nd Inf. Co.C
Tindal, Emanuel SC 21st Inf. Co.I Cpl.
Tindal, George W. MS 29th Inf. Co.G
Tindal, Henry L. SC Inf. Hampton Legion Co.C
Tindal, H.F. SC 11th Res. Co.E Cpl.
Tindal, I.J. SC Post Guard Senn's Co.
Tindal, J.A. FL 11th Inf. Co.C
Tindal, James NC Mil. Clark's Sp.Bn. Co.C
Tindal, James SC 26th Inf. Co.A
Tindal, James E. SC Lt.Arty. Garden's Co. (Palmetto Lt.Btty.) Sgt.Maj.
Tindal, J.L. MS 6th Cav. Co.G
Tindal, J.M. TN 22nd (Barteau's) Cav. 1st Co.H
Tindal, John GA 3rd Inf. Co.E
Tindal, John NC 33rd Inf. Co.K
Tindal, John SC Inf. 9th Bn. Co.A
Tindal, John SC 26th Inf. Co.A
Tindal, J.R. TN Inf. Nashville Bn. Cattles' Co.
Tindal, J.W. 10th Conf.Cav. Co.B
Tindal, L.J. SC Inf. 9th Bn. Co.A
Tindal, L.J. SC 26th Inf. Co.A
Tindal, L.R. SC 7th Cav. Co.B
Tindal, Matthew A. VA 15th Inf. Co.D
Tindal, N. SC 2nd St.Troops Co.D Cpl.
Tindal, N. SC 8th Bn.Res. Fishburne's Co.
Tindal, Nehemiah SC 11th Res. Co.I
Tindal, Samuel FL 10th Inf. Co.F
Tindal, Samuel KY 2nd Cav.
Tindal, Samuel H. SC Arty. Bn. Hampton Legion Co.A
Tindal, Solomon SC 21st Inf. Co.I
Tindal, Thomas TX 4th Cav. Co.H
Tindal, William M. MS 15th Inf. Co.E
Tindal, William T. 4th Conf.Inf. Co.D
Tindal, Zachariah A. SC Arty.Bn. Hampton Legion Co.A
Tindale, Henry S. FL 10th Inf. Co.F Sgt.
Tindale, James NC Lt.Arty. 13th Bn. Co.F
Tindale, James M. TN 48th (Voorhies') Inf. Co.H
Tindale, James W. AR 38th Inf. Co.K
Tindale, John W. FL 9th Inf. Co.C
Tindale, Mathew B. FL 9th Inf. Co.A
Tindale, R.M. Gen. & Staff Asst.Surg.
Tindale, Samuel A. MO 10th Cav. Co.I
Tindale, Samuel B. FL 7th Inf. Co.A
Tindale, William NC 12th Inf. Co.M
Tindale, William NC 32nd Inf. Co.B,A
Tindall, Abner G. NC 3rd Arty. (40th St.Troops) Co.A
Tindall, Allen NC 27th Inf. Co.D
Tindall, Austin NC 51st Inf. Co.G
Tindall, B.L. VA 46th Inf. 2nd Co.E
Tindall, B.M. Gen. & Staff Emply. Physician
Tindall, Bryant AL 6th Cav. Co.K
Tindall, Calvin NC 2nd Arty. (36th St.Troops) Co.C
Tindall, C.H. AR 13th Inf. Co.E
Tindall, C.H. KY 7th Mtd.Inf. Co.K
Tindall, Charles NC 3rd Arty. (40th St.Troops) Co.A
Tindall, Charles W. AL 57th Inf. Co.G,E
Tindall, Columbus AR Cav. Wright's Regt. Co.D
Tindall, Costin NC 2nd Jr.Res. Co.A
Tindall, Curtis NC 8th Bn.Part.Rangers Co.B
Tindall, Curtis NC 3rd Arty. (40th St.Troops) Co.A
Tindall, Curtis NC 66th Inf. Co.C
Tindall, David NC 3rd Arty. (40th St.Troops) Co.F
Tindall, David NC 2nd Inf. Co.H
Tindall, D.O. SC 1st Cav. Co.E
Tindall, Elijah W. MS 24th Inf. Co.L
Tindall, Elisha J. TX 4th Cav. Co.H
Tindall, George G. MS 20th Inf. Co.B
Tindall, Henry MS 15th Inf. Co.E

Tindall, Henry C. MO Searcy's Bn.S.S. Co.E Sgt.
Tindall, Henry S. NC 3rd Arty. (40th St.Troops) Co.A
Tindall, H.F. SC 5th Cav. Co.I
Tindall, J.A. TN 9th (Ward's) Cav. Co.A
Tindall, J.A. VA 46th Inf. 2nd Co.E
Tindall, James MS 15th Inf. Co.E
Tindall, James NC 7th Inf. Co.C
Tindall, James NC 44th Inf. Co.C
Tindall, James SC Inf. 9th Bn. Co.A
Tindall, James VA Lt.Arty. Hardwicke's Co.
Tindall, James VA 16th Inf. Co.A
Tindall, James M. TX 16th Cav. Co.E 2nd Lt.
Tindall, James R. NC 3rd Arty. (40th St.Troops) Co.A
Tindall, James S. SC Cav. 14th Bn. Co.A 1st Lt.
Tindall, James W. NC 21st Inf. Co.G Cpl.
Tindall, J.B. SC 5th Cav. Co.G
Tindall, Jesse NC 3rd Inf. Co.D 1st Sgt.
Tindall, Jesse I. NC 3rd Arty. (40th St.Troops) Co.A
Tindall, J.J. SC 23rd Inf. Co.I
Tindall, J.J. SC Inf. Hampton Legion Co.C
Tindall, J.L. MS St.Cav. 2nd Bn. (Harris') Co.B
Tindall, J.L. MS 11th (Cons.) Cav. Co.G
Tindall, J.M. LA 56th Part.Rangers Co.B
Tindall, J.Mc. SC 5th Cav. Co.E
Tindall, John FL Campbellton Boys
Tindall, John NC 8th Bn.Part.Rangers Co.B
Tindall, John NC 3rd Arty. (40th St.Troops) Co.A
Tindall, John NC 55th Inf. Co.A
Tindall, John NC 66th Inf. Co.C
Tindall, John TX 20th Inf. Co.D
Tindall, John VA 2nd St.Res. Co.F
Tindall, John VA 19th Inf. Co.D Sgt.
Tindall, John L. NC 2nd Inf. Co.H
Tindall, John W. MO 9th Inf. Co.H
Tindall, J.R. SC 8th Res.
Tindall, J.R. TN 1st (Feild's) Inf. Co.L
Tindall, J.W. AL 38th Inf. Co.K
Tindall, Leonard TX 4th Cav. Co.H
Tindall, Levi W. MS 2nd Part.Rangers Co.I
Tindall, Levi W. MS 44th Inf. Co.C Cpl.
Tindall, Louis C. VA 56th Inf. Co.D
Tindall, L.W. MS Cav. Yerger's Regt. Co.E 1st Sgt.
Tindall, N. MS 4th Inf. Co.H
Tindall, Nat T. SC 1st (McCreary's) Inf. Co.F
Tindall, O.H. TX 4th Inf. Co.C
Tindall, Osborne TX Inf. Townsend's Co. (Robertson Five S.)
Tindall, Owen S. NC 2nd Arty. (36th St.Troops)
Tindall, Peter NC 8th Sr.Res. Bryan's Co.
Tindall, Peter NC Giddins' Co. (Detailed & Petitioned Men)
Tindall, Robert MS 3rd Inf. (St.Troops) Co.H
Tindall, Robert T. MO 15th Cav. Co.A Music.
Tindall, Robert W. TX 1st Inf. Sgt.
Tindall, Robert W. TX Inf. Riflemen Arnold's Co.
Tindall, R.W. AL 38th Cav. Co.K
Tindall, R.W. SC Inf. Hampton Legion Co.C Cpl.
Tindall, Samuel KY 2nd Mtd.Inf. Co.I
Tindall, Samuel B. AR 7th Inf. Co.A
Tindall, S.H. SC Arty. Manigault's Bn. 1st Co.A, Co.B
Tindall, Solomon SC 7th Inf. 1st Co.L
Tindall, S.P. SC Lt.Arty. 3rd (Palmetto) Bn. Co.B
Tindall, Thomas KY 2nd Mtd.Inf. Co.I
Tindall, Thomas VA 2nd Arty. Co.K
Tindall, Thomas D. AL Eufaula Lt.Arty.
Tindall, Thomas D. VA Inf. 25th Bn. Co.C
Tindall, Thomas P. TX Inf. Townsend's Co. (Robertson Five S.)
Tindall, Thomas W. MS Inf. 3rd Bn. Co.D
Tindall, Thomas W. MS 15th Inf. Co.E
Tindall, W. VA 46th Inf. Co.E
Tindall, Wiley F. FL 9th Inf. Co.A
Tindall, William TX 4th Cav. Co.H
Tindall, William B. GA 42nd Inf. Co.F Cpl.
Tindall, William B. NC 55th Inf. Co.A
Tindall, William D. AL 39th Inf. Co.K
Tindall, William H. TN 9th (Ward's) Cav. Co.H 1st Lt.
Tindall, William S. NC 46th Inf. Co.I
Tindalle, J.W. AR 19th (Dawson's) Inf. Co.B
Tindel, Burrel AL 57th Inf. Co.I Cpl.
Tindel, Charles TN Conscr. (Cp. of Instr.)
Tindel, George Brush Bn.
Tindel, Isaics AR 15th (N.W.) Inf. Co.I
Tindel, J.M. AL 15th Bn.Part.Rangers Co.B
Tindel, J.M. AL Cav. Murphy's Bn. Co.B
Tindel, Jonathan MO 4th Cav. Wallace's Co.
Tindel, J.T. MS 5th Inf. Surg.
Tindell, Augustus TX 18th Cav. Co.A Sgt.
Tindell, David NC 30th Inf. Co.A
Tindell, Green FL Cav. 5th Bn. Co.E
Tindell, H.C. TN 24th Inf. 1st Co.G, Co.B
Tindell, Henry C. TX 17th Cav. Co.D
Tindell, Henry C. TX 17th Cons.Dismtd.Cav. Co.C
Tindell, J. AR 10th Mil. Co.E
Tindell, J. MO 4th Cav. Wallace's Co.
Tindell, James NC 3rd Arty. (40th St.Troops) Co.H
Tindell, James B. GA Arty. 9th Bn. Co.A,E
Tindell, James C. TX 19th Cav. Co.I
Tindell, James M. MO Cav. Wood's Regt. Co.B
Tindell, James R. NC 35th Inf. Co.F Sgt.
Tindell, J. Burrill SC 10th Inf. Co.K
Tindell, Jeremiah NC 38th Inf. Co.D
Tindell, Jesse T. NC 4th Inf. Co.D
Tindell, John AR 15th (N.W.) Inf. Co.I
Tindell, John F. AR 3rd Cav. Co.B Capt.
Tindell, L.R. MO 16th Inf. Co.B
Tindell, M. LA 4th Inf. Co.F
Tindell, Miles S. NC 30th Inf. Co.A
Tindell, Richard NC 3rd Arty. (40th St.Troops) Co.H
Tindell, Robert W. TN 24th Inf. 1st Co.G, Co.B Capt.
Tindell, R.W. TN Inf. 3rd Cons.Regt. Co.K Capt.
Tindell, S.F. TX 20th Cav.
Tindell, William MS 42nd Inf. Co.A
Tinder, --- TN 18th (Newsom's) Cav. Co.F
Tinder, A.J. TN 8th (Smith's) Cav. Co.I
Tinder, Alonzo VA 6th Cav. Co.I
Tinder, Alonzo VA 9th Cav. Co.E
Tinder, Alonzo VA 46th Inf. 1st Co.K
Tinder, Amos E. VA 6th Cav. Co.I
Tinder, Amos E. VA 46th Inf. 1st Co.K
Tinder, A.R. VA 13th Inf. Co.C
Tinder, Edgar A. VA 6th Cav. Co.I
Tinder, George T. VA Lt.Arty. J.S. Brown's Co.
Tinder, George T. VA Lt.Arty. Taylor's Co.
Tinder, George W. MO Robertson's Regt. St.Guard Co.10
Tinder, G.W. MO 5th Cav. Co.D
Tinder, H.F. VA Inf. 4th Bn.Loc.Def. Co.D
Tinder, H.F. VA 46th Inf. 1st Co.K
Tinder, H.F. 1st Conf.Eng.Troops
Tinder, J.A. VA 46th Inf. 1st Co.K
Tinder, James A. VA 9th Cav. Co.E
Tinder, James L. MS 20th Inf. Co.G
Tinder, James R. VA Lt.Arty. Cooper's Co. Sgt.
Tinder, J.D. VA 9th Cav. Co.E
Tinder, John A. VA Lt.Arty. J.S. Brown's Co.
Tinder, John A. VA 7th Inf. Co.C
Tinder, Joseph A. VA 9th Cav. Co.E
Tinder, Joseph A. VA 46th Inf. 1st Co.K
Tinder, N.B. AL 10th Inf. Co.E
Tinder, Richard VA 2nd Bn.Res. Co.H 2nd Lt.
Tinder, Thomas R. VA 6th Cav. Co.I
Tinder, W. AL 36th Inf. Co.D
Tinder, W.C. AL Cav. Forrest's Regt.
Tinder, W.C. TN 34th Inf. Co.B Sgt.
Tinder, William M. VA 47th Inf. 3rd Co.H Sgt.
Tinder, William R. VA 23rd Inf. Co.E
Tindle, C.A. AR Cav. Wright's Regt. Co.C
Tindle, F. LA 2nd Cav. Co.G
Tindle, G.W. TX Cav. 2nd Regt.St.Troops Co.E
Tindle, H. GA 25th Inf. Co.C
Tindle, Jackson AL 37th Inf. Co.E
Tindle, Jackson FL 11th Inf. Co.K
Tindle, James N. TN 2nd (Robison's) Inf. Co.D Cpl.
Tindle, James W. AL Cav. 5th Bn. Hilliard's Legion Co.B
Tindle, James W. AR 17th (Lemoyne's) Inf. Co.B
Tindle, James W. GA Cobb's Legion Co.B
Tindle, J.C. TX 13th Vol. Co.E
Tindle, J.M. AL 13th Bn.Part.Rangers Co.A
Tindle, John MS 8th Cav. Co.K
Tindle, John A. MO 7th Cav. Co.C
Tindle, John A. MO 10th Inf. Co.I
Tindle, John W. MO Inf. 8th Bn. Co.D
Tindle, J.R. NC 25th Inf. Co.F
Tindle, J.W. AR 21st Inf. Co.D
Tindle, Moses FL 6th Inf. Co.C
Tindle, R.G. TN 63rd Inf. Co.B
Tindle, Robert MS 8th Cav. Co.K
Tindle, Robert W. MS 15th Inf. Co.K,E
Tindle, Roderick V. TX 1st (Yager's) Cav. Co.A
Tindle, Roderick V. TX Cav. 3rd (Yager's) Bn. Co.A
Tindle, Samuel AL 54th Inf. Co.E
Tindle, Samuel A. MO 5th Inf. Co.D
Tindle, Samuel C. AL 37th Inf. Co.E
Tindle, S.C. FL 11th Inf. Co.K
Tindle, W.A. AR 1st Vol. Co.F Drum.
Tindle, William AR 7th Cav. Co.B
Tindle, William M. MS 2nd Inf. (A. of 10,000) Co.H
Tindle, William W. KY 4th Cav. Co.A
Tindley, T.N. VA 198th Mil.

Tindly, Martin AL 6th Cav. Co.I
Tindol, A.J. GA Cav. 19th Bn. Co.C
Tindol, A.J. 10th Conf.Cav. Co.H
Tindol, Burrell FL 11th Inf. Co.C
Tindol, H.P. MS 40th Inf. Co.G
Tindol, James LA 9th Inf. Co.F
Tindol, James SC 24th Inf. Co.D
Tindol, J.L. MS 5th Inf. (St.Troops) Co.E
Tindol, John AL 33rd Inf. Co.G
Tindol, John NC Loc.Def. Croom's Co.
Tindol, J.W. SC 20th Inf. Co.D
Tindol, Samuel FL 11th Inf. Co.C
Tindol, Samuel F. MS 14th Inf. Co.F
Tindol, Sebern FL 11th Inf. Co.C
Tindol, W.R. MS 40th Inf. Co.G
Tindry, John MS 24th Inf. Co.K
Tindsley, George W. VA Hvy.Arty. 20th Bn. Co.B
Tine, James GA 31st Inf. Co.I
Tine, Thomas NC 13th Inf.
Tinell, Joseph VA 25th Cav. Co.F
Tineman, P.S AL Cp. of Instr. Talladega
Tinen, J.J. LA Inf.Crescent Regt. Co.H
Tinenbee, J.C. AL 45th Inf. Co.K
Tiner, Benjamin C. AR 9th Inf. Co.F
Tiner, Beny AR Cav. Wright's Regt. Co.D
Tiner, Bythan NC 50th Inf. Co.C
Tiner, Caleb SC 6th Inf. 2nd Co.E
Tiner, Charles H. AL 3rd Inf. Co.I
Tiner, Charles H. TX 31st Cav. Co.C
Tiner, David 1st Seminole Mtd.Vol.
Tiner, Dock S. AR Cav. Wright's Regt. Co.D
Tiner, E. MS 1st Cav.Res. Co.H
Tiner, E. SC 4th St.Troops Co.E
Tiner, George 1st Seminole Mtd.Vol.
Tiner, G.W. MS 4th Inf. Co.I
Tiner, Isaac AR 14th (McCarver's) Inf.
Tiner, Ivory GA 6th Cav. Co.K
Tiner, Jackson Shecoe's Chickasaw Bn.Mtd.Vol. Co.A
Tiner, Jacob AR 2nd Mtd.Rifles Co.B Bugler
Tiner, Jacob H. AR 3rd Inf. Co.D
Tiner, James LA 18th Inf. Co.I
Tiner, James LA Inf.Crescent Regt. Co.E
Tiner, James MS 1st Cav.Res. Co.B
Tiner, James NC 52nd Inf. Co.E
Tiner, James A. GA 38th Inf. Co.F
Tiner, James A. TX 1st Inf. Co.I
Tiner, James H. AR 9th Inf. Co.F
Tiner, James J. LA Lt.Arty. Holmes' Btty. Ord.Sgt.
Tiner, James J. NC 24th Inf. Co.I
Tiner, James P. MS 33rd Inf. Co.A
Tiner, James W. AL 59th Inf. Co.G Cpl.
Tiner, James W. AL 2nd Bn. Hilliard's Legion Vol. Co.D Cpl.
Tiner, J.C. TN 2nd (Smith's) Cav. Thomasin's Co.
Tiner, Jefferson AL Jeff Davis Arty.
Tiner, Jefferson T. AL 31st Inf. Co.F
Tiner, Jesse E. AL 24th Inf. Co.F Sgt.
Tiner, J.F. TX 33rd Cav. Co.G
Tiner, J.J. Exch.Bn. 2nd Co.A,CSA
Tiner, J.L. AR 35th Inf. Co.K
Tiner, J.M. LA 13th Bn. (Part.Rangers) Co.E
Tiner, J.N. TN 22nd Inf. Co.H
Tiner, John AR 62nd Mil. Co.F
Tiner, John D. MS 40th Inf. Co.A
Tiner, John G. AL 59th Inf. Co.G
Tiner, John H. GA 38th Inf. Co.F
Tiner, John M. GA Arty. 11th Bn. (Sumter Arty.) Co.A
Tiner, John P. AR Inf. 2nd Bn. Co.B
Tiner, John P. AR 3rd Inf. Co.I
Tiner, Joshua P.T. GA 38th Inf. Co.F
Tiner, Leroy C. MS 29th Inf. Co.G
Tiner, Lewis AR 62nd Mil. Co.F
Tiner, Lewis GA 2nd Cav. Co.C
Tiner, Lewis 1st Cherokee Mtd.Vol. 2nd Co.G Sgt.
Tiner, Lewis W. MS 10th Inf. New Co.H
Tiner, L.H. GA 2nd Cav. Co.C
Tiner, Liles MO 10th Inf. Co.F
Tiner, Liles C. AR 38th Inf. Co.M
Tiner, L.S. NC Alex. Brown's Co.
Tiner, L.S. NC 2nd Inf. Co.F
Tiner, Luke M. AR 3rd Inf. Co.D
Tiner, Michael LA 6th Inf. Co.B
Tiner, N. TN 12th (Cons.) Inf. Co.D
Tiner, R.A. TX Inf. Cunningham's Co.
Tiner, Ransom NC 24th Inf. Co.I
Tiner, Richard A. TX 31st Cav. Co.C Sgt.
Tiner, Rufus J. GA Arty. 11th Bn. (Sumter Arty.) Co.A
Tiner, S.B. GA 3rd Res. Co.K
Tiner, Seburn 1st Cherokee Mtd.Vol. 2nd Co.G
Tiner, Sidney S. NC 5th Inf. Co.C
Tiner, Simeon FL 10th Inf. Co.C
Tiner, Stephen 1st Choctaw Mtd.Rifles Ward's Co.
Tiner, Thomas FL 1st Inf. New Co.D
Tiner, Thomas J. MS 40th Inf. Co.A Music.
Tiner, T.J. MS Clayton's Co. (Jasper Defend.) Sgt.
Tiner, T.M. MS 1st (Johnston's) Inf. Co.E Cpl.
Tiner, W. TX Inf. Cunningham's Co.
Tiner, W.A.J. FL 1st Inf. New Co.D
Tiner, William TX 2nd Inf. Co.D
Tiner, William B. GA Arty. 11th Bn. (Sumter Arty.) Co.D,A
Tiner, William L. TN 2nd (Smith's) Cav. Thomason's Co.
Tiner, William W. TX 6th Inf. Co.E
Tiner, Wilson FL 8th Inf. Co.K
Tiner, W.R. MS 1st (Johnston's) Inf. Co.E
Tinery, John AL 15th Inf. Co.C
Tinery, L.W. TN 21st (Wilson's) Cav. Co.D,C
Tinery, L.W. TN 21st & 22nd (Cons.) Cav. Co.F
Tines, James N. VA 1st Arty. Co.E
Tines, Jos. T. VA Hvy.Arty. Wright's Co.
Tines, L. MS Cav. 3rd Bn. (Ashcraft's) Co.C
Tines, L. MS Cav. Ham's Regt. Co.F
Tines, William H. MS 29th Inf. Co.G
Tinesley, G.W. AL 12th Cav. Co.F
Tiney, E. TN 34th Inf. Co.K
Tiney, H.C. TX 17th Cav. Co.D
Tiney, J.C. TN 34th Inf. Co.K
Ting, John H. AL 5th Cav. Co.G
Tingen, A. NC 7th Sr.Res. Davies' Co.
Tingen, Benjamin T. NC 24th Inf. Co.H
Tingen, Garrette R. NC 15th Inf. Co.E
Tingen, John R. NC 24th Inf. Co.H
Tingen, Joseph P. NC 24th Inf. Co.H Music.
Tingen, Starling H. NC 24th Inf. Co.H
Tingen, Zachariah H. NC 24th Inf. Co.H
Tinges, Charles S. MD Arty. 4th Btty.
Tingi, Solomon AL Randolph Cty.Res. J. Hightower's Co.
Tingle, A.J. AL Cp. of Instr. Talladega
Tingle, A.J. NC 1st Arty. (10th St.Troops) Co.I
Tingle, Andrew J. AL 22nd Inf. Co.E
Tingle, Andrew J. NC 67th Inf. Co.B
Tingle, Archibald D. GA 32nd Inf. Co.H
Tingle, Benjamin LA 31st Inf. Co.H
Tingle, Benjamin F. MS 13th Inf. Co.F,D
Tingle, B.F. AL 12th Cav. Co.D Sgt.
Tingle, B.F. MS 46th Inf. Co.I Capt.
Tingle, Birney S. NC 3rd Inf. Co.I
Tingle, Charles F. MS 40th Inf. Co.E
Tingle, Cyrus AL 3rd Res. Co.G
Tingle, D.P.B. MD 1st Inf. Co.G
Tingle, F.M. AL 31st Inf. Co.A
Tingle, Gideon NC 1st Arty. (10th St.Troops) Co.B
Tingle, Henry H. LA 12th Inf. Co.H
Tingle, Jacob C. AL 28th Inf. Co.F
Tingle, J.A. KY 4th Cav. Co.I
Tingle, J.A. KY 5th Mtd.Inf. Co.E
Tingle, James KY 4th Cav. Co.I Sgt.
Tingle, James NC 1st Arty. (10th St.Troops) Co.I
Tingle, James L. GA 32nd Inf. Co.H
Tingle, Jesse S. AL 36th Inf. Co.H
Tingle, J.F. GA 45th Inf. Co.I
Tingle, John D. NC 1st Arty. (10th St.Troops) Co.B
Tingle, John W. NC 3rd Arty. (40th St.Troops) Co.D
Tingle, Joseph B. NC 3rd Arty. (40th St.Troops) Co.D
Tingle, Josiah NC 1st Arty. (10th St.Troops) Co.B
Tingle, Levi W. NC 1st Arty. (10th St.Troops) Co.B
Tingle, McCarroll GA 32nd Inf. Co.H
Tingle, Reuben KY 4th Cav. Co.I Cpl.
Tingle, Reuben KY 5th Mtd.Inf. Co.E
Tingle, Richard H. NC 31st Inf. Co.K Sgt.
Tingle, Roland KY 4th Cav. Co.F,I
Tingle, Roland KY 5th Mtd.Inf. Co.E
Tingle, Samuel KY 4th Cav. Co.A
Tingle, S.W. GA 32nd Inf. Co.H
Tingle, Thomas LA 28th (Gray's) Inf. Co.I
Tingle, Thomas M. AL Lt.Arty. 2nd Bn. Co.F
Tingle, Thomas N. MD 1st Inf. Co.D
Tingle, Thomas N. VA 39th Inf. Co.B Cpl.
Tingle, Thomas N. Eng.,CSA Asst.Eng.
Tingle, T.W. MS 3rd Inf. Co.D
Tingle, W. MD Inf. 2nd Bn. Co.G
Tingle, William VA Inf. 4th Bn.Loc.Def. Co.E Cpl.
Tingle, William D. AL 13th Inf. Co.F
Tingle, William P. AL 62nd Inf. Co.K
Tingle, William P.H. MS 40th Inf. Co.E
Tingle, W.P.H. MS 36th Inf. Co.C
Tingler, Enos VA 25th Inf. 1st Co.F
Tingler, George VA 27th Inf. Co.C Cpl.
Tingler, George W. VA 22nd Inf. Co.A
Tingler, Henry VA 22nd Inf. Co.G
Tingler, H.S. VA 20th Cav. Co.H
Tingler, H.S. VA Horse Arty. Lurty's Co.

Tingler, Jacob VA 10th Bn.Res. Co.C
Tingler, Jacob VA 25th Inf. 1st Co.E, 2nd Co.E
Tingler, James AR 14th (McCarver's) Inf. Co.C
Tingler, James AR 21st Inf. Co.A
Tingler, John C. VA 22nd Inf. Co.C
Tingler, Nelson AR Cav. 1st Bn. (Stirman's) Co.C
Tingler, Richard VA 10th Bn.Res. Co.B
Tingler, S. TN 19th & 20th (Cons.) Cav. Co.C
Tingler, Zebadiah VA 46th Mil. Co.B
Tinin, Ferdinand MO 2nd Cav. Co.F,A 1st Lt.
Tininmon, G.W. AR 32nd Inf. Co.E
Tink, Hugh F. VA 14th Cav. Co.I Sgt.
Tink, W. GA Inf. 27th Bn. (NonConscr.) Co.A
Tinken, C.H. SC 1st Arty. Co.C
Tinker, A. AR 8th Cav. Co.E
Tinker, Benjamin TN 5th (McKenzie's) Cav. Co.A
Tinker, E. MO 15th Cav. Co.B
Tinker, Francis TN 26th Inf. Co.C
Tinker, Francis M. MO 10th Inf. Co.G
Tinker, Henderson GA 21st Inf. Co.H
Tinker, Henderson TN Lt.Arty. Barry's Co.
Tinker, Huston 3rd Conf.Cav. Co.A
Tinker, J.A. MO 12th Inf. Co.H
Tinker, Jacob GA 21st Inf. Co.H
Tinker, James GA Cav. 21st Bn. Co.H
Tinker, James P. NC 64th Inf. Co.K
Tinker, James W. GA 21st Inf. Co.H
Tinker, J.E. 2nd Cherokee Mtd.Vol. Co.F Cpl.
Tinker, Jesse NC 64th Inf. Co.K
Tinker, Jesse TN 3rd (Lillard's) Mtd.Inf. Co.F
Tinker, Jesse TN 19th Inf. Co.B
Tinker, John LA Mil.Conf.Guards Regt. Co.C
Tinker, John 1st Cherokee Mtd.Vol. 1st Co.C
Tinker, John P. NC 64th Inf. Co.K
Tinker, Joseph GA Inf. 18th Bn. (St.Guards) Adam's Co.
Tinker, Nathaniel TN 2nd (Smith's) Cav. Lea's Co.
Tinker, Nathaniel R. AL 9th (Malone's) Cav. Co.I Cpl.
Tinker, Obediah TN 2nd (Smith's) Cav. Lea's Co.
Tinker, Philip NC 64th Inf. Co.K
Tinker, Robert L. TN 19th Inf. Co.B
Tinker, Samuel TN 5th (McKenzie's) Cav. Co.F
Tinker, Smith TN 2nd (Smith's) Cav. Lea's Co.
Tinker, Smith 3rd Conf.Cav. Co.A Cpl.
Tinker, W.C. GA Mtd.Inf. (Pierce Mtd.Vol.) Hendry's Co.
Tinker, William AL 5th Inf. New Co.D
Tinker, William GA 39th Inf. Co.D
Tinker, William MO 10th Inf. Co.G
Tinker, William TX 13th Vol. 2nd Co.D
Tinker, William James TX 20th Cav. Co.D
Tinker, W.J. Brush Bn.
Tinker, W.R. TN 15th Inf. Co.G
Tinkey, Aaron AR 2nd Cav. 1st Co.A Sgt.
Tinkey, Aaron AR Cav. 6th Bn. Co.C Cpl.
Tinkle, C.H. AR 38th Inf. Co.E
Tinkle, George L. TX 19th Inf. Co.H
Tinkle, G.W. AR 38th Inf. Co.E
Tinkle, Jerry B. MS 1st Bn.S.S. Co.A
Tinkle, Jesse MS 25th Inf. Co.I
Tinkle, R.F. TN 15th (Stewart's) Cav. Co.B
Tinkle, R.F. TN 20th (Russell's) Cav. Co.D
Tinkle, R.F. TN 47th Inf. Co.K
Tinkle, Robert MO Cav. Freeman's Regt. Co.A
Tinkle, Robert S. MO 4th Cav. Co.I
Tinkle, Thaddeus AR 3rd Cav. Co.C
Tinkle, T.W. TN 47th Inf. Co.B
Tinkler, D. SC 6th Res. Co.C
Tinkler, Daniel SC 5th St.Troops Co.L
Tinkler, Daniel H. SC 23rd Inf. Co.F
Tinkler, G.S. SC Inf. 3rd Bn. Co.G
Tinkler, James L. TX 19th Cav.
Tinkler, J.C. SC 6th Inf. 1st Co.D, 2nd Co.G Cpl.
Tinkler, J.W. TX 5th Cav. Co.A
Tinkler, Lawrence D. SC Inf. 7th Bn. (Enfield Rifles) Co.H
Tinkler, R.A. SC 6th Inf. 1st Co.D, 2nd Co.G
Tinkler, William SC Inf. 3rd Bn. Co.G
Tinkler, W.J. SC 25th Mil.
Tinkley, J.E. AL 5th Inf. Co.C
Tinler, Charles VA 46th Inf. Co.L
Tinley, Andrew J. VA 45th Inf. Co.C
Tinley, David GA Inf. (Richmond Factory Guards) Barney's Co.
Tinley, David W. GA 48th Inf. Co.I Cpl.
Tinley, James GA 2nd Bn.S.S. Co.C
Tinley, Jesse GA Cav. Allen's Co.
Tinley, Jesse GA Lt.Arty. Fraser's Btty.
Tinley, J.J. GA 2nd Inf. Co.G
Tinley, John GA Cav. Allen's Co.
Tinley, John GA Lt.Arty. Ritter's Co.
Tinley, John GA Inf. 1st Loc.Troops (Augusta) Co.H
Tinley, John MD Arty. 3rd Btty.
Tinley, Joshua J. GA Inf. 2nd Bn. Co.C
Tinley, William W. GA 48th Inf. Co.I
Tinley, W.V. GA 48th Inf. Co.I
Tinley, W.W. GA Lt.Arty. Fraser's Btty.
Tinlin, Edward MO Inf. 1st Bn. Co.C
Tinline, H. VA 1st Res. Co.A
Tin lubbee Choctaw Inf. Wilkins' Co.
Tinly, Mark AL 19th Inf. Co.I
Tinman, E.G. AL 26th (O'Neal's) Inf. Co.H
Tinn, --- Gen. & Staff AASurg.
Tinnel, Francis H. VA 8th Cav. Co.B
Tinnel, Joseph VA 157th Mil. Co.A
Tinnell, Ben F. VA Inf. 23rd Bn. Co.G
Tinnell, Francis M. VA Inf. 23rd Bn. Co.G
Tinnell, J.C. KY Morehead's Regt. (Part. Rangers) Co.C
Tinnell, Joseph VA Arty. Wise Legion
Tinnell, Robert KY 6th Mtd.Inf. Co.D
Tinnell, Winston VA 14th Cav. Co.M
Tinnell, Winston VA Cav. 36th Bn. Co.B
Tinnelle, George C. TX Waul's Legion Co.C
Tinnen, David G. MS 6th Inf. Co.B
Tinnen, H.L. AR 4th St.Inf. Co.C Capt.
Tinnen, J.F. TN 51st (Cons.) Inf. Co.H Cpl.
Tinnen, P.P. AL 8th Inf. Co.C
Tinnen, Thomas D. NC 24th Inf. Co.A
Tinnen, William H. AR 1st Mtd.Rifles Co.E
Tinnen, William N. TN 12th (Green's) Cav. Co.I
Tinner, Allen MO 4th Cav. Co.C
Tinner, Ashley NC 1st Inf. Co.B
Tinner, J.S. MS 8th Inf. Co.D
Tinner, William TX Inf. 1st St.Troops Stevenson's Co.F
Tinner, W.M. TN 12th (Green's) Cav. Co.D
Tinnerly, Patrick NC 6th Inf. Co.A
Tinnery, James M. TN Holman's Bn.Part.Rangers Co.D
Tinney, --- TX Coopwood's Spy Co.
Tinney, A.J. TX 13th Vol. Co.E
Tinney, F.M. VA 25th Inf. 2nd Co.C Cpl.
Tinney, Francis M. VA Inf. 9th Bn. Duffy's Co.C
Tinney, George W. GA Phillips' Legion Co.D
Tinney, Griffin L. TN 34th Inf. Co.D
Tinney, H. GA 1st (Fannin's) Res. Co.K
Tinney, Henry GA Siege Arty. 28th Bn. Co.F
Tinney, Isaac AL 41st Inf. Co.E
Tinney, Jacob TX 4th Cav. Co.A
Tinney, John AR 1st Mtd.Rifles Co.G Cpl.
Tinney, John GA Arty. 9th Bn.
Tinney, John GA 55th Inf. Co.I
Tinney, John TX 3rd Inf. Co.I
Tinney, John VA 1st Arty. Co.F
Tinney, John VA 32nd Inf. Co.G
Tinney, Jordon A. TX Cav. Martin's Regt. Co.K Cpl.
Tinney, Joseph T. AL 42nd Inf. Co.G
Tinney, J.R. AR 19th (Dawson's) Inf. Co.B
Tinney, J.W. 1st Cherokee Mtd.Vol. 1st Co.D
Tinney, M. MS 15th Inf. Co.D
Tinney, O.B. Gen. & Staff AASurg.
Tinney, Oregon B. NC 28th Inf. Co.G
Tinney, R. GA Inf. 25th Bn. (Prov.Guard) Co.D
Tinney, Robert TN 54th Inf. Hollis' Co.
Tinney, Samuel H. TX 1st (Yager's) Cav. Co.F
Tinney, Samuel H. TX 8th Inf. Co.I
Tinney, T.A. 1st Cherokee Mtd.Vol. 1st Co.D
Tinney, Thermon VA Inf. 9th Bn. Duffy's Co.C
Tinney, Thomas AL Cav. 5th Bn. Hilliard's Legion Co.B
Tinney, Thomas A. TX 8th Inf. Co.I Lt.
Tinney, W.C. GA 1st Cav. Co.B
Tinney, W.C. GA 13th Inf. Co.B
Tinney, W.C. VA 21st Inf. Co.F Cpl.
Tinney, W.E. AR 2nd Mtd.Rifles Co.E Cpl.
Tinney, William GA 24th Inf. Co.F
Tinney, William MS 15th Inf. Co.D
Tinney, William C. VA Inf. 5th Bn. Co.C
Tinney, William E. AR 35th Inf. Co.B
Tinney, W.T. GA 1st Cav. Co.B
Tinnille, W.A. Gen. & Staff Capt.,AAG
Tinnin, Alexander M. TX 22nd Cav. Co.F
Tinnin, B.A. MO 7th Cav. Co.I
Tinnin, Benjamin F. MS 10th Inf. Old Co.I
Tinnin, B.F. MS 28th Cav. Co.G
Tinnin, Christopher J. TX Cav. Martin's Regt. Co.K,I
Tinnin, David TX 29th Cav. Co.G
Tinnin, David L. TX 11th Inf. Co.D
Tinnin, Enoch C. TX 19th Cav. Co.G
Tinnin, Ferdinand MO 7th Cav. Co.A 2nd Lt.
Tinnin, H.P. MS Mtd.Inf. (St.Troops) Maxey's Co.
Tinnin, Hugh 1st Cherokee Mtd.Vol. 2nd Co.A Capt.
Tinnin, Jacob W. AR 14th (Powers') Inf. Co.I Sgt.
Tinnin, Jacob W. AR 27th Inf. Co.H
Tinnin, James MO 8th Cav. Reed's Co.
Tinnin, James D. AR 2nd Inf. Co.I 1st Sgt.
Tinnin, James P. MO 7th Cav. Co.I

Tinnin, James Preston 1st Cherokee Mtd.Vol. 2nd Co.A Music.
Tinnin, J.F. MS 2nd Cav. Co.C
Tinnin, J.F. TN 51st Inf. Co.A
Tinnin, J.J. TX 12th Cav. Co.D
Tinnin, Joseph A. NC 31st Inf. Co.E
Tinnin, J.W. AR 27th Inf. QMSgt.
Tinnin, Lawrence W. TX 32nd Cav. Co.G
Tinnin, Robert D. TX 1st Inf. Co.D 2nd Lt.
Tinnin, R.S. TX 12th Cav. Co.D
Tinnin, T.D. NC 1st Jr.Res. Co.I
Tinnin, W.E. TN 18th Inf. Co.B Cpl.
Tinnin, William TX 29th Cav. Co.G
Tinnin, William TX 6th Inf. Co.G
Tinnin, William J. NC 56th Inf. Co.D Sgt.
Tinning, H.P. MS 3rd (St.Troops) Cav. Co.A Sgt.
Tinnison, James LA 13th Inf. Co.A
Tinnon, David AR Lt.Arty. Etter's Btty.
Tinnon, David GA Inf. 25th Bn. (Prov.Guard) Co.A
Tinnon, David Y. GA 5th Inf. Co.F
Tinnon, E. LA 17th Inf. Co.E
Tinnon, James M. MS 33rd Inf. Co.G Capt.
Tinnon, John TN 9th Inf. Co.C
Tinnon, John W. GA 5th Inf. Co.F
Tinnon, John W. GA Inf. 25th Bn. (Prov.Guard) Co.A
Tinnon, Robert TN 3rd (Forrest's) Cav. Co.G
Tinnon, Robert M. TN 3rd (Clack's) Inf. Co.G
Tinnon, Thomas Lawrence GA Inf. (Loc.Def.) Whiteside's Nav.Bn. Co.A Cpl.
Tinnon, T.L. GA Inf. 1st Bn. (St.Guards) Co.B
Tinnon, V.H. GA Lt.Arty. (Arsenal Btty.) Hudson's Co.
Tinnon, W.A. MS Inf. 7th Bn. Cpl.
Tinnon, W.A. TN 19th (Biffle's) Cav. Co.D 1st Lt.
Tinns, William TN 41st Inf. Co.D
Tinny, Addison B. TX 36th Cav. Co.B
Tinny, F.M. TX Cav. Border's Regt. Co.C
Tinny, Griffin TX 36th Cav. Co.B
Tinny, Henry GA 10th Cav. (St.Guards) Co.I
Tinny, Joseph GA 1st Cav. Co.B
Tinny, Wiley C. AL 41st Inf. Co.B,I
Tinon, David Conf.Inf. 1st Bn. 2nd Co.A
Tinon, John W. Conf.Inf. 1st Bn. 2nd Co.A
Tinor, G.B. TN 44th (Cons.) Inf.
Tinsbloom, James S. NC 3rd Bn.Sr.Res. Co.C
Tinsbloom, John VA 55th Inf. Co.D
Tinsbloom, John L. VA 55th Inf. Co.F
Tinsbloom, Thomas TN 7th Inf. Co.K
Tinsbloom, William VA 55th Inf. Co.D
Tinsdale, H.M. Hosp.Stew.
Tin shin na 1st Creek Mtd.Vol. Co.E
Tinsin, --- TX 1st (McCulloch's) Cav. Co.A
Tinsler, H.C. LA 1st (Nelligan's) Inf. Co.K
Tinsley, Abner R. VA 58th Inf. Co.C
Tinsley, A.D. TX Inf. 2nd St.Troops Surg.
Tinsley, A.D. VA 74th Mil. Co.E Cpl.
Tinsley, Adolphus VA Cav. 40th Bn. Co.A
Tinsley, A.G. MS 5th Inf. (St.Troops) Co.I
Tinsley, Alex VA 16th Inf. Asst.Surg.
Tinsley, Alexander Gen. & Staff Asst.Surg.
Tinsley, Alfred VA Inf. 25th Bn. Co.E
Tinsley, Alfred H. VA 38th Inf. Co.D
Tinsley, Andrew J. GA 6th Inf. Co.D
Tinsley, Andrew J. GA 53rd Inf. Co.K
Tinsley, A.R. GA 8th Inf. Co.B
Tinsley, A.R. GA 8th Inf. (St.Guards) Co.I Cpl.
Tinsley, A.R. GA Conscr.
Tinsley, Asa B. GA 44th Inf. Co.G
Tinsley, Augustine Wood AL 4th Inf. Co.D
Tinsley, Augustus VA Cav. 34th Bn. Co.B
Tinsley, Augustus VA Cav. 36th Bn. Co.C
Tinsley, A. Wood VA 4th Cav. Co.C
Tinsley, B. MS 1st (Patton's) Inf. Co.E
Tinsley, B.A. SC 16th Inf. Co.G Cpl.
Tinsley, Benjamin VA Cav. Hounshell's Bn. Gwinn's Co.
Tinsley, Benjamin F. MS 9th Inf. Old Co.E
Tinsley, B.F. MS 2nd Part. Co.A
Tinsley, B.F. MS 18th Cav. Co.F
Tinsley, B.F. MS 1st (Patton's) Inf. Co.I Cpl.
Tinsley, Burrell MS 35th Inf. Co.A
Tinsley, Burrell W. TN 14th Inf. Co.B
Tinsley, C. AL 63rd Inf. Co.E
Tinsley, Calvin SC 13th Inf. Co.F Cpl.
Tinsley, C.B. AL 5th Inf.
Tinsley, C.C. KY Lt.Arty. Cobb's Co.
Tinsley, C.C. VA 2nd St.Res. Co.F Jr.2nd Lt.
Tinsley, C.D. SC 5th St.Troops Co.D
Tinsley, C.D. VA 53rd Inf. Co.D
Tinsley, Cephas VA 74th Mil. Co.C 1st Sgt.
Tinsley, Charles AR 30th Inf. Co.F
Tinsley, Charles SC 1st Arty. Co.G
Tinsley, Charles A. VA Courtney Arty.
Tinsley, Charles A. VA Lt.Arty. Weisiger's Co.
Tinsley, Charles A. VA 16th Inf. Co.I
Tinsley, Charles B. MS 13th Inf. Co.C
Tinsley, Christopher C. KY 4th Mtd.Inf. Co.A
Tinsley, Clement C. VA 1st Inf. Co.I Sgt.
Tinsley, Clifford N. VA 2nd Cav. Co.E Sgt.
Tinsley, C.N. TN 8th Inf. Co.G
Tinsley, Cornelius D. VA Inf. 5th Bn. Co.C
Tinsley, C.T. VA 1st (Farinholt's) Res. Co.H
Tinsley, David C. VA 2nd Cav. Co.E
Tinsley, David H. NC 1st Inf. Co.B
Tinsley, D.C. AR 24th Inf. Co.A
Tinsley, Dedwood KY 9th Mtd.Inf. Co.C
Tinsley, E. SC 1st Arty. Co.D
Tinsley, Eber SC 13th Inf. Co.F,C
Tinsley, Edward M. VA Hvy.Arty. 20th Bn. Co.D
Tinsley, Edward M. VA 51st Inf. Co.G
Tinsley, Elijah SC 3rd Res. Co.G
Tinsley, F.G. MS 6th Cav. Co.G
Tinsley, F.J. MS 1st (Patton's) Inf. Co.I
Tinsley, F.J. MS 5th Inf. (St.Troops) Co.I 1st Lt.
Tinsley, Fountain G. TX 36th Cav. Co.G
Tinsley, F.P. VA 3rd (Chrisman's) Bn.Res. Co.E
Tinsley, Francis A. NC 6th Cav. (65th St.Troops) Co.E
Tinsley, Frank A. NC Cav. 7th Bn. Co.D,E
Tinsley, George SC 1st St.Troops Co.H
Tinsley, George F. KY 2nd Cav. Co.F
Tinsley, George F. VA 2nd Cav. Co.E
Tinsley, George M. VA 3rd Res. Co.A
Tinsley, George R. VA 52nd Inf. Co.E
Tinsley, George W. VA 38th Inf. 2nd Co.I
Tinsley, G.F. GA 31st Inf. Co.B
Tinsley, Golden MS 10th Inf. New Co.A
Tinsley, G.P. TN 12th Inf. Co.A
Tinsley, G.P. TN 12th (Cons.) Inf. Co.A Cpl.
Tinsley, Green P. TN 19th & 20th (Cons.) Cav. Co.K 2nd Lt.
Tinsley, Griffin C. LA 8th Cav. Co.E Sgt.
Tinsley, G.S. NC 62nd Inf. Co.K
Tinsley, G.W. AR 8th Cav. Co.D
Tinsley, H. VA 14th Inf. Co.C
Tinsley, H.B. TN 4th (McLemore's) Cav. Co.D
Tinsley, H.B. VA 28th Inf. Co.F
Tinsley, H.C. MO Cav. Williams' Regt. Co.F Sgt.
Tinsley, H.C. VA Inf. 26th Bn. Co.F
Tinsley, Henry VA 6th Cav. Co.I
Tinsley, Henry C. VA 1st Arty. Co.D Sgt.
Tinsley, Henry G. MS 35th Inf. Co.A
Tinsley, H.G. TN 4th (Murray's) Cav. Co.D
Tinsley, H.G. 1st Conf.Cav. 2nd Co.C
Tinsley, H.L. SC 18th Inf. Co.C
Tinsley, Homer VA 14th Inf. Co.B
Tinsley, Howard GA 4th Inf. AQM
Tinsley, Howard GA Cook's Brig. Capt.,AQM
Tinsley, I.N. GA 18th Inf. Co.A Cpl.
Tinsley, Ira SC 1st Arty. Co.B
Tinsley, Isaac AL 55th Vol. Co.C
Tinsley, Isaac GA Cherokee Legion (St.Guards) Co.K
Tinsley, Isaac VA 14th Cav. 1st Co.F
Tinsley, Isaac VA Cav. 36th Bn. Co.E
Tinsley, Isaac VA Inf. 1st Bn. Co.C
Tinsley, Isaac VA 22nd Inf. Swann's Co.
Tinsley, Isaac VA 59th Inf. 2nd Co.K
Tinsley, Isaac D. VA Hvy.Arty. 19th Bn. Co.D
Tinsley, Isaac D. VA 13th Inf. 2nd Co.E
Tinsley, J. TN 8th Inf. Co.A
Tinsley, J. VA 46th Inf. Co.E
Tinsley, J.A. MO Lt.Arty. Barret's Co.
Tinsley, James SC Lt.Arty. 3rd (Palmetto) Bn. Co.H
Tinsley, James SC 1st (Butler's) Inf. Co.I
Tinsley, James SC 5th Inf. 1st Co.K
Tinsley, James SC 5th St.Troops Co.G 2nd Lt.
Tinsley, James SC 7th Res. Co.A Cpl.
Tinsley, James SC 16th Inf. Co.G
Tinsley, James SC Cav.Bn. Holcombe Legion Co.D
Tinsley, James TX 29th Cav. Co.D
Tinsley, James VA 11th Cav. Co.F
Tinsley, James VA Hvy.Arty. 10th Bn. Co.C
Tinsley, James VA Hvy.Arty. 19th Bn. Co.D
Tinsley, James A. MO 3rd Inf. Co.K 1st Lt.
Tinsley, James C. VA 54th Inf. Co.E
Tinsley, James E. AL 31st Inf. Co.A
Tinsley, James G. MS 35th Inf. Co.A
Tinsley, James G. VA 1st Arty. Co.K
Tinsley, James G. VA Arty. L.F. Jones' Co.
Tinsley, James K.P. SC Inf. Holcombe Legion Co.C
Tinsley, James L. TX 9th Cav. Co.A
Tinsley, James W. AL 6th Cav. Co.A 1st Cpl.
Tinsley, James W. VA 7th Inf. Co.C
Tinsley, J.B. TN 3rd (Forrest's) Cav. Co.B
Tinsley, J.B., Jr. VA 3rd Inf.Loc.Def. Co.A
Tinsley, J.C. SC Lt.Arty. Jeter's Co. (Macbeth Lt.Arty.)
Tinsley, J.D. VA 3rd Res. Co.A
Tinsley, Jeff M. GA 3rd Inf. Co.A

Tinsly, George SC 3rd Res. Co.D
Tinsly, J.M. VA 42nd Inf. Co.K Cpl.
Tinsly, John C. GA 12th Mil.
Tinsly, W.T. SC 9th Res. Co.B
Tinsman, Francis M. VA 8th Inf. Co.F Sgt.
Tinsman, John M. VA 8th Inf. Co.F
Tinsman, Lud VA 122nd Mil. Co.C
Tinsman, Samuel VA 27th Inf. 1st Co.H
Tinson, H. AR 6th Inf. Co.I
Tinson, Jacob K. VA 6th Cav. Co.K
Tinthicum, H.W. AR Cav. McGehee's Regt. Co.B 1st Sgt.
Tintlenot, Henry AL 2nd Cav. Co.B
Tio, Clement F. LA 30th Inf. Co.D
Tiomey, Thomas LA Mil. Chalmette Regt. Co.C
Tipens, Pleasant SC 3rd Res. Co.E
Tipet, Isham 1st Conf.Cav. 1st Co.D
Tipett, P. KY 8th Mtd.Inf. Co.A
Tipett, Simeon R. LA 28th (Gray's) Inf. Co.H
Tipett, William J. LA 28th (Gray's) Inf. Co.H
Tipkey, Charles 1st Creek Mtd.Vol. Co.M 1st Sgt.
Tipko, Henry AR 1st (Colquitt's) Inf. Co.I,K
Tipler, T.D. MS 7th Cav. Co.B
Tipler, Washington MS 7th Cav. 1st Co.H,G 2nd Lt.
Tipmos, S.J. GA 28th Inf. Co.E
Tipp, W. TX Cav. Hardeman's Regt. Co.D
Tipped, Mathews MO Cav. Jackman's Regt. Co.I,D
Tippen, D.J. GA 7th Inf. (St.Guards) Co.C Sgt.
Tippen, George McD. LA 28th (Gray's) Inf. Co.F 3rd Lt.
Tippen, George W. GA Cherokee Legion (St.Guards) Co.D
Tippen, G.W. GA Phillips' Legion Co.E
Tippen, James W. GA Phillips' Legion Co.C,I
Tippen, John M. GA Cherokee Legion (St.Guards) Co.C
Tippen, William GA Cherokee Legion (St.Guards) Co.C
Tippen, William MO Inf. 2nd Regt.St.Guard Col.
Tippens, A.C. GA Inf. Alexander's Co.
Tippens, James G. TX 1st Inf. Co.H
Tippens, James T. GA 50th Inf. Co.A
Tippens, P. SC Rutledge Mtd.Riflemen & Horse Arty. Trenholm's Co.
Tippens, Pleasant SC 1st St.Troops Co.H
Tippens, Silas GA 36th (Broyles') Inf. Co.D
Tippens, W.H. LA 1st Cav. Robinson's Co.
Tippens, William AL 54th Inf. Co.I
Tippens, W.W. GA 41st Inf. Co.K,C
Tipper, A. LA Mil. 4th Regt.Eur.Brig. Co.D Cpl.
Tipper, James AL 56th Part.Rangers Co.G
Tipper, John W. GA 20th Inf. Co.B
Tipper, J.W. AL 13th Bn.Part.Rangers Co.C
Tipper, William AR 15th (Josey's) Inf. Co.E
Tipperer, C.R. GA 5th Inf.
Tippet, George F. MS 1st Cav.Res. Co.A
Tippet, G.W. MO Inf. 4th Regt.St.Guard Co.A
Tippet, J.F.M. GA Inf. 5th Bn. (St.Guards) Co.E
Tippet, J.F.M. 10th Conf.Cav. Co.G
Tippet, J.H. MO Cav. Slayback's Regt. Co.I Lt.
Tippet, Joseph MS 37th Inf. Co.K
Tippet, L.M. NC 1st Inf. Co.I
Tippet, Matthew N. NC 24th Inf. Co.K
Tippet, Morrow Virgil TX 20th Cav. Co.D
Tippet, M.T. TN 49th Inf. Co.H
Tippet, Simon R. LA 18th (Gray's) Inf. Co.H
Tippet, W.C. TN 28th (Cons.) Inf. Co.C
Tippet, W.H. LA Cav. Nutt's Co. (Red River Rangers)
Tippet, William NC 28th Inf. Co.E Cpl.
Tippet, William C. TN 28th Inf. Co.K
Tippet, William H. AL 47th Inf. Co.B
Tippet, William J. GA 18th Inf. Co.I
Tippet, W.L. TN Lt.Arty. Phillips' Co.
Tippett, Abner NC 3rd Arty. (40th St.Troops) Co.K
Tippett, C.C. KY 10th (Johnson's) Cav. Co.A
Tippett, Daniel NC 44th Inf. Co.A
Tippett, D.F. NC 14th Inf. Co.D
Tippett, Francis M. AL 47th Inf. Co.B
Tippett, George W. MD 1st Inf. Co.C
Tippett, Henry KY 7th Mtd.Inf. Co.B
Tippett, Henry J. MO 3rd Cav. Co.A
Tippett, Hesekiah NC 6th Cav. (65th St.Troops) Co.E,A
Tippett, Hezekiah NC Cav. 7th Bn. Co.A
Tippett, H.M. TX 33rd Cav. Co.D
Tippett, H.M. TX St.Troops Hampton's Co.
Tippett, James B. MD 1st Inf. 2nd Co.H
Tippett, James F. AL 47th Inf. Co.B
Tippett, James L. MS 8th Inf. Co.K
Tippett, J.B. GA 50th Inf. Co.D Sgt.
Tippett, J.D. NC 39th Inf. Co.B
Tippett, J.H. KY 10th (Johnson's) Cav. Co.A
Tippett, J.M. AL 17th Inf. Co.K
Tippett, John TN 35th Inf. Co.E
Tippett, John H. VA 6th Cav. Co.K
Tippett, Jonathan NC 21st Inf. Co.A
Tippett, Jones KY 8th Cav.
Tippett, Josias MO Lt.Arty. 3rd Btty. 1st Sgt.
Tippett, J.W. GA 8th Cav. Old Co.D
Tippett, J.W. GA 62nd Cav. Co.D
Tippett, Leeandus A. AR 27th Inf. Co.K
Tippett, M.A.K. MD 1st Cav. Co.B
Tippett, Mathew AR 27th Inf. Co.K
Tippett, R. TX St.Troops Hampton's Co.
Tippett, Robert D. TX 4th Cav. Co.C
Tippett, Robert F. MO Searcy's Bn.S.S. Co.F
Tippett, Seburn T. TX 17th Cav. Co.F Sgt.
Tippett, Simeon NC 21st Inf. Co.A
Tippett, S.T. TX 17th Cons.Dismtd.Cav. Co.F
Tippett, Thomas E. VA Cav. 35th Bn. Co.A
Tippett, Travis NC 48th Inf. Co.B
Tippett, William TX 10th Cav. Co.B
Tippett, William T. NC 39th Inf. Co.B Sgt.
Tippett, W.Y. MO Inf. 4th Regt.St.Guard Co.A 3rd Lt.
Tippetts, J.M.P. TN 20th Inf. Co.D
Tippin, Benjamin SC 13th Inf. Co.B
Tippin, E.A. AL Gid Nelson Lt.Arty.
Tippin, G.M.D. LA 13th Bn. (Part.Rangers) Co.E
Tippin, J. GA 32nd Inf. Co.I
Tippin, J.B. GA 3rd Bn. (St.Guards) Co.E
Tippin, Mathew T. TX 21st Cav. Co.K Sgt.
Tipping, James VA 3rd Bn. Valley Res. Co.B
Tipping, W.H. TX 11th Cav. Co.E
Tippings, Robert J. TX 27th Cav. Co.H
Tippings, T.S. SC 17th Inf. Co.F
Tippins, A. AL 48th Inf. Co.E,C
Tippins, A.C. FL 1st Inf. New Co.H 1st Lt.
Tippins, B.B. MS 16th Inf. Co.H
Tippins, D. GA Inf. 4th Bn. (St.Guards) Co.B
Tippins, Damarcus GA 11th Cav. Co.D
Tippins, D.W. FL 1st Inf. New Co.H 2nd Lt.
Tippins, George TX Vol. Rainey's Co.
Tippins, George W.C. 1st Conf.Inf. 2nd Co.H
Tippins, James J. GA 43rd Inf. Co.I
Tippins, J.E. FL 1st Inf. New Co.H Cpl.
Tippins, J.G. TX Vol. Rainey's Co.
Tippins, J.J. GA Inf. 25th Bn. (Prov.Guard) Co.B
Tippins, J.J. GA 64th Inf. Co.B Sgt.
Tippins, John B. GA 43rd Inf. Co.B
Tippins, John W. GA 47th Inf. Co.G
Tippins, J.U. GA Cav. 1st Bn. Walthour's Co.
Tippins, Lavitus GA 11th Cav. Co.D
Tippins, Lusius A.H. GA 47th Inf. Co.G
Tippins, P. SC 16th Inf. Co.F
Tippins, P.G. GA Cav. 20th Bn. Co.B
Tippins, Philip GA 54th Inf. Co.K,F
Tippins, Philip G. GA 47th Inf. Co.G Capt.
Tippins, Phillip P. GA 1st Reg. Co.H
Tippins, P.H.M. FL 1st Inf. New Co.H 1st Sgt.
Tippins, V. GA Inf. 4th Bn. (St.Guards) Co.B
Tippins, W. GA Inf. 4th Bn. (St.Guards) Co.B
Tippins, W.E. GA Cav. 1st Bn. Walthour's Co.
Tippins, W.H. TN Arty. Ramsey's Btty.
Tippins, William H. GA 1st Reg. Co.E
Tippit, A.B. LA 27th Inf. Co.E
Tippit, Andrew J. LA 28th (Gray's) Inf. Co.D Sgt.
Tippit, E.J. LA 27th Inf. Co.E
Tippit, Elisha H. LA 12th Inf. Co.B
Tippit, George F. TN Arty. Marshall's Co.
Tippit, James L. MS 27th Inf. Co.B
Tippit, John W. LA 12th Inf. Co.B
Tippit, L.B. LA 27th Inf. Co.E
Tippit, Thomas NC 21st Inf. Co.L
Tippit, William J. MS 8th Inf. Co.K
Tippit, William L. LA 1st Hvy.Arty. (Reg.) Co.H Cpl.
Tippit, William T. LA 12th Inf. Co.B
Tippit, W.J. MS 27th Inf. Co.B
Tippitt, E.S. TN 51st (Cons.) Inf. Co.A
Tippitt, J.A. LA 17th Inf. Co.H
Tippitt, James R. LA 9th Inf. Co.A
Tippitt, J.C. TN 51st (Cons.) Inf. Co.A
Tippitt, J.F.M. GA Cav. 19th Bn. Co.B
Tippitt, J.L. MS 29th Inf. Co.B
Tippitt, John F. MO Searcy's Bn.S.S. Co.F
Tippitt, J.P. TN 8th (Smith's) Cav. Co.A
Tippitt, Lott W. NC 3rd Inf. Co.E Sgt.
Tippitt, William L. LA 9th Inf. Co.A
Tippitt, W.J. GA 45th Inf. Co.C Sgt.
Tipps, Barny M. TN 37th Inf. Co.D Sgt.
Tipps, C. TX Cav. Morgan's Regt.
Tipps, C.C. TX 11th Inf. Co.B
Tipps, C.C. Morgan's Co.B,CSA
Tipps, Dudley TN 17th Inf. Co.E
Tipps, G. TN 17th Inf. Co.E
Tipps, George L. TN 34th Inf. 2nd Co.C Cpl.
Tipps, George S. TN 41st Inf. Co.G 2nd Lt.
Tipps, George W. TN 41st Inf. Co.G Cpl.
Tipps, G.H. TN 17th Inf. Co.E
Tipps, Jacob TN 17th Inf. Co.E Sgt.

Tipps, Jacob S. TX 11th Inf. Co.B Capt.
Tipps, James C. TN 41st Inf. Co.G
Tipps, J.F. TN 17th Inf. Co.E Sgt.
Tipps, J.F. TN 34th Inf. 2nd Co.C
Tipps, J.N. TN 17th Inf. Co.E
Tipps, John TN 41st Inf. Co.G
Tipps, John F. TN 41st Inf. Co.G
Tipps, Leander TN 34th Inf. 2nd Co.C
Tipps, Mike TN 17th Inf. Co.E
Tipps, Thomas J. TN 41st Inf. Co.G 3rd Lt.
Tipps, W.C. TN 17th Inf. Co.E Sgt.
Tipps, William J. TN 41st Inf. Co.G
Tipps, W.P. TN 35th Inf. Co.L Ch.Music.
Tipps, W.P. TN 36th Inf. Co.L Drum.
Tippun, --- TX Cav. 4th Regt.St.Troops Co.I
Tippy, John KY 7th Mtd.Inf. Co.F
Tips, G. TX Lt.Arty. Dege's Bn. Co.D Artif.
Tips, Gustav TX 8th Field Btty. Artif.
Tips, Gustav H. TX 1st (McCulloch's) Cav. Co.B
Tips, W. TX Lt.Arty. Dege's Bn. Sgt.
Tips, Walter TX 6th Field Btty. 2nd Lt.
Tips, W.P. TN Inf. 3rd Cons.Regt. Co.A
Tipson, Lotwick TN 37th Inf. Co.I
Tiptin, A.H. 3rd Conf.Cav. Co.E
Tiptin, Edward 3rd Conf.Cav. Co.E
Tiptin, George TN 59th Mtd.Inf. Co.F
Tipton, --- AL 50th Inf. Sgt.
Tipton, --- GA 2nd Bn.Troops & Defences (Macon) Co.C
Tipton, A.A. TX 28th Cav. Co.B
Tipton, A.B. TN 63rd Inf. Co.D
Tipton, Abe TX Cav. McCord's Frontier Regt. Co.I
Tipton, A.C. LA 8th Cav. Co.I
Tipton, A.D. NC 64th Inf. Co.K
Tipton, A.J. NC 1st Cav. (9th St.Troops) Co.K
Tipton, Alfred GA 1st Reg. Co.H,G
Tipton, Andrew A. TX 17th Cav. 1st Co.I
Tipton, Andrew J. AL 50th Inf. Co.C Sgt.
Tipton, Benjamin AR 27th Inf. Co.I
Tipton, Benjamin NC 64th Inf. Co.K
Tipton, Benjamin TN 59th Mtd.Inf. Co.I
Tipton, B.F. NC 18th Inf. Co.F
Tipton, Bradford Mead's Conf.Cav. Co.C
Tipton, B.W. AL 56th Part.Rangers Co.I
Tipton, B.W. AL 55th Vol. Co.I
Tipton, Calvin LA 28th (Gray's) Inf. Co.B
Tipton, C.C. GA 60th Inf. Co.I,C
Tipton, Charles TN 22nd Inf. Co.I Sgt.
Tipton, Charles G. FL 11th Inf. Co.F Sgt.
Tipton, C.J. AL 4th (Russell's) Cav. Co.K
Tipton, C.J. TN 3rd (Forrest's) Cav. 1st Co.F
Tipton, David GA 6th Cav. Co.K
Tipton, David NC 29th St.Troops Co.G
Tipton, David Mc. NC 58th Inf. Co.B
Tipton, D.B. TN 8th (Smith's) Cav. Co.A
Tipton, D.B. TN 34th Inf. Co.K
Tipton, D.C. GA 11th Inf. Co.F
Tipton, D. Jasper AL 26th Inf. Co.D
Tipton, D.J.D. MO St.Guard Lt.
Tipton, D.L. TN 15th Inf. Co.E Cpl.
Tipton, E. Benjamin AL 4th (Russell's) Cav. Co.C
Tipton, Edmond TN 26th Inf. Co.F
Tipton, Edward C. NC 1st Inf.
Tipton, Electus MO 1st N.E. Cav. Co.F
Tipton, Eli TX 20th Inf. Co.E
Tipton, Ellridge L. TN 37th Inf. Co.F 2nd Lt.
Tipton, E.M. TX 20th Inf. Co.H
Tipton, Emberson L. 1st Conf.Inf. 2nd Co.E
Tipton, Emory VA 64th Mtd.Inf. Co.C
Tipton, Enoch C. AL 19th Inf. Co.H
Tipton, Esrom MO Cav. Snider's Bn. Co.B
Tipton, Evan VA 50th Inf. Co.I
Tipton, F. AL 1st Bn.Cadets Co.B
Tipton, Frank TX Inf. Rutherford's Co.
Tipton, George AR 11th & 17th Cons.Inf. Co.I
Tipton, George KY 2nd (Duke's) Cav. Co.F
Tipton, George A. TN 19th Inf. Co.G Sgt.
Tipton, George W. AR 17th (Griffith's) Inf. Co.F
Tipton, George W. KY 7th Cav. Co.B
Tipton, George W. TX 17th Cav. 1st Co.I
Tipton, G.L. TN 63rd Inf. Co.D
Tipton, G.W. AR 34th Inf. Co.I
Tipton, G.W. GA 60th Inf. Co.C
Tipton, G.W. TX 28th Cav. Co.B
Tipton, H. AL 35th Inf. Co.F
Tipton, Harvy GA 11th Inf. Co.G
Tipton, H.B. Mead's Conf.Cav. Co.C
Tipton, H.C. MS 10th Inf. New Co.A Hosp.Stew.
Tipton, H.D. TN 34th Inf. Co.K Capt.
Tipton, Henry MS 9th Inf. Hosp.Stew.
Tipton, Henry C. TX 12th Cav. Co.C
Tipton, Hiram LA 28th (Gray's) Inf. Co.F
Tipton, Isaac TX 18th Inf. Co.G
Tipton, Isaiah FL 1st Inf. Old Co.D,H
Tipton, Isaiah FL 5th Inf. Co.C
Tipton, Isham TX 15th Inf. Co.A Jr.2nd Lt.
Tipton, J. VA 23rd Cav. Co.D
Tipton, J.A. MS Cav. Davenport's Bn. (St.Troops) Co.B
Tipton, Jackson GA 11th Inf. Co.D
Tipton, Jacob NC 39th Inf. Co.E
Tipton, Jacob NC 58th Inf. Co.G
Tipton, Jacob NC Inf. Thomas Legion
Tipton, Jacob VA 8th Bn.Res. Co.A
Tipton, Jacob VA 64th Mtd.Inf. Co.C
Tipton, Jacob E. TX 7th Cav. Co.F
Tipton, Jacob J. TN 59th Mtd.Inf. Co.A
Tipton, Jacob R. VA 23rd Cav. Co.D
Tipton, James AR 11th & 17th Cons.Inf. Co.I Cpl.
Tipton, James VA 4th Res. Co.E,G
Tipton, James VA 64th Mtd.Inf. Co.C
Tipton, James J. AL Nitre & Min. Corps Young's Co.
Tipton, James M. AR 17th (Griffith's) Inf. Co.F Cpl.
Tipton, James M. TN 26th Inf. Co.K 2nd Lt.
Tipton, Jason V. FL 5th Inf. Co.I
Tipton, J.C. TN 2nd (Ashby's) Cav. Co.K
Tipton, J.C. TN Cav. 5th Bn. (McClellan's) Co.E
Tipton, J.C. TN 15th (Cons.) Cav. Co.F
Tipton, Jerry MO 1st N.E. Cav. Co.F
Tipton, J.F. AL 26th Inf. Co.C
Tipton, J.F. TN 18th Inf. Co.K 1st Sgt.
Tipton, J.G. KY 2nd (Duke's) Cav. Co.B
Tipton, J.G. TN 34th Inf. Co.K Cpl.
Tipton, J.H. AL Cav. Lewis' Bn. Co.C
Tipton, J.H. AR 15th (Johnson's) Inf. Co.C
Tipton, J.H. Mead's Conf.Cav. Co.C
Tipton, J.J. Mead's Conf.Cav. Co.A 1st Sgt.
Tipton, J.L. TN 5th (McKenzie's) Cav. Co.H
Tipton, J.M. AL 25th Inf. Co.F Cpl.
Tipton, J.M. AR 34th Inf. Co.I
Tipton, J.N. TN 18th Inf. Co.K
Tipton, John AL 4th (Russell's) Cav. Co.K
Tipton, John AL Inf. 2nd Regt. Co.K
Tipton, John AL 18th Inf. Co.F
Tipton, John KY 2nd (Duke's) Cav. Co.F
Tipton, John MS 32nd Inf. Co.K
Tipton, John NC 58th Inf. Co.G 1st Lt.
Tipton, John TN 3rd (Forrest's) Cav. 1st Co.F
Tipton, John TX 20th Inf. Co.F
Tipton, John A. TN 19th Inf. Co.G
Tipton, John B. AL 19th Inf. Co.B
Tipton, John C. GA 11th Inf. Co.D
Tipton, John C. VA 50th Inf. Co.H
Tipton, John D. NC 58th Inf. Co.G Cpl.
Tipton, John E. TX 12th Cav. Co.C
Tipton, John H. MS 26th Inf. Co.H
Tipton, John S. GA 5th Inf.
Tipton, John S. GA 51st Inf. Co.D
Tipton, John S. LA 12th Inf. Co.H
Tipton, John S. MO 1st N.E. Cav.
Tipton, John T. MS 9th Inf. Old Co.E
Tipton, John T. MO 5th Inf. Co.H
Tipton, John W. TX 20th Inf. Co.H
Tipton, Jonathan NC 58th Inf. Co.G
Tipton, Joseph AR 31st Inf. Co.G
Tipton, Joseph TN 3rd (Clack's) Inf.
Tipton, Joseph TN 15th Inf. Co.E Ord.Sgt.
Tipton, Joseph TN 59th Mtd.Inf. Co.I Sgt.
Tipton, Joseph S. VA 24th Inf. Co.C
Tipton, J.P. AL Inf. 2nd Regt. Co.K
Tipton, J.T. MS 10th Inf. New Co.A
Tipton, J.W. AL 2nd Cav. Co.F
Tipton, J.W. AR 1st (Dobbin's) Cav. Co.F
Tipton, J.W. MS 6th Cav. Co.C
Tipton, Lafayette AL 4th (Russell's) Cav. Co.C
Tipton, LaFayette AL Inf. 2nd Regt. Co.K
Tipton, L.C. AR 30th Inf. Co.C
Tipton, L.D. TX 29th Cav. Co.H
Tipton, Lorenzo D. TN 36th Inf. Co.D
Tipton, L.W. NC 64th Inf. Co.K
Tipton, M. TX Cav. Waller's Regt. Goode's Co.
Tipton, Marion NC 64th Inf. Co.L
Tipton, M.D. TX 20th Inf. Co.H
Tipton, Oliver H. TX Cav. Martin's Regt. Co.I
Tipton, P. AR Cav. 6th Bn. Co.E
Tipton, Pleas TN 7th (Duckworth's) Cav. Co.H
Tipton, Pleas TN 15th (Cons.) Cav. Co.F
Tipton, Pleas TN Cav. Nixon's Regt. Co.A
Tipton, Pleas TN 4th Inf. Co.K Cpl.
Tipton, Pleasant M. TX 31st Cav. Co.B
Tipton, Q.A. TN 15th (Cons.) Cav. Co.C Cpl.
Tipton, R. AL Mil. 4th Vol. Co.G Sgt.
Tipton, R. AR 1st (Dobbin's) Cav. Co.F Cpl.
Tipton, Randolph C. GA 57th Inf. Co.A
Tipton, Reuben MO 1st Inf. Co.G
Tipton, Reuben NC 64th Inf. Co.K
Tipton, Reubin AR 1st (Dobbin's) Cav. Co.B
Tipton, R.H. TN 15th Inf. Co.E Sgt.
Tipton, Richard AL 4th Cav. Co.K
Tipton, R.M. GA 2nd Inf. Co.D
Tipton, Robert J. TN 19th Inf. Co.B 1st Lt.
Tipton, Rufus M. VA 37th Inf. Co.H
Tipton, S. MS 6th Cav. Co.B

Tipton, S. MS Cav. Davenport's Bn. (St.Troops) Co.A
Tipton, Samuel MO 5th Inf. Co.H,G
Tipton, Samuel NC Cav. 7th Bn. Co.C
Tipton, Samuel NC 39th Inf. Co.H
Tipton, Samuel NC Walker's Bn. Thomas' Legion Co.H
Tipton, Samuel H. MO 4th Cav. Co.I
Tipton, Samuel Houston TX 15th Cav. Co.F Cpl.
Tipton, Samuel J. AL 19th Inf. Co.H,I Cpl.
Tipton, Samuel P. MS 10th Inf. New Co.A
Tipton, Sanders NC 64th Inf. Co.K
Tipton, S.B. MO 11th Inf. Co.I
Tipton, S.C. AL 48th Inf. Co.D
Tipton, Seaborn GA 3rd Res. Co.B
Tipton, Sebron NC 29th Inf. Co.G
Tipton, S.H. MO Inf. Winston's Regt. Co.A
Tipton, S.H. TX Granbury's Cons.Brig. Co.F Cpl.
Tipton, Shadrac L. MS St.Cav. Perrin's Bn. Co.G
Tipton, Sherman C.T. AL 19th Inf. Co.B
Tipton, Simeon AL 18th Inf. Co.F
Tipton, S.L. TN 34th Inf. Co.K
Tipton, S.P. GA 39th Inf. Co.K
Tipton, S.S. MS Inf. 2nd St.Troops Co.G
Tipton, Steven NC 64th Inf. Co.K
Tipton, Sumill NC 6th Cav. (65th St.Troops) Co.C
Tipton, Temple H. AL May's Home Guards
Tipton, Thomas GA 14th Inf. Co.G
Tipton, Thomas MO 4th Cav. Co.I
Tipton, Thomas NC 64th Inf. Co.A
Tipton, Thomas TN 19th Inf. Co.B
Tipton, Thomas G. NC 58th Inf. Co.G,B Cpl.
Tipton, Thomas J. GA 39th Inf.
Tipton, Thomas J. MS 18th Inf. Co.A
Tipton, Thomas J. MO 16th Inf. Co.B
Tipton, Thomas J. TX 28th Cav. Co.I
Tipton, T.J. GA Cav. 6th Bn. (St.Guards) Co.B
Tipton, T.J. MO Inf. Winston's Regt. Co.A
Tipton, T.J. TN 34th Inf. Co.K Cpl.
Tipton, T.J. TX 18th Inf. Co.G
Tipton, T.S. TX Cav. Bourland's Regt. Co.E
Tipton, T.T. AL 35th Inf. Co.F
Tipton, T.T. TN 34th Inf. Co.K
Tipton, Valentine NC 16th Inf. Co.C
Tipton, W. AL 35th Inf. Co.F Sgt.
Tipton, W. KY 3rd Bn.Mtd.Rifles Co.B
Tipton, W.A. AL 30th Inf. Co.C
Tipton, W.B. TN 22nd Inf. Co.I Cpl.
Tipton, W.B. Gen. & Staff 1st Lt.,ADC
Tipton, W.E. TX 17th Cons.Dismtd.Cav. Co.B
Tipton, W.E. TX 12th Inf. Co.E
Tipton, W.H. TN 2nd (Ashby's) Cav. Co.K 2nd Lt.
Tipton, W.H. TN Cav. 5th Bn. (McClellan's) Co.E
Tipton, Wilburn NC 16th Inf. Co.C
Tipton, Wiley NC Walker's Bn. Thomas' Legion Co.B
Tipton, Wiley VA 51st Inf. Co.A
Tipton, William AR 17th (Griffith's) Inf. Co.F
Tipton, William AR 38th Inf. Co.A
Tipton, William GA 39th Inf. Co.I
Tipton, William MS 12th Cav. Co.E
Tipton, William MO 1st N.E. Cav. Co.H
Tipton, William MO Cav. Snider's Bn. Co.B
Tipton, William NC 58th Inf. Co.B
Tipton, William NC Walker's Bn. Thomas' Legion Co.E
Tipton, William TX Cav. Well's Bn. Co.A
Tipton, William VA Arty. Bryan's Co.
Tipton, William VA 50th Inf. Co.G Lt.
Tipton, William VA 50th Inf. Co.I
Tipton, William B. KY 8th Cav. Co.I Capt.
Tipton, William C. MS 13th Inf. Co.I
Tipton, William E. TX 15th Cav. Co.B
Tipton, William J. AR 1st Mtd.Rifles Co.E
Tipton, William J. AR 45th Cav. Co.H
Tipton, William K. AL 21st Inf. Co.B
Tipton, William L. VA 29th Inf. Co.D Capt.
Tipton, William M. MO Cav. Poindexter's Regt.
Tipton, William M. TN 5th (McKenzie's) Cav. Co.H
Tipton, William M. TN 47th Inf. Co.E
Tipton, William M. VA 25th Cav. Co.A
Tipton, William R. AL Arty. 1st Bn. Co.E
Tipton, William R. VA 24th Inf. Co.E Sgt.
Tipton, William W. AL 50th Inf. Co.C
Tipton, W.J. MS 10th Cav. Co.B
Tipton, W.S. TN 3rd (Lillard's) Mtd.Inf. Co.A
Tiptus, John NC 58th Inf. Co.D
Tirada, J.B. LA Arty. Guyol's Co. (Orleans Arty.)
Tirade, Charles LA Mil. Mooney's Co. (Saddlers Guards)
Tiragollo, J. LA Mil. 4th Regt. French Brig. Co.1
Tiraud, J.B. LA Mil. 3rd Regt. French Brig. Co.4
Tircuit, Clement LA Mil. St.James Regt. Co.E Cpl.
Tircuit, E. LA 1st Cav. Co.I Sgt.
Tircuit, N. LA 30th Inf. Co.F
Tircuit, Telisp LA Mil. St.James Regt. Co.E
Tirddell, James GA Cobb's Legion Co.C
Tire, John M. VA 25th Inf. 2nd Co.I
Tirey, Benjamin MO 1st N.E. Cav.
Tirey, Jonathan AL 32nd Inf. Co.K
Tirey, Joseph KY 13th Cav. Co.H
Tirey, Joseph TN 4th Inf. Co.E
Tirpin, Pleasant L. AR 31st Inf. Co.A
Tirrell, V.A. TN 19th & 20th (Cons.) Cav. Co.E
Tirroa, Juan TX 3rd Inf. Co.G
Tirry, Adam KY 7th Cav. Co.D,I
Tirus, Joe B. LA 12th Inf. Co.H Cpl.
Tisclar, Theophile LA Mil. LaFourche Regt.
Tisdal, C.C. SC Lt.Arty. 3rd (Palmetto) Bn. Co.E
Tisdal, Leborn MS Cav. 17th Bn. Co.F
Tisdal, S.J. SC Lt.Arty. 3rd (Palmetto) Bn. Co.E
Tisdal, Wrem NC 7th Inf. Co.E
Tisdale, --- TX Cav. Mann's Regt. Co.D
Tisdale, Albert AR 2nd Cav. Co.E
Tisdale, Alex NC Jones' Co. (Supp.Force) Cpl.
Tisdale, Andrew J. VA 13th Inf. Co.D
Tisdale, Barney NC 12th Inf. Co.M
Tisdale, Barney NC 32nd Inf. Co.B
Tisdale, Benjamin N. VA 21st Inf. Co.C Sgt.
Tisdale, B.F. AL 46th Inf. Co.C
Tisdale, B.F. LA Mil.Conf.Guards Regt. Co.B
Tisdale, B.T. AL 23rd Inf. Co.B
Tisdale, B.W. AL 15th Bn.Part.Rangers Co.E
Tisdale, B.W. AL 56th Part.Rangers Co.E
Tisdale, C.C. AL 8th Inf. Co.F
Tisdale, Charles B. TX 32nd Cav. Co.H,E Music.
Tisdale, Charles H. VA Conscr. Cp.Lee
Tisdale, Charles W. VA 14th Inf. Co.E Sgt.
Tisdale, Christopher C. VA 21st Inf. Co.C Sgt.
Tisdale, C.W. VA Hvy.Arty. Wright's Co.
Tisdale, Daniel W. VA 20th Inf. Co.C
Tisdale, David M. TN 20th Inf. Co.D 1st Lt.
Tisdale, D.M. SC 9th Inf. Co.D
Tisdale, D.M. SC Palmetto S.S. Co.E Cpl.
Tisdale, Edward H. AR 19th (Dockery's) Inf. Cons.Co.E,D 2nd Lt.
Tisdale, E.K. LA Washington Arty.Bn. Co.5
Tisdale, Elijah W. MS 8th Inf. Co.K
Tisdale, F.M. TN 24th Inf. Co.B
Tisdale, Foster P. MS 20th Inf. Co.I
Tisdale, F.P. MS 8th Inf. Co.G
Tisdale, Francis M. AR 3rd Inf. Co.G
Tisdale, Frederick J. NC 5th Cav. (65th St.Troops) Co.B
Tisdale, George F. NC 3rd Arty. (40th St.Troops) Co.K
Tisdale, George F. NC 61st Inf. Co.C Sr. 2nd Lt.
Tisdale, Geo. H. AL Inf. 6th Regt. Band Instructor
Tisdale, George R. VA 21st Inf. Co.C Sgt.
Tisdale, George W. NC 12th Inf. Co.H
Tisdale, Henry MS Cav. 6th Bn. Prince's Co.
Tisdale, Henry TX 12th Inf. Co.I
Tisdale, Henry TX Waul's Legion Co.B
Tisdale, Henry VA Hvy.Arty. 10th Bn. Co.A
Tisdale, Henry M. VA 9th Cav. Co.G
Tisdale, Henry M. VA 20th Inf. Co.B
Tisdale, Henry W. VA 9th Inf. 1st Co.H
Tisdale, Henry William TX 2nd Inf. Co.A
Tisdale, H.S. AL 15th Bn.Part.Rangers Co.E
Tisdale, H.S. AL 56th Part.Rangers Co.E
Tisdale, Hy TX Inf. Timmons' Regt. Co.A
Tisdale, Isaac D. MS 27th Inf. Co.G
Tisdale, J. GA Cav. 23rd Regt. Co.F
Tisdale, J. VA 23rd Cav. Co.F
Tisdale, J. VA Cav. 41st Bn. Co.F
Tisdale, Jackson D. MS 1st Lt.Arty. Co.C
Tisdale, James NC 12th Inf. Co.H
Tisdale, James NC 32nd Inf. Co.H
Tisdale, James SC Lt.Arty. 3rd (Palmetto) Bn. Co.G
Tisdale, James VA 52nd Inf. Co.C
Tisdale, James L. MS 35th Inf. Co.A
Tisdale, James S. VA Lt.Arty. Snead's Co.
Tisdale, James W. GA 51st Inf. Co.K
Tisdale, James W. MO Cav. Poindexter's Regt. Co.A
Tisdale, J.E. TX 17th Inf. Co.F
Tisdale, Jesse L. KY 2nd Mtd.Inf.
Tisdale, J.F. TX Cav. McCord's Frontier Regt. Co.C
Tisdale, J.G. SC 4th Cav. Co.I
Tisdale, J.G. SC Cav. 12th Bn. Co.B
Tisdale, J.G. SC 1st (Hagood's) Inf. Co.E Sgt.
Tisdale, J.H. AR 38th Inf. Co.G
Tisdale, J.H. SC 2nd Arty. Co.D
Tisdale, J.H. VA 34th Inf. Co.B

Tisdale, J.J. AL 15th Bn.Part.Rangers Co.C
Tisdale, J.J. AL 56th Part.Rangers Co.C
Tisdale, J.J. MS 10th Cav. Co.F
Tisdale, J.J. VA Inf. 25th Bn. Co.D
Tisdale, J.L. KY Morgan's Men Co.H
Tisdale, J.M. SC 5th Bn.Res. Co.B
Tisdale, J.O. MS 36th Inf. Co.B
Tisdale, John KY 3rd Mtd.Inf. Co.F Cpl.
Tisdale, John MO 8th Cav. Co.A
Tisdale, John TX 12th Inf. Co.I
Tisdale, John TX Inf. Timmons' Regt. Co.A
Tisdale, John TX Waul's Legion Co.B
Tisdale, John A. MS Cav. 3rd Bn.Res. Co.E 1st Sgt.
Tisdale, John B. AL Mil. 2nd Regt.Vol. Co.A 2nd Lt.
Tisdale, John G. KY 6th Mtd.Inf. Co.F,E
Tisdale, John H. NC 20th Inf. Co.K Sgt.
Tisdale, John J. AL 15th Bn.Part.Rangers Co.E
Tisdale, John S. MO Cav. 3rd Bn. Surg.
Tisdale, John S. SC 2nd Arty. Co.D Cpl.
Tisdale, John Y. SC 2nd Arty. Co.D
Tisdale, Joseph LA 5th Inf. Co.F
Tisdale, Joseph MS 8th Inf. Co.G
Tisdale, Joseph MS 20th Inf. Co.I
Tisdale, Joseph W. MS 16th Inf. Co.E
Tisdale, J.P. AL 46th Inf. Co.C
Tisdale, J.P. MS 3rd Inf. Co.D
Tisdale, J.R. TX 32nd Cav. Co.E
Tisdale, J. Singleton MS 35th Inf. Co.A,K
Tisdale, J.W. AR 19th (Dockery's) Inf. Co.E
Tisdale, J.W. TX 12th Inf. Co.I
Tisdale, Kann W. MO Searcy's Bn.S.S. Co.B
Tisdale, Lemuel VA 13th Inf. Co.D
Tisdale, L.J. VA 34th Inf. Co.B
Tisdale, Marshall AL 17th Inf. Co.B
Tisdale, Mathew NC 13th Inf. Sgt.
Tisdale, M.J. SC 4th St.Troops Co.I
Tisdale, M.J. SC 5th Bn.Res. Co.B
Tisdale, N. LA 30th Inf. Co.A
Tisdale, Nathan NC 3rd Arty. (40th St.Troops) Co.H Sgt.
Tisdale, Nathan NC Lt.Arty. 13th Bn. Co.F Sgt.
Tisdale, Nathan NC 2nd Inf. Co.I
Tisdale, Nicholas NC 12th Inf. Co.H
Tisdale, Orlando GA 1st Inf. Co.H
Tisdale, Orlando C. 1st Conf.Inf. 2nd Co.H
Tisdale, Ren AR 1st Mtd.Rifles Co.E
Tisdale, Renison W. VA 9th Inf. 1st Co.H
Tisdale, Renison W. VA 59th Inf. 2nd Co.H Sgt.
Tisdale, R.H. SC 4th St.Troops Co.I
Tisdale, Richard LA 5th Inf. Co.F
Tisdale, Richard H. MO Searcy's Bn.S.S. Co.B
Tisdale, Richard T. VA 34th Inf. Co.B 2nd Lt.
Tisdale, R.M. SC Arty. Fickling's Co. (Brooks Lt.Arty.)
Tisdale, Robert TX 32nd Cav. Co.H,E
Tisdale, Robert VA Lt.Arty. Pegram's Co.
Tisdale, Robert S., Jr. SC 2nd Arty. Co.D
Tisdale, Robert S., Sr. SC 2nd Arty. Co.D
Tisdale, R.S. SC 4th Cav. Co.I Sgt.
Tisdale, R.S. SC Cav. 12th Bn. Co.B Sgt.
Tisdale, R.S. SC 2nd Res.
Tisdale, Rufus M. AL 25th Inf. Co.B
Tisdale, Runion W. VA Inf. 28th Bn. Co.C Cpl.
Tisdale, S. MS 27th Inf. Co.G
Tisdale, Samuel AL Inf. 1st Regt. Co.B
Tisdale, Samuel AL 17th Inf. Co.B
Tisdale, Sherill TN 7th (Duckworth's) Cav. Co.E
Tisdale, Shirley AR 25th Inf. Co.A
Tisdale, S.J. AL 23rd Inf. Co.C
Tisdale, S.W. TN 14th (Neely's) Cav. Co.F 1st Sgt.
Tisdale, Thomas TN 3rd (Forrest's) Cav. Co.E
Tisdale, Thomas B. NC 30th Inf. Co.I Jr.2nd Lt.
Tisdale, T.J. SC Lt.Arty. 3rd (Palmetto) Bn. Co.G
Tisdale, T.J. SC 23rd Inf. Co.I
Tisdale, Victor R. LA Washington Arty.Bn. Co.3
Tisdale, W.B. TX 32nd Cav. Co.E
Tisdale, W.G. AR 11th Inf. Co.C
Tisdale, W.H. MS 8th Inf. Co.G
Tisdale, W.H. Gen. & Staff Asst.Surg.
Tisdale, W.H.H. TN 14th (Neely's) Cav. Co.F Sgt.
Tisdale, William MO Lt.Arty. 4th (Harris') Field Btty.
Tisdale, William MO Inf. 5th Regt.St.Guard Co.A
Tisdale, William A. MS 40th Inf. Co.A Cpl.
Tisdale, William A. MS Clayton's Co. (Jasper Defend.)
Tisdale, William C. VA 9th Cav. Co.G Bugler
Tisdale, William D. AR 12th Bn.S.S. Co.B Sr.2nd Lt.
Tisdale, William D. AR 15th (Josey's) Inf. Co.B Cpl.
Tisdale, William H. TN Lt.Arty. Polk's Btty.
Tisdale, William H. VA 9th Cav. Co.G Sgt.
Tisdale, William M. MS 30th Inf. Co.A
Tisdale, William S. AR 3rd Inf. Co.G
Tisdale, William T. TX Cav. Morgan's Regt. Co.A
Tisdale, W.J. AL 15th Bn.Part.Rangers Co.E
Tisdale, W.J. AL 56th Part.Rangers Co.E
Tisdale, W.P. MS Inf. 2nd St.Troops Co.O 1st Sgt.
Tisdale, Wren NC 47th Inf. Co.A
Tisdale, W.S. MS 5th Inf. (St.Troops) Co.H Sgt.
Tisdale, W.W. SC 1st (Hagood's) Inf. 1st Co.E
Tisdale, W.W. SC 25th Inf. Co.C
Tisdale, W.W. VA 1st (Farinholt's) Res. Co.K
Tisdale, Zachary T. MS Cav. 3rd Bn.Res. Co.E
Tisdall, George W. KY 8th Cav. Co.A
Tisdall, James W. MO Cav. Snider's Bn. Co.B
Tisdall, J.L. TN 9th (Ward's) Cav. Co.A
Tisdall, John KY 7th Mtd.Inf. Co.C
Tisdall, John LA 13th Inf. Co.C
Tisdel, Franklin AL 33rd Inf. Co.F
Tisdel, John MS 2nd Cav. Co.E
Tisdell, John W. AR 1st (Crawford's) Cav. Co.B
Tisdell, Kelly NC 3rd Arty. (40th St.Troops) Co.D
Tisdell, Lafayette NC 32nd Inf. Co.D,E
Tisdell, Louis VA 19th Inf. Co.K
Tisdell, T. MO 12th Inf. Co.G
Tisdell, William H. GA Inf. 10th Bn. Co.C
Tisdell, Willis VA 19th Inf. Co.K
Tise, Charles NC 58th Inf. Co.F
Tise, Jacob NC 7th Sr.Res. Clinard's Co.
Tise, James GA Inf. 1st Loc.Troops (Augusta) Co.E,B
Tise, Solomon NC 7th Sr.Res. Clinard's Co., Holland's Co. 3rd Lt.
Tise, W. TX Inf. 1st St.Troops Biehler's Co.A
Tisen, James GA 11th Cav. (St.Guards) Godfrey's Co.
Tisenger, Peter NC 4th Sr.Res. Co.A
Tisenger, William G. NC 7th Inf. Co.C
Tis e poh che 1st Creek Mtd.Vol. Co.G
Tiser, William H.G. NC 5th Cav. (63rd St.Troops) Co.F
Tisero, Berta GA Inf. 10th Bn. Co.D
Tish ah ho tubbee 1st Choctaw & Chickasaw Mtd.Rifles 2nd Co.K
Tishand, Stephen LA 13th Inf. Co.I
Tisher, David AR 2nd Inf. Co.H Cpl.
Tisher, Thomas Conf.Cav. Baxter's Bn. Co.C
Tisho 1st Choctaw & Chickasaw Mtd.Rifles 2nd Co.C, 1st Co.E
Tishohamby Deneale's Regt. Choctaw Warriors Co.B
Tishohinlubbee John 1st Choctaw & Chickasaw Mtd.Rifles Maytubby's Co.
Tishohintubbe 1st Choctaw Mtd.Rifles Co.D
Tisho Hombi 1st Choctaw Mtd.Rifles Co.K
Tishuah Deneale's Regt. Choctaw Warriors
Tisinger, A. NC 3rd Jr.Res. Co.B
Tisinger, David VA 12th Cav. Co.K
Tisinger, David VA 136th Mil. Co.D
Tisinger, David H. GA 3rd Cav. Co.C,K
Tisinger, D.F. AL Lt.Arty. 20th Bn. Co.A
Tisinger, George VA Rockbridge Cty.Res. Donald's Co.
Tisinger, Isaac VA 12th Cav. Co.K
Tisinger, Robert NC 67th Inf. Co.H
Tisinger, William VA 136th Mil. Co.D
Tisney, W. AL 20th Inf.
Tison, A. GA Inf. 40th Bn. Co.D
Tison, Aaron GA 50th Inf. Co.I
Tison, Adam FL 1st Cav. Co.C
Tison, Adam FL Inf. 2nd Bn. Co.C
Tison, Adam FL 10th Inf. Co.H
Tison, A.G. GA 10th Inf. 2nd Lt.
Tison, C. GA 5th Cav. Co.I
Tison, Cicero GA 11th Inf. Co.B
Tison, D.H. SC Manigault's Bn.Vol. Co.A
Tison, Eason GA Siege Arty. 28th Bn. Co.C AASurg.
Tison, E.U. GA 51st Inf. Co.B
Tison, F.M. GA 59th Inf. Co.F
Tison, F.M. GA Inf. Collier's Co.
Tison, Fr. M. GA 10th Inf. 1st Lt.
Tison, George FL 8th Inf. Co.K
Tison, George N. GA 5th Cav. Co.I
Tison, George W. GA 46th Inf. Co.B
Tison, Golphin N. FL Inf. 2nd Bn. Co.B
Tison, Henry C. GA 9th Inf. Co.K
Tison, H.H. GA 63rd Inf. Co.K
Tison, H.L. GA Arty. 11th Bn. (Sumter Arty.) Co.B Sgt.
Tison, Isaac FL 1st Cav. Co.B
Tison, Isaac P. GA Siege Arty. 28th Bn. Co.A,C QMSgt.
Tison, Isaac P. GA 51st Inf. Co.B
Tison, J.A. GA Tiller's Co. (Echols Lt.Arty.)
Tison, J.A. SC Part.Rangers Kirk's Co. Sgt.
Tison, James H. GA 50th Inf. Co.I
Tison, James T. AL 13th Inf. Co.A

Tison, J.E. FL 2nd Cav. Co.K
Tison, J.E. GA 4th (Clinch's) Cav. Co.H
Tison, J.E. GA 1st Reg.
Tison, J.E. GA 61st Inf. Co.C
Tison, J.G. GA Inf. Bard's Co. Cpl.
Tison, Joab GA 11th Inf. Co.B
Tison, Joab R. GA 13th Inf. Co.E 1st Sgt.
Tison, John AR 25th Inf. Co.B
Tison, John A. SC 11th Inf. Co.D QMSgt.
Tison, John L. GA Arty. 11th Bn. (Sumter Arty.) Co.A
Tison, John L. GA 12th Inf. Co.A
Tison, John W. FL 8th Inf. Co.K
Tison, Josephus C. AR 1st (Crawford's) Cav. Co.C Jr.2nd Lt.
Tison, Josephus C. AR 4th Inf. Co.D Capt.
Tison, J.P. GA 1st Reg. Co.I
Tison, J.W. FL 1st (Res.) Inf. Co.A
Tison, Lawrence H. FL Inf. 2nd Bn. Co.B
Tison, L.S. LA Inf.Cons.Crescent Regt. Co.I
Tison, Mathew GA 11th Cav. (St.Guards) Godfrey's Co.
Tison, M.W. GA Cav. 15th Bn. (St.Guards) Allen's Co.
Tison, Onias GA 46th Inf. Co.B
Tison, P. GA 46th Inf. Co.B
Tison, Perry SC Part.Rangers Kirk's Co.
Tison, Pleasant GA 11th Cav. (St.Guards) Godfrey's Co.
Tison, R.H. TX 3rd (Kirby's) Bn.Vol. Co.B,A
Tison, Robert W. GA 51st Inf. Co.B
Tison, S. GA 32nd Inf. Co.E
Tison, Samuel L. GA Arty. 11th Bn. (Sumter Arty.) Co.B Sgt.
Tison, Seaborn GA 4th (Clinch's) Cav. Co.F,H
Tison, S.H. MS 2nd St.Cav. Co.K Cpl.
Tison, Simeon GA 4th (Clinch's) Cav. Co.F,H
Tison, Theodore MO 4th Cav. Co.D
Tison, W.A. GA 4th (Clinch's) Cav. Co.H
Tison, W.H. FL Inf. 2nd Bn. Co.C
Tison, W.H.H. MS 32nd Inf. Col.
Tison, William FL 1st Cav. Co.C
Tison, William GA 11th Cav. (St.Guards) Godfrey's Co.
Tison, William D. TX 2nd Cav. Co.E
Tison, William H. FL Inf. 2nd Bn. Co.C
Tison, William H. TX 2nd Inf. Co.B Sgt.
Tison, William H.H. MS 19th Inf. Co.K Capt.
Tison, William L. GA 9th Inf. Co.H Sgt.
Tison, William O. FL 2nd Cav. Co.F
Tison, William T. TX 13th Cav. Co.E
Tison, W.J. GA Arty. 11th Bn. (Sumter Arty.) Co.B
Tisserand, Etienne LA 13th Inf. Co.D
Tisserant, Alexander LA 2nd Cav. Co.D
Tissereau, Bertrand GA 20th Inf. Co.A Music.
Tissot, A.L. LA 22nd Inf. Co.B Capt.
Tissot, George LA C.S. Zouave Bn. Co.B
Tissot, J. LA C.S. Zouave Bn. Co.B
Tissot, L. LA Mil. 1st Chasseurs a pied Co.4 Cpl.
Tistoska, --- NC Inf. Thomas Legion
Titanus, Jerry VA 1st St.Res. Co.F
Titcomb, Beniah AR Lt.Arty. Etter's Btty. Sgt.
Titcomb, Francis AL Lt.Arty. 2nd Bn. Co.E 2nd Lt.
Titcomb, Francis AL St.Arty. Co.D 1st Lt.
Titcomb, G.W. GA 1st (Symons') Res. Co.B Cpl.
Tites, J.E. GA 30th Inf. Co.E
Titford, K.J. AL 5th Cav. Co.I
Titghman, William NC Mil. Clark's Sp.Bn. Co.A
Tithew tubbee Deneale's Regt. Choctaw Warriors Co.E
Tither, J. MO 5th Inf. Co.B
Titherington, James D. TN 14th Inf. Co.F
Titherington, R.M. Gen. & Staff Surg.
Titjen, J.H. SC Inf. 1st (Charleston) Bn. Co.F
Title, T.L. MS 26th Inf. Co.H
Titler, John TX Cav. Martin's Regt. Co.F
Titlow, Frederick VA 36th Inf. 2nd Co.B
Titlow, Henry J. VA 1st Lt.Arty. Co.B
Titman, Abraham P. NC 16th Inf. Co.M
Titmash, Richard C. VA Hvy.Arty. 10th Bn. Co.D
Titshaw, Anderson GA 13th Cav. Co.D
Titshaw, L.W.C. GA 9th Inf. Co.C
Titshaw, M.A. GA 9th Inf. (St.Guards) Co.F
Titstone, R. GA 29th Inf. Co.G
Titsworth, Albert NC 13th Inf. Co.E
Titsworth, Elbert SC 1st Arty. Co.F
Titsworth, Elisha TN 23rd Inf. Co.E
Titsworth, E.N. AR Gipson's Bn.Mtd.Riflemen Capt.
Titsworth, E.N. AR Cav. Gordon's Regt. Co.K Capt.
Titsworth, F.J. TN 23rd Inf. Co.C
Titsworth, H.S. MO 5th Cav. Co.H Capt.
Titsworth, J.M. TX 1st Bn.S.S. Co.B
Titsworth, John F. AR Cav. Harrell's Bn. Co.B Cpl.
Titsworth, John P. TN Inf. 1st Bn. (Colms') Co.C 1st Lt.
Titsworth, O. AR 58th Mil. Co.E
Titsworth, R.A. KY 8th Mtd.Inf. Co.C
Titsworth, Sanders AR 27th Inf. Co.A
Titsworth, Simon AR 17th (Griffith's) Inf. Co.G 3rd Lt.
Titsworth, Simon AR 35th Inf. Co.K 2nd Lt.
Titsworth, W.J. AR 5th Mil. Co.I
Titt, Cornelius A. FL Cadets Military Inst.
Tittard, Pre. LA Mil. 4th Regt. French Brig. Co.7
Titterington, Daniel TX 30th Cav. Co.I
Titterington, John AZ Cav. Herbert's Bn. Oury's Co. Cpl.
Tittle, A. TN 22nd (Barteau's) Cav. Co.C
Tittle, Adam TN 8th (Smith's) Cav. Co.F
Tittle, Adam E.W. 1st Choctaw & Chickasaw Mtd.Rifles 1st Co.I
Tittle, Archibald TX 2nd Cav. Co.D Sgt.
Tittle, A.S. AR 2nd Cav. Co.G Sgt.
Tittle, Baxter S. TN 63rd Inf. Co.I
Tittle, Charles GA 34th Inf. Co.F
Tittle, David TN 63rd Inf. Co.I
Tittle, Franklin MS 24th Inf. Co.C
Tittle, George TX 24th Cav. Co.D
Tittle, George 10th Conf.Cav. Co.B
Tittle, George W. TN Lt.Arty. Kain's Co.
Tittle, George W. TN 60th Mtd.Inf. Co.A
Tittle, G.W. GA 42nd Inf. Co.K
Tittle, G.W. MS St.Cav. Perrin's Bn. Co.H Sr.2nd Lt.
Tittle, James KY 4th Mtd.Inf. Co.F
Tittle, James MS 11th (Perrin's) Cav. Co.C
Tittle, James F. TX 19th Cav. Co.A
Tittle, James M. GA 45th Inf. Co.E
Tittle, James S.C. TN 63rd Inf. Co.I
Tittle, J.B. TX 18th Inf. Co.A
Tittle, J. Frank TX 12th Cav. Co.I
Tittle, J.J. AR Inf. Hardy's Regt. Torbett's Co.
Tittle, John E. TX 11th Field Btty. (Howell's Co.,Lt.Arty.)
Tittle, John J. MS 24th Inf. Co.C
Tittle, John H. MS 30th Inf. Co.G
Tittle, John L. TX Cav. Baird's Regt. Co.D
Tittle, John L. TX Cav. Ragsdale's Bn. 2nd Co.C Cpl.
Tittle, J.S. MS 15th Inf. Co.A
Tittle, L.A. TN 63rd Inf. Co.I Cpl.
Tittle, L.P. GA 18th Inf. Co.G
Tittle, McAnnie MS 24th Inf. Co.C
Tittle, McCarrey MS 24th Inf. Co.C
Tittle, M. Camie MS 24th Inf. Co.C
Tittle, Robert W. TX 3rd Cav. Co.H
Tittle, S. TN 22nd (Barteau's) Cav. Co.C
Tittle, S.C. TN 35th Inf. Co.A,E
Tittle, T. MS 2nd (Davidson's) Inf. Co.E
Tittle, Thomas MO 1st N.E. Cav. Co.K
Tittle, Tillmann TN 8th (Smith's) Cav. Co.E
Tittle, William AL Cav. 5th Bn. Hilliard's Legion Co.B
Tittle, William GA 6th Inf. Co.B Cpl.
Tittle, William MO 8th Inf. Co.H
Tittle, William 10th Conf.Cav. Co.B
Tittle, William C. MS 5th Inf. Co.F
Tittle, Zachariah W. TX 14th Cav. Co.E
Tittsworth, David R. VA 25th Cav. Co.D
Tittsworth, George W. TN 61st Mtd.Inf. Co.E
Tittsworth, John B. TN 61st Mtd.Inf. Co.E
Tittsworth, Levi TX 11th Field Btty.
Titus, B. AL 8th Inf. Co.H
Titus, Benjamin F. AL 5th Bn.Vol. Co.D
Titus, B.O. MO 6th Cav. Co.D
Titus, E.B. TX 34th Cav. Co.K Capt.
Titus, Ebb TN 3rd (Forrest's) Cav. Co.A
Titus, F.J.M. TX 1st Bn.S.S. Co.B
Titus, Frank MO Cav. Hobb's Co.
Titus, Frank TX 1st Inf. Co.H
Titus, James E. TX 15th Cav. Co.C
Titus, James T. TN 3rd (Forrest's) Cav. Co.A Cpl.
Titus, James T. TN Inf. 154th Sr.Regt. 1st Co.B Cpl.
Titus, J.G. TX Cav. Morgan's Regt. Co.E
Titus, J.H. NC 27th Inf. Co.I
Titus, J.L. MO 1st & 4th Cons.Inf. Co.H
Titus, J.L. MO 4th Inf. Co.K
Titus, John TN 4th (Murray's) Cav. Co.G
Titus, John F. TN Inf. 154th Sr.Regt. 1st Co.B
Titus, John H. MO 3rd Inf. Co.D Sgt.
Titus, John L. MS 12th Cav. Co.H
Titus, John L. LA Mil. Lewis Guards
Titus, John T. TN 3rd (Forrest's) Cav. Co.A
Titus, Melzar TX 1st (McCulloch's) Cav. Co.G
Titus, Melzar TX 1st (Yager's) Cav. Co.G
Titus, Melzor TX Cav. 8th (Taylor's) Bn. Co.A
Titus, Noah MO 1st Cav. Co.F
Titus, Robert B. TX 16th Cav. Co.A Sgt.
Titus, T. Trans-MS Conf.Cav. 1st Bn. Co.B
Titus, T.H. TX Cav. Baylor's Regt. Co.K

Titus, Turner TX 11th Cav. Co.A
Titus, William VA Cav. 35th Bn. Co.A
Titus, William J. MS 5th Inf. Co.H
Titus, William S. Conf.Inf. 1st Bn. 2nd Co.E
Titus, W.S. AL Inf. 2nd Regt. Co.I Cpl.
Titymouse, M. NC 2nd Jr.Res. Co.G
Tives, B.F. TX Inf. 1st St.Troops Saxton's Co.
Tivey, Joseph A. TX 31st Cav. Co.C 1st Lt.
Tivis, H.M. MO 9th Inf. Co.H
Tivis, James H. AZ Cav. Herbert's Bn. Swope's Co. 1st Lt.
Tivis, S.M. MO 9th Inf. Co.H
Tizly, Jacob LA 18th Inf. Co.D
Tizzell, Jacob Brush Bn.
Tlausnar, John AL 6th Cav. Co.A
Tle yer ser 1st Cherokee Mtd.Rifles Co.D Bugler
Tlos tah ner 1st Cherokee Mtd.Rifles Co.E
Tlo yer ker 1st Cherokee Mtd.Rifles Co.A
Tlur wi key 1st Creek Mtd.Vol. Co.F 1st Lt.
To, Rosendo LA Mil. 5th Regt.Eur.Brig. (Spanish Regt.) Co.4
Toad, William A. MS 4th Inf. Co.A
Toadvine, A.R. LA 1st Cav. Co.E
Toadvine, D.A. LA 16th Inf. Co.A
Toal, Charles MS 19th Inf. Co.A
Toal, R.E. MS 2nd Cav. Co.H
Toal, Robert E. VA 59th Inf. 2nd Co.F
Toalman, William H. AR 2nd Inf. Co.H
Toalson, Thomas MO Cav. Poindexter's Regt.
Toalson, Thomas MO St.Guard
Toalson, Thomas B. MO St.Guard
Tobacco, J.D. 2nd Cherokee Mtd.Vol. Co.I
Tobacco, John 1st Cherokee Mtd.Vol. 1st Co.A, 2nd Co.B
Tobal, M. LA 27th Inf. Co.K
Tobar, D. TX Cav. Benavides' Regt. Co.D
Tobar, Henriquez TX Cav. Benavides' Regt. Co.D
Tobar, Sabas TX 3rd Inf. 1st Co.C
Tobb, John N. AL 55th Vol. Co.D
Tobbert, George C. AL 4th (Russell's) Cav.
Tobby, Samuel B. 1st Choctaw & Chickasaw Mtd.Rifles 3rd Co.D 2nd Lt.
Tobbort, Phillip H. AL 39th Inf. Co.F
Tobe 1st Creek Mtd.Vol. Co.E
Tobee 1st Creek Mtd.Vol. 2nd Co.C
Tobel, Charles LA 13th Inf. Co.D
Tobelman, Hy TX 1st Hvy.Arty. Band Band M.
Tober, Daris TX Cav. Ragsdale's Bn. 1st Co.A
Tober, Henriques TX Cav. Ragsdale's Bn. 1st Co.A
Tobert, E. TX 26th Cav. Co.E
Tobey 1st Creek Mtd.Vol. 1st Co.C
Tobey, Fredrick A. NC 58th Inf. Co.A Capt.
Tobey, Salathial H. GA 1st Inf. Capt.
Tobey, S.H. GA Inf. 17th Bn. (St.Guards) Fay's Co.
Tobey, S.H. TN Inf. 3rd Bn. Co.E 1st Lt.
Tobey, S.H. Smith's Staff Capt.,AAG
Tobey, Stephen H. AR Cav. 1st Bn. (Stirman's) Co.G,F 1st Lt.
Tobi, E. 1st Seminole Mtd.Vol.
Tobias, A.L. SC Mil.Arty. 1st Regt. Regt.QM
Tobias, Benjamin R. AL 57th Inf. Co.B
Tobias, C.H. SC 6th Inf. 2nd Co.K
Tobias, C.H. SC 9th Inf. Co.C,D Cpl.
Tobias, C.L. AL Cav. Barbiere's Bn. Brown's Co.
Tobias, F.W. SC 21st Inf. Co.C
Tobias, F.W. SC 25th Inf. Co.I
Tobias, I.H. SC 25th Inf. Co.I
Tobias, I.N. SC 25th Inf. Co.I
Tobias, James SC 3rd Regt.Res.
Tobias, J.B. SC 6th Inf. 2nd Co.K
Tobias, J.B. SC 9th Inf. Co.C,D
Tobias, J.H. SC 21st Inf. Co.C
Tobias, J.L. SC Mil.Arty. 1st Regt. Walter's Co.
Tobias, J.N. SC 6th Inf. 2nd Co.K
Tobias, J.N. SC 23rd Inf. Co.I
Tobias, John E AL 46th Inf. Co.C
Tobias, J.S. SC 25th Inf. Co.I
Tobias, J.W. SC 21st Inf. Co.C
Tobias, J.W. SC 25th Inf. Co.I
Tobias, M. AL 1st Cav.
Tobias, P. LA Mil.Squad. Guides d'Orleans
Tobias, Philipp TX 1st Hvy.Arty. Co.C
Tobias, S.R. SC 6th Inf. 2nd Co.K Sgt.
Tobias, S.R. SC 9th Inf. Co.C,D
Tobias, T. AL Mil. 2nd Vol. Co.C
Tobias, T.E. SC 21st Inf. Co.C
Tobias, T.E. SC 25th Inf. Co.I Cpl.
Tobias, T.J. SC 25th Inf. Co.I
Tobias, T.N. SC 25th Inf. Co.I
Tobias, W.E. AL 33rd Inf. Co.E Sgt.
Tobias, William M. SC 25th Inf. Co.I
Tobias, W.M. SC 6th Inf. 2nd Co.K
Tobias, W.M. SC 23rd Inf. Co.I
Tobias, W.R. AL 46th Inf. Co.C
Tobin, --- MS 11th Inf. Co.F
Tobin, --- TX 1st Inf.
Tobin, --- VA Cav. 32nd Bn. Co.B
Tobin, A. LA 18th Inf. Co.F
Tobin, Albert VA 10th Inf. Co.K
Tobin, C. VA Inf. 25th Bn. Co.D
Tobin, C.F. SC 8th Bn.Res. Co.C
Tobin, Charles VA 57th Inf. Co.F
Tobin, D. TX 35th (Brown's) Cav. Co.A
Tobin, Dan J. TX Cav. Ragsdale's Bn. Co.A 2nd Lt.
Tobin, Daniel TX 36th Cav. Co.H
Tobin, David TX 13th Vol. 2nd Co.G,C
Tobin, Edward SC Mil. 1st Regt. (Charleston Res.) Co.A
Tobin, Edward VA 2nd Inf. Co.E
Tobin, E.T. AL 8th Inf. Co.I Cpl.
Tobin, F.O. AL St.Arty. Co.D
Tobin, George KY 2nd (Duke's) Cav. Co.H
Tobin, George KY Horse Arty. Byrne's Co. Sgt.
Tobin, H. LA Mil.Cont.Cadets
Tobin, Henry LA Inf.Crescent Regt. Co.C
Tobin, J. LA Lt.Arty. LeGardeur, Jr.'s Co. (Orleans Guard Btty.)
Tobin, J. VA 27th Inf. 2nd Co.H
Tobin, James MO 1st Cav. Co.E
Tobin, James TX 5th Cav. Co.G Far.
Tobin, James VA 14th Inf. Co.I 2nd Lt.
Tobin, James VA Prov.Guard Avis' Co.
Tobin, J.E. SC 2nd St.Troops Co.E
Tobin, J.J. AR 26th Inf. Asst.Surg.
Tobin, J.M. MO 1st & 3rd Cons.Cav.
Tobin, John GA 1st (Olmstead's) Inf. Co.D
Tobin, John GA 2nd Bn.S.S. Co.C
Tobin, John KY 2nd Cav. Co.D
Tobin, John KY Horse Arty. Byrne's Co.
Tobin, John LA 1st (Nelligan's) Inf. Co.C
Tobin, John LA 6th Inf. Co.E Sgt.Maj.
Tobin, John LA Mil.Cont.Regt. Kirk's Co.
Tobin, John MS 20th Inf. Co.F,K
Tobin, John SC Sea Fencibles Symons' Co.
Tobin, John TN Lt.Arty. Polk's Btty.
Tobin, John TN 2nd (Walker's) Inf. Co.D
Tobin, John TX 16th Inf. Co.H
Tobin, John VA 10th Inf. Co.K
Tobin, John J. TN Arty. Marshall's Co.
Tobin, John J. VA Hvy.Arty. A.J. Jones' Co.
Tobin, John J. Gen. & Staff Asst.Surg.
Tobin, John P. TN Inf. 3rd Bn. Co.C
Tobin, Langdon SC 2nd Arty. Co.A Cpl.
Tobin, L.C. SC 2nd Arty. Co.A Cpl.
Tobin, M. LA Mil. Chalmette Regt. Co.B
Tobin, Matthew MS 17th Inf. Co.I
Tobin, M.G. SC 2nd Arty. Co.A
Tobin, Michael VA Inf. 1st Bn. Co.D
Tobin, N.G. TX Cav. Mann's Regt. Capt.
Tobin, Nicholas GA 19th Inf. Co.G
Tobin, Nicholas TN 2nd (Walker's) Inf. Co.H
Tobin, Nicholas 9th Conf.Inf. Co.F
Tobin, Patrick TN 7th (Duckworth's) Cav. Co.B
Tobin, Patrick VA 10th Inf. 2nd Co.C
Tobin, Phillip AR 35th Inf. Co.G
Tobin, Richard AL Lt.Arty. 2nd Bn. Co.B
Tobin, Richard LA 5th Inf. Old Co.A
Tobin, Richard LA 6th Inf. Co.I,A
Tobin, Richard TX Vol. Duke's Co.
Tobin, T.A. SC 3rd Inf. Co.A Ord.Sgt.
Tobin, Thomas MS 6th Inf. Co.E
Tobin, Thomas MS 17th Inf. Co.B
Tobin, Thomas F. TN Lt.Arty. Tobin's Co. Capt.
Tobin, W.H. AR Cav. Gordon's Regt. Asst.Surg.
Tobin, W.H. Gen. & Staff Surg.
Tobin, William SC 1st (McCreary's) Inf. Co.K
Tobin, William TN 2nd (Walker's) Inf. Co.D
Tobin, William TX 3rd Inf. 1st Co.A
Tobin, Wm. C. Gen. & Staff Capt.,AAAG
Tobin, William G. TX 1st (McCulloch's) Cav. Co.D Capt.
Tobin, William G. TX 2nd Cav. Co.F Capt.
Tobin, William G. TX 36th Cav. Co.I
Tobin, William J. VA 10th Inf. Co.K
Toblemann, F. LA Mil. 3rd Regt. 1st Brig. 1st Div. Co.G Capt.
Tobler, Aaron VA 45th Inf. Co.I
Tobler, Albert TX 17th Inf. Co.I
Tobler, Alex. VA 45th Inf. Co.G
Tobler, Hiram B. VA 6th Bn.Res. Co.A
Tobler, J. LA 19th Inf. Co.G
Tobler, Jacob SC 1st Arty. Co.K
Tobler, Jacob VA Cav. 47th Bn. Co.C
Tobler, Jessey VA Loc.Def. Earhart's Co.
Tobler, John GA 36th (Villepigue's) Inf. Co.I
Tobler, John VA 45th Inf. Co.I
Tobler, John VA Loc.Def. Earhart's Co.
Tobler, John Jacob GA 10th Inf. Co.I
Tobler, Jonas VA 63rd Inf. Co.H
Tobler, Stephen VA 29th Inf. Co.B
Tobley, David 1st Choctaw & Chickasaw Mtd.Rifles Co.A
Tobly, Davis 1st Choctaw Mtd.Rifles Ward's Co.

Tobly, Samuel B. 1st Choctaw & Chickasaw Mtd.Rifles 2nd Co.H 2nd Lt.
Toby, Avery TX 15th Cav. Co.D
Toby, Avry TX 17th Cons.Dismtd.Cav. Co.H
Toby, John LA Arty. Castellanos' Btty.
Toby, N. MS 2nd (Quinn's St.Troops) Inf. Co.H
Toby, S. GA Cav. 8th Bn. (St.Guards) Co.A
Toby, Samuel TX 15th Cav. Co.D
Toby, Samuel TX 17th Cons.Dismtd.Cav. Co.H
Toby, Simeon, Jr. Adams' Staff Capt.,ADC
Toby, Stephen H. AR Inf. Williamson's Bn. Co.D 3rd Lt.
Toby, Stephen H. Stirman's Regt.S.S. Co.F Jr.2nd Lt.
Toby, W. MS 2nd (Quinn's St.Troops) Inf. Co.H
Toca, --- LA Miles' Legion Boones' Btty.
Toca, A. LA 22nd Inf. Co.B
Toca, A. LA Mil. Orleans Guards Regt. Co.K
Toca, O. LA Lt.Arty. Bridges' Btty.
Toca, Octave SC Arty. Manigault's Bn. 1st Co.A, Co.D
Toca, S. LA Lt.Arty. 2nd Field Btty.
Toca, S. LA Inf. 1st Sp.Bn. (Rightor's) Co.F Cpl.
Toca, Septime LA Lt.Arty. LeGardeur, Jr.'s Co. (Orleans Guard Btty.)
Toca, T. LA Lt.Arty. 2nd Field Btty. 2nd Lt.
Tocharwer 1st Creek Mtd.Vol. 1st Co.C
To cher la ner 1st Cherokee Mtd.Rifles Co.A Cpl.
Tochorn, Charles LA French Co.
Tochry, T. KY 6th Mtd.Inf. Co.E
Tochterman, Joseph LA Miles' Legion Co.A
Tochtermann, Chs. LA Mil. 4th Regt.Eur.Brig. Co.D
Tocker, Joshua TN Cav. Cox's Bn. Co.A
Tocksey, William E. VA 59th Mil. Hunter's Co.
To clee 1st Creek Mtd.Vol. 1st Co.C
To co co we 1st Creek Mtd.Vol. Co.E
Tocoser Emathla 1st Seminole Mtd.Vol.
Tocoser Fixics 1st Seminole Mtd.Vol.
Tocoser Harjo 1st Creek Mtd.Vol. 1st Co.C 1st Lt.
To co ser Harjo 1st Seminole Mtd.Vol.
To co ser 1st Seminole Mtd.Vol.
Tod, J.E. AR 1st Mtd.Rifles Co.F
Todd, --- TX Cav. Mann's Regt. Co.D
Todd, A. AL Coosa Guards J.W.Suttles' Co.
Todd, A.A. AL 50th Inf. Co.B
Todd, Aaron MS 8th Inf. Co.K
Todd, Aaron TN 23rd Inf. 1st Co.F, Co.H Sgt.
Todd, Aaron M. TN 23rd Inf. Co.B
Todd, A.C. NC 68th Inf. Co.D
Todd, A.C. SC Lt.Arty. M. Ward's Co. (Waccamaw Lt.Arty.)
Todd, Adam C. AR 1st (Colquitt's) Inf. Co.I Sgt.
Todd, Adam P. VA 20th Cav. Co.D
Todd, Addison VA 10th Inf. Co.G
Todd, A.E. GA 22nd Inf. Co.B
Todd, A.F. TN 20th (Russell's) Cav. Co.C
Todd, A.F. TN 12th Inf. Co.F
Todd, A.F. TN 12th (Cons.) Inf. Co.B
Todd, A.G. SC 10th Inf. 2nd Co.G
Todd, A.H. MO 1st & 3rd Cons.Cav. Co.I,E 2nd Lt.
Todd, A.H. TX 20th Cav. Co.D
Todd, A.H. Gen. & Staff 1st Lt.,ADC
Todd, A.J. AL 6th Cav. Co.F
Todd, A.J. GA 13th Cav. Co.C
Todd, A.J. MO Cav. Freeman's Regt. Co.G
Todd, A.L. AL Gid Nelson Lt.Arty.
Todd, Albert H. MO 1st Cav. Co.I 2nd Lt.
Todd, Albert H. VA 3rd Cav. Co.K
Todd, Albert H. VA 23rd Inf. Co.I
Todd, Alexander AR 1st (Dobbin's) Cav. Co.D
Todd, Alexander AR 8th Inf. New Co.H
Todd, Alexander S. LA Inf.Cons.Crescent Regt. Co.H
Todd, Algernal VA 37th Inf. Co.C
Todd, Andrew GA 5th Inf.
Todd, Andrew MO 2nd Cav. Co.D
Todd, Andrew A. TN 5th (McKenzie's) Cav. Co.I Cpl.
Todd, Andrew J. MS 19th Inf. Co.G Sgt.
Todd, Andrew J. MO 3rd Cav. Co.D
Todd, Andrew J. MO 1st Inf.
Todd, Andrew Jackson MO 8th Inf. Co.G
Todd, Andrew K. TX 13th Cav. Co.D
Todd, Andrew W. AL 1st Bn. Hilliard's Legion Vol. Co.C
Todd, Aquilla NC 5th Sr.Res. Co.F Cpl.
Todd, A.R. TN 23rd Inf. 1st Co.F, Co.H
Todd, A.S. LA Arty. King's Btty.
Todd, Atha AL Cav. 24th Bn. Co.B
Todd, Augustus NC 11th (Bethel Regt.) Inf. Co.C
Todd, A.W. AL 60th Inf. Co.K
Todd, A.W. SC 14th Inf. Co.F
Todd, B. KY 1st (Butler's) Cav. Co.F
Todd, B.A. MS Condrey's Co. (Bull Mtn. Invinc.)
Todd, Benjamin VA 109th Mil. 1st Co.A, 2nd Co.A
Todd, Benjamin A. AL 42nd Inf. Co.K
Todd, Benjamin D. TN 54th Inf. Co.E
Todd, Benjamin F. AL 6th Cav. Co.E,C
Todd, Bernard VA 3rd (Archer's) Bn.Res. Co.D 1st Lt.
Todd, Bernard VA Second Class Mil. Wolff's Co. Sgt.
Todd, Bernard H. VA Lt.Arty. Jeffress' Co. 1st Lt.
Todd, Berry NC 31st Inf. Co.E,D
Todd, B.F. GA 13th Cav. Co.C
Todd, B.F. GA Cobb's Legion Co.H
Todd, Bryant NC 1st Inf. Co.A
Todd, Bryant NC 31st Inf. Co.D
Todd, B.T. TN 27th Inf. Co.K
Todd, Burton AL 13th Inf. Co.F
Todd, B.W. GA 23rd Inf. Co.I Cpl.
Todd, C. AL 2nd Cav. Co.K Far.
Todd, C. FL 1st Inf.
Todd, C.A. AL 7th Inf. Co.D
Todd, C.H. LA 6th Inf. Surg.
Todd, C.H. TN 8th (Smith's) Cav. Co.G
Todd, C.H. VA 13th Inf. Surg.
Todd, Charles GA 25th Inf. Co.B
Todd, Charles MS 6th Inf. Co.I Sgt.
Todd, Charles MS 14th (Cons.) Inf. Co.C Sgt.
Todd, Charles B. NC 34th Inf. Co.G Sgt.Maj.
Todd, Charles D. GA 61st Inf. Co.B
Todd, Charles H. Gen. & Staff Surg.
Todd, Charles L. VA Lt.Arty. R.M Anderson's Co. Sgt.
Todd, Charles L. VA 2nd St.Res. Co.F,A
Todd, Charles W. GA 26th Inf. Co.B
Todd, Charley B. AL 38th Inf. Co.F
Todd, C.M. AL 1st Cav. Co.G 1st Sgt.
Todd, C.M.B. KY 4th Mtd.Inf. Co.D
Todd, Corneluis P. AL 34th Inf. Co.G
Todd, C.R. VA Lt.Arty. Pollock's Co.
Todd, C.W. TN 23rd Inf. 1st Co.F, Co.H 1st Lt.
Todd, Cyrus MO Inf. Perkins' Bn. Co.E
Todd, D. AR Inf. Hardy's Regt. Co.I
Todd, D.A. TX 4th Inf. Co.B
Todd, Daucy NC 5th Sr.Res. Co.H
Todd, David AL 2nd Cav. Co.F
Todd, David NC 5th Cav. (63rd St.Troops) Co.H
Todd, David NC 33rd Inf. Co.C
Todd, David VA 20th Cav. Co.I
Todd, David H. LA 21st (Patton's) Inf. Co.A Capt.
Todd, David H. SC 1st (Orr's) Rifles Co.E
Todd, David L. Gen. & Staff Asst.Surg.
Todd, David S. NC 34th Inf. Co.G
Todd, Davidson TX Inf. 2nd St.Troops Co.D
Todd, David W. AL 24th Inf. Co.I
Todd, D.E. NC Cav. 12th Bn. Co.B
Todd, Dennis SC 10th Inf. 2nd Co.G
Todd, D.H. KY 1st Inf. 1st Lt.
Todd, D.H. Recruits W.B. Ochiltree's Detach. Lt.
Todd, D.L. LA 1st Cav. Co.G
Todd, D.L. LA 18th Inf. Co.H
Todd, Drury SC 1st (McCreary's) Inf. Co.B
Todd, D.W. SC 10th Inf. 2nd Co.G
Todd, E.B. MO Searcy's Bn.S.S. Co.D Bvt.2nd Lt.
Todd, Edmund GA Cav. 1st Bn. Hopkin's Co., Brailsford's Co.
Todd, Edmund GA 5th Cav. Co.H
Todd, Edward W. SC 23rd Inf. Co.D 1st Sgt.
Todd, E.G. GA 45th Inf. Co.F Sgt.
Todd, E.G. VA Inf. 2nd Bn.Loc.Def. Co.D
Todd, E.H. AL 6th Cav. Co.A
Todd, E.H. TN 18th (Newsom's) Cav. Co.D Cpl.
Todd, E.H. TN 19th & 20th (Cons.) Cav. Co.H
Todd, E.K. AL 6th Cav. Co.D
Todd, Elbert NC 2nd Inf. Co.B Sgt.
Todd, Eli AL 22nd Inf. Co.D
Todd, Elias VA 32nd Inf. 2nd Co.K
Todd, Elias VA 115th Mil. Co.A
Todd, Elijah S. MO 1st N.E. Cav.
Todd, Elisha NC 11th (Bethel Regt.) Inf. Co.C Ch.Music.
Todd, Elisha SC 10th Inf. Co.M
Todd, E.M. Gen. & Staff Maj.,CS
Todd, E.W. SC Inf. 1st (Charleston) Bn. Co.B
Todd, Ewing MO 1st N.E. Cav. Co.I
Todd, F.M. AL 28th Inf. Co.B
Todd, Frank TN 12th Inf. Music.
Todd, Frank M. GA 51st Inf. Co.I
Todd, Freeman H. GA 5th Inf. Co.D Cpl.
Todd, George GA 21st Inf. Co.F
Todd, George TN Inf. 3rd Bn. Co.G
Todd, George VA 9th Cav. Co.B
Todd, George VA 54th Mil. Co.A

Todd, George C. NC 34th Inf. Co.G Cpl.
Todd, George F. GA 4th Inf. Co.D Capt.
Todd, George H. NC 46th Inf. Co.A
Todd, George K. VA 15th Inf. Surg.
Todd, George M. VA 6th Inf. Co.G
Todd, George N. NC 34th Inf. Co.G Sgt.
Todd, George R. AR 7th Inf. Co.B Capt.
Todd, George R. TN 26th Inf. Co.E 1st Sgt.
Todd, George R.C. VA Lt.Arty. Cayce's Co.
Todd, Geo. R.C. Gen. & Staff Surg.
Todd, George T. TX 1st Inf. Co.A Capt.
Todd, George W. MS 3rd (St.Troops) Cav. Co.B 1st Sgt.
Todd, George W. MO Quantrill's Co. 2nd Lt.
Todd, George W. VA 46th Inf. Co.A
Todd, G.J. MO 3rd & 5th Cons.Inf. Co.H
Todd, G.R. GA 32nd Inf. Co.F
Todd, G.R. GA 59th Inf. Co.E
Todd, Green V. NC 34th Inf. Co.G Sgt.
Todd, G.T. Gen. & Staff Surg.
Todd, G.W. KY 2nd Bn.Mtd.Rifles Co.C Cpl.
Todd, G.W. LA 2nd Inf. Co.C
Todd, H. SC 8th Res.
Todd, H.A. NC 12th Inf. Co.H
Todd, Hardy AL 44th Inf. Co.A
Todd, Hardy H. GA 48th Inf. Co.A 1st Lt.
Todd, Harrison TN 23rd Inf. 1st Co.F, Co.H Cpl.
Todd, Harvey W. MS 13th Inf. Co.D
Todd, Hastings M. AL 13th Inf. Co.C Sgt.
Todd, Haywood NC Cav. 12th Bn. Co.B
Todd, H.C. AL 2nd Cav. Co.F Music.
Todd, H.C. SC Inf. Hampton Legion Co.D
Todd, H.C. SC Palmetto S.S. Co.C
Todd, H. Cater SC 4th Inf. Co.B
Todd, Henry MO Cav. Freeman's Regt. Co.D
Todd, Henry A. NC 32nd Inf. Co.H 1st Sgt.
Todd, Henry H. MO 3rd Inf. Co.G
Todd, Henry R. MO 3rd Inf. Co.C
Todd, Henry R. NC 31st Inf. Co.H Sgt.
Todd, Henry S. VA 6th Inf. Co.G
Todd, Henry S. VA 9th Inf. Co.B 1st Lt.
Todd, Herman AL City Troop (Mobile) Arrington's Co.A
Todd, H.H. NC Inf. 13th Bn. Co.B Cpl.
Todd, H.H. NC 66th Inf. Co.B
Todd, Hilliard SC 1st Arty. Co.K
Todd, Hilliard SC Arty. Manigault's Bn. 1st Co.B
Todd, H.J. SC 10th Inf. 2nd Co.G
Todd, H.J. SC 26th Inf. Co.K
Todd, H.J. TX 14th Inf. Co.E
Todd, H.L. MO 6th Cav. Co.K
Todd, Houston GA 12th Inf. Co.D
Todd, H.P. SC Lt.Arty. 3rd (Palmetto) Bn. Co.G
Todd, H.P. SC 12th Inf. Co.E
Todd, Hugh MO Inf. Perkins' Bn. Co.E Cpl.
Todd, H.W. MS 2nd Cav. Co.B 1st Lt.
Todd, I.M. Conf.Cav. Wood's Regt. Co.I
Todd, Isaac MO 16th Inf. Co.B
Todd, Isaac VA 22nd Cav. Co.A
Todd, Isaac H. MS 15th Inf. Co.I
Todd, Isaac H. SC 1st (McCreary's) Inf. Co.F
Todd, Isaac McD. NC McDugald's Co.
Todd, J. AL 37th Inf. Co.D
Todd, J. AL 51st (Part.Rangers) Co.D,I
Todd, J. AR Inf. Hardy's Regt. Co.I
Todd, J. GA 12th Inf.
Todd, J. LA Mil.Conf.Guards Regt. Co.C
Todd, J. TX 1st Inf. 2nd Co.K
Todd, J.A. GA Inf. 1st Loc.Troops (Augusta) Co.B Cpl.
Todd, J.A. MS 41st Inf. Co.B
Todd, J.A. NC 37th Inf. Co.C
Todd, J.A. SC Arty. Manigault's Bn. Co.E
Todd, Jackson VA Mil. Grayson Cty.
Todd, Jacob GA 26th Inf. Co.G
Todd, Jacob H. VA 14th Inf. Co.I
Todd, Jacob W. VA 59th Mil. Hunter's Co.
Todd, James KY 2nd Bn.Mtd.Rifles Co.C
Todd, James LA 2nd Cav. Co.C Cpl.
Todd, James LA 21st (Kennedy's) Inf. Co.F
Todd, James MS 8th Inf. Co.K
Todd, James MS 21st Inf. Co.C
Todd, James MO 7th Cav. Co.F
Todd, James MO 9th Inf. Co.A,B Sgt.
Todd, James MO Inf. Clark's Regt. Co.A Sgt.
Todd, James MO Inf. Perkins' Bn. Co.E Sgt.
Todd, James NC 31st Inf. Co.H
Todd, James SC Mil.Arty. 1st Regt. Co.C
Todd, James SC Inf. 1st (Charleston) Bn. Co.C
Todd, James SC 27th Inf. Co.H
Todd, James TX 32nd Cav. Co.K 1st Lt.
Todd, James TX 1st Inf. Co.A
Todd, James TX Cadet
Todd, James 1st Chickasaw Inf. McCord's Co.
Todd, James A. AL 47th Inf. Co.K Capt.
Todd, James A. GA Cav. 7th Bn. (St.Guards) Co.A Cpl.
Todd, James A. MO 16th Inf. Co.D
Todd, James A. NC 34th Inf. Co.G Cpl.
Todd, James A. SC Hvy.Arty. Gilchrist's Co. (Gist Guard)
Todd, James A. SC 20th Inf. Co.E
Todd, James A. Gen. & Staff Surg.
Todd, James B. MO 1st Cav. Co.I
Todd, James C. NC 34th Inf. Co.G Capt.
Todd, James D. GA 40th Inf. Co.A
Todd, James E. NC 31st Inf. Co.H Capt.
Todd, James E. SC 1st (Orr's) Rifles Co.C
Todd, James E. VA 16th Cav. Co.A Sgt.
Todd, James E. VA Cav. Ferguson's Bn. Stevenson's Co. Sgt.
Todd, James E. VA 72nd Mil.
Todd, James G. VA Lt.Arty. Douthat's Co.
Todd, James H. GA 51st Inf. Co.A
Todd, James H. GA Cobb's Legion Co.B
Todd, James H. NC Inf. 13th Bn. Co.B
Todd, James H. NC 66th Inf. Co.B
Todd, James I. NC 1st Cav. (9th St.Troops) Co.D
Todd, James J. MS 15th Inf. Co.I
Todd, James L. TN Cav. 16th Bn. (Neal's) Co.E
Todd, James L. TN 29th Inf. Co.H
Todd, James M. AL 9th Inf. Co.E Capt.
Todd, James M. GA 45th Inf. Co.B
Todd, James M. KY 5th Mtd.Inf. Co.C
Todd, James M. SC 10th Inf. 2nd Co.G
Todd, James M. TN 18th Inf. Co.D
Todd, James T. SC 2nd Bn.S.S. Co.A
Todd, James T. SC 4th Inf. Co.B
Todd, James T. SC Palmetto S.S. Co.C
Todd, James T. 7th Conf.Cav. Co.E
Todd, James W. AR 2nd Mtd.Rifles Co.G
Todd, Jarret W. MO Cav. Slayback's Regt. Co.E
Todd, Jarrett MO 1st Cav. Co.I 2nd Lt.
Todd, J.A.S. Gen. & Staff,PACS Surg.
Todd, J.B. MS 5th Cav. Co.H
Todd, J.C. TN 14th (Neely's) Cav. Co.B
Todd, J.C. TX Jamison Res. Co.A
Todd, J.D. GA 63rd Inf. Co.D
Todd, Jesse AR Inf. Cocke's Regt. Co.D
Todd, Jesse MO Searcy's Bn.S.S.
Todd, J.F. AR 11th Inf. Co.G
Todd, J.F. AR 11th & 17th Cons.Inf. Co.G
Todd, J.F. KY 8th Mtd.Inf. Co.A
Todd, J.G. MO Inf. 3rd Bn. Co.E
Todd, J.G. MO 6th Inf. Co.C
Todd, J.H. AR 2nd Cav. Co.F
Todd, J.I. SC 10th Inf. 2nd Co.G Sgt.
Todd, J.J. SC Arty. Manigault's Bn. 1st Co.B Music.
Todd, J.J. SC Inf. 9th Bn. Co.A
Todd, J.J. SC 26th Inf. Co.A
Todd, J.J. TX 32nd Cav. Co.F
Todd, J.K. AR 2nd Cav. Co.D
Todd, J.L.B. GA Siege Arty. 28th Bn. Co.B
Todd, J.M. AL City Troops (Mobile) Arrington's Co.A
Todd, J.M. AL Mil. 4th Vol. Co.E
Todd, J.M. AL 14th Inf. Co.E
Todd, J.M. GA Cav. 1st Bn. Brailsford's Co.
Todd, J.M. GA 5th Cav. Co.H
Todd, J.M. MS 6th Cav. Co.C
Todd, J.M. MS 12th Cav. Co.L
Todd, J.M. MS Cav. Davenport's Bn. (St.Troops) Co.A,C
Todd, J.M. MS 24th Inf. Co.F
Todd, J.M. MO Cav. Fristoe's Regt. Co.D
Todd, J.M. TN 21st (Wilson's) Cav. Co.K 1st Sgt.
Todd, J.M. TN 21st (Wilson's) Cav. Co.K Sgt.Maj.
Todd, J.M. TN 21st & 22nd (Cons.) Cav. Co.F
Todd, J.M. TN 5th Inf. 1st Co.H, 2nd Co.E
Todd, J.M. TX 28th Cav. Co.E
Todd, J.M. TX 35th (Likens') Cav. Co.G
Todd, J.M. 7th Conf.Cav. Co.L
Todd, J.M. 15th Conf.Cav. Co.F
Todd, Joab C. GA 22nd Inf. Co.B
Todd, John AL 6th Inf. Co.M
Todd, John AL 8th Inf. Co.E Sgt.
Todd, John AL 44th Inf. Co.A
Todd, John GA 13th Cav. Co.F
Todd, John KY 4th Mtd.Inf. Co.G
Todd, John MS 9th Cav. Co.B
Todd, John MS 24th Inf. Co.F
Todd, John MO 1st N.E. Cav. Co.L
Todd, John MO 10th Cav. Co.C
Todd, John NC 43rd Inf. Co.C
Todd, John TN Inf. 22nd Bn. Co.B
Todd, John TN 38th Inf. Co.B
Todd, John TN 45th Inf. Co.I
Todd, John TX 1st Hvy.Arty. Co.K
Todd, John VA 20th Cav. Co.I
Todd, John A. GA Inf. Cobb's Guards Co.B
Todd, John A.N. NC 13th Inf. Co.B Music.
Todd, John B. AL St.Arty. Co.C Capt.
Todd, John B. MS 17th Inf. Co.B
Todd, John C. AL 14th Inf. Co.A Cpl.
Todd, John C. NC 1st Cav. (9th St.Troops) Co.D

Todd, John C.C. FL 7th Inf. Co.G Music.
Todd, John C.C. FL Brig.Band,CSA Music.
Todd, John D. TX 28th Cav. Co.K
Todd, John E. AR 4th Inf. Co.C 1st Sgt.
Todd, John F. AL Cav. 5th Bn. Hilliard's Legion Co.D
Todd, John F. 10th Conf.Cav. Co.D
Todd, John H. AR Inf. Hardy's Regt. Co.K
Todd, John H. SC 10th Inf. 2nd Co.G
Todd, John H. TN 18th Inf. Co.A
Todd, John H. VA 62nd Mtd.Inf. 2nd Co.B
Todd, John J. GA Siege Arty. 28th Bn. Co.F
Todd, John K. 1st Conf.Eng.Troops Co.K Sgt.
Todd, John L. NC 34th Inf. Co.G Sgt.
Todd, John L. NC 34th Inf. Co.G
Todd, Jno. M. MS 12th Cav. Co.L
Todd, John M. TN 5th (McKenzie's) Cav. Co.I
Todd, John M. VA 3rd Inf.Loc.Def. Co.F
Todd, John N. SC 1st (Orr's) Rifles Co.E Sgt.
Todd, John P. LA 3rd (Harrison's) Cav. Co.C
Todd, John R. VA 54th Mil. Co.A
Todd, John S. GA 22nd Inf. Co.H
Todd, Johnson H. GA 59th Inf. Co.E
Todd, John T. SC 1st (McCreary's) Inf. Co.F
Todd, John Thomas MS 34th Inf. Co.C
Todd, John W. LA 5th Cav. Capt.,ACS
Todd, John W. MO 1st Cav. Co.I
Todd, John W. NC 13th Inf. Co.B 1st Sgt.
Todd, John W. TN Cav. 11th Bn. (Gordon's) Co.E 2nd Lt.
Todd, John W. VA Lt.Arty. R.M. Anderson's Co.
Todd, John W.S. NC 34th Inf. Co.G
Todd, Jonathan E. SC 10th Inf. Co.M Cpl.
Todd, Joseph GA 55th Inf. Co.K
Todd, Joseph KY 3rd Mtd.Inf. Co.B
Todd, Joseph MS Inf. Cooper's Co. Cpl.
Todd, Joseph, Jr. MS Inf. Cooper's Co.
Todd, Joseph MO Inf. Perkins' Bn. Co.E Sgt.
Todd, Joseph NC 17th Inf. (2nd Org.) Co.D
Todd, Joseph SC 10th Inf. Co.B
Todd, Joseph SC 26th Inf. Co.K
Todd, Joseph, Jr. VA 6th Bn.Res. Co.G Cpl.
Todd, Joseph VA 39th Mil.
Todd, Joseph Gen. & Staff Hosp.Stew.
Todd, Joseph A.S. FL 2nd Inf. Co.E
Todd, Joseph B. NC 1st Cav. (9th St.Troops) Co.D 1st Lt.
Todd, Joseph B. NC 37th Inf. Co.B 1st Lt.
Todd, Joseph D. SC 10th Inf. Co.C
Todd, Joseph E. AL 10th Cav. Co.G
Todd, Joseph E. AL 50th Inf. Co.B
Todd, Joseph H. AL 61st Inf. Co.F
Todd, Joseph T. SC 14th Inf. Co.F
Todd, Josephus GA 41st Inf. Co.F
Todd, Joseph W. NC 1st Cav. (9th St.Troops) Co.D 1st Lt.
Todd, Joshua AL City Troop (Mobile) Arrington's Co.A
Todd, Joshua KY 8th Mtd.Inf. Co.E
Todd, Joshua 15th Conf.Cav. Co.F
Todd, J.R. NC 1st Arty. (10th St.Troops) Co.A
Todd, J.R. SC 9th Res. Co.E
Todd, J.R. SC Inf. 9th Bn. Co.A
Todd, J.R. SC 26th Inf. Co.A
Todd, J.R. TN 13th Inf. Co.G Cpl.
Todd, J.R. TX 14th Inf. Co.I
Todd, J.R. Nitre & Min. Bureau War Dept.,CSA Capt.
Todd, J.S. MS 8th Cav. Co.K
Todd, J.S. Gen. & Staff Asst.Surg.
Todd, J.T. MS 38th Cav. Co.B
Todd, J.T. SC Arty. Manigault's Bn. 1st Co.B
Todd, Julius J. FL 10th Inf. Co.B Sgt.
Todd, Julius J. Sig. Corps,CSA
Todd, J.W. KY 3rd Mtd.Inf. Co.B
Todd, J.W. SC Cav. 2nd Bn.Res. Co.G Sgt.
Todd, J.W. SC Cav. Tucker's Co.
Todd, J.W. SC Arty. Manigault's Bn. 1st Co.B
Todd, J.W. TX 2nd Cav. Co.E
Todd, J.W. TX St.Troops Teel's Co.
Todd, L.A. AL 14th Inf. Co.E
Todd, Lack W. MO 1st N.E. Cav.
Todd, Lawson N. NC 34th Inf. Co.G
Todd, Leander A. NC 28th Inf. Co.I 3rd Lt.
Todd, Lemuel M. SC 10th Inf. 2nd Co.G
Todd, Levi TN 23rd Inf. 1st Co.F, Co.H Lt.
Todd, Levi F. SC 1st (McCreary's) Inf. Co.F
Todd, Lewis AL 13th Inf. Co.E,D
Todd, Lewis NC 1st Arty. (10th St.Troops) Co.E Cpl.
Todd, Lewis NC 11th (Bethel Regt.) Inf. Co.C Sgt.
Todd, Lewis J. AL Cav. 5th Bn. Hilliard's Legion Co.D Far.
Todd, Lewis J. MO Cav. Freeman's Regt. Co.B Lt.
Todd, Lewis J. 10th Conf.Cav. Co.D Far.
Todd, L.J. AR Cav. Gordon's Regt. Co.B
Todd, L.J. MO 12th Cav. Co.K
Todd, L.L. TX 10th Cav. Co.K 2nd Lt.
Todd, L.M. TX 10th Cav. Co.K Capt.
Todd, Lorenzo D. NC 20th Inf. Co.D Cpl.
Todd, Louis B. TX 1st Inf. Co.A Sgt.
Todd, M. AL 62nd Inf. Co.C
Todd, M.A. AL 14th Inf. Co.E
Todd, Marcus B. MO 2nd Cav. 3rd Co.K
Todd, Marcus B. MO 9th Inf. Co.G
Todd, Marcus L. MO 1st Cav. Co.I,E 1st Lt.
Todd, Marcus L. MO 1st & 3rd Cons.Cav. Co.E 1st Lt.
Todd, Marion AL 18th Inf. Co.I,A
Todd, Marius P. VA 5th Cav. Co.E Capt.
Todd, M.B. MO St.Guard Cornet Band
Todd, McD.L. FL 2nd Cav. Co.G
Todd, Meriman MD Cav. 2nd Bn. Co.C Sgt.
Todd, Merriman MO 1st N.E. Cav. Co.A
Todd, Milo G. NC 14th Inf. Co.I
Todd, Moses S. MS 14th Inf. Co.A
Todd, M.V. MS 44th Inf. Co.D
Todd, N.C. SC 3rd Inf. Co.I
Todd, N.C. SC 9th Res. Co.D
Todd, N.C. SC 20th Inf. Co.F
Todd, Nehemiah J. NC 11th (Bethel Regt.) Inf. Co.C Music.
Todd, Neviah MO Inf. Perkins' Bn. Co.E
Todd, N.H. KY 9th Cav. Co.C
Todd, N.K. LA Arty. 1st Field Btty. Cpl.
Todd, O.B. KY 4th Cav. Co.C
Todd, O.B. VA 9th Cav. Co.E
Todd, O.C. KY 19th (Johnson's) Cav. New Co.I
Todd, Overton C. MO Cav. Slayback's Regt. Co.A Sgt.
Todd, Patrick P.L. FL 2nd Inf. Co.C Capt.
Todd, Peter G. TX 14th Cav. Co.E
Todd, Peter V. SC 7th Cav. Co.F
Todd, P.H. MS 18th Cav.
Todd, Pinckney P. SC 10th Inf. Co.B Cpl.
Todd, P.L. TN 4th Inf. Co.D
Todd, Polk NC 2nd Jr.Res. Co.H
Todd, P.P. SC Inf.Bn. Co.B Cpl.
Todd, Preston VA 5th Inf. Co.C
Todd, Preston VA 5th Inf. Co.I
Todd, P.T. MO Inf. 3rd Bn. Co.F
Todd, P.T. MO 6th Inf. Co.H
Todd, P.V. SC Cav. 19th Bn. Co.D
Todd, R.H. GA Inf. 25th Bn. (Prov.Guard) Co.B
Todd, R. Henry NC 53rd Inf. Co.B Cpl.
Todd, Richard VA 13th Inf. Co.G
Todd, Richard F. GA 5th Inf. Co.B
Todd, Richard L. VA 9th Cav. Co.E Cpl.
Todd, R.J. SC Arty. Manigault's Bn. 1st Co.B
Todd, R.J. SC Inf. 3rd Bn. Co.E
Todd, R.J. SC 26th Inf. Co.K
Todd, R.L. MO Cav. Ford's Bn. Co.B
Todd, R.L. NC 11th (Bethel Regt.) Inf. Co.D
Todd, Robert AL 26th (O'Neal's) Inf. Co.K Sgt.
Todd, Robert SC 1st (Butler's) Inf. Co.I
Todd, Robert TX 12th Inf. Co.I
Todd, Robert VA 109th Mil. 1st Co.A, 2nd Co.A
Todd, Robert F. SC 4th Inf. Co.I
Todd, Robert F. SC Palmetto S.S. Co.I Cpl.
Todd, Robert J. NC 37th Inf. Co.I
Todd, Robert K. VA Lt.Arty. Jeffress' Co.
Todd, Robert M. VA 55th Inf. Co.I
Todd, Robert R.P. MO Inf. 8th Bn. Co.B
Todd, Robert S. MS 12th Inf. Co.A
Todd, Robinson A. Gen. & Staff ACS
Todd, Royal VA 1st St.Res. Co.A
Todd, R.P. SC 3rd Inf. Co.G Lt.Col.
Todd, R.S. VA 5th Cav. Co.K
Todd, R.T. AL 26th (O'Neal's) Inf. Co.K 1st Lt.
Todd, Rufus H. MO St.Guard
Todd, R.W. MO 6th Cav. Co.K
Todd, S.A. SC 3rd Inf. Co.I
Todd, Samuel TN 16th (Logwood's) Cav. Co.F Cpl.
Todd, Samuel TN 54th Inf. Co.G
Todd, Samuel C. TN Lt.Arty. Barry's Co.
Todd, Samuel G. AL 4th Inf. Co.A
Todd, Samuel M. LA 3rd (Harrison's) Cav. Co.K Capt.
Todd, Samuel M. LA Inf. 1st Sp.Bn. (Rightor's) Co.A Capt.
Todd, Samuel W. AL 16th Inf. Co.C
Todd, Saul W. MS 1st Cav. Co.C
Todd, S.B. LA Inf. 7th Bn. Co.A
Todd, S.B. LA Inf.Crescent Regt. Co.H
Todd, S.B. TN 3rd (Forrest's) Cav. Co.E
Todd, S.D. SC 10th Inf. 2nd Co.G
Todd, S.D. SC 26th Inf. Co.K
Todd, S.D. SC Palmetto S.S. Co.M
Todd, S.E. NC 1st Inf. (6 mo. '61) Co.C
Todd, S.E. NC 53rd Inf. Co.B
Todd, S.J. MS 2nd Cav. Co.B
Todd, S.J. MS 8th Inf. Co.B
Todd, S.J. MS 22nd Inf.
Todd, S.J. SC 10th Inf. 2nd Co.G
Todd, S.R. SC Bn.St.Cadets Co.B

Todd, Strother H. MO Douglas' Regt. Corn's Co.
Todd, T. GA 47th Inf. Co.C
Todd, T.D. SC 3rd St.Troops Co.D
Todd, Thaddeus S. SC 1st (McCreary's) Inf. Co.F
Todd, Theodore GA 41st Inf. Co.F
Todd, Thomas AL 2nd Cav. Co.F
Todd, Thomas AL 44th Inf. Co.A
Todd, Thomas LA 4th Inf. Co.G
Todd, Thomas MO 16th Inf. Co.D Sgt.
Todd, Thomas B.F. GA Cobb's Legion Co.H
Todd, Thomas C. KY 4th Mtd.Inf. Co.G,D
Todd, Thomas C. SC 1st (Orr's) Rifles Co.E
Todd, Thomas F. GA 16th Inf. Co.H
Todd, Thomas Hart Benton MO 1st Cav. Co.I Sgt.
Todd, Thomas J. KY 10th (Johnson's) Cav. Co.E
Todd, Thomas J. TX 28th Cav. Co.A 1st Lt.
Todd, Thomas J. VA Hvy.Arty. 19th Bn. Co.B
Todd, Thomas J. VA Lt.Arty. Parker's Co. Cpl.
Todd, Thomas K. MS 2nd Inf. Co.D
Todd, Thomas L. GA 27th Inf. Co.E Cpl.
Todd, Thomas P. MS Bradford's Co. (Conf. Guards Arty.)
Todd, Thomas R. MD 1st Inf. Co.E
Todd, Thomas W. VA Lt.Arty. Jeffress' Co. Sgt.
Todd, T.J. AR 11th Inf. Co.G
Todd, T.K. MS 3rd Cav. Co.G
Todd, T.L. SC 14th Inf. Co.F
Todd, T.P. MS 1st Cav. Co.K
Todd, T.W. MO Inf. Perkins' Bn. Capt.
Todd, Vincent MS 46th Inf. Co.I
Todd, W. AL 1st Bn.Cadets Co.B
Todd, W. FL 1st (Res.) Inf. Co.L
Todd, W. KY 8th Mtd.Inf. Co.A
Todd, W. TN 12th (Green's) Cav. Co.F
Todd, W. TX Cav. Hardeman's Regt. Co.G
Todd, W.A. TN 8th (Smith's) Cav. Co.G
Todd, Walker TN 2nd (Robison's) Inf. Co.F
Todd, Walker TN 18th Inf. Co.A
Todd, W.B. MO 2nd Cav. Co.G
Todd, W.B. VA 24th Bn.Part.Rangers Co.A
Todd, W.D. AR 37th Inf. Co.E
Todd, W.E. GA 5th Cav. Co.H
Todd, Wesley F. SC 10th Inf. 2nd Co.G
Todd, Westwood A. VA 12th Inf. Co.E,A
Todd, Westwood A. Weisiger's Brig. 2nd Lt., Ord.Off.
Todd, W.F. TN 61st Mtd.Inf. Co.K
Todd, W.H. AL Vol. Meador's Co.
Todd, W.H. MO Searcy's Bn.S.S. Co.E Capt.
Todd, W.H. SC Lt.Arty. M. Ward's Co. (Waccamaw Lt.Arty.)
Todd, W.H. TN 15th (Stewart's) Cav. Co.G
Todd, W.H. TN 46th Inf. Co.E
Todd, W.H. TN 47th Inf. Co.C
Todd, W.H. TN 51st (Cons.) Inf. Co.B
Todd, W.H. VA 2nd Inf.Loc.Def. Co.E
Todd, W.H. VA Inf. 6th Bn.Loc.Def. Co.B
Todd, W.H.L. TN 27th Inf. Co.H Sgt.
Todd, Wiley VA 4th Res. Co.B
Todd, Wiley J. NC 2nd Inf. Co.B
Todd, William AL Cav. Callaway's Co.
Todd, William AL 4th Res. Co.H
Todd, William AL 34th Inf. Co.E 2nd Lt.
Todd, William AR Cav. Gordon's Regt. Co.C
Todd, William GA 4th Inf. Co.B
Todd, William GA 7th Inf. Co.B
Todd, William KY 3rd Mtd.Inf. Co.B
Todd, William MO 1st N.E. Cav.
Todd, William MO Inf. Perkins' Bn. Co.E
Todd, William NC 5th Cav. (63rd St.Troops) Co.H
Todd, William NC 1st Arty. (10th St.Troops) Co.C
Todd, William NC 1st Inf. (6 mo. '61) Co.C
Todd, William NC 22nd Inf. Co.I
Todd, William NC 46th Inf. Co.A
Todd, William SC 2nd Inf. Co.H
Todd, William TN 3rd (Forrest's) Cav. Co.K
Todd, William TN 19th Inf. Co.I
Todd, William TX 4th Inf. Co.E
Todd, William TX 12th Inf. Co.I
Todd, William VA 32nd Inf. 2nd Co.K
Todd, William VA 115th Mil. Co.A
Todd, William VA Mil. Grayson Cty.
Todd, William A. MS 15th Inf. Co.I
Todd, William A. MS 24th Inf. Co.K
Todd, William A. NC 22nd Inf. Co.A
Todd, William A. SC 6th Cav. Co.E
Todd, William A. SC 12th Inf. Co.K Cpl.
Todd, William A. VA 10th Cav. Co.G
Todd, William B. LA 5th Inf. Co.D
Todd, William B. MS 18th Inf. Co.A
Todd, William B. MS 22nd Inf. Co.G
Todd, William B. VA 9th Cav. Co.E
Todd, William C. SC 1st (Orr's) Rifles Co.E
Todd, William C. TN 21st (Wilson's) Cav. Co.E
Todd, William C. TN Cav. Newsom's Regt. Co.C
Todd, William D. AR Cav. Wright's Regt. Co.G
Todd, William D. LA 14th Inf. Co.I
Todd, William E. GA Cav. 1st Bn. Brailsford's Co.
Todd, William E. LA 30th Inf. Co.C,B
Todd, William E. LA Inf.Crescent Regt. Co.C
Todd, William F. AL 28th Inf. Co.B
Todd, William H. AL 8th (Livingston's) Cav. Co.O
Todd, William H. AL Cav. Moses' Squad. Co.A
Todd, William H. AL 9th Inf. Co.I,E 1st Lt.
Todd, William H. GA 48th Inf. Co.A Cpl.
Todd, William H. MD Cav. 2nd Bn. Co.C
Todd, William H. MS 1st Cav. Co.I
Todd, William H. MO 1st Cav. Co.I Sgt.
Todd, William H. MO 2nd Cav. 3rd Co.K
Todd, William H. MO 6th Cav. Co.K Sgt.Maj.
Todd, William H. NC 1st Inf. (6 mo. '61) Co.L
Todd, William H. NC 11th (Bethel Regt.) Inf. Co.C 1st Lt.
Todd, William H. SC Inf. Hampton Legion Co.A
Todd, William H.B. SC 1st (Orr's) Rifles Co.E Cpl.
Todd, William J. AL Lt.Arty. 2nd Bn. Co.A
Todd, William J. AR 4th Inf. Co.C
Todd, William J. MS 17th Inf. Co.F
Todd, William J. TN 2nd (Robison's) Inf. Co.F Sgt.
Todd, William J. TN 23rd Inf. Co.B
Todd, William L. MO 1st Cav. Co.I
Todd, William L. MO 1st & 3rd Cons.Cav. Co.E
Todd, William M. GA 1st (Fannin's) Res. Co.H
Todd, William M. MS 2nd Inf. (A. of 10,000) Co.H Cpl.
Todd, William M. TN 41st Inf. Co.C
Todd, William O. NC 31st Inf. Co.H Sgt.
Todd, William R. GA 48th Inf. Co.C
Todd, Wm. R. TX 37th Cav. Co.B,C
Todd, William R. VA Lt.Arty. R.M. Anderson's Co.
Todd, William Richards MS Bradford's Co. (Conf.Guards Arty.)
Todd, William Rubin MO 8th Inf. Co.I
Todd, William T. NC 4th Inf. Co.F
Todd, William T. SC 10th Inf. Co.M
Todd, William T.P. TN 5th (McKenzie's) Cav. Co.I
Todd, William W. GA 61st Inf. Co.B
Todd, William W. SC 11th (McCreary's) Inf. Co.F
Todd, Willis AL Cav. 24th Bn. Co.B
Todd, Willis AL 34th Inf. Co.E
Todd, Willis L. SC 10th Inf. Co.C
Todd, Wilson NC 2nd Inf. Co.B
Todd, Wilson TN 23rd Inf. Co.H
Todd, W.J. TN 27th Inf. Co.E
Todd, W.L. NC 5th Cav. (63rd St.Troops) Co.F
Todd, W.M. LA Inf. 1st Sp.Bn. (Rightor's) Co.A
Todd, W.M. TN 4th Cav. Co.D
Todd, W.M. TN 23rd Inf. Co.H
Todd, W.O. KY Lt.Arty. Cobb's Co., Co.A
Todd, W.R. AL 6th Cav. Co.D
Todd, W.R. MO Cav. Fristoe's Regt. Co.D
Todd, W.R. MO 11th Inf. Co.C Lt.
Todd, W.R. TX 3rd Cav. Co.D Cpl.
Todd, W.R. TX 9th (Young's) Inf. Co.B
Todd, W.R. VA 3rd Inf.Loc.Def. Co.C 1st Lt.
Todd, W.S. MO Cav. Fristoe's Regt. Co.C
Todd, W.T. TN 45th Inf. Co.I
Todd, W.W. GA 1st (Fannin's) Res. Co.K
Todd, Wyley VA 2nd St.Res. Co.B
Todd, Zachariah VA 32nd Inf. 2nd Co.K
Todd, Zachariah VA 115th Mil. Co.A
Todder, F. AR Inf. Hardy's Regt. Co.H
Todder, Thomas AR Inf. Hardy's Regt. Co.H
Toddi, W.H. GA 3rd Cav. Co.D
Toddy, Joseph KY 3rd Cav. Co.K
Tode, C. SC Mil.Arty. 1st Regt. Co.A
Todford, W.L. MS Cav. Yerger's Regt. Co.E
Todhunter, Edwin M. KY Capt.,ACS
Todhunter, R. Taylor's Corps Capt.,AAG
Todzers, J.W. LA 2nd Cav. Co.I
Toel, T.F. LA 21st (Kennedy's) Inf. Co.D Music.
Toel, William LA 22nd Inf. Jones' Co.
Toell, Thomas F. MS 2nd Cav. Co.C
Toell, Thomas F. MS 24th Inf. Co.D,I
Toemel, T. LA 22nd Inf. Co.B
Toemel, T. LA 22nd (Cons.) Inf. Co.B
Toepfer, E. TX 3rd Inf. 2nd Co.A
Toepperwein, E.A. TX Lt.Arty. Dege's Bn.
Toepperwein, E.A.F. TX 6th Field Btty.
Toepperwein, Gustav TX 36th Cav. Co.F Music.
Toepperwein, Herman TX 36th Cav. Co.F Music.
Toepperwein, Paul TX 36th Cav. Music.
Toese, William J. VA 3rd Lt.Arty. (Loc.Def.) Co.C

Toffier, Antoine LA Mil.Cav.Squad. (Iberville Ind.Rangers)
Toffier, A.W. AR Arty. West's Btty.
Toffier, W.A. LA Mil.Cav.Squad. (Iberville Ind.Rangers)
Toffier, William A. LA 2nd Cav. Co.I Cpl.
Tofohr, Fredrick LA 1st Hvy.Arty. (Reg.) Co.G
Toft, C.E. MS 10th Cav. Co.K
Togg, I. TN 38th Inf. Co.B
Toghman, Henry NC 1st Inf. Co.H
Toglia, P. SC Mil.Arty. 1st Regt. Walter's Co.
Toglio, Peter SC 5th Cav. Co.G
Toglio, Peter SC Cav. 17th Bn. Co.B
Togni, Antoine LA Mil. 3rd Regt. French Brig. Co.5 Sr.2nd Lt.
Togni, J.B. SC 1st Regt. Charleston Guard Co.D
Togniero, G. SC 1st Regt. Charleston Guard Co.D
Tognini, George LA Mil. 1st Regt. 2nd Brig. 1st Div. Co.C
To go not chee 1st Creek Mtd.Vol. Co.M
Toh cul kay 1st Creek Mtd.Vol. Co.E
Toher, Thomas V. GA 1st Reg. Co.L Cpl.
Toh hees kih NC Inf. Thomas Legion Co.B
Tohnotubbee 1st Choctaw & Chickasaw Mtd.Rifles 3rd Co.K
Tohr, J.L. TN Jackson's Cav. Co.D
Toh tul li key 1st Creek Mtd.Vol. Co.H
Tohubby Deneale's Regt. Choctaw Warriors Co.C
Tohunee, William 1st Cherokee Mtd.Vol. 2nd Co.H
Tohwekeleh, Aleck 1st Choctaw & Chickasaw Mtd.Rifles Co.G
Tokchetubbee 1st Choctaw Mtd.Rifles Co.H
Tokko, Harrison 1st Choctaw & Chickasaw Mtd.Rifles 2nd Co.D,C
Tolan, James AL 2nd Cav. Co.I
Tolan, James AL Cav. Hardie's Bn.Res. Co.A Sgt.
Tolan, John LA 6th Inf. Co.F
Tolan, T.J. MS 46th Inf. Co.D
Tolan, William AR 15th (N.W.) Inf. Co.D
Tolancourth, Dominique LA 10th Inf. Co.I
Toland, Abraham AL 32nd Inf. Co.E
Toland, A.P. GA 2nd Cav. Co.F
Toland, D.W. TN 24th Bn.S.S. Co.B
Toland, E. GA Lt.Arty. Pritchard's Co. (Washington Arty.)
Toland, E. GA 36th (Villepigue's) Inf. Co.F
Toland, E. SC 18th Inf. Asst.Surg.
Toland, E. TN Arty. Marshall's Co.
Toland, E. TN Lt.Arty. Scott's Co.
Toland, E. 1st Conf.Inf. 1st Co.F
Toland, Elihu SC 6th Cav. Co.E
Toland, Elihu SC 18th Inf. Asst.Surg.
Toland, Elihu Gen. & Staff Surg.
Toland, G.W. TN 24th Bn.S.S. Co.B Sgt.
Toland, Hugh MS 30th Inf. Co.A
Toland, Hugh C. MS 20th Inf. Co.C
Toland, James GA 3rd Res. Co.B
Toland, James M. AL 32nd Inf. Co.D
Toland, Jesse MS 12th Inf. Co.I
Toland, J.F. GA 7th Inf. (St.Guards) Co.F
Toland, J.F. TX 5th Inf. Co.E
Toland, J.J. AR 6th Inf. Co.B
Toland, J.J. MS Adams' Co. (Holmes Cty.Ind.)
Toland, J.L. TX Cav. Waller's Regt. Co.B
Toland, John TN 3rd (Lillard's) Mtd.Inf. Co.A 2nd Lt.
Toland, John Vaughn's Staff 2nd Lt.,ADC
Toland, John F. AL 22nd Inf. Co.A
Toland, John S. GA Inf. 1st Loc.Troops (Augusta) Co.I
Toland, John S. SC 13th Inf. Co.D
Toland, Joseph H. TX 35th (Brown's) Cav. Co.G Sgt.
Toland, Joseph H. TX 13th Vol. 2nd Co.G 1st Sgt.
Toland, J.W. MS 26th Inf. Co.H
Toland, R.G. TN 10th (DeMoss') Cav. Co.F
Toland, R.G. TN Cav. Napier's Bn. Co.C
Toland, R.S. TX 5th Inf. Co.E
Toland, R.W. SC 5th Cav. Co.E
Toland, T.M. AR 19th (Dawson's) Inf. Co.C
Toland, T.W. 2nd TX Cav. McCord's Frontier Regt. Co.I
Toland, Walter H. SC 4th Inf. Co.J
Toland, W.F. AL 22nd Inf. Co.B Cpl.
Toland, W.H. SC Inf. Hampton Legion Co.I
Toland, Wm. AL Cp. of Instr. Talladega
Toland, William D. MS 30th Inf. Co.A
Trappe Harjo 1st Seminole Mtd.Vol.
Tolar, A.H. NC 2nd Arty. (36th St Troops) Co.B
Tolar, Alfred H. NC 18th Inf. Co.K Capt.
Tolar, B.S. FL 6th Inf. Co.A
Tolar, Haynes NC 2nd Arty. (36th St.Troops) Co.B
Tolar, Haynes L. NC 18th Inf. Co.K
Tolar, Hiram NC 51st Inf. Co.I
Tolar, I.S. SC 21st Inf. Co.K Sgt.
Tolar, Isaiah MS 7th Inf. Co.G
Tolar, J. MS 7th Cav. Co.G
Tolar, J.A. MS 38th Cav. Co.A
Tolar, James TX 25th Cav. Co.A
Tolar, J.C. AR 8th Cav. Co.F
Tolar, J.K. MS 3rd Inf. (St.Troops) Co.G
Tolar, J.M. NC 2nd Arty. (36th St.Troops) Co.C
Tolar, J.M. NC Lt.Arty. 13th Bn. Co.C Bugler
Tolar, John H. SC 1st (Orr's) Rifles Co.H 1st Lt.
Tolar, John R. NC 2nd Bn.Loc.Def.Troops Co.A Laborer
Tolar, J.W. MS 7th Cav. Co.G
Tolar, J.W. MS 7th Inf. Co.G
Tolar, M.A. NC Lt.Arty. 13th Bn. Co.C Sgt.
Tolar, Matthew A. NC 2nd Arty. (36th St.Troops) Co.C Sgt.
Tolar, Needham S. NC 2nd Arty. (36th St.Troops) Co.B
Tolar, R.E. SC 18th Inf. Co.I
Tolar, Robert M. NC 2nd Arty. (36th St.Troops) Co.B
Tolar, Robert M. NC 51st Inf. Co.I
Tolar, Sampson B. NC 18th Inf. Co.K
Tolar, S.B. NC 2nd Arty. (36th St.Troops) Co.B
Tolar, Simeon R. NC 3rd Inf. Co.C Cpl.
Tolar, Thomas B. SC 10th Inf. Co.B
Tolar, Thomas J. NC 2nd Bn.Loc.Def.Troops Co.A Laborer
Tolar, T.J. TN 49th Inf. Co.G
Tolar, W.A. MS 11th (Perrin's) Cav. Co.G
Tolar, William MS Home Guards Barnes' Co.
Tolar, William A. GA Cobb's Legion Co.G
Tolar, W.J. NC Lt.Arty. 13th Bn. Co.C
Tolar, W.J. SC 10th Inf. Co.B Capt.
Tolar, W.T. MS 9th Inf. Co.A
Tolbart, W.W. TN 27th Inf. Co.A
Tolberson, William MO 1st N.E. Cav. Co.B
Tolbert, A. GA Inf. 27th Bn. (NonConscr.) Co.E
Tolbert, A. MS 13th Inf.
Tolbert, A.C. GA 40th Inf. Co.A
Tolbert, A.F. AR 27th Inf. Co.E
Tolbert, A.J. GA Cav. 10th Bn. (St.Guards) Co.A
Tolbert, A.J. GA 18th Inf. Co.C
Tolbert, Allen GA 17th Inf. Co.C Cpl.
Tolbert, A.M. KY 2nd (Woodward's) Cav. Co.D
Tolbert, Andrew J. GA 41st Inf. Co.B
Tolbert, Ben SC 5th St.Troops Co.B
Tolbert, Benjamin SC 18th Inf. Co.K
Tolbert, Benjamin H. GA 40th Inf. Co.I
Tolbert, B.H. GA 12th Cav. Co.C
Tolbert, B.H. GA 1st Inf. Co.K
Tolbert, B.H. NC 14th Inf. Co.H
Tolbert, B.J. GA 23rd Inf. Co.G
Tolbert, C.C. GA Cav. 9th Bn. (St.Guards) Co.B
Tolbert, Charles AR 11th Inf. Co.G,I
Tolbert, Charles LA Pointe Coupee Arty.
Tolbert, Charles W. VA 108th Mil. Co.D
Tolbert, Chesley M. VA Lt.Arty. 13th Bn. Co.B
Tolbert, David AR 18th Inf. Co.A
Tolbert, David GA 41st Inf. Co.H
Tolbert, David MS 5th Inf. Co.I
Tolbert, David VA Cav. 47th Bn. Co.B Sgt.
Tolbert, Davis VA 26th Cav. Co.H Sgt.
Tolbert, Doctor NC 44th Inf. Co.F
Tolbert, Edward AL 31st Inf. Co.D
Tolbert, E.H. GA 30th Inf. Co.C
Tolbert, Elias SC 2nd Cav. Co.I
Tolbert, E.N. GA 23rd Inf. Co.G
Tolbert, Ephraim NC Walker's Bn. Thomas' Legion Co.B
Tolbert, F. VA 5th Bn.Res. Co.A
Tolbert, Franklin NC 44th Inf. Co.F
Tolbert, George T. LA Inf. 11th Bn. Co.D Sgt.
Tolbert, George W. MS 10th Inf. New Co.D
Tolbert, George W. NC 35th Inf. Co.K
Tolbert, George W. SC 2nd Cav. Co.I
Tolbert, G.M. GA 8th Inf. Co.H
Tolbert, G.W. GA 18th Inf. Co.H
Tolbert, G.W. MS 9th Inf. Co.G
Tolbert, H. AL 31st Inf. Co.D
Tolbert, Harmon V. GA 17th Inf. Co.C
Tolbert, Harrison F. NC 28th Inf. Co.D
Tolbert, H.D. TN 17th Inf. Co.G
Tolbert, Henry L. AL 4th (Russell's) Cav.
Tolbert, H.H. AR 27th Inf. Co.E
Tolbert, H.L. AL 23rd Inf. Co.G
Tolbert, H.L. AL 31st Inf. Co.D
Tolbert, H.R. MS 9th Inf. Co.I
Tolbert, H.R. MS 41st Inf. Co.C
Tolbert, H.S. GA 23rd Inf. Co.G 1st Lt.
Tolbert, Hyram VA 57th Inf. Co.D
Tolbert, Isaiah AL 1st Regt.Conscr. Co.E
Tolbert, J. NC 1st Arty. (10th St.Troops) Co.E
Tolbert, J. NC 2nd Conscr.
Tolbert, J.A. AL 11th Cav. Co.B
Tolbert, J.A. GA 23rd Inf. Co.G Sgt.
Tolbert, James AR Dunnington's Nav.Btty.
Tolbert, James MS 3rd Cav.Res. Co.F
Tolbert, James NC 5th Sr.Res. Co.C

Tolbert, James TN 8th Inf. Co.G
Tolbert, James VA 7th Inf. Co.G
Tolbert, James VA Inf. 23rd Bn. Co.E
Tolbert, James A. GA 20th Inf. Co.D
Tolbert, James A. SC 15th Inf. Co.I
Tolbert, James C. GA 35th Inf. Co.A
Tolbert, James C. GA Inf. Taylor's Co.
Tolbert, James F. SC 19th Inf. Co.G
Tolbert, James H. TN 28th (Cons.) Inf. Maj.
Tolbert, James J. AL 10th Inf. Co.G
Tolbert, James M. GA 34th Inf. Co.B Cpl.
Tolbert, James M. NC 26th Inf. Co.G
Tolbert, James R. TN 28th Inf. Co.E,I Maj.
Tolbert, J.E.P. GA 23rd Inf. Co.G Cpl.
Tolbert, Jeremiah VA 57th Inf. Co.I
Tolbert, Jerry E. MS 11th Inf. Co.G
Tolbert, Jerry T. MS 1st Bn.S.S. Co.D Sgt.
Tolbert, Jesse GA Inf. White's Co.
Tolbert, J.H. MS 5th Inf. (St.Troops) Co.C Cpl.
Tolbert, J.H. MS Hall's Co.
Tolbert, J.M. FL 2nd Inf. Co.D 2nd Lt.
Tolbert, J.M. GA 39th Inf. Co.E Cpl.
Tolbert, J.M. VA 17th Cav. Co.G
Tolbert, John AR 45th Cav. Co.F
Tolbert, John GA Inf. Athens Reserved Corps
Tolbert, John TN 16th Inf. Co.K
Tolbert, John TX Cav. Hardeman's Regt. Co.D
Tolbert, John VA 33rd Inf. Co.E
Tolbert, John C. NC 52nd Inf. Co.I
Tolbert, John H. FL 5th Inf. Co.B Capt.
Tolbert, John H. TX 16th Cav. Co.D Capt.
Tolbert, John J. NC 25th Inf. Co.G
Tolbert, John J. VA 5th Bn.Res. Co.E
Tolbert, John M. AL 21st Inf. Co.C
Tolbert, John N. VA 7th Inf. Co.B
Tolbert, John R. SC 2nd Cav. Co.I Bvt.2nd Lt.
Tolbert, John W. GA 34th Inf. Co.E
Tolbert, Joseph W. SC 15th Inf. Co.I
Tolbert, Josiah GA 23rd Inf. Co.G
Tolbert, Josiah P. NC 28th Inf. Co.K
Tolbert, Josiah T. GA 16th Inf. Co.A
Tolbert, J.P. LA 31st Inf. Co.E
Tolbert, J.P. TX Cav. Hardeman's Regt. Co.D
Tolbert, J.S. LA Mil. Claiborne Regt. Co.A
Tolbert, J.W. MS 9th Inf. Co.I
Tolbert, J.W. MS 41st Inf. Co.C
Tolbert, J.W. TX 1st Inf. Co.F
Tolbert, L. AR 1st (Dobbin's) Cav. Co.B
Tolbert, L. TX 24th & 25th Cav. (Cons.) Co.I
Tolbert, Levi GA Inf. (Madison Cty. Home Guard) Milner's Co.
Tolbert, Lewis AR 32nd Inf. Co.B
Tolbert, L.F. TN 21st (Carter's) Cav. Co.A
Tolbert, Mathew AL 1st Inf. Co.A
Tolbert, Milton NC 44th Inf. Co.F
Tolbert, Nathan 1st Choctaw & Chickasaw Mtd.Rifles 2nd Co.C Sgt.
Tolbert, Nicholas MS 16th Inf. Co.F
Tolbert, O. GA Inf. 27th Bn. (NonConscr.) Co.E
Tolbert, Oliver M. VA 50th Inf. Co.L
Tolbert, O.M. VA Inf. 23rd Bn. Co.E
Tolbert, Osbern H. GA 34th Inf. Co.B
Tolbert, P. MS 4th Cav. Co.I
Tolbert, P.H. GA 1st Cav. Co.D Sgt.
Tolbert, Pinkney T. NC 28th Inf. Co.E
Tolbert, P.W. MS 2nd Part.Rangers Co.I
Tolbert, P.W. MS 28th Cav. Co.G
Tolbert, R.C. TX 8th Cav. Co.K
Tolbert, R.H. GA 56th Inf. Co.I
Tolbert, R.J. LA 31st Inf. Co.D
Tolbert, Robert M. NC 44th Inf. Co.F
Tolbert, Salathiel VA 20th Cav. Co.D
Tolbert, Samuel SC 22nd Inf. Co.E
Tolbert, Shadrick MO Cav. Freeman's Regt. Co.C
Tolbert, Silas AL 36th Inf. Co.F
Tolbert, S.R. MS 31st Inf. Co.G
Tolbert, S.T. LA 5th Cav. Co.H
Tolbert, T.B. AR 27th Inf. Co.E
Tolbert, Thomas SC 12th Inf. Co.E
Tolbert, Thomas TN 23rd Inf. Co.K
Tolbert, Thomas B. MO Inf. 8th Bn. Co.B
Tolbert, Thomas B. MO 9th Inf. Co.F
Tolbert, Thomas C. NC 25th Inf. Co.G
Tolbert, Thomas M. GA Inf. Alexander's Co.
Tolbert, Thomas N. SC 2nd Cav. Co.I Cpl.
Tolbert, Thomas W. LA 28th (Gray's) Inf. Co.F
Tolbert, Tilmon SC 12th Inf. Co.E
Tolbert, T.R. MS 35th Inf. Co.G
Tolbert, W.A. GA 37th Inf. Co.E
Tolbert, W.A. GA 54th Inf. Co.I Cpl.
Tolbert, W.A. MS 35th Inf. Co.G
Tolbert, W.C. AR 7th Inf. Co.I
Tolbert, W.G. MS Cav. (St.Troops) Gamblin's Co.
Tolbert, W.H. LA Inf.Crescent Regt. Co.H
Tolbert, W.H. LA Inf.Cons.Crescent Regt. Co.G
Tolbert, W.H. SC 1st Cav. Co.G
Tolbert, W.H. TX 29th Cav. Co.K Cpl.
Tolbert, Whitson NC 44th Inf. Co.F
Tolbert, William AL 18th Inf. Co.B
Tolbert, William AR 25th Inf. Co.D
Tolbert, William GA Cav. 9th Bn. (St.Guards) Co.B
Tolbert, William NC 47th Inf. Co.A
Tolbert, William TN 8th Inf. Co.G
Tolbert, William TX Cav. Hardeman's Regt. Co.A
Tolbert, William A. GA Inf. 9th Bn. Co.B
Tolbert, William A. NC 34th Inf. Co.K
Tolbert, William J. NC 25th Inf. Co.G
Tolbert, William R. VA Cav. Hounshell's Bn. Huffman's Co.
Tolbert, W.K. SC 1st Cav. Co.G Sgt.
Tolbert, W.M. GA 24th Inf. Co.E
Tolbird, James M. LA 31st Inf. Co.K
Tolbird, William LA 31st Inf. Co.K
Tolbot, Charles AR 17th (Griffith's) Inf. Co.A
Tolbot, John F. NC 43rd Inf. Co.E
Tolbot, W.B. MS Inf. 1st Bn.St.Troops (12 mo. '62-3) Co.A
Tolbott, C.L. LA Mil. Chalmette Regt. Co.F
Tolbott, George H. VA 2nd Arty. Co.A
Tolbott, L.W. TN 3rd (Forrest's) Cav. Co.C Bvt.2nd Lt.
Tolbott, Thomas SC 22nd Inf. Co.E
Tolburt, J. AL 11th Inf.
Tolburt, J.J. NC 23rd Inf.
Tolburt, Samuel A. AL 25th Inf. Co.I
Tolbut, A. MS Inf. 2nd St.Troops Co.H Cpl.
Tolbut, J.S. MS Inf. 2nd St.Troops Co.H
Tolby, George W. VA 6th Inf. Co.I
Tolby, William H. VA 6th Inf. Co.I
Tolds, John H. MO 1st N.E. Cav. Co.L
Tole, Allen MO 3rd Inf. Co.A Sgt.
Tole, William LA 1st Hvy.Arty. (Reg.) Co.H
Toledano, Ben LA Millaudon's Co. (Jefferson Mtd.Guards,Co.B)
Toledano, E.A. LA Arty. Watson Btty. 1st Lt.
Toledano, Ernest LA Washington Arty.Bn. Co.3
Toledano, J.P. LA Mil. Chalmette Regt. Co.K
Toledano, J.R. LA Mil. Orleans Guards Regt. Co.E 1st Lt.
Toledano, Oswald J. LA Washington Arty.Bn. Co.3
Toledano, W.Y. VA 3rd Inf.Loc.Def. Co.D
Toledo, Pablo TX Cav. Baird's Regt. Co.H
Toledo, Pablo TX Cav. Ragsdale's Bn. 1st Co.C
Tolee, William A. VA 3rd Res. Co.A
Tolef, J.S. LA Miles' Legion Co.E
Tolegros, Joseph LA Mil. Chalmette Regt. Co.K
Toleman, Henry H. AR 2nd Inf. Co.H
Toleman, William VA 55th Inf. Co.L
Toleman, William VA 92nd Mil. Co.A
Tolen, Edward GA 5th Inf. Co.K
Tolen, Jonathan GA 64th Inf. Co.B
Tolen, Peter MO 11th Inf. Co.H
Tolen, Woodson GA Inf. 10th Bn. Co.C,E
Toler, A. NC Lt.Arty. 13th Bn. Co.C.E
Toler, Absalom VA Cav. 36th Bn. Co.B
Toler, A.C. MO 2nd Cav. Co.E
Toler, A.C. MO Cav. 3rd Regt.St.Guard Co.C
Toler, A.E. TX 9th (Young's) Inf. Co.C
Toler, Alsey K. GA 35th Inf. Co.K
Toler, Andrew VA Inf. 45th Bn. Co.B 1st Sgt.
Toler, Caleb NC 8th Inf. Co.B Sgt.
Toler, Callum VA Cav. 40th Bn. Co.A
Toler, Callum J. VA 59th Inf. 3rd Co.D 1st Sgt.
Toler, Calvin R. NC 24th Inf. Co.E
Toler, Charles VA Inf. 45th Bn. Co.D
Toler, David NC 1st Arty. (10th St.Troops) Co.F
Toler, David T. NC 55th Inf. Co.G Cpl.
Toler, D.E. VA 4th Cav. Co.G
Toler, Francis A. AL 39th Inf. Co.F
Toler, Frank AL 22nd Inf. Co.F
Toler, Frederick H. VA 17th Inf. Co.G
Toler, George M. VA 41st Inf. Co.B
Toler, George W. GA 48th Inf. Co.F,A
Toler, G.W. GA 59th Inf. Co.D
Toler, G.W. TN 49th Inf. Co.B
Toler, G.W. Inf. Bailey's Cons.Regt. Co.D Sgt.
Toler, H. GA Cav. 19th Bn. Co.D
Toler, H. MO Cav. Williams' Regt. Co.I
Toler, Henry NC 24th Inf. Co.I
Toler, Henry VA Inf. 45th Bn. Co.D
Toler, Henry C. VA 14th Inf. Co.D
Toler, Henry H. MS 16th Inf. Co.B
Toler, Henry P. GA 48th Inf. Co.A
Toler, H.H. VA 1st Inf. Co.H
Toler, Hiram J. AR 9th Inf. Co.G
Toler, H.R. GA 10th Inf. McNeal's Co.
Toler, James TX 3rd (Kirby's) Bn.Vol. Co.C
Toler, James VA Inf. 45th Bn. Co.D
Toler, James A. GA 48th Inf. Co.F
Toler, James D. VA 41st Inf. Co.B
Toler, James Harrison MS 33rd Inf. Co.K
Toler, James M. AR 9th Inf. Co.G
Toler, James R. VA Inf. 45th Bn. Co.D
Toler, James W. VA 24th Cav. Co.B
Toler, James W. VA Cav. 40th Bn. Co.B

Toler, J.C. GA 1st (Olmstead's) Inf. Claghorn's Co.
Toler, J.C. 10th Conf.Cav. Co.B
Toler, J.E. MS 15th Inf. Co.C
Toler, J.F. VA 3rd Inf.Loc.Def. Co.K
Toler, J.H. TN 49th Inf. Co.C
Toler, J.H. Inf. Bailey's Cons.Regt. Co.F
Toler, J.L. MO Cav. Jackman's Regt. Co.D
Toler, J.M. VA Lt.Arty. Montgomery's Co.
Toler, J.M. VA Inf. 25th Bn.
Toler, Joel GA Arty. (Chatham Arty.) Wheaton's Co.
Toler, Joel GA 1st (Olmstead's) Inf. Claghorn's Co.
Toler, John VA Inf. 1st Bn.Loc.Def. Co.F
Toler, John VA 22nd Inf. Co.G
Toler, John C. GA Arty. (Chatham Arty.) Wheaton's Co.
Toler, John D. VA 38th Inf. Co.H
Toler, John J. VA 57th Inf. Co.E
Toler, John M. VA Cav. 1st Bn. (Loc.Def. Troops) Co.C
Toler, John M. VA 4th Cav. Co.F
Toler, John T. TX 15th Cav. Co.A Black.
Toler, John W. FL 6th Inf. Co.A
Toler, John W. VA 19th Cav. Co.B
Toler, John W. VA 2nd Arty. Co.H
Toler, John W. VA Inf. 22nd Bn. Co.H
Toler, John W. VA Inf. 25th Bn. Co.C
Toler, Joseph J. AR 9th Inf. Co.G
Toler, Joseph L. MS 4th Inf. Co.B
Toler, J.S. AL 29th Inf. Co.A
Toler, J.S. TX 27th Cav. Co.K
Toler, Larkin FL 6th Inf. Co.A
Toler, Lemuel VA 53rd Inf. Co.H
Toler, Mathew H. TX Inf. Griffin's Bn. Co.C
Toler, Mathias NC 8th Inf. Co.B
Toler, M.H. TX 21st Inf. Co.C
Toler, Nelson W. VA 6th Cav. Co.K
Toler, Patrick Conf.Cav. Wood's Regt. 1st Co.A
Toler, Peter G. VA 58th Inf. Co.F 1st Sgt.
Toler, Peyton H. VA 57th Inf. Co.E
Toler, P.T. GA 55th Inf. Co.I
Toler, R.H. MS 39th Inf. Co.A
Toler, Richard M. VA 2nd St.Res. Co.A
Toler, Robert AL 41st Inf. Co.C
Toler, Robert MS Lt.Arty. Lomax's Co.
Toler, Robert 2nd Conf.Eng.Troops Co.H
Toler, Robert E. SC 21st Inf. Co.G
Toler, Robert T.L. VA 24th Cav. Co.B
Toler, Robert T.L. VA Cav. 40th Bn. Co.B
Toler, Robert T.L. VA Goochland Lt.Arty.
Toler, Robert W. VA 15th Inf. Co.C
Toler, Samuel A. VA 18th Inf. Co.E
Toler, Samuel D. VA 57th Inf. Co.E
Toler, Saunders NC 2nd Inf. Co.H
Toler, Stephen SC 4th St.Troops Co.F
Toler, T. GA 47th Inf. Co.C
Toler, T. NC Mil. Clark's Sp.Bn. Co.D
Toler, Thomas NC 1st Arty. (10th St.Troops) Co.B
Toler, Thomas NC 24th Inf. Co.E Cpl.
Toler, Thomas C. MS 7th Inf. Co.C Cpl.
Toler, Thomas J. LA 1st Cav. Co.G
Toler, Thomas J. LA Inf.Cons.Crescent Regt. Co.H
Toler, Thomas T. NC 8th Inf. Co.B
Toler, Thomas T. VA 12th Inf. Co.K Sgt.
Toler, Thomas W. VA 12th Inf. Co.C
Toler, T.J. LA 1st Engd.P. Co.I
Toler, T.J. LA Inf.Crescent Regt. Co.H
Toler, Tobias NC Bass' Co.
Toler, W. GA Inf. Collier's Co.
Toler, W.F. MS 7th Inf. Co.C
Toler, W.H. AR 50th Mil. Co.B
Toler, W.H. LA 12th Inf. 2nd Co.M
Toler, W.H. TX 3rd (Kirby's) Bn.Vol. Co.C
Toler, W.H. Conf.Arty. R.C.M. Page's Bn. 2nd Lt.
Toler, William MO 11th Inf. Co.K
Toler, William VA 57th Inf. Co.D
Toler, William B.L. VA 2nd Bn.Res. Co.A 2nd Lt.
Toler, William D. VA 58th Inf. Co.B
Toler, William E. MO Cav. Williams' Regt. Co.I
Toler, William F. KY 4th Mtd.Inf. Co.K Cpl.
Toler, William G. VA 10th Cav. Co.I 3rd Lt.
Toler, William H. LA 14th Inf. Co.C Maj.
Toler, William H. NC 24th Inf. Co.A
Toler, William H. VA Lt.Arty. Montgomery's Co. Sr.2nd Lt.
Toler, William H. VA Lt.Arty. Montgomery's Co.
Toler, William H. VA 58th Inf. Co.F
Toler, William H. Conf.Arty. Nelson's Bn. Co.B Sr.2nd Lt.
Toler, William J. GA 35th Inf. Co.K
Toler, William J. VA 2nd Cav. Co.B
Toler, William J. VA Lt.Arty. Hardwicke's Co.
Toler, William L. GA 14th Inf. Co.F
Toler, William L. VA 18th Inf. Co.E
Toler, William L. VA 41st Inf. Co.B Sgt.
Toler, William M. AL 20th Inf. Co.I
Toler, William W. VA Lt.Arty. Montgomery's Co.
Toler, W.J. GA 9th Inf. Co.C
Toler, W.J. MS 1st (King's) Inf. (St.Troops) Co.H
Toler, W.J. VA 4th Cav. Co.G
Toler, W.L. GA 18th Inf. Co.A
Toler, Wyatte H. VA 22nd Inf. Co.G Sgt.
Toler, Zachariah NC 24th Inf. Co.C
Tolerson, John SC 20th Inf. Co.A
Toles, Charles KY 9th Cav. Co.I
Toles, Daniel GA 32nd Inf. Co.E
Toles, John H. AL 55th Vol. Co.K Sgt.
Toles, N. AL 29th Inf. Co.C
Toles, T. MO 6th Cav. Co.K
Toles, T.O. VA 3rd Cav. Co.G
Toley, Watt AL 43rd Inf. Co.G
Tolf, Charles LA 12th Inf.
Tolger, Gerhardt VA 1st Inf. Co.K
Toliafero, A.P. LA 8th Cav. Co.B
Toliaferro, Baldwin D. TN 6th Inf. Co.H
Toliaferro, Thornton AL Rebels
Tolifaro, J.E TN 18th (Newsom's) Cav. Co.C
Tolin, Dennis AL 2nd Cav. Co.D Sgt.
Tolin, Peter AR 35th Inf. Old Co.F
Tolison, Edward SC 3rd Res. Co.C
Tolison, John MS 14th Inf. Co.B
Tolivar, Angel LA Mil. 5th Regt.Eur.Brig. (Spanish Regt.) Co.6 Sgt.
Toliver, A.J. MO 11th Inf. Co.F
Toliver, Allen NC 61st Inf. Co.I
Toliver, Andrew NC 61st Inf. Co.I
Toliver, Andrew B. TX 24th Cav. Co.C
Toliver, Benjamin F. TX 13th Vol. 2nd Co.C
Toliver, C. AR 37th Inf. Co.D Sgt.
Toliver, Calaway J. NC 22nd Inf. Co.F
Toliver, Calvin J. NC 22nd Inf. Co.F Sgt.
Toliver, C.H. MO 11th Inf. Co.F Sgt.
Toliver, Drury S. NC 37th Inf. Co.K
Toliver, D.S. VA 21st Cav. 2nd Co.I
Toliver, Granvill H. NC 22nd Inf. Co.F
Toliver, G.W. TX Cav. Barnes' Regt. Sgt.
Toliver, H.M. TN 30th Inf. Co.K
Toliver, Hugh KY 5th Mtd.Inf. Co.A
Toliver, Jacob NC 61st Inf. Co.I
Toliver, Jacob NC McMillan's Co.
Toliver, Jacob F. NC 37th Inf. Co.K
Toliver, James A. TX 13th Vol. 2nd Co.C Sgt.
Toliver, J.E. AL 27th Inf. Co.D
Toliver, Jesse NC 61st Inf. Co.I
Toliver, J.F. VA 21st Cav. 2nd Co.I
Toliver, J.H. MO 11th Inf. Co.F
Toliver, J.H. TX 30th Cav. Co.F
Toliver, J.O. TX Cav. McCord's Frontier Regt. Co.E
Toliver, John TX 19th Inf. Co.B
Toliver, John VA Cav. 37th Bn. Co.D
Toliver, John M. NC 22nd Inf. Co.F Cpl.
Toliver, Joseph TX 9th Cav. Co.D
Toliver, J.S. TN 4th (McLemore's) Cav. Co.I
Toliver, J.T. TN 30th Inf. Co.K
Toliver, J.W. TX Cav. Barnes' Regt. Sgt.
Toliver, Nathan D. TN Lyon's Cav. J.C. Stone's Co.A Sgt.
Toliver, Richard TN 44th (Cons.) Inf. Co.K
Toliver, R.K. MO 2nd Inf. Co.D
Toliver, Solomon NC 61st Inf. Co.I
Toliver, W.G. VA 21st Cav. 2nd Co.I Cpl.
Toliver, William KY 5th Mtd.Inf. Co.A
Toliver, William MO 11th Inf. Co.F Sgt.
Toliver, W.J. MO 11th Inf. Co.F Cpl.
Tolker, --- VA 2nd St.Res. Co.L
Toll, Charles H. Gen. & Staff Capt.,CS
Toll, D.G. MS 7th Cav. Surg.
Toll, Thomas KY 8th Cav. Co.F 1st Lt.
Toll, Wilson B. MO 3rd Cav. Co.E
Tollan, --- TX Cav. Mann's Regt. Co.D
Tolland, H.B. AR 33rd Inf. Co.E
Tolland, W.H. AL 37th Inf. Co.K
Tollar, W.H. LA 9th Inf. Co.K
Tollard, William A. GA 15th Inf. Co.C
Tollat, David GA Inf. 40th Bn. Co.B
Tolle, E. TX 36th Cav. Co.F
Tolle, Ferdinand LA 20th Inf. Co.A 2nd Lt.
Tolle, Harry TX 36th Cav. Co.F
Tolle, Jacob LA 3rd Inf. Co.B
Tolle, James T. KY 6th Mtd.Inf. Co.F,D Ch.Music.
Tolle, J.C. MS Conscr.
Tolle, John T. KY 6th Mtd.Inf. Co.F,E
Tolle, Nat W. TX 9th Cav. Co.A
Tolle, N.D. TX 29th Cav. Co.K
Tolle, P.H. FL 2nd Inf. Co.H
Tolle, S.C. MS Lt.Arty. English's Co.
Tolle, Shelby C. GA 36th (Villepigue's) Inf. Co.G
Toller, Absalom S. VA 60th Inf. Co.F
Toller, Bennett L. VA 60th Inf. Co.F

Toller, James TX 24th & 25th Cav. (Cons.) Co.B
Toller, Jesse AR 10th Mil. Co.B Cpl.
Toller, Jesse L. AR 34th Inf. Co.H Sgt.
Toller, J.L. MS 15th Inf. Co.A
Toller, John VA 1st Cav.St.Line Co.A
Toller, William LA 2nd Cav. Co.F
Toller, W.W. AR 35th Inf. Co.H
Tollerson, A.J. GA 32nd Inf. Co.H
Tollerson, B.F. GA Lt.Arty. 12th Bn. 3rd Co.C
Tollerson, B.M. GA 53rd Inf. Co.A
Tollerson, C.C. AR 1st (Monroe's) Cav. Co.F
Tollerson, D.R. AR 1st (Monroe's) Cav. Co.F
Tollerson, Elijah L. GA 32nd Inf. Co.H
Tollerson, H.A. 1st Conf.Inf. 2nd Co.C
Tollerson, J. GA 5th Res. Co.C
Tollerson, James MS 13th Inf. Co.G
Tollerson, James B. SC 18th Inf. Co.F
Tollerson, James H. AR 33rd Inf. Co.H
Tollerson, John 1st Conf.Inf. 2nd Co.C
Tollerson, J.P. KY 7th Cav. Co.G
Tollerson, R.M. SC 18th Inf. Co.F
Tolleson, A.J. SC 5th Inf. 1st Co.F
Tolleson, A.J. SC Palmetto S.S. Co.D Sgt.
Tolleson, Alfred J. SC Inf. Holcombe Legion Co.C 1st Lt.
Tolleson, A.O. GA 7th Inf. (St.Guards) Co.E Cpl.
Tolleson, H. GA 3rd Bn. (St.Guards) Co.G
Tolleson, J. MS 12th Cav. Co.B
Tolleson, J.A. GA 7th Inf. (St.Guards) Co.E Sgt.
Tolleson, James A. SC Inf. Holcombe Legion Co.C Capt.
Tolleson, J.B. SC 7th Res. Lt.Col.
Tolleson, J. Belton SC Inf. Holcombe Legion Co.C
Tolleson, J.D. SC 3rd Inf. Co.I
Tolleson, Jerremy SC 3rd Inf. Co.I
Tolleson, Jesse AL 31st Inf. Co.D
Tolleson, Jesse SC 3rd Inf. Co.I
Tolleson, John SC 3rd Inf. Co.I
Tolleson, John SC 5th St.Troops Co.G
Tolleson, J.W. SC Inf. Holcombe Legion Co.C Ord.Sgt.
Tolleson, J.W. VA 2nd St.Res. Co.A
Tolleson, Robert M. SC 5th Inf. 1st Co.G, 2nd Co.C
Tolleson, T.W. GA Siege Arty. 28th Bn. Co.F
Tolleson, T.W. SC 2nd Rifles Co.C
Tolleson, Wesley J. MS 26th Inf. Co.D
Tolleson, William SC 1st (McCreary's) Inf. Co.C
Tolleson, Wm. D. SC 13th Inf. Co.I
Tollesson, Jesse GA 7th Inf. Co.A
Tollet, John TN 13th (Gore's) Cav. Co.I
Tollet, John TX 22nd Cav. Co.G
Tollet, Scot TN 13th (Gore's) Cav. Co.I
Tollett, A. AR 1st (Monroe's) Cav. Co.D
Tollett, Ferdnand AR 34th Inf. Co.A
Tollett, Henry G. TN 2nd (Ashby's) Cav. Co.F
Tollett, Henry G. TN Cav. 4th Bn. (Branner's) Co.F
Tollett, James AR Inf. Hardy's Regt. Co.I
Tollett, John H. AR Inf. 8th Bn. Co.C
Tollett, John H. AR 25th Inf. Co.F
Tollett, Mark TX 36th Cav. Co.C
Tollett, M.W. AR 19th (Dawson's) Inf. Co.G
Tollett, Wesley TX 36th Cav. Co.C
Tollett, William W. TN 28th Inf. Co.A
Tollett, W.W. TN 28th (Cons.) Inf. Co.B
Tollett, W.W. TX 10th Cav. Co.A
Tolley, Alexander VA 60th Inf. Co.K
Tolley, Archibald T. VA 58th Inf. Co.C
Tolley, Charles W. VA 58th Inf. Co.G
Tolley, Christopher W. VA 30th Bn.S.S. Co.A
Tolley, David NC 6th Inf. Co.E
Tolley, David TN 50th Inf. Co.I
Tolley, E.D. VA 34th Inf. Co.G
Tolley, James B. VA 10th Bn.Res. Co.B
Tolley, James P. VA Rockbridge Cty.Res. Hutcheson's Co.
Tolley, John LA 10th Inf. Co.D
Tolley, John D. TN 8th Inf. Co.K 1st Lt.
Tolley, John H. VA 34th Inf. Co.C
Tolley, Joseph P. VA 10th Bn.Res. Co.B
Tolley, Joseph P. VA Rockbridge Cty.Res. Hutcheson's Co.
Tolley, Joseph R. NC 58th Inf. Co.A
Tolley, O.L. VA 34th Inf. Co.G
Tolley, Preston VA 58th Inf. Co.C
Tolley, William TN 1st (Carter's) Cav. Co.M
Tolley, William P. VA 27th Inf. Co.D Cpl.
Tollifer, M.J. MO Cav. 6th Regt.St.Guard Co.D
Tollins, William TN Conscr. (Cp. of Instr.)
Tollison, Abraham SC Inf. Hampton Legion Co.E
Tollison, A.Y. AL 31st Inf. Co.D Sgt.
Tollison, Burtis TN Inf. 1st Bn. (Colms') Co.B
Tollison, Daniel SC 16th Inf. Co.E
Tollison, E.B. AR 3rd Cav. 3rd Co.E Cpl.
Tollison, Edward SC 1st St.Troops Co.G
Tollison, Edward SC 16th Inf. Co.E
Tollison, Elijah MS 40th Inf. Co.D
Tollison, E.T. SC Inf. Hampton Legion Co.E
Tollison, Francis M. SC Inf. Hampton Legion Co.E
Tollison, H. TX Lavaca Cty. Minute Men 3rd Ord.
Tollison, Healey A. GA Cobb's Legion Co.K
Tollison, Henry GA 2nd Res. Co.D
Tollison, J.A.J. AL 31st Inf. Co.D
Tollison, James AR 1st (Dobbin's) Cav. Co.D
Tollison, James TN Inf. 1st Bn. (Colms') Co.B
Tollison, James O. GA 19th Inf. Co.F
Tollison, Jesse GA 45th Inf. Co.I
Tollison, John AR Lt.Arty. Thrall's Btty.
Tollison, John B. AR 4th Inf. Kelley's Co.
Tollison, John B. AR 16th Inf. Co.H
Tollison, L. MS 38th Cav. Co.G
Tollison, L. 20th Conf.Cav. 2nd Co.I
Tollison, Levi MS 1st (King's) Inf. (St.Troops) Co.H
Tollison, Levi SC Lt.Arty. 3rd (Palmetto) Bn. Co.B
Tollison, Levi SC Loc.Def.Troops Shiver's Co.
Tollison, Matt TN Inf. 22nd Bn. Co.A
Tollison, M.C. AR 1st Mtd.Rifles Co.D
Tollison, N. TN 84th Inf. Co.B
Tollison, P. AR 3rd Cav. Earls' Co.
Tollison, Shelby U. AR 4th Inf. Kelley's Co.
Tollison, Shelby U. AR 16th Inf. Co.H Cpl.
Tollison, Solomon TN Inf. 1st Bn. (Colms') Co.B
Tollison, Solomon TN 50th (Cons.) Inf. Co.H
Tollison, Thomas SC 16th Inf. Co.E
Tollison, T.M. SC 2nd Inf. Co.D,B
Tollison, T.P. SC 7th Inf. 2nd Co.F Sgt.
Tollison, W.A. SC 16th Inf. Co.E
Tollison, W.H. MS 38th Cav. Co.G
Tollison, William MS 2nd St.Cav. Co.E.A
Tollison, William L. AR Cav. 1st Bn. (Stirman's) Co.H
Tollison, William L. TX 27th Cav. Co.B
Tollison, William P. AR 15th (Josey's) Inf. Co.C
Tollison, W.J. AR Inf. Hardy's Regt. Co.G
Tollit, Ennis AR Inf. Hardy's Regt. Co.G
Tollit, John 1st Conf.Cav. 2nd Co.D
Tolliver, Creed NC 1st Cav. (9th St.Troops) Co.G
Tolliver, Henry TN 24th Inf. Co.A
Tolliver, J. KY 9th Cav. Co.D
Tolliver, Jesse VA Inf. 45th Bn. Co.C
Tolliver, Joseph VA 6th Cav. Co.F
Tolliver, Joseph M. TX 19th Cav. Co.F
Tolliver, Newman TN 7th Inf. Co.K 1st Lt.
Tolliver, Thomas G. AL 16th Inf. Co.F
Tolliver, William N. AL 16th Inf. Co.F
Tollman, John MO Inf. 4th Regt.St.Guard Co.D
Tollman, John VA 51st Inf. Co.I
Tollock, P. NC 13th Inf. Co.I
Tollocut, A. LA Mil. 1st Regt. 2nd Brig. 1st Div. Co.D
Tollott, John TX Cav. 2nd Regt.St.Troops Co.I
Tolls, Charles R. KY 2nd Mtd.Inf. Co.I
Tolls, John MO 1st N.E. Cav. Co.A
Tolls, Shelby C. 1st Conf.Inf. 1st Co.G
Tolls, Thomas KY 2nd (Duke's) Cav. Co.A
Tolls, Thomas M. KY 2nd Mtd.Inf. Co.I
Tolls, T.J. MO 6th Cav. Co.K
Tollston, William TX Cav. Bourland's Regt. Co.D
Tolly, D.T. VA Lt.Arty. Wright's Co.
Tolly, E.C. MD 1st Cav. Co.A
Tolly, Edward C. VA 19th Cav. Co.B
Tolly, G.F. SC Palmetto S.S. Co.C
Tolly, H. GA 15th Inf. Co.C
Tolly, I.M. VA 1st Bn.Res. Co.E Sgt.
Tolly, James KY 12th Cav. Co.E
Tolly, James TN 50th Inf. Co.I
Tolly, J.S. 1st Choctaw Mtd.Rifles Co.K 1st Lt.
Tolly, Marion VA Inf. 26th Bn. Co.C
Tolly, M.W. TN 24th Inf. Co.I
Tolly, Sanders NC 58th Inf. Co.A
Tolly, Swinfield NC 58th Inf. Co.A
Tolly, William NC 58th Inf. Co.A
Tolly, William TN 63rd Inf. Co.I
Tolman, J.G. MS 21st Inf. Co.E
Tolman, J.P. AL 13th Inf. 2nd Co.G Cpl.
Tolman, J.W. GA 22nd Inf. Co.E Sgt.
Tolmey, Thomas AR Lt.Arty. Key's Btty.
Tolon, A.C. AL 22nd Inf. Co.B
Toloner, Eli NC 5th Sr.Res. Co.B
Tolse, Octave LA Mil. Assumption Regt. Co.C
Tolson, A. TX 2nd Inf. Co.I
Tolson, Albert MD Arty. 1st Btty.
Tolson, Albert VA 1st Arty. Co.C
Tolson, Albert VA 1st Inf. Co.F
Tolson, Alfred C. MD 1st Cav. Co.B
Tolson, Benjamin F. MO 1st N.E. Cav. Co.L
Tolson, B.G. SC 1st Bn.S.S. Co.B Sgt.
Tolson, B.G. SC 27th Inf. Co.F Sgt.
Tolson, C.C. TX Cav. Bone's Co.

Tolson, Charles E. MD 1st Cav. Co.B
Tolson, Daniel VA 9th Cav. Co.A
Tolson, Exum NC 44th Inf. Co.B
Tolson, Frank A. MD Inf. 2nd Bn. Co.C
Tolson, F.T. AR Cav. Nave's Bn. Co.B
Tolson, George MO Cav. Snider's Bn. Co.B
Tolson, George B. MO Inf. Perkins' Bn. Co.E
Tolson, George L. AR 9th Inf. Co.C 3rd Lt.
Tolson, George W. GA 1st (Olmstead's) Inf. Co.G
Tolson, George W. SC 2nd Arty. Co.D
Tolson, George W. SC Arty. Gregg's Co. (McQueen Lt.Arty.)
Tolson, George W. SC Arty. Manigault's Bn. 1st Co.C
Tolson, Green MO Cav. Freeman's Regt. Co.C
Tolson, G.W. SC 8th Inf. Co.H Cpl.
Tolson, James KY 5th Mtd.Inf. Co.D
Tolson, James A. VA 9th Cav. Co.A
Tolson, James H. NC 1st Arty. (10th St.Troops) Co.I 2nd Lt.
Tolson, James H. NC 67th Inf. Co.A Capt.
Tolson, James P. AR 2nd Inf. Co.G
Tolson, J.D. Gen. & Staff Capt.,QM
Tolson, J.N. GA 63rd Inf. Co.C
Tolson, John NC 3rd Arty. (40th St.Troops) Co.D
Tolson, John H. MO Searcy's Bn.S.S. Co.I
Tolson, John N. VA 4th Cav. Co.A
Tolson, Joseph W. TX 18th Inf. Co.F
Tolson, J.R. GA 11th Cav. (St.Guards) Smith's Co.
Tolson, Moses NC 43rd Inf. Co.E
Tolson, P.E. SC Lt.Arty. Wagener's Co. (Co.A, German Arty.)
Tolson, Peter TX 11th Cav. Co.D
Tolson, Stephen KY 3rd Mtd.Inf. Co.I
Tolson, T.B. MS 35th Inf. Co.H
Tolson, Thomas MO Cav. Snider's Bn. Co.B
Tolson, Thomas H. MD Inf. 2nd Bn. Co.C 2nd Lt.
Tolson, Thomas J. NC 3rd Cav. (41st St.Troops) Co.E
Tolson, Thomas J. NC 67th Inf. Co.A
Tolson, Thomas T. Gen. & Staff AASurg.
Tolson, William GA Arty. 9th Bn. Co.C
Tolson, William NC Mil. Clark's Sp.Bn. Co.D
Tolson, William TX 13th Vol. Co.F
Tolson, William VA 9th Cav. Co.A
Tolson, William Conf.Reg.Inf. Brooks' Bn. Co.C
Tolson, William A. NC 1st Arty. (10th St.Troops) Co.G
Tolson, William D. TX 22nd Cav. Co.H
Tolson, William F. MS 14th Inf. Co.G Capt.
Tolsprich, Cyrus B. MO 16th Inf. Co.A 2nd Lt.
Tolston, Andrew J. NC 8th Inf. Co.C
Tolston, Benjamin TX Cav. Bourland's Regt. Co.D Jr.2nd Lt.
Tolston, B.G. SC Inf. 6th Bn. Co.B
Tolston, B.G. SC Vol. Manigault's Bn. Co.D
Tolston, C.C. TX Cav. 2nd Regt.St.Troops Co.A
Tolston, C.C. TX Cav. Terry's Regt. Co.C
Tolston, D.R. AR 2nd Cav. Co.D
Tolston, George W. NC 17th Inf. (1st Org.) Co.A
Tolston, George W. NC 32nd Inf. Co.B
Tolston, G.L. AR 2nd Cav. Co.D Sgt.
Tolston, Joseph NC 8th Inf. Co.C
Tolston, Moses GA 43rd Inf. Co.F
Tolston, William H. NC 33rd Inf. Co.B
Tolty, Patrick I. AR 2nd Inf.
Tolty, Robert VA 5th Cav. Co.K
Tolty, S.R. Morgan's,CSA Pilot
Tolubbee 1st Choctaw & Chickasaw Mtd.Rifles 3rd Co.F
Tolund, James M. MS 2nd Inf. Co.K
Toly, S., Jr. LA Mil.Conf.Guards Regt. Co.B Sgt.
Tom (Colored) KY 7th Mtd.Inf. Co.B Cook
Tom MS 20th Inf. Co.B Cook
Tom (Negro) SC Hvy.Arty. Gilchrist's Co. (Gist Guard) Music.
Tom SC Lt.Arty. Walter's Co. (Washington Arty.) Col'd Cook
Tom TN 1st Hvy.Arty. Co.K
Tom TX Cav. McCord's Regt. Co.F
Tom (Negro Boy) TX 20th Inf. Co.B Cook
Tom VA Inf. 25th Bn. Co.G Cook
Tom 1st Cherokee Mtd.Rifles Co.A
Tom 1st Cherokee Mtd.Rifles Co.D
Tom (Indian) 1st Cherokee Mtd.Vol.
Tom 1st Creek Mtd.Vol. 1st Co.C
Tom 1st Seminole Mtd.Vol.
Tom, D.O. NC 4th Sr.Res. Co.D
Tom, Dudley TX 33rd Cav. Co.F,D
Tom, George W. TX 33rd Cav. Co.D
Tom, George W. TX Cav. McCord's Frontier Regt. 1st Co.A
Tom, Houston TX 6th Inf. Co.E 1st Lt.
Tom, James H. TX 26th Cav. Co.C,I 2nd Lt.
Tom, J.C. TX 21st Cav. Co.F Cpl.
Tom, Josiah 1st Choctaw & Chickasaw Mtd.Rifles 2nd Co.D
Tom, Simpson TX Cav. McCord's Frontier Regt. Co.L
Tom, T.J. MS 13th Inf. Co.H
Tom, William Deneale's Regt. Choctaw Warriors
Tom, Williamson 1st Choctaw & Chickasaw Mtd.Rifles 1st Co.E
Tom, W.R. TX 26th Cav. Co.I
Toma, John LA 13th Inf. Co.D
Tomalson, Claiborne VA 6th Inf. Co.I
Toman, W.H.R. VA 25th Inf. 2nd Co.H
Tomar, George TN 15th Inf. Co.I
Tomas, Charles KY 11th Cav. Co.A
Tomas, Edward C. VA 40th Inf.
Tomas, Franco LA Mil. 5th Regt.Eur.Brig. (Spanish Regt.) Co.8
Tomas, Joseph TN 11th (Holman's) Cav. Co.H
Tomasi, Felice LA Mil. 6th Regt.Eur.Brig. (Italian Guards Bn.) Co.4
Tomasi, Jean LA Mil. 6th Regt.Eur.Brig. (Italian Guards Bn.) Co.4
Tomassee 1st Creek Mtd.Vol. Co.B
Tomassee 1st Seminole Mtd.Vol.
Tomb, Joseph AR Inf. Cocke's Regt. Co.G Sgt.
Tomb, S.J. SC 18th Inf. Co.B Capt.
Tomb, S. Julius SC 1st Inf. Co.E
Tombarel, Auguste LA Mil. 2nd Regt. French Brig. Co.6
Tombelin, W.J. AR 15th (Josey's) Inf. 1st Co.C Sgt.
Tomberlain, D.B. TN 25th Inf. Co.C Cpl.
Tomberlin, A. VA Cav. 34th Bn. Co.D
Tomberlin, Bennett TX 36th Cav. Co.K
Tomberlin, David AL 17th Bn.S.S. Co.A
Tomberlin, David AL 19th Inf. Co.G
Tomberlin, D.J. AL 45th Inf. Co.A
Tomberlin, Durias NC 4th Sr.Res. Co.I
Tomberlin, Elisha N. AR Inf. Hardy's Regt. Co.A
Tomberlin, E.M. NC 1st Cav. (9th St.Troops) Co.C
Tomberlin, George W. GA Arty. 9th Bn. Co.C
Tomberlin, G.J. NC 62nd Inf. Co.F
Tomberlin, Henry W. GA 49th Inf. Co.E
Tomberlin, Hosea J. NC 53rd Inf. Co.I
Tomberlin, Jacob S. NC 53rd Inf. Co.I
Tomberlin, James FL 2nd Cav. Co.G,A
Tomberlin, James FL Cav. 5th Bn. Co.E Cpl.
Tomberlin, James NC 16th Inf. Co.G
Tomberlin, James VA Cav. 34th Bn. Co.D
Tomberlin, James W. TN 32nd Inf. Co.H
Tomberlin, James W. TN 35th Inf. 2nd Co.F
Tomberlin, J.E. AR 1st (Monroe's) Cav. Co.G
Tomberlin, J.E. NC 62nd Inf. Co.F
Tomberlin, John GA 65th Inf. Co.G
Tomberlin, John NC 50th Inf. Co.G
Tomberlin, John A. GA 49th Inf. Co.E Sgt.
Tomberlin, John H. NC 50th Inf. Co.K Cpl.
Tomberlin, John W. GA 49th Inf. Co.E Bvt.2nd Lt.
Tomberlin, Josiah G. NC 53rd Inf. Co.I
Tomberlin, M. GA 5th Res. Co.I
Tomberlin, Moses GA 1st (Symons') Res. Co.G
Tomberlin, M.S. NC 1st Bn.Jr.Res. Co.C
Tomberlin, Reuben S. NC Hvy.Arty. 10th Bn. Co.C
Tomberlin, Simon D. NC Hvy.Arty. 10th Bn. Co.C Cpl.
Tomberlin, S.W. AL Inf. 1st Regt. Co.H
Tomberlin, S.W. AL 45th Inf. Co.A
Tomberlin, Thomas W. NC Hvy.Arty. 10th Bn. Co.C
Tomberlin, V.B. NC 50th Inf. Co.G
Tomberlin, William FL 9th Inf. Co.D
Tomberlin, William GA 27th Inf. Co.I
Tomberlin, William GA 29th Inf.
Tomberlin, William H. FL 6th Inf. Co.B
Tomberlin, William M. NC 53rd Inf. Co.I
Tomberlin, W.R. MS 32nd Inf. Co.F,A
Tomberlin, Wright GA Cav. 22nd Bn. (St.Guards) Co.D Sgt.
Tomberlins, B.O. GA 5th Res. Co.I
Tomberlinson, H. AL 8th Inf. Co.A
Tom Billy 1st Choctaw & Chickasaw Mtd.Rifles 2nd Co.D
Tomblin, Abner TN 25th Inf. Co.C
Tomblin, Corbin B. VA Arty. J.W. Drewry's Co. Hosp.Stew.
Tomblin, David J. VA 46th Inf. 1st Co.G
Tomblin, Derias B. TN 25th Inf. Co.C Cpl.
Tomblin, Garland G. VA 46th Inf. 1st Co.G
Tomblin, George H. TN 28th Inf. Co.K
Tomblin, H.L. VA 46th Inf. 1st Co.G,I
Tomblin, Isaac TN 25th Inf. Co.C
Tomblin, J. VA Cav. Swann's Bn. Carpenter's Co.
Tomblin, J.A. GA 24th Inf. Co.I Cpl.
Tomblin, Jahazah 3rd Conf.Cav. Co.I
Tomblin, James P. VA 19th Cav. Co.K

Tomblin, John MO St.Guard
Tomblin, John MO St.Guard
Tomblin, John VA 3rd Res. Co.A
Tomblin, John T. GA 24th Inf. Co.I
Tomblin, Joseph S. VA 46th Inf. 1st Co.G, Co.I
Tomblin, Preston VA 3rd Res. Co.A
Tomblin, Samuel P. GA 43rd Inf. Co.F
Tomblin, Snowden VA 122nd Mil. Co.C
Tomblin, Solomon S. GA 35th Inf. Co.E
Tomblin, T.W. VA 46th Inf. 1st Co.G
Tomblin, T.W. VA 46th Inf. 2nd Co.I
Tomblin, W.D. NC 2nd Jr.Res. Co.F
Tomblin, William VA 122nd Mil. Co.C
Tomblin, William D. AL 18th Inf. Co.L
Tomblin, W.O. VA 46th Inf. 1st Co.G, Co.I
Tomblinson, D. TX 13th Vol. Co.G
Tomblinson, David MO Inf. 8th Bn. Co.C
Tomblinson, Jack TX 5th Inf. Co.I,G
Tomblinson, James AL 8th Inf. Co.A
Tomblinson, J.B. TX 5th Inf. Co.G
Tomblinson, J.N. AR 1st Vol. Co.I
Tomblinson, John KY 10th Cav. Co.G
Tomblinson, R.L. SC 18th Inf. Co.H Sgt.
Tomblinson, W.E. TN Cav. Nixon's Regt. Co.G
Tombolin, Alford, Jr. VA 129th Mil. Carter's Co.
Tombolin, Alford, Sr. VA 129th Mil. Carter's Co.
Tombolin, James VA 129th Mil. Carter's Co.
Tombolin, Moses VA 129th Mil. Carter's Co.
Tombolin, W.P. GA 11th Cav. Co.H
Tombs, Anderson MO Inf. 8th Bn. Co.B
Tombs, Anderson MO 9th Inf. Co.F
Tombs, A.S. KY 3rd Cav. Co.C
Tombs, B. AL 32nd Inf. Co.B
Tombs, George TX Cav. 3rd (Yager's) Bn. Co.D
Tombs, George W. MS 36th Inf. Co.K
Tombs, G.W. TX 1st (Yager's) Cav. Co.D
Tombs, J.H. TN 21st (Wilson's) Cav. Co.A
Tombs, J.L. TN Inf. Sowell's Detach.
Tombs, Joel TN 45th Inf. Co.K
Tombs, John TN 31st Inf. Co.C
Tombs, John VA Horse Arty. Jackson's Co.
Tombs, John F. TN 45th Inf. Co.K
Tombs, Jno. H. VA Mtd.Guard 5th Congr.Dist.
Tombs, John H. VA 18th Inf. Co.D
Tombs, Nathen AR 31st Inf. Co.H
Tombs, R.S. MS 36th Inf. Co.K
Tombs, S.G. LA 14th (Austin's) Bn.S.S. Co.B QMSgt.
Tombs, T.H. TX 30th Cav. Co.D
Tombs, William TN Arty. Capt.
Tombs, William TX 8th Inf. Co.E
Tombs, William L. VA 7th Inf. Co.I
Tombulain, J. KY 12th Cav. Co.F
Tomby, John L. MS 22nd Inf. Capt.
Tomby, W.A. GA 21st Inf. Co.F
Tom co chut nee 1st Creek Mtd.Vol. Co.B
Tome, A.G. VA 3rd Res. Co.H
Tomelson, Joseph D. VA 135th Mil. Co.D,I
Tomelson, W.E. TN Inf. Sowell's Detach. Cpl.
Tomer, Samuel VA 58th Mil. Co.E
Tomerlin, J.M. TX 17th Inf. Co.K
Tomerlin, J.W. TN Inf. 4th Cons.Regt. Co.H
Tomerlin, Samuel M. MO 12th Inf. Co.K
Tomerlin, William TX 36th Cav. Co.I
Tomerlin, William J. TX 3rd Inf. Co.I
Tomerson, W.R. TN 7th Inf. Co.H
Tomervilly, W.T. TN 4th Inf.
Tomes, --- VA VMI Co.C
Tomes, Edward TN Inf. 22nd Bn. Co.C
Tomes, Henry TN Inf. 22nd Bn. Co.C
Tomes, Joseph VA 46th Inf. 2nd Co.I
Tomey, W.P. AL 44th Inf. Co.C
Tom e ya ho la 1st Creek Mtd.Vol. Co.A 1st Sgt.
Tomey chuper 1st Creek Mtd.Vol. Co.K
Tomey Larney 1st Creek Mtd.Vol. Co.K Music.
Tom George 1st Seminole Mtd.Vol.
Tomihintubby Deneale's Regt. Choctaw Warriors Co.C
Tomilinson, W.P. AR 5th Inf.
Tomin, Calvin TN 28th Inf. Co.E
Tomins, George GA Inf. 1st Loc.Troops (Augusta) Co.D,B
Tom Isam 1st Choctaw Mtd.Rifles
Tomisich, Vincent AL 21st Inf. Co.A
Tomison, William A. TX Waul's Legion Co.F
Tomissee, O. Trans-MS Conf.Cav. 1st Bn. Co.B
Tom James 1st Choctaw & Chickasaw Mtd.Rifles Co.A
Tomkies, A.J. VA Vol. Binford's Co.
Tomkies, Augustine J. VA Lt.Arty. 12th Bn. 2nd Co.A
Tomkies, Augustine J. VA Lt.Arty. Sturdivant's Co.
Tomkies, E.A. MD Arty. 3rd Btty.
Tomkies, John H. Gen. & Staff Chap.
Tomkies, L.L. LA 27th Inf. Co.G
Tomkies, Thomas W. VA Lt.Arty. 12th Bn. 2nd Co.A
Tomkies, Thomas W. VA Lt.Arty. Sturdivant's Co.
Tomkin, J.M. AL 7th Cav. Co.H
Tomkins, --- TX Cav. Mann's Regt. Co.F Cpl.
Tomkins, A.J. AR 45th Cav. Co.H
Tomkins, Albert VA Cav. 37th Bn. Co.D
Tomkins, D.C. SC 14th Inf. Co.K Capt.
Tomkins, E.A. GA Lt.Arty. Ritter's Co.
Tomkins, George TX Inf. 1st St.Troops Wheat's Co.A, Whitehead's Co.
Tomkins, J. NC 56th Inf. Co.A
Tomkins, Janes AL 30th Inf. Co.F
Tomkins, J.H. TX 35th (Brown's) Cav. Co.A
Tomkins, J.M. GA Cav. 7th Bn. (St.Guards) Co.G
Tomkins, John A. TN Cav. 7th Bn. (Bennett's) Co.A
Tomkins, John F. GA Inf. 3rd Bn. Co.F
Tomkins, J.P. NC 52nd Inf. Co.C Cpl.
Tomkins, Kinnis M. SC 10th Inf. Co.C
Tomkins, Silus AR 45th Cav. Co.H
Tomkins, Socrates SC 15th Inf. Co.K
Tomkins, S.S. SC 24th Inf. Co.K Capt.
Tomkins, Stephen SC 14th Inf. Co.K
Tomkins, William SC 10th Inf. Co.M
Tomkins, William SC 15th Inf. Co.K
Tomkins, W.M. AR 45th Cav. Co.H
Tomlan, E.A. GA Inf. 40th Bn. Co.A
Tomland, Garley GA 1st Cav. Co.D
Tomler, M. GA Inf. 2nd Bn. (St.Guards) Co.A
Tomlin, A. MS 2nd Cav.Res. Co.G Cpl.
Tomlin, A. MS 10th Cav. Co.E
Tomlin, A.A. GA 1st Cav. Co.K
Tomlin, A.J. GA 44th Inf. Co.I
Tomlin, Amos F. AL 47th Inf. Co.E 1st Sgt.
Tomlin, Amos F. GA 6th Cav. Co.H 1st Sgt.
Tomlin, Amos S. NC 4th Inf. Co.C
Tomlin, A.R. NC 4th Inf. Co.H Cpl.
Tomlin, Arken A. GA 1st (Ramsey's) Inf. Co.A
Tomlin, B. VA 46th Inf. Co.I
Tomlin, Calvin TN 18th Inf. Co.E
Tomlin, Charles GA 22nd Inf. Co.C
Tomlin, Christian KY 4th Cav. Co.D
Tomlin, Corbin B. VA Hvy.Arty. Epes' Co.
Tomlin, Corbin Braxton VA 12th Inf. Co.B
Tomlin, Crawford GA 32nd Inf. Co.C
Tomlin, David J. AL 33rd Inf. Co.I
Tomlin, E. LA 13th Bn. (Part.Rangers) Co.B
Tomlin, Edwin A. GA 40th Inf. Co.I
Tomlin, Eli J. GA Cav. 1st Bn.Res. Co.C
Tomlin, Ermond VA 13th Inf. 2nd Co.E
Tomlin, Francis M. AL 13th Inf. Co.I
Tomlin, Francis M. AR 24th Inf. Co.B
Tomlin, Francis M. AR Inf. Hardy's Regt. Co.B
Tomlin, George TN 20th Inf. Co.H
Tomlin, George W. MO 3rd Cav. Co.C
Tomlin, George Washington TN 6th Inf. Co.H Music.
Tomlin, G.W. GA 10th Cav. (St.Guards) Co.E Cpl.
Tomlin, H.A. NC 3rd Jr.Res. Co.F
Tomlin, H.B. VA 53rd Inf. Col.
Tomlin, Henry E. KY 4th Cav. Co.D
Tomlin, Hezekiah GA 4th Res. Co.I
Tomlin, Hiram LA Washington Arty.Bn. Co.5 Cpl.
Tomlin, Hugh W. NC 33rd Inf. Co.A
Tomlin, Isaac GA 32nd Inf. Co.A
Tomlin, Isaac P. MS 40th Inf. Co.K
Tomlin, J. NC 1st Cav. (9th St.Troops) Co.C
Tomlin, J. VA 46th Inf. Co.I
Tomlin, Jacob B. GA 43rd Inf. Co.F
Tomlin, Jacob S. AL 57th Inf. Co.E
Tomlin, James GA 22nd Inf. Co.C
Tomlin, James MS 40th Inf. Co.K
Tomlin, James VA 13th Inf. 2nd Co.E
Tomlin, James M. GA 46th Inf. Co.D
Tomlin, James M. MS 40th Inf. Co.K
Tomlin, J.D. MO Robertson's Regt.St.Guard Co.C
Tomlin, J.E. AL 26th (O'Neal's) Inf. Co.K Sgt.
Tomlin, J.E. KY 2nd (Duke's) Cav. Co.G
Tomlin, Jesse FL 11th Inf. Co.I
Tomlin, Jesse A.B. AL 33rd Inf. Co.I
Tomlin, J.G. VA 2nd Cav. Co.G
Tomlin, J.H. GA 22nd Inf. Co.C
Tomlin, J.H. GA 46th Inf. Co.D
Tomlin, J.H. NC 4th Sr.Res. Co.D
Tomlin, J.J. GA 11th Cav. Co.K
Tomlin, J.M. NC 20th Inf. Co.B
Tomlin, John GA 32nd Inf. Co.C
Tomlin, John MO Cav. Poindexter's Regt.
Tomlin, John MO Cav. Snider's Bn. Co.B
Tomlin, John TN 21st Cav. Co.A
Tomlin, John VA 3rd Inf. 2nd Co.I
Tomlin, John F. NC Cav. 15th Bn. Co.A
Tomlin, John G. LA Inf. 1st Sp.Bn. (Wheat's) New Co.E 1st Sgt.
Tomlin, John G. VA Hvy.Arty. 19th Bn. Co.D
Tomlin, John H. AL 33rd Inf. Co.I
Tomlin, John H. VA 15th Inf. Co.I

Tomlin, John L.G. AL 15th Inf. Co.E
Tomlin, John R. MO 1st Inf. Co.I
Tomlin, John T. GA Cherokee Legion (St.Guards) Co.A Cpl.
Tomlin, Joseph GA 6th Cav. Co.G
Tomlin, Josiah S. AL 58th Inf. Co.K
Tomlin, Josiah S. GA 2nd Bn.S.S. Co.E
Tomlin, J.W. TN 18th (Newsom's) Cav. Co.I
Tomlin, J.W. TN 19th & 20th (Cons.) Cav. Co.C
Tomlin, J.W. TN 51st (Cons.) Inf. Co.D
Tomlin, M. GA 6th Res. Co.H
Tomlin, Marshal NC 42nd Inf. Co.D
Tomlin, Milton L. GA 44th Inf. Co.I
Tomlin, Mordecai TN 32nd Inf. Co.D
Tomlin, N.B. MS 11th Inf. Co.B
Tomlin, Newton J. GA 44th Inf. Co.I
Tomlin, N.H. LA 3rd Inf. Co.H Sgt.
Tomlin, Nicholas H. MS 1st Cav. Co.E
Tomlin, Nicholas H. TN 1st Cav.
Tomlin, O. VA 13th Inf. 2nd Co.E
Tomlin, Patrick GA 32nd Inf. Co.A
Tomlin, Pearce GA 1st Cav. Co.B
Tomlin, Perry NC 5th Sr.Res. Co.I
Tomlin, P.L. AR 15th (Johnson's) Inf. Co.A Cpl.
Tomlin, R.G. GA Cav. 10th Bn. (St.Guards) Co.E
Tomlin, Robert GA 12th Cav. Co.L
Tomlin, Robert C. VA 4th Cav. Co.G
Tomlin, Robert H. MS 40th Inf. Co.K
Tomlin, R.W. GA 22nd Inf. Co.C
Tomlin, Sam TX 29th Cav. Co.D
Tomlin, Sherrod AL 2nd Bn. Hilliard's Legion Vol. Co.C
Tomlin, Thomas VA 13th Inf. 2nd Co.E
Tomlin, Thomas G. VA Hvy.Arty. 19th Bn. Co.D
Tomlin, T.W. NC 6th Cav. (65th St.Troops) Co.B
Tomlin, Wesley AL 10th Cav. Co.B
Tomlin, William TN 13th (Gore's) Cav. Co.F
Tomlin, William A. NC 38th Inf. Co.B
Tomlin, William A. VA 3rd Inf. Co.C
Tomlin, William J. AL 57th Inf. Co.D Cpl.
Tomlin, William L. NC Cav. McRae's Bn. Co.E Sgt.
Tomlin, William T. NC Mallett's Bn. (Cp.Guard) Co.B
Tomlin, William R. AL 27th Inf. Co.H
Tomlin, William S. GA 36th (Broyles') Inf. Co.E Sgt.
Tomlin, Winford S. GA 36th (Broyles') Inf. Co.E Sgt.
Tomlin, W.J. GA 56th Inf. Co.K Sgt.
Tomlin, W.L. AR 1st (Monroe's) Cav. Co.B
Tomlin, Woodward GA 32nd Inf. Co.C
Tomlingson, John GA 1st Cav. Co.H
Tomlinson, --- TX 5th Cav. Co.B
Tomlinson, A. TX 25th Cav. Co.G
Tomlinson, A.A. TX 35th (Likens') Cav. Co.A Jr.2nd Lt.
Tomlinson, A.A. TX 12th Inf. Co.E Capt.
Tomlinson, Aaron GA 29th Inf. Co.H Music.
Tomlinson, A.J. GA Phillips' Legion Co.D 2nd Lt.
Tomlinson, A.J. TX 3rd Inf. Co.G
Tomlinson, Alexander R. VA 50th Inf. 1st Co.G
Tomlinson, Alex R. VA 63rd Inf. 1st Co.I, Co.E Sgt.
Tomlinson, Ambrose VA Lt.Arty. Arch. Graham's Co.
Tomlinson, A.N. VA Arty. Bryan's Co.
Tomlinson, Andrew J. LA 19th Inf. Co.B
Tomlinson, Andrew N. VA Lt.Arty. 13th Bn. Co.B
Tomlinson, Andrew N. VA 22nd Inf. Co.F
Tomlinson, Anthony GA Arty. (Chatham Arty.) Wheaton's Co.
Tomlinson, Anthony GA 1st (Olmstead's) Inf. Claghorn's Co.
Tomlinson, A.R. VA Inf. 54th Bn. Co.A 1st Sgt.
Tomlinson, Archibald MS 21st Inf. Co.L Sgt.
Tomlinson, Augustus AL Cav. Lenoir's Ind.Co. Capt.
Tomlinson, B. NC Allen's Co. (Loc.Def.)
Tomlinson, Barnes NC 55th Inf. Co.A
Tomlinson, B.E. TX 20th Inf. Co.K
Tomlinson, Benjamin H. LA 12th Inf. Co.B
Tomlinson, B.H. GA Ind.Cav. (Res.) Humphrey's Co.
Tomlinson, Brazill B. MS 11th Inf. Co.E
Tomlinson, Burgess VA 4th Inf. Co.F
Tomlinson, C. AL 9th (Malone's) Cav. Co.E
Tomlinson, Camilous VA 58th Inf. Co.F
Tomlinson, C.C. AL 2nd Cav. Co.F
Tomlinson, C.C. AL 1st Bn. Hilliard's Legion Vol. Co.D
Tomlinson, Charles LA 2nd Inf. Co.G Music.
Tomlinson, Charles TX 8th Inf. Co.D
Tomlinson, Clement M. SC Lt.Arty. Kelly's Co. (Chesterfield Arty.)
Tomlinson, C.R. NC Allen's Co. (Loc.Def.) Cpl.
Tomlinson, D. AR 38th Inf. Co.K
Tomlinson, Daniel AL 13th Inf. Co.K 1st Sgt.
Tomlinson, Daniel L. GA 6th Inf. Co.D
Tomlinson, Daniel P. GA 32nd Inf. Co.H
Tomlinson, Daniel W. AL Cav. 5th Bn. Hilliard's Legion Co.A
Tomlinson, David AR 1st Cav. Co.E
Tomlinson, David AR 8th Inf. New Co.B
Tomlinson, David VA 11th Bn.Res. Co.E
Tomlinson, David VA 108th Mil. Co.A
Tomlinson, David B. MO Tracy's Regt. Co.H
Tomlinson, Dred KY 2nd (Woodward's) Cav. Co.C
Tomlinson, D.W. 10th Conf.Cav. Co.A Sgt.
Tomlinson, E. GA 6th Inf. (St.Guards) Co.I
Tomlinson, E. LA Mil. 1st Native Guards
Tomlinson, E. NC 6th Sr.Res. Co.C
Tomlinson, Eason T. NC 55th Inf. Co.A
Tomlinson, Edgar M. GA 1st (Olmstead's) Inf. Gallie's Co.
Tomlinson, Edward R. VA 16th Inf. Co.C
Tomlinson, Edwin VA 58th Inf. Co.F
Tomlinson, E.J. TX 32nd Cav. Co.F
Tomlinson, Elias TN 20th (Russell's) Cav. Co.I
Tomlinson, Elijah TN 8th (Smith's) Cav. Co.C
Tomlinson, Elijah A. TN 55th (McKoin's) Inf. Co.F
Tomlinson, Emmitt KY 5th Mtd.Inf. Co.D
Tomlinson, Enoch GA 50th Inf. Co.G Sgt.
Tomlinson, Eppi NC 53rd Inf. Co.C Lt.
Tomlinson, E.S. GA 2nd Cav. Co.F
Tomlinson, F.G. AR 12th Cav. Co.D
Tomlinson, F.M. AR Mtd.Vol. Baker's Co.
Tomlinson, F.M. TN 22nd (Barteau's) Cav. Co.H
Tomlinson, G. GA 10th Inf. Co.A
Tomlinson, Garry NC 55th Inf. Co.A
Tomlinson, George H. MS 41st Inf. Co.D 1st Sgt.
Tomlinson, George W. VA 49th Inf. Co.I
Tomlinson, G.H. TN 6th Inf. Co.A
Tomlinson, Grifford GA 29th Inf. Co.H
Tomlinson, G.T. GA 6th Inf. Co.D
Tomlinson, H. GA Inf. Fuller's Co.
Tomlinson, H. MS Inf. 2nd St.Troops Co.M
Tomlinson, H.A. AR 19th (Dockery's) Inf. Co.G Sgt.
Tomlinson, Harris GA 50th Inf. Co.G
Tomlinson, H.C. AR 4th Inf. Co.I
Tomlinson, H.C. AR Inf. Hardy's Regt. Co.E
Tomlinson, H.C. KY 2nd (Woodward's) Cav. Co.C
Tomlinson, Henry VA 50th Inf. Co.A
Tomlinson, Henry M. SC Lt.Arty. Kelly's Co. (Chesterfield Arty.) Cpl.
Tomlinson, Henry M. VA 25th Inf. 2nd Co.F
Tomlinson, Hiram NC 37th Inf. Co.A
Tomlinson, H.L. MS 1st Bn.S.S. Co.C
Tomlinson, H.M. MS 3rd Inf. (A. of 10,000) Co.C
Tomlinson, H.M. MS 17th Inf. Co.F
Tomlinson, H.N. NC 38th Inf. Co.H
Tomlinson, I. MO Cav. William's Regt. Co.G
Tomlinson, I.C. GA 27th Inf. Sgt.
Tomlinson, Ira SC 4th St.Troops Co.I
Tomlinson, Ira SC Inf. 6th Bn. Co.B
Tomlinson, Ira SC 26th Inf. Co.H
Tomlinson, Ira SC Manigault's Bn.Vol. Co.D
Tomlinson, Isaac VA 6th Inf. Co.I
Tomlinson, Isaac F. AR 18th Inf. Co.D Music.
Tomlinson, J. SC Arty. Manigault's Bn. Co.A
Tomlinson, J. SC Arty. Melchers' Co. (Co.B,German Arty.)
Tomlinson, J. TN 13th Inf. Co.B
Tomlinson, J.A. VA Arty. Bryan's Co.
Tomlinson, Jabes VA 37th Inf. Co.F
Tomlinson, Jacob H. MO Parsons' Regt.
Tomlinson, James AL 3rd Bn.Res. Co.C
Tomlinson, James GA 4th (Clinch's) Cav. Co.H
Tomlinson, James GA Inf. 10th Bn. Co.C
Tomlinson, James LA 2nd Cav. Co.F
Tomlinson, James LA 8th Cav. Co.E
Tomlinson, James TN 8th (Smith's) Cav. Co.C
Tomlinson, James TN 55th (McKoin's) Inf. Co.F
Tomlinson, James TX 1st Hvy.Arty. Co.K
Tomlinson, James TX 5th Inf. Co.D
Tomlinson, James TX 20th Inf. Co.B
Tomlinson, James VA 48th Inf. Co.A Sgt.
Tomlinson, James D. VA 58th Inf. Co.F
Tomlinson, James F. MS 2nd (Davidson's) Inf. Co.G
Tomlinson, James L. GA 14th Inf. Co.C
Tomlinson, James M. GA 4th Inf. Co.B
Tomlinson, James M. GA 12th Inf. Co.A Sgt.
Tomlinson, James M. NC 5th Inf. Co.C Sgt.

Tomlinson, James M. TN Cav. Newsom's Regt. Co.B 1st Lt.
Tomlinson, James R. MS 2nd Inf. (A. of 10,000) Co.A
Tomlinson, James R. MS 30th Inf. Co.B
Tomlinson, James R. TN 48th (Voorhies') Inf.
Tomlinson, James S. NC 5th Inf. Co.I
Tomlinson, James W. KY 6th Cav. Co.I 1st Lt.
Tomlinson, James W. KY 4th Mtd.Inf. Co.D 1st Sgt.
Tomlinson, James W. LA 2nd Cav. Co.I
Tomlinson, James W. VA Lt.Arty. Arch. Graham's Co.
Tomlinson, James W. VA 12th Inf. 2nd Co.I
Tomlinson, J.C.C. SC Inf. 6th Bn. Co.B Bvt.2nd Lt.
Tomlinson, J.C.C. SC 26th Inf. Co.H 1st Lt.
Tomlinson, J.C.C. SC Manigault's Bn.Vol. Co.D
Tomlinson, J.E. LA 3rd Inf. Co.E
Tomlinson, Jeptha E. LA 12th Inf. Co.A
Tomlinson, Jerome AL Jeff Davis Arty.
Tomlinson, Jesse W. LA 30th Inf. Co.I,C
Tomlinson, J.F. AR 18th Inf. Co.D Music.
Tomlinson, J.F. MS 7th Cav. Co.K
Tomlinson, J.H. AR 32nd Inf. Co.B
Tomlinson, J.H. GA 3rd Cav. Co.H
Tomlinson, J.H. MO 9th Bn.S.S. Co.A
Tomlinson, J.H. TN 20th (Russell's) Cav. Co.I
Tomlinson, J.J. GA 1st Cav. Co.G
Tomlinson, J.J. TN 50th Inf. Co.B
Tomlinson, J.K. TX Cav. 4th Regt.St.Troops Co.C
Tomlinson, J.K.P. MS 1st Bn.S.S. Co.C
Tomlinson, J.M. NC 38th Inf. Co.H
Tomlinson, J.M. TN 21st (Wilson's) Cav. Co.G 1st Lt.
Tomlinson, John AR Cav. McGehee's Regt. Co.B
Tomlinson, John GA 11th Cav. (St.Guards) Staten's Co. 3rd Lt.
Tomlinson, John GA 29th Inf. Co.K
Tomlinson, John KY 8th Mtd.Inf. Co.A
Tomlinson, John NC 2nd Jr.Res. Co.H
Tomlinson, John TN 31st Inf. Co.D
Tomlinson, John TX 5th Inf. Co.D
Tomlinson, John A. MS 28th Cav. Co.D
Tomlinson, John A. TN Cav. Newsom's Regt. Co.B
Tomlinson, John A. Ferguson's Staff 1st Lt.
Tomlinson, John E. MS Cav. 24th Bn. Co.E Sgt.
Tomlinson, John E. MS Cav. Brown's Co. (Foster Creek Rangers)
Tomlinson, John F. LA 19th Inf. Co.B
Tomlinson, John G. GA 4th (Clinch's) Cav. Co.I 1st Sgt.
Tomlinson, John G. GA 29th Inf. Co.H Sgt.
Tomlinson, John H. GA 6th Cav. Co.G,H Cpl.
Tomlinson, John H. NC 33rd Inf. Co.A
Tomlinson, John H. NC 53rd Inf. Co.C Lt.
Tomlinson, John I. GA 19th Inf. Co.G
Tomlinson, John J.W. SC 12th Inf. Co.A 1st Sgt.
Tomlinson, John M. NC 3rd Arty. (40th St.Troops) Co.G
Tomlinson, John P. GA 19th Inf. Co.G Band Music.
Tomlinson, John R. KY 5th Mtd.Inf. Co.D
Tomlinson, John T. NC Vol. Lawrence's Co. 1st Sgt.
Tomlinson, John T. 7th Conf.Cav. Co.H 3rd Lt.
Tomlinson, John W. GA Inf. 10th Bn. Co.C
Tomlinson, John W. TN 50th Inf. Co.H
Tomlinson, John W. VA 58th Inf. Co.F
Tomlinson, Jonas GA 29th Inf. Co.K 2nd Lt.
Tomlinson, Jonathan NC 55th Inf. Co.A
Tomlinson, Joseph AL Cav. Hardie's Bn.Res. Co.E
Tomlinson, Joseph AR 2nd Inf. Co.A
Tomlinson, Joseph AR Inf. Hardy's Regt. Co.A
Tomlinson, Joseph GA 50th Inf. Co.G 1st Lt.
Tomlinson, Joseph TN 6th (Wheeler's) Cav. Co.H
Tomlinson, Joseph VA Arty. Bryan's Co.
Tomlinson, Joseph VA Inf. 26th Bn. Co.D
Tomlinson, Joseph A. TX 18th Inf. Co.E 1st Sgt.
Tomlinson, Joseph H. TN 28th Inf. Co.F
Tomlinson, J.S. AL 17th Inf. Co.H
Tomlinson, J.W. TX 34th Cav. Co.I 1st Lt.
Tomlinson, Larry D. NC 4th Cav. (59th St.Troops) Co.H
Tomlinson, L.D. TX 12th Inf. Co.F
Tomlinson, Lenard H. GA 29th Inf. Co.K
Tomlinson, Levin GA 29th Inf. Co.H
Tomlinson, Lewis D.W. NC 56th Inf. Co.A
Tomlinson, L.H. AR 4th Inf. Co.I
Tomlinson, L.R. NC 1st Jr.Res. Co.F
Tomlinson, M.A. LA 3rd Inf. Co.E
Tomlinson, Manson VA 4th Inf. Co.H
Tomlinson, Martin TX Cav. Hardeman's Regt. Co.A
Tomlinson, M.B. TN 3rd (Clack's) Inf. Co.F 1st Sgt.
Tomlinson, M.B. TN Inf. 4th Cons.Regt. Co.K
Tomlinson, Merritt B. TN 48th (Voorhies') Inf. Co.F 2nd Lt.
Tomlinson, Morrison NC 43rd Inf. Co.C
Tomlinson, Moses GA 29th Inf. Co.H
Tomlinson, N. AR 17th (Lemoyne's) Inf. Co.A
Tomlinson, Naan FL 2nd Inf. Co.K
Tomlinson, Naon FL 1st Cav. Co.I
Tomlinson, Nathan NC 2nd Cav. (19th St.Troops) Co.E
Tomlinson, Nathaniel VA 21st Mil. Co.B
Tomlinson, Nathaniel M. NC 50th Inf. Co.C
Tomlinson, Needham GA 50th Inf. Co.G Cpl.
Tomlinson, Noah NC 4th Inf. Co.H
Tomlinson, N.R. AL 2nd Cav. Co.F
Tomlinson, O.G. TX 17th Cons.Dismtd.Cav. Co.F
Tomlinson, P. MS 6th Inf. Co.E
Tomlinson, Paul T. MS Cav. 24th Bn. Co.E 2nd Lt.
Tomlinson, Paul T. MS Arty. (Seven Stars Arty.) Roberts' Co.
Tomlinson, R. SC Vol. Manigault's Bn. Co.D 2nd Lt.
Tomlinson, Ralph C. VA Inf. 5th Bn.Loc.Def. Mech.
Tomlinson, Reece SC Inf. 6th Bn. Co.B 1st Lt.
Tomlinson, Reece SC 26th Inf. Co.H Capt.
Tomlinson, R.H. GA Ind.Cav. (Res.) Humphrey's Co.
Tomlinson, R.H. VA Hvy.Arty. Allen's Co.
Tomlinson, Richard H. NC Inf. 13th Bn. Co.D
Tomlinson, Richard H. NC 66th Inf. Co.K
Tomlinson, R.J. SC 20th Inf. Co.N Cpl.
Tomlinson, Robert SC 9th Inf. Co.D
Tomlinson, Robert VA 4th Inf. Co.H
Tomlinson, Robert VA 50th Inf. Co.F
Tomlinson, Robert J. AL Cav. 5th Bn. Hilliard's Legion Co.A
Tomlinson, Robert S. GA 6th Inf. Co.D
Tomlinson, S. GA Siege Arty. 28th Bn. Co.I
Tomlinson, S.A. AR 6th Inf. New Co.F,C
Tomlinson, S.A. AR 12th Inf. Co.D
Tomlinson, Samuel FL 5th Inf. Co.C
Tomlinson, Samuel GA 29th Inf. Co.K
Tomlinson, Samuel G. TX 18th Inf. Co.E
Tomlinson, S.B. TN 50th Inf. Co.I
Tomlinson, S.G. GA 1st Cav. Co.G Sgt.
Tomlinson, Sherrod GA 29th Inf. Co.H Sgt.
Tomlinson, Sidney H. TX 34th Cav. Co.D
Tomlinson, S.R. GA 28th Inf.
Tomlinson, T.B. VA Hvy.Arty. Allen's Co.
Tomlinson, T.G. TX Cav. Saufley's Scouting Bn. Co.F 2nd Lt.
Tomlinson, Thomas GA 50th Inf. Co.G
Tomlinson, Thomas MS 1st Bn.S.S. Co.C
Tomlinson, Thomas MO 11th Inf. Co.C
Tomlinson, Thomas VA 36th Inf. Co.F
Tomlinson, Thomas VA 48th Inf. Co.A
Tomlinson, Thomas B. VA 20th Inf. Co.C
Tomlinson, Thomas G. TX Cav. Baylor's Regt. Co.G 2nd Lt.
Tomlinson, Thomas M. GA 44th Inf. Co.E
Tomlinson, T.J. TN 20th (Russell's) Cav. Co.I Sgt.
Tomlinson, T.J. TX 26th Cav. 2nd Co.G
Tomlinson, T.J. VA 19th Inf. Co.I
Tomlinson, T.M. GA Lt.Arty. Ritter's Co.
Tomlinson, T.M. GA 6th Inf. (St.Guards) Co.I
Tomlinson, T.M. GA 42nd Inf. Co.H
Tomlinson, Van AR 35th Inf. Co.I
Tomlinson, W. FL 2nd Inf. Co.K
Tomlinson, W. GA Inf. 18th Bn. Co.A
Tomlinson, W. SC 5th Bn.Res. Co.B
Tomlinson, W.A. GA 1st (Ramsey's) Inf. Co.F
Tomlinson, Waller KY 8th Mtd.Inf. Co.A
Tomlinson, W.C. 10th Conf.Cav. Co.A
Tomlinson, W.D. SC Inf. 6th Bn. Co.B
Tomlinson, W.D. SC 26th Inf. Co.H
Tomlinson, W.D. SC Vol. Manigault's Bn. Co.D
Tomlinson, W.D. TN 50th Inf. Co.I
Tomlinson, W.H. AR 38th Inf. Co.K
Tomlinson, Wilfred T. GA 66th Inf. Co.E
Tomlinson, William AL 1st Inf. Co.E
Tomlinson, William AL 1st Inf. Co.I Cpl.
Tomlinson, William AL 16th Inf. Co.D
Tomlinson, William FL 1st Cav. Co.I Cpl.
Tomlinson, William GA Inf. 10th Bn. Co.C
Tomlinson, William LA 13th Bn. (Part.Rangers) Co.E
Tomlinson, William MO 8th Cav. Co.I
Tomlinson, William NC 4th Cav. (59th St.Troops) Co.H
Tomlinson, William NC 53rd Inf. Co.K
Tomlinson, William NC Loc.Def. Croom's Co. Music.
Tomlinson, William TX 1st Hvy.Arty. Co.I

Tomlinson, William TX 15th Inf. 1st Co.D
Tomlinson, William TX 20th Inf. Co.B
Tomlinson, William VA 21st Cav. Co.I
Tomlinson, William VA 58th Inf. Co.F
Tomlinson, William VA Mil. Washington Cty.
Tomlinson, William 4th Conf.Eng.Troops Co.E Artif.
Tomlinson, William A. GA Lt.Arty. Scogin's Btty. (Griffin Lt.Arty.)
Tomlinson, William B. AL 17th Inf. Co.A
Tomlinson, William C. AL Cav. 5th Bn. Hilliard's Legion Co.A
Tomlinson, William C. VA Arty. Bryan's Co.
Tomlinson, William C. VA 108th Mil. Co.A
Tomlinson, William E. TN 48th (Nixon's) Inf. Co.E Sgt.
Tomlinson, William E. TN 54th Inf. Dooley's Co. Cpl.
Tomlinson, William G. MS 32nd Inf. Co.H
Tomlinson, William H. NC 61st Inf. Co.D
Tomlinson, William H. NC 66th Inf. Co.K
Tomlinson, Wm. J. AL 15th Inf. Co.D Cpl.
Tomlinson, William J. GA 6th Inf. Co.D
Tomlinson, William J. GA Phillips' Legion Co.D
Tomlinson, William J. VA 57th Inf. Co.I
Tomlinson, William M. GA 14th Inf. Co.C Color Sgt.
Tomlinson, William M. VA 63rd Inf. Co.E
Tomlinson, Wm. M. Gen. & Staff AASurg.
Tomlinson, William P. AR 18th (Marmaduke's) Inf. Co.E
Tomlinson, William P. 3rd Conf.Inf. Co.E
Tomlinson, William S. MS 1st Bn.S.S. Co.C
Tomlinson, William S. MS 22nd Inf. Co.B
Tomlinson, William T. GA 11th Cav. (St.Guards) Johnson's Co. Cpl.
Tomlinson, Willie W. NC 55th Inf. Co.A
Tomlinson, W.L. GA 10th Mil.
Tomlinson, W.R. TN 24th Bn.S.S. Co.B
Tomlinson, W.T. AR 1st (Dobbin's) Cav. Co.B
Tomlison, John L. NC 1st Arty. (10th St.Troops) Co.G
Tomlison, William GA Inf. 8th Bn. Co.C
Tom Loman 1st Choctaw & Chickasaw Mtd.Rifles 2nd Co.I
Tomma, Van B. AL 3rd Bn. Hilliard's Legion Vol. Co.B
Tomme 1st Creek Mtd.Vol. Co.M
Tomme, David D. AR 4th Inf. Co.K Sgt.
Tomme, Joseph, A. AR 5th Inf. Co.C
Tomme, Marshal M. GA 41st Inf. Co.E Cpl.
Tomme, O.V. GA 27th Inf. Co.G,K
Tomme, Richard A. AL 13th Inf. Co.E
Tomme, Richard A. GA 7th Inf. Co.F
Tomme, Robert S. AL 13th Inf. Co.E 2nd Lt.
Tomme, Robert S. GA Cobb's Legion Co.B
Tomme, S.H. LA 17th Inf. Co.E
Tomme, Thomas V. AR 33rd Inf. Co.K
Tomme, William W. AR Inf. 2nd Bn. Co.B 1st Sgt.
Tomme, William W. AR 3rd Inf. Co.I Sgt.
Tomme, William W. GA 19th Inf. Co.F Sgt.
Tomme, W.W. AR 6th Inf. 1st Co.B Sgt.
Tommehario 1st Creek Mtd.Vol. 1st Co.C Music.
Tomme hujo 1st Creek Mtd.Vol. 2nd Co.D
Tommey, A.H. GA 13th Inf. Co.B
Tommey, Augustus C. GA Arty. 11th Bn. (Sumter Arty.) Co.A Sgt.
Tommey, Christopher C. AL 3rd Inf. Co.I
Tommey, George H. FL 9th Inf. Co.K
Tommey, Henry C. AL 3rd Inf. Co.I
Tommey, John LA 2nd Inf. Co.C
Tommie 1st Creek Mtd.Vol. 2nd Co.C
Tommie, A.B. AL 15th Inf. Co.E
Tommie, A.V. GA 3rd Cav. Co.D
Tommie, James R. AR 9th Inf. Co.E
Tommie, William E. GA 27th Inf. Co.K Sgt.
Tommus, R.W. GA 2nd Regt.St.Line Co.I
Tommy 1st Creek Mtd.Vol. Co.B Sgt.
Tommy 1st Creek Mtd.Vol. Co.H
Tommy 1st Seminole Mtd.Vol.
Tommy, Edwin V. GA 64th Inf. Co.E Sgt.
Tommy, James LA Mil. 3rd Regt. 1st Brig. 1st Div. Co.K
Tommy, John LA 20th Inf. Co.A,E,D
Tommy, John VA Cav. Ferguson's Bn. Nounnan's Co. Cpl.
Tommy cho no ke 1st Creek Mtd.Vol. Co.A
Tommy Harjo 1st Creek Mtd.Vol. Co.H, 2nd Co.D
Tommy Harjo 1st Creek Mtd.Vol. Co.K
Tommy Harjo 1st Seminole Mtd.Vol.
Tommy Harjo, No.2 1st Seminole Mtd.Vol.
Tommy Larney 1st Creek Mtd.Vol. Co.F
Tommy Tustanuegee 1st Seminole Mtd.Vol.
Tommy Tustanuggee 1st Seminole Mtd.Vol. Sgt.
Tommy Tustenuggee 1st Seminole Mtd.Vol.
Tommy Yoholar 2nd Creek Mtd.Vol. Co.E
Tomney, Barney TN 36th Inf. 3rd Co.F
Tomney, Francis VA 4th Inf. Co.A
Tomney, Patrick TX 2nd Inf. Co.E
Tomochee 1st Seminole Mtd.Vol.
Tomnoi hubbi 1st Choctaw Mtd.Rifles Co.K
Tompkill, James TN 10th Inf. Co.F
Tompkin, J.W. TN 4th (McLemore's) Cav. Co.B
Tompkins, --- AL 25th Inf. Co.G
Tompkins, --- VA 13th Inf. Co.K
Tompkins, A.C. VA 2nd Cav. Co.K
Tompkins, A.G. LA 4th Inf. Co.C
Tompkins, A.G. TN 45th Inf. Co.C
Tompkins, A.J. TN 13th (Gore's) Cav. Co.A,B
Tompkins, Albert G. TN 18th Inf. Co.C
Tompkins, Albin G. MS 1st Lt.Arty. Co.E Sgt.
Tompkins, Alfred FL 9th Inf. Co.B
Tompkins, Alfred NC McMillan's Co.
Tompkins, Ambrose R. MO Cav. Wood's Regt. Co.B Jr.2nd Lt.
Tompkins, Ambrose R. MO 5th Regt.St.Guards Co.A Lt.
Tompkins, Augustus TX 25th Cav. Co.H
Tompkins, Benjamin B. VA 30th Inf. Co.G
Tompkins, Benjamin F. VA 32nd Inf. Co.E
Tompkins, Bennett VA Cav. 40th Bn. Co.F
Tompkins, B.F. VA 64th Mtd.Inf. Co.H
Tompkins, C. VA 3rd Inf.Loc.Def. 1st Co.G
Tompkins, Camel TN 13th (Gore's) Cav. Co.B
Tompkins, C.H. VA Lt.Arty. 38th Bn. Co.B
Tompkins, Charles C. AL 8th Inf. Co.E
Tompkins, Charles G. VA 1st Arty. Co.H,F Ord.Sgt.
Tompkins, Charles G. VA Arty. C.F. Johnston's Co. Sgt.Maj.
Tompkins, Clarence W. VA 24th Cav. Co.F
Tompkins, Cornelius SC 10th Inf. 2nd Co.G
Tompkins, Cornelius P. VA 53rd Inf. Co.E
Tompkins, C.Q. VA Inf. 3rd Kanawha Regt. Col.
Tompkins, C.Q. VA 22nd Inf. Col.
Tompkins, C.Q. Gen. & Staff, Inf. Col.
Tompkins, C.W. VA Cav. 40th Bn. Co.F
Tompkins, Daniel SC Inf. Hampton Legion Co.B
Tompkins, David GA 9th Inf. Co.F Sgt.
Tompkins, David C. TX 13th Cav. Co.K Sgt.
Tompkins, D.C. TX 1st Inf. Co.F
Tompkins, Delaney E. TX 13th Cav. Co.K
Tompkins, D.F. LA 17th Inf. Co.E Cpl.
Tompkins, Donald FL Inf. 2nd Bn. Co.C
Tompkins, Donald FL 3rd Inf. Co.I
Tompkins, Donald FL 8th Inf. Co.F
Tompkins, D.W. SC Arty. Manigault's Bn. 1st Co.B
Tompkins, D.W.M. SC 10th Inf. 2nd Co.G
Tompkins, E. AL 6th Cav. Co.B
Tompkins, E.B. SC Arty. Manigault's Bn. 1st Co.B
Tompkins, Edmond G. VA 21st Inf. Co.F
Tompkins, Edmund T. VA 42nd Inf. Co.G Sgt.
Tompkins, Edward R. VA Lt.Arty. Pollock's Co.
Tompkins, E.G. VA Cav. 1st Bn. Co.A
Tompkins, E.G. VA 3rd Inf.Loc.Def. Co.A Sgt.
Tompkins, E.J. TX 1st Inf. Co.F
Tompkins, Eleazar T. VA 6th Inf. Ferguson's Co.
Tompkins, Eleazar T. VA 12th Inf. Co.H
Tompkins, Eubanks GA 4th Inf. Co.E
Tompkins, Eubanks GA Cobb's Legion Co.D
Tompkins, E.W. AL 4th Res. Co.I
Tompkins, F.H. MS 21st Inf. Co.L
Tompkins, F.O. VA 3rd Res. Co.A
Tompkins, F.O. Gen. & Staff Asst.Surg.
Tompkins, Frank TX Cav. Madison's Regt. Co.E
Tompkins, Frank A. GA 5th Inf. Co.D 1st Lt.
Tompkins, Frank A. Gen. & Staff, Medical Dept. Asst.Surg.
Tompkins, Frank W. AR 2nd Cav. Co.C
Tompkins, George F. FL 5th Inf. Co.B
Tompkins, George G. VA 38th Inf. Co.H
Tompkins, George H. MS 1st Lt.Arty. Co.G Sr.1st Lt.
Tompkins, George H. VA Cav. 1st Bn. Co.A
Tompkins, George H. VA Inf. 2nd Bn.Loc.Def. Co.D
Tompkins, George N. MS 24th Inf. Co.K
Tompkins, George W. LA Prestize Res.Corps
Tompkins, George W. TX 14th Cav. Co.H Sgt.
Tompkins, G.G. VA 1st Inf. Co.H
Tompkins, G.H. MS Lt.Arty. Culbertson's Btty. Lt.
Tompkins, Giles FL Inf. 2nd Bn. Co.C
Tompkins, G.S. TX 13th Cav. Co.K
Tompkins, G.W. NC 3rd Cav. (41st St.Troops) Co.A
Tompkins, H.B. VA 3rd Inf.Loc.Def. Co.D
Tompkins, H.C. VA 4th Cav. Co.B
Tompkins, H. Clay VA Inf. 22nd Bn. Co.A 2nd Lt.
Tompkins, Henry B. AL 22nd Inf. Co.G Capt.
Tompkins, Henry B. AL 39th Inf. Adj.
Tompkins, Henry B. Gen. & Staff 1st Lt.,Adj.
Tompkins, Henry C. FL 1st Cav. Co.A

Tompkins, Henry C. FL Milton Lt.Arty. Dunham's Co.
Tompkins, Herbert B. AR 3rd Inf. Co.A 1st Sgt.
Tompkins, Herbert B. VA 23rd Inf. Co.H
Tompkins, Herbert B. VA 46th Inf. 2nd Co.A
Tompkins, J. GA 3rd Cav. Co.H
Tompkins, J. GA 4th (Clinch's) Cav. Co.D
Tompkins, J. GA Cav. Floyd's Co.
Tompkins, J. MS 14th Inf. Co.F
Tompkins, J. TX 21st Inf. Co.K
Tompkins, J. VA 18th Inf. Co.F
Tompkins, J. VA Conscr. Cp.Lee Co.B
Tompkins, J.A. AL 8th Inf. Co.I
Tompkins, J.A. VA 5th Cav. Co.I
Tompkins, James AL 42nd Inf. Co.E
Tompkins, James SC 10th Inf. Co.C Cpl.
Tompkins, James TN 18th Inf. Co.K
Tompkins, James A. FL 2nd Cav. Co.B
Tompkins, James E. TN 45th Inf. Co.C
Tompkins, James E. VA 11th Inf. Co.B
Tompkins, James G. VA 30th Inf. Co.G Sgt.
Tompkins, James H. TN 2nd (Robison's) Inf. Co.E 1st Sgt.
Tompkins, James H.F. VA 24th Cav. Co.F 1st Sgt.
Tompkins, James H.F. VA Lt.Arty. Parker's Co.
Tompkins, James H.F. VA 17th Inf. Co.K 2nd Lt.
Tompkins, James L. TX 35th (Brown's) Cav. Co.E Capt.
Tompkins, James L. VA 42nd Inf. Co.B 1st Lt.
Tompkins, Jas. L. VA 54th Inf. Sgt.Maj.
Tompkins, James M. AL 5th Bn.Vol. Co.A
Tompkins, James S. SC Inf. Hampton Legion Co.B
Tompkins, James S. TN 2nd (Robison's) Inf. Co.I Bvt.2nd Lt.
Tompkins, James S. VA Lt.Arty. Clutter's Co.
Tompkins, James T. FL 1st Cav. Co.A
Tompkins, James T. LA 1st Cav. Co.A
Tompkins, James W. MS 23rd Inf. Co.D
Tompkins, J.B. LA 3rd Inf. Co.H Cpl.
Tompkins, J.B. SC Lt.Arty. 3rd (Palmetto) Bn. Co.H
Tompkins, J.B. SC 10th Inf. 2nd Co.G
Tompkins, J.B. SC 16th Inf. Co.K
Tompkins, J.E. VA 1st St.Res. Co.E
Tompkins, J.E. VA Conscr.Cp.Lee
Tompkins, J.H. TX 13th Vol. 1st Co.B
Tompkins, J.H. VA 3rd Inf.Loc.Def. Co.C,D Sgt.
Tompkins, J.J. AL 4th Res. Co.F
Tompkins, J.J. TN 8th Inf. Co.D Sgt.
Tompkins, J.M. KY 8th Mtd.Inf. Co.A
Tompkins, J.M. LA Inf.Cons.Crescent Regt. Co.I
Tompkins, J.M. TX 11th Inf. Co.E
Tompkins, J.M. VA 1st St.Res. Co.A
Tompkins, J.N.C. MO 4th Inf. Co.E
Tompkins, J.N.C. Gen.& Staff 2nd Lt.,Dr.M.
Tompkins, John AL Gorff's Co. (Mobile Pulaski Rifles)
Tompkins, John AR Lt.Arty. Key's Btty.
Tompkins, John GA 48th Inf. Co.E
Tompkins, John SC 7th Inf. 1st Co.G
Tompkins, John SC Inf. 9th Bn. Co.D
Tompkins, John SC 14th Inf. Co.K
Tompkins, John SC 26th Inf. Co.E
Tompkins, John TN 2nd (Walker's) Inf. Co.D
Tompkins, John TX 9th Cav. Co.I
Tompkins, John VA 1st Inf. Co.C
Tompkins, John 9th Conf.Inf. Co.D
Tompkins, John A. TN 22nd (Barteau's) Cav. Co.D,E
Tompkins, John C. MO Cav. Poindexter's Regt.
Tompkins, John C. MO St.Guard
Tompkins, John F. GA Lt.Arty. Howell's Co.
Tompkins, John F. VA 2nd Arty. Co.A 2nd Lt.
Tompkins, John F. VA Lt.Arty. Arch. Graham's Co. Cpl.
Tompkins, John F. VA Inf. 22nd Bn. Co.A Capt.
Tompkins, John Fitz VA Cav. 40th Bn. Co.F 1st Sgt.
Tompkins, John H. FL 7th Inf. Co.C Chap.
Tompkins, John L. GA 2nd Mil. Co.G
Tompkins, John M. VA 30th Inf. Co.G
Tompkins, John S. SC 10th Inf. Co.C Cpl.
Tompkins, John T. 1st Conf.Eng.Troops Co.B
Tompkins, John W. FL 3rd Inf. Co.I
Tompkins, John W. FL 8th Inf. Co.F
Tompkins, John W. FL 9th Inf. Co.B
Tompkins, John W. FL 10th Inf. Co.E
Tompkins, John W. SC Inf. Hampton Legion Co.B Cpl.
Tompkins, Joseph AL 51st (Part.Rangers) Co.F
Tompkins, Joseph AL 42nd Inf. Co.G
Tompkins, Joseph VA 41st Inf. 1st Co.G
Tompkins, Joseph VA 61st Inf. Co.I
Tompkins, Joseph J. MO 2nd Inf. Co.A
Tompkins, J.S. AL 5th Cav. Co.E
Tompkins, J.W. GA 28th Inf. Co.B
Tompkins, J.W. SC 1st (Butler's) Inf. Co.C
Tompkins, J.W. SC 16th Inf. Co.K
Tompkins, J.W. TX 2nd Inf. Co.C
Tompkins, J.W. Gen. & Staff AASurg.
Tompkins, Kenneth M. SC 10th Inf. Co.C
Tompkins, L. GA 4th (Clinch's) Cav. Co.D Cpl.
Tompkins, Leander L. MS 1st Lt.Arty. Co.C
Tompkins, Lexington E. SC 10th Inf. Co.C
Tompkins, L.W. AR 20th Inf. Co.E Cpl.
Tompkins, Mathew W. GA 4th Inf. Co.E 2nd Lt.
Tompkins, M.D. NC 3rd Cav. (41st St.Troops) Co.A
Tompkins, Merida W. GA 31st Inf. Co.D
Tompkins, M.W. GA 54th Inf. Co.B
Tompkins, M.W. VA Arty. L.F. Jones' Co.
Tompkins, Nell H. AL 3rd Inf. Co.D
Tompkins, Nicholas GA Lt.Arty. 12th Bn. 2nd Co.A
Tompkins, Nicholas GA 7th Inf. Co.F
Tompkins, Parmelee AL 18th Inf. Co.B
Tompkins, R. GA 4th (Clinch's) Cav. Co.D Sgt.
Tompkins, R. GA 4th (Clinch's) Cav. Co.D
Tompkins, R. GA 4th (Clinch's) Cav. Co.E
Tompkins, R. Augustus SC Inf. Hampton Legion Co.B Capt.
Tompkins, Ray GA 4th (Clinch's) Cav. Co.D
Tompkins, R.F. GA Lt.Arty. 12th Bn. 1st Co.A
Tompkins, R.F. GA 63rd Inf. Co.A
Tompkins, Richard H. VA 30th Inf. Co.G
Tompkins, Robert GA Lt.Arty. Howell's Co.
Tompkins, Robert VA 32nd Inf. Co.E
Tompkins, Robert A. VA 3rd Inf.Loc.Def. Co.D Capt.
Tompkins, Robert A. VA 23rd Inf. Co.H Capt.
Tompkins, Robert E. VA 30th Inf. Co.G
Tompkins, Robert W. SC Inf. Hampton Legion Co.B Capt.
Tompkins, Robert W. VA 58th Inf. Co.I
Tompkins, R.V. TX 2nd Inf. Co.C Sgt.
Tompkins, Samuel AL 42nd Inf. Co.E
Tompkins, Samuel VA 54th Mil. Co.C,D
Tompkins, Samuel G. SC 10th Inf. 2nd Co.G Cpl.
Tompkins, Samuel S. SC 5th Res. Co.K
Tompkins, Samuel T. LA 12th Inf. Co.C
Tompkins, S.B. GA 28th Inf. Co.B
Tompkins, S.B.W. GA 46th Inf. Co.C
Tompkins, S.F. GA 8th Cav. New Co.E
Tompkins, S.F. GA Cav. 20th Bn. Co.C
Tompkins, S.F. GA Lt.Arty. Howell's Co.
Tompkins, S.H. AL 18th Inf. Co.G
Tompkins, Silas B. MS 20th Inf. Co.H
Tompkins, S. James SC Inf. Hampton Legion Co.B
Tompkins, S.L. FL 2nd Inf. Co.L
Tompkins, S.P. MS 12th Cav. Co.A Sgt.
Tompkins, S.S. SC 2nd St.Troops Co.I
Tompkins, Stephen AL Recruits
Tompkins, Stephen A. SC 1st (McCreary's) Inf. Co.G Hosp.Stew.
Tompkins, S.W. TN 9th (Ward's) Cav. Co.A
Tompkins, S.Y. AL Cav. Barlow's Co.
Tompkins, S.Y. 15th Conf.Cav. Co.C
Tompkins, T. MO 1st Inf. Co.D
Tompkins, T. VA Cav. Davis' Bn. Co.C 1st Lt.
Tompkins, T.B. GA 45th Inf. Co.A 2nd Lt.
Tompkins, T.B. LA 5th Cav. Co.E Capt.
Tompkins, T. Clanton SC 1st Inf. Co.H
Tompkins, T.H. FL 2nd Inf. Co.L
Tompkins, Theod MO Inf. 1st Bn. Co.C
Tompkins, Thomas KY 8th Mtd.Inf. Co.A
Tompkins, Thomas SC Cav. 4th Bn. Co.A
Tompkins, Thomas B. AL 23rd Inf. Co.A
Tompkins, Thomas B. LA 8th Inf. Co.G 2nd Lt.
Tompkins, Thomas G. VA 9th Inf. Co.G
Tompkins, Thomas W. TX 11th (Spaight's) Bn.Vol. Co.C
Tompkins, Turner C. SC 1st (McCreary's) Inf. Co.G Sgt.
Tompkins, T.W. TX 21st Inf. Co.E
Tompkins, T.W. VA 15th Cav. Co.B
Tompkins, Uell H. AL 59th Inf. Co.I 2nd Lt.
Tompkins, Uell H. AL Arty. 4th Bn. Hilliard's Legion Co.A Cpl.
Tompkins, W. GA 14th Inf. Co.E
Tompkins, W. VA 1st St.Res. Co.C
Tompkins, W.B. VA 2nd Inf.Loc.Def. Co.B
Tompkins, W.B. VA Inf. 2nd Bn.Loc.Def. Co.D
Tompkins, W.C. LA Mil. 2nd Regt. 3rd Brig. 1st Div. QM
Tompkins, W.C. MS Inf. 2nd Bn. Co.F
Tompkins, W.C. MS 48th Inf. Co.F
Tompkins, W.D. VA 1st St.Res. Co.I
Tompkins, W.D. VA 2nd St.Res.
Tompkins, Wesley K. VA Lt.Arty. 13th Bn. Co.A Hosp.Stew.
Tompkins, W.G.S. GA 2nd Cav. (St.Guards) Co.F

Tompkins, W.G.S. MS 2nd Cav. Co.D
Tompkins, W.H. AL Inf. 2nd Regt. Co.E
Tompkins, W.H. SC Lt.Arty. 3rd (Palmetto) Bn. Co.H
Tompkins, W.H. SC 16th Inf. Co.K
Tompkins, William GA 3rd Inf. Co.A
Tompkins, William LA 11th Inf. Co.E
Tompkins, William LA 13th Inf. Co.I
Tompkins, William MS 7th Inf. Co.I
Tompkins, William TN 60th Mtd.Inf. Co.D
Tompkins, William Conf.Inf. 8th Bn. Co.C
Tompkins, William A. GA 2nd Inf. Co.D
Tompkins, William B. VA Hvy.Arty. 18th Bn. Co.E
Tompkins, William B. VA 49th Inf. Co.C Sgt.Maj.
Tompkins, William B. VA 60th Inf. Co.E
Tompkins, William D. VA 14th Inf. Co.B Capt.
Tompkins, William H. VA Cav. 36th Bn. Co.A
Tompkins, William H. VA Lt.Arty. Pollock's Co.
Tompkins, Wm. M. AL 31st Inf.
Tompkins, William M. GA 4th Bn.S.S. Co.A
Tompkins, William M. VA 1st Arty. Co.K
Tompkins, William P. GA 28th Inf. Co.B
Tompkins, William P. FL 2nd Cav. Co.B 1st Sgt.
Tompkins, William P. FL 10th Inf. Co.B
Tompkins, Wm. R. Gen. & Staff Asst.Surg.
Tompkins, William S. GA 2nd Cav. (St.Guards) Co.G Cpl.
Tompkins, William S. MO Cav. Wood's Regt. Co.B
Tompkins, William T. VA 19th Inf. Co.C
Tompkins, William Y. AL 53rd (Part.Rangers) Co.B Bugler
Tompkins, Willis SC 10th Inf. Co.C
Tompkins, Wilson VA Lt.Arty. 13th Bn. Co.A
Tompkins, W.J. AL 1st Cav. 2nd Co.C 1st Black.
Tompkins, W.J. AR 7th Inf. Co.D
Tompkins, W.R. AL 12th Inf. Co.F
Tompkins, W.R. VA Inf. 25th Bn. Co.G Sgt.
Tompkins, W.S. MO St.Guard
Tompkins, W.T. AR 32nd Inf. Co.K 2nd Lt.
Tompkins, W.T. VA 24th Cav. Co.F
Tompkins, W.W. GA Inf. 3rd Bn. Co.G
Tompkins, W.W. VA 3rd Res. Co.H
Tompley, Victerine LA Ogden's Cav. Co.A
Tomplin, Humphrey A. NC 8th Bn.Jr.Res. Co.A
Tomplin, O. VA Cav. Swann's Bn. Carpenter's Co.
Tompson, A. VA 4th Cav. Co.B
Tompson, C. AR 38th Inf. Co.K
Tompson, Charles GA Cobb's Legion Co.D
Tompson, Charles W. MS 3rd Inf. Co.E Cpl.
Tompson, Daniel A. AR 27th Inf. Co.K
Tompson, Edward VA Cav. Mosby's Regt. (Part.Rangers) Co.A
Tompson, Elisha GA Lt.Arty. King's Btty.
Tompson, F. MO 15th Cav. Co.B
Tompson, Frederick G. MO Cav. Schnabel's Bn.
Tompson, George W. MS 20th Inf. Co.I
Tompson, George W. VA 87th Mil. Co.D
Tompson, G.F. MS 38th Cav. Co.G
Tompson, Green B. AR 27th Inf. Co.K
Tompson, H.C. VA 3rd Res. Co.A
Tompson, J. AL Cav. Moreland's Regt. Co.F
Tompson, J. AL 15th Inf. Co.A
Tompson, J. MS 6th Cav. Co.C
Tompson, J. TX 6th Field Btty.
Tompson, J. TX Lt.Arty. Dege's Bn.
Tompson, J.A. SC 7th Inf. 2nd Co.E
Tompson, James SC 7th Inf. 2nd Co.E
Tompson, James P. AR Cav. Carlton's Regt. Co.D
Tompson, John MS 12th Cav. Co.I
Tompson, John TN Inf. Sowell's Detach.
Tompson, John E. FL Cav. 5th Bn. Co.G
Tompson, John T. VA 61st Inf. Co.H
Tompson, J.S. NC 4th Inf. Co.A
Tompson, L. MS 6th Cav. Co.C
Tompson, R. AL Cav. Moreland's Regt. Co.F
Tompson, S. GA 35th Inf. Co.C
Tompson, Samuel MO Cav. Freeman's Regt. Co.D
Tompson, Samuel H. AR 6th Inf. Co.C Sgt.
Tompson, Sidny NC 6th Cav. (65th St.Troops) Co.H
Tompson, T. TN 6th Inf. Co.F
Tompson, Thomas M. NC 15th Inf. Co.B
Tompson, T.W. AR 1st Vol. Anderson's Co.
Tompson, W. MS Yerger's Co. (St.Troops)
Tompson, William AL 62nd Inf. Co.E
Tompson, William NC 6th Cav. (65th St.Troops) Co.H
Tompson, William B. SC Inf. Hampton Legion Co.C
Tompson, William B. VA Cav. Mosby's Regt. (Part.Rangers) Co.A,B
Tompson, William J. AL 11th Inf. Co.I
Tompson, W.R. AL Cav. Hardie's Bn.Res. Co.K
Toms, Anderson MO 5th Cav. Co.H
Toms, Anderson MO 15th Cav. Co.C
Toms, Chasteine VA 47th Mil.
Toms, Edward AR 3rd Cav. Co.G
Toms, Edward H. AR 19th Inf. Co.A Cpl.
Toms, Garland VA 46th Inf. 1st Co.G
Toms, George W. AR 2nd Inf. New Co.C
Toms, George W. VA 34th Inf. Co.I
Toms, James F. NC 34th Inf. Co.C
Toms, James M. NC 1st Cav. (9th St.Troops) Co.K
Toms, James M. NC 12th Inf. Co.E
Toms, James S. VA 20th Cav. Co.D,E
Toms, Jasper KY 9th Mtd.Inf. Co.G Cpl.
Toms, J.B. VA 58th Inf. Co.B
Toms, John C. NC 34th Inf. Co.C
Toms, L. NC 1st Bn.Jr.Res. Co.B
Toms, Marion C. NC 1st Inf. (6 mo. '61) Co.E
Toms, Marion C. NC 60th Inf. Co.A Capt.
Toms, Naaman VA 46th Inf. 1st Co.G
Toms, Nathan NC 17th Inf. (1st Org.) Co.I
Toms, Nathan NC 68th Inf.
Toms, Richard VA 41st Inf. Co.F
Toms, Richard H. VA 12th Inf. Co.G
Toms, Thomas F. NC 18th Inf. Co.E
Toms, Wilton VA 46th Inf. 1st Co.G
Toms, Zachariah NC Lt.Arty. 13th Bn. Co.A
Toms, Zachariah NC 17th Inf. (1st Org.) Co.I
Toms, Zachariah NC 17th Inf. (2nd Org.) Co.L
Tomsett, J.B. AR Inf. Cocke's Regt. Co.E
Tomsett, Martin AR 6th Inf. Co.E
Tomsett, Martin AR Inf. Cocke's Regt. Co.E
Tomson 1st Seminole Mtd.Vol.
Tomson, A.W. SC 18th Inf. Surg.
Tomson, Thomas AL 38th Inf. Co.K
Tom Wesley 1st Choctaw & Chickasaw Mtd. Rifles Maytubbey's Co. Cpl.
Tomy, James LA 1st Inf.
Tonack, John TX 2nd Inf.
Tonage, David MS 2nd (Quinn's St.Troops) Inf. Co.D
Tonahill, Jesse MS 21st Inf. Co.I
To nah yoh 1st Cherokee Mtd.Rifles McDaniel's Co.
Tonard, William FL Cav. 3rd Bn. Co.B
Tonart, C. AL 1st Hvy.Arty. Co.I
Tonart, Francis FL 1st Inf. Old Co.K, New Co.A Sgt.
Tonart, P. AL 62nd Inf. Co.B
Tonart, S. AL 62nd Inf. Co.B
Tonart, W. AL 15th Cav. Co.D
Tonart, William 15th Conf.Cav. Co.D
Ton a tae ton l 1st Cherokee Mtd.Rifles Co.H
Toncha, J. 1st Chickasaw Inf. Minnis' Co.
Toncrey, Elijah H. TX 6th Cav. Co.K
Toncuno, Antoine LA 28th (Thomas') Inf. Co.H
Tondee, Robert P. GA 1st (Olmstead's) Inf. Davis' Co.
Tondee, Robert P. GA 17th Inf. Co.B Capt.
Tondee, William H. GA 17th Inf. Co.B 2nd Lt.
Tondre, Celleste TX 17th Field Btty.
Tondre, Fr. TX 33rd Cav. Co.F
Tondrel, --- TX Cav. Mann's Regt. Co.G
Tone, J.F. AL 48th Inf. Co.G
Tonehochett, Charles LA Miles' Legion Co.F
Tonell, A. AL Coosa Guards J.W. Suttles' Co.
Tonell, J.J. AL Coosa Guards J.W. Suttles' Co.
Tonella, Joseph TN 15th Inf. Co.K
Tone O Tubbee 1st Choctaw Mtd.Rifles Co.H
Toner, A. LA 1st Cav. Co.F
Toner, Benjamin P. VA 3rd Res. Co.C
Toner, Bernard MS 12th Inf. Co.E Sgt.
Toner, James M. KY 14th Cav.
Toner, John LA 20th Inf. Co.H
Toner, John H. AL Lt.Arty. 2nd Bn. Co.E
Toner, Joseph MS 12th Inf. Co.E
Toner, Thomas MO Dorsey's Regt.
Toner, Thomas Clark's Regt.
Toner, William C. MS 46th Inf. Co.G
Tonery, Barton MO Lt.Arty. Landis' Co.
Tonery, Martin MO Lt.Arty. Landis' Co.
To ney 1st Creek Mtd.Vol. Co.A
Toney 1st Seminole Mtd.Vol.
Toney, --- TN 16th Inf. Co.C
Toney, A. NC 16th Inf. Co.I
Toney, A.C. VA Inf. 22nd Bn. Co.A
Toney, Adam VA 22nd Inf. Co.I Sgt.
Toney, A.K. AR Inf. 4th Bn. Co.A
Toney, Albert NC 62nd Inf. Co.F
Toney, Alonzo KY 2nd Bn.Mtd.Rifles Co.D
Toney, Alonzo VA 8th Cav. Co.K
Toney, Augustus C. GA 41st Inf. Co.I
Toney, Aurelius C. VA 44th Inf. Co.C
Toney, Benjamin MS 2nd Cav. Co.K
Toney, C. AL 26th (O'Neal's) Inf. Co.I
Toney, Carey VA 22nd Inf. Co.I
Toney, Charles MO 8th Cav. Co.B,G
Toney, Charles P. GA 1st (Ramsey's) Inf. Co.K
Toney, Charles P. GA 45th Inf. Co.B 1st Lt.

Toney, C. Samuel LA 9th Inf. Co.I
Toney, C.W. GA Inf. 25th Bn. (Prov.Guard) Co.G Music.
Toney, D.F. GA 24th Inf. Co.D
Toney, D.F. GA Inf. 25th Bn. (Prov.Guard) Co.A
Toney, Doctor F. GA 44th Inf. Co.D
Toney, Ed TX 18th Cav. Co.B
Toney, Edward SC 1st Inf. Co.H
Toney, Edward SC 7th Inf. 1st Co.H, 2nd Co.H Sgt.
Toney, Edward SC 19th Inf. Co.B
Toney, Edward TX Cav. Baylor's Regt. Co.D
Toney, Edward W. SC Inf.Bn. Co.C
Toney, E.N. VA Inf. 25th Bn. Co.D
Toney, E.W. AL Cav. Callaway's Co.
Toney, Frederick VA 22nd Inf. Co.I
Toney, George J. SC 14th Inf. Co.D
Toney, George M. VA Cav. 39th Bn. Co.D
Toney, George M. VA 21st Inf. Co.E
Toney, George M. VA Inf. 25th Bn. Co.C
Toney, George T. MO 11th Inf. Co.F
Toney, George W. NC 62nd Inf. Co.F
Toney, George W. VA 17th Cav. Co.E Sgt.
Toney, George W. VA 24th Inf. Co.G
Toney, Harris GA 1st Cav. Co.D
Toney, Harris LA 1st Cav. Co.D
Toney, Harris J. GA 2nd Cav. (St.Guards) Co.G
Toney, Harris J. GA 41st Inf. Co.H
Toney, Henry LA 20th Inf. Co.C
Toney, Henry MS 2nd Cav. Co.K
Toney, Henry MO 2nd Cav. Co.C
Toney, Henry MO Cav. 3rd Bn. Co.F
Toney, Henry C. VA 3rd Cav. Co.G
Toney, H.J. GA 19th Inf. Co.E
Toney, H.M. GA 2nd Inf. Co.I
Toney, Hopkins MO 1st Inf. Co.E
Toney, Hugh VA 36th Inf. 1st Co.C, 2nd Co.D Capt.
Toney, H.Y. MS Inf. 1st Bn.St.Troops (12 mo. '62-3) Co.D
Toney, J.A. AL 26th Inf. Co.C Sgt.
Toney, James AR 8th Inf. New Co.H
Toney, James GA 38th Inf. Co.K Fifer
Toney, James MS 39th Inf. Co.B
Toney, James H. MO Cav. Fristoe's Regt. Co.F
Toney, James M. GA 19th Inf. Co.E
Toney, James M. GA 44th Inf. Co.D
Toney, James W. Hvy.Arty. DeGournay's Bn. Co.D
Toney, James William LA 20th Inf. Co.C
Toney, Japser N. TX Cav. Baylor's Regt. Co.A
Toney, Jasper N. GA 8th Inf. (St.Guards) Co.D
Toney, J.D. GA 38th Inf. Co.I
Toney, Jefferson NC 62nd Inf. Co.F
Toney, Jesse VA Cav. Hounshell's Bn. Thurmond's Co.
Toney, J.J. VA 1st (Farinholt's) Res. Co.I
Toney, J.M. AL 4th (Russell's) Cav. Co.F
Toney, J.M. SC 2nd Arty. Co.A
Toney, John NC 50th Inf. Co.G
Toney, John VA Inf. 4th Bn.Loc.Def. Co.F
Toney, John A. AR 18th Inf. Co.B Sgt.
Toney, John C. MO 6th Cav. Co.B Capt.
Toney, John C. VA 21st Inf. Co.E
Toney, John Cary VA 44th Inf. Co.C,I
Toney, John G. VA 30th Bn.S.S. Co.A Color Sgt.
Toney, John M. GA Arty. 9th Bn. Co.B
Toney, John P. AL 20th Inf. Co.E Cpl.
Toney, John P. TN 13th (Gore's) Cav. Co.G
Toney, John P. VA 22nd Inf. Co.I Capt.
Toney, John R. VA 41st Inf. Co.B Cpl.
Toney, John T. LA 27th Inf. Co.I
Toney, John W. LA 9th Inf. Co.I
Toney, Joseph W. VA 18th Inf. Co.F
Toney, Joseph W. VA 41st Inf. Co.K
Toney, J.P. AL 53rd (Part.Rangers) Co.A
Toney, J.P. TN 8th Inf. Co.F
Toney, J.T. GA 24th Inf. Co.A
Toney, J.T. VA 1st (Farinholt's) Res. Co.I
Toney, J.W. LA Cav. 18th Bn. Co.G Sgt.
Toney, L.E. SC 2nd Arty. Co.E
Toney, Lemuel G.B. VA 58th Inf. Co.E
Toney, Levi 1st Cherokee Mtd.Vol. 1st Co.B, 2nd Co.H
Toney, Marcus SC 2nd Cav. Co.I
Toney, Marcus B. TN 1st (Feild's) Inf. Co.B
Toney, Marion VA 30th Bn.S.S. Co.A
Toney, Mark M. MO Cav. 1st Regt.St.Guard Co.A
Toney, Mark M. MO 8th Cav. Co.C
Toney, Matthew R.J. GA 21st Inf. Co.C
Toney, M.B. TN 1st (Feild's) & 27th Inf. (Cons.) Co.B
Toney, Michael MO Inf. 4th Regt.St.Guard Co.D
Toney, Napoleon KY 2nd Bn.Mtd.Rifles Co.D
Toney, Napoleon VA 8th Cav. Co.K
Toney, Nimrod H. MO Cav. Fristoe's Regt. Co.F
Toney, Overton G. VA 36th Inf. 1st Co.B, 2nd Co.D
Toney, Patrick H. VA Hvy.Arty. 10th Bn. Co.D
Toney, Peu. GA 19th Inf. Co.E
Toney, Poindexter, Jr. VA 22nd Inf. Co.I
Toney, Poindexter, Sr. VA 22nd Inf. Co.I
Toney, R. SC 7th Inf. Co.M
Toney, R.A. VA Hvy.Arty. Coffin's Co.
Toney, R.D. VA Hvy.Arty. Coffin's Co.
Toney, Richard A. LA 1st Hvy.Arty. (Reg.) Co.C
Toney, Richard A. VA 20th Inf. Co.D
Toney, Riley A. VA 44th Inf. Co.C
Toney, R.J. LA 1st Hvy.Arty. (Reg.) Co.I
Toney, R.J. VA Hvy.Arty. Coffin's Co.
Toney, Robert VA 8th Cav. Co.G
Toney, Robert VA Cav. Hounshell's Bn. Thurmond's Co.
Toney, Robert VA Inf. 45th Bn. Co.F
Toney, Robert L. LA 16th Inf. Co.B
Toney, Samuel A. VA 21st Inf. Co.E
Toney, Seaborne E. GA 30th Inf. Co.E
Toney, Sidney GA 8th Inf. (St.Guards) Co.D
Toney, Squier VA 129th Mil. Carter's Co.
Toney, Squire VA 1st Cav. Co.G
Toney, S.S. GA 5th Inf. Co.D
Toney, S.S. GA 5th Res. Co.D
Toney, Stephen W. VA 2nd Arty. Co.K
Toney, Stephen W. VA Inf. 25th Bn. Co.C
Toney, T.E. AR Inf. 4th Bn. Co.A
Toney, T.E. AR 36th Inf. Co.K
Toney, Thomas KY 2nd (Duke's) Cav. Co.L Capt.
Toney, Thomas W. NC 16th Inf. Co.K
Toney, Vincent A. GA Arty. 9th Bn. Co.B Cpl.
Toney, Waddy M. MS 33rd Inf. Co.I
Toney, Walter L. TN 28th Inf. Co.D, 2nd Co.H
Toney, W.C. LA 3rd (Wingfield's) Cav. Co.A
Toney, W.H. MO Inf. 3rd Regt.St.Guard Co.H 2nd Lt.
Toney, W. Henry GA 1st (Ramsey's) Inf. Co.K
Toney, Wm. AL 15th Inf. Co.K
Toney, William LA 3rd (Wingfield's) Cav. Co.A
Toney, William MS 2nd Cav. Co.K
Toney, William SC 7th Res. Co.G
Toney, William TX Cav. Morgan's Regt. Co.C
Toney, William C. LA 9th Inf. Co.I
Toney, William F. AL 39th Inf. Co.F
Toney, William H. MO Cav. 1st Regt.St.Guard Co.A Comsy.
Toney, William H. MO 8th Cav. Co.I,C Sgt.
Toney, William J. VA 2nd Cav. Co.D
Toney, William L. AL 7th Cav. Co.B,I
Toney, William L. MO 1st Inf. Co.E
Toney, William T. GA 36th (Broyles') Inf. Co.G
Toney, William T. TX 13th Cav. Co.B
Toney, William W. AL 4th Inf. Co.B
Toney, William W. VA 3rd Res. Co.D
Toney, W.J. GA 18th Inf. Co.K
Toney, W.J. NC 62nd Inf. Co.F
Toney, W.L. MO 1st & 4th Cons.Inf. Co.F
Toney, W.P. VA 41st Inf. Co.B
Toney, W.W. AL 53rd (Part.Rangers) Co.A 1st Lt.
Tong, Andrew MO 12th Inf. Co.F 1st Sgt.
Tong, Elijah W. MO 3rd Cav. Co.B
Tong, H.W. TX Cav. Morgan's Regt. Co.A
Tong, William W. MO 3rd Inf. Co.B
Tongate, Willett KY 4th Cav. Co.A,H
Tongblood, A. KY 1st (Butler's) Cav.
Tonge, E. TN 3rd (Clack's) Inf. Co.I
Tonge, H.A. AL 37th Inf. Co.A Sgt.
Tonge, Richard MD 1st Cav. Co.K
Tonge, Richard MD Cav. 2nd Bn. Co.K
Tonge, Richard H. MD 1st Inf. Co.C
Tonge, Rich. H. VA Horse Arty. D. Shank's Co. Cpl.
Tonge, W.G.D. MD 1st Cav.
Tonge, William D.G. VA 13th Inf. Co.G
Tonget, Tom KY 1st (Butler's) Cav. Co.G
Tonglet, John LA Mil. 4th Regt. 2nd Brig. 1st Div. Co.H 1st Lt.
Tonglet, John 14th Conf.Cav. Co.H
Tongreen, J. LA Mil. 3rd Regt. 3rd Brig. 1st Div. Co.E
Tongue, Henry M. VA Cav. 39th Bn. Co.B Cpl.
Tongue, James MD 1st Inf. 2nd Co.H
Tongue, James MD Weston's Bn. Co.D
Tongue, Johnzie VA 4th Cav. Co.H
Tongue, Thomas W. VA Cav. Mosby's Regt. (Part.Rangers) Co.D
Tongue, Willis NC 34th Inf. Co.E
Toniar, Jacob TX Lt.Arty. Jones' Co.
Tonis, Hardin VA 3rd Bn. Valley Res. Co.D
Tonis, Henry LA 22nd Inf. Co.B
Tonis, Henry LA 22nd (Cons.) Inf. Co.B
Tonkaway 1st Seminole Mtd.Vol.
Tonkin, John TN 43rd Inf. Co.A Capt.
Tonkin, John W. NC 54th Inf. Co.A
Tonkin, L.E. VA 22nd Inf. Co.E

Tonkin, William F. VA 9th Inf. Co.G Capt.
Tonkins, Ambrose VA 19th Cav. Co.B
Tonkins, John J. VA 19th Cav. Co.B Cpl.
Tonnahill, Davis MS 30th Inf. Co.H
Tonner, Thomas MS 21st Inf. Co.L Cpl.
Tonnes, H. AL Chas. A. Herts' Co.
Tonnies, Auguste LA 13th Inf. Co.H
Tonnoffski, George L. NC 17th Inf. (2nd Org.) Co.I
Tonnon, Hugh A. MO 4th Cav. Co.C
Tonor, John AL 21st Inf. Co.B
Tonsmire, Henry LA 1st Hvy.Arty. (Reg.) Co.A
Tonstall, A. AL 7th Cav. Co.D
Tonstall, Peyton R. AL City Troop (Mobile) Arrington's Co.
Ton tar co sa na 1st Creek Mtd.Vol. Co.E
Tontenot, H. LA Siege Train Bn. Co.D
Tonton, M.W. MD 1st Cav. Co.E
Tonubbee 1st Choctaw Mtd.Rifles Co.F
Tonville, W.T. MO Inf. 5th Regt.St.Guard Co.D
Tony MS 20th Inf. Co.G Negro Cook
Tony, B. MS 22nd Inf. Co.C
Tony, Benjamin MS 39th Inf. Co.B
Tony, Charles W. GA 38th Inf. Co.K Music.
Tony, George 1st Cherokee Mtd.Rifles Co.C Sgt.
Tony, George 1st Cherokee Mtd.Vol. 1st Co.B, 2nd Co.D
Tony, Jesse A. AR Cav. Harrell's Bn. Co.C
Tony, John LA 13th Inf. Co.D
Tony, Joseph N. MO 8th Cav. Co.H
Tony, J.T. VA Lt.Arty. 1st Bn. Co.B
Tony, Nathaniel F. AR 33rd Inf. Co.C
Tony, Pat MS 20th Inf. Co.K
Tony, R.C. VA 129th Mil. Carter's Co.
Tony, Sidney P. VA 41st Inf. Co.B
Tony, T.E. AR 13th Mil. Co.G
Tony, William R. AR Cav. Harrell's Bn. Co.C
Tony, W.L. MO 1st & 4th Cons.Inf. Co.F
Tonyes, Louis SC Arty.Bn. Hampton Legion Co.A
Toobey, F.F. LA 19th Inf. Co.D
Too che 1st Cherokee Mtd.Rifles Co.H
Toocheestehor, Aleck Tuyonehala NC Inf. Thomas Legion Co.B
Tood, A.W. AL 18th Inf. Co.I
Tood, E.M. Johnson's A. Maj.,CS
Tood, Julius J. FL 1st Inf. Old Co.H
Toodick, Joseph TX Cav. Ragsdale's Bn. Co.B
Toodle, George AL Cav. Murphy's Bn. Co.B
Toodle, George MS Cav. 17th Bn. Co.A
Toodle, George 15th Conf.Cav. Co.G
Toohey, Charles VA Inf. 1st Bn. Co.A
Toohey, Hugh TN 10th Inf. Co.K
Toohey, James LA Mil. 1st Regt. 3rd Brig. 1st Div. Co.A
Toohey, Mike TN 2nd (Walker's) Inf. Co.G
Toohey, Patrick LA 6th Inf. Co.F Cpl.
Toohey, Peter AL 9th Inf. Co.B
Toohey, Thomas MS 21st Inf. Co.L
Toohig, John LA Mil. C.S. Zouave Bn.
Took, --- TX Cav. Mann's Regt. Co.I
Took, Allen GA Cav. 29th Bn. Co.D
Took, Charlton C. GA 1st (Ramsey's) Inf. Co.E
Took, J.W. FL 2nd Inf. Co.B
Tooke, Abram J. GA 11th Cav. (St.Guards) Groover's Co.
Tooke, A.J. GA Cav. 29th Bn. Co.C
Tooke, E. Blake LA 9th Inf. Co.C Sgt.
Tooke, Henry T. LA 9th Inf. Co.C Band
Tooke, H.V. LA 5th Cav. Co.E
Tooke, H.V. LA 13th Bn. (Part.Rangers) Co.F
Tooke, James A. LA 12th Inf. Co.B Music.
Tooke, James T. GA 12th (Wright's) Cav. (St.Guards) Wright's Co.
Tooke, James T. GA Inf. 10th Bn. Co.C Sgt.Maj.
Tooke, James W. LA 12th Inf. Co.B
Tooke, J.F. LA 13th Bn. (Part.Rangers) Co.F
Tooke, J.J. GA 46th Inf. Co.C Sgt.
Tooke, J.N. GA 46th Inf. Co.C
Tooke, John FL 5th Inf. Co.E
Tooke, John F. LA 5th Cav. Co.E
Tooke, John G. FL 9th Inf. Co.A
Tooke, Joseph G. TX 9th (Nichols') Inf. Co.F
Tooke, Joseph G. TX 13th Vol. Co.F
Tooke, J.T. GA 2nd Mil. Co.G
Tooke, Lovard T. TX 5th Cav. Co.A Sgt.
Tooke, T.B. LA Res.Corps 1st Lt.
Tooke, Thomas A. LA 9th Inf. Co.C Sgt.
Tooke, W.A. GA Inf. 5th Bn. (St.Guards) Co.D
Tooke, W.C. Nitre & Min. Bureau War Dept., CSA Detailed Man
Tooke, William A. GA 3rd Inf. Co.E Sgt.
Tooke, William J. GA Siege Arty. 28th Bn. Co.F Lt.
Tooke, William J. GA Inf. 2nd Bn. Co.B
Tooke, William S. GA Arty. 9th Bn. Co.C
Tooker, Charles NC 3rd Inf. Co.I Sgt.
Tool, A.W. AL 20th Cav. Lee's Co.
Tool, Berry TN 62nd Mtd.Inf. Co.B
Tool, Edward SC 2nd Arty. Co.H
Tool, F.M. GA 13th Inf. Co.G
Tool, Garret LA 21st (Patton's) Inf. Co.C
Tool, Irwin GA 19th Inf. Co.G
Tool, Irwin GA 55th Inf. Co.E
Tool, J.A. AL Lt.Arty. Tarrant's Btty.
Tool, J.A. GA 55th Inf. Co.E
Tool, Jasper SC 14th Inf. Co.H
Tool, J.E. AL St.Res. Elliby's Co.
Tool, J.J. GA 55th Inf. Co.E
Tool, John FL 11th Inf. Co.I
Tool, John E. FL 2nd Cav. Co.E
Tool, John R. TN 55th (McKoin's) Inf. Day's Co.
Tool, J.R. AL Lt.Arty. Tarrant's Btty.
Tool, Julius L. SC 1st (McCreary's) Inf. Co.A
Tool, Luke GA 51st Inf. Co.D
Tool, M. LA 3rd Inf. Co.G
Tool, Michael O. VA 20th Inf. Co.A
Tool, Nathaniel SC 2nd Arty. Co.G
Tool, P. GA 55th Inf. Co.E
Tool, Thomas MS 13th Inf. Co.F
Tool, W.G. GA Cav. 20th Bn. Co.A,D
Tool, William R. AL 44th Inf. Co.A
Toolar, William FL Cav. 3rd Bn. Co.A
Toolar, William 15th Conf.Cav. Co.A
Toolase, W. MO Cav. 2nd Regt.St.Guard Co.E
Toole, A. GA Cav. 29th Bn. Co.G
Toole, Adrian V. GA Arty. (Chatham Arty.) Wheaton's Co.
Toole, Adrian V. GA 1st (Olmstead's) Inf. Claghorn's Co.
Toole, Barckley W. TN 39th Mtd.Inf. Co.B Surg.
Toole, Benjamin F. GA 4th Inf. Co.K
Toole, Benjamin F. SC 2nd Arty. Co.A Sgt.
Toole, B.F. SC 1st Cav. Co.C Cpl.
Toole, Bithan NC 50th Inf. Co.D Cpl.
Toole, B.J. SC 2nd Arty. Co.A
Toole, B.J. SC Inf. Holcombe Legion Co.D
Toole, B.W. Gen. & Staff Surg.
Toole, C. SC 1st (Hagood's) Inf. 2nd Co.B
Toole, Calvin FL 6th Inf. Co.D
Toole, Calvin J. FL 6th Inf. Co.G
Toole, Calvin J. FL Campbellton Boys
Toole, C.D. SC 2nd Arty. Co.E
Toole, C.J. GA 6th Res. Co.B
Toole, David SC 2nd Arty. Co.G
Toole, David E. AR 1st (Colquitt's) Inf. Co.I
Toole, D.E. TN 3rd (Forrest's) Cav.
Toole, Dixon L. MS 21st Inf. Co.F
Toole, Edward SC Co.A
Toole, E.G. SC 1st Cav. Co.C
Toole, Eli TX 3rd Inf. Co.I Capt.
Toole, George W. AL Lt.Arty. 2nd Bn. Co.F
Toole, George W. GA 1st Reg. Co.G
Toole, G.F. SC 2nd Arty. Co.B,H
Toole, H. SC 14th Inf. Co.H
Toole, Hezekiah J.J. FL 6th Inf. Co.D
Toole, Hezekiah J.J. FL Campbellton Boys
Toole, H.P. TX 5th Inf. Co.A
Toole, Irving L. FL Campbellton Boys
Toole, Isaac L. GA 1st (Olmstead's) Inf. Stiles' Co.
Toole, Isaac L. GA Inf. 18th Bn. Co.B
Toole, Isaac M. FL 6th Inf. Co.G Sgt.
Toole, James GA Cav. 29th Bn. Co.B
Toole, James GA Siege Arty. Campbell's Ind.Co.
Toole, James GA 63rd Inf. Co.F Asst.Cook
Toole, James TX 26th Cav. Co.A 2nd Lt.
Toole, James VA 49th Inf. Co.H
Toole, James C. LA 16th Inf. Co.D
Toole, James I. MS 21st Inf. Co.F
Toole, James M. GA Cobb's Legion Co.I
Toole, Jasper L. SC 2nd St.Troops Co.K
Toole, J.E. TN 2nd (Ashby's) Cav. Co.K
Toole, J.M. FL Campbellton Boys
Toole, J.M. GA 48th Inf. Co.K
Toole, John LA Hvy.Arty. 8th Bn. Co.C
Toole, John LA 14th Inf. Co.D
Toole, John TX 3rd Inf. 1st Co.A Music.
Toole, John A. VA 9th Cav. Co.H Cpl.
Toole, John E. AL Cav. Barbiere's Bn. Goldsby's Co.
Toole, John E. TN 39th Mtd.Inf. Co.B Capt.
Toole, John L. VA 10th Cav. Co.F
Toole, Jonathan Gen. & Staff Contr.Physician
Toole, Joseph T. MS 21st Inf. Co.F
Toole, J.T. GA 1st (Symons') Res. Co.A
Toole, L. GA Siege Arty. Campbell's Ind.Co.
Toole, Lavareh H. GA 3rd Inf. Co.E Cpl.
Toole, L.B. SC 1st Cav. Co.K,C Sgt.
Toole, Luke GA Cav. 29th Bn. Co.B
Toole, M. SC Inf. 1st (Charleston) Bn. Co.C
Toole, M. SC 27th Inf. Co.H
Toole, Martin AR 2nd Inf. Co.B
Toole, Martin GA 30th Inf. Co.D
Toole, Martin TN 10th Inf. Co.B
Toole, Michael LA Inf. 16th Bn. (Conf.Guards Resp.Bn.) Co.B
Toole, Michael VA 27th Inf. Co.B Cpl.

Toole, M.S. SC 2nd Arty. Co.E
Toole, Oliver GA Conscr.
Toole, Patrick TN 15th Inf. Co.B
Toole, R.F. MS Lt.Arty. 14th Bn. Co.C
Toole, R.F. MS Lt.Arty. Merrin's Btty.
Toole, R.J. Maning SC 14th Inf. Co.H
Toole, Robert F. MS 23rd Inf. Co.K
Toole, Samuel TN 3rd (Lillard's) Mtd.Inf. Co.E Lt.Col.
Toole, Stephen SC Inf. Holcombe Legion Co.D
Toole, W.A. MS Lt.Arty. 14th Bn. Co.C
Toole, W.A. MS Lt.Arty. Merrin's Btty.
Toole, Warren SC 2nd Arty. Co.H
Toole, W.G. GA 16th Inf. Co.K 1st Lt.
Toole, William MS 1st (King's) Inf. (St.Troops) Co.H
Toole, William MO Robertson's Regt.St.Guard Co.3
Toole, William TN Conscr. (Cp. of Instr.)
Toole, William F. GA 20th Inf. Co.A
Toole, Wm. J. Gen. & Staff AASurg.
Toole, William T. GA 4th Inf. Co.K 2nd Lt.
Too lees tee 1st Cherokee Mtd.Rifles Co.D
Toolet, H. GA 1st Inf.
Tooley, Charles AL 46th Inf. Co.E
Tooley, Charles N. AL 3rd Inf. Co.G
Tooley, E.H. LA Lt.Arty. Holmes' Btty. QMSgt.
Tooley, E.H. LA Inf. 1st Sp.Bn. (Rightor's) Co.F
Tooley, E.H. LA 18th Inf. Co.B
Tooley, E.H. LA Inf.Crescent Regt. Co.E 1st Sgt.
Tooley, E.H. Exch.Bn. 2nd Co.A,CSA 1st Sgt.
Tooley, G.H. AR 7th Inf. Co.E Cpl.
Tooley, H. LA 18th Inf. Co.K
Tooley, I.P. MS 12th Inf. Co.H,C
Tooley, Isaac T. VA 15th Cav. Co.B
Tooley, J. AR 58th Mil. Co.C Sgt.
Tooley, James T. TN 8th Inf. Co.I
Tooley, J.F. LA Inf.Cons.Crescent Regt. Co.A
Tooley, John AL 46th Inf. Co.E
Tooley, John LA 13th Inf. Co.H
Tooley, John R. TN 44th (Cons.) Inf. Co.H
Tooley, J.S. 1st Choctaw Mtd.Rifles Co.K Lt.
Tooley, J.T. LA 25th Inf. Co.F
Tooley, J.W. TX 5th Inf. Co.I
Tooley, L. MO Searcy's Bn.S.S.
Tooley, Michael MS 29th Inf. Co.C
Tooley, R.H. GA Hvy.Arty. 22nd Bn. Co.A
Tooley, Thomas AR 35th Inf. Old Co.F
Tooley, Thomas KY 5th Mtd.Inf. Co.K
Tooley, Thomas KY 9th Mtd.Inf. Co.K
Tooley, Thomas LA 8th Inf. Co.G
Tooley, Thomas NC 17th Inf. (1st Org.) Co.E
Tooley, T.M. MO 11th Inf. Co.H
Tooley, W.H. MO 6th Cav. Co.K
Tooly, Andrew J. NC 17th Inf. (2nd Org.) Co.B
Tooly, John M. LA 11th Inf. Co.F
Tooly, William B. NC 17th Inf. (2nd Org.) Co.B Cpl.
Toom, George S. AL 25th Inf. Co.G
Tooman, James VA Lt.Arty. Brander's Co.
Tooman, John F. VA Inf. 23rd Bn. Co.D
Toomann, J. LA Mil. Chalmette Regt. Co.K
Toombes, A.G. MS 7th Cav. 1st Co.I
Toombes, J.J. TN 40th Inf. Co.F
Toombs, --- LA 20th Inf. Co.K
Toombs, Albert G. MS Hamer's Co. (Salem Cav.)
Toombs, Albert G. MS 2nd Inf. Co.D
Toombs, Allen H. AR 1st (Colquitt's) Inf. Co.H Cpl.
Toombs, Allen T. MS 1st Lt.Arty. Co.I
Toombs, A.T. TN 4th Inf. Co.I
Toombs, B.B. VA Inf. 44th Bn. Co.C
Toombs, Calvin M. Conf.Cav. Wood's Regt. Co.E
Toombs, Charles W. VA Inf. 22nd Bn. Co.E
Toombs, C.M. MS Scouts Montgomery's Co.
Toombs, C.W. VA 2nd Arty. Co.E
Toombs, D.S. TN 19th (Biffle's) Cav. Co.I
Toombs, Edman TN 19th (Biffle's) Cav. Co.I
Toombs, G. LA 20th Inf. Co.H
Toombs, G. Bradford's Corps Scouts & Guards Co.B
Toombs, Gabriel VA 47th Inf. 3rd Co.H
Toombs, Galusha B. VA 19th Inf. Co.B
Toombs, George W. MS 18th Inf. Co.E
Toombs, George W. VA 13th Inf. Co.D
Toombs, Green TN 10th (DeMoss') Cav. Co.H
Toombs, Horace B. AR 1st (Colquitt's) Inf. Co.H
Toombs, J. TX 32nd Cav. Co.B
Toombs, James LA 3rd (Harrison's) Cav. Co.F
Toombs, James A. LA 11th Inf. Co.E
Toombs, James L. TN 48th (Voorhies') Inf. Co.K
Toombs, Jas. W. GA 47th Inf. Co.B
Toombs, J.H. Eng.,CSN 3rd Asst.Eng.
Toombs, J.L. TN 48th (Nixon's) Inf. Co.C
Toombs, Joel TN 1st Cav.
Toombs, Jordan VA Lt.Arty. Thornton's Co. Cpl.
Toombs, J.W. TN 47th Inf. Co.B
Toombs, Marshall TX 8th Inf. Co.E
Toombs, R.A. VA 7th Inf. Co.I
Toombs, Richard VA 56th Inf. Co.G
Toombs, Robert GA 3rd Cav. (St.Guards) Col.
Toombs, Robert TN 9th (Ward's) Cav. Co.F
Toombs, Robt. Gen. & Staff Brig.Gen.
Toombs, S.G. LA 11th Inf. Co.I Cpl.
Toombs, Thomas MS 18th Cav. Co.A Sgt.
Toombs, Thomas VA Lt.Arty. Thornton's Co.
Toombs, Thomas C. VA 60th Inf. Co.F
Toombs, Thomas L. VA 59th Inf. 3rd Co.D
Toombs, W.E. Hosp.Stew.
Toombs, William VA Lt.Arty. Thornton's Co.
Toombs, William VA 47th Inf. 3rd Co.H
Toombs, William E. VA 30th Inf. Co.A
Toombs, Wm. E. Gen. & Staff Hosp.Stew.
Toombs, William F. MS 18th Inf. Co.E
Toombs, William H. VA 9th Cav. Co.B Sgt.
Toomer, --- SC 4th St.Troops Co.A
Toomer, Alexander NC 3rd Arty. (40th St.Troops) Co.B Sgt.
Toomer, A.V. SC 10th Inf. 1st Co.G
Toomer, Benjamin AL 4th Res. Co.G Capt.
Toomer, Benj. AL Mil. 89th Vol. Lt.Col.
Toomer, Benjamin AL Loc.Def. & Sp.Serv. Toomer's Co. Capt.
Toomer, Benjamin H. AL Lt.Arty. 2nd Bn. Co.C 1st Sgt.
Toomer, B.F. MS 24th Inf. Co.F Capt.
Toomer, B.H. AR Lt.Arty. 5th Btty. 1st Sgt.
Toomer, Charles O. AL 41st Inf. Co.F Bvt.2nd Lt.
Toomer, Edward T. AL 3rd Inf. Co.B 2nd Lt.
Toomer, E.P. SC Inf. 1st (Charleston) Bn. Co.D
Toomer, E.P. SC 3rd St.Troops QMSgt.
Toomer, E.P. SC Mil. 17th Regt. QMSgt.
Toomer, Fred A. GA Lt.Arty. 14th Bn. Co.A
Toomer, Fred A. GA Lt.Arty. Havis' Btty. Surg.
Toomer, Fred A. Conf.Arty. Palmer's Bn. Asst.Surg.
Toomer, Fred A. Gen. & Staff Surg.
Toomer, F.S. SC 1st Mtd.Mil. Anderson's Co.
Toomer, F.S. SC 5th Cav. Co.C
Toomer, F.S. SC Mil.Cav. Rutledge's Co.
Toomer, F. Stall SC Cav. 17th Bn. Co.D
Toomer, H. Lawrens Conf.Cav. Raum's Co.
Toomer, James H. VA 16th Inf. Co.C 1st Sgt.
Toomer, James H. Eng.,CSA 1st Lt.
Toomer, J.C. VA 18th Cav. Co.G Sgt.
Toomer, J.L. AL 3rd Cav. Co.E
Toomer, J.N. AL 3rd Cav. Co.E
Toomer, John AL Mil. 2nd Regt.Vol. Co.B
Toomer, John A. AR 1st Mtd.Rifles Co.H
Toomer, John C. NC 5th Inf. Co.D Sgt.
Toomer, Joshua AR 7th Cav. Co.D Sgt.Maj.
Toomer, Joshua, Jr. AR 15th (N.W.) Inf. Co.D
Toomer, J.W. SC 3rd Cav. Co.H
Toomer, Sheldon AL 3rd Inf. Co.F
Toomer, Sheldon Gen. & Staff Capt.,AQM
Toomer, Thomas T. AL 1st Bn.Cadets Co.A Cpl.
Toomer, W.G. NC Hvy.Arty. 10th Bn. AQM
Toomer, W.G. Hoke's Div. Capt.,Asst.Ch.QM
Toomer, W.H. AL 4th Res. Co.G
Toomer, W.H. AL Loc.Def. & Sp.Serv. Toomer's Co.
Toomer, Wiley G. AL 3rd Inf. Co.A
Toomer, Wiley M. MS Cav. 17th Bn. Co.D
Toomer, Wm. H. AL 89th Mil. Co.C Capt.
Toomey, Allen J. TN 62nd Mtd.Inf. Co.C Cpl.
Toomey, C.C. MD 1st Cav. Co.K
Toomey, Cornelius AL 12th Inf. Co.C
Toomey, Cornelius VA Inf. 1st Bn. Co.D
Toomey, Daniel GA Lt.Arty. Ritter's Co. Ord.Sgt.
Toomey, Daniel MD Arty. 3rd Btty. Btty.Sgt.
Toomey, Daniel TX 1st Hvy.Arty. 2nd Co.F
Toomey, Daniel TX 2nd Inf. Odlum's Co.
Toomey, David AL 21st Inf. Co.A Cpl.
Toomey, Dennis TX St.Troops Edgar's Co.
Toomey, Edward TN Lt.Arty. Scott's Co.
Toomey, J. VA Inf. 25th Bn. Co.E
Toomey, James GA 26th Inf. Co.K
Toomey, James LA 1st (Strawbridge's) Inf. Co.G,E
Toomey, James NC 55th Inf. Co.D
Toomey, James NC Inf. Thomas Legion Co.I
Toomey, James M. TN 59th Mtd.Inf. Co.B
Toomey, Jerry VA 1st Inf. Co.B
Toomey, J.J. LA Mil. Beauregard Bn. Co.C
Toomey, John LA Pointe Coupee Arty.
Toomey, John MS Inf. 2nd Bn. Co.G
Toomey, John MS 21st Inf. Co.B
Toomey, John MS 48th Inf. Co.G.
Toomey, J.T. MS Inf. 2nd St.Troops Co.B

Toomey, Lalley P. VA Cav. Mosby's Regt. (Part.Rangers) Co.H
Toomey, Lawrence LA 5th Inf. Co.I
Toomey, L.P. LA 2nd Inf. Co.I
Toomey, Mark Antony AL 20th Inf. Co.H Sgt.
Toomey, Michael VA 18th Inf. Co.B
Toomey, Michael C. NC 13th Inf. Co.E
Toomey, O.M. 4th Conf.Inf. Co.B
Toomey, Patrick AL 6th Inf. Co.K
Toomey, Richard A. TN 6th (Wheeler's) Cav. Co.I
Toomey, Stephen AL 24th Inf. Co.B Cpl.
Toomey, Thomas TN 62nd Mtd.Inf. Co.C
Toomey, William TX Cav. McCord's Frontier Regt. Co.D
Toomey, W.J. AR 30th Inf. Co.B 1st Lt.
Toomley, Benjamin AR 26th Inf. Co.C Bvt.2nd Lt.
Toomps, William E. VA 3rd (Chrisman's) Bn.Res. Co.F
Tooms, Isaac TX 5th Cav. Co.H
Tooms, William F. NC 58th Inf. Co.E
Toomy, Dennis TX 1st Field Btty.
Toomy, James KY 8th Bn.Mtd.Rifles Co.A
Toomy, James LA 1st Cav. Co.E,G
Toomy, Jeremiah MS Inf. 2nd Bn. Co.A
Toomy, Jeremiah MS 48th Inf. Co.A
Toomy, Jeremiah VA 26th Inf. 1st Co.B
Toomy, Robert MS 35th Inf. Co.E
Toomy, Thomas F. 4th Conf.Inf. Co.F
Toomy, Thomas H. 4th Conf.Inf. Co.F
Toon, A. NC 66th Inf. Co.I
Toon, Archibald NC McDugald's Co.
Toon, James AL 4th Inf. Co.K
Toon, James J. NC 20th Inf. Co.K
Toon, J.P. TN 8th Inf. Co.C
Toon, L.H. TN 4th Inf. Co.B Cpl.
Toon, Luther NC 51st Inf. Co.H
Toon, Tarner A. TN 44th Inf. Co.G
Toon, Thomas F. NC 20th Inf. Co.K Col.
Toon, Thos. F. Gen. & Staff Brig.Gen.
Toon, W.H. Gen. & Staff 2nd Lt.,Dr.M.
Toon, William H. AL 4th (Russell's) Cav. Co.G
Toon, William H. NC 20th Inf. Co.K Maj.
Toon, William L. AL 50th Inf. Co.B
Too nah wee 1st Cherokee Mtd.Rifles Co.G
Toone, Coleman AR 37th Inf. Co.K
Toone, Ed. H. VA 38th Inf. 1st Co.I 2nd Lt.
Toone, George S.H. TN 53rd Inf. Co.A
Toone, George W. AL Lt.Arty. Ward's Btty. Cpl.
Toone, George W. AR 26th Inf. Co.F
Toone, George W. TX 9th Field Btty.
Toone, G.H. AL 11th Cav. Co.E
Toone, G.S. AL 35th Inf. Co.G
Toone, James AR 2nd Cav. Co.E
Toone, James L. VA 21st Inf. Co.C
Toone, James T. VA 3rd Cav. Co.A Sgt.
Toone, Jasper R. AR 1st (Colquitt's) Inf. Co.F
Toone, John VA 56th Inf. Co.A
Toone, John W. TN 4th Inf. Co.B
Toone, Lewis L. VA 8th Inf. Co.A
Toone, Mumford S. VA 3rd Cav. Co.A
Toone, Reps L. VA 3rd Cav. Co.A
Toone, Tavner AR Inf. 4th Bn. Co.B,E Capt.
Toone, Toleman AR 50th Mil. Co.A 2nd Lt.
Toone, W.H. AR 5th Inf. Co.A
Toone, William AL 9th Inf. Co.H
Toone, William J. VA 34th Inf. Co.B Sgt.
Tooney, Michael AL 54th Inf. Co.C
Toonhair, John LA 8th Inf. Co.I
Too Nie 1st Cherokee Mtd.Rifles Co.C
Toonie, George 1st Cherokee Mtd.Rifles Co.B
Toonie, William 1st Cherokee Mtd.Rifles Co.G
Too nie ah 1st Cherokee Mtd.Rifles Co.C
Too ni ee 1st Cherokee Mtd.Vol. 2nd Co.F
Too nigh yeh NC Inf. Thomas Legion 2nd Co.A
Toonowih NC Inf. Thomas Legion Co.B
Toops, James AR 62nd Mil. Co.F Cpl.
Toops, T. LA Inf.Cons. 18th Regt. & Yellow Jacket Bn. Co.K
Too quah tah, Ned 1st Cherokee Mtd.Rifles McDaniel's Co.
Tooraen, Charles E. LA 4th Inf. Co.D Capt.
Too se wae e tah 1st Cherokee Mtd.Rifles Co.A
Tooshe, John R. NC 32nd Inf. Co.I
Toos too NC Inf. Thomas Legion Co.B
Toot, Charles H. MS 12th Inf. Co.B
Toot, John S. VA 3rd Cav. Co.C
Toot, William A. VA 11th Inf. Co.G
Tooten, A.F. MO Robertson's Regt.St.Guard Co.11
Tooten, Walter NC 3rd Cav. (41st St.Troops) Co.E
Toothacre, Charles C. VA Lt.Arty. Garber's Co. Artif.
Toothaker, J.E. TX 21st Inf. Co.A
Toothaker, Jesse E. TX 11th (Spaight's) Bn.Vol. Co.A
Toothman, Asbury VA Cav. 46th Bn. Co.C Sgt.
Toothman, Benjamin VA 20th Cav. Co.G Sgt.
Toothman, Charles A. VA 14th Cav. Co.D
Toothman, Charles A. VA Inf. 26th Bn. Co.G Sgt.
Toothman, Charles A. VA 59th Inf. 2nd Co.B
Toothman, Davis VA 31st Inf. Co.A 1st Lt.
Toothman, Edward L. VA 31st Inf. Co.A
Toothman, Marshal N. VA 135th Mil. Co.F
Toothman, M.N. VA 14th Cav. Co.A
Toothman, Newton VA 36th Inf. Co.A
Toothman, Robert VA 14th Cav. Co.D
Toothman, Robert A. VA Inf. 26th Bn. Co.G
Toothman, Robert A. VA 59th Inf. 2nd Co.B
Toothman, T.F. VA 17th Cav. Co.F Sgt.
Toothman, Thornton VA 14th Cav. Crawford's Co. Sgt.
Tootin, Robert FL 1st Inf. Old Co.H
Tootle, Capel GA 47th Inf. Co.G Sgt.
Tootle, Columbus GA 47th Inf. Co.G 2nd Lt.
Tootle, Enoch GA 47th Inf. Co.G
Tootle, James H. GA 61st Inf. Co.B
Tootle, Jeremiah GA 47th Inf. Co.G 2nd Lt.
Tootle, John GA 25th Inf. Co.K
Tootle, John E. SC Lt.Arty. 3rd (Palmetto) Bn. Co.F
Tootle, Martin G. GA 61st Inf. Co.H Sgt.
Tootle, Obadiah SC Lt.Arty. 3rd (Palmetto) Bn. Co.F
Tootle, Robert GA Hvy.Arty. 22nd Bn. Co.F
Tootle, Simeon GA 47th Inf. Co.G
Tootle, William W. FL 2nd Inf. Co.I
Tooton, Elihu MS 2nd St.Cav. Co.F
Toots, William AL 30th Inf. Co.H
Tootte, G.W. MS 9th Cav. Co.A
Tooty, Robert T. VA 1st Inf. Co.B
Toowohnaenertooguarlah 1st Cherokee Mtd.Rifles Co.G
To path lar 1st Creek Mtd.Vol. Co.E
Tope, James TX 2nd Cav. Co.K
Toper, A.B. GA 8th Cav. Co.H
Toper, F.E. GA 8th Cav. Co.H
Toper, T.H. NC Cav. 16th Bn. Co.C
Topham, George W. LA 7th Inf. Co.A
Topham, George W. VA 2nd Inf.Loc.Def. Co.D
Topham, George W. VA Inf. 6th Bn.Loc.Def. Co.B,A
Topham, Harry LA Scouts Vinson's Co.
Topham, James H. VA 12th Inf. Co.B
Topham, John P. MS 12th Inf. Co.G
Topham, T.D. TN 25th Inf. Co.B
Topham, William MS Lt.Arty. (Brookhaven Lt.Arty.) Hoskins' Btty.
Topham, W.L. GA 18th Inf. Co.K
Tophan, James VA Inf. 4th Bn.Loc.Def. Co.F 1st Sgt.
Tophan, William LA Arty. 1st Field Btty.
Topin, Sostho LA Mil. St.James Regt. Co.E
Toplar, B.W. AL 6th Cav. Co.A
Tople 1st Seminole Mtd.Vol.
Topler 1st Seminole Mtd.Vol.
Topley, J.C. GA 14th Inf. Co.F Cpl.
Topliffe, George H. VA 49th Inf. Co.C
Toplin, W.T. MS 38th Cav. Co.E
Topp, A. MS 11th (Cons.) Cav. Co.G Cpl.
Topp, Alison MS St.Cav. 2nd Bn. (Harris') Co.B
Topp, Charles VA Cav. 36th Bn. Co.D Sgt.
Topp, Charles VA 27th Inf. Co.G
Topp, E.L. TN 2nd (Walker's) Inf. Co.H 2nd Lt.
Topp, Eugene TN 1st (Feild's) Inf. Co.K Sgt.
Topp, Harvey E. MS 19th Inf. Co.K 1st Lt.
Topp, Harvey E. MS 31st Inf. Co.G Maj.
Topp, H.C. Buckner Guards
Topp, Hugh C. MS 14th Inf. Co.K
Topp, Hugh C. Sig.Corps,CSA
Topp, James E. MS 41st Inf. Co.L Music.
Topp, J.E. MS 11th (Cons.) Cav. Co.G
Topp, J.E. TX St.Troops Hampton's Co.
Topp, Robert MS 10th Inf. Old Co.D
Topp, Robert C. MS 2nd Inf. Co.G
Topp, Robert C. MS 13th Inf. Co.H Capt.
Topp, Robert C. Gen. & Staff Capt.,Comsy.
Topp, R.S. NC 8th Inf. Co.D
Topp, Thomas C. TX 8th Inf. Co.C
Topp, Thomas M. 1st Conf.Eng.Troops Co.G,C Capt.
Topp, W. VA 2nd St.Res. Co.I
Topp, Walter R. TN 53rd Inf. 1st Lt.,Adj.
Topp, W.H. Gen. & Staff Maj.,CS
Topp, William VA Lt.Arty. E.J. Anderson's Co.
Topp, William H. MS 2nd Inf. Co.G Sgt.
Topp, William H. MS 31st Inf. Co.G
Topp, W.R. TN 2nd Cav. Co.B
Toppass, George KY Arty. Corbett's Co.
Toppel, --- LA 13th Inf. Co.F
Topper, P. VA 6th Cav. Co.D
Toppin, Henry MO 16th Inf. Co.I
Toppin, James VA 54th Mil. Co.E,F
Toppin, Jonas VA 7th Cav. Co.H
Toppin, Jonas VA 146th Mil. Co.C
Toppin, Smith VA 41st Inf. 1st Co.G

Toppin, Smith VA 61st Inf. Co.I Sgt.
Toppin, Thomas VA 7th Cav. Co.B
Toppin, Thomas H. VA 146th Mil. Co.C
Toppin, William VA 7th Cav. Co.H
Topping, Charles W. VA 32nd Inf. Co.A
Topping, Daniel J. NC 33rd Inf. Co.H
Topping, Edward VA 109th Mil. Co.B, 2nd Co.A Sgt.
Topping, Garrett VA 115th Mil. Co.A Cpl.
Topping, George VA 32nd Inf. 2nd Co.I
Topping, George VA 115th Mil. Co.C
Topping, James N. VA 1st Arty. Co.G
Topping, James N. VA 32nd Inf. 1st Co.I
Topping, James S. VA 32nd Inf. Co.E
Topping, Marcellus VA 32nd Inf. 2nd Co.I
Topping, Marcellus VA 115th Mil. Co.C
Topping, Nathan B. NC 33rd Inf. Co.H Sgt.
Topping, Parker VA 115th Mil. Co.C
Topping, Robert N. VA 3rd Cav. Co.B
Topping, Samuel F. NC 44th Inf. Co.C 2nd Lt.
Topping, T.H. Hosp.Stew.
Topping, Thomas H. Gen.& Staff Hosp.Stew.
Topping, William LA 21st (Patton's) Inf. Co.I
Topping, William A.G.W. VA 115th Mil. Co.A 1st Lt
Topps, David MS 14th Inf. Co.K Cook
Topson, A.M. MS Cav. (St.Troops) Gamblin's Co.
Topson, N. MS Cav. (St.Troops) Gamblin's Co.
Torance, Samuel W. NC 55th Inf. Co.C
Toranelli, David LA 10th Inf. Co.I
Toras, John LA Bn.Defend. Sgt.
Torbeck, H.B. VA 1st St.Res. Co.I
Torbeck, R. VA 1st Res. Co.I
Torbert, A.T. TN Inf. 154th Sr.Regt. Co.G
Torbert, A.T.A. Gen. & Staff, Arty. 1st Lt.
Torbert, A.W.G. AL 34th Inf. Black's Co. 1st Lt.
Torbert, B.E. GA 32nd Inf. Co.I
Torbert, Charles L. AL 63rd Inf. Co.C Sgt.
Torbert, Hugh L. MS 17th Inf. Co.A
Torbert, H.W. TX Cav. (Dismtd.) Chisum's Regt. Co.I
Torbert, James B. GA 12th (Robinson's) Cav. (St.Guards) Co.G Cpl.
Torbert, James M. GA 17th Inf. Co.A Cpl.
Torbert, John O. GA 2nd Bn.S.S. Co.B Sgt.
Torbert, John O. GA 5th Inf. Co.K,L Sgt.
Torbert, L.L. AL 34th Inf. Black's Co. 1st Sgt.
Torbert, Samuel TX 3rd Cav. Co.G
Torbert, William H. TX 12th Cav. Co.I
Torbert, William L. GA 12th Inf. Co.A
Torbet, F.J. LA 19th Inf. Co.C
Torbet, Frank GA Inf. 1st Bn. Co.C Ord.Sgt.
Torbet, F.T. GA Inf. (Columbus) Arsenal Bn. Co.B
Torbett, Allen TN 19th Inf. Co.G
Torbett, D.A. GA 32nd Inf. Co.I Sgt.
Torbett, D.R. GA Inf. City Bn. (Columbus) Co.A
Torbett, G. AR 10th Mil. Co.C Cpl.
Torbett, G.A. AR 19th (Dawson's) Inf. Co.H Capt.
Torbett, G.A. AR Inf. Hardy's Regt. Torbett's Co. Capt.
Torbett, G.C. AR Cav. Gordon's Regt. Co.E
Torbett, Horace R. TN Inf. 1st Bn. (Colms') Co.A
Torbett, Howard A. AL Mil. 4th Vol. Co.C
Torbett, H.R. TN 35th Inf. Co.G
Torbett, Hugh TN Sullivan Cty.Res. (Loc. Def.Troops) White's Co.
Torbett, Isaac TN Arty. Ramsey's Btty.
Torbett, James B. GA 2nd Bn.S.S. Co.C
Torbett, James H. TX 20th Cav. Co.F
Torbett, James H. TX 10th Inf. Co.C Ord.Sgt.
Torbett, J.B. AR 11th Inf. Co.C 3rd Lt.
Torbett, J.F. GA 32nd Inf. Co.H
Torbett, Joseph TN Arty. Ramsey's Btty.
Torbett, Rush B. TX 16th Cav. Co.G
Torbett, Samuel B. TN 4th Cav. Co.H
Torbett, Samuel P. TX 1st Inf. Co.H 2nd Lt.
Torbett, William F. TN 60th Mtd.Inf.
Torbett, William F. TN Sullivan Cty.Res. (Loc.Def.Troops) White's Co.
Torbett, W.L. GA 31st Inf. Co.F
Torbett, W.W. TN 37th Inf. Co.G 3rd Lt.
Torbetts, John B. AR Inf. Cocke's Regt. Co.I Capt.
Torbeson, J.K.P. TN 3rd (Forrest's) Cav. Co.C
Torbit, --- TX Cav. Morgan's Regt. Co.A
Torbit, F.M. MS 41st Inf. Co.E
Torbitt, Henri M.L. GA Inf. 2nd Bn. Co.A
Torbitt, John TN Detailed Conscr. Co.B
Torbitt, John C. GA 11th Inf. Co.G Sgt.
Torbitt, Robert W. GA Siege Arty. 28th Bn. Co.E
Torbitt, S.M.B. 1st Conf.Cav. 2nd Co.K
Torbitt, T.F. TN 19th Inf. Co.D
Torbitt, U.S. SC 2nd Cav. Co.D
Torbush, James GA Cav. Roswell Bn. Co.B
Torcher, George MO 15th Cav. Co.A
Tor chu lay Nah 1st Cherokee Mtd.Rifles Co.B
Torcksey, W.E. VA 14th Inf. Co.I
Torean, John T. VA Hvy.Arty. Wright's Co.
Toregane, Michel LA Mil. 1st Native Guards
Toregane, Oscar LA Mil. 1st Native Guards
Torel, D.W. NC 23rd Inf. Co.H
Torence, Charles AR 33rd Inf. Co.G
Torence, James AR 33rd Inf. Co.G
Torence, Washington W. AR 33rd Inf. Co.G
Tores, Aut. LA Mil. St.James Regt. Co.G
Tores, Jose TX 11th Inf. Co.A
Toretta, Francis LA 5th Inf. Co.I
Torey, Jasper N. VA 37th Inf. Co.G
Torey, N.B. LA Hvy.Arty. 2nd Bn. Co.C Cpl.
Torgee, George W. VA Lt.Arty. 38th Bn. Co.D
Torian, C.C. TN Inf. 3rd Cons.Regt. Ord.Sgt.
Torian, Chris C. TN 4th Inf. Co.A Ord.Sgt.
Torian, George L. NC 35th Inf. Co.E 2nd Lt.
Torian, J. VA 53rd Inf. Co.G
Torian, Jack KY 12th Cav. Co.B
Torian, James KY 1st (Helm's) Cav. Co.A
Torian, James A. TN 4th Inf. Co.A
Torian, Leonard B. VA 3rd Cav. Co.C
Torian, P. VA 6th Cav. Co.G
Torian, P.A. TN Inf. 3rd Cons.Regt. Co.D 1st Sgt.
Torian, Paul VA Inf. 25th Bn. Co.D
Torian, Peter A. TN 4th Inf. Co.A 1st Sgt.
Torian, R.A. NC 7th Sr.Res. Davie's Co.
Torian, Richard P. VA 6th Cav. Co.G
Torian, R.S. KY 12th Cav. Co.B
Torian, T. TN 12th (Cons.) Inf. Co.C
Torian, Thomas TN 22nd Inf. Co.A
Torian, Thomas P. KY 1st (Helm's) Cav. Co.A
Torian, William VA 3rd Inf. 2nd Co.K
Torian, William B. TX Cav. Waller's Regt. Co.D
Torian, W.S. TN 22nd Inf. Co.A
Torigano, Colastus LA Mil. 1st Native Guards
Tork, E.F. SC Mil.Arty. 1st Regt. Werner's Co.
Tork, W. TX 22nd Inf. Co.F
Tor kin a 1st Creek Mtd.Vol. Co.E
Torksay, Newbern E. VA 59th Mil. Riddick's Co.
Torksey, John NC 32nd Inf. Co.I
Torksey, John B. NC 56th Inf. Co.A
Torksey, John J. NC 56th Inf. Co.A
Torksey, Newbern C. VA 16th Inf. Co.B
Torksey, Thomas W. VA 16th Inf. Co.A
Torlay, --- SC 27th Inf.
Torlay, A.G. SC 24th Inf. Co.A
Torlay, H. SC Inf. 1st (Charleston) Bn. Co.B
Torlay, J.B. SC 1st Regt.Charleston Guard Co.A
Torlay, J. Edmond SC 2nd Arty. Co.A 1st Lt.
Torlay, Samuel B. GA 63rd Inf.
Torley, Alford VA Inf. 1st Bn.Loc.Def. Co.A Cpl.
Torley, C.B. SC Mil. 1st Regt.Rifles Chichester's Co.
Torley, H. SC 23rd Inf. Co.C
Torm, --- TX 2nd Inf. Co.K
Torman, James VA 60th Inf. Co.K
Tormay, Patrick TN 6th Inf. Co.H
Tormey, Frank A. MD Arty. Holbrook's Btty. Lt.
Tormey, Frank A. MD 1st Inf. Co.F 2nd Lt.
Tormey, Frank A. TN 42nd Cav. Capt.
Tormey, John LA 10th Inf. Co.D
Tormey, John NC 12th Inf. Co.G Capt.
Tormey, John VA 16th Cav. Co.K Cpl.
Tormey, Michael VA 14th Inf. Co.I
Tornes, George S. VA 2nd Cav. Co.H
Tornes, Henry C. VA 2nd Cav. Co.H
Tornes, Pleasant A. VA 2nd Cav. Co.H
Tornette, F. LA 10th Inf. Co.G
Torney, John TN 2nd (Robison's) Inf. Co.E
Torney, R.D. MS Cav. Powers' Regt. Co.E
Tornie, F.W.E. LA Mil. 4th Regt.Eur.Brig. Co.A 1st Sgt.
Torno, Charles R. TN 34th Inf. 1st Co.C Sgt.
Tornow, C.R. NC 35th Inf. Co.E
Torns, Thomas J. LA 12th Inf. Co.B
Torny, G.W. VA 86th Mil. Co.D
Toro, Franco. LA Mil. 5th Regt.Eur.Brig. (Spanish Regt.) Co.4
Toronelli, Giovanni LA Mil. 6th Regt.Eur.Brig. (Italian Guards Bn.) Co.1
Torp, S. Conf.Inf. 8th Bn. Co.E
Torpey, James LA 6th Inf. Co.K
Torpey, John AL 17th Inf. Co.F Music.
Torpey, John LA Inf. 9th Bn. Chinn's Co.
Torpi, Thomas LA 30th Inf. Co.G
Torpie, James MD Cav. 2nd Bn. Co.A
Torpie, Thomas LA 13th Inf. Co.H
Torpie, Thomas LA 20th Inf. Co.G,I,H Sgt.
Torpy, John LA 7th Inf. Co.D 1st Lt.
Torr, J. LA 25th Inf. Co.H
Torrain, J.A. KY 4th Mtd.Inf. Co.A
Torrance, Cuthbert GA Cobb's Legion Co.F

Torrance, David GA 35th Inf. Co.E
Torrance, George NC 1st Inf. (6 mo. '61) Co.B
Torrance, H.B. TX 23rd Cav. Co.K
Torrance, Hugh MS Hamer's Co. (Salem Cav.)
Torrance, J.E. TN Lt.Arty. Scott's Co.
Torrance, John A. NC 7th Inf. Co.D 1st Lt.
Torrance, John A. NC 37th Inf. Co.C Sgt.Maj.
Torrance, J.W. GA Inf. 27th Bn. Co.E
Torrance, M. TX 1st Hvy.Arty. Co.F
Torrance, Middleton GA 35th Inf. Co.E
Torrance, R.H. VA 4th Cav. Co.B
Torrance, R.H. VA Inf. 1st Bn.Loc.Def. Co.A
Torrance, Robert D. GA 6th Inf. (St.Guards) Co.F Sgt.
Torrance, S. 1st Conf.Eng.Troops
Torrance, William NC 1st Inf. (6 mo. '61) Co.B
Torrance, William C. AL 15th Bn.Part.Rangers Co.A Cpl.
Torrance, William Hamp GA 4th Inf. Co.H
Torrannelli, Sor LA 30th Inf. Co.D
Torrans, John TX 23rd Cav. Co.F
Torrans, Samuel C. NC 1st Cav. (9th St.Troops) Co.I Sgt.
Torray, --- TX Lt.Arty. Dege's Bn.
Torre, Guiseppe LA Mil. 6th Regt.Eur.Brig. (Italian Guards Bn.) Co.2 Sgt.
Torre, Luigi LA Mil. 6th Regt.Eur.Brig. (Italian Guards Bn.) Co.1 1st Sgt.
Torre, Pietro LA Mil. 6th Regt.Eur.Brig. (Italian Guards Bn.) Co.3
Torre, S. SC Mil. 16th Regt. Robinson's Co.
Torregano, Jean LA 10th Inf. Co.G
Torregrona, E. LA Mil. Orleans Guards Regt. Co.H
Torrell, James F. GA 47th Inf. Co.A
Torrence, Abram P. NC 37th Inf. Co.C 2nd Lt.
Torrence, A.C. LA Mil.Conf.Guards Regt. Co.A
Torrence, Andrew J. GA 1st Cav. Co.E,F
Torrence, C.C. TX 27th Cav. Co.K
Torrence, C.E. NC 23rd Inf. Co.H
Torrence, Charles L. NC 5th Cav. (63rd St.Troops) Co.F
Torrence, C.T. GA Inf. 27th Bn. Co.E
Torrence, David B. MO 4th Cav. Co.I Cpl.
Torrence, E.I. TX Waul's Legion Co.C
Torrence, E.J. TX Cav. Waller's Regt. Co.C
Torrence, E.J. TX 9th (Nichols') Inf. Co.G
Torrence, G.A. NC 4th Inf. Co.B
Torrence, George AL Mil. 2nd Regt.Vol. Co.F
Torrence, H.A. NC 23rd Inf. Co.H Sgt.
Torrence, H.B. TN 2nd (Forrest's) Cav. Co.D
Torrence, H.M. AL Cav. Roddey's Escort
Torrence, Hugh A. NC 28th Inf. Co.B Sgt.
Torrence, Hugh H. MS 34th Inf. Co.K
Torrence, Hugh L.W. NC 37th Inf. Co.C
Torrence, J. GA Inf. 40th Bn. Co.A
Torrence, James H. NC 37th Inf. Co.C
Torrence, James H. NC 48th Inf. Co.C
Torrence, J.D. NC 23rd Inf. Co.H
Torrence, J.E. MS Lt.Arty. (Warren Lt.Arty.) Swett's Co.
Torrence, J.H. TN 3rd (Forrest's) Cav. Co.D
Torrence, John AR 1st Cav. Co.B
Torrence, John A. MO 8th Inf. Co.C
Torrence, John A. 4th Conf.Eng.Troops Co.C
Torrence, John N. NC 49th Inf. Co.H Capt.
Torrence, Joseph H. VA Horse Arty. Shoemaker's Co.
Torrence, J.T. GA 1st Cav.
Torrence, L. NC 23rd Inf. Co.H Cpl.
Torrence, L.C. NC 23rd Inf. Co.H
Torrence, Levi N. MO 8th Cav. Co.D 1st Sgt.
Torrence, M.L. AR 2nd Mtd.Rifles Co.B
Torrence, Oni W. NC 16th Inf. Co.M
Torrence, R.A. TX 8th Cav. Co.H
Torrence, Richard T. AL Lt.Arty. 2nd Bn. Co.F
Torrence, Richmond P. NC 32nd Inf. Co.I
Torrence, R.R. NC 15th Inf. Co.M
Torrence, R.S. NC 23rd Inf. Co.H
Torrence, R.T. GA Lt.Arty. 14th Bn. Co.D,F
Torrence, R.T. GA Lt.Arty. King's Btty.
Torrence, Samuel L.H. NC 34th Inf. Co.D Sgt.
Torrence, Thomas J. LA 9th Inf. Co.A
Torrence, Thomas N. NC 4th Inf. Co.B
Torrence, Thomas O. NC 34th Inf. Co.F
Torrence, W.H. MS Inf. 2nd St.Troops Co.H
Torrence, William GA Lt.Arty. King's Btty.
Torrence, William B. NC 18th Inf. Co.B
Torrence, William H. AL Lt.Arty. Lee's Btty.
Torrence, William H. GA Cav. 7th Bn. (St.Guards) Co.C Cpl.
Torrence, William H. VA 11th Inf. Co.A
Torrence, William L. NC 23rd Inf. Co.K 1st Lt.
Torrence, William W. NC 37th Inf. Co.C Cpl.
Torrence, W.J. TX 27th Cav. Co.K
Torrence, W.M. NC 49th Inf. Co.H
Torrence, W.W. GA Lt.Arty. 14th Bn. Co.D,F
Torrence, W.W. GA 5th Inf. Co.K
Torrens, A. Mareri LA Mil. 5th Regt.Eur.Brig. (Spanish Regt.) Co.1
Torrens, T.K. NC 2nd Arty. (36th St.Troops) Co.A
Torrent, Fletcher TN 25th Inf. Co.C
Torrent, J. SC Inf. 1st (Charleston) Bn. Co.E
Torrent, Patrick H. MS Cav. Duncan's Co. (Tishomingo Rangers)
Torrent, Samuel AL 12th Cav. Co.A
Torrenti, Giacomo LA Mil. 6th Regt.Eur.Brig. (Italian Guards Bn.) Co.3
Torrents, S. AR 15th (Johnson's) Inf. Co.A
Torres, --- TX Cav. Mann's Regt. Co.G
Torres, Angel C. TX 1st (McCulloch's) Cav. Co.D Far.
Torres, Antonio TX Cav. Benavides' Regt. Co.I
Torres, Anto. LA Mil. 5th Regt.Eur.Brig. (Spanish Regt.) Co.9
Torres, Epemenio TX 3rd Inf. 1st Co.C
Torres, Francisco TX 3rd Inf. Co.F
Torres, G. LA Mil. 1st Chasseurs a pied Co.8
Torres, Jacinto TX 3rd Inf. 1st Co.C Sgt.
Torres, J.B. LA 1st Hvy.Arty. (Reg.) Co.I
Torres, Jose LA Mil. 5th Regt.Eur.Brig. (Spanish Regt.) Co.9 Cpl.
Torres, Joseph LA 8th Inf. Co.I
Torres, Julius LA 22nd Inf. D.H. Marks' Co.
Torres, Manana TX Cav. Benavides' Regt. Co.I
Torres, Merriday LA 8th Inf. Co.I
Torres, Modesta TX 33rd Cav. Co.B
Torres, R. LA Mil. 5th Regt.Eur.Brig. (Spanish Regt.) Co.2
Torres, Severiano TX Cav. Madison's Regt. Co.E
Torres, Trinidad TX 33rd Cav. 1st Co.I
Torres, Trinidad TX 8th Field Btty.
Torresse, Justave LA Mil. 1st Native Guards
Torrey, G.W. AL 40th Inf. Co.K Ord.Sgt.
Torrey, H.C. NC 22nd Inf. Co.A
Torrey, James A. MS 1st Lt.Arty. Co.K
Torrey, James F. MS 12th Inf. Co.H
Torrey, James F. MS 19th Inf. Co.D
Torrey, James Ferdinand MS 1st Lt.Arty. Co.A
Torrey, J.F. Conf.Inf. Tucker's Regt. Co.H
Torrey, L.E. LA 2nd Cav. Co.G
Torrey, R.D. MS Inf. 2nd Bn. (St.Troops) Co.F
Torrey, Robert D. MS Inf. 2nd Bn. (St.Troops) Co.F 2nd Lt.
Torrey, S. MS 4th Cav. Co.H
Torrey, Samuel MS 28th Cav. Co.E Cpl.
Torrey, Samuel H. LA Mil. 1st Regt. 3rd Brig. 1st Div. AQM,PM
Torrey, S.H. AR Cav. Gordon's Regt. Co.D Sgt.
Torrey, Sylvester MS Cav. Hughes' Bn. Co.B
Torrey, T.H. MS 4th Cav. Co.H Cpl.
Torrey, T.H. MS Cav. Hughes' Bn. Co.B
Torrez, Sebero TX Cav. Ragsdale's Bn. 1st Co.C
Torri, Joseph LA 18th Inf. Co.F
Torri, Joseph LA Inf.Cons. 18th Regt. & Yellow Jacket Bn. Co.F
Torrie, T. AL 26th (O'Neal's) Inf. Co.I
Torrince, James GA Lt.Arty. 14th Bn. Co.F
Torrince, James GA Lt.Arty. King's Btty.
Torrington, J. MD Arty. 4th Btty.
Torrington, John SC Hvy.Arty. 15th (Lucas') Bn. Co.C
Torrington, John SC Arty. Childs' Co.
Torrington, John SC Arty. Lee's Co.
Torrison, Thomas N. VA Cav. 35th Bn. Co.C
Torriss, J.G. Eng.,CSA
Torry, Abraham TX 1st (McCulloch's) Cav. Co.B
Torry, Abraham TX 8th Field Btty. Cpl.
Torry, G.G. MS Cav. Shelby's Co. (Bolivar Greys)
Torry, James A. TN 1st Hvy.Arty. Co.K
Torry, J.C. AL 11th Inf. Co.I
Torry, John A. TN 1st Hvy.Arty. Co.K Cpl.
Torry, John A. TN Collin's Regt.
Torry, N.B. LA Inf.Cons.Crescent Regt. Co.K
Torry, Richard S. MS Cav. Jeff Davis legion Co.D
Torry, Vernon AL 49th Inf. Co.C
Torry, W.F. SC 24th Inf. Co.G
Torsch, John W. MD Inf. 2nd Bn. Co.E Capt.
Torsch, J.W. MD Walters' Co. (Zarvona Zouaves) 2nd Lt.
Torsch, J.W. VA 47th Inf. Co.H 2nd Lt.
Torshea, J. AL 12th Inf. Co.E
Torsher, Harris AL 29th Inf. Co.D
Tort, R.M. AL Mil. 4th Vol. Co.F
Tort, T.C. AL Mil. 4th Vol. Co.F
Tortell, Jim H. TX 17th Cons.Dismtd.Cav. Co.D Ord.Sgt.
Torto, L. AR Cav. Crabtree's (46th) Regt. Co.A Cpl.
Tortoricei, Giuseppie AL 21st Inf. Co.G
Tortoricio, F. LA Mil. Lewis Guards
Torwood, Samuel AL 43rd Inf. Co.C
Tory, James NC 45th Inf. Co.C
Toryan, R.W. MO 1st & 4th Cons.Inf. Co.C

Toryan, R.W. MO 4th Inf. Co.C
Toryen Nee See 1st Cherokee Mtd.Rifles McDaniel's Co.
Tosa, Dominick VA Lt.Arty. Garber's Co.
To sarquash 1st Seminole Mtd.Vol.
Tosey, Patrick LA 6th Inf. Co.G
Tosh, Charles W. MS 44th Inf. Co.K
Tosh, C.W. MS 9th Bn.S.S. Co.B
Tosh, Daniel VA 57th Inf. Co.D Cpl.
Tosh, Daniel A. TN 35th Inf. Co.B
Tosh, James T. VA 16th Inf. Lt.,Adj.
Tosh, James T. Gen. & Staff 1st Lt.,ADC
Tosh, Josiah VA 63rd Inf. Co.B
Tosh, Jules AL 12th Inf. Co.I
Tosh, Martin 9th Conf.Inf. Co.H
Tosh, Samuel H. VA 18th Inf. Co.I
Tosh, Tascoe TN Inf. 22nd Bn. Co.E
Tosh, William VA 57th Inf. Co.D
Tosh, William L. VA Lt.Arty. Griffin's Co. Sgt.
Tosh, William L. VA 9th Inf. 1st Co.A Cpl.
Tosh, Winborn R. VA 53rd Inf. Co.B
Toslu, J.P. VA 13th Cav.
Tossaux, James NC 3rd Arty. (40th St.Troops)
Tosse, A. LA Mil. 4th Regt. French Brig. Co.4 Sgt.
Tosse, W.R. TN 40th Inf. Co.F
Tosserick, William MS Henley's Co. (Henley's Invinc.)
Tossett, W. AL 2nd Inf. Co.B
Tosso, H. LA Mil. 1st Chasseurs a pied Co.2
Tosto, George NC Lt.Arty. 13th Bn. Co.F
Tosto, Joseph NC 3rd Arty. (40th St.Troops) Co.H
Tostsick, William LA 17th Inf. Co.B
Tot, John NC Mil. Clark's Sp.Bn. Co.L
Tote, Joseph MO Cav. Schnabel's Bn. Co.B
Tote kis Harjo 1st Seminole Mtd.Vol.
Toten, --- TX 19th Cav. Co.I
Toten, Absolom TX 19th Cav. Co.I
Toten, G.W. AL 12th Cav. Co.E
Totham, Daniel LA 1st (Nelligan's) Inf. Co.C
Totham, Daniel LA Inf. 1st Sp.Bn. (Rightor's) New Co.C Cpl.
Tother, Gerhard VA Inf. 4th Bn.Loc.Def. Co.C
Tothero, David MO 6th Cav. Co.I Cpl.
Totherow, George NC 11th (Bethel Regt.) Inf. Co.I
Totherrow, John T. NC 18th Inf. Co.B
Toton, D.P. NC 33rd Inf. Co.C
Toton, William TX Cav. Wells' Regt. Co.A
Totta, Asa TN Inf. Sowell's Detach.
Tottan, John H. NC 3rd Inf. Co.D
Totten, Benjamin MS 44th Inf. Co.H Sgt.
Totten, C.S. NC 5th Cav. (63rd St.Troops) Co.D
Totten, D.L. NC 5th Cav. (63rd St.Troops) Co.D
Totten, D.L. NC 4th Bn.Jr.Res. Co.D
Totten, Edward L. VA 7th Inf. Co.B
Totten, George M. KY 10th Cav. Co.D
Totten, Henry C. NC 13th Inf. Co.A
Totten, J.Y. Gen. & Staff Capt.,QM
Totten, James VA Arty. Kevill's Co.
Totten, James VA 33rd Inf. Co.F
Totten, J.A. TX 2nd Inf. Co.C
Totten, John C., Jr. NC 13th Inf. Co.A,F
Totten, Leroy L.M. NC 13th Inf. Co.A
Totten, Samuel GA 19th Inf.
Totten, Samuel VA Hvy.Arty. 18th Bn. Co.B
Totten, S.T. VA 21st Cav. 2nd Co.E
Totten, Thomas AL 4th Inf. Co.K
Totten, Thomas MO Arty. Lowe's Co. Sgt.
Totten, Thomas NC 13th Inf. Co.A
Totten, Thomas R. NC 5th Cav. (63rd St.Troops) Co.D Cpl.
Totten, Thomas R. TN 2nd (Smith's) Cav.
Totten, William VA 16th Cav. Co.F
Totten, William VA Cav. Caldwell's Bn. Taylor's Co.
Totten, William E. VA Inf. 45th Bn. Co.E
Totten, William R. NC 13th Inf. Co.K 2nd Lt.
Tottenham, James LA 20th Inf. Co.H, Old Co.B
Tottenham, J.W. TX 35th (Brown's) Cav. 2nd Co.B
Totter, James S. AL 6th Inf. Co.B
Tottey, James F. AR 7th Inf. Co.B
Tottle, J. LA 3rd Inf. Co.B
Totton, A.G. KY 9th Cav. Co.G
Totton, George VA 6th Cav. Co.B
Totton, Samuel VA 54th Mil. Co.A
Totton, Silas S. TX 31st Cav. Co.D 1st Lt.
Totton, William B. AR 1st (Colquitt's) Inf. Co.F
Totton, W.J. GA Inf. 14th Bn. (St.Guards) Co.D
Totton, W.J. KY 9th Cav. Co.G
Totty, A.O. TX 3rd Cav. Co.G
Totty, Asa TN 42nd Inf. Co.B
Totty, Asa TN 48th (Voorhies') Inf. Co.D
Totty, B.A. TN 5th Inf. 2nd Co.C Sgt.
Totty, Eli VA Lt.Arty. Pegram's Co.
Totty, Eli VA 12th Inf. Branch's Co.
Totty, Eli VA 16th Inf. Co.K
Totty, Eli VA 41st Inf. Co.C
Totty, F.M. TX Cav. Bourland's Regt. Co.E Capt.
Totty, George W. VA 9th Inf. Co.C
Totty, Henry GA 21st Inf. Co.D
Totty, Henry GA Inf. 25th Bn. (Prov.Guard) Co.G
Totty, J. AR Cav. McGehee's Regt. Co.G
Totty, James B. AR 8th Inf. New Co.F
Totty, James B. AR 14th (McCarver's) Inf. Co.B
Totty, James F. TX 25th Cav. Co.D
Totty, James H. VA Hvy.Arty. Epes' Co.
Totty, J.B. AR Cav. Crabtree's (46th) Regt. Co.A
Totty, J.E. TX Cav. Bourland's Regt. Co.E 1st Lt.
Totty, John VA 9th Inf. Co.C
Totty, John VA Second Class Mil. Hobson's Co. Cpl.
Totty, John H. GA 1st Reg. Co.E Sgt.
Totty, John H. VA 1st Arty. Co.I
Totty, John H. VA Lt.Arty. 38th Bn. Co.B
Totty, John Whitfield TN Cav. 9th Bn. (Gantt's) Co.D
Totty, Jones TN Cav. 9th Bn. (Gantt's) Co.D
Totty, Louis P. TX 14th Cav. Co.F 1st Lt.
Totty, R.B. VA Mtd.Guard 4th Congr.Dist.
Totty, Richard VA 41st Inf. Co.B
Totty, Richard B. VA Arty. J.W. Drewry's Co.
Totty, Robert T. VA Lt.Arty. Cayce's Co.
Totty, Samuel VA 41st Inf. Co.C
Totty, T.H. AR Cav. McGehee's Regt. Co.G
Totty, Theodius AR 1st (Colquitt's) Inf. Co.K
Totty, Thomas VA Arty. J.W. Drewry's Co.
Totty, Thomas H. VA Horse Arty. E. Graham's Co.
Totty, Thomas S. TN 11th Inf. Co.E
Totty, Thomas W. VA 15th Inf. Co.D
Totty, T.S. TN Inf. 2nd Cons.Regt. Co.C
Totty, W. TX 18th Inf. Co.C
Totty, William G. VA 12th Inf. Co.B
Totty, William H. TN Cav. 9th Bn. (Gantt's) Co.D Cpl.
Totty, William W. VA 19th Inf. Co.C Sgt.
Totty, Zachariah TN 10th (DeMoss') Cav. Co.G
Totty, Zachariah TN 42nd Inf. Co.B
Totubbee 1st Choctaw Mtd.Rifles Co.G
Totubbee 1st Choctaw & Chickasaw Mtd.Rifles 2nd Co.H
Toty, Asa TN 48th (Nixon's) Inf. Co.D
Touart, Jos. AL 21st Inf. Co.E Sgt.
Touart, L. AL 21st Inf. Co.K
Toucet, Cenon LA Mil. 5th Regt.Eur.Brig. (Spanish Regt.) Co.2
Touchard, F.A. LA Mil. 2nd Regt. French Brig. Co.H
Touchastoon, Charles GA 11th Cav. (St.Guards) Staten's Co.
Touchberry, James J. SC Inf. Hampton Legion Co.C
Touchberry, Joseph E. SC Inf. Hampton Legion Co.C
Touchberry, W.J. SC 4th Cav. Co.D
Touchberry, W.T. SC 23rd Inf. Co.I
Touchea, Charles LA 13th Inf. Co.D
Touchett, Alexander LA 1st Hvy.Arty. (Reg.) Co.I
Touchett, Theosime LA 1st Hvy.Arty. (Reg.) Co.I
Touchett, Valerien LA 1st Hvy.Arty. (Reg.) Co.I
Touchlien, W.T. SC 4th Cav. Co.D
Touchstone, Alexander AR Cav. Wright's Regt. Co.C
Touchstone, Allen D. AR 8th Inf. Old Co.B Lt.
Touchstone, B. AR Cav. Carlton's Regt.
Touchstone, B.B. GA 3rd Bn. (St.Guards) Co.G
Touchstone, Ben GA Inf. 25th Bn. Co.A
Touchstone, B.R. GA 38th Inf. Co.N
Touchstone, Charles S. GA 29th Inf. Co.K
Touchstone, D. AR Cav. Carlton's Regt.
Touchstone, D. TX 12th Cav. Co.C
Touchstone, Daniel AL 4th Res. Co.G
Touchstone, Daniel TN 32nd Inf. Co.A
Touchstone, D.J. GA 10th Cav. (St.Guards) Co.F
Touchstone, D.J. GA 6th Inf. (St.Guards) Co.K
Touchstone, Elijah J. AR Cav. Wright's Regt. Co.B
Touchstone, E.P. SC 4th Cav. Co.G
Touchstone, E.P. SC 1st Arty. Co.K
Touchstone, Frank GA Inf. 1st Loc.Troops (Augusta) Co.B
Touchstone, George W. AR 3rd Inf. Co.D
Touchstone, H. TX 25th Cav. Co.I
Touchstone, Hardy GA 29th Inf. Co.G
Touchstone, Henry H. GA 51st Inf. Co.G
Touchstone, I.D. 2nd Conf.Eng.Troops Co.D
Touchstone, Isaac GA 51st Inf. Co.G
Touchstone, J. SC 11th Inf. Sheridan's Co.
Touchstone, Jackson J. AR 9th Inf. Old Co.B, Co.G Sgt.

Touchstone, James GA 51st Inf. Co.G
Touchstone, James GA 60th Inf. 1st Co.A
Touchstone, James 1st Conf.Inf. 2nd Co.H
Touchstone, James A. AR 9th Inf. Co.K
Touchstone, James C. LA 12th Inf. Co.E
Touchstone, James L. AL 32nd Inf. Co.A Cpl.
Touchstone, James M. GA 5th Inf. Co.D
Touchstone, James R. AR 9th Inf. Old Co.B
Touchstone, James T. GA 11th Cav. (St.Guards) Johnson's Co. Sgt.
Touchstone, J.D. MS 39th Inf. Co.F
Touchstone, Jesse A. TX 12th Cav. Co.C
Touchstone, J.H. MO 5th Cav. Co.I
Touchstone, J.H. MO Lt.Arty. Von Phul's Co.
Touchstone, J.L. GA Hvy.Arty. 22nd Bn. Co.A
Touchstone, J.L. GA 42nd Inf. Co.G
Touchstone, John GA Inf. 1st Loc.Troops (Augusta) Co.D,B
Touchstone, John GA 51st Inf. Co.G
Touchstone, John SC 4th Cav. Co.G
Touchstone, John SC Cav. 10th Bn. Co.C
Touchstone, John SC 1st Arty. Co.K
Touchstone, John E. MS 12th Inf. Co.D
Touchstone, John W. VA 31st Mil. Co.E
Touchstone, Joseph L. GA 5th Inf. Co.D
Touchstone, Joseph L. GA Inf. 25th Bn. (Prov.Guard) Co.A
Touchstone, Joseph L. Conf.Inf. 1st Bn. 2nd Co.A
Touchstone, J.P. MS Home Guards Barnes' Co. 3rd Lt.
Touchstone, J.S. LA 19th Inf. Co.K
Touchstone, J.S. LA Inf.Crescent Regt. Co.A
Touchstone, J.W. GA 51st Inf. Co.G
Touchstone, L.H. GA 29th Inf. Co.K
Touchstone, L.J. AL 21st Inf. Co.E
Touchstone, Pembroke S. AR 3rd Inf. Co.D 1st Lt.
Touchstone, R. GA 29th Inf.
Touchstone, R.R. GA 30th Inf. Co.N
Touchstone, Solomon GA Cav. Roswell Bn. Co.C,A Jr.2nd Lt.
Touchstone, Stephen GA 1st Bn.S.S. Co.D
Touchstone, Stephen GA 29th Inf. Co.H
Touchstone, Stephen TN 32nd Inf. Co.A
Touchstone, Stephen Gen. & Staff Hosp.Stew.
Touchstone, Thomas F. GA 8th Inf. Co.F
Touchstone, T.N. MS 11th (Perrin's) Cav. Co.G
Touchstone, T.N. MS 46th Inf. Co.B
Touchstone, W. TX 12th Cav. Co.C
Touchstone, William H. GA Inf. 1st Conf.Bn. Co.D
Touchstone, William H. GA 30th Inf. Co.E
Touchstone, William M. GA 5th Inf. Co.D
Touchstone, William M. Conf.Inf. 1st Bn. 2nd Co.A
Touchstone, W.M. GA Inf. 25th Bn. (Prov. Guard) Co.A
Touchstone, W.P. AR 1st (Monroe's) Cav. Co.B
Touchstone, W.W. AR 24th Inf. Co.E
Touchton, John W. GA 10th Inf. Co.C
Touchtone, C.S. GA 4th (Clinch's) Cav. Co.H
Touchtone, H.H. GA 47th Inf. Co.C
Touchtone, T.N. MS 4th Cav. Co.A
Touchtone, W. GA 4th (Clinch's) Cav. Co.H
Touchtone, William TX Bean's Bn.Res.Corps Wilson's Co.
Touell, M. MS Inf. 2nd Bn. Co.E
Tougher, W. MS 2nd St.Cav. Co.G
Touhey, James KY 2nd Mtd.Inf. Co.D
Touhey, James TN 15th Inf. 2nd Co.F
Touhey, Jeremiah TN 2nd (Walker's) Inf. Co.D
Touhey, John NC 3rd Cav. (41st St.Troops) Co.G
Touhey, T.M. SC Mil. 16th Regt. Jones' Co. Sgt.
Toujousse, St. LA Mil. 3rd Regt. French Brig. Co.7
Toulant, A.R. Conf.Inf. Tucker's Regt. Co.H 2nd Lt.
Toulego, H. LA Mil. 3rd Regt. French Brig. Co.4
Touler, William W. AL Inf. 1st Regt. Co.A
Toulin, Desiré LA Conscr.
Touller, B. NC 31st Inf. Co.G
Touller, Frank LA Mil. Chalmette Regt. Co.I
Toulme, John V. MS 3rd Inf. Co.F Capt.
Toulmin, Adolph AL 1st Bn.Cadets Co.A
Toulmin, Harry F. AL 3rd Inf. Co.A
Toulmin, Harry T. AL 22nd Inf. Co.H Col.
Toulmin, John F. AL 21st Inf. Co.K,B 1st Lt.
Toulmin, John Francis AL 3rd Inf. Co.E
Toulmin, M. AL 1st Regt.Mobile Vol. Co.A
Toulmin, M. AL Mil. 2nd Regt.Vol. Co.D
Toulmon, J. AL 33rd Inf. Co.I
Toulous, O. LA 18th Inf.
Toulouse, --- LA Mil. 2nd Regt. French Brig. Co.2
Toulson, Elijah MO 9th (Elliott's) Cav. Co.D
Toulson, John W. VA 40th Inf. Co.G
Toulson, Oscar J. VA 40th Inf. Co.C
Toulson, Thomas R. VA 40th Inf. Co.G
Toulson, William GA Lt.Arty. Howell's Co. Sgt.
Toulson, William H.H. MO 9th (Elliott's) Cav. Co.D
Toumay, C.C. MD 1st Cav. Co.K
Toumbs, Buckner H. MS 10th Inf. Old Co.H
Toumbs, J.R.J. TN 33rd Inf. Co.F
Toumey, Sylvester MD 1st Inf. Co.E
Tounds, J.W. GA Cav. 12th Bn. (St.Guards) Co.E
Tounley, Mounterville LA 28th (Gray's) Inf. Co.K
Tounly, B.J. GA 43rd Inf. Co.I
Tounny, William G. LA 31st Inf. Co.I
Touns, G.W. AL Cav. Hardie's Bn.Res. Co.G
Touns, H.T. MS 4th Cav. Co.F
Touns, Thomas AR 35th Inf. Co.G
Tounsell, John MS Lt.Arty. (Brookhaven Lt.Arty.) Hoskins' Btty.
Tounsend, Adolphus L. NC 16th Inf. Co.I
Tounsend, Andrew J. MS Adair's Co. (Lodi Co.) Sgt.
Tounsend, Francis C. NC 16th Inf. Co.I
Tounsend, I. FL Sp.Cav. 1st Bn.
Tounsend, Robert P. NC 16th Inf. Co.I
Tounsend, V.A. MS 5th Cav. Co.A
Tounsley, G.M. Conf.Arty. Palmer's Bn. Music.
Toupenay, A. LA Mil. 3rd Regt. French Brig. Co.6
Toupes, J. Conf.Lt.Arty. 1st Reg.Btty. Cpl.
Toupiner, Oswald LA Mil. 2nd Regt. French Brig. Co.6
Toups, --- TX 8th Inf.
Toups, Demosthenes TX 5th Inf. Co.F
Toups, Drozin LA 4th Inf. Co.E
Toups, F. LA Mil.Cav. (Chasseurs Jefferson) Cagnolatti's Co.
Toups, Felician LA 26th Inf. Co.I
Toups, George LA 26th Inf. Co.H
Toups, J.A. LA Mil. Terrebonne Regt.
Toups, Jack LA Mil. LaFourche Regt.
Toups, J. Emile LA 26th Inf. Co.I
Toups, Joseph TX Cav.St.Troops Doughty's Co.
Toups, Joseph TX 8th Inf. Co.D
Toups, Joseph P. LA 18th Inf. Co.G
Toups, J.P. LA Inf.Cons. 18th Regt. & Yellow Jacket Bn. Co.F
Toups, Louis LA 26th Inf. Co.I
Toups, L. Ozeme LA 26th Inf. Co.D
Toups, Onesino LA 26th Inf. Co.D
Toups, Ozeme LA 26th Inf. Co.I
Toups, Pierre LA 26th Inf. Co.D
Toups, Prosper LA 26th Inf. Co.I
Toups, Severe LA Mil. LaFourche Regt.
Toups, Tart LA Mil. LaFourche Regt.
Toups, Terence LA 26th Inf. Co.I
Toups, Theophile LA Inf. 16th Bn. (Conf.Guards Resp.Bn.)
Toupse, Adrien LA 30th Inf. Co.H,G
Toupse, Drauzin LA 30th Inf. Co.H
Toupse, Enee LA 30th Inf. Co.H,G
Toupse, Felicien LA 30th Inf. Co.H,G
Tour Enah 1st Seminole Mtd.Vol.
Tourcian, Theogne LA Pointe Coupee Arty.
Tourminelle, J. LA 22nd Inf. Old Co.A
Tournade, Jules LA Arty. Castellanos' Btty.
Tournade, Jules LA 12th Inf. Co.B
Tournade, Julius LA 15th Inf. Co.D
Tournai, E. LA Mil. 1st Regt. 2nd Brig. 1st Div. Co.B
Tournay, L. LA Mil. 3rd Regt. French Brig. Co.8 Sgt.
Tournay, Michel VA Inf. 4th Bn.Loc.Def. Co.A
Tournay, P. AL 6th Inf. Co.K
Tourne, A. LA Mil. 1st Regt. French Brig. Co.2
Tourne, E. LA Mil. Orleans Guards Regt. Co.C 2nd Lt.
Tourne, F.N. LA Mil. Jackson Rifle Bn.
Tourne, N. LA Mil. 3rd Regt.Eur.Brig. (Garde Francaise) Co.7
Tourner, J.R. GA Inf. 2nd Bn. (St.Guards) Co.A Sgt.
Tourney, Dan TN 10th Inf.
Tourney, Frank A. MO Lt.Arty. 3rd Field Btty.
Tournie, A. LA Mil. 4th Regt. French Brig. Co.6
Tournillion, P.H. LA 2nd Cav. Co.H Sgt.
Tournley, Robert AL 5th Inf.
Tournoi, A. LA Mil. 1st Regt. French Brig. Co.1
Tourpain, G. MS 12th Inf. Co.B
Tourriet, O. LA Mil. LaFourche Regt.
Tourtarel, John B. LA Cav. Greenleaf's Co. (Orleans Lt.Horse)
Tourtarelle, J.B. LA Mil. Orleans Guards Regt. Co.D
Tourte, B. LA Mil. 3rd Regt. French Brig. Co.6
Tourte, G. LA Mil. 1st Regt. French Brig. Co.6
Tourte, Michel LA Mil. 6th Regt.Eur.Brig. (Italian Guards Bn.) Co.5
Toury, Edward NC 58th Inf. Co.F

Toury, J.M. MS 2nd St.Cav. Co.F
Tous, Herrman LA 21st (Kennedy's) Inf. Co.F
Tousan, Joseph TX 11th (Spaight's) Bn.Vol. Co.B
Tousend, G. AL 1st Regt. Mobile Vol. Co.K
Tousley, Charles B. AL 4th Inf. Co.G
Tousley, J.B. LA 1st Cav. Co.E
Touso, A. GA 41st Inf.
Touson, J.W. VA 4th Cav. Co.H
Toussaint, Auguste LA Mil. 1st Native Guards
Toussaint, Auguste LA Mil. 1st Native Guards Cpl.
Toussaint, F. LA Mil. 4th Regt. French Brig. Co.3
Toussaint, Henry LA Mil. 1st Regt. French Brig. Co.7
Toussaint, Joseph LA Mil. 1st Native Guards
Tout, John KY 2nd Bn.Mtd.Rifles Co.B
Toutant, A.J. Beauregard's Staff Maj.,ADC
Toutant, R. LA Lt.Arty. Bridges' Btty.
Toutant, R. SC Arty. Manigault's Bn. 1st Co.A, Co.D
Toutcheck, Belizaire LA Conscr.
Toutcheck, Cesare LA Conscr.
Toutcheck, Charles LA Conscr.
Toutcheck, Dolze LA Conscr.
Toutcheck, Drauzin LA Conscr.
Toutcheck, Pierre LA Conscr.
Toutchstone, James M. GA Inf. 25th Bn. (Prov.Guard) Co.A
Touya, Baptiste LA Mil. 1st Regt. French Brig. Co.7
Touya, E. LA Mil. 3rd Regt. French Brig. Co.6
Touya, M. LA Mil. 3rd Regt. French Brig. Co.5 Cpl.
Touya, M. LA Mil. 4th Regt. French Brig. Co.6
Touyal, J. Pierre LA Mil. 2nd Regt. French Brig. Co.5
Touzan, D. LA Mil. 3rd Regt. French Brig. Co.3 Sgt.
Touzannes, J. LA Inf.Cons. 18th Regt. & Yellow Jacket Bn. Co.B
Touzannes, Joseph LA 18th Inf. Co.E
Touzard, George VA Inf. 4th Bn.Loc.Def. Co.A
Touzet, B. LA Mil. 1st Regt. French Brig. Co.4
Tovent, W.H. AL 28th Inf. Co.K
Tovey, Henry M. SC Lt.Arty. Walter's Co. (Washington Arty.)
Tovey, J. LA 13th Inf. Co.G
Tovovich, Lazure LA Mil. 4th Regt.Eur.Brig. Cognevich's Co.
Tow, Albert H. VA 29th Inf. Co.E Sgt.
Tow, Alford NC 60th Inf. Co.F
Tow, Andrew TN Cav. 5th Bn. (McClellan's) Co.E
Tow, Andy TN 2nd (Ashby's) Cav. Co.K
Tow, H. GA 7th Cav. Co.B
Tow, Henry GA Cav. 21st Bn. Co.C
Tow, H.L. TN 2nd (Smith's) Cav. Thomasin's Co.
Tow, James GA 23rd Inf. Co.B
Tow, James TX 17th Inf. Co.E
Tow, J.F. TX 17th Inf. Co.E
Tow, John C. AL 49th Inf. Co.G
Tow, John H. VA 29th Inf. Co.E
Tow, Joseph SC 1st (Hagood's) Inf. 2nd Co.F
Tow, Mattison NC 60th Inf. Co.F
Tow, Moses NC 5th Inf. Co.B
Tow, Reuben T. NC 25th Inf. Co.H
Tow, Samuel M. NC 25th Inf. Co.H
Tow, Samuel M. NC 60th Inf. Co.D
Tow, Shadrack NC 1st Cav. (9th St.Troops) Co.G
Tow, William H. VA 29th Inf. Co.E
Tow, William H. VA Mil. Carroll Cty.
Towa 1st Seminole Mtd.Vol.
Tow aka 1st Seminole Mtd.Vol.
Towantabbee Deneale's Regt. Choctaw Warriors Co.A
Towberman, George VA 2nd Inf. Co.I Cpl.
Towe, James W. NC 8th Inf. Co.I
Towe, John TN 59th Mtd.Inf. Co.D
Towe, William TN 59th Mtd.Inf. Co.D
Towel, Dan GA 5th Inf. Co.K
Towell, --- LA Mil.Cont.Regt. Capt.
Towell, Daniel LA 5th Inf. Co.B
Towell, Isaac TN 7th (Duckworth's) Cav. Co.I
Towell, Isaac D. AR 16th Inf. Co.A
Towell, J.I. AR 10th Mil. Co.D 2nd Lt.
Towell, John LA Mil. McPherson's Btty. (Orleans Howitzers)
Towell, John LA 5th Inf. Old Co.A
Towell, John LA Inf. 16th Bn. (Conf.Guards Resp.Bn.) Co.B
Towell, John LA Mil. Irish Regt. Co.F
Towell, John 1st Cherokee Mtd.Vol. 1st Co.F, 2nd Co.H
Towell, John W. AR 16th Inf. Co.A
Towell, J.R.G. GA 18th Inf. Co.B
Towell, J.W. AR 10th Mil. Co.D 1st Lt.
Towell, M. MS 48th Inf. Co.E
Towell, Owen LA 5th Inf. Old Co.A, Co.K
Towell, Patrick VA Inf. 1st Bn. Co.A
Towell, S.C. TX 11th Cav. Co.F Cpl.
Towell, Stephen LA 7th Inf. Co.E
Towell, W.A. AR Cav. Gordon's Regt. Co.D
Towell, William AR 10th Mil. Co.D Cpl.
Towell, William LA Mil. Irish Regt. Co.G Capt.
Towell, William A. NC 5th Inf. Co.H
Towell, William A. NC 23rd Inf. Co.F
Towels, T. TN 14th (Neely's) Cav. Co.H
Towens, F. TX Waul's Legion Co.G
Toweny, J.B. AL 30th Inf. Co.C
Tower, Alvah MO 12th Inf. Co.F
Tower, Ben TX Cav. Ragsdale's Bn. Co.D Cpl.
Tower, Charles AL Cav. Murphy's Bn. Co.B
Tower, Charles 15th Conf.Cav. Co.G
Tower, Charles H. VA 46th Inf. 2nd Co.A
Tower, F.R. LA Maddox's Regt.Res.Corps Co.B
Tower, G. GA 29th Inf. Co.I
Tower, Isaac N. MS 1st (King's) Inf. (St.Troops) Co.A 1st Sgt.
Tower, Isaac N. MS 6th Inf. Co.G 1st Sgt.
Tower, Isaac S. VA 1st Inf. Co.B 1st Sgt.
Tower, J.G. Gen. & Staff AASurg.
Tower, J.N. MS 3rd (St.Troops) Cav. Co.E
Tower, J.R. AL 6th Inf. Co.A
Tower, J.S. VA Inf. 5th Bn.Loc.Def. Co.H 2nd Lt.
Tower, L.B. GA 45th Inf. Co.E
Tower, L.B. GA 48th Inf. Co.E
Tower, Michael GA 1st (Olmstead's) Inf. Gordon's Co.
Tower, Michael GA 63rd Inf. Co.B
Tower, Stephen AL 36th Inf. Co.G
Towers, A.B. SC 1st St.Troops Co.C 1st Sgt.
Towers, A.B. SC Post Guard Senn's Co.
Towers, A.J. GA 29th Inf.
Towers, A.W. AR 30th Inf. Co.H
Towers, B.F. GA 6th Cav. Co.C
Towers, B.F. GA Smith's Legion Co.E Cpl.
Towers, C.D. FL 1st Inf. Old Co.G Cpl.
Towers, Charles L. FL 2nd Cav. Co.E Sgt.
Towers, Chatham M. VA 25th Cav. Co.F
Towers, C.M. VA 23rd Cav. Co.F Cpl.
Towers, C.M. VA Cav. 41st Bn. Co.F Cpl.
Towers, C.M. VA 25th Inf. 2nd Co.E
Towers, D.R. GA 8th Inf. Co.H 2nd Lt.
Towers, G.D. AL 1st Cav. 1st Co.B
Towers, George VA 16th Cav. Co.F
Towers, H. FL Lt.Arty. Perry's Co.
Towers, Isaac 7th Conf.Cav. Co.B,L
Towers, J.A. GA 31st Inf. Co.I Sgt.
Towers, James E. VA 10th Cav. Co.F
Towers, James E. VA 1st Inf. Co.H
Towers, J.B. AR 30th Inf. Co.I
Towers, J.H. GA 4th Mil. Co.A
Towers, J.N.K. MS 10th Inf. Co.D Sr.2nd Lt.
Towers, Jock GA 4th Bn.S.S. Co.C 1st Lt.
Towers, Joel GA Inf. 9th Bn. Co.A
Towers, John MS Inf. 3rd Bn. Co.D
Towers, John H. VA 27th Inf. Co.G
Towers, John N. LA 6th Cav. Co.I
Towers, John R. GA 8th Inf. Co.E Col.
Towers, J.W. Mead's Conf.Cav. Co.H Sgt.
Towers, L.C. MS Inf. 2nd Bn. Co.B
Towers, L.C. MS 13th Inf. Co.I
Towers, L.C. MS 48th Inf. Co.B
Towers, Richard LA 13th Inf. Co.H
Towers, R.J. GA 6th Cav. Co.C
Towers, S. G. GA 36th Inf. Co.F Cpl.
Towers, W.B.F. GA Cav. 10th Bn. (St.Guards) Co.D
Towers, W.H. TX 4th Inf. Cpl.
Towers, William AL Gorff's Co. (Mobile Pulaski Rifles)
Towers, William TN 37th Inf. Co.K
Towers, William VA 59th Inf. 3rd Co.F
Towers, William VA 60th Inf. 1st Co.H
Towers, William A. GA Cav. Gartrell's Co.
Towers, William A. GA 4th Inf. Co.D
Towers, William B. GA Cav. Gartrell's Co.
Towers, William M. GA Cav. Gartrell's Co.
Towery, A. AR 31st Inf. Co.D
Towery, A.C. MS 5th Inf. Co.A
Towery, A.D. AR 36th Inf. Co.D
Towery, A.J. AR 31st Inf. Co.D
Towery, A.J. AR 36th Inf. Co.D
Towery, Bartlett NC 32nd Inf. Co.D,E
Towery, Bartlett NC 34th Inf. Co.F
Towery, Edward L. AR 33rd Inf. Co.A
Towery, E.U. MS 2nd St.Cav. Co.F
Towery, George W. NC 49th Inf. Co.K
Towery, G.W. AR 10th Inf. Co.C
Towery, G.W. MS 31st Inf. Co.C
Towery, G.W. TN 8th Inf. Co.E
Towery, G.W. Exch.Bn. 2nd Co.A,CSA
Towery, Isaac GA Floyd Legion (St.Guards) Co.A
Towery, Isaac A. NC 1st Arty. (10th St.Troops) Co.C

Towery, James GA 6th Cav. Co.F
Towery, James M. TN 3rd (Lillard's) Mtd.Inf. Co.G Cpl.
Towery, Jeptha TN 8th Inf. Co.E
Towery, J.M. MS 5th Inf. Co.A
Towery, John TN Park's Co.
Towery, John J. AR 1st (Crawford's) Cav. Co.C
Towery, Joseph NC 34th Inf. Co.F
Towery, Joseph NC 49th Inf. Co.K
Towery, M.J. MS 43rd Inf. Co.A
Towery, Samuel NC 18th Inf. Co.A
Towery, Samuel 3rd Conf.Eng.Troops Co.H
Towery, Wade H. MS 5th Inf. Co.A Cpl.
Towery, W.E. AR 36th Inf. Co.L
Towery, William TN Inf. 4th Cons.Regt. Co.A
Towery, William TN 37th Inf. Co.K
Towery, W.W. MO Lt.Arty. Barret's Co.
Towes, J.H. GA 5th Inf. Co.H
Towey, H. TX 8th Inf. Co.I
Towey, J.P. AL Cav. Moreland's Regt. Co.E Sgt.
Towey, Louis NC 7th Inf. Co.D Music.
Towhig, John LA Mil. Brenan's Co. (Co.A, Shamrock Guards) Sgt.
Towie, John 1st Cherokee Mtd.Rifles Co.A Sgt.
Towie, John 1st Cherokee Mtd.Rifles Co.D
Towih, John NC Inf. Thomas Legion Co.B
Towill, Mark W. VA 55th Inf. Co.H Sgt.
Towill, Matthew T. VA 55th Inf. Co.I
Towill, Richard J. VA 55th Inf. Co.I 2nd Lt.
Towill, Richard J. VA 109th Mil. Co.B 2nd Lt.
Towill, Thomas A. VA 55th Inf. Co.C,I
Towland, Thomas MO 6th Cav. Co.I
Towland, W.C. SC Inf. Hampton Legion Co.I
Towle, S.I. MS 16th Inf. Co.I
Towle, William B. VA 3rd Res. Co.E 1st Sgt.
Towlen, W.H. SC Inf. 13th Bn. Co.E
Towler, A.G. VA 1st (Farinholt's) Res. Co.B
Towler, Andrew J. GA 42nd Inf. Co.H
Towler, Benjamin J. GA 11th Inf. Co.H
Towler, B.J. GA 16th Inf. Co.F Cpl.
Towler, C. MO 12th Cav. Co.E
Towler, David M. GA 42nd Inf. Co.H
Towler, H. AL 8th Inf. Co.B
Towler, H.C. VA Inf. 4th Bn.Loc.Def. Co.B
Towler, Henry C. VA 46th Inf. 2nd Co.C
Towler, James J. GA 42nd Inf. Co.H,F
Towler, J.M. GA 16th Inf. Co.F
Towler, J.M. GA 42nd Inf. Co.C
Towler, John H. VA 46th Inf. 2nd Co.C
Towler, John Wenman VA 53rd Inf. Co.I
Towler, Joseph F. VA 46th Inf. 2nd Co.C 2nd Lt.
Towler, Joseph L. VA 38th Inf. Co.B
Towler, Joseph M. Gen. & Staff Surg.
Towler, Joshua VA 46th Inf. 2nd Co.C
Towler, J.R. AL 15th Inf. Co.K
Towler, J.W. VA 46th Inf. 2nd Co.H
Towler, Timothy GA 47th Inf. Co.C
Towler, T.M. TX 20th Inf. Co.F
Towler, William, Sr. VA 46th Inf. 2nd Co.C
Towler, William H. VA Lt.Arty. 13th Bn. Co.B
Towler, William L. GA 48th Inf. Co.F
Towler, William W. AL 3rd Bn. Hilliard's Legion Vol. Co.F
Towler, W.W. AL 60th Inf. Co.D
Towles, Adam T. GA 30th Inf. Co.A Capt.
Towles, Albert AL 7th Inf. Co.A
Towles, Albert AL 47th Inf. Co.I Capt.
Towles, Charles M. LA 1st Cav. Co.B Sgt.
Towles, Daniel F. GA 1st (Olmstead's) Inf. Co.K Sgt.
Towles, D.F. GA Hvy.Arty. 22nd Bn. Co.B
Towles, Edward SC 15th Inf. Co.K
Towles, Edwin L. VA 30th Inf. Co.C
Towles, F.W. GA 1st (Olmstead's) Inf. Co.K
Towles, George R. VA 15th Inf. Co.G
Towles, G.G. TX Waul's Legion Co.B
Towles, G.W. AL 14th Inf. Co.E 2nd Lt.
Towles, Henry KY 2nd (Duke's) Cav. Co.E
Towles, Henry A. GA 1st (Olmstead's) Inf. Co.K
Towles, Henry L. VA 92nd Mil. Co.C
Towles, Herbert H. MO 15th Cav. Co.A
Towles, I.R. TX 11th Inf. Co.G 1st Sgt.
Towles, James NC 14th Inf. Co.K
Towles, James H. GA 1st (Olmstead's) Inf. Co.F,K
Towles, J.C. MD 1st Cav. Co.C
Towles, J.H. TX Inf. Timmons' Regt. Co.A
Towles, John TX 37th Cav. Co.A
Towles, John C. TX 10th Inf. Co.E
Towles, John C. VA 9th Cav. Co.D
Towles, John C. VA 92nd Mil. Co.C
Towles, John H. TX Waul's Legion Co.B
Towles, John M. FL Sp.Cav. 1st Bn. Co.A Sgt.
Towles, John S. AL 7th Inf. Co.A
Towles, John S. KY 2nd Cav. Co.G Cpl.
Towles, John T. KY 4th Mtd.Inf. Co.E
Towles, John T. MS 21st Inf. Co.D 3rd Sgt.
Towles, John T.M. MS 29th Inf. Co.C
Towles, John Vivian VA 4th Cav. Co.A Cpl.
Towles, Joseph H. VA 7th Inf. Co.C Hosp.Stew.
Towles, J.S. KY 2nd (Duke's) Cav. Co.F
Towles, J.T. TN Cav. Nixon's Regt. Co.C
Towles, Lumbert M. VA 40th Inf. Co.H
Towles, M. MS Inf. 4th St.Troops Co.C
Towles, Mildridge MS Lt.Arty. (The Hudson Btty.) Hoole's Co.
Towles, O.D. AL 7th Inf. Co.A
Towles, O.D. AL 17th Inf. Co.E
Towles, Oliver VA 15th Cav. Co.D
Towles, Oliver G. GA 1st (Olmstead's) Inf. Co.K
Towles, Philip S. LA 1st Cav. Co.A
Towles, Portens Gen. & Staff AASurg.
Towles, Ralph S. SC 14th Inf. Co.K
Towles, R.M. MS 12th Inf. Co.F
Towles, Robert C. VA 4th Cav. Co.A Sgt.
Towles, S.B. MS 7th Inf. Co.I
Towles, Seth GA 6th Inf. (St.Guards) Co.B Sgt.
Towles, T. MS 12th Inf. Co.F
Towles, Thomas J. TX 3rd Cav. Co.G 2nd Lt.
Towles, Thomas O. VA 3rd Cav. Co.G
Towles, Thomas R. MS 24th Inf. Co.K Cpl.
Towles, Thomas R. VA 13th Inf. Co.A
Towles, T.P. VA 9th Cav. Co.D
Towles, William VA 30th Inf. Co.B
Towles, William C. MS 21st Inf. Co.D
Towles, William E. LA Washington Arty.Bn. Co.1
Towles, William R. AL 37th Inf. Co.G
Towles, William R. MS 33rd Inf. Co.G
Towles, W.K. MO 6th Cav. Co.K Cpl.
Towles, W.R. AL Vol. Meador's Co.
Towles, W.W. AL 14th Inf. Co.E
Towley, James MO Cav. 2nd Regt. St.Guard Co.F
Towls, G.G. TX Inf. Timmons' Regt. Co.A
Towls, J.M. NC 1st Jr.Res. Co.D Sgt.
Towls, John W. TN 35th Inf. 2nd Co.A Capt.
Towls, William MS 18th Cav. Co.H
Towlster, Thomas TN 21st Inf. Co.F
Towlster, Thomas 9th Conf.Inf. Co.C Cpl.
Towmann, Henry LA Mil. Chalmette Regt. Co.H
Town 1st Seminole Mtd.Vol.
Town, Edwin C. MO Cav. 3rd Bn. Co.C
Town, T.J. TN 12th (Green's) Cav. Co.A
Town, W.B. TN 35th Inf. Co.H
Town, William LA Inf. 9th Bn.
Towndsend, Littleton D. GA 22nd Inf. Co.K Cpl.
Towndsend, Olum L. GA 22nd Inf. Co.K
Towne, George D. Eng.,CSA
Towner, A. MS 4th Cav. Co.F
Towner, A. MS Cav. Hughes' Bn. Co.E
Towner, Albert MS Cav. Powers' Regt. Co.K Capt.
Towner, G.B. NC 2nd Jr.Res. Co.D
Towner, George GA 1st (Olmstead's) Inf. Co.E
Towner, J.A. LA 18th Inf. Co.C
Towner, James L. VA 2nd Inf. Co.B
Towner, John A. MS 27th Inf. Co.E
Towner, Thomas H. VA 2nd Inf. Co.B 1st Sgt.
Towner, William L. MS 6th Inf. Co.E Capt.
Towners, D.L. AL 47th Inf. Co.F
Townes, A.D. VA 1st St.Res. Co.F
Townes, Alexander S. SC Inf. Hampton Legion Co.F
Townes, Daniel C. VA 38th Inf. Co.A Capt.
Townes, E.D. TX Cav. 4th Bn.St.Troops Maj.
Townes, E.W. TN 20th (Russell's) Cav. Co.B
Townes, E.W. TN 12th (Cons.) Inf. Co.G Cpl.
Townes, E.W. TN 22nd Inf. Co.G Cpl.
Townes, G.H. TN 12th Inf. Co.I
Townes, H.C. VA 3rd Cav. Co.A
Townes, Henry VA 20th Inf. Co.G
Townes, James A. MS 1st Cav. Co.D
Townes, James E. NC 12th Inf. Co.D,B Sgt.
Townes, J.E. VA 3rd Cav. Co.A
Townes, J.E. VA 3rd Inf.Loc.Def. Co.I
Townes, J.M. TN 12th Inf. Co.I
Townes, John VA 3rd (Archer's) Bn.Res. Co.E
Townes, John C. MS 22nd Inf. Co.G
Townes, John L. MS 29th Inf. Co.E
Townes, John P. AR 25th Inf. Co.G Sgt.
Townes, John T. SC 4th Inf. Co.J
Townes, J.W. GA 3rd Cav. Co.I
Townes, M.C. TN 20th (Russell's) Cav. Co.B
Townes, Nathaniel W. TX 9th Cav. Col.
Townes, Robert T. TN Lt.Arty. Huggins' Co.
Townes, Samuel A. SC 2nd Inf. Co.B Sgt.
Townes, S.T. TN 12th Inf. Co.I
Townes, Stephen H. VA 38th Inf. Co.A Cpl.
Townes, W. TX 1st Inf.
Townes, W.A. SC 3rd Res. Co.B
Townes, W.H. NC 55th Inf. Co.D 1st Lt.
Townes, William, Jr. VA 38th Inf. Co.G Capt.
Townes, William H. NC 12th Inf. Co.D,B Sr.2nd Lt.
Towney, Isaac S. VA 24th Bn.Part.Rangers Cpl.
Towney, Jacob VA 86th Mil. Co.D

Towney, W.A. AL 30th Inf. Co.A Sgt.
Toweless, R. TN 22nd (Barteau's) Cav. Co.H Lt.
Townley, --- AL 22nd Inf. Co.A
Townley, ---, 1st AL 22nd Inf. Co.A
Townley, A.J. AL 4th Inf. Co.K
Townley, A.J. 1st Conf.Cav. Co.K
Townley, Berry MO 4th Cav. Co.D
Townley, Caleb B. KY 2nd Mtd.Inf. Co.E Cpl.
Townley, Daniel K. AL 47th Inf. Co.G
Townley, G.W. LA Inf.Cons.Crescent Regt. Co.O
Townley, James M. AL Cp. of Instr. Talladega
Townley, J.M. AL 22nd Inf. Co.A
Townley, John AL 13th Bn.Part.Rangers Co.A Sgt.
Townley, John B. VA 47th Mil. Capt.
Townley, J.R. AL 13th Bn.Part.Rangers Co.A
Townley, M.J. GA 42nd Inf. Co.A
Townley, M.T.D. 1st Conf.Eng.Troops Co.B
Townley, Patrick LA 10th Inf. Co.B
Townley, Richmond AL 10th Inf. Co.B
Townley, Robert AL 13th Bn.Part.Rangers Co.A
Townley, Robert TN 22nd (Barteau's) Cav. 1st Co.H
Townley, Stephen AL 30th Inf. Co.K
Townley, Steven M. TX 22nd Cav. Co.E
Townley, Thomas P. GA Inf. 2nd Bn. (St.Guards) New Co.D
Townley, W. TX Inf. Timmons' Regt. Co.D
Townley, W. TX Waul's Legion Co.F
Townley, Wiley A. GA 42nd Inf. Co.A
Townley, William D. TX 22nd Cav. Co.E
Townlin, James W. AR 8th Inf. New Co.G
Townlin, James W. AR 14th (McCarver's) Inf. Co.H
Townlin, William N. TX 27th Cav. Co.I
Townly, J.J. GA 8th Inf. (St.Guards) Co.E
Townly, J.L. TN 46th Inf. Co.A
Townly, John TN 22nd (Barteau's) Cav. 1st Co.H Sgt.
Townly, J.R. TN 22nd (Barteau's) Cav. 1st Co.H
Townly, R. TN 22nd (Barteau's) Cav. 1st Co.H 2nd Lt.
Townly, Richmond AL 13th Bn.Part.Rangers Co.A 2nd Lt.
Townly, T.M. GA Inf. 17th Bn. (St.Guards) Stocks' Co.
Towns, Absolom G. GA 44th Inf. Co.H
Towns, A.D. VA 3rd Inf.Loc.Def. Co.F
Towns, A.J. GA Cav. 15th Bn. (St.Guards) Jones' Co.
Towns, A.J. GA 10th Mil.
Towns, A.L. LA Lt.Arty. 1st Bn. Co.2
Towns, A.L. TX 37th Cav. Co.D
Towns, Augustus R. GA 2nd Cav. (St.Guards) Co.E
Towns, B. LA 17th Inf. Co.G
Towns, B.D. AL 47th Inf. Co.C
Towns, Chas. A. MS 30th Inf. Co.A 2nd Lt.
Towns, David GA 3rd Inf. Co.D
Towns, David H. TX 21st Cav. Co.D Sgt.
Towns, D.R. GA 3rd Cav. Co.I
Towns, E.L. TN 30th Inf. Co.G
Towns, E.W. SC 3rd Cav. Co.K
Towns, G. GA 5th Res. Co.E
Towns, George W. GA 4th Inf. Co.E
Towns, G.H. TN 12th (Cons.) Inf. Co.I
Towns, Gideon P. GA 49th Inf. Co.B
Towns, G.M.D. MO 11th Inf. Co.K
Towns, G.P. GA 5th Res. Co.D
Towns, H. TN 20th Inf. Co.E
Towns, H.A. TX 20th Inf. Co.E
Towns, H.C. GA 13th Inf. Co.K
Towns, Henry MS 2nd (Quinn's St.Troops) Inf. Co.B
Towns, Henry F.S. MS 21st Inf. Co.C
Towns, H.H. AL 14th Inf. Co.H
Towns, H.H. GA 13th Inf. Co.K
Towns, H.H. SC 2nd Arty. Co.H
Towns, H.T. MS Cav. Hughes' Bn. Co.E
Towns, I. Newton AL 58th Inf. Co.I,B
Towns, J. GA 5th Res. Co.E
Towns, James A. MS Cav. 1st Bn. (Miller's) Cole's Co.
Towns, James L. AL Lt.Arty. Clanton's Btty.
Towns, James W. 10th Conf.Cav. Co.E
Towns, J.H. GA Arty. Lumpkin's Co.
Towns, J.H. GA 9th Inf. (St.Guards) Co.H
Towns, J.M. GA 27th Inf. Co.K,H
Towns, J.M. TN 12th (Cons.) Inf. Co.I
Towns, J.O. GA 2nd Cav. (St.Guards) Co.H 2nd Lt.
Towns, John GA 49th Inf. Co.B
Towns, John C. MS 30th Inf. Co.A 2nd Lt.
Towns, John E. VA 136th Mil. Co.A Capt.
Towns, John E. VA 146th Mil. Co.G 1st Sgt.
Towns, John R. GA Cobb's Legion Co.G
Towns, John R. TX 5th Inf. Co.K Cpl.
Towns, John W. GA Siege Arty. 28th Bn. Co.H
Towns, Joseph R. AR 9th Inf. Co.G
Towns, J.P. AR 1st Mtd.Rifles Co.K
Towns, J.S. AL 9th Inf. Co.D
Towns, J.S. MS 17th Inf. Co.E
Towns, J.T. SC Inf. 13th Bn. Co.E Cpl.
Towns, J.T. SC Inf. Hampton Legion Co.I
Towns, J.T. VA 4th Inf. Co.B
Towns, J.W. AL Cav. 5th Bn. Hilliard's Legion Co.E
Towns, J.W. TN 20th Inf. Co.I
Towns, M.C. TN 19th & 20th (Cons.) Cav. Co.B
Towns, M.O. KY 9th Mtd.Inf. Co.C Sgt.
Towns, Peter GA Inf. 27th Bn. Co.C
Towns, P.T. GA 66th Inf. Co.H,I
Towns, R. GA 62nd Cav. Co.A Capt.
Towns, R. GA 9th Inf. (St.Guards) Co.H
Towns, R.A. GA Cav. 1st Bn.Res. Stark's Co. Sgt.
Towns, Randolph GA 62nd Cav. Co.A Capt.
Towns, Reason A. GA 5th Inf. Co.B
Towns, R.H. GA Cav. 15th Bn. (St.Guards) Jones' Co.
Towns, R.H. GA 10th Inf. 1st Sgt.
Towns, Richard TN 18th Inf. Co.C
Towns, S. GA 5th Res. Co.D
Towns, S.T. TN 12th (Cons.) Inf. Co.I
Towns, T. LA 3rd (Wingfield's) Cav. Co.I
Towns, W. LA 3rd (Wingfield's) Cav. Co.I
Towns, W.A. MS Cav. Hughes' Bn. Co.E
Towns, W.A. SC 1st St.Troops Co.K
Towns, W.B. MS 3rd Cav. Co.C 1st Lt.
Towns, W.B. MS 3rd Inf. (St.Troops) Co.B
Towns, W.B. MS Conscr.
Towns, W.H. AL 34th Inf. Co.E
Towns, W.H. TN 12th (Green's) Cav. Co.E Cpl.
Towns, William TN 12th (Green's) Cav. Co.A
Towns, William TN Lt.Arty. McClung's Co.
Towns, William TN 30th Inf. Co.D
Towns, William A. Conf.Cav. Wood's Regt. 2nd Co.M
Towns, William B. GA 41st Inf. Co.E
Towns, William H. MS 34th Inf. Co.E
Towns, William H. GA 4th Res. Co.I
Towns, William H. GA 7th Inf. (St.Guards) Co.E
Towns, William M. LA 1st Cav. Co.C
Towns, William S. TN 15th Cav. Co.D
Towns, William S. TN 30th Inf. Co.G 2nd Lt.
Towns, W.J. TX 20th Inf. Co.E
Towns, W.O. AL 14th Inf. Co.H
Towns, W.S. KY 5th Cav. Co.D
Towns, W.S. TN 1st Cav. Co.D
Townsand, Abraham KY Cav. 2nd Bn. (Dortch's) Co.C
Townsand, A.J. AR Inf. Cocke's Regt. Co.E
Townsand, A.T. MS Cav. 3rd Bn.Res. Co.B
Townsand, Benjamin F. FL 5th Inf. Co.E,D
Townsand, D.R. AL St.Res. Co.A
Townsand, E.L. TX 22nd Inf. Co.E Cpl.
Townsand, Elijah, Jr. FL 7th Inf. Co.B Cpl.
Townsand, Fineis LA 8th Inf. Co.H
Townsand, G.C. KY 2nd (Duke's) Cav. Co.K
Townsand, James AR 2nd Cav. Co.B
Townsand, James Jefferson AL 16th Inf. Co.E
Townsand, J.C. TN 10th (DeMoss') Cav. Co.A
Townsand, John W. TN 10th (DeMoss') Cav. Co.A Bvt.2nd Lt.
Townsand, Jordon W. VA 57th Inf. Co.D
Townsand, Joseph M. AL 16th Inf. Co.E,D
Townsand, J.W. GA 56th Inf. Co.H
Townsand, Levi D. NC 58th Inf. Co.D
Townsand, S. TX 33rd Cav. Cpl.
Townsand, Samuel W. AL 17th Inf. Co.B
Townsand, Sherwood W. TN Cav. 17th Bn. (Sanders') Co.C
Townsand, S.W. MS 10th Cav. Co.F
Townsand, William AL 8th Cav. Co.I
Townsand, William H. GA 36th (Broyles') Inf. Co.I Cpl.
Townsden, Thomas VA Arty. Kevill's Co.
Townsed, John MO Cav. Wood's Regt. Co.H
Townsel, --- TN 34th Inf. Co.F
Townsell, M.L. NC 26th Inf. Co.F
Townsell, William P. NC 26th Inf. Co.F
Townsen, Ed TX 17th Cav. Co.B
Townsen, Joshua AR 2nd Mtd.Rifles Co.D
Townsen, Lewis VA 30th Bn.S.S. Co.C
Townsend, --- FL Harrison's Co. (Santa Rosa Guards) Sgt.
Townsend, --- TX 33rd Cav. Co.B
Townsend, --- TX Waul's Legion Co.H
Townsend, A. FL 11th Inf. Co.E
Townsend, A. KY Morgan's Men Co.G
Townsend, A. LA 3rd Inf. Co.K
Townsend, A. MS 7th Cav. Co.C Cpl.
Townsend, A. MS 3rd Inf. (St.Troops) Co.H
Townsend, A. TX 7th Cav. Co.E
Townsend, A.B. TX 17th Inf. Co.C
Townsend, A.C. MS 2nd Cav. Co.K Sgt.

Townsend, A.C. MS Inf. 1st Bn.St.Troops (30 days '64) Co.C
Townsend, Adam J. AL 43rd Inf. Co.H Sgt.
Townsend, Adolphus FL 7th Inf. Co.B
Townsend, A.J. MS Cav. 3rd (St.Troops) Co.A
Townsend, A.J. MS 1st (King's) Inf. (St.Troops) Co.I
Townsend, A.J. MS Inf. 1st Bn.St.Troops (30 days '64) Co.C
Townsend, A.J. MS 4th Inf. Co.E
Townsend, A.J. MS 15th Inf. Co.B
Townsend, A.J. TN 24th Inf. 2nd Co.G
Townsend, A.J. TX 17th Inf. Co.C
Townsend, A.L. TN Lt.Arty. Scott's Co. Sgt.
Townsend, Albert AR 2nd Cav.
Townsend, Albert VA 19th Cav. Co.A
Townsend, Albert VA 3rd Cav. & Inf.St.Line Co.A
Townsend, Albert A. VA 19th Cav. Co.K Cpl.
Townsend, Alexander NC 18th Inf. Co.D
Townsend, Alfred NC 7th Inf. Co.F
Townsend, Alfred NC 8th Sr.Res. McLean's Co.
Townsend, Alfred KY 4th Mtd.Inf. Co.G,D
Townsend, Allen MS 4th Inf. Co.E
Townsend, A.M. TN 42nd Inf. 2nd Co.H
Townsend, Amos SC 18th Inf. Co.F
Townsend, Andrew C. AL 12th Inf. Co.K 1st Lt.
Townsend, Andrew J. GA Cosncr.
Townsend, Andrew J. MS Cav. 1st Bn. (Miller's) Co.E
Townsend, Andrew J. MS 11th (Perrin's) Cav. Co.K
Townsend, Andrew J. MS 35th Inf. Co.B
Townsend, Andrew J. MS 40th Inf. Co.E
Townsend, Andrew W. AR Inf. 8th Bn.
Townsend, Andrew W. AR 25th Inf. Co.F Bvt.2nd Lt.
Townsend, A.P. MS 4th Inf. Co.E
Townsend, Augustus C. MS 1st (Patton's) Inf. Co.C
Townsend, Auzza MS 1st Cav.
Townsend, A.W. AR Mil. Borland's Regt. Peyton Rifles
Townsend, A.W. KY 10th (Johnson's) Cav. Co.A
Townsend, A.W. MS 2nd Cav. Co.K
Townsend, B.D. TX 36th Cav.
Townsend, Benjamin GA Cav. 1st Bn. Hopkins' Co.
Townsend, Benjamin GA 5th Cav. Co.K
Townsend, Benjamin GA 11th Inf. Co.G
Townsend, Benjamin F. FL 3rd Inf. Co.F
Townsend, Benjamin F. NC 43rd Inf. Co.H
Townsend, Benjamin F. TX 2nd Inf.
Townsend, Benjamin Franklin MS Inf. 1st St.Troops Co.D
Townsend, Benjamin J. NC 28th Inf. Co.E Sgt.
Townsend, Benjamin R. AL Recruits
Townsend, Benj. R. AL Cp. of Instr. Talladega
Townsend, B.F. AL 11th Cav. Co.C
Townsend, B.F. AL 27th Inf. Co.A
Townsend, B.F. FL 11th Inf. Co.E
Townsend, B.J. AL Conscr.
Townsend, B.J. TX 36th Cav. Co.H
Townsend, B.L. AL 26th Inf. Co.A
Townsend, B.M. AL Cav. Forrest's Regt. A. Fancher's Co.
Townsend, B.R. AL Mil. 4th Vol. Moore's Co. Cpl.
Townsend, Caleb GA 6th Cav. Co.I
Townsend, C.B. TX 33rd Cav. Co.F
Townsend, C.C. AL 8th Inf. Co.K
Townsend, C.H. LA 2nd Inf. Co.H Cpl.
Townsend, C.H. VA 1st (Farinholt's) Res. Co.K
Townsend, Charles FL 2nd Cav. Co.H,B
Townsend, Charles FL 3rd Inf. Co.F
Townsend, Charles GA Cav. 6th Bn. (St.Guards) Co.C Cpl.
Townsend, Charles MO Cav. Williams' Regt. Co.E
Townsend, Charles NC 51st Inf. Co.E
Townsend, Charles C. NC 20th Inf. Co.A
Townsend, Charles E. TX 36th Cav.
Townsend, Chas. F. FL 2nd Cav. Co.H
Townsend, Charles N. TN 1st (Turney's) Inf. Co.A
Townsend, Charles Pinckney SC 8th Inf. Co.G Capt.
Townsend, Chas. S. FL 3rd Inf. Co.F
Townsend, Chickering T. VA 16th Inf. 2nd Co.H, Co.G
Townsend, Chickren VA 39th Inf. Co.H
Townsend, C.L. FL Lt.Arty. Dyke's Co.
Townsend, C.L. FL Conscr.
Townsend, Clark AL 54th Inf. Co.I Cook
Townsend, Collin VA 4th Cav. Co.C
Townsend, C.R. AL 2nd Cav. Co.D
Townsend, D. GA Inf. 8th Bn. Co.E
Townsend, Daniel NC 8th Sr.Res. McNeill's Co.
Townsend, Daniel SC 3rd Cav. Co.I
Townsend, David GA 20th Inf. Co.F
Townsend, D.C. TN 8th (Smith's) Cav. Co.A
Townsend, D.E. TX 5th Inf. Co.E
Townsend, Debery NC Detailed Men Cumberland Cty.Bn. Co.A
Townsend, D.H. TX 14th Inf. Co.F
Townsend, D. Henry MS 40th Inf. Co.E
Townsend, D.J. SC Cav. Walpole's Co.
Townsend, E. AL Cp. of Instr. Talladega
Townsend, E. GA 8th Inf. Co.I
Townsend, E.C. MS 2nd Cav. Co.D
Townsend, E.C. TX 36th Cav. Co.I
Townsend, Edmond MO St.Guard 1st Sgt.
Townsend, Edmund L. MO 5th Inf. Co.E
Townsend, Edward FL 7th Inf.
Townsend, Edward GA 23rd Inf. Co.E Sgt.
Townsend, E.E. GA 42nd Inf. Band Music.
Townsend, E.J. KY 5th Mtd.Inf.
Townsend, E.J. KY 9th Mtd.Inf. Co.G
Townsend, E.L. AL 54th Inf.
Townsend, Eli C. NC 2nd Cav. (19th St.Troops) Co.F
Townsend, Elijah LA 31st Inf. Co.E
Townsend, Elijah NC 43rd Inf. Co.H
Townsend, E.R. MS 28th Cav. Co.C
Townsend, E.W. TN 19th Inf. Co.F
Townsend, F. SC 6th Inf. 2nd Co.K
Townsend, F.A. MS 28th Cav. Co.B
Townsend, F.A. SC 7th Inf. 1st Co.G, 2nd Co.G, Co.D
Townsend, Floyd NC 51st Inf. Co.F
Townsend, F.M. FL Lt.Arty. Dyke's Co. Cpl.
Townsend, F.M. MO 6th Cav. Co.D
Townsend, F.M. NC Detailed Men Cumberland Cty.Bn. Co.A
Townsend, F.M. SC 21st Inf. Co.L
Townsend, F.M. TN 24th Inf. 2nd Co.G
Townsend, Francis LA 22nd (Cons.) Inf. Co.I
Townsend, Francis M. MS 40th Inf. Co.E
Townsend, Frank AL Lt.Arty. 2nd Bn. Co.E
Townsend, Fuller C. NC 51st Inf. Co.E
Townsend, G. LA Mil.Conf.Guards Regt. Co.H
Townsend, G. MO 12th Inf. Co.A
Townsend, G.B. MS 35th Inf. Co.H
Townsend, George AL 1st Bn.Cadets Co.B
Townsend, George NC 37th Inf. Co.E
Townsend, George TX 26th Cav. Co.K
Townsend, George VA 17th Inf. Co.I 1st Sgt.
Townsend, George VA 56th Inf. Co.A
Townsend, George F. VA 48th Inf. Co.I
Townsend, George S. TN 4th Inf. Co.A
Townsend, George W. TN 7th (Duckworth's) Cav. Co.B
Townsend, George W. TN 4th Inf. Co.I
Townsend, George W. TN 42nd Inf. Co.G
Townsend, George W. VA Inf. 4th Bn.Loc.Def. Co.E
Townsend, George W. VA Inf. 22nd Bn. Co.B
Townsend, George W. VA 57th Inf. Co.D
Townsend, G.F. GA 48th Inf. Co.I
Townsend, Gideon MO 15th Cav. Co.A Sgt.
Townsend, Gideon Sap. & Min.,CSA
Townsend, G.M. MS Inf. 1st Bn.St.Troops (30 days '64) Co.C
Townsend, Greenberry SC 10th Inf. Co.K Sgt.
Townsend, G.W. AL 41st Inf. Co.H
Townsend, G.W. AR 50th Mil. Co.G
Townsend, G.W. GA 19th Inf. Co.E
Townsend, H. AL Cp. of Instr. Talladega
Townsend, Harris AL 17th Inf. Co.E
Townsend, Harris TX Cav. Good's Bn. Co.A 1st Lt.
Townsend, Harvey VA 22nd Cav. Co.C
Townsend, H.C. VA Lt.Arty. R.M. Anderson's Co. Cpl.
Townsend, Henry AL 40th Inf. Co.F
Townsend, Henry AL Cp. of Instr. Talladega
Townsend, Henry C. GA 48th Inf. Co.F
Townsend, Henry E. SC 8th Inf. Co.G Sgt.
Townsend, Henry J. TX 27th Cav. Co.C
Townsend, Henry J. VA Hvy.Arty. 10th Bn. Co.E
Townsend, H.F. FL 4th Inf. ACS
Townsend, H.G. MO 4th Cav. Co.I
Townsend, H.G. Jones' Staff,CSA Capt.,ACS
Townsend, Hiram KY 2nd Bn.Mtd.Rifles Co.A Sgt.
Townsend, Hiram KY 5th Mtd.Inf. Co.C
Townsend, H.J. AR 8th Inf. New Co.E
Townsend, H.L. TX 5th Cav. Co.A
Townsend, H.S. GA 49th Inf. Co.F
Townsend, I. GA Inf. Athens Reserved Corps
Townsend, Ira KY 2nd (Woodward's) Cav. Co.D
Townsend, Ira TN 9th (Ward's) Cav.
Townsend, Ira TN Cav. McCann's Squad.
Townsend, Isaac LA 7th Inf. Co.B
Townsend, Isaac N. GA 48th Inf. Co.F
Townsend, Israel FL 11th Inf. Co.E
Townsend, J. AL 5th Cav. Co.L

Townsend, J. AL 44th Inf. Co.F
Townsend, J.A. AR 19th (Dawson's) Inf. Co.D
Townsend, J.A. Wheeler's Scouts,CSA
Townsend, Jabus R. LA 31st Inf. Co.E
Townsend, Jackson NC 51st Inf. Co.E
Townsend, Jackson J. GA Cobb's Legion Co.A
Townsend, Jacob NC 50th Inf.
Townsend, Jacob NC 58th Inf. Co.D
Townsend, James AL 26th (O'Neal's) Inf. Co.A
Townsend, James AR 18th Inf. Co.K
Townsend, James FL 8th Inf. Co.H
Townsend, James GA Cav. 1st Bn. Hopkins' Co.
Townsend, James LA 14th Inf. Co.F
Townsend, James LA 18th Inf. Co.H
Townsend, James LA Inf.Cons. 18th Regt. & Yellow Jacket Bn. Co.H
Townsend, James SC 7th Inf. 1st Co.B, 2nd Co.B, Co.F Capt.
Townsend, James TN Cav. 16th Bn. (Neal's) Co.E
Townsend, James TX 12th Cav. Co.D
Townsend, James TX 21st Cav. Co.B
Townsend, James VA 19th Cav. Co.F
Townsend, James VA 62nd Mtd.Inf. 2nd Co.D
Townsend, James VA 2nd Cav.St.Line McNeel's Co.
Townsend, James C. VA 57th Inf. Co.D
Townsend, James E. AL 7th Inf. Co.K
Townsend, James J. AL 10th Cav.
Townsend, James J. MS 48th Inf. Co.B
Townsend, James L. AR 1st (Colquitt's) Inf. Co.B
Townsend, James R. MS 15th Inf. Co.I
Townsend, James R. VA Lt.Arty. Jeffress' Co.
Townsend, James S. AL 1st Inf.
Townsend, James S. GA 26th Inf. Co.B Sgt.
Townsend, James S. NC 23rd Inf. Co.A
Townsend, James T. KY 2nd (Duke's) Cav. Co.B
Townsend, James T. NC 44th Inf. Co.H Capt.
Townsend, James W. GA Inf. 8th Bn. Co.E Cpl.
Townsend, Jaques FL 7th Inf. Co.B Sgt.
Townsend, J.B. TX 9th (Nichols') Inf. Co.A
Townsend, J.C.G. TN 1st Hvy.Arty. 2nd Co.A, 1st Co.C
Townsend, J.D. AR 21st Inf. Co.D
Townsend, J.E. TX 17th Inf. Co.I
Townsend, Jefferson A. NC 60th Inf. Co.D
Townsend, Jefferson C. AL 17th Inf. Co.I
Townsend, Jesse AL Lt.Arty. Phelan's Co.
Townsend, Jesse AL Lt.Arty. 2nd Bn. Co.F
Townsend, J.F. NC Detailed Men Cumberland Cty.Bn. Co.A
Townsend, J.F. SC 3rd Cav. Co.I
Townsend, J.F. SC 7th Inf. 2nd Co.B 1st Lt.
Townsend, J. Fletcher SC 2nd Inf. Co.F
Townsend, J.H. FL Lt.Arty. Dyke's Co.
Townsend, J.H. LA Miles' Legion Co.E,A
Townsend, J.H. MS 38th Cav. Co.G
Townsend, J.H. MO 15th Cav. Co.A
Townsend, J.H. SC 3rd Cav. Co.I
Townsend, J.J. GA 19th Inf. Co.E
Townsend, J.J. GA 56th Inf. Co.E
Townsend, J.L. TX 5th Cav. Co.A
Townsend, J.L. TX 1st Inf.
Townsend, J.M. TN 7th (Duckworth's) Cav. Co.B
Townsend, J.M. TN 16th (Logwood's) Cav. Co.I
Townsend, Joel NC 58th Inf. Co.D
Townsend, Joel A. TX 5th Cav. Co.I
Townsend, John AL 28th Inf. Co.H
Townsend, John AL 54th Inf. Co.I Cook
Townsend, John FL 7th Inf. Co.F
Townsend, John KY 2nd (Duke's) Cav. Co.B
Townsend, John MS Cav. Powers' Regt. Co.A Sgt.
Townsend, John MS 1st (Percy's) Inf. Co.A
Townsend, John MS 39th Inf. Co.E
Townsend, John MO 6th Cav. Co.D
Townsend, John NC 24th Inf. Co.A
Townsend, John TX Cav. Steele's Command Co.D
Townsend, John A. AL 32nd Inf. Co.E
Townsend, John B. MS Inf. 5th Bn. Co.B
Townsend, John B. MS 27th Inf. Co.K
Townsend, John C. NC 37th Inf. Co.E
Townsend, John D. AR 17th (Lemoyne's) Inf. Co.B
Townsend, John D. TX 26th Cav. Co.A
Townsend, John E. MO Cav. Jackman's Regt. Co.E
Townsend, John F. AL 33rd Inf. Co.G
Townsend, John H. AL 3rd Bn. Hilliard's Legion Vol. Co.C
Townsend, John J. TN 25th Inf. Co.A
Townsend, John J. VA 3rd Arty. Co.A
Townsend, John J. VA Hvy.Arty. Epes' Co.
Townsend, John L. GA 19th Inf. Co.G
Townsend, John L. GA 22nd Inf. Co.K
Townsend, John M. AR 3rd Inf. Co.H
Townsend, John R. TX Cav. Mann's Regt. Co.A
Townsend, John R. TX Cav. Mann's Bn. Co.A
Townsend, John S. AR 23rd Inf. Co.E Cpl.
Townsend, John T. LA 19th Inf. Co.K
Townsend, John T. NC 24th Inf. Co.H 2nd Lt.
Townsend, John T. VA 18th Inf. Co.B
Townsend, John V. SC 15th Inf. Co.A
Townsend, John W. AR 1st (Colquitt's) Inf. Co.B
Townsend, John W. NC 8th Sr.Res. McLean's Co., McNeill's Co.
Townsend, John W. TX Cav. Martin's Regt. Co.F,I
Townsend, John W. VA 21st Mil. Co.B
Townsend, John W. VA 34th Inf. Co.A
Townsend, Joseph FL 11th Inf. Co.E
Townsend, Joseph A. MS 15th Inf. Co.E
Townsend, Joseph A. MS 30th Inf. Co.C 2nd Lt.
Townsend, Joseph F. MS 15th Inf. Co.B Capt.
Townsend, Joseph H. NC 25th Inf. Co.H
Townsend, Joseph H. SC 14th Inf. Co.I
Townsend, Joseph J. GA 5th Inf. Co.B
Townsend, Joseph M. AL 7th Cav.
Townsend, Joseph M. TX 27th Cav. Co.D Far.
Townsend, Joseph M. TX Cav. Mann's Regt. Co.A
Townsend, Joseph M. TX Cav. Mann's Bn. Co.A
Townsend, Joseph P. VA 59th Inf. 2nd Co.H
Townsend, Josephus C. VA Inf. 9th Bn. Co.B
Townsend, Josephus C. VA 25th Inf. 2nd Co.G Cpl.
Townsend, Joshua B. NC 60th Inf. Co.D
Townsend, Joshua M. SC Inf. 3rd Bn. Co.A Capt.
Townsend, Josiah AL 41st Inf. Co.H
Townsend, Josiah GA 4th (Clinch's) Cav. Co.G,K
Townsend, Josiah GA Cav. Hendry's Co. (Atlantic & Gulf Guards)
Townsend, J.P. TN 1st Hvy.Arty. 1st Co.C, Co.A,L, 3rd Co.B
Townsend, J.P. TX 12th Inf. Co.K
Townsend, J.R. TX 26th Cav. 1st Co.G
Townsend, J.R. TX Waul's Legion Co.D
Townsend, J.S. AL 62nd Inf. Co.C
Townsend, J.T. TX Waul's Legion Co.D
Townsend, J.V. SC 1st Bn.S.S. Co.A
Townsend, J.V. SC 3rd Inf. Co.G
Townsend, J.W. MS 2nd Cav. Co.K
Townsend, J.W. MS 28th Cav. Co.B
Townsend, J.W. MS Lt.Arty. 14th Bn. Co.C
Townsend, J.W. TX 14th Inf. Co.F Cpl.
Townsend, L. FL 2nd Inf.
Townsend, L. LA 17th Inf. Co.H
Townsend, L.A. FL 11th Inf. Co.E
Townsend, Larkin NC 58th Inf. Co.D
Townsend, L.C. MS 2nd Cav. Co.K Sgt.
Townsend, Levi N. VA 19th Cav. Co.K
Townsend, Light FL 11th Inf. Co.E
Townsend, Light S. TX Cav. Baylor's Regt. Co.A
Townsend, L.J. SC 7th Cav. Co.G
Townsend, L.M. MS 3rd (St.Troops) Cav. Co.E
Townsend, L.M. MS Cav. Powers' Regt. Co.A
Townsend, L.M. MS 1st (King's) Inf. (St.Troops) Co.C
Townsend, L.M. MS 1st (Percy's) Inf. Co.A
Townsend, Loo ney 1st Cherokee Mtd.Rifles Co.A
Townsend, Lorenzo D. FL 7th Inf. Co.B Cpl.
Townsend, Lot AR Cav. McGehee's Regt. Co.B
Townsend, Lot GA 50th Inf. Co.H Capt.
Townsend, Lovick AL 32nd Inf. Co.G
Townsend, L.R. MS 4th Inf. Co.E Capt.
Townsend, L.W. MS 9th Cav. Co.E
Townsend, M. TX 33rd Cav. Co.K
Townsend, M. TX 4th Inf. Co.H
Townsend, M. TX Waul's Legion Co.F
Townsend, Madison W. TX Inf. Griffin's Bn. Co.D
Townsend, Manson G. GA 42nd Inf. Co.F,B
Townsend, Martin W. TX 16th Inf. Co.G
Townsend, Matthew MO 5th Inf. Co.E Capt.
Townsend, McQueen NC 18th Inf. Co.D
Townsend, Miles NC 58th Inf. Co.D
Townsend, M.J. MS Cav. 3rd (St.Troops) Co.I
Townsend, M.J. MS Inf.1st Bn.St.Troops (12 mo. '62-3) Co.A
Townsend, M.M. TX Inf. Timmons' Regt. Co.C
Townsend, Moses S. TX Inf. Griffin's Bn. Co.D 2nd Lt.
Townsend, M.Q. AL Res. Belzer's Co.
Townsend, M.W. TX 13th Vol. Co.A
Townsend, N. AL 2nd Cav. Co.K
Townsend, Nat FL 1st Inf. New Co.I
Townsend, N.B. AR 19th (Dawson's) Inf. Co.D
Townsend, Nebo TN Cav. 16th Bn. (Neal's) Co.E
Townsend, Neill NC 18th Inf. Co.D 1st Lt.

Townsend, Nelson LA Miles' Legion Co.G
Townsend, Newton MO 6th Cav. Co.D
Townsend, Noah MO 15th Cav. Co.A
Townsend, Noah MO 12th Inf. Co.A
Townsend, Noah NC 1st Inf. Co.E
Townsend, Noah NC 7th Inf. Co.F
Townsend, N.T. LA 17th Inf. Co.C
Townsend, O.E. MS 4th Inf. Co.E 3rd Lt.
Townsend, O.L. GA Arty. 9th Bn. Co.B
Townsend, P. MO St.Guard
Townsend, Paul VA 36th Inf. Co.A
Townsend, Peter N. KY 1st Inf. Co.H
Townsend, P.F. AL Lt.Arty. Lee's Btty.
Townsend, P.H. TN 17th Inf. Co.F
Townsend, P.H. TN 51st (Cons.) Inf. Co.G
Townsend, Philip AL 3rd Inf. Co.G
Townsend, Philip NC 60th Inf. Co.H Sgt.
Townsend, Phillip A. AL 63rd Inf. Co.B 2nd Lt.
Townsend, P.J. MS 2nd Cav. Co.K Cpl.
Townsend, P.J. MS 22nd Inf. Cpl.
Townsend, P.P. NC 2nd Jr.Res. Co.E
Townsend, R.G. AR Cav. Gordon's Regt. Co.F
Townsend, R.H. TN 6th Inf. Co.E
Townsend, Richard NC 3rd Arty. (40th St.Troops) Co.E
Townsend, Richard W. MS St.Cav. Perrin's Bn. Co.B Cpl.
Townsend, Right MS Cav. Dunn's Co. (MS Rangers)
Townsend, Robert KY 2nd (Duke's) Cav. Co.B
Townsend, Robert MS Inf. 2nd Bn. Co.H
Townsend, Robert MS 48th Inf. Co.H
Townsend, Robert VA 3rd Cav. Co.C Cpl.
Townsend, Robert A. VA 7th Inf. Co.H
Townsend, Robert E. SC 21st Inf. Co.F 1st Lt.
Townsend, Robert M. GA 60th Inf. Co.D
Townsend, Robert P. AL 20th Inf. Co.H
Townsend, Robert R. AR 1st (Colquitt's) Inf. Co.G
Townsend, R.W. MS 5th Cav. Co.G Cpl.
Townsend, R.W. MS 1st (King's) Inf. (St.Troops) Co.H
Townsend, R.W. TN 8th (Smith's) Cav. Co.A
Townsend, S. MO Robertson's Regt.St.Guard Co.H
Townsend, S. TX Cav. 3rd Regt.St.Troops Capt.
Townsend, S.A. FL 11th Inf. Co.E
Townsend, Samuel FL 11th Inf. Co.E
Townsend, Samuel A. FL 3rd Inf. Co.G,H
Townsend, Samuel L. TX Waul's Legion Co.D
Townsend, Samuel M. AR 2nd Mtd.Rifles Co.C
Townsend, Samuel P. AL 20th Inf. Co.H
Townsend, Sanders SC 6th Cav. Co.C,A,D
Townsend, S.B. TX 33rd Cav. Co.K Cpl.
Townsend, S.B.F. GA 49th Inf. Co.F
Townsend, S.C. VA 2nd Arty. Co.E
Townsend, S.G. GA 13th Inf. Co.D 2nd Lt.
Townsend, S.G. MS 2nd Part.Rangers Co.L
Townsend, S.H. FL 11th Inf. Co.E
Townsend, S.H. LA 8th Cav. Co.D Sgt.
Townsend, Shep. H. LA 2nd Inf. Co.D
Townsend, Silas MS Inf. 1st Bn.St.Troops (30 days '64) Co.C
Townsend, Silas C. VA Inf. 22nd Bn. Co.E
Townsend, S.J. TX Waul's Legion Co.D
Townsend, S.M. AR 2nd Inf. Co.C
Townsend, S.M. AR 37th Inf. Co.K
Townsend, S.M. TX 26th Cav. 1st Co.G
Townsend, S.M. TX Waul's Legion Co.D Sgt.
Townsend, Sol. R. NC 28th Inf. Co.E 2nd Lt.
Townsend, S.S. VA 2nd Arty. Co.E
Townsend, Stape TX 9th (Nichols') Inf. Co.F
Townsend, Stephen S. VA Inf. 22nd Bn. Co.E
Townsend, T. MO Robertson's Regt.St.Guard Co.4
Townsend, T.B. TX Inf. Timmons' Regt. Co.G
Townsend, T.B. TX Waul's Legion Co.A
Townsend, T.G. TX Inf. Griffin's Bn. Co.D
Townsend, T.G. TX Inf. Timmons' Regt. Co.H
Townsend, Thomas AR 8th Inf. New Co.A
Townsend, Thomas LA 27th Inf. Co.K
Townsend, Thomas A. AR 1st (Colquitt's) Inf.
Townsend, Thomas A. VA 47th Mil.
Townsend, Thomas B. MS 10th Inf. Old Co.E
Townsend, Thomas B. MS 27th Inf. Co.K
Townsend, Thomas E. TN 2nd (Robison's) Inf. Co.C
Townsend, Thomas G. TX Inf. Timmon's Regt. Co.H
Townsend, Thomas J. VA 57th Inf. Co.D
Townsend, Thomas S. TX 7th Inf. Co.E 1st Lt.
Townsend, T.M. TX Cav. Benavides' Regt. Co.F
Townsend, T.N. MS 40th Inf. Co.E
Townsend, T.S. Inf. Bailey's Cons.Regt. Co.A
Townsend, V.D. FL 2nd Inf. Co.C
Townsend, W. GA 36th (Villepigue's) Inf. Co.K
Townsend, W. LA 27th Inf. Co.B
Townsend, W. NC 4th Cav. (59th St.Troops) Co.A
Townsend, W. SC 6th Inf. 2nd Co.K
Townsend, Wales LA Inf. 11th Bn. Co.D
Townsend, Wales LA Inf.Cons.Crescent Regt. Co.B
Townsend, Wales J. LA 19th Inf. Co.H
Townsend, Walter KY 9th Cav. Co.C
Townsend, W.B. AL Cty.Mil.
Townsend, W.C. MS Cav. Yerger's Regt. Co.A
Townsend, W.H. AL Cp. of Instr. Talladega
Townsend, W.H. AR 18th Inf. Co.C Sgt.
Townsend, W.H. AR 32nd Inf. Co.B
Townsend, W.H. AR 36th Inf. Co.K Capt.
Townsend, W.H. GA 42nd Inf. Co.I
Townsend, W.H. SC Arty. Stuart's Co. (Beaufort Vol.Arty.)
Townsend, W.H. SC 11th Inf. Co.A
Townsend, W.H. VA Mil. Washington Cty.
Townsend, William AL 44th Inf. Co.F
Townsend, William AR 18th Inf. Co.K
Townsend, William AR Inf. Hardy's Regt. Co.K
Townsend, William FL Cav. 3rd Bn. Co.C 2nd Lt.
Townsend, William FL Lt.Arty. Dyke's Co.
Townsend, William KY 5th Mtd.Inf. Co.D Cpl.
Townsend, William MS 40th Inf. Co.E
Townsend, William MO 2nd Cav. Co.E Cpl.
Townsend, William MO Cav. 3rd Regt.St.Guard Co.C
Townsend, William MO 11th Inf. Co.C Sgt.
Townsend, William NC 18th Inf. Co.D
Townsend, William SC 13th Inf. Co.F
Townsend, William TN 59th Mtd.Inf. Co.E
Townsend, William TX 21st Cav. Co.C
Townsend, William TX 11th (Spaight's) Bn.Vol. Co.B
Townsend, William TX 16th Inf. Co.I
Townsend, William 15th Conf.Cav. Co.E 2nd Lt.
Townsend, William 1st Conf.Inf. 1st Co.K
Townsend, William A. AR Lt.Arty. Wiggins' Btty. Cpl.
Townsend, William A. FL 1st Cav. Co.D
Townsend, William A. TX 33rd Cav. Co.K
Townsend, William B. MO 7th Cav. Co.D,K 1st Lt.
Townsend, William D. VA 31st Inf. Co.E
Townsend, William Finis MO 8th Inf. Co.F Sgt.
Townsend, William H. VA 41st Inf. Co.K
Townsend, William H.L. FL 1st Cav. Co.A Jr.2nd Lt.
Townsend, William M. TX 18th Cav. Co.D Cpl.
Townsend, William N. VA 14th Cav. Crawford's Co.
Townsend, William N. VA 17th Cav. Co.F
Townsend, William O. VA Arty. Paris' Co.
Townsend, William P. TX 4th Inf. Co.C Capt.
Townsend, William P. TX Inf. Townsend's Co. (Robertson Five S.) Capt.
Townsend, William R. MS 15th Inf. Co.B
Townsend, William R. MO Cav. 2nd Regt. St.Guard Co.F
Townsend, William T. VA 31st Inf. Co.G
Townsend, William W. TX 27th Cav. Co.D Capt.
Townsend, W.M. MS 5th Inf. (St.Troops) Co.A
Townsend, W.N. TN Lt.Arty. Lynch's Co.
Townsend, W.P. MS Cav. 1st Bn. (Montgomery's) St.Troops Hammond's Co.
Townsend, W.P. Gen. & Staff, Cav. Col.
Townsend, Wright A. TX 22nd Inf. Co.H
Townsend, W.S. AL 8th Inf. Co.K
Townsend, W.S. AR 19th (Dawson's) Inf. Co.D
Townsend, W.S. SC 24th Inf. Co.B Cpl.
Townsend, W.S. SC 26th Inf. Co.D
Townsend, W.S. TX Inf. Timmons' Regt. Co.C
Townsend, W.S. TX Waul's Legion Co.F
Townsend, W.T. SC Inf.Bn. Co.F
Townsend, W. Thomas SC 19th Inf. Co.G
Townsend, W.W. AR 50th Mil. Co.G
Townsend, W.W. TX Cav. Steele's Command Co.B Capt.
Townsend, Z. AL Cav. Hardie's Bn.Res. Co.C
Townsend, Z.E. MS Lt.Arty. Lomax's Co.
Townsend, Z.E. MS 1st (King's) Inf. (St.Troops) Co.H Cpl.
Townsends, I. Fort's Scouts,CSA
Townsends, Joseph AL 54th Inf. Co.I Cook
Townsends, Prince AL 54th Inf. Co.I Cook
Townsens, John GA 1st Inf. (St.Guards) Sgt.
Townshend, Ed D. NC 44th Inf. Co.B
Townshend, James 20th Conf.Cav. 2nd Co.I
Townshend, Jno. H. Gen. & Staff 1st Lt.,ADC
Townshend, Thomas J. VA 38th Inf. Co.A
Townshend, William L.S. NC 8th Inf. Co.C 1st Lt.
Townshend, Wm. L.S. Gen. & Staff AQM
Townsley, Erasmas MO 2nd Inf. Co.B
Townsley, George M. GA Lt.Arty. 14th Bn. Co.A
Townsley, George M. GA Lt.Arty. Havis' Btty.
Townsley, George W. MO 10th Inf. Co.D Cpl.

Townsley, John TN 21st Inf. Co.H
Townsley, J.Y. TN 62nd Mtd.Inf. Co.F
Townsley, Louis O. AL Mobile City Troop 1st Lt.
Townsley, L.S. GA Lt.Arty. Havis' Btty.
Townsley, Lyman B. GA 2nd Bn.S.S. Co.A
Townsley, Lyman B. GA 5th Inf. Co.I,M Cpl.
Townsley, Samuel MO Cav. Jackman's Regt. Co.E
Townsley, Samuel A. GA 4th Inf. Co.K
Townsley, Samuel A. GA 64th Inf. Co.G Capt.
Townsley, Thomas W. VA 30th Bn.S.S. Co.C,D
Townsley, Thomas W. VA 166th Mil. Co.D 2nd Lt.
Townsley, W.A. TN 62nd Mtd.Inf. Co.F
Townsley, W.A. TX 16th Inf. Co.G
Townsley, W.A. TX 17th Inf. Co.F
Townsley, W.W. TN 19th (Biffle's) Cav. Co.B
Townson, --- LA 12th Inf. Co.L
Townson, Aaron E. NC 28th Inf. Co.C
Townson, Andrew TN 13th (Gore's) Cav. Co.D
Townson, Caleb GA 52nd Inf. Co.G
Townson, David VA 10th Bn.Res. Co.D
Townson, D.H. MS 46th Inf. Co.H
Townson, H. MS 11th Perrin's Cav. Co.K
Townson, H.W. TX 29th Cav. Co.G
Townson, J.C. GA 12th Cav. Co.A Cpl.
Townson, J.J. GA 12th Cav. Co.E
Townson, Robert MS 4th Inf. Co.E
Townson, Solomon NC 28th Inf. Co.C
Townson, T.W. MS 46th Inf. Co.I
Townson, William GA 6th Cav. Co.I
Townson, William GA 52nd Inf. Co.G
Townson, William MS 46th Inf. Co.I
Townson, William 3rd Conf.Eng.Troops Co.H
Townspeare, T.P. GA 48th Inf. Co.K
Townsworth, Sidney MO Cav. Poindexter's Regt.
Townt, S.C. VA 1st Cav. Co.A
Towrey, A.D. AR 47th (Crandall's) Cav. Lay's Co.
Towrey, Henry TN 5th (McKenzie's) Cav. Co.A
Towrey, H.M. 1st Conf.Cav. 2nd Co.K
Towrey, J.K. 1st Conf.Cav. 2nd Co.K
Towry, A. NC 4th Inf. Co.H
Towry, Aaron McF. NC 34th Inf. Co.C
Towry, Ed I. AR 4th Inf. Co.I
Towry, Isaac AL 4th Inf. Co.H
Towry, Isaac NC 15th Inf. Co.D
Towry, Isaac NC 49th Inf. Co.B
Towry, Isham J. TN 44th (Cons.) Inf. Co.E
Towry, Isham J. TN 55th (McKoin's) Inf. Co.H
Towry, Jackson NC 1st Arty. (10th St.Troops) Co.C
Towry, James MS 5th Inf. Co.A
Towry, James N. GA 11th Cav. Co.C
Towry, J.B. AL Cp. of Instr. Talladega Co.C
Towry, J.H. NC 12th Inf. Co.E
Towry, John AR 4th Inf. Co.I
Towry, John TN 9th Inf. Co.E
Towry, John H. AR 4th Inf. Co.I
Towry, John M. AR 4th Inf. Co.I
Towry, John Parker NC 56th Inf. Co.I
Towry, Joseph NC 15th Inf. Co.D
Towry, Joseph NC 49th Inf. Co.A
Towry, J.R. NC 49th Inf. Co.B
Towry, Lewis McCurry NC 56th Inf. Co.I
Towry, Martin S. NC 49th Inf. Co.A
Towry, M.J. MS Inf. 1st Bn. Ray's Co.
Towry, R.C. TN 3rd (Lillard's) Mtd.Inf. Co.G
Towry, R.P. NC 15th Inf. Co.D
Towry, R.P. NC 49th Inf. Co.B
Towry, Silas AR 4th Inf. Co.I
Towsend, William R. GA 48th Inf. Co.F
Towsey, G.W. AR 15th Inf. Co.C
Towsey, W.S. TX 1st Hvy.Arty. Co.H
Towsley, John T. LA 1st Cav. Co.D
Towson, Daniel J. MS 30th Inf. Co.F 2nd Lt.
Towson, Daniel J. MS Conscr.
Towson, James E. VA 3rd Inf.Loc.Def. Co.D 1st Lt.
Towson, James E., Jr. VA 17th Inf. Co.G Capt.
Towson, J.D. GA 62nd Cav. Co.K
Towson, John AL 5th Cav. Co.L
Towson, Suttle VA 9th Cav. Co.A
Towson, Thomas GA 49th Inf. Co.G
Towson, Thomas VA 9th Cav. Co.A Capt.
Towson, William M. TX 17th Cav. Co.A
Towson, W.J.M. TX 17th Cons.Dismtd.Cav. Co.A
Towstey, L.H. Brush Bn.
Toxey, Appleton AL 43rd Inf. Co.H Cpl.
Toxey, C. AL 19th Inf. Asst.Surg.
Toxey, C. AL 25th Inf. Asst.Surg.
Toxey, Caleb Gen. & Staff Surg.
Toxey, W. AL 50th Inf. Asst.Medical Off.
Toxey, William AL 25th Inf. Surg.
Toxey, William NC 58th Inf. Surg.
Toxey, William Gen. & Staff Surg.
Toxon, Henry, Jr. AL 8th Inf. Co.D Cpl.
Toxson, Ed LA 10th Inf. Co.D
Toy, C.H. GA 53rd Inf. Chap.
Toy, C.H. VA Lt.Arty. Grandy's Co. Cpl.
Toy, C.H. Gen. & Staff Chap.
Toy, George AL Eufaula Lt.Arty.
Toy, George AL Inf. 1st Regt. Co.A
Toy, H.D. KY 2nd Cav. Co.C
Toy, Henry GA 19th Inf. Co.A
Toy, Henry D. GA Arty. 9th Bn. Co.A,E
Toy, Henry D. VA Ind.Cav. Co.A
Toy, James VA 61st Inf. Co.A Music.
Toy, James M. GA Inf. Hull's Co. Sgt.
Toy, John GA Inf. Hull's Co.
Toy, John W. VA 7th Inf. Co.H
Toy, Joseph L. MD Inf. 2nd Bn. Co.A
Toy, Patrick MS Inf. Comfort's Co.
Toy, Patrick Cav. 1st Conf.Reg. Co.A
Toy, Thomas B. MD Arty. 4th Btty.
Toy, William GA Inf. 3rd Bn. Co.G
Toy, William GA 4th Bn.S.S. Co.A
Toyaneete NC Inf. Thomas Legion 2nd Co.A Cpl.
Toyarteesee chee wa looke 1st Cherokee Mtd.Rifles Co.B
Toye, R.G. SC 25th Inf. Co.H 1st Sgt.
Toye ne sie 1st Cherokee Mtd.Rifles Co.E
Toysey, James VA 23rd Cav. Co.M
Tozer, Samuel TN 12th (Cons.) Inf. Co.H
Tozer, Samuel TN 22nd Inf. Co.B
Trabb, T. LA Mil. 2nd Regt. 3rd Brig. 1st Div. Co.K
Traber, D.R. VA 45th Inf.
Traber, Joseph TX Cav. Mann's Regt. Co.A
Traber, Joseph TX 6th Inf. Co.A
Traber, Lewis GA 42nd Inf. Co.I
Trabold, Frederick LA 1st (Strawbridge's) Inf. Co.A,C
Trabor, William KY 7th Cav. Co.H
Trabue, A.J. TN Cav. 11th Bn. (Gordon's) Co.C Cpl.
Trabue, A.M. VA Conscr.Cp.Lee Co.B
Trabue, Charles LA 1st (Nelligan's) Inf. Sgt.
Trabue, Charles C. VA Lt.Arty. R.M. Anderson's Co. Sgt.
Trabue, Charles C. Gen. & Staff 1st Lt.,Dr.M.
Trabue, G.W., Jr. KY 7th Cav. Co.K 3rd Lt.
Trabue, John VA Hvy.Arty. Read's Co.
Trabue, John P. VA 4th Cav. Co.B
Trabue, John P. VA Arty. Dance's Co.
Trabue, J.W. TN Inf. 3rd Bn. Co.D
Trabue, Presley KY 4th Mtd.Inf. Co.C
Trabue, Q.C. KY 7th Cav. Co.H Cpl.
Trabue, Quintus C. KY 1st Inf. Co.K
Trabue, Robert P. KY 4th Mtd.Inf. Col.
Trabue, R.W. TN 1st Hvy.Arty. Co.L, 3rd Co.A Sgt.
Trabue, T.E. TN Hvy.Arty. Johnston's Co.
Trabue, Thomas E. TN 3rd (Forrest's) Cav. Co.A
Trabur, Lewis AL 7th Inf. Co.C
Trace, J. VA 24th Cav.
Tracewell, S.C. AR 35th Inf. Co.G
Tracey, A. Edward SC 1st (Butler's) Inf. Co.E Sgt.
Tracey, Andrew J. Conf.Cav. Raum's Co. Cpl.
Tracey, Asa MO 1st Cav. Co.G
Tracey, Benjamin W. KY 2nd Cav. Co.C
Tracey, Dennis TN 1st (Feild's) Inf. Co.A
Tracey, D.R. TN 26th Inf. Co.F
Tracey, Edward GA 1st (Olmstead's) Inf. Read's Co., Co.E
Tracey, Edward G. VA 30th Bn.S.S. Co.B 2nd Lt.
Tracey, F.S. SC 7th Cav. Co.G
Tracey, F.S. SC 3rd Res. Co.B
Tracey, G.B. LA 3rd Inf. Co.I
Tracey, Green B. LA 17th Inf. Co.K
Tracey, Harvey S. VA 30th Bn.S.S. Co.B
Tracey, Henry P. LA 6th Inf. Co.F Drum.
Tracey, J. GA Conscr.
Tracey, James LA Inf.Crescent Regt. Co.A
Tracey, James TN 2nd (Walker's) Inf. Co.B
Tracey, J.D. AL Cav. Hardie's Bn.Res.
Tracey, J.D. MS Lt.Arty. (Jefferson Arty.) Darden's Co.
Tracey, Joel N. VA 8th Inf. Co.A
Tracey, John AL Inf. 2nd Regt. Co.H
Tracey, John LA 6th Cav. Co.C
Tracey, John Conf.Inf. 1st Bn. Co.I
Tracey, John W. VA Mil. Stowers' Co. 2nd Lt.
Tracey, Louis F. TN 5th Cav. Co.D,G
Tracey, M. AR Mil. Borland's Regt. Peyton Rifles
Tracey, M.O. LA 13th Inf. Co.B,A,D,E,I Maj.
Tracey, Nathan K. LA 8th Inf. Co.E
Tracey, P. LA 11th Inf. Co.K
Tracey, Peter LA 13th Inf. Co.A
Tracey, Richard LA 7th Inf. Co.B
Tracey, Roland VA 30th Bn.S.S. Co.B
Tracey, Rowland J. VA 151st Mil. Co.C
Tracey, Ryland VA 8th Inf. Co.F
Tracey, T.C. KY Cav. 3rd Bn. 1st Lt.

Tracey, W.H. GA Inf. 2nd Bn. (St.Guards) Co.C
Tracey, William LA 17th Inf. Co.K
Tracey, William LA 18th Inf. Co.E
Tracey, William 4th Conf.Eng.Troops
Tracey, William E. AR 1st (Colquitt's) Inf. Co.B
Tracey, Wilson AR Cav. 1st Bn. (Stirman's) Co.H
Trachier, W.E. SC 22nd Inf. Co.D
Trachy, E. AL St.Arty. Co.C
Trachy, Edward AL Mil. 3rd Vol. Co.A
Tracker 1st Cherokee Mtd.Rifles Co.F
Tracker 1st Cherokee Mtd.Vol. 2nd Co.E
Tracker, Philip AL Conscr.
Tracking Wolf David 1st Cherokee Mtd.Rifles Co.G
Trackman, Fred Conf.Inf. Tucker's Regt. Co.C
Tracy, --- VA 2nd St.Res. Co.D
Tracy, A. AR 18th (Marmaduke's) Inf. Co.H Sgt.
Tracy, A.J. 3rd Conf.Inf. Co.E Lt.
Tracy, Alexander MO 5th Cav. Co.G
Tracy, Americus D. TN 48th (Nixon's) Inf. Co.K Sgt.
Tracy, Americus D. TN 54th Inf. Co.G Cpl.
Tracy, Anderson C. AL 55th Vol. Co.J,K Cpl.
Tracy, Andrew P. TN 7th Inf. Co.A
Tracy, Asa W. KY 6th Mtd.Inf. Co.E
Tracy, B. VA 1st St.Res. Co.C
Tracy, B.A. KY 7th Cav. Co.G Capt.
Tracy, B.A. Gen. & Staff Capt.,AQM
Tracy, B.H. TX 20th Inf. Co.E Cpl.
Tracy, B.H. TX 22nd Inf. Co.F
Tracy, Blount TX 5th Inf. Co.K Cpl.
Tracy, Buford A. KY 11th Cav. Co.G Capt.
Tracy, C. GA 6th Inf. Lt.
Tracy, C. VA Inf. 2nd Bn.Loc.Def. Co.G
Tracy, C. Tracy's Staff 1st Lt.,ADC
Tracy, Carlos Gen. & Staff, Military Court Col.
Tracy, C. Columbus GA 2nd Cav. Co.G
Tracy, Charles MO Inf. 3rd Regt.St.Guard Co.F 1st Lt.
Tracy, Chris VA 2nd Inf.Loc.Def. Co.I
Tracy, David D. GA 1st Reg. Co.F Sgt.
Tracy, Denis LA Mil. Bonnabel Guards
Tracy, D.R. TN 24th Inf. Co.F
Tracy, E.D. AL 12th Inf. Lt.Col.
Tracy, E.D., Jr. GA Cav. 20th Bn. Go.G 1st Sgt.
Tracy, E.D., Jr. GA Cav. 21st Bn. Co.D Sgt.
Tracy, Edward LA 11th Inf. Co.B
Tracy, Edward LA 20th Inf. New Co.E, Co.A
Tracy, Edward TN 10th Inf.
Tracy, Edward D. AL 4th Inf. Co.I Capt.
Tracy, Edward D. AL 19th Inf. Lt.Col.
Tracy, Edward G. VA 60th Inf. 2nd Co.H
Tracy, E.L. Gen. & Staff Brig.Gen.
Tracy, Francis VA 27th Inf. Co.B
Tracy, Frank M. SC 5th Inf. 1st Co.E, 2nd Co.H
Tracy, Frederick S. SC 2nd Inf. Co.B
Tracy, F.S. SC Rutledge Mtd.Riflemen & Horse Arty. Trenholm's Co.
Tracy, G.B. TN 48th (Nixon's) Inf. Co.K 1st Lt.
Tracy, George GA 51st Inf. Co.H
Tracy, Green B. TN 54th Inf. Co.G
Tracy, Hendenan G. KY 6th Mtd.Inf. Co.E,C Sgt.
Tracy, Henry LA 21st (Kennedy's) Inf. Co.C
Tracy, Henry S. TX 13th Vol. 2nd Co.C
Tracy, Henry W. Price's Div. Maj.,ACS
Tracy, Ivan MO 4th Cav. Co.I
Tracy, Jacob J.H. VA 108th Mil. Co.C, Lemons' Co. 1st Sgt.
Tracy, James GA Inf. 17th Bn. (St.Guards) Stocks' Co.
Tracy, James MS 22nd Inf. Co.C Jr.2nd Lt.
Tracy, James A. VA 19th Cav. Co.F
Tracy, James A. VA 31st Inf. Co.G
Tracy, James K. Polk KY 9th Mtd.Inf. Co.K
Tracy, James L. MO 1st Cav. Hosp.Stew.
Tracy, James L. MO 1st & 3rd Cons.Cav. Hosp.Stew.
Tracy, James L. MO 2nd Inf. Hosp.Stew.
Tracy, James L. MO 3rd Inf. Co.G
Tracy, James M. GA Conscr.
Tracy, James N. MO 5th Inf. Co.I 1st Lt.
Tracy, James W. NC 37th Inf. Asst.Surg.
Tracy, James W. Gen. & Staff Surg.
Tracy, Jasper N. AL 55th Vol. Co.B Cpl.
Tracy, J.B. GA 1st Inf. (St.Guards)
Tracy, J.E. TN 8th (Smith's) Cav. Co.D
Tracy, Jean N. AL 3rd Bn. Hilliard's Legion Vol. Co.F
Tracy, Jeremiah KY 5th Mtd.Inf. Co.K
Tracy, Jeremiah J.H. VA Lt.Arty. G.B. Chapman's Co.
Tracy, Jeremiah P. KY 9th Mtd.Inf. Co.K
Tracy, Jesse H. AR 14th (Powers') Inf. Co.F Sgt.Maj.
Tracy, Jesse H. MO 4th Cav. Co.I Lt.
Tracy, J.F. AR 8th Inf. New Co.C Capt.
Tracy, J.G. TX Waul's Legion Co.B
Tracy, J.H. AR 8th Cav. Co.G 1st Lt.
Tracy, J.H., Jr. AR 8th Cav. Co.G Cpl.
Tracy, J.H. MO Cav. Fristoe's Regt. Lt.Col.
Tracy, J.H. MO Cav. Fristoe's Regt. Co.A 3rd Lt.
Tracy, J.N. AL 54th Inf. Cpl.
Tracy, J.N. AL 60th Inf. Co.D
Tracy, John FL Lt.Arty. Perry's Co.
Tracy, John GA 1st Btty. Co.A
Tracy, John NC 55th Inf. Co.I
Tracy, John SC 15th Inf. Co.H
Tracy, John VA 19th Cav. Co.F
Tracy, John VA Cav. 46th Bn. Co.A
Tracy, John VA 62nd Mtd.Inf. Co.D
Tracy, John B. SC 5th Inf. 2nd Co.H
Tracy, John C. MO Inf. 3rd Regt.St.Guard Lt.Col.
Tracy, John C. MO 5th Inf. Co.I
Tracy, John C. Gen. & Staff Col.
Tracy, John J. VA 2nd Cav.St.Line McNeel's Co.
Tracy, John P. GA 2nd Cav. Co.G
Tracy, John P. VA 19th Cav. Co.H
Tracy, Joseph H. MO 3rd Cav. Co.K Cpl.
Tracy, J.P. KY 5th Mtd.Inf. Co.K
Tracy, J.W. AR 1st (Dobbin's) Cav. Co.D Cpl.
Tracy, J.W. AR 8th Inf. New Co.C
Tracy, J.W. NC 14th Inf. Surg.
Tracy, Lucian P. FL Lt.Arty. Perry's Co. Cpl.
Tracy, M. AR 13th Mil. Co.A
Tracy, M. AR Willett's Co.
Tracy, McDonald GA 23rd Inf. Co.A
Tracy, M.D. MS 19th Inf. Co.I Cpl.
Tracy, Michael VA 15th Inf. Co.F
Tracy, Nathaniel GA 1st Cav. Co.A 2nd Lt.
Tracy, Nathaniel GA Floyd Legion (St.Guards) Co.G
Tracy, Nathaniel TN 5th (McKenzie's) Cav. Co.C
Tracy, Nathaniel G. AR 27th Inf. Co.H
Tracy, Nathaniel H. AR 14th (Powers') Inf. Co.F 1st Lt.
Tracy, Nathaniel H. MO 3rd Cav. Co.K Cpl.
Tracy, N.B. TN 48th (Nixon's) Inf. Co.K
Tracy, Ned LA Mil. Bonnabel Guards
Tracy, N.F. TN 19th (Biffle's) Cav. Co.B
Tracy, N.F. TN 3rd (Clack's) Inf. Co.K
Tracy, N.G. MO Cav. Fristoe's Regt. Co.A Cpl.
Tracy, N.H. AR 8th Cav. Co.G
Tracy, N.H. MO Cav. Fristoe's Regt. Co.A Capt.
Tracy, N.H. TN 63rd Inf. Co.H
Tracy, Obediah KY 11th Cav. Co.C
Tracy, Obediah KY 7th Mtd.Inf. Co.C
Tracy, P. GA 6th Inf. Maj.
Tracy, P. GA 27th Inf. Maj.
Tracy, Patrick GA Hvy.Arty. 22nd Bn. Co.E Sgt.
Tracy, Patrick GA 1st (Olmstead's) Inf. Guilmartin's Co.
Tracy, Patrick GA 20th Inf. Co.A
Tracy, Patrick GA 25th Inf. Co.A
Tracy, Peter LA 20th Inf. Co.K,A
Tracy, Phillip TN 10th Inf. Co.B
Tracy, R. TN 4th (McLemore's) Cav. Co.C
Tracy, R.E. MO Inf. Winston's Regt. Co.A
Tracy, Richard E. MO 4th Cav. Co.I
Tracy, Richard E. MO St.Guard
Tracy, Rowland J. VA 11th Bn.Res. Co.D
Tracy, Solomon KY 4th Mtd.Inf. Co.H Cpl.
Tracy, T. LA Mil. Fire Bn. Co.B QM
Tracy, T.A. TN 8th (Smith's) Cav. Co.D
Tracy, Taylor KY 11th Cav. Co.C 2nd Lt.
Tracy, Taylor KY 7th Mtd.Inf. Co.C
Tracy, Thomas LA Inf. 1st Sp.Bn. (Wheat's) Co.C
Tracy, Thomas MO 5th Cav. Co.G
Tracy, Thomas MO Inf. 3rd Regt.St.Guard Co.F 3rd Lt.
Tracy, Thomas SC 1st Arty. Co.D Artif.
Tracy, Thomas TN 11th Inf. Co.G
Tracy, Thomas Conf.Lt.Arty. 1st Reg.Btty.
Tracy, Thomas Inf. School of Pract. Powell's Command Powell's Detach.
Tracy, Thomas E. VA Cav. 37th Bn. Co.G
Tracy, Thomas J. MO 5th Inf. Co.I 1st Lt.
Tracy, Tom LA 15th Inf. Co.K Color Sgt.
Tracy, W. TX Inf. Timmons' Regt. Co.D
Tracy, W.E. AR 12th Inf. Co.B
Tracy, William AL 9th Inf. Co.B
Tracy, William GA 36th (Broyles') Inf. Co.D Cpl.
Tracy, William MO 5th Cav. Co.G
Tracy, William MO 5th Inf. Co.I
Tracy, William SC 1st (McCreary's) Inf. Co.K Cpl.
Tracy, William TX 28th Cav. Co.E
Tracy, William TX 8th Inf. Co.F
Tracy, William TX 9th (Nichols') Inf.
Tracy, William TX Waul's Legion Co.F Cpl.

Tracy, William VA 31st Inf. Co.G
Tracy, William A. LA 1st (Nelligan's) Inf. Co.G
Tracy, William H. KY 2nd Mtd.Inf. Co.C
Tracy, William W. SC 18th Inf. Co.A
Tracy, Wilson TX 27th Cav. Co.B
Tracy, Winton B. VA 8th Cav. Co.F 2nd Lt.
Tracy, W. Irvin FL 10th Inf. Co.D
Tradaway, A. LA Mil. Lartigue's Co. (Bienville Guards)
Tradaway, J. LA Mil. Lartigue's Co. (Bienville Guards)
Tradenick, Nicholas P. NC 13th Inf. Co.B
Trader, --- GA 8th Inf. Co.C
Trader, A.W. KY 10th (Johnson's) Cav. New Co.B,C
Trader, Benjamin GA 10th Inf. Co.K
Trader, D.C. TN Inf. 3rd Bn. Co.A
Trader, George GA Inf. 1st Loc.Troops (Augusta) Co.E
Trader, George VA 9th Inf. Co.B
Trader, George VA 55th Inf. Co.H Cpl.
Trader, George W. NC 2nd Inf. Co.I
Trader, H.C. Gen. & Staff Capt.,Comsy.
Trader, Henry G. NC Lt.Arty. 3rd Bn. Capt.,AQM
Trader, Henry G. NC 8th Inf. Capt.
Trader, H.G. Gen. & Staff Capt.,AQM
Trader, J. GA 8th Inf. Co.C
Trader, James GA Inf. 3rd Bn. Co.H
Trader, James MS 22nd Inf. Co.I
Trader, James VA 109th Mil. 1st Co.A
Trader, James D. VA 55th Inf. Co.I
Trader, James D. VA 109th Mil. Co.B, 2nd Co.A
Trader, James H. VA 20th Cav. Co.H
Trader, James H. VA 39th Inf. Co.H
Trader, James H. VA 46th Inf. 4th Co.F
Trader, James H. VA 55th Inf. Co.H
Trader, James M. MS 9th Inf. New Co.E Sgt.
Trader, James M. MS 10th Inf. Old Co.C Cpl.
Trader, J.D.C. GA 3rd Inf. Co.I
Trader, John VA 55th Inf. Co.H
Trader, Josephus VA 26th Inf. Co.D
Trader, Leonard H. VA 55th Inf. Co.C Cpl.
Trader, R.E. GA Inf. (RR Guards) Preston's Co. Cpl.
Trader, Richard A. VA 55th Inf. Co.H
Trader, Thomas G. VA 55th Inf. Co.I Sgt.
Trader, Thomas G. VA 109th Mil. Co.B, 2nd Co.A Cpl.
Trader, Thomas W. VA 24th Cav. Co.D
Trader, Thomas W. VA Cav. 40th Bn. Co.D
Trader, William H. AR 5th Inf. Co.A Capt.
Trader, William J. VA 39th Inf. Co.E
Trader, William J. VA 46th Inf. 4th Co.F
Trader, William N. VA 26th Inf. Co.D
Trader, W.W. MO 11th Inf. Co.E
Traderhopf, G.N. NC Walker's Bn. Thomas' Legion
Tradewell, A.G. NC Troops Second Class Dr.M.
Tradewell, A.G. SC 7th Cav. Co.D Sgt.
Tradewell, A.G. SC Cav.Bn. Holcombe Legion Co.B Sgt.
Tradewell, F.A. SC Inf. 3rd Bn. Co.F
Tradewell, F.A. SC 4th St.Troops Co.D 1st Sgt.
Tradewell, F.A. SC 5th Bn.Res. Co.F 2nd Lt.
Tradewell, James W. SC Cav.Bn. Holcombe Legion Co.E
Tradewell, J.W. SC 7th Cav. Co.H
Tradewell, William FL 1st Inf. Old Co.A
Tradewell, William MS Cav. Powers' Regt. Co.G 1st Sgt.
Tradine, A.R. LA 3rd (Wingfield's) Cav. Co.D
Tradwell, John C. MS 25th Inf. Co.A Cpl.
Trady, O.C. GA 4th Inf.
Traelay, J.P. LA 6th Cav. Co.B
Traffanstadt, William A. NC 5th Cav. (63rd St.Troops) Co.K
Traffensteadt, Reuben NC 57th Inf. Co.E
Traffensted, John 3rd Conf.Cav. Co.I
Traffenstedt, Absalom NC 49th Inf. Co.I
Traffenstedt, Daniel NC 49th Inf. Co.I
Traffenstedt, J.M. 3rd Conf.Cav. Co.I
Traffenstedt, Joseph NC 57th Inf. Co.B
Traffenstedt, Levi NC 46th Inf. Co.K
Traffenstedt, Noah NC 49th Inf. Co.I
Traffenstedt, Peter NC 38th Inf. Co.F
Traffenstedt, William NC 38th Inf. Co.F Cpl.
Trafick, A.M. AR 10th Inf. 2nd Lt.
Trafinsted, Joseph H. NC 25th Inf. Co.H
Trafton, Albert C. MO 1st Inf. Co.B
Trafton, B.E. TX 12th Cav. Co.A
Trafton, John NC 17th Inf. (1st Org.) Co.E
Trafton, L.W. KY 10th (Johnson's) Cav. New Co.H Adj.
Trafton, L.W. Gen. & Staff AQM
Trafton, M. TX 12th Cav. Co.A
Trafton, Phillip NC 32nd Inf. Co.I
Trafton, Samuel L. TX 31st Cav. Co.D Cpl.
Trafton, Thomas B. NC 32nd Inf. Co.I
Trager, B.J. TN 12th Cav. Co.G
Trager, Michael LA 2nd Inf. Co.I
Tragine, J.P. TN 8th Inf. Co.A
Tragle, William LA Mil. 4th Regt. 3rd Brig. 1st Div. Co.C
Tragler, W.C.T. AL 23rd Inf. Co.F
Traham, James LA Inf. 16th Bn. (Conf.Guards Resp.Bn.)
Traham, Onizine LA 7th Cav. Co.D
Trahan, A. LA 26th Inf. Co.A
Trahan, Belonie LA 26th Inf. Co.A
Trahan, Camille TX 11th (Spaight's) Bn.Vol. Co.E
Trahan, D. LA Inf.Cons. 18th Regt. & Yellow Jacket Bn. Co.E
Trahan, D. LA 26th Inf. Co.A
Trahan, Don Louis LA Conscr.
Trahan, Doris TX Cav. Waller's Regt. Co.A
Trahan, Dorsoles LA 18th Inf. Co.D
Trahan, E. LA 4th Inf. Co.F
Trahan, E. LA Inf.Cons. 18th Regt. & Yellow Jacket Bn. Co.E
Trahan, E. TX 21st Inf. Co.B
Trahan, Emile LA 18th Inf. Co.D
Trahan, Eugene LA 1st Hvy.Arty. (Reg.) Co.D
Trahan, F. LA 7th Cav. Co.D
Trahan, Francois F. LA Conscr.
Trahan, G.H. LA 2nd Res.Corps Co.K
Trahan, H. LA 2nd Res.Corps Co.A
Trahan, H. LA Miles' Legion Co.E
Trahan, Henriart LA 26th Inf. Co.E
Trahan, J. LA 4th Inf. Co.F
Trahan, J.E. LA 4th Inf. Co.F
Trahan, Jean LA 10th Inf. Co.K
Trahan, John LA Mtd.Part.Rangers Bond's Co.
Trahan, Joseph LA 7th Cav. Co.D
Trahan, Joseph LA Mtd.Part.Rangers Bond's Co. Cpl.
Trahan, Joseph LA 8th Inf. Co.C
Trahan, Joseph LA 18th Inf. Co.G
Trahan, Joseph LA 30th Inf. Co.E
Trahan, Julian LA Inf.Cons. 18th Regt. & Yellow Jacket Bn. Co.A
Trahan, Lastie LA Inf. Weatherly's Bn. Co.E
Trahan, Lawrence LA 1st Hvy.Arty. (Reg.) Co.D
Trahan, Leo TX 11th (Spaight's) Bn.Vol. Co.E
Trahan, Martial LA 2nd Res.Corps Co.K
Trahan, Martin LA 7th Cav. Co.C
Trahan, Maximillien LA 26th Inf. Co.A
Trahan, Maximillien LA 2nd Res.Corps Co.K
Trahan, Maximillion LA 2nd Res.Corps Co.D
Trahan, M. Seville LA 26th Inf. Co.H Sgt.
Trahan, O. LA Inf. 10th Bn. Co.F
Trahan, O. TX 21st Inf. Co.B
Trahan, Onesiphere LA 26th Inf. Co.H
Trahan, O.P. LA Inf.Cons. 18th Regt. & Yellow Jacket Bn. Co.K
Trahan, Oscar TX 11th (Spaight's) Bn.Vol. Co.E
Trahan, Ozan TX Cav. Ragsdale's Bn. Co.A
Trahan, Ozeine LA 26th Inf. Co.H
Trahan, P. LA Inf.Cons. 18th Regt. & Yellow Jacket Bn. Co.E
Trahan, P. LA Inf.Cons. 18th Regt. & Yellow Jacket Bn. Co.I
Trahan, P. TX 11th (Spaight's) Bn.Vol. Co.E
Trahan, Paulin LA Conscr.
Trahan, Pierre LA 18th Inf. Co.F
Trahan, Pierre M. LA 26th Inf. Co.E
Trahan, Placide LA 18th Inf. Co.K
Trahan, P.O. LA Mtd.Part.Rangers Bond's Co.
Trahan, Remond LA 26th Inf. Co.E
Trahan, T. LA 4th Inf. Co.F
Trahan, Theogene LA 1st Hvy.Arty. (Reg.) Co.I
Trahan, Therence LA 18th Inf. Co.K
Trahan, Ursin LA 18th Inf. Co.E
Trahan, V. LA Inf. 10th Bn. Co.E Cpl.
Trahan, V. LA Inf.Cons. 18th Regt. & Yellow Jacket Bn. Co.E,D Cpl.
Trahan, W. LA 7th Cav. Co.C
Trahand, Ferdinand LA 18th Inf. Co.G
Trahand, Ferdinand LA Inf.Cons. 18th Regt. & Yellow Jacket Bn. Co.G
Trahant, C. LA Inf.Cons. 18th Regt. & Yellow Jacket Bn. Co.C
Trahant, Ceolvide LA 18th Inf. Co.A
Trahant, J.B. LA 18th Inf. Co.D
Trahant, Martial LA Inf. 1st Sp.Bn. (Rightor's) Co.E
Trahant, Prudent LA 18th Inf. Co.D
Trahant, S. LA 18th Inf. Co.A
Trahant, Victor LA 18th Inf. Co.D
Trahern, W.E. VA Loc.Def. Durrett's Co.
Trahern, William E. LA 6th Inf. Co.I Cpl.
Trahin, Joseph E. MO 3rd Cav. Co.K Capt.
Trahin, T.J. GA 10th Inf. Co.C Cpl.
Trahn, John LA 18th Inf. Co.G
Trahn, Joseph LA 7th Cav. Co.B
Trahn, L. LA 18th Inf. Co.I

Trahn, L. LA Inf.Cons. 18th Regt. & Yellow Jacket Bn. Co.I
Trahn, O. LA Inf. Weatherly's Bn. Co.A
Trahon, Honore LA Res.Corps Co.E
Trahon, Joseph LA Inf.Cons. 18th Regt. & Yellow Jacket Bn. Co.D
Trahon, Sarazin LA Inf.Cons. 18th Regt. & Yellow Jacket Bn. Co.A
Trahorn, A. TX 11th (Spaight's) Bn.Vol. Co.C,B
Trahorn, A. TX 13th Vol. 4th Co.I
Traigre, Nicholas A. LA 7th Inf. Co.B
Traiham, Nimrod AL 16th Inf. Co.E
Trail, A.J. TN Inf. 4th Cons.Regt. Co.E
Trail, Barton VA 17th Cav. Co.H
Trail, Beverly L. AL 6th Inf. Co.K
Trail, Beverly L. VA Lt.Arty. W.P. Carter's Co.
Trail, B.L. VA Inf. 1st Bn.Loc.Def. Co.F
Trail, Charles H. VA 1st Inf. Chamber's Co.
Trail, Charles H. VA 2nd Inf. Co.K
Trail, Charles M. MD Inf. 2nd Bn. Co.A
Trail, Charles R. TN 29th Inf. Co.D
Trail, Creed V. VA 57th Inf. Co.C
Trail, D. AR 1st (Dobbin's) Cav. Co.B
Trail, Daniel VA 57th Inf. Co.C
Trail, Daniel M. VA 24th Inf. Co.D
Trail, David SC Inf. Holcombe Legion Co.A Cpl.
Trail, David M. FL 7th Inf. Co.F
Trail, Fleming VA 57th Inf. Co.C
Trail, Fleming B. VA Cav. 37th Bn. Co.B
Trail, Franklin D. AL 16th Inf. Co.F
Trail, Friar TN 35th Inf. 2nd Co.K
Trail, Friar TN 41st Inf. Co.F Sgt.
Trail, George J. VA 21st Cav. 2nd Co.G
Trail, G.P. SC Inf. Holcombe Legion Co.A
Trail, Henry NC 5th Cav. (63rd St.Troops)
Trail, Jacob VA 11th Bn.Res. Co.D
Trail, James TN Inf. 1st Bn. (Colms') Co.D
Trail, James VA 50th Inf. Co.E
Trail, James A. TN 26th Inf. Co.D
Trail, James A. TN 29th Inf. Co.D
Trail, John B. AR 1st (Colquitt's) Inf. Co.G
Trail, John B. TN 29th Inf. Co.D Sgt.
Trail, Lewis VA 60th Inf. 2nd Co.H
Trail, Lewis W. MD 1st Cav. Co.D Sgt.
Trail, Lorenzo D. GA 1st Reg. Co.F
Trail, Peter VA Inf. 23rd Bn. Co.E
Trail, Robert MO 11th Inf. Co.E
Trail, Samuel GA 51st Inf. Co.F
Trail, Samuel M. VA 11th Bn.Res. Co.D
Trail, Samuel M. VA 60th Inf. Co.F
Trail, Thomas VA 63rd Inf. Co.A
Trail, Thomas C. VA Cav. 37th Bn. Co.G
Trail, W.C. TN 7th (Duckworth's) Cav. Co.L
Trail, William MO 1st Inf. Co.C
Trail, William F. MO 1st Inf. Co.G
Trail, William H. TN 41st Inf. Co.F
Trail, William V. VA 57th Inf. Co.C
Traile, David C. AR 18th Inf. Co.G
Trailer, Enos AR 35th Inf. Old Co.F
Trailer, I. MS Cav. 2nd Bn.Res. Co.B Sgt.
Trailer, J.B. NC 3rd Inf. Co.C
Trailer, J.J. Bradford's Corps Scouts & Guards Co.B
Trailer, John AL Cp. of Instr. Talladega
Trailer, John Judson MS 16th Inf. Co.F
Trailer, Joseph VA 6th Inf. Weisiger's Co.
Trailer, Richard AL 12th Inf. Co.C
Trailer, T.P. VA 23rd Cav. Co.F
Trailer, W. TN 3rd (Forrest's) Cav. Co.H
Trailor, --- TX Cav. Mann's Bn. Cox's Co.
Trailor, H.H. TN 4th Inf. Co.I
Trailor, J.T. MS 8th Cav. Co.I
Trailor, W.A. KY 1st (Butler's) Cav. Co.E
Traimum, George AL 1st Bn. Hilliard's Legion Vol. Co.B
Train, A.J. SC 2nd Inf. Co.F
Train, George W. LA 1st Hvy.Arty. (Reg.) Co.H 1st Sgt.
Train, H. LA 22nd Inf. Co.B
Train, H. LA Mil. Orleans Guards Regt. Co.H
Train, Henry LA 1st Cav. Co.D
Train, H.F. SC 1st Mtd.Mil. Kirk's Co.
Train, Jules LA 1st Cav. Co.D
Train, Jules LA Mil. Orleans Guards Regt. Co.H Cpl.
Train, Marcus C. MO St.Guards 1st Bn. Lt.
Trainam, A.J. SC 2nd Cav. Co.F
Trainem, Joseph AL 17th Inf. Co.C
Trainer, Alferd TN 10th Inf. Co.F
Trainer, Arthur NC 2nd Inf. Co.A
Trainer, Arthur NC 61st Inf. Co.G
Trainer, Barney VA Lt.Arty. Woolfolk's Co.
Trainer, Bennett M. MS 9th Inf. Old Co.G Music.
Trainer, Bernard VA 1st Inf. Chamber's Co.
Trainer, Bernard J. VA Lt.Arty. Parker's Co.
Trainer, B.F. VA 60th Inf. Co.A
Trainer, B.J. VA 2nd St.Res. Co.A
Trainer, Burnet VA 56th Inf. Co.C
Trainer, Charles LA 1st Hvy.Arty. (Reg.) Co.C
Trainer, David J. TX 15th Cav. Co.A
Trainer, Francis A. VA 51st Inf. Co.C
Trainer, Franklin VA 5th Inf. Co.H
Trainer, George W. VA 52nd Inf. Co.C
Trainer, Henry MO 6th Cav. Co.B,D
Trainer, J. LA Mil. 3rd Regt. 3rd Brig. 1st Div. Co.G
Trainer, James GA 19th Inf. Co.B
Trainer, James LA 30th Inf. Co.C
Trainer, James Conf.Lt.Arty. 1st Reg.Btty.
Trainer, James K. VA 36th Inf. Co.F
Trainer, James M. TX 3rd Inf. Co.I Capt.
Trainer, James M. VA 5th Inf. Co.G
Trainer, Jehu VA 25th Inf. 2nd Co.F Ord.Sgt.
Trainer, J.H. MS Lt.Arty. 14th Bn. Co.B
Trainer, John A. VA 5th Inf. Co.G
Trainer, Michael TN 19th Inf. Co.E
Trainer, Morgan B. VA 25th Inf. 2nd Co.F
Trainer, Morgan B. VA 162nd Mil. Co.C
Trainer, Samuel TX 15th Cav. Co.D
Trainer, Samuel E. TX 15th Cav. Co.A
Trainer, Thomas GA Inf. 23rd Bn.Loc.Def. Co.B
Trainer, Thomas LA 14th Inf. Co.F
Trainer, Thomas MS 28th Cav. Co.A
Trainer, Thomas MS 1st Lt.Arty. Co.G
Trainer, Thomas MS 16th Inf. Co.G
Trainer, Thomas C. GA Lt.Arty. (Jo Thompson Arty.) Hanleiter's Co.
Trainer, Thomas C. GA 38th Inf. Co.M Sgt.
Trainer, Wiley AR 1st Mtd.Rifles Co.A
Trainer, William AL 18th Inf. Co.D
Trainer, William SC 4th Cav. Co.D
Trainer, William SC 1st Arty. Co.E
Trainer, William VA Horse Arty. McClanahan's Co.
Trainer, William A. VA 25th Inf. 2nd Co.F
Trainer, William A. VA 162nd Mil. Co.C
Trainer, William F. GA Inf. 1st Loc.Troops (Augusta) Co.H
Trainer, William R. TX 3rd Inf. Co.I Sgt.
Trainer, William T. MS 14th Inf. Co.F
Trainer, W.R. TX Inf. Cunningham's Co.
Trainham, Andrew J. VA 56th Inf. Co.F
Trainham, Christopher C. VA 56th Inf. Co.F Hosp.Stew.
Trainham, David C. VA 56th Inf. Co.C
Trainham, Elias S. VA 13th Inf. Co.C 1st Lt.
Trainham, F.G. MS 2nd Cav. Co.I
Trainham, F.G. MS 1st (Patton's) Inf. Co.B
Trainham, J.B. Conf.Lt.Arty. Richardson's Bn. Co.A
Trainham, J.H. TN 9th Inf. Co.K
Trainham, John SC 3rd Res. Co.K
Trainham, John M. VA 44th Inf. Co.D
Trainham, John W. VA Hvy.Arty. 10th Bn. Co.C
Trainham, John W.T. SC 6th Cav. Co.K
Trainham, L.D. VA 12th Inf. Co.D
Trainham, W.H. VA 2nd St.Res. Co.G
Trainham, W.T. TN 15th (Cons.) Cav. Co.G
Trainnum, Benjamin J. VA Lt.Arty. Taylor's Co.
Trainnum, Charles H. VA Lt.Arty. Taylor's Co.
Trainor, Arthur NC 3rd Arty. (40th St.Troops) Co.H
Trainor, Bernard TN 2nd (Robison's) Inf. Co.E
Trainor, Bernard VA 2nd Inf. Co.K
Trainor, E. MD Cav. 2nd Bn.
Trainor, George E.N.H. GA 30th Inf. Co.F
Trainor, George W. MS 15th Inf. Co.B
Trainor, G.W. MS 4th Inf. Co.E
Trainor, Henry LA 25th Inf. Co.A
Trainor, James LA 20th Inf. Co.G
Trainor, James LA Herrick's Co. (Orleans Blues)
Trainor, James H. MO Thompson's Command
Trainor, John LA 13th Inf. Co.H
Trainor, John LA 20th Inf. Co.H 2nd Lt.
Trainor, John TX 5th Inf. Co.B
Trainor, John O. LA 6th Inf. Co.C Sgt.
Trainor, Michael LA 14th Inf. Co.H
Trainor, Patrick AL 24th Inf. Co.B Cpl.
Trainor, Patrick MS 18th Cav. Co.K
Trainor, William T. MS 15th Inf. Co.B
Trainum, A.J. SC Cav. 4th Bn. Co.A
Trainum, A.S. VA 1st St.Res. Co.D
Trainum, Benjamin J. VA Lt.Arty. 12th Bn. Co.C
Trainum, Charles VA 21st Inf. Co.F
Trainum, Charles H. VA Lt.Arty. 12th Bn. Co.C
Trainum, Charles L. VA 55th Inf.
Trainum, David C. VA Prov.Guard Avis' Co.
Trainum, Edward C. VA 15th Inf. Co.A
Trainum, Garland A. VA Lt.Arty. 12th Bn. Co.C
Trainum, H.C. VA 82nd Mil. Co.D
Trainum, James F. AL 17th Inf. Co.C
Trainum, Jeremiah SC 3rd Res. Co.H
Trainum, J.W. AL 5th Inf. New Co.F
Trainum, Levi VA 5th Inf. Co.G,K
Trainum, Mathew L. VA 14th Inf. Co.E
Trainum, Samuel AL 5th Inf. New Co.F
Trainum, T.H. MS Cav. 3rd Bn.Res. Co.B

Trainum, William T. AL Arty. 4th Bn. Hilliard's Legion Co.A,D
Trainum, W.G. AL 59th Inf. Co.H
Traisurra, Manuel LA Mil. 5th Regt.Eur.Brig. (Spanish Regt.) Co.7
Trait, Isaac VA Cav. Hounshell's Bn. Huffman's Co.
Traitwick, J.T. AL 15th Inf. Co.M,L
Traker, Steph VA Mil. Wythe Cty.
Trakin, O. LA Miles' Legion Co.E
Trale, William TN 12th (Green's) Cav. Co.I
Tralere, J.E. MS Inf. 2nd St.Troops Co.D
Traley, Thomas D. NC 4th Sr.Res. Co.B
Trall, J.A. MS Inf. 3rd Bn. (St.Troops) Co.F
Trall, L. AL 26th Inf. Co.I
Trall, L. LA Mil. 3rd Regt. 3rd Brig. 1st Div. Co.C
Trallace, E.B. GA 27th Inf. Co.C
Trallar, Faustine MO 6th Inf. Co.I
Traller, Faustin MO Lt.Arty. 1st Btty. Artif.
Trallinger, E.H. AR Cav. Gordon's Regt. Co.F
Tralor, B.H. TX Cav. 2nd Regt.St.Troops Co.C Cpl.
Tralor, Megarnine 10th Conf.Cav. Co.B
Tralor, Murph. B. 10th Conf.Cav. Co.B
Traly, Samuel H. AR 45th Res.Corps
Tramall, Augustus GA 1st (Olmstead's) Inf. Co.B
Trambell, Thomas TN 35th Inf. Co.L
Tramel, A.B. LA Inf. Jeff Davis Regt. Co.J Cpl.
Tramel, C. SC 3rd Bn.Res. Co.A
Tramel, Dawson AL 1st Inf. Co.I
Tramel, Dennis AR 2nd Cav.
Tramel, Edward A. AL 45th Inf. Co.K
Tramel, Franklin AL 19th Inf. Co.F
Tramel, Harry T. AL 18th Inf. Co.L
Tramel, John AL Cav. Moreland's Regt. Co.H
Tramel, John GA 11th Inf. Co.B
Tramel, John M. GA 22nd Inf. Co.F
Tramel, Joseph F. MS 42nd Inf. Co.F
Tramel, Joshua C. TN Cav. Allison's Squad. Co.B
Tramel, J.R. AR Cav. Gordon's Regt. Co.I
Tramel, L. LA 3rd Inf. Co.E
Tramel, M.J. GA 40th Inf. Co.E
Tramel, Peter AR 19th (Dawson's) Inf. Co.E
Tramel, P.L. SC 1st (Hagood's) Inf. 2nd Co.F
Tramel, Thomas J. LA Inf. 11th Bn. Co.E
Tramel, Thomas W. MS 42nd Inf. Co.F
Tramel, W.C. LA 28th (Gray's) Inf. Co.H
Tramel, William AL 53rd (Part.Rangers) Co.F
Tramel, William TN 38th Inf. 2nd Co.K
Tramel, Wilson SC 1st St.Troops Co.H
Tramell, A.J. AR 12th Inf. Co.F Cpl.
Tramell, C.C. TN 50th Inf. Co.C
Tramell, Craven NC 62nd Inf. Co.K
Tramell, David AL 30th Inf. Co.C
Tramell, Derias NC 64th Inf. Co.N
Tramell, George VA 8th Inf. Co.G
Tramell, J.C. AL Cav. Moreland's Regt. Co.H
Tramell, John TN Inf. 22nd Bn. Co.K
Tramell, John R. GA 4th Inf. Co.D
Tramell, Marshall MS 10th Inf. New Co.F
Tramell, Nathan A. VA 48th Inf. Co.I
Tramell, Phillip VA Cav. Mosby's Regt. (Part.Rangers) Co.B
Tramell, Pulaski AL 6th Cav. Co.C
Tramell, Thomas TN 36th Inf. Co.L
Tramer, George TX 2nd Cav.
Tramil, A.F. AL 34th Inf. Co.D
Tramil, D.H. GA Cav. 22nd Bn. (St.Guards) Co.F
Tramil, R. AL 34th Inf.
Tramil, Selcurk TN 14th Inf. Co.K
Tramill, Shadie C. AL 24th Inf. Co.D 2nd Lt.
Tramill, Shadie C. AL 28th Inf. Co.A
Trammel, A.B. AR 27th Inf. Co.E
Trammel, A.B. LA 17th Inf. Co.B
Trammel, Albert O. GA 8th Inf. (St.Guards) Co.F Cpl.
Trammel, Alexander MO 10th Inf. Co.E Capt.
Trammel, Alexander SC 4th Inf. Co.F
Trammel, Andrew J. VA 57th Inf. Co.I
Trammel, B.E.W. SC Palmetto S.S. Co.I
Trammel, B.F. GA 11th Cav. Co.B,C
Trammel, C.H. GA 8th Inf. Co.K
Trammel, Daniel M. AL 29th Inf. Co.K
Trammel, David M. VA 14th Inf. Co.H
Trammel, Dennis TN 2nd (Smith's) Cav.
Trammel, D.H. GA Cav. 19th Bn. Co.B Sgt.
Trammel, D.Mc. MS 43rd Inf. Co.F
Trammel, Ed.W. AL 1st Regt.Conscr. Co.C
Trammel, Frank AR 17th (Griffith's) Inf. Co.B 1st Lt.
Trammel, G. AL 1st Cav. Co.E
Trammel, H. GA 30th Inf. Co.B
Trammel, Horton MO Inf. Clark's Regt. Co.D
Trammel, Horton Conf.Cav. Clarkson's Bn. Ind.Rangers Co.B
Trammel, Isaac TN 16th Inf. Co.H
Trammel, J. AL Inf. 2nd Regt.
Trammel, Jacob H. GA 11th Cav. Co.E
Trammel, Jacob V. NC 6th Cav. (65th St.Troops) Co.A
Trammel, Jacob V. NC Cav. 7th Bn. Co.A
Trammel, James NC 49th Inf. Co.K
Trammel, James M. AL Cav. 5th Bn. Hilliard's Legion Co.A
Trammel, James W. GA 62nd Cav. Co.A
Trammel, James W. GA 9th Inf. Co.G
Trammel, Jerry, Sr. SC 22nd Inf. Co.H
Trammel, J.F. AL 12th Inf. Co.E
Trammel, J. Felix AL 30th Inf. Co.C
Trammel, J.J. TX Cav. Waller's Regt. Goode's Co. Jr.2nd Lt.
Trammel, John B. MO 5th Inf. Co.B Cpl.
Trammel, John H. AL 29th Inf. Co.K,D 2nd Lt.
Trammel, John T. AR 15th (N.W.) Inf. Co.A
Trammel, John W. AL 16th Inf. Co.C
Trammel, J.T. AL 30th Inf. Co.C
Trammel, J.T. GA 5th Inf. (St.Guards) Allums' Co.
Trammel, J.Y. AL 4th Res. Co.E
Trammel, Kennedy MO 8th Cav. Co.C
Trammel, L. Brush Bn.
Trammel, Merideth TN 61st Mtd.Inf. Co.D
Trammel, Nevel GA 11th Cav. Co.B,C
Trammel, N.Y. TX Waul's Legion Co.B
Trammel, P. TX 23rd Cav. Co.D
Trammel, Peter AR Hardy's Regt. Co.K
Trammel, Peter GA Cav. Corbin's Co.
Trammel, Phillip VA 2nd Cav. Co.H
Trammel, Samuel NC 49th Inf. Co.K
Trammel, Thomas NC 49th Inf. Co.K
Trammel, Thomas Gen. of Staff, A. of N.VA Capt.,AQM
Trammel, Thomas O. SC 2nd Rifles Co.H
Trammel, W.H. GA 31st Inf. Co.A
Trammel, W.H. SC 1st (McCreary's) Inf. Co.H
Trammel, William MS 25th Inf. Co.B
Trammel, William SC 5th St.Troops Co.H
Trammel, William SC 9th Res. Co.I
Trammel, William VA Cav. Mosby's Regt. (Part.Rangers) Co.A
Trammel, William 2nd Conf.Inf. Co.B
Trammel, W.J. TX 22nd Inf. Co.I
Trammel, W.M. Gen. & Staff AASurg.
Trammell, A. SC 22nd Inf. Co.H
Trammell, A. SC Inf. Hampton Legion Co.K Sgt.
Trammell, A.A. GA 5th Inf. (St.Guards) Johnston's Co.
Trammell, A.D. GA 5th Inf. (St.Guards) Johnston's Co.
Trammell, Adrian O. NC Inf. 2nd Bn. Co.E
Trammell, A.J. GA 28th Inf. Co.G
Trammell, Alex SC Inf. 13th Bn. Co.D
Trammell, Augustus 1st Conf.Inf. Co.B
Trammell, Benjamin F. MS 2nd Inf. Co.K
Trammell, Benjamin P. SC 4th Inf. Co.F
Trammell, B.F. SC 1st (Hagood's) Inf. 2nd Co.F
Trammell, B.P. SC Inf. 13th Bn. Co.D
Trammell, B.P. SC 22nd Inf. Co.H Cpl.
Trammell, B.P. SC Inf. Hampton Legion Co.K
Trammell, Chas. H. GA Conscr.
Trammell, Charles M. 1st Conf.Inf. Co.B Cpl.
Trammell, Clabourn P. SC 4th Inf. Co.F
Trammell, C.M. TX 10th Cav. Co.G Capt.
Trammell, C.P. SC Inf. 13th Bn. Co.D
Trammell, C.P. SC 16th Inf. Co.K Cpl.
Trammell, C.P. SC 16th & 24th (Cons.) Inf. Co.B Cpl.
Trammell, C.P. SC Inf. Hampton Legion Co.K
Trammell, Cullen A. GA 21st Inf. Co.I
Trammell, D. AL 34th Inf. Co.K
Trammell, D. FL 11th Inf. Co.C
Trammell, David AL 63rd Inf. Co.A
Trammell, David GA Inf. 9th Bn. Co.E
Trammell, David GA 37th Inf. Co.H
Trammell, David C. AR 1st (Crawford's) Cav. Co.A
Trammell, Dawson MS 44th Inf. Co.I
Trammell, D.C. TN 1st Hvy.Arty. Co.A
Trammell, Dennis AR 1st (Crawford's) Cav. Co.A
Trammell, Dennis M. AL 58th Inf. Co.F
Trammell, D.H. 10th Conf.Cav. Co.G
Trammell, Dillard M. MO 6th Div.St.Guards Asst.Comsy. of Subs.
Trammell, D.J. TX 15th Cav. Co.E
Trammell, D.L. MS 10th Inf. Co.B
Trammell, D.O. GA 3rd Res. Co.F
Trammell, Dock W. 1st Conf.Inf. Co.B Cpl.
Trammell, E.C. GA 53rd Inf. Co.K
Trammell, E.D. AR Res.Corps
Trammell, Elias E. TX 16th Cav. Co.F Cpl.
Trammell, Elisha S. GA Phillips' Legion Co.D
Trammell, Erastus V. TX 27th Cav. Co.G
Trammell, E.S. GA 1st Cav. Co.B
Trammell, F.B. SC Inf. 13th Bn. Co.D
Trammell, F.B. SC 22nd Inf. Co.H

Trammell, F.B. SC Inf. Hampton Legion Co.K Cpl.
Trammell, Fleming SC 16th Inf. Co.H
Trammell, Fleming B. SC 4th Inf. Co.F
Trammell, F.M. AR 1st (Crawford's) Cav. Co.A
Trammell, Frank E. AR 11th & 17th Cons.Inf. Co.I 1st Lt.
Trammell, G. AR 34th Inf. Co.K
Trammell, G. AR Inf. 8th Bn. Co.C
Trammell, G.A. 1st Conf.Inf. Co.B
Trammell, George W. AR 25th Inf. Co.F
Trammell, George W. TX 10th Cav. Co.G Cpl.
Trammell, Granville W. VA 18th Inf. Co.I
Trammell, G.W. LA 26th Inf. Co.G
Trammell, H. GA 30th Inf. Co.A
Trammell, Harrison AL 22nd Inf. Co.K
Trammell, H.C. TX 9th (Young's) Inf. Co.D
Trammell, Henry 1st Conf.Inf. Co.B
Trammell, H.M. TX 8th Cav. Co.E
Trammell, H.S. AR 35th Inf. Co.K
Trammell, Isaac F. NC Inf. 2nd Bn. Co.H
Trammell, Isaac L. GA 11th Inf. Co.E
Trammell, Jackson P. GA 44th Inf. Co.D
Trammell, Jacob L. GA 1st Reg. Co.H Cpl.
Trammell, James A. LA 12th Inf. Co.B
Trammell, James M. GA Siege Arty. 28th Bn. Co.E
Trammell, James R. NC 25th Inf. Co.E
Trammell, Jasper J. GA 36th (Broyles') Inf. Co.G Capt.
Trammell, J.B. SC Lt.Arty. 3rd (Palmetto) Bn. Co.I
Trammell, J.D. AR 34th Inf. Co.G Sgt.
Trammell, J.D. TN 35th Inf. Co.E Sgt.
Trammell, J.E. GA 65th Inf. Co.B
Trammell, J.E. GA Smith's Legion Co.C Cpl.
Trammell, Jerry, Jr. SC 22nd Inf. Co.H
Trammell, J.H. AR 1st (Crawford's) Cav. Co.A
Trammell, J.H. GA 11th Inf. Co.E
Trammell, J.J. AL 48th Inf. Co.H
Trammell, J.J. TX Loc.Def.Troops McNeel's Co. (McNeel Coast Guards)
Trammell, John AL Arty. 1st Bn. Co.A,D
Trammell, John AR 34th Inf. Co.G
Trammell, John TX 22nd Cav. Co.D
Trammell, John VA Cav. 35th Bn. Co.A
Trammell, John A. GA 21st Inf. Co.I
Trammell, John B. GA 2nd Inf. Co.E 2nd Lt.
Trammell, John E. VA 8th Inf. Co.G
Trammell, John H. AL Inf. 1st Regt. Co.F
Trammell, John J. LA 9th Inf. Co.A
Trammell, John J. LA 12th Inf. Co.B
Trammell, John M. AL 37th Inf. Co.B 2nd Lt.
Trammell, John V. AL 6th Inf. Co.L
Trammell, John W. GA 1st Cav. Co.B Capt.
Trammell, John W. KY 2nd Cav. Co.D
Trammell, John W. TX 15th Cav. Co.I Sgt.
Trammell, Joseph M. AR 10th (Witt's) Cav.
Trammell, J.R. AR 34th Inf. Co.G
Trammell, J.R. AR 51st Mil. Co.G
Trammell, J.R. GA 5th Inf. (St.Guards) Johnston's Co.
Trammell, J.T. TX 13th Vol. 2nd Co.G
Trammell, J.W. GA 8th Cav. Co.A
Trammell, J.W. GA 64th Inf. Co.A Cpl.
Trammell, L.B. VA Cav. Mosby's Regt. (Part.Rangers) Co.A
Trammell, L.D. AL 51st (Part.Rangers) Co.F
Trammell, Levi GA 36th (Villepigue's) Inf. Co.B
Trammell, Levi 1st Conf.Inf. Co.B
Trammell, L.N. GA 39th Inf. QM
Trammell, L.N. Gen. & Staff Capt.,AQM
Trammell, M.C. TX 19th Inf. Co.K
Trammell, Mercer M. GA 24th Inf. Co.G Capt.
Trammell, Milton H. GA 42nd Inf. Co.C 2nd Lt.
Trammell, Montraville P. NC 25th Inf. Co.E
Trammell, M.P. NC Inf. 2nd Bn. Co.H
Trammell, R.E. TX 8th Cav. Co.E
Trammell, R.J. GA 8th Inf. Co.D 1st Lt.
Trammell, Robert GA 1st Cav. Co.D Capt.
Trammell, Shadrick TN 35th Inf. Co.E
Trammell, T.B. MS 1st Cav. Co.A
Trammell, Thomas AL 47th Inf. Co.E
Trammell, Thomas LA 8th Inf. Co.G
Trammell, Thomas H. GA 30th Inf.
Trammell, Thomas J. AL Cav. Lewis' Bn. Co.E Sgt.
Trammell, Thomas J. GA 30th Inf. Co.B
Trammell, Thomas M. KY 6th Mtd.Inf. Co.F
Trammell, Thomas R. GA 2nd Inf. Co.E
Trammell, Thomas R. GA 11th Inf. Co.E Capt.
Trammell, T.J. AL Cp. of Instr. Talladega
Trammell, T.J. SC 16th Inf. Co.H
Trammell, T.J. TX 10th Cav. Co.G
Trammell, Van B. 1st Conf.Inf. Co.B
Trammell, W.B. NC 32nd Inf. Co.B
Trammell, W.C. AR 1st (Monroe's) Cav. Co.B
Trammell, W.C. SC Inf. 13th Bn. Co.D
Trammell, W.C. SC Inf. Hampton Legion Co.K
Trammell, W.F. AL 1st Cav. 2nd Co.C Cpl.
Trammell, W.H.H. GA 8th Inf. Co.D
Trammell, William AL 22nd Inf. Co.K
Trammell, William LA 2nd Inf. Co.A
Trammell, William MO 16th Inf. Co.E
Trammell, William A. NC 39th Inf. Co.I
Trammell, William C. SC 4th Inf. Co.F Cpl.
Trammell, William H. TX Waul's Legion Co.C
Trammell, William H. VA 6th Bn.Res. Co.C
Trammell, William M. LA Inf.Cons.Crescent Regt. Co.F
Trammell, William R. AL 39th Inf. Co.F
Trammell, William R. AL 62nd Inf. Co.D
Trammell, William S. LA 31st Inf. Co.E
Trammell, W.P. TX Cav. Baird's Regt. Co.H
Trammell, W.T. GA 3rd Bn. (St.Guards) Co.F
Trammell, Z.B. 8th (Wade's) Conf.Cav. Co.K
Trammill, David C. AR 33rd Inf. Co.C
Trammill, James M. TN 14th Inf. Co.L
Trammill, John AL 11th Inf. Co.K Cpl.
Trammill, Shade C. AL 11th Inf. Co.K
Trammill, W.H. GA Inf. 27th Bn. (NonConscr.) Co.B Cpl.
Trammon, John T. AR 36th Inf. Co.G
Tramnel, J. GA 8th Inf. Co.F
Tramp, John GA 18th Inf. Co.K
Trampel, Berry E.W. SC 4th Inf. Co.I
Tramus, Juan TX Cav. Benavides' Regt. Co.C
Tramwell, E.B. NC 45th Inf. Co.I
Tranbarger, David VA 37th Inf. Co.A
Tranbarger, William TN Cav. 12th Bn. (Day's) Co.A
Trance, R. AR Cav. McGehee's Regt. Co.A
Tranchibois, E. LA 2nd Cav. Co.A
Trand, Placide LA Miles' Legion Co.F
Traner, A.J. TX 5th Inf. Co.E Cpl.
Traner, Fleming R. VA 108th Mil. Co.B
Traner, James E. AR 7th Inf. Co.K
Traner, Robert C. VA 11th Bn.Res. Co.B
Trange, R.B. MO Cav. Coffee's Regt. Co.F
Tranham, A.F. VA 59th Inf. Co.H
Tranniz, L. TX Cav. Baird's Regt. Co.F
Tranick, L.W. AL Vol. Goldsmith's Ind.Co.
Tranie, A. NC 23rd Inf.
Tranill, --- AL Cav. Hardie's Bn.Res. D. McClellan's Co.
Trank, August TX Inf. Griffin's Bn. Co.F
Trankle, John N. LA 1st (Strawbridge's) Inf. Co.C
Trannell, J. AL Cav. Hardie's Bn.Res. D. McClellan's Co.
Tranquilino, T. SC 1st Regt. Charleston Guard Co.I
Transmontana, Rosolino LA Mil. 6th Regt. Eur.Brig. (Italian Guards Bn.) Co.2 1st Lt.
Transon, Amos E. NC 52nd Inf. Co.K Sgt.
Transon, Carles NC 33rd Inf. Co.H
Transon, C.E. NC 26th Inf. Music.
Transon, Ed. T. TN 7th (Duckworth's) Cav. Co.F,L
Transon, E.L. NC 9th Bn.S.S. Co.A Music.
Transon, E.L. NC 21st Inf. Co.B Drum.
Transon, J.A. NC 26th Inf. Music.
Transon, Lewis NC 57th Inf. Co.D
Transon, Owen C. NC 21st Inf. Co.K
Transon, Reuben NC 21st Inf. Co.K
Trant, --- TX 4th Inf.
Trant, Edward L. VA Mtd.Res. Rapphannock Dist. Sale's Co.
Trant, George R. VA 10th Cav. Co.G
Trant, John H. VA 9th Cav. Co.H
Trant, R. TX 25th Cav. Smith's Co.
Trant, Richard TX Cav. Waller's Regt. Co.C
Trant, Samuel TX Cav. Madison's Regt. Co.B
Trantham, A. AR 2nd Cav. Co.B
Trantham, A.D. AR 30th Inf. Co.L,A
Trantham, B. MO Cav. Freeman's Regt. Co.K
Trantham, Caleb TN 39th Mtd.Inf. Co.A Drum Maj.
Trantham, Daniel J. NC 42nd Inf. Co.A
Trantham, David A. NC 29th Inf. Co.H
Trantham, David C. MS 1st Lt.Arty. Co.C Cpl.
Trantham, Francis H. NC 54th Inf. Co.A Sgt.
Trantham, George J. MS 33rd Inf. Co.I
Trantham, Green AR 27th Inf. Co.E
Trantham, H. AR 2nd Cav. Co.B
Trantham, H.A. NC 1st Jr.Res. Co.C
Trantham, Ira AR 27th Inf. Co.E
Trantham, J. AR 2nd Cav. Co.B
Trantham, John AR 30th Inf. Co.L,A,F
Trantham, John GA 4th Res. Co.B
Trantham, John NC 11th (Bethel Regt.) Inf. Co.K
Trantham, Joseph NC 11th (Bethel Regt.) Inf. Co.K
Trantham, J.V. NC Inf. Thomas Legion Co.I
Trantham, J.W. AR 5th Inf. Co.H
Trantham, Martin MO 11th Inf. Co.K Cpl.
Trantham, Milton H. MS Lt.Arty. (The Hudson Btty.) Hoole's Co. 2nd Lt.
Trantham, N.J. TN 7th (Duckworth's) Cav. Co.I

Trantham, T.A. AR 5th Inf. Co.E
Trantham, T.H. AR 2nd Vol. Co.B
Trantham, Thomas P. AR 25th Inf. Co.D 1st Sgt.
Trantham, T.P. MO 7th Cav. Co.K
Trantham, W.C. TN 31st Inf. Co.G Sgt.
Trantham, W.D. SC 2nd Inf. Co.G
Trantham, W.D. SC 5th Bn.Res. Co.D
Trantham, William GA 30th Inf. Co.H
Trantham, William P. FL 1st Cav. Co.C
Tranthan, J.F. AR 5th Inf. Co.E
Tranum, Fitz M. Gen. & Staff,PACS 2nd Lt.,Dr.M.
Tranum, Fitzpatrick M. AL 3rd Inf. Co.C
Tranum, Fitzpatrick M. AL Conscr. Echols' Co. 2nd Lt.
Tranum, F.M. AL Cav. Thomas' Regt. Adj.
Tranum, W.T. AL Conscr. & Res.Bn. Co.G 2nd Lt.
Tranun, W.T. Gen. & Staff, Inf. 2nd Lt.
Tranwerk, Robert MS 6th Inf. Co.G
Trapani, F. LA Arty. Guyol's Co. (Orleans Arty.)
Traper, W. VA 13th Cav.
Trapier, B.D. SC 5th Bn.Res. Co.D
Trapier, E.S. SC Lt.Arty. Parker's Co. (Marion Arty.)
Trapier, E.S. SC 2nd Inf. Co.I
Trapier, Jas. H. Gen. & Staff Brig.Gen.
Trapier, Pierre D. 2nd Conf.Eng.Troops Co.F
Trapier, T.D. SC Lt.Arty. Parker's Co. (Marion Arty.)
Trapier, W.H. SC 1st Regt. Charleston Guard Co.H
Trapier, W.W. SC Lt.Arty. Parker's Co. (Marion Arty.)
Trapnall, A. GA Cav. 2nd Bn. Co.C
Trapnall, A. GA 5th Cav. Co.E
Trapnall, J. GA 5th Cav. Co.E
Trapnell, John P. GA 48th Inf. Co.H Cpl.
Trapnell, Joseph MD 1st Cav. Co.D
Trapnell, Joseph VA 7th Cav. Co.G
Trapnell, William W. FL 8th Inf. Co.G Cpl.
Trapp, A.C. GA 56th Inf. Co.I
Trapp, A.D. AL 10th Cav. Co.F
Trapp, A.D. AR 2nd Mtd.Rifles Co.E
Trapp, A.D. MS 43rd Inf. Co.F
Trapp, Allen SC Inf. 7th Bn. (Enfield Rifles) Co.B
Trapp, Asa GA 40th Inf. Co.F
Trapp, Benjamin F. MS 11th (Perrin's) Cav. Co.A
Trapp, B.W. SC 12th Inf. Co.F
Trapp, Charles A. VA 6th Inf. Co.C
Trapp, C.O. SC 4th St.Troops Co.H
Trapp, C.O. SC 6th Res. Co.I Cpl.
Trapp, Daniel GA Floyd Legion (St.Guards) Co.K
Trapp, Frank J. MO 1st Inf. Co.D Cpl.
Trapp, James MO Cav. Fristoe's Regt. Co.C
Trapp, James F. GA 13th Inf. Co.F
Trapp, James T. TN 8th Cav. Co.K
Trapp, James T. TN 35th Inf. 1st Co.I 1st Sgt.
Trapp, J.C. AL 10th Cav. Co.F
Trapp, Jeremiah 1st Conf.Inf. 2nd Co.G
Trapp, Jerry GA 40th Inf. Co.C Cpl.
Trapp, J.M. TN 35th Inf. 1st Co.I, Co.G,E 1st Sgt.
Trapp, John MO Cav. Fristoe's Regt.
Trapp, John A. TN 28th (Cons.) Inf. Co.I Cpl.
Trapp, John C. MS 43rd Inf. Co.F,G
Trapp, John C. 1st Conf.Inf. 2nd Co.G
Trapp, L.B. GA 1st Reg. Co.B
Trapp, Levi SC Inf. 7th Bn. (Enfield Rifles) Co.C
Trapp, L.H. SC 6th Cav. Co.C
Trapp, L.H. SC Inf. 3rd Bn. Co.G Sgt.
Trapp, L.H. SC 4th St.Troops Co.H
Trapp, L.H. SC 25th Mil.
Trapp, L.J. MS 1st (Pattons') Inf. Co.H
Trapp, L.J. MS 43rd Inf. Co.G Sgt.
Trapp, Michael VA Cav. Mosby's Regt. (Part. Rangers)
Trapp, M.V. TN 28th (Cons.) Inf. Co.I
Trapp, Robert W. GA 6th Inf. (St.Guards) Co.F
Trapp, Sydenham B. GA Siege Arty. 28th Bn. Co.C
Trapp, Thomas GA 40th Inf. Co.A
Trapp, Thomas MS 3rd Inf. (A.of 10,000) Co.A
Trapp, T.L. MS 10th Cav. Co.C
Trapp, Tolliver GA 29th Inf. Co.D
Trapp, U.C. SC Cav. 4th Bn. Co.B Sgt.
Trapp, Uriah C. SC 2nd Cav. Sgt.
Trapp, W.C. SC 25th Mil.
Trapp, W.H. SC 6th Cav. Co.C
Trapp, William D. TN 35th Inf. 1st Co.D
Trapp, William H. SC 4th St.Troops Co.H
Trapp, William J. GA 29th Inf. Co.D
Trapp, William S. GA 56th Inf. Co.I
Trappe, Frederick TX Comal Res.
Trappe, L.J. AL 10th Cav. Co.F
Trappe, Sydneham B. GA 5th Inf. Co.F,A
Trapshire, H. MO 10th Inf. Co.A
Trarey, R.J. AL 5th Inf. Co.D
Trark, J.H. Ford's Staff 2nd Lt.
Trasantas, Ramon LA Mil. 5th Regt.Eur.Brig. (Spanish Regt.) Co.9
Trash, Benjamin AL 3rd Inf. Co.I
Trash, J.W. AL Conscr. & Res.Bn.
Trasiar, H.P. MO Cav. Hunter's Regt.
Trask, E. LA 3rd (Wingfield's) Cav. Co.I
Trask, Elias S. MS 15th Inf. Co.F
Trask, James Henry TX 2nd Cav. Co.I,D
Trask, Leander B. GA 25th Inf. Co.H
Trask, Leander B. GA 28th Inf. Co.H
Trask, W.E. LA 4th Inf. New Co.G
Trask, William E. AR 2nd Inf. Co.A
Trask, William L. Conf.Cav. Raum's Co.
Trask, W.L. NC Wallace's Co. (Wilmington RR Guard)
Trasper, I. MO 1st & 4th Cons.Inf. Co.G
Trassy, L.A. SC Hvy.Arty. 15th (Lucas') Bn. Co.A
Trastour, Auguste LA Arty. 1st Field Btty.
Trastour, E.J. LA Mil. Chalmette Regt. Co.G
Trastour, Ernest J. LA 13th Inf. Co.G,H
Trater, John GA 48th Inf. Co.I
Tratham, W.J. AR 2nd Inf. Co.B
Trather, W.D. AL 92nd Inf. Co.F
Tratt, Robert MS 1st Lt.Arty. Co.K
Traub, Jacob LA 20th Inf. New Co.B
Traub, Jacob LA 21st (Kennedy's) Inf. Co.C
Traub, Joseph LA 1st (Strawbridge's) Inf. Co.A,C
Traub, Joseph LA 21st (Kennedy's) Inf. Co.A
Traub, Philip LA 20th Inf. Co.D
Traub, Solomon GA 21st Inf. Co.B
Traube, Charles LA 22nd Inf. Wash. Marks' Co.
Trauber, Henry KY 2nd (Duke's) Cav. Co.B
Trauber, W. TN 42nd Inf. Co.C
Traublefield, A.M. AR 10th Inf. Co.E
Traugh, F. LA Mil. 3rd Regt. French Brig. Co.7
Traugh, Jacob VA Horse Arty. Lurty's Co. Artif.
Traughber, E. MO Cav. Stallard's Co.
Traughber, Emanuel MO 5th Cav. Co.D
Traughber, M.S. MO Inf. Clark's Regt. Co.C
Traughber, W.B. MO Inf. Clark's Regt. Co.C
Traughber, William TN 22nd (Barteau's) Cav. Co.F
Traughber, William R. TX Arty. Douglas' Co.
Traughear, Jonathan LA Herrick's Co. (Orleans Blues)
Traul, C. LA 21st (Kennedy's) Inf. Co.F
Traulman, Peter NC 4th Sr.Res. Co.F
Traum, W.T. AR 8th Inf. Co.C Lt.
Traur, W.W. Gen. & Staff Hosp.Stew.
Trauson, D.J. TN 7th (Duckworth's) Cav. Co.F
Traut, Daniel K. AL Cav. 4th Bn. (Love's) Co.B Cpl.
Traut, S. TX Cav. Durant's Co.
Trauth, J.A. LA Mil. Chalmette Regt. Co.A
Trautham, B.G. MO 8th Inf. Co.B
Trautham, B.G. MO 8th Inf. Co.F
Trautham, Daniel MS 7th Inf. Co.B
Trautham, David NC 62nd Inf. Co.H
Trautham, S.H. AR 1st (Monroe's) Cav. Co.E
Trautham, Thomas S. NC 25th Inf. Co.H Sgt.
Trauthram, S.H. AR 50th Mil. Co.C
Trauthram, T.H. AR 50th Mil. Co.C
Trautman, William VA 59th Inf. 3rd Co.D
Trautwein, A. TX 3rd Inf. 2nd Co.C Sgt.
Trautwein, A. TX Conscr.
Trautwein, William TX 4th Cav. Co.C
Travathan, Medic W. NC 3rd Arty. (40th St.Troops) Co.F
Travelle, Jasper SC Cav.Bn. Holcombe Legion Co.D
Travellstead, Charles MO Cav. Preston's Bn. Co.C
Travelsletts, Peter NC 16th Inf. Co.L
Traveno, L. TX Cav. Cater's Bn. Co.C 1st Lt.
Traver, William Lee AL 6th Cav. Co.B
Travers, E. LA Inf.Cons. 18th Regt. & Yellow Jacket Bn. Co.H 2nd Cpl.
Travers, Edward LA 18th Inf. Co.I,D
Travers, Edward MS 1st Cav. Co.K
Travers, Ernest LA 22nd Inf. Wash. Marks' Co.
Travers, F. LA Mil. Fire Bn. Co.B
Travers, Frank AR Lt.Arty. Key's Btty. Music.
Travers, James H. NC 2nd Cav. (19th St.Troops) Co.G
Travers, J.H. MD Cav. 2nd Bn. Co.F
Travers, John GA 6th Inf. Co.A
Travers, John LA Inf. 1st Sp.Bn. (Wheat's) Co.B
Travers, John LA Mil. Stanley Guards Co.B
Travers, John MS 44th Inf. Co.L Sgt.
Travers, John SC 1st Arty. Co.B
Travers, John TN 2nd (Walker's) Inf. Co.G

Travers, John VA 10th Cav. Co.D
Travers, John M. MD Cav. 2nd Bn. Co.C
Travers, John M. MD 1st Inf. Co.D
Travers, John M. VA Lt.Arty. Brander's Co.
Travers, Michael VA 17th Inf. Co.G
Travers, Middleton TX Cav. Madison's Regt. Co.F
Travers, Payne VA 9th Cav. Co.I
Travers, William J. TN 41st Inf.
Traverso, Antonio LA 10th Inf. Co.I
Traversso, Antonio LA Mil. 6th Regt.Eur.Brig. (Italian Guards Bn.) Co.1
Traveza, Morris AL 48th Mil. Co.A
Travice, D.C. MS 11th Inf. Co.E
Travick, G.W. GA Cav. 29th Bn. Co.A
Travick, R.G. AL 24th Inf. Co.G
Travillain, P.N. TN Cav. 12th Bn. (Day's) Co.D
Travillian, C.J. AL 47th Inf. Co.F Lt.
Travillian, E.H. VA 5th Cav. Co.I
Travillian, E.H. VA 3rd Lt.Arty. Co.F
Travillian, H.N. VA 2nd Cav. Co.K
Travillian, Joab TN 61st Mtd.Inf. Co.F
Travillian, Joseph TN 61st Mtd.Inf. Co.F
Travillian, Thomas E. MS 12th Inf. Co.K
Travillian, William VA 21st Mil. Co.D
Travillion, Joseph T. TN 1st (Carter's) Cav. Co.K
Travillion, Meekins C. NC 4th Inf. Co.G
Travillion, William T. TN 1st (Carter's) Cav. Co.K
Travin, Alfred F. GA 29th Inf. Co.H
Travin, Anson GA 29th Inf. Co.K
Travinio, Gragario TX Cav. Baylor's Regt. Co.B
Travino, --- TX 8th Inf.
Travino, Francisco TX 3rd Inf. Co.G
Travino, Rafel TX 3rd Inf. Co.G
Travis, A. GA 8th Inf. (St.Guards) Asst.Surg.
Travis, A. MO 3rd Cav. Co.F
Travis, A. TX Cav. Baird's Regt. Co.E
Travis, A.F. TN 28th (Cons.) Inf. Co.G
Travis, A.F. TN 84th Inf. Co.C
Travis, A.J. TN 17th Inf. Co.E
Travis, Albert AR 32nd Inf. Ord.Sgt.
Travis, Alexander LA Mil. British Guard Bn. Hamilton's Co.
Travis, Alford H. TN 34th Inf. 2nd Co.C
Travis, Amos TX 20th Cav. Co.B
Travis, B. LA 3rd (Wingfield's) Cav. Co.D
Travis, Benjamin AR 30th Inf. Co.D
Travis, Benjamin NC 5th Cav. (63rd St.Troops) Co.G
Travis, Benjamin F. TX Cav. Martin's Regt. Co.B
Travis, B.F. TN 31st Inf. Co.A Cpl.
Travis, B.M. GA 2nd Cav. Co.F
Travis, Burton J. VA 41st Inf. Co.A Cpl.
Travis, Butler B. TN 19th Inf. Co.D
Travis, C. TX 1st Hvy.Arty. Co.D
Travis, C.H. AL Mil. 2nd Regt.Vol. Co.C
Travis, C.H. AL 40th Inf. Co.A
Travis, Charles GA 2nd Cav. Co.E Sgt.
Travis, Charles KY Cav. Housby's Regt. Co.A
Travis, Charles KY 4th Mtd.Inf. Co.H
Travis, Charles TN 34th Inf. Co.G
Travis, Christian Inf. School of Pract. Powell's Detach. Co.C
Travis, C.S. MS 9th Cav. Co.D
Travis, C.S. MS Cav. 17th Bn. Co.F
Travis, Daniel TN 3rd (Forrest's) Cav. Co.C
Travis, David TN 21st Inf. Co.I
Travis, David TN 39th Mtd.Inf. Co.I
Travis, Dennard VA 6th Inf. Co.A
Travis, D.G. TN 8th (Smith's) Cav. Co.E,B,H
Travis, D.R. AR 5th Inf. Co.I
Travis, D.S. TN 17th Inf. Co.E
Travis, E. TN 2nd (Ashby's) Cav. Co.G
Travis, Ed C. LA Inf.Cons. 18th Regt. & Yellow Jacket Bn. Co.H
Travis, Ed R. AR 2nd Cav. Co.C Sgt.
Travis, Edward AR 1st (Colquitt's) Inf. Co.K
Travis, Edward W. VA Inf. 5th Bn. Co.A
Travis, E.F. AL 22nd Inf. Adj.
Travis, Elbert MS Cav. 3rd Bn.Res. Co.E
Travis, Elias F. Gen. & Staff Capt.,AAG
Travis, Ellis NC 5th Inf. Co.I
Travis, E.W. VA 3rd Cav. 2nd Co.I
Travis, Ezechial S. MS 27th Inf. Co.G
Travis, Ezekiel MS 24th Inf. Co.G
Travis, F. AR 18th (Marmaduke's) Inf. Co.B
Travis, Frank Gen. & Staff 1st Lt.,QM
Travis, Franklin NC 5th Inf. Co.I
Travis, F.W. TN 35th Inf. Co.G
Travis, G. TX 1st Hvy.Arty. Co.D
Travis, George A. VA 41st Inf. Co.A
Travis, G.W. Inf. Bailey's Cons.Regt. Co.C
Travis, H.C. GA 63rd Inf. Co.G
Travis, H.C. KY 6th Cav.
Travis, H.D. LA 4th Inf. Co.I
Travis, Henderson TX 20th Inf. Co.F
Travis, Henry TX 4th Inf. Co.H Cpl.
Travis, Henry C. KY 6th Mtd.Inf. Co.K,E,A
Travis, I.H. TN 3rd (Forrest's) Cav. Co.D
Travis, I.H. VA Hvy.Arty. Coleman's Co.
Travis, J. LA 22nd (Cons.) Inf. Co.F Cpl.
Travis, J. Bradford's Corps Scouts & Guards Co.B
Travis, James KY 1st (Helm's) Cav. Old Co.G
Travis, James KY 7th Cav. Co.F 3rd Lt.
Travis, James LA 31st Inf. Co.I
Travis, James MO Inf. 5th Regt.St.Guard Co.D
Travis, James TN 3rd (Forrest's) Cav. Co.C
Travis, James TN 14th (Neely's) Cav. Co.K
Travis, James TN 39th Mtd.Inf. Co.I
Travis, James TX 20th Inf. Co.K
Travis, James VA Inf. 21st Bn. Co.B
Travis, James VA 64th Mtd.Inf. Co.B
Travis, James E. TN 20th (Russell's) Cav. Co.I
Travis, James E. TN 7th Inf. Co.H
Travis, James F.M. NC 5th Inf. Co.I 2nd Lt.
Travis, James H. VA 57th Inf. Co.I
Travis, James L. TN 16th (Logwood's) Cav. Co.C
Travis, James M. AL 4th Res. Co.D
Travis, James M. TN 34th Inf. 2nd Co.C 1st Lt.
Travis, James R. VA 9th Inf. Co.B
Travis, James S. NC 5th Inf. Co.I
Travis, James T. GA 2nd Cav. (St.Guards) Co.E
Travis, James T. GA 6th Regt.St.Line Co.D
Travis, J.A.P. TX 20th Inf. Co.I Sgt.
Travis, J.E. MS 39th Inf. Co.H
Travis, Jessee W. AL 36th Inf. Co.F
Travis, J.H. TN 28th Cav. Co.B
Travis, J.H. TN 9th Inf. Co.G
Travis, J.M. TX 20th Inf. Co.F
Travis, Jo. VA Inf. 44th Bn. Co.C
Travis, John KY 2nd (Duke's) Cav. Co.A
Travis, John KY 14th Cav. Co.B
Travis, John MO 2nd N.E. Cav. (Franklin's Regt.) Co.B
Travis, John TN 34th Inf. Co.G
Travis, John TX 1st Inf. Co.F
Travis, John TX 9th (Nichols') Inf. Co.D
Travis, John VA Lt.Arty. Clutter's Co.
Travis, John VA 23rd Inf. Co.G
Travis, John VA 64th Mtd.Inf. Co.G
Travis, John A. MS 24th Inf. Co.G Sgt.
Travis, John A. MS 27th Inf. Co.H
Travis, John E. GA 1st (Fannin's) Res. Co.F,I
Travis, John Q. MS 16th Inf. Co.E 3rd Lt.
Travis, John R. VA Inf. 21st Bn. Co.B Cpl.
Travis, John T. MO Lt.Arty. Landis' Co.
Travis, John T. MO 2nd Inf. Co.A
Travis, John T. VA 17th Inf. Co.H
Travis, John W. MS 9th Inf. Old Co.E
Travis, John W. MS 10th Inf. New Co.A
Travis, John W. VA 18th Inf. Co.A Sgt.
Travis, Joseph N. TN 3rd (Lillard's) Mtd.Inf. Co.A Cpl.
Travis, Josiah R. VA 5th Cav. Co.C
Travis, Josiah R. VA 18th Inf. Co.A
Travis, J.P. TX Cav. Giddings' Bn. Co.A 2nd Lt.
Travis, J.V. TN 2nd (Ashby's) Cav. Co.H
Travis, J.V. TN Cav. 4th Bn. (Branner's) Co.A
Travis, J.W. KY 6th Mtd.Inf. Co.I
Travis, J.W. TN 19th & 20th (Cons.) Cav. Co.A
Travis, J.W. TN 5th Inf. 2nd Co.I
Travis, Levi NC 46th Inf. Co.K
Travis, Levi TN 39th Mtd.Inf. Co.I Cpl.
Travis, Lomia MS 27th Inf. Co.H
Travis, Ludson W. TX 19th Cav. Co.H
Travis, Luke GA 1st (Symons') Res. Co.K
Travis, L.W. TN 3rd (Forrest's) Cav. Co.D
Travis, L.W. TN 7th (Duckworth's) Cav. Co.H Sgt.
Travis, Mark B. AL 4th Inf. Co.E Bvt.2nd Lt.
Travis, Mich AL 1st Regt.Mobile Vol. British Guard Co.A
Travis, Michael LA Mil. 3rd Regt. 1st Brig. 1st Div. Co.K
Travis, Milton TN 39th Mtd.Inf. Co.I
Travis, M.M. GA 13th Inf. Co.F 1st Sgt.
Travis, N.A. MS 9th Inf. Co.A
Travis, Nelson NC 12th Inf. Co.A
Travis, Nicholas N. MS 7th Inf. Co.C
Travis, Pinkney H. NC 5th Inf. Co.I
Travis, R. MS 2nd St.Cav. Co.G
Travis, Rezin T. AR 17th (Lemoyne's) Inf. Co.F
Travis, Rezin T. AR 21st Inf. Co.E 1st Sgt.
Travis, Richard N. MS 11th Inf. Co.E
Travis, Robert H. MO 2nd Inf. Co.C
Travis, R.W. GA Cav. 1st Bn.Res. Stark's Co.
Travis, R.W. NC 3rd Cav. (41st St.Troops) Co.C
Travis, S. AL St.Res. Sgt.
Travis, Samuel TN 19th Inf. Co.D
Travis, Samuel 3rd Conf.Eng.Troops Co.B
Travis, Sanford V. AL 10th Inf. Co.B
Travis, Sanford V. AL 28th Inf. Co.H
Travis, Seth MS 9th Cav. Co.G Cpl.
Travis, Seth MS 5th Inf. (St.Troops) Co.B
Travis, Severn B. VA 39th Inf. Co.C

Travis, Simpson LA 11th Inf. Co.E Sgt.
Travis, Simpson LA 14th (Austin's) Bn.S.S. Co.A Cpl.
Travis, T.A. AL 36th Inf. Co.A Sgt.
Travis, T.C. GA 12th Cav. Co.K
Travis, Thaddeus AL 22nd Inf. Co.A 2nd Lt.
Travis, Thomas MS 4th Inf. Co.G
Travis, Thomas VA 39th Inf. Co.B,K
Travis, Thomas B. NC 5th Inf. Co.I
Travis, Thomas C. MS Cav. 4th Bn. Sykes' Co.
Travis, Thomas C. 8th (Wade's) Conf.Cav. Co.G Cpl.
Travis, Thomas S. GA 2nd Cav. Co.E
Travis, Thompson NC 5th Inf. Co.I
Travis, W.A. TN 8th (Smith's) Cav. Co.E
Travis, W.B. AL Mil. 2nd Regt.Vol. Co.D
Travis, W.C. MS 26th Inf. Co.A
Travis, W.E. KY 12th Cav. Co.H Sgt.
Travis, W.G. MS 27th Inf. Co.G
Travis, William AL 21st Inf. Co.E Drum Maj.
Travis, William AR 5th Inf. Co.I
Travis, William MS 5th Inf. (St.Troops) Co.B
Travis, William MS 18th Inf. Co.I
Travis, William MO Cav. Clardy's Bn. Co.C
Travis, William SC 1st Arty. Co.I
Travis, William TN 39th Mtd.Inf. Co.I
Travis, William TX 20th Inf. Co.F
Travis, William VA Inf. 21st Bn. Co.B
Travis, William VA 64th Mtd.Inf. Co.B
Travis, William 14th Conf.Cav. Co.C
Travis, William Bradford's Corps Scouts & Guards Co.B
Travis, William A. AL 3rd Inf. Co.F
Travis, William A. KY 12th Cav. Co.H Sgt.
Travis, William A. NC 45th Inf. Co.H
Travis, William A. TN 2nd (Smith's) Cav.
Travis, William B. MS Inf. 1st St.Troops Co.D
Travis, William E. TN 5th Inf. Col.
Travis, Wm. E. Gen. & Staff Col.,TX Commissioner
Travis, William H. TN 34th Inf. Co.G
Travis, William H. VA 42nd Inf. Co.A
Travis, William J. MS 2nd (Quinn's St.Troops) Inf. Co.E
Travis, William J. VA 56th Inf. Co.F
Travis, William Rufus NC 5th Inf. Co.I
Travis, William S. VA 6th Inf. Co.A
Travis, William W. GA Mil. 12th Regt. Co.A
Travis, Wilson MS 33rd Inf. Co.B
Travis, W.J. TN 34th Inf. 2nd Co.C
Travis, W.R. MS 33rd Inf. Co.B
Travis, W.W. TX 10th Cav. Co.E
Travise, G.W. TN 49th Inf. Co.H
Travise, P.O. TN 14th Inf. Co.K
Travise, Presley O. KY 11th Cav.
Trawalter, Niclaus TX 3rd Inf. Co.H
Trawber, William TN Cav. 7th Bn. (Bennett's) Co.D
Traweck, D.B. MS 5th Cav. Co.E,I
Traweek, A.B. MS 40th Inf. Co.D
Traweek, A.B. MS Inf. Comfort's Co.
Traweek, C.C. TX 5th Inf. Co.C
Traweek, George AL 11th Inf. Co.I Capt.
Traweek, George L. AL 11th Inf. Co.I
Traweek, G.S. AL 11th Inf. Co.I Sgt.
Traweek, Henry P. TX Inf. Whaley's Co.
Traweek, H.P. TX 5th Inf. Co.C
Traweek, Isreal C. AL 44th Inf. Co.A
Traweek, Ripley J. AL 17th Inf. Co.C
Traweek, Robert C. TX 19th Cav. Co.C
Traweek, Simon P. AL 11th Inf. Co.I
Traweek, W.C. MS 46th Inf. Co.B
Trawek, L.M. 15th Conf.Cav. Co.I
Trawic, C.L. SC 20th Inf. Co.L Cpl.
Trawich, Henry MS 3rd Cav. Co.C,B,D
Trawich, S.R. AR 21st Mil. Co.D
Trawick, A.B. MS 5th Cav. Co.I
Trawick, Abner R. GA 5th Inf. Co.H,E
Trawick, A.J. GA Lt.Arty. 12th Bn. 3rd Co.B Music.
Trawick, A.J. GA 1st (Ramsey's) Inf. Co.E
Trawick, Alexander NC Hvy.Arty. 1st Bn. Co.A
Trawick, Alphon H. GA 49th Inf. Co.C
Trawick, A.M. AR 16th Inf. Co.F 2nd Lt.
Trawick, B.A. TN 28th (Cons.) Inf. Co.A Sgt.
Trawick, Benjamin GA 2nd Bn.S.S. Co.A
Trawick, Benjamin A. TN 28th Inf. Co.G
Trawick, Benjamin L. GA 5th Inf. Co.H,M
Trawick, B.F. NC 2nd Jr.Res. Co.F
Trawick, C.A. GA 10th Cav. Co.K
Trawick, C.C. MS 6th Cav. Co.G
Trawick, C.C. MS 5th Inf. (St.Troops) Co.C
Trawick, C.C. TX 7th Inf. Co.G
Trawick, C.L. SC Cav. 19th Bn. Co.E
Trawick, David NC Hvy.Arty. 1st Bn. Co.A
Trawick, D.L. AR 37th Inf. Co.B
Trawick, E.M. TN 13th (Gore's) Cav. Co.K
Trawick, Eugene GA Cav. 29th Bn. Co.H,G
Trawick, F.P. AL 11th Inf. Co.B
Trawick, Francis D.M. AL 6th Inf. Co.B
Trawick, Frank TN 55th (Brown's) Inf. Co.H
Trawick, George A. AL Arty. 1st Bn. Co.E
Trawick, George J. AL 6th Inf. Co.A,B
Trawick, G.W. AL 38th Inf. Co.I
Trawick, G.W. AR 10th Inf. Co.C Cpl.
Trawick, Henry AL St.Res. Palmer's Co.
Trawick, H.F. TX Inf. 1st St.Troops White's Co.D
Trawick, H.F. TX 20th Inf. Co.G
Trawick, H.H. TN 28th (Cons.) Inf. Co.E Cpl.
Trawick, H.H. TN 84th Inf. Co.A Cpl.
Trawick, H.J. AL 53rd (Part.Rangers) Co.D
Trawick, Hugh W. MS 6th Inf. Co.G
Trawick, Ira Y. AL Jeff Davis Arty.
Trawick, Isaac GA 50th Inf. Co.F
Trawick, J. AL 15th Inf. Co.D
Trawick, J.A. MS 6th Inf. Co.K
Trawick, J.A. MS 46th Inf. Co.F
Trawick, James AL 40th Inf. Co.H Sgt.
Trawick, James AL 41st Inf. Co.F Music.
Trawick, James AR 36th Inf. Co.D
Trawick, James M. NC 1st Inf. Co.I Cpl.
Trawick, James P. GA Inf. 27th Bn. Co.C Cpl.
Trawick, Jesse AL Arty. 1st Bn. Co.E
Trawick, Jesse T. GA 1st (Ramsey's) Inf. Co.E
Trawick, J.G. AR 10th Inf. Co.C
Trawick, J.L. AL 1st Cav. 2nd Co.A Sgt.
Trawick, J.N. AL 15th Inf. Co.G Cpl.
Trawick, John GA Cav. 7th Bn. (St.Guards) Co.E
Trawick, John TX 13th Cav. Co.A
Trawick, J.S. AL Mil. 4th Vol. Co.D
Trawick, J.S. AL 4th Res. Co.F
Trawick, J.T. 4th Conf.Inf. Co.B
Trawick, J.W. GA Cav. 22nd Bn. (St.Guards) Co.F
Trawick, J.W. MS 1st Cav. Co.H
Trawick, L.N. AL 17th Inf. Co.C 2nd Lt.
Trawick, L.N. AL 38th Inf. Co.B
Trawick, M. AL 38th Inf. Co.B
Trawick, Martin W. MS 1st (Percy's) Inf. Co.A Sgt.
Trawick, Mose GA Lt.Arty. 12th Bn. 3rd Co.B
Trawick, M.T. AL Lt.Arty. 20th Bn. Co.B
Trawick, Orthnold GA 50th Inf. Co.F
Trawick, P. SC Mil.Arty. 1st Regt. Co.C
Trawick, Peter SC 24th Inf. Co.B
Trawick, R.H. AL 15th Cav. Co.I
Trawick, R.J. AL 5th Inf. New Co.D
Trawick, Robert AL Mil. 4th Vol. Co.D
Trawick, Robert MS 36th Inf. Co.E
Trawick, Robert B. AL 41st Inf. Co.F
Trawick, Robert E. AL 3rd Bn. Hilliard's Legion Vol. Co.A
Trawick, Stephen T. TX 13th Cav. Co.F
Trawick, Thomas A. AL 6th Inf. Co.B
Trawick, Thomas P. AL 41st Inf. Co.F
Trawick, Washington B. AL Jeff Davis Arty.
Trawick, W.C. MS 4th Cav. Co.A
Trawick, William AL 15th Inf. Co.E
Trawick, William AL 57th Inf. Co.E
Trawick, W.J. AL 59th Inf. Co.E
Trawick, W.J. AL Arty. 4th Bn. Hilliard's Legion Co.B,E
Trawick, W.R. AL 53rd (Part.Rangers) Co.D
Trawick, W.S. AL 5th Inf. New Co.I,G
Trax, Alexander VA 1st Arty. Co.F
Trax, Elias VA 24th Bn.Part.Rangers Cropper's Co.
Trax, Louis LA 6th Inf. Co.G
Traxler, James SC 24th Inf. Co.C
Traxler, J.D. SC 11th Inf. Co.H
Traxler, John W. MS 46th Inf. Co.D
Traxler, Thomas E.D. MS 39th Inf. Co.G
Traxler, William SC Mil. 18th Regt. Co.E
Traxler, William B. SC 1st (Butler's) Inf. Co.A
Traye, Francis FL 1st Cav. Co.D Cpl.
Trayer, Charles H. VA Lt.Arty. Garber's Co.
Trayer, James VA Horse Arty. McClanahan's Co.
Trayer, John W. VA 7th Bn.Res. Co.D
Trayer, S.A. VA Horse Arty. McClanahan's Co.
Trayer, Silas VA Horse Arty. McClanahan's Co.
Trayer, Silas A. VA Lt.Arty. Garber's Co.
Trayer, Silas A. VA 62nd Mtd.Inf. Co.A
Trayer, Silas A. 1st Conf.Eng.Troops Co.G Cpl.
Trayhern, James F. VA Cav. 41st Bn. Trayhern's Co. Capt.
Trayhern, J.F. VA Cav. 35th Bn. Co.D Capt.
Trayhon, James T. VA Cav. Mosby's Regt. (Part.Rangers) Co.C
Trayler, A.A. VA Second Class Mil. Wolff's Co.
Trayler, David MS Inf. 1st Bn.St.Troops (30 days '64) Co.B
Trayler, E.A. GA 13th Inf. Co.D
Trayler, G.W. SC 4th Inf. Co.G Cpl.
Trayler, H.G. VA 26th Inf. Co.G
Trayler, James TX 11th Cav. Co.I
Trayler, J.J. MS 20th Inf. Co.I
Trayler, J.L. GA 46th Inf. Co.A
Trayler, J.M. MS 39th Inf. Co.F

Trayler, John GA 3rd Res. Co.I
Trayler, John M. FL 4th Inf. Co.I
Trayler, John W. VA 53rd Inf. Co.B
Trayler, J.R. NC Lt.Arty. 3rd Bn. Co.C
Trayler, N.B. MS Cav. Powers' Regt. Sgt.Maj.
Trayler, Pleasant W. AL 44th Inf. Co.A
Trayler, P.M. MS 8th Inf. Co.K
Trayler, W.A. GA 13th Inf. Co.D
Trayler, W.A. VA Inf. 44th Bn. Co.A
Trayler, William M. FL 4th Inf. Co.I
Trayler, Willis MS Cav. Powers' Regt. Co.H
Trayler, Z.T. VA 44th Inf. Co.E
Traylor, --- TX Cav. Mann's Regt. Co.K
Traylor, A. VA Inf. 44th Bn. Co.A Sgt.
Traylor, A.A. SC 7th Inf. 2nd Co.C, Co.G
Traylor, A.A. VA 3rd (Archer's) Bn.Res. Co.D
Traylor, A.H. TX 5th Inf. Co.D
Traylor, A.J. LA 6th Inf. Co.A Cpl.
Traylor, Albert T. SC 7th Inf. 1st Co.C, 2nd Co.C 1st Lt.
Traylor, Alexander VA 12th Inf. Co.D,C,K
Traylor, Alexander A. TX 22nd Cav. Co.D
Traylor, A.M. NC 30th Inf. Co.G
Traylor, Amos TX 27th Cav. Co.E
Traylor, Augustus G. GA 4th Inf. Co.D
Traylor, B.A. TX Cav. Baylor's Regt. Co.K
Traylor, B.B. VA Arty. J.W. Drewry's Co.
Traylor, Benjamin B. VA 41st Inf. 2nd Co.E
Traylor, Benjamin F. VA 20th Inf. Co.I
Traylor, Calvin VA Arty. J.W. Drewry's Co.
Traylor, Champion T. FL Cav. 5th Bn. Co.E
Traylor, Charles L. NC 30th Inf. Co.G
Traylor, Charles L. VA 23rd Inf. Co.B
Traylor, Charles W. VA 17th Cav. Co.C Cpl.
Traylor, C.T. TX 27th Cav. Co.E
Traylor, D. TX 22nd Inf. Co.A
Traylor, David LA 7th Inf. Co.K
Traylor, David A. VA 13th Cav. Co.E
Traylor, David H. MS 2nd Inf. Co.C Cpl.
Traylor, D.E. MS 1st (Percy's) Inf. Co.K
Traylor, D.E. MS 39th Inf. Co.G
Traylor, Edward VA 14th Inf. Co.D
Traylor, Edward L. MS Inf. 3rd Bn. Co.A
Traylor, E.H. LA 13th Bn. (Part.Rangers) Co.C
Traylor, Enos MO 11th Inf. Co.H
Traylor, E.O. VA Lt.Arty. 12th Bn. Co.B
Traylor, E.O. VA Inf. 1st Bn.Loc.Def. Co.C 3rd Lt.
Traylor, F.M. LA 6th Inf. Co.A Asst.Surg.
Traylor, F.M. Gen. & Staff Asst.Surg.
Traylor, Francis M. AL 44th Inf. Co.K
Traylor, Gaston LA 7th Inf. Co.K
Traylor, G.D. LA 13th Bn. (Part.Rangers) Co.C
Traylor, George TX Cav. Benavides' Regt. Co.G
Traylor, George F. GA 4th Inf. Co.D Cpl.
Traylor, George J. AL 13th Inf. Co.C
Traylor, George M. GA 4th Inf. Co.D Cpl.
Traylor, George W. GA 4th Inf. Co.D
Traylor, George W. LA 31st Inf. Co.I 1st Sgt.
Traylor, George W. VA Inf. 5th Bn. Co.E
Traylor, Greene D. LA 12th Inf. Co.L
Traylor, G.W. MS 39th Inf. Co.A
Traylor, G.W. SC Inf. 13th Bn. Co.B
Traylor, G.W. SC Inf. Hampton Legion Co.I Cpl.
Traylor, G.W. TX 22nd Inf. Co.A 3rd Lt.
Traylor, Harrison A. VA 41st Inf. 2nd Co.E
Traylor, Henry A. VA 44th Inf. Co.H
Traylor, Henry Clay VA 12th Inf. 2nd Co.I
Traylor, Henry W. MS 36th Inf. Co.A Cpl.
Traylor, Henry W. VA Inf. 44th Bn. Co.E
Traylor, Hill M. GA 4th Inf. Co.B Sgt.
Traylor, I.H. LA 3rd Inf. Co.B
Traylor, Irby H. GA 12th (Robinson's) Cav. (St.Guards) Co.G
Traylor, J. MS 3rd Inf. (St.Troops) Co.D 1st Sgt.
Traylor, J. TX 22nd Inf. Co.A
Traylor, J. VA 3rd (Archer's) Bn.Res. Co.E
Traylor, Jackson KY 5th Cav. Co.B
Traylor, James AL Cav. Musgrove's Bn. Co.E
Traylor, James TX 12th Cav. Co.H
Traylor, James A. VA Inf. 5th Bn. Co.A
Traylor, James A. VA 41st Inf. Co.D
Traylor, James A. VA 53rd Inf. Co.H
Traylor, James B. AL 36th Inf. Co.K
Traylor, James M. MS 16th Inf. Co.F
Traylor, James M. TX Cav. Sutton's Co.
Traylor, James W. MS 21st Inf. Co.F Sgt.
Traylor, J.B. AL 9th Inf. Co.B
Traylor, J.B. AL 26th (O'Neal's) Inf. Co.E
Traylor, J.B. VA 13th Cav. Co.E
Traylor, J.D. TX 20th Inf. Co.G
Traylor, J.E. AL 34th Inf. Co.C
Traylor, Jeremiah M. AL Cav. 5th Bn. Hilliard's Legion Co.B
Traylor, J.H. LA 12th Inf. Co.F
Traylor, J.H. TX 5th Inf. Co.D
Traylor, J.H. TX 20th Inf. Co.G
Traylor, J.J. MS 1st Cav.Res. Co.A 1st Sgt.
Traylor, J.L. VA Lt.Arty. 38th Bn. Co.C
Traylor, J.M. TX 11th (Spaight's) Bn.Vol. Co.B
Traylor, J.M. TX 13th Vol. 4th Co.I
Traylor, J.M. 10th Conf.Cav. Co.B
Traylor, John AL 13th Inf. Co.E
Traylor, John LA 13th Bn. (Part.Rangers) Co.F
Traylor, John VA Inf. Lyneman's Co.
Traylor, John A. LA 12th Inf. Co.L
Traylor, John A. TX 27th Cav. Co.E
Traylor, John B. VA 24th Cav. Co.A
Traylor, John B. VA Cav. 40th Bn. Co.A
Traylor, John C. GA 20th Inf. Co.E
Traylor, John H. GA 4th Inf. Co.B
Traylor, John H. VA Hvy.Arty. 18th Bn. Co.C
Traylor, John H. VA 14th Inf. Co.A Cpl.
Traylor, John M. FL Cav. 5th Bn. Co.E
Traylor, John T. GA 4th Inf. Co.D
Traylor, John T. VA 9th Inf. Co.C
Traylor, John W. AR 19th (Dockery's) Inf. Co.B
Traylor, John W. VA Horse Arty. Shoemaker's Co. Cpl.
Traylor, John W. VA Inf. 5th Bn. Co.E
Traylor, John W. VA 42nd Inf. Co.D
Traylor, Joseph VA Courtney Arty.
Traylor, Joseph VA Lt.Arty. Weisiger's Co.
Traylor, Joseph VA 16th Inf. Co.I
Traylor, Joseph H. VA Arty. J.W. Drewry's Co.
Traylor, Joseph J. AL 44th Inf. Co.K
Traylor, J.R. LA 6th Inf. Co.A
Traylor, J.R. TX 1st Hvy.Arty. Co.K
Traylor, J.U. AL 46th Inf.
Traylor, J.W. LA 3rd Inf. Co.I
Traylor, L.A. TX 20th Inf. Co.G
Traylor, Larkin 8th (Wade's) Conf.Cav. Co.B
Traylor, Lemoine VA 23rd Inf. Co.B
Traylor, L.M. TN 10th (DeMoss') Cav. Co.G
Traylor, L.M. TN Cav. Napier's Bn. Co.D
Traylor, L.M. TN 11th Inf. Co.I 2nd Lt.
Traylor, Loyd AL Cp. of Instr. Talladega
Traylor, L.S. AL Cp. of Instr. Talladega
Traylor, L.T. VA 1st (Farinholt's) Res. Co.G
Traylor, L.W. TX 32nd Cav. Co.A
Traylor, M. FL Conscr.
Traylor, Mijamon B. AL Cav. 5th Bn. Hilliard's Legion Co.B
Traylor, Miles T. VA Inf. 5th Bn. Co.E
Traylor, Milton V. VA 23rd Inf. Co.B
Traylor, M.J. VA 37th Inf. Co.A
Traylor, Moses FL Cav. 5th Bn. Co.A,E
Traylor, N.B. MS 1st (Percy's) Inf. Co.K
Traylor, N.B. MS 39th Inf. Co.G Cpl.
Traylor, Norborne T. VA 12th Inf. Co.K
Traylor, O.C. TX 11th Cav. Co.H
Traylor, Pascal TX 6th Inf. Co.H
Traylor, P.R. TX Cav. Baylor's Regt. Co.K
Traylor, P.R. TX Inf. Rutherford's Co.
Traylor, P.W. AL Jeff Davis Arty.
Traylor, Randolph MS Cav. Gibson's Co.
Traylor, Richard AL Cp. of Instr. Talladega
Traylor, R.M. TN 3rd (Forrest's) Cav. Co.E
Traylor, R.M. TN 14th (Neely's) Cav. Co.F
Traylor, Robert VA 12th Inf. Co.F
Traylor, Robert B. LA 12th Inf. Co.F
Traylor, Robt. C. VA Inf. 44th Bn. Co.E
Traylor, Robert J. TX 6th Cav. Co.E
Traylor, S. TN Cav. Napier's Bn. Co.D
Traylor, S.A. TX 35th (Brown's) Cav. Co.A Sgt.
Traylor, S.A. TX 13th Vol. 1st Co.B, 2nd Co.B
Traylor, Simpson E. LA 31st Inf. Co.I Jr.2nd Lt.
Traylor, S.M. TN 10th (DeMoss') Cav. Co.G
Traylor, Stephen TN 10th (DeMoss') Cav. Co.G Cpl.
Traylor, Tay AL 28th Inf. Co.B
Traylor, Taylor VA Inf. 44th Bn. Co.E
Traylor, T.B. TN 10th (DeMoss') Cav. Co.F
Traylor, T.B. TN Cav. Napier's Bn. Co.C
Traylor, T.G. GA 32nd Inf. Co.I Cpl.
Traylor, Theophilus VA Hvy.Arty. 10th Bn. Co.A
Traylor, Theophilus VA 74th Mil. Co.E
Traylor, Thomas SC 6th Inf. 1st Co.C, 2nd Co.H
Traylor, Thomas VA Hvy.Arty. 18th Bn. Co.C
Traylor, Thomas VA 1st Inf. Co.D
Traylor, Thomas VA 12th Inf. Co.K
Traylor, Thomas VA 14th Inf. Co.I
Traylor, Thomas B. TN 11th Inf. Co.A 2nd Lt.
Traylor, Thomas E. VA 1st Inf. Co.I Sgt.
Traylor, Thomas G. AL Jeff Davis Arty. Cpl.
Traylor, Thomas J. TX 27th Cav. Co.E
Traylor, Thomas M. VA 5th Cav. Co.D Sgt.
Traylor, Thomas M. VA 13th Cav. Co.B Sgt.
Traylor, Thomas M. VA 3rd Inf.Loc.Def. Co.I Lt.
Traylor, Thomas P. AL 3rd Inf. Co.K Sgt.
Traylor, Thomas W. MS 2nd Inf. Co.C Sgt.
Traylor, Thomas W. TN 1st (Feild's) Inf. Co.I
Traylor, T.J. TX 22nd Inf. Co.A Cpl.
Traylor, W. SC 3rd Regt.Res.
Traylor, W.A. TX 5th Inf. Co.D

Traylor, Washington AL 3rd Res. Co.E
Traylor, W.H. AL 26th (O'Neal's) Inf. Co.E,F
Traylor, W.H. SC 6th Inf. 2nd Co.H
Traylor, Willard VA 9th Inf. Co.C
Traylor, William AL Cav. Musgrove's Bn. Co.E
Traylor, William AL Cp. of Instr. Talladega
Traylor, William AR 1st Mtd.Rifles Co.C
Traylor, William AR 2nd Mtd.Rifles Co.A
Traylor, William LA 9th Inf. Co.E
Traylor, William TX 11th Cav. Co.A
Traylor, William TX Cav. Waller's Regt. Co.A
Traylor, William VA Hvy.Arty. 18th Bn. Co.C
Traylor, William VA 12th Inf. Co.K
Traylor, William 10th Conf.Cav. Co.B
Traylor, William A. VA 9th Inf. Co.C
Traylor, William A. VA 1st Loc.Guard Co.G
Traylor, William D. VA Arty. J.W. Drewry's Co.
Traylor, William H. VA 14th Inf. Co.I
Traylor, William L. TX 25th Cav. Co.C
Traylor, William L. TX 9th (Nichols') Inf. Co.A
Traylor, William P. AR 3rd Cav. Co.H
Traylor, William P. GA 60th Inf. Co.B
Traylor, William P. LA 3rd Inf. Co.B Cpl.
Traylor, Winfield S. SC 5th Inf. 1st Co.H, 2nd Co.B Sgt.
Traylor, Winston VA 41st Inf. Co.D
Traylor, W.J. VA Inf. 1st Bn. Co.A Sgt.
Traylor, W.N. LA 27th Inf. Co.B Jr.2nd Lt.
Traylor, W.P. VA 14th Inf. Co.D
Traylor, W.R. MS 39th Inf. Co.G 1st Sgt.
Traylor, W.S. TN 10th (DeMoss') Cav. Co.G
Traylor, W.S. TN Cav. Napier's Bn. Co.D
Traylor, W.T. SC 12th Inf. Co.A
Trayman, J.W. VA 4th Cav.
Traymart, T.M. VA 24th Cav. Co.B
Traymor, G.W. AL 12th Inf. Co.B
Trayner, William VA 62nd Mtd.Inf. 1st Co.A
Traynham, A.J. SC Lt.Arty. 3rd (Palmetto) Bn. Co.I
Traynham, B.F. MS 10th Inf. New Co.I Cpl.
Traynham, David J. VA 59th Inf. 3rd Co.E Sgt.
Traynham, David P. VA 3rd Cav. Co.H
Traynham, D.J. VA Hvy.Arty. Wright's Co.
Traynham, James H. SC 16th Inf. Co.F 1st Lt.
Traynham, J.H. TX 20th Inf. Co.B
Traynham, J.J. SC 16th Inf. Co.E
Traynham, John SC 16th Inf. Co.E Cpl.
Traynham, John B. VA Lt.Arty. Penick's Co. Cpl.
Traynham, Madison L. VA 23rd Inf. Co.A
Traynham, Nimrod SC 6th Cav. Co.A
Traynham, Nimrod SC 16th Inf. Co.E
Traynham, Robert L. VA 23rd Inf. Co.A
Traynham, Thomas B. VA 3rd Cav. Co.C Sgt.
Traynham, T.W. SC 1st St.Troops Co.G
Traynham, T.W. SC 3rd Res. Co.C 1st Sgt.
Traynham, T.W. SC 16th Inf. Co.E
Traynham, T.W. SC Inf. Hampton Legion Co.E
Traynham, William B. NC 20th Inf. Co.B Sgt.
Traynham, W.T. GA Conscr.
Traynham, W.T. 3rd Conf.Eng.Troops Co.H
Traynick, J.P. TN 21st & 22nd (Cons.) Cav. Co.I
Traynnan, W.L. GA 16th Inf. Co.H
Traynor, E.W.H. GA 6th Inf. (St.Guards) Co.I
Traynor, James GA 2nd Inf. Co.B
Traynor, James P. TN Lt.Arty. Barry's Co.
Traynor, John VA 59th Inf. 3rd Co.D
Traynor, John D. TN 2nd (Ashby's) Cav. Co.H 1st Lt.
Traynor, John D. TN Cav. 4th Bn. (Branner's) Co.A
Traynor, M.T. TN 3rd (Clack's) Inf. Co.D
Traynor, Patrick LA 1st (Strawbridge's) Inf. Co.B
Traynum, Henry C. VA 55th Inf. Co.M
Traynum, J.P. SC 22nd Inf. Co.G
Trayton, J.W. VA 46th Inf. Co.G
Traytor, William GA 20th Inf. Co.I
Trayvick, Lewis AL 33rd Inf. Co.B
Trayweek, Robert AL 41st Inf. Co.G
Trayweek, T.M. AL 2nd Cav. Co.E
Traywick, A.C. AR Lt.Arty. Marshall's Btty.
Traywick, Alfriend H. GA Cav. 7th Bn. (St.Guards) Co.B
Traywick, Allen C. AR 1st Cav. Co.G Sgt.
Traywick, Allen P. NC Hvy.Arty. 10th Bn. Co.C
Traywick, A.R. 3rd Conf.Eng.Troops Co.C
Traywick, Bryant LA 15th Inf. Co.G
Traywick, Bryant S. NC Hvy.Arty. 10th Bn. Co.C Sgt.
Traywick, Charles A. AL 6th Inf. Co.F
Traywick, Charles M. TN 55th (McKoin's) Inf. James' Co.
Traywick, C.W. AR 8th Inf. New Co.E
Traywick, F.B. NC McLean's Bn.Lt.Duty Men Co.A
Traywick, George W. AL 33rd Inf. Co.B
Traywick, H. AL Cav. Musgrove's Bn. Co.E
Traywick, Harrison AL 63rd Inf. Co.A
Traywick, Henry S. NC 33rd Inf. Co.E
Traywick, Jackson AL 47th Inf. Co.E
Traywick, James S. AL Recruits
Traywick, J.B. NC 6th Inf. Co.B
Traywick, J.C. AL 59th Inf. Co.K
Traywick, J.C. AL 2nd Bn. Hilliard's Legion Vol. Co.B
Traywick, J.L. MS 6th Cav. Co.D,E
Traywick, J.L. MS Cav. Davenport's Bn. (St.Troops) Co.C Sgt.
Traywick, J.M. AL 59th Inf. Co.E
Traywick, J.O. AL 5th Inf. New Co.I
Traywick, John AL 6th Cav. Co.H
Traywick, John TN 10th (DeMoss') Cav. Co.K
Traywick, John TN Greer's Regt.Part.Rangers Co.A
Traywick, John J. AL 58th Inf. Co.K
Traywick, John J. GA 2nd Bn.S.S. Co.E
Traywick, Moses L. AL 13th Inf. Co.H
Traywick, O.L. MS 4th Cav. Co.F
Traywick, O.L. MS 1st (King's) Inf. (St.Troops) Co.G Sgt.
Traywick, Peter L. MS 3rd (St.Troops) Cav. Co.F 3rd Lt.
Traywick, R. AL 15th Inf. Co.G
Traywick, R.G. AL 34th Inf. Co.A
Traywick, R.G. GA 29th Inf. Co.F
Traywick, Richard AL 34th Inf. Co.G
Traywick, Robert AL Recruits
Traywick, Robert FL Cav. 3rd Bn. Co.D
Traywick, Robert 15th Conf.Cav. Co.I
Traywick, Samuel C. NC 23rd Inf. Co.A Sgt.
Traywick, T.B. AL 38th Inf. Co.I
Traywick, T.D. AR 37th Inf. Co.D
Traywick, T.J. AL 59th Inf. Co.E
Traywick, William C. GA 2nd Bn.S.S. Co.E
Traywick, William H. AL 8th Inf. Co.A
Trazelais, Manuel LA Pointe Coupee Arty.
Traznham, J.J. SC 16th & 24th (Cons.) Inf. Co.F
Treacbear, W. LA Mil. 1st Regt. French Brig. Co.2
Treacil, August LA 14th Inf. Co.D
Treack, Jacob Conf.Inf. 8th Bn. Co.E
Treacy, Michael MS 22nd Inf. Co.C
Treadaway, --- TX Cav. Good's Bn. Co.B
Treadaway, A. NC 5th Sr.Res. Co.B
Treadaway, Andrew J. GA 21st Inf. Co.G
Treadaway, Benjamin MS Inf. 1st Bn. Ray's Co.
Treadaway, Bennet MS Inf. 1st Bn. Ray's Co.
Treadaway, Bennett MS 43rd Inf. Co.A
Treadaway, Cornelius AL 55th Vol. Co.B
Treadaway, D. Al 12th Cav. Co.G
Treadaway, Daniel L. GA Cherokee Legion (St.Guards) Co.H
Treadaway, David C. MS 35th Inf. Co.B
Treadaway, David F. NC 64th Inf. Co.C
Treadaway, E. MS 1st (King's) Inf. (St.Troops) Co.H
Treadaway, Elijah MS 32nd Inf. Co.K
Treadaway, Elius AL 55th Vol. Co.B
Treadaway, Erwin N. NC 29th Inf. Co.C
Treadaway, Ezekiel P. AR 1st (Crawford's) Cav. Co.A
Treadaway, F.M. AL 26th (O'Neal's) Inf. Co.C 1st Lt.
Treadaway, F.M. AR 5th Inf. Co.E
Treadaway, Frederick SC 1st (McCreary's) Inf. Co.C
Treadaway, George GA Lt.Arty. 14th Bn. Co.F Cpl.
Treadaway, George GA Lt.Arty. King's Btty. Cpl.
Treadaway, George Taylor SC 4th Inf. Co.E
Treadaway, G.T. SC 22nd Inf. Co.K Cpl.
Treadaway, Henry AR 27th Inf. Co.I
Treadaway, Henry C. AL 17th Inf. Co.G
Treadaway, Iverson B. SC 6th Inf. 2nd Co.D 1st Sgt.
Treadaway, James GA 51st Inf. Co.C Cpl.
Treadaway, James MS 5th Inf. Co.A
Treadaway, James NC 64th Inf. Co.C
Treadaway, James VA 59th Inf. 1st Co.F
Treadaway, James A. NC 43rd Inf. Co.H
Treadaway, James C. NC 43rd Inf. Co.H
Treadaway, J.C. GA 45th Inf. Co.A
Treadaway, J.C. GA 46th Inf. Co.E
Treadaway, J.D. GA Lt.Arty. 14th Bn. Co.D
Treadaway, J.D. GA Lt.Arty. King's Btty.
Treadaway, J.E. SC 22nd Inf. Co.K
Treadaway, Jesse G. AR 1st (Colquitt's) Inf. Co.C
Treadaway, Jesse W. GA 1st Inf. Co.E
Treadaway, J.M. SC 22nd Inf. Co.K
Treadaway, John NC 37th Inf. Co.D
Treadaway, John R. TN 43rd Inf. Co.B
Treadaway, John T. NC 43rd Inf. Co.H
Treadaway, John W. MO Lt.Arty. McDonald's Co.
Treadaway, Joseph TN 43rd Inf. Co.B
Treadaway, Joseph B. AL Lt.Arty. 2nd Bn. Co.F

Treadaway, J.P. GA Smith's Legion Stiff's Co.E
Treadaway, J.W. MO 6th Inf. Co.D
Treadaway, Levi TN 43rd Inf. Co.B
Treadaway, Lewis L. NC 43rd Inf. Co.H
Treadaway, Madison M. NC 29th Inf. Co.C Sgt.
Treadaway, Moses NC 37th Inf. Co.F
Treadaway, M.V. AR 27th Inf. Co.I
Treadaway, R. AL 12th Cav. Co.G
Treadaway, R.C. GA Inf. 1st City Bn. (Columbus) Co.B
Treadaway, R.C. GA 46th Inf. Co.C
Treadaway, Richard A. MS 5th Inf. Co.D
Treadaway, Richard F. MS 35th Inf. Co.B
Treadaway, S.B. GA 22nd Inf. Co.G 1st Lt.
Treadaway, Stephen AL 26th (O'Neal's) Inf. Co.C
Treadaway, Thomas MS 2nd Cav. Co.I
Treadaway, Thomas MS 6th Inf. Co.D
Treadaway, Thomas MS 43rd Inf. Co.G
Treadaway, Thomas John GA 1st Reg. Co.H
Treadaway, William MS 2nd St.Cav. Co.F
Treadaway, William SC 19th Inf. Co.B
Treadaway, William M. SC 22nd Inf. Co.K
Treadaway, William T. MS 35th Inf. Co.A Cpl.
Treadeway, Elijah MS 26th Inf. Co.G
Treadeway, T. NC 1st Jr.Res. Co.I
Treadgill, Samuel G. MS 2nd Part.Rangers Co.A
Treadgill, William H. TN 27th Inf. Co.I
Treadiway, Iverson B. SC 9th Inf. Co.H Cpl.
Treadway, A.T. AR 30th Inf. Co.F
Treadway, Benjamin F. VA 6th Bn.Res. Co.H
Treadway, B.F. MS 35th Inf. Co.B
Treadway, D. MO 9th Inf. Co.E
Treadway, Daniel H. AL 55th Vol. Co.B
Treadway, Drury MO 1st N.E. Cav. Co.F
Treadway, Drury MO Inf. Clark's Regt. Co.H
Treadway, D.T. GA 3rd Cav. Co.A,K
Treadway, E. MS 5th Cav. Co.I
Treadway, E.A.J. AR 10th Inf. Co.C
Treadway, Eli NC 26th Inf. Co.D
Treadway, Elias AL 27th Inf. Co.B
Treadway, F.M. TN Cav. 16th Bn. (Neal's) Co.A
Treadway, Francis M. AL Cp. of Instr. Talladega
Treadway, George W. AL 17th Inf. Co.G
Treadway, G.W. AL 7th Cav. Co.I,C
Treadway, Henry NC 58th Inf. Co.L
Treadway, Henry C. MO 3rd Inf. Co.A
Treadway, I. MO 9th (Elliott's) Cav. Co.H
Treadway, Irvin MO 9th Inf. Co.E
Treadway, Irvin MO Inf. Clark's Regt. Co.H
Treadway, Irwin MO 1st N.E. Cav. Co.F
Treadway, James VA 60th Inf. Co.C
Treadway, James J. TN 60th Mtd.Inf. Co.A
Treadway, James M. AL 17th Inf. Co.G
Treadway, J.D. MO 9th Inf. Co.E
Treadway, J.M. GA Floyd Legion (St.Guards) Co.E
Treadway, John VA 129th Mil. Wilkinson's Co.
Treadway, John D. MO 2nd Inf. Co.G
Treadway, John D. MO Inf. Clark's Regt. Co.H
Treadway, John Dooley AR 36th Inf. Co.G
Treadway, J.W. MS 40th Inf. Co.D
Treadway, M.H. Gen. & Staff Adj.
Treadway, Moses X. TN Cav. 7th Bn. (Bennett's) Co.A 1st Sgt.
Treadway, M.X. TN 22nd (Barteau's) Cav. Co.D
Treadway, N.J. SC 2nd Rifles Co.K
Treadway, N.T. MS 35th Inf. Co.A Cpl.
Treadway, Richard AL Green's Regt. Conscr.
Treadway, Richard MO 7th Cav. Co.K
Treadway, Richard TX 5th Inf. Co.K
Treadway, Thomas MO 4th Cav. Co.H
Treadway, Thomas Jefferson AR 1st (Dobbin's) Cav. Co.E,G
Treadway, William MS St.Cav. 2nd Bn. (Harris') Co.C
Treadway, William NC 58th Inf. Co.L
Treadway, William J. TN Cav. 9th Bn. (Gantt's) Co.E
Treadway, William T. MS 6th Inf. Co.D
Treadway, W.M. GA Inf. 23rd Bn.Loc.Def. Sims' Co.
Treadwell, --- TN Hvy.Arty. Johnston's Co.
Treadwell, --- TX Cav. Border's Regt. Co.B
Treadwell, --- TX Cav. McCord's Frontier Regt. Co.F Cpl.
Treadwell, A.C. TN 7th (Duckworth's) Cav. Co.B
Treadwell, A.G. SC 1st Inf. Co.A
Treadwell, A.H. GA 32nd Inf. Co.H
Treadwell, Albert O. AL 6th Inf. Co.I Cpl.
Treadwell, Amos AR 45th Mil. Co.G 1st Lt.
Treadwell, B.A. AL 46th Inf. Co.K
Treadwell, B.D. TN 1st Cav. 2nd Lt.
Treadwell, B.D. TN 7th (Duckworth's) Cav. Co.A
Treadwell, Benjamin F. TX 17th Cav. Co.H Cpl.
Treadwell, B.W. MS 3rd Inf. (St.Troops) Co.F Capt.
Treadwell, C.A. AL 21st Inf. Co.C
Treadwell, Columbus AL 46th Inf. Co.K
Treadwell, D. AL 12th Cav. Co.G
Treadwell, D. MS 36th Inf. Co.E
Treadwell, Dan TN 19th (Biffle's) Cav. Co.I Sgt.
Treadwell, David AL 7th Inf. Co.B 2nd Lt.
Treadwell, David MS 33rd Inf. Co.F Sgt.
Treadwell, David TX 26th Cav. Co.B
Treadwell, D.C. AR Inf. Crawford's Bn. Co.B
Treadwell, Dodd D. NC 20th Inf. Co.I
Treadwell, Edward TX 36th Cav. Co.D
Treadwell, E.E. AL 48th Inf. Co.K
Treadwell, Eli GA Inf. 23rd Bn.Loc.Def. Pendergrass' Co.
Treadwell, Eluctius W. AL 19th Inf. Co.H
Treadwell, F.M. TN 7th (Duckworth's) Cav. Co.A
Treadwell, F.S. GA 18th Inf. Co.B Capt.
Treadwell, Gustavus A. TX 17th Cav. Co.H Sgt.
Treadwell, Hardy GA Inf. Ezzard's Co.
Treadwell, Hardy GA Cobb's Legion Co.A Sgt.
Treadwell, Haywood NC 61st Inf. Co.G
Treadwell, H.B. GA 16th Inf. Co.F
Treadwell, Henry B. GA Inf. 10th Bn. Co.D Chap.
Treadwell, Henry B. Gen. & Staff Chap.
Treadwell, Henry R. TX 19th Cav. Co.D
Treadwell, H.R. TN 50th Inf. Co.C
Treadwell, H.R. TN 50th (Cons.) Inf. Co.C
Treadwell, Isaac GA 9th Inf. (St.Guards) Co.G
Treadwell, Isaac GA Phillips' Legion Co.F
Treadwell, Isaac MS 24th Inf. Co.F
Treadwell, Isaac MS 27th Inf. Co.E
Treadwell, James AR 9th Inf. Co.A
Treadwell, James MS 22nd Inf. Co.K
Treadwell, James TX 13th Cav. Co.F Sgt.
Treadwell, James A. GA Inf. 2nd Bn. Co.A
Treadwell, James C. NC 60th Inf. Asst.Surg.
Treadwell, James M. LA 19th Inf. Co.A
Treadwell, James T. MS Bradford's Co. (Conf.Guards Arty.)
Treadwell, Jasper GA Cav. Nelson's Ind.Co.
Treadwell, J.C. AR 1st (Colquitt's) Inf. Co.D
Treadwell, J.C. GA 4th Bn.S.S. Asst.Surg.
Treadwell, J.C. 2nd Conf.Inf. Co.A Sgt.
Treadwell, J. Clarence Gen. & Staff Asst.Surg.
Treadwell, J.H. GA 16th Inf. Co.F
Treadwell, J.H. MS 4th Inf. Co.E Cpl.
Treadwell, J.H. TX 4th Inf. Co.I
Treadwell, J.J. GA 4th Res. Co.C
Treadwell, John AL 2nd Bn. Hilliard's Legion Vol. Co.A
Treadwell, John AR 18th (Marmaduke's) Inf. Co.I
Treadwell, John MS Cav. 1st Bn. (Montgomery's) St.Troops Co.C
Treadwell, John A. GA 18th Inf. Co.B
Treadwell, John J. TX 25th Cav. Co.D
Treadwell, John R. AR 18th Inf. Co.D
Treadwell, John R. NC 51st Inf. Co.K
Treadwell, J.R. AR 2nd Cav. Co.G
Treadwell, J.S. AL 59th Inf. Co.F
Treadwell, J.W. SC 1st Inf. Co.A
Treadwell, L. AL 12th Cav. Co.G
Treadwell, N.H. LA 13th Bn. (Part.Rangers) Co.E
Treadwell, R.L. TX 22nd Inf. Co.D
Treadwell, Robert A. TN 7th (Duckworth's) Cav. Co.A,B
Treadwell, S.A. GA 16th Inf. Co.F
Treadwell, Smith TX 14th Cav. Co.G
Treadwell, Stephen G. GA 32nd Inf. Co.H 2nd Lt.
Treadwell, Stephen T. GA 7th Inf. (St.Guards) Co.I
Treadwell, Steven G. AL Inf. 1st Regt. Co.G
Treadwell, Terry GA 15th Inf. Co.I
Treadwell, Thomas GA 4th Res. Co.C
Treadwell, W. TX 25th Cav. Co.E
Treadwell, W.A. GA 16th Inf. Co.F
Treadwell, W.B. SC 2nd Arty. Co.C
Treadwell, W.E. GA 18th Inf. Co.B
Treadwell, W.H. LA 8th Cav. Co.C 1st Lt.
Treadwell, Wilbur F. AL 6th Inf. Co.I 1st Sgt.
Treadwell, William FL 1st (Res.) Inf. Co.D
Treadwell, William LA 1st Cav. Co.I,C
Treadwell, William A. TX 19th Cav. Co.D
Treadwell, Winston W. TX 12th Cav. Co.F Cpl.
Treadwell, W.J. MS 27th Inf. Co.E
Treadwell, W.L. MS 2nd Part.Rangers Co.L
Treadwell, W.L. TN 7th (Duckworth's) Cav. Co.A
Treadwell, W.L. TX 19th Inf. Co.H
Treadwell, W.S. TX Cav. McCord's Frontier Regt. Co.F
Treadwell, Zed B. GA 2nd Cav. (St.Guards) Co.I
Treaker, Theodore TX Cav. Waller's Regt. Menard's Co.
Treakle, Albert MD 1st Cav. Co.K

Treakle, Albert VA 1st Cav. 2nd Co.K
Treakle, Emmett S. MD 1st Cav. Co.A
Treakle, H.C. VA 54th Mil. Co.C,D
Treakle, Henry VA 9th Cav. Co.I
Treakle, Henry VA 25th Mil. Co.A Cpl.
Treakle, Henry W. VA 40th Inf. Co.H Cpl.
Treakle, James C. VA 25th Mil. Co.A
Treakle, J.H. VA 9th Cav. Co.D
Treakle, John H. VA 40th Inf. Co.H
Treakle, John H. VA 92nd Mil. Co.A
Treakle, John P. VA 40th Inf. Co.I
Treakle, Samuel C. VA 40th Inf.
Treakle, Samuel C. VA 55th Inf. Co.L
Treakle, Samuel C. VA 92nd Mil. Co.A
Treakle, Thornton B. VA 55th Inf. Co.L Cpl.
Treakle, Thornton B. VA 92nd Mil. Co.B
Treakle, William T. VA 55th Inf. Co.L
Treakle, William T. VA 92nd Mil. Co.B,A
Treanor, Francis AL 4th Inf. Co.F
Treanor, George Gen. & Staff, Adj.Gen.Dept. Maj.
Treanor, James TN 11th Inf. Co.G
Treanor, J.D. TN Cav. 1st Bn. (McNairy's) Co.A
Treanor, J. Duke TN 8th (Smith's) Cav. Co.K Sgt.
Treanor, John GA 1st (Olmstead's) Inf. Gordon's Co.
Treanor, John GA 63rd Inf. Co.F
Treanor, John O. TN 1st (Feild's) Inf. Co.B
Treanor, Thomas GA 1st (Olmstead's) Inf. Co.C, Way's Co. Sgt.
Treanum, C.F. VA 3rd Bn. Valley Res. Co.B
Treas, H.J. MO 16th Inf. Co.K
Treas, P. AR 12th Bn.S.S. Co.C
Treas, R. AR 12th Bn.S.S. Co.C
Trease, William 3rd Conf.Eng.Troops Co.D
Treat, A. AL 1st Bn.Cadets Co.A
Treat, A.J. AR 14th (Powers') Inf. Co.H Cpl.
Treat, Edwin M. AL 21st Inf. Co.A
Treat, E.E. AR 27th Inf. Co.E
Treat, E.H. AL 1st Bn.Cadets Co.B,A
Treat, Elijah AR 14th (Powers') Inf. Co.H
Treat, E.M. MS 14th Inf. Co.K
Treat, F.W. SC 7th Inf. 1st Co.I
Treat, George TX 1st Hvy.Arty. Co.H
Treat, H. AR 10th (DeWitt's) Cav.
Treat, H. AR 15th (N.W.) Inf. Buck's Co.
Treat, Hezekiah VA 6th Bn.Res. Co.I
Treat, Hiram AR 14th (Powers') Inf. Co.H
Treat, Ignatius AR 27th Inf. Co.E
Treat, Ignitus MO Cav. Schnabel's Bn. Co.B
Treat, James M. AR 27th Inf. Co.E
Treat, James William AR 18th (Marmaduke's) Inf. Co.I
Treat, Jesse AR 15th Mil. Co.G Cpl.
Treat, John AR 27th Inf. Co.E Sgt.
Treat, John B. AR 18th (Marmaduke's) Inf. Co.I
Treat, John P. AR 27th Inf. Co.F
Treat, John S. AL Lt.Arty. 2nd Bn. Co.E 2nd Lt.
Treat, John W. AR 27th Inf. Co.F
Treat, M. AL 1st Regt. Mobile Vol. Baas' Co.
Treat, Richard AR 14th (Powers') Inf. Co.H
Treat, Richard AR 27th Inf. Co.F
Treat, Samuel AR 27th Inf. Co.E
Treat, William AR 27th Inf. Co.E
Treat, William Hamilton AL 3rd Inf. Co.E,K Cpl.
Treatman, William LA C.S. Zouave Bn. Co.B
Treavathan, A.G. TN 20th Inf.
Treavey, Daniel J. VA Lt.Arty. Arch. Graham's Co.
Treavey, J.C. VA 12th Cav. Capt.,Asst.Surg.
Treavey, Robert MO 2nd Inf. Co.C Cpl.
Treay, Francis GA 1st (Olmstead's) Inf. Co.G
Trebbell, M.D.L. TN 40th Inf. Co.D
Trebbett, John P. VA 7th Cav. Preston's Co. Cpl.
Trebble, Abraham J. GA 2nd Res. Co.K
Trebble, G.W. TX 6th & 15th (Cons.) Vol. Asst.Surg.
Trebble, G.W. TX 10th Inf. Asst.Surg.
Trebble, J.B. GA 9th Inf. (St.Guards) Co.F
Trebble, W.H. GA 9th Inf. (St.Guards) Co.F
Trebes, August TX 36th Cav. Co.F Cpl.
Trebes, Ernst TX 36th Cav. Co.F
Treble, Charles W. LA 1st (Nelligan's) Inf. Co.A,I
Treble, Stephen Milton SC 19th Inf. Co.I 1st Lt.
Trebosul, J.T. TX Cav. Waller's Regt. Menard's Co.
Trebouilles, J. LA Mil. 3rd Regt. French Brig. Co.6
Trecher, William B. TX Cav. 3rd (Yager's) Bn. Co.A
Trechfield, T.M. TN 2nd Cav. Co.H
Trecky, John LA Miles' Legion Co.E
Trecott, H. LA Mil. 4th Regt. 2nd Brig. 1st Div. Co.E
Trecy, Henry LA Inf. 7th Bn. Co.C
Tredaway, Andrew GA 6th Inf. Co.F
Tredaway, D.T. AR 10th Inf. Co.C Sgt.
Tredaway, F.M. AR 10th Inf. Co.C
Tredaway, G.W. MS 2nd Cav. Co.H
Tredaway, J.H. AL 12th Inf. Co.D
Tredaway, Joseph NC 64th Inf. Co.A,G
Tredaway, Joseph NC 64th Inf. Co.D
Tredaway, Lloyd B. GA 17th Inf. Co.H
Tredaway, L.G. AR 10th Inf. Co.C
Tredaway, R. AR 5th Inf. Co.D
Tredaway, Robert TN 59th Mtd.Inf. Co.D
Tredaway, S.S. MO 7th Cav. Co.B
Tredaway, W.B. AR 5th Inf. Co.E
Tredder, A. TX Waul's Legion Co.C
Tredder, J. TX Waul's Legion Co.C
Treddy, C.W. AR 24th Inf. Co.E
Treddy, George NC 42nd Inf. Co.I
Tredell, J. GA Cobb's Legion
Tredenice, N. NC 1st Inf. Co.C
Tredenick, L.P. SC 2nd Arty. Co.E
Tredenick, Richard NC 11th (Bethel Regt.) Inf. Co.H
Tredenick, Richard W. NC 5th Cav. (63rd St.Troops) Co.F
Tredennick, J.R. NC 1st Cav. (9th St.Troops) Co.C Far.
Tredennick, N.P. NC 1st Cav. (9th St.Troops) Co.C
Tredennick, W.S. NC 1st Cav. (9th St.Troops) Co.C
Treder, F. LA Mil. Orleans Fire Regt. Co.I Commanding Off.
Treder, Richard LA 20th Inf. Co.D, Old Co.B
Tredewick, John R. NC 1st Inf. (6 mo. '61) Co.B
Tredewick, W.S. NC 1st Inf. (6 mo. '61) Co.B
Tredway, Daniel B. TN 5th (McKenzie's) Cav. Co.H
Tredway, Henry NC 37th Inf. Co.K
Tredway, J. MS 22nd Inf. Co.K
Tredway, John NC 37th Inf. Co.K
Tredway, John TN 5th (McKenzie's) Cav. Co.H Cpl.
Tredway, Moses E. VA 2nd Arty. Co.H 2nd Lt.
Tredway, T. VA 1st Cav. Co.B
Tredway, T.B. VA Inf. Montague's Bn. Co.B Cpl.
Tredway, Thomas B. VA 53rd Inf. Co.I Sgt.
Tredway, William M., Jr. VA 53rd Inf. Co.I Capt.
Tredway, William M., Jr. VA Inf. Montague's Bn. Co.B Cpl.
Tredway, William W. NC 26th Inf. Co.A
Tredwell, Daniel TN 19th (Biffle's) Cav. Co.I Sgt.
Tredwell, Egbert A. TX 2nd Cav. Co.A
Tredwell, H.C. TN 11th Inf. Co.H
Tredwell, Henry B. GA Inf. 2nd Bn. Co.B
Tredwell, John AL 59th Inf. Co.F
Tredwell, John TN 7th (Duckworth's) Cav. Co.L
Tredwell, L.M. AL 6th Cav. Co.A
Tredwell, Thomas J. GA 10th Cav. (St.Guards) Co.F
Tredwell, William B. FL 5th Inf. Co.D
Tree, Josep FL McBride's Co. (Indians)
Treeble, E.W. MO 15th Cav. Co.M
Treece, Arch T. TX Cav. Ragsdale's Bn. 2nd Co.C
Treece, Ben 3rd Conf.Inf. Co.A
Treece, David NC 57th Inf. Co.G
Treece, G.B. AR 45th Mil. Co.C
Treece, I.C. KY 7th Cav. Co.A
Treece, Jacob AL 54th Inf. Co.K
Treece, J.C. NC 5th Inf. Co.F
Treece, John E. AL 58th Inf. Co.I
Treece, John Riley TN 37th Inf. Co.K
Treece, Jonathan AL 22nd Inf. Co.E
Treece, J.P. AL Lt.Arty. Phelan's Co.
Treece, T.G. AL Lt.Arty. Phelan's Co.
Treece, William AL Lt.Arty. Phelan's Co.
Treehy, Lawrence VA Inf. 22nd Bn. Co.G
Treels, J. TN Cav. Nixon's Regt. Co.A
Treeman, C.C. GA Arty. Lumpkin's Co.
Treen, William VA 32nd Inf. 2nd Co.I
Treeney, William Conf.Reg.Inf. Brooks' Bn. Co.B Sgt.
Treer, John AR 45th Mil. Co.D
Trees, Crawford TX 19th Cav. Co.B
Trees, Jacob AL 49th Inf. Co.G
Trees, J.C. 1st Conf.Cav. 2nd Co.B
Trees, J.P. AR 26th Inf. Co.G
Treese, Ben AR 18th (Marmaduke's) Inf. Co.I
Treese, Daniel AR 18th (Marmaduke's) Inf. Co.I
Treese, M.D. TN Lt.Arty. Rice's Btty.
Treese, Peter NC 8th Inf. Co.K
Treese, Pleasant TN 60th Mtd.Inf. Co.H
Treese, William AR 18th (Marmaduke's) Inf. Co.I
Treet, J.P. AR 45th Mil. Co.A 1st Lt.
Treet, Richard MO Cav. Fristoe's Regt. Co.D
Treewolla, James KY 7th Mtd.Inf. Co.C

Treewolla, Joseph KY 7th Mtd.Inf. Co.C
Treewolla, N.J. KY 7th Mtd.Inf. Co.C Ord.Sgt.
Treffeich, Emanuel TX Inf. Cunningham's Co.
Treffelstaff, Jacob TN 19th Inf. Co.B
Trefflich, Emanuel TX 36th Cav. Co.F
Tregle, H.D. LA Mil. LaFourche Regt.
Treglone, R.M. GA 56th Inf. Co.I
Trego, John D. MD 1st Inf. Co.D
Tregoe, John MD Arty. 4th Btty.
Trehame, John B. AL 32nd Inf. Co.K
Trehern, David MS 27th Inf. Co.L
Trehern, John R. VA 59th Inf. 3rd Co.F Jr.2nd Lt.
Trehern, Richard AL Lt.Arty. 2nd Bn. Co.F
Trehey, Thomas LA Inf. A.J. Gibbs' Co.
Trehune, W.B. Nitre & Min. Bureau War Dept.,CSA
Trehurn, John R. SC 1st (Butler's) Inf. Co.A
Trehurn, John R. SC 1st Inf. Co.M
Trehurn, John R. VA 60th Inf. 1st Co.H
Trehurn, Littleton W. VA 39th Inf. Co.A 2nd Lt.
Treibig, B. TX Waul's Legion Co.C
Treichel, F. TX 1st Regt.St.Troops Co.E
Treille, H. Conf.Lt.Arty. Richardson's Bn. Co.B 2nd Lt.
Treille, Hubert LA Arty. Landry's Co. (Donaldsonville Arty.) Sr.2nd Lt.
Trejo, Catarino TX Cav. Ragsdale's Bn. 1st Co.C
Trejo, Christoval TX 3rd Inf. 1st Co.C
Trejo, Tircio TX Cav. Ragsdale's Bn. 1st Co.C
Trelford, Alexander LA Inf.Crescent Regt. Co.C 2nd Lt.
Trell, Henry TX 4th Cav. Co.C
Trellue, Levi W. LA Arty. 1st Field Btty. Sgt.
Trellue, M.G. LA Cav. Greenleaf's Co. (Orleans Lt.Horse)
Trellue, M.L. TN 12th (Cons.) Inf. Co.C 1st Sgt.
Trellue, M.L. TN 22nd Inf. Co.A Ord.Sgt.
Trellue, N.B. LA Cav. Greenleaf's Co. (Orleans Lt.Horse)
Trellue, N.B. TN 12th (Cons.) Inf. Co.C Music.
Trellue, N.B. TN 22nd Inf. Co.A Sgt.
Treloar, John W. NC 1st Jr.Res. Co.H Sr.2nd Lt.
Treloar, J.W. NC 1st Inf. (6 mo. '61) Co.C
Tremain, S.E. LA 27th Inf. Co.C
Tremble, --- TX Cav. Hardeman's Regt. Co.F Cpl.
Tremble, Fred W. TX 2nd Cav. Co.B
Tremble, G.W. MS Cav. (St.Troops) Gamblin's Co.
Tremble, James W. MS Cav. Yerger's Regt. Co.C
Tremble, J.N. MO Cav. Ford's Bn. Co.A 1st Lt.
Tremble, John LA 4th Cav. Co.A
Tremble, John TX Cav. Benavides' Regt. Co.C
Tremble, John K. Gen. & Staff Surg.
Tremble, Joseph MS 25th Inf. Co.H Cpl.
Tremble, Joseph H. MS 1st Bn.S.S. Co.D Cpl.
Tremble, Joseph L. GA 20th Inf. Co.C
Tremble, Lenard AR 9th Inf. Co.G Cpl.
Tremble, Marcus L. MS 2nd Inf. Co.A
Tremble, Robert C. MS 2nd Inf. Co.A
Tremble, T.L. TX 1st (Yager's) Cav. Co.C
Treme, E. LA Arty. Guyol's Co. (Orleans Arty.)
Treme, John E. LA Washington Arty.Bn. Co.3
Tremenlet, A.C. LA Mil. Orleans Guards Regt. Co.F
Tremer, William VA Inf. 25th Bn. Music.
Tremer, William Post Band Cp.Lee,CSA Music.
Tremmell, A. AL 8th Inf. Co.I
Tremmell, M.M. GA 11th Inf. Co.G
Tremmer, P.H. Thomas' Brig. AAG
Tremmer, William VA 1st Inf.
Tremmiel, F. LA Mil. Orleans Fire Regt. Co.I
Tremolet, O. MO Lt.Arty. Barret's Co.
Tremoulet, --- LA Mil. 1st Chasseurs a pied Co.1
Tremoulet, B. LA Lt.Arty. LeGardeur, Jr.'s Co. (Orleans Guard Btty.) Cpl.
Tremoulet, B. MO Lt.Arty. Barret's Co.
Tremoulet, H. LA Lt.Arty. LeGardeur, Jr.'s Co. (Orleans Guard Btty.)
Trenaburge, L.W. MO Inf. 4th Regt.St.Guard Fife Maj.
Trenary, Benjamin VA 6th Cav. Co.D
Trenary, Benjamin F. VA 2nd Inf. Co.C
Trenary, Edward S. VA 6th Cav. Co.A
Trenary, J. VA 3rd Bn. Valley Res. Co.B
Trenary, James VA 51st Mil. Co.A
Trenary, J. Marshall VA 5th Inf. Co.L
Trenary, John VA 52nd Inf. Co.C Sgt.
Trenary, John B. VA 1st Cav. Co.A
Trenary, John B. VA 51st Mil. Co.C 1st Lt.
Trenary, J.S. VA Cav. Mosby's Regt. (Part. Rangers) Co.C
Trenary, Richard TN 9th (Ward's) Cav. Co.F
Trenary, Robert E. VA 5th Inf. Co.L 2nd Lt.
Trenary, Samuel N. VA 51st Mil. Co.C
Trenary, Thomas TN 9th (Ward's) Cav. Co.F
Trenchard, Francis B. AL Lt.Arty. 2nd Bn. Co.E Cpl.
Trenchard, Leonard A. AL Lt.Arty. 2nd Bn. Co.E
Trenchard, Manuel J. AL Lt.Arty. 2nd Bn. Co.E
Trenchard, Nathan MO 3rd Div.St.Guards Lt.
Trenckman, A. TX 1st Inf. Co.C,B
Trenckmann, H. TX Inf. Timmons' Regt. Co.B
Trenckmann, Herrm TX 4th Cav. Co.G
Trenckmann, J.E. TX Inf. Timmons' Regt. Co.B 2nd Lt.
Trenckmann, Otto TX 4th Cav. Co.G
Trende, F. TX Waul's Legion Co.C
Trenford, A.G. VA 3rd Res. Co.I
Trenholm, A.G. SC Mil. Trenholm's Co.
Trenholm, A.G. SC Rutledge Mtd.Riflemen & Horse Arty. Trenholm's Co.
Trenholm, C. SC Mil. Charbonnier's Co.
Trenholm, Charles L. SC Cav. Walpole's Co.
Trenholm, C.L. SC 1st Regt. Charleston Guard Co.H
Trenholm, E.D. SC 4th Cav. Co.K
Trenholm, E.L. SC Rutledge Mtd.Riflemen & Horse Arty. Trenholm's Co.
Trenholm, F.H. Hill's Staff 1st Lt.
Trenholm, G.A., Jr. SC 7th Cav. Co.B
Trenholm, G.A., Jr. SC Rutledge Mtd.Riflemen & Horse Arty. Trenholm's Co.
Trenholm, G.A., Jr. Sig.Corps,CSA
Trenholm, George A., Jr. SC Mil. Trenholm's Co.
Trenholm, P.C. SC Mil.Arty. 1st Regt. Palmer's Co. Cpl.
Trenholm, P.C. SC Inf. 1st (Charleston) Bn. Co.E Ord.Sgt.
Trenholm, P.C. SC 27th Inf. Co.A Ord.Sgt.
Trenholm, S.D. SC 7th Cav. Co.B
Trenholm, W.F. SC Cav. 19th Bn. Lt.Col.
Trenholm, William L. SC Rutledge Mtd.Riflemen & Horse Arty. Trenholm's Co. Capt.
Trenholm, W.L. SC 7th Cav. Co.B Capt.
Trenholm, W.L. SC Mil. Trenholm's Co. Capt.
Trenkitt, W.R. TN Conscr. (Cp. of Instr.)
Trenkle, Jacob TX 3rd Inf. Co.E,B Cpl.
Trenkmann, Ernst TX Waul's Legion Co.D Jr.2nd Lt.
Trenkmann, H. TX 4th Inf. (St.Troops) Co.A
Trennelly, C.D. AL 21st Inf. Co.C
Trennis, E.B. VA 15th Cav. Co.H
Trenor, F.M. VA 22nd Inf. Co.C
Trenor, Garwood H. VA 36th Inf. 2nd Co.H, Co.F
Trenor, George W. VA 28th Inf. Co.B
Trenor, Napoleon B. MS 3rd Inf. Co.D Color Cpl.
Trenor, Van Buren VA 24th Inf. Co.F
Trenor, William H.H. VA 28th Inf. Co.B
Trenor, William M. VA 24th Inf. Co.F
Trensan, Rufus NC 26th Inf. Co.D
Trent, Alexander AR 8th Inf. Old Co.E
Trent, Alexander VA 129th Mil. Buchanon's Co.
Trent, A.M. VA 42nd Inf. Co.I
Trent, Andrew J. AL 13th Inf. Co.K
Trent, Archibald P. VA 28th Inf. Co.I
Trent, Archibald P. VA 54th Inf. Co.E
Trent, Arch P. VA 157th Mil. Co.A
Trent, Benjamin VA 28th Inf. Co.I
Trent, Benjamin H. VA Lt.Arty. Hardwicke's Co.
Trent, Berry VA 58th Inf. Co.E
Trent, Booker T. VA 56th Inf. Co.I
Trent, C. TN 28th (Cons.) Inf. Co.C Sgt.
Trent, Clinton TN 28th Inf. Co.K Sgt.
Trent, Collin S. VA 2nd Arty. Co.A
Trent, Collin S. VA Inf. 22nd Bn. 1st Co.A
Trent, David GA 1st Inf. (St.Guards) Co.A
Trent, Edward L. SC Hvy.Arty. 15th (Lucas') Bn. Co.A
Trent, Edw. P. AL 19th Inf. Co.G
Trent, Eli VA Inf. 45th Bn. Co.B
Trent, Eli VA 129th Mil. Buchanon's Co.
Trent, E.P. VA Inf. 1st Bn.Loc.Def. Co.F
Trent, Fleming VA Inf. 45th Bn. Co.E
Trent, F.W. VA 8th Inf. Co.G
Trent, G. GA 18th Inf.
Trent, George VA Lt.Arty. Pegram's Co. Sgt.
Trent, George VA 12th Inf. Branch's Co.
Trent, George VA 16th Inf. Co.K
Trent, George W. VA 10th Cav. Co.C
Trent, George W. VA Lt.Arty. Montgomery's Co.
Trent, George W. VA Lt.Arty. J.D. Smith's Co.
Trent, George W. VA 11th Inf. Co.E
Trent, G.W. TX 17th Inf. Co.E
Trent, Henry VA Hvy.Arty. 19th Bn. 3rd Co.C Ch.Cook
Trent, Henry VA 4th Res. Co.B
Trent, Henry C. MO Searcy's Bn.S.S. Co.C

Trent, H.H. MO 6th Cav. Co.G
Trent, H.J. LA 2nd Inf. Co.C
Trent, Isaac VA 37th Inf. Co.H
Trent, Isaac VA 50th Inf. 1st Co.G
Trent, Isaiah KY 5th Mtd.Inf. Co.B
Trent, J. VA 11th Inf. Co.B
Trent, Jackson B. AL Cav. Lenoir's Ind.Co.
Trent, Jacob MO Cav. Williams' Regt. Co.I Cpl.
Trent, James VA 10th Cav. Co.C,A
Trent, James L. NC 18th Inf. Co.G
Trent, James L. 1st Conf.Eng.Troops Co.F
Trent, James M. VA Lt.Arty. J.D. Smith's Co.
Trent, James M. VA 4th Inf. Co.L
Trent, James M. VA 16th Inf. 2nd Co.B
Trent, James P. VA 4th Inf. Co.F
Trent, J.C. VA 3rd Cav. Co.G
Trent, Jesse VA 166th Mil. Co.D,H
Trent, J.H. AR 35th Inf. Co.E
Trent, J.M. VA 36th Inf. Co.A
Trent, John MS 2nd Part.Rangers Co.L,D 2nd Lt.
Trent, John TN 7th (Duckworth's) Cav. Co.A Sr.2nd Lt.
Trent, John TX 13th Cav. Co.C
Trent, John VA 21st Cav. 2nd Co.G
Trent, John VA 24th Inf. Co.B
Trent, John VA 37th Inf. Co.F
Trent, John VA 42nd Inf. Co.G
Trent, John VA 46th Inf. 2nd Co.B
Trent, John VA 50th Inf. 1st Co.G
Trent, John VA 63rd Inf. 1st Co.I, Co.E Cpl.
Trent, John VA 166th Mil. Co.D,H Cpl.
Trent, John E. VA 11th Inf. Co.F
Trent, John H. VA Lt.Arty. J.D. Smith's Co.
Trent, John H. VA Lt.Arty. Wimbish's Co.
Trent, John T. VA 42nd Inf. Co.A
Trent, John W. VA 46th Inf. 2nd Co.B
Trent, Jonathan VA 57th Inf. Co.K
Trent, Joseph MO Robertson's Regt.St.Guard Co.5
Trent, Joseph G. VA 42nd Inf. Co.A Sgt.
Trent, Joshua AR 2nd Cav. Co.A
Trent, J.P. AL 3rd Cav. Co.I
Trent, J.P. VA 7th Cav. Preston's Co.
Trent, J.P. VA 14th Cav. Co.G
Trent, J.T. TN 7th (Duckworth's) Cav. Co.C
Trent, J.W. MO 2nd Inf. Co.A
Trent, J.W.M. AR 2nd Cav. Co.A
Trent, J.W.M. AR 34th Inf. Co.A
Trent, Lewis VA 63rd Inf. Co.E
Trent, Milton G. VA 8th Cav. Co.C
Trent, Milton G. VA Mil. Grayson Cty.
Trent, N.B. LA 14th Inf. Co.F,D
Trent, N.B. 8th (Wade's) Conf.Cav. Co.B
Trent, Peter F. VA 3rd Cav. Co.G
Trent, Peterfield Gen. & Staff Surg.
Trent, Phleganon VA 129th Mil. Buchanon's Co.
Trent, Pleasant VA 8th Inf. Co.G
Trent, P.W. NC 2nd Cav. (19th St.Troops) Co.B
Trent, R.E. VA 36th Inf. Co.A
Trent, Richard B., Jr. VA 3rd Cav. Co.G
Trent, Robert H. TN 28th Inf. Co.K
Trent, Roland H. VA 34th Inf. Co.C
Trent, S.A. AL 19th Inf. Co.G
Trent, Stephen A. VA 1st Arty. Co.K
Trent, Stephen A. VA Arty. L.F. Jones' Co.
Trent, S.W. VA Lt.Arty. R.M. Anderson's Co.
Trent, T. TN 5th Inf. 2nd Co.K
Trent, Tazewell VA Hvy.Arty. 18th Bn. Co.D
Trent, Taz. M. VA Hvy.Arty. Patteson's Co.
Trent, T.B. AL 55th Vol. Co.A Sgt.
Trent, T.H. VA Conscr. Cp.Lee
Trent, Thomas VA 3rd Cav. Co.E
Trent, Thomas VA 21st Cav. 2nd Co.G
Trent, Thomas VA 3rd Res. Co.E
Trent, Thomas VA Inf. 26th Bn. Co.C
Trent, Thomas VA 42nd Inf. Co.D
Trent, Thomas VA 59th Inf. 2nd Co.D
Trent, Thomas W. VA 16th Inf. Co.A
Trent, Thomas W. VA 57th Inf. Co.A QMSgt.
Trent, Timothy VA Hvy.Arty. Patteson's Co.
Trent, W.C. AR Cav. Gordon's Regt. Co.F
Trent, W.G. TN Inf. 3rd Cons.Regt. Co.D
Trent, W.G. TN 5th Inf. 1st Co.H, 2nd Co.E Sgt.
Trent, William AL 15th Inf. Co.F
Trent, William VA 11th Inf. Co.K
Trent, William VA 24th Inf. Co.B
Trent, William VA 28th Inf. Co.I
Trent, William VA 42nd Inf. Co.A Sgt.
Trent, William VA 59th Inf. 2nd Co.C
Trent, William E. VA 24th Inf. Co.B
Trent, William F. 1st Conf.Eng.Troops Co.G
Trent, William H. VA 2nd Cav. Co.H Capt.,AQM
Trent, William H. VA 21st Inf. Co.A
Trent, William H. VA 42nd Inf. Co.G
Trent, William J. VA 11th Inf. Co.F
Trent, William J. VA 38th Inf. Co.K
Trent, William J. VA 51st Inf. Co.K
Trent, William T. VA 4th Inf. Co.F
Trent, Willis W. MO Inf. 2nd Regt.St.Guard Co.G Capt.
Trent, Zachariah VA Hvy.Arty. 18th Bn. Co.D
Trent, Zachariah VA Hvy.Arty. Patteson's Co.
Trenta, Raphael LA 10th Inf. Co.I
Trenter, George VA 77th Mil. Co.A
Trenter, R. VA 77th Mil. Co.B
Trentham, A.J. NC Inf. 2nd Bn. Co.G
Trentham, A.J. TN Cav. 16th Bn. (Neal's) Co.C
Trentham, Caleb L. NC Inf. Thomas Legion Co.F Drum.
Trentham, G.J. MS 37th Inf. Co.I
Trentham, H.M. MS 10th Inf. New Co.I
Trentham, James NC 60th Inf. Co.C
Trentham, James M. TN Cav. 16th Bn. (Neal's) Co.C
Trentham, John TN 6th (Wheeler's) Cav. Co.K
Trentham, John TX 18th Cav. Co.D Sgt.
Trentham, John TX Cav. Baird's Regt. Co.G
Trentham, John J. TN 1st Cav.
Trentham, J.W. TN Lt.Arty. Rice's Btty.
Trentham, Lien TN 6th (Wheeler's) Cav. Co.K
Trentham, Merritt NC 29th Inf. Co.H
Trentham, W.C. MS 10th Cav. Co.H
Trentham, W.C. Conf.Cav. Baxter's Bn. Co.A
Trentham, William M. TN Cav. 16th Bn. (Neal's) Co.C
Trentham, Zachariah T. 1st Cherokee Mtd.Vol. 2nd Co.K
Trenti, R. VA 2nd St.Res. Co.K
Trentiss, H.E. VA 16th Inf. Co.G
Trenton, John B. VA 13th Inf. Co.I
Trents, August TX 13th Vol. Co.K Sgt.
Trenum, Burbridge B. VA 7th Cav. Co.F
Trenum, John W. VA 14th Inf. Co.C
Treosher, A. LA Mil. Fire Bn. Co.D
Treosher, C. LA Mil. Fire Bn. Co.D
Treosher, E. LA Mil. Fire Bn. Co.D
Trepagneer, G. LA Arty. 5th Field Btty. (Pelican Lt.Arty.)
Trepagnier, A. LA Dreux's Cav. Co.A
Trepagnier, A. LA Arty. 5th Field Btty. (Pelican Lt.Arty.)
Trepagnier, A. LA Inf.Cons. 18th Regt. & Yellow Jacket Bn. Co.B 1st Cpl.
Trepagnier, Alfred LA 18th Inf. Co.E Cpl.
Trepagnier, D. LA Ogden's Cav.
Trepagnier, D. LA Arty. 5th Field Btty. (Pelican Lt.Arty.)
Trepagnier, E.F. LA Arty. 5th Field Btty. (Pelican Lt.Arty.)
Trepagnier, E.H. LA Mil. St.John the Baptist Res.Guards 1st Lt.
Trepagnier, F. LA 18th Inf. Co.G
Trepagnier, F.E. LA Cav. Greenleaf's Co. (Orleans Lt.Horse)
Trepagnier, F.O. LA 30th Inf. Co.G,F Capt.
Trepagnier, F.O. LA Mil. Orleans Guards Regt. Co.A 3rd Lt.
Trepagnier, Francis LA 18th Inf. Co.G
Trepagnier, Francois LA Mil. 1st Native Guards
Trepagnier, Leon LA 18th Inf. Co.G
Trepagnier, N. LA Mil.Cav. (Chasseurs Jefferson) Cagnolatti's Co.
Trepagnier, N. LA 30th Inf. Co.A Capt.
Trepagnier, Paul LA 18th Inf. Co.E
Trepagnier, Paul E. LA 18th Inf. Co.E
Trepagnier, P.E. LA Inf.Cons. 18th Regt. & Yellow Jacket Bn. Co.B
Trepagnier, S.B. LA 1st Cav. Co.C
Trepagnier, T. LA Lt.Arty. LeGardeur, Jr.'s Co. (Orleans Guard Btty.) 2nd Lt.
Trepaignier, Felix LA 13th Inf. Co.E Sgt.
Trepani, Stefano LA Mil. 6th Regt.Eur.Brig. (Italian Guards Bn.) Co.2
Trepanier, P. LA 22nd (Cons.) Inf. Co.E
Trepannier, T. MO Lt.Arty. Barret's Co. 2nd Lt.
Trepaynier, Gustave LA Mil. St.James Regt. Co.E Cpl.
Trepest, August TX 1st (McCulloch's) Cav. Co.D
Trephagen, H.T. LA Arty. Hutton's Co. (Crescent Arty.,Co.A) Sgt.
Treppe, R.P. VA 37th Inf. Co.G
Trerigne, R. LA Mil. 1st Native Guards
Tresalie, Moris LA 19th Inf. Co.G
Trescasas, James LA Mil. 5th Regt.Eur.Brig. (Spanish Regt.) Co.5
Trescases, Nicolas LA Mil. 6th Regt.Eur.Brig. (Italian Guards Bn.) Co.5
Tresch, --- LA Mil. 3rd Regt.Eur.Brig. (Garde Francaise) Euler's Co.
Tresch, John LA C.S. Zouave Bn. Co.A,B
Tresch, SeBastian LA C.S. Zouave Bn. Co.A
Tresche, B. LA Arty. Landry's Co. (Donaldsonville Arty.)
Tresche, B. Conf.Lt.Arty. Richardson's Bn.
Trescot, George E. NC 37th Inf. Surg.
Trescott, Austin A. MS 21st Inf. Co.A

Trescott, E. SC 11th Inf. Co.A
Trescott, E.B. SC Arty. Stuart's Co. (Beaufort Vol.Arty.)
Trescott, Geo. E. Gen. & Staff Surg.
Trescott, J.C. Gen. & Staff Surg.
Trescott, Wm. H. Gen. & Staff Vol.ADC
Trescutt, A.A. AL 21st Inf. Co.A
Trese, John E. AL 38th Inf. Co.I
Tresher, Ch. LA Mil. Chalmette Regt. Co.G Sgt.
Tresher, William B. TX 1st (Yager's) Cav. Co.A
Treshler, Cazalano TX 8th Inf. Co.E
Tresler, Edward NC 24th Inf. Co.K
Tresler, J.S. TN Inf. 154th Sr.Regt. Co.A 1st Sgt.
Tresneu, M.U. AL 3rd Bn.Res. Co.F
Tresper, Walter C. FL 9th Inf. Co.A
Trespognet, Jean LA Mil. 4th Regt. French Brig. Co.5
Tressam, John TX 21st Cav. Co.H Bugler
Tressam, John TX 24th Cav. Co.A Bugler
Tressam, John TX 5th Inf. Co.A
Tressan, John AR Inf. Hardy's Regt. Co.K
Tressel, S.W. MO Lt.Arty. H.M. Bledsoe's Co.
Tresser, John G. TN 28th Cav. Co.C
Tressler, Oliver LA Arty. Green's Co. (LA Guard Btty.)
Trest, James R. MS 37th Inf. Co.K
Trest, John D. MS 9th Cav. Co.G
Trest, Peter N. MS 37th Inf. Co.K Cpl.
Trest, Richard C. MS 37th Inf. Co.K,E
Trest, Samuel C. MS Inf. 7th Bn. Co.C
Trest, William B. MS 37th Inf. Co.K
Trest, W.R. AL 4th Inf. Co.K
Trestler, Oliver LA Inf. 1st Sp.Bn. (Wheat's) New Co.D
Trestwell, William N. AL 10th Cav. Co.H
Tresvant, W.H. SC 4th Cav. Co.C
Treswant, L.C. Hamilton's Arty. Ord.Sgt.
Trett, Isaac VA 64th Mtd.Inf. Co.I
Trett, William FL 8th Inf. Co.C
Trett, Zion VA 64th Mtd.Inf. Co.I
Tretter, --- TX Cav. Ragsdale's Bn. Co.E
Treuett, E.J. GA 1st (Olmstead's) Inf. Co.K
Treumeo, Gregore TX 17th Field Btty.
Treutel, Pierre Sap. & Min. Gallimard's Co.,CSA 1st Sap.
Trevatham, William M. TX 22nd Inf. Co.D
Trevathan, A.G. TN 5th Inf. 2nd Co.F
Trevathan, A.G. TN 46th Inf. Co.C 2nd Lt.
Trevathan, Francis M. MO 9th Inf. Co.I
Trevathan, Frank M. MO Inf. 8th Bn. Co.E
Trevathan, Franklin M. MO Cav. 11th Regt. St.Guard Co.F Capt.
Trevathan, H.H. TN 46th Inf. Co.D
Trevathan, John TX 7th Cav. Co.E
Trevathan, John W. NC 17th Inf. (2nd Org.) Co.D
Trevathan, Mathew G. NC 2nd Inf. Co.B
Trevathan, R.E. AR 21st Mil. Co.D
Trevathan, R.E. AR 36th Inf. Co.E
Trevathan, Robert H. NC 5th Cav. (63rd St.Troops) Co.B
Trevathan, Sanders M. NC 2nd Inf. Co.B
Trevathan, Sanders M. NC 55th Inf. Co.A
Trevathan, Thomas TX 7th Cav. Co.E
Trevathan, Thomas B. KY 2nd Mtd.Inf. Co.A
Trevathan, V.C. TN 5th Inf. 2nd Co.I
Trevathan, W.H. 7th Conf.Cav. Co.F
Trevathan, William C. NC 5th Cav. (63rd St.Troops) Co.B Sgt.
Trevathan, William H. NC 15th Inf. Co.K
Trevena, William VA Lt.Arty. Cayce's Co.
Trevenia, Charles TX Cav. Madison's Regt. Co.A
Trevenie, Jesus TX 8th Inf. Co.H
Trevenio, Carlo TX 8th Inf. Co.I
Trevenio, Jesus TX 36th Cav. Co.E,H
Trevenio, Oliverio TX 8th Inf.
Trevenio, Thomas TX 8th Inf. Co.I
Treveno, Leonardo TX Conscr.
Trevet, L.H. SC Post Guard Senn's Co. Drum.
Trevett, J. SC 6th Res. Co.I
Trevett, J.W. SC 24th Inf. Co.G
Trevett, L.H. SC 6th Res. 1st Sgt.
Trevett, William 2nd Cherokee Mtd.Vol. Co.D
Trevey, Adam S. VA 1st Cav. Co.C
Trevey, Andrew A. VA 28th Inf. Co.A
Trevey, Cyrus W. VA 1st Cav. Co.C
Trevey, D.A. VA 4th Inf. Co.I
Trevey, David A. VA 1st Cav. Co.C
Trevey, Jacob M. VA 5th Inf. Co.C Capt.
Trevey, Joseph VA 14th Cav. Co.H
Trevey, William B. VA 28th Inf. Co.A Cpl.
Trevi, A.A. VA 3rd Res. Co.K
Trevilean, J.G. Gen. & Staff Surg.
Trevilian, A.S. Conf.Hvy.Arty. Montague's Bn. Co.A
Trevilian, John G. VA Lt.Arty. Leake's Co.
Trevilian, John G. VA 38th Inf. Surg.
Trevilian, William C. VA 24th Cav. Co.D
Trevilian, William C. VA Cav. 40th Bn. Co.D
Treville, G. VA 21st Cav. Co.G
Trevillian, Augustine S. VA 34th Inf. Co.A
Trevillian, B.T. VA 24th Cav. Co.F
Trevillian, Buckner T. VA 30th Inf. Co.E Sgt.
Trevillian, Charles B. VA 4th Cav. Co.F 1st Lt.
Trevillian, D.H. VA Inf. 1st Bn. Co.C
Trevillian, E.C. VA 19th Inf. Co.D
Trevillian, Garrett C. VA 46th Inf. Co.D
Trevillian, James GA 59th Inf. Co.K
Trevillian, Jas. G. Gen. & Staff Surg.
Trevillian, John VA Lt.Arty. Kirkpatrick's Co.
Trevillian, John VA Lt.Arty. Nelson's Co.
Trevillian, P.B. MS Inf. 2nd Bn. (St.Troops) Co.F
Trevillian, Thomas B. VA 24th Cav. Co.F
Trevillian, T.J.M. VA 15th Cav. Co.B
Trevillion, A.L. MS Inf. 2nd Bn. (St.Troops) Co.C
Trevillion, Francis A. TX 9th Cav. Co.K 1st Sgt.
Trevillion, J.A.W. TX 23rd Cav. Co.G
Trevinia, Lorenzo TX 2nd Cav. Co.B Sgt.
Trevinio, Clemento TX 8th Inf. Co.E
Trevinio, Lorenzo TX Cav. L. Trevinio's Co. Capt.
Trevino, Anastasio TX Part.Rangers Thomas' Co.
Trevino, Andreas TX 3rd Inf. Co.D
Trevino, Bonifacio TX Cav. 3rd (Yager's) Bn. Rhodes' Co.
Trevino, Cesario TX 33rd Cav. 1st Co.H
Trevino, Demasio TX 3rd Inf. 1st Co.C
Trevino, Eugenio TX 33rd Cav. 1st Co.H
Trevino, Eujenio TX Cav. Benavides' Regt. Co.A
Trevino, Jose TX 33rd Cav. 1st Co.H
Trevino, Jose TX Cav. Benavides' Regt. Co.A
Trevino, Jose TX Part.Mtd.Vol. Trevino's Squad
Trevino, Juan LA 30th Inf. Co.D
Trevino, Justo TX Part.Mtd.Vol. Trevino's Squad Capt.
Trevino, L. TX Cav. Cater's Bn. Capt.
Trevino, Lesario TX Cav. Ragsdale's Bn. 1st Co.A
Trevino, Logngino TX 33rd Cav. 1st Co.I
Trevino, Longino TX Cav. Benavides' Regt. Co.B
Trevino, Manuel TX 33rd Cav. 1st Co.H
Trevino, Manuel TX Cav. Benavides' Regt. Co.A
Trevino, Martin TX Part.Mtd.Vol. Trevino's Squad
Trevino, Pedro TX 33rd Cav. 1st Co.I 2nd Lt.
Trevino, Polonario TX 33rd Cav. 1st Co.H
Trevino, Sesario TX Cav. Benavides' Regt. Co.A
Trevino, Ygnacio TX Part.Mtd.Vol. Trevino's Squad
Trevino, Yndalecio TX Cav. 3rd (Yager's) Bn. Rhodes' Co. 2nd Lt.
Trevitt, James B. AL 31st Inf. Co.A
Trevitt, J.F. TN Sullivan Cty.Res. (Loc.Def. Troops) Trevitt's Co. Capt.
Trevitt, John E. TN Sullivan Cty.Res. (Loc. Def.Troops) Trevitt's Co.
Trevors, George W. KY 10th Cav. Co.C
Trevy, Andrew J. VA Lt.Arty. Kirkpatrick's Co.
Trevy, G.W. VA Burks' Regt.Loc.Def. McCue's Co.
Trew, B.M. 3rd Conf.Cav. Co.H
Trew, Harrison MO 12th Cav. Co.H
Trew, James C. TN 1st (Turney's) Inf. Co.B
Trew, J.C. TN Conscr. (Cp. of Instr.) Co.B
Trew, Jesse J. TN 59th Mtd.Inf. Co.A
Trew, T.J. TN 1st (Carter's) Cav. Co.C
Trew, William TN Conscr. (Cp. of Instr.) Co.B
Trewaller, H.L. MS 3rd Cav. Co.D
Trewell, A.B. TX Inf. Timmons' Regt. Co.D
Trewett, Elijah AL 24th Inf. Co.E
Trewett, Foster SC Lt.Arty. 3rd (Palmetto) Bn. Co.E
Trewett, H.M. AR 45th Mil. Co.B 1st Sgt.
Trewett, James MS 35th Inf. Co.G
Trewett, R. SC Lt.Arty. 3rd (Palmetto) Bn. Co.E
Trewhitt, S.W. GA 12th Cav. Co.E Sgt.
Trewit, Lewis SC 19th Inf. Co.H Cpl.
Trewitt, Andrew J. TX Cav. 8th (Taylor's) Bn. Co.E
Trewitt, Henry F. KY Cav. Buckner Guards
Trewitt, Henry F. TN 28th Inf. Co.A 1st Lt.
Trewitt, H.F. TN 28th (Cons.) Inf. Co.A 1st Lt.
Trewitt, Ira GA 51st Inf. Co.F Cpl.
Trewitt, Joseph FL 11th Inf. Co.K
Trewitt, Pinckney P. TN Inf. 1st Bn. (Colms') Co.D 2nd Lt.
Trewitt, William H. NC Cav. 7th Bn. Co.B
Trewolla, Alfred P. VA Lt.Arty. 38th Bn. Co.C
Trewolla, Samuel P. VA Lt.Arty. 38th Bn. Co.C
Trexler, Adam NC 6th Inf. Co.G
Trexler, Alex NC 57th Inf. Co.K

Trexler, Alfred M. NC 1st Arty. (10th St.Troops) Co.D
Trexler, Benjamin C. NC 42nd Inf. Co.B
Trexler, Caleb C. NC 57th Inf. Co.C
Trexler, David NC 1st Arty. (10th St.Troops) Co.D
Trexler, David L. NC 14th Inf. Co.I
Trexler, D.M. NC 42nd Inf. Co.B
Trexler, Henry A. NC 42nd Inf. Co.D
Trexler, Hiram A. NC 4th Inf. Co.K
Trexler, Ignatius VA 5th Cav. Co.I
Trexler, J. SC Mil. 18th Regt. Co.A
Trexler, Jacob NC 57th Inf. Co.F
Trexler, James NC 42nd Inf. Co.D
Trexler, James M. NC 1st Arty. (10th St.Troops) Co.D
Trexler, Jesse L. NC 1st Arty. (10th St.Troops) Co.D
Trexler, J.K. AR 23rd Cav. Co.D
Trexler, John NC 57th Inf. Co.K
Trexler, John H. NC 21st Inf. Co.A
Trexler, John W. NC 46th Inf. Co.A
Trexler, Marcus NC 6th Inf. Co.G
Trexler, Moses NC 4th Sr.Res. Co.B
Trexler, Peter M. NC 1st Arty. (10th St.Troops) Co.D
Trexler, Rufus NC 46th Inf. Co.B
Trexler, Warren NC 57th Inf. Co.K
Trexler, William H. NC 38th Inf. Co.A
Trexler, William L. AR 1st (Dobbin's) Cav. Co.G Cpl.
Trexler, William R. NC 5th Inf. Co.L
Trexler, Willis NC 43rd Inf. Co.I
Trexley, Alexander NC 18th Inf. Co.H
Trexley, John NC 18th Inf. Co.H
Trexley, Warren NC 18th Inf. Co.H
Treybig, F. TX Inf. Timmons' Regt. Co.B
Treybig, Fred TX Waul's Legion Co.E Cpl.
Treywand, George S. Gen. & Staff Capt.,Asst.Surg.
Trezevant, E.B. TN 7th (Duckworth's) Cav. Co.A 3rd Lt.
Trezevant, E.B. TN 10th (DeMoss') Cav. Lt.Col.
Trezevant, E.B. Gen. & Staff Adj.
Trezevant, F. SC Mil. 17th Regt. Rogers' Co.
Trezevant, Geo. S. Gen. & Staff Asst.Surg.
Trezevant, James D. SC 1st Cav. Co.E Capt.
Trezevant, James H. LA 1st (Strawbridge's) Inf. Co.A,D Capt.
Trezevant, John F. LA 31st Inf. Co.C
Trezevant, John P. TN Inf. 154th Sr.Regt. Co.L Cpl.
Trezevant, John T. TN 4th Inf. Co.A
Trezevant, J.P. Fowlke's Staff Maj.,Comsy. of Subs.
Trezevant, J.T. SC Charleston Arsenal Bn. Maj.
Trezevant, J.T. Conf.Inf. Tucker's Regt. Co.B 2nd Lt.
Trezevant, J.T. Gen. & Staff, Arty. Maj.
Trezevant, L.C. TN Arty. Ramsey's Btty.
Trezevant, L.C. Conf.Inf. Tucker's Regt. Co.K 2nd Lt.
Trezevant, L. Cruger Conf.Inf. Tucker's Regt. Co.K 2nd Lt.
Trezevant, L.E. TX 26th Cav. Co.I Capt.
Trezevant, Lewis C. TN 4th Inf. Co.A
Trezevant, M.B. TN 4th Inf. Co.A
Trezevant, M.B. TN 40th Inf. Co.C 3rd Lt.
Trezevant, M.B. TN 42nd Inf. 2nd Co.E 2nd Lt.
Trezevant, N.W. LA 6th Cav. Co.G
Trezevant, P. SC Mil. 17th Regt. Rogers' Co.
Trezevant, Peter J. SC 2nd Cav. Co.H
Trezevant, R. TN Inf. 154th Sr.Regt. Co.L
Trezevant, R.B. AR 21st Inf. Co.G Capt.
Trezevant, R.B. Gen. & Staff, Comsy.Dept. Capt.,Comsy.
Trezevant, T.B. Gen. & Staff Capt.,AAG
Trezvant, J. Howell SC Cav.Bn. Hampton Legion Co.D Cpl.
Triall, Stephen L. VA 44th Inf. Co.K
Triay, Gillermo LA Mil. 5th Regt.Eur.Brig. (Spanish Regt.) Co.7,10 Cpl.
Triay, Henry GA 1st Inf. Co.I
Triay, J. LA Mil. Orleans Guards Regt. Co.E
Triay, John GA 1st Bn.S.S. Co.A
Triay, John GA 1st (Olmstead's) Inf. Co.D
Triay, Jose LA Mil. 5th Regt.Eur.Brig. (Spanish Regt.) Co.1,5
Triay, Lorenzo LA Mil. 5th Regt.Eur.Brig. (Spanish Regt.) Co.3
Triay, Peter FL 8th Inf. Co.D
Triay, Rafael LA Mil. 5th Regt.Eur.Brig. (Spanish Regt.) Co.5
Triay, Victorino FL 8th Inf. Co.D
Tribbell, E.W. MO St.Guard
Tribbett, Andrew VA Rockbridge Cty.Res. Miller's Co.
Tribbett, Andrew D. VA 27th Inf. 2nd Co.H, Co.G Cpl.
Tribbett, Francis M. VA Lt.Arty. Donald's Co.
Tribbett, George G. VA 14th Cav. Co.G
Tribbett, George G. VA Rockbridge Cty.Res. Miller's Co.
Tribbett, J.F. VA 14th Cav. Co.C
Tribbett, J.F. VA Rockbridge Cty.Res. Bacon's Co.
Tribbett, John P. VA 14th Cav. Co.G Sgt.
Tribbett, John P. VA 4th Inf. Co.H
Tribbett, Joseph F. VA 4th Inf. Co.H
Tribbett, Robert VA Cav. 46th Bn. Co.E
Tribbett, Robert R. VA Lt.Arty. Donald's Co.
Tribbett, Wilkinson W. Hosp.Stew.
Tribbett, William M. VA 4th Inf. Co.H Cpl.
Tribbett, William W. VA 1st Cav. Co.C
Tribbett, W.W. Gen. & Staff Hosp.Stew.
Tribble, A.H. KY 11th Cav. Co.B Capt.
Tribble, A.J. AR 26th Inf. Co.I
Tribble, A.K. SC 7th Cav. Co.E
Tribble, A.K. SC 9th Res. Co.F Capt.
Tribble, A.K. SC Cav.Bn. Holcombe Legion Co.C
Tribble, Alea KY 2nd (Duke's) Cav. Co.F 1st Lt.
Tribble, Alex. TX Vol. Benton's Co.
Tribble, Alexander KY 6th Cav. Co.A
Tribble, Alexander KY 3rd Bn.Mtd.Rifles Co.C
Tribble, Alfred L. AR 9th Inf. Old Co.B
Tribble, Allen TN 34th Inf. Chap.
Tribble, Allen Gen. & Staff Chap.
Tribble, Andrew J. VA 26th Inf. Co.K
Tribble, Andrew P. MO 1st Cav. Co.A Sgt.
Tribble, Augustus F. AR 26th Inf. Co.A
Tribble, Benjaman J. NC Inf. 2nd Bn. Co.D
Tribble, Benjamin F. AR 3rd Inf. Co.D
Tribble, Benjamin J. GA Phillips' Legion Co.L,C
Tribble, Benjamin Silas TN 40th Inf. Co.A
Tribble, B.F. AR 15th (Johnson's) Inf. Co.C
Tribble, C.E. SC 27th Inf. Co.G
Tribble, Clay KY 12th Cav. Co.E
Tribble, C.W. SC Cav.Bn. Holcombe Legion Co.C
Tribble, Daniel J. AR Cav. Wright's Regt. Co.B
Tribble, D.F. TN 8th (Smith's) Cav. Co.D
Tribble, Dudley KY 7th Cav. Co.A 2nd Lt.
Tribble, Dudley KY 11th Cav. Co.B 2nd Lt.
Tribble, E. LA 2nd Inf. Co.F Sgt.
Tribble, E.A. MO 12th Inf. Co.C Sgt.
Tribble, E.F. GA Inf. 23rd Bn.Loc.Def. Cook's Co.
Tribble, E.K. SC Inf. 3rd Bn. Co.D
Tribble, E.K. SC Post Guard Senn's Co.
Tribble, Elijah GA 29th Inf. Co.B
Tribble, Eugene W. MO 6th Inf. Co.C
Tribble, E.W. Exch.Bn. 2nd Co.C,CSA
Tribble, George T. VA 26th Inf. Co.K
Tribble, George T. VA 38th Inf. Co.F
Tribble, George W. AR 9th Inf. Old Co.B
Tribble, George W. TX 6th Inf. Asst.Surg.
Tribble, Geo. W. Gen. & Staff Asst.Surg.
Tribble, G.W. MS 32nd Inf. Co.B
Tribble, G.W. TX Granbury's Cons.Brig. Asst.Surg.
Tribble, Haney TN 7th Inf. Co.D
Tribble, H.J. GA 32nd Inf. Co.A,D
Tribble, James KY 11th Cav. Co.B
Tribble, James TN 30th Inf. Co.I
Tribble, James H. GA 19th Inf. Co.A
Tribble, James M. MS 27th Inf. Co.D Sgt.
Tribble, James R. GA Cherokee Legion (St.Guards) Co.B
Tribble, James S. AL Lt.Arty. 2nd Bn. Co.A
Tribble, James W. SC Cav.Bn. Holcombe Legion Co.C
Tribble, James W. VA 26th Inf. Co.K
Tribble, J.B. GA Cav. 9th Bn. (St.Guards) Co.C Sgt.
Tribble, J.B. TX 15th Inf. Co.B
Tribble, J.C. SC 3rd Inf. Co.A
Tribble, J.C. TN 1st (Carter's) Cav. Co.K
Tribble, Jefferson R. MS 44th Inf. Co.E
Tribble, J.E.P. GA Arty. Lumpkin's Co.
Tribble, Jesse SC 2nd Rifles Co.A Cpl.
Tribble, J.F. AR 8th Inf. New Co.I
Tribble, J.J. GA Cherokee Legion (St.Guards) Co.K Cpl.
Tribble, J.K. AR 2nd Inf. Co.G
Tribble, John AL 27th Inf. Co.I
Tribble, John C. GA 56th Inf. Co.F Sgt.
Tribble, John C. SC Cav.Bn. Holcombe Legion Co.C
Tribble, John D. AR 26th Inf. Co.B
Tribble, John J. GA 3rd Inf. Co.I Cpl.
Tribble, John J. TN 1st (Turney's) Inf. Co.D 1st Lt.
Tribble, John L. MO St.Guard
Tribble, John R. GA Inf. 10th Bn. Co.C
Tribble, John T. MO 1st Cav. Co.I
Tribble, Joseph MS 5th Cav. Co.C
Tribble, Joseph MO 1st Cav. Co.A
Tribble, Joseph VA 2nd Bn.Res. Co.C

Tribble, J.P. SC 20th Inf. Co.E
Tribble, J.R. GA 9th Inf. Co.K
Tribble, J.R. SC Cav. 2nd Bn.Res. Co.H 2nd Lt.
Tribble, J.T. GA 8th Inf. Co.B
Tribble, J.W. SC 7th Cav. Co.E
Tribble, J.W. TN 5th Inf. 1st Co.F, 2nd Co.E
Tribble, Lemuel N. GA 34th Inf. Co.G
Tribble, Lemuel Richardson SC 4th Inf. Co.K
Tribble, Lemuel W. MS 15th Inf. Co.D 2nd Lt.
Tribble, Lemuel W. SC 4th Inf. Co.J 3rd Lt.
Tribble, Lemuel W. SC 20th Inf. Co.E
Tribble, L.N. GA 39th Inf. Co.A
Tribble, L.R. SC 2nd Rifles Co.D Cpl.
Tribble, Marion AR 26th Inf. Co.B
Tribble, M.C. MS 22nd Inf. Co.A
Tribble, M.M. MS 1st Bn.S.S. Co.C
Tribble, Moses C. MS 1st Bn.S.S. Co.D
Tribble, M.P. SC 7th Cav. Co.E
Tribble, M.P. SC 3rd Inf. Co.A
Tribble, M.P. SC Cav.Bn. Holcombe Legion Co.C
Tribble, N.R. AR 6th Inf. Co.K 1st Lt.
Tribble, P.A. SC 2nd Cav. Co.G
Tribble, P.A. SC 7th Inf. 1st Co.B Cpl.
Tribble, Peter VA 26th Inf. Co.K
Tribble, P.H. TN Inf. 23rd Bn. Co.C Sgt.
Tribble, R. TX 22nd Inf. Co.K
Tribble, Reuben G. TX 21st Cav. Co.H
Tribble, Reuben W. GA 29th Inf. Co.B
Tribble, Richard L. MS 1st Bn.S.S. Co.D
Tribble, R.L. MS 22nd Inf. Co.A
Tribble, R.O. SC 1st St.Troops Co.E Capt.
Tribble, R.O. SC 2nd Rifles Co.D
Tribble, Robert LA Cav. Cole's Co.
Tribble, Robert D. AL 4th Inf. Co.F
Tribble, Robert E. MS 1st Lt.Arty. Co.G Cpl.
Tribble, Robert E. MS 10th Inf. Old Co.I
Tribble, R.W. MS 6th Cav. Co.C
Tribble, R.W. MS 8th Cav. Co.I
Tribble, R.W. SC 7th Inf. 1st Co.B
Tribble, Samuel KY 1st Bn.Mtd.Rifles Co.E 2nd Lt.
Tribble, S.H. AR 8th Inf. New Co.I Cpl.
Tribble, S.M. SC 5th Res. Co.A 1st Sgt.
Tribble, S.T. GA 32nd Inf. Co.A
Tribble, Stephen LA Cav. Cole's Co.
Tribble, Stephen D. GA 36th (Broyles') Inf. Co.C
Tribble, Stephen H. AR 2nd Inf. Co.F
Tribble, Stephen M. SC 20th Inf. Co.E
Tribble, T. MS 29th Inf. Co.B
Tribble, Thomas GA 32nd Inf. Co.A
Tribble, Thomas C. GA Cherokee Legion (St.Guards) Co.K 1st Sgt.
Tribble, Thomas J. AR 26th Inf. Co.B
Tribble, Thomas J. VA 47th Inf. 2nd Co.K
Tribble, Thomas W. MS 1st Bn.S.S. Co.C
Tribble, T.J. MO 4th Inf. Co.I
Tribble, W. MS 3rd Cav. Co.K
Tribble, W.G. NC 1st Inf. Co.H
Tribble, W.H. GA 2nd Cav. Co.D
Tribble, W.H. TX 15th Inf. Co.B
Tribble, Wiley L. TN 1st (Turney's) Inf. Co.D Sgt.
Tribble, Wiley P. GA Cav. 20th Bn. Co.G
Tribble, Wiley P. GA Cav. 21st Bn. Co.D
Tribble, William MS 29th Inf. Co.B
Tribble, William C. GA Cherokee Legion (St.Guards) Co.B
Tribble, William C. MS 18th Inf. Co.C
Tribble, William H. MS 17th Inf. Co.F
Tribble, William H. TN 2nd (Smith's) Cav.
Tribble, William M. SC 1st (Orr's) Rifles Co.G Band
Tribble, William M. VA 9th Inf. 2nd Co.A
Tribble, W.P. GA 64th Inf. Co.E
Tribble, Z.C. AR 8th Inf. New Co.D
Tribbles, Albert G. AL 4th Cav.
Tribby, James VA 2nd Inf. Co.H
Tribby, James W. VA Cav. 35th Bn. Co.A
Tribby, John T. VA Cav. 35th Bn. Co.A
Tribert, Charles Kellersberg's Corps Sap. & Min.,CSA Artif.
Tribette, William H. VA Cav. 35th Bn. Co.C
Tribig, Benjamin TX Inf. Timmons' Regt. Co.K
Tribit, John E. NC 37th Inf. Co.E
Tribite, John TN 60th Mtd.Inf. Co.E
Trible, A.K. SC 3rd Inf. Co.B Sgt.
Trible, C.B. AR 19th (Dockery's) Inf. Co.H
Trible, D. AL 35th Inf. Co.D
Trible, D.J. AR 24th Inf. Co.E
Trible, J.A. SC 9th Res. Co.K
Trible, James GA 36th (Broyles') Inf. Co.C
Trible, James F. VA 23rd Inf. Co.G
Trible, John MS 1st Lt.Arty.
Trible, John VA 13th Cav. Co.B
Trible, J.R. MS T.P. Montgomery's Co.
Trible, J.W. AR Inf. Hardy's Regt. Co.G
Trible, P.H. TN 17th Inf. Co.A
Trible, Robert AR 47th (Crandall's) Cav. Williams' Co.
Trible, W.B. GA 10th Cav.
Trible, William AR 24th Inf. Co.E
Tribout, C. TX 9th (Nichols') Inf. Co.G
Tribout, Charles 4th Conf.Eng.Troops Co.E Artif.
Triboutt, Jules LA Mil. 1st Regt. French Brig. Co.6
Tribue, Grandison 3rd Conf.Eng.Troops Co.A Artif.
Tribute, John TN 60th Mtd.Inf. Co.E
Tric, Thomas SC 6th Res. Co.I
Trice, A.A. VA 4th Cav. Co.F
Trice, Addison L. VA 13th Inf. Co.D
Trice, Addison L. VA 56th Inf. Co.C Cpl.
Trice, A.J. KY 3rd Mtd.Inf. Co.F
Trice, A.J. VA 2nd St.Res. Co.I
Trice, Alfred W. VA 56th Inf. Co.C
Trice, A.M. VA 1st Bn.Res. Co.C Lt.
Trice, Anderson TN 53rd Inf. Co.I
Trice, B.A. GA 54th Inf. Co.B Cpl.
Trice, Benjamin AL 3rd Inf. Co.I
Trice, Benjamin A. GA Inf. 3rd Bn. Co.D
Trice, Benjamin A. GA 4th Bn.S.S. Co.B
Trice, B.F. VA Cav. Mosby's Regt. (Part. Rangers) Co.F
Trice, B.F. VA 20th Inf. Co.F
Trice, C.D. KY 2nd (Woodward's) Cav. Co.A
Trice, C.H. AL Cp. of Instr. Talladega
Trice, Charles H. TN 53rd Inf. Co.I 2nd Lt.
Trice, C.W. Inf. Bailey's Cons.Regt. Co.B
Trice, C.W. TX 7th Inf. Co.A
Trice, D.A. VA 3rd Bn. Valley Res. Co.B
Trice, Dabney A. VA 13th Inf. Co.D Sgt.
Trice, Daniel AL 13th Bn.Part.Rangers Co.B
Trice, Daniel AL 56th Part.Rangers Co.F
Trice, David A. VA 23rd Inf. Co.G Sgt.
Trice, David A. VA Inf. 25th Bn. Co.E
Trice, Edward TN 53rd Inf. Co.I
Trice, Edward VA 53rd Inf.
Trice, Edward G. VA 26th Inf. Co.C
Trice, Elvin AL 25th Inf. Co.C
Trice, Ezekiel FL 3rd Inf. Co.D
Trice, F. KY 3rd Mtd.Inf. Co.H
Trice, F.M. AL 8th Inf. Co.B
Trice, Francis M. AL 12th Inf. Co.I
Trice, George H. VA 9th Mil. Co.A
Trice, George H. VA 26th Inf. Co.I
Trice, G.W. TN Cav. Woodward's Co.
Trice, Harrison A. TN 14th Inf. Co.L Sgt.
Trice, Henry H. TN 14th Inf. Co.L Sgt.
Trice, H.H. AL 25th Inf. Co.C 2nd Lt.
Trice, James MS Cav. Yerger's Regt. Co.A Cpl.
Trice, James C. VA 9th Mil. Co.B
Trice, James C. VA 87th Mil.
Trice, James E. TN 14th Inf. Co.L
Trice, James F. AR 25th Inf. Co.H
Trice, James F. GA Inf. 3rd Bn. Co.D
Trice, James G. GA 13th Inf. Co.D Sgt.
Trice, James H. TX 28th Cav. Co.I
Trice, James K.P. TN 53rd Inf. Co.K
Trice, James M. MS 10th Cav. Co.G
Trice, James M. VA 4th Cav. Co.F Cpl.
Trice, James Monroe VA 13th Inf. Co.D
Trice, James T. AL 27th Inf. Co.A Sgt.
Trice, James T. AL 55th Vol. Co.I
Trice, James V. GA 46th Inf. Co.I
Trice, James W. VA 26th Inf. Co.I
Trice, J.C. AR 19th (Dockery's) Inf. Co.I
Trice, J.C. GA Arty. Maxwell's Regt.Lt.Btty.
Trice, J.C. GA 54th Inf. Co.I
Trice, J.D. MO 5th Cav. Co.C
Trice, J.D. TX 7th Inf. Co.A
Trice, Jessee F. AL 18th Bn.Vol. Co.E,B
Trice, J.J. TX 1st Inf. Co.E
Trice, J.J. VA Arty. B.H. Smith's Co.
Trice, J.J. VA Inf. 25th Bn. Co.E
Trice, J.L. MS 2nd St.Cav. Co.H
Trice, J.M. MS Cav. 1st Bn. (Montgomery's) St.Troops Hammond's Co. Cpl.
Trice, J.M. MS Cav. Yerger's Regt. Co.A
Trice, J.M. MS Lt.Arty. (Jefferson Arty.) Darden's Co.
Trice, J.N. TN 37th Inf. Co.I
Trice, John TN 11th (Holman's) Cav. Co.C
Trice, John VA Mtd.Res. Rappahannock Dist. Sale's Co.
Trice, John VA Res.Forces Clark's Co.
Trice, John C. GA Lt.Arty. Barnwell's Btty. Cpl.
Trice, John E. TN 14th Inf. Co.L
Trice, John F. VA 26th Inf. Co.I
Trice, John Fox VA 9th Mil. Co.A
Trice, John J. VA Lt.Arty. 1st Bn. Co.D
Trice, John L. KY 4th Mtd.Inf. Co.G Capt.
Trice, John L. VA 13th Inf. Co.D
Trice, John M. GA Lt.Arty. Scogin's Btty. (Griffin Lt.Arty.)
Trice, John M. MS 20th Inf. Co.G
Trice, John M. MS 35th Inf. Co.F

Trice, Joseph VA 9th Mil. Co.A
Trice, Joseph VA 55th Inf. Co.F
Trice, Joseph A. AL 19th Inf. Co.C
Trice, J.T. GA 32nd Inf. Co.I
Trice, J.T. GA 46th Inf. Co.I
Trice, J.T. MS 9th Bn.S.S. Co.A
Trice, J.T. MS 29th Inf. Co.I
Trice, J.T. TN 42nd Inf. 1st Co.I Cpl.
Trice, J.W. MS 1st (Patton's) Inf. Halfacre's Co.
Trice, L.A. TN 4th (McLemore's) Cav. Co.C 2nd Lt.
Trice, L.A. TN 8th (Smith's) Cav. Co.D,B,A
Trice, Lawrence A. VA 26th Inf. Co.I
Trice, Lemuel F. VA 8th Inf. Co.H
Trice, Leroy F. VA Lt.Arty. Arch. Graham's Co.
Trice, L.F. VA Mtd.Res. Rappahannock Dist. Sale's Co.
Trice, L.F. VA 53rd Inf. Co.H
Trice, L.F. VA 61st Mil. Co.C
Trice, L.F. VA Conscr. Cp.Lee Co.B
Trice, L.S. AL 8th Inf. Co.F
Trice, Luther J. FL 3rd Inf. Co.D
Trice, M.A. AL Cp. of Instr. Talladega
Trice, Morgan A. MS 2nd Inf. Co.H
Trice, N.W. TN Cav. Woodward's Co.
Trice, Philip P. VA 26th Inf. Co.I Sgt.
Trice, Phillip J. VA 44th Inf. Co.D
Trice, P.J. AR 30th Inf. Co.E Sgt.Maj.
Trice, R.H. VA 4th Cav. Co.F
Trice, Richard A. VA 4th Cav. Co.F Cpl.
Trice, Richard A. VA 23rd Inf. Co.G 2nd Lt.
Trice, R.L. MS 10th Cav. Co.C
Trice, R.L. MS 41st Inf. Co.E Bvt.2nd Lt.
Trice, Robert C. VA Lt.Arty. Thornton's Co.
Trice, Robert M. VA 55th Inf. Co.B
Trice, Robert N. VA Arty. Fleet's Co.
Trice, Robert N. VA 13th Inf. Co.D
Trice, Ro. M. VA Lt.Arty. Woolfolk's Co.
Trice, Samuel TN 53rd Inf. Co.K Sgt.
Trice, Simeon TN 53rd Inf. Co.K
Trice, Simon B. TX 6th Cav. Co.G Black.
Trice, S.J. 15th Conf.Cav. Co.K
Trice, Stephen J. AL Cav. Murphy's Bn. Co.D
Trice, T. VA Cav. 40th Bn. Co.E
Trice, T.A. VA Arty. Dance's Co.
Trice, Tandy Smith Gen. & Staff Asst.Surg.
Trice, T.C. GA 13th Inf. Co.D
Trice, T.E. 15th Conf.Cav. Co.K
Trice, T.F. AL 8th Inf. Co.B
Trice, T.G. VA 4th Cav. Co.F
Trice, Thomas VA 24th Cav. Co.E
Trice, Timoleon G. VA 44th Inf. Co.D
Trice, T.M. KY 7th Mtd.Inf. Co.G
Trice, Troup E. AL Cav. Murphy's Bn. Co.D
Trice, T.S. FL 5th Inf. Asst.Surg.
Trice, T. Smith FL 5th Inf. Co.C
Trice, W.B. GA Cav. 1st Bn.Res. McKinney's Co.
Trice, W.B. GA 32nd Inf. Co.I
Trice, W.H. AL 23rd Inf. Co.B
Trice, W.H. AL 48th Inf. Co.C
Trice, W.H. TN 50th Inf. Co.E Cpl.
Trice, W.H. TN 50th (Cons.) Inf. Co.E Cpl.
Trice, William GA Cav. 1st Bn.Res. Co.C
Trice, William VA Res.Forces Thurston's Co.
Trice, William A. TN 41st Inf. Co.B
Trice, William A. VA 23rd Inf. Co.G 2nd Lt.
Trice, William A. VA Inf. 25th Bn. Co.E
Trice, William B. AL 54th Inf. Co.F 2nd Lt.
Trice, William B. GA 12th (Robinson's) Cav. (St.Guards) Co.G
Trice, William B. 4th Conf.Inf. Co.F 1st Sgt.
Trice, Wm. H. VA Mtd.Res. Rappahannock Dist. Sale's Co.
Trice, William H. VA Res.Forces Clark's Co.
Trice, Wm. J. VA Lt.Arty. W.P. Carter's Co.
Trice, William N. TN 49th Inf. Co.A
Trice, William N. Inf. Bailey's Cons.Regt. Co.G
Trice, William R. AL 19th Inf. Co.B Capt.
Trice, William R. TX 1st (McCulloch's) Cav. Co.C
Trice, William R. TX 9th Cav. Co.A
Trice, William T. AR Cav. 6th Bn. Co.C
Trice, Winter VA 55th Inf. Co.F
Trice, W.J. VA 4th Cav. Co.F
Trice, W.J. VA Lt.Arty. W.P. Carter's Co.
Trice, W.L. TN 21st (Wilson's) Cav. Co.F,C Sgt.
Trice, W.T. TN 3rd (Forrest's) Cav. Co.C Sgt.
Tricey, John VA 2nd Inf. Co.E
Triche, Annace Conf.Lt.Arty. Richardson's Bn. Co.B
Triche, Armace LA Arty. Landry's Co. (Donaldsonville Arty.)
Triche, Dorville LA 18th Inf. Co.G
Triche, Dorville LA Inf.Cons. 18th Regt. & Yellow Jacket Bn. Co.F
Triche, Joachim LA 18th Inf. Co.G
Triche, Jouchim LA Inf.Cons. 18th Regt. & Yellow Jacket Bn. Co.F
Triche, L.A. LA 2nd Cav. Co.H
Triche, Lucien LA Mil. St.John the Baptist Res.Guards
Triche, P.E. LA Lt.Arty. LeGardeur, Jr.'s Co. (Orleans Guard Btty.)
Triche, P. Elphige LA 26th Inf. Co.C
Triche, Victorin LA 18th Inf. Co.E
Trichel, A. LA 18th Inf. Co.C
Trichel, Eustache LA 3rd Inf. Co.D
Trichel, F.F. LA 2nd Cav. Co.C
Trichel, Gervais L. LA 3rd Inf. Co.D 1st Lt.
Trichel, Gilbert LA Inf.Cons.Crescent Regt. Co.K Sgt.
Trichel, John C. LA 3rd Inf. Co.G Lt.
Trichel, Leonard LA Maddox's Regt.Res.Corps Co.B
Trichel, S. LA 3rd Inf. Co.G
Trichel, Severin LA Maddox's Regt.Res.Corps Co.B
Trichell, Gilbert LA Inf. 11th Bn. Co.B Sgt.
Trichell, Henry F. LA 28th (Thomas') Inf. Co.B
Trichell, J.B.S. LA 3rd Inf. Co.G
Trick, John AL 1st Regt.Conscr. Co.C
Trick, John LA 20th Inf. Co.A
Trick, John LA 21st (Kennedy's) Inf. Co.C
Trick, T. KY 7th Cav. Co.K
Trickel, Lucien LA 2nd Cav. Co.D
Tricker, J.S. VA 15th Inf. Co.C
Tricker, Richard NC 1st Inf. Co.H Cpl.
Tricker, Robert VA 25th Mil. Co.B
Tricker, Stanfield VA 25th Mil. Co.C
Tricket, A. AR Cav. Gordon's Regt. Co.I
Trickett, Charles AR 1st (Colquitt's) Inf. Co.B
Trickett, M.E. VA 20th Cav. Co.A
Trickett, Michael VA 19th Cav. Co.D
Trickett, William S. VA Cav. 46th Bn. Co.C Cpl.
Trickey, A.J. TX 29th Cav. Co.D
Trickey, John LA 1st Hvy.Arty. (Reg.) Co.I
Trickey, John 14th Conf.Cav. Co.B
Trickey, William AL 18th Inf. Co.B
Trickey, William T. MS 17th Inf. Co.A
Tricklene, W.F. FL 8th Inf. Co.A
Tricky, John AL 14th Inf. Co.B
Trico, Nathaniel TN 14th Inf. Co.D
Tricom, P.E. LA Mil. Orleans Guards Regt. Co.C
Tricon, H. LA Mil. 3rd Regt.Eur.Brig. (Garde Francaise) Co.1
Tricon, Henry LA Mil. 3rd Regt. 1st Brig. 1st Div. Co.I
Tricon, Paul F. LA 7th Inf. Co.H
Tricon, Pierre O. LA Col.,QMGen.
Tricot, Charles LA Mil. 1st Regt. French Brig. Co.8 Sgt.
Tricou, P.P. LA Mil. Orleans Guards Regt. Co.D
Tricy, Andrew GA 1st Inf. Co.I
Triddle, John W. KY 2nd Cav.
Tridel, Samuel B. FL 7th Inf. Co.A
Trideria, S. AL 12th Inf. Co.A
Triece, Daniel A. AL 10th Inf. Co.A
Triece, George NC 42nd Inf. Co.H
Triece, Greene NC 42nd Inf. Co.H
Triel, J. LA Mil. 1st Chasseurs a pied Co.7
Triel, T. LA Mil. 1st Chasseurs a pied Co.7
Trier, Lewis KY Lt.Arty. Green's Btty.
Trier, Lewis TN 1st (Feild's) Inf. Co.D
Trierweiler, B. LA 3rd Inf. Co.F
Triesch, Adolph TX 36th Cav. Co.F Sgt.
Triesch, William TX 36th Cav. Co.F
Triest, George FL 7th Inf. Co.G
Triest, Jacob GA 1st (Olmstead's) Inf. Co.G
Triest, M. SC Mil. 16th Regt. Triest's Co. Capt.
Triest, M. SC 16th & 24th (Cons.) Inf. QMSgt.
Triest, M. SC 24th Inf. QMSgt
Trieves, Robert D. MS 13th Inf. Co.G Cpl.
Trieves, Robert D. Sig.Corps,CSA
Triford, William VA 6th Inf. 1st Co.B, Co.D
Triger, Peter VA 25th Cav. Co.G
Triger, Steven VA 25th Cav. Co.G
Trigett, William S. VA 20th Cav. Co.C
Trigg, --- TX Cav. Mann's Regt. Co.C
Trigg, A. 1st Chickasaw Inf. White's Co. Cpl.
Trigg, Abram MS 13th Inf. Co.B
Trigg, Abram B. MS VA 37th Inf. Co.K
Trigg, A.C. KY 2nd (Duke's) Cav. Co.C
Trigg, A.J. TN 11th (Holman's) Cav. Co.E
Trigg, A.L. Gen. & Staff Asst.Surg.
Trigg, Allen MS 13th Inf. Co.B
Trigg, A.L. AR 8th Cav. Asst.Surg.
Trigg, A.L. AR 6th Inf. Asst.Surg.
Trigg, Alexander NC 29th Inf. Co.H
Trigg, Allen MS 46th Inf. Co.A
Trigg, Benjamin F. TN 53rd Inf. Co.D Cpl.
Trigg, C.J. TN Holman's Bn.Part.Rangers Co.C
Trigg, Daniel MO 5th Cav. Co.D 2nd Lt.
Trigg, E. AL 4th Res. Co.B
Trigg, E.S. AL 1st Regt. Mobile Vol. Baas' Co.
Trigg, Frank MO Inf. 6th Regt.St.Guard Co.C
Trigg, Frank J. MS 1st Lt.Arty. Co.A

Trigg, Gilbert R. MS 41st Inf. Co.G
Trigg, Gilbert R. TN 41st Inf. Co.G Cpl.
Trigg, Guy S. VA 22nd Cav. Co.G 1st Sgt.
Trigg, H.A. KY 7th Cav. Co.A
Trigg, H.A. TX Cav. Gano's Squad. Co.A
Trigg, Haden A. KY 3rd Cav. Co.A
Trigg, Henry GA 4th (Clinch's) Cav. Co.F
Trigg, Henry GA Lt.Arty. Clinch's Btty.
Trigg, James TN Douglass' Bn.Part.Rangers Perkins' Co.
Trigg, James A. TN 11th (Holman's) Cav. Co.I
Trigg, James M. MS 2nd Inf. (A. of 10,000) Co.A
Trigg, James M. MS 11th Inf. Co.G
Trigg, James T. TN Inf. 154th Sr.Regt. Co.E Cpl.
Trigg, J.E.C. KY Williams' Btty.
Trigg, J.M. KY 3rd Cav. Co.C
Trigg, John AR 31st Inf. Co.E 1st Lt.
Trigg, John A. MO 2nd Cav. Co.C
Trigg, John H. TN Cav. 7th Bn. (Bennett's) Co.D
Trigg, John H. TN Inf. 154th Sr.Regt. Co.E 2nd Lt.
Trigg, John J. MS 13th Inf. Co.B
Trigg, John M. KY 2nd (Duke's) Cav. Co.C
Trigg, John S. TN 45th Inf. Co.K Cpl.
Trigg, John T. AR Lt.Arty. Trigg's Btty. Capt.
Trigg, John W. TX Cav. (Dismtd.) Chisum's Regt. Co.G 1st Lt.
Trigg, John W. TX Cav. Gano's Squad. Co.A 2nd Lt.
Trigg, Joseph T. KY 2nd Mtd.Inf. Co.G
Trigg, J.T. AR Mil. Borland's Regt. Woodruff's Co.
Trigg, J.T. TN Inf. 2nd Cons.Regt. Co.B Cpl.
Trigg, J.W. KY 7th Cav. Co.A 2nd Lt.
Trigg, R.C. VA 54th Inf. Col.
Trigg, Robert C. VA 4th Inf. Co.G Capt.
Trigg, S.L. TN 12th Inf. Co.H Sgt.
Trigg, S.L. TN 12th (Cons.) Inf. Co.K
Trigg, Stephen MS 13th Inf. Co.B
Trigg, Stephen C. MO 15th Cav.
Trigg, Stephen C. MO 3rd Inf. Co.C
Trigg, Thomas KY 2nd Mtd.Inf. Co.D
Trigg, Thomas MS Inf. 2nd St.Troops Co.B
Trigg, Thomas K. VA 37th Inf. Co.K Sgt.
Trigg, T.K. VA 1st Cav. 2nd Co.D
Trigg, W.C. MS Inf. 1st Bn. Co.C
Trigg, W.C. MS 15th Inf. Co.K
Trigg, Will MO Robertson's Regt.St.Guard Co.3 1st Sgt.
Trigg, William AL 55th Vol. Co.B
Trigg, William C. AR 36th Inf. Co.D Cpl.
Trigg, William I. MS 46th Inf. Co.A Sgt.
Trigg, William K. VA 11th Inf. Co.G
Trigg, William W. TN Inf. 154th Sr.Regt. Co.E
Trigg, W.N. TN 41st Inf. Co.G
Trigg, W.R. Gen. & Staff A.Post Adj.
Trigg, W.S. AL Cav. Holloway's Co.
Trigg, W.S. AL 38th Inf. Co.G Sgt.
Trigg, Wyndham R. MS 28th Cav. Co.D Sgt.
Trigger, Benjamin VA 25th Mil. Co.A
Trigger, C. SC 1st St.Troops Co.E
Trigger, Henry C. VA 9th Cav. Co.I
Trigger, Henry C. VA 25th Mil. Co.C Cpl.
Trigger, James VA 30th Inf. Co.B
Trigger, John VA 15th Cav. Co.E
Trigger, John VA Cav. 15th Bn. Co.D
Trigger, John VA 25th Mil. Co.A
Trigger, John Sig.Corps,CSA
Trigger, John L. VA 9th Cav. Co.I
Trigger, John L. VA 25th Mil. Co.B
Trigger, L.C. VA 15th Cav. Co.E
Trigger, Lemuel VA Cav. 15th Bn. Co.D
Trigger, Leonard VA Cav. 15th Bn. Co.D
Trigger, Leonard C. VA 25th Mil. Co.B
Trigger, Lewis VA Cav. 15th Bn. Co.D
Trigger, Lewis VA 25th Mil. Co.B
Trigger, Stanfield VA Lt.Arty. Pollock's Co.
Trigger, Stanfield VA 25th Mil. Co.B
Triggers, Jeremiah VA 47th Inf. Co.B
Triggle, B. GA 2nd Cav.
Triggle, M.F. GA 13th Inf. Co.G
Triggs, Harrison P. VA 2nd Inf. Co.E
Triggs, J.H. MO 2nd Cav. Co.C
Triggs, William AL 4th Cav. Co.B
Trigle, Aug TX 2nd Inf. Co.F
Trigloam, James H. TX 1st (Yager's) Cav. Co.A Sgt.
Triglome, James H. TX Cav. 3rd (Yager's) Bn. Co.A Cpl.
Trijo Catalino TX Cav. Madison's Regt. Co.E
Trilby, John KY 2nd Bn.Mtd.Rifles Co.C
Triley, Francis M. MS Cav. 1st Bn. (Miller's) Co.A
Trillar, Faustine MO Lt.Arty. Parsons' Co. Artif.
Triller, Alexander T. MO 8th Cav. Co.A
Triller, Austin MO Inf. 4th Regt.St.Guard Co.E
Trim, Charles A. AL 41st Inf. Co.B
Trim, C.P. TN 38th Inf. Co.G
Trim, James TX Inf. 1st Bn. (St.Troops) Co.B
Trim, J.H. TX Cav. 2nd Regt.St.Troops Co.K
Trim, J.L. AL 41st Inf. Co.B Sgt.
Trim, John TX 12th Cav. Co.A
Trim, P.R. MS 1st Lt.Arty. Co.I
Trim, Preston MS Cav. 24th Bn. Co.E,B
Trim, Samuel H. AL 41st Inf. Co.B
Trim, T. TX 13th Vol. Co.G
Trim, Thomas NC 7th Sr.Res. Davie's Co.
Trim, Turner TX Cav. 1st Regt.St.Troops Co.B
Trim, William R. MS Cav. 24th Bn. Co.E Sgt.
Trim, William R. MS Arty. (Seven Stars Arty.) Roberts' Co. Sgt.
Trim, William W. MS 42nd Inf. Co.F
Trim, Wisdom TX 22nd Inf. Co.K
Trim, W.J. SC Inf. 1st (Charleston) Bn. Co.A Bvt.2nd Lt.
Trimaitte, Pierre LA Mil. 1st Regt. French Brig. Co.6
Triman, Edward GA 46th Inf. Co.E
Trimble, --- TX Cav. McCord's Frontier Regt. Co.I
Trimble, A.D. TN 8th Bn. Capt.
Trimble, Adolphus L. MS 19th Inf. Co.D
Trimble, A.J. AR 2nd Cav. Co.C
Trimble, A.J. TX 15th Inf. Co.A
Trimble, Alfred MS 21st Inf. Co.D
Trimble, A.M. TX 23rd Cav. Co.C
Trimble, Charles AL Cav. Forrest's Regt.
Trimble, Charles TN 19th & 20th (Cons.) Cav. Ord.Sgt.
Trimble, Charles P. GA Arty. 9th Bn. Co.B
Trimble, Charles Y. KY 2nd (Duke's) Cav. Co.K
Trimble, Columbus VA 8th Cav. Co.C
Trimble, C.S. AL 11th Cav. Co.F
Trimble, C.S. AL 9th Inf. Co.F
Trimble, C.S. TN 18th (Newsom's) Cav. Co.E Ord.Sgt.
Trimble, C.S. TN 19th & 20th (Cons.) Cav. Co.E
Trimble, Draper VA 20th Cav. Co.D
Trimble, Edwin KY 10th (Diamond's) Cav. Co.A Lt.Col.
Trimble, Edwin KY 5th Mtd.Inf. Co.E 1st Lt.
Trimble, E.R. AR 1st Inf. Co.D
Trimble, F. LA 3rd (Harrison's) Cav. Co.I
Trimble, Felix H. LA Lovell's Scouts
Trimble, Finis E. AR 8th Cav. Co.H
Trimble, F.E.P. AR 1st (Dobbin's) Cav. Co.C
Trimble, F.E.P. AR 5th Inf. Co.B
Trimble, F.M. TN 63rd Inf. Co.H
Trimble, F.M. TX 5th Cav. Co.D
Trimble, Francis M. VA 31st Inf. Co.H
Trimble, Francis M. VA 162nd Mil. Co.A
Trimble, Frederick W. TX Cav. Ragsdale's Bn. Co.B 1st Lt.
Trimble, G.A. VA 63rd Inf. Co.C
Trimble, Garland A. VA 29th Inf. Co.C, 2nd Co.F 1st Sgt.
Trimble, General S. GA 7th Inf. (St.Guards) Co.D
Trimble, General S. GA 30th Inf. Co.H
Trimble, George J. GA 42nd Inf. Co.F
Trimble, Green W. MS Gage's Co. (Wigfall Guards) 1st Lt.
Trimble, G.W. AR 37th Inf. Co.K
Trimble, G.W. MS 1st Cav. Co.F
Trimble, Harvey VA 162nd Mil. Co.A
Trimble, Hastin GA 7th Inf. (St.Guards) Co.D
Trimble, Hastin M. GA 30th Inf. Co.G
Trimble, Henry H. VA 55th Inf. Co.D
Trimble, Henry T. KY 4th Mtd.Inf. Co.B
Trimble, Henry T. MS Lt.Arty. (Issaquena Arty.) Graves' Co.
Trimble, H.S. TX Cav. McCord's Frontier Regt. Co.H
Trimble, I.H. MS 22nd Inf. Co.A 4th Cpl.
Trimble, Isaac P. TX 7th Inf. Co.K
Trimble, Isaac R. Gen. & Staff Maj.Gen.
Trimble, J. MO Cav. Schnabel's Bn. Co.B Sgt.
Trimble, J.A. MO 1st & 3rd Cons.Cav.
Trimble, James KY 1st Bn.Mtd.Rifles Co.D
Trimble, James TN 20th Inf. Co.C
Trimble, James F. KY 1st (Butler's) Cav. Co.H
Trimble, James H. AR 27th Inf. Co.E
Trimble, James L. TX 10th Inf. Co.I
Trimble, James M. TX 36th Cav. Co.K Sgt.
Trimble, James T. GA Arty. 9th Bn. Co.B
Trimble, James W. VA 5th Inf. Co.F Cpl.
Trimble, J.B. KY 3rd Mtd.Inf. Co.G
Trimble, J.H. GA 18th Inf. Co.B
Trimble, J.H. TX 11th Cav. Co.E
Trimble, J.L. GA 2nd Mil. Co.G
Trimble, J.M. AR 13th Mil. Co.F
Trimble, J.M. AR 37th Inf. Co.K
Trimble, J.M. TX 7th Inf. Co.E 1st Sgt.
Trimble, John GA 2nd Cav. (St.Guards) Co.K
Trimble, John TX 29th Cav. Co.D

Trimble, John TX St.Troops Gould's Co. (Clarksville Lt.Inf.)
Trimble, John A. AR 30th Inf. Co.E Capt.
Trimble, John A. MO 1st Cav. Co.D
Trimble, John A. TN 40th Inf. Co.F 3rd Lt.
Trimble, John B. TX 16th Inf. Co.I
Trimble, John D. MD Arty. 1st Btty.
Trimble, John D. VA 5th Inf. Co.F Cpl.
Trimble, John G. TX 33rd Cav. Co.A
Trimble, John H. AR 8th Cav. Co.H 1st Lt.
Trimble, John H. TX 3rd Cav. Co.I
Trimble, John H. TX 27th Cav. Co.F
Trimble, John J. MO 10th Inf. Co.B
Trimble, John P. MS Lt.Arty. (Jefferson Arty.) Darden's Co.
Trimble, John T. GA 35th Inf. Co.D
Trimble, Joseph AR 27th Inf. Co.A
Trimble, Joseph A. VA 5th Inf. Co.F
Trimble, Joseph L. GA 12th (Wright's) Cav. (St.Guards) Stapleton's Co.
Trimble, Josephus GA Inf. 8th Bn. Co.D 2nd Lt.
Trimble, Joseph W. MS 19th Inf. Co.D 1st Cpl.
Trimble, Julius B. AL 3rd Inf. Co.I
Trimble, L. TX 1st Inf. Co.E
Trimble, M. 8th (Wade's) Conf.Cav. Co.B
Trimble, M.A. VA 8th Cav. Co.I Cpl.
Trimble, Marcellus A. AL 47th Inf. Co.D
Trimble, Martin M. VA 29th Inf. Co.C Sgt.
Trimble, M.J. GA 2nd Res. Co.H
Trimble, Moses H. GA 30th Inf. Co.H
Trimble, Moses M. GA 4th Inf. Co.B
Trimble, M.R. AR 7th Inf. Co.H
Trimble, M.T. MO Cav. Schnabel's Bn. Co.B
Trimble, Nathaniel W. TN 7th Inf. Co.B
Trimble, Peter J. KY 1st Bn.Mtd.Rifles Co.D
Trimble, Philip M. GA 30th Inf. Co.H Sgt.
Trimble, R.C. TX Cav. Benavides' Regt. Co.B
Trimble, R.L. KY 5th Mtd.Inf. Co.I
Trimble, Robert LA 3rd (Harrison's) Cav. Co.I
Trimble, Robert E. AR 14th (Powers') Inf. Co.H Capt.
Trimble, Robert S. MO Cav. Freeman's Regt. Capt.
Trimble, R.W. AR 1st (Colquitt's) Inf. Chap.
Trimble, R.W. Gen. & Staff Chap.
Trimble, Spugel TX 8th Inf. Co.F
Trimble, Thomas KY 1st (Butler's) Cav. Co.A
Trimble, Thomas KY 10th (Johnson's) Cav. Co.H
Trimble, Thomas J. TX 17th Cav. Co.B
Trimble, W.A. MS Lt.Arty. (Jefferson Arty.) Darden's Co.
Trimble, W.F. TX 33rd Cav. Co.A
Trimble, W.H. GA 18th Inf. Co.B Sgt.
Trimble, W.H. TX 9th (Young's) Inf. Co.H
Trimble, William AR 1st (Monroe's) Cav. Co.E
Trimble, William AR 14th (Powers') Inf. Co.C
Trimble, William KY 3rd Mtd.Inf. Co.K Sgt.
Trimble, William TX 1st Bn.S.S. Co.D
Trimble, William 8th (Wade's) Conf.Cav. Co.B
Trimble, William Conf.Cav. Wood's Regt. 1st Co.A
Trimble, William D. VA 31st Mil. Co.E
Trimble, William H. KY 5th Mtd.Inf. Co.A
Trimble, William J. AR 27th Inf. Co.H Cpl.
Trimble, William S. GA 4th Inf. Co.B Sgt.
Trimble, William W. KY 8th Cav. Co.I
Trimble, W.J. TX 15th Inf. Co.A
Trimble, W.R. AL 7th Cav. Co.F
Trimble, W.W. GA 1st Cav. Co.G,I
Trimble, W.W. TX 11th Cav. Co.E
Trimble, W.W. TX 32nd Cav. Co.C Cpl.
Trimbler, George W. AL Inf. 1st Regt. Co.I
Trimbo, Andrew LA 1st Cav. Co.K,E
Trimbol, T.J. KY 3rd Bn.Mtd.Rifles
Trimer, Newton J. TX 22nd Cav. Co.I
Trimier, Cought AL 9th Inf. Co.K
Trimier, Stanly C. VA Lt.Arty. W.P. Carter's Co.
Trimm, Edward H. MS Cav. Powers' Regt. Co.E,F
Trimm, J.A. TX Cav. Bourland's Regt. Co.H
Trimm, J.H. TX cav. Bourland's Regt. Co.H
Trimm, Robert B. NC 50th Inf. Co.A Sgt.
Trimm, W. TX 13th Vol. 2nd Co.H
Trimm, W.J. SC 27th Inf. Co.I 2nd Lt.
Trimmel, --- TX Cav. Ragsdale's Bn. Co.E
Trimmell, John R. TX 31st Cav. Co.C Sgt.
Trimmer, A.B. TX 22nd Cav. Co.I Sgt.
Trimmer, Frank M. SC 13th Inf. Co.I
Trimmer, George W. VA Hvy.Arty. 10th Bn. Co.A
Trimmer, James AL 4th (Russell's) Cav. Co.H
Trimmer, James FL 11th Inf. Co.K
Trimmer, James VA Hvy.Arty. 10th Bn. Co.A
Trimmer, James VA 62nd Mtd.Inf. 2nd Co.L
Trimmer, James H. VA 23rd Cav. Co.C,B,D
Trimmer, Joseph H. VA Hvy.Arty., 10th Bn. Co.A
Trimmer, Thomas VA Cav. 1st Bn. (Loc.Def. Troops) Co.C
Trimmer, William AL 15th Inf. Co.G
Trimmer, William H. FL Lt.Arty. Abell's Co. 2nd QMSgt.
Trimmer, William H. FL 1st Inf. Old Co.B
Trimmier, Frank M. SC 13th Inf. Co.I Capt.
Trimmier, John GA 22nd Inf. Co.D Sgt.
Trimmier, M.T. GA Cav. (St.Guards) Bond's Co.
Trimmier, Robert B. GA 36th (Villepigue's) Inf. Co.B Music.
Trimmier, Robert B. 1st Conf.Inf. Co.B 2nd Lt.
Trimmier, S.L. 3rd Conf.Cav. Co.E 1st Lt.
Trimmier, Theodore G. AL 41st Inf. Co.A Lt.Col.
Trimmier, Thomas J. TX 15th Inf. Co.B
Trimmier, William H. SC Inf. Holcombe Legion Co.C 1st Lt.
Trimmier, William T. GA 36th (Villepigue's) Inf. Co.B
Trimmier, William T. 1st Conf.Inf. Co.B
Trimnal, C.C. SC 20th Inf. Co.G
Trimnal, Joseph B. SC 19th Inf. Co.E Cpl.
Trimnal, Lewis S. SC 19th Inf. Co.E Cpl.
Trimnal, R.G. SC 7th Cav. Co.E
Trimnal, Robert J. SC 19th Inf. Co.E
Trimnal, T.J.F. SC Lt.Arty. Garden's Co. (Palmetto Lt.Btty.)
Trimnall, George W. KY 2nd (Duke's) Cav. Co.E
Trimnall, G.R. SC Cav.Bn. Holcombe Legion Co.C
Trimnell, B.W. AL 8th Inf. Co.H
Trimnell, S. VA Cav. Mosby's Regt. (Part. Rangers) Co.B
Trimuel, C.C. SC 2nd Inf. Co.G
Trimure, Pagar TN 42nd Inf. 1st Co.H
Trimyer, George N. VA 55th Inf. Co.G
Trimyer, George W. VA Res.Forces Thurston's Co.
Trimyer, Miles R. VA 55th Inf. Co.G
Trimyer, P.H. VA Res.Forces Thurston's Co.
Trimyer, William L. VA 109th Mil. 1st Co.A
Trinchard, Felix F. LA Mil. 2nd Regt. 3rd Brig. 1st Div. Co.G 2nd Lt.
Trinchard, Joseph LA 18th Inf. Co.I
Trinchard, L.A. LA Mil. 2nd Regt. 3rd Brig. 1st Div. Co.G Capt.
Trinchard, M.J. LA Mil. 2nd Regt. 3rd Brig. 1st Div. Co.H 2nd Lt.
Trinchieri, Leopoldo LA 30th Inf. Co.D Ens.
Trine, Jonathan J. AL 23rd Inf. Co.A
Trines, J.E. AR Cav. McGehee's Regt. Co.H
Tringer, J.H. SC 3rd Inf.
Trinida, Domingo TX Cav. Ragsdale's Bn. Co.B
Trinidad, E.B. LA 7th Cav. Co.E Capt.
Trinkle, A.E. VA 7th Cav. Preston's Co.
Trinkle, A.E. VA 14th Cav. Co.G
Trinkle, Charles AR 15th (Josey's) Inf. Co.E
Trinkle, Elbert F.S. VA 4th Inf. Co.C
Trinkle, Jacob VA Inf. 7th Bn.Loc.Def. Co.C
Trinkle, Jacob VA 151st Mil. Co.C
Trinks, Ernst TX 2nd Inf. Co.B
Trinn, B.L. NC 35th Inf. Co.E
Trinnaman, J. LA Mil. Lewis Guards
Trinor, J.C. LA Siege Train Bn. Co.D
Trinsett, F.H. TX 33rd Cav. Co.F
Trint, Andrew J. TX 1st (McCulloch's) Cav. Co.C Sgt.
Trintham, William GA Inf. 25th Bn. (Prov. Guard) Co.G
Trinty, Redman LA 13th Inf. Co.D
Trinum, William TN 45th Inf. Co.B
Trip, D.H. MO 7th Cav.
Trip, E.T. Mead's Conf.Cav. Co.H
Trip, James MS 18th Inf. Co.K
Tripher, S.T. AL 5th Inf. Co.B
Tripiovich, Giov LA Mil. 4th Regt.Eur.Brig. Cognevich's Co.
Tripland, George LA Mil. British Guard Bn. Coburn's Co.
Tripland, W.T. AL 19th Inf. Co.A
Tripler, Charles VA 54th Mil. Co.E,F
Triplet, Abner MO 2nd Cav. Co.F
Triplet, Abner MO 7th Cav. Co.B
Triplet, Abner NC 58th Inf. Co.H
Triplet, Alfred NC 66th Inf. Co.G
Triplet, B.T. AR 11th Inf. Co.E
Triplet, Dan TN 40th Inf. Co.G
Triplet, D.T. AR 15th (Johnson's) Inf. Co.D
Triplet, Elbert NC 54th Inf. Co.G
Triplet, F.M. MS 35th Inf. Co.I
Triplet, Franklin MS 20th Inf. Co.G
Triplet, Irwin NC 35th Inf. Co.B
Triplet, James TN 3rd (Lillard's) Mtd.Inf. Co.H,K Cpl.
Triplet, J.J. TN 19th Inf. Co.H
Triplet, John TN 3rd (Lillard's) Mtd.Inf. Co.G 2nd Lt.
Triplet, J. Wesley AL 37th Inf. Co.B

Triplet, L.H. NC 37th Inf. Co.B
Triplet, Ross NC Inf. Thomas Legion
Triplet, W.D. MS 14th (Cons.) Inf. Co.E Sgt.
Triplet, William KY 5th Mtd.Inf. Co.E
Triplet, William NC 5th Sr.Res. Co.K
Triplet, William T. NC 37th Inf. Co.F
Triplet, W.T. AL 14th Inf. Co.D
Triplett, --- VA VMI Co.C Sgt.
Triplett, A. MS 28th Cav. Co.I
Triplett, A. MS 1st (King's) Inf. (St.Troops) Co.K
Triplett, Abner NC 26th Inf. Co.I
Triplett, Absolom MO 15th Cav. Co.C
Triplett, A.H. TX 15th Cav. Co.C
Triplett, Albert F. VA 8th Inf. Co.B
Triplett, Alexander H. TX 27th Cav. Co.D,M
Triplett, Anthony VA 18th Cav. Co.A
Triplett, Asa L. NC 26th Inf. Co.C
Triplett, B. KY 9th Cav. Co.A
Triplett, B.A. VA Cav. Mosby's Regt. (Part. Rangers) Co.C
Triplett, Benjamin A. VA 8th Inf. Co.B
Triplett, B.F. TX 3rd Cav. Co.A
Triplett, B.T. AR 11th & 17th Cons.Inf. Co.E
Triplett, Calvin NC 37th Inf. Co.B
Triplett, C.B. TN 24th Bn.S.S. Co.A
Triplett, C.D. AL 6th Inf. Co.C
Triplett, Charles AR 1st (Dobbin's) Cav. Co.D
Triplett, Charles VA Cav. 35th Bn. Co.E
Triplett, Charles B. TN 4th Cav.
Triplett, Clayton F. NC 1st Cav. (9th St.Troops) Co.D
Triplett, Daniel VA 33rd Inf. Co.D
Triplett, Daniel H. TX 21st Cav. Co.G
Triplett, D.F. TN 4th Cav. Co.D
Triplett, E.B. VA 22nd Inf. Co.E
Triplett, Edward W. NC 29th Inf. Co.H
Triplett, Edwin VA 31st Mil. Co.G
Triplett, Elbert NC 26th Inf. Co.C
Triplett, Elbert G. NC 56th Inf. Co.C
Triplett, Eli FL Cav. 5th Bn. Co.F
Triplett, Ely FL 8th Inf. Co.A
Triplett, E.M. VA 18th Cav. Co.D
Triplett, Franklin LA Inf. 11th Bn. Co.C
Triplett, Franklin LA Inf.Cons.Crescent Regt. Co.F
Triplett, Franklin TN 36th Inf. Co.C 2nd Lt.
Triplett, Franklin M. NC 37th Inf. Co.B
Triplett, Fredrick G. MO 4th Cav. Co.G
Triplett, G. MO 4th Cav. Co.G
Triplett, George VA Cav. 35th Bn. Co.B
Triplett, George VA Cav. Mosby's Regt. (Part.Rangers) Co.B
Triplett, George W. MS 11th (Perrin's) Cav. Co.D Cpl.
Triplett, George W. MS Inf. 1st Bn.St.Troops (12 mo. '62-3) Co.C
Triplett, George W. NC 37th Inf. Co.B
Triplett, George W. TX 22nd Cav. Co.C
Triplett, G.L.F. MO St.Guard
Triplett, Glover B. MS 11th Inf. Co.E Cpl.
Triplett, Green TX 11th Inf. Co.K
Triplett, G.S.P. VA 4th Cav. Co.G
Triplett, G.W. MS St.Cav. Perrin's Bn. Co.C
Triplett, G.W. Gen. & Staff Maj.,QM
Triplett, Hedgeman VA 22nd Inf. Co.E
Triplett, H.F. VA Horse Arty. D. Shanks' Co.
Triplett, Hilary S. NC 26th Inf. Co.C
Triplett, Jackson NC 54th Inf. Co.G
Triplett, Jackson VA 31st Mil. Co.F
Triplett, James GA 3rd Cav. (St.Guards) Co.D
Triplett, James MS 20th Inf. Co.D
Triplett, James MO Cav. 3rd Bn. Co.F Cpl.
Triplett, James MO 7th Cav. Haislip's Co.
Triplett, James VA Res. Keyser's Co.
Triplett, James D. VA Lt.Arty. 12th Bn. 1st Co.A
Triplett, James H. NC 1st Inf. (6 mo. '61) Co.E
Triplett, James H. NC 11th (Bethel Regt.) Inf. Co.K 1st Sgt.
Triplett, James H. NC 42nd Inf. Co.K
Triplett, James H. TX 27th Cav. Co.D
Triplett, James H. VA 31st Mil. Co.G
Triplett, James P. VA Cav. Mosby's Regt. (Part.Rangers) Co.F
Triplett, James W. VA 2nd Inf. Co.A
Triplett, Jasper MO 7th Cav. Haislip's Co.
Triplett, Jasper VA 18th Cav. Co.A Sgt.
Triplett, Jasper W. VA 62nd Mtd.Inf. 2nd Co.H Cpl.
Triplett, Jeremiah TN 36th Inf. Co.D
Triplett, Jesse F. NC 26th Inf. Co.C 1st Sgt.
Triplett, Jesse O. NC 58th Inf. Co.M,G Cpl.
Triplett, Joel NC 1st Cav. (9th St.Troops) Co.D
Triplett, John MS 35th Inf. Co.D
Triplett, John MO 8th Cav. Co.I
Triplett, John MO Cav. Snider's Bn. Co.C
Triplett, John TN 24th Bn.S.S. Co.A
Triplett, John TN 62nd Mtd.Inf. Co.D Adj.
Triplett, John VA 23rd Cav. Co.I
Triplett, John VA VMI Co.C Sgt.
Triplett, John E. VA Cav. McNeill's Co.
Triplett, John H. KY 1st Inf. Co.G 2nd Lt.
Triplett, Jno. R. Gen. & Staff 2nd Lt.,Dr.M.
Triplett, John W. NC 53rd Inf. Co.K Sgt.
Triplett, Joseph VA Cav. McNeill's Co.
Triplett, J.R. VA VMI Co.C Sgt.
Triplett, J.W. NC 26th Inf. Co.C
Triplett, Leonidas, Jr. VA 7th Cav. Co.A Sgt.
Triplett, Leonidas VA 17th Inf. Co.B
Triplett, Lindsey TN 63rd Inf. Co.K
Triplett, Lorenzo D. NC 37th Inf. Co.B
Triplett, Louis W. TN 36th Inf. Co.C
Triplett, M. KY Capt.
Triplett, Manley VA Cav. 35th Bn. Co.F,C
Triplett, Marshal VA 22nd Inf. Co.E Capt.
Triplett, Marshall VA Cav. Mosby's Regt. (Part.Rangers) Maj.
Triplett, Mc. NC 5th Sr.Res. Co.K
Triplett, Moses NC 26th Inf. Co.C
Triplett, Moses NC 53rd Inf. Co.K
Triplett, Nathan NC 5th Sr.Res. Co.A
Triplett, Nathaniel B. VA 33rd Inf. Co.D
Triplett, Nimrod NC 1st Cav. (9th St.Troops) Co.D
Triplett, Nimrod TN 24th Bn.S.S. Co.A
Triplett, Nimrod VA 51st Mil. Co.F
Triplett, Nimrod D. MS 14th Inf. Co.F Sgt.
Triplett, Noah NC 54th Inf. Co.G
Triplett, O.R. VA 18th Cav. Co.A
Triplett, Otway VA 31st Mil. Co.G
Triplett, Perry C. AR 1st Mtd.Rifles Co.K
Triplett, Pickens L. NC 37th Inf. Co.F Comsy. Sgt.
Triplett, Reuben VA Cav. Mosby's Regt. (Part.Rangers) Co.B
Triplett, Richard C. VA 6th Cav. Co.F 2nd Lt.
Triplett, Richard C. VA Cav. Mosby's Regt. (Part.Rangers) Co.B Sgt.
Triplett, S.B. KY 5th Cav. Co.B QMSgt.
Triplett, S.B. VA Cav. Mosby's Regt. (Part. Rangers) Co.C Cpl.
Triplett, S.B. VA 8th Inf. Co.B
Triplett, Sidney NC 53rd Inf. Co.K
Triplett, S.R. MS 46th Inf. Co.K
Triplett, T.H. VA 23rd Cav. Co.A Capt.
Triplett, T.H. VA Cav. 35th Bn. Co.C
Triplett, T.H. 15th Conf.Cav. Co.A 1st Lt.
Triplett, Thomas NC 5th Sr.Res. Co.A
Triplett, Thomas SC 3rd Bn.Res. Co.E
Triplett, Thomas VA 6th Cav. Co.F
Triplett, Thomas VA Cav. 41st Bn. Co.A Capt.
Triplett, Thomas H. FL 2nd Inf. Co.M
Triplett, Thomas H. LA 17th Inf. Co.I 1st Lt.
Triplett, Thomas H. NC 58th Inf. Co.K,M,G
Triplett, Thomas H. VA 18th Cav. Co.D, 1st Co.G Capt.
Triplett, Thomas H. VA 62nd Mtd.Inf. Co.M 1st Lt.
Triplett, Thomas K. FL Cav. 3rd Bn. Co.A 1st Lt.
Triplett, Thornton VA Hvy.Arty. 19th Bn. 3rd Co.C Capt.
Triplett, Thornton VA 3rd Inf.Loc.Def. Co.C Capt.
Triplett, Tolbert NC 1st Cav. (9th St.Troops) Co.A
Triplett, Troy KY 5th Mtd.Inf. Co.C
Triplett, W. NC 26th Inf. Co.C
Triplett, W. Gen. & Staff AACS
Triplett, Wellington TX 21st Cav. Co.G 1st Lt.
Triplett, W.H. LA 7th Inf. A.Surg.
Triplett, W.H. MS St.Cav. Perrin's Bn. Co.C
Triplett, W.H. MS 27th Inf. Co.E
Triplett, W.H. VA 10th Inf. Asst.Surg.
Triplett, W.H. Gen. & Staff Asst.Surg.
Triplett, William KY 13th Cav. Co.F
Triplett, William NC 53rd Inf. Co.K
Triplett, William NC 58th Inf. Co.D
Triplett, William TX 11th Inf. Co.I
Triplett, William VA 18th Cav. Co.F
Triplett, William 1st Cherokee Mtd.Rifles Co.B
Triplett, William B. VA 18th Cav. Co.D 2nd Lt.
Triplett, William B. VA 17th Inf. Co.B
Triplett, William B. VA 62nd Mtd.Inf. Co.M 2nd Lt.
Triplett, William G. MO Inf. 8th Bn. Co.A
Triplett, William G. MO 9th Inf. Co.A
Triplett, William H. MS 11th (Perrin's) Cav. Co.D
Triplett, William H. VA 4th Cav. Co.H
Triplett, William L. TX 18th Cav. Co.G Cpl.
Triplett, William Mc. VA 22nd Inf. Co.D,E Cpl.
Triplett, W.P. AL St.Arty. Co.D
Triplett, W.P. TN 2nd (Walker's) Inf. Co.B Capt.
Triplette, James MO 3rd Cav. Co.F Cpl.
Triplette, Jeremiah VA 51st Mil. Co.F
Triplette, L. TX 11th Cav. Co.B Cpl.
Triplit, C.T. AL Lt.Arty. Tarrant's Btty.
Triplit, S.R. MS 4th Cav. Co.G

Triplitt, Darby NC 37th Inf.
Triplitt, James W. NC 37th Inf. Co.B
Tripod, A.P. GA Arty. (Macon Lt.Arty.) Slaten's Co. Bugler
Tripp, Aaron W. TN 44th (Cons.) Inf. Co.B
Tripp, Andrew J. MS 24th Inf. Co.F
Tripp, Arthur NC 20th Inf. Co.I
Tripp, Benjamin F. NC 50th Inf. Co.E
Tripp, B.F. NC 8th Bn.Part.Rangers Co.D
Tripp, B.F. NC 68th Inf. Co.C
Tripp, B.F. NC Bass' Co.
Tripp, B.R. SC Lt.Arty. 3rd (Palmetto) Bn. Co.A
Tripp, Bryant NC 8th Inf. Co.G
Tripp, Caleb NC 3rd Inf. Co.D
Tripp, Charles LA C.S. Zouave Bn. Co.D
Tripp, Charles MD Cav. 2nd Bn.
Tripp, Charles NC 4th Inf. Co.I Sgt.
Tripp, Christopher MO 4th Inf. Co.A
Tripp, C.J. TX 11th Cav. Co.I
Tripp, Clarence A. NC 24th Inf. Asst.Surg.
Tripp, Clarence A. Gen. & Staff Asst.Surg.
Tripp, C.N. TX Inf. 2nd St.Troops Co.B
Tripp, C.P. 10th Conf.Cav. Co.H
Tripp, Curtis NC 2nd Arty. (36th St.Troops) Co.K
Tripp, David H. AR 17th (Lemoyne's) Inf. Co.E
Tripp, D.H. AR 21st Inf. Co.I
Tripp, E. SC 1st St.Troops Co.B
Tripp, Edward GA Cav. 22nd Bn. (St.Guards) Co.G
Tripp, Edward NC 4th Inf. Co.I,E 2nd Lt.
Tripp, Elias SC 3rd Res. Co.K
Tripp, Elias SC 4th Inf. Co.G
Tripp, Elias SC 5th Mil. Beat Co.4
Tripp, Francis M. TN 44th Inf. Co.I
Tripp, Francis M. TN 44th (Cons.) Inf. Co.A
Tripp, Furnifold NC 8th Inf. Co.G
Tripp, George W. GA Inf. 1st Loc.Troops (Augusta) Co.I
Tripp, Hiram J. MO 4th Inf. Co.A
Tripp, H.M. MO 5th Cav. Co.H
Tripp, J. GA 5th Res. Co.I
Tripp, James GA Cav. 22nd Bn. (St.Guards) Co.G Cpl.
Tripp, James GA Lt.Arty. Anderson's Btty.
Tripp, James A. TN 1st (Turney's) Inf. Co.H
Tripp, James B. GA 28th Inf. Co.A
Tripp, James H. TN 44th Inf. Co.I
Tripp, James H. TN 44th (Cons.) Inf. Co.A
Tripp, J.B. SC Lt.Arty. 3rd (Palmetto) Bn. Co.A
Tripp, J.C. NC Mallett's Bn. Co.F
Tripp, Jerry NC 11th (Bethel Regt.) Inf. Co.G
Tripp, J.H. GA Phillips' Legion Co.C
Tripp, J.J. SC 7th Inf. Co.A Cpl.
Tripp, John NC 8th Inf. Co.G
Tripp, John NC 27th Inf. Co.C
Tripp, John NC 44th Inf. Co.D
Tripp, John K. GA Phillips' Legion Co.C
Tripp, John R. GA 54th Inf. Co.C,E
Tripp, John W. MS 40th Inf. Co.H,I
Tripp, Jonathan W. NC 44th Inf. Co.K
Tripp, J.P. GA Phillips' Legion Co.C
Tripp, J.R. SC 4th Cav. Co.C
Tripp, J.R. SC Cav. 10th Bn. Co.B
Tripp, J.R. SC 4th Inf. Co.D
Tripp, J.R. SC Inf. 13th Bn. Co.A
Tripp, J. Robert SC 1st (Butler's) Inf. Co.E,D
Tripp, J.W. AL 4th (Russell's) Cav. Co.B
Tripp, Landon F. TN 54th Inf. Co.E
Tripp, Leon NC 67th Inf. Co.I
Tripp, Madison B. TN 1st (Turney's) Inf. Co.H Ord.Sgt.
Tripp, Moses NC Hvy.Arty. 10th Bn. Co.B
Tripp, N. TX 9th (Young's) Inf. Co.H Sgt.
Tripp, O.R. SC 3rd Res. Co.F Cpl.
Tripp, Reading NC Mallett's Bn. Co.F
Tripp, R.H. GA Phillips' Legion Co.C,I
Tripp, R.H. SC 4th Cav. Co.C
Tripp, Richard H. GA 2nd Cav. Co.C
Tripp, Richard H. GA Cherokee Legion (St.Guards) Co.D
Tripp, Samuel J. NC 3rd Cav. (41st St.Troops) Co.K
Tripp, Samuel J. NC 17th Inf. (1st Org.) Co.K
Tripp, T.A. TN 9th Inf. Co.L,D
Tripp, Thomas NC 67th Inf. Co.E
Tripp, Thomas TN Inf. Spencer's Co.
Tripp, Thomas H. TN 44th Inf. Co.E
Tripp, Thomas H. TN 44th (Cons.) Inf. Co.B
Tripp, T.N. AR 17th (Lemoyne's) Inf. Co.E
Tripp, T.N. AR 21st Inf. Co.I
Tripp, Tolman MO 9th (Elliott's) Cav. Co.E
Tripp, Walter NC 8th Inf. Co.G
Tripp, Walter W. MO 4th Inf. Co.A
Tripp, W.B. GA 3rd Inf. Co.F
Tripp, W.F. TN 19th (Biffle's) Cav. Co.D
Tripp, W.F. TN Lt.Arty. Tobin's Co. Cpl.
Tripp, W.H. KY 3rd Mtd.Inf. Co.I,D
Tripp, W.H. TN 44th (Cons.) Inf. Co.B
Tripp, William NC 11th (Bethel Regt.) Inf. Co.G
Tripp, William NC 50th Inf. Co.E
Tripp, William SC 4th Inf. Co.G
Tripp, William B. GA 3rd Cav. Co.F
Tripp, William C. TN 44th (Cons.) Inf. Co.B Cpl.
Tripp, William H. NC 3rd Arty. (40th St.Troops) Co.B Capt.
Tripp, William H. NC 2nd Inf. Co.A
Tripp, William H. NC 8th Inf. Co.G
Tripp, William M. GA Phillips' Legion Co.C
Tripp, W.J. 10th Conf.Cav. Co.H
Tripp, W.R. TN 14th (Neely's) Cav. Co.K 1st Sgt.
Tripp, W.R. TN 9th Inf. Co.A 1st Lt.
Trippe, Albert GA Inf. 2nd Bn. Co.B
Trippe, Albert E. Gen. & Staff, Prov.A. 2nd Lt.
Trippe, Andrew C. MD Inf. 2nd Bn. Co.A
Trippe, Andrew J. MS 27th Inf. Co.E
Trippe, C.P. GA Cav. 19th Bn. Co.C
Trippe, David L. GA 21st Inf. Co.I
Trippe, D.H. MO Cav. 3rd Regt. St.Guard Co.C
Trippe, E.F. GA Inf. 5th Bn. (St.Guards) Co.E
Trippe, E.M. GA 18th Inf. Co.I
Trippe, George E. MS 27th Inf. Co.E
Trippe, Henry W. GA 1st Reg. Co.K 2nd Lt.
Trippe, James M. GA 2nd Cav. Co.A
Trippe, J.E. GA Lt.Arty. Anderson's Btty.
Trippe, J.H. AL 55th Vol. Surg.
Trippe, J.M. GA 7th Cav. Co.C
Trippe, John F. GA 2nd Cav. Co.A 2nd Lt.
Trippe, John F. GA 5th Inf. Co.F
Trippe, John F. GA 12th Inf. Co.I
Trippe, John H. GA Inf. 1st Loc.Troops (Augusta) Co.C
Trippe, Jno. Henry Gen & Staff Surg.
Trippe, John M. GA Cav. 24th Bn. Co.B
Trippe, John R. GA 9th Inf. Co.F Sgt.
Trippe, King H. GA 20th Inf. Co.A
Trippe, Robert P. GA 8th Inf. (St.Guards) Co.D
Trippe, Samuel L. MS 40th Inf. Co.H
Trippe, Samuel W. AR 2nd Mtd.Rifles Co.F
Trippe, Samuel W. AR 37th Inf. Co.H Cpl.
Trippe, T.H. GA Cav. 10th Bn. (St.Guards) Co.D Jr.2nd Lt.
Trippe, W. AL Cp. of Instr. Talladega Co.B
Trippe, W.F. AL Gid Nelson Lt.Arty. Cpl.
Trippe, W.F. AL Mil. 4th Vol. Modawell's Co.
Trippe, William B. AL 19th Inf. Co.H 1st Lt.
Trippe, William H. AL 55th Vol. Co.J,K Bvt.2nd Lt.
Trippe, William J. VA 41st Inf. Co.B
Trippe, W.J. GA Cav. 19th Bn. Co.C
Trippe, W.J.P. GA 8th Inf. Co.D Cpl.
Trippet, Aaron TX 29th Cav. Co.B
Trippet, Caleb VA 19th Cav. Co.A
Trippet, P. VA 19th Cav. Co.A 2nd Lt.
Trippett, C. KY
Trippett, Caleb VA 3rd Cav. & Inf.St.Line Co.A
Trippett, Franklin VA 3rd Cav. & Inf.St.Line Co.A
Trippett, Phillip VA 3rd Cav. & Inf.St.Line Co.A Cpl.
Trippett, W.W. TX 29th Cav. Co.B
Tripple, Charles VA Hvy.Arty. 20th Bn. Co.B
Tripple, Charles VA 6th Inf. Co.H
Tripple, Charles VA 38th Inf. 2nd Co.I
Tripple, William VA 6th Inf. 1st Co.B Cpl.
Tripplet, Philip VA 62nd Mtd.Inf. 2nd Co.L
Tripps, L. MO 7th Cav. Co.I
Triquet, V. LA Mil. 3rd Regt.Eur.Brig. (Garde Francaise) Co.7
Tritt, James C. GA 20th Inf. Co.C
Trisconi, Giovanni LA Mil. Cazadores Espanoles Regt. Co.F
Trish, Conrad AR 35th Inf. Co.C
Trish, Henry AR 35th Inf. Co.C Music.
Trisler, H.A. LA Inf. 1st Sp.Bn. (Rightor's) Co.D
Trisler, W.A. LA 25th Inf. Co.F
Trisler, W.H. LA 17th Inf. Co.E
Trissier, J. LA Mil. French Co. of St.James
Trissler, H.C. 15th Inf. Co.I Cpl.
Trist, Beingier LA 1st (Strawbridge's) Inf. Co.H 2nd Lt.
Trist, Hore B. GA Arty. (Chatham Arty.) Wheaton's Co.
Trist, Hore B. GA 1st (Olmstead's) Inf. Claghorn's Co.
Trist, Hore B. Gen. & Staff Surg.
Trist, J.B. LA Inf. Crescent Regt. Co.B
Trist, N.B. LA Cav. Greenleaf's Co. (Orleans Lt.Horse)
Trist, N.B. Gen. & Staff, Arty. & Ord. Capt.
Trist, N.P. Gen. & Staff 1st Lt.,ADC
Tritall, J.C. TX 10th Cav. Co.B
Tritely, Louis MO St.Guard
Tritt, Alexander VA 64th Mtd.Inf. Co.I
Tritt, Alexander L. VA Inf. 21st Bn. Co.A
Tritt, Alexander L. VA 64th Mtd.Inf. Co.A
Tritt, Archibald C. NC Inf. Thomas Legion Co.F
Tritt, A.W. NC 6th Cav. (65th St.Troops) Co.A

Tritt, A.W. NC Cav. 7th Bn. Co.A
Tritt, A.W. NC Inf. Thomas Legion Co.F
Tritt, Elcany NC 37th Inf. Co.G
Tritt, George W. NC 37th Inf. Co.G Sgt.
Tritt, Henry F. NC 2nd Cav. (19th St.Troops) Co.A
Tritt, Henry F. NC 37th Inf. Co.G
Tritt, Isaac VA 94th Mil. Co.A
Tritt, Jacob VA 64th Mtd.Inf. Co.G
Tritt, Jacob VA 94th Mil. Co.A
Tritt, James VA Inf. 21st Bn. Co.A
Tritt, James VA 64th Mtd.Inf. Co.A
Tritt, James VA 64th Mtd.Inf. Co.G
Tritt, James VA 94th Mil. Co.A
Tritt, John VA 64th Mtd.Inf. Co.I
Tritt, John VA 94th Mil. Co.A
Tritt, Lafayette NC 62nd Inf. Co.I
Tritt, Samuel VA 64th Mtd.Inf. Co.F
Tritt, William VA 64th Mtd.Inf. Co.G 2nd Lt.
Tritt, William VA 94th Mil. Co.A
Tritt, William L. NC 37th Inf. Co.G Cpl.
Tritt, William R. VA 94th Mil. Co.A
Tritt, W.L. NC 18th Inf. Co.D
Tritte, Jacob S. NC 22nd Inf. Co.A
Tritty, W.W. SC 16th & 24th (Cons.) Inf. Co.E Sgt.
Trivathan, F.M. MO Inf. 8th Bn. Co.E
Trivathon, W.H. 8th (Dearing's) Conf.Cav. Co.G
Triver, D. AR 2nd Cav.
Trivet, Lewis W. NC 58th Inf. Co.M,G Cpl.
Trivet, Riley NC 58th Inf. Co.D
Trivett, A. NC Allen's Co. (Loc.Def.)
Trivett, Jesse NC 58th Inf. Co.I
Trivett, John NC 42nd Inf. Co.B
Trivett, Lazarus NC 58th Inf. Co.I,D
Trivett, Lindsy AR 14th (Powers') Inf. Co.F
Trivett, S. NC Allen's Co. (Loc.Def.)
Trivett, Thomas NC 37th Inf. Co.A
Trivett, W. NC Allen's Co. (Loc.Def.)
Trivett, William P. NC 6th Cav. (65th St.Troops) Co.D
Triviett, Isaiah NC Cav. 5th Bn. Co.D
Triviett, Morgan NC Cav. 5th Bn. Co.C,D
Triviett, William H. NC Cav. 5th Bn. Co.D
Trivillian, James M. VA 49th Inf. 3rd Co.G
Trivillion, John C. TN 17th Inf. Co.D
Trivina, John TX 25th Cav. Co.D
Trivis, John A. TN 35th Inf. Co.E
Trivitt, Andrew NC 2nd Inf. Co.G
Trivitt, Elisha NC 58th Inf. Co.D
Trivitt, Isah NC 6th Cav. (65th St.Troops) Co.D
Trivitt, Joel NC 58th Inf. Co.D
Trivitt, Morgan NC 6th Cav. (65th St.Troops) Co.D
Trivono, Polito TN 15th Inf. Co.D
Trivvet, Pinkney NC 42nd Inf. Co.F
Trixler, R.A. NC 1st Detailed Men Co.H
Troat, John VA 11th Bn.Res. Co.B
Trobaugh, Daniel H. AL 16th Inf. Co.C
Trobaugh, H.R. TN 51st (Cons.) Inf. Co.H
Trobaugh, James TN 16th Inf. Co.K
Trobaugh, John VA 3rd (Chrisman's) Bn.Res. Co.A
Trobaugh, John VA 58th Mil. Co.C
Trobaugh, J.W. NT 51st (Cons.) Inf. Co.H Sgt.
Trobaugh, Quincey VA 58th Mil. Co.C
Trobaugh, R.H. TN 9th Inf. Co.C Cpl.
Trobaugh, Thomas B. TN 12th (Green's) Cav. Co.C
Trobaugh, W.A. TN 51st Inf. Co.K 1st Sgt.
Trobaugh, W.A. TN 51st (Cons.) Inf. Co.G Sgt.
Trobaugh, William H. VA Prov.Guard Avis' Co.
Trobell, B.W. Gen. & Staff Lt.Col.
Trobony, George A. TN 61st Mtd.Inf. Co.C
Trobor, J.A. VA 12th Cav. Co.H
Trobough, A.H. TN 9th Inf. Co.C
Trobough, Alexander TN 61st Mtd.Inf. Co.C
Trobough, H.R. TN 51st Inf. Co.A
Trobough, Isaac D. MO 10th Inf. Co.G
Trobough, James TN 51st Inf. Co.A 2nd Lt.
Trobough, J.M. TN 61st Mtd.Inf. Co.C
Trobough, W.F. TN Inf. 2nd Cons.Regt. Co.E
Trobough, William F. TN 29th Inf. Co.I
Trocker, William MO 4th Inf. Co.D
Trocksol, D. VA 3rd Bn. Valley Res. Co.D
Trocy, Campbell GA 6th Inf. Lt.
Troejee, F.A. LA 3rd Inf. Co.F
Troell, Albert B. AL 45th Inf. Co.B Sgt.
Troenille, M. LA Mil. 4th Regt.Eur.Brig. Co.A
Troester, Jacob VA Lt.Arty. E.J. Anderson's Co.
Troeter, George VA 5th Cav. Co.I
Troeter, George VA 1st Arty. Co.H
Troeter, Lewis C. VA 19th Inf. Co.A
Trogden, A.D. NC 6th Inf. Co.I
Trogden, Alfred W. TN 11th Inf. Co.A
Trogden, Andrew P. TN 34th Inf. Co.G,A Sgt.Maj.
Trogden, A.P. TN Inf. 1st Cons.Regt. Co.I
Trogden, Arthur TN 13th (Gore's) Cav. Co.A
Trogden, Charles TN Inf. 22nd Bn. Co.E
Trogden, E.R. NC 1st Jr.Res. Co.F
Trogden, H.K. NC Inf. 2nd Bn. Co.F
Trogden, James TN Inf. 22nd Bn. Co.E
Trogden, Milliken TN Lt.Arty. Lynch's Co.
Trogden, Robert TX 17th Inf. Co.K
Trogden, U.C. GA 64th Inf. Co.I
Trogden, Wiley H. TN 34th Inf. Co.G,B
Trogdon, Abijah NC 6th Sr.Res. Co.A
Trogdon, H.C. NC 22nd Inf. Co.M
Trogdon, Henry K. NC 13th Inf. Co.A
Trogdon, Jeremiah NC 22nd Inf. Co.M
Trogdon, John S. NC Inf. Hall's Bn.
Trogdon, J.W. TN 24th Bn.S.S. Co.C Cpl.
Trogdon, Linden A. NC 22nd Inf. Co.M
Trogdon, Reuben NC 22nd Inf. Co.I
Trogdon, Robert TX 12th Cav. Co.D
Trogdon, Samuel NC 22nd Inf. Co.M
Trogdon, Solomon NC 22nd Inf. Co.M
Trogdon, Stephen W. NC 22nd Inf. Co.M Sgt.
Trogdon, William VA Cav. Swann's Bn. Vincent's Co. Sgt.
Troglin, Lee TN 16th Inf. Co.G
Troglin, Nathan TN 16th Inf. Co.G
Troguille, Joseph LA 26th Inf. Co.D
Trojs, Effiscio LA 10th Inf. Co.I
Trokes, W.C. AL Mil. 2nd Regt.Vol. Co.F
Trolender, J.H. AR 11th Inf. Co.K
Trolinger, Jacob H. NC 13th Inf. Co.K Cpl.
Trolinger, James F. VA 4th Inf. Co.C
Trolinger, John NC 57th Inf. Co.I
Trolinger, John T. NC 6th Inf. Co.F Sgt.
Trolinger, J.T. VA Inf. 7th Bn.Loc.Def. Co.C 1st Lt.
Trolinger, Lem AL 5th Cav. Co.K
Trolinger, Samuel MO 5th Inf. Co.H
Trolinger, William H. MO Cav. 2nd Regt. St.Guard QM
Trolinger, William H. VA 54th Inf. Co.F
Trollenger, Bomar SC Inf. Holcombe Legion Co.C
Trollinger, A.B. SC 1st (Butler's) Inf. Co.F
Trolinger, Calvin D. TN 1st (Feild's) Inf. Co.I
Trollinger, F. NC 7th Sr.Res. Bradshaw's Co.
Trollinger, Hosey SC 1st (Butler's) Inf. Co.F
Trollinger, John H. NC 2nd Bn.Loc.Def.Troops Co.E
Trollinger, W.H. 3rd Conf.Eng.Troops Co.A
Trollinger, William SC 1st (Butler's) Inf. Co.F
Trollinger, William P. AR Cav. Harrell's Bn. Co.B
Trolman, H.T. AL 35th Inf. Co.E
Trolt, W.G. SC Mil. 1st Regt. (Charleston Res.) Co.C
Trom, John D. MS 12th Inf. Co.H
Trombly, Abraham AL 18th Inf. Co.H
Trombon, W.J. AL 40th Inf. Co.H
Trombowsky, Gustav TX 1st Hvy.Arty. Co.C
Tromel, John TN 4th (Murray's) Cav. Co.E
Trommerhouser, J. GA Inf. 1st Loc.Troops (Augusta) Co.B
Trommerhouser, Joseph GA 44th Inf. Co.K
Trommershausser, Philip J. GA 3rd Inf. Co.C
Tromridge, G. SC 13th Inf. Co.K
Tromson, F. LA Mil. 4th Regt. French Brig. Co.3 Sgt.
Tronabage, J.P. AL 17th Inf. Co.K
Tronard, C. LA Mil. Orleans Guards Regt. Co.A
Tronchet, H. LA Mil. Orleans Guards Regt. Co.A
Trone, Henry VA 4th Cav. Co.A
Trone, Joseph LA 18th Inf. Co.G
Trone, Joseph LA Inf.Cons. 18th Regt. & Yellow Jacket Bn. Co.F
Trone, J.W. TN 21st Inf. Co.B
Trone, Peter H. MO 5th Cav. Co.C Black.
Tronson, J. TX 2nd Inf. Co.I
Trook, B.F. VA 18th Cav. 1st Co.G
Trook, B.F. VA Cav. 41st Bn. Co.A
Trook, K.C.A. AL 23rd Inf.
Trook, Lemuel P. VA 23rd Cav. Co.I
Trook, Paul W. VA 146th Mil. Co.D
Trook, Thomas VA 12th Cav. Co.F
Trook, Thomas VA 136th Mil. Co.H
Trook, Thomas M. VA 7th Cav. Gilmor's Co.
Troombly, Robert D. AL Cav.Res. Brooks' Co.
Troop, B.F. VA 23rd Cav. Co.A
Troop, Frank C.A. TN 23rd Inf. Co.B
Troop, James M. AL 55th Vol. Co.G Sgt.
Troop, James M. TN 42nd Inf. 1st Co.H Sgt.
Troop, John G. TN 8th Inf. Co.I Cpl.
Troop, J.R. TN Cav. Jackson's Co.
Troop, T.R. AL 55th Vol. Co.G
Troop, William C. AL 55th Vol. Co.G
Troott, John NC Pris.Guards Howard's Co.
Tropolett, Robert SC 1st Arty. Co.H
Tropp, John A. TN 84th Inf. Co.E
Tropp, Martin MO 4th Cav. Co.C
Tropp, M.V. TN 84th Inf. Co.E
Trosclair, --- LA Mil. 1st Chasseurs a pied Co.8 Cpl.
Trosclair, Aug LA 30th Inf. Co.F

Trosclair, Eugene LA 26th Inf. Co.I
Trosclair, J.J. LA 22nd Inf. Gomez's Co.
Trosclair, Joseph LA 26th Inf. Co.I
Trosclair, L.A. AL 21st Inf. Co.K
Trosclair, L.A. LA Mil. 1st Chasseurs a pied Co.5 1st Lt.
Trosclair, L.A. LA Mil. Jackson Rifle Bn.
Trosclair, Ladislas LA 8th Inf. Co.C
Trosclair, Leufroy LA 26th Inf. Co.I
Trosclair, Lovincy LA 26th Inf. Co.I
Troskoluski, J. GA Inf. (Loc.Def.) Whiteside's Nav.Bn. Co.B
Trosper, J.A. TN 15th (Cons.) Cav. Co.H
Trosper, James M. TX 2nd Cav. 1st Co.F
Trosper, James M. TX 28th Cav. Co.K 1st Lt.
Trosper, J.J. MO 1st & 4th Cons.Inf. Co.G
Trosper, J.J. MO St.Guards Sanders' Co.
Trosper, J.J. Exch.Bn. 2nd Co.C,CSA
Trosper, J.P. TN 12th Inf. Co.G
Trosper, J.P. TN 12th (Cons.) Inf. Co.E
Tross, Jacob VA 2nd Cav. Co.C
Trossh, Martin MO Cav. Preston's Bn. Co.C
Trost, Harman 4th Conf.Eng.Troops Co.E
Trost, Harmon Kellersberg's Corps Sap. & Min.,CSA
Trostman, J. TX 1st Hvy.Arty. Co.D
Trostman, J. TX 2nd Inf.
Troswell, W.H. TN 9th (Ward's) Cav. Co.B
Troth, Benjamin Z. VA 7th Inf. Co.E
Troth, Jacob VA Hvy.Arty. 18th Bn. Co.E
Troth, Robert S. LA 5th Cav. Lt.
Troth, R.S. LA Ogden's Cav. Lt.
Troth, R.S. 14th Conf.Cav. Co.G
Trothe, Alfred AL Inf. 2nd Regt. Co.E Sgt.
Trothe, Alfred Conf.Inf. 1st Bn. 2nd Co.C
Trothschild, Joseph MO Lt.Arty. Landis' Co.
Trotman, Alexander C. NC 5th Inf. Co.B,F 2nd Lt.
Trotman, Colin GA 21st Inf. Co.I
Trotman, Daniel W. NC 52nd Inf. Co.C Cpl.
Trotman, D.W. LA Arty. Hutton's Co. (Crescent Arty.,Co.A)
Trotman, E. Gen. & Staff Asst.Surg.
Trotman, Elkanah J. AL 50th Inf. Co.E
Trotman, George D. NC 2nd Cav. (19th St.Troops) Co.C
Trotman, J. LA Mil. 1st Regt. French Brig. Co.2
Trotman, Jacob GA 31st Inf. Co.G
Trotman, James E. NC 52nd Inf. Co.C
Trotman, John M. NC 5th Inf. Co.B
Trotman, Joseph W. NC 11th (Bethel Regt.) Inf. Co.F Sgt.
Trotman, J.R. MS Inf. 1st Bn.St.Troops (12 mo. '62-3) Co.B
Trotman, Lee MS 1st Cav. Co.D
Trotman, Melkijah B. AL 4th Inf. Co.F
Trotman, Napoleon B. NC Lt.Arty. 13th Bn. Co.A
Trotman, Riddick NC 2nd Cav. (19th St.Troops) Co.C
Trotman, Riddick J. VA Inf. Cohoon's Bn. Co.D
Trotman, S. AL 5th Cav. Co.D
Trotman, S. TN Patterson's Regt.
Trotman, Spivy NC 5th Inf. Co.H
Trotman, T. GA 1st Reg. Co.K
Trotman, T.B. AL 4th Cav. Co.A
Trotman, Thomas GA Siege Arty. 28th Bn. Co.G
Trotman, Thomas C. GA Siege Arty. 28th Bn. Co.G
Trotman, Wiley M. GA 17th Inf. Co.I
Trotman, William T. MS 1st (Foote's) Inf. (St.Troops) Co.B
Trotman, Y.P. AL 7th Inf. Co.D
Trotman, Y.P. AL 35th Inf. Co.E 2nd Lt.
Trotmon, Lee MO 1st Cav. Co.D
Trott, --- AL 20th Inf. Co.C Sgt.
Trott, Athlen NC 3rd Cav. (41st St.Troops) Co.H
Trott, Ben 1st Cherokee Mtd.Vol. Hosp.Stew.
Trott, Benjamin MS 32nd Inf. Co.G
Trott, Benjamin F. AL 20th Inf. Co.D,H Sgt.
Trott, B.F. AL Cav. 24th Bn. Co.B
Trott, B.F. AL 12th Inf. Co.A
Trott, Brice W. NC 3rd Cav. (41st St.Troops) Co.H 2nd Lt.
Trott, C.W. AR 30th Inf. Co.G
Trott, George L. LA 1st (Nelligan's) Inf. Co.I 2nd Lt.
Trott, Henry NC 58th Inf. Co.E
Trott, Hy TX 1st Hvy.Arty. Co.G
Trott, J.A. AR Lt.Arty. (Helena Arty.) Clarkson's Btty. Cpl.
Trott, Jackson NC 4th Sr.Res. Co.B
Trott, James NC Walker's Bn. Thomas' Legion 2nd Co.D
Trott, James E. AR 34th Inf. AQM
Trott, James E. Gen. & Staff Capt.,AQM
Trott, James F. MS 2nd Inf. Co.A
Trott, James F. MS 26th Inf. Co.B 1st Sgt.
Trott, James J. 1st Cherokee Mtd.Vol. 1st Co.C
Trott, J.H. NC 57th Inf. Co.K Sgt.
Trott, Jim 1st Cherokee Mtd.Vol. Co.J
Trott, J.O. AL Lt.Arty. Goldthwaite's Btty.
Trott, John TN 41st Inf. Co.F
Trott, John C. AL 20th Inf. Co.D,H
Trott, John Henry NC 42nd Inf. Co.A
Trott, John Jemison AL Lt.Arty. 2nd Bn. Co.D
Trott, J.T. TN 1st (Carter's) Cav. Co.E
Trott, Michael TN 41st Inf. Co.F
Trott, Michael TN 44th (Cons.) Inf. Co.A
Trott, Newton NC 3rd Inf. Co.G
Trott, T.B. 1st Cherokee Mtd.Vol. 2nd Co.I
Trott, T.B. 2nd Cherokee Mtd.Vol. Co.D
Trott, Wiley AL 62nd Inf. Co.A,D
Trott, William J. NC 3rd Cav. (41st St.Troops) Co.B
Trott, William P. TX Cav. Ragsdale's Bn. 2nd Co.C Cpl.
Trott, William P. 4th Conf.Eng.Troops
Trott, Willis NC 57th Inf. Co.K
Trotter, A.B.C. SC 7th Inf. Co.A
Trotter, Alexander MS 14th Inf. Co.D 1st Lt.
Trotter, Alex. MS 14th (Cons.) Inf. Co.E Capt.
Trotter, Alex G. NC 53rd Inf. Co.B
Trotter, A.P. MS 2nd Cav. 2nd Co.G
Trotter, A.P. MS 5th Cav. Co.B
Trotter, A.S. VA 19th Cav. Co.H
Trotter, B.C. GA Phillips' Legion Co.C
Trotter, Ben TN 10th (DeMoss') Cav. Co.E
Trotter, Benjamin F. AL 10th Inf. Co.I
Trotter, Benjamin F. AR Cav. McGehee's Regt. Co.A
Trotter, Benn F. MS 18th Inf. Co.I
Trotter, Bolden AR 15th (N.W.) Inf. Co.C
Trotter, Butler SC 2nd Rifles Co.B
Trotter, B.W. MS 1st (King's) Inf. (St.Troops) Co.D
Trotter, B.W. MS Inf. 1st Bn.St.Troops (30 days '64) Co.F
Trotter, C.T. NC 16th Inf. Co.H Sgt.
Trotter, C.T. TN 4th (McLemore's) Cav. Co.E
Trotter, David MS Inf. 3rd Bn. Co.B
Trotter, D.H. AL 14th Inf. Co.B
Trotter, D.T. VA Mil. 42nd Regt.
Trotter, E. TN 16th (Logwood's) Cav. Co.I
Trotter, Elias N. GA Phillips' Legion Co.C
Trotter, E.T. TN 51st Inf. Co.C
Trotter, E.T. TN 51st (Cons.) Inf. Co.I
Trotter, F.B. SC 1st Cav. Co.C
Trotter, F.M. SC 4th Bn.Res. Co.A
Trotter, George NC 46th Inf. Co.F
Trotter, George I. VA 18th Inf. Co.A Cpl.
Trotter, George W. SC 6th Cav. Co.B
Trotter, George W. TN 11th Inf. Co.I
Trotter, Green S. AR Inf. Whittington's Bn. Co.A
Trotter, G.T. AR 24th Inf. Co.E
Trotter, G.W. TN Inf. 1st Cons.Regt. Co.E
Trotter, G.W. TN 9th Inf. Co.A
Trotter, H. SC 1st Cav. Co.F
Trotter, H. TN 19th (Biffle's) Cav. Co.E
Trotter, Harrison AR Cav. Harrell's Bn. Co.D Cpl.
Trotter, Harrison AR 27th Inf. Co.D Sgt.
Trotter, Harvey TX 4th Cav. Co.E
Trotter, Harvy TX 12th Inf. Co.F
Trotter, H.C. GA 3rd Bn.S.S. Co.B Cpl.
Trotter, H.C. TN 4th Cav. Co.E
Trotter, H.C. TN Lt.Arty. Huggins' Co.
Trotter, Henry GA 24th Inf. Co.G
Trotter, Henry C. TX 16th Cav. Co.D
Trotter, Henry O. TX 6th Cav. Co.D
Trotter, Isam G. GA 51st Inf. Co.E Cpl.
Trotter, Isham E. VA 56th Inf. Co.E Sgt.
Trotter, James AR 27th Inf. Co.D Capt.
Trotter, James MS 2nd Cav.Res. Co.A,K
Trotter, James H. VA 36th Inf. 2nd Co.E
Trotter, James R. GA 24th Inf. Co.K
Trotter, James R. GA Phillips' Legion Co.C Sgt.
Trotter, James W.B. VA 5th Inf. Co.E Cpl.
Trotter, J.B. NC 21st Inf. Co.K
Trotter, J.B. NC 45th Inf. Co.G
Trotter, J.D. MS 9th Inf. New Co.I Sgt.
Trotter, J.D. MS 9th Bn.S.S. Co.A 3rd Lt.
Trotter, J.D. TN 9th Inf. 1st Lt.
Trotter, J.E. MS Lt.Arty. Turner's Co.
Trotter, J.H. VA 18th Cav. Co.H
Trotter, J.J. NC 2nd Jr.Res. Co.B 2nd Lt.
Trotter, J.J. TN 11th Inf. Co.I
Trotter, J.M. TN 50th Inf. Co.K
Trotter, J.M. TN 50th (Cons.) Inf. Co.G
Trotter, John AR 47th (Crandall's) Cav. Co.K
Trotter, John AR 26th Inf. Co.H
Trotter, John GA Inf. 1st Loc.Troops (Augusta) Co.H
Trotter, John MO Cav. Snider's Bn. Co.C
Trotter, John M. NC 52nd Inf. Co.B Cpl.
Trotter, John W. AL 6th Inf. Co.C
Trotter, Joseph J. NC 20th Inf. Co.C
Trotter, Joseph M. MS 42nd Inf. Co.A
Trotter, Joseph W. MS 3rd Inf. Co.C
Trotter, J.P. MS 5th Cav. Co.B Capt.

Trotter, J.P. MS Cav. Dunn's Co. (MS Rangers) Sgt.
Trotter, J.R. GA Inf. 4th Bn. (St.Guards) Co.B
Trotter, J.R. SC Inf. Hampton Legion Co.I
Trotter, J.S. SC 4th Inf. Co.H
Trotter, J.S. VA Cav. 37th Bn. Co.B
Trotter, J.W. AR 10th Mil. Co.F
Trotter, J.W. MS 2nd Cav. Co.G
Trotter, J.W. MS 5th Cav. Co.B
Trotter, J.W. MS Cav. Dunn's Co. (MS Rangers)
Trotter, J.W. MS 1st (Percy's) Inf. Co.D
Trotter, J.W. TX 1st Inf. Co.C Sgt.
Trotter, L. SC 5th Mil. Beat Co.3
Trotter, L.D. AL 5th Cav. Co.K
Trotter, Marion MS 15th Inf. Co.E
Trotter, Milledge SC 22nd Inf. Co.A
Trotter, M.L. MS 28th Cav. Co.B
Trotter, Nepolian B. MS 24th Inf. Co.D
Trotter, N.N. LA Lt.Arty. Fenner's Btty.
Trotter, Peter D. VA 38th Inf. Co.K 1st Sgt.
Trotter, P.L. SC 4th Cav. Co.C
Trotter, R. KY 4th Cav. Co.E 2nd Lt.
Trotter, Reuben SC 1st Arty. Co.E
Trotter, Richard B. TN 9th Cav. Co.E
Trotter, Robert SC 3rd Res. Co.H
Trotter, Robert TX 16th Cav. Co.D Cpl.
Trotter, Robert B. GA 24th Inf. Co.G 2nd Lt.
Trotter, Robert L. MS 13th Inf. Co.G 1st Lt.
Trotter, Rufus J. TX 4th Cav. Co.E 2nd Lt.
Trotter, Rufus W. MS 30th Inf. Co.C
Trotter, R.W. MS 2nd Cav. 2nd Co.G
Trotter, R.W. MS 5th Cav. Co.B
Trotter, S. NC 7th Sr.Res. Boon's Co.D
Trotter, Sam TX 9th Cav. Co.I
Trotter, S.C. AR 19th (Dawson's) Inf. Co.F
Trotter, Sylvanus TN 14th Inf. Co.G,B
Trotter, T.B. NC 1st Inf. (6 mo. '61) Co.C 2nd Lt.
Trotter, T.H. VA Inf. 44th Bn. Co.C Sgt.
Trotter, Thomas B. NC 53rd Inf. Co.B Cpl.
Trotter, Thomas J. MS 15th Inf. Co.B
Trotter, Thomas R. AR 5th Inf. Co.K Cpl.
Trotter, Thomas R. AR 26th Inf. Co.A
Trotter, Thomas R. TN 5th (McKenzie's) Cav. Co.E
Trotter, Thomas R. VA 21st Inf. Co.G
Trotter, Tilghman H. AL 61st Inf. Co.A Cpl.
Trotter, Tillman R. MS Lt.Arty. Stanford's Co. 2nd Lt.
Trotter, Tillman R. MS 15th Inf. Surg.
Trotter, Tilman H. AL 1st Regt.Conscr. Co.D
Trotter, T.L. MS 34th Inf. Co.C 3rd Lt.
Trotter, T.R. Gen. & Staff Surg.
Trotter, W. AL Mil. 1st Regt. Co.B
Trotter, W.A. MS Inf. 7th Bn. Co.D Capt.
Trotter, W.D. AR 24th Inf. Co.E Capt.
Trotter, W.D. AR Inf. Hardy's Regt. Co.B Capt.
Trotter, W.D. MS Part.Rangers Armistead's Co.
Trotter, W.D. MS 15th Inf. Co.B
Trotter, W.D. TN 24th Bn.S.S. Co.A
Trotter, W.G. TN 1st (Carter's) Cav. Co.C
Trotter, W.H. TN 3rd (Forrest's) Cav. Co.F
Trotter, William AL 31st Inf. Co.I
Trotter, William AL 48th Inf. Co.B
Trotter, William AR 15th (N.W.) Inf. Co.I
Trotter, William LA 3rd (Wingfield's) Cav. Co.E
Trotter, William LA 4th Inf. Old Co.G
Trotter, William SC 2nd Rifles Co.K,E
Trotter, William TN 50th Inf. Co.A
Trotter, William A. MS 13th Inf. Co.G 1st Sgt.
Trotter, William A. NC 6th Cav. (65th St.Troops) Co.A Sgt.
Trotter, William A. NC Cav. 7th Bn. Co.A Sgt.
Trotter, William A. TN 2nd (Robison's) Inf. Co.G
Trotter, William A. VA Loc.Def. Scott's Co.
Trotter, William G. TN 59th Mtd.Inf. Co.H 1st Sgt.
Trotter, William Henry MS 2nd Part.Rangers Co.C
Trotter, William M. GA Phillips' Legion Co.C
Trotter, William M. MS 15th Inf. Co.E
Trotter, William S. KY 4th Mtd.Inf. Co.H Sgt.
Trotter, William W. AL 6th Inf. Co.A
Trotter, William W. FL Cav. 5th Bn. Co.E
Trotter, W.J. TN Inf. 2nd Cons.Regt. Co.I Cpl.
Trotter, W.J. TN 50th (Cons.) Inf. Co.A
Trotter, W.M. AL 48th Inf. Co.G
Trotter, W.P. SC 2nd Arty. Co.K
Trotter, W.P. SC Hvy.Arty. 15th (Lucas') Bn. Co.A
Trotter, W.S. Central Div. KY Sap. & Min.,CSA
Trotter, W.W. AL Cav. Chisolm's Co.
Trotter, W.W. AL Lt.Arty. 20th Bn. Co.K
Trotti, F.B. SC 1st Cav. Co.K,C
Trotti, Frank B. SC Hvy.Arty. Mathewes' Co.
Trotti, James H. TX 13th Cav. Co.G Cpl.
Trotti, Joshua F. TX 13th Cav. Co.G
Trotti, Lawrence J. SC Hvy.Arty. Mathewes' Co. Cpl.
Trotti, L.J. SC Arty. Manigault's Bn. Co.C Cpl.
Trotti, S.W. SC Arty. Stuart's Co. (Beaufort Vol.Arty.)
Trotti, T.B. SC Arty. Manigault's Bn. Co.C
Trottie, John L. TX 13th Cav. Co.H
Trotting Wolfe 1st Cherokee Mtd.Rifles Co.K 2nd Lt.
Trotts, J.W. MO Inf. 1st Bn.St.Guard Co.D Capt.
Trouard, A. LA Mil.Cav. (Chasseurs Jefferson) Cagnolatti's Co.
Trouard, A. LA Arty. 5th Field Btty. (Pelican Lt.Arty.)
Trouard, A.L. LA Inf.Cons.Crescent Regt. Co.E Cpl.
Trouard, Alfred, Jr. LA 18th Inf. Co.E
Trouard, D. LA Mil.Cav. (Chasseurs Jefferson) Cagnolatti's Co.
Trouard, L. LA Mil.Cav. (Chasseurs Jefferson) Cagnolatti's Co.
Trouard, O. LA Arty. 5th Field Btty. (Pelican Lt.Arty.)
Trouard, Prosper LA 7th Cav. Co.H 2nd Lt.
Trouard, Prosper LA 31st Inf. Co.A
Troublefield, A.D. SC 2nd Inf. Co.D,B
Troublefield, A.D. SC Cav.Bn. Holcombe Legion Co.A
Troublefield, M. NC 3rd Jr.Res. Co.F
Troublefield, Marcus NC 8th Bn.Jr.Res. Co.A
Troublefield, Peter B. NC 38th Inf. Co.C Capt.
Troublefield, T.J. SC 2nd Inf. Co.D
Troublefield, William B. SC 2nd Inf. Co.D,B
Troublefield, W.P. SC Lt.Arty. Garden's Co. (Palmetto Lt.Btty.)
Trouche, --- 2nd Conf.Eng.Troops Co.F Sgt.
Trouche, A.F. SC Inf. 1st (Charleston) Bn. Co.D Sgt.
Trouche, A.F. SC 27th Inf. Co.D Sgt.
Trouche, C.A. SC Arty. Manigault's Bn. 1st Co.A
Trouell, Y.F. TX 10th Cav. Co.D
Trough, G. NC 22nd Inf. Co.A
Troughear, Jonathan LA 20th Inf. Co.G
Trouilly, C. LA Mil. 2nd Regt. French Brig. Co.4
Troup, Flornoy TX 13th Vol. Co.E
Troup, Frank AR Lt.Arty. Key's Btty. Cpl.
Troup, George FL 5th Inf. Co.C
Troup, Jacob GA 49th Inf. Co.F
Troup, John L. LA 14th Inf. Co.I
Troup, John M. MS 2nd Part.Rangers Co.A Cpl.
Troup, J.R. Gen. & Staff, Adj.Gen.Dept. Capt.
Troup, Louis VA 110th Mil. Saunders' Co.
Troup, Marcus M. MS 20th Inf. Co.B
Troup, M.M. MS Cav. 4th Bn. Co.C Sgt.
Troup, M.M. 8th (Wade's) Conf.Cav. Co.E 1st Sgt.
Troup, P. GA 1st Troops & Defences (Macon) Co.H
Troup, Peter GA 49th Inf. Co.F
Troup, Robert Gen. & Staff 1st Lt.,ADC
Troup, Thomas MO 1st N.E. Cav. Co.D
Troup, W.J. MS Inf. 2nd St.Troops Co.K
Troup, W.W. MS Inf. 2nd St.Troops Co.K 1st Lt.
Troupe, George W. AR 18th (Marmaduke's) Inf. Co.F
Troupe, J. TX 8th Inf. Co.A
Troupe, James TX Arty. 4th Bn.
Troupe, J.M. MS 7th Cav. Co.F,A
Troupt, Jacob VA 57th Inf. Co.B
Trousdale, --- TX 14th Field Btty.
Trousdale, A.C. TN 46th Inf. Co.A
Trousdale, Alexander TN 5th Inf. Co.A, 2nd Co.G
Trousdale, Alexander P. LA Arty. 1st Field Btty. Cpl.
Trousdale, Benjamin F. AL 35th Inf. Co.A
Trousdale, C.W. KY Morgan's Men Co.E 1st Lt.
Trousdale, C.W. TN 9th (Ward's) Cav. Co.A 1st Lt.
Trousdale, David TN 48th (Voorhies') Inf. Co.E 2nd Lt.
Trousdale, D.B. LA Hvy.Arty. 2nd Bn. Co.D Sgt.
Trousdale, D.R. LA 18th Inf. Co.D Sgt.
Trousdale, F.G. TN 5th Inf. 2nd Co.G, Co.A
Trousdale, F.G. TN 46th Inf. Co.A
Trousdale, Isaac W. TN 48th (Voorhies') Inf. Co.E
Trousdale, Jas. AL 9th (Malone's) Cav. Co.E
Trousdale, James TX 10th Cav. Co.A
Trousdale, James M. LA Scouts Vinson's Co. Sgt.
Trousdale, James M. TN 5th Inf. Co.A 1st Lt.
Trousdale, James M. TX 35th (Brown's) Cav. Co.H

Trousdale, James M. TX 13th Vol. 2nd Co.A
Trousdale, J.C. MS 2nd Cav. Co.D Cpl.
Trousdale, J.M. TX 14th Field Btty.
Trousdale, John A. TX 35th (Brown's) Cav. Co.H
Trousdale, John A. TX 13th Vol. 2nd Co.A
Trousdale, John B. MO 1st Inf. Co.I
Trousdale, John H. TN Cav. 7th Bn. (Bennett's) Co.E
Trousdale, Julius A. TN 2nd (Robison's) Inf. Co.I,E
Trousdale, L. AL 9th (Malone's) Cav. Co.E
Trousdale, Leon Gen. & Staff, Adj.Gen.Dept. Capt.
Trousdale, T.F. TN 48th (Voorhies') Inf. Co.E
Trousdale, T.J. TN 48th (Voorhies') Inf. Co.E
Trousdale, W.C. TN 28th (Cons.) Inf. Co.G Capt.
Trousdale, William C. TN 28th Inf. Co.G Capt.
Trousdale, William F. AL 9th (Malone's) Cav. Co.E 1st Lt.
Trousdale, William H. TN 48th (Voorhies') Inf. Co.E
Trousdale, William L. TN 8th (Smith's) Cav. Co.C
Trousdale, William W. TN 7th Inf. Co.A
Trousdale, Wilson TN Cav. 9th Bn. (Gantt's) Co.B
Trousdale, Wilson TN 48th (Voorhies') Inf. Co.E
Trousdale, W.L. TN 4th (Murray's) Cav. Co.H Sgt.
Trout, A.J. VA Inf. 1st Bn.Loc.Def. Co.A
Trout, Ambrose TN 59th Mtd.Inf. Co.C
Trout, Andrew VA 166th Mil. Co.B
Trout, Andrew J. VA 166th Mil. Co.A Cpl.
Trout, Archibald W. VA 22nd Inf. Co.K
Trout, Archibald W. VA 54th Inf. Co.K
Trout, Benjamin F. GA Cav. 9th Bn. (St.Guards) Co.C
Trout, Benjamin F. GA 41st Inf. Co.B
Trout, B.F. TX Inf. 1st Bn. (St.Troops) Co.A
Trout, B.F. TX Inf. Rutherford's Co. 2nd Lt.
Trout, Bird TN Cav. 7th Bn. (Bennett's) Co.F
Trout, Bird TN 22nd (Barteau's) Cav. Co.G
Trout, C. TN Inf. 3rd Cons.Regt. Co.D
Trout, C. TN 5th Inf. 2nd Co.K
Trout, C.H. TX 8th Inf. Co.I Sgt.
Trout, C.H. TX Inf. 24th Bn. (St.Troops)
Trout, Charles TN 2nd (Robison's) Inf. Co.H
Trout, Charles A. VA Cav. 36th Bn. Co.A
Trout, Christopher C. GA 1st Reg. Co.F
Trout, D. TN 19th & 20th (Cons.) Cav. Co.E
Trout, D. TN 20th (Russell's) Cav. Co.C
Trout, Daniel B. KY 4th Cav. Co.A
Trout, David VA 157th Mil. Co.B Sgt.
Trout, D.V. GA Inf. 25th Bn. (Prov.Guard) Co.B
Trout, Edmund P. AL 19th Inf. Co.G
Trout, Edward MO 11th Inf. Co.K
Trout, Elihu TN 9th (Ward's) Cav. Co.E
Trout, Elijah TN 9th (Ward's) Cav. Co.E
Trout, E.P. GA Cav. 6th Bn. (St.Guards) Co.G Cpl.
Trout, E. Stribling VA 52nd Inf. Co.H Capt.
Trout, G.A. MO 6th Cav. Co.I
Trout, Gaither NC 50th Inf. Co.I
Trout, George 2nd Cherokee Mtd.Vol. Co.G
Trout, George M. AR 19th (Dawson's) Inf. Co.A
Trout, George M. TX 16th Cav. Co.D
Trout, George P. GA 43rd Inf. Co.H,G
Trout, George W. VA 28th Inf. Co.B
Trout, Gideon GA Phillips' Legion Co.M
Trout, Giles GA Cav. 9th Bn. (St.Guards) Co.C
Trout, Green N. GA 21st Inf. Co.B Sgt.
Trout, G.W. AR Inf. Hardy's Regt. Torbett's Co.
Trout, H.C. TN 46th Inf. Co.H
Trout, Henderson GA Inf. (Mell Scouts) Wyly's Co.
Trout, Henry C. GA 22nd Inf. Co.B
Trout, Henry S. VA 28th Inf. Co.I 2nd Lt.
Trout, J.A. VA 22nd Inf. Co.H
Trout, Jackson GA Floyd Legion (St.Guards) Co.B Capt.
Trout, Jacob TN 12th Inf. Co.F
Trout, Jacob TN 12th (Cons.) Inf. Co.B
Trout, James VA 22nd Cav. Co.D
Trout, James C. AR 3rd Cav. Co.I
Trout, James C. TX 6th Cav. Co.D
Trout, James M. NC 18th Inf. Co.E
Trout, James P. TN Cav. 12th Bn. (Day's) Co.B Sgt.
Trout, James R. VA 10th Inf. Co.B
Trout, James S. VA 33rd Inf. Co.C Capt.
Trout, James W. VA 24th Inf. Co.B
Trout, J.H. AR Inf. Cocke's Regt. Co.D
Trout, J.L. TN 59th Mtd.Inf. Co.A
Trout, J.M. GA Lt.Arty. Van Den Corput's Co. Cpl.
Trout, J.M. GA Inf. 3rd Bn. Co.A
Trout, J.M. GA 15th Inf. Co.C
Trout, John TN Cav. 12th Bn. (Day's) Co.A
Trout, John VA Inf. 26th Bn. Co.I
Trout, John F. AR 19th (Dawson's) Inf. Co.A
Trout, John H. TN 25th Inf. Co.I Cpl.
Trout, John H. TX 16th Cav. Co.D
Trout, John R. KY 3rd Cav. Co.C,G Sgt.
Trout, John W. GA 16th Inf. Co.G
Trout, John W. VA 46th Inf. 2nd Co.K
Trout, Joseph B. AR 33rd Inf. Co.I
Trout, Joseph C. 1st Conf.Eng.Troops Co.G Sgt.
Trout, Joseph O. AR 19th (Dawson's) Inf. Co.A
Trout, J.W. VA 5th Cav. Co.D
Trout, J.W. 1st Conf.Inf. 2nd Co.K
Trout, L. SC Lt.Arty. Walter's Co. (Washington Arty.)
Trout, L. TN 1st Hvy.Arty. 3rd Co.A
Trout, Leland TN Hvy.Arty. Johnston's Co.
Trout, Leland TN 1st (Feild's) Inf.
Trout, L.M. TX 11th Cav. Co.F
Trout, Marcus KY 3rd Mtd.Inf. Co.G
Trout, M.D. TN 55th (McKoin's) Inf. Day's Co.
Trout, Noah S. NC 62nd Inf. Co.B
Trout, Norman VA 62nd Mtd.Inf. Co.E
Trout, O.H. TX Inf. 1st Bn. (St.Troops) Co.A
Trout, Patten TN 9th (Ward's) Cav. Co.E
Trout, Perry G. AL 19th Inf. Co.D
Trout, P.G. TX Inf. Chambers' Bn.Res.Corps Co.A
Trout, P.H. VA Mil. 160th Regt. Co.A Capt.
Trout, R.D. AR 34th Inf. Co.F
Trout, R.O. AR Cav. Gordon's Regt. Co.G
Trout, Robert GA 47th Inf. Co.I
Trout, Robert G. GA 41st Inf. Co.B
Trout, Robert W. GA Cherokee Legion (St.Guards) Co.D
Trout, R.T. TN 35th Inf. 1st Co.D Sgt.
Trout, S. TN 5th Inf. 2nd Co.K
Trout, Samuel KY 12th Cav. Co.A,C
Trout, Sanford C. GA 8th Inf. Co.E
Trout, S.C. GA 1st Cav. Co.C
Trout, Sidney A. AR 47th (Crandall's) Cav. Co.B
Trout, Stephen A. AL 19th Inf. Co.G
Trout, T.B. Gen. & Staff Maj.,CS
Trout, Thomas MO 7th Cav. Co.G
Trout, T.P. GA 13th Cav. Co.G
Trout, W. TN 19th & 20th (Cons.) Cav. Co.E
Trout, Walter C. GA 43rd Inf. Co.H
Trout, Walton GA 18th Inf.
Trout, W.B.F. AR 3rd Cav. Co.K
Trout, W.G. NC 1st Bn.Jr.Res. Co.B 1st Sgt.
Trout, William MD Cav. 2nd Bn. Co.C
Trout, William TN 2nd (Ashby's) Cav. Co.K
Trout, William TN Cav. 2nd Bn. (Biffle's) Co.F
Trout, William VA 5th Cav. Co.D Black.
Trout, William VA 157th Mil. Co.B
Trout, William D. VA 10th Inf. Co.B 2nd Lt.
Trout, William D. VA 28th Inf. 2nd Co.C
Trout, William F. VA 54th Inf. Co.K
Trout, William H. GA 24th Inf. Co.D
Trout, William H. NC 62nd Inf. Co.B
Trout, William H. TN Cav. 12th Bn. (Day's) Co.B
Trout, William H. VA Inf. 25th Bn. Co.E
Trout, William P. GA 8th Inf. Co.E
Trout, William R. GA 16th Inf. Co.G
Trout, W.P. TN 12th (Cons.) Inf. Co.D
Trout, W.P. TN 22nd Inf. Co.K
Trout, W.S. AL 45th Inf. Co.G
Trout, W.S. TN 45th Inf. Co.G
Trout, W.S. TN 47th Inf. Co.K
Trout, W.S. TX 10th Cav. Co.A 1st Lt.
Trout, W.W. SC Lt.Arty. Walter's Co. (Washington Arty.)
Trout, W.W. TN 1st Hvy.Arty. 3rd Co.A
Trout, W.W. TN Hvy.Arty. Johnston's Co.
Troute, J.F. AR Inf. Hardy's Regt. Co.A Cpl.
Troutman, A. 1st Conf.Cav. 1st Co.A
Troutman, Aaron C. GA 3rd Cav. Co.E
Troutman, Adam NC 5th Inf. Co.B
Troutman, Adam A. TN 39th Mtd.Inf. Co.E
Troutman, Adam C. NC 48th Inf. Co.C
Troutman, Adam W. NC 48th Inf. Co.C 2nd Lt.
Troutman, A.H. Gen. & Staff AQM
Troutman, Alfred NC 33rd Inf. Co.D
Troutman, Augustus D. NC 2nd Cav. (19th St.Troops) Co.B
Troutman, Caleb M. NC 5th Inf. Co.B
Troutman, Charles MS 9th Inf. New Co.H
Troutman, Charles A. NC 48th Inf. Co.C
Troutman, Daniel A. NC 48th Inf. Co.C
Troutman, Daniel O. NC 1st Arty. (10th St.Troops) Co.D
Troutman, David AL 13th Inf. Co.G
Troutman, David F. NC 33rd Inf. Co.A Cpl.
Troutman, Ed MO 16th Inf. Co.E
Troutman, F.A. Cobb's Staff Capt.,QM
Troutman, F.M. KY 2nd (Duke's) Cav. Co.D
Troutman, George NC 4th Cav. (59th St.Troops) Co.E
Troutman, George W. GA Inf. 2nd Bn. Co.C
Troutman, George W. NC 58th Inf. Co.B

Troutman, Green NC 42nd Inf. Co.D
Troutman, H.A. GA Arty. (Macon Lt.Arty.) Slaten's Co. Jr.1st Lt.
Troutman, Henry M. NC 7th Inf. Co.I
Troutman, Henry M. NC 8th Bn.Jr.Res. Co.A
Troutman, Henry M. NC 42nd Inf. Co.D
Troutman, Hiram A. GA Inf. 2nd Bn. Co.C Sgt.Maj.
Troutman, H.M. NC 5th Inf. Co.B
Troutman, J. SC 1st Regt. Charleston Guard Co.G
Troutman, James MO 6th Cav. Co.D
Troutman, James W. NC Walker's Bn. Thomas' Legion Co.G
Troutman, James W. TN 1st (Carter's) Cav. Co.H
Troutman, J.C. TN Conscr. (Cp. of Instr.)
Troutman, J.D. SC 2nd Arty. Co.C
Troutman, J.F. GA 12th (Robinson's) Cav. (St.Guards) Co.C Sgt.
Troutman, J. Monroe NC 35th Inf. Co.K
Troutman, John NC 2nd Cav. (19th St.Troops) Co.G
Troutman, John NC 52nd Inf. Co.I
Troutman, John A. NC 33rd Inf. Co.A
Troutman, John B. NC 48th Inf. Co.C
Troutman, John J. NC 4th Inf. Co.C Sgt.
Troutman, Jonas NC Walker's Bn. Thomas' Legion 2nd Co.D
Troutman, Joseph AL 24th Inf. Co.D
Troutman, Joseph NC 5th Inf. Co.F
Troutman, M. MO 12th Inf. Co.F
Troutman, M. NC 4th Cav. (59th St.Troops) Co.A
Troutman, M.B. NC 4th Inf. Co.K
Troutman, M.L. GA Floyd Legion (St.Guards) Co.E Capt.
Troutman, M.L. GA Smith's Legion Co.F
Troutman, M.M. NC Mallett's Bn. (Cp.Guard) Co.D
Troutman, Newton AL 17th Inf. Co.C
Troutman, P.L. KY 6th Mtd.Inf. Co.H
Troutman, Rufus NC 1st Arty. (10th St.Troops) Co.D
Troutman, Rufus P. NC 1st Arty. (10th St.Troops) Co.D
Troutman, Sol. H. AL 17th Inf. Co.C
Troutman, Thomas GA 3rd Cav. Co.B Sgt.
Troutman, Thomas J. NC 52nd Inf. Co.I
Troutman, Travis NC 49th Inf. Co.C
Troutman, W.A. AL 8th Inf. Co.E
Troutman, W.A. NC 8th Inf. Co.H
Troutman, W.H. NC 8th Inf. Co.H
Troutman, William KY 6th Mtd.Inf. Co.H
Troutman, William NC 46th Inf. Co.K
Troutman, William VA 46th Inf.
Troutt, A.J. TN 1st (Carter's) Cav. Co.E
Troutt, E. TN 20th Inf. Co.F
Troutt, Henry S. VA 22nd Inf. Co.C 2nd Lt.
Troutt, Jeremiah TN 20th Inf. Co.F Cpl.
Troutt, J.P. TN 13th (Gore's) Cav. Co.F
Troutt, J.R. KY 3rd Mtd.Inf. Co.G 1st Sgt.
Trouty, J.W. MO Cav. Coleman's Regt. Co.K 1st Sgt.
Trover, A. TX Waul's Legion Co.E
Trovillian, B. VA Cav. 40th Bn. Co.F
Trow, N. NC 67th Inf. Co.I
Trow, Th. NC 67th Inf. Co.D
Trowbridge, A.B. MS 1st Lt.Arty. Co.G Artif.
Trowbridge, Almarin GA Cobb's Legion Co.E
Trowbridge, Francis VA 22nd Cav. Co.E
Trowbridge, Isaac LA 2nd Cav. Co.C
Trowbridge, James Conf.Cav. Wood's Regt. Co.L
Trowbridge, J.T. KY 1st (Butler's) Cav. Co.I
Trowbridge, J.W. TX 1st Inf. Co.E
Trowbridge, J.W. Sig.Corps,CSA
Trowbridge, Newman LA Arty. 1st Field Btty.
Trowbridge, S.F. SC Post Guard Senn's Co.
Trowbridge, W. TN Inf. 3rd Bn. Co.B
Trowbridge, William GA Cav. Allen's Co.
Trowell, A.B. TX 11th (Spaight's) Bn.Vol. Co.F
Trowell, A.B. TX 21st Inf. Ens.
Trowell, A.B. TX Waul's Legion Co.F
Trowell, H. GA Lt.Arty. Clinch's Btty.
Trowell, J. SC 3rd Cav. Co.F
Trowell, J.H. TX 14th Inf. Co.F
Trowell, John GA 4th (Clinch's) Cav. Co.F
Trowell, John SC 11th Inf. Co.K
Trowell, John A. GA 2nd Inf. 1st Co.B
Trowell, John A. GA 26th Inf. Co.E
Trowell, John H. TX 35th (Likens') Cav. 1st Lt.
Trowell, John H. TX 37th Cav. Co.K 1st Lt.
Trowell, Jonas SC 3rd Cav. Co.F
Trowell, Joseph E. GA 2nd Inf. 1st Co.B
Trowell, Joseph E. GA 26th Inf. Co.E
Trowell, J.P. GA Cav. 2nd Bn. Co.A
Trowell, J.P. GA 5th Cav. Co.I
Trowell, J.W. GA 50th Inf. Co.I
Trowell, N.J. FL 2nd Cav. Co.B Cpl.
Trowell, Thomas J. SC 3rd Cav. Co.E
Trowell, Thomas S. GA 2nd Inf. 1st Co.B
Trowell, Thomas S. GA 26th Inf. Co.E
Trowell, T.J. SC 2nd Cav. Co.B
Trowell, W.H. MO 4th Inf. Co.B
Trower, George D. VA 39th Inf. Co.B
Trower, Harvey MO Inf. Clark's Regt. Co.G
Trower, Harvey Conf.Cav. Clarkson's Bn. Ind. Rangers Co.D Cpl.
Trower, John MO 11th Inf. Co.C
Trower, Monroe MO 11th Inf. Co.C
Trower, Preston VA 39th Inf. Co.K
Trower, Preston E. VA Hvy.Arty. 19th Bn. 3rd Co.E
Trower, W.H VA 54th Mil. Co.G
Trower, William MO 11th Inf. Co.C Capt.
Trower, William H. VA Cav. Young's Co. Sgt.
Trowers, Alonzo VA Cav. Mosby's Regt. (Part.Rangers) Co.F
Trowers, William H. VA 6th Inf. Co.F
Trowt, W. TN 20th (Russell's) Cav. Co.C
Troxall, James VA 30th Bn.S.S. Co.E
Troxclair, A.S. LA Mil. St.James Regt. Co.F 1st Lt.
Troxclair, Nicolas LA Mil. St.James Regt. Co.F
Troxclair, Onesiphor LA Mil. St.James Regt. Co.F
Troxdell, Rice Conf.Cav. 6th Bn. Co.G
Troxel, Abraham VA 89th Mil. Co.H
Troxell, Amos VA 52nd Inf. Co.H
Troxell, David VA 52nd Inf. Co.H
Troxell, Eli AL 18th Bn.Vol. Co.C
Troxell, F. VA Lt.Arty. Barr's Co.
Troxell, Francis VA Horse Arty. Jackson's Co.
Troxell, Granvill MS 12th Inf.
Troxell, Granville KY 7th Cav. Co.F
Troxell, Granville KY 11th Cav. Co.F
Troxell, Jacob AL 18th Bn.Vol. Co.C
Troxell, James AL 18th Bn.Vol. Co.C Sgt.
Troxell, James KY 8th Cav. Co.F
Troxell, James TN 42nd Inf. 1st Co.E Sgt.
Troxell, James VA Lt.Arty. Barr's Co.
Troxell, Jeremiah VA 52nd Inf. Co.H
Troxell, John G. VA 52nd Inf. Co.I
Troxell, J.W. AR 31st Inf. Co.G
Troxell, W.C. AR 30th Inf. Co.K
Troxell, W.H. AL 18th Bn.Vol. Co.C
Troxle, William TN 1st Hvy.Arty. 2nd Co.C, 3rd Co.B
Troxler, Adam MS 18th Cav. Co.C
Troxler, Adam N. NC 54th Inf. Co.F
Troxler, A.J. TN Inf. 23rd Bn. Co.C
Troxler, Anderson TN 17th Inf. Co.B
Troxler, Benjamin F. NC 47th Inf. Co.K
Troxler, Calvin NC 13th Inf. Co.I
Troxler, Daniel NC 1st Inf. Co.A
Troxler, Emile LA 26th Inf. Co.D Cpl.
Troxler, Feircy LA 30th Inf. Co.F
Troxler, George NC 13th Inf. Co.I
Troxler, George R. NC 5th Cav. (63rd St.Troops) Co.I
Troxler, George S. NC 53rd Inf. Co.A
Troxler, G.R. TN Cav. Jackson's Co.
Troxler, G.R. TN 17th Inf. Co.B
Troxler, H. LA Arty. 5th Field Btty. (Pelican Lt.Arty.)
Troxler, H.C. TN Cav. Jackson's Co.
Troxler, Jacob NC 53rd Inf. Co.A
Troxler, James F. NC 47th Inf. Co.K
Troxler, J.C. TN 17th Inf. Co.B
Troxler, John NC 45th Inf. Co.D
Troxler, J.R. NC 5th Cav. (63rd St.Troops) Co.I
Troxler, Louis LA 30th Inf. Co.F
Troxler, L.W. TN 17th Inf. Co.B
Troxler, M. TN Cav. Jackson's Co.
Troxler, Madison NC 45th Inf. Co.D
Troxler, Martin NC 7th Inf. Co.E
Troxler, Martin NC 45th Inf. Co.D
Troxler, Moses TN 17th Inf. Co.B
Troxler, Moses P. TN 17th Inf. Co.B
Troxler, M.P. TN Cav. Jackson's Co.
Troxler, Peter NC 4th Bn.Jr.Res. Co.B
Troxler, Peter TN 17th Inf. Co.B
Troxler, P.P. NC 3rd Jr.Res. Co.B
Troxler, Samuel W. TN 41st Inf. Co.K
Troxler, S.W. TN 17th Inf. Co.B
Troxler, W. NC 3rd Jr.Res. Co.B
Troxler, William NC 4th Bn.Jr.Res. Co.B
Troxler, William NC 53rd Inf. Co.A
Troxsel, Andrew VA 7th Bn.Res. Co.D
Troxter, William S. TN Inf. 23rd Bn. Co.C Sgt.
Troxtill, William H. AL 33rd Inf.
Troxton, William C. AR 10th (DeWitt's) Cav.
Troxwell, C. MS 12th Inf. Co.K
Troxwell, Francis VA 6th Bn.Res. Co.I
Troxwell, George W. VA 6th Bn.Res. Co.I
Troxwell, J.B. LA 9th Inf. Co.B
Troxwell, John VA 37th Inf. Co.F
Troxwell, Mat AR 11th & 17th Cons.Inf. Co.H
Troxwell, Matt AR 17th (Griffith's) Inf. Co.H
Troy, A.A. NC 8th Inf. Co.E 1st Sgt.

Troy, Alexander A. NC Hvy.Arty. 1st Bn. Co.C
Troy, Daniel AL 1st Regt. Mobile Vol. British Guard Co.A
Troy, Daniel S. AL 60th Inf. Lt.Col.
Troy, Daniel S. AL 1st Bn. Hilliard's Legion Vol. Co.A Maj.
Troy, Dennis TN 2nd (Walker's) Inf. Co.F
Troy, Edmond NC 51st Inf. Co.A
Troy, G. LA Arty. Hutton's Co. (Crescent Arty.,Co.A)
Troy, James TN 12th Inf. Co.A
Troy, James TN 12th (Cons.) Inf. Co.A
Troy, Jerry AL 21st Inf.
Troy, John TN 12th Inf. Co.A
Troy, John TN 12th (Cons.) Inf. Co.A
Troy, John B., Jr. NC 46th Inf. Co.G
Troy, Larry VA 1st Inf. Chambers' Co.
Troy, Lawrence VA 2nd Inf. Co.K
Troy, Marcus L. VA 21st Cav. Co.K
Troy, M.D. NC 48th Inf. Hosp.Stew.
Troy, M.M. NC 26th Inf. Co.E
Troy, M.M. NC 46th Inf. Co.G
Troy, M.M. NC 48th Inf. Co.G Asst.Surg.
Troy, M.M. Gen. & Staff Hosp.Stew.
Troy, R. AL 62nd Inf. Co.I
Troy, Robert Preston NC 46th Inf. Co.G Capt.
Troy, Thomas LA 14th Inf. Co.F
Troy, Thomas SC Inf.Loc.Def. Estill's Co.
Troy, Thomas J. SC 1st Arty. Co.G
Troy, Thomas Settle NC 46th Inf. Co.G 2nd Lt.
Troy, T.J. GA Inf. 1st Loc.Troops (Augusta) Co.I
Troyler, Duncan NC 38th Inf. Co.E
Troylin, W. NC 1st Jr.Res. Co.E
Troyman, Travis MO Cav. 1st Regt.St.Guard Adj.
Troys, Effisio LA Mil. 6th Regt.Eur.Brig. (Italian Guards Bn.) Co.1 QM
Troywick, H.O. AR Mil. Borland's Regt. Woodruff's Co.
Trozland, William VA Cav. Swann's Bn. Vincent's Co.
Truack, R. MS 42nd Inf. Co.G
Truax, A.M. TX 5th Inf. Co.F
Truax, P.J. MO 12th Cav. Co.G 1st Sgt.
Trube, --- TX 2nd Inf. Co.D
Trube, Charles F. TX 1st Hvy.Arty. Co.C
Trube, John C. TX Cav. Waller's Regt. Menard's Co.
Truby, James B. LA Cav. Lott's Co. (Carroll Drag.)
Truce, D.A. AL 9th Inf.
Truce, Peter AR 20th Inf. Co.E
Truce, Peter NC 28th Inf. Co.D
Truce, Richard AR 20th Inf. Co.E
Truch, Manuel LA Mil. 5th Regt.Eur.Brig. (Spanish Regt.) Co.10 Capt.
Truchelet, Eugene GA 47th Inf. Music.
Truchelut, Charles J. GA Inf. 18th Bn. Co.B
Truchelut, Eugene GA 25th Inf. Band Music.
Truchelut, Henry GA 1st (Olmstead's) Inf. Stiles' Co.
Truchelut, Henry GA Inf. 18th Bn. Co.B
Trucks, B.F. AR 18th Inf. Co.D
Trucks, David B. AL 44th Inf. Co.F
Trucks, Davidson VA 4th Inf. Co.A
Trucks, F.M. AL 44th Inf. Co.F
Trucks, Jackson AL 44th Inf. Co.F
Trucks, J.C. AL 29th Inf. Co.H,K
Trucks, Johnson AR Inf. Hardy's Regt. Co.A
Trucks, Josiah MS 2nd Cav. Co.F
Trucks, Josiah MS 14th Inf. Co.B
Trucks, M. AL 44th Inf.
Trucks, William AR Inf. Hardy's Regt. Co.A
Trudau, R.R. LA Mil. Brig.Gen.
Trudean, L.J. LA Inf. 1st Sp.Bn. (Rightor's) Co.A
Trudeau, James LA Legion Brig. Gen.
Trudeau, J.E. LA Dreux's Cav. Co.A
Trudeau, J.E. LA Legion Brig. ADC
Trudeau, Josech E. LA 4th Inf. Co.F
Trudeau, Just LA Mil. Chalmette Regt. Co.C
Trudeau, L. LA Lt.Arty. Holmes' Btty.
Trudeau, L.I. LA Arty. Watson Btty.
Trudeau, Louis MS Lt.Arty. (The Hudson Btty.) Hoole's Co.
Trudeau, M. LA 20th Inf. Co.C
Trudeau, M. LA 21st (Kennedy's) Inf. Co.C
True, A.B. KY 5th Cav. Co.E
True, A.H. MO 1st & 4th Cons.Inf. Co.D
True, Alfred MO Cav. Snider's Bn. Co.C
True, Andrew J. MO 1st Cav. Co.D Sgt.
True, Andrew J. MO Inf. 8th Bn. Co.A
True, Andrew J. MO 9th Inf. Co.A
True, David AR 16th Inf. Co.G
True, David AR 35th Inf. Co.B
True, David H., Jr. TN 54th Inf. Co.G
True, D.H. TN Cav. Nixon's Regt. Co.H
True, D.H. TN 48th (Nixon's) Inf. Co.K Cpl.
True, Dolpin VA Lt.Arty. 38th Bn. Co.C
True, Edward VA Cav. Young's Co.
True, Elija KY 8th Cav. Co.A Cpl.
True, Elijah KY 3rd Cav. Co.A
True, Elijah KY 3rd Bn.Mtd.Rifles Co.A
True, Fountain G. KY 1st Bn.Mtd.Rifles Co.E
True, Fountain G. KY 3rd Bn.Mtd.Rifles Co.E
True, Henry NC 35th Inf. Co.E
True, H.M. AL 8th (Livingston's) Cav. Co.B
True, Irvine AR 35th Inf. Co.B
True, J.A. AL Cp. of Instr. Talladega Asst.Eng.Off.
True, James H. SC 12th Inf. Co.C Sgt.
True, J.K. MS 8th Cav. Co.B Cpl.
True, J.K. MS 28th Cav. Co.E Cpl.
True, J.M. VA Loc.Def. Wood's Co.
True, John MO St.Guard
True, John A. AL 11th Inf. Co.B Cpl.
True, John H. NC 15th Inf. Co.G
True, John L. MS Inf. 2nd Bn. Co.D
True, John L. MS 48th Inf. Co.D
True, John L. MS K. Williams' Co. (Gray's Port Greys)
True, John M. VA 19th Inf. Co.B
True, John W. MS 33rd Inf. Co.C Sr.2nd Lt.
True, Joseph VA 30th Inf. 1st Co.I
True, Joseph VA 47th Inf. 3rd Co.I
True, Joseph A. VA 30th Inf. Co.D Cpl.
True, J.T. TN 51st Inf. Co.A
True, J.W. AL 4th (Russell's) Cav. Co.E Sgt.
True, J.W. TN 49th Inf. Co.K
True, J.W. Inf. Bailey's Cons.Regt. Co.E
True, L. VA Loc.Def. Wood's Co.
True, Leonidas P. TN 54th Inf. Co.G
True, Levi VA 38th Inf. Co.E
True, Levi VA 57th Inf. Co.I
True, Lewis J. VA 38th Inf. Co.E
True, L.P. TN 48th (Nixon's) Inf. Co.K
True, N.P. TN 3rd (Clack's) Inf. Co.K
True, P.G. TN 12th (Green's) Cav. Co.E
True, P.G. TN 16th (Logwood's) Cav. Co.I
True, R.M. KY 1st (Butler's) Cav. Co.C Cpl.
True, R.M. KY 3rd Cav. Grant's Co. Cpl.
True, Robert KY 12th Cav. Co.B,A
True, Robert KY 1st Bn.Mtd.Rifles Co.B
True, Robert TN 12th (Green's) Cav. Co.I
True, Salon MO 1st N.E. Cav.
True, Thomas VA 11th Cav. Co.F
True, Thomas G. VA 25th Inf. 1st Co.G
True, Thomas J. VA 18th Cav. 2nd Co.G
True, Thomas K. TN 54th Inf. Ives' Co.
True, T.J. TN 51st (Cons.) Inf. Co.H
True, T.K. TN 48th (Nixon's) Inf. Co.I
True, William L. AL 11th Inf. Co.B
Trueaud, Benjamin LA 2nd Res.Corps Co.A
Trueblood, Isaac NC 18th Inf. Co.K
Trueblood, J. NC 7th Sr.Res. Johnston's Co.C Cpl.
Trueblood, John AR 14th (Powers') Inf. Co.K
Trueblood, Joshua L. NC 27th Inf. Co.F
Trueblood, Samuel NC Lt.Arty. 13th Bn. Co.A
Trueblood, Samuel VA Lt.Arty. 12th Bn. Co.B
Trueblood, Zachariah VA 135th Mil. Co.D
Truehart, Adolphus H. VA Cav. 1st Bn. (Loc.Def.Troops) Co.C
Truehart, A.H. VA 2nd St.Res. Co.C
Truehart, Charles AL 8th Inf. Asst.Surg.
Truehart, Charles W. VA Inf. Hutter's Co.
Truehart, Dan'l. Gen. & Staff, Arty. 1st Lt.
Truehart, James NC 1st Cav. (9th St.Troops) Co.I
Truehart, N.P. NC 35th Inf. Co.I
Truehart, William A. VA Inf. 1st Bn.Loc.Def. Co.F,E 2nd Lt.
Trueheart, Adolphus H. VA 15th Inf. Co.H
Trueheart, Charles W. VA Lt.Arty. Arch. Graham's Co.
Trueheart, Chas. W. Gen. & Staff Asst.Surg.
Trueheart, D. AL Gid Nelson Lt.Arty.
Trueheart, Daniel Gen. & Staff, Arty. Maj.
Trueheart, G.W. TN Inf. 154th Sr.Regt. Co.G
Trueheart, Henry M. VA Cav. McNeill's Co.
Trueheart, James L. TX Res.Corps
Trueheart, J.G. MD Cav. 2nd Bn. Co.A
Trueheart, J.H. VA 15th Inf. Co.A
Trueheart, J.L. TX 30th St.Troops Co.A 1st Lt.
Trueheart, John H. VA Arty. Paris' Co.
Trueheart, Lewis T. VA 46th Inf. 2nd Co.A
Trueheart, S.D. TN 38th Inf. Co.I
Trueheart, William C. VA 3rd Cav. Co.K
Trueheart, William C. VA 23rd Inf. Co.I 1st Lt.
Truel, William D. VA 15th Inf. Co.E
Truel, William R. TN 63rd Inf. Co.C Lt.
Truell, G.W. AL Coosa Guards J.W. Suttles' Co.
Truell, Peter TX 5th Cav. Co.G
Truelock, --- TX 1st Inf. Co.C
Truelove, Benjamin J. GA 1st (Ramsey's) Inf. Co.H
Truelove, B.J. SC Hvy.Arty. 15th (Lucas') Bn. Co.A
Truelove, Elijah AL 8th Inf. Co.C
Truelove, Elijah GA Phillips' Legion Co.A,G

Truelove, Henry H. KY 4th Cav. Co.A
Truelove, James R. TX 14th Cav. Co.F 2nd Lt.
Truelove, J.B. MS 10th Cav. Co.F
Truelove, Jefferson MS 20th Inf. Co.I
Truelove, Jefferson MS 37th Inf. Co.I
Truelove, J.H. MO 9th Inf. Co.C
Truelove, J.H. MO Inf. Clark's Regt. Co.B
Truelove, John AR 51st Mil. Co.H Drum.
Truelove, John G. NC 28th Inf. Co.F 1st Lt.
Truelove, Major W. GA 43rd Inf. Co.K
Truelove, Marion GA 11th Cav. Co.B
Truelove, M.F. MO 7th Cav. Co.D
Truelove, Timothy TX 17th Cav. Co.C
Truelove, T.J. MS 20th Inf. Co.I
Truelove, T.M. MS 41st Inf. Co.F
Truelove, W.A.J. MS 2nd Cav. Co.B
Truelove, Willburn GA 1st (Ramsey's) Inf. Co.H
Truelove, W.J. SC Hvy.Arty. 15th (Lucas') Bn. Co.B
Truelove, W.T. KY 4th Cav. Co.A
Trueluck, A.J. FL Inf. 2nd Bn. Co.C
Trueluck, D.M. AL 6th Inf. Co.B
Trueluck, H.H. FL Inf. 2nd Bn. Co.C
Trueluck, J.G. FL 1st (Res.) Inf. Co.L
Trueman, --- AL 25th Inf. Co.H
Trueman, Barnabas VA 14th Cav. Co.L
Trueman, Claiborne T. VA 5th Bn.Inf. Co.D
Trueman, George MS 44th Inf. Co.B Sgt.
Trueman, J. AR 2nd Inf.
Trueman, J. MO 5th Cav. Co.H
Trueman, Jackson VA 1st Inf. Co.C
Trueman, John VA Lt.Arty. Parker's Co.
Trueman, John VA 52nd Mil. Co.B
Trueman, John H. LA 13th Inf. Co.G
Trueman, John L. VA Hvy.Arty. 10th Bn. Co.E
Trueman, Mathew T. VA Hvy.Arty. 10th Bn. Co.E
Trueman, Oliver VA Inf. 28th Bn. Co.D
Trueman, Oliver VA 59th Inf. 3rd Co.I
Trueman, Richard VA Inf. 5th Bn. Co.D
Trueman, Richard VA 53rd Inf. Co.A
Trueman, Richard W. VA Inf. 25th Bn. Co.F
Trueman, Robert H. VA Inf. 25th Bn. Co.F
Trueman, T.Y.P. LA Mil. Beauregard Bn.
Trueman, Wm. MO Lt.Arty. 1st Btty.
Trueman, William VA 2nd St.Res. Co.F Sgt.
Trueman, William J. VA Inf. 25th Bn. Co.F
Trueman, W.T. VA 2nd St.Res. Co.A 1st Sgt.
Truesdale, J.C. SC Cav. 10th Bn. Co.D
Truesdale, J.C. SC 12th Inf. Co.I
Truesdale, John AR Cav. Gordon's Regt. Co.G
Truesdale, J.R. SC 4th St.Troops Co.B
Truesdale, Samuel R. MO 3rd Cav. Co.A
Truesdale, S.J. TX 17th Inf. Co.F
Truesdale, S.P. SC 1st Inf. Co.M
Truesdale, Stephen P. SC 1st (McCreary's) Inf. Co.I
Truesdale, Z.T. SC 4th Cav. Co.H
Truesdel, H. SC 7th Cav. Co.K Sgt.
Truesdel, H. SC 2nd Inf. Co.G
Truesdel, J.C. SC 4th Cav. Co.H
Truesdel, J.E. SC 2nd Inf. Co.G Capt.
Truesdel, J.T. SC 7th Cav. Co.K
Truesdel, William J. SC 2nd Inf. Co.G Cpl.
Truesdel, W.M. SC 2nd Inf. Co.G
Truesdel, W.M. SC 6th Inf. 2nd Co.C
Truesdell, Burrell SC 2nd Inf. Co.G
Truesdell, D.B.F. SC 23rd Inf. Co.B Sgt.
Truesdell, G.C. SC 17th Inf. Co.E 2nd Lt.
Truesdell, J.C. SC Arty. Melchers' Co. (Co.B,German Arty.)
Truesdell, John R. SC 1st Cav. Co.H
Truesdell, J.T. SC 1st Inf. Co.N
Truesdell, J.T. SC 2nd Inf. Co.G
Truesdell, Victor AR 2nd Inf. Co.F Sgt.
Truet, Alfred NC 53rd Inf. Co.A
Truet, E.J. GA Inf. Grubbs' Co.
Truet, Elijah M. NC 39th Inf. Co.C
Truet, Henry SC Inf. 9th Bn. Co.F
Truet, M.B. AL 14th Inf. Co.B
Truett, A. MO Lt.Arty. H.M. Bledsoe's Co.
Truett, Ambrose TN 6th (Wheeler's) Cav. Co.E
Truett, Charles L. NC Inf. Thomas Legion Co.I
Truett, Dan SC 4th St.Troops Co.E
Truett, Daniel SC Inf. 9th Bn. Co.F
Truett, E. AL 22nd Inf. Co.C
Truett, Edmond AL 60th Inf. Co.K
Truett, E.J. SC 8th Inf. Co.E
Truett, Elijah F. AL 38th Inf. Co.I
Truett, Elisha AL 32nd Inf. Co.D,C
Truett, E.T. MS 11th (Perrin's) Cav. Co.H
Truett, F.A. TN 20th Inf. Co.H
Truett, Felix G. TN Lt.Arty. Baxter's Co.
Truett, George GA 4th Res. Co.A
Truett, George F. NC 1st Arty. (10th St.Troops) Co.I
Truett, George W. GA 1st (Fannin's) Res. Co.C
Truett, G.W. AL 32nd Inf. Co.D Cpl.
Truett, Harrison NC 45th Inf. Co.H
Truett, Henry AL 60th Inf. Co.K
Truett, Henry J. NC 1st Inf. Co.B
Truett, H.H. AL 19th Inf. Co.A
Truett, J. AL 22nd Inf. Co.E
Truett, J.A. MS 1st Cav.Res. Co.C
Truett, Jacob GA 29th Inf. Co.K
Truett, James FL 1st Inf. New Co.E
Truett, James MS 35th Inf. Co.E
Truett, James TX 6th Cav. Co.B 2nd Lt.
Truett, James A.F. SC 14th Inf. Co.A
Truett, James E. AR 2nd Mtd.Rifles Co.B
Truett, James E. AR 35th Inf. Co.H Capt.
Truett, Jasper N. NC 6th Cav. (65th St.Troops) Co.G,C
Truett, J.C. SC 4th St.Troops Co.E
Truett, J.H. GA Siege Arty. 28th Bn. Co.B
Truett, Joel S. AL 32nd Inf. Co.A,B 2nd Lt.
Truett, John AL 32nd Inf. Co.D
Truett, John FL 1st Inf. New Co.E
Truett, John MO 1st N.E. Cav. Co.K
Truett, John NC 6th Cav. (65th St.Troops) Co.C
Truett, John A. MO Lt.Arty. H.M. Bledsoe's Co.
Truett, John C. GA 3rd Cav. Co.D
Truett, John E. GA 3rd Cav. Co.D
Truett, Joseph NC 31st Inf. Co.K
Truett, Joseph L. NC 16th Inf. Co.A
Truett, J.T. AL 3rd Inf. Co.L
Truett, J.T. AL 60th Inf. Co.K
Truett, J.T. TN 20th Inf. Co.H
Truett, J.W. AL 14th Inf. Co.I
Truett, J.W. TN 6th (Wheeler's) Cav. Co.E
Truett, M.V. AL 14th Inf. Co.I
Truett, Noel R. FL 1st Inf. New Co.E
Truett, P.P. GA 17th Inf. Co.H Sgt.
Truett, R.W. GA Inf. 9th Bn. Co.E
Truett, Silas M. NC Inf. Thomas Legion Co.A Cpl.
Truett, S.J. GA 46th Inf. Co.E 2nd Lt.
Truett, Thomas F. TX 13th Cav. Co.G Capt.
Truett, Turner MO Lt.Arty. H.M. Bledsoe's Co.
Truett, W. MO Lt.Arty. H.M. Bledsoe's Co.
Truett, W.F. AL 60th Inf. Co.K Cpl.
Truett, W.H. AL 60th Inf. Co.K
Truett, W.H. TX 13th Cav. Co.G
Truett, William FL 3rd Inf. Co.K
Truett, William FL 8th Inf. Co.C
Truett, William MO 1st N.E. Cav.
Truett, William SC Inf. 9th Bn. Co.F
Truett, William C. AR 15th Mil. Co.C
Truett, William C. AR 35th Inf. Co.H
Truett, William H. MS 36th Inf. Co.I
Truett, William H. NC Inf. Thomas Legion Co.I
Truett, William L. TN 6th (Wheeler's) Cav. Co.E
Truett, W.M. SC 26th Inf. Co.G
Truett, W.P. GA 1st (Olmstead's) Inf. Co.K
Truett, Zeteric P. GA 20th Inf. Co.E
Truette, John S. AL 39th Inf. Co.H
Truffant, Seth LA Mil.Mtd.Rangers Plaquemines
Truffy, James A. AL 62nd Inf. Co.B
Trugott, F. MO St.Guard
Truhart, A.H. VA 46th Inf. 2nd Co.K
Truhart, W.H. VA 2nd St.Res. Co.C Sgt.
Truit, Alfred M. TX 28th Cav. Co.A QM
Truit, D. GA 28th Inf. Co.C
Truit, E.E. SC 4th Bn.Res. Co.B
Truit, E.K. TX 11th Cav. Co.C
Truit, F.M. TX 12th Inf. Co.I
Truit, George W. TX 14th Cav. Co.D Sgt.
Truit, James T. AL 1st Bn. Hilliard's Legion Vol. Co.C
Truit, James W. TX 28th Cav. Co.A Bugler
Truit, Jesse MS 5th Inf. (St.Troops) Co.I Sgt.
Truit, John W.A. NC 44th Inf. Co.G
Truit, J.W. MS 14th Inf. Co.H
Truit, Levi M. TX 28th Cav. Co.A Capt.
Truit, M.C. GA 3rd Inf. Co.D
Truit, Sidney SC Arty. Manigault's Bn. 2nd Co.C
Truit, Spencer NC 3rd Arty. (40th St.Troops) Co.H
Truit, Walton F. AL 1st Bn. Hilliard's Legion Vol. Co.C
Truit, W.H. TX 11th (Spaight's) Bn.Vol. Co.B
Truit, W.W. TN 15th (Cons.) Cav. Co.D,E
Truitlin, John F. AL 15th Inf. Lt.Col.
Truitt, A.J. TX Waul's Legion Co.B
Truitt, Alex F. KY 4th Cav.
Truitt, Alexander F. KY 2nd (Duke's) Cav. Co.F Cpl.
Truitt, A.M. Gen. & Staff Capt.,AQM
Truitt, A.S. TN 3rd (Forrest's) Cav. 1st Co.E Capt.
Truitt, A.T. SC 21st Inf. Co.B
Truitt, B.A. Gen. & Staff Cadet
Truitt, B.G. GA 55th Inf. Co.A
Truitt, C.D. GA 3rd Cav. Co.D Sgt.
Truitt, Charles FL 1st Inf. New Co.E
Truitt, Charles L. NC 6th Cav. (65th St.Troops) Co.B
Truitt, Charles L. NC Cav. 7th Bn. Co.B
Truitt, Daniel SC 26th Inf. Co.G

Truitt, David GA 38th Inf. Co.C
Truitt, E. TX 14th Inf. Co.I
Truitt, Edmond AL 1st Bn. Hilliard's Legion Vol. Co.C
Truitt, Edward W. MS 40th Inf. Co.E
Truitt, E.R. TX 14th Inf. Co.I
Truitt, F.D. TX 10th Cav. Co.G
Truitt, F.M. TX Waul's Legion Co.B
Truitt, Francis D. TX 14th Cav. Co.D
Truitt, George W. NC 62nd Inf. Co.D
Truitt, Henry AL 1st Bn. Hilliard's Legion Vol. Co.C
Truitt, Henry SC 26th Inf. Co.G
Truitt, H.H. AL 46th Inf. Co.D
Truitt, H.M. AR 7th Cav. Co.C
Truitt, H.N. AL 46th Inf. Co.D
Truitt, J. MS 8th Inf.
Truitt, James TX 3rd Cav. Co.E
Truitt, James TX 15th Cav. Co.D
Truitt, James TX 27th Cav. Co.A 1st Sgt.
Truitt, James C. GA Cobb's Legion Co.A Sgt.
Truitt, James M. GA Lt.Arty. 14th Bn. Co.C Jr.1st Lt.
Truitt, James M. GA Lt.Arty. Ferrell's Btty. Jr.1st Lt.
Truitt, James R. GA Arty. 11th Bn. (Sumter Arty.) New Co.C
Truitt, James R. GA Cobb's Legion Co.A Black.
Truitt, James V. GA 38th Inf. Co.C Cpl.
Truitt, Jasper H. NC Cav. 7th Bn. Co.C
Truitt, J.C. SC 1st Inf. Co.B
Truitt, J.H. TX 3rd Cav. Co.E 2nd Lt.
Truitt, J.M. TN 24th Inf. 1st Co.H
Truitt, John MO 11th Inf. Co.F
Truitt, John NC Cav. 7th Bn. Co.C
Truitt, John D. SC 14th Inf. Co.A
Truitt, John M. AL 46th Inf. Co.D Cpl.
Truitt, John R. NC Walker's Bn. Thomas' Legion Co.E
Truitt, John S. AL 17th Bn.S.S. Co.B
Truitt, John W. GA 30th Inf. Co.G 1st Sgt.
Truitt, John W. NC 62nd Inf. Co.D
Truitt, Joseph TN 1st (Feild's) Inf. Co.D
Truitt, Joseph H. GA 31st Inf. Co.H Cpl.
Truitt, Joseph L. NC 39th Inf. Co.K
Truitt, Joseph L. NC Inf. Thomas Legion 1st Co.A
Truitt, J.R. GA 64th Inf. Co.B
Truitt, J.T. MO Robertson's Regt.St.Guard Co.2
Truitt, J.T. TN 9th Cav. Co.G
Truitt, J.W. MS 40th Inf. Co.E
Truitt, Lewis NC 45th Inf. Co.G
Truitt, L.P. SC 21st Inf. Co.B,K
Truitt, Nathan A. GA 41st Inf. Co.E
Truitt, Nathan D. GA 41st Inf. Co.E
Truitt, Permenta M. TX Cav. Baylor's Regt. Co.C 2nd Lt.
Truitt, P.M. TX 15th Cav. Co.D Jr.2nd Lt.
Truitt, Richard W. GA 37th Inf. Band Music.
Truitt, R.K. TX 12th Cav. Co.K
Truitt, Samuel C. GA 4th Inf. Co.B
Truitt, Silas M. NC 16th Inf. Co.A
Truitt, Silas M. NC 39th Inf. Co.K 1st Lt.
Truitt, Thomas NC 45th Inf. Co.G
Truitt, Thomas NC 53rd Inf. Co.A
Truitt, Thomas A. AL 57th Inf. Co.E
Truitt, Thomas S. TX Waul's Legion Co.B
Truitt, Tilmon A.S. GA 55th Inf. Co.K
Truitt, T.J. GA Cav. 19th Bn. Co.D
Truitt, Warner S. MO Lt.Arty. 1st Btty.
Truitt, Warren S. MO 1st N.E. Cav. Arnold's Co.
Truitt, Warren S. MO 5th Inf. Co.H
Truitt, W.G.M. AL 5th Cav. Co.L
Truitt, Wiley N. MS 22nd Inf. Co.G
Truitt, William AL 46th Inf. Co.D
Truitt, Wm. MO Lt.Arty. H.M. Bledsoe's Co.
Truitt, William NC 2nd Inf. Co.G
Truitt, William SC 26th Inf. Co.G
Truitt, William TN 2nd (Smith's) Cav.
Truitt, William H. AL 1st Bn. Hilliard's Legion Vol. Co.C
Truitt, William P. AL 3rd Bn. Hilliard's Legion Vol. Co.F
Truitt, William P. GA 38th Inf. Co.C
Truitt, William W. MS 1st (Johnston's) Inf. Co.G
Truitt, Willis C. NC 45th Inf. Co.G
Truitt, W.P. AL 60th Inf. Co.D
Truitte, Joseph AL Cav. Lewis' Bn. Co.A
Trujio, Jesus TX 3rd Inf. 1st Co.A
Truland, J.G. MO Lt.Arty. Barret's Co. Artif.
Truland, John G. MS Inf. 5th Bn. Co.B
Truland, John G. MS 27th Inf. Co.K
Truler, J. TX Waul's Legion Co.C
Trulieb, Peter GA 25th Inf. Co.C
Trull, Andrew G. NC 48th Inf. Co.A
Trull, Benjamin R. NC Inf. Thomas Legion Co.C Cpl.
Trull, Branch H.M. NC Inf. Thomas Legion Co.C Cpl.
Trull, Calvin NC 53rd Inf. Co.I Sgt.
Trull, Charles E. NC Hvy.Arty. 10th Bn. Co.C
Trull, D.C. FL Cav. 3rd Bn. Co.D
Trull, D.C. 15th Conf.Cav. Co.I
Trull, Edward E. MS 31st Inf. Co.C
Trull, G.W. GA 32nd Inf. Co.G
Trull, G.W. TX 11th (Spaight's) Bn.Vol. Co.B
Trull, Hampton H. NC 37th Inf. Co.D
Trull, Jacob G. AL 41st Inf. Co.G Sgt.
Trull, James H. NC 53rd Inf. Co.I Cpl.
Trull, James L. KY 2nd Cav.
Trull, James R. NC Inf. Thomas Legion Co.C
Trull, James T. NC Hvy.Arty. 10th Bn. Co.C,D
Trull, J.B. TX Waul's Legion Co.A 1st Lt.
Trull, Jesse TX Cav. Ragsdale's Bn. 2nd Co.F
Trull, J.J. AL 23rd Inf. Co.A
Trull, John MS 6th Cav. Co.L
Trull, John H. MS 8th Cav. Co.E
Trull, John J. NC 53rd Inf. Co.I
Trull, John W. MS 24th Inf. Co.L
Trull, John W. NC 25th Inf. Co.F
Trull, J.W. AR 10th Inf. Co.D
Trull, K.P. MS 1st (Patton's) Inf. Co.B
Trull, K.P. MS 43rd Inf. Co.C
Trull, Levi MS 13th Inf. Co.H
Trull, Lewellen AL 8th Cav. Co.K
Trull, Nelson S. NC 39th Inf. Co.I
Trull, S. AL 26th (O'Neal's) Inf. Co.I
Trull, Salathiel TN 10th (DeMoss') Cav. Co.H
Trull, S.J. MS Inf. 3rd Bn. (St.Troops) Co.B
Trull, T.H. TX 11th (Spaight's) Bn.Vol. Co.B
Trull, Thomas G. NC Inf. Thomas Legion Co.C
Trull, Thomas S. NC 37th Inf. Co.D Cpl.
Trull, William A. NC Walker's Bn. Thomas' Legion Co.A
Trull, William H. NC 37th Inf. Co.D
Trull, William J. AL 41st Inf. Co.G
Trull, William R. NC Inf. Thomas Legion Co.C 1st Lt.
Truller, J. TX 30th Cav. Co.F Sgt.
Trullier, Jean LA 18th Inf. Co.A
Trullsem, J.M. MS 11th Inf. Co.H
Trulock, A.J. GA 3rd Res. Co.I
Trulock, Charles GA 50th Inf. Co.F
Trulock, Gordon B. GA 1st (Ramsey's) Inf. Co.G
Trulock, R.L. GA 3rd Res. Co.I
Trulock, Zimmerman GA 50th Inf. Co.F Sgt.
Trulove, B. MS 9th Cav. Co.E
Trulove, F. MO Beck's Co.
Trulove, George A. MS 43rd Inf. Co.H
Trulove, J. MO Beck's Co.
Trulove, Jefferson MS 3rd Inf. Co.D
Trulove, John B. TN Cav. 17th Bn. (Sanders') Co.B
Trulove, J.R. AL 10th Cav. Co.F 1st Lt.
Trulove, J.R. MS 2nd Cav. Co.I Sgt.
Trulove, R.S. NC 31st Inf. Co.I
Trulove, Thomas D. NC 31st Inf. Co.I
Trulove, Timothy NC 50th Inf. Co.H
Trulove, William GA 66th Inf. Co.H Cpl.
Truluce, John GA Inf. 5th Bn. (St.Guards) Co.E
Truluck, Andrew J. FL 10th Inf. Co.H
Truluck, Arthur FL 6th Inf. Co.C
Truluck, David M. FL 6th Inf. Co.B
Truluck, E.P. SC Inf. 6th Bn. Co.B
Truluck, E.P. SC 26th Inf. Co.H
Truluck, E.P. SC Manigault's Bn.Vol. Co.D Cpl.
Truluck, G.B. GA Cav. 29th Bn. Co.F
Truluck, Gordon B. GA 50th Inf. Co.F
Truluck, J. GA 3rd Res. Co.D
Truluck, Jason FL 5th Inf. Co.B
Truluck, J.F. FL 10th Inf. Co.A
Truluck, J.P. SC Inf. 6th Bn. Co.B
Truluck, J.P. SC 26th Inf. Co.H Cpl.
Truluck, J.P. SC Manigault's Bn.Vol. Co.D
Truluck, J.T. SC Inf. 6th Bn. Co.B
Truluck, J.T. SC 26th Inf. Co.H
Truluck, J.T. SC Manigault's Bn.Vol. Co.D
Truluck, R. FL 11th Inf. Co.I
Truluck, William GA 17th Inf. Co.D
Truly, Bennet R. AR 3rd Inf. Co.A
Truly, F.C. LA Inf. Jeff Davis Regt. Co.J Cpl.
Truly, James B. MS 2nd Part.Rangers Co.B Cpl.
Truly, John H. AR 1st Mtd.Rifles Co.A
Truly, Joshua S. AR Inf. 8th Bn. Co.B 1st Lt.
Truly, R.H. LA 3rd (Harrison's) Cav. 2nd Lt.
Truly, R.H. MS 1st Lt.Arty. Co.K QMSgt.
Truly, Samuel M. AL 45th Res.Corps
Truly, William P. AR Inf. 1st Bn. Co.B Sgt.
Truman, A.J. TX 33rd Cav. Co.A
Truman, Barnabas VA 17th Cav. Co.I
Truman, Charles MO 1st N.E. Cav. Co.A
Truman, Charles MO 2nd N.E. Cav. (Franklin's Regt.) Co.B
Truman, Frank KY 9th Mtd.Inf. Co.K
Truman, Franklin KY 5th Mtd.Inf. Co.K
Truman, Frank M. MO 1st N.E. Cav. Co.A
Truman, J. VA 12th Cav. Co.G

Truman, James AR 13th Inf.
Truman, John LA 1st Hvy.Arty. (Reg.) Co.B
Truman, Joseph KY 9th Mtd.Inf. Co.K
Truman, J.W. GA Inf. 14th Bn. (St.Guards) Co.D
Truman, J.W. GA 29th Inf. Co.D
Truman, L.W. MO 5th Cav. Co.D
Truman, Robert VA 19th Cav. Co.K
Truman, Shedrick VA 19th Cav. Co.H
Truman, S.P. FL 1st (Res.) Inf.
Truman, Thomas AL 45th Inf. Co.G
Truman, Thomas J. VA 56th Inf. Co.K
Truman, William MS 35th Inf. Co.I
Truman, William VA 56th Inf. Co.K
Truman, William P. VA 3rd Lt.Arty. (Loc.Def.) Co.H
Truman, W.L. MO Lt.Arty. Walsh's Co.
Truman, W.R. VA 4th Cav. Co.F
Trumble, James T. TN 10th Inf. Co.D Sgt.
Trumble, Martin VA 17th Inf. Co.D
Trumble, W.H.A. TX Conscr.
Trumbly, A. LA Inf.Cons. 18th Regt. & Yellow Jacket Bn. Co.E
Trumbo, Andrew J. VA 25th Inf. 2nd Co.K
Trumbo, A.S. SC 25th Inf. Co.B
Trumbo, Benjamin VA 7th Cav. Co.B
Trumbo, C.O. SC Lt.Arty. J.T. Kanapaux's Co. (Lafayette Arty.)
Trumbo, C.O. SC Mil. Charbonnier's Co. Cpl.
Trumbo, Elijah VA 46th Mil. Co.B
Trumbo, Elijah VA 62nd Mtd.Inf. 2nd Co.I
Trumbo, George VA 25th Inf. 1st Co.E
Trumbo, George VA 62nd Mtd.Inf. 2nd Co.I
Trumbo, James S. VA 46th Mil. Co.B
Trumbo, James S. VA 62nd Mtd.Inf. 2nd Co.K 1st Sgt.
Trumbo, John KY 9th Cav. Co.F
Trumbo, John A. KY 5th Mtd.Inf. Co.H Sgt.
Trumbo, John D. VA 25th Inf. 2nd Co.E
Trumbo, John D. VA 62nd Mtd.Inf. 2nd Co.K
Trumbo, Morgan VA Cav. McNeill's Co.
Trumbo, Oliver KY 10th (Johnson's) Cav. New Co.F
Trumbo, Samuel VA 46th Mil. Co.B
Trumbull, Brisbane M. Gen. & Staff, PACS 2nd Lt.
Trumbull, Charles W. FL 9th Inf. Co.C Cpl.
Trumbull, Edwin R. AR 1st Mtd.Rifles Co.D
Trumbull, J.A. TX 8th Cav. Co.B
Trumbull, John D. NC 11th (Bethel Regt.) Inf. Co.C
Trumbull, Robert MO 1st & 4th Cons.Inf. Co.G Music.
Trumbull, T. AL 21st Inf. Co.F
Trumbull, V. VA 5th Cav. 2nd Co.F
Trumbull, V. VA 11th Cav. Co.I
Trumley, Andrew TX 26th Cav. Co.K
Trummel, A.B. LA McArthur's Co. (Sabine Rifles)
Trummel, W.H. SC 1st (Orr's) Rifles Co.A
Trummell, D.M. MO St.Guard
Trummell, James H. MS 29th Inf. Co.B
Trummell, William AR 17th (Griffith's) Inf. Co.C
Trummell, William H. VA 16th Inf. Co.C
Trummn, C.W. AL 60th Inf. Co.H
Trump, Charles LA 4th Inf. Co.B
Trump, David C. VA 11th Inf. Co.F
Trump, Harman MO 16th Inf. Co.I
Trump, Henry C. VA 30th Bn.S.S. Co.A
Trump, Jacob MO Cav. 2nd Regt.St.Guard Co.B
Trump, J.B. MO 16th Inf. Co.B
Trump, John TX 2nd Inf. Co.H
Trump, John H. VA Inf. 45th Bn. Co.C
Trump, Russell G. VA 30th Bn.S.S. Co.A
Trump, Samuel H. VA 42nd Inf. Co.K Color Cpl.
Trump, William VA 11th Inf. Co.F
Trumper, Mark MO 5th Inf. Co.B Capt.
Trunbow, Ambrose TN Lt.Arty. Morton's Co.
Trunch, --- VA 55th Inf. Co.B
Trundall, Richard NC 18th Inf. Co.A
Trundle, B.H. VA 46th Inf. Co.A
Trundle, D.L. GA 12th Cav. Co.E
Trundle, James H. TX Cav. Good's Bn. Co.B
Trundle, J.H. VA Cav. 35th Bn. Co.B
Trundle, J.N. MO 5th Cav. Co.H
Trundle, John MO 16th Inf. Co.A
Trundle, J.W. GA 12th Cav. Co.E
Trundle, Robert GA 12th Cav. Co.E
Trundle, Samuel H. VA Cav. Mosby's Regt. (Part.Rangers) Co.B
Trundle, Thomas MO 16th Inf. Co.A
Trundle, W.C. TN 39th Mtd.Inf. Co.A 1st Lt.
Trunell, J.W. GA 39th Inf. Co.F
Trunin, John TX 36th Cav. Co.I
Trunley, George J. AL 10th Inf. Sgt.Maj.
Trunnel, William VA Cav. Mosby's Regt. (Part.Rangers) Co.D 2nd Lt.
Trunnell, J.W. AR Cav. Harrell's Bn. Co.D
Truntham, T.P. AR Inf. Kuykendall's Co.
Trunzler, Joseph LA Inf. 1st Sp.Bn. (Wheat's) Old Co.D Cpl.
Trunzler, Joseph LA Inf. 7th Bn. Co.B Cpl.
Trunzler, Joseph LA 15th Inf. Co.I Sgt.
Truot, Sebastian LA Mil. 5th Regt.Eur.Brig. (Spanish Regt.) Co.3
Trup, Thomas AL 7th Cav. Co.A
Trupes, J.B. NC 28th Inf. Co.G Cpl.
Trupill, J.M. MS 46th Inf. Co.F
Trupill, J.S. AL Talladega Cty.Res. J. Lucius' Co.
Trureaud, L. LA Mil. Chalmette Regt.
Trusby, B.L. MS 31st Inf. Co.D
Trusdale, C.W. Maples' Staff 1st Lt.,AAAG
Trusdel, J.R. SC 5th Bn.Res. Co.E
Trusdel, Zack SC 5th Bn.Res. Co.D
Trusell, Victor AR 21st Inf. Co.H Sgt.
Truseler, G.W. TN 61st Mtd.Inf. Co.K
Trusheim, H. GA Lt.Arty. 12th Bn. 2nd Co.D Sgt.
Trusheim, John VA Horse Arty. E. Graham's Co. Sgt.
Trusillow, William SC 11th Inf. 2nd Co.F Music.
Trusky, Charles LA Mil. 4th Regt. 1st Brig. 1st Div. Co.A
Trusle, Richard VA Rockbridge Cty.Res. Donald's Co.
Trusle, Simson KY 11th Cav. Co.A
Trusler, James W. VA 25th Inf. 2nd Co.D
Trusler, L.W. TN 63rd Inf. Co.E
Trusley, John TN 19th Inf. Co.D
Trusloe, George VA 47th Inf. Co.A
Trusloe, John VA 47th Inf. Co.A
Trusloe, Stephen VA 25th Mil. Co.C
Truslon, Joseph VA Inf. 2nd Bn.Loc.Def. Co.F
Truslow, --- AR Inf. Cocke's Regt. Chap.
Truslow, George W. VA 50th Inf. Co.I
Truslow, Henry B. VA 36th Inf. 2nd Co.B
Truslow, Hezekiah VA Lt.Arty. Rives' Co.
Truslow, Huz Conf.Lt.Arty. Stark's Bn. Co.C
Truslow, J.A. GA 3rd Res. Co.B
Truslow, James H. VA 30th Inf. 2nd Co.I
Truslow, J.B. VA 14th Cav. Co.D
Truslow, J.F. MO QM Dept.St.Guard Clerk
Truslow, J.F. Gen. & Staff Chap.
Truslow, John AR 2nd Inf. Old Co.C
Truslow, John L. VA 26th Cav. Co.B
Truslow, John L. VA Cav. 46th Bn. Co.B
Truslow, Joseph VA Lt.Arty. Rives' Co.
Truslow, Joseph VA 2nd Inf.Loc.Def. Co.H
Truslow, Joseph Conf.Lt.Arty. Stark's Bn. Co.C
Truslow, Joseph B. VA Cav. Moorman's Co. Cpl.
Truslow, Stephen A. VA 30th Inf. Co.K
Truslow, William VA 54th Inf. Co.I
Truss, A. AL Talladega Cty.Res. Cunningham's Co.
Truss, Benjamin AL 20th Inf. Co.C Lt.
Truss, C.C. AL 17th Inf. Co.F
Truss, C.C. AL 58th Inf. Co.C
Truss, Charles E. TX 15th Cav. Co.G
Truss, Enos AL 10th Inf. Co.A
Truss, F. AL Talladega Cty.Res. Cunningham's Co.
Truss, G.N. AL 10th Inf. Co.E Sgt.
Truss, G.W. AL Cav. Barbiere's Bn. Truss' Co.
Truss, G.W. AL 13th Inf. Co.E
Truss, Henry W. AL Cp. of Instr. Talladega
Truss, James D. AL 10th Inf. Co.F Capt.
Truss, J.D. AL 51st (Part.Rangers) Co.F
Truss, John, Jr. AL 10th Inf. Co.B Sgt.
Truss, John VA 12th Cav. Co.A
Truss, John W. AL Gid Nelson Lt.Arty.
Truss, John W. TX 12th Cav. Co.D Cpl.
Truss, Josiah MS 31st Inf. Co.D
Truss, J.S. AL 55th Vol. Co.F
Truss, J.W. AL 18th Inf. Co.C
Truss, Marion S. 8th (Wade's) Conf.Cav. Co.A
Truss, M.D. AL 18th Inf. Co.L
Truss, Milton AL 10th Inf. Co.E
Truss, M.S. AL 31st Inf. Co.G
Truss, Samuel AL 20th Inf. Co.C
Truss, S.W. AL 10th Inf. Co.E Cpl.
Truss, T.F. AL 10th Inf. Co.E
Truss, Thomas AL 18th Inf. Co.L
Truss, Thomas K. AL Cav. Barbiere's Bn. Truss' Co. Capt.
Truss, Thos. W. AL 6th Cav. Co.A
Truss, T.J. TX Inf. 1st St.Troops White's Co.D
Truss, T.T. AL 51st (Part.Rangers) Co.F
Truss, T.W. AL 51st (Part.Rangers) Co.A
Truss, W. AL Talladega Cty.Res. Cunningham's Co.
Trussel, D.K. MS 31st Inf. Co.I
Trussel, Eli TN 35th Inf. Co.L
Trussel, Eli TN 36th Inf. Co.L
Trussel, Henry MO 1st N.E. Cav. Co.C
Trussel, J.J. SC Mil. 16th Regt. Lawrence's Co.
Trussel, J.T. MS 4th Inf. Co.A

Trussel, Richard T. MO 1st N.E. Cav. Co.C
Trussel, W.A. FL 1st (Res.) Inf. Co.L Sgt.
Trussel, William B. MS 11th (Perrin's) Cav. Co.C
Trussell, Armsted KY 11th Cav. Co.A
Trussell, Benjamin F. MS 40th Inf. Co.E
Trussell, Charles VA 122nd Mil. Co.E
Trussell, Charles G. GA 3rd Inf. Co.F
Trussell, Charles W. VA 12th Cav. Co.B Sgt.
Trussell, Charles W. VA 2nd Inf. Co.A Sgt.
Trussell, Christopher LA Arty. Moody's Co. (Madison Lt.Arty.)
Trussell, D. GA 3rd Res. Co.H
Trussell, Daniel L. GA 35th Inf. Co.C
Trussell, D.L. GA Lt.Arty. (Arsenal Btty.) Hudson's Co.
Trussell, E. MS 40th Inf. Co.G
Trussell, Edward Sap. & Min. Flynn's Co.,CSA Cpl.
Trussell, Edward C. VA 12th Cav. Co.B
Trussell, Edward C. VA 2nd Inf. Co.A
Trussell, Edward J. MS 8th Inf. Co.F
Trussell, Elisha C. MS 37th Inf. Co.I 1st Lt.
Trussell, F.A. GA 10th Cav. (St.Guards) Co.D
Trussell, G.B. AL Cav. Barbiere's Bn. Bowie's Co.
Trussell, G.B. AL Cav. Hardie's Bn.Res. Co.C
Trussell, H.C. GA 32nd Inf. Co.B
Trussell, Henry Harrison LA 28th (Gray's) Inf. Co.F
Trussell, Henry P. MO 9th Bn.S.S. Co.D
Trussell, Howard VA 8th Inf. Co.F Sgt.
Trussell, J. AL 25th Inf. Co.H
Trussell, James AL 30th Inf. Co.H
Trussell, James AL Cp. of Instr. Talladega
Trussell, James LA 12th Inf. Co.B
Trussell, James MS 6th Cav. Co.D
Trussell, James MS 8th Cav. Co.K
Trussell, James M. MS 1st (Patton's) Inf. Co.I
Trussell, James M. VA 2nd Inf. Co.H
Trussell, James O. MO 12th Cav. Co.B
Trussell, James R. MS 31st Inf. Co.I
Trussell, James T. VA 12th Cav. Co.B
Trussell, James T. VA 2nd Inf. Co.A
Trussell, James W. GA 51st Inf. Co.D
Trussell, J.K. MS Lt.Arty. 14th Bn. Co.C
Trussell, J.K. MS Lt.Arty. Merrin's Btty.
Trussell, J.M., Sr. MS Cav. Knox's Co. (Stonewall Rangers)
Trussell, J.M. MS 37th Inf. Co.I Cpl.
Trussell, John LA 12th Inf. Co.B
Trussell, John LA 28th (Gray's) Inf. Co.F
Trussell, John VA Lt.Arty. Clutter's Co.
Trussell, John F.H. MS 1st (Patton's) Inf. Co.K
Trussell, John F.H. MS 37th Inf. Co.I 2nd Lt.
Trussell, John H. GA Cav. 29th Bn. Co.E
Trussell, John W. AL 46th Inf. Co.F
Trussell, John W. GA 32nd Inf. Co.B 1st Lt.
Trussell, John W. LA 12th Inf. Co.K
Trussell, John W. MS 8th Inf. Co.I
Trussell, J.S. AL Cp. of Instr. Talladega
Trussell, J.W. GA 10th Inf. Co.A
Trussell, Levi VA 51st Inf. Co.E
Trussell, Moses AL 2nd Cav. Co.A
Trussell, Moses AL 7th Inf. Co.B
Trussell, Moses VA 12th Cav. Co.B
Trussell, R.L. GA 32nd Inf. Co.B Cpl.
Trussell, Samuel VA 11th Cav. Co.K Cpl.
Trussell, Samuel VA 51st Mil. Co.D
Trussell, Samuel VA 122nd Mil. Co.C
Trussell, Samuel M. VA Cav. 39th Bn. Co.A
Trussell, T. TN Inf. Harman's Regt. Co.A
Trussell, Thomas W. VA 1st Cav. Co.A Capt.
Trussell, W.C. MS 37th Inf. Co.I Cpl.
Trussell, W.F. MO Lt.Arty. H.M. Bledsoe's Co.
Trussell, W.H. GA Lt.Arty. Croft's Btty. (Columbus Arty.)
Trussell, William LA 28th (Gray's) Inf. Co.F
Trussell, William SC Hvy.Arty. 15th (Lucas') Bn. Co.A
Trussell, William W. MS 30th Inf. Co.I
Trussle, Armstead KY 7th Cav. Co.A
Trussle, J.A.J. MS 13th Inf. Co.C
Trussle, O.S. MO 12th Cav. Co.B
Trussle, Peter GA Lt.Arty. Daniell's Btty.
Trussle, Simpson A. KY 7th Cav. Co.A
Trussle, William SC 6th Res. Co.A Cpl.
Trussley, James TN 1st (Carter's) Cav. Co.E
Trust, F.A. LA Mil.Conf.Guards Regt. Co.A
Trust, George VA Horse Arty. D. Shanks' Co.
Trust, Guillermo LA Mil. 5th Regt.Eur.Brig. (Spanish Regt.) Co.4
Trust, John L. LA 5th Inf. Co.F
Truster, H.B. AR 62nd Mil. Co.E 2nd Lt.
Truston, C.P. Gen. & Staff, QM Dept.
Trusty, B.L. MS 2nd Inf. (A. of 10,000) Co.G
Trusty, B.L. MS 31st Inf. Co.D
Trusty, F.J. MS Cav. Yerger's Regt. Co.E
Trusty, Francis M. MS 8th Cav. Co.C
Trusty, H.B. AR 35th Inf. Co.C
Trusty, Jackson MO 2nd Inf. Co.F
Trusty, James W. MS 15th Inf. Co.F
Trusty, J.F. MS 8th Cav. Co.C Cpl.
Trusty, John KY 2nd (Duke's) Cav. Co.A
Trusty, John MS 4th Inf. Co.D
Trusty, John T. MS 15th Inf. Co.F,I Sgt.
Trusty, J.W. MS Cav. Hughes' Bn. Co.H
Trusty, J.W. MS 2nd Inf. (A. of 10,000) Co.G
Trusty, R.B. TN 33rd Inf. Co.F
Trusty, W. MS Cav. Yerger's Regt. Co.E
Trusty, William GA 52nd Inf. Co.F
Trusty, William TN 6th (Wheeler's) Cav. Co.D
Trusty, William TN 35th Inf. 1st Co.I, Co.G
Trusty, William C. MS 8th Cav. Co.C
Trusty, W.M. KY 10th (Johnson's) Cav. Co.K
Trustz, Jackson MO 8th Inf. Co.C
Truth, G.M. TN 44th (Cons.) Inf.
Truthman, Aloys TN 15th Inf. Co.K 1st Lt.
Truwit, James M. SC 14th Inf. Co.G 1st Lt.
Truxdale, Jackson MS 25th Inf. Co.K Sgt.
Truxell, Andrew J. VA 11th Inf. Co.A
Truxell, Andrew J. 3rd Conf.Eng.Troops Co.A Artif.
Truxell, John D. TN 5th (McKenzie's) Cav. Co.H
Truxell, John D. TN Lt.Arty. Morton's Co. Cpl.
Truxell, John D. Conf.Arty. Marshall's Co.
Truxell, Joseph E.M. TN 5th (McKenzie's) Cav. Co.H
Truxillio, John LA 1st Hvy.Arty. (Reg.) Co.B
Truxillo, A. LA Inf. Jeff Davis Regt. Co.F 2nd Lt.
Truxillo, Andro LA 26th Inf. Co.C
Truxillo, Antoine LA 28th (Thomas') Inf. Co.H
Truxillo, Denis LA 28th (Thomas') Inf. Co.H Cpl.
Truxillo, E.H. LA 28th (Gray's) Inf. Sgt.
Truxillo, F. LA Arty. Hutton's Co. (Crescent Arty.,Co.A) Cpl.
Truxillo, Fleurentine LA 28th (Thomas') Inf. Co.H
Truxillo, Lucien LA 2nd Cav. Co.H Cpl.
Truxillo, Manuel R. LA 2nd Cav. Co.H
Truxillo, Philipp LA 28th (Thomas') Inf. Co.H Sgt.
Truxillo, Sosthene LA 2nd Cav. Co.H
Truxwell, Granville NC 64th Inf. Co.N
Try, Elbert AR 2nd Vol. Co.D
Tryal, Styles NC 17th Inf. (1st Org.) Co.E
Trye, William L. AL 1st Bn. Hilliard's Legion Vol. Co.B
Tryer, Edward GA 4th Inf. Co.E
Tryer, W. TX Cav. Coopwood's Spy Co.
Tryer, W.M. GA 51st Inf. Co.K
Tryon, B.S. AL 8th Cav. Co.H
Tryon, D.C. SC 7th Cav. Co.K
Tryon, E.C. TX Cav. 6th Bn. Co.D
Tryon, Frank KY 2nd Mtd.Inf. Co.E Capt.
Tryon, J.C. TN Lt.Arty. Rice's Btty.
Tryon, Thomas AR 23rd Inf. Co.E
Tryon, W.A. TX 2nd Cav. Co.C
Tryon, W.A. TX 15th Field Btty. QMSgt.
Tryon, W.A. TX 5th Inf. Co.A
Trywell, R. GA Inf. 27th Bn. Co.F
Tschady, Melchior TN 15th Inf. Co.K,I
Tschalter, Frederick Inf. School of Pract. Powell's Detach. Co.C
Tschiedel, J. TX 3rd Inf. 2nd Co.A Bugler
Tschiffely, Elgar L. MD 1st Cav. Co.A
Tschoepe, Rudolph TX 12th Field Btty. Bugler
Tschudi, Melchior TN 15th Inf. Co.H
Tschudy, Matthias TN 19th Inf. Co.I
Tschumi, Nicholas TX Inf. Griffin's Bn. Co.F
Tshear, Napoleon AR 3rd Inf. Co.H 1st Sgt.
Tshipowada, Joseph NC 5th Inf. Co.A
Tshusky, Wm. VA 2nd Regt.Res. Co.A Sgt.
Tuart, Louis AL 1st Regt. Mobile Vol. Co.A
Tubb, --- TX Cav. Mann's Regt. Co.G
Tubb, A. MS 2nd St.Cav. Co.H
Tubb, Abraham S. MS 2nd Inf. Co.K
Tubb, Andrew P. AL 28th Inf. Co.A
Tubb, A.W. MS 43rd Inf. Co.C
Tubb, B.A. LA 13th Bn. (Part.Rangers) Co.A
Tubb, Benjamin TX 13th Cav. Co.A
Tubb, Benjamin F. MS Inf. 5th Bn. Co.B
Tubb, Benjamin F. MS 27th Inf. Co.K
Tubb, Benson MS 14th Inf. Co.E
Tubb, Benson MS 43rd Inf. Co.C
Tubb, Daniel F. AL 43rd Inf. Co.H
Tubb, David J. TX 26th Cav. Co.D
Tubb, E. AL Cp. of Instr. Talladega
Tubb, Eli LA 17th Inf. Co.C
Tubb, F.T. AL 8th Inf. Co.A
Tubb, George TN 34th Inf. Co.D
Tubb, George R. TX 28th Cav. Co.L Cpl.
Tubb, George W. AL 8th Inf. Co.A Sgt.
Tubb, George W. MS 14th Inf. Co.E
Tubb, G.K. TX Cav. Morgan's Regt. Co.C Cpl.
Tubb, G.W. MS 23rd Inf. Co.A
Tubb, H. MS 9th Bn.S.S. Co.C
Tubb, Henry MS 7th Inf. Co.I

Tubb, H.J. TX 25th Cav. Co.E
Tubb, Isaac D. AL 28th Inf. Co.A
Tubb, James MS 10th Cav. Co.F
Tubb, James, Jr. MS 14th Inf. Co.E
Tubb, James, Sr. MS 14th Inf. Co.E Cpl.
Tubb, James TX 20th Inf. Co.K
Tubb, James C. AL 58th Inf. Co.I
Tubb, James M. TX 13th Cav. Co.A
Tubb, J.C. AL 11th Inf.
Tubb, J.C. GA 55th Inf. Co.I
Tubb, Jeptha MS 6th Cav. Co.E Cpl.
Tubb, Jeptha MS 43rd Inf. Co.C
Tubb, Jepther MS Inf. 3rd Bn. (St.Troops) Co.B Sgt.
Tubb, Jesse E. TX 13th Cav. Co.A
Tubb, J.H.P. AR 38th Inf. Co.E
Tubb, J.L. MS 12th Cav. Co.G
Tubb, J.M.L. MS 43rd Inf. Co.C
Tubb, J.N. 2nd Conf.Inf. Co.B Cpl.
Tubb, Job AL 62nd Inf. Co.D,B
Tubb, John MS 14th Inf. Co.E Cpl.
Tubb, John, Jr. MS 43rd Inf. Co.C
Tubb, John TN 34th Inf. Co.D
Tubb, John B. TN Cav. 11th Bn. (Gordon's) Co.F 1st Sgt.
Tubb, John B. TN Cav. Allison's Squad. Co.A
Tubb, John L. MS 43rd Inf. Co.C
Tubb, John N. MS 25th Inf. Co.B Cpl.
Tubb, Joseph LA 6th Inf. Co.A
Tubb, Joseph MS 14th Inf. Co.E
Tubb, J.P. MS 2nd St.Cav. Co.F,H
Tubb, J.S. MS 2nd St.Cav. Co.H
Tubb, J.W. AR 20th Inf. Co.C
Tubb, J.W. TN 10th (DeMoss') Cav. Co.F
Tubb, J.W. TN Cav. Napier's Bn. Co.C
Tubb, Kitchen P. AL 20th Inf. Co.F
Tubb, Lee TX 5th Inf. Co.C 1st Sgt.
Tubb, Lee TX Inf. Whaley's Co. 2nd Lt.
Tubb, Lewis LA 6th Inf. Co.A
Tubb, Lion AL 20th Inf. Co.F
Tubb, Nathan M. AL 28th Inf. Co.A
Tubb, Nicholas MS 14th Inf. Co.E 2nd Lt.
Tubb, N.M. AL 41st Inf. Co.E Sgt.
Tubb, N.T. TN 10th (DeMoss') Cav. Co.F
Tubb, Perry LA 31st Inf. Co.H
Tubb, R.B. AL 40th Inf. Co.H
Tubb, Reuben D. AL 24th Inf. Co.H
Tubb, Reuben S. AL 62nd Inf. Co.D
Tubb, Reuben W. TN Cav. Allison's Squad. Co.A
Tubb, Richard AL 20th Inf. Co.F
Tubb, Richard B. AL Mil. 4th Vol. Co.C
Tubb, Robert H. AL 62nd Inf. Co.D Cpl.
Tubb, Samuel AL 20th Inf. Co.F
Tubb, Samuel TN 10th (DeMoss') Cav. Co.E
Tubb, W. AL 7th Cav. Co.A
Tubb, W.A.C. TN 50th (Cons.) Inf. Co.E
Tubb, W.C. TN 40th Inf. Co.E
Tubb, W.E. LA 1st Hvy.Arty. (Reg.) Co.E
Tubb, William AL Cp. of Instr. Talladega
Tubb, William L. MS 14th Inf. Co.E
Tubb, William R. TN 7th Inf. Co.B
Tubb, William W. AL 41st Inf. Co.E
Tubb, William W. TN 34th Inf. Co.D
Tubbee Choctaw Inf. Wilkins' Co.
Tubbee, Ho. Deneale's Regt. Choctaw Warriors
Tubbee, Sam Deneale's Regt. Choctaw Warriors Co.C
Tubberville, A.H. LA 3rd Inf. Co.B
Tubberville, D.R. AL 11th Cav. Co.I
Tubberville, E.C. AR 6th Inf. Old Co.D
Tubberville, William AR 2nd Mtd.Rifles Co.F
Tubberville, William AR 12th Inf. Co.C Cpl.
Tubbeville, Willis H. LA 31st Inf. Co.I
Tubbs, A.J. TN 10th (DeMoss') Cav. Co.C
Tubbs, Andrew TN 53rd Inf. Co.F
Tubbs, Ballis TN 51st (Cons.) Inf. Co.A
Tubbs, Benson MS 2nd St.Cav. Co.F
Tubbs, C.W. TN 1st Hvy.Arty. 2nd Co.C
Tubbs, C.W. TN 51st (Cons.) Inf. Co.A
Tubbs, David D. MS 19th Inf. Co.F
Tubbs, D.C. AR 30th Inf. Co.F
Tubbs, D.C. MO Cav. Slayback's Regt. Co.B
Tubbs, D.L. AL 13th Bn.Part.Rangers Co.C
Tubbs, D.L. AL 56th Part.Rangers Co.G
Tubbs, D.S. AL 21st Inf. Co.A Music.
Tubbs, E. TN 51st (Cons.) Inf. Co.A
Tubbs, G.A. TN 51st (Cons.) Inf. Co.A Sgt.
Tubbs, George LA 5th Cav. Co.I Cpl.
Tubbs, George MS 29th Inf. Co.A
Tubbs, G.R. TX Inf. Timmons' Regt. Co.I
Tubbs, G.W. TX 29th Cav. Co.I
Tubbs, J. TX 7th Inf. Co.H
Tubbs, J. TX 9th (Nichols') Inf. Co.E
Tubbs, J.A. MS 1st (King's) Inf. (St.Troops) D. Love's Co.
Tubbs, James MS Cav. 2nd Bn.Res. Co.C 1st Lt.
Tubbs, James MS 9th Cav. Co.E
Tubbs, James TN Cav. 17th Bn. (Sanders') Co.B
Tubbs, James TX 1st Inf. Co.H
Tubbs, James TX Vol. Rainey's Co.
Tubbs, James A. MS 19th Inf. Co.D
Tubbs, James L. MS 43rd Inf. Co.C
Tubbs, J.B. TN 6th (Wheeler's) Cav. Co.D
Tubbs, Jenus TN 5th Inf. 2nd Co.H
Tubbs, J.F. AL 41st Inf. Co.C
Tubbs, J.F. MS 37th Inf. Co.D
Tubbs, J.G. MS 37th Inf. Co.D
Tubbs, J.J. AR 2nd Cav. Co.E
Tubbs, J.M. TN 13th (Gore's) Cav. Co.K
Tubbs, John AL 40th Inf. Co.C
Tubbs, John MS 2nd Cav. Co.I
Tubbs, John MS 19th Inf. Co.F
Tubbs, John TX 1st (Yager's) Cav. Co.A
Tubbs, John TX Cav. 3rd (Yager's) Bn. Co.A
Tubbs, John TX 18th Cav. Co.H Cpl.
Tubbs, John TX 22nd Inf. Co.D
Tubbs, John A. AL 6th Inf. Co.E
Tubbs, John B. TX 14th Field Btty.
Tubbs, John C. TX Cav. Morgan's Regt. Co.D
Tubbs, John L. TX Inf. Griffin's Bn. Co.A Capt.
Tubbs, John N. MS 43rd Inf. Co.C Cpl.
Tubbs, John W. LA 19th Inf. Co.C
Tubbs, Jones TN 51st (Cons.) Inf. Co.A
Tubbs, J.P. TN 4th (McLemore's) Cav. Co.C
Tubbs, J.S. TX 10th Cav. Co.G
Tubbs, J.W. MO Cav. Fristoe's Regt. Co.D
Tubbs, L.C. TN 51st (Cons.) Inf. Co.A
Tubbs, Lemuel TN 27th Inf. Co.A
Tubbs, Len TN 27th Inf. Co.D
Tubbs, Manuel TN 5th Inf. 2nd Co.H
Tubbs, Marion MS 43rd Inf. Co.G
Tubbs, Matthew MS 12th Inf. Co.I Sgt.
Tubbs, R.C. TX 15th Cav. Co.C
Tubbs, Robert AL 18th Bn.Vol. Co.E,C
Tubbs, Robert TX 18th Cav. Co.H
Tubbs, Robert TX Cav. Morgan's Regt. Co.D
Tubbs, Robert TX 4th Inf. Co.K
Tubbs, Robert H. MS 29th Inf. Co.A
Tubbs, Robert P. AL Lt.Arty. Phelan's Co.
Tubbs, Sam TN Cav. Napier's Bn. Co.B
Tubbs, Samuel AL 6th Inf. Co.E
Tubbs, Samuel AR 1st (Colquitt's) Inf. Co.E
Tubbs, Samuel AR 24th Inf. Co.E
Tubbs, Samuel AR Inf. Hardy's Regt. Co.B 1st Sgt.
Tubbs, Samuel TX 16th Inf. Co.F
Tubbs, S.J. AR Inf. 1st Bn. Co.E
Tubbs, T.D. TX Cav. Border's Regt. Co.A 2nd Lt.
Tubbs, Thomas D. TX 13th Cav. Co.F
Tubbs, Thomas D. TX 22nd Inf. Co.D Jr.2nd Lt.
Tubbs, Thornton G. MO Cav. Preston's Bn. Co.B
Tubbs, T.J. TX Waul's Legion Co.C
Tubbs, W. AR 1st (Monroe's) Cav. Co.L
Tubbs, W.A.C. TN 50th Inf. Co.E
Tubbs, William AL 21st Inf. Co.F
Tubbs, William MS Inf. 3rd Bn. Co.I
Tubbs, William MO 6th Cav.
Tubbs, William MO 7th Cav. Co.D Cpl.
Tubbs, William MO 6th Inf. Co.I
Tubbs, William MO 10th Inf. Co.B
Tubbs, William TX 20th Cav. Co.C
Tubbs, William TX 35th (Brown's) Cav. Co.F
Tubbs, William TX Cav. Benavides' Regt. Co.C
Tubbs, William TX 13th Vol. 1st Co.H
Tubbs, William T. TN 50th Inf. Co.H
Tubbs, Willis AR 1st (Monroe's) Cav. Co.L
Tubbs, W.J. AR 18th Inf. Co.C
Tubbs, W.R. TN 13th (Gore's) Cav. Co.K
Tubbs, W.W. MS 43rd Inf. Co.C
Tubbs, W.W. 1st Conf.Cav. 1st Co.K
Tubby, A. TX 18th Inf. Co.A
Tubby, Bixen Deneale's Regt. Choctaw Warriors
Tubby, Fokelin Deneale's Regt. Choctaw Warriors
Tubby, John 1st Creek Mtd.Vol. Co.M
Tubby, Richard E. VA 108th Mil. McNeer's Co.
Tubby, Thomas P. MO Cav. 2nd Regt.St.Guard Co.D
Tuber, Charles TX Inf. 1st St.Troops Stevenson's Co.F
Tuberty, Martin TN 21st Inf. Co.E
Tuberty, Patrick GA 1st (Olmstead's) Inf. Co.B
Tuberville, A.J. TX 7th Cav. Co.D
Tuberville, D.G. AL 22nd Inf. Co.C
Tuberville, Eldridge P. AR 33rd Inf. Co.D
Tuberville, G.E.H. SC Cav. Tucker's Co.
Tuberville, G.H. SC 7th Cav. Co.F
Tuberville, J.M. AL 25th Inf. Co.A
Tuberville, John AL 4th Cav. Co.H
Tuberville, John AL 40th Inf. Co.H
Tuberville, Joseph AR 33rd Inf. Co.D
Tuberville, Sam F. Gen. & Staff Capt.,AQM
Tuberville, William AR 6th Inf. New Co.F

Tubman, Albert Magruder VA 17th Inf. Co.E 1st Lt.
Tubman, A.M. VA 26th Cav. Co.A Lt.
Tubman, C. TN Arty. Ramsey's Btty.
Tubman, Charles LA 1st Cav. Robinson's Co.
Tubman, Chs. LA Mtd.Rifles Miller's Ind.Co.
Tubman, Oscar VA Hvy.Arty. 18th Bn. Co.E Sgt.
Tubman, Richard MD 1st Cav. Co.G
Tubra, H.O. LA 6th Cav. Co.C
Tubran, E. LA Mil. 1st Regt. French Brig. Co.2 Cpl.
Tubre, Henry O. LA 6th Inf. Co.C 1st Sgt.
Tubs, Hugh AL Cav. Moreland's Regt. Co.I
Tubs, James AL 55th Vol. Co.I
Tubs, Jesse TX 11th Cav. Co.K
Tucchetubbe 1st Choctaw & Chickasaw Mtd.Rifles 3rd Co.K
Tuchen, G.A. AL 8th Inf. Co.H
Tucholke, Alexander LA 1st (Strawbridge's) Inf. Co.A,F
Tuchstine, William GA 11th Cav. (St.Guards) Johnson's Co.
Tuchtone, G.W. GA 54th Inf. Co.K
Tuck, Alonzo C. AL 10th Inf. Co.F
Tuck, Anderson VA 53rd Inf. Co.D Cpl.
Tuck, Andrew J. VA 20th Inf. Co.K
Tuck, Andrew J. VA 59th Inf. 3rd Co.C
Tuck, Ashley D. AL 20th Inf. Co.E
Tuck, B. VA 14th Inf. Co.I
Tuck, Benjamin F. GA 42nd Inf. Co.I
Tuck, Bennett D. GA 38th Inf. Co.N
Tuck, B.M. GA Arty. Lumpkin's Co.
Tuck, B.M. MS 35th Inf. Co.G
Tuck, C.A. NC 35th Inf. Co.E Sgt.
Tuck, C.H. AL 51st (Part.Rangers) Co.F
Tuck, Charles P. TN 32nd Inf. Co.K
Tuck, C.L. AR 1st Mtd.Rifles Co.B
Tuck, C.T. TN Inf. 4th Cons.Regt. Co.H
Tuck, David TN 5th (McKenzie's) Cav. Co.K
Tuck, Davis VA 14th Inf. Co.B
Tuck, Detrien P. VA 3rd Inf. 2nd Co.K Cpl.
Tuck, E.A. TN 27th Inf. Co.E 2nd Lt.
Tuck, Edward A. VA 14th Inf. Co.K Capt.
Tuck, Edward C. MO 5th Inf. Co.C Cpl.
Tuck, Edward I. NC 24th Inf. Co.H
Tuck, Edward J. VA Lt.Arty. W.P. Carter's Co.
Tuck, Elijah B. AL 10th Inf. Co.F Sgt.
Tuck, Emilus P. NC 15th Inf. Co.G
Tuck, E. Prentiss 7th Conf.Cav. 1st Co.I
Tuck, George VA 14th Inf. Co.B
Tuck, George P. VA 53rd Inf. Co.H
Tuck, George S. VA 2nd Arty. Co.G
Tuck, George S. VA 87th Mil. Co.C
Tuck, George W. GA 11th Inf. Co.H
Tuck, George W. LA 1st (Strawbridge's) Inf. Co.G
Tuck, George W. VA 24th Cav. Co.B
Tuck, George W. VA Cav. 40th Bn. Co.B
Tuck, George W. VA 20th Inf. Co.H
Tuck, G.S. VA Res.Forces Thurston's Co.
Tuck, G.W. VA Inf. 25th Bn. Co.D
Tuck, H.C. TX 1st Bn.S.S. Co.D
Tuck, Henry MO 11th Inf. Co.G Cpl.
Tuck, Henry D. AL 49th Inf. Co.E Sgt.
Tuck, Hiram N. MO 5th Inf. Co.C
Tuck, James VA Inf. 25th Bn. Co.G
Tuck, James VA 53rd Inf. Co.H
Tuck, James E. VA Hvy.Arty. Wright's Co. Cpl.
Tuck, James I. GA Cobb's Legion Co.C
Tuck, James R. AL 30th Inf. Co.A
Tuck, James T. VA Lt.Arty. W.P. Carter's Co.
Tuck, James W. GA 42nd Inf. Co.G
Tuck, J.D. MS Inf. 1st Bn. Co.C
Tuck, J.E. Gen. & Staff, Ord.Dept.
Tuck, J.H. TN 47th Inf. Co.H
Tuck, John GA Arty. Lumpkin's Co.
Tuck, John B. AR 1st Mtd.Rifles Co.B
Tuck, John C. VA Lt.Arty. W.P. Carter's Co.
Tuck, John F. VA 53rd Inf. Co.D
Tuck, John H. AR 34th Inf. Co.F
Tuck, John H. VA 53rd Inf. Co.G
Tuck, John R. GA 40th Inf. Co.I,C
Tuck, John T. GA 11th Inf. Co.H
Tuck, John W. AR 47th (Crandall's) Cav.
Tuck, Joseph VA 53rd Inf. Co.G
Tuck, Joseph VA 53rd Inf. Co.H
Tuck, Joseph D. VA 14th Inf. Co.B
Tuck, Joseph E. GA 3rd Inf. Co.K
Tuck, Joseph P. VA 14th Inf. Co.K Cpl.
Tuck, Joseph R. AL 31st Inf. Co.G
Tuck, Josiah L. GA 11th Inf. Co.H
Tuck, J.R. GA Arty. Lumpkin's Co.
Tuck, J.W. VA 1st (Farinholt's) Res. Co.E
Tuck, Lewis M. VA 9th Cav. Co.H
Tuck, M.C. VA 10th Cav. Co.D
Tuck, Moses TN 26th Inf. Co.A
Tuck, Moses TN Conscr. (Cp. of Instr.)
Tuck, M.P. VA 24th Cav. Co.F
Tuck, Nat NC 54th Inf. Co.D
Tuck, Patrick H. VA 53rd Inf. Co.D
Tuck, Paul L. VA 3rd Inf. 2nd Co.K
Tuck, Paul P. VA 3rd Inf. 2nd Co.K Sgt.
Tuck, Phal VA 1st (Farinholt's) Res. Co.E
Tuck, Phaltile M. VA 3rd Inf. 2nd Co.K 1st Lt.
Tuck, Phaltile R.T. VA 3rd Inf. 2nd Co.K
Tuck, Phaltile W.S. VA 3rd Inf. 2nd Co.K Sgt.
Tuck, Powell, Sr. VA 3rd Inf. 2nd Co.K
Tuck, R. VA 2nd St.Res. Co.B
Tuck, R.A.C. AR 50th Mil. Co.G
Tuck, R.B. AL Inf. 1st Regt. Co.A
Tuck, R.B. VA 14th Inf. Co.K
Tuck, R.C. VA 1st (Farinholt's) Res. Co.E Sgt.
Tuck, R.H. SC Inf. Holcombe Legion Co.C Sgt.
Tuck, Richard VA 53rd Inf. Co.H
Tuck, Richard VA Res.Forces Clark's Co.
Tuck, Richard B. VA Hvy.Arty. Wright's Co.
Tuck, Richard F. VA 6th Cav. Co.G
Tuck, Richard H. VA 3rd Inf. 2nd Co.K Capt.
Tuck, Richard M. VA 2nd Arty. Co.G Sgt.
Tuck, Richard M. VA Inf. 22nd Bn. Co.G Sgt.
Tuck, Richard M. VA 87th Mil. Co.C Cpl.
Tuck, Richard S.T. VA 3rd Inf. 2nd Co.K
Tuck, Robert AR 12th Bn.S.S.
Tuck, Robert TX Vol. Teague's Co. (So.Rights Guards) 2nd Lt.
Tuck, Robert A.C. AR 25th Inf. Co.H
Tuck, Robert E. SC Palmetto S.S. Co.K
Tuck, Robert J. GA Carlton's Co. (Troup Cty.Arty.)
Tuck, Robert N. GA Inf. Fuller's Co.
Tuck, R.W. VA Lt.Arty. Otey's Co.
Tuck, R.W. VA Inf. 25th Bn. Co.G
Tuck, Samuel SC Palmetto S.S. Co.K
Tuck, Samuel H. MO 5th Inf. Co.C Cpl.
Tuck, Seaborn G. GA 11th Inf. Co.H 1st Lt.
Tuck, Stephen H. VA 14th Inf. Co.B
Tuck, Thomas GA 40th Inf. Co.K
Tuck, Thomas TN 1st (Feild's) Inf. Co.F
Tuck, Thomas TN Inf. 1st Cons.Regt. Co.B
Tuck, Thomas VA 14th Inf. Co.B
Tuck, Thomas VA 21st Inf. Co.H
Tuck, Thomas VA 47th Inf. 3rd Co.H
Tuck, Thomas M. GA 3rd Inf. Co.K
Tuck, Thomas R. GA Cobb's Legion Co.C
Tuck, T.J. VA Inf. 4th Bn.Loc.Def. Co.B
Tuck, T.M. SC Inf. Holcombe Legion Co.C
Tuck, W. VA 115th Mil. Co.D
Tuck, W.A. NC 23rd Inf. Co.I
Tuck, William NC Mallett's Bn. (Cp.Guard)
Tuck, William TN 1st (Feild's) Inf. Co.F
Tuck, William A. TN 38th Inf. Co.F
Tuck, William B. GA Cobb's Legion Co.H
Tuck, William C. VA Lt.Arty. W.P. Carter's Co.
Tuck, William H. VA 53rd Inf. Co.H
Tuck, William J. GA Phillips' Legion Co.B,H
Tuck, William J. SC Inf. Holcombe Legion Co.C
Tuck, William M. VA 3rd Inf. 2nd Co.K 2nd Lt.
Tuck, William R. GA 51st Inf. Co.K
Tuck, William T. VA 1st Arty. Co.D
Tuck, William Thomas VA 59th Inf. 3rd Co.F
Tuck, William Thomas VA 60th Inf. 1st Co.H
Tuck, W.J. GA Cav. Dorough's Bn.
Tuck, W.J. SC 7th Res. Co.M
Tuck, W.L. TX 32nd Cav. Co.D
Tuck, W.R. GA Arty. Lumpkin's Co.
Tuck, W.S. VA 1st (Farinholt's) Res. Co.E
Tuck, W.T. AL 8th (Hatch's) Cav. Co.D
Tuck, W.T. AL Lt.Arty. Tarrant's Btty.
Tuck a batchee Harjo 1st Creek Mtd.Vol. Co.B
Tucke, E. Prentiss NC 2nd Cav. (19th St.Troops) Co.E 2nd Lt.
Tucke, I.N. Lidell's Staff ADC
Tucke, William NC 37th Inf. Co.A
Tuckelton, G.W. GA 54th Inf.
Tucker, --- AL 6th Inf. Co.F
Tucker, --- AL 15th Inf. Co.D
Tucker, --- MS 2nd Part.Rangers Co.C
Tucker, --- MO 5th Cav. Co.I
Tucker, --- NC 54th Inf. Co.I
Tucker, --- TX Cav. Mann's Regt. Co.H
Tucker, --- TX Cav. McCord's Frontier Regt. Co.K
Tucker, A. AL 23rd Inf. Co.F
Tucker, A. AR Lt.Arty. Hart's Btty.
Tucker, A. NC 51st Inf. Co.B
Tucker, A. TN 1st (Feild's) Inf. Co.L Sgt.
Tucker, A. TN 1st (Feild's) & 27th Inf. (Cons.) Co.I
Tucker, A. TN Inf. 1st Cons.Regt. Co.I
Tucker, A. TN 44th (Cons.) Inf. Co.G
Tucker, A. TX Cav. 3rd Regt.St.Troops Townsend's Co.
Tucker, A. TX Cav. Terry's Regt. Co.K Sgt.
Tucker, A.A. GA 55th Inf. Co.K
Tucker, A.A. LA 27th Inf. Co.A
Tucker, A.A. VA 39th Mil. Co.B
Tucker, Aaron NC 52nd Inf. Co.F
Tucker, Aaron TX 19th Cav. Co.E

Tucker, Aaron C. VA 22nd Inf. Co.A
Tucker, A.B. GA 5th Res. Co.B
Tucker, A.B. VA 1st (Farinholt's) Res. Co.H
Tucker, Abner TN 18th Inf. Co.F
Tucker, A.C. SC 24th Inf. Co.I
Tucker, A.C. TN 40th Inf. Co.G
Tucker, A.C. VA 2nd Arty. Co.I 1st Lt.
Tucker, Adam M. NC 33rd Inf. Co.C
Tucker, Addison D. MO 1st Cav. Co.C Sgt.
Tucker, Addison D. MO Inf. 8th Bn. Co.A
Tucker, Addison D. MO 9th Inf. Co.A
Tucker, Adikus J. VA Inf. 1st Bn.Loc.Def. Co.C,E
Tucker, Adolphus F. MS 17th Inf. Co.F
Tucker, A.E. TN 5th Inf. 2nd Co.K 1st Lt.
Tucker, A.F. LA 19th Inf. Co.I
Tucker, A.F. LA 27th Inf. Co.G
Tucker, A.F. MS 18th Cav. Co.C
Tucker, A.F. MS 25th Inf. Co.I
Tucker, A.F. 2nd Conf.Inf. Co.I
Tucker, A.G. MS 8th Inf. Co.K
Tucker, A.H. GA 42nd Inf. Co.I
Tucker, A.I. TN 6th (Wheeler's) Cav. Co.K
Tucker, A.J. AL 7th Cav. Co.A
Tucker, A.J. AL 29th Inf. Co.A
Tucker, A.J. GA 12th Cav. Co.L
Tucker, A.J. GA 38th Inf.
Tucker, A.J. SC 5th Cav. Co.B
Tucker, A.J. TN 30th Inf. Co.D
Tucker, A.J. TX 11th Inf. Co.A
Tucker, A.K. VA 2nd Arty. Co.E
Tucker, Albert MD 1st Cav. Co.F
Tucker, Albert TX 4th Inf. (St.Troops) Co.E
Tucker, Albert VA Hvy.Arty. 20th Bn. Co.E
Tucker, Albert VA 12th Inf. Co.D,C
Tucker, Albert A. VA 12th Inf. Co.A Music.
Tucker, Albert G. MS Inf. 7th Bn. Co.C
Tucker, Albert J. VA Hvy.Arty. 19th Bn. 2nd Co.C
Tucker, Albert S. VA 9th Inf. 2nd Co.H 1st Lt.
Tucker, Albert S. VA 12th Inf. 1st Co.I 1st Lt.
Tucker, Albert W. NC 6th Inf. Co.H
Tucker, Alex TN 27th Inf. Co.E
Tucker, Alexander AL 24th Inf. Co.I
Tucker, Alexander AL 34th Inf. Co.G
Tucker, Alexander TN 39th Mtd.Inf. Co.B
Tucker, Alexander TN 43rd Inf. Co.G
Tucker, Alexis TX Cav. Mann's Regt. Co.A
Tucker, Alexis TX Cav. Mann's Bn. Co.A
Tucker, Alford AR Cav. Davies' Bn. Co.D
Tucker, Alfred TN Inf. Nashville Bn. Cattle's Co.
Tucker, Alfred A. LA Cav. Cole's Co.
Tucker, Alfred B. Gen. & Staff Surg.
Tucker, Alfred J. TN 19th (Biffle's) Cav. Co.I
Tucker, Alfred J. TN 19th Inf. Co.I
Tucker, Alfred T. NC 43rd Inf. Co.K
Tucker, Allen AR 27th Inf. New Co.B
Tucker, Allen AR Inf. Adams' Regt. Moore's Co.
Tucker, Allen VA Inf. 25th Bn. Co.G
Tucker, Allen E. AL 38th Inf. Co.B
Tucker, Allen J. TX 12th Inf. Co.G
Tucker, Allen J. VA 15th Inf. Co.H
Tucker, Allen S. MS 1st Lt.Arty. Co.D
Tucker, Allen S. MS 33rd Inf. Co.F Cpl.
Tucker, Alonzo W. FL 8th Inf. Co.K
Tucker, Alpheus G. LA 7th Inf. Co.K Capt.
Tucker, Alpheus L. VA Lt.Arty. French's Co.
Tucker, Alpheus L. VA Arty. Wise Legion
Tucker, Alvin TN 32nd Inf. Co.I
Tucker, Alvin H. GA 36th (Broyles') Inf. Co.F
Tucker, Alvin T. AL 28th Inf. Co.H
Tucker, A.M. VA 3rd Lt.Arty. (Loc.Def.) Co.C
Tucker, A. Marion VA Arty. Dance's Co.
Tucker, Ambrose TX 30th Cav. Co.B Bugler
Tucker, Amon. VA 11th Inf. Co.B
Tucker, Amos B. TX 16th Cav. Co.H
Tucker, Amus MS 23rd Inf. Co.G
Tucker, Anderson NC 22nd Inf. Co.I
Tucker, Anderson TN 41st Inf. Co.A,D
Tucker, Andrew NC 2nd Inf. Co.K
Tucker, Andrew NC 43rd Inf. Co.F
Tucker, Andrew VA 28th Inf. Co.B
Tucker, Andrew C. MO 12th Inf. Co.K
Tucker, Andrew H. NC 31st Inf. Co.H Sgt.
Tucker, Andrew J. GA 12th Inf. Co.I Bvt.2nd Lt.
Tucker, Andrew J. TN 55th (McKoin's) Inf. Co.F
Tucker, Andrew J. TX 30th Cav. Co.G
Tucker, Andrew S. VA 6th Inf. Co.K
Tucker, A.O. AL 45th Inf. Co.F
Tucker, A.P. TX 9th (Young's) Inf. Co.F
Tucker, Arch AL 55th Vol. Co.E
Tucker, Archer VA Cav. 39th Bn. Co.D
Tucker, Archer VA 3rd (Archer's) Bn.Res. Co.B
Tucker, Archer B. VA Inf. 5th Bn. Co.D
Tucker, Archer B. VA 53rd Inf. Co.A
Tucker, Archibald TN 44th Inf. Co.B Sgt.
Tucker, Arden C. NC 17th Inf. (2nd Org.) Co.K Sgt.
Tucker, Armistead R. VA Inf. 22nd Bn. Co.E
Tucker, Arthur NC 44th Inf. Co.I
Tucker, Atticus J. VA 1st Inf. Co.G 2nd Lt.
Tucker, Atticus J. VA 41st Inf. Co.B 1st Lt.
Tucker, Augustus GA 6th Cav. Co.I
Tucker, A.W. AL 8th (Livingston's) Cav. Co.C
Tucker, A.W. AL 8th Inf. Co.C
Tucker, A.W. TX 2nd Inf. Co.C
Tucker, Azriah TN 55th (McKoin's) Inf. Bound's Co. Cpl.
Tucker, B. AR 1st Mtd.Rifles Co.G
Tucker, B. AR 18th (Marmaduke's) Inf. Co.H
Tucker, B. VA 3rd Res. Co.K
Tucker, B. 3rd Conf.Inf. Co.E
Tucker, Banister AR Cav. Gordon's Regt. Co.B
Tucker, Banister AR 15th Mil. Co.D
Tucker, Barnard H. AR 3rd Inf. Co.E Capt.
Tucker, B.C. MS 18th Cav. Co.G
Tucker, B.C. 1st Conf.Cav. 2nd Co.E
Tucker, B.D. VA Lt.Arty. 13th Bn. Co.A
Tucker, B.D. VA 3rd Inf.Loc.Def. 1st Co.G, 2nd Co.G, Co.B
Tucker, B.E. VA 14th Inf. Co.F
Tucker, Ben AL Cp. of Instr. Talladega
Tucker, Ben F. VA Lt.Arty. R.M. Anderson's Co.
Tucker, Benjamin AL 28th Inf. Co.H
Tucker, Benjamin NC 55th Inf. Co.E
Tucker, Benjamin VA 15th Cav. Co.G
Tucker, Benjamin VA Cav. 15th Bn. Co.D Cpl.
Tucker, Benjamin VA 19th Cav. Co.D
Tucker, Benjamin VA 1st St.Res. Co.C
Tucker, Benjamin VA 41st Mil. Co.C Cpl.
Tucker, Benjamin VA 55th Inf. Co.A
Tucker, Benjamin E. FL 2nd Cav. Co.C,F
Tucker, Benjamin F. GA 42nd Inf. Co.G
Tucker, Benjamin F. MS 30th Inf. Co.A
Tucker, Benjamin F. MO 9th Bn.S.S. Co.F
Tucker, Benjamin F. NC 42nd Inf. Co.B
Tucker, Benjamin F. NC 42nd Inf. Co.D
Tucker, Benjamin F. TX 18th Inf. Co.E 2nd Lt.
Tucker, Benjamin Johnson MS 7th Cav. Co.E
Tucker, Benjamin P. VA Inf. 22nd Bn. Co.D
Tucker, Bentley H. VA 56th Inf. Co.K Sgt.
Tucker, Beriah B. VA 20th Inf. Co.I Cpl.
Tucker, Beriah B. VA 59th Inf. 3rd Co.B
Tucker, Beverly VA Cav. 1st Bn. (Loc.Def. Troops) Co.A
Tucker, B.F. AL 33rd Inf. Co.E
Tucker, B.F. SC 1st (McCreary's) Inf. Co.F
Tucker, B.F. TN Inf. 23rd Bn. Co.E
Tucker, B.K. GA 8th Inf. Co.D Sgt.
Tucker, B.L. AR 9th Inf. Co.K
Tucker, B.L. TN 50th Inf. Co.K 1st Sgt.
Tucker, B.M. VA VMI Co.C
Tucker, B.P. TX 11th Field Btty.
Tucker, B.R. AL 23rd Inf. Co.C Cpl.
Tucker, Branch TN 39th Mtd.Inf. Co.G 1st Lt.
Tucker, B.S. SC 1st Cav. Co.G
Tucker, B.S., Jr. VA Cav. Swann's Bn. Watkins' Co.
Tucker, B. St.George FL 10th Inf. Surg.
Tucker, B. St.George VA 41st Inf. Asst.Surg.
Tucker, B. St.Geo. Gen. & Staff Surg.
Tucker, Burdine T. GA 41st Inf. Co.K
Tucker, Burwell P. VA 2nd Arty. Co.D
Tucker, B.W. LA Inf. 9th Bn. Co.C Cpl.
Tucker, Byrd L. TN Cav. 2nd Bn. (Biffle's) Co.F
Tucker, C. AL 9th (Malone's) Cav. Co.H
Tucker, C. FL 11th Inf.
Tucker, C.A. NC 2nd Cav. (19th St.Troops) Co.F
Tucker, C.A. NC 5th Cav. (63rd St.Troops) Co.I
Tucker, Calaway G. TN 32nd Inf. Co.A Capt.
Tucker, Calvin LA 7th Inf. Co.K
Tucker, Calvin NC 51st Inf. Co.B Sgt.
Tucker, Calvin TN 12th (Green's) Cav. Co.E
Tucker, Calvin J. TX Cav. Madison's Regt. Co.D
Tucker, Calvin M. NC 45th Inf. Co.D
Tucker, Carroll TN 53rd Inf. Co.G 2nd Lt.
Tucker, Cary W. AL 46th Inf. Co.B
Tucker, C.E. NC 53rd Inf. Co.I
Tucker, C.E. TN 23rd Inf. Co.D
Tucker, C.H. TN 61st Mtd.Inf. Co.G
Tucker, C.H. VA 19th Inf. Co.H
Tucker, Charles AR 27th Inf. Co.G
Tucker, Charles FL 5th Inf. Co.I Cpl.
Tucker, Charles FL Norwood's Co. (Home Guards)
Tucker, Charles VA Lt.Arty. Cayce's Co.
Tucker, Charles A. NC 12th Inf. Co.D,B
Tucker, Charles C. AR 33rd Inf. Co.C
Tucker, Charles E. NC 43rd Inf. Co.K
Tucker, Charles E. TN 2nd (Smith's) Cav.
Tucker, Charles E. VA 60th Inf. Co.K Capt.
Tucker, Charles H. AL 39th Inf. Co.E
Tucker, Charles H. VA 19th Inf. Co.I

Tucker, Charles H. VA 34th Inf. Co.C
Tucker, Charles J. NC 33rd Inf. Co.C
Tucker, Charles J. VA 19th Inf. Co.I Cpl.
Tucker, Charles W. SC Hvy.Arty. 15th (Lucas') Bn. Co.C
Tucker, Charles W. SC Arty. Lee's Co.
Tucker, Charles William SC Arty. Childs' Co.
Tucker, Chiswell D. VA 34th Inf. Co.C
Tucker, Christopher VA 22nd Inf. Co.E
Tucker, Christopher B. VA 19th Cav. Co.H
Tucker, C.I. LA 26th Inf. Co.I Capt.
Tucker, Citt C. GA 3rd Cav. (St.Guards) Co.B
Tucker, C.J. MO Cav. Fristoe's Regt. Co.L
Tucker, C.J. NC 7th Sr.Res. Clinard's Co.
Tucker, C.J. VA 6th Cav. Co.G
Tucker, C.L. 8th (Wade's) Conf.Cav. Co.E
Tucker, Clayton W. MS 5th Inf. Co.F Cpl.
Tucker, Clayton W. MS 14th Inf. Co.G
Tucker, Clem MO Cav. 3rd Regt.St.Guard Co.D
Tucker, Clem J. TX Cav. Hardeman's Regt. Co.B
Tucker, Clement L. MO Lt.Arty. Parsons' Co.
Tucker, Clement L. MO 6th Inf. Co.I
Tucker, Clinton M. TN 24th Inf. 2nd Co.G
Tucker, C.M. GA 3rd Res. Co.C Sgt.
Tucker, C.M. GA 9th Inf. (St.Guards) Co.A
Tucker, C.N. TX 7th Inf. Co.B
Tucker, Coke AL 45th Inf. Co.F
Tucker, Cole LA 12th Inf. Co.E
Tucker, Cornelius TN 18th (Newsom's) Cav. Co.D
Tucker, Cornelius VA 2nd Arty. Co.I
Tucker, Cornelius VA Inf. 22nd Bn. Co.G
Tucker, Cornelius R. MS 31st Inf. Co.D
Tucker, Cornelius V. VA Cav. 40th Bn. Co.C
Tucker, Cornelius W. VA Arty. Dance's Co.
Tucker, Crawford GA 1st Reg. Co.F 2nd Lt.
Tucker, C.V. VA 24th Cav. Co.C
Tucker, C.W. AL 23rd Inf. Co.F
Tucker, C.W. GA 12th Cav. Co.G
Tucker, C.W. GA 13th Inf. Co.K
Tucker, C.W. GA 36th (Broyles') Inf. Co.F
Tucker, C.W.C. GA 4th Cav. (St.Guards) Pirkle's Co.
Tucker, D. AR 51st Mil. Co.E
Tucker, D. MS 41st Inf. Co.B
Tucker, D. SC 11th Inf. Asst.Surg.
Tucker, D. VA 2nd St.Res. Co.I Cpl.
Tucker, Daniel AL 40th Inf. Co.D
Tucker, Daniel GA 31st Inf. Co.A
Tucker, Daniel GA 61st Inf. Co.A
Tucker, Daniel GA 64th Inf. Co.D
Tucker, Daniel KY 4th Mtd.Inf.
Tucker, Daniel MS Cav. 3rd Bn. (Ashcraft's) Co.B
Tucker, Daniel MS 18th Cav. Co.I
Tucker, Daniel MS Lt.Arty. (Issaquena Arty.) Graves' Co.
Tucker, Daniel VA 25th Cav. Co.H
Tucker, Daniel VA 64th Mtd.Inf. Co.A
Tucker, Daniel Marine Brig. Capt.
Tucker, Daniel F. AL Lt.Arty. Tarrant's Btty.
Tucker, Daniel H. AL 55th Vol. Co.B
Tucker, Daniel J. NC Inf. 2nd Bn. Co.E
Tucker, Daniel M. NC 42nd Inf. Co.H Cpl.
Tucker, Daniel Santford MS Inf. 1st St.Troops Co.D
Tucker, Daniel W. LA 31st Inf. Co.H
Tucker, Daniel W. VA Arty. Dance's Co.
Tucker, Darlin NC 52nd Inf. Co.A
Tucker, Darling NC 4th Sr.Res. Co.F
Tucker, David AL 8th Inf. Co.A Cpl.
Tucker, David AR 1st Mtd.Rifles Co.H
Tucker, David AR 9th Inf. Co.F
Tucker, David TN 8th Inf. Chap.
Tucker, David 1st Cherokee Mtd.Rifles McDaniel's Co.
Tucker, David C. NC 52nd Inf. Co.G
Tucker, David H. Gen. & Staff,PACS Surg.
Tucker, David W. TN 55th (McKoin's) Inf. Bound's Co. Sgt.
Tucker, D.B. VA 1st (Farinholt's) Res. Co.E
Tucker, DeJarnet SC 1st Arty. Co.A
Tucker, Demsey NC 26th Inf. Co.B
Tucker, D.H. TN 3rd (Clack's) Inf. Co.A
Tucker, Dickson TN 21st (Wilson's) Cav. Co.A
Tucker, Dixon AL 1st Cav. Co.K
Tucker, D.J. AL 3rd Inf. Co.A
Tucker, D.J. AL 3rd Res. Co.A
Tucker, D.J. GA 2nd Cav. (St.Guards) Co.B
Tucker, D.J. GA Inf. 26th Bn. Co.B
Tucker, D.J. TX 4th Inf. Co.H
Tucker, D.L. AR 1st (Dobbin's) Cav. Co.D
Tucker, D.L. MS Cav. 17th Bn. Co.A
Tucker, D.N. TN 33rd Inf. Co.I
Tucker, Doceor P. AR 15th (N.W.) Inf. Co.C
Tucker, D.T. TN 43rd Inf. Co.I
Tucker, Dudley F. TX 6th Cav. Co.K
Tucker, D.W. TN 16th Inf. Co.B Ord.Sgt.
Tucker, D.W. TN 44th (Cons.) Inf. Co.G
Tucker, E. AL 62nd Inf. Co.F
Tucker, E. LA 27th Inf. Co.A
Tucker, E. TN 22nd (Barteau's) Cav. Co.G
Tucker, E. VA 3rd (Archer's) Bn.Res. Co.B
Tucker, E.A. FL Inf. 2nd Bn. Co.C
Tucker, E.A. FL 2nd Inf. Co.C
Tucker, E.A. TN 27th Inf. Co.H
Tucker, E.A. VA 3rd (Archer's) Bn.Res. Co.B
Tucker, E.B. VA 2nd St.Res. Co.C
Tucker, E.B. VA 3rd Inf.Loc.Def. Co.F
Tucker, Ebenezer D. TX 9th Field Btty.
Tucker, Ed AR Inf. 4th Bn. Co.A
Tucker, E.D. AR 10th Mil. Co.B
Tucker, Ed. AR 35th Inf. Co.A
Tucker, E.D. LA 6th Cav. Co.D
Tucker, Ed. MS 26th Inf. Co.A
Tucker, Edmond NC 46th Inf. Co.F Cpl.
Tucker, Edmond P. VA Hvy.Arty. 19th Bn. Co.D Sgt.
Tucker, Edward MS 2nd Cav. Co.C
Tucker, Edward TN 42nd Inf. 1st Co.F
Tucker, Edward VA 18th Cav. Co.C
Tucker, Edward VA Lt.Arty. Jeffress' Co.
Tucker, Edward B. VA Inf. 45th Bn. Co.B
Tucker, Edward D. FL 8th Inf. Co.K
Tucker, E.F. GA 2nd Cav. Co.D
Tucker, E.F. TN Cav. Jackson's Co.
Tucker, E.J. MS 2nd Inf. (A. of 10,000) Co.F
Tucker, Eli GA 32nd Inf. Co.K Sgt.
Tucker, Eli TN Inf. Tackitt's Co.
Tucker, Elias AL 49th Inf. Co.F
Tucker, Elias AR 1st (Colquitt's) Inf. Co.F
Tucker, Eli B. VA 53rd Inf. Co.D
Tucker, Eligha B. VA 50th Inf. Co.I
Tucker, Elijah FL 10th Inf. Co.F
Tucker, Elijah GA 4th (Clinch's) Cav. Co.F,H
Tucker, Elijah GA 12th Cav. Co.G
Tucker, Elijah MO Inf. 1st Regt.St.Guard Co.L 1st Lt.
Tucker, Elijah SC 5th Cav. Co.K
Tucker, Elijah SC 5th St.Troops Co.M
Tucker, Elijah SC 18th Inf. Co.A
Tucker, Elijah TN 18th Inf. Co.A
Tucker, Elijah TX 10th Inf. Co.E Cpl.
Tucker, Elijah 1st Cherokee Mtd.Vol. 2nd Co.B
Tucker, Elijah A. FL 10th Inf. Co.B Sgt.
Tucker, Elijah D. FL 8th Inf. Co.G
Tucker, Elisha GA Inf. 10th Bn. Co.B
Tucker, Elisha GA 49th Inf. Co.F
Tucker, Elisha MO 12th Cav. Co.E
Tucker, Ellis MS 33rd Inf. Co.F
Tucker, Ellis TX 16th Cav. Co.I
Tucker, Elzy W. TN 54th Inf. Co.G
Tucker, E.M. TX 12th Inf. Co.E
Tucker, Enoch AL 3rd Res. Co.A
Tucker, Enoch TN Cav. Nixon's Regt. Co.H
Tucker, Enoch I. MS 40th Inf. Co.I
Tucker, Enoch T. TN 34th Inf. Co.B
Tucker, E.P. MO Cav. Schnabel's Bn. Co.C
Tucker, Ephraim A. NC 1st Jr.Res. Co.G 2nd Lt.
Tucker, Eppes AL 45th Inf. Co.F
Tucker, Eppes GA Inf. 1st City Bn. (Columbus) Co.C
Tucker, E.R. GA 3rd Bn. (St.Guards) Co.C Sgt.
Tucker, E.R. TN 1st (Feild's) Inf. Co.I
Tucker, Erasmus VA Cav. McNeill's Co.
Tucker, Erasmus VA 14th Mil. Co.C
Tucker, Erastus B. VA 12th Inf. Co.C Cpl.
Tucker, E.S. TX Cav. 1st Bn.St.Troops Co.F
Tucker, E.S. TX 14th Inf. Co.H Drum.
Tucker, E.T. TX Cav. Baird's Regt. Co.B
Tucker, E.T. TX 5th Inf. Co.F
Tucker, Ethan VA Cav. 46th Bn. Co.C
Tucker, Everett J. MS 40th Inf. Co.C Sgt.
Tucker, E.W. NC 53rd Inf. Co.G 1st Sgt.
Tucker, E.W. NC 54th Inf. Co.G
Tucker, E.W. TN 48th (Nixon's) Inf. Co.K
Tucker, E.W. VA 19th Cav. Co.D
Tucker, E.W. Conf.Cav. Wood's Regt. Co.H
Tucker, Exton AL 12th Inf. Co.D Capt.
Tucker, F. MS 2nd Cav. Co.D
Tucker, F. VA 3rd Res. Co.G
Tucker, F.A. MS 18th Cav. Co.F
Tucker, F.A. VA 3rd Inf.Loc.Def. Co.F
Tucker, F.E. GA Inf. (Express Inf.) Witt's Co.
Tucker, Felix TX 2nd Cav. Co.D
Tucker, Ferdinand N. GA 2nd Inf. Co.C
Tucker, F.F. MO Cav. Fristoe's Regt. Co.L
Tucker, F.H. TX 3rd Cav. Co.E
Tucker, F.H. TX 1st Inf. 2nd Co.K Lt.
Tucker, F.M. AR 1st (Monroe's) Cav. Co.K
Tucker, F.M. AR 9th Inf. New Co.I Cpl.
Tucker, F.M. AR 11th Inf. Co.H
Tucker, F.M. AR 19th (Dockery's) Inf. Co.A
Tucker, F.M. LA 3rd Inf. Co.E Sgt.
Tucker, F.M. MS 25th Inf. Co.F
Tucker, F.M. MO 1st Inf. Co.C
Tucker, F.M. SC 18th Inf. Co.E Capt.
Tucker, F.M. TN 31st Inf. Co.C
Tucker, F.M. VA 10th Cav. Co.B Cpl.

Tucker, F.M. 2nd Conf.Inf. Co.G
Tucker, Francis TN 8th Inf. Co.K
Tucker, Francis J. NC 12th Inf. Co.F
Tucker, Francis M. LA 31st Inf. Co.H
Tucker, Francis M. MS 25th Inf. Co.G
Tucker, Francis M. MO 8th Cav. Co.F
Tucker, Frank AR 7th Mil. Co.B
Tucker, Frank MS 3rd Inf. Co.A Sgt.
Tucker, Frank TN 18th Inf. Co.A
Tucker, Frank TN 40th Inf. Co.I
Tucker, Frank E. MD Arty. 1st Btty.
Tucker, Frank J. TX Cav. Hardeman's Regt. Co.B
Tucker, Franklin AR Inf. 4th Bn. Co.A
Tucker, Franklin GA 14th Inf. Co.E
Tucker, Franklin NC 42nd Inf. Co.B
Tucker, Franklin V. TN Inf. Tackitt's Co.
Tucker, Fred VA Inf. Lyneman's Co.
Tucker, Frederick GA 49th Inf. Co.F
Tucker, G. TN 12th (Green's) Cav. Co.G
Tucker, G. TN 12th (Green's) Cav. Co.I
Tucker, G. 1st Cherokee Mtd.Vol. 1st Co.B
Tucker, Gabriel SC Lt.Arty. 3rd (Palmetto) Bn. Co.G,K
Tucker, Gabriel SC 8th Res.
Tucker, Gabriel H. NC Inf. 2nd Bn. Co.A
Tucker, Gallant TN 25th Inf. Co.F
Tucker, Gardner R. AR 7th Inf. Co.I Sgt.
Tucker, Gardner R. MO 10th Inf. Co.F Cpl.
Tucker, Garret L. VA 52nd Inf. Co.E
Tucker, G.D. LA 27th Inf. Co.G
Tucker, G.D. Inf. Bailey's Cons.Regt. Co.B
Tucker, G.E. GA 8th Cav. Co.G
Tucker, G.E. GA 62nd Cav. Co.G
Tucker, G.E. TN 40th Inf. Co.G
Tucker, George AL 56th Part.Rangers Co.E
Tucker, George AL 32nd Inf. Co.F Cpl.
Tucker, George AL 55th Vol. Co.E
Tucker, George AR 37th Inf. Co.K
Tucker, George AR 50th Mil. Co.G
Tucker, George GA 3rd Inf. Co.E
Tucker, George GA 46th Inf. Co.G
Tucker, George LA 27th Inf. Co.I Maj.
Tucker, George NC 46th Inf. Co.K
Tucker, George SC Cav. 17th Bn. Co.D Sgt.
Tucker, George SC 9th Res. Co.H
Tucker, George TN 5th (McKenzie's) Cav. Co.D Sgt.
Tucker, George TX 12th Inf. Co.G
Tucker, George VA 10th Inf. Co.L
Tucker, George VA 59th Inf. 3rd Co.I
Tucker, George 3rd Conf.Cav. Co.D
Tucker, George Gen. & Staff Maj.,QM
Tucker, George B. SC 9th Res. Co.G
Tucker, George B. VA 9th Inf. 2nd Co.H Cpl.
Tucker, George B. VA 12th Inf. 1st Co.I
Tucker, George D. TX 7th Inf. Co.D
Tucker, George H. MS Inf. 3rd Bn. Co.A
Tucker, George L. TN Cav. 5th Bn. (McClellan's) Co.A 2nd Lt.
Tucker, George L. TN Lt.Arty. Barry's Co.
Tucker, George M. AL 1st Regt.Conscr. Co.K
Tucker, George M. AL 25th Inf. Co.A Cpl.
Tucker, George M. NC 12th Inf. Co.K
Tucker, George M. VA Hvy.Arty. Allen's Co.
Tucker, George M. VA 20th Inf. Co.C
Tucker, George N. TN 44th (Cons.) Inf. Co.F
Tucker, George N. VA 82nd Mil. Co.C
Tucker, George P. GA 21st Inf. Co.B
Tucker, George T. NC 37th Inf. Co.D
Tucker, George T. VA 38th Inf. Co.G
Tucker, George W. AL Arty. 1st Bn. Co.F
Tucker, George W. AL 22nd Inf. Co.B
Tucker, George W. AL 27th Inf. Co.B
Tucker, George W. AL 49th Inf. Co.E Sgt.
Tucker, George W. AL 54th Inf. Co.I
Tucker, George W. AL 63rd Inf. Co.C Cpl.
Tucker, George W. AR Cav. Reves' Co.
Tucker, George W. GA 11th Cav. (St.Guards) Tillman's Co.
Tucker, George W. GA 24th Inf. Co.A
Tucker, George W. GA 39th Inf. Co.G
Tucker, George W. MS Inf. 3rd Bn. Co.F Cpl.
Tucker, George W. MS 9th Inf. New Co.I
Tucker, George W. MS 9th Bn.S.S. Co.C
Tucker, George W. MS 10th Inf. New Co.E
Tucker, George W. MS 17th Inf. Co.B
Tucker, George W. MO Cav. 2nd Bn.St.Guard Co.B 1st Sgt.
Tucker, George W. MO 11th Inf. Co.E
Tucker, George W. TN Hvy.Arty. Caruthers' Btty.
Tucker, George W. TN 53rd Inf. Co.C Cpl.
Tucker, George W. TN 55th (Brown's) Inf.
Tucker, George W. VA 3rd Lt.Arty. Co.C
Tucker, George W. VA Inf. 28th Bn. Co.D
Tucker, George W., Jr. VA 34th Inf. Co.F
Tucker, George W. VA 36th Inf. 2nd Co.C 2nd Lt.
Tucker, George W. VA 38th Inf. Co.F
Tucker, George W. VA Inf. 44th Bn. Co.B
Tucker, George W., Jr. A.P. Hill's Couriers Sgt.
Tucker, George W.S. NC 12th Inf. Co.F
Tucker, G.G. VA 3rd (Archer's) Bn.Res. Co.B
Tucker, G.H. AL 11th Inf. Co.A
Tucker, G.H. TN 2nd (Ashby's) Cav. Co.A
Tucker, Gideon TN 18th Inf. Co.F
Tucker, Gideon TN 44th Inf. Co.I
Tucker, Gideon TN 44th (Cons.) Inf. Co.A
Tucker, G.J. SC 1st Mtd.Mil. Smith's Co. Cpl.
Tucker, G.K. 1st Conf.Cav. 1st Co.D
Tucker, G.L. TN 22nd (Barteau's) Cav. Co.K
Tucker, G.L. TN 27th Inf. Co.C
Tucker, G.M. MO 11th Inf. Co.E Cpl.
Tucker, G.M. TN 3rd (Forrest's) Cav. Co.I
Tucker, G.M. TN 12th (Green's) Cav. Co.H
Tucker, G. Picket SC Inf. Hampton Legion Co.B Sgt.
Tucker, G.R. MS 1st (Patton's) Inf. Co.E
Tucker, G.R. MS 37th Inf. Co.I
Tucker, G.R. MO Cav. Freeman's Regt. Co.D
Tucker, Granville TN Cav. 2nd Bn. (Biffle's) Co.F Bugler
Tucker, Granville TN Cav. Jackson's Co.
Tucker, Gratton VA 4th Cav. Co.C
Tucker, Green TN 7th (Duckworth's) Cav. Co.B
Tucker, Green C. GA 44th Inf. Co.B
Tucker, Green H. TN 4th (McLemore's) Cav. Co.G
Tucker, G.S. Conf.Cav. Wood's Regt. 2nd Co.F
Tucker, G.T. SC 23rd Inf. Co.I
Tucker, G.W. AL 31st Inf. Co.B
Tucker, G.W. GA Inf. 27th Bn. (NonConscr.) Co.B
Tucker, G.W. MS 2nd Cav. Co.E
Tucker, G.W. MO 15th Cav. Co.C
Tucker, G.W. MO 11th Inf. Co.D
Tucker, G.W. NC 12th Inf. Co.K
Tucker, G.W. TN 17th Inf. Co.F
Tucker, G.W. TN 20th Inf. Co.I
Tucker, G.W. TN 36th Inf. Co.B Cpl.
Tucker, G.W. TX 37th Cav. 2nd Co.I
Tucker, G.W. TX 18th Inf. Co.H Sgt.
Tucker, H. AL 15th Cav. Co.A
Tucker, H. AR 7th Mil. Co.E
Tucker, H. GA 54th Inf.
Tucker, H. GA Inf. Collier's Co.
Tucker, H. SC 7th Cav. Co.G
Tucker, H. SC Mil.Arty. 1st Regt. Werner's Co.
Tucker, H. SC Lt.Arty. Wagener's Co. (Co.A, German Arty.)
Tucker, H. SC Inf. Hampton Legion Co.I
Tucker, H. TN 26th Inf. Co.C
Tucker, H. TX Cav. 3rd Regt.St.Troops Townsend's Co.
Tucker, Hampton AR 2nd Inf. Co.G
Tucker, Hampton B. SC 24th Inf. Co.I
Tucker, Hard TN 11th (Holman's) Cav. Co.K
Tucker, Hard TN Holman's Bn.Part.Rangers Co.D
Tucker, Harden E. NC 38th Inf. Co.I
Tucker, Hardin TN 6th (Wheeler's) Cav. Co.K
Tucker, Hardy AR Lt.Arty. Zimmerman's Btty.
Tucker, Hardy AR 15th (N.W.) Inf. Co.D
Tucker, Hardy G. MS 39th Inf. Co.G
Tucker, Harrison VA 39th Mil. Co.B
Tucker, Harrison VA 41st Inf. Co.C
Tucker, Harrison S. TN 44th Inf. Co.B
Tucker, Hartwell M. GA 20th Inf. Co.A 1st Sgt.
Tucker, Haywood TN 46th Inf. Co.B
Tucker, H.C. GA 13th Inf. Co.H 1st Sgt.
Tucker, H.C. GA 42nd Inf. Co.F
Tucker, H.C. TN 15th (Stewart's) Cav. Co.F
Tucker, H.C. 1st Conf.Cav. 2nd Co.E
Tucker, Henry GA 35th Inf. Co.H
Tucker, Henry KY 5th Mtd.Inf. Co.E
Tucker, Henry KY Inf. Ficklin's Bn. Marshall's Co.
Tucker, Henry MO Cav. Ford's Bn. Co.E
Tucker, Henry MO Lt.Arty. Parsons' Co.
Tucker, Henry NC Hvy.Arty. 10th Bn. Co.B
Tucker, Henry NC 5th Sr.Res. Co.H
Tucker, Henry NC 12th Inf. Co.H Sgt.
Tucker, Henry NC 46th Inf. Co.F
Tucker, Henry SC 1st (Butler's) Inf. Co.A
Tucker, Henry SC 5th Inf. 1st Co.F Cpl.
Tucker, Henry SC Inf. Hampton Legion Co.K
Tucker, Henry SC Palmetto S.S. Co.D
Tucker, Henry TX 14th Cav. Co.B 2nd Lt.
Tucker, Henry B. AL 11th Inf. Co.A
Tucker, Henry H. GA 28th Inf. Co.H
Tucker, Henry H. TX 13th Cav. Co.D
Tucker, Henry H. TX 16th Cav. Co.H 1st Lt.
Tucker, Henry L. AL 43rd Inf. Co.A
Tucker, Henry M. SC Inf. 9th Bn. Co.D Lt.
Tucker, Henry P. VA Lt.Arty. Brander's Co.
Tucker, Henry S. GA 50th Inf. Co.H Sgt.
Tucker, Henry T. MS 9th Inf. Old Co.E
Tucker, Henry T. MS 10th Inf. New Co.A
Tucker, Henry T. VA 56th Inf. Co.K Cpl.
Tucker, Henry T. Gen. & Staff Capt.,QM

Tucker, Henry W. AL 6th Inf. Co.C
Tucker, H.H. GA 59th Inf. Co.D
Tucker, H.H. TX Vol. Teague's Co. (So.Rights Guards)
Tucker, Hillery TX Cav. Mann's Regt. Co.A
Tucker, Hillery TX Cav. Mann's Bn. Co.A
Tucker, Hillery VA 53rd Inf. Co.C
Tucker, Hillory VA Inf. 5th Bn. Co.C
Tucker, Hinton G. VA 3rd Cav. Co.H
Tucker, Hiram AR Inf. 4th Bn. Co.A
Tucker, Hiram GA 1st Inf.
Tucker, Hiram TN 2nd (Ashby's) Cav. Co.E
Tucker, Hiram TN Cav. 4th Bn. (Branner's) Co.D
Tucker, Hiram H. TN 5th (McKenzie's) Cav. Co.G
Tucker, H.J. MS 18th Cav. Co.H
Tucker, H.L. AL 26th (O'Neal's) Inf. Co.H
Tucker, H.L. AR 27th Inf. Co.G
Tucker, H.L. MS Cav. 3rd Bn.Res. Co.D
Tucker, H.L. MS Inf. 2nd Bn. (St.Troops) Co.F
Tucker, H.M. SC 7th Cav. Co.A 1st Lt.
Tucker, H.M. SC Cav. Tucker's Co.
Tucker, H.M. SC 26th Inf. Co.E 1st Lt.
Tucker, Horten TN Cav. Newsom's Regt. Co.G
Tucker, Howel H. TN 32nd Inf. Co.A 2nd Lt.
Tucker, H.R. TX 4th Cav. Co.B
Tucker, I. MS Inf. 1st St.Troops Co.I
Tucker, I.J. MS 37th Inf. Co.I
Tucker, I.M.B. LA Maddox's Regt.Res.Corps Co.B
Tucker, I.R. TX 35th (Brown's) Cav. Co.F
Tucker, Ira AR 1st (Crawford's) Cav. Co.I
Tucker, Isaac MS 35th Inf. Co.E
Tucker, Isaac TN 62nd Mtd.Inf. Co.F
Tucker, Isaac Lt.Arty. Dent's Btty.,CSA
Tucker, Isaac M. AR Inf. Clayton's Co. Sgt.
Tucker, Isaac M. AR 27th Inf. Co.B 1st Lt.
Tucker, Isaac M. MO 10th Inf. Co.F 1st Sgt.
Tucker, Isadore TX 5th Inf. Co.B
Tucker, I.W. MS Lt.Arty. (Issaquena Arty.) Graves' Co.
Tucker, J. AL Coosa Guards J.W. Suttles' Co.
Tucker, J. AR 4th Inf. Co.A
Tucker, J. AR 19th Inf. Co.A
Tucker, J. GA 10th Mil.
Tucker, J. GA Lt.Arty. Barnwell's Btty.
Tucker, J. KY 3rd Mtd.Inf. Co.G
Tucker, J. SC Mil. 16th Regt. Robinson's Co. Cpl.
Tucker, J. TN 15th (Cons.) Cav. Co.I
Tucker, J. TN 20th Inf. Co.E
Tucker, J. TN 29th Inf.
Tucker, J. TX Cav. Giddings' Bn. Weisiger's Co.
Tucker, J.A. AL 29th Inf. Co.K
Tucker, J.A. AL 46th Inf. Co.B
Tucker, J.A. AR 18th Inf. Co.K
Tucker, J.A. AR 34th Inf. Co.B
Tucker, J.A. GA 63rd Inf. Co.D
Tucker, J.A. MS 7th Cav. Co.C
Tucker, J.A. MS 2nd (Davidson's) Inf. Co.I
Tucker, J.A. NC 4th Bn.Jr.Res. Co.D
Tucker, J.A. NC 43rd Inf. Co.A
Tucker, J.A. SC 1st Cav. Co.I
Tucker, J.A. VA 2nd Arty. Co.E
Tucker, Jackson J. AL 3rd Res. Co.D
Tucker, Jacob AL 55th Vol. Co.B
Tucker, Jacob GA 49th Inf. Co.F
Tucker, Jacob NC 33rd Inf. Co.C
Tucker, Jacob VA 10th Cav. Co.A Cpl.
Tucker, Jacob VA 19th Cav. Co.D
Tucker, Jacob VA 31st Inf. Co.A
Tucker, Jacob M. TN 39th Mtd.Inf. Co.D Cpl.
Tucker, Jacob N. TN 3rd (Clack's) Inf. Co.A
Tucker, James AL 3rd Cav. Co.B
Tucker, James AL 11th Inf. Co.D
Tucker, James AL 36th Inf. Co.H
Tucker, James AL 49th Inf. Co.F
Tucker, James AL Cp. of Instr. Talladega
Tucker, James AR Lt.Arty. Wiggins' Btty.
Tucker, James AR Inf. 4th Bn. Co.A
Tucker, Jas. AR 13th Inf. Co.H
Tucker, James FL 8th Inf. Co.A
Tucker, James FL 8th Inf. Co.H Capt.
Tucker, James GA 3rd Res. Co.C
Tucker, James GA 11th Inf. Co.E
Tucker, James GA 49th Inf. Co.F
Tucker, James KY Lt.Arty. Cobb's Co.
Tucker, James KY 4th Mtd.Inf. Co.D
Tucker, James LA 10th Inf. Co.F
Tucker, James MS 3rd Inf. Co.K
Tucker, James MS 39th Inf. Co.G
Tucker, James MO 6th Cav. Co.C
Tucker, James MO Cav. Fristoe's Regt. Co.A
Tucker, James MO Inf. 4th Regt.St.Guard Co.A
Tucker, James NC 58th Inf. Co.G,M
Tucker, James SC 22nd Inf. Co.D
Tucker, James TN 16th (Logwood's) Cav. Co.E
Tucker, James TN 1st (Feild's) Inf. Co.H
Tucker, James TN 1st (Turney's) Inf. Co.B
Tucker, James TX 15th Cav. Co.C Capt.
Tucker, James TX 8th Field Btty. 1st Lt.
Tucker, James TX Lt.Arty. Dege's Bn. Co.C 1st Lt.
Tucker, James VA Lt.Arty. Brander's Co. Cpl.
Tucker, James VA 82nd Mil. Co.D
Tucker, James Conf.Cav. Wood's Regt. 1st Co.M
Tucker, James Gen. & Staff AAQM
Tucker, James A. AL 11th Cav. Co.B
Tucker, James A. AL 39th Inf. Co.B
Tucker, James A. AL 43rd Inf. Co.A
Tucker, James A. AR 9th Inf. Old Co.B, Co.F
Tucker, James A. LA 13th Inf. Co.G,E
Tucker, James A. SC Inf. Holcombe Legion Co.I
Tucker, James A. VA 17th Cav. Co.A
Tucker, James A. VA 3rd Inf. Co.A
Tucker, James A. VA 45th Inf. Co.D
Tucker, James A. VA 61st Inf. Co.H
Tucker, James B. AL 6th Cav. Co.M
Tucker, James B. AL 16th Inf. Co.B
Tucker, James B. AR 2nd Inf. Co.F
Tucker, James B. AR 33rd Inf. Co.G
Tucker, James B. NC Inf. 2nd Bn. Co.A 1st Lt.
Tucker, James B. SC 5th Inf. 1st Co.A
Tucker, James C. TX 16th Cav. Co.H
Tucker, James D. AL 6th Inf. Co.C
Tucker, James D. AL 11th Inf. Co.A
Tucker, James D. GA 53rd Inf. Co.I
Tucker, James D. TN 24th Inf. Co.K
Tucker, James D. VA Hvy.Arty. 10th Bn. Co.E
Tucker, James E. MO 6th Cav. Co.A Sgt.
Tucker, James E. VA 2nd Cav. Co.K
Tucker, James E. VA 2nd Arty. Co.D
Tucker, James E. VA Arty. Paris' Co.
Tucker, James E. VA Inf. 22nd Bn. Co.D
Tucker, James E. VA 56th Inf. Co.K
Tucker, James E. VA 61st Inf. Co.B Sgt.
Tucker, James F. FL 9th Inf. Co.D Capt.
Tucker, James F. LA 13th & 20th Inf. Co.K
Tucker, James F. Gen. & Staff 2nd Lt.,Dr.M.
Tucker, James G. VA 53rd Inf. Co.F 1st Sgt.
Tucker, James G. VA Inf. Montague's Bn. Co.C Sgt.
Tucker, James H. AL 42nd Inf. Co.G
Tucker, James H. NC 12th Inf. Co.I
Tucker, James H. TN 24th Inf. Co.I
Tucker, James H. TN 62nd Mtd.Inf. Co.B
Tucker, James H. VA 11th Cav. Co.D
Tucker, James H. VA 2nd Arty. Co.E
Tucker, James J. AR 4th Inf. Co.E
Tucker, James J. NC 56th Inf. Co.G
Tucker, James John NC 17th Inf. (1st Org.) Co.C
Tucker, James K.P. GA 27th Inf. Co.E
Tucker, James L. AL 37th Inf. Co.E
Tucker, James L. GA 13th Inf. Co.E Sgt.Maj.
Tucker, James L. GA 34th Inf. Co.D Cpl.
Tucker, James L. MS 17th Inf. Co.B
Tucker, James L. MO 12th Cav. Co.D Capt.
Tucker, James L. TN Lt.Arty. Burroughs' Co.
Tucker, James M. AL 6th Cav. Co.A
Tucker, James M. AL 45th Inf. Co.F
Tucker, James M. AR 2nd Inf. Co.K
Tucker, James M. AR 4th Inf. Co.E
Tucker, James M. AR 15th Mil. Co.C Cpl.
Tucker, James M. AR 26th Inf. Co.H
Tucker, James M. FL 7th Inf. Co.F
Tucker, James M. GA 1st Reg. Co.K
Tucker, James M. GA 2nd Inf.
Tucker, James M. GA 35th Inf. Co.G
Tucker, James M. MS 7th Cav. Co.I
Tucker, James M. NC 44th Inf. Co.F
Tucker, James M. TX 8th Cav. Co.B
Tucker, James M. TX 16th Cav. Co.B 2nd Lt.
Tucker, James M. TX 18th Inf. Co.D AQM
Tucker, James M. VA 22nd Inf. Co.B Sgt.
Tucker, James M. VA 3rd Cav. & Inf.St.Line Co.A
Tucker, James M. Gen. & Staff Capt.,AQM
Tucker, James Monroe LA 8th Inf. Co.A
Tucker, James O.A. AL 46th Inf. Co.B
Tucker, James P. MO 2nd Cav. 3rd Co.K
Tucker, James P. NC 1st Cav. (9th St.Troops) Co.H Sgt.
Tucker, James P. NC 8th Sr.Res. Broadhurst's Co.
Tucker, James P. NC Inf. 13th Bn. Co.B Sgt.
Tucker, James P. NC 66th Inf. Co.B Music.
Tucker, James P. TN 9th Inf. Co.B
Tucker, James P. VA 6th Cav. Co.G
Tucker, James P. VA 9th Inf. 2nd Co.H
Tucker, James P. VA 38th Inf. Co.F
Tucker, James R. FL Cav. 3rd Bn. Co.A Bvt.2nd Lt.
Tucker, James R. VA 41st Inf. 2nd Co.E
Tucker, James R. 15th Conf.Cav. Co.A 1st Lt.
Tucker, James R.P. GA Inf. 9th Bn. Co.B
Tucker, James R.P. GA 37th Inf. Co.E
Tucker, James R.W. GA 41st Inf. Co.F Sgt.
Tucker, James S. MS 8th Inf. Co.I

Tucker, James S. MS 14th Inf. Co.G
Tucker, James T. AL 21st Inf. Co.B
Tucker, James T. FL 2nd Inf. Co.K 2nd Lt.
Tucker, James T. TN 2nd (Robison's) Inf. Co.B
Tucker, James T. VA 56th Inf. Co.K
Tucker, James W. GA 63rd Inf. Co.A
Tucker, James W. MS 40th Inf. Co.C
Tucker, James W. TN 8th Inf.
Tucker, James W. VA 18th Cav. Co.B Cpl.
Tucker, James W. VA 38th Inf. Co.F
Tucker, James W. VA 62nd Mtd.Inf. 1st Co.G Cpl.
Tucker, James William TX 2nd Cav. Co.A
Tucker, J.A.P. AL 23rd Inf. Co.F
Tucker, Jarrott TN 4th (McLemore's) Cav. Co.G Sgt.
Tucker, Jasper GA 61st Inf. Co.A Cpl.
Tucker, J.B. AL Coosa Guards J.W. Suttles' Co.
Tucker, J.B. LA 2nd Inf. Co.A
Tucker, J.B. MS Blythe's Bn. (St.Troops) Co.A
Tucker, J.B. NC 4th Sr.Res. Co.H
Tucker, J.B. SC Palmetto S.S. Co.A
Tucker, J.B. TN 9th Inf. Co.K
Tucker, J.B. TN 12th (Cons.) Inf. Co.G
Tucker, J.B. TX 7th Cav. Co.I
Tucker, J.B. TX Vol. Teague's Co. (So.Rights Guards)
Tucker, J.C. AL 4th Inf. Co.D,B
Tucker, J.C. MS 3rd Inf. (A. of 10,000) Co.G
Tucker, J.C. MS Blythe's Bn. (St.Troops) Co.A
Tucker, J.C. MS Res.Corps Withers' Co.
Tucker, J.C. NC 44th Inf. Co.H
Tucker, J.C. TX 10th Field Btty.
Tucker, J.C. 1st Conf.Cav. 2nd Co.E
Tucker, J.D. AL 8th (Livingston's) Cav. Co.C
Tucker, J.D. AL 9th Inf. Co.F
Tucker, J.D. AL 33rd Inf. Co.E
Tucker, J.D. AL 45th Inf. Co.B
Tucker, J.D. AR 36th Inf. Co.B
Tucker, J.D. TN 45th Inf. Co.H
Tucker, J.E. AL 5th Cav. Co.H
Tucker, J.E. AL 6th Cav. Co.F
Tucker, J.E. FL 2nd Inf. Co.C
Tucker, J.E. TX 9th (Young's) Inf. Co.H
Tucker, Jef. AL 26th (O'Neal's) Inf. Co.C
Tucker, Jeff AL 12th Inf. Co.F
Tucker, Jeff KY 6th Cav. Co.B
Tucker, Jeptha TX 7th Cav. Co.I
Tucker, Jeremiah TX 16th Cav. Co.F Bugler
Tucker, Jeremiah D. MS 40th Inf. Co.H Cpl.
Tucker, Jeremiah L. AL 23rd Inf. Co.C Cpl.
Tucker, Jerry MS Cav. Jeff Davis Legion Co.E
Tucker, Jerry MS Inf. 2nd Bn. Co.K
Tucker, Jerry MS 48th Inf. Co.K
Tucker, Jerry TX 24th Cav. Co.G
Tucker, Jerry 1st Cherokee Mtd.Rifles Co.H
Tucker, Jery M. AR 33rd Inf. Co.A
Tucker, Jesse AR Lt.Arty. Owen's Btty.
Tucker, Jesse TN 23rd Inf. Co.B
Tucker, Jesse B. FL 9th Inf. Co.C
Tucker, Jesse B. FL Parsons' Co.
Tucker, Jesse B. LA Inf. 4th Bn. Co.C Sgt.
Tucker, Jesse B. VA 31st Inf. Co.A
Tucker, Jesse D. NC 46th Inf. Co.F Ord.Sgt.
Tucker, Jessee AL 55th Vol. Co.B
Tucker, Jessee NC 6th Sr.Res. Co.A
Tucker, Jessee W. AL 1st Regt.Conscr. Co.A
Tucker, Jesse H. FL 9th Inf. Co.C
Tucker, Jesse H. FL Parsons' Co.
Tucker, Jesse M. NC 37th Inf. Co.D
Tucker, Jesse T. VA 3rd Lt.Arty. (Loc.Def.) Co.C
Tucker, Jesse T. VA 59th Inf. 3rd Co.I
Tucker, Jesse W. AL 57th Inf. Co.K
Tucker, J.F. AL 8th Cav. Co.A
Tucker, J.F. AL 40th Inf. Co.G
Tucker, J.F. LA 25th Inf. Co.K
Tucker, J.F. TN 40th Inf. Co.I
Tucker, J.G. LA Mil.Conf.Guards Regt. Co.E
Tucker, J.G. SC 5th Cav. Co.C
Tucker, J.G. VA Inf. 44th Bn. Co.C
Tucker, J.H. AR Lt.Arty. Owen's Btty.
Tucker, J.H. LA 27th Inf. Co.G 1st Lt.
Tucker, J.H. MS 12th Cav. Co.E
Tucker, J.H. MS 28th Cav. Co.H
Tucker, J.H. MS 39th Inf.
Tucker, J.H. NC Mallett's Bn. Co.A
Tucker, J.H. SC 19th Inf. Co.G
Tucker, J.H. TN 20th Inf. Co.D
Tucker, J.H. VA 1st (Farinholt's) Res. Co.D Cpl.
Tucker, J.H. VA Inf. 1st Bn. Co.B
Tucker, J.H. VA Conscr. Cp.Lee Co.A
Tucker, J.H. 15th Conf.Cav. Co.A
Tucker, J.H. Gen. & Staff AQM
Tucker, J.H.F. AR 1st (Monroe's) Cav. Co.G
Tucker, J.H.F. TN 40th Inf. Co.G
Tucker, J.I. TN 3rd (Forrest's) Cav. 1st Co.E
Tucker, J.J. SC 14th Inf. Co.I
Tucker, J.J. TX 31st Cav. Co.H
Tucker, J.K. TN 10th (DeMoss') Cav. Co.K
Tucker, J.K.P. KY 3rd Bn.Mtd.Rifles Co.B Cpl.
Tucker, J.K.P. TN 19th (Biffle's) Cav. Co.D
Tucker, J.K.P. TN 21st & 22nd (Cons.) Cav. Co.F
Tucker, J.L. AL 13th Inf. Co.A
Tucker, J.L. AL 21st Inf. Co.C
Tucker, J.L. AR 21st Mil. Co.G Cpl.
Tucker, J.L. GA 25th Inf. Co.C 3rd Lt.
Tucker, J.L. GA 42nd Inf. Co.E Sgt.
Tucker, J.L. MO Quantrill's Co. Sgt.
Tucker, J.L. VA Cav. 35th Bn. Co.C
Tucker, J.M. AL 8th (Livingston's) Cav. Co.C
Tucker, J.M. AL 5th Inf. New Co.I
Tucker, J.M. AL 17th Inf. Co.F
Tucker, J.M. AR 1st (Monroe's) Cav. Co.G
Tucker, J.M. AR 8th Cav. Co.D 3rd Lt.
Tucker, J.M. AR Cav. Gordon's Regt. Co.E
Tucker, J.M. AR 11th Inf. Co.G Sgt.
Tucker, J.M. AR 11th Inf. Co.H
Tucker, J.M. AR 11th & 17th Cons.Inf. Co.G Sgt.
Tucker, J.M. AR 35th Inf. Co.H
Tucker, J.M. GA 16th Inf. Co.F Sgt.
Tucker, J.M. GA 32nd Inf. Co.A
Tucker, J.M. MS 4th Inf. Co.E
Tucker, J.M. MS 15th Inf. Co.E,B
Tucker, J.M. MO 11th Inf. Co.D
Tucker, J.M. NC 13th Inf. Co.A,F
Tucker, J.M. SC 2nd Arty. Co.I
Tucker, J.M. TN 18th Inf. Co.H
Tucker, J.M. TX 7th Cav. Co.C Sgt.
Tucker, J.M. TX 10th Cav. Co.D 1st Sgt.
Tucker, J.M. TX Cav. Terry's Regt. Co.B
Tucker, J.M. VA 1st (Farinholt's) Res. Co.B
Tucker, J.M. Exch.Bn. Co.E,CSA
Tucker, J.M.H. GA 54th Inf. Co.G
Tucker, J.N. AL 8th (Livingston's) Cav. Co.C
Tucker, J.N. AR Cav. Gordon's Regt. Co.C
Tucker, J.N. AR 10th Mil. Co.E Sgt.
Tucker, J.N. TN 47th Inf. Co.H
Tucker, J.N. TX 5th Cav. Co.F Sgt.
Tucker, J.O. MS 6th Cav. Co.K
Tucker, Joel 15th Conf.Cav. Co.A
Tucker, Joel A. NC 53rd Inf. Co.G
Tucker, Joel B. VA 21st Inf. Co.H
Tucker, Joel H. FL Cav. 3rd Bn. Co.A
Tucker, Joel P. VA 38th Inf. Co.F
Tucker, John AL 1st Cav. 2nd Co.E
Tucker, John AL 8th (Livingston's) Cav. Co.C
Tucker, John AL 8th Inf. Co.A
Tucker, John AR 1st (Monroe's) Cav. Co.F
Tucker, John AR Inf. Adams' Regt. Moore's Co.
Tucker, John GA 11th Cav. (St.Guards) Tillman's Co. Ens.
Tucker, John, Jr. GA Cav. 16th Bn. (St.Guards) Co.G
Tucker, John GA 12th Mil. 1st Lt.
Tucker, John GA 50th Inf. Co.H Bvt.2nd Lt.
Tucker, John GA 54th Inf. Co.E
Tucker, John GA 64th Inf. Co.I
Tucker, John Weems' Detach.Cp.Guard
Tucker, John LA 1st Inf. Co.E
Tucker, John LA 21st (Kennedy's) Inf. Co.E
Tucker, John MS 9th Cav. Co.D
Tucker, John MS 11th (Perrin's) Cav. Co.G
Tucker, John MS Cav. Ham's Regt. Co.G
Tucker, John MS 1st Lt.Arty. Co.K
Tucker, John MS Inf. 7th Bn. Co.C
Tucker, John MS 11th Inf. Co.A
Tucker, John MS 17th Inf. Co.K
Tucker, John MO 1st Cav. Co.D
Tucker, John MO 6th Cav. Co.C
Tucker, John MO Lt.Arty. Parsons' Co.
Tucker, John MO 6th Inf. Co.I
Tucker, John MO 10th Inf. Co.E
Tucker, John NC 24th Inf. Co.F
Tucker, John NC 57th Inf. Co.B
Tucker, John NC Mallett's Bn. (Cp.Guard)
Tucker, John SC 5th Cav. Co.B
Tucker, John SC Cav. 17th Bn. Co.C
Tucker, John SC 1st (Butler's) Inf. Co.A
Tucker, John SC 8th Res.
Tucker, John SC 21st Inf. Co.I
Tucker, John TN 19th & 20th (Cons.) Cav. Co.E
Tucker, John TN 1st Hvy.Arty. 2nd Co.B
Tucker, John TN 1st (Feild's) Inf. Co.L
Tucker, John TN 27th Inf. Co.C
Tucker, John TN 28th Inf. Co.I,E
Tucker, John TN 28th (Cons.) Inf. Co.D
Tucker, John TN 37th Inf. Co.B
Tucker, John TN 48th (Voorhies') Inf. Co.K
Tucker, John TN 63rd Inf. Co.H
Tucker, John TN Miller's Co. (Loc.Def.Troops) Sgt.
Tucker, John TX 7th Cav. Co.C
Tucker, John TX 11th (Spaight's) Bn.Vol. Co.E
Tucker, John TX 21st Inf. Co.B
Tucker, John TX Waul's Legion Co.F
Tucker, John VA Lt.Arty. Brander's Co.
Tucker, John VA 22nd Inf. Co.K

Tucker, John 1st Cherokee Mtd.Rifles Co.B Black.
Tucker, John Conf.Inf. Tucker's Regt. Co.C
Tucker, John A. AL 37th Inf.
Tucker, John A. GA 12th Cav. Co.L
Tucker, John A. GA 21st Inf. Co.B Capt.
Tucker, John A. LA 9th Inf. Co.I
Tucker, John A. MO 12th Cav. Co.D Cpl.
Tucker, John A. NC 42nd Inf. Co.B
Tucker, John A. TN 11th (Holman's) Cav. Co.G
Tucker, John A. TN Holman's Bn.Part.Rangers Co.B
Tucker, John A. VA Inf. 22nd Bn. Co.B Capt.
Tucker, John A. VA Inf. 22nd Bn. Co.E
Tucker, John A. VA 23rd Inf. Co.K 2nd Lt.
Tucker, John A.P. AL 46th Inf. Co.B
Tucker, John B. AR 17th (Griffith's) Inf. Co.B 1st Lt.
Tucker, John B. MS 28th Cav. Co.H Capt.
Tucker, John B. NC 44th Inf. Co.A 1st Lt.
Tucker, John B. TN 8th Cav. Co.B
Tucker, John B. TX 8th Cav. Co.B
Tucker, John B. TX 2nd Inf. Co.A 2nd Lt.
Tucker, John C. MS 39th Inf. Co.I Cpl.
Tucker, John C. NC 52nd Inf. Co.G
Tucker, John C. TN 32nd Inf. Co.E
Tucker, John D. FL 7th Inf. Co.B
Tucker, John D. NC 46th Inf. Co.C
Tucker, John D. TN 3rd (Clack's) Inf. Co.F
Tucker, John D. VA 56th Inf. Co.K
Tucker, John E. AL 29th Inf. Co.K
Tucker, John E. VA 5th Cav. Co.B
Tucker, John E. VA 24th Cav. Co.D
Tucker, John E. VA Cav. 40th Bn. Co.D
Tucker, John E.A. GA 7th Inf. Co.I
Tucker, John F. AL 14th Inf. Co.A
Tucker, John F. MO 4th Cav. Co.I Cpl.
Tucker, John F. TN 2nd (Ashby's) Cav. Co.A
Tucker, John F. TN 5th (McKenzie's) Cav. Co.C
Tucker, John F. NC 4th Sr.Res. Co.F
Tucker, John F. TN Inf. Nashville Bn. Fulcher's Co.
Tucker, John H. GA 61st Inf. Co.A
Tucker, John H. MS Inf. 3rd Bn. Co.A
Tucker, John H. MS 10th Inf. New Co.I 2nd Lt.
Tucker, John H. MO 12th Cav. Co.D
Tucker, John H. NC 12th Inf. Co.H
Tucker, John H. SC 7th Cav. Co.A Capt.
Tucker, John H. SC Cav. Tucker's Co. Capt.
Tucker, John H. VA 3rd Cav. 2nd Co.I
Tucker, John H. VA 61st Inf. Co.B 1st Sgt.
Tucker, John H. Forrest's Scouts T. Henderson's Co.,CSA
Tucker, Jno. H. Gen. & Staff AASurg.
Tucker, John J. GA 1st (Symons') Res. Co.G
Tucker, John J. GA 9th Inf. Co.H
Tucker, John J. GA 60th Inf. Co.A Capt.
Tucker, John J. LA Miles' Legion Co.B
Tucker, John J. MO Inf. 5th Regt.St.Guard Co.E Capt.
Tucker, John J. NC Inf. 2nd Bn. Co.E Capt.
Tucker, John J. VA 19th Cav. Co.B Cpl.
Tucker, John L. GA Inf. 3rd Bn. Co.G
Tucker, John L. GA 42nd Inf. Co.G
Tucker, John M. AL 41st Inf. Co.E
Tucker, John M. GA 6th Inf. (St.Guards) Co.F
Tucker, John M. NC 42nd Inf. Co.B
Tucker, John M. VA 3rd Cav. Co.A
Tucker, John M. VA 41st Inf. Co.B Capt.
Tucker, John M. Gen. & Staff Capt.
Tucker, John N. MS 18th Inf. Co.G
Tucker, John N. VA Cav. 46th Bn. Co.C
Tucker, John N. VA 21st Inf. Co.H
Tucker, John O. MS St.Cav. Perrin's Bn. Co.F
Tucker, John O. NC 42nd Inf. Co.H
Tucker, John P. NC Mil. 66th Bn. J.H. Whitman's Co.
Tucker, John P. NC McMillan's Co.
Tucker, John P. TN 9th Inf.
Tucker, John P. VA 9th Inf. 2nd Co.H
Tucker, John P. VA 12th Inf. 1st Co.I
Tucker, John R. GA 28th Inf. Co.A Capt.
Tucker, John R. KY 2nd (Duke's) Cav. Co.H,E
Tucker, John R. NC 37th Inf. Co.B
Tucker, John R.A. FL 7th Inf. Co.A 1st Sgt.
Tucker, John R.C. TN 53rd Inf. Co.A
Tucker, John R.V. AL 57th Inf. Co.F
Tucker, John S. AL Inf. 1st Regt. Co.E
Tucker, John S. AL 5th Inf. New Co.D
Tucker, John S. GA Cherokee Legion (St.Guard) Co.C,B Sgt.
Tucker, John S. MS Cav. Jeff Davis Legion Co.E
Tucker, John S. MO 3rd Inf. Co.H 1st Sgt.
Tucker, John S. VA Hvy.Arty. 19th Bn. Co.D
Tucker, John S. VA Inf. 5th Bn.Loc.Def. Co.D Capt.
Tucker, John S. Gen. & Staff, Arty. Capt.
Tucker, John T. AL 32nd Inf. Co.G
Tucker, John T. AR Inf. Crawford's Bn. Co.B
Tucker, John T. GA 38th Inf. Co.A,D
Tucker, John T. MO Cav. Preston's Bn. Co.B
Tucker, John T. TN 7th (Duckworth's) Cav. Co.B
Tucker, John T. TN 1st (Feild's) Inf. Co.H 1st Sgt.
Tucker, John T. VA 56th Inf. Co.K
Tucker, John W. GA 1st (Ramsey's) Inf. Co.B
Tucker, John W. GA 50th Inf. Co.E Cpl.
Tucker, John W. GA 57th Inf. Co.G,A
Tucker, John W. GA 59th Inf. Co.D
Tucker, John W. LA 13th Inf. Co.G
Tucker, John W. LA 17th Inf. Co.A
Tucker, John W. MD Arty. 1st Btty.
Tucker, John W. MS 17th Inf. Co.B
Tucker, John W. MO 15th Cav. Co.C
Tucker, John W. MO Inf. 8th Bn. Co.E
Tucker, John W. MO 9th Inf. Co.I Cpl.
Tucker, John W. NC 2nd Cav. (19th St.Troops) Co.F
Tucker, John W. NC 3rd Inf. Co.B
Tucker, John W. NC 37th Inf. Co.B
Tucker, John W. NC 45th Inf. Co.D
Tucker, John W. TN 10th (DeMoss') Cav. Co.B Sgt.
Tucker, John W. TN 7th Inf. Co.H
Tucker, John W. TN 24th Bn.S.S. Co.A
Tucker, John W. TN 32nd Inf. Co.A
Tucker, John W. TX 6th Cav. Co.H
Tucker, John W. TX Cav. Wells' Bn. Co.B
Tucker, John W. VA 2nd Cav. Co.I
Tucker, John W. VA 18th Inf. Co.A
Tucker, John W. 3rd Conf.Cav. Co.F
Tucker, John Wesley LA 12th Inf. Co.A
Tucker, John William TX 18th Cav. Co.E
Tucker, Jonathan TN 19th Inf. Co.I
Tucker, Jonus KY 4th Mtd.Inf. Co.G
Tucker, Jong W. AR Cav. Gordon's Regt. Co.E
Tucker, Jordan AL Cav. Moreland's Regt. Co.B
Tucker, Jordan FL 2nd Cav. Co.I 1st Lt.
Tucker, Jordan FL 1st Inf. Old Co.F,H
Tucker, Joseph AL 7th Cav. Co.H
Tucker, Joseph AL 9th (Malone's) Cav. Co.H
Tucker, Joseph AL Cav. Moreland's Regt. Co.I
Tucker, Joseph AL Lt.Arty. 2nd Bn. Co.A
Tucker, Joseph AL 37th Inf. Co.E Sgt.
Tucker, Joseph, Jr. AR 11th & 17th Cons.Inf. Co.I
Tucker, Joseph, Sr. AR 11th & 17th Cons.Inf. Co.I
Tucker, Joseph FL 2nd Cav. Co.G
Tucker, Joseph FL Cav. 5th Bn. Co.A
Tucker, Joseph NC 2nd Cav. (19th St.Troops) Co.A
Tucker, Joseph NC 14th Inf. Co.A
Tucker, Joseph SC Mil. 18th Regt. Co.E
Tucker, Joseph TN 29th Inf. Co.K
Tucker, Joseph TN 62nd Mtd.Inf. Co.A
Tucker, Joseph TX 7th Cav. Co.I
Tucker, Joseph TX 19th Cav. Co.E
Tucker, Joseph TX 27th Cav. Co.C
Tucker, Joseph VA Lt.Arty. Woolfolk's Co.
Tucker, Joseph VA 56th Inf. Co.K
Tucker, Joseph A. Conf.Cav. Wood's Regt. 2nd Co.M
Tucker, Joseph B., Jr. AR 17th (Griffith's) Inf. Co.B
Tucker, Joseph B., Sr. AR 17th (Griffith's) Inf. Co.B
Tucker, Joseph B. GA 5th Inf. Co.D Sgt.
Tucker, Joseph C. MS 2nd Res.Corps Co.J
Tucker, Joseph C. TX 9th (Young's) Inf. Co.F
Tucker, Joseph C. VA 26th Inf. Co.C Sgt.
Tucker, Joseph D.A. Gen. & Staff Hosp.Stew.
Tucker, Joseph H. GA 9th Inf. Co.F
Tucker, Joseph J. MS 24th Inf. Co.E Cpl.
Tucker, Joseph J. 7th Conf.Cav. 1st Co.I, Co.H
Tucker, Joseph K. NC 4th Cav. (59th St.Troops) Co.E Chap.
Tucker, Joseph L. KY 6th Mtd.Inf. Co.B Sgt.
Tucker, Joseph M. GA 11th Inf. Co.C Sgt.
Tucker, Joseph P. LA 18th Inf. Co.G 2nd Lt.
Tucker, Joseph R. AR 2nd Inf. Co.G
Tucker, Joseph R. GA 7th Inf. Co.I
Tucker, Joseph R. SC 7th Cav. Co.A 2nd Lt.
Tucker, Joseph R. SC Cav. Tucker's Co. Bvt.2nd Lt.
Tucker, Joseph R. Sig.Corps,CSA
Tucker, Jos. T. KY 2nd (Duke's) Cav. Col.
Tucker, Joseph T. KY 11th Cav. Col.
Tucker, Joseph T. MO Cav. Clardy's Bn. Bumbaugh's Co. 3rd Lt.
Tucker, Joseph T. VA 18th Cav. Co.B
Tucker, Joseph T. VA 62nd Mtd.Inf. 1st Co.G
Tucker, Joseph Taylor MO 3rd Cav. Co.B
Tucker, Joseph V.A. VA 12th Inf. Co.E
Tucker, Joseph W. FL 9th Inf. Co.I
Tucker, Joseph W. MS 27th Inf. Co.H
Tucker, Joseph W. MS 29th Inf. Co.H
Tucker, Joseph W. NC 3rd Arty. (40th St.Troops) Co.A

Tucker, Joseph W. VA 1st Cav. Co.G
Tucker, Joseph Y. TX Cav. Gidding's Bn. Weisiger's Co.
Tucker, Joshua AL 4th Inf. Co.H
Tucker, Joshua L. NC 55th Inf. Co.E
Tucker, Joshua W. 7th Conf.Cav. 1st Co.I, Co.H
Tucker, Josiah A.S. AL 37th Inf. Co.I
Tucker, Josiah M. AR Cav. 1st Bn. (Stirman's) Co.A
Tucker, Josiah M. AR 7th Inf. Co.I 1st Lt.
Tucker, J.P. AL 1st Cav. 1st Co.C
Tucker, J.P. GA Lt.Arty. Daniell's Btty.
Tucker, J.P. GA Reg.Lt.Arty. Maxwell's Bn. Co.B
Tucker, J.P. KY 7th Mtd.Inf. Co.G
Tucker, J.P. MS 32nd Inf. Co.H
Tucker, J.P. SC 1st St.Troops Co.C
Tucker, J.P. SC 24th Inf. Co.F 2nd Lt.
Tucker, J.P. SC Inf. Hampton Legion Co.I
Tucker, J.P. TN 7th (Duckworth's) Cav. Co.F
Tucker, J.P. TN 12th (Cons.) Inf. Co.D
Tucker, J.P. TN 22nd Inf. Co.H
Tucker, J. Pinkney NC 46th Inf. Co.K
Tucker, J.R. AR 7th Mil. Co.B
Tucker, J.R. GA Inf. 9th Bn. Co.C
Tucker, J.R. GA 37th Inf. Co.F 1st Lt.
Tucker, J.R. GA 54th Inf. Co.H Capt.
Tucker, J.R. MS 9th Inf. New Co.H
Tucker, J.R. SC Cav. 14th Bn. Co.B Far.
Tucker, J.R. SC 2nd Arty. Co.C
Tucker, J.R. TN 55th (Brown's) Inf. Co.C 1st Sgt.
Tucker, J.R. TX 30th Cav. Co.B Cpl.
Tucker, J.R. TX St.Troops Hampton's Co.
Tucker, J.R.V. AL 8th Cav. Co.C
Tucker, J.S. AL 29th Inf. Co.D,A Sgt.
Tucker, J.S. AR 37th Inf. Co.K
Tucker, J.S. MS Cav. 17th Bn. Co.D
Tucker, J.S. NC Mallett's Bn. (Cp.Guard) Co.D
Tucker, J.S. TN 43rd Inf. Co.I
Tucker, J.S. VA 3rd Res. Co.A
Tucker, J.S. Gen. & Staff, Ord.Dept. Clerk
Tucker, J.T. AL 50th Inf. Cpl.
Tucker, J.T. AR 19th (Dawson's) Inf. Co.H,K
Tucker, J.T. GA 45th Inf. Co.D
Tucker, J.T. NC 23rd Inf. Co.C
Tucker, J.T. SC Inf. Hampton Legion Co.H
Tucker, J.T. TN 19th & 20th (Cons.) Cav. Co.F
Tucker, J.T. TN 20th (Russell's) Cav. Co.A
Tucker, J.T. TX 6th Inf. Co.G 1st Sgt.
Tucker, J.T. VA 5th Cav. Co.C
Tucker, J.T. VA 18th Inf. Co.F
Tucker, J.T. VA 19th Inf. Co.I
Tucker, J.T. VA Inf. 28th Bn. Co.D
Tucker, J.T. VA Loc.Def. Tayloe's Co.
Tucker, J.T. 7th Conf.Cav. Co.K Cpl.
Tucker, J. Thomas GA 2nd Res. Co.B
Tucker, Judson VA 15th Inf. Co.H
Tucker, Julius VA 10th Cav. Co.G, 1st Co.E Capt.
Tucker, Julius G. Conf.Inf. Tucker's Regt. Col.
Tucker, Junius F. TN 1st (Feild's) Inf. Co.H Music.
Tucker, J.W. AL 5th Cav. Co.I
Tucker, J.W. AL 29th Inf. Co.D,A Cpl.
Tucker, J.W. AL 31st Inf. Co.A Cpl.
Tucker, J.W. AL 43rd Inf. Co.K
Tucker, J.W. AL 47th Inf. Co.K
Tucker, J.W. AL 1st Bn. Hilliard's Legion Vol. Co.D
Tucker, J.W. AL Cp. of Instr. Talladega
Tucker, J.W. AR 2nd Cav. Co.D
Tucker, J.W. AR 6th Inf. Co.A
Tucker, J.W. AR 15th Mil. Co.C 1st Lt.
Tucker, J.W. GA 13th Inf. Co.H
Tucker, J.W. GA 18th Inf. Co.K
Tucker, J.W. MS Blythe's Bn. (St.Troops) Co.A
Tucker, J.W. MS Res.Corps Withers' Co.
Tucker, J.W. TN 22nd (Barteau's) Cav. Co.K
Tucker, J.W. TN 22nd Inf. Co.G
Tucker, J.W. TN 49th Inf. Co.D
Tucker, J.W. TX 17th Cons.Dismtd.Cav. 1st Co.G
Tucker, J.W. VA 7th Cav. Co.H
Tucker, J.W. TX 7th Cav. Co.I
Tucker, J.W. VA Conscr. Cp.Lee Co.B
Tucker, J.W. Brush Bn.
Tucker, J.W. Gen. & Staff Chap.
Tucker, J.W.S. SC 8th Bn.Res. Co.C
Tucker, J.W.T. AR 58th Mil. Co.C
Tucker, Keeton M. MS 9th Inf. New Co.D
Tucker, Keton M. MS 10th Inf. Old Co.D, Co.E
Tucker, Kilba NC 51st Inf. Co.B
Tucker, Killian NC 44th Inf. Co.F
Tucker, King MO 8th Cav. Co.B
Tucker, King MO Cav. 2nd Regt.St.Guard Co.A
Tucker, King MO 15th Cav. Co.B
Tucker, K.W. AR 27th Inf. New Co.B Cpl.
Tucker, L. AR 37th Inf. Co.K
Tucker, L. MS 18th Inf. Co.C
Tucker, L. SC Lt.Arty. J.T. Kanapaux's Co. (Lafayette Arty.)
Tucker, L.A. GA Cav. 16th Bn. (St.Guards) Co.G
Tucker, L.A. GA Cav. 29th Bn. Co.E
Tucker, Lafayette TX 30th Cav. Co.G
Tucker, Landon SC Mtd.Inf. 1st Regt. Co.C
Tucker, L.B. AR 7th Mil. Co.E
Tucker, L.B. MS 9th Cav. Co.A
Tucker, L.B. MS Cav. 17th Bn. Co.A
Tucker, L.C. AL 7th Cav. Co.C
Tucker, L.C. AR 35th Inf. Co.H
Tucker, L.D. AL 21st Inf. Co.K
Tucker, L.D. NC 12th Inf. Co.H
Tucker, L.E. VA 32nd Inf. Co.F
Tucker, Legrand M. VA 41st Inf. Co.C
Tucker, Lemuel NC Cav. 12th Bn. Co.B
Tucker, Lemuel VA 41st Inf. Co.B
Tucker, Lemuel D. NC 30th Inf. Co.I
Tucker, Lemuel T. TX 2nd Cav. Co.I
Tucker, Lemuel T. TX 31st Cav. Co.C
Tucker, Leonard B. NC 46th Inf. Co.C
Tucker, Leonard G. NC 42nd Inf. Co.H
Tucker, Leonard P. SC 20th Inf. Co.E
Tucker, Leonidas AR 2nd Inf. Co.G
Tucker, Leonidas R. VA Lt.Arty. Parker's Co.
Tucker, Leonidas H. VA Horse Arty. E. Graham's Co.
Tucker, Leroy GA 22nd Inf. Co.G
Tucker, Leroy GA Inf. 25th Bn. (Prov.Guard) Co.C
Tucker, Leroy TN 3rd (Lillard's) Mtd.Inf. Co.G
Tucker, Leroy G. GA 5th Inf. Co.F
Tucker, Levi NC 42nd Inf. Co.H
Tucker, Levi TN 11th (Holman's) Cav. Co.K
Tucker, Levi TN Holman's Bn.Part.Rangers Co.D
Tucker, Levi TN 1st (Feild's) Inf. Co.K
Tucker, Levi 1st Cherokee Mtd.Rifles McDaniel's Co.
Tucker, Levi 1st Cherokee Mtd.Vol. 2nd Co.I
Tucker, Levi 2nd Cherokee Mtd.Vol. Co.D
Tucker, Levi 1st Choctaw & Chickasaw Mtd.Rifles 1st Co.E Cpl.
Tucker, Levi Shecoe's Chickasaw Bn.Mtd.Vol. Co.A
Tucker, Levi C. AR Cav. 1st Bn. (Stirman's) Co.A
Tucker, Levi M. Gen. & Staff 1st Lt.,AADC, AAAG
Tucker, Levi T. NC 33rd Inf. Co.A
Tucker, Lewis GA 38th Inf. Co.H
Tucker, Lewis NC 23rd Inf. Co.A
Tucker, Lewis NC 43rd Inf. Co.H
Tucker, Lewis SC 11th Inf. Co.C
Tucker, Lewis SC 23rd Inf. Co.D
Tucker, Lewis J. TN 25th Inf. Co.F
Tucker, Lewis W. VA 56th Inf. Co.G
Tucker, L.G. AR 8th Cav. Co.D
Tucker, L.G. AR 27th Inf. Co.G
Tucker, L.H. MO Robertson's Regt.St.Guard Co.5 Cpl.
Tucker, L.H. VA 10th Cav. 2nd Co.E
Tucker, Littleberry NC 54th Inf. Co.K Sgt.
Tucker, Littlebury VA 3rd Res. Co.A
Tucker, Littleton VA 14th Cav. Co.G, 2nd Co.F
Tucker, L.M. KY 6th Mtd.Inf. Co.B 1st Lt.
Tucker, L.M. NC 23rd Inf. Co.C
Tucker, L.M. VA 3rd (Archer's) Bn.Res. Co.B
Tucker, L.M. Gen. & Staff Cadet
Tucker, Lorenzo L. VA 3rd Cav. Co.C
Tucker, Lot AR 32nd Inf. Co.G Music.
Tucker, L.P. AL 20th Inf. Co.A
Tucker, L.T. NC 1st Jr.Res. Co.G
Tucker, Lucien Q. GA 57th Inf. Co.C Capt.
Tucker, Lunsford MS Inf. 1st Bn.St.Troops (12 mo. '62-3) Co.B
Tucker, Luther FL Military Inst. Cadets
Tucker, Luther B. AR 1st S.S. Co.C
Tucker, L.W. AR Cav. Gordon's Regt. Co.B Sgt.
Tucker, L.W. AR 15th Mil. Co.I 1st Lt.
Tucker, M. AL St.Arty. Co.C
Tucker, M. NC 57th Inf. Co.B
Tucker, M. TN 6th (Wheeler's) Cav. Co.L
Tucker, M. VA 82nd Mil. Co.D
Tucker, M.A. TN 55th (Brown's) Inf. Co.C 1st Lt.
Tucker, Marion J. TN 9th Inf. Co.K,D
Tucker, Martin S. TX 22nd Cav. Co.K
Tucker, Martin V. TN 44th Inf. Co.I
Tucker, Martin V. TN 44th (Cons.) Inf. Co.A
Tucker, Mathew AL Jeff Davis Arty.
Tucker, Mathew GA 12th Mil.
Tucker, Mathew GA 49th Inf. Co.F
Tucker, Mathew TN 3rd (Clack's) Inf. Co.H
Tucker, Mathew L. AL 6th Inf. Co.A,K,H
Tucker, Matthew GA 11th Cav. (St.Guards) Tillman's Co.
Tucker, Matthew M. AL 43rd Inf. Co.A
Tucker, Matt W. MO 1st Inf. Co.G

Tucker, M.C. VA Inf. 25th Bn. Co.F
Tucker, McCarty W. GA 6th Inf. Co.K
Tucker, McDan TN Inf. 23rd Bn. Co.A
Tucker, M.D. AR 11th & 17th Cons.Inf. Co.I Sgt.
Tucker, M.D. AR 35th Inf. Co.D
Tucker, M.D. TX 4th Cav. Co.A
Tucker, Meridith NC 14th Inf. Co.A
Tucker, M.F. NC 2nd Jr.Res. Co.F
Tucker, Micajah GA 11th Cav. (St.Guards) Godfrey's Co.
Tucker, Miles VA 19th Inf. Co.I
Tucker, Miles C. VA Lt.Arty. Woolfolk's Co.
Tucker, Miles S. VA Inf. 25th Bn. Co.A
Tucker, Miles T. VA Inf. 5th Bn. Co.C
Tucker, Miles T. VA 53rd Inf. Co.C
Tucker, Milton TX 16th Cav. Co.H
Tucker, Milton TX 12th Inf. Co.G
Tucker, Milton A. TX 15th Cav. Co.F,B Sgt.
Tucker, Milton A. TX 10th Inf. Co.B
Tucker, Milton P. GA 55th Inf. Co.K Capt.
Tucker, M.J. GA 54th Inf. Co.E
Tucker, M.J. TN 19th (Biffle's) Cav. Co.D
Tucker, M.L. MS 2nd St.Cav. Co.E
Tucker, M.N. AL 23rd Inf. Co.C
Tucker, Monroe M. NC 7th Inf. Co.B
Tucker, Montgomery TN 60th Mtd.Inf. Co.I
Tucker, Moses AL 26th (O'Neal's) Inf. Co.H
Tucker, Moses GA 54th Inf. Co.A
Tucker, Moses G. NC 38th Inf. Co.B
Tucker, Moses W. MS Inf. 3rd Bn. Co.F
Tucker, M.T. GA 2nd Brig.St.Troops Capt.
Tucker, M.V. MS Inf. 7th Bn. Co.C
Tucker, M.W. NC 27th Inf. Co.H
Tucker, Napoleon B. TX 36th Cav. Co.E,I
Tucker, Nathan VA 19th Cav. Co.D
Tucker, Nathaniel NC 44th Inf. Co.H
Tucker, Nathaniel TN 8th Inf. Co.K
Tucker, Nathaniel C. NC 2nd Cav. (19th St.Troops) Co.F 2nd Lt.
Tucker, Nathaniel W. LA 7th Inf. Co.K Cpl.
Tucker, Nelson AR 32nd Inf. Co.A
Tucker, Neri AL 45th Inf. Co.F Capt.
Tucker, Newman TX 10th Inf. Co.B 1st Sgt.
Tucker, N.H. AL 63rd Inf. Co.E
Tucker, Nicholus L. MS 1st (Johnston's) Inf. Co.C
Tucker, Noah GA Arty. Maxwell's Reg.Lt.Btty.
Tucker, Noah GA 38th Inf. Co.B
Tucker, Noah NC 54th Inf. Co.G
Tucker, Norman T. AR 2nd Inf. Co.G
Tucker, N.W. NC 68th Inf.
Tucker, O.G. LA 1st Hvy.Arty. (Reg.) Co.I
Tucker, Oliver G. LA Arty. Kean's Btty. (Orleans Ind.Arty.)
Tucker, Oliver J. LA C.S. Zouave Bn. Co.A
Tucker, Oliver P. TN 16th Inf. Co.B Sgt.
Tucker, O.M. GA 5th Res. Co.L
Tucker, O.N. GA 36th (Broyles') Inf. Co.D
Tucker, O.P. KY 13th Cav. Co.D
Tucker, Othello W. VA 12th Inf. Co.C
Tucker, O.W. AR Inf. Cocke's Regt. Co.E
Tucker, Owen LA 27th Inf. Co.B
Tucker, Owen NC 12th Inf. Co.C
Tucker, Owen NC 30th Inf. Co.E
Tucker, Owen H. TN 44th Inf. Co.E
Tucker, Owen H. TN 44th (Cons.) Inf. Co.B
Tucker, Owen H. VA 28th Inf. Co.B 2nd Lt.
Tucker, P. GA 4th (Clinch's) Cav. Co.D
Tucker, P. VA 1st (Farinholt's) Res. Co.K
Tucker, P. VA 2nd St.Res. Co.H
Tucker, Pascal D. MS 15th Inf. Co.D
Tucker, Paschal MS Cav. 2nd Bn.Res. Co.I
Tucker, Patrick H. LA 15th Inf. Co.G
Tucker, Paul AR Lt.Arty. Zimmerman's Btty.
Tucker, Paul VA Hvy.Arty. 19th Bn. Co.D
Tucker, P.B. AR 27th Inf. Co.G
Tucker, P.B. MO Cav. Ford's Bn. Co.A
Tucker, P.D. TX Inf. 1st Bn. (St.Troops) Co.E
Tucker, P.D. TX 3rd (Kirby's) Bn.Vol. Co.B
Tucker, P. Drake TX 17th Inf. Co.F
Tucker, P.E. Conf.Cav. Wood's Regt. 2nd Co.F 1st Lt.
Tucker, Perry AL 33rd Inf. Co.E Cpl.
Tucker, Peter SC 8th Bn.Res. Co.C
Tucker, Peter A. VA Lt.Arty. Jeffress' Co.
Tucker, Peter J. GA Cav. 24th Bn. Co.A
Tucker, P.H. LA 19th Inf. Co.E
Tucker, P.H. LA Inf. Pelican Regt. Co.A
Tucker, Philip GA 62nd Cav. Co.G
Tucker, Pickens L. SC 24th Inf. Co.I Cpl.
Tucker, Pinckney C. AR 2nd Mtd.Rifles Co.F
Tucker, Pinkney NC 22nd Inf. Co.I
Tucker, Pinkney C. AR 37th Inf. Co.H
Tucker, P.J. GA 7th Cav. Co.G
Tucker, Pleasant M. AL 21st Inf. Co.G
Tucker, Pleasant M. AL Conscr. Echols' Co.
Tucker, Pleasant T. FL 9th Inf. Co.C
Tucker, P.M. AL 1st Regt.Conscr. Co.K
Tucker, P.M. AL Mil. 4th Vol. Modawell's Co.
Tucker, P.M. MS Cav. 2nd Bn.Res. Adj.
Tucker, P.N. AL 29th Inf. Co.I
Tucker, Powhattan F. LA 25th Inf. Co.C
Tucker, Q.P. AR 19th (Dockery's) Inf. Co.A
Tucker, R., Jr. GA 4th (Clinch's) Cav. Co.F,H Sgt.
Tucker, R., Sr. GA 4th (Clinch's) Cav. Co.F,K
Tucker, R. LA Mil. 3rd Regt. 1st Brig. 1st Div. Co.F
Tucker, R. NC 22nd Inf. Co.I
Tucker, R. SC 1st (Butler's) Inf. Co.A
Tucker, R. TX 26th Cav. Co.H
Tucker, R.A. AL 14th Inf. Co.B
Tucker, R.A. AR 19th (Dawson's) Inf. Co.H,K
Tucker, R.A. AR 35th Inf. Co.I Sgt.
Tucker, R.A. MS 2nd St.Cav. Co.E
Tucker, R.A. VA 1st (Farinholt's) Res. Co.E
Tucker, R.A. VA 32nd Inf. Co.F
Tucker, Rains TX 10th Field Btty.
Tucker, Raleigh W. VA 38th Inf. Co.F
Tucker, R.B. TN Lt.Arty. McClung's Co. Cpl.
Tucker, R.B. VA Cav. Mosby's Regt. (Part. Rangers) Co.D
Tucker, R.C. AL 2nd Cav. Co.H
Tucker, R.D. SC 2nd Rifles Co.F Sgt.
Tucker, R.D. TX 1st Inf. 2nd Co.K
Tucker, R.E. VA 3rd Cav. Co.I
Tucker, R.E. VA 9th Inf. 2nd Co.A
Tucker, Reuben AR 37th Inf. Co.G
Tucker, Reuben GA 1st (Fannin's) Res. Co.G
Tucker, Reuben TN 18th (Newsom's) Cav. Co.D
Tucker, Reuben H. AL 6th Inf. Co.A,K
Tucker, R.F. GA 41st Inf. Co.I
Tucker, R.G. TN 13th Inf. Co.G
Tucker, R.H. GA 53rd Inf. Co.A
Tucker, R.H. TN 10th (DeMoss') Cav. Co.D Sgt.
Tucker, R.H. TN Cav. Napier's Bn. Co.A Sgt.
Tucker, Richard GA 49th Inf. Co.F 2nd Lt.
Tucker, Richard GA 50th Inf. Co.H Sgt.
Tucker, Richard NC 6th Sr.Res. Co.A
Tucker, Richard VA Cav. 39th Bn. Co.D
Tucker, Richard VA Inf. 5th Bn. Co.D
Tucker, Richard VA 38th Inf. Co.C
Tucker, Richard VA 53rd Inf. Co.A
Tucker, Richard M. GA 38th Inf. Co.B
Tucker, Richard M. VA 20th Inf. Co.I
Tucker, Richard M. VA 59th Inf. 3rd Co.B Cpl.
Tucker, Richard T. VA 26th Inf. Co.K
Tucker, R.J. GA 39th Inf. Co.K
Tucker, R.J. SC 1st Arty. Co.K
Tucker, R.L. VA 3rd Inf.Loc.Def. Co.A
Tucker, R.M. AL 14th Inf. Co.A Cpl.
Tucker, Robert AL 1st Regt.Conscr. Co.A
Tucker, Robert AL Cp. of Instr. Talladega Co.B
Tucker, Robert AR 27th Inf. New Co.B Sgt.
Tucker, Robert AR Inf. Adams' Regt. Moore's Co.
Tucker, Robert KY 2nd (Woodward's) Cav. Co.F
Tucker, Robert KY 1st Inf. Co.B
Tucker, Robert SC 4th Cav. Co.A Sgt.
Tucker, Robert SC 6th Cav. Co.G
Tucker, Robert SC Cav. 12th Bn. Co.A
Tucker, Robert TX Cav. Giddings' Bn. (Weisiger's Co.)
Tucker, Robert VA 2nd St.Res. Co.C
Tucker, Robert VA 30th Bn.S.S. Co.F 1st Lt.
Tucker, Robert, Jr. Conf.Cav. Wood's Regt. 2nd Co.F 2nd Lt.
Tucker, Robert A. AR Cav. 1st Bn. (Stirman's) Co.A
Tucker, Robert A. AR Inf. Crawford's Bn. Co.B
Tucker, Robert A. KY 8th Cav. Co.B
Tucker, Robert A. NC 52nd Inf. Co.G
Tucker, Robert B. NC 13th Inf. Co.G
Tucker, Robert B. NC 37th Inf. Co.H Sgt.
Tucker, Robert B. VA Lt.Arty. Kirkpatrick's Co. Sgt.
Tucker, Robert C. VA Lt.Arty. French's Co.
Tucker, Robert C. VA 9th Inf. Co.D
Tucker, Robert E. VA 26th Inf. Co.K
Tucker, Robert F. AL 37th Inf. Co.D
Tucker, Robert F. AR 9th Inf. Co.K Ord.Sgt.
Tucker, Robert H. AL 16th Inf. Co.B
Tucker, Robert H. MS Inf. 2nd Bn. Co.D Cpl.
Tucker, Robert H. MS 48th Inf. Co.D Sgt.
Tucker, Robert H. TN 6th (Wheeler's) Cav. Co.K
Tucker, Robert H. VA 9th Inf. 2nd Co.H 2nd Lt.
Tucker, Robert H. VA 12th Inf. 1st Co.I 2nd Lt.
Tucker, Robert H. Gen. & Staff Capt.,ACS
Tucker, Robert J. GA Lt.Arty. Guerard's Btty.
Tucker, Robert J. MO 9th (Elliott's) Cav. Co.A Capt.
Tucker, Robert L. MS 1st Cav.Res. Co.I 1st Sgt.
Tucker, Robert L. VA 1st Inf. Co.G
Tucker, Robert P. MS Cav. 3rd Bn.Res. Co.E
Tucker, Robertson VA 9th Inf. 2nd Co.A

Tucker, Robert W. MS 9th Inf. Old Co.E
Tucker, Robert W. MS 10th Inf. New Co.A
Tucker, Robert W. VA Inf. 1st Bn. Co.E
Tucker, Roden A. Trans-MS Conf.Cav. 1st Bn. Co.E
Tucker, Rodolphus GA Lt.Arty. (Jackson Arty.) Massenburg's Btty.
Tucker, Rowan NC 20th Inf. Co.B
Tucker, R.P. AR Cav. Gordon's Regt. Co.E
Tucker, R.P. AR 35th Inf. Co.H
Tucker, R.P. VA Hvy.Arty. Allen's Co.
Tucker, R.R. SC 3rd Cav. Co.B
Tucker, R.S. AR Inf. Adams' Regt. Moore's Co.
Tucker, R.T. AL 8th (Livingston's) Cav. Co.C
Tucker, Rudolphus S. GA 45th Inf. Co.A
Tucker, Rufus J. MS 26th Inf. Co.I
Tucker, Rufus S. NC 3rd Cav. (41st St.Troops) Co.I Capt.
Tucker, R.W. MS Inf. 1st Bn. Polk's Co.
Tucker, R.W. MS Burt's Ind.Co. (Dixie Guards)
Tucker, R.W. TN 20th (Russell's) Cav. Co.G
Tucker, R.W. TN 16th Inf. Co.B
Tucker, R.W. VA Loc.Def. Chappell's Co. Sgt.
Tucker, R.Y. NC 12th Inf. Co.F
Tucker, S. AL 9th (Malone's) Cav. Co.G
Tucker, S. AR Inf. Cocke's Regt. Co.B
Tucker, S. GA 54th Inf. Co.A
Tucker, S. MS 9th Inf. New Co.I
Tucker, S. TN 22nd (Barteau's) Cav. Co.I
Tucker, S.A. AL 11th Inf. Co.A
Tucker, S.A. AL 45th Inf. Co.B
Tucker, Samuel FL 10th Inf. Co.F
Tucker, Samuel GA 39th Inf. Co.G
Tucker, Samuel TX 17th Cav. Co.I
Tucker, Samuel TX 17th Cons.Dismtd.Cav. Co.K
Tucker, Samuel TX 14th Inf. 1st Co.K
Tucker, Samuel TX 18th Inf. Co.L
Tucker, Samuel VA Hvy.Arty. 20th Bn. Co.B
Tucker, Samuel VA 38th Inf. 2nd Co.I
Tucker, Samuel C. FL 2nd Cav. Co.F
Tucker, Samuel D. NC 25th Inf. Co.E
Tucker, Samuel E. VA 53rd Inf. Co.A Cpl.
Tucker, Samuel E. VA Inf. Montague's Bn. Co.A
Tucker, Samuel H. TN 44th Inf. Co.B
Tucker, Samuel J. AL 18th Inf. Co.L
Tucker, Samuel J. VA 31st Inf. Co.A
Tucker, Samuel L. GA 38th Inf. Co.B
Tucker, Samuel L. TN 1st (Turney's) Inf. Co.E
Tucker, Samuel M. AR Lt.Arty. Rivers' Btty.
Tucker, Samuel M. TN 45th Inf. Co.I
Tucker, Samuel T. VA Cav. McNeill's Co.
Tucker, Samuel W. VA Goochland Lt.Arty.
Tucker, S.B. VA Inf. Lyneman's Co.
Tucker, S.D. VA 56th Inf.
Tucker, S.H. TN Cav. 11th Bn. (Gordon's) Co.A
Tucker, S.H. TN 28th Cav. Co.C 1st Sgt.
Tucker, Shepherd AR 26th Inf. Co.A
Tucker, S.I. MS Grace's Co. (St.Troops)
Tucker, Sidney G. VA Horse Arty. E. Graham's Co. Cpl.
Tucker, Silas AL Inf. 1st Regt. Co.B
Tucker, Silas MS 6th Cav. Co.B
Tucker, Silas Conf.Inf. Tucker's Regt. Co.I Cpl.
Tucker, Silas A. TX 16th Cav. Co.H Cpl.
Tucker, Silas M. TX 4th Cav. Co.A
Tucker, Simeon LA 12th Inf. Co.L
Tucker, S.J. AL 58th Inf. Co.G
Tucker, S.J. MS 36th Inf. Co.I
Tucker, S.J. MS 41st Inf. Co.B
Tucker, S.L. GA Lt.Arty. Daniell's Btty. Cpl.
Tucker, S.L. GA Arty. Maxwell's Reg.Lt.Btty.
Tucker, S.L. GA Reg.Lt.Arty. Maxwell's Bn. Co.B
Tucker, S.L. GA 49th Inf. Co.D
Tucker, S.L. TX 32nd Cav. Co.K
Tucker, S.L. VA Hvy.Arty. Allen's Co.
Tucker, S.L. VA 20th Inf. Co.C
Tucker, S.M. LA 4th Inf. Co.C
Tucker, S.M. MS Cav. 3rd Bn. (Ashcraft's) Co.F Cpl.
Tucker, S.M. MS Cav. Davenport's Bn. (St.Troops) Co.A
Tucker, S.M. MS Cav. Ham's Regt. Co.E
Tucker, S.M. MS Inf. 2nd St.Troops Co.E
Tucker, S.M. MS Inf. 7th Bn. Co.C
Tucker, S.M. TX 7th Cav. Co.D Sgt.
Tucker, Smith G. VA Arty. Dance's Co.
Tucker, Sol TN 25th Inf. Co.G
Tucker, Sol A. MS Cav. Jeff Davis Legion Co.E
Tucker, Solimon GA 49th Inf. Co.F
Tucker, Solomon GA 11th Cav. (St.Guards) Godfrey's Co.
Tucker, Solomon TN 23rd Inf. Co.G
Tucker, Solomon P. AL 43rd Inf. Co.A
Tucker, S.R. MS 8th Inf. Co.G
Tucker, S.T. AL 14th Inf. Co.C Cpl.
Tucker, S.T. AL St.Troops
Tucker, Stephen GA Inf. 10th Bn. Co.D
Tucker, Stephen TN 47th Inf. Co.K Cpl.
Tucker, Stephen A. AL 37th Inf. Co.D
Tucker, Stephen J. VA 22nd Inf. Co.A
Tucker, Stephen M. NC 45th Inf. Co.D
Tucker, Stephen T. AL 6th Inf. Co.C 2nd Lt.
Tucker, Sterling GA Inf. 14th Bn. (St.Guards) Co.A
Tucker, Sterling TX 22nd Cav. Co.E,F
Tucker, St.George VA 15th Inf. Co.E Lt.Col.
Tucker, S.W. LA 25th Inf. Co.D
Tucker, S.W. MO 2nd Inf. Co.I
Tucker, S.W. TN 15th Inf. Co.E
Tucker, Sydney AR 50th Mil. Co.G
Tucker, Sylvester J. VA Lt.Arty. Parker's Co. Sr.1st Lt.
Tucker, Sylvester J. VA 1st Inf. Co.G 1st Lt.
Tucker, Sylvester J. VA Inf. 1st Bn.Loc.Def. Co.E Capt.
Tucker, Sylvester J. Conf.Arty. Nelson's Bn. Co.D Sr.1st Lt.
Tucker, T. GA 4th (Clinch's) Cav. Co.H
Tucker, T. SC Lt.Arty. 3rd (Palmetto) Bn. Co.H,I
Tucker, T.A. MS 35th Inf. Co.D
Tucker, Taylor MO Cav. 3rd Regt.St.Guard Co.A
Tucker, Taylor MO Cav. Clardy's Bn. Co.C 3rd Lt.
Tucker, T.B. MO 11th Inf. Co.D
Tucker, T.B. TN 6th (Wheeler's) Cav. Co.K Sgt.
Tucker, T.B. TN Cav. 11th Bn. (Gordon's) Co.A
Tucker, T.B. TN 3rd (Clack's) Inf. Co.F Sgt.
Tucker, T.D. MS 3rd (St.Troops) Cav. Co.G
Tucker, T.E. 4th Conf.Inf. Co.F
Tucker, Telem H. TN 24th Inf. Co.K
Tucker, T.G. TN Inf. Nashville Bn. Fulcher's Co.
Tucker, T.H. AR 26th Inf. Co.K
Tucker, T.H. GA 59th Inf. Co.D
Tucker, T.H. MO 7th Cav. Co.F,G
Tucker, T.H. MO 8th Cav. Co.G
Tucker, T.H. TN 16th Inf. Co.B
Tucker, T.H. TN 43rd Inf. Co.I
Tucker, Theophilus I. VA 18th Inf. Co.G Sgt.
Tucker, Thomas AL Cav.Res. Brooks' Co.
Tucker, Thomas AL 12th Inf. Co.I
Tucker, Thomas AL 29th Inf. Co.C
Tucker, Thomas AL 31st Inf. Co.H
Tucker, Thomas AL 50th Inf. Co.E
Tucker, Thomas AR 7th Cav. Co.G
Tucker, Thomas FL 9th Inf. Co.I
Tucker, Thomas LA 21st (Kennedy's) Inf. Co.E
Tucker, Thomas MS 5th Inf. (St.Troops) Co.H
Tucker, Thomas MS Inf. (Res.) Berry's Co.
Tucker, Thomas MO 7th Cav. Co.G
Tucker, Thomas NC 5th Cav. (63rd St.Troops) Co.B
Tucker, Thomas NC 12th Inf. Co.K
Tucker, Thomas TN 1st (Feild's) Inf. Co.L
Tucker, Thomas TN 45th Inf. Co.I
Tucker, Thomas TN 46th Inf. Co.B
Tucker, Thomas TN 60th Mtd.Inf. Co.D
Tucker, Thomas TX 1st (Yager's) Cav. Co.I
Tucker, Thomas VA Lt.Arty. 38th Bn. Co.C
Tucker, Thomas VA 1st (Farinholt's) Res. Co.B
Tucker, Thomas A. AL 6th Inf. Co.C
Tucker, Thomas A. TN 20th (Russell's) Cav. Co.G
Tucker, Thomas A. VA 1st Cav. Co.A
Tucker, Thomas C. TX 6th Cav. Co.H AQMSgt.
Tucker, Thomas D. NC 57th Inf. Co.B
Tucker, Thomas E. AL 3rd Cav. Co.A 1st Cpl.
Tucker, Thomas E. MS 11th Inf. Co.B
Tucker, Thomas E. MS 13th Inf. Co.B
Tucker, Thomas E. Conf.Cav. Wood's Regt. Co.C
Tucker, Thomas F. TX 17th Cav. Co.E Capt.
Tucker, Thomas F. TX 17th Cons.Dismtd.Cav. Col.
Tucker, Thomas G. VA Lt.Arty. Kirkpatrick's Co.
Tucker, Thomas G. VA 19th Inf. Co.I
Tucker, Thomas G. VA 54th Inf. Co.E
Tucker, Thomas H. AL 43rd Inf. Co.B
Tucker, Thomas H. GA 14th Inf. Co.F
Tucker, Thomas H. VA 53rd Inf. Co.H
Tucker, Thomas H. VA Res.Forces Thurston's Co.
Tucker, Thomas J. AL 6th Inf. Co.C
Tucker, Thomas J. AR 1st (Dobbin's) Cav. Co.B
Tucker, Thomas J. AR 2nd Inf. Co.G
Tucker, Thomas J. AR 26th Inf. Co.A
Tucker, Thomas J. GA 10th Cav. (St.Guards) Co.B
Tucker, Thomas J. GA Siege Arty. 28th Bn. Co.H
Tucker, Thomas J. MS 35th Inf. Co.D
Tucker, Thomas J. MO Lt.Arty. 13th Btty.
Tucker, Thomas J. TN 1st (Feild's) Inf. Co.I

Tucker, Thomas J. TX 22nd Inf. Co.E
Tucker, Thomas J. VA 1st Arty.
Tucker, Thomas J. VA 2nd Cav. Co.E
Tucker, Thomas J. VA 3rd Lt.Arty. (Loc.Def.) Co.C
Tucker, Thomas J. VA Arty. Dance's Co.
Tucker, Thomas J. VA 18th Inf. Co.A
Tucker, Thomas J.W. VA 60th Inf. Co.K
Tucker, Thomas L. TN 11th (Holman's) Cav. Co.G
Tucker, Thomas L. TN Holman's Bn. Part.Rangers Co.B
Tucker, Thomas M. SC 14th Inf. Co.I Cpl.
Tucker, Thomas M. TN 3rd (Clack's) Inf. Co.E Maj.
Tucker, Thomas M. VA Arty. Paris' Co. Sr.1st Lt.
Tucker, Thomas N. AL 37th Inf. Co.I
Tucker, Thomas S. NC 4th Inf. Co.C
Tucker, Thomas W. AL 11th Inf. Co.A
Tucker, Thomas W. GA 1st Reg. Co.M
Tucker, Thompson W. FL 3rd Inf. Co.H Cpl.
Tucker, Tilghlman M. MS 17th Inf. Co.C Cpl.
Tucker, T.J. AR 2nd Inf. Co.I
Tucker, T.J. AR 18th Inf. Co.G
Tucker, T.J. GA 20th Inf. Music.
Tucker, T.J. MS 5th Inf. Co.C
Tucker, T.J. NC 7th Sr.Res. Williams' Co.
Tucker, T.J., Sr. TX Cav. Baird's Regt. Co.A
Tucker, T.M. AR 1st (Monroe's) Cav. Co.K
Tucker, T.M. AR 11th Inf. Co.H
Tucker, T.M. GA 28th Inf. Co.A Bvt.2nd Lt.
Tucker, T.O. TN 12th (Cons.) Inf. Co.F
Tucker, T.O. TN 22nd Inf. Co.D
Tucker, Tom NC Mallett's Bn. (Cp.Guard) Co.D
Tucker, Tony FL 8th Inf. Co.K
Tucker, T.P. GA 8th Cav. Co.G
Tucker, T.P. NC 46th Inf. Co.K
Tucker, T.S. FL 10th Inf. Love's Co.
Tucker, T.S.B. Gen. & Staff 1st Lt.,ADC
Tucker, T.T. GA 7th Inf. (St.Guards) Co.F
Tucker, T.T. MS 8th Inf. Co.I
Tucker, T.T. TN 40th Inf. Co.G
Tucker, T.W. GA 44th Inf. Co.H
Tucker, Uriah A. VA 31st Inf. Co.A
Tucker, V.D. TX 23rd Cav. Co.F
Tucker, Vincent W. TX Cav. Hardeman's Regt. Co.B
Tucker, W. AL 1st Bn.Cadets Co.A
Tucker, W. AR Lt.Arty. Hart's Btty.
Tucker, W. AR Mil. Desha Cty.Bn.
Tucker, W. GA 1st Inf. Capt.
Tucker, W. GA 3rd Res. Co.E
Tucker, W. MS 22nd Inf. Co.E
Tucker, W. TN Cav. Napier's Bn. Co.A
Tucker, W. TN 47th Inf. Co.H
Tucker, W. TX 20th Cav. Co.H
Tucker, W. VA 21st Cav. 2nd Co.G
Tucker, W.A. GA Inf. Exempts Roberts' Co. 1st Lt.
Tucker, W.A. MS 5th Inf. Co.C
Tucker, W.A. MS 44th Inf. Co.H
Tucker, W.A. TN 2nd Cav. Co.E
Tucker, W.A. TN 9th Inf. Co.B Sgt.
Tucker, W.A. TN 23rd Inf. Co.D
Tucker, W.A. TN Inf. 23rd Bn. Co.E
Tucker, W.A. TN 51st Inf. Co.C 1st Sgt.
Tucker, W.A. TN 51st (Cons.) Inf. Co.I
Tucker, W.A. VA Conscr. Cp.Lee Co.B
Tucker, Walter E. MS 10th Inf. Co.A
Tucker, Walter J. VA Inf. 25th Bn. Co.C
Tucker, Walter S. VA 3rd Cav. Co.C 2nd Lt.
Tucker, Washington FL 5th Inf. Co.I
Tucker, Washington TX 22nd Inf. Co.G
Tucker, W.B. AR Inf. Cocke's Regt. Co.F
Tucker, W.B. TN 20th Inf. Co.E
Tucker, W.B. TX Cav. 1st Regt.St.Troops Co.B
Tucker, W.B. VA 1st (Farinholt's) Res. Co.H
Tucker, W.C. KY 12th Cav. Co.G Cpl.
Tucker, W.C. LA 3rd Inf. Co.E
Tucker, W.C. MS Inf. 3rd Bn. (St.Troops) Co.D
Tucker, W.C. TN Lt.Arty. Rice's Btty.
Tucker, W.C. TN 51st (Cons.) Inf. Co.A
Tucker, W.C. TN 52nd Inf. Co.A
Tucker, W.C. Exch.Bn. Co.E,CSA
Tucker, W.D. AL 16th Inf.
Tucker, W.D. KY 4th Cav. Co.H
Tucker, W.D. MO Quantrill's Co.
Tucker, W.D. NC 67th Inf. Co.D
Tucker, W.D. TN Inf. 154th Sr.Regt. Asst.Surg.
Tucker, W.D. VA 51st Inf. Co.G
Tucker, W.E. AL 5th Cav. Co.A Cpl.
Tucker, W.E. MS 14th Inf. Co.H
Tucker, W.E. NC 17th Inf. (1st Org.) Co.L
Tucker, W.E. VA 2nd Inf.Loc.Def. Co.G
Tucker, W.E. VA Inf. 2nd Bn.Loc.Def. Co.A
Tucker, Wesley VA 19th Cav. Co.B
Tucker, Wesley H. VA 38th Inf. Co.F
Tucker, W.F. MS 41st Inf. Col.
Tucker, W.F. TN 8th (Smith's) Cav. Co.A Cpl.
Tucker, W.F. TN Conscr. (Cp. of Instr.)
Tucker, W.G. AR 1st (Monroe's) Cav. Co.L
Tucker, W.G. GA 15th Inf.
Tucker, W.G. NC 2nd Cav. (19th St.Troops) Co.F
Tucker, W.H. AL 3rd Res. Co.C
Tucker, W.H. AR 1st (Monroe's) Cav. Co.K
Tucker, W.H. GA Cav. 9th Bn. (St.Guards) Co.B
Tucker, W.H. GA 10th Inf. Co.A
Tucker, W.H. GA 60th Inf. Co.C
Tucker, W.H. GA 63rd Inf. Co.C
Tucker, W.H. MS 3rd Cav. Co.E
Tucker, W.H. SC 1st Mtd.Mil. Screven's Co.
Tucker, W.H. SC 7th Cav. Co.A QMSgt.
Tucker, W.H. SC Cav. Tucker's Co. Lance Cpl.
Tucker, W.H. SC Lt.Arty. J.T. Kanapaux's Co. (Lafayette Arty.)
Tucker, W.H. TN 7th (Duckworth's) Cav. Co.F
Tucker, W.H. TN 14th Cav. Co.C
Tucker, W.H. TX 12th Cav. Co.B
Tucker, W.H.H. 1st Conf.Cav. 2nd Co.A
Tucker, W.H.H. Horse Arty. White's Btty.
Tucker, Whil TN 11th Inf. Co.H
Tucker, Whiten D. VA 58th Inf. Co.C
Tucker, Whitten D. VA Loc.Def. Bosher's Co.
Tucker, W.H.J. AR 2nd Cav. Co.D
Tucker, Wilburn F. TN 1st (Turney's) Inf. Co.H
Tucker, Wiley AL 27th Inf. Co.B
Tucker, Wiley VA Hvy.Arty. 19th Bn. Co.D
Tucker, William AL 7th Cav. Co.D
Tucker, William AL 56th Part.Rangers Co.K
Tucker, William AL 5th Inf. New Co.A
Tucker, Wm. AL 21st Inf. Co.C
Tucker, William AL 29th Inf. Co.D Music.
Tucker, William AL 38th Inf. Co.H
Tucker, William AL 55th Vol. Co.E
Tucker, William AL 63rd Inf. Co.C
Tucker, William AR 7th Cav. Co.E
Tucker, Wm. AR 1st (Colquitt's) Inf. Co.D
Tucker, William AR 11th & 17th Cons.Inf. Co.I
Tucker, William AR 17th (Griffith's) Inf. Co.B
Tucker, William AR 35th Inf. Co.A Cpl.
Tucker, William AR 37th Inf. Co.K Cpl.
Tucker, William AR Inf. Adams' Regt. Moore's Co.
Tucker, William GA 12th Cav. Co.L
Tucker, William GA Cav. 29th Bn. Co.F Sgt.
Tucker, William GA 39th Inf. Co.B
Tucker, William KY 8th Cav. Co.C
Tucker, William KY 9th Cav. Co.H
Tucker, William MS 2nd Cav. Co.C
Tucker, William MS 9th Inf. Old Co.K Capt.
Tucker, William MS 13th Inf. Co.K
Tucker, William MS 33rd Inf. Co.F
Tucker, William MS Moseley's Regt.
Tucker, William MO 1st N.E. Cav. Co.A
Tucker, William MO 5th Cav.
Tucker, William MO 12th Cav. Co.A
Tucker, William MO Cav. Fristoe's Regt. Co.G
Tucker, William MO 1st & 4th Cons.Inf. Co.I
Tucker, William MO 4th Inf. Co.D
Tucker, William MO Thompson's Command
Tucker, William NC 3rd Inf. Co.D
Tucker, William NC 5th Sr.Res. Co.A
Tucker, William NC 23rd Inf. Co.A
Tucker, William NC 30th Inf. Co.E,F
Tucker, William NC 33rd Inf. Co.C
Tucker, William NC 44th Inf. Co.A
Tucker, William NC 51st Inf. Co.B
Tucker, William SC 2nd Cav. Co.C
Tucker, William SC Cav. 4th Bn. Co.B
Tucker, William TN 6th (Wheeler's) Cav. Co.C
Tucker, William TN 7th (Duckworth's) Cav. Co.D
Tucker, William TN 10th (DeMoss') Cav. Co.D
Tucker, William TN 19th & 20th (Cons.) Cav. Co.E
Tucker, William TN 34th Inf. Co.H
Tucker, William TX 22nd Cav. Co.E Cpl.
Tucker, William TX Cav. Wells' Bn. Co.A
Tucker, William TX 11th Inf. Co.I
Tucker, William TX 20th Inf. Co.K
Tucker, William VA Lt.Arty. 38th Bn. Co.C
Tucker, William VA 10th Inf. Co.L
Tucker, William VA 30th Bn.S.S. Co.E
Tucker, William VA 34th Inf. Co.C
Tucker, William VA 51st Inf. Co.K
Tucker, William VA 74th Mil. Co.E
Tucker, William VA 82nd Mil. Co.C
Tucker, William Conf.Cav. Wood's Regt. 2nd Co.F
Tucker, William A. AL 4th Cav. Co.M
Tucker, William A. AL 14th Inf. Co.D Cpl.
Tucker, William A. GA 3rd Bn. (St.Guards) Co.H
Tucker, William A. KY 2nd (Woodward's) Cav. Co.E,A
Tucker, William A. TN 43rd Inf. Co.F Cpl.
Tucker, William A. VA 59th Inf. 3rd Co.E Sgt.
Tucker, William A. VA 59th Inf. 2nd Co.H

Tucker, William A.L. GA 64th Inf. Co.I
Tucker, William B. AL 44th Inf. Co.A
Tucker, William B. MO 11th Inf. Co.E
Tucker, William B. SC 2nd Rifles Co.F
Tucker, William B. VA 4th Inf. Co.G Cpl.
Tucker, William C. TN 13th Inf. Co.D,A
Tucker, William D. AL 16th Inf. Co.C
Tucker, William D. GA 3rd Inf. Co.E
Tucker, William D. TN 1st (Feild's) Inf. Co.G
Tucker, Wm. D. Gen. & Staff Surg.
Tucker, William Dallas VA Arty. Dance's Co.
Tucker, William E. GA Cav. Hall's Co.
Tucker, William E. GA 42nd Inf. Co.E,A Sgt.
Tucker, William E. NC 47th Inf. Co.B
Tucker, William E. SC Lt.Arty. 3rd (Palmetto) Bn. Kanapaux's Co.
Tucker, William F. AR 12th Bn.S.S. Co.C Sr.2nd Lt.
Tucker, William F. AR 18th Inf. Co.D
Tucker, William F. GA 44th Inf. Co.H
Tucker, William F. MS 11th Inf. Co.H Capt.
Tucker, William F. TN 3rd (Clack's) Inf. Co.A Sgt.
Tucker, William F. TN 39th Mtd.Inf. Co.G Sgt.
Tucker, William F. Johnson's Staff Brig.Gen.
Tucker, William F. Johnson's Staff Capt.,AAG
Tucker, William G. AR 1st (Monroe's) Cav. Co.L
Tucker, William G. TN 34th Inf. Co.G
Tucker, William H. AL 3rd Bn.Res. Jackson's Co.
Tucker, William H. AL 14th Inf. Co.B N.C.S. Sgt.Maj.
Tucker, William H. AR 19th (Dawson's) Inf. Co.H
Tucker, William H. AR 27th Inf. New Co.B
Tucker, William H. KY 2nd (Duke's) Cav. Co.C
Tucker, William H. LA 7th Inf. Co.K Hosp.Stew.
Tucker, William H. SC 3rd Cav. Co.C
Tucker, William H. SC Cav.Mil. 4th Regt. Howard's Co.
Tucker, William H. TN 54th Inf. Hollis' Co.
Tucker, William H. TX 28th Cav. Co.G Capt.
Tucker, William H. VA Hvy.Arty. 20th Bn. Co.B
Tucker, William H. VA 18th Inf. Co.A
Tucker, William H. VA 20th Inf. Co.C
Tucker, William H. VA 20th Inf. Co.I
Tucker, William H. VA 22nd Inf. Co.A
Tucker, William H. VA Inf. 26th Bn. Co.B
Tucker, William H. VA 30th Bn.S.S. Co.A
Tucker, William H. VA 38th Inf. 2nd Co.I
Tucker, William H. VA 51st Inf. Co.G
Tucker, William H. VA 59th Inf. 3rd Co.B
Tucker, William H. VA 135th Mil. Co.D
Tucker, William H. Conf.Cav. Wood's Regt. Co.K
Tucker, Wm. H. Gen. & Staff Asst.Surg.
Tucker, William Henry 1st Conf.Eng.Troops Co.F
Tucker, William J. GA 45th Inf. Co.D
Tucker, William J. GA 50th Inf. Co.E
Tucker, William J. GA Cobb's Legion Co.A
Tucker, William J. KY 2nd Mtd.Inf. Co.G
Tucker, William J. NC 12th Inf. Co.C
Tucker, William J. SC 20th Inf. Co.E
Tucker, William J. TX 13th Cav. Co.D 2nd Lt.
Tucker, William Jackson GA 20th Inf. Co.K
Tucker, William L. GA 16th Inf. Co.F
Tucker, William L. TX Cav. Martin's Regt. Co.K
Tucker, William M. AR 7th Inf. Co.I
Tucker, William M. AR 27th Inf. Co.E,H
Tucker, William M. GA Inf. 10th Bn. Co.D
Tucker, William M. MS 21st Inf. Co.K
Tucker, William M. MO Lt.Arty. Farris' Btty. (Clark Arty.)
Tucker, William M. NC 12th Inf. Co.E
Tucker, William M. TN 1st (Feild's) Inf. Co.G
Tucker, William M. TN 34th Inf. 2nd Co.C
Tucker, William M. TN 48th Inf. Co.H
Tucker, William M. TN 53rd Inf. Co.C
Tucker, William M. VA 9th Inf. 1st Co.H
Tucker, William M. VA Inf. 28th Bn. Co.C
Tucker, William M. VA 42nd Inf. Co.D
Tucker, William M. VA 59th Inf. 2nd Co.H
Tucker, William M. Stuart Horse Arty. Johnson's Btty.,CSA
Tucker, William Mc. TN 44th Inf. Co.I
Tucker, William Mc. TN 44th (Cons.) Inf. Co.A
Tucker, William N. AR 27th Inf. Co.H
Tucker, William P. LA 9th Inf. Co.E Cpl.
Tucker, William P. NC 62nd Inf. Co.C
Tucker, William P. VA 26th Inf. Co.C
Tucker, William R. AL 28th Inf. Co.E 2nd Lt.
Tucker, William R. GA 20th Inf. Co.A
Tucker, William R. NC Jones' Co. (Supp.Force)
Tucker, William R. TN 45th Inf. Co.I
Tucker, William R. VA Lt.Arty. Jeffress' Co.
Tucker, William R. VA 14th Inf. Co.F
Tucker, William S. GA 41st Inf. Co.K,E
Tucker, William S. VA Inf. 5th Bn. Co.C
Tucker, William S. VA 53rd Inf. Co.C
Tucker, William S. VA 53rd Inf. Co.F Cpl.
Tucker, William S. VA Inf. Montague's Bn. Co.C
Tucker, Williamson TN Miller's Co. (Loc.Def.Troops)
Tucker, William T. GA 6th Inf. Co.K
Tucker, William T. VA 5th Cav. Co.H
Tucker, William T. VA Arty. Dance's Co.
Tucker, William W. AL 28th Inf. Co.H
Tucker, William W. FL 1st Inf. Old Co.I, New Co.C 1st Lt.
Tucker, William W. GA 3rd Inf. Co.L
Tucker, William W. GA 35th Inf. Co.D
Tucker, William W. LA 16th Inf. Co.C
Tucker, William W. NC 67th Inf. Co.I 2nd Lt.
Tucker, William W. TX 10th Cav. Co.E
Tucker, William W. VA 12th Inf. Co.A
Tucker, Willis C. AL 49th Inf. Co.F
Tucker, Willis P. VA 2nd Cav. Co.B
Tucker, Willis W. VA 3rd Inf. Co.A Cpl.
Tucker, Willoughby FL 10th Inf. Co.D
Tucker, Wilson AR 36th Inf. Co.F
Tucker, Wilson M. TN 1st (Feild's) Inf. Co.G
Tucker, Winfree VA 74th Mil. Co.E
Tucker, W.J. AR 10th (Witt's) Cav. Co.C
Tucker, W.J. FL Cav. 5th Bn. Co.H
Tucker, W.J. FL Inf. 2nd Bn. Co.C
Tucker, W.J. FL 9th Inf. Co.E
Tucker, W.J. SC 4th Cav. Co.A
Tucker, W.J. TN 16th (Logwood's) Cav. Co.D
Tucker, W.J. TN 15th Inf. Co.E
Tucker, W.J. TN 33rd Inf. Co.H
Tucker, W.J. TX 26th Cav. Co.H
Tucker, W.J. TX Cav. Madison's Regt. Co.B
Tucker, W.J. VA 5th Cav. Co.C
Tucker, W.L. LA Ogden's Cav. Co.F
Tucker, W.L. MS 4th Cav. Co.D
Tucker, W.L. MS Cav. Hughes' Bn. Co.C
Tucker, W.L. TX Cav. McCord's Frontier Regt. Co.E Cpl.
Tucker, W.M. GA Arty. St.Troops Pruden's Btty. Cpl.
Tucker, W.M. TN 45th Inf. Co.K
Tucker, W.M. TX 13th Vol. 1st Co.K Sgt.
Tucker, W.M. VA 2nd Cav. Co.G
Tucker, W.N. TX 9th Cav. Co.B
Tucker, W.N. TX Waul's Legion Co.H
Tucker, Woodson SC 1st (Butler's) Inf. Co.A,K
Tucker, W.P. AL 4th Inf. Co.D
Tucker, W.P. AL Cp. of Instr. Talladega Co.D
Tucker, W.P. GA 2nd Cav. Co.D
Tucker, W.P. SC 1st (Butler's) Inf. Co.E Sgt.
Tucker, W.R. SC 3rd Cav. Co.B
Tucker, Wright GA 21st Inf. Co.B
Tucker, Wright NC 2nd Inf. Co.K
Tucker, W.S. AL 38th Inf. Co.B
Tucker, W.S. SC 1st Mtd.Mil. Smith's Co. 2nd Lt.
Tucker, W.S. TN 20th (Russell's) Cav. Co.I
Tucker, W.T. AL 34th Inf. Co.A
Tucker, W.T. AL Seldon's Bn. Co.I
Tucker, W.T. GA 7th Cav. Co.D
Tucker, W.T. GA Cav. 24th Bn. Co.C
Tucker, W.T. SC 1st St.Troops Co.C
Tucker, W.T. VA 8th Inf. Co.G
Tucker, W. Thomas KY 3rd Mtd.Inf. Co.E
Tucker, W.W. AL 24th Inf. Co.F
Tucker, W.W. AL 45th Inf. Co.F
Tucker, W.W. FL 2nd Cav. Co.F
Tucker, W.W. GA 66th Inf.
Tucker, W.W. MS 9th Bn.S.S. Co.A Capt.
Tucker, W.W. MO 8th Cav. Co.H
Tucker, W.W. VA 39th Mil. Co.B
Tucker, Wyatt VA Hvy.Arty. 19th Bn. Co.D
Tucker, Wyatt VA 19th Inf. Co.I
Tucker, Yancy TN 29th Inf. Co.K
Tucker, Young KY 12th Cav. Co.E
Tucker, Z. LA Inf. 9th Bn. Co.D
Tucker, Z. SC 27th Inf. Co.I
Tucker, Zachariah AL 23rd Inf. Co.C
Tucker, Zebulon B. TN 1st (Turney's) Inf. Co.A Cpl.
Tucker, Zephaniah NC 58th Inf. Co.C,D
Tucker, Zepheniah H. NC Cav. 5th Bn. Co.C Cpl.
Tucker, Zepheniah H. NC 6th Cav. (65th St.Troops) Co.C Cpl.
Tucker, Zill TX 10th Cav. Co.H
Tucket, J.C. AL 30th Inf. Co.E
Tuckett, T.A. Gen. & Staff Capt.,AAAG
Tuckette, John G. SC 2nd Cav. Co.H
Tuckey, --- 1st Seminole Mtd.Vol.
Tuckey, H. GA 30th Inf. Co.I
Tuckey, W.J. GA Inf. Athens Reserved Corps
Tuckness, Thomas TN 16th (Logwood's) Cav. Co.I
Tucks, C. TX 5th Field Btty. Cpl.

Tucks, C. TX Lt.Arty. Dege's Bn. Cpl.
Tucks, W.R. GA Cav. Dorough's Bn.
Tucks Se 1st Cherokee Mtd.Rifles Co.H
Tuckweller, Absalom VA 97th Mil. Co.K
Tuckwiler, Crawford VA 22nd Inf. Co.E
Tuckwiller, Henry VA 97th Mil. Co.F
Tuckwiller, John VA 60th Inf. Co.E
Tuckwiller, M. VA 22nd Inf. Co.B
Tuckwiller, William VA 2nd Inf. Co.E
Tuckwiller, William VA 97th Mil. Co.F
Tucons, C. MO 8th Cav. Reed's Co.
Tudale, C.W. VA Hvy.Arty. Wright's Co.
Tuder, B.F. TX 9th (Young's) Inf. Co.K
Tuder, F.C. VA 32nd Inf. Co.F
Tuder, John D. MS 2nd St.Cav. Co.A
Tuder, R.S. VA 32nd Inf. Co.F
Tuder, Thomas B. MS 11th Inf. Co.A
Tuder, W.D. MS 10th Inf. New Co.K 1st Sgt.
Tuder, William B. TN 63rd Inf. Co.B
Tuder, Woodward S. MS 2nd St.Cav. Co.A
Tudgele, William J. LA 31st Inf. Co.E
Tudis, A.D. AL 42nd Inf. Co.D
Tudor, Abrose KY 8th Mtd.Inf. Co.E Cpl.
Tudor, Charles KY 7th Cav. Co.F
Tudor, Cyrus VA 61st Inf. Co.G
Tudor, H. MS 7th Cav. Co.H
Tudor, Henderson TN Inf. 22nd Bn. Co.D
Tudor, Henry TX Cav. 3rd (Yager's) Bn. Co.B
Tudor, Hezekiah GA Inf. 1st Loc.Troops (Augusta) Co.H
Tudor, H.L. MS 7th Cav. Co.H
Tudor, J. TN 15th (Cons.) Cav. Co.E,D
Tudor, J.A. MS 7th Cav. Co.H
Tudor, James TN Inf. 22nd Bn. Co.D
Tudor, James C. VA Loc.Def. Chappell's Co.
Tudor, James R. VA 12th Inf. Co.F
Tudor, J.D. TX 29th Cav. Co.C
Tudor, John TN 51st (Cons.) Inf. Co.A
Tudor, John TN 52nd Inf. Co.A
Tudor, John G. MS 2nd Inf. Co.F
Tudor, Joseph VA Hvy.Arty. 18th Bn. Co.C
Tudor, Lord AL 95th Mil. Co.D
Tudor, Nicholas F.M. TX 10th Inf. Co.K
Tudor, Raiford GA 28th Inf. Co.C
Tudor, Richard VA 12th Inf. Co.K Sgt.
Tudor, Robert VA 12th Inf. 2nd Co.I
Tudor, R.R. MO Inf. Clark's Regt. Co.A
Tudor, R.W. MO 9th Inf. Co.B
Tudor, T.B. MS Cav. Street's Bn.
Tudor, T.B. MS 4th Inf.
Tudor, T.B. TN 15th (Cons.) Cav. Co.E,D
Tudor, Theophilus VA 61st Inf. Co.G
Tudor, Thomas B. MS 23rd Inf. Co.G Sgt.
Tudor, T.W. TN 15th (Cons.) Cav. Co.E,D
Tudor, William GA Inf. 1st Loc.Troops (Augusta) Co.E,B
Tudor, William D. MS 23rd Inf. Co.G Cpl.
Tudor, William E. VA 16th Inf. Co.E
Tudor, William Henry VA Inf. 1st Bn. Co.E
Tudor, William J. VA 12th Inf. Co.F
Tudson, Josephus 1st Choctaw & Chickasaw Mtd.Rifles 2nd Co.K
Tudury, Anthony LA Mil. 5th Regt.Eur.Brig. (Spanish Regt.) Co.5
Tudury, R. LA Mil. 5th Regt.Eur.Brig. (Spanish Regt.) Co.1
Tueger, William P. MS Cav. 13th Regt. Co.B
Tuel, Isaac S. VA 19th Inf. Co.F
Tuel, James S. GA 9th Inf. (St.Guards) Co.B
Tuel, Socrates VA Cav. 35th Bn. Co.F
Tuel, W.H. TX 10th Cav. Co.D Sgt.
Tuell, A.J. SC Cav. DeSaussure's Squad.
Tuell, A.J. SC Hvy.Arty. 15th (Lucas') Bn. Co.B
Tuell, C.C. 3rd Conf.Eng.Troops Co.E
Tuell, George W. MO 9th Bn.S.S. Co.A Sgt.
Tuell, Nathaniel O. GA Cherokee Legion (St.Guards) Co.D Jr.2nd Lt.
Tuell, R.A. GA 28th Inf. Co.F 2nd Lt.
Tuell, S.S. LA 15th Inf. Co.I
Tuening, George W. VA 162nd Mil. Co.A
Tuening, John W. VA 162nd Mil. Co.C
Tueo, Martin LA 2nd Cav. Co.C
Tuereau, Fred LA 13th Inf. Co.H
Tuergens, William TX 1st Hvy.Arty. Co.C
Tuerill, Stephen LA Miles' Legion
Tuey, J.B. LA 6th Cav. Co.I Sgt.
Tuey, Michael 9th Conf.Inf. Co.E
Tuffer, J.A. MS 2nd St.Cav. Co.G
Tuffley, John TX Cav. Waller's Regt. Co.C
Tuffley, Simon TX Inf. 1st St.Troops Stevenson's Co.F
Tuffts, David F. AR Lt.Arty. Thrall's Btty. QMSgt.
Tuft, J.B. Gen. & Staff Surg.
Tuft, W.B. VA 54th Mil. Co.G
Tufts, A.W. LA Inf.Crescent Regt. Co.C
Tufts, B.M. GA Cav. 8th Bn. (St.Guards) Co.A
Tufts, Charles E. VA Goochland Lt.Arty. Cpl.
Tufts, Joseph T.A. GA Inf. 2nd Bn. Co.C Ord.Sgt.
Tufts, O. GA Cav. 1st Bn.Res. Tufts' Co. Capt.
Tufts, O. GA Cav. 8th Bn. (St.Guards) Co.A 1st Sgt.
Tufts, Orris GA Inf. 2nd Bn. Co.C
Tufts, William VA Lt.Arty. Clutter's Co.
Tugg, A. GA 26th Inf. Co.F
Tuggle, Adam G. GA 35th Inf. Co.H Cpl.
Tuggle, Alexander C. GA 8th Inf. (St.Guards) Co.B
Tuggle, Anderson GA 35th Inf. Co.H
Tuggle, Anderson VA 24th Inf. Co.I
Tuggle, Augustus W. GA 3rd Inf. Co.C
Tuggle, Bennett S. GA 66th Inf. Co.E Cpl.
Tuggle, Charles M. GA 35th Inf. Co.H
Tuggle, Charles M. GA 35th Inf. Co.H Capt.
Tuggle, Edward B. GA 3rd Inf. Co.C Sgt.
Tuggle, Edward Y. VA Hvy.Arty. 19th Bn. Co.A
Tuggle, E.H. AL 13th Bn.Part.Rangers Co.C
Tuggle, E.H. AL 56th Part.Rangers Co.G
Tuggle, George MS 46th Inf. Co.H
Tuggle, George M. GA 35th Inf. Co.H Sgt.
Tuggle, G.R. TN 13th Inf. Co.C
Tuggle, Henry H. GA 35th Inf. Co.H
Tuggle, Henry L. VA Hvy.Arty. Kyle's Co.
Tuggle, Henry P. TX 10th Inf. Co.I
Tuggle, Henry T. VA Hvy.Arty. 19th Bn. Co.A
Tuggle, H.L. VA 3rd Res. Co.I
Tuggle, James KY 6th Cav. Co.B
Tuggle, James KY 13th Cav. Co.K
Tuggle, James MO 4th Cav. Co.F Sgt.
Tuggle, James TN 63rd Inf. Co.C
Tuggle, James 3rd Conf.Eng.Troops Co.A
Tuggle, James B. AR Cav. Carlton's Regt. Co.G
Tuggle, James B. AR 1st (Colquitt's) Inf. Co.K Sgt.
Tuggle, J.B. GA 5th Inf. Co.G
Tuggle, J.B. GA Inf. 25th Bn. (Prov.Guard) Co.E
Tuggle, J.C. AR 1st Vol. Co.I 1st Sgt.
Tuggle, J.C. AR 38th Inf. Co.K
Tuggle, John LA 11th Inf. Co.H
Tuggle, John MS 21st Inf. Co.C
Tuggle, John VA 60th Inf. 2nd Co.H
Tuggle, John VA 151st Mil. Co.D
Tuggle, John B. GA 5th Inf. Co.G
Tuggle, John F. GA 13th Inf. Co.G
Tuggle, John N. VA Conscr. Cp.Lee
Tuggle, John P. GA Inf. 27th Bn. Co.F,D
Tuggle, Joseph AL 56th Part.Rangers Co.G
Tuggle, Joseph T. TN 13th Inf. Co.C
Tuggle, Joseph W. AL 50th Inf. Co.I
Tuggle, Joseph W. TN 38th Inf. 1st Co.H
Tuggle, J.W. GA 10th Cav. (St.Guards) Co.H
Tuggle, J.W. GA Inf. (Express Inf.) Witt's Co.
Tuggle, J.W. TX 29th Cav. Co.D
Tuggle, Leroy GA 27th Inf. Co.F Cpl.
Tuggle, Lewis GA 27th Inf. Co.F
Tuggle, Lewis VA Inf. 26th Bn. Co.C
Tuggle, Lewis A. VA 60th Inf. 2nd Co.H
Tuggle, Manning J. GA 35th Inf. Co.H
Tuggle, Milton B. GA Cav. 7th Bn. (St.Guards) Co.D Cpl.
Tuggle, Milton B. GA 3rd Inf. Co.C
Tuggle, M.T. GA Arty. 8th Regt. Co.A
Tuggle, N. GA Arty. Lumpkin's Co.
Tuggle, Nathaniel VA 42nd Inf. Co.H
Tuggle, Newton M. LA 9th Inf. Co.A
Tuggle, N.M. TX 21st Inf. Co.E
Tuggle, P.P. TN 13th Inf. Co.C
Tuggle, Ransom TX 1st (McCulloch's) Cav. Co.G Surg.
Tuggle, Ransom Gen. & Staff AASurg.
Tuggle, Richard H. AR 26th Inf. Co.B
Tuggle, Richard W. VA 3rd Cav. Co.E
Tuggle, Robert GA 5th Res. Co.E
Tuggle, Robert GA 8th Inf. Co.K
Tuggle, Robert TX 13th Vol. 1st Co.K
Tuggle, Robert TX 15th Inf. 2nd Co.F 1st Lt.
Tuggle, Robert J. GA 7th Inf. (St.Guards) Co.B Capt.
Tuggle, Robert L. AR 3rd Inf. Co.C
Tuggle, R.P. GA Inf. 27th Bn. Co.F
Tuggle, Russell A. GA 35th Inf. Co.H
Tuggle, Samuel R. VA 44th Inf. Co.G
Tuggle, Sanford GA 35th Inf. Co.H
Tuggle, Thomas J. MS 13th Inf. Co.F
Tuggle, Thomas S. GA Arty. Baker's Co.
Tuggle, T.J. TN 13th Inf. Co.C Cpl.
Tuggle, Toliver GA 10th Cav. (St.Guards) Co.H
Tuggle, Walter C. AL St.Arty. Co.A Cpl.
Tuggle, W.H. MO 1st & 3rd Cons.Cav. Co.K Cpl.
Tuggle, William MS 46th Inf. Co.F
Tuggle, William MO 2nd Inf. Co.E
Tuggle, William VA 58th Inf. Co.H
Tuggle, William A. VA 18th Inf. Co.F
Tuggle, William B. GA 3rd Inf. Co.C Cpl.
Tuggle, William C. GA Arty. (Chatham Arty.) Wheaton's Co.

Tuggle, William C. GA 1st (Olmstead's) Inf. Claghorn's Co.
Tuggle, William H. GA 13th Cav. Co.D
Tuggle, William H. GA 8th Inf. Co.K
Tuggle, William L. GA Cav. 7th Bn. (St.Guards) Co.D Sgt.
Tuggle, William O. GA 4th Inf. Co.B
Tuggle, William O. KY 14th Cav. Co.B Sgt.
Tuggle, William T. AR 3rd Inf. Co.C
Tuggle, William T. TX 12th Inf. Co.H Cpl.
Tuggle, W.O. Nitre & Min. Bureau War Dept., CSA 2nd Lt.
Tuggle, Woodward GA 35th Inf. Co.H
Tuggles, William H. MO 1st Cav. Co.K
Tugle, W.R. AR 26th Inf.
Tugman, Benjamin F. NC 58th Inf. Co.I
Tugman, James M. NC 37th Inf. Co.B
Tugman, J.J. NC 5th Sr.Res. Co.I
Tugmon, Mecager NC 37th Inf.
Tugwell, Benjamin S. LA 31st Inf. Co.I Cpl.
Tugwell, H.H. TN 31st Inf. Co.D
Tugwell, John T. NC 44th Inf. Co.D
Tugwell, John W. AR 8th Inf. New Co.F
Tugwell, Levi NC 27th Inf. Co.E
Tugwell, Levi NC 44th Inf. Co.D
Tugwell, Robbert AR 1st Vol. Co.B
Tugwell, Robert AR 27th Inf. Co.G
Tugwell, Robert NC 44th Inf. Co.D
Tugyler, T.J. TX Cav. 2nd Bn.St.Troops Wilson's Co.
Tuhner, John LA 8th Inf. Co.I
Tuhri, M. LA Mil. 2nd Regt. 2nd Brig. 1st Div. Co.F
Tuillier, Amede LA 1st Hvy.Arty. (Reg.) Co.A
Tuillier, Forrester LA 1st Hvy.Arty. (Reg.) Co.A
Tuillier, Lawrence LA 1st Hvy.Arty. (Reg.) Co.A
Tuillier, Mayence LA 1st Hvy.Arty. (Reg.) Co.A
Tuillier, Oscar LA 1st Hvy.Arty. (Reg.) Co.A
Tuilloway, L. GA Inf. 2nd Bn. (St.Guards) Co.A
Tuisdle, --- TN 16th (Logwood's) Cav. Co.I
Tuisley, I.H. LA Inf.Cons.Crescent Regt. Co.F
Tuit, Michael MD 1st Inf. Co.G
Tuite, Andrew SC 1st (Butler's) Inf. Co.E
Tuite, John A. NC 3rd Cav. (41st St.Troops) Co.F
Tuitu, B.G.A. SC 11th Inf. Co.E
Tujacque, --- LA Mil. 2nd Regt. French Brig. Co.1
Tujague, Alexander LA Mil. 1st Regt. French Brig. Co.6,10
Tujague, F. LA Mil. 1st Regt. French Brig. Co.6
Tujague, Frois LA Mil. 3rd Regt.Eur.Brig. (Garde Francaise) Co.4
Tujague, J.M. LA Mil. 1st Regt. French Brig. Co.3
Tujague, Joseph LA Mil. 3rd Regt.Eur.Brig. (Garde Francaise) Frois' Co.
Tuke, H. MS 44th Inf. Co.A
Tuke, Henry SC 1st (Butler's) Inf. Co.C
Tuke, J.H. AL 6th Inf. Co.K
Tuker, C.E. MS 18th Cav. Co.H
Tukobbi, William 1st Choctaw Mtd.Rifles Co.K
Tul, I.J. AL Coosa Guards J.W. Suttles' Co.
Tul, W.H. AL Coosa Guards J.W. Suttles' Co.
Tulaird, J. GA 43rd Inf. Co.C
Tulane, Alonzo J. VA 6th Inf. Co.A
Tulane, Arthur VA Inf. 4th Bn.Loc.Def. Co.C
Tulane, Horatio B. AL 3rd Inf. Co.I
Tulbert, J.R. VA Inf. 1st Bn.Loc.Def. Co.F
Tulbeth, J.C. VA Mil. Carroll Cty.
Tulbird, W.F. AL 8th Inf. Co.E
Tulburt, B.F. AL 22nd Inf. Co.F
Tulburt, J.L. NC 66th Inf. Co.G
Tulburt, Joshua C. VA 29th Inf. 2nd Co.F
Tuley, Charles M.M. TN 1st (Turney's) Inf. Co.K 1st Sgt.
Tuley, F.M. MS 1st Cav. Co.H
Tuley, M.B. TX Conscr.
Tuley, W.H. MO 6th Cav. Co.K
Tuley, Wright W. TN 1st (Turney's) Inf. Co.K
Tulford, Arthur Thomas GA 54th Inf. Co.C Sgt.
Tulgham, James T. MS 10th Inf. Old Co.E
Tulghan, Allen AL Cp. of Instr. Talladega
Tulghum, R.T. Gen. & Staff 1st Lt.,ADC
Tulhar, 1st Creek Mtd.Vol. Co.K
Tulington, A.J. TN 8th Cav. Co.A
Tulis, John B. MO 2nd N.E. Cav. (Franklin's Regt.)
Tuliver 1st Creek Mtd.Vol. Co.F
Tulk, H.T. MO 3rd & 5th Cons.Inf. Co.F
Tulk, Jacob TN 62nd Mtd.Inf. Co.D
Tulks, T.A. AL 51st (Part.Rangers)
Tull, Charles S. MO 1st Cav. Co.G
Tull, D.G. Gen. & Staff Asst.Surg.
Tull, Dudley G. MS 2nd Part.Rangers Co.H 1st Sgt.
Tull, Dudley G. TN Cav. 1st Bn. (McNairy's) Co.C
Tull, E.A. AR 1st (Monroe's) Cav. Co.H 1st Lt.
Tull, F.M. AR 35th Inf. Co.A
Tull, F.M. GA 8th Cav. Co.G Sgt.
Tull, F.M. GA 62nd Cav. Co.G Sgt.
Tull, Francis M. GA 1st (Ramsey's) Inf. Co.C
Tull, Francis S. GA 36th (Villepigue's) Inf. Co.I Capt.
Tull, Frank MS 24th Inf. Co.G
Tull, Frederick GA Lt.Arty. (Jo Thompson Arty.) Hanleiter's Co.
Tull, Frederick KY 1st (Helm's) Cav. Co.F
Tull, Frederick KY 6th Mtd.Inf. Co.B
Tull, George W. TX 15th Cav. Co.I
Tull, G.W. Brush Bn.
Tull, H.J. MS 7th Cav. 1st Co.H
Tull, Isaac W. TX 10th Inf. Co.D
Tull, Isaac W. TX 12th Inf. Co.L
Tull, J. TN 51st (Cons.) Inf. Co.C
Tull, J.A. 4th Conf.Inf. Co.K
Tull, J.L. KY 6th Mtd.Inf. Co.C
Tull, John AR 11th & 17th Cons.Inf. Co.I
Tull, John AR 17th (Griffith's) Inf. Co.F
Tull, John AR 35th Inf. Co.A
Tull, John A. TN 42nd Inf. Co.D
Tull, John F. LA 9th Inf. Co.G
Tull, John G. TX 15th Cav. Co.F
Tull, Justus H. LA 9th Inf. Co.G Sgt.
Tull, Lemuel H. NC 3rd Inf. Co.E
Tull, Lemuel H. NC 66th Inf. Co.I
Tull, L.G.S.J. TX 7th Inf. Co.G
Tull, L.H. AR 11th Inf. Co.A
Tull, L.H. AR 11th & 17th Cons.Inf. Co.A Cpl.
Tull, L.H. NC 8th Bn.Part.Rangers Co.F
Tull, Martin L. Gen. & Staff, QM Dept.
Tull, Samuel LA Inf. 1st Bn. (St.Guards) Co.B
Tull, T.M. AR 1st (Monroe's) Cav. Co.H
Tull, W.B. LA 9th Inf. Co.G
Tull, W.C. KY 2nd (Woodward's) Cav. Co.G
Tull, W.D. TN 47th Inf. Co.K
Tull, William AR 11th & 17th Cons.Inf. Co.I
Tull, William AR 17th (Griffith's) Inf. Co.F
Tull, William AR 35th Inf. Co.A
Tull, Willis C. KY 1st (Helm's) Cav. New Co.A
Tullabouque, S. 1st Chickasaw Inf. Hanes' Co.
Tullas, Albert TX 13th Cav. Co.K
Tullas, Henry LA 5th Cav. Co.I
Tullas, Joseph LA 5th Cav. Co.I
Tullas, Robert LA 5th Cav. Co.I
Tullas, Silas A. LA 5th Cav. Co.I
Tullas, W.B. AL 4th Res. Co.H 1st Sgt.
Tullatubba, C. 1st Chickasaw Inf. Minnis' Co.
Tullen, John AR 21st Inf. Co.H
Tullent, T.H. MS Cav. 2nd Bn.Res. Co.F
Tuller, A. AL 33rd Inf. Co.H
Tuller, A.B. TX 12th Inf. Co.D
Tuller, Daniel TX Inf. 1st St.Troops Wheat's Co.A
Tuller, R. AL 1st Regt. Mobile Vol. Baas' Co.
Tuller, W.H. GA 3rd Bn. (St.Guards) Co.E
Tuller, W.H. GA Inf. (Express Inf.) Witt's Co.
Tulley, B. LA Conscr.
Tulley, George W. AR 5th Inf. Co.K
Tulley, Jno. LA Inf.Cons. 18th Regt. & Yellow Jacket Bn. Co.E
Tulley, John MD Cav. 2nd Bn. Co.D
Tulley, John VA 1st St.Res. Co.C
Tulley, John W. TX 27th Cav. Co.I,N
Tulley, L.D. AL 60th Inf. Co.K
Tulley, M. FL 9th Inf. Co.E
Tulley, M. GA 2nd Bn. Troops & Defences (Macon) Co.C
Tulley, Michael GA 1st (Olmstead's) Inf. Co.A
Tulley, Owen TN 15th Inf. Co.C
Tulley, Patrick LA Mil. Barr's Ind.Co. (Blakesley Guards)
Tulley, R.S. KY 2nd (Duke's) Cav. Co.B Cpl.
Tulley, Rufus KY 1st Inf. Co.K
Tulley, T.S. GA 24th Bn.Part.Rangers Co.A 2nd Lt.
Tulley, W.C. AL 6th Inf. Co.E
Tulley, William TN 51st (Cons.) Inf. Co.A
Tulley, William C. Inf. School of Pract. Powell's Detach. Co.B
Tulley, William J. SC Inf. Hampton Legion Co.B
Tulley, W.M. TN 52nd Inf. Co.D Sgt.
Tullford, Joseph VA 54th Mil. Co.C,D
Tulli, E.M. SC Mil.Arty. 1st Regt. Pope's Co.
Tullier, Dorval LA 4th Inf. Co.H
Tullier, J.B. LA 30th Inf. Co.I,B
Tullier, Portalis LA 4th Inf. Co.H
Tullier, Ulysse LA 4th Inf. Co.H
Tullis, A. GA 13th Cav. Co.K
Tullis, A.D. TX 18th Inf. Co.D 1st Sgt.
Tullis, B.A. AL 33rd Inf. Co.K
Tullis, C. LA 28th (Gray's) Inf. Co.C
Tullis, Claiborn MS 5th Inf. (St.Troops) Co.G
Tullis, Edmund AR 10th Inf. Co.D 3rd Lt.
Tullis, Eli Conf.Cav. Wood's Regt. 1st Co.A
Tullis, E.M. SC 1st Arty. Co.A
Tullis, George W. MS 15th Inf. Co.I
Tullis, G.G. TX Inf. Timmons' Regt. Co.I
Tullis, G.G. TX Waul's Legion Co.E

Tullis, Jackson MS 5th Inf. (St.Troops) Co.G
Tullis, James LA 27th Inf. Co.E
Tullis, James TX Waul's Legion Co.E
Tullis, James M. AL 33rd Inf. Co.K Cpl.
Tullis, James M. GA 2nd Cav. Co.G
Tullis, James M. GA 12th Inf. Co.K
Tullis, James M. GA 46th Inf. Co.F
Tullis, Jesse LA 12th Inf. 2nd Co.M, Co.D
Tullis, Jessee LA 9th Inf. Co.K
Tullis, J.M. TX Inf. Timmons' Regt. Co.I
Tullis, John LA Arty. Watson Btty.
Tullis, John A. GA 47th Inf. Co.I Sgt.
Tullis, John C. GA 5th Res. Co.E
Tullis, John W. AL Lt.Arty. Hurt's Btty. 1st Lt.
Tullis, J.R. LA 1st Hvy.Arty. (Reg.) Co.G
Tullis, J.T. LA 9th Inf. Co.K
Tullis, Lehn MS 2nd Cav. Co.A
Tullis, Marion LA 9th Inf. Co.K
Tullis, Marion LA 12th Inf. 2nd Co.M, Co.D
Tullis, Moses TN 5th (McKenzie's) Cav. Co.A
Tullis, N. GA 13th Cav. Co.K
Tullis, P.A. GA 54th Inf. Co.I
Tullis, Richard MS 4th Cav. Co.A
Tullis, Richard MS 46th Inf. Co.B
Tullis, R.W. GA 47th Inf. Co.I Cpl.
Tullis, Stephen GA 1st (Symons') Res. Co.C
Tullis, Thomas E. AL 46th Inf. Co.C
Tullis, Thomas E. Gen. & Staff Surg.
Tullis, Thomas J. LA 1st Hvy.Arty. (Reg.) Co.H
Tullis, T.J. LA 17th Inf. Co.C
Tullis, W.B. AL 46th Inf. Co.C
Tullis, William MS Cav. 1st Bn. (McNair's) St.Troops Co.A
Tullis, William MS Inf. 1st Bn.St.Troops (12 mo. '62-3) Co.E 1st Sgt.
Tullis, William MS Home Guards Barnes' Co. 1st Sgt.
Tullis, William J. GA 24th Inf. Co.F
Tullis, William J. TX Cav. Martin's Regt. Co.D
Tullis, Wm. J. TX 11th Field Btty.
Tullis, W.R. GA 1st Reg. Co.F
Tullit, James LA 2nd Res.Corps Co.K
Tulliy, M. LA Arty. 8th Bn.
Tullman, William AL Cav. Hardie's Bn.Res. Co.K
Tulloaf Harjo 2nd Creek Mtd.Vol. Co.E
Tulloch, David NC 13th Inf. Co.K
Tulloch, James NC 13th Inf. Co.K
Tulloch, James W. VA Inf. 22nd Bn. Co.H
Tulloch, John SC 1st Arty. Co.C
Tulloch, John J. VA Inf. 22nd Bn. Co.H
Tulloch, John R. NC 13th Inf. Co.K
Tullock, A.J. MO 12th Inf. Co.C Cpl.
Tullock, C.T. MO 10th Inf. Co.F
Tullock, C.T. MO 12th Inf. Co.C
Tullock, E.M. TN 29th Inf. Co.F
Tullock, Mot TN Inf. 2nd Cons.Regt. Co.E
Tullock, Samuel MO 12th Inf. Co.C
Tulloh, J.J. VA 2nd Arty. Co.H
Tulloh, Joseph L. VA 13th Inf. Co.D
Tulloh, J.W. VA 2nd Arty. Co.H
Tulloh, Newton W. VA 23rd Inf. Co.E
Tulloh, Noah H. VA 23rd Inf. Co.E
Tullons, Richard TX 2nd Cav. Co.K
Tullop, Joseph D. VA Lt.Arty. 12th Bn. 1st Co.A
Tullors, J.C. TN 1st Hvy.Arty. Co.K
Tullos, A. TX Cav. Terry's Regt. Co.H
Tullos, A.G. MS 1st Lt.Arty. Co.C
Tullos, A.J. AR 36th Inf. Co.C
Tullos, Alfred MS 8th Inf. Co.E
Tullos, A.M. MS 8th Inf. Co.E
Tullos, Anselm N. TX Cav. 6th Bn. Co.A
Tullos, A.W. MS Inf. 1st Bn.St.Troops (12 mo. '62-3) Co.C
Tullos, C.W. MS 8th Inf. Co.C
Tullos, C.W. MS 46th Inf. Co.H
Tullos, Daniel Norviel LA 28th (Gray's) Inf. Co.F
Tullos, George S. TX Cav. 1st Regt.St.Troops Co.C 1st Lt.
Tullos, G.M. TX 7th Cav. Co.E
Tullos, Henry LA 13th Bn. (Part.Rangers) Co.E
Tullos, Howard LA 3rd (Wingfield's) Cav. Co.A
Tullos, J.A. MS 1st Lt.Arty. Co.C
Tullos, J.A. TX 7th Cav. Co.E Cpl.
Tullos, J.A. TX Cav. Terry's Regt. Co.H
Tullos, Jackson MS 3rd (St.Troops) Cav. Co.K
Tullos, James B. TX Cav. 6th Bn. Co.A Cpl.
Tullos, J.B. TX 7th Cav. Co.E
Tullos, J.H. TX 7th Cav. Co.E
Tullos, J.M. MS 8th Inf. Co.E
Tullos, J.N. MS 1st Lt.Arty. Co.C
Tullos, John B. TX Cav. 6th Bn. Co.A
Tullos, John Thomas LA 28th (Gray's) Inf. Co.F
Tullos, Joseph LA 13th Bn. (Part.Rangers) Co.E
Tullos, Joseph MS 6th Inf. Co.C
Tullos, Joseph A. TX Cav. 6th Bn. Co.A Capt.
Tullos, Marion TX Cav. 6th Bn. Co.A Cpl.
Tullos, Martin Abraham AL 28th (Gray's) Inf. Co.F Cpl.
Tullos, Newton Newkirk LA 28th (Gray's) Inf. Co.F
Tullos, S.A. LA 13th Bn. (Part.Rangers) Co.E
Tullos, S.F. TX 7th Cav. Co.E 1st Lt.
Tullos, Shederick J. MS 33rd Inf. Co.A Cpl.
Tullos, Stephen F. TX Cav. 6th Bn. Co.A 1st Lt.
Tullos, Stephen J. MS 33rd Inf. Co.A
Tullos, Stephen J. TX Cav. 6th Bn. Co.A 2nd Lt.
Tullos, Wade A. TX Cav. 6th Bn. Co.A
Tullos, Wash. LA 8th Cav. Co.E
Tullos, William TX Cav. 6th Bn. Co.A
Tullos, William A. MS 33rd Inf. Co.A Sgt.
Tullos, William H. TX Cav. 6th Bn. Co.A
Tullos, William J. TX Cav. 6th Bn. Co.A Cpl.
Tullos, William Riley LA 28th (Gray's) Inf. Co.F
Tullos, Willoughby, Jr. TX Cav. 6th Bn. Co.A
Tullos, W.J. TX 7th Cav. Co.E Far.
Tulloss, J.C. TN 4th (McLemore's) Cav. Co.F
Tulloss, Jo P. TN Cav. 1st Bn. (McNairy's) Co.C
Tulloss, Joseph TN Lt.Arty. Winston's Co. Sgt.
Tulloss, Joseph D. VA Lt.Arty. Utterback's Co. QMSgt.
Tulloss, Jos. D. Gen. & Staff AQM
Tulloss, Samuel C. TN 4th (McLemore's) Cav. Co.F 3rd Lt.
Tulloss, Thomas TN 4th (McLemore's) Cav. Co.F Sgt.
Tulloss, William H. VA 11th Inf. Co.I
Tullous, W. TX 1st Inf. Co.M
Tullows, Jackson W. MS 8th Inf. Co.C
Tullows, Stephen MS 8th Inf. Co.C
Tullus, C.N. LA 27th Inf. Co.F
Tullus, J.R. MS Cav. Williams' Co.
Tullus, S.J. MS 3rd Inf. (A. of 10,000) Co.A
Tullus, W.A. MS 3rd Inf. (A. of 10,000) Co.A
Tully, A.D. VA 6th Inf. Co.D
Tully, A.J. MS Cav. Yerger's Regt. Sgt.Maj.
Tully, A.J. Gen. & Staff Capt.,Vol.ADC
Tully, Andrew LA Maddox's Regt.Res.Corps Co.B
Tully, A.P. FL Wauchilla Mil. Sgt.
Tully, Bernard GA 1st (Olmstead's) Inf. Stiles' Co.
Tully, Bernard GA Inf. 18th Bn. Co.B,C
Tully, Benjamin KY 9th Cav. Co.H Sgt.
Tully, Benjamin Young KY 4th Cav. Co.H
Tully, Bernard LA 8th Inf. Co.K
Tully, Britton AL Cav. Forrest's Regt.
Tully, Britton TN 18th (Newsom's) Cav. Co.F
Tully, C.F. VA Inf. 22nd Bn. Co.H
Tully, Charles A.J. NC 44th Inf. Co.A
Tully, Elijah R. VA 32nd Inf. 2nd Co.H
Tully, George W. FL 1st Cav. Co.F
Tully, George W. FL 4th Inf. Co.I
Tully, Howard LA Washington Arty.Bn. Co.3
Tully, J.A. GA 18th Inf. Co.A
Tully, James LA Washington Arty.Bn. Co.3
Tully, James M. VA 22nd Inf. Co.H
Tully, James W. GA 49th Inf. Co.D Sgt.
Tully, John AR Inf. 8th Bn. Co.B Sgt.
Tully, John LA 18th Inf. Co.H 1st Sgt.
Tully, John MS 1st Lt.Arty. Co.H
Tully, John TN 10th Inf. Co.E
Tully, John E. TX 22nd Cav. Co.H
Tully, John F. FL 2nd Inf. Co.C Music.
Tully, John F. SC 1st Arty. Co.F
Tully, John W. KY 4th Mtd.Inf. Co.H
Tully, John Y. MS 12th Inf. Co.G
Tully, Joseph FL 4th Inf. Co.K
Tully, Joseph MS 8th Cav. Co.D
Tully, L.B. TN 12th Inf. Co.I
Tully, L.B. TN 12th (Cons.) Inf. Co.I
Tully, Lovet A. SC Inf. Hampton Legion Co.B 1st Lt.
Tully, M. LA Mil. Bragg's Bn. Fowler's Co.
Tully, M. VA 22nd Inf. Co.H
Tully, M.D. TX Cav. Bourland's Regt. Co.E
Tully, Michael LA Mil. Stanley Guards Co.B
Tully, P. AL 21st Inf. Co.E
Tully, Pat KY 10th Cav. Co.A
Tully, Patrick GA 1st (Olmstead's) Inf. Co.A
Tully, Patrick GA 1st (Olmstead's) Inf. Co.E
Tully, Patrick GA 63rd Inf. Co.A
Tully, Patrick LA Lewis Regt. Co.B
Tully, Patrick LA Mil. Stanley Guards Co.B
Tully, Patrick A. LA 18th Inf. Co.I
Tully, Richard VA 10th Cav. Co.H
Tully, Thomas B. AL Inf. 1st Regt. Co.D
Tully, Thomas B. VA 6th Inf. 2nd Co.B
Tully, W.C. FL 2nd Cav. Co.D
Tully, W.C. TX 23rd Cav. Co.B Cpl.
Tully, W.F. MS 18th Cav. Co.A
Tully, William GA 1st (Olmstead's) Inf. Gallie's Co.
Tully, William TX 1st Hvy.Arty.
Tully, William VA Hvy.Arty. 10th Bn. Co.E
Tully, William VA Inf. 25th Bn. Co.E

Tully, William VA 34th Inf. Fray's Co.
Tully, William Conf.Inf. Tucker's Regt. Co.K
Tully, William C. FL 1st Cav. Co.F
Tully, William S. TX 18th Inf. Co.E
Tulmars Emertha 1st Creek Mtd.Vol. Co.B
Tulmars Fixico 1st Creek Mtd.Vol. Co.B
Tulmars see 1st Creek Mtd.Vol. Co.F
Tulmo chris Fixico 1st Creek Mtd.Vol. Co.B
Tulmo chussee 1st Creek Mtd.Vol. 1st Co.C Sgt.
Tulmo chussee 1st Creek Mtd.Vol. Co.F
Tulmochussee 2nd Creek Mtd.Vol. Co.A 2nd Lt.
Tulmus Hargo 1st Creek Mtd.Vol. Co.G
Tulner, J.H. VA 3rd Res. Co.H
Tulsee Fixeco 1st Creek Mtd.Vol. Co.F
Tulsee Micco 1st Seminole Mtd.Vol. Cpl.
Tulsee Yo Hola 1st Seminole Mtd.Vol. Capt.
Tulse Hajo 1st Creek Mtd.Vol. Co.F
Tulton, Elias AR 17th (Lemoyne's) Inf. Co.D
Tulty, Samuel K. GA 47th Inf. Co.H 1st Sgt.
Tulwa Fixico 1st Seminole Mtd.Vol. Sgt.
Tulwa Harjo 1st Seminole Mtd.Vol. Sgt.
Tul wa mek Ko 1st Seminole Mtd.Vol.
Tulwar Fixico 1st Creek Mtd.Vol. Co.A
Tulwar Fixico 1st Creek Mtd.Vol. Co.L
Tulwar Harjo 1st Creek Mtd.Vol. Co.G
Tulwar Yarholar 2nd Creek Mtd.Vol. Co.E
Tulwiller, T.H. Gen. & Staff Capt.,QM
Tuly, L.R.P. TN 32nd Inf. Co.A
Tum, G.W. GA 27th Inf. Co.F Cpl.
Tumage, Cicero AR 33rd Inf. Co.F
Tumage, L. SC 21st Inf. Co.F
Tumbelty, Dennis LA 5th Inf. Co.B
Tumberland, William GA Lt.Arty. 14th Bn. Co.G
Tumberlin, George W. GA Arty. 9th Bn. Co.C
Tumberlin, William GA Lt.Arty. Anderson's Btty.
Tumberlinson, James AL 8th Inf. Co.A
Tumbler, Peter NC 17th Inf. (1st Org.) Co.E
Tumbler, Peter NC 32nd Inf. Co.H
Tumbler, Peter NC 56th Inf. Co.A Sgt.
Tumbleson, George VA Inf. 4th Bn.Loc.Def. Co.E 2nd Lt.
Tumbleson, George W. VA 6th Inf. Co.H
Tumbleston, C.A. SC 1st Cav. Co.I
Tumbleston, C.A. SC 1st Mtd.Mil. Smith's Co.
Tumbleston, Charles SC 1st Mtd.Mil. Smith's Co.
Tumbleston, Charles SC 5th Cav. Co.C
Tumbleston, Charles SC Cav. 17th Bn. Co.D
Tumbleston, E. SC 5th Cav. Co.C
Tumbleston, Evan SC Cav. 17th Bn. Co.D
Tumbleston, H. SC 2nd St.Troops Co.H
Tumbleston, H.C. SC 11th Inf. Co.C
Tumbleston, Ivan SC 1st Mtd.Mil. Smith's Co. Sgt.
Tumbleston, J.J. SC 1st Cav. Co.I
Tumbleston, J.R. SC Cav. 17th Bn. Co.D
Tumbleston, J.T. SC 11th Inf. 1st Co.I
Tumbleston, N. SC 1st Cav. Co.I
Tumbleston, Nathaniel SC 1st Mtd.Mil. Smith's Co.
Tumbleston, Richard SC 1st Mtd.Mil. Smith's Co.
Tumbleston, R.P. SC 1st Cav. Co.I
Tumbleston, William AR 15th Mil. Co.I
Tumbleston, William SC 1st Mtd.Mil. Smith's Co. Cpl.
Tumbleston, William M. SC 1st Cav. Co.C
Tumbleston, William M. SC 5th Cav. Co.C
Tumbleston, W.M. SC Cav. 17th Bn. Co.D
Tumblian, William H. TN 4th (McLemore's) Cav. Co.B
Tumblin, D.H. GA 11th Inf. Co.A
Tumblin, H.H. SC 14th Inf. Co.E
Tumblin, James VA 11th Cav. Co.K
Tumblin, James M. NC 45th Inf. Co.A
Tumblin, James M. SC 14th Inf. Co.E
Tumblin, John AL 15th Inf. Co.E
Tumblin, John SC Inf. 3rd Bn. Co.E
Tumblin, John SC 14th Inf. Co.E
Tumblin, John SC Inf. Hampton Legion Co.D
Tumblin, John SC Inf. Hampton Legion Co.E
Tumblin, John H. FL 8th Inf. Co.I Sgt.
Tumblin, Samuel H. NC 22nd Inf. Co.H
Tumblin, Samuel W. FL 8th Inf. Co.I
Tumblin, Silas J. SC 14th Inf. Co.E Cpl.
Tumblin, S.W. SC 4th Bn.Res. Co.E
Tumblin, W.D. AL 58th Inf. Co.A
Tumblin, William MS 23rd Inf. Co.I
Tumblin, William VA 11th Cav. Co.K
Tumblin, William W. FL Inf. 2nd Bn. Co.B 2nd Lt.
Tumbling, John TX Cav. Hardeman's Regt. Co.H
Tumblinson, Perry MO Cav. Williams' Regt. Co.E
Tumbllen, V. Gillum's Regt. Co.F
Tumbo, James AR 14th Powers' Inf. Co.C 2nd Lt.
Tumbow, J.F. MO Cav. Coleman's Regt. Co.F
Tumbreton, George A. NC 1st Inf. Co.E
Tumbro, Alexander D. NC 4th Inf. Co.D Capt.
Tumbro, James R. NC 4th Inf. Co.D Sgt.
Tumell, A. TX Cav. Giddings' Bn. Pickerell's Co.
Tumelty, Thomas W. SC Sea Fencibles Symons' Co. 2nd QM
Tumeony, J.J. LA Mil.Crescent Cadets
Tumey, C.H. TX Cav. Benavides' Regt. Co.A
Tumi, Juan LA Mil. 5th Regt.Eur.Brig. (Spanish Regt.) Co.9
Tumkit, Robert SC Hvy.Arty. Gilchrist's Co. (Gist Guard)
Tumlenson, D. TX Cav. 1st Regt.St.Troops Co.F
Tumlin, A.J. GA 23rd Inf. Co.F,D
Tumlin, F.M. AL 16th Inf. Co.D
Tumlin, Francis E. GA 1st Inf. Co.D
Tumlin, Francis M. AL Inf. 1st Regt. Co.D Sgt.
Tumlin, George H. TN 7th Inf. Co.B
Tumlin, George W. GA Inf. 17th Bn. (St.Guards) McCarty's Co. Sgt.
Tumlin, G.W. GA 27th Inf. Co.D
Tumlin, Henry I. GA 2nd Cav. (St.Guards) Co.I Sgt.
Tumlin, H.J. GA 1st Cav. Co.H
Tumlin, Isaac GA Phillips' Legion Co.B
Tumlin, James S. GA 1st Cav. Co.H 1st Sgt.
Tumlin, James S. GA 2nd Cav. (St.Guards) Co.I Capt.
Tumlin, Jasper N. GA 1st Inf. Co.A
Tumlin, J.F. GA 1st Inf. (St.Guards) Co.F
Tumlin, Joseph B. GA 43rd Inf. Co.F
Tumlin, J.W. GA 47th Inf. Co.B
Tumlin, Levi GA 43rd Inf. Co.F Sgt.
Tumlin, Lewis GA Cav. 10th Bn. (St.Guards) Co.C
Tumlin, Lewis GA 38th Inf. Co.I
Tumlin, Lewis W. AL 16th Inf. Co.C,D
Tumlin, L.L. GA Ind.Cav. (Res.) Humphrey's Co.
Tumlin, Newton J. GA Floyd Legion (St.Guards) Co.G,C Cpl.
Tumlin, Reuben GA Arty. 9th Bn. Co.B Cpl.
Tumlin, Samuel S. GA 14th Inf. Co.K
Tumlin, Snowden VA 11th Cav. Co.K
Tumlin, Thomas GA Cav. 10th Bn. (St.Guards) Co.E 2nd Lt.
Tumlin, V.M. GA 1st Cav. Co.H 1st Lt.
Tumlin, V.M. GA 19th Inf. Co.K Sgt.
Tumlin, William FL 10th Inf. Co.G 2nd Lt.
Tumlin, William GA 43rd Inf. Co.F
Tumlin, William SC 9th Res. Co.A
Tumlin, William M. GA 1st Cav. Co.H Capt.
Tumlin, William M. GA 19th Inf. Co.K 2nd Lt.
Tumlinson, Abner T. TX Cav. Ragsdale's Bn. Co.D
Tumlinson, Alexander AL 31st Inf. Co.K
Tumlinson, David MO Robertson's Regt. St.Guard Co.11
Tumlinson, Henry TX Cav. McDowell's Co.
Tumlinson, James L. TX 1st (McCulloch's) Cav. Co.I
Tumlinson, James R. TX 10th Cav. Co.A
Tumlinson, John TX Cav. Madison's Regt. Co.A
Tumlinson, Joseph TX 36th Cav. Co.K
Tumlinson, Joseph H. GA Inf. 3rd Bn. Co.C
Tumlinson, Peter TX 36th Cav. Co.K
Tumlinson, Sylvester MS Inf. 3rd Bn. (St.Troops) Co.E
Tumlinson, Wiley A. AR Inf. Cocke's Regt. Co.K Capt.
Tumlinson, William O. TX 36th Cav. Co.K
Tumlinstan, A.J. AR 9th Inf. New Co.B
Tumlison, J.L. TX 6th Inf. Co.C Cpl.
Tumlison, John H. TX 6th Inf. Co.C Sgt.
Tumm, Hiram GA Cav. Corbin's Co.
Tumm, J.C. GA Cav. Corbin's Co.
Tumm, W.T. GA Cav. Corbin's Co.
Tummins, James Wheeler's Scouts,CSA
Tummoney, John LA 14th Inf. Co.H Cpl.
Tumoine, A.J. LA Mil. Beauregard Regt. Co.C
Tumpton, Robert SC 1st (Butler's) Inf. Co.D
Tumstall, --- VA Arty.Detach. VMI
Tunage, H.N. TN 12th (Green's) Cav. Co.H
Tunage, R.H.C. 3rd Conf.Eng.Troops Co.H
Tunan, Calvin H. TN 1st Cav.
Tunbridge, John S. VA Lt.Arty. Parker's Co.
Tundy, T.Z. KY 3rd Mtd.Inf. Co.D
Tune, A. VA 1st (Farinholt's) Res. Co.E
Tune, Charles W. VA 1st Arty. 3rd Co.C Sgt.
Tune, Charles W. VA Lt.Arty. 1st Bn. Co.C Sgt.
Tune, Charles W. VA 14th Inf. 1st Co.G Cpl.
Tune, C.W. VA Arty. Young's Co. Sgt.
Tune, Edward J. VA 37th Mil. Co.E 1st Lt.
Tune, Elias K. VA 3rd Cav. Co.H
Tune, Elias K. VA 1st Arty. 3rd Co.C
Tune, Elias K. VA 14th Inf. 1st Co.G Cpl.
Tune, George W. MO 8th Inf. Co.E

Tune, George W. TN 41st Inf. Co.F
Tune, G.W. TN 45th Inf. Co.C
Tune, H. TN 20th Inf. Co.E
Tune, Henry C. VA 40th Inf. Co.B
Tune, James TN 19th (Biffle's) Cav. Co.C
Tune, J.H. AL Cav. Co.H
Tune, J.L. AR 30th Inf. Co.D
Tune, Jno. AL 36th Inf. Co.H
Tune, John TN Lt.Arty. Phillips' Co.
Tune, John VA 55th Inf. Co.G
Tune, Joseph S. VA Lt.Arty. 1st Bn. Co.C
Tune, J.S. VA 1st Arty. 3rd Co.C
Tune, J.S. VA Arty. Young's Co.
Tune, Lewis H. TN 45th Inf. Co.C 2nd Lt.
Tune, Lewis T. GA 6th Inf. Co.G
Tune, Nathaniel B. GA 6th Inf. Co.G
Tune, Samuel E. VA 15th Cav. Co.G
Tune, Samuel E. VA Cav. 15th Bn. Co.D
Tune, Samuel E. VA 41st Mil. Co.C Asst.Comsy.
Tune, Samuel T. KY 1st Bn.Mtd.Rifles Co.D Cpl.
Tune, Samuel T. KY 3rd Bn.Mtd.Rifles Co.F
Tune, Thomas AL 20th Inf. Co.H
Tune, Thomas MO 8th Inf. Co.E
Tune, Thomas NC 2nd Arty. (36th St.Troops) Co.F
Tune, Thomas M. TN 3rd (Clack's) Inf. Co.D Sgt.
Tune, Thomas S. VA 40th Inf. Co.B Sgt.
Tune, T.T. TN 19th (Biffle's) Cav. Co.C
Tune, William MS 3rd Inf. Co.C
Tune, William MO 8th Inf. Co.E
Tune, William NC 2nd Arty. (36th St.Troops) Co.F
Tune, William H. TN 3rd (Clack's) Inf. Co.C
Tune, William K. VA 14th Inf. Co.H
Tune, William L. VA 1st Arty. 3rd Co.C
Tune, William L. VA Lt.Arty. 1st Bn. Co.C
Tune, William N. GA 6th Inf. Co.G
Tune, William N. GA 45th Inf. Co.E
Tune, William T. TN 3rd (Clack's) Inf. Co.D
Tune, W.J. AL 36th Inf. Co.F
Tune, W.K. VA 53rd Inf. Co.F
Tuneison, H.T. AL Cav. Moreland's Regt. Co.G
Tunell, G.W., Jr. AL Coosa Guards J.W. Suttles' Co.
Tunes, William MS 9th Inf. Co.C
Tunett, J.A. MS 3rd Inf. (A. of 10,000) Co.A
Tungate, James KY 6th Cav.
Tungate, Nicholas KY 6th Cav.
Tungate, W.R. AR 2nd Cav. Co.G
Tunget, Larkin VA 57th Inf. Co.K
Tungett, J.N. KY 4th Cav. Co.A,H
Tungett, William H. TN 53rd Inf. Co.C 2nd Lt.
Tuning, A.W. VA 18th Cav. 2nd Co.G
Tuning, Benjamin F. VA 25th Inf. 1st Co.G
Tuning, B.F. VA 18th Cav. 2nd Co.G
Tuning, Harrison VA Cav. Swann's Bn. Co.D
Tuning, W.H. VA 9th Cav. Co.E
Tunis, John E. VA 54th Mil. Co.A
Tunis, John O. MD 1st Cav. Co.B
Tunis, Lewis VA 16th Inf. 1st Co.H
Tunis, Lewis VA 54th Mil. Co.A
Tunis, Lewis E. VA 6th Inf. Vickery's Co.
Tunis, Theoph MD 1st Cav. Co.B
Tunison, C.M. AL 30th Inf. Co.G
Tunison, George GA Inf. 27th Bn. Co.F
Tunison, George H. GA 66th Inf. Co.G
Tunkesley, George AR 32nd Inf. Co.C
Tunley, James TN 2nd (Ashby's) Cav.
Tunlin, Wm. Gen. & Staff, QM Dept Agent
Tunlison, G.C. VA 46th Inf. 2nd Co.D
Tunly, M. KY 1st (Helm's) Cav. New Co.G
Tunnage, Emanuel FL 6th Inf. Co.E
Tunnage, John GA 46th Inf. Co.B
Tunnal, G.F. MS 43rd Inf. Co.B
Tunnard, Alexander LA 1st Cav. Co.B
Tunnard, F.D. LA 3rd Inf. Co.K 2nd Lt.
Tunnard, W.F. LA 3rd Inf. Maj.
Tunnard, W.H. LA 3rd Inf. Co.K ACSSgt.
Tunnaye, James L. AR 1st (Crawford's) Cav. Co.H
Tunndle, William H. VA Cav. Mosby's Regt. (Part.Rangers) Co.A
Tunnel, Alexander E. TN 5th (McKenzie's) Cav. Co.H
Tunnel, Ashley D. MS 29th Inf. Co.I
Tunnel, E.C. MO 6th Inf. Co.G
Tunnel, Isaac TN Sullivan Cty.Res. (Loc.Def.Troops) Trevitt's Co. Cpl.
Tunnel, James A. TX 22nd Inf. Co.H
Tunnel, John TX 17th Cons.Dismtd.Cav. Co.A
Tunnel, Martin L. TX 22nd Inf. Co.I
Tunnel, Peyton MS 8th Cav. Co.D,B
Tunnel, William S. VA 46th Inf. 4th Co.F Cpl.
Tunnelhill, William C. AR 1st Cav. Co.E
Tunnell, A.N. VA 32nd Inf. Co.A
Tunnell, Dallas W. MS 29th Inf. Co.I
Tunnell, D.P. TX 9th (Young's) Inf. Co.I 2nd Lt.
Tunnell, George T. VA 32nd Inf. 2nd Co.K
Tunnell, Henry B. VA Lt.Arty. 13th Bn. Co.C
Tunnell, James TN 59th Mtd.Inf. Co.K
Tunnell, Jesse M. TX Cav. Madison's Regt. Co.F
Tunnell, John TN 50th Inf. Co.D
Tunnell, John TN 59th Mtd.Inf. Co.K
Tunnell, John P. MS 6th Cav. Morgan's Co.
Tunnell, John P. MS 12th Cav. Co.C
Tunnell, John P. MS 24th Inf. Co.C
Tunnell, John S. AL Inf. 1st Regt. Co.F,K Cpl.
Tunnell, Joseph AL Inf. 1st Regt. Co.K
Tunnell, J.S. SC 7th Inf. 1st Co.L, Co.A
Tunnell, L.C. MS St.Cav. 2nd Bn. (Harris') Co.C
Tunnell, Marcillon L. NC 15th Inf. Co.I
Tunnell, M.L. TX 20th Inf. Co.D
Tunnell, Perry W. TX 6th Cav. Co.E
Tunnell, P.G. MS 31st Inf. Co.H
Tunnell, Reuben S. TX 3rd Cav. Co.K 3rd Lt.
Tunnell, S.C. MS 2nd St.Cav. Co.H
Tunnell, S.M. MS 1st (Patton's) Inf. Co.B
Tunnell, Stephen MS 43rd Inf. Co.A
Tunnell, Thomas L. MS 43rd Inf. Co.B
Tunnell, W.G. TX 12th Cav. Co.F
Tunnell, William NC 3rd Arty. (40th St.Troops) Co.D
Tunnell, William S. VA 39th Inf. Co.F Cpl.
Tunner, Elijah VA 22nd Inf. Co.E
Tunner, John VA 22nd Inf. Co.E
Tunnil, Josiah T. TX 14th Cav. Co.B 1st Lt.
Tunnil, Perry O. TX 14th Cav. Co.B
Tunnil, William B. TX 14th Cav. Co.B
Tunnill, George T. VA 115th Mil. Co.A
Tunnison, P.T. LA Mil.Conf.Guards Regt. Co.D
Tunno, Wm. M. Gen. & Staff Asst.Comsy.
Tunrage, H.M. AR 50th Mil. Co.B
Tunstall, --- VA VMI Co.B
Tunstall, A.H. VA Lt.Arty. Thornton's Co.
Tunstall, A.H. VA Inf. 44th Bn. Co.E
Tunstall, A. Hoomes VA 30th Inf. Co.F
Tunstall, Alexander, Jr. VA 6th Inf. Co.G Adj.
Tunstall, Alex'r. Gen. & Staff 1st Lt.,Adj.
Tunstall, B.S. LA Hvy.Arty. 2nd Bn. Co.C
Tunstall, David P. AR 45th Cav. Co.E
Tunstall, D.P. AR 7th Inf. Co.E 1st Sgt.
Tunstall, E.H. MS 28th Cav. Co.I
Tunstall, E.S. AL 15th Cav. Co.F
Tunstall, E.S. AL 23rd Inf. Co.I 2nd Lt.
Tunstall, E.S. 15th Conf.Cav. Co.F
Tunstall, George D. NC 47th Inf. Co.G 1st Lt.
Tunstall, George N. VA Lt.Arty. Otey's Co.
Tunstall, George N. VA Inf. 5th Bn.Loc.Def. Co.A
Tunstall, George N. VA 18th Inf. Co.K
Tunstall, George W. NC 46th Inf. Co.C
Tunstall, G.W. AL 2nd Cav. Co.I Ord.Sgt.
Tunstall, G.W. TN 8th Inf. Co.I Cpl.
Tunstall, Harrison M. AR 45th Cav. Co.E 3rd Lt.
Tunstall, H.M. AR 7th Inf. Co.E Sgt.Maj.
Tunstall, James L. AL 62nd Inf. Co.K 2nd Lt.
Tunstall, J.B. NC 23rd Inf. Co.G
Tunstall, John L. Conf.Inf. Tucker's Regt. Co.I 1st Lt.
Tunstall, J.P. TX 33rd Cav. Co.A
Tunstall, J.R. TX Cav. Baird's Regt. Co.C Sgt.
Tunstall, L.C. NC 47th Inf. Co.G
Tunstall, Lewis H. VA 30th Inf. Co.E Sgt.
Tunstall, Miles C. VA Hvy.Arty. A.J. Jones' Co. 2nd Lt.
Tunstall, Nathaniel NC 12th Inf. Co.C
Tunstall, Nathaniel R. NC 15th Inf. Co.L
Tunstall, N.R. NC 32nd Inf. Co.K
Tunstall, P.A. VA 34th Inf. Co.B Sgt.
Tunstall, Percy R. NC 31st Inf. Co.F Sgt.
Tunstall, P.Q. TX 33rd Cav. Co.A
Tunstall, P.R. 15th Conf.Cav. Co.F
Tunstall, Pryor Q. TX Cav. Baird's Regt. Co.C Capt.
Tunstall, R.A. NC 12th Inf. Co.D
Tunstall, R.B. VA 54th Mil. Co.A
Tunstall, R.C. VA Lt.Arty. Thornton's Co.
Tunstall, Thomas Lomax's Staff Capt.,AQM
Tunstall, Thomas B. NC 46th Inf. Co.C
Tunstall, Thomas J. NC 3rd Cav. (41st St.Troops) AQM
Tunstall, Thomas J. TN 23rd Inf. 2nd Co.A
Tunstall, Thomas J. VA 18th Inf. Co.A
Tunstall, Thomas T. MO 1st Inf. Co.D,G 2nd Lt.
Tunstall, Thomas T. MO 1st & 4th Cons.Inf. Co.G 2nd Lt.
Tunstall, Wiley C. AL 5th Inf. New Co.D 3rd Lt.
Tunstall, William H. NC 57th Inf. Co.H Sgt.Maj.
Tunstall, William R. VA 52nd Mil. Co.B
Tunstall, W.J. SC 7th Inf. 1st Co.L, 2nd Co.L
Tunstall, W.J. SC 26th Inf. Co.H

Tunstall, W.J. SC Manigault's Bn.Vol. Co.D
Tunstill, J.A. TN 40th Inf. Co.E
Tunstill, James D. VA 18th Inf. Co.G
Tunstill, John G. AR 37th Inf. Co.G
Tunstill, John W. VA 18th Inf. Co.G Cpl.
Tunstill, Josephus M. VA 18th Inf. Co.G
Tunstill, Stokes AL 9th (Malone's) Cav. Co.D
Tunstill, William H. AL 7th Cav. Co.D
Tunstills, W.S. AR 37th Inf. Co.A
Tun Suy lee, James 1st Cherokee Mtd.Rifles Co.B
Tunulle, A.S. GA Cav. 12th Bn. (St.Guards) Co.A
Tuohey, Patrick J. LA 14th Inf. Co.C
Tuomey, Thomas LA 22nd Inf. Wash. Marks' Co.
Tuomey, Thomas P. MS Cav. 24th Bn. Co.A
Tuomey, Timothy J. SC 15th Inf. Co.A
Tuomy, T.J. TX Cav. Wells' Regt. Co.G
Tuoy, E. TX Inf. 1st St.Troops Biehler's Co.A
Tupan, Joseph LA Mil. Terrebonne Regt.
Tupe, Joseph TX 25th Cav. Co.D
Tupman, Benjamin W. KY 2nd (Duke's) Cav. Co.I
Tupman, Benjamin W. KY 4th Cav.
Tupman, G. Swann KY 5th Mtd.Inf. Co.A Cpl.
Tupman, John H. VA 55th Inf. Co.F 2nd Lt.
Tupman, Paul M. VA 55th Inf. Co.F
Tupman, Samuel L. KY 9th Cav. Co.G
Tupman, Wash C. KY 2nd Mtd.Inf. Co.H
Tupman, W.S. VA 2nd St.Res. Co.B 2nd Lt.
Tupman, W.T. KY 2nd (Duke's) Cav. Co.I
Tupp, G.H. TX 10th Cav. Co.G
Tupp, William AR 15th Mil. Co.H
Tupper, C.F. MS 28th Cav. Co.D
Tupper, C.P. TX Cav. Bourland's Regt. Co.K
Tupper, F. SC Mil.Arty. 1st Regt. Tupper's Co.
Tupper, F.A. GA 1st (Symons') Res. Co.A
Tupper, Frederick GA 1st (Olmstead's) Inf. Screven's Co. Cpl.
Tupper, Frederick GA Inf. 18th Bn. Co.A 2nd Lt.
Tupper, Frederick SC Lt.Arty. Parker's Co. (Marion Arty.) Cpl.
Tupper, George SC 5th Cav. Co.D Capt.
Tupper, George SC Cav. 17th Bn. Co.A 1st Lt.
Tupper, H.A. GA 9th Inf. Chap.
Tupper, H. Allen Gen. & Staff Chap.
Tupper, H.C. Brantley's Brig. Capt.,AAG
Tupper, Henry C. MS 24th Inf. Co.E Capt.
Tupper, J., Jr. SC Inf. 1st (Charleston) Bn. Co.D
Tupper, James, Jr. SC 1st Regt. Charleston Guard Co.H
Tupper, James, Jr. SC 27th Inf. Co.D 1st Lt.
Tupper, James SC Inf. Hampton Legion Co.A
Tupper, S.Y. SC 1st Regt. Charleston Guard Co.H Capt.
Tupper, T.C. Gen. & Staff Maj.Gen.
Tupper, Tristram, Jr. SC Lt.Arty. Parker's Co. (Marion Arty.) Cpl.
Tupper, William SC Inf. Hampton Legion Co.A
Tupper, William T. SC 1st (McCreary's) Inf. Co.L
Tupper, W.T. SC 4th Cav. Co.K
Tur, --- MS 46th Inf. Co.B
Tur, A. LA Mil. 5th Regt.Eur.Brig. (Spanish Regt.) Co.1
Tur, Bartolme LA Mil. 5th Regt.Eur.Brig. (Spanish Regt.) Co.6
Turaro, H. LA 26th Inf. Co.B
Turay, W. GA 1st Inf.
Turbaville, M.D. SC Cav. 19th Bn. Co.D
Turbaville, M.D. SC Cav. Rodgers' Co.
Turbefield, James NC 11th (Bethel Regt.) Inf. Co.H
Turbell, Dilliard F. TN 4th Cav. Co.D
Turberg, --- LA Mil. 1st Regt. French Brig. Co.12
Turberg, --- LA Mil. 3rd Regt.Eur.Brig. (Garde Francaise) Euler's Co.
Turbert, Adolphe LA 28th (Thomas') Inf. Co.D
Turberton, B. AR 3rd Inf. (St.Troops) Co.A
Turbervill, J.H. MO Lt.Arty. Barret's Co.
Turbervill, W. AL Lt.Arty. 2nd Bn. Co.D
Turberville, A.H. LA Mil.Cav. (Jeff Davis Rangers) Norwood's Co.
Turberville, A.H. LA 27th Inf. Co.A
Turberville, Baily P. MS 18th Inf. Co.D
Turberville, Benjamin C. TN Cav. 9th Bn. (Gantt's) Co.D
Turberville, B.F. LA 4th Inf. Co.K
Turberville, C.O. AR 5th Inf. Co.A
Turberville, J. AL 17th Inf. Co.H
Turberville, J. 2nd Conf.Eng.Troops Co.C
Turberville, James KY 12th Cav. Co.D Sgt.
Turberville, James MS 18th Inf. Co.D
Turberville, James TX 12th Inf. Co.B
Turberville, James E. AL 54th Inf. Co.F
Turberville, James E. 4th Conf.Inf. Co.F
Turberville, J.C. LA 12th Inf. Co.I
Turberville, Jesse Franklin AL Lt.Arty. 2nd Bn. Co.D
Turberville, J.H. AL Lt.Arty. 2nd Bn. Co.D
Turberville, J.J. TN 48th (Voorhies') Inf. Co.B
Turberville, John G. AR 1st (Crawford's) Cav. Co.A
Turberville, Johnson AL 3rd Bn.Res. Co.C
Turberville, J.W. MS 12th Cav. Co.C 1st Sgt.
Turberville, Peter SC 10th Inf. Co.D
Turberville, P.P. AL 11th Cav. Co.F
Turberville, Ransom SC 10th Inf. Co.I Sgt.
Turberville, Solomon SC 1st Inf. Co.K
Turberville, Thomas TN Cav. 11th Bn. (Gordon's) Co.D
Turberville, W.A. MS 33rd Inf. Co.A
Turbeville, A.B. SC 23rd Inf. Co.H
Turbeville, Asa SC 21st Inf. Co.I
Turbeville, B. AL 6th Inf. Co.E
Turbeville, E. Clay. MS 11th Inf. Co.I Sgt.Maj.
Turbeville, Fountain M. VA Lt.Arty. Penick's Co.
Turbeville, Frank SC 10th Inf. Co.D
Turbeville, George SC 25th Inf. Co.D Cpl.
Turbeville, G.W. SC 23rd Inf. Co.H
Turbeville, J. AL Inf. 1st (Loomis') Bn. Co.A
Turbeville, James SC Arty. Manigault's Bn. 1st Co.C
Turbeville, James 3rd Conf.Cav. Co.D
Turbeville, James E. MS 6th Cav.
Turbeville, James H. TN 5th Inf. 1st Co.C 1st Sgt.
Turbeville, J.B. TX Arty. Douglas' Co.
Turbeville, Jesse T. AL 36th Inf. Co.F
Turbeville, J.M. SC 25th Inf. Co.D
Turbeville, John SC 3rd St.Troops Co.C Cpl.
Turbeville, John T. TN 5th Inf. 2nd Co.G
Turbeville, John W. LA 12th Inf. Co.I
Turbeville, Joseph L. TN 11th Inf. Co.A
Turbeville, J.W. MS 6th Cav. Morgan's Co. 1st Sgt.
Turbeville, J.W. SC Arty. Gregg's Co. (McQueen Lt.Arty.)
Turbeville, L. AL 36th Inf. Co.F
Turbeville, P. SC 25th Inf. Co.D
Turbeville, Richard SC Arty. Gregg's Co. (McQueen Lt.Arty.)
Turbeville, Richard SC Arty. Manigault's Bn. 1st Co.C
Turbeville, R.M. Arsenal Bn. Co.A,CSA
Turbeville, Samuel SC 3rd St.Troops Co.C
Turbeville, Samuel F. Gen. & Staff AQM
Turbeville, Samuel H. TN 5th Inf. 1st Co.C AQM
Turbeville, Solomon SC 1st (McCreary's) Inf. Co.E
Turbeville, Stephen SC 10th Inf. Co.F
Turbeville, Stephen SC Inf.Bn. Co.A
Turbeville, W. AL 36th Inf. Co.F
Turbeville, W.B. AL Lt.Arty. 2nd Bn. Co.D
Turbeville, W.H. TN 5th Inf. 1st Co.C
Turbeville, William SC 23rd Inf. Co.H Sgt.
Turbeville, William SC 26th Inf. Co.E
Turbeville, Willis SC 10th Inf. Co.D
Turbeville, Willis SC Inf.Bn. Co.A
Turbey, J.F. AR 6th Inf. Co.B
Turbin, E. 1st Conf.Cav. Co.G,I
Turbinville, Calvin SC 8th Inf. Co.I
Turbit, Frank LA Inf.Cons.Crescent Regt. Co.H
Turbiville, Charles P. VA 20th Inf. Co.K Sgt.
Turbiville, Charles R. VA 10th Cav. Co.D
Turbiville, C.O. Gen. & Staff Capt.,AAG
Turbiville, C.P. VA 46th Inf. Co.F
Turbiville, F.M. VA 59th Inf. 3rd Co.E Sgt.
Turbiville, James MS 10th Inf. Old Co.K
Turbiville, Joseph W. VA 59th Inf. 3rd Co.C
Turbiville, J.W. VA Lt.Arty. Motley's Co. Cpl.
Turbiville, W.D. FL 1st (Res.) Inf. Co.E Capt.
Turbody, D. LA Mil. 3rd Regt. 3rd Brig. 1st Div. Co.D
Turbot, James LA Miles' Legion Co.H
Turbanell, Lafayett MO Inf. 1st Regt.St.Guard Co.E
Turbutton, W.B. TN 55th (Brown's) Inf. Ford's Co.
Turbville, Price Richard TN 3rd (Forrest's) Cav. Steele's Co., Co.A,B
Turbwill, James E. MS Cav. 1st Bn. (Montgomery's) St.Troops Co.C
Turbwill, James E. MS Cav. Yerger's Regt. Co.F
Turbwille, C.O. AR 30th Inf. Co.D
Turby, N. NC 23rd Inf.
Turbyfield, Franklin W. NC 23rd Inf. Co.K
Turbyfield, Jackson NC 49th Inf. Co.I
Turbyfield, James P. NC 58th Inf. Co.B
Turbyfield, John NC 16th Inf. Co.C
Turbyfield, Thomas A. NC 12th Inf. Co.A
Turbyfield, William GA 4th Res. Co.B
Turbyfield, W.O. NC 12th Inf. Co.A
Turbyfill, A.J. GA 4th Res. Co.B
Turbyfill, Elam A. NC 28th Inf. Co.C

Turbyfill, Elkana NC 28th Inf. Co.C Cpl.
Turbyfill, John L. NC 28th Inf. Co.C Music.
Turbyfill, Jonas A. NC 28th Inf. Co.C
Turbyfill, Lawson GA 4th Res. Co.B
Turbyfill, Malcom M. GA Carlton's Co. (Troup Cty.Arty.)
Turbyfill, Marcus NC 23rd Inf. Co.B Sgt.
Turbyfill, S.H. SC 1st St.Troops Co.G
Turbyfill, Sidney W. SC 2nd Cav. Co.E
Turbyfill, T.P. SC Inf. Hampton Legion Co.E
Turbyville, David KY 3rd Mtd.Inf. Co.D
Turbyville, Lafayette MO 7th Cav. Ward's Co.
Turbyville, Richard MO 7th Cav. Ward's Co.
Turcaud, J. LA Lt.Arty. LeGardeur, Jr.'s Co. (Orleans Guard Btty.)
Turce, R.P. MS 15th Inf. Co.I
Turck, J.R. LA Mil.Conf.Guards Regt. Co.I
Turck, Martin SC 1st (McCreary's) Inf. Co.I
Turcle, William MS 43rd Inf. Co.C
Turcott, L.B. MS Lt.Arty. Turner's Co.
Turcott, W.H. MS Lt.Arty. Turner's Co.
Turcotte, James LA Mil. British Guard Bn. Kurczyn's Co. 2nd Lt.
Turdan, W.T. GA 29th Inf. Co.H
Turdell, James MS 33rd Inf. Co.I
Tureand, --- LA 1st Hvy.Arty. (Reg.)
Tureand, Geo. N. Gen. & Staff Lt.,ADC
Tureaud, Emile LA 1st Cav. Co.A
Tureaud, James W. LA 1st Cav. Co.A
Tureaud, L. LA Lt.Arty. Holmes' Btty.
Tureaud, L. LA Arty. Watson Btty.
Tureman, F.S. MS Cav. Jeff Davis Legion Co.D Sgt.
Tureman, James D. AL 5th Bn.Vol. Co.A
Tureman, P.S. AL 19th Inf. Co.G 1st Sgt.
Tureman, P.S. AL 40th Inf. Co.C Sgt.
Tureman, T.T.P. LA Mil. 3rd Regt. 3rd Brig. 1st Div. Co.G 1st Lt.
Tureman, T.Z.P. LA Cav. Greenleaf's Co. (Orleans Lt.Horse)
Tureman, W.S. MO Lt.Arty. H.M. Bledsoe's Co. Sgt.
Tureman, Zack, Jr. AL 5th Inf. New Co.G
Turentine, C.F. AR 23rd Inf. Co.F
Turentine, F.J. AR 23rd Inf. Co.F Sgt.
Turentine, J.F. TN 12th Inf. Co.F
Turentine, Joseph AR Inf. Cocke's Regt. Co.E
Turentine, Joseph A. AR 12th Inf. Co.G
Turentine, J.P. AR 23rd Inf. Co.F
Turentine, Roan J. TN 47th Inf. Co.E
Turey, E.S. AR 10th Inf. Co.I
Turgean, C.L. LA Lt.Arty. Bridges' Btty.
Turgean, C.L. SC Arty. Manigault's Bn. 1st Co.B, Co.D
Turgeau, Laroque LA 22nd Inf.
Turgeau, L.L. LA Mil. Orleans Guards Regt. Co.D
Turgerson, O. TX Cav. 2nd Regt.St.Troops Co.G
Turgis, Isidore F. Gen. & Staff Chap.
Turgis, J.F. LA 30th Inf. Chap.
Turgurson, J.B. AR Cav. Crabtree's (46th) Regt. Co.A
Turhune, B. GA Ind.Cav. (Res.) Humphrey's Co.
Turiford, J.W. Conf.Cav. Wood's Regt. 1st Co.G
Turil, R.N. VA 18th Cav.
Turill, T.M. AL 36th Inf. Co.A
Turir, J.E. GA 24th Inf. Co.D
Turk, --- TX Cav. Mann's Regt. Co.H
Turk, A.L. VA Baldwin's Mtd.Regt.Loc.Def. A.L. Turk's Co. Capt.
Turk, Albarin M. MO Inf. 8th Bn. Co.E
Turk, Albarino M. MO 9th Inf. Co.I
Turk, Alex VA 1st Cav. Co.E
Turk, Charles T. AL 63rd Inf. Co.C
Turk, D.A. AL 10th Inf. Co.D
Turk, DeWitt C. VA 1st Cav. Co.E
Turk, Ernest LA 7th Inf. Co.E
Turk, George W. AL Lt.Arty. Kolb's Btty.
Turk, Hiram K. 1st Cherokee Mtd.Vol. 2nd Co.K
Turk, H.K. MO 6th Cav. Co.H
Turk, Hugh F. VA Cav. 39th Bn. Co.C Sgt.
Turk, James TX Cav. Mann's Bn. Cox's Co.
Turk, James A. KY 3rd Mtd.Inf. Co.D 1st Lt.
Turk, James A. VA Rockbridge Cty.Res. Bacon's Co.
Turk, James A. Lyon's Brig. Capt.,Insp.Gen.
Turk, James G. VA Patrol Guard 11th Congr. Dist. (Mtd.)
Turk, James G. VA 52nd Inf. Co.C Sgt.
Turk, James L. AL 3rd Cav. Co.G 4th Sgt.
Turk, James L. AL 19th Inf. Co.I
Turk, James W. GA 8th Inf. (St.Guards) Co.D
Turk, James W. VA 45th Inf. Co.D
Turk, James W.B. TN 59th Mtd.Inf. Co.A Cpl.
Turk, John AL 4th Res. Co.H
Turk, John AL 46th Inf. Co.D
Turk, John F. GA 7th Inf. Co.D
Turk, John G. GA 45th Inf. Co.D Sgt.
Turk, John M. AL 5th Bn.Vol. Co.B 2nd Lt.
Turk, John M. AL 5th Bn.Vol. Co.B Hosp.Stew.
Turk, John N. GA 24th Inf. Co.A Capt.
Turk, Jonathan GA 44th Inf. Co.B
Turk, K.C. KY 6th Mtd.Inf. Co.C
Turk, Mason Conf.Reg.Inf. Brooks' Bn. Co.E
Turk, Milton GA 7th Inf. (St.Guards) Co.E Cpl.
Turk, N. MO 6th Cav. Co.H
Turk, N.B. KY 2nd (Duke's) Cav. Co.I
Turk, N.G. MO 11th Inf. Co.A
Turk, Randolph Gen. & Staff Capt.,QM
Turk, Samuel B. KY 4th Mtd.Inf. Co.F
Turk, T.B. KY 6th Mtd.Inf. Co.C
Turk, T.H. KY 7th Mtd.Inf. Co.C
Turk, Theodocius W. GA Cav. 7th Bn. (St.Guards) Co.C Sgt.
Turk, Theodosius W. AL 4th Inf. Co.E
Turk, Thomas A. Gen. & Staff AQM
Turk, Thomas L. AL 3rd Inf. Co.C
Turk, Thomas L. GA Cav. 29th Bn. Co.E
Turk, T.W. AL 2nd Cav. Co.H
Turk, W.F. TN 63rd Inf. Co.D Music.
Turk, W.H. GA 24th Inf. Co.A
Turk, William AL 2nd Cav. Co.H
Turk, William VA 7th Bn.Res. Co.D
Turk, William H. TX 2nd Cav. Co.D Sgt.
Turk, William T. GA 7th Inf. Co.D
Turk, W.R. VA 3rd Res. Co.D Sgt.
Turker, William B. AR 15th Mil. Co.C
Turkes, Charles AR Willett's Co.
Turket, J. SC Cav. 4th Bn. Co.B
Turket, J.A. SC Cav. 10th Bn. Co.A Sgt.
Turket, J.E. AL 30th Inf. Co.G
Turket, Warren SC Inf. 3rd Bn. Co.G
Turkett, Ausbur R. AL 19th Inf. Co.E
Turkett, J.A. SC 4th Cav. Co.B Sgt.
Turkett, J.H.G. TN 7th Inf. Asst.Surg.
Turkett, J.H.G. Gen. & Staff Asst.Surg.
Turkett, John H. SC Cav.Bn. Hampton Legion Co.D
Turkett, J.W. GA 12th Cav. Co.A
Turkett, T.W. SC 24th Mil.
Turkett, W.A. AL 14th Inf. Co.I
Turkett, William GA Lt.Arty. 14th Bn. Co.B
Turkett, William GA Lt.Arty. Anderson's Btty.
Turkett, William J. AL 19th Inf. Co.E
Turkey, James FL 10th Inf. Co.C
Turkin, Henry AL 12th Inf. Co.C
Turkington, F.G. MS 48th Inf. Co.I 2nd Lt.
Turknett, James A. FL 2nd Cav. Co.K
Turknett, John P. MS 20th Inf. Co.G
Turknett, L. FL 2nd Cav. Co.K
Turknett, Lawrence FL Cav. Pickett's Co. 1st Sgt.
Turknett, Thomas F. MS 20th Inf. Co.G
Turknett, Wiley J. MS 20th Inf. Co.G
Tur koo ner Harjo 1st Creek Mtd.Vol. Co.K
Turla, E. LA Mil. 1st Chasseurs a pied Co.8
Turla, James MO 8th Cav. Co.D
Turla, L. LA Mil. 1st Chasseurs a pied Co.8
Turla, Manuel LA 8th Inf. Co.B Sgt.
Turla, S. LA Mil. 1st Chasseurs a pied Co.8
Turle, B. LA Mil. 2nd Regt. 2nd Brig. 1st Div.
Turley, A. TN 1st (Turney's) Inf. Co.K
Turley, Allen TX 15th Cav. Co.H
Turley, Archibald TX 37th Cav. Co.B
Turley, Benjamin F. MO Cav. Coffee's Regt. Co.H
Turley, B.F. Shecoe's Chickasaw Bn.Mtd.Vol. Co.A
Turley, C.A. TX Kennard's Bn.Res.Corps Co.D Capt.
Turley, C.G. TN 41st Inf. Co.A
Turley, Charles A. MO 5th Inf. Co.A
Turley, Clabourn C. VA 22nd Inf. Co.A
Turley, Cornelius GA 4th Inf. Co.D
Turley, Eber MO 3rd Cav. Co.C
Turley, F.F. MO 6th Cav. Co.K 1st Sgt.
Turley, G.A. MO 5th Cav. Co.D
Turley, G.A. MO Cav. Stallard's Co.
Turley, George W. TX 15th Cav. Co.H
Turley, G.S. TX 4th Cav. Co.F
Turley, G.S. TX Cav. Terry's Regt. Co.E
Turley, G.T. MO 12th Inf. Co.H
Turley, Hosea H. GA 56th Inf. Co.F
Turley, J. MO 2nd Cav. Co.E
Turley, James AR Cav. Nave's Bn. Co.C
Turley, James Shecoe's Chickasaw Bn.Mtd.Vol. Co.A 2nd Lt.
Turley, James M. AL 6th Inf. Co.L
Turley, James M. MO Cav. Wood's Regt. Co.K
Turley, James P. TX 11th Cav. Co.C Cpl.
Turley, James S. VA 29th Inf. Co.H
Turley, Jessey MO Cav. Clardy's Bn. Co.A
Turley, J.M. TX 4th Inf. (St.Troops) Co.C
Turley, Joel Benton NC 50th Inf. Co.C Cpl.
Turley, John MO 11th Inf. Co.I
Turley, John TN 3rd (Clack's) Inf. Co.K
Turley, John A. TN 1st (Carter's) Cav. Co.C 1st Lt.

Turley, Joseph MO Cav. 2nd Regt.St.Guard Co.F Cpl.
Turley, J.W. GA Inf. 18th Bn. (St.Guards) Co.D
Turley, Lafayette AL 13th Inf. Co.I
Turley, Nathaniel GA 7th Inf. Co.H
Turley, Patterson D. VA 25th Inf. 1st Co.H 3rd Lt.
Turley, P.D. VA 11th Cav. Co.B
Turley, P.D. VA 62nd Mtd.Inf. Co.B 2nd 2nd Lt.
Turley, Perrey MO Cav. Clardy's Bn. Co.A
Turley, Peter MO 5th Cav. Co.A
Turley, R.D. GA Inf. 17th Bn. (St.Guards) Stocks' Co.
Turley, Rees VA 45th Inf. Co.G
Turley, Reese T. VA Inf. 45th Bn. Co.B
Turley, Rees T. VA 29th Inf. Co.H
Turley, Richard A. VA Cav. Mosby's Regt. (Part.Rangers) Co.A
Turley, Sampson AR 36th Inf. Co.E
Turley, Sampson MO Cav. Coffee's Regt. Co.H Cpl.
Turley, Sanford KY 13th Cav. Co.B
Turley, Sanford G. KY 2nd (Woodward's) Cav. Co.B
Turley, Silas VA Cav. 34th Bn. Co.B
Turley, Solomon VA Inf. 45th Bn. Co.B
Turley, Solomon C. VA 29th Inf. Co.I
Turley, Thomas VA 22nd Cav. Co.F Jr.2nd Lt.
Turley, Thomas VA Inf. 23rd Bn. Co.C
Turley, Thomas B. TN Inf. 154th Sr.Regt. Co.L
Turley, Thomas B. VA 22nd Inf. Co.A
Turley, Thomas W. AR 3rd Inf. Co.G
Turley, T.W. LA 3rd Inf. Co.E
Turley, Walker MO Robertson's Regt.St.Guard Co.9
Turley, W.E. TN Lt.Arty. Huggins' Co.
Turley, W.F. LA 25th Inf. Co.D
Turley, William AL 5th Inf. New Co.I
Turley, William GA 20th Inf. Co.D
Turley, William NC 24th Inf. Co.E
Turley, William C. MO 5th Inf. Co.A
Turley, William J. KY 5th Cav. Co.D
Turley, William M. TX 34th Cav. Co.B
Turley, William P. VA 58th Mil. Co.D
Turley, Willis MO 3rd Cav. Co.E
Turley, W.O. MO 12th Inf. Co.H
Turlin, Wm. LA 1st (Strawbridge's) Inf. Co.D
Turlington, A.J. TN 16th Inf. Co.K
Turlington, Alexander D. NC Hvy.Arty. 10th Bn. Co.B Sgt.
Turlington, C.E. FL 11th Inf. Co.E
Turlington, Frederick VA 2nd Inf. Co.F
Turlington, George W. VA 39th Inf. Co.I
Turlington, H.T. GA Lt.Arty. 12th Bn. 3rd Co.E
Turlington, James VA 32nd Inf. 2nd Co.K
Turlington, James VA 115th Mil. Co.B
Turlington, James H. NC 2nd Bn.Loc.Def. Troops Co.E
Turlington, James L. AL 45th Inf. Co.A
Turlington, J.M. AL Lt.Arty. Kolb's Btty.
Turlington, J.M. AL 59th Inf. Co.E
Turlington, J.M. AL Arty. 4th Bn. Hilliard's Legion Co.B,E
Turlington, John NC 56th Inf. Co.B
Turlington, John E. VA 26th Inf. Co.E
Turlington, John J. TN 16th Inf. Co.K Cpl.
Turlington, John W. VA 59th Mil. Hunter's Co.
Turlington, Randall NC Hvy.Arty. 10th Bn. Co.B 1st Lt.
Turlington, Robert VA 32nd Inf. Co.E
Turlington, R.S. AL Lt.Arty. Kolb's Btty.
Turlington, R.S. AL Arty. 4th Bn. Hilliard's Legion Co.B,E Cpl.
Turlington, W.F. AL 5th Inf. New Co.A
Turlington, William NC Cumberland Cty.Bn. Detailed Men Co.B
Turlington, William A. NC 32nd Inf. Co.G
Turlington, William D. TN 16th Inf. Co.K Capt.
Turlington, William F. AL 39th Inf. Co.B
Turlington, William T. VA 1st Arty. Co.A,F
Turlington, William T. VA 32nd Inf. 1st Co.K
Turlley, W.O. AR 21st Inf. Co.A
Turlow, D. GA 24th Inf. Co.C
Turlton, Jeff TN 12th (Green's) Cav. Co.H
Turly, C.A. GA 56th Inf. Co.F
Turly, J.A. LA 25th Inf. Co.D
Turly, Job W. MO Inf. 1st Regt.St.Guard Co.C 1st Lt.
Turly, Louis AL 36th Inf. Co.E
Turly, O.G. MO Cav. 2nd Regt.St.Guard Co.F Capt.
Turly, William P. VA 10th Inf. Co.D
Turlyfill, Wilson AL 49th Inf. Co.E
Turman, Abner B. TX 2nd Cav. Co.G
Turman, A.J. TX 18th Inf. Co.E
Turman, Alfred P. AL 16th Inf. Co.K
Turman, Barnard P. VA 54th Inf. Co.G 1st Sgt.
Turman, B.B. TN 24th Inf. 1st Co.H
Turman, Benjamin E. VA 54th Inf. Co.B
Turman, Carroll AR 35th Inf. Co.G
Turman, Charles VA 54th Inf. Co.G
Turman, David MS 1st (Patton's) Inf. Co.G
Turman, David M. MS 31st Inf. Co.C
Turman, Early P. MS 1st Lt.Arty. Co.C
Turman, Elijah VA 4th Res. Co.H,I
Turman, Elijah VA 54th Inf. Co.B
Turman, G.C. MS 2nd St.Cav. Co.B
Turman, George E. GA 15th Inf. Co.C,F
Turman, George H. VA 54th Inf. Co.G Capt.
Turman, George J. AL Vol. Lee, Jr.'s Co.
Turman, George J. AL 1st Bn. Hilliard's Legion Vol. Co.E
Turman, George W. AL Cav. Lewis' Bn. Co.A
Turman, G.T. AL 33rd Inf. Co.F
Turman, Hiram W. TX 22nd Inf. Co.H
Turman, J. TX 35th (Brown's) Cav. Co.E
Turman, Jacob VA 54th Inf. Co.B
Turman, James AL Cav. Lewis' Bn. Co.A
Turman, James MS Bradford's Co. (Conf.Guards Arty.)
Turman, James M. AL Vol. Lee, Jr.'s Co.
Turman, James M. MS 43rd Inf. Co.A
Turman, James M. TX 2nd Cav. Co.G
Turman, J.B. TX Cav. 2nd Bn.St.Troops Co.A
Turman, J.B. TX 18th Inf. Co.F
Turman, J.G. TN 24th Bn.S.S. Co.A
Turman, J.J. GA 7th Inf. (St.Guards) Co.L Sgt.
Turman, J.M. AL 45th Inf. Co.C
Turman, Joel L. TX 18th Inf. Co.F
Turman, John B. TX Cav. Baylor's Regt. Co.K
Turman, Joseph P. VA 54th Inf. Co.D Cpl.
Turman, Kerney TN 24th Inf. 1st Co.H, Co.I
Turman, Mahlon VA 54th Inf. Co.B
Turman, Mason P. MS 42nd Inf. Co.G
Turman, M.C. GA 55th Inf. Co.B
Turman, Neal TX 9th (Young's) Inf. Co.D
Turman, R.F. MS 12th Cav. Co.F
Turman, Richard MS 6th Cav. Co.K
Turman, Simon FL 1st Cav. Co.F
Turman, Simon FL 7th Inf. Co.E 1st Lt.
Turman, T.G. TX 10th Cav. Co.A 1st Sgt.
Turman, Thomas TN 24th Inf. 1st Co.H
Turman, Thomas M. GA 15th Inf. Co.C,F
Turman, T.T. AL 33rd Inf. Co.F Sgt.
Turman, W.H.H. TX 10th Cav. Co.A
Turman, William AL 33rd Inf. Co.F
Turman, William TX Cav. 2nd Bn.St.Troops Co.A
Turman, William TX 18th Inf. Co.F
Turman, William R. GA 1st (Ramsey's) Inf. Co.B 2nd Lt.
Turman, William W. GA 52nd Inf. Co.K Cpl.
Turmann, William TX Inf. Timmons' Regt. Co.B
Turmon, L.D. AL 26th (O'Neal's) Inf. Co.H
Turmon, Robert AL 26th (O'Neal's) Inf. Co.H
Turmy, T.P. AR 18th (Marmaduke's) Inf. Co.E
Turnage, Albert LA 16th Inf. Co.D
Turnage, Albert J. MS 7th Inf. Co.I
Turnage, Alex TN 22nd (Barteau's) Cav. Co.D
Turnage, Alexander TN Cav. 7th Bn. (Bennett's) Co.C
Turnage, Amos NC 8th Inf. Co.G Sgt.
Turnage, Amos NC 17th Inf. (1st Org.) Co.C Cpl.
Turnage, B. MS 11th (Perrin's) Cav. Co.A
Turnage, Benjamin W. NC 17th Inf. (2nd Org.) Co.K Sgt.
Turnage, B.F. SC 8th Inf. Co.C
Turnage, C. MS 1st Cav.Res. Co.E
Turnage, C.B. TN 18th Co.K
Turnage, Charles NC 4th Inf. Co.I
Turnage, David TN 18th Inf. Co.K
Turnage, D.E. TN 38th Inf. Co.I
Turnage, Dillard SC 8th Inf. Co.B
Turnage, E. GA 6th Cav.
Turnage, Elisha MS 40th Inf. Co.B
Turnage, Elisha B. TX 13th Vol. 2nd Co.A,F
Turnage, E.M. MS 28th Cav. Co.K
Turnage, Exum NC 3rd Arty. (40th St.Troops) Co.F
Turnage, F.D. MS 46th Inf. Co.B
Turnage, Gaston LA 16th Inf. Co.D
Turnage, George H. MS 1st Lt.Arty. Co.K
Turnage, Henry TN 9th (Ward's) Cav. Co.C
Turnage, Henry 7th Conf.Cav. 2nd Co.I
Turnage, Henry C. NC 55th Inf. Co.E Music.
Turnage, Hiram LA 16th Inf. Co.D Jr.2nd Lt.
Turnage, I.D. TN 51st Inf. Co.A
Turnage, Irwin AL 40th Inf. Co.F
Turnage, Isaac NC 43rd Inf. Co.K
Turnage, James NC Hvy.Arty. 10th Bn. Co.B 1st Sgt.
Turnage, James NC 44th Inf. Co.I
Turnage, James B. LA 5th Cav. Co.K Sgt.
Turnage, James G. GA 46th Inf. Co.C
Turnage, James P. SC 4th St.Troops Co.K
Turnage, James W. GA 22nd Inf. Co.F
Turnage, James W. TN 7th Inf. Co.C
Turnage, J.D. TN 51st (Cons.) Inf. Co.H

Turnage, J.E. GA Inf. City Bn. (Columbus) Co.C
Turnage, Jesse J. NC 2nd Inf. Co.C
Turnage, J.L. AR 6th Inf. New Co.F Cpl.
Turnage, J.L. TN 51st Inf. Co.A
Turnage, J.N. TN 7th (Duckworth's) Cav. Co.B
Turnage, John LA 1st (Nelligan's) Inf. Co.B
Turnage, John SC 7th Inf. 1st Co.C, 2nd Co.C, Co.G
Turnage, John TN 51st (Cons.) Inf. Co.H
Turnage, John F. NC 61st Inf. Co.E
Turnage, John W. NC 2nd Inf. Co.C
Turnage, Joseph NC 3rd Arty. (40th St.Troops) Co.F
Turnage, Joseph NC 3rd Inf. Co.A Music.
Turnage, Joseph TN Inf. 154th Sr.Regt. Co.A Sgt.
Turnage, Joseph J. NC 8th Inf. Co.G Sgt.
Turnage, Joseph W. GA Arty. 9th Bn. Co.C
Turnage, J.P. SC 21st Inf. Co.E
Turnage, J.W. AL 3rd Cav. Co.A
Turnage, J.W. TN 18th Inf. Co.K
Turnage, J.W. Conf.Cav. Wood's Regt. Co.C
Turnage, J.W. 4th Conf.Inf. Co.F
Turnage, Larkin S. GA Arty. 9th Bn. Co.C
Turnage, Luke NC 26th Inf. Co.K
Turnage, Luke SC 20th Inf. Co.N
Turnage, M. NC Cav. 16th Bn. Co.F
Turnage, Mills P. MS 7th Inf. Co.I
Turnage, Moses 7th Conf.Cav. Co.H
Turnage, M.P. MS 9th Inf. Co.A
Turnage, Newton F. TX 35th (Brown's) Cav. Co.H
Turnage, Newton F. TX 13th Vol. 2nd Co.A
Turnage, N.F. TX Cav. Waller's Regt. Goode's Co.
Turnage, Oster GA 28th Inf. Co.C
Turnage, Peter A. SC 6th Cav. Co.K Cpl.
Turnage, Peter A. SC 8th Inf. Co.B 1st Lt.
Turnage, R. TN 7th (Duckworth's) Cav. Co.I
Turnage, R.B. SC 21st Inf. Co.E
Turnage, Richard H.C. AR 26th Inf. Co.B
Turnage, Robert D. MS 3rd Inf. Co.I
Turnage, Robert NC 33rd Inf. Co.K
Turnage, Silvester B. NC Mil. Clark's Sp.Bn. Rountree's Co.
Turnage, T.G. TN Inf. 3rd Bn. Co.D
Turnage, Thomas F. GA Arty. 9th Bn. Co.C
Turnage, Thomas J. GA 2nd Res. Co.C
Turnage, W.A. SC 21st Inf. Co.D
Turnage, W.A. TN 9th Inf. Co.C
Turnage, W.H. MS 35th Inf. Co.G
Turnage, W.H. 2nd Conf.Eng.Troops Co.D
Turnage, William AR 8th Inf. New Co.E Capt.
Turnage, William MS 7th Inf. Co.I
Turnage, William MS 9th Inf. Co.A
Turnage, William TX 35th (Brown's) Cav. Co.H
Turnage, William B. MS 1st Lt.Arty. Co.D
Turnage, William B. NC 38th Inf. Co.C
Turnage, William H. AL 3rd Inf. Co.B
Turnage, William H. LA 25th Inf. Co.I
Turnage, William H. SC 21st Inf. Co.D
Turnage, William M. TX 13th Vol. 2nd Co.A
Turnage, William S. TN 9th (Ward's) Cav. Co.C
Turnage, W.O. AL 12th Inf. Co.C
Turnam, T.S. AR 34th Inf. Co.G
Turnay, T.P. AR 5th Inf. Co.B
Turnban, James B. MS 48th Inf.
Turnbaugh, George H. KY Lt.Arty. Green's Btty.
Turnbaugh, L.W. MO St.Guard Fife Maj.
Turnbaugh, T.B. MO Inf. 4th Regt.St.Guard Adj.
Turnbeaugh, Eli AR 3rd Inf. (St.Troops) Co.E
Turnbeaugh, Samuel AR 11th & 17th Cons.Inf. Co.I
Turnbeaugh, Samuel AR 17th (Griffith's) Inf. Co.B
Turnbeaugh, Samuel AR 35th Inf. Co.A
Turnbel, J.E. TX Conscr.
Turnbenville, J. AL 21st Inf. Co.D
Turnbill, James NC 64th Inf. Co.H
Turnbille, John Y. TN Cav. 12th Bn. (Day's) Co.B
Turnbo, A.A. MS 5th Cav. Co.D Capt.
Turnbo, Andrew D. MS 21st Inf. Co.G 2nd Lt.
Turnbo, East TN 19th (Biffle's) Cav. Co.H
Turnbo, James M. TN Cav. 2nd Bn. (Biffle's) Co.B
Turnbo, James M. TN 6th (Wheeler's) Cav. Co.G
Turnbo, J.B. AR 13th Inf. Co.F
Turnbo, Joseph TN 19th (Biffle's) Cav. Co.H
Turnbo, Silas C. AR 27th Inf. Co.A
Turnboe, Joseph E. AR 3rd Inf. Co.A Sgt.
Turnbough, Benjamin F. TX 11th Cav. Co.A
Turnbough, Eli AR 34th Inf. Co.D
Turnbough, George AR 35th Inf. Co.D 2nd Lt.
Turnbough, J.M. AR 11th Inf. Co.E
Turnbough, J.M. AR 11th & 17th Cons.Inf. Co.E
Turnbough, Jms. TX 29th Cav. Co.H
Turnbough, John MO Lt.Arty. 3rd Field Btty. Cpl.
Turnbough, Joseph MO Lt.Arty. 3rd Field Btty.
Turnbough, J.W. AR 11th Inf. Co.E
Turnbough, J.W. AR 11th & 17th Cons.Inf. Co.E
Turnbough, Madison C. AR 15th Inf. Co.D
Turnbough, Madison C. TX 16th Cav. Co.A
Turnbough, P.C. MS Inf. 7th Bn. Co.G
Turnbough, Robert W. MO 1st N.E. Cav.
Turnbough, Samuel MO 9th Bn.S.S. Co.A
Turnbough, W.D.L. AL Cp. of Instr. Talladega
Turnbough, W.J. MS 8th Inf. Co.C
Turnbow, A.J. TX 17th Inf. Co.G
Turnbow, Andrew TN 48th (Nixon's) Inf. Co.A
Turnbow, Andy A. TN 48th (Voorhies') Inf. Co.B
Turnbow, Calvin TN 3rd (Clack's) Inf. Co.H
Turnbow, George AR 31st Inf. Co.E
Turnbow, George TN 3rd (Clack's) Inf. Co.C
Turnbow, J.A. TN 3rd (Clack's) Inf. Co.C
Turnbow, J.A. TN 48th (Nixon's) Inf. Co.A Cpl.
Turnbow, James TX 17th Cav. Co.A
Turnbow, James TX 37th Cav. 2nd Co.D, Co.H
Turnbow, James A. TN 48th (Voorhies') Inf. Co.B
Turnbow, James M. AL 4th Inf. Co.G 2nd Lt.
Turnbow, John L. TN 48th (Voorhies') Inf. Co.E
Turnbow, William AR Cav. 1st Bn. (Stirman's) Co.B
Turnbow, Williford AL Mil. 4th Vol. Co.C
Turnbow, W.J. AL 7th Cav. Co.B
Turnbrough, W.D.L. AL Cav. Hardie's Bn.Res. Co.F
Turnbull, Adam 4th Conf.Eng.Troops 2nd Lt.
Turnbull, Adam Eng.,CSA 1st Lt.
Turnbull, Alexander MO Inf. 1st Regt.St.Guard Co.E
Turnbull, A.M. MS Cav. Semple's Co.
Turnbull, Andrew, Jr. Gen. & Staff Vol.ADC
Turnbull, B. SC 23rd Inf. Co.A
Turnbull, B.M. LA Mil.Conf.Guards Regt. Co.D
Turnbull, B.M. Gen. & Staff 2nd Lt.,Dr.M.
Turnbull, Charles F. Sig.Corps,CSA
Turnbull, Chas. F. Gen. & Staff ADC
Turnbull, Charles J. AR 25th Inf. Col.
Turnbull, Daniel 1st Choctaw Mtd.Rifles Ward's Co.
Turnbull, Daniel J., Jr. Sig.Corps,CSA
Turnbull, E.H.B. MS 1st Lt.Arty. Co.G
Turnbull, F.A. AL 21st Inf. Co.F,D
Turnbull, F.J. MO Lt.Arty. Barret's Co. Sgt.
Turnbull, George W. AL 7th Cav. Co.H
Turnbull, Graeme MD 1st Cav. Co.C 2nd Lt.
Turnbull, G.W. AL 21st Inf. Co.F
Turnbull, H.A. GA 12th Inf. Co.I
Turnbull, James Horse Arty. White's Btty.
Turnbull, James F. LA 5th Inf. Co.D
Turnbull, James H. GA 2nd Cav. Co.D
Turnbull, J.B. GA Arty. Lumpkin's Co. Sgt.
Turnbull, J.F. TX 9th Cav. Co.E Sgt.
Turnbull, J.J. GA Arty. Lumpkin's Co. Sgt.
Turnbull, John SC 7th Cav. Co.H
Turnbull, John SC Cav.Bn. Holcombe Legion Co.E
Turnbull, John D. MO Lt.Arty. 1st Btty.
Turnbull, John P. 1st Choctaw Mtd.Rifles Co.B 1st Lt.
Turnbull, John R. NC 12th Inf. Co.F Capt.
Turnbull, Joseph MO Lt.Arty. 3rd Btty.
Turnbull, Junius FL 2nd Inf. Co.M 1st Sgt.
Turnbull, J.W. AL 21st Inf. Co.F
Turnbull, L. GA 12th Inf. Co.I
Turnbull, L. GA 26th Inf. Co.H
Turnbull, L.G. MS 28th Cav. Co.D
Turnbull, R.H. LA 3rd (Wingfield's) Cav. Co.E 2nd Lt.
Turnbull, Richard FL 1st Inf. Old Co.I Bvt.2nd Lt.
Turnbull, Rob LA Mil.Conf.Guards Regt. Co.F
Turnbull, Robert H. LA 4th Inf. Old Co.G 2nd Lt.
Turnbull, Samuel, Jr. FL 5th Inf. Co.A 1st Lt.
Turnbull, Simeon 1st Choctaw & Chickasaw Mtd.Rifles 2nd Co.I
Turnbull, Theodore FL Cav. 5th Bn. Co.C
Turnbull, Theodore FL 1st Inf. Old Co.I Sgt.
Turnbull, Theodore FL 5th Inf. Co.A 1st Sgt.
Turnbull, Thomas P. SC 2nd Cav. Co.A
Turnbull, William AL 21st Inf. Co.F
Turnbull, William GA 4th Res. Co.C
Turnbull, William GA 43rd Inf. Co.E
Turnbull, W.W. GA 42nd Inf. Co.H
Turndon, A. AR 19th (Dawson's) Inf. Co.B
Turnedge, Philip AL Eufaula Lt.Arty.
Turneer, Andy NC 56th Inf. Co.F
Turneesee Johnson 1st Cherokee Mtd.Rifles Co.I

Turnell, Charles LA Mil. 3rd Regt. 1st Brig. 1st Div. Co.K
Turnell, George W. VA 9th Inf. 1st Co.A
Turnell, G.W. VA 5th Cav. Co.D 1st Lt.
Turnell, James W. GA 3rd Inf. Co.L
Turnell, John T. GA 3rd Inf. Co.L 2nd Lt.
Turnell, J.S. VA 5th Cav. Co.D 1st Sgt.
Turnell, Ralph LA Washington Arty.Bn. Co.3
Turnell, Robert GA 9th Inf. (St.Guards) Co.G
Turnell, Scott VA 2nd Cav. Co.I
Turnell, Thomas T. VA 4th Cav. & Inf.St.Line 1st Co.I Sgt.
Turnell, T.T. VA 21st Cav. Co.B Sgt.
Turnell, William F. GA 3rd Inf. Co.L,G
Tur ne nall C 1st Cherokee Mtd.Rifles McDaniel's Co.
Turner, --- AL 10th Inf. Co.C
Turner, --- AR 26th Inf. Asst.Surg.
Turner, --- MO St.Guard Lt.
Turner, --- TX Cav. Border's Regt. Co.D
Turner. --- TX Cav. Good's Bn. Co.A
Turner, --- TX Cav. Mann's Regt. Co.H
Turner, --- TX Cav. McCord's Frontier Regt. Co.K
Turner, --- TX Cav. Steele's Command Co.D
Turner, --- VA Inf. 3rd Kanawha Regt. Capt.
Turner, --- VA 55th Inf. Co.G
Turner, --- VA VMI Co.A
Turner, --- VA VMI Co.C
Turner, A. AL 12th Cav. Co.G
Turner, A. AL Mil. 4th Vol. Modawell's Co.
Turner, A. FL Cav. 5th Bn. Co.B
Turner, A. GA 12th (Robison's) Cav. (St.Guards) Co.I
Turner, A. GA Inf. 27th Bn. (NonConscr.) Co.C Sgt.
Turner, A. GA 47th Inf. Co.C
Turner, A. GA Inf. (Loc.Def.) Whiteside's Nav.Bn. Co.A
Turner, A. KY 7th Mtd.Inf. Co.D
Turner, A. MS 38th Cav. Co.G
Turner, A. MS 44th Inf. Co.G
Turner, A. TN 7th (Duckworth's) Cav. White's Co.
Turner, A. TN 51st Inf. Co.H
Turner, A.A. AR 1st (Monroe's) Cav. Co.B
Turner, A.A. GA Arty. 11th Bn. (Sumter Arty.) Co.A
Turner, A.A. GA 63rd Inf. Co.G
Turner, Aaron AL 3rd Bn.Res. Co.B
Turner, Aaron SC Inf. 9th Bn. Co.C
Turner, Aaron SC 26th Inf. Co.D
Turner, Aaron M. TX 13th Cav. Co.I
Turner, A.B. AR 1st (Monroe's) Cav. Co.B
Turner, A.B. AR 2nd Cav. 1st Lt.
Turner, A.B. AR 24th Inf. Co.D Cpl.
Turner, A.B. GA 48th Inf. Co.H
Turner, A.B. TX 3rd Cav. Co.B
Turner, Abe A. GA 37th Inf. Co.K
Turner, Abel 15th Conf.Cav. Co.G
Turner, Abel T. NC 1st Inf. Co.D
Turner, Abner GA 66th Inf. Co.B Cpl.
Turner, Abner TN 48th (Nixon's) Inf. Co.A
Turner, Abner TN 48th (Voorhies') Inf. Co.B
Turner, Abner A. GA 8th Inf. (St.Guards) Co.G
Turner, Abraham AL 25th Inf. Co.H
Turner, Abraham KY 5th Mtd.Inf. Co.I
Turner, Abraham KY 9th Mtd.Inf. Co.I
Turner, Abraham S. MS 16th Inf. Co.A Sgt.
Turner, Abram GA 37th Inf. Co.K
Turner, Abram 1st Chickasaw Inf. Milam's Co.
Turner, Absalom AL 43rd Inf. Co.A
Turner, Absalom GA Cobb's Legion Co.L
Turner, Absalom VA 6th Cav. Co.B
Turner, Absalom D. TX 13th Cav. Co.B
Turner, A.C. AL 11th Cav. Co.I,K
Turner, A.C. GA Cav. 29th Bn. Co.H
Turner, A.C.R. LA 1st (Nelligan's) Inf. Co.B
Turner, A.D. AL Cp. of Instr. Talladega
Turner, Adam SC Inf. 9th Bn. Co.F
Turner, Aden P. MS 12th Cav. Co.B 1st Sgt.
Turner, Adin W. FL Cav. Pickett's Co. Sgt.
Turner, Admire VA 28th Inf. Co.G
Turner, Adolphis P. SC 2nd Cav. Co.C
Turner, Adolphus VA 3rd Inf. 2nd Co.I
Turner, A.E. NC 61st Inf. Co.G
Turner, A.E. VA 10th Cav. Co.K
Turner, A.F. TN 11th (Holman's) Cav. Co.D
Turner, A.F. TN Douglass' Bn.Part.Rangers Lytles' Co.
Turner, A.G. GA Arty. Lumpkin's Co. Bvt.2nd Lt.
Turner, A.G. GA 9th Inf. (St.Guards) Co.H Sgt.
Turner, A.G. MS Inf. 7th Bn. Co.A
Turner, A.G. TX 3rd Cav. Co.E
Turner, A.G. TX 17th Inf. Co.E
Turner, A.H. MS Inf. 7th Bn. Co.A
Turner, A.H. VA 57th Inf. Co.A
Turner, A.J. AL 8th Inf.
Turner, A.J. AL 11th Inf. Co.I
Turner, A.J. AL 48th Inf. Co.D Sgt.
Turner, A.J. AR 26th Inf. Co.I
Turner, A.J. GA 13th Inf. Co.F
Turner, A.J. GA 56th Inf. Co.C
Turner, A.J. MS 1st (Johnston's) Inf. Co.B
Turner, A.J. MS 37th Inf. Co.D
Turner, A.J. MO Inf. Winston's Regt. Co.A Cpl.
Turner, A.J. NC 58th Inf. Co.M,G Cpl.
Turner, A.J. NC 64th Inf. Co.H
Turner, A.J. TN 10th (DeMoss') Cav. Co.G
Turner, A.J. TN 20th (Russell's) Cav. Co.K
Turner, A.J. TN Inf. 3rd Cons.Regt. Co.F
Turner, A.J. TN 50th Inf. Co.B
Turner, A.J. TX 35th (Brown's) Cav. Co.E
Turner, A.J. VA 5th Inf. Music.
Turner, A.J. 15th Conf.Cav. Co.F
Turner, A.J. Shecoe's Chickasaw Bn.Mtd.Vol.
Turner, A.K. MS 1st (King's) Inf. (St.Troops) Co.B Cpl.
Turner, A.K. MS Yerger's Co. (St.Troops)
Turner, A.L. SC 22nd Inf. Co.H
Turner, Albert TN 43rd Inf. Co.K
Turner, Albert VA 17th Inf. Co.E
Turner, Albert C. VA Inf. 5th Bn. Co.D Cpl.
Turner, Albert C. VA 53rd Inf. Co.A
Turner, Albert G. MO 1st Cav. Co.K
Turner, Albert G. MO 10th Cav. Co.K 2nd Lt.
Turner, Albert G. TN 20th Inf. Co.A
Turner, Albert T. AR 33rd Inf. Co.D Sgt.
Turner, Aleck O. TN 4th Inf. Co.E Cpl.
Turner, Alec L.R. MS 14th Inf. Co.A
Turner, Alex GA 23rd Inf. Co.H
Turner, Alex NC Mallett's Bn. (Cp.Guard)
Turner, Alex VA 29th Inf. Co.D
Turner, Alexander AL 34th Inf. Breedlove's Co.
Turner, Alexander GA 35th Inf. Co.C
Turner, Alex. LA 7th Inf. Co.C
Turner, Alexander LA 27th Inf. Co.C
Turner, Alexander MO 4th Cav. Co.F,G
Turner, Alexander NC 1st Arty. (10th St.Troops) Co.D
Turner, Alexander NC 3rd Arty. (40th St.Troops) Co.G
Turner, Alexander NC 44th Inf. Co.A
Turner, Alexander TN 15th (Stewart's) Cav. Co.G
Turner, Alexander VA 63rd Inf. Co.G, 2nd Co.I Sgt.
Turner, Alexander VA Mil. Carroll Cty.
Turner, Alexander C. MS 11th Inf. Co.K
Turner, Alexander K. MS 2nd Part.Rangers Co.I 1st Sgt.
Turner, Alexander W. GA 59th Inf. Co.I
Turner, Alexander W. VA 14th Inf. Co.B 1st Lt.
Turner, Alex K. MS Graves' Co. (Copiah Horse Guards)
Turner, Alford AL 19th Inf. Co.B
Turner, Alford C. GA Arty. 9th Bn. Co.A,E
Turner, Alfred AL 50th Inf.
Turner, Alfred NC 4th Inf. Co.C
Turner, Alfred TN 51st (Cons.) Inf. Co.D
Turner, Alfred VA Cav. 41st Bn. Co.G
Turner, Alfred VA 2nd Inf.Loc.Def. Co.K
Turner, Alfred VA Inf. 2nd Bn.Loc.Def. Co.B
Turner, Alfred VA 57th Inf. Co.B
Turner, Alfred J. MS 43rd Inf. Co.H Cpl.
Turner, Alfred L. AR 33rd Inf. Co.G
Turner, Alfred W. GA Inf. 11th Bn. (St.Guards) Co.A Cpl.
Turner, Allen AL Inf. 1st Regt. Co.A
Turner, Allen AL 24th Inf. Co.F
Turner, Allen MS 3rd Cav. Co.D
Turner, Allen MS 16th Inf. Co.F
Turner, Allen TN 17th Inf.
Turner, Allen H. VA 19th Inf. Co.D Sgt.
Turner, Allen S. GA 24th Inf. Co.B AQM
Turner, Allen S. DuBose's Brig. Capt.,AQM
Turner, Allen Y. MS 43rd Inf. Co.H
Turner, Alonzo TX Cav. Martin's Regt. Co.A Cpl.
Turner, Alonzo VA 11th Inf. Co.A
Turner, Alonzo D. GA Inf. 10th Bn. Co.A
Turner, Alpheus SC 13th Inf. Co.F
Turner, A.M. FL Vol. Harrison's Co.
Turner, A.M. GA 13th Inf. Co.A
Turner, A.M. GA 23rd Inf. Co.F
Turner, A.M. GA Floyd Legion (St.Guards) Co.B Sgt.
Turner, A.M. GA Phillips' Legion Co.B
Turner, A.M.C. SC Lt.Arty. Jeter's Co. (Macbeth Lt.Arty.)
Turner, Americus V. NC 38th Inf. Co.G
Turner, Amos J. AL 60th Inf. Co.G
Turner, Amos J. AL 3rd Bn. Hilliard's Legion Vol. Co.E
Turner, A.N. GA 44th Inf. Co.K
Turner, A.N. SC 6th Inf. 1st Co.I Cpl.
Turner, A.N. SC 18th Inf. Co.K
Turner, Anderson VA Hvy.Arty. 19th Bn. Co.D Drum.

Turner, Anderson VA Hvy.Arty. Kyle's Co.
Turner, Andrew AR Cav. Gordon's Regt. Co.K
Turner, Andrew TN Cav. 12th Bn. (Day's) Co.D
Turner, Andrew TN 43rd Inf. Co.F
Turner, Andrew 3rd Conf.Eng.Troops Co.D
Turner, Andrew C. MO Inf. Perkins' Bn. Co.F
Turner, Andrew H. VA 57th Inf. Co.B
Turner, Andrew J. AL 5th Inf. Co.A
Turner, Andrew J. AL 6th Inf. Co.G
Turner, Andrew J. AL 37th Inf. Co.H
Turner, Andrew J. AL 44th Inf. Co.I
Turner, Andrew J. AL 57th Inf. Co.A
Turner, Andrew J. FL 9th Inf. Co.A
Turner, Andrew J. GA 20th Inf. Co.D Cpl.
Turner, Andrew J. GA 30th Inf. Co.I
Turner, Andrew J. MO 3rd Cav. Co.K
Turner, Andrew J. MO 4th Cav. Co.I Cpl.
Turner, Andrew J. NC 4th Inf. Co.E
Turner, Andrew J. NC 22nd Inf. Co.M
Turner, Andrew J. NC 43rd Inf. Co.A
Turner, Andrew J. NC 66th Inf. Co.E
Turner, Andrew J. TN 24th Inf. Co.I
Turner, Andrew J. TN 35th Inf. Co.B Sgt.
Turner, Andrew J. VA 8th Bn.Res. Co.B
Turner, Andrew J. VA 97th Mil. Co.E
Turner, Andrus J. AL 9th Inf. Co.C
Turner, Anguish MS 24th Inf. Co.L
Turner, Ansolem A. VA 58th Inf. Co.D
Turner, A.P. GA 6th Inf. (St.Guards) Co.E 1st Lt.
Turner, A.P. MS 12th Cav. Co.B Sgt.
Turner, A.P. TX 28th Cav. Co.I
Turner, A.P. TX 12th Inf. Co.E
Turner, A.R. AR 24th Inf. Co.D 2nd Lt.
Turner, A.R. SC 18th Inf. Co.K
Turner, A.R. TN 14th (Neely's) Cav. Co.B
Turner, Archibald GA 7th Inf. Co.K
Turner, Archibald LA Inf. 11th Bn. Co.F
Turner, Archibald VA Loc.Def. Bosher's Co.
Turner, Archibald H. KY Cav. 2nd Bn. (Dortch's) Co.C
Turner, Archibald J. MS 11th Inf. Co.K
Turner, Aretas NC 27th Inf. Co.D
Turner, Aretus GA Siege Arty. 28th Bn. Co.D
Turner, Arthur AL 21st Inf. Co.K
Turner, Arthur GA 64th Inf. Co.G
Turner, Arthur MO 1st Inf. Co.C
Turner, Arthur C. FL 7th Inf. Co.B
Turner, Arual AL 57th Inf. Co.B
Turner, A.S. AL 6th Inf. Co.F
Turner, A.S. TX Cav. Ragsdale's Bn. 2nd Co.C
Turner, Asbery NC Hoskins' Co. (Loc.Def.)
Turner, Asbery W. AL 1st Bn. Hilliard's Legion Vol. Co.C
Turner, Asbury GA 10th (St.Guards) Cav. Co.F
Turner, Asbury VA Lt.Arty. Waters' Co.
Turner, Asbury A. GA 1st (Ramsey's) Inf. Co.K Cpl.
Turner, A.T. GA 3rd Cav. Co.B
Turner, A.T. GA Brooks' Co. (Terrell Lt.Arty.)
Turner, A.T. GA Inf. (Muscogee Guards) Thornton's Co.
Turner, A.T. LA 15th Inf. Co.E N.C.S. 1st Lt.
Turner, A.T. MS Inf. 2nd St.Troops Co.A
Turner, A.T. SC 1st Cav. Co.F
Turner, A.T. SC Hvy.Arty. 15th (Lucas') Bn. Co.A
Turner, A. Thomas SC 16th Inf. Co.K
Turner, Atkins W. VA 59th Mil. Riddick's Co.
Turner, Augustus NC 24th Inf. Co.I
Turner, Augustus H. VA Hvy.Arty. 19th Bn. Co.A
Turner, Augustus J. TX 22nd Cav. Co.F
Turner, Augustus R. AR 9th Inf. Co.D
Turner, Austin AL Conscr. Echols' Co.
Turner, Austin H. AL 1st Regt.Conscr. Co.E
Turner, Austin H. AL 21st Inf. Co.H
Turner, A.V. MS 23rd Inf. Co.I
Turner, A.W. AL 60th Inf. Co.K
Turner, A.W. FL 2nd Cav. Co.K
Turner, A.W. FL Cav. 3rd Bn. Co.B
Turner, A.W. GA 48th Inf. Co.H
Turner, A.W. KY 3rd Mtd.Inf. Co.B
Turner, A.W. MO 10th Inf. Co.A,E 2nd Lt.
Turner, A.W. TX 7th Cav. Co.E
Turner, A.W. 15th Conf.Cav. Co.D
Turner, A.Y. MS 1st (Johnston's) Inf. Co.B
Turner, A.Y. SC 6th Inf. 1st Co.D, 2nd Co.G
Turner, B. AL 8th Inf. Co.F
Turner, B. GA 5th Res. Co.F
Turner, B. GA Inf. 27th Bn. (NonConscr.) Co.C
Turner, B. MS Yerger's Co. (St.Troops)
Turner, B. MO Cav. Ford's Bn. Co.B
Turner, B. NC 7th Sr.Res. Fisher's Co. 1st Lt.
Turner, B. SC 5th Mil. Beat Co.4
Turner, B. SC 6th Inf. 2nd Co.K
Turner, B. TX Cav. 3rd Bn. (St.Troops) 1st Lt.
Turner, B.A. AR 8th Cav. Peoples' Co.
Turner, B.A. AR 30th Inf. Co.I Cpl.
Turner, B.A. TN 40th Inf. Co.F
Turner, Balis AR 27th Inf. New Co.B
Turner, Balis M. GA 52nd Inf. Co.H
Turner, Banard TN 3rd (Lillard's) Mtd.Inf. Co.G
Turner, Bartlett KY 3rd Mtd.Inf. Co.H
Turner, Barton Y. AR 2nd Inf. Old Co.E Capt.
Turner, Bart Y. AR 1st (Dobbin's) Cav. Swan's Co. 1st Lt.
Turner, B.B. GA 39th Inf. Co.K
Turner, B.B. TX 26th Cav. Co.E
Turner, B.D. AR Inf. Cocke's Regt. Co.B
Turner, B.D. SC Inf. 7th Bn. (Enfield Rifles) Co.F
Turner, Beauford A. MS 19th Inf. Co.B 1st Sgt.
Turner, Belton O. SC 9th Inf. Co.I
Turner, Ben TN 40th Inf. Co.B
Turner, Ben. F. TN Cav. 2nd Bn. (Biffle's) 1st Lt.
Turner, Ben F. TX 22nd Inf. Co.C 1st Sgt.
Turner, Benjamin AL 10th Inf. Co.F
Turner, Benjamin FL 2nd Cav. Co.B
Turner, Benjamin FL Cav. Pickett's Co. Sgt.
Turner, Benjamin FL 10th Inf. Co.C
Turner, Benjamin GA 39th Inf. Co.D
Turner, Benjamin GA 41st Inf. Co.K
Turner, Benjamin LA 11th Inf. Co.E 2nd Lt.
Turner, Benjamin NC 35th Inf. Co.K
Turner, Benjamin NC 53rd Inf. Co.D
Turner, Benjamin TN 1st Cav. Co.A Capt.
Turner, Benjamin TN Arty. Ramsey's Btty. Sgt.
Turner, Benjamin TX 4th Inf. Co.C 1st Lt.
Turner, Benjamin TX Inf. Townsend's Co. (Robertson Five S.) 2nd Lt.
Turner, Benjamin VA Lt.Arty. Jeffress' Co.
Turner, Benjamin VA Lt.Arty. Thornton's Co.
Turner, Benjamin VA 40th Inf. Co.C Sgt.
Turner, Benjamin Trans-MS Conf.Cav. 1st Bn. Co.E
Turner, Benjamin A. AR 23rd Inf. Co.I
Turner, Benjamin B. AL 3rd Bn. Hilliard's Legion Vol. Co.E
Turner, Benjamin C. FL 7th Inf. Co.D
Turner, Benjamin C. TX 21st Cav. Co.G
Turner, Benjamin D. LA 1st Hvy.Arty. (Reg.) Co.I Sgt.
Turner, Benjamin D. LA Miles' Legion Sgt.
Turner, Benjamin D. VA 44th Inf. Co.D 1st Sgt.
Turner, Benjamin D. McRae's Brig. & Churchill's Brig. Capt.,AIG
Turner, Benjamin F. AR 35th Inf. Co.E Sgt.
Turner, Benjamin F. MS 1st Lt.Arty. Co.A
Turner, Benjamin F. MO 1st N.E. Cav.
Turner, Benjamin F. SC 4th Inf. Co.F
Turner, Benjamin F. VA 3rd Inf. 2nd Co.I
Turner, Benjamin F. VA 7th Inf. Co.C
Turner, Benjamin F. VA 22nd Inf. Co.H Sgt.
Turner, Benjamin F. VA Inf. 45th Bn. Co.E 2nd Lt.
Turner, Benjamin F.P. SC 6th Inf. 1st Co.K Cpl.
Turner, Benjamin H. AL 17th Inf. Co.I 1st Sgt.
Turner, Benjamin H. FL 2nd Inf. Co.G
Turner, Benjamin M. FL 4th Inf. Co.K
Turner, Benjamin M. GA Inf. 3rd Bn. Co.D 1st Lt.
Turner, Benjamin M. GA 4th Bn.S.S. Co.B,C Capt.
Turner, Benjamin R. AL 51st (Part.Rangers) Co.A
Turner, Benjamin R. AL 2nd Inf. Co.A
Turner, Benjamin R. VA 2nd Cav. Co.F
Turner, Benjamin W. AL 30th Inf. Co.E
Turner, Berry GA Inf. 11th Bn. (St.Guards) Co.A
Turner, Berry A. MS 1st Bn.S.S. Co.C
Turner, Berry F.P. SC 6th Cav. Co.A
Turner, Beverly B. VA 9th Cav. Co.H
Turner, Beverly B. Lee's Staff Lt.,ADC
Turner, B.F. AL 3rd Res. Co.F
Turner, B.F. GA 4th (Clinch's) Cav. Co.F Sgt.
Turner, B.F. GA Cav. 20th Bn. Co.A,F
Turner, B.F. GA 19th Inf.
Turner, B.F. GA 27th Inf. Co.H
Turner, B.F. KY 2nd Mtd.Inf. Co.K
Turner, B.F. SC Inf. 13th Bn. Co.D Cpl.
Turner, B.F. SC 22nd Inf. Co.H
Turner, B.F. SC Inf. Hampton Legion Co.K
Turner, B.F. VA 8th Cav. Co.I
Turner, B.F.P. SC Inf. 13th Bn. Co.A
Turner, B.H. FL 2nd Cav. Co.K
Turner, B.H. GA Inf. 11th Bn. (St.Guards) Co.D
Turner, B.H. GA Cherokee Legion (St.Guards) Co.B
Turner, B.J. GA 11th Cav. Co.K
Turner, B.J. SC Inf. 7th Bn. (Enfield Rifles) Co.F,A Cpl.
Turner, B.J. TX 3rd Cav. Co.B
Turner, B.L. AL 53rd (Part.Rangers) Co.D
Turner, B.L. GA 3rd Res. Co.G
Turner, B.L. LA 6th Cav. Co.F
Turner, B.O. SC Inf. 1st (Charleston) Bn. Co.G
Turner, B.O. SC 27th Inf. Co.K,I

Turner, Boswell AL 3rd Cav. Co.A
Turner, Boswell Conf.Cav. Wood's Regt. Co.C
Turner, Bradshaw B. VA Lt.Arty. Nelson's Co.
Turner, B.S. GA 18th Inf. Co.K
Turner, B.S. GA 56th Inf. Co.C
Turner, B.S. NC 4th Sr.Res. Co.C
Turner, B.S. TN 7th (Duckworth's) Cav. Co.I
Turner, B.S. TN 35th Inf. Co.E 2nd Lt.
Turner, C. FL 2nd Inf. Co.D
Turner, C. GA Cav. Ragland's Co.
Turner, C. MO 1st N.E. Cav. Co.I
Turner, C. SC 2nd Inf. Co.K
Turner, C. TN Arty. Marshall's Co. 2nd Lt.
Turner, C. Inf. Bailey's Cons.Regt. Co.A
Turner, C.A. MS 34th Inf. Co.C
Turner, C.A. TX 7th Inf. Co.H
Turner, Cader M. AL Inf. 1st Regt. Co.E
Turner, Calhoun TX Cav. Davis' Bn. Sgt.
Turner, Calhoun H. GA Cobb's Legion Co.B
Turner, Callihill M. VA 42nd Inf. Co.F
Turner, Calvin LA 16th Inf. Co.G
Turner, Calvin TX 31st Cav. Co.A
Turner, Calvin C. AL 30th Inf. Co.B
Turner, Calvin S. TX 36th Cav. Co.E 2nd Lt.
Turner, Carr P. VA 57th Inf. Co.B Sgt.
Turner, Caspar AL 58th Inf. Co.I
Turner, C.B. AL 60th Inf. Co.K
Turner, C.B. VA 21st Cav. 2nd Co.D
Turner, C.B. 4th Conf.Eng.Troops Sgt.
Turner, C.B. Hosp.Stew.
Turner, C.C. TX 10th Cav. Co.D
Turner, C.C. TX 12th Inf. Co.A
Turner, C.D. AL 41st Inf. Co.K
Turner, Cecinna V. VA 9th Inf. Co.C
Turner, Cemsey SC 7th Res. Co.G
Turner, C.F. LA 8th Cav. Co.A Cpl.
Turner, C.F. NC 57th Inf. Co.I Cpl.
Turner, C.H. AL 49th Inf. Co.C
Turner, C.H. GA 11th Cav. Co.K
Turner, C.H. GA Cobb's Legion Co.G
Turner, C.H. TX 5th Inf. Co.K
Turner, Charles AL 24th Inf. Co.D
Turner, Charles GA 4th (Clinch's) Cav.
Turner, Charles GA 7th Inf. (St.Guards) Co.D
Turner, Charles MS Inf. 2nd St.Troops Co.B
Turner, Charles MO Cav. Snider's Bn. Co.A
Turner, Charles TN 10th Inf. Co.B Sgt.
Turner, Charles VA 22nd Inf. Co.H
Turner, Charles VA 40th Inf. Co.C
Turner, Charles VA 47th Inf. Co.B
Turner, Charles VA 54th Inf. Co.H
Turner, Charles A. AL 43rd Inf. Co.A
Turner, Charles A. FL 9th Inf. Co.B
Turner, Charles B. AR 30th Inf. Co.E
Turner, Charles B. VA 9th Cav. Co.C
Turner, Chas. B. Gen. & Staff Hosp.Stew.
Turner, Charles E. AL Lt.Arty. 2nd Bn. Co.B
Turner, Charles E. GA Inf. 3rd Bn. Co.D
Turner, Charles E. GA 4th Bn.S.S. Co.C
Turner, Charles E. VA 58th Inf. Co.I
Turner, Charles H. LA 6th Inf. Co.H Cpl.
Turner, Charles H. VA 11th Inf. Co.H
Turner, Charles K. LA Inf.Crescent Regt. Co.K
Turner, Charles K. MO Cav. 3rd Regt.St.Guard Co.C
Turner, Charles L. AL Cav. Murphy's Bn. Co.C
Turner, Charles L. 15th Conf.Cav. Co.H
Turner, Charles M. MO 8th Cav. Co.G
Turner, Charles M. TX 20th Inf. Co.H
Turner, Charles M. VA 4th Inf. Co.G
Turner, Charles O. SC 10th Inf. Co.B
Turner, Charles T. VA Hvy.Arty. 19th Bn. Co.A
Turner, Charles W. VA Lt.Arty. W.P. Carter's Co.
Turner, Charles W. VA 5th Inf. Co.L
Turner, Charles W. Conf.Inf. 8th Bn. Co.E 2nd Lt.
Turner, Chesley TN Inf. 1st Bn. (Colms') Co.C 2nd Lt.
Turner, Chesley TN 28th (Cons.) Inf. Co.I
Turner, Chesley TN 84th Inf. Co.E Cpl.
Turner, Chester VA 25th Cav. Co.E
Turner, Chester B. VA 11th Inf. Co.F
Turner, Chesterfield NC 20th Inf. Co.K
Turner, Christopher A. AR 32nd Inf. Co.A 2nd Lt.
Turner, Christopher C. VA 16th Inf. Co.F
Turner, Christopher S. NC 56th Inf. Co.G
Turner, Cicero NC 2nd Bn.Loc.Def.Troops Co.B Music.
Turner, Cicero NC 20th Inf. Faison's Co.
Turner, Cicero NC 30th Inf. Co.A Drum.
Turner, Cicero NC 66th Inf. Co.D
Turner, C.J. GA Cav. 29th Bn. Co.A
Turner, C.J. GA 24th Inf. Co.G
Turner, C.J. SC Palmetto S.S.
Turner, C.K. TX 9th Field Btty.
Turner, C.L. GA Inf. 1st Loc.Troops (Augusta) Co.I
Turner, C.L. SC Inf. Holcombe Legion Co.A Cpl.
Turner, C.L. VA Wade's Regt.Loc.Def. Co.D
Turner, Claibourn AR 26th Inf. Co.F
Turner, Clark P. VA 57th Inf. Co.B
Turner, Clark West MS 34th Inf. Co.C
Turner, Claud C. SC 5th Inf. 1st Co.F, 2nd Co.I 2nd Lt.
Turner, Clayton MO 6th Cav. Co.K
Turner, C.M. GA 2nd Res. Co.I
Turner, C.M. VA 8th Cav. 2nd Co.D
Turner, C.N. TN Cav. Napier's Bn. Co.E
Turner, C.O. SC 7th Inf. 1st Co.L
Turner, Columbus C. GA 4th Bn.S.S. Co.C 1st Sgt.
Turner, Columbus C. LA 17th Inf. Co.I 1st Sgt.
Turner, Columbus H. MO 3rd Cav. Co.F 1st Sgt.
Turner, Columbus L. NC 33rd Inf. Co.A 2nd Lt.
Turner, Columbus M. GA Phillips' Legion Co.B,H
Turner, Cooper MO Inf. Clark's Regt. Co.A
Turner, Copeland B. AL 1st Bn. Hilliard's Legion Vol. Co.C
Turner, Cornelius FL Inf. 2nd Bn. Co.A
Turner, Cornelius FL 10th Inf. Co.I
Turner, Cornelius C. GA Cobb's Legion Co.H
Turner, Cornelius J. GA Siege Arty. 28th Bn. Co.C
Turner, Cornelius L. MO St.Guard
Turner, C.P. NC 17th Inf. (2nd Org.) Co.L
Turner, C.R. TN 11th (Holman's) Cav. Co.D
Turner, C.R. TN Douglass' Bn.Part.Rangers Lytles' Co.
Turner, Cread O. TN 1st (Turney's) Inf. Co.K
Turner, Creed VA Cav. 35th Bn. Co.C
Turner, Creed O. VA 51st Inf. Co.D
Turner, C.S. GA 56th Inf. Co.D Cpl.
Turner, C.T. KY 12th Cav. Co.H
Turner, C.T. KY 7th Mtd.Inf. Co.G
Turner, C.T. VA Lt.Arty. Cayce's Co.
Turner, Curtis GA 8th Inf. Co.G
Turner, C.V. GA Cav. Nelson's Ind.Co.
Turner, C.W. GA 10th Cav. (St.Guards) Co.K
Turner, C.W. KY 5th Cav. Co.C
Turner, C.W. TX 12th Cav. Co.D
Turner, Cyrus KY 11th Cav. Co.G
Turner, Cyrus LA 16th Inf. Co.A
Turner, D. AL Mil. 2nd Regt.Vol. Co.F
Turner, D. AL 44th Inf. Co.K
Turner, D. FL 2nd Cav. Co.H
Turner, D. GA 10th Inf. Co.A
Turner, D. LA 8th Cav. Co.A
Turner, D. SC 16th & 24th (Cons.) Inf. Co.C
Turner, D. TX 29th Cav. Co.K
Turner, D. TX 20th Inf. Co.E
Turner, D. VA 72nd Mil.
Turner, Dan F. TX Cav. Madison's Regt. Co.G
Turner, Daniel GA 64th Inf. Co.G
Turner, Daniel NC 2nd Inf. Co.E
Turner, Daniel SC 19th Inf. Co.F
Turner, Daniel SC 24th Inf. Co.B
Turner, Daniel SC Inf.Bn. Co.E
Turner, Daniel TX 14th Cav. Co.I
Turner, Daniel TX 15th Cav. Co.C
Turner, Daniel C. GA 44th Inf. Co.H
Turner, Daniel H. AL 4th Inf. Co.I 2nd Lt.
Turner, Daniel H. MS 48th Inf. Co.I
Turner, Daniel H. VA 16th Inf. Co.F
Turner, Daniel M. AL 4th Inf. Co.C
Turner, Darling SC 19th Inf. Co.K
Turner, David AL 13th Inf. Co.E
Turner, David AL 20th Inf. Co.B
Turner, David AL 41st Inf. Co.E
Turner, David AL Cp. of Instr. Talladega
Turner, David FL 8th Inf. Co.G
Turner, David GA Cav. 9th Bn. (St.Guards) Co.D
Turner, David GA Lt.Arty. Howell's Co.
Turner, David GA Inf. 3rd Bn. Co.H
Turner, David GA 17th Inf. Co.K
Turner, David MS 1st Cav.Res. Co.H Sgt.
Turner, David NC 3rd Cav. (41st St.Troops) Co.B
Turner, David NC 5th Inf. Co.H
Turner, David NC 6th Inf. Co.F
Turner, David NC 48th Inf. Co.I
Turner, David NC 55th Inf. Co.F
Turner, David VA 1st St.Res. Co.F
Turner, David 7th Conf.Cav. Co.A
Turner, David A.J. AL 4th Inf. Co.D Sgt.
Turner, David B. FL 9th Inf. Co.I
Turner, David C. AL 5th Bn.Vol. Co.B 2nd Lt.
Turner, David C. TN 28th Inf. Co.A
Turner, David C. VA 36th Inf. 2nd Co.G
Turner, David D. TX 15th Cav. Co.F
Turner, David H. NC 28th Inf. Co.C
Turner, David J. NC 27th Inf. Co.D
Turner, David M. FL 2nd Cav. Co.C
Turner, David S. GA 37th Inf. Co.K
Turner, David S. MS 11th Inf. Co.E

Turner, David T. GA 44th Inf. Co.A
Turner, David T. TN 33rd Inf. Co.B 1st Sgt.
Turner, David W. NC 12th Inf. Co.C
Turner, David W. NC 51st Inf. Co.C
Turner, Davis SC 11th Inf. Co.C
Turner, D.B. GA Lt.Arty. Howell's Co.
Turner, D.C. AL 15th Bn.Part.Rangers Co.B
Turner, D.C. AR Mtd.Vol. (St.Troops) Abraham's Co.
Turner, D.C. GA 13th Inf. Co.A Sgt.
Turner, DeLaura GA Cav. Nelson's Ind.Co.
Turner, Dempsey F. LA 27th Inf. Co.C
Turner, Dennis GA 56th Inf. Co.C Cpl.
Turner, Dennis LA 1st Inf. Co.C Sgt.
Turner, Dennis F. AL 1st Regt.Conscr. Co.E
Turner, Dennis M. GA 49th Inf. Co.F
Turner, Derescus VA 21st Cav. 1st Co.E
Turner, D.F. AL 3rd Bn.Res. Co.H
Turner, D.G. VA 1st (Farinholt's) Res. Co.E
Turner, D.H. AR 2nd Cav. 1st Co.A
Turner, Dillard TN 11th Inf. Co.C
Turner, Dixon L. MS St.Cav. Perrin's Bn. Co.A
Turner, D.J. KY 3rd Mtd.Inf. Co.F
Turner, D.M. AL 4th Inf. Co.B
Turner, D.M. MD Weston's Bn. Co.D
Turner, D.M. MS 1st Cav.Res. Co.F
Turner, D.R. GA Cav. 9th Bn. (St.Guards) Co.B
Turner, Drury NC 34th Inf. Co.F,H
Turner, D.S. AR 15th (Johnson's) Inf. Co.E
Turner, Dugald M. NC 18th Inf. Co.G
Turner, Duncan FL 11th Inf. Co.C,L
Turner, Duncan M. MD 1st Cav. Co.B Sgt.
Turner, Duncan M. MD 1st Inf. 2nd Co.H
Turner, D.W. NC 30th Inf. Co.E
Turner, D.W. NC 35th Inf. Co.K
Turner, D.W. TN 14th (Neely's) Cav. Co.B Sgt.
Turner, D.W. TN 51st (Cons.) Inf. Co.B 1st Sgt.
Turner, D.W. TX 17th Inf. Co.E
Turner, D.W. VA 62nd Mtd.Inf. Co.G
Turner, D.W. 2nd Conf.Eng.Troops Co.C
Turner, E. FL 2nd Cav. Co.K
Turner, E. GA Cav. Nelson's Ind.Co.
Turner, E. GA 59th Inf. Co.C
Turner, E. LA Inf. 4th Bn. Co.D
Turner, E. SC 6th Cav. Co.H
Turner, E. SC 23rd Inf. Co.E
Turner, E. TX 12th Cav. Co.G
Turner, E. VA 62nd Mtd.Inf. 2nd Co.H
Turner, E.B. LA 4th Inf. Co.D
Turner, E.B. MS 23rd Inf. Co.I
Turner, Ebenezer AL 33rd Inf. Co.G
Turner, Ebenezer W. GA 6th Inf. Co.C
Turner, E.B.S. TX 14th Inf. Co.G
Turner, E.C. AL 25th Inf. Co.H Capt.
Turner, E.C. VA 19th Inf. Co.A Sgt.
Turner, E.D. AL Inf. 1st Regt. Co.F
Turner, E.D. AR 7th Mil. Co.A
Turner, E.D. AR 34th Inf. Co.G
Turner, E.D. LA Inf.Crescent Regt. Co.E
Turner, E.D. NC 43rd Inf. Co.I
Turner, E.D. SC Lt.Arty. 3rd (Palmetto) Bn. Co.E
Turner, Edmund VA 34th Inf. Co.K
Turner, Edmund P. VA 3rd Cav. Co.F
Turner, Ed. P. TN 24th Inf. Comsy.
Turner, Ed. W. MS Cav. Jeff Davis Legion Co.C
Turner, Edward NC 4th Inf. Co.G
Turner, Edward NC 37th Inf. Co.G
Turner, Edward TN 19th (Biffle's) Cav. Co.H Sgt.
Turner, Edward VA 1st St.Res. Co.C 2nd Lt.
Turner, Edward VA 3rd Inf. Co.G
Turner, Edward VA 42nd Inf. Co.A
Turner, Edward A. TN 7th Inf. Co.H
Turner, Edward C. GA 1st (Fannin's) Res. Co.G Cpl.
Turner, Edward J. NC 57th Inf. Co.B
Turner, Edward J. VA 57th Inf. Co.B
Turner, Edward L. VA 5th Cav. (12 mo. '61-2) Co.F
Turner, Edward L. VA 13th Cav. Co.F
Turner, Edward P. VA 3rd Inf. Co.G
Turner, Edward P. Gen. & Staff Lt.Col.,AAG
Turner, Edward R. KY 5th Mtd.Inf. Co.D Sgt.
Turner, Edward V. VA 5th Cav. Co.D
Turner, Edward W. NC 51st Inf. Co.H,A
Turner, Edwin FL Cav. Pickett's Co.
Turner, Edwin VA 57th Inf. Co.G
Turner, Edwin A. GA 10th Cav. (St.Guards) Co.A Sgt.
Turner, Edwin C. AL 3rd Cav. Co.G 1st Sgt.
Turner, Edwin C. AL Inf. 6th (McClellan's) Bn. Co.D Capt.
Turner, E.E. AL Cav. Hardie's Bn.Res. Co.A
Turner, E.J. SC Lt.Arty. 3rd (Palmetto) Bn. Culpeper's Co.
Turner, E.J. SC Lt.Arty. 3rd (Palmetto) Bn. Co.E
Turner, E.J. TN 9th Inf. Co.K
Turner, E.J.B. TX 1st Inf. Co.E
Turner, E.J.B. VA 21st Cav. Co.A 2nd Lt.
Turner, E.L. AL 63rd Inf. Co.K
Turner, E.L. TN 10th & 11th (Cons.) Cav. Co.D
Turner, E.L. TX 1st Hvy.Arty. Co.H,F
Turner, Eli NC 6th Sr.Res. Co.A
Turner, Elias FL 7th Inf. Co.D
Turner, Elias GA 65th Inf. Co.A
Turner, Elias GA Smith's Legion Co.B
Turner, Elias TN 24th Inf. Co.I
Turner, Elias D. AR Cav. Gordon's Regt. Co.K 3rd Lt.
Turner, Elias L. GA 36th (Broyles') Inf. Co.A
Turner, Elihu AL 36th Inf.
Turner, Elihu GA Conscr.
Turner, Elihu B. AR 11th Inf. Co.I
Turner, Elijah AL 28th Inf. Co.G
Turner, Elijah MO Cav. Poindexter's Regt.
Turner, Elijah NC 16th Inf. Co.G
Turner, Elijah F. GA 42nd Inf. Co.D
Turner, Elijah L. GA 42nd Inf. Co.K,C
Turner, Elijah M. AL 10th Inf. Co.A
Turner, Elijah P. TX 4th Field Btty.
Turner, Elisha AL 10th Inf. Co.F
Turner, Elisha GA 7th Cav. Co.E
Turner, Elisha GA Cav. 21st Bn. Co.B
Turner, Elisha TX 15th Cav. Co.C Cpl.
Turner, Elisha M. NC 3rd Cav. (41st St.Troops) Co.K
Turner, Elisha P. MS 30th Inf. Co.D
Turner, Elisha W. AL Mil. 4th Vol. Co.B
Turner, Ellis GA 61st Inf. Co.A
Turner, Ellis SC 12th Inf. Co.K
Turner, E.M. AL Inf. 1st Regt. Co.E Capt.
Turner, E.M. AL 9th Inf.
Turner, E.M. AL 15th Inf. Co.D
Turner, E.M. AL 26th (O'Neal's) Inf. Co.F Capt.
Turner, E.M. LA Res.Corps
Turner, E.M. TX 18th Inf. Co.H Cpl.
Turner, Emmett C. VA 3rd Cav. & Inf.St.Line Co.A
Turner, E.N. NC 14th Inf. Co.E
Turner, Enoch NC 28th Inf. Co.K
Turner, Enoch L. MS 43rd Inf. Co.H
Turner, Enos MO 9th Bn.S.S. Co.A
Turner, E.P. MS 4th Inf. Co.K
Turner, Eph. L. TN 1st (Feild's) Inf. Co.I
Turner, Ephraim MO Inf. Clark's Regt. Co.A
Turner, Ephraim NC 44th Inf. Co.G
Turner, Ephraim A. NC 6th Inf. Co.H
Turner, E.R. AL Cav. Forrest's Regt. 2nd Lt.
Turner, E.R. TN 18th (Newsom's) Cav. Co.E 2nd Lt.
Turner, E.R. TX 12th Cav. Co.G
Turner, E.S. GA Cherokee Legion (St.Guards) Co.F Sgt.
Turner, Esquire NC 42nd Inf. Co.F
Turner, E.T. AL 41st Inf. Co.K
Turner, Eugene LA 1st Hvy.Arty. (Reg.) Co.H
Turner, Evan LA 1st Cav. Co.C Cpl.
Turner, Evans NC 6th Inf. Co.C 2nd Lt.
Turner, Everett NC 5th Cav. (63rd St.Troops) Co.C
Turner, E.W. AL 8th (Livingston's) Cav. Co.A
Turner, E.W. AL 42nd Inf. Co.H
Turner, E.W. SC Inf. Holcombe Legion Co.C
Turner, E.Y. MS 28th Cav. Co.G
Turner, E.Y. MS Inf. 1st Bn.St.Troops (12 mo. '62-3) Co.D
Turner, F. AL Talladega Cty.Res. Cunningham's Co.
Turner, F. TN 16th (Logwood's) Cav. Co.E
Turner, F. VA 8th Cav. Co.B
Turner, F. VA 24th Cav. Co.B Capt.
Turner, F. VA Lt.Arty. Parker's Co.
Turner, F. 2nd Conf.Inf. Co.A
Turner, F.A. AL 20th Inf. Co.B 1st Lt.
Turner, F.A. AL 30th Inf. Co.C 1st Lt.
Turner, F.A. TX Inf. Chambers' Bn.Res.Corps Co.B 1st Lt.
Turner, F.D. AR 6th Inf. Co.C
Turner, F.D. MS 20th Inf. Co.B
Turner, F.D. VA 3rd Inf.Loc.Def. Co.K
Turner, F.E. GA 55th Inf. Co.C
Turner, F.E. MS Cav. Powers' Regt. Co.B
Turner, F.E. MS 39th Inf. Co.H
Turner, Felix AR 5th Inf. Co.D 2nd Lt.
Turner, Ferdinand G. NC 28th Inf. Co.D
Turner, F.F. GA 63rd Inf. Co.I
Turner, F.G. AL 4th Inf. Co.D
Turner, F.G. MO 10th Inf. Co.A
Turner, F.H. SC 13th Inf. Co.I Capt.
Turner, Fielden M. SC 13th Inf. Co.I
Turner, Fielden S. SC 9th Inf. Co.I Cpl.
Turner, Fielding AL St.Arty. Co.D
Turner, Fielding TN 16th Inf. Co.A
Turner, F.J. FL Inf. 2nd Bn. Co.A
Turner, F.J. TX 16th Cav. Co.I
Turner, Flavious J. MS 8th Inf. Co.E
Turner, Flemin E. VA 31st Inf. Co.D Sgt.

Turner, Fleming GA 1st (Fannin's) Res. Co.H,I Sr.2nd Lt.
Turner, Fleming VA 54th Inf. Co.I
Turner, F.M. AL 25th Inf. Co.H
Turner, F.M. AL 42nd Inf. Co.H
Turner, F.M. AL Cp. of Instr. Talladega
Turner, F.M. GA Phillips' Legion Co.B
Turner, F.M. MO Cav. Wood's Regt. Co.F Jr.2nd Lt.
Turner, F.M. NC 16th Inf. Co.I
Turner, F.M. TN 6th Inf. Co.B
Turner, F.M. TN 12th Inf. Co.C
Turner, F.M. TX Cav. Baird's Regt. Co.F
Turner, F.M. VA Lt.Arty. W.P. Carter's Co.
Turner, F.M. VA 110th Mil. Saunders' Co.
Turner, F.M. 20th Conf.Cav. 2nd Co.H
Turner, F.P. TN 9th (Ward's) Cav. Kirkpatrick's Co.
Turner, F.P. TN 24th Inf. Co.C
Turner, F.P. VA 36th Inf. 2nd Co.E Capt.
Turner, F.P. Long's Staff Maj.,Ch.QM
Turner, Francis LA 28th (Thomas') Inf. Co.G 1st Lt.
Turner, Francis MS 7th Inf. Co.B
Turner, Francis MS 25th Inf. Co.A
Turner, Francis MS Inf. (Red Rebels) D.J. Red's Co.
Turner, Francis TN 2nd (Smith's) Cav.
Turner, Francis C. TN 1st (Turney's) Inf. Co.F
Turner, Francis M. AL Inf. 1st Regt. Co.E
Turner, Francis M. GA 39th Inf. Co.B
Turner, Francis M. GA Smith's Legion Co.D
Turner, Francis M. MS 1st Bn.S.S. Co.B
Turner, Francis M. MS 22nd Inf. Co.B
Turner, Francis M. MS 43rd Inf. Co.H
Turner, Francis M. NC 49th Inf. Co.F
Turner, Francis M. TX 27th Cav. Co.G Cpl.
Turner, Francis M. VA Lt.Arty. Leake's Co.
Turner, Francis M. VA 11th Inf. Co.H
Turner, Francis M. VA 57th Inf. Co.C
Turner, Frank LA Inf. 4th Bn. Co.B
Turner, Frank TN 12th (Cons.) Inf. Co.B
Turner, Frank TX 10th Cav. Co.A
Turner, Frank J. MS 21st Inf. Co.C
Turner, Franklin LA 4th Cav. Co.B
Turner, Franklin NC 7th Inf. Co.B
Turner, Franklin TX 9th Field Btty.
Turner, Franklin VA Cav. 39th Bn. Co.C
Turner, Franklin VA 13th Inf. 1st Co.E
Turner, Franklin VA 33rd Inf. Co.H
Turner, Franklin P. VA 36th Inf. Co.E Capt.
Turner, Frank M. MO 3rd Cav. Co.F Jr.2nd Lt.
Turner, Frank Y. MS 19th Inf. Co.K
Turner, Fred AL 9th Inf. Co.K
Turner, Frederick VA 166th Mil. Taylor's Co.
Turner, Fred P. AL Lt.Arty. Tarrant's Btty. Sgt.
Turner, Fredrick GA 13th Inf. Co.F
Turner, Fritz TX 2nd Cav. Co.D
Turner, F.S. SC 2nd Cav. Co.C
Turner, F.T. GA Inf. Bard's Co.
Turner, F.W. TX 2nd Inf. Co.I
Turner, G. AL 15th Inf. Co.A
Turner, G. TX 26th Cav. Co.E
Turner, G.A. VA 10th Cav. Co.K Sgt.
Turner, Gaston NC 31st Inf. Co.D
Turner, Gaston W. AL 47th Inf. Co.H 2nd Lt.
Turner, G.B. AR 1st (Dobbin's) Cav. Co.K
Turner, G.B. GA Inf. 1st Conf.Bn. Co.B
Turner, G.B. TN 21st & 22nd (Cons.) Cav. Co.B
Turner, G.B. TN 24th Bn.S.S. Co.A
Turner, G.C. GA Phillips' Legion Co.I
Turner, G.C. VA 5th Bn.Res. Co.G 2nd Lt.
Turner, G.D. MS Lt.Arty. Turner's Co.
Turner, G.D. VA Lt.Arty. W.P. Carter's Co.
Turner, George AR 16th Inf. Co.B Capt.
Turner, George FL 9th Inf. Co.B
Turner, George GA Hvy.Arty. 22nd Bn. Co.D
Turner, George GA Siege Arty. 28th Bn. Co.D
Turner, George GA Arty. (Chatham Arty.) Wheaton's Co. Cpl.
Turner, George GA 1st (Olmstead's) Inf. Claghorn's Co.
Turner, George GA 7th Inf. (St.Guards) Co.F
Turner, George GA 31st Inf. Co.C
Turner, George GA Inf. (Ogeechee Minute Men) Garrison's Co.
Turner, George LA Arty. Moody's Co. (Madison Lt.Arty.)
Turner, George LA Conscr.
Turner, George MO 1st N.E. Cav. Co.O
Turner, George MO 9th Bn.S.S. Co.D Sgt.
Turner, George MO 10th Inf. Co.B
Turner, George NC 27th Inf. Co.D
Turner, George NC 37th Inf. Co.F
Turner, George NC 44th Inf. Co.C
Turner, George NC 54th Inf. Co.E
Turner, George NC 60th Inf. Co.H
Turner, George NC 61st Inf. Co.E
Turner, George SC 1st (Butler's) Inf. Co.G
Turner, George SC 7th Res. Co.C
Turner, George TN 13th (Gore's) Cav. Co.I
Turner, George TN 21st & 22nd (Cons.) Cav. Co.G
Turner, George TX 12th Cav. Co.D
Turner, George TX 21st Cav. Co.K
Turner, George TX Cav. Baylor's Regt. Co.D
Turner, George VA Cav. 32nd Bn. Co.A
Turner, George VA Cav. 37th Bn. Co.K
Turner, George VA Inf. 6th Bn.Loc.Def. Co.C
Turner, George VA 15th Inf. Co.G
Turner, George VA 25th Mil. Co.A
Turner, George Gen. & Staff, Adj.Gen.Dept. Capt.
Turner, George A. LA Washington Arty.Bn. Co.5 Driver
Turner, Geo. A. MO St.Guard QM
Turner, George A. NC 53rd Inf. Co.C Cpl.
Turner, George A. TX 17th Cons.Dismtd.Cav. Co.E
Turner, George A. TX 18th Cav. Co.E
Turner, George A. Gen. & Staff Maj.,QM
Turner, George D. AL Lt.Arty. 2nd Bn. Co.B 2nd Lt.
Turner, George D. GA 2nd Cav. (St.Guards) Co.E
Turner, George D. NC 3rd Cav. (41st St.Troops) Co.C
Turner, George D. SC 18th Inf. Co.H
Turner, George E. AL 3rd Inf. Co.B
Turner, George E. VA 5th Cav. Co.K
Turner, George E. VA 15th Cav. Co.I
Turner, George G. GA 1st (Fannin's) Res. Co.E Sgt.
Turner, George H. AR Inf. Clayton's Co.
Turner, George H. MS 2nd Inf. Co.C
Turner, George H. VA 15th Cav. Co.K
Turner, George H. 1st Conf.Eng.Troops Co.C
Turner, George K. VA 28th Inf. Co.G
Turner, George L. NC 28th Inf. Co.C
Turner, George L. TN 11th Inf. Co.A
Turner, George L. TX Cav. Benavides' Regt. Co.G Sgt.
Turner, George M. AR 1st (Crawford's) Cav. Co.A
Turner, George M. GA 1st (Olmstead's) Inf. Stiles' Co. 1st Sgt.
Turner, George M. GA Inf. 18th Bn. Co.B,C 1st Lt.
Turner, George M. VA 9th Inf. Co.K
Turner, George P. KY 1st (Butler's) Cav. Co.B
Turner, George P. NC 8th Bn.Part.Rangers Co.A
Turner, George Q. TX 8th Cav. Co.C
Turner, George R. SC 2nd Cav. Co.C
Turner, George R. VA 3rd Inf. Co.G
Turner, George R. 1st Conf.Inf. 2nd Co.F
Turner, George S. AL 8th Cav. Co.H
Turner, George T. GA 1st (Olmstead's) Inf. Gallie's Co.
Turner, George T. GA 46th Inf. Co.A
Turner, George T. VA 3rd Inf.Loc.Def. Co.A
Turner, George T. VA 26th Inf. Co.G Cpl.
Turner, George T. VA 30th Inf. Co.E
Turner, George T. VA 51st Inf. Co.D
Turner, George W. AL Mil. 4th Vol. Gantt's Co.
Turner, George W. AL 6th Inf. Co.G
Turner, George W. AL 18th Inf. Co.L
Turner, George W. AL 21st Inf. Co.A
Turner, George W. AL Recruits
Turner, George W. FL Cav. 3rd Bn. Co.A
Turner, George W. FL 1st Inf. New Co.C
Turner, George W. GA Inf. 1st Loc.Troops (Augusta) Co.D Sgt.
Turner, George W. GA 3rd Inf. Co.G
Turner, George W. GA 14th Inf. Co.D
Turner, George W. GA 20th Inf. Co.D
Turner, George W. MS Inf. 1st Bn.St.Troops (30 days '64) Co.G
Turner, George W. MS 13th Inf. Co.D
Turner, George W. MS 40th Inf. Co.A
Turner, George W. MO 5th Inf. Co.H
Turner, George W. NC 4th Cav. (59th St.Troops) Co.A
Turner, George W. NC 7th Inf. Co.E
Turner, George W. NC 20th Inf. Co.A
Turner, George W. NC 42nd Inf. Co.F
Turner, George W. NC 50th Inf. Co.F Music.
Turner, George W. SC 2nd Arty. Co.B,K
Turner, George W. SC 27th Inf. Music.
Turner, George W. TN Inf. 1st Bn. (Colms') Co.C
Turner, George W. TN Inf. 154th Sr.Regt. Co.E Ch.Music.
Turner, George W. TX 4th Cav. Co.A
Turner, George W. TX 22nd Cav. Co.H
Turner, George W. TX 28th Cav. Co.I Sgt.
Turner, George W. TX 20th Inf. Co.D
Turner, George W. VA 3rd Cav. Co.F
Turner, George W. VA 6th Cav. Co.D,B
Turner, George W. VA 11th Cav. Co.C
Turner, George W. VA 22nd Cav. Co.H
Turner, George W. VA Cav. 36th Bn. Co.B

Turner, George W. VA Lt.Arty. 12th Bn. 2nd Co.A
Turner, George W. VA Hvy.Arty. A.J. Jones' Co. 1st Sgt.
Turner, George W. VA Lt.Arty. Sturdivant's Co.
Turner, George W. VA 2nd Inf. Co.C
Turner, George W. VA 3rd Inf. Co.D
Turner, George W. VA 3rd Inf. Co.G 2nd Lt.
Turner, George W. VA 6th Inf. Co.C
Turner, George W. VA 6th Inf. 2nd Co.E Sgt.
Turner, George W. VA 23rd Inf. Co.E
Turner, George W. VA Inf. 28th Bn. Co.D
Turner, George W. VA 48th Inf. Co.D
Turner, George W. VA 56th Inf. Co.H
Turner, George W. VA 59th Inf. 3rd Co.I
Turner, George W. VA 63rd Inf. Co.K
Turner, George W. President's Guard,CSA
Turner, Gerald VA 3rd Inf. Co.G
Turner, G.F. AR 24th Inf. Co.D
Turner, G.F. AR Inf. Hardy's Regt. Co.C
Turner, G.F. MS 38th Cav. Co.G
Turner, G.G. GA 10th Inf. Co.H
Turner, G.H. AL 48th Inf. Co.C
Turner, G.H. AL 60th Inf. Co.K
Turner, G.H. GA Cav. 9th Bn. (St.Guards) Co.D Ens.
Turner, Gideon MS Inf. 1st St.Troops Co.G
Turner, Gideon MS Inf. 3rd Bn. (St.Troops) Co.E
Turner, Gideon T. MS 11th (Perrin's) Cav. Co.H
Turner, Gilbert H. TN 17th Inf. Co.F
Turner, Gilford B. LA 12th Inf. Co.C
Turner, G.J. AL 53rd (Part.Rangers) Co.D Sgt.
Turner, G.J. AR 10th Mil. Co.C
Turner, G.J. NC 3rd Cav. (41st St.Troops) Co.B
Turner, G.K. Hoke's Div. Surg.
Turner, G. Kempton VA 11th Inf. Co.E
Turner, G.M. SC 17th Inf. Co.E
Turner, G.M. TX 15th Cav. Co.K
Turner, G.M. VA 1st Inf. Co.B
Turner, G.M. VA 11th Inf. Co.G
Turner, Goodwyn A. VA 61st Inf. Co.G
Turner, Goslin MO Inf. Perkins' Bn. Co.F Cpl.
Turner, G. Paul M. MS 5th Cav. Co.I Capt.
Turner, G.R. NC 49th Inf. Co.H
Turner, G.R. 4th Conf.Eng.Troops Co.B
Turner, Granville TN Cav. 7th Bn. (Bennett's) Co.B
Turner, Granville TN 22nd (Barteau's) Cav. Co.E
Turner, Granvill T. VA 28th Inf. Co.G
Turner, Green B. AL Vol. Lee, Jr.'s Co.
Turner, Green B. GA Lt.Arty. Scogin's Btty. (Griffin Lt.Arty.)
Turner, Green B. TX 3rd Cav. Co.B
Turner, Green B. 1st Conf.Inf. 2nd Co.F
Turner, Green B.H. GA 63rd Inf. Co.H
Turner, Green F. GA 30th Inf. Co.B Sgt.
Turner, Green R. AR Inf. 4th Bn. Co.C
Turner, G.S. TX 5th Inf. (St.Troops) Martindale's Co.
Turner, G.T. AL Cav. Moreland's Regt. Co.I
Turner, G.T. FL 1st (Res.) Inf.
Turner, G.T. TN 11th Inf. Co.C
Turner, Gustus M. TX 31st Cav. Co.C
Turner, G.W. AL 53rd (Part.Rangers) Co.G
Turner, G.W. AL 1st Regt. Mobile Vol. Co.A
Turner, G.W. AL 20th Inf. Co.B
Turner, G.W. AL 40th Inf. Co.I
Turner, G.W. AL Cp. of Instr. Talladega
Turner, G.W. AR 7th Mil. Co.E Sgt.
Turner, G.W. AR 15th (N.W.) Inf. Co.I
Turner, G.W. AR 25th Inf. Co.E
Turner, G.W. GA 8th Cav.
Turner, G.W. GA Tiller's Co. (Echols Lt.Arty.)
Turner, G.W. GA Inf. 1st City Bn. (Columbus) Co.C
Turner, G.W. GA 5th Inf. Co.H
Turner, G.W. GA Inf. 25th Bn. (Prov.Guard) Co.B
Turner, G.W. GA 64th Inf. Co.F
Turner, G.W. LA 28th (Gray's) Inf. Co.E
Turner, G.W. MS 9th Cav. Co.A
Turner, G.W. MS Inf. 1st Bn.St.Troops (12 mo. '62-3) Co.B
Turner, G.W. MS 8th Inf. Co.A
Turner, G.W. MS 24th Inf. Co.A
Turner, G.W. MO 5th Cav. Co.H
Turner, G.W. MO Cav. Freeman's Regt. Co.B 3rd Lt.
Turner, G.W. MO Lt.Arty. Farris' Btty. (Clark Arty.)
Turner, G.W. MO 8th Inf. Co.F Sgt.
Turner, G.W. SC 5th Cav. Co.I
Turner, G.W. SC Cav. 14th Bn. Co.D
Turner, G.W. SC Inf. 1st (Charleston) Bn.
Turner, G.W. SC 5th Res. Co.D 1st Lt.
Turner, G.W. SC 7th Inf. 1st Co.G
Turner, G.W. SC 7th Res. Co.L
Turner, G.W. SC 10th Inf. Co.F
Turner, G.W. SC 18th Inf. Co.K
Turner, G.W. SC 27th Inf. Co.F
Turner, G.W. TN 10th (DeMoss') Cav. Co.F Sgt.
Turner, G.W. TN 15th Cav. Co.G Sgt.
Turner, G.W. TN 21st (Wilson's) Cav. Co.B Cpl.
Turner, G.W. TN Cav. Napier's Bn. Co.C
Turner, G.W. TN 13th Inf. Co.H 1st Lt.
Turner, G.W. TN 16th Inf. Co.B 2nd Lt.
Turner, G.W. TX 10th Cav. Co.D
Turner, G.W. 15th Conf.Cav. Co.A
Turner, H. GA Cav. Logan's Co. (White Cty. Old Men's Home Guards)
Turner, H. GA 47th Inf. Co.K
Turner, H. LA 3rd (Wingfield's) Cav. Co.H
Turner, H. MS 4th Cav. Co.F
Turner, H. MS Inf. 1st Bn.St.Troops (12 mo. '62-3) Co.E
Turner, H. NC 12th Inf. Co.H
Turner, H. TN 22nd Inf. Co.B
Turner, H. TN 84th Inf. Co.B
Turner, H. TX Cav. Terry's Regt. Co.F
Turner, H.A. AR 8th Inf. New Co.I
Turner, H.A. SC Inf.Loc.Troops
Turner, Hadarezer B. NC 5th Inf. Co.C Cpl.
Turner, Haderezer B. NC 3rd Cav. (41st St.Troops) Co.D
Turner, Ham MS 1st (Percy's) Inf. Co.I
Turner, Hamilton MS 2nd Part.Rangers Co.D,F
Turner, Hanbury D. AR 23rd Inf. Co.E Cpl.
Turner, Harden VA 63rd Inf. Co.A
Turner, Harden J. VA 53rd Inf. Co.E
Turner, Hardin NC 21st Inf. Co.L
Turner, Hardway A. VA 14th Inf. Co.B
Turner, Hardy B. NC 3rd Arty. (40th St.Troops) Co.A
Turner, Hardy B. NC 32nd Inf. Lenoir Braves 1st Co.K
Turner, Hardy W. AL Inf. 1st Regt. Co.G
Turner, Harry S. AL 4th (Roddey's) Cav. Co.C
Turner, Harvey SC 7th Inf. 1st Co.F, 2nd Co.F
Turner, Hasiel NC 55th Inf. Co.D
Turner, H.B. AL 5th Cav. Co.G
Turner, H.C. AL 60th Inf. Co.K
Turner, H.C. AR Cav. Gordon's Regt. Co.H
Turner, H.C. GA 27th Inf. Co.H
Turner, H.C. MS 1st Cav.Res. Co.K,I
Turner, H.C. NC 50th Inf. Co.F Music.
Turner, H.C. TN 18th (Newsom's) Cav. Co.C,G
Turner, H.C. TN 19th & 20th (Cons.) Cav. Co.B
Turner, H.C. TN 55th (McKoin's) Inf. Bound's Co.
Turner, H.D. AL Cav. (St.Res.) Young's Co.
Turner, H.D. AR 20th Inf. Co.K
Turner, H.D. TX 15th Inf. Co.B Cpl.
Turner, H.E. SC Inf. Hampton Legion Co.H
Turner, Hector NC 27th Inf. Surg.
Turner, Hector Gen. & Staff Surg.
Turner, Henly S. AR 9th Inf. Co.D
Turner, Henry AL 53rd (Part.Rangers) Co.D
Turner, Henry AL 21st Inf. Co.I
Turner, Henry GA 4th (Clinch's) Cav. Co.G
Turner, Henry GA 1st Bn.S.S. Co.B
Turner, Henry GA Inf. 11th Bn. (St.Guards) Co.A
Turner, Henry GA 26th Inf. Co.K
Turner, Henry GA 36th (Broyles') Inf. Co.B
Turner, Henry GA 56th Inf. Co.D
Turner, Henry KY 8th Cav. Co.G
Turner, Henry KY 11th Cav. Co.C
Turner, Henry LA 1st (Nelligan's) Inf. Howell's Co. Sgt.
Turner, Henry LA Inf. 9th Bn. Co.B
Turner, Henry LA 28th (Thomas') Inf. Co.G Sgt.
Turner, Henry MS 32nd Inf. Co.C,G Cpl.
Turner, Henry MO 1st N.E. Cav. Co.O
Turner, Henry MO 4th Inf. Co.C
Turner, Henry NC 4th Inf. Co.G
Turner, Henry NC 30th Inf. Co.B
Turner, Henry NC 31st Inf. Co.D
Turner, Henry NC 43rd Inf. Co.E
Turner, Henry NC 46th Inf. Co.C
Turner, Henry NC Mallett's Bn. (Cp.Guard) Co.A
Turner, Henry SC 3rd Res. Co.I
Turner, Henry TN 16th Inf. Co.H
Turner, Henry TN 43rd Inf. Co.A
Turner, Henry TN 48th (Nixon's) Inf. Co.G
Turner, Henry TN 59th Mtd.Inf. Co.F
Turner, Henry TX 28th Cav. Co.L
Turner, Henry TX Cav. Morgan's Regt. Co.C
Turner, Henry TX 20th Inf. Co.H
Turner, Henry VA 6th Cav. Co.C
Turner, Henry VA Lt.Arty. Thornton's Co.
Turner, Henry VA 9th Inf. Co.E Sgt.
Turner, Henry VA 49th Inf. 1st Co.G
Turner, Henry Morgan's,CSA
Turner, Henry A. SC 5th Inf. 1st Co.K, 2nd Co.K Sgt.

Turner, Henry A. VA 3rd Inf. 2nd Co.I
Turner, Henry B. AL 29th Inf. Co.A Maj.
Turner, Henry B. AR 20th Inf. Co.A Sgt.
Turner, Henry B. MS 22nd Inf. Co.F
Turner, Henry C. AL 1st Bn. Hilliard's Legion Vol. Co.C
Turner, Henry C. AR 6th Inf. Co.I
Turner, Henry C. KY 1st Bn.Mtd.Rifles Co.B
Turner, Henry C. KY 5th Mtd.Inf. Co.B
Turner, Henry C. MS 1st Lt.Arty. Co.C
Turner, Henry C. NC 28th Inf. Co.K 2nd Lt.
Turner, Henry C. NC 52nd Inf. Co.I Sgt.Maj.
Turner, Henry C. VA 24th Inf. Co.H
Turner, Henry G. NC 23rd Inf. Co.H Capt.
Turner, Henry H. AR 23rd Inf. Co.B Sgt.
Turner, Henry H. NC 4th Inf. Co.C
Turner, Henry H. VA 5th Cav. (12 mo. '61-2) Co.H
Turner, Henry H. VA 13th Cav. Co.A
Turner, Henry J. TX 14th Cav. Co.C
Turner, Henry J. VA Lt.Arty. 38th Bn. Co.A
Turner, Henry L. VA Vol. Taylor's Co.
Turner, Henry M. NC 44th Inf. Co.C
Turner, Henry M. VA 24th Cav. Co.A
Turner, Henry M. VA Lt.Arty. W.P. Carter's Co.
Turner, Henry N. LA 12th Inf. Co.L
Turner, Henry P. AL 4th Inf. Co.I Sgt.
Turner, Henry P. MS 1st Lt.Arty. Co.C Capt.
Turner, Henry R. MO Lt.Arty. 3rd Btty.
Turner, Henry T. TN 12th (Cons.) Inf. Co.H
Turner, Henry T. VA 28th Inf. Co.I
Turner, Henry T. VA 41st Inf. Co.H
Turner, Henry V. VA 9th Cav. Co.C
Turner, Henson GA 1st (Fannin's) Res. Co.I Sgt.
Turner, Herod TN Cav. 7th Bn. (Bennett's) Co.B
Turner, Heron TN 22nd (Barteau's) Cav. Co.E
Turner, Hezekiah MS 11th Inf. Co.G
Turner, Hezekiah VA 3rd Cav. Co.F
Turner, Hezekiah VA 7th Cav. Co.A
Turner, Hezekiah VA 1st St.Res. Co.C
Turner, H.F. AL 5th Inf. New Co.A
Turner, H.F. GA Inf. 1st City Bn. (Columbus) Co.A
Turner, H.G. AL Mil. 2nd Regt.Vol. Co.B
Turner, H.G. AL 42nd Inf. Co.I
Turner, H.G. GA Inf. 18th Bn. Co.B
Turner, H.G.B. GA 43rd Inf. Co.A
Turner, H.H. AR 15th (N.W.) Inf. Co.I Jr.2nd Lt.
Turner, H.H. GA Tiller's Co. (Echols Lt.Arty.)
Turner, H.H. MS 7th Cav. Co.E
Turner, H.H. MS 23rd Inf. Co.B
Turner, H.H. SC Inf. 1st (Charleston) Bn. Co.B,G
Turner, H.H. SC 13th Inf. Co.E Sgt.
Turner, H.H. SC 27th Inf. Co.K
Turner, H.H. TX 12th Cav. Co.D 1st Sgt.
Turner, H.H. VA 10th Cav. Co.D
Turner, H.H. VA Hvy.Arty. Allen's Co.
Turner, Hilary M. MO 4th Cav. Co.I
Turner, Hilliard NC 66th Inf. Co.K
Turner, Hilliard A. GA 44th Inf. Co.A
Turner, Hiram SC Inf. Hampton Legion Co.D
Turner, Hiram M. VA Hvy.Arty. 19th Bn. Co.A
Turner, Hiram M. VA Hvy.Arty. Kyle's Co.
Turner, H.J. AL 3rd Inf. Co.L
Turner, H.J. AL 6th Inf. Co.L
Turner, H.J. GA 19th Inf. Co.H
Turner, H.J. TN 47th Inf. Co.C
Turner, H.L. MS Cav. Jeff Davis Legion Co.C
Turner, H.L. MS Inf. 1st Bn. Co.D
Turner, H.L. MS 10th Inf. New Co.K
Turner, H.L. MO Cav. Wood's Regt. Co.F 1st Lt.
Turner, H.L. TN 28th Cav. Surg.
Turner, H.L. TN 23rd Inf. Co.I
Turner, H.L. TX 23rd Cav. Co.A
Turner, H.L. Gen. & Staff Surg.
Turner, H.M. GA 13th Inf. Co.A
Turner, H.M. NC 17th Inf. (2nd Org.) Co.K
Turner, H.M. SC 1st (Hagood's) Inf. 2nd Co.E
Turner, H.M. SC 13th Inf. Co.E
Turner, H.M. TX Inf. 3rd St.Troops Co.F
Turner, Hovce MO 6th Cav. Co.K
Turner, H.R. AL 8th Inf. Co.G
Turner, H.R. GA Cav. 29th Bn. Co.G
Turner, H.R. NC 54th Inf. Co.G
Turner, H.R. SC 7th Inf. 1st Co.H, Co.A
Turner, H.R. SC Inf. Hampton Legion Co.G
Turner, H.S. GA 64th Inf. Co.B
Turner, H.T. KY Arty. Corbett's Co.
Turner, Hud MO 6th Cav. Co.K
Turner, Hugh TN 9th Inf. Co.G
Turner, Hugh C. NC 1st Cav. (9th St.Troops) Co.A Cpl.
Turner, Hugh G. SC Lt.Arty. 3rd (Palmetto) Bn. Co.F
Turner, H.W. AR 27th Inf. Co.I
Turner, H.W. MS Inf. 3rd Bn. Co.E
Turner, H.W. NC 3rd Inf. Co.B
Turner, H.W. NC 8th Sr.Res. McNeill's Co.
Turner, H.W. NC Allen's Co. (Loc.Def.)
Turner, H.W. TN 24th Bn.S.S. Co.A
Turner, I.B. 8th (Wade's) Conf.Cav. Co.C
Turner, I.E. MS 6th Cav. Co.L
Turner, I.J. KY 12th Cav. Co.A Cpl.
Turner, Ike N.M. TX 5th Inf. Co.K Capt.
Turner, I.P. AL 2nd Cav. Co.D
Turner, Ira SC 2nd Inf. Co.F
Turner, Ira SC 7th Inf. 2nd Co.G
Turner, Irby H. GA 44th Inf. Co.K Sgt.
Turner, Irijah VA 61st Inf. Co.F
Turner, Isaac MS 43rd Inf. Co.G
Turner, Isaac NC Cav. 7th Bn. Co.D
Turner, Isaac NC 60th Inf. Co.G
Turner, Isaac TN 3rd (Lillard's) Mtd.Inf. Co.D
Turner, Isaac TN 35th Inf. 1st Co.I Cpl.
Turner, Isaac VA 146th Mil. Co.C
Turner, Isaac A. TN 63rd Inf. Co.B
Turner, Isaac J. FL 8th Inf. Co.E
Turner, Isaac N. MS 34th Inf. Co.E
Turner, Isaac N. MO 9th Bn.S.S. Co.E
Turner, Isaac P. AR 24th Inf. Co.G
Turner, Isaac P. AR Inf. Hardy's Regt. Co.G
Turner, Isaiah TN 35th Inf. 1st Co.A
Turner, Isham GA 10th Cav. Co.D
Turner, Isham 7th Conf.Cav. Co.D Cpl.
Turner, Israel M. MS 24th Inf. Co.E
Turner, Ivy B. NC 20th Inf. Co.I
Turner, I.W. VA Lt.Arty. Griffin's Co.
Turner, Izeur AL 46th Inf. Co.H
Turner, J. AL 3rd Inf. Co.D
Turner, J. AL 10th Inf.
Turner, J. AL 37th Inf. Co.A
Turner, J. AL 69th Regt. Co.B
Turner, J. AR 58th Mil. Co.D
Turner, J. FL Cav. 5th Bn. Co.H
Turner, J. GA Cav. Logan's Co. (White Cty. Old Men's Guards)
Turner, J. GA 1st Reg. Co.H
Turner, J. GA 1st Reg. Co.I
Turner, J. GA 5th Res. Co.F
Turner, J. GA 5th Res. Co.K
Turner, J. GA Inf. 27th Bn. (NonConscr.) Co.C
Turner, J. GA 47th Inf. Co.C
Turner, J. LA 1st (Strawbridge's) Inf. Co.E
Turner, J. MS 5th Inf. (St.Troops) Co.E
Turner, J. MO 1st Cav.
Turner, J. NC 5th Sr.Res. Co.I
Turner, J. SC Lt.Arty. 3rd (Palmetto) Bn. Co.A
Turner, J. SC Lt.Arty. 3rd (Palmetto) Bn. Culpeper's Co.
Turner, J. SC 1st (Butler's) Inf. Co.G
Turner, J. SC 1st Mil. 4th Regt.
Turner, J. SC 7th Inf. Co.B
Turner, J. SC 10th Inf. Co.I
Turner, J. TN 50th Inf. Co.K Sgt.
Turner, J. TX Cav. Mann's Regt. Co.I
Turner, J. TX 4th Inf. Co.G
Turner, J. VA 12th Cav. Co.G
Turner, J. VA 55th Inf. Co.K
Turner, J.A. AL 1st Cav. 2nd Co.A Cpl.
Turner, J.A. AL 3rd Cav. Co.A
Turner, J.A. AL 7th Cav. Co.C,F
Turner, J.A. AL 51st (Part.Rangers) Co.C
Turner, J.A. AL Cav. Barbiere's Bn. Co.B
Turner, J.A. AL Gid Nelson Lt.Arty.
Turner, J.A. AL 22nd Inf. Co.H Sgt.
Turner, J.A. AL Talladega Cty.Res. D.M. Reid's Co.
Turner, J.A. AR 15th (N.W.) Inf. Co.I
Turner, J.A. AR 19th (Dawson's) Inf. Co.I Capt.
Turner, J.A. AR 27th Inf. Co.I
Turner, J.A. AR 34th Inf. Co.I
Turner, J.A. GA Lt.Arty. Ritter's Co.
Turner, J.A. GA 5th Res. Co.A
Turner, J.A. GA 8th Inf. (St.Guards) Co.K
Turner, J.A. MS 14th Inf. Co.E
Turner, J.A. MO 10th Inf. Co.B
Turner, J.A. TN 12th Inf. Co.D
Turner, J.A. TN 12th (Cons.) Inf. Co.E
Turner, J.A. TN 20th Inf. Co.F
Turner, J.A. VA 46th Inf. Co.F
Turner, J.A. VA 67th Mil. Co.B
Turner, J.A. 7th Conf.Cav. Co.M
Turner, J.A. Gen. & Staff Ord.Sgt.
Turner, Jackson E. GA 61st Inf. Co.D
Turner, Jacob AL 33rd Inf. Co.D
Turner, Jacob NC 27th Inf. Co.F
Turner, Jacob SC 6th Cav. Co.D Sgt.
Turner, Jacob TN 46th Inf. Co.E
Turner, Jacob VA 7th Cav. Co.B
Turner, Jacob VA 61st Inf. Co.F
Turner, Jacob C. VA 9th Inf. Co.B
Turner, Jacob H. AL 3rd Inf. Co.B
Turner, Jacob P. GA 57th Inf. Co.F
Turner, Jacob W. VA 26th Inf. Co.G 1st Sgt.
Turner, James AL 15th Bn.Part.Rangers Co.B

Turner, James M. AR 35th Inf. Co.G
Turner, James M. GA 2nd Cav. Co.D
Turner, James M. GA 38th Inf. Co.B
Turner, James M. GA 44th Inf. Co.H
Turner, James M. MS 1st Lt.Arty. Co.D
Turner, James M. MS 2nd Part.Rangers Co.K,H
Turner, James M. MS 1st (Johnston's) Inf. Co.F
Turner, James M. MS 15th Inf. Co.I
Turner, James M. MS 19th Inf. Co.K
Turner, James M. MS 40th Inf. Co.E
Turner, James M. NC 4th Inf. Co.B
Turner, James M. SC Arty. Fickling's Co. (Brooks Lt.Arty.)
Turner, James M. SC 2nd Inf. Co.K
Turner, James M. SC 3rd St.Troops Co.B
Turner, James M. SC 9th Inf. Co.I Cpl.
Turner, James M. TN 1st Cav. Co.E
Turner, James M. TN 1st (Feild's) Inf. Co.B
Turner, James M. TX 18th Cav. Co.B
Turner, James M. VA 2nd Cav. Co.F
Turner, James M. VA Lt.Arty. Hankins' Co.
Turner, James M. VA 16th Inf. Co.F Cpl.
Turner, James M. VA 45th Inf. Co.I
Turner, James M. VA 59th Inf. 3rd Co.C
Turner, James N. NC 2nd Cav. (19th St.Troops) Co.B Capt.
Turner, James N. TN 2nd (Robison's) Inf. Co.I Sgt.
Turner, James N. Eng. 2nd Lt.
Turner, James P. AL 3rd Cav. Co.A
Turner, James P. GA 4th (Clinch's) Cav. Co.F,H Capt.
Turner, James P. GA 64th Inf. Co.G
Turner, James P. NC 45th Inf. Co.D
Turner, James P. NC 55th Inf. Co.B
Turner, James P. SC 17th Inf. Co.F
Turner, James P. VA 48th Inf. Co.D
Turner, James Polk GA Phillips' Legion Co.B
Turner, James R. AL 33rd Inf. Co.H
Turner, James R. KY 6th Cav. Co.C
Turner, James R. NC 4th Cav. (59th St.Troops) Co.B
Turner, James R. NC 45th Inf. Co.A
Turner, James R. TN 4th Inf.
Turner, James R. TN 34th Inf. Co.B,E,G
Turner, James R. VA Lt.Arty. J.S. Brown's Co.
Turner, James R. VA Lt.Arty. Taylor's Co.
Turner, James R. VA 51st Inf. Co.D
Turner, James R. VA 57th Inf. Co.K
Turner, James S. AR 20th Inf. Co.A
Turner, James S. GA 4th Inf. Co.I
Turner, James T. AL 61st Inf. Co.E
Turner, James T. KY Cav. 1st Bn. Co.A
Turner, James T. LA 27th Inf. Co.C
Turner, James T. SC 16th Inf. Co.G Sgt.
Turner, James T. TN 9th Cav.
Turner, James T. TN 47th Inf. Co.E
Turner, James T. TX 9th Cav. Co.D
Turner, James T. VA 8th Cav. 2nd Co.D
Turner, James T. VA Lt.Arty. Hankins' Co.
Turner, James T. VA 34th Inf. Co.I
Turner, James W. AL 25th Inf. Co.I
Turner, James W. AL Cp. of Instr. Talladega
Turner, James W. GA 55th Inf. Co.K
Turner, James W. GA 66th Inf. Co.B
Turner, James W. KY 9th Cav. Co.B
Turner, James W. MS Cav. Ham's Regt. Co.E Sgt.
Turner, James W. MS 4th Inf. Co.H
Turner, James W. MO 1st Cav. Co.D
Turner, James W. NC 2nd Arty. (36th St.Troops) Co.B
Turner, James W. NC Inf. 2nd Bn. Co.E
Turner, James W. VA 3rd Lt.Arty. (Loc.Def.) Co.H
Turner, James W. VA Lt.Arty. Clutter's Co.
Turner, James W. VA Goochland Lt.Arty.
Turner, James W. VA 20th Inf. Co.I
Turner, James W. VA 20th Inf. Co.K
Turner, James W. VA 54th Inf. Co.F
Turner, James W. VA 56th Inf. Co.C Cpl.
Turner, James W. VA 59th Inf. 3rd Co.B Cpl.
Turner, James W. VA 59th Inf. 3rd Co.C
Turner, James SC 19th Inf. Co.A
Turner, Jarvis AL 1st Regt. Mobile Vol. Co.E
Turner, Jarvis AL 4th Res. Co.C
Turner, Jasper GA 32nd Inf. Co.B
Turner, Jasper TN 48th (Nixon's) Inf. Co.A
Turner, Jasper TN 48th (Voorhies') Inf. Co.B
Turner, Jasper TN Inf. Sowell's Detach.
Turner, Jasper M. GA 3rd Inf. Co.H
Turner, Jasper M. 2nd Conf.Eng.Troops Co.G Sgt.
Turner, Jasper N. GA 6th Inf. Co.B
Turner, J.B. AL Cav. Hardie's Bn.Res. Co.C Cpl.
Turner, J.B. AL Lt.Arty. Kolb's Btty.
Turner, J.B. AL 10th Inf. Co.C
Turner, J.B. AL 34th Inf. Co.A
Turner, J.B. AL 34th Inf. Co.G
Turner, J.B. AL Res. J.G. Rankin's Co. Sgt.
Turner, J.B. GA 1st (Fannin's) Res. Co.B
Turner, J.B. GA 3rd Inf. Co.G Cpl.
Turner, J.B. GA Inf. 23rd Bn.Loc.Def. Cook's Co.
Turner, J.B. GA 24th Inf. Co.G
Turner, J.B. LA Miles' Legion Co.C Capt.
Turner, J.B. MS 8th Cav. Co.D,C
Turner, J.B. MS 28th Cav. Co.K
Turner, J.B. MS 4th Inf. Co.F
Turner, J.B. NC 5th Inf. Co.C
Turner, J.B. NC 12th Inf. Co.C
Turner, J.B. SC 5th Cav. Co.K
Turner, J.B. SC 6th Cav. Co.H
Turner, J.B. SC Inf. Hampton Legion Co.D
Turner, J.B. TN 13th Inf. Co.K
Turner, J.B. TN Inf. 22nd Bn. Co.B
Turner, J.B. TX 12th Cav. Co.D
Turner, J.B. VA Lt.Arty. Cooper's Co.
Turner, J.B. VA Lt.Arty. Penick's Co.
Turner, J.B. VA 29th Inf. Co.A
Turner, J.B. 8th (Wade's) Conf.Cav. Co.I
Turner, J.B. Gen. & Staff Asst.Surg.
Turner, J.C. AL 4th (Russell's) Cav. Co.F
Turner, J.C. AL St.Arty. Co.D Sgt.
Turner, J.C. AL Mil. 2nd Regt.Vol. Co.F Sgt.
Turner, J.C. FL 1st Inf. New Co.C
Turner, J.C. GA 27th Inf. Co.H
Turner, J.C. MS Cav. 2nd Bn.Res. Co.B
Turner, J.C. MS 3rd Inf. Co.D 1st Lt.
Turner, J.C. NC 4th Cav. (59th St.Troops) Co.I
Turner, J.C. NC Cav. 12th Bn. Co.B
Turner, J.C. NC 1st Inf. Co.K
Turner, J.C. NC 5th Inf. Co.K
Turner, J.C. SC 2nd Cav. Co.G
Turner, J.C. SC 1st (Hagood's) Inf. 2nd Co.I
Turner, J.C. SC 6th Inf. 2nd Co.B
Turner, J.C. SC 18th Inf. Co.K Cpl.
Turner, J.C. SC Inf. Holcombe Legion Co.G
Turner, J.C. TN 3rd (Forrest's) Cav. Co.E
Turner, J.C. TN 11th (Holman's) Cav. Co.C
Turner, J.C. TN 13th Inf. Co.H
Turner, J.C. TN 33rd Inf. Co.H
Turner, J.C. TX Cav. Baird's Regt. Co.G
Turner, J.C. TX Baylor's Cav. Co.F
Turner, J.C. TX Cav. Crump's Regt. Co.D 2nd Lt.
Turner, J.C. Gen. & Staff Capt.,AQM
Turner, J. Calvin SC 9th Inf. Co.I
Turner, J. Calvin VA 7th Cav. Co.E
Turner, J. Carr AR 1st (Dobbin's) Cav. Co.A 1st Lt.
Turner, J. Claudius 8th (Dearing's) Conf.Cav. Co.B
Turner, J.D. AL 53rd (Part.Rangers) Co.G,I Sgt.
Turner, J.D. AL St.Arty. Co.C
Turner, J.D. AR 1st (Monroe's) Cav. Co.H
Turner, J.D. GA 2nd Cav. (St.Guards) Co.K
Turner, J.D. FL Cav. 3rd Bn. Co.A
Turner, J.D. GA 13th Inf. Co.B
Turner, J.D. LA LA & Govt.Employees Regt. Co.D 2nd Lt.
Turner, J.D. MS 6th Cav. Co.E 1st Lt.
Turner, J.D. MS 24th Inf. Co.A
Turner, J.D. NC Mallett's Bn. Co.E
Turner, J.D. SC 2nd St.Troops Co.I
Turner, J.D. SC 13th Inf. Co.C
Turner, J.D. SC 22nd Inf. Co.I Sgt.
Turner, J.D. TX 7th Cav. Co.E Sgt.
Turner, J.D. TX 10th Cav. Co.K
Turner, J.D. Gen. & Staff AASurg.
Turner, J.E. AL 59th Inf. Co.H
Turner, J.E. GA Lt.Arty. 12th Bn.
Turner, J.E. LA 6th Cav. Co.K
Turner, J.E. MS 28th Cav. Co.K
Turner, J.E. MS 23rd Inf. Co.B
Turner, J.E. SC Lt.Arty. 3rd (Palmetto) Bn. Co.A,I,H 2nd Lt.
Turner, J.E. SC 1st (Butler's) Inf. Co.I
Turner, J.E. SC 1st (McCreary's) Inf. Campbell's Co.
Turner, J.E. TN 42nd Inf. Co.C 2nd Lt.
Turner, J.E. VA 11th Cav.
Turner, Jefferson KY 10th (Diamond's) Cav. Co.A
Turner, Jefferson VA 54th Inf. Co.H
Turner, Jefferson J. AL 47th Inf. Co.F
Turner, Jefferson J. GA Cobb's Legion Co.C Artif.
Turner, Jefferson J. TX 22nd Cav. Co.H
Turner, Jefferson M. SC 1st Arty. Co.C
Turner, Jeptha AR 24th Inf. Co.G
Turner, Jeptha SC 5th St.Troops Co.E
Turner, Jeptha SC 22nd Inf. Co.F
Turner, Jeremiah TN 7th Inf. Co.F
Turner, Jesse FL 9th Inf. Co.D 2nd Lt.
Turner, Jesse GA 65th Inf. Co.F
Turner, Jesse MO Robertson's Regt.St.Guard Co.C

Turner, Jesse SC 2nd Arty. Co.K
Turner, Jesse SC 21st Inf. Co.A
Turner, Jesse TN 3rd (Clack's) Inf. Co.C 3rd Lt.
Turner, Jesse TN 48th (Nixon's) Inf. Co.I
Turner, Jesse TN 54th Inf. Ives' Co.
Turner, Jesse VA 22nd Cav. Co.K
Turner, Jesse VA Lt.Arty. Cayce's Co.
Turner, Jesse VA 16th Inf. Co.D
Turner, Jesse VA 25th Mil. Co.C
Turner, Jesse 10th Conf.Cav. Co.B
Turner, Jessee GA Cav. Corbin's Co.
Turner, Jesse R. AL 44th Inf. Co.I
Turner, Jesse S. GA 65th Inf. Co.B Sgt.
Turner, Jessie F. TX Cav. Baylor's Regt. Co.H
Turner, J.F. AL 44th Inf. Co.K
Turner, J.F. AR 19th (Dawson's) Inf. Co.K
Turner, J.F. GA 7th Inf. (St.Guards) Co.F
Turner, J.F. NC 1st Inf. Co.B Sgt.
Turner, J.F. SC 15th Inf. Co.F
Turner, J.F. VA 4th Cav. Co.K Sgt.
Turner, J.F.V. SC 12th Inf. Co.I
Turner, J.G. AL 6th Cav. Co.E
Turner, J.G. AR 8th Cav. Peoples' Co.
Turner, J.G. AR 2nd Inf. Co.E
Turner, J.G. AR 2nd Vol. Co.D
Turner, J.G. AR 14th (McCarver's) Inf. Co.K
Turner, J.G. AR 21st Inf. Co.F Cpl.
Turner, J.G. GA 3rd Inf. Co.G
Turner, J.G. GA 27th Inf. Co.H Sgt.
Turner, J.G. GA 40th Inf. Co.E
Turner, J.G. KY 7th Mtd.Inf. Co.D
Turner, J.G. SC 2nd St.Troops Co.K
Turner, J.G. SC 9th Res. Co.K
Turner, J.G. SC 27th Inf. Co.D
Turner, J.G. SC Inf. Holcombe Legion Co.D
Turner, J.G. TN 6th (Wheeler's) Cav. Co.D Cpl.
Turner, J.G. TN 1st (Feild's) Inf. Co.I
Turner, J.G. TN Inf. 154th Sr.Regt. Co.I
Turner, J.G. Gen. & Staff Surg.
Turner, J.H. AL Mil. 4th Vol. Gantt's Co.
Turner, J.H. AL 4th Inf.
Turner, J.H. AL 40th Inf. Co.I
Turner, J.H. AL 48th Inf. Co.E,I Cpl.
Turner, J.H. AR Cav. Gordon's Regt. Co.D
Turner, J.H. GA 5th Res. Co.D
Turner, J.H. GA 27th Inf. Co.H
Turner, J.H. GA 53rd Inf. Co.H
Turner, J.H. KY Morgan's Men Co.I
Turner, J.H. LA 17th Inf. Co.D
Turner, J.H. MS 10th Cav. Co.K
Turner, J.H. MS 12th Cav. Co.C
Turner, J.H. MS 5th Inf. (St.Troops) Co.H Cpl.
Turner, J.H. MS 43rd Inf. Co.F
Turner, J.H. SC 26th Inf. Co.B 2nd Lt.
Turner, J.H. SC Inf. Holcombe Legion Co.A Cpl.
Turner, J.H. TN 10th (DeMoss') Cav. Co.F
Turner, J.H. TN 51st Inf. Co.A
Turner, J.H. Conf.Inf. 8th Bn. Co.E
Turner, J.H. Gen. & Staff Capt.,AQM
Turner, J. Henry MD Inf. 2nd Bn. Co.B
Turner, J.I. SC 22nd Inf. Co.G
Turner, Jim M. TX 17th Cons.Dismtd.Cav. Sgt.Maj.
Turner, J.J. AL 7th Cav. Co.C
Turner, J.J. AL Inf. 1st (Loomis') Bn. Co.A 1st Lt.
Turner, J.J. AL 23rd Inf. Co.H
Turner, J.J. AL 24th Inf. Co.K
Turner, J.J. AL 25th Inf. Co.A 1st Lt.
Turner, J.J. AR 12th Inf. Co.F
Turner, J.J. GA 59th Inf. Co.I,B
Turner, J.J. KY 3rd Cav. Grant's Co.
Turner, J.J. KY 8th Mtd.Inf. Co.B
Turner, J.J. MS 7th Cav. Co.G
Turner, J.J. MS Scouts Morphis' Ind.Co.
Turner, J.J. MS 1st (Percy's) Inf. Co.I
Turner, J.J. MS 2nd Inf. Co.C
Turner, J.J. MS 9th Inf. Co.F
Turner, J.J. MS 40th Inf. Co.C
Turner, J.J. NC Inf. 2nd Bn. Co.F
Turner, J.J. NC 3rd Bn.Sr.Res. Williams' Co.
Turner, J.J. NC Townsend's Co. (St.Troops)
Turner, J.J. TN 10th (DeMoss') Cav. Co.E
Turner, J.J. TN Cav. Napier's Bn. Co.B
Turner, J.J. VA 11th Inf. Co.A
Turner, J.J. Gillum's Regt. Co.D
Turner, J.J. Gen. & Staff Surg.
Turner, J.K. AL 7th Inf. Co.E
Turner, J.K. AR 11th & 17th Cons.Inf. Co.A,B
Turner, J.K. AR 62nd Mil. Co.E 1st Sgt.
Turner, J.K. 8th (Wade's) Conf.Cav. Co.B
Turner, J.K.P. TN 4th Inf. Co.B
Turner, J.L. AL 5th Inf. New Co.I
Turner, J.L. AL 46th Inf. Co.H
Turner, J.L. AR 7th Mil. Co.E
Turner, J.L. GA 1st (Symons') Res. Co.E
Turner, J.L. GA 1st Troops & Defences (Macon) Co.G
Turner, J.L. KY 1st (Butler's) Cav. Co.D
Turner, J.L. KY 3rd Cav. Grant's Co.
Turner, J.L. MS 5th Inf. Co.C
Turner, J.L. MS 13th Inf. Co.E
Turner, J.L. NC 2nd Cav. (19th St.Troops) Co.H
Turner, J.L. SC 4th Cav. Co.I
Turner, J.L. SC Cav. 12th Bn. Co.B
Turner, J.L. SC Lt.Arty. 3rd (Palmetto) Bn. Co.E
Turner, J.L. TN 15th (Cons.) Cav. Co.A
Turner, J.L. TN 46th Inf. Co.K
Turner, J.L. VA 5th Cav. Co.G
Turner, J.L. 7th Conf.Cav. Co.F
Turner, J.L. Gen. & Staff, Ord.Dept.
Turner, J.M. AL Arty. 1st Bn. Co.B
Turner, J.M. AR 10th Mil.
Turner, J.M. GA 4th (Clinch's) Cav.
Turner, J.M. GA 12th Cav. Co.H
Turner, J.M. GA Inf. 1st Loc.Troops (Augusta) Co.G
Turner, J.M. GA 1st (Olmstead's) Inf. Stiles' Co. Sgt.
Turner, J.M. GA Inf. 18th Bn. Co.B Sgt.
Turner, J.M. GA Inf. City Bn. (Columbus) Co.C
Turner, J.M. KY 7th Mtd.Inf. Co.G
Turner, J.M. MS 2nd (Quinn's St.Troops) Inf. Co.I
Turner, J.M. MS 9th Inf. Co.K
Turner, J.M. MS 41st Inf. Co.E Cpl.
Turner, J.M. SC 2nd Arty. Co.G
Turner, J.M. SC 5th Inf. 2nd Co.I
Turner, J.M. TN 1st (Feild's) & 27th Inf. (Cons.) Co.B
Turner, J.M. TX 9th Cav. Co.F
Turner, J.M. TX 17th Cons.Dismtd.Cav. 1st Co.G
Turner, J.M. TX 6th Inf. Co.G Cpl.
Turner, J.M. TX 8th Inf.
Turner, J.M. 1st Conf.Cav. 1st Co.H
Turner, J.M., Jr. Gen. & Staff,PACS Surg.
Turner, J.McL. VA 6th Cav. 1st Co.E Sgt.
Turner, J.M.V. TX 6th Inf. Co.G
Turner, J.N. GA 53rd Inf. Co.H
Turner, J.N. NC 55th Inf. Co.D
Turner, J.N. VA 57th Inf. Co.A
Turner, J.N.W. SC 6th Cav. Co.G
Turner, Jo MS 6th Inf. Co.K
Turner, J.O.A. GA 13th Inf. Co.F
Turner, Job GA Cav. 20th Bn. Co.A,D
Turner, Job GA Siege Arty. 28th Bn. Co.K
Turner, Joe MO Inf. Clark's Regt. Co.C
Turner, Joel AL 6th Cav. Co.A
Turner, Joel NC 3rd Bn.Sr.Res. Williams' Co.
Turner, Joel SC 1st (Hagood's) Inf. 2nd Co.I
Turner, Joel, Jr. SC 3rd St.Troops Co.B
Turner, Joel SC 23rd Inf. Co.E
Turner, Joel VA Inf. 21st Bn. Co.B Sgt.
Turner, Joel VA 64th Mtd.Inf. Co.B Sgt.
Turner, Joel A. NC 15th Inf. Co.M
Turner, Joel A. NC 32nd Inf. Co.I
Turner, Joel A. VA 13th Cav. Co.F
Turner, Joel L. GA 3rd Cav. (St.Guards) Co.A 1st Lt.
Turner, John AL 12th Inf. Co.E
Turner, John AL 23rd Inf. Co.B Sgt.
Turner, John AL 23rd Inf. Co.D Sgt.
Turner, John AL 23rd Inf. Co.F
Turner, John AL 30th Inf. Co.H
Turner, John AL 34th Inf. Co.I
Turner, John AL 39th Inf. Co.C
Turner, John AL 58th Inf. Co.A
Turner, John AL City Guards Lockett's Co.
Turner, John AR Cav. Gordon's Regt. Co.K
Turner, John AR 7th Mil. Co.E
Turner, John AR 8th Inf. New Co.F
Turner, John AR 14th (McCarver's) Inf. Co.E
Turner, John AR 27th Inf. Co.A
Turner, John FL 4th Inf. Co.I
Turner, John FL 9th Inf. Co.D
Turner, John GA 7th Cav. Co.E
Turner, John GA Cav. 7th Bn. (St.Guards) Co.E Sgt.
Turner, John GA Hawkins' Cav.
Turner, John GA Lt.Arty. Van Den Corput's Co.
Turner, John GA 1st (Olmstead's) Inf. Way's Co.
Turner, John GA 2nd Inf.
Turner, John GA 2nd Res. Co.E
Turner, John GA 5th Res. Co.E
Turner, John GA 6th Inf. (St.Guards) Pittman's Co.
Turner, John GA Inf. 11th Bn. (St.Guards) Co.B
Turner, John GA Inf. 11th Bn. (St.Guards) Co.C
Turner, John GA 17th Inf. Co.F Cpl.
Turner, John GA 63rd Inf. Co.I Cpl.
Turner, John KY 1st (Helm's) Cav. New Co.G
Turner, John KY 6th Cav. Co.K
Turner, John KY 10th Cav. Co.I Cpl.
Turner, John KY 11th Cav. Co.B
Turner, John LA 13th Bn. (Part.Rangers) Co.E
Turner, John LA 1st (Nelligan's) Inf. Co.B Cpl.

Turner, John LA 1st (Strawbridge's) Inf. Co.F,E
Turner, John LA 8th Inf. Co.D
Turner, John LA 11th Inf. Co.L
Turner, John LA 16th Inf. Co.E
Turner, John LA 20th Inf. New Co.E
Turner, John MS 2nd St.Cav. Co.L
Turner, John MS 11th (Perrin's) Cav. Co.F
Turner, John MS 18th Cav. Co.C
Turner, John MS Cav. Buck's Co.
Turner, John MS Lt.Arty. (Brookhaven Lt.Arty.) Hoskins' Btty.
Turner, John MS 1st (Patton's) Inf. Co.B
Turner, John MS 21st Inf. Co.H
Turner, John MS 35th Inf. Co.E
Turner, John MO 7th Cav. Co.C
Turner, John MO Cav. Jackman's Regt. Co.B
Turner, John MO 1st & 4th Cons.Inf. Co.C
Turner, John MO 4th Inf. Co.C
Turner, John MO 11th Inf. Co.K
Turner, John MO Inf. Clark's Regt. Co.A Sgt.
Turner, John NC 4th Cav. (59th St.Troops) Co.B
Turner, John NC 6th Cav. (65th St.Troops) Co.B
Turner, John NC Cav. 7th Bn. Co.B
Turner, John NC 8th Bn.Part.Rangers Co.A,C
Turner, John NC 2nd Arty. (36th St.Troops) Co.H
Turner, John NC 3rd Arty. (40th St.Troops) Co.H
Turner, John NC 3rd Arty. (40th St.Troops) Co.K
Turner, John NC 1st Inf. Co.K
Turner, John NC 3rd Bn.Sr.Res. Durham's Co.
Turner, John NC 7th Inf. Co.E
Turner, John NC 12th Inf. Co.A
Turner, John NC Inf. 13th Bn. Co.C
Turner, John NC 20th Inf. Co.A
Turner, John NC 28th Inf. Co.C
Turner, John NC 31st Inf. Co.G
Turner, John NC 32nd Inf. Co.D,E
Turner, John NC 47th Inf. Co.A
Turner, John NC 55th Inf. Co.B
Turner, John NC 57th Inf. Co.I
Turner, John NC 58th Inf. Co.F Cpl.
Turner, John NC 61st Inf. Co.C
Turner, John NC 66th Inf. Co.D
Turner, John NC Jones' Co. (Supp.Force) 1st Lt.
Turner, John NC Inf.Sr.Res. 5th Congr.Dist. 1st Lt.
Turner, John SC 6th Cav. Co.H
Turner, John SC Cav. 19th Bn. Co.E
Turner, John SC 1st (Butler's) Inf. Co.H
Turner, John SC 1st St.Troops Co.F
Turner, John SC 2nd Rifles Co.A
Turner, John SC 6th Inf. 2nd Co.G
Turner, John SC 12th Inf. Co.K Cpl.
Turner, John SC Mil. 16th Regt. Sigwald's Co.
Turner, John SC 18th Inf. Co.K
Turner, John SC 19th Inf. Co.D
Turner, John SC 20th Inf. Co.L
Turner, John SC 24th Inf. Co.A Cook
Turner, John SC 24th Inf. Co.B
Turner, John TN 6th (Wheeler's) Cav. Co.I
Turner, John TN 21st (Wilson's) Cav. Co.G
Turner, John TN Cav. Newsom's Regt. Co.D
Turner, John TN 3rd (Lillard's) Mtd.Inf. Co.D
Turner, John TN 10th Inf. Sgt.
Turner, John TN 21st Inf. Co.H
Turner, John TN 22nd Inf. Co.B
Turner, John TN 29th Inf. Co.I
Turner, John TN 43rd Inf. Co.C Sgt.
Turner, John TN 61st Mtd.Inf. Co.K,I
Turner, John TX 20th Cav. Co.D
Turner, John TX 21st Cav. Co.K
Turner, John TX 28th Cav. Co.L
Turner, John TX Cav. Baylor's Regt. Co.F
Turner, John TX Cav. Bourland's Regt. Co.D
Turner, John TX Cav. Bourland's Regt. Co.E
Turner, John TX Cav. Morgan's Regt. Co.C
Turner, John TX Inf. 1st St.Troops Saxton's Co.
Turner, John TX Inf. 1st St.Troops White's Co.D
Turner, John TX 6th Inf. Co.C
Turner, John TX 12th Inf. Co.E
Turner, John TX 15th Inf.
Turner, John VA 7th Cav. Co.I
Turner, John VA 22nd Cav. Co.K
Turner, John VA Cav. 41st Bn. Co.C
Turner, John VA Hvy.Arty. 19th Bn. Co.A
Turner, John VA 1st St.Res. Co.F
Turner, John VA 28th Inf. Co.I Cpl.
Turner, John VA 39th Inf. Co.H
Turner, John VA 54th Inf. Co.H
Turner, John VA 58th Inf. Co.A
Turner, John Conf.Lt.Arty. 1st Reg.Btty.
Turner, John Conf.Inf. 8th Bn. Co.C Cpl.
Turner, John 9th Conf.Inf. Co.C
Turner, John 3rd Conf.Eng.Troops Co.H
Turner, John A. AL 19th Inf. Co.I
Turner, John A. AL 20th Inf. Co.E,A
Turner, John A. AR 3rd Inf. Co.F
Turner, John A. AR 11th Inf. Co.B
Turner, John A. AR 11th & 17th Cons.Inf. Co.A,B
Turner, John A. AR Inf. Hardy's Regt. Co.I Capt.
Turner, John A. LA 1st Cav. Robinson's Co. Jr.1st Lt.
Turner, John A. LA Miles' Legion Co.A Cpl.
Turner, John A. MO Cav. Wood's Regt. Co.E Cpl.
Turner, John A. NC 8th Inf. Co.G
Turner, John A. TN Arty. Ramsey's Btty. 1st Lt.
Turner, John A. VA 10th Cav. Co.K
Turner, John A. VA 11th Cav. Co.A Capt.
Turner, John A. VA Lt.Arty. Garber's Co.
Turner, John A. VA 1st Inf. Co.A
Turner, John A. VA Inf. 1st Bn. Co.B Capt.
Turner, John A. VA 3rd Inf.Loc.Def. Co.A
Turner, John A. VA 12th Inf. Co.G
Turner, John A. VA 20th Inf. Co.K
Turner, John A. VA 59th Inf. 3rd Co.C
Turner, Johnathan FL 7th Inf. Co.D
Turner, Johna W. KY 7th Cav. Co.D
Turner, John B. AL 15th Inf. Co.C
Turner, John B. AL 59th Inf. Co.D
Turner, John B. AL Arty. 4th Bn. Hilliard's Legion Co.B
Turner, John B. NC 4th Inf. Co.H
Turner, John B. TN 1st (Feild's) Inf. Co.B
Turner, John B. TN 2nd (Robison's) Inf. Co.K
Turner, John B. TN 4th Inf. Co.I Capt.
Turner, John B., Jr. TN 4th Inf. Co.I
Turner, John B. VA Lt.Arty. B.Z. Price's Co.
Turner, John B. VA 11th Inf. Co.H
Turner, John B. 1st Choctaw & Chickasaw Mtd.Rifles 1st Co.K Sgt.
Turner, John Brown Gen. & Staff AAAG
Turner, John C. GA 3rd Cav. (St.Guards) Co.F Capt.
Turner, John C. GA 7th Inf. Co.K
Turner, John C. GA 36th (Broyles') Inf. Co.B
Turner, John C. MS 23rd Inf. Co.D Capt.
Turner, John C. MS 40th Inf. Co.K
Turner, John C. MO Inf. Perkins' Bn. Co.B 2nd Lt.
Turner, John C. NC 4th Inf. Co.C 2nd Lt.
Turner, John C. SC 8th Inf. Co.I
Turner, John C. TX 29th Cav. Co.F Cpl.
Turner, John C. TX 1st Hvy.Arty. Co.D
Turner, John C. VA 8th Cav. 2nd Co.D
Turner, John D. AL Lt.Arty. 2nd Bn. Co.E
Turner, John D. AR Cav. Gordon's Regt. Co.E
Turner, John D. AR 2nd Inf. Co.B
Turner, John D. SC 19th Inf. Co.F
Turner, John D. TN 10th Cav. Co.C
Turner, John D. VA 25th Cav. Co.E
Turner, John D. VA 24th Inf. Co.B
Turner, John E. AL Arty. 1st Bn. Co.A Sgt.
Turner, John E. AL 39th Inf. Co.I
Turner, John E. AL Arty. 4th Bn. Hilliard's Legion Co.A,D
Turner, John E. GA Carlton's Co. (Troup Cty.Arty.)
Turner, John E. MS 1st Cav. Co.I Capt.
Turner, John E. MS Cav. 1st Bn. (Miller's) Cole's Co. Cpl.
Turner, John E. MS St.Cav. 2nd Bn. (Harris') Asst.Surg.
Turner, John E. MO Inf. 8th Bn. Co.F
Turner, John E. NC 2nd Arty. (36th St.Troops) Co.G
Turner, John E. NC 2nd Inf. Co.G
Turner, John E. TN 51st (Cons.) Inf. Co.B
Turner, John E. TN 59th Mtd.Inf. Co.K
Turner, John F. AL 61st Inf. Co.B
Turner, John F. AR 3rd Inf. Co.I
Turner, John F. AR 37th Inf. Co.E Cpl.
Turner, John F. GA Seige Arty. 28th Bn. Co.E
Turner, John F. LA 1st (Nelligan's) Inf. Co.I Sgt.Maj.
Turner, John F. MO 11th Inf. Co.H
Turner, John F. NC 26th Inf. Co.D
Turner, John F. SC 15th Inf. Co.D
Turner, John F. TX Cav. 2nd Regt.St.Troops Co.D
Turner, John F. VA 3rd Inf. Co.G
Turner, John F. VA 39th Inf. Co.B
Turner, John G. AL 4th (Roddey's) Cav. Wisdom's Co.
Turner, John G. AR 26th Inf. Co.I
Turner, John G. GA Inf. 10th Bn. Co.A
Turner, John G. SC Inf. 1st (Charleston) Bn. Co.D
Turner, John H. AL 4th Cav. Co.I
Turner, John H. AL 17th Inf. Co.I
Turner, John H. AL 29th Inf. Co.A Cpl.
Turner, John H. AL 37th Inf. Co.I,D
Turner, John H. AL 50th Inf. Co.F
Turner, John H. AR 10th Mil. Co.C
Turner, John H. GA Arty. 9th Bn. Co.A,E

Turner, John H. GA 16th Inf. Co.F
Turner, John H. GA 38th Inf. Co.B Sgt.
Turner, John H. GA 41st Inf. Co.C
Turner, John H. GA 48th Inf. Co.D
Turner, John H. KY 2nd Cav. Co.D
Turner, John H. LA 31st Inf. Co.K
Turner, John H. MS 6th Cav. Morgan's Co.
Turner, John H. MS 24th Inf. Co.L
Turner, John H. SC Inf. 9th Bn. Co.B Lt.
Turner, John H. TN Cav. Napier's Bn. Co.E
Turner, John H. TN 30th Inf. Co.E Capt.
Turner, John H. VA 1st St.Res. Co.B
Turner, John H. VA 11th Inf. Co.A
Turner, John H. VA 46th Inf. 2nd Co.F Sgt.
Turner, John H. VA 58th Inf. Co.D Cpl.
Turner, John I. MO Lt.Arty. Landis' Co.
Turner, John J. FL 7th Inf. Co.D 1st Sgt.
Turner, John J. GA 44th Inf. Co.A
Turner, John J. GA 56th Inf. Co.K
Turner, John J. KY 5th Cav. Co.G
Turner, John J. KY 8th Cav.
Turner, John J. NC 1st Inf. Co.E
Turner, John J. NC 2nd Bn.Loc.Def.Troops Co.F
Turner, John J. NC 14th Inf. Co.A
Turner, John J. NC 46th Inf. Co.G Sgt.
Turner, John J. TN 1st (Turney's) Inf. Co.C,F
Turner, John J. VA 5th Cav. (12 mo. '61-2) Co.F
Turner, John J. VA 13th Cav. Co.F Cpl.
Turner, John J. VA 24th Cav. Co.A
Turner, John J. VA Cav. 40th Bn. Co.A
Turner, John J. VA 4th Inf. Co.H
Turner, John K. AL Cav. Falkner's Co.
Turner, John K. SC 26th Inf. Co.C
Turner, John L. FL 7th Inf. Co.H Cpl.
Turner, John L. GA Lt.Arty. 12th Bn. 3rd Co.B
Turner, John L. MS 43rd Inf. Co.H
Turner, John L. MO 3rd Cav. Co.F
Turner, John L. SC 2nd Inf. Co.B Sgt.
Turner, John L. SC 5th Inf. 1st Co.D, 2nd Co.D
Turner, John L. SC 6th Inf. 1st Co.K
Turner, John L. SC 10th Inf. Co.B
Turner, John L. SC Palmetto S.S. Co.A
Turner, John L. VA 53rd Inf. Co.E
Turner, John L. Inf. School of Pract. Powell's Detach. Powell's Co.
Turner, John M. AL Arty. 1st Bn. Co.D
Turner, John M. GA Inf. 3rd Bn. Co.D
Turner, John M. GA 4th Bn.S.S. Co.C 2nd Lt.
Turner, John M. LA Inf.Cons.Crescent Regt. Co.O
Turner, John M. MO 5th Inf. Co.F
Turner, John M. NC 34th Inf. Co.F Cpl.
Turner, John M. NC 43rd Inf. Co.A
Turner, John M. SC 13th Inf. Co.F
Turner, John M. TN 9th (Ward's) Cav. Co.C
Turner, John M. VA 29th Inf. Co.B
Turner, John McLeod NC 7th Inf. Co.F Lt.Col.
Turner, John N. MS Cav. Ham's Regt. Co.A Cpl.
Turner, John N. SC 1st (Orr's) Rifles Co.H
Turner, John P. AL 18th Inf. Co.L
Turner, John P. AL 58th Inf. Co.G
Turner, John P. AR 7th Mil. Co.D Capt.
Turner, John P. GA 21st Inf. New Co.E
Turner, John P. MS 2nd Inf. (A. of 10,000) Co.A
Turner, John P. MO 10th Inf. Co.E
Turner, John P. NC Inf. 2nd Bn. Co.D
Turner, John P. VA 10th Cav. Co.K
Turner, John P. VA Lt.Arty. B.Z. Price's Co.
Turner, John P. VA 6th Inf. Co.C
Turner, John Q. AL 53rd (Part.Rangers) Co.D
Turner, John R. AL 34th Inf. Co.G
Turner, John R. GA Inf. 3rd Bn. Co.D
Turner, John R. GA 14th Inf. Co.K
Turner, John R. MO 3rd Inf. Co.F
Turner, John R. TX 10th Cav. Co.C
Turner, John R. VA Lt.Arty. Parker's Co.
Turner, John R. VA 11th Inf. Co.F Sgt.
Turner, John R. VA 12th Inf. Co.C,E Cpl.
Turner, John R. VA 17th Inf. Co.K 2nd Lt.
Turner, John Robert MS 34th Inf. Co.C 2nd Lt.
Turner, John S. AR 37th Inf. Co.F
Turner, John S. FL 7th Inf. Co.K
Turner, John S. GA 4th Mil.
Turner, John S. NC 1st Cav. (9th St.Troops) Co.F Cpl.
Turner, John S. NC 4th Cav. (59th St.Troops) Co.E
Turner, John S. SC 2nd Inf. Co.F
Turner, John S. SC 5th Inf. 1st Co.A
Turner, John S. TN 44th Inf. Co.E Cpl.
Turner, John S. TN 44th (Cons.) Inf. Co.B
Turner, John S. TN Inf. Spencer's Co.
Turner, John S. VA 8th Cav. Co.A
Turner, John S. VA Lt.Arty. Cayce's Co.
Turner, John S. VA Inf. 5th Bn. Co.F Cpl.
Turner, John S. VA Loc.Def. Scott's Co.
Turner, Johnson C. GA 30th Inf. Co.B
Turner, John T. MS 14th Inf. Co.A
Turner, John T. NC 22nd Inf. Co.M Cpl.
Turner, John T. TX 9th Field Btty.
Turner, John T. VA 3rd Inf. 2nd Co.I
Turner, John T. VA 4th Res. Co.A
Turner, John T. VA 24th Inf. Co.H
Turner, John T. Wheeler's Scouts,CSA
Turner, John W. AL 31st Inf. Co.I
Turner, John W. AL 43rd Inf. Co.K
Turner, John W. AL 63rd Inf. Co.D
Turner, John W. AR 1st Mtd.Rifles Co.A 2nd Lt.
Turner, John W. FL 1st (Res.) Inf. Co.A 2nd Lt.
Turner, John W. FL 2nd Inf. Co.E
Turner, John W. FL 7th Inf. Co.I
Turner, John W. GA 4th Bn.S.S. Ord.Sgt.
Turner, John W. GA Inf. 9th Bn. Co.D
Turner, John W. GA 29th Inf. Co.D Capt.
Turner, John W. GA 36th (Broyles') Inf. Co.F
Turner, John W. GA 44th Inf. Co.D
Turner, John W. GA 46th Inf. Co.G
Turner, John W. GA 50th Inf. Co.I
Turner, John W. LA Hvy.Arty. 2nd Bn. Co.A
Turner, John W. MS Cav. 4th Bn. Sykes' Co.
Turner, John W. MS Cav. Jeff Davis Legion Co.C QMSgt.
Turner, John W. MS 11th Inf. Co.E
Turner, John W. NC 6th Sr.Res. Co.K
Turner, John W. NC 7th Inf. Co.B
Turner, John W. NC 11th (Bethel Regt.) Inf. Co.E
Turner, John W. NC Inf. 13th Bn. Co.D
Turner, John W. NC 14th Inf. Co.C Sgt.
Turner, John W. NC 43rd Inf. Co.I
Turner, John W. NC 51st Inf. Co.A
Turner, John W. NC 54th Inf. Co.K
Turner, John W. SC 19th Inf. Co.F Capt.
Turner, John W. SC Inf. Hampton Legion Co.B
Turner, John W. TN 60th Mtd.Inf. Co.H
Turner, John W. VA 3rd Lt.Arty. (Loc.Def.) Co.D
Turner, John W. VA Hvy.Arty. 10th Bn. Co.C 1st Lt.
Turner, John W. VA Hvy.Arty. 19th Bn. Co.A
Turner, John W. VA Hvy.Arty. 20th Bn. Co.A
Turner, John W. VA 3rd Inf. Co.D
Turner, John W. VA 16th Inf. Co.B
Turner, John W. (of M.) VA 16th Inf. Co.B
Turner, John W. VA 38th Inf. Co.A
Turner, John W. VA 44th Inf. Co.A
Turner, John W. VA 58th Inf. Co.B
Turner, John W. VA 61st Inf. Co.F
Turner, John W. 8th (Wade's) Conf.Cav. Co.G
Turner, John W. Conf.Cav. Wood's Regt. Co.L 2nd Lt.
Turner, John W. 1st Conf.Inf. 2nd Co.G
Turner, John William NC 6th Inf. Co.C
Turner, John W.M. NC 54th Inf. Co.I Ord.Sgt.
Turner, Jonah KY 1st (Helm's) Cav.
Turner, Jonathan SC 22nd Inf. Co.H
Turner, Jonathan TN 4th Cav. Co.H
Turner, Jones J. MO 1st Cav. Co.F
Turner, Jones L. TN 1st (Turney's) Inf. Co.C,F
Turner, J.O.P. GA 56th Inf. Co.D
Turner, Jordan AL 28th Inf. Co.H
Turner, Jordan VA 12th Cav. Co.G
Turner, Jordan VA 48th Inf. Co.E Sgt.
Turner, Jordan VA 61st Inf. Co.F
Turner, Jordan A. VA 3rd Inf. 2nd Co.I
Turner, Joseph AL 15th Inf. Co.A
Turner, Joseph AL 51st Part.Rangers Co.E
Turner, Joseph GA 1st Cav. Co.A
Turner, Joseph KY 4th Cav. Co.I Sgt.
Turner, Joseph LA 3rd Inf. Co.B
Turner, Joseph LA 25th Inf. Co.A
Turner, Joseph LA 27th Inf. Co.C
Turner, Joseph MO 8th Inf. Co.H
Turner, Joseph SC 1st Cav. Co.H
Turner, Joseph SC 3rd Bn.Res. Co.A
Turner, Joseph SC 23rd Inf. Co.H
Turner, Joseph TN 4th (Murray's) Cav. Co.G
Turner, Joseph TN Inf. 22nd Bn. Co.G
Turner, Joseph TX 19th Cav. Co.K
Turner, Joseph TX 5th Inf. Co.K Jr.2nd Lt.
Turner, Joseph VA 3rd Inf. Co.G
Turner, Joseph VA Inf. 26th Bn. Co.I
Turner, Joseph VA 58th Mil. Co.I
Turner, Joseph VA Loc.Def. Bosher's Co.
Turner, Joseph 3rd Conf.Cav. Co.A
Turner, Joseph 20th Conf.Cav. 2nd Co.H
Turner, Joseph A. GA 2nd Mil.
Turner, Joseph A. VA Hvy.Arty. 10th Bn. Co.A
Turner, Joseph A. VA Hvy.Arty. Kyle's Co.
Turner, Joseph A. VA Inf. 5th Bn. Co.F
Turner, Joseph A. VA 41st Inf. N.C.S. Sgt.Maj.
Turner, Joseph A. VA Mil. Scott Cty.
Turner, Joseph B. AL 3rd Cav. Co.A Ord.Sgt.
Turner, Joseph B. AL 12th Cav. Co.F Sgt.

Turner, Joseph B. GA 52nd Inf. Co.I
Turner, Joseph B. SC Inf. Holcombe Legion Co.I
Turner, Joseph B. Conf.Cav. Wood's Regt. Co.C Cpl.
Turner, Joseph D. FL 1st Inf. Old Co.I, New Co.C Capt.
Turner, Joseph E. FL 2nd Inf. Co.E
Turner, Joseph E. NC 35th Inf. Co.B Sgt.
Turner, Joseph E. TX Cav. 6th Bn. Co.A
Turner, Joseph F. AL 17th Inf. Co.C
Turner, Joseph H. VA 3rd Inf. Co.G
Turner, Joseph H. VA 38th Inf. Co.C,K
Turner, Joseph H. VA 41st Inf. Co.H
Turner, Joseph H. 1st Conf.Inf. 2nd Co.E
Turner, Joseph J. GA 12th (Robinson's) Cav. (St.Guards) Co.A Cpl.
Turner, Joseph J. MS 15th Inf. Co.A
Turner, Joseph L. LA 3rd (Harrison's) Cav. Co.E Sgt.
Turner, Joseph M. TX 12th Inf. Co.A
Turner, Joseph McLeod MS Cav. Jeff Davis Legion Co.F 2nd Lt.
Turner, Jos. O. KY 1st (Helm's) Cav. Co.B
Turner, Joseph P. MS 2nd Inf. Co.C
Turner, Joseph R. AL 60th Inf. Co.E
Turner, Joseph R. AL 3rd Bn. Hilliard's Legion Vol. Co.A
Turner, Joseph R. GA 1st (Fannin's) Res. Co.H,I
Turner, Joseph S. MS 28th Cav. Co.K
Turner, Joseph S. VA 62nd Mtd.Inf. 2nd Co.M
Turner, Joseph S. 3rd Conf.Eng.Troops Co.B
Turner, Joseph T. VA Lt.Arty. Pegram's Co.
Turner, Joseph T. VA 12th Inf. Co.D,E
Turner, Joseph T. VA 54th Inf. Co.I
Turner, Josephus NC 12th Inf. Co.A
Turner, Josephus NC 32nd Inf. Co.D,E
Turner, Joseph W. VA Lt.Arty. W.P. Carter's Co. Cpl.
Turner, Joshua AL Randolph Cty.Res. D.A. Self's Co.
Turner, Joshua GA 24th Inf. Co.C
Turner, Joshua KY 4th Cav. Co.I Sgt.
Turner, Joshua SC 5th Res. Co.B
Turner, Joshua SC Inf. Holcombe Legion Co.F
Turner, Joshua VA 30th Inf. Co.E
Turner, Joshua C. TX 10th Cav. Co.K
Turner, Josiah AL 34th Inf. Breedlove's Co.
Turner, Josiah, Jr. NC 2nd Cav. (19th St.Troops) Co.K Capt.
Turner, Josiah VA Arty. (Loc.Def. & Sp.Serv.) Lanier's Co.
Turner, Josiah VA 6th Inf. Co.C
Turner, Josiah VA 21st Inf. Co.I
Turner, Josiah VA 24th Inf. Co.H
Turner, J.P. GA Siege Arty. Campbell's Ind.Co.
Turner, J.P. GA Inf. 26th Bn. Co.B
Turner, J.P. GA 32nd Inf. Co.I
Turner, J.P. GA 44th Inf. Co.F
Turner, J.P. MS 1st (Johnston's) Inf. Co.B
Turner, J.P. MS 4th Inf. Co.H
Turner, J.P. SC 13th Inf. Co.E Sgt.
Turner, J.P. TN 50th Inf. Co.K
Turner, J.P. TN 50th (Cons.) Inf. Co.G
Turner, J.P. TX 10th Field Btty.
Turner, J.P. TX 22nd Inf. Co.F
Turner, J.P. Conf.Cav. Wood's Regt. Co.C
Turner, J.P. Gen. & Staff AQM
Turner, J.R. AL 56th Part.Rangers Co.B
Turner, J.R. AL Cav. Murphy's Bn. Co.D
Turner, J.R. AL 18th Inf. Co.H
Turner, J.R. FL 8th Inf.
Turner, J.R. FL Conscr.
Turner, J.R. GA Arty. Maxwell's Reg.Lt.Btty.
Turner, J.R. GA 39th Inf. Co.K
Turner, J.R. GA 46th Inf. Co.G
Turner, J.R. GA 56th Inf. Co.C
Turner, J.R. MS 2nd Inf. Co.K
Turner, J.R. MS Inf. 2nd Bn. Co.I
Turner, J.R. MS 48th Inf. Co.I
Turner, J.R. MO 16th Inf. Co.D
Turner, J.R. MO Todd's Co.
Turner, J.R. NC 3rd Jr.Res. Co.K
Turner, J.R. NC 4th Bn.Jr.Res. Co.D
Turner, J.R. SC 5th Cav. Co.I
Turner, J.R. SC 3rd Bn.Res. Co.C
Turner, J.R. SC 11th Res. Co.E 1st Sgt.
Turner, J.R. TN 24th Bn.S.S. Co.A Cpl.
Turner, J.R. VA 8th Cav. Co.G
Turner, J.R.J. TN 18th (Newsom's) Cav. Co.D
Turner, J. Russell MS 7th Cav. Co.D Sgt.
Turner, J.S. AL 3rd Res. Co.C
Turner, J.S. GA Lt.Arty. Daniell's Btty.
Turner, J.S. GA 1st (Olmstead's) Inf. Co.F Capt.
Turner, J.S. GA 1st (Olmstead's) Inf. Co.K
Turner, J.S. GA 13th Inf. Co.B
Turner, J.S. GA 25th Inf. Pritchard's Co. 1st Lt.
Turner, J.S. GA 44th Inf. Co.A
Turner, J.S. GA Smith's Legion Co.C Sgt.
Turner, J.S. MS 9th Cav. Co.D
Turner, J.S. MS 7th Inf. Co.K
Turner, J.S. MS 14th (Cons.) Inf. Co.B
Turner, J.S. MS 32nd Inf. Co.B
Turner, J.S. MS 46th Inf. Co.I Sgt.
Turner, J.S. NC Allen's Co. (Loc.Def.)
Turner, J.S. SC 2nd Cav. Co.G
Turner, J.S. SC 5th St.Troops Co.A Sgt.
Turner, J.S. TN 4th Inf. Co.H
Turner, J.S. TN 16th Inf. Co.E
Turner, J.S. TN 51st (Cons.) Inf. Co.B
Turner, J.S. TN 52nd Inf. Co.B
Turner, J.S. TX 12th Cav. Co.D
Turner, J.S. TX 5th Inf. (St.Troops) Martindale's Co.
Turner, J.T. AL 18th Inf. Co.F
Turner, J.T. GA Inf. 1st City Bn. (Columbus) Co.C
Turner, J.T. MS 4th Inf. Co.H 3rd Sgt.
Turner, J.T. MS Walsh's Co. (Muckalusha Guards)
Turner, J.T. MO 1st Cav. Co.I
Turner, J.T. MO 1st & 3rd Cons.Cav. Co.E
Turner, J.T. MO 16th Inf. Co.I
Turner, J.T. SC Lt.Arty. 3rd (Palmetto) Bn. Co.H,I Sgt.
Turner, J.T. TN 10th (DeMoss') Cav. Co.F
Turner, J.T. TN 11th (Holman's) Cav. Co.D
Turner, J.T. TN Cav. Napier's Bn. Co.E
Turner, J.T. TX Arty. Douglas' Co.
Turner, J.T. VA 4th Res. Co.A
Turner, J.T. VA 20th Inf.
Turner, J.T. Gen. & Staff AASurg.
Turner, J.T.B. SC 13th Inf. Co.C
Turner, Judson GA 61st Inf. Co.G,K
Turner, Julian S. NC 2nd Cav. (19th St.Troops) Co.K 2nd Lt.
Turner, Julius GA Hvy.Arty. 22nd Bn. Co.B
Turner, Julius GA 25th Inf. 1st Co.K
Turner, Julius TX 18th Cav. Witt's Co.
Turner, Julius C. GA 12th Inf. Co.C
Turner, Junius TX 18th Cav. Co.E
Turner, Junius D. NC 31st Inf. Co.D 1st Sgt.
Turner, J.V. GA 63rd Inf. Co.G
Turner, J.W. AL 6th Cav. Co.C
Turner, J.W. AL 7th Cav. Co.C
Turner, J.W. AL Inf. 1st Regt. Co.B Sgt.
Turner, J.W. AL 1st Regt. Mobile Vol. Butt's Co.
Turner, J.W. AL Inf. 2nd Regt. Co.E
Turner, J.W. AR Inf. Hardy's Regt. Co.C Cpl.
Turner, J.W. GA Inf. 1st Conf.Bn. Co.C
Turner, J.W. GA 5th Res. Co.G
Turner, J.W. GA Inf. 8th Bn. Co.G
Turner, J.W. GA 11th Mil.
Turner, J.W. GA Inf. 27th Bn. (NonConscr.) Co.A Sgt.
Turner, J.W. GA 28th Inf. Co.B
Turner, J.W. GA 37th Inf. Co.G
Turner, J.W. GA 54th Inf. Ord.Sgt.
Turner, J.W. GA 54th Inf. Co.C
Turner, J.W. GA Inf. (NonConscr.) Howard's Co.
Turner, J.W. KY 7th Cav. Co.E
Turner, J.W. MS 28th Cav. Co.B
Turner, J.W. MS Part.Rangers Armistead's Co.
Turner, J.W. MS 1st (Johnston's) Inf. Co.B
Turner, J.W. MS Inf. 1st Bn.St.Troops (30 days '64) Co.C Jr.2nd Lt.
Turner, J.W. MS 39th Inf. Co.K
Turner, J.W. MO 3rd Cav. Co.A
Turner, J.W. MO 5th Cav. Co.A
Turner, J.W. MO 9th Inf. Co.B
Turner, J.W. MO Inf. Clark's Regt. Co.A
Turner, J.W. NC 6th Sr.Res. Co.D Capt.
Turner, J.W. NC Mil. 1st Regt. W.D. Crowder's Co.
Turner, J.W. NC 12th Inf. Co.C
Turner, J.W. NC Snead's Co. (Loc.Def.)
Turner, J.W. TN 3rd (Forrest's) Cav. 1st Co.B
Turner, J.W. TN 13th Inf. Co.H
Turner, J.W. TN 49th Inf. Co.C 1st Sgt.
Turner, J.W. Inf. Bailey's Cons.Regt. Co.F 1st Sgt.
Turner, J.W. TX 11th Cav. Co.E
Turner, J.W. TX Cav. Madison's Regt. Co.B
Turner, J.W. TX 9th (Young's) Inf. Co.D
Turner, J.W. VA 3rd Inf.Loc.Def. Co.C
Turner, J.W. VA 16th Inf. Co.D
Turner, J.W. VA 28th Inf. Co.G
Turner, J.W. VA Inf. 28th Bn. Co.D
Turner, J.W. VA 59th Inf. 3rd Co.I
Turner, J.W.F. MS Lt.Arty. 14th Bn. Co.C Bugler
Turner, J.W.H. VA 62nd Mtd.Inf. 2nd Co.M
Turner, J.W.R. LA 31st Inf. Co.D
Turner, J.Y. AR 12th Inf. Co.F
Turner, K. NC 1st Jr.Res. Co.D
Turner, K. SC 1st Inf. Co.O
Turner, Kemsey SC 5th St.Troops Co.F
Turner, Kenyon GA 20th Inf. Co.D
Turner, L. FL Cav. 5th Bn. Co.G

Turner, L. GA 40th Inf. Co.G
Turner, L. KY 2nd (Woodward's) Cav. Co.G
Turner, L. KY 5th Cav. Co.G
Turner, L. KY 7th Mtd.Inf. Co.D
Turner, L. MS Cav. 1st Bn. (Montgomery's) St.Troops Co.C
Turner, L. MS 12th Cav. Co.K
Turner, L. MS 1st (King's) Inf. (St.Troops) D. Love's Co.
Turner, L. SC 1st St.Troops Co.B
Turner, L. SC 1st Bn.S.S. Co.C
Turner, L. SC 7th Inf. Co.F
Turner, L. SC 11th Inf. Co.G
Turner, L. SC 23rd Inf. Co.E
Turner, L. SC 27th Inf. Co.G
Turner, L. TN 6th Inf. Co.L
Turner, L. TN 51st Inf. Co.F
Turner, L. TN 55th (Brown's) Inf. Ford's Co.
Turner, L. TX Cav. Border's Regt. Co.D
Turner, L.A. GA Ind.Cav. (Res.) Humphrey's Co. Cpl.
Turner, L.A. LA Inf. 4th Bn. Co.B
Turner, Laban C. NC 28th Inf. Co.C
Turner, Larkin AL 47th Inf. Co.F
Turner, Larkin B. VA 3rd Res. Co.B
Turner, Larkin J. AR 14th (McCarver's) Inf. Co.H
Turner, Larkin J. GA 7th Inf. Co.K
Turner, Larkin J. MO Cav. Freeman's Regt. Co.A Cpl.
Turner, Larkin J.A. GA 56th Inf. Co.I
Turner, Larkin T. MS 5th Inf. Co.D
Turner, Lawrence T. GA 1st (Olmstead's) Inf. Gordon's Co.
Turner, Lawrence T. GA 63rd Inf. Co.F 1st Lt.
Turner, Lawson TX 8th Cav. Co.A
Turner, L.B. FL 2nd Inf. Co.A
Turner, L.B. KY 1st Inf. Co.F
Turner, L.B. MS 4th Inf. Co.A
Turner, L.D. MS 1st Cav.Res. Co.F
Turner, L.D. MS 5th Cav. Co.E
Turner, L.D. MS 40th Inf. Co.D
Turner, L.D. SC Cav. 4th Bn. Co.B
Turner, L.D. Sig.Corps,CSA
Turner, L. Dion MS 15th Inf. Co.E
Turner, L.E. MS 3rd Cav. Co.K
Turner, Leander GA Smith's Legion Co.C
Turner, Leander M. GA 65th Inf. Co.B Cpl.
Turner, Leander S. TN 2nd (Smith's) Cav.
Turner, Lee KY 8th Mtd.Inf. Co.G 2nd Lt.
Turner, Lee L. SC 13th Inf. Co.E,I
Turner, Leland VA 47th Inf. 3rd Co.H
Turner, Lemuel SC 2nd Rifles Co.B
Turner, Lemuel SC 3rd Res. Co.H
Turner, Lemuel L. GA 21st Inf. New Co.C, Co.D
Turner, Lemuel S. MS 22nd Inf. Co.D
Turner, Lemuel W. GA Inf. 11th Bn. (St.Guards) Co.C
Turner, Lenard MS Cav. 17th Bn. Co.F
Turner, Lenard J. AR 11th & 17th Cons.Inf. Co.K
Turner, Lenard J. AR 17th (Griffith's) Inf. Co.D
Turner, Leo. VA 12th Cav. Co.B
Turner, Leonard AR Lt.Arty. Wiggins' Btty.
Turner, Leonard MS 9th Cav. Co.D
Turner, Leonard K. MO Searcy's Bn.S.S. Cone's Co.
Turner, Leonidas NC 15th Inf. Co.C
Turner, Leroy AL 16th Inf. Co.K
Turner, Lesiel TX 22nd Inf. Co.H
Turner, Leslie A.W. NC 48th Inf. Co.A Capt.
Turner, Levi AL 61st Inf. Co.A
Turner, Levi GA 12th (Robinson's) Cav. (St.Guards) Co.H Cpl.
Turner, Levi GA 55th Inf. Co.H
Turner, Levi NC 4th Inf. Co.K
Turner, Levi H. TX Cav. Morgan's Regt. Co.B
Turner, Levi J.W. GA Cobb's Legion Co.F
Turner, Levi M. GA 41st Inf. Co.F
Turner, Levi M. GA 55th Inf. Co.K
Turner, Levin T. AL 23rd Inf. Co.A
Turner, Levy SC 24th Inf. Co.B
Turner, Lewis AL 4th (Russell's) Cav. Co.G
Turner, Lewis MS Cav. 1st Bn. (McNair's) St.Troops Co.A
Turner, Lewis MS 18th Cav. Co.K
Turner, Lewis MS 41st Inf. Co.E
Turner, Lewis NC 1st Inf. (6 mo. '61) Co.I
Turner, Lewis SC 2nd Rifles Co.B
Turner, Lewis VA Lt.Arty. Hankins' Co.
Turner, Lewis VA 3rd Inf. 1st Co.I
Turner, Lewis C. VA 13th Inf. 1st Co.B, 2nd Co.B Sgt.
Turner, Lewis D. SC 2nd Cav. Co.C
Turner, Lewis H. SC 10th Inf. Co.I Cpl.
Turner, Lewis H. VA 28th Inf. Co.G
Turner, Lewis P. NC 6th Inf. Co.H
Turner, Lewis T. Gen. & Staff Surg.
Turner, Lewis W. MS 43rd Inf. Co.H,A
Turner, Linzy SC 10th Inf. Co.D
Turner, Littleberry AL 44th Inf. Co.K
Turner, Littleberry AL 61st Inf. Co.B
Turner, Littleton LA 16th Inf. Co.E
Turner, Livingstone LA Inf. 11th Bn. Co.B
Turner, L.J. AR Cav. Gordon's Regt. Co.K
Turner, L.J. AR 7th Mil. Co.E 1st Lt.
Turner, L.J. SC 5th Inf. 2nd Co.I 1st Lt.
Turner, L.J. TN 15th (Cons.) Cav. Co.A
Turner, L.J. TN 12th Inf. Co.D
Turner, L.J. TN 12th (Cons.) Inf. Co.E
Turner, L.M. AL 58th Inf. Co.I
Turner, L.M. GA 64th Inf. Co.E
Turner, L.M. MS Inf. 3rd Bn. Co.E
Turner, L.M. VA 1st (Farinholt's) Res. Co.E
Turner, Loderwick GA 64th Inf. Co.G Cpl.
Turner, Logan VA 9th Cav. Co.H
Turner, Logan VA 34th Inf. Co.K
Turner, Logan VA 53rd Inf. Co.D
Turner, Lorenzo FL 4th Inf. Co.A
Turner, Lorenzo J. TX 19th Cav. Co.F
Turner, Losson J. SC 9th Inf. Co.I 1st Sgt.
Turner, Louis TX 27th Cav. Co.D Ch.Music.
Turner, Louis TX Cav. Hardeman's Regt. Co.B Music.
Turner, Louis VA 44th Inf. Co.D
Turner, L.R. VA 3rd Res. Co.H Sgt.
Turner, L. Richard AL 1st Inf. Co.C,G
Turner, L.S. NC Mil. Clark's Sp.Bn. Co.K
Turner, L.T., Jr. GA 1st (Symons') Res. Co.A 3rd Lt.
Turner, L.T. MS 3rd Inf. Co.E
Turner, Lucius GA Inf. 1st Loc.Troops (Augusta) Co.D
Turner, Lucius G. GA 3rd Inf. Co.G
Turner, Luke GA 3rd Cav. (St.Guards) Co.C
Turner, Luke GA 61st Inf. Co.G
Turner, Luther MS 26th Inf. Co.A
Turner, Luther TN 18th (Newsom's) Cav. Co.I
Turner, Luther TN 19th & 20th (Cons.) Cav. Co.C
Turner, L.W. AL 63rd Inf. Co.E 2nd Lt.
Turner, L.W. MS 14th (Cons.) Inf. Co.K
Turner, L.W. TN 16th (Logwood's) Cav. Co.E
Turner, L.W. TN 47th Inf. Co.K
Turner, L.W.J. GA 27th Inf. Co.H
Turner, Lycurgus NC 6th Inf. Co.C Sgt.
Turner, Lynch MO 3rd Inf. Co.C Sgt.
Turner, Lynch Gen. & Staff Capt.,Comsy.
Turner, Lysander NC 47th Inf. Co.G Sgt.
Turner, M. AL Cav. Moreland's Regt. Co.I
Turner, M. GA 18th Inf. Co.K
Turner, M. MS 22nd Inf. Co.G
Turner, M. MS 35th Inf. Co.K
Turner, M. NC 15th Inf. Co.C
Turner, M. TX Cav. Border's Regt. Co.D
Turner, M. TX Inf. 1st St.Troops Whitehead's Co.
Turner, M. VA 7th Cav. Co.F
Turner, M. VA 12th Cav. Co.F
Turner, M. VA 45th Inf. Co.E
Turner, M.A. AL 11th Inf. Co.K
Turner, M.A. AL Cp. of Instr. Talladega Co.D
Turner, M.A. MS 8th Inf. Co.G
Turner, M.A. NC 66th Inf. Co.C
Turner, Madison F. AR 12th Inf. Co.H Sgt.
Turner, Magill VA 1st Cav. Co.F
Turner, Maltire TN 29th Inf. Co.I
Turner, Malvin TN Cav. 12th Bn. (Day's) Co.F
Turner, Mansel AL Cav. Hardie's Bn.Res. Co.C
Turner, Mansel AL Morris' Co. (Mtd.)
Turner, Mansfield MS 10th Cav. Co.C
Turner, Manson AR 24th Inf. Co.G
Turner, Manson GA 44th Inf. Co.G
Turner, Marcellus A. VA 2nd Arty. Co.A
Turner, Marcellus A. VA Inf. 22nd Bn. Co.A Sgt.
Turner, Marcellus G. TX 1st (Yager's) Cav. Capt.
Turner, Marcellus G. TX Cav. 3rd (Yager's) Bn. Co.C 2nd Lt.,AQM
Turner, Marcus GA 45th Inf. Co.I
Turner, Marcus SC 13th Inf. Co.C
Turner, Marcus D. TX 10th Cav. Co.C
Turner, Marcus H. GA 3rd Cav. Co.F
Turner, Marcus J. GA Inf. 25th Bn. (Prov. Guard) Co.A
Turner, Marcus J. Conf.Inf. 1st Bn. 2nd Co.A
Turner, Marcus L. TN 14th Cav. Co.F
Turner, Marion GA 6th Cav. Co.I
Turner, Marion NC 37th Inf. Co.B
Turner, Marion TX 15th Cav.
Turner, Marion TX 28th Cav. Co.I
Turner, Mark A. AL 63rd Inf. Co.D
Turner, Mark A. GA Arty. 11th Bn. (Sumter Arty.) Co.B
Turner, Mark C. NC 3rd Bn.Sr.Res. Williams' Co.
Turner, Martain C. GA 23rd Inf. Co.F

Turner, Martin GA 13th Inf. Co.A
Turner, Martin GA 43rd Inf. Co.A
Turner, Martin SC 19th Inf. Co.K
Turner, Martin SC 25th Inf. Co.D
Turner, Martin TX 2nd Cav. Co.K
Turner, Martin VA 5th Cav. Co.F
Turner, Martin VA 136th Mil. Co.C
Turner, Martin C. VA 23rd Inf. Co.A 1st Lt.
Turner, Martin G. MS 16th I nf. Co.F Cpl.
Turner, Martin L. VA Lt.Arty. 12th Bn. Co.C
Turner, Martin L. VA 44th Inf. Co.D
Turner, Martin V. TX 22nd Inf. Co.H
Turner, Martin W. SC 3rd St.Troops Co.B
Turner, Mastin NC 55th Inf. Co.D Cpl.
Turner, Mat A. TN Cav. 11th Bn. (Gordon's) Co.E
Turner, Mathew GA 48th Inf. Co.H
Turner, Mathew VA Lt.Arty. 12th Bn. Co.B
Turner, Mathew Gen. & Staff Asst.Surg.
Turner, Mathew J. TN 44th (Cons.) Inf. Co.E Sgt.
Turner, Mathew J. TN 55th (McKoin's) Inf. Co.F
Turner, Mathias VA 31st Inf. Co.H
Turner, Mathias C. AL 2nd Cav. Co.H
Turner, Mathias F. VA 62nd Mtd.Inf. 2nd Co.A
Turner, Matt AL 22nd Inf. Asst.Surg.
Turner, Matthew NC Hvy.Arty. 10th Bn. Co.C
Turner, Matthew C. FL 9th Inf. Co.G
Turner, Matthias VA 162nd Mil. Co.C
Turner, M.B. NC 37th Inf. Co.F
Turner, M.C. AL 5th Cav. Co.H
Turner, M.C. GA 39th Inf. Co.F
Turner, M.C. GA 56th Inf. Co.I
Turner, M.C. GA 65th Inf. Co.C
Turner, M.C. GA Smith's Legion Co.D
Turner, M.C. MS 5th Inf. Co.A
Turner, M.C. MS 9th Bn.S.S. Co.C
Turner, M.C. MS 26th Inf. Co.B,K
Turner, M.C. TX Cav. 1st Regt.St.Troops Co.A
Turner, McCager GA 2nd Inf. Co.F
Turner, M.D. AR 20th Inf. Co.K
Turner, M.D. GA 7th Cav. Co.I Sgt.
Turner, M.D. GA Cav. 24th Bn. Co.D Sgt.
Turner, M.D. GA Lt.Arty. 12th Bn. 3rd Co.B
Turner, M.D. GA 7th Inf. (St.Guards) Co.G
Turner, M.D. MO 16th Inf. Co.I
Turner, M.D. SC 26th Inf. Co.C
Turner, Meadows VA 16th Cav. Co.C
Turner, Meadows VA Cav. Caldwell's Bn. Hankins' Co.
Turner, Memory VA 5th Inf. Music.
Turner, Memory C. TX 17th Cav. Co.F 1st Lt.
Turner, Mercer W. TN 1st (Turney's) Inf. Co.F Cpl.
Turner, Meshach VA 57th Inf. Co.B
Turner, Meshack VA 64th Mil. Hunley's Co.
Turner, M.H. GA 23rd Inf. Co.I
Turner, M.H. GA 54th Inf. Co.K
Turner, M.H. SC Inf. 33rd Regt. Co.K
Turner, M.H. TX Cav. 1st Regt.St.Troops Co.G
Turner, M.H. TX 13th Vol. Co.G Music.
Turner, Micajah GA 56th Inf. Co.G
Turner, Miles J. GA 30th Inf. Co.A
Turner, Miles S. TN 8th Cav. Co.G Sgt.
Turner, Milligan TN 2nd (Smith's) Cav. Rankin's Co.
Turner, Milligan TN 4th (McLemore's) Cav. Co.H
Turner, Milligan TN Inf. 84th Regt. Co.H
Turner, Mills MO 8th Inf. Co.G
Turner, Mills VA 61st Inf. Co.H
Turner, Milton GA Cav. 29th Bn. Co.A
Turner, Milton J. VA 58th Inf. Co.I Sgt.
Turner, Milton L. GA 1st Reg. Co.K
Turner, M.J. GA 5th Inf. Co.K
Turner, M.J. TN 8th (Smith's) Cav. Co.A Ord.Sgt.
Turner, M.J. TN 16th (Logwood's) Cav. Co.D
Turner, M. John FL 1st Inf. Old Co.I,C 2nd Lt.
Turner, M.L. MS Cav. Powers' Regt. Co.K 1st Lt.
Turner, M.L. MS 6th Inf. Co.K
Turner, M.L. MS 14th (Cons.) Inf. Co.B
Turner, M.L. NC Inf. 2nd Bn. Co.D
Turner, M.L. TN 20th (Russell's) Cav. Co.K
Turner, M.L. TX 17th Inf. Co.F,B
Turner, M.L. VA Lt.Arty. Leake's Co.
Turner, M.L. VA 53rd Inf. Co.E
Turner, M.M. FL 1st (Res.) Inf.
Turner, Morgan KY 13th Cav. Co.F
Turner, Moses GA 1st (Fannin's) Res. Co.H,I
Turner, Moses SC 1st Arty. Co.I
Turner, Moses VA 7th Cav. Co.B
Turner, Moses P. KY 3rd Bn.Mtd.Rifles Co.E Cpl.
Turner, Moton E. AL 13th Inf. Co.G
Turner, M.P. GA 1st (Fannin's) Res. Co.H
Turner, M.P. Gen. & Staff Capt.
Turner, M.S. GA 1st Inf. (St.Guards) Co.G
Turner, M.S. NC 22nd Inf. Co.M
Turner, M.S. TX 8th Cav. Co.A Sgt.
Turner, M.S. TX 23rd Cav. Co.B
Turner, M.T. GA 44th Inf. Co.A
Turner, M.T. TN 3rd (Forrest's) Cav. Co.B
Turner, M.T. TX 16th Cav. Co.H
Turner, Mulligan TN 3rd (Forrest's) Cav.
Turner, Murphy MS 4th Inf. Co.A
Turner, M.V. NC 15th Inf. Co.C,D
Turner, N. AL Talladega Cty.Res. R.N. Ware's Cav.Co.
Turner, N. AL Mil. 2nd Regt.Vol. Co.F
Turner, N. MS 3rd Cav. Co.K
Turner, N. SC Cav. 10th Bn. Co.B Teamster
Turner, Nath GA 13th Inf. Co.F
Turner, Nathan GA 42nd Inf. Co.D 2nd Lt.
Turner, Nathan B. AR 6th Inf. Co.C Sgt.
Turner, Nathan B. FL 9th Inf. Co.G,A
Turner, Nathan E. FL 1st Inf. Old Co.I, New Co.C Sgt.
Turner, Nathaniel B. GA Inf. 10th Bn. Co.A Music.
Turner, Nathan J. MO 3rd Cav. Co.F
Turner, N.B. AL 34th Inf. Co.A
Turner, N.B. AR 27th Inf. Co.I Cpl.
Turner, N.B. AR Inf. Cocke's Regt. Co.C
Turner, N.E. SC 6th Cav. Co.D
Turner, Ned TN 6th (Wheeler's) Cav. Co.E
Turner, Nelson TX 30th Cav. Co.K
Turner, Nelson VA 24th Inf. Co.K
Turner, Nelson VA 63rd Inf. Co.D Cpl.
Turner, Newberry AL 13th Inf. Co.E
Turner, Newberry MS 44th Inf. Co.I
Turner, Newton TN 1st (Feild's) Inf. Co.F
Turner, Newton A. VA Lt.Arty. Cooper's Co.
Turner, N.F. SC 17th Inf. Co.H
Turner, Nicholas Lt.Arty. Dent's Btty.,CSA
Turner, Nicholas G. NC 1st Cav. (9th St.Troops) Co.A 1st Sgt.
Turner, Noah NC 22nd Inf. Co.B
Turner, Noah A. GA 1st (Ramsey's) Inf. Co.E
Turner, Noah E. NC 16th Inf. Co.G
Turner, Noah R. 10th Conf.Cav. Co.C
Turner, Noel AL Cav. Murphy's Bn. Co.B
Turner, Noel 15th Conf.Cav. Co.G
Turner, Noel M. AL Vol. Lee, Jr.'s Co.
Turner, N.R. AL 10th Inf. Co.C
Turner, N.T. LA 8th Cav. Co.I
Turner, O. AR Lt.Arty. Hart's Btty.
Turner, O. FL Cav. Smith's Co. (Marianna Drag.)
Turner, O.B. TN 10th (DeMoss') Cav. Co.G
Turner, O.B. TN Cav. Napier's Bn. Co.D
Turner, Obediah AL 29th Inf. Co.C Cpl.
Turner, Obediah VA 8th Cav. Co.A
Turner, Obediah VA 53rd Inf. Co.A
Turner, O.C. AL 9th Inf. Co.C
Turner, O.D. TN 11th (Holman's) Cav. Co.L
Turner, Ogden LA 8th Cav. Co.I
Turner, Oliver TX 20th Inf. Co.C
Turner, Oliver J. TX 2nd Cav. Co.B Sgt.
Turner, O.P. GA 52nd Inf. Co.D
Turner, Orlando FL Cav. 5th Bn. Co.G
Turner, Oscar F. TN 4th Inf. Co.I 1st Lt.
Turner, O.W. AL 21st Inf. Co.E
Turner, O.W. GA 31st Inf. Co.E
Turner, Owen FL 10th Inf. Co.D
Turner, P. AL St.Arty. Co.C
Turner, P. AL 6th Inf. Co.K
Turner, P. LA 3rd (Wingfield's) Cav. Chap.
Turner, P. MO Cav. Williams' Regt. Co.G
Turner, P. TX Cav. Bone's Co. Cpl.
Turner, P. TX Cav. Border's Regt. Co.K
Turner, P. TX 6th Field Btty.
Turner, P. TX Lt.Arty. Dege's Bn.
Turner, Pascal D. MS 2nd Part.Rangers Co.I Cpl.
Turner, Paschal TX 27th Cav. Co.G
Turner, Paschal R. TX 18th Cav. Co.B
Turner, Paschal R. TX 37th Cav. 2nd Co.I Capt.
Turner, Patrick LA Mil. Bragg's Bn. Schwartz's Co. Sgt.
Turner, P.C. SC Lt.Arty. 8th (Palmetto) Bn. Co.E
Turner, P.D. MS 7th Inf. Co.F Cpl.
Turner, P.D. TX Cav. Ragsdale's Bn. 2nd Co.C
Turner, Peel NC 26th Inf. Co.H
Turner, Penington T. TX 28th Cav. Co.I
Turner, Permenter NC Cav. 5th Bn. Co.A
Turner, Perry AL 32nd & 58th (Cons.) Inf.
Turner, Perry AL 58th Inf. Co.I
Turner, Perry GA 41st Inf. Co.K
Turner, Persons W. AL 4th Inf. Co.I
Turner, Peter GA 13th Inf. Co.F
Turner, Peter KY 14th Cav. Co.G
Turner, Peter LA 30th Inf. Co.H
Turner, Peter TX Cav. 2nd Regt.St.Troops Co.B 1st Lt.
Turner, Peter E. GA 36th (Villepigue's) Inf. Co.D
Turner, Peter E. MS 9th Inf. New Co.G Cpl.

Turner, Peter R. GA 55th Inf. Co.H
Turner, Peyton VA 16th Cav. Co.C
Turner, Peyton VA Cav. Caldwell's Bn. Hankins' Co.
Turner, Peyton S. GA 44th Inf. Co.A
Turner, P.G. GA 10th Cav. (St.Guards) Co.K
Turner, Phails NC Jones' Co. (Supp.Force)
Turner, Philemon SC 22nd Inf. Co.H
Turner, Philip M. AL 48th Inf. Co.G
Turner, Philip M. NC Inf. Thomas Legion Co.E
Turner, Phleming D. TX Cav. Madison's Regt. Co.G Capt.
Turner, Pickens T. SC 20th Inf. Co.A
Turner, Pinckney SC 15th Inf. Co.A
Turner, Pinkney NC 13th Inf. Co.F
Turner, P.J. GA Cav. 29th Bn.
Turner, Pleasant TN 30th Inf. Co.G
Turner, P.M. MS 9th Cav. Co.E
Turner, P.M. MS 31st Inf. Co.A
Turner, P.M. TN Cav. 17th Bn. (Sanders') Co.B
Turner, P.M. VA 50th Inf. Co.F
Turner, P.N. NC 15th Inf. Co.F 1st Lt.
Turner, P.P. VA 5th Cav. Co.G
Turner, P.P. VA 15th Cav. Co.B
Turner, P.R. TX 17th Cons.Dismtd.Cav. 1st Co.G
Turner, Preston MO Inf. Clark's Regt. Co.G
Turner, Preston Conf.Cav. Clarkson's Bn. Ind.Rangers Co.D
Turner, Preston H. NC 14th Inf. Co.H Sgt.Maj.
Turner, Preston H. NC 28th Inf. Co.K 1st Lt.
Turner, Price GA 39th Inf. Co.A
Turner, P.S. AR 7th Inf. Co.G
Turner, P.W. SC 18th Inf. Co.K Cpl.
Turner, R. AL Cav. Moreland's Regt. Co.F
Turner, R. AL 8th Inf.
Turner, R. AL 36th Inf. Co.E
Turner, R. AL Talladega Cty.Res. W.Y. Hendrick's Co.
Turner, R. AL Talladega Cty.Res. W. Steed's Co.
Turner, R. AR 1st (Monroe's) Cav. Co.H
Turner, R. FL 2nd Cav. Co.K
Turner, R. NC 31st Inf. Co.E
Turner, R. SC Mil. 1st Regt. (Charleston Res.) Co.B
Turner, R. SC 23rd Inf. Co.E
Turner, R. SC Palmetto S.S. Co.D
Turner, R.A. GA 2nd Cav. Co.I
Turner, R.A. NC 23rd Inf. Co.G
Turner, R.A. SC 1st Arty. Co.H
Turner, R.A. SC Inf. Holcombe Legion Co.K Music.
Turner, Raleigh H. GA 27th Inf. Co.K Comsy.Sgt.
Turner, Ramson MS 44th Inf. Co.E 1st Lt.
Turner, Randolph SC 7th Res. Co.G
Turner, Randolph SC Inf. Holcombe Legion Co.I Ch.Music.
Turner, Randolph R. NC 17th Inf. (1st Org.) Co.H
Turner, Ransom H. MS 1st Lt.Arty. Co.C Sgt.
Turner, Ransom H. MS 15th Inf. Co.D
Turner, Rasmus TN 13th (Gore's) Cav. Co.B
Turner, Raymond S. GA 43rd Inf. Co.K
Turner, R.B. AR 6th Inf. Old Co.F
Turner, R.B. NC 4th Sr.Res. Co.H
Turner, R.B. SC 15th Inf. Co.I
Turner, R.B. SC 26th Inf. Co.C
Turner, R.B. Sig.Corps,CSA
Turner, R.C. KY 12th Cav. Co.B
Turner, R.C. NC 2nd Jr.Res. Co.D
Turner, R.C. TN 11th (Holman's) Cav. Co.D
Turner, R.C. TX 9th Cav. Co.F Sgt.
Turner, R.C. TX Inf. Chambers' Bn.Res.Corps Co.A
Turner, R.D. MO Inf. Winston's Regt. Co.A
Turner, R.E. GA 18th Inf. Co.A
Turner, R.E. SC Lt.Arty. 3rd (Palmetto) Bn. Co.E
Turner, Resin LA 4th Inf. Co.D Capt.
Turner, Reuben KY 7th Cav. Co.B 2nd Lt.
Turner, Reuben KY 11th Cav. Co.B
Turner, Reuben NC 60th Inf. Co.H
Turner, Reuben TX Cav. 6th Bn. Co.A
Turner, Reuben D. VA 30th Inf. Co.E
Turner, Reuben F. GA 40th Inf. Co.G
Turner, Reuben H. KY Horse Arty. Byrne's Co.
Turner, Reubin MO 1st N.E. Cav. Co.D Cpl.
Turner, R.F. AL 8th (Hatch's) Cav. Co.D
Turner, R.F. SC 23rd Inf. Co.I
Turner, R.F. TN 33rd Inf. Co.H
Turner, R.G. GA 54th Inf. Co.E Sgt.
Turner, R.G. MS 1st Cav. Co.I
Turner, R.G. TN 10th (DeMoss') Cav. Co.E
Turner, R.G. Gen. & Staff Surg.
Turner, R.G.W. TX 19th Inf. Co.H
Turner, R.H. AL 1st Cav. 1st Co.K
Turner, R.H. FL Cav. 3rd Bn. Co.B
Turner, R.H. GA Lt.Arty. Daniell's Btty.
Turner, R.H. GA Arty. Maxwell's Reg.Lt.Btty.
Turner, R.H. LA 8th Cav. Co.I Capt.
Turner, R.H. LA 27th Inf. Co.F
Turner, R.H. MS Cav. 1st Bn. (Miller's) Cole's Co.
Turner, R.H. MS Inf. 7th Bn. Co.A Cpl.
Turner, R.H. SC Lt.Arty. Wagener's Co. (Co.A,German Arty.)
Turner, R.H. SC 10th Inf. Co.F
Turner, R.H. Trans-MS Conf.Cav. 1st Bn. Co.B
Turner, R.H. 15th Conf.Cav. Co.D 2nd Lt.
Turner, Rhodes SC 22nd Inf. Co.H
Turner, Rice R. TX 11th Inf. Co.B 2nd Lt.
Turner, Richard AL Cav. Forrest's Regt.
Turner, Richard GA 1st (Olmstead's) Inf. Co.C
Turner, Richard MO Inf. Perkins' Bn. Co.E
Turner, Richard NC 11th (Bethel Regt.) Inf. Co.G
Turner, Richard NC 18th Inf. Co.A
Turner, Richard NC 35th Inf. Co.B
Turner, Richard NC Erwin's Bn.Sr.Res. Co.B 2nd Lt.
Turner, Richard SC 23rd Inf. Co.D
Turner, Richard TX 25th Cav. Co.I
Turner, Richard TX 5th Inf. Co.C
Turner, Richard VA 39th Inf. Co.H
Turner, Richard A. MS 27th Inf. Co.E
Turner, Richard A. VA 58th Inf. Co.B
Turner, Richard G. TX 35th (Brown's) Cav. Co.D Surg.
Turner, Richard G. TX 13th Vol. 1st Co.I Sgt.
Turner, Richard H. NC 27th Inf. Co.F
Turner, Richard H. NC 46th Inf. Co.C
Turner, Richard L. GA 35th Inf. Co.I
Turner, Richard M. VA 24th Cav. Co.A
Turner, Richard M. VA Cav. 40th Bn. Co.A
Turner, Richard S. VA 55th Inf. Co.G
Turner, Richardson NC 1st Jr.Res. Co.D
Turner, Richard W. LA 19th Inf. Co.A Col.
Turner, Richmond R. VA Inf. 5th Bn. Co.C
Turner, Right AL Loc.Def. & Sp.Serv. Toomer's Co.
Turner, Riley FL 8th Inf. Co.F
Turner, Riley F. GA 56th Inf.
Turner, R.J. SC Lt.Arty. 3rd (Palmetto) Bn. Co.C
Turner, R.J. SC Inf. 7th Bn. (Enfield Rifles) Co.F,A
Turner, R.J. TN Cav. Napier's Bn. Co.B
Turner, R.J. TN 5th Inf. Asst.Surg.
Turner, R.K. NC 22nd Inf. Co.K
Turner, R.L. AR 11th Inf. Co.G
Turner, R.L. AR 33rd Inf. Co.B
Turner, R.L. GA Cav. 6th Bn. (St.Guards) Co.F
Turner, R.L. GA 37th Inf. Co.E
Turner, R.L. MS 8th Cav. Co.I
Turner, R.L. MS 48th Inf. Co.D
Turner, R.L. VA 19th Cav. Co.G Cpl.
Turner, R.M. AL 8th Inf. Co.G
Turner, R.M. AR 3rd Cav. Co.B
Turner, R.M. GA 56th Inf. Co.B
Turner, R.M. SC Inf. 7th Bn. (Enfield Rifles) Co.D
Turner, R.N. SC Lt.Arty. 3rd (Palmetto) Bn. Co.E Cpl.
Turner, Robinson MS Packer's Co. (Pope Guards)
Turner, Robert AL 12th Inf. Co.D
Turner, Robert AL 16th Inf. Co.C
Turner, Robert AL 22nd Inf. Co.K
Turner, Robert FL 8th Inf. Co.G 1st Sgt.
Turner, Robert KY 11th Cav. Co.B
Turner, Robert LA 7th Inf. Co.E
Turner, Robert NC 24th Inf. Co.A
Turner, Robert SC 6th Cav. Co.B
Turner, Robert SC 2nd Arty. Co.K
Turner, Robert SC 3rd St.Troops Co.C
Turner, Robert SC 5th St.Troops Co.K
Turner, Robert TN 7th (Duckworth's) Cav. Co.I
Turner, Robert TX 32nd Cav. Co.C
Turner, Robert VA 56th Inf. Co.F
Turner, Robert A. GA 52nd Inf. Co.I
Turner, Robert A. SC Inf. Hampton Legion Co.B Sgt.
Turner, Robert A. TX Cav. 6th Bn. Co.A
Turner, Robert A. VA Lt.Arty. Douthat's Co.
Turner, Robert A. VA 3rd Inf. Co.G
Turner, Robert B. MO 1st Inf. Co.G 1st Lt.
Turner, Robert B. TN 4th Inf. Co.I
Turner, Robert B. VA 23rd Inf. Co.E
Turner, Robert B. VA 30th Bn.S.S. Co.B
Turner, Robert B. 1st Conf.Inf. 2nd Co.E
Turner, Robert D. MO 4th Cav. Co.I
Turner, Robert E. VA 12th Inf. Co.C
Turner, Robert G. TN 14th Inf. Co.F
Turner, Robert G. VA 1st Arty. Co.D
Turner, Robert G. VA Lt.Arty. 1st Bn. Co.D
Turner, Robert G. VA 6th Inf. Co.H
Turner, Robert G. VA 28th Inf. Co.G
Turner, Robt. G. Gen. & Staff Capt.,ACS
Turner, Robert H. KY 7th Cav. Co.B

Turner, Robert H. MS 3rd Cav. Co.K Capt.
Turner, Robert H. MS Inf. 2nd Bn. Co.D
Turner, Robert H. MS 48th Inf. Co.D
Turner, Robert H. TX 22nd Cav. Co.C Cpl.
Turner, Robert H. VA 17th Inf. Co.B QM
Turner, Robert H. Corse's Brig. Maj.,QM
Turner, Robert J. AL 58th Inf. Asst.Sgt.
Turner, Robert J. TN 1st (Feild's) Inf. Co.I
Turner, Robert J. VA Horse Arty. E. Graham's Co.
Turner, Robert J. VA 9th Inf. 2nd Co.H Cpl.
Turner, Robert J. Cheatham's Div. Asst.Surg.
Turner, Robert K. VA 44th Inf. Co.D,I Cpl.
Turner, Robert L. MS Inf. 2nd Bn. Co.D
Turner, Robert L. VA Cav. 46th Bn. Co.E
Turner, Robert M. GA 41st Inf. Co.F
Turner, Robert M. SC 12th Inf. Co.H
Turner, Robert N. AR 3rd Cav. Co.K,B Sgt.
Turner, Robert O. MO 3rd Inf. Co.C
Turner, Robert P. TN 4th (McLemore's) Cav. Co.A
Turner, Robert R. AR 24th Inf. Co.G
Turner, Robert S. NC 35th Inf. Co.B
Turner, Robert T. NC 60th Inf. Co.G
Turner, Robert T. SC 1st Arty. Co.G
Turner, Robert W. AR 1st (Colquitt's) Inf. Co.E
Turner, Robert W. TX 11th Inf. Co.H 2nd Lt.
Turner, Robert W. VA 16th Inf. Co.E
Turner, Robinson E. TN 1st (Turney's) Inf. Co.F
Turner, R.P. GA 2nd Cav. (St.Guards) Co.A
Turner, R.P. KY 8th Mtd.Inf. Co.B
Turner, R.P. MS Cav. Drane's Co. (Choctaw Cty.Res.)
Turner, R.P. SC 2nd Arty. Co.K
Turner, R.P. SC 7th Inf. 1st Co.G
Turner, R.R. SC 2nd St.Troops Co.D
Turner, R.R. TX 19th Inf. Co.H Cpl.
Turner, R.S. AL Mil. 2nd Regt.Vol. Co.E
Turner, R.T. AL 8th (Hatch's) Cav. Co.D
Turner, R.T. LA 8th Cav. Co.I
Turner, Rudolph R. NC 1st Arty. (10th St.Troops) Co.K Cpl.
Turner, Rufus LA 16th Inf. Co.E
Turner, Rufus TX Cav. Morgan's Regt. Co.E
Turner, Rufus VA 12th Inf. Co.D 2nd Lt.
Turner, Rufus K. NC 16th Inf. Co.K
Turner, Russel GA 4th (Clinch's) Cav. Co.G
Turner, R.W. SC 6th Cav. Co.I
Turner, R.W. TX 11th Inf. Co.A Ord.Sgt.
Turner, R.W. VA 1st (Farinholt's) Res. Co.K
Turner, S. AL Cav. Barbiere's Bn. Co.B
Turner, S. AL 7th Inf. Co.F
Turner, S. AR 32nd Inf. Co.C
Turner, S. GA 5th Res. Co.D
Turner, S. GA 5th Res. Co.K
Turner, S. GA Inf. (E. to W. Point Guards) Matthews' Co.
Turner, S. MS 1st (King's) Inf. (St.Troops) D. Love's Co.
Turner, S. MS 9th Bn.S.S. Co.C
Turner, S. MO 1st N.E. Cav. Co.I
Turner, S. SC Lt.Arty. 3rd (Palmetto) Bn. Co.H
Turner, S. SC Lt.Arty. 3rd (Palmetto) Bn. Co.I
Turner, S. SC 7th Inf. Co.G
Turner, S. TX 5th Inf.
Turner, S. Horse Arty. White's Btty.
Turner, S.A. AR Inf. Cocke's Regt. Co.K 2nd Lt.
Turner, S.A. 2nd Conf.Eng.Troops Co.D Artif.
Turner, Sam AL 11th Inf. Co.D
Turner, Sam TN 19th & 20th (Cons.) Cav. Co.B
Turner, Sampson GA 13th Inf. Co.F
Turner, Samuel AL 5th Cav. Co.H
Turner, Samuel AL 18th Inf. Co.L
Turner, Samuel AL 34th Inf. Breedlove's Co.
Turner, Samuel AR 17th (Lemoyne's) Inf. Co.C Cpl.
Turner, Samuel AR 17th (Lemoyne's) Inf. Co.D Sgt.
Turner, Samuel AR 21st Inf. Co.C
Turner, Samuel GA 18th Inf. Co.I
Turner, Samuel GA 38th Inf. Co.E
Turner, Samuel GA 55th Inf. Co.H
Turner, Samuel GA 61st Inf. Co.D
Turner, Samuel GA Phillips' Legion Co.D
Turner, Samuel MS 3rd Cav. Co.B Cpl.
Turner, Samuel MS 5th Inf. Co.A
Turner, Samuel MO Cav. Snider's Bn. Co.D
Turner, Samuel TN 3rd (Clack's) Inf. Co.H
Turner, Samuel TN 61st Mtd.Inf. Co.K
Turner, Samuel TX 22nd Cav. Co.B
Turner, Samuel TX 22nd Cav. Co.E
Turner, Samuel TX 23rd Cav. Co.I
Turner, Samuel TX 34th Cav. Co.G
Turner, Samuel TX 20th Inf. Co.D
Turner, Samuel VA 61st Inf. Co.F
Turner, Samuel A. AR 21st Inf. Co.H
Turner, Samuel C. TN 18th (Newsom's) Cav. Co.C,G Cpl.
Turner, Samuel C. VA 12th Inf. Co.D
Turner, Samuel Coote AL 3rd Inf. Co.E
Turner, Samuel D. NC 27th Inf. Co.K Music.
Turner, Samuel F. SC 2nd Cav. Co.C
Turner, Sam'l. F. Gen. & Staff Surg.
Turner, Samuel H. NC 28th Inf. Co.A
Turner, Samuel H. VA Cav. 36th Bn. Co.A
Turner, Samuel H. VA Hvy.Arty. 19th Bn. Co.A
Turner, Samuel H. VA Hvy.Arty. Kyle's Co.
Turner, Samuel H. VA Lt.Arty. J.D. Smith's Co.
Turner, Samuel H. VA 45th Inf. Co.I
Turner, Samuel J. VA 51st Inf. Co.G
Turner, Samuel L. GA 62nd Cav. Co.K Capt.
Turner, Samuel L. GA 44th Inf. Co.E
Turner, Samuel P. KY 13th Cav. Co.B
Turner, Samuel S. SC Cav. 17th Bn. Co.B
Turner, Samuel S. VA 58th Inf. Co.E Capt.
Turner, Samuel T. AR 6th Inf. Co.I Surg.
Turner, Samuel William TX 20th Cav. Co.D
Turner, Sanford D. TX 13th Cav. Co.C
Turner, Saul W. TX Cav. 2nd Regt.St.Troops Co.D
Turner, Sawyer LA 17th Inf. Co.D
Turner, S.B. SC 7th Cav. Co.K
Turner, S.B. TX 11th (Spaight's) Bn.Vol. Co.D
Turner, S.C. SC 1st Mtd.Mil. Heyward's Co.
Turner, S. Camull TN 27th Inf. Co.B
Turner, Scott MS 1st Cav. Co.I
Turner, Scott MS Cav. 1st Bn. (Miller's) Cole's Co.
Turner, Scott MS St.Cav. 2nd Bn. (Harris') Co.B Jr.2nd Lt.
Turner, Scott MS 11th (Cons.) Cav. Co.G 2nd Lt.
Turner, Scott MS 10th Inf. Old Co.D
Turner, S.D. GA 12th Cav. Co.B
Turner, S.D. SC 23rd Inf. Co.E
Turner, S.E. AL 44th Inf. Co.I
Turner, S.E. TX Cav. (Dismtd.) Chisum's Regt. Co.F
Turner, Seaborn J. LA 28th (Gray's) Inf. Co.K
Turner, Seaborn K. GA Lt.Arty. Scogin's Btty. (Griffin Lt.Arty.)
Turner, S.F. VA 4th Res. Co.H
Turner, S.G. GA 6th Inf. Co.H
Turner, S.G. TN 14th (Neely's) Cav. Co.B Sgt.
Turner, S.G. TN 51st (Cons.) Inf. Co.B
Turner, S.H. SC Cav. 4th Bn. Co.A
Turner, Shadrack R. GA 2nd Cav. (St.Guards) Co.G
Turner, Shadric TN Cav. 7th Bn. (Bennett's) Co.E
Turner, Shadroch AR 33rd Inf. Co.D
Turner, Sidney VA 21st Inf. Co.H
Turner, Silas MS 1st (Johnston's) Inf. Co.A
Turner, Silas M. MS 11th Inf. Co.A
Turner, Sim MS Blythe's Bn. (St.Troops) Co.A
Turner, Simeon NC 8th Bn.Part.Rangers Co.C
Turner, Simeon NC 66th Inf. Co.D
Turner, Simeon P. GA 2nd Cav. Co.A
Turner, Simon MS Part.Rangers Armistead's Co. Cpl.
Turner, Simon SC 16th Inf. Co.A
Turner, Simon SC 16th Inf. Co.H 2nd Lt.
Turner, Simon B. AL 44th Inf. Co.K
Turner, Simon B. AL 61st Inf. Co.B
Turner, Simpson AR 10th Inf. Co.E
Turner, S.J. VA 11th Inf. Co.G
Turner, S.L. GA 8th Cav. Co.K Capt.
Turner, S.M. GA 36th (Broyles') Inf. Co.E
Turner, S.M. MS 9th Cav. Co.E
Turner, Smith GA Cav. 22nd Bn. (St.Guards) Co.D
Turner, Smith GA 27th Inf. Co.F
Turner, Smith R. AR 6th Inf. New Co.D
Turner, Smith S. VA 17th Inf. Co.B 1st Lt.
Turner, S.O. MS Inf. 7th Bn. Co.A
Turner, Solomon SC 10th Inf. Co.D
Turner, S. Otis GA Cobb's Legion
Turner, S.P. VA Inf. 26th Bn. Co.C
Turner, S.P. VA 166th Mil. Taylor's Co.
Turner, S.R. AR 12th Inf. Co.H
Turner, S.R. GA Mil. 37th Regt. Co.F 2nd Lt.
Turner, S.S. NC Mil. 1st Regt. W.D. Crowder's Co.
Turner, S.S. SC 5th Cav. Co.G
Turner, S.S. SC Inf. 1st (Charleston) Bn. Co.A
Turner, S.S. TN 3rd (Forrest's) Cav. Co.B
Turner, S.S. Sig.Corps,CSA
Turner, S.T. GA 4th Res. Co.B
Turner, Starling SC 6th Cav. Co.B
Turner, St. Clair VA 162nd Mil. Co.C
Turner, Stephen GA 1st (Ramsey's) Inf. Co.F
Turner, Stephen GA Cobb's Legion Co.B,G
Turner, Stephen MO 11th Inf. Co.K
Turner, Stephen SC 10th Inf. Co.D
Turner, Stephen TN 24th Inf. Co.D
Turner, Stephen VA 19th Inf. Co.H
Turner, Stephen VA 61st Inf. Co.F
Turner, Stephen A. AL 34th Inf. Co.G

Turner, Stephen A. GA 1st (Olmstead's) Inf. Co.K,F
Turner, Stephen C. TX 29th Cav. Co.G
Turner, Stephen C. VA 54th Inf. Co.I
Turner, Stephen D. NC 1st Arty. (10th St.Troops) Co.H
Turner, Stephen E. GA 49th Inf. Co.E
Turner, Stephen H. VA Hvy.Arty. 19th Bn. Co.D Sgt.
Turner, Stephen L. TN 7th Inf. Co.H
Turner, Stephen R. NC 37th Inf. Co.I Cpl.
Turner, Stephen S. 1st Conf.Inf. 2nd Co.F
Turner, Stephen W. VA 56th Inf. Co.B 2nd Lt.
Turner, Sterling GA 3rd Cav. Co.I
Turner, Sterling SC 4th Inf. Co.G
Turner, Sterling SC Inf. 13th Bn. Co.B
Turner, Sterling G. GA 4th Inf. Co.B
Turner, Sterling G. GA 19th Inf. Adj.
Turner, Sterling T. TN 43rd Inf. Co.F Capt.
Turner, Stuart C. VA 29th Inf. Co.D
Turner, Stringfellow SC Arty. Manigault's Bn. 1st Co.A
Turner, Sumpter LA Washington Arty.Bn. Co.1 Cpl.
Turner, Sumpter SC 6th Cav. Co.B
Turner, Sumpter S. LA Washington Arty.Bn. Co.6 Can.
Turner, S.V. TX Cav. Wells' Regt. Co.K
Turner, S.W. GA 10th Cav. Co.K
Turner, S.W. MS 4th Inf. Co.H Cpl.
Turner, S.W. TX 10th Cav. Co.G
Turner, S.W. TX 13th Vol. Co.H
Turner, S.W. TX Inf. Chambers' Bn.Res.Corps Co.A
Turner, T. AR 1st Mtd.Res. Co.C
Turner, T. GA 5th Res. Co.D
Turner, T. GA 5th Res. Co.F
Turner, T. GA Inf. 27th Bn. (NonConscr.) Co.C
Turner, T. GA 48th Inf. Co.I
Turner, T. LA Washington Arty.Bn. Co.5
Turner, T. MS 8th Inf. Asst.Surg.
Turner, T. MO St.Guard
Turner, T. NC 7th Sr.Res. Boon's Co.
Turner, T. SC 1st Cav. Co.C
Turner, T. TN 14th (Neely's) Cav. Surg.
Turner, T. TN Cav. Napier's Bn. Co.E
Turner, T. TX Inf. Timmons' Regt. Co.D
Turner, T. Stewart's Staff Lt.Gen.
Turner, T. Gillum's Regt. Co.F
Turner, T.A. MS 1st Cav.Res. Co.E
Turner, T.A. NC 1st Regt.Vol. C.M. Avery's Co., Co.G
Turner, T.A. TN 42nd Inf. 1st Co.H
Turner, T.A. VA 42nd Inf. Co.G
Turner, T.B. GA 13th Cav. Co.C
Turner, Talbot GA 6th Inf. (St.Guards) Pittman's Co.
Turner, Talbot GA 30th Inf. Co.I
Turner, Taylor SC 1st (Hagood's) Inf. 2nd Co.K Drum.
Turner, Tazewell A. VA 51st Inf. Co.H
Turner, T.B. AR 35th Inf. Co.G
Turner, T.B. LA 2nd Cav. Co.H
Turner, T.B. MS 4th Inf. Co.F
Turner, T.B. TX 3rd Cav. Co.H
Turner, T.B. TX Inf. 3rd St.Troops Co.F
Turner, T. Barnes LA 2nd Inf. Co.H
Turner, T.C. TX 5th Inf.
Turner, T.C. VA 21st Inf. Co.I
Turner, T.E. TN 17th Inf. Co.E
Turner, T.F. GA 3rd Res. Co.C
Turner, T.G. AL 12th Inf. Lt.Col.
Turner, T.H. GA Hvy.Arty. 22nd Bn. Co.B
Turner, T.H. MO 9th Inf. Lt.Col.
Turner, T.H. SC Inf. 1st (Charleston) Bn. Co.G Sgt.
Turner, T.H. SC 13th Inf. Co.I 2nd Lt.
Turner, T.H. SC 27th Inf. Co.K Sgt.
Turner, T.H. TN 14th (Neely's) Cav. Co.B Capt.
Turner, T.H. TN 15th (Stewart's) Cav. Co.G
Turner, T.H. 1st Conf.Inf. 1st Co.D Sgt.
Turner, Thaddeus S. MO 2nd Cav. Co.A
Turner, Thaddeus S. MO 3rd Cav. Co.A Cpl.
Turner, Thaddeus S. MO Cav. 3rd Bn. Co.C
Turner, Theodore VA 22nd Inf. Co.H
Turner, Theo H. SC Inf. Hampton Legion Co.A
Turner, Theophilus H. GA 36th (Villepigue's) Inf. Co.D Sgt.
Turner, Thos. AL 53rd (Part.Rangers)
Turner, Thomas AL 38th Inf. Co.B
Turner, Thomas AL 45th Inf. Co.I
Turner, Thomas AR Cav. 1st Bn. (Stirman's) Co.F
Turner, Thomas AR 2nd Mtd.Rifles Co.C
Turner, Thomas AR 10th Mil. Co.C
Turner, Thomas AR 16th Inf. Co.F
Turner, Thomas FL Lt.Arty. Perry's Co.
Turner, Thomas FL 1st Inf. Old Co.K, New Co.A
Turner, Thomas FL 2nd Inf. Co.L
Turner, Thomas FL 3rd Inf. Co.B
Turner, Thomas GA Cav. 9th Bn. (St.Guards) Co.A
Turner, Thomas GA 1st Inf. (St.Guards) Co.H
Turner, Thomas GA 11th (St.Troops) Co.B
Turner, Thomas GA 64th Inf. Co.A
Turner, Thomas GA Floyd Legion (St.Guards) Co.K 1st Sgt.
Turner, Thomas KY 2nd (Duke's) Cav. Co.K
Turner, Thomas MS Part.Rangers Armistead's Co.
Turner, Thomas MS Lt.Arty. Lomax's Co.
Turner, Thomas MS 7th Inf. Asst.Surg.
Turner, Thomas MS 26th Inf. Co.A
Turner, Thomas MS 41st Inf. Asst.Surg.
Turner, Thomas MS 44th Inf. Asst.Surg.
Turner, Thomas MO 2nd Cav. Co.G Lt.
Turner, Thomas MO Searcy's Bn.S.S. Co.E
Turner, Thomas MO Cav. Williams' Regt. Co.C Ord.Sgt.
Turner, Thomas NC 1st Arty. (10th St.Troops) Co.K
Turner, Thomas NC 22nd Inf. Co.M
Turner, Thomas NC 46th Inf. Co.I
Turner, Thomas SC Lt.Arty. 3rd (Palmetto) Bn. Co.C
Turner, Thomas SC Lt.Arty. Beauregard's Co.
Turner, Thomas SC 4th Bn.Res. Co.D
Turner, Thomas SC 7th Inf. Co.D
Turner, Thomas SC 9th Res. Co.K
Turner, Thomas SC Inf. Holcombe Legion Co.H
Turner, Thomas TN 4th (Murray's) Cav. Co.K
Turner, Thomas TN 5th Inf. 2nd Co.B
Turner, Thomas TN 7th Inf. Surg.
Turner, Thomas TN Inf. 22nd Bn. Co.F
Turner, Thomas TN 44th (Cons.) Inf. Co.D
Turner, Thomas VA 1st Cav. 2nd Co.K
Turner, Thomas VA Cav. 47th Bn. Co.C
Turner, Thomas VA Goochland Lt.Arty.
Turner, Thomas VA Lt.Arty. Penick's Co.
Turner, Thomas VA 3rd (Archer's) Bn.Res. Co.E Cpl.
Turner, Thomas VA 36th Inf. 3rd Co.I Cpl.
Turner, Thomas VA 45th Inf. Co.F
Turner, Thomas VA 61st Inf. Co.C
Turner, Thomas VA 61st Inf. Co.G
Turner, Thomas VA Wade's Regt.Loc.Def. Co.A
Turner, Thomas Gen. & Staff Lt.,ADC
Turner, Thomas Gen. & Staff Asst.Surg.
Turner, Thomas A. AR 8th Inf. New Co.F
Turner, Thomas A. AR 14th (McCarver's) Inf. Co.E
Turner, Thomas A. NC 5th Inf. Co.C
Turner, Thomas A. TN 42nd Inf. Co.C,G
Turner, Thomas A. TX 15th Cav. Co.F 1st Sgt.
Turner, Thomas A. VA 24th Inf. Co.K
Turner, Thomas B. MO 3rd Cav. Co.F
Turner, Thomas B. NC 5th Inf. Co.I
Turner, Thomas B. VA 7th Cav. Co.A
Turner, Thomas B. VA 8th Inf. Co.B
Turner, Thomas B. VA 17th Inf. Co.A
Turner, Thomas C. GA 6th Inf. Co.A Cpl.
Turner, Thomas C. GA 12th Inf. Co.C Cpl.
Turner, Thomas C. GA 42nd Inf. Co.D
Turner, Thomas C. TX Waul's Legion Co.E
Turner, Thomas D. SC 10th Inf. Co.F
Turner, Thomas E. AL 1st Inf. Co.A
Turner, Thomas E. AL 15th Inf. Co.A
Turner, Thomas E. AL 18th Inf. Co.A
Turner, Thomas E. MS 31st Inf. Co.B
Turner, Thomas E. VA 32nd Inf. 2nd Co.K
Turner, Thomas E. VA 115th Mil. Co.D
Turner, Thomas H. SC 6th Res. Co.G
Turner, Thomas H. TN 1st (Turney's) Inf. Co.F Ord.Sgt.
Turner, Thomas H. TN 53rd Inf. Co.E
Turner, Thomas H. VA Horse Arty. G.W. Brown's Co.
Turner, Thomas H. VA 34th Inf. Co.C
Turner, Thomas Henry Gen. & Staff Surg.
Turner, Thomas J. AL 10th Inf. Co.A
Turner, Thomas J. AR 1st (Crawford's) Cav. Co.K
Turner, Thomas J. AR 4th Inf. Co.K
Turner, Thomas J. AR 25th Inf. Co.K
Turner, Thomas J. AR Inf. Clayton's Co.
Turner, Thomas J. GA Cav. 29th Bn. Co.E
Turner, Thomas J. GA 21st Inf. Co.I
Turner, Thomas J. GA 41st Inf. Co.B
Turner, Thomas J. LA 21st (Patton's) Inf. Co.C
Turner, Thomas J. MS 13th Inf. Co.A
Turner, Thomas J. MO 10th Inf. Co.F
Turner, Thomas J. NC 13th Inf. Co.A
Turner, Thomas J. TX Cav. Giddings' Bn. Onin's Co.
Turner, Thomas J. VA 38th Inf. Co.A Capt.
Turner, Thomas J. 1st Conf.Inf. 2nd Co.F Cpl.
Turner, Thos. J. Gen. & Staff Asst.Surg.
Turner, Thos. J. Gen. & Staff 1st Lt.,ADC
Turner, Thomas J. Gen. & Staff Capt.,ACS

Turner, Thomas K. MS 11th Inf. Co.G
Turner, Thomas M. GA 3rd Cav. (St.Guards) Co.H
Turner, Thomas M. GA 6th Inf. Co.A
Turner, Thomas M. GA Inf. 9th Bn. Co.D 2nd Lt.
Turner, Thomas M. MS 48th Inf. Co.I Sgt.
Turner, Thomas M. TN 34th Inf. Co.B,E Cpl.
Turner, Thomas M. VA Horse Arty. 20th Bn. Co.A Music.
Turner, Thomas M. VA 4th Inf. Co.I
Turner, Thomas M. Gen. & Staff Lt.,ADC
Turner, Thomas N. 1st Conf.Inf. 2nd Co.F
Turner, Thomas O. FL 1st Inf. Old Co.H
Turner, Thomas O. FL 7th Inf. Co.D 1st Cpl.
Turner, Thomas P. TX 16th Cav. Co.B
Turner, Thomas P. VA Lt.Arty. Jeffress' Co.
Turner, Thos. P. Gen. & Staff Maj.
Turner, Thomas R. GA 45th Inf. Co.D Cpl.
Turner, Thomas R. TX 31st Cav. Co.A
Turner, Thomas S. LA Washington Arty.Bn. Co.1 Cpl.
Turner, Thomas S. VA Cav. 39th Bn. Co.B 1st Lt.
Turner, Thomas S. Cav. Lee's Escort Capt.
Turner, Thomas T. AL 3rd Bn. Hilliard's Legion Vol. Co.E
Turner, Thomas T. FL 7th Inf. Co.D Sgt.
Turner, Thomas T. TX 14th Cav. Co.I
Turner, Thomas T. Ewell's Staff Capt.,ADC
Turner, Thomas W. AL 47th Inf. Co.K
Turner, Thomas W. TX Cav. 6th Bn. Co.A
Turner, Thomas W. VA 17th Inf. Co.F
Turner, Thompson SC 18th Inf. Co.A
Turner, Thompson B. MS 8th Cav. Co.C 2nd Lt.
Turner, Timothy GA 4th (Clinch's) Cav. Co.G
Turner, T.J. AL 8th (Hatch's) Cav. Co.E
Turner, T.J. AR 8th Cav. Peoples' Co.
Turner, T.J. GA Lt.Arty. 12th Bn. Co.B
Turner, T.J. GA 10th Inf. Co.B
Turner, T.J. LA 1st (Nelligan's) Inf. Co.C
Turner, T.J. MS 3rd Cav.Res. Co.G
Turner, T.J. MS 5th Inf. Co.D
Turner, T.J. MO 10th Inf. Co.A
Turner, T.J. NC 2nd Inf.
Turner, T.J. SC 2nd Arty. Co.B
Turner, T.J. SC 5th Inf. 2nd Co.K
Turner, T.J. SC 6th Inf. 2nd Co.F
Turner, T.J. SC 13th Inf. Co.I,F
Turner, T.J. TN 11th (Holman's) Cav. Co.D
Turner, T.J. TN Douglass' Bn.Part.Rangers Lytle's Co.
Turner, T.K. GA 52nd Inf. Co.B
Turner, T.L. AL 18th Inf. Co.G
Turner, T.L. MS Inf. 2nd St.Troops Co.A
Turner, T.M. AR Inf. Cocke's Regt. Co.C
Turner, T.M. MS Inf. 2nd Bn. Co.I Cpl.
Turner, T.M. TN 4th (McLemore's) Cav. Co.B Cpl.
Turner, T.M. VA 14th Cav. Music.
Turner, T.N. Sig.Corps,CSA
Turner, Tobe AR 37th Inf. Co.G
Turner, Tolbert GA 45th Inf. Co.I
Turner, T.P. SC Hvy.Arty. Gilchrist's Co. (Gist Guard)
Turner, T.P. SC Arty. Manigault's Bn. Co.E
Turner, T.P. TX 33rd Cav. Co.D
Turner, T.P. VA 4th Cav. Co.G
Turner, T.P. VA 24th Cav. Co.G
Turner, T.P. VA 52nd Mil.
Turner, Truman AL Cav. Forrest's Regt.
Turner, T.T. GA Cav. 12th Bn. (St.Guards) Co.D
Turner, T.T. SC 5th St.Troops Co.D
Turner, T.W. GA 38th Inf. Co.I
Turner, U.M. VA 17th Cav. Co.K Ord.Sgt.
Turner, U.M. VA 3rd Inf.Loc.Def. Co.E 2nd Lt.
Turner, Uriel M. VA 31st Inf. Co.C Capt.
Turner, V. TN 14th (Neely's) Cav. Co.H
Turner, V.B. KY 10th (Diamond's) Cav. Co.L
Turner, V.B. TX Cav. Hardeman's Regt. Co.A
Turner, V.E. Early's Div. Capt.,AQM
Turner, Velerius VA 9th Inf. Co.C
Turner, Vines VA 56th Inf. Co.E Cpl.
Turner, Vines E. NC 23rd Inf. Co.G Capt.,AQM
Turner, Virginius B. TX 35th (Brown's) Cav. Co.D Jr.2nd Lt.
Turner, Virginius B. TX 13th Vol. 1st Co.I Cpl.
Turner, V.M. GA Tiller's Co. (Echols Lt.Arty.) Cpl.
Turner, W. AL 3rd Cav. Co.A
Turner, W. AL Arty. 1st Bn. Co.B
Turner, W. AL Mil. 2nd Regt.Vol. Co.E
Turner, W. AL 19th Inf. Co.I
Turner, W. AR Cav. Davies' Bn. Co.C
Turner, W. KY 7th Mtd.Inf. Co.C
Turner, W. SC Inf. 1st (Charleston) Bn. Co.G
Turner, W. SC 23rd Inf. Co.E
Turner, W. TN 15th (Cons.) Cav. Co.A
Turner, W. TX 24th & 25th Cav. (Cons.) Co.B
Turner, W. TX 25th Cav. Co.A
Turner, W. TX Cav. Border's Regt. Co.D
Turner, W. TX 10th Field Btty.
Turner, W. TX Inf. 1st St.Troops Whitehead's Co.
Turner, W.A. AL Gid Nelson Lt.Arty.
Turner, W.A. AL 13th Inf. Co.F
Turner, W.A. AL 14th Inf. Co.C
Turner, W.A. AL 26th (O'Neal's) Inf. Co.F
Turner, W.A. GA 2nd Cav. (St.Guards) Co.D
Turner, W.A. MS 2nd Cav. Co.F
Turner, W.A. MS 28th Cav. Co.K
Turner, W.A. MS 4th Inf. Co.F
Turner, W.A. MS 6th Inf. Co.C
Turner, W.A. MS 36th Inf. Co.D
Turner, W.A. MS 37th Inf. Co.D
Turner, W.A. SC 2nd Arty. Co.K
Turner, W.A. TN 8th (Smith's) Cav. Co.C
Turner, W.A. TN 12th Inf. Co.C
Turner, W.A. VA 4th Cav. Co.B
Turner, Waddy SC 1st Arty. Co.G
Turner, Wade 3rd Conf.Cav. Co.A
Turner, Wade A. GA 27th Inf. Co.H Lt.
Turner, Walter AR 8th Inf. New Co.I
Turner, Walter M. TX 37th Cav. Co.C Cpl.
Turner, Walter S. NC 30th Inf. Co.I Music.
Turner, Warren G. NC 6th Inf. Co.E 1st Lt.
Turner, Washington R. VA Inf. 25th Bn. Co.C
Turner, Washington R. VA 51st Inf. Co.E
Turner, W.B. AR 15th (Johnson's) Inf. Co.A
Turner, W.B. FL 2nd Cav. Co.H
Turner, W.B. GA 8th Inf. (St.Guards) Co.H Sgt.
Turner, W.B. GA 27th Inf. Co.E
Turner, W.B. TX 10th Cav. Co.C
Turner, W.B. TX 10th Cav. Co.E Sgt.
Turner, W.B. TX Cav. Hardeman's Regt. Co.A
Turner, W.B. VA Cav. Mosby's Regt. (Part. Rangers) Co.B
Turner, W.B. VA 1st (Farinholt's) Res. Co.K Sgt.
Turner, W.C. AL 48th Inf. Co.E
Turner, W.C. FL 1st (Res.) Inf. Co.K
Turner, W.C. GA 56th Inf. Co.C
Turner, W.C. LA Mil. Beauregard Bn.
Turner, W.C. MS 37th Inf. Co.D Capt.
Turner, W.C. SC 2nd Arty. Co.G
Turner, W.C. SC 1st (Hagood's) Inf. 1st Co.G
Turner, W.C. SC 22nd Inf. Co.G
Turner, W.C. SC Inf. Hampton Legion Co.K
Turner, W.C. TN 19th (Biffle's) Cav. Co.L
Turner, W.C. TX Cav. Border's Regt. Co.H
Turner, W.D. AL 32nd Inf. Co.H
Turner, W.D. GA Inf. 1st Loc.Troops (Augusta) Co.E
Turner, W.D. GA 4th Inf. Co.E
Turner, W.D. LA Inf. 4th Bn. Co.E Cpl.
Turner, W.D. LA Inf. Pelican Regt. Co.G Cpl.
Turner, W.D. MS 1st Cav. Co.I
Turner, W.D. MS 11th (Cons.) Cav. Co.G
Turner, W.D. MS 32nd Inf. Co.D Sgt.
Turner, W.D. MO 3rd Inf. Co.G
Turner, W.D. TN 10th (DeMoss') Cav. Co.E
Turner, W.D. TN Cav. Napier's Bn. Co.B
Turner, W.D. VA 2nd Cav. Co.E
Turner, W.D. VA 2nd St.Res. Co.C
Turner, W. Dallas GA Phillips' Legion Co.B
Turner, W.E. GA 2nd Inf. Co.D
Turner, W.E. MS 4th Inf. Co.H
Turner, W.E. NC 3rd Jr.Res. Co.B
Turner, W.E. NC 4th Bn.Jr.Res. Co.B
Turner, W.E. SC 6th Inf. 1st Co.H, 2nd Co.B Sgt.
Turner, W.E. SC Inf. Holcombe Legion Co.A
Turner, W.E. TN 14th (Neely's) Cav. Co.I
Turner, W.E. TN 16th (Logwood's) Cav. Co.H
Turner, W.E. TX 1st Inf. Co.E
Turner, Wesley GA Inf. 9th Bn. Co.D
Turner, Wesley TX 4th Inf. Co.G
Turner, Wesley TX 12th Inf. Co.D
Turner, Wesley C. MS 15th Inf. Co.G
Turner, Wesley G. MO 2nd Cav. Co.C
Turner, Wesley J. NC 6th Inf. Co.A
Turner, West E. AR 32nd Inf. Co.A
Turner, W.F. AL 41st Inf. Co.K
Turner, W.F. GA 2nd Cav. (St.Guards) Co.A
Turner, W.F. MS Lt.Arty. Merrin's Btty. Bugler
Turner, W.F. MO 9th Inf. Co.B
Turner, W.F. MO Inf. Clark's Regt. Co.A
Turner, W.F. SC 5th Bn.Res. Co.D
Turner, W.F. TX 25th Cav. Co.A
Turner, W.F. TX Cav. Hardeman's Regt. Co.A
Turner, W.G. AR 3rd Cav. Co.A
Turner, W.G. GA 3rd Cav. (St.Guards) Co.C
Turner, W.G. GA 10th Cav. (St.Guards) Co.K
Turner, W.G. GA 39th Inf. Co.C
Turner, W.G. GA 56th Inf. Co.F
Turner, W.G. MS 8th Cav. Co.B Sgt.
Turner, W.G. MS 8th Cav. Co.C

Turner, W.G. MS 9th Cav. Co.A
Turner, W.G. MS Cav. 17th Bn. Co.A
Turner, W.G. MS 28th Cav. Co.E 1st Sgt.
Turner, W.G. MS 3rd Inf. (St.Troops) Co.K Capt.
Turner, W.G. TN 4th (McLemore's) Cav. Co.B
Turner, W.H. AL 13th Bn.Part.Rangers Co.A
Turner, W.H. AL 1st Regt.Conscr. Co.K
Turner, W.H. AL 18th Inf. Co.F
Turner, W.H. AR 45th Cav. Co.I
Turner, W.H. AR 4th Inf. Co.I
Turner, W.H. GA Cav. 15th Bn. (St.Guards) Wooten's Co.
Turner, W.H. GA 1st (Olmstead's) Inf. Stiles' Co.
Turner, W.H. GA Inf. 2nd Bn. (St.Guards) Co.C
Turner, W.H. GA 8th Inf. Co.H
Turner, W.H. GA Inf. 9th Bn. Co.E
Turner, W.H. GA 10th Inf. Co.A
Turner, W.H. GA 10th Mil.
Turner, W.H. GA 19th Inf. Co.A
Turner, W.H. GA 37th Inf. Co.H
Turner, W.H. GA 54th Inf. Co.C 1st Sgt.
Turner, W.H. GA Cobb's Legion Co.F
Turner, W.H. LA 1st Cav. Co.I
Turner, W.H. LA 8th Cav. Co.A
Turner, W.H. MS Inf. 3rd Bn. Co.E 1st Cpl.
Turner, W.H. MS Inf. 7th Bn. Co.A 1st Sgt.
Turner, W.H. MS 34th Inf. Co.C
Turner, W.H. MO 1st N.E. Cav. Co.I
Turner, W.H. SC 6th Cav. Co.B
Turner, W.H. SC 2nd Arty. Co.E
Turner, W.H. SC 14th Inf. Co.K
Turner, W.H. TN 22nd (Barteau's) Cav. 1st Co.H
Turner, W.H. TX 34th Cav. Co.G
Turner, W.H. TX 1st Inf.
Turner, W.H. TX 5th Inf. Co.K
Turner, W.H. VA Inf. 6th Bn.Loc.Def. Co.A
Turner, W.H. Mead's Conf.Cav. Co.E
Turner, W.H.H. GA Inf. 18th Bn. Co.A,B
Turner, W.H.H. VA 2nd Inf.Loc.Def. Co.D
Turner, Whitfield AL 21st Inf. Co.K
Turner, Wiley NC 4th Sr.Res. Co.H
Turner, Wiley SC 3rd Res. Co.I
Turner, Wiley TX 10th Field Btty.
Turner, Wiley L. AL Lt.Arty. 2nd Bn. Co.E
Turner, Wiley L. AL 3rd Inf. Co.H
Turner, Wiley Redmon MS Inf. 1st Bn. Co.D
Turner, Wiley T. MS 8th Inf. Co.G
Turner, Wiley Z.T. TN Cav. Newsom's Regt. Co.G
Turner, Wilford NC 4th Inf. Co.C
Turner, Wilford D. AL 33rd Inf. Co.C
Turner, Wilford D. TN 33rd Inf. Co.C
Turner, Wilham AL 7th Cav. Co.K
Turner, William AL 15th Bn.Part.Rangers Co.D
Turner, William AL 53rd (Part.Rangers) Co.E
Turner, William AL 56th Part.Rangers Co.D
Turner, William AL Cav. Hardie's Bn.Res. Co.B
Turner, William AL 1st Regt. Mobile Vol. Butt's Co.
Turner, William AL Mil. 2nd Regt.Vol. Co.F Cpl.
Turner, William AL Mil. 4th Vol. Co.K
Turner, William AL 15th Inf. Co.C
Turner, William AL 17th Inf. Co.A
Turner, William AL 21st Inf. Co.E
Turner, William AL 23rd Inf. Co.H
Turner, William AL 30th Inf. Co.E
Turner, William AL 46th Inf. Co.G
Turner, William AL 55th Vol. Co.A
Turner, William AL Cp. of Instr. Talladega
Turner, William AR 1st Mtd.Rifles Co.A
Turner, William AR Cav. Gordon's Regt. Co.K
Turner, Wm. AR 4th St.Inf. Co.E 2nd Lt.
Turner, William AR 32nd Inf. Co.C
Turner, William AR 37th Inf. Co.G
Turner, William FL Cav. 3rd Bn. Co.D
Turner, William FL Lt.Arty. Dyke's Co.
Turner, William FL 1st (Res.) Inf. Co.K
Turner, William GA Siege Arty. 28th Bn. Co.A
Turner, William GA 2nd Res. Co.G
Turner, William GA 9th Inf. Co.E
Turner, William GA 12th Inf. Co.F
Turner, William GA 17th Inf. Co.E
Turner, Wm. GA 28th Inf. Co.A
Turner, William GA 29th Inf. Co.A
Turner, William GA 46th Inf. Music.
Turner, William GA Smith's Legion Co.D
Turner, William KY 11th Cav. Co.B
Turner, William KY 3rd Mtd.Inf. Co.B
Turner, William KY 4th Mtd.Inf. Co.C
Turner, William LA 3rd (Wingfield's) Cav. Co.K Capt.
Turner, William LA 8th Cav. Co.A
Turner, William LA 2nd Inf. Co.G
Turner, William LA 8th Inf. Co.G
Turner, William LA 9th Inf. Co.I 1st Lt.
Turner, William LA 10th Inf. Co.H
Turner, William MS 1st Cav.Res. Co.H
Turner, William MS 3rd Cav.
Turner, William MS Cav. 3rd Bn.Res. Co.E
Turner, William MS 7th Cav. Co.G,A
Turner, William MS 9th Cav. Co.D
Turner, William MS Cav. 17th Bn. Co.F
Turner, William MS 18th Cav. Co.B
Turner, William MS 18th Cav. Co.E
Turner, William MS 29th Inf. Co.F
Turner, William MS 32nd Inf. Co.A
Turner, William MS 44th Inf. Co.G
Turner, William MO Cav. Fristoe's Regt. Co.G
Turner, William MO 1st Inf. Co.C
Turner, William MO 2nd Inf. Co.B
Turner, William MO Inf. 8th Bn. Co.F
Turner, William NC 6th Cav. (65th St.Troops) Co.G
Turner, William NC 7th Sr.Res. Bradshaw's Co.
Turner, William NC 12th Inf. Co.M
Turner, William NC 13th Inf. Co.D
Turner, William NC 15th Inf. Co.C
Turner, William NC 21st Inf. Co.L
Turner, William NC 32nd Inf. Co.B,A
Turner, William NC 33rd Inf. Co.F
Turner, William NC 37th Inf. Co.I
Turner, William NC 44th Inf. Co.B
Turner, William NC 56th Inf. Co.D 2nd Lt.
Turner, William NC Loc.Def. Croom's Co.
Turner, William NC Home Guards Co.A
Turner, William SC Arty. Manigault's Bn. 1st Co.B,C
Turner, William SC 2nd Arty. Co.E
Turner, William SC 1st (Orr's) Rifles Co.L
Turner, William SC 1st Bn.S.S. Co.C
Turner, William SC 2nd St.Troops Co.K
Turner, William SC 3rd Res. Co.F
Turner, William SC 4th St.Troops Ch.Music.
Turner, William SC 7th Inf. 2nd Co.G
Turner, William SC 8th Bn.Res. Co.C
Turner, William SC 18th Inf. Co.E
Turner, William SC 20th Inf. Co.A, Arty.Co.
Turner, William SC 20th Inf. Co.A
Turner, William SC 24th Inf. Co.B
Turner, William SC 27th Inf. Co.K
Turner, William SC Post Guard Senn's Co.
Turner, William SC Inf. Holcombe Legion Co.I
Turner, William TN 9th (Ward's) Cav. Co.C
Turner, William TN 15th (Cons.) Cav. Co.K
Turner, William TN 19th & 20th (Cons.) Cav. Co.B
Turner, William TN Arty. Marshall's Co.
Turner, William TN Lt.Arty. Scott's Co.
Turner, William TN Lt.Arty. Weller's Co. Cpl.
Turner, William TN Inf. 1st Cons.Regt. Co.G
Turner, William TN Inf. 1st Bn. (Colms') Co.C
Turner, William TN 3rd (Lillard's) Mtd.Inf. Co.D
Turner, William TN 25th Inf. Co.E Capt.
Turner, William TN 26th Inf. Co.K
Turner, William TN 28th (Cons.) Inf. Co.I
Turner, William TN Inf. 154th Sr.Regt. Co.I
Turner, William TX 7th Cav. Co.K Cpl.
Turner, William TX Trevino's Squad.Part. Mtd.Vol. 1st Sgt.
Turner, William TX 5th Inf. Co.D
Turner, William TX 13th Vol. 2nd Co.B,H Cpl.
Turner, William TX Loc.Def.Troops Merriman's Co. (Orange Cty.Coast Guards)
Turner, William VA Cav. 1st Bn. (Loc.Def. Troops) Co.B Sgt.
Turner, William VA 7th Cav. Co.A Capt.
Turner, William VA 11th Cav. Co.A
Turner, William VA 15th Cav.
Turner, William VA 25th Cav. Co.F
Turner, William VA Cav. 35th Bn. Co.C
Turner, William VA Lt.Arty. Brander's Co.
Turner, William VA Inf. 1st Bn.Loc.Def. Co.E
Turner, William VA Inf. 2nd Bn.Loc.Def. Co.A
Turner, William VA 3rd Inf.Loc.Def. Co.K
Turner, William VA 12th Inf. Co.D
Turner, William VA Inf. 23rd Bn. Co.A
Turner, William VA 24th Inf. Co.H
Turner, William VA 25th Inf. 1st Co.E
Turner, William VA 26th Inf. Co.D
Turner, William VA 30th Inf. Co.E
Turner, William VA 57th Inf. Co.B
Turner, William VA 61st Inf. Co.G
Turner, William VA 166th Mil. Taylor's Co. Cpl.
Turner, William VA Prov.Guard Avis' Co.
Turner, William 1st Conf.Cav. 2nd Co.G
Turner, William 15th Conf.Cav. Co.I
Turner, William 2nd Conf.Inf. Co.D
Turner, William Conf.Reg.Inf. Brooks' Bn. Co.B
Turner, William A. AL Arty. 1st Bn. Co.D,E
Turner, William A. AL Cav. 5th Bn. Hilliard's Legion Co.C
Turner, William A. FL 6th Inf. Co.H
Turner, William A. GA 7th Inf. Co.C 1st Lt.
Turner, William A. GA 30th Inf. Co.B
Turner, William A. KY 4th Cav. Co.E

Turner, William A. MS 8th Cav. Co.C
Turner, William A. MS 1st Lt.Arty. Co.E
Turner, William A. MS 14th Inf. Co.B Cpl.
Turner, William A. MS 15th Inf. Co.G
Turner, William A. MS 40th Inf. Co.E
Turner, William A. MO 3rd Cav. Co.G 1st Lt.
Turner, William A. NC 34th Inf. Co.F
Turner, William A. TX 6th Cav. Co.G Cpl.
Turner, William A. VA Hvy.Arty. 19th Bn. Co.A
Turner, William A. VA Lt.Arty. W.P. Carter's Co. Sgt.
Turner, William A. VA Hvy.Arty. Kyle's Co.
Turner, William A. VA 9th Inf. Co.C
Turner, William A. VA Inf. 26th Bn. Co.F
Turner, William A. VA 58th Inf. Co.K
Turner, William A. VA 59th Inf. 3rd Co.I
Turner, William A. 10th Conf.Cav. Co.C
Turner, William A. 1st Choctaw & Chickasaw Mtd.Rifles 1st Co.K
Turner, William B. AR 35th Inf. Co.H
Turner, William B. GA 2nd Res. Co.K Cpl.
Turner, William B. GA Inf. 11th Bn. (St.Guards) Co.B
Turner, William B. MS Lt.Arty. Turner's Co. Capt.
Turner, William B. TX 31st Cav. Co.A
Turner, William B. TX 1st Hvy.Arty. Co.G
Turner, William B. VA 17th Inf. Co.B
Turner, William B. VA 20th Inf. Co.K
Turner, William B. VA 23rd Inf. Co.E
Turner, William B. VA Inf. 23rd Bn. Co.F
Turner, William B. VA 24th Inf. Co.B Sgt.
Turner, William B. 1st Conf.Inf. 2nd Co.E
Turner, William B. 1st Conf.Inf. 2nd Co.F
Turner, William Butler TX 20th Cav. Co.D
Turner, William C. GA 7th Inf. Co.I
Turner, William C. GA 21st Inf. New Co.E
Turner, William C. MS 1st (Patton's) Inf. Co.A
Turner, William C. MS 5th Inf. Co.F
Turner, William C. MS 41st Inf. Co.F Cpl.
Turner, William C. MO 15th Cav. Co.B
Turner, William C. NC Cav. 14th Bn. Sgt.
Turner, William C. NC Inf. 2nd Bn. Co.D
Turner, William C. TX Cav. Mann's Bn. Cox's Co.
Turner, William D. AR 17th (Lemoyne's) Inf. Co.C Cpl.
Turner, William D. AR 21st Inf. Co.C
Turner, William D. MS 9th Inf. Old Co.A
Turner, William D. MS 15th (Cons.) Inf. Co.K
Turner, William D. MS 22nd Inf. Co.D Sgt.
Turner, William D. NC 4th Cav. (59th St.Troops) Co.E
Turner, William D. VA 2nd Cav. Co.E
Turner, William D. VA Lt.Arty. Fry's Co. Sgt.
Turner, William D. VA Lt.Arty. Turner's Co. Cpl.
Turner, William D. VA 57th Inf. Co.B 1st Sgt.
Turner, William D. VA Arty. Wise Legion Cpl.
Turner, William D. 1st Conf.Inf. 2nd Co.G Cpl.
Turner, William E. AL 7th Cav. Co.E
Turner, William E. GA Inf. (Jones Hussars) Jones' Co.
Turner, William E. MS 2nd Inf. Co.A Cpl.
Turner, William E. NC 22nd Inf. Co.G
Turner, William E. SC 1st (Orr's) Rifles Co.H
Turner, William E. VA 18th Inf. Co.B
Turner, William F. AL 43rd Inf. Co.A
Turner, William F. GA 4th Res. Co.A 3rd Lt.
Turner, William F. MS 9th Inf. Old Co.A
Turner, William F. NC 7th Inf. Co.F
Turner, William F. VA Cav. 7th Regt. Co.A Capt.
Turner, William G. GA 27th Inf. Co.H
Turner, William G. TX 3rd Regt.Res.Corps Co.C Lt.
Turner, William G. VA 14th Cav. Co.G, 2nd Co.F
Turner, William H. AL 3rd Inf. Co.H
Turner, William H. AL 37th Inf. Co.H
Turner, Wm. H. AL 54th Inf. Co.G
Turner, William H. AR 1st (Crawford's) Cav. Co.E
Turner, William H. AR 20th Inf. Co.A 1st Lt.
Turner, William H. GA 2nd Bn.S.S. Co.E
Turner, William H. GA 7th Inf. Co.D Sgt.
Turner, William H. GA 13th Inf. Co.F
Turner, William H. GA Inf. 25th Bn. (Prov. Guard) Co.A
Turner, William H. GA 36th (Villepigue's) Inf. Co.D
Turner, William H. MS 12th Inf. Co.K
Turner, William H. MS 16th Inf. Co.B
Turner, William H. MS 16th Inf. Co.F
Turner, William H. MS 30th Inf. Co.H
Turner, William H. MS 40th Inf. Co.C
Turner, William H. MO 1st Cav. Co.G
Turner, William H. NC 31st Inf. Co.D
Turner, William H. NC 34th Inf. Co.F
Turner, William H. NC 56th Inf. Co.E Cpl.
Turner, William H. TX 22nd Cav. Co.E
Turner, William H. TX 9th (Young's) Inf. Co.I
Turner, William H. VA Cav. Mosby's Regt. (Part.Rangers) Co.B
Turner, William H. VA Lt.Arty. Hankins' Co.
Turner, William H. VA Lt.Arty. Turner's Co. Capt.
Turner, William H. VA Arty. Wise Legion 1st Lt.
Turner, William H. VA 24th Inf. Co.G
Turner, William H. Conf.Inf. 1st Bn. 2nd Co.A
Turner, William H. 1st Cherokee Mtd.Vol. 2nd Co.F 1st Lt.
Turner, William H.H. VA 10th Cav. Co.D
Turner, William I. NC 21st Inf. Co.L
Turner, William J. AR 1st (Colquitt's) Inf. Co.H
Turner, William J. AR 17th (Lemoyne's) Inf. Co.D
Turner, William J. AR 21st Inf. Co.H
Turner, William J. AR 25th Inf. Co.K
Turner, William J. FL 1st (Res.) Inf. Co.C 2nd Lt.
Turner, William J. FL 8th Inf. Co.K Capt.
Turner, William J. GA Lt.Arty. Hamilton's Co.
Turner, William J. GA Lt.Arty. Milledge's Co.
Turner, William J. GA 1st Reg. Co.A Music.
Turner, William J. GA 2nd Inf. Co.E
Turner, William J. GA 35th Inf. Co.B
Turner, William J. GA 38th Inf. Co.B
Turner, William J. GA 42nd Inf. Co.K
Turner, William J. GA Inf. (Muscogee Guards) Thornton's Co.
Turner, William J. KY 4th Cav. Co.D Sgt.
Turner, William J. KY 4th Cav. Co.I 2nd Lt.
Turner, William J. KY Horse Arty. Byrne's Co.
Turner, William J. LA Inf. 11th Bn. Co.C
Turner, William J. NC 2nd Arty. (36th St.Troops) Co.H
Turner, William J. SC 6th Cav. Co.B
Turner, William J. SC Horse Arty. (Washington Arty.) Vol. Hart's Co.
Turner, William J. SC Inf. 3rd Bn. Co.F
Turner, William J. SC 7th Res. Co.M
Turner, William J. TN 1st (Feild's) Inf. Co.G
Turner, William J. VA 23rd Inf. Co.E
Turner, William J. VA 53rd Inf. Co.D Capt.
Turner, William J. VA 57th Inf. Co.F
Turner, William K. MS 30th Inf. Co.A
Turner, William L. LA 1st (Nelligan's) Inf. Howell's Co. 1st Sgt.
Turner, William L. MD Inf. 2nd Bn. Co.B
Turner, William L. NC 7th Inf. Co.F
Turner, William L. SC 18th Inf. Co.A Sgt.
Turner, William L. VA 9th Inf. Co.E Sgt.
Turner, William L. VA 57th Inf. Co.G
Turner, William Lewis TX 20th Cav. Co.C Capt.
Turner, William M. AL 4th Inf. Co.D
Turner, William M. GA 1st Bn.S.S.
Turner, William M. GA Inf. 8th Bn. Co.G
Turner, William M. GA 12th Inf. Co.E
Turner, William M. GA 65th Inf. Co.C
Turner, William M. MS 8th Cav. Co.K,C
Turner, William M. MS 27th Inf. Co.F Cpl.
Turner, William M. MS 31st Inf. Co.D
Turner, William M. NC 24th Inf. Co.C
Turner, William M. NC 47th Inf. Co.A
Turner, William M. NC Walker's Bn. Thomas' Legion Co.E
Turner, William M. VA 3rd Inf. Co.E
Turner, William M. VA 17th Inf.
Turner, William M. 1st Conf.Inf. 2nd Co.H
Turner, Wm. M. Gen. & Staff, Medical Dept. Asst.Surg.
Turner, William N. GA Siege Arty. 28th Bn. Co.D
Turner, William P. AL 3rd Res. Co.D
Turner, William P. AL 10th Inf. Co.I
Turner, Wm. P. AL 16th Inf. Co.C
Turner, Wm. P. GA 37th Inf. Co.G Cpl.
Turner, William P. MS Inf. 2nd Bn. Co.A,F
Turner, William P. MS 35th Inf. Co.B
Turner, William P. MS 48th Inf. Co.A,F
Turner, William P. NC Inf. Thomas Legion Co.G
Turner, William P. TX 13th Cav. Co.B
Turner, William P. TX Cav. Baylor's Regt. Co.E
Turner, William P. VA 26th Inf. 1st Co.B
Turner, William P. Gillum's Regt. Whitaker's Co.
Turner, William R. AL 22nd Inf. Co.H
Turner, William R. AL Vol. Rabby's Coast Guard Co. No.1
Turner, William R. GA 49th Inf. Co.F
Turner, William R. GA 64th Inf. Co.D
Turner, William R. VA 2nd Inf. Co.E,C
Turner, William R. VA 19th Inf. Co.H
Turner, William R. Sig.Corps,CSA
Turner, William S. AL 4th Inf. Co.I
Turner, William S. AR 33rd Inf. Co.B
Turner, William S. GA 17th Inf. Co.K

Turner, William S. LA 28th (Gray's) Inf. Co.G 1st Lt.
Turner, William S. MS 27th Inf. Co.C
Turner, William S. MO Cav. 1st Regt.St.Guard Co.C
Turner, William S. NC 11th (Bethel Regt.) Inf. Co.E 1st Lt.
Turner, William S. NC 53rd Inf. Co.C
Turner, Wm. S. Gen. & Staff 1st Lt.,Adj.
Turner, William T. AL 4th Inf. Co.D 1st Lt.
Turner, William T. GA 27th Inf. Co.E
Turner, William T. KY 7th Cav. Co.D
Turner, William T. SC 19th Inf. Co.K Cpl.
Turner, William T. TX 14th Cav. Co.I Cpl.
Turner, William T. VA 8th Cav. Co.B
Turner, William T. VA Cav. Mosby's Regt. (Part.Rangers) Co.A 1st Lt.
Turner, William T. VA 15th Inf. Co.B
Turner, William T. VA 30th Inf. Co.E
Turner, William V. VA 3rd Inf. Co.D
Turner, William W. GA 12th (Robinson's) Cav. (St.Guards) Co.E Cpl.
Turner, William W. GA 3rd Inf. Co.B Adj.
Turner, William W. GA 4th Inf. Co.B
Turner, William W. GA 5th Inf. Co.E
Turner, William W. GA 41st Inf. Co.E Sgt.
Turner, William W. GA 41st Inf. Co.H Cpl.
Turner, William W. GA Inf. Athens Reserved Corps
Turner, William W. SC 2nd Inf. Co.E
Turner, William W. TX Cav. Martin's Regt. Co.I
Turner, William W. TX Inf. Griffin's Bn. Co.A
Turner, William W. VA 22nd Cav. Co.K
Turner, William W. VA Cav. 39th Bn. Co.C
Turner, William W. VA Cav. 46th Bn. Co.B Sgt.
Turner, William W. VA Cav. Mosby's Regt. (Part.Rangers) Co.H
Turner, William W. VA Hvy.Arty. A.J. Jones' Co.
Turner, William W. VA Horse Arty. Shoemaker's Co.
Turner, William W. VA 1st Inf. Co.D
Turner, William W. VA 38th Inf. Co.C 1st Sgt.
Turner, William Y. TN Cav. 2nd Bn. (Biffle's) Co.F
Turner, Willis TN 24th Inf. Co.I Cpl.
Turner, Willis Wheeler's Scouts,CSA
Turner, Willis W. VA 38th Inf. Co.K
Turner, Wilson VA 21st Cav. 1st Co.E
Turner, Wilson VA 54th Inf. Co.F
Turner, Wilson VA 72nd Mil.
Turner, Wilson T. VA 58th Inf. Co.D
Turner, Winguit H. GA 5th Inf. Co.E
Turner, W.J. AL 58th Inf. Co.I
Turner, W.J. AR 1st Mtd.Rifles Co.K
Turner, W.J. AR 18th Inf. Co.G 1st Lt.
Turner, W.J. AR 24th Inf. Co.D Cpl.
Turner, W.J. AR Inf. Cocke's Regt. Co.K Cpl.
Turner, W.J. GA Inf. 1st Loc.Troops (Augusta) Co.F
Turner, W.J. LA Inf.Cons.Crescent Regt. Co.F Sgt.
Turner, W.J. MS Inf. 1st Bn.St.Troops (30 days '64) Co.G
Turner, W.J. MO St.Guard 2nd Lt.
Turner, W.J. TN Cav. Williams' Co. Sgt.
Turner, W.J. TX 25th Cav. Co.D
Turner, W.J. TX 28th Cav. Co.G
Turner, W.J.F. TN Lt.Arty. McClung's Co. Bugler
Turner, W.K. MS 24th Inf. Co.B
Turner, W.L. AL 7th Cav. Co.D
Turner, W.L. AL 34th Inf. Co.A
Turner, W.L. GA 40th Inf. Co.E
Turner, W.L. GA Inf. 40th Bn. Co.F
Turner, W.L. SC 2nd Cav. Co.G
Turner, W.L. SC 5th Inf. 1st Co.A
Turner, W.L. TN 8th (Smith's) Cav. Co.D
Turner, W.L. TX Inf. Timmons' Regt. Co.F
Turner, W.L. 1st Conf.Cav. 1st Co.H
Turner, W.L. Gen. & Staff Capt.,AIG
Turner, W.M. AL Arty. 1st Bn. Co.D
Turner, W.M. AL 1st Bn.Cadets Co.D
Turner, W.M. MS 6th Cav. Co.E
Turner, W.M. SC Cav. 4th Bn. Co.A
Turner, W.M. SC 16th Inf. Co.C
Turner, W.M. TN 50th Inf. Co.K
Turner, W.M.C. AR 45th Cav. Co.I
Turner, W.M.P. TN 1st (Carter's) Cav. Co.K
Turner, W.N. AR 24th Inf. Co.E
Turner, W.N. GA 35th Inf. Co.I
Turner, W.N. KY 9th Cav. Co.C
Turner, W.N. SC Cav. 4th Bn. Co.A
Turner, W.N. SC 1st St.Troops Co.H
Turner, W.P. AR Inf. Hardy's Regt. Co.I
Turner, W.P. GA 11th Cav. Co.E
Turner, W.P. GA Inf. 9th Bn. Co.D
Turner, W.P. GA Inf. (GA Defend.) Chapman's Co.
Turner, W.P. MS Cav. 24th Bn. Co.D
Turner, W.P. MS Cav. Hughes' Bn. Co.C
Turner, W.P. NC 4th Cav. (59th St.Troops) Co.A
Turner, W.P. NC 23rd Inf. Co.A
Turner, W.P. SC 1st Arty. Co.F Cpl.
Turner, W.P. SC 3rd Res. Co.G
Turner, W.P. TN 23rd Inf. Co.D
Turner, W.P. VA 5th Cav. Co.D
Turner, W.P. 2nd Conf.Eng.Troops Co.D
Turner, W.P.H. VA 17th Inf. Co.A
Turner, W.R. AL 27th Inf. Co.A
Turner, W.R. AR 30th Inf. Co.H
Turner, W.R. KY 12th Cav. Co.B
Turner, W.R. MS Inf. 3rd Bn. Co.I
Turner, W.R. MS 6th Inf. Co.C
Turner, W.R. MS 10th Inf. New Co.K
Turner, W.R. TN 10th (DeMoss') Cav. Co.G
Turner, W.R. TX 12th Inf. Co.E 1st Lt.
Turner, W.R. VA 3rd Res. Co.A
Turner, W.R.B. LA 4th Inf. Co.D
Turner, W.S. AL 1st Cav. Co.G
Turner, W.S. AL 18th Inf. Co.F
Turner, W.S. AR 1st (Dobbin's) Cav. Co.K
Turner, W.S. FL Cav. 3rd Bn. Co.B
Turner, W.S. MS Part.Rangers Armistead's Co.
Turner, W.S. MS 4th Inf. Co.H
Turner, W.S. MS 39th Inf. Co.I Sgt.
Turner, W.S. MO 2nd & 6th Cons.Inf. Co.A
Turner, W.S. SC 6th Inf. 1st Co.A, 2nd Co.F
Turner, W.S. SC 23rd Inf. Co.E
Turner, W.S. TX 14th Inf. Co.F
Turner, W.T. AL Cav. 24th Bn. Co.A
Turner, W.T. AL Mil. 2nd Regt.Vol. Co.C Cpl.
Turner, W.T. AL 28th Inf. Co.H
Turner, W.T. AL 33rd Inf. Co.H
Turner, W.T. GA 8th Inf. (St.Guards) Co.K Cpl.
Turner, W.T. KY 5th Mtd.Inf. Co.A
Turner, W.T. MS 2nd Cav.Res. Co.I
Turner, W.T. NC 1st Arty. (10th St.Troops) Co.F
Turner, W.T. SC Hvy.Arty. Mathewes' Co.
Turner, W.T. TX 2nd Inf. Co.D
Turner, W.T. TX 2nd Inf. Co.E
Turner, W.T. Gen. & Staff Hosp.Stew.
Turner, W.V. TN 50th Inf. Co.B Asst.Surg.
Turner, W.W. AL 4th (Russell's) Cav. Co.A
Turner, W.W. AR 2nd Inf. Co.H
Turner, W.W. FL 2nd Cav. Co.K
Turner, W.W. GA Cav. 15th Bn. (St.Guards) Wooten's Co.
Turner, W.W. GA Arty. St.Troops Pruden's Btty.
Turner, W.W. MS 21st Inf. Co.C
Turner, W.W. NC Mallett's Bn. (Cp.Guard) Co.D
Turner, W.W. SC 8th Inf. Co.C
Turner, W.W. TN 13th Inf. Co.H
Turner, W.W. TX 10th Cav. Co.D Ord.Sgt.
Turner, W.W. TX Cav. Giddings' Bn. Carrington's Co.
Turner, W.W. VA Hvy.Arty. 18th Bn. Co.E
Turner, W.W. VA Loc.Def. Durrett's Co.
Turner, W.W. 4th Conf.Eng.Troops Co.I
Turner, W.Y. TN 6th (Wheeler's) Cav. Co.B
Turner, Wythe R. VA Lt.Arty. Hardwicke's Co. Sgt.
Turner, Y.B. TN 7th (Duckworth's) Cav. Co.I
Turner, Y.D. TN 1st Hvy.Arty. 1st Co.C, 2nd Co.A
Turner, Z. MS 22nd Inf. Co.H
Turner, Zebulon K.D. VA 3rd Inf. Co.G Sgt.
Turner, Z.T. VA 5th Bn.Res. Co.A Sgt.
Turney, A.A. AR 36th Inf. Co.D
Turney, A.C. AR 27th Inf. Co.F
Turney, A.D. MS 18th Cav. Co.H
Turney, A.D. MS 28th Cav. Co.F
Turney, A.D. MS 1st Bn.S.S. Co.A
Turney, A.D. MS 25th Inf. Co.I
Turney, Albert TN 1st (Turney's) Inf. Co.K
Turney, Albert G. TX 17th Cav. Co.K 1st Lt.
Turney, Boman AR 14th (Powers') Inf. Co.K
Turney, Bowman AR 18th (Marmaduke's) Inf. Co.I
Turney, D. TX 33rd Cav. Co.G
Turney, Daniel E. KY 2nd Mtd.Inf. Co.G,I 1st Lt.
Turney, Daniel H. TX 3rd Cav. Co.C
Turney, E.D. AL 1st Cav. 1st Co.C
Turney, E.D. AL 5th Cav. Co.L
Turney, George AR 14th (Powers') Inf. Co.K
Turney, George MO Cav. Jackman's Regt. Co.G
Turney, George TN Lt.Arty. Phillips' Co.
Turney, G.H. TX 9th (Nichols') Inf. Co.B
Turney, G.H. TX 18th Inf. Co.K
Turney, G.W. AR 16th Inf. Co.D
Turney, Henry AL 5th Cav. Co.G
Turney, Henry KY 9th Cav. Co.C
Turney, Henry KY 2nd Mtd.Inf.
Turney, Henry L. TN 1st (Turney's) Inf. Co.K

Turney, H.L. Gen. & Staff Hosp.Stew.
Turney, H.L.W. TN Cav. 1st Bn. (McNairy's) Co.E
Turney, H.L.W. TN 22nd (Barteau's) Cav. Co.C 1st Lt.
Turney, Hopkins L. TN 1st (Turney's) Inf. Co.C,I
Turney, I.G. 2nd Conf.Inf. Co.I
Turney, I.R. 2nd Conf.Inf. Co.I
Turney, Isaac MS 1st (King's) Inf. (St.Troops) Co.D
Turney, J. TX 15th Inf. Co.B
Turney, Jacob B. TN 1st (Turney's) Inf. Co.K Capt.
Turney, James TN 1st (Turney's) Inf. Co.K
Turney, James M. TN Cav. Allison's Squad. Co.A
Turney, J.B. AR Cav. Harrell's Bn. Co.G Capt.
Turney, J.B.R. AR 18th (Marmaduke's) Inf. Co.I
Turney, J.C. TX 15th Inf. 1st Co.E, Co.B
Turney, J.F. AL 12th Cav. Co.E
Turney, J.H. MS 28th Cav. Co.F
Turney, J.M. GA 38th Inf. Co.H
Turney, Joel T. TN 1st (Turney's) Inf. Co.K
Turney, John SC 5th Inf. 1st Co.B, 2nd Co.F
Turney, John C. AR 14th (Powers') Inf. Co.K
Turney, John F. AL 12th Inf. Co.H
Turney, John W. AR 10th Inf. Co.G Cpl.
Turney, Joseph AR 10th Inf. Co.C
Turney, Joseph D. TX Inf. Yarbrough's Co. (Smith Cty.Lt.Inf.)
Turney, Josiah S. AR 14th (Powers') Inf. Co.K
Turney, J.R. MS 25th Inf. Co.I
Turney, J.S. AR Lt.Arty. Zimmerman's Btty.
Turney, J.W. AL 12th Cav. Co.E
Turney, M. TX Cav. Baird's Regt. Co.G
Turney, Miller TN 1st (Turney's) Inf. Co.C Capt.
Turney, Miller Gen. & Staff Capt.,AQM
Turney, N.S TX 15th Inf. 1st Co.E, Co.B
Turney, P.B.R. 3rd Conf.Inf. Co.A Cpl.
Turney, Peter TN 1st (Turney's) Inf. Col.
Turney, P.G. AR 10th (Witt's) Cav. Co.G
Turney, P.G. AR 10th Inf. Co.A
Turney, Richard LA 21st (Kennedy's) Inf. Co.C
Turney, Richard TX Cav. Baird's Regt. Co.G
Turney, Russell AR 10th Inf. Co.A
Turney, S.W. AR Cav. Harrell's Bn. Co.D
Turney, Thomas FL 2nd Inf. Co.G
Turney, Thomas TN 7th (Duckworth's) Cav. Co.E
Turney, Thomas TN 60th Mtd.Inf. Co.I
Turney, T.P. 3rd Conf.Inf. Co.E
Turney, Vincent M. VA 45th Inf. Co.E
Turney, W.A. AR 10th Inf. Co.A
Turney, W.H. MO Cav. Woodson's Co.
Turney, William TX 6th Cav. Co.A
Turney, William TX 37th Cav. Co.A
Turney, William A. AR 10th Inf. Co.E
Turney, William T. FL 2nd Inf. Co.G Cpl.
Turney, W.I. AR Cav. Harrell's Bn. Co.D
Turney, W.J. AR 16th Inf. Co.D 1st Sgt.
Turney, W.J. SC 2nd Cav. Co.G
Turney, W.J. SC 2nd Rifles Co.A
Turnham, J.C. AL 21st Inf. Co.G
Turnham, Joseph C. AL 1st Regt.Conscr. Co.A
Turnham, Joseph C. AL Conscr. Echols' Co.
Turnham, R.C. TX 5th Inf. Co.G
Turnham, R.P. TX Cav. Border's Regt. Co.D
Turnham, Thomas J. AL Inf. Co.C
Turnham, T.J. AL 2nd Bn. Hilliard's Legion Vol. Co.F
Turnham, W.H. AR 34th Inf. Co.G
Turnhill, E.C. AL Hvy.Arty. 1st Bn. Co.E
Turnill, J. AL 4th Cav. Co.H
Turnipseed, Andrew J. AL 6th Cav. Co.F
Turnipseed, C. Bookster AL 24th Inf. Co.C,A
Turnipseed, C.P. MS 1st (Percy's) Inf. Co.F Capt.
Turnipseed, C.P. MS 33rd Inf. Co.E Ord.Sgt.
Turnipseed, D.B. MS 36th Inf. Co.K
Turnipseed, D.C. AL 1st Bn.Cadets Co.A
Turnipseed, E. FL 7th Inf. Co.H
Turnipseed, E. SC 12th Inf. Surg.
Turnipseed, E.B. Gen. & Staff Surg.
Turnipseed, Edward SC Inf. 7th Bn. (Enfield Rifles) Co.C
Turnipseed, Emanuel A. FL 9th Inf. Co.G 1st Sgt.
Turnipseed, F. Adam GA 2nd Res. Co.B
Turnipseed, F.B. AL 2nd Cav. Co.D
Turnipseed, Fielcher H. GA Inf. 2nd Bn. Co.D
Turnipseed, George S. MS 5th Inf. Co.D
Turnipseed, G.M. MS 33rd Inf. Co.K
Turnipseed, G.S. AL Lt.Arty. Clanton's Btty.
Turnipseed, G.W. GA 2nd Cav. Co.F
Turnipseed, Harmon W. GA 1st (Ramsey's) Inf. Co.A
Turnipseed, Harmon W. GA 53rd Inf. Co.G Sgt.
Turnipseed, Harris W. MS 33rd Inf. Co.E
Turnipseed, Henry W. MS 16th Inf. Co.H
Turnipseed, H.W. MS 1st (Percy's) Inf. Co.F
Turnipseed, H.W. MS 22nd Inf. Co.G
Turnipseed, J.A. AL 19th Inf. Co.D Cpl.
Turnipseed, Jacob W. GA Inf. 2nd Bn. Co.D
Turnipseed, James A. AL 11th Inf. Co.H
Turnipseed, James A. AL 40th Inf. Co.G
Turnipseed, J.B. MS 5th Cav. Co.D
Turnipseed, J.B. MS 5th Inf. Co.D
Turnipseed, J.D. AL Lt.Arty. Clanton's Btty.
Turnipseed, Jesse C. GA 44th Inf. Co.A
Turnipseed, J.O. SC 3rd Inf. Co.E
Turnipseed, John AL Cav. 24th Bn. Co.C
Turnipseed, John AL 1st Bn. Hilliard's Legion Vol. Co.G Sgt.
Turnipseed, John A. AL 40th Inf. Co.G Sgt.
Turnipseed, John A.F. GA 19th Inf. Co.D
Turnipseed, John H. MS 33rd Inf. Co.K
Turnipseed, John M. MS 5th Inf. Co.D Sgt.
Turnipseed, John T. AL Lt.Arty. Clanton's Btty.
Turnipseed, John W. AL 11th Inf. Co.H
Turnipseed, John W. GA 44th Inf. Co.A
Turnipseed, J.T. GA 9th Inf. Co.G
Turnipseed, J.U. SC 12th Inf. Co.D
Turnipseed, J.W. SC 12th Inf. Co.F
Turnipseed, Nathaniel C. GA 44th Inf. Co.A
Turnipseed, R.A. GA 9th Inf. Co.D Col.
Turnipseed, Richard A. GA Inf. Cobb Guards Co.B Capt.
Turnipseed, R.W. GA Hvy.Arty. 22nd Bn. Co.A
Turnipseed, T.H. AL 40th Inf. Co.G
Turnipseed, T.L. MS 3rd (St.Troops) Cav. Co.K
Turnipseed, W.F. MS Inf. Lewis' Co.
Turnipseed, William W. GA Inf. 2nd Bn. Co.D
Turnipseed, W.O. AL 51st (Part.Rangers) Co.A
Turnipseed, Z.F. GA 53rd Inf. Co.G
Turnish, H.S. GA Cav. 29th Bn.
Turnlaw, J.A. TN 24th Inf. Co.I
Turnley, George Isbell AL 10th Inf. Co.G
Turnley, G.W. TN Inf. 154th Sr.Regt. 2nd Co.B
Turnley, I.T. LA 28th (Gray's) Inf. Co.B
Turnley, James W. VA Courtney Arty.
Turnley, Joseph TN 39th Mtd.Inf. Co.E
Turnley, J.W. AL 9th Inf. Co.D Sgt.
Turnley, J.W. AR 6th Inf. Co.K Sgt.
Turnley, Luther W. VA Inf. 5th Bn.Loc.Def.
Turnley, N.G. Gen. & Staff Hosp.Stew.
Turnley, P.L. GA Floyd Legion (St.Guards) Co.A 1st Sgt.
Turnley, W.H. LA 8th Cav. Co.F
Turnley, William F. VA Lt.Arty. Parker's Co.
Turnley, William H. TN 49th Inf. Co.A
Turnley, William H. Inf. Bailey's Cons.Regt. Co.G QMSgt.
Turnly, John VA 13th Cav. Co.K
Turnly, William H. KY 2nd Cav.
Turnmire, David L. NC 37th Inf. Co.B
Turnmire, J.N. NC 26th Inf. Co.I
Turnmire, John NC 26th Inf. Co.I
Turnmire, John N. NC 58th Inf. Co.H Cpl.
Turnmire, Joseph A. NC 58th Inf. Co.H
Turnmire, Larkin G. NC 1st Cav. (9th St.Troops) Co.D
Turnmire, Larkin G. NC 37th Inf. Co.C
Turnmire, Peter W. NC 37th Inf. Co.B
Turnner, G.W. SC 2nd Cav. Co.G
Turnney, Dennis TN 10th Inf. Co.D
Turnoh wai lah ne 1st Cherokee Mtd.Rifles Co.G
Turnor, James G. GA 12th Inf. Co.C
Turnor, Richard F. GA 12th Inf. Co.C
Turnover 1st Cherokee Mtd.Vol. 2nd Co.B
Turnover, Davis 1st Cherokee Mtd.Rifles Co.D
Turn Over, Isaac 1st Cherokee Mtd.Rifles Co.D
Turnover Joseph 1st Cherokee Mtd.Vol. 2nd Co.E
Turnover Tyes kie 1st Cherokee Mtd.Rifles Co.I
Turnow, Charles C. VA 34th Inf. Co.C
Turnstall, W.J. SC Inf. 6th Bn. Co.B
Turntine, James AR Cav. Gordon's Regt. Co.D
Turnun, J.W. AL 8th (Livingston's) Cav. Co.B
Turnuphowa 1st Choctaw Mtd.Rifles Co.E
Turny, J.A. TX 18th Inf. Co.K
Turpan, Joseph TN 28th Inf. Co.B
Turpe, Richard TX 3rd Inf. Co.H
Turpen, John MO Cav. Coleman's Regt. Co.C
Turpen, John 1st Cherokee Mtd.Vol. 1st Co.G
Turpen, J.W. TX Cav. (Dismtd.) Chisum's Regt. Co.B
Turpen, Richard TN 22nd Inf. Co.I
Turpen, William TN 22nd Inf. Co.I
Turpin, A.B. VA Cav. 32nd Bn. Co.A
Turpin, A.J. GA 13th Inf. Co.F
Turpin, A.J. TN 25th Inf. Co.B
Turpin, A. Jackson MS 33rd Inf. Co.I
Turpin, Al. VA Inf. 22nd Bn. Co.G
Turpin, Alfred S. VA 57th Inf. Co.I
Turpin, Allen P. GA 65th Inf. Co.I
Turpin, Ambrose J. GA 24th Inf. Co.E
Turpin, Andrew KY 7th Cav. Co.F
Turpin, Andrew KY 11th Cav. Co.F
Turpin, Andrew J. GA 7th Inf. (St.Guards) Co.D

Turpin, Andy J. MS 2nd Inf. (A. of 10,000) Co.A
Turpin, Archer MS Lt.Arty. (Jefferson Arty.) Darden's Co.
Turpin, Archie B. VA 5th Cav. Co.E
Turpin, Berry KY 2nd Mtd.Inf. Co.I
Turpin, B.R. GA 8th Cav. New Co.E Sgt.
Turpin, B.R. GA Cav. 20th Bn. Co.C Sgt.Maj.
Turpin, Caswell VA 2nd Cav. Co.A
Turpin, Charles AL Cav. Shockley's Co.
Turpin, Charles TX 4th Inf. Cpl.
Turpin, Charles P. MS 9th Inf. New Co.E 2nd Lt.
Turpin, Charles P. MS 10th Inf. Old Co.F Sgt.
Turpin, C.M. MO 5th Cav. Co.I Capt.
Turpin, Elisha S. VA Cav. 1st Bn. (Loc.Def. Troops) Co.A
Turpin, Elisha S. VA Cav. 40th Bn. Co.B
Turpin, Emerson KY 7th Mtd.Inf. Co.H
Turpin, E.S. LA Washington Arty.Bn. Co.5
Turpin, E.S. VA Hvy.Arty. 18th Bn. Co.B
Turpin, F.M. MS St.Cav. 3rd Bn. (Cooper's) 1st Co.A
Turpin, G.B. GA Cav. 8th Bn. (St.Guards) Co.A
Turpin, G.D. VA 51st Inf. Co.G,H
Turpin, George GA 52nd Inf. Co.F
Turpin, George A. VA Cav. 41st Bn. Co.F Cpl.
Turpin, George B. GA Inf. 2nd Bn. Co.C 2nd Lt.
Turpin, George B. GA 45th Inf. AQM
Turpin, George B. Gen. & Staff Capt.,QM
Turpin, George N. VA 5th Cav. Co.E
Turpin, George V. VA 23rd Cav.
Turpin, George Washington VA 2nd Cav. Co.G
Turpin, G.V. TX 11th Inf. Co.H
Turpin, H. Allen NC 16th Inf. Co.A Cpl.
Turpin, Henry TN Inf. 23rd Bn. Co.C
Turpin, Henry A. NC 39th Inf. Co.K Cpl.
Turpin, Henry A. NC 62nd Inf. Co.C
Turpin, Henry A. NC Inf. Thomas Legion 1st Co.A
Turpin, Henry B. TX 19th Cav. Cpl.
Turpin, Henry W. Gen. & Staff AASurg.
Turpin, Horace VA 24th Cav. Co.B
Turpin, Horace VA Cav. 40th Bn. Co.B
Turpin, J. LA Mil. 1st Native Guards
Turpin, J. MO 11th Inf. Co.G
Turpin, Jackson F. GA Inf. 1st Loc.Troops (Augusta) Co.A Cpl.
Turpin, James MO 1st Cav. Burns' Co.
Turpin, James NC 16th Inf. Co.A
Turpin, James NC 39th Inf. Co.K
Turpin, James VA 1st Cav. Co.C
Turpin, James VA 28th Inf. Co.A,E
Turpin, James A. VA Horse Arty. Shoemaker's Co.
Turpin, James F. TX 12th Cav. Co.C Sgt.
Turpin, James H. GA 24th Inf. Co.E
Turpin, James H. MO Cav. 1st Regt.St.Guard Co.E
Turpin, James H. MO 5th Cav. Co.E
Turpin, James M. LA 3rd (Wingfield's) Cav. Co.H
Turpin, James M. VA 34th Inf. Co.G
Turpin, James P. VA 36th Inf. 2nd Co.H
Turpin, James P. VA 86th Mil. Co.F,B
Turpin, James R. VA 5th Bn.Res. Co.C
Turpin, James T. MO 4th Cav. Co.E
Turpin, James W. KY 4th Cav. Co.E
Turpin, J.C. Gen. & Staff Asst.Surg.
Turpin, Jesse GA Inf. 3rd Bn. Co.G 2nd Lt.
Turpin, Jesse GA 4th Bn.S.S. Co.A 2nd Lt.
Turpin, Jesse M. Gen. & Staff Capt.,Ord.Off.
Turpin, J.G. LA 3rd Inf. Co.E 1st Lt.
Turpin, J.G. VA 3rd (Archer's) Bn.Res. Co.B
Turpin, J.M. GA Cav. 20th Bn. Co.C Capt.
Turpin, J.M. GA Inf. 1st Loc.Troops (Augusta) Barnes' Lt.Arty.Co.
Turpin, John KY 10th (Johnson's) Cav. New Co.B Cpl.
Turpin, John LA Washington Arty.Bn. Co.1
Turpin, John MS 7th Inf. Co.H
Turpin, John MO St.Guard
Turpin, John NC 62nd Inf. Co.C Capt.
Turpin, John VA 5th Cav. 3rd Co.F
Turpin, John VA 50th Inf. Co.F
Turpin, John A. VA 4th Cav. Co.E
Turpin, Johnathan MO 10th Inf. Co.A
Turpin, John C. GA 13th Inf. Co.I
Turpin, John C. VA Hvy.Arty. 20th Bn. Co.D
Turpin, John D. VA 34th Inf. Co.G
Turpin, John G. VA Inf. 22nd Bn. ACS
Turpin, John G. Gen. & Staff Capt.,Comsy.
Turpin, John H. AL 28th Inf. Co.B Capt.
Turpin, John J. GA 65th Inf. Co.I
Turpin, John O. VA 5th Cav. Co.E
Turpin, John S. VA 59th Inf. 3rd Co.D
Turpin, John T. MO 2nd Inf. Co.B
Turpin, John T. VA Inf. 25th Bn. Co.C
Turpin, Joseph GA Inf. (Mell Scouts) Wyly's Co.
Turpin, Joseph F. TX 19th Inf. Co.B
Turpin, L. Sanford VA Loc.Def. Bosher's Co.
Turpin, Mathew W. TN 41st Inf. Co.K
Turpin, M.D. NC 53rd Inf. Co.H
Turpin, M.D.L. 1st Conf.Cav. Co.I Cpl.
Turpin, Miles GA Lt.Arty. 12th Bn. 1st Co.A
Turpin, Miles GA 1st (Ramsey's) Inf. Co.D
Turpin, Miles GA 63rd Inf. Co.A
Turpin, Miles VA 1st St.Res. Co.D
Turpin, Nash VA 1st Cav. Co.C
Turpin, Paul J. VA 58th Inf. Co.C Sgt.
Turpin, P.B. KY 7th Cav. Co.A Sgt.Maj.
Turpin, Percival B. KY 3rd Cav. Co.A Sgt.Maj.
Turpin, Peter VA 28th Inf. Co.F
Turpin, Philip VA 28th Inf. Co.F
Turpin, R.C. VA Rockbridge Cty.Res. Bacon's Co. Capt.
Turpin, R.G. AR 27th Inf. New Co.B
Turpin, R.G. VA 2nd Cav. Co.G
Turpin, Richard KY 7th Cav. Co.F
Turpin, Richard MD Cav. 2nd Bn. Co.D
Turpin, Richard C. VA 5th Inf. Co.B
Turpin, Richard C. VA 27th Inf. 2nd Co.H
Turpin, Richard F. KY 6th Cav. Co.D,F
Turpin, Richard L. VA 34th Inf. Co.G 1st Lt.
Turpin, Richmon TN 15th (Stewart's) Cav. Co.C
Turpin, Robert KY 6th Cav. Jewett's Co. Sgt.
Turpin, Robert H. VA 58th Inf. Co.C Sgt.
Turpin, Samuel KY 7th Cav. Co.F
Turpin, Samuel KY 11th Cav. Co.F
Turpin, Sanford VA Lt.Arty. 38th Bn. Co.D
Turpin, S.E. LA Hvy.Arty. 2nd Bn. Co.D
Turpin, S.W. MS Lt.Arty. (Jefferson Arty.) Darden's Co.
Turpin, S.W. Lee's Corps Asst.Surg.
Turpin, T. AR 1st (Monroe's) Cav. Co.H
Turpin, T. MS 8th Cav. Co.K
Turpin, T.E. VA 2nd Cav. Co.G
Turpin, Th. Ed. VA 50th Inf. Co.F
Turpin, Thomas MO 1st N.E. Cav.
Turpin, Thomas MO 2nd N.E. Cav. (Franklin's Regt.) Co.B 1st Lt.
Turpin, Thomas MO 4th Cav. Co.B
Turpin, Thomas MO Cav. Poindexter's Regt.
Turpin, Thomas TN 7th Inf. Co.E
Turpin, Thomas VA 28th Inf. Co.F
Turpin, Thomas L. VA 59th Inf. 3rd Co.D Drum.
Turpin, Thomas N. VA 58th Inf. Co.C 2nd Lt.
Turpin, Thomas W. MS 2nd Inf. (A. of 10,000) Co.A
Turpin, Thomas W. MS 33rd Inf. Co.I
Turpin, T.J. SC 3rd Res. Co.E
Turpin, T.M. VA 28th Inf. Co.E
Turpin, T.M. VA 34th Inf. Co.G
Turpin, T.W. MS 22nd Inf. Co.G
Turpin, W. LA 18th Inf. Co.I
Turpin, W.A. VA 5th Cav. Co.D
Turpin, Walter E. VA 54th Inf. Co.A
Turpin, Walter G. Eng.,CSA Capt.
Turpin, W.B. MO 8th Inf. Co.B
Turpin, W.B.C. AL 6th Inf. Co.K
Turpin, W.C. TX 11th Inf. Co.H
Turpin, W.E. GA Inf. 1st Loc.Troops (Augusta) Barnes' Lt.Arty.Co.
Turpin, W.H., Jr. GA Cav. 2nd Bn. Co.D
Turpin, W.H. GA Inf. 1st Loc.Troops (Augusta) Barnes' Lt.Arty.Co.
Turpin, W.H. Gen. & Staff Capt.,Vol.ADC
Turpin, White LA Inf.Crescent Regt. Co.B Cpl.
Turpin, White LA Inf.Cons.Crescent Regt. Co.C
Turpin, White MS Lt.Arty. (Jefferson Arty.) Darden's Co.
Turpin, William AR Cav. Harrell's Bn. Co.B
Turpin, William MO 2nd Cav. Co.C
Turpin, William MO 12th Cav. Co.B
Turpin, William MO 2nd Inf. Co.A,I
Turpin, William TN 15th (Stewart's) Cav. Co.H
Turpin, William TN 37th Inf. Co.K
Turpin, William A. VA Lt.Arty. 38th Bn. Co.D
Turpin, William A. VA 51st Inf. Co.G Sgt.
Turpin, William A. VA 57th Inf. Co.I
Turpin, William C. TX 28th Cav. Co.K
Turpin, William H. GA Cav. 20th Bn. Co.C
Turpin, William H. GA Lt.Arty. Pritchard's Co. (Washington Arty.)
Turpin, William H. GA 12th Inf. Co.A 2nd Lt.
Turpin, William H. TN Arty. Marshall's Co.
Turpin, William H. VA 1st St.Res. Co.D
Turpin, William H. VA 53rd Inf. Co.D
Turpin, William Henry GA 20th Inf. Co.K Music.
Turpin, William L. VA 2nd Cav. Co.A
Turpin, William M. VA 60th Inf. Co.G Sgt.
Turpin, William P. AR 2nd Vol. Co.A
Turpin, William P. SC 2nd Inf. Co.B
Turpin, William R. MO Cav. 1st Regt.St.Guard Co.E
Turpin, William R. VA Lt.Arty. Hardwicke's Co.

Turpin, W.M. MS St.Cav. 3rd Bn. (Cooper's) 1st Co.A
Turpin, W.M. TX 1st Bn.S.S. Co.A
Turpin, Woodson MO Cav. Snider's Bn. Co.D
Turpin, Woodson MO Cav. Wood's Regt. Co.B Sgt.
Turpin, Woodson MO St.Guard
Turpin, W.P. AR 32nd Inf. Co.C
Turpin, W.R. TN 15th (Cons.) Cav. Co.F
Turpison, W.M. TX 35th (Brown's) Cav. 2nd Co.B
Turquah, George 1st Cherokee Mtd.Vol. 2nd Co.B
Turquais, Pierre LA 10th Inf. Co.F
Turquet, Osborne AL 17th Bn.S.S. Co.A
Turquet, W. GA 44th Inf. Co.G
Turquett, J.M. AR 19th (Dawson's) Inf. Co.B
Turquett, Thomas J. GA 13th Inf. Co.F
Turquit, A.F. AL 19th Inf. Co.E
Turrance, W.J. AL 1st Cav. Co.K
Turrell, Barron MD 1st Cav. Co.D
Turren, A.D. AL 12th Cav. Co.G
Turrentine, A.A. AR 1st (Colquitt's) Inf. Co.I
Turrentine, Absalom AR 16th Inf. Co.C
Turrentine, Addison AR 19th (Dawson's) Inf. Co.B
Turrentine, A.J. MS 2nd Part.Rangers Co.K
Turrentine, Andrew J. MS 12th Inf. Co.F
Turrentine, Charles F. AR 15th (Josey's) Inf. Co.A
Turrentine, Charles W. MS 12th Inf. Co.F
Turrentine, D.A. AR 12th Inf. Co.G Cpl.
Turrentine, Daniel AR 12th Inf. Co.G Sr.2nd Lt.
Turrentine, Daniel AR Logan's Cons.Regt. Co.K 2nd Lt.
Turrentine, Daniel C. AL 48th Inf. Co.G QM
Turrentine, D.C. Gen. & Staff Capt.,QM
Turrentine, Felix J. AR 15th (Josey's) Inf. Co.A
Turrentine, F.J. AL Cav. Hardie's Bn.Res.
Turrentine, James AR 1st Mtd.Rifles Co.C
Turrentine, James AR 7th Cav. Co.M
Turrentine, James GA 8th Inf. (St.Guards) Co.A
Turrentine, James A. AR 15th (Josey's) Inf. Co.A
Turrentine, James A. VA 5th Cav. (12 mo. '61-2) Co.G
Turrentine, James A. VA 13th Cav. Co.I
Turrentine, James L. AL 48th Inf. Co.G
Turrentine, John AR Inf. Cocke's Regt. Co.E
Turrentine, John GA Inf. 27th Bn. (NonConscr.) Co.B
Turrentine, John James TN 40th Inf. Co.A 1st Lt.
Turrentine, John R. AL Lt.Arty. Hurt's Btty.
Turrentine, Joseph TX 17th Cav. 1st Co.I
Turrentine, Joseph TX 18th Inf. Co.A Cpl.
Turrentine, Joseph S. NC 1st Inf. Co.D
Turrentine, J.R. GA Lt.Arty. (Jackson Arty.) Massenburg's Btty.
Turrentine, M.B. TX 1st Inf.Co.E
Turrentine, M.H. NC 2nd Arty. (36th St.Troops) Co.D Sgt.
Turrentine, M.H. NC 31st Inf. 2nd Lt.
Turrentine, Miles AR 1st (Colquitt's) Inf. Co.I
Turrentine, Newton M. MS 12th Inf. Co.F
Turrentine, Samuel W. NC 6th Inf. Co.B
Turrentine, S.M. AR 2nd Cav. Co.C
Turrentine, S.M. AR 24th Inf. Co.E Sgt.
Turrentine, Thomas AR 7th Cav. Co.M
Turrentine, Thomas J. AL Lt.Arty. Ward's Btty.
Turrentine, T.J. AR Inf. Cocke's Regt. Co.E
Turrentine, W.B. Gen. & Staff Hosp.Stew.
Turrentine, W.F. NC 57th Inf. Co.A
Turrentine, William E. AR 34th Inf. Co.A
Turrentine, William G. NC 2nd Arty. (36th St.Troops) Co.D
Turrentine, William S. AR 15th (Josey's) Inf. Co.A
Turrentine, W.L.T. AR Inf. Hardy's Regt. Co.G Sgt.
Turrenton, John J. AL 54th Inf. Co.B 1st Lt.
Turrh, L.D. Brush Bn.
Turrill, J.C. KY 5th Cav. Co.E 3rd Lt.
Turrner, Thomas J. NC 50th Inf. Co.F
Turro, Pablo LA Mil. Cazadores Espanoles Regt. Co.1
Turron, F.L. LA 5th Inf. Co.D
Turski, Francis VA 11th Inf. Co.E
Tursstall, Percil R. NC 17th Inf. (1st Org.) Co.G
Turtan, G. GA Inf. 1st Bn. (St.Guards) Co.E
Turtan, George GA Inf. City Bn. (Columbus) Co.A
Turtman, H. SC 1st Regt. Charleston Guard Co.G
Turton, Benjamin F. MD 1st Cav. Co.E Sgt.
Turton, M.W. MD 1st Cav. Co.E
Turtoy, William KY 5th Cav. Co.A
Turtoy, William J. KY 5th Cav. Co.D
Turvaville, Joseph W. GA 17th Inf. Co.I
Turvaville, Tapley C. AL 51st (Part.Rangers) Co.A
Turvaville, Tapley C. AL 2nd Inf. Co.A
Turvaville, T.C. AL 31st Inf. Co.A
Turver, Tilman L. AR 23rd Inf. Co.H Sr.2nd Lt.
Turveyville, William AL 23rd Inf. Co.E
Turville, Charles LA Miles' Legion Co.H
Turvin, D.E. TX 26th Cav. Co.I
Turvin, D.J. FL Cav. 3rd Bn. Co.C
Turvin, D.J. 15th Conf.Cav. Co.E
Turvin, Elija 15th Conf.Cav. Co.I
Turvin, G.W. TX 20th Inf. Co.G
Turvor, T.W. MS 2nd Cav. Co.A
Turwell, S.W. NC 25th Inf.
Turwood, L.A. GA 11th Cav. Co.D
Tury, Henry GA 63rd Inf. Co.I
Tuscan, W. VA 46th Inf. Co.B
Tuscano, Santiago TX Cav. 1st Bn.St.Troops Co.A
Tuscans, P. TX 17th Cons.Dismtd.Cav. Co.G
Tusche, H. LA Mil. 4th Regt.Eur.Brig. Co.F
Tuscooner 1st Creek Mtd.Vol. Co.H 2nd Lt.
Tuselier, Alfred A. LA Mil. Orleans Guards Regt. Co.C
Tush, Moses NC 5th Sr.Res. Co.H
Tusha, Eliga GA 2nd Cav. Co.E
Tusha, Henry LA Mil. 4th Regt. 1st Brig. 1st Div. Co.B
Tushakaruttah 1st Choctaw Mtd.Rifles Ward's Co.
Tushf, Jerry GA 47th Inf.
Tush kam ba, William 1st Choctaw & Chickasaw Mtd.Rifles 2nd Co.K
Tushkoonta, Thomas 1st Choctaw & Chickasaw Mtd.Rifles Co.G
Tushkoontah, Jonas 1st Choctaw & Chickasaw Mtd.Rifles Co.G
Tushkoyah 1st Choctaw & Chickasaw Mtd.Rifles Co.G
Tushpahtubbee 1st Choctaw & Chickasaw Mtd.Rifles Co.G
Tush par tubbee 1st Choctaw Mtd.Rifles Co.H
Tusing, Charles VA 18th Cav. Co.H
Tusing, Christian VA 62nd Mtd.Inf. 2nd Co.H
Tusing, Elijah VA 11th Cav. Co.C
Tusing, Gideon P. VA 8th Bn.Res. Co.C Sgt.
Tusing, Henry VA 7th Cav. Co.K
Tusing, Israel VA 8th Bn.Res. Co.C
Tusing, Jeremiah P. VA 33rd Inf. Co.E
Tusing, Jeremiah P. VA 146th Mil. Co.C
Tusing, John VA 23rd Cav. Co.I
Tusing, Moses VA 146th Mil. Co.B
Tusing, Nicholas VA 8th Bn.Res. Co.C
Tusing, Nickolas VA 97th Mil. Co.C
Tusing, Noah VA 18th Cav. Co.K
Tusing, S. VA 82nd Mil. Co.D
Tusing, Samuel VA 10th Inf. Co.L
Tusing, Solomon VA 8th Bn.Res. Co.C
Tusing, William VA 18th Cav. Co.H
Tusing, William VA 14th Mil. Co.F
Tuske he ne har 1st Creek Mtd.Vol. Co.H Cpl.
Tuskeheneher 2nd Creek Mtd.Vol. Co.E
Tuskey 1st Creek Mtd.Vol. Co.B
Tuskiah Harjo 1st Seminole Mtd.Vol.
Tuskiah Micco 1st Seminole Mtd.Vol.
Tuskis, C. AR 13th Mil. Co.A
Tuslen, C.E. AL Conscr.
Tusmage, J.D. TN 7th Cav. Co.I Cpl.
Tusner, J.F. TN 9th Inf. Co.C
Tusner, W.M. TN 12th Cav. Co.I
Tussee Kiah Harjo 2nd Creek Mtd.Vol. Co.E
Tusse kiah Harjo 1st Creek Mtd.Vol. Co.H
Tus sekiah hat ke 1st Creek Mtd.Vol. Co.G
Tussey, David NC 48th Inf. Co.H
Tussey, F.H. NC 48th Inf. Co.H Sgt.
Tussneau, William KY 2nd Cav. Co.I
Tusson, J.B. LA Inf.Cons.Crescent Regt. Co.G
Tusson, John B. LA Inf.Crescent Regt. Co.D Sgt.
Tusson, Leonee LA 5th Inf. Co.D Sgt.Maj.
Tusson, Rene LA 5th Inf. New Co.A Sgt.
Tustannsagee 1st Seminole Mtd.Vol.
Tustanucogee 1st Seminole Mtd.Vol. Capt.
Tusten, John L. MS 20th Inf. Co.C,A QMSgt.
Tustenuc Harjockee 1st Seminole Mtd.Vol.
Tustenucochee 1st Seminole Mtd.Vol. 1st Lt.
Tustenuggee 1st Seminole Mtd.Vol.
Tusternug co che 1st Creek Mtd.Vol. Co.H
Tuster nug ke 1st Creek Mtd.Vol. Co.A
Tuster nuy emer thia 1st Creek Mtd.Vol. Co.A
Tustin, H.T. SC 1st Cav. Co.A
Tustin, John L. MS 30th Inf. Co.H Jr.2nd Lt.
Tustin, Samuel MS 28th Cav. Co.F
Tustonugge 1st Creek Mtd.Vol. 1st Co.C
Tustumuggachee 2nd Creek Mtd.Vol. Co.E
Tustun oko che 1st Creek Mtd.Vol. Co.A
Tustunug Chupco 2nd Creek Mtd.Vol. Co.E
Tustunuggee Yarhar 2nd Creek Mtd.Vol. Co.B Capt.
Tuswochee 1st Seminole Mtd.Vol.
Tus Ya holo 1st Creek Mtd.Vol. Co.I
Tutarow, Thomas P. 7th Conf.Cav. Co.G,M

Tutch, M.M. GA 12th Mil.
Tutchstone, B.R. GA Inf. 25th Bn. (Prov.Guard) Co.A
Tute, Edward LA 20th Inf. Co.G
Tute, Edward LA Herrick's Co. (Orleans Blues)
Tute, W.L. TN 10th (DeMoss') Cav. Co.F
Tuten, Abram M. GA 1st (Olmstead's) Inf. 1st Co.A
Tuten, Abram M. GA 1st Bn.S.S. Co.B
Tuten, A.G. SC 1st Mtd.Mil. Martin's Co.
Tuten, A.G. SC Lt.Arty. J.T. Kanapaux's Co. (Lafayette Arty.)
Tuten, A.J. SC 5th Cav. Co.B
Tuten, A.J. SC 11th Inf. 2nd Co.F
Tuten, Alexander A. GA 4th (Clinch's) Cav. Co.G Cpl.
Tuten, Alexander A. GA 26th Inf. Co.K
Tuten, Artemas FL 1st Inf. Old Co.G
Tuten, Artemus FL 6th Inf. Co.C
Tuten, B. SC Cav. 19th Bn. Co.A
Tuten, B. SC Part.Rangers Kirk's Co.
Tuten, Charles D. FL 1st Inf. Old Co.F, New Co.B Sgt.
Tuten, Claudius Erastus AL Lt.Arty. 2nd Bn. Co.D
Tuten, David J. GA 27th Inf. Co.I
Tuten, David R. GA 47th Inf. Co.F Sgt.
Tuten, Evan H. FL 2nd Inf. Co.G
Tuten, Evan Hudson FL 3rd Inf. Co.K
Tuten, F.J. SC 1st Mtd.Mil. Blakewood's Co. Cpl.
Tuten, Frederick J. SC 3rd Cav. Co.E
Tuten, George W. SC 3rd Cav. Co.C
Tuten, George W. SC Mil.Cav. 4th Regt. Howard's Co.
Tuten, Green A. SC 11th Res. Co.I
Tuten, G.W. AR 30th Inf. Co.D
Tuten, G.W. SC 1st Mtd.Mil. Screven's Co.
Tuten, H. SC Part.Rangers Kirk's Co.
Tuten, Hardy P. GA 1st (Olmstead's) Inf. 1st Co.A
Tuten, Hardy P. GA 1st Bn.S.S. Co.B
Tuten, H.P. FL 2nd Cav. Co.F
Tuten, Isaac SC 3rd Cav. Co.C Sgt.
Tuten, Isaac SC Mil.Cav. 4th Regt. Howard's Co.
Tuten, Isham W. SC 5th Cav. Co.B
Tuten, Isham W. SC Cav. 17th Bn. Co.C
Tuten, Isom W. SC 1st (Butler's) Inf. Co.C
Tuten, J.A. SC 1st Mtd.Mil. Anderson's Co. Cpl.
Tuten, J.A. SC Lt.Arty. J.T. Kanapaux's Co. (Lafayette Arty.)
Tuten, J.A. SC 24th Inf. Co.D
Tuten, James C. GA 47th Inf. Co.F
Tuten, James R. GA 4th (Clinch's) Cav. Co.G
Tuten, James S. SC 3rd Cav. Co.E
Tuten, J.C. GA 4th (Clinch's) Cav. Co.I
Tuten, J.C.C. SC 5th Cav. Co.B Cpl.
Tuten, J.C.C. SC Cav. 17th Bn. Co.C Cpl.
Tuten, Jefferson N. SC 1st (McCreary's) Inf. Co.H
Tuten, Jesse J. SC 1st (McCreary's) Inf. Co.H
Tuten, J.G. SC 3rd Cav. Co.F
Tuten, J.H. SC 1st Mtd.Mil. Blakewood's Co.
Tuten, J.H. SC Cav. 19th Bn. Co.C
Tuten, Jiant SC 1st Mtd.Mil. Smart's Co.
Tuten, J.J. SC 1st Mtd.Mil. Screven's Co.
Tuten, J.J. SC 24th Inf. Co.D
Tuten, John SC 1st Mtd.Mil. Screven's Co. Sgt.
Tuten, John A. SC 5th Cav. Co.C
Tuten, John B. GA 4th (Clinch's) Cav. Co.G
Tuten, John B. SC 3rd Cav. Co.E
Tuten, John H. SC 3rd Cav. Co.E
Tuten, Jonathan SC 1st Mtd.Mil. Screven's Co.
Tuten, Joseph FL Cav. 5th Bn. Co.F
Tuten, Joseph M. GA 1st Bn.S.S. Co.B
Tuten, Joseph W. Mil.Cav. 4th Regt. Howard's Co.
Tuten, J.T. SC 1st Mtd.Mil. Smart's Co. Sgt.
Tuten, J.T. SC 3rd Cav. Co.F
Tuten, J.W. SC 1st Mtd.Mil. Smart's Co.
Tuten, J.W. SC 5th Cav. Co.B
Tuten, J.W. SC 5th Cav. Co.B Cpl.
Tuten, J.W. SC Cav. 17th Bn. Co.C
Tuten, J.W. SC Cav. 19th Bn. Co.A Sgt.
Tuten, J.W. SC Part.Rangers Kirk's Co. Sgt.
Tuten, J.W. SC 24th Inf. Co.A
Tuten, N.B. VA Inf. 26th Bn. Co.G
Tuten, N.B. Gen. & Staff AASurg.
Tuten, Noah B. NC 4th Inf. Co.I 2nd Lt.
Tuten, Patrick H. FL 2nd Cav. Co.F
Tuten, Patrick H. TX 19th Cav. Co.H
Tuten, Redding G. NC 4th Inf. Co.I Sgt.
Tuten, Redding R. NC 4th Inf. Co.I 1st Lt.
Tuten, Robert J. FL 8th Inf. Co.C Cpl.
Tuten, T. GA 5th Cav. Co.C
Tuten, Thomas SC 3rd Cav. Co.C
Tuten, Thomas SC 5th Cav. Co.C
Tuten, Thomas SC Lt.Arty. 3rd (Palmetto) Bn. Co.F
Tuten, Thomas A.E. NC 3rd Arty. (40th St.Troops) Co.I 2nd Lt.
Tuten, Thomas P. GA 1st (Olmstead's) Inf. Co.K
Tuten, Thomas S. SC 11th Inf. Co.E 1st Lt.
Tuten, T.P. GA Cav. 2nd Bn. Co.E
Tuten, T.W. SC Mtd.Mil. Scott's Co. Cpl.
Tuten, W.H. SC 1st Mtd.Mil. Blakewood's Co.
Tuten, W.H. SC Cav. 19th Bn. Co.C
Tuten, W.H. SC Part.Rangers Kirk's Co.
Tuten, William H. SC 3rd Cav. Co.E
Tuten, William J. SC 3rd Cav. Co.C
Tuten, William J. Mil.Cav. 4th Regt. Howard's Co.
Tuten, William L. GA 4th (Clinch's) Cav. Co.G
Tuten, William S. GA 1st (Olmstead's) Inf. 1st Co.A
Tuten, William S. GA 1st Bn.S.S. Co.B
Tuten, Wilson NC 3rd Arty. (40th St.Troops) Co.B
Tuten, W.J. SC 1st Mtd.Mil. Screven's Co.
Tuten, W.R. FL 2nd Inf. Co.F
Tuter, Henderson MS 2nd Inf. (A. of 10,000) Co.G Sgt.
Tuter, Henry MS 2nd Inf. (A. of 10,000) Co.G
Tuter, H.L. MS 2nd Inf. (A. of 10,000) Co.G
Tuter, J.A. MS 2nd Inf. (A. of 10,000) Co.G
Tuter, James A. NC 3rd Inf. Co.K
Tuter, J.A.W. MS 2nd Inf. (A. of 10,000) Co.G
Tuter, J.D. MS 7th Cav. Co.H
Tuter, Jefferson MS 2nd Inf. (A. of 10,000) Co.G
Tuter, Owen MS 2nd Inf. (A. of 10,000) Co.G
Tuter, Pickard VA Inf. 23rd Bn. Co.B
Tuterton, A. FL Cav. 5th Bn. Cpl.
Tutherford, Thomas H. VA Hvy.Arty. Bowyer's Co. (Botetourt Arty.)
Tuthero, Silas NC 1st Cav. (9th St.Troops) Co.K
Tutherow, A.M. NC 1st Cav. (9th St.Troops) Co.K
Tutherow, John NC 1st Cav. (9th St.Troops) Co.K
Tuthy, Henry TN 12th (Green's) Cav. Co.C
Tutile, John NC 48th Inf. Co.K
Tutin, T.W. SC 1st Mtd.Mil. Scott's Co. Cpl.
Tutle, David TX 16th Cav. Co.G
Tutle, J.L. GA Cav. 2nd Bn. Co.B
Tutle, J.L. GA 5th Cav. Co.F
Tutle, Pink TX Cav. 1st Bn.St.Troops Co.D
Tutle, Robert GA 7th Cav. Co.E
Tutle, W.A. TX Cav. 1st Bn.St.Troops Co.D
Tutle, W.A. TX Cav. 1st Bn.St.Troops Co.D 2nd Lt.
Tutle, William GA 7th Cav. Co.E
Tutler, R.S. GA 28th Inf. Co.C
Tutley, John Brush Bn.
Tutman, Samuel KY 5th Cav. Co.G
Tuton, Evans FL 3rd Inf. Co.K
Tuton, H.C. NC 3rd Arty. (40th St.Troops) Co.F
Tuton, J.A. FL 1st (Res.) Inf. Co.F
Tuton, James L. TX 6th Inf. Co.C 2nd Lt.
Tuton, J.C. SC 1st (Butler's) Inf. Co.G
Tuton, John NC 8th Inf. Co.A
Tuton, John SC Cav. 17th Bn. Co.D
Tuton, Richard M.J. NC 3rd Arty. (40th St.Troops) Co.F
Tuton, Thomas SC Cav. 17th Bn. Co.D
Tuton, Walter J. NC 3rd Inf. Co.A
Tuton, Warry J. NC 3rd Arty. (40th St.Troops) Co.F
Tuton, William VA Arty. Fleet's Co.
Tuton, William VA Lt.Arty. Woolfolk's Co.
Tuton, William VA 55th Inf. Co.B
Tuton, William G. FL 2nd Inf. Co.E
Tuton, W.J. NC 1st Arty. (10th St.Troops) Co.B
Tutor, Abner V. VA 63rd Inf. Co.C
Tutor, A.H. MS 17th Inf. Co.K
Tutor, A.V. VA Inf. 54th Bn. Co.C
Tutor, Balard VA Cav. 34th Bn. Co.K
Tutor, Charles N. MS 2nd Cav. Co.F
Tutor, C.M. MS 22nd Inf.
Tutor, Hendon D. MS 17th Inf. Co.K
Tutor, James A. NC 31st Inf. Co.I
Tutor, James A.W. MS 17th Inf. Co.K
Tutor, J.H. NC 31st Inf. Co.I
Tutor, John 20th Conf.Cav. Co.M Cpl.
Tutor, John A. MS 1st Cav.
Tutor, John Harris MS 8th Cav. Co.A
Tutor, J.W. MS 8th Cav. Co.E
Tutor, Owen NC 31st Inf. Co.I
Tutor, Pickard VA 36th Inf. 2nd Co.I
Tutor, Reuben NC 31st Inf. Co.I
Tutor, Richard VA Cav. 34th Bn. Co.K
Tutor, Robert MO Cav. 3rd Regt.St.Guard Co.E
Tutor, Samuel A. VA 56th Inf. Co.B Sgt.
Tutor, Thomas N. GA 21st Inf. Co.G
Tutor, W.H. MS Cav. Hughes' Bn. Co.F
Tutor, William H. VA 2nd Arty. Co.D
Tutor, William O. NC 31st Inf. Co.I Jr.2nd Lt.
Tutor, William W. VA Inf. 22nd Bn. Co.D 2nd Lt.

Tutorow, A.P. 7th Conf.Cav. Co.G,M
Tutrow, A.P. NC Cav. 16th Bn. Co.E
Tutrow, Thomas J. VA 10th Cav. Co.B
Tutt, A.B. GA 8th Inf. Co.C
Tutt, Andrew M. MO St.Guard Maj.,Prov.Marsh.
Tutt, Benjamin MO Cav. Schnabel's Bn.
Tutt, B.F. GA Inf. 1st Loc.Troops (Augusta) Barnes' Lt.Arty.Co.
Tutt, C.G. SC Wilson's Cav.
Tutt, Davis K., Jr. AR 27th Inf. Co.A
Tutt, Edmond L. AR 2nd Mtd.Rifles Co.C
Tutt, Edward L. AR 10th (Witt's) Cav. Co.F
Tutt, Flournoy B. SC Cav.Bn. Hampton Legion Co.A
Tutt, Hansford TX 29th Cav. Co.E 3rd Lt.
Tutt, H.B. GA 28th Inf. Co.C 1st Lt.
Tutt, Henry C. MO 10th Cav. Co.H
Tutt, Henry D. TX 6th Cav. Co.G
Tutt, Henry W. GA Floyd Legion (St.Guards) Co.C Sgt.
Tutt, H.W. GA Brown's Cav.
Tutt, James B. TX 7th Inf. Co.K
Tutt, James H. AR 14th (Powers') Inf. Co.K Cpl.
Tutt, James M. MO 9th Inf. Chap.
Tutt, James V. AL 8th (Hatch's) Cav. Co.C Capt.
Tutt, James V. AL 5th Inf. New Co.E 2nd Lt.
Tutt, J.B. GA 3rd Cav. (St.Guards) Co.I
Tutt, Jefferson MO 4th Cav. Co.I
Tutt, J.M. MO Inf. Clark's Regt. Chap.
Tutt, J.M. Gen. & Staff Chap.
Tutt, John MS Cav. Jeff Davis Legion Co.A
Tutt, John C. TX 5th Inf. Co.F
Tutt, John G. MS 28th Cav. Co.D
Tutt, John S. AR 16th Inf. 1st Lt.,Adj.
Tutt, John S. Gen. & Staff 1st Lt.,Adj.
Tutt, John Z. AL 8th (Hatch's) Cav. Co.C 2nd Lt.
Tutt, J.S. MO 3rd Inf. Co.D
Tutt, Julian GA Lt.Arty. Barnwell's Btty.
Tutt, L.C. AL Cav. Roddey's Escort Sgt.
Tutt, L.P. VA Horse Arty. G.W. Brown's Co.
Tutt, M.R. MO Dorsey's Regt. Co.D
Tutt, P.B. TX 19th Inf. Co.I
Tutt, R.C. AR 18th Inf. Co.I
Tutt, R.H. TX 19th Inf. Co.I Cpl.
Tutt, Robert H. GA 48th Inf. Co.I
Tutt, Samuel S. AR 14th (Powers') Inf. Co.B Sgt.
Tutt, Sidney AR 18th Inf. Co.I
Tutt, Sidney O.P. AR 33rd Inf. Co.B
Tutt, Thomas E. LA 10th Inf. Co.E
Tutt, Thomas J. GA Lt.Arty. 12th Bn. Co.F Bvt.2nd Lt.
Tutt, Thomas J. GA 1st (Ramsey's) Inf. Co.D
Tutt, Thos. N. AR 18th Inf. Co.I
Tutt, W. KY Lt.Arty. Cobb's Co.
Tutt, W.F. LA Inf.Crescent Regt. Co.B
Tutt, W.H. GA Inf. 1st Loc.Troops (Augusta) Barnes' Lt.Arty.Co.
Tutt, William KY 2nd Cav. Co.F
Tutt, William TX 31st Cav. Co.B
Tutt, William D. AL 17th Inf. Co.G 1st Lt.
Tutt, William D. GA 5th Inf. Co.A Cpl.
Tutt, William E. MO Inf. 4th Regt.St.Guard QM
Tutt, Wm. E. Gen. & Staff Capt.,ACS,AQM
Tutt, William F. LA Washington Arty.Bn. Co.5
Tutt, William G. MO 2nd Inf. Co.H
Tutt, William H. KY 2nd Bn.Mtd.Rifles Co.A,E
Tutt, William W. GA 21st Inf. Old Co.E 2nd Lt.
Tutt, William W. GA Smith's Legion Co.G 2nd Lt.
Tuttarow, George W. NC 13th Inf. Co.F
Tuttarow, John V. NC 13th Inf. Co.F
Tutten, C. GA 47th Inf. Co.F
Tuttenton, James NC 44th Inf. Co.G
Tutterow, H. NC 4th Sr.Res. Co.A
Tutterow, Samuel NC 4th Sr.Res. Co.A
Tutterow, William N. NC 42nd Inf. Co.F
Tutterow, William W. NC 42nd Inf. Co.F
Tutterow, W.W. NC 4th Sr.Res. Co.A
Tutterson, William NC 1st Bn.Jr.Res. Co.E
Tuttle, --- LA 1st (Strawbridge's) Inf. Co.E
Tuttle, --- MS 4th Inf.
Tuttle, --- TX Cav. Border's Regt. Co.K Sgt.
Tuttle, --- TX Cav. Mann's Regt. Co.I
Tuttle, Abraham NC 27th Inf.
Tuttle, Abraham H. NC 33rd Inf. Co.I
Tuttle, A.G. AL 45th Inf. Co.K
Tuttle, A.G. NC 21st Inf. Co.G
Tuttle, Andrew J. GA 9th Inf. Co.G 1st Sgt.
Tuttle, B. MS 39th Inf. Co.K
Tuttle, B. Marcus NC 1st Cav. (9th St.Troops) Co.D
Tuttle, Calvin NC 52nd Inf. Co.D
Tuttle, Charles MD 1st Inf. Co.D Music.
Tuttle, Charles E. AL Inf. 1st Regt. Co.K 2nd Lt.
Tuttle, Christopher C. TN 3rd (Lillard's) Mtd.Inf. Co.D Music.
Tuttle, Columbus A. NC 26th Inf. Co.F
Tuttle, Daniel TX Cav. 1st Bn.St.Troops Co.D Sgt.
Tuttle, Daniel W. GA 2nd Bn.S.S. Co.C
Tuttle, David AL Arty. 1st Bn. Co.F
Tuttle, Dewitt P. NC 52nd Inf. Co.D Sgt.
Tuttle, D.H. SC 11th Inf. Co.G
Tuttle, D.K. Nitre & Min. Bureau War Dept., CSA 1st Lt.
Tuttle, D.M. SC 11th Inf. Co.G
Tuttle, D.S. AL 56th Part.Rangers Co.B
Tuttle, D.S. LA 17th Inf. Co.I
Tuttle, E.B. Gen. & Staff Capt.,Comsy.
Tuttle, Edward GA Cav. 29th Bn. Co.F
Tuttle, Edwin D. VA 26th Inf. Co.G
Tuttle, E.E. GA Cav. 12th Bn. (St.Guards) Co.A
Tuttle, Ezra B. VA 14th Inf. Co.A ACS
Tuttle, Francis J. NC 2nd Inf. Co.G
Tuttle, Francis M. MO 1st Cav. Co.E
Tuttle, Francis M. MO 5th Cav. Co.E
Tuttle, Gabe NC 13th Inf. Co.A
Tuttle, George C. VA 4th Inf. Co.L
Tuttle, George G. GA Inf. 1st Loc.Troops (Augusta) Co.B,K
Tuttle, George K. AR 8th Inf. New Co.B
Tuttle, George W. TX Waul's Legion Co.D Sgt.
Tuttle, George Washington MO 8th Inf. Co.C
Tuttle, Gerome GA 4th Inf. Co.H
Tuttle, Gideon J. NC 52nd Inf. Co.D
Tuttle, G.W. TX Waul's Legion Co.D Cpl.
Tuttle, Henry MO 2nd Inf. Co.D
Tuttle, Henry A. Conf.Inf. Tucker's Regt. Co.C
Tuttle, J. SC 1st (Butler's) Inf. Co.G Music.
Tuttle, J.A. GA Inf. 2nd Bn. (St.Guards) Old Co.D
Tuttle, J.A. GA 47th Inf. Co.B
Tuttle, James KY 14th Cav. Co.E
Tuttle, James MO 2nd & 6th Cons.Inf. Co.F
Tuttle, James NC 22nd Inf. Co.G
Tuttle, James TN 20th Inf. Co.F
Tuttle, James B. TN 1st (Turney's) Inf. Co.K
Tuttle, James H. MO 2nd Inf. Co.C
Tuttle, James H. TX 16th Cav. Co.G Capt.
Tuttle, James M. KY 7th Cav. Co.E
Tuttle, James M. NC 21st Inf. Co.G
Tuttle, Jefferson G. NC 52nd Inf. Co.D
Tuttle, Jerome GA Inf. 3rd Bn. Co.E
Tuttle, Jerome GA 37th Inf. Co.C
Tuttle, Jerome VA 26th Inf. Co.G
Tuttle, John MO 8th Inf. Co.C
Tuttle, John NC 21st Inf. Co.D
Tuttle, John TN 55th (McKoin's) Inf. Day's Co.
Tuttle, John A. NC 26th Inf. Co.F
Tuttle, John C. NC 21st Inf. Co.I Sgt.
Tuttle, John E. SC 8th Bn.Res. Fishburne's Co.
Tuttle, John F. NC 32nd Inf. Co.A,B
Tuttle, John H. NC Inf. 72nd Regt. Co.B
Tuttle, John T. NC 12th Inf. Co.M
Tuttle, John W. GA Cav. 21st Bn. Co.B
Tuttle, John W. NC 21st Inf. Co.G
Tuttle, John W. NC 52nd Inf. Co.D Sgt.
Tuttle, John W. TN 8th Cav. Co.D
Tuttle, Joseph MO 8th Inf. Co.C
Tuttle, Joseph SC 3rd St.Troops Co.A
Tuttle, J.S. LA 30th Inf. Co.I
Tuttle, J.W. TX Cav. (Loc.Def.) Durant's Co.
Tuttle, J.W. TX Cav. Madison's Regt. Co.B
Tuttle, Levi W. Gen. & Staff Surg.
Tuttle, Marcus G. NC 3rd Jr.Res. Co.G 1st Lt.
Tuttle, Marcus G. NC 8th Bn.Jr.Res. Co.C 1st Lt.
Tuttle, Marshall TX 36th Cav. Co.A
Tuttle, Martin NC 1st Arty. (10th St.Troops) Co.I
Tuttle, Martin NC 2nd Arty. (36th St.Troops) Co.A
Tuttle, Martin Lee NC 2nd Inf. Co.G
Tuttle, M.D.L. LA 14th Inf. Co.C
Tuttle, Miles V. NC 21st Inf. Co.G
Tuttle, M.T. NC 7th Sr.Res. Watts' Co.
Tuttle, N. TX Cav. 3rd Regt.St.Troops Kelly's Co.
Tuttle, O.T. SC 11th Inf. Co.G
Tuttle, Peter H. NC 52nd Inf. Co.D
Tuttle, Robert GA Cav. 21st Bn. Co.B
Tuttle, Romulus M. NC 26th Inf. Co.F Capt.
Tuttle, S. NC 21st Inf. Co.G
Tuttle, Solomon TN 45th Inf. Co.I
Tuttle, Thomas MO Cav. Fristoe's Regt. Co.E
Tuttle, Thomas MO 8th Inf. Co.C
Tuttle, Thomas TN Lt.Arty. Burroughs' Co.
Tuttle, Thomas VA Inf. Mileham's Co.
Tuttle, Thomas A. MO 2nd Inf. Co.C
Tuttle, Thomas Forsyth NC 7th Sr.Res. Clinard's Co., Holland's Co.
Tuttle, Thomas H. NC 21st Inf. Co.I
Tuttle, Thomas J. NC 21st Inf. Co.G
Tuttle, Thomas Stokes NC 7th Sr.Res. Watts' Co., Holland's Co.

Tuttle, Thomas W. GA 37th Inf. Co.C
Tuttle, Thornton NC 21st Inf. Co.G
Tuttle, T.W. GA 5th Res. Co.A
Tuttle, W.B. AL 31st Inf. Co.C
Tuttle, W.B. NC 21st Inf. Co.G
Tuttle, William GA Inf. 18th Bn. (St.Guards) Adam's Co.
Tuttle, William MO Cav. Fristoe's Regt. Co.E
Tuttle, William MO 8th Inf. Co.C
Tuttle, William NC 3rd Arty. (40th St.Troops) Co.D
Tuttle, William SC 8th Bn.Res. Fishburne's Co.
Tuttle, William A. AL Lt.Arty. 2nd Bn. Co.A
Tuttle, William A. NC 22nd Inf. Co.A 2nd Lt.
Tuttle, William A. TX 17th Cav. Co.E
Tuttle, William B. MO 2nd Inf. Co.C
Tuttle, William H. TX Cav. Hardeman's Regt. Co.B
Tuttle, William H. VA Cav. 37th Bn. Co.D
Tuttle, William J. MS 21st Inf. Co.K
Tuttle, William M. NC 21st Inf. Co.G
Tuttle, W.P. MO Lt.
Tuttle, W.P. TX 5th Inf. Co.G
Tuttle, W.T. AL 23rd Inf. Co.H
Tuttleton, B.C. TN 28th (Cons.) Inf. Co.H
Tuttleton, David E. TN Inf. 1st Bn. (Colms') Co.B
Tuttleton, John W. TN Inf. 1st Bn. (Colms') Co.B
Tuttleton, J.W. TN 28th (Cons.) Inf. Co.H
Tutton, --- TX Cav. Mann's Regt. Co.K
Tutton, Elias J. AR 21st Inf. Co.H
Tutton, J.B. AR 3rd Cav. Co.K
Tutton, J.B. Exch.Bn. 2nd Co.A,CSA
Tutton, Joseph B. AR 21st Inf. Co.H
Tutton, W.L. MS Rogers' Co.
Tutwater, George W. VA 52nd Inf. Co.C
Tutwater, W.H. VA 52nd Inf. Co.F
Tutwiler, --- VA VMI Co.D
Tutwiler, Addison VA 10th Cav. Co.H
Tutwiler, Addison VA 25th Inf. 1st Co.I
Tutwiler, C.H. VA 59th Inf. 3rd Co.F
Tutwiler, Charles VA 46th Inf. 2nd Co.E
Tutwiler, Charles H. VA 20th Inf. Co.E
Tutwiler, Charles H. VA Inf. 25th Bn. Co.B
Tutwiler, Edward VA 58th Mil. Co.D
Tutwiler, Edward H. VA 19th Cav. Co.H
Tutwiler, Eli VA 9th Bn.Res. Co.C
Tutwiler, Eli VA 58th Mil. Co.D
Tutwiler, George H. VA 25th Inf. 1st Co.I
Tutwiler, George W. VA 5th Inf. Co.C
Tutwiler, H.A. Sig.Corps,CSA Sgt.
Tutwiler, Harvey VA 25th Inf. 1st Co.I
Tutwiler, Henry P. VA Lt.Arty. Ancell's Co.
Tutwiler, Henry P. VA Inf. 25th Bn. Co.C
Tutwiler, Jacob VA 25th Inf. 1st Co.I
Tutwiler, Jacob O. VA 2nd Inf. Co.A,H
Tutwiler, J.B. VA 46th Inf. 2nd Co.E
Tutwiler, Joseph L. VA 1st Cav. Co.I
Tutwiler, Marion L. VA Lt.Arty. Ancell's Co.
Tutwiler, Marion L. VA Lt.Arty. Snead's Co.
Tutwiler, Martin VA 114th Mil. Co.B
Tutwiler, Noah A. VA 58th Mil. Co.D
Tutwiler, Peter C. VA 5th Inf. Co.C
Tutwiler, Peter C. VA 58th Mil. Co.D
Tutwiler, Philip VA 58th Mil. Co.D
Tutwiler, Richard P. VA Lt.Arty. Snead's Co.
Tutwiler, Robert VA 1st Cav. Co.I
Tutwiler, Robert P. AL 11th Inf. Co.B
Tutwiler, Robert P. VA 15th Cav. Co.B Jr.2nd Lt.
Tutwiler, Robert R. VA 25th Inf. 1st Co.I
Tutwiler, Samuel VA 7th Bn.Res. Co.B Capt.
Tutwiler, Samuel F. Gen. & Staff Capt.,AQM
Tutwiler, Samuel H. VA 52nd Inf. Co.A
Tutwiler, S.K. TX 8th Cav. Co.F
Tutwiler, Thos. H. Gen. & Staff QM
Tutwiler, Wesley C. VA Lt.Arty. Ancell's Co.
Tutwiler, William MD 1st Cav. Co.A
Tutwiler, William VA 6th Inf. Co.G
Tutwiler, William VA 25th Inf. 1st Co.I Cpl.
Tutwiler, William H. VA 5th Inf. Co.C
Tutwiller, E.S. Gen. & Staff Capt.,QM
Tutwiller, H. VA 18th Cav. 2nd Co.E
Tutzer, Peter AR 37th Inf. Co.E
Tuyes, Jules LA Mil. Orleans Guards Regt. Co.D 1st Lt.
Twachtman, Herman SC Arty. Bachman's Co. (German Lt.Arty.)
Twachtman, Herman SC Arty.Bn. Hampton Legion Co.B
Twaddle, Jacob C. TX 6th Cav. Co.G
Twain, C.F. MS 22nd Inf. Co.K Sgt.
Twanis, James AL 42nd Inf. Co.A
Twaits, James S. TX Cav. 3rd (Yager's) Bn. Co.A Sgt.
Twebough, Archibald J. MO 3rd Cav. Co.K
Twebough, Solomon MO 3rd Cav. Co.K Sgt.
Twedy, Jacob GA 2nd Inf. Co.A
Tweed, Iame H. NC 58th Inf. Co.H Sgt.
Tweed, James H. NC 60th Inf. Co.F Sgt.
Tweed, N.M. VA Lt.Arty. 12th Bn. Co.B
Tweed, Robert LA Mil.Conf.Guards Regt. Co.D
Tweed, Thomas W. NC 60th Inf. Co.F
Tweed, T.W. NC 58th Inf. Co.H
Tweedell, James A. GA 50th Inf. Co.D
Tweedell, John T. AL 44th Inf. Co.I 1st Lt.
Tweedell, Lewis H. GA 42nd Inf. Co.D
Tweedell, Marion J. GA 38th Inf. Co.K
Tweedle, A. TN 12th Inf. Co.E
Tweedle, Alexander TN Arty. Marshall's Co.
Tweedle, Finus TX 16th Cav. Co.E
Tweedle, James GA 2nd Bn.S.S. Co.A Cpl.
Tweedle, James W. MO 1st N.E. Cav. Co.A
Tweedle, J.C. AR 37th Inf. Co.H
Tweedle, Richard AR 2nd Cav. Co.C
Tweedle, Robert M. GA 2nd Res. Co.K
Tweedle, Thomas J. GA 23rd Inf. Co.H
Tweedle, William TX 9th (Young's) Inf. Co.I
Tweedle, William H. AR 2nd Mtd.Rifles Co.E
Tweedy, Edmund A. VA 11th Inf. Co.C Cpl.
Tweedy, Ephraim GA Cobb's Legion Co.A 1st Lt.
Tweedy, Fayette B. VA 11th Inf. Co.C
Tweedy, F.W. GA 64th Inf. Co.C
Tweedy, George D. VA 11th Inf. Co.C
Tweedy, George W. NC 17th Inf. (1st Org.) Co.F
Tweedy, George W. NC 17th Inf. (2nd Org.) Co.A
Tweedy, Hardy NC 17th Inf. (2nd Org.) Co.A
Tweedy, Harvey NC 17th Inf. (2nd Org.) Co.A
Tweedy, Henry H. NC 1st Inf. Co.H
Tweedy, I.W. MO Cav. Fristoe's Regt. Co.K
Tweedy, Jacob K. GA Inf. White's Co.
Tweedy, James GA 42nd Inf.
Tweedy, James G. NC 1st Inf. Co.H Sgt.
Tweedy, James Madison GA 20th Inf. Co.K
Tweedy, J.K. GA 9th Inf. (St.Guards) Culp's Co.
Tweedy, John W. AR 38th Inf. Co.C Sgt.
Tweedy, Joseph MO 4th Cav. Co.E
Tweedy, Joseph MO Cav. Coleman's Regt. Co.A
Tweedy, Joseph B. VA 11th Inf. Co.H
Tweedy, Joseph W. AR 38th Inf. Co.C
Tweedy, J.S. AR 47th (Crandall's) Cav. Co.D Cpl.
Tweedy, Milton GA Lt.Arty. 12th Bn. 3rd Co.C Sgt.
Tweedy, R.A. AR 38th Inf. Co.C,E
Tweedy, R.A. MO 15th Cav. Co.G Sgt.
Tweedy, R.C. AR 15th (N.W.) Inf. Co.I Capt.
Tweedy, R.C. AR Inf. Williamson's Bn. Co.A Capt.
Tweedy, R.E. VA 2nd Cav. Co.I
Tweedy, Robert AR 7th Inf. Co.E
Tweedy, Robert C. VA 11th Inf. Co.C
Tweedy, Robert W. VA 13th Inf. 2nd Co.B Sgt.
Tweedy, Smith P., Jr. VA 11th Inf. Co.C
Tweedy, Thomas T. AL 9th Inf. Co.H
Tweedy, T.T. AL 9th Inf. Co.F
Tweedy, W. SC Mil.Arty. 1st Regt. Walter's Co.
Tweedy, W. SC Charleston Arsenal Bn. Co.B Capt.
Tweedy, William T. GA 4th Inf. Co.G
Tweedy, William W. NC 1st Inf. Co.H
Tweetly, J. Brush Bn.
Tweitman, J.H. SC Inf. 1st (Charleston) Bn. Co.F Cpl.
Twelley, William R. GA Mil. Lee's Bn. Co.K
Twells, George LA Inf. McLean's Co. 3rd Lt.
Twhie, John MS 10th Inf. Old Co.H
Twichel, A.F. TX 25th Cav. Co.F
Twichel, A.T. TX 3rd (Kirby's) Bn.Vol. Co.C
Twichell, Albert H. SC 13th Inf. Co.C
Twichell, B.F. TX 25th Cav. Co.F
Twichell, C. Carter LA Washington Arty.Bn. Co.2 Cpl.
Twichell, H. Tracy LA Washington Arty.Bn. Co.2
Twichell, Jerome AR 8th Inf. New Co.E
Twichell, Seth TX 28th Cav. Co.M
Twichell, Seth TX 14th Inf. 2nd Co.K
Twicher, James LA Mil. Beauregard Bn. Co.D Marker
Twiddy, Benjamin A. NC 12th Inf. Co.L
Twiddy, Benjamin A. NC 32nd Inf. Co.F,A
Twiddy, David MO 4th Cav. Co.E
Twiddy, James NC 17th Inf. (2nd Org.) Co.H
Twiddy, John J. NC 17th Inf. (2nd Org.) Co.H
Twiddy, Joseph NC 1st Inf. Co.G
Twiddy, Levi NC 17th Inf. (2nd Org.) Co.H
Twiddy, Uriah NC 12th Inf. Co.L
Twiddy, Uriah NC 32nd Inf. Co.F,A
Twidwell, T.Z. MS 8th Cav. Co.K
Twif, J.D. MO 1st & 3rd Cons.Cav.
Twiford, D. AL 40th Inf. Co.H
Twiford, D. AL 63rd Inf. Co.K Cpl.
Twiford, George W. KY 7th Mtd.Inf. Co.H Sgt.
Twiford, Henry V. VA 6th Inf. 2nd Co.B Cpl.
Twiford, James H. VA 5th Cav. (12 mo. '61-2) Co.B

Twiford, James H. VA Cav. 14th Bn. Co.C
Twiford, James H. VA 39th Inf. Co.I
Twiford, John W. MS 1st Cav.
Twiford, John W. Conf.Cav. Raum's Co.
Twiford, Purnell O. VA 39th Inf. Co.F
Twiford, Purnel O. VA 46th Inf. 4th Co.F Cpl.
Twiford, Revell D. VA 1st Arty. Co.I Driver
Twiford, Rivel VA Vol. Binford's Co. Cpl.
Twiford, William H. VA 39th Inf. Co.F
Twiford, William H. VA 46th Inf. 4th Co.F
Twigg, Jerry TN 1st Hvy.Arty. Co.F
Twigg, J.H. TN 4th Inf. Co.E
Twigg, Samuel H. VA Hvy.Arty. A.J. Jones' Co.
Twigg, Wm. MO St.Guard
Twiggs, Alfred GA Inf. (Anderson Guards) Anderson's Co.
Twiggs, David E. Gen. & Staff Maj.Gen.
Twiggs, G.W. GA Cav. Allen's Co.
Twiggs, H.D.D. GA 1st Reg. Co.G,D Lt.Col.
Twiggs, H.D.D. Gen. & Staff Capt.
Twiggs, J. MS Inf. 2nd Bn. Co.E
Twiggs, J. MS 48th Inf. Co.E
Twiggs, James TX 27th Cav. Co.B
Twiggs, J.E. LA 4th Inf. Co.A
Twiggs, J.M. GA 23rd Inf. Co.G
Twiggs, John D. SC 1st Cav. Co.C Lt.Col.
Twiggs, Joseph A. SC 1st Cav. Co.C,K
Twiggs, Richard LA C.S. Zouave Bn. Co.D
Twiggs, Richard T. VA Lt.Arty. Page's Co.
Twiggs, W.D.D. GA Arty. Maxwell's Reg. Lt.Btty. Lt.
Twiggs, William NC 6th Inf. Co.D
Twiggs, William A. GA 52nd Inf. Co.H
Twilla, Henry C. TN 53rd Inf. Co.F
Twillegar, George E. TX 10th Inf. Co.C
Twilleger, G.E. TX Cav. Benavides' Regt. Co.D
Twilley, --- AL 25th Inf. Co.F
Twilley, Benjamin F. MD Inf. 2nd Bn. Co.G
Twilley, Benjamin F. VA 16th Inf. 2nd Co.H Cpl.
Twilley, Elias P. TN 24th Inf. Co.I
Twilley, George H. MD Inf. 2nd Bn. Co.C
Twilley, George W. GA 20th Inf. Co.I Cpl.
Twilley, Henry GA Inf. 1st Loc.Troops (Augusta) Co.G
Twilley, Henry GA 6th Inf. Co.A
Twilley, James GA 7th Inf. Co.C
Twilley, James W. GA 42nd Inf. Co.D,E
Twilley, Jesse AL 28th Inf. Co.F
Twilley, J.S. AL 25th Inf. Co.F Cpl.
Twilley, J.T. AL 25th Inf. Co.F
Twilley, J.W. AL 25th Inf. Co.F
Twilley, J.W. AR 8th Cav. Co.D
Twilley, Thomas C. AL 46th Inf. Co.G,C
Twilley, W.R. GA Cav. 9th Bn. (St.Guards) Co.F Sgt.
Twillie, Henry GA 54th Inf. Co.H
Twilligear, George E. TX 12th Cav. Co.A
Twilly, Benjamin F. VA 39th Inf. Co.L
Twilly, George Thomas VA 12th Cav. Co.I
Twilly, James T. GA 17th Inf. Co.H
Twilly, W.B. TN 10th (DeMoss') Cav. Co.A
Twilly, William GA Inf. 1st City Bn. (Columbus) Co.F
Twine, W.M. MS Cav. 3rd Bn.Res. Co.C 1st Sgt.
Twiner, B.W. MS 1st Lt.Arty. Co.F
Twiner, J.A. MS 4th Cav. Co.C
Twiner, J.A. MS Cav. Hughes' Bn. Co.A
Twiner, J.A. MS 1st Lt.Arty. Co.I
Twiner, James MS 46th Inf. Co.C
Twiner, James M. MS 18th Inf. Co.B
Twiner, J.D. MS Cav. 24th Bn. Co.F
Twiner, John T. MS 1st Lt.Arty. Co.I
Twiner, Joseph A. Conf.Cav. Wood's Regt. Co.K
Twiner, Mack MS 36th Inf. Co.G
Twiner, M.C. MS Cav. 24th Bn. Co.B
Twiner, M.H. MS 1st Lt.Arty. Co.F
Twiner, W.M. MS Inf. 2nd Bn. (St.Troops) Co.B 2nd Lt.
Twiner, W.M. Conf.Cav. Wood's Regt. Co.K
Twingler, N.J. GA 12th Inf. Co.F
Twining, Isaac AL Inf. 1st Regt. Co.D
Twinney, William A. MO 1st N.E. Cav. Co.L
Twisdale, Alexander G. NC 43rd Inf. Co.G
Twisdale, D.M. TN 7th (Duckworth's) Cav. Co.B
Twisdale, George W. VA 14th Inf. Co.E
Twisdale, G.T. TN 9th Inf. Co.C
Twisdale, James H. NC 1st Jr.Res. Co.A Cpl.
Twisdale, John E. VA 87th Mil. Co.C
Twisdale, John W. VA 53rd Inf. Co.H
Twisdale, Pleasant A. NC 12th Inf. Co.C
Twisdell, F.M. TN 7th Cav. Co.D
Twissdale, W.W. VA Loc.Def. Durrett's Co.
Twist, M.T. GA 49th Inf. Co.C 2nd Lt.
Twister 1st Cherokee Mtd.Rifles Co.C
Twister 2nd Cherokee Mtd.Vol. Co.I
Twitty, A.M. SC 1st (Butler's) Inf. Co.G
Twitty, A.M. SC 2nd Inf. Co.H
Twitty, Andrew J. GA 2nd Cav. Co.C
Twitty, Charles R. SC 16th Inf. Co.A 1st Sgt.
Twitty, Decatur I. NC 6th Cav. (65th St.Troops) Co.D 1st Lt.
Twitty, D.J. SC 5th St.Troops Co.E
Twitty, D.J. SC 7th Res. Co.L
Twitty, F.R. SC 5th Bn.Res. Co.E
Twitty, Francis L. NC 34th Inf. Co.C Ens.
Twitty, G.W. AR Lt.Arty. Owen's Btty.
Twitty, G.W. SC 12th Inf. Co.E
Twitty, Henry F. NC 12th Inf. Co.C
Twitty, Hiram B. TX Cav. Baylor's Regt. Co.D Sgt.
Twitty, James K.P. TN 17th Inf. Co.C
Twitty, James R. NC 16th Inf. Co.G
Twitty, James T. TN 31st Inf.
Twitty, J.B. GA Inf. (Mitchell Home Guards) Brooks' Co.
Twitty, John AL 9th Inf. Co.H
Twitty, John E. NC 12th Inf. Co.C Sgt.
Twitty, John W. SC 4th Cav. Co.H
Twitty, L.H. TN Lt.Arty. Huggins' Co.
Twitty, L.H. TN 17th Inf. Co.H
Twitty, Patrick H. TN 17th Inf. Co.C
Twitty, P.B. SC Lt.Arty. 3rd (Palmetto) Bn. Co.G
Twitty, Peter S. GA 4th Inf. Co.K Sgt.
Twitty, Peter W. GA 2nd Cav. Co.C Capt.
Twitty, Peter W. GA 18th Inf. Co.D 2nd Lt.
Twitty, P.L. TN 28th (Cons.) Inf. Co.E Cpl.
Twitty, P.L. TN 84th Inf. Co.A Cpl.
Twitty, P.T. SC Lt.Arty. 3rd (Palmetto) Bn. Co.G
Twitty, R.C. NC 1st Cav. (9th St.Troops) Co.E Adj.
Twitty, Reuben GA 8th Inf. Co.C
Twitty, Robert C. NC 12th Inf. Co.C Sr.2nd Lt.
Twitty, S.C. TN 40th Inf. Co.E 1st Lt.
Twitty, Smith C. AL 54th Inf. Co.I Capt.
Twitty, Theophilus B. NC 34th Inf. Hosp.Stew.
Twitty, Thomas TX 2nd Cav. 1st Co.F
Twitty, Thomas TX Cav. Morgan's Regt. Co.I
Twitty, Thomas W. TN 32nd Inf. Co.G Cpl.
Twitty, W. AL Cav. Moreland's Regt. Co.F
Twitty, W.C. Gen. & Staff Capt.,AQM
Twitty, William B. SC 12th Inf. Co.I Sgt.
Twitty, William C. TX 11th Cav. Co.B Capt.
Twitty, William C. TX Cav. Bourland's Regt. AQM
Twitty, William L. NC 34th Inf. Co.C
Twitty, Willis W. MS 26th Inf. Co.A
Twitty, W.W. SC Lt.Arty. 3rd (Palmetto) Bn. Co.H
Twitty, Wynn TN 53rd Inf. Co.B
Twity, Lewis M. SC Inf. 7th Bn. (Enfield Rifles) Co.D Cpl.
Twity, Watson W. SC 16th Inf. Co.A
Twohey, Francis MO 1st Inf. Co.A Cpl.
Twohig, John MS 7th Inf. Co.B
Twohy, John MS 9th Inf. New Co.B
Twoieg, John MS 12th Inf. Co.C
Twoley, Isaac T. VA 5th Cav. Co.I
Twombly, William O. GA 4th (Clinch's) Cav. Co.K,B
Twombly, William O. GA 26th Inf. Atkinson's Co.B
Twomey, Cornelius GA 5th Inf. Co.C
Twomey, James VA 27th Inf. Co.B Cpl.
Twomey, Morris D. TN 48th (Voorhies') Inf. Co.I 2nd Lt.
Twomy, Cornelius LA 20th Inf. Co.G Music.
Twony, John LA 10th Inf. Co.K
Twyford, J.C. TN 38th Inf. Co.I
Twyford, John P. KY 4th Mtd.Inf. Co.I
Twyford, Revel T. VA Lt.Arty. 38th Bn. Co.B
Twyford, William KY 6th Cav. Co.H,C
Twyford, W.S. TN 38th Inf. Co.I
Twyman, --- TX Cav. Steele's Command Co.B
Twyman, Anthony VA Cav. 39th Bn. Co.C
Twyman, Buford KY 5th Cav. Co.A
Twyman, Buford VA 9th Cav. Co.E
Twyman, D.L. MO 11th Inf. Co.I
Twyman, Frank K.B. MO Unassign.Conscr.
Twyman, H.D. GA Inf. 1st Conf.Bn. Co.E Capt.
Twyman, Horace D. GA 1st Bn.S.S. Co.A Capt.
Twyman, James W. VA 3rd Inf.Loc.Def. Co.D Sgt.
Twyman, James W. VA 82nd Mil. Col.
Twyman, John J. VA 9th Cav. Co.E
Twyman, John W. KY Recruit
Twyman, John W. TN 6th (Wheeler's) Cav. Co.I
Twyman, J.W. TX 11th Cav. Co.E
Twyman, J.W. VA 4th Cav. Co.C
Twyman, R.D. KY 4th Mtd.Inf. Co.E
Twyman, R.G. AR 5th Inf. Co.D 1st Lt.
Twyman, Smith VA 1st Bn.Res. Co.H
Twyman, Travis J. VA 19th Inf. Co.E Cpl.
Twyman, Tucker A. VA Cav. 35th Bn. Co.F
Twyman, Walker G. VA 19th Inf. Co.B Cpl.

Twyman, Wesley R. VA 9th Cav. Co.E Sgt.
Twyman, William S. VA 109th Mil. 1st Co.A
Twyman, W.J. AR 1st (Monroe's) Cav. Co.H 1st Sgt.
Twyman, W. Redd KY 5th Cav. Co.A
Twyman, W. Redd TN 9th (Ward's) Cav. Kirkpatrick's Co.
Twymman, B. VA 8th Cav. Co.L Cpl.
Twynham, William D. VA 32nd Inf. 2nd Co.I
Twyning, Isaac AL Lt.Arty. 2nd Bn. Co.B
Tyack, J.L. NC 23rd Inf. Co.I
Tyack, Joseph L. VA 11th Inf. Co.I QMSgt.
Tyce, Andrew J. GA 31st Inf. Co.B
Tyce, John GA Floyd Legion (St.Guards) Co.K
Tyce, Moses NC 2nd Arty. (36th St.Troops) Co.E
Tyce, Moses NC 20th Inf. Co.C
Tycer, J.A. AR 36th Inf. Co.H
Tycer, Lewis A. AR 36th Inf. Co.H
Tycer, Richard William LA 16th Inf. Co.D
Tycer, R.W. LA Ogden's Cav. Co.E
Tycer, R.W. 14th Conf.Cav. Co.H
Tydings, Charles B. KY 9th Cav. Asst.Surg.
Tydings, Chas. B. Gen. & Staff Asst.Surg.
Tydings, J.H. KY 2nd (Duke's) Cav. Co.A
Tydings, Joseph M. KY 9th Mtd.Inf. Co.B
Tydwell, J. MS 3rd Cav. Co.I
Tydwell, R.A. MS 3rd Cav. Co.I
Tye, Anthony MS 21st Inf. Co.C
Tye, B.F. AL 45th Inf.
Tye, Cullen MS 6th Cav. Co.D
Tye, Cullen MS Cav. Davenport's Bn. (St.Troops) Co.C
Tye, Drury 3rd Conf.Eng.Troops Co.A Artif.
Tye, Enoch MO 1st Cav.
Tye, Enoch MO 9th (Elliott's) Cav. Co.B
Tye, F. FL Cav. 5th Bn.
Tye, Franklin FL 6th Inf.
Tye, Franklin GA Inf. 2nd Bn. Co.B Sgt.
Tye, G.B. GA 45th Inf. Co.F
Tye, George M. MO 1st Cav. Sgt.
Tye, George M. MO 9th (Elliott's) Cav. Co.B
Tye, Henry AR 1st (Monroe's) Cav. Co.K
Tye, Henry M. GA 51st Inf. Co.G
Tye, H.H. KY 6th Cav. Co.B
Tye, James H. GA Inf. 13th Bn. (St.Guards) Guerry's Co.
Tye, James H. GA 51st Inf. Co.G
Tye, James M. GA 51st Inf. Co.H
Tye, James T. GA 51st Inf. Co.E
Tye, J.H. AR 35th Inf. Old Co.F
Tye, J.H. GA Inf. 27th Bn. (NonConscr.) Co.D
Tye, J.N. KY 6th Cav. Co.B
Tye, John AR Cav. Harrell's Bn. Co.A
Tye, John AR 14th (Powers') Inf. Co.G
Tye, John GA 61st Inf. Co.F Cpl.
Tye, John MS 30th Inf. Co.F
Tye, John TN Lt.Arty. Barry's Co.
Tye, John F. MS 1st Lt.Arty. Co.I 1st Lt.
Tye, John H. MO 11th Inf. Co.H
Tye, John W. TN Conscr. (Cp. of Instr.)
Tye, Joshua KY 6th Cav. Co.B
Tye, Joshua B. KY 10th Cav. Co.K
Tye, J.S. AR Inf. Cocke's Regt. Co.G
Tye, Lewis M. GA 10th Cav. (St.Guards) Co.B
Tye, Milton M. AL 53rd (Part.Rangers) Co.B Cpl.
Tye, P.F. GA Cav. 1st Bn.Res. Co.A
Tye, Reuben GA Inf. 13th Bn. (St.Guards) Guerry's Co.
Tye, R.S. TX 14th Inf. Co.F
Tye, Samuel Miller GA 36th (Broyles') Inf. Co.H
Tye, Thomas MS 20th Inf. Co.C
Tye, Thomas TN 2nd (Walker's) Inf. Co.I
Tye, Thomas F. MO 1st Cav. Cpl.
Tye, Thomas F. MO 9th (Elliott's) Cav. Co.B
Tye, Thomas J. AR 14th (Powers') Inf. Co.G
Tye, T.J. AR Inf. Cocke's Regt. Co.G
Tye, W.B. NC 1st Cav. (9th St.Troops) Co.C
Tye, William AR 20th Inf. Co.I
Tye, William MO Inf. Clark's Regt. Co.I
Tye, William Conf.Cav. Clarkson's Bn. Ind. Rangers Co.C
Tye, William A. NC 56th Inf. Co.K
Tye, William A. 2nd Conf.Eng.Troops Co.G Artif.
Tye, William E. GA 55th Inf. Co.A
Tye, William M. TN Lt.Arty. Barry's Co.
Tye, William M. TN Conscr. (Cp. of Instr.)
Tyeall, James 1st Cherokee Mtd.Rifles McDaniel's Co.
Tyeer, Jonatha E. MS 30th Inf. Co.F
Tyen, Edward FL Inf. 2nd Bn. Co.C
Tyen, Edward FL 10th Inf. Co.H
Tyer 1st Cherokee Mtd.Rifles McDaniel's Co.
Tyer, A. GA 1st (Symons') Res. Co.F
Tyer, Columbus MO 16th Inf. Co.A
Tyer, C.S. AR 30th Inf. Co.B
Tyer, D.A. MS 3rd Cav. Co.F
Tyer, D.A. MS 18th Cav. Co.A
Tyer, Henry Clay MS 34th Inf. Co.C
Tyer, Hillary FL 1st Cav. Co.K Cpl.
Tyer, Isham, Sr. GA Mayer's Co. (Appling Cav.)
Tyer, James R. NC 27th Inf. Co.E 2nd Lt.
Tyer, Jason GA 54th Inf. Co.F
Tyer, Jesse FL Inf. 2nd Bn. Co.B
Tyer, Jessee FL 9th Inf. Co.E
Tyer, John FL 1st Cav. Co.G
Tyer, John E. NC 27th Inf. Co.E Sgt.
Tyer, J.W. AR 30th Inf. Co.B Sgt.
Tyer, J.W. AR 30th Inf. Co.D
Tyer, M. AR 30th Inf. Co.B
Tyer, Perry MO Robertson's Regt.St.Guard Co.8
Tyer, Pleasant G. MS 34th Inf. Co.C
Tyer, R.G. AR 31st Inf. Co.H Sgt.
Tyer, Thomas R. KY 2nd Mtd.Inf. Co.G
Tyer, Thomas R. KY 4th Mtd.Inf. Co.G,I
Tyer, T.P. MO 9th Inf. Co.B
Tyer, T.P. MO Inf. Clark's Regt. Co.A
Tyer, William LA 1st Hvy.Arty. (Reg.) Co.E
Tyer, William MO Robertson's Regt.St.Guard Co.8 Cpl.
Tyer, William H. MS 11th Inf. Co.G
Tyer, William P. MO 5th Inf. Co.B Sgt.
Tyer, W.P. NC 5th Cav. (63rd St.Troops) Co.I
Tyer Mouse 1st Cherokee Mtd.Rifles Co.D
Tyers, Joshua P. AL 1st Cav. Co.I
Tyers, Lewis G. GA 6th Inf. Co.H Cpl.
Tyers, W.J. AR 1st Inf. Co.D
Tyert, S.G. MO Cav. Freeman's Regt. Co.G
Tyes, Peter F. GA 6th Inf. (St.Guards) Co.H
Tyffer, J.R. TX Granbury's Cons.Brig. Co.C
Tyffer, William TX Granbury's Cons.Brig. Co.C
Tygart, Elihu L. GA 29th Inf. Co.G
Tyger, Leonidas VA 3rd Res. Co.E
Tyger, Mark 1st Cherokee Mtd.Vol. 1st Co.F, 2nd Co.H Ord.Sgt.
Tyger, Wheeler 1st Cherokee Mtd.Rifles Co.D 1st Sgt.
Tyger Looney 1st Cherokee Mtd.Vol. 1st Co.E, 2nd Co.C
Tygert, T.B. Conf.Cav. Baxter's Bn. Co.A
Tygret, James M. AL 30th Inf. Co.E
Tygret, John A. VA 79th Mil. Co.5
Tygret, William R. VA 52nd Inf. Co.E
Tygrett, J.A. VA Inf. 26th Bn. Co.B
Tykes, C.T. GA 20th Inf. Co.G Sgt.
Tykl, Henry NC 18th Inf.
Tylar, Wilson AL Res.
Tylee, Charles A. SC Lt.Arty. 3rd (Palmetto) Bn. Co.F Sgt.
Tylee, John W.L. SC Lt.Arty. Walter's Co. (Washington Arty.)
Tylee, J.W.L. SC Mil.Arty. 1st Regt. Walter's Co.
Tylee, N., Jr. SC Mil.Arty. 1st Regt. Walter's Co.
Tylee, William MD 1st Inf. Co.B
Tylee, William C. SC 1st (Butler's) Inf. Co.D
Tyler, --- TX 1st (Yager's) Cav. Co.F
Tyler, --- TX 33rd Cav. Co.D
Tyler, A. GA Inf. 27th Bn. (NonConscr.) Co.B
Tyler, Aaron F. SC 1st (McCreary's) Inf. Co.A
Tyler, A.C. TX 5th Cav. Co.E
Tyler, A.F. KY 3rd Bn.Mtd.Rifles Co.A
Tyler, A.G. AL 39th Inf.
Tyler, A.H. AR 38th Inf. Co.C
Tyler, A.I. Conf.Cav. Raum's Co.
Tyler, A.J. GA 54th Inf. Co.G
Tyler, A.J. VA Cav. 1st Bn. (Loc.Def.Troops) Co.C
Tyler, A.L. AR 32nd Inf. Co.B
Tyler, Albert MD 1st Cav. Co.D
Tyler, Albert VA 11th Cav. Co.H
Tyler, Albert E. 1st Conf.Eng.Troops Co.A
Tyler, Alfred Gen. & Staff ADC
Tyler, Algernon VA Lt.Arty. Taylor's Co.
Tyler, Algernon VA 41st Inf. Co.B
Tyler, Allen VA 6th Inf. Co.C
Tyler, Allen VA 32nd Inf. Co.E
Tyler, Allen R. GA 35th Inf. Co.I
Tyler, Alonzo VA 46th Inf. 2nd Co.A
Tyler, A.M. NC 6th Cav. (65th St.Troops) Co.C
Tyler, Ambrose VA 25th Cav. Co.C
Tyler, A.R. MS Conscr.
Tyler, Asbury AR 16th Inf. Co.G Sgt.
Tyler, Augustas AR 17th (Lemoyne's) Inf. Co.A Sgt.
Tyler, Augustine MS 18th Inf. Co.I Sgt.
Tyler, Augustus AR 21st Inf. Co.D Capt.
Tyler, Augustus F. KY 1st Bn.Mtd.Rifles Co.A
Tyler, Barker KY 12th Cav. Co.D
Tyler, Bazel W. MO 10th Inf. Co.I
Tyler, Ben MO Cav. 2nd Regt.St.Guard Co.D Capt.
Tyler, Benjamin MO Capt.
Tyler, Benjamin VA 6th Bn.Res. Co.H
Tyler, Benjamin F. AR 25th Inf. Co.A
Tyler, Benjamin R. VA 26th Inf. Co.C
Tyler, Benjamin R. VA 52nd Mil. Co.A
Tyler, B.F. SC 1st Cav. Co.C

Tyler, B.F. 2nd Conf.Eng.Troops Co.A
Tyler, Brinkly H. TX 4th Cav. Co.F Sgt.
Tyler, Brittain C. GA 1st Inf. (St.Guards) Co.H 2nd Lt.
Tyler, Caleb GA 36th (Broyles') Inf. Co.G
Tyler, Caleb 1st Conf.Inf. Co.B
Tyler, Calvin AR 3rd Cav. 2nd Co.E, Co.I Sgt.
Tyler, Calvin VA Inf. 1st Bn.Loc.Def. Co.C
Tyler, C.E. VA 4th Cav. Co.H
Tyler, C.H. KY 5th Cav. Co.A
Tyler, Charles AR 15th (Johnson's) Inf. Co.F
Tyler, Charles GA Lt.Arty. Ritter's Co.
Tyler, Charles GA 5th Inf. (St.Guards) Russell's Co.
Tyler, Charles KY 5th Cav. Co.A
Tyler, Charles MD Arty. 3rd Btty.
Tyler, Charles MO 5th Cav. Co.A
Tyler, Charles MO Arty. Jos. Bledsoe's Co. Cpl.
Tyler, Charles MO 50th Inf. Co.E 2nd Lt.
Tyler, Charles E. VA Cav. Mosby's Regt. (Part.Rangers) Co.B
Tyler, Charles E. VA 49th Inf. Co.A 2nd Lt.
Tyler, Chas. H. Gen. & Staff, Inf. Capt.
Tyler, Chas. W. TN 10th (DeMoss') Cav. Co.E Capt.
Tyler, Clarence W. KY 2nd Cav. Co.A
Tyler, Clarence W. NC 18th Inf. Co.I
Tyler, C.M. KY 12th Cav. Co.E
Tyler, C.P. MS Lt.Arty. 14th Bn. Co.C
Tyler, C.R. TN 15th Inf. Co.D
Tyler, C.W. MS 20th Inf. Co.D Sgt.
Tyler, C.W. MS 41st Inf. Co.I Sgt.
Tyler, D. TX 12th Cav. Co.B
Tyler, Dabney VA 49th Inf. Co.I
Tyler, Daniel VA 17th Cav. Co.F
Tyler, Daniel VA 52nd Inf. Co.H
Tyler, Daniel Z.B. AL Lt.Arty. Hurt's Btty.
Tyler, David C. NC 17th Inf. (2nd Org.) Co.C
Tyler, David L. VA 15th Inf. Co.I
Tyler, D.C. GA 1st Inf. (St.Guards) Co.H
Tyler, DeWitt MS Cav. Buck's Co.
Tyler, D.G. VA Rockbridge Cty.Res. Bacon's Co.
Tyler, D. Gardner VA Lt.Arty. Arch. Graham's Co.
Tyler, D.H. AR 27th Inf. Co.D
Tyler, D.S. SC 2nd Arty. Co.C
Tyler, D.S. SC 11th Res. Co.G Capt.
Tyler, E. TX 9th Cav. Co.H
Tyler, E.B. SC 2nd Arty. Co.H
Tyler, E.B. SC 8th Bn.Res. Co.C
Tyler, Ed M. LA LA & Govt.Employees Regt. Co.H Capt.
Tyler, Edmund A. VA 8th Inf. Co.D Cpl.
Tyler, Edward GA 22nd Inf. Co.F
Tyler, Edward TX 13th Cav. Co.C
Tyler, Edward VA Inf. 5th Bn.Loc.Def.
Tyler, Edwin AR 3rd Cav. 2nd Co.E, Co.I
Tyler, E.G. VA Arty. B.H. Smith's Co.
Tyler, E.G. VA 3rd Inf.Loc.Def. Co.B
Tyler, E.H. Lt.Col.
Tyler, Elbert VA 6th Bn.Res. Co.H
Tyler, Elias SC Inf. 9th Bn. Co.G
Tyler, Elias SC 26th Inf. Co.K
Tyler, Elias H. GA 26th Inf. Co.H
Tyler, Elisha SC Arty. Manigault's Bn. 1st Co.B Bugler
Tyler, Elisha SC 1st (McCreary's) Inf. Co.F
Tyler, Elisha VA 13th Cav. Co.C
Tyler, Erastus G. VA Lt.Arty. 1st Bn. Co.D
Tyler, F.A. MS 3rd Cav. Co.K
Tyler, F.A. TN Inf. 3rd Bn. Co.E
Tyler, Felix VA Lt.Arty. Montgomery's Co.
Tyler, Fielden B. VA Hvy.Arty. 20th Bn. Co.D Cpl.
Tyler, Fleming VA Lt.Arty. Montgomery's Co.
Tyler, F.M. AL 25th Inf. Co.A
Tyler, F.M. AR 1st Mtd.Rifles Co.K
Tyler, F.M. LA 2nd Cav. Co.G
Tyler, Francis M. AR 25th Inf. Co.A
Tyler, Francis M. GA 14th Inf. Co.C 1st Sgt.
Tyler, Franklin AR 25th Inf. Co.A
Tyler, Frank M. TX 18th Inf. Co.D
Tyler, F.S. GA Inf. 9th Bn. Co.E
Tyler, Gardner Gen. & Staff 2nd Lt.,Dr.M.
Tyler, George MD 1st Cav. Co.D
Tyler, George MD 1st Inf. Co.A Sgt.
Tyler, George MS Cav.Brig.Res.
Tyler, George VA 9th Cav. Co.H
Tyler, George Johnson's Staff Capt.,AAG
Tyler, George B. AR 10th Cav. Co.A
Tyler, George Bailey VA 8th Inf. Co.C QMSgt.
Tyler, George C. VA Lt.Arty. Woolfolk's Co.
Tyler, George C. VA 46th Inf. 2nd Co.A
Tyler, George E. MO 2nd Cav. New Co.H
Tyler, George E. TN Lt.Arty. Palmer's Co.
Tyler, George N. VA Inf. 21st Bn. Co.E Capt.
Tyler, George N. VA 64th Mtd.Inf. Co.K Capt.
Tyler, Geo. N. VA Mil. 139th Regt. Co.E Capt.
Tyler, George P. VA Lt.Arty. 38th Bn. Co.C Cpl.
Tyler, George W. GA 14th Inf. Co.C
Tyler, George W. LA 28th (Thomas') Inf. Co.I
Tyler, George W. MS 29th Inf. Co.G
Tyler, George W. MO 2nd Cav. Co.B
Tyler, Grafton, Jr. MD Arty. 1st Btty.
Tyler, Grafton Conf.Arty. Braxton's Bn. 1st Lt., Adj.
Tyler, Grafton Gen. & Staff 1st Lt.,Adj.
Tyler, Grayson VA 17th Inf. Co.F Lt.Col.
Tyler, Gustavus VA 7th Cav. Co.E
Tyler, Gustavus VA 17th Inf. Co.B Cpl.
Tyler, G.W. AL 3rd Cav. Co.G
Tyler, G.W. AL 3rd Inf. Co.G
Tyler, G.W. AL 25th Inf. Co.A
Tyler, G.W. GA 5th Res. Co.C
Tyler, G.W. MO Cav. 2nd Regt.St.Guard Co.E 2nd Lt.
Tyler, H.A. KY 12th Cav. Co.A Capt.
Tyler, H.A. SC 3rd Inf. Ord.Sgt.
Tyler, H.A. TN 5th Inf. 2nd Co.K Sgt.
Tyler, H.C. MS Cav. Gartley's Co. (Yazoo Rangers) Capt.
Tyler, H.C. VA Lt.Arty. Woolfolk's Co.
Tyler, H.C. Gen. & Staff 1st Lt.,Prov.Marsh.
Tyler, H.E. LA 7th Cav. Co.A
Tyler, Henry KY 8th Mtd.Inf. Co.G
Tyler, Henry MS Cav. 2nd Bn.Res. Co.I Sgt.
Tyler, Henry MS Scouts Montgomery's Co.
Tyler, Henry MO 4th Cav. Co.H,B
Tyler, Henry MO Mtd.Inf. Boone's Regt.
Tyler, Henry NC 16th Inf.
Tyler, Henry VA Lt.Arty. Parker's Co.
Tyler, Henry VA 16th Inf. Co.B
Tyler, Henry A. SC 8th Inf. Co.F Ord.Sgt.
Tyler, Henry C. MS 18th Inf. Co.D 1st Lt.
Tyler, Henry C. VA 24th Cav. Co.A
Tyler, Henry C. VA Cav. 40th Bn. Co.A
Tyler, Henry C. VA 74th Mil. Co.E
Tyler, Henry N. AL Lt.Arty. Hurt's Btty.
Tyler, Hick AL 4th (Russell's) Cav. Co.I
Tyler, Hickman AL 35th Inf.
Tyler, Hickman AL 49th Inf.
Tyler, Hiram A. TN 34th Inf. Co.B
Tyler, H.L. MS 16th Inf. Co.F
Tyler, H.M. TN 5th Inf. 2nd Co.D
Tyler, H.N. MS 18th Inf. Co.I
Tyler, Hugh SC 1st (Hagood's) Inf. 1st Co.E
Tyler, Hugh SC 1st (McCreary's) Inf. Co.F
Tyler, Hugh SC 25th Inf. Co.C
Tyler, Ira W. MS 1st Lt.Arty. Co.L Cpl.
Tyler, Isaac LA 26th Inf. Co.H
Tyler, Isaac B. VA Cav. 46th Bn. Co.A
Tyler, Isaac G. NC 2nd Arty. (36th St.Troops) Co.A
Tyler, Isam MO 15th Cav. Co.E
Tyler, Isham AR 25th Inf. Co.A
Tyler, Ishem AR 38th Inf. Co.H
Tyler, J. LA Inf. Pelican Regt. Co.G
Tyler, J. LA Sabine Res.
Tyler, J.A. 7th Conf.Cav. Co.D
Tyler, Jack AR 7th Inf. Co.F
Tyler, Jackson SC 26th Inf. Co.K
Tyler, Jacob S. VA 15th Inf. Co.D
Tyler, James AL 38th Inf. Co.B
Tyler, James AR 7th Inf. Co.F
Tyler, James AR 27th Inf. Co.A
Tyler, James AR 33rd Inf. Co.F
Tyler, James AR 38th Inf. Co.H
Tyler, James GA 1st (Olmstead's) Inf. Co.I
Tyler, James LA 2nd Cav. Co.B
Tyler, James MO 9th (Elliott's) Cav.
Tyler, James MO 15th Cav. Co.G,D
Tyler, James MO Cav. Schnabel's Bn.
Tyler, James NC 2nd Arty. (36th St.Troops) Co.A
Tyler, James VA 20th Cav. Co.E
Tyler, James VA Hvy.Arty. 18th Bn. Co.E
Tyler, James VA Inf. 25th Bn. Co.E
Tyler, James A. VA Lt.Arty. Douthat's Co.
Tyler, James E. VA 19th Cav. Co.F
Tyler, James E. VA Lt.Arty. Brander's Co. 2nd Lt.
Tyler, James E. VA 1st Inf. Co.A
Tyler, James E. VA 12th Inf. Co.G Capt.
Tyler, James E. VA 21st Inf. Co.F
Tyler, James E. VA 2nd Cav.St.Line McNeel's Co.
Tyler, James F. VA 37th Inf. Co.K
Tyler, James H. GA 2nd Cav. Co.G
Tyler, James H. Sig.Corps,CSA
Tyler, James K.P. MS 1st Lt.Arty. Co.L
Tyler, James M. AR 25th Inf. Co.A
Tyler, James M. MS 15th Inf. Co.E
Tyler, James M. VA Lt.Arty. Parker's Co. Sgt.
Tyler, James M. VA 17th Inf. Co.B
Tyler, James P. TN 5th Inf. 2nd Co.K Cpl.
Tyler, James P. VA Courtney Arty.

Tyler, James Rochelle VA Inf. 1st Bn. Co.B 1st Lt.
Tyler, James S. VA Hvy.Arty. A.J. Jones' Co.
Tyler, James W. SC 1st (McCreary's) Inf. Co.A
Tyler, J.B. AR 6th Inf. Co.A
Tyler, J.B. TN 21st Inf. Co.C
Tyler, J.C. AR 15th (Johnson's) Inf. Co.E
Tyler, J.C. SC 2nd Arty. Co.H
Tyler, Jefferson AR 25th Inf. Co.A
Tyler, Jesse L. KY 6th Cav. Co.D,G
Tyler, J.F. AL 57th Inf. Co.A
Tyler, J.F. MS Condrey's Co. (Bull Mtn.Invinc.)
Tyler, J.F. Lee's Div. Ord.Sgt.
Tyler, J.F.M. AL 30th Inf. Co.F
Tyler, J.H. VA Lt.Arty. R.M. Anderson's Co.
Tyler, J.H. VA 60th Inf.
Tyler, J.H. Stuart Horse Arty.,CSA Deserter
Tyler, J.J. MO 1st Regt.St.Guards Co.A
Tyler, J.L.W. TN 28th Inf. Co.I
Tyler, J.M. AL 20th Inf. Co.G
Tyler, J.M. AR 38th Inf. Co.H Cpl.
Tyler, J.M. MS Cav. 1st Bn. (McNair's) St.Troops Co.C
Tyler, J.M. SC 8th Bn.Res. Co.C
Tyler, J.M. TN 14th Inf. Co.K,A
Tyler, J.M. VA Cav. 39th Bn. Co.D
Tyler, J. Monroe MO Inf. 3rd Bn. Co.E 1st Sgt.
Tyler, J. Monroe MO 6th Inf. Co.C 2nd Lt.
Tyler, J.N. VA Cav. 1st Bn. (Loc.Def.Troops) Co.C
Tyler, J.N.N. AR 50th Inf. Co.C
Tyler, Jobe GA Inf. (Jasper & Butts Cty.Guards) Lane's Co.
Tyler, Job M., Jr. GA 4th Inf. Co.G
Tyler, John AL 7th Inf.
Tyler, John AL 9th Inf. Co.B
Tyler, John AL 42nd Inf. Co.K
Tyler, John AL 63rd Inf. Co.D
Tyler, John AR 7th Inf. Co.F
Tyler, John AR 14th (Powers') Inf. Co.A
Tyler, John AR 27th Inf. Co.A
Tyler, John GA 37th Inf.
Tyler, John GA 42nd Inf. Co.E
Tyler, John LA Mil. 3rd Regt. 2nd Brig. 1st Div.
Tyler, John LA 11th Inf. Co.E
Tyler, John LA 12th Inf. Co.D
Tyler, John MS 38th Cav. Co.D
Tyler, John MS Condrey's Co. (Bull Mtn. Invinc.)
Tyler, John MO 3rd Cav. Co.A Sr.2nd Lt.
Tyler, John NC 1st Inf. Co.F
Tyler, John NC 18th Inf. Co.D
Tyler, John NC 50th Inf. Co.B
Tyler, John TN 3rd (Forrest's) Cav. Co.G
Tyler, John TN 12th (Cons.) Inf. Co.D
Tyler, John TN 22nd Inf. Co.K
Tyler, John TN 29th Inf.
Tyler, John TX 28th Cav. Co.I Far.
Tyler, John TX Cav. Hardeman's Regt. Co.G 1st Lt.
Tyler, John TX 3rd Inf. Co.D
Tyler, John VA Hvy.Arty. 18th Bn. Co.E
Tyler, John VA 6th Bn.Res. Co.H
Tyler, John VA 21st Inf. Co.F Sgt.
Tyler, John 1st Choctaw & Chickasaw Mtd.Rifles 2nd Co.D
Tyler, John Conf.Inf. Tucker's Regt. Co.E
Tyler, John Gen. & Staff Maj.,AAG
Tyler, John A. TX 17th Inf. Co.I
Tyler, John A. VA 24th Cav. Co.B
Tyler, John A. VA Cav. 40th Bn. Co.B
Tyler, John A. VA Inf. 21st Bn. Co.A
Tyler, John Alexander VA Lt.Arty. Arch. Graham's Co.
Tyler, John B. MD 1st Cav. Co.D
Tyler, John B. VA Horse Arty. Shoemaker's Co.
Tyler, John B. VA Lt.Arty. Thompson's Co.
Tyler, John E. GA Lt.Arty. Milledge's Co.
Tyler, John E. MD 1st Inf. Co.A
Tyler, John F. TX 8th Cav. Co.I
Tyler, John H. VA Lt.Arty. Brander's Co. 1st Lt.
Tyler, John H. VA 1st St.Res. Co.A,F Sgt.
Tyler, John H. VA 23rd Inf. Co.H
Tyler, John H. VA Inf. 25th Bn. Co.F
Tyler, John H. VA 59th Inf. 3rd Co.D
Tyler, John J. GA 14th Inf. Co.C
Tyler, John J. MO Lt.Arty. 1st Btty. Cpl.
Tyler, John J. MO Lt.Arty. Landis' Co.
Tyler, John J. SC 2nd Arty. Co.A
Tyler, John J. VA 13th Inf. Co.C
Tyler, John J. VA 15th Inf. Co.D
Tyler, John O. MS 20th Inf. Co.D
Tyler, John P. AL 26th (O'Neal's) Inf. Co.C Sgt.
Tyler, John Python Gen. & Staff Maj.,QM
Tyler, John R. MS 15th Inf. Co.E Cpl.
Tyler, John S. TN 40th Inf. Co.D
Tyler, John S. VA Lt.Arty. W.P. Carter's Co.
Tyler, John S. VA 39th Inf. Co.L 2nd Lt.
Tyler, John T. GA Cav. Hughes' Regt.
Tyler, John T. LA 12th Inf. Co.B
Tyler, John T. TN Lt.Arty. Huggins' Co.
Tyler, John T. TN 37th Inf. Co.A
Tyler, John T. VA Inf. 2nd Bn.Loc.Def. Co.C
Tyler, John T. VA 34th Inf. Co.H
Tyler, John W. AR Cav. Davies' Bn. Co.C,D
Tyler, John W. AR 3rd Inf. Co.F
Tyler, John W. GA 2nd Cav. Co.G
Tyler, John W. VA 56th Inf. Co.H
Tyler, Joseph KY 2nd (Duke's) Cav. Co.F
Tyler, Joseph NC 4th Cav. (59th St.Troops) Co.I
Tyler, Joseph NC Cav. 12th Bn. Co.B
Tyler, Joseph NC 8th Inf. Co.I
Tyler, Joseph TN Cav. 9th Bn. (Gantt's) Co.A
Tyler, Joseph TX 8th Inf. Co.E
Tyler, Joseph VA 9th Cav. Co.E
Tyler, Joseph 8th (Dearing's) Conf.Cav. Co.B
Tyler, Joseph A. LA 12th Inf. Co.A
Tyler, Joseph B. GA 2nd Cav. Co.G
Tyler, Joseph F. VA 24th Cav. Co.B
Tyler, Joseph F. VA Cav. 40th Bn. Co.B
Tyler, Joseph F. VA Courtney Arty.
Tyler, Joseph K. MO Inf. 3rd Regt.St.Guard Co.H 1st Lt.
Tyler, Joseph L. SC 2nd Arty. Co.H Sgt.
Tyler, Joseph W. VA 57th Inf. Co.H Cpl.
Tyler, Joshua M. SC 2nd St.Troops Co.K
Tyler, J.P. AR Cav. Harrell's Bn. Co.D
Tyler, J.P. AR 27th Inf. Co.D
Tyler, J.R. GA 23rd Inf. Co.A Capt.
Tyler, J.S. AR 15th (Johnson's) Inf. Co.B
Tyler, J.T. SC 2nd Arty. Co.H
Tyler, J.T. TN 47th Inf. Co.K
Tyler, J.T. VA 2nd Inf.Loc.Def. Co.A
Tyler, J.U. KY Cav. 2nd Bn. (Dortch's) Co.B
Tyler, Julius H. VA 16th Inf. Co.B
Tyler, J.W. KY 7th Cav. Co.H
Tyler, J.W. KY 12th Cav. Co.E
Tyler, J.W. LA 17th Inf. Co.I
Tyler, J.W. LA 28th (Thomas') Inf. Co.I
Tyler, J.W. MS 39th Inf. Co.F
Tyler, J.W. SC 2nd Arty. Co.B
Tyler, J.W. TN 24th Inf. 1st Co.H, Co.I Cpl.
Tyler, J.W. VA 18th Cav. Co.I
Tyler, J.W. VA 13th Inf. Co.A
Tyler, J.W. VA 62nd Mtd.Inf. 1st Co.D
Tyler, L. AR 38th Inf. Co.H
Tyler, Lafayett AR 25th Inf. Co.A
Tyler, Lafayette AR 1st Mtd.Rifles Co.K
Tyler, L.D. NC Lt.Arty. 13th Bn. Co.B
Tyler, Lane C. GA 1st Inf. Co.C
Tyler, Lewis SC 10th Inf. 2nd Co.G
Tyler, Lewis A. VA 26th Inf. Co.C Sgt.
Tyler, Lewis M. TX 6th Cav. Co.K,D
Tyler, L.M. LA 19th Inf. Co.K Cpl.
Tyler, Louis MS 36th Inf.
Tyler, L.S. SC 5th Cav. Co.I
Tyler, Lucius A. NC Lt.Arty. 3rd Bn. Co.B,C
Tyler, Lucius A. NC 1st Inf. Co.F
Tyler, Luke FL 7th Inf. Co.G
Tyler, Luther R. NC 4th Cav. (59th St.Troops) Co.D Sgt.
Tyler, Lyttleton VA 4th Cav. Co.H
Tyler, M.A. NC Mallett's Bn. Co.D
Tyler, M.A. 20th Conf.Cav. 1st Co.H
Tyler, Martin V. MS 2nd Part.Rangers Co.A Cpl.
Tyler, M.B. KY Jessee's Bn.Mtd.Riflemen Co.C
Tyler, M.B. KY Part.Rangers Rowan's Co.
Tyler, M.B. VA Lt.Arty. 12th Bn. Co.B
Tyler, Melvin R. MS 42nd Inf. Co.A
Tyler, M.F. TN 18th (Newsom's) Cav. Co.D
Tyler, M.F. TN 46th Inf. Co.F 2nd Lt.
Tyler, M.J. VA 2nd Inf.Loc.Def. Co.C
Tyler, M.M. SC 22nd Inf. Co.I
Tyler, Moses NC 3rd Inf. Co.A
Tyler, Moses SC 10th Inf. 2nd Co.G
Tyler, Moses B. TX 4th Cav. Co.F
Tyler, M.V. SC 1st Cav. Co.C
Tyler, Napoleon B. NC 17th Inf. (2nd Org.) Co.C
Tyler, Nat VA 46th Inf. Lt.Col.
Tyler, Nath. LA 2nd Cav. Co.G
Tyler, Nathan NC 2nd Cav. (19th St.Troops) Co.A Cook
Tyler, Nathan A. NC 1st Inf. Co.D Sgt.
Tyler, Nathan L. MO Cav. 3rd Regt.St.Guard Co.B Maj.
Tyler, Nehemiah W. MS 1st Lt.Arty. Co.L,E
Tyler, N.J. VA 1st Cav.
Tyler, N.W. AR Cav. Harrell's Bn. Co.D
Tyler, N.W. AR 27th Inf. Co.D
Tyler, O.A. GA 19th Inf. Co.E Cpl.
Tyler, O.H. Gen. & Staff,PACS Col.
Tyler, Peter AR 14th (Powers') Inf. Co.D
Tyler, P.H. TX Inf. 3rd St.Troops Co.C
Tyler, Philip MO 15th Cav. Co.B,A
Tyler, Phillip MO 3rd Cav. Co.B
Tyler, Pierson J. VA 6th Inf. Co.C
Tyler, P.J. GA 36th (Broyles') Inf. Co.G

Tyler, Pleasant AL 4th (Russell's) Cav. Co.H
Tyler, Porter AR Cav. Davies' Bn. Co.C
Tyler, P.S. AR 7th Inf. Co.H
Tyler, P.S. AR 27th Inf. Co.I Cpl.
Tyler, R. AL 38th Inf. Co.B
Tyler, R.C. AR 8th Inf. New Co.D
Tyler, R.C. TN 15th Inf. Col.
Tyler, R.C. Gen. & Staff Capt.,QM
Tyler, R.D. VA 2nd St.Res. Co.I
Tyler, R.E. SC 1st Cav. Co.C
Tyler, Redwin W. MS 14th Inf. Co.D
Tyler, Reuben A. VA 24th Cav. Co.A
Tyler, Reuben A. VA Cav. 40th Bn. Co.B
Tyler, R.F. SC 2nd Inf. Co.D
Tyler, R.F. SC 21st Inf. Co.L
Tyler, R.G. TN 1st Hvy.Arty. Co.L
Tyler, Richard B. VA Lt.Arty. Utterback's Co. Cpl.
Tyler, Richard L. AL Lt.Arty. Hurt's Btty.
Tyler, Richard L. AL 24th Inf. Co.H 2nd Lt.
Tyler, Richard L. VA 58th Inf. Co.F
Tyler, Richard R. FL Cav. Pickett's Co.
Tyler, Richard R. FL 10th Inf. Co.I
Tyler, Richard R. VA Lt.Arty. Nelson's Co.
Tyler, Richard R.R. FL Inf. 2nd Bn. Co.A
Tyler, Richmond FL 10th Inf. Co.A Sgt.
Tyler, R.K. MO 6th Cav. Co.K Sgt.
Tyler, R.L. TX 4th Inf. Co.H Sgt.
Tyler, Robert KY 2nd (Duke's) Cav. Co.A
Tyler, Robert KY Cav. 2nd Bn. (Dortch's) Co.A 1st Lt.
Tyler, Robt. KY 14th Cav. Co.D 1st Lt.
Tyler, Robert KY 9th Mtd.Inf. Co.B Cpl.
Tyler, Robert TN 5th Inf. 2nd Co.K
Tyler, Robert VA Lt.Arty. 38th Bn. Co.C
Tyler, Robert VA 3rd Inf.Loc.Def. Co.F
Tyler, Robert Morgan's Staff 2nd Lt.,ADC
Tyler, Robert C. LA 12th Inf. Co.B
Tyler, Robert E. VA 21st Inf. Co.F
Tyler, Robert H. VA 8th Inf. Co.C Capt.
Tyler, R.P. LA 13th Bn. (Part.Rangers) Co.A
Tyler, R.P. TX 12th Cav. Co.I
Tyler, S. VA Inf. 2nd Bn.Loc.Def. Co.A
Tyler, Samuel VA 48th Inf. Cadet
Tyler, Samuel Eng.,CSA Asst.Eng.
Tyler, Samuel G. VA Lt.Arty. 38th Bn. Co.C
Tyler, Samuel L. MO 2nd Inf. Co.H Cpl.
Tyler, Samuel L. TX Cav. Baylor's Regt. Co.E
Tyler, Samuel P. VA Hvy.Arty. 19th Bn. Co.D
Tyler, Samuel S. AL 24th Inf. Co.H
Tyler, S.C. AL Inf. 2nd Regt. Co.K
Tyler, S.J. MS 28th Cav. Co.C
Tyler, S.L. SC 2nd Arty. Co.C
Tyler, Spencer C. AL 48th Inf. Co.E 1st Lt.
Tyler, Stanley R. VA Lt.Arty. 13th Bn. Co.A
Tyler, Stanly B. VA 3rd Inf.Loc.Def. Co.I Cpl.
Tyler, Stephen J. FL 9th Inf. Co.D,E Cpl.
Tyler, Sylvester N. VA 12th Inf. Co.G
Tyler, Sylvester N. VA 15th Inf. Co.B Cpl.
Tyler, T. SC 1st Regt. Charleston Guard Co.D
Tyler, T. SC 13th Inf. Surg.
Tyler, T. VA 2nd St.Res. Co.I
Tyler, Taywell Gen. & Staff,PACS Surg.
Tyler, Tazewell NC 18th Inf. Surg.
Tyler, Tazewell VA Inf. 22nd Bn. Asst.Surg.
Tyler, Tazewell Gen. & Staff Surg.
Tyler, T.B. SC 20th Inf. Co.I
Tyler, Thomas AR 3rd Inf. Co.H
Tyler, Thomas GA 1st Reg. Co.L Drum.
Tyler, Thomas GA 8th Inf. (St.Guards) Co.D Cpl.
Tyler, Thomas LA Cav. 18th Bn. Co.E
Tyler, Thomas VA Cav. 32nd Bn. Co.A
Tyler, Thomas VA Hvy.Arty. A.J. Jones' Co.
Tyler, Thomas VA 52nd Mil. Co.B
Tyler, Thomas A. VA Courtney Arty.
Tyler, Thomas B. SC 2nd St.Troops Co.G Capt.
Tyler, Thomas E. VA Lt.Arty. 12th Bn. Co.C
Tyler, Thomas E. VA Lt.Arty. Taylor's Co.
Tyler, Thomas F. TX 8th Inf. Co.E
Tyler, Thomas G. MS 28th Cav. Co.C Cpl.
Tyler, Thomas J. AR 38th Inf. Co.H Sgt.
Tyler, Thomas J. MS 42nd Inf. Co.A
Tyler, Thomas R. VA 57th Inf. Co.H
Tyler, Thomas S. TN 27th Inf. Co.I Sgt.
Tyler, Thomas W. SC 5th Cav. Co.I Capt.
Tyler, Thomas W. VA 5th Cav. Co.E
Tyler, Thompson VA 46th Inf. Comsy.Sgt.
Tyler, T.I. MO 12th Inf. Co.G
Tyler, T.J. TX Conscr.
Tyler, T.R. AR 27th Inf. Co.D
Tyler, T.S. TN 3rd (Forrest's) Cav. Co.G
Tyler, T.W. SC Cav. 14th Bn. Co.D 1st Lt.
Tyler, U.L. SC 20th Inf. Co.D
Tyler, W. MO St.Guard
Tyler, W. TX Cav. Wells' Regt. Co.D
Tyler, W.A. AL 4th Cav. Co.G
Tyler, W.A. GA 12th Cav. Co.G
Tyler, Walker W. VA Hvy.Arty. 20th Bn. Co.D
Tyler, Walter AL 49th Inf. Co.A
Tyler, Walter Exch.Bn. Co.E,CSA
Tyler, Walter B. VA Lt.Arty. Carpenter's Co.
Tyler, Warren MS 1st Lt.Arty. Co.L
Tyler, Warren M. LA 2nd Cav. Co.F
Tyler, Washington AR 1st Mtd.Rifles Co.K
Tyler, Washington AR 25th Inf. Co.A
Tyler, Washington VA 2nd Arty. Co.G
Tyler, Washington VA Inf. 22nd Bn. Co.G
Tyler, Washington VA 87th Mil. Co.D
Tyler, Washington H. VA Hvy.Arty. 10th Bn. Co.A 2nd Lt.
Tyler, Washington L. VA Arty. Paris' Co.
Tyler, Wat 1st Choctaw Mtd.Rifles Co.H Sgt.
Tyler, W.B. AL 9th Inf. Co.C
Tyler, W.C. AL 4th Cav. Co.B
Tyler, W.C. SC 8th Bn.Res. Co.D
Tyler, W.C. VA 2nd St.Res. Co.I
Tyler, W.E. MS 3rd (St.Troops) Cav. Co.G
Tyler, W.E. VA 1st Inf. Co.B
Tyler, Wesley GA 66th Inf. Co.F
Tyler, W.G. AR 7th Inf. Co.H
Tyler, W.G. AR 27th Inf. Co.I Sgt.
Tyler, W.H. AL 34th Inf. Co.D
Tyler, W.H. GA Inf. Clemons' Co.
Tyler, W.H. GA Conscr.
Tyler, W.H. VA 2nd Inf.Loc.Def. Co.A
Tyler, W.H. VA Inf. 2nd Bn.Loc.Def. Co.C
Tyler, W.I. TX 17th Inf. Co.C
Tyler, Wiley MS 18th Inf. Co.F
Tyler, William AL 42nd Inf. Co.K
Tyler, William AL Coosa Guards J.W. Suttles' Co.
Tyler, William AR 34th Inf. Co.G
Tyler, William GA 43rd Inf. Co.B
Tyler, William MS 38th Cav. Co.D
Tyler, William MS Condrey's Co. (Bull Mtn. Invinc.)
Tyler, Wm. MO St.Guard
Tyler, William SC 2nd Arty. Co.H
Tyler, William VA Lt.Arty. Brander's Co.
Tyler, William VA Inf. 4th Bn.Loc.Def. Co.C
Tyler, William VA 82nd Mil. Co.C
Tyler, William VA Mil. Scott Cty.
Tyler, Wm. Gen. & Staff AQM
Tyler, William A. VA 28th Inf. Co.K Cpl.
Tyler, William B. MO 9th (Elliott's) Cav. Co.F
Tyler, William C. TN Cav. 9th Bn. (Gantt's) Co.C Sgt.
Tyler, William C. VA 37th Inf. Co.A Cpl.
Tyler, William D. MS 15th Inf. Co.E
Tyler, William G. TX 6th Inf. Co.C
Tyler, William H. AR Lt.Arty. Rivers' Btty.
Tyler, William H. KY 5th Cav. Co.A
Tyler, William H. SC 1st (McCreary's) Inf. Co.A
Tyler, William H. VA 24th Cav. Co.A
Tyler, William H. VA Cav. 40th Bn. Co.A
Tyler, William H. VA Hvy.Arty. 20th Bn. Co.D 1st Sgt.
Tyler, William H. VA Lt.Arty. Cayce's Co.
Tyler, William H. VA Lt.Arty. Woolfolk's Co.
Tyler, William H. VA 1st St.Res. Co.I
Tyler, William H.H. AR 25th Inf. Co.A
Tyler, William J. GA 4th Inf. Co.G
Tyler, William J. MS 11th Inf. Co.F
Tyler, Wm. J. VA 48th Inf. Co.A
Tyler, William L. TX 5th Cav. Co.E
Tyler, William M. GA 1st (Symons') Res. Co.E
Tyler, William M. GA 12th Inf. Co.I
Tyler, William M. MS Cav. 24th Bn. Co.B
Tyler, William M. MS 42nd Inf. Co.A
Tyler, William N. VA Hvy.Arty. 10th Bn. Co.C
Tyler, William R. VA Goochland Lt.Arty.
Tyler, William R. VA 12th Inf. Branch's Co. Cpl.
Tyler, William R. VA 16th Inf. Co.K Cpl.
Tyler, William S. FL Cav. Pickett's Co.
Tyler, William S. TX 22nd Cav. Co.B
Tyler, William T. AL 20th Inf. Co.C,G
Tyler, William T. GA 2nd Cav. Co.G
Tyler, William T. MS 16th Inf. Co.E Comsy.
Tyler, William T. TN 28th (Cons.) Inf. Co.A
Tyler, Willis SC 1st (McCreary's) Inf. Co.F
Tyler, Winfield MD 1st Cav. Co.F
Tyler, Winfield S. VA Lt.Arty. Utterback's Co.
Tyler, W.J. MS 18th Inf. Co.I
Tyler, W.J. TX 25th Cav. Co.K Cpl.
Tyler, W.J. TX 9th (Nichols') Inf. Co.E
Tyler, W.M. MS 38th Cav. Co.I
Tyler, W.N. VA Inf. 2nd Bn.Loc.Def. Co.C
Tyler, W.S. AL 32nd Inf. Co.I
Tyler, W.T. AR 27th Inf. Co.K
Tyler, W.T. GA 11th Inf. Co.C
Tyler, W.T. 7th Conf.Cav. Co.D
Tyler, W.W. SC 1st Arty. Co.F
Tyler, W.W. SC 2nd Arty. Co.A
Tyler, W.W. TX 7th Cav. Co.E
Tyler, W.W. VA 2nd Inf.Loc.Def. Co.A
Tyler, W.W. VA Conscr. Cp.Lee Co.A
Tyler, W.W. Gen. & Staff 1st Lt.
Tyler, Z.B. TX St.Troops Gould's Co. (Clarksville Lt.Inf.)

Tyler, Zenas B. TX 9th Field Btty. Sr.1st Lt.
Tylor, Charles MO Lt.Arty. 2nd Field Btty. Sgt.
Tylor, E. SC 3rd St.Troops Co.D
Tylor, J.C. TN 1st (Turney's) Inf. Co.H
Tylor, J.W. MS 36th Inf. Co.B Cpl.]
Tylor, L.D. NC 2nd Arty. (36th St.Troops) Co.B
Tylor, Thomas M. VA 26th Inf. Co.H
Tylor, W.W. SC 11th Res. Co.A Cpl.
Tylton, T.T. AL 21st Inf. Co.C Music.
Tyman, R.B. KY 9th Cav. Co.E
Tymes, George W. TN 2nd (Ashby's) Cav. Co.H
Tymes, George W. TN Cav. 4th Bn. (Branner's) Co.A
Tymes, James TN Cav. 4th Bn. (Branner's) Co.A
Tymes, Robert M. AR 15th Inf. Co.E
Tyms, A. TN 2nd (Ashby's) Cav. Co.H
Tyms, James TN 2nd (Ashby's) Cav. Co.H
Tynan, Francis T. VA 3rd Inf. Co.H 1st Sgt.
Tynan, Frank M. LA 1st Hvy.Arty. (Reg.) Co.E
Tynan, John LA 5th Inf. Co.K
Tynan, John TX 8th Cav. Co.G
Tynan, John 9th Conf.Inf. Co.D Sgt.
Tynan, William LA Mil. 2nd Regt. 2nd Brig. 1st Div. Co.C
Tynch, A.G. TN Cav. 16th Bn. (Neal's) Co.D Sgt.
Tynch, Josephus NC 4th Cav. (59th St.Troops) Co.I
Tynch, Josephus NC Cav. 12th Bn. Co.B
Tynch, Josephus 8th (Dearing's) Conf.Cav. Co.B
Tyndal, Joshua NC 2nd Arty. (36th St.Troops) Co.D
Tyndal, Stready NC 2nd Arty. (36th St.Troops) Co.D
Tyndall, J.M. MO 2nd Inf. Co.D
Tyndall, Mark A. VA 10th Cav. Co.A 1st Lt.
Tyne, Edward FL 11th Inf. Co.D
Tyne, W. GA Arty. Maxwell's Reg.Lt.Btty.
Tyne, William AL 21st Inf. Co.B
Tyne, William TN 2nd (Walker's) Inf. Co.I Cpl.
Tyne, William 9th Conf.Inf. Co.F
Tyne, William H. GA 3rd Inf. Co.E Sgt.
Tyner, A. 1st Cherokee Mtd.Vol. 1st Co.B
Tyner, A.C. 1st Cherokee Mtd.Vol. 1st Co.B Cpl.
Tyner, A.M. 3rd Conf.Cav. Co.C
Tyner, Barnette T. FL 7th Inf. Co.G
Tyner, Benjamin NC 3rd Inf. Co.F
Tyner, Caleb SC 9th Inf. Co.G
Tyner, Cicero AR Inf. Hardy's Regt. Co.A
Tyner, David M. GA 4th Inf. Co.G
Tyner, David Y. FL 7th Inf. Co.G
Tyner, Edward J. FL 1st Cav. Co.G
Tyner, Elijah S. AL 17th Inf. Co.B
Tyner, Enock AR Inf. 2nd Bn. Co.B
Tyner, E.P. GA 52nd Inf. Co.C Sr.2nd Lt.
Tyner, Ezekiel SC Lt.Arty. 3rd (Palmetto) Bn. Co.E
Tyner, Ezekiel SC 21st Inf. Co.G
Tyner, Franklin AL 29th Inf. Co.A
Tyner, George LA 22nd (Cons.) Inf. Co.C
Tyner, George R. AL Pris.Guard Freeman's Co. Music.
Tyner, George S. GA 9th Inf. Co.D
Tyner, George W. NC 56th Inf. Co.E
Tyner, G.J. TX 9th Cav. Co.C
Tyner, G.W. GA 4th Res. Co.E
Tyner, Hugh SC 21st Inf. Co.G
Tyner, Isaac N. AR 14th (McCarver's) Inf. Co.D
Tyner, Jackson FL 9th Inf. Co.I
Tyner, Jackson MO Cav. Fristoe's Regt. Co.I
Tyner, James TN 19th Inf. Co.I Music.
Tyner, James VA Lt.Arty. Fry's Co.
Tyner, James A. GA 24th Inf. Co.B
Tyner, James C. 3rd Conf.Cav. Co.C
Tyner, James L. MS 29th Inf. Co.G
Tyner, James M. MS 1st Lt.Arty. Co.D
Tyner, James Q. GA 24th Inf. Co.D
Tyner, James W. FL 4th Inf. Co.E
Tyner, J.C. TN 49th Inf. Co.I Sgt.
Tyner, Jesse FL 2nd Cav. Co.B
Tyner, J.H. GA 3rd Cav. (St.Guards) Co.B
Tyner, J.J. GA Inf. 14th Bn. (St.Guards) Co.H
Tyner, J.J. GA 27th Inf. Co.K
Tyner, J.M. TN 31st Inf. Co.E
Tyner, John SC 21st Inf. Co.G
Tyner, John F. GA 1st (Ramsey's) Inf. Co.H
Tyner, John F. GA 52nd Inf. Co.C,I Sgt.
Tyner, John J. FL 2nd Cav. Co.C
Tyner, John J. FL 7th Inf. Co.G
Tyner, John W. Inf. Bailey's Cons.Regt. Co.D
Tyner, Joseph D. MS 9th Cav. Co.G
Tyner, Joshua E. GA 24th Inf. Co.B
Tyner, Josiah A. AL 17th Inf. Co.B,C
Tyner, J.P. MS 2nd (Quinn's St.Troops) Inf. Co.G
Tyner, J.S. GA Cav. 6th Bn. (St.Guards) Co.E
Tyner, J.S. 1st Conf.Cav. 2nd Co.K Capt.
Tyner, J.T. AR 15th (Josey's) Inf. 1st Co.C Cpl.
Tyner, J.W. TN 49th Inf. Co.I
Tyner, Keeland GA 3rd Cav. (St.Guards) Co.G
Tyner, Keeland S. AL 13th Inf. Co.G
Tyner, L.J. 3rd Conf.Cav. Co.I
Tyner, M.V. GA 32nd Inf. Co.A
Tyner, M.V. 2nd Conf.Eng.Troops Co.E
Tyner, Nicholas NC 51st Inf. Co.F
Tyner, Patrick LA Mil. 1st Regt. 2nd Brig. 1st Div. Co.E
Tyner, Richard GA 1st Reg. Co.I,H
Tyner, R.J. GA 32nd Inf. Co.A
Tyner, R.J. 2nd Conf.Eng.Troops Co.E Sgt.
Tyner, Ruben 2nd Cherokee Mtd.Vol. Co.H
Tyner, Samuel AL Mil. 4th Vol. Gantt's Co. Cpl.
Tyner, Samuel A. SC Hvy.Arty. 15th (Lucas') Bn. Co.A 1st Sgt.
Tyner, Seborn 2nd Cherokee Mtd.Vol. Co.H
Tyner, Simeon FL 8th Inf. Co.A
Tyner, S.J. GA Inf. 14th Bn. (St.Guards) Co.H
Tyner, S.J. KY Lt.Arty. Green's Btty. QMSgt.
Tyner, S.J. LA 22nd Inf. QMSgt.
Tyner, S.J. LA 22nd (Cons.) Inf. Co.B QMSgt.
Tyner, Stewart FL 8th Inf. Co.K
Tyner, T.C. AL 17th Inf. Co.C
Tyner, T.C. GA 1st (Fannin's) Res. Co.D
Tyner, T.J. KY Lt.Arty. Green's Btty. Cpl.
Tyner, Tom LA 22nd Inf. Cpl.
Tyner, Tom LA 22nd (Cons.) Inf. Co.B Cpl.
Tyner, W.C. AL Pris.Guard Freeman's Co.
Tyner, W.D.H. AL Pris.Guard Freeman's Co.
Tyner, Wiley GA 52nd Inf. Co.C
Tyner, Wiley J. NC 51st Inf. Co.E
Tyner, William GA 12th Cav. Co.D
Tyner, William LA Washington Arty.Bn. Co.5 Driver
Tyner, William NC 51st Inf. Co.F
Tyner, William VA 54th Mil. Co.G
Tyner, William E. FL 9th Inf. Co.G
Tyner, William W. GA 24th Inf. Co.B
Tyner, Willis K. FL 2nd Cav. Co.B 1st Bugler
Tyner, W.L. 3rd Conf.Cav. Co.B
Tyner, W.R. AL Pris.Guard Freeman's Co.
Tynes, Achilles J. VA 8th Cav. Co.H Capt.,ACS
Tynes, A.J. Gen. & Staff Capt.,Comsy.
Tynes, Henry LA Inf. 11th Bn. Co.C Cpl.
Tynes, Henry LA Inf.Cons.Crescent Regt. Co.F
Tynes, Henry C. AR 26th Inf. Co.A
Tynes, H.L. VA VMI Co.A
Tynes, Isaac J. VA 3rd Cav. Co.H 1st Lt.
Tynes, J.A. VA Hvy.Arty. Wright's Co. Sgt.Maj.
Tynes, James VA 9th Inf. Co.F
Tynes, James L. MS Cav. 1st Bn. (McNair's) St.Troops Co.C 2nd Lt.
Tynes, James M. MS 19th Inf. Co.K Bvt.2nd Lt.
Tynes, Jeremiah MS 19th Inf. Co.K Bvt.2nd Lt.
Tynes, Joel A. VA 14th Inf. Co.H 2nd Lt.
Tynes, John B. MS Lt.Arty. (The Hudson Btty.) Hoole's Co.
Tynes, John C. NC Lt.Arty. 3rd Bn. Co.C
Tynes, John H. LA Inf. 11th Bn. Co.E 1st Lt.
Tynes, John N. VA Hvy.Arty. 10th Bn. Co.E
Tynes, John P. VA Hvy.Arty. Wright's Co.
Tynes, J.W. MS 38th Cav. Co.I
Tynes, M.E. MS 33rd Inf. Co.B
Tynes, Minor E. MS 33rd Inf. Co.C 1st Lt.
Tynes, R.H. TX 7th Cav. Co.E
Tynes, Robert H. VA 59th Mil. Hunter's Co.
Tynes, Robert M. MS 26th Inf. Co.G
Tynes, S.A. SC Cav. DeSaussure's Squad.
Tynes, Samuel LA 4th Inf. Co.B
Tynes, T.F. MS 2nd (Quinn's St.Troops) Inf. Co.A
Tynes, T.F. 20th Conf.Cav. 2nd Co.H
Tynes, Thomas H. VA Hvy.Arty. 10th Bn. Co.E
Tynes, Thomas H. VA Lt.Arty. Hankins' Co.
Tynes, Thomas J. VA 6th Cav. Co.G
Tynes, T.J. VA Hvy.Arty. Wright's Co.
Tynes, W.H. MS 9th Bn.S.S. Co.C
Tynes, William TN 1st (Feild's) Inf. Co.C
Tynes, William D. MS 19th Inf. Co.K
Tynes, William F. VA 3rd Cav. Co.H Sgt.
Tynes, William F. VA 1st Arty. 3rd Co.C Cpl.
Tynes, Wm. F. VA Hvy.Arty. Wright's Co.
Tynes, William F. VA 14th Inf. 1st Co.G
Tynes, William T. VA 11th Inf. Co.C Cpl.
Tynin, Edward FL 1st Cav. Co.E
Tynon, John TN 2nd (Walker's) Inf. Co.E Cpl.
Tynor, T. GA 11th Inf.
Tyns, B.F. TN 6th Inf. Co.A
Tyns, James MS Cav. (St.Troops) Gamblin's Co. Sgt.
Tyor, W. GA 21st Inf. Co.D
Type, Horace TN Lt.Arty. Huggins' Co.
Tyra, Alfred NC 1st Cav. (9th St.Troops) Co.D
Tyra, E.H. MS 10th Cav. Co.B Capt.
Tyra, E.H. MS 32nd Inf. Co.F
Tyra, Jesse V. MS 32nd Inf. Co.K
Tyra, John W. KY 13th Cav. Co.H

Tyra, Joseph KY 13th Cav. Co.H
Tyra, J.R. TN 2nd (Robison's) Inf.
Tyra, J.S. MS 32nd Inf. Co.F Cpl.
Tyra, J.V. AL Cav. 8th Regt. (Livingston's) Co.G
Tyra, Paterson KY 13th Cav. Co.H
Tyra, T.J. TX 22nd Inf. Co.G
Tyra, William KY 10th (Diamond's) Cav. Co.E
Tyrant, J.M. GA 1st Inf.
Tyre, Albert AR 19th (Dawson's) Inf. Co.E
Tyre, Alexander MS 18th Cav. Co.I Sr.2nd Lt.
Tyre, Benjamin FL 2nd Cav. Co.H
Tyre, Berrian GA 4th (Clinch's) Cav. Co.F
Tyre, Calvin GA Lt.Arty. 12th Bn. 3rd Co.E
Tyre, Charles P. TX 13th Cav. Co.C
Tyre, Christopher SC 9th Inf. Co.B
Tyre, D. GA 7th Cav. Co.G
Tyre, D.A. AR Cav. McGehee's Regt. Co.A
Tyre, D.A. MS 34th Inf. Co.C 1st Sgt.
Tyre, Daniel GA 4th (Clinch's) Cav. Co.A
Tyre, Daniel GA Cav. 24th Bn. Co.A
Tyre, David GA 4th (Clinch's) Cav. Co.A
Tyre, Durant A. MS 11th Inf. Co.G
Tyre, George NC 54th Inf. Co.G
Tyre, Harvey TN 43rd Inf. Co.G
Tyre, H.C. MS 2nd St.Cav. Co.D
Tyre, Isaac FL 3rd Inf. Co.K
Tyre, Isham GA 4th (Clinch's) Cav. Co.A
Tyre, Isham GA 4th Inf.
Tyre, Isham GA 54th Inf.
Tyre, James A. VA 10th Bn.Res. Co.E 2nd Lt.
Tyre, Jessee FL 10th Inf. Co.G
Tyre, J.H. TN 21st & 22nd (Cons.) Cav. Co.K
Tyre, John FL 10th Inf. Co.D Cpl.
Tyre, John MO 12th Cav. Co.C Cpl.
Tyre, John H. TN 22nd (Barteau's) Cav. Co.G Cpl.
Tyre, John T. TX 13th Cav. Co.C
Tyre, Joseph NC 37th Inf. Co.G
Tyre, Joseph W. AR 13th Inf. Co.K Cpl.
Tyre, J.R. TX 11th Inf. Co.H
Tyre, J.S. MS 2nd Cav. Co.I
Tyre, J.T. TX 28th Cav. Co.L
Tyre, J.W. 4th Conf.Eng.Troops
Tyre, Lewis FL 5th Inf. Co.B
Tyre, Lewis TX Inf. Griffin's Bn. Co.C
Tyre, Nathanael FL 5th Inf. Co.F
Tyre, R.J. TN 4th (Murray's) Cav. Co.H
Tyre, S. AR 30th Inf. Co.I
Tyre, Samuel S. MS 2nd Inf. (A. of 10,000) Co.A
Tyre, Solomon FL 1st (Res.) Inf. Co.B
Tyre, Solomon FL 10th Inf. Co.B
Tyre, S.S. MS 34th Inf. Co.C
Tyre, Thomas B. NC 3rd Cav. (41st St.Troops) Co.I
Tyre, W. GA 7th Cav. Co.G
Tyre, William GA Cav. 24th Bn. Co.A
Tyre, William TX 19th Cav. Co.I
Tyre, William H. FL 9th Inf. Co.E
Tyre, William H. MO 3rd Inf. Co.C
Tyre, William W. AR 13th Inf. Co.K
Tyree, A.G. VA 22nd Inf. Co.C
Tyree, A.H. VA 2nd St.Res. Co.C
Tyree, A.H. VA 2nd Inf.Loc.Def. Co.F
Tyree, A.H. VA Inf. 6th Bn.Loc.Def. Co.C
Tyree, Alexander VA 3rd Res. Co.H
Tyree, Alexander N. VA 22nd Inf. Co.G
Tyree, Alonzo VA 53rd Inf. Co.B
Tyree, Alonzo VA Inf. Tomlin's Bn. Co.A Cpl.
Tyree, Andrew J. VA Lt.Arty. Kirkpatrick's Co.
Tyree, Andrew W. VA Inf. 25th Bn. Co.E
Tyree, A.P. VA 2nd Inf.Loc.Def. Co.F
Tyree, A.P. VA Inf. 6th Bn.Loc.Def. Co.C
Tyree, Archibald W. GA 21st Inf. Co.F Sgt.
Tyree, Augustus VA 34th Inf. Co.C
Tyree, A.W. VA 3rd Inf.Loc.Def. Co.K
Tyree, C.H. TN 19th (Biffle's) Cav. Co.A Sgt.
Tyree, Charles D. VA 11th Inf. Co.A
Tyree, Charles H. VA 11th Inf. Co.A,E 1st Lt.
Tyree, C.T. VA 49th Inf. Co.B
Tyree, Cyrus D. VA 3rd Cav. 1st Co.I
Tyree, Daniel AR 20th Inf. Co.B
Tyree, David A. VA Arty. (Loc.Def. & Sp.Serv.) Lanier's Co.
Tyree, David A. VA 2nd St.Res. Co.F
Tyree, David A. VA 38th Inf. Co.E
Tyree, David A. VA 53rd Inf. Co.B
Tyree, David A. VA Inf. Tomlin's Bn. Co.A
Tyree, D.W. TN 55th (Brown's) Inf. Co.H
Tyree, Ed VA 2nd St.Res. Co.C
Tyree, Edward P. TN Cav. 7th Bn. (Bennett's) Co.C Capt.
Tyree, E.P. Cheatham's Staff Maj.,AQM
Tyree, G.D. VA 3rd Res. Co.I
Tyree, George TN 7th Inf. Co.C
Tyree, George D. VA Hvy.Arty. 19th Bn. Co.A
Tyree, George P. VA 49th Inf. Co.I
Tyree, George R. TN 37th Inf. Co.C
Tyree, George R. VA 2nd Inf.Loc.Def. Co.D
Tyree, George R. VA Inf. 6th Bn.Loc.Def. Co.A
Tyree, George W. VA 3rd Cav. Co.F Sgt.
Tyree, George W. VA 3rd Cav. 1st Co.I Sgt.
Tyree, George W. VA 5th Cav. Co.H
Tyree, George W. VA 49th Inf. Co.I
Tyree, Giles VA 24th Inf. Co.B
Tyree, Giles VA 36th Inf. 2nd Co.B
Tyree, H.C. VA 21st Inf. Co.F Cpl.
Tyree, Henry R. VA 53rd Inf. Co.E
Tyree, Herod S. VA 49th Inf. Co.I
Tyree, H.J. VA 24th Cav. Co.H
Tyree, H.J. VA Cav. 32nd Bn. Co.B
Tyree, J.A. VA 2nd St.Res. Co.F Sgt.
Tyree, Jackson J. AR 24th Inf. Co.F
Tyree, Jackson J. AR Inf. Hardy's Regt. Co.D
Tyree, Jacob VA 3rd Res. Co.A
Tyree, Jacob VA 49th Inf. Co.B,I
Tyree, James AL 3rd Bn.Res. Appling's Co.
Tyree, James Gen. & Staff,PACS, QM Dept.
Tyree, James H. VA Lt.Arty. 38th Bn. Co.B Cpl.
Tyree, James S. VA Hvy.Arty. A.J. Jones' Co.
Tyree, James S. VA 53rd Inf. Co.E
Tyree, James T. VA 1st Inf. Co.I
Tyree, Jerome B. Morgan's,CSA
Tyree, Jesse LA Inf. 4th Bn. Co.E
Tyree, J.F. AR 13th Mil. Co.A
Tyree, J.H. 2nd Conf.Eng.Troops Co.C
Tyree, J.M. VA Lt.Arty. Lamkin's Co.
Tyree, Joe P. TN 2nd (Robison's) Inf. Co.I Capt.
Tyree, John TN Cav. 7th Bn. (Bennett's) Co.E
Tyree, John VA 53rd Inf. Co.B
Tyree, John VA Inf. Tomlin's Bn. Co.A
Tyree, John Conf.Cav. Wood's Regt. Co.I
Tyree, John A. VA 1st Inf. Co.I 2nd Lt.
Tyree, John A. VA 79th Mil. Co.2
Tyree, John B. AR 24th Inf. Co.F
Tyree, John B. AR Inf. Hardy's Regt. Co.D
Tyree, John H. VA 1st Arty. Co.I
Tyree, John H. VA 51st Inf. Co.E Cpl.
Tyree, John J. VA 49th Inf. Co.I
Tyree, John M. VA 22nd Inf. Co.C Sgt.
Tyree, John P. TN 4th Inf. Co.F
Tyree, John R. VA Hvy.Arty. 20th Bn. Co.A,E
Tyree, John R. VA 11th Inf. Co.A
Tyree, John R. VA 44th Inf. Co.A
Tyree, John W. VA Hvy.Arty. 19th Bn. Co.D Cpl.
Tyree, John W. VA Lt.Arty. Rives' Co.
Tyree, Joseph VA 49th Inf. Co.I
Tyree, Joseph M. VA 22nd Inf. Co.C
Tyree, Joseph P. TN 2nd (Robison's) Inf. Co.I Capt.
Tyree, J.P. 8th (Wade's) Conf.Cav. Co.K
Tyree, J.S. VA 19th Inf. Co.I
Tyree, Larken F. VA 52nd Inf. Co.K
Tyree, L.H. TN 19th & 20th (Cons.) Cav. Co.B
Tyree, L.H. TN 20th (Russell's) Cav. Co.D
Tyree, Llewellyn VA 49th Inf. Co.I
Tyree. Lucas P. VA 19th Inf. Co.H
Tyree, Marshal L. VA 49th Inf. Co.I
Tyree, Meridith G. VA 10th Cav. Co.K
Tyree, Nathan J. VA Lt.Arty. Kirkpatrick's Co.
Tyree, Paulus P. VA 49th Inf. Co.I
Tyree, Pizarro T. VA 49th Inf. Co.H
Tyree, Reuben VA 51st Inf. Co.G
Tyree, R.F. VA Lt.Arty. Parker's Co.
Tyree, Richard C. VA Lt.Arty. Kirkpatrick's Co.
Tyree, Richard J. VA 2nd Cav. Co.B
Tyree, Richard T. VA 53rd Inf. Co.B
Tyree, Richard T. VA Inf. Tomlin's Bn. Co.A
Tyree, R.J. TN 8th (Smith's) Cav. Co.C
Tyree, Robert F. VA 1st Inf. Co.G Sgt.
Tyree, Robert L. VA Hvy.Arty. 19th Bn. Co.D
Tyree, Robert N. VA 49th Inf. Co.I
Tyree, Robert W. TX 34th Cav. Co.H
Tyree, R.T. TN Inf. 1st Bn. (Colms') Co.A Sgt.
Tyree, Samuel VA Cav. Hounshell's Bn. Co.A
Tyree, Samuel VA 22nd Inf. Co.C 1st Sgt.
Tyree, Samuel B. VA 11th Inf. Co.G
Tyree, Simeon KY 4th Mtd.Inf. Co.H
Tyree, Stephen J. AR 24th Inf. Co.F
Tyree, Stephen J. TX 34th Cav. Co.H
Tyree, Thomas H. VA 49th Inf. Co.H
Tyree, Thomas J. TN 19th (Biffle's) Cav. Co.A
Tyree, Thomas M. VA Hvy.Arty. 19th Bn. Co.D
Tyree, Thomas M. VA 38th Inf. Co.E Capt.
Tyree, T.R. TN 50th (Cons.) Inf. Co.B Sgt.
Tyree, W.H. VA 3rd Res. Co.A
Tyree, William KY 7th Cav. Co.D
Tyree, William MO 16th Inf. Co.I
Tyree, William VA 25th Cav. Co.A
Tyree, William VA 3rd Inf.Loc.Def. 2nd Co.G
Tyree, William VA 22nd Inf. Co.C Capt.
Tyree, William VA 59th Inf. 2nd Co.B
Tyree, William A. VA 49th Inf. Co.I
Tyree, William B. VA 13th Cav. Co.G
Tyree, William D.R. VA Lt.Arty. 13th Bn. Co.C
Tyree, William D.R. VA 11th Inf. Co.A
Tyree, William F. VA 2nd Inf.Loc.Def. Co.D

Tyree, William F. VA Inf. 6th Bn.Loc.Def. Co.A
Tyree, William H. VA Lt.Arty. Kirkpatrick's Co.
Tyree, William H. VA 46th Inf. 2nd Co.A Sgt.
Tyree, William J. VA 2nd St.Res. Co.F
Tyree, William N. VA 14th Cav. Co.A
Tyree, William W. VA 22nd Inf. Co.G Music.
Tyree, Woodson A. VA 22nd Inf. Co.C 1st Lt.
Tyree, W.T. AR 32nd Inf. Co.G
Tyree, W.W. VA 10th Cav. Co.A
Tyrel, William Conf.Reg.Inf. Brooks' Bn. Co.C
Tyrell, Patrick VA 1st Inf. Co.C
Tyrell, W.H. NC McLean's Bn.Lt.Duty Men Co.B
Tyrer, James VA 8th Inf. Co.E
Tyrer, Robert KY 9th Mtd.Inf. Co.C Cpl.
Tyrer, Thomas VA Inf. 4th Bn.Loc.Def. Co.A
Tyrey, James E. TN 2nd (Smith's) Cav.
Tyrey, M.D.L. AR Lt.Arty. Zimmerman's Btty.
Tyrie, S.J. AR Lt.Arty. Hart's Btty.
Tyris, W.F. VA Hvy.Arty. Wright's Co.
Tyrone, Adam LA 28th (Gray's) Inf. Co.F
Tyrone, Adolphus L. MS 42nd Inf.
Tyrone, A.L. MS 8th Cav. Co.H
Tyrone, A.L. MS 28th Cav. Co.L
Tyrone, C.M. AL 9th (Malone's) Cav. Co.C Sgt.
Tyrone, D.A. TN 40th Inf. Co.E
Tyrone, Hartwell H. MS 22nd Inf. Co.A
Tyrone, Henry Clay LA 28th (Gray's) Inf. Co.F
Tyrone, H.G. MS Cav. 1st Bn. (McNair's) St.Troops Co.B
Tyrone, H.G. 2nd (Quinn's St.Troops) Inf. Co.A
Tyrone, James H. MS 14th Inf. Co.I
Tyrone, J.C. MS Cav. 1st Bn. (McNair's) St.Troops Co.C
Tyrone, Jerome C. MS 7th Inf. Co.G
Tyrone, J.H. MS 43rd Inf. Co.L
Tyrone, Parkman MS 7th Inf. Co.G
Tyrone, Parkman MS 22nd Inf. Co.A
Tyrone, W.T. MS 2nd (Quinn's St.Troops) Inf. Co.A
Tyrons, Samuel NC 3rd Inf.
Tyrre, J.W. VA Hvy.Arty. 20th Bn. Co.A
Tyrrell, Edward A. NC 1st Arty. (10th St.Troops) Co.H
Tyrrell, J. LA 13th & 20th Inf. Co.E
Tyrrell, John AL Inf. 1st Regt. Co.D
Tyrrell, John LA 13th Inf. Co.I,E
Tyrrell, John MS 9th Inf. New Co.C
Tyrrell, John TX Cav. Ragsdale's Bn. Co.B
Tyrrell, Pulaski TX 12th Cav. Co.E
Tyrrell, T. AR Lt.Arty. 5th Btty.
Tyrrell, Thomas AL Lt.Arty. 2nd Bn. Co.C
Tyrrell, William NC 7th Sr.Res. Fisher's Co., Bradshaw's Co.
Tyrrer, James R. AR Inf. 8th Bn. 1st Co.C
Tyrrer, James R. AR 25th Inf. Co.F
Tyrril, Nicholas 1st Choctaw & Chickasaw Mtd.Rifles 2nd Co.H
Tyruss, H. LA 18th Inf. Co.I
Tysant, R.B. SC Mil. 15th Regt. QM
Tysen, Alexander GA 40th Inf. Co.D
Tysen, J.R. NC 17th Inf. (1st Org.) Co.C
Tyser, James VA 59th Inf. 3rd Co.D Sgt.
Tyser, M.W. GA 55th Inf.
Tysinger, Alexander NC 14th Inf. Co.B
Tysinger, Alexander NC 21st Inf. Co.A
Tysinger, Andrew NC 4th Bn.Jr.Res. Co.B
Tysinger, Daniel NC 14th Inf. Co.F
Tysinger, David VA 7th Cav. Co.C
Tysinger, D.C. VA 4th Cav. Co.C
Tysinger, Farley NC 14th Inf. Co.B
Tysinger, G. VA 10th Bn.Res. Co.B
Tysinger, Henry H. NC 42nd Inf. Co.E
Tysinger, Isaac VA 7th Cav. Co.C
Tysinger, James NC 7th Inf. Co.F
Tysinger, John NC 22nd Inf. Co.L
Tysinger, Peter N. NC 14th Inf. Co.I 1st Sgt.
Tysinger, Robert NC 1st Inf.
Tysinger, Robert NC 66th Inf. Co.G
Tysinger, Robert S. GA 6th Inf. (St.Guards) Co.D
Tysinger, Solomon NC 48th Inf. Co.K
Tysinger, William NC 42nd Inf. Co.E Sgt.
Tysinger, William NC 48th Inf. Co.B
Tysinger, William VA 8th Bn.Res. Co.D
Tysinger, William E. VA 1st Inf. Co.H Capt.
Tyson, A. GA 1st Troops & Defences (Macon) Co.G
Tyson, A. NC Inf. 2nd Bn. Co.B
Tyson, Aaron AL 38th Inf. Co.I
Tyson, Aaron NC 2nd Bn.Loc.Def.Troops Co.B
Tyson, A.B. AL 46th Inf. Co.I
Tyson, Abner G. NC 24th Inf. Co.G Music.
Tyson, Abraham NC 2nd Arty. (36th St.Troops) Co.H
Tyson, Aderson NC 17th Inf. (1st Org.) Co.I
Tyson, A.J. AL 8th Inf. Co.C
Tyson, A.J. MS Cav. Dunn's Co. (MS Rangers)
Tyson, A.J. NC 6th Sr.Res. Co.I
Tyson, Albert NC 26th Inf. Co.K
Tyson, Alexander GA 10th Cav. (St.Guards) Co.I
Tyson, Alexander GA 41st Inf. Co.G Sgt.
Tyson, Allen NC Cav. 16th Bn. Co.F
Tyson, Allen NC Vol. Lawrence's Co.
Tyson, Allen 7th Conf.Cav. 1st Co.I, Co.H
Tyson, Allenson L. MS 36th Inf. Co.G
Tyson, Allinson MS 10th Inf. Old Co.H
Tyson, Andrew J. NC 2nd Bn.Loc.Def.Troops Co.F
Tyson, Andrew J. NC 44th Inf. Co.D
Tyson, A.P. AL 7th Cav. Co.F,A
Tyson, Arch NC 17th Inf. (1st Org.) Co.C
Tyson, Archibald NC 8th Inf. Co.E
Tyson, Archibald NC 54th Inf. Co.C
Tyson, Archibald NC 55th Inf. Co.E Music.
Tyson, Archibald J. GA 6th Inf. Co.F
Tyson, Arnold GA 37th Inf. Co.K
Tyson, B. MS 5th Cav. Co.G
Tyson, Bartlet Y. NC 2nd Cav. (19th St.Troops) Co.I 2nd Lt.
Tyson, Basil VA 89th Mil. Co.H
Tyson, B.C. KY 9th Mtd.Inf. Co.G Cpl.
Tyson, Benjamin NC 67th Inf. Co.G
Tyson, Benjamin Franklin TN 2nd (Walker's) Inf. Co.E
Tyson, Benjamin H. SC 5th Cav. Co.E
Tyson, Benjamin J. AR 33rd Inf. Co.B
Tyson, Benjamin Y. MS 31st Inf. Co.I
Tyson, B.F. AL 45th Inf. Co.G
Tyson, B.F. GA 3rd Res. Co.I
Tyson, B.F. NC 1st Jr.Res. Co.F
Tyson, B.F. NC 27th Inf. Co.H
Tyson, B.G. MS 12th Cav. Co.I
Tyson, B.H. SC 20th Inf. Co.O
Tyson, B.H. SC Inf. Hampton Legion Co.A
Tyson, Blooming G. MS 15th Inf. Co.D
Tyson, Blooming G. MS 24th Inf. Co.K
Tyson, Cammel GA Cav. 2nd Bn. Co.A
Tyson, Charles NC 44th Inf. Co.C Music.
Tyson, Clement GA 41st Inf. Co.G Sgt.
Tyson, Cornelius NC 3rd Inf. Co.C
Tyson, Daniel NC 51st Inf. Co.H
Tyson, Dawson P. NC 26th Inf. Co.H
Tyson, E. TN 51st Inf. Co.D Sgt.
Tyson, Ed TN 51st (Cons.) Inf. Co.F
Tyson, Enoch GA 17th Inf. Co.B
Tyson, F.M. GA 62nd Cav. Co.A
Tyson, George FL 9th Inf. Co.G
Tyson, George NC 3rd Inf. Co.A
Tyson, George N. GA Cav. 2nd Bn. Co.A
Tyson, George W. LA Inf.Crescent Regt. Co.F 2nd Lt.
Tyson, George W. NC 32nd Inf. Co.I
Tyson, G.G. KY 12th Cav. Co.B 2nd Lt.
Tyson, G.G. MS 28th Cav. Co.B
Tyson, G.G. MS 4th Inf. Co.E Music.
Tyson, G.G. Forrest's Scouts A. Harvey's Co.,CSA
Tyson, Gideon A. NC 2nd Arty. (36th St.Troops) Co.H
Tyson, G.M. KY 12th Cav. Co.B,D Sgt.
Tyson, G.W. LA Inf.Cons.Crescent Regt. Co.G,O 1st Lt.
Tyson, G.W. NC 15th Inf. Co.M
Tyson, Harvey NC 31st Inf. Co.B
Tyson, Henry GA 26th Inf. Co.I
Tyson, Henry C. AL 6th Inf. Co.A
Tyson, Henry C. NC 26th Inf. Co.H
Tyson, Henry F. GA 14th Inf. Co.C Sgt.
Tyson, H.H. AL 33rd Inf. Co.K
Tyson, Hiram P. AL 6th Inf. Co.C
Tyson, Houston MS Cav. 3rd Bn. (Ashcraft's) Co.D
Tyson, Howard R. GA 14th Inf. Co.D
Tyson, J. MS 5th Inf. (St.Troops) Co.H
Tyson, J. NC 7th Bn.Jr.Res. Co.C
Tyson, Jackson A. MS 15th Inf. Co.D
Tyson, Jacob GA 2nd Res. Co.B
Tyson, James NC 18th Inf. Co.B
Tyson, James NC 26th Inf. Co.H
Tyson, James A. TN 6th Inf. Co.K
Tyson, James C. GA 25th Inf. Co.D 2nd Lt.
Tyson, James E. MO 7th Cav. Co.G
Tyson, James M. AR 2nd Mtd.Rifles Co.B
Tyson, James N. TN 14th Inf. Co.B Cpl.
Tyson, James O. MS 19th Inf. Co.I 3rd Lt.
Tyson, James R. AR 17th (Lemoyne's) Inf. Co.B
Tyson, Jason AR 1st (Monroe's) Cav. Co.K
Tyson, J.C. TX 3rd Cav. Co.A Cpl.
Tyson, J.D. GA 1st (Fannin's) Res. Co.C
Tyson, J.D. GA 1st (Fannin's) Res. Co.F 1st Sgt.
Tyson, J.E. TX 33rd Cav. Co.G Sgt.
Tyson, Jehu GA 64th Inf. Co.A
Tyson, J.G. LA Res.Corps
Tyson, J.L. AL 40th Inf. Co.E
Tyson, J.M. TN Inf. 4th Cons.Regt. Co.G Cpl.
Tyson, J.M. TN 49th Inf. Co.G

Tyson, J.M. Inf. Bailey's Cons.Regt. Co.C
Tyson, Joab 7th Conf.Cav. 1st Co.I, Co.H
Tyson, Joel NC 17th Inf. (2nd Org.) Co.K
Tyson, Joel NC 42nd Inf. Co.C
Tyson, John AR 4th Inf. Co.D
Tyson, John AR 26th Inf. Co.C
Tyson, John GA 29th Inf. Co.G
Tyson, John GA Cobb's Legion Co.F 1st Lt.
Tyson, John LA 3rd (Wingfield's) Cav. Co.K
Tyson, John MS 28th Cav. Co.B
Tyson, John NC 23rd Inf. Co.A
Tyson, John A. NC 26th Inf. Co.K
Tyson, John D. NC 26th Inf. Co.H
Tyson, John E. MS Applewhite's Co. (Vaiden Guards)
Tyson, John H. TX 5th Cav. Co.E
Tyson, John L. GA 4th (Clinch's) Cav. Co.F,H Cpl.
Tyson, John M. AR Cav. Gordon's Regt. Co.B
Tyson, John S. GA Hvy.Arty. 22nd Bn. Co.D
Tyson, John W. MS 31st Inf. Co.I
Tyson, John W. VA 7th Inf. Co.A,E
Tyson, John W. VA 28th Inf. Co.F
Tyson, Jonah GA 1st (Fannin's) Res. Co.C
Tyson, Joseph NC 5th Cav. (63rd St.Troops) Co.A
Tyson, Joseph NC 31st Inf. Co.A
Tyson, Joseph VA 13th Inf. 2nd Co.E
Tyson, Joseph N. FL 9th Inf. Co.B
Tyson, Joseph W. NC 51st Inf. Co.H
Tyson, Joshua NC 18th Inf. Co.B
Tyson, Josiah GA 1st (Fannin's) Res. Co.F
Tyson, J.P. 10th Conf.Cav. Co.A
Tyson, J.R. GA 1st (Symons') Res. Co.H
Tyson, J.R. GA 13th Inf. Co.E 1st Sgt.
Tyson, J.R. TX 2nd Regt.St.Troops Co.G
Tyson, J.W. 1st Conf.Inf. 2nd Co.C
Tyson, Lazarus NC 18th Inf. Co.B
Tyson, Lemuel NC 55th Inf. Co.E
Tyson, Levi MS 36th Inf. Co.G
Tyson, Lewis VA 67th Mil. Co.E
Tyson, Lucian P. NC 26th Inf. Co.H Sgt.
Tyson, Luther VA 9th Inf. Co.G
Tyson, Madison L. GA 41st Inf. Co.G 2nd Lt.
Tyson, Madison L. GA Cobb's Legion Co.F 2nd Lt.
Tyson, Martin V. NC 14th Inf. Co.C
Tyson, M.E. GA 10th Mil.
Tyson, Meredith VA 30th Inf. Co.A
Tyson, Merritt NC 6th Sr.Res. Co.I
Tyson, M.L. AR 11th Inf. Co.I
Tyson, M.L. AR 11th & 17th Cons.Inf. Co.C Cpl.
Tyson, Neal MO Lt.Arty. McDonald's Co.
Tyson, Neil AR 5th Inf. Co.E
Tyson, Neil MO 6th Inf. Co.D
Tyson, Noah FL 1st (Res.) Inf. Co.G
Tyson, Noah NC 8th Inf. Co.G
Tyson, Noah NC Loc.Def. Croom's Co.
Tyson, P. GA 1st (Symons') Res. Co.F
Tyson, P.F. 10th Conf.Cav. Co.A
Tyson, Priestly SC 1st (Butler's) Inf. Co.A
Tyson, R.H. TX Waul's Legion Co.A
Tyson, Richard MD Arty. 3rd Btty.
Tyson, Richard L. NC 17th Inf. (2nd Org.) Co.K Sgt.
Tyson, R.L. NC 67th Inf.
Tyson, Robert AR 21st Inf. Co.D
Tyson, S. GA 54th Inf.
Tyson, S. NC 67th Inf. Co.G
Tyson, Samuel L. GA 1st (Ramsey's) Inf. Co.G
Tyson, Samuel V. NC Vol. Lawrence's Co.
Tyson, S.E. AR Cav. 1st Bn. (Stirman's) Co.G
Tyson, Seth NC 55th Inf. Co.E
Tyson, Seth H. NC Vol. Lawrence's Co.
Tyson, Seth H. 7th Conf.Cav. Co.H
Tyson, S.H. GA 3rd Res. Co.I
Tyson, S.H. NC Cav. 16th Bn. Co.F
Tyson, Shem NC 8th Inf. Co.G
Tyson, S.M. LA 17th Inf. Co.F
Tyson, S.M. TX 3rd Cav. Co.A
Tyson, Thomas GA 25th Inf. Co.D
Tyson, Thomas MS 3rd Cav. Co.D
Tyson, Thomas NC 33rd Inf. Co.E
Tyson, Thomas F. NC 33rd Inf. Co.E
Tyson, Thomas H. NC 7th Bn.Jr.Res. Co.C
Tyson, Thomas J. GA 1st (Ramsey's) Inf. Co.E
Tyson, Thomas M. NC 2nd Cav. (19th St.Troops) Co.E Cpl.
Tyson, Thomas O. 7th Conf.Cav. Co.E
Tyson, Thomas S. AR 1st (Colquitt's) Inf. Co.I
Tyson, Thomas U. MS 34th Inf. Co.D
Tyson, T.J. GA Lt.Arty. 12th Bn. 3rd Co.B
Tyson, T.J. TX 1st Hvy.Arty. Co.H
Tyson, T.S. AR 20th Inf. Chap.
Tyson, T.S. MS Inf. 3rd Bn. (St.Troops) Co.C
Tyson, U.N. AR 18th Inf. Co.I Sgt.
Tyson, Uriah AL 32nd & 58th (Cons.) Inf.
Tyson, Uriah NC 3rd Arty. (40th St.Troops) Co.C
Tyson, W.F. NC 4th Cav. (59th St.Troops) Co.A
Tyson, W.H. FL 1st (Res.) Inf. Co.G
Tyson, W.H. MS 1st Lt.Arty. Co.H
Tyson, W.H.H. NC 15th Inf. Co.M 2nd Lt.
Tyson, William AR Cav. Gordon's Regt. Co.B
Tyson, William FL 10th Inf. Co.H
Tyson, William GA 59th Inf. Co.A
Tyson, William GA Inf. (Wright Loc.Guards) Holmes' Co.
Tyson, William GA Cobb's Legion Co.F 2nd Lt.
Tyson, William KY 9th Cav. Co.E
Tyson, William NC 8th Inf. Co.E
Tyson, William VA 67th Mil. Co.E
Tyson, William A. GA 44th Inf. Co.E
Tyson, William A. NC 4th Cav. (59th St.Troops) Co.H Cpl.
Tyson, William G. NC 31st Inf. Co.B
Tyson, William G. VA 5th Cav. (12 mo. '61-2) Co.B
Tyson, William G. VA Cav. 14th Bn. Co.A
Tyson, William G. VA 15th Cav. Co.F
Tyson, William Gaston KY Cav. 2nd Bn. (Dortch's) Co.B
Tyson, William H. NC 32nd Inf. Co.I Capt.
Tyson, William J. AR 19th (Dockery's) Inf. Co.F Capt.
Tyson, William J. NC 24th Inf. Co.G
Tyson, William J. Gen. & Staff Capt., Prov.Marsh.
Tyson, William L. MS 11th Inf. Co.K
Tyson, William L. MS 15th Inf. Co.B Bvt.2nd Lt.
Tyson, William M. AR 17th (Lemoyne's) Inf. Co.B
Tyson, William M. AR 21st Inf. Co.D
Tyson, William S. FL 7th Inf. Co.H
Tyson, William S. TN 14th Inf. Co.B
Tyson, William Thomas NC 38th Inf. Co.E Cpl.
Tyson, W.J. LA 27th Inf. Co.F
Tyson, W.J. MS Cav. 24th Bn. Co.E
Tyson, W.L. MS 28th Cav. Co.B
Tyson, W.L. Forrest's Scouts A. Harvey's Co.,CSA Bvt.2nd Lt.
Tyson, W.P. MS 3rd Inf. (St.Troops) Co.B
Tyson, W.R. GA 39th Inf. Co.A
Tyson, Wright SC 9th Inf. Co.B
Tyson, Wright C. SC Inf. 7th Bn. (Enfield Rifles) Co.H
Tyson, W.S. MS Cav. 3rd Bn.Res. Co.A
Tyson, W.S. TX 5th Cav. Co.D Far.
Tyson, W.T. GA 1st Inf. (St.Guards) Co.F Sgt.
Tyson, W.V. MS 28th Cav. Co.A
Tysone, J.C. 14th Conf.Cav. Co.K
Tysor, Edwin L. NC 48th Inf. Co.G 2nd Lt.
Tysor, Henry D. NC 3rd Cav. (41st St.Troops) Co.E
Tysor, Jordan NC 26th Inf. Co.H
Tysor, Joseph C. NC 3rd Cav. (41st St.Troops) Co.D
Tysor, Joseph C. NC 15th Inf. Co.M Cpl.
Tysor, Joseph C. NC 32nd Inf. Co.I Cpl.
Tysor, Josiah NC 5th Cav. (63rd St.Troops) Co.E 2nd Lt.
Tysor, Lewis B. NC 26th Inf. Co.H
Tysor, L.G. NC 53rd Inf. Co.C
Tysor, M.W. GA 53rd Inf.
Tysor, Thomas B. NC 15th Inf. Co.M
Tysor, Thomas B. NC 32nd Inf. Co.I Cpl.
Tyus, A.J. AL 14th Inf. Co.H 1st Lt.
Tyus, Albertus J. GA 12th (Robinson's) Cav. (St.Guards) Co.G 1st Sgt.
Tyus, Benjamin R. TX 15th Cav. Co.F Capt.
Tyus, Benjamin R. TX 6th & 15th (Cons.) Vol. Co.F Capt.
Tyus, C. GA Cobb's Legion Co.D
Tyus, Clem AL 29th Inf. Co.H Cpl.
Tyus, D.H. AL Arty. 1st Bn. Co.B
Tyus, Donaldson H. AL 6th Inf. Co.G Sgt.
Tyus, Fitz J. AL Mil. 4th Vol. Co.B
Tyus, F.J. AL Arty. 1st Bn. Co.B
Tyus, F.W. TN 38th Inf. 2nd Co.A
Tyus, George W. AL 6th Inf. Co.G
Tyus, James E. TN 38th Inf. 2nd Co.A
Tyus, James H. GA 17th Inf. Co.E
Tyus, James R. AL 6th Inf. Co.G
Tyus, James R. AR Cav. Carlton's Regt. Co.D
Tyus, John AL Mil. 4th Vol. Co.B 2nd Lt.
Tyus, John E. TN 31st Inf. Co.D Cpl.
Tyus, John L. GA 1st (Ramsey's) Inf. Co.K Cpl.
Tyus, John T. GA 6th Inf. Co.A
Tyus, Joseph B. TX 15th Cav. Co.F Jr.2nd Lt.
Tyus, Joseph B. TX 6th & 15th (Cons.) Vol. Co.F 2nd Lt.
Tyus, Joseph B. TX 9th (Nichols') Inf. Co.F
Tyus, Joseph M. AL 6th Inf. Co.G
Tyus, Joseph T. VA 41st Inf. Co.A
Tyus, Joshua N. GA 17th Inf. Co.E Capt.
Tyus, Joshua N. GA 17th Inf. Co.E
Tyus, Joshua R. AL 6th Inf. Co.G
Tyus, Lewis GA 6th Inf. Co.A
Tyus, L.G. GA 8th Cav. Co.A

Tyus, Phillip G. FL Inf. 2nd Bn. Co.E Sgt.
Tyus, Phillip G. FL 11th Inf. Co.A
Tyus, Robert B. AR 34th Inf. ACS
Tyus, Robert B. Gen. & Staff Capt.,ACS
Tyus, T.E. TN 31st Inf. Co.D
Tyus, W.A. GA 8th Cav. Co.A
Tyus, William A. GA 62nd Cav. Co.A Bugler
Tyus, William D. AL Mil. 4th Vol. Co.B
Tyus, William H. GA 6th Inf. Co.A
Tyus, William J. AR 1st Mtd.Rifles Co.D
Tyus, William J. Gen. & Staff Maj.,AAG

U

U., John TX Cav. Wells' Regt. Co.D
Ubanks, B.J. SC 14th Inf. Co.H
Ubbee 1st Choctaw & Chickasaw Mtd.Rifles Co.G
Ubbey, Minton Deneale's Regt. Choctaw Warriors Co.D 1st Lt.
Ubera, F. LA Mil. Cazadores Espanoles Regt. Co.1
Uberchlag, B. LA Mil. 4th Regt. French Brig. Co.3
Uberchlag, F. LA Mil. 4th Regt. French Brig. Co.3
Ubi, Stephen 1st Choctaw Mtd.Rifles Co.E
Ubletz, R. TX Waul's Legion Co.D
Uche, Sandy 1st Cherokee Mtd.Vol. Co.E
Uchee, John 1st Creek Mtd.Vol. Co.E
Uckert, F. TX Inf. Timmons' Regt. Co.K
Uckert, Hermann TX 16th Inf. Co.F
Uckert, Wilhelm TX 16th Inf. Co.F
Udah, Auguste LA Hvy.Arty. 8th Bn. Co.C
Udee, Forrest LA 3rd Inf. Co.B Cpl.
Uden, G. TX 14th Inf. Co.A Cpl.
Uden, T.H. TX 14th Inf. Co.A
Udurley, Moses VA Lt.Arty. 38th Bn. Co.B
Ueckert, C.L. TX Cav. Waller's Regt. Co.C Cpl.
Ueckert, F. TX Waul's Legion Co.B
Ueckert, W. TX Inf. Timmons' Regt. Co.K
Uehlinger, John TX 1st (Yager's) Cav. Co.F
Uekert, C. TX 9th (Nichols') Inf. Co.G
Uekert, F. TX 9th (Nichols') Inf. Co.G
Uell, James A. VA 63rd Inf. Co.E
Uesdon, Theodore LA 6th Inf. Co.B
Uewen, Martin LA 13th Inf. Co.F
Ufal Tustemeggee 1st Seminole Mtd.Vol. Sgt.
Ufala 1st Creek Mtd.Vol. Co.A
Ufaula Fixico 2nd Creek Mtd.Vol. Co.E
Ufferman, W. Conf.Reg.Inf. Brooks' Bn. Co.A
Ufford, Eugene GA 6th Inf. (St.Guards) Co.I
Ugarte, B. LA Mil. 5th Regt.Eur.Brig. (Spanish Regt.) Co.5
Uguet, Jayme LA Mil. 5th Regt.Eur.Brig. (Spanish Regt.) Co.3
Uhalt, R. LA Mil. 1st Regt. French Brig. Co.3
Uhel, William MS 38th Cav. Co.B
Uhink, William AL 1st Cav. 1st Co.B
Uhink, William GA 36th (Villepigue's) Inf. Co.B
Uhl, Alex TX 14th Field Btty.
Uhl, Alexander TX Conscr.
Uhl, Christian LA Mil.Cont.Regt. Lang's Co.
Uhl, Gust TX 3rd Inf. Co.B 2nd Lt.
Uhl, J.K. TX 12th Cav. Co.F
Uhl, Samuel TX 12th Cav. Co.F
Uhl, Thomas TX 6th Cav. Co.F
Uhl, Zack TN 15th Cav. Co.A,K
Uhle, Fred LA Mil. Chalmette Regt. Co.D
Uhlenburg, H. MS 1st Lt.Arty. Co.I
Uhler, Jackson MS 16th Inf. Co.F
Uhler, Napoleon AL 21st Inf. Co.H
Uhler, Uriah MS 18th Inf. Co.C
Uhles, Alexander W. TN Cav. 7th Bn. (Bennett's) Co.B
Uhles, A.W. TN 22nd (Barteau's) Cav. Co.E
Uhles, David VA 38th Inf. Co.B Cpl.
Uhles, Fred TN 31st Inf. Co.A
Uhles, J.H. TN 31st Inf. Co.A
Uhles, William TN 9th (Ward's) Cav. Co.D
Uhlfelder, Myer AL Res. Belser's Co.
Uhlhorn, Charles L. LA Arty. Green's Co. (LA Guard Btty.)
Uhlhorn, J.H.K. MD Weston's Bn. Co.A
Uhlhorn, John H. MD 1st Inf. Co.C Sgt.
Uhlhorn, John H. VA Cav. 1st Bn. (Loc.Def. Troops) Co.A
Uhlhorn, Theodore G. LA Arty. Green's Co. (LA Guard Btty.)
Uhlichobe 1st Choctaw & Chickasaw Mtd.Rifles Co.A
Uhlinger, Henry LA Mil. 1st Regt. 3rd Brig. 1st Div. Co.E
Uhlman, Reinhard LA 1st Hvy.Arty. (Reg.) Co.K
Uhlrich, Richard AL 55th Vol. Co.F Music.
Uhls, Jacob M. TN 24th Inf. Co.C
Uhls, J.M. TN 24th Inf. Co.C Capt.
Uhr, Charles TX 33rd Cav. Co.B
Uhr, Matthew TX 15th Cav. Co.D
Uhrig, Phillip KY 2nd Mtd.Inf. Co.E
Uhrmacher, George LA Mil. 3rd Regt. 1st Brig. 1st Div. Co.I
Uhsley, L. VA Hvy.Arty. 19th Bn. Co.A
Uhte, F. LA Mil. Orleans Fire Regt. Co.I
Ui Key Key Chi 1st Squad. Cherokee Mtd.Vol. Co.A
Uink, William AR Lt.Arty. Wiggins' Btty.
Uitz, G.T. KY Jessee's Bn.Mtd.Riflemen Co.B
Uitz, Thomas J. KY Cav. 1st Bn. Co.B
Uitz, Thomas J. KY 4th Cav. Co.K Sgt.
Ujiffy, G.H. TX Inf. 1st St.Troops Martin's Co.A
Uker, William FL 3rd Inf. Co.D
Ukerich, Louis SC Mil. 1st Regt. (Charleston Res.) Co.F
Ulbreht, Charles TN Inf. 3rd Bn. Co.F
Uldrick, John E. SC 1st (Orr's) Rifles Co.B
Uldrick, Nathaniel T. AL 47th Inf. Co.D
Uldrix, William P. GA 23rd Inf. Co.E
Ulen, H.C. TN 47th Inf. Co.F Cpl.
Ulen, Henry Clay KY 2nd Mtd.Inf. Co.C Cpl.
Ulen, John R. KY 7th Mtd.Inf. Co.C 2nd Lt.
Ulen, N.C. TN Inf. 47th Regt. Co.F Cpl.
Ulery, Harison VA 114th Mil. Co.K
Ulhman, J. AL Mil. 4th Vol. Co.I
Ulhorn, Joseph MD Cav. 2nd Bn. Co.C
Ulhorn, Joseph VA 13th Inf. Co.G
Ulhorn, T.G. LA Mil. Crescent Cadets
Ulh pisah, Thomas 1st Choctaw Mtd.Rifles Co.K
Ulick, J. AL 1st Bn.Cadets Co.A
Ulinan, Th. TX Inf. Timmons' Regt. Co.K
Ulit, William TX 36th Cav. Co.F
Ulke, Theodore AL Gorff's Co. (Mobile Pulaski Rifles)
Ulke, Theodore VA 10th Cav. 1st Co.E Music.
Ulland, P.P. TX 24th & 25th Cav. (Cons.) Co.B
Ulla tees kih NC Inf. Thomas Legion Co.B
Ulla tees ky 1st Cherokee Mtd.Rifles Co.K
Uller, Isreal J. GA 12th Inf. Co.A
Uller, John AL 32nd Inf. Co.F
Ullery, Elias VA 13th Inf. Co.K
Ullman, Jacob VA 49th Inf. Co.C
Ullman, Jacob B. TN Cav. 4th Bn. (Branner's) Co.E
Ullman, Joseph KY 3rd Mtd.Inf. Co.K
Ullman, L.M. AL 5th Inf. Co.D
Ullman, Samuel MS 16th Inf. Co.G
Ullman, William 8th (Wade's) Conf.Cav. Co.A
Ullmann, Christ LA Mil. Fire Bn. Co.C
Ullmann, Gottlob TX 17th Inf. Co.H
Ullrich, August TX 15th Field Btty.
Ullrich, W. NC 18th Inf. Co.A
Ullrick, F.A. AL Gorff's Co. (Mobile Pulaski Rifles)
Ullrick, John TX Inf. 1st St.Troops Sheldon's Co.B
Ullum, John VA 7th Cav. Co.F
Ulm, F.A. GA Lt.Arty. Barnwell's Btty.
Ulm, F.A. GA Arty. Maxwell's Reg.Lt.Btty.
Ulm, Francis A. GA 3rd Cav. (St.Guards) Co.I
Ulm, Jacob LA 4th Inf. Co.D
Ulm, J.B. SC 2nd Cav. Co.A QM,Comsy.
Ulm, K.M. SC 1st Bn.S.S. Co.H
Ulm, K.M. SC 27th Inf. Co.E
Ulm, L. LA Mil. 1st Chasseurs a pied Co.5
Ulm, Lawrence LA 13th Inf. Co.A
Ulm, Michael LA 20th Inf. Co.I
Ulm, Philip LA Mil. 3rd Regt. 1st Brig. 1st Div. Co.H
Ulma, J.V. AR Inf. Cocke's Regt. Co.D
Ulman, Adolph MS Inf. 2nd Bn. Co.E Sgt.
Ulman, J. KY 3rd Cav. Co.D
Ulman, J.B. TN 2nd (Ashby's) Cav. Co.I
Ulman, M. AL Mil. 4th Vol. Co.K Cpl.
Ulmann, A. MS 48th Inf. Co.E Sgt.
Ulme, Thomas M. SC 4th Inf. Co.F
Ulmer, --- LA Mil. 1st Regt. French Brig. Co.5,12
Ulmer, --- LA Mil. 3rd Regt.Eur.Brig. (Garde Francaise) Euler's Co.
Ulmer, A.C. SC 8th Bn.Res. Fishburne's Co.
Ulmer, Adam SC 1st (Hagood's) Inf. 1st Co.B, 2nd Co.B
Ulmer, Adam TX 13th Vol. 2nd Co.I,B
Ulmer, A.J. MS 8th Inf. Co.E
Ulmer, A.J. MS 40th Inf. Co.A

Ulmer, A.J. 15th Conf.Cav. Co.G Sgt.
Ulmer, Charles P. FL 3rd Inf. Co.H Cpl.
Ulmer, Christin AL 1st Regt. Mobile Vol. Butt's Co.
Ulmer, Christian AL 4th Res. Co.A
Ulmer, C.W. SC Cav. 19th Bn. Co.C
Ulmer, David H. MS 40th Inf. Co.A
Ulmer, D.C. SC 1st (Butler's) Inf. Co.C
Ulmer, F.F. SC 25th Inf. Co.F
Ulmer, F.H. MS 1st (Johnston's) Inf. Co.I
Ulmer, F.H. MS 22nd Inf. Co.D
Ulmer, F.H. MS 40th Inf. Co.A
Ulmer, G. LA Mil.Squad. Guides d'Orleans Cavalier
Ulmer, G. LA Mil. 3rd Regt. 1st Brig. 1st Div. Co.G
Ulmer, G.B. SC 3rd Cav. Co.A
Ulmer, G.B. SC Arty. Bachman's Co. (German Lt.Arty.)
Ulmer, George LA C.S. Zouave Bn. Co.A,B
Ulmer, George C. GA 1st (Olmstead's) Inf. Gordon's Co.
Ulmer, George C. GA 63rd Inf. Co.F
Ulmer, George L. SC 1st (Hagood's) Inf. 1st Co.D
Ulmer, George W. GA Cav. 21st Bn. Co.C
Ulmer, G.L. SC 25th Inf. Co.F
Ulmer, G.W. GA 7th Cav. Co.B
Ulmer, H.D. SC Cav. 19th Bn. Co.A
Ulmer, H.D. SC Part.Rangers Kirk's Co.
Ulmer, Henry LA 22nd Inf. Co.B Sgt.
Ulmer, H.F. MS 40th Inf. Co.A
Ulmer, H.L. SC 1st Mtd.Mil. Green's Co. Cpl.
Ulmer, H. Martin SC 17th Inf. Co.H Capt.
Ulmer, I.B. AL 3rd Cav. Co.A
Ulmer, I.B. Conf.Cav. Wood's Regt. Co.C 1st Sgt.
Ulmer, Jacob LA 10th Inf. Co.F Sgt.
Ulmer, Jacob J. AR 1st Mtd.Rifles Co.I
Ulmer, James J. AL 3rd Cav. Co.D
Ulmer, James M. MS 40th Inf. Co.A Sgt.
Ulmer, James M. SC 17th Inf. Co.H Cpl.
Ulmer, J.B. SC 17th Inf. Co.H
Ulmer, J.F. MS 40th Inf. Co.A
Ulmer, J.J. AL Cp. of Instr. Talladega
Ulmer, John AL Mil. T. Hunt's Co.
Ulmer, John AR 34th Inf. Co.D
Ulmer, John FL Cav. 3rd Bn. Co.A 2nd Lt.
Ulmer, John GA 47th Inf. Co.E Cpl.
Ulmer, John LA Mil. Fire Bn. Co.C
Ulmer, John 15th Conf.Cav. Co.A Capt.
Ulmer, John 1st Choctaw & Chickasaw Mtd.Rifles 3rd Co.D
Ulmer, John M. AL 43rd Inf. Co.A
Ulmer, John W. MS 16th Inf. Co.F Cpl.
Ulmer, John W. MS 20th Inf. Co.I
Ulmer, Joseph AL 6th Inf. Co.I
Ulmer, Joseph L. FL 3rd Inf. Co.D Sgt.
Ulmer, Joseph T. GA Cav. 2nd Bn. Co.D
Ulmer, J.T. GA 5th Cav. Co.A
Ulmer, L.G. SC 24th Inf. Co.E
Ulmer, Malcolm C. MS Cav. Jeff Davis Legion Co.F
Ulmer, M.M. SC 2nd Arty. Co.I
Ulmer, M.M. SC 1st (Hagood's) Inf. 2nd Co.B
Ulmer, M.W. SC 3rd Cav. Co.A
Ulmer, M.W. SC 2nd Inf. Co.K
Ulmer, N.B. MS 40th Inf. Co.A
Ulmer, N.M. GA Cav. 2nd Bn. Co.A
Ulmer, N.M. GA 5th Cav. Co.I
Ulmer, Noah M. GA Cav. 1st Bn. Lamar's Co., Brailsford's Co. Cpl.
Ulmer, Peter SC 2nd St.Troops Co.H
Ulmer, Peter L. AL 3rd Cav. Co.D
Ulmer, P.L. Exch.Bn. 1st Co.A,CSA
Ulmer, R.H. MS Inf. 7th Bn. Co.A
Ulmer, Robert C. AR 25th Inf. Co.B
Ulmer, S.S. SC 2nd Arty. Co.I
Ulmer, S.V. FL 2nd Cav. Co.D
Ulmer, Thomas SC 11th Inf. 2nd Co.F
Ulmer, Thomas W. SC 1st (Hagood's) Inf. 1st Co.D
Ulmer, T.I. MS 6th Cav. Co.G Cpl.
Ulmer, T.W. SC 25th Inf. Co.F Cpl.
Ulmer, W.H. GA Hvy.Arty. 22nd Bn. Co.B
Ulmer, William A. MS 13th Inf. Co.K
Ulmer, William H. AL 3rd Cav. Co.F
Ulmer, W.M. MS 9th Cav. Co.G
Ulmer, W.P. Molette AL 3rd Cav. Co.D
Ulmer, W.T. SC 2nd St.Troops Co.E
Ulmo, J.H. SC Mil.Arty. 1st Regt. Tupper's Co.
Ulmo, M. GA Cav. Waring's Co.
Ulmo, Marcial GA Cav. 2nd Bn. Co.D
Ulmo, W.C. SC Mil.Arty. 1st Regt. Tupper's Co.
Ulmore, J.F. MS 44th Inf. Co.A
Ulms, J.O. GA Hvy.Arty. 22nd Bn. Co.B
Uln, M. LA Mil. 4th Regt. 2nd Brig. 1st Div. Co.C
Ulnaunt, Adolphus MS Page's Co. (Lexington Guards)
Ulock, J.M. NC 28th Inf. Co.B
Ulph pis a tobi 1st Choctaw Mtd.Rifles Co.K
Ulrey, Isaac MO Robertson's Regt.St.Guard Co.1
Ulrich, --- TX 3rd Inf. Co.K
Ulrich, August TX Cav. Ragsdale's Bn. Co.E
Ulrich, C. TX Inf. 4th Bn. (Oswald's) Co.B
Ulrich, Charles Conf.Inf. Tucker's Regt. Co.C
Ulrich, F. LA Mil. 4th Regt.Eur.Brig. Co.A
Ulrich, John FL Milton Lt.Arty. Dunham's Co.
Ulrich, L. LA Mil. 4th Regt.Eur.Brig. Co.E
Ulrich, L. TX 24th & 25th Cav. (Cons.) Co.B
Ulrich, L. TX 3rd (Kirby's) Bn.Vol. Co.C Cpl.
Ulrich, Louis TX 25th Cav. Co.F
Ulrich, M. LA Mil. Fire Bn. Co.E
Ulrich, P. LA Mil.Conf.Guards Regt. Band
Ulrick, John VA 3rd (Chrisman's) Bn.Res. Co.B
Ulrick, John VA 9th Bn.Res. Co.D
Ulrick, John VA 58th Mil. Co.E
Ulrug, Philip GA 57th Inf. Co.H
Ulry, David MO Cav. Slayback's Regt. Co.F
Ulry, Isaac MO 5th Cav. Co.H
Ulser, J.B. AL 50th Inf. Co.I
Ulstrop, --- LA Mil. 3rd Regt. 1st Brig. 1st Div. Co.I
Ul tee Ske 1st Cherokee Mtd.Rifles Co.H
Ul te Skee 1st Cherokee Mtd.Vol. 2nd Co.E
Ults, George SC 14th Inf. Co.B
Ultz, John P. KY 5th Cav. Co.G
Ulum, John VA 77th Mil. Co.C
Ulvy, Sebastian MS 21st Inf. Co.I
Uly cully Gray 1st Creek Mtd.Vol. Co.M
Ulysse, Charles LA Mil. 1st Native Guards
Umaran, J. LA Lt.Arty. LeGardeur, Jr.'s Co. (Orleans Guard Btty.)
Umaran, Joseph LA Mil. Chalmette Regt. Co.H
Umbach, Charles A.H. GA 1st (Olmstead's) Inf. Co.I Capt.
Umbargar, Lorenzo D. VA Mil. Wythe Cty.
Umbargar, William VA Mil. Wythe Cty.
Umbarger, Abram N. VA 4th Inf. Co.D
Umbarger, Alexander VA 45th Inf. Co.B
Umbarger, Alexander VA 45th Inf. Co.D
Umbarger, Alx VA Loc.Def. Patterson's Co.
Umbarger, Andrew VA 36th Inf. 2nd Co.G
Umbarger, Casper Y. VA 50th Inf. Cav.Co.B
Umbarger, Charles E. VA 4th Inf. Co.A,D
Umbarger, Charles W. VA 51st Inf. Co.C Cpl.
Umbarger, Daniel VA 51st Inf. Co.C
Umbarger, Edward H. VA 51st Inf. Co.C
Umbarger, Eley VA 45th Inf. Co.D
Umbarger, Eph VA Mil. Wythe Cty.
Umbarger, Ephraim T. VA 4th Inf. Co.D
Umbarger, Frank T. VA 51st Inf. Co.C
Umbarger, George H. VA Loc.Def. Patterson's Co.
Umbarger, Harvey VA 45th Inf. Co.B
Umbarger, Henry VA 36th Inf. 2nd Co.G
Umbarger, H.M. VA 21st Cav. 2nd Co.E
Umbarger, Isaac M. VA 51st Inf. Co.C
Umbarger, James A. VA Cav. 47th Bn. Co.B
Umbarger, James A. VA Loc.Def. Patterson's Co.
Umbarger, James D. VA 51st Inf. Co.C
Umbarger, James H. VA 4th Inf. Co.B
Umbarger, James H. VA 4th Inf. Co.G
Umbarger, James L. VA 4th Inf. Co.A,D
Umbarger, James L.Y. VA 45th Inf. Co.D
Umbarger, James R. VA 21st Cav. Co.B, 2nd Co.E Sgt.
Umbarger, Jehiel F. VA 51st Inf. Co.C 1st Lt.
Umbarger, John VA 36th Inf. 2nd Co.G
Umbarger, John VA 63rd Inf. Co.H
Umbarger, John VA Mil. Wythe Cty.
Umbarger, John D. VA 64th Mtd.Inf. Co.G Sgt.
Umbarger, John F. VA 51st Inf. Co.F Sgt.
Umbarger, John H. VA 30th Bn.S.S. Co.D Cpl.
Umbarger, John P. VA 63rd Inf. Co.H
Umbarger, Joseph B. VA 4th Inf. Co.D
Umbarger, J.P. TX 5th Inf. Co.B
Umbarger, J.S. TN 4th (McLemore's) Cav. Co.I
Umbarger, J.W. TN 61st Mtd.Inf. Co.E
Umbarger, Levi VA 4th Res. Co.E
Umbarger, Michael F. VA 45th Inf. Co.D Cpl.
Umbarger, N.B. VA 30th Bn.S.S. Co.D
Umbarger, Peter VA 198th Mil.
Umbarger, R. VA Mil. Wythe Cty.
Umbarger, Rufus VA 21st Cav. Co.K
Umbarger, Rufus E. VA 51st Inf. Co.C
Umbarger, Stephen VA 1st Inf. Co.K
Umbarger, Stephen G. TX 22nd Cav. Co.F
Umbarger, T.P. VA Loc.Def. Patterson's Co.
Umbarger, W.H. VA 4th Res. Co.E
Umbarger, William VA 11th Bn.Res. Co.A
Umbarger, William VA 36th Inf. 2nd Co.G Sgt.
Umbarger, William VA 45th Inf. Co.B
Umbarger, William VA Loc.Def. Patterson's Co.
Umbarger, William A. VA 51st Inf. Co.C Sgt.
Umbarger, William H., Jr. VA 4th Res. Co.E
Umbarger, William S. VA 4th Inf. Co.D

Umberfield, --- TX Cav. Border's Regt. Co.K
Umberfield, G. TX 26th Cav. Co.E
Umberger, Joseph W. VA 51st Inf. Co.C
Umberger, Samuel AR 7th Inf. Co.I
Umberson, R.W. TX 4th Inf. Co.E
Umberson, W. TX 22nd Inf. Co.B
Umberson, W.F. TX 15th Inf. Co.K
Umbland, Jacob TX 20th Inf. Co.B
Umble, James MO 9th Bn.S.S. Co.D
Umbles, R. AR 21st Mil. Co.E
Umdenstock, W. TX Inf. 2nd St.Troops Co.H
Umfleet, Jonathan TN Lt.Arty. Burroughs' Co.
Umflett, Lewis NC 33rd Inf. Co.E
Umforg, C. SC Mil. 16th Regt. Steinmeyer, Jr.'s Co. Sgt.
Umfress, M. MS Cav. 3rd Bn. (Ashcraft's) Co.A
Umfress, William H. MS 17th Inf. Co.E
Umfreys, Monroe GA Cherokee Legion (St.Guards) Co.C
Umfries, C. MS Cav. Davenport's Bn. (St.Troops) Co.A
Umgelder, F. TX 3rd (Kirby's) Bn.Vol. Co.A
Umgelter, Frederick TX 16th Inf. Co.F Sgt.
Umhalt, Julius TN Inf. 3rd Bn. Co.G
Umhow, John AR 5th Inf. Co.I
Umina, Antonio LA Mil. 6th Regt.Eur.Brig. (Italian Guards Bn.) Co.2
Uminsky, H. GA 36th (Villepigue's) Inf. Co.H Sgt.
Uminsky, Henry 1st Conf.Inf. Co.B, 2nd Co.F
Umlang, E. TX Waul's Legion Co.E
Umlenhour, Jacob VA 2nd Inf. Co.F Cpl.
Umpenour, Jacob VA 31st Mil. Co.D
Umpflet, Elisha NC 33rd Inf. Co.E
Umpflet, Thomas NC 33rd Inf. Co.E
Umphflet, L.B. AR 15th Mil. Co.D
Umphies, G.B. AL 25th Inf. Co.A
Umphlet, Bryant NC 52nd Inf. Co.C
Umphlet, Edmond NC 5th Inf. Co.H
Umphlet, Jesse NC 5th Inf. Co.H
Umphlet, William NC 5th Inf. Co.H
Umphlett, J. TN 19th & 20th (Cons.) Cav. Co.C 1st Sgt.
Umphlett, Job TN 18th (Newsom's) Cav. Co.K Ord.Sgt.
Umphlett, Job TN 38th Inf. Co.E Capt.
Umphlett, William H. VA 3rd Inf. Co.F
Umphres, M.C. MS 10th Cav. Co.B
Umphress, John R. AL 47th Inf. Co.B
Umphrey, Benjamin B. TN Inf. 1st Bn. (Colms') Co.B
Umphrey, Berry VA Lt.Arty. G.B. Chapman's Co.
Umphrey, Edward LA 14th Inf. Co.F
Umphrey, John GA 60th Inf. Co.E
Umphrey, John TX 19th Inf. Co.K Sgt.
Umphrey, John L. GA 40th Inf. Co.F Sgt.
Umphrey, Lewis GA 6th Cav.
Umphrey, William GA 40th Inf. Co.F 3rd Lt.
Umphrey, Zebulum AR 19th (Dawson's) Inf. Co.K
Umphreys, --- TX Cav. Mann's Regt. Co.G
Umphreys, Gaston GA 24th Inf. Co.G Sgt.
Umphreys, George M. MO 4th Cav. Co.F
Umphreys, Wade LA Inf.Crescent Regt. Co.A
Umphreys, William MO 4th Cav. Co.F
Umphreys, William C. VA 20th Cav. Co.I
Umphries, A. GA 36th (Broyles') Inf. Co.B
Umphries, Jacob NC 21st Inf. Co.C
Umphries, J.C. LA Inf.Crescent Regt. Co.B
Umphries, John GA 51st Inf. Co.C
Umphries, John MS 5th Inf.
Umphries, John TX 33rd Cav. Co.D
Umphries, John VA 61st Inf. Co.D
Umphries, Samuel VA 5th Cav. Co.G
Umphries, Wesley TX 16th Cav. Co.F
Umphries, W.S. VA 4th Inf. Co.I
Umphris, J.C. TN 38th Inf. 2nd Co.K Sgt.
Umphris, Nathan SC 4th St.Troops Co.C
Umphris, Nathaniel SC 4th St.Troops Co.C
Umphris, William AL 19th Inf. Co.G
Umphriss, Richard H. LA 8th Inf. Co.F
Umphriss, Samuel C. GA 47th Inf. Co.D
Umphrys, Andrew KY 5th Mtd.Inf. Co.E
Umpley, J.B. AL Cav. Hardie's Bn.Res.
Umprey, J.W. TN 51st (Cons.) Inf. Co.A
Umpstadt, W.J. MO 9th Bn.S.S. Co.C
Umstadt, W.J. MO 16th Inf. Co.D
Umstadter, Michael VA 6th Inf. Co.G
Umstadter, Michael VA 54th Mil. Co.E,F
Umstead, A. NC 1st Jr.Res. Co.I
Umstead, Alvis K. NC 6th Inf. Co.B 1st Lt.
Umstead, George W. NC 6th Inf. Co.B Sgt.
Umstead, J.M. TN 12th Inf. Co.K Sgt.
Umstead, John W. NC 2nd Cav. (19th St.Troops) Co.K
Umstead, Joseph R. NC 2nd Cav. (19th St.Troops) Co.K Sgt.Maj.
Umstead, Kenneth R. NC 6th Inf. Co.B Sgt.
Umstead, W.F. AL 92nd Inf. Co.K
Umsted, A.C. KY 2nd Bn.Mtd.Rifles Co.B
Umsted, D.W. NC Lt.Arty. 13th Bn. Co.E
Umsted, George W. FL 5th Inf. Co.B
Umsted, Henry NC Inf. 13th Bn. Co.A
Umsted, Henry L. NC 66th Inf. Co.A
Umsted, J. NC Lt.Arty. 13th Bn. Co.E
Umsted, James M. TN 12th (Cons.) Inf. Co.K
Umsted, William D. AR 1st (Crawford's) Cav. Co.A 3rd Lt.
Umstot, Conrad G. VA 11th Cav. Co.D Sgt.
Umstott, Conrad VA 77th Mil. Co.B, Blue's Co.
Umstott, John VA 77th Mil. Co.C
Umstott, S. VA 77th Mil. Co.B
Unah, John 1st Creek Mtd.Vol. Co.A
Unce, Christopher TX 3rd Inf. 1st Co.A, Co.D
Uncell, J.H. KY 2nd (Duke's) Cav. Co.K
Unchick, John TX 2nd Inf. Co.B
Uncil, George C. AR 4th Inf. Co.H
Uncill, William AR 1st Vol. Kelsey's Co.
Uncke, August. LA Mil. 3rd Regt. 2nd Brig. 1st Div.
Uncle, Elijah KY 7th Mtd.Inf. Co.K
Uncle, Elisha KY 7th Mtd.Inf. Co.K
Underdown, John W. NC 26th Inf. Co.F
Underdown, Joseph K. TN 32nd Inf. Co.K
Underdown, Stephen NC 5th Sr.Res. Co.D
Underdown, William NC 26th Inf. Co.F
Underdunk, William VA 67th Mil. Co.A
Undereinn, J. AL 1st Regt. Mobile Vol. Baas' Co.
Underhill, A.E. TN 18th Inf. Co.D
Underhill, D.H. TN 24th Inf. 1st Co.H, Co.I
Underhill, E.M. AL Inf. 65th Regt. Col.
Underhill, Felix KY 7th Mtd.Inf. Co.C
Underhill, Francis VA 54th Mil. Co.C,D
Underhill, G.T. MS 1st (King's) Inf. (St.Troops) Co.D
Underhill, Henry FL 10th Inf. Co.E
Underhill, J. FL 2nd Cav. Co.K
Underhill, J. FL Cav. 5th Bn. Co.H
Underhill, J.A. VA 3rd (Archer's) Bn.Res. Co.A
Underhill, James A. VA Hood's Bn.Res. Tappey's Co.
Underhill, J.D. NC 31st Inf. Co.H
Underhill, Jerry FL 7th Inf. Co.B
Underhill, J.N. TX 19th Inf. Co.C Cpl.
Underhill, John FL 7th Inf. Co.E
Underhill, John FL 8th Inf. Co.K
Underhill, John NC Hvy.Arty. 1st Bn. Co.C
Underhill, John J. NC 2nd Inf. Co.C
Underhill, M.A. MO Cav. 3rd Bn. Co.F
Underhill, Marian W. TN Cav. 9th Bn. (Gantt's) Co.D
Underhill, Martin A. MO 10th Cav. Co.H
Underhill, Michael E. VA Hvy.Arty. 19th Bn. Co.B
Underhill, Michael E. VA 39th Inf. Co.A
Underhill, R.B. MO Cav. 3rd Bn. Co.G Sgt.
Underhill, Robert TX 24th Cav. Co.C
Underhill, R.V. MO 12th Inf. Co.I Sgt.
Underhill, S.M. Lee's Staff Lt.,ADC
Underhill, T.G. MS Hall's Co. Cpl.
Underhill, Thomas J. AR Lt.Arty. Rivers' Btty.
Underhill, W. NC Mil. Clark's Sp.Bn. Co.D
Underhill, William FL 2nd Cav. Co.K
Underhill, William GA 8th Cav. Old Co.I
Underhill, William GA 62nd Cav. Co.I
Underhill, William MO 11th Inf. Co.K
Underhill, William H. NC 12th Inf. Co.G Sgt.
Understull, Frits MO 10th Cav. Co.E
Underwald, --- TX Cav. Baird's Regt. Co.C
Underwood, A. TN 48th (Nixon's) Inf. Co.B
Underwood, Aaron M. AL 20th Inf. Co.K
Underwood, A.B. 1st Conf.Cav. 2nd Co.K
Underwood, Abe GA 21st Inf. Co.B
Underwood, Abe NC 2nd Cav. (19th St.Troops) Co.F
Underwood, Abner GA Inf. 8th Bn. Co.D 2nd Lt.
Underwood, Abner J. GA 18th Inf. Co.F
Underwood, Acy J. NC 51st Inf. Co.D
Underwood, Adam H. AL Eufaula Lt.Arty.
Underwood, A.G. LA Mil. Claiborne Regt. Co.A
Underwood, A.H. AL Mil. 4th Vol. Gantt's Co.
Underwood, A.H. AL 40th Inf. Co.H
Underwood, A.J. AL 22nd Inf. Co.K Sgt.
Underwood, A.J. GA 18th Inf. Co.K
Underwood, A.J. MS 10th Cav. Co.B
Underwood, A.J. MS 32nd Inf. Co.K
Underwood, A.J. NC 31st Inf. Co.H
Underwood, A.J. TX 25th Cav. Co.B
Underwood, A.J. Conf.Lt.Arty. Stark's Bn. Co.D
Underwood, Albert SC 1st Arty. Co.A
Underwood, Albert G. MS 26th Inf. Co.G 1st Sgt.
Underwood, Alex AL 26th Inf. Co.H
Underwood, Alexander TN 19th Inf. Co.K
Underwood, Alfred TN 33rd Inf. Co.C
Underwood, Alfred VA 51st Inf. Co.H
Underwood, Alfred M. MO 8th Inf. Co.H
Underwood, Allen KY 2nd Bn.Mtd.Rifles Co.B

Underwood, Alvin C. GA Cobb's Legion Co.C
Underwood, Alvin P. TN 19th Inf. Co.K
Underwood, A.M. LA Inf. 9th Bn. Co.B
Underwood, Anderson TN 48th (Voorhies') Inf. Co.A
Underwood, Andrew MS 24th Inf. Co.D,E
Underwood, Andrew J. MS 26th Inf. Co.G
Underwood, Andrew J. TN 59th Mtd.Inf. Co.H
Underwood, Andrew J. VA Lt.Arty. French's Co.
Underwood, Andrew J. VA 44th Inf. Co.B
Underwood, Andrew J. VA Arty. Wise Legion
Underwood, Archer NC 5th Inf. Co.C
Underwood, Armstead S. MS 22nd Inf. Co.E Cpl.
Underwood, A.T. TN 45th Inf. Co.E
Underwood, Augustus AL Rebels
Underwood, A.V. AL 5th Cav. Co.K
Underwood, A.W. TX 5th Inf. Co.D
Underwood, B. NC 47th Inf. Co.C
Underwood, Benajah GA 22nd Inf. Co.B Cpl.
Underwood, Benjamin NC 7th Inf. Co.C
Underwood, Benjamin TN Inf. 1st Bn. (Colms') Co.B
Underwood, Benjamin F. AL 19th Inf. Co.E
Underwood, Benjamin F. GA 45th Inf. Co.B
Underwood, Benjamin M. GA 11th Inf. Co.E
Underwood, Benjamin W. AL 3rd Inf. Co.D
Underwood, B.F. AL 15th Bn.Part.Rangers Co.A
Underwood, B.F. AL 56th Part.Rangers Co.A
Underwood, B.F. GA Cav. 21st Bn. Co.E
Underwood, B.F. GA 9th Inf. (St.Guards) Co.C
Underwood, B.G. MS 6th Cav. Co.F 1st Lt.
Underwood, B.G. MS Inf. 3rd Bn. (St.Troops) Co.F
Underwood, Burwell VA 42nd Inf. Co.B
Underwood, Bushrod VA Cav. Mosby's Regt. (Part.Rangers) Co.A
Underwood, Bushrod VA Lt.Arty. 38th Bn. Co.A
Underwood, Bushrod VA Lt.Arty. Rogers' Co.
Underwood, Charles Conf.Inf. Tucker's Regt. Co.F 1st Sgt.
Underwood, Charles E. GA 31st Inf. Co.D
Underwood, Chet AR 7th Cav. Co.D
Underwood, Chet H. AR 1st Mtd.Rifles Co.H
Underwood, Clemons MO Cav. 3rd Bn. Co.G Sgt.
Underwood, Clint AL 26th (O'Neal's) Inf. Co.H Cpl.
Underwood, Colvin TN 45th Inf. Co.B
Underwood, Creed VA Cav. 37th Bn. Co.G
Underwood, Creed VA 24th Inf. Co.A
Underwood, C.T. NC 1st Jr.Res. Co.C Cpl.
Underwood, D. AR 62nd Mil. Co.F
Underwood, D. TX 20th Inf. Co.I
Underwood, D.A. MS 2nd St.Cav. Co.H
Underwood, D.A. MS Inf. 1st Bn. Co.A
Underwood, D.A. MS 41st Inf. Co.G
Underwood, Daniel J. AL Cp. of Instr. Talladega
Underwood, Daniel R. NC 30th Inf. Co.A
Underwood, David KY 2nd (Duke's) Cav. Co.C
Underwood, David NC 1st Arty. (10th St.Troops) Co.C
Underwood, David H. GA Cav. 16th Bn. (St.Guards) Co.C Sgt.
Underwood, Davidson A. NC 42nd Inf. Co.C Maj.
Underwood, D.E. GA 3rd Bn.S.S. Co.A
Underwood, DeWitt B. NC 1st Inf. Co.D
Underwood, D.H. GA 18th Inf. Co.K
Underwood, D.L. GA 18th Inf. Co.H
Underwood, D.L. GA 23rd Inf. Co.I
Underwood, D.R. GA Inf. 12th Bn. Co.B
Underwood, D.W. NC 1st Jr.Res. Co.E
Underwood, Ed KY 6th Mtd.Inf. Co.D
Underwood, Edmond TN 39th Mtd.Inf. Co.B
Underwood, Edward AR 1st (Dobbin's) Cav. Co.K
Underwood, E.H. GA 6th Cav. Co.B
Underwood, E.H. GA Smith's Legion Co.D
Underwood, E.J. GA 18th Inf. Co.E
Underwood, E.J. KY 12th Cav. Co.A
Underwood, Elbert SC Hvy.Arty. 15th (Lucas') Bn. Co.A
Underwood, Elbert R. GA 57th Inf. Co.C
Underwood, Elias KY 6th Mtd.Inf. Co.D
Underwood, Elias MO 15th Cav. Co.I 2nd Lt.
Underwood, Elijah V. AR 3rd Inf. Co.I
Underwood, Elisha P. TN 45th Inf. Co.E
Underwood, E.M. GA 8th Inf. Co.D
Underwood, E.M. GA 23rd Inf. Co.I
Underwood, Eml VA 166th Mil. Taylor's Co.
Underwood, Enoch D. NC 25th Inf. Co.C
Underwood, Enoch F. AL 44th Inf. Co.A
Underwood, E.O. MS 18th Cav.
Underwood, E.O. TN 4th Inf. Co.D
Underwood, Ephram MO 5th Inf. Co.K
Underwood, Epriam MO Inf. 1st Bn. Co.A
Underwood, E.R. TN Lt.Arty. Barry's Co.
Underwood, E.W. KY 12th Cav. Co.A,B,D
Underwood, F. GA Lt.Arty. 12th Bn. 3rd Co.B
Underwood, F.G. AL 22nd Inf. Co.C
Underwood, F.G. AL 25th Inf. Co.B
Underwood, Finis TN 1st Hvy.Arty. 2nd Co.C, 3rd Co.A, Co.L
Underwood, Fleming G. MO 1st N.E. Cav. Co.D,G
Underwood, Fleming G. MO Cav. 3rd Bn. Co.G
Underwood, F.M. AL 22nd Inf. Co.B
Underwood, F.M. MO Inf. 4th Regt.St.Guard Co.B
Underwood, F.M. MO 6th Inf. Co.D
Underwood, F.M. TN 43rd Inf. Co.H
Underwood, F.M. TX 17th Cav. 2nd Co.I
Underwood, F.M. TX 14th Inf. 1st Co.K
Underwood, Francis TN Inf. 1st Cons.Regt. Co.G
Underwood, Francis TN 28th Inf. Co.F
Underwood, Francis TN 28th (Cons.) Inf. Co.B
Underwood, Francis M. TX 18th Inf. Co.L
Underwood, Frank TN 13th (Gore's) Cav. Co.A
Underwood, Frank TN 16th Inf. Co.G
Underwood, Franklin GA Inf. Alexander's Co.
Underwood, Frank M. MO 2nd Cav. Co.E
Underwood, Frank M. MO 8th Cav. Co.A
Underwood, Frede VA 4th Res. Co.I
Underwood, Frederick MO 10th Inf. Co.I
Underwood, Freeling H. KY 12th Cav.
Underwood, F.W. GA 18th Inf. Co.H
Underwood, F.W. GA 23rd Inf. Co.I
Underwood, G.A. GA 54th Inf. Co.H
Underwood, G.A. LA 31st Inf. Co.D
Underwood, G.C. GA 1st Bn.S.S. Co.B
Underwood, George NC 18th Inf. Co.E
Underwood, George TN 24th Inf. 1st Co.G
Underwood, George C. NC 26th Inf. Co.G 2nd Lt.
Underwood, George E. MS 12th Inf. Co.G
Underwood, George W. MO Inf. 8th Bn. Co.F
Underwood, G.F. GA 8th Cav. Co.F Cpl.
Underwood, G.F. GA 62nd Cav. Co.F
Underwood, G.L. GA 18th Inf. Co.K Sgt.
Underwood, Gustavus A. GA 1st Bn.S.S. Co.C
Underwood, G.W. AL 5th Cav. Co.K
Underwood, G.W. AL Cav. Moreland's Regt. Co.E
Underwood, G.W. AR 2nd Cav. Co.E
Underwood, G.W. MS 26th Inf. Co.A,K
Underwood, G.W. MO 15th Cav. Co.I Capt.
Underwood, H. KY 10th (Johnson's) Cav. New Co.B
Underwood, H. 1st Chickasaw Inf. Hansell's Co.
Underwood, H.C. AL 26th (O'Neal's) Inf. Co.H
Underwood, Henry GA 35th Inf. Co.E
Underwood, Henry NC 5th Sr.Res. Co.H
Underwood, Henry NC 38th Inf. Co.B Fifer
Underwood, Henry VA Cav. Swann's Bn. Sweny's Co.
Underwood, Henry J. VA Lt.Arty. G.B. Chapman's Co.
Underwood, H.F. GA Lt.Arty. 12th Bn. Co.B
Underwood, H.F. LA 5th Cav. Co.D 2nd Lt.
Underwood, H.F. LA 13th Bn. (Part.Rangers) Co.E
Underwood, H.H. KY 2nd (Woodward's) Cav. Co.C
Underwood, H.H. TN 50th Inf. Co.A
Underwood, Hiram AL 12th Cav. Co.E
Underwood, H.J. VA 166th Mil. Co.H
Underwood, H.M. LA 6th Cav. Co.C
Underwood, H.N. GA 1st Cav. Co.H
Underwood, H.P. MS 41st Inf. Co.G
Underwood, H.V. AR 1st Mtd.Rifles Co.K
Underwood, H.V. AR 7th Inf. Co.D
Underwood, H.V. AR 25th Inf. Co.G Sgt.
Underwood, I. GA 1st Cav. Co.A
Underwood, Isaac A. TX 29th Cav. Co.E
Underwood, Isaac W. TX 8th Inf. Co.K
Underwood, Isaac W. VA 12th Inf. Co.D
Underwood, Isaiah GA 12th Inf. Co.C
Underwood, Isam VA 59th Inf. 2nd Co.I
Underwood, Isham VA 57th Inf. Co.C
Underwood, J. GA Inf. City Bn. (Columbus) Co.B
Underwood, J. MS 3rd (St.Troops) Cav. Co.E
Underwood, J. MS Cp.Guard (Cp. of Instr. for Conscr.)
Underwood, J.A. GA 9th Inf. Co.K
Underwood, Jack GA 18th Inf. Co.K
Underwood, Jacob NC 8th Sr.Res. Bryan's Co.
Underwood, Jacob S. NC 1st Arty. (10th St.Troops) Co.C
Underwood, J.A.F. AL 33rd Inf. Co.F
Underwood, James AL 20th Inf. Co.D
Underwood, James GA 46th Inf. Co.D
Underwood, James MS 1st Cav.Res. Co.A
Underwood, James MS 22nd Inf. Co.E
Underwood, James MS 33rd Inf. Co.B Sgt.
Underwood, James MO 16th Inf. Co.A Cpl.

Underwood, James NC 6th Sr.Res. Co.H
Underwood, James TX 1st Hvy.Arty. Co.A
Underwood, James VA Inf. 23rd Bn. Co.G
Underwood, James Gen. & Staff AAG
Underwood, James A. VA 60th Inf. 2nd Co.H
Underwood, James A.S. TN 39th Mtd.Inf. Co.F
Underwood, James B. GA Inf. 8th Bn. Co.D
Underwood, James B. GA 43rd Inf. Co.K
Underwood, James B. GA 49th Inf. Co.C Sgt.
Underwood, James B. LA 17th Inf. Co.A Sgt.
Underwood, James C. AR 2nd Inf. Co.F Cpl.
Underwood, James D. GA 1st (Olmstead's) Inf. 1st Co.A
Underwood, James D. GA 1st Bn.S.S. Co.B
Underwood, James D. TX 19th Cav. Co.E
Underwood, James H. AR 15th (Josey's) Inf. Co.A Cpl.
Underwood, James H. TX 16th Cav. Co.I
Underwood, James H. TX 5th Inf. Co.C
Underwood, James H. VA 8th Cav. Co.F
Underwood, James H. VA Lt.Arty. French's Co.
Underwood, James H. VA Arty. Wise Legion
Underwood, James H. Conf.Lt.Arty. Stark's Bn. Co.D
Underwood, James J. AR 17th (Lemoyne's) Inf. Co.F 2nd Lt.
Underwood, James J. TN 48th (Voorhies') Inf. Co.A
Underwood, James L. TX 2nd Cav. Co.G
Underwood, James M. FL 2nd Inf. Co.I 1st Lt.
Underwood, James M. GA 10th Inf. Co.F Sgt.
Underwood, James M. LA 8th Cav. Co.E Cpl.
Underwood, James M. NC 38th Inf. Co.E
Underwood, James M. NC 45th Inf. Co.G
Underwood, James N. MS Inf. 3rd Bn. (St.Troops) Co.B
Underwood, James R. TN 22nd Cav.
Underwood, James W. NC 1st Arty. (10th St.Troops) Co.C
Underwood, J.B. AL 7th Cav. Co.F,A
Underwood, J.B. GA Arty. 11th Bn. (Sumter Arty.) Co.B
Underwood, J.B. GA Inf. 40th Bn. Co.E
Underwood, J.B. AASurg.
Underwood, J.C. MO 15th Cav. Co.I
Underwood, J.C. TX 12th Inf. Co.A 1st Lt.
Underwood, J.C. VA Lt.Arty. Hankins' Co.
Underwood, J.C. Gen. & Staff Surg.
Underwood, J.D. AL 33rd Inf. Co.F
Underwood, J.D. GA 54th Inf. Co.C
Underwood, J.D. MO Cav. Freeman's Regt. Co.B
Underwood, J.E. GA 52nd Inf. Co.H 2nd Lt.
Underwood, J.E. TN 24th Inf. Co.A
Underwood, Jedon R. NC 1st Arty. (10th St.Troops) Co.C
Underwood, Jesse NC Walker's Bn. Thomas' Legion 2nd Co.D
Underwood, Jesse VA 42nd Inf. Co.B
Underwood, Jesse VA 59th Inf. 2nd Co.I
Underwood, Jesse VA 60th Inf. 2nd Co.H
Underwood, J.F. AL Cav. 24th Bn. Co.C
Underwood, J.F. AR 12th Bn.S.S. Co.B
Underwood, J.F. MO 12th Cav. Co.E
Underwood, J.G. AR 7th Inf. Co.D
Underwood, J.G. AR 24th Inf. Co.E
Underwood, J.G. AR Inf. Hardy's Regt. Co.B
Underwood, J.G. TN 42nd Inf. 1st Co.F
Underwood, J.H. GA Hvy.Arty. 22nd Bn. Co.B
Underwood, J.H. LA Inf. 4th Bn. Co.E
Underwood, J.H. LA Inf. Pelican Regt. Co.G
Underwood, J.H. MO Inf. 1st Bn.St.Guard Co.D 3rd Lt.
Underwood, J.H. MO Inf. 5th Regt.St.Guard Co.D 3rd Lt.
Underwood, J.H. VA 13th Cav. Co.K
Underwood, J.H. Brush Bn.
Underwood, J.I. AR 21st Inf. Co.E 2nd Lt.
Underwood, J.J. AL 15th Inf. Co.I
Underwood, J.J. AR 2nd Cav. Co.G
Underwood, J.J. MS 1st (King's) Inf. (St.Troops) Co.A
Underwood, J.J. SC 6th Cav. Co.H
Underwood, J.J. SC 20th Inf.
Underwood, J.J. TN 31st Inf. Co.A
Underwood, J.L. AL 30th Inf. Chap.
Underwood, J.L. VA Loc.Def. Morehead's Co.
Underwood, J.M. AL 5th Cav. Co.K Capt.
Underwood, J.M. TN 33rd Inf. Co.E
Underwood, J.M. TN 48th (Nixon's) Inf. Co.B Sgt.Maj.
Underwood, J.N. GA 23rd Inf. Co.E,I
Underwood, J.N. GA 44th Inf. Co.A
Underwood, Joe TX 13th Vol. 2nd Co.H
Underwood, Joel LA 13th Bn. (Part.Rangers) Co.E
Underwood, Joel MS 28th Cav. Co.H
Underwood, Joel B. LA 5th Cav. Co.I
Underwood, John AL Arty. 1st Bn. Co.B
Underwood, John AL Arty. 1st Bn. Co.C
Underwood, John AL Mil. 4th Vol. Co.B
Underwood, John AL 19th Inf. Co.H
Underwood, John AR 21st Inf. Co.E Sgt.
Underwood, John AR 37th Inf. Co.A
Underwood, John FL 11th Inf. Co.L Cpl.
Underwood, John GA 12th Cav. Co.C 1st Sgt.
Underwood, John GA 4th Inf. Co.I
Underwood, John GA 18th Inf. Co.K Cpl.
Underwood, John GA 52nd Inf. Co.H
Underwood, John GA Floyd Legion (St.Guards) Co.A
Underwood, John LA Cav. 18th Bn. Co.F 1st Lt.
Underwood, John MS Inf. 7th Bn. Co.G
Underwood, John MO 12th Cav. Co.A
Underwood, John NC 1st Inf. Co.D
Underwood, John NC 7th Inf. Co.C
Underwood, John TN 11th Cav. Co.D
Underwood, John TN 5th Inf. 2nd Co.F
Underwood, John TN 24th Inf. Co.A
Underwood, John TN 29th Inf. Co.K
Underwood, John VA Cav. Hounshell's Bn. Huffman's Co.
Underwood, John VA Cav. Thurmond's Co.
Underwood, John VA Lt.Arty. Hankins' Co. Sgt.
Underwood, John VA 3rd Inf. 1st Co.I
Underwood, John VA 54th Inf. Co.H
Underwood, John Gen. & Staff Chap.
Underwood, John A. NC 30th Inf. Co.H Cpl.
Underwood, John A.B. AL 11th Inf. Co.K
Underwood, John C. TN Cav. 9th Bn. (Gantt's) Co.F
Underwood, John C. Gen. & Staff, Eng. Rec. 1st Lt.
Underwood, John D. NC 16th Inf. Co.M
Underwood, John D. TX 15th Inf. Co.C
Underwood, John E. GA 2nd Inf. Co.E
Underwood, John F. AL Stewart's Detach. Loc.Def.
Underwood, John F. AR 17th (Lemoyne's) Inf. Co.F Sgt.
Underwood, John F. GA 20th Inf. Co.G Sgt.
Underwood, John F. VA 16th Inf. Co.A
Underwood, John G. TX 17th Cav. Co.I
Underwood, John G. TX 14th Inf. 1st Co.K
Underwood, John G. TX 18th Inf. Co.L
Underwood, John H. AL Cav. Holloway's Co. Cpl.
Underwood, John H. GA 4th Res. Co.H
Underwood, John H. GA 16th Inf. Co.I
Underwood, John H. NC 28th Inf. Co.D
Underwood, John J. AL 26th (O'Neal's) Inf. Co.H
Underwood, John L. AL 20th Inf. Co.I Sgt.Maj.
Underwood, John M. GA 23rd Inf. Co.H
Underwood, John N. MO 10th Cav. Co.G
Underwood, John P. GA 1st Cav. Co.H
Underwood, John R. VA 20th Cav. Co.H
Underwood, John T. GA 14th Inf. Co.F
Underwood, John T. VA 24th Inf. Co.A
Underwood, John W. AL Gid Nelson Lt.Arty.
Underwood, John W. GA 49th Inf. Co.A
Underwood, John W. MO Lt.Arty. 1st Btty.
Underwood, John W. Conf.Cav. Wood's Regt. 1st Co.A
Underwood, John W. Gillum's Regt. Whitaker's Co.
Underwood, John Z. LA 9th Inf. Co.G 2nd Lt.
Underwood, John Z. Conf.Cav. Powers' Regt. Co.I 1st Lt.
Underwood, Jonathan TN 33rd Inf. Co.C
Underwood, Jordan O. NC 1st Arty. (10th St.Troops) Co.C
Underwood, Joseph AL 7th Cav. Co.C,A
Underwood, Joseph AL 6th Inf.
Underwood, Joseph AL 50th Inf. Co.K
Underwood, Joseph TN 23rd Inf. 1st Co.F, Co.H
Underwood, Joseph TN 29th Inf. Co.E Sgt.
Underwood, Joseph TN 38th Inf. 1st Co.K
Underwood, Joseph TN 60th Mtd.Inf. Co.L
Underwood, Joseph TX 5th Cav. Co.B
Underwood, Joseph VA 24th Inf. Co.A
Underwood, Joseph B. NC 20th Inf. Faison's Co. Sgt.
Underwood, Joseph B. NC 51st Inf. Co.K Capt.
Underwood, Joseph B. NC 61st Inf. Co.A
Underwood, Joseph B. SC 1st Arty. Co.C
Underwood, Joseph C. MO 4th Cav. Co.F
Underwood, Joseph W. AL 17th Inf. Co.D
Underwood, Joseph W. LA 28th (Gray's) Inf. Co.E
Underwood, Joseph W. TX 17th Cav. Co.I
Underwood, Joseph W. TX 18th Inf. Co.L
Underwood, Joshua VA 24th Inf. Co.A
Underwood, Joshua VA 57th Inf. Co.C
Underwood, Joshua J. GA 57th Inf. Co.C Sgt.
Underwood, J.P. TN 3rd (Lillard's) Mtd.Inf. Co.G
Underwood, J.R. AL 28th Inf. Co.D

Underwood, J.R. GA 1st Cav. Co.G,I
Underwood, J.R. GA Arty. 11th Bn. (Sumter Arty.) Co.D,B
Underwood, J.R. TN 21st (Carter's) Cav. Co.A Sgt.
Underwood, J.R.G. GA Lt.Arty. 12th Bn. 3rd Co.B
Underwood, J.T. AL 5th Inf. Co.B
Underwood, J.T. GA Lt.Arty. 12th Bn. 3rd Co.B
Underwood, J.T. TN 33rd Inf. Co.C
Underwood, J.W. GA Phillips' Legion Co.C
Underwood, J.W. KY 12th Cav. Co.A,B
Underwood, J.W. LA 6th Cav. Co.C
Underwood, J.W. TN 21st & 22nd (Cons.) Cav. Co.K
Underwood, J.W. TN 22nd (Barteau's) Cav. Co.B
Underwood, J.W. TN 46th Inf. Co.C
Underwood, J.W. TX 14th Inf. 1st Co.K
Underwood, Killis AL 16th Inf. Co.E
Underwood, Kirby NC Inf. Thomas Legion Co.D
Underwood, Lawson GA Inf. Alexander's Co.
Underwood, L.B. TX 7th Cav. Co.D
Underwood, L.B. TX 17th Cons.Dismtd.Cav. Co.K
Underwood, L.B. TX 14th Inf. 1st Co.K
Underwood, L.C. MS 3rd Cav. 2nd Lt.
Underwood, Leonard AR 16th Inf. Co.B
Underwood, Leonard B. TX 18th Inf. Co.L
Underwood, Lewis MS 2nd Cav.Res. Co.A
Underwood, Lewis M. NC 6th Cav. (65th St.Troops) Co.B Cpl.
Underwood, Lewis M. NC Cav. 7th Bn. Co.B Cpl.
Underwood, L.H. MS Inf. 2nd St.Troops Co.K
Underwood, Lindsay J. VA Lt.Arty. French's Co.
Underwood, L.J. GA 20th Inf. Co.D
Underwood, L.J. KY 2nd (Woodward's) Cav. Co.C
Underwood, Luke T. VA 7th Bn.Res. Co.D
Underwood, M. AL 25th Inf. Co.K
Underwood, M. AR 21st Inf. Co.E
Underwood, M. LA Ogden's Cav. Co.K
Underwood, M. LA Mil. Moreau Guards
Underwood, M. TN 3rd (Clack's) Inf. Co.A
Underwood, M. VA 19th Cav. Co.I
Underwood, M. VA 21st Cav. Co.B
Underwood, M. 15th Conf.Cav. Co.C
Underwood, Marshall AL City Troop (Mobile) Arrington's Co.A
Underwood, Martin VA 57th Inf. Co.C
Underwood, Mathew AL 22nd Inf. Co.K
Underwood, Mathis GA 17t Inf. Co.C Cpl.
Underwood, M.B. GA 19th Inf. Co.G
Underwood, Minter AR 17th (Lemoyne's) Inf. Co.F
Underwood, M.J. TN 48th (Voorhies') Inf. Co.A
Underwood, M.V. TN 43rd Inf. Co.I Cpl.
Underwood, N. LA Mil. McPherson's Btty. (Orleans Howitzers)
Underwood, Nathan G. TX 18th Inf. Co.L
Underwood, Nelson KY 9th Mtd.Inf. Co.H
Underwood, Nelson MO 10th Cav. Co.G
Underwood, Nelson TN 1st (Carter's) Cav. Co.B,E
Underwood, N.G. TX 14th Inf. 1st Co.K
Underwood, Paul MS 2nd (Quinn's St.Troops) Inf. Co.D
Underwood, Peter VA 8th Cav. Co.H
Underwood, Peter VA 151st Mil. Co.D
Underwood, P.H. GA Inf. 25th Bn. (Prov.Guard) Co.E
Underwood, Phillip S. MO 1st N.E. Cav. Co.A
Underwood, Pleasant VA 57th Inf. Co.C
Underwood, P.M. FL 2nd Inf. Co.F
Underwood, Polk GA Inf. Alexander's Co.
Underwood, R. GA Lt.Arty. 12th Bn. 3rd Co.B
Underwood, R.C. MS 36th Inf. Co.D
Underwood, Reuben NC 1st Arty. (10th St.Troops) Co.C
Underwood, Reuben H. TX 13th Cav. Co.D
Underwood, Reuben S. AL 6th Inf. Co.G
Underwood, Richard NC 1st Arty. (10th St.Troops) Co.G
Underwood, Richard TN Lt.Arty. Morton's Co.
Underwood, Richard G. VA 54th Inf. Co.H
Underwood, Richard H. MS 20th Inf. Co.B
Underwood, Richard P. MS 3rd Inf. Co.C
Underwood, Richard R. NC 4th Inf. Co.D
Underwood, Richard T. MS 24th Inf. Co.D
Underwood, Richard W. VA 3rd Inf. Co.E
Underwood, R.J. VA 2nd Cav. Co.F
Underwood, R.K. MO Cav. Freeman's Regt. Co.B
Underwood, R.M. TN 1st (Carter's) Cav. Co.B
Underwood, R.M. 1st Conf.Cav. 2nd Co.K
Underwood, Robert MS Inf. 7th Bn. Co.G
Underwood, Robert D. LA 12th Inf. Co.C
Underwood, Robert D. MS 8th Inf. Co.G
Underwood, Robert F.T. MS 41st Inf. Co.G
Underwood, R.R. AL Cav. Barlow's Co.
Underwood, R.R. AL 6th Inf. Co.K
Underwood, R.R. AL 3rd Bn. Hilliard's Legion Vol. Co.D
Underwood, R.R. AL Conscr.
Underwood, R.R. 15th Conf.Cav. Co.C
Underwood, R.S. TX 13th Vol. 2nd Co.D
Underwood, R.S. TX 22nd Inf. Co.I Cpl.
Underwood, R.T. MO 6th Cav. Co.F
Underwood, Rufus J. AL 45th Inf. Co.I Sgt.
Underwood, R.W. GA 23rd Inf. Co.I
Underwood, R.W. GA 48th Inf. Co.A Cpl.
Underwood, R.W. VA 13th Cav. Co.E
Underwood, S. GA 3rd Res. Co.H 3rd Lt.
Underwood, S. NC 7th Sr.Res. Bradshaw's Co.A
Underwood, Samuel TN 39th Mtd.Inf. Co.B
Underwood, Samuel VA 8th Inf. Co.G
Underwood, Samuel VA 22nd Inf. Co.G
Underwood, Samuel VA 166th Mil. Taylor's Co.
Underwood, Samuel A. TX 2nd Cav. 1st Co.F
Underwood, Samuel A. TX Cav. Morgan's Regt. Co.I
Underwood, Samuel C. NC 20th Inf. Co.B
Underwood, Samuel L. VA Cav. Mosby's Regt. (Part.Rangers) Co.A
Underwood, Samuel S. VA Cav. 46th Bn. Co.A
Underwood, S.D. AR 2nd Inf. Co.F
Underwood, Seaborn B. GA 57th Inf. Co.I,K
Underwood, Seborn NC Walker's Bn. Thomas' Legion Co.A
Underwood, Seburn LA 5th Cav. Co.I
Underwood, Simpson VA Loc.Def. Dulany's Co.
Underwood, S.L. TN 43rd Inf. Co.H
Underwood, S.M. NC 1st Cav. (9th St.Troops) Co.C
Underwood, Stephen GA 18th Inf. Co.K
Underwood, Stephen LA 1st (Strawbridge's) Inf. Co.H
Underwood, Sylvanus G. AL Cav. Holloway's Co.
Underwood, Sylvanus G. AL 8th Inf. Co.D
Underwood, T. GA Inf. 1st Bn. (St.Guards) Co.E
Underwood, T.B. TN Cav. 1st Bn. (McNairy's) Co.C 2nd Lt.
Underwood, T.C. GA 18th Inf. Co.K 2nd Lt.
Underwood, T.G. GA Cherokee Legion (St.Guards) Co.C 1st Lt.
Underwood, Thomas AL 8th (Livingston's) Cav. Co.C
Underwood, Thomas AL 22nd Inf. Co.C
Underwood, Thomas AR 1st Mtd.Rifles Co.E
Underwood, Thomas FL 1st Cav. Co.C
Underwood, Thomas GA 42nd Inf. Co.I
Underwood, Thomas GA 64th Inf. Co.E 1st Sgt.
Underwood, Thomas MO 2nd Cav. Co.E
Underwood, Thomas MO Cav. 3rd Regt. St.Guard Co.C
Underwood, Thomas NC Walker's Bn. Thomas' Legion 2nd Co.D
Underwood, Thomas TN 8th (Smith's) Cav. Co.G
Underwood, Thomas TN 16th Inf. Co.I
Underwood, Thomas TN Inf. 22nd Bn. Co.E
Underwood, Thomas TN Conscr. (Cp. of Instr.)
Underwood, Thomas VA 15th Cav. Co.B
Underwood, Thomas VA 9th Inf. 2nd Co.A
Underwood, Thomas VA Conscr. Cp.Lee Co.A
Underwood, Thomas VA Conscr. Cp.Lee Co.B
Underwood, Thomas VA Mil. Washington Cty.
Underwood, Thomas B. GA 57th Inf. Co.K Sgt.
Underwood, Thomas B. TN 22nd (Barteau's) Cav. Co.B Capt.
Underwood, Thomas H. AL 19th Inf. Co.H
Underwood, Thomas J. GA Inf. 4th Bn. (St.Guards) Co.H
Underwood, Thomas J. GA 52nd Inf. Co.H
Underwood, Thomas J. NC 6th Cav. (65th St.Troops) Co.D,E
Underwood, Thomas J. NC Cav. 7th Bn. Co.D,E
Underwood, Thomas J. NC 47th Inf. Co.K
Underwood, Thomas S. LA 17th Inf. Co.K
Underwood, Thomas W. AL 43rd Inf. Co.C
Underwood, Thomas W. TN 50th Inf. Co.A
Underwood, Threewit 2nd Conf.Eng.Troops Co.G
Underwood, T.J. TN Cav. 1st Bn. (McNairy's) Co.D Cpl.
Underwood, Tom MO Inf. 5th Regt.St.Guard Co.D
Underwood, T.T. GA 19th Inf. Co.G
Underwood, U. VA Cav. Mosby's Regt. (Part.Rangers) Co.A
Underwood, Uriah NC 8th Sr.Res. Kelly's Co.
Underwood, W. AL 10th Inf. Co.K
Underwood, W. TX 7th Cav. Co.D
Underwood, W. TX 11th Cav. Co.F Capt.
Underwood, W.A. MS 36th Inf. Co.D
Underwood, W.A. TN 24th Inf. Co.A
Underwood, Washington Q. MS 19th Inf. Co.K

Underwood, Watt 1st Choctaw & Chickasaw Mtd.Rifles Co.A
Underwood, W.B. TN 50th Inf. Co.A
Underwood, W.C. MS 6th Inf. Co.E Cpl.
Underwood, W.C. MO 1st Brig.St.Guard
Underwood, W.C. TX 13rd Vol. 2nd Co.D
Underwood, W.E. TN 30th Inf. Co.K Cpl.
Underwood, W.G. AR 8th Inf. New Co.A
Underwood, W.H. FL Inf. 2nd Bn. Co.C Sgt.
Underwood, W.H. GA Arty. 11th Bn. (Sumter Arty.) Co.D,B
Underwood, W.H. NC 31st Inf. Co.H
Underwood, W.H. TX 17th Cons.Dismtd.Cav. Co.K
Underwood, W.H. TX 14th Inf. 1st Co.K
Underwood, Wiley L. GA 61st Inf. Co.D,K
Underwood, William AL 5th Cav. Co.B
Underwood, William AL 16th Inf. Co.I
Underwood, William AL 46th Inf.
Underwood, William AL 47th Inf. Co.E
Underwood, William AR 2nd Cav. Co.G
Underwood, William AR 21st Inf. Co.E Cpl.
Underwood, William GA 12th Cav. Co.E
Underwood, William GA 23rd Inf. Co.I
Underwood, William GA 46th Inf. Co.D
Underwood, William GA 65th Inf. Co.F
Underwood, William GA Cherokee Legion (St.Guards) Co.G
Underwood, William GA Phillips' Legion Co.C
Underwood, William KY Fields' Co. (Part. Rangers)
Underwood, William MO 15th Cav. Co.I 3rd Lt.
Underwood, William MO Inf. 8th Bn. Co.F Cpl.
Underwood, William NC 6th Sr.Res. Co.I
Underwood, William NC 16th Inf. Co.M
Underwood, William TN 39th Mtd.Inf. Co.F
Underwood, William TX 9th Cav. Co.B
Underwood, William VA 21st Cav. 2nd Co.G
Underwood, William A. MS 22nd Inf. Co.E Lt.
Underwood, William A. VA 24th Inf. Co.A
Underwood, William B. AR 2nd Inf. Co.F
Underwood, William B. AR 31st Inf. Co.K
Underwood, William B. GA Phillips' Legion Co.C
Underwood, William B. VA 28th Inf. Co.I
Underwood, William B. VA 57th Inf. Co.C
Underwood, William C. GA 34th Inf. Co.D
Underwood, William H. AR 17th (Lemoyne's) Inf. Co.F Cpl.
Underwood, William H. FL 10th Inf. Co.H 1st Sgt.
Underwood, William H. NC 1st Cav. (9th St.Troops) Co.B
Underwood, William H. TX 18th Inf. Co.L
Underwood, William H. VA 17th Inf. Co.E
Underwood, William J. AL 10th Cav. Co.A
Underwood, William J. GA 3rd Cav. Co.B Capt.
Underwood, William J. GA 1st Inf. (St.Guards) Co.H 1st Lt.
Underwood, William J. GA Inf. 2nd Bn. Co.A Cpl.
Underwood, William J. GA 4th Inf. Co.F 1st Sgt.
Underwood, William J. GA 18th Inf. Co.K
Underwood, William J. GA 57th Inf. Co.K
Underwood, William J. TX 29th Cav. Co.E Sgt.
Underwood, William J. VA 9th Inf. Co.F
Underwood, William K. MS 19th Inf. Co.K
Underwood, William L. MS 6th Cav. Morgan's Co. Cpl.
Underwood, William L. TN 2nd (Robison's) Inf. Co.D
Underwood, William L. VA 1st Inf. Co.G
Underwood, William L. VA 12th Inf. Co.K
Underwood, William L. VA 24th Inf. Co.A
Underwood, William M. NC Hvy.Arty. 10th Bn. Co.D,C Cpl.
Underwood, William M. NC 26th Inf. Co.B
Underwood, William N. GA 31st Inf. Co.D
Underwood, William P. 1st Choctaw & Chickasaw Mtd.Rifles 1st Co.I Cpl.
Underwood, William R. MO 4th Cav. Co.K Lt.
Underwood, William R. VA 50th Inf. Co.K
Underwood, William S. KY 5th Cav. Co.E,H
Underwood, William S. VA 5th Cav. (12 mo. '61-2) Co.F
Underwood, William S. VA 13th Cav. Co.G
Underwood, William T.E. LA 11th Inf. Co.G
Underwood, William W. GA 23rd Inf. Co.H Jr.2nd Lt.
Underwood, William W. NC 27th Inf. Co.B
Underwood, Willis NC 4th Sr.Res. Co.G,K
Underwood, Winfield W.L. GA 57th Inf. Co.C
Underwood, W.J. AL 6th Cav. Co.G
Underwood, W.J. GA 1st (Cons.) Inf. Co.H
Underwood, W.J. TN 16th Inf. Co.I
Underwood, W.J. TN 43rd Inf. Co.H
Underwood, W.J.E. LA 14th Inf. Co.G Sgt.
Underwood, W.K. MS 2nd (Davidson's) Inf. Co.A
Underwood, W.L. MS 12th Cav. Co.C Cpl.
Underwood, W.L. MS Inf. 3rd Bn. (St.Troops) Co.B
Underwood, W.M. GA 19th Inf. Co.G
Underwood, W.M. GA 23rd Inf. Co.I
Underwood, W.N. Horse Arty. White's Btty.
Underwood, Woodson J. TN Inf. 22nd Bn.
Underwood, W.P. AL 5th Cav. Co.K
Underwood, W.P. AL 10th Cav.
Underwood, W.P. AL 26th (O'Neal's) Inf. Co.H
Underwood, W.R. MS 5th Inf. (St.Troops) Co.A
Underwood, W.S. TN 61st Mtd.Inf. Co.G
Underwood, W.S. VA Lt.Arty. Hankins' Co.
Underwood, W.T. TN 15th Inf. Co.E
Undewood, R.H. NC 30th Inf. Co.E
Undirnee, Oscar VA 6th Cav. Co.K
Undra, Byron VA 6th Cav. Co.K
Undrimer, P. AL 48th Mil. Co.A
Unery, William F. LA 28th (Gray's) Inf. Co.C
Unfill, F.A. GA 7th Cav. Lt.Col.
Unfleet, Jonathan VA Inf. Mileham's Co.
Unfug, Casper SC Hvy.Arty. Gilchrist's Co. (Gist Guard)
Ungar, Lawrence NC 50th Inf. Co.G
Unger, David W. SC Arty. Bachman's Co. (German Lt.Arty.)
Unger, E.L. LA Mil. 3rd Regt. 3rd Brig. 1st Div. Co.B 1st Lt.
Unger, George LA Mil. Mooney's Co. (Saddlers Guards)
Unger, H. LA Mil. 1st Regt. 2nd Brig. 1st Div.
Unger, Henry TX 4th Cav. Co.C
Unger, Henry E. SC 5th Cav. Co.F
Unger, James D. MS 15th Inf. Co.C
Unger, John VA 89th Mil. Co.B
Unger, John J. SC 5th Cav. Co.F
Unger, John J. SC Cav. 14th Bn. Co.C
Unger, John W. VA 89th Mil. Co.C Capt.
Unger, Joshua NC 16th Inf. Co.E
Unger, Moses VA 89th Mil. Co.C
Unger, Nicholas, Jr. VA 89th Mil. Co.C
Unger, Patrick D. SC Cav. 14th Bn. Co.C Cpl.
Unger, Phillip MO Cav. Slayback's Regt. Co.G
Unger, Sol AL 15th Bn.Part.Rangers Co.B
Unger, Solomon AL Inf. 1st Regt. Co.D
Unger, Solomon AL 8th Inf. Co.E
Unger, Solomon MS 9th Inf. New Co.C
Unger, Washington, Jr. VA 89th Mil. Co.B
Unger, William VA 31st Mil. Co.H
Ungerer, J.I. MO 1st Inf. Chap.
Ungerer, J.J. KY 3rd Mtd.Inf. Chap.
Ungerer, J.J. Gen. & Staff Chap.
Unglebee, William VA 33rd Inf. Co.F
Unglesbee, William VA 18th Cav. Co.K
Unglesbee, William VA 114th Mil. Co.G
Unhill, W. NC Cav. 16th Bn. Co.I
Uniacke, James AL Cav. Murphy's Bn. Co.B
Uniacke, James AL Mil. 3rd Vol. Co.A
Union, John F. FL 3rd Inf. Co.K
Unis, Charles GA 1st (Olmstead's) Inf. Co.K
Unkel, W.F. MD Walters' Co. (Zarvona Zouaves) Cpl.
Unkles, William F. MD Inf. 2nd Bn. Co.E
Unland, William VA Inf. 4th Bn.Loc.Def. Co.C
Unley, Lewis TN 15th (Stewart's) Cav. Co.G
Unmack, Henry LA 7th Inf. Co.H
Unrah, Edward AL Lt.Arty. 2nd Bn. Co.E
Unroe, Adam VA 1st Cav. Co.C
Unroe, Adam VA 18th Cav. Co.H
Unrue, Henry VA 11th Inf. Co.K
Unruh, Charles N. VA 40th Inf. Co.K 1st Sgt.
Unrut, Ed AL 24th Inf. Co.A
Unseld, John G. VA 2nd Inf. Co.B
Unsell, Alfread LA Inf. 9th Bn. Co.A
Unsell, Alfred LA 5th Cav. Co.D
Unsom, T.A. MS 38th Cav. Co.B
Unsworth, J. Eng.,CSA
Untereiner, P. AL 1st Regt. Mobile Vol. Co.E
Unthank, Calvin KY 13th Cav. Co.H
Unthank, Calvin VA 25th Cav. Co.G
Unthank, Calvin VA 64th Mtd.Inf. Co.H
Unthank, Melton TN 2nd (Ashby's) Cav. Co.D
Un thar pee 1st Creek Mtd.Vol. Co.F
Unusey 1st Creek Mtd.Vol. 1st Co.C
Upatter 1st Creek Mtd.Vol. Co.K
Upchurch, A. AL 42nd Inf. Co.B Sgt.
Upchurch, A. TX Arty. 4th Bn. Co.A
Upchurch, A. TX 8th Inf. Co.A
Upchurch, A.B. NC 1st Inf. Co.G
Upchurch, A.H. NC 23rd Inf. Co.G
Upchurch, A.H. TN 17th Inf. Co.K
Upchurch, A.J. AL 20th Inf. Co.E
Upchurch, A.J. NC 1st Cav. (9th St.Troops) Co.E
Upchurch, A.J. NC 43rd Inf. Co.C
Upchurch, Albert E. NC 55th Inf. Co.A Capt.
Upchurch, Almarine G. Conf.Cav. Wood's Regt. 2nd Co.G
Upchurch, A.N. NC 39th Inf. Co.I
Upchurch, Ansel M. NC 58th Inf. Co.H

Upchurch, A.R. AL 1st Bn. Hilliard's Legion Vol. Co.C
Upchurch, Archibald M.D. NC 15th Inf. Co.E
Upchurch, A.V. GA 19th Inf. Co.G
Upchurch, B. MS 8th Inf. Co.D
Upchurch, B.A.A.B. NC Lt.Arty. 13th Bn. Co.B
Upchurch, Ben NC 6th Sr.Res. Co.I
Upchurch, Benjamin AR 31st Inf. Co.C
Upchurch, Benjamin MS 9th Inf. New Co.G
Upchurch, Benjamin NC 2nd Arty. (36th St.Troops) Co.C
Upchurch, Benjamin NC 66th Inf. Co.B
Upchurch, Benjamin N. MS 8th Inf. Co.D
Upchurch, Benjamin W. NC Inf. 13th Bn. Co.B
Upchurch, Bennett A.A.B. NC 2nd Arty. (36th St.Troops) Co.B
Upchurch, Berry AL 17th Inf. Co.E
Upchurch, B.H. TN 20th (Russell's) Cav. Co.F
Upchurch, B.J. NC 1st Inf. Co.G
Upchurch, B.N. MS Inf. 7th Bn. Co.E
Upchurch, Britton AR 1st (Crawford's) Cav. Co.A
Upchurch, Burkley NC 47th Inf. Co.B
Upchurch, Burt AL Inf. 2nd Regt. Co.B
Upchurch, Burt AL 37th Inf. Co.G Capt.
Upchurch, Burtin AL 42nd Inf. Co.B 2nd Lt.
Upchurch, C. AL 37th Inf. Co.G 1st Sgt.
Upchurch, C. AL 1st Bn. Hilliard's Legion Vol. Co.C
Upchurch, C. GA 3rd Res. Co.H Sgt.
Upchurch, C. GA 8th Inf. (St.Guards) Co.K Sgt.
Upchurch, C. MS Rogers' Co.
Upchurch, C. NC 1st Jr.Res. Co.H
Upchurch, Calvin AL Inf. 2nd Regt. Co.B
Upchurch, Calvin FL 8th Inf. Co.G
Upchurch, Calvin KY 5th Mtd.Inf. Co.G
Upchurch, Calvin W. NC 1st Inf. Co.I Cpl.
Upchurch, Carter TN 25th Inf. Co.G
Upchurch, C.B. AL 43rd Inf. Co.C
Upchurch, C.E. GA 53rd Inf. Co.F
Upchurch, C.H. AR 25th Inf. Co.G
Upchurch, C.H. TN 4th Cav. Co.K
Upchurch, C.H. TN 8th Cav. Co.G
Upchurch, Charles D. NC Snead's Co. (Loc.Def.)
Upchurch, Churchwill MS Inf. (Res.) Berry's Co.
Upchurch, Claiborn D. GA 66th Inf. Co.E
Upchurch, Corbin AL 42nd Inf. Co.B 1st Sgt.
Upchurch, Cyrus TX 21st Cav. Co.A
Upchurch, Dal. H. NC 31st Inf. Co.H Cpl.
Upchurch, Dallas H. NC 1st Inf. Co.I
Upchurch, Daniel NC 34th Inf. Co.I
Upchurch, David H. AR 36th Inf. Co.F
Upchurch, Davis H. AR 31st Inf. Co.C Sgt.
Upchurch, E.S. GA 13th Inf. Co.D
Upchurch, F.M. GA 53rd Inf. Co.F
Upchurch, Frank M. TN 5th Inf. 2nd Co.G
Upchurch, George W. TN 46th Inf. Co.A
Upchurch, G.H. AR 1st (Monroe's) Cav. Co.E
Upchurch, Green Berry NC 33rd Inf. Co.D
Upchurch, G.W. TN Inf. 3rd Cons.Regt. Co.D
Upchurch, G.W. TN 5th Inf. Co.A, 2nd Co.G
Upchurch, Hansel NC 8th Sr.Res. Daniel's Co. Sgt.
Upchurch, Harbord M. AL 17th Inf. Co.E
Upchurch, Henry GA 13th Inf. Co.D
Upchurch, Henry A. MO 8th Cav. Co.B,A
Upchurch, Henry R. TN 4th Cav. Co.I
Upchurch, H.K. KY 10th Cav. Co.I
Upchurch, H.R. TN Arty. Marshall's Co.
Upchurch, H.R. TN 16th Inf. Co.A
Upchurch, H.T. GA Inf. 25th Bn. (Prov.Guard) Co.D
Upchurch, I.S. NC 16th Inf. Co.G
Upchurch, J.A. TN 22nd Inf. Co.F 1st Sgt.
Upchurch, Jack MS 39th Inf. Co.I
Upchurch, James GA 3rd Inf. Co.G
Upchurch, James NC 35th Inf. Co.D
Upchurch, James TN Inf. 22nd Bn. Co.C
Upchurch, James A. TX 18th Cav. Co.C Black.
Upchurch, James A. TX 30th Cav. Co.I Black.
Upchurch, James B. TX 3rd Inf. Co.H
Upchurch, James C. TX 13th Vol. 3rd Co.I
Upchurch, James K. AL 1st Bn. Hilliard's Legion Vol. Co.C
Upchurch, James M. GA 44th Inf. Co.A
Upchurch, James M. TN 43rd Inf. Co.C
Upchurch, James M. TX 37th Cav. Co.F
Upchurch, James W. NC 1st Inf. Co.I Sgt.
Upchurch, Jasper GA 44th Inf. Co.A
Upchurch, J.C. TX 20th Inf. Co.G
Upchurch, J.F. NC 4th Bn.Jr.Res. Co.D
Upchurch, J.F. NC 8th Bn.Part.Rangers
Upchurch, J.F. TN 20th (Russell's) Cav. Co.F
Upchurch, J.F. TN 46th Inf. Co.B 2nd Lt.
Upchurch, J.H. NC 6th Inf. Co.I Sgt.
Upchurch, J.K. AL 60th Inf. Co.K Cpl.
Upchurch, J.K. SC 1st Arty. Co.K
Upchurch, J.K. TN 35th Inf. 2nd Co.A
Upchurch, J.M. GA 8th Inf. (St.Guards) Co.K 1st Sgt.
Upchurch, J.M. GA 53rd Inf. Co.B
Upchurch, J.M. NC 3rd Cav. (41st St.Troops) Co.I
Upchurch, J.M. TX Cav. (Loc.Def.) Durant's Co. Sgt.
Upchurch, J.M. TX Cav. Madison's Regt. Co.B Sgt.
Upchurch, J.M. TX Cav. Terry's Regt. Co.A
Upchurch, J.N. NC 1st Cav. (9th St.Troops) Co.E Cpl.
Upchurch, Job MO Inf. 4th Regt.St.Guard Co.C
Upchurch, John AL 42nd Inf. Co.B,D
Upchurch, John C. AL 20th Inf. Co.E,A Cpl.
Upchurch, John C. GA Cobb's Legion Co.B Cpl.
Upchurch, John T. TN 5th Inf. 2nd Co.G
Upchurch, John W. NC 47th Inf. Co.B
Upchurch, Joseph AR 19th (Dockery's) Inf. Co.C
Upchurch, Joseph NC 47th Inf. Co.H Cpl.
Upchurch, Joseph E. GA 56th Inf. Co.C Sgt.
Upchurch, Joshua TN 44th (Cons.) Inf. Co.C
Upchurch, Joshua S. TN 55th (McKoin's) Inf. Dillehay's Co.
Upchurch, J.R. VA 7th Inf. Co.F
Upchurch, Jubal NC 47th Inf. Co.E
Upchurch, J.W. AL 17th Inf. Co.E
Upchurch, J.W. GA 39th Inf. Co.C
Upchurch, J.W. GA 56th Inf. Co.C
Upchurch, J.W. LA 2nd Inf. Co.K
Upchurch, J.W. NC 32nd Inf. Co.D
Upchurch, J. William TN 35th Inf. 2nd Co.A
Upchurch, K.B. AL 5th Cav. Co.C
Upchurch, L. AL 17th Inf. Co.E
Upchurch, L.A. GA 44th Inf. Co.A
Upchurch, Lawrence MS 29th Inf. Co.H
Upchurch, L.H. GA 44th Inf. Co.B
Upchurch, Lindaman NC 1st Inf. Co.G
Upchurch, M. AL 46th Inf. Co.K,C
Upchurch, M. MS Inf. 3rd Bn. (St.Troops) Co.E
Upchurch, M. TX Cav. 3rd Bn.St.Troops Co.D 2nd Lt.
Upchurch, N.P. MS Inf. 7th Bn. Co.E
Upchurch, N.S. FL 2nd Cav. Co.K
Upchurch, O. TX Cav. Terry's Regt. Co.A
Upchurch, O.H. NC 1st Jr.Res. Co.G
Upchurch, Oliver H.P. TX 10th Inf. Co.A
Upchurch, Oliver P. NC 47th Inf. Co.A
Upchurch, Oliver P.H. TX 37th Cav. Co.F
Upchurch, Osburn AL 60th Inf. Co.K
Upchurch, Osburn AL 1st Bn. Hilliard's Legion Vol. Co.C
Upchurch, Parker NC 47th Inf. Co.H
Upchurch, P.B. NC 15th Inf. Co.D
Upchurch, Richard NC 26th Inf. Co.F
Upchurch, Richard NC 47th Inf. Co.B
Upchurch, R.L. TN 45th Inf. Co.C
Upchurch, Robert LA Res.Corps Kennedy's Co.
Upchurch, Robert J. AL 11th Inf. Co.C
Upchurch, Ross TN 4th (Murray's) Cav. Co.E
Upchurch, S. TX 7th Cav. Co.G
Upchurch, Sidney NC 3rd Bn.Sr.Res. Durham's Co.
Upchurch, Sion M. NC 55th Inf. Co.A Cpl.
Upchurch, S.W. AR Lt.Arty. Zimmerman's Btty. Sgt.
Upchurch, T.C. AR 24th Inf. Co.C
Upchurch, T.C. AR Inf. Hardy's Regt. Co.F Sgt.
Upchurch, T.H. AL 8th (Hatch's) Cav. Co.D
Upchurch, Thomas NC 7th Inf. Co.G
Upchurch, Thomas TN 4th Cav. Co.K
Upchurch, Thomas TN 4th (Murray's) Cav. Co.E
Upchurch, Thomas TN 8th Cav. Co.C
Upchurch, Thomas TN Inf. 22nd Bn. Co.C
Upchurch, Thomas TN Inf. 22nd Bn. Co.K
Upchurch, Thomas A. AR 36th Inf. Co.F
Upchurch, Thomas C. TN 35th Inf. 2nd Co.A
Upchurch, Thomas J. NC 47th Inf. Co.H
Upchurch, T. Ross TN Inf. 22nd Bn. Co.K
Upchurch, T.S. TN 17th Inf. Co.K
Upchurch, Vinson P. AL 17th Inf. Co.E
Upchurch, W. GA 4th Res. Co.F
Upchurch, W. TX Cav. 3rd Regt.St.Troops Townsend's Co.
Upchurch, W.A. KY 7th Mtd.Inf. Co.D
Upchurch, W.A. NC Mallett's Bn. (Cp.Guard) Co.E
Upchurch, W.B. GA 56th Inf. Co.C
Upchurch, Wesley NC 5th Sr.Res. Co.K
Upchurch, Wesley NC 7th Inf. Co.G
Upchurch, W.G. TN 7th (Duckworth's) Cav. Co.I
Upchurch, Will H. NC 26th Inf. Co.F
Upchurch, Wm. AL 5th Cav. Co.C
Upchurch, William GA Cav. 1st Bn.Res. Stark's Co.

Upchurch, William GA 10th Cav. (St.Guards) Co.B
Upchurch, William NC 35th Inf. Co.D
Upchurch, William NC 50th Inf. Co.I
Upchurch, William TN 10th Inf. Co.I
Upchurch, William TX Cav. Mann's Regt. Co.A
Upchurch, William TX Cav. Mann's Bn. Co.A
Upchurch, William A. AR 36th Inf. Co.F
Upchurch, William H. NC 15th Inf. Co.E
Upchurch, William R. NC 52nd Inf. Co.I Cpl.
Upchurch, William S. NC 58th Inf. Co.H
Upchurch, Williford NC 6th Inf. Co.I
Upchurch, Winship NC 6th Inf. Co.I
Upchurch, Winslow NC 6th Inf. Co.I
Upchurch, W.L. 7th Conf.Cav. Co.L
Upchurch, W.W. TN 45th Inf. Co.C
Upcraft, Charles GA Hvy.Arty. 22nd Bn. Co.E
Updegraff, David D. GA Inf. 2nd Bn. Co.A Cpl.
Updegrove, George AL 11th Inf. Co.K
Updike, --- VA 42nd Inf. Co.K
Updike, Abner VA 58th Inf. Co.D
Updike, Abraham VA 49th Inf. Co.D 2nd Lt.
Updike, Abraham VA 146th Mil. Co.K Capt.
Updike, Aman VA 146th Mil. Co.K
Updike, Amon VA 28th Inf. 2nd Co.C
Updike, Amon W. VA 53rd Inf. Co.I
Updike, Benjamin F. VA 6th Cav. Co.B,I
Updike, C.F.M. VA 8th Inf. Co.E
Updike, Christopher VA Hvy.Arty. 10th Bn. Co.B
Updike, Daniel VA 11th Inf. Co.B
Updike, D.J. VA 10th Cav. Co.E
Updike, Elija KY 7th Cav. Co.K
Updike, Elijah KY 3rd Cav. Co.C Teamster
Updike, Fielden W. VA 146th Mil. Co.K
Updike, Garnett VA 14th Inf. Co.B
Updike, George VA 146th Mil. Co.K
Updike, Isaac VA Lt.Arty. Pollock's Co.
Updike, James G. VA 4th Inf. Co.H Capt.
Updike, J.G. VA Rockbridge Cty.Res. Miller's Co. Capt.
Updike, John B. VA 49th Inf. Co.D Capt.
Updike, John T. VA 14th Inf. Co.B
Updike, Lafayette VA 146th Mil. Co.H 2nd Lt.
Updike, N.B. VA 1st Bn.Res. Co.I,E
Updike, Samuel VA 8th Bn.Res. Co.A
Updike, Samuel VA 58th Inf. Co.A
Updike, W.H. KY 7th Cav. Co.K
Updike, William VA Cav. 47th Bn. Co.C
Updike, William A. VA 14th Inf. Co.B
Updike, William D. VA 58th Inf. Co.A Cpl.
Updike, William H. KY 3rd Cav. Co.C
Updyke, William J. AL 3rd Res. Co.I
Upemhuck, M. AL 19th Inf. Co.A
Upgrapht, Charles GA 1st Reg. Co.I
Uphaw, J.H. MS 9th Inf. Co.K
Uphoff, Henry AR 35th Inf. Co.C
U pitch chee 1st Creek Mtd.Vol. Co.E
Upp, Samuel VA 3rd (Chrisman's) Bn.Res. Co.B
Upp, Samuel VA 9th Bn.Res. Co.C
Upperman, H. MS 2nd (Quinn's St.Troops) Inf. Co.C
Upperman, J.H. NC Inf. 13th Bn. Co.B
Upperman, John H. NC 66th Inf. Co.B QMSgt.
Upperman, William A. VA 16th Cav. Co.B
Uppes, George H. VA Lt.Arty. Garber's Co.
Uppletree, William VA 62nd Mtd.Inf. Co.G
Upright, Eli NC 6th Inf. Co.G
Upright, J.A. NC 17th Inf. (2nd Org.) Co.B
Upright, J.C. NC 2nd Jr.Res. Co.B
Upright, John NC 4th Sr.Res. Co.B
Upright, Samuel S. NC 4th Sr.Res. Co.B
Upright, William H. NC 42nd Inf. Co.G
Upshan, H. KY 7th Cav. Co.K
Upshaur, Leroy AL 60th Inf. Co.H
Upshaw, Adkin AL 4th (Russell's) Cav. Co.E
Upshaw, A.L. GA 1st Cav. Co.B
Upshaw, Drury MS 46th Inf. Co.A Cpl.
Upshaw, Edward W. MS 17th Inf. Maj.
Upshaw, E.W. Gen. & Staff Maj.
Upshaw, Forister GA 13th Inf. Co.B
Upshaw, Garland GA 13th Inf. Co.B
Upshaw, George A. TX 10th Inf. Co.K Sgt.
Upshaw, George H. AL 1st Bn. Hilliard's Legion Vol. Co.B
Upshaw, George M. GA 9th Inf. Co.C
Upshaw, George W. VA Mil. 6th Regt. Col.
Upshaw, G.M. GA Inf. 25th Bn. (Prov.Guard) Co.G
Upshaw, Henry H. TX 34th Cav. Co.A
Upshaw, H.S. KY 7th Mtd.Inf. Co.C
Upshaw, Isaac D. AL 47th Inf. Co.G Sgt.
Upshaw, J.A. GA 1st Cav. Co.B
Upshaw, James AR 34th Inf. Co.K
Upshaw, James GA Cobb's Legion Co.F
Upshaw, James MO 15th Cav. Co.G Cpl.
Upshaw, James M. VA Lt.Arty. Thornton's Co. Cpl.
Upshaw, James R. Price's Div. Maj.
Upshaw, J.B. AL 12th Inf. Co.F
Upshaw, J.C. GA 13th Inf. Co.B
Upshaw, J.D. AL Randolph Cty.Res. J. Hightower's Co.
Upshaw, J.J. GA Cav. 10th Bn. (St.Guards) Co.A
Upshaw, J.M. GA Brooks' Co. (Terrell Lt.Arty.) Sgt.
Upshaw, J.M. GA 3rd Bn.S.S. Co.A 1st Sgt.
Upshaw, J.M. GA 18th Inf. Co.H
Upshaw, John TN 15th (Stewart's) Cav. Co.B
Upshaw, John R. GA 1st Cav. Co.B
Upshaw, John R. GA 7th Inf. Co.F
Upshaw, John U. GA Siege Arty. 28th Bn. Co.G
Upshaw, Joseph H. AL Cav. Moses' Squad. Co.B
Upshaw, Joseph T. GA 30th Inf. Co.K
Upshaw, J.S. GA Cav. 10th Bn. (St.Guards) Co.D
Upshaw, J.S. GA 12th Cav. Co.L
Upshaw, J.W. LA Inf. 4th Bn. Co.D
Upshaw, Lee AL 1st Bn. Hilliard's Legion Vol. Co.B
Upshaw, Lee AR 34th Inf. Co.K
Upshaw, Marshall E. GA 55th Inf. Co.K
Upshaw, M.E. GA 13th Inf. Co.B Sgt.
Upshaw, M.E. MS Adams' Co. (Holmes Cty.Ind.)
Upshaw, R. GA 14th Inf. Co.B
Upshaw, R.L. TX 16th Inf. Adj.
Upshaw, Roberson GA 1st Cav. Co.B
Upshaw, Robert A. GA 9th Inf. Co.C
Upshaw, Robert H. VA 9th Cav. Co.B
Upshaw, Samuel C. MS 17th Inf. Co.B 2nd Lt.
Upshaw, Samuel C. TX Waul's Legion Co.E 1st Lt.
Upshaw, S.W. MS Adams' Co. (Holmes Cty.Ind.)
Upshaw, T.A. MS Inf. 7th Bn. Co.A
Upshaw, Thomas A. LA 9th Inf. Co.H 1st Lt.
Upshaw, Thomas E. VA 13th Cav. Co.C Lt.Col.
Upshaw, Thomas L. TN Inf. 3rd Bn. Co.B
Upshaw, T.L. GA 1st Cav. Co.K,B
Upshaw, T.L. MS 2nd Part.Rangers Co.L
Upshaw, T.L. TN 7th (Duckworth's) Cav. Co.A
Upshaw, Turner L. GA 7th Inf. Co.A
Upshaw, W. GA 5th Res. Co.E
Upshaw, W.E. LA Inf. 4th Bn. Co.D
Upshaw, William AL 5th Inf. Co.K
Upshaw, William MS 12th Cav. Co.E
Upshaw, William MS 1st (Percy's) Inf. Co.B
Upshaw, William E. Blake's Scouts,CSA
Upshaw, William J. VA 3rd Cav. Co.D
Upshaw, William L. GA 40th Inf. Co.I
Upshaw, William M. GA 7th Inf. Co.A
Upshaw, Wm. T. GA 9th Inf. Co.C
Upshaw, William W. LA 9th Inf. Co.H Cpl.
Upshaw, Wilson GA Cav. 7th Bn. (St.Guards) Co.C
Upshaw, W.J. Gen. & Staff,PACS Asst.Surg.
Upshaw, W.T. Gen. & Staff Surg.
Upsher, J.N. VA VMI Co.G Cadet
Upsher, John B. NC 1st Detailed Men Co.H Jr.2nd Lt.
Upsher, Thomas H. Gen. & Staff,PACS Asst.Surg.
Upsher, T.W. NC 2nd Cav. (19th St.Troops) Asst.Surg.
Upshire, Avin MD Cav. 2nd Bn. Co.B Sgt.
Upshire, Thomas TN Inf. 23rd Bn. Co.D
Upshow, Alex. W. LA 31st Inf. Co.I
Upshur, Abel P. VA 1st Arty. Co.B Cpl.
Upshur, A.P. VA Lt.Arty. 1st Bn. Co.B Cpl.
Upshur, A.P. VA Arty. Richardson's Co. Cpl.
Upshur, Caleb L. VA 9th Inf. Co.F 1st Lt.
Upshur, J.N. VA VMI Co.C
Upshur, John B. VA Lt.Arty. Moore's Co.
Upshur, John B. Conf.Lt.Arty. Richardson's Bn. Co.D
Upshur, J.W. VA 3rd Inf.Loc.Def. Co.C
Upshur, L. MS Conscr.
Upshur, R.S. LA Mil. Lewis Guards
Upshur, Thos. Harold W. Gen. & Staff Asst.Surg.
Upshur, Thomas H.W. VA 3rd Inf. Asst.Surg.
Upshur, Thomas T. VA Cav. 39th Bn. Co.B
Upshur, Thomas T. VA 39th Inf. Co.A
Upshur, Thomas W. VA Lt.Arty. Moore's Co.
Upshur, Thomas W. Conf.Lt.Arty. Richardson's Bn. Co.D
Upshur, T.W. VA 54th Mil. Co.G
Upshur, Wm. G. Gen. & Staff Asst.Surg.
Upson, H.M. SC 6th Inf. 2nd Co.I
Upson, John D. FL 2nd Cav. Co.C
Upstett, F. TX 6th Inf. Co.B
Upstine, H. TX 5th Cav. Co.F
Uptegrove, J.E. SC Cav. 12th Bn. Co.C
Uptegrove, William VA 77th Mil. Co.C
Uptergrove, E.F. AR 8th Inf. New Co.D
Uptgrove, Elisha TN 27th Inf. Co.A

Upthegrove, Daniel TX 9th (Young's) Inf. Co.A
Uptin, Francis M. TN 25th Inf. Co.B Cpl.
Upton, A. VA 5th Inf. Co.H
Upton, A.J. TN 22nd (Barteau's) Cav. Co.K
Upton, Alvis NC Inf. 2nd Bn. Co.F
Upton, A.W. TN 13th (Gore's) Cav. Co.A
Upton, Benjamin GA Inf. 14th Bn. (St.Guards) Co.H Sgt.
Upton, Benjamin B. NC 50th Inf. Co.G
Upton, Benjamin F. MO Cav. Wood's Regt. Co.D
Upton, Benjamin H. GA 3rd Inf. Co.E
Upton, Boyd F. NC 18th Inf. Co.F
Upton, Braxton MO 1st N.E. Cav. Co.D
Upton, Daniel MO 3rd Cav. Co.K
Upton, Daniel M. TN 1st Hvy.Arty. 2nd Co.B, 3rd Co.A, Co.L 1st Lt.
Upton, D.H. NC 11th (Bethel Regt.) Inf. Co.D
Upton, D.M. MO 15th Cav. Co.H
Upton, D.M. TN 15th Inf. Co.E
Upton, E. MO 4th Inf. Co.K
Upton, E. TX 2nd Inf. Co.I
Upton, Edward NC 50th Inf. Co.G
Upton, Eli GA 19th Inf. Co.E
Upton, Elisha MO 1st & 4th Cons.Inf. Co.H,K
Upton, E.P. TX Cav. (Loc.Def.) Upton's Co. Capt.
Upton, F.M. MS 1st Cav. Co.F
Upton, F.M. MS 41st Inf. Co.D
Upton, F.M. TN Arty. Marshall's Co.
Upton, F.M. TN Lt.Arty. Polk's Btty.
Upton, Franklin GA 11th Inf. Co.I
Upton, Frank P. LA 18th Inf. Co.I
Upton, G. GA 55th Inf.
Upton, George MO Inf. 8th Bn. Co.C
Upton, George MO 9th Inf. Co.G
Upton, George VA 60th Inf. Co.I
Upton, George 3rd Conf.Cav. Co.B Cpl.
Upton, George G. VA 30th Bn.S.S. Co.C,D Cpl.
Upton, George G. VA 166th Mil. B.G. Lively's Co.D
Upton, George W. MO 7th Div.St.Guards
Upton, Giles TX 1st (McCulloch's) Cav. Co.C
Upton, G.S. GA 2nd Inf. Co.I
Upton, G.W. GA Inf. 14th Bn. (St.Guards) Co.H
Upton, G.W. MS 8th Inf. Co.C
Upton, G.W. TN 48th (Voorhies') Inf. Co.H
Upton, Harvey J. VA Lt.Arty. G.B. Chapman's Co.
Upton, Hiram N. MO 1st Cav. Co.C Capt.
Upton, H.K. MO 1st & 4th Cons.Inf. Co.C
Upton, H.K. MO 4th Inf. Co.C
Upton, Isom NC 13th Inf. Co.K
Upton, James AL 8th Cav. Co.F
Upton, James AL 9th (Malone's) Cav. Co.B
Upton, James AL Lt.Arty. Hurt's Btty.
Upton, James AR 2nd Inf. Co.D
Upton, James MO 1st N.E. Cav. Price's Co.M
Upton, James NC 6th Sr.Res. Co.D
Upton, James B. MS 11th (Perrin's) Cav. Co.K
Upton, James B. NC 12th Inf. Co.I
Upton, James J. AL Lt.Arty. Phelan's Co.
Upton, James H. VA 166th Mil. Co.A,B 1st Sgt.
Upton, James K.P. MO 5th Inf. Co.A
Upton, James M. AR 27th Inf. Old Co.C, Co.D
Upton, James P. GA 54th Inf. Co.H
Upton, J.B. MS 1st Cav.Res. Co.D
Upton, J.D. TN 1st Hvy.Arty. 2nd Co.B Maj.
Upton, Jerry AR 1st (Dobbin's) Cav. Co.B
Upton, J.M. MO 5th Inf. Co.G
Upton, Job MO 3rd Cav. Co.K
Upton, Job MO 4th Inf. Co.C
Upton, John AL 8th (Livingston's) Cav. Co.F
Upton, John MO Cav. Fristoe's Regt. Co.A
Upton, Jno. MO St.Guard
Upton, John NC 32nd Inf. Co.I
Upton, John TN 51st (Cons.) Inf. Co.F
Upton, John 3rd Conf.Cav. Co.B
Upton, John A. AL Lt.Arty. Phelan's Co.
Upton, John C. TX 5th Inf. Co.B Lt.Col.
Upton, John G. MO 5th Inf. Co.A Cpl.
Upton, John M. MO 3rd Cav. Co.F
Upton, John M. MO 10th Inf. Co.D
Upton, John W. TX 12th Cav. Co.C
Upton, Jordan GA 11th Inf. Co.I
Upton, Joseah E. NC Currituck Guard J.W.F. Bank's Co.
Upton, Joseph NC 39th Inf. Co.K
Upton, Joseph NC 54th Inf. Co.D
Upton, Joseph C. VA 53rd Inf. Co.A
Upton, Joseph C. VA Inf. Montague's Bn. Co.A
Upton, Joseph E. NC 4th Cav. (59th St.Troops) Co.G
Upton, Joseph J. NC 17th Inf. (2nd Org.) Co.E
Upton, J.S.B. TN 2nd (Ashby's) Cav. Co.A
Upton, J.S.B. TN Cav. 5th Bn. (McClellan's) Co.A
Upton, L.A. VA Lt.Arty. Fry's Co.
Upton, L.A. VA Arty. Wise Legion
Upton, L.B. TN 2nd (Ashby's) Cav. Co.A Sgt.
Upton, L.B. TN Cav. 5th Bn. (McClellan's) Co.A Cpl.
Upton, Lewis VA Horse Arty. Jackson's Co.
Upton, Lewis VA 151st Mil. 1st Co.E 1st Sgt.
Upton, Lewis E. MO Cav. Wood's Regt. Co.D
Upton, Lewis E. MO 8th Inf. Co.C
Upton, Lorenzo D. MO 10th Cav. Co.I
Upton, Lorenzo D. MO 5th Inf. Co.A
Upton, Loyd A. VA Lt.Arty. Turner's Co.
Upton, Nelson TN 12th Inf. Co.F
Upton, Peter AR 1st Cav. Co.D
Upton, R. Exch.Bn. Co.D,CSA Sgt.
Upton, R.A. TX Cav. Waller's Regt. Co.E
Upton, R.B. VA 2nd St.Res. Co.C
Upton, R.M. GA 2nd Inf. Co.I
Upton, Robert AL 49th Inf. Co.G Sgt.
Upton, Robert NC 18th Inf. Co.F
Upton, Robert NC 46th Inf. Co.B
Upton, Robert R. VA Lt.Arty. Montgomery's Co.
Upton, Samuel E. TX Cav. Waller's Regt. Co.E
Upton, S.J. GA Inf. 1st Bn. (St.Guards) Co.D
Upton, T.E. MO Cav. Coleman's Regt. Co.D
Upton, Thomas NC 13th Inf. Co.K
Upton, Thomas TN 2nd (Ashby's) Cav. Co.G
Upton, Thomas TN Cav. 4th Bn. (Branner's) Co.B
Upton, Thomas TN 7th (Duckworth's) Cav. Co.E
Upton, Thomas TN 62nd Mtd.Inf. Co.C
Upton, Thomas VA Cav. 34th Bn. Co.K
Upton, Thomas H. MO 5th Inf. Co.A
Upton, Thomas W. VA 38th Inf. Co.F
Upton, Tobias SC 1st Arty. Co.F
Upton, W. TX 5th Cav. Co.K
Upton, W.B. AL 48th Inf. Co.A
Upton, W.F. TX 9th (Nichols') Inf. Co.F 2nd Lt.
Upton, William AR 38th Inf. Co.H
Upton, William MS 6th Cav. Co.E
Upton, William A. TN 2nd (Ashby's) Cav. Co.G Bvt.2nd Lt.
Upton, William A. TN Cav. 4th Bn. (Branner's) Co.B 2nd Lt.
Upton, William A. Vaughn's Staff Vol.ADC
Upton, William E. TN 25th Inf. Co.D
Upton, William F. TX Cav. Mann's Regt. Co.H Lt.Col.
Upton, William H. AL 49th Inf. Co.G
Upton, William L. MO 5th Cav. Co.E
Upton, William R. GA 2nd Cav. Co.G
Upton, William R. TX 9t (Nichols') Inf. Co.G 1st Sgt.
Upton, Willis VA 61st Inf. Co.C
Upton, W.M. GA Inf. 1st City Bn. (Columbus) Co.D
Upton, W.R. TX Waul's Legion Co.A 2nd Lt.
Upton, W.T. LA 27th Inf. Co.H
Urback, Charles LA Inf.Crescent Regt. Co.D
Urback, Charles LA Inf.Cons.Crescent Regt. Co.G
Urbaine, Charles LA 22nd Inf. Wash. Marks' Co.
Urban, C.F. LA 12th Inf. Co.A
Urban, Charles T. LA Arty. Kean's Btty. (Orleans Ind.Arty.)
Urban, Joe TX 13th Vol. 3rd Co.A
Urban, John TX 21st Cav. Co.I Black.
Urban, Joseph TX Arty. 4th Bn. Co.A
Urban, Joseph TX Inf. Griffin's Bn. Co.D
Urban, Michael LA 14th Inf. Co.K Sgt.
Urban, Michael TX 3rd Inf. Co.K
Urbancyzk, John TX 8th Field Btty.
Urbanks, Benjamin NC 67th Inf. Co.E
Urbanskey, John TX Lt.Arty. Dege's Bn.
Urbantke, Gustav TX Waul's Legion Co.C
Urbauczh, M. TX Cav. Baird's Regt. Co.C
Urbesa, Jose R. LA Mil. 5th Regt.Eur.Brig. (Spanish Regt.) Co.4
Urbezo, C. LA Mil. 1st Chasseurs a pied Co.8
Urbezo, P. LA Mil. 1st Chasseurs a pied Co.8
Urby, S.C. AR 2nd Vol. Co.C
Urcery, W.H. TN 10th (DeMoss') Cav. Co.I
Uren, Joseph VA Lt.Arty. Cayce's Co.
Urey, Levi NC 4th Sr.Res. Co.F
Urey, Thomas T. MS 27th Inf. Co.E
Urey, W.G. AR 15th (Johnson's) Inf. Co.K
Urguahart, John AL 36th Inf. Co.E
Urguhart, John AL 34th Inf. Co.H
Urguhart, Norman B. FL 2nd Cav. Co.A
Urgwhart, Robert T. GA Inf. 1st Loc.Troops (Augusta) Co.B Sgt.
Urigh, Philip KY 9th Mtd.Inf. Co.H
Urista, Julian TX 8th Inf. Co.E
Urles, I.R. AL 28th Inf. Co.G
Urley, John GA 12th Cav. Co.C Sgt.
Urls, William VA 25th Cav. Co.G
Urlson, J.H. MD 1st Cav. Lt.
Urmston, W.D. MO St.Guard QM

Urner, Lewis H. VA Lt.Arty. B.Z. Price's Co. Sgt.
Urner, Lewis H. VA Lt.Arty. W.H. Rice's Co. Sgt.
Urner, William P. MS Cav. Jeff Davis Legion Co.B
Uroile, T. LA 2nd Res.Corps Co.A
Uron, G.P. NC 1st Jr.Res. Co.A Cpl.
Urp, Peleg VA Inf. 23rd Bn. Co.A
Urp, Philip VA Inf. 23rd Bn. Co.A
Urp, William G. VA Inf. 23rd Bn. Co.A Cpl.
Urquahart, A. AL 1st Cav. 2nd Co.E
Urquhart, Aaron AL St.Res.
Urquehart, D.W. TX 11th Inf. Co.E
Urqueheart, H.A. GA 2nd Cav. (St.Guards) Co.F
Urquhart, Aaron AL 22nd Inf. Co.A
Urquhart, A.B. VA 13th Cav. Co.A
Urquhart, Ansalem B. VA 5th Cav. (12 mo. '61-2) Co.H
Urquhart, Anselm B. VA 6th Inf. Co.G
Urquhart, Benjamin F. AL 6th Inf. Co.B
Urquhart, Benjamin F. AL 39th Inf. Co.G
Urquhart, Burgess VA Lt.Arty. 12th Bn. 2nd Co.A
Urquhart, Burgess VA Lt.Arty. Sturdivant's Co.
Urquhart, Charles F., Jr. VA 3rd Inf. Co.D Capt.
Urquhart, C.V. LA Mil. 1st Native Guards
Urquhart, David Gen. & Staff, Adj.Gen.Dept. Lt.Col.
Urquhart, D.M. AL 4th Res. Co.F
Urquhart, George AL Inf. 1st Regt. Co.G
Urquhart, George LA 30th Inf. Co.F
Urquhart, G.S. VA Conscr. Cp.Lee Co.A
Urquhart, G.S. Gen. & Staff 2nd Lt.,Dr.M.
Urquhart, G.W. FL Conscr.
Urquhart, H.B. VA 6th Inf. Co.G
Urquhart, Henry A. GA 41st Inf. Co.D
Urquhart, Henry B. VA 5th Cav. (12 mo. '61-2) Co.H
Urquhart, J.A. McHenry AR 2nd Mtd.Rifles Hawkins' Co.
Urquhart, James LA Mil. Orleans Guards Regt. Co.F
Urquhart, James B. VA 5th Cav. (12 mo. '61-2) Co.H
Urquhart, James B. VA 6th Inf. Co.G
Urquhart, J. Capers FL 8th Inf. Co.C
Urquhart, J.N. AL 32nd Inf. Co.E
Urquhart, John J. VA 42nd Inf. Co.D
Urquhart, Joseph W. VA 5th Cav. (12 mo. '61-2) Co.H
Urquhart, Joseph W. VA 13th Cav. Co.A,H
Urquhart, Joseph W. VA 6th Inf. Co.G Cpl.
Urquhart, Jos. W. Gen. & Staff Maj.,Comsy.
Urquhart, K.D. VA 2nd Cav. Co.G
Urquhart, Kenneth M. VA 9th Inf. Co.E
Urquhart, Mathew A. GA 12th Cav. Co.H
Urquhart, Murdock M. VA Lt.Arty. 12th Bn. 2nd Co.A
Urquhart, Murdock M. VA Lt.Arty. Sturdivant's Co.
Urquhart, R.D. LA Mil. Orleans Guards Regt. Co.F
Urquhart, Robert AL 22nd Inf. Co.A
Urquhart, Robert, Jr. LA Cav. Greenleaf's Co. (Orleans Lt.Horse)
Urquhart, Robert, Jr. LA Washington Arty.Bn. Co.2
Urquhart, Robert F. GA 25th Inf. Co.H
Urquhart, S.J. GA Cav. 29th Bn. Co.H
Urquhart, Thomas H. VA 6th Inf. Surg.
Urquhart, Thos. H. Gen. & Staff Surg.
Urquhart, Thomas N. VA 13th Cav. Co.A
Urquhart, T.N. AL 12th Inf. Co.D Music.
Urquhart, W. LA Mil. Orleans Guards Regt. Co.F
Urquhart, W.H. AL 22nd Inf. Co.K
Urquhart, W.H. GA 59th Inf. Co.G
Urquhart, William AL Lt.Arty. Kolb's Btty.
Urquhart, William VA 5th Cav. (12 mo. '61-2) Co.H
Urquhart, William C. VA 13th Cav. Co.A
Urquhart, William J. VA 9th Inf. Co.D
Urquhart, W.N. GA 53rd Inf. Co.D
Urquhart, Yolvington T. GA 51st Inf. Co.A
Urquheart, J.A. McHenry TX 27th Cav. Co.A 2nd Lt.
Urrey, Washington AR 33rd Inf. Co.F
Urrey, W.G. AR 11th & 17th (Cons.) Inf. Co.C
Urril, --- AL 6th Inf. Co.B
Urry, A.J. AR 26th Inf. Co.G Sgt.
Urry, F.M. AR 26th Inf. Co.G
Urry, William 3rd Conf.Eng.Troops Co.H
Ursary, J.B. MS 3rd (St.Troops) Cav. Co.D
Urseau, A. LA Mil. 2nd Regt. French Brig. Co.4
Urser, Calvin LA 25th Inf. Co.C
Ursery, Alexander A. AL 3rd Res. Co.E
Ursery, Andrew J. AR 1st (Crawford's) Cav. Co.D
Ursery, Andrew J. AR 33rd Inf. Co.D
Ursery, A.T. AR 15th (Johnson's) Inf. Co.B
Ursery, Calvin J. AL 3rd Res. Co.F
Ursery, E.M. TX 18th Inf. Co.D
Ursery, George NC 2nd Arty. (36th St.Troops) Co.B
Ursery, Isaah AR 33rd Inf. Co.D Cpl.
Ursery, James R. MS 2nd Inf. (A. of 10,000) Co.H
Ursery, Jeff MS Lt.Arty. 14th Bn. Co.B
Ursery, John AR 23rd Inf. Co.C
Ursery, John SC 20th Inf. Co.A
Ursery, John C. SC Inf. Hampton Legion Co.G
Ursery, John T. VA 55th Inf. Co.D
Ursery, Jonathan D. MS 19th Inf. Co.G
Ursery, J.R. MS 28th Cav. Co.H
Ursery, Milton J. AL 3rd Res. Co.E
Ursery, M.S. TX 12th Cav. Co.G Cpl.
Ursery, O'Bannon SC 2nd St.Troops Co.K
Ursery, P. GA 1st (Symons') Res. Co.F
Ursery, Phillip LA 6th Inf. Co.A
Ursery, Ransom G. AL 43rd Inf. Co.I
Ursery, Richard LA 6th Inf. Co.A
Ursery, Robert F. AR 1st (Crawford's) Cav. Co.D
Ursery, Samuel M. AL 5th Inf. Co.E
Ursery, T.B. AR Inf. Cocke's Regt. Co.C
Ursery, William A. AR Lt.Arty. Rivers' Btty.
Ursery, William R. MO 1st Cav. Co.E
Ursey, Wm. AL Cp. of Instr. Talladega
Ursive, David GA 28th Inf. Co.A
Ursory, Edward G. AL 4th Inf. Co.C
Ursry, John TN 6th Inf. Co.B
Ursry, L.F. TX 24th Cav. Co.I
Urssey, J. TN 19th (Biffle's) Cav. Co.I
Ursuelos, Sosteno Conf.Lt.Arty. Davis' Co.
Ursurey, W.G. AR 15th Inf. Co.F Cpl.
Ursy, Jess MS Lt.Arty. Yates' Btty.
Ur tah ol tah 1st Cherokee Mtd.Rifles McDaniel's Co.
Urton, John VA 11th Cav. Co.A
Urton, John W. VA 11th Cav. Co.D
Ururiy, A.M. AR 23rd Inf. Co.F
Urvin, Rigdon P. TX 22nd Cav. Co.I
Urwich, Barnett FL 2nd Inf. Co.G
Urwin, James M. NC 8th Inf. Co.K
Ury, Andrew J. NC 52nd Inf. Co.A
Ury, Daniel J. NC 57th Inf. Co.H
Ury, Green George NC 20th Inf. Co.B
Ury, Jacob NC 42nd Inf. Co.H
Ury, Jacob NC 57th Inf. Co.H
Ury, J.G. NC 2nd Jr.Res. Co.E
Ury, M.G. AR 11th Inf. Co.H
Ury, Stephen S. TX Cav. 2nd Regt.St.Troops Co.I 3rd Lt.
Usary, J.W. SC 3rd Res. Co.K
Usary, William H. TN 13th Inf. Co.L
Usaw, John TN 29th Inf. Co.A
Uscery, Dempse TN 31st Inf. Co.B
Uscery, J.M. TN 31st Inf. Co.B
Uscery, Warren C. TN 31st Inf. Co.B
Uscery, William C. TN 31st Inf. Co.B
Uscey, Joseph MS 42nd Inf. Co.F
Use, Alfred LA Mil. LaFourche Regt.
Use, J.B. LA 26th Inf. Co.F
Usedom, Theodore VA Lt.Arty. Sturdivant's Co.
Usedom, Theodore W. VA Lt.Arty. 12th Bn. 2nd Co.A N.C.S. Sgt.Maj.
Uselton, B.D. TN 18th Inf. Co.F Cpl.
Uselton, J.B. TN Inf. 4th Cons.Regt. Co.F
Uselton, J.B. TN 18th Inf. Co.F
Uselton, John W. AL 50th Inf. Co.I
Uselton, John W. TN 38th Inf. 1st Co.H
Uselton, John W. TN 44th (Cons.) Inf. Co.A
Uselton, P.G. TN 44th (Cons.) Inf. Co.D
Uselton, W.S. AR Cav. Gordon's Regt. Co.K
Usener, John D. TX 2nd Cav. Co.E
Useri, C.J. LA 11th Inf. Co.G
Usery, A. AL 63rd Inf. Co.I
Usery, Albert NC 43rd Inf. Co.K
Usery, Benjamin LA 27th Inf. Co.F
Usery, Butler MS 12th Cav. Co.F
Usery, D.C. 1st Cherokee Mtd.Vol. 2nd Co.I
Usery, Dempsey TN 18th (Newsom's) Cav. Co.D,B
Usery, Dempsey TN Cav. Newsom's Regt. Co.E
Usery, George NC Lt.Arty. 13th Bn. Co.B
Usery, G.H. MS 34th Inf. Co.C
Usery, Green B. GA 59th Inf. Co.F
Usery, Hampton NC Hvy.Arty. 10th Bn. Co.C
Usery, Hampton NC 49th Inf. Co.K
Usery, Hiram NC Hvy.Arty. 10th Bn. Co.D
Usery, Isaac 1st Cherokee Mtd.Vol. 2nd Co.I
Usery, J. AR 1st (Dobbin's) Cav. Co.C
Usery, James GA 59th Inf. Co.F
Usery, James NC 28th Inf. Co.E
Usery, James 1st Cherokee Mtd.Vol. 2nd Co.I
Usery, J.C. AL 45th Inf. Co.E
Usery, J.M. MS Inf. 3rd Bn. (St.Troops) Co.D Cpl.
Usery, John TN Cav. Newsom's Regt. Co.E

Usery, John 1st Cherokee Mtd.Vol. 2nd Co.I
Usery, John Calvin MS 34th Inf. Co.C
Usery, Philip 1st Cherokee Mtd.Vol. 2nd Co.I
Usery, Warren C. TN Cav. Newsom's Regt. Co.E
Usery, W.D. SC 2nd Inf. Co.H
Usery, William AR 30th Inf. Co.G
Usery, William 1st Cherokee Mtd.Vol. 1st Co.I, 2nd Co.I 1st Sgt.
Usery, William, Jr. 1st Cherokee Mtd.Vol. 2nd Co.I
Usery, William C. TN Cav. Newsom's Regt. Co.E
Usher, C.C. NC 3rd Cav. (41st St.Troops) Co.A
Usher, Charles SC 24th Inf. Co.B
Usher, David C. TX 9th Cav. Co.I Sgt.
Usher, E.C. GA Cav. Allen's Co.
Usher, Edwin T. NC 2nd Bn.Loc.Def.Troops Co.B,F Cpl.
Usher, Edwin T. NC 61st Inf. Co.A
Usher, F.C. TN Inf. 1st Cons.Regt. Co.H
Usher, Frank C. TN 1st (Feild's) Inf. Co.B Cpl.
Usher, Frederick GA 3rd Cav. Co.E
Usher, George D. GA 3rd Cav. Co.E
Usher, G.W. SC 22nd Inf. Co.E
Usher, Henry GA Cav. Allen's Co.
Usher, Henry GA 63rd Inf. Co.E
Usher, Henry LA Inf. McLean's Co. Cpl.
Usher, Henry VA 59th Inf. 2nd Co.A
Usher, James GA 5th Cav. Co.F
Usher, J.J. GA Cav. 2nd Bn. Co.A
Usher, J.J. GA 5th Cav. Co.I
Usher, John GA 5th Inf. (St.Guards) Russell's Co.
Usher, John B. NC 28th Inf. Co.E
Usher, John C. SC Inf. 7th Bn. (Enfield Rifles) Co.C
Usher, John D. MS 2nd Inf. Co.G 1st Lt.
Usher, John D. MS 22nd Inf. Co.G 1st Lt.
Usher, John P. LA 10th Inf. Co.H Sgt.
Usher, John W. SC 22nd Inf. Co.E
Usher, Joseph GA Cav. 2nd Bn. Co.B
Usher, Joseph GA 5th Cav. Co.F
Usher, J.W. AR Lt.Arty. 5th Btty.
Usher, Memucan SC 21st Inf. Co.F
Usher, Noah SC 4th St.Troops Co.F
Usher, Oswald E. GA Cobb's Legion Co.E
Usher, Robert TX 22nd Inf. Co.F
Usher, Samuel SC 1st (Butler's) Inf. Co.A,K
Usher, S.E. GA 5th Cav. Co.F
Usher, T.H. GA 7th Cav. Co.B
Usher, T.H. GA Cav. 21st Bn. Co.C
Usher, Thomas GA 47th Inf. Co.I
Usher, W.B. MS 3rd Inf. (St.Troops) Co.G
Usher, W.H. GA Cav. 2nd Bn. Co.B
Usher, William GA Cav. 2nd Bn. Co.B
Usher, William GA 5th Cav. Co.F
Usher, William H. GA 5th Cav. Co.F
Usi, Leo. LA 26th Inf. Co.K
Usina, --- GA 1st Reg.
Usina, Domingo FL 3rd Inf. Co.B
Usina, John FL Inf. 2nd Bn. Co.B Sgt.
Usina, Michael FL 3rd Inf. Co.B
Usina, Michael S. FL 3rd Inf. Co.B
Usina, M.S. GA 1st (Cons.) Inf. Co.K
Usinger, G.J. TX 9th (Young's) Inf. Co.D
Usleton, Alfred TN 17th Inf. Co.G
Usleton, Joseph TN 4th (McLemore's) Cav. Co.E
Usley, A.J. VA 3rd Cav. Co.C Cpl.
Usly 1st Creek Mtd.Vol. 2nd Co.C
Usom, Jehu TN 43rd Inf. Co.D
Usra, John NC Inf. Thomas Legion Co.K
Usrea, Nathaniel T. TN 11th Inf. Co.F
Usred, M.B. GA 26th Inf.
Usrey, Alexander TN 17th Inf. Co.D
Usrey, Jacob TN 17th Inf. Co.D
Usrey, John R. KY 2nd Mtd.Inf. Co.D
Usrey, Randolph AL 56th Part.Rangers Co.K
Usrey, Richard L. KY 2nd Mtd.Inf. Co.D 1st Lt.
Usrey, Samuel W. NC 2nd Inf. Co.E
Usrey, W.B. AR 2nd Cav. Co.G
Usry, Benjamin TX 15th Cav. Co.F,B
Usry, Daniel F. GA 48th Inf. Co.A
Usry, Daniel W. NC 46th Inf. Co.E
Usry, D.W. NC Mallett's Bn. Co.E
Usry, George J. GA Cav. 7th Bn. (St.Guards) Co.G Cpl.
Usry, Hampton NC 37th Inf. Co.D
Usry, Hampton NC 42nd Inf. Co.H
Usry, Hampton NC 45th Inf. Co.K
Usry, James D. AL 10th Inf. Co.D
Usry, James M. GA 22nd Inf. Co.B
Usry, J.F. GA Cav. 7th Bn. (St.Guards) Co.G 1st Lt.
Usry, J. Freeman NC 46th Inf. Co.E Cpl.
Usry, J.G. GA Inf. 5th Bn. (St.Guards) Co.D
Usry, J.L. GA 8th Cav. Co.F
Usry, J.L. GA 62nd Cav. Co.F
Usry, J.N. AL 10th Inf. Co.D
Usry, John B. MS Packer's Co. (Pope Guards) Drum.
Usry, John L. TN 19th Inf. Co.A
Usry, Joshua F. GA Cobb's Legion Co.A
Usry, J.W. GA Cav. 7th Bn. (St.Guards) Co.G
Usry, N.M. AL Cav. Hardie's Bn.Res. Co.A
Usry, R.L. GA 8th Cav. Co.F
Usry, R.L. GA 62nd Cav. Co.F
Usry, Robert C. AL 10th Inf. Co.D
Usry, Thomas NC 23rd Inf. Co.E
Usry, Thomas NC 37th Inf. Co.D
Usry, Thomas TN 60th Mtd.Inf. Co.D
Usry, Thomas TX 35th (Likens') Cav. Co.I
Usry, Thomas J. MS Packer's Co. (Pope Guards)
Usry, W.A. AL 10th Inf. Co.D
Usry, W.C. MS 29th Inf. Co.D
Usry, W.D. NC 48th Inf. Co.H
Usry, W.D. NC Mallett's Bn. Co.D
Usry, William J. AL 39th Inf. Co.K
Usry, William T. AL 10th Inf. Co.D
Usry, W.J. GA Conscr.
Ussary, Alexander AL 20th Inf. Co.E
Ussary, F.W. AR Mil. Desha Cty.Bn.
Ussary, John SC 2nd Inf. Co.A
Ussary, William J. AR 1st (Crawford's) Cav. Co.A Sgt.
Usselton, John W. TN 44th Inf. Co.H
Usselton, R.W. TX 10th Cav. Co.B
Ussen, Warren TN 3rd (Forrest's) Cav.
Usser, Peter KY 12th Cav. Co.G
Usser, Whig KY 12th Cav. Co.G
Usserey, H.L. GA 5th Res. Co.A
Usserry, Miles NC 3rd Arty. (40th St.Troops) Co.D
Ussery, Angus P. SC 1st (McCreary's) Inf. Co.A
Ussery, A.P. FL 2nd Inf. Co.B
Ussery, B.W. Gen. & Staff Surg.
Ussery, Charles E. GA 15th Inf. Co.H Cpl.
Ussery, D. GA Lt.Arty. Ritter's Co.
Ussery, E.P. TN 3rd (Clack's) Inf. Co.D
Ussery, F.C.P. TX 2nd Inf. Co.C
Ussery, Frank MS Cav. Duncan's Co. (Tishomingo Rangers)
Ussery, George G. MS 24th Inf. Co.D 1st Lt.
Ussery, G.H. TN 3rd (Clack's) Inf. Co.H
Ussery, Henry NC 56th Inf. Co.B
Ussery, Henry TN 18th (Newsom's) Cav. Co.I
Ussery, Henry R. MS 24th Inf. Co.D
Ussery, I.B. AL 14th Inf. Co.F
Ussery, James B. NC 35th Inf. Co.B
Ussery, James M. SC 1st (McCreary's) Inf. Co.A
Ussery, James R. AR 1st (Colquitt's) Inf. Co.I,A
Ussery, J.B. 4th Conf.Inf. Co.I
Ussery, J.C. MS 14th (Cons.) Inf. Co.I
Ussery, J.E. AL 42nd Inf. Co.F
Ussery, Jesse R. NC 43rd Inf. Co.H
Ussery, J.G. GA 12th (Robinson's) Cav. (St.Guards) Co.C
Ussery, J.G. MS 43rd Inf. Co.F
Ussery, J.L. AR 15th (Josey's) Inf. 1st Co.C
Ussery, J.M. TX 32nd Cav. Co.I
Ussery, John GA 45th Inf. Co.F
Ussery, John NC 44th Inf. Co.F
Ussery, John B. GA 49th Inf. Co.A 1st Sgt.
Ussery, John C. AL 37th Inf. Co.H
Ussery, John C. MS 43rd Inf. Co.F
Ussery, John C. NC 23rd Inf. Co.D Sgt.Maj.
Ussery, John M. LA Inf.Cons.Crescent Regt. Co.E
Ussery, John M. MS 24th Inf. Co.D Sgt.
Ussery, Joseph TN 23rd Inf. Co.B
Ussery, Joseph W. SC 1st (McCreary's) Inf. Co.A 2nd Lt.
Ussery, J.R. TX 33rd Cav. Co.D
Ussery, J.W. GA 63rd Inf. Co.D
Ussery, Leander F. MS 2nd Inf. Co.K
Ussery, L.F. AL Cav. Moreland's Regt. Co.H 1st Lt.
Ussery, L.F. MS Cav. Jeff Davis Legion Co.B Sgt.
Ussery, M.A. MS 19th Inf. Co.H Cpl.
Ussery, Martin A. NC 38th Inf. Co.E
Ussery, Martin V.B. MS 12th Inf. Co.F
Ussery, Morgan AR 19th (Dockery's) Inf. Co.E 1st Sgt.
Ussery, Morgan L. AR 9th Inf. Co.F
Ussery, Moses A. AR 15th (Josey's) Inf. Co.A
Ussery, Murphey NC 48th Inf. Co.E
Ussery, O. SC Cav. 19th Bn. Co.C
Ussery, O. SC Part.Rangers Kirk's Co.
Ussery, Peter LA 1st Cav. Co.K
Ussery, P.H. TX 32nd Cav. Co.I
Ussery, R.D. AR 10th Inf. Co.C
Ussery, Samuel A. GA 57th Inf. Co.D
Ussery, Seth AR Cav. Harrell's Bn. Co.A
Ussery, S.M. MS 44th Inf. Co.A
Ussery, S.W. SC 1st (McCreary's) Inf. Co.A
Ussery, T.B. SC Inf. 1st (Charleston) Bn. Co.F
Ussery, T.B. SC 27th Inf. Co.C

Ussery, T.F. AL 14th Inf. Co.F Sgt.
Ussery, Theodore B. SC 1st (Butler's) Inf. Co.A
Ussery, Thomas SC 2nd Arty. Co.B
Ussery, T.J. AL 22nd Inf. Co.B
Ussery, T.J. AL Cp. of Instr. Talladega
Ussery, T.J. 4th Conf.Inf. Co.I
Ussery, W. GA 5th Res. Co.I
Ussery, W.C. TN 13th Inf. Co.L
Ussery, W.C. TX 32nd Cav. Co.I
Ussery, Welcome GA 5th Res. Co.G
Ussery, W.H. TN 19th (Biffle's) Cav. Co.I
Ussery, William AR Cav. Harrell's Bn. Co.A Sgt.
Ussery, William GA 3rd Inf. Co.F
Ussery, William GA 45th Inf. Co.F
Ussery, William LA 2nd Inf. Co.K
Ussery, William MS 24th Inf. Co.D,E
Ussery, William NC 35th Inf. Co.B
Ussery, William D. NC 43rd Inf. Co.H
Ussery, W.J. GA 5th Res. Co.I Sgt.
Ussery, W.O. SC 11th Res. Co.B
Ussery, W.R. MO 1st & 3rd Cons.Cav. Co.E
Ussery, W.R. TN 42nd Inf. Surg.
Ussery, W.T. AR 10th Inf. Co.F,C Bvt.2nd Lt.
Ussery, Zachariah GA 45th Inf. Co.F Cpl.
Ussey, Augustus AR Cav. Harrell's Bn. Co.A
Ussey, John AR 2nd Inf. Co.K
Ussleton, Jeremiah TN 23rd Inf. 1st Co.F, Co.H
Ussleton, John Wesley MS 15th Bn.S.S. Co.A
Ussleton, J.W. MS 15th Bn.S.S. Co.A
Ussleton, P.G. MS 15th Bn.S.S. Co.A
Ussleton, P.G. TN 44th Inf. Co.A
Ussrey, G.H. Central Div. KY Sap. & Min.,CSA
Ussry, Maliches G. GA 21st Inf. Co.F
Ussury, Samuel SC 2nd Rifles Co.L
Ussy, George J. GA 22nd Inf. Co.B
Ustel, H. KY Cav. 2nd Bn. (Dortch's) Co.A
Ustick, James C. AL 5th Inf. New Co.G
Ustick, James L. AL 5th Inf. New Co.G
Ustick, Thomas MO 5th Cav. Co.B
Ustinick, John TX 20th Inf. Co.A
Usurey, Martin V. GA 26th Inf. Co.A
Usury, G.J. GA 2nd Inf. Co.C
Ute, Adam LA 21st (Kennedy's) Inf. Co.F
Utell, John LA Mil. 5th Regt.Eur.Brig. (Spanish Regt.) Co.5
Utes, John SC 1st (McCreary's) Inf. Co.I
Utesey, W.L. AL 32nd Inf. Co.F Sgt.
Utesler, J.W. AR 15th (N.W.) Inf. Co.K
Utesy, Jacob AL 45th Inf. Co.A Music.
Uthoff, Henry LA Mil.Cont.Regt. Mitchell's Co.
Utler, Thomas A. VA Cav. 41st Bn. Co.F
Utley, A. KY 10th (Johnson's) Cav. Co.K
Utley, A.C. NC Snead's Co. (Loc.Def.)
Utley, A.J. TN 49th Inf. Co.I
Utley, Alexander KY 10th (Johnson's) Cav. Co.A Capt.
Utley, A.Q. TX 29th Cav. Co.H
Utley, Benjamin F. MO 5th Inf. Co.D
Utley, B.L. TN 5th Inf. 2nd Co.H 1st Lt.
Utley, Britton S. NC 26th Inf. Co.D Sgt.
Utley, B.W. AR 32nd Inf. Co.K
Utley, Charles R. VA 20th Inf. Co.D
Utley, Charles R. VA 59th Inf. 3rd Co.B
Utley, Daniel KY 4th Mtd.Inf. Co.B
Utley, D.T. AR 37th Inf. Co.B Sgt.
Utley, E. KY 12th Cav. Co.E,F
Utley, Francis M. MS 26th Inf. Co.F
Utley, Gaston NC 47th Inf. Co.C Cpl.
Utley, George W. AR Cav. Gordon's Regt. Co.C
Utley, Green B. GA 48th Inf. Co.D Cpl.
Utley, G.W. TN 5th Inf. 2nd Co.H
Utley, Henry GA 48th Inf. Co.D
Utley, Henry C. NC 3rd Inf. Co.F Music.
Utley, Henry C. NC 5th Sr.Res. Co.E
Utley, Henry C. VA 3rd Lt.Arty. (Loc.Def.) Co.C
Utley, Henry C. VA Hvy.Arty. Wilkinson's Co.
Utley, H.L. GA 32nd Inf. Co.C
Utley, J.A. TN 10th (DeMoss') Cav. Co.K 2nd Lt.
Utley, Jacob W. NC 35th Inf. Co.D
Utley, James W.F. NC 26th Inf. Co.D
Utley, Jasper T. NC Hvy.Arty. 1st Bn. Co.D Music.
Utley, J.B. TN 19th & 20th (Cons.) Cav. Co.B
Utley, J.B. TN 20th (Russell's) Cav. Co.D
Utley, J.D. AR 31st Inf. Co.D Cpl.
Utley, J.H. AL Cav. Forrest's Regt.
Utley, J.H. TN 19th & 20th (Cons.) Cav. Co.E
Utley, J.K. KY 7th Mtd.Inf. Co.B
Utley, J.L. GA 32nd Inf. Co.C
Utley, J.M. NC 3rd Cav. (41st St.Troops) Co.I
Utley, J.M. NC 26th Inf. Co.D
Utley, John A. NC 1st Inf. (6 mo. '61) Co.D
Utley, John C. AR 16th Inf. Co.B
Utley, John J. NC 31st Inf. Co.D
Utley, John P. MS 9th Inf. New Co.I
Utley, John R. NC 14th Inf. Co.E
Utley, John W. AR 16th Inf. Co.B Capt.
Utley, Joseph S. AR Cav. 1st Bn. (Stirman's) Co.A
Utley, L.F. TN 47th Inf. Co.F
Utley, M. KY 10th (Johnson's) Cav. Co.D
Utley, Mack G. NC 3rd Cav. (41st St.Troops) Co.I
Utley, Martin V. AR 16th Inf. Co.A
Utley, Mirabeau NC 1st Arty. (10th St.Troops) Co.K
Utley, Morris NC 6th Sr.Res. Co.K
Utley, Moses C. NC 2nd Arty. (36th St.Troops) Co.C
Utley, Moses C. NC 2nd Bn.Loc.Def.Troops Co.A
Utley, Quinton NC 31st Inf. Co.C 1st Lt.
Utley, Robert G. AR 3rd Inf. Co.L Cpl.
Utley, S. NC 1st Jr.Res. Co.D
Utley, Samuel AL Lt.Arty. 2nd Bn. Co.B
Utley, S.M. NC Mil. 1st Regt. W.D. Crowder's Co. 1st Sgt.
Utley, S.M. NC 6th Sr.Res. Co.K
Utley, S.W. AR 62nd Mil. Co.F Sgt.
Utley, T.B. TN 10th (DeMoss') Cav. Co.K 1st Sgt.
Utley, T.B. TN 20th (Russell's) Cav. Co.D
Utley, T.B. TN 21st & 22nd (Cons.) Cav. Co.F Sgt.
Utley, Thomas TX 9th Cav. Co.D 1st Lt.
Utley, Thomas J. NC 3rd Cav. (41st St.Troops) Co.I 1st Lt.
Utley, T.J. TN 18th Inf. Co.B
Utley, T.J. VA 1st (Farinholt's) Res. Co.I
Utley, T.L. TX Cav. Waller's Regt. Co.F
Utley, W.H. KY 2nd (Woodward's) Cav. Co.G Cpl.
Utley, W.H. NC 31st Inf. Co.C
Utley, W.H. TN 12th Inf. Co.H
Utley, W.H. TX Granbury's Cons.Brig. Co.B
Utley, William KY 7th Mtd.Inf. Co.D 2nd Lt.
Utley, William KY 8th Mtd.Inf. Co.E
Utley, William NC 30th Inf. Co.H
Utley, William NC 31st Inf. Co.D
Utley, William F. NC 26th Inf. Co.D Sgt.
Utley, William H. KY 7th Cav. Co.D 2nd Lt.
Utley, William H. NC 3rd Cav. (41st St.Troops) Co.I
Utley, William H. TX 7th Inf. Co.B
Utley, William J. NC 15th Inf. Co.B
Utley, William L. TN 6th Inf. Co.K Sgt.
Utley, William T. TN 12th Inf. Co.H
Utley, W.J. AL Cav. Forrest's Regt.
Utley, W.J. NC Snead's Co. (Loc.Def.)
Utley, W.J. TN 18th (Newsom's) Cav. Co.H
Utley, W.T. TN 12th (Cons.) Inf. Co.K
Utly, Addison C. NC 31st Inf. Co.C
Utly, A.J. Inf. Bailey's Cons.Regt. Co.D
Utly, Gaston T. NC 31st Inf. Co.C
Utly, John TN 5th Inf. 2nd Co.H
Utly, William A. MO 7th Cav. Old Co.A
Utman, H. AL 10th Inf. Co.G
Utsey, C.J.D. SC 11th Inf. Co.H
Utsey, D.D. SC 11th Inf. Co.H
Utsey, D.M. SC 24th Inf. Co.C Cpl.
Utsey, D.W. SC 11th Inf. Co.H Sgt.
Utsey, G.C. SC 4th Cav. Co.G
Utsey, G.C. SC Cav. 10th Bn. Co.C
Utsey, Govan AL 7th Inf. Co.E
Utsey, Govan V. AL Cav. 4th Bn. (Love's) Co.B
Utsey, G.V. MS Cav. Jeff Davis Legion Co.I
Utsey, Isaac SC 11th Inf. Co.H
Utsey, J.C. SC 6th Cav. Co.F
Utsey, J.C. SC 11th Inf. Co.H
Utsey, John AL Inf. 1st Regt. Co.H
Utsey, John SC 24th Inf. Co.C
Utsey, John J. AL 38th Inf. Co.C
Utsey, J.R. SC 11th Inf. Co.H
Utsey, J.R.S. SC 2nd Inf. Co.C
Utsey, Pompey AL Inf. 1st Regt. Co.H
Utsey, W.M. SC 3rd Cav. Co.B
Utsler, Abraham AR 15th (N.W.) Inf. Co.C
Utsman, William AR 23rd Inf. Co.C
Utt, George W. MO 16th Inf. Co.D
Utt, James H. VA 63rd Inf. Co.G, 2nd Co.I
Utt, James S. VA 5th Inf. Co.F
Utt, John VA 5th Inf. Co.F
Utt, John P. TX Cav. Martin's Regt. Co.F
Utt, King MO Cav. Wood's Regt. Co.K
Utt, Thomas MO Cav. Snider's Bn. Co.A
Utt, Thomas MO Inf. Clark's Regt. Co.H
Utt, Thomas H. VA 63rd Inf. Co.G
Utt, Thomas H. VA Mil. Carroll Cty.
Utt, William MO Cav. Snider's Bn. Co.A
Utt, William MO 2nd Inf.
Utt, William MO Inf. 3rd Bn. Co.A
Utt, William MO 6th Inf. Co.E
Utt, William MO Inf. Clark's Regt. Co.H
Utt, William L. VA 24th Inf. Co.C
Utt, William T. VA 24th Inf. Co.C
Ut tah wohs ki Scontie 1st Cherokee Mtd.Rifles Co.B

Utter, Bryant VA 19th Cav. Co.C
Utter, Bryant VA 20th Cav. Co.F
Utter, Bryant VA 3rd Cav. & Inf.St.Line Co.D
Utter, J.Y. GA 6th Cav. Co.I 1st Lt.
Utter, Marian VA 19th Cav. Co.C
Utter, Marion VA 20th Cav. Co.F
Utter, Marion VA 3rd Cav. & Inf.St.Line Co.D
Utter, Nicholas VA 21st Cav. Co.A
Utter, Samuel VA 19th Cav. Co.C
Utter, Thomas A. VA 23rd Cav. Co.F
Utterback, Addison W. VA Lt.Arty. 12th Bn. 1st Co.A Jr.1st Lt.
Utterback, Addison W. VA Lt.Arty. Utterback's Co. Capt.
Utterback, Arthur W. VA 34th Mil. Co.B Cpl.
Utterback, B.D. VA Cav. Mosby's Regt. (Part.Rangers) Co.H
Utterback, C. VA 13th Inf. 2nd Co.B
Utterback, F. VA 8th Inf. Co.B
Utterback, Grandison KY 6th Mtd.Inf. Co.G Capt.
Utterback, H.C. TN 3rd (Clack's) Inf. Black.
Utterback, Irvin MO 1st N.E. Cav. White's Co. Sgt.
Utterback, James H. KY 7th Mtd.Inf. Co.G Drum.
Utterback, James M. KY 5th Mtd.Inf. Co.A
Utterback, John VA 20th Cav. Co.D
Utterback, John VA Cav. 35th Bn. Co.F
Utterback, John S. KY 5th Cav. Co.H
Utterback, John W. KY 1st (Butler's) Cav.
Utterback, John W. KY 5th Cav. Co.F
Utterback, John W. VA 8th Inf. Co.K
Utterback, J.V. VA 25th Inf. 2nd Co.A,D
Utterback, Owen MO 9th Bn.S.S. Co.E
Utterback, Robert E. VA 4th Cav. Co.D Maj.
Utterback, S.P. MO 9th Inf. Co.C
Utterback, S.T. MO Inf. Clark's Regt. Co.B
Utterback, W.F. MO 3rd & 5th Cons.Inf. Sgt.
Utterback, W.H. VA 11th Cav. Co.I
Utterback, William F. MO 2nd Inf. Co.G 1st Sgt.
Utterback, William H. VA 5th Cav. 2nd Co.F
Utterbuck, Henry MO 1st N.E. Cav. White's Co.
Utterbuck, Saunder MO 1st N.E. Cav. White's Co.
Utterbuck, William MO 1st N.E. Cav. White's Co. Cpl.
Uttey, John MS 18th Cav. Co.A
Uttley, W.H. TN 19th (Biffle's) Cav. Co.K
Uttley, William T. TN Cav. Newsom's Regt. Co.B
Uttz, A.J. VA 82nd Mil. Co.C
Uttz, Joseph P. VA 82nd Mil. Co.C
Uttz, Oliver VA 82nd Mil. Co.C
Utz, A.S. VA Cav. Mosby's Regt. (Part.Rangers) Co.D
Utz, A.S. VA 82nd Mil. Co.A 2nd Lt.
Utz, Augustus S. VA Lt.Arty. Utterback's Co.
Utz, Burr D. VA 4th Cav. Co.D
Utz, Calvin VA 4th Inf. Co.I
Utz, Charles VA Burks' Regt.Loc.Def. McCue's Co.
Utz, Charles M. VA Burks' Regt.Loc.Def. Price's Co.
Utz, Edwin VA 1st Bn.Res. Co.H
Utz, G.A. VA 4th Cav. Co.C
Utz, George VA 1st Bn.Res. Co.H
Utz, George A. VA 82nd Mil. Co.A
Utz, George S. VA 49th Inf. 3rd Co.G
Utz, George W. VA Lt.Arty. Brander's Co.
Utz, George W. VA 7th Inf. Co.K Sgt.
Utz, G.T. KY Corbin's Men
Utz, G.W. VA 4th Cav. Co.C
Utz, G.W. VA 82nd Mil. Co.D
Utz, Henry T. VA 10th Inf. Co.L
Utz, Henry T. VA 82nd Mil. Co.A
Utz, H.S. LA 3rd (Harrison's) Cav. Co.C
Utz, James MO Lt.Arty. Von Phul's Co.
Utz, James F. LA 2nd Inf. Co.B Capt.
Utz, James M. MO Inf. 8th Bn. Co.C
Utz, James M. MO 9th Inf. Co.G
Utz, James S. VA 1st Arty. Co.D 2nd Lt.
Utz, J.C. VA Cav. Mosby's Regt. (Part.Rangers) Co.E
Utz, J.H. VA 4th Cav. Co.C
Utz, John A. VA 6th Cav. Co.B
Utz, John J. VA 7th Cav. Co.A
Utz, John J. VA 13th Inf. 1st Co.B Cpl.
Utz, John S. VA 4th Cav. Co.C
Utz, Joseph TX Waul's Legion Co.F
Utz, Joseph P. VA Lt.Arty. 12th Bn. 1st Co.A
Utz, Joseph P. VA Lt.Arty. Utterback's Co.
Utz, Lewis A. VA 49th Inf. 3rd Co.G
Utz, Malory W. VA 34th Inf. Fray's Co.D
Utz, M.H. VA 10th Inf. Co.L
Utz, Michael VA 1st Bn.Res. Co.H
Utz, Morgan VA Burks' Regt.Loc.Def.
Utz, R.E. VA 4th Cav. Co.C
Utz, Robert VA 1st Bn.Res. Co.H
Utz, Robert O. VA 34th Inf. Fray's Co.D Cpl.
Utz, Toliver S. VA Lt.Arty. 12th Bn. 1st Co.A
Utz, Toliver S. VA Lt.Arty. Utterback's Co.
Utz, W. MS Cav. 3rd Bn.Res. Co.B
Utz, W.H. VA 4th Cav. Co.C
Utz, William M. VA 157th Mil. Co.A
Utze, John P. KY 3rd Cav. Co.E
Utzfeldt, Henry TX Inf. 1st St.Troops Sheldon's Co.B
Utzman, Frank TX 7th Inf. Co.I Drum.
Utzman, Jacob TX 19th Inf. Co.I
Utzman, J.L. TX 4th Inf. Co.I Music.
Utzman, John NC Mil. 66th Bn. J.H. Whitman's Co.
Utzman, Robert M. NC 1st Inf. Co.H,A
U un tah 1st Creek Mtd.Vol. Co.E
Uzec, Henry Conf.Lt.Arty. 1st Reg.Btty.
Uzee, Arthur LA 1st Hvy.Arty. (Reg.) Co.C
Uzee, Forest LA 22nd Inf. Wash. Marks' Co. Cpl.
Uzee, Forrest LA 30th Inf. Co.E
Uzee, Henry LA 30th Inf. Co.E
Uzee, Joseph LA Inf.Cons.Crescent Regt. Co.E
Uzee, Valere LA 30th Inf. Co.G,H
Uzee, Vinot LA 1st Hvy.Arty. (Reg.) Co.C
Uzle, H.T. Conf.Cav. Wood's Regt. 2nd Co.D
Uzzel, David NC 33rd Inf. Co.A
Uzzel, E.B. TX 4th Inf. (St.Troops) Co.D
Uzzell, Benjamin NC 47th Inf. Co.G
Uzzell, Elisha NC 55th Inf. Co.G
Uzzell, James NC 1st Cav. (9th St.Troops) Co.H
Uzzell, James NC Loc.Def. Griswold's Co.
Uzzell, James SC Lt.Arty. 3rd (Palmetto) Bn. Co.K
Uzzell, James E. NC 47th Inf. Co.G Sgt.
Uzzell, James N. NC 3rd Bn.Sr.Res. Co.C
Uzzell, James T. NC 3rd Arty. (40th St.Troops) Co.A Cpl.
Uzzell, John NC 61st Inf. Co.C
Uzzell, Joshua NC 1st Cav. (9th St.Troops) Co.H
Uzzell, J.T. NC 32nd Inf. Lenoir Braves 1st Co.K
Uzzell, Lemuel TX 13th Vol. 1st Co.I
Uzzell, Major NC 3rd Arty. (40th St.Troops) Co.K
Uzzell, Major NC Mil. Clark's Sp.Bn. Co.D
Uzzell, Major NC 61st Inf. Co.C
Uzzell, Major D. NC 1st Cav. (9th St.Troops) Co.H
Uzzell, Mathew NC 8th Bn.Part.Rangers Co.F Cpl.
Uzzell, Mathew NC 66th Inf. Co.I Cpl.
Uzzell, M.E. NC Loc.Def. Griswold's Co.
Uzzell, M.M. TX 24th Cav. Co.A
Uzzell, M.M. TX 24th & 25th Cav. (Cons.) Co.A 2nd Lt.
Uzzell, M.M. TX Cav. Mann's Regt. Co.A 2nd Lt.
Uzzell, Richard NC 1st Arty. (10th St.Troops) Co.F
Uzzell, Robert T. VA Hood's Bn.Res. Tappey's Co.
Uzzell, Thomas M. TN 53rd Inf. Co.E
Uzzell, Thomas W. NC 8th Bn.Part.Rangers Co.F Sgt.
Uzzell, Thomas W. NC 66th Inf. Co.I Sgt.
Uzzell, W.F. AR 5th Inf. Co.I
Uzzell, William KY 8th Mtd.Inf. Co.F
Uzzell, William NC 3rd Arty. (40th St.Troops) Co.K
Uzzell, William NC Mil. Clark's Sp.Bn. Co.D
Uzzell, William NC 61st Inf. Co.C
Uzzell, William Gray NC 5th Inf. Co.G
Uzzell, William H. VA 9th Inf. 2nd Co.A
Uzzell, William J. VA Horse Arty. E. Graham's Co.
Uzzell, W.J. VA 3rd (Archer's) Bn.Res. Co.A
Uzzelle, T. NC 67th Inf. Co.B
Uzzle, --- SC 2nd Inf. Co.E
Uzzle, C.D. TX 20th Inf. Co.G
Uzzle, E.B. TX 20th Inf. Co.G
Uzzle, Henry T. MS Part.Rangers Smyth's Co.
Uzzle, James TX 35th (Brown's) Cav. Co.A
Uzzle, James TX 13th Vol. 1st Co.B
Uzzle, Lemuel TX 35th (Brown's) Cav. Co.A
Uzzle, Matthew NC Loc.Def. Croom's Co.
Uzzle, Thomas NC Loc.Def. Croom's Co.
Uzzle, W.W. TX 35th (Brown's) Cav. Co.A
Uzzle, W.W. TX 13th Vol. 1st Co.B

V

Vaas, H.E. TX 22nd Inf. Co.K Band Ch.Music.
Vable, Alfred LA 6th Inf. Co.C
Vable, Alphonse LA Inf.Cons.Crescent Regt. Co.H
Vable, Honore LA 6th Inf. Co.C
Vacaro, Philip KY 9th Mtd.Inf. Co.B ACS
Vacaro, Philip Gen. & Staff Capt.,CS
Vacarro, B. TN Inf. 154th Sr.Regt. Co.L Sgt.
Vacarro, C.N TN Inf. 154th Sr.Regt. Co.L
Vaccaro, A.B. TN 3rd (Forrest's) Cav. Co.B
Vacors, Benjamin GA 10th Inf.
Vacovan, D. Eng.,CSA
Vacter, Rodney VA Cav. Swann's Bn. Co.H
Vaddegan, Edward SC 27th Inf. Co.C
Vaden, Algernon S. VA Inf. 5th Bn. Co.B
Vaden, Allen TX 9th (Young's) Inf. Co.G 1st Sgt.
Vaden, B.F. Conf.Cav. Powers' Regt. Co.E
Vaden, Charles B. VA 4th Cav. Co.B Jr.2nd Lt.
Vaden, Charles B. VA 3rd Inf.Loc.Def. Co.A
Vaden, Cornelius J. VA Hvy.Arty. Epes' Co.
Vaden, C.W. TN 45th Inf. Co.A
Vaden, Daniel VA Hvy.Arty. 20th Bn. Co.E Music.
Vaden, D.J. TN 24th Bn.S.S. Co.B
Vaden, Dodson VA Hood's Bn.Res. Co.B
Vaden, Edward VA Inf. 4th Bn.Loc.Def. Co.C,A
Vaden, F. TN 9th Inf. Co.K
Vaden, F.M. AL 27th Inf. Co.B
Vaden, F.O.Q.A. TN 15th (Stewart's) Cav. Co.B Sgt.
Vaden, French TX 3rd Inf. Co.D Sgt.
Vaden, George P. VA Lt.Arty. 38th Bn. Co.B
Vaden, George R. VA 9th Inf. 1st Co.H
Vaden, George T. VA 41st Inf. 2nd Co.G
Vaden, George W. VA 16th Inf. Co.F
Vaden, G.L. GA 38th Inf. Co.H
Vaden, G.M. VA 18th Inf. Co.I
Vaden, G.N. TN 24th Bn.S.S. Co.B
Vaden, G.R. LA 25th Inf. Co.D
Vaden, Granville VA Lt.Arty. Motley's Co.
Vaden, G.W. VA 6th Cav. Co.C
Vaden, H.C. TN 12th (Green's) Cav. Co.G
Vaden, Henry M. VA Inf. 5th Bn. Co.A 2nd Lt.
Vaden, J.A. TN 31st Inf. Co.A
Vaden, James TN 13th (Gore's) Cav. Co.K
Vaden, James A. VA Lt.Arty. Weisiger's Co. 1st Sgt.
Vaden, James A. VA 6th Inf. Weisiger's Co. Sgt.
Vaden, James A. VA 16th Inf. Co.I 1st Sgt.
Vaden, James M. VA 4th Inf. Co.E
Vaden, James W. TN 9th (Ward's) Cav. Co.D
Vaden, James W. TX 11th Cav. Co.C Sgt.
Vaden, John AL Cav. Forrest's Regt.
Vaden, John B. AR Lt.Arty. Wiggins' Btty. Bugler
Vaden, John H. TN 32nd Inf. Co.K
Vaden, John H. VA 54th Inf. Co.E
Vaden, John T. VA 14th Inf. Co.I Sgt.
Vaden, John Willis VA 12th Inf. 2nd Co.I,D
Vaden, Joseph D. TN 4th (McLemore's) Cav. Co.A
Vaden, L. VA Inf. 44th Bn. Co.C
Vaden, Leonidas TX 1st (McCulloch's) Cav. Co.K
Vaden, Leonidas TX 1st (Yager's) Cav. Co.I
Vaden, Leonidas TX Cav. 8th (Taylor's) Bn. Co.D
Vaden, L.I. TX Cav. McCord's Frontier Regt. Co.D
Vaden, L.J. TX 9th (Young's) Inf. Co.G Sgt.
Vaden, Michael W. VA 4th Cav. Co.B
Vaden, M.W. AL 27th Inf. Co.I Bvt.2nd Lt.
Vaden, N.B. TN 45th Inf. Co.A
Vaden, Olerver TX 10th Cav. Co.B
Vaden, Page H. VA Inf. 5th Bn. Co.E
Vaden, Paul TN 13th (Gore's) Cav. Co.K
Vaden, Paul C. TN 9th (Ward's) Cav. Co.D
Vaden, Paul C. TN 12th (Cons.) Inf. Co.C
Vaden, Peter F. VA Hvy.Arty. 20th Bn. Co.E 1st Lt.
Vaden, Peter F. VA Lt.Arty. Jeffress' Co.
Vaden, P.F. VA Lt.Arty. Parker's Co.
Vaden, Robert MO 7th Cav. Co.I
Vaden, Robert VA 54th Mil. Co.G
Vaden, Samuel E. VA 4th Cav. Co.B
Vaden, Samuel E. VA Lt.Arty. R.M. Anderson's Co.
Vaden, Sam'l E. VA Lt.Arty. R.M. Anderson's Co.
Vaden, T. VA Inf. 44th Bn. Co.A
Vaden, Thad. TN Inf. 2nd Cons.Regt. Co.B
Vaden, Thaddeus TN Inf. 154th Sr.Regt. Co.D Cpl.
Vaden, Thomas VA 21st Cav. 2nd Co.D
Vaden, Thomas VA Lt.Arty. Cayce's Co.
Vaden, Thomas VA Lt.Arty. Utterback's Co.
Vaden, T.J. TN 10th (DeMoss') Cav. Co.F
Vaden, T.J. TN Cav. Napier's Bn. Co.C
Vaden, W. AL 11th Cav. Co.F
Vaden, W.A. VA 23rd Cav. Co.C
Vaden, W.A. VA Cav. 41st Bn. 2nd Co.H
Vaden, W.E. VA Cav. 37th Bn. Co.K
Vaden, W.H. VA 59th Inf. 3rd Co.E
Vaden, Wiley L. VA 6th Inf. Ferguson's Co.
Vaden, Wiley L. VA 12th Inf. Co.H
Vaden, William AL 6th Co.A
Vaden, William A. VA 4th Cav. Co.B
Vaden, William H. NC 13th Inf. Co.A Cpl.
Vaden, William H. TX 32nd Cav. Co.B 1st Lt.
Vaden, William W. TN 9th (Ward's) Cav. Co.D
Vaden, William W. TN 28th Inf. Co.G 3rd Lt.
Vaden, William W. TX Cav. Martin's Regt. Co.B Sgt.
Vaden, W.N. TN 17th Inf. Co.F
Vaden, W.P. AR 12th Inf. Co.H 1st Sgt.
Vaden, W.W. TN 28th (Cons.) Inf. Co.G 2nd Lt.
Vadier, Napoleon B. MO 9th Inf. Co.F
Vadrine, U. LA Inf.Crescent Regt. Co.C
Vael, Patrick LA Mil. 4th Regt. 1st Brig. 1st Div. Co.F
Vahey, Michael LA 7th Inf. Co.D
Vahl, A.L. LA Mil. 4th Regt. French Brig. Co.4
Vahl, F.W. Hermann TX 5th Field Btty.
Vahl, J. LA Mil. Moreau Guards Cpl.
Vahl, M. LA Mil. Orleans Fire Regt. Co.H
Vahl, N. LA Mil. Fire Bn. Co.A
Vahl, William TN Inf. 3rd Bn. Co.F Music.
Vahl, X. LA Mil. Fire Bn. Co.A
Vahldreck, T.H. TX Inf. Adner's Bn.Res.Corps Co.B
Vahldrick, F.H. TX 14th Field Btty.
Vahlmann, J. LA Mil. 4th Regt.Eur.Brig. Co.A
Vahrenkamp, Carl LA 20th Inf. Co.D
Vahy, John LA 20th Inf. Co.G Sgt.
Vaiden, Algernon S. VA 53rd Inf. Co.E 2nd Lt.
Vaiden, A.S. VA 5th Cav. Co.H
Vaiden, Baily P. AR 37th Inf. Co.F
Vaiden, C.M. MS Applewhite's Co. (Vaiden Guards)
Vaiden, Edward J. VA Hvy.Arty. A.J. Jones' Co.
Vaiden, Galba VA 3rd Cav. Co.F
Vaiden, Galba VA 5th Cav. Co.B
Vaiden, George R. VA Inf. 28th Bn. Co.C
Vaiden, George R. VA 59th Inf. 2nd Co.H
Vaiden, George W. VA 52nd Mil. Co.A Capt.
Vaiden, Henry VA Inf. 1st Bn.Loc.Def. Co.E,D
Vaiden, H.F. TN 2nd Cav.
Vaiden, Jacob VA 52nd Mil. Co.A 1st Lt.
Vaiden, James M. VA 36th Inf. Co.F
Vaiden, J.B. AL Mil. Co.E Capt.
Vaiden, J.C. Gen. & Staff Asst.Surg.
Vaiden, John B. VA 3rd Cav. Co.F,D
Vaiden, John H. VA Hvy.Arty. 18th Bn. Co.C
Vaiden, John H. VA Hvy.Arty. A.J. Jones' Co.
Vaiden, John S. VA 52nd Mil. Co.A
Vaiden, John W. VA Hvy.Arty. 18th Bn. Co.C
Vaiden, L. VA Hvy.Arty. 18th Bn. Co.C
Vaiden, Melville VA 3rd Cav. Co.F Capt.
Vaiden, Micajah VA 3rd Cav. Co.F
Vaiden, Page H. VA 53rd Inf. Co.B
Vaiden, Volosko VA 5th Cav. Co.H
Vaiden, Vulosko VA 3rd Cav. Co.F, 1st Co.I
Vaiden, Vulosko VA 52nd Mil. Maj.
Vaiden, W.E. VA Inf. 4th Bn.Loc.Def. Co.F
Vaiden, William VA 1st St.Res. Co.D
Vaiden, William B. VA 5th Cav. Co.H
Vaiden, William Benjamin VA 3rd Cav. 1st Co.I
Vaigneur, John SC 1st Mtd.Mil. Kirk's Co.
Vaigneur, John SC 11th Inf. Co.E
Vaigneur, John H. SC 3rd Cav. Co.C

Vaigneur, John H. SC Mil.Cav. 4th Regt. Howard's Co.
Vaigneur, Lewis S. SC 3rd Cav. Co.C
Vaigneur, Lewis S. SC 11th Inf. Co.E
Vaigneur, S.H. SC 1st Mtd.Mil. Kirk's Co.
Vaigneur, S. Henry SC 3rd Cav. Co.C
Vail, --- AL Inf. 1st (Loomis') Bn. Co.E
Vail, Andrew J. AR Lt.Arty. Thrall's Btty.
Vail, Edward P. VA 6th Bn.Res. Co.E 1st Sgt.
Vail, H. GA 8th Cav. Old Co.I
Vail, Henry AL 5th Inf. Co.H
Vail, Henry NC Mil. 16th Regt.
Vail, Henry VA 41st Inf. 1st Co.E Cpl.
Vail, I.M. MS 11th Inf. Co.I
Vail, Irving M. MS 6th Cav. Co.H
Vail, J. TX Nolan's Mtd.Co. (Loc.Def.)
Vail, J.A. VA 45th Inf. Co.A
Vail, James AR 2nd Inf. Co.E,D
Vail, James A. VA 16th Cav. Co.F
Vail, James W. AR Inf. Cocke's Regt. Co.C
Vail, J.B. AL 5th Inf. Co.E
Vail, J.C. AL 5th Inf. Co.E
Vail, J.H. AL 5th Inf. Co.H
Vail, J.L. AR 30th Inf. Co.M
Vail, John VA 32nd Inf. 2nd Co.H
Vail, John R. KY 4th Cav.
Vail, John R. KY 4th Mtd.Inf. Co.B
Vail, John R. MS Lt.Arty. (Issaquena Arty.) Graves' Co.
Vail, Joseph NC 17th Inf. (2nd Org.) Co.G
Vail, Josephus NC 1st Bn.
Vail, J.T. TN 15th (Cons.) Cav. Co.C
Vail, J.W. AL 8th Cav. Co.A
Vail, J.W. AL 5th Inf. Co.E
Vail, L.C. AL 21st Inf. Co.K
Vail, L.G. TN 1st Hvy.Arty. Co.L
Vail, Lovick AL 21st Inf. Co.D Cpl.
Vail, Lovitt C. AL 3rd Inf. Co.B
Vail, Thomas L. NC 1st Cav. (9th St.Troops) Co.H 1st Lt.
Vail, W. AL Cp. of Instr. Talladega Co.D
Vail, W.H. MS 35th Inf. Co.G
Vail, William Benners AL 3rd Inf. Co.E
Vail, William H. VA 21st Mil. Co.D,C
Vail, W.L. AL 5th Inf. Co.E
Vail, W.M. AL 25th Inf. Co.E
Vaile, E.W. TN 13th Inf. Co.F Cpl.
Vaile, Henry GA 62nd Cav. Co.I
Vaile, Jesse M. AL 11th Inf. Co.I
Vailes, Benjamin LA 11th Inf. Co.E
Vailes, Henry GA Inf. 1st Loc.Troops (Augusta) Co.B
Vailes, W.B. TX 29th Cav. Co.H
Vailes, William B. AR 34th Inf. Co.G
Vailles, Charles VA 46th Inf. Co.L
Vailleux, Henry LA Mil. LaFourche Regt.
Vails, A.J. LA Inf.Cons.Crescent Regt. Co.A
Vails, Alexander TN Cav. Newsom's Regt. Co.H
Vails, James J. AL 41st Inf. Co.I
Vails, John GA 43rd Inf. Co.F
Vails, John M. AL 5th Inf. Co.E
Vails, R.C. LA Inf.Cons.Crescent Regt. Co.A
Vails, W. AL Pickens Cty.Supp.Force Allen's Co.
Vaines, Isaac FL 10th Inf. Co.A
Vainhoi, A. NC 3rd Jr.Res. Co.B
Vainright, John E. NC 17th Inf. (2nd Org.) Co.K
Vainright, William NC 33rd Inf. Co.B
Vainwright, Daniel NC 42nd Inf. Co.B
Vainwright, Daniel NC 61st Inf. Co.H
Vainwright, James NC 17th Inf. (2nd Org.) Co.A
Vaio, Onezian LA Siege Train Bn. Co.D
Vairin, Augustus L.P. MS 2nd Inf. Co.B,L 1st Sgt.
Vairin, Julius LA Mil.Conf.Guards Regt. Co.H 2nd Lt.
Vairin, Justus LA Mil.Conf.Guards Regt. Co.I
Vaitzenager, John LA 1st (Strawbridge's) Inf. Co.E
Valade, Y. LA Unassign.
Valadie, --- LA Mil. 1st Regt. French Brig. Co.C
Valandingham, George LA 1st Cav. Robinson's Co.
Valandingham, George MS 8th Cav. Co.B Cpl.
Valandingham, George MS 28th Cav. Co.E Cpl.
Valandingham, George TN Arty. Ramsey's Btty.
Valandingham, J.S. Gen. & Staff Asst.Surg.
Valandingham, Manly NC Hvy.Arty. 1st Bn. Co.C
Valandingham, Oliver E. VA 55th Inf. Co.K
Valantine, John VA 6th Cav. Co.C
Valck, Charles VA 15th Inf. Co.K
Valdes, Antonio TX Trevino's Squad. Part. Mtd.Vol.
Valdes, C.L. AL 1st Bn.Cadets Co.A
Valdes, J.D. LA Mil. 5th Regt.Eur.Brig. (Spanish Regt.) Co.1
Valdewaire, Celestin LA 13th Inf. Co.F
Valdez, Ambrosia TX 1st (McCulloch's) Cav. Co.D
Valdez, D. TX St.Troops Teel's Co.
Valdez, Emiterio TX Cav. Benavides' Regt.
Valdez, Eugenio TX 3rd Inf. Co.G
Valdez, Ignacio TX 8th Inf. Co.C
Valdez, Jose M. TX 2nd Cav. 2nd Co.F
Valdez, Jose Maria TX 1st (McCulloch's) Cav. Co.D
Valdez, Jose Maria TX 3rd Inf. Co.F
Valdez, Jose Maria TX 8th Inf. Co.H
Valdez, Nicanor TX 33rd Cav. Co.B
Valdin, Thomas GA 53rd Inf. Co.F
Valdneer, William VA 21st Cav. 2nd Co.I
Valdwin, J.M. TX 4th Inf. (St.Troops) Co.C
Vale, --- TX Lt.Arty. Dege's Bn.
Vale, H. NC Mil. Clark's Sp.Bn. Co.D
Vale, Henry GA 3rd Inf. Co.G
Vale, Henry LA 28th (Gray's) Inf. Co.A
Vale, J.L. AR 23rd Inf. Co.G
Vale, John K. MS 14th Inf. Co.I
Vale, Josephus AL Lt.Arty. Lee's Btty.
Vale, L.G. TN Arty. Stewart's Co.
Vale, Peter VA Loc.Def.
Valega, Nichol LA 11th Inf. Co.B
Valega, Nicholas LA 1st Cav. Co.A
Valencia, A. Pons LA Mil. 5th Regt.Eur.Brig. (Spanish Regt.) Co.3 Capt.
Valent, Juan LA Mil. 5th Regt.Eur.Brig. (Spanish Regt.) Co.3
Valentein, J.B. TN 51st (Cons.) Inf. Co.F
Valentin, Oscar LA Mil. 1st Native Guards
Valentine, Albert AR 20th Inf. Co.A
Valentine, Alexander AR 36th Inf. Co.H
Valentine, Alexander MS 17th Inf. Co.F
Valentine, Andrew VA 62nd Mtd.Inf. 2nd Co.E 2nd Lt.
Valentine, A.R. GA 1st Cav. Co.G
Valentine, Armstead GA Cav. Gartrell's Co.
Valentine, B. MS Inf. 2nd St.Troops Co.G
Valentine, Benjamin MS Cav. 1st Bn. (McNair's) St.Troops Co.A
Valentine, Benjamin J. MO 4th Cav. Co.I
Valentine, Benjamin S. NC 1st Inf. (6 mo. '61) Co.F
Valentine, Benjamin S. NC 2nd Bn.Loc.Def. Troops Co.C
Valentine, Benjamin T.T. AL 24th Inf. Co.C
Valentine, B.J. MO Inf. Winston's Regt. Co.A
Valentine, Caspar SC Lt.Arty. 3rd (Palmetto) Bn. Co.D
Valentine, Charles VA Inf. 4th Bn.Loc.Def. Co.A
Valentine, Charles Conf.Inf. 8th Bn. Co.B
Valentine, D. GA 14th Inf. Co.B
Valentine, Daniel TX 13th Vol. 3rd Co.I
Valentine, Daniell GA Inf. 2nd Bn. Co.C
Valentine, David MS 14th Inf. Co.G
Valentine, D.N. TN Cav. Williams' Co.
Valentine, E. TX 2nd Inf. Co.G
Valentine, Edmond MO Inf. 1st Bn. Co.B
Valentine, Edward D. VA 12th Inf. Co.F
Valentine, E.W. VA 11th Inf. Co.G
Valentine, George MD 1st Cav. Co.C
Valentine, George G. VA 5th Inf. Co.E
Valentine, G.F. GA Inf. 25th Bn. (Prov.Guard) Co.F
Valentine, G.W. NC 68th Inf. Co.A
Valentine, H. SC Inf. 1st (Charleston) Bn. Co.D
Valentine, Henry GA 12th Inf. Co.I
Valentine, Henry VA 14th Cav. Co.E
Valentine, Hezekiah SC 11th Inf. 1st Co.I, 2nd Co.I
Valentine, Isaac J. AL 39th Inf. Co.I
Valentine, J. MS Inf. 2nd St.Troops Co.G
Valentine, J. MS Inf. 3rd Bn. (St.Troops) Co.E
Valentine, Jacob S. SC 1st (Butler's) Inf. Co.F,G Capt.
Valentine, James AL 11th Cav. Co.I
Valentine, James LA 6th Inf. Co.I
Valentine, James TN 1st (Feild's) Inf. Co.G
Valentine, James TX 15th Cav. Co.F
Valentine, James H. AL 25th Inf. Co.K
Valentine, James H. NC Vol. Lawrence's Co.
Valentine, James H. 7th Conf.Cav. Co.H
Valentine, James T. VA 55th Inf. Co.A
Valentine, J.B. TN 51st Inf. Co.D
Valentine, J.C. AL 42nd Inf. Co.B
Valentine, J.D. SC Inf. 1st (Charleston) Bn. Co.D Cpl.
Valentine, J.E. AR 21st Mil. Co.D
Valentine, Jesse AR 7th Mil. Co.C
Valentine, Jessee M. FL 7th Inf. Co.C
Valentine, J.G. MO Inf. Winston's Regt. Co.A
Valentine, J.H. NC 4th Bn.Jr.Res. Co.C Sgt.
Valentine, J.K. GA 6th Cav. Co.G Ch.Bugler
Valentine, J.K. GA Smith's Legion Co.G
Valentine, John AR 7th Mil. Co.C
Valentine, John GA 11th Cav. (St.Guards) Staten's Co.
Valentine, John GA Inf. 2nd Bn. Co.C
Valentine, John GA 12th Inf. Co.I

Valentine, John GA 49th Inf. Co.H
Valentine, John KY 9th Cav. Co.E
Valentine, John LA 10th Inf. Co.B
Valentine, John LA Inf.Cons.Crescent Regt. Co.A
Valentine, John TX 21st Cav. Co.E
Valentine, John TX 2nd Field Btty.
Valentine, John TX 13th Vol. 3rd Co.I
Valentine, John VA 19th Inf.
Valentine, John Conf.Cav. Wood's Regt. Co.I
Valentine, John B. LA Washington Arty.Bn. Co.4 Sgt.
Valentine, John C. MD Arty. 4th Btty.
Valentine, John C. MS 11th (Perrin's) Cav. Co.E
Valentine, John C. VA 5th Inf. Co.E
Valentine, John F. FL Lt.Arty. Abell's Co.
Valentine, John G. MO 4th Cav. Co.I
Valentine, John H. MS 17th Inf. Co.B
Valentine, John J. AL Lt.Arty. 2nd Bn. Co.A
Valentine, John W. KY 1st (Helm's) Cav. Capt.
Valentine, John W. GA 30th Inf. Co.F
Valentine, John W. MS 24th Inf. Co.B
Valentine, John W. VA 13th Inf. Co.D
Valentine, Joseph NC 32nd Inf. Co.C,D Sgt.
Valentine, Joseph SC 11th Inf. 1st Co.I, 2nd Co.I
Valentine, Joseph VA 11th Inf. Co.G
Valentine, Joseph J. NC 17th Inf. (2nd Org.) Co.D
Valentine, J.S. LA 19th Inf. Co.I 1st Sgt.
Valentine, J.S. LA Inf. Pelican Regt. Co.A 1st Sgt.
Valentine, J.S. TX 7th Inf. Co.F
Valentine, J.T. VA 3rd Inf.Loc.Def. Co.A
Valentine, J.W. KY 12th Cav. Co.B
Valentine, J.W. LA 19th Inf. Co.C
Valentine, L. LA 8th Cav. Co.D
Valentine, Lewis GA 49th Inf. Co.H
Valentine, L.W. SC 1st (Hagood's) Inf. 2nd Co.A
Valentine, M. LA Mil. Orleans Fire Regt. Co.H
Valentine, Mark LA 3rd (Harrison's) Cav. Co.E 2nd Lt.
Valentine, M.S., Jr. VA 1st St.Res. Co.I
Valentine, M.V.B. TN 46th Inf. Co.D 1st Lt.
Valentine, Nathaniel R. MS 17th Inf. Co.F
Valentine, Norman LA 27th Inf. Co.G
Valentine, P. TN 51st Inf. Co.D Cpl.
Valentine, P. TX 14th Field Btty.
Valentine, Paul MS 6th Cav. Co.I
Valentine, Paul TN 51st (Cons.) Inf. Co.F
Valentine, Peter AR 6th Inf. Music.
Valentine, Peter TN 4th Cav.
Valentine, Philo G. Gen. & Staff Asst.Surg.
Valentine, Raphael VA 33rd Inf. Co.C
Valentine, Reuben LA Conscr.
Valentine, R.F.J. VA 24th Cav. Co.B
Valentine, R.H. NC Lt.Arty. 13th Bn. Co.C
Valentine, Richard H. MS 7th Inf. Co.F
Valentine, Richard J. VA Lt.Arty. 13th Bn. Co.A
Valentine, Robert H.C. NC 2nd Bn.Loc.Def. Troops Co.E Cpl.
Valentine, Robert S. VA 46th Inf. 2nd Co.A
Valentine, S. SC Mil. 2nd Regt. Co.B
Valentine, Samuel VA Cav. 47th Bn. Co.A
Valentine, Samuel O. VA Inf. 25th Bn. Co.C
Valentine, Samuel T. VA 5th Inf. Co.E
Valentine, Samuel T. VA Prov.Guard Avis' Co.
Valentine, Silas M. MS 14th Inf. Co.G
Valentine, Starkey A. NC 17th Inf. (2nd Org.) Co.D
Valentine, Thomas TX 20th Cav. Co.K
Valentine, Thomas VA 12th Inf. Co.B
Valentine, Thomas E. VA 15th Inf. Co.A
Valentine, Thomas R. TN 46th Inf. Co.D Sgt.
Valentine, Tilman TX 15th Cav. Co.F
Valentine, T.S. TN 46th Inf. Co.D
Valentine, W. TX 4th Cav. Co.B
Valentine, Washington W. SC 1st (Hagood's) Inf. 1st Co.A
Valentine, W.B. MS Inf. 7th Bn. Co.F
Valentine, W.H. LA Mil. St.James Regt. Co.F
Valentine, W. Houston TN 5th Inf. 2nd Co.G
Valentine, William VA Inf. 5th Bn.Loc.Def. Co.B Sr.2nd Lt.
Valentine, William VA 46th Inf. Co.L
Valentine, William VA 59th Inf. 3rd Co.F Sgt.
Valentine, William VA 60th Inf. 1st Co.H
Valentine, William G. VA Lt.Arty. Parker's Co.
Valentine, William J. Conf.Cav. Wood's Regt. Co.E
Valentine, W.J. AL 57th Inf. Co.H
Valentine, W.L. MS 44th Inf. Co.B
Valentine, W.P. MS Inf. 7th Bn. Co.F
Valentine, W.P. NC 3rd Bn.Sr.Res. Williams' Co.
Valentine, W.W. SC 2nd Arty. Co.C Cpl.
Valentino, Gabriel GA 7th Inf. Co.B Cpl.
Valentino, Lewis GA 7th Inf. Co.K Music.
Valenza, Antonio LA Mil. 6th Regt.Eur.Brig. (Italian Guards Bn.) Co.4
Valenzano, Giuseppe LA Mil. 6th Regt.Eur.Brig. (Italian Guards Bn.) Co.1
Valenzia, Salvatore LA Mil. 6th Regt.Eur.Brig. (Italian Guards Bn.) Co.1
Valenzuela, Incarnacion TX 3rd Inf. Co.G
Valer, S.A. MS 35th Inf. Co.C
Valerian, Charles TX Cav. Ragsdale's Bn. Co.A
Valerien, Vallot LA Inf. 10th Bn. Co.C
Valery, B. LA 26th Inf. Co.G
Valery, John LA 28th (Gray's) Inf. Co.G
Valery, Lucien LA Inf.Cons.Crescent Regt. Co.N
Valery, Oscar LA Mil. 1st Native Guards
Vales, James GA 3rd Inf. Co.G
Vales, John M. LA 9th Inf. Co.H
Vales, W. Henry H. TN 11th Inf. Co.E
Valet, Desir LA Mil. 1st Native Guards
Valeton, Alcide LA 22nd Inf. Co.B
Valeton, Alcide LA 22nd (Cons.) Inf. Co.B
Valeton, O. LA Mil. Chalmette Regt. Co.G Capt.
Valeton, Oscar LA 22nd (Cons.) Inf. Co.E,B
Valevini, S. LA Mil. 3rd Regt. French Brig. Co.8
Valiade, William Conf.Reg.Inf. Brooks' Bn. Co.F
Valiant, R.J. AR 2nd Cav. Co.G
Valiant, Thomas R. MD 1st Inf. 2nd Co.H
Valiant, W.A. AR 2nd Cav. Co.G 2nd Lt.
Valiant, William TN 27th Inf. Co.C
Valient, William R. AR 24th Inf. Co.C
Valienti, Antonio LA Mil. Cazadores Espanoles Regt. Co.2
Valin, Ambroise LA 28th (Thomas') Inf. Co.K
Valincio, Florencio AZ Cav. Herbert's Bn. Oury's Co.
Valines, Adderson AR 7th Cav. Co.G
Valines, Joel AR 7th Cav. Co.G
Valines, Patrick H. VA 1st Arty. Co.E
Valines, Watson B. VA 41st Inf. Co.F
Valish, G. LA Mil. 3rd Regt.Eur.Brig. (Garde Francaise) Co.3
Valk, Charles VA 59th Inf. 3rd Co.F 1st Lt.
Valk, Jno. M.E. Gen. & Staff A.Brig.QM
Valker, Conrad KY 1st Inf. Music.
Valker, J. FL 7th Inf. Music.
Valker, John C. KY 6th Mtd.Inf. Co.G Music.
Valker, W. SC 2nd St.Troops Co.I
Vall, Frederick LA 1st Hvy.Arty. (Reg.) Co.F
Vall, W.W. GA 59th Inf. Co.C
Vallandigham, I.S. Conf.Arty. McIntosh's Bn. Asst.Surg.
Vallandigham, J.L. MD 1st Cav. Co.B
Vallandigham, J.L. MD Arty. 4th Btty.
Vallandigham, J.T. Gen. & Staff, A. of N.VA Asst.Surg.
Vallandigham, M.J. NC 46th Inf. Co.C
Vallandingham, A. AR Inf. McNair's Brig.
Vallandingham, George LA Arty. Barlow's Btty. 1st Lt.
Vallandingham, George MO 3rd Inf. Co.F
Vallandingham, George T. KY 5th Cav. Co.E Cpl.
Vallandingham, John LA Inf. 4th Bn. Co.A
Vallandingham, J.W. AL 15th Inf. Co.E
Vallandingham, Lawson VA 40th Inf. Co.G
Vallandingham, O.C. MS Cav. Powers' Regt. Co.B
Vallandingham, P. GA 12th Mil. Sgt.
Vallandingham, Pickard KY Cav. 1st Bn. Co.B
Vallandingham, Pickard KY 4th Cav. Co.B
Vallandingham, R.C. VA 37th Mil. 2nd Co.B
Vallandingham, Richard KY 5th Mtd.Inf. Co.E 3rd Lt.
Vallandingham, Richard MO 11th Inf. Co.H
Vallandingham, Richard L. MO 3rd Inf. Co.F Sgt.
Vallandingham, William NC Jones' Co. (Supp.Force)
Vallandingham, W.N. AR 36th Inf. Co.E Cpl.
Vallasana, Refugio TX 3rd Inf. Co.F Cpl.
Vallatte, C. LA Mil. 4th Regt. French Brig. Co.6
Valle, --- LA Mil. 1st Chasseurs a pied Co.1
Valle, Angelo LA Mil. 6th Regt.Eur.Brig. (Italian Guards Bn.) Co.3
Valle, Francis MO 7th Cav. Co.I 1st Lt.
Valle, Francis MO Inf. 5th Regt.St.Guard Co.C 2nd Lt.
Valle, Frank MO 8th Cav. Co.G Capt.
Valle, Geo. LA Mil. 5th Regt.Eur.Brig. (Spanish Regt.) Co.8
Valle, Girolamo LA Mil. 6th Regt.Eur.Brig. (Italian Guards Bn.) Co.3
Valle, Henry MO 12th Inf. Co.C Sgt.
Valle, Jerome C. MO Cav. 3rd Regt.St.Guard Co.A
Vallean, John R. GA 63rd Inf. Co.B
Vallean, J.R. GA Conscr.
Valleau, William N. GA 29th Inf. Hosp.Stew.
Valleau, W.N. GA Inf. 18th Bn. Co.B
Vallee, E.J. Trans-MS Conf.Cav. 1st Bn. Co.B

Vallely, Thomas VA Lt.Arty. King's Co.
Vallentine, Edward VA Burks' Regt.Loc.Def.
Vallentine, G.W. MO 7th Cav. Co.G
Vallentine, John C. MS St.Cav. Perrin's Bn. Co.F
Vallentine, John E. VA 1st St.Res. Co.D
Vallentine, J.W. KY 1st Inf. Co.A
Vallentine, Levi AL Cav. Lewis' Bn. Co.B
Valler, Charles LA 12th Inf. Co.H
Vallery, Casemire LA 1st Hvy.Arty. (Reg.) Co.D
Vallery, E. LA 26th Inf. Co.D
Vallery, Francois LA 1st Hvy.Arty. (Reg.) Co.D
Vallery, James LA 28th (Gray's) Inf. Co.G
Vallery, Joachin LA 1st Hvy.Arty. (Reg.) Co.D
Vallery, Valcour LA 28th (Gray's) Inf. Co.G
Vallet, Joseph MS 18th Inf. Co.E
Valleton, J.R. GA Pioneer Corps
Vallette, A.P. LA 30th Inf. Co.A Sgt.
Vallette, F., Jr. LA Arty. Watson Btty. Cpl.
Vallette, G.E. TN Inf. 1st Cons.Regt. Co.H Sgt.
Vallette, G. Edward TN 1st (Feild's) Inf. Co.A Sgt.
Vallette, O.F. LA 30th Inf. Co.A Capt.
Vallette, V. TN Inf. 1st Cons.Regt. Co.H
Vallette, Victor TN 1st (Feild's) Inf. Co.A
Valley, Henry MO 6th Cav. Co.G Cpl.
Valley, John FL 1st Cav. Co.D
Valley, John TN 10th Inf. Co.D
Valli, Silvester TX Cav. 3rd (Yager's) Bn. Rhodes' Co.
Valliant, Edwin S. MD Inf. 2nd Bn. Co.C
Valliant, F. MS 12th Cav. AQM
Valliant, F. MS 28th Cav. Co.D
Valliant, George E.W. MD 1st Inf. Co.E
Valliant, John D. MS 6th Cav. Co.C
Valliant, John D. MS 8th Cav. Co.G Sgt.
Valliant, John D. MS 17th Inf. Co.A
Valliant, J.T. AR 11th Inf. Co.E Hosp.Stew.
Valliant, J.T. AR 11th & 17th (Cons.) Inf. Co.E
Valliant, Leroy B. MS 22nd Inf. Co.I Capt.
Valliant, W.A. TX 5th Inf. Co.G
Valliant, William W. Gen. & Staff Capt.,AIG
Valliant, W.R. AR 11th Inf. Co.E
Vallie, C.C. MO Cav. 1st Bn.St.Guard Co.C 1st Lt.
Vallie, J. MO Inf. 1st Bn.St.Guard Co.C 2nd Lt.
Vallie, Joseph LA Mil. 5th Regt.Eur.Brig. (Spanish Regt.) Co.5
Vallingdingham, William C. TX Cav. 2nd Regt. St.Troops Co.E
Vallinger, Simon LA Mil. Mooney's Co. (Saddlers Guards)
Vallis, A.E. MO Cav. 1st Bn.St.Guard Co.C Capt.
Vallmont, D. LA Miles' Legion Co.E
Vallod, Eli AL 48th Mil. Co.D
Valloff, William A. LA Inf. 7th Bn. Co.A
Valloft, W.A. LA Mil. 3rd Regt. 2nd Brig. 1st Div. Co.A 1st Lt.
Vallon, --- LA Mil. 3rd Regt.Eur.Brig. (Garde Francaise) Co.5 Sgt.
Vallon, John Randolph TN 6th Inf. Co.H
Vallot, Treville LA Inf. 10th Bn. Co.C
Vallotton, J.R. GA Cav. Allen's Co.
Valloy, B. LA Mil. Chalmette Regt. Co.C
Valls, Andrew R. LA 7th Inf. Co.H
Valls, Bartolome LA Mil. 5th Regt.Eur.Brig. (Spanish Regt.) Co.2
Valls, G. LA Mil. 5th Regt.Eur.Brig. (Spanish Regt.) Co.1
Vallsen, W.N. GA Inf. 1st Conf.Bn. Hosp.Stew.
Valmour, --- LA Mil. 1st Native Guards
Valois, Numa LA Miles' Legion Co.B
Valois, V. LA Mil. 1st Chasseurs a pied
Valores, Joseph AL 95th Mil. Co.D
Valory, Bartolomi LA Mil. Chalmette Regt. Co.F
Valsin, Vincent LA Miles' Legion Co.F
Valverde, John TX 1st (Yager's) Cav. Co.E
Valverde, John TX Cav. 8th (Taylor's) Bn. Co.C
Valverde, William AL Cav. Murphy's Bn. Co.B
Valverde, William 15th Conf.Cav. Co.G
Valverthe, Francisco TX 2nd Cav. Co.K
Valyer, William SC 2nd Inf.
Vam, C.D. AL 2nd Cav. Co.H
Vam, J.E. GA 3rd Inf. Co.K
Vamadon, J. AL 16th Inf. Co.G
Vamble, F.A. TX Conscr.
Vampelt, David VA 3rd Bn. Valley Res. Co.B
Vampton, T.D. MO 8th Inf. 2nd Lt.
Vamster, Valentine LA 13th Inf. Co.D Sgt.
Van, Abraham VA 136th Mil. Co.D
Van, Edward VA Inf. 2nd Bn.Loc.Def. Co.B
Van, Eli VA 136th Mil. Co.F
Van, G.P. TN 7th Cav. Co.E
Van, Hector 4th Conf.Eng.Troops
Van, Jesse TN 17th Inf. Co.D
Van, Jesse TN 32nd Inf. Co.K
Van, J.S. TN 12th (Green's) Cav. Co.D
Van, L.E. AL 63rd Inf. Co.F
Van, Lewis MS Inf. 2nd St.Troops Co.F
Van, Lewis MS Inf. 7th Bn. Co.C
Van, N.P. AL 19th Inf. Co.C
Van, Sanders AL 33rd Inf. Co.E
Van, S.R. AL 4th Res. Co.H
Van, S.T. AR Cav. Gordon's Regt. Co.B
Van, William TX 9th Cav. Co.I
Van, William F. MS 29th Inf. Co.G
Van, W.W. TX 5th Cav. Co.I
Vanadore, David J. SC 20th Inf. Co.E
Vanaken, John E. VA 4th Inf. Co.B
Van Alamann, Joseph Conf.Lt.Arty. 1st Reg.Btty.
Van Allen, George W. TX 1st (Yager's) Cav. Co.A 1st Lt.
Van Allen, George W. TX Cav. 3rd (Yager's) Bn. Co.A
Van Alman, Fred Conf.Lt.Arty. 1st Reg.Btty.
Vanalstine, George TX 12th Cav. Co.K
Van Alstine, James H. AL Lt.Arty. Lee's Btty.
Van Alstine, James H. Conf.Lt.Arty. Stark's Bn. Co.A
Van Alstine, J.T. AR 2nd Inf. Co.I
Van Alstyne, Fred TX 13th Vol. 2nd Co.C
Vanalstyne, J. TX 4th Inf. (St.Troops) Co.D
Vanalstyne, W.A. TX Inf. 1st St.Troops Sheldon's Co.B
Van Amburg, Charles VA 23rd Cav. Co.M
Vanamheven, T. LA 18th Inf. Co.C
Van Ammige, Stacey NC Wallace's Co. (Wilmington RR Guard)
Van Amringe, C.S. NC 61st Inf. Co.G
Van Amringe, Stacey NC 61st Inf. Co.G Capt.
Vanandale, J. VA 2nd Inf. Co.D
Vanandell, Jeremiah VA 7th Cav. Co.K
Vanandngham, M. NC Wallace's Co. (Wilmington RR Guard)
Vanansdale, Ulysses MO 8th Cav. Co.C 2nd Lt.
Van Antwerp, G. Gen. & Staff Hosp.Stew.
Van Antwerp, George AL 21st Inf. Co.A
Vanarian, William LA 16th Inf. Co.E
Van Arsdale, Cornelius C. KY Cav. 2nd Bn. (Dortch's) Co.B
Vanarsdale, Isaac M. KY 2nd Cav. Co.F
Vanarsdale, J. VA 67th Mil. Co.A
Vanarsdale, John KY 6th Cav. Co.D
Vanarsdale, Lucas MS Nash's Co. (Leake Rangers)
Vanarsdale, Robert W. KY 6th Cav. Co.B
Vanarsdale, R.V. TX 13th Vol. 2nd Co.B
Vanarsdale, William KY 6th Cav. Co.G
Vanarsdall, J.K. TX 5th Cav. Co.A
Vanarsdell, J.M. KY Morgan's Men Co.E
Vanarsdell, Milton KY 9th Cav. Co.F 1st Sgt.
Vanarsdell, R.C. MS 6th Inf. Co.C Sgt.
Vanartsdalen, George SC Arty. Bachman's Co. (German Lt.Arty.) Cpl.
Van Artsdalen, G.W. SC Arty.Bn. Hampton Legion Co.B Cpl.
Vanasseur, D.F. LA Arty. 5th Field Btty. (Pelican Lt.Arty.)
Vanatta, James TN 7th Inf. Co.A Sgt.
Vanatta, McAdoo TN 2nd (Smith's) Cav.
Vanatta, William S. AR 21st Inf. Co.A Sr.2nd Lt.
Vanatter, J. VA 1st Inf. Co.D
Vanatter, James VA Inf. 45th Bn. Co.E
Vanatter, Jefferson VA 36th Inf. Co.D
Vanatter, John VA Inf. 45th Bn. Co.E
Vanausdal, Thomas MO Inf. Perkins' Bn. Co.A
Vanawlman, Fred AR Mil. Desha Cty.Bn.
Van Badenhausen, Chs. Gen. & Staff, Inf. 1st Lt.,MSK
Vanbeck, A.H. LA 15th Inf. Co.E
Van Benthuysen, A.C. Gen. & Staff
Van Benthuysen, F. LA Mil.Conf.Guards Regt. Co.E
Van Benthuysen, G.E. TX 1st Hvy.Arty. Co.B Cpl.
Van Benthuysen, Jeff D. LA Inf. 1st Sp.Bn. (Rightor's) Co.B Cpl.
Van Benthuysen, Jefferson D. LA 6th Inf. Co.G Capt.
Van Benthuysen, W. LA Mil. 2nd Regt. 3rd Brig. 1st Div. Maj.
Van Benthuysen, W. Gen. & Staff Capt.,AQM
Van Bergen, V. TX 5th Inf. Co.A
Vanbeuren, William H. VA 59th Inf. 2nd Co.B
Van Bibber, Andrew D. VA 22nd Inf. Co.D
Van Bibber, F.J. LA Lt.Arty. 3rd Btty. (Benton's)
Van Bibber, F.J. LA Mil.Conf.Guards Regt. Co.G
Vanbibber, Jacob TX 27th Cav. Co.C
Van Bibber, James M.R. VA 22nd Inf. Co.D Sgt.
Van Bibber, John C. VA 22nd Inf. Co.D
Van Bibber, Nathaniel B. VA 22nd Inf. Co.D
Vanbibber, S. MO St.Guard
Van Bibber, Samuel LA 27th Inf. Co.I
Vanbibber, Samuel C. MO 1st Cav. Co.K
Van Biber, Samuel MO 4th Inf. Co.C

Vanbiber, Sandy TX 15th Cav. Co.H
Van Biel, Nathaniel GA 1st (Symons') Res. Co.K
Van Blarcore, Isaac Conf.Inf. Tucker's Regt. Co.D
Vanbokelee, H.H. NC 7th Sr.Res. Johnston's Co.
Van Bokkelen, John F.S. NC 3rd Inf. Co.D Capt.
Vanboskirk, Richard AR 15th (Josey's) Inf. Co.A
Vanbrackle, H.D. GA 7th Cav. Co.K
Vanbrackle, H.D. GA Hardwick Mtd.Rifles Co.A
Vanbrackle, Henry D. GA 25th Inf. Co.B Sgt.
Vanbrackle, J.E. GA 7th Cav. Co.K 3rd Lt.
Vanbrackle, J.E. GA Hardwick Mtd.Rifles Co.A Sgt.
Vanbrackle, J.E. GA 25th Inf. Co.B
Van Bremer, Sam TX 8th Inf. Co.A
Van Bremer, Samuel TX 6th Inf. Co.D
Van Bruner, J. Gen. & Staff 1st Lt.,Ord.Off.
Van Brunt, F. GA Cav. 20th Bn. Co.A,F
Van Brunt, James C. FL Kilcrease Lt.Arty.
Vanbrunt, J.C. FL Lt.Arty. Dyke's Co.
Vanbrunt, Richard FL 1st Mil.
Vanbrunt, T.S. GA 13th Cav.
Vanburan, David VA 108th Mil. Co.F
Vanburan, George TX 12th Cav. Co.H
Van Buren, B.B. VA Inf. 5th Bn.Loc.Def. Co.E 2nd Lt.
Van Buree, Benjamin B. VA 21st Inf. Co.F
Van Buren, David VA Inf. 26th Bn. Co.F,H
Van Buren, D.H. GA Inf. 18th Bn. (St.Guards) Adam's Co.
Van Buren, D. Halsey GA Inf. 1st Loc.Troops (Augusta) Co.K
Van Buren, George KY 2nd Mtd.Inf. Co.H
Van Buren, H. TX Lt.Arty. H. Van Buren's Co. Lt.
Van Buren, Hamlet TN 27th Inf. Co.I
Vanburen, J.M. VA 2nd St.Res. Co.G Sgt.
Van Buren, John H. VA Inf. 26th Bn. Co.H
Van Buren, William H. VA Inf. 26th Bn. Co.G
Van Buskirk, Clinton P. VA 13th Inf. Co.H Music.
Vanbussum, Philip KY 4th Mtd.Inf. Co.C 1st Sgt.
Van Bussum, Philip VA Cav. 35th Bn. Co.B
Vanc, I.S. KY 13th Cav. Co.D
Vancamblin, Eug. LA Mil. 4th Regt. 1st Brig. 1st Div. Co.D
Van Camp, Daniel H. TN 10th Inf. Co.D Cpl.
Van Camp, Eugene B. VA 6th Cav. Co.F Sgt.
Vancamp, H. MO 9th (Elliott's) Cav. Co.E
Vancannon, John W. NC 51st Inf. Co.A
Vance, A. MS 1st Cav.Res. Co.D
Vance, A. MS 9th Cav. Co.A
Vance, A. TN Cav. 17th Bn. (Sanders') Co.A
Vance, A.A. VA Inf. 45th Bn. Co.E
Vance, A.B. MS 3rd Cav. Co.K
Vance, A.B. MS 8th Cav. Co.B
Vance, A.B. MS McCord's Co. (Slate Springs Co.)
Vance, Abner VA 22nd Cav. Co.I
Vance, Abner VA 129th Mil. Carter's Co.
Vance, A.C. MS 22nd Inf. Co.K
Vance, Adam VA Arty. Bryan's Co.
Vance, Adam VA Inf. 26th Bn. Co.C
Vance, Adam VA 59th Inf. 1st Co.B
Vance, Adam VA 60th Inf. Co.A
Vance, Adam 3rd Conf.Eng.Troops Co.E Artif.
Vance, Adam J. VA 135th Mil. Co.D
Vance, Addison VA Cav. 34th Bn. Co.D
Vance, Adison VA 129th Mil. Carter's Co.
Vance, A.H. KY 10th (Diamond's) Cav. Co.I
Vance, A.J. MS 38th Cav. Co.D
Vance, A.J. VA 10th Inf. Co.D
Vance, A.J. VA 129th Mil. Carter's Co.
Vance, Alex MS 2nd Cav. Co.B
Vance, Alexander VA 22nd Cav. Co.G
Vance, Alexander VA Cav. 34th Bn. Co.C
Vance, Alexander VA Inf. 21st Bn. 2nd Co.F
Vance, Alexander VA 33rd Inf. Co.B
Vance, Alexander VA 51st Inf. Co.A Sgt.
Vance, Anderson H. AR 38th Inf. Co.F
Vance, Andrew TN 14th Inf. Co.I
Vance, Archibald C. TN 2nd (Robison's) Inf. Co.H
Vance, Archibald H. VA 10th Inf. Co.D
Vance, Augustus C. VA 108th Mil. Co.F, Lemons' Co.
Vance, Barnabas H. MS 43rd Inf. Co.D
Vance, B.B. TN 7th Inf.
Vance, Benjamin F. AL Eufaula Lt.Arty. Cpl.
Vance, Benjamin L. KY 1st (Butler's) Cav. Co.B
Vance, Buren NC 6th Inf. Co.H
Vance, C. TX Cav. Morgan's Regt. Co.E
Vance, Caleb F. FL 7th Inf. Co.I
Vance, Calvin W. SC 2nd Inf. Co.F
Vance, Caperton VA Lt.Arty. G.B. Chapman's Co.
Vance, C.B. MS Lt.Arty. 14th Bn. Co.A Capt.
Vance, C.E. FL 9th Inf. Co.F
Vance, Charles FL 9th Inf. Co.F
Vance, Charles VA 14th Cav. Co.D
Vance, Charles VA Inf. 45th Bn. Co.E 1st Sgt.
Vance, Charles VA 129th Mil. Buchanon's Co.
Vance, Charles R. TN 19th Inf. Co.K
Vance, Charles R. TN Conscr. (Cp. of Instr.)
Vance, Charles S. VA 25th Inf. 1st Co.G
Vance, C.H.R. LA 17th Inf. Co.A
Vance, Christopher R. MO 3rd Inf. Co.B
Vance, C.L. MS 24th Inf. Co.H,I
Vance, C.V. VA 60th Inf. Co.A
Vance, Cyrus VA Vol. Vance's Co. Capt.
Vance, Daniel GA Inf. 1st City Bn. (Columbus) Co.C
Vance, Daniel TN 18th Inf. Co.A
Vance, Daniel A. VA Lt.Arty. G.B. Chapman's Co.
Vance, Daniel A. VA 108th Mil. Co.A
Vance, Daniel W. FL 7th Inf. Co.I
Vance, David LA Inf. 1st Sp.Bn. (Wheat's) New Co.D
Vance, David TN 1st (Carter's) Cav. Co.K
Vance, David TN 39th Mtd.Inf. Co.E Cpl.
Vance, David TN 63rd Inf. Co.B
Vance, David TX 20th Inf. Co.G
Vance, David D. VA 29th Inf. 1st Co.F
Vance, David D. VA 64th Mtd.Inf. Co.H
Vance, David E. MO 1st N.E. Cav.
Vance, David F. TX 36th Cav. Co.E QMSgt.
Vance, David M. VA 51st Inf. Co.A Cpl.
Vance, Davidson TX 16th Inf. Co.C
Vance, D.B. TN 4th (McLemore's) Cav. Co.B
Vance, D.B. TN 18th Inf. Co.A
Vance, D.F. TN 13th (Gore's) Cav. Co.B
Vance, D.J. MS 8th Inf. Co.B
Vance, D.L. AR 1st (Monroe's) Cav. Co.G 1st Lt.
Vance, D.S. AR Mtd.Vol. Hooker's Co.
Vance, D.S. AR 32nd Inf. Co.C
Vance, D.W. TX 26th Cav. Co.H
Vance, D.W. TX 2nd Inf. Co.D
Vance, E.D. AL Inf. 2nd Regt. Co.B
Vance, Edward MS 41st Inf. Co.C
Vance, Edward E. KY 3rd Cav. Co.D
Vance, Eli TN 39th Mtd.Inf. Co.E,H Sgt.
Vance, Eli VA 1st Cav.St.Line Co.A
Vance, Eli D. AL 40th Inf. Co.B 2nd Lt.
Vance, Elihu LA 28th (Gray's) Inf. Co.G
Vance, Elihu VA Cav. 46th Bn. Co.A
Vance, Elijah KY 10th (Diamond's) Cav. Co.I
Vance, Elijah VA Cav. 34th Bn. Co.C
Vance, Elijah VA Inf. 21st Bn. 2nd Co.F
Vance, Emmett B. VA 50th Inf. 1st Co.G
Vance, Emmett B. VA 63rd Inf. 1st Co.I, Co.E Ens.
Vance, Finis C. TX 19th Cav. Co.G
Vance, Fleming NC 58th Inf. Co.A
Vance, Francis VA Cav. 34th Bn. Co.D
Vance, Francis M. AL 20th Inf. Co.B Adj.
Vance, Frank FL Inf. 2nd Bn. Co.E
Vance, G. MS 1st Cav.Res. Co.C
Vance, Gains B. AR 14th (McCarver's) Inf. Co.F
Vance, Gaston NC 6th Inf. Co.E
Vance, G.B. AR 21st Inf. Co.B
Vance, George KY Cav. 2nd Bn. (Dortch's) Co.B
Vance, George KY 3rd Cav. Co.K
Vance, George MS 31st Inf. Co.C
Vance, George MS McCord's Co. (Slate Springs Co.)
Vance, George SC 7th Inf. 1st Co.I, 2nd Co.I
Vance, George VA 10th Bn.Res. Co.D
Vance, George 1st Chickasaw Inf. Hansell's Co. Sgt.
Vance, George Conf.Reg.Inf. Brooks' Bn. Co.B
Vance, George W. AR 14th (McCarver's) Inf. Co.F
Vance, George W. GA Lt.Arty. 12th Bn. 2nd Co.A
Vance, George W. MS 30th Inf. Co.H
Vance, George W. VA 63rd Inf. Co.A
Vance, G.M. MS 3rd Cav. Co.K
Vance, G. McD. AR 1st Mtd.Rifles Co.B
Vance, G.W. AR 5th Inf. Co.D Cpl.
Vance, G.W. KY 6th Cav. Co.I
Vance, G.W. KY 7th Cav. Co.C Sgt.
Vance, G.W. KY Morgan's Men Beck's Co.
Vance, G.W. MS Cav. 4th Bn. Co.A
Vance, G.W. SC Palmetto S.S. Co.F
Vance, G.W. 8th (Wade's) Conf.Cav. Co.C
Vance, H.A. MS 46th Inf. Co.K
Vance, Harvey VA 22nd Cav. Co.D
Vance, Henry LA 28th (Gray's) Inf. Co.G
Vance, Henry LA 31st Inf. Co.G
Vance, Henry NC 4th Inf.
Vance, Henry NC 10th Regt.
Vance, Henry VA 19th Cav. Co.G
Vance, Henry VA Cav. 41st Bn. 2nd Co.H
Vance, Henry VA 33rd Inf. Co.D

Vance, Henry P. VA Hvy.Arty. 10th Bn. Co.A
Vance, Henry R. VA Lt.Arty. G.B. Chapman's Co.
Vance, Henry R. VA 108th Mil. Co.B, Lemons' Co.
Vance, Henry W. VA 108th Mil. Co.B
Vance, H.H. VA 51st Inf. Co.A Sgt.
Vance, H.J. TN 3rd (Forrest's) Cav. 1st Co.E
Vance, H.M.N. LA Hvy.Arty. 2nd Bn. Co.D
Vance, Hua TN 63rd Inf. Co.G
Vance, H.W. VA Inf. 26th Bn. Co.D
Vance, Isaac TN Detailed Conscr. Co.A
Vance, Isham W. TN 18th Inf. Co.A
Vance, J. KY Morgan's Men Co.E
Vance, J. TX 2nd Cav. Co.G
Vance, J.A. TX Cav. Hardeman's Regt. Co.H
Vance, Jack VA Cav. 41st Bn. 2nd Co.H
Vance, Jackson AL Inf. 1st Regt. Co.G
Vance, Jackson VA Cav. 34th Bn. Co.D
Vance, Jackson VA 33rd Inf. Co.D
Vance, Jacob R. VA Lt.Arty. G.B. Chapman's Co.
Vance, Jacob R. VA 108th Mil. Co.D, McNeer's Co.
Vance, J.A.J. MS 7th Cav. Co.G
Vance, James GA 61st Inf. Co.I
Vance, James KY 4th Cav. Co.D
Vance, James MS 2nd Cav. Co.B
Vance, James MS 3rd Inf. (St.Troops) Co.E
Vance, James TN 2nd (Smith's) Cav.
Vance, James TN 8th (Smith's) Cav. Co.E
Vance, James VA 14th Cav. Co.D
Vance, James VA Cav. 34th Bn. Co.B Sgt.
Vance, James VA 6th Bn.Res. Co.E
Vance, James, Jr. VA 37th Inf. Co.K Capt.
Vance, James Gen. & Staff 1st Lt.,Adj.
Vance, James A. MS 43rd Inf. Co.D
Vance, James B. TN Cav. 7th Bn. (Bennett's) Co.F Sgt.
Vance, James G. TX 6th Cav. Co.A 2nd Lt.
Vance, James G. TX Cav. (Dismtd.) Chisum's Regt. Maj.
Vance, James H. GA 21st Inf. Co.F
Vance, James H. KY 10th (Diamond's) Cav. Co.I
Vance, James H. MS 29th Inf. Co.F
Vance, James H. NC 64th Inf. Co.N
Vance, James H. TN 4th (McLemore's) Cav. Co.B
Vance, James H. TN Cav. 16th Bn. (Neal's) Co.G Lt.
Vance, James H. VA 7th Cav. Co.F
Vance, James H. VA 22nd Cav. Co.I Sgt.
Vance, James H. VA 63rd Inf. Co.A
Vance, James K. MS 15th Inf. Co.E,B
Vance, James K. TN Res.
Vance, James M. MS 2nd Part.Rangers Co.H
Vance, James M. MS 2nd Inf. (A. of 10,000) Co.H
Vance, James M. MS 30th Inf. Co.H
Vance, James M. TN Cav. 7th Bn. (Bennett's) Co.D,F
Vance, James M. TN 22nd (Barteau's) Cav. Co.F
Vance, James M. TN 3rd (Clack's) Inf. Co.A Sgt.
Vance, James R. VA 20th Cav. Co.A
Vance, James W. VA 25th Inf. 1st Co.G
Vance, J.B. KY 6th Mtd.Inf. Co.C
Vance, J.B. MS 2nd Cav. Co.E Capt.
Vance, J.B. TN 22nd (Barteau's) Cav. Co.G
Vance, J.B. TX 17th Inf. Co.C
Vance, J.C. GA 2nd Res. Co.G
Vance, J.C. MS Lt.Arty. 14th Bn. Co.A Sgt.
Vance, J.C. MS Lt.Arty. Yates' Btty. Sgt.
Vance, J.C. MS 9th Inf. Old Co.H
Vance, J.C. NC 1st Cav. (9th St.Troops) Co.C
Vance, J.D. MS Lt.Arty. 14th Bn. Co.A Capt.
Vance, J.D. MS 9th Inf. Old Co.H 2nd Lt.
Vance, J.D. TN 21st & 22nd (Cons.) Cav. Co.B,K
Vance, J.E. TN 9th (Ward's) Cav. Co.F,A
Vance, Jefferson W. VA 33rd Inf. Co.B
Vance, Jesse B. MS 31st Inf. Co.C
Vance, J.H. GA Inf. 25th Bn. (Prov.Guard) Co.B
Vance, J.H. LA 6th Cav. Co.H
Vance, J.H. TN Cav. 16th Bn. (Neal's) Co.E
Vance, J.J. TX 26th Cav. Co.H
Vance, J.K. SC 1st St.Troops Co.F
Vance, J.K. Gen. & Staff AQM
Vance, J.L. AL Cav. Hardie's Bn.Res. Co.C
Vance, J.L.C. 2nd Conf.Eng.Troops Co.B Cpl.
Vance, J.M. AL 8th (Livingston's) Cav. Co.A,F Cpl.
Vance, J.M. MS 7th Cav. Co.G
Vance, J.M. TN 22nd (Barteau's) Cav. Co.G
Vance, J.M. TX 32nd Cav. Co.B
Vance, J.N. MS 4th Inf. Co.F,H
Vance, J.N. MS 30th Inf. Co.D
Vance, John GA 63rd Inf. Co.B,D
Vance, John MS Cav. 2nd Bn.Res. Co.F
Vance, John MS 14th Inf. Co.H
Vance, John NC 5th Inf. Co.D
Vance, John NC 28th Inf. Co.G
Vance, John NC 58th Inf. Co.A
Vance, John TN 43rd Inf. Co.H
Vance, John VA Cav. Swann's Bn. Vincent's Co.
Vance, John VA Lt.Arty. G.B. Chapman's Co.
Vance, John VA 18th Inf. Co.G
Vance, John VA 51st Inf. Co.A
Vance, John VA 63rd Inf. Co.A
Vance, John VA 129th Mil. Buchanon's Co. Cpl.
Vance, John Conf.Reg.Inf. Brooks' Bn. Co.F
Vance, John A. TN 32nd Inf. Co.E Cpl.
Vance, John A. VA 46th Mil. Co.B
Vance, John A. VA 48th Inf. Co.I 1st Sgt.
Vance, John B. MS 2nd Inf. Co.H 2nd Lt.
Vance, John B. MS 2nd (Davidson's) Inf. Co.E 1st Lt.
Vance, John B. TN 16th Inf. Co.F Capt.
Vance, John C. SC 2nd Inf. Co.F
Vance, John C.K. AL 13th Inf. Co.K
Vance, John C.K. AL 19th Inf. Co.I
Vance, John C.K. 1st Conf.Inf. 2nd Co.C
Vance, John D. MS 30th Inf. Co.H
Vance, John D. TN Cav. 7th Bn. (Bennett's) Co.F
Vance, John D. TN 22nd (Barteau's) Cav. Co.G
Vance, John D. VA Lt.Arty. G.B. Chapman's Co.
Vance, John D. VA 108th Mil. Co.B
Vance, John E. KY 3rd Cav. Co.D
Vance, John Edward KY 7th Cav. Co.D
Vance, John F. AR 11th & 17th (Cons.) Inf. Co.B
Vance, John F. MS 4th Cav. Co.E
Vance, John G. VA Inf. 21st Bn. 2nd Co.F
Vance, John H. KY 12th Cav.
Vance, John H. TN 18th Inf. Co.A
Vance, John J. NC 58th Inf. Co.E
Vance, John L. AR 14th (McCarver's) Inf. Co.F
Vance, John L. AR 21st Inf. Co.B
Vance, John L. GA Arty. 11th Bn. (Sumter Arty.) New Co.C
Vance, John L. GA 9th Inf. Co.A
Vance, John M. AL Lt.Arty. 2nd Bn.
Vance, John M. TN Cav. 16th Bn. (Neal's) Fitzgerald's Co. 1st Lt.
Vance, John W. KY Mail Carrier
Vance, John W. MS Lt.Arty. Stanford's Co.
Vance, John W. MS 24th Inf. Co.A Cpl.
Vance, John W. MS 29th Inf. Co.I
Vance, John W. NC 58th Inf. Co.A
Vance, John W. NC 64th Inf. Co.N 1st Lt.
Vance, John W. TX Cav. Morgan's Regt. Co.E
Vance, John W. VA 108th Mil. Co.F
Vance, Joseph MS McCord's Co. (Slate Springs Co.)
Vance, Joseph VA 36th Inf.
Vance, Joseph VA Inf. 45th Bn. Co.E
Vance, Joseph VA 129th Mil. Buchanon's Co. Cpl.
Vance, Joseph J. AL 19th Inf. Co.I
Vance, Joseph W. KY 3rd Cav. Co.D
Vance, Joseph W. KY 7th Cav. Co.D
Vance, Joshua T. MS 30th Inf. Co.D
Vance, Josiah G. NC 56th Inf. Co.G
Vance, J.P. KY 3rd Mtd.Inf. Co.H
Vance, J.P. LA 8th Cav. Co.H
Vance, J.P. LA 28th (Gray's) Inf. Co.B
Vance, J.P. TN 63rd Inf. Co.E
Vance, J.S. KY 3rd Bn.Mtd.Rifles Co.B
Vance, J.T. TX 6th Cav. Co.B,A
Vance, J.W. AL 19th Inf. Co.C
Vance, J.W. GA 43rd Inf. Co.E
Vance, J.W. MS 3rd Cav.
Vance, J.W. MS Inf. 2nd St.Troops Co.H
Vance, J.W. SC Bn.St.Cadets Co.B
Vance, Kinson M. MS 6th Inf. Co.G
Vance, L. TN 12th (Green's) Cav. Co.A
Vance, Lawson W. VA 64th Mtd.Inf. Co.H
Vance, Levi VA Inf. 45th Bn. Co.E
Vance, Levi VA 46th Mil. Co.B
Vance, Levi VA 129th Mil. Buchanon's Co.
Vance, Lewis NC 58th Inf. Co.A
Vance, Lewis VA Cav. 34th Bn. Co.D
Vance, Lewis VA 129th Mil. Carter's Co.
Vance, L.H. GA Inf. 27th Bn. (NonConscr.) Co.A
Vance, L.H. GA 37th Inf. Co.B
Vance, L.H. GA 54th Inf. Co.E
Vance, L.H. GA Inf. (NonConscr.) Howard's Co.
Vance, L.S. NC 26th Inf. Co.F
Vance, Marion MO Cav. Freeman's Regt. Co.D
Vance, Martin V. AR 14th (McCarver's) Inf. Co.F
Vance, Martin V. AR 21st Inf. Co.B
Vance, Marvel VA 36th Inf. 2nd Co.D
Vance, M.D. AR 11th Inf. Co.A Lt.Col.

Vance, Meekin VA Cav. 34th Bn. Co.D
Vance, M.J. AR 47th (Crandall's) Cav. Co.D
Vance, M.J. AR 32nd Inf. Co.G
Vance, M.M. MS 3rd Inf. (St.Troops) Co.E
Vance, M.V. MO Cav. Fristoe's Regt. Co.I
Vance, Newton TN 13th (Gore's) Cav. Co.E Cpl.
Vance, Peter KY 4th Cav. Co.D
Vance, Phillip M. AL 11th Inf. Co.F 1st Lt.
Vance, Quill KY 1st (Butler's) Cav.
Vance, R.B. VA 36th Inf. Co.D
Vance, R.E. MS 3rd Inf. (St.Troops) Co.E
Vance, Reuben VA 46th Mil. Co.B
Vance, Reuben M. AL Inf. 1st Regt. Co.G
Vance, R.H. MS 24th Inf. Co.A 1st Lt.
Vance, Richard NC 7th Inf. Co.D
Vance, Richard TX 13th Cav. Co.A
Vance, Richard VA Cav. 34th Bn. Co.D
Vance, Richard VA 188th Mil.
Vance, Richard VA 5th Cav.Arty. & Inf.St.Line Co.I
Vance, Richard 1st Cherokee Mtd.Vol. 2nd Co.D Cpl.
Vance, Richard 2nd Cherokee Mtd.Vol. Co.D
Vance, Richard B. TN 18th Inf. Co.A
Vance, Rienzi H. MS 29th Inf. Co.I Sgt.
Vance, R.M. MS 3rd Cav. Co.K
Vance, R.M. MS 3rd Inf. (St.Troops) Co.E
Vance, R.M. MS McCord's Co. (Slate Springs Co.)
Vance, R.M. SC 3rd Inf. Co.F
Vance, R.M. SC 14th Inf. Co.F
Vance, Robert AR 1st (Crawford's) Cav. Co.B
Vance, Robert LA 9th Inf. Co.H
Vance, Robert MS 5th Inf. (St.Troops) Co.C
Vance, Robert MS 46th Inf. Co.I
Vance, Robert MO 9th Bn.S.S. Co.A Sgt.
Vance, Robert B. NC 29th Inf. Col.
Vance, Robert B. NC Western Dist. Brig.Gen.
Vance, S. LA 6th Cav. Co.H
Vance, S. TX 26th Cav. Co.H
Vance, Samuel FL 9th Inf. Co.F
Vance, Samuel MS 10th Inf. Old Co.H
Vance, Samuel MO 1st Cav. Co.D
Vance, Samuel TN 1st (Carter's) Cav. Co.F
Vance, Samuel TN 2nd (Walker's) Inf. Co.F Capt.
Vance, Samuel VA 33rd Inf. Co.E
Vance, Samuel C. NC 6th Inf. Co.E 3rd Lt.
Vance, Samuel E. TN 19th Inf. Co.C
Vance, Samuel G. SC 16th Inf. Co.E
Vance, Samuel G. MS 13th Inf. Co.G
Vance, Samuel G. VA 10th Inf. 1st Co.C, Co.F
Vance, Samuel J. FL 7th Inf. Co.I
Vance, Samuel L. AR 14th (McCarver's) Inf. Co.F
Vance, Samuel L. AR 21st Inf. Co.B
Vance, Samuel P. MS 31st Inf. Co.C
Vance, Samuel W. AL 11th Inf. Co.G Sgt.
Vance, S.E., Sr. AR 32nd Inf. Co.C
Vance, S.F. SC 3rd Inf. Co.A,I
Vance, S.G. MS Lt.Arty. Turner's Co.
Vance, S.G. SC 16th & 24th (Cons.) Inf. Co.F
Vance, Silas 3rd Conf.Cav. Co.D
Vance, S.L. MO Cav. Freeman's Regt. Co.D Sgt.
Vance, S.L. TN 29th Inf. Co.I
Vance, S.N. TN 2nd (Ashby's) Cav. Co.E
Vance, Solomon MO 7th Cav. Co.C
Vance, Solomon TN 63rd Inf. Co.E
Vance, T. TN Cav. 17th Bn. (Sanders') Co.A
Vance, Thomas MS 2nd Part.Rangers Co.A
Vance, Thomas MS Mtd.Inf. (St.Troops) Maxey's Co.
Vance, Thomas MS 1st (King's) Inf. (St.Troops) Co.G
Vance, Thomas MS 46th Inf. Co.I Cpl.
Vance, Thomas TN 2nd (Smith's) Cav.
Vance, Thomas TN 8th (Smith's) Cav. Co.E
Vance, Thomas TX 6th Cav. Co.B
Vance, Thomas VA 6th Bn.Res. Co.E
Vance, Thomas D. NC 58th Inf. Co.A
Vance, Thomas J. AL Inf. 1st Regt. Co.G
Vance, Thomas J. LA 1st (Nelligan's) Inf. Co.A
Vance, Thomas J. TN 4th (McLemore's) Cav. Co.B
Vance, Thomas J. VA 12th Inf. Asst.Surg.
Vance, Thomas J. VA 16th Inf. Asst.Surg.
Vance, Thos. J. Gen. & Staff Asst.Surg.
Vance, Thomas R. TX 6th Cav. Co.A
Vance, Tillman NC 6th Inf. Co.E
Vance, T.J. AL 31st Inf. Co.H
Vance, T.J. AL 57th Inf. Co.A
Vance, T.J. LA 28th (Gray's) Inf. Co.A
Vance, T.J. MS 4th Inf. Co.E
Vance, T.J. MS 5th Inf. (St.Troops) Co.A
Vance, T.M. TN 8th (Smith's) Cav. Co.E
Vance, W., Jr. VA Cav. Swann's Bn. Carpenter's Co.
Vance, W., Sr. VA Cav. Swann's Bn. Carpenter's Co.
Vance, W.A. SC 3rd Inf. Co.F Sgt.
Vance, W.A. TN 26th Inf. Co.B,H
Vance, Walter J. AR 3rd Cav. Co.I 3rd Lt.
Vance, Warren AL 15th Inf. Co.E
Vance, Wayne AL 15th Inf. Co.E
Vance, W.C. MS Cav. 3rd Bn.Res. Co.A
Vance, W.C. TN 22nd (Barteau's) Cav. Co.G
Vance, W.C. Gen. & Staff Orderly Sgt.
Vance, W.D. LA Inf.Crescent Regt. Co.B
Vance, W.D. SC 16th Inf. Co.E 1st Lt.
Vance, William AL 41st Inf. Co.F
Vance, William AR 1st Mtd.Rifles Co.I
Vance, William AR 1st Vol. Co.B
Vance, William GA 21st Inf. Co.F
Vance, William KY 10th (Diamond's) Cav. Co.G
Vance, William MS 31st Inf. Co.C
Vance, William NC 58th Inf. Co.A
Vance, William TN 12th (Cons.) Inf. Co.A
Vance, William TN 61st Mtd.Inf. Co.I
Vance, William TN 63rd Inf. Co.E
Vance, William VA Lt.Arty. G.B. Chapman's Co.
Vance, William VA 27th Inf. Co.A
Vance, William VA 36th Inf. 2nd Co.B
Vance, William, Jr. VA 162nd Mil. Co.A
Vance, William VA 166th Mil. R.G. Lively's Co.
Vance, William A. NC 58th Inf. Co.A 3rd Lt.
Vance, William C. AR 9th Inf. Co.E Cpl.
Vance, William C. MS 15th Inf. Co.E
Vance, William C. SC 2nd Inf. Co.F,D Capt.
Vance, William C. TN Cav. 7th Bn. (Bennett's) Co.F 1st Sgt.
Vance, William D. SC 1st Inf. Co.L
Vance, William D. TX 2nd Cav. Co.H,C Cpl.
Vance, William D. TX Cav. (Dismtd.) Chisum's Regt. Co.D Jr.2nd Lt.
Vance, William H. KY 10th (Diamond's) Cav. Co.I
Vance, William H. KY 5th Mtd.Inf. Co.C
Vance, William H. NC 56th Inf. Co.K
Vance, William H. TN 18th Inf. Co.A
Vance, William H. TX 36th Cav. Co.E Cpl.
Vance, William H. VA Inf. 21st Bn. 2nd Co.F
Vance, William H. VA 31st Inf. 2nd Co.B
Vance, William J.C. TX 17th Cav. Co.C Cpl.
Vance, William L. TX 17th Cav. Co.E 2nd Lt.
Vance, William P. NC 25th Inf. Co.F
Vance, William V. AL 40th Inf. Co.B
Vance, Wistley P. TN 4th (McLemore's) Cav. Co.K
Vance, W.O. MO 12th Inf. Co.F
Vance, W.R. KY 12th Cav. Co.A
Vance, W.T. KY 7th Mtd.Inf. Co.G
Vance, W.T. MS 8th Inf. Co.B
Vance, Zebulon B. NC 26th Inf. Col.
Vance, Zebulon Baird NC 14th Inf. Co.F Capt.
Vancell, --- MO Beck's Co. Sgt.
Vancell, Benjamin MO Cav. Snider's Bn. Co.D
Vancetavern, A.P. VA 108th Mil. Lemons' Co.
Vancetavern, Hudson VA 108th Mil. Co.F, Lemons' Co.
Vancetavern, William C. VA 108th Mil. Co.F
Vancey, James VA Cav. 34th Bn. Co.C
Vanciel, T.B. MO 2nd Inf. Co.B
Vancil, Alfred AR 25th Inf. Co.G
Vancil, Anderson VA 4th Res. Co.H
Vancil, James AR 13th Inf. Co.F
Vancil, James TX 9th Cav. Co.G 1st Sgt.
Vancil, James 2nd Conf.Eng.Troops Sgt.
Vancil, T.B. MO 2nd Inf. Co.B
Vancil, T.J. TX 9th Cav. Co.G
Vancil, William VA 54th Inf. Co.A
Van Clay, M. Cherokee Regt. Miller's Co. Cpl.
Vanclean, G.M. MO 3rd Cav. Co.I
Vancleave, Courteous TX 2nd Cav. Co.I
Vancleave, Daniel B. MS 3rd Inf. Co.I
Vancleave, D.B. Conf.Cav. Wood's Regt. Co.K
Vancleave, George W. TX 22nd Cav. Co.D Sgt.
Vancleave, G.M. MO 6th Cav. Co.A
Vancleave, Henry AL 9th Inf. Co.K Sgt.
Vancleave, Henry TN 46th Inf. Co.H
Vancleave, J. MS 10th Inf. Old Co.K
Vancleave, James AR Cav. Wright's Regt. Co.G
Van Cleave, James H. MO Lt.Arty. 1st Field Btty.
Vancleave, Jesse KY 8th Mtd.Inf. Co.D Sgt.
Vancleave, J.J. TN 5th Inf. 2nd Co.I
Vancleave, J.M. TN 35th Inf. 2nd Co.I Capt.
Vancleave, J.M. TX 12th Inf. Co.C Sgt.
Vancleave, J.N. TN 46th Inf. Co.G
Vancleave, John B. KY 8th Cav. Co.K
Vancleave, John M. TN 41st Inf. Co.H 1st Lt.
Van Cleave, Joshua TN 23rd Inf. Co.G
Vancleave, J.P. TN 51st (Cons.) Inf. Co.B
Vancleave, J.U. MO 6th Cav. Co.A
Vancleave, J.W. KY 8th Cav. Co.K
Vancleave, Mathew TX 2nd Cav. Co.H
Vancleave, Mathias M. TX Inf. Griffin's Bn. Co.B
Van Cleave, M.R. MS 1st Lt.Arty. Co.I

Vancleave, Nathaniel M. Conf.Cav. Wood's Regt. Co.K Bugler
Vancleave, Newton J. TN 41st Inf. Co.H Sgt.
Van Cleave, N.M. MS 1st Lt.Arty. Co.I
Vancleave, P. TX 2nd Inf. Co.E
Vancleave, Peter TX 12th Inf. Co.C
Van Cleave, R.A. MS 1st Lt.Arty. Co.I
Vancleave, Samuel J. TX Inf. Griffin's Bn. Co.B
Vancleave, S.N. TN 46th Inf. Co.G Sgt.
Van Cleave, Thomas AL 4th (Russell's) Cav.
Vancleave, Thomas Y. TN 41st Inf. Co.H
Vancleave, T.V. MS 39th Inf. Co.I
Vancleave, T.Y. TN 3rd (Clack's) Inf. Co.H
Vancleave, W.B. TN 46th Inf. Co.G Capt.
Vancleave, W.G. TX 12th Inf. Co.C Capt.
Vancleave, William AL 4th (Russell's) Cav.
Vancleave, William G. TN 41st Inf. Co.H
Vancleave, William G. TX 22nd Cav. Co.D Cpl.
Vancleave, William W. TX Inf. Griffin's Bn. Co.B
Vancleave, W.J. KY 3rd Mtd.Inf. Co.H
Vancleve, Alfred TX 3rd Inf. Co.E
Vancleve, Elijah MO Robertson's Regt.St.Guard Co.1
Vancleve, E.S. TX 4th Cav. Co.E
Vancleve, Henry H. TX 13th Vol. 3rd Co.I
Van Cleve, James H. MO 3rd Inf. Co.A
Vancleve, James P. TN 9th Cav.
Van Cleve, J.B. KY 3rd Cav. Co.K
Vancleve, J.M. MO 6th Cav. Co.A
Vancleve, Jonathan MS 39th Inf. Co.I
Vancleve, Jonathan TX 33rd Cav. Co.C
Vancleve, P. TX Home Guards Killough's Co.
Vanclieve, Henry H. TX 3rd Inf. Co.H
Van Colln, Philip LA Washington Arty.Bn. Co.4,2
Vancott, W.A. TN 2nd (Walker's) Inf. Co.A
Vancott, William A. LA 1st Inf.
Vancourt, --- MO 4th Cav. Co.D
Vancourt, D. LA 21st (Kennedy's) Inf. Co.E 1st Lt.
Vancresson, L. LA Mil. 1st Native Guards
Van Culin, J.H. TN Inf. 3rd Bn. Co.E
Vancurn, J.M. AL 63rd Inf. Co.I
Vancuron, James M. AL 3rd Res. Co.F
Vand, R.L. AL 36th Inf.
Vandae, William F. VA 19th Cav. Co.C
Vandagriff, James R. AL 18th Inf. Co.C
Van Dailey, John GA 4th (Clinch's) Cav. Co.F
Vandaily, John GA Lt.Arty. Clinch's Btty. Artif.
Vandal, William VA 30th Bn.S.S. Co.F
Vandall, William F. VA Cav. 46th Bn. Co.D
Vandall, William F. VA 3rd Cav. & Inf.St.Line Co.D
Vandalsen, Eliphalet C. Conf.Cav. Wood's Regt. 2nd Co.G 3rd Lt.
Van Dan Corput, J.H.G. AL 10th Inf. Co.G
Vandaveer, James AR 1st Field Btty.
Vandeburg, Herbert TN 10th Inf. Co.C
Vandeford, C. MS Cav. Davenport's Bn. (St.Troops) Co.A
Vandeford, O.B. AL 4th Inf. Co.D
Vandegaer, J.B. LA Inf. 16th Bn. (Conf.Guards Resp.Bn.) Co.B
Vandegar, A. LA Miles' Legion Co.D
Vandeger, A. LA 15th Bn.S.S. (Weatherly's) Co.B
Van de Graaf, A. Sebastian AL 5th Bn.Vol. Co.A Maj.
Van De Graaff, J.S. GA 27th Inf. Co.K
Van De Graaff, William J. MS 31st Inf. 1st Lt.,Adj.
Vandegraft, J.H. AL Cav. Barbiere's Bn. Truss' Co.
Vandegrieff, A.J. LA Inf. 16th Bn. (Conf.Guards Resp.Bn.) Co.A
Vandegriff, A.J. LA Mil. Lewis Guards 1st Sgt.
Vandegriff, Berry B. GA 39th Inf. Co.G
Vandegriff, Charles VA 3rd Res. Co.K
Vandegriff, I. GA Siege Arty. Campbell's Ind.Co.
Vandegriff, John AR 1st (Dobbin's) Cav. Co.C
Vandegrift, A.B. AL 18th Inf. Co.C Cpl.
Vandegrift, C.C. AL 2nd Cav. Co.B Comsy. Sgt.
Vandegrift, Charles VA Burks' Regt.Loc.Def. Sprinkle's Co.
Vandegrift, Christian W. VA 19th Inf. Co.A Sgt.
Vandegrift, Griffin L. VA Burks' Regt.Loc.Def. Sprinkle's Co.
Vandegrift, G.W. AL Cav. Barbiere's Bn. Co.E
Vandegrift, J.H. AL 18th Inf. Co.C Jr.2nd Lt.
Vandegrift, J.L. AL 18th Inf. Co.C Sgt.
Vandegrift, John W. VA 54th Inf. Co.K
Vandegrift, J.R. GA 2nd Inf. Co.H
Vandegrift, M.B. VA 14th Cav. Co.A
Vandegrift, Nathaniel D. VA 2nd Cav. Co.I Sgt.
Vandegrift, Robert C. VA 19th Inf. Co.A
Vandegrift, Robert C. 1st Conf.Eng.Troops Co.G Sgt.
Vandegrift, Stewart VA Burks' Regt.Loc.Def.
Vandegrift, W.H. VA 17th Cav. Co.H
Vandegrift, William H. MS 25th Inf. Co.F
Vandegrift, William L. VA 18th Cav. Co.C Cpl.
Vandegrift, William L. VA 13th Inf. Co.I
Vandegrifte, William F. AL 58th Inf. Co.G Sgt.
Vandegroft, J.S. TX 1st Inf. Co.E
Vanden, F.M. KY 2nd Bn.Mtd.Rifles Co.A Sgt.
Vanden, Lewis KY 4th Mtd.Inf. Co.I
Vanden, M.W. AL 37th Inf. Co.I
Vandenberg, C.G. 1st Conf.Inf. 1st Co.F
Vandenberg, J. LA 3rd (Harrison's) Cav. Co.C
Vandenberg, J.G. GA 5th Inf. Co.I
Vandenberg, Joseph TX 1st (Yager's) Cav. Co.B Cpl.
Vandenberg, Joseph TX Cav. 3rd (Yager's) Bn. Co.B Cpl.
Vanden Bossche, J.B. LA Mil. 3rd Regt. Eur.Brig. (Garde Francaise)
Vandenburg, C.G. MS 28th Cav. Co.A
Vandenburg, James Conf.Inf. Tucker's Regt. Co.I
Vandencoop, J.H.J. AL 9th Inf.
Van Den Corput, Felix GA Lt.Arty. Van Den Corput's Co. QMSgt.
Van Den Corput, Felix GA Inf. 3rd Bn. Co.A QMSgt.
Van Den Corput, G. GA Lt.Arty. Van Den Corput's Co.
Van Den Corput, Jules V. GA Inf. 3rd Bn. Co.A
Van Den Corput, Max GA Lt.Arty. Van Den Corput's Co. Capt.
Van Den Corput, Max GA Inf. 3rd Bn. Co.A 1st Lt.
Vandenherreweghen, Jean LA Mil. 3rd Regt. Eur.Brig. (Garde Francaise) Co.9
Vandenherreweghen, Jean LA C.S. Zouave Bn. Co.B,A 2nd Lt.
Vandenour, Jacob TN Cav. Newsom's Regt.
Vandenton, J.C. VA 6th Cav. Co.A
Vander Horst, A. Gen. & Staff, Adj.Gen.Dept. Maj.
Vander, T.S. GA 43rd Inf. Co.F
Vanderbelt, William S. VA 1st Arty. Co.I
Vanderbelt, W.S. VA 1st St.Res. Co.A
Vanderberg, C.G. GA 36th (Villepigue's) Inf. Co.F
Vanderberg, James VA 38th Inf. 2nd Co.I
Vanderberg, W.J. TX 18th Cav. Co.B
Vanderberry, James VA 6th Inf. Co.C
Vanderberry, Thomas VA 12th Inf. 1st Co.I
Vanderbilt, A.D. AR Mtd.Vol. (St.Troops) Abraham's Co.
Vanderbilt, A.D. AR 20th Inf. Co.K
Vanderbilt, A.H. AR 26th Inf. Co.G
Vanderbosche, Henry LA 14th Inf. Co.D
Vanderburg, Alfred NC 7th Inf. Co.B
Vanderburg, Amzi NC 33rd Inf. Co.A
Vanderburg, F.M. NC 2nd Jr.Res. Co.E
Vanderburg, Francis NC 49th Inf. Co.C
Vanderburg, Francis M. NC 33rd Inf. Co.A
Vanderburg, J. NC 2nd Jr.Res. Co.B
Vanderburg, John J. NC 7th Inf. Co.B
Vanderburg, J.Q. Conf.Cav. Wood's Regt. Co.K
Vanderburg, J.S. LA Inf. 4th Bn. Co.C Sgt.
Vanderburg, Julius NC 17th Inf. (2nd Org.) Co.L
Vanderburg, Loveless NC 7th Inf. Co.B
Vanderburg, N. MS Inf. 2nd Bn. (St.Troops) Co.E
Vanderburg, Rufus K.W. LA 12th Inf. Co.K Music.
Vanderburg, William C. NC 33rd Inf. Co.A
Vanderburgh, R.K.W. Band Featherston's Brig.
Vanderbury, James VA Hvy.Arty. 20th Bn. Co.B
Vanderdoes, P.A. LA 26th Inf. Co.I
Vanderenter, John MO 9th Bn.S.S. Co.E
Vanderest, W.P. AL Maj.,AQM
Vanderford, A.A. SC 21st Inf. Co.D 2nd Lt.
Vanderford, Adriel B. MS Cav. 4th Bn. Roddey's Co.
Vanderford, Aquilla MS 17th Inf. Co.D
Vanderford, A.T. TN Lt.Arty. Rice's Btty.
Vanderford, Beley P. AR 1st (Colquitt's) Inf. Co.G
Vanderford, Charles F. Gen. & Staff, A. of TN Capt.,Asst.Ch.Ord.Off.
Vanderford, Dudley SC 5th Inf. 1st Co.D, 2nd Co.D
Vanderford, H.A. MS 18th Cav. Co.A
Vanderford, Hampton SC 15th Inf. Co.H
Vanderford, J.A. MS Cav. 24th Bn. Co.D
Vanderford, J.A. 20th Conf.Cav. Co.F
Vanderford, James MS 17th Inf. Co.D
Vanderford, James A. AR 5th Inf. Co.C
Vanderford, J.N. LA Inf.Crescent Regt. Co.B
Vanderford, John AR 23rd Inf. Co.I
Vanderford, John MS Cav. Davenport's Bn. (St.Troops) Co.A
Vanderford, John MS Cav. Ham's Regt. Co.A

Vanderford, John B. NC 61st Inf. Co.F
Vanderford, John J. MS 12th Inf. Co.I
Vanderford, John J. MS 26th Inf. Co.F
Vanderford, John T. GA 13th Cav. Co.H
Vanderford, Joseph J. NC 52nd Inf. Co.B
Vanderford, K.Y. MS 12th Inf. Co.I
Vanderford, N. TN Lt.Arty. Rice's Btty.
Vanderford, Oliver H.P. AL 55th Vol. Co.J
Vanderford, R.A. GA 16th Inf. Co.B Sgt.
Vanderford, Richard A. GA Inf. 3rd Bn. Co.C
Vanderford, Richard A. GA 3rd Bn.S.S. Co.C
Vanderford, S. SC 2nd Bn.S.S. Co.B
Vanderford, S. SC 18th Inf. Co.B
Vanderford, S.J. TN Lt.Arty. Rice's Btty.
Vanderford, S.J. TN 38th Inf. 1st Co.A
Vanderford, Stephen NC 61st Inf. Co.F
Vanderford, Thos. AL Cp. of Instr. Talladega
Vanderford, Thomas J. MS 26th Inf. Co.B
Vanderford, Thompson AL 31st Inf. Co.A
Vanderford, T.J. MS 32nd Inf. Co.I Music.
Vanderford, William SC 15th Inf. Co.H
Vanderford, William B. NC 52nd Inf. Co.B
Vanderford, W.J. SC 15th Inf. Co.H
Vandergaer, J.P. LA Inf.Cons.Crescent Regt. Co.A
Vandergraft, John LA 11th Inf. Co.E
Vandergraft, W.H. VA 14th Cav. 1st Co.F
Vandergrass, J. LA 13th Inf. Co.E
Vandergrieft, Nathaniel MS 2nd Part.Rangers Co.G
Vandergrif, Joseph TN Cav. Newsom's Regt. Co.D
Vandergriff, C.P. GA 2nd Res. Co.D
Vandergriff, Frank TN 1st (Carter's) Cav. Co.B Cpl.
Vandergriff, George VA 54th Inf. Co.K
Vandergriff, G.W. TX 2nd Inf. Co.A
Vandergriff, J. TN 17th Cav. Co.C
Vandergriff, James AR 2nd Mtd.Rifles Co.I
Vandergriff, James AR Cav. Gordon's Regt. Co.I
Vandergriff, James LA 21st (Patton's) Inf. Co.E
Vandergriff, James W. GA 2nd Res. Co.D
Vandergriff, John D. FL Milton Lt.Arty. Dunham's Co.
Vandergriff, John T. GA 41st Inf. Co.B
Vandergriff, Joseph LA 10th Inf. Co.C
Vandergriff, Joseph TN 18th (Newsom's) Cav. Co.C
Vandergriff, J.W. MO 15th Cav. Co.E
Vandergriff, Lafayette TN 16th Inf. Co.F
Vandergriff, Martin GA Smith's Legion Ralston's Co.
Vandergriff, Martin V. GA 6th Cav. Co.D
Vandergriff, N. MS 3rd Cav. Co.G
Vandergriff, W.C. GA Lt.Arty. (Arsenal Btty.) Hudson's Co.
Vandergriff, William AR 35th Inf. Co.F
Vandergriff, William LA 1st (Strawbridge's) Inf. Co.C Sgt.
Vandergriff, William E. MS 34th Inf. Co.K
Vandergriff, W.J. TN 18th Inf. Co.I
Vandergrift, A.B. AL 32nd & 58th (Cons.) Inf. Capt.
Vandergrift, A.B. AL 58th Inf. Co.G Capt.
Vandergrift, Andrew J. TN 39th Mtd.Inf. Co.F
Vandergrift, E. NC 44th Inf. Co.F
Vandergrift, Gilbert TN 2nd (Walker's) Inf. Co.B
Vandergrift, James A. GA 2nd Inf. Co.H
Vandergrift, John VA 3rd Res. Co.B
Vandergrift, Mahlon V. VA Cav. Moorman's Co.
Vandergrift, Marshall Conf.Reg.Inf. Brooks' Bn. Co.C
Vandergrift, R.L. TN 4th (McLemore's) Cav. Co.I
Vandergrift, Thomas VA 157th Mil. Co.A
Vandergrift, W. VA 22nd Inf. Co.H
Vandergrift, W.H. VA Cav. 36th Bn. Co.E
Vandergrift, William NC 44th Inf. Co.F
Vandergriph, E.A. GA Smith's Legion Co.D
Vandergrist, Enoch LA 11th Inf. Co.B
Vanderherreweghen, John TX Waul's Legion Co.B Lt.
Vanderhider, Henry TX 4th Cav. Co.B
Vanderhorn, Joseph LA 21st (Kennedy's) Inf. Co.F
Vanderhorst, L. SC Mil.Cav. Rutledge's Co.
Vander Horst, Lewis SC 4th Cav. Co.K
Vanderhorst, Robert SC 11th Inf. Co.C Music.
Vanderhuff, William TX 2nd Cav. 1st Co.F
Vanderhuff, William TX Cav. Morgan's Regt. Co.I
Vanderhurst, Michael M. TX 6th Cav. Co.G Chap.
Vander Hurst, Wm. M. Gen. & Staff Chap.
Vanderipe, James FL 1st Cav. Co.K
Vanderipe, William FL 7th Inf. Co.K
Vanderlehr, A. VA Inf. 4th Bn.Loc.Def. Co.C
Vanderlice, J. AL 3rd Inf. Co.K
Vanderlier, Joseph VA 10th Cav. Co.C
Vanderlin, --- LA Mil. 2nd Regt. 3rd Brig. 1st Div. Co.F
Vanderlip, Elias VA 10th Cav. Co.A,D Cpl.
Vanderman, Peter KY Morgan's Men Beck's Co.
Vanderolice, --- LA 20th Inf. Co.I
Vanderpool, Abraham TX 16th Cav. Co.A
Vanderpool, Cameron TN 2nd (Robison's) Inf. Co.C
Vanderpool, C.C. TN Cav. Allison's Squad. Co.C
Vanderpool, Cornelius VA 50th Inf. 1st Co.G
Vanderpool, Cornelius VA 63rd Inf. 1st Co.I, Co.F 1st Lt.
Vanderpool, E. TX Cav. Baird's Regt. Co.A
Vanderpool, G.A. AR Cav. Crabtree's (46th) Regt. Co.A
Vanderpool, Gustavus AR 8th Inf. New Co.H
Vanderpool, Hezekiah KY 5th Mtd.Inf. Co.B,I
Vanderpool, H.L. TX 12th Inf. Co.E Sgt.
Vanderpool, James TX Loc.Def.Troops McNeel's Co. (McNeel Coast Guards)
Vanderpool, Jerry AR 62nd Mil. Co.A
Vanderpool, J.H. VA 72nd Mil.
Vanderpool, John H. VA 22nd Cav. Co.E Cpl.
Vanderpool, L. SC 2nd Bn.S.S. Co.A
Vanderpool, Little B. MS 1st Lt.Arty. Co.A
Vanderpool, P. VA 63rd Inf. Co.F
Vanderpool, P. VA Mil. Washington Cty.
Vanderpool, Pleasant VA Inf. 23rd Bn. Co.A
Vanderpool, Samuel MO 16th Inf. Co.C
Vanderpool, William MO 1st Inf. Co.F
Vanderport, Henry VA 21st Cav. Co.A
Vandershuer, Charles LA 20th Inf. New Co.B
Vandershuer, Charles LA 21st (Kennedy's) Inf. Co.C
Vanderslice, --- AL Mobile City Troop
Vanderslice, Benjamin TX 17th Cav. Co.K
Vanderslice, Benjamin TX 17th Cons. Dismtd.Cav. Co.K
Vanderslice, B.F. AL 2nd Cav. Co.B
Vanderslice, Franklin AL 24th Inf. Co.K
Vanderslice, Franklin MS 44th Inf. Co.I
Vanderslice, George C. VA 49th Inf. 3rd Co.G Capt.
Vanderslice, Henry LA 11th Inf. Co.I
Vanderslice, James AL 51st (Part.Rangers) Co.I
Vanderslice, Jesse MS 8th Inf. Co.E
Vanderslice, J.F. AL 42nd Inf. Co.I
Vanderslice, J.G. VA 49th Regt. Co.I,G Capt.
Vanderslice, J.H. TX Cav. (Dismtd.) Chisum's Regt. Co.H
Vanderslice, John AR 3rd Inf. Co.I
Vanderslice, Joseph AL 3rd Res. Co.K
Vanderslice, Mac. MS 44th Inf. Co.I
Vanderslice, Mackiah AL 24th Inf. Co.K
Vanderslice, Reinard AL 24th Inf. Co.K
Vanderslice, Rhinard MS 44th Inf. Co.I
Vanderslice, T.F. TX 7th Inf. Co.H
Vanderslice, Washington AL 24th Inf. Co.K,C
Vanderslice, Washington MS 44th Inf. Co.I
Vanderslice, W.J. TX 7th Inf. Co.H
Vanderstracten, --- LA Mil. 2nd Regt. French Brig. Co.1
Vanderstrocten, A. LA Mil. Orleans Guards Regt. Co.K
Vandervander, J.R. MS Cav. Jeff Davis Legion Co.C
Vandervanter, John LA Pointe Coupee Arty.
Vanderveer, A.H. LA 18th Inf. Co.E
Vanderveer, A.H. LA Inf.Crescent Regt. Co.F
Vanderveer, G. TX 16th Inf. Co.A
Vanderveer, W.B. AL Lt.Arty. Goldthwaite's Btty.
Vanderveer, William J. TX 1st (Yager's) Cav. Co.B
Van Derveer, W.P. Gen. & Staff Maj.,AQM
Vanderven, J.J. AL 18th Inf. Co.A 1st Lt.
Vanderventer, H. VA Cav. 47th Bn. Co.A
Vanderventer, James VA Lt.Arty. 1st Bn. Co.D
Vanderventer, J.M. VA 26th Cav. Co.G
Vanderventer, John VA Cav. 1st Bn. Co.C
Vanderventer, T.J. VA 50th Inf. Co.B
Vanderver, Asbury MO 1st Cav. Co.D 1st Lt.
Vanderver, E. AL 35th Inf. Co.B
Vanderver, E. KY 3rd Mtd.Inf. Co.I
Vanderver, E. MS Moore's Co. (Palo Alto Guards)
Vanderver, Gilbert AR 31st Inf. Co.A
Vanderver, Hallingswth AL 19th Inf. Co.E
Vanderver, M. TX Cav. Baird's Regt. Co.E
Vanderver, S.G. MS 1st Lt.Arty. Co.B
Vanderver, William W. AL 19th Inf. Co.E
Vanderver, W.T. KY 3rd Mtd.Inf. Co.I,K
Vandervier, Thomas P. AL 28th Inf. Co.C
Vanderville, G.W. TN 51st Inf. Co.C
Vanderville, G.W. TN 51st (Cons.) Inf. Co.I
Vanderville, J. TN 51st (Cons.) Inf. Co.I Surg.
Vanderville, T.J. Gen. & Staff Surg.
Vanderville, T.P. TN 51st Inf. Co.C

Vandervoort, Benjamin O. TX 8th Inf. Co.I Music.
Vandervoort, C. TX 8th Inf. Co.G Music.
Vandervoort, R.B. TX 8th Inf. Co.I
Vandervort, J.C. KY 3rd Mtd.Inf. Co.D
Vandervort, William NC 23rd Inf. Co.H
Vanderwall, Matthew LA 5th Inf. Co.C Cpl.
Vanderwerth, John TX 4th Cav. Co.G
Vanderwood, B.O. TX Inf. 24th Bn.
Vandestracten, J.B. LA Mil. 1st Regt. French Brig. Co.4
Vandevander, Andrew VA 62nd Mtd.Inf. 2nd Co.D
Vandevander, H. MS Inf. 2nd St.Troops Co.C Sgt.
Van Devander, I.R. MS 11th (Perrin's) Cav. Co.B
Vandevander, R.S. MS Inf. 2nd St.Troops Co.C
Vandevander, W.W. MS Cav. Jeff Davis Legion Co.C
Vandevanter, Cornelius VA 17th Inf. Co.C
Vandevanter, D.H. VA Cav. Mosby's Regt. (Part.Rangers) Co.H
Vandevanter, I.C. VA Cav. Mosby's Regt. (Part.Rangers) Co.D
Vandevanter, L.C. VA Cav. Mosby's Regt. (Part.Rangers) Co.D
Vandevanter, T.H. VA Cav. Mosby's Regt. (Part.Rangers) Co.A
Vandevanter, Townsend H. VA Cav. 35th Bn. Co.A
Vandevanter, William VA Cav. Mosby's Regt. (Part.Rangers) Co.D
Vandeveer, C.G. TX Cav. McCord's Frontier Regt. Co.K
Vandeveer, Charles S. TX Cav. Waller's Regt. Co.E
Vandeveer, J. AL 19th Inf. Co.E
Vandeveer, John J. TX Arty. 4th Bn. Co.A 2nd Lt.
Vandeveer, W.H. AL 19th Inf. Co.E
Vandeveer, William TX Cav. 3rd (Yager's) Bn. Co.B
Vandevender, Adam VA 46th Mil. Co.B
Vandevender, Adam VA 62nd Mtd.Inf. 2nd Co.C
Vandevender, Addison VA 31st Inf. Co.F
Vandevender, Albert MO 1st N.E. Cav. Price's Co.M, White's Co.
Vandevender, Alonzo C. MS Inf. 3rd Bn. Co.C
Vandevender, Andrew VA 25th Inf. 2nd Co.F
Vandevender, Archer MO 1st N.E. Cav. Price's Co.M
Van Devender, Charles VA Cav. Mosby's Regt. (Part.Rangers) Co.F
Vandevender, G.A. VA 20th Cav. Co.H Sgt.
Vandevender, George VA 10th Bn.Res. Co.D
Vandevender, George VA 162nd Mil. Co.A
Vandevender, Isaac VA 25th Inf. 1st Co.E
Vandevender, Isaac VA 62nd Mtd.Inf. 2nd Co.C
Vandevender, Isaac C. VA 62nd Mtd.Inf. 2nd Co.C
Vandevender, J. VA 62nd Mtd.Inf.
Vandevender, Jacob VA 31st Inf. 1st Co.B
Vandevender, Jacob E. VA 62nd Mtd.Inf. 2nd Co.D
Vandevender, J.C. MS Cav. Jeff Davis Legion Co.C
Vandevender, John MO 1st N.E. Cav. Price's Co.M
Vandevender, Josiah VA 31st Inf. Co.F
Vandevender, J.S. MS Cav. Jeff Davis Legion Co.C
Vandevender, R. MS 46th Inf. Co.K
Van Devender, Samuel C. MS 35th Inf. Co.A
Van Devender, S.C. MS 1st (Patton's) Inf. Co.I Cpl.
Van Devender, S.C. MS 46th Inf. Co.K
Vandevender, Solomon VA 62nd Mtd.Inf. 2nd Co.D
Vandevender, William C. VA 31st Inf. 1st Co.B
Vandevender, William H. VA 25th Inf. 2nd Co.G, 2nd Co.D
Vandeventer, A.C. VA 62nd Mtd.Inf. Co.C
Vandeventer, Alexander MO Cav. 3rd Bn. Co.D
Vandeventer, Alexander S. VA 50th Inf. Co.B Col.
Vandeventer, Edward E. VA 1st Inf. Co.I
Vandeventer, Elijah MO 9th Bn.S.S. Co.E
Vandeventer, Houston VA 25th Cav. Co.G
Vandeventer, Houston VA 50th Inf. Co.B Sgt.
Vandeventer, Isaac VA 6th Cav. Co.A
Vandeventer, Isaac VA 8th Inf. Co.A
Vandeventer, J. TX 24th & 25th Cav. (Cons.) Co.H
Vandeventer, J. TX 25th Cav. Co.B
Vandeventer, James MO 3rd Inf. Co.B
Vandeventer, James VA 1st Arty. Co.F,D
Vandeventer, James VA 32nd Inf. Co.G
Vandeventer, J.C. VA Cav. 47th Bn. Co.A
Vandeventer, J.M. VA 24th Cav.
Van Deventer, Joe VA Cav. Mosby's Regt. (Part.Rangers) Co.D
Vandeventer, John T. TN 60th Mtd.Inf. Co.D
Vandeventer, Larkin VA 25th Cav. Co.G
Vandeventer, Larkin VA 50th Inf. Co.B
Vandeventer, Larkin VA 64th Mtd.Inf. Co.B
Vandeventer, Robert VA 48th Inf. Co.G
Vandeventer, Thomas J. VA 25th Cav. Co.B,G
Vandeventer, William VA 25th Cav. Co.G
Vandeventer, William VA 62nd Mtd.Inf. 2nd Co.C
Vandever, Elihu TN 28th (Cons.) Inf. Co.H
Vandever, Elijah MO 1st Cav. Co.B
Vandever, George AR Cav. Gordon's Regt. Co.G
Vandever, H.P. GA 66th Inf. Co.H
Vandever, J. AL 19th Inf. Co.E
Vandever, J.M. AL Cav. Moreland's Regt. Co.H
Vandever, Johnson AL 19th Inf. Co.E 1st Sgt.
Vandever, J.R. TN 12th Inf. Co.I
Vandever, J.W. AR Capt.,En.O.
Vandever, Louis MO Thompson's Command
Vandever, M.D. GA 4th Cav. (St.Guards) Cannon's Co.
Vandever, Noah AR 3rd Cav. Co.D
Vandever, P.J. TN 23rd Inf. Co.B
Vandever, P.V. TN 23rd Inf. Co.B
Van Dever, Robert K. MO 1st Cav. Co.H Cpl.
Vandever, Thomas M. GA 16th Inf. Co.E
Vandever, Turner TN 6th (Wheeler's) Cav. Co.K
Vandever, W.B. SC 3rd Res. Co.H
Vandever, William SC 5th Mil. Beat Co.3
Vandevere, H. VA 2nd Cav. Co.I
Vandevere, Joel A. AL 1st Cav. Co.G
Vandevier, A.J. GA 28th Inf. Co.G
Vandevier, Elijah M. MO 1st Cav. Co.B
Vandevier, E.M. MO 1st & 3rd Cons.Cav. Co.B
Vandevier, J.F. AR 32nd Inf. Co.C,I Sgt.
Vandevier, J.G. AL 12th Inf. Co.C
Vandevire, B.P. GA 1st Mil. Co.I
Vandevire, J.T. SC Mil. 1st Regt. Co.B
Vandevner, B.C. MS 26th Inf. Co.G
Vandevner, Benjamin C. MS 32nd Inf. Co.K
Vandevner, James K. MS 32nd Inf. Co.K
Van De Voort, William P. TN 13th Inf. Co.C
Vandewater, V. Conf.Cav. Wood's Regt. 1st Co.A
Vandford, A.T. MS 2nd (Davidson's) Inf. Potts' Co.
Vandford, Perry AL 9th (Malone's) Cav. Co.M Sgt.
Vandier, John H. AL Talladega Cty.Res. J. Henderson's Co.
Vandiererse, S.W. AL 34th Inf. Co.H
Vandifer, Wesley C. MO 8th Inf. Co.D
Vandiford, A.T. MS 6th Cav. Co.B
Vandiford, A.T. MS Cav. Davenport's Bn. (St.Troops) Co.A
Vandiford, Jackson NC 44th Inf. Co.D
Vandiford, J.D. MS 6th Cav. Co.B
Vandiford, John NC 44th Inf. Co.D
Vandiford, R.P. MS 6th Cav. Co.B
Vandiford, R.P. MS Cav. Davenport's Bn. (St.Troops) Co.A
Vandiford, S.G. NC 61st Inf. Co.F
Vandiford, T.B. NC 61st Inf. Co.F
Vandiford, William NC 44th Inf. Co.D
Vandigriff, J.W. GA 53rd Inf. Co.F Capt.
Vandigriff, W.B. GA Cav. 16th Bn. (St.Guards) Co.E
Vandigrift, W.H. TN 2nd (Walker's) Inf. Co.B
Vandike, Andrew VA 45th Inf. Co.A
Vandike, Emanuel NC 58th Inf. Co.M,G
Vandike, George L. NC 58th Inf. Co.I Sgt.
Vandike, J.H. SC 5th St.Troops Co.E
Vandike, J.H. SC 7th Res. Co.L Capt.
Vandike, Robert VA 45th Inf. Co.A
Vandike, T. Nixon TN 63rd Inf. Co.D
Vandike, Walter VA Cav. 34th Bn. Co.C
Vandike, Walter VA Inf. 21st Bn. 2nd Co.F
Vandike, William MO Cav. Wood's Regt. Co.B
Vandike, William VA Cav. 34th Bn. Co.C
Vandike, William VA Inf. 21st Bn. 2nd Co.F
Vandikes, David KY 10th (Diamond's) Cav. Co.G
Vandikes, Walter KY 10th (Diamond's) Cav. Co.G
Vandikes, William KY 10th (Diamond's) Cav. Co.G
Vandine, Isaiah VA 19th Cav. Co.C
Vandine, Isaiah VA 22nd Inf. Co.B
Vandine, Isham C. VA 22nd Inf. Co.A,B
Vandingham, G.W. MO 3rd Inf. Co.F
Vandiver, A.C. MS 23rd Inf. Co.E 1st Lt.
Vandiver, A.F. GA Inf. 1st Loc.Troops (Augusta) Co.K
Vandiver, A.F. SC 5th Res. Co.C
Vandiver, Asa P. GA 11th Inf. Co.A
Vandiver, Ashberry MO 10th Cav. Co.K Capt.

Vandiver, A.W. LA 1st Cav. Co.G
Vandiver, A.W. SC 2nd Rifles Co.F 1st Lt.
Vandiver, C.C. GA 18th Inf. Co.C
Vandiver, Charles H. VA 7th Cav. Co.F 2nd Lt.
Vandiver, D.M. AL 18th Inf. Co.I
Vandiver, Edwin SC 22nd Inf. Co.G
Vandiver, E.H. MS 23rd Inf. Co.E
Vandiver, Elam SC 1st (Orr's) Rifles Co.L 2nd Lt.
Vandiver, E.M. AL 26th (O'Neal's) Inf. Co.A Capt.
Vandiver, E.M. TN 28th Inf. Co.A
Vandiver, E.W. SC 7th Inf. 1st Co.B, 2nd Co.B
Vandiver, G.A. GA Inf. 11th Bn. (St.Guards) Co.D
Vandiver, George T. MD 1st Cav. Co.E
Vandiver, George V. GA Inf. 11th Bn. (St.Guards) Co.D
Vandiver, George V. GA 24th Inf. Co.G Sgt.
Vandiver, George W. SC 1st (Orr's) Rifles Co.L
Vandiver, Hack TN 18th (Newsom's) Cav. Co.I
Vandiver, Hack TN 19th & 20th (Cons.) Cav. Co.C
Vandiver, Harris A. SC 1st (Orr's) Rifles Co.L Band Cpl.
Vandiver, Henry C. SC Inf. Holcombe Legion Co.B
Vandiver, Hezekiah R. SC 2nd Rifles QMSgt.
Vandiver, H.P. GA Lt.Arty. 12th Bn. 2nd Co.A
Vandiver, H.P. GA Inf. 4th Bn. (St.Guards) Co.G
Vandiver, H.R. SC 1st (Orr's) Rifles Co.D Sgt.
Van Diver, Hunter GA Phillips' Legion Co.C
Vandiver, James C. TN 28th Inf. Co.A
Vandiver, James E. AR Inf. 2nd Bn. Co.B
Vandiver, James J. GA 38th Inf. Co.G
Vandiver, James M. SC 1st St.Troops Co.F
Vandiver, James M. SC 5th Res. Co.A
Van Diver, James S. AL 26th (O'Neal's) Inf. Co.A
Vandiver, Jasper N. SC 1st (Orr's) Rifles Co.L
Vandiver, J.B. SC Inf. 7th Bn. (Enfield Rifles) Co.H
Vandiver, J.D. GA 43rd Inf. Co.F
Vandiver, Jeptha AL Lt.Arty. 2nd Bn. Co.F
Vandiver, Jeptha M. SC 2nd Rifles Co.K 3rd Lt.
Vandiver, J.J. AL 25th Inf. ACS
Vandiver, J.L. AL Cp. of Instr. Talladega
Vandiver, John TN 12th (Cons.) Inf. Co.I 1st Sgt.
Vandiver, John Lambkin SC 4th Inf. Co.D
Vandiver, John S. SC 1st (Orr's) Rifles Co.L
Vandiver, John W. AL 18th Inf. Co.I
Vandiver, Jol J. Gen. & Staff Capt.,Comsy.
Vandiver, Joseph L. VA Cav. McNeill's Co. Sgt.
Vandiver, Joseph L. VA 77th Mil. Maj.
Vandiver, J.S. GA 43rd Inf. Co.F
Vandiver, J.W. SC 1st Bn.S.S. Co.C
Vandiver, J.W. SC 27th Inf. Co.G
Vandiver, J.W. SC Inf. Holcombe Legion Co.B
Vandiver, L. KY Morgan's Men Co.D
Vandiver, Lafayette KY 10th (Johnson's) Cav. New Co.F
Vandiver, Lafayette KY Horse Arty. Byrne's Co.
Vandiver, L.D. GA Cav. 6th Bn. (St.Guards) Co.C 1st Sgt.
Vandiver, M. AR 1st (Monroe's) Cav. Co.F
Vandiver, Marcus L. GA 24th Inf. Co.G
Vandiver, Mathew AR 2nd Mtd.Rifles Co.F
Vandiver, Mathew SC 1st (Orr's) Rifles Co.L
Vandiver, Mathew SC 4th Inf. Co.B
Vandiver, Newton C. MO 10th Inf. Co.C
Vandiver, O.K. SC Inf. Holcombe Legion Co.B
Vandiver, P.W. GA 43rd Inf. Co.F
Vandiver, Richard TN 42nd Inf. 1st Co.I
Vandiver, Richard B. AR 8th Inf. New Co.E
Vandiver, Robert MO 5th Cav. Co.H
Vandiver, T.G. AL 41st Inf. Co.K
Vandiver, Thomas A. GA 3rd Cav. (St.Guards) Co.E
Vandiver, Thomas E. TX 15th Cav. Co.H
Vandiver, Thomas E.C. SC Palmetto S.S. Co.I
Vandiver, Thomas G. AL 43rd Inf. Co.I
Vandiver, Van C. MS 32nd Inf. Co.K
Vandiver, W.C. TN 48th (Nixon's) Inf. Co.K
Vandiver, W.E.C. GA 56th Inf. Co.D
Vandiver, W.G. KY 4th Cav. Co.E
Vandiver, W.H. MS 10th Cav. Co.A
Vandiver, W.H. MS 44th Inf. Co.F
Vandiver, Whitfield AL 19th Inf. Co.E
Vandiver, William C. TN 54th Inf. Co.G
Vandiver, William H. MS 9th Cav. Co.F
Vandiver, William H. TN Cav. 17th Bn. (Sanders') Co.C
Vandiver, William M. AL Lt.Arty. 2nd Bn. Co.F
Vandiver, William S. SC 1st (Orr's) Rifles Co.G
Vandiver, William T. GA 26th Inf. Co.I
Vandivere, George VA Cav. McNeill's Co.
Vandivere, George W. GA 13th Cav. Co.G
Vandivere, Samuel W. GA 34th Inf. Co.A,H
Vandivier, Daniel N. GA 24th Inf. Co.K
Vandivier, George AR 4th Inf. Co.C Cpl.
Vandivier, James J. GA 28th Inf. Co.G
Vandivier, J.P. TX 9th (Nichols') Inf. Co.G
Vandivier, Peter S. GA Inf. 4th Bn. (St.Guards) Co.A
Vandivier, Peter S. GA 24th Inf. Co.H
Vandivier, Thomas GA 28th Inf. Co.G Sgt.
Van Diviere, A.P. GA 3rd Bn.S.S. Co.B
Van Diviere, M.L. GA 3rd Bn.S.S. Co.B
Vandiviere, S.H. GA 52nd Inf. Lt.Col.
Vandle, Joseph D. VA 60th Inf. Co.B
Vandle, Joseph Dan VA 46th Inf. 1st Co.C
Vandle, Thomas VA 11th Bn.Res. Co.C
Van Dohlan, D. GA 7th Cav. Co.A
Van Dohlan, Diederick GA 36th (Villepigue's) Inf. Co.F
Van Dohlan, J. MS Lt.Arty. Turner's Co.
Van Dohlan, Jacob GA 36th (Villepigue's) Inf. Co.F
Van Dohlen, C.A. SC Cav. 17th Bn. Co.B
Van Dohlen, C.A. SC Mil. 1st Regt.Rifles Chichester's Co.
Van Dohlen, D. GA Cav. 21st Bn. Co.A
Van Dohlen, Diederick 1st Conf.Inf. 1st Co.F
Van Dohlen, Jacob GA Lt.Arty. Pritchard's Co. (Washington Arty.) Sgt.
Van Dohlen, Jacob 1st Conf.Inf. 1st Co.F
Van Dolan, George TX 8th Inf. Co.E Sgt.
Van Doorn, Charles A. AL 24th Inf. Co.K
Van Doren, C.A. MS 44th Inf. Co.G,I
Van Doren, Meverell VA 1st Cav. Co.B
Vandoren, Micajah MO 15th Cav. Co.M
Vandorf, Edward LA O'Hara's Co. (Pelican Guards,Co.B)
Vandorford, V. MS 2nd (Davidson's) Inf. Potts' Co.
Van Dorn, Earl Gen. & Staff Maj.Gen.
Van Dorn, Moses M. TX 35th (Brown's) Cav. Co.D
Van Dorp, Edward TX 1st Field Btty.
Van Dorp, Edward 1st Conf.Reg.Cav. Co.A
Vandover, A. AR 30th Inf. Co.B
Vandover, Caleb MO 10th Inf. Co.I Sgt.
Vandover, G.W. AL 27th Inf. Co.K
Vandover, Horatio F. TX 2nd Cav. Co.G Cpl.
Vandover, James AR 11th & 17th (Cons.) Inf. Co.H
Vandover, James AR 17th (Griffith's) Inf. Co.H
Vandover, J.J. AR 30th Inf. Co.B
Vandover, J.M. AR 1st (Monroe's) Cav. Co.D Cpl.
Vandover, John MO 10th Inf. Co.G
Vandover, John MO 12th Inf. Co.K
Vandover, John R. MO 10th Inf. Co.I 1st Sgt.
Vandover, L. MO 15th Cav. Co.H
Vandover, M.H. MO 12th Inf. Co.K
Vandover, W. Lafayette AL 43rd Inf. Co.G
Vandrell, Bartholemy LA Mil. 4th Regt. 3rd Brig. 1st Div. Co.H 3rd Lt.
Vandrey, Jules, Jr. LA 1st (Nelligan's) Inf. Co.C
Vandry, Jules, Jr. LA Inf. 1st Sp.Bn. (Rightor's) New Co.C
Vandry, William T. LA 1st (Nelligan's) Inf. Co.C
Vandry, William T. LA Inf. 1st Sp.Bn. (Rightor's) New Co.C QMSgt.
Van Dusen, H. TX 4th Inf. Co.C
Van Dusen, H. TX Inf. Townsend's Co. (Robertson Five S.)
Vanduver, R.E. AL 55th Vol. Co.I
Van Duyn, S.P. NC 61st Inf. Co.D
Vanduyne, Anderson AR 17th (Lemoyne's) Inf. Co.F
Vanduzer, William T. GA 3rd Cav. (St.Guards) Co.H
Vandver, George TN 28th Inf. Co.A
Vandy, J. LA Cav. Hugh's Bn. 1st Lt.
Vandyck, J.D. TN Inf. 4th Cons.Regt. Co.G
Vandyck, John TN 7th (Duckworth's) Cav. Co.G
Vandyck, John C. TX 16th Cav. Co.H Cpl.
Vandyck, R.S. TN 7th (Duckworth's) Cav. Co.G Cpl.
Van Dyck, R.S. TN 15th (Stewart's) Cav. Co.B 2nd Lt.
Vandyck, W.H. TN 46th Inf. Co.D 1st Sgt.
Vandyck, William O. TN 7th (Duckworth's) Cav. Co.G
Vandygriff, James A. AR 15th (N.W.) Inf. Co.A
Vandygrift, John W. AR 1st Vol. Co.B
Vandygroft, John KY 2nd Mtd.Inf. Co.C
Van Dyke,--- TX Cav. 4th Regt.St.Troops Co.K
Vandyke, Albert MS 28th Cav. Co.K
Vandyke, A.M. TN 13th Inf. Co.I
Vandyke, August MS 16th Inf. Co.I
Vandyke, Benjamin GA 52nd Inf. Co.C
Vandyke, Benjamin F. TX 36th Cav. Co.E
Vandyke, Benjamin T. GA 1st St.Troops Co.K
Van Dyke, Benjamin W. GA 43rd Inf. Co.F
Vandyke, C.E. TN 21st (Wilson's) Cav. Co.H

Vandyke, Charles KY 10th (Diamond's) Cav. Co.I Cpl.
Vandyke, Charles R. GA 4th Inf. Co.F
Vandyke, David H. GA 3rd Cav. Co.F
Vandyke, D.B. TN 55th (Brown's) Inf. Co.F
Vandyke, I.N. TN 13th Inf. Co.I
Van Dyke, J. VA Vol. Binford's Co. Sgt.
Vandyke, James MS 1st (Patton's) Inf. Co.A
Vandyke, James VA Lt.Arty. Jeffress' Co.
Vandyke, James A. GA 4th Inf. Co.F
Vandyke, James A. MS 12th Inf. Co.G
Vandyke, J.D. TN 55th (Brown's) Inf. Co.F
Vandyke, J.E. TX 23rd Cav. Co.K Sgt.
Van Dyke, John TX Waul's Legion Co.A
Van Dyke, John M. TN 59th Mtd.Inf. Co.A Capt.
Vandyke, Jno. S. Forrest's Cav. Lyon's Escort,CSA
Vandyke, Joseph F. MS 12th Inf. Co.G
Vandyke, Joshua NC 34th Inf. Co.F
Vandyke, L.S. NC 23rd Inf. Co.H
Van Dyke, M.H. Gen. & Staff Contr.Surg.
Van Dyke, R.S. TN 1st (Carter's) Cav. Co.C Maj.
Van Dyke, R.S. TN 15th (Cons.) Cav. Co.A 2nd Lt.
Van Dyke, William D. TN 59th Mtd.Inf. Co.A ACS
Van Dyke, William D. Gen. & Staff Capt.,ACS
Vandyke, William L. GA 4th Inf. Co.F
Vandyke, William R. NC 55th Inf. Co.C
Vandyn, James AR Inf. Cocke's Regt. Co.F
Vandyne, A. AR Lt.Arty. Zimmerman's Btty.
Vandyne, James AR Inf. Cocke's Regt. Co.B
Vane, L.W. 7th Conf.Cav. Co.K
Vane, W.N. NC Cav. 15th Bn. Co.C
Van Eaton, Barton R. VA 10th Cav. Co.B
Van Eaton, F.M. NC 57th Inf. Co.A
Van Eaton, H.S. Gen. & Staff Capt.,ACS
Van Eaton, Hy S. MS 16th Inf. Co.K
Van Eaton, James M. NC 42nd Inf. Co.F Cpl.
Van Eaton, Joseph L. NC 39th Inf. Co.E 1st Lt.
Van Eaton, McDonald NC 2nd Cav. (19th St.Troops) Co.B
Van Eaton, McDonald VA 10th Cav. Co.B
Van Eaton, Richard T. NC 57th Inf. Co.H
Van Eden, Charles SC 7th Cav. Co.A
Van Eden, Charles SC Cav. Tucker's Co.
Vanee John 1st Chickasaw Inf. Gregg's Co.
Van Eitzen, H. SC 1st Regt. Charleston Guard Co.G
Vane Johnson 2nd Cherokee Mtd.Vol. Co.B
Van Ekelen, C. Metzler Gen. & Staff,PACS Dr.M.
Vaneo, Cornelis TX Cav. Benavides' Regt. Co.D Sgt.
Van Epps, A.S. AL City Troop (Mobile) Arrington's Co.A
Van Epps, A.S. AL Mil. 2nd Regt.Vol. Co.C
Van Epps, A.S. 15th Conf.Cav. Co.F
Van Epps, George C. TN 19th Inf. Co.A,E
Vanerson, F.T. TN Inf. 3rd Cons.Regt. Co.F 2nd Lt.
Vanes, Cornelius TX Cav. Ragsdale's Bn. 1st Co.A Sgt.
Vanes, Zachariah MO 4th Cav. Co.B
Vanesler, J. MO Inf. 3rd Bn. Co.E
Vaness, Cornelio TX Cav. Benavides' Regt. Co.D Sgt.
Vaness, T.F. TN 5th Inf. Co.G
Vaness, William SC 23rd Inf. Co.H
Vanestle, Joseph MO 10th Cav. Co.I
Vanestler, John MO 6th Inf. Co.C
Vanfelson, C.A. VA 3rd Inf.Loc.Def. Co.A,K,B
Vanfleet, A.L. MS 25th Inf. Co.F
Vanfleet, A.L. 2nd Conf.Inf. Co.F 1st Lt.
Van Fleet, Henry MO Cav. Freeman's Regt. Capt.
Vanford, F. FL 15th Regt. Co.H
Van Forsen, A.W. VA 5th Bn.Res. Co.D
Vanforsen, G.R. AR Mil. Desha Cty.Bn.
Vanfossen, Alexander Y. VA 7th Bn.Res. Co.D
Vanfossen, C.H. AL Lt.Arty. 2nd Bn. Co.C
Vanfossen, Charles VA 7th Bn.Res. Co.D
Van Fossen, Jacob VA Prov.Guard Avis' Co.
Vanfossen, Jacob B. VA 5th Inf. Co.F
Van Fossen, James A. VA Prov.Guard Avis' Co.
Vanfossen, James W. VA 5th Inf. Co.F
Van Fossen, J.C. VA 14th Cav. Co.I
Van Fossen, J.C. VA 17th Cav. Capt.,AQM
Van Fossen, J.C. Gen. & Staff AQM
Vanfossen, Nathan H. KY 4th Mtd.Inf. Co.I Sgt.
Vanfossen, William E. VA 52nd Inf. Co.F
Van Gardner, T.H. NC 12th Inf. Co.A
Van Geisen, Henry MS Cav. Jeff Davis Legion Co.F
Vangelder, J. AR Cav. McGehee's Regt. Co.E
Van Giesen, H. VA 6th Cav. 1st Co.E
Van Giesen, Uriah GA Inf. 2nd Bn. Co.B
Vangilder, John MO 8th Cav. Co.D,K
Vangine, B.F. AR 20th Inf. Co.I
Vangine, Paul AR 20th Inf. Co.I
Van Hagan, H.W. AL 2nd Cav. Co.C Sgt.
Vanhagan, John B. AL 32nd Inf. Co.G
Vanhagen, A. Conf.Inf. Tucker's Regt. Co.I
Van Hagen, John TX Cav. Morgan's Regt. Co.A
Vanham, Joseph TX 21st Cav. Co.E
Vanhan, F.B. AL Jeff Davis Arty.
Vanhay, Norman NC 1st Cav. (9th St.Troops) Co.B
Van Heck, Chs. LA Mil. 3rd Regt.Eur.Brig. (Garde Francaise) Co.9
Vanhee, Julius LA 13th Inf.
Van Heemskerck, William A. TX 1st Hvy.Arty. Co.E 2nd Lt.
Vanheis, --- LA 1st (Strawbridge's) Inf. Co.C
Van Hick, Laurent LA Mil. 3rd Regt.Eur.Brig. (Garde Francaise)
Vanhille, L. LA 2nd Res.Corps Co.H
Vanhille, Louis LA 18th Inf. Co.B
Vanholland, H.W. SC Mil. 1st Regt. (Charleston Res.) Co.F
Vanhook, A. KY Morgan's Men Co.E
Vanhook, A.F. AR 10th Inf. Co.H
Vanhook, Albert G. NC 6th Cav. (65th St.Troops) Co.C,G Cpl.
Van Hook, Albert G. NC Cav. 7th Bn. Co.C Cpl.
Vanhook, Ambrose KY 9th Cav. Co.F
Vanhook, Andrew KY 6th Cav. Co.C
Vanhook, G.W. AR 20th Inf. Co.F
Van Hook, Henry C. TX 17th Inf. Co.A
Vanhook, Henry T. KY Cav. 1st Bn. Co.A
Vanhook, Isaac N. NC 39th Inf. Co.B Sgt.
Van Hook, James NC 6th Inf. Co.B
Vanhook, James H. KY 1st Bn.Mtd.Rifles Co.A Cpl.
Vanhook, J.G. AR 3rd Cav. Co.B
Van Hook, J.H. TX 14th Inf. Co.A 1st Lt.
Vanhook, J.N. TN 45th Inf. Co.B
Van Hook, John C. NC 50th Inf. Co.A Lt.Col.
Van Hook, John L. MS 2nd Cav. Co.B
Vanhook, John L. MS 2nd Inf. Co.B
Vanhook, John R. NC 39th Inf. Co.B Cpl.
Vanhook, Joseph TN 49th Inf. Co.K
Vanhook, Joseph C. KY 6th Cav. Co.C
Vanhook, J.W. TN 11th Inf. Co.F
Vanhook, Lafayette VA 63rd Inf. Co.B
Vanhook, N.M. NC 39th Inf. Co.I Sgt.
Van Hook, Robert KY 2nd Cav. Co.B
Vanhook, Robert KY 6th Cav. Co.B
Vanhook, Robert E. NC 15th Inf. Co.G,E
Vanhook, S.S. TN 24th Bn.S.S. Co.A
Vanhook, Thomas KY 3rd Bn.Mtd.Rifles Co.A
Vanhook, W.D. AR 3rd Cav. Co.B
Vanhook, William KY 6th Cav. Co.B
Vanhook, William VA 63rd Inf. Co.B
Vanhook, William VA Mil. Washington Cty.
Vanhook, William H. KY Cav. 1st Bn. Co.A Capt.
Vanhook, William H. KY 1st Bn.Mtd.Rifles Co.A Bvt.2nd Lt.
Van Hook, William L. MS 14th Inf. Co.K
Van Hook, W.T. NC 39th Inf. Co.B
Vanhoon, Anthony VA 63rd Inf. Co.A
Van Hoovebuke, Ed. LA Mil. 3rd Regt.Eur.Brig. (Garde Francaise)
Vanhoos, John A. 1st Conf.Cav. 2nd Co.G Sgt.
Vanhoos, Sidney 1st Chickasaw Inf. Milam's Co.
Vanhoose, A.H. AL 1st Bn.Cadets Co.A
Van Hoose, Ellison Y. TN 1st (Feild's) Inf. Co.G
Van Hoose, George V. TN 1st (Feild's) Inf. Co.G
Van Hoose, G.W. AR 11th & 17th (Cons.) Inf. Co.K,H Capt.
Van Hoose, G.W. AR 17th (Griffith's) Inf. Co.D Capt.
Van Hoose, H.B. AR 11th & 17th (Cons.) Inf. Co.K Sgt.
Van Hoose, H.B. AR 17th (Griffith's) Inf. Co.D Sgt.
Van Hoose, Isaac W. TN 1st (Feild's) Inf. Co.G
Van Hoose, V.C. AL 51st (Part.Rangers) Co.G Sgt.
Van Hoose, Z. Gen. & Staff AASurg.
Vanhooser, A.J. TN Inf. 1st Cons.Regt. Co.K
Vanhooser, A.J. TN 16th Inf. Co.E Cpl.
Vanhooser, A.V. TN 16th Inf. Co.E Cpl.
Vanhooser, A.V. TN 35th Inf. 1st Co.D, 2nd Co.A
Vanhooser, B.P. TN 13th (Gore's) Cav. Co.G
Vanhooser, F.F. TN 28th (Cons.) Inf. Co.D Sgt.
Vanhooser, Frank F. TN 28th Inf. Co.B,I Sgt.
Vanhooser, H.A. TN 16th Inf. Co.E Cpl.
Vanhooser, I.J. TN 35th Inf. 1st Co.D
Vanhooser, Ira MS 15th Inf. Co.H
Vanhooser, Isaac TN Inf. 22nd Bn. Co.D
Van Hooser, Isaac TX 2nd Inf. Co.D
Vanhooser, Isaac M. TN 16th Inf. Co.E

Vanhooser, John TN Inf. 1st Cons.Regt. Co.K Sgt.
Van Hooser, John TN 4th Inf. Co.A
Vanhooser, John TN 8th Inf. Co.K Cpl.
Vanhooser, John TN 16th Inf. Co.E Sgt.
Vanhooser, John TN 28th (Cons.) Inf. Co.D
Vanhooser, John TN 35th Inf. Co.E
Vanhooser, L.L. TN Inf. 1st Cons.Regt. Co.K 2nd Lt.
Vanhooser, L.L. TN 16th Inf. Co.E 2nd Lt.
Vanhooser, Moses P. TX 6th Cav. Co.E
Vanhooser, Nelson TN Inf. 22nd Bn. Co.D
Van Hooser, V.A. AL 26th (O'Neal's) Inf. Co.H
Vanhooser, William B. TN 28th Inf. Co.B,I
Van Hooser, William J. MO 9th Bn.S.S. Co.A
Vanhooser, W.J. TN 11th (Holman's) Cav. Co.H
Vanhoover, R. MS Conscr.
Vanhoozer, Ambrose Branter TX 20th Cav. Co.C
Vanhoozer, Eli TN 44th (Cons.) Inf. Co.F
Vanhoozer, Jacob TN 44th Inf. Co.G 2nd Lt.
Vanhoozer, J.L. AR 3rd Cav. Earl's Co.
Van Hoozer, Joseph TN 32nd Inf.
Vanhoozer, Robert S. MS 15th Inf. Co.H
Vanhoozer, Sampson TN 32nd Inf. Co.E
Vanhoozer, T.H. MS 2nd Cav. Co.E
Vanhoozer, Thomas H.B. MS 15th Inf. Co.H
Vanhoozer, William Carroll TX 20th Cav. Co.C Sgt.
Vanhoozer, William H. TN 32nd Inf. Co.E Cpl.
Vanhoozin, Robert S. MS K. Williams' Co. (Gray's Port Greys)
Vanhorn, Abe MO 9th Inf. Co.E
Vanhorn, Abe. MO Inf. Clark's Regt. Co.H
Vanhorn, A.J. AL 48th Inf. Co.A Cpl.
Vanhorn, Arnold A. SC 14th Inf. Co.I
Vanhorn, B.F. VA 8th Inf. Co.G
Vanhorn, Burr W. VA 6th Cav. Co.H
Van Horn, C.E. TX 26th Cav. Co.A Cpl.
Vanhorn, Craven O. VA 8th Inf. Co.F Sgt.
Vanhorn, Edward C. VA Cav. Mosby's Regt. (Part.Rangers) Co.B
Vanhorn, Edward O. VA 1st Cav. Co.H
Vanhorn, E.O. VA 11th Cav. Co.K
Vanhorn, Franklin B. MS 8th Cav. Co.C
Vanhorn, F.S. TN Lt.Arty. Rice's Btty. Cpl.
Vanhorn, F.S. TN 38th Inf. 1st Co.A Cpl.
Vanhorn, George KY 2nd (Duke's) Cav. Co.G
Vanhorn, George D. AR 7th Inf. Co.E
Van Horn, George D. MS Lt.Arty. (Warren Lt.Arty.) Swett's Co.
Vanhorn, George R. MO 4th Cav. Co.K,D
Van Horn, H.A. AL St.Arty. Co.C
Van Horn, James F. MS Cav. Garland's Bn. Co.C
Van Horn, James F. 14th Conf.Cav. Co.C
Vanhorn, James R. VA 8th Inf. Co.F
Vanhorn, J.D. FL Cav. 3rd Bn. Co.A
Van Horn, J.D. 15th Conf.Cav. Co.A
Vanhorn, J.E. SC 4th Bn.Res. Co.B
Vanhorn, John LA 15th Inf. Co.E
Vanhorn, John F. MO 4th Cav. Co.K,D
Vanhorn, John G. SC 14th Inf. Co.I Sgt.
Van Horn, John L. NC 32nd Inf. Co.A
Vanhorn, John M. VA 7th Cav. Co.F
Vanhorn, John N. VA 20th Cav. Co.D
Vanhorn, Joseph NC 1st Inf. Co.H
Van Horn, Joseph A. NC 16th Inf. Co.E
Vanhorn, Joseph E. SC 14th Inf. Co.I
Vanhorn, Nicholas GA 24th Inf. Co.I
Van Horn, R.E. AL 21st Inf. Co.I
Van Horn, Robert MO Cav. 3rd Bn. Co.F
Vanhorn, Robert S. VA 6th Cav. Co.B
Vanhorn, S. VA 2nd Inf.Loc.Def. Co.D
Vanhorn, Samuel NC 1st Inf. Co.H
Vanhorn, Samuel VA 12th Cav. Co.G 1st Sgt.
Vanhorn, Samuel VA 34th Mil. Co.D Cpl.
Vanhorn, Shelley VA 10th Cav. Co.A Sgt.
Van Horn, Shelly VA Inf. 6th Bn.Loc.Def. Co.A
Van Horn, Thomas NC 32nd Inf. Co.F,A
Vanhorn, Thomas A. VA 17th Cav. Co.B
Vanhorn, Tray A. MO 1st N.E. Cav. Co.C
Vanhorn, W. AR Mil. Desha Cty.Bn. 2nd Lt.
Vanhorn, Washington VA 31st Inf. Co.D Sgt.
Van Horn, William GA Hvy.Arty. 22nd Bn. Co.C
Vanhorn, William MS 29th Inf. Co.H
Vanhorn, William 3rd Conf.Eng.Troops Co.G Cpl.
Vanhorn, William A. MS 15th Inf. Co.H
Vanhorn, William H. MO 4th Cav. Co.K,D
Vanhorn, William P. MS 29th Inf. Co.D
Vanhorne, David NC 58th Inf. Co.A
Van Horne, H.A. AL Mil. 3rd Vol. Co.A
Van Horne, L. TN 7th (Duckworth's) Cav. Co.C Cpl.
Van Horne, T. KY Morgan's Men Co.C
Vanhosier, Willis AR 23rd Inf. Co.B
Van Houten, Charles E. MS Lt.Arty. (Madison Lt.Arty.) Richards' Co.
Van Houten, Edwin AL Inf. 1st Regt. Co.B
Van Houten, Edwin Lt.Arty. Dent's Btty.,CSA Bugler
Van Houten, Jonathan B. TX 8th Cav. Co.H
Van Houton, C.L. LA Inf.Crescent Regt. Co.F
Van Houton, C.S. LA 18th Inf. Co.C
Vanhouton, Daniel GA 1st (Fannin's) Res. Co.A Sgt.
Van Houton, James H. GA 1st (Olmstead's) Inf. Co.C Sgt.
Vanhowton, G.W. TX 4th Cav. Co.B
Vanhoy, Amos NC 28th Inf. Co.K
Vanhoy, Edward F. NC 66th Inf. Co.G
Vanhoy, E.H. TX 12th Cav. Co.C
Van Hoy, Henry NC 6th Inf. Co.F
Vanhoy, J.F. NC 57th Inf. Co.K
Vanhoy, J.F. 2nd Cherokee Mtd.Vol. Co.A 2nd Lt.
Vanhoy, J.L. NC Allen's Co. (Loc.Def.)
Vanhoy, John A. NC 3rd Inf.
Vanhoy, Robert TN 1st (Carter's) Cav. Co.E
Vanhoy, William NC 66th Inf. Co.G
Van Hughes, Martin MS 1st Lt.Arty. Co.C
Van Huss, Anthony VA 6th Bn.Res. Co.H,F
Vanhuss, David B. VA 37th Inf. Co.H
Vanhuss, D.H. VA 30th Bn.S.S. Co.E
Vanhuss, Finly TX 16th Cav. Co.E
Vanhuss, John M. VA 25th Cav. Co.H
Vanhuss, John M. VA 30th Bn.S.S. Co.E
Vanhuss, John M. VA Mil. Washington Cty.
Vanhuss, Michael VA 25th Cav. Co.H
Vanhuss, Solomon VA 25th Cav. Co.H
Vanhuss, Valentine VA 25th Cav. Co.H
Vanhuss, Valentine VA 30th Bn.S.S. Co.E
Vanhuss, Valentine VA Mil. Washington Cty.
Vanhuss, V.V. TN 61st Mtd.Inf. Co.D
Vanhuss, William VA 25th Cav. Co.H
Vanhuss, William A. VA 25th Cav. Co.H
Vanhuten, R. TX 25th Cav. Co.H
Vanible, W.L. VA Richmond Cadets
Vanice, George B. MO Cav. Wood's Regt. Co.K,G
Vanice, H. MO 4th Cav. Co.G
Vanier, A. LA 13th Inf. Co.C
Vanier, J.P. VA 18th Inf. Co.E
Vanison, L. TX Inf. 1st Bn. (St.Troops) Co.E
Van James, W. AL 17th Inf. Co.K
Van Jugen, J.S. LA 1st Cav. Co.B
Vankirk, Henry KY 2nd Bn.Mtd.Rifles Co.B
Vankirk, John MS 1st Cav. Co.C,G
Van Kirk, John TX Inf. 1st Bn. Co.B
Vankirk, John TX Inf. Rutherford's Co.
Vankirk, William J. MO Cav. 2nd Regt.St.Guard Co.E Adj.
Vankirk, William J. MO Cav. 3rd Bn. Co.B Capt.,AQM
Vankirk, W.J. MO 2nd Cav. AQM
Vankirk, W.J. MO 5th Inf. Co.C
Vankirk, W.J. Gen. & Staff Capt.,AQM
Vanknapp, Miles NC Inf. 2nd Bn. Co.H
Vankuren, Augustus LA Mil. Bragg's Bn. Schwartz's Co.
Vanlandigham, William E. AR Cav. Harrell's Bn. Co.C
Vanlandingham, David VA 37th Mil. Co.D
Vanlandingham, E. GA 12th Mil. Capt.
Vanlandingham, Edward GA 11th Cav. (St.Guards) McGriff's Co. Sgt.
Vanlandingham, E.P. LA Ogden's Cav. Co.C
Vanlandingham, E.P. 14th Conf.Cav. Co.G
Vanlandingham, Ewel VA 37th Mil. Co.D
Vanlandingham, George KY 4th Cav. Co.C
Vanlandingham, H.J. MS 35th Inf. Co.D 1st Sgt.
Van Landingham, James MS 11th (Perrin's) Cav. Co.D
Vanlandingham, James D. MS 42nd Inf. Co.G Sgt.
Vanlandingham, James M. FL 7th Inf. Co.C 1st Lt.
Vanlandingham, James M. MS 26th Inf. Co.B
Vanlandingham, J.E. FL Cav. 5th Bn. Co.D
Vanlandingham, John N. GA 3rd Inf. Co.F
Vanlandingham, John T. GA 3rd Inf. Co.F
Vanlandingham, J.T.C. SC 12th Inf. Co.I
Vanlandingham, Moses E. MS 42nd Inf. Co.G
Vanlandingham, N.B. SC 12th Inf. Co.I Capt.
Vanlandingham, O. LA Ogden's Cav. Co.F
Vanlandingham, O. MS Cav. Hughes' Bn. Co.C
Vanlandingham, O. VA Cav. 15th Bn. Co.B
Vanlandingham, O.C. 14th Conf.Cav. Co.G
Vanlandingham, Peter GA 11th Cav. (St.Guards) McGriff's Co. Sgt.
Vanlandingham, Richard C. VA 40th Inf. Co.F
Vanlandingham, R.P. NC 12th Inf. Co.C Sgt.
Vanlandingham, Sion C. FL 7th Inf. Co.D Capt.
Vanlandingham, S.J. MS 35th Inf. Co.D
Vanlandingham, Spencer VA 15th Cav. Co.D
Vanlandingham, Spencer VA Cav. 15th Bn. Co.B
Vanlandingham, Spencer VA 37th Mil. Co.D
Vanlandingham, Thomas O. VA 15th Cav. Co.G

Vanlandingham, Thomas O. VA Cav. 15th Bn. Co.D Sgt.
Vanlandingham, Thomas O. VA 41st Mil. Co.C Cpl.
Vanlandingham, T.J. AR 45th Cav. Co.L
Vanlandingham, W.C. AR 2nd Cav.
Vanlandingham, Wesley C. AR 2nd Cav.
Vanlandingham, William VA 37th Mil. Co.D
Vanlandingham, William VA 40th Inf. Co.C
Vanlandingham, W.K. GA 63rd Inf. Co.D
Vanlandingham, W.L. AL 25th Inf. Co.K
Vanlandingham, W.T. SC 4th Cav. Co.H
Vanlear, Ausbert G.L. VA 5th Inf. Co.F
Vanlear, Charles A. VA 33rd Inf. Co.I Cpl.
Van Lear, Edward F. VA 10th Inf. Co.G Sgt.
Van Lear, G.W. MO St.Guard
Van Lear, Harden A. VA 7th Bn.Res. Co.A 1st Lt.
Van Lear, James P. VA 23rd Cav. Co.B Sgt.
Van Lear, James P. VA Cav. 41st Bn. Co.B Sgt.
Van Lear, James P. VA 25th Inf. 2nd Co.D
Van Lear, J.L. MO 6th Cav. Co.G
Vanleer, Joseph H. TN 1st (Feild's) Inf. Co.B 1st Lt.
Van Leer, Rush Frazier's Staff Capt.,Ch.Eng.
Vanlempat, John Conf.Inf. Tucker's Regt. Co.D
Vanlendryham, George MS 3rd Inf. (St.Troops) Co.E
Van Lew, John N. VA 18th Inf. Co.C
Vanlier, John VA 14th Cav. Co.C
Vanloan, Abram H. GA Arty. 9th Bn. Co.A
Vanmata, Ere MO 4th Inf. Co.F,H
Van Matre, David S. VA Horse Arty. Jackson's Co. 2nd Lt.
Van Meeter, Isaac AL 8th Inf. Co.E
Van Meeter, S. VA 14th Inf. Co.B
Vanmeter, A. Morgan VA 1st Cav. Co.F
Vanmeter, Beall VA 33rd Inf. Co.F
Vanmeter, Benjamin F. VA 31st Inf. Co.K
Vanmeter, Charles W. VA 7th Cav. Co.F
Vanmeter, Colgan MO 5th Cav. Co.C
Vanmeter, Daniel VA 46th Mil. Co.C
Van Meter, David MO 1st N.E. Cav.
Van Meter, David MO Cav. Woodson's Co.
Vanmeter, David C. VA 11th Cav. Co.B
Vanmeter, D.G. VA 7th Cav. Co.F
Vanmeter, D.R. KY 1st (Helm's) Cav. New Co.A Sgt.
Van Meter, D.S. TN 50th Inf. 2nd Lt.
Vanmeter, Edward P. VA 7th Cav. Co.F
Vanmeter, Garrett I. VA 25th Inf. 2nd Co.E
Vanmeter, Isaac VA 7th Cav. Co.F
Vanmeter, Isaac VA 11th Cav. Co.B
Vanmeter, Isaac N. VA 25th Inf. 1st Co.H
Vanmeter, J.A. MS 28th Cav. Co.D
Vanmeter, Jacob VA 46th Mil. Co.C
Van Meter, James S.E. VA 122nd Mil. Co.A
Vanmeter, Jasper N. AR 36th Inf. Co.A
Vanmeter, John MO 5th Cav. Co.I 3rd Lt.
Van Meter, John M. KY 8th Cav. Co.E Sgt.
Vanmeter, John S. KY 8th Cav. Co.E
Vanmeter, Joseph VA 2nd Inf. Co.H
Vanmeter, Joseph VA 25th Inf. 2nd Co.E 3rd Lt.
Vanmeter, Joseph B. VA 1st Cav. Co.F
Vanmeter, L.M. KY 9th Cav. Co.E 2nd Lt.
Vanmeter, Milton VA 7th Cav. Co.F
Vanmeter, Morgan VA 2nd Inf. Co.H
Vanmeter, M.P. AR 7th Inf. Co.K Sgt.
Vanmeter, Oliver MO 5th Cav. Co.C
Vanmeter, Samuel MO 5th Cav. Co.C
Vanmeter, Solomon VA 62nd Mtd.Inf. 2nd Co.B
Vanmeter, William KY 3rd Mtd.Inf.
Vanmeter, William C. VA 18th Cav. Co.H
Vanmeter, William C. VA 25th Inf. 2nd Co.E,D
Vanmeter, William H. KY 6th Mtd.Inf. Co.H
Vanmeter, W.P. TX 17th Inf. Co.D Sgt.
Vanmetre, David A. VA 62nd Mtd.Inf. 2nd Co.I
Vanmetre, David A. VA 25th Inf. 1st Co.E
Vanmetre, David P. VA 7th Cav. Co.F
Van Metre, Abraham TX 4th Field Btty.
Vanmetre, James L.E. VA 11th Cav. Co.C Sgt.
Vanmetre, James W. VA 122nd Mil. Co.F
Vanmetre, R. Beall VA 7th Cav. Co.F
Van Morgan, S. AL 4th Cav. Surg.
Vann, --- TX Cav. Mann's Regt. Co.C
Vann, A. GA 54th Inf. Co.A
Vann, A.J. AL 50th Inf. Co.C
Vann, Albert NC 4th Cav. (59th St.Troops)
Vann, Albert NC Cav. 12th Bn. Co.C
Vann, Albert NC Lt.Arty. 3rd Bn. Co.C,B
Vann, Albert C. NC 3rd Arty. (40th St.Troops) Co.B
Vann, Alexander AL 33rd Inf. Co.B
Vann, Alfred H. VA 9th Inf. Co.I
Vann, A.M. GA 6th Cav. Co.G
Vann, A.M. GA Smith's Legion Co.G
Vann, Andrew GA 50th Inf. Co.E Sgt.
Vann, Andrew TN 3rd (Forrest's) Cav. 1st Co.E
Vann, Appling GA 4th Inf. Co.C Cpl.
Vann, Arnold S. AL 53rd (Part.Rangers) Co.B
Vann, Asa GA 20th Inf. Co.A
Vann, Asbury J. GA 1st Inf. (St.Guards)
Vann, Benjamin T. GA 64th Inf. Co.C
Vann, B.F. AL 12th Cav. Co.F
Vann, C. GA 15th Mil. Co.C
Vann, C. 1st Cherokee Mtd.Vol. 1st Co.B
Vann, Calvin AL 1st Bn. Hilliard's Legion Vol. Co.B
Vann, Calvin GA 20th Inf. Co.A
Vann, Charles M. GA 12th Mil. Co.F,H
Vann, Chester R. NC 51st Inf. Co.K 1st Sgt.
Vann, C.K. AL Cav. Hardie's Bn.Res. Co.G
Vann, Clemm 1st Cherokee Mtd.Rifles Co.K
Vann, Daniel NC 56th Inf. Co.B
Vann, David AL 12th Inf. Co.B
Vann, David 1st Cherokee Mtd.Vol. 2nd Co.H,B
Vann, David 2nd Cherokee Mtd.Vol. Co.F Sgt.
Vann, David 1st Creek Mtd.Vol. 2nd Co.D
Vann, D.D. GA 6th Cav. Co.G
Vann, Dempsey NC 5th Inf. Co.G
Vann, D.J. FL Conscr.
Vann, D.R. 2nd Cherokee Mtd.Vol. Co.K 1st Lt.
Vann, D.W. 1st Cherokee Mtd.Vol. 1st Co.D
Vann, E. 1st Cherokee Mtd.Vol. 1st Co.B 2nd Lt.
Vann, Edward GA 26th Inf. Co.I
Vann, Edward K. GA Cav. 29th Bn. Co.C Sgt.
Vann, Edward T. AL 40th Inf. Co.A
Vann, Elias GA 49th Inf. Co.A
Vann, Ephraim 1st Cherokee Mtd.Vol. 2nd Co.F
Vann, Ephraim 2nd Cherokee Mtd.Vol. Co.D
Vann, E.T. AL Cav. Barbiere's Bn. Truss' Co.
Vann, E.T. AL 17th Inf. Co.F
Vann, E.W. FL 5th Inf. Co.E
Vann, E.W. FL 8th Inf. Co.A
Vann, E.W. FL 11th Inf. Co.G
Vann, Flopper 1st Cherokee Mtd.Vol. 2nd Co.B
Vann, George W. FL 10th Inf. Co.D
Vann, George W. NC 5th Cav. (63rd St.Troops) Co.C
Vann, George W. NC Inf. Thomas Legion Co.K
Vann, George W. Mead's Conf.Cav. Co.E Cpl.
Vann, G.W. AL 37th Inf. Co.F N.C.S. QMSgt.
Vann, H. KY 12th Cav. Co.E
Vann, Henry NC 46th Inf. Co.I
Vann, Henry NC Giddins' Co. (Detailed & Petitioned Men)
Vann, J. SC 12th Inf. Co.C
Vann, Jacob AL 3rd Inf. Co.E
Vann, Jacob M. AL 13th Inf.
Vann, James AL 18th Inf. Co.F
Vann, James GA Cav. 19th Bn. Co.A
Vann, James TN 35th Inf. 2nd Co.A
Vann, James 1st Cherokee Mtd.Rifles Co.E Capt.
Vann, James B. AL 11th Inf. Asst.Surg.
Vann, James H. NC 1st Cav. (9th St.Troops) Co.B
Vann, James I. AL 56th (Part.Rangers) Co.E
Vann, James J. GA 51st Inf. Co.A
Vann, James S. 1st Cherokee Mtd.Rifles Adj.
Vann, Jas. S. Gen. & Staff 1st Lt.,Adj.
Vann, James W. AL 19th Inf. Co.C Sgt.
Vann, James W. GA 14th Inf. Co.F
Vann, Jasper L.C. AL Cp. of Instr. Talladega
Vann, J.B. AL Cp. of Instr. Talladega
Vann, J. Byrd Gen. & Staff Asst.Surg.
Vann, J.D. GA 6th Cav. Co.G
Vann, J.E. FL Lt.Arty. Dyke's Co.
Vann, J.E. MS 2nd Cav. Co.D
Vann, J.E. SC 4th St.Troops Co.E
Vann, Jeremiah E. SC 21st Inf. Co.G
Vann, Jesse 1st Cherokee Mtd.Rifles Co.E
Vann, Jesse 1st Cherokee Mtd.Rifles Co.F
Vann, Jesse 2nd Cherokee Mtd.Vol. Co.I
Vann, Jessee AR 38th Inf. Co.F
Vann, J.F. TX 4th Inf. (St.Troops) Co.E
Vann, J.H. AL 13th Inf. Co.C
Vann, J.I. AL 15th Bn.Part.Rangers Co.E
Vann, J.K. AL Cav. Barbiere's Bn. Truss' Co.
Vann, J.L. GA Lt.Arty. Croft's Btty. (Columbus Arty.) Cpl.
Vann, J.M. AL 15th Inf. Co.A Ord.Sgt.
Vann, J.M. NC 8th Sr.Res. Kelly's Co.
Vann, J.O. MS 2nd Cav. Co.D
Vann, Joe G. 2nd Cherokee Mtd.Vol. Co.D
Vann, Joel NC 56th Inf. Co.B
Vann, John AR Cav. McGehee's Regt. Co.A Cpl.
Vann, John FL Inf. 2nd Bn. Co.E
Vann, Jno. GA 45th Inf. Co.A
Vann, John GA 50th Inf. Co.E
Vann, John 1st Cherokee Mtd.Vol. 1st Co.C
Vann, John 2nd Cherokee Mtd.Vol. Co.I Maj.
Vann, John 2nd Cherokee Mtd.Vol. Co.K Cpl.
Vann, John 1st Creek Mtd.Vol. 2nd Co.D
Vann, John Canadian Dist. Cherokee Nation,CSA Prov.Marsh.
Vann, John C. AL 50th Inf.
Vann, John D. AR 36th Inf. Co.F
Vann, John H. AL 37th Inf. Co.A

Vann, John H. Mead's Conf.Cav. Co.E Sgt.
Vann, John J. NC 20th Inf. Faison's Co.
Vann, John J. NC 61st Inf. Co.A
Vann, John N. MS Inf. 7th Bn. Co.E
Vann, John R. NC 1st Inf. Co.F
Vann, John R. NC 51st Inf. Co.A
Vann, John R. NC 61st Inf. Co.A
Vann, Johnson 2nd Cherokee Mtd.Vol. Co.F
Vann, John W. FL 5th Inf. Co.E Cpl.
Vann, John W. GA 59th Inf. Co.D
Vann, John W. TN 7th Inf. Co.G
Vann, Jo P. AR 37th Inf. Co.E Capt.
Vann, Joseph NC 4th Cav. (59th St.Troops) Co.K
Vann, Joseph NC Cav. 12th Bn. Co.A
Vann, Joseph TX 13th Cav. Co.A Cpl.
Vann, Joseph 8th (Dearing's) Conf.Cav. Co.A
Vann, Joseph 1st Cherokee Mtd.Rifles Co.K Cpl.
Vann, Joseph 1st Cherokee Mtd.Vol. 2nd Co.F
Vann, Joseph 1st Cherokee Mtd.Vol. 2nd Co.H
Vann, Joseph L. AL 6th Cav. Co.H,F 2nd Lt.
Vann, Joseph L. AL 3rd Inf. Co.D
Vann, Joseph P. AL 40th Inf. Co.A
Vann, Joseph T. SC 18th Inf. Co.I
Vann, Josh 1st Creek Mtd.Vol. 2nd Co.D
Vann, Joshua 1st Creek Mtd.Vol. 2nd Co.H
Vann, Josiah 1st Cherokee Mtd.Rifles Co.K
Vann, J.W. AL 25th Inf. Co.D Sgt.
Vann, Lazarus N. AR 15th (Josey's) Inf. Co.F 1st Lt.
Vann, Lemuel D. NC 1st Inf. (6 mo. '61) Co.D
Vann, Lemuel D. NC 11th (Bethel Regt.) Inf. Co.G
Vann, Leonard FL Inf. 2nd Bn. Co.E
Vann, Leonard FL 11th Inf. Co.A
Vann, Lewis GA 57th Inf. Co.A
Vann, M. AL 45th Inf. Co.C
Vann, Macklin M. AL 50th Inf. Co.C
Vann, Marion NC 3rd Inf. Co.D Cpl.
Vann, Marshal NC 38th Inf. Co.C
Vann, Martin 1st Creek Mtd.Vol. 2nd Co.C 1st Lt.
Vann, Mills Le VA Inf. Cohoon's Bn. Co.D
Vann, M.K. AL Cav. Barbiere's Bn. Truss' Co.
Vann, Moses AL 18th Inf. Co.A
Vann, Moses 2nd Cherokee Mtd.Vol. Co.I
Vann, M.R. AL 13th Inf. Co.E
Vann, Quinton H. TX 4th Inf. Co.A
Vann, R.D. GA 28th Inf. Co.A
Vann, Reuben GA 66th Inf. Co.D
Vann, Richard NC Cav. 12th Bn. Co.C
Vann, Richard 8th (Dearing's) Conf.Cav. Co.C
Vann, R.J. AL Inf. 1st (Loomis') Bn. Co.D
Vann, R.J. AL 25th Inf. Co.D
Vann, Robert 1st Cherokee Mtd.Vol. 1st Co.I, 2nd Co.I Sgt.
Vann, Robert J. AL 20th Inf. Co.C
Vann, Robt. J. AL Cp. of Instr. Talladega Co.H
Vann, Robert T. TN 39th Mtd.Inf. Co.A Cpl.
Vann, R.S. SC 2nd Arty. Co.I
Vann, Rufus NC Mil. Clark's Sp.Bn. Co.L
Vann, Samuel GA 59th Inf. Co.D
Vann, Samuel D. AR Cav. McGehee's Regt. Co.A Cpl.
Vann, Samuel R. AL 6th Inf. Co.B
Vann, Simpon T. AR 1st Cav. Co.B
Vann, Simpson T. AR 1st Inf. Co.B
Vann, S.K. AL 19th Inf. Co.C,K
Vann, S.R. GA 28th Inf. Co.A
Vann, S.T. AL 17th Inf. Co.F
Vann, Tahtanor 1st Cherokee Mtd.Vol. 2nd Co.H,B
Vann, T.C. TN 8th Inf. Co.B Wagon M.
Vann, T.E. FL Lt.Arty. Dyke's Co.
Vann, Thaddeus E. NC 3rd Arty. (40th St.Troops) Co.B
Vann, Thomas AR 8th Cav. Co.A
Vann, Thomas AR Inf. 4th Bn. Co.E Cpl.
Vann, Thomas NC Unassign.Conscr.
Vann, Thomas J. AL 4th Inf. Co.K Sgt.
Vann, Thomas J. FL 1st Inf. Old Co.F,H
Vann, Thomas J. FL 5th Inf. Co.E 1st Lt.
Vann, Thomas J. SC 1st (Hagood's) Inf. 1st Co.B, 2nd Co.K Cpl.
Vann, Thomas N. NC 3rd Inf. Co.E
Vann, Thomas R. AL Cav. Hardie's Bn.Res. Co.C
Vann, Thomas S. TX 4th Inf. Co.A
Vann, T.J. AL 49th Inf. Co.H
Vann, Valentine NC 3rd Arty. (40th St.Troops) Co.H
Vann, Valentine NC 61st Inf. Co.G
Vann, W.A. NC 13th Inf. Chap.
Vann, W.D. AL 19th Inf. Co.C
Vann, W.E. AL 33rd Inf. Co.E
Vann, Webster 2nd Cherokee Mtd.Vol. Co.D
Vann, Wiley GA 54th Inf. Co.A
Vann, Wiley GA 64th Inf. Co.B
Vann, William AR 38th Inf. Co.F
Vann, William NC 1st Cav. (9th St.Troops) Co.B Cpl.
Vann, William NC 4th Cav. (59th St.Troops) Co.K 2nd Lt.
Vann, William NC Cav. 12th Bn. Co.A 3rd Lt.
Vann, William TN 32nd Inf. Co.K
Vann, William 8th (Dearing's) Conf.Cav. Co.A 2nd Lt.
Vann, William 1st Cherokee Mtd.Vol. 1st Co.B Cpl.
Vann, William 2nd Cherokee Mtd.Vol. Co.F
Vann, William 1st Creek Mtd.Vol. 2nd Co.D
Vann, William A. Gen. & Staff Chap.
Vann, William H. AR 5th Inf. Co.I
Vann, William H., Jr. NC McDugald's Co.
Vann, William H., Sr. NC McDugald's Co.
Vann, William H. VA 9th Inf. Co.I
Vann, William H. 8th (Wade's) Conf.Cav. Co.A
Vann, William J. AL 19th Inf. Co.C
Vann, William K. NC 2nd Inf. Co.C
Vann, William L. AL 19th Inf. Co.C
Vann, William N. AL 30th Inf. Co.C
Vann, Wm. N. AL 30th Inf. Co.E
Vann, William T. NC 51st Inf. Co.A Cpl.
Vann, William W. MS 42nd Inf. Co.H
Vann, W.J. NC 2nd Jr.Res. Co.A
Vann, W.K. GA 6th Cav. Co.G
Vann, W.M. AL 23rd Inf. Co.C
Vann, W.S. AR 50th Mil. Co.A
Vann, W.W. TX Waul's Legion Co.G Sgt.
Vann, W.W. Exch.Bn. 1st Co.B,CSA Cpl.
Vann, Yahtunnu 1st Creek Mtd.Vol. 2nd Co.D
Vann, Z. MS 10th Inf. Old Co.D
Vann, Zachariah MS 13th Inf. Co.G
Van Name, M. LA 2nd Cav.
Vanname, Peter M. VA 1st Arty. Co.F,K
Vanname, Peter M. VA Arty. L.F. Jones' Co.
Vanname, Peter M. VA 32nd Inf. Co.G
Vannap, Miles NC Cav. 5th Bn. Co.A
Vannason, Adrian B. VA Cav. 5th Regt. Co.F
Vannatta, William S. AR 14th (McCarver's) Inf. Co.C
Vannatter, James J. VA 129th Mil. Chambers' Co., Avis' Co.
Vannatter, Jefferson VA 129th Mil. Chambers' Co., Avis' Co.
Vannatter, Jeremiah J. VA 129th Mil. Chambers' Co., Avis' Co.
Vannatter, John, Jr. VA 129th Mil. Chambers' Co., Avis' Co.
Vannatter, Lewis VA 129th Mil. Chambers' Co., Avis' Co.
Vannatter, Patterson VA 129th Mil. Avis' Co.
Vannatter, Samuel P. VA 129th Mil. Chambers' Co.
Vannatter, Theodore VA 129th Mil. Chambers' Co., Avis' Co.
Vannatti, E. MO 1st & 4th Cons.Inf. Co.E
Vannauker, John Conf.Reg.Inf. Brooks' Bn. Co.F
Vannay, Charles LA 25th Inf. Co.F,D
Vannay, J.W. TX 10th Cav. Co.A
Vannay, Lewis W. NC Cav. 5th Bn. Co.D
Vannay, Neal C. NC Cav. 5th Bn. Co.D
Vannerson, A.B. VA 5th Cav. Co.F Sgt.
Vannerson, Frank TN 35th Inf. 1st Co.D, Co.G,B 2nd Lt.
Vannerson, J.H. TN 35th Inf. QMSgt.
Vannerson, John T. VA 15th Inf. Co.H Capt.
Vannerson, Julian VA Inf. 25th Bn. Co.C 1st Sgt.
Vannerson, Lucian TX Inf. Rutherford's Co.
Vannerson, Robert KY 1st (Butler's) Cav. Sgt.
Vannerson, Robert TN 16th Inf. Co.C
Van Ness, H. AL Cav. Forrest's Regt. Capt.
Vanness, Henry AL 2nd Inf. Co.A Capt.
Vanness, Henry MS Cav. 4th Bn. Roddey's Co.
Van Ness, James H. VA 15th Cav. Co.D
Van Ness, James K. SC Hvy.Arty. Mathewes' Co.
Van Ness, J. Armistead TX 6th Cav. Co.H
Van Ness, J.I. VA 3rd Inf.Loc.Def. Co.B
Vanness, T.E. MO 6th Cav. Co.I
Van Ness, William TX 5th Cav. Co.G
Vanness, William P. VA 9th Cav. Co.K
Van Ness, William P. VA 41st Mil. Co.B Comsy.
Vannest, John MO 6th Cav. Co.E Cpl.
Vanneter, A.P. VA 7th Cav. Co.F
Vannetre, A.M. VA 67th Mil. Co.C
Vannetre, J.M. VA 67th Mil. Co.D
Vannettee, W. MO 4th Inf. Co.H
Vanney, Asa M. LA 6th Inf. Co.C
Vanney, Harman LA 25th Inf. Co.C
Vanney, Harman LA Inf. Pelican Regt. Co.C
Vanni, --- LA Mil. 1st Chasseurs a pied Co.8 Cpl.
Vanni, J. VA 2nd St.Res. Co.K
Vannice, John KY 4th Cav. Co.E,F
Vannier, J. TX 25th Cav. Co.I
Vannoge, Charles TX 15th Inf. Co.C
Vannop, Miles NC 64th Inf. Co.F 2nd Lt.
Vannorden, A. AL Gid Nelson Lt.Arty.

Vannorden, P.G. AL Gid Nelson Lt.Arty.
Van Norman, A.L. MS 32nd Inf. Co.E
Vannorman, Andrew J. MS 22nd Inf. Co.E
Vannorman, Antoine L. MS 22nd Inf. Co.E
Van Norman, Garnett B. MS 7th Inf. Co.C
Van Norman, P.B. LA 4th Inf. Co.K
Van Norman, Samuel T. MS 7th Inf. Co.C
Vannorstale, Thomas LA 20th Inf. Co.F
Vannort, James VA 97th Mil. Co.L Cpl.
Vannort, James E. VA 7th Cav. Co.D
Vannort, Levi D. VA 17th Cav. Co.B
Vannort, William D. VA 17th Cav. Co.B
Vannort, William H. MO 4th Cav. Co.F,D
Vannortrick, Oliver NC 33rd Inf. Co.B
Vannoshdall, --- MO Cav. 2nd Regt.St.Guard Co.F
Van Nostrand, E.M. LA 6th Cav. Co.A Sgt.
Vannote, Robert Conf.Inf. 8th Bn. Co.F Cpl.
Vannoy, A. NC 18th Inf. Co.G
Vannoy, A.J. NC Mil. 66th Bn. J.H. Whitman's Co.
Vannoy, Alexander W. NC 1st Inf. Co.B
Vannoy, A.M. LA Arty. 1st Field Btty.
Vannoy, A.M. MO 1st & 4th Cons.Inf. Co.I
Vannoy, A.M. MO 4th Inf. Co.I
Vannoy, A.N. TX 7th Cav. Co.I
Vannoy, Anderson M. NC 1st Inf. Co.B
Vannoy, Andrew NC 4th Bn.Jr.Res. Co.B
Vannoy, B.P. LA 16th Inf. Co.K
Vannoy, C.C. TX Cav. Sutton's Co.
Vannoy, Columbus F. NC 56th Inf. Co.G
Vannoy, Elijah R. NC 52nd Inf. Co.F 1st Sgt.
Vannoy, Harvey S. NC 1st Inf. Co.B
Vannoy, Henry S. MD 1st Cav. Co.B
Van Noy, J. LA 18th Inf. Co.A
Vannoy, J.A. SC 1st Regt. Charleston Guard Co.I Sgt.
Vannoy, James A. NC 53rd Inf. Co.K Music.
Vannoy, James H. NC 37th Inf. Co.A Sgt.
Vannoy, James H. TX Cav. Martin's Regt. Co.B
Vannoy, James R. NC Cav. 5th Bn. Co.D
Vannoy, James R. NC 56th Inf. Co.G
Vannoy, Jesse NC 5th Sr.Res. Co.A 1st Sgt.
Vannoy, Jesse F. NC Cav. 5th Bn. Co.D
Vannoy, Jesse F. TN 41st Inf. Co.F
Vannoy, Jesse S. LA 6th Inf. Co.C
Vannoy, J.H. AL 2nd Cav. Co.D
Vannoy, John TX 32nd Cav. Co.F
Vannoy, John TX Cav. Baylor's Regt. Co.G
Vannoy, John TX Vol. Teague's Co. (So.Rights Guards) Sgt.
Vannoy, John H. NC 2nd Cav. (19th St.Troops) Co.B
Vannoy, John H. TX 13th Cav. Co.D
Vannoy, John H. TX 37th Cav. Co.E
Vannoy, Joseph C. LA Scouts Ind.Co.
Vannoy, Lewis W. NC 6th Cav. (65th St.Troops) Co.D,B
Vannoy, Mason, Jr. TN 1st (Feild's) Inf. Co.C
Vannoy, Thomas J. NC 37th Inf. Co.F Sgt.
Van Noy, Thomas J. TX 9th (Young's) Inf. Co.D Capt.
Vannoy, William NC 58th Inf. Co.G
Vannoy, William H. NC 58th Inf. Co.G
Vannoy, William O. NC 6th Cav. (65th St.Troops) Co.B
Vannoy, William O. TX 15th Cav. Co.E
Vannoy, William W. NC 1st Inf. Co.B 2nd Lt.
Van Nuss, A. TX 15th Field Btty.
Van Olar, Peter MS 29th Inf. Music.
Van Olker, Piere MS 24th Inf. Music.
Vanoni, Bartol LA Mil. Cazadores Espanoles Regt. Co.F
Vanorden, John W. MS 33rd Inf. Co.E
Vanorden, J.W. MS 22nd Inf. Co.G
Van Orman, S.T. MS 9th Inf. Co.A 1st Sgt.
Van Orsdale, Michael LA 11th Inf. Co.I
Van Orsdale, Thomas J. LA 11th Inf. Co.I
Vanorsdoll, Isaac M. VA 89th Mil. Co.B
Vanorsdoll, William VA 89th Mil. Co.A
Vanorsdoll, William G. VA 89th Mil. Co.B
Van Osdall, E. LA 4th Inf. Co.K
Van Osdall, J. LA 4th Inf. Co.K
Van Osdall, M. LA 4th Inf. Co.K
Van Osdol, Henry 1st Choctaw & Chickasaw Mtd.Rifles Co.A 1st Lt.
Van Osten, Robert L. KY 1st Inf. Co.I Capt.
Van Osten, Robert L. LA 1st (Nelligan's) Inf. Co.H 1st Lt.
Van Ostrand, H.Q. LA Mil.Conf.Guards Regt. Co.D
Vanotter, Jeff VA Inf. 1st Bn. Co.A
Vanover, Charles NC Cav. 5th Bn. Co.C
Vanover, Charles NC 6th Cav. (65th St.Troops) Co.H,C
Vanover, Charles NC 58th Inf. Co.D
Vanover, Charles J. NC 1st Arty. (10th St.Troops) Co.I
Vanover, C.J. NC 2nd Arty. (36th St.Troops) Co.A
Vanover, Elijah VA Inf. French's Bn. Co.D
Vanover, Eli S. VA 50th Inf. Co.H
Vanover, Jacob NC 1st Arty. (10th St.Troops) Co.I
Vanover, Jacob NC 2nd Arty. (36th St.Troops) Co.A
Vanover, John NC 26th Inf. Co.A
Vanover, Richard VA 21st Cav. Co.K
Vanover, Samuel TX 10th Inf. Co.I
Vanover, William VA 21st Cav. Co.K
Vanover, William VA 50th Inf. Co.H
Vanover, William P. VA 21st Cav. Co.K
Vanoy, --- TX Cav. Mann's Regt. Co.D
Vanoy, A.M. VA Scott's Bn.Loc.Def. 3rd Cpl.
Vanoy, Cornelius GA 1st Reg. Co.G
Vanoy, Cornelius TN 13th (Gore's) Cav. Co.G
Vanoy, David TN 13th (Gore's) Cav. Co.G
Vanoy, Henry H. MS 44th Inf. Co.E
Vanoy, James TN 25th Inf. Co.G Sgt.
Vanoy, Jesse D. NC 6th Cav. (65th St.Troops) Co.D
Vanoy, John VA 36th Inf. 2nd Co.E
Vanpatern, R. SC 3rd Inf. Co.D
Van Patten, Adam E. SC 14th Inf. Co.E
Van Patten, Alfred AZ Cav. Herbert's Bn. Oury's Co. Cpl.
Van Patten, Eugene AZ Cav. Herbert's Bn. Oury's Co. Bugler
Van Patten, V.V. SC 23rd Inf. Co.B
Vanpeet, J.H. VA 11th Cav. Co.G
Van Peet, J.J. TN Arty. Bibb's Co.
Van Pelt, Abe MS 26th Inf. Co.A
Vanpelt, Abe MS 32nd Inf. Co.H
Van Pelt, Abraham GA Floyd Legion (St.Guards) Co.C
Vanpelt, Abraham C. AL Arty. 1st Bn. Co.F
Van Pelt, A.D. VA 10th Inf. 2nd Co.C
Vanpelt, A.J. TX 12th Cav. Co.G
Vanpelt, A.J. VA 9th Bn.Res. Co.C
Van Pelt, A.J. VA Mil. 145th Regt. Lt.Col.
Vanpelt, Alex. M. VA 31st Inf. 2nd Co.B Sgt.
Van Pelt, Amsi C. GA 35th Inf. Co.I
Vanpelt, Andrew J. AR 36th Inf. Co.F
Van Pelt, Andrew J. VA 1st Cav. Co.I
Vanpelt, Andrew J. VA 10th Inf. Co.H
Vanpelt, B.A. TN Cav. 17th Bn. (Sanders') Co.A
Vanpelt, Benjamin A. AL 9th (Malone's) Cav. Co.F
Van Pelt, Benjamin S. VA 1st Cav. Co.I
Vanpelt, Benj. S. VA 24th Bn.Part.Rangers Co.C
Van Pelt, Calvin TN 6th Inf. Co.I
Vanpelt, Charles NC 52nd Inf. Co.A
Vanpelt, David VA 39th Inf. Co.E
Vanpelt, David A. TX 2nd Cav. Co.C
Vanpelt, D.H. VA 9th Bn.Res. Co.C
Vanpelt, F. SC 6th Inf. 1st Co.G, 2nd Co.F
Vanpelt, Franklin NC 7th Inf. Co.H
Vanpelt, George G. TX 2nd Cav. Co.C Sgt.
Van Pelt, H. VA Cav. 35th Bn. Co.C
Vanpelt, Henry VA 58th Mil. Co.H,E
Vanpelt, H.H. VA 3rd Bn. Valley Res. Co.B
Vanpelt, I.N. NC 1st Cav. (9th St.Troops) Co.C
Vanpelt, Ira VA Hood's Bn.Res. Tappey's Co.
Van Pelt, James TX 36th Cav. Co.H
Vanpelt, James H. VA 10th Inf. Co.H
Vanpelt, James S. NC 7th Inf. Co.H
Van Pelt, James S. NC 7th Inf. Co.I Sgt.
Vanpelt, Jesse VA 27th Inf.
Vanpelt, J.J. TN Conscr.
Van Pelt, J.K. TN 6th Inf. Co.C
Vanpelt, J.K.P. AR 45th Cav. Co.D
Van Pelt, John GA 6th Inf.
Van Pelt, John GA Floyd Legion (St.Guards) Co.C
Vanpelt, John TN 2nd (Robison's) Inf. Co.B
Vanpelt, John VA Cav. McNeill's Co.
Van Pelt, John V. Eng.,CSA
Vanpelt, Joseph H. VA 5th Inf. Co.L
Vanpelt, J.R. NC 17th Inf. (2nd Org.) Co.L
Van Pelt, J.T. KY 4th Cav. Co.K 2nd Lt.
Van Pelt, J.V. LA 4th Inf. Co.F
Van Pelt, J.V. LA Inf.Crescent Regt. Co.B
Van Pelt, J.V. LA Inf.Cons.Crescent Regt. Co.C
Vanpelt, J.W. TN Inf. 3rd Cons.Regt. Co.D
Vanpelt, J.W. TN 4th Inf. Co.C
Vanpelt, Martin H. VA 10th Inf. Co.H
Van Pelt, Morgan VA 5th Cav. Co.G
Vanpelt, Morgan F. VA 10th Inf. Co.H
Van Pelt, N.B. VA 17th Cav. Co.H
Van Pelt, Newton GA 6th Cav. Co.H
Van Pelt, Newton GA Floyd Legion (St.Guards) Co.C
Van Pelt, Newton B. VA Prov.Guard Avis' Co. Cpl.
Van Pelt, Robert VA Lt.Arty. Arch. Graham's Co.
Vanpelt, Samuel E. NC 7th Inf. Co.H Cpl.
Vanpelt, S.E. SC 6th Inf. 1st Co.G, 2nd Co.F
Vanpelt, Simon TX 2nd Cav. Co.C
Van Pelt, Simon TX 36th Cav. Co.H

Vanpelt, Sinclare H. VA 31st Inf. Co.B
Vanpelt, Thomas S. NC 52nd Inf. Co.A Sgt.
Vanpelt, W.H. MS 7th Cav. 1st Co.I,C
Vanpelt, William GA Cav. 6th Bn. (St.Guards) Co.F
Van Pelt, William TN 6th Inf. Co.I
Vanpelt, William B. TX 2nd Cav. Co.C
Vanpelt, William C. NC 52nd Inf. Co.A
Van Pelt, William F. TX 2nd Cav. Co.K
Vanpelt, William H. VA 18th Cav. Co.G
Vanpelt, Wm. H. VA 2nd Inf. Co.C
Vanpelt, Wm. H. VA Mil. 145th Regt. Huff's Co. 1st Lt.
Vanpelt, William S. VA 97th Mil. Co.D
Vanpelts, W.H.F. MS 2nd Cav. Co.C
Vanpet, W.S. VA 9th Bn.Res. Co.C
Vanpett, William VA 3rd (Chrisman's) Bn.Res. Co.B
Vanpool, O. TX Cav. (Dismtd.) Chisum's Regt. Co.K
Vanpool, Obed. TX 12th Cav. Co.G 1st Lt.
Van Pool, W. TX Inf. Houston Bn. Capt.
Van Pragg, Henry A. AL Inf. 1st Regt. Co.E Jr.2nd Lt.
Vanransler, Willian H. LA 1st Hvy.Arty. (Reg.) Co.F Sgt.
Vanrenan, John VA 19th Cav. Co.F
Van Rice, A. GA 2nd Cav. 2nd Lt.
Van Rich, Lorenzo AL 36th Inf.
Vanrickle, W. MO 35th Inf.
Van Ripen, Jerry LA 20th Inf. Co.G
Van Riper, D.W. SC Mil. 16th Regt. Lawrence's Co. Sgt.
Van Riper, H. SC Inf. 1st (Charleston) Bn. Co.B
Van Riper, H. SC 27th Inf. Co.B
Van Riper, J.A. MS 21st Inf. Co.C
Van Riper, James M. TX 31st Cav. Co.C Cpl.
Van Riper, Jeremiah LA 1st Hvy.Arty. (Reg.) Co.I
Van Riper, Jeremiah LA Miles' Legion Co.A
Van Riper, Jerry LA Inf. 1st Sp.Bn. (Wheat's) New Co.D
Van Riper, John VA 1st Inf. Co.D
Vanrompey, Henry LA 10th Inf. Co.G Sgt.
Van Ronkel, J. LA 22nd (Cons.) Inf. Co.A
Van Ronkel, Jo TN Inf. 3rd Bn. Co.D
Van Rooten, C. LA Mil. Delery's Co. (St.Bernard Horse Rifles Co.)
Van Rooten, H. LA Mil. Delery's Co. (St.Bernard Horse Rifles Co.)
Van Rorder, Otto TX Inf. 24th Bn.
Vanruff, D. LA Mil. 3rd Regt. 3rd Brig. 1st Div. Co.F 3rd Lt.
Van Ruyssevelde, G. LA Mil. 3rd Regt.Eur.Brig. (Garde Francaise)
Vansandt, A.J. AL 34th Inf. Co.B Sgt.
Vansandt, George AR 2nd Mtd.Rifles Co.D
Vansandt, George W. AL 32nd Inf. Co.I 1st Sgt.
Vansandt, George W. AL 32nd & 58th (Cons.) Inf. 1st Sgt.
Vansandt, J. AL 34th Inf. Co.B
Vansandt, John W. MO Cav. Wood's Regt. Co.D
Vansandt, W. Mc. AL 34th Inf. Co.B
Vansant, A. SC 7th Inf. Co.H
Vansant, A. SC 15th Inf. Co.C
Vansant, Eli GA 56th Inf. Co.A
Vansant, Emanuel GA 56th Inf. Co.A
Vansant, H.E. SC Inf.Bn. Co.D Capt.
Vansant, Henry Earlyburry SC 19th Inf. Co.D 2nd Lt.
Vansant, Huston SC 13th Inf. Co.K
Vansant, James P. MS 16th Inf. Co.H
Vansant, John GA 36th (Broyles') Inf. Co.A
Vansant, John GA 56th Inf. Co.A
Vansant, John B. MD Arty. 4th Btty.
Vansant, J.T. SC 7th Inf. Co.E
Van Sant, J.W. SC 14th Inf. Co.B
Vansant, Noah GA 56th Inf. Co.A
Vansant, T. AR 35th Inf. Co.G
Vansant, Thomas B. LA 21st (Patton's) Inf. Co.E
Vansant, Wilks GA 30th Inf. Co.C
Vanschuyber, Edward TN 10th Inf. Co.B
Vanse, A.E. FL Cav. 5th Bn. Co.D
Vanse, Charles FL 9th Inf. Co.F
Vanse, J. GA 29th Inf. Co.I
Vanse, James B. NC 3rd Arty. (40th St.Troops) Co.A
Vanse, Samuel FL 9th Inf. Co.F
Vansel, Edward MO 15th Cav. Co.E
Vansell, T.B. MO 2nd Inf. Co.B
Vansenen, John VA 2nd Cav.St.Line McNeel's Co.
Vansener, John VA 20th Cav. Co.E
Vanshaw, W. TX Cav. 1st Regt.St.Troops Co.F
Van Shedroy, G.M. TX 28th Cav. Co.E
Vansiccel, W.G. MO 6th Cav. Co.B
Vansickle, E.A. MO Cav. 1st Bn.St.Guard Co.E 1st Lt.
Vansickle, E.S. TX 10th Cav. Co.E Ord.Sgt.
Vansickle, Henry AR 19th (Dockery's) Inf. Co.E
Vansickle, John TX 26th Cav. Co.C
Vansickle, Miles AR 3rd Cav. Co.F
Vansickle, S.H. TX 32nd Cav. Co.B
Vansickle, T.J. TX 9th (Young's) Inf. Co.F
Vansickle, William AR 3rd Cav. Co.F
Vansickle, W.K. TX 16th Cav. Co.H
Vansickler, James C. VA 6th Cav. Co.A
Vansickler, J.B. VA 8th Inf. Co.E
Vansickler, J.C. VA 8th Inf. Co.E
Vansickler, John A. VA 8th Inf. Co.E
Vansickler, P.F. VA 8th Inf. Co.E
Vansickler, R.W. VA 8th Inf. Co.E Sgt.
Van Sickles, Isaac AZ Cav. Herbert's Bn. Oury's Co. Cpl.
Vansickles, William G. MO 1st N.E. Cav. Co.B
Vansicle, William MO 2nd N.E. Cav. (Franklin's Regt.) Co.B
Van Simpler, V. GA Lt.Arty. Clinch's Btty.
Van Sindenen, W. TX 35th (Likens') Cav. Co.F
Vanskike, Henry MO 10th Inf.
Vanskike, W.H. MO Inf. Clark's Regt. Co.A
Vanskike, William MO 3rd Inf. Co.K
Vanskyke, Henry MO Cav. Freeman's Regt.
Vanslooten, J. LA Mil.Conf.Guards Regt. Co.G
Vanslute, N. GA Siege Arty. 28th Bn. Co.C
Vanslyke, Jesse MS Inf. 1st Bn.St.Troops (30 days '64) Co.H
Van Solingen, H.M. LA Mil. 2nd Regt. 3rd Brig. 1st Div. Co.K Capt.
Vanson, A. TX 13th Vol. Co.K
Vanstavern, Benjamin VA Inf. 26th Bn. Co.F
Vanstavern, Benjamin VA 108th Mil. Co.A
Vanstavern, Erasmus N. VA 36th Inf. Co.F
Vanstavern, Hudson VA Lt.Arty. G.B. Chapman's Co.
Vanstavern, N. VA 22nd Inf. Co.H,K
Vanstone, R. LA 3rd Inf. Co.F
Vanstory, John NC 4th Bn.Jr.Res.
Vanstory, John NC 8th Inf. Co.I
Vanstory, John T. NC 2nd Cav. (19th St.Troops) Co.F
Vanstory, Lindsay M. NC 14th Inf. Co.B
Vanstory, Pinckney NC 2nd Cav. (19th St.Troops) Co.F Sgt.
Vanstory, Samuel A. AL 6th Inf. Co.K
Vanswarenger, Thos. 2nd Conf.Inf. Co.C
Vansyckle, Samuel LA 9th Inf. Co.D
Vanszant, S.L. MO Cav. Schnabel's Bn. Co.B
Vant, Samuel MO 2nd Cav. Co.D
Van Tarnot, J.W. LA Bienville Res.
Van Tassel, James SC 2nd Arty. Co.C
Van Tassel, James A. SC 1st (Hagood's) Inf. 1st Co.A
Vanter, J.D. TN Lt.Arty. Morton's Co.
Vantier, D. 14th Conf.Cav. Co.H
Vantine, Marcus DeL. TX 14th Cav. Co.F
Vantine, T.J. TX Cav. (Dismtd.) Chisum's Regt.
Vanto, T.O. TX Cav. 6th Bn. Co.B
Vantoller, David MO 1st N.E. Cav.
Vantramp, H. MO 1st & 4th Cons.Inf. Co.E
Vantreas, John L. TN Cav. Allison's Squad.
Vantrease, Andrew TN 23rd Inf. 1st Co.A, Co.B
Vantrease, G.W. TN Cav. Allison's Squad. Co.B
Vantrease, Jackson TN Cav. Allison's Squad. Co.B
Vantrease, Jacob TN Cav. Allison's Squad. Co.B
Vantrease, James W. KY 1st (Butler's) Cav. Co.E
Vantrease, Rich TN 4th (McLemore's) Cav. Co.C
Vantrece, Thomas TN 6th Inf. Co.C
Vantreece, Benjamin F. TN 6th Inf. Co.C
Vantreece, B.F. TN Cav. Newsom's Regt.
Vantreece, B.F. TN 31st Inf. Co.B
Vantrees, Emanuel KY 5th Mtd.Inf. Co.F Cpl.
Vantrees, Nicholas TN 24th Inf. Co.F
Vantrees, Wash TN 24th Inf. Co.F
Vantreese, J.H. TN 51st (Cons.) Inf. Co.F
Vantreese, W.A. TN 31st Inf. Co.B
Vantrese, R. TN 18th (Newsom's) Cav. Co.K
Vantrice, J.L. TN 4th (McLemore's) Cav. Co.C Bugler
Vantrice, Nicholas TN 4th (McLemore's) Cav. Co.C Cpl.
Vantrice, R. TN 19th & 20th (Cons.) Cav. Co.C
Vantrimp, J.P. MO 16th Inf. Co.B
Vantromps, H. MO 4th Inf. Co.H
Vantrot, Gustavus AL Lt.Arty. 2nd Bn. Co.E Cpl.
Vantroy, John NC Allen's Co. (Loc.Def.) Music.
Vantz, John GA 1st (Olmstead's) Inf. Gordon's Co.
Vanvackenburg, F.D. GA Inf. 2nd Bn. (St.Guards) Co.C
Van Vacter, C. VA 59th Inf. 2nd Co.D Cpl.
Vanvacter, Joseph E. VA 2nd Inf. Co.A
Vanvacter, Joseph W. VA 8th Cav. Co.I
Vanvacter, Rodney VA Cav. Swann's Bn. Co.H
Vanvacter, Syms VA Cav. Swann's Bn. Co.H

Van Vactor, Cyrus VA Inf. 26th Bn. Co.D,H
Vanvactor, Joseph L. VA 12th Cav. Co.A
Van Valkenberg, George S. GA Inf. 2nd Bn. Co.B
Van Valkenburg, James D. GA 61st Inf. Co.I Maj.
Van Valkenburgh, Frank D. AR 5th Inf. Co.C
Van Valkenburgh, G.S. AR 1st (Monroe's) Cav. Co.B Capt.
Van Valkenburgh, J. GA Inf. 2nd Bn. (St.Guards) Co.A
Vanvaxter, J.T. VA Cav. 37th Bn. Co.H
Van Vechten, D.H. TX 20th Inf. Co.C
Vanvecoven, A. LA 9th Inf. Co.B
Vanveghten, H.W. GA Inf. (GA Defend.) Chapman's Co.
Vanvelt, John MS 2nd Part.Rangers Co.B
Vanvickle, Jackson MO 10th Inf. Co.A
Vanvickle, John AR 36th Inf. Co.F
Van Vickle, John TX 15th Cav. Co.G,B
Vanvickle, William MO 5th Inf. Co.A
Van Victor, B.F. MO 1st N.E. Cav.
Vanvirt, Jordan MS 34th Inf. Co.K
Van Vlack, William TX 5th Cav. Co.C
Van Vleck, A. TN Arty. Marshall's Co. 2nd Lt.
Van Vleck, Geo. W. TX St.Troops Brig.Gen.
Van Vleck, J.L. TX 1st Inf. Co.F
Van Vleet, Francis Conf.Reg.Inf. Brooks' Bn. Co.E Sgt.
Van Vleit, Francis Conf.Reg.Inf. Brooks' Bn. Co.E Sgt.
Van Voores, Charles Conf.Inf. 8th Bn. Co.E
Van Vorice, Stephen MS 4th Cav. Co.C
Van Voris, Stephen MS Cav. Hughes' Bn. Co.A
Vanvort, Isaac VA 54th Mil. Co.E,F
Van Vranken, H.N. TN 6th Inf. Co.F,H
Van Wagner, R. Sig.Corps,CSA
Van Wagner, Rupert TX 13th Vol. 3rd Co.A
Van Wagner, Rupert TX Inf. Griffin's Bn. Co.D
Van Wart, Walter SC Cav.Bn. Holcombe Legion Co.B
Vanway, D.C. TX 27th Cav. Co.F
Vanway, H.T. TX Cav. Border's Regt. Co.F
Vanway, Jacob AR Lt.Arty. Rivers' Btty. QMSgt.
Vanway, Richard TX Cav. Wells' Regt. Co.H
Vanwenkle, Andrew TX Cav. Madison's Regt. Co.D
Van Wert, N. LA Siege Train Bn. Co.E
Van Wert, Walter SC 4th St.Troops Co.G
Van Wester, W. GA 40th Inf. Co.D
Van Wickle, Charles R. LA 1st Cav. Co.A
Vanwie, W. LA 3rd (Wingfield's) Cav. Co.D
Vanwinkle, Andrew J. TX 18th Cav. Co.D
Van Winkle, B.A. Brush Bn.
Van Winkle, D.L. TX Cav. Terry's Regt. Co.E
Vanwinkle, D.L. TX 4th Inf. Co.H
Van Winkle, J. AR 20th Inf. Co.F
Van Winkle, J. SC Mil. 1st Regt. (Charleston Res.) Co.C
Vanwinkle, J.A. AR 10th Inf. Co.H
Van Winkle, J.A. MS 18th Inf. Co.H
Vanwinkle, James TX Cav. Madison's Regt. Co.G
Vanwinkle, James B. MS 31st Inf. Co.D Cpl.
Vanwinkle, J.L. AR Cav. Gordon's Regt. Co.B
Vanwinkle, John AR 1st (Crawford's) Cav. Co.E
Van Winkle, John SC 1st Regt. Charleston Guard Co.A
Vanwinkle, W.H. AR Inf. Cocke's Regt. Co.B
Vanwinkle, W.H.H. AR 10th Inf. Co.H
Van Winkler, Wiley R. MO Cav. Schnabel's Bn.
Van Wirt, George Conf.Reg.Inf. Brooks' Bn. Co.E
Van Woert, N. LA Mtd.Part.Rangers Bond's Co. 1st Sgt.
Van Wort, George Conf.Reg.Inf. Brooks' Bn. Co.E
Van Wort, N. LA Lt.Arty. 2nd Field Btty.
Van Wyck, S.M. Gen. & Staff Surg.
Vany, C.M. AL 4th (Russell's) Cav. Co.D
Van York, E. TX Inf. 1st St.Troops Stevenson's Co.F
Van Yorx, Edmund TX Lt.Arty. H. Van Buren's Co. 1st Sgt.
Vanzandt, David W. MO Cav. Wood's Regt. Co.E
Vanzandt, George W. AL 30th Inf. Co.B Jr.2nd Lt.
Vanzandt, Giles P.K. MO Inf. 8th Bn. Co.E
Vanzandt, H.T. AL 34th Inf. Co.G
Vanzandt, Isaac MS 31st Inf. Co.I 1st Lt.
Van Zandt, Isaac L. TX 7th Inf. Co.D
Vanzandt, Isaiah AR 15th (N.W.) Inf. Emergency Co.I
Vanzandt, James AR 15th (N.W.) Inf. Emergency Co.I
Vanzandt, J.G. MS 4th Cav. Co.A
Vanzandt, J.L. MS 46th Inf. Co.B
Van Zandt, J.L. Inf. Bailey's Cons.Regt. Co.B
Vanzandt, John R. TX 10th Cav. Co.I
Van Zandt, K.M. TX 7th Inf. Co.D Maj.
Vanzandt, T.H. AR 15th (N.W.) Inf. Emergency Co.I
Vanzant, Benjamin F. AR 14th (McCarver's) Inf. Co.F
Vanzant, B.F. AR 8th Cav. Co.D
Vanzant, B.F. AR 1st S.S. Co.B
Vanzant, B.F. AR 21st Inf. Co.B
Vanzant, B.T. AR 12th Bn.S.S. Co.B
Vanzant, Daniel GA 1st Bn.S.S. Co.B
Vanzant, D.J. AL Cav. Lewis' Bn. Co.D
Vanzant, D.J. FL 2nd Cav. Co.K
Vanzant, Enoch C. NC 57th Inf. Co.H
Vanzant, E.W. GA Inf. 25th Bn. (Prov.Guard) Co.E
Vanzant, Garret FL 5th Inf. Co.B Capt.
Vanzant, G.W. AR 8th Cav. Co.G
Vanzant, Harrison MO 1st N.E. Cav. Co.B Cpl.
Vanzant, H.G. GA 3rd Res. Co.A
Vanzant, Hiram GA 6th Inf. (St.Guards) Co.B Cpl.
Vanzant, Isaac MS 15th Inf. Co.I 2nd Lt.
Vanzant, Isaac TN 17th Inf. Co.E
Vanzant, Isaac TN 41st Inf. Co.G
Van Zant, Isaac A. GA 52nd Inf. Co.H 1st Lt.
Vanzant, Jacob H. TN 41st Inf. Co.G
Vanzant, James AL 3rd Inf. Co.H
Vanzant, James AR 8th Cav. Co.D
Vanzant, James MO 11th Inf. Co.C,I
Vanzant, James VA 25th Cav. Co.B
Vanzant, James E. AR 14th (McCarver's) Inf. Co.F
Vanzant, James E. AR 21st Inf. Co.B
Vanzant, Jerome M. MO 3rd Cav. Co.K Jr.2nd Lt.
Vanzant, J.L. LA 4th Inf. Old Co.G
Vanzant, J. Layfayette SC 1st (Orr's) Rifles Co.F
Vanzant, John AR 8th Cav. Co.D
Vanzant, John AR 7th Inf. Co.I
Vanzant, John AR 14th (McCarver's) Inf. Co.F
Vanzant, John AR 21st Inf. Co.B
Vanzant, John TX 23rd Cav. Co.H Cpl.
Vanzant, John L. MS 2nd Inf. Co.G
Vanzant, John W. MO 3rd Cav. Co.K
Vanzant, Joseph KY 10th Cav. Co.H
Vanzant, Leander NC 37th Inf. Co.K
Vanzant, Martin AR 35th Inf. Co.I
Vanzant, Obed AL 26th Inf. Co.B
Vanzant, R.J. AR Cav. Harrell's Bn. Co.D
Vanzant, Robert AR 34th Inf. Co.C
Vanzant, Samuel AR 27th Inf. Co.A Cpl.
Vanzant, Samuel H. AL 11th Inf. Co.H 1st Lt.
Vanzant, Starling NC 37th Inf. Co.A
Vanzant, Thomas MO 11th Inf. Co.C
Vanzant, W. AR Prov.Guard Co.A
Vanzant, W.G. AL 56th Part.Rangers Co.I
Vanzant, W.G. AL 43rd Inf. Co.H
Vanzant, William VA 23rd Cav. Co.D
Vanzant, William T. GA Inf. 10th Bn. Co.D
Vanzant, W.L. GA Inf. 25th Bn. (Prov.Guard) Co.E 1st Sgt.
Vanzant, W.M. FL 2nd Cav. Co.K
Vanzantt, George W. MO 4th Cav. Co.I
Vanzent, J.F. AR Inf. Cocke's Regt. Co.C
Vanzent, Joseph KY 1st (Helm's) Cav. Old Co.G, Co.A
Vanzile, William A. MS 21st Inf. Co.A
Van Zyndregt, John LA 21st (Patton's) Inf. Co.A
Varalle, John TN Arty. Fisher's Co.
Varalman, Augustus D. AL 9th Inf. Co.H
Varar, J.F. MO Cav. 2nd Regt.St.Guard Co.E
Varble, Isaac KY 2nd (Duke's) Cav. Co.A
Varbridge, Charles MS 29th Inf. Co.C
Varbrough, T.G. AR Cav. McGehee's Regt. Co.C
Vardaman, C.C. GA 46th Inf. Co.E
Vardaman, E.P. 2nd Conf.Eng.Troops Sgt.
Vardaman, Ephraim P. TX 6th Cav. Co.D Cpl.
Vardaman, James A. GA 35th Inf. Co.K Sgt.
Vardaman, James J. AL 10th Inf. Co.K
Vardaman, James M. AL Cav. 5th Bn. Hilliard's Legion Co.C Music.
Vardaman, James M. 10th Conf.Cav. Co.C Bugler
Vardaman, J.F. MS Inf. 2nd Bn. (St.Troops) Co.F Cpl.
Vardaman, John F. AL Cav. 5th Bn. Hilliard's Legion Co.E,C
Vardaman, P.L. AL 34th Inf. Co.B
Vardaman, Sanford AL Cp. of Instr. Talladega
Vardaman, Simeon V. GA 6th Inf. Co.D
Vardaman, S.M. GA 53rd Inf. Co.K
Vardaman, S.V. GA Inf. (St.Armory Guards) Green's Co. 1st Sgt.
Vardaman, Thomas W.R. AL 10th Inf. Co.K
Vardaman, T.W. AL 10th Inf. Co.K
Vardaman, Washington B. AL 10th Inf. Co.K Music.
Vardaman, William F. AL 14th Inf. Co.G

Vardaman, William S. TX 27th Cav. Co.D,M 1st Sgt.
Vardaman, W.P. AL 10th Inf. Co.K
Vardaman, Jeremiah T. TX 6th Cav. Co.D
Vardel, John T. TN 18th Inf. Co.H
Vardell, --- SC 23rd Inf. Capt.
Vardell, Henry T. GA Inf. 2nd Bn. Co.B Sgt.
Vardell, H.T. GA Arty. (Macon Lt.Arty.) Slaten's Co. Sgt.
Vardell, L. AR 21st Mil. Co.G
Vardell, Lafayette AR 36th Inf. Co.B
Vardell, Milton G. AL 17th Inf. Co.B 2nd Lt.
Vardell, R.B. TN 22nd (Barteau's) Cav. Co.H
Vardell, R.B. TN 2nd (Robison's) Inf. Co.H
Vardell, Thomas L. MO 1st Inf. Co.B
Vardell, Thomas S. AL 6th Inf. Co.M
Vardell, T.Z. TN 4th (McLemore's) Cav. Co.E
Vardell, W.A. TN 20th Inf. Co.E
Vardell, W.G. SC 23rd Inf. AQM
Vardell, W.G. Gen. & Staff, A. of TN Maj.,QM
Vardeman, A. Bradford's Corps Scouts & Guards Co.A
Vardeman, A.A. MS Cav. 24th Bn. Co.E
Vardeman, Ayers A. MS Arty. (Seven Stars Arty.) Roberts' Co.
Vardeman, George W. MS Arty. (Seven Stars Arty.) Roberts' Co.
Vardeman, G.S. MS 1st (King's) Inf. (St.Troops) Co.B
Vardeman, G.W. MS Cav. 24th Bn. Co.E
Vardeman, J.A. GA 53rd Inf. Co.K
Vardeman, James AL 3rd Bn. Hilliard's Legion Vol. Co.C
Vardeman, James TX 18th Cav. Co.H
Vardeman, J.B. TX 20th Inf. Co.K
Vardeman, J.E. GA 2nd Inf. Co.B
Vardeman, Jesse M. TX Cav. Martin's Regt. Co.K,I Cpl.
Vardeman, John F. 10th Conf.Cav. Co.C Sgt.
Vardeman, John H. 2nd Conf.Eng.Troops Co.G Sgt.
Vardeman, N. GA Inf. (NonConscr.) Howard's Co.
Vardeman, Noah GA Inf. 27th Bn. (NonConscr.) Co.B Sgt.
Vardeman, Noah GA 37th Inf. Co.K
Vardeman, Peter KY 7th Cav. Co.B
Vardeman, Peter TX Cav. Gano's Squad. Co.B
Vardeman, Samuel M. GA Inf. 3rd Bn. Co.C
Vardeman, T.L. AL 1st Cav. 2nd Co.A
Varden, E.S. VA Loc.Def. Wood's Co.
Varden, George P. VA 1st Arty. Co.I
Varden, James AR Mil. Desha Cty.Bn.
Varden, James H. AR 26th Inf. Co.E
Varden, J.B. TN 10th (DeMoss') Cav. Co.F
Varden, J.B. TN Cav. Napier's Bn. Co.C Sgt.
Varden, Joseph AR Cav. Wright's Regt. Co.D
Varden, T.J. TN 10th (DeMoss') Cav. Co.F
Varden, T.J. TN Cav. Napier's Bn. Co.C
Varden, T.J. TN 50th Inf. Co.G
Varden, T.J. TN 50th (Cons.) Inf. Co.G
Varden, W. AR Mil. Desha Cty.Bn.
Varden, William AL Cp. of Instr. Talladega
Varden, William AR 26th Inf. Co.E
Varden, W.M. AL 4th Inf. Co.H
Varden, W.M. AL Cp. of Instr. Talledega Co.C Cpl.
Varderman, Bishop GA 2nd Inf. Co.B
Varderman, J.F. AL 60th Inf. Co.B
Varderman, J.M. AL 60th Inf. Co.B
Vardiman, James TX Cav. Morgan's Regt. Co.D
Vardin, Thomas J. TX 8th Cav. Co.D
Vardin, W. AL Cp. of Instr. Talladega Co.D,C Cpl.
Varding, Elisha TN Lt.Arty. Baxter's Co.
Vardman, J.H. Trans-MS Conf.Cav. 1st Bn. Co.A
Vareen, J.D. SC Post Guard Senn's Co.
Varen, L. TX Inf. 1st St.Troops Biehler's Co.A
Varenholt, F. LA Mil. Fire Bn. Co.C
Vares, J.F. GA 52nd Inf. Co.K
Varet, Louis LA Arty. Castellanos' Btty.
Varga, --- TX Lt.Arty. Dege's Bn.
Varga, Alexander TX 3rd Inf. Co.I
Varga, Alex. D. TX 8th Field Btty.
Varga, John TX 3rd Inf. Co.H
Varga, Joseph H. TX 8th Field Btty. Sgt.
Varga, Paul TX 5th Cav. Co.D
Vargas, Benito TX Cav. Ragsdale's Bn. 1st Co.A Cpl.
Vargas, Felipe TX 8th Inf. Co.C Sgt.
Vargas, Felipe TX Cav. Benavides' Regt. Co.C Sgt.
Vargas, Florencio TX Cav. Ragsdale's Bn. 1st Co.A
Vargas, Manl. LA Mil. 5th Regt.Eur.Brig. (Spanish Regt.) Co.8
Varger, J.N. MS 29th Inf. Co.F
Varhall, B. AL 25th Inf. Co.A
Varhian, J.P. TN 19th & 20th (Cons.) Inf. Co.A
Varin, E. GA 20th Inf. Co.I
Varin, Paul TX 5th Inf. Co.F
Varine, John T. NC 18th Inf. Co.C
Varish, Nathan AL 33rd Inf. Co.I
Varker, James NC 54th Inf. Co.A
Varker, William NC 7th Inf. Co.D
Varlet, --- Gen. & Staff
Varlet, Edouard LA Miles' Legion Co.K
Varley, John TN 10th Inf. Co.D Sgt.
Varlin, W. LA 5th Inf. Co.C
Varliss, --- TX Cav. Wells' Regt.
Varn, Aaron SC 11th Inf. Co.K
Varn, Aaron B. GA 47th Inf. Co.F
Varn, A.E. SC 1st Mtd.Mil. Smart's Co. 1st Lt.
Varn, A.E. SC 3rd Cav. Co.D
Varn, Andrew L. FL 1st Cav. Co.D
Varn, Carson W. SC 17th Inf. Co.H,G
Varn, C.W. SC 5th Cav. Co.I
Varn, Daniel R. GA 47th Inf. Co.F
Varn, G. SC 11th Inf. Co.K
Varn, G.W. SC 5th Cav. Co.I
Varn, G.W. SC 17th Inf. Co.H
Varn, H.D. SC Mil. 14th Regt. Co.K
Varn, J. SC 11th Res. Co.E
Varn, Jacob E. FL 7th Inf. Co.A
Varn, J.L. GA Cav. 20th Bn. Co.A
Varn, John A. SC Mil. 18th Regt. Co.D Capt.
Varn, John W. SC 17th Inf. Co.H,G
Varn, Josiah FL 1st Cav. Co.K
Varn, Josiah FL 7th Inf. Co.E
Varn, J.W. SC 5th Cav. Co.I
Varn, P.M. SC Cav. 19th Bn. Co.C
Varn, P.M. SC Part.Rangers Kirk's Co.
Varn, P.M.E. SC 24th Inf. Co.E
Varn, R.A. LA 9th Inf. Co.H
Varn, R.A. SC 5th Cav. Co.I
Varn, S.G. GA 4th (Clinch's) Cav. Co.H
Varn, T.J. GA Lt.Arty. Clinch's Btty.
Varn, W.D.L. SC 3rd Cav. Co.A
Varn, William B. FL 7th Inf. Co.E
Varn, William D.L. SC 1st (McCreary's) Inf. Co.A
Varn, William T. GA 1st (Symons') Res. Co.G Sgt.
Varn, W.T. GA 6th Res. Co.H
Varnadere, Samuel SC 5th St.Troops Co.A
Varnado, Allen MS Cav. 24th Bn. Co.F
Varnado, Charles 14th Conf.Cav. Co.K
Varnado, Ellis M. MS 33rd Inf. Co.B Music.
Varnado, E.M. MS 22nd Inf. Co.F Lt.
Varnado, F.H. MS Inf. 3rd Bn. Co.E Cpl.
Varnado, Frank M. MS 33rd Inf. Co.K
Varnado, G.R. LA 3rd (Wingfield's) Cav. Co.E
Varnado, G.W. LA 3rd (Wingfield's) Cav. Co.A 1st Lt.
Varnado, H.C. MS 39th Inf. Co.K
Varnado, James L. MS 33rd Inf. Co.B 1st Sgt.
Varnado, J.E. MS 2nd (Quinn's St.Troops) Inf. Co.H
Varnado, M.A. LA 3rd (Wingfield's) Cav. Co.C 2nd Lt.
Varnado, M.A. MS Inf. 3rd Bn. Co.E
Varnado, M.J. LA Inf. 9th Bn. Co.B
Varnado, P.H. LA 3rd (Wingfield's) Cav. Co.C
Varnado, R.H. MS 33rd Inf. Co.B Cpl.
Varnado, Samuel MS Cav.Part.Rangers Rhodes' Co.
Varnado, Samuel 14th Conf.Cav. Co.F
Varnado, S.H. MS 39th Inf. Co.K
Varnado, V.V. LA 3rd (Wingfield's) Cav. Co.K Sgt.
Varnado, William L. MS 22nd Inf. Co.E
Varnado, W.N. LA 3rd (Wingfield's) Cav. Co.C
Varnadoe, Andrew J. GA 61st Inf. Co.B
Varnadoe, A.P. GA 23rd Inf. Co.F
Varnadoe, C.C. GA 8th Cav. New Co.I Cpl.
Varnadoe, C.C. GA Cav. 20th Bn. Co.D
Varnadoe, Francis M. MS 22nd Inf. Co.E
Varnadoe, H. MS 1st (King's) Inf. (St.Troops) Co.B
Varnadoe, Henry SC 15th Inf. Co.E
Varnadoe, James O. GA 26th Inf. Co.B
Varnadoe, Jeff M. LA 16th Inf. Co.B
Varnadoe, M. GA 46th Inf. Co.H
Varnadoe, N.A. LA 3rd (Wingfield's) Cav. Co.C
Varnadoe, N.B. LA 3rd (Wingfield's) Cav. Co.C
Varnadoe, Obediah GA 20th Inf. Co.H
Varnadoe, Thomas L. GA 20th Inf. Co.H
Varnadoe, William GA Cav. 22nd Bn. (St.Guards) Co.I
Varnadon, J.A.C. SC 8th Bn.Res. Fishburne's Co.
Varnadon, Samuel SC 3rd Bn.Res. Co.E
Varnador, Henry GA Mayer's Co. (Appling Cav.)
Varnadore, Adam SC 23rd Inf. Co.F
Varnadore, A.J. GA 19th Inf. Co.B
Varnadore, Benjamin F. AR Lt.Arty. Thrall's Btty.
Varnadore, Charles SC 3rd Cav. Co.A

Varnadore, Early L. GA Siege Arty. 28th Bn. Co.C
Varnadore, Elias GA 10th Inf. Co.H
Varnadore, G.W. SC 23rd Inf. Co.F
Varnadore, H. SC 24th Inf. Co.E
Varnadore, H.C. SC 2nd St.Troops Co.H
Varnadore, H.C. SC 11th Res. Co.D
Varnadore, Henry GA Sharp's Bn. Co.H
Varnadore, Henry J. GA 50th Inf. Co.H
Varnadore, Isaiah AL 16th Inf. Co.G
Varnadore, J.C. TX Cav. 1st Regt.St.Troops Co.C 2nd Lt.
Varnadore, J.H. GA 12th Inf. Co.F Sgt.
Varnadore, J.M. SC 3rd Cav. Co.A
Varnadore, John SC 3rd Inf. Co.G
Varnadore, John C. TX 13th Cav. Co.B
Varnadore, Leonard FL 2nd Cav. Co.C
Varnadore, Miles SC 3rd Cav. Co.A
Varnadore, Robert GA 51st Inf. Co.C
Varnadore, Robert SC 23rd Inf. Co.F
Varnadore, Samuel GA 25th Inf. Co.K
Varnadore, Samuel SC 23rd Inf. Co.F
Varnadore, Thomas AL 15th Inf. Co.D
Varnadore, Thompson SC 6th Inf. 1st Co.C
Varnadore, Wesley A. GA 11th Inf. Co.B
Varnadore, William SC 11th Inf. Co.E Music.
Varnal, Kinchen NC 17th Inf. (2nd Org.) Co.I
Varnall, Joseph H. KY 1st (Helm's) Cav. Old Co.G, Co.A
Varnam, Spires NC 54th Inf. Co.C
Varnan, S. AL Talladega Cty.Res. D.B. Brown's Co.
Varnarsdale, Cornelius C. AR 3rd Inf. Co.H
Varnasdoll, Jeremiah VA 27th Inf. 1st Co.H
Varnburg, Frank GA 1st Inf. (St.Guards) Co.F Sgt.
Varncunon, J. NC 1st Jr.Res. Co.E,F
Varndoe, T.L. GA Mil. Coast Guard Bn.
Varne, A.J. GA 11th Cav. (St.Guards) Godfrey's Co.
Varnedoe, C.C. GA Cav. 1st Bn. Winn's Co., Walthour's Co.
Varnedoe, C.C. GA 5th Cav. Co.G
Varnedoe, E.S. GA 1st Reg. Co.B
Varnedoe, J.O. GA Cav. 1st Bn. Winn's Co., Walthour's Co. Cpl.
Varnedoe, J.O. GA 5th Cav. Co.G Sgt.
Varnedoe, L.L. GA Cav. 20th Bn. Co.B QM
Varnedoe, L.L. Gen. & Staff,PACS Capt.,AQM
Varnedoe, R.A. GA Cav. 1st Bn. Walthour's Co.
Varnedon, Leonard FL 7th Inf. Co.D
Varnel, John TN 36th Inf. Co.C
Varnell, Albert GA 1st Inf. (St.Guards) Co.I
Varnell, Ben TX Cav. 3rd (Yager's) Bn. Co.B
Varnell, Benjamin TX 1st (Yager's) Cav. Co.B
Varnell, D.F. MS 1st Lt.Arty. Co.F
Varnell, D.F. MS Horse Arty. Cook's Co.
Varnell, D.F. MS 3rd Inf. Co.C
Varnell, D.F. MS 12th Inf. Co.C
Varnell, E. MS 6th Inf. Co.K
Varnell, E. MS 14th (Cons.) Inf. Co.B
Varnell, F.M. 1st Conf.Cav. 2nd Co.K
Varnell, F.W. TX 1st Inf. Co.L
Varnell, George MS 25th Inf. Co.F
Varnell, Henry S. LA 12th Inf. Co.D
Varnell, H.F. TN 43rd Inf. Co.H
Varnell, James L. MS 38th Cav. Co.I
Varnell, James P. AL 16th Inf. Co.C Cpl.
Varnell, J.H. KY 4th Cav. Co.C Sgt.
Varnell, John AR 8th Inf. New Co.I
Varnell, Josiah TN 35th Inf. 3rd Co.F
Varnell, M.P. GA 1st Inf. (St.Guards) Co.I
Varnell, Powhattan TX 19th Cav. Co.D
Varnell, Ransom AL 43rd Inf. Co.B
Varnell, R.H. GA Phillips' Legion Co.B
Varnell, Richard A. MS 16th Inf. Co.K
Varnell, R.N. TN 5th (McKenzie's) Cav. Co.A
Varnell, R.P. TX 28th Cav. Co.H Cpl.
Varnell, W.C. AR 8th Cav. Co.C
Varnell, W.C. 1st Conf.Cav. 2nd Co.K
Varnell, W.E. GA Phillips' Legion Co.B
Varnell, William AL 9th (Malone's) Cav. Co.E
Varnell, William Hunter KY 9th Mtd.Inf. Co.H Cpl.
Varnell, William Hunter TX Inf. W. Cameron's Co. Cpl.
Varnell, William J. AR 24th Inf. Co.F
Varnell, William K. AR 9th Inf. Co.C
Varnell, William P. AR 9th Inf. Co.G
Varnell, W.K. AR 2nd Cav. Co.D Bvt.2nd Lt.
Varnell, Z.N. TN 5th (McKenzie's) Cav. Co.A
Varnelle, J.L. MS Inf. 1st Bn.St.Troops (30 days '64) Co.B Cpl.
Varner, --- VA Horse Arty. Jackson's Co. Sgt.
Varner, A.A. MO 12th Inf. Co.I 1st Sgt.
Varner, Adison M. MS 20th Inf. Co.H
Varner, A.H. AR 6th Inf. Co.E
Varner, A.J. GA 45th Inf. Co.I
Varner, Alexander MO 1st N.E. Cav. Co.H
Varner, Alford J. MS 20th Inf. Co.H
Varner, Alison M. MS 39th Inf. Co.C
Varner, Amos NC 46th Inf. Co.G
Varner, Andrew NC 6th Inf. Co.A
Varner, Andrew SC 3rd Inf. Co.D
Varner, Andrew W. VA 5th Inf. Co.B Cpl.
Varner, Andrew W. VA 27th Inf. 2nd Co.H 2nd Lt.
Varner, A.T. MS 2nd Cav.
Varner, B. NC 2nd Jr.Res. Co.G
Varner, Benjamin VA 162nd Mil. Co.A
Varner, Benjamin VA 31st Inf. Co.H
Varner, Benjamin A. LA 31st Inf. Co.K
Varner, Benjamin R. GA 25th Inf. Co.G Sgt.
Varner, B.F. AL 4th Inf. Co.D
Varner, C.A. AL 8th (Livingston's) Cav. Co.C
Varner, Calvin Milton NC 7th Inf. Co.H
Varner, C.C. NC 6th Sr.Res. Co.F
Varner, Chas. VA 27th Inf. Co.H
Varner, Charles A. AL 6th Inf. Co.M
Varner, Charles H. GA Arty. 11th Bn. (Sumter Arty.) Co.A Cpl.
Varner, Charles H. GA Siege Arty. 28th Bn. Co.A
Varner, Christian VA 46th Mil. Co.A
Varner, Columbus W. KY 1st (Butler's) Cav. Co.B
Varner, Cornelius NC 6th Sr.Res. Co.A,D
Varner, C.P. SC 3rd Inf. Co.K Sgt.
Varner, C.W. KY 3rd Bn.Mtd.Rifles Co.B
Varner, Daniel VA Inf. 26th Bn. Co.E
Varner, Daniel VA 62nd Mtd.Inf. 2nd Co.K
Varner, Daniel, Jr. VA 162nd Mil. Co.A
Varner, Daniel S. VA 31st Inf. Co.E
Varner, David VA 31st Inf. Co.E
Varner, David A. VA 25th Inf. 2nd Co.I
Varner, David D. GA 24th Inf. Co.B
Varner, David G. NC 5th Cav. (63rd St.Troops) Co.K
Varner, David K. VA 97th Mil. Co.F 2nd Lt.
Varner, Dex VA 25th Cav. Co.H
Varner, Dexterity VA 64th Mtd.Inf. Co.K
Varner, D.J. NC 56th Inf. Co.K
Varner, E. MS 46th Inf. Co.G
Varner, E. SC Lt.Arty. Jeter's Co. (Macbeth Lt.Arty.)
Varner, E. 2nd Conf.Eng.Troops Co.D
Varner, E.C. NC 1st Arty. (10th St.Troops) Co.E
Varner, Edward F. AL 3rd Inf. Co.C
Varner, E.G. MS 14th Inf. Co.E
Varner, E.G. MS 41st Inf. Co.E
Varner, Eli F. LA Inf. 4th Bn. Co.F
Varner, Eliha SC Lt.Arty. Jeter's Co.
Varner, Elijah FL 6th Inf. Co.F
Varner, Emanuel VA 8th Bn.Res. Co.B
Varner, E.P. AL Cav. 24th Bn. Co.C Sgt.
Varner, Ernsley NC 5th Inf. Co.I
Varner, Ervin MO 1st N.E. Cav. Co.E
Varner, E.T. MS 41st Inf. Co.E Cpl.
Varner, F. AR Cav. Wright's Regt. Co.C
Varner, F. MO 2nd Cav. Co.E
Varner, F. Conf.Cav. Wood's Regt. Co.H
Varner, F.A. MS 10th Cav. Co.F
Varner, F.M. AL 15th Bn.Part.Rangers Co.C
Varner, Francis MO Cav. 3rd Regt.St.Guard Co.E
Varner, Frank AL 4th Inf. Co.D
Varner, F.W. AL 56th Part.Rangers Co.C
Varner, George AL Mtd.Res. Logan's Co.
Varner, George TN Cav. 16th Bn. (Neal's) Co.E
Varner, George VA 25th Inf. 2nd Co.F
Varner, George M. GA Arty. 9th Bn. Co.A
Varner, George W. AL 8th Inf. Co.H
Varner, George W. GA Arty. 11th Bn. (Sumter Arty.) Co.A
Varner, George W. NC 6th Inf. Co.I
Varner, George W. TN Cav. 12th Bn. (Day's) Co.B
Varner, George W. TN 29th Inf. Co.H
Varner, Giles J. LA 9th Inf. Co.F
Varner, G.J. LA 1st (Nelligan's) Inf. Co.H
Varner, G.W. GA 11th Cav. Co.A
Varner, H. LA 22nd (Cons.) Inf. Co.F
Varner, H. LA 27th Inf. Co.B
Varner, Henry VA 31st Inf. Co.E
Varner, Henry H. VA 52nd Inf. Co.C
Varner, Hiram GA 40th Inf. Co.H
Varner, H.M. GA Arty. (Macon Lt.Arty.) Slaten's Co. Lt.
Varner, Isaac TN 2nd (Ashby's) Cav. Co.B
Varner, Isaac TN Cav. 5th Bn. (McClellan's) Co.C
Varner, J. AL 7th Cav. Co.D
Varner, J. FL 1st (Res.) Inf. Co.K
Varner, J.A. GA Arty. (Macon Lt.Arty.) Slaten's Co.
Varner, J.A. MS Rogers' Co.
Varner, Jacob TN 3rd (Lillard's) Mtd.Inf. Co.F
Varner, Jacob TN 19th Inf. Co.H
Varner, Jacob VA 10th Cav. Co.H
Varner, James AL 5th Inf. Co.K

Varner, James AL 6th Inf. Co.M
Varner, James GA Inf. 9th Bn. Co.C
Varner, James NC 5th Inf. Co.I
Varner, James H. AL 11th Inf. Co.A
Varner, James H. LA 31st Inf. Co.K
Varner, James M. GA 40th Inf. Co.F
Varner, J.B. SC 2nd Cav. Co.D 2nd Lt.
Varner, J.B. SC Cav. 4th Bn. Co.D 3rd Lt.
Varner, Jefferson M. GA 6th Inf. Co.D 2nd Lt.
Varner, Jesse NC 46th Inf. Co.G
Varner, Jessee AL 11th Inf. Co.A
Varner, J.F. LA 9th Inf. Co.B
Varner, J.F. LA 19th Inf. Co.K
Varner, J.G. NC 5th Inf. Co.K
Varner, J.M. GA Inf. 27th Bn. (NonConscr.) Co.B
Varner, J.N. SC Inf. Holcombe Legion Co.A
Varner, Joel VA Mil. 127th Regt.
Varner, Joel T. FL 6th Inf. Co.F Cpl.
Varner, John AL 13th Inf. Co.H
Varner, John GA 5th Res. Co.E Sgt.
Varner, John LA Inf.Cons.Crescent Regt. Co.N
Varner, John MO 5th Cav. Co.G
Varner, John NC 7th Inf. Co.F
Varner, John SC Lt.Arty. Jeter's Co. (Macbeth Lt.Arty.)
Varner, John SC Mil. 18th Regt. Co.F
Varner, John A. GA Inf. 2nd Bn. Co.C
Varner, John A. VA 4th Inf. Co.I
Varner, John C. GA 6th Inf. Co.D 1st Lt.
Varner, John F. VA 31st Inf. Co.H
Varner, John F. VA 162nd Mil. Co.A
Varner, John G. NC 46th Inf. Co.G
Varner, John L. GA Arty. 9th Bn. Co.D
Varner, John L. NC 37th Inf. Co.C
Varner, John P. NC 5th Inf. Co.I
Varner, John P. VA 31st Inf. Co.G Cpl.
Varner, John R. AL 11th Inf. Co.A
Varner, John W. AL 2nd Bn. Hilliard's Legion Vol. Co.B
Varner, John W. GA Inf. 9th Bn. Co.C
Varner, John W. VA 19th Cav. Co.I Cpl.
Varner, Jonah FL 6th Inf. Co.F
Varner, Joseph TX 17th Inf. Co.K
Varner, Joseph F. TX 4th Cav. Co.F
Varner, Joseph L. GA Inf. 5th Bn. (St.Guards) Co.B Cpl.
Varner, Joseph W. AR Cav. Wright's Regt. Co.K
Varner, J.R. SC 3rd Inf. Co.K
Varner, J.T. GA 1st Cav. Co.I
Varner, J.T. SC 18th Inf. Co.E
Varner, J.W. AL 59th Inf. Co.K
Varner, J.W. SC 3rd Inf. Co.D
Varner, L. AR 51st Mil. Co.E
Varner, Lewis F. GA 11th Cav. Co.A
Varner, Louis AR 34th Inf. Co.D
Varner, M.A. MS 14th Inf. Co.E
Varner, M.A. MS 41st Inf. Co.E 1st Sgt.
Varner, M.C. NC 22nd Inf. Co.L
Varner, M.D. 1st Conf.Cav. 2nd Co.G
Varner, Mige SC 3rd Inf. Co.D
Varner, M.S. SC 18th Inf. Co.E
Varner, M.T. SC 2nd Bn.S.S. Co.B Cpl.
Varner, M.T. SC 11th Inf. Co.B
Varner, Nathan NC 46th Inf. Co.G
Varner, Nicholas R. KY 5th Mtd.Inf. Co.F
Varner, Noah KY 6th Cav. Co.B
Varner, Noah KY 9th Cav. Co.H
Varner, Peter NC 7th Inf. Co.F
Varner, Peter VA 62nd Mtd.Inf. 2nd Co.D
Varner, P.F. SC 8th Bn.Res. Co.A Cpl.
Varner, Philip VA 11th Cav. Co.E
Varner, Philip VA 46th Mil. Co.A
Varner, P.L. SC Mil. 18th Regt. Co.F
Varner, R. MO 12th Inf.
Varner, Rankin A. NC 52nd Inf. Co.H
Varner, Reuben VA 3rd (Chrisman's) Bn.Res. Co.C
Varner, Reuben VA 8th Bn.Res. Co.B
Varner, Reuben VA 97th Mil. Co.K
Varner, R.K. AL 16th Inf. Co.D Cpl.
Varner, R.L. AL Lowndes Rangers Vol. Fagg's Co.
Varner, R.L. AL 1st Bn. Hilliard's Legion Vol. Co.D
Varner, Robert MO 2nd Cav. Co.E
Varner, Robert MO Cav. 3rd Regt.St.Guard Co.C Cpl.
Varner, Robert P. GA 24th Inf. Co.A
Varner, Roddy SC 9th Res. Co.I
Varner, Rody SC 5th St.Troops Co.H
Varner, R.P. GA 43rd Inf. Co.D
Varner, Samuel AL 4th Inf. Co.D
Varner, Samuel AL 11th Inf. Co.A
Varner, Samuel VA 64th Mtd.Inf. 2nd Co.F
Varner, Samuel D. GA Cav. Allen's Co.
Varner, Sam'l D. Gen. & Staff Capt.,QM
Varner, Solomon 1st Conf.Eng.Troops Co.C
Varner, T.H. GA 2nd Cav. (St.Guards) Co.D
Varner, Thomas SC 18th Inf. Co.E
Varner, Thomas H. GA 2nd Cav. Co.I
Varner, Thomas J. AL 3rd Inf. Co.C
Varner, Thomas J. AL Conscr. & Res.Bn. Co.A 2nd Lt.
Varner, Thomas J. MS 17th Inf. Co.C
Varner, T.J. LA Inf. 1st Sp.Bn. (Rightor's) Co.D Cpl.
Varner, W. NC 1st Arty. (10th St.Troops) Co.E
Varner, W.A. GA 63rd Inf. Co.I
Varner, W.A. NC 29th Inf. Co.D
Varner, Wade SC Inf.Loc.Def. Estill's Co.
Varner, Walter MO Cav. 3rd Regt.St.Guard Co.E
Varner, Washington VA 31st Inf. Co.E
Varner, Watson TN Cav. 12th Bn. (Day's) Co.B
Varner, Watson TN Cav. 16th Bn. (Neal's) Co.E
Varner, W.D. GA 19th Inf. Co.G
Varner, W.E. NC 1st Arty. Co.E
Varner, W.F. TX 22nd Inf. Co.F
Varner, W.H. GA 40th Inf. Co.F
Varner, William AR 34th Inf. Co.D
Varner, William GA 43rd Inf. Co.L,C
Varner, William GA 60th Inf. Co.B
Varner, William MS 20th Inf. Co.H
Varner, William NC 22nd Inf. Co.K
Varner, William NC 45th Inf. Co.K
Varner, William TN 5th (McKenzie's) Cav. Co.A
Varner, William VA 25th Inf. 1st Co.F
Varner, William VA 62nd Mtd.Inf. 2nd Co.F
Varner, William VA 162nd Mil. Co.A
Varner, William E. GA Lt.Arty. Scogin's Btty. (Griffin Lt.Arty.) Cpl.
Varner, William F. VA 31st Inf. Co.H
Varner, William M. GA 2nd Cav. (St.Guards) Co.D
Varner, William P. NC Inf. 2nd Bn. Co.F
Varner, William R. MS 29th Inf. Co.A Sgt.
Varner, William S. GA 7th Inf. Co.D Cpl.
Varner, William S. 1st Conf.Inf. 2nd Co.F 2nd Lt.
Varner, W.S. 1st Conf.Eng.Troops Co.B
Varner, W. Wade SC Mil. Charbonnier's Co.
Varner, Zeus NC 6th Sr.Res. Co.A
Varnerot, Adolphe LA Mil. 1st Regt. French Brig. Co.6
Varnes, Henry FL 9th Inf. Co.D
Varnes, J. SC 2nd St.Troops Co.C
Varnes, William FL 10th Inf. Co.A
Varnes, W.M. SC 1st Bn.S.S. Co.A
Varnes, W.M. SC 20th Inf. Co.B
Varnes, W.M. SC 27th Inf. Co.E
Varney, Benton AL Unassign.Conscr.
Varney, Ed TX Cav. 3rd Regt.St.Troops Co.A
Varney, J. AL 7th Cav. Co.I
Varney, John H. VA Inf. 45th Bn. Co.B
Varney, John W. VA Lt.Arty. Carpenter's Co.
Varney, John W. VA Lt.Arty. Cutshaw's Co.
Varney, Joseph L. GA 5th Inf. Co.F
Varney, M.B. VA Inf. 45th Bn. Co.B
Varnhouse, John W. VA Horse Arty. McClanahan's Co.
Varnidoe, John M. GA 4th (Clinch's) Cav. Co.B
Varnier, Edward VA 9th Inf. Co.C 2nd Lt.
Varnier, Hiram VA Arty. J.W. Drewry's Co. Sgt.
Varnier, John W. VA 9th Inf. Co.C Sgt.
Varnier, Robert VA 9th Inf. Co.C
Varnier, William W. VA Arty. J.W. Drewry's Co. Sgt.
Varning, R.J. FL 2nd Inf. Co.E
Varnnom, William C. GA 6th Inf. (St.Guards) Co.C
Varnom, William C. GA 6th Inf. (St.Guards) Co.C
Varnon, Alonzo AL Cp. of Instr. (Talladega)
Varnon, A.W. AL 40th Inf. Co.H
Varnon, B. LA 27th Inf. Co.K
Varnon, David H. AL 59th Inf. Co.C
Varnon, David H. AL 2nd Bn. Hilliard's Legion Vol. Co.F
Varnon, Elijah H. AL Inf. 1st Regt. Co.D Cpl.
Varnon, F.H. AR Cav. McGehee's Regt. Co.C
Varnon, J.H. AL 25th Inf. Co.G
Varnon, John B. MS 1st Lt.Arty.
Varnon, John T. KY 2nd Mtd.Inf. Co.H Jr.2nd Lt.
Varnon, McB. AL 62nd Inf. Co.B,E
Varnon, William LA 27th Inf. Co.K
Varnon, William M. TX 10th Inf. Co.C
Varnon, W.M. TX 12th Cav. Co.A
Varnor, L.D. AL Cav. Hardie's Bn.Res. S.D. McClellan's Co.
Varnovis, James I. AL 25th Inf. Co.G
Varns, Isaac FL 1st Cav. Co.D
Varns, J. FL Inf. 2nd Bn. Co.A
Varnum, A.D. AL 46th Inf. Co.I
Varnum, Alexander NC 54th Inf. Co.C
Varnum, Colin GA 25th Inf. Co.E
Varnum, Colon S. AL 61st Inf. Co.K 1st Sgt.
Varnum, C.S. GA 38th Inf. 2nd Co.I Sgt.

Varnum, C.S. GA 60th Inf. 2nd Co.A Sgt.
Varnum, George W. NC 21st Inf. Co.C
Varnum, James M. MS 2nd Inf. Co.D
Varnum, Jasper AL 20th Inf. Co.C
Varnum, J.B. MO Lt.Arty. 3rd Field Btty.
Varnum, J.M. GA 13th Cav. Co.I
Varnum, J.M. MS 10th Cav. Co.H
Varnum, J.M. Conf.Cav. Baxter's Bn. Co.A
Varnum, John AL 50th Inf. Co.A
Varnum, John L. TN Lt.Arty. Burroughs' Co.
Varnum, Joseph B. VA Lt.Arty. 38th Bn. Co.D
Varnum, Marion AL 10th Inf. Co.D
Varnum, Meredith MS 34th Inf. Co.H
Varnum, Oliver NC Hvy.Arty. 1st Bn. Co.C,D
Varnum, Oliver NC 24th Inf. Co.G
Varnum, Thomas TX 12th Cav. Co.A
Varny, James MS 43rd Inf. Co.A
Varomore, Alford MO Cav. Ford's Bn. Co.C
Varonee, C.B. SC Inf. 3rd Bn. Co.G
Varramon, B.F. AL 29th Inf. Co.D
Varrera, Jesus TX Cav. Benavides' Regt. Co.C
Varrera, Jesus TX 8th Inf. Co.C
Varrnea, Victoriano TX Cav. Ragsdale's Bn. 1st Co.A
Varrow, Pat. TX 35th (Brown's) Cav. Co.C
Varrun, C. KY 2nd Cav. Co.G
Varsant, A.R. AL 34th Inf. Co.B
Varser, John P. TX 16th Inf. Co.G Cpl.
Varser, William H. VA 14th Inf. Co.A
Varser, William H. VA 59th Mil. Riddick's Co. Cpl.
Varterling, Fred LA Mil. Fire Bn. Co.D
Varterling, H. LA Mil. Fire Bn. Co.D
Varts, H.H. LA Arty. 7th Regt. Co.K
Varvel, Isaac H. MO 1st Cav. Co.C
Varvel, William KY 9th Cav. Co.E
Varvell, James W. KY 5th Mtd.Inf. Co.C
Varwell, James AR 1st Mtd.Rifles Co.G
Vasant, Wastley MO Cav. Fristoe's Regt. Co.A
Vasbinder, Eugene B. TX 2nd Inf. Co.E
Vasbinder, Lemuel J. TX 8th Inf. Co.F
Vasbinder, Leonard B. TX 8th Inf. Co.F
Vasbinder, Virgil TX Cav. 6th Bn. Co.B
Vascer, James TN 62nd Mtd.Inf. Co.C Cpl.
Vascer, John TN 62nd Mtd.Inf. Co.C Sgt.
Vascocu, D.V. LA 27th Inf. Co.K
Vascocue, J.L. LA Inf.Cons.Crescent Regt. Co.L
Vascoe, John LA 9th Inf. Co.F
Vascoen, J.O. LA 2nd Cav. Co.B
Vascoene, P. LA 2nd Cav. Co.C
Vaseur, C. AR Mil. Desha Cty.Bn.
Vaseur, Eugene AR Mil. Desha Cty.Bn.
Vaseur, John B. LA 1st Hvy.Arty. (Reg.) Co.D
Vaseur, N. AR Mil. Desha Cty.Bn.
Vasey, J.T. MO 16th Inf. Co.G
Vasey, P. LA Mil. 4th Regt. 1st Brig. 1st Div. Co.A
Vasey, William SC Inf. Holcombe Legion Co.B
Vashon, George S. VA Inf. 25th Bn. Co.A
Vason, J.M. AL 4th Res. Co.H
Vason, Joseph GA Cobb's Legion Co.G 1st Lt.
Vason, Marcellus E. GA 4th Inf. Co.E
Vason, Marcellus E. Gen. & Staff Asst.Surg.
Vason, M.E. VA 46th Inf. Asst.Surg.
Vason, William J. GA Cav. 19th Bn. Co.D Capt.
Vason, William J. GA Inf. 1st Loc.Troops (Augusta) Co.A
Vason, William J. GA 4th Inf. Co.E 2nd Lt.
Vason, W.J. 10th Conf.Cav. Co.I Col.
Vasque, Charles A.F. VA Arty. Paris' Co.
Vasquez, Cristobal TX 8th Inf. Co.H
Vasquez, Jose TX 8th Inf. Co.C
Vasquez, Juan TX 3rd Inf. Co.F
Vasquez, Pamfilo TX 3rd Inf. Co.F
Vasquez, Policarpio TX 3rd Inf. Co.F
Vasquez, Zacharias TX 3rd Inf. Co.F
Vass, A.C. VA Inf. 26th Bn. Co.C
Vass, A.F. LA Washington Arty.Bn. Co.4
Vass, Alx NC 4th Bn.Jr.Res. Co.B
Vass, Alexander TN 4th (McLemore's) Cav. Co.I
Vass, Alexander TN 16th Inf. Co.K
Vass, Anderson C. VA 108th Mil. Co.B, Lemons' Co.
Vass, Benjamin W. VA Lt.Arty. Ellett's Co. Sgt.
Vass, C. VA 59th Inf. 1st Co.B
Vass, Charles VA Arty. Bryan's Co.
Vass, Curtis VA 60th Inf. Co.A
Vass, Curtiss VA Inf. 23rd Bn.
Vass, Douglas AL 3rd Inf. Co.A Sgt.
Vass, Douglas AL 21st Inf. QM
Vass, Ed C. VA 19th Cav. Co.G
Vass, Elijah VA Cav. Hounshell's Bn. Co.A
Vass, Elijah VA 166th Mil. Co.D
Vass, George F. VA 13th Inf. 1st Co.B
Vass, George W. VA 60th Inf. Co.E
Vass, Henry VA Hvy.Arty. 20th Bn. Co.E Cpl.
Vass, H.J.C. VA Lt.Arty. Ellett's Co. Cpl.
Vass, H.P. AL Mil. 2nd Regt.Vol. Co.E
Vass, H. Penrose AL 21st Inf. Co.K 1st Sgt.
Vass, James VA 4th Cav. Co.H
Vass, James VA 13th Inf. 1st Co.B
Vass, James L. VA 36th Inf. 2nd Co.C 2nd Lt.
Vass, James P. VA 15th Inf. Co.E
Vass, James S. FL 3rd Inf. Co.K
Vass, Jeremiah VA 54th Inf. Co.G
Vass, J.F. FL 2nd Inf. Co.C
Vass, J.H. VA Cav. Swann's Bn. Watkins' Co.
Vass, John VA 11th Bn.Res. Co.C
Vass, John L. VA 108th Mil. Co.C
Vass, John W. VA Lt.Arty. Ellett's Co.
Vass, Joseph A. VA 15th Inf. Co.E
Vass, L.C. VA 27th Inf. Chap.
Vass, L.C. Gen. & Staff Chap.
Vass, Lee E. VA 7th Inf. Co.D
Vass, Mathew E. VA 36th Inf. 2nd Co.C
Vass, Pembrook VA 30th Bn.S.S. Co.C,D Sgt.
Vass, Philip VA Lt.Arty. Lowry's Co.
Vass, Philip N. VA 166th Mil. Co.B,D
Vass, R.C. LA 11th Inf. Co.L 1st Lt.
Vass, R.C. LA 20th Inf. New Co.E 1st Lt.
Vass, R.C. VA Cav. Hounshell's Bn. Gwinn's Co.
Vass, Rice C. VA Lt.Arty. Lowry's Co.
Vass, Rice C. VA 11th Bn.Res. Co.C
Vass, Rice Curtis VA 8th Cav. 1st Co.D
Vass, Stephen T. VA 18th Inf. Co.A
Vass, T.D. VA 4th Cav. Co.H
Vass, Thomas VA Lt.Arty. French's Co.
Vass, Thomas VA Arty. Wise Legion
Vass, Thomas Conf.Lt.Arty. Stark's Bn. Co.D
Vass, Thomas J. VA 15th Inf. Co.E Cpl.
Vass, Thornton VA 34th Mil. Co.D
Vass, T.M. VA 23rd Cav. Co.C
Vass, T.M. VA 3rd Inf.Loc.Def. Co.A
Vass, W.A. 2nd Conf.Eng.Troops Co.B
Vass, William VA 7th Inf. Co.C
Vass, William VA 166th Mil. Co.B
Vass, William A. VA Lt.Arty. French's Co. Artif.
Vass, William E. VA 36th Inf. 2nd Co.C
Vass, William H. TX 8th Inf. Co.I
Vass, W.R.C. VA 7th Inf. Co.D Cpl.
Vassallo, Antonio LA Mil. 6th Regt.Eur.Brig. (Italian Guards Bn.) Co.1
Vassar, George L. GA 15th Inf. Co.F
Vassar, George W. MS 20th Inf. Co.C
Vassar, G.L. GA 38th Inf. Co.H
Vassar, John AR 14th (Powers') Inf. Co.K
Vassar, John J. GA 38th Inf. Co.H 1st Lt.
Vassar, T.Z.B. SC Manigault's Bn.Vol. Co.D
Vassau, Idolph TN 40th Inf. Co.F
Vassau, Zam TN 40th Inf. Co.F
Vassaux, Gista AR 8th Cav. Peoples' Co.
Vasse, George W. SC 5th Inf. 1st Co.G
Vasse, John T. SC 5th Inf. 1st Co.G
Vasse, Sanford P. MO 10th Cav. Co.C
Vasser, C.W. MS 5th Cav. Co.C
Vasser, C.W. MS 28th Cav. Co.C
Vasser, D. AR 7th Inf. Co.F
Vasser, D. MO 12th Inf. Co.G,C
Vasser, Daniel MO 11th Inf. Co.C
Vasser, Daniel L. VA 3rd Inf. 2nd Co.K
Vasser, Ealy A. SC 20th Inf. Co.G
Vasser, Elijah J. MS 14th Inf. Co.I 2nd Lt.
Vasser, E.J. MS 43rd Inf. Co.L
Vasser, E.M. AL Mil. 4th Vol. Co.G
Vasser, E.M. Gen. & Staff,PACS Asst.Surg.
Vasser, Franklin VA 9th Inf. Co.B
Vasser, George R. AL 2nd Cav. Co.B
Vasser, George W. MS 30th Inf. Co.K
Vasser, George W. Gen. & Staff Asst.Surg.
Vasser, H. AL 33rd Inf. Co.A 1st Lt.
Vasser, H. TN 13th Inf. Co.G
Vasser, Harry MS 15th Bn.S.S. Co.B 1st Lt.
Vasser, J.A. VA 1st (Farinholt's) Res. Co.D
Vasser, James TN 2nd (Ashby's) Cav. Co.K
Vasser, James TN Cav. 5th Bn. (McClellan's) Co.E
Vasser, James TN 8th (Smith's) Cav. Co.E
Vasser, James H. NC 32nd Inf. Co.B,C
Vasser, J.F. AR 2nd Cav. Co.F
Vasser, John VA 34th Inf. Co.E
Vasser, Joseph NC 32nd Inf. Co.B,C
Vasser, J.P. MS 15th Bn.S.S. Co.B
Vasser, J.S. TX 12th Inf. Co.E
Vasser, Levi MO 1st Cav. Co.H
Vasser, Levi C. VA 16th Inf. Co.E
Vasser, Morgan AR 33rd Inf. Co.H Cpl.
Vasser, N. FL 4th Inf. Nichols' Co.
Vasser, R.H. 1st Chickasaw Inf. Hansell's Co.
Vasser, Richard A. GA Cobb's Legion Co.C
Vasser, Robert MO 12th Inf. Co.G
Vasser, Robert R. AL 29th Inf. Co.G Music.
Vasser, R.R. SC Lt.Arty. Garden's Co. (Palmetto Lt.Btty.)
Vasser, T.Z.B. SC Inf. 6th Bn. Co.B
Vasser, T.Z.B. SC 26th Inf. Co.H Cpl.

Vasser, Wade H. MS 24th Inf. Co.E
Vasser, W.H. Gen. & Staff Capt.,Asst.Comsy.
Vasser, William FL Cav. 4th Regt.
Vasser, William TN 8th (Smith's) Cav. Co.G
Vasser, William A. AR 14th (Powers') Inf. Co.K
Vasser, William H. MS 14th Inf. ACS
Vasser, William J. AR 14th (Powers') Inf. Co.K
Vasserer, Gus. AR Mil. Desha Cty.Bn.
Vassersvi, J. LA 8th Cav. Co.B
Vasseur, Pierre LA 8th Cav. Co.B
Vasseur, U. LA 2nd Res.Corps Co.A
Vassey, Charles TN 6th Inf. Co.G
Vassey, John SC Palmetto S.S. Co.M Cpl.
Vassey, Jonas SC Palmetto S.S. Co.M
Vasso, James VA 28th Inf. Co.H
Vassor, Benjamin NC 54th Inf. Co.D
Vassor, Edwin NC Lt.Arty. 3rd Bn. Co.A
Vassor, Henry B. NC Lt.Arty. 3rd Bn. Co.A
Vassor, James H. NC 12th Inf. Co.N
Vassor, Joseph NC 12th Inf. Co.N
Vassor, William J. NC Lt.Arty. 3rd Bn. Co.A
Vassore, Charles W. MS 3rd Cav.
Vassy, Levi SC 7th Res. Co.C
Vassy, Levy SC 5th St.Troops Co.G
Vastal, J.R. TX 25th Cav. Co.A
Vaton, T.T. VA 44th Inf. Co.B
Vator, Alphonse LA 7th Cav. Co.G
Vatt, G.I.M. AL 58th Inf. Co.B
Vatter, Ls. LA 2nd Res.Corps Co.B 1st Lt.
Vauclin, Louis LA C.S. Zouave Bn. Co.B
Vaucon, Lastele LA 18th Inf. Co.A
Vaucon, Lastele LA Inf.Cons. 18th Regt. & Yellow Jacket Bn. Co.A
Vaudelet, S. LA Mil. 3rd Regt. French Brig. Co.4
Vanderdos, Philip A. LA 21st (Patton's) Inf. Co.I
Vauderson, J.M. SC 14th Inf. Co.A
Vandeville, S.J. Gen. & Staff Surg.
Vaudran, --- LA Mil. 2nd Regt. French Brig. Co.4
Vaudry, Jules, Sr. LA Arty. Beauregard Bn.Btty.
Vaudry, Jules MS Cav. Hughes' Bn. Co.G 1st Lt.
Vaudry, W.T. LA Lt.Arty. Fenner's Btty.
Vaugalin, Henry F. LA Mil. Orleans Fire Regt. Co.F
Vaugolin, Chas. LA Arty. 8th Bn. Co.3
Vaugen, Sidney W. VA 33rd Inf. Co.H
Vaugh, A.C. TN 40th Inf. Co.F
Vaugh, Alfred SC 24th Inf. Co.E
Vaugh, Allen Mead's Conf.Cav. Co.A
Vaugh, A.M. TN Holman's Bn.Part.Rangers Co.A
Vaugh, C. MS 35th Inf. Co.H
Vaugh, C.S. VA 3rd Cav.
Vaugh, F.R. TN 7th Cav. Co.I
Vaugh, Frederick TX Cav. Ragsdale's Bn. Co.B
Vaugh, F.W. GA 38th Inf. Co.C
Vaugh, H.W. TN 7th (Duckworth's) Cav. White's Co. Black.
Vaugh, James KY 1st (Butler's) Cav. Co.B
Vaugh, James D. VA 24th Cav. Co.B
Vaugh, Jesse H. TX Cav. McCord's Frontier Regt. 2nd Co.A
Vaugh, John MO Cav. Preston's Bn.
Vaugh, John TN Cav. 16th Bn. (Neal's) Co.F
Vaugham, F.G. TX 17th Inf. Co.K
Vaugham, William TN 21st (Wilson's) Cav. Co.K
Vaughan, --- FL 1st Inf. Co.D
Vaughan, --- VA 11th Inf. Co.E
Vaughan, A. AL 5th Cav. Co.E
Vaughan, A. AL 7th Inf. Co.F
Vaughan, A. GA 38th Inf. Co.H
Vaughan, A. MS 11th Inf. Co.L Cpl.
Vaughan, A. MO Inf. 6th Regt.St.Guard Co.G
Vaughan, A. NC 5th Cav. (63rd St.Troops) Co.K
Vaughan, Aaron VA 22nd Cav. Co.G
Vaughan, A.B. VA 1st (Farinholt's) Res. Co.E
Vaughan, Abner P. 8th (Wade's) Conf.Cav. Co.G
Vaughan, Abner W. TN 6th (Wheeler's) Cav. Co.C
Vaughan, Abner W. TN Cav. 11th Bn. (Gordon's) Co.C
Vaughan, Abraham VA 16th Cav. Co.E Cpl.
Vaughan, A.C. TN 34th Inf. Co.D 3rd Lt.
Vaughan, Adoniram E. VA 55th Inf. Co.H Sgt.
Vaughan, A.F. MO 2nd Inf. Co.I,E
Vaughan, A.F. VA 44th Inf. Co.H
Vaughan, A.H. AR 15th (Johnson's) Inf. Co.D Sgt.
Vaughan, A.H. TN 11th Inf. Co.H 2nd Lt.
Vaughan, A.J. AR Cav. Gordon's Regt. Co.A
Vaughan, A.J. GA Cav. 10th Bn. (St.Guards) Co.E
Vaughan, A.J. TN 22nd (Barteau's) Cav. Co.H
Vaughan, A.J., Jr. TN 13th Inf. Co.E Col.
Vaughan, A.J. TN 40th Inf. Co.F,H
Vaughan, A.J. VA 18th Inf. Co.D
Vaughan, A.J. Gen. & Staff Capt.,QM
Vaughan, A.N. TX 5th Inf. Co.F
Vaughan, A.R. TX Cav. Benavides' Regt. Co.B
Vaughan, A.R. TX 5th Inf. Co.F
Vaughan, A.R. VA 3rd Cav. Co.B Cpl.
Vaughan, A.S. Bradford's Corps Scouts & Guards
Vaughan, A.W. GA 38th Inf. Co.H
Vaughan, Albert VA 97th Mil. Co.L
Vaughan, Albert F. VA Inf. 5th Bn. Co.A
Vaughan, Albert G. TX 6th Cav. Co.G
Vaughan, Alexander AL 34th Inf. Co.E
Vaughan, Alexander NC 23rd Inf. Co.G
Vaughan, Alexander VA Hvy.Arty. 18th Bn. Co.C
Vaughan, Alex. VA 1st (Farinholt's) Res. Co.F
Vaughan, Alexander VA 3rd Inf. Co.C
Vaughan, Alexander VA 3rd (Archer's) Bn.Res. Co.E Sgt.
Vaughan, Alexander VA 51st Inf. Co.K
Vaughan, Alex. B. NC 6th Inf. Co.H
Vaughan, Alfred TN Cav. 4th Bn. (Branner's) Co.E Sgt.
Vaughan, Alfred J. VA 1st Inf. Co.G
Vaughan, Allen F. AL 4th Inf. Co.A
Vaughan, Alonzo NC 54th Inf. Co.F Hosp.Stew.
Vaughan, Amzi M. AL 20th Inf. Co.F
Vaughan, Andrew A. MS 24th Inf. Co.G Cpl.
Vaughan, Andrew C. TN Holman's Bn. Part.Rangers Co.B
Vaughan, Andrew J. NC 2nd Cav. (19th St.Troops) Co.C
Vaughan, Andrew J. VA Cav. 39th Bn. Co.D
Vaughan, Andrew J. Gen. & Staff Maj.,Comsy.
Vaughan, Archibald A.E. GA Inf. (Franklin Cty.Guards) Kay's Co.
Vaughan, Archibald M. MS Cav. 24th Bn. Co.E Sgt.
Vaughan, Asa AL 11th Inf. Co.D
Vaughan, Asa VA 1st (Farinholt's) Res. Co.A
Vaughan, Asa VA 1st (Farinholt's) Res. Co.F
Vaughan, Asa VA 14th Inf. Co.E
Vaughan, Asa J. VA 59th Inf. 2nd Co.H
Vaughan, Asa W. VA Lt.Arty. 12th Bn. 2nd Co.A
Vaughan, Asa W. VA Lt.Arty. Sturdivant's Co.
Vaughan, Augustus AR 4th Inf. Co.B
Vaughan, Augustus Gillum's Regt. Co.G Sgt.
Vaughan, Azariah NC 14th Inf. Co.B
Vaughan, B.A. KY 1st (Butler's) Cav. Co.A
Vaughan, B.A. Gen. & Staff Surg.
Vaughan, Barrington A. SC Inf. 3rd Bn. Co.C
Vaughan, B.B. VA 1st Cav. Co.G
Vaughan, Benjamin AR 17th (Griffith's) Inf. Co.H Sgt.
Vaughan, Benjamin GA 52nd Inf. Co.K
Vaughan, Benjamin NC 17th Inf. (2nd Org.) Co.C
Vaughan, Benjamin SC 1st St.Troops Co.K
Vaughan, Benjamine AL Cav. 5th Bn. Hilliard's Legion Co.E
Vaughan, Benjamin F. MS 19th Inf. Co.B Cpl.
Vaughan, Benjamin J. VA 40th Inf. Co.A
Vaughan, Benjamin R. AR 33rd Inf. Co.K
Vaughan, Benjamin T. AL 36th Inf. Co.G
Vaughan, B.F. GA 18th Inf. Co.E Sgt.
Vaughan, B.F. TN 41st Inf. Co.E
Vaughan, B.F. VA 4th Cav. Co.G
Vaughan, B.J. VA 1st St.Res. Co.F
Vaughan, B. Kelly SC 22nd Inf. Co.B Sgt.
Vaughan, B.O. VA 1st (Farinholt's) Res. Co.F Sgt.
Vaughan, Bogan D. MS 44th Inf. Co.C
Vaughan, B.R. MS Blythe's Bn. (St.Troops) Co.B
Vaughan, Brad AR 33rd Inf. Co.K
Vaughan, C. AL Cav. Co.E
Vaughan, C. AL 1st Bn.Cadets Co.B
Vaughan, C. GA Inf. 1st Loc.Troops (Augusta) Co.I
Vaughan, C. MO Cav. Williams' Regt. Co.H Sgt.
Vaughan, C. VA Inf. 25th Bn. Co.E
Vaughan, Cadmus VA Lt.Arty. Jeffress' Co.
Vaughan, Calvin TN 34th Inf. Co.D
Vaughan, C.B. AL St.Mil. Co.A
Vaughan, C.C.P. SC 16th & 24th (Cons.) Inf. Co.E
Vaughan, C.C. Pinkney SC 16th Inf. Co.B
Vaughan, Cecil C. VA 5th Cav. (12 mo. '61-2) Co.H
Vaughan, Cecil C. VA 13th Cav. Co.A
Vaughan, C.H. TN 4th (McLemore's) Cav. Co.B
Vaughan, Charles MO 8th Cav. Co.H Jr.2nd Lt.
Vaughan, Charles NC 33rd Inf. Co.K
Vaughan, Charles B. MS 1st Lt.Arty. Co.I
Vaughan, Charles C. AL 6th Inf. Co.L
Vaughan, Charles C. VA 5th Cav. (12 mo. '61-2) Co.H
Vaughan, Charles H. VA 2nd Bn.Res. Co.B Capt.

Vaughan, Charles H. VA 26th Inf. Co.K
Vaughan, Charles R. VA 21st Mil. Co.D
Vaughan, Charles T. VA 3rd Inf. Co.C Cpl.
Vaughan, Charles V. VA 18th Inf. Co.C
Vaughan, Cincinatus S. VA 13th Cav. Co.F
Vaughan, Cincinnatus B. VA 4th Cav. Co.G
Vaughan, Cincinnatus Stith VA 5th Cav. (12 mo. '61-2) Co.F
Vaughan, Clifford AL 56th Part.Rangers Co.B Cpl.
Vaughan, Clifford P. AL 15th Bn.Part.Rangers Co.B Cpl.
Vaughan, Clinton Gillum's Regt. Whitaker's Co.
Vaughan, Columbus M. KY 7th Mtd.Inf. Co.B
Vaughan, Cornelius G. VA 19th Inf. Co.E
Vaughan, C.P. AL Cav. Murphy's Bn. Co.B
Vaughan, C.T. GA Cav. Dorough's Bn.
Vaughan, C.V. VA Arty. Lanier's Co.
Vaughan, C.W. AR 19th (Dawson's) Inf. Co.B
Vaughan, D. MS 2nd Part. Co.A
Vaughan, D. VA 1st (Farinholt's) Res. Co.A
Vaughan, Daniel S. VA Cav. 47th Bn. Co.C
Vaughan, David GA 52nd Inf. Co.K
Vaughan, David MO 8th Inf. Co.B,F
Vaughan, David MO Robertson's Regt.St.Guard Co.1
Vaughan, David NC 23rd Inf. Co.E
Vaughan, David NC Mil. Clark's Sp.Bn. Rountree's Co., Co.C
Vaughan, David A. Gen. & Staff AASurg.
Vaughan, David L. TN 4th (McLemore's) Cav. Co.F
Vaughan, David Y. SC 16th Inf. Co.B
Vaughan, D.B. MS 7th Cav. Co.E
Vaughan, D.C. MS Lt.Arty. (Jefferson Arty.) Darden's Co.
Vaughan, D.C. NC 35th Inf. Co.E
Vaughan, DeJohnson TN 7th Inf. Co.I
Vaughan, D.F. MO 1st Brig.St.Guard
Vaughan, D.K. GA 52nd Inf. Co.K
Vaughan, D.K. SC 15th Inf. Co.K
Vaughan, D.L. SC 16th Inf. Co.F
Vaughan, D.M. MS Morgan's Co. (Morgan Riflemen)
Vaughan, Dow NC 23rd Inf. Co.E
Vaughan, D.T. SC 22nd Inf. Co.A 2nd Lt.
Vaughan, E. LA 3rd (Harrison's) Cav. Co.I
Vaughan, E.A. NC 2nd Cav. (19th St.Troops) Co.H
Vaughan, E.A. VA 1st (Farinholt's) Res. Co.E
Vaughan, E.A. VA 28th Inf. Co.I
Vaughan, E.B. AL 50th Inf. Co.F,G Capt.
Vaughan, E.B. NC Inf. Whitfield's Bn. Co.F
Vaughan, E.B. VA 24th Cav. Sgt.Maj.
Vaughan, Ebenezer H. MS 2nd Inf. Co.G
Vaughan, E.C. AR Cav. Gordon's Regt. Co.K
Vaughan, Edgar H. VA 6th Cav. Co.G Sgt.
Vaughan, Edgar L. VA 5th Cav. (12 mo. '61-2) Co.H
Vaughan, Edgar L. VA 13th Cav. Co.A
Vaughan, Edmund D. TN 4th (McLemore's) Cav. Co.B
Vaughan, Ed. R. MS 1st Lt.Arty. Co.B
Vaughan, Edward A. VA 14th Inf. Co.E
Vaughan, Edward S. VA Lt.Arty. Grandy's Co.
Vaughan, E.E. GA 7th Inf. Co.I Sgt.
Vaughan, E.F. SC 18th Inf. Co.B Sgt.
Vaughan, E.H. MS Wilson's Co. (Ponticola Guards)
Vaughan, E.H. SC Lt.Arty. 3rd (Palmetto) Bn. Co.C
Vaughan, E.H. TN 22nd (Barteau's) Cav. Co.D
Vaughan, E.H. 8th (Dearing's) Conf.Cav. Co.C
Vaughan, E.J. VA 9th Inf. 2nd Co.A
Vaughan, E.L. AR 10th Inf. Co.E Col.
Vaughan, Elias VA 63rd Inf. 1st Co.A, Co.B,E
Vaughan, Elias H. NC Cav. 12th Bn. Co.C
Vaughan, Elias H. NC Cav. 16th Bn. Co.G
Vaughan, Elias H. NC 12th Inf. Co.O
Vaughan, Elias H. NC 32nd Inf. Co.C,D
Vaughan, Elias W. VA Lt.Arty. Douthat's Co.
Vaughan, Elisha T. NC 1st Cav. (9th St.Troops) Co.B
Vaughan, E.M. MS 5th Inf. Co.B
Vaughan, Emmett R. AL 32nd Inf. Co.A
Vaughan, Enoch VA 38th Inf. 1st Co.I
Vaughan, E.P. TN 10th (DeMoss') Cav. Co.D
Vaughan, E.P. TN Inf. 4th Cons.Regt. Co.G Cpl.
Vaughan, E.R. AL Cav. Murphy's Bn. Co.B
Vaughan, Erasmus GA Inf. (Baldwin Inf.) Moore's Co.
Vaughan, F. AL Mil. 4th Vol. Co.G
Vaughan, F., Jr. AL 38th Inf. Co.H
Vaughan, F. AL St.Mil. Co.A
Vaughan, F. AR Lt.Arty. Marshall's Btty.
Vaughan, F. LA Inf.Crescent Regt. Co.A
Vaughan, F.C. NC 12th Inf. Co.F
Vaughan, F.D. FL 1st Inf. New Co.K
Vaughan, F.H. GA 62nd Cav. Co.L
Vaughan, Fielding NC 23rd Inf. Co.G 1st Sgt.
Vaughan, F.L. MS 8th Cav. Co.I
Vaughan, F.M. MO 12th Cav. Co.D
Vaughan, F.O. SC 2nd Inf. Co.D
Vaughan, Francis VA 16th Inf. Co.D
Vaughan, Francis L. VA 12th Inf. Co.B
Vaughan, Francis M. VA 5th Cav. (12 mo. '61-2) Co.H
Vaughan, Francis M. VA 13th Cav. Co.A Cpl.
Vaughan, Francis M. VA 3rd Inf. Co.D Sgt.
Vaughan, Frank VA 1st Cav. Co.G
Vaughan, Frank C. MS 2nd Cav. Co.F
Vaughan, Fred B. AL Jeff Davis Arty. Cpl.
Vaughan, Fred H. VA 24th Cav. Co.K
Vaughan, Fred H. 8th (Dearing's) Conf.Cav. Co.E
Vaughan, Frederick B. AL 28th Inf. Co.I 1st Sgt.
Vaughan, Fredrick A. AL 6th Cav. Co.E
Vaughan, G. VA 3rd Res. Co.K
Vaughan, G.A. AR 12th Inf. Co.G
Vaughan, G.B. KY Jessee's Bn.Mtd.Riflemen Co.B Sgt.
Vaughan, G.B. LA 3rd Inf. Co.B
Vaughan, George MS Inf. 3rd Bn. (St.Troops) Co.D
Vaughan, George MO Cav. Williams' Regt. Co.E
Vaughan, George VA 51st Inf. Co.K
Vaughan, George A. TN Cav. 5th Bn. (McClellan's) Co.D
Vaughan, George A. 7th Conf.Cav. Co.B
Vaughan, George B. KY Cav. 1st Bn. Co.B
Vaughan, George B. KY 4th Cav. Co.B
Vaughan, George D. VA 4th Cav. Co.G
Vaughan, George H. MO Inf. 3rd Bn. Co.D Sgt.
Vaughan, George H. MO Inf. 4th Bn.St.Guard Co.D
Vaughan, George H. MO 6th Inf. Co.F Sr.2nd Lt.
Vaughan, George H. MO St.Guard Div.P.M.Dept. Clerk
Vaughan, George M. MS 31st Inf. Co.E
Vaughan, George M. MO 8th Inf. Co.H Hosp.Stew.
Vaughan, George M. TN 34th Inf. Co.D 2nd Lt.
Vaughan, George M. VA 24th Cav. Co.B 1st Sgt.
Vaughan, George M. VA Cav. 40th Bn. Co.B 1st Sgt.
Vaughan, George P. SC 1st (Orr's) Rifles Co.A
Vaughan, George S.E. MO 1st N.E. Cav.
Vaughan, George T. MO Inf. 8th Bn. Co.E 1st Lt.
Vaughan, George T. MO 9th Inf. Co.I 1st Lt.
Vaughan, George W. AL Lt.Arty. 2nd Bn. Co.F 1st Lt.
Vaughan, George W. AR 3rd Cav. Co.K
Vaughan, George W. AR 15th (N.W.) Inf. Co.F
Vaughan, George W. GA Cobb's Legion Co.E,F
Vaughan, George W. MS Inf. 2nd Bn. Co.K
Vaughan, George W. MS 48th Inf. Co.K
Vaughan, George W. MO Inf. 4th Regt.St.Guard Co.D Capt.
Vaughan, George W. TN Cav. 16th Bn. (Neal's) Co.F
Vaughan, George W. TN 1st (Turney's) Inf. Co.B
Vaughan, George W. VA 9th Cav. Co.G
Vaughan, George W. VA Horse Arty. E. Graham's Co. Cpl.
Vaughan, George W. VA 3rd Res. Co.D
Vaughan, George W. VA 20th Inf. Co.K
Vaughan, George W. VA 55th Inf. Co.H Sgt.
Vaughan, George W. VA 59th Inf. 3rd Co.C
Vaughan, George W. 8th (Wade's) Conf.Cav. Co.F
Vaughan, Giles N. AL 43rd Inf. Co.A
Vaughan, G.J. 8th (Wade's) Conf.Cav. Co.H Sgt.
Vaughan, G.M. AR 12th Inf. Co.G
Vaughan, G.W. GA 6th Cav. Co.G
Vaughan, G.W. GA Smith's Legion Co.G
Vaughan, G.W. MS Standefer's Co.
Vaughan, G.W. TN 20th Inf. Co.H
Vaughan, G.W. TN 22nd Inf. Co.H
Vaughan, G.W. Gen. & Staff AASurg.
Vaughan, G.Y. NC 3rd Cav. (41st St.Troops)
Vaughan, H. Gen. & Staff Surg.
Vaughan, Hartwell AL 28th Inf. Co.C
Vaughan, HayWood TN 13th Inf. Co.K
Vaughan, H.B. VA Cav. Swann's Bn. Vaughan's Co. Capt.
Vaughan, H.C. AL 7th Cav. Co.F 1st Lt.
Vaughan, H.C. 4th Conf.Inf. Co.K
Vaughan, H.E. SC 21st Inf. Co.K
Vaughan, Henry AL Cav. Callaway's Co.
Vaughan, Henry GA 62nd Cav. Co.L
Vaughan, Henry NC 1st Jr.Res. Co.K
Vaughan, Henry TN 4th (McLemore's) Cav. Co.F

Vaughan, Henry VA 24th Cav. Co.I
Vaughan, Henry VA 2nd Arty. Co.G
Vaughan, Henry VA 47th Inf. Co.E
Vaughan, Henry 8th (Dearing's) Conf.Cav. Co.D
Vaughan, Henry A. GA 66th Inf. Co.E
Vaughan, Henry A. MS Cav. 24th Bn. Co.E
Vaughan, Henry B., Jr. TN 2nd (Robison's) Inf. Co.I
Vaughan, Henry B. Gen. & Staff Asst.Surg.
Vaughan, Henry G. SC 16th Inf. Co.I 1st Sgt.
Vaughan, Henry J. NC 7th Inf. Co.D
Vaughan, Henry J. 1st Conf.Eng.Troops Co.G Artif.
Vaughan, Henry T. AR 4th Inf. Co.B Sgt.
Vaughan, Henry T. MO 1st Cav. Co.K
Vaughan, Henry W. AL 9th Cav. Co.F 1st Sgt.
Vaughan, Henry W. AL 28th Inf. Co.I
Vaughan, Henry W. AL Cp. of Instr. Talladega
Vaughan, H.H. GA Phillips' Legion Co.B,H
Vaughan, H.I. AL 23rd Inf. Co.B
Vaughan, Hicks AL 9th Inf. Co.K
Vaughan, Hilry D. NC 54th Inf. Co.D
Vaughan, H.J. 3rd Conf.Cav. Co.D
Vaughan, H.K. AL 23rd Inf. Sgt.Maj.
Vaughan, Horace D. FL Lt.Arty. Perry's Co.
Vaughan, Horace G. FL Lt.Arty. Perry's Co.
Vaughan, Howard VA 3rd Cav. Co.B
Vaughan, Howard T. VA 32nd Inf. Co.E Music.
Vaughan, H.R. AL 46th Inf. Co.F Sgt.Maj.
Vaughan, H.R. VA 3rd Inf.Loc.Def. Co.I
Vaughan, H.S. SC Lt.Arty. 3rd (Palmetto) Bn. Co.C
Vaughan, H.S. SC 21st Inf. Co.K
Vaughan, H.T. MO 1st & 3rd Cons.Cav. Co.F
Vaughan, Hugh R. MS 18th Inf. Co.B Capt.
Vaughan, H.W. AL 8th (Hatch's) Cav. Co.F Sgt.
Vaughan, H.W. SC 4th Cav. Co.G
Vaughan, H.W. SC Cav. 10th Bn. Co.C
Vaughan, I.C. AL 9th (Malone's) Cav. Co.G Sgt.
Vaughan, I.L. MO Robertson's Regt.St.Guard Co.11
Vaughan, Isaac Cole GA 38th Inf. Co.G 1st Lt.
Vaughan, J. AR Cav. McGehee's Regt. Co.G
Vaughan, J. AR Lt.Arty. Marshall's Btty.
Vaughan, J. FL 1st Inf. Co.D Sgt.
Vaughan, J. TX Cav. Border's Regt. Co.H
Vaughan, J.A. AL 8th (Hatch's) Cav. Co.C
Vaughan, J.A. AR 15th (Johnson's) Inf. Co.A
Vaughan, J.A. GA 4th Cav. (St.Guards) Cartledge's Co.
Vaughan, J.A. SC 16th Inf. Co.E
Vaughan, Jackson FL Lt.Arty. Perry's Co.
Vaughan, Jackson VA 29th Inf. Co.E
Vaughan, James AR 30th Inf. Co.F
Vaughan, James GA 18th Inf. AQM
Vaughan, James GA 61st Inf. Co.E
Vaughan, James LA Hvy.Arty. 8th Bn. Co.3
Vaughan, James LA Mil. Fire Bn. Co.G
Vaughan, James LA Inf. Jeff Davis Regt. Co.F
Vaughan, James MS 10th Cav. Co.H Sgt.
Vaughan, James MS 18th Inf. Co.B Sgt.
Vaughan, James MS 30th Inf. Co.E Cpl.
Vaughan, James NC 1st Cav. (9th St.Troops) Co.B
Vaughan, James NC 64th Inf. Co.M
Vaughan, James TN Cav. 16th Bn. (Neal's) Co.F
Vaughan, James TN Lt.Arty. Winston's Co.
Vaughan, James TX 7th Cav. Co.I
Vaughan, James TX Granbury's Cons.Brig. Co.B Cpl.
Vaughan, James VA 30th Inf. Co.H
Vaughan, James Conf.Cav. Baxter's Bn. Co.A Sgt.
Vaughan, James Conf.Cav. Wood's Regt. 2nd Co.F
Vaughan, Jas. Gen. & Staff Capt.,QM
Vaughan, James A. AL 3rd Cav. Co.C,B
Vaughan, James A. AL 6th Cav. Co.A
Vaughan, James A. AL Inf. 1st Regt. Co.D
Vaughan, James A. FL 1st Inf. New Co.K
Vaughan, James Alexander MS Arty. (Seven Stars Arty.) Roberts' Co.
Vaughan, James B. MS 15th Inf. Co.B Cpl.
Vaughan, James C. GA 23rd Inf. Co.C Jr.2nd Lt.
Vaughan, James C. MS 1st (Johnston's) Inf. Co.C
Vaughan, James C. VA Lt.Arty. 38th Bn. Co.B
Vaughan, James C. VA 34th Inf. Co.A Cpl.
Vaughan, James C. VA 59th Mil. Riddick's Co. Sgt.
Vaughan, James D. VA Cav. 1st Bn. Adj.
Vaughan, James D. VA 3rd Cav. Co.E
Vaughan, James D. VA 19th Cav. Co.I 2nd Lt.
Vaughan, James D. Gen. & Staff 1st Lt.,Adj.
Vaughan, James E. TN 13th (Gore's) Cav. Co.E
Vaughan, James E. VA 53rd Inf. Co.K
Vaughan, James F. KY 4th Cav. Co.C
Vaughan, James F. KY 9th Cav. Co.F
Vaughan, James F. KY 13th Cav. Co.B
Vaughan, James F. TN 23rd Inf. Co.E
Vaughan, James G. MD Cav.Bn. Co.D
Vaughan, James G. VA 9th Inf. 1st Co.H
Vaughan, James G. VA 28th Bn.Inf. Co.C
Vaughan, James G. VA 59th Inf. 2nd Co.H
Vaughan, James G. VA 82nd Mil. Co.C 1st Lt.
Vaughan, James H. AR 33rd Inf. Co.K
Vaughan, James H. TN 21st Inf.
Vaughan, James H. VA 1st Arty. 3rd Co.C
Vaughan, James H. VA Hvy.Arty. 18th Bn. Co.A
Vaughan, James H. VA 108th Mil. Co.B
Vaughan, James J. AL 11th Inf. Co.C Sgt.
Vaughan, James J. VA Hvy.Arty. Coleman's Co.
Vaughan, James L. KY 1st Inf. Co.H
Vaughan, James M. AR 25th Inf. Co.B
Vaughan, James M. NC 66th Inf. Co.I
Vaughan, James M. TN 23rd Inf. Co.C
Vaughan, James M. VA 3rd Cav. Co.B
Vaughan, James M. VA 56th Inf. Co.A
Vaughan, James N. AL Lt.Arty. Ward's Btty.
Vaughan, James O. MS 2nd St.Cav. Co.F
Vaughan, James P. KY 7th Mtd.Inf. Co.B Sgt.
Vaughan, James T. MS 9th Inf. Old Co.A 1st Lt.
Vaughan, James T. TN 18th Inf. Co.K
Vaughan, James T. VA 1st Inf. Co.H Lt.
Vaughan, James T. VA 14th Inf. 2nd Co.G
Vaughan, James T. VA Inf. 25th Bn. Co.A 1st Lt.
Vaughan, James T. VA 38th Inf. 1st Co.I
Vaughan, James W. GA 61st Inf. Co.E 1st Lt.
Vaughan, James W. VA 4th Cav. Co.G
Vaughan, James W. VA Horse Arty. E. Graham's Co.
Vaughan, James W. VA Inf. 5th Bn. Co.E
Vaughan, James W. VA 53rd Inf. Co.B
Vaughan, Jasper AR 1st (Colquitt's) Inf. Co.G
Vaughan, Jasper N. TN 23rd Inf. Co.E,C
Vaughan, J.B. AL 46th Inf. Co.D
Vaughan, J.B. TN 22nd Inf. Co.H
Vaughan, J.B. TN 23rd Inf. Co.E Cpl.
Vaughan, J.C. GA 4th Cav. (St.Guards) Cartledge's Co. Sgt.
Vaughan, J.C. TN Cav. 4th Bn. (Branner's) Co.D
Vaughan, J.C. TX 7th Inf. Co.I
Vaughan, J.C. Forrest's Cav. Lyon's Escort,CSA
Vaughan, J.D. VA Cav. 40th Bn. Co.B
Vaughan, J.E. AL 28th Inf. Co.K
Vaughan, J.E. TN 22nd Inf. Co.F
Vaughan, Jefferson Conf.Reg.Inf. Brooks' Bn. Co.B
Vaughan, Jerome B. MS 2nd Part.Rangers Co.D,F
Vaughan, Jerre AL 4th Inf. Co.B
Vaughan, Jesse GA 1st (Olmstead's) Inf. Co.K
Vaughan, Jesse J. NC 4th Cav. (59th St.Troops) Co.D
Vaughan, Jesse T. NC Lt.Arty. 3rd Bn. Co.B,C Cpl.
Vaughan, Jesse T. NC 17th Inf. (2nd Org.) Co.C
Vaughan, J.F. AL 12th Cav. Co.D
Vaughan, J.F. AR 21st Inf. Co.F Sgt.Maj.
Vaughan, J.F. KY 14th Cav. Co.B
Vaughan, J.G. MS 22nd Inf. Co.H
Vaughan, J.H. SC 16th & 24th (Cons.) Inf. Co.A Cpl.
Vaughan, J.H. TN 31st Inf. Co.K Sgt.
Vaughan, J.H. VA Arty. Young's Co.
Vaughan, Jim FL 2nd Cav. Co.I
Vaughan, J.J. KY 12th Cav. Co.B
Vaughan, J.J. NC 3rd Bn.Sr.Res. Williams' Co.
Vaughan, J.J. TN 31st Inf. Co.K
Vaughan, J.J. VA 1st (Farinholt's) Res. Co.B Sgt.
Vaughan, J.L. AL 7th Cav. Co.F
Vaughan, J.L. KY 9th Mtd.Inf. Co.H
Vaughan, J.L. LA 3rd Inf. Co.I
Vaughan, J. Lewis MS 12th Inf. Co.H 1st Lt.
Vaughan, J.M. MS 26th Inf. Co.D,K
Vaughan, J.M. SC 16th Inf. Co.F
Vaughan, J.M. SC 16th & 24th (Cons.) Inf. Co.A
Vaughan, J. Marshal TX 2nd Cav. 1st Co.F Sgt.
Vaughan, J. Marshall TX Cav. Morgan's Regt. Co.I Sgt.
Vaughan, J.N. MS Mtd.Inf. (St.Troops) Maxey's Co. Cpl.
Vaughan, J.N. MS Lt.Arty. 14th Bn. Co.A
Vaughan, J.O. VA 1st (Farinholt's) Res. Co.D Cpl.
Vaughan, J.O. VA 53rd Inf. Co.E
Vaughan, Joel SC Inf. 1st (Charleston) Bn. Co.B
Vaughan, Joel SC 14th Inf. Co.C
Vaughan, Joel SC 27th Inf. Co.B
Vaughan, John AL 6th Cav. Co.H
Vaughan, John AL 4th Res. Co.H

Vaughan, John AR Lt.Arty. Thrall's Btty. Bugler
Vaughan, John GA 5th Res. Co.G
Vaughan, John GA 52nd Inf. Co.K
Vaughan, John LA Home Guards
Vaughan, John NC 2nd Bn.Loc.Def.Troops Co.E
Vaughan, John NC 3rd Inf. Co.A
Vaughan, John NC 64th Inf. Co.M
Vaughan, John SC 1st St.Troops Co.K
Vaughan, John SC 3rd Res. Co.A
Vaughan, John TN Cav. 16th Bn. (Neal's) Co.F
Vaughan, John TN Lt.Arty. Burroughs' Co.
Vaughan, John TN 4th Inf. Co.C
Vaughan, John TX 13th Cav. Co.A
Vaughan, John VA 25th Cav. Co.A
Vaughan, John VA 14th Inf. Co.E
Vaughan, John VA 63rd Inf. Co.G
Vaughan, John A. AL Inf. 1st Regt. Co.A Bvt.2nd Lt.
Vaughan, John A. TN 42nd Inf. 1st Co.I
Vaughan, John A. 8th (Wade's) Conf.Cav. Co.I 1st Lt.
Vaughan, John B. VA Cav. 40th Bn. Co.C
Vaughan, John B. VA 1st Inf. Co.A Sgt.
Vaughan, John B. VA Inf. 5th Bn.Loc.Def. Co.C Maj.
Vaughan, John B. VA 12th Inf. Co.G Sgt.
Vaughan, John C. TN 2nd (Ashby's) Cav. Co.E
Vaughan, John C. TN 3rd (Lillard's) Mtd.Inf. Col.
Vaughan, John C. Conf.Hvy.Arty. Montague's Bn. Co.C
Vaughan, John D. TN 4th (McLemore's) Cav. Co.B
Vaughan, John D. TN 18th Inf. Co.K Sgt.
Vaughan, John F. MO Cav. Wood's Regt. Co.K
Vaughan, John H. SC Lt.Arty. 3rd (Palmetto) Bn. Co.G
Vaughan, John H. SC 16th Inf. Co.F Cpl.
Vaughan, John H. VA 3rd Cav. Co.E
Vaughan, John H. VA Lt.Arty. 1st Bn. Co.C
Vaughan, John J. FL 1st Inf. Old Co.H, New Co.K 2nd Lt.
Vaughan, John J. GA 61st Inf. Co.E
Vaughan, John J. VA Lt.Arty. Pegram's Co.
Vaughan, John J. VA 12th Inf. Co.D,C
Vaughan, John J. 1st Conf.Eng.Troops Co.A
Vaughan, John L. VA 56th Inf. Co.B
Vaughan, Jno. M. LA Lovell Scouts Lt.
Vaughan, John M. MS 19th Inf. Co.K
Vaughan, John M. VA 10th Cav. Co.D 2nd Lt.
Vaughan, John M. VA 1st Inf. Co.G
Vaughan, John P. TN 1st (Feild's) Inf. Co.F
Vaughan, John R. VA 24th Cav. Co.C Cpl.
Vaughan, John S. MS 1st (Patton's) Inf. Co.K
Vaughan, Johnson TN 3rd (Forrest's) Cav. 1st Lt.
Vaughan, Johnson VA 6th Cav. Co.B
Vaughan, John T. GA 7th Inf. Co.G 1st Lt.
Vaughan, John T. NC 1st Cav. (9th St.Troops) Co.B
Vaughan, John T. NC 12th Inf. Co.O
Vaughan, John T. NC 32nd Inf. Co.C,D
Vaughan, John T. VA Lt.Arty. 38th Bn. Co.C
Vaughan, John T. VA Hvy.Arty. A.J. Jones' Co.
Vaughan, John W. AL 44th Inf. Co.K
Vaughan, John W. MO Inf. 2nd Regt.St.Guard Co.C,I 1st Lt.
Vaughan, John W. TN 44th (Cons.) Inf. Co.I
Vaughan, John W. VA 3rd Cav. Co.B
Vaughan, John W. VA Hvy.Arty. Epes' Co.
Vaughan, John W. VA Inf. 5th Bn. Co.B
Vaughan, John W. VA 9th Inf. 1st Co.H
Vaughan, John W. VA Inf. 28th Bn. Co.C
Vaughan, John W. VA 59th Inf. 2nd Co.H
Vaughan, John W. VA 97th Mil. Co.G
Vaughan, John W. VA Burks' Regt.Loc.Def.
Vaughan, John W. Gen. & Staff Surg.
Vaughan, Jonathan AL 36th Inf.
Vaughan, Joseph MO 9th (Elliott's) Cav. Co.I
Vaughan, Joseph SC 3rd Inf. Co.K
Vaughan, Joseph VA 38th Inf. Co.F
Vaughan, Joseph A. MS Cav. 24th Bn. Co.E
Vaughan, Joseph E. NC 17th Inf. (1st Org.) Co.D
Vaughan, Jos. H. Gen. & Staff Surg.
Vaughan, Joseph L. NC 2nd Cav. (19th St.Troops) Co.F Music.
Vaughan, Joseph N. VA Mtd.Guard 4th Congr.Dist.
Vaughan, Joseph P. MO Inf. 3rd Bn. Co.E
Vaughan, Joseph T. VA 97th Mil. Co.L
Vaughan, Joseph W. TN Holman's Bn. Part.Rangers Co.B
Vaughan, Joseph W. VA 48th Inf. Co.B Sgt.
Vaughan, Joshua NC 66th Inf. Co.I
Vaughan, Joshua B. VA Inf. 26th Bn. Co.D
Vaughan, Josiah VA 2nd Arty. Co.E 1st Lt.
Vaughan, Josiah B. AR 2nd Mtd.Rifles Co.H Capt.
Vaughan, J.P. GA 27th Inf. Co.G
Vaughan, J.P. SC 16th Inf. Co.F
Vaughan, J.P. SC 16th & 24th (Cons.) Inf. Co.A
Vaughan, J.R. AL 5th Cav.
Vaughan, J.R. KY 12th Cav. Co.B Sgt.
Vaughan, J.R. TN 23rd Inf. Co.E
Vaughan, J.R.T. AR 24th Inf. Co.I
Vaughan, J.S. MS Lt.Arty. (Jefferson Arty.) Darden's Co. 1st Sgt.
Vaughan, J.S. VA 1st (Farinholt's) Res. Co.E Cpl.
Vaughan, J.T. NC 3rd Bn.Sr.Res. Williams' Co.
Vaughan, J.T. TN Cav. 16th Bn. (Neal's) Co.B 1st Lt.
Vaughan, J.T. VA 11th Inf. Co.A
Vaughan, J.V. AL St.Mil. Co.A
Vaughan, J.W. AR 2nd Mtd.Rifles Co.D
Vaughan, J.W. AR 13th Mil. Co.F Capt.
Vaughan, J.W. GA Cav. 22nd Bn. (St.Guards) Co.B 1st Lt.
Vaughan, J.W. GA 7th Inf. Co.G
Vaughan, J.W. TN 45th Inf. Co.F
Vaughan, J.W. Inf. Bailey's Cons.Regt. Co.A
Vaughan, J.W. TX 7th Cav. Co.I
Vaughan, J.W. TX 7th Inf. Co.I Cpl.
Vaughan, J.W. VA Lt.Arty. Thornton's Co.
Vaughan, L.A. MS 1st (Patton's) Inf. Co.H
Vaughan, L.A. MS 43rd Inf. Co.G
Vaughan, L.A. VA Res.Forces Thurston's Co. Sgt.
Vaughan, L.B. VA 4th Cav. Co.G
Vaughan, Lemuel E. NC 24th Inf. Co.D
Vaughan, Leroy SC 2nd Rifles Co.B Cpl.
Vaughan, Lewis LA Inf.Cons. 18th Regt. & Yellow Jacket Bn. Co.A
Vaughan, Lewis SC 1st (Orr's) Rifles Co.L
Vaughan, L.F. TX 19th Inf. Co.D Sgt.
Vaughan, L.M. SC 2nd Inf. Co.A
Vaughan, Lorenzo D. VA 6th Bn.Res. Co.G
Vaughan, Luther B. VA 15th Inf. Co.C
Vaughan, M. MS Inf. 2nd St.Troops Co.L Capt.
Vaughan, Madison P. VA 18th Inf. Co.C 2nd Lt.
Vaughan, Manoah V. LA 31st Inf. Co.B Sgt.
Vaughan, Marion TN 35th Inf. 2nd Co.F
Vaughan, Martin VA 56th Inf. Co.A
Vaughan, Matthew AL 45th Inf. Co.G
Vaughan, Maurice NC 17th Inf. (1st Org.) Chap.
Vaughan, Maurice H. NC 3rd Inf. Chap.
Vaughan, Maurice H. Gen. & Staff Chap.
Vaughan, M.B. GA 38th Inf. Co.H
Vaughan, McDonald GA Inf. 1st Loc.Troops (Augusta) Co.H
Vaughan, M.D. MS 1st Cav. Co.E
Vaughan, M.D. TN 22nd (Barteau's) Cav. Co.D
Vaughan, M.H. AR 10th Inf. Co.E Capt.
Vaughan, Michael GA 5th Inf. Co.C
Vaughan, Michael A. AL 6th Cav. Co.K 2nd Cpl.
Vaughan, M.M. TN 22nd (Barteau's) Cav. Co.D
Vaughan, Monroe NC 6th Inf. Co.B Cpl.
Vaughan, M.P. SC 4th Cav. Co.G
Vaughan, M.P. SC Cav. 10th Bn. Co.C
Vaughan, M.R. TN 23rd Inf. Co.E
Vaughan, Murphy TX 32nd Cav. Co.F
Vaughan, N. VA 1st Inf. Co.H
Vaughan, Napoleon W. VA Arty. Paris' Co.
Vaughan, N.B. MO 3rd Inf. Co.F
Vaughan, N.C. TN 10th & 11th (Cons.) Cav. Co.D
Vaughan, N.D. AL 20th Inf. Co.E
Vaughan, Newton AL 4th Inf. Co.H
Vaughan, N.H. VA 9th Cav. Co.G
Vaughan, N.J. AR 20th Inf. Co.K
Vaughan, N.M NC 1st Jr.Res. Co.B
Vaughan, N.M. NC 23rd Inf. Co.E
Vaughan, O. AR Cav. McGehee's Regt. Co.G
Vaughan, O. LA Inf.Crescent Regt. Co.A
Vaughan, O.F. VA 3rd (Archer's) Bn.Res. Co.A
Vaughan, Offord NC 35th Inf. Co.I
Vaughan, Oliver H. VA 2nd Inf. Co.F Sgt.
Vaughan, P. KY 7th Mtd.Inf. Co.B
Vaughan, P.A. AR 1st Cav. Co.E
Vaughan, Paschal D. SC 16th Inf. Co.I Sgt.
Vaughan, Patrick TX 19th Cav. Co.H
Vaughan, Peter TN 17th Inf. Co.F
Vaughan, Peter E. VA Hvy.Arty. Epes' Co.
Vaughan, Peter F. GA 52nd Inf. Co.K
Vaughan, Peter G. VA 14th Inf. 2nd Co.G Jr.2nd Lt.
Vaughan, Peter G. VA 38th Inf. 1st Co.I
Vaughan, Peter W. MO 9th Inf. Co.I
Vaughan, P.J. LA 2nd Inf. Co.G
Vaughan, P.J. VA 21st Cav. Co.A
Vaughan, Plutarch AL 28th Inf. Co.E
Vaughan, P. Turner AL 4th Inf. Co.C 2nd Lt.
Vaughan, Q.D. KY 7th Mtd.Inf. Co.C
Vaughan, R. AR 37th Inf. Co.C Sgt.
Vaughan, R. MS 2nd St.Cav. Co.B

Vaughan, Raleigh T. VA 53rd Inf. Co.G Sgt.
Vaughan, Randolph B. VA 3rd Inf. Co.D
Vaughan, R.B.M. SC 27th Inf. Co.B
Vaughan, R.D. MS Lt.Arty. 14th Bn. Co.B
Vaughan, Reuben T. AR 25th Inf. Co.B
Vaughan, R.F. TN 45th Inf. Co.D
Vaughan, R.F. VA 4th Cav. Co.F
Vaughan, R.F. VA Lt.Arty. Grandy's Co. 1st Sgt.
Vaughan, R.F. Conf.Lt.Arty. Richardson's Bn. Co.C
Vaughan, R.H. SC Lt.Arty. 3rd (Palmetto) Bn. Co.E,G,K Cpl.
Vaughan, R.H. TN 23rd Inf. Co.E Cpl.
Vaughan, Richard SC 6th Cav. Co.F
Vaughan, Richard VA Lt.Arty. Thornton's Co.
Vaughan, Richard VA 3rd Inf. 2nd Co.K, Co.G
Vaughan, Richard B. TN 11th Cav.
Vaughan, Richard J. MS 31st Inf. Co.K Sgt.
Vaughan, Richard M. NC 1st Cav. (9th St.Troops) Co.B
Vaughan, Richard N.C. SC 5th Inf. 1st Co.A
Vaughan, Richard S. 8th (Dearing's) Conf.Cav. Co.E
Vaughan, Richard W. VA Courtney Arty. 3rd Lt.
Vaughan, R.L. GA 62nd Cav. Co.L
Vaughan, R.L. VA 22nd Inf. Co.D
Vaughan, R.M. GA 7th Inf. Co.G
Vaughan, R.N.C. SC Palmetto S.S. Co.A
Vaughan, Robert SC Inf. 1st (Charleston) Bn. Co.B
Vaughan, Robert VA 24th Cav. Co.B Sgt.
Vaughan, Robert VA Cav. 40th Bn. Co.B Cpl.
Vaughan, Robt. Gen. & Staff Capt.,Comsy.
Vaughan, Robert B.M. SC 7th Res. Co.E
Vaughan, Robert C. VA 4th Inf. Co.D 1st Lt.
Vaughan, Robert F. VA 6th Inf. Vickery's Co. Cpl.
Vaughan, Robert F. VA 16th Inf. 1st Co.H Sgt.
Vaughan, Robert H. VA 3rd Cav. Co.B
Vaughan, Robert H. VA Courtney Arty. 1st Lt.
Vaughan, Robert H. Gen. & Staff Capt.,ACS
Vaughan, Robert J. MO 4th Inf. Co.F Cpl.
Vaughan, Robert L. GA 38th Inf. Co.K
Vaughan, Robert O. VA Arty. Kevill's Co.
Vaughan, Robert O. VA 12th Inf. Co.D Cpl.
Vaughan, Robert P. VA 1st Inf. Co.G
Vaughan, Robert S. MS Cav. 24th Bn. Co.E
Vaughan, Robert S. VA 20th Inf. Co.K Sgt.
Vaughan, Robert S. VA 55th Inf. Co.A
Vaughan, Robert S. VA 59th Inf. 3rd Co.C 1st Sgt.
Vaughan, Robert Singleton MS Arty. (Seven Stars Arty.) Roberts' Co. Cpl.
Vaughan, Robert W. VA 14th Inf. 2nd Co.G
Vaughan, Roger C. TN 18th Inf. Co.C
Vaughan, Rolin 8th (Wade's) Conf.Cav. Co.I
Vaughan, Roscoe T. VA 53rd Inf. Co.E
Vaughan, R.P. AR 17th (Lemoyne's) Inf. Co.E
Vaughan, R.S. VA 46th Inf. Co.F
Vaughan, R.T. GA Tiller's Co. (Echols Lt.Arty.)
Vaughan, R.T. KY 7th Mtd.Inf. Co.B
Vaughan, R.T. SC 16th Inf. Co.F
Vaughan, Rufus A. TN 60th Mtd.Inf. Co.D Sgt.
Vaughan, Rufus Y. NC 6th Inf. Co.H
Vaughan, Russel T. GA 61st Inf. Co.E
Vaughan, R.W. VA 38th Inf. 1st Co.I
Vaughan, Samuel NC 3rd Arty. (40th St.Troops) Co.G
Vaughan, Samuel NC 64th Inf. Co.M
Vaughan, Samuel TN Cav. 16th Bn. (Neal's) Co.F
Vaughan, Samuel C. AL 6th Cav. Co.E,C Capt.
Vaughan, Samuel E. AL 44th Inf. Co.K Cpl.
Vaughan, Samuel F. MO Inf. 8th Bn. Co.E Sgt.
Vaughan, Samuel F. MO 9th Inf. Co.I Sgt.
Vaughan, Samuel L. SC 13th Inf. Co.B
Vaughan, Samuel O. MO Inf. 8th Bn. Co.A
Vaughan, Samuel O. MO 9th Inf. Co.A
Vaughan, Samuel W. VA 2nd Arty. Co.E
Vaughan, Sanford 15th Conf.Cav. Co.G
Vaughan, S.C. AR 15th Mil. Co.H
Vaughan, S.C. MS 43rd Inf. Co.B Cpl.
Vaughan, S.C. MS 44th Inf. Co.A
Vaughan, S.C. 8th (Wade's) Conf.Cav. Co.I 2nd Lt.
Vaughan, S.D. SC 24th Inf. Co.E
Vaughan, Seamore VA 5th Cav. (12 mo. '61-2) Co.H
Vaughan, Seymore VA 13th Cav. Co.A
Vaughan, Sidney AR 7th Inf. Co.G
Vaughan, Silas AR 14th (McCarver's) Inf. Co.I
Vaughan, Silas MO 12th Cav. Co.D
Vaughan, Silas VA 49th Inf. 3rd Co.G
Vaughan, Sim E. VA 22nd Cav. Co.G
Vaughan, Simpson NC 1st Inf. Co.D
Vaughan, S.L. SC 16th Inf. Co.F
Vaughan, S.L. VA 14th Inf. Co.F
Vaughan, S.M. VA Mil. Wythe Cty.
Vaughan, S. Marshall VA 4th Inf. Co.A
Vaughan, Spencer VA 9th Inf. 2nd Co.A
Vaughan, Spencer C. VA 18th Inf. Co.D
Vaughan, S.R. VA 1st (Farinholt's) Res. Co.E,A
Vaughan, S.S. TN 1st (Feild's) Inf. Co.F
Vaughan, Stephen MS 20th Inf. Co.I
Vaughan, Stephen SC 24th Inf. Co.E
Vaughan, Stephen B. VA 4th Inf. Co.F
Vaughan, Stephen E.H. VA Lt.Arty. Jeffress' Co.
Vaughan, S.W. AR 37th Inf. Co.A Maj.,Surg.
Vaughan, S.W. VA Inf. 25th Bn. Co.D
Vaughan, S.W. Gen. & Staff Surg.
Vaughan, T. TN Inf. 4th Cons.Regt. Co.F
Vaughan, T.A. TN 45th Inf. Co.D
Vaughan, T.A. VA Inf. 1st Bn. Co.D
Vaughan, T.A. VA 57th Inf. Co.H
Vaughan, Tac TX 4th Inf. Co.C
Vaughan, T.B. MS 33rd Inf. Co.F
Vaughan, T.D. MS Lt.Arty. 14th Bn. Co.A
Vaughan, Thomas KY 2nd (Duke's) Cav. Co.I
Vaughan, Thomas NC 31st Inf. Co.G
Vaughan, Thomas SC 2nd St.Troops Co.H
Vaughan, Thomas SC 16th Inf. Co.F
Vaughan, Thomas TN 4th (McLemore's) Cav. Co.F
Vaughan, Thomas TN 18th Inf. Co.K
Vaughan, Thomas TX 6th Field Btty.
Vaughan, Thomas VA 5th Cav. (12 mo. '61-2) Co.H
Vaughan, Thomas VA 46th Inf. Co.F
Vaughan, Thomas A. VA 9th Inf. 1st Co.H
Vaughan, Thomas A. VA Inf. 28th Bn. Co.C
Vaughan, Thomas A. VA 59th Inf. 2nd Co.H
Vaughan, Thomas C. GA 62nd Cav. Co.L
Vaughan, Thomas H. VA 3rd Cav. Co.E 1st Sgt.
Vaughan, Thomas J. MS 34th Inf. Co.F
Vaughan, Thomas J. TN 53rd Inf. Co.E
Vaughan, Thomas J. VA 16th Cav. Co.A
Vaughan, Thomas J. VA Cav. Ferguson's Bn. Stevenson's Co.
Vaughan, Thomas J. VA 1st Arty. Co.E
Vaughan, Thomas J. VA 59th Inf. 3rd Co.E
Vaughan, Thomas J. VA 59th Mil. Hunter's Co.
Vaughan, Thomas J. VA 63rd Inf. Co.D
Vaughan, Thomas P. MS 2nd Cav. Co.F
Vaughan, Thomas P. VA 20th Inf. Co.K
Vaughan, Thomas P. VA 59th Inf. 3rd Co.C
Vaughan, Thompson MS 34th Inf. Co.C
Vaughan, Tilman W. VA 23rd Inf. Co.E
Vaughan, Timothy NC 15th Inf. Co.A
Vaughan, Tolaver R. SC 16th Inf. Co.I
Vaughan, T.R. TN 15th (Cons.) Cav. Co.I Cpl.
Vaughan, Travis VA 3rd Cav. Co.E 1st Lt.
Vaughan, T.S. AR 1st (Monroe's) Cav. Co.D Cpl.
Vaughan, Turner NC Cav. 12th Bn. Co.A
Vaughan, Turner 8th (Dearing's) Conf.Cav. Co.A
Vaughan, T.Y. NC 23rd Inf. Co.E
Vaughan, Vespasian VA 1st Regt.Mtd.Guards Co.F
Vaughan, Vespasian VA 55th Inf. Co.H Sgt.
Vaughan, V.H. AL 1st Cav. 1st Co.K
Vaughan, Victor V. VA 14th Inf. Co.E Cpl.
Vaughan, Vincent MS Gordon's Co. (Loc.Guard Wilkinson Cty.)
Vaughan, V.V. VA 2nd Inf.Loc.Def. Co.B Capt.
Vaughan, V.V. VA Inf. 2nd Bn.Loc.Def. Co.D Capt.
Vaughan, W. AR 12th Inf. Co.I
Vaughan, W. MS 5th Inf. (St.Troops) Co.A
Vaughan, W. MS 6th Inf. Co.K
Vaughan, W.A. GA 9th Inf. Co.C
Vaughan, W.A. MO Cav. Ford's Bn. Co.B
Vaughan, W.A. TN 47th Inf. Co.B
Vaughan, Warren T. NC 4th Cav. (59th St.Troops) Co.B
Vaughan, Washington VA 29th Inf. Co.E
Vaughan, W.B. AL 9th Inf. Co.F Cpl.
Vaughan, W.B. AL 45th Inf. Co.C
Vaughan, W.B. VA Conscr. Cp.Lee Co.A
Vaughan, W.B. Gen. & Staff 1st Lt.,Adj.
Vaughan, W.C. SC 18th Inf. Co.F
Vaughan, W.D. AL 5th Cav. Co.E
Vaughan, W.D. GA 44th Inf. Co.G
Vaughan, W.E. AR 7th Mil. Co.C
Vaughan, W.E. MS 44th Inf. Co.A
Vaughan, W.E. MO 3rd & 5th Cons.Inf.
Vaughan, W.H. GA 38th Inf. Co.H
Vaughan, W.H. KY Jessee's Bn.Mtd.Riflemen Co.B Capt.
Vaughan, W.H. MS 29th Inf. Co.F
Vaughan, W.H. MO 12th Cav. Co.E
Vaughan, W.H. TX Cav. Madison's Regt. Co.C
Vaughan, W.H. VA 24th Cav. Co.B
Vaughan, W.H. VA 1st (Farinholt's) Res. Co.A
Vaughan, Wilborn GA 52nd Inf. Co.K
Vaughan, Wiley C. AL 41st Inf. Co.H
Vaughan, William AL 63rd Inf. Co.K

Vaughan, William AL Rives' Supp.Force 9th Congr.Dist.
Vaughan, William GA 61st Inf. Co.E
Vaughan, William MS 46th Inf. Co.K
Vaughan, William NC 4th Cav. (59th St.Troops) Co.B
Vaughan, William NC 1st Jr.Res. Co.A
Vaughan, William NC 1st Jr.Res. Co.B
Vaughan, William NC 6th Inf. Co.B
Vaughan, William NC 8th Inf. Co.F
Vaughan, William SC Lt.Arty. 3rd (Palmetto) Bn. Co.B
Vaughan, William SC 1st (Butler's) Inf. Co.F
Vaughan, William SC 7th Res. Co.E Cpl.
Vaughan, William SC 13th Inf. Co.H,B
Vaughan, William TN Cav. 5th Bn. (McClellan's) Co.D
Vaughan, William VA 4th Inf. Co.A
Vaughan, William VA 12th Inf. 1st Co.I
Vaughan, William VA Inf. 44th Bn. Co.E
Vaughan, William VA 72nd Mil.
Vaughan, William VA Hood's Bn.Res.
Vaughan, William Conf.Cav. 6th Bn. Co.B Capt.
Vaughan, William A. VA Cav. Ferguson's Bn. Stevenson's Co.
Vaughan, William A. VA 53rd Inf. Co.H
Vaughan, William A. VA 56th Inf. Co.E
Vaughan, Wm. A. Gen. & Staff AAAG
Vaughan, William B. MS Inf. 3rd Bn. (St.Troops) Co.B Cpl.
Vaughan, William B. VA 3rd Cav. Co.E
Vaughan, William C. AL Rives' Supp.Force 9th Congr.Dist.
Vaughan, William C. MS 43rd Inf. Co.E
Vaughan, William C. TN 59th Mtd.Inf. Co.A 1st Lt.
Vaughan, William E. MO 1st & 4th Cons.Inf. Co.B,C
Vaughan, William E. MO 4th Inf. Co.F Sgt.
Vaughan, William E. NC 17th Inf. (1st Org.) Co.L Sgt.
Vaughan, William F. VA Cav. 37th Bn. Co.H
Vaughan, William G. GA 1st (Olmstead's) Inf. Co.C
Vaughan, William H. AL 50th Inf. Co.A
Vaughan, William H. NC 14th Inf. Co.E Music.
Vaughan, William H. VA 3rd Cav. Co.F
Vaughan, William H. VA 5th Cav. (12 mo. '61-2) Co.H
Vaughan, Wm. H. VA Lt.Arty. Jeffress' Co.
Vaughan, William H. VA 3rd Inf. 2nd Co.K
Vaughan, William H. VA 9th Inf. 1st Co.H, 2nd Co.H
Vaughan, William H. VA 19th Inf. Co.A
Vaughan, William H. VA Inf. 28th Bn. Co.C
Vaughan, William H. VA 30th Inf. Co.H
Vaughan, William H. VA 34th Inf. Co.K
Vaughan, William H. VA 55th Inf. Co.C
Vaughan, William H. VA 59th Inf. 2nd Co.H
Vaughan, William H. 1st Conf.Eng.Troops Co.I
Vaughan, William J. NC 12th Inf. Co.O
Vaughan, William J. NC 32nd Inf. Co.C,D
Vaughan, William J. VA 19th Inf. Co.E
Vaughan, William J. VA 56th Inf. Co.B
Vaughan, William J.D. SC 5th Inf. 1st Co.A
Vaughan, William K. VA 24th Inf. Co.C
Vaughan, William L. GA 13th Cav. Co.E
Vaughan, William L. VA 19th Inf. Co.G
Vaughan, William L. VA 32nd Inf. Co.C
Vaughan, William M. MO 3rd Inf. Co.F Cpl.
Vaughan, William M. TX 7th Cav. Co.I
Vaughan, William P. AL 6th Cav. Co.K 2nd Sgt.
Vaughan, William P. AL 32nd Inf. Co.A
Vaughan, William P. SC 1st (Orr's) Rifles Co.A
Vaughan, William P. TN 54th Inf. Co.G
Vaughan, William R. AL 10th Inf. Co.I
Vaughan, William R. GA 61st Inf. Co.E Cpl.
Vaughan, William R. SC 13th Inf. Co.H,B Cpl.
Vaughan, William R. VA 3rd Cav. Co.B Capt.
Vaughan, Wm. R. Gen. & Staff Surg.
Vaughan, William S. GA 1st (Fannin's) Res. Co.G
Vaughan, William S. VA 3rd Inf. Co.D
Vaughan, William S. VA 59th Inf. 3rd Co.B
Vaughan, William T. NC 43rd Inf. Co.D Cpl.
Vaughan, William T. TN 1st (Turney's) Inf. Co.B
Vaughan, William T. VA 3rd Cav. Co.E
Vaughan, William T. VA Hvy.Arty. 18th Bn. Co.C 1st Sgt.
Vaughan, William T. VA 53rd Inf. Co.C
Vaughan, William T. VA Inf. Montague's Bn. Co.D
Vaughan, William W. GA 38th Inf. Co.H
Vaughan, William W. VA 1st Cav. 2nd Co.D
Vaughan, Wilton VA 30th Inf. Co.H
Vaughan, W.J. SC 7th Cav. Co.C
Vaughan, W.L. GA 48th Inf. Co.G
Vaughan, W.L. VA 3rd Res. Co.D
Vaughan, W.M. SC 5th St.Troops Co.M
Vaughan, Wood G. MS 19th Inf. Co.F Capt.
Vaughan, W.P. SC 3rd Res. Co.B
Vaughan, W.P. TN 48th (Nixon's) Inf. Co.K
Vaughan, W.R. AR 15th Mil. Co.H
Vaughan, W.R. GA 10th Inf. Co.I
Vaughan, W.R. TN 4th Inf. Co.K
Vaughan, W.R. TN 22nd Inf. Co.F
Vaughan, W.R. VA 16th Inf. Surg.
Vaughan, W.S. LA 27th Inf. Co.A
Vaughan, W.S. SC Inf. 1st (Charleston) Bn. Co.B,G
Vaughan, W.S. SC 27th Inf. Co.K
Vaughan, W.T. KY 12th Cav. Co.B Cpl.
Vaughan, W.T. NC 12th Inf. Co.F
Vaughan, W.W. AL 44th Inf.
Vaughan, Zephaniah D. VA 61st Inf. Co.F
Vaughen, J.C. TN 22nd Inf. Co.E
Vaughen, R.W. TX Cav. McCord's Frontier Regt. Co.I
Vaughen, W.R. TN 22nd Inf. Co.E Cpl.
Vaughn, --- AL 25th Inf. Co.I
Vaughn, --- AL 62nd Inf. Co.H
Vaughn, --- AR 3rd Inf. (St.Troops) Stuart's Co.
Vaughn, --- MO Quantrill's Co.
Vaughn, A. AL Cav. Barbiere's Bn. Co.G
Vaughn, A. MS 36th Inf. Co.C
Vaughn, A. MO Cav. Snider's Bn. Co.A
Vaughn, A. NC 4th Sr.Res. Co.D
Vaughn, A. SC 16th & 24th (Cons.) Inf. Co.B
Vaughn, A.A. GA Cobb's Legion Co.G,K
Vaughn, Aaron TN 26th Inf. Co.A
Vaughn, Aaron TN Conscr. (Cp. of Instr.)
Vaughn, A.B. MO Cav. Wood's Regt. Co.H
Vaughn, A.B. NC 60th Inf. Co.I
Vaughn, Abner MS Cav. 4th Bn. Sykes' Co.
Vaughn, Abraham VA Cav. Ferguson's Bn. Spurlock's Co.
Vaughn, Abraham S. VA 4th Inf. Co.F
Vaughn, A.C. TN 11th (Holman's) Cav. Co.G
Vaughn, A.E. MS 8th Inf. Co.H
Vaughn, A.G. MS 3rd Cav. Co.D
Vaughn, A.H. TN 40th Inf. Co.G
Vaughn, A.I. Bradford's Corps Scouts & Guards Co.A
Vaughn, A.J. AL 3rd Inf. Co.K
Vaughn, A.J. GA Cav. 8th Bn. (St.Guards) Co.C
Vaughn, A.J. GA Inf. 25th Bn. (Prov.Guard) Co.B
Vaughn, A.J. GA 34th Inf. Co.K
Vaughn, A.J. KY 8th Mtd.Inf. Co.E
Vaughn, A.J. TN 3rd (Lillard's) Mtd.Inf. AQM
Vaughn, A.J. TX Inf. 1st Bn. Co.F
Vaughn, Albert B. GA 34th Inf. Co.B
Vaughn, Albert W. MS 2nd Inf. Co.D
Vaughn, Alex. VA Hvy.Arty. Allen's Co.
Vaughn, Alexander AL 46th Inf. Co.F
Vaughn, Alexander NC 12th Inf. Co.B,D
Vaughn, Alexander S. NC 52nd Inf. Co.D
Vaughn, Alfred TN 19th Inf. Co.D
Vaughn, Aljowina S. TN 55th (McKoin's) Inf. Co.I
Vaughn, Allen MO Inf. 5th Regt.St.Guard Co.A
Vaughn, Allen MO 10th Inf. Co.E
Vaughn, Allen TN Cav. 12th Bn. (Day's) Co.A Sgt.
Vaughn, Alonzo AL 51st (Part.Rangers) Co.F
Vaughn, A.M. MS 23rd Inf. Co.L
Vaughn, A.M. TN 2nd (Ashby's) Cav. Co.I
Vaughn, A.M. TN Cav. 4th Bn. (Branner's) Co.E Sgt.
Vaughn, A.M. VA 54th Mil. Co.C,D
Vaughn, Amas TN 23rd Inf. Co.C
Vaughn, Ambrose AL 10th Cav. Co.E
Vaughn, A.N. TN 11th (Holman's) Cav. Co.B
Vaughn, Andrew MO Cav. 1st Regt.St.Guard Co.E
Vaughn, Andrew NC 12th Inf. Co.B,D
Vaughn, Andrew VA 4th Res. Co.K
Vaughn, Andrew Conf.Cav. Clarkson's Bn. Ind.Rangers Co.A
Vaughn, Andrew A. MS 27th Inf. Co.L Cpl.
Vaughn, Andrew G. GA 36th (Broyles') Inf. Co.C
Vaughn, Andrew J. MS Inf. 3rd Bn. Co.K 1st Sgt.
Vaughn, Andrew J. VA 36th Inf. Co.F
Vaughn, Anthony VA 7th Cav. Co.E
Vaughn, A.P. TN Cav. Shaw's Bn.
Vaughn, A.R. SC 20th Inf. Co.F
Vaughn, Archibald SC 2nd Cav. Co.F
Vaughn, Archibald SC Inf. Hampton Legion Co.F
Vaughn, Archibald F. MO 1st N.E. Cav.
Vaughn, Archibald M. MS Arty. (Seven Stars Arty.) Roberts' Co.
Vaughn, Arris NC 24th Inf. Co.H
Vaughn, Arthur TN 25th Inf. Co.H Sgt.
Vaughn, Asa GA 52nd Inf. Co.K
Vaughn, Asbury GA 52nd Inf. Co.K
Vaughn, A.T. MS 9th Inf. New Co.A

Vaughn, Augustus J. GA 31st Inf. Co.D Sgt.
Vaughn, Austin VA 47th Inf. Co.G
Vaughn, Avery SC 1st (Orr's) Rifles Co.A
Vaughn, A.W. GA 15th Inf. Co.C
Vaughn, Azariah A. NC 45th Inf. Co.D Sgt.
Vaughn, B. SC 2nd Inf. Co.A
Vaughn, Battle VA Lt.Arty. Thornton's Co.
Vaughn, B.D. KY Morgan's Men Co.G
Vaughn, B.D. KY 8th Mtd.Inf. Co.E Sgt.
Vaughn, Benjamin AL 51st (Part.Rangers) Co.F
Vaughn, Benjamin GA 1st Inf. Co.B
Vaughn, Benjamin D. KY 10th (Johnson's) Cav. Co.C
Vaughn, Benjamin F. GA 5th Inf. Co.G Cpl.
Vaughn, Benjamin F. TN 55th (McKoin's) Inf. McEwen, Jr.'s Co.
Vaughn, Benjamin T. NC 39th Inf.
Vaughn, Berry TN 61st Mtd.Inf. Co.D
Vaughn, Beverly J. NC 21st Inf. Co.G
Vaughn, B.F. AL Cav. Barlow's Co.
Vaughn, B.F. AL Cav. Stuart's Bn. Co.G
Vaughn, B.F. FL Cav. 3rd Bn. Co.B
Vaughn, B.F. KY 10th (Johnson's) Cav. Co.C
Vaughn, B.F. TN Cav. 16th Bn. (Neal's) Co.C
Vaughn, B.F. TN 44th (Cons.) Inf. Co.I Cpl.
Vaughn, B.F. 1st Conf.Cav. 2nd Co.A
Vaughn, B.F. 15th Conf.Cav. Co.D
Vaughn, B.F. Horse Arty. White's Btty.
Vaughn, B.H. LA 25th Inf. Co.F
Vaughn, B.H. LA Inf. Pelican Regt. Co.C
Vaughn, B.L. MO Inf. 5th Regt.St.Guard Co.B
Vaughn, B.O. TN 51st (Cons.) Inf. Co.A
Vaughn, B.R. GA 5th Res. Co.D
Vaughn, B.R. GA Inf. (Baldwin Inf.) Moore's Co.
Vaughn, Burwell VA 135th Mil. Co.I
Vaughn, B.W. NC 1st Arty. (10th St.Troops) Co.E
Vaughn, Byron VA 4th Inf. Co.F
Vaughn, C. AL 50th Inf. Co.A
Vaughn, C. GA Inf. (Baldwin Inf.) Moore's Co.
Vaughn, Calvin AL 9th (Malone's) Cav. Co.K
Vaughn, Calvin TN 9th Inf. Co.B
Vaughn, C.B. GA 38th Inf. Co.F
Vaughn, C.C. TN 6th (Wheeler's) Cav. Co.E Ord.Sgt.
Vaughn, C.F. MO Cav. Pinelly Bn. Co.E
Vaughn, C.F. VA 34th Inf. Co.E
Vaughn, C.H. LA 6th Cav. Co.A Sgt.
Vaughn, C.H. VA 3rd Lt.Arty. Co.G 2nd Lt.
Vaughn, Charles AL Cav. Barbiere's Bn. Goldsby's Co.
Vaughn, Charles GA 8th Inf. Co.G
Vaughn, Charles MO Cav. Clardy's Bn. Co.C
Vaughn, Charles NC 66th Inf. Co.I
Vaughn, Charles TN 6th (Wheeler's) Cav. Co.K
Vaughn, Charles TN Cav. 11th Bn. (Gordon's) Co.A
Vaughn, Charles TX Cav. 6th Bn. Co.B
Vaughn, Charles C. GA 38th Inf. Co.E
Vaughn, Charles E. AR Cav. Wright's Regt. Co.B
Vaughn, Charles E. LA 5th Cav. Co.C
Vaughn, Charles H. AL Cav. Lewis' Bn. Co.D
Vaughn, Charles R. VA 34th Inf. Co.K
Vaughn, Charles S. AL Cav. Lewis' Bn. Co.D
Vaughn, C.J. VA 59th Inf. 3rd Co.E
Vaughn, Claborn GA Cav. 6th Bn. (St.Guards) Co.B
Vaughn, Claborn GA Cobb's Legion Co.E Cpl.
Vaughn, C.M. AR 24th Inf. Co.A
Vaughn, Colvin Mead's Conf.Cav. Co.A
Vaughn, C.P. GA Hvy.Arty. 22nd Bn. Co.A
Vaughn, C.P. GA 60th Inf. 1st Co.A
Vaughn, C.P. NC 31st Inf.
Vaughn, C.P. VA 51st Inf. Co.D
Vaughn, C.P. Conf.Cav. Wood's Regt. Co.L
Vaughn, C.R. AR Inf. 2nd Bn. Co.A 1st Lt.
Vaughn, C.W. AR Inf. Hardy's Regt. Co.G
Vaughn, D. SC Inf. Hampton Legion Co.F
Vaughn, Daniel AL 53rd (Part.Rangers) Co.B
Vaughn, Daniel AR 17th (Griffith's) Inf. Co.G
Vaughn, Daniel VA 45th Inf. Co.D
Vaughn, Daniel M. NC 56th Inf. Co.E
Vaughn, Daniel M. TN 3rd (Lillard's) Mtd.Inf. Co.F
Vaughn, David NC 8th Bn.Part.Rangers Co.B
Vaughn, David NC 39th Inf. Co.H
Vaughn, David NC 66th Inf. Co.C
Vaughn, David SC 1st Cav. Co.G
Vaughn, David SC 1st (Butler's) Inf. Co.I
Vaughn, David SC 19th Inf. Co.H
Vaughn, David TN Cav. 16th Bn. (Neal's) Co.C
Vaughn, David TN 3rd (Clack's) Inf. Co.I
Vaughn, David TX 23rd Cav. Co.B
Vaughn, David L. TN 3rd (Lillard's) Mtd.Inf. Co.B,E
Vaughn, David R. TN 3rd (Lillard's) Mtd.Inf. Co.F,H
Vaughn, David Thomas AL 5th Inf. New Co.B
Vaughn, D.C. MS Scouts Montgomery's Co.
Vaughn, D.C. MS 36th Inf. Co.K
Vaughn, D.C. Bradford's Corps Scouts & Guards Co.A
Vaughn, D.H. LA 13th Bn. (Part.Rangers) Co.D Cpl.
Vaughn, D.H. SC 15th Inf. Co.K
Vaughn, D.M. SC 15th Inf. Co.K
Vaughn, D.N. LA Conscr.
Vaughn, Drewry MS Cav. Russell's Co.
Vaughn, Drury MS 11th (Perrin's) Cav. Co.E
Vaughn, Drury MS 3rd Inf. (St.Troops) Co.I
Vaughn, D.T. SC 22nd Inf. Lt.
Vaughn, E. GA 27th Cav. Co.I
Vaughn, E. KY 8th Mtd.Inf. Co.E
Vaughn, E.C. SC 5th Inf. 1st Co.E, 2nd Co.H
Vaughn, E.C. SC 15th Inf. Co.H
Vaughn, E.D. VA 51st Inf. Co.D Sgt.
Vaughn, Edgar G.W. GA 1st Reg. Co.B
Vaughn, Edward TN 9th (Ward's) Cav. Co.C
Vaughn, Edward B. VA Cav. 40th Bn. Co.B
Vaughn, Edwin C. AL 44th Inf. Co.A
Vaughn, Elias MO Cav. Hunter's Regt.
Vaughn, Elias VA 50th Inf. 1st Co.G
Vaughn, Elijah AR 34th Inf. Co.D
Vaughn, Elijah KY 4th Mtd.Inf. Co.H
Vaughn, Elijah LA 1st Cav. Scott's Co.
Vaughn, Elisha NC 33rd Inf. Co.K
Vaughn, E.M. MS 1st Cav.Res. Co.D
Vaughn, E.M. MS St.Cav. Perrin's Bn. Co.E
Vaughn, E. Millage MS 11th (Perrin's) Cav. Co.K
Vaughn, Enoch TX Cav. 2nd Regt.St.Troops Co.C
Vaughn, Enos MO 3rd Inf. Co.E
Vaughn, E.P. MS 26th Inf. Co.A
Vaughn, E.P. TN Cav. Napier's Bn. Co.A
Vaughn, E.P. TN 46th Inf. Co.K
Vaughn, Ephraim TN 25th Inf. Co.H
Vaughn, E.R. TN Cav. Nixon's Regt. Co.A
Vaughn, E.R. TN 1st (Feild's) Inf. Co.I
Vaughn, Erastus R. VA 36th Inf. 1st Co.C, 2nd Co.D
Vaughn, Evan E. VA 24th Inf. Co.C
Vaughn, E.W. AR 11th Inf. Co.H
Vaughn, F. LA 12th Inf. Co.E
Vaughn, F. VA Cav. Mosby's Regt. (Part. Rangers) Co.E
Vaughn, F.C. SC 6th Inf. 1st Co.E, 2nd Co.I
Vaughn, Felix TX 8th Cav. Co.D
Vaughn, Felix A. GA Arty. 9th Bn. Co.B
Vaughn, F.H. LA 25th Inf. Co.F
Vaughn, F.H. SC Inf. Hampton Legion Co.E
Vaughn, Fielden VA Mil. Grayson Cty.
Vaughn, Fielden C. VA 48th Inf. Co.H
Vaughn, Fielden J. VA 63rd Inf. Co.G
Vaughn, Fielding AL Cav. Barbiere's Bn. Goldsby's Co.
Vaughn, F.J. TX Cav. Good's Bn. Co.A
Vaughn, F.M. GA 2nd Bn. Troops & Defences (Macon) Co.B
Vaughn, F.M. TN 19th (Biffle's) Cav. Co.D
Vaughn, F.M. Conf.Cav. Clarkson's Bn. Ind.Rangers Co.A
Vaughn, F.R. KY 14th Cav. Co.C
Vaughn, Francis M. GA 31st Inf. Co.C
Vaughn, Francis M. NC 21st Inf. Co.G
Vaughn, Francis M. TX 29th Cav. Co.K
Vaughn, Frank TN 8th (Smith's) Cav. Co.A
Vaughn, Frank TN Cav. Nixon's Regt. Co.I
Vaughn, Frank R. LA 7th Inf. Co.I
Vaughn, Fred AL 8th (Hatch's) Cav. Co.F 2nd Lt.
Vaughn, Freling VA Mil. Grayson Cty.
Vaughn, G. MS Inf. 2nd Bn. Co.L
Vaughn, G.A. GA 10th Cav. Co.B
Vaughn, Gabriel MS Inf. 1st St.Troops Co.D
Vaughn, Garrett Conf.Inf. 1st Bn. 2nd Co.A
Vaughn, G.B. KY 3rd Cav. Co.B Sgt.
Vaughn, G.B.W. TX 8th Cav. Co.A
Vaughn, George GA Phillips' Legion Co.C
Vaughn, George MS 48th Inf. Co.L
Vaughn, George TN Cav. 16th Bn. (Neal's) Co.F
Vaughn, George TN 44th (Cons.) Inf. Co.I
Vaughn, George TX 2nd Cav. Co.I
Vaughn, George VA 7th Cav. Co.E Black.
Vaughn, George A. GA 7th Inf. Co.F
Vaughn, George A. MO Mtd.Inf. Boone's Regt. Co.A
Vaughn, George A. TN 2nd (Ashby's) Cav. Co.C Black.
Vaughn, George B. KY 7th Cav. Co.E
Vaughn, George B. KY 3rd Bn.Mtd.Rifles Co.B Sgt.
Vaughn, George D. VA Lt.Arty. Woolfolk's Co. Jr.1st Lt.
Vaughn, George G. TX 12th Inf. Co.H Sgt.
Vaughn, George L. GA 48th Inf. Co.G 1st Lt.
Vaughn, George P. TN 55th (McKoin's) Inf. Co.I
Vaughn, George W. LA 16th Inf. Co.H

Vaughn, George W. MS 10th Inf. Old Co.E Bvt.2nd Lt.
Vaughn, George W. MS 14th Inf. Co.K
Vaughn, George W. MO 4th Cav. Co.I
Vaughn, George W. TN 32nd Inf. Co.H
Vaughn, G.G. TN 5th (McKenzie's) Cav. Co.B
Vaughn, G.M. MS Inf. 1st Bn. Co.C
Vaughn, G.N. AL 3rd Inf. Co.D
Vaughn, G.P. TN 22nd Inf. Co.B
Vaughn, G.R. MS 2nd St.Cav. Co.D
Vaughn, G.W. GA 31st Inf. Co.H
Vaughn, G.W. GA Phillips' Legion Co.E
Vaughn, G.W. TN 8th (Smith's) Cav. Co.D Ord.Sgt.
Vaughn, G.W. TN 12th (Cons.) Inf. Co.D
Vaughn, G.Y. NC 21st Inf. Co.I
Vaughn, H. AL 29th Inf. Co.D
Vaughn, H. GA 38th Inf. Co.H
Vaughn, H.A. AL 3rd Res. Co.G
Vaughn, H.A. TN 31st Inf. Co.I
Vaughn, H.A. VA Inf. 44th Bn. Co.E
Vaughn, Hannibal T. VA 24th Inf. Co.C
Vaughn, Harmin MO 9th Bn.S.S. Co.E Cpl.
Vaughn, Hartwell GA 6th Cav. Co.C
Vaughn, Harvey B. VA 4th Inf. Co.F Sgt.
Vaughn, Harvey S. AL 6th Inf. Co.I
Vaughn, H.B. MS 4th Cav. Co.C
Vaughn, H.B. MS 12th Cav. Co.G
Vaughn, H.B. MS 41st Inf. Co.L
Vaughn, H.B. VA Cav. 37th Bn. Co.H 2nd Lt.
Vaughn, H.C. GA 52nd Inf. Co.K
Vaughn, H.C. TN 8th (Smith's) Cav. Co.D
Vaughn, Henry GA 3rd Cav. Co.D
Vaughn, Henry KY 10th (Johnson's) Cav. Co.C
Vaughn, Henry KY 4th Mtd.Inf. Co.K
Vaughn, Henry MS 22nd Inf. Co.C
Vaughn, Henry TN 1st (Turney's) Inf. Co.I
Vaughn, Henry Horse Arty. White's Btty.
Vaughn, Henry D. LA 5th Cav. Co.C
Vaughn, Henry G. VA 34th Inf. Co.H
Vaughn, Henry J. AL 46th Inf. Co.F
Vaughn, Henry M. TX 28th Cav. Co.I Sgt.
Vaughn, Henry W. GA 42nd Inf. Co.C
Vaughn, H.H. AL 51st (Part.Rangers) Co.I
Vaughn, H.H. AL 25th Inf. Co.I
Vaughn, Hickman Deneale's Regt. Choctaw Warriors Co.B
Vaughn, H.J. TN 42nd Inf. Co.D
Vaughn, H.M. AL 8th Cav. Co.F 1st Sgt.
Vaughn, H.N. VA Cav. 36th Bn. Co.F
Vaughn, H.R. TN 13th (Gore's) Cav. Co.D
Vaughn, H.S. AL Arty. Owens' Bn.
Vaughn, H.S. GA 56th Inf. Co.D Sgt.
Vaughn, H.T. VA 53rd Inf. Co.A
Vaughn, I.L. MS 2nd Cav. Co.I
Vaughn, Ira L. TN Sullivan Cty.Res. (Loc.Def.Troops) White's Co.
Vaughn, Isaac C. GA 38th Inf. Co.G 1st Lt.
Vaughn, Isaac D. GA 31st Inf. Co.F
Vaughn, J. AR 38th Inf. Co.K Cpl.
Vaughn, J. LA 16th Inf. Co.G
Vaughn, J. TN 6th (Wheeler's) Cav. Co.K
Vaughn, J. TN 21st & 22nd (Cons.) Cav. Co.C
Vaughn, J. TN 3rd (Lillard's) Mtd.Inf. Co.B
Vaughn, J. TN Inf. 4th Cons.Regt. Co.H
Vaughn, J. TX Cav. Mann's Regt. Co.K
Vaughn, J.A. AL 55th Vol. Co.D
Vaughn, J.A. AR 27th Inf. Co.G
Vaughn, J.A. MS 25th Inf. Co.B
Vaughn, J.A. MS 37th Inf. Co.D
Vaughn, J.A. SC Lt.Arty. Wagener's Co. (Co.A,German Arty.)
Vaughn, J.A. TX Conscr.
Vaughn, J.A. 2nd Conf.Inf. Co.B
Vaughn, Jackson A. AL 18th Inf. Co.D
Vaughn, Jackson W. MS 21st Inf. Co.K
Vaughn, Jacob AL Inf. 2nd Regt. Co.G
Vaughn, Jacob VA 48th Inf. Co.A
Vaughn, Jacob Conf.Inf. 1st Bn. 2nd Co.E
Vaughn, James AL Cav. Barbiere's Bn. Goldsby's Co.
Vaughn, James AL Lt.Arty. 2nd Bn. Co.A
Vaughn, James GA Cav. 1st Bn.Res. Stark's Co. 2nd Lt.
Vaughn, James GA Cav. 19th Bn. Co.C
Vaughn, James GA 6th Inf. (St.Guards) Co.K
Vaughn, James GA 10th Inf. Co.D
Vaughn, James GA 15th Inf. Co.B
Vaughn, James GA Inf. 27th Bn. Co.C
Vaughn, James GA 63rd Inf. Co.D
Vaughn, James GA 63rd Inf. Co.I
Vaughn, James KY 1st Inf. Co.B
Vaughn, James KY 2nd Mtd.Inf. Co.D
Vaughn, James KY 3rd Mtd.Inf. Co.K Sgt.
Vaughn, James MS 12th Cav. Co.F
Vaughn, James MS 44th Inf. Co.A,F
Vaughn, James MO 12th Cav. Co.E
Vaughn, James MO Mtd.Inf. Boone's Regt.
Vaughn, James MO Searcy's Bn.S.S. Co.B
Vaughn, James NC 33rd Inf. Co.K
Vaughn, James NC 56th Inf. Co.G
Vaughn, James SC 15th Inf. Co.K
Vaughn, James TN 6th (Wheeler's) Cav. Co.K
Vaughn, James TN Cav. 9th Bn. (Gantt's) Co.C
Vaughn, James TN Cav. 16th Bn. (Neal's) Co.F
Vaughn, James TN Cav. Newsom's Regt.
Vaughn, James TN 22nd Inf. Co.C
Vaughn, James TN 44th Inf. Co.H
Vaughn, James TN 61st Mtd.Inf. Co.E
Vaughn, James TX 14th Inf. Co.H Cpl.
Vaughn, James VA Cav. Mosby's Regt. (Part.Rangers) Co.F
Vaughn, James VA Inf. 4th Bn.Loc.Def. Co.A
Vaughn, James 10th Conf.Cav. Co.H
Vaughn, James Lt.Arty. Dent's Btty.,CSA
Vaughn, James A. AL 5th Cav. Co.C
Vaughn, James A. AL 20th Inf. Co.F
Vaughn, James A. TN 39th Mtd.Inf. Co.H
Vaughn, James A. VA 36th Inf. Co.F
Vaughn, James A.J. NC 34th Inf. Co.F
Vaughn, James C. AL 7th Cav. Co.K
Vaughn, James C. MO 5th Inf. Co.I
Vaughn, James C. NC 2nd Bn.Loc.Def.Troops Co.D
Vaughn, James C. Conf.Hvy.Arty. Montague's Bn. Co.A
Vaughn, James D. TN Cav. 11th Bn. (Gordon's) Co.D
Vaughn, James F. AL 10th Inf. Co.H
Vaughn, James F. GA 16th Inf. Co.D
Vaughn, James F. KY Corbin's Men
Vaughn, James F. MO 1st Cav. Co.G Sgt.
Vaughn, James F. TN 1st (Field's) Inf. Co.I
Vaughn, James H. AL Cav. Lewis' Bn. Co.D
Vaughn, James H. KY 2nd Cav. Co.A
Vaughn, James H. SC 7th Inf. 1st Co.F, 2nd Co.F Cpl.
Vaughn, James H. VA 36th Inf. 2nd Co.H Sgt.
Vaughn, James J. GA 42nd Inf. Co.D
Vaughn, James L. GA 64th Inf. Co.H
Vaughn, James L. TX 16th Inf. Co.C 2nd Lt.
Vaughn, James M. AL 53rd (Part.Rangers) Co.B
Vaughn, James M. AL 10th Inf. Co.I
Vaughn, James M. AL 18th Inf. Co.D
Vaughn, James M. GA 36th (Broyles') Inf. Co.C
Vaughn, James M. NC 5th Cav. (63rd St.Troops) Co.D
Vaughn, James M. NC 45th Inf. Co.D Sgt.
Vaughn, James M. NC Jones' Co. (Supp.Force)
Vaughn, James S. GA 1st Inf. Co.H
Vaughn, James T. NC 13th Inf. Co.H
Vaughn, James W. AL 37th Inf. Co.A Cpl.
Vaughn, James W. AR 11th Inf. Co.I
Vaughn, James W. MS 1st Lt.Arty. Co.G
Vaughn, James W. NC 1st Arty. (10th St.Troops) Co.K
Vaughn, Jarret GA Inf. Pool's Co.
Vaughn, Jasper GA 18th Inf. Co.H Sgt.
Vaughn, Jasper MO 3rd Cav. Co.F
Vaughn, Jasper SC 22nd Inf. Co.C
Vaughn, J.B. FL Cav. 3rd Bn. Co.B Capt.
Vaughn, J.B. KY 7th Cav. Co.B
Vaughn, J.B. LA Mil. 2nd Regt. 3rd Brig. 1st Div. Co.I 3rd Lt.
Vaughn, J.B. MS 10th Inf. New Co.I Cpl.
Vaughn, J.B. SC 3rd Inf. Co.D
Vaughn, J.B. TN 12th (Cons.) Inf. Co.D
Vaughn, J.B. TX 20th Inf. Co.E
Vaughn, J.B. 15th Conf.Cav. Co.D Capt.
Vaughn, J.C. AL 5th Inf. Co.B
Vaughn, J.C. KY 12th Cav. Co.D
Vaughn, J.C. MS 41st Inf. Co.B
Vaughn, J.C. MS Moseley's Regt.
Vaughn, J.C. TN 1st Hvy.Arty. 1st Co.A, 2nd Co.C, Co.A
Vaughn, J.C. TN 3rd (Lillard's) Mtd.Inf. Col.
Vaughn, J.C. VA 34th Inf. Co.H
Vaughn, J.C.S. SC 3rd Bn.Res. Co.A
Vaughn, J.D. GA 38th Inf. Co.H
Vaughn, J.D. KY 10th (Johnson's) Cav. New Co.C
Vaughn, J.D. SC 16th & 24th (Cons.) Inf. Co.B
Vaughn, J.D. VA 2nd Inf.
Vaughn, J.E. KY 3rd Mtd.Inf. Co.M
Vaughn, J.E. MS St.Cav. Perrin's Bn. Co.I
Vaughn, J.E. MS Inf. 2nd St.Troops Co.G
Vaughn, J.E. SC 4th St.Troops Co.E
Vaughn, J.E.D. GA 2nd Cav. Co.F 1st Lt.
Vaughn, Jefferson Conf.Reg.Inf. Brooks' Bn. Co.B
Vaughn, Jeremiah TN 25th Inf. Co.K
Vaughn, Jerry H. TN 24th Inf. Co.B
Vaughn, Jerry M. GA 48th Inf. Co.D
Vaughn, Jesse GA 20th Inf. Co.H
Vaughn, Jesse TN Inf. 154th Sr.Regt. Co.K
Vaughn, Jesse S. KY 13th Cav. Co.A
Vaughn, J.F. AR 14th (McCarver's) Inf. Co.K
Vaughn, J.F. MS 10th Inf. New Co.C
Vaughn, J.F. MO Cav. 3rd Bn.
Vaughn, J. Frank TN 1st (Feild's) Inf. Co.I
Vaughn, J.G. TN 14th (Neely's) Cav. Co.B

Vaughn, J.G. TN Cav. Nixon's Regt. Co.D
Vaughn, J.H. AL 6th Cav. Co.C Cpl.
Vaughn, J.H. GA 5th Inf. (St.Guards) Johnston's Co.
Vaughn, J.H. GA 27th Inf. Co.G
Vaughn, J.H. GA 38th Inf. Co.H
Vaughn, J.H. MS 41st Inf. Co.L
Vaughn, J.H. NC Inf. 2nd Bn. Co.E
Vaughn, J.H. SC 4th Cav. Co.H
Vaughn, J.H. SC Cav. 10th Bn. Co.D
Vaughn, J.H. TN Cav. 1st Bn. (McNairy's) Co.A
Vaughn, J.H. TN 11th (Holman's) Cav. Co.D
Vaughn, J.H. Conf.Cav. Wood's Regt. 1st Co.A
Vaughn, J.J. GA 2nd Res. Co.H
Vaughn, J.J. MO 3rd Inf. Co.I 1st Sgt.
Vaughn, J.J. TN 3rd (Lillard's) Mtd.Inf. Co.D
Vaughn, J.J.G. NC 16th Inf. Co.I
Vaughn, J.L. AL Cadet Troop Co.F
Vaughn, J.L. MS St.Cav. Perrin's Bn. Co.E
Vaughn, J.L. TN 12th (Green's) Cav. Co.K
Vaughn, J.L. TN 23rd Inf. Co.E
Vaughn, J.M. MS 5th Inf. (St.Troops) Co.A
Vaughn, J.M. NC 56th Inf. Co.C
Vaughn, J.M. SC Inf. Hampton Legion Co.F
Vaughn, Joel SC Res.
Vaughn, Joel SC 9th Res. Co.A
Vaughn, Joel S. GA 38th Inf. Co.K
Vaughn, John AL 4th Cav. Co.K
Vaughn, John AL 6th Inf. Co.I
Vaughn, John AL Hardy's Co. (Eufaula Minute Men)
Vaughn, John AR Inf. Cocke's Regt. Co.E
Vaughn, John FL 9th Inf. Co.I
Vaughn, John GA 3rd Inf. Co.F
Vaughn, John GA 44th Inf. Co.F
Vaughn, John KY 3rd Cav. Co.A,C
Vaughn, John KY 4th Mtd.Inf. Co.H
Vaughn, John KY 10th (Diamond's) Cav. Co.A,C
Vaughn, John MS Cav. Ham's Regt. Co.G
Vaughn, John MS 26th Inf. Co.E
Vaughn, John MS 36th Inf. Co.C
Vaughn, John MS 40th Inf. Co.C
Vaughn, John MO 7th Cav. Co.D
Vaughn, John MO Cav. Preston's Bn. Co.C
Vaughn, John NC 2nd Inf. Co.I
Vaughn, John NC 21st Inf. Co.H
Vaughn, John NC 22nd Inf. Co.B
Vaughn, John NC 45th Inf. Co.D
Vaughn, John SC 3rd Inf. Co.A
Vaughn, John SC 11th Inf. Co.C
Vaughn, John TN 2nd (Ashby's) Cav. Co.C
Vaughn, John TN Inf. 22nd Bn. Co.D
Vaughn, John TN 29th Inf. Co.K
Vaughn, John TN 32nd Inf. Co.D
Vaughn, John TN 51st (Cons.) Inf. Co.E
Vaughn, John TN 55th (McKoin's) Inf. McEwen, Jr.'s Co.
Vaughn, John TX 13th Cav. Co.A
Vaughn, John TX 23rd Cav. Co.B
Vaughn, John TX Cav. Hardeman's Regt. Co.E
Vaughn, John VA Cav. 37th Bn. Co.H
Vaughn, John VA 3rd Inf. Co.H
Vaughn, John VA 47th Inf. 2nd Co.K
Vaughn, John VA Mil. Grayson Cty.
Vaughn, John A. AL 8th (Hatch's) Cav. Co.C
Vaughn, John A. MO St.Guard Ex.QM
Vaughn, John C. VA 34th Inf. Co.I
Vaughn, John C. 2nd Brig. Smith's Div. Brig.Gen.
Vaughn, John E. GA 3rd Inf. Co.I
Vaughn, John George W. AL 34th Inf. Breedlove's Co.
Vaughn, John H. GA 31st Inf. Co.D
Vaughn, John H. LA 1st Cav. Co.A
Vaughn, John H. TN 2nd (Robinson's) Inf. Co.D
Vaughn, John H. VA 6th Bn.Res. Co.E
Vaughn, John H. VA Inf. 26th Bn. Co.A
Vaughn, John J. GA 21st Inf. Co.A
Vaughn, John L. MS 11th (Perrin's) Cav. Co.K
Vaughn, John M. AL 55th Vol. Co.I
Vaughn, John M. SC 12th Inf. Co.C
Vaughn, John N. MO 9th Bn.S.S. Co.E
Vaughn, John P. AL 53rd (Part.Rangers) Co.B
Vaughn, John S. AL 5th Inf. Co.I
Vaughn, Johnson VA 34th Mil. Co.D
Vaughn, John W. MS 1st (Johnston's) Inf. Co.C
Vaughn, John W. MO 2nd Inf. Co.B Surg.
Vaughn, John W. MO 9th Bn.S.S. Co.E
Vaughn, John W. NC 47th Inf. Co.A
Vaughn, John W. NC 50th Inf. Co.A
Vaughn, John W. TN 10th Cav.
Vaughn, John W. VA 4th Res. Co.K
Vaughn, John W. VA 8th Bn.Res. Co.B
Vaughn, John Z. VA Inf. 23rd Bn. Co.H
Vaughn, John Zebulon NC 21st Inf. Co.I
Vaughn, Joseph GA 28th Inf. Co.G
Vaughn, Joseph MO Cav. Hunter's Regt.
Vaughn, Joseph TN 21st (Carter's) Cav. Co.G
Vaughn, Joseph VA Cav. Swann's Bn. Watkins' Co.
Vaughn, Joseph VA Lt.Arty. Thornton's Co.
Vaughn, Joseph VA 30th Inf. Co.G
Vaughn, Joseph 1st Choctaw & Chickasaw Mtd.Rifles Co.A
Vaughn, Joseph Deneale's Regt. Choctaw Warriors Co.B
Vaughn, Joseph B. VA 4th Inf. Co.F
Vaughn, Joseph E. VA 37th Inf. Co.B
Vaughn, Joseph H. NC 25th Inf. Co.D
Vaughn, Joseph J. SC Inf. Hampton Legion Co.E Cpl.
Vaughn, Joseph M. AL 44th Inf. Co.C
Vaughn, Joseph M. NC 45th Inf. Co.D
Vaughn, Joseph P. MO 6th Inf. Maj.
Vaughn, Joseph W. MS Inf. 3rd Bn. (St.Troops) Co.D
Vaughn, Joseph W. VA 6th Bn.Res. Co.E
Vaughn, Josh MO 7th Cav. Co.C
Vaughn, Joshua GA 15th Inf. Co.B
Vaughn, Joshua NC 2nd Inf. Co.I
Vaughn, Joshua A. VA 42nd Inf. Co.G
Vaughn, Josiah TX 34th Cav. Co.K
Vaughn, J.P. AL 25th Inf. Co.D
Vaughn, J.P. AL 32nd Inf. Co.A
Vaughn, J.P. MS 13th Inf. Co.H
Vaughn, J.P. SC Hvy.Arty. Gilchrist's Co. (Gist Guard)
Vaughn, J.P. TN 14th (Neely's) Cav. Co.E
Vaughn, J.Q. TN 3rd (Lillard's) Mtd.Inf. Co.D
Vaughn, J.R. MS 7th Cav. Co.H
Vaughn, J.R. TN 20th Inf. Co.H
Vaughn, J.R.Z. AR 19th (Dawson's) Inf. Co.I
Vaughn, J.S. AL 42nd Inf. Co.D
Vaughn, J.S. GA 2nd Res. Co.H
Vaughn, J.S. GA 38th Inf. Co.K
Vaughn, J.T. GA Hvy.Arty. 22nd Bn. Co.A Sgt.
Vaughn, J.T. GA 4th Res. Co.C
Vaughn, J.T. GA 60th Inf. 1st Co.A
Vaughn, J.T. SC Arty. Manigault's Bn. Co.E
Vaughn, J.T. TN Cav. 1st Bn. (McNairy's) Co.A
Vaughn, J.T. TN 22nd (Barteau's) Cav. Co.A
Vaughn, J.T. TN 5th Inf. 2nd Co.I
Vaughn, J.T. TN Inf. 23rd Bn. Co.D
Vaughn, J.W. GA Hvy.Arty. 22nd Bn. Co.A
Vaughn, J.W. GA 6th Inf. (St.Guards) Co.K Music.
Vaughn, J.W. GA 56th Inf. Co.G
Vaughn, J.W. GA 60th Inf. 1st Co.A
Vaughn, J.W. KY 10th (Johnson's) Cav. New Co.C
Vaughn, J.W. MS 12th Cav. Co.G Sgt.
Vaughn, J.W. MS Rogers' Co.
Vaughn, J.W. MO 7th Cav. Co.C
Vaughn, J.W. MO 7th Cav. Co.H
Vaughn, J.W. SC Hvy.Arty. Gilchrist's Co. (Gist Guard)
Vaughn, J.W. SC Arty. Manigault's Bn. Co.E
Vaughn, J.W. TN 11th (Holman's) Cav. Co.G Sgt.
Vaughn, J.W. TN 5th Inf. Co.A
Vaughn, J.W. TX Inf. 3rd St.Troops Co.A
Vaughn, J.W. TX 9th (Young's) Inf. Co.F
Vaughn, J.W. VA Mil. 78th Regt. Lt.Col.
Vaughn, J.W.A. TN 49th (Voorhies') Inf. Co.B
Vaughn, J. William TX 2nd Inf. Co.E
Vaughn, Kendrick SC 3rd Res. Co.C
Vaughn, Kindrick SC 1st St.Troops Co.G Sgt.
Vaughn, King David NC 56th Inf. Co.E
Vaughn, L. AL 23rd Inf. Co.C
Vaughn, L.A. MS 1st Cav. Co.K
Vaughn, La. TN 19th Inf. Co.A Cpl.
Vaughn, Lafayette C. TN Cav. 4th Bn. (Branner's) Co.E
Vaughn, L.C. TN 2nd (Ashby's) Cav. Co.I
Vaughn, L.D. AR 14th (McCarver's) Inf. Co.H
Vaughn, L.D. MO 2nd Cav. Co.A Sgt.
Vaughn, Lemuel AL 4th Inf. Co.D
Vaughn, Lemuel SC 2nd Cav. Co.F
Vaughn, Lemuel SC Cav. 4th Bn. Co.A
Vaughn, Leon D. GA Cav. 16th Bn. (St.Guards) Co.B 3rd Lt.
Vaughn, Leroy KY 5th Cav.
Vaughn, Lewis A. AL 33rd Inf. Co.B
Vaughn, Lewis L. VA 18th Inf. Co.B 2nd Lt.
Vaughn, L.F. VA Cav. 37th Bn. Co.D 1st Lt.
Vaughn, L.H. SC 3rd Inf. Co.K
Vaughn, Lorenzo D. AR 8th Inf. New Co.G
Vaughn, M. MS Inf. 1st Bn.St.Troops (12 mo. '62-3) Co.D
Vaughn, M. TN 51st Inf. Co.K
Vaughn, M. TN 51st (Cons.) Inf. Co.G
Vaughn, M. VA 19th Inf.
Vaughn, M. 2nd Conf.Eng.Troops Co.B
Vaughn, Marian TN 53rd Inf. Co.C
Vaughn, Marshall SC Inf. Hampton Legion Co.F
Vaughn, Martin V. TN 16th Cav. Wilson's Co.
Vaughn, Mathew B. TX 13th Cav. Co.C Cpl.
Vaughn, M.B. TX 28th Cav. Co.I

Vaughn, Memory C. GA Phillips' Legion Co.M
Vaughn, M.H. Conf.Cav. Clarkson's Bn. Ind. Rangers Co.A
Vaughn, Mitchell B. NC 45th Inf. Co.E
Vaughn, M.J. LA 4th Inf. Old Co.G
Vaughn, M.L. TN 12th (Green's) Cav. Co.E
Vaughn, M.M. TN 21st & 22nd (Cons.) Cav. Co.D
Vaughn, Monterville P. NC 6th Cav. (65th St.Troops) Co.A,E Sgt.
Vaughn, Montgomery C. KY 2nd Mtd.Inf. Co.A
Vaughn, Montraville P. NC Cav. 7th Bn. Co.A
Vaughn, M.P.G. TN 11th (Holman's) Cav. Co.D
Vaughn, M.R. GA 1st Inf. Co.B
Vaughn, M.R. GA Phillips' Legion Co.C
Vaughn, M.V. TN 51st (Cons.) Inf. Co.K
Vaughn, Nathan TN 1st Hvy.Arty. Co.L
Vaughn, Nathan TX 6th Inf. Co.F
Vaughn, Nathaniel TN 46th Inf. Co.G
Vaughn, Neaser TN 46th Inf. Co.G
Vaughn, Newt I. TN Cav. Nixon's Regt. Co.I Capt.
Vaughn, Newton MS Terry's Co.
Vaughn, Nicholas I. VA 53rd Inf. Co.D
Vaughn, Nicholas L. VA Inf. Montague's Bn. Co.C
Vaughn, N.J. TN 25th Inf. Co.F
Vaughn, Norman SC 3rd Inf. Co.F
Vaughn, Norman SC 9th Res. Co.A
Vaughn, Norman SC 16th Inf. Co.B
Vaughn, N.W. TN Sullivan Cty.Res. (Loc. Def.Troops) White's Co.
Vaughn, Obadiah AR 19th (Dawson's) Inf. Co.H
Vaughn, Oliver GA Inf. Pool's Co.
Vaughn, Oliver VA 12th Cav. Co.F
Vaughn, Owen TX Cav. 6th Bn. Co.B
Vaughn, P. AL 51st (Part.Rangers) Co.I
Vaughn, P. KY Cav. 2nd Bn. (Dortch's) Co.A
Vaughn, Panaval W. NC 56th Inf. Co.G
Vaughn, Parley W. TN 34th Inf. Co.D
Vaughn, P.D. VA Cav. Mosby's Regt. (Part.Rangers) Co.E
Vaughn, Perry SC 22nd Inf. Co.C
Vaughn, Peter D. GA 15th Inf. Co.C
Vaughn, P.H. LA 14th Inf. Co.A
Vaughn, Pinkney MS 2nd Cav. 1st Co.G
Vaughn, Pipkin NC 1st Inf. Co.F
Vaughn, P.T. AL 8th Cav. Co.F Sgt.
Vaughn, Q.C. VA Hood's Bn.Res. Co.B
Vaughn, R. AL 35th Inf. Co.D
Vaughn, Randolph GA 2nd Cav. Co.I
Vaughn, R.B. AL 23rd Inf. Co.I,E 1st Sgt.
Vaughn, R.B. GA 24th Inf. Co.H
Vaughn, R.B. MS 31st Inf. Co.H
Vaughn, R.B.M. SC 5th Cav. Co.K
Vaughn, R.D. AL Cp. of Instr. Talladega Co.B
Vaughn, R.D. AL Conscr. Co.B
Vaughn, Reuben F. MO 4th Cav. Co.E
Vaughn, R.F. VA 13th Inf. Co.B
Vaughn, R.H. AR Inf. Cocke's Regt. Co.K
Vaughn, R.H. LA 9th Inf. Co.K
Vaughn, R.H. LA 12th Inf. 2nd Co.M
Vaughn, R.H. SC Arty. Manigault's Bn. 2nd Co.C
Vaughn, Richard KY 13th Cav. Co.B
Vaughn, Richard NC 31st Inf. Co.A
Vaughn, Richard SC 3rd Res. Co.E
Vaughn, Richard VA 36th Inf. 2nd Co.D, 1st Co.C Cpl.
Vaughn, Richard D. TN 7th Inf. Co.G Sgt.
Vaughn, Richard H. GA 55th Inf. Co.C
Vaughn, Richard H. TN 34th Inf. Co.H
Vaughn, Richard J. SC 5th Inf. 1st Co.E, 2nd Co.H
Vaughn, Richard M. MS 30th Inf. Co.B
Vaughn, Richard N. VA Inf. 25th Bn. Co.F
Vaughn, Richard T. NC 22nd Inf. Co.K
Vaughn, R.L. GA 24th Inf. Co.H
Vaughn, R.L. LA Inf. Pelican Regt. Co.F
Vaughn, R.M. GA Inf. (Baldwin Inf.) Moore's Co.
Vaughn, Robert AL 48th Inf. Co.B
Vaughn, Robert AR 32nd Inf. Co.G
Vaughn, Robert GA 42nd Inf. Co.C
Vaughn, Robert SC 1st St.Troops Co.H
Vaughn, Robert TN 12th (Green's) Cav. Co.D
Vaughn, Robert TN 34th Inf. Co.I
Vaughn, Robert A. AL 35th Inf. Co.D
Vaughn, Robert D.L. GA 24th Inf. Co.H
Vaughn, Robert E. MO 1st Cav. Co.D
Vaughn, Robert E. MO 1st & 3rd Cons.Cav. Co.A
Vaughn, Robert H. TN 4th (McLemore's) Cav. Co.A
Vaughn, Robert J. MO 9th Bn.S.S. Co.E
Vaughn, R.P. AR 21st Inf. Co.I Cpl.
Vaughn, R.P. SC 22nd Inf. Co.A
Vaughn, R.S. NC Inf. 2nd Bn. Co.B
Vaughn, Ruffin NC 2nd Bn.Loc.Def.Troops Co.D
Vaughn, Rufus L. LA Inf. 4th Bn. Co.A
Vaughn, Rufus W. AL 5th Inf. New Co.B
Vaughn, R.W. SC 1st St.Troops Co.H
Vaughn, S. AL 22nd Inf. Co.B
Vaughn, S. AR 13th Inf. Co.B
Vaughn, S. GA 34th Inf. Co.G
Vaughn, S. SC 11th Inf. 1st Co.F
Vaughn, Samuel GA 15th Inf. Co.B Sgt.
Vaughn, Samuel SC Inf. Hampton Legion Co.F
Vaughn, Samuel TN 34th Inf. Co.K 1st Lt.
Vaughn, Samuel VA Cav. 47th Bn. Co.C
Vaughn, Samuel F. MO 16th Inf. Co.B
Vaughn, Samuel T. MS 12th Inf. Co.D
Vaughn, Sanford M. GA St.RR Guards
Vaughn, S.E. AL 25th Inf. Co.K
Vaughn, S.F. GA Floyd Legion (St.Guards) Co.D
Vaughn, S.F. MO 11th Inf. Co.E
Vaughn, S.G. TX 28th Cav. Co.I Jr.2nd Lt.
Vaughn, Sidney TN 44th (Cons.) Inf. Co.I
Vaughn, Silas KY 4th Cav. Co.I
Vaughn, Silas KY 5th Mtd.Inf. Co.E
Vaughn, Sion VA 45th Inf. Co.D
Vaughn, S.J. VA Mtd.Riflemen Balfour's Co.
Vaughn, S.L. GA 18th Inf. Co.H
Vaughn, Smith GA 12th Cav. Co.G
Vaughn, Solomon SC 1st (Orr's) Rifles Co.C
Vaughn, Spencer NC 43rd Inf. Co.K
Vaughn, Stephen AR 1st Inf. Co.G
Vaughn, Stephen AR 19th (Dawson's) Inf. Co.H
Vaughn, Stephen KY 4th Mtd.Inf. Co.H
Vaughn, Stephen LA 1st Cav. Scott's Co.
Vaughn, Stephen MS 15th (Cons.) Inf. Co.I
Vaughn, Stephen NC 2nd Bn.Loc.Def.Troops Co.D
Vaughn, Stephen NC 43rd Inf. Co.K
Vaughn, Stephen TN 6th (Wheeler's) Cav. Co.K
Vaughn, Stephen G. TX 13th Cav. Co.C 1st Sgt.
Vaughn, Strother KY 5th Cav.
Vaughn, Strother KY 10th Cav.
Vaughn, S.V. SC 1st (Orr's) Rifles Co.D
Vaughn, T. MS 35th Inf. Co.K
Vaughn, T. VA 5th Cav. Co.E
Vaughn, T.A.W. MS 38th Cav. Co.D
Vaughn, Taylor MS 11th (Perrin's) Cav. Co.E
Vaughn, Taylor MS Inf. 1st Bn. Co.C
Vaughn, T.C. LA 8th Cav. Co.G
Vaughn, T.H. TX 20th Inf. Co.D
Vaughn, Theofilos TN 19th (Biffle's) Cav. Co.B
Vaughn, Theophilus D. TN 3rd (Clack's) Inf. Co.I
Vaughn, Thomas AL 36th Inf.
Vaughn, Thomas AR 8th Inf. New Co.C
Vaughn, Thomas LA 14th Inf. Co.E
Vaughn, Thomas MS Rogers' Co.
Vaughn, Thomas NC 16th Inf. Co.B
Vaughn, Thomas SC Cav. 4th Bn. Co.A
Vaughn, Thomas SC 8th Bn.Res. Fishburne's Co.
Vaughn, Thomas TN 5th (McKenzie's) Cav. Co.B
Vaughn, Thomas TN 14th (Neely's) Cav. Co.E
Vaughn, Thomas TN 16th (Logwood's) Cav. Co.K Cpl.
Vaughn, Thomas TN Inf. 4th Cons.Regt. Co.F
Vaughn, Thomas TN 22nd Inf. Co.C
Vaughn, Thomas TX 14th Cav. Co.A
Vaughn, Thomas 7th Conf.Cav. 2nd Co.I
Vaughn, Thomas 1st Choctaw & Chickasaw Mtd.Rifles 2nd Co.K 1st Lt.
Vaughn, Thomas H. GA 31st Inf. Co.D Capt.
Vaughn, Thomas J. GA 14th Inf. Co.C
Vaughn, Thomas J. KY 5th Mtd.Inf. Co.K 1st Sgt.
Vaughn, Thomas J. VA Hvy.Arty. 10th Bn. Co.D
Vaughn, Thomas J. VA 9th Inf. Co.D
Vaughn, Thomas L. AL 3rd Inf. Co.D
Vaughn, Thomas M. TX 1st Inf. Co.I
Vaughn, Thomas R. GA Cobb's Legion Co.E
Vaughn, Thomas W. SC 2nd Cav. Co.I
Vaughn, Thomas W. SC Cav.Bn. Hampton Legion Co.A
Vaughn, Tillman AL 51st (Part.Rangers) Co.F
Vaughn, Timothy VA 10th Inf. 2nd Co.C
Vaughn, T.J. AR Cav. Gordon's Regt. Co.A
Vaughn, T.J. GA 7th Cav. Co.A
Vaughn, T.J. GA Cav. 21st Bn. Co.A
Vaughn, T.J. GA 16th Inf. Co.I
Vaughn, T.J. LA 25th Inf. Co.F
Vaughn, T.J. TX Cav. Wells' Regt. Co.K
Vaughn, T.M. TX Inf. Currie's Co.
Vaughn, T.M. VA 34th Inf. Co.G
Vaughn, T.R. GA 56th Inf. Co.F
Vaughn, T.R. VA 4th Res. Co.C
Vaughn, T.S. AL Inf. 1st Regt. Co.C
Vaughn, T.S. TN Inf. 1st Cons.Regt. Co.E
Vaughn, T.S. TN 9th Inf. Co.C
Vaughn, T.S. TN 20th Inf. Co.H
Vaughn, T.S. TX Cav. 6th Bn. Co.B

Vaughn, Turner NC 4th Cav. (59th St.Troops) Co.K
Vaughn, T.W. AL 51st (Part.Rangers) Co.C
Vaughn, T.W. TN 15th (Cons.) Cav. Co.D
Vaughn, Uriah VA 7th Bn.Res.
Vaughn, Urial VA Harper's Res. Co.A
Vaughn, Van Buren TN 52nd Inf. Wilson's Co.
Vaughn, Victor E. GA 1st Reg. Co.L,A Cpl.
Vaughn, W. GA 46th Inf. Co.A
Vaughn, W. GA Inf. (Baldwin Inf.) Moore's Co.
Vaughn, W. NC 3rd Jr.Res. Co.C
Vaughn, W. NC 4th Bn.Jr.Res. Co.C
Vaughn, W. TN 12th (Cons.) Inf. Co.G Cpl.
Vaughn, W. VA 19th Inf. Co.G
Vaughn, W.A. AR 8th Cav. Co.D
Vaughn, Warren LA 16th Inf. Co.F
Vaughn, Warren LA 25th Inf. Co.D
Vaughn, W.B. AL 1st Inf. 3rd Co.G
Vaughn, W.B. AL 8th Inf.
Vaughn, W.B. TN 35th Inf. 2nd Co.A
Vaughn, W.C. GA 52nd Inf. Co.K
Vaughn, W.C. KY 7th Cav. Co.I
Vaughn, W.C. MS Scouts Morphis' Ind.Co.
Vaughn, W.C. SC 13th Inf. Co.I
Vaughn, W.C. VA 46th Inf. Co.D
Vaughn, W.F. AL 41st Inf. Co.H
Vaughn, W.F. AR 11th & 17th (Cons.) Inf. Co.C,D
Vaughn, W.F. TX 26th Cav. Co.H
Vaughn, W.G. GA 1st (Ramsey's) Inf.
Vaughn, W.H. GA Inf. 1st Loc.Troops (Augusta) Co.G
Vaughn, W.H. GA 3rd Res. Co.K
Vaughn, W.H. KY Corbin's Men
Vaughn, Wiley SC 22nd Inf. Co.C
Vaughn, Wiley C. GA 14th Inf. Co.E
Vaughn, William AL 3rd Bn.Res. Co.C
Vaughn, William AR 16th Inf. Co.D
Vaughn, William AR 34th Inf. Co.A
Vaughn, William FL 8th Inf. Co.I
Vaughn, William GA 21st Inf. Co.C
Vaughn, William GA 31st Inf. Co.F
Vaughn, William GA Cherokee Legion (St.Guards) Co.B
Vaughn, William KY 5th Mtd.Inf. Co.B
Vaughn, William LA Inf. 9th Bn. Co.D
Vaughn, William MS 46th Inf. Co.E
Vaughn, William MS 46th Inf. Co.K
Vaughn, William MO Mtd.Inf. Boone's Regt. Co.A
Vaughn, William NC 2nd Cav. (19th St.Troops) Co.D
Vaughn, William NC 8th Bn.Part.Rangers Co.F,D
Vaughn, William NC 25th Inf. Co.H
Vaughn, William NC 39th Inf. Co.H
Vaughn, William NC 43rd Inf. Co.K
Vaughn, William NC 47th Inf. Co.D
Vaughn, William NC 55th Inf. Co.K
Vaughn, William TN 2nd (Ashby's) Cav. Co.C Far.
Vaughn, William TN 4th Cav.
Vaughn, William TN 4th (McLemore's) Cav. Co.I
Vaughn, William TN Cav. 12th Bn. (Day's) Co.D
Vaughn, William TN 16th Cav. Co.B,F
Vaughn, William TN Cav. Newsom's Regt. Co.D
Vaughn, William TN Lt.Arty. Huggins' Co.
Vaughn, William TN 14th Inf. Co.G
Vaughn, William TN 16th Inf. Co.F
Vaughn, William TN 22nd Inf. Co.B
Vaughn, William TN 29th Inf. Co.I
Vaughn, William TN 37th Inf. Co.K Cpl.
Vaughn, William TX 23rd Cav. Co.B
Vaughn, William VA 21st Cav. Co.K
Vaughn, William VA 18th Inf. Co.A
Vaughn, William VA 36th Inf. 2nd Co.B
Vaughn, William Horse Arty. White's Co.
Vaughn, William A. NC 53rd Inf. Co.F
Vaughn, William A. TN 4th (McLemore's) Cav. Co.A
Vaughn, William A. VA 24th Inf. Co.E
Vaughn, William A. VA 24th Inf. Co.K
Vaughn, William A. VA 45th Inf. Co.D
Vaughn, William B. NC 21st Inf. Co.G 1st Sgt.
Vaughn, William C. MS 2nd Inf. Co.E
Vaughn, William D. GA 14th Inf. Co.C
Vaughn, William E. TN Cav. 12th Bn. (Day's) Co.A
Vaughn, William F. AR 11th Inf. Co.I
Vaughn, William F. MO 10th Inf. Co.E,G 1st Lt.
Vaughn, William F. TX 13th Cav. Co.A
Vaughn, William H. AR 1st (Crawford's) Cav. Co.A
Vaughn, William H. GA Lt.Arty. Milledge's Co.
Vaughn, William H. GA 3rd Inf. 1st Co.I
Vaughn, William H. GA 44th Inf. Co.G
Vaughn, William H. NC 66th Inf. Co.I
Vaughn, William H. SC 2nd Rifles Co.L
Vaughn, William H. SC Inf. Hampton Legion Co.E
Vaughn, William H. TN 34th Inf. Co.H
Vaughn, William H. VA 61st Inf. Co.G
Vaughn, William L. NC 34th Inf. Co.F
Vaughn, William M. AL Inf. 1st Regt. Co.K
Vaughn, William M. MS 1st Cav.Res. Co.A Cpl.
Vaughn, William M. MS 3rd Cav.Res. Co.A
Vaughn, William M. TN 5th Inf. 2nd Co.G
Vaughn, William M. TX Cav. 6th Bn. Co.C
Vaughn, William P. KY 2nd (Duke's) Cav. Co.B
Vaughn, William R. KY 3rd Mtd.Inf. Co.M
Vaughn, William R. TX 28th Cav. Co.I 1st Lt.
Vaughn, William S. TX 28th Cav. Co.I
Vaughn, William S. VA Hvy.Arty. 19th Bn. Co.A
Vaughn, William S. VA Hvy.Arty. Kyle's Co.
Vaughn, William S.T. TX 13th Cav. Co.K
Vaughn, William Thomas AL 5th Inf. New Co.B
Vaughn, William W. TX Cav. 3rd (Yager's) Bn. Co.D
Vaughn, Willis FL 7th Inf. Co.C
Vaughn, Willis GA 4th Inf. Co.H
Vaughn, Willis MO Cav. Snider's Bn. Co.A
Vaughn, W.J. SC 4th St.Troops Co.B
Vaughn, W.J. SC Cav.Bn. Holcombe Legion Co.D
Vaughn, W.L. TX 5th Cav. Co.A
Vaughn, W.L. TX Cav. Ragsdale's Bn. Co.C
Vaughn, W.M. AL 36th Inf. Co.K
Vaughn, W.M. MS 1st Cav. Co.A Cpl.
Vaughn, W.M. MS 6th Cav. Co.G
Vaughn, W.M. MS 12th Inf. Co.A
Vaughn, W.M. TN 3rd (Forrest's) Cav. Co.D Cpl.
Vaughn, W.M. TX Cav. Hardeman's Regt. Co.G
Vaughn, Word H. TX 13th Cav. Co.C Cpl.
Vaughn, W.P. GA 3rd Bn.S.S. Co.F
Vaughn, W.P. GA Phillips' Legion Co.D
Vaughn, W.P. MS 2nd Cav. Co.G
Vaughn, W.P. MS 4th Cav. Co.G
Vaughn, W.P. SC 22nd Inf. Co.E
Vaughn, W.R. GA 2nd Inf. Co.A
Vaughn, W.R. TN 11th (Holman's) Cav. Co.D
Vaughn, W.R. TN Douglass' Bn.Part.Rangers Lytle's Co.
Vaughn, W.S. LA 22nd (Cons.) Inf. Co.F
Vaughn, W.S. MS 1st Lt.Arty. Co.F
Vaughn, W.S. NC 1st Bn.Jr.Res. Co.C
Vaughn, W.S. SC Cav. 4th Bn. Co.C
Vaughn, W.T. AL 51st (Part.Rangers) Co.F
Vaughn, W.T. AL 44th Inf. Co.K
Vaughn, W.T. GA 38th Inf. Co.K
Vaughn, W.W. AL 45th Inf. Co.C
Vaughn, W.W. GA 16th Inf. Co.D
Vaughn, W.W. GA 21st Inf. Co.A
Vaughn, W.W. GA 53rd Inf. Co.H
Vaughn, W.W. MS 6th Cav.
Vaughn, W.W. MO 2nd Inf. Co.I
Vaughn, W.W. MO 11th Inf. Co.E
Vaughn, W.W. TX 1st (Yager's) Cav. Co.D
Vaughn, Wyatt GA Inf. (Richmond Factory Guards) Barney's Co.
Vaughn, Z. NC 7th Sr.Res. Davies' Co.
Vaughn, Zachariah TN Cav. Shaw's Bn. Cullen's Co.
Vaughn, Z.C. VA 4th Res.
Vaughn, Z.J. AL 26th (O'Neal's) Inf. Co.K Sgt.
Vaughn, Z.M. AR 27th Inf. Co.G Sgt.
Vaughner, William VA 64th Mtd.Inf. Co.K
Vaughnier, W. GA 12th Mil.
Vaughon, Franklin LA Inf. 11th Bn. Co.D
Vaughon, Franklin LA Inf.Cons.Crescent Regt. Co.B
Vaughon, James A. LA Inf. 11th Bn. Co.D
Vaughon, James A. LA Inf.Cons.Crescent Regt. Co.B
Vaughon, John G. NC 30th Inf. Co.D
Vaughon, Thomas AL 62nd Inf. Co.C
Vaughs, H.W. AR 1st Vol. Surg.
Vaught, A.J. AR 19th (Dawson's) Inf. Co.D
Vaught, A.M. AR 34th Inf. Co.E Sgt.
Vaught, Andrew AR Cav. 1st Bn. (Stirman's) Co.C
Vaught, Andrew P. TN 39th Mtd.Inf. Co.B Sgt.
Vaught, B.B. AR Inf. Hardy's Regt. Co.K
Vaught, B.D. KY 12th Cav. Co.K,D 1st Sgt.
Vaught, Caswell B. AR 4th Inf. Co.C
Vaught, Caswell C. TX 19th Cav. Co.I Sgt.
Vaught, Charles M. Gen. & Staff 1st Lt.,CS
Vaught, Charles N. TN 1st (Feild's) Inf. Co.H
Vaught, Christian L. VA 4th Inf. Co.L
Vaught, Christian L. VA 36th Inf. 2nd Co.H Cpl.
Vaught, Christopher A. VA 29th Inf. Co.B
Vaught, C.L. TN 12th Inf. Co.C 2nd Lt.
Vaught, C.W. TX 8th Cav. Co.K
Vaught, David B. VA 29th Inf. Co.B

Vaught, David B. VA Mil. Carroll Cty.
Vaught, David H. VA Lt.Arty. Lowry's Co.
Vaught, Ephraim VA 5th Bn.Res. Co.B
Vaught, Ephraim VA 29th Inf. Co.B
Vaught, G.C. KY 8th Cav. Co.H
Vaught, George MO Inf. Perkins' Bn.
Vaught, George VA 23rd Cav. Co.D
Vaught, George H. VA 49th Inf. Co.D
Vaught, George W. AL 6th Inf. Co.H
Vaught, George W. VA 29th Inf. Co.B
Vaught, G.M. AR 19th (Dawson's) Inf. Co.D
Vaught, Green C. KY Horse Arty. Byrne's Co. Sgt.
Vaught, Henley J. VA 36th Inf. 2nd Co.H
Vaught, Henry AR 3rd Inf. (St.Troops) Co.E
Vaught, Hiram W. AL 4th (Russell's) Cav. Co.G
Vaught, H.M. AR 19th (Dawson's) Inf. Co.D
Vaught, J. TX 20th Bn.St.Troops Co.A
Vaught, Jackson VA Mil. Grayson Cty.
Vaught, James AR 10th Mil. Co.F
Vaught, James B. LA 25th Inf. Co.A Sgt.
Vaught, James F. VA 28th Inf. Co.B Sgt.
Vaught, James L. AL 4th (Russell's) Cav. Co.G
Vaught, James L. MO 3rd Inf. Co.H
Vaught, James M. VA 29th Inf. Co.B
Vaught, James T. MS Conscr.
Vaught, James Z. VA 29th Inf. Co.B Cpl.
Vaught, J.F. TN 1st (Feild's) & 27th Inf. (Cons.) Co.B
Vaught, J.K. MO 1st Inf. Co.K
Vaught, J.M. TN 55th (Brown's) Inf. Co.D
Vaught, John SC 3rd St.Troops Co.D
Vaught, John F. TN 1st (Feild's) Inf. Co.B
Vaught, John H. VA 36th Inf. 2nd Co.H
Vaught, John W. VA 45th Inf. Co.B Sgt.
Vaught, Jonathan AR Inf. Cocke's Regt. Co.K
Vaught, Joseph MO 10th Inf. Co.G
Vaught, J.S. TX Cav. 1st Bn.St.Troops Co.A
Vaught, Larkin TN 14th Inf. Co.I Cpl.
Vaught, Leroy M. TX 2nd Cav. Co.E
Vaught, Lewis P. VA 4th Inf. Co.F
Vaught, L.M. TX St.Troops Teel's Co.
Vaught, M. LA Lt.Arty. Bridges' Btty.
Vaught, M. SC Lt.Arty. M. Ward's Co. (Waccamaw Lt.Arty.)
Vaught, Miles P. VA Lt.Arty. G.B. Chapman's Co.
Vaught, M.M. FL 5th Inf. Co.E
Vaught, Noah T. VA 29th Inf. Co.B 2nd Lt.
Vaught, P. VA Mil. Wythe Cty.
Vaught, Peter VA 45th Inf. Co.B
Vaught, Pope TX 8th Cav. Co.G
Vaught, Ransom VA 36th Inf. 2nd Co.H
Vaught, Ransum VA 86th Mil. Co.D
Vaught, Riley VA 86th Mil. Co.B,D
Vaught, R.T. TX 12th Inf. Co.B
Vaught, Rufus VA 36th Inf. 2nd Co.H
Vaught, S.F. TN 20th (Russell's) Cav. Co.D
Vaught, S.F. TN 20th (Russell's) Cav. Co.I
Vaught, Silas P. AR 2nd Mtd.Rifles Co.E Cpl.
Vaught, Silas P. AR Cav. Witherspoon's Bn. Co.B 1st Lt.
Vaught, Simeon VA 23rd Cav. Co.D
Vaught, Simeon VA 146th Mil. Co.K
Vaught, Simon TN 15th (Stewart's) Cav. Co.A
Vaught, Stephen E. VA 29th Inf. Co.B
Vaught, Stephen M. TN 20th Inf. Co.H
Vaught, Stephen P. VA 45th Inf. Co.B
Vaught, S.W. SC 7th Inf. 1st Co.L, 2nd Co.L
Vaught, Thomas TN 20th (Russell's) Cav. Co.C
Vaught, Tom TN 19th & 20th (Cons.) Cav. Co.E
Vaught, W.A. MS 6th Cav. Co.I
Vaught, W.C. AR 11th & 17th (Cons.) Inf. Co.I QM Clerk
Vaught, W.C.D. LA Washington Arty.Bn. Co.5 1st Lt.
Vaught, W.H. TX Cav. Terry's Regt. Co.A Sgt.
Vaught, William AL 4th (Russell's) Cav. Co.G
Vaught, William B. FL 2nd Cav. Co.C
Vaught, William E. TN 11th Inf. Co.B
Vaught, William H. TX 37th Cav. Co.F
Vaught, William J. VA 29th Inf. Co.B
Vaught, William M. TX 12th Inf. Co.B
Vaught, William R. VA 36th Inf. 2nd Co.H
Vaught, William T. VA 36th Inf. 2nd Co.H
Vaught, William T. VA 86th Mil. Co.B,D Sgt.
Vaught, Wilson A. VA Inf. 26th Bn. Co.F
Vaught, Wilson A. VA 166th Mil. R.G. Lively's Co. Cpl.
Vaught, W.R. VA 86th Mil. Co.D
Vaught, W.W. AR 11th & 17th (Cons.) Inf. Capt.,AQM
Vaught, W.W. MS 4th Cav. Co.I 2nd Lt.
Vaught, W.W. Gen. & Staff 2nd Lt.,AQM
Vaught, Z.M. MO 6th Cav. Co.E
Vaughten, J.E. TN 55th (Brown's) Inf. Co.G Cpl.
Vaughten, J.T. TN 55th (Brown's) Inf. Co.G Sgt.
Vaughten, P. LA Mil. 4th Regt. 1st Brig. 1st Div. Co.A
Vaughter, A.J. TN 20th (Russell's) Cav. Co.B
Vaughter, Franklin MO 9th Bn.S.S. Co.E
Vaughter, G.L. KY 4th Cav. Co.A
Vaughter, Hiram F. GA 52nd Inf. Co.K
Vaughter, James MO 9th Bn.S.S. Co.E
Vaughter, J.B. TN 4th (McLemore's) Cav. Co.C
Vaughter, Rolly A. MS 13th Inf. Co.A
Vaughter, Samuel H. GA 5th Inf. Co.K 1st Lt.
Vaughter, T.D. TN 22nd Inf. Co.D
Vaughter, W.H. TN 20th (Russell's) Cav. Co.B
Vaughter, William G. TN 7th Inf. Co.G
Vaughter, W.R. TN 22nd Inf. Co.D
Vaughters, Samuel H. GA 52nd Inf. Co.K 1st Lt.
Vaugine, Charles AR 9th Inf. Co.H
Vaugine, C.P. AR 1st (Monroe's) Cav. Co.G
Vaugine, F.G. AR 1st (Monroe's) Cav. Co.G Bvt.2nd Lt.
Vaugine, Joseph AR 18th Inf. Co.E
Vaugine, Mathias AR 9th Inf. Co.H
Vaugine, P.N. AR 1st (Monroe's) Cav. Co.G
Vaugn, A.C. AR 27th Inf. Co.G
Vaugn, Berry GA 34th Inf. Co.G
Vaugn, Charles KY Cav. 2nd Bn. (Dortch's) Co.B,A
Vaugn, James MO Quantrill's Co.
Vaugn, J.D. GA 3rd Inf. Co.A
Vaugn, J.N. LA 13th Bn. (Part.Rangers) Co.F
Vaugn, John GA 34th Inf. Co.G
Vaugn, J.R. SC 4th Bn.Res. Co.A
Vaugn, Mitchel R. GA Inf. 4th Bn. (St.Guards) Co.G
Vaugn, N. GA 52nd Inf. Co.K
Vaugn, R.C. TN 28th Inf. Co.C
Vaugn, Richard TN 20th Inf. Co.D,B
Vaugn, Thomas TN 46th Inf. Co.A
Vaugn, V.R. GA 52nd Inf. Co.K
Vaugn, William LA 13th Bn. (Part.Rangers) Co.F
Vaugn, Willis Deneale's Regt. Choctaw Warriors Co.A
Vaugtt, A.B. FL Cav. 5th Bn. Co.H
Vauguelin, Charles LA C.S. Zouave Bn. Co.A A.Cpl.
Vaules, F.T. TN 2nd Cav.
Vauley, J. AL 48th Inf. Co.K
Vault, W. VA 10th Cav. Co.E
Vaults, Augustus MS 14th Inf. Co.H
Vaultz, A. MS 14th (Cons.) Inf. Co.E
Vaulx, John W. TN 12th (Green's) Cav. Co.I
Vaulx, Joseph, Jr. TN 1st (Feild's) Inf. Co.A Capt.
Vaulx, Joseph, Jr. Cheatham's Div. Lt.Col.
Vaulx, J.W. TN 14th (Neely's) Cav. Co.D
Vaulx, W.C. TN 14th (Neely's) Cav. Co.D
Vaun, George W.W. AL 49th Inf. Co.H
Vaun, James W. AL 49th Inf. Co.H
Vaun, J.F. AL 6th Cav. Co.L
Vaun, John MO 1st N.E. Cav.
Vaun, John T. NC 2nd Cav. (19th St.Troops) Co.C
Vaun, Joseph C. AL 49th Inf. Co.H Lt.
Vaun, Richard NC Cav. 16th Bn. Co.G
Vaun, W.C.H. AL 6th Cav. Co.E
Vaun, William MS 1st (Patton's) Inf. Co.I
Vaun, W.L. AL 4th (Russell's) Cav. Co.D
Vaunasda, --- KY 7th Mtd.Inf.
Vaunghn, George W. NC 64th Inf. Co.M
Vauquehn, Charles AL 24th Inf. Co.G
Vauquehn, Henry LA Mil. 1st Regt. French Brig. Co.7
Vause, Amos R. NC 51st Inf. Co.H
Vause, Charles E. FL 9th Inf. Co.F
Vause, Edward K. NC 18th Inf. Co.C
Vause, Etheldred NC 33rd Inf. Co.K
Vause, Francis M. FL 3rd Inf. Co.D
Vause, Jacob McD. NC 51st Inf. Co.H
Vause, James SC 19th Inf. Co.E
Vause, James B. NC 32nd Inf. Lenoir Braves 1st Co.K
Vause, James W.W. FL 3rd Inf. Co.D
Vause, J.M. GA 28th Inf. Co.I
Vause, Nathan L. NC 51st Inf. Co.H
Vause, Samuel FL 9th Inf. Co.F
Vause, Samuel A. NC 18th Inf. Co.C
Vause, Thomas V. FL 7th Inf.
Vause, W.A. GA 28th Inf. Co.I
Vause, W.D. GA 28th Inf. Co.I
Vauss, L.P. TN 6th (Wheeler's) Cav. Co.F
Vausse, A.E. SC 1st Bn.S.S. Co.B
Vausse, A.E. SC 27th Inf. Co.F
Vausse, J.J. SC 1st Bn.S.S. Co.B
Vausse, J.J. SC 27th Inf. Co.F
Vaut, Henly J. VA 86th Mil. Co.B,D
Vauter, Benson GA 3rd Cav. (St.Guards) Co.H
Vauter, Jeptha KY 5th Cav. Co.H
Vauters, J.N. MS 26th Inf. Co.A
Vautier, Charles LA Pointe Coupee Arty. Cpl.
Vautier, Charles LA Arty. Watson Btty.
Vautier, D. LA Mil. 1st Chasseurs a pied Co.2

Vautier, Joseph LA Pointe Coupee Arty.
Vautier, Joseph LA Mil. 3rd Regt. 2nd Brig. 1st Div. Co.K 1st Orderly
Vautier, P. LA Mil. 4th Regt. French Brig. Co.1
Vautrin, Joseph LA C.S. Zouave Bn. Co.A Cpl.
Vaux, Robert W. SC 21st Inf. Co.A Cpl.
Vaux, R.W. SC Bn.St.Cadets Co.B
Vaux, W.P. SC Cav. Tucker's Co.
Vavasseur, Pierre LA 28th (Thomas') Inf. Co.D
Vavy, Eli Conf.Reg.Inf. Brooks' Bn. Co.D
Vaw, W.B. GA 20th Inf. Co.B
Vawell, H.L. TN 9th Inf. Co.G
Vawell, R.W. TN 9th Inf. Co.G
Vawn, J. GA 19th Inf. Co.F
Vawn, James AL 1st Inf. Co.I
Vawter, A.J. TN 19th & 20th (Cons.) Cav. Co.A
Vawter, A.J. TN 12th Inf. Co.I
Vawter, A.J. TN 12th (Cons.) Inf. Co.I
Vawter, Alex L. NC 21st Inf. Co.K
Vawter, Alpheus KY 4th Cav. Co.A
Vawter, Charles E. VA 27th Inf. Co.D Sgt.
Vawter, Charles E. VA 30th Bn.S.S. Co.D Capt.
Vawter, David M. 1st Choctaw & Chickasaw Mtd.Rifles 1st Co.K Sgt.
Vawter, D.W. TX Cav. Wells' Regt. Co.C Capt.
Vawter, James VA 11th Bn.Res. Co.C
Vawter, James E. MS 12th Inf. Co.I
Vawter, J.C. NC 57th Inf. Co.D
Vawter, John MS 2nd Cav. Co.D
Vawter, John W. VA 27th Inf. Co.D
Vawter, J.R. TX 12th Inf. Co.B
Vawter, J.W. VA 166th Mil. Co.E
Vawter, Lemuel VA 33rd Inf. Co.I
Vawter, Lewis A. VA 27th Inf. Co.D
Vawter, Lewis A. VA 30th Bn.S.S. Co.C Capt.
Vawter, M.G. VA 56th Inf. Co.I
Vawter, R.A. GA 3rd Bn.S.S. Co.F
Vawter, R.A. GA Phillips' Legion Co.M
Vawter, T.D. TN 12th (Cons.) Inf. Co.F
Vawter, T.H. TX 12th Inf. Co.B
Vawter, W.H. TN 19th & 20th (Cons.) Cav. Co.A
Vawter, William TX 12th Inf. Co.B Cpl.
Vawter, William A. Conf.Cav. 6th Bn. Co.G
Vawter, William H. KY 4th Cav. Co.A
Vawter, William J. VA 10th Inf. 1st Co.C
Vawter, W.R. TN 12th (Cons.) Inf. Co.F
Vawters, J.N. MS 32nd Inf. Co.I
Vawters, Marion TX 16th Cav. Co.I
Vawth, J.W. VA 7th Cav. Co.F
Vay, James S. LA 8th Inf. Co.A Jr.2nd Lt.
Vay, Lewis TN Arty. Fisher's Co.
Vayheo, John LA Mil. British Guard Bn. Hamilton's Co.
Vayles, Perry GA 2nd Inf. Co.A
Vayles, William C. AR 4th Inf. Co.F
Vea, William C. VA 7th Inf. Co.I
Veach,--- AL Calhoun Cty.Res. Meharge's Co.
Veach, Benjamin A. TX 30th Cav. Co.A
Veach, E. NC 7th Sr.Res. Clinard's Co.
Veach, F. NC 1st Jr.Res. Co.C
Veach, Frank GA Inf. 3rd Bn. Co.F
Veach, Franklin GA Inf. 3rd Bn. Co.F
Veach, G.W. NC 42nd Inf. Co.D
Veach, H.A. MS 9th Bn.S.S. Co.A
Veach, Jacob VA 11th Cav. Co.E
Veach, Jacob VA 136th Mil. Co.C
Veach, Jacob VA 136th Mil. Co.H
Veach, Jacob VA 146th Mil. Co.D
Veach, James L. NC 38th Inf. Co.B Drum.
Veach, James W. KY 8th Mtd.Inf. Co.A
Veach, Joseph KY 8th Cav. Co.C
Veach, Joseph KY 8th Mtd.Inf. Co.A
Veach, Joseph VA 136th Mil. Co.F
Veach, Joseph P. NC Hvy.Arty. 10th Bn. Co.A
Veach, Joseph R.P. NC Inf. 2nd Bn. Co.F 1st Sgt.
Veach, Lewis VA 33rd Inf. Co.F
Veach, Lewis T. VA Cav. 35th Bn. Co.F
Veach, McKendrie L. NC Hvy.Arty. 10th Bn. Co.A
Veach, McKindree L. NC Inf. 2nd Bn. Co.F
Veach, Samuel J. NC Hvy.Arty. 10th Bn. Co.A
Veach, Stephan AL 55th Inf. Co.D
Veach, Stephen 2nd Conf.Inf. Co.B
Veach, Stephen D. AL 27th Inf. Co.B
Veach, Thomas MO 12th Inf. Co.B
Veach, Thomas K. TN 27th Inf. Co.K
Veach, W.F. NC 1st Bn. Co.A
Veach, Will KY 8th Cav. Co.C
Veach, William D. NC 14th Inf. Co.B
Veach, William E. NC 57th Inf. Co.H
Veach, William T. TN 8th Cav. Co.B
Veahmeier, Wilhelm LA C.S. Zouave Bn. Co.D
Veal, A.J. AL 37th Inf. Drum Maj.
Veal, A.J. AL 54th Inf. Co.D Music.
Veal, A.J. GA 54th Inf. Co.C
Veal, A.J. MO Lt.Arty. Barret's Co.
Veal, A.J. TN 19th & 20th (Cons.) Cav. Co.E
Veal, A.K. GA 2nd St.Line
Veal, Alexander AL Inf. 1st Regt. Co.B Cpl.
Veal, A.L.W. TX 12th Cav. Co.K
Veal, A.M. TX Cav. 4th Regt.St.Troops Capt., AQM
Veal, Amos E. VA Inf. 28th Bn. Co.C Drum.
Veal, Andrew J. TX 19th Cav. Co.D
Veal, Asa GA Lt.Arty. 12th Bn. 3rd Co.C
Veal, Asberry P. GA 4th Res. Co.I
Veal, Augustus D. GA 21st Inf. Co.C
Veal, B. AL 59th Inf. Co.F
Veal, Benjamin AL 2nd Bn. Hilliard's Legion Vol. Co.A
Veal, Benjamin GA Lt.Arty. 14th Bn. Co.B
Veal, Benjamin F. GA Lt.Arty. Anderson's Btty.
Veal, B.F., Jr. GA Lt.Arty. 12th Bn. 3rd Co.C
Veal, B.F. GA 8th Inf. (St.Guards) Co.H
Veal, B.W. GA Lt.Arty. 12th Bn. 3rd Co.E
Veal, Carroll TX 19th Cav. Co.D
Veal, Christopher C. TX 19th Cav. Co.D
Veal, Columbus GA 2nd Res. Co.K
Veal, Dickson TX 19th Cav. Co.D
Veal, Dory KY 8th Cav. Co.A
Veal, E.B. GA 28th Inf. Co.B
Veal, Edward W. GA 42nd Inf. Co.K
Veal, E.H. AL Cav. Forrest's Regt.
Veal, E.H. TN 18th (Newsom's) Cav. Co.E
Veal, E.H. TN 19th & 20th (Cons.) Cav. Co.E
Veal, Elijah A. GA 9th Inf. (St.Guards) DeLaperriere's Co.
Veal, Francis D. AL Inf. 1st Regt. Co.C,F,G
Veal, Francis M. GA 42nd Inf. Co.F
Veal, Franklin TX 4th Inf. Co.F Music.
Veal, George TN Arty. Bibb's Co.
Veal, George H. GA 18th Inf. Co.B
Veal, George W. GA 9th Inf. (St.Guards) Co.G
Veal, George W. GA 10th Inf. Co.D
Veal, George W. GA 49th Inf. Co.C
Veal, G.P. GA 36th (Broyles') Inf. Co.K
Veal, H.B. GA 5th Inf. Co.C
Veal, H.B. GA 5th Res. Co.C
Veal, Henry TN 1st Hvy.Arty. Co.B
Veal, Henry B. GA 42nd Inf. Co.F
Veal, Henry M. GA 42nd Inf. Co.F Cpl.
Veal, Hiram TX 9th Cav. Co.G
Veal, James KY 2nd (Duke's) Cav. Co.D,A
Veal, James KY 8th Cav. Co.A
Veal, James KY 1st Bn.Mtd.Rifles Co.C
Veal, James TX 27th Cav. Co.D
Veal, James VA 5th Cav. (12 mo. '61-2) Co.A
Veal, James VA Cav. 14th Bn. Co.C
Veal, James D. KY 8th Cav. Co.A
Veal, James F. GA 24th Inf. Co.I Cpl.
Veal, Jas. H. GA Lt.Arty. Howell's Co.
Veal, James L. GA 20th Inf. Co.H
Veal, James M. GA 3rd Bn.S.S. Co.E
Veal, James M. GA 24th Inf. Co.I
Veal, James M. GA 49th Inf. Co.C Cpl.
Veal, James M. TX 35th (Brown's) Cav. Co.H
Veal, James M. TX 13th Vol. 2nd Co.A
Veal, James N. TN 39th Mtd.Inf. Co.K
Veal, James O. GA Inf. 4th Bn. (St.Guards) Co.C
Veal, James W. GA Inf. 3rd Bn. Co.E
Veal, Jarett N. 10th Conf.Cav. Co.B
Veal, Jarrett M. AL Cav. 5th Bn. Hilliard's Legion Co.B
Veal, J.E. GA Floyd Legion (St.Guards) Co.I Cpl.
Veal, J.E. VA 3rd Cav. Co.D
Veal, J.H. GA Lt.Arty. Howell's Co.
Veal, J.L. GA 56th Inf. Co.B
Veal, J.M. GA 15th Inf. Co.A Sgt.
Veal, J.M. SC 1st Inf. Co.A
Veal, J.M. SC 7th Regt.Eng. Co.B
Veal, J.O. GA 37th Inf. Co.F
Veal, John AL Randolph Cty.Res. J. Hightower's Co.
Veal, John GA Inf. Arsenal Bn. (Columbus)
Veal, John KY 2nd (Duke's) Cav. Co.D
Veal, John KY 8th Cav. Co.A
Veal, John VA 8th Inf. Co.H
Veal, John C. TX 1st Inf. Co.A
Veal, John M. GA Inf. Taylor's Co. Cpl.
Veal, John Malcomb SC 15th Inf. Co.A Sgt.
Veal, John O. GA 54th Inf. Co.H
Veal, John W. AL Cav. Forrest's Regt.
Veal, John W. GA 36th (Broyles') Inf. Co.K
Veal, John W. KY 8th Cav. Co.A
Veal, Joseph GA 21st Inf. Co.C
Veal, Joseph GA 30th Inf. Co.B
Veal, Joseph T. NC Lt.Arty. 3rd Bn. Co.C
Veal, J.T. GA 18th Inf. Co.B
Veal, J.T. TX Inf. 3rd St.Troops Col.
Veal, J.W. GA Lt.Arty. Howell's Co.
Veal, J.W. TN 18th (Newsom's) Cav. Co.E
Veal, L.C. GA Arty. Lumpkin's Co.
Veal, Levi E. GA 49th Inf. Co.A 1st Lt.
Veal, Littleton GA Inf. 10th Bn. Co.E
Veal, Marquis D.L. GA 3rd Inf. Co.L
Veal, M.D.L. GA 66th Inf. Co.K Cpl.

Veal, Milton KY 8th Cav. Co.A
Veal, Minton G. GA 42nd Inf. Co.F
Veal, Moses TN 39th Mtd.Inf. Co.K
Veal, Newton KY 8th Cav. Co.A
Veal, Reuben H. GA 1st (Ramsey's) Inf. Co.E
Veal, Reuben H. GA 2nd St.Line Co.H
Veal, Richard R. TX Cav. Mann's Regt. Co.A
Veal, Richard R. TX Cav. Mann's Bn. Co.A
Veal, Rufus GA Inf. 10th Bn. Co.D
Veal, Rufus T. TX 27th Cav. Co.D
Veal, Thomas KY 10th (Johnson's) Cav. Co.K
Veal, Thomas TX 19th Inf. Co.D
Veal, Thomas C. SC Arty.Bn. Hampton Legion Co.A Sgt.
Veal, Thomas C. 2nd Conf.Eng.Troops Co.F 1st Lt.
Veal, Thomas J. VA 5th Cav. (12 mo. '61-2) Co.I
Veal, Thomas J. VA Cav. 14th Bn. Co.B
Veal, T.J. GA Arty. (Chatham Arty.) Wheaton's Co.
Veal, T.J. GA 1st (Olmstead's) Inf. Claghorn's Co.
Veal, T.J. GA 48th Inf. Co.E
Veal, T.N. SC 1st Bn.S.S. Co.A
Veal, Uriah W. GA 49th Inf. Co.C
Veal, U.W. GA 6th Inf. (St.Guards) Co.G
Veal, Warren KY 8th Cav. Co.A
Veal, W.H. GA Lt.Arty. Howell's Co.
Veal, W.H. 10th Conf.Cav. Co.A
Veal, William GA 48th Inf. Co.E
Veal, William G. TX 12th Cav. Co.F Capt.
Veal, William H. AL Cav. 5th Bn. Hilliard's Legion Co.A
Veal, William H. GA 21st Inf. Co.C
Veal, William H. GA 65th Inf. Co.F
Veal, William J. GA 36th (Broyles') Inf. Co.K
Veal, William M. GA 6th Inf. (St.Guards) Co.G Cpl.
Veal, W.R. SC 7th Cav. Co.K
Veale, Amos E. VA 59th Inf. 2nd Co.H Drum.
Veale, Dixon TX 12th Cav. Co.A
Veale, James E. VA 3rd Inf. Co.H
Veale, J.H. LA 3rd Inf. Co.H
Veale, John H. LA 2nd Inf. Co.F Cpl.
Veale, Mathew TX 7th Field Btty. Cpl.
Veale, Samuel VA Lt.Arty. Grandy's Co.
Veale, Samuel VA 6th Inf. Vickery's Co.
Veale, Samuel VA 16th Inf. 1st Co.H
Veale, Thomas G. TN Lt.Arty. Burroughs' Co. Cpl.
Veale, Thomas J. VA 15th Cav. Co.I
Veale, William TX 13th Vol. 1st Co.I, Co.E
Vean, Alfred SC Arty. Manigault's Bn. 1st Co.B Cpl.
Veanhoy, Calvin NC 29th Inf. Co.F
Vease, --- TX 2nd Cav. Co.G
Veaser, Francis VA Bushwhacker
Veasey, A.J. AL Conscr.
Veasey, A.J. AR 11th Inf. Co.A
Veasey, A.J. AR 11th & 17th (Cons.) Inf. Co.A
Veasey, Benjamin F. GA 2nd Cav. Co.A
Veasey, Elijah NC 23rd Inf. Co.E
Veasey, George W. AL 3rd Bn.Res. Co.B
Veasey, G.E.B. AR 1st (Monroe's) Cav. Co.B
Veasey, Henry L. AR 1st (Colquitt's) Inf. Co.I Cpl.
Veasey, Jas. M. AL 34th Inf. Co.G
Veasey, James T. AL 61st Inf. Co.B
Veasey, J.M. AR 15th Mil. Co.C
Veasey, J.M. 8th (Wade's) Conf.Cav. Co.I Sgt.
Veasey, John NC 23rd Inf. Co.E
Veasey, Leonidas S. AR 3rd Inf. Co.C
Veasey, Simon C. AL 63rd Inf. Co.A
Veasey, T.C. MS 8th Cav. Co.F
Veasey, Thomas AR 24th Inf. Co.D
Veasey, Wesley T. GA 7th Inf. (St.Guards) Co.I
Veasey, William J. AL 3rd Inf. Co.C
Veasey, William T. AL 3rd Inf. Co.L
Veasey, Y.S. 4th Conf.Eng.Troops Artif.
Veassey, Francis M. GA Cav. 1st Bn.Res. McKinney's Co.
Veasy, S.M. AL 3rd Inf. Co.C
Veatch, Franklin GA 54th Inf. Co.H
Veatch, Fredrick W. MS 22nd Inf. Co.F
Veatch, Fred W. MS 9th Inf. Old Co.I
Veatch, Henry A. MS 9th Inf. Old Co.I
Veatch, I. LA 4th Cav. Co.B
Veatch, Jacob KY 1st Inf. Co.E
Veatch, J.G. MS 9th Inf. Old Co.I
Veatch, John KY 2nd Mtd.Inf. Co.I
Veatch, John MS 18th Cav. Co.F
Veatch, John G. MS 22nd Inf. Co.A,F
Veatch, J.R. KY 12th Cav. Co.I
Veatch, S.H. TX 11th Inf. Co.F
Veator, Edward LA Inf.Cons. 18th Regt. & Yellow Jacket Bn. Co.A
Veau, A. LA Lt.Arty. Bridges' Btty. Cpl.
Veau, Alfred LA Mil. Chalmette Regt. Co.I 1st Lt.
Veau, F. LA 22nd Inf. Co.C,E
Veau, F. LA 22nd (Cons.) Inf. Co.E
Veau, Th. LA Mil. Orleans Guards Regt. Co.E
Veazey, Alcibiade LA 8th Inf. Co.C Cpl.
Veazey, Alcide LA 8th Inf. Co.C
Veazey, Alfred LA 8th Inf. Co.C Sgt.
Veazey, Azenor LA Conscr.
Veazey, Ben NC 55th Inf. Co.K
Veazey, Benjamin NC 3rd Bn.Sr.Res. Durham's Co.
Veazey, B.F. MS 5th Cav. Co.K
Veazey, B.F. MS 18th Cav. Co.G
Veazey, E.F. MS 5th Cav. Co.K Sgt.
Veazey, E.F. MS 18th Cav. Co.G Sgt.
Veazey, Ezekiel MS 30th Inf. Co.D Cpl.
Veazey, F. LA Inf. 10th Bn. Co.B
Veazey, Fieldin L. NC 6th Inf. Co.B
Veazey, Franklin GA 3rd Inf. Co.C
Veazey, Henry C. AL 14th Inf. Co.G 1st Lt.
Veazey, Henry Y. AL 34th Inf. Co.G Sgt.
Veazey, Isaac NC 23rd Inf. Co.E
Veazey, James J. MS 4th Inf. Co.B
Veazey, J.C. MS 18th Cav. Co.G
Veazey, J.F. TN 5th Inf. 1st Co.H,F
Veazey, J.H. MS Lt.Arty. Lomax's Co.
Veazey, J.H. NC Lt.Arty. 13th Bn. Co.E
Veazey, J.J. AL 12th Inf. Co.B
Veazey, J.M. AL 51st (Part.Rangers) Co.I Sgt.
Veazey, John C. TX 7th Field Btty. Artif.
Veazey, John W. TX 35th (Brown's) Cav. Co.C Capt.
Veazey, John W. TX 13th Vol. 1st Co.H Capt.
Veazey, Littleton M. AR 18th Inf. Co.H
Veazey, M.W.B. NC Lt.Arty. 13th Bn. Co.E
Veazey, N. KY 10th (Johnson's) Cav. Co.A
Veazey, Prior G. GA 15th Inf. Co.D 1st Lt.
Veazey, Robert AR 7th Cav. Co.D 1st Sgt.
Veazey, S.H. AL 12th Inf. Co.B
Veazey, Simeon KY 8th Mtd.Inf. Co.A
Veazey, Stiles TX 20th Inf. Co.C
Veazey, T.C. GA 3rd Inf. Co.C
Veazey, Theodore LA Inf. 10th Bn.
Veazey, Thomas J. 7th Conf.Cav. Co.E 1st Sgt.
Veazey, W.A. AL 2nd Cav. Co.G
Veazey, W.C. MS Lt.Arty. Lomax's Co. Sgt.
Veazey, W.C. MS 1st (King's) Inf. (St.Troops) Co.H Sgt.
Veazey, William TX 2nd Inf. Co.D
Veazey, William E. NC 6th Inf. Co.B
Veazey, William H. NC 55th Inf. Co.K
Veazey, William J., Jr. MS 9th Inf. New Co.I
Veazey, William J., Sr. MS 9th Inf. Old Co.I
Veazey, William J. MS 42nd Inf. Co.B
Veazey, William J. Conf.Cav. Wood's Regt. 2nd Co.G Cpl.
Veazey, W.L. AR 5th Inf. Co.F Sgt.
Veazey, Y.S. TX 20th Inf. Co.C Cpl.
Veazez, J. Adolphe LA Conscr.
Veazie, Simeon AR 1st Colquitt's Inf. Co.D
Veazie, W.J. AL 61st Inf. Co.B
Veazsy, J.E. KY 8th Cav. Co.B
Veazy, E. NC 1st Jr.Res. Co.B
Veazy, James LA 31st Inf. Co.E
Veazy, James W. AL 47th Inf. Co.H
Veazy, Jesse H. AL 42nd Inf. Co.E
Veazy, John T.J. AL 57th Inf. Co.C
Veazy, Robert AR Inf. Cocke's Regt. Co.B 1st Lt.
Veazy, S.J. LA 17th Inf. Co.I
Vecner, E.T. MS 12th Cav. Co.C
Vecque, Jules LA C.S. Zouave Bn. Co.B,A 1st Lt.
Vedan, J. SC Mil. 1st Regt. (Charleston Res.) Co.B
Vedder, Albert LA 1st (Strawbridge's) Inf. Co.H
Vedoni, Antoni TX Cav. Benavides' Regt. Co.I Jr.2nd Lt.
Vedot, --- LA Mil. 3rd Regt.Eur.Brig. (Garde Francaise) Co.5
Vedrine, Adolphe LA Miles' Legion Co.H
Vedrines, Henry LA Conscr.
Vedroz, Antoine LA 18th Inf. Co.G
Vedsey, W.C. AL Coosa Guards J.W. Suttles' Co. Sgt.
Veece, J.L.C. TN 44th (Cons.) Inf.
Veech, Joseph TN Cav. 5th Bn. (McClellan's) Co.F
Veech, Moses B. TX 9th (Young's) Inf. Co.B
Veech, Stephen MS 25th Inf. Co.B
Veech, William TX 19th Cav. Co.E
Veers, Charles O. VA Lt.Arty. Arch. Graham's Co.
Vegas, H.C. LA 28th (Gray's) Inf. Co.H
Vegas, John LA Mil. 5th Regt.Eur.Brig. (Spanish Regt.) Co.5
Vegas, P.A. LA 28th (Thomas') Inf. Co.H
Vegas, Paul Gen. & Staff, Ord.Dept.
Vegas, Salvador LA Mil. 5th Regt.Eur.Brig. (Spanish Regt.) Co.6
Vego, J. LA Mil. Chalmette Regt. Co.B
Vegua, C. LA Mil. 1st Native Guards

Vehann, J.L. SC 16th Inf. Co.D
Vehnencamp, Frederick VA 136th Mil. Co.F
Vehon, Thos. A. SC 13th Inf. Co.F
Vehoon, William L. SC 2nd Rifles Co.F
Vehorn, Elias SC 13th Inf. Co.F
Vehorn, W.J. SC 3rd Inf. Co.K
Veich, J.C. GA Inf. 18th Bn. Co.A
Veick, Ransom NC Inf. 10th Bn. Co.B
Veiden, Allen SC 1st St.Troops Co.K
Veigas, Juan TX Cav. Ragsdale's Bn. Co.D
Veigel, T. LA Mil. 3rd Regt. 3rd Brig. 1st Div. Co.G
Veigeld, Edgar M. VA Cav. 35th Bn. Co.F
Veigele, William LA Mil. 4th Regt.Eur.Brig. Co.B
Veigham, D. VA 5th Cav. Co.C
Veigham, J. GA 45th Inf. Co.H
Veil, Benjamin LA Pointe Coupee Arty.
Veil, J. MO 1st N.E. Cav. Co.G
Veil, L. MO 1st N.E. Cav. Co.G
Veil, Thomas GA 60th Inf. Co.I Cpl.
Veil, Thomas MO 1st N.E. Cav. Co.G
Veil, Thomas G. TN 34th Inf. 1st Co.C Cpl.
Veill, B. GA 5th Res. Co.E
Veill, F. LA Mil. 4th Regt. French Brig. Co.3
Veille, John LA 30th Inf. Co.C
Veillere, M. LA Mil. Mtd.Rangers Plaquemines
Veillion, A. LA 30th Inf. Co.A
Veillon, E. LA Mil. Chalmette Regt. Co.K
Veillon, John Bpte. LA 16th Inf. Co.K
Veillon, Onezime, Jr. LA 16th Inf. Co.K
Veillon, P. LA Mil. Chalmette Regt. Co.K
Veillon, Vallerien LA 2nd Res.Corps Co.I
Veillon, Vallery LA Mil. Orleans Arty.
Veilton, I.B. LA Mil. Chalmette Regt. Co.F
Veinstal, Valentine LA 11th Inf. Co.F
Veirs, Charles O. VA 11th Cav. Co.E
Veirs, Elijah VA Cav. 35th Bn. Co.B
Veirs, Elijah VA Cav. 41st Bn. Co.B
Veirs, Henry VA Cav. 41st Bn. Co.D
Veirs, Henry B. VA Cav. 35th Bn. Co.B
Veirs, Hezakiah VA Cav. 35th Bn. Co.D
Veirs, H.W. VA Cav. 35th Bn. Co.D
Veirs, William S. VA Cav. 35th Bn. Co.B
Veiss, H.B. VA Cav. 35th Bn. Co.B
Veit, Johnie GA 1st Reg. Music.
Veit, Maurice LA 20th Inf. Co.F, Old Co.B
Veitch, Daniel MO Inf. 6th Regt.St.Guard Maj.
Veitch, E.W. AL Gid Nelson Lt.Arty.
Veitch, George TN Inf. 154th Sr.Regt.
Veitch, George E. AL Gid Nelson Lt.Arty. Cpl.
Veitch, George W. VA 6th Cav. Co.F 1st Lt.
Veitch, H.F. SC Arty. Stuart's Co. (Beaufort Vol.Arty.)
Veitch, H.F. SC 11th Inf. Co.A
Veitch, Isaac A. VA 6th Cav. Co.F
Veitch, J.C. GA 1st (Olmstead's) Inf. Screven's Co.
Veitch, J.L. TX 4th Cav. Co.K
Veitch, John AL Gid Nelson Lt.Arty.
Veitch, John C. SC 1st (McCreary's) Inf. Co.H
Veitch, J.W. TX 4th Cav. Co.K
Veitch, Richard A. VA 6th Cav. Co.F
Veitch, W.A. TX 4th Cav. Co.K
Veitch, William AL Gid Nelson Lt.Arty.
Veitch, William MS Loundes Cty.Res.
Veith, Ignatz VA 54th Mil. Co.E,F
Veitz, Frank LA 10th Inf. Co.F
Vela, Cristian LA Mil. 5th Regt.Eur.Brig. (Spanish Regt.) Co.3
Vela, Christiano LA Mil. Cazadores Espanoles Regt. Co.5
Vela, Domingo TX 33rd Cav. 1st Co.H
Vela, Jose LA Mil. Cazadores Espanoles Regt. Co.5 Sgt.
Vela, Juan TX Cav. 3rd (Yager's) Bn. Co.A
Veland, Anto LA Mil. Chalmette Regt. Co.G
Velasco, F. LA Mil. 5th Regt.Eur.Brig. (Spanish Regt.) Co.1 Sgt.
Velasco, Faustino LA Mil. 5th Regt.Eur.Brig. (Spanish Regt.) Co.10
Velasques, Jose Maria TX 3rd Inf. 1st Co.C
Velasquez, Antonio TX 3rd Inf. Co.F
Velasquez, P. LA Mil. 1st Chasseurs a pied Co.7
Velati, A. GA 5th Inf. (St.Guards) Everitt's Co.
Velati, A. GA Inf. (GA Defend.) Chapman's Co.
Velazco, Tomas LA Mil. 5th Regt.Eur.Brig. (Spanish Regt.) Co.2
Velker, C. Gen. & Staff, QM Dept.
Vella, Eduardo LA Mil. Cazadores Espanoles Regt. Co.5
Vella, Jose LA Mil. Cazadores Espanoles Regt. Co.5
Vellarial, Recente TX 8th Inf. Co.I
Vellarreal, Cesilio TX Cav. Benavides' Regt. Co.A
Vellastrigo, Jomas TX Cav. Benavides' Regt. Co.A
Vellereau, C. LA Mil. 1st Regt. French Brig. Co.C
Vellines, Flavius L. VA 5th Cav. (12 mo. '61-2) Co.C Sgt.
Vellines, Flavius L. VA 13th Cav. Co.H
Vellines, Isaac VA 9th Inf. Co.E
Vellines, John A. VA Hvy.Arty. 18th Bn. Co.B Cpl.
Vellines, John A. VA 3rd Inf. 2nd Co.I
Vellines, John E.H. VA 3rd Inf. 2nd Co.I
Vellines, Junius VA Hvy.Arty. 19th Bn. Co.A
Vellines, Marsden J. VA 9th Inf. Co.E Sgt.
Vellines, Patrick H. VA 13th Cav. Co.H
Vellines, Peter H. VA 5th Cav. (12 mo. '61-2) Co.C
Vellines, Thomas R. VA 3rd Inf. 2nd Co.I
Vellines, William E. VA 3rd Inf. 2nd Co.I Sgt.
Velmor, Charles LA 22nd Inf. Wash. Marks' Co.
Velp, Bernard LA Mil. 4th Regt. 1st Brig. 1st Div. Co.I
Velrin, S.S. GA 10th Cav. (St.Guards) Co.D
Velshaw, Fred TX 16th Inf. Co.B
Velt, --- LA Mil. 1st Chasseurs a pied Co.1
Velten, W. TX 3rd Inf. Co.B
Veltfort, Richard LA 16th Inf. Co.F Cpl.
Veltmann, Henry TX Res.Corps Co.A
Velton, --- TX Lt.Arty. Dege's Bn.
Velton, Michael TX 8th Field Btty.
Velvin, Andrew C. GA 1st Cav. Co.E 1st Lt.
Velvin, Andrew C. GA 7th Inf. Co.F
Velvin, J.H. GA 19th Inf. Band Music.
Velvin, J.J. GA 56th Inf. Co.I
Velvin, Robert J. VA 41st Inf. Co.H
Velvin, Robert J. 7th Conf.Cav. Co.B,L
Velvin, Sidney S. GA 3rd Cav. Co.B,E
Velvin, William H. VA 41st Inf. Co.H
Venable, A. GA 4th Cav. (St.Guards) Deadwyler's Co.
Venable, A. GA Arty. Lumpkin's Co.
Venable, A. VA Cav. 32nd Bn. Co.B
Venable, A.A. AL 5th Cav. Co.E
Venable, Abraham B. VA 18th Inf. Co.F,D 2nd Lt.
Venable, Abrm. G. MO Searcy's Bn.S.S. Co.C Cpl.
Venable, A.K. VA 2nd Arty. Co.H
Venable, A.K. VA 5th Bn.Res. Co.H Cpl.
Venable, A.K. VA Inf. 22nd Bn. Co.H
Venable, A.L. AL 51st (Part.Rangers) Co.H
Venable, Alfred MO Robertson's Regt.St.Guard Co.1
Venable, Allen NC 21st Inf. Co.H
Venable, Ananias A. AR 15th (Josey's) Inf. Co.C
Venable, Andrew J. AL 9th Inf. Co.F
Venable, Andrew M. VA 64th Mtd.Inf. Co.B
Venable, Andrew R. VA 1st Arty. Co.D Capt.,ACS
Venable, Andrew R. VA Capt.,AQM
Venable, Andrew R. Gen. & Staff Maj.,AIG
Venable, A.R. VA 3rd Cav. Co.K
Venable, Archibald GA Conscr.
Venable, Augustus N. VA 24th Cav. Co.H
Venable, A.V. AL 7th Inf. Co.D
Venable, Benjamin W. MO Searcy's Bn.S.S. Co.C
Venable, B.F. GA Inf. 23rd Bn.Loc.Def. Cook's Co.
Venable, Burton VA 48th Inf. Co.G
Venable, B.W. MO Robertson's Regt.St.Guard Co.7
Venable, C.D. TN 5th Inf. Col.
Venable, Charles GA 13th Cav. Co.I
Venable, Charles GA 41st Inf. Co.A
Venable, Charles S. Gen. & Staff, A. of N.VA Lt.Col.,AAG
Venable, Charles W. VA 3rd Cav. Co.K
Venable, Clemant R. 1st Conf.Eng.Troops Co.H 2nd Lt.
Venable, Clement R. VA 23rd Inf. Co.I Sgt.
Venable, C.W. GA 1st Cav. Co.I
Venable, C.W. VA 8th Cav. Co.A 1st Sgt.
Venable, C.W. Gen. & Staff Capt.,Asst.Comsy.
Venable, David VA 48th Inf. Co.F
Venable, D.C. GA 2nd Res. Co.A
Venable, Drury W. VA 4th Inf. Co.D
Venable, E.K. AL 18th Bn.Vol. Co.A
Venable, Elijah GA 7th Inf. (St.Guards) Co.H
Venable, George P. MO Inf. 6th Regt.St.Guard Co.A 2nd Lt.
Venable, George S. VA Inf. 23rd Bn. Co.F
Venable, George W. AR 36th Inf. Co.F 1st Sgt.
Venable, Gideon VA Cav. 47th Bn. Co.C
Venable, G.M. GA 5th Inf. (St.Guards) Russell's Co.
Venable, Goodrich W. VA Arty. Dance's Co.
Venable, G.S. VA Lt.Arty. King's Co. Cpl.
Venable, G.W. AR 10th (Witt's) Cav. Co.A
Venable, G.W. LA Arty. Watson Btty.
Venable, H.A. Gen. & Staff AASurg.
Venable, Henry VA 23rd Inf. Co.I Sgt.
Venable, Henry D. VA Conscr.
Venable, Hugh TX 3rd Cav. Co.K

Venable, Hugh L. VA 3rd Lt.Arty. (Loc.Def.) Co.C
Venable, Iredell A. NC 2nd Detailed Men Co.C Capt.
Venable, Isaac VA Inf. 21st Bn. 1st Co.D
Venable, Isaac VA 64th Mtd.Inf. Co.C
Venable, Isaac H. AL 6th Inf. Co.K
Venable, Isaac M. NC Inf. Thomas Legion Co.I
Venable, J. NC 18th Inf. Co.I
Venable, J. VA Cav. 40th Bn. Co.E
Venable, James AL 50th Inf. Co.E
Venable, James NC 22nd Inf. Co.I
Venable, James VA 8th Cav. Co.G
Venable, James VA 23rd Cav. Co.D
Venable, James VA Horse Arty. J.W. Carter's Co.
Venable, James C. AL 22nd Inf. Co.H
Venable, James C. AL City Guards Lockett's Co. Sgt.
Venable, James C. AL Cp. of Instr. Talladega
Venable, James E. GA 61st Inf. Co.I
Venable, James H. AR 19th (Dawson's) Inf. Co.F Sgt.
Venable, James H. MO Inf. 4th Regt.St.Guard Co.G 3rd Lt.
Venable, James J. AL 4th Inf. Co.I
Venable, James L. TN 46th Inf. Co.A
Venable, James M. MS 9th Inf. New Co.C
Venable, James M. TN 5th Inf. 2nd Co.G
Venable, James M. VA 12th Inf. Co.E
Venable, James P. AR 8th Cav. Co.E
Venable, James T. VA 17th Inf. Co.B
Venable, James T. VA 51st Mil. Co.A
Venable, James W. VA Cav. O'Ferrall's Bn. Co.B
Venable, James W. VA 22nd Inf. Swann's Co.
Venable, James W. VA 59th Inf. 2nd Co.K
Venable, Jasper AL 4th (Russell's) Cav. Co.I
Venable, J.B. TN 46th Inf. Co.D Cpl.
Venable, J.C. GA Cobb's Legion Co.D
Venable, J.C. 1st Chickasaw Inf. Hansell's Co.
Venable, J.E. VA Cav. 32nd Bn. Co.B
Venable, Jesse E. VA 24th Cav. Co.H Cpl.
Venable, J.F. MO 3rd Inf. Co.I
Venable, J.M. MO 2nd Inf. Co.D
Venable, J.M. TN 46th Inf. Co.A
Venable, John AL 5th Cav. Co.E
Venable, John TN 5th Inf. 2nd Co.G
Venable, John VA Inf. 21st Bn. 2nd Co.C 3rd Lt.
Venable, John VA 48th Inf. Co.B 1st Lt.
Venable, John VA 64th Mtd.Inf. Co.C 2nd Lt.
Venable, John A. GA 43rd Inf. Co.H
Venable, John B. AL 18th Inf. Co.L
Venable, John B. TN 46th Inf. Co.A
Venable, John M. GA 16th Inf. Co.B Capt.
Venable, John M. VA 21st Inf. Co.K 1st Lt.
Venable, John T. NC 21st Inf. Co.F
Venable, John W. MO Searcy's Bn.S.S. Co.C Sgt.
Venable, Joseph AL 8th Inf.
Venable, Joseph AL 9th Inf. Co.F
Venable, Joseph LA 2nd Cav. Co.A
Venable, Joseph NC 22nd Inf. Co.I
Venable, Joseph NC 28th Inf. Co.A
Venable, Joseph H. AR 15th (N.W.) Inf. Co.C Sgt.
Venable, Joseph J. VA Inf. 23rd Bn. Co.F
Venable, Joseph L. VA Inf. 21st Bn. Co.B
Venable, Joseph L. VA 64th Mtd.Inf. Co.K
Venable, Joseph P. VA 41st Inf. 2nd Co.E
Venable, Joseph S. TN 5th Inf. 2nd Co.G
Venable, Joseph T. TN Cav. 16th Bn. (Neal's) Co.F
Venable, Joshua NC 28th Inf. Co.A
Venable, J.P. AR 10th (Witt's) Cav. Co.I
Venable, J.P. AR 10th Inf. Co.B Capt.
Venable, J.P. GA 1st Cav. Co.G,I
Venable, J.R. KY 6th Mtd.Inf. Co.I
Venable, L.B. TX Cav. Bourland's Regt. Co.H Sgt.
Venable, Lewis R. TN 28th Cav. Co.I
Venable, L.R. AR 8th Cav. Co.A Capt.
Venable, L.R. AR 10th Inf. Lt.Col.
Venable, Mathews W. 1st Conf.Eng.Troops Co.H Cpl.
Venable, McDowell R. VA 1st Arty. Co.D
Venable, McDowell R. VA Lt.Arty. Pegram's Co. Sgt.
Venable, M.P. VA 21st Cav. 2nd Co.E
Venable, N. Gen. & Staff Surg.
Venable, Nathaniel E. VA 23rd Inf. Co.I 1st Sgt.
Venable, Nathaniel J. AL 19th Inf. Co.K 2nd Lt.
Venable, N.E. VA Inf. 25th Bn. Co.D Cpl.
Venable, Oliver AL Cp. of Instr. Talladega
Venable, Oscar NC 21st Inf. Co.C
Venable, Paul C. VA 18th Inf. Co.F,D Ord.Sgt.
Venable, Paul C. Cav. Butler's Div. Capt.,Ord.Ch.
Venable, Peyton S. KY Cav. Buckner Guards
Venable, Pittman R. VA Inf. 22nd Bn. Co.E Cpl.
Venable, Pleasant NC 23rd Inf. Co.F,H
Venable, P.S. KY 1st (Helm's) Cav. New Co.G
Venable, Puttman R. VA 2nd Arty. Co.E Cpl.
Venable, Randolph M. MO 12th Cav. Co.H 2nd Lt.
Venable, R.B. AR 19th (Dawson's) Inf. Co.F Sgt.
Venable, R.H. AL 29th Inf. Co.A
Venable, Rial NC 21st Inf. Co.K
Venable, Richard C. GA 2nd Res. Co.A
Venable, Richard J. VA 6th Bn.Res. Co.D
Venable, Richard M. VA 1st Arty. Co.D Cpl.
Venable, Richd. M. Eng.,CSA Maj.
Venable, Richard M. Gen. & Staff 1st Lt.,Adj.
Venable, Richard W. GA 40th Inf. Co.H 1st Sgt.
Venable, R.M. 4th Conf.Eng.Troops Co.C Capt.
Venable, R.N. MS 26th Inf. Surg.
Venable, R.N. MS 27th Inf. Asst.Surg.
Venable, Robert SC 5th Inf. 1st Co.B
Venable, Samuel MO Searcy's Bn.S.S. Co.C
Venable, Silas NC 48th Inf. Co.K
Venable, S.W. VA 13th Cav. Co.E 1st Lt.
Venable, S.W. Johnson's A. Capt.,AQM
Venable, T. AL 35th Inf. Co.G
Venable, T.A.P. AR 10th Inf. Co.I Capt.
Venable, T.B. Lee's Corps Maj.,AAG
Venable, Thomas MO 9th Inf. Co.H
Venable, Thomas VA 22nd Cav. Co.E
Venable, Thomas VA Lt.Arty. Ellett's Co.
Venable, Thomas A. KY 8th Cav. Co.F Cpl.
Venable, Thomas B. NC 24th Inf. Lt.Col.
Venable, T.J. VA 3rd Res. Co.H
Venable, T.W. GA 1st Cav. Co.G,I
Venable, W.G. AL 29th Inf. Co.A Jr.2nd Lt.
Venable, W.G. Nitre & Min. Bureau War Dept.,CSA
Venable, W.H. KY 6th Mtd.Inf. Co.I
Venable, William AR 10th Inf. Sgt.Maj.
Venable, William NC 21st Inf. Co.H
Venable, William TX 26th Cav. Co.D
Venable, William VA 22nd Cav. Co.E
Venable, William VA Mil. Washington Cty.
Venable, William G. AL 35th Inf. Co.G
Venable, William G. VA 18th Inf. Co.F
Venable, William H. VA Inf. 5th Bn. Co.A
Venable, William J. TX 6th Cav. Co.H
Venable, William L. AR 1st (Crawford's) Cav. Co.D
Venable, William L. MO Searcy's Bn.S.S. Co.C
Venable, William L. TX 6th Inf. Co.H
Venable, William M. VA 29th Inf. 2nd Co.F
Venable, William R. MO Searcy's Bn.S.S. Co.C
Venable, Willis E. GA Arty. 9th Bn. Co.D
Venable, W.L. VA Corps Cadets VMI
Venable, Woodson Gen. & Staff, QM Dept. Capt.
Venable, W.T. AL 55th Vol. Co.E 1st Sgt.
Venable, W.T. TN 42nd Inf. 1st Co.K
Venables, John W. LA 16th Inf. Co.F
Venables, N. AL Lt.Arty. Phelan's Co. 2nd Lt.
Venables, N. AL 5th Inf. Co.H Surg.
Venables, Richard S. LA Inf.Crescent Regt. Co.D Capt.
Venables, W.L. TX 28th Cav. Co.B
Venatler, Irvine A. VA Inf. 45th Bn. Co.F Sgt.
Vencen, Eli LA 26th Inf. Co.H
Vencent, A. LA 7th Cav. Co.F
Vencent, D. LA Inf.Cons.Crescent Regt. Co.P
Vencher, J.L. AL 12th Inf. Co.C Lt.
Vencill, George VA Cav. McFarlane's Co.
Vencill, George VA 72nd Mil.
Vencill, Henry VA 72nd Mil.
Vencill, John VA Cav. McFarlane's Co. Sgt.
Vencill, John VA Cav. McFarlane's Co.
Vencill, John VA 72nd Mil.
Vencill, John Conf.Cav. 6th Bn. 1st Sgt.
Vencill, Meshech VA 72nd Mil.
Vencill, Meshick VA Cav. McFarlane's Co.
Vencill, T.D. VA 72nd Mil.
Vencill, William VA Cav. McFarlane's Co. Sgt.
Vencill, William VA Cav. McFarlane's Co.
Vencill, William VA 72nd Mil.
Vencill, William, Jr. VA 72nd Mil.
Vencill, William Conf.Cav. 6th Bn. Sgt.
Vendeford, R.A. GA 16th Inf. Co.B
Venderholder, George KY 1st (Butler's) Cav. Co.H
Venderholder, Lewis KY 1st (Butler's) Cav. Co.H
Vendig, D. TN 9th Inf. Co.C
Vendling, --- LA Mil. 1st Regt. French Brig. Co.5
Vendling, G. LA Mil. 1st Regt. French Brig. Co.5
Vendling, J. LA Mil. 1st Regt. French Brig. Co.5
Vendrick, John FL 6th Inf. Co.A
Vendrick, John NC 7th Inf. Co.C

Vendrick, John A. NC 27th Inf. Co.H Cpl.
Vendrick, Nathan FL 6th Inf. Co.A
Vendrick, W.F. NC 27th Inf. Co.H Sgt.
Vendrick, W.N. FL Cav. 5th Bn. Co.B
Veneble, Isaac NC 1st Inf. Co.I
Veneble, William VA 63rd Inf. Co.F
Venell, Peter VA 2nd Inf.Loc.Def. Co.C
Venerable, A.L. AR 1st (Dobbin's) Cav.
Venerable, A.Y. TN 31st Inf. Co.G
Venerable, Eli MO 4th Inf. Co.D
Venerable, James TN 20th (Russell's) Cav. Co.F
Venerable, John TN 60th Mtd.Inf. Co.B
Venerable, John W. VA 20th Inf. Co.D
Venerable, Joseph AR 2nd Mtd.Rifles Co.I
Venerable, Joseph LA Mtd.Part.Rangers Bond's Co.
Venerable, Joseph T. VA 48th Inf. Co.A
Venn, Albert LA 1st Hvy.Arty. (Reg.) Co.D
Venn, Frank H. MS 17th Inf. Co.B
Venn, Frank H. MS 19th Inf. Co.I Sgt.
Vennard, G. LA 18th Inf. Co.K
Vennard, George H. LA Inf. Crescent Regt. Co.B N.C.S. Sgt.Maj.
Vennard, G.H. LA Inf.Cons.Crescent Regt. Co.C
Venne, U. SC Mil. 1st Regt. (Charleston Res.) Co.D
Vennette, D. LA Mil. Chalmette Regt. Co.E
Venney, Felix V. AR 35th Inf. Co.B
Venning, David B. SC 5th Cav. Co.E
Venning, D.B. SC 2nd Cav. Co.B
Venning, D.B. SC 10th Inf. 1st Co.G Sgt.
Venning, D.B. SC 20th Inf. Co.O Sgt.
Venning, D.B. SC Manigault's Bn.Vol. Co.C
Venning, E. SC 10th Inf. 1st Co.G
Venning, Elias SC 2nd Cav. Co.B
Venning, Elias SC 5th Cav. Co.E 1st Lt.
Venning, Elias SC 20th Inf. Co.O Capt.
Venning, Elias SC Manigault's Bn.Vol. Co.A 1st Lt.
Venning, John SC Lt.Arty. Gaillard's Co. (Santee Lt.Arty.) 1st Lt.
Venning, John SC 10th Inf. 1st Co.G 2nd Lt.
Venning, John SC Manigault's Bn.Vol. Co.B 1st Lt.
Venning, N.B. SC 5th Cav. Co.E Cpl.
Venning, N.B. SC 10th Inf. 1st Co.G 1st Sgt.
Venning, N.B. SC Manigault's Bn.Vol. Co.C Cpl.
Venning, Robert D. FL 2nd Inf. Co.E
Venning, R.S. SC 2nd Cav. Co.B
Venning, R.S. SC Lt.Arty. Gaillard's Co. (Santee Lt.Arty.) Sgt.
Venning, R.S. SC 10th Inf. 1st Co.G
Venning, R.S. SC 20th Inf. Co.O 1st Sgt.
Venning, R.S. SC Manigault's Bn.Vol. Co.B Cpl.
Venning, W.C. SC 6th Cav. Co.C
Venning, W.C. SC 10th Inf. 1st Co.G
Venning, W.C. SC Manigault's Bn.Vol. Co.A 2nd Lt.
Venning, W.C. SC Manigault's Bn.Vol. Co.C
Venning, William C. SC 5th Cav. Co.E 1st Lt.
Venning, William C. SC 5th Res. Co.B 3rd Lt.
Venning, William L. SC Manigault's Bn.Vol. Co.C Lt.
Venning, W.L. SC 10th Inf. 1st Co.G 1st Lt.
Venning, W.L. SC 20th Inf. Co.O
Vennoy, Benjamin VA 3rd Inf. Co.B,C
Veno, Francis NC 1st Arty. (10th St.Troops) Co.C
Veno, George W. NC 5th Inf. Co.A
Veno, John SC 2nd Arty. Co.E
Venot, A. LA Mil. 1st Regt. French Brig. Co.3 Sgt.
Vensant, John AR 7th Inf. Co.C
Vensonau, Victor LA C.S. Zouave Bn. Co.B
Venstein, Joseph LA 8th Inf.
Vent, James P. AR Ringold's Inf.
Venta, Jose de la LA Mil. Cazadores Espanoles Regt. Co.2
Venters, A.J. SC 15th Inf. Co.G
Venters, Augustus AR 3rd Inf. Co.A
Venters, Benjamin F. NC 2nd Cav. (19th St.Troops) Co.G Sgt.
Venters, Benjamin F. NC 61st Inf. Co.B
Venters, B.F. FL 2nd Inf. Co.C
Venters, Brinson NC 35th Inf. Co.A 2nd Lt.
Venters, Daniel C. NC 24th Inf. Co.B
Venters, George M. KY 5th Mtd.Inf. Co.B
Venters, G.W. NC 27th Inf. Co.H
Venters, James NC 35th Inf. Co.A
Ventorine, A. AL Mil. 3rd Vol. Co.A
Ventorino, V. AL 1st Regt. Mobile Vol. Co.C
Ventres, C.A. MO Cav. Hunter's Regt. Co.E
Ventres, Edward MO 8th Inf. Co.E
Ventress, A.J. TN 18th Inf. Co.E
Ventress, George T. LA 13th Bn. (Part.Rangers) Co.F 2nd Lt.
Ventress, James A., Jr. LA 11th Inf. Co.B Capt.
Ventress, Jesse TN 44th Inf. Co.E
Ventress, Jesse TN 44th (Cons.) Inf. Co.B
Ventress, J.L.H. TN 18th Inf. Co.E
Ventress, Peter R. LA Inf. 16th Bn. (Conf. Guards Resp.Bn.) Co.B Cpl.
Ventress, P.R. LA Inf.Cons.Crescent Regt. Co.A Cpl.
Ventress, S.K. AL 5th Inf. New Co.A
Verbuke, T. AL 21st Inf. Co.H
Vercerne, William LA 13th & 20th Inf. Band Music.
Vercher, C. LA 26th Inf. Co.G
Vercher, Charles LA 18th Inf. Co.C
Vercher, G. LA 18th Inf. Co.C
Vercher, Isidore LA 2nd Cav. Co.D
Vercher, J.B. LA 26th Inf. Co.G
Vercher, Jeriva LA Inf. 11th Bn. Co.C
Vercher, Jeriva LA Inf.Cons.Crescent Regt. Co.F
Vercher, Joseph LA 2nd Cav. Co.D
Vercher, Joseph LA Maddox's Regt.Res.Corps Co.B
Vercher, Leandre LA Maddox's Regt.Res.Corps Co.B
Vercher, L.H. TX 7th Inf. Co.C
Vercher, Louis LA 2nd Cav. Co.D
Vercher, M. LA Inf.Cons.Crescent Regt. Co.O,G
Vercher, M. LA Maddox's Regt.Res.Corps Co.B
Vercher, W.J. SC 4th Cav. Co.G
Verdin, A.G. GA 32nd Inf. Co.H
Verdin, Allen SC 16th Inf. Co.I
Verdin, B. TX 20th Inf. Co.E
Verdin, Calvin J. AR Cav. Gordon's Regt. Co.C Cpl.
Verdin, F.G. AR Cav. Gordon's Regt. Co.C
Verdin, John A. AR Inf. Crawford's Bn. Co.A
Verdin, Ledford SC 1st Arty. Co.I
Verdin, Ledford N. SC Inf. Hampton Legion Co.F
Verdin, Paul SC 16th Inf. Co.I Sgt.
Verdin, T.B. AR Cav. Gordon's Regt. Co.C
Verdin, William J. GA 38th Inf. Co.A
Verdin, William J. SC 3rd Cav. Co.C
Verett, Charles P. MS 21st Inf. Co.F
Verge, Henry KY 7th Cav. Co.H
Verge, James R. LA Inf.Crescent Regt. Co.I Cpl.
Verge, J.R. LA 18th Inf. Co.C
Verges, D. LA Mil. Bn.French Vol. Co.7 2nd Lt.
Verges, Jean LA Mil. 3rd Regt.Eur.Brig. (Garde Francaise) Co.4
Vergez, Bernard LA Mil. 3rd Regt.Eur.Brig. (Garde Francaise) Frois' Co.
Vergez, Dgm. LA Mil. 3rd Regt.Eur.Brig. (Garde Francaise) Frois' Co.
Vergez, Francois LA Mil. 3rd Regt.Eur.Brig. (Garde Francaise) Frois' Co.
Vergez, Gme. LA Mil. 3rd Regt.Eur.Brig. (Garde Francaise) Frois' Co.
Vergez, Jn. Mir. LA Mil. 3rd Regt.Eur.Brig. (Garde Francaise) Frois' Co.
Vergez, Pere LA Mil. 3rd Regt.Eur.Brig. (Garde Francaise) Frois' Co. Sgt.
Vergez, Pierre LA Mil. 3rd Regt.Eur.Brig. (Garde Francaise) Frois' Co.
Vergez, Sylvain LA Mil. 3rd Regt.Eur.Brig. (Garde Francaise) Frois' Co. Cpl.
Verhine, W.H. GA Inf. 40th Bn.
Verhine, William H. GA 41st Inf. Co.C
Verhines, A.H. TN 20th (Russell's) Cav. Co.A
Verhines, John P. TN 33rd Inf. Co.D
Verhines, J.P. TN 20th (Russell's) Cav. Co.A
Verial, Clemento TX 8th Inf. Co.E
Verial, Ecletto TX 8th Inf. Co.E
Veringe, Jean LA Mil. 2nd Regt. French Brig. Co.5
Veris, C.O. VA 4th Cav. Co.E
Verlanda, Joseph M. VA Lt.Arty. W.P. Carter's Co.
Verlander, C.F. LA Mil.Conf.Guards Regt. Co.K
Verlander, George W. GA 3rd Bn. (St.Guards) Co.H Cpl.
Verlander, George W. LA Inf. 16th Bn. (Conf.Guards Resp.Bn.) Co.A
Verlander, G.W. GA Inf. Exempts Roberts' Co.
Verlander, Henry M. LA 14th Inf. Co.K Capt.
Verlander, James W. VA Lt.Arty. Parker's Co. Cpl.
Verlander, John L. VA 26th Inf. Co.I
Verlander, Mordecai VA 26th Inf. Co.I Cpl.
Verlander, T.N. VA Lt.Arty. W.P. Carter's Co.
Verlander, W.R. LA Mil. 2nd Regt. 3rd Brig. 1st Div. Co.C 2nd Lt.
Verlaque, Honore LA Mil. 2nd Regt. French Brig. Co.1
Verlaque, Tofield MO Cav. 1st Regt.St.Guard Co.E Cpl.

Verlentine, Joseph AL St.Arty. Co.D
Verlines, John A. VA 54th Mil. Co.E,F
Verling, Joseph LA 5th Inf. Co.C
Verloin, F. LA Mil. Orleans Guards Regt. Co.I,H
Verloin, J. LA Dreux's Cav. Co.A
Verloin, Jules LA Millaudon's Co. (Jefferson Mtd.Guards,Co.B)
Verlouin, O. LA Mil. 3rd Regt. 2nd Brig. 1st Div.
Verman, Moses Mead's Conf.Cav. Co.K
Vermarien, Chs. LA Mil. 3rd Regt.Eur.Brig. (Garde Francaise) Co.9
Verme, Felix AR 51st Mil. Co.B
Vermesse, Agathon LA 14th Inf. Co.B,D
Vermette, H. TX 23rd Cav. Co.K
Vermilion, James R. VA 17th Cav. Co.A
Vermilion, R.A. Sig.Corps,CSA Sgt.
Vermillera, Charles VA Inf. 1st Bn.Loc.Def. Co.E
Vermillera, Philip J. VA 1st Inf. Co.B
Vermillia, Chars VA 18th Bn.Res. Co.E Cpl.
Vermillian, Samuel N. NC Mallett's Co.
Vermillian, Fielding VA 146th Mil. Co.H
Vermillion, Alexander P. VA 9th Inf. Co.K
Vermillion, Benjamin AR 31st Inf. Co.A
Vermillion, Benjamin VA 16th Cav. Co.A
Vermillion, Benjamin F. VA 37th Inf. Co.G 1st Lt.
Vermillion, B.F. MO 3rd Inf. Co.I 2nd Lt.
Vermillion, Dennis VA 9th Inf. Co.K Capt.
Vermillion, E.R. TX Cav. 1st Regt.St.Troops Co.E
Vermillion, F. MO 16th Inf. Co.B
Vermillion, Gilliam S. VA 9th Inf. Co.K
Vermillion, Guiliaume S. Sig.Corps,CSA
Vermillien, Isaac VA 6th Bn.Res. Co.G
Vermillion, James VA 12th Cav. Co.I
Vermillion, James VA 6th Bn.Res. Co.H
Vermillion, James VA 146th Mil. Co.H
Vermillion, James D. VA 48th Inf. Co.E
Vermillion, James H. TX Inf. Griffin's Bn. Co.C
Vermillion, James M. NC 25th Inf. Co.H
Vermillion, James Revson VA 8th Cav. 1st Co.D 1st Sgt.
Vermillion, Jesse VA Cav. Ferguson's Bn. Stevenson's Co. Bugler
Vermillion, Jesse, Jr. VA 72nd Mil.
Vermillion, J.H. TX 9th (Young's) Inf. Co.I
Vermillion, J.H. VA Mil. Scott Cty.
Vermillion, J.L. MS 1st Lt.Arty. Co.B
Vermillion, John MO 9th (Elliott's) Cav. Co.A Sgt.
Vermillion, John MO 11th Inf. Co.C
Vermillion, John VA 9th Inf. Co.K 2nd Lt.
Vermillion, John H. VA 6th Bn.Res. Co.H
Vermillion, John L. VA 15th Cav. Co.H
Vermillion, John M. VA 48th Inf. Co.A Capt.
Vermillion, John S. VA 37th Inf. Co.C Lt.
Vermillion, John W. TN 2nd (Ashby's) Cav. Co.C
Vermillion, John W. TN Cav. 5th Bn. (McClellan's) Co.D
Vermillion, John W. VA 30th Bn.S.S. Co.E
Vermillion, Joseph VA Loc.Def. Morehead's Co.
Vermillion, Joseph H. MO Lt.Arty. 3rd Btty.
Vermillion, Joseph H. MO Arty. Lowe's Co.
Vermillion, Levi H. VA 24th Inf. Co.G
Vermillion, Nelson VA Hvy.Arty. 18th Bn. Co.E
Vermillion, Nelson VA 62nd Mtd.Inf. Co.L
Vermillion, Patrick H. VA 11th Inf. Co.B
Vermillion, P.H. Sig.Corps,CSA Sgt.
Vermillion, R.A. TX 6th Inf. Co.B
Vermillion, R.A. VA 25th Cav. Co.E
Vermillion, Richard VA 9th Inf. Co.D 2nd Lt.
Vermillion, Robert A. VA 11th Inf. Co.B
Vermillion, Samuel N. NC 25th Inf. Co.H
Vermillion, S.H. TX 21st Inf. Co.C
Vermillion, Stephen T. VA 17th Cav. Co.D
Vermillion, Thomas SC 1st (Hagood's) Inf. 2nd Co.F
Vermillion, Thomas M. VA 16th Cav. Co.A
Vermillion, Uriah, Jr. VA 4th Inf. Co.C
Vermillion, W.H. MS 10th Cav. Co.C
Vermillion, W.H. MO 2nd Cav. Co.D
Vermillion, W.M. GA 27th Inf. Co.D
Vermillion, W.T. SC 1st (Hagood's) Inf. 2nd Co.F
Vermilya, Sylvester P. AL 3rd Inf. Co.H 1st Sgt.
Vermilya, T.P. AL 60th Inf. Co.F
Vermosdell, C. LA Miles' Legion Co.K
Vermosdell, James LA Miles' Legion Co.K
Vermosdell, M. LA Miles' Legion Co.K
Vermote, R. TN 5th Cav.
Vermylea, J.S. VA 67th Mil. Co.B
Vernan, J.B. AL 7th Inf. Co.A
Vernan, Samuel VA 50th Inf. Co.C
Vernan, W.B. AR 1st Cav. Co.B
Vernay, Benjamin VA 19th Cav. Co.B
Verneiulle, J. Louis AL Lt.Arty. 2nd Bn. Co.E Cpl.
Vernell, C.C. AL 17th Inf. Co.A
Vernell, J.H. KY 1st Inf. Co.A
Vernelson, John NC 3rd Arty. (40th St.Troops) Co.G
Vernelson, John VA Inf. 4th Bn.Loc.Def. Co.C
Vernelson, J.W. NC 1st Arty. (10th St.Troops) Co.A
Vernen, E.L. AL 51st (Part.Rangers) Co.A
Verner, Adam LA Mil. Chalmette Regt. Co.A
Verner, A.J. MO 1st Inf. 2nd Co.A
Verner, Arthur Cheatham's Div. Pioneer Co.
Verner, Aug AL 21st Inf. Co.H
Verner, E.P. SC 1st St.Troops Co.E 1st Sgt.
Verner, E.T. MS 43rd Inf. Co.C
Verner, F.M. GA Inf. 9th Bn. Co.C
Verner, F.M. GA 37th Inf. Co.F
Verner, Frederick LA 8th Inf. Co.B
Verner, George E. GA 3rd Cav. (St.Guards) Co.E
Verner, G.W. GA 4th Cav. (St.Guards) McDonald's Co. Sgt.
Verner, Hardy 7th Conf.Cav. Co.M
Verner, H.F. GA 2nd Cav. Co.A
Verner, Jacob W. AL 9th Inf. Co.C
Verner, James J. GA 37th Inf. Co.F Sgt.
Verner, J.D. SC 7th Cav. Co.G
Verner, J.D. SC Rutledge Mtd.Riflemen & Horse Arty. Trenholm's Co.
Verner, J.M. GA Inf. 9th Bn. Co.C
Verner, J.T. MS 1st (Patton's) Inf. Co.H
Verner, K.M. AL Mil. 1st Regt. Co.B
Verner, L.E. TX 14th Inf. Co.C
Verner, Lewis F. GA Inf. 4th Bn. (St.Guards) Co.C
Verner, Samuel H. GA 37th Inf. Co.C Sgt.
Verner, S.H. GA Inf. 9th Bn. Co.C Sgt.
Verner, Solomon S. SC Inf. Hampton Legion Co.A Cpl.
Verner, T.T. MS St.Cav. 2nd Bn. (Harris') Co.C
Verner, W.H. SC Cav. 2nd Bn.Res. Co.H 1st Lt.
Verner, William E. MS 43rd Inf. Co.C
Verner, William H. VA 18th Cav. Co.I
Verner, William L. MS 41st Inf. Co.G
Verner, W.L. MS Inf. 1st Bn. Co.A
Vernes, C. LA Mil. 1st Chasseurs a pied Co.2
Vernet, Adam LA 15th Inf. Co.H
Verneth, Mathey AL 1st Regt. Mobile Vol. Co.E
Verneuil, --- LA Mil. 2nd Regt. French Brig. Co.1
Verneuille, A. LA 22nd (Cons.) Inf. Co.E
Verneuille, Henry AL 24th Inf. Co.A
Verneuille, John B. AL 24th Inf. Co.A Sgt.
Verney, Jas. Gen. & Staff Capt.,Comsy.
Verney, John TX 27th Cav. Co.D,M
Vernielle, F. AL Mil. 2nd Regt.Vol. Co.F
Vernigan, G.W. MS 1st Cav. Co.A Cpl.
Vernill, A.M. MS 10th Cav. Co.A
Vernin, Ewel VA 21st Cav. Co.K
Vernnille, A. AL 1st Bn. Cadets Co.B
Vernoble, Richard M. Gen. & Staff, Gen.Serv. Asst.Surg.
Vernom, Ewell VA 45th Inf. Co.E
Vernom, Wiley VA 45th Inf. Co.E
Vernon, --- TX Cav. McCord's Frontier Regt. Co.E Sgt.
Vernon, A. GA 8th Inf. Co.H
Vernon, Abner TN 19th Inf. Co.C
Vernon, A.J. TN 4th Inf. Co.B
Vernon, Alex VA Arty. C.F. Johnston's Co.
Vernon, Alexander VA 1st Arty. Co.H
Vernon, Alexander VA 7th Inf. Co.F
Vernon, A.M. LA Lt.Arty. Bridges' Btty.
Vernon, A.M. SC Lt.Arty. M. Ward's Co. (Waccamaw Lt.Arty.)
Vernon, A.M. SC 2nd Bn.S.S. Co.B
Vernon, A.P. MO 9th (Elliott's) Cav.
Vernon, A.P. TX 29th Cav. Co.B
Vernon, B.T.H. GA 8th Cav. Old Co.D
Vernon, B.T.H. GA 62nd Cav. Co.D
Vernon, B.T.H. NC Cav. 16th Bn. Co.H
Vernon, Christopher C. MS 42nd Inf. Co.H
Vernon, D.A. LA 3rd (Wingfield's) Cav. Co.E
Vernon, David H. GA 4th Bn.S.S. Co.C,H
Vernon, D.H. GA Inf. 9th Bn. Co.A
Vernon, Ebenezer VA 59th Inf. 3rd Co.E
Vernon, Ebenezer R. Cheatham's Div. Asst.Surg.
Vernon, Edward NC 2nd Arty. (36th St.Troops) Co.G
Vernon, E.F. AR 30th Inf. Co.H
Vernon, Eleizer R. AL 2nd Bn. Hilliard's Legion Vol. Co.F
Vernon, E.R. AL 59th Inf. Co.C
Vernon, E.R. TN 4th Inf. Asst.Surg.
Vernon, E.W. AL 5th Inf. New Co.H
Vernon, E.W. AL 63rd Inf. Co.C
Vernon, F.D. GA Cherokee Legion (St.Guards) Co.A Sgt.

Vernon, Franklin D. GA 2nd Inf. Co.F
Vernon, G. TX Cav. McCord's Frontier Regt. Co.E
Vernon, George LA 4th Inf. Co.K
Vernon, George NC 38th Inf. Co.D
Vernon, George NC 45th Inf. Co.F
Vernon, George M. AL 61st Inf. Co.F Sgt.
Vernon, George P. MS Cav. Jeff Davis Legion Co.C
Vernon, Green NC 13th Inf. Co.H
Vernon, H. TN 22nd Inf. Co.H
Vernon, H. TX 4th Cav. Co.D
Vernon, Hardin VA 4th Res. Co.E,G
Vernon, Henry NC 45th Inf. Co.F
Vernon, Henry F. AL 10th Inf. Co.G
Vernon, H.F. Conf.Inf. 1st Bn. 2nd Co.E
Vernon, H.G. LA Cav. 18th Bn. Co.D
Vernon, H.H. TN 12th (Cons.) Inf. Co.D
Vernon, Hiram L. NC 21st Inf. Co.I
Vernon, H.P. LA 27th Inf. Co.H Cpl.
Vernon, Isaac AR 34th Inf. Co.A
Vernon, Isaac E. TX 4th Cav. Co.D
Vernon, Isaac M. VA 1st Bn.Res. Co.H
Vernon, James AR 2nd Inf. Co.D
Vernon, James MS 2nd St.Cav. 1st Co.C
Vernon, James TN 42nd Inf. 2nd Co.F
Vernon, James A. TN 24th Inf. Co.B Cpl.
Vernon, James D. VA 38th Inf. Co.C
Vernon, James H. VA 38th Inf. Co.C Cpl.
Vernon, James H. VA 57th Inf. Co.D
Vernon, James M. MS 6th Cav. Morgan's Co.
Vernon, James M. VA 59th Inf. 3rd Co.E
Vernon, James P. AL Rives' Supp.Force 9th Congr.Dist.
Vernon, James R. AR 3rd Cav. Co.I
Vernon, James W. AR 2nd Inf. Co.C
Vernon, James W. VA 4th Cav. Co.C
Vernon, J.B. AL 7th Cav. Co.F
Vernon, J.B. TN 21st (Wilson's) Cav. Co.C,H
Vernon, J.B. TN 21st & 22nd (Cons.) Cav. Co.F
Vernon, J.C. GA 18th Inf. Co.E
Vernon, Jesse P. AL 20th Inf. Co.D,H Music.
Vernon, J.H. AL Mil. 4th Vol. Modawell's Co.
Vernon, J.H. SC Lt.Arty. M. Ward's Co. (Waccamaw Lt.Arty.) Artif.
Vernon, J.H. TN 21st & 22nd (Cons.) Cav. Co.G
Vernon, J.J. LA 3rd (Wingfield's) Cav. Co.E
Vernon, J.J. LA 4th Inf. Old Co.G, Co.A
Vernon, J.J. MS 5th Cav. Co.A
Vernon, J.J. TN 21st (Wilson's) Cav. Co.F,C
Vernon, J.J. TN 21st & 22nd (Cons.) Cav. Co.G
Vernon, J. Joseph VA 4th Res. Co.F,K
Vernon, J.M. AR 13th Inf. Co.G
Vernon, J.M. MO 2nd Inf. Co.D
Vernon, J.M. MO 3rd & 5th Cons.Inf.
Vernon, J.M. TX 21st Cav. Co.C
Vernon, John GA 20th Inf. Co.D
Vernon, John MS 7th Cav. Co.D
Vernon, John MS 11th Inf. Co.I
Vernon, John NC 4th Bn.Jr.Res. Co.D Sgt.
Vernon, John NC 45th Inf. Co.F,H
Vernon, John TN 3rd (Lillard's) Mtd.Inf. Co.G
Vernon, John TN 42nd Inf. 2nd Co.F
Vernon, John A. TX Arty. 4th Bn. Co.A Capt.
Vernon, John A. TX 8th Inf. Co.A Maj.
Vernon, John C. TN 59th Mtd.Inf. Co.G
Vernon, John E. LA 8th Inf. Co.H
Vernon, John E. LA 2nd Res.Corps Co.I
Vernon, John G. GA Cherokee Legion (St.Guards) Co.B
Vernon, John H. NC 45th Inf. Co.A
Vernon, John M. AL Arty. 1st Bn. Co.F
Vernon, John M. AL 37th Inf. Co.G
Vernon, John Radford NC 22nd Inf. Co.H
Vernon, John S. AR 18th Inf. Co.C Sgt.
Vernon, Joseph MS 6th Cav. Morgan's Co.
Vernon, Joseph MS 12th Cav. Co.C
Vernon, Joseph MS 43rd Inf. Co.L
Vernon, Joseph VA 1st Arty. Co.I
Vernon, Joseph A. LA 16th Inf. Co.B
Vernon, Joseph C. VA Lt.Arty. 38th Bn. Co.B
Vernon, Joseph M. MS 12th Cav. Co.C
Vernon, Joseph S. MS 1st (Johnston's) Inf. Co.H
Vernon, J.P. AL Gid Nelson Lt.Arty.
Vernon, J.S. LA 4th Inf. Old Co.G
Vernon, J.S. MS 7th Inf. Co.H
Vernon, J.W. AR 13th Inf. Co.G
Vernon, J.W. NC 22nd Inf. Co.H
Vernon, L. LA Mil. 3rd Regt. French Brig. Co.3
Vernon, L.B. AL 15th Bn.Part.Rangers Co.A
Vernon, L.B. AL 56th Part.Rangers Co.A
Vernon, Matthew P. TX 22nd Cav. Asst.Surg.
Vernon, M.H. KY 7th Cav. Co.A
Vernon, M.H. TN 4th Inf. Co.B Capt.
Vernon, Miles KY 3rd Cav. Co.A Cpl.
Vernon, Miles MO Cav. 3rd Bn. Co.E
Vernon, Moses AR 36th Inf. Co.G
Vernon, Moses MO 2nd Inf. Co.C
Vernon, Moses C. GA 20th Inf. Co.D
Vernon, M.P. LA 18th Inf. Co.B Asst.Surg.
Vernon, M.W.W. LA 3rd (Wingfield's) Cav. Co.E
Vernon, M.W.W. LA 4th Inf. Old Co.G
Vernon, Nathan H. VA 45th Inf. Co.H
Vernon, Nicholas VA Mil. Carroll Cty.
Vernon, Obadiah C. AL 17th Inf. Co.K
Vernon, Obediah MS 34th Inf. Co.F
Vernon, Obediah C. AL 20th Inf. Co.D
Vernon, O.C. AL 44th Inf. Co.D
Vernon, Peter VA Inf. 23rd Bn. Co.D
Vernon, Reuben W. NC 22nd Inf. Co.H
Vernon, R.G. AL 9th Inf. Co.G
Vernon, R.H. AR 35th Inf. Co.K
Vernon, Richard AR Cav. 1st Bn. (Stirman's) Co.E
Vernon, Richard NC 13th Inf. Co.I
Vernon, Richard NC 22nd Inf. Co.H
Vernon, Richard T. TN 24th Inf. Co.B
Vernon, Robert F.M. GA 20th Inf. Co.D
Vernon, Robert M. GA 37th Inf. Co.D
Vernon, Robt. M. GA 1st St.Line
Vernon, Robert T. VA 5th Cav. Co.C
Vernon, S. NC 22nd Inf. Co.H
Vernon, S.McD. Eng.,CSA 1st Lt.
Vernon, Sam McD. MS 1st Lt.Arty. Co.K Sgt.
Vernon, Samuel P. LA Miles' Legion Co.C
Vernon, T.C. TN Cav. Nixon's Regt. Co.H
Vernon, Thomas AL Cp. of Instr. Talladega
Vernon, Thomas AR Inf. 4th Bn. Co.E
Vernon, Thomas MO 10th Inf. Co.B
Vernon, Thomas TX 23rd Cav. Co.E 2nd Lt.
Vernon, Thomas A. MO 4th Cav. Co.I
Vernon, Thomas H. AL Mil. 4th Vol. Co.A
Vernon, Thomas J. AL 44th Inf. Co.B
Vernon, Tinsley TX 12th Inf. Co.K Hosp.Stew.
Vernon, T.J. AL 20th Inf. Co.D
Vernon, T.J. AR 3rd Inf. Co.K
Vernon, T.J. AR 37th Inf. Co.A 2nd Lt.
Vernon, T.L. Forrest's Scouts T.N. Kizer's Co.,CSA
Vernon, W.A. AR Cav. 1st Bn. (Stirman's) Co.E
Vernon, W.A. AR Cav. Gordon's Regt. Co.F
Vernon, Wesley NC 22nd Inf. Co.H
Vernon, W.H. TN 45th Inf. Co.B Capt.
Vernon, W.H. VA Cav. Mosby's Regt. (Part.Rangers)
Vernon, Wiley VA Cav. 37th Bn. Co.H
Vernon, William AR 1st (Dobbin's) Cav. Co.B
Vernon, William AR 23rd Inf. Co.E
Vernon, William AR 58th Mil. Co.B
Vernon, William LA Arty. Kean's Btty. (Orleans Ind.Arty.)
Vernon, William NC 8th Sr.Res. Gardner's Co. 1st Lt.
Vernon, William NC 45th Inf. Co.F
Vernon, William NC Nelson's Co. (Loc.Def.)
Vernon, William TN 10th Inf. Co.F
Vernon, William TX 17th Cav. Co.H Sgt.
Vernon, William VA Inf. 23rd Bn. Co.D
Vernon, William A. TN 23rd Inf. 1st Co.A, Co.B Capt.
Vernon, William Claiborne LA 28th (Gray's) Inf. Co.F
Vernon, William E. MS 30th Inf. Co.C Cpl.
Vernon, William E. MO Inf. 8th Bn. Co.F
Vernon, William E. MO 9th Inf. Co.K
Vernon, William H. VA Hvy.Arty. 19th Bn. Ord.Off.
Vernon, William H. VA 38th Inf. Co.A
Vernon, William J. AL 8th Cav. Co.B
Vernon, William S. AR 25th Inf. Co.A Cpl.
Vernon, William T. GA 20th Inf. Co.D Cpl.
Vernon, William T. VA 38th Inf. Co.C Sgt.
Vernon, Wilson VA 5th Inf. Co.C
Vernon, W.L. AR Cav. 1st Bn. (Stirman's) Co.E
Vernon, W.L. AR Cav. Gordon's Regt. Co.F 1st Sgt.
Vernon, W.R. SC Bn.St.Cadets Co.B
Vernon, W.R. TX 29th Cav. Co.B
Vernon, W.T. TN 24th Inf. Co.A
Vernon, Wyley VA Cav. Swann's Bn. Watkin's Co.
Vernooy, Thomas TX Inf. 3rd St.Troops Co.H
Vernor, James A. MS 34th Inf. Co.B
Vernor, James H. MS 18th Cav. Co.K
Vernor, Zenas E. MS 2nd Inf. Co.B
Vernoux, --- LA Mil. 2nd Regt. French Brig. Co.1
Vernow, Ebeneger R. TN 4th Inf. A.Surg.
Vernoy, C. TX Inf. 1st St.Troops Martin's Co.A N.C.S. Ord.Sgt.
Vernoy, Daniel NC 54th Inf. Co.G
Vernoy, J. Gen. & Staff Maj.,QM
Vernoy, James AL 15th Inf. A.Comsy.
Vernoy, Robert AR 1st (Monroe's) Cav. Co.C Cpl.
Vernum, G.W. VA Cav. 37th Bn. Co.F
Vernum, John A. VA 13th Inf. Co.G Sgt.
Veron, Ernest LA Mil. 1st Regt. French Brig. Co.6

Veron, H. LA Mil. French Co. of St.James
Veron, Leopold LA Mil. 6th Regt.Eur.Brig. (Italian Guards Bn.) Co.5
Veron, Louis LA Mil. 6th Regt.Eur.Brig. (Italian Guards Bn.) Co.5
Verone, G.W. SC Charleston Arsenal Bn. Co.A Jr.2nd Lt.
Veronee, Cornelious B. GA Inf. 1st Loc.Troops (Augusta) Co.H Capt.
Veronee, Cornelius B. SC 15th Inf. Co.E
Veronee, G.N. SC Mil. 17th Regt. Buist's Co. Sgt.
Veronee, T.W. SC Mil. 17th Regt. Buist's Co. 1st Lt.
Veronee, T. William SC Arty. Manigault's Bn. 1st Co.A 1st Lt.
Veroni, Andrew LA 3rd (Harrison's) Cav. Co.K
Verpillot, F. LA Mil. Lartigue's Co. (Bienville Guards)
Verraden, J. GA 25th Inf. Co.K
Verree, William SC Arty. Stuart's Co. (Beaufort Vol.Arty.)
Verree, William SC 11th Inf. Co.B
Verrell, B.O. SC 1st Cav. Co.A
Verrell, James SC 1st Cav. Co.A
Verrell, Joseph MS 21st Inf. Co.K
Verrell, William J. VA 2nd Inf.Loc.Def. Co.C
Verret, A. LA 30th Inf. Co.A,F
Verret, A.L. LA Inf.Crescent Regt. Co.G
Verret, August LA 28th (Thomas') Inf. Co.H Sgt.
Verret, Augustin LA Conscr.
Verret, C. LA Lt.Arty. 2nd Field Btty.
Verret, Edgar LA 30th Inf. Co.F
Verret, G. LA 3rd (Harrison's) Cav. Co.I
Verret, Gustave LA Conscr.
Verret, H. LA Lt.Arty. 2nd Field Btty.
Verret, H. LA 22nd (Cons.) Inf. Co.E
Verret, Henry LA Pointe Coupee Arty.
Verret, Henry LA 22nd Inf. Co.D
Verret, J. LA Mil. 1st Chasseurs a pied Co.2
Verret, Jules LA Lt.Arty. LeGardeur, Jr.'s Co. (Orleans Guard Btty.)
Verret, Nicholas LA Conscr.
Verret, Numa LA 1st Hvy.Arty. (Reg.) Co.B
Verret, Numa LA 8th Inf. Co.K
Verret, Onil LA Conscr.
Verret, T. LA 3rd (Harrison's) Cav. Co.I
Verret, T.J. LA 30th Inf. Co.F
Verrett, Achille LA 13th Inf. Co.G
Verrett, Aristide A. LA 13th Inf. Co.G,E
Verrett, Gerouis LA 2nd Cav.
Verrett, Joseph LA 2nd Cav. Co.C
Verrette, Edmond FL 3rd Inf. Co.I
Verrette, T.J. LA Mil. Orleans Guards Regt. Co.K
Verrey, Charles A. LA 1st Cav. Co.G
Verrier, Francis LA 5th Inf. Co.G
Verrier, J. LA Mil. 3rd Regt. French Brig. Co.7
Verrier, Th. LA Mil. 1st Regt. French Brig. Co.8
Verrier, Victor LA Mil. 1st Regt. French Brig. Co.8
Verrit, Jules LA Dreux's Cav. Co.A
Verse, J.D. VA 36th Inf. Co.D,K
Verser, Cicero A. VA 18th Inf. Co.F Sgt.
Verser, D.J. TN 6th Inf. Co.K
Verser, Edward P. VA 18th Inf. Co.F
Verser, Fort P. AR 25th Inf. Co.I
Verser, George D. AR Inf. 4th Bn. Co.B
Verser, James NC 43rd Inf. Co.G
Verser, James W. VA 2nd Arty. Co.G
Verser, James W. VA Inf. 22nd Bn. Co.G
Verser, J.L. TN Inf. 3rd Bn. Co.D
Verser, John NC 30th Inf. Co.B
Verser, John A. AR 26th Inf. Co.F
Verser, John A. VA Lt.Arty. Jeffress' Co. Cpl.
Verser, John A. VA Inf. 25th Bn. Co.D Sgt.
Verser, Leroy J. VA 20th Inf. Co.B
Verser, Leroy J. VA Inf. 22nd Bn. Co.B Cpl.
Verser, Nathan AL Cav. Lewis' Bn. Co.E 1st Lt.
Verser, Nathan F. VA Lt.Arty. Jeffress' Co.
Verser, Richard C. VA 18th Inf. Co.C Sgt.
Verser, W.H. VA 1st (Farinholt's) Res. Co.F
Verser, William AR 6th Inf. Co.C
Versey, Simon AR 9th Inf. Old Co.I
Verster, G.W. TN 7th (Duckworth's) Cav. Co.L
Verstille, H.W. AL 60th Inf. Co.D
Verstille, H.W. AL 3rd Bn. Hilliard's Legion Vol. Co.F
Vertegans, Ed G. VA 16th Cav. Co.K 2nd Lt.
Vertegans, Ed. G. VA Cav. Ferguson's Bn. Nounnan's Co.
Vertegans, Edward VA 16th Cav. Chap.
Vertegans, Edward Gen. & Staff Chap.
Vertegans, George S. VA 16th Cav. Co.K
Vertigan, Edward G. VA 8th Cav. Co.E
Vertigan, George S. VA 8th Cav. Co.E
Vertir, A. LA Mil. 4th Regt. French Brig. Co.6
Vertner, A.V. LA 4th Inf. Co.C
Vertner, A.V. Gen. & Staff 1st Lt.,ADC
Vertrecs, William B. MO 5th Inf. Co.F
Vertrees, E.J. KY Cav. Forrest's Regt.
Vertrees, John L. KY 4th Mtd.Inf. Co.A
Vertrees, John L. KY 6th Mtd.Inf. Asst.Surg.
Vertrees, Jno. Luther Gen. & Staff Surg.
Vertrees, Joseph MO Lt.Arty. 3rd Btty.
Vertrese, John MO Cav. Snider's Bn. Co.D
Vertrey, Elza R. KY Cav. Chenoweth's Regt. Co.C
Verts, John W. VA Lt.Arty. Rogers' Co.
Vertz, Jacob LA Mil. Chalmette Regt. Co.C
Verva, Angelo TX 16th Inf. Co.H
Vervant, C. LA Mil. 3rd Regt. 2nd Brig. 1st Div. Co.K Sgt.
Vervet, John LA Mil. LaFourche Regt.
Vescori, Charles LA Mil. 2nd Regt. 2nd Brig. 1st Div. Co.B
Vesey, A.J. AL 12th Inf. Co.F
Vesey, Elijah TX 20th Inf. Co.A
Vesey, F.W. MS 43rd Inf. Co.C Music.
Vesey, George J. AR 5th Inf. Co.I
Vesey, John R. AL 13th Inf. Co.F 1st Sgt.
Vesey, John W. MS 43rd Inf. Co.C Capt.
Vesey, Joseph L. MS 20th Inf. Co.B
Vesey, Marcellus L. MS 14th Inf. Co.I 1st Sgt.
Vesey, Samuel AL 61st Inf. Co.B
Vesey, Thomas B. MS 20th Inf. Co.B
Vesey, V.A. MS 43rd Inf. Co.C
Vesey, V.L. MS 43rd Inf. Co.C 1st Lt.
Vesey, W.H. MS 14th (Cons.) Inf. Co.D
Vesey, Wilmot H. MS 14th Inf. Co.I
Vesey, William J. VA 13th Cav. Co.B
Vesey, William J. VA 9th Inf. Co.F
Vespers, R.W. AL 10th Inf. Co.F
Vesphol, Francis LA Inf. 1st Sp.Bn. (Wheat's) Co.C
Vess, Abram NC 62nd Inf. Co.A
Vess, A.J. NC 6th Inf. Co.K
Vess, Alfred W. GA 34th Inf. Co.G Music.
Vess, Alney B. NC 22nd Inf. Co.K Music.
Vess, Andrew VA 20th Cav. Co.K
Vess, Andrew J. VA 58th Inf. Co.G
Vess, Andrew J. VA Rockbridge Cty.Res. Bacon's Co.
Vess, Augustus TX 9th (Nichols') Inf. Co.C
Vess, A.W. GA Inf. 9th Bn. Co.C
Vess, Crosberry D. VA Lt.Arty. Donald's Co.
Vess, David M. NC 62nd Inf. Co.I
Vess, F.A. TX Inf. Timmons' Regt. Co.F
Vess, F.A. TX Waul's Legion Co.C
Vess, George W. VA 52nd Inf. Co.K
Vess, Harvey VA 58th Inf. Co.G
Vess, Jackson VA 58th Inf. Co.G
Vess, Jacob H. VA 14th Cav. Co.K
Vess, James H. VA Inf. 23rd Bn. Co.D Music.
Vess, James M. NC 29th Inf. Co.E
Vess, John AL 11th Cav. Co.C
Vess, John SC Lt.Arty. 3rd (Palmetto) Bn. Co.H
Vess, John SC 3rd Res. Co.G
Vess, John VA Inf. Lyneman's Co.
Vess, John T. VA 14th Cav. Co.C
Vess, John T. VA 20th Cav. Co.K
Vess, Jonathan TX 2nd Inf. Co.K
Vess, Matthew VA Lt.Arty. Donald's Co. Artif.
Vess, Samuel VA 14th Cav. Co.C
Vess, S.P. TN 1st (Feild's) Inf. Co.F Cpl.
Vess, W.A. TX Inf. Timmons' Regt. Co.F
Vess, William A. VA 14th Cav. Co.C
Vess, William D. TX Cav. Ragsdale's Bn. 2nd Co.C
Vess, William W. TN 25th Inf. Co.K Sgt.
Vess, William W. TN 28th (Cons.) Inf. Co.H,G
Vess, W.W. TN 84th Inf. Co.D
Vess, Z. NC 60th Inf. Co.C
Vess, Z.B. VA 20th Cav. Co.K
Vessati, Charles LA 22nd Inf. Jones' Co.
Vesscher, D.W. GA 12th (Robinson's) Cav. (St.Guards) Co.C
Vesscher, J.G. GA 12th (Robinson's) Cav. (St.Guards) Co.C
Vessel, J.J. AL 1st Cav. Co.G
Vessells, G.W. TN 38th Inf. Co.L
Vessells, J. AL 1st Inf. Co.E
Vessells, James E. TN 38th Inf. Co.L
Vessells, John AR 1st Mtd.Rifles Co.A
Vessels, Andrew J. AL 6th Cav. Co.E,C
Vessels, George AR 32nd Inf. Co.K
Vessels, George W. TN 22nd Inf. Looney's Co.
Vessels, Horace AR 23rd Inf. Co.G
Vessels, I. TN 15th Inf. Co.K
Vessels, J.A. AL 53rd (Part.Rangers) Co.H
Vessels, James TX 31st Cav. Co.A Sgt.
Vessels, James H. GA 44th Inf. Co.G
Vessels, J.C. AL 53rd (Part.Rangers) Co.H
Vessels, Joseph E. TN 22nd Inf. Looney's Co.
Vessels, J.F. AL 18th Inf. Co.F
Vessels, Thomas J. GA 53rd Inf. Co.C Cpl.
Vessels, Thos. S. AL 51st (Part.Rangers) Co.F
Vessels, W.A. AL 58th Inf. Co.I
Vessels, William AL 5th Cav. Co.A

Vessels, Wm. AL 53rd (Part.Rangers) Co.H
Vessels, W.L. GA 19th Inf. Co.E,A
Vessels, W.T. AL 53rd (Part.Rangers) Co.H
Vessey, Barney GA 3rd Cav. Co.I
Vessey, James LA C.S. Zouave Bn. Co.D
Vessier, John LA 13th Inf. Co.B
Vessier, William LA 13th Inf. Co.B,C
Vest, A.H. MO Cav. Ford's Bn. Co.D
Vest, A.L. NC 62nd Inf. Co.F
Vest, Albert H. MO Cav. Wood's Regt. Co.C
Vest, Alexander NC 33rd Inf. Co.I
Vest, Alfred W. GA 15th Inf. Co.B Music.
Vest, Anderson VA 21st Cav. Co.B
Vest, Andrew J. VA Lt.Arty. Arch. Graham's Co.
Vest, Archibald M. AL 9th (Malone's) Cav. Co.K
Vest, Aurelius VA Courtney Arty.
Vest, Aurelius VA Lt.Arty. Weisiger's Co.
Vest, Aurelius VA 6th Inf. Weisiger's Co.
Vest, Aurelius VA 16th Inf. Co.I
Vest, A.W. GA 34th Inf. Co.G Music.
Vest, Benjamin VA 3rd Res. Co.C
Vest, Benjamin VA 4th Cav. & Inf.St.Line 1st Co.I
Vest, Berry VA 21st Cav. Co.B
Vest, C. VA 4th Cav. & Inf.St.Line 1st Co.I
Vest, Calvin C. NC Walker's Bn. Thomas' Legion Co.H
Vest, Calvin C. TN 3rd (Lillard's) Mtd.Inf. Co.C
Vest, Charles B. VA Cav. Mosby's Regt. (Part.Rangers) Co.C
Vest, Charles D. VA 54th Inf. Co.I Cpl.
Vest, Charles F. VA 7th Cav. Co.F
Vest, Charles F. VA 77th Mil. Co.A
Vest, Charles J. VA 60th Inf. Co.I
Vest, Charles O. NC 1st Arty. (10th St.Troops) Co.H
Vest, Charles T. VA 42nd Inf. Co.B
Vest, Chastine H. VA 9th Inf. Co.C
Vest, Crawford E. VA 24th Inf. Co.G
Vest, David VA 20th Cav. Co.I
Vest, David VA 4th Res. Co.E,G
Vest, David VA 51st Inf. Co.B
Vest, D.K. VA Cav. 36th Bn. Co.A
Vest, D.W. VA 7th Bn.Res. Co.D
Vest, E. TX Waul's Legion Co.B
Vest, E.S. AL 2nd Cav. Co.A
Vest, Floyd VA 11th Bn.Res. Co.F
Vest, Floyd J. VA 11th Bn.Res. Co.F
Vest, Francis M. AL 9th (Malone's) Cav. Co.K
Vest, Franklin TN 62nd Mtd.Inf. Co.E
Vest, Geo. S. VA Lt.Arty. R.M. Anderson's Co.
Vest, Georges A. LA Conscr.
Vest, George W. AL 5th Cav. Co.L
Vest, George W. VA 21st Cav. Co.B
Vest, George W. VA 59th Inf. 3rd Co.D
Vest, G.G. MO St.Guard Col.
Vest, G.W. AL 9th (Malone's) Cav. Co.K Sgt.
Vest, Henry C. TN 3rd (Lillard's) Mtd.Inf. Co.C
Vest, Henry L. Stuart Horse Arty.,CSA
Vest, H.H. VA 10th Bn.Res. Co.B
Vest, H.H. VA Rockbridge Cty.Res. Hutcheson's Co.
Vest, Hiram KY 10th (Johnson's) Cav. New Co.G
Vest, H.N. AL 9th (Malone's) Cav. Co.K
Vest, I. LA Thomas' Brig. Ord.Sgt.
Vest, Isaac VA 30th Bn.S.S. Co.D
Vest, Isam LA Hvy.Arty. 8th Bn. Co.3 Sgt.
Vest, Ithmar T. TX 2nd Cav. Co.A
Vest, Jackson VA Inf. 23rd Bn. Co.B,G
Vest, Jackson VA 60th Inf. Co.I
Vest, Jacob H. VA 25th Inf. 1st Co.G
Vest, James AL 9th (Malone's) Cav. Co.K
Vest, James MO 10th Inf. Co.F
Vest, James MO 12th Inf. Co.B
Vest, James NC 5th Cav. (63rd St.Troops) Co.E
Vest, James TX 2nd Cav. Co.A
Vest, James VA 20th Cav. Co.I
Vest, James VA 21st Cav. Co.B
Vest, James VA Cav. Swann's Bn. Sweny's Co.
Vest, James VA 4th Res. Co.H,I
Vest, James A. VA 49th Inf. Co.H
Vest, James H. VA 28th Inf. Co.K
Vest, James J. AL 24th Inf. Co.H
Vest, James J. AR 1st Vol. Co.G Drum Maj.
Vest, James J. VA 60th Inf. Co.I
Vest, James M. VA 54th Inf. Co.I
Vest, James S. TX Waul's Legion Co.A
Vest, J.B. MO Cav. Hicks' Co.
Vest, Jehu VA 60th Inf. Co.I
Vest, J.J. AL 34th Inf. Co.H
Vest, J.K. VA Lt.Arty. E.J. Anderson's Co.
Vest, Joel W. AL 2nd Cav. Co.B
Vest, John AR 8th Inf. Old Co.C
Vest, John SC Lt.Arty. 3rd (Palmetto) Bn. Co.I
Vest, John TN 3rd (Lillard's) Mtd.Inf. Co.C
Vest, John TN 62nd Mtd.Inf. Co.E
Vest, John VA 2nd Cav. Co.C
Vest, John VA 20th Cav. Co.K
Vest, John VA Inf. 25th Bn. Co.B
Vest, John VA Burks' Regt.Loc.Def. Ammen's Co.
Vest, John VA Inf. Lyneman's Co.
Vest, John A. AL 14th Cav. Co.A
Vest, John A. MS 16th Inf. Co.H
Vest, John A. VA 7th Cav. Co.F
Vest, John D. TN 50th Inf. Co.I
Vest, John E. VA 54th Inf. Co.I
Vest, John F. MO 1st Cav. Co.C Cpl.
Vest, John H. VA 1st Arty. Co.K Sgt.
Vest, John J. MS 26th Inf. Co.D Cpl.
Vest, John J. VA 60th Inf. Co.I
Vest, John M. VA 22nd Inf. Co.E
Vest, John R. VA 42nd Inf. Co.C
Vest, John S. TX Cav. (Dismtd.) Chisum's Regt. Co.D 1st Lt.
Vest, John W. TX 13th Cav. Co.A
Vest, John W. VA Arty. Dance's Co.
Vest, John W. VA 20th Inf. Co.D
Vest, Jonathan AL 7th Cav.
Vest, Joseph F. VA Inf. 5th Bn.Loc.Def. Co.F
Vest, J.T. VA Inf. 5th Bn.Loc.Def. Co.D 2nd Lt.
Vest, J.V. AR 31st Inf. Co.F
Vest, J.W. VA 60th Inf. Co.K
Vest, Lewis H. MD Inf. 2nd Bn. Co.C
Vest, O.R. AL 31st Inf. Co.G
Vest, P. TN 62nd Mtd.Inf. Co.E
Vest, Peter VA Inf. 5th Bn.Loc.Def. Co.D
Vest, Peter R. VA Inf. 1st Bn. Co.A
Vest, Peter R. VA 54th Inf. Co.B
Vest, Philip G. VA 7th Cav. Preston's Co.
Vest, Philip G. VA 14th Cav. Co.G
Vest, Philip G. VA 4th Inf. Co.H
Vest, R.F. TN 5th (McKenzie's) Cav. Co.E
Vest, Richard S. Gen. & Staff Contr.Surg.
Vest, R.L. AR 10th Mil. Co.E
Vest, Robert AL 9th (Malone's) Cav. Co.K
Vest, Robert VA 1st Bn.Res. Co.D 3rd Lt.
Vest, Robert E. VA 9th Inf. Co.C
Vest, S.A. AL Cav. Roddey's Escort
Vest, Samuel NC 33rd Inf. Co.G
Vest, Samuel, Jr. VA 20th Cav. Co.I
Vest, Samuel, Sr. VA 20th Cav. Co.I
Vest, Samuel VA 57th Inf. Co.C 1st Sgt.
Vest, Samuel A. AL Cav. Roddey's Escort
Vest, S.C. MS Inf. 7th Bn. Co.C
Vest, Silas NC 29th Inf. Co.B,K
Vest, S.M. VA 49th Inf. Co.H
Vest, S.W. VA 20th Cav.
Vest, Tarleton W. VA 9th Inf. Co.C
Vest, Taylor MO Cav. Slayback's Regt.
Vest, Thomas TN 62nd Mtd.Inf. Co.E
Vest, Thomas A. VA Cav. Mosby's Regt. (Part.Rangers) Co.C
Vest, Thomas J. VA 2nd Arty. Co.A
Vest, Thomas J. VA Hvy.Arty. 18th Bn. Co.D
Vest, Thomas J. VA Inf. 22nd Bn. Co.A
Vest, Thomas J. VA 34th Inf. Norton's Co. Cpl.
Vest, Thomas P. TN 5th (McKenzie's) Cav. Co.E
Vest, Thomas R. VA 4th Inf. Co.H
Vest, W. VA 11th Bn.Res. Co.F
Vest, Walker W. VA Government Guard S.F. Sutherland's Co.
Vest, Washington VA 21st Cav. Co.B
Vest, W.E. NC 3rd Jr.Res. Co.B
Vest, W.E. NC 4th Bn.Jr.Res. Co.B
Vest, Wesley W. NC 21st Inf. Co.K
Vest, William TN 17th Inf. Co.G
Vest, William VA 21st Cav. Co.B
Vest, William VA 52nd Inf. Co.E
Vest, William B. VA Hvy.Arty. 18th Bn. Co.D
Vest, William G. VA 60th Inf. Co.I
Vest, William H. VA 13th Inf. Co.C
Vest, William H. VA 23rd Inf. Co.A N.C.S. Sgt.Maj.
Vest, William H. VA 42nd Inf. Co.C
Vest, William R. VA 60th Inf. Co.I Cpl.
Vest, William T. NC Walker's Bn. Thomas' Legion Co.H
Vest, Willis M. VA 57th Inf. Co.C Sgt.
Vest, Wiseman TN 5th Inf. 2nd Co.D
Vest, W.M. TX 32nd Cav. Co.I
Vest, W.R. GA 60th Inf. Co.I
Vestal, A.A. AR 3rd Cav. Co.H
Vestal, Abram B. NC 26th Inf. Co.E
Vestal, A.J. TN Inf. 2nd Cons.Regt. Co.B
Vestal, A.J. TN 51st Inf. Co.F
Vestal, Albert M. TX 21st Cav. Co.D
Vestal, Allen AR 15th (N.W.) Inf. Co.K
Vestal, A.M. TX 12th Inf. Co.F
Vestal, Bartholomew D. AL 47th Inf. Co.A
Vestal, Bud TN Cav. 9th Bn. (Gantt's) Co.G
Vestal, Charles W. TN 48th (Voorhies') Inf. Co.K Capt.
Vestal, C. Marion NC 22nd Inf. Co.L 1st Sgt.
Vestal, D.A. NC 9th Bn.S.S. Co.A Cpl.
Vestal, D.A. NC 21st Inf. Co.B

Vestal, Daniel L. NC 48th Inf. Co.G
Vestal, G.A. MO 10th Cav. Co.A
Vestal, George S. NC 54th Inf. Co.H
Vestal, George W. TN 32nd Inf. Co.H
Vestal, G.W. AR 3rd Cav. Co.H
Vestal, G.W. AR 6th Inf. Co.B
Vestal, Henderson TN 1st (Feild's) Inf. Co.G
Vestal, Henry T. NC 26th Inf. Co.G
Vestal, Hezekiah H. NC 26th Inf. Co.E
Vestal, H.T. NC 54th Inf. Co.H
Vestal, Isaac NC 5th Sr.Res. Co.H
Vestal, James M. TN 32nd Inf. Co.H
Vestal, James R. NC 26th Inf. Co.G
Vestal, James R. VA 37th Inf. Co.H
Vestal, Jay TN Cav. 9th Bn. (Gantt's) Co.G
Vestal, Jeremiah GA 2nd Inf. Co.E
Vestal, Jesse VA Inf. 1st Bn. Co.E
Vestal, J.H. AR Cav. Gordon's Regt. Co.B
Vestal, J.H. AR 15th Mil. Co.D
Vestal, J.M. AR Cav. Gordon's Regt. Co.G
Vestal, J.M. NC 28th Inf. Co.I
Vestal, J.M. TN Lt.Arty. Sparkman's Co. Cpl.
Vestal, Joab R. TX 21st Cav.
Vestal, John NC 3rd Jr.Res. Co.B
Vestal, John NC 4th Bn.Jr.Res. Co.B
Vestal, John VA 37th Inf. Co.H
Vestal, John A. NC 3rd Cav. (41st St.Troops) Co.D
Vestal, John A. NC 54th Inf. Co.K
Vestal, John B. NC 38th Inf. Co.B
Vestal, John C. TN 48th (Nixon's) Inf. Co.G
Vestal, John C. VA 37th Inf. Co.H
Vestal, John R. NC 3rd Inf. Co.H
Vestal, John S. TX 21st Cav. Co.D Sgt.
Vestal, Joseph S. AR 15th (N.W.) Inf. Co.A Sgt.
Vestal, J.S. AR Cav. Gordon's Regt. Co.G Cpl.
Vestal, J.T. TN Arty. Ramsey's Btty.
Vestal, J.T. TN 37th Inf. Co.G
Vestal, J.W. NC 9th Bn.S.S. Co.A
Vestal, J.W. 1st Cherokee Mtd.Vol. 2nd Co.E
Vestal, Larkin H. NC 28th Inf. Co.F
Vestal, Leonidas M. NC Hvy.Arty. 10th Bn. Co.A
Vestal, Lindsey C. NC Hvy.Arty. 10th Bn. Co.A 1st Sgt.
Vestal, Lodric B. VA 37th Inf. Co.H
Vestal, Martin B.V. NC 28th Inf. Co.I
Vestal, Miles J. NC 28th Inf. Co.I Sgt.
Vestal, Murphy E. NC 26th Inf. Co.G
Vestal, Nathan NC 48th Inf. Co.G
Vestal, Neal H. VA 37th Inf. Co.H
Vestal, N.G. TN 1st Hvy.Arty. 2nd Co.C Cpl.
Vestal, Oren D. NC 26th Inf. Co.E
Vestal, R.B. AR 19th (Dockery's) Inf. Co.C Sgt.
Vestal, Robert TN Arty. Ramsey's Btty. Sgt.
Vestal, Robert VA 52nd Inf. Co.I
Vestal, R.S. NC 38th Inf. Co.A
Vestal, Sion L. VA Mil. Washington Cty.
Vestal, T.A. MS Standefer's Co. 2nd Lt.
Vestal, Thomas TX 29th Cav. Co.G
Vestal, Thomas J. VA 37th Inf. Co.H
Vestal, Tilman R. TN 14th Inf. Co.I
Vestal, W.A. LA 2nd Cav. Co.G
Vestal, W.D. TX 5th Cav. Co.K Black.
Vestal, W.F. NC 26th Inf. Co.G
Vestal, William NC 9th Bn.S.S. Co.A
Vestal, William TN Inf. 3rd Cons.Regt. Co.H
Vestal, William TN 19th Inf. Co.E,H
Vestal, William B. TX 1st (McCulloch's) Cav. Co.K
Vestal, William B. TX 1st (Yager's) Cav. Co.I
Vestal, William B. TX Cav. 8th (Taylor's) Bn. Co.D
Vestal, William P.D. NC 21st Inf. Co.B
Vestal, W.P.D. NC 9th Bn.S.S. Co.A
Vestal, W.W. GA 8th Inf. Co.F
Vestall, Olliver NC Mallett's Bn. Co.A
Vestander, C. LA Mil. 2nd Regt. 2nd Brig. 1st Div. Co.C
Vestel, A.A. AR 6th Inf. Co.G Sgt.
Vestel, Asberry MO 11th Inf. Co.H
Vestel, James H. NC 44th Inf. Co.D
Vestel, John GA 52nd Inf. Co.H
Vestel, John C. TN 54th Inf. Co.B
Vestele, A. 10th Conf.Cav. Co.B
Vestell, Joseph NC 5th Sr.Res. Co.E
Vester, Benjamin F. TX 13th Vol. 1st Co.H
Vester, D.Y. TN 55th (Brown's) Inf. Co.B
Vester, J.B. MO 15th Cav. Co.L
Vester, J.C. TN 55th (Brown's) Inf. Co.B
Vester, Robert MS 2nd Inf. Co.F
Vesterling, A. AL Cav. Murphy's Bn. Co.C
Vesterling, A. 15th Conf.Cav. Co.H
Vestial, Adolphus G. NC Hvy.Arty. 10th Bn. Co.A
Vestill, A.J. TN 51st (Cons.) Inf. Co.F
Vestill, Andrew J. NC 2nd Cav. (19th St.Troops) Co.I
Vesting, Adolph GA Cav. 2nd Bn. Co.F
Vesting, Adolph GA 5th Cav. Co.B
Vesting, Adolph GA 47th Inf. Co.E
Vestle, Denis A. MD 1st Cav. Co.A
Vestol, John B. NC 28th Inf. Co.I
Vestring, Baptist LA Mil. 3rd Regt. 1st Brig. 1st Div. Co.I
Vestus, Nathan NC 1st Arty. (10th St.Troops) Co.D
Vestus, Nathan H. NC 3rd Arty. (40th St.Troops) Co.G
Vestz, W. SC Lt.Arty. 3rd (Palmetto) Bn. Culpeper's Co.
Veticut, Joseph T. Conf.Inf. 8th Bn.
Vetor, Joseph LA 7th Cav. Co.E
Vetsworth, --- VA 2nd Inf. Co.E
Vetta, Allis LA 10th Inf. Co.I
Vette, G. LA Mil. 1st Regt. French Brig. Co.3
Vetter, H. TX 2nd Inf. Co.I
Vetter, J. TX Cav. 2nd Regt.St.Troops Co.E
Vetter, J. TX Cav. Waller's Regt. Dunn's Co.
Vetter, J. TX Inf. 1st St.Troops Martin's Co.
Vetter, John LA 2nd Cav. Co.C
Vetter, Jno. VA Cav. 35th Bn. Co.D
Vetter, John G. TX 22nd Cav. Co.A
Vetters, Charles LA 4th Inf. Co.B
Vetters, Jacob VA Cav. 35th Bn. Co.A
Vetters, John VA 5th Inf. Co.A
Vetters, John VA 136th Mil. Co.C
Vetters, William VA 2nd Inf. Co.K
Vetters, William, Jr. VA 136th Mil. Co.C
Vetters, W.J. FL 1st Cav.
Vettertoe, A.G. NC 64th Inf. Co.L
Vettitoe, A.G. AR Cav. Gordon's Regt. Co.B
Vettla, James AL 20th Inf. Co.I
Veuleman, John MO 5th Inf. Co.G
Veulemans, Joseph LA 3rd Inf. Co.G
Veyman, J.R. GA 21st Inf. Co.E
Veyon, Alphonse LA 1st Hvy.Arty. (Reg.) Co.D
Veyual, Jean LA Mil. 2nd Regt. French Brig. Co.6
Vezey, James TX Inf. 1st St.Troops Sheldon's Co.B
Vezzy, William H. AL 12th Inf. Co.B
Vhintubbee 1st Choctaw Mtd.Rifles Co.F
Via, A. VA 21st Cav. 2nd Co.G
Via, A. VA 4th Cav. & Inf.St.Line 1st Co.I
Via, Anderson VA 57th Inf. Co.C
Via, Andrew KY 12th Cav. Co.A,D
Via, Andrew J. VA 15th Inf. Co.I
Via, A.R. TN 9th Inf. Co.I
Via, C.F. VA 88th Mil.
Via, Charles E. VA Lt.Arty. 12th Bn. 2nd Co.A
Via, Charles E. VA Lt.Arty. Sturdivant's Co.
Via, Charles F. VA Lt.Arty. 12th Bn. 2nd Co.A
Via, Charles F. VA Lt.Arty. Sturdivant's Co.
Via, Charles H. VA Cav. 37th Bn. Co.A
Via, Chesly C. VA Lt.Arty.Carpenter's Co.
Via, Clifton VA 26th Inf.
Via, D. VA 88th Mil.
Via, Dabney J. VA Lt.Arty. 12th Bn. 2nd Co.A
Via, Dabney J. VA Lt.Arty. Sturdivant's Co.
Via, Daniel VA 3rd Res. Co.I
Via, David VA Lt.Arty. B.Z. Price's Co.
Via, David VA Lt.Arty. W.H. Rice's Co.
Via, David VA 97th Mil. Co.B
Via, David G. VA Hvy.Arty. 18th Bn. Co.B
Via, Dillard VA 9th Inf. Co.B
Via, Dillard VA 57th Inf. Co.H
Via, D.J. VA 88th Mil.
Via, Doctor G. VA 51st Inf. Co.D
Via, E.D. VA 51st Inf. Co.H 1st Lt.
Via, Edward VA 56th Inf. Co.K Sgt.
Via, F.M. VA 14th Cav. Co.D 2nd Lt.
Via, Francis M. VA 59th Inf. 2nd Co.B
Via, George VA 3rd Res. Co.I
Via, George M. VA 1st Arty. Co.H
Via, George M. VA Arty. C.F. Johnston's Co.
Via, G.S. VA 54th Inf. Co.H
Via, Harrison VA 56th Inf. Co.K 2nd Lt.
Via, Horace W. VA Lt.Arty. 12th Bn. 2nd Co.A
Via, Horace W. VA Lt.Arty. Sturdivant's Co.
Via, H.W. VA 88th Mil.
Via, I.H. VA 88th Mil.
Via, Isaac VA Lt.Arty. Fry's Co.
Via, Isaac VA 57th Inf. Co.K
Via, Jackson VA 36th Inf. 2nd Co.B 1st Lt.
Via, James VA 14th Cav. Co.D
Via, James VA 21st Cav. 2nd Co.G
Via, James VA 42nd Inf. Co.H
Via, James VA 74th Mil. Co.E Cpl.
Via, James Archibald VA 1st Inf. Co.H Cpl.
Via, James E. VA 51st Inf. Co.C
Via, James F. VA 10th Cav.
Via, James G. VA Loc.Def. Mallory's Co.
Via, James R. VA 51st Inf. Co.D
Via, James T. VA 23rd Cav. Co.M
Via, James T. VA 1st Inf. Co.G
Via, James T. VA 135th Mil. Co.B
Via, James W. VA 19th Inf. Co.B
Via, Jesse VA 12th Inf. Co.D

Via, J.H. LA LA & Government Employees Regt. Co.G 1st Lt.
Via, J.L. KY 12th Cav. Co.A
Via, John VA 21st Cav. 2nd Co.G
Via, John VA 22nd Inf. Taylor's Co.
Via, John H. AL Lt.Arty. 2nd Bn. Co.E Cpl.
Via, John J. VA 60th Inf. Co.E
Via, John R. VA Lt.Arty. 12th Bn. 2nd Co.A
Via, John R. VA Lt.Arty. Sturdivant's Co.
Via, John W. VA Lt.Arty. 12th Bn. 2nd Co.A
Via, John W. VA Lt.Arty. Sturdivant's Co.
Via, John W. VA 57th Inf. Co.H
Via, Joseph VA 17th Cav. Co.E
Via, Joseph VA 54th Inf. Co.H
Via, J.R. VA 88th Mil.
Via, J.T. MD 1st Cav. Co.G
Via, J.W. VA 13th Inf. Co.F
Via, J.W. VA 88th Mil.
Via, Larkin T. VA 54th Inf. Co.H
Via, Lewis VA 49th Inf. Co.I
Via, Lilburn H. VA 46th Inf. 1st Co.G
Via, Lyman VA Lt.Arty. Carrington's Co. Guidon
Via, Manoali G. VA 56th Inf. Co.H
Via, Pete VA 60th Inf. Co.D
Via, Pleasant TN 47th Inf. Co.D
Via, Pleasant A. VA 19th Inf. Co.I
Via, Pleasant M. VA Lt.Arty. 12th Bn. 2nd Co.A
Via, Pleasant M. VA Lt.Arty. Sturdivant's Co.
Via, Reuben VA Lt.Arty. Fry's Co.
Via, Robert TN 20th (Russell's) Cav. Co.I
Via, Robert C. VA 7th Inf. Co.I
Via, Samuel VA 49th Inf. Co.I
Via, Samuel VA 57th Inf. Co.C Sgt.
Via, Samuel E. VA 57th Inf. Co.K
Via, Samuel J. VA Prov.Guard Avis' Co.
Via, S.J. VA 46th Inf. 1st Co.G
Via, Sparrel VA 36th Inf. 2nd Co.B
Via, T.H. VA 10th Cav. Co.F
Via, Thomas D. VA 7th Inf. Co.I
Via, Thomas G. MO 4th Cav. Co.D Sgt.
Via, Thompson S. VA 57th Inf. Co.H Sgt.
Via, T.N. KY 7th Mtd.Inf. Co.B
Via, T.T. VA 1st Res. Co.A
Via, T.T. VA 88th Mil.
Via, W. KY 12th Cav. Co.I
Via, Waller T. VA 56th Inf. Co.H
Via, Walter T. VA Goochland Lt.Arty.
Via, W.B. VA 10th Cav. Co.K
Via, Wesley A. MO 10th Inf. Co.D
Via, Wesley T. VA 25th Inf. 2nd Co.H Cpl.
Via, W.H. VA 56th Inf. Co.H
Via, Wiley A. VA 57th Inf. Co.K
Via, William VA 7th Bn.Res. Co.D
Via, William VA 19th Inf. Co.I
Via, William VA Inf. 25th Bn. Co.G
Via, William VA Rockbridge Cty.Res. Hutcheson's Co.
Via, William A. VA 17th Cav. Co.E
Via, William A. VA 52nd Inf. Co.A
Via, William B. VA 42nd Inf. Co.G
Via, William F. VA 57th Inf. Co.H
Via, William H. VA Lt.Arty. Lamkin's Co.
Via, W.R. VA 2nd Cav. Co.K
Viacava, --- VA 2nd St.Res. Co.A
Viade, Juan LA Mil. 5th Regt.Eur.Brig. (Spanish Regt.) Co.5
Viade, R. LA Mil. Cazadores Espanoles Regt. Co.1 Cpl.
Viade, Tomas LA Mil. Cazadores Espanoles Regt. Co.2 Cpl.
Vial, A. LA Lt.Arty. LeGardeur, Jr.'s Co. (Orleans Guard Btty.) Bugler
Vial, A.J. MO Lt.Arty. Barret's Co.
Vial, C.S. VA 42nd Inf. Co.F
Vial, F. TX 9th (Nichols') Inf. Co.G
Vial, F. TX Waul's Legion Co.A
Vial, Joseph LA C.S. Zouave Bn. Co.C Cpl.
Vial, Peter VA 1st St.Res. Co.A
Viala, B. LA Mil. 1st Regt. French Brig. Co.3
Viala, H. LA Arty. 5th Field Btty. (Pelican Lt.Arty.)
Viala, J.L. LA Mil. 1st Regt. French Brig. Co.3
Viala, Philogene LA Arty. Landry's Co. (Donaldsonville Arty.) Cpl.
Viala, Theogene LA 1st Cav. Co.A
Viale, H. LA Mil. Terrebonne Regt.
Viallon, P. LA Arty. Guyol's Co. (Orleans Arty.)
Viallon, Paul LA Lt.Arty. LeGardeur, Jr.'s Co. (Orleans Guard Btty.)
Viallon, P. Nicolet LA Inf. 7th Bn. Co.A
Vialon, Paul LA 30th Inf. Co.G
Viands, Henry VA 18th Cav. Co.D
Vianes, --- VA 46th Inf. Co.G
Vians, Henry VA Cav. 41st Bn. Trayhern's Co.
Viar, A.J. TN 62nd Mtd.Inf. Co.F
Viar, David VA Loc.Def. Bosher's Co.
Viar, George W. VA 24th Inf. Co.E
Viar, George W. VA 54th Inf. Co.I
Viar, H.W. VA Res.Forces Thurston's Co.
Viar, Isaac S. VA 54th Inf. Co.I
Viar, J.A. VA Wade's Regt.Loc.Def. Co.D
Viar, Jacob VA Lt.Arty. 38th Bn. Co.D Driver
Viar, Jesse W. VA 1st Inf. Co.H
Viar, John VA 22nd Cav. Co.H
Viar, John VA 4th Inf. Co.D
Viar, Lowery VA 22nd Cav. Co.H
Viar, Riley TN 62nd Mtd.Inf. Co.F
Viar, Robert TN 62nd Mtd.Inf. Co.F Cpl.
Viar, Robert VA Inf. Lyneman's Co.
Viar, Samuel VA 54th Inf. Co.C
Viar, Samuel 3rd Conf.Eng.Troops Co.A Artif.
Viar, Thomas G. MO Cav. Freeman's Regt. Co.F
Viar, William VA 54th Inf. Co.I
Viar, William H. VA 15th Inf. Co.I
Viar, William M. VA 22nd Cav. Co.H
Viar, William M. VA 30th Bn.S.S. Co.D
Viarant, H. LA Mil. Orleans Guards Regt. Co.C
Viarant, J.L. LA Mil. Orleans Guards Regt. Co.C
Viard, Benjamin SC 1st Mtd.Mil. Smith's Co.
Viard, Benjamin SC 5th Cav. Co.C
Viard, Benjamin SC Cav. 17th Bn. Co.D
Viard, P.B. AL 1st Bn. Hilliard's Legion Vol. Co.A
Viars, Amos L. VA 29th Inf. Co.A
Viars, Amos L. VA 45th Inf. Co.K
Viars, Amos L. VA 63rd Inf. 2nd Co.I
Viars, Anderson T. VA 24th Inf. Co.K
Viars, Henry W. VA Lt.Arty. W.P. Carter's Co.
Viars, Isaac KY 5th Mtd.Inf. Co.D
Viars, James V. VA 22nd Cav. Co.K
Viars, John B. VA 24th Inf. Co.E
Viars, Lafayette VA 24th Inf. Co.K
Viars, Richard KY 5th Mtd.Inf. Co.D
Viars, Thomas VA 24th Inf. Co.K
Viars, William S. VA 63rd Inf. Co.D
Viary, Joseph H. TN 7th Inf. Co.G
Vias, Samuel VA 2nd Cav. Co.H
Viasca, J. LA Mil. Orleans Guards Regt. Co.B
Viass, Matthew VA 3rd Cav. & Inf.St.Line Co.A
Viaten, Joseph LA Inf. 10th Bn. Co.F
Viator, Alphonse LA Conscr.
Viator, Andre LA Conscr.
Viator, Antoine LA 7th Cav. Co.K
Viator, Antoine LA Inf. 10th Bn. Co.C
Viator, Antoine LA Conscr.
Viator, Beatist LA 7th Cav. Co.H
Viator, Edoward LA Conscr.
Viator, Emanuel LA Conscr.
Viator, Hervillien LA Conscr.
Viator, Joseph LA Conscr.
Viator, Lassatire LA Inf. 10th Bn. Co.C
Viator, Manuel LA Inf. 10th Bn. Co.C
Viator, Theogene LA Conscr.
Viator, Trinecourt LA 7th Cav. Co.G
Viator, Vileor LA Conscr.
Viator, William LA Inf. 10th Bn. Co.C
Viaunet, B. LA Mil. 3rd Regt. French Brig. Co.8
Viavant, A. LA Mil. 4th Regt. 2nd Brig. 1st Div. Co.I 1st Lt.
Viavant, A., Jr. LA Cav. Greenleaf's Co. (Orleans Lt.Horse) Sgt.
Viavant, A., Jr. LA Mil. Orleans Guards Regt. Co.D
Viavant, H. LA 22nd Inf. Co.C
Viavant, H. LA 22nd (Cons.) Inf. Co.E
Vibbart, James H. TN 1st (Turney's) Inf. Co.B
Vibbert, Horace D. LA 11th Inf. Co.I
Vic, R. TN 19th & 20th (Cons.) Cav. Co.E
Vicain, E. LA 1st Inf. Co.B
Vicar, William B. VA 41st Inf. Co.F
Vicare, D. LA Inf.Cons.Crescent Regt. Co.L
Vicario, Diego LA 30th Inf. Co.D,G Cpl.
Vicaro, Joseph LA 4th Inf. Co.D
Vicars, E.H. GA 16th Inf. Co.F
Vicars, Ferdinand A. AR 8th Inf. New Co.E Lt.
Vicars, F.J. VA Mil. Scott Cty.
Vicars, Francis M. VA 19th Cav. Co.G
Vicars, Henry VA 25th Cav. Co.B,K
Vicars, Jacob TN Cav. 16th Bn. (Neal's) Co.B
Vicars, Jacob TN 62nd Mtd.Inf. Co.K
Vicars, Joel VA Mil. Scott Cty.
Vicars, Joel VA St.Line
Vicars, John VA 25th Cav. Co.H
Vicars, John VA 48th Inf. Co.G
Vicars, John VA 72nd Mil.
Vicars, John W. AR 24th Inf. Co.F
Vicars, Joseph TN 35th Inf. 1st Co.A, Co.B
Vicars, Peter VA 72nd Mil.
Vicars, Robert TN Cav. 16th Bn. (Neal's) Co.B
Vicars, Robert TN 62nd Mtd.Inf. Co.K
Vicars, Samuel VA 72nd Mil.
Vicars, Thomas VA Mil. Scott Cty.
Vicars, W.H. TN Cav. 16th Bn. (Neal's) Co.B
Vicars, William VA 72nd Mil.
Vicars, William, Jr. VA 72nd Mil.
Viccellio, H. VA Inf. Montague's Bn. Co.B
Viccillio, Henry VA 53rd Inf. Co.I
Vice, --- GA 19th Inf. Co.K Cpl.

Vice, Columbus B. LA 28th (Gray's) Inf. Co.C
Vice, George TN 19th (Biffle's) Cav. Co.A
Vice, George P. SC 5th Cav. Co.E
Vice, G.P. SC Manigault's Bn.Vol. Co.A
Vice, James SC 2nd St.Troops Co.C
Vice, James VA 42nd Inf. Co.H
Vice, J.D.F. SC Manigault's Bn.Vol. Co.A
Vice, J.E. TX 32nd Cav. Co.F
Vice, J.H. AL Cav. Hardie's Bn.Res. S.D. McClellan's Co.
Vice, J.M. SC 5th Cav. Co.E
Vice, Jno. AL 8th (Hatch's) Cav. Co.E Drum.
Vice, John D.F. SC 5th Cav. Co.E
Vice, John R. AL 8th (Hatch's) Cav. Co.K
Vice, John R. AL 17th Inf. Co.C,E
Vice, J.R., Jr. AL 8th Inf. Co.E
Vice, L.H. AL 5th Bn.Vol. Co.C
Vice, Mansfield KY 2nd Bn.Mtd.Rifles Co.B
Vice, Memory AL Cp. of Instr. Talladega
Vice, W. SC 2nd St.Troops
Vicens, Guillermo LA Mil. 5th Regt.Eur.Brig. (Spanish Regt.) Co.2
Vicente, John H. SC 1st (Butler's) Inf. Co.G Sgt.
Vicentini, Felipe LA Mil. 5th Regt.Eur.Brig. (Spanish Regt.) Co.9
Viceroy, Calvin GA 24th Inf. Co.G
Viceroy, William D. AL 16th Inf. Co.K
Vicery, Frank MO 8th Cav. Co.I
Vich, J.A. MS 8th Inf. Co.H
Vicheler, T.G. VA 49th Inf.
Vick, --- TX 33rd Cav. Co.F
Vick, A. LA 13th Bn. (Part.Rangers) Co.B
Vick, A.B. SC 5th Inf. 2nd Co.D
Vick, Abel J. NC 47th Inf. Co.A
Vick, Abraham AL 26th Inf.
Vick, Absalom NC 35th Inf. Co.C Sgt.
Vick, A.F. MS 3rd Inf. (A. of 10,000) Co.C
Vick, Albert AR 19th (Dawson's) Inf. Co.A
Vick, Albert SC 1st (Butler's) Inf. Co.A,K
Vick, Alexander AL 5th Cav. Co.B
Vick, Alexander AL 41st Inf. Co.H
Vick, Alexander AL 43rd Inf. Co.I
Vick, Alexander W. TN 7th Inf. Capt.,AQM
Vick, Alex W. Heth's Div. Maj.,Div.QM
Vick, Allen F. MS 34th Inf. Co.E
Vick, A.M. GA 12th Cav. Co.B
Vick, A.N. AL Cp. of Instr. Talladega
Vick, Andrew J. VA 5th Cav. (12 mo. '61-2) Co.H
Vick, Andrew J. VA 13th Cav. Co.A Sgt.
Vick, Anthony W. VA 41st Inf. Co.H
Vick, A.R. MS 10th Inf. New Co.I 1st Sgt.
Vick, B. NC 2nd Jr.Res. Co.G
Vick, B.B. TN 50th Inf. Co.D
Vick, Benjamin F. AL 42nd Inf. Co.C
Vick, Benjamin F. VA Hvy.Arty. 18th Bn. N.C.S. A.Hosp.Stew.
Vick, Benjamin H. NC 30th Inf. Co.I
Vick, Benjamin J. AR 14th (Powers') Inf. Co.K
Vick, Benjamin T. VA 41st Inf. Co.H
Vick, Berry TX 19th Inf. Co.D
Vick, Britton C. NC 1st Inf. Co.F
Vick, Burton NC 17th Inf. (2nd Org.) Co.C
Vick, Bushrod W. NC 7th Inf. Co.E 2nd Lt.
Vick, C. MS 24th Inf. Co.G
Vick, Calvin TN 26th Inf. Co.C
Vick, Charles J. AL 27th Inf. Co.B
Vick, Chris TX 13th Vol. 2nd Co.H
Vick, Clement L. SC Lt.Arty. Kelly's Co. (Chesterfield Arty.)
Vick, C.T. AL 38th Inf. Co.I
Vick, C.T. TX 21st Cav. Co.F
Vick, Cullen TX 21st Cav. Co.F
Vick, C.W. TN Inf. 4th Cons.Regt. Co.E
Vick, David NC 1st Arty. (10th St.Troops) Co.A
Vick, David NC 3rd Arty. (40th St.Troops) Co.G
Vick, David NC 4th Inf. Co.F
Vick, David NC 17th Inf. (1st Org.) Co.C
Vick, Davis VA 3rd Inf. Co.G
Vick, Demboriah W. GA 50th Inf. Co.C
Vick, D.H. MS Inf. 1st Bn. Co.C
Vick, D.L. KY 1st (Helm's) Cav. New Co.A
Vick, E. AL 4th Inf. Co.B
Vick, E. AL 45th Inf. Co.F
Vick, Eaton TN 14th Inf. Co.D
Vick, E.C. TX Cav. 2nd Regt.St.Troops Co.C
Vick, Edmond M. NC 32nd Inf. Co.B,C
Vick, Edmund M. AL 6th Inf. Co.I Sgt.
Vick, Edward C. NC 7th Inf. Co.E
Vick, Edward N. VA Inf. Cohoon's Bn. Co.A,B
Vick, Edward S. MS 19th Inf. Co.G
Vick, E.J. TN Inf. 4th Cons.Regt. Co.E
Vick, E.J. TN 26th Inf. Co.C
Vick, Elias VA 41st Inf. Co.H
Vick, Elias R. NC 1st Inf. Co.F
Vick, Elijah NC 27th Inf. Co.K
Vick, Elisha NC 12th Inf. Co.O
Vick, Elisha NC 32nd Inf. Co.C,D
Vick, Eli W. MS 34th Inf. Co.E
Vick, E.M. NC 12th Inf. Co.N
Vick, Emanuel AL 3rd Res. Co.B,K
Vick, Enoch B. NC 44th Inf. Co.D
Vick, E.R. AL 23rd Inf. Co.A
Vick, E.T. AL Inf. 2nd Regt. Co.D
Vick, E.T. AL 38th Inf. Co.I
Vick, Exum R. NC 30th Inf. Co.I
Vick, George AL 29th Inf. Co.E
Vick, George AL Cp. of Instr. Talladega
Vick, George W. AL 43rd Inf. Co.A
Vick, G.W. AL 5th Cav. Co.F
Vick, H. MS Inf. 2nd Bn. Co.L
Vick, Hartwell D. MS 48th Inf. Co.L
Vick, H.C. AR 15th Mil. Co.C
Vick, H. Clay AR Cav. 1st Bn. (Stirman's) Co.F
Vick, Henry AL 32nd Inf. Co.I
Vick, Henry AL 41st Inf. Co.H
Vick, Henry TX Cav. 2nd Regt.St.Troops Co.C
Vick, H.H. TX 8th Inf. Co.F
Vick, Howell G. VA 12th Inf. 2nd Co.I
Vick, Howell R. MS 18th Cav. Co.A
Vick, H.P. TX Inf. 2nd St.Troops Co.A
Vick, Hudson NC 3rd Bn.Sr.Res. Williams' Co.
Vick, Hudson NC 47th Inf. Co.A
Vick, I.K. TX 1st Inf. 2nd Co.K Chap.
Vick, Iredell R. AR 3rd Inf. Co.C
Vick, Isaac H. MS 5th Inf. (St.Troops) Co.D
Vick, J. GA 41st Inf. Co.C
Vick, J. NC 2nd Jr.Res. Co.K
Vick, J.A. AL 62nd Inf. Co.C,B
Vick, Jacob MS 40th Inf. Co.D
Vick, James AR Cav. 1st Bn. (Stirman's) Co.F
Vick, James AL Mil. 2nd Regt.Vol. Co.C
Vick, James GA Cav. 20th Bn. Co.A,E
Vick, James KY 3rd Cav. Co.B
Vick, James NC 12th Inf. Co.H
Vick, James NC 32nd Inf. Co.H
Vick, James VA 3rd Inf. Co.G
Vick, James VA 9th Inf. Co.B
Vick, James VA 12th Inf. Co.K
Vick, James VA 59th Inf. 3rd Co.F
Vick, James A. MS Inf. 7th Bn. Co.E
Vick, James B. VA 5th Cav. (12 mo. '61-2) Co.H
Vick, James B. VA 13th Cav. Co.A
Vick, James E. VA 41st Inf. Co.H
Vick, James F. NC 30th Inf. Co.I
Vick, James L. NC 17th Inf. (2nd Org.) Co.I
Vick, Jasper MS 2nd Inf. (A. of 10,000) Co.G
Vick, Jasper MS 42nd Inf. Co.F
Vick, J.B. GA Inf. 8th Bn. Co.F
Vick, J.B. NC 2nd Jr.Res. Co.G 1st Sgt.
Vick, J.E., Jr. VA Res.
Vick, Jesse TX 20th Inf. Co.K
Vick, Jesse Brush Bn.
Vick, Jesse E. VA Hvy.Arty. 18th Bn. Co.A Cpl.
Vick, Jesse G.W. NC 7th Inf. Co.E Sgt.
Vick, Jesse V. NC 61st Inf. Co.H
Vick, J.F. AL 62nd Inf. Co.I
Vick, J.H.W. LA 8th Inf. Co.G
Vick, J.J. MS Lt.Arty. 14th Bn. Co.B
Vick, J.J. NC 3rd Bn.Sr.Res. Co.A
Vick, J.M.H. VA 20th Inf. Co.C
Vick, J.M.H. VA Inf. 28th Bn. Co.D
Vick, Joel T. TN 48th (Voorhies') Inf. Co.B
Vick, John MS 5th Cav. Co.H
Vick, John MS 18th Cav. Co.C
Vick, John MS St.Troops (Peach Creek Rangers) Maxwell's Co.
Vick, John NC 35th Inf. Co.C
Vick, John NC 47th Inf. Co.A
Vick, John TN 35th Inf. 3rd Co.F
Vick, John TN 50th Inf. Co.D
Vick, John VA Inf. 44th Bn. Co.B
Vick, John A. MS 14th Inf. Co.A
Vick, John B. NC Cav. 12th Bn. Co.C
Vick, John B. NC Cav. 16th Bn. Co.G
Vick, John B. VA 41st Inf. Co.H
Vick, John B. 8th (Dearing's) Conf.Cav. Co.C
Vick, John H. VA 41st Inf. Co.H
Vick, John M. VA 3rd Lt.Arty. (Loc.Def.) Co.D
Vick, John N. NC 8th Bn.Part.Rangers Co.D,F Sgt.
Vick, John N. NC 50th Inf. Co.E
Vick, John N.B. NC 66th Inf. Co.I
Vick, John R. AL 9th Inf. Co.D
Vick, John T. VA 41st Inf. Co.H
Vick, John W. NC 14th Inf. Co.A
Vick, John W. TN 54th Inf. Co.E
Vick, Joseph LA 13th Inf. Co.G
Vick, Joseph NC 7th Inf. Co.E
Vick, Joseph J. NC 12th Inf. Co.H
Vick, Joseph J. NC 30th Inf. Co.I
Vick, Joshua D. TN 44th (Cons.) Inf. Co.C
Vick, Joshua W. NC 7th Inf. Co.E Capt.
Vick, Josiah NC 1st Jr.Res. Co.A
Vick, Josiah NC 47th Inf. Co.D
Vick, Josiah D. TN 55th (McKoin's) Inf. James' Co.

Vick, Josiah J.B. NC 2nd Cav. (19th St.Troops) Co.E Capt.
Vick, Josiah S. TN 50th Inf. Co.H
Vick, J.R. AL 62nd Inf. Co.H
Vick, J.R. Gen. & Staff Chap.
Vick, J.S. AL 23rd Inf. Co.A
Vick, J.S. SC 1st (Butler's) Inf. Co.A,K
Vick, J.T. LA 1st Cav. Co.K
Vick, J.T. TN 48th (Nixon's) Inf. Co.A
Vick, Julius MS 13th Inf. Co.E Cpl.
Vick, J.W. TN 48th (Nixon's) Inf. Co.K
Vick, J.W. TX 21st Cav. Co.F
Vick, L. AL 4th Inf. Co.B
Vick, Lawrence AL 1st Cav. 1st Co.K
Vick, Lawson AR Inf. 2nd Bn. Co.C
Vick, Lawson AR 3rd Inf. Co.G
Vick, L.B.F. MS Inf. 3rd Bn. (St.Troops) Co.E Sgt.
Vick, Levi AL 5th Cav. Co.B
Vick, Lorenzo NC 30th Inf. Co.F
Vick, L.W. AL 31st Inf. Co.I Capt.
Vick, M.H. GA 10th Inf.
Vick, M.P. MS Inf. 7th Bn. Co.E
Vick, Nathan TN 49th Inf. Co.A
Vick, Nathan Inf. Bailey's Cons.Regt. Co.G
Vick, Nathan G. TN 13th (Gore's) Cav. Co.C
Vick, Nathan W. NC 8th Inf. Co.C
Vick, Nathan W. NC 33rd Inf. Co.E
Vick, Newton AL 25th Inf. Co.B
Vick, Otto AL 6th Inf. Co.G
Vick, P.E. NC 8th Bn.Part.Rangers Co.D
Vick, Peter AL 32nd Inf. Co.I
Vick, Peter MS Lt.Arty. 14th Bn. Co.B
Vick, Pinckney TN 50th Inf. Co.D Teamster
Vick, R. TN 13th (Gore's) Cav. Co.C
Vick, Redin A. NC 43rd Inf. Co.E
Vick, Richard H. VA 6th Inf. Co.K
Vick, R.J. MS 10th Inf. New Co.I
Vick, Robartus TN 28th Inf. Co.B
Vick, Robert NC 4th Inf. Co.F
Vick, Robert NC 17th Inf. (1st Org.) Co.C
Vick, Robert C. NC 39th Inf. Co.D
Vick, Robert C. TN 53rd Inf. Co.I
Vick, R.R. AL 62nd Inf. Co.C
Vick, Samuel MS Lt.Arty. 14th Bn. Co.B
Vick, Samuel NC Inf. 13th Bn. Co.D
Vick, Samuel NC 51st Inf. Co.A
Vick, Samuel VA 41st Inf. Co.H
Vick, Samuel D. LA 27th Inf. Co.C Sgt.
Vick, Samuel D. MS 40th Inf. Co.D
Vick, Samuel S. NC 12th Inf. Co.H Capt.
Vick, Shanley NC 2nd Arty. (36th St.Troops) Co.D
Vick, Sidney TN 38th Inf. Co.C
Vick, S.J. MS Lt.Arty. Yates' Btty.
Vick, Sydney TN 39th Mtd.Inf. Co.I
Vick, Tamlin H.M. VA Hvy.Arty. Coleman's Co.
Vick, T. Cicero NC 12th Inf. Co.H Sgt.
Vick, T.E. TX 9th (Nichols') Inf. Co.B Sgt.
Vick, T.E. TX 18th Inf. Co.K Jr.2nd Lt.
Vick, Thaddeus W. AR 3rd Inf. Co.C
Vick, Thomas MS Inf. 2nd St.Troops Co.G
Vick, Thomas TX 20th Inf. Co.H
Vick, Thomas B. VA 3rd Inf. Co.G
Vick, Thomas B. VA 32nd Inf. Co.E
Vick, Thomas E. LA 4th Inf. Co.E Maj.
Vick, Thomas E. TX 17th Inf. Surg.
Vick, Thomas W. TN 42nd Inf. 2nd Co.F
Vick, T.J. AL 23rd Inf. Co.A
Vick, V.C. TX 20th Inf. Co.K
Vick, W.A. TN 45th Inf. Co.H Cpl.
Vick, W.A. TX 1st Inf. Co.M
Vick, Walter C. KY 1st Inf. Co.K
Vick, W.B. SC 23rd Inf. Co.A
Vick, W.D. TN 50th Inf. Co.D
Vick, Wesley J. TN 53rd Inf. Co.I Sgt.
Vick, Wesley J. TX 5th Inf. Co.B
Vick, W.F. TX 21st Cav. Co.E
Vick, W.H. AL 29th Inf. Co.E
Vick, W.H. AL Unassign.Recruit
Vick, W.H. KY 1st (Butler's) Cav. Co.A
Vick, W.H. MS Inf. 1st Bn. Co.C
Vick, William NC 30th Inf. Co.F
Vick, William SC 20th Inf. Co.G
Vick, William TX 20th Inf. Co.G
Vick, William TX 21st Cav. Co.E
Vick, William TX 1st Hvy.Arty. Co.G
Vick, William VA 12th Inf. Co.K
Vick, William A. MS 14th Inf. Co.A Sgt.
Vick, William B. NC 3rd Arty. (40th St.Troops) Co.F
Vick, William B. SC 4th St.Troops Co.K
Vick, William C. KY 1st Inf. Co.K
Vick, William D. NC 5th Inf. Co.G
Vick, William E. SC Lt.Arty. Kelly's Co. (Chesterfield Arty.)
Vick, William H. AL 43rd Inf. Co.B,A
Vick, William H. MS 17th Inf. Co.G
Vick, William H. NC 12th Inf. Co.O
Vick, William H. NC 30th Inf. Co.I
Vick, William H. NC 32nd Inf. Co.C,D
Vick, William H. VA 41st Inf. Co.H
Vick, William J. AR 23rd Inf. Co.E
Vick, William J. LA 27th Inf. Co.C
Vick, William P. NC Cav. 12th Bn. Co.C 1st Sgt.
Vick, William P. NC 15th Inf. Co.A 2nd Lt.
Vick, William R. VA 3rd Inf. Co.D
Vick, William S. NC 2nd Arty. (36th St.Troops) Co.D
Vick, William S. TN 53rd Inf. Co.I
Vick, William T. MS 40th Inf. Co.D
Vick, Willie R. NC 30th Inf. Co.I
Vick, Willis TN 6th Inf. Co.A
Vick, W.J. GA 24th Inf. Co.B
Vick, W.J. TN 54th Inf. Co.E
Vick, W.S. TN 38th Inf. Co.E
Vickar, J. KY 12th Cav. Co.E
Vickard, A. LA Ogden's Cav. Co.G
Vickars, A.K.P. AL 14th Inf. Co.H
Vickars, Eason A. LA 27th Inf. Co.C
Vickars, Jackson MO Cav. 3rd Bn. Co.F
Vickars, James VA 28th Inf. Co.B
Vickars, J.M. MS Blythe's Bn. (St.Troops) Co.A
Vickars, Thomas VA 64th Mtd.Inf. Co.H
Vicker, --- TX 25th Cav. Co.E
Vicker, A. VA 61st Inf. Co.B
Vicker, A.M. FL 1st Cav.
Vicker, Bangrac LA Mil. Chalmette Regt. Co.G
Vicker, Silas TX 30th Cav. Co.A
Vicker, Thomas A. MO St.Guard
Vickerey, Azel TX 14th Cav. Co.I
Vickerey, Levi TX 14th Cav. Co.I
Vickerey, Richard GA 50th Inf. Co.B
Vickers, --- GA 19th Inf. Co.E
Vickers, A.B. SC Lt.Arty. 3rd (Palmetto) Bn. Co.A QMSgt.
Vickers, Absolem M. GA 9th Inf. (St.Guards) Co.G
Vickers, Albert TN 14th Inf. Co.E
Vickers, Alexander R. NC 50th Inf. Co.G
Vickers, A.M. GA 1st Lt.Duty Men Co.A
Vickers, Andrew FL 1st (Res.) Inf. Co.F
Vickers, Andrew J. AL 12th Inf. Co.I
Vickers, Andrew J. GA 2nd Cav. Co.I
Vickers, Andrew J. NC 1st Cav. (9th St.Troops) Co.F
Vickers, A. Newton TX 10th Inf. Co.I
Vickers, A.T. AL 46th Inf. Co.D 1st Lt.
Vickers, Benjamin C. TN 4th Inf. Co.A
Vickers, Benjamin F. AL 6th Inf. Co.E
Vickers, Benjamin F. AL 12th Inf. Co.I
Vickers, B.H.D. AL 14th Inf. Co.H
Vickers, Caleb Z. TX 36th Cav. Co.E,A
Vickers, Charles C. VA 36th Inf. 2nd Co.B
Vickers, Charles L. VA 8th Cav. Co.G
Vickers, Christopher W. TX 36th Cav. Co.C
Vickers, C.L. VA 1st Cav.St.Line Co.B
Vickers, C.S. GA 7th Inf. Co.G Cpl.
Vickers, D. FL Cav. 5th Bn. Co.D
Vickers, D. GA 50th Inf. Co.D
Vickers, David H. TN 14th Inf. Co.G
Vickers, David P. TX 10th Inf. Co.I
Vickers, D.C. VA Mil. Scott Cty.
Vickers, Demarkus M.R. AL 20th Inf. Co.B,C
Vickers, E. TN 21st & 22nd (Cons.) Cav. Co.F
Vickers, Edward S. TN 21st (Wilson's) Cav. Co.E
Vickers, Elijah GA 50th Inf. Co.I
Vickers, Elijah M. TN 21st (Wilson's) Cav. Co.E
Vickers, Eli M. TX 10th Inf. Co.I
Vickers, E.N. NC 53rd Inf. Co.B
Vickers, Ephraim FL 2nd Cav. Co.D
Vickers, F.B. MS 9th Inf. New Co.D
Vickers, F.E. TX 24th Cav. Co.C 1st Sgt.
Vickers, F.L. MO St.Guard W.H. Taylor's Co.
Vickers, Floyd S. VA 36th Inf. 2nd Co.B
Vickers, Francis M. LA 19th Inf. Co.B Cpl.
Vickers, Francis M. VA 22nd Inf. Swann's Co.
Vickers, Francis M. VA Inf. 25th Bn. Co.C
Vickers, Francis M. VA 59th Inf. 2nd Co.K
Vickers, George AL 4th Res. Co.F
Vickers, George F. NC 4th Cav. (59th St.Troops) Co.E Sgt.
Vickers, G.W. TN 49th Inf. Co.H
Vickers, G.W. Inf. Bailey's Cons.Regt. Co.C
Vickers, H. GA Cav. 20th Bn. Co.A
Vickers, H. GA 50th Inf. Co.D
Vickers, Harris FL 1st (Res.) Inf. Co.F
Vickers, Henry GA 8th Cav. New Co.D
Vickers, Henry KY 9th Mtd.Inf. Co.C
Vickers, Henry C. MO Cav. Hunter's Regt. Co.F
Vickers, Henry L. TN 3rd (Forrest's) Cav. Co.B Capt.
Vickers, Henry Owens MO 4th Cav. Co.A
Vickers, Henry P. TX 15th Cav. Co.K
Vickers, Henry P. TX 10th Inf. Co.I
Vickers, H.F. LA 27th Inf. Co.B Sgt.
Vickers, Hiram NC 6th Inf. Co.C Sgt.
Vickers, H.T. GA 7th Inf. Co.G

Vickers, J. GA Inf. 18th Bn. Co.A
Vickers, J. GA 50th Inf. Co.D
Vickers, J. LA Mil. 1st Regt. 2nd Brig. 1st Div. Co.B
Vickers, Jacob GA 53rd Inf. Co.A
Vickers, James AL Inf. 1st Regt. Co.F
Vickers, James VA 8th Cav. Co.G Sgt.
Vickers, James A. TX 36th Cav. Co.A
Vickers, James K.P. AL 46th Inf. Co.D
Vickers, James L. FL 6th Inf. Co.G
Vickers, James L. FL Campbellton Boys
Vickers, James M. AL Inf. 1st Regt. Co.A
Vickers, James M. LA 8th Inf. Co.E
Vickers, James R. AL Mil. 4th Vol. Co.A
Vickers, James R. AL 38th Inf. Co.H
Vickers, James W. VA 4th Inf. Co.C
Vickers, J.C. GA Inf. 23rd Bn.Loc.Def. Pendergrass' Co.
Vickers, J.C. GA 44th Inf.
Vickers, J.C. TN 23rd Inf. Co.H
Vickers, J.D. GA 59th Inf. Co.D
Vickers, Jefferson MS 3rd (St.Troops) Cav. Co.I
Vickers, Jefferson MS Inf. 1st Bn.St.Troops (12 mo. '62-3) Co.D Cpl.
Vickers, Jesse AL 6th Cav. Co.E
Vickers, J.F. GA 2nd St.Line Co.K
Vickers, J.H. AR 45th Cav. Co.H
Vickers, J. Hiram AL Lt.Arty. Goldthwaite's Btty.
Vickers, J.J. MS 2nd St.Cav. Co.H
Vickers, J.J. MS 6th Cav. Co.B
Vickers, J.J. TN 16th Inf. Co.H
Vickers, J.M. AL Lt.Arty. Kolb's Btty.
Vickers, J.M. AL St.Guards
Vickers, J.M. FL St.Guards
Vickers, J.N. GA 50th Inf. Co.G
Vickers, J.N. NC 50th Inf. Co.G
Vickers, Joel W. AL 12th Inf. Co.I
Vickers, John FL 2nd Cav. Co.D
Vickers, John GA Arty. Lumpkin's Co.
Vickers, John MS 20th Inf. Co.H
Vickers, John NC 2nd Inf. Co.K
Vickers, John NC 3rd Bn.Sr.Res. Durham's Co.
Vickers, John TN Lt.Arty. Tobin's Co.
Vickers, John TN 18th Inf. Co.I
Vickers, John VA 36th Inf. 2nd Co.B
Vickers, John, Jr. VA 64th Mtd.Inf. Co.H
Vickers, John, Sr. VA 64th Mtd.Inf. Co.H
Vickers, John VA 1st Cav.St.Line Co.B
Vickers, John A. NC 7th Inf. Co.B Cpl.
Vickers, John C. VA Lt.Arty. Lowry's Co.
Vickers, John H. VA 8th Cav. Co.G Sgt.
Vickers, John H. VA 22nd Inf. Swann's Co.
Vickers, John H. VA 59th Inf. 2nd Co.K
Vickers, John L. LA 19th Inf. Co.B 1st Sgt.
Vickers, John T. VA Inf. 45th Bn. Co.A
Vickers, John W. GA 9th Inf. (St.Guards) Co.G
Vickers, John W. GA 44th Inf. Co.C
Vickers, John W. VA 8th Cav. Co.G
Vickers, Jonathan GA 34th Inf. Co.H Cpl.
Vickers, Joseph G. NC 28th Inf. Co.G
Vickers, Joshua TN 44th Inf. Co.G
Vickers, Joshua TN 44th (Cons.) Inf. Co.B
Vickers, J.R. AL 42nd Inf. Co.H
Vickers, J.R. GA 59th Inf. Co.D
Vickers, J.W. AL Cav. 4th Bn. (Love's) Co.A
Vickers, J.W. NC 50th Inf. Co.G
Vickers, L. GA Cav. 20th Bn. Co.A
Vickers, L. TN 12th (Green's) Cav. Co.F
Vickers, Lawrence B. VA 39th Inf. Co.E
Vickers, Levi AR Cav. Gordon's Regt. Co.E
Vickers, Levi MO 6th Cav. Co.E
Vickers, Lewis GA 8th Cav. New Co.D
Vickers, Lewis F. VA 36th Inf. 2nd Co.B Sgt.
Vickers, L.F. MO 6th Cav. Co.E
Vickers, Linsey NC 1st Inf. Co.B
Vickers, M. GA Cav. 29th Bn. Co.C
Vickers, M. GA 50th Inf. Co.D
Vickers, Martin L. NC 4th Cav. (59th St.Troops) Co.E
Vickers, Mathew GA Inf. 29th Bn.
Vickers, M.H. LA 18th Inf. Co.C
Vickers, M.L. GA 16th Inf. Co.F
Vickers, Moses NC Inf. 13th Bn. Co.A
Vickers, Moses NC 66th Inf. Co.A
Vickers, M.W. AL 32nd Inf. Co.F
Vickers, Nich AL 1st Regt. Mobile Vol. British Guard Co.A
Vickers, P. FL 2nd Cav. Co.D
Vickers, Pleasant N. GA 12th Mil. Cpl.
Vickers, P.N. GA 5th Cav.
Vickers, P.N. GA 11th Cav. (St.Guards) MacIntyre's Co.
Vickers, Redding TX 1st Res.Corps Co.B
Vickers, Richard H. MS 11th Inf. Co.F
Vickers, Riley NC 3rd Bn.Sr.Res. Durham's Co.
Vickers, Rome G. GA 3rd Inf. Co.H Cpl.
Vickers, Samuel MS Cav. 24th Bn. Co.B
Vickers, Samuel MS 2nd (Quinn's St.Troops) Inf. Co.C
Vickers, Samuel TN 62nd Mtd.Inf. Co.F
Vickers, Silas W. GA 42nd Inf. Co.G
Vickers, Simeon VA 4th Res. Co.C
Vickers, Sion MS 20th Inf. Co.H
Vickers, T.B. MS Cav. 2nd Bn.Res. Co.I
Vickers, T.H. KY 12th Cav. Co.G
Vickers, Thomas AL 37th Inf. Co.E
Vickers, Thomas LA 21st (Patton's) Inf. Co.D
Vickers, Thomas MO Cav. 1st Regt.St.Guard Co.C
Vickers, Thomas MO 6th Cav. Co.E
Vickers, Thos. MO St.Guard
Vickers, Thomas NC 6th Inf. Co.C
Vickers, Thomas A. MO 8th Inf. Co.G
Vickers, Thomas J. NC 50th Inf. Co.G
Vickers, Thomas J. TX 19th Inf. Co.F 1st Sgt.
Vickers, T.J. AL 32nd Inf. Co.F Cpl.
Vickers, T.J. GA 16th Inf. Co.F
Vickers, T.J. TX 14th Inf. Co.H Ord.Sgt.
Vickers, T.M. MO Cav. 5th Regt.St.Guard Asst.Surg.
Vickers, T.S. MO 9th (Elliott's) Cav.
Vickers, W.A. GA 7th Inf. Co.G
Vickers, W.A. NC 49th Inf. Co.H
Vickers, W.A. VA Loc.Def. Jordan's Co.
Vickers, Washington A. MD Inf. 2nd Bn. Co.G,A
Vickers, Washington M. NC 56th Inf. Co.E
Vickers, W.B. NC 50th Inf. Co.G
Vickers, W.C. AL 38th Inf. Co.G
Vickers, W.E. GA 1st Inf. Co.C
Vickers, W.H. GA 53rd Inf. Co.A
Vickers, W.H. TN 8th Cav. Co.K
Vickers, W.H. TX Cav. McCord's Frontier Regt. Co.G Cpl.
Vickers, Wiley GA Cav. 20th Bn. Co.G Cpl.
Vickers, Wiley GA Cav. 21st Bn. Co.D Cpl.
Vickers, William GA 44th Inf. Co.D
Vickers, William GA 61st Inf. Co.A
Vickers, William MD Inf. Barry's Co.
Vickers, William VA Inf. 21st Bn. 2nd Co.E
Vickers, William VA 30th Bn.S.S. Co.A
Vickers, William VA 64th Mtd.Inf. Co.E
Vickers, William VA 189th Mil. Co.C
Vickers, William A. AL 10th Inf. Co.H
Vickers, William A. TN 14th Inf. Co.E
Vickers, William D. NC 56th Inf. Co.E
Vickers, William H. TN Inf. 1st Bn. (Colms') Co.A
Vickers, William H. VA 8th Cav. Co.G 1st Sgt.
Vickers, William H. VA 22nd Inf. Swann's Co.
Vickers, William H. VA 59th Inf. 2nd Co.K Cpl.
Vickers, William H. VA 64th Mtd.Inf. Co.H
Vickers, William H. VA Mil. Scott Cty.
Vickers, William M. TN 44th Inf. Co.G
Vickers, William M. TN 44th (Cons.) Inf. Co.F
Vickers, William R. TX 6th Inf. Co.E Sgt.
Vickers, William Riley NC 6th Inf. Co.C
Vickers, William T. VA 4th Inf. Co.C,D Sgt.
Vickers, W.J. MS Res.Corps Withers' Co.
Vickers, W.M. LA 19th Inf. Co.B
Vickers, W.R. LA 27th Inf. Co.I
Vickers, W.R. TX Granbury's Cons.Brig. Co.A Sgt.
Vickers, W.S. TN 16th Inf. Co.H
Vickers, W.T. TN 8th Inf. Co.C
Vickers, Y.J. AL 15th Inf. Co.G
Vickers, Young GA 1st (Symons') Res. Co.K
Vickert, S. LA Mil. Orleans Guards Regt. Co.I
Vickery, --- TX Cav. 4th Regt.St.Troops Co.F
Vickery, Aaron TX 20th Inf. Co.E
Vickery, A.B. AR 30th Inf. Co.E
Vickery, Alfred J. MS 29th Inf. Co.D
Vickery, A.W. TX 20th Inf. Co.E
Vickery, B.B. GA Inf. 25th Bn. (Prov.Guard) Co.A
Vickery, Berry B. GA 5th Inf.
Vickery, Charles MS 28th Cav. Co.D
Vickery, Christopher H. NC 18th Inf. Co.I
Vickery, Daniel GA Inf. 27th Bn. (NonConscr.) Co.E Sgt.
Vickery, Daniel TX 10th Cav. Co.B
Vickery, Daniel H. MO 1st N.E. Cav. Co.E
Vickery, Davis GA 12th Cav. Co.H
Vickery, D.J. GA 3rd Res. Co.F 1st Sgt.
Vickery, Eli GA 14th Inf. Co.G
Vickery, Elisha AL 43rd Inf. Co.F
Vickery, Ephriam FL Inf. 2nd Bn. Co.E
Vickery, Franklin AL 61st Inf. Co.D Cpl.
Vickery, G.B. SC 12th Inf. Co.I
Vickery, George GA Inf. 27th Bn. (NonConscr.) Co.E
Vickery, George F. TX 21st Cav. Co.D
Vickery, George W. AL 33rd Inf. Co.D
Vickery, Gilford R. MS 29th Inf. Co.D
Vickery, G.W. AR 24th Inf. Co.K
Vickery, G.W. SC Palmetto S.S. Co.M
Vickery, H. GA 54th Inf. Co.D
Vickery, H. TX 20th Inf. Co.E

Vickery, Hezekiah GA 50th Inf. Co.I
Vickery, H.H. TX 11th Field Btty.
Vickery, J. GA 4th (Clinch's) Cav. Co.E
Vickery, Jackson GA 1st (Fannin's) Res. Co.I
Vickery, Jacob VA 6th Inf. Vickery's Capt.
Vickery, Jacob VA 16th Inf. 1st Co.H Capt.
Vickery, James A. GA 3rd Cav. (St.Guards) Co.A
Vickery, James E. GA 3rd Cav. (St.Guards) Co.A
Vickery, James P. GA 15th Inf. Co.H 1st Sgt.
Vickery, James Percy GA 15th Inf. Co.H Cpl.
Vickery, James S. TX 10th Cav. Co.B
Vickery, J.B. AL 2nd Cav. Co.K
Vickery, J.B. MS 43rd Inf. Co.A
Vickery, J.C. GA 43rd Inf. Co.B
Vickery, J.C. GA Cobb's Legion Co.B
Vickery, J.C. TX 19th Inf. Co.E
Vickery, J.D. GA 5th Inf. Co.C
Vickery, J.E. GA 5th Inf. Co.D Cpl.
Vickery, J.G. MS 1st (Patton's) Inf. Co.I
Vickery, J.H. GA 11th Inf. Co.H
Vickery, J.H. TX 2nd Cav. Co.G
Vickery, J.J. AL 17th Inf. Co.H
Vickery, J.J. GA Inf. 3rd Bn. Co.H
Vickery, J.N. AL 12th Inf. Co.H
Vickery, J.N. MS 27th Inf. Co.B
Vickery, John AL 3rd Inf. Co.H
Vickery, John AL 12th Inf. Co.E
Vickery, John G. MS 35th Inf. Co.A
Vickery, Jonathan H. GA 3rd Cav. (St.Guards) Co.A
Vickery, Joseph T. GA 37th Inf. Co.K
Vickery, J.R. AL 23rd Inf. Co.F
Vickery, J.S. AL 2nd Cav. Co.K
Vickery, J.T. TN Lt.Arty. Rice's Btty.
Vickery, J.W. FL Cav. 3rd Bn. Co.B
Vickery, J.W. MO Cav. Ford's Bn. Co.F
Vickery, J.W. SC Palmetto S.S. Co.M
Vickery, J.W. 15th Conf.Cav. Co.D
Vickery, Leroy J. MS 40th Inf. Co.E Cpl.
Vickery, L.G. TX 7th Cav. Co.K
Vickery, Miles A. NC 32nd Inf. Co.E,F
Vickery, M.L. AL 18th Inf. Co.H
Vickery, M.T. TX 4th Cav. Co.F
Vickery, Phil GA 11th Cav. Co.H
Vickery, R.E. TN 16th Inf. Co.B
Vickery, Robert GA 26th Inf. Co.G Sgt.
Vickery, Shadrach MO 1st N.E. Cav. Co.E
Vickery, Solomon GA 26th Inf. Co.G
Vickery, T.E. GA 1st Inf. Co.C
Vickery, Thomas MO Cav. Ford's Bn. Co.F
Vickery, Thomas E. GA 3rd Cav. (St.Guards) Co.A
Vickery, Thomas M. GA 35th Inf. Co.I Cpl.
Vickery, Vance TX 20th Inf. Co.E,A
Vickery, W.H. TX Cav. 1st Regt.St.Troops Co.F
Vickery, William FL Cav. 3rd Bn. Co.B
Vickery, William GA 3rd Cav. (St.Guards) Co.A
Vickery, William GA 21st Inf. Co.A
Vickery, William GA Inf. 27th Bn. (NonConscr.) Co.E
Vickery, William GA 50th Inf. Co.K
Vickery, William GA 54th Inf. Co.D
Vickery, William 15th Conf.Cav. Co.D
Vickery, William C. FL 8th Inf. Co.E
Vickery, William D. AL 16th Inf. Co.K
Vickery, William S. TX 21st Cav. Co.D
Vickery, W.J. GA 3rd Bn.S.S. Co.B Cpl.
Vickery, W.J. TX Cav. Morgan's Regt. Co.H
Vickery, W.S. TX 17th Inf. Co.I
Vickerz, Halcher AL 6th Cav. Co.D
Vickes, Jesse H. NC 56th Inf. Co.H
Vickey, W.W. TX Cav. Baird's Regt. Co.G
Vickley, David S. KY 2nd Mtd.Inf. Co.G
Vickley, James P. TN 3rd (Forrest's) Cav.
Vickman, Charles TX Inf. 1st St.Troops Stevenson's Co.F
Vickmeyer, William LA Arty. Kean's Btty. (Orleans Ind.Arty.)
Vicknair, Adolph LA Mil. LaFourche Regt.
Vicknair, Clairville LA Mil. St.John the Baptist Res.Guards
Vicknair, E. LA 18th Inf. Co.A Cpl.
Vicknair, E. LA 22nd Inf. Co.E
Vicknair, Edward LA St.John the Baptist Res. Guards
Vicknair, Emile LA Mil. LaFourche Regt.
Vicknair, Felix LA 18th Inf. Co.A
Vicknair, Francois LA 4th Inf. Co.E
Vicknair, Franklin LA Mil. LaFourche Regt.
Vicknair, Henry LA Mil. St.John the Baptist Res.Guards
Vicknair, Jacques LA Mil. St.John the Baptist Res.Guards
Vicknair, Jean Bapt. LA Mil. St.John the Baptist Res.Guards
Vicknair, Joseph LA Mil. St.John the Baptist Res.Guards
Vicknair, Louis LA Inf. 9th Bn. Co.D
Vicknair, Onesephon LA Mil. St.John the Baptist Res.Guards
Vicknair, P. LA 22nd (Cons.) Inf. Co.E
Vicknair, Paul LA Inf. 9th Bn. Co.D
Vicknair, Paul S. LA Inf. 9th Bn. Co.D
Vicknair, Udger LA Mil. St.John the Baptist Res.Guards
Vicknair, Ulger LA Mil. St.John the Baptist Res.Guards
Vicknaire, E. LA Inf.Cons. 18th Regt. & Yellow Jacket Bn. Co.C
Vickner, Achile LA 28th (Thomas') Inf. Co.E
Vickner, Alexander LA 28th (Thomas') Inf. Co.E
Vickner, Edouard LA 28th (Thomas') Inf. Co.E
Vickney, --- AL 33rd Inf. Cpl.
Vicknoir, Emile LA 30th Inf. Co.H
Vicknoir, Ernest LA 30th Inf. Co.H
Vickory, Alfred H. TX 22nd Inf. Co.H
Vickory, Calaway GA 59th Inf. Co.G
Vickory, David FL 5th Inf. Co.E
Vickory, E.A. TN 19th Inf. Co.D
Vickory, Elias GA 4th Res. Co.E
Vickory, G.B. FL Inf. 2nd Bn. Co.D
Vickory, G.V. FL 5th Inf. Co.D
Vickory, J.D. AL 33rd Inf. Co.D Sgt.
Vickory, J.H. GA 11th Cav. Co.H
Vickory, John FL 1st Cav. Co.B
Vickory, John TN 3rd (Lillard's) Mtd.Inf. Co.I
Vickory, John M. GA 35th Inf. Co.B
Vickory, M.C. AL 18th Inf. Co.H
Vickory, Middleton TN Lt.Arty. Baxter's Co.
Vickory, N.D. AL 33rd Inf. Co.D
Vickory, Scott GA 60th Inf. Co.I
Vickory, S.M. MS 8th Cav. Co.C
Vickory, Thomas S. GA 4th Res. Co.E
Vickory, William B. NC 3rd Arty. (40th St.Troops) Co.D
Vickory, William S. GA 24th Inf. Co.C
Vickrey, Absalom AR 8th Inf. New Co.F
Vickrey, Absalom AR 14th (McCarver's) Inf. Co.B
Vickrey, Burnett TN 24th Inf. Co.A
Vickrey, George F. TX 17th Inf. Co.I
Vickrey, H.B. NC 1st Jr.Res. Co.F Sgt.
Vickrey, John TN 20th Inf. Co.G
Vickrey, John F. GA 9th Inf. Co.G
Vickrey, J.W. MO 5th Cav. Co.K
Vickrey, S.D. MO 5th Cav. Co.K
Vickrey, T.H. GA 39th Inf. Co.D
Vickrey, Thomas GA Inf. 9th Bn. Co.A
Vickrey, William H. TN Inf. Tackitt's Co.
Vickrey, W.S. MO 5th Cav. Co.K
Vickroy, John MO Cav. Freeman's Regt. Co.E
Vickry, A.H. TX 10th Cav. Co.B
Vickry, C. MS 32nd Inf. Co.F
Vickry, Calvin GA Inf. 4th Bn. (St.Guards) Co.C
Vickry, Cuyler GA 54th Inf. Co.D
Vickry, D.G. TN 7th Inf. Co.G
Vickry, G.B. FL 10th Inf. Co.K
Vickry, James AR 19th (Dawson's) Inf. Co.K
Vickry, James H. GA 37th Inf. Co.D
Vickry, James W. NC 48th Inf. Co.F
Vickry, J.B. GA 87th Inf. Co.D
Vickry, John GA 64th Inf. Co.E
Vickry, John H. LA 2nd Cav. Co.F
Vickry, M.N. GA 87th Inf. Co.D
Vickry, Nimrod J. GA 30th Inf. Co.H
Vickry, Thomas GA 34th Inf. Co.G
Vickry, Thomas J. LA 2nd Cav. Co.F
Vickry, William NC 48th Inf. Co.F
Vickry, William TN 20th Inf. Co.G Sgt.
Vickry, William L. LA 2nd Cav. Co.F
Vicks, J.J. MS Lt.Arty. Yates' Btty.
Vicks, J.L. AR 30th Inf. Co.H
Vicks, W. TN 14th (Neely's) Cav. Co.K
Vickus, A.J. MS 6th Inf. Co.H
Vicors, Johnathan GA 6th Inf. Co.B
Vicory, Francis MO Inf. 5th Regt.St.Guard Co.D Cpl.
Vicory, James B. AR 3rd Inf. Co.H
Vicory, James C. GA 41st Inf. Co.H Cpl.
Vicory, J.B. AR Inf. 2nd Bn. Co.A
Vicory, Joseph GA 20th Inf. Co.G
Vicory, Wilb 1st Cherokee Mtd.Vol. 1st Co.C
Vicry, B.F. AR 23rd Inf. Co.H
Victery, D.C. TX 20th Inf. Co.E
Victor, --- LA Mil. 1st Regt. 2nd Brig. 1st Div. Co.B
Victor, --- LA Mil. 3rd Regt. French Brig. Co.5
Victor, Alfred TX 10th Inf. Co.F
Victor, Arthur Joseph LA Mil. 1st Native Guards
Victor, A.W. TX 17th Cons.Dismtd.Cav. Co.D
Victor, Celistan MS 3rd Inf. Co.G
Victor, Charles Stevenson's Div. QM Dept. Capt.
Victor, George N. KY 1st Inf. Co.D Sgt.
Victor, George W. KY Morehead's Regt. (Part.Rangers) Co.A
Victor, G.W. MS 7th Cav. 2nd Co.G 1st Sgt.
Victor, H. LA Mil. 4th Regt. French Brig. Co.4
Victor, Henry Clay VA 11th Inf. Co.A

Victor, Jely LA 13th Inf. Co.D
Victor, John W. KY 4th Cav. Co.D
Victor, J.W. TN 14th (Neely's) Cav. Co.A 1st Sgt.
Victor, Levi GA 42nd Inf. Co.E
Victor, Nicholas LA Mil. 1st Native Guards
Victor, Octavius AL 13th Inf. Co.A Sgt.
Victor, Philip M. KY 1st Inf. Co.D 1st Lt.
Victor, Ph. M. KY Morehead's Regt. (Part. Rangers) Co.A
Victor, Pierre LA Mil. 2nd Regt. French Brig. Co.5
Victor, Robert 1st Choctaw & Chickasaw Mtd.Rifles 2nd Co.H
Victor, S. KY 1st (Butler's) Cav. Co.C
Victor, S. LA 5th Inf. Co.A
Victor, T. GA 66th Inf. Co.B
Victor, Thomas L. MO 6th Cav. Co.E
Victor, T.L. MO St.Guard W.H. Taylor's Co.
Victor, William TX 16th Cav. Co.K
Victori, Martin LA Mil. 5th Regt.Eur.Brig. (Spanish Regt.) Co.10
Victorious, Morris GA 1st (Olmstead's) Inf. Co.G
Victory, James GA 1st Inf. Co.B
Victory, James MO 7th Cav. Co.F
Victory, John TX 1st Inf. Co.B Sgt.
Victory, John E. MO Lt.Arty. Landis' Co.
Victory, Martin LA Mil. 5th Regt.Eur.Brig. (Spanish Regt.) Co.8
Victory, Middleton GA 38th Inf. Co.K
Victory, William AR 36th Inf. Co.F
Victry, James MO 8th Cav. Co.G
Vidal, A.J. SC Lt.Arty. Parker's Co. (Marion Arty.)
Vidal, A.J. TX 33rd Cav. Co.A
Vidal, E. LA Mil. Orleans Guards Regt. Co.K Sgt.
Vidal, Ernest LA Washington Arty.Bn. Co.3
Vidal, Ernest LA 5th Inf. Co.D
Vidal, F. LA Mil. 1st Native Guards
Vidal, J. SC Mil. 16th Regt. Robinson's Co.
Vidal, J.F. LA Mil. 1st Native Guards
Vidal, Juan LA Mil. 5th Regt.Eur.Brig. (Spanish Regt.) Co.2
Vidal, Juan LA Mil. Cazadores Espanoles Regt. Co.5
Vidal, Juan Masdivevasti LA Mil. 5th Regt. Eur.Brig. (Spanish Regt.) Co.4
Vidal, M. LA Mil. 1st Regt. French Brig. Co.6
Vidal, M. LA Mil. French Brig. Capt.,ADC
Vidal, S. LA Mil. 5th Regt.Eur.Brig. (Spanish Regt.) Co.2
Vidanani, Atanacio TX Cav. Benavides' Regt. Co.I Jr.2nd Lt.
Vidato, Thomas TN 51st (Cons.) Inf. Co.C
Vidau, P. LA Mil. 4th Regt. French Brig. Co.3
Vidaurri, Atanacio TX Cav. Benavides' Regt. Co.D Jr.2nd Lt.
Videau, Alf LA Mil. 1st Chasseurs a pied Co.5
Videau, P. LA Mil. 3rd Regt. French Brig. Co.4 Cpl.
Videl, J. AL Cav. Barlow's Co.
Videl, John 15th Conf.Cav. Co.C
Viderro, C. AL 3rd Cav. Co.E
Videto, John TN 8th (Smith's) Cav. Co.L
Videtoe, T.W. TN 52nd Inf. Co.C Sgt.
Videtto, Henry A. GA 32nd Inf. Co.K 1st Lt.
Videtto, Peyton L. SC 3rd Cav. Co.K
Vidine, A. LA Inf. Weatherly's Bn. Co.B
Vidirin, Joseph LA Inf. Weatherly's Bn. Co.B
Vidito, J. KY 10th (Johnson's) Cav. Co.E
Viditoe, G.T. KY 10th (Johnson's) Cav. New Co.B
Viditoe, J.H. KY 10th (Johnson's) Cav. Co.B
Vidler, James 14th Conf.Cav. Co.G
Vidler, J.S. LA Ogden's Cav. Co.C
Vidmer, George AL 21st Inf Adj.
Vidmer, George Gen. & Staff 1st Lt.,Adj.
Vidmer, John AL 3rd Inf. Co.K
Vidmer, John AL 36th Inf. Co.I 2nd Lt.
Vidmer, John Gen. & Staff Capt.,AAG
Vidor, Charles TX 1st Inf. Co.L
Vidor, Charles Gen. & Staff Capt.,AQM
Vidovich, Steffano LA Mil. 6th Regt.Eur.Brig. (Italian Guards Bn.) Co.4
Vidraine, Vahmon LA Miles' Legion Co.A
Vidrin, S. LA Inf. Weatherly's Bn. Co.B
Vidrine, Alcin LA 16th Inf. Co.K
Vidrine, Aurelie LA 28th (Thomas') Inf. Co.K
Vidrine, C. LA 26th Inf. Co.A
Vidrine, Edmond LA 3rd (Harrison's) Cav. Co.K
Vidrine, Eloi, Jr. LA 28th (Thomas') Inf. Co.K Cpl.
Vidrine, Eloir LA 2nd Res.Corps Co.I
Vidrine, Emile LA Miles' Legion Co.H
Vidrine, H. LA 15th Bn.S.S. (Weatherly's) Co.D
Vidrine, J.B. LA 6th Inf. Co.C
Vidrine, Jean Bapt. LA 2nd Res.Corps Co.I
Vidrine, Jules LA 2nd Cav. Co.A
Vidrine, L. LA 2nd Cav. Co.A
Vidrine, Leon LA Mil. Chalmette Regt. Co.F
Vidrine, Leon A. LA 16th Inf. Co.K
Vidrine, Leone LA Inf. Weatherly's Bn. Co.D
Vidrine, O. LA Inf.Crescent Regt. Co.A
Vidrine, P. LA Inf. Weatherly's Bn. Co.B
Vidrine, Pierre LA Inf. Weatherly's Bn. Co.D
Vidrine, S. LA Miles' Legion Co.H
Vidrine, Theodule A. LA 8th Inf. Co.F
Vidrine, Y. LA Inf. Weatherly's Bn. Co.C Sgt.
Vidrine, Y. LA Miles' Legion Co.H
Vidrine, Z. LA Inf. Weatherly's Bn. Co.B
Vidrine, Zelien LA Miles' Legion Co.H
Viebahn, William LA 20th Inf. Co.A
Viebahn, William LA 21st (Kennedy's) Inf. Co.C Sgt.
Viebruck, John D. TX 2nd Inf. Co.F
Viedrine, Pierre LA 8th Cav. Co.B
Viegee, Pierre LA Arty. 1st Field Btty.
Viehmeyster, William VA 10th Cav. Co.A
Viel, P. LA Mil. 3rd Regt.Eur.Brig. (Garde Francaise) Co.5
Viel, Thomas KY Horse Arty. Byrne's Co.
Vielar, John Conf.Inf. Tucker's Regt. Co.D
Viele, J.L. GA 20th Inf. Co.H
Viele, William B. FL 1st Inf. Co.C
Vieneger, John TX Cav. Baylor's Regt. Co.F
Vienne, Adolph LA 2nd Cav. Co.C
Vienne, Francois LA 2nd Cav. Co.B
Vienne, Francois LA Maddox's Regt.Res.Corps Co.B
Vienne, Henry LA Pointe Coupee Arty. Cpl.
Vienne, Henry LA Arty. Watson Btty.
Vienne, James LA 30th Inf. Co.F 1st Lt.
Vienne, James LA Mil. Orleans Guards Regt. Co.D
Vienne, J.G. LA Mil. Orleans Guards Regt. Co.D
Vienne, J.G. SC Arty. Manigault's Bn. 1st Co.A,D 1st Lt.
Vienne, Jules LA Inf.Crescent Regt. Co.D Capt.
Vienne, L.G. LA 30th Inf. Co.F,D 2nd Lt.
Vienne, P.A. LA Mil. Orleans Guards Regt. Co.D Cpl.
Vienni, John G. LA Lt.Arty. Bridges' Btty. 1st Lt.
Vienuava, Santago TX Cav. Benavides' Regt. Co.D
Vier, C. GA 23rd Inf. Co.B 1st Lt.
Vier, Darius MO 1st N.E. Cav.
Vier, D.W. MO 9th Bn.S.S. Co.D
Vier, Edward VA 34th Inf. Co.C Cpl.
Vier, Lewis VA 21st Cav. 1st Co.E
Viera, Antonio AL 21st Inf. Co.B
Vierd, Peter SC 11th Inf. Co.G
Viereck, H. TX 4th Inf. Co.F
Viereck, John VA 1st Inf. Co.K
Vierick, H. TX 7th Field Btty.
Vierick, John VA Inf. Lyneman's Co.
Viering, H. LA Dreux's Cav. Co.A
Viering, Henry LA Mil. Fire Bn. Co.G
Vierlieng, F.A. LA 30th Inf. Co.C,F Sgt.
Viern, E. NC 10th Sgt.
Vierra, Louis LA Mil. 1st Native Guards
Viers, B.P. LA 4th Inf. New Co.G
Viers, Charles O. VA Cav. Mosby's Regt. (Part.Rangers) Co.F
Viers, Elisha MO Inf. 3rd Bn. Co.B
Viers, Elisha MO 6th Inf. Co.A Cpl.
Viers, Hezekiah W. VA Cav. 41st Bn. Trayhern's Co.
Viers, H.K. LA 4th Inf. Co.I 1st Sgt.
Viers, John H. KY 6th Mtd.Inf. Co.H
Viers, J.W. LA 4th Inf. New Co.G
Viers, Matheson VA 19th Cav. Co.B
Viers, Richard J. VA Res.Forces Thurston's Co.
Viers, Thomas TN Inf. 1st Bn. (Colms') Co.A
Viers, William VA Cav. 40th Bn. Co.E
Viers, William H. MO 15th Cav. Co.H
Viers, William H. VA 24th Cav. Co.E
Viers, William M. NC 34th Inf. Co.A
Viers, William S. VA 21st Cav.
Viery, Daniel G. TN 7th Inf. Co.F
Vies, Emile LA 26th Inf. Co.H
Viest, James TX Waul's Legion Co.A
Viet, J.W. TX Cav. Giddings' Bn. Pickerell's Co.
Viet, M. LA Mil.Cont.Cadets
Vigain, Charles 1st Conf.Cav. 2nd Co.A Sgt.
Vigaine, Charles KY 7th Cav. Co.F
Vigal, George M. GA 1st Reg. Co.L Sgt.
Vigal, John A. NC 33rd Inf. Asst.Surg.
Vigal, John Adams Gen. & Staff Asst.Surg.
Vigar, John E. VA 5th Inf. Co.I 2nd Lt.
Vigar, John H. VA 5th Inf. Co.I Sgt.
Vigar, William A. VA 23rd Cav. Co.B
Vige, E.P. LA 28th (Thomas') Inf. Co.I
Vige, Julien LA Mil. 4th Regt.Eur.Brig. Co.5
Vigee, Charles LA 15th Inf. Co.C
Vigelow, G. TX 2nd Inf. Co.K
Vigeneau, Octave LA Miles' Legion Co.A

Viger, Charles F. LA 1st Hvy.Arty. (Reg.) Co.D
Vight, James GA 62nd Cav. Co.L
Vight, John GA 62nd Cav. Co.L
Vigier, Maximilian LA 15th Inf. Co.C,G
Vigier, Rosemont LA 2nd Cav. Co.I
Vigil, A.G. LA Prov.Regt. Legion Co.2 Capt.
Vigil, A. Gomzalez LA Mil. Jackson Rifle Bn. Capt.
Vigis, Thomas GA Cobb's Legion Co.B
Viglini, John P. LA 3rd Inf. Co.K Capt.
Viglini, J.P. Gen. & Staff, QM Dept. Capt.
Vignan, Pierre LA Mil. 3rd Regt.Eur.Brig. (Garde Francaise) Frois' Co.
Vignand, A. LA Mil. 1st Regt. 2nd Brig. 1st Div. Co.A
Vignand, J.A. LA Arty. Guyol's Co. (Orleans Arty.)
Vignaud, A. LA Lt.Arty. LeGardeur, Jr.'s Co. (Orleans Guard Btty.)
Vignaud, A. LA 8th Inf. Co.B
Vignaud, A. LA 22nd Inf. Co.E
Vignaud, A. LA 22nd (Cons.) Inf. Co.E
Vignaud, A. LA Mil. Orleans Guards Regt. Co.K
Vignaud, B. LA Mil. 3rd Regt. French Brig. Co.1
Vignaud, Etienne LA Mil. 1st Native Guards
Vignaud, J.H. LA Dreux's Cav. Co.A
Vignaud, Joseph LA Mil. 1st Native Guards
Vignaud, L. LA Mil. 3rd Regt. French Brig. Co.2,6
Vignaud, V. LA Mil. Orleans Guards Regt. Co.D
Vigne, A. LA Mil. 1st Regt. French Brig. Co.5
Vigne, John VA Hvy.Arty. Epes' Co.
Vigneali, S. LA Mil. 4th Regt. French Brig. Co.7
Vigneau, M. LA Mil. 3rd Regt. French Brig. Co.8
Vigneaud, H. LA Mil. 3rd Regt. 2nd Brig. 1st Div. Co.G Capt.
Vigner, Fred VA 10th Cav. 1st Co.E
Vignerie, J.P. 4th Conf.Eng.Troops Lt.
Vigneron, --- LA Mil. 2nd Regt. French Brig. Co.4
Vignerot, H. LA Mil. 3rd Regt. 2nd Brig. 1st Div. Co.A
Vignes, Adolphe LA Mil. Knaps' Co. (Fausse River Guards)
Vignes, Albert LA Pointe Coupee Arty.
Vignes, Albert LA Mil. Knaps' Co. (Fausse River Guards)
Vignes, Alcei LA Pointe Coupee Arty.
Vignes, Arnold LA 4th Inf. Co.D
Vignes, Edwin LA Pointe Coupee Arty.
Vignes, Eugine LA 1st Cav. Co.I
Vignes, J. LA Mil. 3rd Regt. French Brig. Co.6
Vignes, Jean LA Mil. 6th Regt.Eur.Brig. (Italian Guards Bn.) Co.5
Vignes, Joseph LA Pointe Coupee Arty.
Vignes, Joseph LA Mil. Knaps' Co. (Fausse River Guards)
Vignes, Joseph D. LA 4th Inf. Co.F
Vignie, E. LA Arty. Guyol's Co. (Orleans Arty.)
Vigo, Dominique LA 24th Inf. Co.B 1st Sgt.
Vigo, J. LA Lt.Arty. Bridges' Btty.
Vigo, J. LA Mil. Orleans Fire Regt. Hall's Co.
Vigo, Joseph SC Arty. Manigault's Bn. 1st Co.B,D
Vigo, Paul LA Lt.Arty. Fenner's Btty.
Vigo, Paul 14th Conf.Cav. Co.H
Vigo, P.J. LA Inf. 1st Sp.Bn. (Rightor's) Co.F
Vigo, R. AL 1st Regt. Mobile Vol. Co.C
Viguni, G. AL 21st Inf. Co.G
Vigus, A.P. TN Inf. 154th Sr.Regt. Co.D
Vigus, Frank W. TN Inf. 154th Sr.Regt. Co.D
Vigus, I.H. 3rd Conf.Eng.Troops Co.H Sgt.Maj.
Vigus, James H. TN Inf. 154th Sr.Regt. Co.D
Vigus, James H. Eng.Dept. Polk's Corps A. of TN Sap. & Min. Co.,CSA
Vigus, John J. VA 19th Inf. Co.D
Vije, Onesime LA Miles' Legion Co.D
Vila, Joel LA Mil. 5th Regt.Eur.Brig. (Spanish Regt.)
Vila, Jose LA Mil. 5th Regt.Eur.Brig. (Spanish Regt.) Co.7
Vila, M. LA Mil. 5th Regt.Eur.Brig. (Spanish Regt.) Co.1
Vila, Santiago LA Mil. 5th Regt.Eur.Brig. (Spanish Regt.) Co.3
Vilain, Adolphe LA Mil. 6th Regt.Eur.Brig. (Italian Guards Bn.) Co.5
Vildcas, --- TX Cav. Ragsdale's Bn. Co.A
Vildebill, C. GA Inf. 17th Bn. (St.Guards) Fay's Co.
Vilebert, W. Sap. & Min.,CSA
Viles, Anthony GA Cav. 6th Bn. (St.Guards) Co.E
Viles, Jacob TN 3rd (Lillard's) Mtd.Inf. Co.A
Viles, James SC 2nd St.Troops
Viles, J.E. GA 10th Inf. Co.E
Viles, Joseph TX 23rd Cav. Co.B
Viles, L.A. TX 29th Cav. Co.C
Viles, Levi VA 64th Mtd.Inf. Co.K
Viley, John R. Gen. & Staff Maj.,QM
Viley, John W. KY 2nd Mtd.Inf. Co.B
Vilkin, Louis LA Mil. 3rd Regt. 1st Brig. 1st Div. Co.E
Villa, Eduardo LA Mil. 5th Regt.Eur.Brig. (Spanish Regt.) Co.6 1st Lt.
Villa, George LA 22nd (Cons.) Inf. Co.H
Villa, J. LA Mil. 3rd Regt. French Brig. Co.3
Villa, J. LA 22nd Inf. Co.E
Villa, J. LA 22nd (Cons.) Inf. Co.E
Villa, J.L. LA Mil. Chalmette Regt. Co.H
Villa, Jose LA Mil. 5th Regt.Eur.Brig. (Spanish Regt.) Co.6 Sgt.
Villa, Joseph LA 1st Hvy.Arty. (Reg.) Co.I
Villa, Joseph LA Arty. Castellanos' Btty. Sgt.
Villa, V. AL 1st Regt. Mobile Vol. Baas' Co.
Villabonga, J.A. GA 7th Cav. Co.F
Villalonga, J.A. GA Cav. 21st Bn. Co.B,E
Villalonga, Jno. L. Gen. & Staff Maj.,Comsy.
Villalonga, Juluis A. GA 1st (Olmstead's) Inf. Gallie's Co.
Villannes, Jose LA Mil. 5th Regt.Eur.Brig. (Spanish Regt.) Co.A
Villanueva, Antonio LA 30th Inf. Co.D
Villanueva, Candelario TX 3rd Inf. Co.F
Villanueva, Flario LA Mil. 5th Regt.Eur.Brig. (Spanish Regt.) Co.A
Villanueva, Santiago TX 3rd Inf. Co.F
VillaPonteaux, J.B. SC 26th Inf. Co.F
Villar, A. FL 2nd Inf. Co.A
Villar, Jose LA Mil. 5th Regt.Eur.Brig. (Spanish Regt.) Co.3 Cpl.
Villar, M. TN 42nd Inf. 2nd Co.E Cpl.
Villar, Martin MS 10th Inf. Old Co.C, New Co.F
Villar, Martin TN 40th Inf. Co.C
Villarana, Fele P. LA 5th Inf. Co.F Bugler
Villaraso, E. LA Lt.Arty. Bridges' Btty. Cpl.
Villaraso, J.M. LA Lt.Arty. Bridges' Btty. Cpl.
Villard, Antoine LA 13th Inf. Co.I
Villard, J.B. 14th Conf.Cav. Co.D
Villard, T.D. SC Prov.Guard Hamilton's Co. 1st Sgt.
Villard, Thomas D. SC 6th Cav. Co.B
Villard, Thomas D. SC 19th Inf. Co.F 2nd Lt.
Villareal, Feliciana TX Cav. Benavides' Regt. Co.I 5th Sgt.
Villareal, Andreas TX Trevino's Squad.Part.Mtd.Vol.
Villareal, Antonio TX 3rd Inf. Co.F.
Villareal, Cesilio TX 33rd Cav. 1st Co.H Cpl.
Villareal, Indelacio TX 33rd Cav. 1st Co.H
Villareal, Martin TX 3rd Inf. Co.F
Villareal, Ventura TX 3rd Inf. Co.A
Villaret, B. LA Mil. 1st Regt. French Brig. Co.3
Villarial, Nasceno TX 8th Inf. Co.I
Villarrubia, E. LA Arty. Guyol's Co. (Orleans Arty.) 1st Sgt.
Villarrubia, J. LA Arty. Guyol's Co. (Orleans Arty.) Ord.Sgt.
Villars, Ad. LA Lt.Arty. Bridges' Btty.
Villars, Ad. LA 30th Inf. Co.F
Villars, Adolph SC Arty. Manigault's Bn. 1st Co.A,D
Villars, Alb. LA Lt.Arty. Bridges' Btty.
Villars, Albert LA 30th Inf. Co.F
Villars, Albert SC Arty. Manigault's Bn. Co.D
Villars, D. LA Arty. Guyol's Co. (Orleans Arty.)
Villars, D. LA Lt.Arty. LeGardeur, Jr.'s Co. (Orleans Guard Btty.)
Villars, D. LA 30th Inf. Co.F
Villars, Gaston LA 30th Inf. Co.F
Villars, J.C. LA 30th Inf. Co.F
Villars, J.T. LA Lt.Arty. Bridges' Btty.
Villars, J.T. SC Arty. Manigault's Bn. 1st Co.A,D
Villars, L.A. LA Mil. Orleans Guards Regt. Co.F,B
Villasana, Frank P. LA Washington Arty.Bn. Co.1 Ch.Bugler
Villastrigo, Tomas TX 33rd Cav. 1st Co.H
Villato, Jarvis LA Miles' Legion Co.A
Villaume, Dominique LA Arty. Kean's Btty. (Orleans Ind.Arty.) Cpl.
Villaumme, D. LA C.S. Zouave Bn. Co.C 2nd Lt.
Villavaro, E. LA Mil. Orleans Guards Regt. Co.B,F
Villavaro, J.E. LA Mil. Orleans Guards Regt. Co.B
Villavaro, L. LA Mil. Orleans Guards Regt. Co.B
Villavaso, A.E. LA Arty. 5th Field Btty. (Pelican Lt.Arty.)
Villavaso, Alfred LA Mil. St.James Regt. Co.E
Villavaso, Aug. LA Mil. St.James Regt. Gaudet's Co.

Villavaso, Emil SC Arty. Manigault's Bn. 1st Co.A,D
Villavaso, J.M. LA Mil. Delery's Co. (St.Bernard Horse Rifles Co.) Marechal logis Chef
Villavaso, Martin SC Arty. Manigault's Bn. 1st Co.A,D Cpl.
Villavaso, Ml. LA Mil. Delery's Co. (St.Bernard Horse Rifles Co.)
Villavaso, N. LA Lt.Arty. 6th Field Btty. (Grosse Tete Flying Arty.)
Villavaso, P. LA Arty. 5th Field Btty. (Pelican Lt.Arty.)
Villavaso, Paul LA Mil. St.James Regt. Gaudet's Co.
Villa y Alvarez, J. LA Mil. 5th Regt.Eur.Brig. (Spanish Regt.) Co.1
Villa y Columbo, J. LA Mil. 5th Regt.Eur.Brig. (Spanish Regt.) Co.1
Villebois, Jules LA 13th Inf. Co.E
Villegas, Fernando LA Mil. 5th Regt.Eur.Brig. (Spanish Regt.) Co.4
Villegas, Jose LA Mil. 5th Regt.Eur.Brig. (Spanish Regt.) Co.3
Villegas, R. TX Cav. Ragsdale's Bn. 1st Co.A
Villemain, A. LA 22nd (Cons.) Inf. Co.C
Villemain, L. LA Mil. 1st Chasseurs a pied Co.2
Villemain, L. LA 22nd Inf. Co.C
Villemaine, Leon LA Mil. Mooney's Co. (Saddlers Guards)
Villeman, J. LA Mil. 1st Chasseurs a pied Co.5
Villembet, J. LA Mil. 4th Regt. French Brig. Co.6 1st Sgt.
Villement, Francois J. LA 16th Inf. Co.D
Villemont, T.J. LA Mil. Chalmette Regt. Co.D
Villeneuve, A. LA 30th Inf. Co.B
Villeneuve, Joseph H. SC 21st Inf. Co.D 1st Lt.
Villepigue, F.L. FL Kilcrease Lt.Arty. Capt.
Villepigue, James I. SC 2nd Inf. Capt.,QM
Villepigue, John B. GA 36th (Villepigue's) Inf. Lt.Col.
Villepigue, John B. SC Cav. DeSaussure's Squad. Co.A Capt.
Villepigue, Jno. B. Gen. & Staff Brig.Gen.
Villepigue, P.B. SC 27th Inf. Co.I
Villepontoux, Benjamin SC Vol. Simons' Co. 1st Sgt.
Viller, L. LA Mil. 3rd Regt. French Brig. Co.3
Villere, A.L. LA Mil. Orleans Guards Regt. Co.E
Villere, C. LA Lt.Arty. Bridges' Btty.
Villere, C. SC Arty. Manigault's Bn. 1st Co.A,D
Villere, Charles LA 1st Cav. Co.I 2nd Lt.
Villere, Cyril LA Mil. Delery's Co. (St.Bernard Horse Rifles Co.) 4th Brig.
Villere, Denis LA Mil. Delery's Co. (St.Bernard Horse Rifles Co.)
Villere, E. LA Mil. Mtd.Rangers Plaquemines
Villere, E. LA Mil. Orleans Guards Regt. Co.A Sgt.
Villere, E.C. LA Inf.Cons. 18th Regt. & Yellow Jacket Bn. Co.B
Villere, Edmond LA Mil. Delery's Co. (St.Bernard Horse Rifles Co.)
Villere, Ereville LA Mil. Delery's Co. (St.Bernard Horse Rifles Co.) 3rd Marechal
Villere, Ernest C. LA 18th Inf. Co.E
Villere, J. LA Mil. Mtd.Rangers Plaquemines
Villere, L. LA Mil. Mtd.Rangers Plaquemines
Villere, L.C. LA Mil. Mtd.Rangers Plaquemines
Villere, L.C. LA Inf.Cons. 18th Regt. & Yellow Jacket Bn. Co.B,G Cpl.
Villere, Leonce C. LA 18th Inf. Co.E Cpl.
Villere, O. LA Dreux's Cav. Co.A
Villere, Phillippe LA Mil. Delery's Co. (St.Bernard Horse Rifles Co.)
Villeret, Charles LA 2nd Cav. Co.K
Villeret, F. Gen. & Staff Asst.Surg.
Villeret, Frederick F. AL Eufaula Lt.Arty.
Villeret, Jean Bapt. LA 2nd Cav. Co.K
Villerett, Frederic AL 54th Inf. Asst.Surg.
Villerett, Frederick AL Inf. 1st Regt. Co.B
Villerett, M. LA 4th Inf. Co.F
Villerial, J. TX Cav. Ragsdale's Bn. 1st Co.A
Villermot, Elie LA Mil. 1st Regt. French Brig. Co.6
Villero, Frederico LA Mil. 5th Regt.Eur.Brig. (Spanish Regt.) Co.4
Villers, Charles I. Beauregard's Staff Col.,ADC
Villers, W. TX Cav. Baird's Regt. Co.G
Villesariez, Constantini LA 10th Inf. Co.I
Villeuame, Nicolas LA 21st (Kennedy's) Inf. Co.D
Villey, John R. Gen. & Staff, A. of TN Maj.,Disbursing QM
Villiam, Stephen AL 1st Cav. Co.E
Villian, A. LA 15th Inf. Co.E
Villian, R.R. TX 7th Cav.
Villiard, George W. GA 11th Inf. Co.A
Villiard, William H.H. GA Inf. 8th Bn. Co.B
Villieaux, Upton AL 1st Cav. Co.D
Villims, James W. NC 24th Inf. Co.A
Villims, John S. VA 9th Inf. Co.E
Villines, D.M. TN 30th Inf. Co.K
Villines, F.M. AR 27th Inf. Co.F Sgt.
Villines, Robert AR 3rd Inf. Co.A
Villines, T.G. TN 30th Inf. Co.K
Villinger, M. MS Inf. 2nd Bn. Co.E
Villiot, Giuseppe LA Mil. 6th Regt.Eur.Brig. (Italian Guards Bn.) Co.3 Capt.
Villiot, J. LA Mil. 1st Regt. 2nd Brig. 1st Div. Co.B
Villipeague, Charles 7th Conf.Cav. Co.A
Villipigne, A. GA Inf. 1st Loc.Troops (Augusta) Co.D
Villipigue, F.L. FL Lt.Arty. Dyke's Co. Sr.1st Lt.
Villipigue, Jas. J. Gen. & Staff Capt.,AQM
Villipigue, John T. SC Inf. 7th Bn. (Enfield Rifles) Co.G
Villmeret, C. LA Lt.Arty. 2nd Field Btty.
Villneuve, G. LA Mil. 4th Regt. French Brig. Co.3
Villoe, S.A. AL 1st Cav. Co.E
Villuyhoff, W.F. MO Arty.Regt.St.Guard Co.B 1st Lt.
Vilmeur, --- LA Mil. 2nd Regt. French Brig. Co.1
Vilmon, W.L. VA 49th Inf. Co.B
Vilmont, John N. LA Conscr.
Vilmont, Jules LA 18th Inf. Co.A
Vilmor, C.W. LA Mil. Chalmette Regt. Co.H
Vilmore, Charles LA 14th (Austin's) Bn.S.S. Co.B
Vilmore, F. LA 16th Inf. Co.D
Vilneuve, A. LA 30th Inf. Co.G
Vilneuve, Augustave 14th Conf.Cav. Co.D
Vilt, Henry SC 1st (Butler's) Inf. Co.G
Vilus, W. GA Inf. Collier's Co.
Vilus, W.J. GA Inf. Collier's Co. Sgt.
Viment, Louis LA Mil. 4th Regt. 1st Brig. 1st Div. Co.G
Vimerson, Jacob LA 13th Inf. Co.A
Vimmel, J. NC 2nd Inf. Co.B
Vimprenne, Louis LA Mil. St.John the Baptist Res.Guards
Vimprenne, M. LA Mil. St.John the Baptist Res.Guards
Vimprenne, Quesime LA Mil. St.John the Baptist Res.Guards
Vimprenne, Rupert LA Mil. St.John the Baptist Res.Guards
Vimprenne, Ulysse LA Mil. St.John the Baptist Res.Guards
Vin, Martin VA 3rd Res. Co.B
Vinagum, Daniel V. NC 13th Inf. Co.F
Vinagum, Thomas V. NC 13th Inf. Co.F
Vinant, John MO 2nd & 6th Cons.Inf.
Vinay, C. LA Mil. 3rd Regt.Eur.Brig. (Garde Francaise) Co.1
Vincamp, Uriah AL Lt.Arty. 2nd Bn. Co.E
Vince, James MS 38th Cav. Co.I
Vince, J.R. MS 7th Inf. Co.H
Vince, M. VA Cav. 34th Bn. Co.D
Vince, Pinkney SC 5th Res. Co.K
Vince, R.W. LA 3rd (Wingfield's) Cav. Co.C
Vince, T.G. SC 7th Cav. Co.G
Vince, T.G. SC Rutledge Mtd.Riflemen & Horse Arty. Trenholm's Co.
Vince, T.G. SC Mil. 1st Regt.Rifles Palmer's Co.
Vince, William SC 7th Cav. Co.G
Vince, William SC Rutledge Mtd.Riflemen & Horse Arty. Trenholm's Co.
Vince, William A. TX 1st (McCulloch's) Cav. Co.C Black.
Vincell, H. KY 10th (Johnson's) Cav. Co.E
Vincen, C.W. MS 15th Inf. Co.D
Vincen, David TN Inf. Sowell's Detach.
Vincen, E.P. AL 15th Inf. Co.C
Vincen, J. GA 28th Inf. Co.C
Vincen, J. MS 10th Cav. Co.K
Vincen, J.L. GA 41st Inf. Co.A
Vincen, J.W. GA 34th Inf. Co.F
Vincen, L. AR 15th (Johnson's) Inf. Co.A
Vincen, Powhatan VA Inf. 25th Bn. Co.B
Vincen, Wade H. MS 25th Inf. Co.D
Vincent, --- LA Mil. 3rd Regt.Eur.Brig. (Garde Francaise) Co.1
Vincent, A. AL 23rd Inf. Co.A Sgt.
Vincent, A.A. GA Cav. 10th Bn. (St.Guards) Co.A Sgt.
Vincent, A.A. TX Cav. Wells' Regt. Co.H
Vincent, Aaron AL 46th Inf. Co.A Sgt.
Vincent, A.B. AL 3rd Inf. Co.C
Vincent, Adolph LA Conscr.
Vincent, A.F. TN 11th (Holman's) Cav. Co.H
Vincent, A.F. TN Douglass' Bn.Part.Rangers Coffee's Co.
Vincent, A.G. LA 2nd Cav. Co.K 1st Lt.
Vincent, A.G. LA Mil. 4th Regt. 3rd Brig. 1st Div. Co.B 3rd Lt.

Vincent, A.J. 8th Conf.Cav. Co.H
Vincent, Albert AL 6th Inf. Co.I
Vincent, Alexis LA 1st Hvy.Arty. (Reg.) Co.D
Vincent, Allen SC 5th Inf. 1st Co.E, 2nd Co.H
Vincent, Andrew J. TN 3rd (Lillard's) Mtd.Inf. Co.I
Vincent, A.P. AR 11th Cav. Co.A
Vincent, A.P. TX 7th Inf. Co.H
Vincent, Ash KY 2nd (Duke's) Cav. Co.B
Vincent, A.W. LA 17th Inf. Co.G 2nd Jr.Lt.
Vincent, B. GA 54th Inf. Co.A
Vincent, Bailey LA 2nd Cav. Co.G
Vincent, Benjamin J. VA 41st Inf. 2nd Co.E
Vincent, Benjamin W. NC 1st Arty. (10th St.Troops) Co.K
Vincent, Berry TN 1st (Feild's) Inf. Co.D
Vincent, B.F. MS Detailed Conscr.
Vincent, B.S. TN 23rd Inf. 2nd Co.F
Vincent, B.W. AL 45th Inf. Co.D
Vincent, C. VA 54th Inf. Co.G
Vincent, C.A. GA 9th Inf. (St.Guards) Co.C Sgt.
Vincent, Carl MO 8th Inf. Co.C 1st Sgt.
Vincent, Carlo AL 95th Mil. Co.D
Vincent, C.C. VA 3rd (Archer's) Bn.Res. Co.A
Vincent, C.C. VA 39th Mil. Co.B
Vincent, C.E. AL 1st Regt. Mobile Vol. Co.A
Vincent, C.E. AL Mil. 2nd Regt.Vol. Co.D
Vincent, Charles LA 6th Inf. Co.A
Vincent, Charles LA Conscr.
Vincent, Charles D. GA Inf. Athens Reserved Corps
Vincent, Charles S. MS 2nd Inf. Co.C
Vincent, Christopher C. MO Cav. Preston's Bn. Co.A Cpl.
Vincent, Christopher H. KY Fields' Co. (Part.Rangers)
Vincent, Columbus P. AL 23rd Bn.S.S. Co.G
Vincent, Corneluis VA 23rd Cav. Co.D
Vincent, C.P. AL 1st Bn. Hilliard's Legion Vol. Co.G
Vincent, C.S. GA Hvy.Arty. 22nd Bn. Co.B
Vincent, Daniel GA 54th Inf. Co.B
Vincent, Daniel SC Mil. Charbonnier's Co.
Vincent, Daniel TN 41st Inf. Co.B
Vincent, David GA 28th Inf. Co.C Cpl.
Vincent, David TN 3rd (Forrest's) Cav. 1st Co.E
Vincent, David TN 48th (Nixon's) Inf. Co.A
Vincent, David TN 48th (Voorhies') Inf. Co.B
Vincent, David P. AL Recruits
Vincent, D.H. AL 30th Inf. Co.F
Vincent, D.H. AL 36th Inf. Co.I
Vincent, D.J. NC 2nd Arty. (36th St.Troops) Co.F
Vincent, Drew NC 55th Inf. Co.E
Vincent, D.T. AL Cav. 24th Bn. Co.A Sgt.
Vincent, D.T. AL Mil. 4th Vol. Moore's Co. 1st Sgt.
Vincent, E.A. AL 2nd Inf. Co.H
Vincent, Edmond AR 7th Inf.
Vincent, Edwin A. AL 4th (Roddey's) Cav.
Vincent, E.J. AL 59th Inf. Co.B
Vincent, Eli MO 8th Cav. Co.I
Vincent, Elial TN 43rd Inf. Co.D 2nd Lt.
Vincent, Elias VA Cav. Swann's Bn. Vincent's Co. Capt.
Vincent, Elihue MO 2nd Cav. Co.F 2nd Lt.
Vincent, E.M. AL 63rd Inf. Co.A,C
Vincent, E.R. AL 12th Cav. Co.D
Vincent, Erastus AL 19th Inf. Co.D
Vincent, Eugene LA 1st Hvy.Arty. (Reg.) Co.D
Vincent, Eugene LA Mil. 1st Native Guards
Vincent, Eugene LA 13th Inf. Co.I
Vincent, F. LA Mil. 3rd Regt. French Brig. Co.2 Cpl.
Vincent, F. SC 1st Regt. Charleston Guard Co.D
Vincent, Farro TX 7th Field Btty. Cpl.
Vincent, Ferril TX 35th (Brown's) Cav. Co.E
Vincent, Fletcher VA 20th Cav. Co.B QMSgt.
Vincent, Francis M. AL 5th Bn.Vol. Co.B
Vincent, Francois LA C.S. Zouave Bn. Co.A
Vincent, G. LA Mil. 1st Regt. 2nd Brig. 1st Div. Co.A 1st Lt.
Vincent, G. LA Mil.Conf.Guards Regt. Co.B
Vincent, George MO 16th Inf. Co.K
Vincent, George TN 3rd (Clack's) Inf. Co.C
Vincent, George Conf.Cav. Clarkson's Bn. Ind.Rangers Co.B
Vincent, George M. GA 30th Inf. Co.H
Vincent, George S. TX 24th Cav. Co.D
Vincent, George W. AL 2nd Cav. Co.A
Vincent, German LA 2nd Cav. Co.A
Vincent, G.G. GA 39th Inf. Co.F,G
Vincent, Giles M. TX 16th Inf. Co.C
Vincent, G.W. AL 31st Inf.
Vincent, H. AL 18th Inf. Co.F
Vincent, H. SC 25th Inf. Co.E
Vincent, Harvey B. AL 4th Inf. Co.A
Vincent, Henry MO 10th Inf. Co.G Cpl.
Vincent, Henry TX 33rd Cav. Co.I
Vincent, Henry P. LA 12th Inf. Co.L Music.
Vincent, Hemeginz TX Inf. Griffin's Bn. Co.F
Vincent, Howard E. SC Lt.Arty. Parker's Co. (Marion Arty.)
Vincent, Howell NC Walker's Bn. Thomas' Legion Co.B
Vincent, Hugh TN 3rd (Lillard's) Mtd.Inf. Co.I
Vincent, I. TX 11th (Spaight's) Bn.Vol. Co.E
Vincent, Ike H. AL 47th Inf. Co.I Capt.
Vincent, Isaac GA Inf. 23rd Bn.Loc.Def. Cook's Co.
Vincent, Isaac H. AL 7th Inf. Co.A Sgt.
Vincent, Isaac S. GA 3rd Inf. Co.L Capt.
Vincent, Isaac T. SC 12th Inf. Co.I
Vincent, Isaac T. VA 19th Cav. Co.D
Vincent, Isaac W. AL 1st Regt.Conscr. Co.D
Vincent, J. GA 8th Inf. Co.H
Vincent, J. TX 5th Cav. Co.I
Vincent, J.A. TN 3rd (Clack's) Inf. Co.E
Vincent, James AL 62nd Inf. Co.H
Vincent, James AL Calhoun Cty.Res. A. Bryant's Co.
Vincent, James GA Floyd Legion (St.Guards) Co.F Cpl.
Vincent, James MO 10th Inf. Co.B
Vincent, James NC 17th Inf. (1st Org.) Co.C
Vincent, James TN Inf. 1st Bn. (Colms') Co.E
Vincent, James VA Cav. Swann's Bn. Vincent's Co.
Vincent, James B. NC 7th Inf. Co.D
Vincent, James C. TN Inf. 1st Bn. (Colms') Co.D
Vincent, James C. TN 50th (Cons.) Inf. Co.K Sgt.
Vincent, James C. TX 1st (Yager's) Cav. Co.C 1st Lt.
Vincent, James C. TX Cav. 3rd (Yager's) Bn. Co.C 2nd Lt.
Vincent, James F. LA 2nd Inf. Co.H
Vincent, James H. NC 32nd Inf. Co.B,C
Vincent, James H. 1st Cherokee Mtd.Vol. 2nd Co.K
Vincent, James L. GA 63rd Inf. Co.E
Vincent, James L. MO 10th Inf. Co.G
Vincent, James W. AL 61st Inf. Co.B
Vincent, James W. KY Morehead's Regt. (Part.Rangers) Co.A
Vincent, J.B. LA C.S. Zouave's Bn. Co.A
Vincent, J.B. NC 2nd Cav. (19th St.Troops) Co.H
Vincent, J.C. SC Rhett's Co.
Vincent, J. Calhoun SC 5th Inf. 1st Co.E, 2nd Co.H
Vincent, Jesse NC 8th Inf. Co.G
Vincent, Jesse SC Lt.Arty. 3rd (Palmetto) Bn. Co.H,I
Vincent, Jesse TN 60th Mtd.Inf. Co.H
Vincent, J.F. AL 44th Inf. Co.D
Vincent, J.H. NC 22nd Inf. Co.E
Vincent, J.H. TN 19th (Biffle's) Cav. Co.E
Vincent, J.J. AL 3rd Cav. Co.F
Vincent, J.J. AL 5th Cav. Co.F
Vincent, J.J. AL 23rd Inf. Co.A
Vincent, J.J. GA Arty. Lumpkin's Co.
Vincent, J.J. MO 16th Inf. Co.E
Vincent, J.L. KY 1st (Butler's) Cav. Co.B
Vincent, J.L. LA Arty. 5th Field Btty. (Pelican Lt.Arty.)
Vincent, J.L. LA 30th Inf. Co.F
Vincent, J.M. TX 37th Cav. Co.D
Vincent, J.O. KY 12th Cav. Co.B
Vincent, John AL 48th Inf. Co.F
Vincent, John KY 1st (Butler's) Cav. Co.B
Vincent, John LA 9th Inf. Co.F
Vincent, John MO 10th Inf. Co.G
Vincent, John MO St.Guard
Vincent, John SC 1st Arty. Co.F
Vincent, John TN 3rd (Clack's) Inf. Co.C
Vincent, John TN 3rd (Lillard's) Mtd.Inf. Co.I
Vincent, John TN 44th (Cons.) Inf. Co.G
Vincent, John VA 2nd St.Res. Co.E
Vincent, John B. VA 41st Inf. 2nd Co.E 1st Lt.
Vincent, John H. GA 1st (Olmstead's) Inf. Co.K
Vincent, John H. TN 53rd Inf. Co.E
Vincent, John J. MS 11th Inf. Co.F
Vincent, John J. VA 31st Inf. Co.A
Vincent, John P. VA 19th Inf. Co.C
Vincent, John R. AL 3rd Res. Co.E
Vincent, John T. NC 6th Inf. Co.K Sgt.
Vincent, John T. VA 14th Cav.
Vincent, John W. TN 3rd (Lillard's) Mtd.Inf. Co.I
Vincent, Joseph LA 7th Cav. Co.A
Vincent, Joseph LA 2nd Res.Corps Co.K
Vincent, Joseph LA Inf. 19th Bn. Co.F
Vincent, Joseph LA Mil.Conf.Guards Regt. Co.G
Vincent, Joseph NC 1st Jr.Res. Co.K
Vincent, Joseph E. KY 1st (Butler's) Cav. Co.B 2nd Lt.
Vincent, Joseph R. NC Lt.Arty. 3rd Bn. Co.A
Vincent, Joseph S. NC 6th Inf. Co.K Capt.

Vincent, Josephus TN 33rd Inf. Co.H Sgt.
Vincent, Josiah GA 6th Inf. (St.Guards) Co.G
Vincent, Josiah SC Inf. 7th Bn. (Enfield Rifles) Co.D
Vincent, J.T. AL 40th Inf. Co.H Sgt.
Vincent, J.U. GA Cav. 10th Bn. (St.Guards) Co.A
Vincent, Julius MS 1st (King's) Inf. (St.Troops) Co.K
Vincent, J.W. LA 3rd (Wingfield's) Cav. Co.D
Vincent, J.W. NC 1st Cav. (9th St.Troops) Co.H
Vincent, L. VA Cav. Swann's Bn. Vincent's Co. Cpl.
Vincent, Lasty TX Loc.Def.Troops Merriman's Co. (Orange Cty. Coast Guards)
Vincent, Levi GA 23rd Inf. Co.A Cpl.
Vincent, Levi NC 6th Cav. (65th St.Troops) Co.B
Vincent, Louis LA Washington Arty.Bn. Co.5
Vincent, Louis LA Inf.Crescent Regt. Co.B
Vincent, L.W. GA 12th (Robinson's) Cav. (St.Guards) Co.C
Vincent, M. GA 19th Inf. Co.A
Vincent, M. LA Inf.Cons.Crescent Regt. Co.N
Vincent, Martin LA 1st Hvy.Arty. (Reg.) Co.D
Vincent, Moses TN 24th Inf. Co.A
Vincent, Moses TN 43rd Inf. Co.D
Vincent, Nat B. GA 44th Inf. Co.F
Vincent, Nathaniel LA 2nd Cav. Co.A
Vincent, Nehemiah TN 42nd Inf. Co.G
Vincent, O.B. KY 12th Cav. Co.B Cpl.
Vincent, O.B. TN 31st Inf. Co.K
Vincent, Obediah VA 31st Inf. Co.A
Vincent, P. KY 12th Cav. Co.E
Vincent, Peleg VA 1st St.Res. Co.A
Vincent, Perry NC 1st Inf. Co.F
Vincent, Peter VA 1st St.Res. Co.A
Vincent, Peyton AL Cav. Hardie's Bn.Res. Co.A
Vincent, Pierre LA 10th Inf. Co.K Sgt.
Vincent, R. AL 12th Cav. Co.F
Vincent, R. AR 2nd Inf. Co.C
Vincent, R. SC 7th Inf. Co.I
Vincent, R.B. MS Inf. 1st Bn.St.Troops (30 days '64) Co.H
Vincent, Richard VA 49th Inf. Co.D
Vincent, Robert A. VA 22nd Inf. Co.D
Vincent, R.S. LA 14th Inf. Co.E Cpl.
Vincent, R.T. GA Inf. 9th Bn. Co.C Cpl.
Vincent, S. TX 21st Inf. Co.B
Vincent, S. VA Cav. Swann's Bn. Vincent's Co.
Vincent, Samuel TN 43rd Inf. Co.D
Vincent, Severrain TX 13th Vol. 3rd Co.K
Vincent, S.J. SC 4th St.Troops Co.B
Vincent, S.J. SC 5th Bn.Res. Co.E Sgt.
Vincent, Solomon Y. TN 1st (Feild's) Inf. Co.D
Vincent, T.C. TX 20th Inf. Co.C
Vincent, Thomas AL 50th Inf. Co.B
Vincent, Thomas LA 2nd Cav.
Vincent, Thomas LA 7th Cav. Co.A
Vincent, Thomas MS 1st (Johnston's) Inf. Co.C
Vincent, Thomas NC 45th Inf. Co.C
Vincent, Thomas SC 11th Res. Co.I
Vincent, Thomas TN 19th (Biffle's) Cav. Co.D
Vincent, Thomas TX 20th Cav. Co.K
Vincent, Thomas TX Loc.Def.Troops Merriman's Co. (Orange Cty. Coast Guards)
Vincent, Thomas E. TN 44th Inf. Co.H
Vincent, Thomas J. GA 30th Inf. Co.H
Vincent, Thomas L. MS 27th Inf. Co.L
Vincent, Thomas N. GA 22nd Inf. Co.G
Vincent, T.J. MS 1st (Johnston's) Inf. Co.D
Vincent, U. LA 7th Cav. Co.A
Vincent, U. LA Mil. 2nd Regt. French Brig. Co.4
Vincent, Uclisse LA 1st Hvy.Arty. (Reg.) Co.D
Vincent, V. LA Inf. 16th Bn. (Conf.Guards Resp.Bn.) Co.C
Vincent, V. TX 6th Field Btty.
Vincent, V. TX Lt.Arty. Dege's Bn. Co.D
Vincent, Valentine LA 28th (Thomas') Inf. Co.F
Vincent, Vulsa LA 7th Cav. Co.G
Vincent, W. KY Cav. 2nd Bn. (Dortch's) Co.D Sgt.
Vincent, W. LA 3rd (Wingfield's) Cav. Co.D
Vincent, W. SC 1st (Butler's) Inf. Co.G
Vincent, W.A. AL 38th Inf. Co.H
Vincent, W.A. TN 24th Inf. Co.A
Vincent, Walter F. NC 15th Regt.Res.
Vincent, Washington AR 1st Cav. Co.A
Vincent, W.B. AL 6th Inf. Co.I 2nd Lt.
Vincent, W.C. GA 2nd Inf. Co.A
Vincent, W.D. KY 9th Cav. Co.G
Vincent, W.E. SC 4th Cav. Co.K
Vincent, Wesley C. GA Inf. 2nd Bn. Co.A
Vincent, W.H. AL 56th Part.Rangers Co.A
Vincent, W.H. AL 8th Inf. Co.C
Vincent, W.H. AL 55th Vol. Co.A
Vincent, W.H. KY 12th Cav. Co.B
Vincent, W.H. 2nd Conf.Inf. Co.D
Vincent, William AL 19th Inf. Co.H 2nd Lt.
Vincent, William KY 5th Mtd.Inf.
Vincent, William MO 1st N.E. Cav. Co.I
Vincent, William MO 10th Inf. Co.B
Vincent, William SC 13th Inf. Co.I
Vincent, William TX 11th (Spaight's) Bn.Vol. Co.E
Vincent, William TX 21st Inf. Co.B
Vincent, William VA 17th Inf. Co.E
Vincent, William A. AL Mil. 4th Vol. Co.A
Vincent, William A. LA 12th Inf. Co.B
Vincent, William C. AR 1st (Dobbin's) Cav. Co.B
Vincent, William D. AL 6th Inf. Co.I
Vincent, Wm. E. SC 4th Cav. Co.K
Vincent, William G. LA 2nd Cav. Col.
Vincent, William G. LA 1st (Nelligan's) Inf. Col.
Vincent, William H. GA 3rd Inf. Co.K
Vincent, William H. LA 31st Inf. Co.A
Vincent, William H. VA 31st Inf. Co.A
Vincent, William J. GA 22nd Inf. Co.G
Vincent, William J. TN 3rd (Lillard's) Mtd.Inf. Co.I Sgt.
Vincent, William M. VA 49th Inf. Co.D
Vincent, William P. AL Cav. Lewis' Bn. Co.E
Vincent, William P. LA Res.Corps Scott's Co.
Vincent, William T. GA 4th Inf. Co.G Sgt.
Vincent, William T. KY Cav. 1st Bn. Sgt.
Vincent, Willis TN 48th (Voorhies') Inf. Co.B
Vincent, Willis H. FL 1st Inf. Old Co.H, New Co.K Sgt.
Vincent, Willis P. AL 24th Inf. Co.K
Vincent, W.J. AL 9th Inf. Co.F
Vincent, W.J. SC Inf. 1st (Charleston) Bn. Co.E
Vincent, W.J. SC 27th Inf. Co.A
Vincent, W.L. GA Arty. St.Troops Pruden's Btty.
Vincent, W.M. AL 3rd Bn.Res. Jackson's Co.
Vincent, W.T. KY 1st (Helms') Cav. Co.E 3rd Lt.
Vincent, W.T. KY 8th Cav. Co.H
Vincent, W.T. KY Morgan's Men Co.D Sgt.
Vincent, W.W. AL 12th Cav. Co.F
Vincents, H. GA Lt.Arty. (Arsenal Btty.) Hudson's Co.
Vinciad, J.J. TX Cav. Wells' Regt. Co.D
Vincient, Honesean LA Miles' Legion Co.F
Vincient, James H. NC 12th Inf. Co.N
Vincient, Powell P. TX 5th Cav. Co.I
Vincil, James D. VA 45th Inf. Co.K
Vincil, William VA Cav. 34th Bn. Co.I Forage M.
Vincil, William D. VA 50th Inf. Co.H Cpl.
Vincill, John Conf.Cav. 6th Bn.
Vincill, Meshecth Conf.Cav. 6th Bn.
Vincine, --- NC 54th Inf. Co.I
Vincint, David TN 19th (Biffle's) Cav. Co.H
Vincint, R.W. TN 19th (Biffle's) Cav. Co.H
Vincon, B. AL 13th Inf. Co.H
Vincon, T.B. AL 9th Inf. Co.F
Vinds, Henry VA 136th Mil. Co.D
Vine, B.M. TN Inf. Nashville Bn. Felts' Co.
Vine, C.F. TN 61st Mtd.Inf. Co.I
Vine, George AL 36th Inf. Co.D
Vine, George VA Lt.Arty. G.B. Chapman's Co.
Vine, John GA 1st (Olmstead's) Inf. Gordon's Co.
Vine, John GA 63rd Inf. Co.K,D
Vine, P.A. VA 19th Inf. Co.I
Vine, Silas VA 11th Bn.Res. Co.C
Vine, W.A. TX 1st (Yager's) Cav. Co.H
Vine, William MS 12th Cav. Co.I
Vine, William A. TX Cav. 8th (Taylor's) Bn. Co.E
Vineberg, C. TX 1st Hvy.Arty. Co.B
Vineberg, H. TX 1st Hvy.Arty. Co.B
Vineberg, L. TX 1st Hvy.Arty. Co.B
Vinegar, August LA 11th Inf. Co.K
Vineing, Jackson GA 36th (Villepigue's) Inf. Co.C
Vineing, J.H. GA 50th Inf. Co.G
Viner, Benjamin GA 55th Inf. Co.H 2nd Lt.
Viner, Thomas SC 1st (Hagood's) Inf. 2nd Co.B
Vines, Alexander M. NC 8th Inf. Co.C
Vines, Andrew AL 18th Inf. Co.G,E
Vines, Andrew J. VA 27th Inf. 2nd Co.H
Vines, A.S. TN 1st (Carter's) Cav. Co.M
Vines, B. AL 18th Inf. Co.G
Vines, Benjamin R. TX 9th Cav. Co.I
Vines, Bennett AL 28th Inf. Co.H
Vines, B.M. AL 48th Inf. Co.I
Vines, B.M. TN 1st (Feild's) Inf. Co.L
Vines, Charles NC 30th Inf. Co.F 2nd Lt.
Vines, Charles NC 43rd Inf. Co.E 1st Lt.
Vines, Charles N. 7th Conf.Cav. Co.B,L
Vines, Chesley D. AL 61st Inf. Co.E
Vines, C.L. 7th Conf.Cav. 2nd Co.I
Vines, C.O. AL 6th Cav. Co.A
Vines, Columbus W. VA 5th Inf. Co.G
Vines, C.W. NC 12th Inf. Co.D,B
Vines, Daniel AL 28th Inf. Co.L

Vines, David C. VA 50th Inf. Co.F Sgt.
Vines, D.W. LA 19th Inf. Co.C
Vines, Eli AL 18th Inf. Co.G
Vines, Enoch AL 28th Inf. Co.H
Vines, G.B. AL 63rd Inf. Co.H
Vines, George W. AL 6th Cav. Co.C
Vines, George W. AL 28th Inf. Co.H
Vines, Geo. W. VA Hvy.Arty. 20th Bn. Co.D
Vines, G.M. 1st Conf.Eng.Troops Co.D
Vines, G.W. AL 34th Inf. Co.D
Vines, Henry NC 2nd Arty. (36th St.Troops) Co.G
Vines, Henry NC 61st Inf. Co.G
Vines, Hosea AL 28th Inf. Co.H
Vines, H.T. AL 18th Inf. Co.G
Vines, H.W. GA Inf. Collier's Co.
Vines, Isaac N. VA 5th Inf. Co.E Cpl.
Vines, J. AL 22nd Inf. Co.G
Vines, J. AL 63rd Inf. Co.H
Vines, J. LA Inf. Pelican Regt. Co.F 1st Sgt.
Vines, J. MS 2nd St.Cav. Co.H
Vines, Jackson LA Inf. 4th Bn. Co.D
Vines, James AL 18th Inf. Co.G
Vines, James AL 31st Inf. Co.G,C
Vines, James AR Inf. 4th Bn. Co.A
Vines, James SC 19th Inf. Co.D
Vines, James SC Inf.Bn. Co.D
Vines, James VA 3rd Res. Co.H
Vines, James F. GA 52nd Inf. Co.K
Vines, James H. VA 52nd Inf. 2nd Co.B
Vines, Jas. P. AR 11th Inf. Co.E
Vines, James P. GA 30th Inf. Co.K
Vines, James W. VA Lt.Arty. Lowry's Co.
Vines, James W. VA 5th Inf. Co.E Sgt.
Vines, Jeff VA 12th Cav. Co.A
Vines, J.H.M. AL 34th Inf. Co.D
Vines, John AL 18th Inf. Co.G
Vines, John AR 11th Inf. Co.E
Vines, John AR 11th & 17th (Cons.) Inf. Co.E
Vines, John LA Inf. 4th Bn. Co.D
Vines, John A. NC 43rd Inf. Co.E Capt.
Vines, John A. TX 9th Cav. Co.I
Vines, John A. 7th Conf.Cav. Co.B,L
Vines, John D. AL 10th Inf. Co.B
Vines, John M. TX 2nd Cav. 1st Co.F
Vines, John M. TX Cav. Morgan's Regt. Co.I Sgt.
Vines, Joseph AL 18th Inf. Co.G
Vines, Joseph AR 5th Mil. Co.I 1st Sgt.
Vines, Joseph MO 3rd Inf. Co.I Cpl.
Vines, Joseph W. AR 35th Inf. Co.G
Vines, Joshua N. AL 28th Inf. Co.G
Vines, J.T. GA 4th Res. Co.K
Vines, J.V. AL 8th Inf. Co.A
Vines, J.W. AL 53rd (Part.Rangers) Co.H
Vines, J.W. GA 19th Inf. Co.I
Vines, Lee LA 2nd Cav. Co.D,B
Vines, Levi AL 28th Inf. Co.H
Vines, Luis LA Mil. Cazadores Espanoles Regt. Co.5
Vines, Major C. VA 52nd Inf. Co.G
Vines, McDaniel AL 28th Inf. Co.H
Vines, M.L. VA Harper's Regt.Res. Co.A
Vines, P.H. GA 7th Inf. (St.Guards) Co.B
Vines, Phillip GA 1st (Fannin's) Res. Co.K Cpl.
Vines, Phillip GA 1st (Fannin's) Res. Co.K
Vines, R.N. LA 19th Inf. Co.C
Vines, Samuel R. NC 3rd Arty. (40th St.Troops) Co.D
Vines, Silvester AL 28th Inf. Co.H
Vines, S.S. VA 166th Mil. R.G. Lively's Co.
Vines, Thomas AL Inf. 1st Regt. Co.A
Vines, Thomas MS 3rd Cav. Co.H
Vines, Thomas MS 8th Cav. Co.C
Vines, Thomas MS 29th Inf. Co.D
Vines, Thomas NC 17th Inf. (1st Org.) Co.K
Vines, Thomas G. TX 18th Inf. Co.H
Vines, W. AL Cav. Barbiere's Bn. Truss' Co.
Vines, W. AR 13th Mil. Co.E
Vines, Washington LA 19th Inf. Co.C
Vines, W.B. AL 63rd Inf. Co.H,I
Vines, W.D. AL 28th Inf. Co.H
Vines, W.H. AL Inf. 1st Regt. Co.A
Vines, W.H. TX 18th Inf. Co.H
Vines, W.H. Gen. & Staff, QM Dept.
Vines, Wiley AL 28th Inf. Co.H
Vines, Willaby AL Cp. of Instr. Talladega
Vines, William AL 17th Inf. Co.C
Vines, William AL 18th Inf. Co.G
Vines, William, Jr. AL 29th Inf. Co.H
Vines, William AL 31st Inf. Co.G,C
Vines, William AL 58th Inf. Co.E Cpl.
Vines, William LA Desoto Res.
Vines, William TN 27th Inf. Co.I
Vines, William VA 50th Inf. Co.F Cpl.
Vines, William A.J. AL 21st Inf. Co.F
Vines, William E. AR Cav. Gordon's Regt. Co.H Sgt.
Vines, William H. MO Cav. Slayback's Regt. Co.E
Vines, William H. VA 14th Cav. Co.H Sgt.
Vines, William Henry AL Arty. 1st Bn. Co.F
Vines, William J. AL 19th Inf. Co.C
Vines, William J. GA Sharp's Bn. Co.C,F
Vines, William J. VA 52nd Inf. 2nd Co.B
Vines, William O. GA 30th Inf. Co.K
Vines, William T. NC 20th Inf. Co.C
Vines, Willoughby AL Cp. of Instr. Talladega
Vines, W. Pinckney SC 1st (McCreary's) Inf. Co.G
Vinesett, Johnson SC 18th Inf. Co.K
Vinesett, William AR 18th Inf. Co.G
Vinet, Antonio LA Mil. 5th Regt.Eur.Brig. (Spanish Regt.) Co.4
Vinet, F.E. LA Mil. Lartigue's Co. (Bienville Guards)
Vinet, J. AL 21st Inf. Co.K
Vinet, John B. Eng.,CSA Capt.
Vinet, Jno. B. Gen. & Staff Capt.,AAQM
Vinet, Jules LA Mil. 3rd Regt. 1st Brig. 1st Div. Co.A 1st Lt.
Vinet, Jules LA 30th Inf. Co.F
Vinet, Nicholas Valery LA Mil. Orlean's Arty.
Vinet, V. LA Mil. 1st Chasseurs a pied Co.4
Vinett, Daniel LA 15th Inf. Co.H Cpl.
Vinett, William J. AR 1st Cav. Co.B
Vinette, D. LA Mil. Chalmette Regt. Co.K
Viney, A.J. AR 19th (Dawson's) Inf. Co.I
Vineyard, A.G. FL 7th Inf. Co.I
Vineyard, A.J. GA 2nd Cav. Co.F
Vineyard, A.R. MS 1st Cav. Co.D
Vineyard, Benjamin N. TX 29th Cav. Co.A Cpl.
Vineyard, B.R. MS 23rd Inf. Co.I
Vineyard, C.P. VA 36th Inf. 2nd Co.K
Vineyard, Daniel TN 59th Mtd.Inf. Co.I
Vineyard, Elisha M. VA 25th Cav. Co.D
Vineyard, E.M. VA Mil. Scott Cty.
Vineyard, George TX 1st (Yager's) Cav. Co.B
Vineyard, George TX Cav. 3rd (Yager's) Bn. Co.B
Vineyard, George S. GA 24th Inf. Co.F
Vineyard, George W. VA 48th Inf. Co.H
Vineyard, Isaac W. VA 157th Mil. Co.B
Vineyard, Jacob C. TN 59th Mtd.Inf. Co.I
Vineyard, James N. GA 2nd Cav. (St.Guards) Co.E
Vineyard, Jessee AL 3rd Bn.Res. Co.B
Vineyard, J.H. GA Phillips' Legion Co.F
Vineyard, J.L. AL Cp. of Instr. Talladega
Vineyard, John TN 21st Inf. Co.H
Vineyard, John H. AR 1st (Dobbin's) Cav. Co.B
Vineyard, John M. AL 37th Inf. Co.D
Vineyard, Johon KY Cav. 2nd Bn. (Dortch's) Co.A
Vineyard, Joseph AL 13th Inf. Co.F
Vineyard, Joshua M. MS 14th Inf. Co.H Sgt.
Vineyard, Lycurgus MO 3rd Inf. Co.D
Vineyard, M.H. TN Inf. 2nd Cons.Regt. Co.K
Vineyard, M.H. TN 11th Inf. Co.K
Vineyard, M.T. MO 12th Inf. Co.C
Vineyard, Nathnaiel W. GA 7th Inf. Co.A
Vineyard, N.H. TN 2nd (Ashby's) Cav. Co.H
Vineyard, Nicholas G. TN 2nd (Ashby's) Cav. Co.G
Vineyard, N.J. VA 157th Mil. Co.A
Vineyard, N.O. TX Cav. 3rd (Yager's) Bn. Co.B
Vineyard, N.O. TX 8th Inf. Co.G
Vineyard, Owen N. TX 1st (Yager's) Cav. Co.B
Vineyard, R.A. VA Inf. 26th Bn. Co.I 1st Sgt.
Vineyard, Robert VA 14th Cav. Co.E
Vineyard, Samuel C. TX 8th Inf. Co.E,F,G 1st Lt.
Vineyard, Samuel F. GA Phillips' Legion Co.F
Vineyard, S.P. GA 24th Inf. Co.F
Vineyard, T.A. GA 18th Inf. Co.G
Vineyard, T.B. TN 34th Inf. Co.D
Vineyard, Thomas B. AL 4th Inf. Co.K
Vineyard, W.F. GA 4th Res. Co.B
Vineyard, William J. AR 25th Inf. Co.K Sgt.
Vineyard, William J. VA 48th Inf. Co.H
Vineyard, William T. TN 21st (Carter's) Cav. Co.E
Vineyard, Willis AL 13th Inf. Co.F
Vineyard, W.T. TN 3rd (Lillard's) Mtd.Inf. Co.H
Vingard, J.H. FL 10th Inf. Co.B
Vinier, John TX 25th Cav. Co.H
Vinig, --- LA 13th Inf. Co.F
Vinin, M.C. TX 9th (Nichols') Inf. Co.K
Vining, A.M. GA Lt.Arty. 12th Bn. 3rd Co.B
Vining, A.S. GA Cav. (St.Guards) Bond's Co. Sgt.
Vining, B.F. Inf. Bailey's Cons.Regt. Co.B 2nd Lt.
Vining, B.F. TX 7th Inf. Co.E Capt.
Vining, Casley L. GA 39th Inf. Co.C
Vining, D.J. TN Lt.Arty. Scott's Co.
Vining, D.M. GA Inf. (GA RR Guards) Porter's Co.
Vining, Edmund C. TX 4th Cav. Co.D

Vining, E.G.N. LA 3rd (Wingfield's) Cav. Co.F,D
Vining, E.H. GA 42nd Inf. Co.E Conscr.
Vining, Elijah GA 12th Inf. Co.G
Vining, E.M. GA Inf. (Newton Factory Employees) Russell's Co.
Vining, F. LA Miles' Legion Co.F,C
Vining, F.M. LA 13th Bn. (Part.Rangers) Co.E
Vining, Francis J. GA 2nd Bn.S.S. Co.B 1st Lt.
Vining, Francis J. GA 5th Inf. Co.K,L 1st Lt.
Vining, George B. AL Inf. 1st Regt. Co.I
Vining, George J. AR 9th Inf. Old Co.I
Vining, Jackson L. GA 57th Inf. Co.F
Vining, James GA 30th Inf. Co.C
Vining, James C. AL 39th Inf. Co.A
Vining, James C. GA Inf. 1st City Bn. (Columbus) Co.C
Vining, James E. LA 28th (Gray's) Inf. Co.I
Vining, James P. GA 29th Inf. Co.H
Vining, J. Benson LA 27th Inf. Co.H
Vining, J.C. GA Inf. 1st City Bn. (Columbus) Co.A
Vining, Jehu S. AL Cp. of Instr. Talladega Co.B,D
Vining, J.F. GA Inf. (Newton Factory Employees) Russell's Co. Cpl.
Vining, J.G. GA Lt.Arty. Daniell's Btty.
Vining, J.J. GA 29th Inf. Co.H
Vining, J.L. GA 4th (Clinch's) Cav. Co.F,H
Vining, J.M. TX 4th Cav. Co.K Sgt.
Vining, John C. GA 13th Cav. Co.C
Vining, John L. GA 40th Inf. Co.I
Vining, John N. MS 17th Inf. Co.K
Vining, John S. AL 4th Inf. Co.I,C
Vining, John S. GA 46th Inf. Co.A
Vining, Jones GA 29th Inf. Co.H
Vining, Josiah GA 28th Inf.
Vining, Josiah K. GA 26th Inf. Co.D
Vining, J.R. TX Cav. Baird's Regt. Co.A
Vining, J.S. AL Cp. of Instr. Talladega Co.B
Vining, J.T. GA 4th (Clinch's) Cav. Co.F,H
Vining, Judson H. GA 29th Inf. Co.H
Vining, J.V. GA 29th Inf. Co.H
Vining, J.W. TX 28th Cav. Co.B
Vining, O.K. LA Mil.Conf.Guards Regt. Co.C
Vining, Oregon J. AR 3rd Inf. Co.C
Vining, Richard J. TX Cav. Baylor's Regt. Co.A
Vining, Shad AL 3rd Res. Co.K
Vining, S.R. LA 16th Inf. Co.A
Vining, T.B. GA 60th Inf. Co.E
Vining, T.G. LA Mil. Chalmette Regt. Co.C Cpl.
Vining, Thomas A. LA Pointe Coupee Arty.
Vining, Thomas G. LA 16th Inf. Co.F Sgt.
Vining, Washington F. GA 57th Inf. Co.F
Vining, William GA 18th Inf. Co.H
Vining, William M. GA 57th Inf. Co.F
Vinion, D.N. GA 48th Inf. Co.K
Vinis, M.V. AR Mil. Borland's Regt. King's Co.
Vink, William NC Cumberland Cty.Bn. Detailed Men Co.A
Vinling, F.J. LA Mil. 3rd Regt.Eur.Brig. (Garde Francaise) Co.4
Vinna, S. LA Mil. 1st Regt. 2nd Brig. 1st Div. Co.B
Vinne, Peter VA Horse Arty. G.W. Brown's Co.
Vinnett, Manuel LA 7th Inf. Co.A
Vinnier, A. LA 13th Inf. Co.C
Vinning, B.F. AL 50th Inf. Co.F
Vinning, Edmund TX 22nd Inf. Co.E
Vinning, G. SC Lt.Arty. Wagener's Co. (Co.A, German Arty.)
Vinning, James LA 7th Inf. Co.K
Vinning, R.V. TX Cav. Baird's Regt. Co.A
Vinning, T.L. LA 4th Inf. New Co.G
Vinsan, John NC 67th Inf. Co.D
Vinsant, George W. TN 59th Mtd.Inf. Co.G Cpl.
Vinsant, Hiram J. TN 59th Mtd.Inf. Co.G
Vinsant, Isaiah B. AR 35th Inf. Co.G
Vinsant, John AR 35th Inf. Co.G
Vinsant, Robert W. 1st Conf.Inf. Co.B, 2nd Co.D
Vinsant, W.H. SC 7th Inf. 2nd Co.E
Vinsar, W. TN 21st Cav. Co.E
Vinscons, S.D. GA 45th Inf. Co.A
Vinsen, John TN 55th (Brown's) Inf. Co.H
Vinsen, W.H. GA 36th (Broyles') Inf. Co.D
Vinsent, H.E. GA 11th Inf. Co.H
Vinsent, J.S. AL 13th Inf. Co.F
Vinsickle, T.C. TX 31st Inf. Co.E
Vinsin, G. AL 20th Inf. Co.B
Vinsler, Corrod Conf.Cav. Clarkson's Bn. Ind. Rangers Co.B
Vinson, --- MS 7th Cav. Co.I
Vinson, --- NC 27th Inf. Co.H
Vinson, --- TN 3rd (Forrest's) Cav. Co.E
Vinson, --- TX Cav. Mann's Regt. Co.I
Vinson, A. TX 7th Cav. Co.D
Vinson, A.B. GA 8th Cav. Old Co.I
Vinson, A.B. GA 62nd Cav. Co.I
Vinson, Abraham TX 1st Inf. Co.C
Vinson, A.D. GA Cav. 19th Bn. Co.E Far.
Vinson, A.D. 10th Conf.Cav. Co.K
Vinson, Addison H. TX 14th Cav. Co.C
Vinson, Alexander NC 35th Inf. Co.I
Vinson, Alfred D. LA Scouts Vinson's Co.
Vinson, Ali VA Cav. 34th Bn. Co.B
Vinson, Andrew NC 67th Inf. Co.I
Vinson, Andrew J. AL 6th Inf. Co.F
Vinson, Andrew J. GA 7th Inf. (St.Guards) Co.I
Vinson, A.P. AR 1st (Monroe's) Cav. Co.H
Vinson, A.P. SC 2nd Inf. Co.C,K Capt.
Vinson, Armistead M. TX 10th Inf. Co.I
Vinson, Bailie P.L. LA Scouts Vinson's Co. Capt.
Vinson, Baldridge LA Arty. 1st Field Btty. Cpl.
Vinson, Bartlett C. TN 43rd Inf. Co.K
Vinson, Ben TN 5th Inf. 2nd Co.F
Vinson, Benjamin GA 26th Inf. Co.I
Vinson, B.F. AL 46th Inf. Co.K
Vinson, B.F. TN 8th (Smith's) Cav. Co.E
Vinson, B.F. TX 30th Cav. Co.E
Vinson, B.P. LA Inf. 1st Sp.Bn. (Rightor's) Co.F
Vinson, B.P. TN 50th Inf. Co.D
Vinson, B.P.L. LA 11th Inf. Co.D 2nd Lt.
Vinson, Briant AL 34th Inf. Black's Co.
Vinson, Bryant GA 6th Inf. Co.C Sgt.
Vinson, Christopher C. MO 4th Cav. Co.A Cpl.
Vinson, C.S. 1st Choctaw & Chickasaw Mtd.Rifles 1st Co.E
Vinson, D. AL 2nd Cav. Co.G
Vinson, Daniel GA 8th Cav. Co.G 2nd Lt.
Vinson, Daniel GA 62nd Cav. Co.G 2nd Lt.
Vinson, Daniel GA 6th Inf. Co.C
Vinson, Daniel GA 56th Inf. Co.B
Vinson, Daniel NC 35th Inf. Co.I
Vinson, Daniel J. NC 1st Arty. (10th St.Troops) Co.F
Vinson, David SC 20th Inf. Co.A
Vinson, David J. TN 1st (Turney's) Inf. Co.B
Vinson, David T. AR 27th Inf. Co.A Sgt.
Vinson, D.D. SC 1st (McCreary's) Inf.
Vinson, D.H. GA Lt.Arty. 12th Bn. 3rd Co.E
Vinson, Drewry D. NC 1st Inf. Co.F
Vinson, D.T. GA 8th Cav. Old Co.I
Vinson, D.T. GA 62nd Cav. Co.I
Vinson, Ed J. AL Arty. 1st Bn. Co.C,E
Vinson, Edward J. AL 2nd Bn. Hilliard's Legion Vol. Co.E 1st Sgt.
Vinson, E.H. GA 17th Inf. Co.K
Vinson, E.J. AL 53rd (Part.Rangers) Co.C
Vinson, Eli AL 49th Inf. Co.C Cpl.
Vinson, Eliab H. AR 13th Inf. Co.K
Vinson, Elihu MO 7th Cav. Haislip's Co.I Jr.2nd Lt.
Vinson, Elijah GA 57th Inf. Co.F
Vinson, Elijah NC Loc.Def. Griswold's Co.
Vinson, Elijah H. GA 3rd Cav. Co.F
Vinson, E.S. AL 22nd Inf. Co.E
Vinson, Exum NC 12th Inf. Co.O Cpl.
Vinson, Exum NC 32nd Inf. Co.C,D 2nd Lt.
Vinson, F. 1st Chickasaw Inf. Hansell's Co.
Vinson, F. Conf.Inf. Tucker's Regt. Co.G
Vinson, F.C. AL Leighton Rangers 1st Lt.
Vinson, F.M. TN Inf. 3rd Bn. Co.E
Vinson, Francis M. VA 8th Cav. Co.K Sgt.
Vinson, G. AL 2nd Cav. Co.G
Vinson, G. AL 22nd Inf. Co.G
Vinson, G.B. NC Cav. 16th Bn. Co.G
Vinson, G.D. TN 18th Inf. Co.F
Vinson, George TN 45th Inf. Co.B,D
Vinson, George B. NC 15th Inf. Co.A
Vinson, George H. GA 62nd Cav. Co.E
Vinson, George W. AR 33rd Inf. Co.G
Vinson, George W. GA 38th Inf. Co.B
Vinson, George W. LA 11th Inf. Co.D
Vinson, George W. NC 26th Inf. Co.G
Vinson, G.H. GA 8th Cav. Old Co.E
Vinson, G.H. NC Cav. 16th Bn. Co.A
Vinson, G.L. GA 12th (Robinson's) Cav. (St.Guards) Co.B,C
Vinson, Grun B. AL 15th Inf. Co.C
Vinson, G.W. TX 22nd Inf. Co.F Sgt.
Vinson, H. SC 7th Res. Co.E
Vinson, Harrison SC 18th Inf. Co.B
Vinson, H.C. AL Cav. Moreland's Regt. Co.A
Vinson, H.C. GA 13th Inf. Co.G 1st Sgt.
Vinson, H.D. MS 14th Inf. Co.C
Vinson, Henry TN 17th Inf. Co.K
Vinson, Henry TX Cav. 2nd Bn.St.Troops Hubbard's Co.
Vinson, Henry Conf.Cav. Wood's Regt. Co.E
Vinson, Henry B. GA 6th Inf. Co.C Cpl.
Vinson, Henry C. GA 4th Inf. Co.H
Vinson, Henry G.W. AL 2nd Bn. Hilliard's Legion Vol. Co.A
Vinson, Henry H. TX 2nd Cav. Co.A
Vinson, H.G.W. AL 59th Inf. Co.F
Vinson, H.H. AL 40th Inf. Co.D Cpl.
Vinson, Homer R. TX 5th Cav. Co.H
Vinson, Hugh AL 19th Inf. Co.H

Vinson, H.W. TX 22nd Inf. Co.F,E 2nd Lt.
Vinson, I.E. MO Cav. Fristoe's Regt. Co.G
Vinson, Isaac GA Carlton's Co. (Troup Cty.Arty.)
Vinson, Isaac GA 2nd Inf. Stanley's Co.
Vinson, Isaac GA 51st Inf. Co.F
Vinson, Isaac GA 56th Inf. Co.B
Vinson, Isaac N. GA 6th Inf. Co.C Sgt.
Vinson, J. LA 2nd Inf. Co.H
Vinson, J. LA Red River S.S.
Vinson, J.A. TN 16th Inf. Co.D
Vinson, Jacob K. VA 6th Cav. Co.H
Vinson, James AR 7th Inf. Co.F
Vinson, James GA 8th Cav. Old Co.E
Vinson, James GA 62nd Cav. Co.E
Vinson, James GA 31st Inf. Co.A Cpl.
Vinson, James GA 55th Inf. Co.A
Vinson, James NC Cav. 16th Bn. Co.A
Vinson, James SC 15th Inf. Co.H
Vinson, James TN 8th (Smith's) Cav. Co.E
Vinson, James TN 14th (Neely's) Cav. Co.G
Vinson, James TN 4th Inf. Co.B
Vinson, James TN 33rd Inf. Co.B
Vinson, James TN 50th Inf. Co.D Sgt.
Vinson, James VA 8th Cav. Co.K
Vinson, James VA 1st Cav.St.Line Co.A
Vinson, James B. KY 7th Mtd.Inf. Co.B
Vinson, James F. AL 34th Inf. Black's Co.
Vinson, James F. GA 11th Inf. Co.F
Vinson, James H. AL 8th Inf. Co.C
Vinson, James J. AR Lt.Arty. Wiggins' Btty.
Vinson, James J. AR 7th Inf. Co.B
Vinson, James L. MO 2nd Cav. Co.F
Vinson, James M. AL 2nd Cav. Co.A Sgt.
Vinson, James M. AL 6th Inf. Co.F
Vinson, James M. AR 4th Inf. Co.G
Vinson, James M. TN 4th Inf. Co.E
Vinson, James W. NC 26th Inf. Co.D 2nd Lt.
Vinson, James W. SC 5th Cav. Co.K
Vinson, J.B. AL Arty. 1st Bn. Co.F
Vinson, J.B. TX 13th Vol. Co.H
Vinson, J.C. AR 7th Inf. Co.F Cpl.
Vinson, J.D. AL 11th Cav. Co.H
Vinson, J.D. AL Leighton Rangers Sgt.
Vinson, J.E. AL Cav. Moreland's Regt. Co.I
Vinson, J.E. AL 29th Inf. Co.G
Vinson, Jess AL Cav. Moreland's Regt. Co.A
Vinson, Jesse SC 7th Res. Co.M
Vinson, Jesse SC Inf. Holcombe Legion Co.C
Vinson, Jethro GA 51st Inf. Co.F
Vinson, J.F. AL 25th Inf. Co.D
Vinson, J.F. TN 38th Inf. 2nd Co.K Cpl.
Vinson, J.J. AR Cav. Crabtree's (46th) Regt. Co.F
Vinson, J.J. GA 9th Inf. (St.Guards) Co.G
Vinson, J.L. AL Cav. Moreland's Regt. Co.D
Vinson, J.L. AL 35th Inf. Co.B
Vinson, J.L. MS Inf. 1st Bn.St.Troops (30 days '64) Co.A 3rd Lt.
Vinson, J.L. MS 6th Inf. Music.
Vinson, J.M. TN 33rd Inf. Co.E
Vinson, J.M. TX 12th Cav. Co.K
Vinson, J.N.B. MS 10th Inf. New Co.C
Vinson, Joel T. GA 20th Inf. Co.B
Vinson, John AL Cav. Lenoir's Ind.Co.
Vinson, John AL 48th Inf. Co.F
Vinson, John AL Leighton Rangers
Vinson, John GA 3rd Cav. Co.I
Vinson, John MO 7th Cav. Haislip's Co.
Vinson, John MO Lt.Arty. Landis' Co.
Vinson, John MO 2nd Inf. Co.H
Vinson, John NC 8th Sr.Res. Gardner's Co.
Vinson, John NC 26th Inf. Co.G
Vinson, John TN 14th (Neely's) Cav. Co.G
Vinson, John TN Cav. Newsom's Regt. Co.H
Vinson, John TN 55th (McKoin's) Inf. Bound's Co.
Vinson, John A. GA Floyd Legion (St.Guards) Co.K Cpl.
Vinson, John B. MS Inf. 3rd Bn. Co.C
Vinson, John B. TX 14th Cav. Co.C
Vinson, John E. AL 4th Inf. Co.H
Vinson, John F. GA 57th Inf. Co.F Capt.
Vinson, John H. LA 13th Inf. Co.G,C
Vinson, John M. MO Cav. Preston's Bn. Co.B
Vinson, John P. GA Inf. 14th Bn. (St.Guards) Co.E
Vinson, John P. GA 26th Inf. Co.I
Vinson, John P. GA 57th Inf. Co.I
Vinson, John P. VA 29th Inf. Co.D
Vinson, John R. AL 59th Inf. Co.B Sgt.
Vinson, John R. AL 2nd Bn. Hilliard's Legion Vol. Co.E Sgt.
Vinson, John T. SC 20th Inf. Co.A
Vinson, John W. GA 17th Inf. Co.K
Vinson, John W. GA 54th Inf. Co.F
Vinson, John W. GA 57th Inf. Co.D
Vinson, John W. GA 57th Inf. Co.F
Vinson, John W. MS 26th Inf. Co.D
Vinson, Joseph TN 50th Inf. Co.D
Vinson, Joseph 7th Conf.Cav. Co.F
Vinson, Joseph 8th (Dearing's) Conf.Cav. Co.G
Vinson, Joseph B. AR 7th Inf. Co.F Cpl.
Vinson, Joseph S. GA 26th Inf. Co.I
Vinson, Joshua A. VA Cav. 35th Bn. Co.B
Vinson, Josiah AR 19th (Dockery's) Inf. Co.B
Vinson, Josiah FL 8th Inf. Co.B
Vinson, Josiah GA 3rd Inf. Co.F
Vinson, Josiah GA 6th Inf. Co.C
Vinson, J.P. AL 34th Inf. Black's Co.
Vinson, J.R. AL 56th (Part.Rangers) Co.B
Vinson, J.S. GA 8th Cav. Co.G
Vinson, J.S. GA Cav. 8th Bn. (St.Guards) Co.B
Vinson, J.S. GA 62nd Cav. Co.G
Vinson, J.S. TN 50th Inf. Co.D
Vinson, J.S. TN 50th (Cons.) Inf. Co.D Sgt.
Vinson, J.T. AL 20th Inf. Co.D 1st Sgt.
Vinson, J.T. AL 30th Inf. Co.C
Vinson, J.T. GA 63rd Inf. Co.E
Vinson, J.V. LA 17th Inf. Co.G
Vinson, J.W. AL 12th Inf. Co.E
Vinson, J.W. AL 46th Inf. Co.K
Vinson, J.W. GA 6th Inf. (St.Guards) Co.A 2nd Lt.
Vinson, J.W. MS 46th Inf. Co.G
Vinson, J.W. SC 7th Cav. Co.B
Vinson, J.W. SC 2nd Inf. Co.C Cpl.
Vinson, J.W. SC 15th Inf. Co.H
Vinson, J.W. SC Bn.St.Cadets Co.A
Vinson, L. AL 9th Inf. Co.F
Vinson, L. AL 15th Inf. Co.L Sgt.
Vinson, Lafayette VA 8th Cav. Co.K
Vinson, L.D. LA 2nd Cav. Co.C
Vinson, L.D. LA 2nd Res.Corps Co.A
Vinson, Leonard AL 7th Cav.
Vinson, Levin J.H. GA 57th Inf. Co.I 1st Lt.
Vinson, L.G. GA 6th Inf. Co.C
Vinson, Littleton SC 15th Inf. Co.H
Vinson, Liven G. GA 57th Inf. Co.F
Vinson, L.J. GA 23rd Inf. Co.B
Vinson, L.J.H. GA 57th Inf. Co.G
Vinson, M. LA 13th Bn. (Part.Rangers) Co.D
Vinson, M. TN Cav. Nixon's Regt. Co.D
Vinson, M. TN 6th Inf. Co.K
Vinson, Marion LA 5th Cav. Co.C
Vinson, Mat TN 14th (Neely's) Cav. Co.G Cpl.
Vinson, Matthew NC 1st Arty. (10th St.Troops) Co.F
Vinson, Micager W. AL 17th Inf. Co.E
Vinson, Milton W. AL 16th Inf. Co.E Sgt.
Vinson, M.O. KY 7th Mtd.Inf. Co.B
Vinson, Moses GA 9th Inf. (St.Guards) Co.G Sgt.
Vinson, M.W. AL Inf. 1st Regt. Co.H Music.
Vinson, Nathan MS Inf. 7th Bn. Co.E
Vinson, Nathan NC 1st Arty. (10th St.Troops) Co.F
Vinson, Nathan 2nd Conf.Eng.Troops Co.D
Vinson, Nathan H. GA 3rd Cav. Co.F
Vinson, Newborn GA 57th Inf. Co.F,E
Vinson, Nicholas W. AL Cav. 4th Bn. (Love's) Co.B Jr.2nd Lt.
Vinson, Nicholas W. AL Inf. 1st Regt. Co.F Cpl.
Vinson, N.L. SC 18th Inf. Co.B
Vinson, N.W. MS Cav. Jeff Davis Legion Co.I 2nd Lt.
Vinson, O. MS 41st Inf. Co.F
Vinson, Obadiah GA Carlton's Co. (Troup Cty.Arty.)
Vinson, Obadiah GA 2nd Inf. Stanley's Co.
Vinson, P.A. AL 34th Inf. Black's Co.
Vinson, Phillip MS 18th Inf. Co.I
Vinson, P.J. AL Arty. 1st Bn. Co.F
Vinson, R. AL 3rd Inf. Co.H
Vinson, R. AR Inf. 2nd Bn. Lt.
Vinson, R. MS 18th Inf. Co.I
Vinson, R.B. MS 46th Inf. Co.G
Vinson, R.H. AL 31st Inf. Co.H
Vinson, Richard SC 15th Inf. Co.F
Vinson, Richard L. NC 17th Inf. (2nd Org.) Co.C
Vinson, R.N. MO 15th Cav. Co.H Sgt.
Vinson, Robert AL 63rd Inf. Co.B
Vinson, Robert AR 38th Inf. Co.E
Vinson, Robert LA 4th Inf. New Co.G
Vinson, Robert B. GA 64th Inf. Co.H
Vinson, Robert B. LA 5th Cav. Co.K 1st Sgt.
Vinson, R.T. LA Washington Arty.Bn. Co.5
Vinson, Rufus L. AL 13th Inf. Co.H Music.
Vinson, S. TN 20th Inf. Co.E
Vinson, Samuel NC 2nd Arty. (36th St.Troops) Co.C
Vinson, Samuel S. VA 8th Cav. Co.K 1st Lt.
Vinson, Sanford F. AL 63rd Inf. Co.D Cpl.
Vinson, Sevang LA 7th Cav. Co.B
Vinson, S.H. MS 28th Cav. Co.G
Vinson, Spiers D. GA 61st Inf. Co.B Cpl.
Vinson, S.S. Gen. & Staff, QM Dept. Lt.,AAQM
Vinson, T.B. TN 50th Inf. Co.D

Vinson, T.C. AR Cav. Crabtree's (46th) Regt. Co.F
Vinson, T.C. AR 7th Inf. Co.B
Vinson, T.D.A. TN 60th Mtd.Inf. Co.I
Vinson, T.F. AL Cav. Moreland's Regt. Co.A
Vinson, Thomas AL Recruits
Vinson, Thomas GA 6th Inf. Co.H
Vinson, Thomas KY 8th Mtd.Inf. Co.D
Vinson, Thomas NC 2nd Jr.Res. Co.A
Vinson, Thomas TN 8th (Smith's) Cav. Co.E
Vinson, Thomas TX 2nd Cav. Co.A
Vinson, Thomas B. Sig.Corps,CSA
Vinson, Thomas J. GA 66th Inf. Co.D
Vinson, Thomas J. NC Loc.Def. Griswold's Co. Sgt.
Vinson, Thomas L. AL 40th Inf. Co.D Jr.2nd Lt.
Vinson, Thomas Morgan AL 46th Inf. Co.A
Vinson, Thomas W. AL 34th Inf. Black's Co.
Vinson, Thomas W. GA 57th Inf. Co.F
Vinson, T.J. AL 59th Inf. Co.B
Vinson, T.L. AL 19th Inf. Co.E 1st Lt.
Vinson, Tolbert F. MS 26th Inf. Co.E
Vinson, U.T. NC 1st Arty. (10th St.Troops) Co.F
Vinson, Van LA Washington Arty.Bn. Co.1 Sgt.
Vinson, Van LA Inf. 1st Sp.Bn. (Rightor's) Co.F
Vinson, W. MS 37th Inf. Co.D
Vinson, W. TX 12th Inf. Co.A
Vinson, W. VA 25th Inf. Co.A
Vinson, W.A. SC 22nd Inf. Co.E
Vinson, Washington G. TX 17th Cav. Co.F
Vinson, W.D. AL Cav. Moreland's Regt. Co.A
Vinson, W.G. TX 17th Cons.Dismtd.Cav. Co.F
Vinson, W.H. TX 35th (Brown's) Cav. 2nd Co.B
Vinson, W.H. TX 1st Inf. Co.C
Vinson, Wiley TX 20th Cav. Co.H,D Cpl.
Vinson, Wiley TX Cav. Martin's Regt. Co.K
Vinson, William AL Inf. 1st Regt. Co.B
Vinson, William MS Inf. 1st Bn.St.Troops (30 days '64) Co.A Cpl.
Vinson, William MS 8th Inf. Co.D
Vinson, William NC 32nd Inf. Co.C,D
Vinson, William SC 5th Cav. Co.K
Vinson, William SC 18th Inf. Co.B
Vinson, William A. MS 2nd Inf. Co.C
Vinson, William D. GA 57th Inf. Co.F Cpl.
Vinson, William H. AL 39th Inf. Co.K
Vinson, William H. NC 32nd Inf. Co.C,D
Vinson, William J. AL 15th Cav.
Vinson, William J. AL Arty. 1st Bn. Co.E
Vinson, William J. TN 21st (Wilson's) Cav. Co.E
Vinson, William P. LA 5th Cav. Co.C
Vinson, William P. LA 13th Bn. (Part.Rangers) Co.D
Vinson, William W. GA 2nd Res. Co.K
Vinson, Willis P. AL 34th Inf. Co.K
Vinson, W.J. SC 5th Cav. Co.K
Vinson, W.J. TN 21st & 22nd (Cons.) Cav. Co.F
Vinson, W.L. GA 8th Cav. Co.G 1st Sgt.
Vinson, W.L. GA 62nd Cav. Co.G 1st Sgt.
Vinson, W.L. TN 50th Inf. Co.D
Vinson, W.M. MS 34th Inf. Co.C
Vinson, W.P. GA Troops
Vinson, W.R. AL 40th Inf. Co.D
Vinson, W.R. KY Lt.Arty. Cobb's Co.
Vinson, Wright GA 57th Inf. Co.F Sgt.
Vinson, W.T. AR 3rd Inf. (St.Troops) Stuart's Co. Sgt.
Vinson, W.W. AL 45th Inf. Co.D
Vinson, W.W. AR 15th (N.W.) Inf. Co.D Sgt.
Vinson, Y.A. TX 17th Cons.Dismtd.Cav. Co.F
Vinson, Y.D. NC 8th Bn.Part.Rangers Co.F
Vinson, Y.D. NC 1st Arty. (10th St.Troops) Co.B
Vinson, Y.D. NC 66th Inf. Co.I
Vinson, Young A. TX 17th Cav. Co.F
Vinson, Z.T. GA 8th Cav. Co.G
Vinson, Z.T. GA 62nd Cav. Co.G
Vinston, Jesse TN 3rd (Lillard's) Mtd.Inf. Co.A
Vinsut, J. LA Mil. 1st Chasseurs a pied Co.7
Vint, Beniah VA 5th Inf. Co.I
Vint, Esau VA 18th Cav. 2nd Co.G Cpl.
Vint, Esau VA 31st Inf. 2nd Co.B
Vint, George VA 18th Cav. 2nd Co.G
Vint, James AR Inf. Cocke's Regt. Co.B
Vint, James M. VA 52nd Inf. Co.C
Vint, John VA 25th Inf. 1st Co.E
Vint, John VA 62nd Mtd.Inf. 2nd Co.I
Vint, Josiah VA 18th Cav. 2nd Co.G
Vint, Josiah VA 5th Inf. Co.I Cpl.
Vint, Martin MO Cav. Freeman's Regt. Co.A
Vint, Osburn VA 62nd Mtd.Inf. 2nd Co.K
Vint, R.J. VA 17th Cav. Co.H
Vint, Thomas AR 10th Inf. Co.H
Vint, William, Jr. VA 18th Cav. 2nd Co.G
Vint, William, Sr. VA 18th Cav. 2nd Co.G
Vint, William H. VA 46th Mil. Co.B
Vint, William H. VA 62nd Mtd.Inf. 2nd Co.I
Vinton, A. FL Inf. 2nd Bn. Co.A
Vinton, I. VA 59th Inf. Co.A
Vinton, J.F. TX 9th Cav. Co.C
Vinton, John R. TX 33rd Cav. Co.A 2nd Lt.
Vinton, Morrimore GA 24th Inf.
Vintor, Theogene LA Inf. 10th Bn. Co.F
Vintry, Charles H. FL Cav. 5th Bn. Co.B
Vintzaut, G.F. MS 6th Inf. Co.H
Vinyard, A.J. LA Inf. 9th Bn. Co.D
Vinyard, A.J. 14th Conf.Cav. Co.H
Vinyard, Augustus LA 7th Inf. Co.K Sgt.
Vinyard, B. MS Cav. Ham's Regt. Co.G
Vinyard, C.O. TX 20th Inf. Co.A
Vinyard, C.W. LA Ogden's Cav. Co.E
Vinyard, C.W. 14th Conf.Cav. Co.H
Vinyard, E.N. 14th Conf.Cav. Co.H
Vinyard, Ezra O. VA Hvy.Arty. 10th Bn. Co.B
Vinyard, Eugene LA Inf. 9th Bn. Co.D
Vinyard, G. MS Cav. Davenport's Bn. (St.Troops) Co.B 3rd Lt.
Vinyard, Ganum M. TN Cav. 12th Bn. (Day's) Co.E Sgt.
Vinyard, Henry LA 9th Inf.Bn. Co.D
Vinyard, Housten TN 1st (Carter's) Cav. Co.E
Vinyard, Jacob MO 3rd Inf. Co.A
Vinyard, James L. TN 20th Inf. Co.G
Vinyard, James R. GA 39th Inf. Co.F
Vinyard, Jesse TX Cav. Baird's Regt. 2nd Lt.
Vinyard, J.M. Central Div. KY Sap. & Min.,CSA
Vinyard, Joab E. VA 28th Inf. Co.I
Vinyard, John GA Lt.Arty. Milledge's Co.
Vinyard, John 9th Conf.Inf. Co.C
Vinyard, John H. VA Hvy.Arty. 10th Bn. Co.B
Vinyard, Jonathan AR 17th (Lemoyne's) Inf. Co.E
Vinyard, Joseph AL 47th Inf. Co.B
Vinyard, Lycurgus MO 11th Inf. Co.H
Vinyard, Mathew E. LA 7th Inf. Co.K
Vinyard, M.E. 14th Conf.Cav. Co.H
Vinyard, Michael MO 3rd Inf. Co.A
Vinyard, Nicholas G. TN Cav. 4th Bn. (Branner's) Co.B Sgt.
Vinyard, N.J. VA 28th Inf. Co.I
Vinyard, Noah H. TN Cav. 4th Bn. (Branner's) Co.A
Vinyard, Noah H. TN 37th Inf. Co.D
Vinyard, Robert A. VA 28th Inf. Co.I
Vinyard, Thomas J. TN 42nd Inf. Co.B
Vinyard, William TN Cav. 12th Bn. (Day's) Co.E
Vinyard, William J. AL 47th Inf. Co.B
Vinzandt, E.H. MS 8th Inf. Co.A
Vinzant, A.L. TX Cav. 6th Bn. Co.A
Vinzant, A.S. TX Cav. Border's Regt. Co.A
Vinzant, Ed. TX 7th Cav. Co.E Far.
Vinzant, George GA 4th (Clinch's) Cav. Co.E
Vinzant, G.T. GA 36th (Broyles') Inf. Co.G
Vinzant, G.W. AR 14th (Powers') Inf. Co.F
Vinzant, James J. FL 2nd Inf. Co.H
Vinzant, John FL 1st Cav. Co.A Sgt.
Vinzant, John TX 7th Cav. Co.E
Vinzant, John R. AL 12th Cav. Co.E
Vinzant, John T. AL 5th Inf. Co.C,H Cpl.
Vinzant, J.W.G. AL 13th Bn.Part.Rangers Co.C,E
Vinzant, Robert W. GA 36th (Villepigue's) Inf. Co.B
Vinzant, William MS 3rd (St.Troops) Cav. Co.K Capt.
Vinzant, William B. FL 2nd Cav. Co.F
Vinzant, Wyley AL 4th (Russell's) Cav. Co.D
Viohl, H. SC Mil.Arty. 1st Regt. Harms' Co.
Viohl, H. SC 1st Regt. Charleston Guard Co.G
Violet, A.V. AL 1st Bn.Cadets Co.B,A,C
Violet, H. MO 12th Cav. Co.I
Violet, John W. TN Cav. 7th Bn. (Bennett's) Co.B
Violet, John W. VA 51st Mil. Co.C
Violett, E.S. MO Lt.Arty. Farris' Btty. (Clark Arty.)
Violett, James Elijah VA 7th Cav. Co.A
Violett, John E. AR 15th (Josey's) Inf. Co.B Cpl.
Violett, J.W. TN 22nd (Barteau's) Cav. Co.E
Violett, Thomas KY 4th Cav. Co.C
Violett, W.A. Gen. & Staff AQM
Violett, William H. VA 11th Cav. Co.B
Violett, William M. KY 4th Cav. Co.I
Violett, William M. VA 4th Cav. Co.D
Violette, William A. TX 15th Cav. Co.G
Viosca, J., Jr. LA Mil. Orleans Guards Regt. Co.H Capt.
Viosca, Joaquin LA Mil. 5th Regt.Eur.Brig. (Spanish Regt.) Co.5
Viosca, Ramon LA Mil. 5th Regt.Eur.Brig. (Spanish Regt.) Co.2
Viot, Ernest LA Mil. 2nd Regt. French Brig. Co.6
Vipperman, Emanuel J. VA 48th Inf. Co.F
Vipperman, George W. VA 48th Inf. Co.F

Vipperman, John H. VA 72nd Mil.
Vipperman, William A. VA 72nd Mil.
Vippirman, Nicholas T. VA 24th Inf. Co.I
Virden, A. MS 1st (King's) Inf. (St.Troops) Co.E
Virden, E. GA Cav. Nelson's Ind.Co.
Virden, E. GA Cav. Ragland's Co.
Virden, Henderson AR Cav. Gordon's Regt. Co.C
Virden, H.W. GA Cav. Nelson's Ind.Co.
Virden, James M. GA Lt.Arty. Guerard's Btty.
Virden, John GA 37th Inf. Co.C
Virden, M.F. LA 29th Inf. Co.G
Virden, M.W. KY 2nd Mtd.Inf. Co.B
Virden, Peter MS 1st (King's) Inf. (St.Troops) Co.E
Virden, P.J. SC 16th & 24th (Cons.) Inf. Co.D Sgt.
Virden, P.L.S. MS 3rd (St.Troops) Cav. Co.C
Virden, S. GA Cav. Nelson's Ind.Co.
Virden, S. GA Cav. Ragland's Co.
Virden, Thomas GA 32nd Inf. Co.I
Virden, William KY 2nd Cav. Co.F
Virden, William VA 14th Cav. Co.A
Virdin, Felix G. AR 15th (N.W.) Inf. Co.E
Vire, Berrel VA 146th Mil. Co.B
Vire, Burwell VA 33rd Inf. Co.E
Vires, Amos L. NC 34th Inf. Co.A
Vires, James KY 5th Mtd.Inf. Co.A
Vires, John KY 5th Mtd.Inf. Co.A
Vires, John TN 51st (Cons.) Inf. Co.C
Vires, Peter TN 62nd Mtd.Inf. Co.C
Vires, Randall KY 5th Mtd.Inf. Co.A
Vires, Robert VA 32nd Inf. 2nd Co.K
Virett, L.E. LA 4th Inf. Co.K
Virgan, U. LA C.S. Zouave Bn. Co.G
Virgeley, Barney GA 8th Inf. Co.B
Virgilio, Luciano LA Mil. 6th Regt.Eur.Brig. (Italian Guards Bn.) Co.4
Virgin, Charles S. GA 61st Inf. Co.I Capt.
Virgin, Edward F. LA 15th Inf. Co.K,G
Virgin, E.F. LA Inf. 7th Bn. Co.C
Virgin, Frederick B. GA Inf. 2nd Bn. Co.C Cpl.
Virgin, F.W. TN 15th Inf. Co.D
Virgin, J.L. KY 12th Cav. Co.I Cpl.
Virgin, John D. KY 7th Mtd.Inf. Co.F
Virgin, John W. TN 14th Inf. Co.C
Virgin, Samuel AR Cav. Harrell's Bn. Co.D
Virgin, Samuel MO Inf. 8th Bn. Co.E
Virgin, Samuel MO 9th Inf. Co.I
Virgin, Saml. MO St.Guard
Virgin, Uriah LA Inf. 7th Bn. Co.C Cpl.
Virgin, Uriah LA 15th Inf. Co.K 1st Sgt.
Virgin, W.H. GA Arty. (Macon Lt.Arty.) Slaten's Co.
Virgin, William TN 13th Inf. Co.E
Viries, Philip GA 1st Res. Co.K Cpl.
Virinn, Justus VA 3rd Inf.Loc.Def. Co.D
Virnelson, Joseph VA Inf. 4th Bn.Loc.Def. Co.A 2nd Lt.
Virnelson, Joseph E. VA 9th Inf. Co.G
Virnelson, Thomas VA Inf. 4th Bn.Loc.Def. Co.A
Virnelson, Thomas H. VA Lt.Arty. Moore's Co.
Virnelson, Thomas H. VA Lt.Arty. Thompson's Co.
Virnelson, William B. VA 9th Inf. Co.G
Virnelson, William L.D. VA 9th Inf. Co.G
Virnillion, Richard VA Lt.Arty. Thompson's Co.
Virres, J. AL 50th Inf. Co.F
Virtch, R.A. VA 11th Cav. Co.K
Virth, C. LA Mil. 3rd Regt.Eur.Brig. (Garde Francaise) Co.5
Virth, R. LA Mil. 3rd Regt.Eur.Brig. (Garde Francaise) Co.5
Virtress, J.S. Gen. & Staff Asst.Surg.
Virtue, Edward J., Jr. LA Washington Arty.Bn. Co.5
Virtue, Edward J., Jr. LA 1st (Strawbridge's) Inf. Co.A,C
Visage, J. GA Cav. 1st Bn.Res. Tufts' Co.
Visage, J. LA 13th Bn. (Part.Rangers) Co.B
Visage, James NC 39th Inf. Co.A
Visage, James T. TN 43rd Inf. Co.A0
Visage, J.J. TX Inf. Cotton's Co.
Visage, John GA 6th Inf. Co.C
Visage, John NC 39th Inf. Co.A
Visage, Pleast B. 3rd Conf.Eng.Troops Co.A
Visage, Samuel LA 5th Cav. Co.B
Visant, Edward AR Arty. 7th Field Btty. 2nd Lt.
Visant, G.W. MO Cav. Fristoe's Regt. Co.A
Visard, Michael MS Griffin's Co. (Madison Guards)
Visark, E. AR Mil. Borland's Regt. Woodruff's Co.
Visart, Edward AR Lt.Arty. Zimmerman's Btty. 2nd Lt.
Vise, Calvin AL 44th Inf. Co.I
Vise, C.M. SC Lt.Arty. Jeter's Co. (Macbeth Lt.Arty.)
Vise, Elias J. AL 41st Inf. Co.B
Vise, George W. AL 41st Inf. Co.B
Vise, Hosea M. AL 44th Inf. Co.I
Vise, James E. SC 3rd Inf. Co.K,I Cpl.
Vise, J.E. SC 1st (Hagood's) Inf. 2nd Co.H 2nd Lt.
Vise, J.E. SC 27th Inf. Co.G
Vise, John R. SC 9th Res. Co.I
Vise, John R. SC 18th Inf. Co.E
Vise, John S. SC Lt.Arty. Jeter's Co. (Macbeth Lt.Arty.)
Vise, Starlin AL 44th Inf. Co.I
Viser, J.M. TX 23rd Cav. Co.G Cpl.
Viser, P.H. TX 23rd Cav. Co.G
Viser, Washington J. TX 35th (Brown's) Cav. Co.K
Viser, Washington J. TX 13th Vol. 3rd Co.I
Viser, William TN Cav. 9th Bn. (Gantt's) Co.F
Viser, William W. TX Cav. 6th Bn. Co.B Maj.
Vishman, F.J. MS Cav. Yerger's Regt. QMSgt.
Vishure, J. MS Inf. 2nd Bn. Co.E
Visor, George FL 2nd Inf. Co.A
Visor, John TX 11th Cav. Co.D
Vissage, John J. SC 1st (Orr's) Rifles Co.F Cpl.
Vissage, Pleas B. GA 55th Inf. Co.H
Vissage, William GA 54th Inf. Co.A
Vistall, J.W. NC 1st Inf. Co.A
Vital, H. LA Arty. Guyol's Co. (Orleans Arty.)
Vital, Lesco LA C.S. Zouave Bn. Co.B Cpl.
Vitale, B. LA Mil. 3rd Regt.Eur.Brig. (Garde Francaise) Co.3
Vitatoe, G.W. TN 51st (Cons.) Inf. Co.C
Vitatoe, Hiram TN 17th Inf. Co.K
Vitator, H. GA Cav. 6th Bn. (St.Guards) Co.E
Vitch, David LA Inf. 10th Bn. Co.H
Vite, Chunn GA 10th Inf. Co.D
Viterre, --- LA Mil. 3rd Regt.Eur.Brig. (Garde Francaise) Co.5
Vitetoe, M.V. AL 23rd Inf. Co.K
Vitetoe, Thomas TN 61st Mtd.Inf. Bundren's Co.
Vititoe, Samuel F. MO 11th Inf. Co.A
Vititoe, W.H. AR 47th (Crandall's) Cav. Brown's Co. 2nd Lt.
Vititon, Daniel MO 6th Cav. Co.I 1st Sgt.
Vitry, Ch. LA Mil. 3rd Regt. French Brig. Co.3
Vittatoe, Hiram TN 25th Inf. Co.G
Vittatoe, James TN 17th Inf. Co.K
Vittatoe, William TN 17th Inf. Co.K
Vitter, A. LA Mil. Squad. Guides d'Orleans
Vitter, Conrad MS 9th Inf. Co.G
Vittetoe, John KY 1st Inf. Co.G
Vittetoe, John TN 5th (McKenzie's) Cav. Co.A
Vittetoe, J.R. AR 1st (Monroe's) Cav. Co.A
Vittetoe, W.H. AR 2nd Mtd.Rifles Co.C
Vittinghoff, F. LA 22nd Inf. Co.B
Vittinghoff, F. LA 22nd (Cons.) Inf. Co.B
Vittinghoff, Frederick AL 12th Inf. Co.C
Vittinghoff, Wm. F. MO St.Guard 1st Lt.
Vittitoe, James H. KY 2nd (Duke's) Cav. Co.C
Vittitoe, William TN 59th Mtd.Inf. Co.I
Vittiton, Fred TX 9th Cav. Co.C Cpl.
Vittiton, Quincy TX Cav. 2nd Regt.St.Troops Co.B
Vittitow, C.C. TX 9th Cav. Co.C
Vittitow, H.T. TX 9th Cav. Co.K
Vittoe, J.T. TN 4th Cav. Co.L
Vity, C. LA Mil. 2nd Regt. French Brig. Co.4
Vivant, Louis, Jr. LA Mil. 1st Native Guards
Viven, Francis L. TX 5th Inf. Co.A
Viver, Michael Conf.Inf. 8th Bn.
Viveraux, P.H. TX 3rd Cav. Co.I
Viverett, James MS 6th Cav. Co.G
Viverett, J.M. TN 18th Inf. Co.K
Viverett, J.N. TN 45th Inf. Co.H
Viverett, L.L. MS Inf. 1st Bn.St.Troops (30 days '64) Co.E
Viverett, P.H. TN 45th Inf. Co.H 1st Lt.
Viverett, Thomas TN 18th Inf. Co.K
Viverett, W.M. TN 18th Inf. Co.K
Vives, Damian LA Mil. 5th Regt.Eur.Brig. (Spanish Regt.) Co.2
Vives, Edouard LA 28th (Thomas') Inf. Co.H 1st Lt.
Vives, Geronimo LA Mil. 5th Regt.Eur.Brig. (Spanish Regt.) Co.2
Vives, Joseph LA 2nd Cav. Co.I
Vives, Juan M. LA Mil. Cazadores Espanoles Regt. Co.2
Vivett, Thomas TN 18th Inf. 2nd Lt.
Vivett, Thomas Morgan's,CSA 2nd Lt.
Vivez, H. LA 2nd Cav. Co.H
Vivian, A.F. TX 1st (Yager's) Cav. Co.B
Vivian, A.F. TX Cav. 3rd (Yager's) Bn. Co.B
Vivian, C.W. TX 30th Cav. Co.B
Vivian, Flavel W. TX 6th Cav. Co.G Cpl.
Vivian, F.M. TX Cav. 3rd (Yager's) Bn. Co.B
Vivian, Harvey B. MO 9th Bn.S.S. Co.F Cpl.
Vivian, Henry J. MO 12th Cav. Co.B Maj.
Vivian, I. MO St.Guard Capt.
Vivian, John TX Cav. Waller's Regt. Co.D Cpl.
Vivian, Robert MO Inf. Perkins' Bn. Co.B
Vivian, T.M. TX Granbury's Cons.Brig. Co.D

Vivier, Ed Conf.Inf. 8th Bn. Co.E
Vivion, Frank M. TX 1st (Yager's) Cav. Co.B
Vivion, H.C. MO 2nd Cav. Co.C
Vivion, H.C. TX 25th Cav. Co.D Sgt.
Vivion, H.J. MO 2nd Inf. Maj.
Vivion, John F. TX Cav. Benavides' Regt. Co.G
Vivion, Milton KY 11th Cav. Co.C Sgt.
Vivion, Thacker MS Cav. Vivion's Co. Capt.
Vivion, Thomas TX 10th Inf. Co.F
Vivions, Milton H. KY 7th Cav. Co.C
Vivitt, M.T. TN 4th (McLemore's) Cav. Co.C
Vivitt, W.D. TN 4th (McLemore's) Cav. Co.C
Vivrett, Elisha B. TN 21st Cav.
Vivrett, J.A. TN 45th Inf. Co.F
Vivrett, James NC 3rd Bn.Sr.Res. Williams' Co.
Vivrett, James Morgan's,CSA
Vivrett, James D. TN 21st Cav.
Vivrett, John B. TN 7th Bn. Co.I
Vivrett, John L. TN 12th Cav.
Vivrett, John L. TN 7th Inf. Co.I
Vivrett, John L. Wheeler's Scouts,CSA
Vivrett, John W. TN 7th Inf. Co.I 2nd Lt.
Vivrett, Rufus A. TN 21st Cav. 3rd Lt.
Vivrett, Rufus F. TN 7th Inf. Co.I Cpl.
Vivrett, Thomas TN 7th Inf. Co.I Sgt.
Vivrett, Thomas TN 45th Inf. Co.H
Vivrett, W.B. TN 45th Inf. Co.F Ord.Sgt.
Vivrett, William H. TN 7th Inf. Co.I 3rd Lt.
Vix, --- LA Mil. 2nd Regt. French Brig. Co.1
Vix, F. LA Mil. 3rd Regt.Eur.Brig. (Garde Francaise) Co.1 Cpl.
Vix, William H. TN 33rd Inf. Co.I
Vixen, J. GA 10th Inf. Co.H
Vize, Charles KY 6th Mtd.Inf. Co.H
Vizer, J.H. MS 3rd Cav. Co.I
Vizers, Jno. A. Gen. & Staff Surg.
Vizier, Felix LA 27th Inf. Co.D
Vizier, L. MS Mil. 4th Cav. Co.I 2nd Lt.
Vizzard, M. MS 18th Inf. Co.I
Vlemmikx, Jean LA C.S. Zouave Bn. Co.B
Vocaline, Charles SC Lt.Arty. Beauregard's Co.
Vocelle, A. SC 1st Regt. Charleston Guard Co.G
Vocelle, A. SC Mil. 16th Regt. Eason's Co.
Vocelle, A. SC 25th Inf. Co.E
Vocelle, Joseph GA 26th Inf. Co.A
Vocelle, L. GA 4th (Clinch's) Cav. Co.D
Vocelle, Leon SC 25th Inf. Co.E Cpl.
Vocnear, Philip VA 6th Inf. 1st Co.B, Co.D
Vocus, E.O. GA 44th Inf. Co.I
Voebel, Charles LA Mil. Fire Bn. Co.A
Voebel, Daniel LA Mil. 4th Regt.Eur.Brig. Co.D
Voege, A. SC Mil.Arty. 1st Regt. Werner's Co.
Voege, A. SC Lt.Arty. Wagener's Co. (Co.A, German Arty.)
Voegele, Jacob LA Mil.Cont.Regt. Lang's Co.
Voegelin, Frederick AL St.Arty. Co.A
Voegelin, Philip C. AL Lt.Arty. Tarrant's Btty.
Voegler, E.A. VA Cav. 1st Bn. (Loc.Def. Troops) Co.A
Voekel, Christian LA 20th Inf. Old Co.B, Co.D
Voelkel, J. TX 4th Inf. Co.F
Voelkel, J. TX Waul's Legion Co.H
Voelkel, John LA Mil. Fire Bn. Co.C
Voelkel, John TX 4th Cav. Co.G
Voelkel, William TX 4th Cav. Co.G
Voelker, Henry MS Inf. 1st Bn.St.Troops (12 mo. '62-3) Co.E
Voelker, W. GA Inf. 1st Loc.Troops (Augusta) Co.I
Voelkner, Julius Gen. & Staff Asst.Surg.
Voerge, S.F. LA 21st (Kennedy's) Inf. Co.D
Vogar, W.A. VA Cav. 41st Bn. Co.B
Vogel, Adolf LA Mil.Cont.Regt. Lang's Co.
Vogel, Amand LA Mil. 4th Regt.Eur.Brig. Co.D
Vogel, Augustus MS 14th Inf. Co.K
Vogel, C. TX 17th Inf. Co.F
Vogel, Casper V. TX Waul's Legion Co.E
Vogel, D. NC Mil. Clark's Sp.Bn. Co.B
Vogel, Ernst TX 4th Field Btty.
Vogel, Ferdinand TX Cav. 3rd (Yager's) Bn. Co.A
Vogel, G. LA Mil. 1st Regt. 2nd Brig. 1st Div. Co.D
Vogel, Henry LA 11th Inf. Co.F,A
Vogel, Henry LA 14th (Austin's) Bn.S.S. Co.A
Vogel, Jacob AL Cp. of Instr. Talladega
Vogel, Jacob Gen. & Staff, Ord.Dept.
Vogel, John A. VA 1st Lt.Arty. Co.B Black.
Vogel, John A. VA Lt.Arty. J.S. Brown's Co.
Vogel, John G. LA 28th (Thomas') Inf. Co.C
Vogel, Joseph LA 1st Hvy.Arty. (Reg.) Co.F
Vogel, K. TX 26th Cav. 1st Co.G
Vogel, K. TX 9th (Nichols') Inf. Atchison's Co.
Vogel, L. GA 32nd Inf. Co.E
Vogel, M.A. LA Miles' Legion Co.E
Vogel, Paul LA 4th Inf. Co.B Sgt.
Vogel, Philip TX Waul's Legion Co.E
Vogel, W. LA 21st (Patton's) Inf. Co.H
Vogel, W.H. SC 1st Inf. Co.A
Vogel, William LA 6th Inf. Co.G Cpl.
Vogel, William H. SC 1st (McCreary's) Inf. Co.C
Vogelberg, Louis SC 25th Inf. Co.E
Vogelgesang, Augustus LA 20th Inf. Co.A Cpl.
Vogelgsang, Fred GA 4th Inf. Co.K
Vogelin, Frederick AL 44th Inf. Co.G
Vogelin, Henry AL 4th Inf. Co.A
Vogelin, Henry LA 1st (Strawbridge's) Inf. Co.E,F
Vogelsang, E. TX 3rd Inf. 2nd Co.A
Vogelsang, Ernst TX 20th Inf. Co.A
Vogelsang, Frederick TX 20th Inf. Co.A
Vogelsang, Paul TX 4th Cav. Co.G 1st Lt.
Vogelsang, Theodore TX 20th Inf. Co.A
Vogelskamp, Henry LA 20th Inf. Old Co.B
Voges, Anton TN Inf. 3rd Bn. Co.F
Voges, Fr. TX Comal Res. Cpl.
Vogg, Charles TX 6th Inf. Co.D Cpl.
Vogg, Fredrick TX 8th Inf. Co.A
Voght, Adam H. SC 1st (McCreary's) Inf. Co.H
Voght, F. SC 1st Regt. Charleston Guard Co.G
Voght, Frederick E. MD 1st Inf. Co.F Sgt.
Voght, L. SC Mil. 18th Regt. Co.D Cpl.
Voght, Valley LA 1st Hvy.Arty. (Reg.) Co.C
Vogle, Augustus MS 11th Inf. Co.F
Vogle, Charles VA 20th Cav. Co.K
Vogle, Fred LA 15th Inf. Co.A
Vogle, John A. MD Inf. 2nd Bn. Co.K
Vogle, John A. VA 2nd Inf. Co.K
Vogle, Levi TN Lt.Arty. Lynch's Co.
Vogler, Augustus NC 57th Inf. Co.D
Vogler, C.F. SC 25th Inf. Co.E
Vogler, E.M.H. NC 33rd Inf. Co.H
Vogler, George E. NC 2nd Inf. Co.I
Vogler, Henry VA Conscr.
Vogler, J.C. NC 33rd Inf. Co.G
Vogler, J.L. NC 21st Inf. Co.K
Vogler, John E. 7th Conf.Cav. Co.G
Vogler, Joseph LA 6th Inf. Co.G
Vogler, J.R. NC 9th Bn.S.S. Co.B 2nd Lt.
Vogler, J.R. Early's Div. Capt.,AQM
Vogler, Julius R. NC 21st Inf. Co.E AQM
Vogler, Mathew D. 7th Conf.Cav. Co.G
Vogler, S.F. NC 33rd Inf. Co.H
Vogler, William F. NC 21st Inf. Co.D
Vogles, John H. GA 43rd Inf. Co.F
Voglesang, H. TX 24th Cav. Co.I
Vogt, A. MS 4th Cav. Co.F
Vogt, Ben TX 8th Inf. Co.E
Vogt, Charles LA 1st Hvy.Arty. (Reg.) Music.
Vogt, Charles LA 8th Inf. Co.B Band Music.
Vogt, D.A. SC 18th Inf. Asst.Surg.
Vogt, Daniel A. FL 7th Inf. Co.G
Vogt, Dan'l A. Gen. & Staff Asst.Surg.
Vogt, F.P. SC 27th Inf. Co.G
Vogt, F.W. SC 2nd Cav. Co.D
Vogt, F.W. SC Cav. 4th Bn. Co.D Sgt.Maj.
Vogt, H.L. TX 3rd Inf. 2nd Co.C Sgt.
Vogt, John Inf. School of Pract. Powell's Detach. Co.C
Vogt, L.C. SC 25th Inf. Co.F
Vogt, Leonidas SC Lt.Arty. J.T. Kanapaux's Co. (Lafayette Arty.)
Vogt, M.A. SC 1st (McCreary's) Inf. Co.B Cpl.
Vogt, M.A. SC 1st Inf. Co.L
Vogt, P. TX 3rd Inf. Co.B
Vogt, T. LA Mil. Orleans Fire Regt. Co.G
Vogt, Thomas P. SC Inf. Hampton Legion Co.E
Vogts, Deiderick TX 13th Vol. 2nd Co.B Sgt.
Voguel, A. LA Mil. 1st Regt. French Brig. Co.5
Vogues, Henry LA Mil. 1st Regt. 3rd Brig. 1st Div.
Voguet, Paul LA Mil. 6th Regt.Eur.Brig. (Italian Guards Bn.) Co.5
Vohiah, Noah NC 2nd Jr.Res. Co.I
Voice, H. VA 10th Cav. Co.D
Voie, G.P. TN 3rd (Forrest's) Cav. Lt.
Voigdt, Frederick TX Comal Res.
Voight, A. TX 6th Inf. Co.B
Voight, C. SC 1st Regt. Charleston Guard Co.D 2nd Lt.
Voight, E. TX 1st Hvy.Arty. Co.A
Voight, Fr. TX 12th Inf. Co.G,B Capt.
Voight, Henry GA Arty. Baker's Co. Sgt.
Voight, Henry TX 12th Inf. Co.G Music.
Voight, James VA 41st Inf. Co.I Sgt.
Voight, John T. VA 14th Inf. Co.I
Voight, John T. VA 59th Mil. Hunter's Co.
Voight, Lewis VA 1st Arty. Co.H
Voight, Robert TX Inf. Timmons' Regt. Co.K Capt.
Voight, T.F. Conf.Cav. Wood's Regt. 2nd Co.F
Voight, William D. VA Arty. Paris' Co.
Voights, John SC 3rd Cav. Co.G Cpl.
Voigler, Henry VA 1st Inf. Co.G
Voigt, Chs. LA Mil. 3rd Regt. 3rd Brig. 1st Div. Co.H
Voigt, Charles F. LA 16th Inf. Co.B
Voigt, Edward TX 26th Cav. Co.B
Voigt, F.E. TX St.Troops Hampton's Co.
Voigt, Frederick TX Inf.Riflemen Arnold's Co.

Voigt, G. TX Cav. Baird's Regt. Co.G
Voigt, Gottlieb TX 4th Cav. Co.G
Voigt, Henry TX Cav. 8th (Taylor's) Bn. Co.C
Voigt, Henry TX Waul's Legion Co.E Cpl.
Voigt, J.M. TX St.Troops Hampton's Co.
Voigt, Julius Conf.Inf. Tucker's Regt. Co.C
Voigt, Lewis A. LA 16th Inf. Co.B Sgt.
Voigt, Robert TX Waul's Legion Co.C Capt.
Voigt, William Conf.Inf. 8th Bn. Co.D
Voiland, --- LA Mil. 2nd Regt. French Brig. Co.4
Voiles, John AR 4th Inf. Co.I
Voiles, John B. GA 22nd Inf. Co.A
Voiles, Nathaniel GA 14th Inf. Co.D
Voiles, Nicholas P. TX Cav. 2nd Regt.St.Troops Co.D Cpl.
Voiles, N.J. AR 24th Inf. Co.H
Voiles, O.F. TX 29th Cav. Co.K
Voiles, Perry GA Inf. 4th Bn. (St.Guards) Co.C
Voiles, Robert VA Lt.Arty. Douthat's Co.
Voiles, Rudolphus TX 37th Cav. Co.B
Voiles, Samuel TX 37th Cav. Co.B
Voiles, William AR 38th Inf. Co.H
Voiles, W.J. GA 4th Res. Co.G
Voils, G.W. MS 10th Cav. Co.B
Voils, John J. NC 84th Inf. Co.D
Voils, Perry GA 66th Inf. Co.H
Voils, W.J. MS 10th Cav. Co.B
Voinet, D. GA Inf. 18th Bn. (St.Guards) Co.B
Voipe, A.M. TX 19th Inf. Co.F
Voiron, Theophile LA Mil. 2nd Regt. French Brig.
Voirs, James T. KY 2nd Bn.Mtd.Rifles Co.C
Voisin, A. LA Mil. 3rd Regt.Eur.Brig. (Garde Francaise) Co.3
Voisin, A.D. LA 30th Inf. Co.F
Voisin, Ate. LA Mil. French Co. of St.James
Voisin, F. LA Mil. 4th Regt. French Brig. Co.3
Voisin, Ferrand LA Mil. 1st Native Guards
Voisin, H.D. LA Mil. Chalmette Regt. QMSgt.
Voisin, J.A. LA 27th Inf. Co.D
Voisin, Leonard LA 26th Inf. Co.H
Voit, E. TX 17th Cons.Dismtd.Cav. Co.B
Voit, J. TX 6th Inf. Co.B
Voit, J.A. AR 19th (Dawson's) Inf. Co.F Cpl.
Voit, J.A. AR Inf. Crawford's Bn. Co.A Cpl.
Voladeir, Jean LA Mil. 2nd Regt. French Brig. Co.5 1st Lt.
Volaire, E. LA 22nd Inf. Co.D Sr.1st Lt.
Voland, John VA 59th Inf. 3rd Co.D
Voland, Philipp Conf.Lt.Arty. 1st Reg.Btty.
Volant, Francois SC Lt.Arty. 3rd (Palmetto) Bn. Co.D
Volant, Francis VA 41st Inf. 2nd Co.E
Volard, S.V. GA 5th Inf. (St.Guards) Brooks' Co.
Volaski, J. SC Mil. 1st Regt. (Charleston Res.) Co.B
Volaski, Revd J. SC 1st Regt.Charleston Guard Co.G
Volaskie, J. SC 5th Res. Co.B
Volbrecht, Cheidas LA C.S. Zouave Bn. Co.B
Volcan, George AL 89th Mil. Co.G
Volcar, J. LA Mil. Orleans Guards Regt. Co.B
Volcar, Justin LA Mil. Orleans Guards Regt. Co.B
Volck, Fred. VA Loc.Def. Sutherland's Co. 2nd Sgt.
Volckmann, D. LA Mil. 1st Regt. 2nd Brig. 1st Div. Co.E
Voldrick, A. AL 35th Inf. Co.C
Voleaux, Edmond LA 7th Inf. Co.G
Volentine, Andrew J. MS 27th Inf. Co.B
Volentine, Daniel TX 35th (Brown's) Cav. Co.I
Volentine, Henry LA Hvy.Arty. 2nd Bn. Co.D
Volentine, James M. AL Vol. Lee, Jr's Co.
Volentine, James M. AR 33rd Inf. Co.K
Volentine, J.C. MS 46th Inf. Co.H
Volentine, Jerry W. LA 9th Inf. Co.A
Volentine, J.F. LA 3rd (Wingfield's) Cav. Co.G
Volentine, John TX 35th (Brown's) Cav. Co.I
Volentine, John C. LA 2nd Inf. Co.C Cpl.
Volentine, John G. NC 4th Inf. Co.F
Volentine, R.H. MS 27th Inf. Co.B
Volentine, R.H. MS 46th Inf. Co.H
Volentine, Robert TN Conscr. (Cp. of Instr.)
Volentine, S. LA 31st Inf. Co.F
Volentine, Samuel GA 56th Inf. Co.E
Volentine, T.A. LA 31st Inf. Co.F
Volentine, Thomas TN 51st (Cons.) Inf. Co.K
Volentine, Thomas TX 20th Cav. Co.K
Volentine, William TN Conscr. (Cp. of Instr.)
Volentine, William T. MS 27th Inf. Co.B
Volentine, W.T. MS Inf. 2nd Bn. (St.Troops) Co.C
Volger, G. GA 1st (Symons') Res. Co.I Cpl.
Volger, Gustav GA Inf. 1st Loc.Troops (Augusta) Co.A
Volgermott, Aaron Conf.Inf. Tucker's Regt. Co.C
Volintine, L. Andrew LA Inf. 11th Bn. Co.A
Voliva, Asa NC 33rd Inf. Co.H
Voliva, Jasper NC 33rd Inf. Co.H
Voliva, Joseph P. NC 1st Arty. (10th St.Troops) Co.K
Voliva, William P. NC 3rd Arty. (40th St.Troops) Co.I
Volivia, Asa NC Part.Rangers Swindell's Co.
Volk, Charles H. TX Cav. Waller's Regt. Co.E
Volk, Christian TX 1st Hvy.Arty. Co.G
Volkart, John AL 21st Inf. Co.B
Volkart, Joseph AL 32nd Inf. Co.K Cpl.
Volkel, J.J. TX Waul's Legion Co.E Sgt.
Volkel, T. Exch.Bn. 1st Co.C,CSA
Volker, Charles GA 4th Inf. Co.E
Volker, John Vendel LA Mil. Chalmette Regt. Co.C
Volker, William GA Inf. 1st Loc.Troops (Augusta) Co.B
Volkhereit, James MO 1st Cav. Co.B
Volkman, A. LA Mil. Chalmette Regt. Co.D Sgt.
Volkman, Charles VA 3rd Inf.Loc.Def. Co.D
Volkman, Charles VA Inf. 4th Bn.Loc.Def. Co.C
Volkman, Charles W. VA 3rd Inf. Co.H
Volkner, Henry MS Inf. (Res.) Berry's Co.
Volland, Philip Inf. School of Pract. Powell's Detach. Co.A
Vollandt, C. LA 5th Inf. Band Band Leader
Vollentine, Isaac J. LA 39th Inf. Co.F
Vollentine, J.I. MS Inf. 7th Bn. Co.F Sgt.
Vollentine, M.B. MS Inf. 7th Bn. Co.F Cpl.
Vollentine, Robert TN Lt.Arty. Kain's Co.
Vollentine, William TN Lt.Arty. Kain's Co.
Vollenweder, Jacob LA 5th Inf. Co.D Sgt.
Vollers, Charles F. TX 8th Inf. Co.B
Vollers, Charles Frederick TX Arty. 4th Bn. Co.B
Vollers, Hanke NC 18th Inf. Co.A 1st Lt.
Vollers, Luhr NC 18th Inf. Co.A Sgt.
Vollinger, M. MS 48th Inf. Co.E
Vollman, Fred LA Inf. 4th Bn. Co.A
Vollmar, Jacob TX Conscr.
Vollmer, Fred TN 7th (Duckworth's) Cav. Co.C
Vollmer, Henry TX 1st Hvy.Arty. Co.C
Vollmer, John TX 36th Cav. Co.H Sgt.
Vollmers, Charles LA Mil. Chalmette Regt. Co.A 3rd Lt.
Vollrath, J. SC Lt.Arty. Wagener's Co. (Co.A,-German Arty.)
Vollsath, Conrad LA Mil. Mech.Guard
Volmer, Chr. SC 3rd Cav. Co.G 2nd Lt.
Volmer, Claus SC Mil.Cav. Theo. Cordes' Co. 1st Sgt.
Volmer, David TN 2nd (Walker's) Inf. Co.K Cpl.
Volmer, John GA Arty. Baker's Co.
Volmer, Louis AR 1st Mtd.Rifles Co.G
Volmering, --- LA 13th Inf. Co.F
Volnuth, Charles LA Mil. Chalmette Regt. Co.F
Volpert, M. TX 3rd Inf. Co.B
Volrath, H. LA Mil. Chalmette Regt. Co.D
Volst, G. TX 6th Inf. Co.I Sgt.
Voltaire, Jacques LA Mil. 1st Native Guards
Voltairis, Lorenzo TX Cav. Madison's Regt. Co.A
Voltz, Benjamin F. AL 13th Inf. Co.A Cpl.
Voltz, Charles AL 1st Regt. Mobile Vol. Co.E
Voltz, Frederick LA Mil. 2nd Regt. 2nd Brig. 1st Div. Co.I
Voltz, Henry E. AL 3rd Cav. Co.C
Voltz, John W. AL 3rd Cav. Co.C Capt.
Voltz, Joseph AL 1st (Strawbridge's) Inf. Co.F
Voltz, L. LA Mil. Fire Bn. Co.E
Voltz, Solomon VA Cav. 36th Bn. Co.D
Voltz, Solomon VA 27th Inf. Co.G Sgt.
Voltz, Westley AL 3rd Cav. Co.C Cpl.
Voluntine, A. AL 23rd Inf. Co.K
Voluntine, Andrew J. GA 14th Inf. Co.B
Voluntine, J. Mead's Conf.Cav. Co.K
Voluntine, James AL 24th Inf. Co.E
Voluntine, John NC 62nd Inf. Co.A
Voluntine, John F. GA 14th Inf. Co.B
Voluntine, Joseph TX 4th Cav. Co.B
Voluntine, Lewis GA 1st Bn.S.S. Co.C
Voluntine, Silas GA 14th Inf. Co.B
Voluntine, William 1st Cherokee Mtd.Vol. 1st Co.K
Voluntine, W.N. GA Phillips' Legion Co.E
Volz, Andrew LA Mil. 3rd Regt. 1st Brig. 1st Div. Co.E
Volz, Chs. LA Mil. Orleans Fire Regt. Co.A
Volz, M. LA Mil. 1st Regt. 3rd Brig. 1st Div. Co.G
Vombacher, Cd. LA Mil. 4th Regt. French Brig. Co.7
Von Amelunxen, Thomas LA Inf.Crescent Regt. Co.B
Vonan, Joseph LA 13th Inf. Co.B,C
Vonberger, Henry VA Lt.Arty. Brander's Co.
Von Bern, Aug LA Mil. Chalmette Regt. Co.I

Von Bern, William LA Mil. Chalmette Regt. Co.I
Von Borcke, Hercs Gen. & Staff Maj.,AAG
Von Butler, Charles LA 8th Inf. Co.A
Voncannon, Abram B. NC 52nd Inf. Co.F
Voncannon, Henry C. MS 19th Inf. Co.F
Voncannon, John NC 52nd Inf. Co.B
Voncannon, John W. MS 19th Inf. Co.F
Von Cannon, Noah NC 5th Inf. Co.A
Voncannon, William C. MO 5th Inf. Co.D
Vonchanan, J.F. MO 5th Inf. Co.C
Vondelehr, John VA 10th Cav. Co.A
Vonder, Cyrus E. GA 35th Inf. Co.C Lt.
Vonder, Hoehl D. VA 2nd St.Res. Co.H 2nd Lt.
Vonderbeck, George LA Mil. Irish Regt. Co.B
Vonder Dicken, Otto TX 3rd Inf. Co.K Sgt.
Vonder Heydt, Theo LA Mil. 4th Regt.Eur.Brig. Co.D
Vonderluth, E.H. GA 9th Inf. (St.Guards) Co.H
Vondersmith, James F. TX 17th Cav. Co.H
Vondersmith, J.P. TX Cav. 1st Bn.St.Troops Co.A
Vonder Wall, Gerh Pet TN 15th Inf. Co.K
Vondhriele, J.D. MS 9th Inf. New Co.E
Von Dohelen, C.A. SC 2nd Arty. Co.F
Von Dohlen, C.A. SC 5th Cav. Co.G
Von Dohlen, Nic SC Arty.Bn. Hampton Legion Co.B
Vondrehl, John MS 10th Inf. Old Co.K
Vondy, James TX 11th (Spaight's) Bn.Vol. Co.A
Vondy, James TX 21st Inf. Co.A
Von Eaton, John I. NC 13th Inf. Co.F Sgt.
Von Eaton, Samuel P. NC 13th Inf. Co.F
Von Eberstein, William H. NC 1st Arty. (10th St.Troops) Co.K Sgt.
Von Eberstein, William H. NC 61st Inf. Sgt.Maj.
Von Eitzen, H. SC Mil.Arty. 1st Regt. Werners' Co.
Von Eitzen, H. SC Lt.Arty. Wagener's Co. (Co.A,German Arty.)
Von Eye, E. LA Mil. Chalmette Regt. Co.G
Von Glahen, C. SC 23rd Inf. Co.B
Von Glahn, C. SC 23rd Inf. Co.B
Von Glahn, Christopher NC Hvy.Arty. 1st Bn. Co.A 1st Sgt.
Von Glahn, Christopher NC 18th Inf. Co.A Cpl.
Von Glahn, Henry NC Cav. (Loc.Def.) Howard's Co. 3rd Lt.
Von Hadeln, Frederick W. SC 1st (Orr's) Rifles Co.C
Von Hadeln, Henry SC 1st (Orr's) Rifles Co.C Music.
Von Haden, E.H. SC 1st (Orr's) Rifles Band
Von Harden, W.J. MS 4th Cav. Co.I
Von Harten, E. TX 1st Hvy.Arty. Co.E Maj.
Von Hasseln, A. SC 3rd Cav. Co.G
Von Hasseln, A. SC 15th Inf. Co.F,D
Vonhooser, John TN 28th Inf. Co.I
Von Hornberger, J. LA Mil. 2nd Regt. 3rd Brig. 1st Div. Co.F
Vonhouer, William VA Horse Arty. Shoemaker's Co.
Von Hutton, William B. TX 1st Inf. Co.L
Voniche, Alfonzo A. LA 1st Cav. Co.C
Vonkannan, James F. MO Cav. 3rd Bn. Co.B QMSgt.
Von Kietzel, Albert TX 1st Field Btty.
Von Kohlintz, George F. SC Cav. 17th Bn. Co.A
Von Kolnitz, George F. SC 5th Cav. Co.D
Von Lahoche, T., Jr. LA Mil.Crescent Cadets
Von Landgraff, Anton LA 20th Inf. Co.C Sgt.
Von Lehe, D. SC Mil.Arty. 1st Regt. Werner's Co.
Von Lehe, D. SC Lt.Arty. Wagener's Co. (Co.A,German Arty.)
Von Lehe, J.C. SC Lt.Arty. Wagener's Co. (Co.A,German Arty.)
Von Lehee, John C. SC 1st (McCreary's) Inf. Co.F
Von Lingteg, H. SC 1st Regt. Charleston Guard Co.G
Von Muller, Mau LA 13th Inf. Co.E
Vonn, R.B. MS 11th (Perrin's) Cav. Co.A
Vonn, W.F. AR Cav. McGehee's Regt. Co.I
Von Newton, John H. SC Arty. Bachman's Co. (German Lt.Arty.) Sgt.
Von Olker, Peter AL Cav. Lenoir's Ind.Co. 1st Bugler
Vonon, R.P. VA Cav. Swann's Bn. Vincent's Co. Sgt.
Von Phul, B. Gen. & Staff 1st Lt.,Dr.M.
Von Phul, Ben MO Lt.Arty. Von Phul's Co. 1st Lt.
Von Phul, Francis Price's Div. ADC
Von Phul, Wm. Gen. & Staff Lt.,Ord Off.
Von Roeder, Joachim TX 36th Cav. Co.G Sgt.
Von Roeder, Louis TX 36th Cav. Co.G
Von Rordorf, L. TX 14th Field Btty.
Von Rosenberg, Alexander TX 5th Field Btty. Sgt.
Von Rosenberg, John Eng.,CSA Lt.
Von Rosenburg, E. TX Waul's Legion Co.E Sgt.
Von Rosenburg, W. TX Lt.Arty. Dege's Bn. Co.A
Von Rosenberg, Walter TX 5th Field Btty. Cpl.
Von Santen, F. SC Mil.Arty. 1st Regt. Walter's Co., Co.C 1st Lt.
Von Santen, Frederick SC Lt.Arty. Walter's Co. (Washington Arty.) Sr.2nd Lt.
Von Schellenberg, A. LA 20th Inf. Co.D 1st Lt.
Von Schmelling, Wedig Price's Staff Col.
Vonschmitts, Sterling B. TN 50th Inf. Co.H
Von Stein, Emile TX Inf.Res. Co.A
Von Steinaecker, Henry VA 2nd Inf. Co.K
Von Strantz, Benno LA 1st Hvy.Arty. (Reg.) Co.B
Vonstratton C. SC 2nd St.Troops Co.I
Von Stratton, Charles SC 5th Res. Co.C
Von Terrell, Samuel M. MO 1st N.E. Cav.
Von Terrell, S.B. GA 1st (Olmstead's) Inf. Co.D
Von Terrell, S.B. TX 4th Inf. Co.I Sgt.
Von Thun, Henry LA Mil.Cont.Regt. Mitchell's Co.
Vontrees, A.J. TN 8th (Smith's) Cav. Co.K
Vontrese, William A. TN 21st (Wilson's) Cav. Co.E
Vontress, Ed H. TX Cav. Morgan's Regt. Co.A Capt.
Vonviller, Jacob LA Arty. Kean's Btty. (Orleans Ind.Arty.)
Von Viller, Jacob LA C.S. Zouave Bn. Co.B
Von Wamer, A. Conf.Inf. 8th Bn. Co.E
Von Warmel, A. Conf.Inf. 8th Bn. Co.E
Von Zinken, Leon LA 13th Inf. Col.
Von Zinken, Leon LA 20th Inf. Col.
Vooly, R. AR 15th (Josey's) Inf. Co.E
Voorhees, Aaron L. MS Cav. 4th Bn. Co.A
Voorhees, Abraham VA 2nd Inf. Co.D,C
Voorhees, A.L. 8th (Wade's) Conf.Cav. Co.C QMSgt.
Voorhees, Alfred H. Hood's A. Surg.,Medical Insp.
Voorhees, George LA Lt.Arty. Fenner's Btty.
Voorhees, George F. VA 2nd Inf. Co.D Sgt.
Voorhees, George F. VA 27th Inf. 1st Co.H Sgt.
Voorhees, H.V.H. AL 1st Regt. Mobile Vol. Baas' Co.
Voorhees, Jacob TN 10th Inf. Co.F
Voorhees, Jacob F. VA 2nd Inf. Co.B
Voorhees, J.L. TX Cav. Baird's Regt. Co.B
Voorhees, John VA 2nd Inf. Co.D
Voorhees, John VA 27th Inf. 1st Co.H
Voorhees, John V.C. LA Inf. 4th Bn. Co.F Jr.2nd Lt.
Voorhees, Samuel W. TN Cav. 2nd Bn. (Biffle's) Co.B
Voorheis, C.D. TX Cav. Baird's Regt. Co.B
Voorheis, C.K. TN 4th Inf. Co.E
Voorheis, C.V. TN 4th Inf. Co.H,E
Voorheis, F.F. KY 1st Inf. Co.E
Voorheis, John S. VA 10th Cav. Co.H
Voorhies, A.H. NC 29th Inf. A.Medical Director
Voorhies, A.H. TN 10th Inf. Surg.
Voorhies, A.M. Gen. & Staff Surg.
Voorhies, C.H. Buford's Staff 1st Lt.,ADC
Voorhies, C.V. Forrest's Scouts T. Henderson's Co.,CSA
Voorhies, D.L. TN 19th (Biffle's) Cav. Co.A
Voorhies, E. LA 25th Inf. Co.F
Voorhies, Felix LA 8th Inf. Co.C
Voorhies, Frank LA 2nd Cav. Co.I
Voorhies, George LA Inf. 1st Sp.Bn. (Rightor's) Co.F
Voorhies, George T. LA 1st Cav. Co.G
Voorhies, G.F. LA 2nd Cav. Co.G
Voorhies, G.P. KY 2nd Cav.
Voorhies, H. LA 1st Cav. Co.G
Voorhies, H.H. Forrest's Scouts T. Henderson's,CSA Sgt.
Voorhies, James TX 19th Cav. Co.E Sgt.
Voorhies, J.L. TX 16th Inf. Co.A
Voorhies, M. LA Mil. Orleans Guards Regt. Co.B,F
Voorhies, O. LA Mil. Orleans Guards Regt. Maj.
Voorhies, Octave Gen. & Staff Maj.,AAG
Voorhies, William LA 2nd Cav. Co.G Sgt.
Voorhies, William M. TN 1st (Feild's) Inf. Co.H
Voorhies, William M. TN 48th (Voorhies') Inf. Co.K Col.
Voorhis, Robert Gen. & Staff Maj.,AAAG
Voorhis, Samuel W. TN 19th (Biffle's) Cav. Co.A
Voorrhees, John H. AL Inf. 1st Regt. Co.F
Voortman, A.G. TX 2nd Inf. Co.C
Voorvart, William LA 10th Inf. Co.A
Voosborn, B. NC 22nd Inf. Co.K
Voose, James VA Inf. Cohoon's Bn. Co.A
Voose, T. NC 33rd Inf. Co.G

Vopel, Theodore TX 3rd Inf. Co.B
Vorass, Robert GA 3rd Cav. Co.E
Vorbeck, John TX 24th & 25th Cav. (Cons.) Co.H
Vorbeck, John TX 25th Cav. Co.I
Vorchan, Ferdinand VA 56th Inf. Co.H
Vordell, William G. TX 12th Cav. Co.F 1st Lt.,Adj.
Vordenbaumen, H. TX Inf. Houston Bn. Co.D
Vordenbaumen, H.W. TX 1st Hvy.Arty. Co.C
Vordenbaumen, H.W. TX St.Troops Atkins' Co.
Vordenbaumen, Hy TX 1st Hvy.Arty. Co.C
Vordenbimon, --- TX Cav. Border's Regt. Co.A
Vorderharr, F. LA Mil. Squad. Guides d'Orleans
Vore, Israel 1st Choctaw & Chickasaw Mtd.Rifles 3rd Co.K
Vore, Israel G. 1st Cherokee Mtd.Rifles QM
Vore, Israel G. Gen. & Staff Maj.,QM
Voreager, John TX 2nd Cav. Co.E
Vores, Robert VA 115th Mil. Co.A
Vorhall, J.B. KY Corbin's Men
Vorhees, J. VA Cav. Mosby's Regt. (Part. Rangers) Co.C
Vorhes, John VA 67th Mil. Co.E
Vorin, Alford TX 18th Cav. Co.B Ens.
Vorin, Charles TX 18th Cav. Co.B Sgt.
Voris, William TX Cav. Madison's Regt. Co.E
Voris, William H. TX 2nd Cav. Co.E Cpl.
Vormickle, A. TX 26th Cav. Co.C
Vornedoe, L.L. Gen. & Staff Capt.,AAQM
Vorner, G.W. TN 22nd (Barteau's) Cav. Co.C
Vorner, Johnson F. GA 9th Inf. (St.Guards) Co.F 2nd Bvt.Lt.
Vorner, M.D. TN 21st (Wilson's) Cav. Co.H Sgt.
Vornhohl, --- TX 4th Inf. Co.F
Vorns, I. FL 1st (Res.) Inf. Co.I
Vorns, John AR 1st (Dobbin's) Cav.
Vorous, John A. VA Cav. 39th Bn. Co.A
Vorris, John KY 4th Cav. Co.F
Vorsell, J. LA 25th Inf. Co.F
Vortees, W.E. SC 2nd St.Troops Co.I
Vorters, George L. TN 45th Inf. Co.G
Vorters, N. MS 6th Cav. Co.B
Vorters, N. MS Cav. Davenport's Bn. (St.Troops) Co.A
Vortner, Andrew AL 61st Inf. Co.E,C
Vorz, Thomas SC Inf.Loc.Def. Estill's Co.
Vosberg, F. LA 18th Inf. Co.C
Vosberg, Samuel, Jr. LA 7th Inf. Co.A
Vosburg, Charles C. MS 22nd Inf. Co.G
Vosburg, Charles C. MS 30th Inf. Co.A
Vosburg, F. LA Inf.Crescent Regt. Co.I
Vosburg, James H. LA Pointe Coupee Arty.
Vosburg, William TX 11th (Spaight's) Bn.Vol. Co.B
Vosburg, William, Jr. TX 11th (Spaight's) Bn.Vol. Co.B
Vosburg, William TX 11th (Spaight's) Bn.Vol. Co.E
Vosburg, William H. TX 13th Vol. Co.K
Vosburg, William H. TX 21st Inf. Co.B
Vosburg, William M. MS 21st Inf. Co.L Capt.
Vosburg, William W. LA 1st Cav. Co.I
Vosburgh, B.H. TX 16th Inf. Co.F
Vosburgh, Eugene TX 13th Vol. Co.H
Vosburgh, William B. TX 16th Inf. Co.F
Vose, C. SC 1st Mtd.Mil. Anderson's Co. 1st Sgt.
Vose, C. SC Mil. 18th Regt. Co.E
Vose, E.J. MS 7th Cav. Co.H
Vose, Henry J. LA Mil.Conf.Guards Regt. Co.E Cpl.
Vose, J.G. SC 1st Mtd.Mil. Anderson's Co.
Vose, J.G. SC Arty. Manigault's Bn. 1st Co.A
Vosemus, O.D. KY 2nd (Duke's) Cav. Co.G
Vosier, A.F. TX 14th Inf. Co.H 1st Sgt.
Vosmus, Oran D. LA 5th Inf. Co.D
Voss, A. TX 35th (Brown's) Cav. Co.A
Voss, A. TX Nolan's Mtd.Co. (Loc.Def.)
Voss, A. TX Cav. Waller's Regt. Goode's Co.
Voss, A. TX 13th Vol. 1st Co.B
Voss, Adrian L. NC 21st Inf. Co.E
Voss, Albert C. VA 6th Inf. Co.G
Voss, Albert G. NC 2nd Cav. (19th St.Troops) Co.H
Voss, A.S. NC 6th Inf. Co.F
Voss, Aug. AR 13th Mil. Co.A
Voss, August AL 1st Regt.Conscr. Co.E
Voss, August LA Miles' Legion Co.C
Voss, Bedford B. VA 38th Inf. Co.E
Voss, C.H. AL 8th Cav. Co.H,E
Voss, Charles H. 8th (Wade's) Conf.Cav. Co.H
Voss, C.R. TN 15th (Cons.) Cav. Co.G
Voss, C.R. TN 1st Hvy.Arty. 2nd Co.B Jr. 1st Lt.
Voss, Daniel AR Cav. Gordon's Regt. Co.E
Voss, Daniel AR 15th Mil. Co.A 3rd Lt.
Voss, Douglass Gen. & Staff Capt.,QM
Voss, Edward C. VA 108th Mil. Co.F, Lemons' Co. Sgt.
Voss, Edward W. TN 1st (Feild's) Inf. Co.H
Voss, Eli TN 48th (Nixon's) Inf. Co.H
Voss, Eli TN 54th Inf. Co.C Sgt.
Voss, F. SC Mil. 1st Regt. (Charleston Res.) Co.B
Voss, Ferdinand Conf.Inf. Tucker's Regt. Co.C
Voss, Fields M. TX 4th Cav. Co.F
Voss, Frank AR 34th Inf. Co.H
Voss, Frank KY 7th Cav. Co.B
Voss, Frank MD Weston's Bn. Co.A
Voss, Franklin MD 1st Inf. Co.C
Voss, Franklin VA Inf. Hutter's Co.
Voss, Fred TX Inf. 1st St.Troops Sheldon's Co.B
Voss, G.C. TX 9th (Young's) Inf. Co.G
Voss, Gerhard NC Hvy.Arty. 1st Bn. Co.A
Voss, H. VA 23rd Cav. Co.C
Voss, Henry LA Miles' Legion Co.C
Voss, Henry TX 17th Inf. Co.H Music.
Voss, H.O. TN Arty. Ramsey's Btty. Sgt.
Voss, I.E. TN 11th Inf. Co.K
Voss, J.A. TX 13th Vol. 2nd Co.B
Voss, James TN 1st Hvy.Arty. Co.G 1st Lt.
Voss, James VA 6th Inf. Co.D
Voss, James A. GA Cobb's Legion Co.E
Voss, James O. VA Lt.Arty. B.Z. Price's Co.
Voss, James R. TN Cav. Nixon's Regt. Co.G Capt.
Voss, James R. TN 46th (Nixon's) Inf. Co.H 1st Lt.
Voss, James R. TN 54th Inf. Co.C 1st Lt.
Voss, John AR 31st Inf. Co.E 2nd Lt.
Voss, John FL 9th Inf. Co.E
Voss, John TN 15th (Cons.) Cav. Co.A
Voss, John TN Jackson's Cav.
Voss, John TN 6th Inf. Co.A
Voss, John A. GA Cobb's Legion Co.E
Voss, John B. TX 18th Cav. Co.A
Voss, John C. MS 16th Inf. Co.K Cpl.
Voss, John C. VA Inf. 21st Bn. Co.B 1st Sgt.
Voss, John C. VA 64th Mtd.Inf. Co.B Sgt.
Voss, John E. LA 3rd Inf. Co.D
Voss, John E. TN 2nd (Robison's) Inf. Co.B
Voss, John G. NC 18th Inf. Co.A
Voss, John M. NC 6th Inf. Co.F
Voss, John W. AR Cav. Gordon's Regt. Co.E
Voss, J.R. TN Cav. Nixon's Regt. Co.G Capt.
Voss, J.W. TN 16th (Logwood's) Cav. Co.G
Voss, Leroy TN Cav. Nixon's Regt. Co.G
Voss, Leroy TN 48th (Nixon's) Inf. Co.H
Voss, Leroy TN 54th Inf. Co.C
Voss, L.P. TN 19th (Biffle's) Cav. Co.E
Voss, Nat GA Cav. Roswell Bn. Co.B Sgt.
Voss, Otto LA 1st Cav. Robinson's Co., Co.K Sgt.
Voss, Philip P. VA 23rd Inf. Co.E
Voss, Pinckney N. AL 39th Inf. Co.I
Voss, Pinkney N. AL 22nd Inf. Co.G Cpl.
Voss, P.T. VA 17th Inf.
Voss, R. FL Cav. 5th Bn. Co.H
Voss, Richard FL 3rd Inf. Co.B
Voss, Robert TN 1st Hvy.Arty. 2nd Co.B 1st Lt.
Voss, Samuel NC 6th Inf.
Voss, Sceam VA 20th Inf. Co.E
Voss, Silvestus R. MS 3rd Inf. Co.C Cpl.
Voss, T. SC 4th St.Troops Co.A
Voss, Thomas TN 15th (Cons.) Cav. Co.C
Voss, Thomas TN 15th (Stewart's) Cav. Co.B
Voss, Uriah GA 12th Cav. Co.L
Voss, Uriah GA 7th Inf. Co.C
Voss, W.A. TN 19th (Biffle's) Cav. Co.H
Voss, W.C. TN 16th (Logwood's) Cav. Co.G
Voss, W.D. AR 19th (Dockery's) Inf. Co.G
Voss, W.E. TN 19th (Biffle's) Cav. Co.H
Voss, Wiley TX 12th Cav. Co.C
Voss, Wiley TX 18th Cav. Co.A
Voss, William LA Mil. 4th Regt. 2nd Brig. 1st Div. Co.G Capt.
Voss, William TX 17th Inf. Co.H Sgt.
Voss, William 14th Conf.Cav. Co.H
Voss, William A. GA Cobb's Legion Co.E
Voss, William H. NC 21st Inf. Co.D Sgt.
Voss, William H. VA 38th Inf. Co.E
Voss, William J. MO 3rd Cav. Co.H
Voss, William M. VA 18th Inf. Co.A
Voss, William T. AL 3rd Cav. Co.G
Voss, W.J. TN 6th Inf. Co.A
Voss, W.O. LA Miles' Legion Co.A
Voss, Zillman TN 14th (Neely's) Cav. Co.C Capt.
Voss, Zilman TN 51st (Cons.) Inf. Co.F
Voss, Zilmon TN Cav. Nixon's Regt. Co.B Capt.
Voss, Zilmon TN 51st Inf. Co.D
Voss, Z.S. TN 15th (Cons.) Cav. Co.G
Voss, Z.S. TN 1st Hvy.Arty. 2nd Co.B Sr.1st Lt.
Voss, Z. Taylor TN 2nd (Robison's) Inf. Co.B
Vossall, Fritz LA Mil. Lafayette Arty.
Votan, A. MO Lt.Arty. 3rd Field Btty.

Votan, John MO 16th Inf. Co.F
Votaw, Landon J. TX 5th Cav. Co.I
Votaw, T. TX 21st Cav. Co.C
Votaw, Thomas F. TX 24th Cav. Co.H 1st Sgt.
Votaw, T.O. TX 22nd Inf. Co.B
Votow, William TX 5th Cav. Co.D
Votry, Nelson Conf.Inf. Tucker's Regt. Co.D
Votto, Joseph AL 32nd Inf. Co.C
Voucher, Wm. FL 3rd Inf. Co.D
Voudry, John TX Cav. Ragsdale's Bn. Co.E
Vouel, Martin V. TN Cav. Newsom's Regt. Co.B
Vouenburg, G. LA 8th Cav. Co.G
Vough, Jacob Forrest's Scouts T. Henderson's,CSA
Vougher, S. AL Talladega Cty.Res. Cunningham's Co.
Voughn, S.C. MS 22nd Inf.
Vouinaz, Nicolo LA Mil. 4th Regt.Eur.Brig. Cognevich's Co.
Voung, J.T. TN 51st (Cons.) Inf. Co.C
Voweel, R. TX Cav. Wells' Regt. Co.G
Vowel, D.W. AL 30th Inf. Co.C
Vowel, J.L. MO 16th Inf. Co.D
Vowel, John MS 14th Inf. Co.F
Vowel, Thomas J. MS 4th Inf.
Vowel, Van MS 35th Inf. Co.I
Vowel, Vimpard MS 35th Inf. Co.I
Vowel, William L. VA Inf. 25th Bn.
Vowel, W.R. TN 31st Inf. Co.K
Vowell, --- TX Cav. Good's Bn. Co.B
Vowell, Adolphus H. AR 6th Inf. New Co.D
Vowell, A.H. AR 12th Inf. Co.I
Vowell, Andrew J. LA Inf.Cons.Crescent Regt. Co.F
Vowell, Edward P. VA Cav. Young's Co.
Vowell, E.L. TN 21st (Wilson's) Cav. Co.G
Vowell, Fines E. TX 34th Cav. Co.C
Vowell, Finis E. TX 16th Cav. Co.A
Vowell, Harrison W. TX 11th Cav. Co.A
Vowell, H.L. TN Cav. Newsom's Regt.
Vowell, James KY 2nd (Woodward's) Cav. Co.C
Vowell, J.C. AL 17th Inf. Co.E
Vowell, John W. AL 18th Inf. Co.I
Vowell, John W. TX 34th Cav. Co.C
Vowell, Jos. C. AL Cp. of Instr. Talladega
Vowell, Joseph H. AR 1st (Colquitt's) Inf. Co.C
Vowell, J.R. TN 20th Inf. Co.H
Vowell, J.R. TX 4th Inf. Co.K
Vowell, Levi M. TX 34th Cav. Co.C
Vowell, Lit TN 21st (Wilson's) Cav. Co.G
Vowell, Litt TN Cav. Newsom's Regt. Co.B Cpl.
Vowell, Mart TN 21st (Wilson's) Cav. Co.G
Vowell, Martin KY 2nd (Woodward's) Cav. Co.C
Vowell, Nathaniel MS 24th Inf. Co.H,I
Vowell, Richard H. VA 34th Inf. Co.F
Vowell, R.W. TN 31st Inf. Co.K
Vowell, Thomas J. MS 14th Inf. Co.F
Vowell, William LA Inf. 11th Bn. Co.C
Vowell, William LA Inf.Cons.Crescent Regt. Co.F
Vowell, William A. TX 22nd Cav. Co.F
Vowell, William A. TX 34th Cav. Co.C
Vowell, William L. TN 11th Cav. Co.B
Vowell, W.N. AR 2nd Mtd.Rifles Hawkins' Co.
Vowell, W.N. TX 27th Cav. Co.A
Vowell, W.R. TN 9th Inf. Co.G
Vowells, Hamilton G. LA 12th Inf. Co.C 2nd Lt.
Vowells, Henry N. MS 20th Inf. Co.A
Vowels, A.D.J. AR 7th Inf. Co.H
Vowels, Andrew J. LA 12th Inf. Co.C
Vowels, James N. VA Patrol Guard 11th Congr.Dist. (Mtd.)
Vowels, Philip D. VA 27th Inf. Co.A Cpl.
Vowels, Phillip D. VA Lt.Arty. Carpenter's Co.
Vowels, Vinyard MS 14th Inf. Co.F
Vowels, Volentine MS 14th Inf. Co.F
Vowenckle, H.W. TX 2nd Cav. Co.D
Vowles, D.W. Gen. & Staff, Adj.Gen.Dept. Capt.
Vowles, Richard S. VA 49th Inf. Co.C Cpl.
Vowles, Weedon F. VA 49th Inf. Co.C
Vox, --- TX Cav. 4th Cav. St.Troops Co.F
Voyce, Frederick VA Cav. Mosby's Regt. (Part.Rangers)
Voyle, H. LA 13th Inf. Co.E
Voyle, Joseph LA 1st Hvy.Arty. (Reg.) Co.A
Voyles, Alonzo F. TX 22nd Cav. Co.D,I
Voyles, A.M. MS 26th Inf. Co.H
Voyles, Amos GA 29th Inf. Co.B
Voyles, A.P. TX Cav. 2nd Regt.St.Troops Co.D
Voyles, Benson GA 4th Cav. (St.Guards) McDonald's Co.
Voyles, E.E. MS 32nd Inf. Co.I
Voyles, Elijah TX 7th Inf. Co.K
Voyles, Elijah TX 14th Inf. Co.F
Voyles, Enoch NC 39th Inf. Co.C,G 2nd Lt.
Voyles, Franklin GA 34th Inf. Co.E
Voyles, Harvey MS 26th Inf. Co.H
Voyles, Henry GA 4th Cav. (St.Guards) McDonald's Co.
Voyles, Ira GA 34th Inf. Co.E
Voyles, Ira GA 39th Inf. Co.A
Voyles, Jackson A. GA 24th Inf. Co.I
Voyles, Jacob C. AR 33rd Inf. Co.I
Voyles, J.E. AR 33rd Inf. Co.I
Voyles, J.M. MS 26th Inf. Co.H Sgt.
Voyles, John GA 24th Inf. Co.I
Voyles, John TX 31st Cav. Co.H
Voyles, John C. AR 37th Inf. Co.F
Voyles, John N. GA 20th Inf. Co.D
Voyles, Levi GA 34th Inf. Co.E
Voyles, Newton J. AR 33rd Inf. Co.I
Voyles, Oscar F. TX 22nd Cav. Co.D
Voyles, Oscar T. TX Cav. 2nd Regt.St.Troops Co.D
Voyles, Rudolph TX 22nd Cav. Co.I
Voyles, William TX 31st Cav. Co.H
Voyles, William C. AR 37th Inf. Co.F Cpl.
Voyles, William E. TN 19th Inf. Co.F
Voyls, --- TX Cav. Good's Bn. Co.E
Voyls, Jobbery GA 55th Inf. Co.D
Voyt, Alb MS 3rd (St.Troops) Cav. Co.A
Vrear, B.F. AR 1st (Monroe's) Cav. Co.K
Vredenburgh, W.H. LA Mil. Orleans Guards Regt. Co.F
Vreeland, C.A. Morgan's Co.B,CSA Sgt.
Vreeland, Charles LA 1st Cav. Co.K
Vreeland, J.W. AL Mil. 2nd Regt.Vol. Co.F
Vreeland, J.W. AL Mobile Fire Bn. Mullany's Co. 1st Lt.
Vreeland, W.R. LA Dreux's Cav. Co.A
Vreeland, W.R. LA Inf.Crescent Regt. Co.G
Vreen, Charles J. NC Moseley's Co. (Sampson Arty.)
Vreen, Pinckney NC Moseley's Co. (Sampson Arty.)
Vrestridge, B.B. AL 3rd Res. Co.I
Vrick, Ranson NC 20th Inf. Co.B
Vroman, George SC Lt.Arty. 3rd (Palmetto) Bn. Co.B Far.
Vroman, George S. LA 1st Hvy.Arty. (Reg.) Co.K
Vroom, W.L. GA 1st (Symons') Res. Co.C
Vrooman, Josiah A. AL 3rd Inf. Co.H
Vucalovich, Pietro LA Mil. 4th Regt.Eur.Brig. Cognevich's Co.
Vueve, A. GA Inf. 18th Bn. (St.Guards) Co.E
Vul, T. LA Mil. 1st Regt. French Brig. Co.6
Vulgarnot, Moses VA 67th Mil. Co.C
Vulgarnott, Aaron VA 67th Mil. Co.C
Vulky, E. LA Mil. 4th Regt. 2nd Brig. 1st Div. Co.F
Vulrath, Phil LA Mil. 4th Regt. 2nd Brig. 1st Div. Co.C
Vuncannon, Alson G. NC 3rd Inf. Co.H
Vuncannon, Daniel NC 6th Sr.Res. Co.A
Vuncannon, Henry NC 46th Inf. Co.F
Vuncannon, James F. NC 44th Inf. Co.H
Vuncannon, J.P. NC 30th Inf. Co.C
Vuncannon, William NC Inf. 2nd Bn. Co.F
Vuncannon, William NC 3rd Inf. Co.C
Vuncannon, William NC 3rd Inf. Co.H
Vuncanon, Eli MO 6th Cav. Co.B
Vuncanon, George T. NC Hvy.Arty. 10th Bn. Co.D
Vuncanon, I.J.M. NC 1st Inf. Co.F
Vuncanon, Jesse NC Hvy.Arty. 10th Bn. Co.A,D
Vuncanon, William A. NC 26th Inf. Co.H
Vinkannan, Benjamin F. MO Cav. 3rd Bn. Co.B
Vurdy, Oscar TX 19th Cav. Co.E
Vurge, --- KY Cav. 2nd Bn. (Dortch's) Co.B
Vurnon, D.H. AL 6th Cav. Co.A
Vuroine, A. LA 2nd Res.Corps Co.A
Vuscowich, S. AL 21st Inf. Co.H
Vust, John Jacob LA Mil. 4th Regt. 1st Brig. 1st Div. Co.D
Vyers, Robert F. VA 24th Cav. Co.C
Vyle, Joseph LA Arty. Kean's Btty. (Orleans Ind.Arty.)
Vyness, Henry AL Cav. Moreland's Regt. Co.B

W

W., B. NC 4th Cav. (59th St.Troops) Co.H
W'ton'lis., B. LA 28th (Gray's) Inf. Co.C
Waage, A. LA Mil. 3rd Regt. 1st Brig. 1st Div. Co.C Sgt.
Waal, J. LA Mil. 4th Regt. French Brig. Co.4
Waarters, G.W. GA Cav. Hall's Co.
Waax, John LA 1st (Nelligan's) Inf. Co.E
Wabalt, S. LA Mil. 3rd Regt. 3rd Brig. 1st Div. Co.F
Wabars, A.H. AL 25th Inf. Co.C
Wabbington, William LA 1st Hvy.Arty. (Reg.) Co.C
Wabbington, William LA Hvy.Arty. 8th Bn. Co.2
Wabeck, John VA 23rd Cav. Co.F
Waber, Joel M. LA 28th (Gray's) Inf. Co.G
Waber, Paul Conf.Inf. 8th Bn. Co.D
Waber, Simon TX 4th Inf. Co.F
Wabington, A.J. MS 38th Cav. Co.G
Wabington, George MS 35th Inf. Co.K
Wableton, A.J. MS 4th Inf. Co.A
Wableton, F.B. MS 4th Inf. Co.A
Wableton, G.W. MS 4th Inf. Co.A
Wabrey, P. GA Cobb's Legion
Wabuyan, C. AL 42nd Inf. Capt.
Waby, J.S. AL 1st Inf. Co.E
Wacacy, Zone Shecoe's Chickasaw Bn.Mtd.Vol. Co.A Sgt.
Wacaser, David GA 66th Inf. Co.H
Wacaser, Sidney S. GA 47th Inf. Co.B
Wacaster, Abraham NC 11th (Bethel Regt.) Inf. Co.I
Wacaster, Adolphus NC 1st Inf. (6 mo. '61) Co.K
Wacaster, Adolphus NC 11th (Bethel Regt.) Inf. Co.I
Wacaster, Cowis NC 2nd Jr.Res. Co.C
Wacaster, Elijah NC 58th Inf. Co.G
Wacaster, Hassel NC 58th Inf. Co.G
Wacaster, Hiram GA 16th Inf. Co.H
Wacaster, Jacob NC 58th Inf. Co.A
Wacaster, James AR 33rd Inf. Co.I
Wacaster, John GA Floyd Legion (St.Guards) Co.B
Wacaster, Levi NC 34th Inf. Co.E
Wacaster, Phillip MS 11th (Perrin's) Cav. Co.F
Wacaster, Phillip MS 12th Cav. Co.C
Wacaster, Samuel GA 24th Inf. Co.H
Wacaster, Stephen M. NC 49th Inf. Co.A
Wacaster, William W. NC 49th Inf. Co.A
Waccarlay, H. AR Lt.Arty. Zimmerman's Btty.
Waces, Jarus B. MS 23rd Inf. Co.H
Wacey, George TX 3rd Inf. Co.D
Wachen, B. LA Mil. 3rd Regt. French Brig. Co.3 Sgt.
Wachenfeld, William LA 20th Inf. Co.D,C
Wachenheimer, Simon TN 43rd Inf. Co.A
Wacher, George AL 8th Inf. Co.A
Wacher, Philip MS 11th Inf. Co.K,I
Wachob, Arthur Mc. FL 8th Inf. Co.E
Wachob, Francis M. FL 8th Inf. Co.E
Wachob, Joseph F. FL 8th Inf. Co.E
Wachsmuth, Fred TX 1st Hvy.Arty. Co.C
Wachter, Frederick LA 6th Inf. Co.H
Wachter, Gottfried KY 14th Cav.
Wachter, Jacob VA 1st Inf. Co.K
Wachter, Jakob VA Hvy.Arty. Read's Co.
Wachther, Jacob VA Hvy.Arty. 19th Bn. Co.B
Wacker, C.F. TX 16th Inf. Co.C Sgt.
Wacker, John TX Waul's Legion Co.D
Wacker, L. SC Mil.Arty. 1st Regt. Harms' Co.
Wacker, Lewis SC 3rd Cav. Co.G Cpl.
Wackerly, H.H. MO 6th Cav. Co.F
Wackernah, Chris G. AL 24th Inf. Co.D
Wacksman, E. LA 3rd Inf. Co.I
Wackter, Isaac TX 2nd Cav. Co.I
Wacom 1st Choctaw & Chickasaw Mtd.Rifles 2nd Co.I
Wacter, D.S. GA 45th Inf. Co.K
Wacter, Henry AL 39th Inf. Co.A
Wacter, H.G. MS 2nd (Quinn's St.Troops) Inf. Co.F
Wacter, J.H. MS 7th Inf. Co.A
Wacter, J.J. MS Inf. 1st Bn.St.Troops (12 mo. '62-3) Co.E
Wacter, J.J. SC Lt.Arty. 3rd (Palmetto) Bn. Co.B
Wacter, J.J. TX 1st Inf. Co.F
Wacter, John W. 14th Conf.Cav. Co.B
Wacter, J.R. MS 2nd (Quinn's St.Troops) Inf. Co.F
Wacter, J.R. 14th Conf.Cav. Co.I
Wacter, R.C. SC Inf. 7th Bn. (Enfield Rifles) Co.E
Wactor, A. 20th Conf.Cav. 2nd Co.H
Wactor, G.L. SC 20th Inf. Co.D
Wactor, J.W. GA 5th Res. Co.D
Wactor, J.W. MS Cav. Garland's Bn. Co.B
Wactor, R.C. SC 7th Cav. Co.I
Wactor, Rufus C. SC 20th Inf. Co.G
Wacum John 1st Choctaw Mtd.Rifles Co.D
Wacum Sam 1st Choctaw Mtd.Rifles Co.D Cpl.
Wadavick, J. TX 2nd Inf. Co.I
Waddail, J.N. GA 38th Inf. Co.E
Waddail, Thomas E. GA 7th Inf. Co.K
Wadde, William GA 5th Inf. (St.Guards) Rucker's Co.
Waddeal, J. GA 1st Reg. Co.D
Waddel, Albert P. MS 24th Inf. Co.B
Waddel, E.P. GA Cav. 16th Bn. (St.Guards) Co.E
Waddel, George TN 13th Inf. Co.H,L Sgt.
Waddel, Henry TN 50th (Cons.) Inf. Co.H
Waddel, Isaac TN 10th (DeMoss') Cav. Co.K
Waddel, J. NC 1st Jr.Res. Co.I
Waddel, J.C. SC 3rd Res. Co.E
Waddel, J.G. TN 13th Inf. Co.L
Waddel, John SC 13th Inf. Co.C
Waddel, Meredith NC 26th Inf. Co.C
Waddel, Robert TN 2nd (Ashby's) Cav. Co.D
Waddel, Willie TN 10th (DeMoss') Cav. Co.K
Waddell, A.A. VA Lt.Arty. Carrington's Co.
Waddell, Abel I. MS 30th Inf. Co.D
Waddell, Abel W. TX 16th Cav. Co.K
Waddell, Abner C. AL 5th Inf. New Co.D
Waddell, Adolphus A. NC 14th Inf. Co.C Cpl.
Waddell, A.J. SC 2nd Cav. Co.G
Waddell, Alfred KY Fields' Co. (Part.Rangers)
Waddell, Alfred NC Mil. Clark's Sp.Bn. A.R. Davis' Co.
Waddell, Alfred H. GA Floyd Legion (St.Guards) Co.G
Waddell, Alfred M. NC 3rd Cav. (41st St.Troops) Lt.Col.
Waddell, Alfred V. NC 15th Inf. Co.I
Waddell, Alphard L. GA 10th Cav. (St.Guards) Co.D
Waddell, Andrew J. VA 56th Inf. Co.G
Waddell, B.B. Gen. & Staff Capt.,Comsy.
Waddell, B.J. AL 25th Inf. Co.I
Waddell, Captain AL 6th Inf. Co.D
Waddell, Carr B. MO Inf. 3rd Bn. Co.C
Waddell, Carr B. MO 6th Inf. Co.B
Waddell, C.B. MO St.Guard
Waddell, Charles E. VA 12th Inf. Co.A Capt.
Waddell, Charles M. GA 1st Lt.Duty Men Co.A
Waddell, Charles P. VA Inf. 22nd Bn. Co.B
Waddell, David VA 51st Inf. Co.F
Waddell, D.B. AL 15th Inf. Co.G Capt.
Waddell, D.B. Gen. & Staff 1st Lt.,Adj.
Waddell, D.C. NC 1st Inf. Co.G
Waddell, D.C. NC 15th Inf. Co.D
Waddell, DeBerniere AL 6th Inf. Co.F,K Sr.2nd Lt.
Waddell, D.S. Gen. & Staff Dr. on Ex.Board
Waddell, Duncan C. NC 11th (Bethel Regt.) Inf. Co.G 1st Lt.
Waddell, E. TX 15th Inf. Co.I
Waddell, E. VA Arty. 1st Regt. Hosp.Stew.
Waddell, E. Burke MS Cav. Stockdale's Bn. Co.B 1st Sgt.
Waddell, Edward B. AL 4th Inf. Co.C 1st Sgt.
Waddell, Edward L. VA 5th Inf. Co.L Jr.2nd Lt.
Waddell, Edward W. TX Lt.Arty. Hughes' Co.
Waddell, Elam B. AR 2nd Inf. Co.H Ch.Bugler
Waddell, Elcanah VA 50th Inf. Co.C
Waddell, Ellison S. SC 13th Inf. Co.B
Waddell, Ellison S. SC 22nd Inf. Co.C
Waddell, Estelle MS 18th Inf. Co.D
Waddell, Everett NC 8th Sr.Res. Daniel's Co.
Waddell, F.A., Jr. Gen. & Staff 2nd Lt.,Dr.M.
Waddell, F.N. NC Inf.,PACS 2nd Lt.
Waddell, Francis M. MS Cav. Stockdale's Bn. Co.B

Waddell, Francis N. VA 41st Inf. 2nd Co.G 2nd Lt.
Waddell, Frederick S. LA 16th Inf. Co.C Sgt.
Waddell, George GA Inf. 18th Bn. Co.A Music.
Waddell, George NC 31st Inf. Co.C
Waddell, George W. SC 14th Inf. Co.E
Waddell, G.H. SC 7th Inf. 1st Co.B
Waddell, G.H. Gen. & Staff Asst.Surg.
Waddell, Guion W. NC 27th Inf. Co.G
Waddell, G.W. SC Arty. Zimmerman's Co. (Pee Dee Arty.)
Waddell, Harvey TN 1st Hvy.Arty. 2nd Co.C
Waddell, Henry TN Inf. 1st Bn. (Colms') Co.B
Waddell, Henry C. VA Inf. 22nd Bn. Co.G
Waddell, Henry W. VA 20th Inf. Co.B
Waddell, H.G. Sig.Corps,CSA
Waddell, H.J. AR 38th Inf. Co.H
Waddell, Hugh F. LA 3rd (Wingfield's) Cav. Co.G 1st Lt.
Waddell, Hugh Y. LA 3rd Inf. Co.D Sgt.
Waddell, Jacob GA Siege Arty. 28th Bn. Co.D Cpl.
Waddell, J. Alex Gen. & Staff Surg.
Waddell, Jas. AR 2nd Inf. Co.H
Waddell, James GA 12th Inf. Co.D
Waddell, James KY 2nd Mtd.Inf. Co.G
Waddell, James MS 34th Inf. Co.I
Waddell, James MO 1st Inf. Co.F Cpl.
Waddell, James VA Cav. 41st Bn. Co.G
Waddell, James A. VA Inf. 22nd Bn. Co.B
Waddell, James D. GA 20th Inf. Co.D Col.
Waddell, James D. LA 1st (Strawbridge's) Inf. Co.B Cpl.
Waddell, James D. SC 19th Inf. Co.F 2nd Lt.
Waddell, James D. SC Inf.Bn. Co.E 1st Lt.
Waddell, James F. AL Lt.Arty. 20th Bn. Co.A Maj.
Waddell, James F. AL 6th Inf. Co.C Capt.
Waddell, James H. MS 18th Inf. Co.D
Waddell, James H. NC 5th Cav. (63rd St.Troops) Co.D Sgt.
Waddell, James H. VA 1st Arty. Co.D
Waddell, James H. VA 26th Inf. Co.A Adj.
Waddell, Jas. H. Gen. & Staff 1st Lt.,Adj.
Waddell, James L. VA Inf. 22nd Bn. Co.B Sgt.
Waddell, James M. AL 61st Inf. Co.B
Waddell, James M. TX 8th Cav. Co.G
Waddell, James P. SC 14th Inf. Co.E
Waddell, James R. GA 29th Inf. Co.D
Waddell, J.C. SC Lt.Arty. 3rd (Palmetto) Bn. Co.H
Waddell, Jesse GA 40th Inf. Co.G Cpl.
Waddell, J.F. TX 4th Cav. Co.F
Waddell, J.F. TX 13th Vol. 1st Co.H
Waddell, J.H. MS 23rd Inf. Co.K
Waddell, J.K. AR 12th Inf. Co.K
Waddell, J.M. NC 1st Jr.Res. Co.D
Waddell, John GA Inf. 27th Bn. (NonConscr.) Co.C
Waddell, John MS 12th Inf. Co.B Cpl.
Waddell, John VA Cav. 41st Bn. Co.G
Waddell, John VA Inf. 6th Bn.Loc.Def. Co.B
Waddell, John Drayton's/Frost's/Clark's Brig. Maj.,CS
Waddell, John A. NC 4th Inf. Co.C Cpl.
Waddell, John E. VA 1st Arty. Co.D
Waddell, John J. VA 23rd Inf. Co.I
Waddell, John O. GA Carlton's Co. (Troop Cty.Arty.) Sgt.
Waddell, John O. GA 2nd Inf. Stanley's Co.
Waddell, John O. GA 20th Inf. Adj.
Waddell, John T. MS 16th Inf. Co.G 1st Sgt.
Waddell, John T. VA 23rd Inf. Co.E
Waddell, Joseph TX Cav. 1st Regt.St.Troops Co.C
Waddell, Joseph VA Cav. Ferguson's Bn. Morris' Co.
Waddell, Joseph H. AR 2nd Inf. Co.H
Waddell, Joseph L. MO 5th Cav. Co.F
Waddell, J.W. TX St.Troops Edgar's Co.
Waddell, L., Jr. VA Patrol Guard 11th Congr.Dist. (Mtd.)
Waddell, L. VA 52nd Inf. Surg.
Waddell, L. VA 62nd Mtd.Inf.
Waddell, Larry NC 15th Inf. Co.I
Waddell, Larry NC Mil. Clark's Sp.Bn. A.R. Davis' Co.
Waddell, Littlebury A. VA 3rd Cav. Co.D Sgt.
Waddell, Livingston Gen. & Staff Surg.
Waddell, Lyttleton, Jr. VA Lt.Arty. Garber's Co. QMSgt.
Waddell, Maurice LA 1st Hvy.Arty. (Reg.) Co.C,B
Waddell, Montg P. LA Hvy.Arty. 8th Bn. Co.3
Waddell, Morgan AL Cav. Hardie's Bn.Res. Co.A
Waddell, N. MS 2nd St.Cav.Res. Co.G
Waddell, Newton M. AL Cav. Bowie's Co.
Waddell, N.T. SC 15th Inf. Co.D
Waddell, Owen A. MO Inf. 3rd Regt.St.Guard Co.E 3rd Lt.
Waddell, Owen A. MO 5th Inf. Co.A Maj.
Waddell, Phillip SC Cav. 4th Bn. Co.C
Waddell, R.B. SC Lt.Arty. 3rd (Palmetto) Bn. Co.B Sr.1st Lt.
Waddell, R.H. MS 20th Inf. Co.K 2nd Lt.
Waddell, R.H. VA 23rd Cav. Co.D
Waddell, Richard NC 2nd Arty. (36th St.Troops) Co.D
Waddell, Richard SC 5th St.Troops Co.M
Waddell, Robert MS 15th Inf. Co.G
Waddell, Robert A. VA Courtney Arty.
Waddell, Robert A. VA 1st St.Res. Co.D
Waddell, Robert M. AL 28th Inf. Co.I Cpl.
Waddell, Samuel V. SC 14th Inf. Co.E
Waddell, S.B. TN 13th Inf. Co.H
Waddell, S.D. AL 5th Cav. Co.G
Waddell, Simeon H. GA 10th Cav. (St.Guards) Co.D
Waddell, T.D. NC Mil. Clark's Sp.Bn. Co.B
Waddell, T.D. TN 27th Inf. Co.H Cpl.
Waddell, T.D. Gen. & Staff Hosp.Stew.
Waddell, T.E. SC 16th Inf. Co.C 1st Sgt.
Waddell, Thomas LA 1st (Strawbridge's) Inf. Co.C
Waddell, Thomas LA Res.Corps
Waddell, Thomas NC 53rd Inf. Co.C
Waddell, Thomas VA 16th Cav. Co.C
Waddell, Thomas J. AL 11th Inf. Co.D
Waddell, Thomas P. SC 14th Inf. Co.E
Waddell, T.J. Hosp.Stew.
Waddell, T.W. AL 24th Inf. Co.G
Waddell, T.W. AL 34th Inf. Co.A
Waddell, Vann NC 8th Inf. Co.E
Waddell, V.B. TN Cav. Nixon's Regt. Co.A Capt.
Waddell, V.B. TN 4th Inf. Co.A Cpl.
Waddell, V.B. Gen. & Staff Capt.,AAAG
Waddell, V.J. MS 28th Cav. Co.E
Waddell, W.B. SC 14th Inf. Co.E
Waddell, W.D. VA 1st Inf. Co.H
Waddell, Welly MS Cav. Stockdale's Bn. Co.B
Waddell, W.F. NC 3rd Arty. (40th St.Troops) Co.I
Waddell, W.H. GA 9th Inf. (St.Guards) Co.H 1st Sgt.
Waddell, W.H. NC 57th Inf. Co.B
Waddell, William AR Cav. Wright's Regt. Co.I
Waddell, William TN 20th (Russell's) Cav. Co.B
Waddell, William TX 27th Cav. Co.F
Waddell, William A. TX 16th Cav. Co.K Cpl.
Waddell, William H. VA 62nd Mtd.Inf.
Waddell, William Henry GA Arty. Moore's Btty. Can.
Waddell, William J. GA 46th Inf. Co.B,G
Waddell, William J. NC Inf. 2nd Bn. Co.H
Waddell, William M. TX 13th Cav. Co.C
Waddell, William R. SC 14th Inf. Co.E
Waddell, William T. AL 6th Inf. Co.F
Waddell, William W. MS Cav. Jeff Davis Arty. Co.F Cpl.
Waddell, William W. VA 6th Cav. 1st Co.E
Waddell, Willis E. TN Lt.Arty. Palmer's Co.
Waddell, W.M. TX 28th Cav. Co.I
Waddell, W.M. TX Inf. Currie's Co. 1st Sgt.
Waddell, W.R. NC 23rd Inf. Co.A
Waddell, W.S. TX Cav. Waller's Regt. Dunn's Co.
Waddell, W.T. VA 2nd Arty. Co.G
Waddell, W.T. VA 34th Inf. Co.B
Waddell, W.W. LA 8th Cav. Co.G Sgt.
Waddell, W.W. TN 20th (Russell's) Cav. Co.B Cpl.
Wadden, N. MO Inf. 3rd Bn. Co.B
Wadden, Nicholes MO 6th Inf. Co.A
Waddey, Charles S. GA Arty. 11th Bn. (Sumter Arty.) New Co.C
Waddey, George E. GA Inf. 2nd Bn.
Waddey, William VA Loc.Def. Henderson's Co.
Waddiell, Alfred KY 5th Mtd.Inf. Co.K 1st Sgt.
Waddill, A.D. VA 14th Inf. Co.H
Waddill, A.D. VA 23rd Inf. Co.E
Waddill, Alfred GA 1st Bn.S.S. Co.I
Waddill, A.M. Gen. & Staff Lt.Col.
Waddill, Charles SC Inf. Holcombe Legion Co.E
Waddill, Charles M. VA 38th Inf. Co.A Ord.Sgt.
Waddill, Charles T. VA Lt.Arty. 38th Bn. Co.D
Waddill, Dudly M. TX 16th Cav. Co.E 2nd Lt.
Waddill, Edmund M. NC 2nd Cav. (19th St.Troops) Co.D Sgt.
Waddill, Edward C. VA 6th Cav. Co.G
Waddill, E.T. VA Conscr. Cp.Lee
Waddill, Francis F. VA 18th Inf. Co.K
Waddill, G.D. LA 3rd Inf. Co.K
Waddill, G.D. Gen. & Staff Hosp.Stew.
Waddill, George C. LA Inf. 4th Bn. Co.A Maj.
Waddill, George G. TX 5th Cav. Co.A
Waddill, George M. VA 53rd Inf. Co.K Maj.
Waddill, George M. VA Conscr.

Waddill, George W. NC 2nd Arty. (36th St.Troops) Co.B
Waddill, George W. NC Lt.Arty. 13th Bn. Co.B
Waddill, G.W. SC 1st (McCreary's) Inf. Co.D
Waddill, H.C. VA 2nd Arty. Co.E
Waddill, H.J. AR 18th Inf. Co.F
Waddill, James AL 54th Inf. Co.I
Waddill, James NC 43rd Inf. Co.I
Waddill, James NC 44th Inf. Co.E
Waddill, James A. VA 23rd Inf. Co.B Sgt.
Waddill, James B. AR 1st (Colquitt's) Inf. Co.G
Waddill, James C. NC 43rd Inf. Co.I
Waddill, James H. NC 2nd Cav. (19th St.Troops) Co.F Sgt.
Waddill, James M. NC 2nd Arty. (36th St.Troops) Co.B
Waddill, James T. VA 18th Inf. Co.G
Waddill, J.J. SC Inf. Holcombe Legion Co.E
Waddill, J.M. NC Lt.Arty. 13th Inf. Co.B
Waddill, J.M. TX Cav. Morgan's Regt. Co.G
Waddill, J.O. Gen. & Staff 1st Lt.,Adj.
Waddill, John, Jr. NC 2nd Arty. (36th St.Troops) Co.G
Waddill, John A. AL 6th Inf. Co.I
Waddill, John A. VA Lt.Arty. Parker's Co.
Waddill, John B. NC 14th Inf. Co.C Cpl.
Waddill, John M. AR 1st (Colquitt's) Inf. Co.G Cpl.
Waddill, John M. LA Inf. 4th Bn. Co.E
Waddill, John M. NC 46th Inf. Co.C 2nd Lt.
Waddill, John M. VA 18th Inf. Co.A
Waddill, John M. Gen. & Staff AASurg.
Waddill, John S. AR 18th Inf. Co.C
Waddill, John T. NC 43rd Inf. Co.I
Waddill, J.W. AR 10th Inf. Co.H Cpl.
Waddill, Littlebury G. VA 3rd Cav. 1st Co.I, Co.F
Waddill, Noel SC Inf. Holcombe Legion Co.E
Waddill, Phillip SC Inf. Holcombe Legion Co.E
Waddill, Pleasant A. GA Hvy.Arty. 22nd Bn. Co.B Cpl.
Waddill, Pleasant A. GA 25th Inf. 1st Co.K Cpl.
Waddill, R.O. VA 2nd St.Res. Co.F Cpl.
Waddill, Robt. Gen. & Staff 2nd Lt.,Dr.M.
Waddill, Robert A. LA 3rd (Wingfield's) Cav. Co.G
Waddill, Robert A. LA 4th Inf. Co.F
Waddill, Samuel H. VA 56th Inf. Co.K
Waddill, S.D. TX Waul's Legion Co.D 1st Sgt.
Waddill, S.J. AR 37th Inf. Co.C
Waddill, T.D. LA 2nd Inf. Co.H 2nd Lt.
Waddill, Thomas TX 29th Cav. Co.D
Waddill, Thomas H. LA 2nd Inf. Co.E Lt.
Waddill, Thompson F. VA 53rd Inf. Co.K 2nd Lt.
Waddill, Vinkler J. MS Inf. 3rd Bn. Co.K
Waddill, W.H. TX Cav. Morgan's Regt. Co.G
Waddill, William AL St.Res. 1st Lt.
Waddill, William NC 43rd Inf. Co.I
Waddill, William D. VA 53rd Inf. Co.A
Waddill, William D. VA Inf. Montague's Bn. Co.A
Waddill, William F. VA 2nd Arty. Co.E
Waddill, William F. VA 18th Inf. Co.G
Waddill, William H. VA Inf. Montague's Bn. Co.A
Waddill, William R. NC 43rd Inf. Co.H
Waddill, William W. MS 16th Inf. Co.E
Waddill, W.L. VA Lt.Arty. R.M. Anderson's Co. Artif.
Waddill, W.R. SC Inf. Holcombe Legion Co.E
Waddille, J.J. LA 3rd (Wingfield's) Cav. Co.G Sgt.
Waddille, John H. VA 1st Arty. Co.B
Waddille, John H. VA Lt.Arty. 1st Bn. Co.B
Waddille, John H. VA Arty. Richardson's Co.
Wadding, C. SC 1st Regt. Charleston Guard Co.G
Waddington, F.J. MS Cav. Hughes' Bn. Co.C
Waddle, Abraham AR 17th (Griffith's) Inf. Co.B
Waddle, A.J. KY 7th Mtd.Inf. Co.I Sgt.
Waddle, A.J. SC 3rd Inf. Co.G,D
Waddle, A.J. TX 12th Inf. Co.K
Waddle, A.L. GA 1st Cav. Co.E,F
Waddle, Al C. VA Inf. 23rd Bn. Co.G
Waddle, Alfred H. NC 16th Inf. Co.B
Waddle, Alfred H. 1st Conf.Inf. 2nd Co.G
Waddle, Alson NC 37th Inf. Co.K
Waddle, Andrew J. TN Cav. 12th Bn. (Day's) Co.B
Waddle, Augustus A. AL 41st Inf. Co.B Sgt.
Waddle, Beverly AL 8th Inf. Co.A
Waddle, Beverly L. AL 11th Inf. Co.K 2nd Lt.
Waddle, Calvin VA 21st Cav. 2nd Co.E
Waddle, Calvin VA 36th Inf. 2nd Co.G
Waddle, Canuel D. NC 49th Inf. Co.B
Waddle, Charles R. MS 13th Inf. Co.C
Waddle, Daniel VA Loc.Def. Patterson's Co.
Waddle, D.M. TX 37th Cav. 2nd Co.I
Waddle, Eber MS 42nd Inf. Co.K
Waddle, Elkanah VA 22nd Cav. Co.F
Waddle, Ellison TX 37th Cav. 2nd Co.I
Waddle, Ephraim VA 11th Bn.Res. Co.A
Waddle, Felix GA 34th Inf. Co.F
Waddle, F.M. GA 1st (Fannin's) Res. Co.E
Waddle, F.M. MS 4th Cav. Co.B
Waddle, F.M. TN 17th Inf. Co.H
Waddle, Francis M. VA 51st Inf. Co.C
Waddle, Franklin SC 2nd Rifles Co.E
Waddle, George GA 1st Inf. (St.Guards) Co.G Cpl.
Waddle, George TN 41st Inf. Co.C Sgt.
Waddle, George W. GA Lt.Arty. King's Btty.
Waddle, Granville VA 198th Mil.
Waddle, Green NC 60th Inf. Co.B
Waddle, G.W. GA Lt.Arty. 14th Bn. Co.D
Waddle, G.W. GA Lt.Arty. Havis' Btty.
Waddle, H.A. TN 21st (Wilson's) Cav. Co.C
Waddle, Hardy GA 65th Inf. Co.E
Waddle, Harmon J. AR 38th Inf. Co.H
Waddle, Henry A. TN 1st (Feild's) Inf. Co.C
Waddle, H.I. MO Cav. Snider's Bn. Co.B Sgt.
Waddle, Hughston NC 37th Inf. Co.K Sgt.
Waddle, Huston VA 21st Cav. 2nd Co.I Jr.2nd Lt.
Waddle, I.A. MO Cav. Snider's Bn. Co.B
Waddle, Isaac TN 3rd (Forrest's) Cav.
Waddle, Isaac VA Cav. 47th Bn. Co.B
Waddle, Jacob D. AR 7th Inf. Co.A,K
Waddle, James AR 8th Cav. Co.A
Waddle, James TN 6th (Wheeler's) Cav. Co.E
Waddle, James TN 16th (Logwood's) Cav. Co.F
Waddle, James VA 25th Cav. Co.A
Waddle, James VA 22nd Inf. Co.D
Waddle, James VA Mil. Stowers' Co.
Waddle, James A. AL 25th Inf. Co.I Sgt.
Waddle, James A. VA 11th Bn.Res. Co.E
Waddle, James H. VA 34th Inf. Co.A
Waddle, James H. Conf.Hvy.Arty. Montague's Bn. Co.A
Waddle, James M. AR 36th Inf. Co.F
Waddle, James W. VA 4th Cav. Co.K
Waddle, James W. VA Cav. Mosby's Regt. (Part.Rangers) Co.B
Waddle, J.B. TN 21st (Wilson's) Cav. Co.C
Waddle, J.B. TN 21st & 22nd (Cons.) Cav. Co.G
Waddle, J.B. TN 55th (Brown's) Inf. Co.F 1st Lt.
Waddle, J.B. TX 9th Cav. Co.E Sgt.
Waddle, Jefferson VA 9th Inf. Co.I,A
Waddle, Jesse AL St.Res. Palmer's Co.
Waddle, Jesse MS 10th Cav. Co.A
Waddle, Jesse TN Cav. 17th Bn. (Sanders') Co.C
Waddle, J.F.M. NC 60th Inf. Co.B
Waddle, J.K. AR 20th Inf. Co.C
Waddle, John AL 29th Inf. Co.A
Waddle, John GA 24th Inf. Co.K
Waddle, John B. TN 25th Inf. Co.G
Waddle, John E. NC 60th Inf. Co.B
Waddle, John M. VA 5th Cav. Co.E,C
Waddle, John R. MS 3rd Cav.Res. Co.F
Waddle, John R. VA 21st Mil. Co.D
Waddle, Joseph VA Cav. Caldwell's Bn. Hankins' Co.
Waddle, Joseph VA 45th Inf. Co.A
Waddle, Joseph Maynard AL Lt.Arty. 2nd Bn. Co.D
Waddle, Joseph S. VA 151st Mil. Co.F
Waddle, J.T. SC 3rd Inf. Co.G
Waddle, J.W. SC 3rd Inf. Co.G
Waddle, J.W. TN 19th & 20th (Cons.) Cav. Co.D
Waddle, J.W. VA 6th Cav. Co.F
Waddle, L. VA Cav. Swann's Bn. Sweny's Co.
Waddle, Lansom H. VA 45th Inf. Co.C
Waddle, L.C. GA 1st Cav. Co.E,F
Waddle, Lewis C. TN Cav. 12th Bn. (Day's) Co.E
Waddle, Malachi GA 28th Inf. Co.E
Waddle, M.D. AL 25th Inf. Co.I
Waddle, Michael VA 198th Mil.
Waddle, Michael VA Mil. Stowers' Co.
Waddle, Morris LA Inf. 9th Bn. Co.D
Waddle, M.P. MS 43rd Inf. Co.B
Waddle, N. MS 6th Cav. Co.B
Waddle, N. MS Cav. Davenport's Bn. (St.Troops) Co.A,B
Waddle, Nat TX 37th Cav. 2nd Co.I
Waddle, Newton VA 45th Inf. Co.F
Waddle, Newton M. 8th (Wade's) Conf.Cav. Co.A
Waddle, Patrick GA 24th Inf. Co.K
Waddle, R. MS 33rd Inf. Co.A
Waddle, Richard SC 5th Inf. 1st Co.C
Waddle, Richard J. AL 8th Inf. Co.A Sgt.
Waddle, S.D. TN 14th (Neely's) Cav. Co.B
Waddle, S.D. TN Inf. 1st Cons.Regt. Co.I Cpl.
Waddle, S.D. TN 14th Inf. Co.B
Waddle, Thomas AR 2nd Mtd.Rifles Co.A
Waddle, Thomas GA 34th Inf. Co.F Cpl.

Waddle, Thomas VA 188th Mil. Co.C
Waddle, Thomas P. MS 42nd Inf. Co.K
Waddle, T.W. AR 10th Inf. Co.C 2nd Lt.
Waddle, W. AL 62nd Inf. Co.C
Waddle, W. AR 7th Inf. Co.F 2nd Lt.
Waddle, W. AR 36th Inf. Co.H
Waddle, W. NC Mil. 30th Regt. Co.C
Waddle, W.G. VA 51st Inf. Co.F
Waddle, W.H. AR 45th Cav. Co.K
Waddle, W.H. TX 17th Inf. Co.B
Waddle, William AL 41st Inf. Co.B
Waddle, William NC 58th Inf. Co.L 1st Sgt.
Waddle, William TN 19th & 20th (Cons.) Cav. Co.B,A
Waddle, William TN 44th (Cons.) Inf. Co.I
Waddle, William VA 17th Cav. Co.A
Waddle, William VA 8th Inf. Co.I
Waddle, William A. TN 1st (Turney's) Inf. Co.G
Waddle, William B. VA 151st Mil. Co.C
Waddle, William G. VA Cav. 34th Bn. Co.A
Waddle, William P. AR Inf. Hardy's Regt. Co.E
Waddle, William R. VA 16th Cav. Co.I,C
Waddle, William S. TN 11th (Holman's) Cav. Co.I
Waddle, William S. TN 55th (McKoin's) Inf. McEwen, Jr.'s Co.
Waddle, William T. VA 24th Cav. Co.D Cpl.
Waddle, William T. VA Cav. 40th Bn. Co.D Cpl.
Waddle, William T. VA 34th Inf. Co.A
Waddle, William T. Conf.Hvy.Arty. Montague's Bn. Co.A
Waddle, Willis TN 16th (Logwood's) Cav. Co.F
Waddle, W.R. NC 6th Inf. Co.B
Waddle, W.T. GA 13th Inf. Co.B 2nd Music.
Waddle, W.T. TN 19th & 20th (Cons.) Cav. Co.E
Waddle, W.T. TN 20th (Russell's) Cav. Co.H Sgt.
Waddley, W.B. TN 27th Inf. Co.F
Waddlington, --- LA 22nd (Cons.) Inf. Cpl.
Waddlington, Thomas MS Cav. 6th Bn. Prince's Co.
Waddlington, William KY 3rd Mtd.Inf. Co.E
Waddlington, William K. MS Cav. 6th Bn. Prince's Co.
Waddll, W.P. AR Inf. Hardy's Regt. Co.E
Waddly, Henry TN 27th Inf. Co.F Cpl.
Waddock, Patrick AL 24th Inf. Co.B
Waddy, A.J. Gen. & Staff,PACS Capt.
Waddy, Dennis 1st Chickasaw Inf. Wallace's Co. Cpl.
Waddy, George E. GA 6th Inf. (St.Guards) Co.I
Waddy, George M. VA Lt.Arty. 13th Bn. Co.A
Waddy, George R. VA 55th Inf. Co.L Capt.
Waddy, George R. VA 92nd Mil. Co.A
Waddy, George T. VA 1st Inf. Co.C
Waddy, George T. VA 23rd Inf. Co.G Sgt.Maj.
Waddy, I.R. Beauregard's Staff Lt.Col., Ch.Ord.Off.
Waddy, Jackson KY 3rd Mtd.Inf. Co.A
Waddy, Jas. C. Gen. & Staff Capt.
Waddy, James E. GA Arty. 11th Bn. (Sumter Arty.) New Co.C
Waddy, James E. GA 9th Inf. Co.A N.C.S. ACS
Waddy, John H. TN 32nd Inf. Co.D 2nd Lt.
Waddy, John P. VA 23rd Inf. Co.G Sgt.
Waddy, Joseph W. VA 23rd Inf. Co.A 2nd Lt.
Waddy, M. TN 47th Inf. Co.H
Waddy, Nelson H. VA 23rd Inf. Co.A
Waddy, W. VA Cav. Mosby's Regt. (Part. Rangers)
Waddy, W.B. VA 9th Cav. Co.D
Waddy, William VA 23rd Inf. Co.G
Waddy, William C. TN 4th (McLemore's) Cav. Co.F Sgt.
Wade, --- AL 22nd Inf. Co.G
Wade, --- GA Inf. 27th Bn. (NonConscr.) Co.B
Wade, A. AR 1st (Monroe's) Cav. Co.G
Wade, A. LA 26th Inf. Co.G
Wade, A. TN 20th (Russell's) Cav. Co.D
Wade, Absalom VA Hvy.Arty. 19th Bn. Co.D
Wade, A.C. MS Inf. 2nd St.Troops Co.L
Wade, A.J. AL 9th Inf. Co.C
Wade, Alex TN 7th (Duckworth's) Cav. Co.G
Wade, Alex TX 24th Cav. Co.F
Wade, Alexander LA 10th Inf. Co.K
Wade, Alex. TN 19th & 20th (Cons.) Cav. Co.B
Wade, Alexander VA 46th Inf. Co.G
Wade, Alfred MS Cav. Powers' Regt. Co.A
Wade, Alfred MS 1st (Percy's) Inf. Co.H
Wade, Alfred TN Inf. 22nd Bn. Co.C
Wade, Alfred TN 29th Inf. Co.C
Wade, Alfred VA 135th Mil. Co.A
Wade, Alfred 1st Choctaw Mtd.Rifles Co.C Capt.
Wade, Alfred H. VA Inf. 26th Bn. Co.E
Wade, Alfred J. MS Inf. 3rd Bn. Co.K
Wade, Alfred J. VA 20th Inf. Co.F
Wade, Alfred J. VA 57th Inf. Co.A
Wade, Alfred L. NC 22nd Inf. Co.E
Wade, Alfred R. MO Inf. 8th Bn. Co.D
Wade, Alfred R. MO 9th Inf. Co.H
Wade, Algernal S. VA 12th Cav. Co.B
Wade, Algernon S. VA 5th Inf. Co.B Sgt.
Wade, Algernon S. VA 27th Inf. 2nd Co.H Sgt.
Wade, Allen TN 33rd Inf. Co.F Cpl.
Wade, Allen A. NC 3rd Cav. (41st St.Troops) Co.D Cpl.
Wade, Anderson J. VA 135th Mil. Co.A
Wade, Andrew E. FL 1st Cav. Co.K
Wade, Andrew J. AR Lt.Arty. Key's Btty.
Wade, Andrew J. GA 1st Cav. Co.A
Wade, Andrew J. TX 30th Cav. Co.I
Wade, Andrew P. VA 57th Inf. Co.G
Wade, Anson O. VA 14th Cav. Co.I
Wade, A.P. GA Mtd.Inf. (Pierce Mtd.Vol.) Hendry's Co.
Wade, A.P. GA Lt.Arty. Ritter's Co.
Wade, A.P. VA 10th Cav. Co.C
Wade, A.R. MS Lt.Arty. (Jefferson Arty.) Darden's Co.
Wade, Aretus J. NC 51st Inf. Co.B Sgt.
Wade, Asa AR Inf. Cocke's Regt. Co.B Sgt.
Wade, Asa D. AR Cav. 1st (Stirman's) Bn. 1st Lt.
Wade, Asa P. GA Inf. 8th Bn. Co.D
Wade, Ashly T. GA 59th Inf. Co.F
Wade, Augustus GA Inf. 26th Bn. Co.A
Wade, A.W. AL 9th (Malone's) Cav. Co.B
Wade, A.W. SC 1st Cav. Co.D
Wade, A.W. Lt.Arty. Dent's Btty.,CSA
Wade, B.A. AL 22nd Inf. Co.G
Wade, Barksdale AR 5th Inf. Co.C
Wade, B.B. AL 38th Inf. Co.D
Wade, Benjamin MS 1st Lt.Arty. Co.H 1st Lt.
Wade, Benjamin MS 1st (Patton's) Inf. Co.A Jr.2nd Lt.
Wade, Benjamin VA 2nd Cav. Co.I
Wade, Benjamin C. NC 24th Inf. Co.H
Wade, Benjamin F. MS 10th Inf. Old. Co.C, New Co.H
Wade, Benjamin F. NC 5th Inf. Co.K
Wade, Benjamin F. VA Cav. 36th Bn. Co.A
Wade, Benjamin F. VA 19th Inf. Co.C
Wade, Benjamin H. VA 57th Inf. Co.G Lt.Col.
Wade, Benjamin O. NC 2nd Cav. (19th St.Troops) Co.I
Wade, Benjamin O. NC 12th Inf. Co.F Lt.Col.
Wade, Benjamin S. AL Inf. 1st Regt. Co.D
Wade, Benjamin S. Lt.Arty. Dent's Btty.,CSA
Wade, B.F. AR 26th Inf. Co.K Sgt.
Wade, B.F. GA 40th Inf. Co.I
Wade, B.F. MS 5th Inf. Co.A
Wade, B.F. TN Inf. 23rd Bn. Co.D
Wade, B.F. VA 5th Bn.Res. Co.G 2nd Lt.
Wade, Billy 1st Choctaw & Chickasaw Mtd.Rifles 2nd Co.H, 3rd Co.D
Wade, Blaney W. TN Lt.Arty. Morton's Co.
Wade, Blany W. TN 32nd Inf. Co.B
Wade, Blunt 1st Choctaw & Chickasaw Mtd.Rifles Co.A
Wade, B.N. AL 23rd Inf. Co.H
Wade, Bradly VA 6th Inf. Co.C
Wade, Breckenridge VA Horse Arty. Shoemaker's Co.
Wade, B.S. MS 5th Inf. Co.A
Wade, Burnal H. MS 31st Inf. Co.K
Wade, B.W. TN 6th (Wheeler's) Cav. Co.K
Wade, B.W. VA 56th Inf. Sgt.
Wade, B.W. Morgan's,CSA
Wade, B.Y. Conf.Cav. Wood's Regt. 2nd Co.A
Wade, C.A. Gen. & Staff Asst.Surg.
Wade, Calvin J. GA 12th Inf. Co.F
Wade, Calvin L. MS 18th Inf. Co.G Sgt.
Wade, Carroll AR 12th Inf. Co.E Cpl.
Wade, Carter NC 5th Sr.Res. Co.B 2nd Lt.
Wade, Castleton VA 57th Inf. Co.G
Wade, C.C. GA 13th Inf. Co.G
Wade, C.E. AR 7th Inf. Co.E
Wade, Charles GA 3rd Inf. Co.D
Wade, Charles MS 44th Inf. Co.A
Wade, Charles TN 3rd (Forrest's) Cav. Co.G Sgt.
Wade, Charles TN 12th (Green's) Cav. Co.A
Wade, Charles VA 10th Bn.Res. Co.D 2nd Lt.
Wade, Charles VA 162nd Mil. Co.C
Wade, Charles VA Conscr.
Wade, Charles A. TX 2nd Cav. Co.A Surg.
Wade, Charles A. VA Hvy.Arty. 18th Bn. Co.C
Wade, Charles A. VA 53rd Inf. Co.C
Wade, Charles A. VA Inf. Montague's Bn. Co.D
Wade, Charles A.C. VA 6th Cav. Co.F
Wade, Charles B. AL 63rd Inf. Co.C
Wade, Charles B. TN Holman's Bn.Part.Rangers Co.B
Wade, Charles B. VA 9th Cav. Oliver's Co.
Wade, Charles C. VA 135th Mil. Co.A
Wade, Charles E. MD Inf. 2nd Bn. Co.C,F
Wade, Charles E. VA Inf. 25th Bn. Co.B

Wade, Charles H. TN 35th Inf. Co.E 1st Sgt.
Wade, Charles H. VA Inf. 26th Bn. Co.E
Wade, Charles N. GA 65th Inf. Co.K
Wade, Charles R. AL Arty. 1st Bn. Co.E
Wade, Charles R. AL 3rd Bn. Hilliard's Legion Vol. Co.F
Wade, Charles R. TN 45th Inf. Co.C
Wade, Charles R. VA 42nd Inf. Co.K
Wade, Charley A. GA 48th Inf. Co.K
Wade, Chidley VA 115th Mil. Co.B
Wade, Christopher B. VA 60th Inf. Co.E
Wade, Christopher B. VA 135th Mil. Co.A
Wade, Christopher C. NC 23rd Inf. Co.C
Wade, Cicero M. TN 1st (Turney's) Inf. Co.E Cpl.
Wade, Clark M. NC 51st Inf. Co.C
Wade, Clayton TN 47th Inf. Co.A
Wade, Clem W. TN Holman's Bn.Part.Rangers Co.B
Wade, C.N. TN 12th Inf. Co.G 1st Lt.
Wade, C.N. TN 12th (Cons.) Inf. Co.E Capt.
Wade, Cooper Calloway AL 49th Inf. Co.C
Wade, Council GA 45th Inf. Co.C
Wade, C.R. Lt.Arty. Dent's Btty.,CSA
Wade, Craven A. TN 34th Inf. Co.I Sgt.
Wade, C.W. GA 5th Inf. (St.Guards) Rucker's Co.
Wade, C.W. TN 11th (Holman's) Cav. Co.G
Wade, Dallas AL 11th Cav. Co.I
Wade, D. Allen TX 35th (Brown's) Cav. Co.G
Wade, Daniel AR 1st (Colquitt's) Inf. Co.B
Wade, Daniel FL Inf. 2nd Bn. Co.E
Wade, Daniel KY 10th (Johnson's) Cav. Co.D
Wade, Daniel KY Horse Arty. Byrne's Co.
Wade, Daniel E. MS 8th Inf. Co.D
Wade, Daniel F. TN 3rd (Clack's) Inf. Co.C Capt.
Wade, Daniel G. VA 2nd Cav. Co.F
Wade, Daniel G. VA Lt.Arty. J.D. Smith's Co.
Wade, Daniel G. Conf.Arty. Lewis' Bn. Co.A
Wade, Daniel W. MS Inf. 7th Bn. Co.C Sgt.
Wade, David TN 55th (McKoin's) Inf. James' Co.
Wade, David VA 25th Cav. Surg.
Wade, David VA 54th Inf. Surg.
Wade, David Gen. & Staff Surg.
Wade, David A. TX 13th Vol. 2nd Co.D,I,G
Wade, David B. VA 25th Inf. 2nd Co.F
Wade, David D. VA 52nd Mil. Co.B
Wade, David H. AL Inf. 2nd Regt. Co.H Cpl.
Wade, David H. Conf.Inf. 1st Bn. 2nd Co.E
Wade, David S. MO 12th Cav. Co.B
Wade, David W. MS 23rd Inf. Co.H 1st Sgt.
Wade, D.B. MS Lt.Arty. (Jefferson Arty.) Darden's Co.
Wade, D.B. TN 51st Inf. Co.D 1st Lt.
Wade, D.B. TN 51st (Cons.) Inf. Co.F
Wade, D.E. AL 34th Inf. Co.F
Wade, D.E. GA 52nd Inf. Co.B
Wade, D.H. GA Inf. 8th Bn. Co.D
Wade, D.H. NC 66th Inf. Co.C Music.
Wade, D.M. GA Cav. 29th Bn. Co.H
Wade, Dock GA 6th Inf. Co.I
Wade, Drew H. NC 8th Bn.Part.Rangers Co.B
Wade, Dunbar MS Lt.Arty. (Jefferson Arty.) Darden's Co. Sgt.
Wade, Duncan B. NC 51st Inf. Co.K
Wade, D.W. AL 10th Inf. Co.F
Wade, D.W. MS Inf. 1st Bn. Johnston's Co.
Wade, E. AL 11th Cav. Co.A
Wade, E. GA 8th Cav. New Co.I
Wade, E. MS 5th Inf. (St.Troops) Co.I
Wade, E. Conf.Cav. Baxter's Bn. 2nd Co.B
Wade, Eastman 1st Choctaw & Chickasaw Mtd.Rifles 2nd Co.D
Wade, E.B. MS Inf. 7th Bn. Co.C
Wade, E.B. TN 18th Inf. Co.C
Wade, E.B. VA 21st Cav. 2nd Co.G
Wade, Ebenezer TX 10th Inf. Co.K
Wade, E.C. GA Inf. 18th Bn. Co.B Sgt.
Wade, E.D. NC 5th Inf. Co.I
Wade, Ed F. AL 11th Cav. Co.I,K Sgt.
Wade, Edward VA 2nd Inf.Loc.Def. Co.E 1st Lt.
Wade, Edward VA Inf. 6th Bn.Loc.Def. Co.B 1st Lt.
Wade, Edward Deneal's Regt. Choctaw Warriors Co.D
Wade, Edward J. GA 13th Cav. Co.E,H
Wade, Edward K. TN 18th Inf. Co.C
Wade, Edward O. GA 48th Inf. Co.K
Wade, Edward P. AL 11th Cav. Co.L
Wade, Edward W. AL 62nd Inf. Co.D Sgt.
Wade, Edwin W. VA Cav. 1st Bn. Co.A
Wade, Edwin W. VA Lt.Arty. R.M. Anderson's Co.
Wade, E.H. AL 9th (Malone's) Cav. Co.F
Wade, E.H. AL 19th Inf. Co.A
Wade, E.H. AL 46th Inf. Co.K
Wade, E.J. FL 1st (Res.) Inf. Co.H Sgt.
Wade, E.K. TN 45th Inf. Co.C
Wade, Elbert C. VA 18th Inf. Co.I
Wade, Eli VA 54th Inf. Co.D Sgt.
Wade, Elias TN 44th (Cons.) Inf. Co.C Sgt.
Wade, Elias TN 55th (McKoin's) Inf. James' Co.
Wade, Elijah AL 25th Inf. Co.A
Wade, Elijah GA Cav. 20th Bn. Co.D
Wade, Eli Riley TN 55th (McKoin's) Inf. James' Co.
Wade, Elisha W. VA 3rd Inf. 2nd Co.K
Wade, Elza J. NC 13th Inf. Co.E
Wade, Emanuel C. GA Inf. 18th Bn. Co.B
Wade, Enoch D. GA 38th Inf. Co.K
Wade, E.P. NC 28th Inf. Co.E
Wade, E.P. TX 30th Cav. Co.H Sgt.
Wade, Ephraim MS 36th Inf. Co.G Sgt.
Wade, E.R. TN 13th (Gore's) Cav. Co.K
Wade, E.T. AL 1st Regt.Conscr. Co.B
Wade, E.T. SC 1st Cav. Co.D
Wade, Ethelbert Barksdale Gen. & Staff Lt.,ADC
Wade, Evans MS 40th Inf.
Wade, E.W. VA 3rd Inf.Loc.Def. Co.F
Wade, F. TN Cav. Nixon's Regt. Co.I
Wade, Farley B., Jr. TN 1st (Turney's) Inf. Co.I Cpl.
Wade, F.H. MS 18th Inf. Co.D
Wade, F.H. TX Arty. Douglas' Co.
Wade, F.M. AL 26th (O'Neal's) Inf. Co.I
Wade, F.M. AR 1st Inf. Co.E Sgt.
Wade, F.M. AR 27th Inf. Co.E
Wade, F.M. GA 38th Inf. Co.K
Wade, F.M. LA 27th Inf. Co.K
Wade, F.M. TN 3rd (Forrest's) Cav. Co.D
Wade, F.M. TX Cav. Giddings' Bn. Weisiger's Co.
Wade, F.M. Exch.Bn. 3rd Co.B,CSA Sgt.
Wade, Fountain P. TN 32nd Inf. Co.G Capt.
Wade, Francis AL 12th Cav. Co.I
Wade, Francis M. AL 21st Inf. Co.A
Wade, Frank H. TX 4th Inf. Co.H
Wade, Franklin GA Cobb's Legion Co.C
Wade, Franklin M. LA Inf. 11th Bn. Co.A
Wade, F.S. LA McNelly's Scouts Sgt.
Wade, F.S. TX 4th Cav. Co.E
Wade, G. TX 9th (Young's) Inf. Co.F
Wade, General J. TN Cav. 4th Bn. (Branner's) Co.C
Wade, George AR Lt.Arty. Key's Btty.
Wade, George AR 1st Inf. Co.D
Wade, George AR Inf. 1st Bn. Co.I
Wade, George KY 14th Cav. Co.B
Wade, George LA Mil. 4th Regt. 1st Brig. 1st Div. Co.H
Wade, George TN 4th (McLemore's) Cav. Co.E
Wade, George TN 51st (Cons.) Inf. Co.K
Wade, George A. MD Inf. 2nd Bn. Co.C,F
Wade, George A. VA Inf. 25th Bn. Co.B
Wade, George A. Conf.Cav. Wood's Regt. Co.I
Wade, George B. KY 2nd (Duke's) Cav. Co.C
Wade, George H. AR 2nd Cav. Co.C Cpl.
Wade, George H. GA 51st Inf. Co.D
Wade, George McD. SC 15th Inf. Co.A
Wade, George P. KY Morgan's Men Co.D,C
Wade, George R. MS 9th Inf. Old Co.F
Wade, George T. SC 12th Inf. Co.I 1st Sgt.
Wade, George W. GA 8th Inf. Co.G
Wade, George W. GA 18th Inf. Co.K
Wade, George W. GA 38th Inf. Co.K Music.
Wade, George W. NC 63rd Inf. Co.I,A
Wade, George W. TN 48th (Voorhies') Inf. Co.I
Wade, George W. TX 6th Cav. Co.H
Wade, Geo. W. VA 3rd Arty. Co.D
Wade, Geo. W. VA Hvy.Arty. 20th Bn. Co.E
Wade, George W. VA Hvy.Arty. A.J. Jones' Co.
Wade, George W. VA 3rd Res. Co.C
Wade, George W. VA 19th Inf. Co.I
Wade, George W. VA Inf. 26th Bn. Co.G
Wade, G.H. TN 43rd Inf. Co.D
Wade, G.J. TN 2nd (Ashby's) Cav. Co.D
Wade, G.M. GA 64th Inf. Co.D
Wade, G.Mc. TX 12th Inf. Co.I
Wade, G.P. KY Cav. 2nd Bn. (Dortch's) Co.A Lt.
Wade, Gran C. TN 43rd Inf. Co.D
Wade, Granville M. AR 13th Inf. Co.B
Wade, Granville N. TN 13th Inf. Co.D,A
Wade, Green B. AL Cav. Bowie's Co.
Wade, Green B. GA 59th Inf. Co.F.
Wade, G.W. GA Cav. 19th Bn. Co.C Cpl.
Wade, G.W. GA 66th Inf. Co.I
Wade, G.W. TN 10th (DeMoss') Cav. Co.I
Wade, G.W. TN 19th & 20th (Cons.) Cav. Co.A
Wade, G.W. TN 20th (Russell's) Cav. Co.A
Wade, G.W. TN 12th (Cons.) Inf. Co.D
Wade, G.W. TN 22nd Inf. Co.H Cpl.
Wade, G.W. VA Inf. 26th Bn. Co.B
Wade, G.W. 10th Conf.Cav. Co.H Cpl.
Wade, H. GA 2nd Cav. Co.F
Wade, H. GA Cobb's Legion Co.C
Wade, H. MS 2nd St.Cav. Co.E

Wade, H. SC 2nd Cav. Co.F
Wade, H. TN 21st & 22nd (Cons.) Cav. Co.C
Wade, H. VA Inf. 26th Bn.
Wade, H. Gen. & Staff Capt.,ACS
Wade, Hamilton D. VA 7th Cav. Preston's Co. 2nd Lt.
Wade, Hamilton D. VA 4th Inf. Co.G Capt.
Wade, Hamilton L. GA 9th Inf.
Wade, Hampton AR 3rd Cav. Co.B
Wade, Hampton SC 7th Inf. 1st Co.F
Wade, Hampton TN 28th Inf. Co.G
Wade, Hamton KY 8th Mtd.Inf. Co.B Cpl.
Wade, Hamton C. AL 38th Inf. Co.F
Wade, Herman S. NC 22nd Inf. Co.E
Wade, Harris GA 7th Inf. (St.Guards) Co.K Cpl.
Wade, Harris GA 35th Inf. Co.F
Wade, Harrison VA 135th Mil. Co.A
Wade, Harvey David MO 8th Inf. Co.H,K Ord.Sgt.
Wade, Harvey S. VA 21st Cav. 2nd Co.G
Wade, H.C. AR 7th Inf. Co.K
Wade, Henderson S. MS 38th Cav. Co.A
Wade, Henry GA 3rd Inf. Co.D
Wade, Henry GA 9th Inf. (St.Guards) Co.B
Wade, Henry GA 40th Inf. Co.D
Wade, Henry GA 60th Inf. Co.B
Wade, Henry LA 16th Inf. Co.H
Wade, Henry MO Lt.Arty. H.M. Bledsoe's Co.
Wade, Henry MO 2nd Cav. Co.E
Wade, Henry SC 2nd Cav. Co.F
Wade, Henry SC Cav. 4th Bn. Co.A
Wade, Henry, Jr. TN Inf. 154th Sr.Regt. Co.G 1st Sgt.
Wade, Henry TX 6th Cav. Co.B Capt.
Wade, Henry VA 22nd Cav. Co.F
Wade, Henry VA 42nd Inf. Co.A
Wade, Henry C. VA 25th Cav. Co.E
Wade, Henry C. VA 4th Inf. Co.G
Wade, Henry C. VA 54th Inf. Co.E Adj.
Wade, Henry F., Jr. LA Hvy.Arty. 8th Bn. Co.D Capt.
Wade, Henry F., Jr. MS 39th Inf. Co.B Capt.
Wade, Henry H. MS 40th Inf. Co.A
Wade, Henry H. TX 4th Cav. Co.H
Wade, Henry H. VA 19th Cav. Co.I
Wade, Henry J. GA Cav. 2nd Bn. Co.D
Wade, Henry J. GA 40th Inf. Co.I Sgt.
Wade, Henry P. TN Holman's Bn.Part.Rangers Co.B
Wade, Henry R. NC 4th Cav. (59th St.Troops) Co.D
Wade, Henry S.M. GA 43rd Inf. Co.D
Wade, Hezekiah GA 50th Inf. Co.F
Wade, Hezekiah A. VA 12th Inf. Co.A
Wade, H.H. TX 12th Inf. Co.B
Wade, Hiram AL 46th Inf. Co.F
Wade, H.J. TN 22nd (Barteau's) Cav. Co.H
Wade, H.J. GA 5th Cav. Co.A
Wade, H.K. AL 30th Inf. Co.G
Wade, H.M. KY 3rd Mtd.Inf. Co.G Cpl.
Wade, H.M. VA 15th Cav. Co.B
Wade, Horace M. VA 12th Cav. Co.I Cpl.
Wade, Howard VA 20th Cav. Co.C
Wade, Howard VA 25th Inf. 2nd Co.F
Wade, H.R. TN 33rd Inf. Co.F
Wade, H.R. 3rd Conf.Eng.Troops Co.B
Wade, H.R. Eng.Dept. Polk's Corps A. of TN Sap. & Min. Co.,CSA
Wade, I.A. Conf.Cav. Wood's Regt. Co.I
Wade, I.R. MS Cav. Hughes' Bn. Co.B
Wade, I.R. Conf.Cav. Wood's Regt. 2nd Co.A
Wade, Isaac C. MS 40th Inf. Co.A
Wade, Isaac J. MS 40th Inf. Co.A
Wade, Isham H. TN 28th Inf. Co.F 1st Sgt.
Wade, Isom TN 5th Cav.
Wade, J. AL 1st Regt. Mobile Vol. Bass' Co.
Wade, J. AL 15th Inf. Co.A
Wade, J. GA 1st Cav. Co.A
Wade, J. NC 17th Inf. (2nd Org.) Co.L
Wade, J.A. NC 3rd Jr.Res. Co.H
Wade, J.A. TX 7th Inf. Co.D
Wade, J.A. Gen. & Staff AASurg.
Wade, J.A.C. GA 15th Inf. Co.H
Wade, Jacob VA 50th Inf. Co.H
Wade, Jacob B. VA 27th Inf. Co.C
Wade, Jacob S. TX 3rd Cav. Co.F
Wade, James AL 5th Cav. Co.H
Wade, James AL Cp. of Instr. Talladega
Wade, James GA 51st Inf. Co.C
Wade, James KY 3rd Cav. Co.H
Wade, James KY 11th Cav. Co.B
Wade, James KY Horse Arty. Byrne's Co.
Wade, James KY 7th Mtd.Inf. Co.B
Wade, James LA 1st Cav. Co.A
Wade, James LA 8th Cav. Co.E
Wade, James LA 14th Inf. Co.G
Wade, James MS Cav. Ham's Regt. Co.D
Wade, James MS Inf. 2nd Bn. Co.A
Wade, James MS Inf. 7th Bn. Co.C 1st Sgt.
Wade, James MS 48th Inf. Co.A
Wade, James MO 1st N.E. Cav. Co.L
Wade, James SC 2nd Cav. Co.B
Wade, James TN 48th (Voorhies') Inf. Co.K
Wade, James TN 51st Inf. Co.A Cpl.
Wade, James TN 51st (Cons.) Inf. Co.H
Wade, James VA Inf. 1st Bn.Loc.Def. Co.E
Wade, James VA 26th Inf. 1st Co.B
Wade, James VA 46th Inf. 1st Co.G
Wade, James 3rd Conf.Inf. Co.C
Wade, James 1st Choctaw & Chickasaw Mtd.Rifles Co.A Cpl.
Wade, James Gen. & Staff, Comsy.Dept. Capt.
Wade, James A. GA Cav. 29th Bn. Co.E
Wade, James A. GA 41st Inf. Co.K
Wade, James A. NC 7th Bn.Jr.Res. Co.A
Wade, James A. VA 2nd Cav. Co.F
Wade, James A. VA Inf. 26th Bn. Co.E
Wade, James A. VA 42nd Inf. Co.A
Wade, James B. GA Tiller's Co. (Echols Lt.Arty.) Sr.2nd Lt.
Wade, James B. GA 59th Inf. Co.F
Wade, James B. MO Cav. 3rd Bn. Co.C
Wade, James B. MO Cav. Wood's Regt. Co.B
Wade, James C. GA 3rd Inf. Co.B Sgt.
Wade, James C. GA 3rd Bn.S.S. Co.B Sgt.
Wade, James C. GA 24th Inf. Co.A
Wade, James C. NC 15th Inf. Co.A 1st Sgt.
Wade, James C. SC 2nd Rifles Co.H
Wade, James F. GA 48th Inf. Co.K
Wade, James F. MS 1st Bn.S.S. Co.B
Wade, James F. MS Inf. (Red Rebels) D.J. Red's Co.
Wade, James H. AL 1st Cav. 2nd Co.E
Wade, James H. AL 43rd Inf. Co.K
Wade, James H. GA Cav. 12th Bn. (St.Guards) Co.C
Wade, James H. MS 25th Inf. Co.A
Wade, James H. NC 27th Inf. Co.C
Wade, James H. TN 41st Inf. Co.B Sgt.
Wade, James H. TX 10th Cav. Co.G
Wade, James I. MS Inf. 1st Bn. Johnston's Co.
Wade, James K. MS 1st Lt.Arty. Co.L
Wade, James K. TN 53rd Inf.
Wade, James L. MS 2nd Inf. Co.H
Wade, James L.C. NC 42nd Inf. Co.B
Wade, James M. AL 36th Inf. Co.K
Wade, James M. NC 25th Inf. Co.C
Wade, James M. TN 43rd Inf. Co.C 1st Sgt.
Wade, James M. VA 4th Inf. Co.G 1st Lt.
Wade, James N. VA 28th Inf. Co.F Cpl.
Wade, James O. NC 2nd Arty. (36th St.Troops) Co.G
Wade, James P. AL 44th Inf. Co.K
Wade, James P. AL 51st Part.Rangers Co.D
Wade, James P. AL Cp. of Instr. Talladega
Wade, James P. MO Inf. Perkins' Bn. Co.F
Wade, James R. NC 8th Bn.Part.Rangers Co.B Cpl.
Wade, James S. GA Lt.Arty. Guerard's Btty.
Wade, James S. TN 1st (Feild's) Inf. Co.F Cpl.
Wade, James T. LA 12th Inf. Co.E
Wade, James T. MO 5th Inf. Co.H
Wade, James W. AR 4th Inf. Co.K Sgt.
Wade, James W. GA 2nd Inf. 1st Co.B
Wade, James W. GA 26th Inf. Co.E
Wade, James W. NC 2nd Cav. (19th St.Troops) Co.H,G
Wade, James W. NC 3rd Arty. (40th St.Troops) Co.H
Wade, James W. NC Lt.Arty. 13th Bn. Co.F
Wade, James W. NC 28th Inf. Co.E
Wade, James W. TN 38th Inf.
Wade, James W. TX Cav. 3rd Regt.St.Troops Co.A 2nd Lt.
Wade, James W. TX 12th Cav. Co.I
Wade, Jas. W. Gen. & Staff Capt.,Comsy.
Wade, Jarrett TN 5th (McKenzie's) Cav. Co.D,C Bugler
Wade, Jarrett TN 63rd Inf. Co.H
Wade, J.A.S. TN 12th (Green's) Cav. Co.A
Wade, Jasper N. AL Cav. Bowie's Co.
Wade, Jasper N. GA 43rd Inf. Co.K
Wade, Jasper N. 8th (Wade's) Conf.Cav. Co.A 2nd Lt.
Wade, J.B. MO Lt.Arty. 1st Btty.
Wade, J.B. TX 34th Cav. Co.K 1st Lt.
Wade, J.C. AL Cav. Barbiere's Bn. Bowie's Co.
Wade, J.C. SC 11th Res. Co.F Sgt.
Wade, J.C. TN 46th Inf. Co.F Sgt.
Wade, J.C. VA 3rd Res. Co.H
Wade, J.D. AR 38th Inf. Co.K
Wade, J.D. GA 12th (Wright's) Cav. (St.Guards) Stubb's Co.
Wade, J.D. GA 1st Reg. Co.B
Wade, J.D. MS 2nd Cav. AQM
Wade, J.D. TX Inf. Cunningham's Co. Sgt.
Wade, J.D. Gen. & Staff Capt.,QM
Wade, J. Dallas AL 10th Cav. Co.I
Wade, J.E. VA 10th Cav. Co.K
Wade, J.E. VA 42nd Inf. Co.K

Wade, Jerry 1st Choctaw & Chickasaw Mtd.Rifles Co.A
Wade, Jerry 1st Choctaw & Chickasaw Mtd.Rifles 2nd Co.C
Wade, Jerry 1st Choctaw & Chickasaw Mtd.Rifles 2nd Co.D Capt.
Wade, Jesse GA Lt.Arty. Anderson's Btty.
Wade, Jesse GA 1st Inf. (St.Guards) Co.I
Wade, Jesse GA 7th Inf. (St.Guards) Co.K
Wade, Jesse GA 18th Inf. Co.D
Wade, Jesse SC 7th Inf. Co.G
Wade, Jesse TX 20th Inf. Co.A
Wade, Jesse VA 8th Cav. 2nd Co.D
Wade, Jesse 1st Choctaw & Chickasaw Mtd.Rifles 2nd Co.H
Wade, Jesse L. VA 36th Inf. Co.A
Wade, Jessy GA 8th Inf. Co.G
Wade, J.F. TN 3rd (Forrest's) Cav. Co.D
Wade, J.F. TN 8th (Smith's) Cav. Co.A
Wade, J.F. TN 12th (Green's) Cav. Co.G Cpl.
Wade, J.G. TN 45th Inf. Co.H Cpl.
Wade, J.G. TX Cav. 1st Bn.St.Troops Co.A 2nd Lt.
Wade, J.H. GA 10th Mil.
Wade, J.H. MS 2nd St.Cav. Co.E
Wade, J.H. SC 16th Inf. Co.G
Wade, J.H. TN 28th (Cons.) Inf. Co.B 1st Sgt.
Wade, J.J. AR Inf. Cocke's Regt. Co.G
Wade, J.J. VA 3rd Res. Co.G
Wade, J.J. Gen. & Staff Surg.
Wade, J.K. GA 12th (Robinson's) Cav. (St.Guards) Co.H
Wade, J.K.P. KY 12th Cav. Co.A
Wade, J.K.P. KY 8th Mtd.Inf. Co.B
Wade, J.L. GA 8th Inf. Co.H
Wade, J.L. TN 47th Inf. Co.B 1st Sgt.
Wade, J.M. GA 13th Inf. Sgt.
Wade, J.M. GA 18th Inf. Co.B
Wade, J.M. MS 43rd Inf. Co.F
Wade, J.M. TX Cav. Border's Regt. Co.B
Wade, J.M. VA 36th Inf. ACS
Wade, J.M. VA Arty. Wise Legion
Wade, J.N. AR 5th Inf.
Wade, Joel AL 36th Inf. Co.K
Wade, Joel AL Cp. of Instr. Talladega
Wade, John AL 8th (Hatch's) Cav. Co.K
Wade, John AR 17th (Griffith's) Inf. Co.F Music.
Wade, John AR Inf. Cocke's Regt. Co.B
Wade, John GA Siege Arty. 28th Bn. Co.F
Wade, John GA Inf. 3rd Bn. Co.B
Wade, John GA Inf. 3rd Bn. Co.F
Wade, John GA 37th Inf. Co.B
Wade, John KY 7th Cav. Co.H
Wade, John LA 6th Inf. Co.C
Wade, John MS 2nd Cav.Res. Co.E,D
Wade, John NC 13th Inf. Co.D
Wade, John, Jr. SC 16th Inf. Co.G
Wade, John TN 1st Cav. Co.A
Wade, John TN 48th (Voorhies') Inf.
Wade, John VA 2nd Cav. Co.I
Wade, John Conf.Lt.Arty. Davis' Co. Cpl.
Wade, John A. MS Cav. 24th Bn. Co.C
Wade, John A. MS Arty. (Seven Stars Arty.) Roberts' Co. Sgt.
Wade, John A. VA 24th Cav. Co.B
Wade, John A. VA Cav. 40th Bn. Co.B
Wade, John A. VA Goochland Lt.Arty.
Wade, John A. VA Inf. 25th Bn. Co.B
Wade, John A. VA 36th Inf. 2nd Co.E
Wade, John B. TN 6th (Wheeler's) Cav. Co.C
Wade, John B. TN Cav. 11th Bn. (Gordon's) Co.C
Wade, John B. TN Lt.Arty. Huggins' Co.
Wade, John C. NC 4th Cav. (59th St.Troops) Co.B
Wade, John C. NC 13th Inf. Co.D
Wade, John C. VA Horse Arty. G.W. Brown's Co.
Wade, John C. VA 3rd Inf.Loc.Def. Co.E Capt.
Wade, John C. VA 4th Inf. Co.G Capt.
Wade, John C. VA 4th Res. Co.H
Wade, John D. VA 42nd Inf. Co.F
Wade, John D. VA 46th Inf. 1st Co.G Cpl.
Wade, John E. AR Inf. 4th Bn. Co.B
Wade, John E. GA 61st Inf. Co.F Sgt.
Wade, John E. TN 55th (McKoin's) Inf. Duggan's Co.
Wade, John F. TN 4th (McLemore's) Cav. Co.A
Wade, John F. TN Cav. Jackson's Co.
Wade, John G. KY 3rd Mtd.Inf. Co.E Cpl.
Wade, John G. VA Cav. 1st Bn. Co.A Sgt.
Wade, John G. VA 14th Cav. Co.D Cpl.
Wade, John G. VA Inf. 1st Bn. Co.B
Wade, John G. VA Mil. 179th Regt. Capt.,AQM
Wade, John H. AL St.Res. Palmer's Co.
Wade, John H. AL 27th Inf. Co.H
Wade, John H. GA Arty. 9th Bn. Co.B
Wade, John H. GA 2nd Res. Co.C
Wade, John H. GA Cobb's Legion Co.G
Wade, John H. LA 31st Inf. Co.A Bvt.2nd Lt.
Wade, John H. MO 4th Inf.
Wade, John H. MO 8th Inf. Co.F
Wade, John H. NC 2nd Inf. Co.I
Wade, John H. VA 10th Cav. Co.K Cpl.
Wade, John J. VA Hvy.Arty. 19th Bn. Co.D
Wade, John J. VA 34th Inf. Co.H
Wade, John J. VA 54th Inf. Co.E Lt.Col.
Wade, John Lewis NC 51st Inf. Co.I
Wade, John M. FL 11th Inf. Co.H
Wade, John M. GA Cav. 12th Bn. (St.Guards) Co.C
Wade, John M. GA 36th (Villepigue's) Inf. Co.C Drum.
Wade, John M. GA 61st Inf. Co.F Sgt.
Wade, John M. MS 9th Inf. New Co.G Music.
Wade, John M. NC 3rd Inf. Co.F Music.
Wade, John M. TN 2nd (Ashby's) Cav. Co.D
Wade, John M. TN Cav. 4th Bn. (Branner's) Co.C
Wade, John M. TX 20th Inf. Co.K Cpl.
Wade, John P. AL 63rd Inf. Co.A
Wade, John R. GA 47th Inf. Co.D Cpl.
Wade, John R. MD Arty. 1st Btty.
Wade, John R. NC Inf. Thomas Legion Co.C
Wade, John R. VA 24th Inf. Co.B
Wade, John Rives SC 9th Inf. Co.A Sr.2nd Lt.
Wade, John S. AL 57th Inf. Co.D
Wade, Johnston MO 3rd Cav. Co.E
Wade, John T. VA Lt.Arty. French's Co.
Wade, John T. VA 38th Inf. Co.F
Wade, John T. VA 59th Inf. 3rd Co.D
Wade, John T.S. VA 4th Inf. Co.G
Wade, John V. NC 52nd Inf. Co.E Cpl.
Wade, John W. AR 8th Cav. Co.D 1st Lt.
Wade, John W. AR 9th Inf. Co.C
Wade, John W. AR 14th (McCarver's) Inf. Co.C
Wade, John W. AR 14th (Powers') Inf. Co.C 2nd Lt.
Wade, John W. GA 1st Inf. (St.Guards) Co.E
Wade, John W. MO 10th Inf. Co.A
Wade, John W. NC 1st Cav. (9th St.Troops) Co.B
Wade, John W. TX 3rd Cav. Co.C
Wade, John W. TX 22nd Cav. Co.D,I
Wade, John W. VA 5th Inf. Co.D
Wade, John W. VA Inf. 22nd Bn. Co.H
Wade, John William MS Inf. 1st St.Troops Co.G
Wade, Joseph AL Cav. Lewis' Bn. Co.C
Wade, Joseph LA 27th Inf. Co.C
Wade, Joseph MS Cav. 3rd Bn.Res. Co.B
Wade, Joseph MS 15th Inf. Co.I
Wade, Joseph MS 21st Inf. Co.E
Wade, Joseph A. VA 3rd Inf. Co.A
Wade, Joseph C. AL Cav. Barbiere's Bn. Co.F
Wade, Joseph D. TX 4th Inf. Co.F AQM
Wade, Joseph D. VA 24th Cav. Co.A
Wade, Joseph D. VA Cav. 40th Bn. Co.A
Wade, Joseph E. NC 62nd Inf. Co.I,A
Wade, Joseph H. NC 54th Inf. Co.D
Wade, Joseph H. VA 10th Cav. Co.C
Wade, Joseph J. MS 38th Cav. Surg.
Wade, Joseph N. AR 18th (Marmaduke's) Inf. Co.E
Wade, Joseph T. TN 44th (McKoin's) Inf. Duggan's Co. Sgt.
Wade, Josh GA Lt.Arty. 14th Bn. Co.D
Wade, Josh GA Lt.Arty. King's Btty.
Wade, Joshua AR 30th Inf. Co.M,B Cpl.
Wade, Joshua VA 9th Inf. Co.B
Wade, Josiah TN 55th (McKoin's) Inf. James' Co.
Wade, Josiah D. VA Hvy.Arty. 10th Bn. Co.A
Wade, J.P. VA Cav. 1st Bn. Co.A
Wade, J.R. GA 1st Reg. Co.G Cpl.
Wade, J.R. MS 6th Cav. Co.F
Wade, J.R., Jr. MS Lt.Arty. (Jefferson Arty.) Darden's Co.
Wade, J.R. MS 43rd Inf. Co.F
Wade, J.R. NC 66th Inf. Co.C Cpl.
Wade, J.R. NC Mil. Clark's Sp.Bn. Co.C
Wade, J.R. SC 4th Cav. Co.H
Wade, J.R. SC 12th Inf. Co.I 2nd Lt.
Wade, J.R. VA Inf. 25th Bn. Co.D
Wade, J.R. 20th Conf.Cav. 2nd Co.H 2nd Lt.
Wade, J. Reeves SC 4th Cav. Co.H
Wade, J.S. AL 53rd (Part.Rangers) Co.D
Wade, J.S. TX 4th Cav. Co.E
Wade, J.S. VA 42nd Inf. Co.K
Wade, J.W. AL 53rd (Part.Rangers) Co.F
Wade, J.W. AL 21st Inf. Co.C
Wade, J.W. AR 21st Inf. Co.A 2nd Lt.
Wade, J.W. FL 1st (Res.) Inf. Co.H
Wade, J.W. GA Lt.Arty. Clinch's Btty.
Wade, J.W. MS 6th Cav. Co.E
Wade, J.W. MS 5th Inf. (St.Troops) Co.G Cpl.
Wade, J.W. MS 15th Inf. Co.C Asst.Comsy.
Wade, J.W. TN 17th Inf. Co.B
Wade, J.W. TN 18th Inf. Co.C
Wade, J.W. TX 9th Cav. Co.B
Wade, J.W. TX 10th Field Btty.

Wade, J.W. VA 2nd Arty. Co.H
Wade, Kincheon SC 2nd Bn.S.S. Co.A
Wade, Kinchon SC Arty. Manigault's Bn. 1st Co.B
Wade, L. AL 11th Cav. Co.K
Wade, L.A. NC 51st Inf. Co.K
Wade, Lawrence MS Lt.Arty. (Jefferson Arty.) Darden's Co.
Wade, L.B. TN 2nd (Smith's) Cav. Thomasson's Co.
Wade, L.E. MS 11th (Perrin's) Cav. Co.F
Wade, Ledwell VA 74th Mil. Co.E
Wade, Lemuel N. NC 2nd Cav. (19th St.Troops) Co.G
Wade, Leonidas 1st Choctaw & Chickasaw Mtd.Rifles Co.G
Wade, Leroy GA 47th Inf. Co.D
Wade, Levi G. GA 36th (Broyles') Inf. Co.G
Wade, Lewis C. AL Lt.Arty. Hurt's Btty.
Wade, Lewis E. GA 12th Inf. Co.F
Wade, Lewis H. FL 5th Inf. Co.A
Wade, Lidwell J. VA Hvy.Arty. A.J. Jones' Co.
Wade, Littleton R. NC 32nd Inf. Co.E
Wade, Loyd H. GA Arty. 9th Bn. Co.B
Wade, L.R. AL 19th Inf. Co.G 1st Lt.
Wade, L.R. GA 18th Inf. Co.M 1st Lt.
Wade, L.R. GA 28th Inf. Co.F Capt.
Wade, L.S. TN 19th & 20th (Cons.) Cav. Co.K Cpl.
Wade, L.S. TN 12th Inf. Co.H 2nd Lt.
Wade, L.S. TN 12th (Cons.) Inf. Co.K 2nd Lt.
Wade, Lucius P. NC 57th Inf. Co.C Cpl.
Wade, Luke VA 59th Inf. 1st Co.G
Wade, Luke R. VA 6th Cav. 2nd Co.E
Wade, Lusby VA Loc.Res.
Wade, Luther R. VA 52nd Inf. Co.I
Wade, Lycurgus S. MS 2nd Part.Rangers Co.E Sgt.
Wade, M. KY 3rd Bn.Mtd.Rifles Co.B
Wade, M.A. TX Cav. 3rd (Yager's) Bn. Co.D
Wade, Marion TX 3rd Cav. Co.C
Wade, Marshal VA 2nd Cav. Co.D Capt.
Wade, Marshall M. MS 31st Inf. Co.I
Wade, Martin KY 9th Cav. Co.B
Wade, Martin L. KY 1st (Helm's) Cav. Co.B
Wade, Martin T. VA Hvy.Arty. A.J. Jones' Co.
Wade, Mat G. VA Lt.Arty. Carrington's Co.
Wade, Matthew D. AL 49th Inf. Co.G
Wade, M.C. AL 9th (Malone's) Cav. Co.D Sgt.
Wade, M.C. GA 1st (Olmstead's) Inf. Co.G Sgt.Maj.
Wade, M.C. SC 16th Inf. Co.G
Wade, McGrady TX 20th Cav. Co.B
Wade, M.D. SC 1st Arty. Co.F
Wade, Micajah G. GA 27th Inf. Co.D
Wade, Micajah T. MS Arty. (Seven Stars Arty.) Roberts' Co. Sr.2nd Lt.
Wade, Mikael J. AL 12th Inf. Co.H
Wade, Mike VA Inf. 1st Bn.Loc.Def. Co.C
Wade, Miles P. VA 59th Inf. 3rd Co.D
Wade, Milo P. AL 6th Inf. Co.F
Wade, Milton C. GA Hvy.Arty. 22nd Bn. Co.C 1st Lt.
Wade, Milton T. AL 4th (Russell's) Cav.
Wade, Mitchel A. VA 59th Inf. 3rd Co.D
Wade, Mitchell G. GA 11th Inf. Co.A
Wade, M.J. LA Inf. 7th Bn. Co.A
Wade, M.J. LA 15th Inf. Co.K
Wade, M.M. GA Conscr.
Wade, M.M. MS 4th Inf. Co.G
Wade, Morgan VA Inf. 26th Bn. Co.E
Wade, Moses T. NC 12th Inf. Co.D,B
Wade, M.W. SC 4th Cav. Co.B
Wade, N. GA 40th Inf. Co.E
Wade, N. MS 12th Cav. Co.I
Wade, Nathaniel GA 54th Inf. Co.H
Wade, Needham B. TN 34th Inf. Co.I
Wade, Newton GA Inf. 8th Bn. Co.D
Wade, Newton TN 3rd (Forrest's) Cav. Co.G
Wade, Newton TN 12th (Green's) Cav. Co.A
Wade, N.L. VA 6th Cav. Co.G
Wade, Noah F. MO 10th Inf. Co.D
Wade, Norval G. MS 8th Inf. Co.E Cpl.
Wade, Norvell G. TX 17th Cav. Co.H
Wade, Nowland D. GA 51st Inf. Co.K Sgt.
Wade, N.T. MS 18th Inf. Co.I
Wade, O. KY Morgan's Men Beck's Co.
Wade, O.B. TX Cav. 2nd Bn.St.Troops Wilson's Co.
Wade, Obediah KY 5th Cav. Co.E
Wade, O.H. TN 12th (Green's) Cav. Co.G Jr.2nd Lt.
Wade, O.H. TN 47th Inf. Co.G
Wade, Oran TX 17th Inf. Co.D Jr.2nd Lt.
Wade, Owen, Jr. VA Inf. 7th Bn.Loc.Def. Co.C
Wade, Owen VA 64th Mtd.Inf. Franklin's Co.
Wade, P. SC Mil.Arty. 1st Regt. Parker's Co.
Wade, P.A. SC Lt.Arty. Parker's Co. (Marion Arty.)
Wade, Patrick TN 34th Inf. Co.F Music.
Wade, Patrick H. GA Lt.Arty. (Arsenal Btty.) Hudson's Co.
Wade, P.E. MS 43rd Inf. Co.F
Wade, Perry GA 64th Inf. Co.C Cpl.
Wade, Perry H. GA 5th Cav. Cpl.
Wade, Peter D. VA 42nd Inf. Co.F
Wade, Peter G. LA 12th Inf. Co.C,E
Wade, Peyton L. GA 1st Reg. Co.M,K 1st Lt.
Wade, Peyton W. GA 6th Inf. Co.G
Wade, P.G. LA 3rd (Harrison's) Cav. Co.E
Wade, P.H. GA Inf. (Loc.Def.) Hamlet's Co.
Wade, P.H. KY 12th Cav. Co.A
Wade, P.H. KY 8th Mtd.Inf. Co.B
Wade, Pickens Choctaw Inf. Wilkins' Co.
Wade, Pinkney NC 33rd Inf. Co.K
Wade, P.J. AL Cav. Moreland's Regt. Co.C
Wade, P.L. GA 1st Inf. (St.Guards) Co.I
Wade, P.L. TN 18th Inf. Co.C
Wade, P.L. TN 23rd Inf. 2nd Co.F
Wade, Pleasant MO 12th Cav. Co.B
Wade, Pleasant NC 2nd Arty. (36th St.Troops) Co.B
Wade, Pleasant NC Lt.Arty. 13th Bn. Co.B
Wade, Pleasant J. AL 14th Cav. Co.A
Wade, Polk D. KY 7th Cav. Co.G
Wade, Pope KY 11th Cav. Co.H
Wade, P.R. MS 6th Cav. Co.F Sgt.
Wade, P.T. TX Cav. 3rd Regt.St.Troops Co.A
Wade, P.T. TX 24th Cav. Co.F Sgt.
Wade, R. AL 30th Inf. Co.H
Wade, R. MO Lt.Arty. H.M. Bledsoe's Co.
Wade, R. SC 11th Inf. Co.G
Wade, R.A. GA 32nd Inf. Co.B
Wade, R.A. MS 18th Cav. Co.A
Wade, R.A. TN 5th Inf. 2nd Co.B
Wade, Ramey J. GA 52nd Inf. Co.A
Wade, Ranson C. LA Cav. Cole's Co.
Wade, R.C. TN 7th (Duckworth's) Cav. Co.F
Wade, R.C. 3rd Conf.Eng.Troops Co.C
Wade, R.C. Forrest's Scouts T. Henderson's Co.,CSA
Wade, R.D. NC Wallace's Co. (Wilmington RR Guard)
Wade, Reuben SC 3rd Res. Co.G
Wade, R.H. AL 5th Inf. New Co.I
Wade, R.H. KY 7th Mtd.Inf. Co.H
Wade, R.H. MS 2nd (Davidson's) Inf. Co.F
Wade, R.H. NC 21st Inf. Co.G
Wade, R.H. TN 12th Inf. Co.G 1st Sgt.
Wade, R.H. TN 12th (Cons.) Inf. Co.E Sgt.
Wade, R.H. TX 4th Inf. Co.I
Wade, Richard LA 8th Inf. Co.H
Wade, Richard TN 1st (Carter's) Cav. Co.E
Wade, Richard VA Inf. Cohoon's Bn. Co.B
Wade, Richard C. AL 3rd Bn.Res. Co.B 2nd Lt.
Wade, Richard F. AR 23rd Inf. Co.C
Wade, Richard J. SC 14th Inf. Co.H Sgt.
Wade, Richard M. TX 15th Cav. Co.B
Wade, Riley TN 44th (Cons.) Inf. Co.C
Wade, R.J. VA 3rd Res. Co.G
Wade, R.L. Gen. & Staff Capt.,Vol.ADC
Wade, R.M. GA Cav. 2nd Bn. Co.B
Wade, R.M. GA Hvy.Arty. 22nd Bn. Co.D Cpl.
Wade, R.N. GA Cav. 1st Bn.Res. Co.E
Wade, Robert GA 1st Reg. Co.L 2nd Lt.
Wade, Robert GA 8th Inf. Co.E 2nd Lt.
Wade, Robert VA Cav. 47th Bn. Co.A Sgt.
Wade, Robert VA Hvy.Arty. A.J. Jones' Co.
Wade, Robert VA Inf. 1st Bn. Co.D
Wade, Robert VA Inf. 5th Bn. Co.D
Wade, Robert VA 53rd Inf. Co.E
Wade, Robert VA 110th Mil. Saunder's Co.
Wade, Robert C. TN 47th Inf. Co.G
Wade, Robert D. VA 18th Inf. Co.B 2nd Lt.
Wade, Robert G. NC 17th Inf. (2nd Org.) Co.F
Wade, Robert H. LA 25th Inf. Co.A
Wade, Robert H. MS 31st Inf. Co.K
Wade, Robert H. NC 23rd Inf. Co.I
Wade, Robert J. SC 16th Inf. Co.G
Wade, Robert L. VA Rockbridge Cty.Res. Miller's Co.
Wade, Robert M. GA 7th Inf. (St.Guards) Co.K
Wade, Robert T. VA Hvy.Arty. 18th Bn. Co.D
Wade, Robert W. VA Cav. 35th Bn. Co.A
Wade, Robert W. VA Hvy.Arty. 10th Bn. Co.B Cpl.
Wade, Robinson 1st Choctaw & Chickasaw Mtd.Rifles 2nd Co.K
Wade, R. Oscar VA 23rd Cav. Co.M Cpl.
Wade, R.T. TN 14th (Neely's) Cav. Co.H
Wade, R.T. VA 3rd Arty. Co.H
Wade, R.W. GA Cav. 29th Bn. Co.H Capt.
Wade, R.W. LA 17th Inf. Co.I
Wade, S. TN 21st & 22nd (Cons.) Cav. Co.C
Wade, S. Bradford's Corps Scouts & Guards Co.A
Wade, S.A. AL 4th (Roddey's) Cav. Co.F
Wade, S.A. MS 10th Cav. Co.B
Wade, S.A. TN 45th Inf. Co.H 1st Lt.
Wade, Samuel AL 15th Inf. Co.E
Wade, Samuel VA 46th Inf. Co.G

Wade, Samuel A. VA 94th Mil. Co.A
Wade, Samuel B. FL Inf. 2nd Bn. Co.E
Wade, Samuel E. AL 34th Inf.
Wade, Samuel I. VA 2nd Cav. Co.F
Wade, Samuel M. MS 29th Inf. Co.H
Wade, S.B. MS 7th Inf. Co.C
Wade, Seaborn H. GA Hvy.Arty. 22nd Bn. Co.C,E
Wade, Seaborn H. GA Inf. 1st Loc.Troops (Augusta) Co.B Sgt.
Wade, Seat LA 3rd Inf. Co.H
Wade, Seaton MS Inf. 3rd Bn. Co.K Cpl.
Wade, Seaton H. MS 18th Inf. Co.H
Wade, Sebron L. MS 15th Inf. Co.A
Wade, Sidney S. VA 59th Inf. 3rd Co.E
Wade, Sidney S. VA Inf. Gregory's Co.
Wade, Silas 1st Choctaw Mtd.Rifles Co.B
Wade, Silas 1st Choctaw & Chickasaw Mtd.Rifles 2nd Co.B
Wade, Simpson 1st Choctaw Mtd.Rifles Co.I
Wade, S.J. MS Inf. 7th Bn. Co.C
Wade, S.L. MS 1st Cav.Res. Co.G
Wade, S.L. MS 1st (Percy's) Inf. Co.I
Wade, S.M. MS Inf. 2nd St.Troops Co.L
Wade, S.M. TN 22nd (Barteau's) Cav. Co.H
Wade, Solomon GA Lt.Arty. Van Den Corput's Co.
Wade, Solomon GA Inf. 3rd Bn. Co.A
Wade, Solomon VA Cav. Ferguson's Bn. Ferguson's Co., Parks' Co.
Wade, Spottswood P. VA 28th Inf. Co.D
Wade, S.R. MO 5th Cav. Co.H Sgt.
Wade, S.S. VA 14th Cav. Co.I
Wade, S.S. VA Inf. 25th Bn. Co.G
Wade, Stephen F. NC 22nd Inf. Co.E
Wade, Stephen G. GA Phillips' Legion Co.E
Wade, Summy 1st Choctaw & Chickasaw Mtd.Rifles 3rd Co.E 2nd Lt.
Wade, S.W. TX Cav. Benavides' Regt. Co.F
Wade, T. TN 3rd (Forrest's) Cav.
Wade, T.B. GA 1st Inf. (St.Guards) Co.C
Wade, T.B. TN 3rd (Clack's) Inf. Co.F Sgt.
Wade, T.B. 3rd Conf.Cav. Co.C
Wade, Telemicus Weir TX 20th Cav. Co.B,A 2nd Lt.
Wade, Terry U. TX 6th Cav. Co.B 1st Lt.
Wade, T.H. GA Siege Arty. 28th Bn. Co.B
Wade, T.H. KY 2nd Cav.
Wade, T.H. MS 38th Cav. Co.G 2nd Lt.
Wade, Thaddeus M. VA 28th Inf. Co.D
Wade, Thaddeus O. VA 2nd Inf.Loc.Def.
Wade, Thomas AL Inf. 1st Regt. Co.C
Wade, Thomas AL 12th Inf. Co.H
Wade, Thomas AL 16th Inf. Co.A
Wade, Thomas AL 27th Inf. Co.H
Wade, Thomas GA 5th Cav. Co.B
Wade, Thomas MS Inf. 2nd St.Troops Co.L
Wade, Thomas NC Loc.Def. Croom's Co.
Wade, Thomas TX Cav. 2nd Regt.St.Troops Co.F
Wade, Thomas TX Cav. Border's Regt. Co.D
Wade, Thomas TX Cav. Wells' Regt. Co.B
Wade, Thomas VA 22nd Cav. Co.F
Wade, Thomas VA 24th Cav. Co.A
Wade, Thomas, Jr. VA 25th Cav. Co.F
Wade, Thomas VA Cav. 40th Bn. Co.A
Wade, Thomas B. GA 8th Inf.
Wade, Thomas B. MO Inf. Perkins' Bn. Co.F 2nd Lt.
Wade, Thomas B. TN 11th (Holman's) Cav. Co.G
Wade, Thomas B. VA 5th Inf.
Wade, Thomas C. TN 18th Inf. Co.C
Wade, Thomas F. AR 2nd Inf. Co.A Cpl.
Wade, Thos. F. Gen. & Staff Chap.
Wade, Thomas G. GA 12th Mil.
Wade, Thomas G. TN 44th Inf. Co.E
Wade, Thomas H. AL 11th Inf. Co.A
Wade, Thomas H. AL Cp. of Instr. Talladega
Wade, Thomas H. GA 21st Inf. Co.D
Wade, Thomas H. MS 4th Inf. Co.B
Wade, Thomas H. SC 15th Inf. Co.A
Wade, Thomas J. LA 12th Inf. Co.E
Wade, Thomas J. MS 2nd Inf. Co.A
Wade, Thomas J. TN 1st (Feild's) Inf. Co.I
Wade, Thomas J. TX 12th Cav. Co.D
Wade, Thomas J. VA 157th Mil. Co.A
Wade, Thomas L. MS Applewhite's Co. (Vaiden Guards)
Wade, Thomas L. VA 25th Cav. Co.F Sgt.
Wade, Thomas L. VA 6th Bn.Res. Co.C
Wade, Thomas M. VA Lt.Arty. Arch. Graham's Co.
Wade, Thomas M. VA 18th Inf. Co.I
Wade, Thomas W. AR 18th (Marmaduke's) Inf. Co.G
Wade, Thomas W. GA Cav. 2nd Bn. Co.F
Wade, Tindsley D. TX 16th Inf. Co.C
Wade, T.J. AL Cav. Moreland's Regt. Co.B 1st Lt.
Wade, T.J. GA 3rd Cav. Co.B
Wade, T. Jefferson GA 4th Inf. Co.F
Wade, T.L. TN 8th (Smith's) Cav. Co.B
Wade, T.M. MS 1st Bn. Sgt.
Wade, T.M. MS 5th Inf. (St.Troops) Co.G Cpl.
Wade, Tom W. TN 31st Inf. Co.C
Wade, T.P. GA Inf. 1st Loc.Troops (Augusta) Co.G
Wade, T.P. TN 12th (Green's) Cav. Co.G
Wade, T.R. TN 47th Inf. Co.A
Wade, Triplett L. TN Cav. 5th Bn. (McClellan's) Co.F
Wade, T.S. VA 19th Cav. Chap.
Wade, T.U. TX 15th Cav. Co.D
Wade, T.W. 3rd Conf.Inf. Co.G Sgt.
Wade, Tyler GA Inf. 11th Bn. (St.Guards) Co.B
Wade, W. AR Cav. McGehee's Regt. Co.F
Wade, W.A. TN Inf. Spencer's Co.
Wade, Walter P. NC 29th Inf. Co.E
Wade, Walter W. MS Page's Co. (Lexington Guards)
Wade, Washington 1st Choctaw & Chickasaw Mtd.Rifles Co.A
Wade, Washington J. AL 39th Inf. Co.E
Wade, Watson R. MS 15th Inf. Co.A
Wade, W.B. TX Cav. (Dismtd.) Chisum's Regt.
Wade, W.D. MS Inf. 3rd Bn. Co.K
Wade, W.D. SC 1st Cav. Co.C
Wade, W.D. SC 4th Cav. Co.B
Wade, W.D. SC Cav. 10th Bn. Co.A
Wade, W.D. SC 2nd Arty. Co.E
Wade, W.D. SC Inf. Hampton Legion Co.C
Wade, W.D. TN Inf. Spencer's Co.
Wade, W.E. MD Cav. 2nd Bn. Co.A
Wade, W.E. TN 12th (Green's) Cav. Co.G
Wade, W.E. TN 4th Inf. Co.H
Wade, W.E. TN 12th (Cons.) Inf. Co.D
Wade, W.E. TN 22nd Inf. Co.H
Wade, W.E. TN 47th Inf. Co.G
Wade, W.E. VA Cav. Mosby's Regt. (Part. Rangers) Co.A
Wade, Webb TN Inf. 22nd Bn. Co.C,B Sgt.
Wade, W.F. AL 38th Inf. Co.D
Wade, W.G. GA 15th Inf. Co.H
Wade, W.G. TN Lt.Arty. Kain's Co.
Wade, W.G. TN Conscr. (Cp. of Instr.)
Wade, W.H. AR 38th Inf. Co.K
Wade, W.H. FL 1st Inf. Old Co.G
Wade, W.H. GA 24th Inf. Co.K
Wade, W.H. MS Inf. 3rd Bn. (St.Troops) Co.A
Wade, W.H. NC 11th (Bethel Regt.) Inf. Co.B
Wade, W.H. NC 14th Inf. Co.D
Wade, W.H. TN Arty. Bibb's Co.
Wade, W.H. TN 4th Inf. Co.F
Wade, W.H. TN 45th Inf. Co.C 1st Sgt.
Wade, William AL 12th Cav. Co.E
Wade, William AL 53rd (Part.Rangers) Co.A
Wade, William AR 2nd (Dobbin's) Cav.
Wade, William AR 18th Inf. Co.G
Wade, William GA Lt.Arty. 14th Bn. Co.B
Wade, William GA Lt.Arty. Anderson's Btty.
Wade, William GA Arty. (Chatham Arty.) Wheaton's Co.
Wade, William GA 1st (Olmstead's) Inf. Claghorn's Co., Gallie's Co.
Wade, William GA 18th Inf. Co.G
Wade, William GA 37th Inf. Co.B
Wade, William GA 43rd Inf. Co.I
Wade, William GA Conscr.
Wade, William LA Hvy.Arty. 2nd Bn. Co.C
Wade, William MS 17th Inf. Co.I
Wade, William MO Lt.Arty. Walsh's Co. Capt.
Wade, William NC Hvy.Arty. 1st Bn. Co.C
Wade, William NC 45th Inf. Co.I
Wade, William SC 16th Inf. Co.G
Wade, William TN 35th Inf. Co.E
Wade, William TX 17th Cav. Co.D
Wade, William TX 22nd Cav. Co.D,I
Wade, William VA 24th Cav. Co.B
Wade, William VA Hvy.Arty. 10th Bn. Co.C
Wade, William VA Inf. 1st Bn.Loc.Def. Co.E
Wade, William VA 4th Inf. Co.G 1st Lt.,Adj.
Wade, William VA 14th Inf. Co.K
Wade, William VA Inf. Cohoon's Bn. Co.B
Wade, William Brush Bn.
Wade, William Sig.Corps,CSA
Wade, William Gen. & Staff 1st Lt.,Adj.
Wade, William A. AL 38th Inf. Co.E
Wade, William A. NC 32nd Inf. Co.E
Wade, William A. NC 54th Inf. Co.D
Wade, William A. SC Hvy.Arty. 15th (Lucas') Bn. Co.A
Wade, William A. TN 7th Inf. Co.H
Wade, William A. TN 44th (Cons.) Inf. Co.B
Wade, William A. VA Lt.Arty. 12th Bn. Co.C
Wade, William A. VA Inf. 25th Bn. Co.F
Wade, William A. VA 51st Inf. Co.G
Wade, William B. AL 47th Inf. Co.E
Wade, William B. MS 10th Inf. Old Co.D Capt.
Wade, William B. TX 6th Cav. Co.B 1st Sgt.
Wade, William B. 8th (Wade's) Conf.Cav. Col.

Wade, William C. AR 6th Inf. New Co.D
Wade, William C. GA 39th Inf. Co.D
Wade, William C. TN 44th (Cons.) Inf. Co.C Sgt.
Wade, William C. TN 55th (McKoin's) Inf. James' Co.
Wade, William C. VA 8th Inf. Co.B
Wade, William D. AL 13th Inf. Co.F
Wade, William D. TN 44th Inf. Co.E
Wade, William D. TN 44th (Cons.) Inf. Co.B
Wade, William D. VA 24th Cav. Co.A
Wade, William D. VA Cav. 40th Bn. Co.A
Wade, William E. GA 10th Inf. Co.F
Wade, William E. KY 4th Cav. Co.G
Wade, William F. AL 33rd Inf. Co.F
Wade, William F. VA 14th Inf. Co.F
Wade, William G. NC 15th Inf. Co.F
Wade, William G. TX 12th Inf. Co.B
Wade, William H. AL 10th Inf. Co.I
Wade, William H. AL 11th Inf. Co.A
Wade, William H. FL 6th Inf. Co.A
Wade, William H. GA Cav. 12th Bn. (St.Guards) Co.C
Wade, William H. GA 5th Inf. Co.E
Wade, William H. MS 32nd Inf. Co.K
Wade, William H. NC 3rd Bn.Res. Co.C
Wade, William H. NC 8th Sr.Res. Kelly's Co.
Wade, William H. NC 8th Sr.Res. Williams' Co.
Wade, William H. NC 15th Inf. Co.F Music.
Wade, William H. SC 16th & 24th (Cons.) Inf. Co.D
Wade, William H. TN Lt.Arty. Winston's Co. Artif.
Wade, William H. VA 2nd Cav. Co.A
Wade, William H. VA 15th Inf. Co.H
Wade, William H. VA 52nd Inf. Co.H
Wade, William H. VA 53rd Inf. Co.E Cpl.
Wade, William H. VA Inf. Lyneman's Co.
Wade, William J. AR 20th Inf. Co.A
Wade, William J. MO Inf. Perkins' Bn. Co.F
Wade, William Josiah TX 20th Cav. Co.B Black.
Wade, Wm. K. AL Cp. of Instr. Talladega
Wade, William L. 1st Choctaw & Chickasaw Mtd.Rifles 1st Co.K
Wade, William M. AR Willett's Co.
Wade, William M. TN 4th (McLemore's) Cav. Co.A
Wade, William M. TX 10th Inf. Co.K
Wade, William M. VA Courtney Arty.
Wade, William M. VA 16th Inf. Co.F
Wade, William O. VA 25th Cav. Co.F
Wade, William O. VA 28th Inf. Co.E
Wade, William P. GA 1st (Olmstead's) Inf. Co.G
Wade, William P. MO Cav. 3rd Bn. Co.C
Wade, William R. GA 59th Inf. Co.F
Wade, William S. AR 23rd Inf. Co.A 1st Lt.
Wade, William S. GA 54th Inf. Co.G
Wade, William S. VA 5th Inf. Co.D
Wade, William T. AL Cav. Holloway's Co. Sgt.
Wade, William T. AL Jeff Davis Arty.
Wade, William T. KY 3rd Mtd.Inf. Co.H Sgt.
Wade, William T. MO 1st Cav. Co.I
Wade, William T. NC 44th Inf. Co.F 1st Sgt.
Wade, William T. TN 51st (Cons.) Inf. Co.E
Wade, William W. AR 3rd Inf. Co.C
Wade, Willis GA Lt.Arty. Anderson's Btty.
Wade, Willis GA Inf. 3rd Bn. Co.B
Wade, Wilson GA 35th Inf. Co.F
Wade, Winston VA 59th Inf. 3rd Co.E
Wade, W.J. MS 18th Cav. Co.F
Wade, W.L. TN Conscr. (Cp. of Instr.)
Wade, W.M. TN 8th (Smith's) Cav. Co.A
Wade, W.N. VA Inf. 28th Bn. Co.D
Wade, W.N. VA 59th Inf. 3rd Co.I
Wade, W.O. LA 1st (Strawbridge's) Inf. Co.C
Wade, W.O. LA 21st (Kennedy's) Inf. Co.B
Wade, W.O. TX 3rd Cav. Co.C
Wade, Woodson O. TX 17th Cav. Co.D Sgt.
Wade, W.P. GA Inf. 18th Bn. Co.B
Wade, W.P. MO 3rd Cav. Co.C
Wade, W.P. TN 13th Inf. Co.B
Wade, W.R.B. TN 3rd (Clack's) Inf. Co.H
Wade, W.R.B. Central Div. KY Sap. & Min.,CSA
Wade, W.S. AR Cav. McGehee's Regt. Co.D 3rd Lt.
Wade, W.S. AR 26th Inf. Co.K
Wade, W.S. LA Siege Train Bn. Co.C Cpl.
Wade, W.S. LA Mil. Chalmette Regt.
Wade, W.S. MS 41st Inf. Co.L
Wade, W.T. AL 21st Inf. Co.C
Wade, W.T. GA 23rd Inf. Co.H
Wade, W.T. GA 60th Inf. Co.I
Wade, W.T. TN 52nd Inf. Co.H 2nd Lt.
Wade, W.W. AL 9th (Malone's) Cav. Co.I
Wade, W.W. KY 9th Cav. Co.B
Wade, W.W. MS Lt.Arty. (Jefferson Arty.) Darden's Co. QMSgt.
Wade, W.W. MS 12th Inf. Co.B
Wade, W.W. TN 3rd (Forrest's) Cav. Co.I
Wade, W.W. TN 12th (Green's) Cav. Co.G
Wade, W.W. TN 19th & 20th (Cons.) Cav. Co.E
Wade, W.W. TN 20th (Russell's) Cav. Co.H
Wade, W.W. TN 17th Inf. Co.H
Wade, W.W. TX Cav. Waller's Regt. Dunn's Co.
Wade, Z.A. VA 51st Inf. Co.E
Wade, Zachariah B. 1st Conf.Inf. 2nd Co.E
Wade, Z.B. GA 36th (Villepigue's) Inf. Co.C
Wadel, Alexander LA Miles' Legion Co.C
Wadel, H. GA 54th Inf. Co.F
Wadell, Francis M. VA 12th Inf. Co.A
Wadell, W.H. GA 65th Inf. Co.G
Waden, Fred J. AL 22nd Inf. Co.H
Waden, Robert H. VA 54th Mil. Co.G
Wades, Jeames GA 4th Cav. (St.Guards) McDonald's Co.
Wadford, Alexander NC 30th Inf. Co.D,H
Wadford, Alex D. NC 47th Inf. Co.F
Wadford, C.M. SC Inf. 9th Bn. Co.F
Wadford, C.M. SC 14th Inf. Co.A
Wadford, E. FL Conscr.
Wadford, E.F. NC 48th Inf. Co.D
Wadford, H.G. SC Inf. 9th Bn. Co.F
Wadford, J.C. SC Inf. 9th Bn. Co.F
Wadford, Jesse SC Inf. 9th Bn. Co.F
Wadford, J.N. SC 14th Inf. Co.A
Wadford, John SC 14th Inf. Co.A
Wadford, J.R. SC 14th Inf. Co.A
Wadford, Lazarus SC 21st Inf. Co.K
Wadford, Michael FL Inf. 2nd Bn. Co.E
Wadford, N. SC 3rd St.Troops Co.D
Wadford, Nelson SC 8th Inf. Co.E
Wadford, Seaborn GA 48th Inf. Co.I Sgt.
Wadford, S.M. SC Inf. 9th Bn. Co.F
Wadford, W. Fletcher AL 39th Inf. Co.D Sgt.
Wadford, William FL 6th Inf. Co.F
Wadford, William GA Inf. (Richmond Factory Guards) Barney's Co.
Wadford, William NC 14th Inf. Co.E
Wadford, William C. SC 21st Inf. Co.K
Wadgymeir, Arthur Gen. & Staff, Ord. 2nd Lt.
Wadill, James H. MS 31st Inf. Co.A
Wadill, S. TX Cav. Waller's Regt. Dunn's Co.
Wadkin, N.M. AL 15th Inf. Co.F
Wadkins, A.B. MS 4th Inf.
Wadkins, Abner, Jr. GA Smith's Legion Co.B
Wadkins, Abner, Sr. GA Smith's Legion Co.B
Wadkins, Abrahm B. VA 54th Inf. Co.A Cpl.
Wadkins, A.D. AL Cp. of Instr. Talladega
Wadkins, A.J. AL 26th (O'Neal's) Inf. Co.H Cpl.
Wadkins, A.J. TX 14th Inf. Co.H
Wadkins, Albert SC Arty. Fickling's Co. (Brooks Lt.Arty.)
Wadkins, Alva M. NC 18th Inf. Co.H
Wadkins, Ambrose KY 5th Mtd.Inf. Co.C
Wadkins, Ananias TN 40th Inf. Co.A
Wadkins, Andrew AR 8th Inf. New Co.E Lt.
Wadkins, B. AR 2nd Cav. Co.E
Wadkins, B. MO Cav. Slayback's Regt. Co.B
Wadkins, B. NC Lt.Arty. 13th Bn. Co.F
Wadkins, B.E. SC 5th Bn.Res. Co.D
Wadkins, Benet MO Cav. Freeman's Regt. Co.D
Wadkins, Berry NC 1st Jr.Res. Co.D
Wadkins, Bolen NC 3rd Arty. (40th St.Troops) Co.H
Wadkins, Bryant GA 22nd Inf. Co.C
Wadkins, Burden NC 5th Inf. Co.C
Wadkins, Calvin GA 37th Inf. Co.B
Wadkins, Charles H. MS 24th Inf. Co.H,I
Wadkins, D.A. SC 5th Bn.Res. Co.D
Wadkins, Daniel GA 25th Inf. Co.E
Wadkins, Darden H. VA 13th Cav. Co.A
Wadkins, David AL Cav. Moreland's Regt. Co.B
Wadkins, David GA 24th Inf. Co.D
Wadkins, David NC 5th Inf. Co.C
Wadkins, David A. LA 31st Inf. Co.I
Wadkins, David J. GA 3rd Inf. Co.I
Wadkins, D.M. AR Cav. Gordon's Regt. Co.H
Wadkins, E. KY 3rd Bn.Mtd.Rifles Co.B Cpl.
Wadkins, Edward H. MS 17th Inf. Co.H
Wadkins, Enoch TN 41st Inf. Co.B
Wadkins, Ephraim TN 40th Inf. Co.A
Wadkins, Euc. K. AR 33rd Inf. Co.I
Wadkins, F. Gen. & Staff Capt.,QM
Wadkins, Fedrick MO 4th Cav. Co.B
Wadkins, F.M. AL 53rd (Part.Rangers) Co.C Cpl.
Wadkins, Francis M. AR Cav. Gordon's Regt.
Wadkins, G.D. TX 19th Inf. Co.G
Wadkins, General J. AL 33rd Inf. Co.B
Wadkins, George TX 11th Inf.
Wadkins, George E. NC 49th Inf. Co.A
Wadkins, George W. FL 4th Inf. Co.A 3rd Lt.
Wadkins, George W. MS 11th (Perrin's) Cav. Co.B
Wadkins, Geo. W. TX 12th Cav. Co.H
Wadkins, Green W. TX 6th Cav. Co.G
Wadkins, G.W. FL 8th Inf. Co.A Sgt.

Wadkins, G.W. GA 7th Inf. (St.Guards) Co.G
Wadkins, G.W. KY 12th Cav. Co.A
Wadkins, H. GA 5th Res. Co.D
Wadkins, Henry GA Inf. 11th Bn. (St.Guards) Co.B
Wadkins, Henry N. 1st Cherokee Mtd.Vol. 1st Co.K
Wadkins, H.H. SC 4th Bn.Res. Co.D
Wadkins, H.H. SC 9th Res. Co.A
Wadkins, H.N. MO Inf. Clark's Regt. Co.D
Wadkins, Hugh MO Cav. 11th Regt.St.Guard Co.C 2nd Lt.
Wadkins, Isaac AL Arty. 1st Bn. Co.B
Wadkins, J. AR 23rd Inf. Co.I
Wadkins, J. VA Cav. 36th Bn. Co.D
Wadkins, Jackson C. GA 41st Inf. Co.B
Wadkins, Jacob AL 37th Inf. Co.K
Wadkins, Jacob GA 12th Cav. Co.D
Wadkins, James AR 45th Mil. Co.F
Wadkins, James GA 3rd Cav. (St.Guards) Co.E
Wadkins, James GA 10th Cav. Co.A
Wadkins, James 1st Conf.Cav. 2nd Co.B
Wadkins, James 7th Conf.Cav. Co.A
Wadkins, James H. AR 33rd Inf. Co.I
Wadkins, James H. GA 62nd Cav. Co.E
Wadkins, James M. MS 24th Inf. Co.H,I
Wadkins, James M. TN 44th (Cons.) Inf. Co.E
Wadkins, J.B. NC 11th (Bethel Regt.) Inf. Co.D
Wadkins, J.C. GA Inf. 3rd Bn. Co.F
Wadkins, J.E. GA 19th Inf. Co.D
Wadkins, J.F. MS 1st (Patton's) Inf. Co.I
Wadkins, J.J. AL 3rd Res. Co.G
Wadkins, Joel MO 4th Cav. Co.B
Wadkins, John GA 52nd Inf. Co.A
Wadkins, John GA 52nd Inf. Co.H
Wadkins, John KY 5th Mtd.Inf. Co.C
Wadkins, John MS 14th (Cons.) Inf. Co.K
Wadkins, John MO Inf. Perkins' Bn. Co.C
Wadkins, John NC Jones' Co. (Supp.Force)
Wadkins, John SC 1st Arty. Co.K
Wadkins, John A. TX 15th Cav. Co.A
Wadkins, Johnathan W. AR 17th (Lemoyne's) Inf. Co.B
Wadkins, John C. GA 37th Inf. Co.B
Wadkins, John H. NC 3rd Arty. (40th St.Troops) Co.H
Wadkins, John H. NC Lt.Arty. 13th Bn. Co.F Bugler
Wadkins, John M. AR 1st Mtd.Rifles Co.C
Wadkins, John M. KY Cav. 1st Bn. Co.A
Wadkins, John M. NC 49th Inf. Co.A
Wadkins, John W. NC Hvy.Arty. 10th Bn. Co.D,C
Wadkins, John W. NC 54th Inf. Co.G
Wadkins, Joseph GA 7th Inf. (St.Guards) Co.G Cpl.
Wadkins, Joseph GA Smith's Legion Co.B
Wadkins, Joseph KY 5th Mtd.Inf. Co.C
Wadkins, Joseph TN 4th (McLemore's) Cav. Co.E
Wadkins, Joshua GA Smith's Legion Co.B
Wadkins, J.P. TN Inf. Nashville Bn. Cattles' Co. Sgt.
Wadkins, J.R. TX Cav. 1st Regt.St.Troops Co.B
Wadkins, J.S. GA 11th Inf. Co.D
Wadkins, J.S. GA 23rd Inf. Co.D
Wadkins, J.T. AL 29th Inf. Co.I Sgt.
Wadkins, J.T. SC 2nd Rifles Co.B
Wadkins, J.T. TN 40th Inf. Co.A
Wadkins, J.W. KY 7th Cav. Co.B
Wadkins, Kelley R. NC 18th Inf. Co.H
Wadkins, L.C. AL 14th Inf. Co.B
Wadkins, Lemuel GA 36th (Broyles') Inf. Co.B
Wadkins, Lewis GA Inf. 3rd Bn. Co.F
Wadkins, Marion TX 1st (Yager's) Cav. Co.G
Wadkins, Marion TX Cav. 8th (Taylor's) Bn. Co.A
Wadkins, M.C. GA Smith's Legion Co.B
Wadkins, Melville M. GA 37th Inf. Co.B
Wadkins, M.M. GA Inf. 3rd Bn. Co.F
Wadkins, Orien W. NC 3rd Arty. (40th St.Troops) Co.F
Wadkins, P. TX 33rd Cav. Co.K
Wadkins, R.O. AL 8th Inf. Co.E
Wadkins, R.R. NC 4th Bn.Jr.Res. Co.D
Wadkins, Samuel GA 52nd Inf. Co.E
Wadkins, Samuel C. AL 42nd Inf. Co.E
Wadkins, Samuel G. MS 17th Inf. Co.H
Wadkins, S.O. AL Talladega Cty.Res. G.M. Gamble's Co.
Wadkins, S.P. AL Talladega Cty.Res. G.M. Gamble's Co.
Wadkins, S.R. GA 27th Inf. Co.C
Wadkins, Thomas MS Cav. 3rd Bn. (Ashcraft's) Co.D
Wadkins, Thomas SC 4th St.Troops Co.C
Wadkins, Thomas TN 8th (Smith's) Cav. Co.H
Wadkins, T.W. VA Conscr. Cp. Lee
Wadkins, Warren W. NC Walker's Bn. Thomas' Legion Co.B
Wadkins, Washington L. LA 12th Inf. Co.L
Wadkins, W.C. TN 19th & 20th (Cons.) Cav. Co.D
Wadkins, W.C. TN 20th (Russell's) Cav. Co.F
Wadkins, W.F. TN Inf. Nashville Bn. Cattles' Co.
Wadkins, Wiley GA 43rd Inf. Co.K
Wadkins, Wiley SC 4th St.Troops Co.C
Wadkins, William KY 10th (Diamond's) Cav. Co.E
Wadkins, William KY 5th Mtd.Inf. Co.C
Wadkins, William MS Cav. 1st Bn. (Montgomery's) St.Troops Hammond's Co.
Wadkins, William NC Lt.Arty. 13th Bn. Co.F
Wadkins, William C. NC 54th Inf. Co.G
Wadkins, William H. GA 52nd Inf. Co.H
Wadkins, William H. MS 34th Inf. Co.I
Wadkins, William H. NC 42nd Inf. Co.E
Wadkins, William S. MO 4th Cav. Co.E
Wadkins, William W. TX 14th Cav. Co.H
Wadkins, W.J. NC 2nd Inf. Co.H
Wadkins, W.M. GA 23rd Inf. Co.A,B
Wadkins, W.R.D. GA 65th Inf. Co.A
Wadkins, W.W. LA Inf.Cons.Crescent Regt. Co.E
Wadkins, W.W. MS 27th Inf. Co.E
Wadkins, Z. TN 45th Inf. Co.B
Wadland, James H. TN 7th Cav. Co.B
Wadlaw, J.M. MS 7th Cav. Co.F Sgt.
Wadle, Anderson J. VA 25th Cav. Co.I
Wadle, John R. SC 27th Inf. Co.B
Wadle, Josiah VA 64th Mtd.Inf. Co.I
Wadlee, H.S. GA Cobb's Legion Co.C
Wadley, A.W. TN 21st (Wilson's) Cav. Co.H
Wadley, B.F. MO Cav. Snider's Bn. Co.E
Wadley, B.L. KY 7th Mtd.Inf. Co.A Cpl.
Wadley, Caswell H. TN 45th Inf. Co.I Maj.
Wadley, C.T. KY 2nd (Woodward's) Cav. Co.A
Wadley, David C. TN 27th Inf. Co.I
Wadley, D.M. AR 37th Inf. Co.H
Wadley, Felix W. TN 27th Inf. Co.I 2nd Lt.
Wadley, F.M. KY 7th Mtd.Inf. Co.A
Wadley, F.M. MO Cav. Jackman's Regt. Co.C
Wadley, Francis M. MO 3rd Cav. Co.E Sgt.
Wadley, F.W. Forrest's Scouts T.N. Kizer's Co.,CSA
Wadley, G.A. TN 51st Inf. Co.F Sgt.
Wadley, G.G. AR 38th Inf. Co.F
Wadley, G.H. TN 51st (Cons.) Inf. Co.F
Wadley, Henry A. TN 18th (Newsom's) Cav. Co.I
Wadley, H.S. KY 7th Mtd. Inf. Co.A
Wadley, James M. MO Cav. Slayback's Regt. Co.D Sgt.
Wadley, J.E. TN 45th Inf. Co.D
Wadley, J.G. TX 17th Cons.Dismtd.Cav. Co.H
Wadley, J.L. TN 21st (Wilson's) Cav. Co.C Cpl.
Wadley, J.L. TN 51st Inf. Co.F
Wadley, J.L. TN 51st (Cons.) Inf. Co.F
Wadley, John TN 55th (Brown's) Inf. Co.E 1st Lt.
Wadley, Joseph G. TX 15th Cav. Co.F
Wadley, Samuel VA Lt.Arty. Barr's Co.
Wadley, Soloman H. AR 38th Inf. Co.F
Wadley, Thomas J. TN 17th Inf. Co.F
Wadley, W.A. TN 19th & 20th (Cons.) Cav. Co.C
Wadley, Washington GA 1st (Ramsey's) Inf.
Wadley, W.H. 4th Conf.Eng.Troops
Wadley, William MO Inf. Clark's Regt. Co.H
Wadley, William F. MO Cav. Slayback's Regt. Co.D
Wadley, William H. AR 32nd Inf. Co.A
Wadley, William H. AR 36th Inf. Co.H
Wadley, Wm. M. Gen. & Staff,PACS Col.
Wadley, William O. LA 3rd Inf. Co.A
Wadley, William R. TN 27th Inf. Co.I Cpl.
Wadley, William T. AR 27th Inf. Old Co.C
Wadley, W.L. AR Inf. Cocke's Regt. Co.G
Wadley, W.S. AR Cav. Harrell's Bn. Co.D
Wadlington, A. MS Cav. 2nd Bn.Res. Co.I
Wadlington, Augustus B. MS 30th Inf. Co.K Cpl.
Wadlington, B. MS 4th Inf. Co.H
Wadlington, B.J. MS Cav. 3rd Bn.Res. Co.A
Wadlington, C.H. KY 3rd Mtd.Inf. Co.C
Wadlington, D.M. Gen. & Staff Surg.
Wadlington, F. KY 3rd Mtd.Inf. 1st Co.F
Wadlington, F.M. KY Lt.Arty. Cobb's Co.
Wadlington, F.T. AR 2nd Cav. Co.C
Wadlington, George A. VA 57th Inf. Co.D
Wadlington, James C. MS 1st Lt.Arty. Co.L
Wadlington, James C. MS 11th Inf. Co.K
Wadlington, James M. TX 13th Vol. 2nd Co.I,B Cpl.
Wadlington, Julius C. NC 21st Inf. Co.D
Wadlington, M.C. TN Cav. Newsom's Regt. Lipscomb's Co.
Wadlington, O.S. LA 3rd Inf. Co.E
Wadlington, Pat KY 3rd Mtd.Inf. Co.E

Wadlington, Price P. LA Hvy.Arty. 2nd Bn. Co.A
Wadlington, Price P. TN 3rd (Forrest's) Cav. Co.A
Wadlington, Thomas G. LA 14th Inf. Co.I
Wadlington, T.R. MS 28th Cav. Co.B
Wadlington, W. MS 5th Cav. Co.E
Wadlington, W. MS 18th Cav. Co.I
Wadlington, Waymon KY 4th Mtd.Inf. Co.G Sgt.
Wadlington, W. Presley TN 1st (Feild's) Inf. Co.A
Wadlington, W.S. TX Cav. Crump's Regt. Co.A
Wadlow, Charles C. MO Pollock's Regt.
Wadlow, John B. MO Pollock's Regt.
Wadlow, William SC Inf. 3rd Bn. Co.F
Wadly, H.J. AL 31st Inf. Co.E
Wadman, Francis AR 9th Inf. Co.E
Wadray, J.W. SC 1st Regt. Charleston Guard Co.A Sgt.
Wadrope, William NC Cav. 5th Bn. Co.A
Wadsen, W.N. GA 26th Inf. Co.I
Wadsick, F. TX Cav. Mann's Bn. Cox's Co.
Wadson, James S. GA Arty. 9th Bn. Co.B
Wadsow, J.T. TN 5th Inf. Co.L
Wadsworth, --- GA Inf. (NonConscr.) Howard's Co.
Wadsworth, A. GA 5th Inf. Co.B
Wadsworth, A. SC 1st Bn.
Wadsworth, A.H. AL 25th Inf. Co.F
Wadsworth, Alexander NC 26th Inf. Co.H
Wadsworth, Alphonzo GA Inf. 25th Bn. (Prov.Guard) Co.A Music.
Wadsworth, Alphonzo Conf.Inf. 1st Bn. 2nd Co.A
Wadsworth, Andrew J. GA Lt.Arty. Scogin's Btty. (Griffin Lt.Arty.)
Wadsworth, Archibald G. GA Lt.Arty. Scogin's Btty. (Griffin Lt.Arty.)
Wadsworth, B.D. FL 2nd Cav. Co.I
Wadsworth, Benj. AL 15th Inf. Co.G
Wadsworth, Berry AL 15th Inf. Co.G
Wadsworth, C.J. GA Hvy.Arty. 22nd Bn. Co.B Music.
Wadsworth, C.T. AL 33rd Inf. Co.D Sgt.
Wadsworth, D. MS 6th Inf. Co.K
Wadsworth, David AR 35th Inf. Co.E
Wadsworth, D.F. GA Inf. 1st City Bn. (Columbus) Co.B
Wadsworth, D.S. SC Inf. 9th Bn. Co.E,F Capt.
Wadsworth, D.S. SC 26th Inf. Co.F Capt.
Wadsworth, Edward GA Inf. (Loc.Def.) Whiteside's Nav.Bn. Co.A
Wadsworth, Eli GA Cav. Nelson's Ind.Co.
Wadsworth, Eli NC 35th Inf. Co.I
Wadsworth, Enoch NC 1st Arty. (10th St.Troops) Co.B Sgt.
Wadsworth, F.J. GA 27th Inf. Co.G
Wadsworth, F.L. AL 60th Inf. Co.F
Wadsworth, F.L. AL 1st Bn. Hilliard's Legion Vol. Co.A
Wadsworth, Francis L. AL 59th Inf. Co.B 1st Lt.
Wadsworth, Frank GA Cav. Nelson's Ind.Co. Cpl.
Wadsworth, George NC 35th Inf. Co.C
Wadsworth, G.L. NC Mil. Clark's Sp.Bn. Co.B
Wadsworth, H. GA Siege Arty. Campbell's Ind.Co.
Wadsworth, Hiram NC 35th Inf. Co.C
Wadsworth, James A. FL 9th Inf. Co.F
Wadsworth, James B. SC 18th Inf. Co.I
Wadsworth, James C. GA 44th Inf. Co.E
Wadsworth, James F. NC 26th Inf. Co.K
Wadsworth, James M. TX 35th (Brown's) Cav. Co.D
Wadsworth, James W. AL 47th Inf. Co.K
Wadsworth, James W. NC 31st Inf. Co.F
Wadsworth, J.B. SC 8th Inf. Co.E
Wadsworth, J.B. VA 5th Cav. Co.B
Wadsworth, Jesse D. AL 46th Inf. Co.H
Wadsworth, J.G. GA 59th Inf. Co.H
Wadsworth, J.J. NC 61st Inf. Co.E Music.
Wadsworth, J.J. TX 32nd Cav. Co.I
Wadsworth, J.M. SC Lt.Arty. 3rd (Palmetto) Bn. Co.E
Wadsworth, John AL 33rd Inf. Co.D 2nd Lt.
Wadsworth, John AL 40th Inf. Co.F
Wadsworth, John AL Cp. of Instr. Talladega
Wadsworth, John GA 21st Inf. Co.B
Wadsworth, John LA Cav. 18th Bn. Co.A Sgt.
Wadsworth, John NC 48th Inf. Co.E
Wadsworth, John B. NC Inf. 13th Bn. Co.C
Wadsworth, John C. MS 1st Cav. Co.K
Wadsworth, John E. VA Lt.Arty. Moore's Co.
Wadsworth, John M. FL 2nd Inf. Co.L
Wadsworth, John M. FL 10th Inf. Co.C
Wadsworth, John N. AL 15th Inf. Co.F Lt.
Wadsworth, John R. GA Lt.Arty. Scogin's Btty. (Griffin Lt.Arty.)
Wadsworth, John T. Conf.Lt.Arty. Richardson's Bn. Comsy.Sgt.
Wadsworth, John W. LA 9th Inf. Co.I 2nd Lt.
Wadsworth, Joseph C. TX 2nd Cav. Co.I 1st Sgt.
Wadsworth, J.P. AL 63rd Inf. Co.F,H
Wadsworth, J.T. GA Inf. 1st City Bn. (Columbus) Co.B
Wadsworth, J.T. VA Mtd.Riflemen Balfour's Co.
Wadsworth, J.W. FL Lt.Arty. Dyke's Co.
Wadsworth, J.W. TX Cav. McCord's Frontier Regt. Co.F
Wadsworth, L.A. GA Inf. 27th Bn. (NonConscr.) Co.B
Wadsworth, L.H. SC 21st Inf. Co.E Sgt.
Wadsworth, Malchi FL 7th Inf. Co.K
Wadsworth, Malcom S. AL 3rd Cav. Co.H
Wadsworth, Marcus M. TX 35th (Brown's) Cav. Co.D Sgt.
Wadsworth, Micajah J. GA 12th Inf. Co.A
Wadsworth, M.S. GA 45th Inf. Co.E
Wadsworth, M.T. AR 35th Inf. Co.E
Wadsworth, Murdock C. FL 6th Inf. Co.K
Wadsworth, N.B. FL Inf. 2nd Bn. Co.C
Wadsworth, Peter S. NC 26th Inf. Co.H
Wadsworth, Stephen LA Recruit
Wadsworth, T.F. MS 1st Cav. Co.K Sgt.
Wadsworth, Thomas C. FL 3rd Inf. Co.I
Wadsworth, Thomas J. NC 44th Inf. Co.I
Wadsworth, Thomas M. AL 28th Inf. Co.B Sgt.
Wadsworth, Thomas M. TX 35th (Brown's) Cav. Co.D
Wadsworth, T.T. VA Mtd.Riflemen Balfour's Co.
Wadsworth, Vincent C. GA 7th Inf. Co.A
Wadsworth, Vincent E. FL 10th Inf. Co.F
Wadsworth, Walker AL 30th Inf. Co.H
Wadsworth, W.C. GA 27th Inf. Co.G
Wadsworth, W.D. AL Lt.Arty. Goldthwaite's Btty.
Wadsworth, William AL 3rd Cav. Co.H
Wadsworth, William AL 30th Inf. Co.H
Wadsworth, William GA 63rd Inf. Co.E
Wadsworth, William TX 6th Inf. Co.D Cpl.
Wadsworth, William B. TX 17th Cons. Dismtd.Cav. Co.H Sgt.
Wadsworth, William J. NC 46th Inf. Co.H
Wadsworth, William M. GA 45th Inf. Co.E
Wadsworth, William M. MS 16th Inf. Co.A Color Cpl.
Wadsworth, William W. AL 21st Inf. Co.D
Wadsworth, W.J. GA 44th Inf. Co.H
Wadsworth, W.R. MS 1st Lt.Arty.
Wadsworth, W.R. MS Mtd.Inf. (St.Troops) Maxey's Co.
Wadsworth, W.S. GA 45th Inf. Co.E
Wadsworth, W.T. SC Inf. 9th Bn. Co.F 1st Sgt.
Wadsworth, W.W. SC 26th Inf. Co.F
Wadwells, W.W. GA 2nd Cav. Co.K
Wadworth, W.R. 20th Conf.Cav. Co.C
Wadzeck, E.C. TX Cav. Terry's Regt. Co.E Cpl.
Wadzeck, E.C. TX Cav. Waller's Regt. Menard's Co.
Wadzock, Albert L. TX 5th Cav. Co.B
Waebel, John AR 19th Inf. Co.K
Waechtershausen, A. LA Mil. 4th Regt.Eur.Brig. Co.F
Waegner, Charles TX Inf. Timmons' Regt. Co.K Sgt.
Waegner, Charles TX Waul's Legion Co.B Cpl.
Waegner, Fred TX Waul's Legion Co.B
Wael, John VA 1st Inf. Co.E
Waeland, Nicholas TX 3rd Inf. 2nd Co.C
Waelin, D.C. GA 31st Inf.
Waeller, William AR 18th Inf. Co.H
Waesch, August TX 3rd Inf. Co.K
Waeschae, George W. VA 58th Mil. Co.F
Waesche, G.W. VA 6th Cav. Co.D
Waesche, William H. VA 10th Inf. Co.B 1st Lt.
Waesner, Charles F. LA Lewis Regt. Co.B
Waesner, G.W. NC 28th Inf. Co.E
Wafer, Cicero LA 6th Cav. Co.C Sgt.
Wafer, J.T. LA 17th Inf. Co.H
Waffard, Sam NC 6th Sr.Res. Co.C
Waffelaer, A. LA Mil. 3rd Regt.Eur.Brig. (Garde Francaise) 2nd Lt.
Waffelaer, Girard LA Mil. 3rd Regt.Eug.Brig. (Garde Francaise) Co.9
Waffer, William M. AL 55th Vol. Co.E
Wafford, Alexander 2nd Cherokee Mtd.Vol. Co.D Capt.
Wafford, B.J. MS 5th Inf. Co.G
Wafford, C. MS 8th Cav. Co.D
Wafford, Eli AR 11th & 17th (Cons.) Inf. Co.D
Wafford, F. TX 4th Cav. Co.C
Wafford, Green B. TX 4th Cav. Co.A
Wafford, J. AR 1st (Monroe's) Cav. Co.H
Wafford, Jackson B. MO 4th Cav. Co.E
Wafford, James GA 7th Inf. (St.Guards) Co.C
Wafford, James H. TX 36th Cav. Co.B

Wafford, James L. AR Inf. 2nd Bn. Co.B
Wafford, J.B. AR 30th Inf. Co.E
Wafford, J.F. GA Cherokee Legion (St.Guards) Co.K
Wafford, J.G. TX 9th Cav. Co.B
Wafford, John NC 4th Sr.Res. Co.F
Wafford, John A. AR 3rd Cav. Co.I
Wafford, John A. MS 11th (Perrin's) Cav. Co.D
Wafford, John D. GA 38th Inf. Co.N
Wafford, John T. TX 4th Cav. Co.C Sgt.
Wafford, Joseph GA Inf. 40th Bn. Co.E Sgt.
Wafford, Joseph TX 4th Cav. Co.A
Wafford, Joseph L. TX Cav. Hardeman's Regt. Co.E
Wafford, J.T. SC 13th Inf. Co.B
Wafford, J.T. TX Cav. Giddings' Bn. Weisiger's Co.
Wafford, J.W. GA 4th Cav. (St.Guards) Robertson's Co.
Wafford, L.P. TX 2nd Cav. Co.D
Wafford, M. MS 8th Cav. Co.D
Wafford, Marmaduke MS 2nd Inf. Co.K Cpl.
Wafford, M.N. MS 2nd St.Cav. Co.B,F
Wafford, Samuel TX 1st Inf. 2nd Co.K
Wafford, Simeon TN 24th Bn.S.S. Co.A
Wafford, W. TX 4th Cav. Co.C
Wafford, W. TX 16th Inf. Co.H
Wafford, W.H. GA 2nd Cav. Co.H
Wafford, William KY 3rd Cav. Co.G
Wafford, William MO 4th Cav. Co.D Cpl.
Wafford, William F. AR 8th Inf. New Co.E
Wafford, William G. AL 19th Inf. Co.G
Wafford, William H. NC Inf. 2nd Bn. Co.D
Wafford, W.L. MS 2nd St.Cav. Co.B
Wafield, T. VA 49th Inf. Co.I
Waford, E.C. AR 11th Inf. Co.K
Waford, Eli AR 11th Inf. Co.D
Waford, William LA 13th Inf. Co.G
Wagana, C. GA 32nd Inf. Band Music.
Waganon, Thomas A. GA 3rd Cav. Co.G
Wagatha, Adam LA 30th Inf. Co.C,B Cpl.
Wagby, J.L. LA 7th Cav. Asst.Surg.
Wage, John MO 10th Inf. Co.B
Wage, L. MO 10th Inf. Co.B
Wageman, Henry TX 12th Cav. Co.K Cpl.
Wagenbrett, F. TX Inf. 4th Bn. (Oswald's) Co.B Sgt.
Wagener, Bruno John TX Lt.Arty. Hughes' Co.
Wagener, Charles VA 10th Cav. 1st Co.E
Wagener, Daniel TX 8th Inf. Co.K
Wagener, E.R. LA Mil. 4th Regt.Eur.Brig. Co.F Sgt.
Wagener, F.W. SC Mil.Arty. 1st Regt. Werner's Co. 1st Lt.
Wagener, F.W. SC Lt.Arty. Wagener's Co. (Co.A,German Arty.) Capt.
Wagener, G.A. SC Mil.Arty. 1st Regt. Werner's Co.
Wagener, G.A. SC Lt.Arty. Wagener's Co. (Co.A,German Arty.)
Wagener, H. NC 7th Sr.Res. Holland's Co.
Wagener, H. SC Mil.Arty. 1st Regt. Adj.
Wagener, Henry A. SC Arty.Bn. Hampton Legion Co.B 2nd Lt.
Wagener, H.M. AL 31st Inf. Co.G
Wagener, J. SC Mil.Arty. 1st Regt. Werner's Co.
Wagener, J.J. SC Mil.Arty. 1st Regt. Werner's Co.
Wagener, J.J. SC Lt.Arty. Wagener's Co. (Co.A,German Arty.)
Wagener, J.M. TX Conscr.
Wagener, John A. SC Mil.Arty. 1st Regt. Col.
Wagener, John G. NC 18th Inf. Co.A
Wagener, Julius SC Mil.Arty. 1st Regt. Werner's Co.
Wagener, Julius E. TX 8th Inf. Co.K Band Music.
Wagener, Philipp LA Mil.Cont.Regt. Lang's Co.
Wagener, T.D. SC 8th Bn.Res. Co.A
Wagener, William AR 27th Inf. New Co.B
Wagener, William TN 5th (McKenzie's) Cav. Co.C
Wagenfier, Christian LA Mil. 2nd Regt. 3rd Brig. 1st Div. Co.G
Wagenfuehr, Andreas TX 3rd Inf. Co.K
Wagenfuehr, Friedrich TX 3rd Inf. Co.K
Wagenfuhr, --- TX Lt.Arty. Dege's Bn. Sgt.
Wagenfuhr, Frederick TX 8th Field Btty. Sgt.
Wagenspaek, F. LA Inf.Cons. 18th Regt. & Yellow Jacket Bn. Co.B
Wagenspeck, Halbert LA Mil. LaFourche Regt.
Wager, C.C. GA 1st (Fannin's) Res. Co.K
Wager, C.C. GA 1st (Fannin's) Res. Co.K Sgt.
Wager, Charles VA 6th Cav. Co.D
Wager, Charles E. LA Miles' Legion Co.E
Wager, Charles H. VA Mil. 5th Regt. Col.
Wager, Charles H. VA 13th Inf. 2nd Co.B Cpl.
Wager, Daniel LA Miles' Legion Co.C
Wager, E. Gen. & Staff AASurg.
Wager, E. Lee VA Inf. 44th Bn. Surg.
Wager, E. Lee Gen. & Staff Asst.Surg.
Wager, F. LA Miles' Legion Co.C
Wager, James P. VA 13th Inf. 1st Co.E
Wager, Marseille LA Miles' Legion Co.B
Wager, P.B. MS 1st Cav. Co.H
Wager, P.B. Gen. & Staff Capt.,AQM
Wager, Peter B. AR 23rd Inf. Co.G
Wager, Simon 1st Chickasaw Inf. McCord's Co.
Wager, T. AL 47th Inf. Co.G
Wagerman, Henry TX Cav. Hardeman's Regt. Co.F 2nd Lt.
Wages, Aaron SC 6th Inf. 1st Co.F, 2nd Co.I
Wages, A.J. MS 23rd Inf. Co.H
Wages, Allen TN 38th Inf. Co.F Sgt.
Wages, Andrew SC 6th Inf. 1st Co.F, 2nd Co.I
Wages, Andrew J. GA 13th Cav. Co.E,G,H
Wages, Edmund SC Lt.Arty. 3rd (Palmetto) Bn. Co.B
Wages, Edward GA 9th Inf. Co.F
Wages, Elihu SC 6th Res. Co.A
Wages, F.M. GA 8th Inf. (St.Guards) Co.C 3rd Lt.
Wages, Garland SC Hvy.Arty. 15th (Lucas') Bn. Co.B
Wages, George W. SC 23rd Inf. Co.F
Wages, George Washington MS 7th Cav. Co.E
Wages, G.L. MS 2nd St.Cav. Co.E
Wages, Green Lee MS Inf. 3rd Bn. Co.G
Wages, Isaac M. MS 23rd Inf. Co.H
Wages, Isaiah M. MS Inf. 3rd Bn. Co.G
Wages, J. SC 1st Regt. Charleston Guard Co.F
Wages, J. SC 6th Res. Co.A
Wages, James GA 13th Cav. Co.E,G,H
Wages, James MS Cav. Gibson's Co.
Wages, James MS 39th Inf. Co.A,F
Wages, James SC 3rd Bn.Res. Co.E
Wages, James Benjamin MS 7th Cav. Co.E
Wages, James G. MS 31st Inf. Co.K
Wages, James O. SC Hvy.Arty. 15th (Lucas') Bn. Co.B
Wages, J.D. TX 10th Cav. Co.H
Wages, J.E. AL 18th Inf. Co.E
Wages, J.E. SC Mil. 1st Regt. (Charleston Res.) Co.C
Wages, J.J. AR 15th Mil. Co.B
Wages, J.J. GA 8th Inf. (St.Guards) Co.C Cpl.
Wages, J.N. TN 38th Inf. Co.F
Wages, Joel I. TN 38th Inf. Co.F
Wages, John MS St.Cav. 3rd Bn. (Cooper's) Little's Co.
Wages, John MS Inf. 1st Bn.St.Troops (12 mo. '62-3) Co.F
Wages, John MS 39th Inf. Co.A
Wages, John SC 8th Res.
Wages, John SC 14th Inf. Co.B
Wages, John G. MS 23rd Inf. Co.H
Wages, John P. TN 10th Inf. Co.E
Wages, John R. TX 11th Inf. Co.I
Wages, John S. GA 13th Cav. Co.E 1st Cpl.
Wages, Joseph SC 1st (McCreary's) Inf. Co.A
Wages, J.P. MS 23rd Inf. Co.H
Wages, J. Patrick SC 6th Cav. Co.B
Wages, J.W. MS 2nd St.Cav. Co.E
Wages, J. William MS 34th Inf. Co.F
Wages, L. MS 18th Cav.
Wages, Lemuel T. TX 1st (McCulloch's) Cav. Co.I
Wages, Lemuel T. TX 17th Inf. Co.K
Wages, Leroy GA 9th Inf. Co.F Cpl.
Wages, Morgan J. AR 3rd Cav. Co.G
Wages, P. SC 19th Inf. Co.D
Wages, Peter S. MS 23rd Inf. Co.H
Wages, Peter Smith MS 7th Cav. Co.E
Wages, Phillip G. MS Inf. 3rd Bn. Co.G
Wages, Romeo SC Lt.Arty. 3rd (Palmetto) Bn. Co.B
Wages, Trezevant SC Lt.Arty. 3rd (Palmetto) Bn. Co.B
Wages, Trezevant SC Shiver's Co.
Wages, T.W. TN 38th Inf. Co.F
Wages, Wade SC Inf. 3rd Bn. Co.F,K
Wages, William GA 13th Cav. Co.E,G,H
Wages, William MS 7th Cav. Co.E
Wages, William MS 31st Inf. Co.K
Wages, William SC 23rd Inf. Co.F
Wagg, Alfred W. NC 26th Inf. Co.A
Wagg, John D. NC Loc.Def. Lee's Co. (Silver Greys)
Wagg, Samuel P. NC 26th Inf. Co.A Capt.
Waggaman, Eugene LA 10th Inf. Co.I Col.
Waggan, A.A. TX Cav. 1st Bn.St.Troops Co.D
Wagganer, Thomas AL Detailed Conscr.
Waggenbrenner, M. AL Mil. 2nd Regt.Vol. Co.A
Waggener, Adair A. KY 4th Mtd.Inf. Co.F 1st Sgt.
Waggener, Arthur KY 4th Mtd.Inf. Co.F
Waggener, Herman LA Inf. 16th Bn. (Conf. Guards Resp.Bn.) Co.B
Waggener, Jacob C. VA 28th Inf. Co.B

Waggener, James R. Gen. & Staff Chap.
Waggener, Jesse TN 2nd (Ashby's) Cav. Co.D,B
Waggener, Leslie KY 9th Mtd.Inf. Co.A 2nd Lt.
Waggener, Leslie Gen. & Staff 2nd Lt.,Ord.Off.
Waggener, Nathaniel KY 10th Cav. Co.C
Waggener, Thomas M. LA 16th Inf. Co.C
Waggenor, John M. VA 62nd Mtd.Inf. 2nd Co.D
Waggerman, P.H. VA 6th Cav. Co.K
Waggerman, Samuel VA Cav. Mosby's Regt. (Part.Rangers) Co.A
Waggerner, J.L. MS 9th Cav. Co.E
Waggington, James B. VA 51st Mil. Co.G
Waggner, J. GA Cav. 19th Bn. Co.D
Waggner, J. 10th Conf.Cav. Co.I
Waggner, J.M. AL 4th Res. Co.A
Waggner, William R. TN Cav. Jackson's Co.
Waggoman, P.B. MS 6th Inf. Co.E
Waggoner, A.A. TN 14th Inf. Co.E 1st Sgt.
Waggoner, A.G. TN Inf. Spencer's Co.
Waggoner, A.J. MS 27th Inf. Co.E
Waggoner, A.J. TN Cav. 17th Bn. (Sanders') Co.C
Waggoner, A.J. TN Inf. Spencer's Co. Sgt.
Waggoner, Allen VA 63rd Inf. Co.G
Waggoner, Amos H. TN Cav. 2nd Bn. (Biffle's) Co.F
Waggoner, Andrew TN Inf. 23rd Bn. Co.E Sgt.
Waggoner, Andrew TN 44th (Cons.) Inf. Co.B Music.
Waggoner, B. AL 1st Regt.Mobile Vol. Butt's Co.
Waggoner, B.J. MS 27th Inf. Co.E
Waggoner, Booker MS Lt.Arty. (Madison Lt.Arty.) Richards' Co.
Waggoner, Calvin NC 28th Inf. Co.I
Waggoner, Charles Conf.Inf. Tucker's Regt. Co.H
Waggoner, Christian A. NC 46th Inf. Co.B
Waggoner, C.J. TN 11th Inf. Co.I Sgt.
Waggoner, C.L. TN 17th Inf. Co.E
Waggoner, Coalman Hudson LA 28th (Gray's) Inf. Co.F
Waggoner, Daniel NC 22nd Inf. Co.F
Waggoner, Daniel TX 10th Cav. Co.E Music.
Waggoner, Daniel J. TN 8th Inf. Co.K
Waggoner, Daniel N. TN 8th Inf. Co.K
Waggoner, Davault H. NC 60th Inf. Co.A
Waggoner, David KY Fields' Co. (Part.Rangers)
Waggoner, David KY 9th Mtd.Inf. Co.E
Waggoner, David NC 42nd Inf. Co.F
Waggoner, David TN Inf. 23rd Bn. Co.A
Waggoner, David N. VA 16th Cav. Co.I
Waggoner, D.J. KY 9th Mtd.Inf. Co.E
Waggoner, D.J. TN Inf. 23rd Bn. Co.A Cpl.
Waggoner, D.N. TN Inf. 1st Cons.Regt. Co.D
Waggoner, Doct TX 10th Cav. Co.E
Waggoner, E. TN 24th Bn.S.S. Co.A
Waggoner, E.A. TN 4th Inf. Co.L
Waggoner, Edward VA Inf. 4th Bn.Loc.Def. Co.C
Waggoner, Elisha J. AL 44th Inf. Co.B
Waggoner, Emanuel NC 14th Inf. Co.B
Waggoner, E.W. NC 64th Inf. Co.B
Waggoner, F. AL Cav. Forrest's Regt.
Waggoner, F. TN 18th (Newsom's) Cav. Co.A
Waggoner, Felix TN Inf. 23rd Bn. Co.A
Waggoner, Felix M. TN 8th Inf. Co.K
Waggoner, Felix W. TN 8th Inf. Co.K
Waggoner, G. MS Inf. 2nd Bn. (St.Troops) Co.C
Waggoner, George TN Inf. 1st Cons.Regt. Co.D
Waggoner, George A. TN 8th Inf. Co.K
Waggoner, George D. VA 62nd Mtd.Inf. 2nd Co.I Sgt.
Waggoner, George H. TN 8th Inf. Co.K Sgt.
Waggoner, George W. MS 16th Inf. Co.I
Waggoner, George W. TN 8th Inf. Co.K
Waggoner, George W. TN 8th Inf. Co.K Sgt.
Waggoner, George W. TN Inf. 23rd Bn. Co.A Cpl.
Waggoner, George W. TX 16th Inf. Co.D
Waggoner, G.L. TN 19th (Biffle's) Cav. Co.K
Waggoner, G.L. TN 51st (Cons.) Inf. Co.D
Waggoner, G.W. TN Cav. Napier's Bn. Co.E
Waggoner, G.W. TN 17th Inf. Co.E 2nd Lt.
Waggoner, G.W. 3rd Conf.Cav. Co.D Bugler
Waggoner, Henry AL 6th Cav. Co.C
Waggoner, Henry NC 5th Sr.Res. Co.H
Waggoner, Henry NC 22nd Inf. Co.F
Waggoner, Henry NC 44th Inf. Co.H
Waggoner, Henry NC 47th Inf. Co.K
Waggoner, Henry NC Doughton's Co. (Alleghany Gray's)
Waggoner, Henry TN 1st (Feild's) Inf. Co.D
Waggoner, Henry A. TN 8th Inf. Co.K
Waggoner, Henry A. TN Inf. 23rd Bn. Co.A
Waggoner, Henry C. TN 2nd (Robison's) Inf. Co.G
Waggoner, Henry R. NC 22nd Inf. Co.F
Waggoner, H.N. TN 13th Inf. Co.I
Waggoner, H.P. AR 7th Mil. Co.B Cpl.
Waggoner, Isaac T. TN 2nd (Ashby's) Cav. Co.D
Waggoner, J. AL 62nd Inf. Co.C
Waggoner, Jacob NC 14th Inf. Co.B Sgt.
Waggoner, Jacob NC 28th Inf. Co.I
Waggoner, Jacob NC 47th Inf. Co.K Sgt.
Waggoner, Jacob NC 47th Inf. Co.K
Waggoner, Jacob TX 26th Cav. Co.E
Waggoner, Jacob VA 8th Cav. Co.F
Waggoner, Jacob VA 135th Mil. Co.A
Waggoner, Jacob J. VA 77th Mil. Co.C
Waggoner, James NC 34th Inf. Co.A
Waggoner, James NC 44th Inf. Co.G
Waggoner, James A. VA 25th Inf. 2nd Co.K Cpl.
Waggoner, James C. TN 16th Cav.
Waggoner, James F. TX 35th (Brown's) Cav. Co.H
Waggoner, James F. TX 13th Vol. 2nd Co.A
Waggoner, James H. NC 44th Inf. Co.G
Waggoner, James L. TN Cav. 17th Bn. (Sanders') Co.C
Waggoner, James M. AL 11th Inf. Co.F
Waggoner, James M. MS 18th Inf. Co.C
Waggoner, James M. TN 41st Inf. Co.G Sgt.
Waggoner, James R. VA 56th Inf. Chap.
Waggoner, James W. GA Inf. 3rd Bn. Co.D
Waggoner, James W. GA 4th Bn.S.S. Co.B
Waggoner, Jasper A. TN 14th Inf. Co.A Bvt.2nd Lt.
Waggoner, Jasper A. TN Brig. Capt.,AAG
Waggoner, J.C. TN 50th Inf. Co.K
Waggoner, J.D. 8th (Wade's) Conf.Cav. Co.I
Waggoner, Jesse Powell NC 60th Inf. Co.A
Waggoner, J.J. AR Inf. Cocke's Regt. Co.K
Waggoner, J.J. Gen. & Staff, QM Dept. Capt.,AQM
Waggoner, J.L. MS 1st (Johnston's) Inf. Co.I
Waggoner, J.L. TX 16th Inf. Co.D Sgt.
Waggoner, J.M. MS 18th Inf. Co.C
Waggoner, J.M. TN 24th Bn.S.S. Co.B
Waggoner, J.M. Conf.Cav. Wood's Regt. 2nd Co.M
Waggoner, J.O. AR 6th Inf. Old Co.F Cpl.
Waggoner, John AL Lt.Arty. 2nd Bn. Co.D
Waggoner, John MO Lt.Arty. Barret's Co.
Waggoner, John NC 4th Sr.Res. Co.B
Waggoner, John NC 47th Inf. Co.K
Waggoner, John TN 18th (Newsom's) Cav. Co.A
Waggoner, John TN Lt.Arty. Browne's Co.
Waggoner, John B. MO Cav. Ford's Bn. Co.B Cpl.
Waggoner, John B. VA 62nd Mtd.Inf. 2nd Co.D
Waggoner, John B. VA 162nd Mil. Co.A
Waggoner, John H. AR 1st Cav. Co.C Sgt.
Waggoner, John H. NC 22nd Inf. Co.F
Waggoner, John H. NC 34th Inf. Co.A Music.
Waggoner, John H. NC 42nd Inf. Co.F Cpl.
Waggoner, John I. MO 10th Cav. Co.C
Waggoner, John L. NC 21st Inf. Co.K Cpl.
Waggoner, John O. LA 13th Inf. Co.G
Waggoner, John T. TX 31st Cav. Co.E Cpl.
Waggoner, John W. GA Inf. 3rd Bn. Co.D
Waggoner, John W. GA 4th Bn.S.S. Co.B
Waggoner, John W. NC 14th Inf. Co.B
Waggoner, John W. NC 28th Inf. Co.I
Waggoner, Joseph MS 18th Inf. Co.C
Waggoner, Joseph TN 10th Inf. Co.E
Waggoner, Joseph VA 22nd Inf. Swann's Co.
Waggoner, J.P. NC 64th Inf. Co.G
Waggoner, J.R.C. AR 26th Inf. Co.G Sgt.
Waggoner, J.S. AR 19th (Dockery's) Inf. Co.K
Waggoner, J.T. TN 24th Bn.S.S. Co.A 1st Sgt.
Waggoner, L. TX Cav. Border's Regt. Co.C
Waggoner, Lafayette TX 32nd Cav. Co.A
Waggoner, L.C. TN 10th Inf. Co.I Capt.
Waggoner, Levin VA 60th Inf. Co.E
Waggoner, Lewis VA Inf. 26th Bn. Co.G
Waggoner, Lewis B. VA 46th Mil. Co.B Cpl.
Waggoner, Lewis B. VA 62nd Mtd.Inf. 2nd Co.I
Waggoner, Lewis C. TN 10th Inf. Co.I Capt.
Waggoner, L.P. KY 13th Cav. Co.D
Waggoner, L.S. GA 7th Inf. (St.Guards) Co.F Sgt.
Waggoner, Luther TX 23rd Cav. Co.B
Waggoner, Malcom G. TN 41st Inf. Co.G
Waggoner, Martin NC Doughton's Co.(Alleghany Grey's)
Waggoner, Martin E. VA 77th Mil. Co.C
Waggoner, M.G. TN Inf. Spencer's Co.
Waggoner, Middleton C. MO 10th Inf. Co.F
Waggoner, Milton C. AR 14th (McCarver's) Inf. Co.C
Waggoner, Moses NC 44th Inf. Co.H
Waggoner, M.W. AR Inf. Cocke's Regt. Co.K
Waggoner, R. NC 22nd Inf. Co.I
Waggoner, R.A. MO Cav. Ford's Bn. Co.B Sgt.
Waggoner, R.E. AR 21st Inf. Co.A
Waggoner, Riley TN 8th Inf. Co.K
Waggoner, Robert LA Maddox's Regt.Res.Corps Co.B

Waggoner, Robert E. AR 14th (McCarver's) Inf. Co.C Sgt.
Waggoner, Russell A. MS 18th Inf. Co.C
Waggoner, Samuel MO Lt.Arty. 1st Field Btty.
Waggoner, Samuel MO 16th Inf. Co.B
Waggoner, Samuel VA 3rd Cav. & Inf.St.Line Co.D
Waggoner, Samuel H. VA 42nd Inf. Co.G
Waggoner, Samuel M. VA 13th Inf. Co.D
Waggoner, Sidney J. GA Inf. 3rd Bn. Co.D
Waggoner, Sidney J. GA 4th Bn.S.S. Co.B
Waggoner, Solomon VA 162nd Mil. Co.B Sgt.
Waggoner, Stanford H. TN 2nd (Robison's) Inf. Co.G
Waggoner, Stephen TX 18th Cav. Co.E
Waggoner, Sylvester G. MS 18th Inf. Co.C
Waggoner, T. TX Cav. Giddings' Bn. Carr's Co.
Waggoner, T.B. VA 30th Bn.S.S. Co.F
Waggoner, Th. TX Cav. 2nd Regt.St.Troops Co.E
Waggoner, Thomas H. MS 18th Inf. Co.C Sgt.
Waggoner, Thomas J. TN 44th (Cons.) Inf. Co.I
Waggoner, Thomas Jefferson TN 55th (McKoin's) Inf. Co.I
Waggoner, T.J. TN Inf. Nashville Bn. Cattles' Co. Cpl.
Waggoner, T.L. VA Cav. 36th Bn. Co.E Sgt.Maj.
Waggoner, West LA 31st Inf. Co.F Sgt.
Waggoner, W.G. TN 11th (Holman's) Cav. Co.H
Waggoner, W.G. TN Douglass' Bn.Part.Rangers Coffee's Co.
Waggoner, Wiley B. TN 2nd (Robison's) Inf. Co.C
Waggoner, William NC 5th Sr.Res. Co.H
Waggoner, William NC 44th Inf. Co.H
Waggoner, William A. NC 60th Inf. Co.A
Waggoner, William A. TX 10th Cav. Co.I
Waggoner, William D. GA 53rd Inf. Co.I
Waggoner, William H. MS 31st Inf. Co.F
Waggoner, William H. TN 2nd (Robison's) Inf. Co.G
Waggoner, William R. NC 52nd Inf. Co.F
Waggoner, Wilson H. TN 1st (Turney's) Inf. Co.E
Waggoner, W.M. AL 27th Inf. Co.K
Waggoner, W.P. TX 32nd Cav. Co.A
Waggoner, W.T. TN Inf. 154th Sr.Regt. Co.I
Waggoner, W.W. AR 6th Inf. Old Co.F,A Cpl.
Waggoner, W.W. AR 21st Inf. Co.A,D,E
Waggoner, W.W. KY 9th Mtd.Inf. Co.E
Waggoner, W.W. TN Inf. 23rd Bn. Co.A
Waggy, Daniel VA 46th Mil. Co.C
Waggy, George VA 25th Inf. 2nd Co.F
Waggy, George VA 62nd Mtd.Inf. 2nd Co.D Sgt.
Waggy, Henry VA 25th Inf. 2nd Co.F
Waggy, Isaac VA 62nd Mtd. Inf. 2nd Co.K
Waggy, Jacob VA 162nd Mil. Co.C
Waggy, Joel VA 25th Inf. 2nd Co.K
Waggy, Solomon VA 46th Mil. Co.C
Waginer, W.R. TN 59th Mtd.Inf. Co.D
Wagington, G.W. AR 62nd Mil. Co.F
Wagis, Green Lee MS 2nd Cav. Co.E
Wagland, B.C. VA 43rd Inf. Co.C
Waglay, Hinson LA 2nd Cav. Co.B
Waglay, John L. LA 2nd Inf. Co.D
Wagle, R.J. MS 38th Cav. Co.H Sgt.
Wagley, Albert A. TX 29th Cav. Co.D
Wagley, B.F. LA 4th Cav. Co.I
Wagley, B.F. TX 12th Inf. Co.I
Wagley, D.C. TX 9th Cav. Co.E
Wagley, Hinson TX 27th Cav. Co.F
Wagley, Joseph VA 7th Cav. Glenn's Co.
Wagley, S.C. TX 27th Cav. Co.F
Wagley, William TX 34th Cav. Co.K
Wagley, William VA 7th Cav. Glenn's Co.
Wagly, T.J. LA 2nd Cav. Co.B
Wagnan, George LA 14th Inf. Co.A
Wagner, A. LA Mil. 3rd Regt. French Brig. Co.1
Wagner, A. LA 21st (Patton's) Inf. Co.H
Wagner, A.B. MS 13th Inf. Co.I Music.
Wagner, A.C. SC 4th Cav. Co.K
Wagner, A.C. SC Mil.Cav. Rutledge's Co. Sgt.
Wagner, A.C. SC 3rd St.Troops Co.C
Wagner, Adam H. TN Cav. 12th Bn. (Day's) Co.B
Wagner, A.G. TX 33rd Cav. Co.C
Wagner, A.J. AR 5th Mil. Co.E
Wagner, A.J. LA Lt.Arty. LeGardeur, Jr.'s Co. (Orleans Guard Btty.)
Wagner, A.J. LA Mil. Lewis Guards
Wagner, Albert MS 16th Inf. Co.D
Wagner, Albert L. LA 21st (Patton's) Inf. Co.H
Wagner, Alex NC 26th Inf. Co.F
Wagner, Allison NC 35th Inf. Co.K
Wagner, Andrew LA 18th Inf. Co.E
Wagner, Andrew LA Inf.Cons. 18th Regt. & Yellow Jacket Bn. Co.E
Wagner, Andrew NC 45th Inf. Co.D
Wagner, Andrew TN 45th Inf. Co.E Sgt.
Wagner, Andrew J. TN 44th Inf. Co.D
Wagner, Andrew J. TN 44th (Cons.) Inf. Co.D
Wagner, Archibald NC 21st Inf. Co.F
Wagner, August TX Cav. Crump's Regt. Co.H
Wagner, August TX 6th Inf. Co.B Ch.Music.
Wagner, Barnard C. GA Cav. 2nd Bn. Co.D Sgt.
Wagner, B.C. GA 5th Cav. Co.A
Wagner, B.C. GA Cav. Waring's Co.
Wagner, Benjamin NC 28th Inf. Co.C
Wagner, Benjamin F. AL Inf. 1st Regt. Co.A Sgt.
Wagner, B.J. TX 1st Hvy.Arty. Co.B
Wagner, C. MS Inf. 3rd Bn. (St.Troops) Co.C
Wagner, C. NC 1st Jr.Res. Co.I
Wagner, C. SC Mil. Trenholm's Co.
Wagner, C. SC Rutledge Mtd.Riflemen & Horse Arty. Trenholm's Co.
Wagner, C.A. SC 7th Cav. Co.B
Wagner, Carl TX 3rd Inf. Co.K
Wagner, Caspar Conf.Inf. Tucker's Regt. Co.C
Wagner, C.F. AL 12th Inf. Co.F
Wagner, C.H. LA 25th Inf.
Wagner, C.H. MS 34th Inf. Co.D
Wagner, Charles AL 3rd Cav. Co.F Bugler
Wagner, Charles GA 1st Reg. Music.
Wagner, Chs. LA Mil. Lafayette Arty.
Wagner, Charles LA Mil. 1st Regt. 3rd Brig. 1st Div. Co.E
Wagner, Charles LA Inf. 9th Bn. Co.C Sgt.
Wagner, Charles VA 24th Cav. Co.B
Wagner, Charles VA 15th Inf. Co.K
Wagner, Charles Conf.Inf. 8th Bn.
Wagner, Charles G. TX 22nd Inf. Co.K Sgt.
Wagner, Chas. G. Gen. & Staff, Arty. Capt.,MSK
Wagner, Chas. H. Gen. & Staff Asst.Surg.
Wagner, Charles T. AL 3rd Res. Co.H
Wagner, Charles V. VA 7th Cav. Co.G 1st Lt.
Wagner, Christian LA 6th Inf. Co.G Cpl.
Wagner, Christian VA Cav. 1st Bn. Co.B
Wagner, Coleman GA 3rd Cav. (St.Guards) Co.D
Wagner, Conrad VA 2nd Arty. Co.G
Wagner, Conward VA 87th Mil. Co.D
Wagner, Conway VA 2nd Arty. Co.G
Wagner, Conway VA Res.Forces Clark's Co.
Wagner, Daniel R. MS 15th Inf. Co.F Cpl.
Wagner, Daniel W. NC 6th Cav. (65th St.Troops) Co.A,F
Wagner, David GA Arty. St.Troops Pruden's Btty.
Wagner, David NC 6th Cav. (65th St.Troops) Co.F
Wagner, David S. AR 15th (Josey's) Inf. Co.A Cpl.
Wagner, D.B. NC 6th Cav. (65th St.Troops) Co.F,A Sgt.
Wagner, D.R. MS 18th Cav. Co.C Sgt.
Wagner, D.S. NC 6th Sr.Res. Co.I Sgt.
Wagner, E. MS 46th Inf. Co.C
Wagner, E.B. VA 11th Bn.Res. Co.B
Wagner, E.C. LA Mil. 3rd Regt. French Brig. Co.1
Wagner, Edward LA 1st (Strawbridge's) Inf. Co.D
Wagner, Edward P. GA Inf. 2nd Bn. Co.A Sgt.
Wagner, Elijah TN Cav. 12th Bn. (Day's) Co.B
Wagner, Ernest LA 7th Inf. Co.K
Wagner, Ernest LA 20th Inf. Co.I
Wagner, Ernest TX Lt.Arty. Jones' Co.
Wagner, Ernst LA 1st (Strawbridge's) Inf. Co.D
Wagner, F. LA Mil. Squad. Guides d'Orleans Cavalier
Wagner, F. LA Mil. 2nd Regt. 3rd Brig. 1st Div. Co.E 2nd Lt.
Wagner, F. LA Mil. 4th Regt. French Brig. Co.5
Wagner, F. Hosp.Stew.
Wagner, F.H. TX Cav. 6th Bn. Co.C
Wagner, Frank TX 12th Cav. Co.B
Wagner, Frank TX 35th (Likens') Cav. Co.A
Wagner, Frank VA 10th Cav. Co.A
Wagner, Fred Hosp.Stew.
Wagner, Frederick LA Arty. Landry's Co. (Donaldsonville Arty.)
Wagner, Frederick LA C.S. Zouave Bn. Co.A,F Hosp.Stew.
Wagner, Frederick VA 6th Inf. 1st Co.E, Co.D
Wagner, Frederick Gen. & Staff Hosp.Stew.
Wagner, G. SC Lt.Arty. Wagener's Co. (Co.A, German Arty.)
Wagner, G. VA 2nd St.Res. Co.H
Wagner, G.C. LA 17th Inf. Co.D
Wagner, George AL Seawell's Btty. (Mohawk Arty.)
Wagner, George AL 3rd Inf. Co.I
Wagner, George G. AL Lt.Arty. 20th Bn. Co.A
Wagner, George M. MO 4th Cav. Co.I

Wagner, George W. VA Lt.Arty. Hankins' Co.
Wagner, G.W. AR 2nd Inf. Co.D
Wagner, G.W. LA 17th Inf. Co.D
Wagner, H. AL 6th Inf. Co.C
Wagner, H. AR 1st (Colquitt's) Inf. Co.A
Wagner, Hamilton F. GA 5th Inf. Co.I
Wagner, Hans LA 30th Inf. Co.E
Wagner, Henry LA 17th Inf. Co.D
Wagner, Henry MD 1st Cav. Co.K
Wagner, Henry NC 3rd Arty. (40th St.Troops) Co.G
Wagner, Henry VA 58th Mil. Co.H
Wagner, Henry M., Jr. VA 10th Cav. Co.B
Wagner, Herm LA Mil. 4th Regt.Eur.Brig. Co.C
Wagner, H.W. LA Mil. 4th Regt.Eur.Brig. Co.E
Wagner, I.G. NC 21st Inf. Co.H
Wagner, Ignatius MS Inf. 46th Regt. Co.C
Wagner, I.P. NC 10th Cav. Co.B
Wagner, Ireson TN Sullivan Cty.Res. (Loc.Def.Troops) White's Co.
Wagner, Isaac AR Lt.Arty. Thrall's Btty.
Wagner, Isaac R. AR 33rd Inf. Co.I
Wagner, Isaac T. TN 1st Cav. Co.L Sgt.
Wagner, J. GA 22nd Inf. Co.G
Wagner, J. LA 10th Inf. Co.G
Wagner, J. TX 13th Cav. Co.C
Wagner, J.A. VA Cav. 37th Bn. Co.F
Wagner, Jacob LA Arty. Castellanos' Btty.
Wagner, Jacob LA 14th Inf. Co.K
Wagner, Jacob NC 4th Inf. Co.G
Wagner, Jacob TX 15th Inf. 2nd Co.E Music.
Wagner, Jacob VA 10th Bn.Res. Co.D
Wagner, James TN 44th Inf. Co.D Capt.
Wagner, James VA 9th Inf. Co.I
Wagner, James C. TN 60th Mtd.Inf. Co.C
Wagner, James D. 1st Conf.Cav. 2nd Co.G
Wagner, James H. TN 4th (McLemore's) Cav. Co.I
Wagner, Jas. S. AL 19th Inf. Co.B
Wagner, James W. TN 32nd Inf. Co.K
Wagner, J.B. AL 14th Inf. Co.E
Wagner, J.B. MS Inf. 2nd St.Troops Co.B
Wagner, J.B. TN Detailed Conscr. Co.A
Wagner, J.C. GA Arty. St.Troops Pruden's Btty.
Wagner, J.C. TN 16th Cav.
Wagner, Jesse VA 20th Cav. Co.H
Wagner, J.F. NC 5th Inf. Co.K
Wagner, J.H. LA Mil. Orleans Guards Regt. Co.D
Wagner, J.L. TN 13th Inf. Co.A
Wagner, J.M. TN 1st Cav. Co.E,F
Wagner, Johanes LA Mil. Mech.Guard
Wagner, John AR Cav. 1st Bn. (Stirman's) Co.D
Wagner, John GA Cav. 2nd Bn. Co.F
Wagner, John GA 5th Cav. Co.B
Wagner, John GA 25th Inf. Co.C
Wagner, John KY 9th Cav. Co.H
Wagner, John LA 11th Inf. Co.L
Wagner, John LA 13th Inf. Co.A Sgt.
Wagner, John LA 17th Inf. Co.D
Wagner, John LA 17th Inf. Co.K
Wagner, John LA 20th Inf. New Co.E Sgt.
Wagner, John LA 30th Inf. Co.E
Wagner, John MO Cav. 10th Regt.St.Guard Comsy.
Wagner, John MO Inf. Perkins' Bn. Co.I
Wagner, John NC 3rd Arty. (40th StTroops) Co.G
Wagner, John NC 21st Inf. Co.F
Wagner, John TN 23rd Inf. Co.I
Wagner, John TX Cav. 1st Regt.St.Troops Co.D
Wagner, John TX 14th Cav. Co.C
Wagner, John TX 20th Cav. Co.A
Wagner, John TX Inf. 1st St.Troops Stevenson's Co.
Wagner, John VA Cav. 32nd Bn. Co.A Cpl.
Wagner, John VA 1st Inf. Co.K
Wagner, John VA 12th Inf.
Wagner, John A. TX 6th Cav. Co.G
Wagner, John A. VA Arty. Bryan's Co.
Wagner, John A. VA 7th Bn.Res. Co.D
Wagner, John F. GA 14th Inf. Co.I
Wagner, John G. MD 1st Inf. Co.G
Wagner, John G. MD Inf. 2nd Bn. Co.A
Wagner, John L. VA 10th Cav. Co.B
Wagner, John M. TX 6th Inf. Co.E
Wagner, John P. VA 10th Cav. Co.B
Wagner, John P. VA Inf.Res.Corps
Wagner, John T. GA 2nd Cav. Co.C
Wagner, John W. TN 44th Inf. Co.D
Wagner, John W. TN 44th (Cons.) Inf. Co.D
Wagner, John W., Jr. VA 10th Cav. Co.B
Wagner, John W., Sr. VA 10th Cav. Co.B
Wagner, Joseph AR 27th Inf. New Co.B
Wagner, Joseph NC 6th Cav. (65th St.Troops) Co.F
Wagner, Joseph NC 48th Inf. Co.K
Wagner, Joseph TX Cav. Gidding's Bn. Onins' Co.
Wagner, Joseph VA Inf. 26th Bn. Co.A
Wagner, Joseph VA 59th Inf. 2nd Co.K
Wagner, Joseph C. GA 15th Inf. Co.D
Wagner, Joseph L. MD Inf. 2nd Bn. Co.F Sgt.
Wagner, Josiah TN 29th Inf. Co.I 2nd Lt.
Wagner, Josiah J. GA 3rd Inf. Co.B
Wagner, J.P. VA Inf. Lyneman's Co.
Wagner, J.R. KY 12th Cav. Co.H
Wagner, J.W. GA Arty. St.Troops Pruden's Btty.
Wagner, J.W. LA 25th Inf. Co.E
Wagner, J.W. NC Mallett's Co.
Wagner, J.W. TN 4th (Mclemore's) Cav. Co.I
Wagner, J.W. TN 23rd Inf. Co.D
Wagner, L. LA 9th Inf. Co.B
Wagner, L. TX 3rd Inf. Co.B
Wagner, L. VA 2nd St.Res. Co.A
Wagner, Lewis AL City Troop (Mobile) Arrington's Co.A
Wagner, Lewis VA Cav. 40th Bn. Co.A
Wagner, Lewis C. VA 61st Inf. Co.E
Wagner, Lewis P. AL City Troop (Mobile) Arrington's Co.A
Wagner, Lisby TX 10th Cav. Co.A
Wagner, L.J. SC 5th Cav. Co.B
Wagner, L.J. SC Cav. 17th Bn. Co.C
Wagner, Louis MS 16th Inf. Co.A
Wagner, Louis K. VA 12th Inf. Co.K
Wagner, Lucian Q. AL 1st Regt.Conscr. Co.H
Wagner, Lucius Q. AL. Conscr. Echols' Co.
Wagner, M. AR Cav. Crabtree's (46th) Regt. Co.A
Wagner, M. LA Mil. Chalmette Regt. Co.G
Wagner, M. NC 3rd Bn.Sr.Res. Durham's Co. 2nd Lt.
Wagner, Mark H. AR Cav. 1st Bn. (Stirman's) Co.C
Wagner, Martin LA Mil. Mech.Guard
Wagner, Michael AR 4th Inf. Co.G
Wagner, Michael TN 19th Inf. Co.B
Wagner, M.L. TX 1st Inf. Co.L
Wagner, M.L. TX Waul's Legion Co.B
Wagner, N. LA Mil. 3rd Regt. French Brig. Co.3
Wagner, N.M. AL 7th Cav. Co.K
Wagner, Noah P. NC 28th Inf. Co.C
Wagner, O.T. GA 1st (Olmstead's) Inf. Co.D Cpl.
Wagner, P. LA 15th Inf. Co.B
Wagner, P. LA 22nd Inf. Co.E
Wagner, P. LA Mil. Fire Bn. Co.B
Wagner, P. TX 3rd Inf. Co.B Capt.
Wagner, Paul LA Mil. 4th Regt. 1st Brig. 1st Div. Co.H
Wagner, Peter AL 5th Cav.
Wagner, Peter LA 1st Hvy.Arty. (Reg.) Co.I,K
Wagner, Peter LA 6th Inf. Co.K
Wagner, Peter LA 13th Inf. Co.F Sgt.
Wagner, Philip VA Hvy.Arty. 19th Bn. 3rd Co.C
Wagner, Philip VA 58th Mil. Co.F
Wagner, Philip VA 58th Mil. Co.G Sgt.
Wagner, Philip 1st Conf.Eng.Troops Co.D
Wagner, P.L. NC 57th Inf. Co.E
Wagner, Q. LA Mil. 3rd Regt. French Brig. Co.7
Wagner, R. TX 6th Field Btty.
Wagner, R. TX 4th Inf. Co.F
Wagner, R.A. GA 23rd Inf.
Wagner, R.J. NC 1st Jr.Res. Co.C
Wagner, R.M. NC 21st Inf. Co.H
Wagner, Robert Q. AR Cav. 1st Bn. (Stirman's) Co.C Cpl.
Wagner, Samuel VA 19th Cav. Co.C
Wagner, Samuel F. VA 5th Inf. Co.C
Wagner, Samuel J. VA 10th Cav. Co.B
Wagner, S.C. NC 5th Inf. Co.H,K
Wagner, Solomon AR Cav. 1st Bn. (Stirman's) Co.C
Wagner, Solomon TX 4th (McLemore's) Cav. Co.K
Wagner, T.G. MO 12th Cav. Co.A
Wagner, Th. LA Mil. 1st Regt. French Brig. Co.5
Wagner, Theodor LA Mil. 3rd Regt. 3rd Brig. 1st Div. Co.H
Wagner, Thomas LA C.S. Zouave Bn. Co.F
Wagner, Thomas J. LA 17th Inf. Co.K
Wagner, Thomas J. NC 28th Inf. Co.C
Wagner, Thomas M. SC 1st Arty. Co.A,D Lt.Col.
Wagner, T.S. AL 14th Inf. Co.E
Wagner, Uriah VA 20th Cav. Co.D
Wagner, W. LA Mil. 3rd Regt. French Brig. Co.1
Wagner, W. NC 3rd Arty. (40th St.Troops) Co.G
Wagner, W. NC 54th Inf. Co.D
Wagner, Walter M. AL 24th Inf. Co.K Cpl.
Wagner, W.B. AR 1st Inf. Co.C
Wagner, W.F. LA Capt.,AAG
Wagner, W.F. Conf.Cav. Raum's Co.
Wagner, W.H. GA 1st (Ramsey's) Inf. Co.E
Wagner, W.H. MS 2nd St.Cav. Co.E

Wagner, W.H. TN 23rd Inf. Co.D Sgt.
Wagner, William LA 4th Inf. Co.H
Wagner, William LA Mil. Orleans Fire Regt. Co.A
Wagner, William MO 1st N.E. Cav. Co.B 1st Sgt.
Wagner, William TX 1st (Yager's) Cav. Co.A Sgt.
Wagner, William TX 19th Cav. Co.H
Wagner, William VA Cav. Hounshell's Bn. Co.A
Wagner, William B. MS 15th Inf. Co.F QMSgt.
Wagner, William C. MO 6th Inf. Co.D
Wagner, William F. NC 57th Inf. Co.E
Wagner, William G. VA 57th Inf. Co.F
Wagner, William H. GA Lt.Arty. 12th Bn. 3rd Co.B,E Music.
Wagner, William H. GA 6th Inf. Co.H
Wagner, William H. VA 56th Inf. Co.E
Wagner, Wm. Henry Gen. & Staff 1st Lt.,ADC
Wagner, William M. TX 17th Cav. Co.D
Wagner, William M. 1st Conf.Cav. Co.G
Wagner, William P. NC 6th Inf. Co.B
Wagner, William R. TX 19th Cav. Co.H
Wagner, William T. TX Cav. 3rd (Yager's) Bn. Co.A Sgt.
Wagner, W.M. MS 44th Inf. Co.I Cpl.
Wagner, W.M. TX 2nd Inf. Co.I
Wagnier, A.L. TX 9th (Nichols') Inf. Co.G
Wagnier, A.L. TX Waul's Legion Co.A Cpl.
Wagnier, P.H.C. TX 9th (Nichols') Inf. Co.G
Wagnier, P.H.C. TX Inf. Timmons' Regt. Co.G
Wagnier, P.H.C. TX Waul's Legion Co.A
Wagnon, --- AL 11th Cav. Co.F
Wagnon, A. TX 7th Cav. Co.E
Wagnon, A.J. AR 17th (Griffith's) Inf. Co.G
Wagnon, A.J. AR 35th Inf. Co.K
Wagnon, A.J. TX 11th (Spaight's) Bn.Vol. Co.A
Wagnon, Benjamin AR 17th (Griffith's) Inf. Co.G
Wagnon, Benjamin AR 35th Inf. Co.K
Wagnon, Burrell AR 35th Inf. Co.K
Wagnon, Burt AR Cav. 1st Bn. (Stirman's) Co.E
Wagnon, Cecil O. TX 1st Inf. Co.I,M 2nd Lt.
Wagnon, Clarance AR 17th (Lemoyne's) Inf. Co.H
Wagnon, Clarence AR 21st Inf. Co.G
Wagnon, Crumly T. GA Inf. 27th Bn. Co.C
Wagnon, Daniel T. TX Cav. 6th Bn. Co.A 3rd Lt.
Wagnon, D.F. TX 7th Cav. Co.E
Wagnon, D.T. TX 7th Cav. Co.E Sgt.
Wagnon, Edouard LA 8th Inf. Co.C
Wagnon, Eugenius N. GA Phillips' Legion Co.A
Wagnon, F.S. TX 7th Cav. Co.E Cpl.
Wagnon, G.D. LA 2nd Inf. Co.G Cpl.
Wagnon, George TX 1st Inf. Co.M 2nd Lt.
Wagnon, George H. GA 3rd Bn.S.S. Co.E Cpl.
Wagnon, Geo. P. Gen. & Staff Capt.,ACS
Wagnon, George W. TX Cav. Ragsdale's Bn. Co.E Sgt.
Wagnon, G.H. GA Phillips' Legion Co.A
Wagnon, Green W. AR 2nd Inf. Co.H
Wagnon, G.W. LA 28th (Thomas') Inf. Co.F 2nd Lt.
Wagnon, H.D. LA 13th Bn. (Part.Rangers) Co.B
Wagnon, Hinton C. GA 44th Inf. Co.K
Wagnon, James D. GA 3rd Bn.S.S. Co.E
Wagnon, J.H. TX Cav. Terry's Regt. Co.B
Wagnon, J.H. TX Cav. Waller's Regt. Co.E
Wagnon, John LA 14th Inf. Co.A
Wagnon, John TN 3rd (Forrest's) Cav. 1st Co.E
Wagnon, John R. MO 11th Inf. Co.E
Wagnon, John T. AL 29th Inf. Co.G 1st Lt.
Wagnon, John T. VA 3rd Inf.Loc.Def. Co.A
Wagnon, Joseph M. GA 41st Inf. Co.I,B
Wagnon, J.P. GA 9th Inf. (St.Guards) Co.C Cpl.
Wagnon, J.P. LA 13th Bn. (Part.Rangers) Co.B
Wagnon, J.S. TX 28th Cav. Co.F Capt.
Wagnon, J.T. TX 14th Inf. Co.H
Wagnon, J.W. LA 28th (Thomas') Inf. Co.F Sgt.
Wagnon, L.H. AL Cav. 5th Bn. Hilliard's Legion Co.E Cpl.
Wagnon, L.H. 10th Conf.Cav. Co.E Cpl.
Wagnon, Mart. LA 4th Cav. Co.A
Wagnon, M.H. AL 4th (Russell's) Cav. Co.B
Wagnon, M.H. TN 3rd (Forrest's) Cav. 1st Co.E
Wagnon, N.B. LA Inf. 11th Bn. Co.B
Wagnon, N.S. GA Inf. City Bn. (Columbus) Williams' Co.
Wagnon, Peter AR Cav. 6th Bn. Co.B
Wagnon, Pitman M. GA Phillips' Legion Co.A
Wagnon, Pittman M. GA 3rd Bn.S.S. Co.E
Wagnon, S.D. GA 60th Inf. Co.E
Wagnon, Thomas TX 19th Inf. Co.C
Wagnon, W.C. AL 2nd Cav. Co.E
Wagnon, W.C. AL 9th Inf. Co.G
Wagnon, Wesley F. AL 6th Inf. Co.L Cpl.
Wagnon, W.F. AL 53rd (Part.Rangers) Co.A
Wagnon, Wiley H. GA 36th (Villepigue's) Inf. Co.C Sgt.
Wagnon, William AL 4th (Russell's) Cav. Co.B
Wagnon, William TN 3rd (Forrest's) Cav. 1st Co.E
Wagnon, William H. LA 28th (Thomas') Inf. Co.B
Wagnon, William S. GA 44th Inf. Co.K
Wagnon, W.J. LA 28th (Thomas') Inf. Co.F 1st Lt.
Wagnon, W.O. AL 30th Inf. Co.G
Wagnon, W.T. TX 7th Cav. Co.E
Wagnon, W.W. GA 64th Inf. Co.B 1st Lt.
Wagnon, Wyly H. 1st Conf.Inf. 2nd Co.E Sgt.
Wagnor, William S. TX 24th Cav. Co.E
Wagnow, George P. AL 29th Inf. ACS
Wagnur, A.D. TN 16th Inf. Co.A
Wagonan, S.J. AL 9th (Malone's) Cav. Co.H
Wagoner, A.B. NC 26th Inf. Co.F
Wagoner, A.B. VA 8th Inf. Co.F
Wagoner, Absalom VA 77th Mil. Co.C
Wagoner, Adam MS 3rd Inf. Co.K Music.
Wagoner, Adam TN 8th (Smith's) Cav. Co.B
Wagoner, Adam C. VA 36th Inf. 2nd Co.G
Wagoner, A.G. TX 4th Inf. Co.B
Wagoner, A.H. TN 6th (Wheeler's) Cav. Co.B
Wagoner, A.J. Gen. & Staff Maj.,Sp.Agent
Wagoner, Allen VA Mil. Grayson Cty.
Wagoner, Allen P. MS 21st Inf. Co.I
Wagoner, Andrew VA 60th Inf. Co.E
Wagoner, Andrew C. TX 17th Cav. Co.G
Wagoner, Angus TX 10th Cav. Co.E
Wagoner, August 7th Conf.Cav. Co.E
Wagoner, C. MS 1st Cav.Res. Co.E
Wagoner, C.A. NC 42nd Inf. Co.B
Wagoner, Carl VA 24th Bn.Part.Rangers Cropper's Co.
Wagoner, Charles L. TN 44th (Cons.) Inf. Co.B
Wagoner, C.J. NC 57th Inf. Co.C
Wagoner, Cornelius KY 9th Cav. Co.B
Wagoner, D. TN Inf. 4th Cons.Regt. Co.F
Wagoner, D. TX Cav. Bourland's Regt. Co.H
Wagoner, D. Brush Bn.
Wagoner, Daniel, Jr. NC 21st Inf. Co.M Cpl.
Wagoner, Daniel TN 7th Inf. Co.E
Wagoner, Daniel TX Cav. 2nd Regt.St.Troops Co.C
Wagoner, David NC 1st Inf. Co.H
Wagoner, D.B. VA 1st Inf. Co.D
Wagoner, D.J. TN Inf. 4th Cons.Regt. Co.F
Wagoner, D.M. NC 57th Inf. Co.C
Wagoner, D.N. VA Cav. Caldwell's Bn. Graham's Co.
Wagoner, D.R. MS 8th Cav. Co.C 1st Sgt.
Wagoner, E. NC 45th Inf. Co.K
Wagoner, Edward MO Cav. 1st Regt.St.Guard Co.E
Wagoner, E.J. AL 11th Inf. Co.F
Wagoner, Elijah AL 4th (Russell's) Cav.
Wagoner, Elisha LA 27th Inf. Co.H
Wagoner, Franklin P. VA 36th Inf. 2nd Co.G
Wagoner, Fred TN 19th & 20th (Cons.) Cav. Co.C
Wagoner, Frederick VA 9th Inf. Co.F Sgt.
Wagoner, Garret TN 63rd Inf. Co.A
Wagoner, George VA 60th Inf. Co.K
Wagoner, George D. VA 25th Inf. 1st Co.E
Wagoner, George E. VA 36th Inf. 2nd Co.G
Wagoner, George Q. NC 45th Inf. Co.D
Wagoner, George W. LA Mil. C.S. Zouave Bn. Co.H
Wagoner, George W. 1st Cherokee Mtd.Vol. 2nd Co.K
Wagoner, G.M. TN 50th Inf. Co.H
Wagoner, G.W. MO 1st & 4th Cons.Inf. Co.E
Wagoner, G.W. MO 4th Inf. Co.E,H
Wagoner, G.W. TN 51st Inf. Co.H
Wagoner, H.C. LA 4th Inf. Co.I
Wagoner, H.D. NC 26th Inf. Co.A
Wagoner, Henry NC Lt.Arty. 13th Bn. Co.E
Wagoner, Henry NC 9th Bn.S.S. Co.A
Wagoner, Henry NC 54th Inf. Co.H
Wagoner, Henry VA 45th Inf. Co.C
Wagoner, H.J. AR Mil. Borland's Regt. Peyton Rifles Sgt.
Wagoner, Isaac T. TN Cav. 4th Bn. (Branner's) Co.C
Wagoner, J. NC 7th Sr.Res. Clinard's Co.
Wagoner, J. TX Cav. Border's Regt. Co.C
Wagoner, J. 4th Conf.Inf. Co.E
Wagoner, Jacob NC 33rd Inf. Co.D
Wagoner, James AR 17th (Lemoyne's) Inf. Co.A
Wagoner, James MS 15th Inf.
Wagoner, James MO 2nd Inf. Co.F
Wagoner, James TX 15th Cav. Co.C
Wagoner, James E. VA 36th Inf. 2nd Co.G
Wagoner, James F. VA 77th Mil. Co.C
Wagoner, James M. TN 50th Inf. Co.H
Wagoner, James M. TX 3rd Inf. 2nd Co.C
Wagoner, J.E. VA Inf. 1st Bn. Co.A

Wagoner, Jesse B. TN Cav. 4th Bn. (Branner's) Co.C
Wagoner, J.F. MS 41st Inf. Co.C
Wagoner, J.L. MS 10th Cav. Co.F
Wagoner, J.L. MO 11th Inf. Co.A
Wagoner, J.L. NC 4th Sr.Res. Co.D
Wagoner, J.M. NC 18th Inf. Co.K
Wagoner, J.N. Gen. & Staff, QM Dept.
Wagoner, Job NC Home Guards
Wagoner, Joe TX Waul's Legion Co.E
Wagoner, John AL Cav. Forrest's Regt.
Wagoner, John AL 32nd Inf. Co.B
Wagoner, John AR Lt.Arty. Wiggins' Btty.
Wagoner, John MS 9th Inf. Old Co.F
Wagoner, John MO 12th Cav. Co.A
Wagoner, John MO Cav. Snider's Bn. Co.C
Wagoner, John MO Thompson's Command
Wagoner, John NC Lt.Arty. 13th Bn. Co.E
Wagoner, John NC 4th Sr.Res. Co.F
Wagoner, John TX 10th Cav. Co.E
Wagoner, John TX 15th Cav. Co.B
Wagoner, John TX 18th Inf. Co.I Fifer
Wagoner, John VA 60th Inf. Co.G
Wagoner, John 1st Cherokee Mtd.Rifles Co.E
Wagoner, John B. LA 1st Cav. Co.K
Wagoner, John C. TX 3rd Cav. Co.G
Wagoner, John M. VA 31st Inf. Co.E
Wagoner, John M. VA 57th Inf. Co.C
Wagoner, Joseph KY 9th Cav. Co.B
Wagoner, Joseph NC 7th Sr.Res. Holland's Co.
Wagoner, Joseph T. TN 44th (Cons.) Inf. Co.B
Wagoner, Joshua MO 6th Cav. Co.F
Wagoner, J.S. VA 19th Cav. Co.I
Wagoner, J.W. GA 54th Inf. Co.B
Wagoner, J.W. LA 17th Inf. Co.K,F
Wagoner, J.W. NC 1st Inf. (6 mo. '61) Co.B
Wagoner, J.W. TX 10th Cav. Co.K
Wagoner, Laf TX Cav. Martin's Regt. Co.F
Wagoner, Lafayette TX Cav. 2nd Regt.St.Troops Co.E
Wagoner, Lem F. NC 4th Sr.Res. Co.D
Wagoner, L.M. MS 10th Cav. Co.F
Wagoner, Louis P. AL St.Arty. Co.D
Wagoner, L.P. AL Mobile City Troop
Wagoner, Martin NC 22nd Inf. Co.F
Wagoner, Martin TX 1st Field Btty.
Wagoner, Martin TX St.Troops Edgar's Co.
Wagoner, M.C. AR 21st Inf. Co.A
Wagoner, Mebine NC 56th Inf. Co.D
Wagoner, Michel of Fred VA 77th Mil. Co.C
Wagoner, M.M. AR 26th Inf. Co.K
Wagoner, Murray MO Inf. Clark's Regt. Co.I
Wagoner, Murray Conf.Cav. Clarkson's Bn. Ind.Rangers Co.C
Wagoner, Nathaniel B. KY Cav. Sypert's Regt. Co.C
Wagoner, N.S. GA 1st Inf. (St.Guards) Co.C
Wagoner, Peter NC 47th Inf. Co.K
Wagoner, Peter F. NC 34th Inf. Co.B
Wagoner, Philip VA Horse Arty. McClanahan's Co.
Wagoner, P.R. NC 7th Sr.Res. Boon's Co.
Wagoner, Reuben NC 1st Inf. Co.H
Wagoner, Richard MD Inf. 2nd Bn. Co.C
Wagoner, R.J.B. TN 40th Inf. Co.G
Wagoner, Samuel TN Hvy.Arty. Caruthers' Btty.
Wagoner, Samuel VA 60th Inf. Co.G
Wagoner, S.B. TN 6th Inf. Co.L
Wagoner, S.B. TN 55th (Brown's) Inf. Ford's Co.
Wagoner, Simeon NC 42nd Inf. Co.I
Wagoner, Simeon NC 1st Home Guards Co.F Sgt.
Wagoner, Solomon MO Inf. Clark's Regt. Co.I
Wagoner, Solomon TN 4th (McLemore's) Cav. Co.K
Wagoner, Solomon Conf.Cav. Clarkson's Bn. Ind.Rangers Co.C
Wagoner, Stanford H. TN 2nd Robison's Inf. Co.G
Wagoner, T.J. LA 13th Bn. (Part.Rangers) Co.F,C
Wagoner, W. NC 15th Inf. Co.H
Wagoner, W. TX 2nd Inf. Co.K
Wagoner, W. VA 30th Inf. Co.I
Wagoner, Wiley MO Inf. Clark's Regt. Co.I
Wagoner, Wiley Conf.Cav. Clarkson's Bn. Ind.Rangers Co.C
Wagoner, William LA 11th Inf. Co.E
Wagoner, William MO Cav. Clardy's Bn. Co.A,C
Wagoner, William MO Cav. Snider's Bn. Co.C
Wagoner, William NC 9th Bn.S.S. Co.A
Wagoner, William NC 21st Inf. Co.B
Wagoner, William NC 42nd Inf. Co.E
Wagoner, William VA 59th Inf. 2nd Co.A
Wagoner, William C. MO Lt.Arty. McDonald's Co.
Wagoner, William D. VA 6th Bn.Res. Co.G
Wagoner, William P. TN Cav. 2nd Bn. (Biffle's) Co.F Cpl.
Wagoner, Wilson NC Lt.Arty. 13th Bn. Co.E
Wagoner, W.M. AL 3rd Res. Co.C
Wagoner, W.P. TN 6th (Wheeler's) Cav. Co.H,B 1st Lt.
Wagoner, W.P. TX 11th Cav. Co.H
Wagoner, W.P. TX 32nd Cav. Co.A
Wagoner, W.R. NC 4th Inf. Co.G
Wagoner, W.R. VA 21st Cav. 2nd Co.E
Wagoner, W.S. TX 11th Cav. Co.F
Wagoner, W.S. TX 24th & 25th Cav. (Cons.) Co.F
Wagoner, W.W. AR 17th (Lemoyne's) Inf. Co.A
Wagoner, W.W. MO 12th Cav. Co.I Sgt.
Wagram, J. MO Inf. Perkins' Bn.
Wagstaff, Christopher R. VA 56th Inf. Co.A
Wagstaff, Clem. M.G. NC 13th Inf. Co.D
Wagstaff, C.R. VA 9th Cav. Co.G
Wagstaff, C.R. VA Mtd.Guard 5th Congr.Dist.
Wagstaff, Edward T. NC 24th Inf. Co.A
Wagstaff, Emanuel M. NC 14th Inf. Co.K
Wagstaff, E.T. NC 35th Inf. Co.E
Wagstaff, G.C. NC 4th Bn.Jr.Res. Co.C
Wagstaff, George B. VA 9th Cav. Co.G
Wagstaff, George C. NC 3rd Jr.Res. Co.C
Wagstaff, James SC 12th Inf. Co.D
Wagstaff, James R. NC 37th Inf. Co.C
Wagstaff, J.G. SC 24th Inf. Co.H
Wagstaff, J.M. VA 1st (Farinholt's) Res. Co.A
Wagstaff, John F. NC 37th Inf. Co.C
Wagstaff, John R. TN 53rd Inf. Co.K
Wagstaff, John W. NC 1st Inf. Co.C
Wagstaff, Robert D. TN 53rd Inf. Co.I 2nd Lt.
Wagstaff, S. NC Cav. (Loc.Def.) Howard's Co.
Wagstaff, Seymour NC Cav. (Loc.Def.) Howard's Co.
Wagstaff, William TX 28th Cav. Co.A
Wagstaff, William W. TX 28th Cav. Co.A
Wagstaff, W.K. VA 34th Inf. Co.B
Wagster, C. MO Inf. 1st Regt.St.Guard QM
Wagster, D.A. AR 5th Inf. Co.E
Wagster, David TN 12th (Cons.) Inf. Capt.
Wagster, J.C. TN 21st (Wilson's) Cav. Co.K
Wagster, J.C. TN 21st & 22nd (Cons.) Cav. Co.F
Wagster, J.H. TN 12th Inf. Co.A Sgt.
Wagster, J.H. TN 12th (Cons.) Inf. Co.A
Wagster, John MO 2nd Cav. Co.D
Wagster, John MO Inf. 1st Regt.St.Guard Co.E
Wagster, John TN 12th Inf. Co.A
Wagster, John TN 12th (Cons.) Inf. Co.A
Wagster, J.P. AR 30th Inf. Co.L,A
Wagster, J.S. TN 20th (Russell's) Cav. Co.C
Wagster, J.S. TN 4th Inf. Co.K
Wagster, M.B. TN 12th (Cons.) Inf. Co.D
Wagster, M.D. TN 22nd Inf. Co.K
Wagster, R.A. TN 4th Inf. Co.K
Wagster, Robert A. TN 16th (Logwood's) Cav. Co.E
Wagster, Robert L. MO 9th (Elliott's) Cav. Co.H
Wagster, Tho. H. MO 7th Cav. Co.H
Wagster, Thomas MO 2nd Cav. Co.D
Wagster, W.C. TN 8th Inf. Co.C
Wagster, W.C. TN 47th Inf. Co.C
Wagster, William TN 15th (Stewart's) Cav. Co.A
Waguespack, A. LA 30th Inf. Locoul's Co.
Waguespack, Felicien LA Mil. St.James Regt. Co.F 1st Sgt.
Waguespack, Felin LA Mil. St.James Regt. Co.F
Waguespack, Felix LA 18th Inf. Co.E
Waguespack, Felix LA 30th Inf. Locoul's Co.
Waguespack, Florest LA 30th Inf. Locoul's Co.
Waguespack, Florestan LA 30th Inf. Co.G
Waguespack, Floriant LA Mil. St.James Regt. Co.F
Waguespack, J.B. LA 30th Inf. Co.G
Waguespack, J.B. LA Mil. St.James Regt. Co.F Sgt.
Waguespack, Orcillien LA Mil. St.James Regt. Co.F
Waguespack, T.B. LA 30th Inf. Locoul's Co.
Wagworth, A.B. AL 4th Inf. Co.H
Wagworth, T. AL 4th Inf. Co.H
Wahab, Dallas NC 2nd Cav. (19th St.Troops) Co.G Cpl.
Wahab, Henry W. NC 17th Inf. (1st Org.) Co.B
Wahab, James H. NC 17th Inf. (2nd Org.) Co.B Sgt.
Wahab, James H. NC Gibbs' Co. (Loc.Def.) Cpl.
Wahab, Uriah NC 2nd Jr.Res. Co.I Sgt.
Wah ga Cov NC Inf. Thomas Legion 2nd Co.A
Wah ha hoo, Moses NC Inf. Thomas Legion 2nd Co.A
Wah heyuske Blanket 1st Cherokee Mtd.Rifles Co.H
Wah hos seh NC Inf. Thomas Legion Co.B
Wah Jah gee 1st Cherokee Mtd.Rifles Co.K
Wah Kaw chili 1st Osage Bn. Co.A,CSA 2nd Lt.
Wah kay ah 1st Choctaw & Chickasaw Mtd.Rifles 2nd Co.D

Wahl, Anthony LA 21st (Patton's) Inf. Co.E Cpl.
Wahl, Theodore VA 5th Inf. Co.K
Wah la neeteh NC Inf. Thomas Legion 2nd Co.A
Wahlen, Adolph LA Mil. 3rd Regt. 3rd Brig. 1st Div. Co.H
Wahlig, M. LA Mil. 1st Regt. 3rd Brig. 1st Div. Co.G
Wahloo 1st Seminole Mtd.Vol.
Wahlrob, Charles AL 5th Inf. Co.H Music.
Wahlstab, William TX 4th Cav. Co.C
Wahman, J.A. VA 2nd St.Res. Co.C
Wahmann, J.F. VA 2nd St.Res. Co.E Sgt.
Wahmann, J.H. VA 2nd St.Res. Co.E
Wah ner 1st Creek Mtd.Vol. Co.K
Wahrer, Henry LA 2nd Inf. Co.C
Wahrmann, H. TX 4th Inf. Co.C
Wahrmund, Carl TX 1st (Yager's) Cav. Co.E 1st Lt.
Wahrmund, Carl TX Cav. 8th (Taylor's) Bn. Co.C Sgt.
Wahrmund, William TX 1st (Yager's) Cav. Co.E Music.
Wahrmund, William TX Cav. 8th (Taylor's) Bn. Co.C
Wahsha benatinego 1st Osage Bn. Co.B,CSA 2nd Lt.
Wah six cocker 1st Seminole Mtd.Vol.
Wah-skon mon ne 1st Osage Bn. Co.C,CSA 2nd Lt.
Wah tar too Kar, William 1st Cherokee Mtd.Rifles McDaniel's Co.
Wahta Sutteh NC Inf. Thomas Legion 2nd Co.A
Wahtie 1st Cherokee Mtd.Rifles Co.A
Wah ti in joh 1st Osage Bn. Co.C,CSA Capt.
Wahwahseeteh NC Inf. Thomas Legion 2nd Co.A
Wah ya calooneh NC Inf. Thomas Legion Co.B
Wahyahneete, John NC Inf. Thomas Legion Co.B Drum.
Wahyaneete Sicatow ih NC Inf. Thomas Legion Co.B
Wahyelossih NC Inf. Thomas Legion 2nd Co.A
Waibel, Beda TX Scouts Co.D
Waibel, Benjamin TN Inf. 3rd Bn. Co.F
Waibel, Peter TX 2nd Cav. Co.E
Waibel, John AR 24th Inf. Co.K
Waid, Alexander VA 50th Inf. Co.A
Waid, Charles W. VA 2nd Cav. Co.D
Waid, Christopher B. VA Inf. 26th Bn. Co.G Sgt.
Waid, Edmond VA 2nd Cav. Co.D
Waid, Elijah L. AL 28th Inf. Co.B
Waid, George W. VA 2nd Cav. Co.D
Waid, Green Berry 8th (Wade's) Conf.Cav. Co.A
Waid, H. GA 5th Res. Co.D
Waid, J.A. GA 22nd Inf. Co.B
Waid, James VA 42nd Inf. Co.K
Waid, James D. VA 16th Inf. Co.I Capt.
Waid, John B. VA 5th Inf. Co.D
Waid, John C. TN 8th Inf. Co.K
Waid, John H. KY 10th Cav.
Waid, L.B. AL 55th Vol. Co.B
Waid, Luke VA 60th Inf. Co.D
Waid, Simon 1st Choctaw Mtd.Rifles Ward's Co. Sgt.
Waid, S.J. AL 44th Inf. Co.K
Waid, Solomon VA 16th Cav. Co.G
Waid, Thomas AL Randolph Cty.Res. J. Orr's Co.
Waid, William P. MO Cav. Fristoe's Regt. Co.B
Waid, William R. VA 2nd Cav. Co.D
Waid, W.L. TN 8th Inf. Co.D
Waide, A.M. AL Cav. Barbiere's Bn. Bowie's Co.
Waide, E.B. MS 7th Cav. Co.C
Waide, Hampton W. MS 37th Inf. Co.B
Waide, Ringo KY 9th Cav. Co.G
Waide, S.J. MS 7th Cav. Co.C
Waide, W.E. KY 9th Cav. Co.G
Waide, W.H. KY 2nd (Woodward's) Cav. Co.E 1st Lt.
Waide, W.H. TN 3rd (Forrest's) Cav. Co.A 1st Lt.
Waidland, J.B. LA Lt.Arty. 3rd Btty. (Benton's) Cpl.
Waids, R. AL Talladega Cty.Res. B. Stewart's Co.
Waifer, Alexander L. LA 28th (Gray's) Inf. Co.I
Waifer, Wilbur W. LA 28th (Gray's) Inf. Co.I
Waight, E.B. GA 7th Inf. Capt.
Waight, R.W. GA 6th Mil. 1st Lt.
Waightman, David NC 18th Inf. Co.A
Wail, D. LA Mil. 3rd Regt.Eur.Brig. (Garde Francaise) Co.5
Wail, D.A. GA 2nd Inf. Co.B
Wail, James H. TN 35th Inf. Co.E
Wail, John D. VA Hvy.Arty. 19th Bn. Co.A
Wail, William VA 3rd Inf. 2nd Co.I
Wail, William T. LA Mil.Conf.Guards Regt. Co.C Sgt.
Wailes, Albert M. Conf.Cav. Wood's Regt. 1st Co.A
Wailes, B.H. LA 2nd Cav. Co.I
Wailes, B.H. LA Mil.Conf.Guards Regt. Co.E
Wailes, E.H. MS Gordon's Co. (Loc.Guard Wilkinson Cty.)
Wailes, James LA 27th Inf. Co.H
Wailes, James TN 12th (Green's) Cav. Co.D
Wailes, John T. LA 27th Inf. Co.H
Wailes, Levin MS 21st Inf. Co.D
Wailes, William E. AL 3rd Cav. Co.F 2nd Lt.
Wailey, Chas. W. Gen. & Staff, Arty. Capt.
Wails, I.W. LA 1st Cav. Co.K
Wails, J. MS 24th Inf. Co.H,A
Wails, J.M. MS 24th Inf. Co.A,H
Wails, L.A. LA 3rd Cav. Asst.Surg.
Wain, Kennedy W. AL 28th Inf. Co.A
Wain, L.W. VA 3rd Res. Co.G
Wain, R.S. VA 54th Inf. Co.C Sgt.
Wain, Thomas NC 30th Inf. Co.G
Waine, John A. AR 18th (Marmaduke's) Inf. Co.D Sgt.
Waine, R. TX Cav. Bone's Co.
Waine, W.T. MS 6th Cav. Co.E
Wainell, C. VA 28th Inf. Co.C
Wainer, Henry LA 7th Inf. Co.K
Wainfield, R.W. AR 19th (Dawson's) Inf. Co.A
Wainright, A.G. MO St.Guards Bludge's Co.
Wainright, A.J. GA 4th (Clinch's) Cav. Co.A,K,F
Wainright, E. GA Inf. Foulingus' Bn. Sgt.
Wainright, E.G. GA 17th Inf. Co.G
Wainright, E.H. LA 3rd (Wingfield's) Cav. Co.B
Wainright, E.K. GA 4th (Clinch's) Cav. Co.F
Wainright, F. GA 4th (Clinch's) Cav. Co.D
Wainright, F. GA 7th Cav. Co.D
Wainright, F.D. GA 7th Cav. Co.D Sgt.
Wainright, Francis GA 27th Inf. Co.B
Wainright, George KY Cav. 2nd Bn. (Dortch's) Co.A
Wainright, George KY 7th Cav. Co.E
Wainright, George LA 7th Inf. Co.K
Wainright, George W. AR 3rd Inf. Co.L
Wainright, G.W. KY 6th Cav. Co.B
Wainright, H.D. AL Inf. 2nd Regt. Co.C
Wainright, H.D. AL 42nd Inf. Co.A
Wainright, J. FL Cav. 5th Bn. Co.H
Wainright, James NC 8th Inf. Co.G
Wainright, James L. AL 3rd Cav. Co.H Sgt.
Wainright, J.E. GA 50th Inf. Co.B
Wainright, John AL 3rd Cav. Co.H,K
Wainright, John NC 3rd Inf. Co.A
Wainright, John E. GA 26th Inf. Co.G
Wainright, John R. GA 51st Inf. Co.F
Wainright, Joseph GA 4th (Clinch's) Cav. Co.A,K
Wainright, M.V.B. AL Cav. Murphy's Bn. Co.C
Wainright, M.V.B. Conf.Cav. Wood's Regt. Co.I
Wainright, Noah GA 26th Inf. Co.G
Wainright, R.M. Conf.Cav. Wood's Regt. Co.I
Wainright, Robert MO Lt.Arty. Walsh's Co.
Wainright, Robert J. GA 26th Inf. Co.D
Wainright, S. LA 3rd (Wingfield's) Cav. Co.H
Wainright, T.A. NC 43rd Inf. Co.G
Wainright, Warren T. GA 31st Inf. Co.K
Wainright, W.H. GA 4th (Clinch's) Cav. Co.A,K
Wainright, William MS 1st (Percy's) Inf. Co.A
Wainright, William Conf.Cav. Powers' Regt. Co.A
Wainright, William R. GA 26th Inf. Co.G
Wainright, William T.H. SC 19th Inf. Co.E
Wainright, W.J. AR Cav. 1st Bn. (Stirman's) Co.G
Wainright, W.R. GA 50th Inf. Co.B
Wainscot, D.J. MO 9th Inf. Co.E
Wainscot, S.J. TX 34th Cav. Co.B
Wainscott, B. TX Cav. 2nd Regt.St.Troops Co.A
Wainscott, Benton B. TX 14th Cav. Co.F
Wainscott, C.E. TX Conscr.
Wainscott, David I. MO Inf. Clark's Regt. Co.H
Wainscott, D.J. MO Cav. Snider's Bn. Co.E
Wainscott, Ervin Marion MO 5th Inf. Co.C
Wainscott, Ewing M. MO 1st & 3rd Cons.Cav. Co.H
Wainscott, Ewing M. MO Cav. 3rd Bn. Co.B
Wainscott, James MO Cav. Poindexter's Regt.
Wainscott, J.M. MO 3rd Cav. Co.B
Wainscott, Lewis A. MO Cav. 3rd Bn. Co.B
Wainscott, Lewis A. MO 5th Inf. Co.C
Wainscott, S.T. Brush Bn.
Wainscott, W.C. TN 46th Inf. Co.I
Wainscott, W.H. TX Cav. Martin's Regt. Co.A
Wainscott, William NC 18th Inf. Co.B
Wainscott, William G. MO Cav. 3rd Bn. Co.B
Wainscott, William G. MO Inf. 8th Bn. Co.A
Wainscott, William G. MO 9th Inf. Co.A
Wainscott, William S. MO Inf. 3rd Bn. Co.E
Wainscott, William S. MO 5th Inf. Co.C
Wainscott, William S. MO 6th Inf. Co.C

Wainsett, D.G. TN 14th (Neely's) Cav. Co.C Cpl.
Wainstock, --- VA 2nd St.Res. Co.A
Wainwright, --- AL 25th Inf. Co.A
Wainwright, Abraham GA 2nd Res. Co.B
Wainwright, Adolphus LA 7th Inf. Co.G
Wainwright, C.S. AR 8th Inf. New Co.A
Wainwright, Edward J. FL 1st Cav. Co.B Sgt.
Wainwright, E.G. KY 2nd Mtd.Inf. Co.G
Wainwright, Elias K. GA 26th Inf. Co.G
Wainwright, Er. B. Bradford's Corps Scouts & Guards Co.B
Wainwright, F. GA Cav. 24th Bn. Co.A,C
Wainwright, F.D. GA Cav. 24th Bn. Co.A,C Cpl.
Wainwright, Frederick P. LA 21st (Patton's) Inf. Co.A
Wainwright, G. VA 7th Cav. Preston's Co. Cpl.
Wainwright, George AL Arty. 1st Bn. Co.B
Wainwright, George AL 32nd Inf. Co.K
Wainwright, George A. VA 4th Inf. Co.G
Wainwright, George I. MS 37th Inf. Co.B Cpl.
Wainwright, George J. MS 14th Inf. Co.B
Wainwright, George W. VA 14th Cav. Co.G, 2nd Co.F Sgt.
Wainwright, G.W. KY 7th Cav. Co.A
Wainwright, G.W. 14th Conf.Cav. Co.A
Wainwright, Jackson NC 3rd Arty. (40th St.Troops) Co.H
Wainwright, Jacob NC 3rd Arty. (40th St.Troops) Co.F
Wainwright, James GA Mil. Camden Cty. (Mtd.) 1st Lt.
Wainwright, James GA 59th Inf. Co.C
Wainwright, James MS 14th Inf. Co.H
Wainwright, J.C. VA 3rd Cav. Co.B
Wainwright, J.C. VA 32nd Inf. 2nd Co.K
Wainwright, Jesse C. VA 115th Mil. Co.B
Wainwright, John VA Wade's Regt.Loc.Def. Co.A
Wainwright, John F. VA 4th Inf. Co.G
Wainwright, John K. NC 30th Inf. Co.G
Wainwright, John V. MS 37th Inf. Co.B
Wainwright, John W. VA 32nd Inf. Co.F
Wainwright, John W. VA 115th Mil. Co.C Sgt.
Wainwright, Joseph F. AR 1st Vol. Co.G Cpl.
Wainwright, Kinchen NC 3rd Arty. (40th St.Troops) Co.F
Wainwright, L.S. LA 3rd (Wingfield's) Cav. Co.H
Wainwright, Martin G. AR 38th Inf. Co.F Bvt.2nd Lt.
Wainwright, N.P. LA 3rd (Wingfield's) Cav. Co.H
Wainwright, Samuel AR Jackson Cty. Ind.Co.2 Capt.
Wainwright, Samuel G. VA 41st Inf. 2nd Co.E
Wainwright, Solomon VA 32nd Inf. Co.F
Wainwright, W. GA 23rd Inf. Co.G
Wainwright, William MS Cav. Powers' Regt. Co.A
Wainwright, William MS 1st (King's) Inf. (St.Troops) Co.A
Wainwright, William MO Cav. Freeman's Regt. Co.D
Wainwright, William NC 44th Inf. Co.D
Wainwright, William H. VA 4th Res. Co.A
Wainwright, W.W. AL Unassign.Conscr.
Wainwrite, A. GA Cav. 9th Bn. (St.Guards) Co.E
Waiott, J.J. GA Cobb's Legion
Wair, James TN 20th Inf. Co.B
Wair, Jessy K. AR Cav. Wright's Regt. Co.K
Wair, J.P. TX 6th Cav.
Wair, Martin GA 39th Inf. Co.E
Wair, Samuel AR 1st Mtd.Rifles Co.B
Wair, William AR 21st Inf. Co.D Sgt.
Wair, William W. AR 1st Mtd.Rifles Co.B Capt.
Wair, W.W. AR 1st Mtd.Rifles Co.F
Wair, W.W. TN 20th Inf. Co.B Cpl.
Waire, Sam AR 45th Mil. Co.E
Waire, T. Fort's Scouts,CSA
Waiscots, Isaac LA 15th Inf. Co.F
Waisner, Alexander NC 44th Inf. Co.F
Waisner, Brantley NC 44th Inf. Co.F
Waisner, David 1st Conf.Eng.Troops Co.K
Waisner, David W. NC 28th Inf. Co.E
Waisner, Jacob MO 2nd Inf. Co.D
Waisner, Jacob MO 3rd & 5th Cons.Inf.
Waisner, William NC 44th Inf. Co.F
Waison, Absolum MS 14th Inf. Co.B
Waiss, J. SC 4th St.Troops Co.G
Waistcoat, William S. VA 44th Inf. Co.F
Waistcot, Henry LA 15th Inf. Co.F
Waistunna 1st Creek Mtd.Vol. 2nd Co.C
Wait, Abner K. AL 10th Inf. Co.F 2nd Lt.
Wait, B.P. GA 1st (Olmstead's) Inf. Co.F
Wait, B.P. GA 25th Inf. Pritchard's Co.
Wait, Edwin GA 1st (Olmstead's) Inf. Co.F 1st Lt.
Wait, Edwin GA 25th Inf. Pritchard's Co. 1st Sgt.
Wait, E.J. TN 38th Inf. Co.G 1st Lt.
Wait, E.P. GA 5th Cav. Co.A
Wait, G. AL Talladega Cty.Res. D.B. Brown's Co.
Wait, George D. TX 36th Cav. Co.E
Wait, G.H. AR Lt.Arty. Marshall's Btty.
Wait, G.H. AR Willett's Co. Cpl.
Wait, Gilbert MS 8th Inf. Co.E
Wait, J. AL 43rd Inf. Co.C
Wait, James MS 42nd Inf. Co.F
Wait, James W. MS 34th Inf. Co.C
Wait, J.C. GA Inf. (RR Guards) Preston's Co. Cpl.
Wait, Jesse T. GA 36th (Broyles') Inf. Co.D
Wait, Jessie G. AL 10th Inf. Co.F Cpl.
Wait, J.M. TN 38th Inf. Co.G Sgt.
Wait, John F. MS 42nd Inf. Co.F
Wait, John T. MS 8th Inf. Co.E Sgt.
Wait, Joshua SC 5th Res. Co.I,B
Wait, L.J. SC Lt.Arty. Jeter's Co. (Macbeth Lt.Arty.)
Wait, M. LA Mil. 2nd Regt. 2nd Brig. 1st Div. Co.H
Wait, Nicklolas C. GA Cobb's Legion Co.C
Wait, P.D. 2nd Conf.Eng.Troops Co.D Sgt.
Wait, Philip D. GA 1st (Olmstead's) Inf. Gordon's Co.
Wait, Philip D. GA 63rd Inf. Co.F
Wait, Pinkney C. AL 8th (Hatch's) Cav. Co.K
Wait, P.M.B. Conf.Cav. Wood's Regt. 2nd Co.G
Wait, Rasberry MS 8th Inf. Co.E
Wait, Richard H. AL 11th Inf. Co.I
Wait, Rochambeau L. Conf.Cav. Wood's Regt. 2nd Co.G
Wait, Simpson SC 1st St.Troops Co.F
Wait, S.J. MS Cav. 3rd (St.Troops) Co.D
Wait, W. SC 6th (Merriwether's) Bn.St.Res.
Wait, William G. MS 42nd Inf. Co.F
Wait, Zachariah MS 17th Inf. Co.K
Waite, Andrew M. AL Arty. 1st Bn. Co.E
Waite, C. FL Fernandez's Mtd.Co. (Supply Force)
Waite, C. MS 9th Inf. Co.I
Waite, Charles VA 9th Cav. Co.B
Waite, Charles Gen. & Staff Maj.,QM
Waite, P. TX Cav. Benavides' Regt. Co.C
Waite, George B. TN 24th Inf. Co.K
Waite, George W. LA 16th Inf. Co.C
Waite, George W. TN 24th Inf. Co.K
Waite, George W. VA 12th Inf. Co.E
Waite, H. MS 37th Inf. Co.A
Waite, Hinz VA Lt.Arty. Cooper's Co.
Waite, James R. AL 38th Inf. Co.C Cpl.
Waite, Jesse J. GA 30th Inf. Co.D
Waite, J.G. AL Conscr.
Waite, J.M. GA 11th Inf. Co.K
Waite, John H. SC 2nd Rifles Co.A
Waite, Samuel C. VA 22nd Inf. Co.F 2nd Lt.
Waite, Samuel C. VA 108th Mil. Lemons' Co.
Waite, Samuel I. MS 39th Inf. Co.C 2nd Lt.
Waite, S.C. VA Inf. 26th Bn. Co.B Sgt.
Waite, Selathiel VA 30th Inf. Co.C
Waite, S.J. 20th Conf.Cav. Co.G
Waite, Thomas TX 15th Cav. Co.K
Waite, Thomas H. 4th Conf.Inf. Co.F
Waite, V.B. MS 9th Inf. Co.I
Waite, William H, Jr. VA 9th Cav. Co.E Cpl.
Waiter, J. AL 3rd Inf. Co.K
Waiter, W.B. GA 2nd Cav. Co.D Sgt.
Waiters, Thomas GA 20th Inf. Co.A
Waiters, William A. GA 1st Reg. Co.H
Waites, A.R. GA 2nd Res. Co.G Cpl.
Waites, A.R. MS 5th Inf. (St.Troops) Co.I
Waites, Cicero H. TX 19th Cav. Co.D 2nd Lt.
Waites, Edward LA 22nd Inf. Co.B
Waites, Elbridge AR 1st (Colquitt's) Inf. Co.F
Waites, Franklin L. TX 17th Cav. 1st Co.I
Waites, Franklin L. TX 19th Cav. Co.D
Waites, George D. AR 1st (Colquitt's) Inf. Co.H
Waites, H. MS 5th Inf. (St.Troops) Co.D
Waites, Jacob B. TX 15th Cav. Co.E
Waites, John R. TN 28th (Cons.) Inf. Co.K
Waites, W.F. AL St.Res. Palmer's Co. 1st Lt.
Waitman, A. MO 6th Cav. Co.H
Waitman, Jacob TX 16th Inf. Co.I
Waitman, W.H. MO 6th Cav. Co.H
Waitmann, L.V. VA 12th Cav. Co.H
Waits, Abraham AL Lt.Arty. 2nd Bn.
Waits, A.F.M. AR 16th Inf. Co.I
Waits, A.F.M. AR 35th Inf. Co.K
Waits, A.K. AL 40th Inf. Co.H
Waits, Alexander GA Siege Arty. 28th Bn. Co.F
Waits, Alford B. AR 3rd Inf. Co.B
Waits, Anderson F. MS 15th Inf. Co.K
Waits, Andrew F. MS Adair's Co. (Lodi Co.) Sgt.
Waits, Andrew M. GA Lt.Arty. (Jo Thompson Arty.) Hanleiter's Co.
Waits, Andrew M. GA 38th Inf. Co.M

Waits, A.R. GA Inf. (Collier Guards) Collier's Co.
Waits, A.R. GA Inf. Jackson's Co.
Waits, A.R. MS 26th Inf. Co.D Cpl.
Waits, Asberrey L. GA Cherokee Legion (St.Guards) Co.H
Waits, Beaufort SC Inf. Holcombe Legion Co.H
Waits, B.M. AL Inf. 1st Regt. Co.D,F
Waits, Brander B. AR 3rd Inf. Co.F Cpl.
Waits, Burleson W. AL 62nd Inf. Co.G
Waits, C. MS 2nd Inf. Co.E
Waits, Calvin FL 9th Inf. Co.F Cpl.
Waits, Carroll A. MS Cav. Hughes' Bn. Co.H Cpl.
Waits, Daniel D.M. GA 42nd Inf. Co.I Cpl.
Waits, David MO 1st N.E. Cav. Co.A
Waits, Dempsey AR 23rd Inf. Co.G
Waits, Denis C. MS 17th Inf. Co.K
Waits, Denis C. VA Cav. Mosby's Regt. (Part.Rangers)
Waits, Drayton SC Inf. Holcombe Legion Co.H
Waits, E.J. 4th Conf.Inf. Co.B Music.
Waits, F.A. GA Cherokee Legion (St.Guards) Co.H
Waits, F.H. MS 4th Cav. Co.K
Waits, F.M. AR 3rd Cav. Co.D
Waits, Francis M. MS 27th Inf. Co.H
Waits, Francis M. TX Cav. Benavides' Regt. Co.K
Waits, Francis Marion KY Jessee's Bn.Mtd. Riflemen Lt.
Waits, Frank H. AL 38th Inf. Co.C
Waits, Freeling H. MS Cav. Hughes' Bn. Co.H
Waits, George A. MS 26th Inf. Co.D
Waits, George M.T. GA 44th Inf. Co.B
Waits, G.M. AL 34th Inf. Co.C Sgt.
Waits, G.P. AL Inf. 1st Regt. Co.B
Waits, H. MS Inf. 2nd St.Troops Co.H
Waits, Henry MS 5th Cav. Co.G
Waits, Henry MS St.Cav. Perrin's Bn. Co.B
Waits, Henry MS 2nd (Davidson's) Inf. Co.A
Waits, Henry SC 2nd Arty. Co.K
Waits, H.W. AL 26th (O'Neal's) Inf. Co.F
Waits, J. GA Inf. Jackson's Co.
Waits, Jacob MS 37th Inf. Co.I
Waits, James AL Inf. 1st Regt. Co.D
Waits, James AR 16th Inf. Co.I
Waits, James MS 37th Inf. Co.I
Waits, James TX 10th Cav. Co.G
Waits, James C. 3rd Conf.Eng.Troops Co.D
Waits, James M. GA Lt.Arty. (Jo Thompson Arty.) Hanleiter's Co.
Waits, James M. GA 38th Inf. Co.M
Waits, James M. MS 2nd St.Cav. Co.D
Waits, James W. GA 5th Inf. Co.C
Waits, James W. GA 34th Inf. Co.A Cpl.
Waits, J.D. AR 1st Inf. Co.H
Waits, J.H. AL Lt.Arty. 2nd Bn. Co.F
Waits, J.H. AR 37th Inf. Co.G
Waits, J.H. GA Lt.Arty. 14th Bn. Co.F
Waits, John GA 41st Inf. Co.D
Waits, John MS 2nd Inf. Co.E
Waits, John MS 37th Inf. Co.I
Waits, John MS 43rd Inf. Co.K
Waits, John C. GA Floyd Legion (St.Guards) Co.H
Waits, John P. TX 14th Inf. Co.G
Waits, John R. TN 84th Inf. Co.F
Waits, John W. AL 59th Inf. Co.K
Waits, Joseph TX 29th Cav. Co.B 2nd Lt.
Waits, Joseph G. GA 30th Inf. Co.G
Waits, Joseph M. MS 28th Cav. Co.E
Waits, Joseph W. AR 2nd Cav. Co.C
Waits, L. AL 25th Inf. Co.F Sgt.
Waits, Larry AL 46th Inf. Co.G
Waits, Leonidas B. AL 4th Inf. Co.H
Waits, Leroy GA 20th Inf. Co.E
Waits, Levi GA Inf. (Jasper & Butts Cty.Guards) Lane's Co.
Waits, Livingston B. MS 17th Inf. Co.K
Waits, M.A. GA 42nd Inf. Co.H
Waits, Madison GA 7th Inf. Co.H
Waits, Maxey GA 2nd Res. Co.K
Waits, M.B. AL 7th Inf. Co.G
Waits, Newton GA 38th Inf. Co.A
Waits, O.K. AL 25th Inf. Co.F
Waits, Patrick O. MS 9th Inf. Old Co.C Cpl.
Waits, Patrick O. MS 42nd Inf. Co.I Sgt.
Waits, Rasmus AR 2nd Inf. Co.D
Waits, Richard GA Inf. (Jasper & Butts Cty.-Guards) Lane's Co.
Waits, Richd. MS 8th Inf. Co.E
Waits, S.A. MS Inf. 3rd Bn. Co.H
Waits, Samuel AL Talladega Cty.Res. B. Stewart's Co.
Waits, Samuel KY Horse Arty. Byrne's Co.
Waits, Samuel LA Inf. 1st Sp.Bn. (Wheat's) Co.B Sgt.
Waits, Samuel MO Lt.Arty. Barret's Co.
Waits, Samuel SC 2nd Arty. Co.K
Waits, Samuel SC Inf. Holcombe Legion Co.H
Waits, Samuel P. AL 44th Inf. Co.A
Waits, Samuel S. MS 15th Inf. Co.K
Waits, Shelton A. AL 27th Inf. Co.C
Waits, S.M. MS 8th Inf. Co.H Music.
Waits, S.P. AL 7th Cav. Co.A
Waits, S.P. AL 59th Inf. Co.E
Waits, Thomas GA Phillips' Legion Co.F,P
Waits, Thomas K. GA 42nd Inf. Co.I
Waits, W.A. MS 28th Cav. Co.E Sgt.
Waits, W.D. AR Cav. Gordon's Regt. Co.B
Waits, W.H. MS 41st Inf. Co.G
Waits, William AL 12th Cav. Co.G
Waits, William MS 5th Inf. (St.Troops) Co.C
Waits, William MS Rogers' Co.
Waits, William B. GA 44th Inf. Co.B
Waits, William F. FL 7th Inf. Co.H
Waits, William F. FL 9th Inf. Co.K,G
Waits, William H. MS 10th Cav. Co.G
Waits, William P. GA 5th Inf. Co.A
Waits, W.J. FL 1st (Res.) Inf. Co.A
Waits, W.J. 8th (Wade's) Conf.Cav. Co.C
Waits, W.L. TX Arty. Douglas' Co. Cpl.
Waits, W.M. AL Randolph Cty.Res. R.C. Raney's Co.
Waits, W.P. MS 1st Cav. Co.K
Waits, W.S. MS 1st Cav. Co.E
Waits, W.T. MS 18th Cav. Co.C
Waitt, George N. NC 28th Inf. Co.G
Waitt, Horatio A. NC 14th Inf. Co.K
Waitt, J.W. 20th Conf.Cav. Co.M
Waitt, Z. 8th (Wade's) Conf.Cav. Co.E
Waitte, Anderson M. VA 108th Mil. Co.C
Waitz, A. GA Arty. (Macon Lt.Arty.) Slaten's Co. Cpl.
Waitz, Zack MS Cav. 4th Bn. Co.C
Waitze, Augustus AL Inf. 1st Regt. Co.A
Waitzfelder, E. GA Inf. (Milledgeville Guards) Caraker's Co.
Waitzfelder, Elkan GA 1st (Ramsey's) Inf. Co.E
Waitzfelder, L. GA Inf. (Milledgeville Guards) Caraker's Co. 1st Lt.
Wakage Aikin 1st Choctaw & Chickasaw Mtd.Rifles 3rd Co.D
Wakayacha 1st Choctaw & Chickasaw Mtd.Rifles 3rd Co.K
Wakayomebe Deneale's Regt. Choctaw Warriors Co.A
Wake, A.R. TN 10th Inf. Co.F
Wake, John J. VA 109th Mil. Co.B Cpl.
Wakeborn, John O. MS 2nd (Quinn's St.Troops) Inf. Co.E
Wakee, Johnny 1st Seminole Mtd.Vol.
Wakefield, A. SC 16th Inf. Co.K
Wakefield, A. SC 22nd Inf. Co.C Capt.
Wakefield, A. TX 33rd Cav. Co.K
Wakefield, A. TX Cav. Giddings' Bn. Weisiger's Co. Cpl.
Wakefield, A.H. MO Lt.Arty. 1st Btty.
Wakefield, A.J. MS Cav. Hughes' Bn. Co.H
Wakefield, Alex SC 22nd Inf. Co.C
Wakefield, Alex TX Cav. Gidding's Bn.
Wakefield, Alexander H. MO Lt.Arty. 1st Field Btty.
Wakefield, A.R. SC 13th Inf. Co.B 1st Sgt.
Wakefield, B.F. AL 26th (O'Neal's) Inf. Co.C
Wakefield, Charles GA Brooks' Co. (Terrell Lt.Arty.)
Wakefield, Charles N. TN 41st Inf. Co.G Sgt.
Wakefield, D. AL 5th Inf. Co.H Sgt.
Wakefield, F.M. GA Brooks' Co. (Terrell Lt.Arty.)
Wakefield, George N. GA 6th Inf. Co.B
Wakefield, George N. TX 10th Inf. Co.I 2nd Lt.
Wakefield, Harvey AR 2nd Mtd.Rifles Hawkins' Co.
Wakefield, Harvey TX 27th Cav. Co.A
Wakefield, Henry F. TX 18th Cav. Co.G
Wakefield, H.F. TX 15th Cav. Co.C
Wakefield, H.S. SC 14th Inf. Co.I
Wakefield, J. GA Lt.Arty. Pritchard's Co. (Washington Arty.)
Wakefield, J.A. SC 2nd Cav. Co.G
Wakefield, J.A. SC 7th Inf. 1st Co.B
Wakefield, J.A. SC 13th Inf. Co.E
Wakefield, James AL 4th (Russell's) Cav. Co.K Cpl.
Wakefield, James MD Arty. 3rd Btty.
Wakefield, James SC 13th Inf. Co.B Cpl.
Wakefield, James E. SC 2nd Cav. Co.H
Wakefield, James G. KY 9th Mtd.Inf. Co.A
Wakefield, James H. TX 27th Cav. Co.I
Wakefield, James M. AL 41st Inf. Co.K 2nd Lt.
Wakefield, James M. GA 36th (Villepigue's) Inf. Co.D,F
Wakefield, J.H. GA 6th Inf. Co.B
Wakefield, J.H. TX 11th Cav. Co.I
Wakefield, J.M. AL 4th (Russell's) Cav. Co.K
Wakefield, J.M. AL 7th Cav. Co.I

Wakefield, J.M. GA Lt.Arty. Pritchard's Co. (Washington Arty.)
Wakefield, J.M. MS 12th Cav. Co.D
Wakefield, J.M. 1st Conf.Inf. 1st Co.F
Wakefield, John TX 5th Cav. Co.F
Wakefield, John A. AR 25th Inf. Co.K Capt.
Wakefield, John A. GA 39th Inf. Co.D,K
Wakefield, John J. TX 6th Inf. Co.E
Wakefield, John J.W. TN 41st Inf. Co.E
Wakefield, John R. AL 28th Inf. Co.E
Wakefield, John W. GA 36th (Villepigue's) Inf. Co.D,F
Wakefield, John W. SC 14th Inf. Co.I
Wakefield, Judson SC 22nd Inf. Co.C
Wakefield, Julius M. NC 26th Inf. Co.I
Wakefield, J.W. MS 6th Cav. Co.C
Wakefield, J.W. MS Cav. Davenport's Bn. (St.Troops) Co.B
Wakefield, J.W. MS Lt.Arty. Stanford's Co.
Wakefield, J.W. TN 8th Inf. Co.I
Wakefield, J.W. 1st Conf.Inf. 1st Co.F
Wakefield, L.A. SC 7th Inf. Co.I
Wakefield, Lafayette SC 15th Inf. Co.F
Wakefield, Larkin L. TX 27th Cav. Co.I
Wakefield, M. VA Inf. 4th Bn.Loc.Def. Co.C
Wakefield, M.A. AL 4th Inf. Co.K
Wakefield, M.F. AL 5th Inf. New Co.H 1st Sgt.
Wakefield, M.L. AL 4th (Russell's) Cav. Co.K
Wakefield, M.L. TN 3rd (Forrest's) Cav. 1st Co.F
Wakefield, M.S. MS 28th Cav. Co.D
Wakefield, Nelson VA Inf. 1st Bn.Loc.Def. Co.D
Wakefield, O. LA Dreux's Cav. Co.A
Wakefield, Oren VA 13th Cav. Co.E
Wakefield, Owen VA 12th Inf. Co.K
Wakefield, P.J. GA 2nd Inf. Co.E
Wakefield, R.A. NC 58th Inf. Co.H
Wakefield, Richard A. NC 22nd Inf. Co.A
Wakefield, S.A. MS 26th Inf. Co.A
Wakefield, Samuel J. TN 32nd Inf. Co.A
Wakefield, Samuel M. TN 32nd Inf. Co.A
Wakefield, S.D. NC 1st Inf. (6 mo. '61) Co.G
Wakefield, S.D. NC 11th (Bethel Regt.) Inf. Co.B
Wakefield, S.M. AR Inf. Hardy's Regt. Co.I
Wakefield, Sylvester VA 5th Cav. Co.K
Wakefield, Thomas GA Brooks' Co. (Terrell Lt.Arty.)
Wakefield, Thomas GA 47th Inf. Co.I Ens.,ACS
Wakefield, Thomas A. TX 18th Cav. Co.G
Wakefield, Thomas J. GA 2nd Inf. Co.E Sgt.
Wakefield, Thomas M. AL 41st Inf. Co.I
Wakefield, T.J. SC 22nd Inf. Co.C Capt.
Wakefield, W. LA Mil.Conf.Guards Regt. Co.H
Wakefield, W. TX Cav. Giddings' Bn. Weisiger's Co.
Wakefield, W. VA 4th Bn.Res. Co.A
Wakefield, W.A. TX Cav. Giddings' Bn.
Wakefield, W.F. AR Lt.Arty. 5th Btty.
Wakefield, William NC 3rd Cav. (41st St.Troops) Co.F
Wakefield, William Sap. & Min.,CSA
Wakefield, William C. TN 24th Inf. Co.M, 2nd Co.H
Wakefield, Wm. J. AL Cp. of Instr. Talladega
Wakefield, William P. GA 39th Inf. Co.D Sgt.
Wakefield, William T. TN 44th Inf. Co.I
Wakefield, W.R. AL 8th Inf. Co.C
Wakefield, W.S. AL 38th Inf. Co.G
Wakefield, W.T. MS 15th Bn.S.S. Co.A Sgt.
Wakefield, W.T. TN 44th (Cons.) Inf.
Wakeham, Alfred VA Lt.Arty. 1st Bn. Co.D
Wakeham, Alfred VA Lt.Arty. B.H. Smith's Co. Cpl.
Wakeham, J.E. VA Inf. 2nd Bn.Loc.Def. Co.C
Wakeham, John TN 41st Inf. Co.B
Wakeham, John E. VA 1st Arty. Co.D
Wakeham, John E. VA 18th Inf. Co.E Cpl.
Wakeham, John K. VA 1st Arty. Co.D Sgt.
Wakeham, Samuel A. VA 1st Arty. Co.D
Wakeham, William VA 1st Arty. Co.D
Wakeham, William VA Lt.Arty. 1st Bn. Co.D
Wakeham, William VA Lt.Arty. B.H. Smith's Co.
Wakeland, --- LA Mil. 2nd Regt. 2nd Brig. 1st Div. Co.A
Wakeland, F.M. TX 7th Inf. Co.H
Wakeland, H.F. TN 7th (Duckworth's) Cav. Co.G
Wakelee, Augustus TX 1st Inf. Co.L
Wakelee, William L. GA Cav. 2nd Bn. Co.D Sgt.
Wakelee, William L. GA 5th Cav. Co.A Jr.2nd Lt.
Wakeley, W.M. TX 11th Cav. Co.E
Wakely, Thomas L. AL 3rd Cav. Co.G
Wakeman, A.B. FL Inf. 2nd Bn. Co.A
Wakeman, John VA 7th Cav. Co.K
Wakeman, John J. VA 146th Mil. Co.G
Wakenight, J.C. TN 19th Inf. Co.E
Wakenight, John NC 1st Inf. Co.G
Wakenight, John VA 23rd Cav. Co.M
Wakenight, John T. VA 7th Cav. Co.G
Waker, H.S. NC 47th Inf. Co.E
Waker, J.B. GA 66th Inf.
Waker, Michael AL 1st Cav. Co.F
Wakes, George W. VA 5th Inf. Co.A
Wak hah ge 1st Seminole Mtd.Vol.
Wakiah, Davis 1st Choctaw & Chickasaw Mtd.Rifles 2nd Co.H
Wakiah, William 1st Choctaw & Chickasaw Mtd.Rifles 2nd Co.H
Waking, S.L. TX 1st Hvy.Arty. Co.K
Wakins, D.W. MS Inf. 1st St.Troops Co.I
Wakins, L.F. GA Inf. (Muscogee Guards) Thornton's Co.
Wak ke 1st Seminole Mtd.Vol.
Wakley, J.R. AR 19th (Dawson's) Inf. Co.D
Waklin, Martin LA Miles' Legion Co.A Drum.
Waknight, J. MD 1st Cav. Co.G
Wak Se Harjo 1st Seminole Mtd.Vol.
Wakupp, Marshal VA 14th Cav. Co.E
Walace, Andrew H. AR Cav. 1st Bn. (Stirman's) Co.B
Walace, James TN 18th Inf. Co.D
Walace, John J. VA 22nd Cav. Co.F
Walace, M. AR 51st Mil. Co.B
Walace, William MO 11th Inf. Co.G
Walaver, R. TN 12th Inf. Co.B
Walbach, John B. AL 3rd Inf.
Walback, J.J.B. Gen. & Staff 1st Lt.,Dr.M.
Walback, John B. VA Hvy.Arty. 10th Bn. Co.C
Walback, John B. VA Hvy.Arty. Wilkinson's Co.
Walben, J. GA 18th Inf. Co.H
Walberg, Albert VA 1st St.Res. Co.B
Walberg, Lewis MS 10th Inf. Old Co.D
Walberge, A. AL 9th Inf. Co.A
Walbert, C.P. GA 66th Inf. Co.A
Walbert, J.A. KY 2nd (Woodward's) Cav. Co.B Cpl.
Walborn, Jackson MO 2nd Inf. Co.K
Walbour, Fred VA Cav. 40th Bn. Co.A
Walbright, Frederick LA Mil. C.S. Zouave Bn. Co.H
Walbridge, Rufus MO St.Guard
Walbrink, Frank AR 3rd Cav. 3rd Co.E
Walbrink, Frank AR 5th Inf. Co.F
Walburg, Louis MS 9th Bn.S.S. Co.B
Walcer, George MS Inf. 3rd Bn. (St.Troops) Co.E Sgt.
Walch, Andrew VA 6th Inf. Co.B
Walch, Andrew J. NC 6th Cav. (65th St.Troops) Co.G,F
Walch, C. VA 5th Inf. Co.F
Walch, Edward H. VA Loc.Res.
Walch, E.F. SC 11th Inf. Co.A
Walch, J. LA 5th Inf. Co.D
Walch, J.F. AR Mil. Louis' Co.
Walch, John NC 4th Cav. (59th St.Troops) Co.G
Walch, John SC 1st Arty. Co.F
Walch, John TX Cav. Baird's Regt. Co.E
Walch, John L. MO Cav. Slayback's Regt. Co.C
Walch, M. KY Cav. 2nd Bn. (Dortch's) Co.D
Walch, Mathis TX Cav. Terry's Regt. Co.D
Walch, P. GA Inf. 18th Bn. (St.Guards) Co.D
Walch, Phillip TX Waul's Legion Co.E
Walch, P.P. LA Mil.Cont.Regt. Mitchell's Co.
Walch, P.W. LA Mil.Cont.Regt. Mitchell's Co.
Walch, T.C. NC 15th Inf. ACS
Walch, Thomas VA 1st Cav. 2nd Co.K
Walch, Thomas M. TN 14th Inf. Co.D
Walch, William R. TX 1st (Yager's) Cav. Co.G
Walcker, Emil VA 15th Inf. Co.K
Walcot, John V. LA 22nd Inf. Co.B
Walcott, Andrew J. VA 26th Inf. Co.H
Walcott, Dexter TX 35th (Brown's) Cav. Co.D
Walcott, H. FL 1st (Res.)Inf. Co.E
Walcott, H. FL 2nd Inf. Co.D
Walcott, Henry A. AL 41st Inf. Co.C,E Cpl.
Walcott, Horace GA 46th Inf. Co.C
Walcott, J.V. LA 22nd (Cons.) Inf. Co.B
Walcott, M.W. MS Cav. 4th Bn. Co.C
Walcott, M.W. 8th (Wade's) Conf.Cav. Co.E
Walcott, Stephen F. NC 17th Inf. (1st Org.) Co.H
Walcott, T.G. LA 3rd Inf. Co.H 1st Sgt.
Walcott, Theodore G. LA 31st Inf. Co.A
Walcott, William H. TX 19th Cav. Co.A
Wald, A. TN 9th Inf. Co.B Cpl.
Wald, Thomas LA Mil.Cont.Regt. Kirk's Co.
Walde, Charles H. TX 1st (McCulloch's) Cav. Co.C 1st Sgt.
Walde, Charles H. TX Cav. 8th (Taylor's) Bn. Co.E
Walde, Charles H. TX Cav. Baylor's Regt. Co.C
Waldeck, James M. KY 5th Mtd.Inf. Co.A
Waldeck, L. SC 1st (McCreary's) Inf. Co.L
Waldeck, Peter LA 28th (Thomas') Inf. Co.A

Waldeen, J. SC Mil. 16th Regt. Sigwald's Co.
Walden, A. GA 54th Inf. Co.C
Walden, A. MS 6th Cav. Co.D
Walden, A. MS Cav. Davenport's Bn. (St.Troops) Co.C
Walden, Aaron TX Waul's Legion Co.A
Walden, A.B. AL 19th Inf. Co.I
Walden, Able A. AL 11th Inf. Co.I 1st Lt.
Walden, Abner T. GA 51st Inf. Co.K
Walden, Addison KY 2nd Cav. Co.I
Walden, Addison LA 1st Cav. Co.I
Walden, Addison B. KY 6th Cav. Co.G,I
Walden, Adel VA Lt.Arty. 13th Bn. Co.C
Walden, Albert AL 3rd Bn.Res. Co.B
Walden, Alex J. NC 54th Inf. Co.C
Walden, Allen B. GA 60th Inf. Co.K
Walden, Andrew J. KY 8th Cav. Co.B
Walden, Asa NC 37th Inf. Co.D
Walden, A.T. VA 23rd Cav. Co.A Capt.
Walden, Aurilius J. AL Arty. 1st Bn. Co.C
Walden, Austin T. VA 7th Inf. Co.G Capt.
Walden, B.B. GA 46th Inf. Co.A
Walden, Ben TN Lt.Arty. Browne's Co.
Walden, Benjamin AL 29th Inf. Co.K
Walden, Benjamin GA 53rd Inf. Co.F
Walden, Benjamin GA 59th Inf. Co.A
Walden, B.P. LA 13th Bn. (Part.Rangers) Co.A
Walden, B.V. AL 15th Inf. Co.E
Walden, B.W. TN 2nd (Ashby's) Cav. Co.D
Walden, C. AL Cp. of Instr. Talladega
Walden, C. TN 20th Inf. Co.E
Walden, Capel R. GA 51st Inf. Co.K
Walden, C.E. GA 1st (Symons') Res. Co.E
Walden, Charles VA Lt.Arty. 13th Bn. Co.B
Walden, Charles VA 26th Inf. Co.H
Walden, Charles L. LA 16th Inf. Co.E 1st Lt.
Walden, Charles R. GA 49th Inf. Co.E 2nd Lt.
Walden, Charles W. VA 62nd Mtd.Inf. Co.H Cpl.
Walden, C.L. LA Inf.Crescent Regt. Co.K Sgt.
Walden, C.M. VA 1st Cav. 2nd Co.D Cpl.
Walden, C.R. LA Washington Arty.Bn. Co.1
Walden, C.W.H. LA 4th Inf. Co.D
Walden, D. GA 9th Inf. Co.G
Walden, Dan AL Cav. Roddey's Escort Sgt.
Walden, Daniel GA Inf. 11th Bn. (St.Guards) Co.B
Walden, David AL 43rd Inf. Co.H
Walden, David N. AR 33rd Inf. Co.F
Walden, David R. TN 23rd Inf. 1st Co.A Sgt.
Walden, Dennis J. MS 20th Inf. Co.B
Walden, D.J. GA 10th Inf. Co.E
Walden, D.W. GA 10th Inf. Co.E
Walden, Edward VA 7th Inf. Co.G Jr.2nd Lt.
Walden, E.E. GA 6th Res.
Walden, E.G. GA 10th Inf. Co.E
Walden, Elijah H. VA Lt.Arty. 38th Bn. Co.D
Walden, Ellis J. MS 29th Inf. Co.F,A
Walden, Em GA 28th Inf. Co.I 2nd Lt.
Walden, Enos VA 24th Cav. Co.E
Walden, Enos VA Cav. 40th Bn. Co.E
Walden, Enos VA 55th Inf. Co.C
Walden, Erastus Sewell AL Lt.Arty. 2nd Bn. Co.D
Walden, E.S. TN Lt.Arty. Browne's Co.
Walden, Feilden SC 5th Inf. 1st Co.K
Walden, Fielden SC Palmetto S.S. Co.K Sgt.
Walden, F.L. AL 26th Inf. Co.I
Walden, F.M. GA 62nd Cav. Co.F
Walden, Francis M. AL 16th Inf. Co.G
Walden, Francis M. GA 44th Inf. Co.D
Walden, Franklin GA 48th Inf. Co.A
Walden, Franklin VA 5th Cav. Co.E,C
Walden, Frederic AL 19th Inf. Co.I
Walden, G. LA 1st Hvy.Arty. (Reg.) Co.H
Walden, George TN Lt.Arty. Phillips' Co.
Walden, George P. AL 10th Inf. Co.G
Walden, George V. GA 20th Inf. Co.C
Walden, George W. AL 11th Inf. Co.I
Walden, George W. AL 39th Inf. Co.G
Walden, George W. NC 9th Bn.S.S. Co.A
Walden, George W. TN 20th Inf. Co.E Cpl.
Walden, G.E.W. GA 55th Inf. Co.C
Walden, G.G. GA 59th Inf. Co.A Sgt.
Walden, G.L. MS Cav. Yerger's Regt. Co.E
Walden, G.P. AL 19th Inf. Co.I
Walden, G.S. AL Talladega Cty.Res. J. Henderson's Co.
Walden, G.T. TN 38th Inf. Co.C
Walden, G.W. LA 22nd (Cons.) Inf. Co.E
Walden, G.W. NC 2nd Jr.Res. Co.F
Walden, H. AL 12th Inf. Co.F
Walden, Hamilton G.G. AL 10th Inf. Co.G 4th Cpl.
Walden, Hardy J. GA 49th Inf. Co.G
Walden, Henry AL 12th Cav. Co.F
Walden, Henry AL 10th Inf. Co.G,B
Walden, Henry GA 22nd Inf. Co.H
Walden, Henry TN 20th Inf. Co.B
Walden, Henry VA 55th Inf. Co.H
Walden, Henry C. MO 1st Inf. Co.B,C
Walden, Henry W. GA 66th Inf. Co.D
Walden, H.G.G. AL 12th Cav. Co.F
Walden, Isaac GA 22nd Inf. Co.B
Walden, J. GA 5th Res. Co.H
Walden, J. TN 20th Inf. Co.E
Walden, J.A. TN Douglass' Bn.Part.Rangers
Walden, Jacob SC 2nd Arty. Co.B
Walden, Jacob SC 1st Bn.S.S. Co.B
Walden, Jacob SC 27th Inf. Co.F
Walden, James AL Lt.Arty. Hurt's Btty.
Walden, James AL 15th Inf. Co.E
Walden, James AL 41st Inf. Co.H
Walden, James MO 9th Inf. Co.B Cpl.
Walden, James MO Inf. Clark's Regt. Co.A Cpl.
Walden, James SC 1st Bn.S.S. Co.C
Walden, James SC 20th Inf. Co.E
Walden, James SC 22nd Inf. Co.G
Walden, James SC 27th Inf. Co.G
Walden, James TN 51st Inf.
Walden, James A. AR 16th Inf. Co.E,K Capt.
Walden, James A. MO Searcy's Bn.S.S. Co.E Jr.2nd Lt.
Walden, James H. AR 17th (Lemoyne's) Inf. Co.D Cpl.
Walden, James H. AR 21st Inf. Co.H Sgt.
Walden, James H. GA 30th Inf. Co.C Cpl.
Walden, James M. AL 3rd Cav. Co.G
Walden, James P. GA 19th Inf. Co.H
Walden, James S. AL 10th Inf. Co.H
Walden, James T. VA 26th Inf. 2nd Co.B, Co.C
Walden, James W. AL Inf. 1st Regt. Co.B
Walden, James W. KY 13th Cav. Co.E
Walden, Jesse J. GA 1st Reg. Co.L
Walden, J.F. AR 3rd Inf. Co.B
Walden, J.G. AL Cp. of Instr. Talladega Co.A
Walden, J.G. MS 26th Inf. Co.F
Walden, J.H. TN 20th Inf. Co.B
Walden, J.H. VA Lt.Arty. 12th Bn. Co.B
Walden, J.M. GA Lt.Arty. Howell's Co.
Walden, J.M. GA Inf. 14th Bn. (St.Guards) Co.H Capt.
Walden, J.N. MS 2nd (Davidson's) Inf. Co.A
Walden, John AL 10th Cav. Co.F 2nd Lt.
Walden, Jno. AL 26th (O'Neal's) Inf. Co.E 1st Lt.
Walden, John AR 3rd Inf. Co.B
Walden, John GA 22nd Inf. Co.H
Walden, John LA Inf. 1st Sp.Bn. (Wheat's) New Co.D Cpl.
Walden, John MS Inf. 3rd Bn. Co.I
Walden, John VA Cav. 34th Bn. Co.G
Walden, John VA 57th Inf. Co.E
Walden, John VA 109th Mil. Co.B
Walden, John A. MO 6th Cav. Co.K
Walden, John A. MO Searcy's Bn.S.S. Co.F
Walden, John C. GA 57th Inf. Co.E
Walden, John D. GA 44th Inf. Co.D
Walden, John E. AR 18th Inf. Co.H
Walden, John E. VA 3rd Cav. Co.G
Walden, John F. NC 64th Inf. Co.B
Walden, John H. MS 26th Inf. Co.D,K
Walden, John J. AR 33rd Inf. Co.F
Walden, John J. GA 7th Inf. Co.F
Walden, John J. MO 6th Inf. Co.C
Walden, John J. VA 37th Inf. Co.C
Walden, John W. GA 1st (Ramsey's) Inf. Co.H
Walden, John W. NC 48th Inf. Co.E Capt.
Walden, John W. SC Inf. 9th Bn. Co.B
Walden, John W. TN 20th Inf.
Walden, John W. TX 12th Cav. Co.H 2nd Lt.
Walden, John W. VA 13th Inf. 2nd Co.B
Walden, John W. VA 34th Mil. Co.D Capt.
Walden, Jonathan GA 50th Inf. Co.F
Walden, Jordan GA 48th Inf. Co.A Cpl.
Walden, Joseph FL 8th Inf. Co.E
Walden, Joseph Exch.Bn. 2nd Co.A,CSA
Walden, Joseph A. MO 6th Cav. Co.K
Walden, Joseph A. MO St.Guard
Walden, Joseph H. VA 109th Mil. Co.B
Walden, J.T. AL 26th (O'Neal's) Inf. Co.I
Walden, Jurdan AL 27th Inf. Co.G
Walden, J.W. AL 51st (Part.Rangers) Co.C
Walden, J.W. SC 26th Inf. Co.B
Walden, J.W. VA 3rd (Archer's) Bn.Res. Co.D
Walden, J.W. VA Second Class Mil. Wolff's Co.
Walden, K.J.N. GA Inf. 14th Bn. (St.Guards) Co.H
Walden, Kune F. GA 51st Inf. Co.K
Walden, Lary O.G. GA 29th Inf. Co.H
Walden, Lemuel FL 2nd Inf. Co.I
Walden, Lemuel J. FL 6th Inf. Co.A Sgt.
Walden, Lewis GA 48th Inf. Co.A
Walden, Lewis MS 14th Inf. Co.A
Walden, Lewis J. VA 37th Inf. Co.C
Walden, L.G. GA 56th Inf. Co.B
Walden, L.J. FL 10th Inf. Davidson's Co.
Walden, M.F. GA 8th Cav. Co.F
Walden, M.P. AL 15th Inf. Co.H
Walden, N. AL 6th Cav. Co.A
Walden, Nathan TN Cav. Allison's Squad. Co.B

Walden, Nathan A. VA 57th Inf. Co.A
Walden, Newton AL 9th Inf.
Walden, Newton AL 10th Inf. Co.G
Walden, Newton GA 59th Inf. Co.A
Walden, N.J. AL 26th Inf. Co.B
Walden, P.A. TN 41st Inf. Co.I
Walden, Patrick AL 57th Inf. Co.A
Walden, P.D. GA Inf. 25th Bn. (Prov.Guard) Co.B
Walden, Peter AL 19th Inf. Co.I
Walden, R.A. SC Inf. Holcombe Legion Co.C
Walden, R.C. VA Lt.Arty. Ellett's Co. Cpl.
Walden, R.H. MO 9th Inf. Co.B 2nd Lt.
Walden, R.H. MO Inf. Clark's Regt. Co.A 2nd Lt.
Walden, Richard AL 27th Inf. Co.G
Walden, Richard GA Cav. 7th Bn. (St.Guards) Co.G Capt.
Walden, Richard, Jr. GA 48th Inf. Co.A
Walden, Richard LA 5th Cav. Co.C
Walden, Richard TN 44th (Cons.) Inf. Co.I
Walden, Richard E. VA 17th Inf. Co.K
Walden, Richard M. VA Arty. Paris' Co. Cpl.
Walden, Richard N. VA 20th Inf. Co.H
Walden, R.J.N. GA 28th Inf. Co.I
Walden, Robert TN 20th Inf. Co.B
Walden, Robert H. MO Cav. Williams' Regt. Co.K 1st Lt.
Walden, Robert M. MO Cav. Hunter's Regt. Co.B
Walden, R.W. KY 6th Cav. Co.I
Walden, S.A. MS 29th Inf. Co.F Cpl.
Walden, S.A. TN 22nd Cav. Co.D
Walden, S.A. 3rd Conf.Eng.Troops Co.G
Walden, Samuel A. TN 32nd Inf. Co.D
Walden, Samuel P. FL 1st Inf. Old Co.B
Walden, Samuel P. FL 8th Inf. Co.E
Walden, Samuel V. VA Arty. Paris' Co.
Walden, Seaborn GA 13th Cav. Co.F
Walden, Seaborn J. GA 51st Inf. Co.K
Walden, Seth GA 48th Inf. Co.A
Walden, Silvester GA 29th Inf. Co.H
Walden, S.L. AR 12th Inf.
Walden, T. MS Cav. 3rd (St.Troops) Co.K
Walden, T.A. AR Inf. Cocke's Regt. Co.D
Walden, T.B. MS 46th Inf. Co.G
Walden, T.D. GA 5th Inf. Co.A
Walden, T.D. VA 18th Inf. Co.F
Walden, T.E. GA 5th Res. Co.A
Walden, T.E. GA 63rd Inf. Co.B
Walden, T.H. GA 54th Inf. Co.C
Walden, Thomas GA Inf. 14th Bn. (St.Guards) Co.H
Walden, Thomas GA 53rd Inf. Co.F
Walden, Thomas LA Arty. Green's Co. (LA Guard Btty.)
Walden, Thomas LA 1st (Nelligan's) Inf. 1st Co.B
Walden, Thomas VA Cav. 35th Bn. Co.F
Walden, Thomas Andrew TX 20th Cav. Co.D Cpl.
Walden, Thomas B. MS 4th Cav. Co.E
Walden, Thomas B. MS Graves' Co. (Copiah Horse Guards)
Walden, Thomas D. VA 57th Inf. Co.G
Walden, Thomas H. AL 15th Inf. Co.H
Walden, Thomas J. AR 3rd Inf. Co.B
Walden, Tilman GA 17th Inf. Co.I
Walden, T.J. TN 43rd Inf. Co.C
Walden, T.J. VA Cav. 40th Bn. Co.E
Walden, T.T. AL 6th Inf. Co.C
Walden, Uriah GA 4th Cav. (St.Guards) Robertson's Co.
Walden, Uriah GA 24th Inf. Co.G
Walden, W.A. GA 7th Inf. Co.I
Walden, W.A. SC 24th Inf. Co.A
Walden, W.D. AL 2nd Bn. Hilliard's Legion Vol. Co.B Capt.
Walden, W.G. GA 49th Inf. Co.E
Walden, W.H. AL 14th Inf. Co.A
Walden, W.H. TN 7th Cav. Co.I
Walden, W.H. TN Lt.Arty. Phillips' Co. Cpl.
Walden, W.H. TN 9th Inf. Co.L,D
Walden, William AR 3rd Inf. Co.B
Walden, William GA 9th Inf. Co.G
Walden, William GA 65th Inf. Co.E
Walden, William GA 66th Inf. Co.D
Walden, William MO 1st & 3rd Cons.Cav. Co.K
Walden, William MO 9th Inf. Co.B
Walden, William TN Cav. Welcker's Bn. Kincaid's Co.
Walden, William A. SC 5th Inf. 1st Co.K
Walden, William A. SC Palmetto S.S. Co.K
Walden, William C. AL 36th Inf. Co.D
Walden, William E. MO Inf. Clark's Regt. Co.A
Walden, William G. GA 20th Inf. Co.C
Walden, William H. AL 14th Cav. Co.A
Walden, William H. VA Lt.Arty. 38th Bn. Co.D
Walden, William H. VA 20th Inf. Co.E
Walden, William M. NC 53rd Inf. Co.I Sgt.
Walden, William O. VA Cav. Mosby's Regt. (Part.Rangers) Co.G
Walden, William S. NC Hvy.Arty. 10th Bn. Co.C
Walden, William T. VA 20th Inf. Co.F
Walden, William T. VA 57th Inf. Co.A
Walden, William W. GA Lt.Arty. 12th Bn. 2nd Co.A
Walden, William W. GA 30th Inf. Co.C
Walden, W.L. SC 6th Cav. Co.H
Walden, W.W. MS 46th Inf. Co.G
Walden, Z. Turner VA 6th Cav. Co.B
Walder, Charles LA 1st Hvy.Arty. (Reg.) Co.C
Walder, Charles LA 20th Inf.
Walder, Gustave LA 20th Inf. Co.C
Walder, Jacob Inf. School of Pract. Powell's Detach. Co.B
Walder, James A. VA 4th Cav. Co.F
Walder, James A. 1st Conf.Eng.Troops Co.G
Walder, James H. AL Lt.Arty. 20th Bn. Co.A
Walder, James H. AL 6th Inf. Co.F
Walder, John Conf.Reg.Inf. Brooks' Bn. Co.B
Walder, William Conf.Lt.Arty. 1st Reg.Btty.
Walder, W.W. AL 11th Inf. Co.F
Walder, Xavier LA Mil. 2nd Regt. French Brig. Co.5
Walderoon, John VA Regt.Res.
Walders, F. MS 4th Inf. Co.K
Walders, Franklin MS Part.Rangers Armistead's Co.
Waldert, Edward TX 1st Hvy.Arty. Co.C
Waldhauer, David MS Cav. Jeff Davis Legion Co.F Capt.
Waldhauer, David Gen. & Staff AAQM
Waldhauer, E.R. GA Cav. 2nd Bn. Co.A
Waldhauer, E.R. GA 5th Cav. Co.I Cpl.
Waldhouer, David VA 6th Cav. 1st Co.E 1st Lt.
Waldhour, Charles GA 7th Cav. Co.E
Waldhour, Charles GA Cav. 21st Bn. Co.B
Waldhour, D. GA Cav. Waring's Co. 2nd Lt.
Waldhour, Robert GA 7th Cav. Co.E
Waldhour, Robert GA Cav. 21st Bn. Co.B
Waldie, Jas. AR 3rd (Cons.) Inf. Co.1
Waldie, J.C.C. AR 24th Inf. Co.C
Waldie, Polk AR 19th (Dockery's) Inf. Co.K Cpl.
Waldie, Richard S. MS 14th Inf. Co.D
Waldie, S.H. AR 6th Inf. Co.G Jr.2nd Lt.
Waldin, E.R. AL 10th Inf. Co.G
Waldin, Jesse GA 12th Cav. Co.D
Waldin, J.I. AL 15th Inf. Co.E
Waldin, M. 1st Conf.Eng.Troops Co.H
Waldin, Patrick AL 27th Inf. Co.F
Waldin, Richard B. TN 55th (McKoin's) Inf. Co.I
Waldin, Richard M. MS 29th Inf. Co.F Cpl.
Waldin, Robert J. GA 22nd Inf. Co.K
Walding, Benjamin V. AL 27th Inf. Co.H 1st Lt.
Walding, B.V. AL 57th Inf. Co.I 2nd Lt.
Walding, C.H. TX 19th Inf. Co.K
Walding, Henry FL 11th Inf. Co.C
Walding, James A. MS 2nd Inf. Co.D
Walding, John AL 53rd (Part.Rangers) Co.D
Walding, John GA Inf. Co.G
Walding, S. TX 17th Cons.Dismtd.Cav. Co.G
Walding, Sebern FL 11th Inf. Co.C
Walding, William AL 57th Inf. Co.I
Walding, William MO 1st Inf. Co.G
Walding, William MO 1st & 4th Cons.Inf. Co.G
Waldkirch, --- LA Mil. 3rd Regt.Eur.Brig. (Garde Francaise) Euler's Co.
Waldman, Charles LA 6th Inf. Co.G
Waldman, Charles TX 6th Inf. Co.D 1st Sgt.
Waldman, George R. VA Hvy.Arty. 19th Bn. 1st Co.E 2nd Lt.
Waldman, George R. VA 44th Inf. Co.E 2nd Lt.
Waldman, L. AL Res. Belser's Co.
Waldmuller, Charles LA 1st Hvy.Arty. (Reg.) Co.A
Waldner, John GA 1st (Symons') Res. Co.B
Waldo, Charles H. LA Washington Arty.Bn. Co.6 Jr.2nd Lt.
Waldo, Charles M. AL 17th Inf. Co.F
Waldo, David MO 4th Inf. Co.A
Waldo, Isaac C. VA 17th Cav. Co.C Cpl.
Waldo, J. MO Inf. Mitchell's Brig. 1st Lt.,AAAG
Waldo, Jas. W. FL Sp.Cav. 1st Bn. Co.D 2nd Lt.
Waldo, J.C. TN 4th (McLemore's) Cav. Co.I
Waldo, J.C. TN 16th Inf. Co.G
Waldo, Jed. MO Inf. 8th Bn. Adj.
Waldo, Jedediah MO Cav. 2nd Regt.St.Guard Co.C 3rd Lt.
Waldo, Jedediah Drayton's & Frost's Brig. 1st Lt.,AAIG
Waldo, Jeremiah F. MS Bradford's Co. (Conf.Guards Arty.)
Waldo, Jerry MS St.Cav. 2nd Bn. (Harris') Co.A,B

Waldo, J.M. MS 1st Cav. Co.E
Waldo, J.M. TN 15th (Cons.) Cav. Co.D
Waldo, J.N. MS 11th (Cons.) Cav. Co.E
Waldo, John N. MS St.Cav. 2nd Bn. (Harris') Co.A
Waldo, John N. MS 2nd Inf. Co.H
Waldo, Joseph NC 3rd Bn.Sr.Res. Co.C
Waldo, Joseph T. NC 31st Inf. Co.F 1st Sgt.
Waldo, Joseph W. FL 2nd Cav. Co.C Cpl.
Waldo, J.P. MS 1st Cav. Co.E
Waldo, Peter AL 23rd Inf. Co.I,E
Waldo, Richard LA 4th Inf. Co.D Sgt.
Waldo, Samuel P. NC 4th Cav. (59th St.Troops) Co.I
Waldo, S. Pierce NC 3rd Cav. (41st St.Troops) Co.K
Waldo, Thaddeus P. VA 17th Cav. Co.C Capt.
Waldo, W.G. TX Arty. Douglas' Co.
Waldo, Wiley TN 51st (Cons.) Inf. Co.B
Waldo, W.S. NC Inf. 2nd Bn. Co.D Cpl.
Waldon, A.A. AL 7th Inf. Co.B
Waldon, Alexander P. AL 5th Cav. Co.B,D
Waldon, A.J. MS 43rd Inf. Co.L
Waldon, Benjamin MO 5th Cav. Co.G
Waldon, C. MO Cav. Williams' Regt. Co.H
Waldon, Crockett VA 22nd Cav. Co.K
Waldon, F.C. AR 4th Inf. Co.E
Waldon, H. GA 11th Inf. Co.A
Waldon, Henry GA 62nd Cav. Co.B
Waldon, J. AL 10th Inf. Co.G
Waldon, James MO 5th Cav. Co.G
Waldon, James Lt.Arty. Dent's Btty.,CSA
Waldon, James A. AR Inf. 8th Bn. 1st Co.C
Waldon, James A. AR 25th Inf. Co.F
Waldon, J.F. MS 11th (Cons.) Cav. Co.G
Waldon, J.H. GA 4th Res.
Waldon, J.J. MS 32nd Inf. Co.F
Waldon, John AL St.Res. Palmer's Co.
Waldon, John MS 2nd Cav. Co.I
Waldon, John MO Robertson's Regt.St.Guard Co.11
Waldon, John VA 22nd Cav. Co.K
Waldon, John A. TX 35th (Brown's) Cav. Co.G
Waldon, John A. TX 13th Vol. 2nd Co.I,B,G
Waldon, Johnathan GA 5th Cav. Co.C
Waldon, John B. AR 35th Inf. Co.B
Waldon, J.W. GA 65th Inf. Co.E
Waldon, Lewis VA 22nd Cav. Co.K
Waldon, L.O.G. GA 4th (Clinch's) Cav. Co.H
Waldon, M. 1st Conf.Eng.Troops Co.H
Waldon, N.S. GA Cav. 15th Bn. (St.Guards) Co.D
Waldon, Pete LA 2nd Inf. Co.K
Waldon, Peter AL 15th Bn.Part.Rangers Co.B
Waldon, Peter AL 56th Part.Rangers Co.B
Waldon, Richmond GA Cav. 22nd Bn. (St.Guards) Co.D
Waldon, Samuel AR Cav. Gordon's Regt. Co.K
Waldon, S.P. GA Inf. 11th Bn. (St.Guards) Co.A
Waldon, Taylor MO Cav. Williams' Regt. Co.E
Waldon, Thomas AR Cav. Harrell's Bn. Co.B
Waldon, Thomas Shecoe's Chickasaw Bn. Mtd.Vol.
Waldon, T.N. VA 3rd Res. Co.D
Waldon, Uriah TN Cav. 11th Bn. (Gordon's) Co.F
Waldon, W. MO Cav. Wood's Regt. Co.K
Waldon, W. VA 21st Inf. Co.E
Waldon, W.A. VA 3rd Res. Co.C
Waldon, W.H. GA Phillips' Legion Co.D,K
Waldon, William AL 1st Cav. Co.E
Waldon, William AR 35th Inf. Co.B
Waldon, William GA 53rd Inf. Co.D
Waldon, William MO Cav. 3rd Bn. Co.H,K
Waldon, William TN 14th (Neely's) Cav. Co.I Cpl.
Waldon, William E. MO Cav. Williams' Regt. Co.H Cpl.
Waldon, William J. MS 26th Inf. Co.F Cpl.
Waldon, William M. TX 34th Cav. Co.F
Waldon, W. W. AL 17th Inf. Co.E
Waldran, F.M. LA 27th Inf. Co.I
Waldran, John H. AR 21st Inf. Co.H
Waldran, William L. MS 42nd Inf. Co.I 2nd Lt.
Waldrand, Andrew VA 58th Inf. Co.A 1st Lt.
Waldrap, W.D. AL 55th Vol. Cpl.
Waldrass, A.M. LA 12th Inf. Co.A
Waldraup, Noah NC 6th Cav. (65th St.Troops) Co.A
Waldren, Elisha AR 19th (Dawson's) Inf. Co.D
Waldren, Isaac MS 1st Cav. Co.B
Waldren, Isaac VA 42nd Inf. Co.K
Waldren, Jeremiah AR 19th (Dawson's) Inf. Co.D
Waldren, John AR 19th (Dawson's) Inf. Co.D
Waldren, John LA Miles' Legion Co.G
Waldren, John TX 12th Cav. Co.B
Waldren, John VA 42nd Inf. Co.K
Waldren, Moses VA 42nd Inf. Co.K
Waldren, Samuel VA 42nd Inf. Co.K
Waldren, Thomas B. VA 42nd Inf. Co.K
Waldren, W.H. MO 7th Cav. Co.D,I
Waldren, William Z. TN 32nd Inf. Co.C
Waldrep, A.J. GA 13th Inf. Co.C
Waldrep, C.L.B. SC Inf. 13th Bn. Co.B
Waldrep, C.M. AL 16th Inf. Co.I
Waldrep, E. SC Inf. 13th Bn. Co.B Sgt.
Waldrep, Edmond AL 27th Inf. Co.K
Waldrep, Edward AL 16th Inf. Co.I
Waldrep, Edward SC 16th Inf. Co.G
Waldrep, E.N. GA 13th Inf. Co.C
Waldrep, Israel SC Inf. Hampton Legion Co.F
Waldrep, Israel A. SC 16th Inf. Co.A
Waldrep, James H. NC 29th Inf. Co.D
Waldrep, James S.L. GA 17th Inf. Co.B
Waldrep, John H. TX Inf. 1st St.Troops White's Co.D
Waldrep, Joseph SC 16th Inf. Co.G
Waldrep, J.S. GA 13th Inf. Co.C 1st Sgt.
Waldrep, Lewis SC 6th Cav. Co.A
Waldrep, Lewis SC 9th Inf. Co.I
Waldrep, M.C. SC 16th Inf. Co.G
Waldrep, P.J. GA 8th Cav. Co.G
Waldrep, P.J. GA 62nd Cav. Co.G
Waldrep, S.D. TX 5th Inf. Co.K
Waldrep, Simeon AL 16th Inf. Co.I
Waldrep, T.T. GA 64th Inf. Co.G
Waldrep, Vanburen AL 16th Inf. Co.I
Waldrep, Watson AL 27th Inf. Co.K Cpl.
Waldrep, Wiley AL 16th Inf. Co.I
Waldrep, William M. AL Inf. 1st Regt. Co.G
Waldrep, X.L. GA 62nd Cav. Co.A,H
Waldress, A.B. SC 22nd Inf. Co.C
Waldress, W.H. TX Inf. 1st St.Troops Whitehead's Co. Cpl.
Waldress, W.M.G. SC 22nd Inf. Co.C
Waldridge, D.R. LA 31st Inf. Co.F
Waldrip, A.J. TX 10th Cav. Co.A Cpl.
Waldrip, Asa M. LA 12th Inf. Co.H
Waldrip, B.C. MS 6th Inf. Co.E
Waldrip, B.W. SC 27th Inf. Co.G
Waldrip, C.L. Berry SC 4th Inf. Co.G
Waldrip, D.D. SC 16th Inf. Co.K
Waldrip, Edmund SC 4th Inf. Co.G Cpl.
Waldrip, Egbert P.D. GA Inf. 10th Bn. Co.C
Waldrip, Eli GA 43rd Inf. Co.E
Waldrip, Eli E. GA 43rd Inf. Co.E
Waldrip, Ira W. GA 36th (Broyles') Inf. Co.D 1st Sgt.
Waldrip, Isaac W. GA 43rd Inf. Co.B Sgt.
Waldrip, James A. SC 13th Inf. Co.E
Waldrip, James C. AL 51st (Part.Rangers) Co.E
Waldrip, James F. LA 12th Inf. Co.H
Waldrip, James M. MS 34th Inf. Co.I Cpl.
Waldrip, James R. GA 22nd Inf. Co.D
Waldrip, J.C. GA 23rd Inf. Co.F
Waldrip, Jefferson TX 31st Cav. Co.D Cpl.
Waldrip, J.H. MS 4th Inf.St.Troops Co.A
Waldrip, J.L. SC 13th Inf. Co.I
Waldrip, J.M. MS 3rd Inf. (A. of 10,000) Co.G
Waldrip, John AR 19th (Dockery's) Inf. Co.A
Waldrip, John MS 1st Lt.Arty. Co.I
Waldrip, John SC 23rd Inf. Co.F
Waldrip, John TN 54th Inf. Hollis' Co.
Waldrip, John Russel LA 28th (Gray's) Inf. Co.F
Waldrip, Joseph J. MS Lt.Arty. (The Hudson Btty.) Hoole's Co. Sgt.
Waldrip, J.P. AR 12th Bn.S.S. Co.D
Waldrip, J.W. MS 3rd Inf. (A. of 10,000) Co.G
Waldrip, L.B. SC 16th Inf. Co.I
Waldrip, Loren A. GA 40th Inf. Co.E
Waldrip, Loring GA 30th Inf. Co.E
Waldrip, Napoleon Geb. TX 20th Cav. Co.E
Waldrip, N.G. TX 15th Inf. 2nd Co.F
Waldrip, Nimrod S. GA 22nd Inf. Co.D
Waldrip, Sanford B. LA 12th Inf. Co.H
Waldrip, S.B. AL 2nd Cav. Co.G
Waldrip, S.H. TX 13th Vol. 1st Co.K Cpl.
Waldrip, S.H. TX 15th Inf. 2nd Co.F Cpl.
Waldrip, Thomas E. GA 22nd Inf. Co.D
Waldrip, Thomas W. MS Conscr.
Waldrip, W.B. MS 38th Cav. Co.H
Waldrip, W.H. AL 22nd Inf. Co.G
Waldrip, W.H. FL 2nd Cav. Co.I
Waldrip, William FL 4th Inf. Co.C
Waldrip, William FL 5th Inf. Co.E
Waldrip, William TN 54th Inf. Hollis' Co.
Waldrip, William C. GA 43rd Inf. Co.E
Waldrip, William H. FL 1st Inf. Old Co.F
Waldrip, William P. MS Cav. Crumby's Regt. Co.A
Waldrip, W.L. MS 38th Cav. Co.H
Waldrip, W.M. SC 15th Inf. Co.B
Waldrip, W.M. SC 16th Inf. Co.I
Waldrip, W.T. MS 3rd Inf. (A. of 10,000) Co.G
Waldrip, X.L. GA 8th Cav. Co.A
Waldripe, Andrew J. GA 14th Inf. Co.K
Waldrivan, A. NC 57th Inf. Co.D
Waldriven, J.J. NC 57th Inf. Co.D
Waldro, L.C. AR 38th Inf. Co.E

Waldrof, I.J. AL Cav. Moreland's Regt. Co.E
Waldroff, Martin AR Lt.Arty. Rivers' Btty.
Waldrom, C. MS Inf. 2nd St.Troops Co.B
Waldrom, Charles AL 5th Inf. Co.K
Waldrom, Charles AL 6th Inf. Co.M
Waldrom, D.S. MS Inf. 2nd St.Troops Co.B
Waldrom, Henry J. MS 13th Inf. Co.B
Waldrom, James E. MS 13th Inf. Co.B
Waldrom, J.C. LA 1st Cav. Co.F
Waldrom, Joseph TX Cav. Martin's Regt. Co.C
Waldrom, M.A. VA Cav. Hounshell's Bn.
Waldrom, Patrick TN 20th Inf. Co.A
Waldrom, W. TX 9th (Young's) Inf. Co.H
Waldrom, W.H. AL 2nd Cav. Co.H
Waldrom, William B. TX 12th Inf. Co.I Capt.
Waldron, A. AR 15th (Josey's) Inf. 1st Co.C
Waldron, A. GA 48th Inf. Lt.
Waldron, A. TN Inf. 3rd Cons.Regt. Co.I
Waldron, A.B. MS 32nd Inf. Co.E 1st Sgt.
Waldron, Alfred GA Inf. 1st Loc.Troops (Augusta) Co.K
Waldron, Andrew AR 15th (Josey's) Inf. Co.D
Waldron, A.T. VA 42nd Inf. Co.K
Waldron, Benjamin AL Lt.Arty. 2nd Bn. Co.D
Waldron, Benjamin GA 50th Inf. Co.A
Waldron, B.H. TN 19th Inf. Co.E
Waldron, B.J. GA 4th (Clinch's) Cav. Co.K
Waldron, Burwell VA Lt.Arty. Cayce's Co.
Waldron, Burwell VA Lt.Arty. J.R. Johnson's Co.
Waldron, Burwell VA 28th Inf. 1st Co.C
Waldron, C. GA 10th Inf. Co.E
Waldron, C. MS 18th Cav. Co.K,L
Waldron, Daniel FL 7th Inf. Co.E
Waldron, David FL 9th Inf. Co.B
Waldron, David W. VA 54th Inf. Co.C
Waldron, E. FL Lt.Arty. Dyke's Co.
Waldron, E.D. FL 4th Inf. Co.D 1st Sgt.
Waldron, Elias D., Jr. GA 2nd Inf. 1st Co.B
Waldron, Elias D., Jr. GA 26th Inf. Co.E
Waldron, George AR 1st (Monroe's) Cav. Co.C
Waldron, George Conf.Reg.Inf. Brooks' Bn. Co.D
Waldron, George W. GA 50th Inf. Co.A Capt.
Waldron, Gilbert TN 2nd (Walker's) Inf. Co.B
Waldron, G.W. FL 1st (Res.) Inf. Co.B Cpl.
Waldron, Hiram VA 11th Inf. Co.G
Waldron, Isaac MS 7th Cav. Co.D,B
Waldron, J. 9th Conf.Inf. Co.E
Waldron, Jacob VA Lt.Arty. Cayce's Co.
Waldron, Jacob VA Lt.Arty. J.R. Johnson's Co.
Waldron, Jacob VA 28th Inf. 1st Co.C
Waldron, James LA 6th Inf. Co.K
Waldron, James C. FL 5th Inf. Co.B Cpl.
Waldron, James E. MO Cav. Davies' Bn. Co.C
Waldron, James P. TX 14th Cav. Co.H
Waldron, J.H. MO Robertson's Regt.St.Guard Co.1
Waldron, John LA 1st (Strawbridge's) Inf. Co.D
Waldron, John LA 6th Inf. Co.K
Waldron, John TN 2nd (Walker's) Inf. Co.A Cpl.
Waldron, John TN 20th Inf. Co.E
Waldron, John D. VA 38th Inf. Co.B
Waldron, John George Conf.Reg.Inf. Brooks' Bn. Co.D
Waldron, John H. MO Thompson's Command
Waldron, John P. GA Inf. 10th Bn. Co.D
Waldron, Joseph W. TN Cav. 12th Bn. (Day's) Co.E
Waldron, J.P. GA 59th Inf. Co.K
Waldron, J.P. LA Mil.Cont.Regt. Mitchell's Co.
Waldron, J.T. GA 26th Inf. Co.K Sgt.
Waldron, K.S. FL Cav. 5th Bn. Co.G
Waldron, K.S. FL 4th Inf. Co.D
Waldron, Lewis AR Cav. 1st Bn. (Stirman's) Co.E
Waldron, Lewis AR 34th Inf. Co.H Sgt.
Waldron, Leyborn VA 157th Mil. Co.A
Waldron, L.J. VA 16th Cav. Co.A
Waldron, L.P. AR 38th Inf. Co.E
Waldron, M. FL 9th Inf. Co.B
Waldron, M. 1st Conf.Eng.Troops Co.H
Waldron, Malcom GA Inf. 14th Bn. (St.Guards) Co.A
Waldron, Mathew A. VA 45th Inf. Co.H
Waldron, Moses GA 4th (Clinch's) Cav. Co.G
Waldron, Moses VA 34th Inf. Co.H
Waldron, M.T. AL 63rd Inf. Co.F
Waldron, O.A. GA Mtd.Inf. (Pierce Mtd.Vol.) Hendry's Co.
Waldron, Oliver GA 50th Inf. Co.B
Waldron, Paschal VA 34th Inf. Co.H
Waldron, Randal D. GA 50th Inf. Co.A
Waldron, Randol D. GA Cav. (Atlantic & Gulf Guards) Hendry's Co.
Waldron, R.D. GA 7th Cav. Co.G
Waldron, R.D. GA Cav. 24th Bn. Co.A
Waldron, R.H. AR 8th Cav. Peoples' Co.
Waldron, Robert L. VA 11th Inf. Co.G
Waldron, Samuel VA 3rd Res. Co.G
Waldron, Samuel VA 34th Inf. Co.H
Waldron, T.E. GA 13th Inf. Co.B
Waldron, Thomas GA Inf. 2nd Bn. Co.A
Waldron, Thomas G. AL 1st Cav. Sgt.
Waldron, Uriah 1st Cherokee Mtd.Vol. 2nd Co.D
Waldron, W.A. VA 2nd Inf.Loc.Def. Co.F
Waldron, W.A. VA Inf. 6th Bn.Loc.Def. Co.C
Waldron, W.A. VA 42nd Inf. Co.D
Waldron, W.H.C. VA 1st Arty. 3rd Co.C
Waldron, William AR Cav. 1st Bn. (Stirman's) Co.E
Waldron, William VA 34th Inf. Co.H
Waldron, William H. GA 59th Inf. Co.K Bvt.2nd Lt.
Waldron, William H.C. VA Lt.Arty. 1st Bn. Co.C
Waldron, William H.C. VA 18th Inf. Co.I
Waldron, William L. AL Jeff Davis Arty.
Waldron, William L. MS 12th Inf. Co.F
Waldron, William R. VA 37th Inf. Co.A
Waldrond, J. VA 50th Inf. Co.G,B
Waldroofs, Jacob S. NC Mallett's Bn. (Cp.Guard) Co.B
Waldroop, A.I. TN 6th (Wheeler's) Cav. Co.H
Waldroop, David S. NC 39th Inf. Co.I Sgt.
Waldroop, E.D. MS 7th Cav. Co.C,A
Waldroop, J.F. MS Cav. Yerger's Regt. Co.A
Waldroop, Joab M. NC Cav. 7th Bn. Co.A
Waldroop, John GA 52nd Inf. Co.E
Waldroop, John H. NC 6th Cav. (65th St.Troops) Co.B,F
Waldroop, John H. NC Cav. 7th Bn. Co.B
Waldroop, Levi TN 19th (Biffle's) Cav. Co.B
Waldroop, N.S. GA 1st Inf. (St.Guards) Co.F
Waldroop, Thomas NC Cav. 7th Bn. Co.A
Waldroop, William GA 52nd Inf. Co.C
Waldroop, William GA 52nd Inf. Co.H
Waldroop, William E. NC 6th Cav. (65th St.Troops) Co.B
Waldroop, William E. NC Cav. 7th Bn. Co.B
Waldroop, William W. TX 36th Cav. Co.A
Waldroope, Joab M. NC 6th Cav. (65th St.Troops) Co.A,E
Waldroope, Thomas NC 6th Cav. (65th St.Troops) Co.A,E
Waldrop, A. SC Cav. 4th Bn. Co.C
Waldrop, A. SC Lt.Arty. 3rd (Palmetto) Bn. Co.H
Waldrop, Aaron GA Hvy.Arty. 22nd Bn. Co.A
Waldrop, A.B. AL 18th Inf. Co.G
Waldrop, A.B. AL Cp. of Instr. Talladega
Waldrop, Abraham GA 40th Inf. Co.B
Waldrop, A.D. AR 26th Inf. Co.G
Waldrop, A.E. SC 16th Inf. Co.G
Waldrop, A.J. TN 3rd (Clack's) Inf. Co.B
Waldrop, Albert D. AL 28th Inf. Co.H
Waldrop, Alexander NC 16th Inf. Co.I
Waldrop, Alfred M. AL 28th Inf. Co.H
Waldrop, Allen P. AL 9th Inf. Co.I
Waldrop, Anderson NC 39th Inf. Co.A,F
Waldrop, Anderson SC 9th Res. Co.C
Waldrop, Andrew AL 36th Inf. Co.K
Waldrop, Andrew J. GA 42nd Inf. Co.K
Waldrop, Andrew J. MS Cav. 4th Bn. Roddey's Co.
Waldrop, Andrew J. SC 4th Inf. Co.F
Waldrop, Archibald MS 24th Inf. Co.C
Waldrop, A.S. LA 1st Res. Co.I
Waldrop, Asa P. AL Cav. 5th Bn. Hilliard's Legion Co.C
Waldrop, Asa P. 10th Conf.Cav. Co.C
Waldrop, Benjamin F. MS 24th Inf. Co.C Cpl.
Waldrop, B.M. AL 56th Part.Rangers Co.F
Waldrop, B.W. SC 1st Bn.S.S. Co.C
Waldrop, B.W. SC 9th Res. Co.D
Waldrop, B.Z. MS 6th Inf. Co.E
Waldrop, C. TN 59th Mtd.Inf. Co.K
Waldrop, C. VA 1st St.Res. Co.B
Waldrop, Claborn P. LA Inf. 11th Bn. Co.E
Waldrop, C.P. AR 7th Inf. Co.F
Waldrop, D. LA 15th Inf. Co.G
Waldrop, David FL Cav. 3rd Bn. Co.C
Waldrop, David 15th Conf.Cav. Co.E
Waldrop, David F. VA 4th Cav. Co.G
Waldrop, D.D. SC Lt.Arty. 3rd (Palmetto) Bn. Co.A
Waldrop, D.G. AL Talladega Cty.Res. B.H. Ford's Co.
Waldrop, D.H. TN 3rd (Clack's) Inf. Co.B
Waldrop, Drayton SC 2nd St.Troops Co.F
Waldrop, E. AR 32nd Inf. Co.G
Waldrop, E.A. AR 26th Inf. Co.G
Waldrop, E.B. AL 18th Inf. Co.G Sgt.
Waldrop, Edmon W. AL 42nd Inf. Co.K
Waldrop, Edward P. GA Phillips' Legion Co.B,H
Waldrop, Edward W. AL Cav. Forrest's Regt. Fancher's Co.
Waldrop, Elbridge J. AL 10th Inf. Co.B
Waldrop, Eli NC 6th Cav. (65th St.Troops) Co.K
Waldrop, Eli M. NC 60th Inf. Co.G Cpl.

Waldrop, Elisha A. AR 33rd Inf. Co.F
Waldrop, E.M. NC Cav. 7th Bn. Co.D
Waldrop, E.N. GA 2nd Cav. Co.F
Waldrop, E.W. AL Cav. Moreland's Regt. Co.E
Waldrop, F.M. GA Inf. 14th Bn. (St.Guards) Co.H
Waldrop, F.M. VA Inf. 2nd Bn.Loc.Def. Co.D
Waldrop, F.P. TX 17th Inf. Co.C
Waldrop, Francis VA 2nd Bn.Res. Co.B
Waldrop, Francis M. GA 8th Inf. (St.Guards) Co.G
Waldrop, Frank AL 18th Inf. Co.I
Waldrop, Franklin SC 4th Bn.Res. Co.D
Waldrop, Frank M. VA Cav. 1st Bn. Co.A 1st Sgt.
Waldrop, C.C. MS 21st Inf. Co.A
Waldrop, George H. VA 10th Cav. Co.I
Waldrop, George W. GA 59th Inf. Co.A 1st Lt.
Waldrop, George W. LA 28th (Gray's) Inf. Co.C
Waldrop, G.M. TN 3rd (Clack's) Inf. Co.B
Waldrop, Green B. AL 8th Cav. Co.B Sgt.
Waldrop, Greenberry AL 41st Inf. Co.F
Waldrop, G.W. GA Inf. 25th Bn. (Prov.Guard) Co.B
Waldrop, G.W. GA 64th Inf. Co.F
Waldrop, G.W. MS Cp.Guard (Cp. of Instr. for Conscr.)
Waldrop, Harman GA 19th Inf. Co.I
Waldrop, Harrison C. AL Arty. 1st Bn. Co.C
Waldrop, Harrison M. MS 1st (Johnston's) Inf. Co.B 1st Lt.
Waldrop, Harvey GA Cav. Roswell Bn. Co.B Cpl.
Waldrop, H.B. AL 18th Inf. Co.G
Waldrop, Henry AR 2nd Mtd.Rifles Co.E 1st Lt.
Waldrop, Henry Gen. & Staff Capt.,AAG
Waldrop, Hiram R. LA Inf. 11th Bn. Co.E Cpl.
Waldrop, Hiram R. LA Inf.Cons.Crescent Regt. Co.D
Waldrop, H.T. GA 5th Res. Co.D
Waldrop, I. SC 16th Inf. Co.K
Waldrop, I.D. LA Maddox's Regt.Res.Corps Co.B
Waldrop, Iley SC Lt.Arty. 3rd (Palmetto) Bn. Co.H
Waldrop, Isaac J. AL 10th Inf. Co.I
Waldrop, Isham GA 9th Inf. Co.E
Waldrop, J.A. NC Cav. 7th Bn. Co.D
Waldrop, Jacomion A. NC 60th Inf. Co.G
Waldrop, Jacob TN 59th Mtd.Inf. Co.K
Waldrop, James F. SC 20th Inf. Co.F
Waldrop, James K.P. AL 47th Inf. Co.B
Waldrop, James L. AL 31st Inf. Co.G,I
Waldrop, James L. AL Cp. of Instr. Talladega Co.B
Waldrop, James L.H. GA 2nd Cav. Co.H
Waldrop, James W. SC Hvy.Arty. Mathewes' Co.
Waldrop, Jason C. AL 25th Inf. Co.F
Waldrop, Jasper AL 27th Inf. Co.E
Waldrop, Jasper AL 49th Inf. Co.G
Waldrop, Jasper Exch.Bn. Co.D,CSA
Waldrop, Jasper N. TN 55th (Brown's) Inf. Co.F
Waldrop, J.C. MS 21st Inf. Co.A
Waldrop, J.F. MS 2nd Part.Rangers Co.K
Waldrop, J.F. SC 2nd Inf. Co.F
Waldrop, J.G. AL 31st Inf. Co.G
Waldrop, J.H. GA 2nd Cav. Co.F
Waldrop, J.H. TX 22nd Inf. Co.F
Waldrop, J.J. TX Cav. 2nd Regt.St.Troops Co.H
Waldrop, J.L. MS 6th Inf. Co.H
Waldrop, J.M. GA Lt.Arty. 14th Bn. Co.D
Waldrop, J.M. GA Lt.Arty. King's Btty.
Waldrop, J.N. VA 5th Cav. Co.I Sgt.
Waldrop, John MS 7th Cav. Co.K
Waldrop, John VA 1st Arty. Co.K
Waldrop, John VA Arty. L.F. Jones' Co.
Waldrop, John E. AR 37th Inf. Co.H Cpl.
Waldrop, John F. AR 2nd Cav. Co.D
Waldrop, John F. SC 2nd Cav. Co.E
Waldrop, John F. VA 56th Inf. Co.F Cpl.
Waldrop, John H. MS 31st Inf. Co.C
Waldrop, John M. GA 35th Inf. Co.A Sgt.
Waldrop, John R. AL 14th Inf. Co.K
Waldrop, John R. TX 19th Inf. Co.B Cpl.
Waldrop, John T. VA 56th Inf. Co.F
Waldrop, Joseph AR 26th Inf. Co.G
Waldrop, Joseph FL Kilcrease Lt.Arty.
Waldrop, Joseph NC 6th Cav. (65th St.Troops) Co.K
Waldrop, Joseph 1st Conf.Eng.Troops Co.H
Waldrop, Joseph G. NC 6th Cav. (65th St.Troops) Co.D
Waldrop, Joseph M. GA 35th Inf. Co.A Sgt.
Waldrop, Joseph M. GA 40th Inf. Co.G
Waldrop, Joseph S. MS 13th Inf. Co.H
Waldrop, J.P. AR Inf. 1st Bn. Co.D
Waldrop, J.S. TX 20th Inf. Co.E
Waldrop, J.T. GA 2nd Cav. Co.F
Waldrop, J.T. MS 6th Cav. Co.D
Waldrop, J.V.B. AR 37th Inf. Co.G
Waldrop, J.W. TN 31st Inf. Co.E 1st Lt.
Waldrop, L. AL 15th Inf. Co.B
Waldrop, L.A. GA 19th Inf. Co.D Ord.Sgt.
Waldrop, Lank AL 18th Inf. Co.I
Waldrop, Larkin AL 47th Inf. Co.B
Waldrop, Latta J. AL 28th Inf. Co.H
Waldrop, L.B. SC Lt.Arty. 3rd (Palmetto) Bn. Co.H
Waldrop, Lewis NC 39th Inf. Co.A
Waldrop, L.L. GA Phillips' Legion Co.F,P
Waldrop, M.A. VA 4th Cav. Co.G
Waldrop, Matthew N. AL 13th Inf. Co.D
Waldrop, M.B. AL 18th Inf. Co.G Cpl.
Waldrop, M.C. TN 38th Inf. Co.G Sgt.
Waldrop, Miles SC 6th Inf. 1st Co.K
Waldrop, M.J. SC 2nd Inf. Co.F
Waldrop, M.J. SC 9th Res. Co.F
Waldrop, M. Jefferson SC 20th Inf. Co.F
Waldrop, M.P. 3rd Conf.Cav. Co.K
Waldrop, Napoleon B. LA Inf. 11th Bn. Co.E
Waldrop, Napoleon P. Conf.Cav. Wood's Regt. Co.K
Waldrop, Napolian B. LA Inf.Cons.Crescent Regt. Co.D
Waldrop, N.J. AL 51st (Part.Rangers) Co.G
Waldrop, N.J. TN 38th Inf. Co.G
Waldrop, O. TX Cav. Baird's Regt. Co.C
Waldrop, Patrick VA Cav. 40th Bn. Co.A
Waldrop, Pitts C. SC 20th Inf. Co.F
Waldrop, R. AL 13th Bn.Part.Rangers Co.B
Waldrop, Reuben AL 56th Part.Rangers Co.F
Waldrop, Richard W. VA 21st Inf. Co.F N.C.S. Comsy.Sgt.
Waldrop, R.J. AL Cav. Barbiere's Bn. Truss' Co.
Waldrop, R.M. GA Inf. 5th Bn. (St.Guards) Co.F
Waldrop, R.M. Gen. & Staff AASurg.
Waldrop, R.N. 1st Conf.Cav. 1st Co.C
Waldrop, Robert GA Cav. 9th Bn. (St.Guards) Co.F
Waldrop, Robert SC 18th Inf. Co.C
Waldrop, Robert B. VA Lt.Arty. 12th Bn. 2nd Co.A
Waldrop, Robert B. VA Lt.Arty. Sturdivant's Co.
Waldrop, Robert D. SC Inf. 3rd Bn. Co.B 1st Sgt.
Waldrop, Robert W. GA 42nd Inf. Co.D
Waldrop, Ro. J. VA Inf. 25th Bn. Co.E
Waldrop, Samuel AL 23rd Inf. Co.I
Waldrop, Samuel GA 23rd Inf. Co.I
Waldrop, Samuel GA 43rd Inf. Co.C
Waldrop, Samuel J. SC Hvy.Arty. Mathewes' Co.
Waldrop, Samuel M. SC 2nd Cav. Co.E
Waldrop, S.D. VA 5th Cav. Co.I Sgt.
Waldrop, Sebron M. AL 13th Inf. Co.D
Waldrop, S.H. GA 1st Cav. Co.B
Waldrop, S.M. SC Cav. 4th Bn. Co.C
Waldrop, Solomon Roswell GA 52nd Inf. Co.H
Waldrop, Stephen R. MS 11th (Perrin's) Cav. Co.G
Waldrop, Sylvester J. TX 36th Cav. Co.A
Waldrop, T.C. AR 26th Inf. Co.G
Waldrop, T.D. SC 1st St.Troops Co.H
Waldrop, T.H. AL 5th Inf. New Co.A
Waldrop, Theron D. NC 34th Inf. Co.C
Waldrop, Thomas AL 9th Inf. Co.I
Waldrop, Thomas SC 9th Res. Co.H
Waldrop, Thomas SC 18th Inf. Co.C
Waldrop, Thomas F. VA 40th Inf. Co.A
Waldrop, Thomas G. GA 40th Inf. Co.G 1st Lt.
Waldrop, Thomas G. VA 23rd Inf. Co.D
Waldrop, Tilmon W. SC 3rd Res. Co.F
Waldrop, T.J. TN 3rd (Clack's) Inf. Co.B
Waldrop, T.J. TN Inf. 4th Cons.Regt. Co.C
Waldrop, T.M. SC 3rd Inf. Co.F
Waldrop, W. GA 56th Inf. Co.I
Waldrop, W.A. GA 3rd Res. Co.G 2nd Lt.
Waldrop, W.B. TX 3rd Inf. 2nd Co.C
Waldrop, W.B. TX Conscr.
Waldrop, W.C. MS 41st Inf. Co.F 1st Lt.
Waldrop, W.C.P. AL 49th Inf. Co.G,H
Waldrop, W.C.P. Exch.Bn. Co.D,CSA
Waldrop, W.E. AR 1st Inf. Co.H Cpl.
Waldrop, W.E. SC 3rd Inf. Co.F Cpl.
Waldrop, W.E. SC Inf. 3rd Bn. Co.B
Waldrop, W.F. MS 22nd Inf. Co.K Sgt.
Waldrop, W.H. GA 4th Res. Co.A,F
Waldrop, W.H. LA Inf. Pelican Regt. Co.A Sgt.
Waldrop, Wm. AL 15th Inf. Co.D
Waldrop, William GA 2nd Cav. Co.F
Waldrop, William NC 35th Inf. Co.G
Waldrop, William SC 18th Inf. Co.C
Waldrop, William A. VA 26th Inf. Co.H
Waldrop, William C. AL 51st (Part.Rangers) Co.E
Waldrop, William C. AL 10th Inf. Co.B
Waldrop, William D. VA 56th Inf. Co.F
Waldrop, William F. VA 11th Inf. Co.H

Waldrop, William F. VA 56th Inf. Co.F
Waldrop, William H. GA 18th Inf. Co.B
Waldrop, William H. LA 19th Inf. Co.A Sgt.
Waldrop, William H. NC 64th Inf. Co.A
Waldrop, William M. GA 65th Inf. Co.C
Waldrop, William M. MS 6th Inf. Co.D
Waldrop, William R. AL 5th Cav. Co.E
Waldrop, William W. AL 8th Cav. Co.I Sgt.
Waldrop, William W. TN 55th (McKoin's) Inf. Co.F
Waldrop, W.M.G SC Lt.Arty. 3rd (Palmetto) Bn. Co.H
Waldrop, W.P. AR 1st (Crawford's) Cav. Co.K Sgt.
Waldrop, W.T. VA Cav. 37th Bn. Co.B
Waldrop, W.W. KY 9th Mtd.Inf. Co.F
Waldrop, W.W. SC 2nd St.Troops Co.F Cpl.
Waldrop, W.W. SC 9th Res. Co.F
Waldrop, W.W. SC Cav.Bn. Holcombe Legion Co.C Sgt.
Waldrop, W.W. SC Inf. Holcombe Legion Co.G
Waldrop, W.W. TN 19th (Biffle's) Cav. Co.F
Waldrop, W.W. TX 3rd Inf. 2nd Co.C
Waldrope, A.J. SC Inf. 13th Bn. Co.D
Waldrope, A.J. SC Inf. Hampton Legion Co.K
Waldrope, Darius LA 28th (Thomas') Inf. Co.B
Waldrope, John NC 64th Inf. Co.A
Waldrope, Robert SC 5th St.Troops Co.H
Waldrope, Samuel H. LA 28th (Thomas') Inf. Co.B
Waldrope, S.D. VA 3rd Lt.Arty. Co.F
Waldrope, S.S. KY 4th Cav. Co.C
Waldrope, Thomas SC 5th St.Troops Co.H
Waldrope, W.E. SC 2nd Cav. Co.G
Waldrope, William H. SC 5th St.Troops Co.H
Waldroph, R.J. AL 13th Inf. Co.E
Waldropp, John MS 22nd Inf. Co.K
Waldross, G.C. MS 21st Inf. Co.A
Waldross, P. VA Inf. 1st Bn.Loc.Def. Co.C
Waldross, S.R. MS Terrill's Scouts
Waldroup, David T. AL 44th Inf. Co.H
Waldroup, Elias GA 43rd Inf. Co.E
Waldroup, George E. GA Inf. 4th Bn. (St.Guards) Co.H
Waldroup, James AR 33rd Inf. Co.F Sgt.
Waldroup, James H. AR 15th (Johnson's) Inf. Co.F
Waldroup, J.L.H. GA 7th Inf. (St.Guards) Co.F
Waldroup, J.S. AR 20th Inf. Co.K,A
Waldroup, Lazzel J. GA Inf. (Jasper & Butts Cty.Guards) Lane's Co.
Waldroup, Lee J. GA Siege Arty. 28th Bn. Co.E
Waldroup, T.M.D. GA 2nd Res. Co.H
Waldroup, William NC 6th Cav. (65th St.Troops) Co.A,I
Waldroupe, John C. GA 22nd Inf. Co.K
Waldroupe, William G. AL 46th Inf. Co.G
Waldrum, F.M. TX Cav. Bourland's Regt. Co.H
Waldrum, John LA 8th Inf. Co.F Cpl.
Waldrum, John SC 1st Arty. Co.A
Waldrum, J.W. TN 33rd Inf. Co.F
Waldrum, N.M. TX Cav. Hardeman's Regt. Co.A
Waldrum, W.H. AR 20th Inf. Co.C
Waldrum, W.H. LA 6th Cav. Co.A,C
Waldrum, W.N. AR 15th Inf. 2nd Lt.
Waldrun, W.H. LA 31st Inf. Co.E
Waldrup, A. GA 19th Inf.
Waldrup, A. SC 11th Inf. Co.B
Waldrup, A.B. SC 22nd Inf. Co.H
Waldrup, A.B. SC Palmetto S.S. Co.D
Waldrup, Abram TN 1st Hvy.Arty. 2nd Co.A
Waldrup, Anderson SC Inf. Hampton Legion Co.E
Waldrup, B. Charles GA 2nd Res. Co.B
Waldrup, Edward SC Inf. Hampton Legion Co.I Sgt.
Waldrup, Elihu H. GA 2nd Res. Co.I
Waldrup, F. Lafayette NC 39th Inf. Co.B
Waldrup, Francis M. AR 3rd Inf. Co.B
Waldrup, George M. MS 8th Inf. Co.E
Waldrup, George W. GA 5th Inf. Co.A
Waldrup, G.W. GA 11th Cav. Co.H
Waldrup, G.W. MS 40th Inf. Co.A
Waldrup, H. GA Inf. (Anderson Guards) Anderson's Co.
Waldrup, Henry AL 3rd Bn.Res. Co.A
Waldrup, Henry MS 18th Cav. Co.K
Waldrup, Hillory AL 16th Inf. Co.B
Waldrup, Hugh TN 51st (Cons.) Inf. Co.B
Waldrup, Isaac A. NC 39th Inf. Co.B
Waldrup, James SC 1st (Butler's) Inf. Co.B,D
Waldrup, James M. MS 40th Inf. Co.A
Waldrup, James S. SC 7th Res. Co.K
Waldrup, J.B. MS Inf. 2nd St.Troops Co.D
Waldrup, J.C. TX 15th Field Btty.
Waldrup, J.J. GA Cobb's Legion
Waldrup, J.M. GA Inf. (Express Inf.) Witt's Co.
Waldrup, J.M. TN 3rd (Clack's) Inf. Co.B
Waldrup, John MO Inf. 4th Regt.St.Guard Co.E
Waldrup, John SC 3rd Res. Co.D
Waldrup, Joseph MO 8th Cav. Co.G
Waldrup, Joseph R. MS 19th Inf. Co.H Sgt.
Waldrup, J.T. AR 58th Mil. Co.D
Waldrup, J.T. TX 15th Field Btty.
Waldrup, J.W. MS 42nd Inf. Co.I
Waldrup, N. TN 1st Hvy.Arty.
Waldrup, Noah NC Inf. 2nd Bn. Co.H
Waldrup, Patillo C. GA 64th Inf. Co.K
Waldrup, P.C. GA 41st Inf. Co.C
Waldrup, P.W. TX 33rd Cav. Co.B
Waldrup, R. MS 18th Cav. Co.K
Waldrup, Robert SC 9th Res. Co.H
Waldrup, S. MS Cav. Ham's Regt. Co.D
Waldrup, Samuel AL 30th Inf. Co.C
Waldrup, Thomas SC 3rd Res. Co.D
Waldrup, Thomas G. MS 8th Inf. Co.E
Waldrup, W.B. MS 5th Cav. Co.H
Waldrup, W.B. MS 18th Cav. Co.K
Waldrup, W.G. MS 6th Cav. Co.E
Waldrup, W.G. MS 40th Inf. Co.A
Waldrup, W.H. AL 34th Inf. Co.D
Waldrup, W.H. SC 9th Res. Co.H
Waldrup, William GA 1st (Fannin's) Res. Co.H
Waldrup, William MO 8th Cav. Co.G
Waldrup, William A. GA 30th Inf. Co.A
Waldrup, William A. NC 39th Inf. Co.B
Waldrup, William R. GA 42nd Inf. Co.A
Waldrup, Willis C. GA 41st Inf. Co.C
Waldrup, W.K. TN 51st (Cons.) Inf. Co.B
Waldrup, W.T. MS 5th Cav. Co.H
Waldrup, W.T. MS 18th Cav. Co.E
Waldrup, W.T. MS 18th Cav. Co.K
Waldrupe, William MO 8th Cav. Co.A Cpl.
Waldrupe, W.R. GA Inf. 25th Bn. (Prov.Guard) Co.G
Waldrupt, Noah NC Cav. 5th Bn. Co.A
Waldrupt, William NC Cav. 5th Bn. Co.A
Walds, H.C. MS 10th Cav. Co.B
Walds, Henry GA 3rd Cav. Sgt.
Walds, James A. KY 13th Cav. Co.B,E
Waldschmidt, A. TX Cav. Waller's Regt. Menard's Co.
Waldschmidt, Charles TX 36th Cav. Co.F
Waldschmidt, Jacob TX 36th Cav. Co.F
Waldschmidt, Phillip TX 7th Cav. Co.B
Waldum, L. TX Cav. Bourland's Regt. Co.G
Waldwin, Benjamin FL 11th Inf. Co.I
Waldworth James M. TX 35th (Brown's) Cav. Co.D
Waldy, E.D. AL 6th Inf. Co.C
Wale, Josiah AL 3rd Bn.Res. Co.D
Wale, William LA Mil. 1st Native Guards
Walea, A.M.C. GA Inf. (Emanuel Troops) Moring's Co.
Walea, James S. GA 28th Inf. Co.K Lt.
Walea, John G. GA 28th Inf. Co.K 1st Lt.
Walea, T.L. GA 1st Cav. Co.F
Walea, T.L. GA 1st Inf. Co.F
Walea, William W. GA 28th Inf. Co.K
Walers, S. GA 54th Inf. Co.D
Wales, Benjamin LA 13th Inf. Co.E,I
Wales, De. Conf.Inf. 8th Bn. Co.B
Wales, Edward TX 1st Hvy.Arty. Co.B
Wales, George H. VA 54th Mil. Co.G
Wales, James T. TX 12th Cav. Co.I
Wales, J.C. MD Arty. 2nd Btty.
Wales, John E. Conf.Cav. Wood's Regt. 2nd Co.M
Wales, P.G. MS 18th Inf. Co.C 1st Sgt.
Wales, Thomas MS 11th (Perrin's) Cav. Co.G
Wales, W.A. GA Cav. Nelson's Ind.Co.
Wales, W.A. GA Cav. Ragland's Co.
Wales, W.B. LA 1st (Nelligan's) Inf. Co.B
Wales, W.H. VA 54th Mil. Co.G
Wales, William LA 2nd Inf.
Wales, William LA Inf.Cons.Crescent Regt. Co.I
Wales, William A. GA 20th Inf. Co.I Sgt.
Wales, William H. VA 20th Inf. Co.I
Waletubbee 1st Choctaw & Chickasaw Mtd.Rifles 2nd Co.C Sgt.
Waletze, E.G. TX Inf. 2nd St.Troops Co.C
Waley 1st Creek Mtd.Vol. Co.12 Lt.
Waley, C.H. AL 38th Inf. Co.A
Waley, Daird AL 36th Inf. Co.I
Waley, Gideon MS 37th Inf. Co.H
Waley, J. AL Cav. Hardie's Bn.Res. Co.I
Waley, James TX Lt.Arty. Hughes' Co.
Waley, J.T. GA 17th Inf. Co.A
Waley, R.A. GA 48th Inf. Co.A
Waley, Thomas MS 37th Inf. Co.H
Waley, W.J. GA 36th (Villepigue's) Inf. Co.A
Walford, D.D. TN Detailed Conscr. Co.B
Walford, Edward F. VA 1st Arty. Co.K
Walford, Edward F. VA Arty. L.F. Jones' Co.
Walford, Frederick VA 36th Inf. Co.K
Walford, George TN 19th Inf.
Walford, James VA 1st St.Res. Co.C
Walford, M.T. TX 15th Cav. Co.K Sgt.
Walford, N. KY 6th Mtd.Inf. Co.K
Walford, Thomas L. VA 1st St.Res. Co.C

Walford, W.B. Gen. & Staff AASurg.
Walfram, Louis LA Arty. Landry's Co. (Donaldsonville Arty.)
Walgamotte, Thomas L. LA 5th Inf. Co.C
Walge, C. LA Mil. 4th Regt. 3rd Brig. 1st Div. Co.D
Walgrave, Leo AL 10th Inf. Co.B
Walgrave, Leo AL Cp. of Instr. Talladega Asst.Enrolling Off.
Walgreave, Leo AL Cp. of Instr. Talladega Asst.Enrolling Off.
Walhauser, Frank LA 21st (Patton's) Inf. Co.I
Walhorn, --- AL 22nd Inf. Co.F
Walhul, Isaac P. VA 2nd Cav. Co.I
Walice, James NC 4th Sr.Res. Co.G Cpl.
Walidge, W. LA Lewis Regt. Co.G
Walien, William H. AL 47th Inf. Co.D
Walingall, Thomas MO 5th Cav. Co.D
Walis, John TN 33rd Inf. Co.K
Walis, William AR 26th Inf. Co.F
Walison, R. NC 27th Inf. Co.D
Walk, Alexander VA 22nd Cav. Co.G
Walk, Amos VA 29th Inf. Co.D
Walk, Amos VA 63rd Inf. Co.G, 2nd Co.I
Walk, Amos VA Mil. Carroll Cty.
Walk, A.W. TN 7th (Duckworth's) Cav. Co.I Cpl.
Walk, E.H. MS Cav. 3rd (St.Troops) Co.D Cpl.
Walk, E.H. MS 6th Inf. Co.K
Walk, E.H. MS 14th (Cons.) Inf. Co.B
Walk, F.M. 1st Chickasaw Inf. McCord's Co.
Walk, George LA 21st (Patton's) Inf. Co.A
Walk, Geo. W. MS 11th Inf. Co.I
Walk, G.N. MS 20th Inf. Co.F
Walk, G.W. MS 6th Inf. Co.E Cpl.
Walk, J.A. MS 6th Inf. Co.K Cpl.
Walk, J.A. MS 14th (Cons.) Inf. Co.B Cpl.
Walk, James VA 23rd Inf. Co.B
Walk, Jesse F. VA Mil. Wythe Cty.
Walk, J.F. VA 63rd Inf. Co.H
Walk, J.H. TX 1st Hvy.Arty. Co.H Cpl.
Walk, John A. MS 10th Inf. Co.G
Walk, John R. VA 23rd Inf. Co.B
Walk, John R. VA 23rd Inf. Co.C
Walk, John W. MS 37th Inf. Co.E
Walk, J.W. AL 8th Cav. Co.E
Walk, Martin V. VA 29th Inf. Co.D 2nd Lt.
Walk, Richard VA 14th Inf. Co.A
Walk, Thomas B. TN 7th (Duckworth's) Cav. Co.B Cpl.
Walk, William J. AL 8th Cav. Co.D
Walk, William M. VA 22nd Cav. Co.G Sgt.
Walk, William Talbot VA 15th Cav. Co.I
Walke, A.H. VA 5th Cav. Co.G
Walke, Anthony VA 15th Cav. Co.K
Walke, Anthony VA 16th Inf. 2nd Co.H
Walke, A.R.G. MS Cav. 1st Bn. (McNair's) St.Troops Co.C
Walke, A.T. AL 8th (Hatch's) Cav. Co.E
Walke, A.T. AL 62nd Inf. Co.H
Walke, F.A. VA 46th Inf. Surg.
Walke, Francis A. VA 6th Inf. Co.G
Walke, Francis A. Gen. & Staff Surg.
Walke, Isaac T. VA Lt.Arty. Grandy's Co.
Walke, Isaac T. VA 6th Inf. Co.G
Walke, Isaac T. VA Inf. Hutter's Co.
Walke, Isaac T. Gen. & Staff Lt.,Ord.Off.
Walke, J. AL 58th Inf. Co.H
Walke, James H. VA Inf. 4th Bn.Loc.Def. Co.A
Walke, James R. VA 5th Cav. (12 mo. '61-2) Co.A,I Sgt.
Walke, James R. VA Cav. 14th Bn. Co.B
Walke, James R. VA 15th Cav. Co.K
Walke, J.H. VA 1st St.Res. Co.D
Walke, John B. TN Lt.Arty. Burroughs' Co. Sgt.
Walke, John B. TN 34th Inf. 1st Co.C Cpl.
Walke, John P. AL 4th Inf. Co.D Sgt.
Walke, J.Q.A. TX Inf. 1st Bn. Co.D
Walke, J. Wistar Gen. & Staff Surg.
Walke, R. Gen. & Staff Capt.,AAG
Walke, R.D. VA Mtd.Guard 4th Congr.Dist.
Walke, Richard, Jr. VA 6th Inf. Co.G
Walke, R.K. LA Dreux's Cav. Co.A
Walke, R.K. LA Inf.Crescent Regt. Co.K Sgt.
Walke, W.C. TX 5th Inf. Co.D Cpl.
Walke, Wiley W. VA Lt.Arty. 12th Bn. Co.B
Walke, William T. VA 6th Inf. Co.G
Walke, W.T. VA 54th Mil. Co.G
Walke, W. Talbot VA 5th Cav. (12 mo. '61-2) Co.I
Walke, W. Talbot VA Cav. 39th Bn. 1st Lt.,Adj.
Walkel, John B. VA 38th Inf. Co.I
Walkeley, T.L. AL 58th Inf. Co.G
Walken Wolf 2nd Cherokee Mtd.Vol. Co.B
Walker 1st Cherokee Mtd.Rifles Co.A
Walker 1st Cherokee Mtd.Vol. 1st Co.A, 2nd Co.B
Walker 1st Cherokee Mtd.Vol. 2nd Co.H
Walker 2nd Cherokee Mtd.Vol. Co.B
Walker, --- AL Cav. Barbiere's Bn. Goldby's Co.
Walker, --- GA 5th Res. Co.E
Walker, --- TX Cav. 4th Regt.St.Troops Co.D
Walker, --- TX 24th & 25th Cav. (Cons.) Co.E
Walker, --- TX Cav. Bourland's Regt. Co.F
Walker, --- TX Cav. Bourland's Regt. Co.G
Walker, --- TX Cav. Mann's Regt. Co.B
Walker, --- TX Cav. Mann's Regt. Co.F
Walker, --- TX Cav. Mann's Regt. Co.G
Walker, --- TX Cav. Mann's Regt. Co.K
Walker, --- TX Cav. McCord's Frontier Regt. Co.B
Walker, --- TX Cav. McCord's Frontier Regt. Co.F
Walker, --- (1st) TX Cav. McCord's Frontier Regt. Co.B
Walker, --- (2nd) TX Cav. McCord's Frontier Regt. Co.B
Walker, --- (4th) TX Cav. McCord's Frontier Regt. Co.B
Walker, --- TX Inf. 1st Bn. Co.B
Walker, --- VA 15th Inf. Co.K
Walker, --- VA VMI Co.C
Walker, A. AR 45th Cav. Co.C
Walker, A. AR 50th Mil. Co.A
Walker, A. GA 7th Cav. Co.D
Walker, A. GA 12th Cav. Co.K
Walker, A. GA Lt.Arty. 12th Bn. 3rd Co.E
Walker, A. GA Lt.Arty. Howell's Co.
Walker, A. GA Inf. 27th Bn. Co.E
Walker, A. GA 46th Inf. Co.K
Walker, A. LA 6th Cav. Co.A 1st Sgt.
Walker, A. MS 2nd Cav.Res. Co.F
Walker, A. MS 2nd (Quinn's St.Troops) Inf. Co.B
Walker, A. MS 19th Inf.
Walker, A. NC 1st Bn.Jr.Res. Co.D
Walker, A. NC 2nd Inf. Co.E
Walker, A. SC Arty. Stuart's Co. (Beaufort Vol.Arty.)
Walker, A. SC 7th Inf. Co.E
Walker, A. TN Cav. Clark's Ind.Co.
Walker, A. TN 4th Inf.
Walker, A. TN 28th (Cons.) Inf. Co.F Cpl.
Walker, A. TN 84th Inf. Co.B Cpl.
Walker, A. TX 2nd Cav. Co.K Sgt.
Walker, A. TX 24th & 25th Cav. (Cons.) Co.E
Walker, A. TX 25th Cav. Co.G
Walker, A. Gillum's Regt. Co.F
Walker, A.A. AL 7th Cav. Co.F
Walker, A.A. AL Lt.Arty. Kolb's Btty.
Walker, A.A. AL 59th Inf. QMSgt.
Walker, A.A. AL Arty. 4th Bn. Hilliard's Legion QMSgt.
Walker, A.A. MS 32nd Inf. Co.D,B
Walker, A.A. TX Cav. Sutton's Co.
Walker, A.A. TX Lt.Inf. & Riflemen Maxey's Co. (Lamar Rifles)
Walker, Aaron AL 13th Inf.
Walker, Aaron TN 12th (Green's)Cav. Co.I
Walker, Aaron VA 7th Cav. Co.C
Walker, Aaron VA 12th Cav. Co.K
Walker, Aaron VA 21st Mil. Co.A
Walker, Aaron VA 26th Inf. Co.F
Walker, Aaron VA 136th Mil. Co.F
Walker, A.B. AR 19th (Dockery's) Inf. Co.K
Walker, A.B. FL 6th Inf. Co.D
Walker, A.B. TN 40th Inf. Co.G
Walker, A.B. TX 26th Cav. Co.C
Walker, A.B. VA Inf. 1st Bn.Loc.Def. Co.A
Walker, A.B. VA Inf. 25th Bn. Co.E
Walker, A.B. VA 53rd Inf. Co.E
Walker, A.B. VA 87th Mil. Co.D
Walker, Abner NC 7th Sr.Res. Mitchell's Co.
Walker, Abner SC 1st St.Troops Co.H
Walker, Abner SC 3rd Res. Co.E Cpl.
Walker, Abner TX 26th Cav. Co.A
Walker, Abner S. TN 26th Inf. Co.I Cpl.
Walker, Abner W. NC 22nd Inf. Co.G
Walker, Abraham GA 4th (Clinch's) Cav. Co.G
Walker, Abraham GA 26th Inf. Co.K
Walker, Abraham E. AR 8th Inf. New Co.A
Walker, Abraham P. GA 21st Inf. Co.G
Walker, Abraham P. GA 49th Inf. Co.F Cpl.
Walker, Abram AL 43rd Inf. Co.A
Walker, Abram AR 4th Inf. Co.C Sgt.
Walker, Abram G. AR 36th Inf. Co.A
Walker, Abram W. TN 28th (Cons.) Inf. Co.F Sgt.
Walker, Absalom AL 30th Inf. Co.B
Walker, Absalom NC Inf. Conscr.Lt.Duty Bn. Co.D
Walker, Absalom SC 5th Inf. 1st Co.K
Walker, Absalom SC Palmetto S.S. Co.K
Walker, Absalom M. GA 24th Inf. Co.D
Walker, A.C. AL 8th Cav. Co.E
Walker, A.C. AL 40th Inf. Co.K Cpl.
Walker, A.C. AR 7th Cav. Co.G 1st Lt.
Walker, A.C. AR Cav. Gordon's Regt. Co.F
Walker, A.C. GA Inf. 8th Bn. Co.A

Walker, A.C. MS 24th Inf. Co.E 3rd Lt.
Walker, A.C. MS 27th Inf. Co.E
Walker, A.C. NC 51st Inf. Co.K
Walker, A.C. SC 4th Cav. Co.F
Walker, A.C. TX Inf. 3rd St.Troops Co.H
Walker, A.C. TX 8th Inf. Co.G Music.
Walker, A.C. TX 8th Inf. Co.G
Walker, A.D. MS Stricklin's Co. (St.Troops)
Walker, A.D. TX 8th Cav. Co.C Sgt.
Walker, Adam AR 27th Inf. Gaither's Co.
Walker, Addison L. NC 56th Inf. Co.E
Walker, Adelbert KY 6th Mtd.Inf. Co.G Sgt.
Walker, Aderson KY 12th Cav. Co.D
Walker, Adolphus D. VA 6th Cav. Co.H
Walker, Adolphus F. MO 8th Inf. Co.G Cpl.
Walker, A.E. GA 10th Cav. (St.Guards) Co.F
Walker, A.E. GA Lt.Arty. King's Btty.
Walker, A.E. GA 8th Inf. (St.Guards) Co.G
Walker, A.E. NC 6th Cav. (65th St.Troops) Co.K Sgt.
Walker, A.E. SC 11th Inf. Co.K
Walker, A.E. TX 23rd Cav. Co.K
Walker, A.E. TX 32nd Cav. Co.K
Walker, A.F. NC 6th Inf. Co.G
Walker, A.F. SC 17th Inf. Co.A
Walker, A.F. TX Cav. McCord's Frontier Regt. Co.C
Walker, A.G. LA Inf. 16th Bn. (Conf.Guards Resp.Bn.) Co.B
Walker, A.G. MS Grace's Co. (St.Troops)
Walker, Agreal L. MO 16th Inf. Co.H
Walker, A.H. AR 35th Inf. Co.K
Walker, A.H. TN 15th (Cons.) Cav. Co.F 1st Sgt.
Walker, A.H. TN 15th (Stewart's) Cav. Co.C Sgt.
Walker, A.H. TN 12th Inf. Co.B
Walker, A.H. TN 12th (Cons.) Inf. Co.A
Walker, A.H. TN 23rd Inf. Co.C
Walker, A.H.C. GA Inf. 25th Bn. (Prov.Guard) Co.D
Walker, A.H.C. GA 66th Inf. Co.B 2nd Lt.
Walker, A.J. AL 1st Cav. Co.A
Walker, A.J. AL Cav. Hardie's Bn.Res. Co.A
Walker, A.J. AL Cav. Moreland's Regt. Co.H
Walker, A.J. AL Mil. 4th Vol. Co.E
Walker, A.J. AL 6th Inf. Co.I
Walker, A.J. AL 9th Inf. Co.B
Walker, A.J. AL 9th Inf. Co.K
Walker, A.J. AL 14th Inf. Co.I Cpl.
Walker, A.J. AL 21st Inf. Co.F
Walker, A.J. AL 29th Inf. Co.D
Walker, A.J. AR 2nd Inf. Co.H
Walker, A.J. AR 36th Inf. Co.E
Walker, A.J. AR Inf. Cocke's Regt. Co.C,I
Walker, A.J. GA 5th Res. Co.C
Walker, A.J. KY 10th (Johnson's) Cav. New Co.C
Walker, A.J. MS 7th Cav. Co.E
Walker, A.J. MS 46th Inf. Co.H
Walker, A.J. MO 4th Cav. Co.C
Walker, A.J. SC 17th Inf. Co.A
Walker, A.J. TN 30th Inf. Co.H
Walker, A.J. TX Cav. Waller's Regt. Co.E
Walker, A.J. TX 2nd Inf. Co.I
Walker, A.J. TX 15th Inf. 2nd Co.E
Walker, A.J. 1st Conf.Inf. 2nd Co.I
Walker, A.J.B. TN 8th Inf. Co.E Capt.
Walker, A. John Gen. & Staff Capt.,Brig.Ord. Off.
Walker, A.L. MS Cav. 3rd Bn. (Ashcraft's) Co.E
Walker, A.L. TN 8th Inf. Co.E Sgt.
Walker, A.L. TN 63rd Inf. Co.B
Walker, A.L. TX Cav. Mann's Regt. Co.H
Walker, A.L. VA 8th Cav. Co.I
Walker, A.L. VA Inf. 23rd Bn. Co.C Cpl.
Walker, Albany AR 3rd Cav. Co.K
Walker, Albert GA 11th Cav. Co.E
Walker, Albert KY 12th Cav. Co.I
Walker, Albert A. TX 27th Cav. Co.G 1st Lt.
Walker, Albert B. AL 3rd Inf. Co.H,G
Walker, Albert B. SC 10th Inf. Co.A
Walker, Albert B. VA Cav. 46th Bn. Co.C
Walker, Albert G. MS 7th Inf. Co.I Cpl.
Walker, Albert H. NC 1st Cav. (9th St.Troops) Co.K Cpl.
Walker, Albert W. NC 2nd Bn.Loc.Def.Troops Co.C Cpl.
Walker, Alex MS Inf. Comfort's Co.
Walker, Alex VA 60th Inf. Co.A Cpl.
Walker, Alexander AR 8th Inf. New Co.A
Walker, Alexander GA Inf. (Newton Factory Employees) Russell's Co.
Walker, Alexander MS 3rd Inf. Co.A
Walker, Alexander MS 30th Inf. Co.D
Walker, Alexander MO 10th Cav. Co.L
Walker, Alexander NC 2nd Cav. (19th St.Troops) Co.F
Walker, Alexander SC 15th Inf. Co.E
Walker, Alexander TN Inf. 1st Bn. (Colms') Co.C
Walker, Alexander TN 31st Inf. Co.C
Walker, Alexander TN 50th (Cons.) Inf. Co.K
Walker, Alexander TX 2nd Cav. Co.I
Walker, Alexander VA Goochland Lt.Arty.
Walker, Alexander VA 1st Inf. Co.G
Walker, Alexander VA Burks' Regt.Loc.Def. Flaherty's Co.
Walker, Alexander B. TN Cav. 12th Bn. (Day's) Co.B
Walker, Alexander B. VA 2nd Arty. Co.G
Walker, Alexander F. FL 2nd Inf. Co.H Sgt.
Walker, Alexander S. SC 14th Inf. Co.D Hosp.Stew.
Walker, Alexander S. TX 12th Cav. Co.I
Walker, Alexander S. VA 2nd Cav. Co.F 3rd Lt.
Walker, Alexander S. VA 14th Cav. Co.H,B
Walker, Alexander W. NC 13th Inf. Co.K
Walker, Alex D. VA 13th Inf. 2nd Co.E Sgt.
Walker, Alford NC 2nd Home Guards Co.B
Walker, Alfred AL 3rd Inf. Co.D
Walker, Alfred GA 1st Reg. Co.H
Walker, Alfred LA 6th Cav. Co.C Cpl.
Walker, Alfred MS Lt.Arty. (Brookhaven Lt.Arty.) Hoskins' Btty.
Walker, Alfred NC 22nd Inf. Co.L
Walker, Alfred NC 49th Inf. Co.A
Walker, Alfred TN 8th Inf. Co.E
Walker, Alfred TX Res.Corps Co.I
Walker, Alfred B. NC 52nd Inf. Co.K
Walker, Alfred R. MS 2nd Inf. Co.C 2nd Lt.
Walker, Alfred T. TX 17th Cav. Co.K
Walker, Alfred W. FL 3rd Inf. Co.H
Walker, Alfred W. VA 56th Inf. Co.B
Walker, Allen FL 8th Inf. Co.K
Walker, Allen GA 65th Inf. Co.G
Walker, Allen MS 7th Cav. Co.I
Walker, Allen MS Inf. 1st Bn. Polk's Co.
Walker, Allen NC 25th Inf. Co.G
Walker, Allen SC 6th Inf. 2nd Co.F
Walker, Allen TN 24th Bn.S.S. Co.A,C
Walker, Allen B. FL 1st Inf. Old Co.A, New Co.B
Walker, Allen B. FL 5th Inf. Co.C
Walker, Allen C. TX Cav. 3rd (Yager's) Bn. Co.A
Walker, Alonzo E. GA 57th Inf. Co.C Cpl.
Walker, Alphred O.P. AR 8th Inf. New Co.A
Walker, A.M. AL Cav. 24th Bn. Co.A
Walker, A.M. SC 11th Inf. Co.K
Walker, A.M. TX 12th Cav. Co.B Cpl.
Walker, Ambrose N. LA 9th Inf. Co.C Cpl.
Walker, Americus E. GA 19th Inf. Co.G
Walker, Amos TX 35th (Brown's) Cav. Co.G
Walker, Amos TX 13th Vol. 2nd Co.G
Walker, Amos B. AL 28th Inf. Co.L
Walker, Amos J. MS 36th Inf. Co.I
Walker, Amos V. AR 20th Inf. Co.B 1st Sgt.
Walker, A.N. GA 8th Mil.
Walker, A.N. SC 2nd Arty. Co.B
Walker, A.N. SC 11th Inf. Co.K
Walker, A.N. TN 52nd Inf. Co.A Bvt.2nd Lt.
Walker, A.N. VA 11th Inf. Co.G
Walker, Anderson MS 16th Inf. Co.E
Walker, Anderson MO Cav. Poindexter's Regt.
Walker, Anderson L. VA 45th Inf. Co.H
Walker, Anderson W. AL 4th Inf. Co.D
Walker, Andrew AL 4th Inf. Co.D
Walker, Andrew AR 15th (Josey's) Inf. Co.D
Walker, Andrew GA 60th Inf. Co.I Cpl.
Walker, Andrew TN 3rd (Forrest's) Cav. Co.B
Walker, Andrew TN 14th (Neely's) Cav. Co.H Cpl.
Walker, Andrew TN Inf. Nashville Bn. Cattles' Co.
Walker, Andrew TX 9th (Young's) Inf. Co.D Sgt.
Walker, Andrew VA 11th Bn.Res. Co.C
Walker, Andrew VA 29th Inf. Co.C
Walker, Andrew B. VA Inf. 22nd Bn. Co.G
Walker, Andrew J. AL 29th Inf. Co.K
Walker, Andrew J. FL Inf. 2nd Bn. Co.B
Walker, Andrew J. FL 4th Inf. Co.D 1st Sgt.
Walker, Andrew J. GA Siege Arty. 28th Bn. Co.E Sgt.
Walker, Andrew J. MS 24th Inf. Co.C
Walker, Andrew J. MS 33rd Inf. Co.G
Walker, Andrew J. MO Cav. Preston's Bn. Co.C
Walker, Andrew J. NC 35th Inf. Co.F
Walker, Andrew J. TN 9th (Ward's) Cav. Co.B
Walker, Andrew J. TN 41st Inf. Co.D Sgt.
Walker, Andrew J. TX 25th Cav. Co.E
Walker, Andrew J. TX 35th (Brown's) Cav. Co.G
Walker, Andrew J. TX 13th Vol. 2nd Co.G
Walker, Andrew J. VA 37th Mil. Co.A
Walker, Andrew R. MS 2nd Inf. Co.A Capt.
Walker, Andrew W. GA 10th Cav. (St.Guards) Co.B
Walker, Andrew W. GA 19th Inf. Co.G

Walker, Anera AL 50th Inf. Co.G
Walker, Ansel GA Cav. 24th Bn. Co.A,C
Walker, A.P. AL Mil. 2nd Regt.Vol. Co.B
Walker, A.P. KY 9th Mtd.Inf. Co.B
Walker, A.P. MS 13th Inf. Co.G
Walker, A.P. MS 26th Inf. Co.H,K
Walker, A.P. MS 32nd Inf. Co.K
Walker, A.P. MO Cav. 3rd Regt.St.Guard Co.D
Walker, A.P. TN 34th Inf. Co.B
Walker, A.R. KY 10th (Johnson's) Cav. New Co.I
Walker, A.R. KY 8th Mtd.Inf. Co.F
Walker, A.R. NC 50th Inf. Co.G
Walker, Archibald J. FL 3rd Inf. Co.H
Walker, Aris AR 47th (Crandall's) Cav.
Walker, Armstead NC 7th Sr.Res. Clinard's Co., Holland's Co.
Walker, Arther M. NC 7th Inf. Co.K 2nd Lt.
Walker, Arthur GA 12th Inf. Co.H
Walker, Arthur VA 6th Cav. Co.H
Walker, Arthur VA Cav. Mosby's Regt. (Part.Rangers) Co.A
Walker, Arthur E. NC Cav. 5th Bn. Co.B Sgt.
Walker, Arthur G. VA 136th Mil. Co.H
Walker, Arthur H. TX 14th Cav. Co.H
Walker, Arthur M. NC 48th Inf. Co.C Capt.
Walker, A.S. MS Cav. Yerger's Regt. Co.F
Walker, A.S. TN Inf. 4th Cons.Regt. Co.E Cpl.
Walker, A.S. 14th Conf.Cav. Co.C
Walker, Asa GA 60th Inf. Co.H
Walker, Asa MS 21st Inf. Co.F
Walker, Asa MS 29th Inf. Co.H
Walker, Asa MS 39th Inf. Co.A Sgt.
Walker, Asa W. AR 33rd Inf. Co.K
Walker, Asa W. LA 28th (Gray's) Inf. Co.G
Walker, Asher AR 4th Inf. Co.A
Walker, A.T. AR 4th Inf. Co.K
Walker, A.T. FL Cav. 3rd Bn. Co.B
Walker, A.T. GA Cav. 19th Bn. Co.C
Walker, A.T. GA Lt.Arty. Anderson's Btty.
Walker, A.T. GA 49th Inf. Co.H
Walker, A.T. 10th Conf.Cav.
Walker, A.T. 15th Conf.Cav. Co.D
Walker, Atwood C. VA 26th Inf. Co.I 2nd Lt.
Walker, Augustine TX 7th Inf. Co.B
Walker, Augustus C. GA 8th Inf. Co.A
Walker, Augustus S. MS 38th Cav. Co.K
Walker, Aug. W. AR Cav. Wright's Regt. Co.E
Walker, Avery AL 30th Inf. Co.D
Walker, A.W. AL 46th Inf. Co.G Cpl.
Walker, A.W. AR 6th Inf. 1st Co.B
Walker, A.W. LA Mil.Conf.Guards Regt. Co.C
Walker, A.W. MS Inf. 1st Bn. Polk's Co.
Walker, A.W. SC 13th Inf. Co.C
Walker, A.W. TN 16th Inf. Co.G
Walker, A.W. TN Inf. 22nd Bn. Co.D
Walker, Azariah L. MO Lt.Arty. 1st Field Btty.
Walker, Azariah T. NC 45th Inf. Co.E 2nd Lt.
Walker, B. AR 6th Inf. Co.C
Walker, B. NC 7th Sr.Res. Davie's Co.
Walker, B. SC Lt.Arty. Jeter's Co. (Macbeth Lt.Arty.)
Walker, B. VA 9th Cav. Co.I
Walker, B.A. FL 1st Inf. New Co.E
Walker, Balam TN 43rd Inf. Co.H Sgt.
Walker, Bargsdale A. TX 9th Field Btty. Sgt.
Walker, Bartlett J. GA 30th Inf. Co.H
Walker, Bartley GA 6th Inf. (St.Guards) Co.B
Walker, Bartley GA 6th Inf. (St.Guards) Co.C
Walker, B.A.S. VA 60th Inf. Co.A
Walker, B.A.S. VA 166th Mil. Co.D
Walker, Basley J. NC 45th Inf. Co.G
Walker, B.B. AL Mil. 4th Vol. Co.C Cpl.
Walker, B.B. LA 31st Inf. Co.D
Walker, B.B. TX 17th Cons.Dismtd.Cav. Co.F
Walker, B.C. AL 40th Inf. Co.G Cpl.
Walker, B.C. SC 1st St.Troops Co.I
Walker, B.C. SC 7th Inf. Co.A
Walker, B.C. SC 15th Inf. Co.K
Walker, B.C. TN 6th Inf. Co.K
Walker, Ben TX 18th Cav. Co.C,E Sgt.
Walker, Benjamin AL 43rd Inf. Co.H
Walker, Benjamin AR 8th Cav. Co.G
Walker, Benjamin AR 45th Cav. Co.A
Walker, Benjamin AR 9th Inf. New Co.I
Walker, Benjamin KY 9th Mtd.Inf. Co.F Sgt.
Walker, Benjamin LA 6th Cav. Co.C
Walker, Benjamin LA 17th Inf. Co.K
Walker, Benjamin MO 8th Cav. Co.C,D
Walker, Benjamin MO Cav. Preston's Bn.
Walker, Benjamin NC 5th Sr.Res. Co.K
Walker, Benjamin NC 37th Inf. Co.G
Walker, Benjamin TN 1st (Turney's) Inf. Co.H Cpl.
Walker, Benjamin TN 4th Inf. Co.D Cpl.
Walker, Benjamin TN 33rd Inf. Co.H Cpl.
Walker, Benjamin TX 35th (Brown's) Cav. Co.K
Walker, Benjamin VA 60th Inf. Co.A
Walker, Benjamin 2nd Conf.Inf. Co.G
Walker, Benjamin A. SC 5th Cav. Co.H
Walker, Benjamin C. AL 41st Inf. Co.G Cpl.
Walker, Benjamin Drake GA 36th (Villepigue's) Inf. Co.G Sgt.
Walker, Benjamin F. AR 15th (N.W.) Inf. Co.F 1st Lt.
Walker, Benjamin F. FL 5th Inf. Co.K Cpl.
Walker, Benjamin F. GA 1st Bn.S.S. Co.D Sgt.
Walker, Benjamin F. GA 42nd Inf. Co.K 2nd Lt.
Walker, Benjamin F. KY Cav. Sypert's Regt. Co.F
Walker, Benjamin F. LA 28th (Gray's) Inf. Co.G
Walker, Benjamin F. MS 2nd Inf. Co.F
Walker, Benjamin F. MS 15th Inf. Co.H
Walker, Benjamin F. MS 24th Inf. Co.C
Walker, Benjamin F. MS 32nd Inf. Co.F 2nd Lt.
Walker, Benjamin F. MO Cav. 4th Regt.St.Guard Co.A Col.
Walker, Benjamin F. SC 5th Inf. 1st Co.C, 2nd Co.F
Walker, Benjamin F. TX 6th Inf. Co.G
Walker, Benjamin F. VA 59th Inf. 3rd Co.B
Walker, Benjamin F. Conf.Cav. Wood's Regt. Co.B 2nd Lt.
Walker, Benj. F. Gen. & Staff Asst.Surg.
Walker, Benjamin G. MS 1st (Pattons') Inf. Co.C
Walker, Benjamin G. TN 44th (Cons.) Inf. Co.A
Walker, Benjamin H. GA 11th Inf. Co.C
Walker, Benjamin H. NC 11th (Bethel Regt.) Inf. Co.E
Walker, Benjamin H. VA 34th Inf. Co.K 2nd Lt.
Walker, Benjamin J. VA 19th Inf. Co.C
Walker, Benjamin J. VA 53rd Inf. Co.H
Walker, Benjamin L. TN 21st (Wilson's) Cav. Co.E
Walker, Benjamin M. NC 3rd Cav. (41st St.Troops) Surg.
Walker, Benj. M. Gen. & Staff Surg.
Walker, Benjamin P. GA 31st Inf. Co.E
Walker, Benjamin P. VA 4th Inf. Co.D
Walker, Benjamin R. FL 1st Cav. Co.H Bvt.2nd Lt.
Walker, Benjamin R. GA 2nd (Stapleton's) St.Troops Co.B
Walker, Benjamin T. VA 20th Inf. Co.I
Walker, Benjamin W.L. VA 14th Inf. Co.F
Walker, Ben M. MS 1st Cav. Co.F Cpl.
Walker, Bennett GA 49th Inf. Co.B
Walker, Benton TN 16th (Logwood's) Cav. Co.F Sgt.
Walker, Berry AL 26th (O'Neal's) Inf. Co.H
Walker, Berry FL 2nd Inf. Co.I
Walker, Berry GA 4th (Clinch's) Cav. Co.G
Walker, Berry 1st Conf.Cav. 2nd Co.F
Walker, Berryman NC 30th Inf. Co.I
Walker, Beverly C. VA 59th Inf. 3rd Co.E
Walker, B.F. AL 4th (Russell's) Cav. Co.F
Walker, B.F. AL 12th Inf. Co.I
Walker, B.F. AL 14th Inf. Co.D
Walker, B.F. AL Leighton Rangers
Walker, B.F. AR 1st St.Cav. Co.D
Walker, B.F. AR 6th Inf. Co.B,K
Walker, B.F. AR 30th Inf. Co.G
Walker, B.F. FL 2nd Inf. Asst.Surg.
Walker, B.F. GA 12th (Robinson's) Cav. (St.Guards) Co.G
Walker, B.F. GA Inf. 8th Bn. Co.A
Walker, B.F. LA Inf.Crescent Regt. Co.G
Walker, B.F. MS 18th Cav. Co.H
Walker, B.F. MO 11th Inf. Co.G
Walker, B.F. SC Lt.Arty. Beauregard's Co.
Walker, B.F. VA 46th Inf. 2nd Co.H
Walker, B.F. Mead's Conf.Cav. Co.F Cpl.
Walker, B. Frank MO 2nd Inf. Co.C
Walker, B. Franklin AL 49th Inf. Co.D
Walker, B.G. MS 8th Inf. Co.A
Walker, B.G. MS 37th Inf. Co.H Cpl.
Walker, B.H. AL 3rd Inf. Co.I
Walker, B.H. FL 1st Inf.
Walker, B.H. NC 38th Inf. Co.A
Walker, B.H. VA 53rd Inf. Co.E
Walker, Bine B. TX 18th Inf. Co.I
Walker, Bishop TN 8th Inf. Co.K
Walker, B.J. VA Cav. O'Ferrall's Bn. Co.C
Walker, B.L. NC 44th Inf.
Walker, B.L. TN Inf. 23rd Bn. Co.B 1st Sgt.
Walker, B.L. TX Cav. 2nd Regt.St.Troops Co.K
Walker, B.L. TX 22nd Inf. Co.I 3rd Lt.
Walker, B.M. MS 6th Cav. Co.A Sgt.
Walker, B.M. MS Inf. 2nd St.Troops Co.M
Walker, B.M. TX Inf. 2nd St.Troops Co.C
Walker, B.N. MS 5th Inf. (St.Troops) Co.G
Walker, B.P. SC 7th Cav. Co.B
Walker, B.P. VA Conscr.
Walker, B.R. TN 7th (Duckworth's) Cav. Co.M
Walker, Brazilla AL 57th Inf. Co.H
Walker, Broson GA Cav. 19th Bn. Co.A
Walker, Bryant T. SC 19th Inf. Co.F Cpl.
Walker, B.S. TX Inf. 3rd St.Troops Co.F
Walker, B.S. VA 1st (Farinholt's) Res. Co.K

Walker, B.T. TN 1st Cav.
Walker, B.T. TN 31st Inf. Co.C
Walker, Buckley NC 24th Inf. Co.D
Walker, Bud Mead's Conf.Cav. Co.H
Walker, Burrell U. VA 11th Bn.Res. Co.D
Walker, Burrel U. VA 60th Inf. Co.H
Walker, Burton C. SC 5th Res. Co.I
Walker, B.W. AL 2nd Cav. Co.K,F Sgt.
Walker, B.W. SC Inf. Holcombe Legion Co.A
Walker, B.W. TX 11th Cav. Co.K
Walker, B.W. TX 32nd Cav. Co.H
Walker, B.W. Eng.Dept. Polk's Corps A. of TN Sap. & Min. Co.,CSA
Walker, C. AL 15th Inf. Co.C
Walker, C. AL 50th Inf. Co.C
Walker, C. AR Inf. Cocke's Regt. Co.C
Walker, C. GA 66th Inf. Co.H
Walker, C. LA Mil.Cav. (Jeff Davis Rangers) Norwood's Co.
Walker, C. NC 55th Inf. Co.K
Walker, C. TN Lt.Arty. Winston's Co.
Walker, C. TX Cav. Giddings' Bn. Weisiger's Co.
Walker, C. VA 5th Cav. Co.D
Walker, C. VA 45th Inf. Co.G
Walker, C. Gen. & Staff Chap.
Walker, C.A. GA 11th Inf. 3rd Lt.
Walker, Caleb NC 2nd Cav. (19th St.Troops) Co.G
Walker, Calvin AL 2nd Cav. Co.A
Walker, Calvin MS 46th Inf. Co.A Cpl.
Walker, Calvin 2nd Cherokee Mtd.Vol. Co.K,H
Walker, Calvin H. TN 3rd (Clack's) Inf. Col.
Walker, Calvin M. KY 6th Mtd.Inf. Co.G
Walker, Cam. VA Inf. 1st Bn.Loc.Def. Co.F
Walker, Campbell MO 8th Inf. Co.I
Walker, Cap. AL 12th Inf. Co.D
Walker, Carlton LA 1st Hvy.Arty. (Reg.) Co.H,D
Walker, Carroll MS Cav. 3rd Bn. (Ashcraft's) Co.D
Walker, Carter A. NC 3rd Cav. (41st St.Troops) Co.K
Walker, Cary 2nd Cherokee Mtd.Vol. Co.I 1st Lt.
Walker, C.B. AR Inf. Cocke's Regt. Co.C,I
Walker, C.B. GA Lt.Arty. Pritchard's Co. (Washington Arty.)
Walker, C.B. NC 31st Inf. Co.H
Walker, C.B. SC 15th Inf. Co.K
Walker, C.B. 1st Conf.Inf. 1st Co.F
Walker, C.C. AL 37th Inf. Co.H
Walker, C.C. AL 38th Inf. Co.D
Walker, C.C. GA 1st Cav. Co.G Wag.
Walker, C.C. SC Lt.Arty. Beauregard's Co.
Walker, C.C. TN 55th (Brown's) Inf. Co.D
Walker, C.C. TX Arty. Douglas' Co.
Walker, C.C. VA 2nd Cav. Co.H
Walker, C.D. MS 12th Cav. Co.A,H
Walker, C.D. MS 39th Inf. Co.A
Walker, C.D. VA VMI Co.B
Walker, C.E. AL 14th Inf. Co.I
Walker, C.E. GA 39th Inf. Co.F Capt.
Walker, Cephas MS 12th Cav. Co.A
Walker, C.F. LA 9th Inf. Co.K
Walker, C.F. MS 12th Cav. Co.A
Walker, C.H. MS 41st Inf. Co.K Sgt.
Walker, C.H. TX 30th Cav. Co.F
Walker, C.H. VA Cav. Mosby's Regt. (Part. Rangers) Co.C
Walker, C.H. Trans-MS Conf.Cav. 1st Bn. Co.B
Walker, Chales 1st Creek Mtd.Vol. Co.G Cpl.
Walker, Chambers GA 66th Inf. Co.F
Walker, Charles AL Arty. 1st Bn. Co.E
Walker, Charles AL 1st Bn.Cadets Co.A
Walker, Charles GA 49th Inf. Co.K
Walker, Charles NC 1st Arty. (10th St.Troops) Co.K
Walker, Charles TN 26th Inf. Co.I
Walker, Charles TN 43rd Inf. Co.C
Walker, Charles TN Inf. 154th Sr.Regt. Co.H
Walker, Charles TN Inf. 154th Sr.Regt. Co.L Sgt.
Walker, Charles VA Inf. 1st Bn. Co.C
Walker, Charles VA 15th Inf. Co.F
Walker, Charles A. NC Inf. Thomas Legion Co.I
Walker, Charles B. AL Arty. 1st Bn. Co.F
Walker, Chas. B. AL 22nd Inf. Co.A
Walker, Charles B. VA Inf. 4th Bn.Loc.Def. Co.E Sgt.
Walker, Charles B. VA 15th Inf. Co.B
Walker, Charles C. VA Cav. 35th Bn. Co.A
Walker, Charles D. MS 7th Inf. Co.I Cpl.
Walker, Charles E. GA 56th Inf. Co.B 1st Lt.
Walker, Charles E. SC Arty. Manigault's Bn. 1st Co.A
Walker, Charles E. VA 14th Inf. Co.F
Walker, Charles F. AL 8th Inf. Co.G 2nd Lt.
Walker, Charles F. AR 9th Inf. Co.G
Walker, Charles G. LA 5th Inf. New Co.A 1st Lt.
Walker, Charles H. GA 3rd Inf. Co.E
Walker, Charles H. TX 1st (McCulloch's) Cav. Co.C
Walker, Charles H. VA 3rd Cav. Co.D
Walker, Charles H. VA 53rd Inf. Co.K
Walker, Charles H. VA 60th Inf. Co.A Sgt.
Walker, Charles K. GA Inf. 10th Bn. Co.E
Walker, Charles L. GA 26th Inf. Co.F 1st Lt.
Walker, Charles M. TX 1st (Yager's) Cav. Co.C 1st Lt.
Walker, Charles M. TX Cav. 3rd (Yager's) Bn. Co.C 1st Lt.
Walker, Charles M. TX 29th Cav. Co.D
Walker, Charles M. VA 18th Inf. Co.F
Walker, Charles P. AL 3rd Inf. Co.I
Walker, Charles P. VA 2nd Cav. Co.F
Walker, Charles R. GA Cav. 1st Bn. Hopkins' Co. 1st Sgt.
Walker, Charles R. NC 4th Cav. (59th St.Troops) Co.G
Walker, Charles T. GA 4th Inf. Co.K
Walker, Charles T. VA 24th Inf. Co.B
Walker, Charles W. AL 50th Inf. Co.C
Walker, Charles W. AR 34th Inf. Co.A
Walker, Charles W. GA 2nd Cav. Co.C
Walker, Charles W. TX 22nd Cav. Co.E
Walker, Charles W. VA Lt.Arty. G.B. Chapman's Co. Cpl.
Walker, Charles W. VA 32nd Inf. Asst.Surg.
Walker, Charles W. VA 38th Inf. Co.G
Walker, Charles W. VA 108th Mil. Co.G Cpl.
Walker, Chas. W. Gen. & Staff Asst.Surg.
Walker, Chastain C. VA 14th Inf. Co.F
Walker, Chelse VA 32nd Inf. 2nd Co.I Ch.Cook
Walker, Chesley SC 5th Res. Co.I
Walker, Chesley B. NC 16th Inf. Co.D
Walker, Chris TX Inf. 1st St.Troops Sheldon's Co.B
Walker, Chrispia A. VA 60th Inf. 2nd Co.H
Walker, Christia VA 190th Mil. Co.G
Walker, Christian VA 36th Inf. 2nd Co.I
Walker, Christopher NC 30th Inf. Co.B
Walker, Christopher G. MO Cav. Freeman's Regt. Co.F
Walker, Chr. P. VA 3rd Res. Co.B Sgt.
Walker, C.I. SC 10th Inf. Adj.
Walker, Cicero MS 11th Inf. Co.F
Walker, C. Irvine SC Inf.Bn. Lt.Col.
Walker, C.J. SC Arty. Manigault's Bn. Co.E
Walker, C.J. TX 34th Cav. Co.B Sgt.
Walker, C.J. Brush Bn.
Walker, C.J. Gen. & Staff, Adj.Gen.Dept. Lt.Col.
Walker, C.L. GA 10th Mil.
Walker, Clarence V. GA 48th Inf. Co.I 1st Lt.
Walker, Clayton VA 3rd Cav. Co.D
Walker, Clement L. AR Cav. Wright's Regt. Co.F
Walker, Clement L. AR 23rd Inf. Co.G
Walker, Clement W. GA 62nd Cav. Co.A
Walker, Clem L. Eng.,CSA
Walker, Clifford B. GA 36th (Villepigue's) Inf. Co.C,F Cpl.
Walker, Clifton AL 4th Inf. Co.I
Walker, Clifton AL 19th Inf. Adj.
Walker, Clifton Gen. & Staff Capt.,AAG
Walker, Clinton VA Mil. 160th Regt. Capt.
Walker, Clinton M. VA 52nd Inf. Co.F Sgt.
Walker, C.M. TX 27th Cav. Co.A
Walker, C.M. VA 4th Cav. Co.K
Walker, C.M. 14th Conf.Cav.
Walker, C.N. AL 1st Cav. 2nd Co.B Cpl.
Walker, C.N. MS 24th Inf. Co.F 3rd Lt.
Walker, Colton MS 5th Inf. (St.Troops) Co.C
Walker, Columbus AL 2nd Cav. Co.E
Walker, Columbus F. NC Walker's Bn. Thomas Legion Co.B Sgt.Maj.
Walker, Cornelius VA 6th Inf. Co.A
Walker, Cornelius D. AL 36th Inf. Co.A
Walker, Cornelius J. TX 22nd Cav. Co.B
Walker, C.P. TN 5th Inf. 2nd Co.D
Walker, C.P. VA Conscr. Cp.Lee Co.B
Walker, C.R. AL Mil. 4th Vol. Co.H Sgt.
Walker, C.R. GA 5th Cav. Co.K,G 1st Sgt.
Walker, C.R. VA 23rd Inf. Co.E
Walker, C. Radford VA Arty. Paris' Co.
Walker, Crawford NC 3rd Arty. (40th St.Troops) Co.B
Walker, Crawford N. NC 3rd Cav. (41st St.Troops) Co.K Sgt.
Walker, Creed T. AR 15th (Josey's) Inf. Co.B
Walker, C.S. SC 2nd Arty. Co.B
Walker, C.T. GA 12th (Robinson's) Cav. (St.Guards) Co.E Cpl.
Walker, C.T. TN 15th (Stewart's) Cav. Co.B
Walker, Curry AL Inf. 1st Regt. Co.D
Walker, C.V. GA Inf. 1st Loc.Troops (Augusta) Co.G
Walker, C.W. AL 1st Regt. Mobile Vol. Co.B
Walker, C.W. AL 21st Inf. Co.A

Walker, C.W. GA 8th Cav. Co.A
Walker, C.W. GA Inf. (Mitchell Home Guards) Brooks' Co.
Walker, C.W. NC 1st Arty. (10th St.Troops) Co.B
Walker, C.W. SC 6th (Merriwether's) Bn.St.Res. Co.D
Walker, C.W. TX 2nd Cav. 2nd Co.F
Walker, C.W. VA Arty. Bryan's Co.
Walker, C.W. Conf.Lt.Arty. Stark's Bn. Co.B 1st Sgt.
Walker, C.W. Gen. & Staff, QM Dept.
Walker, Cyrus VA 14th Cav. Co.H
Walker, Cyrus C. AL 42nd Inf. Co.K
Walker, D.A. AL Cav. Forrest's Regt.
Walker, D.A. AL 5th Inf. New Co.H 2nd Lt.
Walker, D.A. GA Boddie's Co. (Troup Cty.Ind.Cav.) 1st Sgt.
Walker, D.A. MS 32nd Inf. Co.C
Walker, D.A. SC Mil. 16th Regt. Robinson's Co. Bvt.2nd Lt.
Walker, D.A. TN 18th (Newsom's) Cav. Co.H
Walker, D.A. TX 17th Cons.Dismtd.Cav. Co.F
Walker, Daid MO Cav. Fristoe's Regt. Co.F
Walker, Dale MO 1st Cav. Co.H Sgt.
Walker, Dan TX Cav. McCord's Frontier Regt. Co.B
Walker, Daniel AL 15th Part.Rangers Co.C
Walker, Daniel AL 56th Part.Rangers Co.C
Walker, Daniel GA 3rd Cav. (St.Guards) Co.C
Walker, Daniel GA 43rd Inf. Co.A
Walker, Daniel GA 49th Inf. Co.F
Walker, Daniel MS 7th Inf. Co.I
Walker, Daniel MS 22nd Inf. Co.D
Walker, Daniel MS 36th Inf.
Walker, Daniel NC 12th Inf. Co.L
Walker, Daniel NC 32nd Inf. Co.A
Walker, Daniel SC 2nd St.Troops Co.H
Walker, Daniel SC 8th Bn.Res. Fishburne's Co.
Walker, Daniel SC 11th Res. Co.K
Walker, Daniel SC 15th Inf. Co.E
Walker, Daniel SC 24th Inf. Co.I
Walker, Daniel VA 8th Cav. Co.A
Walker, Daniel 1st Cherokee Mtd.Vol. 2nd Co.B Sgt.
Walker, Daniel A. MS 26th Inf. Co.E Cpl.
Walker, Daniel A. NC Hvy.Arty. 10th Bn. Co.D
Walker, Daniel A. VA Cav. Swann's Bn.
Walker, Daniel F. NC 6th Cav. (65th St.Troops) Co.F,B
Walker, Daniel J. AR 1st Cav. Co.G
Walker, Daniel J. GA 1st Reg. Co.G
Walker, Daniel M. VA 1st Inf. Co.G
Walker, Daniel R. AR 26th Inf. Co.A
Walker, Daniel S. GA 2nd Inf. Co.A
Walker, Daniel W. AL 17th Inf. Co.F
Walker, Daniel W. TN 7th Inf. Co.E
Walker, Darling R. AL 29th Inf. Co.K
Walker, David AR Cav. Davies' Bn. Co.B
Walker, David AR 7th Inf. Co.I
Walker, David AR 33rd Inf. Co.D
Walker, David AR Inf. Adams' Regt. Moore's Co.
Walker, David AR Inf. Cocke's Regt. Co.A
Walker, David FL 1st Res. Co.F 2nd Lt.
Walker, David GA 6th Cav. Co.F
Walker, David GA 11th Cav. Co.C
Walker, David GA 17th Inf. Co.F
Walker, David GA 53rd Inf. Co.C
Walker, David GA Cherokee Legion (St.Guards) Co.E
Walker, David MS Cav. 17th Bn. Co.F
Walker, David MO 1st Inf. Co.A,C 1st Lt.
Walker, David MO 1st & 4th Cons.Inf. Co.A 1st Lt.
Walker, David NC 3rd Bn.Sr.Res. Co.C
Walker, David NC 54th Inf. Co.G
Walker, David NC 58th Inf. Co.F
Walker, David TN 2nd (Ashby's) Cav. Co.I
Walker, David TN Cav. 12th Bn. (Day's) Co.B
Walker, David TN 21st (Wilson's) Cav. Co.I
Walker, David TN 46th Inf. Co.A
Walker, David VA Lt.Arty. Otey's Co.
Walker, David Gen. & Staff, Cav. Col.
Walker, David A. GA 41st Inf. Co.E
Walker, David A. NC 6th Inf. Co.H
Walker, David A. TX 17th Cav. Co.F Sgt.
Walker, David B. TN 29th Inf. Co.H
Walker, David C. KY 7th Cav. Co.K Cpl.
Walker, David C. KY 6th Mtd.Inf. Co.F,I 1st Lt.
Walker, David C. MS 38th Cav. Co.K 1st Lt.
Walker, David C. TN 28th Inf. Co.D,H 3rd Lt.
Walker, David C. TX Granbury's Cons.Brig. Co.D 1st Lt.
Walker, David C. TX 10th Inf. Co.F 1st Lt.
Walker, David C. Gen. & Staff Capt.,QM
Walker, David F. AR 17th (Lemoyne's) Inf. Co.E
Walker, David F. TX 1st Inf. Co.A
Walker, David J. GA 57th Inf. Co.E Sgt.
Walker, David J. NC 2nd Arty. (36th St.Troops) Co.G
Walker, David L. AL 63rd Inf. Co.D
Walker, David L. FL 3rd Inf. Co.G
Walker, David L. NC 39th Inf. Co.H Capt.
Walker, David L. SC 7th Cav. Co.B 2nd Lt.
Walker, David L.M. FL 5th Inf. Co.D
Walker, David M. LA 28th (Gray's) Inf. Co.A Sgt.
Walker, David N. GA 49th Inf. Co.K
Walker, David N. NC 4th Inf. Co.H
Walker, David N. NC 45th Inf. Co.H
Walker, David N. VA Lt.Arty. 13th Bn. Co.A Capt.
Walker, David R. GA 6th Cav. Co.D Cpl.
Walker, David R. GA Smith's Legion Ralston's Co. Cpl.
Walker, David R. VA 56th Inf. Co.B
Walker, David S. FL Kilcrease Lt.Arty.
Walker, David S. FL 5th Inf. Co.A
Walker, David S. TN 25th Inf. Co.D 1st Lt.
Walker, Davidson NC 56th Inf. Co.I
Walker, David T. MS 2nd Inf. Co.C 1st Lt.
Walker, David T. VA 2nd Cav. Co.I
Walker, David W. TX 1st (Yager's) Cav. Co.I
Walker, D.B. GA 59th Inf. Co.B
Walker, D.B. TN 19th & 20th (Cons.) Cav. Co.E
Walker, D.B. TN 12th Inf. Co.C
Walker, D.B. TN 12th (Cons.) Inf. Co.B
Walker, D. Blake GA Lt.Arty. 14th Bn. Co.A Cpl.
Walker, D. Blake GA Lt.Arty. Havis' Btty. Cpl.
Walker, D.C. AR 8th Cav. Co.A
Walker, D.C. KY 8th Cav. Co.K Cpl.
Walker, D.C. MS 2nd St.Cav. Co.I
Walker, D.D. MO Cav. Freeman's Regt. Co.I
Walker, D.D. NC 22nd Inf. Co.B
Walker, D.D. NC 62nd Inf. Co.F 2nd Lt.
Walker, D.D. VA 1st (Farinholt's) Res. Co.C
Walker, Delos G. MS 28th Cav. Co.I
Walker, Dennis FL 1st Inf. New Co.I
Walker, Dennis GA Inf. (Ogeechee Minute Men) Garrison's Co.
Walker, D.F. GA 32nd Inf. Co.I
Walker, D.G. TX Inf. 1st Bn. (St.Troops) Co.C
Walker, D.H. AL 11th Cav. Co.H
Walker, Dick TX 1st Inf. Co.A Music.
Walker, Dickerson H. GA 9th Inf. (St.Guards) Co.F Lt.Col.
Walker, Dillard O. TN 8th Cav. Co.I
Walker, D.K. GA Phillips' Legion Co.E,N
Walker, D.L. FL 4th Inf. Co.D Cpl.
Walker, D.L. MO 1st Cav. Co.H Sgt.
Walker, D.L. SC Rutledge Mtd.Riflemen & Horse Arty. Trenholm's Co. Cpl.
Walker, D.L. TN 19th (Biffle's) Cav. Co.F
Walker, D.L. TX 5th Cav. Co.A Sgt.
Walker, D.M. FL Cadets Military Inst.
Walker, D.M. MS 1st Lt.Arty. Co.F
Walker, D.M. SC 18th Inf. Co.G
Walker, D.M. TX 27th Cav. Co.A
Walker, D.M. TX 1st Inf. Co.E
Walker, D.M. TX 13th Vol. 2nd Co.B
Walker, D.M.L. TN 20th (Russell's) Cav. Co.F
Walker, D.M.L. TN 46th Inf. Co.I
Walker, D.N. MS 4th Cav. Co.I 2nd Lt.
Walker, D.N. TX 28th Cav. Co.C 1st Lt.
Walker, D.N.B. AR 9th Inf. Co.K
Walker, D.N.B. LA 13th Bn. (Part.Rangers) Co.A
Walker, Dock G. TN 32nd Inf. Co.A
Walker, Don F.H. GA 39th Inf. Co.B Sgt.
Walker, Dotson VA 14th Cav. 1st Co.F
Walker, Douglas N. MS 16th Inf. Co.K
Walker, D.P. AL 9th Inf. Co.K
Walker, D.R. AR Cav. 6th Bn. Co.C
Walker, D.R. AR 27th Inf. Old Co.C, Co.D
Walker, Dr. MS 14th Inf. Co.E
Walker, D.R. VA 1st (Farinholt's) Res. Co.C
Walker, D.S. AL 15th Inf. Co.H,L
Walker, D.S. FL Lt.Arty., Dyke's Co.
Walker, Dudley AL 5th Inf. Co.I
Walker, Dudley NC 44th Inf. Co.A
Walker, D.V. AR 34th Inf. Co.F
Walker, D.V. TN 22nd Cav. Co.I
Walker, D.W. AR 2nd Mtd.Rifles Co.K
Walker, D.W. AR Cav. Gordon's Regt. Co.A
Walker, D.W. AL 8th Inf. Co.H
Walker, D.W. MS 6th Inf. Co.H
Walker, D.W. TN 30th Inf. Co.E
Walker, D.W. TX 5th Inf. Co.A
Walker, Dyer VA Arty. Paris' Co.
Walker, E. AL 19th Inf. Co.C
Walker, E. AR 7th Cav. Co.E
Walker, E. AR 11th & 17th (Cons.) Inf. Co.F
Walker, E. AR 27th Inf. New Co.C
Walker, E. FL Conscr.
Walker, E. GA 1st Troops & Defences (Macon) Co.G

Walker, E. GA 64th Inf.
Walker, E. MS Inf. 1st Bn.St.Troops (30 days '64) Co.B
Walker, E. MO St.Guard
Walker, E. NC 5th Sr.Res. Co.C
Walker, E. TN 22nd (Barteau's) Cav. Co.I
Walker, E. TN 51st (Cons.) Inf. Co.A
Walker, E. VA Hvy.Arty. 20th Bn. Co.C Sgt.
Walker, E. VA 1st St.Res. Co.A
Walker, E.A. AL Cav. Forrest's Regt. 1st Lt.
Walker, E.A. AL Cp. of Instr. Talladega Co.C
Walker, E.A. MS 2nd St.Cav. Co.A
Walker, E.A. MS 26th Inf. Co.E Sgt.
Walker, E.A. MS 32nd Inf. Co.C
Walker, E.B. AL 21st Inf. Co.F,C
Walker, E.B. FL Inf. 2nd Bn. Co.D
Walker, E.C. AL 8th Cav. Co.A,C
Walker, E.C. GA 1st Reg. Co.G
Walker, E.C. TN 28th (Cons.) Inf. Co.D 2nd Lt.
Walker, E.D. AL 5th Inf. Co.I
Walker, E.D. NC 3rd Cav. (41st St.Troops) Co.A
Walker, E.D. TX 16th Inf. Co.G
Walker, E.D. TX Inf. Carter's Co.
Walker, Ed TX Inf. Timmons' Regt. Co.G
Walker, Edmond VA 25th Inf. 1st Co.E
Walker, Edmond VA 54th Mil. Co.E,F
Walker, Edmond VA 62nd Mtd.Inf. 2nd Co.I,K
Walker, Edmond 1st Cherokee Mtd.Rifles Co.B
Walker, Edmond J. TX Inf. Griffin's Bn. Co.C
Walker, Edmund N. GA 34th Inf. Co.K Sgt.
Walker, Edmund Rhett Gen. & Staff Surg.
Walker, Edmund W. VA Hvy.Arty. 20th Bn. Co.A Sgt.
Walker, Edmund W. VA 44th Inf. Co.A
Walker, Edward TX 36th Cav. Co.E 1st Lt.
Walker, Edward VA 37th Mil. Co.A
Walker, Edward VA 40th Inf. Co.G
Walker, Edward VA 54th Mil. Co.E,F
Walker, Edward A. TX 13th Vol. 2nd Co.C
Walker, Edward D., Jr. NC 1st Inf. Co.C Sgt.
Walker, Edward G. SC 1st (McCreary's) Inf. Co.G 2nd Lance Cpl.
Walker, Edward G. TX Inf. Griffin's Bn. Co.D
Walker, Edward J. GA 3rd Inf. Co.G Col.
Walker, Edward J. NC 51st Inf. Co.A
Walker, Edward L. TX Cav. Baylor's Regt. Co.B
Walker, Edward M. GA 31st Inf. Co.C,K
Walker, Edward S. TN 59th Mtd.Inf. Co.H Sgt.
Walker, Edward S. VA 24th Cav. Co.E
Walker, Edward S. VA 2nd Arty. Co.D
Walker, Edward S. VA Inf. 22nd Bn. Co.D
Walker, Edward T. VA 58th Inf. Co.A Maj.
Walker, Edwin NC 1st Arty. (10th St.Troops) Co.F
Walker, Edwin SC 1st Mtd.Mil. Green's Co.
Walker, E.F. AR 18th Inf. Co.G
Walker, E.F. MO Inf. 5th Regt.St.Guard Co.D Sgt.
Walker, E.F. NC 11th (Bethel Regt.) Inf. Co.B 3rd Lt.
Walker, E.F. SC Inf. 1st (Charleston) Bn. Co.D
Walker, E.F. SC 27th Inf. Co.D
Walker, E.G. MS 28th Cav. Co.I
Walker, E.G. MO St.Guard Music.
Walker, E.G. TX 12th Cav. Co.B
Walker, E.G. Conf.Cav. Wood's Regt. Co.I
Walker, E.H. AL 14th Inf. Co.H
Walker, E.H. AR Cav. Gordon's Regt. Co.F 3rd Lt.
Walker, E.H. GA 11th Cav. Co.I
Walker, E.H. MS 4th Cav. Co.I
Walker, E.H. TN 5th Inf. Co.A
Walker, E.H. TX 6th Inf. Co.A
Walker, E. Hugh GA 10th Cav. (St.Guards) Co.G
Walker, E.J. GA 6th Cav. Co.C
Walker, E.J. GA Smith's Legion Co.E
Walker, E.J. NC 3rd Jr.Res. Co.D
Walker, E.J. NC 7th Bn.Jr.Res. Co.B
Walker, E.J. TN 2nd (Smith's) Cav. Thomason's Co.
Walker, E.J. TN 15th (Cons.) Cav. Co.K
Walker, E.J. TN 16th (Logwood's) Cav. Co.H
Walker, E.J. TN 16th Inf. Co.B
Walker, E.J. TN 27th Inf. Co.G Ord.Sgt.
Walker, E.J. TN 52nd Inf. Co.G 2nd Lt.
Walker, E.J. TX 20th Cav. Co.A
Walker, E.J. 3rd Conf.Cav. Co.C
Walker, E.L. MS 1st (King's) Inf. (St.Troops) Co.H Cpl.
Walker, E.L. MS 7th Inf. Co.D
Walker, E.L. TX 24th Cav. Co.F,I
Walker, Elbert FL 3rd Inf. Co.I
Walker, Eldridge TN 1st (Carter's) Cav. Co.D
Walker, Elethan C. AL 47th Inf. Co.E
Walker, Eli GA 3rd Inf. Co.A
Walker, Elias FL 1st (Res.) Inf. Co.A
Walker, Elias NC 50th Inf. Co.G
Walker, Elias TN 29th Inf. Co.B
Walker, Elias D. FL 9th Inf. Co.B
Walker, Elias G. AL 3rd Res. Co.K
Walker, Elias M. VA 1st Lt.Arty. Co.B 1st Lt.
Walker, Elias M. VA Lt.Arty. J.S. Brown's Co. 1st Lt.
Walker, Eli H. GA 3rd Inf. Co.B
Walker, Elijah GA 6th Cav. Co.F
Walker, Elijah MS 37th Inf. Co.A
Walker, Elijah NC Hvy.Arty. 1st Bn. Co.B,D
Walker, Elijah NC 50th Inf. Co.I
Walker, Elijah VA 5th Cav. Co.A
Walker, Elijah VA 22nd Inf. Co.E
Walker, Elijah E. AR 8th Inf. Old Co.I
Walker, Elijah F. MO 8th Cav. Co.E 1st Lt.
Walker, Elijah H. VA 11th Inf. Co.K 2nd Lt.
Walker, Elijah M. NC 49th Inf. Co.F
Walker, Elijah R. VA 7th Inf. Co.D Jr.2nd Lt.
Walker, Elisha AL 40th Inf. Co.A
Walker, Elisha FL 1st (Res.) Inf. Co.A
Walker, Elisha GA 14th Inf. Co.F
Walker, Elisha MS 2nd St.Cav. Co.F
Walker, Elisha NC 46th Inf. Co.K
Walker, Elisha C. GA Inf. 10th Bn. Co.E
Walker, Eli W. MO 8th Cav. Co.D
Walker, Eltride Jerry LA Arty. Moody's Co. (Madison Lt.Arty.)
Walker, E.M. NC 1st Inf. (6 mo. '61) Co.B
Walker, E.M. VA Cav. 47th Bn. Co.A Capt.
Walker, Emerson NC 8th Inf. Co.B
Walker, Emile LA Mil. LaFourche Regt.
Walker, Emmetta MS Cav. (St.Troops) Grace's Co.
Walker, Emmett A. MS 24th Inf. Co.H
Walker, E. Newton AL 44th Inf. Co.G
Walker, Enoch NC 8th Inf. Co.B
Walker, Enoch NC 17th Inf. (1st Org.) Co.E
Walker, Enoch VA 26th Inf. Co.F
Walker, Enoch VA Mil. Scott Cty.
Walker, E. Oscar KY 8th Cav. Co.K Sgt.
Walker, E.P. MO 6th Cav. Co.C
Walker, E.P. NC 28th Inf. Co.A
Walker, E.P. SC 7th Inf. 1st Co.B, Co.H
Walker, E.P. SC Inf. 7th Bn. (Enfield Rifles) Co.H Sgt.
Walker, Ephraim AR Cav. Poe's Bn. Co.A
Walker, Ephraim MO Cav. Preston's Bn.
Walker, Ephraim A. AL Inf. 2nd Regt. Co.B 1st Lt.
Walker, Ephraim A. TX Cav. Morgan's Regt. Co.A
Walker, Ephraim E. TX Cav. Baylor's Regt. Co.H
Walker, Ephram AR 11th Inf. Co.F
Walker, Eppa C. VA Cav. 15th Bn. Co.B
Walker, Eppa C. VA 41st Mil. Co.A Cpl.
Walker, Epriam MO 8th Cav.
Walker, E.R. TN Cav. 1st Bn. (McNairy's) Co.D Cpl.
Walker, E.R. TN 22nd (Barteau's) Cav. Co.B
Walker, E.R. TX 4th Inf. Co.A
Walker, Erasmus D. VA 46th Inf. 2nd Co.C
Walker, Erastus T. VA 46th Inf. Co.C
Walker, E.R.J.S.C. VA 2nd Cav. Co.I
Walker, E.S. Brass Band Vaughn's Brig.,CSA Music.
Walker, E.T. GA 5th Res. Co.A,D 1st Lt.
Walker, E.T. TN Inf. 2nd Cons.Regt. Co.B
Walker, E.T. TN 51st Inf. Co.K Hosp.Stew.
Walker, E.T. TN 51st (Cons.) Inf. Co.G
Walker, E.T. VA 34th Inf. Co.E
Walker, Ethelbert O. VA 17th Inf. Co.E
Walker, Euclid KY 6th Mtd.Inf. Co.G Sgt.
Walker, Eugene AL 21st Inf. Co.F
Walker, E.W. AL 37th Inf. Co.E
Walker, E.W. NC 38th Inf. Co.H
Walker, E.W. TN 6th (Wheeler's) Cav. Co.E
Walker, E.W. TN 16th Inf. Co.B Capt.
Walker, E.W. TX 17th Inf. Co.B Sgt.
Walker, Ezekiel GA 4th (Clinch's) Cav. Co.G
Walker, Ezekiel GA 26th Inf. Co.K Cpl.
Walker, Ezkiel MS 8th Inf. Co.G
Walker, F. GA 8th Cav. New Co.D
Walker, F. GA Cav. 20th Bn. Co.A
Walker, F. GA Siege Arty. 28th Bn. Co.K
Walker, F. GA 7th Inf. Co.G
Walker, F. MS Hall's Co.
Walker, F. TN 15th (Cons.) Cav. Co.D,E
Walker, F. TX 1st Hvy.Arty. Co.B
Walker, Fantley MO 3rd Inf. Co.C
Walker, F.B. GA 12th Mil.
Walker, F.B. LA 8th Cav. Co.I
Walker, F.C. VA 82nd Mil. Co.D Sgt.
Walker, F.D. MO Cav. 3rd Bn. Co.E
Walker, F.D. MO 4th Inf. Co.E
Walker, F.D. SC 3rd Cav. Co.H
Walker, F. Douglas SC Inf. Hampton Legion Co.A
Walker, F.E. TX Cav. Baird's Regt. Co.G
Walker, Felix SC 5th Inf. 1st Co.K
Walker, Felix SC Inf. Holcombe Legion Co.A

Walker, Felix SC Palmetto S.S. Co.K
Walker, Felix TX Cav. McCord's Frontier Regt. Co.D
Walker, Felix G. AL 17th Inf. Co.B
Walker, Felix H. GA Inf. 8th Bn. Co.B 1st Sgt.
Walker, Felix P. SC 2nd Cav. Co.I
Walker, Felix P. SC Cav.Bn. Hampton Legion Co.A Sgt.
Walker, Felix R. GA 7th Inf. Co.B
Walker, Felix T. TN 48th (Voorhies') Inf. Co.C 1st Lt.
Walker, F.F. GA 4th (Clinch's) Cav. Co.I
Walker, F.F. GA 59th Inf. Co.B
Walker, F.H. TX 20th Inf. Co.B
Walker, F.H. VA 34th Inf. Co.G
Walker, Fielding SC 5th Inf. 1st Co.K
Walker, F.L. AL 17th Inf. Co.A
Walker, F.L. VA Lt.Arty. Penick's Co. 1st Sgt.
Walker, Fleetwood GA 14th Inf. Co.C Asst.Surg.
Walker, Fleetwood Gen. & Staff Asst.Surg.
Walker, Fleming B. FL 4th Inf. Co.D Sgt.
Walker, Fleming B. GA 11th Cav. (St.Guards) Groover's Co.
Walker, Floid GA Cobb's Legion Co.F,B
Walker, Florence H. VA 57th Inf. Co.D
Walker, Flournoy LA 28th (Gray's) Inf. Co.E
Walker, F.M. AL 53rd (Part.Rangers) Co.H 2nd Lt.
Walker, F.M. AL 4th Res. Co.D Capt.
Walker, F.M. AL 16th Inf. Co.D Capt.
Walker, F.M. AL 40th Inf. Co.A
Walker, F.M. AL Cp. of Instr. Talladega
Walker, F.M. FL 11th Inf. Co.G
Walker, F.M. GA Cav. 10th Bn. (St.Guards) Co.D Sgt.
Walker, F.M. GA Arty. (Chatham Arty.) Wheaton's Co.
Walker, F.M. GA 1st (Olmstead's) Inf. Claghorn's Co.
Walker, F.M. GA 11th Inf. Co.K
Walker, F.M. GA 56th Inf. Co.B
Walker, F.M. GA 65th Inf. Co.H
Walker, F.M. GA Smith's Legion Co.A
Walker, F.M. MS 28th Cav. Co.B
Walker, F.M. TN 35th Inf. Co.B, 1st Co.A
Walker, F.M. TX 17th Cons.Dismtd.Cav. Co.G
Walker, F.M. TX 11th (Spaight's) Bn.Vol. Co.B
Walker, F.M. TX 13th Vol. 4th Co.I
Walker, F.M. Horse Arty. White's Btty. Sgt.
Walker, F.N. SC 3rd Inf. Co.D Capt.
Walker, Francis FL 10th Inf. Co.C
Walker, Francis VA 14th Inf.
Walker, Francis VA 41st Inf. Co.B Asst.Surg.
Walker, Francis Gen. & Staff Asst.Surg.
Walker, Francis M. MS Cav. 24th Bn. Co.A
Walker, Francis M. SC Inf. 3rd Bn. Co.B Cpl.
Walker, Francis M. TN 1st Cav.
Walker, Francis M. TN 19th Inf. Co.I Col.
Walker, Francis M. TN 41st Inf. Co.F
Walker, Francis M. TN 53rd Inf. Co.I Cpl.
Walker, Francis M. VA 55th Inf. Co.H 1st Lt.
Walker, Francis M. TN 59th Mtd.Inf. Co.G
Walker, Frank AR 35th Inf. Co.G
Walker, Frank LA 9th Inf. Co.K
Walker, Frank TN 30th Inf. Co.H
Walker, Frank Conf.Inf. Tucker's Regt. Co.I
Walker, Frank A. NC 13th Inf. Asst.Surg.
Walker, Frank C. LA 12th Inf. 2nd Co.M
Walker, Frank J. GA 6th Inf. (St.Guards) Co.B
Walker, Franklin VA Rockbridge Cty.Res. Bacon's Co.
Walker, Franklin B. GA 39th Inf. Co.G
Walker, Franklin M. AL 49th Inf. Co.D
Walker, Franklin M. SC 14th Inf. Co.A
Walker, Franklin M. TX 11th Cav. Co.A Cpl.
Walker, Franklin T.G. AL 6th Inf. Co.G
Walker, Fred GA 8th Inf. Co.C 2nd Lt.
Walker, Fred NC 15th Inf. Co.K
Walker, Fred TX Lt.Arty. Jones' Co.
Walker, Frederick LA 1st (Strawbridge's) Inf. Co.H
Walker, Frederick NC 56th Inf. Co.I
Walker, Frederick W. TN 59th Mtd.Inf. Co.I Sgt.
Walker, Fredrick A. SC 1st (Butler's) Inf. Co.H
Walker, Freeman FL 5th Inf. Co.G
Walker, Freeman GA 24th Inf. Co.A
Walker, Freeman GA 27th Inf. Co.K 2nd Lt.
Walker, Freeman MS Cav. 2nd Bn.Res. Co.F
Walker, Freeman MS 23rd Inf. Co.A Cpl.
Walker, Freeman SC Lt.Arty. Beauregard's Co.
Walker, F.F. MS 2nd Cav.
Walker, F.W. LA 12th Inf. Co.K
Walker, F.W. MS Cp.Guard (Cp. of Instr. for Conscr.)
Walker, F.W. 3rd Conf.Eng.Troops Co.H
Walker, G. AR Lt.Arty. Hart's Btty.
Walker, G. KY 4th Mtd.Inf. Co.K
Walker, G. LA Hvy.Arty. 2nd Bn. Co.A
Walker, G. LA Washington Arty.Bn. Co.5
Walker, G. LA Mil. 4th Regt.Eur.Brig. Co.B
Walker, G. LA 18th Inf. Co.C
Walker, G. MS 4th Cav. Co.B
Walker, G. MS 6th Inf. Co.H 3rd Lt.
Walker, G. MO 5th Cav. Co.A
Walker, G. NC 7th Sr.Res. Boon's Co.
Walker, G. NC 7th Sr.Res. Bradshaw's Co.
Walker, G. NC 7th Sr.Res. Clinard's Co.
Walker, G. SC 12th Inf. Co.I
Walker, G. SC Mil. 16th Regt. Lawrence's Co.
Walker, G. TX Cav. Baird's Regt. Co.A
Walker, G.A. TN 62nd Mtd.Inf. Co.D Sgt.
Walker, Galveston A. TX 4th Cav. Co.A
Walker, Garland W. AR 33rd Inf. Co.G 2nd Lt.
Walker, Garret LA Inf.Crescent Regt. Co.C
Walker, G.B. AL 26th (O'Neal's) Inf. Co.H
Walker, G.B. GA Conscr.
Walker, G.B. MS 12th Cav. Co.E Capt.
Walker, G.B. MS 2nd (Davidson's) Inf. Co.A
Walker, G.B. MS Inf. 2nd St.Troops Co.M
Walker, G.B. MS 26th Inf. Co.G
Walker, G.B. VA 13th Cav. Co.K
Walker, G.D. GA Cav. Dorough's Bn.
Walker, G.D. GA Phillips' Legion Co.E,N
Walker, G.D. LA Mil. 1st Regt. 2nd Brig. 1st Div. Co.G
Walker, G.D. MS 6th Inf. Co.E
Walker, George AL Cav. Murphy's Bn. Co.D
Walker, George AR 1st (Colquitt's) Inf. Co.K
Walker, George AR 4th Inf. QM
Walker, George AR 7th Inf.
Walker, George AR 35th Inf. Co.D
Walker, George AR 36th Inf. Co.G 1st Lt.
Walker, George AR 51st Mil. Co.E
Walker, George FL 3rd Inf. Co.H
Walker, George FL 10th Inf. Co.F
Walker, George GA 5th Res. Co.D
Walker, George GA 8th Inf. (St.Guards) Co.D
Walker, George KY 2nd (Duke's) Cav. Co.A
Walker, George KY 1st Inf. Co.A
Walker, George KY 6th Mtd.Inf. Co.K 2nd Lt.
Walker, George LA Washington Arty.Bn. Co.4
Walker, George LA Inf. 1st Sp.Bn. (Rightor's) Co.B
Walker, George LA 31st Inf. Co.I
Walker, George MS Inf. 3rd Bn. (St.Troops) Co.G 1st Sgt.
Walker, George MO 7th Cav. Maj.
Walker, George MO 3rd Inf. Co.F
Walker, George NC 2nd Cav. (19th St.Troops) Co.F
Walker, George NC 23rd Inf. Co.D
Walker, George NC 34th Inf. Co.K
Walker, George SC Mil. 16th Regt. Prendergast's Co.
Walker, George SC Inf. Hampton Legion Co.F
Walker, George TN 13th (Gore's) Cav. Co.I
Walker, George TN 35th Inf. Co.C
Walker, George TN 35th Inf. Co.H
Walker, George TN 48th (Nixon's) Inf. Co.F
Walker, George TN 54th Inf. Co.A
Walker, George TX 7th Cav. Co.H Sgt.
Walker, George TX 11th Field Btty.
Walker, George TX 1st Inf. Co.B
Walker, George VA 14th Cav. Co.L
Walker, George VA 17th Cav. Co.I
Walker, George VA 24th Cav. Co.D
Walker, George VA Cav. 40th Bn. Co.D
Walker, George VA 6th Inf. 1st Co.B
Walker, George VA 21st Mil. Co.D
Walker, George VA 22nd Inf. Co.C
Walker, George VA 40th Inf. Co.K Sgt.
Walker, George VA Inf. 45th Bn. Co.D
Walker, George Conf.Inf. 8th Bn. Co.C
Walker, George Morgan's,CSA
Walker, George 1st Cherokee Mtd.Rifles Co.F
Walker, George 1st Cherokee Mtd.Vol. 2nd Co.D
Walker, Geo. Gen. & Staff Capt.,QM
Walker, George A. AL 13th Inf. Co.E
Walker, George A. FL 3rd Inf. Co.A Sgt.
Walker, George A. MO 2nd Cav. 3rd Co.K Cpl.
Walker, George A. NC 27th Inf. Co.G
Walker, George A. VA 12th Cav. Co.B
Walker, George A. VA Lt.Arty. Arch. Graham's Co.
Walker, George A. 7th Conf.Cav. Co.B
Walker, George A.B. GA Inf. 1st Loc.Troops (Augusta) Co.B
Walker, George Alen MS 16th Inf. Co.K
Walker, George B. MS 10th Cav. Co.B,E Capt.
Walker, George B. VA 5th Cav. (12 mo. '61-2) Co.C
Walker, George B. VA Lt.Arty. 13th Bn. Co.B
Walker, George B. VA 6th Inf. Co.G
Walker, George C. GA 4th Inf. Co.B
Walker, George C. VA 4th Cav. Co.B
Walker, George C. VA Cav. Mosby's Regt. (Part.Rangers) Co.A
Walker, George C. VA 60th Inf. 2nd Co.H
Walker, George D. VA Lt.Arty. French's Co.

Walker, George E. LA 12th Inf. Co.B
Walker, George E. VA 20th Inf. Co.C
Walker, George E. VA 21st Inf. Co.K
Walker, George E. Eng.,CSA Capt.
Walker, George F. NC 51st Inf. Co.A Capt.
Walker, George H. LA 1st Hvy.Arty. (Reg.) Surg.
Walker, George H. LA 9th Inf. Co.A
Walker, George H. VA 24th Inf. Co.C 2nd Lt.
Walker, Geo. H. Gen. & Staff, Medical Dept. Surg.
Walker, George J. AL 8th Inf. Co.A
Walker, George J.S. AL Cav. Lewis Bn. Co.D Sgt.
Walker, George L. AR 15th Mil. Co.I Sgt.
Walker, George L. GA 3rd Inf. Co.H
Walker, George M. AL Inf. 1st Regt. Co.H
Walker, George M. GA 7th Inf. Co.A
Walker, George M. MS 2nd Inf. Co.F,D
Walker, George M. SC 1st (McCreary's) Inf. Co.G
Walker, George M. SC 2nd Rifles Co.C
Walker, George M. VA 15th Inf. Co.D
Walker, George M. Sig.Corps,CSA
Walker, George Mc. NC 3rd Arty. (40th St.Troops) Co.C
Walker, George O. SC 6th Inf. 2nd Co.D 2nd Lt.
Walker, George O. SC 9th Inf. Co.H
Walker, George P. FL 1st Cav. Co.H
Walker, George P. GA Arty. (Chatham Arty.) Wheaton's Co.
Walker, George P. GA 32nd Inf. Co.D Cpl.
Walker, George R. FL 5th Inf. Co.F,G 1st Lt.
Walker, George R. GA Inf. 1st Loc.Troops (Augusta) Co.G
Walker, George R. VA Cav. Mosby's Regt. (Part.Rangers) Co.A
Walker, George T. GA Lt.Arty. 14th Bn. Co.A
Walker, George T. GA Lt.Arty. Havis' Btty.
Walker, George T. TX 11th Inf. Co.G Capt.
Walker, George T. VA 11th Inf. Co.C
Walker, George T. VA 34th Inf. Co.C
Walker, George V. GA 53rd Inf. Co.C Sgt.
Walker, George W. AL 25th Inf. Co.F
Walker, George W. AL 32nd Inf. Co.G
Walker, George W. AL 49th Inf. Co.E
Walker, George W. AR 4th Inf. Co.I 2nd Lt.
Walker, George W. AR 11th Inf. Co.B Cpl.
Walker, George W. AR 11th & 17th (Cons.) Inf. Co.A,B Sgt.
Walker, George W. FL 3rd Inf. Co.H
Walker, George W. FL 8th Inf. Co.K
Walker, George W. GA Siege Arty. 28th Bn. Co.E
Walker, George W. GA Lt.Arty. Anderson's Btty.
Walker, George W. GA 5th Inf. Co.K
Walker, George W. GA 31st Inf. Co.C,K Music.
Walker, George W. GA 36th (Villepigue's) Inf. Co.A
Walker, George W. GA 45th Inf. Co.D Cpl.
Walker, George W. GA 47th Inf. Co.F
Walker, George W. GA 49th Inf. Co.F Cpl.
Walker, George W. GA Smith's Legion Co.H
Walker, George W. KY 6th Cav. Co.A,C
Walker, George W. KY 1st Inf. Co.H,A
Walker, George W. LA 19th Inf. Co.B Sgt.
Walker, George W. MS 30th Inf. Co.K Cpl.
Walker, George W. MS 44th Inf. Co.C
Walker, George W. MO Cav. Coffee's Regt. Co.B
Walker, George W. MO 5th Inf. Co.K
Walker, George W. NC 2nd Cav. (19th St.Troops) Co.K
Walker, George W. NC 4th Cav. (59th St.Troops) Co.C
Walker, George W. NC 8th Inf. Co.A Cpl.
Walker, George W. NC 8th Inf. Co.C
Walker, George W. NC 20th Inf. Co.G 3rd Lt.
Walker, George W. NC 42nd Inf. Co.F Cpl.
Walker, George W. SC 5th Inf. 1st Co.B, 2nd Co.F
Walker, George W. TN 2nd (Ashby's) Cav. Co.F Sgt.
Walker, George W. TN Cav. 4th Bn. (Branner's) Co.F
Walker, George W. TN 4th (McLemore's) Cav. Co.D
Walker, George W. TN 9th Cav.
Walker, George W. TN 54th Inf. Childress' Co.
Walker, George W. TX 11th Cav. Co.C,E
Walker, George W. TX 25th Cav. Co.E
Walker, George W. TX Inf. Griffin's Bn. Co.D
Walker, George W. VA 24th Cav. Co.D
Walker, George W. VA Cav. 40th Bn. Co.D
Walker, George W. VA 1st Lt.Arty. Co.B
Walker, George W. VA Lt.Arty. J.S. Brown's Co.
Walker, George W. VA Hvy.Arty. A.J. Jones' Co.
Walker, George W. VA Lt.Arty. Taylor's Co. Cpl.
Walker, George W. VA Inf. 23rd Bn. Co.C Sgt.
Walker, George W. VA 45th Inf. Co.L
Walker, George W. VA Res.Forces Thurston's Co.
Walker, George W. 1st Conf.Inf. Co.A
Walker, George Washington MO Inf. 1st Bn. Co.A
Walker, G.F. AL 50th Inf. Co.H
Walker, G.G. GA 50th Inf. Co.D
Walker, G.G. LA Inf. 10th Bn. Co.G
Walker, G.G. TN 31st Inf. Co.E
Walker, G.H. AL 9th Inf. Co.A
Walker, G.H. AL 31st Inf. Co.C
Walker, G.H. LA 1st Cav. Co.A
Walker, G.H. TX 32nd Cav. Co.F
Walker, G.H. TX 1st Hvy.Arty. Co.D
Walker, G.H. TX 15th Field Btty.
Walker, Gideon TX 15th Cav. Co.K
Walker, Gilbert FL 3rd Inf. Co.I Cpl.
Walker, Gilbert GA 10th Inf. Co.E
Walker, G.J. LA Pointe Coupee Arty.
Walker, G.J.S. AL 5th Inf. New Co.F
Walker, G.L. MO 2nd Cav. Co.D Cpl.
Walker, G.L. MO 9th Bn.S.S. Co.B
Walker, G.L. MO 10th Inf. Co.A,D,B
Walker, G.L. MO 11th Inf. Co.G
Walker, G.M. SC Lt.Arty. Parker's Co. (Marion Arty.)
Walker, G.N. LA 28th (Gray's) Inf. Co.K
Walker, G.O. SC 7th Cav. Co.B
Walker, Goldsmith TX 2nd Cav. Co.K Capt.
Walker, G.P. TN 12th Inf. Co.D
Walker, G.R. TN 12th (Cons.) Inf. Co.E
Walker, Granville MS 17th Inf. Co.F
Walker, Granville VA 44th Inf. Co.B
Walker, Green GA 49th Inf. Co.F
Walker, Green B. LA 9th Inf. Co.A
Walker, Griffin SC Lt.Arty. 3rd (Palmetto) Bn. Co.B
Walker, Griffin SC 4th St.Troops Co.B
Walker, Griffin B. NC 4th Cav. (59th St.Troops) Co.G
Walker, Griffith C. TN Cav. 9th Bn. (Gantt's) Co.E
Walker, G.S. TX Inf. Timmons' Regt. Co.A
Walker, G.S. TX Waul's Legion Co.B
Walker, G.S. VA 3rd Res. Co.H Cpl.
Walker, G.S. Gen. & Staff AASurg.
Walker, G.T. AR Inf. Hardy's Regt. Torbett's Co.
Walker, G.T. GA 8th Inf.
Walker, G.T. NC Mil. Co.A 2nd Lt.
Walker, G.T. SC 2nd Rifles Co.C
Walker, Gus M. GA Lt.Arty. Anderson's Btty.
Walker, G.W. AL Cav. Lewis' Bn. Co.B
Walker, G.W. AL 6th Inf. Co.M
Walker, G.W. AL 34th Inf. Co.B
Walker, G.W. AL 37th Inf. Co.E
Walker, G.W. AL 45th Inf. Co.E
Walker, G.W. AL 54th Inf. Sgt.
Walker, G.W. AL 3rd Bn. Hilliard's Legion Vol. Co.C
Walker, G.W. AR Inf. Cocke's Regt. Co.I
Walker, G.W. GA 10th Cav. (St.Guards) Co.K
Walker, G.W. GA 19th Inf. Co.G Sgt.
Walker, G.W. GA Philips' Legion Co.E
Walker, G.W. KY 10th (Johnson's) Cav. New Co.C
Walker, G.W. KY 3rd Bn.Mtd.Rifles Co.B
Walker, G.W. KY 6th Mtd.Inf. Co.K 2nd Lt.
Walker, G.W. LA Mtd.Rifles Miller's Ind.Co.
Walker, G.W. LA 1st Hvy.Arty. (Reg.) Co.G,B
Walker, G.W. LA 8th Inf. Co.G
Walker, G.W. LA Inf. Pelican Regt. Co.E Sgt.
Walker, G.W. MS 2nd St.Cav. Co.B
Walker, G.W. MS 2nd St.Cav. Co.H
Walker, G.W. MS St.Cav. 3rd Bn. (Cooper's) Little's Co.
Walker, G.W. MS Cav. 3rd Bn.Res. Co.D 2nd Lt.
Walker, G.W. MS St.Cav. Stubbs' Bn. Co.A 2nd Lt.
Walker, G.W., Jr. MS 3rd Inf. Co.A
Walker, G.W. MS Inf. 3rd Bn. (St.Troops) Co.C
Walker, G.W. MS 4th Inf. Co.C
Walker, G.W. MS 6th Inf. Co.H 1st Sgt.
Walker, G.W. MS 24th Inf. Co.C
Walker, G.W. MS 39th Inf. Co.E
Walker, G.W. MS 44th Inf. Co.G
Walker, G.W. MS Home Guards Barnes' Co. 1st Lt.
Walker, G.W. MO 6th Cav. Co.H
Walker, G.W. MO 10th Inf. Co.E
Walker, G.W. NC 1st Arty. (10th St.Troops) Co.E
Walker, G.W. NC 6th Inf. Co.G
Walker, G.W. SC Inf. 1st (Charleston) Bn. Co.D

Walker, G.W. TN 3rd (Forrest's) Cav. 1st Co.E Bugler
Walker, G.W. TN 13th (Gore's) Cav. Co.I
Walker, G.W. TN Inf. 3rd Cons.Regt. Co.A
Walker, G.W. TN 48th (Nixon's) Inf. Co.A
Walker, G.W. TN 48th (Voorhies') Inf. Co.B Cpl.
Walker, G.W. TN 49th Inf. Co.F
Walker, G.W. TX Cav. 2nd Bn.St.Troops Co.A
Walker, G.W. TX 4th Cav. Co.I
Walker, G.W. TX 6th Cav. Co.H
Walker, G.W. TX 26th Cav. Co.I
Walker, G.W. TX 2nd Inf. Co.C
Walker, G.W. TX 4th Inf. Co.B
Walker, G.W. Inf. Bailey's Cons.Regt. Co.C
Walker, G.W. TX 13th Vol. 3rd Co.A
Walker, G.W. TX Inf. Currie's Co.
Walker, G.W. TX Inf. Timmons' Regt. Co.I
Walker, G.W. TX Waul's Legion Co.H Sgt.
Walker, G.W. VA Inf. 4th Bn.Loc.Def. Co.B
Walker, G.W. Exch.Bn. 1st Co.C,CSA Sgt.
Walker, G.W. Gen. & Staff Hosp.Stew.
Walker, G.W.V. VA Cav. 34th Bn. Co.K Cpl.
Walker, H. AL 21st Inf. Co.F
Walker, H. AR 58th Mil. Co.A
Walker, H. GA Siege Arty. 28th Bn. Co.I
Walker, H. GA 50th Inf. Co.D
Walker, H. KY 6th Cav. Co.I
Walker, H. KY 12th Cav. Co.K
Walker, H. MS 3rd (St.Troops) Cav. Co.A
Walker, H. MS 8th Cav. Co.K
Walker, H. MS 5th Inf. (St.Troops) Co.A
Walker, H. MS 34th Inf. Co.I
Walker, H. NC 7th Sr.Res. Johnston's Co.
Walker, H. TN 21st & 22nd (Cons.) Cav. Co.C
Walker, H. TN 16th Inf. Co.I
Walker, H. TN 45th Inf. Co.A
Walker, H. TX 5th Field Btty.
Walker, H. TX Lt.Arty. Dege's Bn.
Walker, H. TX Inf. 1st Bn. (St.Troops) Co.F
Walker, H. TX 13th Vol. Co.G Cpl.
Walker, H. TX 21st Inf. Co.C
Walker, H. VA 54th Mil. Co.E,F
Walker, H. 15th Conf.Cav. Co.F
Walker, H.A. GA 2nd Inf. Co.A
Walker, H.A. SC 22nd Inf. Co.G
Walker, H.A. TN 19th (Biffle's) Cav. Co.C
Walker, Hal T. Gen. & Staff ADC
Walker, Hamilton VA 26th Inf. Co.A
Walker, Hamilton VA 36th Inf. 2nd Co.B
Walker, Hamilton K. FL 3rd Inf. Co.E Capt.
Walker, Hamilton S. VA 55th Inf. Co.H
Walker, Hampton C. MS 2nd Inf. Co.E
Walker, Hardin C. MS 42nd Inf. Co.G
Walker, Hardy C. GA 30th Inf. Co.H
Walker, Hardy F. NC 45th Inf. Co.G 2nd Lt.
Walker, Hardy R. GA 30th Inf. Co.H
Walker, Hardy W. AR 14th (McCarver's) Inf. Co.D Drum.
Walker, Hardy W. AR 21st Inf. Co.K Cpl.
Walker, Harman B. VA 3rd Cav. Co.F
Walker, Harman B. VA 52nd Mil. Co.B
Walker, Harris VA 9th Cav. Co.I
Walker, Harris 1st Choctaw & Chickasaw Mtd.Rifles 2nd Co.C
Walker, Harrison NC 28th Inf. Co.A
Walker, Harrison SC 23rd Inf. Co.F
Walker, Harrison VA 16th Cav. Capt., Asst.Surg.
Walker, Harry VA Inf. 45th Bn. Co.A,K Capt.
Walker, Harry A. TN 48th (Voorhies') Inf. Co.B
Walker, Hartwell NC 44th Inf. Co.B
Walker, Hartwell B. MO Cav. Freeman's Regt. Co.F
Walker, Harvey NC 1st Bn.Jr.Res. Co.B
Walker, Harvey VA 1st Cav.St.Line Co.A Sgt.
Walker, Harvey C. VA 44th Inf. Co.A Sgt.
Walker, H.B. VA 13th Cav. AQM
Walker, H.B.C. VA 1st St.Res. Co.B
Walker, H.C. AL Gid Nelson Lt.Arty.
Walker, H.C. GA 13th Co.K Cpl.
Walker, H.C. LA Lt.Arty. Fenner's Btty. Sgt.
Walker, H.C. LA Inf. 1st Sp.Bn. (Rightor's) Co.A
Walker, H.C. LA 17th Inf. Co.H
Walker, H.C. MO 1st & 4th Cons.Inf. Co.E
Walker, H.C. MO 4th Inf. Co.E
Walker, H.C. NC 1st Cav. (9th St.Troops) Co.F
Walker, H.C. SC Mil.Arty. 1st Regt. Tuppers' Co.
Walker, H.C. TN 51st (Cons.) Inf. Co.A Sgt.
Walker, H.C. TN 52nd Inf. Co.A Sgt.
Walker, H.C. TX 20th Cav. Co.B Bugler
Walker, H.C. TX 26th Cav. Co.E
Walker, H.C. Conf.Cav. Wood's Regt. 2nd Co.F
Walker, H.D. MS Cav. 3rd Bn. (Ashcraft's) Co.F
Walker, H.D. MS 5th Cav. Co.K
Walker, H.D. MS 18th Cav. Co.G
Walker, H.D. MS 1st (Johnston's) Inf. Co.G
Walker, H.D. NC 18th Inf. Co.I
Walker, H.E. TN 9th (Ward's) Cav. Co.F,A
Walker, H.E. TX 4th Inf. Co.I
Walker, Henderson NC 31st Inf. Co.H
Walker, Henderson 1st Choctaw & Chickasaw Mtd.Rifles 2nd Co.H
Walker, Henley LA 12th Inf. Co.D
Walker, Henry AL 32nd Inf. Co.A
Walker, Henry AR 7th Inf. Co.H
Walker, Henry GA 12th Cav. Co.K
Walker, Henry GA Cav. 16th Bn. (St.Guards) Co.C
Walker, Henry GA 21st Inf. Old Co.E
Walker, Henry GA 65th Inf. Co.E
Walker, Henry LA Inf. 1st Bn. (St.Guards)
Walker, Henry MS 9th Cav. Co.G
Walker, Henry MS Lt.Arty. (Brookhaven Lt.Arty.) Hoskins' Btty.
Walker, Henry NC 6th Inf. Co.K
Walker, Henry NC 7th Sr.Res. Fisher's Co. Cpl.
Walker, Henry NC 7th Sr.Res. Mitchell's Co.
Walker, Henry SC Arty. Manigault's Bn.
Walker, Henry SC 1st (Butler's) Inf. Co.A Music.
Walker, Henry SC 1st Bn.S.S. Co.C
Walker, Henry SC Inf. 1st (Charleston) Bn. Co.F 2nd Lt.
Walker, Henry SC 27th Inf. Co.C 2nd Lt.
Walker, Henry TN 22nd (Barteau's) Cav. Co.K Cpl.
Walker, Henry TN 43rd Inf. Co.I
Walker, Henry TX Cav. Bourland's Regt. Co.I,H
Walker, Henry TX 15th Inf. Co.A
Walker, Henry VA 7th Cav. Co.A
Walker, Henry VA Lt.Arty. Hardwicke's Co.
Walker, Henry VA 60th Inf. Co.A
Walker, Henry 15th Conf.Cav. Co.A
Walker, Henry A. MS 9th Cav. Co.G Sgt.
Walker, Henry A. NC 13th Inf. Co.C Adj.
Walker, Henry A. NC 44th Inf. Co.G
Walker, Henry A. SC Inf. Hampton Legion Co.F
Walker, Henry A. VA 108th Mil. Lemans' Co.
Walker, Henry B. TN 1st (Feild's) Inf. Co.D Sgt.
Walker, Henry C. VA 24th Inf. Co.D
Walker, Henry C. VA 53rd Inf. Co.K
Walker, Henry D. NC 4th Cav. (59th St.Troops) Co.C
Walker, Henry G. NC 42nd Inf. Co.D Sgt.
Walker, Henry H. AL 47th Inf. Co.C
Walker, Henry H. GA Lt.Arty. Ferrell's Btty.
Walker, Henry H. MS Lt.Arty. (Brookhaven Lt.Arty.) Hoskins' Btty.
Walker, Henry H. NC 2nd Arty. (36th St.Troops) Co.A
Walker, Henry H. NC Inf. 13th Bn. Co.A
Walker, Henry H. NC 66th Inf. Co.A
Walker, Henry H. TN 6th Inf. Co.H
Walker, Henry H. TX 10th Inf. Co.I Sgt.
Walker, Henry H. VA 55th Inf. Co.H
Walker, Henry J. GA 49th Inf. Co.B
Walker, Henry J. NC 13th Inf. Co.B 3rd Lt.
Walker, Henry J. TN 24th Inf. Co.B
Walker, Henry M. Gen. & Staff 1st Lt.,Adj.
Walker, Henry P. MO 1st N.E. Cav.
Walker, Henry P., Jr. SC Arty. Manigault's Bn. 1st Co.A
Walker, Henry R. VA 40th Inf. Co.K
Walker, Henry S. GA 66th Inf. Co.E
Walker, Henry S. NC 3rd Arty. (40th St.Troops) Co.C
Walker, Henry S. VA Arty. Paris' Co. Sgt.
Walker, Henry T. MS 17th Inf. Co.H
Walker, Henry T. MS Packer's Co. (Pope Guards)
Walker, Henry T. MO Inf. 8th Bn. Co.D 1st Lt.
Walker, Henry W. FL 1st Cav. Co.F
Walker, Henry W. MS 29th Inf. Co.E
Walker, Henry W. TN 48th (Nixon's) Inf. Co.G
Walker, Henry W. VA 4th Bn.Res. Co.C
Walker, Henry W. VA 47th Inf. Co.F
Walker, Heuston C. AR 16th Inf. Co.H
Walker, Hezekiah GA 64th Inf. Co.D
Walker, Hezekiah VA 29th Inf. 2nd Co.F, Co.C
Walker, H.F. SC 2nd Rifles Co.C
Walker, H.G. GA Lt.Arty. Havis' Btty.
Walker, H.G. MS 36th Inf. Co.E
Walker, H.H. AL 5th Bn.Vol. Lt.Col.
Walker, H.H. AL 47th Inf. Co.F Sgt.
Walker, H.H. GA 44th Inf.
Walker, H.H. MS 20th Inf. Co.A
Walker, H.H. TX 9th (Young's) Inf. Co.C
Walker, H.H. TX 22nd Inf. Co.F
Walker, H.H. VA 18th Cav. Co.I
Walker, H.H. VA 40th Inf. Lt.Col.
Walker, H.H. 15th Conf.Cav. Co.K
Walker, H.H. Hill's Corps Brig.Gen.
Walker, H.I. GA 12th (Robinson's) Cav. (St.Guards) Co.E
Walker, Hiram LA 25th Inf. Co.E
Walker, Hiram A. FL 4th Inf. Co.C

Walker, Hiram L. VA 14th Inf. Co.D
Walker, H.J. AR 15th (Josey's) Inf. 1st Co.C
Walker, H.J. AR 18th Inf. Co.A
Walker, H.J. GA 47th Inf. Co.B
Walker, H.L. MO Cav. 1st Regt.St.Guard Co.E
Walker, H.L. 2nd Cherokee Mtd.Vol. Co.C Bn.Dr.M.
Walker, H.M. GA Inf. 8th Bn. Co.C
Walker, H.M. MS Blythe's Bn. (St.Troops) Co.B
Walker, H.N. TN 24th Inf. Co.K
Walker, H.N. VA Inf. 4th Bn.Loc.Def. Co.D
Walker, Hogner 1st Cherokee Mtd.Vol. 2nd Co.E
Walker, Holland W.F. VA 55th Inf. Co.C
Walker, Horatis Perry TX 20th Cav. Co.G
Walker, Houston C. AR 4th Inf. Kelley's Co.
Walker, Howard MS 10th Cav. Co.G
Walker, Howard MS 31st Inf. Co.F
Walker, Howard NC 54th Inf. Co.G
Walker, Howell C. GA 1st Inf. Co.C
Walker, H.P. AL 18th Inf. Co.E,G Capt.
Walker, H.P. GA 28th Inf. Co.C
Walker, H.P. SC Mil. 17th Regt. Buist's Co.
Walker, H.P. TX Cav. Morgan's Regt. Co.F
Walker, H.R. TN 48th (Voorhies') Inf. Co.B Capt.
Walker, H.S. TX 28th Cav. Co.B
Walker, H.S. TX 30th Cav. Co.C
Walker, H.T. AL 25th Inf. Co.F
Walker, H.T. KY 13th Cav. Co.C
Walker, H.T. MO 9th Inf. Co.H 1st Lt.
Walker, H.T. MO Robertson's Regt.St.Guard Co.H Capt.
Walker, H.T. VA Arty. L.F. Jones' Co.
Walker, H.T. VA 3rd Res. Co.D
Walker, H.T.W. FL Inf. 2nd Bn. Co.B
Walker, Hugh B. VA 5th Cav. (12 mo. '61-2) Co.C
Walker, Hugh B. VA 13th Cav. Co.H
Walker, Hugh B. Gen. & Staff, QM Dept. Capt.
Walker, Hugh M. MS 24th Inf. Co.H
Walker, H.W. LA 31st Inf. Co.D
Walker, H.W. MS 6th Cav. Co.F
Walker, H.W. MS Inf. 3rd Bn. (St.Troops) Co.E
Walker, H.W. MS 9th Inf. New Co.A
Walker, H.W. MS 9th Inf. Old Co.G
Walker, H.W. SC Hvy.Arty. Gilchrist's Co. (Gist Guard)
Walker, H.W. SC Arty. Manigault's Bn. Co.E
Walker, H.W. SC 11th Inf. Co.K
Walker, H.W. VA 10th Cav. Co.C
Walker, H.Y. NC 26th Inf. Co.A
Walker, I. MO Cav. Williams' Regt. Co.H Sgt.
Walker, I.A. Gen. & Staff, A. of N.VA Capt.,ACS
Walker, I.B. TX 12th Inf. Co.I
Walker, I.E. TN 35th Inf. Co.B
Walker, Ignatius TX 11th Inf. Co.B Cpl.
Walker, I.J. TN 15th (Cons.) Cav. Co.K
Walker, Ike E. TX 29th Cav. Co.I
Walker, Ike W. 1st Conf.Inf. 1st Co.G
Walker, I.M. Gen. & Staff, Subs.Dept. Capt.,ACS
Walker, I.R. Conf.Cav. Wood's Regt. 2nd Co.D
Walker, Is E. TN Cav. 4th Bn. (Branner's) Co.F
Walker, Is. J. TN 2nd (Ashby's) Cav. Co.F
Walker, Isaac AL 62nd Inf. Co.I
Walker, Isaac AR Inf. Cocke's Regt. Co.A
Walker, Isaac FL 4th Inf. Co.E
Walker, Isaac MS Lt.Arty. Lomax's Co.
Walker, Isaac MO Inf. Perkins' Bn. Co.E
Walker, Isaac TN 1st (Carter's) Cav. Co.L
Walker, Isaac TN Cav. Welcker's Bn. Kincaid's Co., Co.D
Walker, Isaac TN 25th Inf. Co.H
Walker, Isaac TN 35th Inf. 1st Co.A
Walker, Isaac A. LA 27th Inf. Co.C Cpl.
Walker, Isaac C. LA 8th Inf. Co.G
Walker, Isaac C. NC 15th Inf. Co.K Cpl.
Walker, Isaac D. AL 49th Inf. Co.G
Walker, Isaac J. TN Cav. 4th Bn. (Branner's) Co.F
Walker, Isaac W. GA 36th (Villepigue's) Inf. Co.G
Walker, Isaac W. MS 13th Inf. Co.D
Walker, Isaiah VA 3rd Inf. 2nd Co.I
Walker, Isam TX 34th Cav. Co.D Cpl.
Walker, Isham FL 1st Cav. Co.I Bugler
Walker, Isham FL 4th Inf. Co.D
Walker, Isham GA 50th Inf. Co.A
Walker, Isham MS Lt.Arty. (Brookhaven Lt.Arty.) Hoskins' Btty.
Walker, Isham MS 9th Inf. Old Co.D
Walker, Isham 1st Conf.Eng.Troops Co.C Artif.
Walker, Isham D. AL 49th Inf. Co.G Lt.
Walker, Isham J. FL 5th Inf. Co.F,G
Walker, Israel MS 46th Inf. Co.H
Walker, I.T. LA 1st Inf. Co.H
Walker, Ivy MS 8th Inf. Co.A
Walker, Ivy MS 46th Inf. Co.H
Walker, I.W. MS 2nd Cav. Co.B
Walker, I.W. MS 2nd Cav.Res. Co.C
Walker, J. AL 9th (Malone's) Cav. Co.L Cpl.
Walker, J. AL 4th Inf. Co.D
Walker, J. AL 31st Inf. Co.I
Walker, J. AL 35th Inf. Co.C
Walker, J. AL Talladega Cty.Res. G.M. Gamble's Co.
Walker, J. AR 11th & 17th (Cons.) Inf. Co.F
Walker, J. FL 5th Inf. Co.E
Walker, J. GA Cav. 1st Bn. Walthour's Co.
Walker, J. GA 5th Cav. Co.G
Walker, J. GA 7th Cav. Co.D
Walker, J. GA Siege Arty. 28th Bn. Co.I
Walker, J. GA 2nd Bn. Troops & Defences (Macon) Co.D
Walker, J. GA 5th Res. Co.F
Walker, J. GA 5th Res. Co.G
Walker, J. GA 7th Inf. (St.Guards) Co.B
Walker, J. GA Inf. 27th Bn. (NonConscr.) Co.C
Walker, J. GA 39th Inf.
Walker, J. GA 45th Inf. Co.D Cpl.
Walker, J. GA 50th Inf. Co.D
Walker, J. GA 63rd Inf. Co.I
Walker, J. GA Inf. (NonConscr.) Howard's Co.
Walker, J. KY 4th Mtd.Inf. Co.K
Walker, J. LA Inf.Crescent Regt. Co.H
Walker, J. LA Mil. St.John the Baptist Res. Guards 2nd Lt.
Walker, J. SC 1st Cav. Lt.
Walker, J. SC 27th Inf. Co.D
Walker, J. TX 37th Cav. Mullins' Co.
Walker, J. TX 5th Inf. Co.F
Walker, J. TX 18th Inf. Co.F
Walker, J. TX 20th Inf. Co.K
Walker, J. TX Inf. Chambers' Bn.Res.Corps Co.E
Walker, J.A. AL 1st Cav. 2nd Co.D
Walker, J.A. AL 3rd Inf. Co.C
Walker, J.A. AL 14th Inf. Co.I
Walker, J.A. AL 19th Inf. Co.C
Walker, J.A. AL 25th Inf. Co.E
Walker, J.A. AL 29th Inf. Co.D
Walker, J.A. FL 1st Inf. New Co.H Sgt.
Walker, J.A. FL 2nd Inf.
Walker, J.A. GA 1st Cav. Co.K 1st Sgt.
Walker, J.A. GA 4th (Clinch's) Cav. Co.F Sgt.
Walker, J.A. GA 11th Cav.
Walker, J.A. GA 2nd Inf. Co.K
Walker, J.A. GA 5th Res. Co.F
Walker, J.A. GA Inf. 25th Bn. (Prov.Guard) Co.G QMSgt.
Walker, J.A. GA 27th Inf. Co.C
Walker, J.A. GA 48th Inf. Co.K
Walker, J.A. MS Part.Rangers Smyth's Co.
Walker, J.A. MS 10th Inf. New Co.A
Walker, J.A. MO Inf. 1st Regt.St.Guard Co.D Col.
Walker, J.A. SC 5th Cav. Co.I
Walker, J.A. SC Inf. 3rd Bn. Co.C
Walker, J.A. SC 6th Inf. 1st Co.A
Walker, J.A. TN 2nd (Ashby's) Cav. Co.F
Walker, J.A. TN 6th (Wheeler's) Cav. Co.E
Walker, J.A. TN 13th (Gore's) Cav. Co.I
Walker, J.A. TN Inf. 1st Bn. (Colms') Co.C
Walker, J.A. TN 5th Inf. 2nd Co.H
Walker, J.A. TN 12th Inf. Co.H Cpl.
Walker, J.A. TN 12th (Cons.) Inf. Co.K Cpl.
Walker, J.A. TN 16th Inf. Co.B
Walker, J.A. TN 27th Inf. Co.A
Walker, J.A. TX Cav. Waller's Regt. Co.F
Walker, J.A. TX 5th Inf. Co.K
Walker, J.A. VA 2nd St.Res.
Walker, J.A. VA 22nd Inf. Co.E
Walker, J.A. 2nd Conf.Eng.Troops Co.E
Walker, J.A. Exch.Bn. Co.D,CSA
Walker, J. Abner VA 20th Inf. Co.C
Walker, J.A.C. AL 20th Inf. Co.K
Walker, J.A.C. AL 30th Inf. Co.I Cpl.
Walker, Jack TX Inf. Currie's Co.
Walker, Jackson GA Lt.Arty. 14th Bn. Co.D
Walker, Jackson GA Lt.Arty. King's Btty.
Walker, Jackson MO Lt.Arty. 13th Btty.
Walker, Jackson MO 4th Inf. Co.D
Walker, Jackson Conf.Inf. 8th Bn. Co.A
Walker, Jackson Conf.Reg.Inf. Brooks' Bn. Co.A
Walker, Jacob AL 44th Inf. Co.H
Walker, Jacob MO Inf. Perkins' Bn. Co.E
Walker, Jacob NC 6th Inf. Co.K
Walker, Jacob TN 14th Inf. Co.D Cpl.
Walker, Jacob TN 16th Inf. Co.B
Walker, Jacob VA 18th Cav. Co.B
Walker, Jacob VA Inf. 45th Bn. Co.C
Walker, Jacob VA 62nd Mtd.Inf. 1st Co.G
Walker, Jacob VA 190th Mil. Co.E
Walker, Jacob B. VA 10th Cav. Co.K
Walker, Jacob C. SC 2nd Rifles Co.C Cpl.
Walker, Jacob T. AL 4th Cav.
Walker, Jacob W. AR 34th Inf. Co.A Capt.
Walker, James AL 1st Regt. Mobile Vol. British Guard Co.B

Walker, James AL 1st Regt. Mobile Vol. Co.K Cpl.
Walker, James AL 20th Inf. Co.A
Walker, James AL 21st Inf. Co.I
Walker, James AL 58th Inf. Co.D
Walker, James AL 62nd Inf. Co.A
Walker, James AR 1st (Dobbin's) Cav. Co.A
Walker, James AR 1st Mtd.Rifles Co.I
Walker, James AR 7th Cav. Co.G
Walker, James AR 8th Cav. Co.G
Walker, James AR Cav. Gordon's Regt. Co.B
Walker, James AR 5th Inf. Co.E
Walker, James AR 33rd Inf. Co.I
Walker, James AR 35th Inf. Co.G
Walker, James FL Cav. 3rd Bn. Co.B Sgt.
Walker, James FL Lt.Arty. Dyke's Co. Cpl.
Walker, James FL 1st Inf. New Co.I
Walker, James FL 1st Inf. Old Co.K, New Co.K
Walker, James FL 5th Inf. Co.G
Walker, James FL 11th Inf. Co.E
Walker, James GA 1st Cav. Co.G
Walker, James GA Cav. 16th Bn. (St.Guards) Co.D
Walker, James GA Lt.Arty. 12th Bn. 1st Co.A
Walker, James GA Siege Arty. 28th Bn. Co.F
Walker, James GA 3rd Res. Co.C
Walker, James GA 19th Inf. Co.F
Walker, James GA 49th Inf. Co.F Sgt.
Walker, James GA 63rd Inf. Co.A
Walker, James GA Cherokee Legion (St.Guards) Co.B
Walker, James GA Cherokee Legion (St.Guards) Co.E 1st Lt.
Walker, James GA Inf. Dozier's Co. Cpl.
Walker, James KY 8th Cav.
Walker, James LA 12th Inf. Co.D
Walker, James LA 14th Inf. Co.G
Walker, James LA 15th Bn.S.S. (Weatherly's) Co.D
Walker, James LA 20th Inf. Co.K Sgt.
Walker, James LA 21st (Patton's) Inf. Co.G
Walker, James LA 27th Inf. Co.K
Walker, James LA 28th (Gray's) Inf. Co.E
Walker, James LA Inf.Crescent Regt. Co.C
Walker, James MS 12th Inf. Co.I
Walker, James MS 13th Inf. Co.D
Walker, James MS 36th Inf. Co.I
Walker, James MO 9th (Elliott's) Cav. Co.A
Walker, James MO Cav. Freeman's Regt. Co.E
Walker, James MO 1st & 4th Cons.Inf. Co.F
Walker, James MO 4th Inf. Co.A Capt.
Walker, James MO 16th Inf. Co.F
Walker, James NC 3rd Arty. (40th St.Troops) Co.G,H
Walker, James NC 1st Inf. Co.B
Walker, James NC 7th Sr.Res. Clinard's Co.
Walker, James NC 18th Inf. Co.E
Walker, James NC 33rd Inf. Co.D
Walker, James NC 35th Inf. Co.E
Walker, James NC 42nd Inf. Co.E
Walker, James SC 5th Cav. Co.E
Walker, James SC Cav. 14th Bn. Co.D
Walker, James SC 1st Arty. Co.F
Walker, James SC Hvy.Arty. Gilchrist's Co. (Gist Guard)
Walker, James SC Arty. Lee's Co.
Walker, James SC 1st (Butler's) Inf. Co.A
Walker, James SC 1st (Butler's) Inf. Co.F
Walker, James SC 3rd Res. Co.I
Walker, James SC 6th Inf. 1st Co.F, 2nd Co.I
Walker, James SC 19th Inf. Co.K
Walker, James SC 27th Inf. Co.E
Walker, James SC Inf. Hampton Legion Co.F
Walker, James SC Manigault's Bn.Vol. Co.A
Walker, James TN 2nd (Ashby's) Cav. Co.F 1st Lt.
Walker, James TN Cav. 4th Bn. (Branner's) Co.F 1st Lt.
Walker, James TN 9th Cav.
Walker, James TN 9th (Ward's) Cav. Co.I
Walker, James TN 13th (Gore's) Cav. Co.I 1st Lt.
Walker, James TN 19th & 20th (Cons.) Cav. Co.E
Walker, James TN Cav. Nixon's Regt. Co.B Sgt.
Walker, James TN Lt.Arty. Winston's Co. Sgt.
Walker, James TN 2nd (Walker's) Inf. Co.I 1st Lt.
Walker, James TN Inf. 4th Cons.Regt. Co.G
Walker, James TN 5th Inf. Co.H Cpl.
Walker, James TN 6th Inf. Co.K Bvt.2nd Lt.
Walker, James TN 17th Inf. Co.E Cpl.
Walker, James TN 17th Inf. Co.G Cpl.
Walker, James TN 18th Inf. Co.K
Walker, James TN 25th Inf. Co.K 2nd Lt.
Walker, James TN 28th (Cons.) Inf. Co.A Capt.
Walker, James TN 55th (Brown's) Inf. Co.H
Walker, James TN Inf. Nashville Bn. Felt's Co. Cpl.
Walker, James TX 1st (Yager's) Cav. Co.F
Walker, James TX 2nd Cav. Co.D Lt.Col.
Walker, James TX 21st Cav. Co.I Sr.2nd Lt.
Walker, James TX Cav. Giddings' Bn. Carrington's Co.
Walker, James TX 2nd Inf. Co.E
Walker, James TX 10th Inf. Co.D
Walker, James TX 12th Inf. Co.L
Walker, James TX 19th Inf. Co.H
Walker, James TX 20th Inf. Co.B
Walker, James VA 9th Cav. Co.C
Walker, James VA 13th Cav. Co.F
Walker, James VA 16th Cav. Co.G
Walker, James VA Cav. Ferguson's Bn. Spurlock's Co., Parks' Co., Ferguson's Co.
Walker, James VA 1st St.Res. Co.B
Walker, James VA 5th Inf. Co.H
Walker, James VA 6th Inf. Co.C
Walker, James VA 17th Inf. Co.G
Walker, James 15th Conf.Cav. Co.D Sgt.
Walker, James Horse Arty. White's Btty.
Walker, James 2nd Cherokee Mtd.Vol. Co.H Cpl.
Walker, James A. AL Arty. 1st Bn. Co.D
Walker, James A. AL Lt.Arty. 2nd Bn. Co.D
Walker, James A. AL 40th Inf. Co.A
Walker, James A. FL 5th Inf. Co.G 1st Sgt.
Walker, James A. FL 5th Inf. Co.I
Walker, James A. GA 12th Inf. Co.B 2nd Lt.
Walker, James A. GA 45th Inf. Co.K
Walker, James A. GA 49th Inf. Co.B
Walker, James A. MS 38th Cav. Co.H Sgt.
Walker, James A. MS 2nd Inf. Co.E
Walker, James A. MS 9th Inf. New Co.I, Old Co.E,F
Walker, James A. MS 43rd Inf. Co.A
Walker, James A. MO 7th Cav. Maj.
Walker, James A. NC 1st Inf. Co.A Music.
Walker, James A. NC 1st Inf. (6 mo. '61) Co.M
Walker, James A. SC Arty.Bn. Hampton Legion Co.A
Walker, James A. TN 44th Inf. Co.I 1st Lt.
Walker, James A. TN 44th (Cons.) Inf. Co.A 2nd Lt.
Walker, James A. TX 4th Cav. Co.A
Walker, James A. TX 1st Hvy.Arty. Co.H
Walker, James A. TX 9th (Young's) Inf. Co.B
Walker, James A. TX 18th Inf. Co.B
Walker, James A. VA Cav. 37th Bn. Co.A
Walker, James A. VA Hvy.Arty. 20th Bn. Co.A
Walker, James A. VA Lt.Arty. Armistead's Co.
Walker, James A. VA Hvy.Arty. Kyle's Co.
Walker, James A. VA 4th Inf. Co.C Capt.
Walker, James A. VA 19th Inf. Lt.Col.
Walker, James A. VA 61st Mil. Co.H
Walker, Jas. A. Gen. & Staff Chap.
Walker, James A. Gen. & Staff Brig.Gen.
Walker, James Archer TN 13th Inf. Co.K
Walker, James B. FL Inf. 2nd Bn. Co.B
Walker, James B. GA 2nd Inf. Co.A 2nd Lt.
Walker, James B. GA 7th Inf. Co.A
Walker, James B. LA 1st Cav. Co.C
Walker, James B. LA 5th Inf. New Co.A
Walker, James B. LA 12th Inf. Co.D 2nd Lt.
Walker, James B. MS 2nd Inf. Co.C
Walker, James B. MS 24th Inf. Co.H,D
Walker, James B. NC 6th Inf. Co.H Cpl.
Walker, James B. SC Horse Arty. (Washington Arty.) Vol. Hart's Co.
Walker, James B. SC 3rd Bn.Res. Co.B Cpl.
Walker, James B. TN Cav. 16th Bn. (Neal's) Co.C
Walker, James B. TN Holman's Bn.Part.Rangers Co.B
Walker, James B. VA 6th Bn.Res. Co.D Cpl.
Walker, James C. AL Mil. 2nd Regt.Vol. Co.C
Walker, James C. GA Inf. 25th Bn. (Prov.Guard) Co.C
Walker, James C. KY 13th Cav. Co.F Capt.
Walker, James C. LA Cav. Greenleaf's Co. (Orleans Lt.Horse) Cpl.
Walker, James C. MO 8th Cav. Co.D
Walker, James C. NC 30th Inf. Co.A
Walker, James C. SC 1st (McCreary's) Inf. Co.G
Walker, James C. SC 20th Inf. Co.A
Walker, James C. TN 53rd Inf. Co.H
Walker, James C. TX 12th Cav. Co.D 1st Bugler
Walker, James C. TX 18th Cav. Co.K 1st Lt.
Walker, James C. VA 6th Cav. Co.G
Walker, James C. VA 45th Inf. Co.I
Walker, James C. VA 48th Inf. Co.D
Walker, James D. GA 42nd Inf. Co.E 2nd Lt.
Walker, James D. NC 60th Inf. Co.G Sgt.
Walker, James D. TN 28th (Cons.) Inf. Co.K
Walker, James D. VA 2nd Cav. Co.K
Walker, James D. VA 53rd Inf. Co.E
Walker, James E. GA Lt.Arty. Havis' Btty.
Walker, James E. TX 14th Cav. Co.H
Walker, James E. TX Cav. Baylor's Regt. Co.A

Walker, James E. VA 1st Arty. Co.H
Walker, James E. VA 1st St.Res. Co.C,K Sgt.
Walker, James Edward MS Bradford's Co. (Conf.Guards Arty.)
Walker, James F. AL Cav. Lewis' Bn. Co.D 1st Lt.
Walker, James F. AL 6th Inf. Co.C
Walker, James F. GA Siege Arty. 28th Bn. Co.E,F
Walker, James F. GA 36th (Broyles') Inf. Co.F Cpl.
Walker, James F. GA 59th Inf. Co.B
Walker, James F. GA Cobb's Legion Co.B
Walker, James F. MS 1st (Patton's) Inf. Co.B
Walker, James F. MS 24th Inf. Co.C
Walker, James F. MS Blythe's Bn. (St.Troops) Co.A 1st Lt.
Walker, James F. TN 3rd (Clack's) Inf. Co.D
Walker, James F. TX 13th Vol. Co.M Lt.
Walker, James F. TX 15th Inf. 2nd Co.H 1st Lt.
Walker, James G. AL 39th Inf. Co.F Cpl.
Walker, James G. AR 3rd Inf. Co.G
Walker, James G. MS Wilkinson Cty. Minute Men Co.B,A 2nd Lt.
Walker, James G. TX Cav. Ragsdale's Bn. Co.B
Walker, James H. AL 51st (Part.Rangers) Co.C Cpl.
Walker, James H. AL 31st Inf. Co.C
Walker, James H. AR 2nd Inf. Co.A
Walker, James H. AR 27th Inf. Co.E 1st Sgt.
Walker, James H. AR 31st Inf. Co.E 2nd Lt.
Walker, James H. FL 3rd Inf. Co.K
Walker, Jas. H. GA Lt.Arty. Howell's Co.
Walker, James H. GA 11th Inf. Co.D
Walker, James H. KY 4th Mtd.Inf. Co.I Sgt.
Walker, James H. LA 2nd Cav. Co.C
Walker, James H. MS 2nd Inf. Co.D
Walker, James H. MS 16th Inf. Co.K
Walker, James H. NC 1st Cav. (9th St.Troops) Co.F Cpl.
Walker, James H. NC 11th (Bethel Regt.) Inf. Co.E Cpl.
Walker, James H. NC 14th Inf. Co.G Cpl.
Walker, James H. NC 56th Inf. Co.B
Walker, James H. NC 57th Inf. Co.H Cpl.
Walker, James H. TN 2nd (Smith's) Cav.
Walker, James H. TN 4th (McLemore's) Cav. Co.G
Walker, James H. TN 14th Inf. Co.D
Walker, James H. TN 36th Inf. Co.B 2nd Lt.
Walker, James H. TN 43rd Inf. Co.A Sgt.
Walker, James H. VA 9th Inf. Co.K Sgt.
Walker, James H. VA 49th Inf. Co.D
Walker, James H. VA 67th Mil. QM
Walker, James I. FL 1st Cav. Co.D
Walker, James I.A. Early's Div. Brig.Gen.
Walker, James J. AL 63rd Inf. Co.G
Walker, James J. GA 50th Inf. Co.K
Walker, James J. SC 5th Inf. 1st Co.A
Walker, James J. SC Palmetto S.S. Co.A
Walker, James J. TX 9th Cav. Co.K
Walker, James J. TX 37th Cav. Co.G
Walker, James J.F. LA 12th Inf. Co.B
Walker, James K. AL 21st Inf. Co.A
Walker, James K. TX Inf. Griffin's Bn. Co.D
Walker, James L. AL 4th (Russell's) Cav. Co.D
Walker, James L. AL 10th Cav. Co.F
Walker, James L. AL 25th Inf. Co.F
Walker, James L. KY 6th Cav. Co.A
Walker, James L. MS 19th Inf. Co.F Cpl.
Walker, James L. MS 30th Inf. Co.A
Walker, James L. MO 1st Cav. Co.H Cpl.
Walker, James L., Jr. NC 4th Inf. Co.H
Walker, James L., Sr. NC 4th Inf. Co.H
Walker, James L. NC 42nd Inf. Co.G
Walker, James L. SC 6th Cav. Co.G
Walker, James L. TX 18th Inf. Co.K
Walker, James L. VA Hvy.Arty. 20th Bn. Co.D Cpl.
Walker, James M. AL 4th (Russell's) Cav. Co.K Sgt.
Walker, James M. AL Lt.Arty. Clanton's Btty.
Walker, James M. AR 1st Mtd.Rifles Co.A
Walker, James M. AR 14th (McCarver's) Inf. Co.D
Walker, James M. AR 15th (N.W.) Inf. Co.B
Walker, James M. AR 21st Inf. Co.K
Walker, James M. FL 1st Cav. Co.H
Walker, James M. GA 38th Inf. Co.K Cpl.
Walker, James M. GA 46th Inf. Co.I
Walker, James M. GA 56th Inf. Co.B
Walker, James M. KY 1st (Butler's) Cav. Co.G
Walker, James M. KY 9th Mtd.Inf. Co.B
Walker, James M. LA 8th Inf. Co.G
Walker, James M. LA 11th Inf. Co.E
Walker, James M. LA 14th (Austin's) Bn.S.S. Co.A
Walker, James M. LA 28th (Gray's) Inf. Co.E
Walker, James M. LA 28th (Gray's) Inf. Co.K 1st Lt.
Walker, James M. MS 4th Cav. Co.A
Walker, James M. MS Cav. 24th Bn. Co.A
Walker, James M. MS Cav. Street's Bn. Co.A
Walker, James M. MS Lt.Arty. (Brookhaven Lt.Arty.) Hoskins' Btty.
Walker, James M. MS 9th Inf. Old Co.E 1st Lt.
Walker, James M. MS 10th Inf. New Co.A Col.
Walker, James M. MS 43rd Inf. Co.G
Walker, James M. MO 16th Inf. Co.H
Walker, James M. NC 3rd Arty. (40th St.Troops) Co.C
Walker, James M. NC 3rd Arty. (40th St.Troops) Co.I
Walker, James M. NC 4th Inf. Co.A
Walker, James M. NC 6th Inf. Co.G
Walker, James M. NC 48th Inf. Co.C 2nd Lt.
Walker, James M. NC 48th Inf. Co.F Sgt.
Walker, James M. TN 3rd (Forrest's) Cav. 1st Co.F
Walker, James M. TX 13th Cav. Co.G
Walker, James M. TX 15th Cav. Co.G Sgt.
Walker, James M. TX 8th Inf. Co.E Sgt.
Walker, James M. VA 2nd Cav. Co.K
Walker, James M. VA 18th Inf. Co.A Sgt.
Walker, James M. VA 22nd Inf. Co.D
Walker, James M. VA Inf. 26th Bn. Co.E
Walker, James M. VA 59th Inf. 1st Co.F
Walker, James M. VA 60th Inf. Co.B 1st Sgt.
Walker, James M. VA 60th Inf. Co.I
Walker, James Mamucan VA 46th Inf. 1st Co.C Cpl.
Walker, James Monroe NC 3rd Arty. (40th St.Troops) Co.C
Walker, James N. AL 50th Co.C Cpl.
Walker, James N. AR 6th Inf. Co.K
Walker, James O. AL 29th Inf. Co.A
Walker, James O. MS 14th Inf. Co.H
Walker, James O. NC 60th Inf. Co.G Cpl.
Walker, James O. TX 16th Cav. Co.E
Walker, Jas. O.K. MO St.Guard
Walker, James P. AL 17th Inf. Co.G Sgt.
Walker, James P. AL Rives' Supp.Force 9th Congr.Dist.
Walker, James P. GA Inf. 5th Bn. (St.Guards) Co.C 1st Lt.
Walker, James P. MS 9th Inf. Old Co.I
Walker, James P. MO 4th Inf. Co.F Sr.2nd Lt.
Walker, James P. NC 3rd Inf. Co.H
Walker, James P. NC 18th Inf. Co.E
Walker, James P. NC 55th Inf. Co.F
Walker, James P. TN 14th Cav. Co.I Sgt.
Walker, James P. TN 14th (Neely's) Cav. Co.K
Walker, James P. TN 44th Inf. Co.A Sgt.
Walker, James R. AL 4th (Russell's) Cav. Sgt.
Walker, James R. AL 3rd Inf. Co.K
Walker, James R. AL 26th (O'Neal's) Inf. Co.K
Walker, James R. AL 29th Inf. Co.K
Walker, James R. AR 2nd Mtd.Rifles Co.I
Walker, James R. AR 18th Inf. Co.A
Walker, James R. AR Inf. Cocke's Regt. Co.C
Walker, James R. GA Inf. 2nd Bn. Co.B
Walker, James R. GA Inf. 3rd Bn. Co.D
Walker, James R. MS 17th Inf. Co.F 1st Lt.
Walker, James R. TN 41st Inf. Co.D
Walker, James R. TN 44th (Cons.) Inf. Co.D
Walker, James R. VA 9th Inf. Co.B Cpl.
Walker, James R. VA 24th Inf. Co.B
Walker, James R. VA 26th Inf. Co.F
Walker, James R. 1st Conf.Cav. 2nd Co.G
Walker, James S. GA Lt.Arty. Guerard's Btty.
Walker, James S. LA 28th (Gray's) Inf. Co.D
Walker, James S. NC 6th Inf. Co.H
Walker, James S. NC 23rd Inf. Co.F
Walker, James S. TN 3rd (Clack's) Inf. Co.H Capt.
Walker, James S. TN 28th Inf. Co.A Capt.
Walker, James S. TN 42nd Inf. 2nd Co.F
Walker, James S. VA Lt.Arty. Carpenter's Co.
Walker, James S. VA Lt.Arty. Arch. Graham's Co.
Walker, James T. AL Lt.Arty. Tarrant's Btty.
Walker, James T. GA 6th Inf. Co.K
Walker, James T. MO 2nd Cav. 3rd Co.K
Walker, James T. MO Cav. 3rd Bn. Co.D
Walker, James T. NC 34th Inf. Co.I
Walker, James T. NC Jones' Co. (Supp.Force)
Walker, James T. TN 48th (Nixon's) Inf. Co.G
Walker, James T. TN 54th Inf. Co.B
Walker, James T. TX 8th Cav. Co.H 1st Sgt.
Walker, James T. TX 12th Inf. Co.G
Walker, James T. VA 17th Inf. Co.E
Walker, James V. NC Walker's Bn. Thomas' Legion 2nd Co.D Sgt.
Walker, James V. TN 3rd (Lillard's) Mtd.Inf. Co.G 1st Lt.
Walker, James W. AL 4th Inf. Co.C
Walker, James W. AL 32nd Inf. Co.B
Walker, James W. AL 58th Inf. Co.I
Walker, James W. AL 61st Inf. Co.B 1st Sgt.
Walker, James W. FL 3rd Inf. Co.D,H Cpl.
Walker, James W. GA 2nd Bn.S.S. Co.D

Walker, James W. GA 20th Inf. Co.K 1st Lt.
Walker, James W. GA 55th Inf. Co.F Sgt.
Walker, James W. GA 56th Inf. Co.B
Walker, James W. GA Inf. (Express Inf.) Witt's Co. 2nd Lt.
Walker, James W. MO 1st Inf. Co.H
Walker, James W. NC 2nd Cav. (19th St.Troops) Co.A
Walker, James W. NC Cav. 14th Bn. Co.B Sgt.
Walker, James W. NC Hvy.Arty. 10th Bn. Co.C
Walker, James W. NC 13th Inf. Co.K
Walker, James W. NC 49th Inf. Co.A
Walker, James W. NC 50th Inf. Co.G
Walker, James W. TN 53rd Inf.
Walker, James W. TN 59th Mtd.Inf. Co.H
Walker, James W. TX 1st Inf. Co.F
Walker, James W. VA 14th Inf. Co.F
Walker, James W. VA 23rd Inf. Co.D
Walker, James W. VA 34th Inf. Co.K
Walker, James W. Mahone's Div. AADC
Walker, James W. Simms' Brig. Capt.,AAG
Walker, J. And TN Cav. 4th Bn. (Branner's) Co.F
Walker, Japhith MS 7th Cav. Co.I
Walker, Jarrett NC 30th Inf. Co.D
Walker, Jasper GA 50th Inf. Co.A
Walker, Jasper TX 35th (Brown's) Cav. Co.G
Walker, Jasper B. TX 22nd Cav. Co.B
Walker, Jasper W. AL 19th Inf. Co.D
Walker, Jasper W. TN 4th Cav. Co.H
Walker, J.A.T. GA 5th Res. Co.I
Walker, J.B. AR 26th Inf. Co.K
Walker, J.B. GA Cav. 19th Bn. Co.B
Walker, J.B. GA 46th Inf. Co.E Sgt.
Walker, J.B. GA 49th Inf. Co.H
Walker, J.B. GA Phillips' Legion Co.E
Walker, J.B. KY 3rd Mtd.Inf. Co.I
Walker, J.B. KY 7th Mtd.Inf. Co.B
Walker, J.B. MS 2nd St.Cav. Co.A Sgt.
Walker, J.B. MS 38th Cav. Co.D
Walker, J.B. MO 1st & 3rd Cons.Cav. Co.B
Walker, J.B. MO Lt.Arty. Farris' Btty. (Clark Arty.)
Walker, J.B. NC 1st Cav. (9th St.Troops) Co.C
Walker, J.B. NC 56th Inf. Co.K
Walker, J.B. TN 7th (Duckworth's) Cav. Co.E
Walker, J.B. TN 12th (Green's) Cav. Co.D
Walker, J.B. TN 13th Inf. Co.L
Walker, J.B. TN 51st (Cons.) Inf. Co.A
Walker, J.B. TX 13th Cav. Co.D
Walker, J.B. TX Cav. Giddings' Bn. Co.A
Walker, J.B. VA 7th Inf. Co.F Cpl.
Walker, J.B. 10th Conf.Cav. Co.G
Walker, J.B. Hosp.Stew.
Walker, J.C. AL Cav. 24th Bn. Co.A
Walker, J.C. AL 21st Inf. Co.F
Walker, J.C. AR Cav. McGehee's Regt. Co.F
Walker, J.C. AR 19th (Dockery's) Inf. Co.K 3rd Lt.
Walker, J.C. FL Cav. 5th Bn. Co.D 2nd Lt.
Walker, J.C. GA 8th Cav. Co.A
Walker, J.C. GA 9th Inf. (St.Guards) Co.G
Walker, J.C. GA 37th Inf. Co.B Sgt.
Walker, J.C. GA 65th Inf. Co.C Sgt.
Walker, J.C. KY 1st (Butler's) Cav. New Co.H
Walker, J.C. MO Cav. Slayback's Regt. Co.A
Walker, J.C. MO 11th Inf. Co.G
Walker, J.C. SC Hvy.Arty. 15th (Lucas') Bn. Co.C
Walker, J.C. SC 6th Inf. 1st Co.A, 2nd Co.F
Walker, J.C. TN 4th (Murray's) Cav. Co.G
Walker, J.C. TN 12th (Green's) Cav. Co.D Cpl.
Walker, J.C. TN 3rd (Clack's) Inf. Co.I Cpl.
Walker, J.C. TN Inf. 22nd Bn. Co.G
Walker, J.C. TN 35th Inf. 3rd Co.F
Walker, J.C. TX 24th & 25th Cav. (Cons.) Co.I
Walker, J.C. TX 33rd Cav. Co.E
Walker, J.C. TX 4th Inf. Co.I
Walker, J.C. TX 12th Inf. Co.K
Walker, J.C. 3rd Conf.Cav. Co.G
Walker, J.C. 10th Conf.Cav. Co.H
Walker, J.C. Gen. & Staff Asst.Surg.
Walker, J.C.L. GA Siege Arty. 28th Bn. Co.G
Walker, J.D. AL Gid Nelson Lt.Arty.
Walker, J.D. AR 4th St.Inf. Col.
Walker, J.D. GA 16th Inf. Co.K
Walker, J.D. KY 1st Inf. Co.E
Walker, J.D. MS 2nd Cav. Co.C
Walker, J.D. MS 11th (Perrin's) Cav. Co.H
Walker, J.D. NC 32nd Inf. Co.F
Walker, J.D. NC McDugald's Co.
Walker, J.D. SC Lt.Arty. Beauregard's Co.
Walker, J.D. SC 5th Res. Co.D Sgt.
Walker, J.D. SC 24th Inf. Co.E
Walker, J.D. SC Palmetto S.S. Co.H
Walker, J.D. TN 21st (Wilson's) Cav. Co.C,I 3rd Lt.
Walker, J.D. TN 21st & 22nd (Cons.) Cav. Co.G
Walker, J.D. TX 13th Cav. Co.I
Walker, J.D.C. TN 21st (Wilson's) Cav. Co.I
Walker, J.E. AL 13th Bn.Part.Rangers Co.D Far.
Walker, J.E. AL 8th Inf. Co.A
Walker, J.E. AL 27th Inf. Co.D
Walker, J.E. AL 57th Inf. Co.H
Walker, J.E. GA Lt.Arty. 14th Bn. Co.A
Walker, J.E. KY 10th (Johnson's) Cav. New Co.I
Walker, J.E. LA 31st Inf. Co.E
Walker, J.E. SC 11th Inf. Co.K
Walker, J.E. SC 13th Inf. Co.C
Walker, J.E. TN 9th Inf. Co.C
Walker, J.E. TN 50th Inf. Co.D
Walker, J.E. TX 22nd Inf. Co.F
Walker, J.E. TX St.Troops Gould's Co. (Clarksville Lt.Inf.)
Walker, Jefferson NC 57th Inf. Co.I
Walker, Jefferson SC 1st Arty. Co.H
Walker, Jefferson S. TN 2nd (Ashby's) Cav. Co.G
Walker, Jefferson S. TN Cav. 4th Bn. (Branner's) Co.B
Walker, Jenkins D. GA Inf. 1st Loc.Troops (Augusta) Co.G
Walker, Jenk R. AL 8th Inf. Co.D
Walker, Jeptha T. GA 2nd Bn.S.S. Co.B
Walker, Jeptha V. MS 9th Inf. Old Co.G 1st Lt.
Walker, Jeremiah AL 19th Inf. Co.G
Walker, Jeremiah AL 49th Inf. Co.C Cpl.
Walker, Jeremiah FL 1st Cav. Co.D
Walker, Jeremiah KY 13th Cav. Co.I
Walker, Jeremiah KY 5th Mtd.Inf. Co.I
Walker, Jeremiah MS Lt.Arty. (Brookhaven Lt.Arty.) Hoskins' Btty.
Walker, Jeremiah NC 37th Inf. Co.G
Walker, Jeremiah NC 50th Inf. Co.G
Walker, Jeremiah TN 5th (McKenzie's) Cav. Co.E Black.
Walker, Jeremiah TN 3rd (Lillard's) Mtd.Inf. Co.A
Walker, Jeremiah A. AL 49th Inf. Co.G
Walker, Jeremiah C. NC 58th Inf. Co.F
Walker, Jeremiah J. GA 30th Inf. Co.B
Walker, Jeremiah P. NC 53rd Inf. Co.K
Walker, Jeremiah W. SC 6th Inf. 2nd Co.D Capt.
Walker, Jerome W. SC 9th Inf. Co.H Capt.
Walker, Jerre NC 7th Sr.Res. Holland's Co.
Walker, Jerry MS 3rd (St.Troops) Cav. Co.G
Walker, Jerry MS Inf. 2nd Bn. (St.Troops) Co.C
Walker, Jerry, Sr. NC 49th Inf. Co.A
Walker, Jerry TX 1st (Yager's) Cav. Co.E
Walker, Jerry C. AL 29th Inf. Co.F
Walker, Jerry L. NC 49th Inf. Co.A Cpl.
Walker, Jerry T. SC 6th Inf. 1st Co.F,A
Walker, Jerry W. TX Cav. 8th (Taylor's) Cav. Co.B,C
Walker, Jesse AL 30th Inf. Co.H
Walker, Jesse GA 5th Res. Co.F
Walker, Jesse GA 46th Inf. Co.K Cpl.
Walker, Jesse MS 39th Inf. Co.F
Walker, Jesse MS Wilkinson Cty. Minute Men Co.B
Walker, Jesse MO 4th Cav. Co.E
Walker, Jesse SC 21st Inf. Co.K,B
Walker, Jesse 1st Choctaw Mtd.Rifles Co.G
Walker, Jesse A. FL 1st Inf. Old Co.I,B
Walker, Jesse A. FL 5th Inf. Co.F,G
Walker, Jesse A. SC Inf. Hampton Legion Co.F
Walker, Jesse A. VA 23rd Inf. Co.D
Walker, Jesse B. GA 65th Inf. Co.F
Walker, Jesse C. FL 2nd Inf. Co.E
Walker, Jesse F. NC 58th Inf. Co.G
Walker, Jesse G. VA Hvy.Arty. 10th Bn. Co.A
Walker, Jesse M. NC 2nd Cav. (19th St.Troops) Co.A,G
Walker, Jesse R. NC 50th Inf. Co.I
Walker, Jesse W. FL 3rd Inf. Co.H
Walker, Jethro P. GA 49th Inf. Co.D 1st Sgt.
Walker, J.E.W. TX 27th Cav. Co.I,A
Walker, Jewel L. GA Inf. 37th Regt. Co.F
Walker, J.F. AL 8th Cav. Co.C Cpl.
Walker, J.F. AL 29th Inf. Co.H Sgt.
Walker, J.F. AL 63rd Inf. Co.F,H
Walker, J.F. AR 4th Inf. Co.K
Walker, J.F. AR 6th Inf. 1st Co.B
Walker, J.F. AR 7th Inf. Co.I
Walker, J.F. GA 4th (Clinch's) Cav. Co.A,K
Walker, J.F. GA Lt.Arty. Howell's Co.
Walker, J.F. GA 1st (Fannin's) Res. Co.B
Walker, J.F. GA 2nd Inf. Co.A
Walker, J.F. GA 5th Res. Co.D
Walker, J.F. GA 10th Inf. Co.A
Walker, J.F. GA 45th Inf. Co.A
Walker, J.F. MS 2nd Part. Co.A
Walker, J.F. MO Robertson's Regt.St.Guard Co.7
Walker, J.F. SC 27th Inf. Co.B,I
Walker, J.F. TX 10th Cav. Co.F Hosp.Stew.
Walker, J.F. TX 23rd Cav. Co.A
Walker, J.F. TX 28th Cav. Co.B

Walker, J.F. TX Cav. Baird's Regt. Co.A
Walker, J.F. VA 8th Inf. Co.G
Walker, J.F. Hoffman's Bn. Chap.
Walker, J. Felix SC 18th Inf. Co.F Capt.
Walker, J.G. AL 7th Cav. Co.H
Walker, J.G. AL 22nd Inf. Co.F
Walker, J.G. AL 24th Inf. Co.K
Walker, J.G. AL 38th Inf. Co.H
Walker, J.G. AR 21st Mil. Co.D
Walker, J.G. AR 36th Inf. Co.E
Walker, J.G. MS 3rd Inf. (St.Troops) Co.A
Walker, J.G. MS 6th Inf. Co.A
Walker, J.G. MS 24th Inf. Co.C Chap.
Walker, J.G. MS 44th Inf. Co.G,J
Walker, J.G. NC 5th Sr.Res. Co.H
Walker, J.G. TX Cav. Bourland's Regt. Co.D
Walker, J.G.B. AL 31st Inf. Co.C,B
Walker, J.H. AL 9th Inf. Co.K
Walker, J.H. AL 19th Inf. Co.C
Walker, J.H. AL 29th Inf. Co.H
Walker, J.H. AR 1st (Dobbin's) Cav. Co.A
Walker, J.H. AR 24th Inf. Co.A
Walker, J.H. FL 1st (Res.) Inf. Co.F
Walker, J.H. GA Cav. Nelson's Ind.Co.
Walker, J.H. GA Cav. Ragland's Co.
Walker, J.H. GA Lt.Arty. Howell's Co.
Walker, J.H. GA 59th Inf. Co.I
Walker, J.H. GA Nitre & Min. Bureau
Walker, J.H. KY 3rd Cav. Co.C
Walker, J.H. KY 3rd Mtd.Inf. Co.C
Walker, J.H. KY 3rd Mtd.Inf. Co.I
Walker, J.H. LA 4th Cav. Co.G
Walker, J.H. LA Inf. 4th Bn. Co.F Capt.
Walker, J.H. MS 4th Cav. Co.B
Walker, J.H. MS Cav. Ham's Regt. Co.E Cpl.
Walker, J.H. MS 1st Inf. Co.H
Walker, J.H. MO 16th Inf. Co.G Sgt.
Walker, J.H. MO Inf. Winston's Regt. Co.A
Walker, J.H. NC 11th (Bethel Regt.) Inf. Co.E
Walker, J.H. NC 14th Inf. Co.F Sgt.
Walker, J.H. SC 4th Bn.Res. Co.D
Walker, J.H. SC 5th St.Troops Co.A
Walker, J.H. SC 6th Res. Co.A
Walker, J.H. SC 14th Inf. Co.G
Walker, J.H. TN 6th (Wheeler's) Cav. Co.E
Walker, J.H. TN 7th (Duckworth's) Cav. Co.G
Walker, J.H. TN 5th Inf. 2nd Co.B Cpl.
Walker, J.H. TN 13th Inf. Co.B
Walker, J.H. TX 2nd Cav. 2nd Lt.
Walker, J.H. TX Cav. Terry's Regt. Co.H
Walker, J.H. TX 12th Inf. Co.E
Walker, J.H. TX 15th Inf. 2nd Co.F
Walker, J.H. VA 3rd Cav. Co.A
Walker, J.H. Conf.Cav. Wood's Regt. 2nd Co.D
Walker, J.H.C. VA 3rd Inf.Loc.Def. Co.K
Walker, J. Henry SC 3rd Inf. Co.D 2nd Lt.
Walker, J.I. FL Sp.Cav. 1st Bn. Co.A
Walker, Jim TX 29th Cav. Co.D
Walker, J.J. AL 12th Cav. Co.A
Walker, J.J. AL 12th Cav. Co.D
Walker, J.J. AL 7th Inf. Co.F
Walker, J.J. AL 19th Inf. Co.F
Walker, J.J. AL 40th Inf. Co.G
Walker, J.J. AR 15th (Johnson's) Inf. Co.E
Walker, J.J. AR Inf. Williamson's Bn. Co.F 2nd Lt.
Walker, J.J. FL Fernandez's Mtd.Co. (Supply Force)
Walker, J.J. FL Kilcrease Lt.Arty.
Walker, J.J. GA 10th Cav. (St.Guards) Co.B
Walker, J.J. GA Boddie's Co. (Troup Cty.Ind.Cav.)
Walker, J.J. GA 5th Res. Co.F Cpl.
Walker, J.J. GA 16th Inf. Co.K
Walker, J.J. GA 23rd Inf. Co.G
Walker, J.J. GA 54th Inf. Co.H Cpl.
Walker, J.J. LA 19th Inf. Co.G 2nd Lt.
Walker, J.J. LA 25th Inf. Co.C
Walker, J.J. LA 30th Inf. Co.F
Walker, J.J. LA Conscr.
Walker, J.J. MS 2nd Cav. Co.A,E
Walker, J.J. NC 1st Inf. Co.I
Walker, J.J. SC 2nd Inf. Co.B
Walker, J.J. TN 4th (McLemore's) Cav. Co.B
Walker, J.J. TN 11th (Holman's) Cav. Co.E
Walker, J.J. TN Holman's Bn.Part.Rangers Co.C
Walker, J.J. VA 3rd Res. Co.D
Walker, J.K. AR 15th (Josey's) Inf. Co.F
Walker, J.K. FL 1st (Res.) Inf. Co.F
Walker, J.K. LA 8th Cav. Co.A
Walker, J.K. MS 18th Cav. Co.H
Walker, J.K. TN 20th (Russell's) Cav. Co.I
Walker, J. Knox TN 2nd (Walker's) Inf. Col.
Walker, J.K.P. TN 4th Inf. Co.K
Walker, J.K.P. TN 47th Inf. Co.C
Walker, J.L. AL Mil. 4th Vol. Co.D
Walker, J.L. AL 21st Inf. Co.F
Walker, J.L. AL 44th Inf. Co.E
Walker, J.L. AL Cp. of Instr. Talladega
Walker, J.L. GA 20th Inf. Co.H
Walker, J.L. GA Phillips' Legion Co.E,N
Walker, J.L. MS 18th Cav. Co.C
Walker, J.L. MS 44th Inf. Co.H
Walker, J.L. MO 4th Inf. Co.D
Walker, J.L. SC 4th Cav. Co.B
Walker, J.L. SC 14th Inf. Co.H
Walker, J.L. SC 16th & 24th (Cons.) Inf. Co.A 1st Lt.
Walker, J.L. SC 23rd Inf. Co.F
Walker, J.L. TN 13th Inf. Co.F 1st Sgt.
Walker, J.L. TN 35th Inf. Co.E
Walker, J.L. TN 49th Inf. Co.D
Walker, J.L. TX Cav. McCord's Frontier Regt. Co.E Sgt.
Walker, J.L. TX Cav. Morgan's Regt. Co.G
Walker, J.L. TX Cav. Ragsdale's Bn. Co.B
Walker, J.L. TX 11th (Spaight's) Bn.Vol. Co.D
Walker, J.L. Hosp.Stew.
Walker, J.M. AL 12th Cav. Co.B
Walker, J.M. AL 23rd Inf. Co.K Cpl.
Walker, J.M. AL 30th Inf. Co.K
Walker, J.M. AL 36th Inf. Co.D 1st Lt.
Walker, J.M. AR 19th (Dockery's) Inf. Co.B
Walker, J.M. AR 26th Inf. Co.A
Walker, J.M. GA 2nd Cav. Co.F
Walker, J.M. GA Lt.Arty. Croft's Btty. (Columbus Arty.)
Walker, J.M. GA 10th Mil.
Walker, J.M. GA 26th Inf. Co.H
Walker, J.M. KY 3rd Mtd.Inf. Co.I,K
Walker, J.M. LA 2nd Inf. Co.I
Walker, J.M. MS 2nd Cav. Co.A
Walker, J.M. MS 7th Cav. Co.H
Walker, J.M. MS 11th (Cons.) Cav. Capt., Comsy.
Walker, J.M. MS Cav. Ham's Regt. Co.A
Walker, J.M. MS Lt.Arty. Lomax's Co.
Walker, J.M. MS 1st (King's) Inf. (St.Troops) Co.F
Walker, J.M. MS Inf. 2nd St.Troops Co.M 1st Sgt.
Walker, J.M. MS Inf. 3rd Bn. (St.Troops) Co.E Sgt.
Walker, J.M. MO 6th Cav. Co.F
Walker, J.M. MO Inf. 5th Regt.St.Guard Co.D
Walker, J.M. NC 6th Inf. Co.H
Walker, J.M. SC Lt.Arty. 3rd (Palmetto) Bn. Co.B
Walker, J.M. SC 5th Res. Co.B
Walker, J.M. SC 12th Inf. Co.I
Walker, J.M. TN 15th (Cons.) Cav. Co.E
Walker, J.M. TN 19th & 20th (Cons.) Cav. Co.K
Walker, J.M. TN 35th Inf. 2nd Co.I
Walker, J.M. TN 55th (Brown's) Inf. Ford's Co.
Walker, J.M. TX Cav. Benavides' Regt. Co.G
Walker, J.M. TX Cav. Morgan's Regt. Co.E Cpl.
Walker, J.M. TX 6th Inf. Co.G
Walker, J.M. VA 1st Cav. Co.L
Walker, J.M. VA 5th Cav. Co.A
Walker, J.M. VA 14th Cav. Co.B
Walker, J.M. VA Cav. Mosby's Regt. (Part. Rangers) Co.C
Walker, J.M. VA 34th Inf. Co.B
Walker, J. Marion AL 31st Inf. Co.A
Walker, J.N. AL 62nd Inf. Co.I
Walker, J.N. AL 1st Bn. Hilliard's Legion Vol. Co.E
Walker, J.N. GA Cav. 2nd Bn. Co.A
Walker, J.N. GA 13th Inf. Co.D Sgt.
Walker, J.N. GA 65th Inf. Co.H
Walker, J.N. KY 12th Cav. Co.C
Walker, J.N. LA 3rd Inf. Co.C
Walker, J.N. LA Inf. 16th Bn. (Conf.Guards Resp.Bn.) Co.B
Walker, J.N. MS 39th Inf. Co.F Cpl.
Walker, J.N. SC 3rd Cav. Co.F
Walker, J.N. SC 2nd Arty. Co.B 1st Lt.
Walker, J.N. TN 5th Inf. 2nd Co.H
Walker, J.N. TN 6th Inf. Co.L
Walker, J.N. TN 49th Inf. Co.D
Walker, J.N. TX 20th Inf. Co.H
Walker, J.O. 2nd Conf.Eng.Troops Co.C Artif.
Walker, J.O. 1st Cherokee Mtd.Vol. 1st Co.B, 2nd Co.G
Walker, Joe H. TN 19th Inf. Co.H
Walker, Joel GA 5th Inf. Co.I
Walker, Joel GA 50th Inf. Co.B Sgt.
Walker, Joel MO 10th Cav. Co.I Cpl.
Walker, Joel MO 2nd Inf. Co.H
Walker, Joel NC 22nd Inf. Co.F
Walker, Joel TN 14th (Neely's) Cav. Co.I,F Sgt.
Walker, Joel VA 28th Inf. Co.A Sgt.
Walker, Joel A. GA 6th Inf. Co.E
Walker, Joel A. GA 45th Inf. Co.K 1st Lt.
Walker, Joel A. VA 45th Inf. 2nd Lt.
Walker, Joel E. FL 1st Inf. New Co.E
Walker, Joel E. FL 1st Inf. Old Co.I, New Co.C
Walker, Joel H. NC 31st Inf. Co.H

Walker, Joel H. VA 53rd Inf. Co.G
Walker, Joel L. GA 57th Inf. Co.F
Walker, Joel P. MS 2nd Cav. Co.C 2nd Lt.
Walker, Joel P. MS 9th Inf. Old Co.E Sgt.
Walker, Joel Peyton MS 13th Inf. Co.F 3rd Lt.
Walker, Joel S. MS 6th Inf. Co.A
Walker, Joel T. VA 55th Inf. Co.H,C Cpl.
Walker, Joel W. AL 2nd Cav. Co.B
Walker, Joel W. GA 4th Inf. Co.D Cpl.
Walker, Joel W. MO 2nd Inf. Co.C
Walker, Joe W. AL Lt.Arty. Ward's Btty.
Walker, John AL 12th Cav. Co.F
Walker, John AL Cav. Forrest's Regt.
Walker, John AL Lt.Arty. 2nd Bn. Co.B
Walker, John AL Lt.Arty. 2nd Bn. Co.E
Walker, John AL 11th Inf. Co.D
Walker, John AL 12th Inf. Co.B
Walker, John AL 13th Inf. Co.B
Walker, John AL 18th Inf. Co.F
Walker, John AL 24th Inf. Co.F
Walker, John AL 30th Inf. Co.H
Walker, John AL 35th Inf. Co.C
Walker, John AL 42nd Inf. Co.F
Walker, John AL 48th Inf. Co.D
Walker, John AL 50th Inf. A.Surg.
Walker, John AL 58th Inf. Co.C
Walker, John AL Coosa Cty.Res. W.W. Griffin's Co.
Walker, John AL Talladega Cty.Res. J. Henderson's Co.
Walker, John AL Cp. of Instr. Talladega
Walker, John AR 7th Cav. Co.K
Walker, John AR 2nd Inf. Co.H
Walker, John AR 6th Inf. New Co.D
Walker, John AR 11th Inf. Co.F
Walker, John AR 31st Inf. Co.K Cpl.
Walker, John AR 35th Inf. Co.G
Walker, John AR Inf. Cocke's Regt. Co.C Cpl.
Walker, John AR Inf. Cocke's Regt. Co.D
Walker, John AR Inf. Williamson's Bn.
Walker, John FL 9th Inf. Co.K
Walker, John GA Cav. 16th Bn. (St.Guards) Co.E
Walker, John GA Cav. 22nd Bn. (St.Guards) Co.I Sgt.
Walker, John GA Cav. 24th Bn. Co.A,C
Walker, John GA 1st (Olmstead's) Inf. Co.G
Walker, John GA 7th Inf.
Walker, John GA 46th Inf. Co.I
Walker, John GA 50th Inf. Co.A
Walker, John KY 2nd (Duke's) Cav. Co.E
Walker, John KY Horse Arty. Byrne's Co.
Walker, John KY 2nd Bn.Mtd.Rifles Co.D
Walker, John LA 1st Hvy.Arty. (Reg.) Co.E Cpl.
Walker, John LA Inf. 1st Sp.Bn. (Wheat's) New Co.D
Walker, John LA 6th Inf. Co.B
Walker, John LA 10th Inf. Co.B,E Sgt.
Walker, John LA 14th Inf. Co.K
Walker, John LA 16th Inf. Co.F,H
Walker, John LA 18th Inf. Co.F
Walker, John LA 20th Inf. Co.K
Walker, John LA 25th Inf. Co.E
Walker, John MS 2nd Part. Co.A
Walker, John MS 8th Cav. Co.A
Walker, John MS 11th (Cons.) Cav. Co.F
Walker, John MS 18th Cav. Co.F
Walker, John MS 2nd Inf. Co.A
Walker, John MS 2nd Inf. Co.E
Walker, John MS 27th Inf. Co.F
Walker, John MS 31st Inf. Co.F
Walker, John MO 1st N.E. Cav. Co.B
Walker, John MO 4th Cav. Co.I
Walker, John MO Cav. Freeman's Regt. Co.C
Walker, John MO Cav. Fristoe's Regt. Co.L
Walker, John MO 4th Inf. Co.F
Walker, John NC Hvy.Arty. 1st Bn. Co.C
Walker, John NC 3rd Bn.Sr.Res. Durham's Co.
Walker, John NC 6th Sr.Res. Co.F
Walker, John NC 11th Bn.Home Guards Co.A Cpl.
Walker, John NC 12th Inf. Co.H
Walker, John NC 22nd Inf. Co.G
Walker, John NC 34th Inf. Co.K
Walker, John NC 42nd Inf. Co.E
Walker, John NC 49th Inf. Co.A
Walker, John NC 54th Inf. Co.G
Walker, John NC 56th Inf. Co.I
Walker, John NC Pris.Guards Howard's Co. Cpl.
Walker, John NC Littlejohn's Bn.R.R. Co.G
Walker, John SC 3rd Cav. Co.D
Walker, John SC Cav. 14th Bn. Co.D
Walker, John SC 1st Arty. Co.A
Walker, John SC Inf. 1st (Charleston) Bn. Co.D
Walker, John SC 3rd Res. Co.I
Walker, John SC 9th Res. Co.I
Walker, John SC 16th Inf. Co.E 2nd Lt.
Walker, John SC 18th Inf. Co.C
Walker, John TN 4th Cav.
Walker, John TN Cav. 4th Bn. (Branner's) Co.D
Walker, John TN 1st Hvy.Arty. 2nd Co.A, Co.C
Walker, John TN Lt.Arty. Winston's Co.
Walker, John TN 2nd (Walker's) Inf. Co.F
Walker, John TN 3rd (Lillard's) Mtd.Inf. Co.G
Walker, John TN Inf. 4th Cons.Regt. Co.G
Walker, John TN 11th Inf. C.D
Walker, John TN 12th (Cons.) Inf. Co.A
Walker, John TN 16th Inf. Co.C
Walker, John TN 18th Inf. Co.E
Walker, John TN 19th Inf. Co.F
Walker, John TN Inf. 23rd Bn. Co.B
Walker, John TN 35th Inf. Co.L
Walker, John TN 43rd Inf. Co.C
Walker, John TN 43rd Inf. Co.H
Walker, John TN 55th (Brown's) Inf. Co.H
Walker, John TX Cav. 3rd (Yager's) Bn. Co.C
Walker, John TX 21st Cav. Co.I Jr.2nd Lt.
Walker, John TX 27th Cav. Co.A
Walker, John TX Cav. Baylor's Regt. Co.C
Walker, John TX Cav. McCord's Frontier Regt. Co.B
Walker, John TX Cav. Morgan's Regt. Co.K
Walker, John TX 1st Field Btty.
Walker, John TX 20th Inf. Co.B
Walker, John TX 22nd Inf. Co.F
Walker, John VA 8th Cav. Co.D
Walker, John VA 17th Cav. Co.G
Walker, John VA Cav. Ferguson's Bn. Ferguson's Co., Parks' Co. Cpl.
Walker, John VA Cav. Hounshell's Bn. Co.A Sgt.
Walker, John VA Cav. Hounshell's Bn. Co.A Cpl.
Walker, John VA Cav. Young's Co.
Walker, John VA Lt.Arty. Moore's Co.
Walker, John VA 1st Inf. Co.I
Walker, John VA 6th Inf. Vickery's Co.
Walker, John VA 21st Mil. Co.E
Walker, John VA 22nd Inf. Co.A
Walker, John VA 30th Inf. Co.I
Walker, John VA 38th Inf. Co.B
Walker, John VA 38th Inf. Co.D
Walker, John VA Inf. 45th Bn. Co.D
Walker, John VA 57th Inf. Co.K
Walker, John Mead's Conf.Cav. Co.A
Walker, John 1st Cherokee Mtd.Rifles Co.F
Walker, John 1st Creek Mtd.Vol. 2nd Co.C
Walker, John Sap. & Min. Flynn's Co.,CSA
Walker, Jno. Gen. & Staff Capt.,Comsy.
Walker, John A. AL 9th Inf. Co.I
Walker, John A. AL 20th Inf. Co.I,H
Walker, John A. AL 39th Inf. Co.B Cpl.
Walker, John A. AL 44th Inf. Co.K
Walker, John A. AR 3rd Inf. Co.C
Walker, John A. AR 3rd Inf. Co.D 2nd Lt.
Walker, John A. AR 14th (McCarver's) Inf. Co.D
Walker, John A. AR 15th (N.W.) Inf. Co.B 2nd Sgt.
Walker, John A. AR 21st Inf. Co.K
Walker, John A. AR 27th Inf. Co.I
Walker, John A. GA 4th Cav. (St.Guards) McDonald's Co.
Walker, John A. GA 4th Res. Co.G 1st Lt.
Walker, John A. GA 31st Inf. A.Comsy.Sgt.
Walker, John A. GA 38th Inf. Co.B
Walker, John A. MS Inf. 1st Bn.St.Troops (12 mo. '62-3) Co.C 3rd Lt.
Walker, John A. MS 6th Inf. Co.H
Walker, John A. MS 15th Inf. Co.A
Walker, John A. MS 16th Inf. Co.E Cpl.
Walker, John A. MO Cav. Freeman's Regt. Co.F
Walker, John A. NC 2nd Cav. (19th St.Troops) Co.I Sgt.
Walker, John A. NC Inf. 13th Bn. Co.A
Walker, John A. NC 66th Inf. Co.A
Walker, John A. SC 5th St.Troops Asst.Surg.
Walker, John A. SC 6th Res. Surg.
Walker, John A. TN Cav. 16th Bn. (Neal's) Co.C
Walker, John A. TN 19th (Biffle's) Cav. Co.A
Walker, John A. TN 21st (Carter's) Cav. Co.G
Walker, John A. TX 4th Inf. Co.H
Walker, John A. VA 9th Cav. Co.G
Walker, John A. VA Lt.Arty. Hardwicke's Co.
Walker, John A. VA 1st Bn.Res. Co.D
Walker, John A. VA 4th Res. Co.F
Walker, John A. VA 21st Inf. Co.C
Walker, John A. VA 22nd Inf. Co.C
Walker, John A. VA 29th Inf. Co.C
Walker, John A. VA 34th Inf. Co.B
Walker, John A. VA Inf. 45th Bn. Co.C
Walker, John A. Gen. & Staff Capt.,ACS
Walker, John Andrew LA 19th Inf. Co.D 2nd Lt.
Walker, Johnathan GA Smith's Legion Anderson's Co. Sgt.
Walker, Johnathan NC 49th Inf. Co.A

Walker, John B. AL 19th Inf. Co.D Cpl.
Walker, John B. AL 35th Inf. Co.A
Walker, John B. AR 18th Inf. Co.H Capt.
Walker, John B. AR Inf. Cocke's Regt. Co.C
Walker, John B., Jr. GA 9th Inf. (St.Guards) Co.B Sgt.
Walker, John B. GA 34th Inf. Co.K
Walker, John B. GA 36th (Broyles') Inf. Co.K
Walker, John B. GA Cobb's Legion Co.G
Walker, John B. MS 1st Lt.Arty. Co.C
Walker, John B. MS 39th Inf. Co.C
Walker, John B. MO 1st Cav. Co.B,C
Walker, John B. NC 30th Inf. Co.I
Walker, John B. NC 34th Inf. Co.B
Walker, John B. NC 62nd Inf. Co.F
Walker, John B. SC 2nd Arty. Co.B
Walker, John B. TN 5th Inf. 2nd Co.H 1st Sgt.
Walker, John B. VA 36th Inf. Co.K
Walker, John C. AL 22nd Inf. Co.H
Walker, John C. AL 29th Inf. Co.F
Walker, John C. AL Cp. of Instr. Talladega
Walker, John C. AR 3rd Inf. Co.C
Walker, John C. GA Cav. 19th Bn. Co.C
Walker, John C. GA Cav. 24th Bn. Co.A Cpl.
Walker, John C. LA 19th Inf. Co.A
Walker, John C. MO 7th Cav. Co.I
Walker, John C. MO 8th Cav. Co.E
Walker, John C. SC Hvy.Arty. 15th (Lucas') Bn. Co.C
Walker, John C. SC 1st (Orr's) Rifles Co.E
Walker, John C. SC 4th St.Troops Co.G Cpl.
Walker, John C. SC Cav.Bn. Holcombe Legion Co.B Cpl.
Walker, John C. TN 4th Inf. Co.D Cpl.
Walker, John C. VA 10th Inf. Co.I
Walker, John Campbell TN 40th Inf. Co.A
Walker, John C.C. GA Inf. 3rd Bn. Co.F Sgt.
Walker, John D. AL 10th Inf. Co.G Sgt.
Walker, John D. AR 33rd Inf. Co.G
Walker, John D. FL 1st Inf. Co.E
Walker, John D. GA 1st Reg. Co.C Maj.
Walker, John D. KY 1st Inf. Co.E
Walker, John D. MO 3rd Cav. Co.H Sgt.
Walker, John D. NC Walker's Bn. Thomas' Legion 2nd Co.D
Walker, John D. TN 27th Inf. Co.D
Walker, John D. TX Cav. Ragsdale's Bn. Co.E
Walker, John E. AL 56th Part.Rangers Co.H,G
Walker, John E. GA Inf. 2nd Bn. Co.A
Walker, John E. MS 22nd Inf. Co.E
Walker, John E. NC 18th Inf. Co.I
Walker, John E. SC 5th Inf. 1st Co.K
Walker, John E. SC Palmetto S.S. Co.K
Walker, John E. VA 52nd Mil. Co.A
Walker, John E. 1st Cherokee Mtd.Vol. 2nd Co.I Ord.Sgt.
Walker, John F. AL 10th Inf. Co.D
Walker, John F. AL 29th Inf. Co.K
Walker, John F. AR 1st (Crawford's) Cav. Co.B
Walker, John F. MO 8th Cav. Co.D
Walker, John F. MO 6th Inf. Co.D
Walker, John F. NC Cav. 15th Bn. Co.A
Walker, John F. TN 53rd Inf. Co.K Chap.
Walker, John F. TX 17th Cav. 1st Co.I
Walker, John F. VA Cav. 35th Bn. Co.A
Walker, John F. VA 25th Inf. 2nd Co.H
Walker, John F. VA 57th Inf. Co.K
Walker, John G. NC 64th Inf. Co.N Sgt.
Walker, John G. SC 1st Cav. Co.G
Walker, John G. TX 8th Cav. Co.K Lt.Col.
Walker, John G. TX 12th Cav. Co.D
Walker, John G. TX Cav. Baylor's Regt. Co.G Sgt.
Walker, John G. Gen. & Staff Maj.Gen.
Walker, John H. AL 29th Inf. Co.K Sgt.
Walker, John H. AL 40th Inf. Co.A
Walker, John H. AL 46th Inf. Co.C
Walker, John H. AR 3rd Inf. Co.B
Walker, John H. GA 4th (Clinch's) Cav.
Walker, John H. GA 11th Cav. (St.Guards) Groover's Co.
Walker, John H. GA Brooks' Co. (Terrell Lt.Arty.)
Walker, John H. GA 32nd Inf. Co.B
Walker, John H. GA 48th Inf. Co.B
Walker, John H. GA 49th Inf. Co.K
Walker, John H. KY 6th Mtd.Inf. Co.F,I
Walker, John H. LA 9th Inf. Co.A
Walker, John H. LA 28th (Gray's) Inf. Co.K Cpl.
Walker, John H. MS 10th Cav. Co.E
Walker, John H. MS 18th Cav. Co.A Sgt.
Walker, John H. MS 1st Lt.Arty. Co.K
Walker, John H. MS 23rd Inf. Co.G
Walker, John H. MS 42nd Inf. Co.I
Walker, John H. MO 3rd Cav.
Walker, John H. MO 8th Cav. Co.D,B
Walker, John H. NC 6th Inf. Co.H
Walker, John H. NC 11th (Bethel Regt.) Inf. Co.E
Walker, John H. SC 5th Res. Co.C Cpl.
Walker, John H. TN 5th Cav. Co.B
Walker, John H. TN 26th Inf. Co.I
Walker, John H. TN 33rd Inf. Co.C
Walker, John H. TX 1st (Yager's) Cav. Co.B
Walker, John H. VA 6th Cav. Co.G
Walker, John H. VA Lt.Arty. E.J. Anderson's Co.
Walker, John H. VA 40th Inf. Co.F
Walker, John H. Conf.Cav. Wood's Regt. 2nd Co.M
Walker, John H. Mead's Conf.Cav. Co.H 2nd Lt.
Walker, John H. 1st Conf.Inf. 2nd Co.G
Walker, John Harkins TN 40th Inf. Co.A
Walker, John H.B. AL 50th Inf. Co.C
Walker, John H.C. NC 56th Inf. Co.D
Walker, John Henry MS 19th Inf. Co.E,A
Walker, John H.H. TN 2nd (Ashby's) Cav. Co.E Sgt.
Walker, John Hurdle NC 6th Inf. Co.H
Walker, John I. SC 2nd Arty. Co.B
Walker, John J. AL 1st Cav. Co.C
Walker, John J. AL Cav. Holloway's Co.
Walker, John J. AL Lt.Arty. 2nd Bn. Co.F
Walker, John J. AR 1st Cav. (St.) Co.G Capt.
Walker, John J. AR 3rd Cav. Co.K 2nd Lt.
Walker, John J. AR 7th Mil. Co.A
Walker, John J. LA Miles' Legion Co.D Cpl.
Walker, John J. MS 2nd St.Cav. Co.E Cpl.
Walker, John J. MS 1st Lt.Arty., Co.L
Walker, John J. MS 23rd Inf. Co.H
Walker, John J. NC 18th Inf. Co.E
Walker, John J. NC 46th Inf. Co.E 1st Lt.
Walker, John J. VA 21st Inf. Co.E 1st Lt.
Walker, John J. VA 56th Inf. Co.D Sgt.
Walker, John J. Gen. & Staff, Comsy.Dept. Maj.
Walker, John Jackson AL 49th Inf. Co.B
Walker, John K. NC 6th Inf. Co.K 1st Sgt.
Walker, John L. AL 3rd Inf. Co.D
Walker, John L. AL 6th Inf. Co.F
Walker, John L. AL 23rd Inf. Co.A
Walker, John L. AL Recruits
Walker, John L. MS 26th Inf. Co.G ACS
Walker, John L. SC 16th Inf. Co.F 3rd Lt.
Walker, John L. VA 3rd Cav. Co.D
Walker, John L. VA 22nd Cav. Co.F
Walker, John L. VA Inf. 26th Bn. Co.C,H
Walker, John L. VA 59th Inf. 2nd Co.I Sgt.
Walker, John L. VA Res.Mil. Co.D
Walker, John L. Gen. & Staff ACS
Walker, John L. Gen. & Staff Hosp.Stew.
Walker, John M. AL 4th Inf. Co.D
Walker, John M. AL 6th Inf. Co.L
Walker, John M. AL 12th Inf. Co.E
Walker, John M. AL 29th Inf. Co.G
Walker, John M. GA 7th Inf. (St.Guards) Co.I
Walker, John M. LA 9th Inf. Co.A
Walker, John M. MS 2nd St.Cav. Co.A
Walker, John M. MS 2nd Inf. Co.A
Walker, John M. MS 4th Inf. Co.I
Walker, John M. NC 2nd Bn.Loc.Def.Troops Co.F 1st Sgt.
Walker, John M. NC 14th Inf. Co.G Sgt.
Walker, John M. NC 48th Inf. Co.C
Walker, John M. SC Inf. 3rd Bn. Co.C
Walker, John M. TX 12th Cav. Co.C
Walker, John M. VA Lt.Arty. French's Co. Cpl.
Walker, John M. VA 6th Bn.Res. Co.B
Walker, John M. VA 21st Mil. Co.D,E
Walker, John M. VA 38th Inf. Co.H
Walker, John M. VA 55th Inf. Co.F
Walker, John M. VA 60th Inf. Co.I Sgt.
Walker, John M. VA Arty. Wise Legion Cpl.
Walker, John M. Gen. & Staff Capt.,Comsy.
Walker, John M.B. GA 21st Inf. Co.K
Walker, John McKenzie VA 8th Cav. 1st Co.D
Walker, John N. AL Cav. Lewis' Bn. Co.D 1st Sgt.
Walker, John N. GA 5th Inf. Co.E
Walker, John N. TX Cav. Morgan's Regt. Co.B
Walker, John N. VA 24th Inf. Co.D
Walker, John O. VA 56th Inf. Co.B Cpl.
Walker, John P. MS 22nd Inf. Co.B
Walker, John P. NC 16th Inf. Co.H
Walker, John P. NC 48th Inf. Co.F
Walker, John P. TN 31st Inf. Co.K
Walker, John P. VA Cav. Mosby's Regt. (Part.Rangers) Co.E
Walker, John P. VA 39th Inf. Co.I Cpl.
Walker, John R. AR 5th Inf. Co.I
Walker, John R. AR 6th Inf. Co.A
Walker, John R. MS 2nd Cav. Co.C
Walker, John R. MS 1st Bn.S.S. Co.A
Walker, John R., Jr. MS 13th Inf. Co.F 1st Lt.
Walker, John R. TX 12th Cav. Co.E
Walker, John R. VA 24th Inf. Co.H
Walker, John R. VA 26th Inf. Co.A
Walker, John R. VA 34th Inf. Co.B 2nd Lt.
Walker, John R.B. NC 5th Inf. Co.A
Walker, John R.B. NC 56th Inf. Co.B

Walker, John S. AR 12th Inf. Co.G Lt.Col.
Walker, John S. AR Inf. Cocke's Regt. Co.C
Walker, John S. GA 3rd Inf. Co.L
Walker, John S. GA Cobb's Legion Co.D
Walker, John S. MS Cav. Ham's Regt. Co.F
Walker, John S. MS 2nd (Davidson's) Inf. Co.D
Walker, John S. MS 34th Inf. Co.H
Walker, John S. TN Inf. 22nd Bn. Co.A Sgt.
Walker, John S. TN 25th Inf. Co.E
Walker, John S. TX 2nd Cav. Co.D
Walker, John S. VA Cav. 35th Bn. Co.A
Walker, John S. VA 11th Inf. Co.I
Walker, John S. VA 13th Inf. 2nd Co.E
Walker, John S. VA 15th Inf. Co.B Maj.
Walker, John S.L. VA 11th Inf. Co.E
Walker, Johnson TX Cav. (Dismtd.) Chisum's Regt. Co.F Jr.2nd Lt.
Walker, Johnson TX 15th Field Btty.
Walker, Johnson TX 14th Inf. Co.I 2nd Lt.
Walker, Johnson S. SC Horse Arty. (Washington Arty.) Vol. Hart's Co.
Walker, Johnson S. SC Arty.Bn. Hampton Legion Co.A QMSgt.
Walker, John T. AR 1st Mtd.Rifles Co.E
Walker, John T. AR 9th Inf. Co.H Cpl.
Walker, John T. AR 25th Inf. Co.E
Walker, John T. AR Inf. Cocke's Regt. Co.A
Walker, John T. AR Inf. Cocke's Regt. Co.C
Walker, John T. GA 2nd Cav. Co.G
Walker, John T. GA Cav. 15th Bn. (St.Guards) Wooten's Co.
Walker, John T. GA Siege Arty. 28th Bn. Co.F
Walker, John T. GA 31st Inf. Co.A
Walker, John T. MO Inf. 5th Regt.St.Guard Co.A
Walker, John T. NC 43rd Inf. Co.G
Walker, John T. SC 5th Inf. 1st Co.K
Walker, John T. SC 6th Inf. 1st Co.A Capt.
Walker, John T. SC 12th Inf. Co.G
Walker, John T. SC Palmetto S.S. Co.K 1st Lt.
Walker, John T. TN Lt.Arty. Baxter's Co.
Walker, John T. TN 3rd (Clack's) Inf. Co.K
Walker, John T. VA 34th Inf. Co.K
Walker, John T. VA 59th Inf. 1st Co.G
Walker, John T. VA 60th Inf. Co.D
Walker, John T. VA 60th Inf. Co.I
Walker, John V. TN 55th (McKoin's) Inf. James' Co.
Walker, John W. AL 4th (Russell's) Cav. Co.K
Walker, John W. AL 12th Cav. Co.A
Walker, John W. AL 3rd Bn. Hilliard's Legion Vol. Co.B
Walker, John W. AR 1st (Crawford's) Cav. Maj.
Walker, John W. AR 8th Inf. New Co.B
Walker, John W. AR 10th Inf. Co.G
Walker, John W. AR 15th (Johnson's) Inf. Co.C 1st Lt.
Walker, John W. GA Cav. 8th Bn. (St.Guards) Co.D
Walker, John W. GA Inf. 1st Loc.Troops (Augusta) Co.A Bvt.2nd Lt.
Walker, John W. GA Inf. 1st Loc.Troops (Augusta) Co.C
Walker, John W. GA 19th Inf. Co.F
Walker, John W. GA 49th Inf. Co.B
Walker, John W. GA 57th Inf. Co.C
Walker, John W. GA 64th Inf. Co.B
Walker, John W. KY 9th Mtd.Inf. Co.B
Walker, John W. LA 6th Cav. Co.C
Walker, John W. LA 7th Inf. Co.I Sgt.
Walker, John W. LA 19th Inf. Co.A Cpl.
Walker, John W. MS 2nd St.Cav. Co.F
Walker, John W. MS 3rd Inf. (St.Troops) Co.C Capt.
Walker, John W. MS 6th Inf. Co.G
Walker, John W. MS 17th Inf. Co.C
Walker, John W. MO 12th Cav. Co.G
Walker, John W. MO Cav. Poindexter's Regt.
Walker, John W. MO Lt.Arty. 3rd Field Btty.
Walker, John W. MO 5th Inf. Co.H
Walker, John W. MO 10th Inf. Co.A
Walker, John W. MO 16th Inf. Co.B
Walker, John W. NC 1st Arty. (10th St.Troops) Co.G Sgt.
Walker, John W. NC 1st Inf. Co.C
Walker, John W. NC 25th Inf. Co.G ACS
Walker, John W. NC 31st Inf. Co.B
Walker, John W. NC 38th Inf. Co.C Sgt.
Walker, John W. NC 42nd Inf. Co.D Cpl.
Walker, John W. NC 66th Inf. Co.G Bvt.2nd Lt.
Walker, John W. TN 4th (McLemore's) Cav. Co.B
Walker, John W. TN 5th (McKenzie's) Cav. Co.E
Walker, John W. TN 18th (Newsom's) Cav. Co.A
Walker, John W. TN 4th Inf. Co.H 2nd Lt.
Walker, John W. TN 7th Inf. Co.E
Walker, John W. TN 18th Inf. Co.G Orderly
Walker, John W. TN 40th Inf. Co.C 1st Lt.
Walker, John W. TN 42nd Inf. 2nd Co.E Capt.
Walker, John W. TN 42nd Inf. 2nd Co.F Capt.
Walker, John W. TN 44th Inf. Co.I Sgt.
Walker, John W. TN 44th (Cons.) Inf. Co.A
Walker, John W. TN 60th Mtd.Inf. Co.H
Walker, John W. TX 14th Cav. Co.H Cpl.
Walker, John W. VA 8th Cav. Co.K
Walker, John W. VA Cav. Hounshell's Bn. Thurmond's Co.
Walker, John W. VA Hvy.Arty. 19th Bn. Co.A
Walker, John W. VA Lt.Arty. Arch. Graham's Co.
Walker, John W. VA 15th Inf. Co.B
Walker, John W. VA 26th Inf. Co.L
Walker, John W. VA 38th Inf. Co.H
Walker, John W. VA 46th Inf. 2nd Co.C
Walker, John W. Gen. & Staff Capt.,Comsy.
Walker, John Willy AL 51st (Part.Rangers) Co.C
Walker, John Wister VA 59th Inf. Surg.
Walker, John Z. TX 16th Inf. Co.I
Walker, Jonah W. AL 13th Inf. Co.E
Walker, Jonathan AL 20th Inf.
Walker, Jonathan TN 63rd Inf. Co.A Sgt.
Walker, Jonathan C. GA 6th Cav. Co.F
Walker, Jonathan Harkness TN 40th Inf. Co.A
Walker, Jonathan L. GA 44th Inf. Co.I
Walker, Jones C. NC 51st Inf. Co.G
Walker, Jones H. NC 45th Inf. Co.H
Walker, Joseph GA 10th Cav. (St.Guards) Co.A Sgt.
Walker, Joseph GA 12th Cav. Co.B
Walker, Joseph GA 7th Inf. (St.Guards) Co.F
Walker, Joseph GA 48th Inf. Co.F
Walker, Joseph GA 49th Inf. Co.F Sgt.
Walker, Joseph KY 12th Cav. Co.I
Walker, Joseph LA Inf. 1st Sp.Bn. (Wheat's) AACS
Walker, Joseph LA 5th Inf. New Co.A Cpl.
Walker, Joseph LA 12th Inf. Co.H
Walker, Joseph LA 15th Inf. Co.B
Walker, Joseph MS 3rd Cav.
Walker, Joseph MS 18th Cav. Co.B
Walker, Joseph MO 1st Brig.St.Guard
Walker, Joseph NC 3rd Inf. Co.E
Walker, Joseph NC 7th Sr.Res. Clinard's Co.
Walker, Joseph NC 11th (Bethel Regt.) Inf. Co.B
Walker, Joseph NC 44th Inf. Co.A
Walker, Joseph NC 58th Inf. Co.K,A Sgt.
Walker, Joseph SC 1st Cav. Co.H
Walker, Joseph SC 5th Inf. 1st Co.K Capt.
Walker, Joseph SC Palmetto S.S. Col.
Walker, Joseph SC Cav.Bn. Holcombe Legion Co.E Teamster
Walker, Joseph TN 14th (Neely's) Cav. Co.F
Walker, Joseph TN 16th Inf. Co.I
Walker, Joseph TX 2nd Inf. Co.I
Walker, Joseph VA 2nd Cav. Co.H
Walker, Joseph VA 19th Inf. Co.C
Walker, Joseph Gen. & Staff Chap.
Walker, Joseph Gen. & Staff Col.
Walker, Joseph A. KY 13th Cav. Co.I,K
Walker, Joseph A. MS 34th Inf. Co.G
Walker, Joseph A. TN Lt.Arty. Kain's Co. Sgt.
Walker, Joseph A. VA 16th Cav. Co.E
Walker, Joseph Asa GA 39th Inf. Co.B
Walker, Joseph B. GA Phillips' Legion Co.A Music.
Walker, Joseph B. MS 16th Inf. Co.B
Walker, Joseph B. Gen. & Staff Hosp.Stew.
Walker, Joseph B.W. GA 30th Inf. Co.D
Walker, Joseph C. GA 62nd Cav. Co.C,A
Walker, Joseph C. KY 10th Cav. Co.I,B
Walker, Joseph C. NC 37th Inf. Co.C
Walker, Joseph E. FL 7th Inf. Co.H
Walker, Joseph H. GA Inf. Fuller's Co. Cpl.
Walker, Joseph H. NC Hvy.Art. 1st Bn. Co.B
Walker, Joseph H. TN 63rd Inf. Co.D Cpl.
Walker, Joseph J. GA 34th Inf. Co.K Sgt.
Walker, Joseph J. TX 1st (McCulloch's) Cav. Co.A
Walker, Joseph J. TX 16th Inf. Co.G
Walker, Joseph L. TN 8th Cav. Co.G
Walker, Joseph L. TX 8th Cav. Co.G,B
Walker, Joseph L. VA 21st Cav. 2nd Co.G
Walker, Joseph L. VA Inf. 57th Regt. Co.F
Walker, Joseph M. NC 1st Inf. Co.A
Walker, Joseph M. NC 1st Inf. Co.C Cpl.
Walker, Joseph M. NC 16th Inf. Co.D
Walker, Joseph Morgan NC 56th Inf. Co.I 1st Lt.
Walker, Joseph N. TN Cav. 9th Bn. (Gantt's) Co.A Capt.
Walker, Joseph R. AL 4th Inf. Co.B
Walker, Joseph R. NC 14th Inf. Co.A
Walker, Joseph S. TX 14th Cav. Co.B
Walker, Joseph T. AL 6th Inf. Co.C
Walker, Joseph T. GA 41st Inf. Co.K
Walker, Joseph T. SC 6th Inf. 1st Co.A
Walker, Joseph W. GA 38th Inf. Co.B
Walker, Joshua AL 3rd Bn.Res. Flemming's Co.

Walker, Joshua GA Cav. 22nd Bn. (St.Guards) Co.H
Walker, Joshua GA 49th Inf. Co.A 2nd Lt.
Walker, Joshua TN 14th Inf. Co.K
Walker, Joshua C. NC 3rd Inf. Asst.Surg.
Walker, Joshua E. VA 14th Inf. Co.F Capt.
Walker, Joshua E. VA 56th Inf. Co.B 1st Lt.
Walker, Josiah GA Inf. 9th Bn. Co.A
Walker, Josiah GA 37th Inf. Co.D
Walker, Josiah MS 8th Inf. Co.G
Walker, Josiah MS 37th Inf. Co.H
Walker, Josiah TN 8th Inf. Co.E
Walker, Josiah VA Cav. 1st Bn. (Loc.Def. Troops) Co.C
Walker, Josiah R. MS Part.Rangers Smyth's Co.
Walker, Jos. R. AL 12th Inf. Co.F
Walker, Jotison TX 2nd Cav. 1st Co.F
Walker, J.P. AL 1st Cav. 2nd Co.E
Walker, J.P. AL 3rd Inf. Co.A
Walker, J.P. AL Mil. 4th Vol. Co.E
Walker, J.P. AL 7th Inf. Co.D 2nd Lt.
Walker, J.P. AL 31st Inf. Co.C
Walker, J.P. AR 8th Inf. New Co.K
Walker, J.P. GA 4th Res. Co.B
Walker, J.P. LA Inf. 1st Bn. (St.Guards)
Walker, J.P. MS 10th Inf. New Co.A
Walker, J.P. SC 3rd Inf. Co.F
Walker, J.P. TN Cav. 16th Bn. (Neal's) Co.B
Walker, J.P. TN 21st (Wilson's) Cav. Co.D
Walker, J.P. TN 21st & 22nd (Cons.) Cav. Co.H
Walker, J.P. TN 9th Inf. Co.G
Walker, J.P. TN Inf. 154th Sr.Regt. Co.E
Walker, J.P. TX 12th Cav. Co.H
Walker, J.P. TX Cav. Mann's Regt. Co.A,E
Walker, J.P. VA 2nd Cav. Co.I
Walker, J.P. Gen. & Staff Capt.,AIG
Walker, J.P.K. GA Inf. 1st Loc.Troops (Augusta) Barnes' Lt.Arty.Co.
Walker, J.R. AL 8th Cav. Co.F
Walker, J.R. AL 13th Bn.Part.Rangers Co.D Sgt.
Walker, J.R. AL 56th Part.Rangers Co.H
Walker, J.R. AL Lt.Arty. 20th Bn. Co.A
Walker, J.R. AL 30th Inf. Co.H
Walker, J.R. AL 44th Inf. Co.B
Walker, J.R. AL 50th Inf. Co.K
Walker, J.R. AR 8th Inf. New Co.H
Walker, J.R. FL 2nd Cav. Co.I
Walker, J.R. GA 4th (Clinch's) Cav. Co.F,H
Walker, J.R. GA Cav. 8th Bn. (St.Guards) Co.D
Walker, J.R. GA Lt.Arty. Clinch's Btty.
Walker, J.R. GA 13th Inf. Co.E
Walker, J.R. KY 10th (Johnson's) Cav. Co.D
Walker, J.R. MS 25th Inf. Co.I
Walker, J.R. MO 9th (Elliott's) Cav. Co.A
Walker, J.R. NC 11th (Bethel Regt.) Inf. Co.B
Walker, J.R. SC 2nd Arty. Co.C
Walker, J.R. TN Arty. Marshall's Co.
Walker, J.R. TN 38th Inf. 1st Co.K
Walker, J.S. AL 4th Cav. Co.A
Walker, J.S. AL 5th Inf. New Co.H
Walker, J.S. GA 3rd Cav. (St.Guards) Co.C
Walker, J.S. GA 5th Res. Co.F
Walker, J.S. GA Inf. 27th Bn. (NonConscr.) Co.A
Walker, J.S. GA 32nd Inf. Co.D
Walker, J.S. GA 56th Inf. Co.B
Walker, J.S. LA Inf. 16th Bn. (Conf.Guards Resp.Bn.) Co.A
Walker, J.S. MO 5th Cav. Co.I
Walker, J.S. NC 22nd Inf. Co.F
Walker, J.S. TN Inf. 4th Cons.Regt. Co.C
Walker, J.S. 8th (Wade's) Conf.Cav. Co.D
Walker, J.S.L. VA 2nd Cav. Co.I
Walker, J.T. AL 4th (Russell's) Cav. Co.E Sgt.
Walker, J.T. AL 25th Inf. Co.F
Walker, J.T. AL Randolph Cty.Res. J. Orr's Co.
Walker, J.T. AR 2nd Inf. Co.I
Walker, J.T. AR 6th Inf. 1st Co.B
Walker, J.T. AR 7th Inf. Co.K
Walker, J.T. AR 19th (Dawson's) Inf. Co.A
Walker, J.T. AR 26th Inf. Co.C
Walker, J.T. AR 31st Inf. Co.A
Walker, J.T. AR Inf. Hardy's Regt. Torbett's Co.
Walker, J.T. GA 11th Inf. Co.K Sgt.
Walker, J.T. GA 46th Inf. Co.B
Walker, J.T. GA 56th Inf. Co.H
Walker, J.T. KY 12th Cav. Co.I
Walker, J.T. NC 12th Inf. Co.C
Walker, J.T. SC 1st Cav. Co.D
Walker, J.T. TN 2nd (Ashby's) Cav. Co.A
Walker, J.T. TN Cav. 5th Bn. (McClellan's) Co.A
Walker, J.T. TN 51st (Cons.) Inf. Co.A 3rd Lt.
Walker, J.T. TX Cav. 1st Regt.St.Troops Co.G
Walker, J.T. TX Cav. Border's Regt. Co.C
Walker, J.T. TX Inf. 1st St.Troops Lawrence's Co.D Cpl.
Walker, J.T. VA 59th Inf. 3rd Co.E
Walker, J. Thompson NC 13th Inf. Co.H
Walker, J.V. MS 32nd Inf. Co.A
Walker, J.V.F. AL Jeff Davis Arty.
Walker, J.W. AL 1st Cav. Co.C
Walker, J.W. AL 4th (Roddey's) Cav.
Walker, J.W. AL 51st (Part.Rangers) Co.D
Walker, J.W. AL Cav. Forrest's Regt.
Walker, J.W. AL 3rd Res.
Walker, J.W. AL 14th Inf. Co.C Cpl.
Walker, J.W. AL 20th Inf. Co.I
Walker, J.W. AL 45th Inf. Co.K
Walker, J.W. AL 50th Inf.
Walker, J.W. AL 60th Inf. Co.A
Walker, J.W. AL 63rd Inf. Co.F,H
Walker, J.W. AL 63rd Inf. Co.G
Walker, J.W. AR 4th St.Inf. Co.F 1st Lt.
Walker, J.W. AR 24th Inf. Co.H Cpl.
Walker, J.W. AR Inf. Hardy's Regt. Co.E Sgt.
Walker, J.W. GA 8th Cav. New Co.D Cpl.
Walker, J.W. GA 10th Cav. (St.Guards) Co.K
Walker, J.W. GA Cav. 20th Bn. Co.A Cpl.
Walker, J.W. GA Arty. 11th Bn. (Sumter Arty.) Co.D 1st Lt.
Walker, J.W. GA Inf. 1st Loc.Troops (Augusta) Dearing's Cav.Co.
Walker, J.W. GA 1st (Ramsey's) Inf.
Walker, J.W. GA Inf. 2nd Bn. (St.Guards) Co.C Cpl.
Walker, J.W. GA 14th Inf. Co.F
Walker, J.W. GA 16th Inf. Co.E
Walker, J.W. GA 19th Inf. Co.H
Walker, J.W. GA 36th (Broyles') Inf. Co.E
Walker, J.W. GA 59th Inf. Co.H Cpl.
Walker, J.W. GA Phillips' Legion Co.G Sgt.
Walker, J.W. KY 12th Cav. Co.D Ord.Sgt.
Walker, J.W. KY 12th Cav. Co.I
Walker, J.W. KY 9th Mtd.Inf. Co.B
Walker, J.W. MS 5th Cav. Co.C,D
Walker, J.W. MS 5th Cav. Co.I
Walker, J.W. MS 28th Cav. Co.F
Walker, J.W. MS 4th Inf. Co.C
Walker, J.W. MS 41st Inf. Co.F
Walker, J.W. MS 41st Inf. Co.K
Walker, J.W. MS Res. Co.C
Walker, J.W. MO Lt.Arty. 3rd Field Btty.
Walker, J.W. MO 10th Inf. Co.A
Walker, J.W. NC 1st Jr.Res. Co.C
Walker, J.W. NC 1st Bn.Jr.Res. Co.D
Walker, J.W. NC 20th Inf. Co.B
Walker, J.W. NC 32nd Inf. Co.B
Walker, J.W. NC 55th Inf. Co.I
Walker, J.W. TN 18th (Newsom's) Cav. Co.H
Walker, J.W. TN 5th Inf. 2nd Co.B
Walker, J.W. TN 12th Inf. Co.B
Walker, J.W. TN 19th Inf. Co.F
Walker, J.W. TN 31st Inf. Co.G Cpl.
Walker, J.W. TN 33rd Inf. Co.E Capt.
Walker, J.W. TN 35th Inf. Co.E
Walker, J.W. TN 55th (Brown's) Inf. Co.H
Walker, J.W. TN 84th Inf. Co.D
Walker, J.W. TX Cav. Bourland's Regt. Co.D
Walker, J.W. TX Cav. Saufley's Scouting Bn. Co.C
Walker, J.W. TX 15th Field Btty.
Walker, J.W. TX 1st Inf. 2nd Co.K
Walker, J.W. TX Inf. 1st St.Troops White's Co.D
Walker, J.W. TX 13th Vol. 1st Co.H
Walker, J.W. TX 15th Inf. Co.A
Walker, J.W. VA 3rd Lt.Arty. (Loc.Def.) Co.D
Walker, J.W. VA Lt.Arty. Penick's Co.
Walker, J.W. VA Inf. 22nd Bn. Co.I
Walker, J.W. VA Inf. 28th Bn. Co.D
Walker, J.W. VA Inf. 44th Bn. Co.D
Walker, J.W. VA 59th Inf. 3rd Co.I
Walker, J.W. VA Loc.Def. Durrett's Co.
Walker, J.W. Comsy.Dept. F Brig.
Walker, J.W. Nitre & Min. Bureau War Dept.,CSA
Walker, J.W. Gen. & Staff Surg.
Walker, J.Y. TN 40th Inf. Co.G
Walker, J.Y. 1st Chickasaw Inf. McCord's Co.
Walker, K. NC 3rd Jr.Res. Co.C
Walker, Kate AL 36th Inf.
Walker, K.L. TX 11th (Spaight's) Bn.Vol. Co.B
Walker, K.L. TX 13th Vol. 4th Co.I
Walker, L. GA 15th Inf. Co.F
Walker, L. LA Inf. 1st Bn. (St.Guards)
Walker, L. MO Arty. Lowe's Co.
Walker, L. TN 21st & 22nd (Cons.) Cav. Co.C
Walker, L. TN 25th Inf. Co.I
Walker, L. TX 12th Cav. Co.K
Walker, L. VA Lt.Arty. Fry's Co.
Walker, L.A. AR 34th Inf. Co.F
Walker, L.A. GA 10th Inf. Co.G
Walker, L.A. VA Arty. C.F. Johnston's Co. Cpl.
Walker, Lafayette GA Inf. 19th Bn. (St.Guards) Co.C
Walker, Lafayette LA 28th (Gray's) Inf. Co.C
Walker, Landon M.E. SC 5th Cav. Co.K

Walker, Landrick A. FL 1st Cav. Co.I
Walker, Landsey L. NC 11th (Bethel Regt.) Inf. Co.E
Walker, Landy L. NC 22nd Inf. Co.G
Walker, Laroy W. MS 26th Inf. Co.B
Walker, Lawrence VA 19th Inf. Co.D Cpl.
Walker, Layson Conf.Cav. Wood's Regt. 2nd Co.F
Walker, L.B. AL Cav. Moreland's Regt. Co.D
Walker, L.B. AL Cav. Moreland's Regt. Co.H
Walker, L.B. SC 11th Inf. Co.K
Walker, L.B. SC 24th Inf. Co.E
Walker, L.B. TN 20th (Russell's) Cav. Co.C
Walker, L.B. TX Cav. Border's Regt. Co.E
Walker, L.B. TX Cav. Waller's Regt. Co.F
Walker, L. Berry FL 1st Inf. Old Co.D, New Co.C
Walker, L.C. GA Inf. 14th Bn. (St.Guards) Co.H
Walker, L.C. NC 37th Inf. Co.G
Walker, L.C. TN 30th Inf. Co.A
Walker, L.C. Trans-MS Conf.Cav. 1st Bn. Co.A
Walker, L.D. AL 6th Cav. Co.A
Walker, L.D. AL Arty. 1st Bn. Co.A
Walker, L.D. TN 12th Inf. Co.G Capt.
Walker, L.D. TN 12th (Cons.) Inf. Co.E Capt.
Walker, L.D. Gen. & Staff,PACS Capt.
Walker, L.E. KY 3rd Cav. Grant's Co.
Walker, L.E. LA 1st Res. Co.K
Walker, L.E. MS 8th Cav. Co.F
Walker, L.E. VA 1st (Farinholt's) Res. Co.C Sgt.
Walker, Leander LA 28th (Gray's) Inf. Co.K
Walker, Leander NC 33rd Inf. Co.D
Walker, Leander TX 29th Cav. Co.B
Walker, Leander T. AL Cav. 8th Regt. (Livingston's) Co.K
Walker, Leander T. AL Cav. Moses' Squad. Co.A
Walker, Leander T. VA 28th Inf. Co.B Cpl.
Walker, Lem AL 21st Inf. Co.F
Walker, Lemard Z. TN 1st Cav.
Walker, Lemuel O. TX 18th Inf. Co.F
Walker, Lenord MO Todd's Co.
Walker, Leonard MS 12th Cav. Co.H
Walker, Leonard MO 5th Inf. Co.H
Walker, Leonard MO Dorsey's Regt.
Walker, Leonard B. TX Cav. Ragsdale's Bn. Co.D
Walker, Leonidas J. NC 37th Inf. Co.D
Walker, Leroy AL 1st Cav. 2nd Co.C Cpl.
Walker, Levi AL 42nd Inf. Co.B,C
Walker, Levi LA Inf. 9th Bn. Co.A
Walker, Levi NC 30th Inf. Co.B
Walker, Levi VA 7th Cav. Co.K
Walker, Levi A. NC 11th (Bethel Regt.) Inf. Co.E
Walker, Levi H. NC 6th Inf. Co.H 1st Lt.
Walker, Levi Jasper NC 13th Inf. Co.B
Walker, Levin LA 25th Inf. Co.E
Walker, Levi S. NC 2nd Cav. (19th St.Troops) Co.K
Walker, Lewellyn J. VA 55th Inf. Co.C
Walker, Lewis GA 7th Cav. Co.C
Walker, Lewis GA Cav. 24th Bn. Co.B
Walker, Lewis NC 22nd Inf. Co.L
Walker, Lewis A. VA 1st Arty. Co.H Cpl.
Walker, Lewis Adams NC 56th Inf. Co.I
Walker, Lewis Archibald KY 9th Mtd.Inf. Co.H
Walker, Lewis Archibald TX Inf. W. Cameron's Co.
Walker, Lewis D. MO Inf. 8th Bn. Co.E Sgt.
Walker, Lewis D. MO 9th Inf. Co.I Sgt.
Walker, Lewis L. NC 22nd Inf. Co.B
Walker, Lewis W. VA 61st Inf. Co.D
Walker, L.F. AL 48th Inf. Co.I
Walker, L.F. FL 2nd Inf. Co.K
Walker, L.F. FL 4th Inf. Co.D
Walker, L.F. VA Cav. Mosby's Regt. (Part. Rangers) Co.E
Walker, L.G. TN 7th (Duckworth's) Cav. Co.D Cpl.
Walker, L.H. LA Lt.Arty. Fenner's Btty.
Walker, L.H. LA Inf. 1st Sp.Bn. (Rightor's) Co.E
Walker, L.H. TN 11th (Holman's) Cav. Co.K Cpl.
Walker, L.H. TN Holman's Bn.Part.Rangers Co.D Cpl.
Walker, Little B. FL 5th Inf. Co.G
Walker, Little B. MS Cav. 1st Bn. (McNair's) St.Troops Co.C
Walker, Littleton E. TX Inf. Griffin's Bn. Co.D
Walker, L.J. SC 7th Cav. Co.B 1st Lt.
Walker, L.J. SC Rutledge Mtd.Riflemen & Horse Arty. Trenholm's Co. 1st Lt.
Walker, L.J. SC Mil. Trenholm's Co. 1st Lt.
Walker, L.K. AR 2nd Inf. Co.K
Walker, L.M. FL 1st (Res.) Inf. Co.F
Walker, L.M. TN 40th Inf. Col.
Walker, L.M. TX 20th Inf. Co.E
Walker, L.M. Gen. & Staff Brig.Gen.
Walker, L.O. MS Cav. Abbott's Co. Cpl.
Walker, L.O. MS Inf. 3rd Bn. (St.Troops) Co.F
Walker, Lorenzo VA 33rd Inf. Co.F
Walker, Lorenzo E. VA 14th Inf. Co.E
Walker, Lou TX 21st Cav. Co.D 1st Lt.
Walker, Louis A. TX 16th Cav. Co.H 1st Lt.
Walker, Love GA 50th Inf. Co.B
Walker, L.P. TN 11th (Holman's) Cav. Co.K
Walker, L.P. TN Holman's Bn.Part.Rangers Co.D
Walker, L.P. TX 12th Cav. Co.B
Walker, L.P. Gen. & Staff Brig.Gen.
Walker, L.R. TN 40th Inf. Co.I 1st Lt.
Walker, L.T. MS 9th Inf. Co.I
Walker, Ludy F. GA 55th Inf. Co.H
Walker, Luther VA 6th Inf. Ferguson's Co. Cpl.
Walker, Luther VA 12th Inf. Co.H Sgt.
Walker, Luther M. VA 30th Inf. Prin.Music.
Walker, L.W. MS 1st Cav. Co.G,F
Walker, L.W. MS 32nd Inf. Co.B
Walker, L.W. VA 3rd Lt.Arty. (Loc.Def.) Co.D
Walker, L.W. VA Inf. 28th Bn. Co.D
Walker, L.W. VA 59th Inf. 3rd Co.I
Walker, L.W.H. AL 25th Inf. Co.F
Walker, M. FL 2nd Cav. Co.I
Walker, M. GA Inf. 27th Bn. (NonConscr.) Co.C
Walker, M. GA 46th Inf. Co.K
Walker, M. LA Mil. 4th Regt. French Brig. Co.7
Walker, M. MO 6th Cav. Co.F
Walker, M. MO Inf. 1st Bn.St.Guard QM
Walker, M. NC 6th Inf. Co.G
Walker, M. TN 3rd (Forrest's) Cav. Co.I
Walker, M. TX 13th Vol. 1st Co.K
Walker, M.A. GA Lt.Arty. Havis' Btty.
Walker, Madison MS 37th Inf. Co.H
Walker, Madison G. KY 2nd (Duke's) Cav. Co.C
Walker, Major D. NC 24th Inf. Co.D
Walker, Malcom MO Inf. 2nd Regt.St.Guard Co.G 2nd Lt.
Walker, Malikiah W. AL 57th Inf. Co.G
Walker, Marcus LA 2nd Cav. Co.C
Walker, Marcus TX 18th Cav. Co.I
Walker, Marcus D.L. GA 2nd Bn.S.S. Co.B
Walker, Marion D. GA Inf. 8th Bn. Co.B
Walker, Mark AL 63rd Inf. Co.C
Walker, Marshall LA 12th Inf. Co.D Sgt.
Walker, Marshall LA 28th (Gray's) Inf. Co.K 1st Lt.
Walker, Marshall E. SC 1st (McCreary's) Inf. Co.G
Walker, Marshall H. NC 6th Inf. Co.H Cpl.
Walker, Martin AL 50th Inf. Co.A Capt.
Walker, Martin MS 5th Inf. (St.Troops) Co.G Cpl.
Walker, Martin TN 44th (Cons.) Inf. Co.G
Walker, Martin VA 21st Mil. Co.A
Walker, Martin VA 32nd Inf. 2nd Co.H
Walker, Martin J. TN 35th Inf. 1st Co.A, Co.B
Walker, Martin T. GA 17th Inf. Co.F
Walker, Mason D. TX 37th Cav. Co.H Sgt.
Walker, Mathew TX 2nd Inf. Co.F
Walker, Mathew VA 5th Cav. 3rd Co.F
Walker, Matt TX 27th Cav. Co.G
Walker, Matthew G. AR 18th Inf. Co.B Cpl.
Walker, M.B. TX 15th Cav. Co.K
Walker, M.C. SC 1st Arty. Co.F
Walker, M.C. TN 31st Inf. Co.G
Walker, M.D. GA 1st Bn.S.S. Co.D
Walker, M.D. TX 31st Cav. Co.I
Walker, M.D.L. TX 4th Cav. Co.K
Walker, M.E. TX 18th Inf. Co.K
Walker, Melville VA 5th Cav. Co.E
Walker, Melville VA 34th Inf. Co.B 2nd Lt.
Walker, Melvin M. VA 21st Inf. Co.C
Walker, Memory NC Walker's Bn. Thomas' Legion Co.B
Walker, M.F. TN 31st Inf. Co.H
Walker, M.F. TX 15th Inf. 2nd Co.F
Walker, M.G. KY 4th Mtd.Inf. Co.K
Walker, M.H. VA 14th Inf. Co.F
Walker, Micajah D. TN 35th Inf. Co.C
Walker, Michael AL 41st Inf. Co.A,H
Walker, Michael FL 3rd Inf. Co.H Cpl.
Walker, Michael F. GA 10th Inf. Co.K
Walker, Michael S. NC 37th Inf. Co.G
Walker, Miller B. TX 10th Cav. Co.I
Walker, Mills M. NC 2nd Arty. (36th St.Troops) Co.E
Walker, Milton SC 19th Inf. Co.C
Walker, Milton M. VA 40th Inf. Co.K
Walker, Milton N. VA Hvy.Arty. 19th Bn. Co.B
Walker, Milton S. SC 14th Inf. Co.D
Walker, Milus F. NC 4th Inf. Co.H Cpl.
Walker, Mims AL 4th Inf. Co.D
Walker, Mims Gen. & Staff 1st Lt.,ADC
Walker, Minor W. FL 1st Inf. Old Co.I,B 1st Sgt.
Walker, Mitchel LA Res.Corps

Walker, Mitchell GA 1st (Olmstead's) Inf. 1st Co.A
Walker, Mitchell GA 1st Bn.S.S. Co.B
Walker, M.J. GA Inf. 19th Bn. (St.Guards) Co.E Sgt.
Walker, M.J. GA 60th Inf. Co.G
Walker, M.J. GA Inf. City Bn. (Columbus) Williams' Co.
Walker, M.L. MS 10th Cav. Co.E 1st Lt.
Walker, M.L. MS 2nd (Davidson's) Inf. Co.A 1st Lt.
Walker, M.L. MS 32nd Inf. Co.F Sgt.
Walker, M.L. SC Lt.Arty. Beauregard's Co.
Walker, M.L. TX 6th Cav. Co.H Sgt.
Walker, M.L. VA 59th Inf. 2nd Co.K Cpl.
Walker, M.M. GA Cav. 15th Bn. (St.Guards) Wooten's Co.
Walker, M.M. VA 8th Cav. 2nd Co.D
Walker, M.M. VA 9th Cav. Co.K
Walker, Monroe KY 6th Mtd.Inf.
Walker, Morgan NC 7th Inf. Co.B
Walker, Morgan VA 12th Cav. Co.B
Walker, Morgan A. NC 57th Inf. Co.F Cpl.
Walker, Moses NC 24th Inf. Co.H
Walker, Moses NC 51st Inf. Co.A
Walker, Moses VA 38th Inf. Co.B
Walker, Moses F. VA 24th Inf. Co.D Cpl.
Walker, Moses J.M. VA 55th Inf. Co.C
Walker, Moses T. TX 11th Inf. Co.K
Walker, M.S. MO 3rd Inf. Co.F
Walker, M.S. NC 1st Arty. (10th St.Troops) Co.G
Walker, M.T. AL 3rd Cav. Co.C
Walker, M.T. AL 40th Inf. Co.G
Walker, M.T. AL St.Troops
Walker, M.T. MS 2nd Cav. Co.B
Walker, M.T. MS 22nd Inf.
Walker, M.T. SC 22nd Inf. Co.G
Walker, M.T. SC Palmetto S.S. Co.K
Walker, Muscoe L. VA Inf. 1st Bn. Co.C
Walker, Muscoe L. VA Inf. 26th Bn. Co.A Sgt.
Walker, Musco L. VA 22nd Inf. Swann's Co.H
Walker, M.V.B. TX 4th Cav. Co.K
Walker, M.V.B. TX 11th Cav. Co.E
Walker, M.W. AL 40th Inf. Co.G
Walker, M.W. FL 1st (Res.) Inf. Co.I
Walker, M.W. GA Lt.Arty. 12th Bn. 2nd Co.D
Walker, M.W. VA 14th Inf. Co.F
Walker, M.W.P. TN 38th Inf. Co.G
Walker, N. SC 2nd Arty. Co.E
Walker, N.A. GA 40th Inf. Co.A
Walker, N.A. MS 2nd Cav. Co.B
Walker, N.A.K. SC 2nd Arty. Co.B Sgt.
Walker, Napoleon B. AL 17th Inf. Co.A
Walker, Napoleon B. AL 22nd Inf. Co.F Cpl.
Walker, Napoleon B. LA 1st Hvy.Arty. (Reg.) Co.H
Walker, Nath SC 1st Bn.S.S. Co.B
Walker, Nathan MO Cav. Poindexter's Regt.
Walker, Nathan B. NC 3rd Bn.Sr.Res. Co.A 2nd Lt.
Walker, Nathan H. VA Lt.Arty. Armistead's Co. 1st Lt.
Walker, Nathan H. VA 61st Mil. Co.H Sgt.
Walker, Nathan H. Conf.Lt.Arty. Stark's Bn. Co.B 2nd Lt.
Walker, Nathaniel NC 24th Inf. Co.A
Walker, Nathaniel SC 2nd Arty. Co.B Sgt.
Walker, Nathaniel SC 14th Inf. Co.H
Walker, Nathaniel TN 4th Cav. Co.E
Walker, Nathaniel VA 33rd Inf. Co.F
Walker, Nathaniel B. FL 2nd Inf. Co.I Capt.
Walker, Nathaniel S. GA 44th Inf. Asst.Surg.
Walker, Nathaniel S. VA Inf. 1st Bn.Loc.Def. Co.D 1st Lt.
Walker, Nathaniel S. Gen. & Staff Surg.
Walker, Nathan S. NC 52nd Inf. Co.B
Walker, Nathan W. VA 18th Inf. Co.I 1st Sgt.
Walker, N.B. AR Mtd.Vol. (St.Troops) Abraham's Co.
Walker, N.B. LA 19th Inf. Co.B
Walker, N.B. LA 25th Inf. Co.E
Walker, N.B. VA Lt.Arty. 13th Bn. Co.B
Walker, N.B. VA 53rd Inf.
Walker, N. Dixon VA Hvy.Arty. 19th Bn. 1st Co.E
Walker, N.E. MS Part.Rangers Smyth's Co.
Walker, N.E. MS 24th Inf. Co.E
Walker, Neadham TN 32nd Inf. Co.G
Walker, Neal AZ Cav. Herbert's Bn. Helm's Co.
Walker, Neal TX 2nd Cav. 2nd Co.F
Walker, Neck AL 3rd Cav. Co.F
Walker, Neel GA 62nd Cav. Co.B
Walker, Nelson S. MS 48th Inf. Co.F Capt.
Walker, Newton GA 1st (Fannin's) Res. Co.C Sgt.
Walker, Newton MS Inf. 1st Bn.St.Troops (12 mo. '62-3) Co.C
Walker, Newton SC 5th Inf. 1st Co.K
Walker, Newton TN 39th Mtd.Inf. Co.A
Walker, Newton A. VA 18th Inf. Co.A
Walker, Newton H. LA 8th Inf. Co.G
Walker, Newton K. VA Lt.Arty. G.B. Chapman's Co.
Walker, Newton S. GA 2nd Cav. (St.Guards) Co.H,K
Walker, N.G. TN 3rd (Clack's) Inf. Co.E 1st Sgt.
Walker, N.H. TN Cav. Nixon's Regt. Co.C Cpl.
Walker, N.H. TX 10th Cav. Co.F
Walker, Nicholas LA 28th (Gray's) Inf. Co.C
Walker, Nicholas O. MS 2nd Cav. Co.F
Walker, N.J. AL Montgomery Guards
Walker, N.J. LA 9th Inf. Co.H Lt.Col.
Walker, N.J. NC 1st Bn.Jr.Res. Cpl.
Walker, N.J. SC 1st Mtd.Mil.
Walker, N.L. 14th Conf.Cav. Co.C
Walker, N.M. GA 13th Inf. Co.D
Walker, Noah GA 1st Cav. Co.K
Walker, Noah VA 18th Cav. Co.H
Walker, Noah VA 14th Mil. Co.D
Walker, Noah VA 62nd Mtd.Inf. 1st Co.G
Walker, Noah B. TN Cav. 7th Bn. (Bennett's) Co.C
Walker, Noah Dixon VA 44th Inf. Co.E 2nd Lt.
Walker, Noah J. NC 43rd Inf. Co.C
Walker, Norman S. VA 15th Inf. Co.B Capt.
Walker, Norman S. Gen. & Staff 1st Lt.,ADC
Walker, N.R. AL 11th Inf. Co.A
Walker, N.R. AL 15th Inf. Co.H
Walker, N.S. MS Inf. 2nd Bn. Co.F 2nd Lt.
Walker, Numa VA Inf. 23rd Bn. Co.B,G
Walker, Numa VA 190th Mil. Co.G
Walker, N.W. GA 13th Inf. Co.D
Walker, Obadiah GA 16th Inf. Co.K
Walker, Obadiah NC 3rd Bn.Sr.Res. Co.A
Walker, Obediah TX 11th Inf. Co.K
Walker, O.C. MO St.Guards
Walker, O.D. TN 16th Inf. Co.G Cpl.
Walker, O.E. MO Cav. 1st Regt.St.Guard Co.E
Walker, O.F. TN 3rd (Forrest's) Cav. Co.B
Walker, O.J. AR 4th Inf. Co.K
Walker, O.K. GA 13th Inf. Co.K Adj.
Walker, Oliver A. FL 8th Inf. Co.K
Walker, Oliver H.P. AL 1st Regt.Conscr. Co.F
Walker, Oliver P. KY Cav. 2nd Bn. (Dortch's) Co.C
Walker, O.M. VA 54th Mil. Co.C,D
Walker, O.P. LA 3rd (Harrison's) Cav. Co.C
Walker, O.P. SC 14th Inf. Co.D
Walker, O.P. TN Cav. Clark's Ind.Co.
Walker, O.P. TN 51st Inf. Co.G
Walker, Orange LA 8th Cav. Co.E
Walker, Orange LA 3rd Inf. Co.I
Walker, Origan M. VA 6th Inf. Co.H
Walker, Orren M. GA 20th Inf. Co.B
Walker, Osburn J. SC 1st (Orr's) Rifles Co.E
Walker, Ossamus S. AL 10th Inf. Co.F Cpl.
Walker, O.W. AL 7th Cav. Co.G
Walker, O.W. AL Mil. 4th Vol. Modawell's Co.
Walker, Owen J. AR 33rd Inf. Co.K
Walker, P. KY 2nd (Duke's) Cav. Co.K
Walker, P. MO 1st N.E. Cav. Co.B
Walker, P. MO 10th Inf. Co.G
Walker, P.A. AL 42nd Inf. Co.K
Walker, P.A. MS 19th Inf. Co.B 2nd Lt.
Walker, P.A. MS 24th Inf. 2nd Lt.
Walker, P.A. TN 12th Inf. Co.D
Walker, P.A. TN 12th (Cons.) Inf. Co.B
Walker, P.A. TX Cav. Giddings' Bn. Carr's Co.
Walker, Paschal Har TX 20th Cav. Co.E
Walker, Patrick LA 1st (Nelligan's) Inf. Co.H
Walker, Patrick H. TX 4th Inf. Co.A Sgt.
Walker, Paul GA 12th Inf. Co.D
Walker, P.C. TX 8th Cav. Co.K
Walker, P.D. TX 13th Vol. 1st Co.K
Walker, P.E. SC 7th Inf. 1st Co.H, Co.A Lt.
Walker, Percival S. VA 16th Cav. Co.E 2nd Lt.
Walker, Perry MO 6th Inf. Co.H
Walker, Perry H. MS 42nd Inf. Co.D
Walker, Persons GA Cobb's Legion Co.A
Walker, Peter AR 5th Inf. Co.E
Walker, Peter LA Mil. 4th Regt.Eur.Brig. Co.D
Walker, Peter MO 1st N.E. Cav. Co.K
Walker, Peter TN 5th (McKenzie's) Cav. Co.G Sgt.
Walker, Peter TX 36th Inf. Co.G
Walker, Peter J. NC 3rd Cav. (41st St.Troops) Co.F
Walker, Peter N. VA 41st Inf. 2nd Co.G
Walker, P.H. KY 1st Inf. Co.I
Walker, P.H. LA Inf.Crescent Regt. Co.A
Walker, P.H. MS Blythe's Bn. (St.Troops) Co.B
Walker, P.H. TN 42nd Inf. Co.B
Walker, P.H. Fort's Scouts,CSA
Walker, Philip AL 29th Inf. Co.K
Walker, Philip VA 146th Mil. Co.E
Walker, Philip H. VA 15th Inf. Co.H
Walker, Phillip MS Lt.Arty. (Madison Lt.Arty.) Richards' Co.

Walker, Phillip TN 20th (Russell's) Cav. Co.C
Walker, Phillip A. TX 13th Cav. Co.F
Walker, Pinkney G.W. NC 45th Inf. Co.E
Walker, P.J. AL 50th Inf. Co.B
Walker, P.J. AR 24th Inf. Co.D
Walker, P.J. AR Inf. Hardy's Regt. Co.C 1st Sgt.
Walker, P.J. FL Lt.Arty. Dyke's Co.
Walker, P.J. FL Kilcrease Lt.Arty. Guidon
Walker, P.J. FL 2nd Inf. Co.K
Walker, P.J. NC 5th Sr.Res. Co.I Sgt.
Walker, Pleasant MO 12th Inf. Co.I
Walker, Pleasant TN 5th (McKenzie's) Cav. Co.G
Walker, Pleasant A. MS 16th Inf. Co.B 2nd Lt.
Walker, P.M. AR 27th Inf. Old Co.C, Co.D
Walker, P.M. MS 2nd St.Cav. Co.K,L
Walker, P.M. MS 7th Cav. Co.E
Walker, P.M. MO 5th Cav. Co.D
Walker, P.M. MO Robertson's Regt.St.Guard Co.12
Walker, Polonzo MO Cav. Hobbs' Co.
Walker, Preston MO Inf. Perkins' Bn. Co.K
Walker, Preston TN 29th Inf. Co.I
Walker, Preston TX 16th Cav. Co.C
Walker, P.S. MS 8th Inf. Co.I
Walker, P.T. AL 9th (Malone's) Cav. Co.C,E
Walker, Purcvell S. VA Cav. Ferguson's Bn. Spurlock's Co. 2nd Lt.
Walker, P.V.B. GA Lt.Arty. 12th Bn. 2nd Co.D
Walker, P.V.B. GA 1st (Ramsey's) Inf. Co.I
Walker, P.W. VA 13th Cav. Co.E
Walker, P.W. VA 5th Bn.Res. Co.A
Walker, R. AL 1st Cav. 2nd Co.A
Walker, R. AL 25th Inf. Co.F
Walker, R. AL 35th Inf. Co.C
Walker, R. AL 38th Inf. Co.H
Walker, R. GA 7th Cav. Co.I
Walker, R. GA 5th Res. Co.F
Walker, R. GA 7th Inf.
Walker, R. GA Inf. 27th Bn. (NonConscr.) Co.C Cpl.
Walker, R. KY Morgan's Men Beck's Co. Cpl.
Walker, R. LA 1st Res. Co.K
Walker, R. SC Lt.Arty. Jeter's Co. (Macbeth Lt.Arty.)
Walker, R. SC 14th Inf. Co.B
Walker, R. TX 37th Cav. Mullins' Co.
Walker, R. TX 5th Field Btty.
Walker, R.A. AL St.Arty. Co.D
Walker, R.A. GA 2nd Inf. Co.D
Walker, R.A. TX Cav. Madison's Regt. Co.B Cpl.
Walker, R.A. TX 9th (Nichols') Inf. Co.K
Walker, R.A. TX Inf. Timmons' Regt. Co.I
Walker, R.A. 7th Conf.Cav. Co.G
Walker, Ralph A. TN 3rd (Lillard's) Mtd.Inf. Co.H
Walker, Randall KY 2nd (Duke's) Cav. Co.H
Walker, Randell KY 5th Cav. Co.H Cpl.
Walker, Ransom AR 11th Cav.
Walker, Ransom NC 8th Inf. Co.F
Walker, Ransome SC 18th Inf. Co.E
Walker, R.A.S. GA 40th Inf. Co.H
Walker, R.B. AL 53rd (Part.Rangers) Co.K
Walker, R.B. AL 18th Inf. Co.F
Walker, R.B. AR 26th Inf. Co.C
Walker, R.B. KY 9th Mtd.Inf. Co.D
Walker, R.B. MS 1st Lt.Arty. Co.H Sgt.
Walker, R.B. MO St.Guard Lt.Col.,Aide
Walker, R.B. TX 23rd Cav. Co.E Sgt.
Walker, R.B. TX 34th Cav. Co.B Sgt.
Walker, R.B. Brush Bn.
Walker, R.C. AL Gid Nelson Lt.Arty.
Walker, R.C. AL Mil. 2nd Regt.Vol. Co.E Cpl.
Walker, R.C. MS 1st Res.Corps
Walker, R.C. TN 4th Inf. Co.B 1st Sgt.
Walker, R.C. TN 51st Inf. Co.G Cpl.
Walker, R.C. TN 51st (Cons.) Inf. Co.G
Walker, Rd. AL 8th Inf. Co.I
Walker, R.D. GA Inf. (Baldwin Inf.) Moore's Co.
Walker, R.D. SC 2nd Inf. Co.I
Walker, R.D. TX 3rd Cav. Co.I Cpl.
Walker, R.D. VA Lt.Arty. Woolfolk's Co.
Walker, R.D.B. SC 11th Inf. 2nd Co.I
Walker, R.E. MS 18th Cav. Co.C
Walker, Redmond G. GA 4th Mil.
Walker, Reese W. VA Lt.Arty. Hardwicke's Co.
Walker, Reuben VA Lt.Arty. B.Z. Price's Co.
Walker, Reuben VA Lt.Arty. W.H. Rice's Co.
Walker, Reuben VA 58th Mil. Co.E
Walker, Reuben B. GA 2nd Bn.S.S. Co.D
Walker, Reuben K. MS Cav. Jeff Davis Legion Co.F
Walker, Reuben Lindsay Gen. & Staff Brig.Gen.
Walker, Reuben Webster TN Cav. 4th Bn. (Branner's) Co.E
Walker, Reziah TN Inf. 1st Bn. (Colms') Co.B,D
Walker, R.F. MS 5th Cav. Co.F
Walker, R.F. MO 3rd Inf. Co.E
Walker, R.F. VA 21st Inf. Co.G
Walker, R.F.M MS 1st Lt.Arty. Co.B
Walker, R.G. LA 15th Inf. Co.I
Walker, R.G. TN 6th (Wheeler's) Cav. Co.E
Walker, R.G. TX 15th Cav. Co.K
Walker, R.H. AL 21st Inf. Co.K
Walker, R.H. AL 30th Inf. Co.K
Walker, R.H. AR 19th (Dockery's) Inf. Co.F
Walker, R.H. LA Inf.Cons.Crescent Regt. Co.K
Walker, R.H. MS 3rd Inf. (St.Troops) Co.C
Walker, R.H. SC 7th Inf. 2nd Co.E
Walker, R.H. TN 2nd (Ashby's) Cav. Co.D
Walker, R.H. TN 30th Inf. Co.A
Walker, R.H. TX 7th Inf. Co.H
Walker, R.H. TX 9th (Young's) Inf. Co.D
Walker, R.H. VA 1st (Farinholt's) Res. Co.A
Walker, Richard AL 15th Inf. Co.F
Walker, Richard AL 39th Inf. Co.G
Walker, Richard AR 2nd Mtd.Rifles Co.F
Walker, Richard GA Cav. 24th Bn. Co.A,C,D
Walker, Richard GA Cav. Newbern's Co. (Coffee Revengers)
Walker, Richard GA 1st (Olmstead's) Inf. 1st Co.A
Walker, Richard GA 1st Bn.S.S. Co.B
Walker, Richard GA 59th Inf. Co.D
Walker, Richard LA Inf.Crescent Regt. Co.C
Walker, Richard MS Inf. 1st Bn.St.Troops Co.H
Walker, Richard MO Inf. 3rd Bn. Co.D
Walker, Richard MO 6th Inf. Co.F
Walker, Richard MO 16th Inf. Co.B Sgt.
Walker, Richard SC 8th Bn.Res. Co.C
Walker, Richard 1st Choctaw & Chickasaw Mtd.Rifles 2nd Co.C Cpl.
Walker, Richard B. VA 15th Inf. Co.D
Walker, Richard C. TX 9th Field Btty. Jr.1st Lt.
Walker, Richard E. MS 9th Inf. Old Co.D
Walker, Richard H. GA 50th Inf. Co.C
Walker, Richard H. TN 2nd (Smith's) Cav.
Walker, Richard H. VA 24th Cav. Co.C
Walker, Richard H. VA Cav. 40th Bn. Co.C
Walker, Richard H. VA 21st Mil. Co.D,E
Walker, Richard M. GA 28th Inf. Co.H
Walker, Richard M. MS 8th Inf. Co.I
Walker, Richard P. GA 44th Inf. Co.K Cpl.
Walker, Richard P. Gen. & Staff AQM
Walker, Richard S. Gen. & Staff Lt.Col.
Walker, Richard T. SC Lt.Arty. Walter's Co. (Washington Arty.)
Walker, Richard W. NC 53rd Inf. Co.K
Walker, Richmond MS 39th Inf. Co.A 1st Lt.
Walker, Richmond D. NC 30th Inf. Co.I
Walker, Riley SC 22nd Inf. Co.F
Walker, Riley T. TX Cav. McCord's Frontier Regt. Co.B
Walker, R.J. AL 18th Inf. Co.G
Walker, R.J. GA 44th Inf. Co.E
Walker, R.J. MS 1st Cav. Co.G
Walker, R.J. MS Cav. Yerger's Regt. Co.B Sgt.
Walker, R.J. MS 44th Inf. Co.A
Walker, R.J. TN Inf. 2nd Cons.Regt. Co.G
Walker, R.J. TN 53rd Inf. Co.I
Walker, R.J. TX 7th Inf. Co.C
Walker, R.J. Gen. & Staff Chap.
Walker, R.K. VA 6th Cav. 1st Co.E
Walker, R.L. AL Gid Nelson Lt.Arty.
Walker, R.L. AL 11th Inf. Co.C
Walker, R.L. TN 9th Inf. Co.C
Walker, R.L. TN 15th Inf. Co.G
Walker, R.L. VA Lt.Arty. Cayce's Co. Capt.
Walker, R.L.D. NC 55th Inf. Co.B
Walker, R.M. AL 4th (Russell's) Cav. Co.F
Walker, R.M. AL 46th Inf. Co.G
Walker, R.M. AR 1st (Monroe's) Cav. Co.D
Walker, R.M. AR Inf. Crawford's Bn. Co.A
Walker, R.M. GA 4th Res. Co.K
Walker, R.M. SC 3rd Cav. Co.F
Walker, R.M. TX Cav. Crump's Regt. Co.D
Walker, Ro Conf.Arty. R.C.M. Page's Bn. 2nd Lt.
Walker, Robert AL Mil. 3rd Vol. Co.E
Walker, Robert AL 9th Inf. Co.K
Walker, Robert AL 12th Inf. Co.D
Walker, Robert AR 34th Inf. Co.B
Walker, Robert GA Cav. 29th Bn. Co.B
Walker, Robert LA Mil. 4th Regt. 1st Brig. 1st Div. Co.I
Walker, Robert LA Inf. 4th Bn. Co.F
Walker, Robert LA 13th Inf. Co.G Cpl.
Walker, Robert LA 13th Inf. Co.I,G
Walker, Robert LA 18th Inf. Co.E Cpl.
Walker, Robert LA 22nd (Cons.) Inf. Co.H
Walker, Robert LA 27th Inf. Co.F
Walker, Robert LA 28th (Gray's) Inf. Co.K
Walker, Robert LA Bickham's Co. (Caddo Mil.)
Walker, Robert MS 1st Cav.Res. Co.E
Walker, Robert MS 15th Inf. Co.B
Walker, Robert MO 1st Cav. Co.C,D
Walker, Robert NC 37th Inf. Co.I

Walker, Robert NC 45th Inf. Co.I
Walker, Robert SC 5th Res. Co.I
Walker, Robert SC 19th Inf. Co.B
Walker, Robert SC 19th Inf. Co.H
Walker, Robert TN 49th Inf. Co.D
Walker, Robert TN 50th Inf. Co.B
Walker, Robert TX 24th Cav. Co.G Sgt.
Walker, Robert VA Cav. Mosby's Regt. (Part.Rangers) Co.B
Walker, Robert VA 22nd Cav. Co.C
Walker, Robert VA Lt.Arty. 13th Bn. Co.B
Walker, Robert VA 21st Inf. Co.H
Walker, Robert VA 30th Inf. Co.C
Walker, Robert Mtd.Spies & Guides Madison's Co.
Walker, Robert Conf.Inf. Tucker's Regt. Co.G Cpl.
Walker, Robert A. AR 15th Inf. Co.F
Walker, Robert A. MS 3rd Inf. Co.D
Walker, Robert A. TX 6th Cav. Co.H
Walker, Robert A. 1st Conf.Inf. 2nd Co.G
Walker, Robert Brown MO 8th Inf. Co.E
Walker, Robert C. VA 3rd Cav. Co.D
Walker, Robert C. VA 26th Inf. 2nd Co.B Cpl.
Walker, Robert C. VA 92nd Mil. Co.A
Walker, Robert D. GA 1st (Olmstead's) Inf. Co.K Capt.
Walker, Robert D. NC 6th Cav. (65th St.Troops) Co.E
Walker, Robert D. NC Cav. 7th Bn. Co.D,E
Walker, Robert D. Gen. & Staff, Comsy.Dept. Capt.
Walker, Robert E. MO 8th Cav. Co.D
Walker, Robert E. NC 1st Arty. (10th St.Troops) Co.G 1st Lt.
Walker, Robt. E. Gen. & Staff 1st Lt.
Walker, Robert F. MO Cav. Freeman's Regt. Co.F
Walker, Robert H. LA Inf. 11th Bn. Co.B
Walker, Robert H. MS 8th Inf. Co.C
Walker, Robert H. TN Cav. 4th Bn. (Branner's) Co.C
Walker, Robert H. TN 19th Inf. Co.E
Walker, Robert H. TX 24th Cav. Co.D 1st Sgt.
Walker, Robert H. VA 55th Inf. Co.C
Walker, Robert J. AL Lt.Arty. 2nd Bn.
Walker, Robert J. MS 6th Inf. Co.G,H
Walker, Robert J. MS 15th Inf. Co.B
Walker, Robert J. TN 41st Inf. Co.H Cpl.
Walker, Robert J. TX 3rd Cav. Co.K
Walker, Robert J. VA Lt.Arty. Snead's Co.
Walker, Robert L. LA 11th Inf. Co.E
Walker, Robert L. NC 6th Inf. Co.K Sgt.
Walker, Robert L. SC 5th Inf. 1st Co.B
Walker, Robt. M. AR 15th (Johnson's) Inf. Co.D Capt.
Walker, Robert M. GA 10th Cav. (St.Guards) Co.B 1st Sgt.
Walker, Robert M. GA 2nd Res. Co.B 1st Lt.
Walker, Robert M. MS 2nd Inf. Co.D
Walker, Robert M. TN 40th Inf. Co.G 1st Lt.
Walker, Robert M. TX Cav. Border's Regt. Co.G
Walker, Robert M. 3rd Conf.Cav. Co.I Sgt.
Walker, Robert P. AL 38th Inf. Co.G
Walker, Robert P. LA 27th Inf. Co.C
Walker, Robert P. TX 7th Cav. Co.H
Walker, Robert P. VA 6th Inf. Co.G
Walker, Robt. P. Gen. & Staff 1st Lt.,ADC
Walker, Robert R. AL 12th Cav. Co.E Sgt.
Walker, Robert R. GA 8th Inf. Co.G
Walker, Robert S. AL Jeff Davis Arty. 2nd Lt.
Walker, Robert S. AL 43rd Inf. Co.I 1st Lt.
Walker, Robert S. AR Lt.Arty. 5th Btty. 2nd Lt.
Walker, Robert S. LA 5th Inf. New Co.A Cpl.
Walker, Robert S. NC 2nd Cav. (19th St.Troops) Co.K
Walker, Robert S. NC 1st Arty. (10th St.Troops) Co.G
Walker, Robert S. TN 53rd Inf. Co.K 2nd Lt.
Walker, Robert T. AR 14th (McCarver's) Inf.
Walker, Robert T. NC 45th Inf. Co.G 2nd Lt.
Walker, Robert T. NC McDugald's Co.
Walker, Robert W. FL 1st Cav. Co.H
Walker, Robert W. MS 34th Inf. Co.I
Walker, Robert W. TX 23rd Cav. Co.E
Walker, Robert W. TX 7th Inf. Co.K 1st Sgt.
Walker, Robert W. VA 19th Cav. Co.E
Walker, Robert W. VA 2nd Arty. Co.D
Walker, Robert W. VA Inf. 22nd Bn. Co.D
Walker, Robert Y. NC 2nd Cav. (19th St.Troops) Co.K
Walker, Robinson D. VA Arty. Fleet's Co.
Walker, Robinson D. VA 55th Inf. Co.B
Walker, Ro. F. VA Lt.Arty. W.P. Carter's Co.
Walker, R.P. MS 2nd Cav. Co.C 1st Sgt.
Walker, R.P. MS 5th Inf. Co.C
Walker, R.P. VA Lt.Arty. Grandy's Co.
Walker, R.R. TX 37th Cav. Co.K
Walker, R.S. MS 28th Cav. Co.C
Walker, R.S. SC 5th Cav. Co.D
Walker, R.S. SC Cav. 17th Bn. Co.A
Walker, R.S. SC Mil.Arty. 1st Regt. Tupper's Co.
Walker, R.S. TN 8th (Smith's) Cav. Co.A Cpl.
Walker, R.S. TN Inf. 4th Cons.Regt. Co.K
Walker, R.S. TN 52nd Inf. Co.A 2nd Lt.
Walker, R.S. TX 5th Field Btty.
Walker, R.S. 1st Conf.Eng.Troops Co.K
Walker, R.T. AR 27th Inf. New Co.C
Walker, R.T. GA 13th Inf. Co.K
Walker, R.T. MS 2nd Cav. Co.C
Walker, R.T. MS 5th Inf. (St.Troops) Co.C
Walker, R.T. SC Mil.Arty. 1st Regt. Walter's Co.
Walker, R.T. TN 46th Inf. Co.K
Walker, R.T. TX Inf. Currie's Co.
Walker, Rudesill F. NC 4th Inf. Co.A
Walker, Ruffin B. LA 7th Inf. Co.H Sgt.
Walker, Rufus AL 38th Inf. Co.D
Walker, Rufus TN 5th (McKenzie's) Cav. Co.A
Walker, Rufus S. TN 48th (Voorhies') Inf. Co.C 2nd Lt.
Walker, Runion A. VA Hvy.Arty. Coleman's Co.
Walker, Russell F. VA 45th Inf. Co.C
Walker, R.W. AR 7th Inf. Co.H
Walker, R.W. KY Cav. 2nd Bn. (Dortch's) Co.D
Walker, R.W. KY 3rd Cav. Co.H Cpl.
Walker, R.W. MS 1st (Johnston's) Inf. Co.E
Walker, R.W. MS Inf. 2nd St.Troops Co.A
Walker, R.W. TN 2nd (Ashby's) Cav. Co.I
Walker, R.W. TN 9th Inf. Co.G
Walker, R.W. TX 14th Inf. Co.I
Walker, S. AL 8th Inf. Co.G
Walker, S. AL 17th Inf. Co.D
Walker, S. AL 25th Inf. Co.E
Walker, S. GA Cav. 20th Bn. Co.E
Walker, S. GA 1st Troops & Defences (Macon) Co.D
Walker, S. GA 7th Inf.
Walker, S. KY 3rd Mtd.Inf. 1st Co.F
Walker, S. LA Inf. 7th Bn. Co.B
Walker, S. MS 46th Inf. Co.H
Walker, S. NC 5th Sr.Res. Co.C
Walker, S. TN 21st & 22nd (Cons.) Cav. Co.A 1st Sgt.
Walker, S.A. AR 4th Inf. Co.K
Walker, S.A. GA 56th Inf. Co.B
Walker, S.A. MS 7th Cav. Co.I
Walker, S.A. MS Taylor's Co. (Boomerangs)
Walker, S.A. NC 31st Inf. Co.B
Walker, S.A. TX 7th Inf. Co.G
Walker, S.A.G. AL 5th Cav. Co.E Sgt.
Walker, Sam KY Lt.Arty. Cobb's Co.
Walker, Samson AR 1st Vol. Simington's Co.
Walker, Samuel AL 50th Inf. Co.K
Walker, Samuel GA 4th Inf. Co.H 2nd Lt.
Walker, Samuel GA 49th Inf. Co.F
Walker, Samuel KY 1st (Butler's) Cav. Co.A
Walker, Samuel LA 13th Inf. Co.G
Walker, Samuel MS 11th (Cons.) Cav. Co.F
Walker, Samuel MS Cav. 17th Bn. Co.A
Walker, Samuel NC 53rd Inf. Co.E 1st Lt.
Walker, Samuel NC Walker's Bn. Thomas' Legion Co.G
Walker, Samuel SC 15th Inf. Co.D
Walker, Samuel TN 1st (Carter's) Cav. Co.A
Walker, Samuel TN 1st (Carter's) Cav. Co.H
Walker, Samuel TN Cav. 1st Bn. (McNairy's) Co.E Cpl.
Walker, Samuel TN 22nd (Barteau's) Cav. Co.C 1st Sgt.
Walker, Samuel TN 1st (Turney's) Inf. Co.H
Walker, Samuel TN 38th Inf. 1st Co.K
Walker, Samuel TN 40th Inf. Co.I 1st Lt.
Walker, Samuel TN 50th Inf. Co.B
Walker, Samuel TX 2nd Cav. Co.K
Walker, Samuel VA 9th Cav. Co.I
Walker, Samuel VA 40th Inf. Co.F
Walker, Samuel VA 40th Inf. Co.K
Walker, Samuel A. SC 14th Inf. Co.G Sgt.
Walker, Samuel A. VA 4th Cav. Co.B
Walker, Samuel A. VA 14th Cav. Co.H
Walker, Samuel B. MS 1st (Johnston's) Inf. Co.C
Walker, Samuel B. MS Inf. 2nd Bn. Co.F 1st Lt.
Walker, Samuel B. MS 48th Inf. Co.F 1st Lt.
Walker, Samuel B. TN Cav. 2nd Bn. (Biffle's) Co.C
Walker, Samuel B. TN 13th Inf. Co.K
Walker, Samuel D.S. LA Inf. 1st Sp.Bn. (Wheat's) Old Co.D Cpl.
Walker, Samuel E. VA 2nd Arty. Co.D
Walker, Samuel E. VA 14th Inf. Co.E
Walker, Samuel E. VA Inf. 22nd Bn. Co.D Sgt.
Walker, Sam'l E. VA Inf. 44th Bn. Co.D
Walker, Samuel F. GA 17th Inf. Co.C
Walker, Samuel F. VA 6th Cav. Co.H
Walker, Samuel F.C. VA Lt.Arty. Brander's Co.
Walker, Samuel H. FL Inf. 2nd Bn. Co.B

Walker, Samuel H. GA 57th Inf. Co.A Cpl.
Walker, Samuel H. VA 7th Cav. Co.D
Walker, Samuel H. VA 14th Inf. 1st Co.G 1st Lt.
Walker, Samuel H. VA 21st Inf. Co.G
Walker, Samuel H. VA 24th Inf. Co.B
Walker, Samuel H. VA 97th Mil. Co.F
Walker, Samuel J. KY 2nd Mtd.Inf. Co.B
Walker, Samuel J. LA 9th Inf. Co.D
Walker, Samuel J. NC 1st Inf. Co.C
Walker, Samuel J. NC 51st Inf. Co.A Cpl.
Walker, Samuel J. VA 40th Inf. Co.F
Walker, Samuel J.B. MS 36th Inf. Co.E Cpl.
Walker, Samuel L. GA Cav. 2nd Bn. Co.B
Walker, Samuel L. MS 9th Inf. Old Co.I Lt.
Walker, Samuel L. MS 42nd Inf. Co.B
Walker, Samuel M.V. VA 5th Inf. Co.C Cpl.
Walker, Samuel N. MS 2nd St.Cav. Co.K Surg.
Walker, Samuel P. AR 15th (Johnson's) Inf. Co.A Capt.
Walker, Samuel P. MS Inf. 5th Bn. Co.A
Walker, Samuel P. MS 43rd Inf. Co.I
Walker, Samuel P. TX 24th Cav. Co.D
Walker, Samuel R. GA 12th (Robinson's) Cav. (St.Guards) Co.E
Walker, Samuel T. VA 10th Inf. Maj.
Walker, Samuel T. Conf.Cav. Wood's Regt. Co.K
Walker, Samuel W. MS Graves' Co. (Copiah Horse Guards)
Walker, Samuel W. MS 16th Inf. Co.B
Walker, Samuel W. MS 36th Inf. Co.G
Walker, Samuel W. NC 4th Inf.
Walker, Sam W. MS 1st (Percy's) Inf. Co.A
Walker, Sanford A. AL 5th Inf. Co.I
Walker, S.B.W. TX 37th Cav. Co.B
Walker, S.C. AL 30th Inf. Co.C
Walker, S.C. LA 28th (Thomas') Inf. Co.F
Walker, S.C. TX 11th Cav. Co.H
Walker, S.D.S. LA Inf. 7th Bn. Co.B Cpl.
Walker, S.D.S. LA 15th Inf. Co.I Sgt.
Walker, S.E. GA 5th Res. Co.D
Walker, Seaborn AL 5th Inf. New Co.I
Walker, Seaborn LA 12th Inf. Co.D
Walker, Seaborn J. GA 9th Inf. (St.Guards) Co.B Cpl.
Walker, Seth B. TX 11th Inf. Co.K
Walker, Seth J. TN 5th (McKenzie's) Cav. Co.D
Walker, Seth M. TN 3rd (Lillard's) Mtd.Inf. Co.H
Walker, S.F. AL 2nd Cav. Co.D
Walker, S.F. AL 42nd Inf. Co.F
Walker, S.F. NC 1st Arty. (10th St.Troops) Co.E
Walker, S.G. LA Inf. 4th Bn. Co.D Sgt.
Walker, S.G. LA Inf. Pelican Regt. Co.F Sgt.
Walker, S.G. NC 12th Inf.
Walker, S.H. AR 12th Inf. Co.G Sgt.
Walker, S.H. KY 7th Cav. Co.K
Walker, S.H. MO 11th Inf. Co.A
Walker, S.H. TN 21st (Wilson's) Cav. Co.I
Walker, S.H. TN 27th Inf. Co.K
Walker, S.H. TX 5th Inf. Co.G
Walker, Shade GA Inf. (Collier Guards) Collier's Co.
Walker, Sidney LA 19th Inf. Co.B
Walker, Sidney NC 47th Inf. Co.K
Walker, Sidney A. NC 44th Inf. Co.G
Walker, Sidney M. TN 44th Inf. Co.E
Walker, Sidney M. TN 44th (Cons.) Inf. Co.B
Walker, Sila D. GA 2nd Inf. Co.B
Walker, Silas AL 15th Inf. Co.C
Walker, Silas KY 5th Mtd.Inf. Co.D
Walker, Silas MO 8th Cav. Co.D
Walker, Silas SC 7th Cav. Co.E 1st Lt.
Walker, Silas SC Cav.Bn. Holcombe Legion Co.C 1st Lt.
Walker, Silas VA 8th Cav. Co.A
Walker, Silas C. MS 38th Cav. Co.K
Walker, Silas D. GA 48th Inf. Co.I
Walker, Silas H. VA 1st Cav. Co.E 2nd Lt.
Walker, Silas J. NC 60th Inf. Co.G
Walker, Silas L. GA 19th Inf. Co.G
Walker, Simeon AL 41st Inf. Co.G
Walker, Simeon AR 9th Inf. Co.D
Walker, Simeon GA Inf. (Muscogee Guards) Thornton's Co.
Walker, Simeon L. KY 8th Cav. Co.K
Walker, Simeon R. AR 1st (Dobbin's) Cav. Co.B
Walker, Simon H. KY 3rd Cav. Co.C
Walker, Singleton V. MS 37th Inf. Co.B
Walker, S.J. AL 4th Res. Co.H
Walker, S.J. FL 1st (Res.) Inf. Co.F 2nd Lt.
Walker, S.J. GA Mil. 8th Regt. Co.K
Walker, S.J. MS Cav. 3rd Bn. (Ashcraft's) Co.D
Walker, S.J. MO Cav. Freeman's Regt. Co.I
Walker, S.J. NC 12th Inf. Co.I
Walker, S.J. SC Mil. Trenholm's Co. Cpl.
Walker, S.J. TN 16th Inf. Co.G
Walker, S.J. TN 26th Inf. Co.E Fifer
Walker, S.J. TX 10th Cav. Co.F 2nd Lt.
Walker, S.L. GA 5th Cav. Co.E
Walker, S.L. GA 53rd Inf. Co.F
Walker, S.L. KY 9th Mtd.Inf. Co.A
Walker, S.M. AL Talladega Cty.Res. G.M. Gamble's Co.
Walker, S.M. TN Inf. Spencer's Co.
Walker, Smith MS 40th Inf. Co.B
Walker, S.N. MS 7th Cav. Co.E
Walker, S. Nic Gen. & Staff Surg.
Walker, Snoden B. NC 3rd Arty. (40th St.Troops) Co.C
Walker, Sol SC Lt.Arty. Beauregard's Co.
Walker, Solomon GA Siege Arty. 28th Bn. Co.K
Walker, Solomon MS 6th Inf. Co.H Cpl.
Walker, S.P. AL 48th Inf. Co.G
Walker, S.P. AR 19th Inf. Co.B
Walker, S.P. GA 59th Inf. Co.G
Walker, S.P. MS 14th (Cons.) Inf. Co.H
Walker, S.P. Humes' Staff Capt.,AAAG
Walker, Spencer AL 5th Cav. Co.E
Walker, S.R. AR 1st Cav. Co.B
Walker, S.R. AR 6th Inf. Co.G
Walker, S.R. TX Loc.Def. Perry's Co. (Fort Bend Scouts) Sgt.
Walker, S.S. GA 46th Inf. Co.H
Walker, S.S. SC 15th Inf. Co.F 1st Lt.
Walker, S.S. Gen. & Staff AQM
Walker, S.T. SC 7th Cav. Co.B Sgt.
Walker, S.T. SC Cav. 19th Bn. Co.C Capt.
Walker, S.T. SC Rutledge Mtd.Riflemen & Horse Arty. Trenholm's Co. Sgt.
Walker, S.T. TN 49th Inf. Co.D
Walker, S.T. Inf. Bailey's Cons.Regt. Co.L
Walker, S.T. TX 24th Cav. Co.B
Walker, Stanley KY 8th Cav. Co.D
Walker, Stephen AR 15th (N.W.) Inf. Emergency Co.I
Walker, Stephen LA 28th (Gray's) Inf. Co.G Cpl.
Walker, Stephen VA 6th Bn.Res. Co.D
Walker, Stephen A. NC 45th Inf. Co.H
Walker, Stephen D. MS 42nd Inf. Co.I
Walker, Stephen D. TX 10th Inf. Co.B Sgt.
Walker, Stephen M. GA 39th Inf. Co.G Fifer
Walker, Stephen W. TN Cav. Welcker's Bn. Kincaid's Co.
Walker, Steven TX 36th Cav. Co.E
Walker, Steven 1st Cherokee Mtd.Vol. 1st Co.E, 2nd Co.A Cpl.
Walker, S.V. MS 34th Inf. Co.B
Walker, S.W. AL 46th Inf. Co.G
Walker, S.W. GA 8th Inf. Co.C Music.
Walker, S.W. GA Inf. 19th Bn. (St.Guards) Co.C
Walker, S.W. NC 1st Cav. (9th St.Troops) Co.E Cpl.
Walker, S.W. TN 43rd Inf. Co.F
Walker, S.W. TX Cav. Wells' Regt. Co.K
Walker, S.W. VA 13th Cav. Co.E
Walker, S.W. Brush Bn.
Walker, Sylvanius LA 15th Inf. Co.I
Walker, Sylvanus LA Inf. 1st Sp.Bn. (Wheat's) Old Co.D
Walker, Sylvester TN 5th (McKenzie's) Cav. Co.G Sgt.
Walker, Sylvester TN 29th Inf. Co.D Cpl.
Walker, S.Z. AL 31st Inf. Co.C,B
Walker, T. GA 8th Cav. New Co.D
Walker, T. MS 2nd Cav. Co.K
Walker, T. MS 46th Inf. Co.H
Walker, T. NC 3rd Inf. Co.A
Walker, T. TX Cav. Baird's Regt. Co.G
Walker, T. VA 1st Cav. Co.E
Walker, T. Sap. & Min.,CSA
Walker, T.A. AL 5th Inf. New Co.I
Walker, T.A. SC 3rd Res. Co.B
Walker, T.A. SC 5th Res. Co.D
Walker, T.A. TN 7th (Duckworth's) Cav. Co.M 1st Sgt.
Walker, T.A. TN 16th (Logwood's) Cav. Co.E
Walker, T.A. TN Lt.Arty. Sparkman's Co. 1st Sgt.
Walker, Talbot AL 3rd Inf. Co.H
Walker, Tandy NC 30th Inf. Co.H
Walker, Tandy SC 3rd Inf. Co.F Capt.
Walker, Tandy TN 41st Inf.
Walker, Tandy VA 24th Inf. Co.A
Walker, Tandy 1st Choctaw & Chickasaw Mtd.Rifles Col.
Walker, Tandy W. GA 40th Inf. Co.C
Walker, Tapley L. GA 21st Inf. Co.C
Walker, Taylor GA Cav. Bond's Co. (St.Guards)
Walker, Taylor 1st Conf.Eng.Troops Co.C
Walker, T.B. GA 2nd Inf. Co.A
Walker, T.B. SC 3rd Bn.Res. Co.B
Walker, T.B. SC 6th Res. Co.H Cpl.
Walker, T.B. SC Manigault's Bn.Vol. Co.C
Walker, T.B. TN 5th (McKenzie's) Cav. Co.A
Walker, T.B. TN 3rd (Clack's) Inf. Co.B
Walker, T.B. TN 31st Inf. Co.C
Walker, T.B. TN 31st Inf. Co.I
Walker, T.B. VA 3rd Lt.Arty. Co.D

Walker, T.B. VA 21st Inf. Co.F Sgt.
Walker, T.C. AL 10th Inf. Co.D
Walker, T.C. AL 27th Inf. Co.E
Walker, T.C. NC 57th Inf. Co.E
Walker, T.C. TN 15th (Cons.) Cav. Co.A
Walker, T.C. TX Arty. Douglas' Co.
Walker, T.C. Mead's Conf.Cav. Co.F
Walker, T. Clark FL Inf. 2nd Bn. Co.A
Walker, T.E. GA 3rd Bn. (St.Guards) Co.F
Walker, T.E. MS 10th Cav. Co.H
Walker, T.E. NC 4th Sr.Res. Co.A
Walker, T.E. Conf.Cav. Baxter's Bn. Co.A
Walker, T.F. GA Cav. 19th Bn. Co.B
Walker, T.G. VA Inf. 25th Bn. Co.G
Walker, T.H. AL 12th Cav. Co.D,B
Walker, T.H. MS 38th Cav. Co.E
Walker, T.H. MS 9th Inf. Old Co.H, New Co.A
Walker, T.H. VA 3rd Cav. Co.H
Walker, Thaddeus M. NC 16th Inf. Co.D Sgt.
Walker, Themp NC 4th Bn.Jr.Res. Co.C
Walker, Theophilus AL 1st Cav. Co.H
Walker, T.H.H. LA Washington Arty.Bn. Co.2
Walker, Thomas AL 4th (Russell's) Cav. Co.I
Walker, Thomas AL 11th Cav. Co.F
Walker, Thomas AL 11th Cav. Co.I
Walker, Thomas AL 29th Inf. Co.F
Walker, Thomas AL 44th Inf. Co.F
Walker, Thomas AL 62nd Inf. Co.D
Walker, Thomas FL 3rd Inf. Co.I
Walker, Thomas FL 8th Inf. Co.C
Walker, Thomas GA 2nd Cav. (St.Guards) Co.A
Walker, Thomas GA 3rd Cav. Co.D
Walker, Thomas GA 1st (Olmstead's) Inf. Co.D
Walker, Thomas GA Inf. 5th Bn. (St.Guards) Co.D Cpl.
Walker, Thomas GA 17th Inf. Maj.
Walker, Thomas GA 20th Inf.
Walker, Thomas GA 26th Inf. Co.B
Walker, Thomas GA 64th Inf. Co.D
Walker, Thomas LA 1st (Nelligan's) Inf. Co.H
Walker, Thomas LA 16th Inf. Co.G
Walker, Thomas LA 17th Inf. Co.A
Walker, Thomas LA Mil. Irish Regt. Co.F
Walker, Thomas MS 1st Cav. Co.F
Walker, Thomas MS 2nd Cav. Co.E
Walker, Thomas MS 5th Cav. Co.D Sgt.
Walker, Thomas MS 34th Inf. Co.I
Walker, Thomas MO Lt.Arty. 13th Btty.
Walker, Thomas MO 1st & 4th Cons.Inf. Co.B
Walker, Thomas MO 4th Inf. Co.F
Walker, Thomas NC 2nd Arty. (36th St.Troops) Co.H
Walker, Thomas NC 1st Jr.Res. Co.B
Walker, Thomas NC Inf. 2nd Bn. Co.H
Walker, Thomas NC 4th Inf. Co.G
Walker, Thomas NC 7th Inf. Co.G
Walker, Thomas NC 34th Inf. Co.I
Walker, Thomas TN 3rd (Lillard's) Mtd.Inf. Co.F
Walker, Thomas TN 21st Inf. Co.A
Walker, Thomas TX 8th Cav. Co.K
Walker, Thomas TX Cav. Frontier Bn. Co.B
Walker, Thomas TX Cav. Mann's Regt. Co.A,E
Walker, Thomas TX Cav. Mann's Bn. Co.A
Walker, Thomas TX Cav. McCord's Frontier Regt. Co.I
Walker, Thomas TX 1st Lt.Arty.
Walker, Thomas TX Arty. Douglas' Co.
Walker, Thomas TX 13th Vol. Co.H
Walker, Thomas VA 2nd Inf.Loc.Def. Co.C
Walker, Thomas VA 2nd Inf.Loc.Def. Co.D
Walker, Thomas VA 3rd Inf. Co.A
Walker, Thomas VA 6th Inf. Co.I
Walker, Thomas VA Inf. 6th Bn.Loc.Def. Co.C,A
Walker, Thomas VA Inf. 25th Bn. Co.G
Walker, Thomas VA 54th Mil. Co.E,F
Walker, Thomas VA 190th Mil. Co.G Sgt.
Walker, Thomas A. GA 12th Inf. Co.G
Walker, Thomas A. MS 11th Inf. Co.E
Walker, Thomas A. VA 3rd Cav. Co.A
Walker, Thomas A. VA Arty. Paris' Co.
Walker, Thomas B. GA 57th Inf. Co.A
Walker, Thomas B. KY 1st (Helm's) Cav. Co.I
Walker, Thomas B. KY 11th Cav. Co.E
Walker, Thomas B. KY 1st Inf. Co.I Sgt.
Walker, Thomas B. MS 34th Inf. Co.E
Walker, Thomas B. VA 24th Inf. Co.D
Walker, Thomas C. LA 14th Inf. Co.F
Walker, Thomas C. NC Walker's Bn. Thomas' Legion Co.G
Walker, Thomas C. TN 1st (Carter's) Cav. Co.H
Walker, Thomas C. VA 55th Inf. Co.F
Walker, Thomas C. VA Res.Forces Thurston's Co.
Walker, Thomas D. AR 33rd Inf. Co.G
Walker, Thomas D. NC 4th Cav. (59th St.Troops) Co.G
Walker, Thomas E. GA Inf. Fuller's Co.
Walker, Thomas E. NC 6th Cav. (65th St.Troops) Co.E,D
Walker, Thomas E. NC Cav. 7th Bn. Co.D,E
Walker, Thomas F. LA 6th Inf. Co.E Capt.
Walker, Thomas F. VA 36th Inf. 2nd Co.G 1st Lt.
Walker, Thomas F. 2nd Vol. Brig. Maj.,AAG
Walker, Thos. F. Gen. & Staff Asst.Surg.
Walker, Thomas G. VA Lt.Arty. Ellett's Co.
Walker, Thomas G. VA 28th Inf. Co.B 1st Sgt.
Walker, Thomas H. AR 1st Vol. Co.F Cpl.
Walker, Thomas H. GA 6th Inf. Co.E Sgt.
Walker, Thomas H. GA 30th Inf. Co.H
Walker, Thomas H. MS 7th Inf. Co.H
Walker, Thomas H. MO Cav. Fristoe's Regt. Co.E
Walker, Thomas H. TN 19th Inf. Co.I Capt.
Walker, Thomas H. VA 2nd Arty. Co.E 1st Sgt.
Walker, Thomas H. VA 18th Inf. Co.I
Walker, Thomas J. AL 10th Inf. Co.G 2nd Lt.
Walker, Thomas J. AL 63rd Inf. Co.G
Walker, Thomas J. GA 31st Inf. Co.C
Walker, Thomas J. GA 57th Inf. Co.C
Walker, Thomas J. LA Inf.Cons.Crescent Regt. Co.H Cpl.
Walker, Thomas J. MS 1st Lt.Arty. Co.D
Walker, Thomas J. MS 3rd Inf. Co.A
Walker, Thomas J. MS 3rd Inf. Co.C
Walker, Thomas J. MS 26th Inf. Co.F
Walker, Thomas J. MO 3rd Inf. Co.C Sgt.
Walker, Thos. J. MO St.Guard
Walker, Thomas J. NC 3rd Cav. (41st St.Troops) Co.K
Walker, Thomas J. TN 6th (Wheeler's) Cav. Co.H
Walker, Thomas J. TN Cav. 7th Bn. (Bennett's) Co.D
Walker, Thomas J. TN 21st (Wilson's) Cav. Co.E
Walker, Thomas J. TN 22nd (Barteau's) Cav. Co.F
Walker, Thomas J. TN Inf. 23rd Bn. Co.D
Walker, Thomas J. TN 41st Inf. Co.F
Walker, Thomas J. TX 17th Cav. Co.I
Walker, Thomas J. TX 18th Inf. Co.L
Walker, Thomas K. SC Inf. Hampton Legion Co.A
Walker, Thomas L. LA 28th (Gray's) Inf. Co.I
Walker, Thomas L. MS 2nd Inf. Co.F
Walker, Thomas L. VA 3rd Cav. Co.D
Walker, Thos. L. Gen. & Staff Pvt.Physician
Walker, Thomas M. NC 4th Inf. Co.A
Walker, Thomas M. SC 1st (McCreary's) Inf. Co.G
Walker, Thomas M. TN Cav. 9th Bn. (Gantt's) Co.E Sgt.
Walker, Thomas M. VA 55th Inf. Co.A
Walker, Thomas N. VA 34th Inf. Co.K Sgt.
Walker, Thomas P. NC 46th Inf. Co.C
Walker, Thomas P. SC 15th Inf. Co.A
Walker, Thomas R. MS 3rd Inf. Co.A Sgt.
Walker, Thomas R. MS 39th Inf. Co.B Cpl.
Walker, Thomas R. TX 13th Cav. Co.F
Walker, Thomas R. TX Cav. Border's Regt. Co.E
Walker, Thomas R. VA 61st Inf. Co.H
Walker, Thomas S. Conf.Inf. 8th Bn. Co.C
Walker, Thomas T. NC 24th Inf. Co.A 1st Sgt.
Walker, Thomas T. TX 1st Bn.S.S. Co.A,E
Walker, Thomas W. KY 8th Cav. Co.K
Walker, Thomas W. MS 2nd Part.Rangers Co.F
Walker, Thomas W. VA 3rd Cav. Co.A Cpl.
Walker, Thomas W. VA 3rd Arty. Co.B
Walker, Thompson L. VA Inf. 23rd Bn. Co.B
Walker, Tilman SC 1st (McCreary's) Inf. Co.G
Walker, Tipton Eng.,CSA Capt.,Asst.Eng.
Walker, T.J. AR 30th Inf. Co.C 2nd Lt.
Walker, T.J. GA 1st (Fannin's) Res. Co.F
Walker, T.J. GA 5th Res. Co.A
Walker, T.J. GA Inf. 19th Bn. (St.Guards) Co.C
Walker, T.J. GA 32nd Inf. Co.B
Walker, T.J. GA 59th Inf. Co.H
Walker, T.J. GA Phillips' Legion Co.A
Walker, T.J. LA 4th Cav. Cpl.
Walker, T.J. LA Miles' Legion Co.D
Walker, T.J. MD Cav. 2nd Bn. Co.D
Walker, T.J. MS 2nd St.Cav. Co.E
Walker, T.J. MS St.Cav. 2nd Bn. (Harris') Co.C
Walker, T.J. MS 7th Cav. Co.I
Walker, T.J. MS 8th Inf. Co.A
Walker, T.J. SC 1st Arty. Co.B
Walker, T.J. SC 6th Inf. 2nd Co.H
Walker, T.J. SC 18th Inf. Co.G
Walker, T.J. TN 7th Cav.
Walker, T.J. TN 21st & 22nd (Cons.) Cav. Co.C
Walker, T.J. TN 21st & 22nd (Cons.) Cav. Co.E Sgt.
Walker, T.J. TN Inf. 1st Cons.Regt. Co.E
Walker, T.J. TN 9th Inf. Co.C
Walker, T.J. TN 24th Inf. Co.I
Walker, T.J. TX 5th Cav. Co.E

Walker, T.J. TX Cav. Giddings' Bn. Pickerell's Co.
Walker, T.J. TX Inf. 1st St.Troops Martin's Co.A
Walker, T.J. TX 14th Inf. 1st Co.K
Walker, T.J. VA Inf. 25th Bn. Co.G
Walker, T.J. VA 42nd Inf. Co.D Sgt.
Walker, T.J. Gen. & Staff AASurg.
Walker, T.L. MO Inf. 1st Regt.St.Guard Co.C 2nd Lt.
Walker, T.L. VA 12th Cav. Co.D
Walker, T.L. VA 82nd Mil. Co.D Clerk
Walker, T.M. GA Inf. 10th Bn. Co.A
Walker, T.M. TN 1st (Carter's) Cav. Co.B
Walker, T.M. TX 2nd Inf. Co.I
Walker, Tos MO Cav. Ford's Bn. Co.F
Walker, T.P. AL Cav. Forrest's Regt.
Walker, T.P. TN 31st Inf. Co.G 2nd Lt.
Walker, T.R. AL 22nd Inf. Co.E
Walker, T.S. AL 25th Inf. Co.F
Walker, T.S. NC Allen's Co. (Loc.Def.)
Walker, T.S. TX 9th (Nichols') Inf. Co.I
Walker, Tuman GA 27th Inf. Co.K
Walker, T.W. AL 36th Inf. Co.B Sgt.
Walker, T.W. GA 1st Cav. Co.A
Walker, T.W. GA Cav. 20th Bn. Co.A
Walker, T.W. MS St.Cav. 2nd Bn. (Harris') Co.C
Walker, T.W. MO Cav. Freeman's Regt. Co.I
Walker, T.W. TN 14th (Neely's) Cav. Co.F
Walker, T.W. TN 22nd (Barteau's) Cav. Co.C
Walker, T.W. TN 8th Inf. Co.H 2nd Lt.
Walker, T.W. VA 14th Inf. Co.F
Walker, T.W. VA Inf. 44th Bn. Co.D
Walker, T.W. Mead's Conf.Cav. Co.H Cpl.
Walker, T.W. 9th Conf.Inf. Co.H
Walker, U. LA 7th Cav. Co.A
Walker, U.G.M. TX 16th Inf. Surg.
Walker, U.G.M. TX Inf. Yarbrough's Co. (Smith Cty.Lt.Inf.) Surg.
Walker, Underwood VA 60th Inf. 2nd Co.H
Walker, Uriah FL 1st Cav. Co.I
Walker, Uriah FL 1st (Res.) Inf. Co.A
Walker, U.V. Gen. & Staff Surg.
Walker, Valentine VA 3rd Cav. Co.D 1st Lt.
Walker, Vance AR 15th (N.W.) Inf. Emergency Co.I
Walker, Vergil NC 20th Inf. Co.E
Walker, Vincent V. AL Cp. of Instr. Talladega Co.B
Walker, Virgil H. NC 52nd Inf. Co.K 2nd Lt.
Walker, Virgil J. TX 5th Inf. Co.C
Walker, W. AL 7th Cav. Co.G
Walker, W. AL 11th Cav. Co.F
Walker, W. AL Talladega Cty.Res. D.M. Reid's Co. Sgt.
Walker, W. AL Cp. of Instr. Talladega
Walker, W. FL Conscr.
Walker, W. KY 1st (Helm's) Cav. Old Co.G
Walker, W. LA 4th Cav. Co.C
Walker, W. MS 41st Inf. Co.C
Walker, W. NC 5th Sr.Res. Co.I
Walker, W. NC 26th Inf. Co.C
Walker, W. SC 1st Cav. Co.C
Walker, W. SC Lt.Arty. 3rd (Palmetto) Bn. Co.G
Walker, W. TN 9th Inf. Co.H
Walker, W. TN Inf. Sowell's Detach.
Walker, W. TX 35th (Brown's) Cav.
Walker, W. TX Inf. Timmons' Regt. Co.G
Walker, W. TX Waul's Legion Co.A
Walker, W. VA 10th Inf. Co.B
Walker, W.A. AL 7th Cav. Co.F,A Sgt.
Walker, W.A. AL 13th Bn.Part.Rangers Co.D
Walker, W.A. AL 56th Part.Rangers Co.H
Walker, W.A. AL 18th Inf. Co.F 1st Lt.
Walker, W.A. GA Cav. 8th Bn. (St.Guards) Co.B
Walker, W.A. GA Lt.Arty. Clinch's Btty.
Walker, W.A. GA Arty.Ind.Co. Cpl.
Walker, W.A. GA Btty.
Walker, W.A. LA 13th Bn. (Part.Rangers) Co.A
Walker, W.A. MS 8th Cav. Co.K
Walker, W.A. MS 3rd Inf. (St.Troops) Co.E
Walker, W.A. MS 15th Bn.S.S. Co.A
Walker, W.A. MS 24th Inf. Co.E
Walker, W.A. NC 4th Inf. Co.C,H
Walker, W.A. NC 11th (Bethel Regt.) Inf. Co.G Sgt.
Walker, W.A. SC 1st Cav. Co.D Lt.Col.
Walker, W.A. SC 2nd Inf. Co.I
Walker, W.A. SC Inf. Hampton Legion Co.H
Walker, W.A. TN 5th (McKenzie's) Cav. Co.E
Walker, W.A. VA 3rd Inf. Co.D
Walker, W.A. 15th Conf.Cav. Co.A
Walker, W.A. 20th Conf.Cav. Co.E
Walker, W.A. Gen. & Staff Maj.,QM
Walker, Wade H. VA Lt.Arty. G.B. Chapman's Co.
Walker, Walter B. AL 47th Inf. Co.C
Walker, Walter J. GA Inf. 10th Bn. Co.D
Walker, Warren Davis SC Inf. Hampton Legion Co.F
Walker, Warren W. SC 13th Inf. Co.A Sgt.
Walker, Wash MO Cav. Fristoe's Regt. Co.E
Walker, Washington GA 49th Inf. Co.E
Walker, Washington NC 49th Inf. Co.A
Walker, Washington VA 18th Cav. Co.K
Walker, Washington H. NC 1st Inf. Co.C
Walker, Washington H. NC 51st Inf. Co.A 3rd Lt.
Walker, Washington L. TN 13th Inf. Co.K
Walker, Washington P. TN 48th (Voorhies') Inf. Co.B
Walker, Watson VA 5th Cav. Co.E
Walker, Watson A. TN 1st Cav.
Walker, W.B. AL 32nd Inf. Co.G
Walker, W.B. AR 48th Cav. Co.D
Walker, W.B. FL 1st (Res.) Inf. Co.I
Walker, W.B. KY 1st (Butler's) Cav. Co.F
Walker, W.B. KY Cav. Thompson's Co.
Walker, W.B. MO 6th Cav. Co.E 1st Sgt.
Walker, W.B. MO 9th (Elliott's) Cav. Co.B 1st Lt.
Walker, W.B. MO Cav. Coleman's Regt. Co.D
Walker, W.B. MO 11th Inf. Co.F
Walker, W.B.H. TN 18th Inf. Co.K
Walker, W.C. AL Arty. 1st Bn. Co.F
Walker, W.C. AR 7th Inf. Co.I
Walker, W.C. GA 63rd Inf. Co.G
Walker, W.C. TX Cav. 2nd Regt.St.Troops Co.C
Walker, W.C. TX 3rd (Kirby's) Bn.Vol. Co.A
Walker, W.D. FL 2nd Cav. Co.H
Walker, W.D. GA Lt.Arty. 12th Bn. 3rd Co.E
Walker, W.D. GA 31st Inf. Co.K
Walker, W.D. GA 59th Inf. Co.B
Walker, W.D. LA 1st (Nelligan's) Inf. Co.E
Walker, W.D. MS 6th Cav. Co.D
Walker, W.D. MS Inf. 2nd Bn. (St.Troops) Co.E
Walker, W.D. SC 16th Inf. Co.F
Walker, W.D. TN Inf. 22nd Bn. Co.G
Walker, W.D. TX 9th Cav. Co.K Cpl.
Walker, W.D. TX 23rd Cav. Co.I Sgt.
Walker, W.D. TX 15th Inf. 2nd Co.F 2nd Lt.
Walker, W.D. VA Res.Forces Clark's Co.
Walker, W.E. AL 17th Inf. Co.D
Walker, W.E. LA 3rd Inf. Co.B
Walker, W.E. LA 22nd (Cons.) Inf. Co.H Cpl.
Walker, W.E. MO 10th Cav. Co.I
Walker, W.E. VA 3rd Cav. Co.A
Walker, W.E. VA Hvy.Arty. Allen's Co.
Walker, Welbern AL 27th Inf. Co.G
Walker, Wellington 1st Choctaw Mtd.Rifles Co.I
Walker, Wesley GA 26th Inf. Co.K
Walker, Wesley MO 7th Cav. Co.H
Walker, Wesley SC 11th Res. Co.F Cpl.
Walker, Wesley TN Inf. 22nd Bn. Co.G
Walker, Wesley A. VA 2nd Arty. Co.D
Walker, Wesley A. VA Inf. 22nd Bn. Co.D
Walker, West MS 9th Inf. New Co.F
Walker, West TN 4th (Murray's) Cav. Co.G
Walker, West TN Inf. 3rd Cons.Regt. Co.A
Walker, West TN 35th Inf. Co.H
Walker, W.F. AL 13th Bn.Part.Rangers Co.B Cpl.
Walker, W.F. AL 56th Part.Rangers Co.F Cpl.
Walker, W.F. GA 2nd Cav. Co.D
Walker, W.F. MS 8th Cav. Co.G
Walker, W.F. SC Inf. Holcombe Legion Co.K
Walker, W.F. TX 1st Inf. Co.B 2nd Lt.
Walker, W.F. VA 8th Inf. Co.E
Walker, W.F., Jr. VA 52nd Mil.
Walker, W.F. Gen. & Staff Surg.
Walker, W.G. AL 14th Inf. Co.H Sgt.
Walker, W.G. MS 46th Inf. Co.E
Walker, W.G. SC 6th Cav. Co.G
Walker, W.G. TN 25th Inf. Co.D
Walker, W.G. TX Cav. Martin's Regt. Co.D 2nd Lt.
Walker, W.G. TX 2nd Inf. Co.I
Walker, W.H. AL 38th Inf. Co.E Sgt.
Walker, W.H. AL Arty. 4th Bn. Hilliard's Legion Co.A
Walker, W.H. GA Lt.Arty. Barnwell's Btty.
Walker, W.H. GA 65th Inf. Co.H
Walker, W.H. KY 9th Mtd.Inf. Co.F
Walker, W.H. LA 1st Hvy.Arty. (Reg.) Co.G,B
Walker, W.H. LA 1st (Nelligan's) Inf. Asst.Surg.
Walker, W.H. MD 1st Inf.
Walker, W.H. MS 2nd St.Cav. Co.H
Walker, W.H. MS 7th Cav. Co.G
Walker, W.H. MS 7th Inf. Co.G
Walker, W.H. MS 9th Inf. New Co.I Cpl.
Walker, W.H. MS Conscr.
Walker, W.H. MO Cav. Woodson's Co.
Walker, W.H. MO 1st Inf. Co.H
Walker, W.H. MO 1st & 4th Cons.Inf. Co.F
Walker, W.H. NC 30th Inf. Co.B
Walker, W.H. NC 56th Inf. Co.H
Walker, W.H. SC 19th Inf. Co.H

Walker, W.H. SC Inf. Holcombe Legion Co.C
Walker, W.H. TN 21st & 22nd (Cons.) Cav. Co.F
Walker, W.H. TN 16th Inf. Co.G
Walker, W.H. TN Inf. 23rd Bn. Co.B
Walker, W.H. TX 10th Cav. Co.C
Walker, W.H. TX 23rd Cav. Co.A Cpl.
Walker, W.H. TX 30th Cav. Co.K Cpl.
Walker, W.H. TX 34th Cav. Co.I
Walker, W.H. TX 10th Field Btty.
Walker, W.H. TX 12th Inf. Co.K
Walker, W.H. VA 3rd Cav. Co.A
Walker, W.H. VA 8th Cav. Co.H
Walker, W.H. VA 13th Cav. Co.I
Walker, W.H. VA Inf. 4th Bn.Loc.Def. Co.F
Walker, W.H.H. TN 51st (Cons.) Inf. Co.A
Walker, W.H.H. TN 52nd Inf. Co.A
Walker, Whitfield AL 3rd Res. Maj.
Walker, Whitfield SC 1st (McCreary's) Inf. Co.B Capt.
Walker, Whitfield SC 1st Inf. Co.L Capt.
Walker, W.H.T. Gen. & Staff Maj.Gen.
Walker, W.I. MS 6th Cav. Co.F
Walker, Wiatt LA 11th Inf. Co.E
Walker, Wiley TX 13th Vol. 2nd Co.I,B
Walker, Wiley VA Cav. 14th Bn. Co.B
Walker, Wiley 3rd Conf.Eng.Troops Co.E Sgt.
Walker, Wiley L. MS 15th Inf. Co.A
Walker, Wiley O. NC 4th Cav. (59th St.Troops) Co.G
Walker, Wiley T. MS 18th Inf. Co.G
Walker, Wiley W. AL 22nd Inf. Co.B
Walker, Wiley W. AR 26th Inf. Co.F
Walker, Wilkerson VA 166th Mil. Taylor's Co.
Walker, Willard SC 7th Inf. 1st Co.C Cpl.
Walker, William AL 4th (Russell's) Cav. Co.E
Walker, William AL 12th Cav. Co.F
Walker, William AL Arty. 1st Bn. Co.A Capt.
Walker, William AL Lt.Arty. 2nd Bn. Co.C
Walker, William AL Mil. 4th Vol. Co.B
Walker, William AL 7th Inf. Co.G
Walker, William AL 10th Inf. Co.F
Walker, William AL 49th Inf. Co.C
Walker, William AL 59th Inf. Co.K
Walker, William AL Talladega Cty.Res. W. Steed's Co.
Walker, William AL 2nd Bn. Hilliard's Legion Vol. Co.B
Walker, William AR 12th Inf. Co.I Sgt.
Walker, William AR 32nd Inf. Co.E Cpl.
Walker, William FL 3rd Inf. Co.F Sgt.
Walker, William GA Cav. 9th Bn. (St.Guards) Co.E
Walker, William GA Hvy.Arty. 22nd Bn. Co.B
Walker, William GA Lt.Arty. 14th Bn. Co.D
Walker, William GA Lt.Arty. King's Btty.
Walker, William GA 1st (Olmstead's) Inf. Co.C
Walker, William GA 3rd Res. Co.F
Walker, William GA 8th Inf. (St.Guards) Co.D
Walker, William GA 18th Inf. Co.F
Walker, William GA 53rd Inf. Co.K
Walker, William GA 57th Inf. Co.C
Walker, William GA Inf. (Ogeechee Minute Men) Garrison's Co.
Walker, Wm. GA 1st St.Line Co.G
Walker, William KY 5th Cav. Co.H
Walker, William KY 11th Cav. Co.E
Walker, William KY 12th Cav. Co.I
Walker, William LA 2nd Inf. Co.B
Walker, William LA 17th Inf. Co.K
Walker, William LA 21st (Kennedy's) Inf. Co.E
Walker, William LA 21st (Patton's) Inf. Co.B Ord.Sgt.
Walker, William LA 27th Inf. Co.I
Walker, William LA 28th (Gray's) Inf. Lt.Col.
Walker, William LA Maddox's Regt.Res.Corps Co.B
Walker, William MS 4th Cav. Co.C
Walker, William MS 18th Cav. Co.C
Walker, William MS Cav. Polk's Ind.Co. (Polk Rangers)
Walker, William MS 1st (Johnston's) Inf. Co.E
Walker, William MS Inf. 2nd Bn. (St.Troops) Co.B
Walker, William MS Inf. 3rd Bn. (St.Troops) Co.C
Walker, William MS 4th Inf. Co.B
Walker, William MS 5th Inf. (St.Troops) Co.A
Walker, William MS 9th Inf. Old Co.A
Walker, William MS 9th Inf. New Co.F
Walker, William MS 9th Inf. Co.H
Walker, William MS 15th Inf. Co.G
Walker, William MS 34th Inf. Co.D Cpl.
Walker, William MO 1st N.E. Cav. White's Co.
Walker, William MO 7th Cav. Co.H
Walker, William MO 15th Cav. Co.A
Walker, William MO Cav. Fristoe's Regt. Co.F
Walker, William MO 11th Inf. Co.I
Walker, Wm. MO St.Guard W.H. Taylor's Co. 2nd Lt.
Walker, William NC 4th Sr.Res. Co.D
Walker, William NC 7th Inf. Co.F
Walker, William NC 7th Sr.Res. Clinard's Co.
Walker, William NC 12th Inf. Co.F
Walker, William NC 31st Inf. Co.H
Walker, William NC 33rd Inf. Co.D
Walker, William NC 34th Inf. Co.K
Walker, William NC 37th Inf. Co.F
Walker, William NC 42nd Inf. Co.E
Walker, William NC 48th Inf. Co.C Sgt.
Walker, William NC 50th Inf. Co.I
Walker, William NC 52nd Inf. Co.C
Walker, William NC 54th Inf. Co.G
Walker, William NC Mallett's Bn. (Cp.Guard) Co.B
Walker, William, Jr. NC Walker's Bn. Thomas' Legion 2nd Co.D
Walker, William, Sr. NC Walker's Bn. Thomas' Legion 2nd Co.D
Walker, William SC 4th Cav. Co.H
Walker, William SC Cav. 10th Bn. Co.D
Walker, William SC Lt.Arty. Beauregard's Co.
Walker, Wm. SC 2nd Inf. Co.I
Walker, William SC 6th Inf. 1st Co.G, 2nd Co.I
Walker, William SC 7th Inf. 2nd Co.F
Walker, William SC 8th Inf.
Walker, Wm. SC 17th Inf.
Walker, William SC 18th Inf. Co.K
Walker, William TN 4th (Murray's) Cav. Co.A
Walker, William TN 9th (Ward's) Cav. Kirkpatrick's Co.I
Walker, William TN 21st & 22nd (Cons.) Cav. Co.C
Walker, William TN 22nd (Barteau's) Cav. Co.K
Walker, William TN 2nd (Robison's) Inf. Co.F
Walker, William TN 3rd (Lillard's) Mtd.Inf. Co.A
Walker, William TN 9th Inf. Co.G
Walker, William TN 17th Inf. Co.I
Walker, William TN 37th Inf. Co.D
Walker, William TN 37th Inf. Co.I
Walker, William TN 42nd Inf. Co.C
Walker, William TN 44th Inf. Co.D Sgt.
Walker, William TN 44th (Cons.) Co.H
Walker, William TN Inf. 154th Sr.Regt. Co.E Cpl.
Walker, William TN Conscr. (Cp. of Instr.)
Walker, William TX 19th Cav. Co.I
Walker, William TX 24th Cav. Co.B
Walker, William TX Cav. Hardeman's Regt. Co.A Cpl.
Walker, William TX Cav. McCord's Frontier Regt. Co.B
Walker, William TX Arty. 4th Bn. Co.A
Walker, William TX 5th Inf. Co.K
Walker, William TX 18th Inf. Co.C
Walker, William TX 20th Inf. Co.C
Walker, William TX 22nd Inf. Co.E
Walker, William VA 4th Cav. Co.C
Walker, William VA 8th Cav. Co.K
Walker, William VA 17th Cav. Co.H
Walker, William VA 22nd Cav. Co.F
Walker, William VA 25th Cav. Co.A
Walker, William VA Cav. 27th Regt. Co.G
Walker, William VA Lt.Arty. Douthat's Co.
Walker, William VA 1st St.Res. Co.K,F
Walker, William VA 33rd Inf. Co.G
Walker, William VA 36th Inf. Co.B
Walker, William VA 50th Inf. Co.D
Walker, William VA 53rd Inf. Co.F
Walker, William, Jr. VA 82nd Mil. Co.D Sgt.
Walker, William VA 151st Mil. Co.D
Walker, William VA 190th Mil. Co.E
Walker, William VA Mil. Scott Cty.
Walker, William 1st Conf.Cav. 2nd Co.D
Walker, William Conf.Inf. 8th Bn. Co.C
Walker, William 1st Cherokee Mtd.Rifles Co.H
Walker, William 1st Creek Mtd.Vol. Co.G
Walker, William Conf.Reg.Inf. Brooks' Bn. Co.F
Walker, William Exch.Bn. Co.E,CSA
Walker, Wm. Gen. & Staff Hosp.Stew.
Walker, William A. AL 4th Cav. Co.K
Walker, William A. AL 53rd (Part.Rangers) Co.B 1st Lt.
Walker, William A. AL Lt.Arty. 20th Bn. Co.A Hosp.Stew.
Walker, William A. AL Inf. 1st Regt. Co.G 1st Lt.
Walker, William A. AL 6th Inf. Co.B
Walker, William A. AL 39th Inf. Co.E 2nd Lt.
Walker, William A. AR Cav. 1st Bn. (Stirman's) Co.A
Walker, William A. FL Cav. 3rd Bn. Co.A
Walker, William A. GA Arty. (Chatham Arty.) Wheaton's Co. Cpl.
Walker, William A. GA 1st (Olmstead's) Inf. Claghorn's Co.
Walker, William A. GA 4th Inf. Co.A
Walker, William A. GA 22nd Inf. Co.F Cpl.
Walker, William A. GA 30th Inf. Co.H
Walker, William A. GA 34th Inf. Co.K Capt.

Walker, William A. LA Pointe Coupee Arty. Sgt.
Walker, William A. MS 20th Inf. Co.K
Walker, William A. NC 1st Arty. (10th St.Troops) Co.G,E
Walker, William A. NC 2nd Inf. Co.I
Walker, William A. NC 13th Inf. Co.K
Walker, William A. NC 22nd Inf. Co.I
Walker, William A. NC 37th Inf. Co.A
Walker, William A. NC 57th Inf. Co.H
Walker, William A. TN Cav. 2nd Bn. (Biffle's) Co.B Cpl.
Walker, William A. TN 4th (McLemore's) Cav. Co.B Black.
Walker, William A. TN 5th (McKenzie's) Cav. Co.E
Walker, William A. TN 6th (Wheeler's) Cav. Co.G
Walker, William A. TN 41st Inf. Co.D
Walker, William A. TN 44th (Cons.) Inf. Co.A
Walker, William A. VA 14th Cav. Co.H,B,C
Walker, William A. VA 28th Inf. Co.G
Walker, William A. VA 34th Inf. Co.G
Walker, William A. VA 42nd Inf. Co.E
Walker, William A.J. LA 28th (Gray's) Inf. Co.D Sgt.
Walker, William A.J. TN 4th Inf. Co.K
Walker, William B. AR 32nd Inf. Co.A
Walker, William B. FL 3rd Inf. Co.H
Walker, William B. GA 5th Inf. Co.G
Walker, William B. NC 32nd Inf. Co.B
Walker, William B. TX 27th Cav. Co.D 2nd Lt.
Walker, William B. TX 4th Inf. Co.A
Walker, William B. VA 59th Inf. 1st Co.F
Walker, William B. VA 60th Inf. Co.C
Walker, William C. KY 9th Mtd.Inf. Co.A
Walker, William C. MS Inf. 7th Bn. Co.E
Walker, William C. MS 31st Inf. Co.F
Walker, William C. MO 8th Cav. Co.D
Walker, William C. NC 29th Inf. Co.A Lt.Col.
Walker, William C. NC 37th Inf. Co.G
Walker, William C. NC Walker's Bn. Thomas' Legion Co.B Lt.Col.
Walker, William C. TN Inf. 1st Bn. (Colms') Co.A
Walker, William C. TN 50th (Cons.) Inf. Co.B
Walker, William D. AL 9th Inf. Co.K 1st Sgt.
Walker, William D. AL 29th Inf. Co.F Sgt.
Walker, William D. MS 1st Bn.S.S. Co.C
Walker, William D. MO 3rd Inf. Co.C
Walker, William D. TN 48th (Voorhies') Inf. Co.B,A 2nd Lt.
Walker, William D. VA 3rd Cav. Co.G
Walker, William E. AL 33rd Inf. Co.I
Walker, William E. GA Cav. Allen's Co. 2nd Lt.
Walker, William E. GA 34th Inf. Co.I
Walker, William E. LA 16th Inf. Co.D Lt.Col.
Walker, William E. MS Inf. 1st Bn.St.Troops (12 mo. '62-3) Co.F
Walker, William E. MO 10th Inf. Co.G 2nd Lt.
Walker, William E. NC 42nd Inf. Co.E
Walker, William E. SC Inf. Hampton Legion Co.D Music.
Walker, Wm. E. VA Mtd.Guard 3rd Congr.Dist.
Walker, William E. VA 19th Cav. Co.H
Walker, William E. VA Lt.Arty. Hardwicke's Co.
Walker, William E. VA Inf. 1st Bn.Loc.Def. Co.F
Walker, William E. VA 14th Inf. Co.F
Walker, William E. VA 17th Inf. Co.E 1st Sgt.
Walker, William F. AL 16th Inf. Co.K
Walker, William F. NC 13th Inf. Co.A
Walker, William F. SC 2nd Rifles Co.A Cpl.
Walker, William F. TN 16th Inf. Co.B
Walker, William F. TX 21st Cav. Co.H
Walker, William F. VA 52nd Mil. Co.A
Walker, William F., Jr. VA 53rd Inf. Co.K
Walker, William F., Sr. VA 53rd Inf. Co.K
Walker, William Franklin VA 10th Cav. Co.C
Walker, William G. GA Inf. 8th Bn. Co.E
Walker, William G. KY 2nd Mtd.Inf. Co.E
Walker, William G. MS 22nd Inf. Co.E Capt.
Walker, William G. NC 47th Inf. Co.D
Walker, William G. VA 6th Inf. Co.H
Walker, William G. VA 38th Inf. Co.B
Walker, William G. Conf.Cav. Wood's Regt. Co.L
Walker, William G.H. TN 50th Inf. Co.F
Walker, William H. AL 4th (Russell's) Cav. Co.I
Walker, William H. AL 10th Inf. Co.F
Walker, William H. AL 29th Inf. Co.A
Walker, William H. AL 59th Inf. Co.I
Walker, William H. AR 8th Inf. New Co.D Sgt.
Walker, William H. AR 16th Inf. Co.H Cpl.
Walker, William H. FL 3rd Inf. Co.D 3rd Lt.
Walker, William H. FL 5th Inf. Co.I Jr.2nd Lt.
Walker, William H. GA Inf. 2nd Bn. Co.B
Walker, William H. GA 21st Inf. Co.F
Walker, William H. GA 45th Inf. Co.B
Walker, William H. GA 49th Inf. Co.K
Walker, William H. LA 9th Inf. Co.D
Walker, William H. LA Conscr.
Walker, William H. MS 1st (Johnston's) Inf. Co.H
Walker, William H. MS 9th Inf. New Co.E
Walker, William H. MS 24th Inf. Co.C
Walker, William H. SC 1st Mtd.Mil. Heyward's Co. Lt.
Walker, William H. SC Cav. Walpole's Co. Sgt.
Walker, William H. SC 5th Inf. 1st Co.K
Walker, William H. TN 3rd (Forrest's) Cav.
Walker, William H. TN Cav. 9th Bn. (Gantt's) Co.E
Walker, William H. TN 13th (Gore's) Cav. Co.H
Walker, William H. TN 21st (Wilson's) Cav. Co.E
Walker, William H. TN 3rd (Lillard's) Mtd.Inf. Co.G
Walker, William H. TN 24th Inf. 2nd Co.H, Co.M Sgt.
Walker, William H. TN 32nd Inf. Co.G
Walker, William H. TN 40th Inf. Co.F 1st Sgt.
Walker, William H. TN Conscr. (Cp. of Instr.) Co.B
Walker, William H. TX 3rd Cav. Co.K
Walker, William H. TX 15th Cav. Co.E
Walker, William H. TX 32nd Cav. Co.H
Walker, William H. VA 6th Cav. Co.I 1st Lt.
Walker, William H. VA 2nd Arty. Co.D
Walker, William H. VA 6th Inf. Ferguson's Co.
Walker, William H. VA 12th Inf. Co.H
Walker, William H., Jr. VA Inf. 22nd Bn. Co.D Sgt.
Walker, William H. VA 34th Inf. Co.K
Walker, William H. VA 59th Inf. 2nd Co.I
Walker, William H. VA 60th Inf. Co.H
Walker, Wm. H. Gen. & Staff Asst.Surg.
Walker, William Harrison KY 9th Mtd.Inf. Co.H Cpl.
Walker, William Harrison TX Inf. W. Cameron's Co. Cpl.
Walker, William H.C. VA 14th Inf. Co.F Hosp.Stew.
Walker, William Henry AL 5th Inf. New Co.G
Walker, William Henry KY 9th Mtd.Inf. Co.H Sgt.
Walker, William Henry MS 27th Inf. Co.F
Walker, William Henry TX Inf. W. Cameron's Co. Sgt.
Walker, William H.H. LA 31st Inf. Co.E
Walker, William H.H. VA Hvy.Arty. 20th Bn. Co.A
Walker, William H.H. VA 44th Inf. Co.A
Walker, William H.R. AR 1st (Crawford's) Cav. Co.E
Walker, William J. AL 38th Inf. Co.B,D
Walker, William J. FL 1st Inf. Old Co.I
Walker, William J. FL 5th Inf. Co.G
Walker, William J. GA 22nd Inf. Co.H Capt.
Walker, William J. LA 12th Inf. Co.D
Walker, William J. LA 27th Inf. Co.C
Walker, William J. MO 10th Inf. Co.A
Walker, William J. NC Hvy.Arty. 1st Bn. Co.B
Walker, William J. NC 6th Inf. Co.K
Walker, William J. NC 14th Inf. Co.G Sgt.
Walker, William J. NC 33rd Inf. Co.F
Walker, William J. TX 1st (Yager's) Cav. Co.C
Walker, William J. TX Cav. 3rd (Yager's) Bn. Co.C
Walker, William J. TX Cav. Martin's Regt. Co.C 2nd Lt.
Walker, William J. TX 10th Inf. Co.F
Walker, William J. VA 19th Inf. Co.D Cpl.
Walker, William J. VA 21st Inf. Co.H
Walker, William J. VA 42nd Inf. Co.C
Walker, William Joseph MS 17th Inf. Co.B Cpl.
Walker, William K. AR 14th (McCarver's) Inf. Co.D
Walker, William K. AR 21st Inf. Co.K
Walker, William L. AL 13th Inf. Co.A
Walker, William L. AR 1st (Crawford's) Cav. Co.A
Walker, William L. GA 12th (Robinson's) Cav. (St.Guards) Co.G
Walker, William L. GA 30th Inf. Co.H
Walker, William L. MS 8th Cav. Co.E Lt.Col.
Walker, William L. MS 7th Inf. Co.H 2nd Lt.
Walker, William L. MS 24th Inf. Co.C 1st Lt.
Walker, Wm. L. NC Currituck Guard J.W.F. Bank's Co.
Walker, William L. SC 2nd Inf. Co.F
Walker, William L. TN 10th Cav.
Walker, William L. TX 35th (Brown's) Cav. Co.D Cpl.
Walker, William L. TX 13th Vol. 2nd Co.C
Walker, William L. VA 24th Cav. Co.C
Walker, William L. VA Cav. 40th Bn. Co.C
Walker, William L. VA 3rd Inf. Loc.Def. Co.B

Walker, William L. VA 21st Mil. Co.D
Walker, William L. VA 59th Inf. 3rd Co.D Jr.2nd Lt.
Walker, William M. AR 7th Inf. Co.H
Walker, William M. GA Arty. 11th Bn. (Sumter Arty.) Co.A
Walker, William M. MO Cav. Freeman's Regt. Co.F
Walker, William M. NC 8th Inf. Co.F 1st Lt.
Walker, William M. NC 13th Inf. Co.K
Walker, William M. NC 22nd Inf. Co.I
Walker, William M. SC 5th Cav. Co.K
Walker, William M. TN Cav. Allison's Squad. Co.A
Walker, William M. TN 41st Inf. Co.D
Walker, William M. VA 16th Cav. Co.C
Walker, William M. VA Lt.Arty. Griffin's Co.
Walker, William M. VA 40th Inf. Co.K
Walker, William M. VA 46th Inf. 2nd Co.A, 4th Co.F
Walker, William M. VA 53rd Inf. Co.K
Walker, William M.R. VA 61st Inf. Co.D
Walker, William N. GA Inf. 1st Conf.Bn. Co.D
Walker, William N. GA 30th Inf. Co.H
Walker, William N. VA 9th Cav. Co.D
Walker, William O. MS 30th Inf. Co.E
Walker, William O. TN 6th (Wheeler's) Cav. Co.E
Walker, William P. AR Cav. Wright's Regt. Co.F
Walker, William P. AR 3rd Inf. Co.C
Walker, William P. GA 3rd Inf. Co.D Cpl.
Walker, William P. MS 6th Inf. Co.G
Walker, William P. TN 35th Inf. Co.L Sgt.
Walker, William P. TX 11th Inf. Co.K,H
Walker, William P. TX 18th Inf. Co.B
Walker, William P. VA 22nd Cav. Co.F
Walker, William P. VA Hvy.Arty. 20th Bn. Co.C
Walker, William P. VA 12th Inf. Co.D
Walker, William P. VA 44th Inf. Co.G Capt.
Walker, William P. VA 79th Mil. Co.4
Walker, William P. VA Loc.Def. Scott's Co.
Walker, William R. AL 37th Inf. Co.D 4th Cpl.
Walker, William R. AL 39th Inf. Co.F
Walker, William R. AL 44th Inf. Co.A
Walker, William R. GA 6th Cav. Co.F
Walker, William R. GA Inf. 4th Bn. (St.Guards) Co.C
Walker, William R. GA 65th Inf. Co.G
Walker, William R. GA Smith's Legion Anderson's Co.
Walker, William R. MS 22nd Inf. Co.E
Walker, William R. MO 11th Inf. Co.K
Walker, William R. NC 3rd Arty. (40th St.Troops) Co.I,C
Walker, William R. NC 8th Inf. Co.F
Walker, William R. NC 56th Inf. Co.D
Walker, William R. TN 25th Inf. Co.K Sgt.
Walker, William R. VA 58th Inf. Co.A
Walker, Wm. R. Gen. & Staff Surg.
Walker, William Ray MO 8th Inf. Co.E 2nd Lt.
Walker, William S. AL 6th Inf. Co.G
Walker, William S. AL 48th Inf. Co.C Capt.
Walker, William S. AR 17th (Griffith's) Inf. Co.I 1st Sgt.
Walker, Williams GA 5th Cav. Co.E
Walker, William S. GA 21st Inf. Co.G 2nd Lt.
Walker, William S. MO 1st Cav. Co.G
Walker, Williams MO Cav. Poindexter's Regt.
Walker, William S. NC 2nd Cav. (19th St.Troops) Co.K Sgt.
Walker, William S. NC 6th Inf. Co.H
Walker, William S. NC 22nd Inf. Co.B
Walker, William S. TN Lyon's Cav. J.C. Stone's Co.A 2nd Lt.
Walker, William S. Gen. & Staff Brig.Gen.
Walker, William S.T. LA 2nd Inf. Co.B
Walker, Williamson TX Cav. Martin's Regt. Co.F
Walker, William T. AL 12th Inf. Co.C
Walker, William T. AL 29th Inf. Co.F
Walker, William T. FL 1st Cav. Co.H,I
Walker, William T. GA 3rd Cav. (St.Guards) Co.F
Walker, William T. GA Inf. 2nd Bn. Co.D Capt.
Walker, William T. GA 3rd Inf. Co.K
Walker, William T. GA 8th Inf. (St.Guards) Co.F Sgt.
Walker, William T. GA Inf. 19th Bn. (St.Guards) Co.C
Walker, William T. MO Cav. 1st Regt.St.Guard Co.C
Walker, William T. NC 6th Inf. Co.H
Walker, William T. TN Cav. 9th Bn. (Gantt's) Co.E
Walker, William T. TN Cav. 16th Bn. (Neal's) Co.C
Walker, William T. VA 22nd Cav. Co.F
Walker, William T. VA Cav. 35th Bn. Co.A
Walker, William T. VA Hvy.Arty. 18th Bn. Co.D
Walker, William T. VA 1st Bn.Res. Co.D
Walker, William T. VA 59th Inf. 2nd Co.A
Walker, William W. AL 13th Inf. Co.H
Walker, Wm. W. AL 38th Inf. Co.A
Walker, William W. AR 1st (Colquitt's) Inf. Co.I
Walker, William W. GA 14th Inf. Co.G
Walker, William W. LA Inf. 1st Sp.Bn. (Wheat's) Co.A 2nd Sgt.
Walker, William W. LA 31st Inf. Co.G
Walker, William W. MS 19th Inf. Co.F Sgt.
Walker, William W. MO Inf. 4th Regt.St.Guard Co.B
Walker, William W. NC 54th Inf. Co.F Sgt.
Walker, William W. SC 14th Inf. Co.H
Walker, William W. TN 4th (McLemore's) Cav. Co.D
Walker, William W. TN 4th Inf. Co.A Sgt.
Walker, William W. TN 7th Inf. Co.C
Walker, William W. TX 36th Cav. Co.A
Walker, William W. VA 2nd Cav. Co.I
Walker, William W. VA Hvy.Arty. 18th Bn. Co.B
Walker, William W. VA Hvy.Arty. 20th Bn. Co.B
Walker, William W. VA Arty. Paris' Co. Sr.2nd Lt.
Walker, William Young MO Lt.Arty. Parsons' Co.
Walker, William Young MO 6th Inf. Co.I
Walker, William Y.S. VA 55th Inf. Co.A
Walker, Willie O. VA 5th Cav. (12 mo. '61-2) Co.I
Walker, Willie O. VA 15th Cav. Co.I
Walker, Willis MS 8th Inf. Co.F
Walker, Willis MS 16th Inf. Co.B
Walker, Willis TN 34th Inf.
Walker, Willis G. TN 24th Bn.S.S. Co.A
Walker, Willis L. MS 27th Inf. Co.D Sgt.
Walker, Willis S. NC 3rd Arty. (40th St.Troops) Co.C
Walker, Willis S. NC 30th Inf. Co.D
Walker, Willis W. AL 33rd Inf. Co.I
Walker, Wilson KY 8th Cav. Co.K
Walker, Wilson MS 2nd Cav. Co.C
Walker, Wilson MS 3rd Cav.Res. Co.F
Walker, Wilson NC 38th Inf. Co.E
Walker, Wilson H. NC 7th Inf. Co.B
Walker, Winbourne TX 1st (McCulloch's) Cav. Co.B
Walker, Winter MS 9th Inf. New Co.H
Walker, Winter MS 10th Inf. Old Co.I
Walker, W.J. AL 12th Cav. Co.D,B
Walker, W.J. AL 12th Inf. Co.E Lt.
Walker, W.J. AR 19th (Dawson's) Inf. Co.C 1st Lt.
Walker, W.J. FL Inf. 3rd Regt. Co.F
Walker, W.J. GA Cav. 1st Bn.Res. McKinney's Co.
Walker, W.J. GA 32nd Inf. Co.K
Walker, W.J. LA Hvy.Arty. 2nd Bn. Co.D
Walker, W.J. MS 2nd Cav. Co.C Cpl.
Walker, W.J. MS 3rd Cav. Co.E Capt.,Adj.
Walker, W.J. MS 1st (Foote's) Inf. (St.Troops) Co.B Cpl.
Walker, W.J. MS Inf. 2nd Bn. (St.Troops) Co.C
Walker, W.J. TN Inf. Crews' Bn. Co.G 1st Lt.
Walker, W.J. TX Cav. 2nd Bn.St.Troops Wilson's Co.
Walker, W.J. TX 10th Cav. Co.D
Walker, W.J. TX 29th Cav. Co.K 1st Lt.
Walker, W.J. TX Cav. Good's Bn. Co.E 1st Lt.
Walker, W.J. VA Inf. 25th Bn. Co.G
Walker, W.J.H. MS 14th (Cons.) Inf. Co.H
Walker, W.J.H. MS 43rd Inf. Co.B
Walker, W. Jordan NC 3rd Cav. (41st St.Troops) Co.H Capt.
Walker, W.J.R. FL 2nd Inf. Co.L Cpl.
Walker, W.J.R. FL 5th Inf. Co.D
Walker, W.J.V. MS Blythe's Bn. (St.Troops) Co.A
Walker, W.K. MS Lt.Arty. English's Co.
Walker, W.K. TX Cav. Madison's Regt. Co.C Sr.2nd Lt.
Walker, W.L. GA Cav. 1st Bn.Res. McKinney's Co.
Walker, W.L. GA 13th Inf. Co.D
Walker, W.L. GA 16th Inf. Co.E
Walker, W.L. GA 31st Inf. Co.C
Walker, W.L. GA Inf. (Express Inf.) Witt's Co.
Walker, W.L. MS 2nd St.Cav. Co.B
Walker, W.L. MS 6th Cav. Lt.Col.
Walker, W.L. MS St.Cav. Perrin's Bn. Co.H Capt.
Walker, W.L. MS 3rd Inf. Co.C
Walker, W.L. TN 12th (Green's) Cav. Co.D Ord.Sgt.
Walker, W.L. TN 16th (Logwood's) Cav. Co.H
Walker, W.M. AL Jeff Davis Arty.
Walker, W.M. AR 27th Inf. New Co.C Sgt.

Walker, W.M. MS St.Troops (Peach Creek Rangers) Maxwell's Co.
Walker, W.M. SC Hvy.Arty. 15th (Lucas') Bn. Co.B
Walker, W.M. SC 3rd Bn.Res. Co.E
Walker, W.M. TN 14th (Neely's) Cav. Co.F
Walker, W.M. TN 15th (Stewart's) Cav. Co.C
Walker, W.M. TN 12th (Cons.) Inf. Co.A Capt.
Walker, W.M. TN Inf. 12th Regt. Co.C Capt.
Walker, W.M. TX 7th Cav. Co.H
Walker, W.M. VA 9th Cav. Co.C
Walker, W.N. KY 3rd Mtd.Inf. Co.I
Walker, W.N. LA 13th Bn. (Part.Rangers) Co.E
Walker, W.N. LA 19th Inf. Co.B
Walker, W.O. AR 2nd Inf. Co.D 2nd Lt.
Walker, Woods A. TN 1st (Carter's) Cav. Co.D
Walker, Woolfolk GA 3rd Cav. Co.I Bvt.2nd Lt.
Walker, Woolfolk GA 12th (Robinson's) Cav. (St.Guards) Co.K
Walker, Woolfolk GA Cav. Pemberton's Co.
Walker, Woolfolk NC Inf. 2nd Bn. Co.E
Walker, Worrell P. NC 30th Inf. Co.I
Walker, W.P. LA 3rd (Harrison's) Cav. Co.C
Walker, W.P. MS 3rd (St.Troops) Cav. Co.K
Walker, W.P. MS Conscr.
Walker, W.P. SC Brabham's Mtd.Inf.
Walker, W.P. TN 3rd (Forrest's) Cav. Co.A
Walker, W.P. TN 18th (Newsom's) Cav. Co.D 2nd Lt.
Walker, W.P. TN 19th & 20th (Cons.) Cav. Co.B 2nd Lt.
Walker, W.P. TN 20th (Russell's) Cav. Co.K
Walker, W.P. TN 6th Inf. Co.L
Walker, W.P. TN 36th Inf. Co.H 2nd Lt.
Walker, W.P. TN 36th Inf. Co.L Sgt.
Walker, W.P. TN 55th (Brown's) Inf. Ford's Co.
Walker, W.P. TX Arty. Douglas' Co.
Walker, W.R. AL 1st Cav. Sgt.
Walker, W.R. AL 51st (Part.Rangers) Co.G Capt.
Walker, W.R. AL 5th Inf. New Co.H Jr.2nd Lt.
Walker, W.R. AL 9th Inf. Co.I
Walker, W.R. GA 27th Inf. Co.E
Walker, W.R. KY 3rd Mtd.Inf. Co.L
Walker, W.R. MS 2nd (Davidson's) Inf. Co.E
Walker, W.R. MS 39th Inf. Co.G
Walker, W.R. MS 41st Inf. Co.F
Walker, W.R. TN 3rd (Clack's) Inf. Co.E
Walker, W.R. TN 12th Inf. Co.E
Walker, Wright W. FL 3rd Inf. Co.D
Walker, Wryley R. NC 53rd Inf. Co.K
Walker, W.S. AL 8th (Hatch's) Cav. Co.I
Walker, W.S. AL 16th Cav. Co.M
Walker, W.S. AR 11th & 17th (Cons.) Inf. Co.K,F 1st Sgt.
Walker, W.S. GA 2nd Inf. Capt.
Walker, W.S. GA Inf. 23rd Bn.Loc.Def. Pendergrass' Co.
Walker, W.S. GA 40th Inf. Co.H
Walker, W.S. GA Inf. 40th Bn. Co.A
Walker, W.S. TN 14th Inf. Co.I
Walker, W.T. AL 7th Cav. Co.H,F,A
Walker, W.T. AL 5th Inf. New Co.D
Walker, W.T. AR Mil. Desha Cty.Bn.
Walker, W.T. GA 2nd Res. Co.G
Walker, W.T. GA 22nd Inf. Co.E
Walker, W.T. GA 32nd Inf. Co.A
Walker, W.T. MS Lt.Arty. Turner's Co.
Walker, W.T. MS 4th Inf. Co.C
Walker, W.T. TN 47th Inf. Co.D
Walker, W.T. TX 11th Cav. Co.H
Walker, W.T. TX 5th Inf. Co.G
Walker, W.T. Gen. & Staff,PACS Surg.
Walker, W.V. TN 33rd Inf. Co.C
Walker, W.W. AL 11th Cav. Co.B Cpl.
Walker, W.W. AL 17th Inf. Co.D
Walker, W.W. AL 46th Inf. Co.G
Walker, W.W. AR 7th Cav. Co.E Sgt.
Walker, W.W. AR 2nd Inf. Co.K
Walker, W.W. AR 19th (Dockery's) Inf. Co.C
Walker, W.W. GA Inf. 18th Bn. Co.B
Walker, W.W. LA 7th Cav. Co.A Cpl.
Walker, W.W. LA 6th Inf. Co.D
Walker, W.W. LA 19th Inf. Co.B
Walker, W.W. MS 28th Cav. Co.G
Walker, W.W. MS 8th Inf. Co.F
Walker, W.W. MO 7th Cav. Co.G
Walker, W.W. SC 13th Inf. Co.A
Walker, W.W. TN 3rd (Forrest's) Cav. Co.D
Walker, W.W. TN 8th (Smith's) Cav. Co.F
Walker, W.W. TN 12th Inf. Co.C Capt.
Walker, W.W. TX 4th Cav. Co.F
Walker, W.W. TX 23rd Cav. Co.K 2nd Lt.
Walker, W.W. TX 32nd Cav. Co.H
Walker, W.W. TX 35th (Likens') Cav. Co.I
Walker, W.W. TX 1st Inf. Co.B
Walker, W.W. TX 1st Bn.S.S. Co.B
Walker, W.W. TX 2nd Inf. Co.K
Walker, W.W. TX 9th (Young's) Inf. Co.B
Walker, W.W. TX 12th Inf. Co.G
Walker, W.W. VA 54th Mil. Co.H
Walker, W.W. Conf.Cav. Wood's Regt. 1st Co.A
Walker, W.W.H. TN 23rd Inf. Co.E
Walker, W.Y. SC Hvy.Arty. 15th (Lucas') Bn. Co.C
Walker, Wyatt B. VA 3rd Cav. Co.D
Walker, Wyatt W. VA Lt.Arty. 13th Bn. Co.B Cpl.
Walker, Wyatt W. VA 53rd Inf. Co.G
Walker, Xenophen L. NC 29th Inf. Co.A Sgt.
Walker, Y.P. TN 49th Inf. Co.D
Walker, Z. MS Yerger's Co. (St.Troops)
Walker, Zachariah A. TN 44th Inf. Co.I
Walker, Zachariah A. TN 44th (Cons.) Inf. Co.A
Walker, Zachariah J. VA 14th Cav. Co.H 2nd Lt.
Walker, Zack H. AR 19th (Dockery's) Inf. Co.G,F
Walker, Zebedee P. VA 53rd Inf. Co.I
Walker, Zebulon AR 7th Inf. Co.A
Walker, Zephaniah NC 58th Inf. Co.G Cpl.
Walker, Z.H. TX 13th Vol. Co.G
Walker, Z.J. VA 17th Cav. Co.F
Walker, Z.P. VA Inf. Montague's Bn. Co.B
Walker, Z.T. GA 31st Inf. Co.K
Walker, Z.W. AR Cav. Gordon's Regt. Co.H Sgt.
Walker Ground Squirrel 1st Cherokee Mtd.Rifles Co.G
Walkers, John M. TX 24th Cav. Co.E
Walkers, William LA 21st (Patton's) Inf. Co.I
Walkert, J.V. AL
Walkin, H.H. GA Cobb's Legion Co.A
Walkin, L.D. AR 11th Cav. Co.H
Walkingstick, John 1st Cherokee Mtd.Rifles Co.E
Walkingstick, Levi 1st Cherokee Mtd.Rifles Co.E Sgt.
Walkingstick, Samuel TN 19th Inf. Co.F
Walkingstick, Samuel TN 43rd Inf. Co.A
Walking Wolf 1st Cherokee Mtd.Rifles Co.K
Walking Wolf 1st Cherokee Mtd.Vol. 1st Co.I
Walkins, Doctor Franklin AL 10th Inf. Co.G
Walkins, George TN Holman's Bn.Part.Rangers Co.B
Walkins, J.B. AL Mil. 4th Vol. Co.I Sgt.
Walkins, J.F. GA 12th Cav. Co.K
Walkins, Martin M. AL 37th Inf. Co.K
Walkins, S.G. MS Moore's Co. (Palo Alto Guards) 1st Lt.
Walkins, T. LA 15th Inf. Co.E
Walkins, William TN Lt.Arty. Burroughs' Co.
Walkins, W.M. GA Inf. 23rd Bn.Loc.Def. Co.A
Walkley, Bryant S. AL 63rd Inf. Co.B Cpl.
Walkley, E.A. AL 8th Inf. Co.B
Walkling, Friedrich AL 20th Inf. Co.A
Walkling, Henry LA 3rd (Harrison's) Cav. Co.K
Walkly, Nelson AL 21st Inf. Co.E
Walks, W.W. VA Inf. 44th Bn. Co.B Sgt.
Walkup, Arthur M. VA Lt.Arty. Douthat's Co.
Walkup, Arthur M. VA Burks' Regt.Loc.Def. Shield's Co.
Walkup, C.G. VA 8th Cav. Co.L Cpl.
Walkup, C.G. VA 14th Cav. Co.A Cpl.
Walkup, C.R. VA 135th Mil. Co.B
Walkup, E.N. TN 8th (Smith's) Cav. Co.E Sgt.
Walkup, Henry C. NC 26th Inf. Co.B
Walkup, Isreal P. NC 26th Inf. Co.B
Walkup, J.A. TN 3rd (Forrest's) Cav. Co.C,E,I
Walkup, James TN 53rd Inf. Co.C
Walkup, James A. TN 32nd Inf. Co.B
Walkup, James C. NC 26th Inf. Co.B
Walkup, James D. VA 11th Inf. Co.K
Walkup, James E. VA 14th Cav. Co.A
Walkup, James McB. VA 14th Cav. Co.A
Walkup, J.J. VA 135th Mil. Co.B
Walkup, J.M. SC 1st (Butler's) Inf. Co.I
Walkup, J.M.B. VA 135th Mil. Co.B
Walkup, John MO 9th Inf. Co.B
Walkup, John MO Inf. Clark's Regt. Co.A
Walkup, John A. VA 53rd Inf. Co.G
Walkup, John B. VA 135th Mil. Co.B
Walkup, Joseph TN 35th Inf. 2nd Co.F
Walkup, Joseph A. VA 14th Cav. Co.A
Walkup, Joseph A. VA 135th Mil. Co.B
Walkup, Joseph W. VA 9th Inf. Chap.
Walkup, Joseph W. Gen. & Staff Chap.
Walkup, J.T. TN 28th (Cons.) Inf. Co.F
Walkup, J.T. TN 84th Inf. Co.B
Walkup, Limon VA 79th Mil. Co.3
Walkup, Marshal VA Inf. 26th Bn. Co.B
Walkup, Matthew H. VA 11th Inf. Co.A
Walkup, M.H. VA 59th Inf. 2nd Co.D 2nd Lt.
Walkup, R.L. TN 8th (Smith's) Cav. Co.E
Walkup, Robert L. TN 2nd (Smith's) Cav.
Walkup, Samuel H. NC 26th Inf. Co.B 1st Sgt.
Walkup, Samuel H. NC 48th Inf. Co.F Col.
Walkup, Samuel H. VA 11th Inf. Co.K Cpl.
Walkup, S.W. VA 135th Mil. Co.B
Walkup, T.H. AR 21st Inf. Co.E Cpl.
Walkup, Thomas VA Inf. 26th Bn. Co.G
Walkup, Thomas VA 79th Mil. Co.3

Walkup, Thomas H. AR 17th (Lemoyne's) Inf. Co.F Cpl.
Walkup, W.H. MO 1st N.E. Cav. Co.O
Walkup, William AR 21st Inf. Co.E
Walkup, William MO 1st N.E. Cav. Price's Co.M, White's Co.
Walkup, William TN 53rd Inf. Co.C
Walkup, William VA 27th Inf. Co.F
Walkup, William E. VA Burks' Regt.Loc.Def. Shield's Co.
Walkup, William H. VA 8th Cav. Co.L
Walkup, William H. VA 14th Cav. Co.A Bvt.2nd Lt.
Walkup, William H. VA 135th Mil. Co.B Sgt.
Walkup, William J. AR 17th (Lemoyne's) Inf. Co.F
Walkup, William M. VA 11th Inf. Co.K 2nd Lt.
Walkup, W.J. TN 8th (Smith's) Cav. Co.E
Wall, --- GA 2nd Regt.St.Line Co.B 2nd Lt.
Wall, A. LA Mil. 4th Regt. French Brig. Co.1
Wall, A. TX 13th Vol. Co.D
Wall, A. 14th Conf.Cav. Co.F
Wall, Aaron N. NC 16th Inf. Co.D
Wall, A.B. NC 38th Inf.
Wall, Able C. MS 22nd Inf. Co.E
Wall, Abraham J. NC 45th Inf. Co.H
Wall, Absolom AL 37th Inf. Co.D
Wall, A.C. NC Cav. McRae's Bn. Co.E
Wall, A.C. NC 21st Inf. Co.H
Wall, A.C. VA 31st Inf. Co.F
Wall, Adam TN 45th Inf. Co.H
Wall, A.E. Gen. & Staff Asst.Surg.,Hosp.Stew.
Wall, A.G. VA 42nd Inf. Co.K
Wall, A.H. Lee's A. Asst.Surg.
Wall, A.J. AR 27th Inf. New Co.B
Wall, A.J. GA Inf. (Milledgeville Guards) Caraker's Co.
Wall, A.L. TX Waul's Legion Co.B
Wall, Albert NC 5th Cav. (63rd St.Troops) Co.D
Wall, Albert SC Inf. 6th Bn. Co.A
Wall, Albert SC 26th Inf. Co.C
Wall, Alexander MS Cav. 6th Bn. Prince's Co.
Wall, Alexander SC 14th Inf. Co.H
Wall, Alexander VA Cav. 35th Bn.
Wall, Allen D. NC 45th Inf. Co.K
Wall, Ambrose VA 7th Inf. Co.H
Wall, Anderson P. TN Cav. 2nd Bn. (Biffle's) Co.C
Wall, Anderson P. TN 6th (Wheeler's) Cav. Co.I Far.
Wall, Andrew B. NC 6th Cav. (65th St.Troops) Co.C,G Cpl.
Wall, Andrew J. GA 17th Inf. Co.B
Wall, Andrew J. NC 21st Inf. Co.H
Wall, Andrew J. VA Hvy.Arty. Wright's Co.
Wall, Andrew J. VA 20th Inf. Co.K
Wall, Anthony LA 21st (Patton's) Inf. Co.E
Wall, A.P. GA 13th Inf. Co.C Sgt.
Wall, A.P.E. MS 28th Cav. Co.A
Wall, Archibald N. GA 61st Inf. Co.E
Wall, Arthur GA 16th Inf. Co.B
Wall, Arthur C. NC 16th Inf. Co.D
Wall, A.S. MS 5th Cav. Co.C
Wall, A.S. MS 28th Cav. Co.B
Wall, Asa Gen. & Staff Surg.
Wall, Augustus VA 17th Inf. Co.H
Wall, Augustus A. AL 3rd Inf. Co.I
Wall, Augustus A. MS 2nd (Davidson's) Inf. Co.D
Wall, Augustus A. MS 34th Inf. Co.H
Wall, Augustus L. TX 1st (McCulloch's) Cav. Co.I
Wall, A.W. GA 62nd Cav. Co.I
Wall, Azariah NC 21st Inf. Co.I
Wall, Bartley B. 14th Conf.Cav. Co.B
Wall, B.B. MS 2nd (Quinn's St.Troops) Inf. Co.F
Wall, B.D. LA 18th Inf. Co.B
Wall, B.D. LA Inf.Cons.Crescent Regt. Co.C 1st Sgt.
Wall, Ben MS 19th Inf. Co.H Music.
Wall, Benjamin MS Part.Rangers Smyth's Co.
Wall, Benjamin MS Inf. 1st Bn.St.Troops (12 mo. '62-3) Co.C
Wall, Benjamin TN Cav. 12th Bn. (Day's) Co.G
Wall, Benjamin D. LA Inf.Crescent Regt. Co.B 1st Sgt.
Wall, Benjamin F. GA 38th Inf. Co.E
Wall, Bennet GA 62nd Cav. Co.I
Wall, Bennet NC 24th Inf. Co.C
Wall, Bent GA 8th Cav. Old Co.I
Wall, Berry VA 12th Inf. Co.D
Wall, B.F. AL 7th Cav. Co.G
Wall, B.G. MS Cav. Part.Rangers Rhodes' Co.
Wall, B.G. 14th Conf.Cav. Co.F
Wall, B.H. SC 5th Inf. 1st Co.C
Wall, Booker NC 13th Inf. Co.I
Wall, B.S. FL 2nd Cav. Co.B
Wall, Burrel SC 1st (Orr's) Rifles Co.C
Wall, Calvin NC 53rd Inf. Co.H
Wall, Calvin J. GA 24th Inf. Co.E Cpl.
Wall, Carey J. NC 16th Inf. Co.D
Wall, Carrey J. GA 2nd Inf. Co.I
Wall, C.C. MS 2nd Part.Rangers Co.L
Wall, C.D. GA Inf. 14th Bn. (St.Guards) Co.G Capt.
Wall, C.H. TX 10th Cav. Co.F
Wall, Chapman M. SC 10th Inf. Co.F
Wall, Charles MO 1st Cav. Co.G
Wall, Charles A. GA 1st (Ramsey's) Inf. Co.E Sgt.
Wall, Charles I. LA Pointe Coupee Arty. Cpl.
Wall, Charles J. SC 11th Res. Co.I
Wall, Charles T. NC 21st Inf. Co.G Sgt.
Wall, Charles V. MS 7th Inf. Co.C
Wall, C.I. GA 34th Inf. Co.E
Wall, Cincinnatus TN 14th Inf. Co.B
Wall, C.J. LA 4th Inf. Old Co.G
Wall, Clem C. TN 12th (Green's) Cav. Scarborough's Co. 2nd Lt.
Wall, Clem H. TN 4th (McLemore's) Cav. Co.A
Wall, Clm. A. TN Cav. 2nd Bn. (Biffle's) Co.C
Wall, C.M. GA 16th Inf. Co.K Sgt.
Wall, C.M. SC Inf.Bn. Co.A
Wall, Columbus S. VA 57th Inf. Co.D
Wall, Conrad AL Cav. 5th Bn. Hilliard's Legion Co.D
Wall, Conrad AL 60th Inf. Surg.
Wall, Conrad AL 1st Bn. Hilliard's Legion Vol. Asst.Surg.
Wall, Conrad Gen. & Staff Surg.
Wall, C.R. GA 5th Inf. Co.A
Wall, C.W. MS Cav. Jeff Davis Legion Co.D
Wall, Daniel NC 23rd Inf. Co.H
Wall, Daniel C. TN 34th Inf. Co.G
Wall, David MS 22nd Inf. Co.E Sgt.
Wall, David NC 45th Inf. Co.G
Wall, David TX
Wall, David 3rd Conf.Eng.Troops Co.D
Wall, David H. FL 3rd Inf. Co.C 2nd Lt.
Wall, Davis H. NC 21st Inf. Co.I
Wall, Delaney NC 17th Inf. (2nd Org.) Co.C
Wall, Dilany NC 17th Inf. (1st Org.) Co.D
Wall, D.J. 14th Conf.Cav. Co.F
Wall, D.K. AR 1st Mtd.Rifles Co.D
Wall, D.R. SC Cav. 4th Bn. Co.D
Wall, Dread AR 27th Inf. New Co.B
Wall, Dred J. NC 21st Inf. Co.C
Wall, Drewry MS 22nd Inf. Co.E
Wall, D.T. AL 1st Cav. Co.B
Wall, D.W. MS Cav. Part.Rangers Rhodes' Co.
Wall, D.W. 14th Conf.Cav. Co.F Sgt.
Wall, Dyer K. GA 57th Inf. Co.D
Wall, E.B. MS Cav. Jeff Davis Legion Co.E
Wall, E.B. VA 29th Inf. Co.F
Wall, E.D. Exch.Bn. Co.D,CSA
Wall, Edward MO 3rd Inf. Co.C
Wall, Edward A. MS 16th Inf. Co.K
Wall, Edward J. MS 8th Inf. Co.G
Wall, Edwin 1st Choctaw Mtd.Rifles Co.G
Wall, Edwin G. VA 18th Inf. Co.D Maj.
Wall, E.G. AL Lt.Arty. Kolb's Btty.
Wall, E.G. Lt.Arty. Dent's Btty.,CSA Cpl.
Wall, E.G. Gen. & Staff Maj.
Wall, E.H. GA Inf. (Milledgeville Guards) Caraker's Co. 3rd Lt.
Wall, E.J. LA 1st (Nelligan's) Inf. Co.B
Wall, Eli Holaway NC 56th Inf. Co.I
Wall, Elijah VA Wade's Regt.Loc.Def. Co.F
Wall, Elijah B. MS 33rd Inf. Co.B
Wall, Elkana NC 33rd Inf. Co.I
Wall, E.M. GA 63rd Inf. Co.E
Wall, Enoch J. AR 2nd Inf. Co.F
Wall, Enoch W. GA Inf. Cobb Guards Co.A
Wall, E.R. TN Inf. 154th Sr.Regt. Co.F Music.
Wall, E.R. TX 23rd Cav. Co.A
Wall, Evy NC 52nd Inf. Co.D
Wall, F.A. MO 3rd St.Guards
Wall, F.A. MO 12th Inf. Co.H Cpl.
Wall, F.F. TN 12th (Green's) Cav. Co.G,H
Wall, F.F. TN 51st Inf. Co.B Sgt.
Wall, F.F. TN 51st (Cons.) Inf. Co.H Sgt.
Wall, F.G. TN 1st (Feild's) & 27th Inf. (Cons.) Co.K
Wall, F.L. MS 4th Cav. Co.I Sgt.
Wall, F.M. AL 56th Part.Rangers Co.C
Wall, F.M. GA 5th Cav. Co.E
Wall, F.M. MS 10th Cav. Co.F
Wall, Francis MS 16th Inf. Co.K
Wall, Francis NC 52nd Inf. Co.D
Wall, Francis G. TN 1st (Feild's) Inf. Co.K
Wall, Francis M. GA Cav. 2nd Bn. Co.D
Wall, Francis M. MS 36th Inf. Co.I
Wall, Frank VA 23rd Inf. Co.H
Wall, Franklin VA 14th Cav. 2nd Co.F
Wall, Franklin VA 4th Inf. Co.L
Wall, Frederick TN 45th Inf. Co.H
Wall, F.W. MS 17th Inf. Co.A
Wall, G.A. NC 21st Inf. Co.F
Wall, Garret KY 7th Cav. Co.A
Wall, Garrett Gen. & Staff Lt.,ADC

Wall, George LA 1st (Strawbridge's) Inf. Co.E,I
Wall, George MS 18th Cav. Co.A
Wall, George MS Cav. Powers' Regt. Co.C
Wall, George VA Lt.Arty. Griffin's Co.
Wall, George G. NC 50th Inf. Co.C
Wall, George J. MO 5th Inf. Co.F
Wall, George W. GA 5th Inf. Co.G
Wall, George W. GA 27th Inf. Co.A
Wall, George W. GA 31st Inf. Co.B
Wall, George W. LA 1st Hvy.Arty. (Reg.) Co.C
Wall, George W. MS 9th Inf. Old Co.D
Wall, George W. MS 11th Inf. Co.I
Wall, George W. MS 16th Inf. Co.C
Wall, George W. MS 21st Inf. Co.F,C Capt.
Wall, George W. NC 13th Inf. Co.H
Wall, George W. TX 37th Cav. Co.B
Wall, George W. VA 136th Mil. Co.E
Wall, G.F.M. GA 2nd Inf. Co.B
Wall, G.H. NC 2nd Jr.Res. Co.K Cpl.
Wall, Gideon AL 37th Inf. Co.C
Wall, G.M. AR 8th Cav. Co.F
Wall, G.R. TN 12th Inf. Co.D
Wall, G.R. TN 12th (Cons.) Inf. Co.E
Wall, G.W. AR 9th Inf. Co.D
Wall, G.W. MS 8th Cav. Co.I
Wall, G.W. MS 1st Res. Co.A
Wall, G.W. MS 24th Inf. Co.C Capt.
Wall, G.W. NC 21st Inf. Co.I
Wall, H.A. TN 49th Inf. Co.E 1st Lt.
Wall, H.A. Inf. Bailey's Cons.Regt. Co.F 3rd Lt.
Wall, Hammett NC 42nd Inf. Co.A
Wall, Hampton MS 33rd Inf. Co.B 1st Lt.
Wall, Hansel J. NC 1st Inf. Co.F
Wall, Hanson D. FL Lt.Arty. Perry's Co.
Wall, Hardy SC 2nd Arty. Co.H
Wall, Hartwell TX 34th Cav. Co.I
Wall, H.C. GA 2nd Inf. Co.B,H
Wall, H.C. NC 4th Cav. (59th St.Troops) Co.A
Wall, H.C. VA 3rd Inf.Loc.Def. Co.A
Wall, H.D. AR 2nd Inf. Co.I
Wall, H.D. LA Lt.Arty. Fenner's Btty.
Wall, Henry LA 15th Inf. Co.A
Wall, Henry MS 18th Cav. Co.K,D
Wall, Henry VA 46th Inf. 1st Co.C
Wall, Henry VA 60th Inf. Co.B
Wall, Henry C. NC 23rd Inf. Co.D Sgt.
Wall, Henry D. VA 60th Inf. 2nd Co.H
Wall, Henry F. TX Cav. 2nd Regt.St.Troops Co.D
Wall, Henry N. LA 31st Inf. Co.G
Wall, H.G. SC 2nd St.Troops Co.D
Wall, H. Gideon SC 3rd Cav. Co.C
Wall, H.H. MS 19th Inf. Co.H
Wall, H.H. MS 33rd Inf. Co.K
Wall, Hillary GA Inf. 19th Bn. (St.Guards) Co.B
Wall, Hillman AL 39th Inf. Co.F
Wall, Hiram G. NC 21st Inf. Co.C
Wall, H.K. AL 53rd (Part.Rangers) Co.H
Wall, H.L. MO 12th Cav. Co.K
Wall, H.M. TN 5th Inf. 2nd Co.B
Wall, Howell C. MS 33rd Inf. Co.B
Wall, Howell G. SC Mil.Cav. 4th Regt. Howard's Co.
Wall, H.T. TN Inf. 4th Cons.Regt. Co.E Cpl.
Wall, H.T. TN 26th Inf. Co.D Cpl.
Wall, Hugh SC Cav. 12th Bn. Co.D
Wall, Hugh G. SC 4th Cav. Co.F
Wall, H.W. SC 26th Inf. Co.C
Wall, H.W. VA 1st (Farinholt's) Res. Co.K
Wall, I.J. LA Inf. 9th Bn. Co.C 1st Lt.
Wall, I.N. TX Cav. Mann's Regt. Co.H 3rd Lt.
Wall, Ira B. LA 19th Inf. Co.G 1st Lt.
Wall, Isaac VA 57th Inf. Co.I
Wall, Isaac H. NC 21st Inf. Co.F
Wall, Isaac N. TX 9th (Nichols') Inf. Co.F Sgt.
Wall, J. AL 10th Inf.
Wall, J. GA Hvy.Arty. 22nd Bn. Co.F
Wall, J.A. AL 4th (Russell's) Cav. Co.F
Wall, J.A. GA Cav. 20th Bn.
Wall, Jack TX 10th Cav. Co.F
Wall, Jackson FL 2nd Cav. Co.B 1st Sgt.
Wall, Jacob VA Cav. 34th Bn. Co.D
Wall, Jacob B. TN 59th Mtd.Inf. Co.G 1st Sgt.
Wall, Jacob C. VA 24th Inf. Co.K
Wall, James AR Cav. Harrell's Bn. Co.B
Wall, James AR 27th Inf. Co.B
Wall, James MS 18th Cav. Co.K
Wall, James MS Lt.Arty. Lomax's Co.
Wall, James MS Res.Corps Co.B
Wall, James NC 1st Inf. Co.I
Wall, James NC 21st Inf. Co.I
Wall, James SC Cav. 4th Bn. Co.D
Wall, James SC Cav. 12th Bn. Co.D
Wall, James TN 10th Inf. Co.I Cpl.
Wall, James TN 21st Inf. Co.I
Wall, James TN 50th Inf. Co.D
Wall, James VA 36th Inf. 2nd Co.B
Wall, James VA Loc.Def. Morehead's Co.
Wall, James Deneale's Regt. Choctaw Warriors Co.A
Wall, James A. GA 10th Inf. Co.F
Wall, James A. MS 36th Inf. Co.I 3rd Lt.
Wall, James A. VA Arty. Forrest's Co.
Wall, James B. GA 48th Inf. Co.G 2nd Lt.
Wall, James B. MS 18th Cav. Co.A Sgt.
Wall, James B. NC 18th Inf. Co.E
Wall, James B. SC 4th Cav. Co.F
Wall, James B. TX 31st Cav. Co.H Cpl.
Wall, James C. SC 10th Inf. Co.F
Wall, James C. VA 36th Inf. Co.F
Wall, James D. MD Arty. 4th Btty. 1st Sgt.
Wall, James E. GA 11th Cav. Co.G
Wall, James E. GA 9th Inf. (St.Guards) Co.G
Wall, James F. VA Cav. 39th Bn. Co.D
Wall, James G. FL 7th Inf. Co.F
Wall, James G. FL 9th Inf. Co.I
Wall, James G. LA 2nd Inf. Co.H
Wall, James G. VA 4th Inf. Co.E 2nd Lt.
Wall, James H. AL 22nd Inf. Co.A 2nd Lt.
Wall, James H. LA 21st (Patton's) Inf. Co.C
Wall, James I. LA Washington Arty.Bn. Co.4
Wall, James J. GA 1st (Olmstead's) Inf. Co.C
Wall, James J. LA Inf. 1st Sp.Bn. (Rightor's) Co.A
Wall, James J. SC 14th Inf. Co.H
Wall, James J.N. TN 6th (Wheeler's) Cav. Co.I 2nd Lt.
Wall, James M. FL 3rd Inf. Co.F Cpl.
Wall, James M. MS 10th Cav. Co.G
Wall, James M. MS 42nd Inf. Co.D
Wall, James M. NC 4th Cav. (59th St.Troops) Co.A 2nd Lt.
Wall, James M. NC 23rd Inf. Co.A Capt.
Wall, James N. GA Inf. 27th Bn. Co.B
Wall, James P. TN 34th Inf. Co.G
Wall, James R. NC 45th Inf. Co.H
Wall, James T. NC 5th Cav. (63rd St.Troops) Co.D Cpl.
Wall, James T. VA 52nd Mil.
Wall, Jason SC 5th St.Troops Co.F
Wall, Jason TX 1st (Yager's) Cav. Co.K
Wall, Jasper GA Inf. 19th Bn. (St.Guards) Co.B
Wall, Jasper MS 8th Cav. Co.K
Wall, J.B. LA 4th Inf. Co.A
Wall, J.B. MS 4th Cav. Co.G
Wall, J.B. MS Cav. Hughes' Bn. Co.F
Wall, J.B. TN 8th (Smith's) Cav. Co.A
Wall, J.B. TN 9th Inf. Co.D
Wall, J.B. VA 3rd Cav. Co.B
Wall, J.B.L. GA 3rd Inf. Co.C
Wall, J.C. AL 8th (Hatch's) Cav. Co.E Sgt.
Wall, J.C. KY Cav. A. Howsley's Bn.
Wall, J.C. MS 3rd Inf. (A. of 10,000) Co.C
Wall, J.C. MS Blythe's Bn. (St.Troops) Co.B
Wall, J.C. NC 31st Inf. Co.B
Wall, J.C. SC 6th Cav. Co.E
Wall, J.C. SC 5th Inf. 2nd Co.K
Wall, J.D. GA 8th Cav. Old Co.I
Wall, J.D. GA 62nd Cav. Co.I
Wall, J.D. NC 33rd Inf. Co.H
Wall, J.D. SC Lt.Arty. J.T. Kanapaux's Co. (Lafayette Arty.)
Wall, J.E. MS 1st (Johnston's) Inf. Co.B
Wall, J.E. SC 24th Inf. Co.D
Wall, Jerome L. AR 2nd Mtd.Rifles Co.A
Wall, Jesse NC 5th Sr.Res. Co.C
Wall, Jesse NC 22nd Inf. Co.I
Wall, Jesse NC 33rd Inf. Co.H
Wall, Jesse SC 5th Inf. 1st Co.C
Wall, Jesse J. TX 7th Inf. Co.K
Wall, J.F. TN 5th Inf. 2nd Co.B
Wall, J.F. TX Cav. 2nd Bn.St.Troops Co.A
Wall, J.G. LA 19th Inf. Surg.
Wall, J.G. MS Cav. Part.Rangers Rhodes' Co.
Wall, J.G. NC 30th Inf. Co.K
Wall, J.G. Gen. & Staff Surg.
Wall, J.H. AL 21st Inf. Co.F
Wall, J.H. AL 22nd Inf. Co.K 2nd Lt.
Wall, J.H. GA 45th Inf. Co.C
Wall, J.H. KY 3rd Mtd.Inf. Co.I
Wall, J.H. MS Lt.Arty. (Warren Lt.Arty.) Swett's Co. Cpl.
Wall, J.H. MS 31st Inf. Co.D
Wall, J.H. TX 11th Cav. Co.F
Wall, J.J. GA 8th Cav. Old Co.I
Wall, J.J. GA 62nd Cav. Co.I
Wall, J.J. MS Cav. 1st Bn. (McNair's) St.Troops Co.E 1st Lt.
Wall, J.J. MS 2nd Part.Rangers Co.L
Wall, J.J. MS 41st Inf. Co.H
Wall, J.J. TN 11th (Holman's) Cav. Co.E
Wall, J.J. TN 13th Inf. Co.A
Wall, J.J. VA 2nd Cav. Co.E
Wall, J.J. Gillum's Regt. Co.H
Wall, J.L. AR 9th Inf. Co.D
Wall, J.L. TX 2nd Cav. Co.A
Wall, J.M. AR 8th Cav. Co.F
Wall, J.M. GA 62nd Cav. Co.I
Wall, J.M. GA Inf. (Milledgeville Guards) Caraker's Co.
Wall, J.M. MS 2nd Cav. Co.E

Wall, J.M. MS 1st (Johnston's) Inf. Co.B
Wall, J.M. MS 12th Inf. Co.F
Wall, J.M. MS Blythe's Bn. (St.Troops) Co.A
Wall, J.M. MO 16th Inf. Co.F 1st Lt.
Wall, J.M. SC 5th Inf. 2nd Co.K
Wall, J.M. TN 5th Inf. 2nd Co.B
Wall, J.N. GA Cav. 22nd Bn. (St.Guards) Co.A
Wall, J.N. NC Cav. McRae's Bn. Co.E
Wall, Joel S. GA 41st Inf. Co.I
Wall, John AL Arty. 1st Bn. Co.D
Wall, John AL 17th Inf. Co.D
Wall, John GA 3rd Bn.S.S. Co.E Sgt.
Wall, John GA 24th Inf. Co.E
Wall, John GA 59th Inf. Co.C
Wall, John LA 28th (Gray's) Inf. Co.B
Wall, John LA C.S. Zouave Bn. Co.A
Wall, John MS Moseley's Regt.
Wall, John MO 12th Inf. Co.H
Wall, John NC 6th Sr.Res. Co.C
Wall, John NC 6th Sr.Res. Co.K
Wall, John NC 27th Inf. Co.E
Wall, John NC 33rd Inf. Co.H
Wall, John NC 47th Inf. Co.E
Wall, John NC 56th Inf. Co.I
Wall, John NC Jones' Co. (Supp.Force)
Wall, John TN 2nd (Walker's) Inf. Co.C
Wall, John TN 14th Inf. Co.E 1st Sgt.
Wall, John TN 21st Inf. Co.I
Wall, John TN 48th (Nixon's) Inf. Co.K
Wall, John VA Inf. 1st Bn. Co.B
Wall, John VA 14th Inf. Co.D
Wall, John VA 57th Inf. Co.D
Wall, John VA 151st Mil. Co.B
Wall, John VA Arty. Wise Legion Sgt.
Wall, John VA Loc.Def. Chappell's Co.
Wall, John 1st Conf.Inf. 2nd Co.K,G
Wall, John 9th Conf.Inf. Co.E Sgt.
Wall, John A. NC 32nd Inf. Co.G
Wall, John A. TX 14th Inf. Co.A
Wall, John B. GA 9th Inf. Co.F Cpl.
Wall, John B. MS 19th Inf. Co.H Capt.
Wall, John B. TN 6th (Wheeler's) Cav. Co.I
Wall, John B. TN 14th Inf. Co.B
Wall, John B. TX 5th Inf. Co.B Sgt.
Wall, John B.L. GA 3rd Bn.S.S. Co.E
Wall, John B.L. GA 24th Inf. Co.E
Wall, Jno. C. AL 8th (Hatch's) Cav. Co.E 1st Sgt.
Wall, John C. SC 3rd Cav. Co.C
Wall, John C. SC Mil.Cav. 4th Regt. Howard's Co.
Wall, John C. TX 13th Cav. Co.B
Wall, John D. AL 60th Inf. N.C.S. Co.C QMSgt.
Wall, John D. AL 3rd Bn. Hilliard's Legion Vol. Co.D QMSgt.
Wall, John D. GA 48th Inf. Co.C
Wall, John D. NC Inf. Thomas Legion Co.D
Wall, John G. LA 8th Inf. Co.E
Wall, John H. GA Brooks' Co. (Terrell Lt.Arty.)
Wall, John H. KY Cav. 2nd Bn. (Dortch's) Co.C 2nd Lt.
Wall, John H. KY 10th Cav. 1st Lt.
Wall, John H. KY Morgan's Men Co.G 1st Lt.
Wall, John H. MS 22nd Inf. Co.E
Wall, John H. MS 33rd Inf. Co.B,K
Wall, John I. MS 2nd Inf. Co.E
Wall, John J. MS 2nd Cav. Co.E
Wall, John J. MS 1st (Percy's) Inf. Co.H
Wall, John J. MS 2nd Inf. Co.F 2nd Lt.
Wall, John J. MS 34th Inf. Co.H Sgt.
Wall, John K. TN 32nd Inf. Co.B
Wall, John M. LA 8th Inf. Co.H,F
Wall, John M. MS 9th Inf. New Co.E
Wall, John M. MS 37th Inf. Co.B
Wall, John M. TN 15th Inf. Co.G Maj.
Wall, John N. LA 11th Inf. Co.F
Wall, John P. FL 9th Inf. Co.A Capt.
Wall, John P. MS 36th Inf. Co.I
Wall, John P. VA 11th Bn.Res. Co.D
Wall, Jno. P. Gen. & Staff Surg.
Wall, John Q. LA Pointe Coupee Arty. 2nd Lt.
Wall, John R. MO 3rd Inf. Co.C
Wall, John R. NC 24th Inf. Co.C
Wall, John S. GA 63rd Inf. Co.K,D
Wall, John S. LA 7th Inf. Co.K
Wall, Johnson TX 16th Cav. Co.A
Wall, Johnson TX Cav. McCord's Frontier Regt. Co.D
Wall, Johnson B. NC 3rd Arty. (40th St.Troops) Co.H
Wall, Johnson B. NC Lt.Arty. 13th Bn. Co.F
Wall, John T. GA 15th Inf. Co.D
Wall, John W. GA 43rd Inf. Co.H
Wall, John W. MS 43rd Inf. Co.G
Wall, John W. TN 26th Inf. Co.D
Wall, John W. TN 54th Inf. Co.G
Wall, Jonathan MS 2nd Cav. Co.E
Wall, Joseph MS 2nd Cav. Co.E
Wall, Joseph NC 6th Sr.Res. Co.K
Wall, Joseph TX 11th Inf. Co.D
Wall, Joseph M. AL 37th Inf. Co.D
Wall, Joseph M. AL 39th Inf. Co.F
Wall, Joseph M. NC 13th Inf. Co.H
Wall, Joseph W. TN 49th Inf. Co.E Capt.
Wall, Joshua VA Cav. 34th Bn. Co.D
Wall, Joshua VA 36th Inf. 1st Co.C, 2nd Co.D
Wall, Joshua T. 1st Conf.Eng.Troops Co.F
Wall, J.Q. TX Waul's Legion Co.B Capt.
Wall, J.R. GA 8th Cav. Old Co.I
Wall, J.R. GA 62nd Cav. Co.I
Wall, J.R. NC 55th Inf. Co.D
Wall, J.R. NC Mil. Clark's Sp.Bn. Co.I
Wall, J.R.P. SC 1st Cav. Co.D
Wall, J.S. GA Inf. (Milledgeville Guards) Caraker's Co.
Wall, J.S. TN 11th (Holman's) Cav. Co.E
Wall, J.T. AR Cav. Harrell's Bn. Co.B
Wall, Julius M. GA 38th Inf. Co.E
Wall, J.W. AR 5th Inf. Co.D
Wall, J.W. MS 2nd Cav. Co.E
Wall, J.W. MS 5th Inf. Co.A
Wall, J.W. NC 21st Inf. Co.F
Wall, J.W. Inf. Bailey's Cons.Regt. Co.F 2nd Lt.
Wall, Kinsion NC 33rd Inf. Co.I
Wall, Lawrence D. FL 2nd Cav. Co.B
Wall, Lawrence H. AR 6th Inf. Co.K Sgt.
Wall, Lawrence W. GA 3rd Cav. Co.A 2nd Lt.
Wall, Lawrence W. GA 1st (Ramsey's) Inf. Co.B 2nd Lt.
Wall, Lazarus SC 2nd Arty. Co.H
Wall, L.C. MS 33rd Inf. Co.B
Wall, L.C. 14th Conf.Cav. Co.F
Wall, Lewis A. KY 1st (Butler's) Cav. Co.G
Wall, L.H. AR 3rd Cav. Co.H
Wall, L.H. NC 21st Inf. Co.I Cpl.
Wall, Litleton M. GA 24th Inf. Co.E
Wall, Little B. NC 18th Inf. Co.E
Wall, Littleton M. GA 3rd Bn.S.S. Co.E
Wall, L.J. SC 21st Inf. Co.I
Wall, L.J. SC Prov.Guard Hamilton's Co.
Wall, L.J. VA 13th Cav. Co.D
Wall, L.M. AR 45th Cav. Co.A
Wall, Logan KY 2nd Cav. Co.C
Wall, Logan TN 14th (Neely's) Cav. Co.F
Wall, Logan H. MS 19th Inf. Co.H
Wall, Louis KY 10th (Johnson's) Cav. New Co.C
Wall, Loven Ross GA 40th Inf. Co.C
Wall, L.P. AL 5th Inf. New Co.D
Wall, L.P. GA 4th Cav. (St.Guards) Cannon's Co.
Wall, L.P. GA 11th Cav. Co.F
Wall, L.P. GA 52nd Inf. Co.F Sr.2nd Lt.
Wall, L.W. GA 27th Inf. Co.A
Wall, L.W. GA 59th Inf. Co.C
Wall, M. AR Inf. Clear Lake Ind.Guards
Wall, M. GA 8th Cav. Old Co.I
Wall, M. GA 19th Inf. Co.A
Wall, Marion J. GA 46th Inf. Co.B
Wall, Marshall S. LA Pointe Coupee Arty. Cpl.
Wall, Martin GA Hvy.Arty. 22nd Bn. Co.E
Wall, Martin GA 1st (Olmstead's) Inf. Guilmartin's Co.
Wall, Martin N. GA 3rd Bn.S.S. Co.E
Wall, Martin N. GA 24th Inf. Co.E
Wall, Mc. GA 62nd Cav. Co.I
Wall, M.C. MS 8th Inf. Co.G
Wall, M.H. SC 24th Inf. Co.D
Wall, M. Henry MS 42nd Inf. Co.D
Wall, Mial NC 3rd Arty. (40th St.Troops) Co.G
Wall, Micajah C. MS 14th Inf. Co.B
Wall, Michael TN 10th Inf. Co.B
Wall, Michael VA Inf. 1st Bn. Co.C
Wall, Miles S. GA 3rd Inf. Co.B Cpl.
Wall, Milton D.C. GA 24th Inf. Co.E
Wall, M.M. NC 7th Sr.Res. Holland's Co.
Wall, M.O. SC 1st Mtd.Mil. Evans' Co.
Wall, M.O. SC 2nd Arty. Co.H
Wall, Morrison G. TN 14th Inf. Co.F
Wall, M.R. GA 53rd Inf. Co.A
Wall, M.S. VA Hvy.Arty. Coffin's Co.
Wall, M.T. NC 1st Inf. Co.C
Wall, M.T. SC 2nd Inf. Co.D
Wall, M.W. NC Cav. McRae's Bn. Co.E
Wall, N. GA 3rd Inf.
Wall, N. TN 14th Inf. Co.B
Wall, N. TN Inf. 23rd Bn. Co.B
Wall, Nace L. GA 3rd Bn.S.S. Co.E
Wall, Nathaniel AL 37th Inf. Co.C
Wall, Nathan T. GA 2nd Cav. Co.G
Wall, Nelson N.L. TN 16th (Logwood's) Cav. Co.K
Wall, Newel J. NC Inf. 2nd Bn. Co.B
Wall, Newel J. NC 21st Inf. Co.H
Wall, Newton TN 11th (Holman's) Cav. Co.E
Wall, N.L. MS Inf. 3rd Bn. (St.Troops) Co.B
Wall, O.C. TN 9th Inf. Co.D
Wall, Octavius MO 3rd Inf. Co.C 1st Sgt.
Wall, Octavius MO St.Guard
Wall, P. LA Mil. 4th Regt. French Brig. Co.7
Wall, P. MS 10th Inf. Co.H

Wall, P. NC 2nd Inf. Co.G 3rd Lt.
Wall, P.A. SC 5th Inf. 2nd Co.K
Wall, Patrick LA 1st Hvy.Arty. (Reg.) Co.H
Wall, Patrick TN 2nd (Robison's) Inf. Co.E Sgt.
Wall, Patrick 3rd Conf.Eng.Troops Co.F
Wall, P.C. MS Inf. 1st Bn.St.Troops (30 days '64) Co.D
Wall, P.J. MO 10th Inf. Co.G
Wall, Preston B. VA 57th Inf. Co.B
Wall, P.S. GA 59th Inf. Co.C
Wall, R. NC 33rd Inf. Co.K
Wall, Radmon MS 20th Inf. Co.B
Wall, R.B. TN 3rd (Forrest's) Cav. Co.D
Wall, R.B. TN 12th Inf. Co.D
Wall, R.B. TN 12th (Cons.) Inf. Co.E Cpl.
Wall, R.B. TX 23rd Cav. Co.A Hosp.Stew.
Wall, R.C. AR Cav. Anderson's Unatt.Bn.
Wall, Redman NC Cav. 12th Bn. Co.C
Wall, Redmund NC 17th Inf. (1st Org.) Co.D
Wall, Redmund NC 17th Inf. (2nd Org.) Co.C
Wall, Reuben NC 1st Jr.Res. Co.D
Wall, R.H. NC 56th Inf. Co.I
Wall, R.H. VA 57th Inf. Co.E
Wall, Richard MS 28th Cav. Co.C Cpl.
Wall, Richard E. VA Hvy.Arty. Wright's Co.
Wall, Richard M. KY 9th Mtd.Inf. Co.D 2nd Lt.
Wall, Rienzi G. FL 1st Inf. Old Co.A
Wall, R.J.F. SC 5th Inf. 2nd Co.K
Wall, R.J.F. SC 13th Inf. Co.F
Wall, R.M. GA 3rd Bn. (St.Guards) Co.G
Wall, Robert KY 3rd Cav. Co.I
Wall, Robert KY 6th Cav. Co.A
Wall, Robert MS 1st Lt.Arty. Co.K
Wall, Robert NC 46th Inf. Co.F
Wall, Robert SC 5th Inf. 1st Co.C
Wall, Robert TN 12th (Cons.) Inf. Co.A
Wall, Robert VA Cav. 39th Bn. Co.D
Wall, Robert J. GA Inf. 1st Loc.Troops (Augusta) Co.F
Wall, Robert J. GA 5th Inf. Co.D
Wall, Robert W. GA Cav. 2nd Bn. Co.D
Wall, Rowan L. FL 7th Inf. Co.I 2nd Lt.
Wall, R.T. TN 5th Inf. 2nd Co.B
Wall, Rufus D. NC 24th Inf. Co.C
Wall, R.W. GA 5th Cav. Co.A
Wall, Samuel B. LA 8th Inf. Co.H
Wall, Samuel B. TN Cav. 1st Bn. (McNairy's) Co.C
Wall, Samuel B. TN 22nd (Barteau's) Cav. Co.B 2nd Lt.
Wall, Samuel C. NC 23rd Inf. Co.A
Wall, Samuel D. MS 16th Inf. Co.K
Wall, Samuel G. KY 10th (Johnson's) Cav. New Co.C Capt.
Wall, Samuel J. NC 3rd Jr.Res. Co.C
Wall, Samuel W. NC 53rd Inf. Co.H,E Sgt.
Wall, Samuel W. SC 10th Inf. Co.F
Wall, S.B. AL 33rd Inf. Co.I
Wall, S.D. AL St.Res.
Wall, Seaburn T. MS 8th Inf. Co.G
Wall, Sebert NC Townsend's Co. (St.Troops)
Wall, Septimus Gen. & Staff, Cav. Capt.
Wall, S.F. LA 3rd (Wingfield's) Cav. Co.E AQM
Wall, S.F. LA 4th Inf. Old Co.G
Wall, S.F. Gen. & Staff, QM Dept. Capt.
Wall, S.H. AR 2nd Inf. Co.I
Wall, S.I. NC 56th Inf. Co.I
Wall, Sidney J. AL 1st Inf. Co.F
Wall, S.J. FL 2nd Cav. Co.B 1st Sgt.
Wall, S.J. GA 1st Reg. Co.A
Wall, S.J. NC 4th Bn.Jr.Res. Co.C
Wall, S.J. SC 11th Inf. 2nd Co.F
Wall, S.L. AR 1st (Monroe's) Cav. Co.G
Wall, S.L. AR 11th Inf. Co.A
Wall, S.L. AR 11th & 17th (Cons.) Inf. Co.A
Wall, S.M. SC Inf.Bn. Co.A Cpl.
Wall, S.T. TX 34th Cav. Co.I
Wall, Stanley NC 21st Inf. Co.H
Wall, Starling NC 45th Inf. Co.G
Wall, Stephen GA Inf. 19th Bn. (St.Guards) Co.A
Wall, Stephen B. SC 10th Inf. Co.L
Wall, Stephen J. FL 1st Inf. Old Co.C Sgt.
Wall, S.V. TN 4th (McLemore's) Cav. Co.F
Wall, S.V. TN 22nd (Barteau's) Cav. Co.B
Wall, S.V. TN 20th Inf. Co.D
Wall, S.W. AL 29th Inf. Co.G
Wall, T.A. AL 53rd (Part.Rangers) Co.C Cpl.
Wall, T.A. AR Cav. Crabtree's (46th) Regt. Co.A
Wall, T.A. GA Cav. 12th Bn. (St.Guards) Co.E Cpl.
Wall, Thempsey 1st Choctaw Mtd.Rifles Co.I
Wall, Tho. J. AL 22nd Inf. Co.K
Wall, Thomas AL St.Arty. Co.A
Wall, Thomas AL 21st Inf. Co.F
Wall, Thomas AL 37th Inf. Co.C
Wall, Thomas GA 1st (Olmstead's) Inf. Co.A
Wall, Thomas GA 46th Inf. Co.B,G
Wall, Thomas LA 5th Inf. Co.C
Wall, Thomas LA 6th Inf. Co.F
Wall, Thomas LA 14th (Austin's) Bn.S.S. Co.B
Wall, Thomas LA Miles' Legion Co.A
Wall, Thomas MS 3rd Cav. Co.G
Wall, Thomas MO 15th Cav. Co.A
Wall, Thomas NC 48th Inf. Co.H
Wall, Thomas TN 14th Inf. Co.E
Wall, Thomas TN 15th Inf. Co.B
Wall, Thomas TN 53rd Inf. Co.K
Wall, Thomas VA 8th Cav. Co.A
Wall, Thomas 1st Choctaw Mtd.Rifles Co.G
Wall, Thomas A. AL 3rd Inf. Co.I
Wall, Thomas C.H. MS 34th Inf. Co.K
Wall, Thomas F. LA 11th Inf. Co.C Sgt.
Wall, Thomas F. MS 12th Inf. Co.E
Wall, Thomas H.W. MS 22nd Inf. Co.F 1st Lt.
Wall, Thomas J. MS 11th Inf. Co.I
Wall, Thomas J. MS 14th Inf. Co.B
Wall, Thomas J. VA 2nd Cav. Co.B
Wall, Thomas M.T. TN Inf. 1st Bn. (Colms') Co.A Sgt.
Wall, Thomas N. TN 54th Inf. Ives' Co.
Wall, Thomas P. FL Lt.Arty. Perry's Co.
Wall, Thomas T. LA Inf. 9th Bn. Co.C 1st Sgt.
Wall, Thornton GA Siege Arty. 28th Bn. Co.D
Wall, T.J. GA 13th Inf. Co.H
Wall, T.J. LA Mil. Beauregard Bn. Co.C
Wall, T.L. KY Cav. Thompson's Co.
Wall, T.M. TX 34th Cav. Co.I
Wall, T.N. MS 2nd Cav. Co.E
Wall, T.P. FL 1st Cav. Co.C Capt.
Wall, Trussell GA 26th Inf. Co.I
Wall, T.T. LA 26th Inf. Co.G
Wall, W. AL 34th Inf. Co.C 2nd Lt.
Wall, W. NC 5th Sr.Res. Co.C
Wall, W. NC 21st Inf. Co.F
Wall, W. TX Cav. 1st Regt.St.Troops Co.F
Wall, W. VA 2nd St.Res. Co.K
Wall, W.A. NC 21st Inf. Co.F
Wall, W.A. TN 3rd (Clack's) Inf. Co.I
Wall, W.A. TX 11th Inf. Co.E
Wall, Walter P. MS 1st Lt.Arty. Co.H
Wall, Warren LA 28th (Gray's) Inf. Co.G
Wall, Watkins W.A. NC 52nd Inf. Co.D
Wall, Watson L. SC 14th Inf. Co.H
Wall, W.B. GA 8th Cav. Old Co.I
Wall, W.B. GA 62nd Cav. Co.I
Wall, W.B. Gen. & Staff Capt.,AQM
Wall, W.C. TN 44th (Cons.) Inf. Co.I
Wall, W.D. NC 21st Inf. Co.F
Wall, W.D. SC Cav. 12th Bn. Co.D Cpl.
Wall, W.D. SC 7th (Ward's) Bn.St.Res. Co.F
Wall, W.D. Gen. & Staff,PACS Hosp.Stew.
Wall, W.E. TX 13th Vol. 1st Co.H
Wall, W.E.G. GA 13th Inf. Co.H
Wall, Wesley NC 52nd Inf. Co.D
Wall, Wesley D. SC 4th Cav. Co.F Cpl.
Wall, Wesley W. LA 19th Inf. Co.G
Wall, W.H. MO 2nd Cav.
Wall, W.H. TN 9th Inf. Co.A Sgt.
Wall, W.H. 9th Conf.Inf. Co.E
Wall, W.H. Gen. & Staff 1st Lt.,Adj.
Wall, Wilburn GA Cav. 6th Bn. (St.Guards) Co.A
Wall, Wiley NC 6th Sr.Res. Co.G
Wall, Wiley 1st Conf.Inf. 2nd Co.D
Wall, William AL 4th (Russell's) Cav. Co.F
Wall, William AL 34th Inf. Co.E
Wall, William AR Cav. Harrell's Bn. Co.B
Wall, William AR 27th Inf. Co.B
Wall, William GA Cav. 7th Bn. (St.Guards) Co.F
Wall, William, Jr. GA 24th Inf. Co.E
Wall, William GA 39th Inf. Co.K
Wall, William KY 1st (Butler's) Cav. Co.G
Wall, William KY 2nd (Duke's) Cav. Co.E Cpl.
Wall, William MS 1st Cav. Co.H Cpl.
Wall, William MS 7th Cav. Co.H Cpl.
Wall, William MS Cav. Vivion's Co.
Wall, William MO 4th Cav. Co.H
Wall, William NC 7th Sr.Res. Watts' Co.
Wall, William NC 31st Inf. Co.H
Wall, William NC 48th Inf. Co.G
Wall, William SC 2nd Arty. Co.H
Wall, William SC 5th Inf. 1st Co.C Sgt.
Wall, William SC Inf. 7th Bn. (Enfield Rifles) Co.D
Wall, William TN 27th Inf. Co.C
Wall, William VA Cav. O'Ferrall's Bn. Co.B Sgt.
Wall, William VA 11th Bn.Res. Co.D Cpl.
Wall, William VA 11th Bn.Res. Co.D
Wall, William VA 17th Inf. Co.K
Wall, William VA 31st Mil. Co.A
Wall, William VA 151st Mil. Co.B
Wall, William A. NC 24th Inf. Co.C
Wall, William B. GA 26th Inf. Co.I
Wall, William B. GA 50th Inf. Co.C
Wall, William B. MS 22nd Inf. Surg.
Wall, William B. MS 33rd Inf. Co.I Surg.
Wall, William B. NC 22nd Inf. Co.M,E

Wall, William B. TX 1st Inf. Co.I 1st Lt.
Wall, William Burgess Gen. & Staff Surg.
Wall, William C. GA Cobb's Legion Co.F
Wall, William C. MS 10th Inf. Old Co.B
Wall, William C. MS 33rd Inf. Co.B Sgt.
Wall, William C. MS 43rd Inf. Co.H
Wall, William C. NC 4th Cav. (59th St.Troops) Co.C
Wall, William C. NC 23rd Inf. Co.D Capt.
Wall, William C. TN 55th (McKoin's) Inf. McEwen, Jr.'s Co.
Wall, William D. GA 26th Inf. Co.K
Wall, William D. GA 57th Inf. Co.I,D
Wall, William D. MS 16th Inf. Co.K
Wall, William D. NC 45th Inf. Co.H Cpl.
Wall, William D. SC 1st (Orr's) Rifles Co.C
Wall, William E. TX 35th (Brown's) Cav. Co.C
Wall, William Evy NC 21st Inf. Co.G
Wall, William G. GA 1st (Ramsey's) Inf. Co.E
Wall, William H. LA Inf.Crescent Regt. Co.C 1st Lt.
Wall, William H. LA Inf.Cons.Crescent Regt. Co.G 1st Lt.
Wall, William H. MS 12th Inf. Co.F 1st Lt.
Wall, William H. NC 24th Inf. Co.C
Wall, William H. TN 8th (Smith's) Cav. Co.K
Wall, William H. VA 41st Inf. 2nd Co.G
Wall, William H. Horse Arty. White's Btty.
Wall, William Hillery TN 2nd (Walker's) Inf. Co.E
Wall, William J. MS 19th Inf. Co.H Capt.
Wall, William J. NC 47th Inf. Co.E
Wall, William J. VA 4th Res. Co.C
Wall, William J. VA 57th Inf. Co.I
Wall, William L. AR 5th Inf. Co.C
Wall, William L. MS 33rd Inf. Co.B Cpl.
Wall, William L. VA 32nd Inf. 2nd Co.H
Wall, William M. NC 16th Inf. Co.D Cpl.
Wall, William N. MS 10th Inf. Old Co.B
Wall, William R. AL 15th Bn.Part.Rangers Co.A
Wall, William S. AL 3rd Inf. Co.I
Wall, William T. GA 56th Inf. Co.B
Wall, William W. FL 9th Inf. Co.C
Wall, William W. FL Parsons' Co.
Wall, Willis AL Gid Nelson Lt.Arty.
Wall, Willis Guilford NC 56th Inf. Co.I Sgt.
Wall, Wilson M. VA 57th Inf. Co.D
Wall, W.J. NC Mallett's Bn. Co.C
Wall, W.J.B. SC 7th Cav. Co.A
Wall, W.J.B. SC Cav. Tucker's Co.
Wall, W.K. MS 5th Cav. Co.E
Wall, W.K. MS 18th Cav. Co.I
Wall, W.L. AR 9th Inf. Co.D
Wall, W.L. GA 59th Inf. Co.C 1st Lt.
Wall, W.M. AL 12th Cav. Co.B
Wall, W.N. MS 2nd Cav. Co.E
Wall, W.P. TN 51st Inf. Co.B 1st Sgt.
Wall, W.R. AL 56th Part.Rangers Co.A
Wall, W.R. AL 4th Inf. Co.F
Wall, W.R. TN 38th Inf. Co.C Cpl.
Wall, Wright AL 11th Inf. Co.E
Wall, W.S. AL 53rd (Part.Rangers) Co.C
Wall, W.T. AR 15th (Johnson's) Inf. Co.C 2nd Lt.
Wall, W.T. TN 12th (Green's) Cav. Co.H
Wall, W.T. TN 51st (Cons.) Inf. Co.I 1st Sgt.
Wall, W.W. LA Inf.Crescent Regt. Co.B
Wall, W.W. MS Cav. 3rd Bn.Res. Co.B
Wall, W.W. MS Inf. 2nd Bn. Co.B
Wall, W.W. MS 48th Inf. Co.B
Wall, W.W. MS Conscr.
Wall, W.W. MO 5th Cav. Co.C
Wall, W.W. VA 23rd Cav. Co.G Sgt.
Wall, Young AL 15th Bn.Part.Rangers Co.C
Wall, Young AL 56th Part.Rangers Co.C Sgt.
Wall, Young MS 10th Cav. Co.F Sgt.
Wall, Zachariah MS 8th Inf. Co.G
Wall, Zachariah L. 1st Conf.Eng.Troops Co.F
Wallace, --- KY 2nd (Duke's) Cav. New Co.D
Wallace, --- NC Inf. Thomas Legion
Wallace, --- SC Mil. 16th Regt. Steinmeyer, Jr.'s Co.
Wallace, --- TX Cav. Bourland's Regt. Co.G
Wallace, --- TX Cav. Mann's Regt. Co.D
Wallace, A. AL 8th Cav. Co.H
Wallace, A. LA 3rd Inf.
Wallace, A. LA 21st (Kennedy's) Inf. Co.D
Wallace, A. LA 31st Inf. Co.D
Wallace, A. SC 4th Bn.Res. Co.E
Wallace, Aaron VA 5th Cav. (12 mo. '61-2) Co.A
Wallace, Aaron VA Cav. 14th Bn. Co.C
Wallace, Aaron G. TN 1st Cav.
Wallace, A.B. AR 1st (Dobbin's) Cav. Co.A
Wallace, Abel B. Gen. & Staff Asst.Surg.
Wallace, Abraham C. KY 13th Cav. Co.A
Wallace, Abraham L. NC Walker's Bn. Thomas' Legion Co.F
Wallace, Abram NC Walker's Bn. Thomas' Legion 1st Co.D
Wallace, Abram TN 1st (Carter's) Cav. Co.I
Wallace, Abram F. AL 17th Inf. Co.C
Wallace, Abram J. TX 5th Cav. Co.K
Wallace, Abram L. TN 5th (McKenzie's) Cav. Co.K
Wallace, A.C. AR 31st Inf. Co.K
Wallace, Addison S. TX 17th Cav. Co.B
Wallace, Adolphus MS 11th (Perrin's) Cav. Co.K
Wallace, A.F. NC 57th Inf. Co.G
Wallace, A.F. NC Hill's Bn.Res. Co.C 1st Lt.
Wallace, A.G. MS 18th Inf. Co.B Music.
Wallace, A.H. TX 12th Cav. Co.C
Wallace, A.H. VA 30th Inf. Co.C
Wallace, A.J. AL Cav. Moreland's Regt. Co.D
Wallace, A.J. AL 5th Cav. Co.B
Wallace, A.J. AL 46th Inf. Co.D
Wallace, A.J. FL Lt.Arty. Dyke's Co.
Wallace, A.J. GA 65th Inf. Co.B
Wallace, A.J. LA 4th Cav.
Wallace, A.J. MS 18th Cav. Co.D
Wallace, A.J. MS 3rd Inf. Co.F
Wallace, A.J. MS 10th Inf. Co.P, New Co.G
Wallace, A.J. MS 23rd Inf. Co.F
Wallace, A.J. MS 34th Inf. Co.I
Wallace, A.J. SC 12th Inf. Co.B
Wallace, A.J. TN 24th Bn.S.S. Co.C
Wallace, A.J. TN 50th (Cons.) Inf. Co.C
Wallace, A. Jackson SC Lt.Arty. Kelly's Co. (Chesterfield Arty.)
Wallace, A.K. NC 50th Inf. Co.G
Wallace, A.L. TX Cav. Wells' Regt. Co.F 2nd Lt.
Wallace, Albert NC 37th Inf. Co.I
Wallace, Albert TN 42nd Inf. 1st Co.E
Wallace, Albert TX Cav. Benavides' Regt. Co.C
Wallace, Albert D. AL 6th Inf. Co.L Cpl.
Wallace, Albert M. GA Cav. Nelson's Ind.Co.
Wallace, Albert S. VA 44th Inf. Co.H Cpl.
Wallace, Albright VA Lt.Arty. Donald's Co. Cpl.
Wallace, Alex LA Mil. 1st Regt. 2nd Brig. 1st Div. Co.G 3rd Lt.
Wallace, Alexander NC 26th Inf. Co.H
Wallace, Alexander NC 35th Inf. Co.B
Wallace, Alexander SC 18th Inf. Co.G
Wallace, Alexander VA 23rd Cav. Co.D
Wallace, Alexander A. VA 4th Inf. Co.H
Wallace, Alexander D. VA 16th Inf. 2nd Co.H, Co.G
Wallace, Alexander L. SC 12th Inf. Co.B Sgt.
Wallace, Alexander Lafayette KY 4th Mtd.Inf. Co.G,K 2nd Lt.
Wallace, Alexander M. GA 1st Reg. Co.L Capt.
Wallace, Alexn. M. GA 36th (Broyles') Inf. Lt.Col.
Wallace, Alexander R. VA Lt.Arty. Pollock's Co.
Wallace, Alfred AR 15th (N.W.) Inf. Emergency Co.I
Wallace, Alfred MS 9th Inf. New Co.A
Wallace, Alfred NC Inf. Thomas Legion Co.K Cpl.
Wallace, Alfred SC 15th Inf. Co.A Asst.Surg.
Wallace, Alfred Gen. & Staff Asst.Surg.
Wallace, Alfred Boyd KY 2nd (Woodward's) Cav. Co.D
Wallace, Alfred D. TN 1st (Feild's) Inf. Co.B
Wallace, Algernon S. AL 44th Inf. Co.B Cpl.
Wallace, Allen NC 35th Inf. Co.K
Wallace, Allen S. TX Cav. Martin's Regt. Co.F
Wallace, Alonzo SC 13th Inf. Co.F
Wallace, Alonzo G. NC 34th Inf. Co.C
Wallace, A.M. AR 19th (Dockery's) Inf. Co.A
Wallace, A.M. GA Cav. Ragland's Co.
Wallace, A.M. MS 10th Inf. Co.P, New Co.G
Wallace, A.M. TN 14th (Neely's) Cav. Co.D
Wallace, Amos TN 13th (Gore's) Cav. Co.A
Wallace, Ananias GA Cav. Roswell Bn. Co.B,A Cpl.
Wallace, Ananias GA 7th Inf. Co.H
Wallace, Anderson GA 4th Cav. (St.Guards) White's Co.
Wallace, Andrew TN 13th (Gore's) Cav. Co.D
Wallace, Andrew B. VA 11th Cav. Co.G
Wallace, Andrew H. MO Cav. Wood's Regt. Co.E
Wallace, Andrew J. AL 36th Inf. Co.G
Wallace, Andrew J. MS 2nd Part.Rangers Co.K,H
Wallace, Archible S. GA Cav. 1st Bn.Res. McKinney's Co.
Wallace, Arthur LA 21st (Patton's) Inf. Co.D Sgt.
Wallace, Arthur VA Lt.Arty. Pollock's Co.
Wallace, A.S. TX 17th Cons.Dismtd.Cav. Co.C Cpl.
Wallace, A.S. TX 22nd Inf. Co.G
Wallace, Asa MS 28th Cav. Co.B
Wallace, Augustus GA 42nd Inf. Co.F
Wallace, Augustus A. GA Cobb's Legion Co.E

Wallace, Augustus H. GA 7th Inf. (St.Guards) Co.K
Wallace, A.W. AL 36th Inf. Co.G
Wallace, A.W. VA 30th Inf. Co.C
Wallace, B. AR Lt.Arty. Hart's Btty.
Wallace, B. AR 24th Inf. Co.H
Wallace, B. NC Mallett's Bn. Co.F
Wallace, B. SC 3rd St.Troops Co.A
Wallace, B. SC 25th Inf. Co.F
Wallace, B.A. TX 2nd Cav. 1st Co.F
Wallace, B.D. GA 4th Cav. (St.Guards) Deadwyler's Co.
Wallace, Beaty SC 17th Inf. Co.D
Wallace, Ben SC Cav. 4th Bn. Co.C 1st Sgt.
Wallace, Benjamin AL 39th Inf. Co.F
Wallace, Benjamin MD Inf. 2nd Bn. Co.D Sgt.
Wallace, Benjamin SC 2nd Cav. Co.E 1st Sgt.
Wallace, Benjamin A. TX Cav. Morgan's Regt. Co.I
Wallace, Benjamin F. LA 31st Inf. Co.I
Wallace, Benjamin F. TN 39th Mtd.Inf. Co.H
Wallace, Benjamin F. TX 15th Cav. Co.F
Wallace, Benjamin F. TX 18th Inf. Co.B
Wallace, Benjamin J. MS Bowen's Co. (Chulahoma Cav.)
Wallace, Benjamin J. MS 19th Inf. Co.I Music.
Wallace, Benjamin Rush TX 3rd Cav. Co.E
Wallace, Benjamin T. GA 45th Inf. Co.E
Wallace, B.F. TN 46th Inf. Co.A
Wallace, B.F. TX 4th Cav. Co.K
Wallace, B.F. TX Granbury's Cons.Brig. Co.F
Wallace, B.G. AL 1st Regt. Mobile Vol. Co.A
Wallace, B.G. AL 4th Res. Co.B
Wallace, B.G. Brush Bn.
Wallace, Bland NC 43rd Inf. Co.A
Wallace, B.M. TX Cav. Saufley's Scouting Bn. Co.F
Wallace, B.R. AL 46th Inf. Co.G
Wallace, Brinson A. GA 22nd Inf. Co.A
Wallace, Bruce MO Robertson's Regt.St.Guard Co.7 Cpl.
Wallace, Bythan NC 24th Inf. Co.I
Wallace, C. AR Lt.Arty. Hart's Btty. Artif.
Wallace, C. AR 24th Inf. Co.C
Wallace, C. LA Mil. 3rd Regt. 1st Brig. 1st Div. Co.H
Wallace, C. LA Inf.Crescent Regt. Co.D
Wallace, C. SC 6th Res. Co.C
Wallace, C.A. NC 3rd Jr.Res. Co.F
Wallace, C.A. SC Lt.Arty. 3rd (Palmetto) Bn. Co.I
Wallace, Caleb M.D. Retributors Young's (5th) Co.
Wallace, Calvin AR 7th Inf. Co.H
Wallace, Calvin LA 28th (Gray's) Inf. Co.D
Wallace, Calvin NC 48th Inf. Co.D
Wallace, Calvin SC 3rd Bn.Res. Co.E
Wallace, Calvin SC 5th St.Troops Co.L
Wallace, Calvin B. TX 17th Cav. Co.H Sgt.
Wallace, Calvin R. NC 2nd Inf. Co.I
Wallace, Campbell TX 18th Inf. Co.C
Wallace, C.B. TX Inf.Riflemen Arnold's Co.
Wallace, C.C. MO Lt.Arty. H.M. Bledsoe's Co. Sgt.
Wallace, C.C. MO St.Guard Cpl.
Wallace, C.C. TN Inf. 3rd Cons.Regt. Co.D
Wallace, C.C. TX 35th (Likens') Cav. Co.C
Wallace, C.C. TX 9th (Young's) Inf. Co.G
Wallace, C.D.E. TN 47th Inf. Co.G
Wallace, C.E. TX 10th Cav. Co.D
Wallace, Ceaur AR 15th (Johnson's) Inf. Co.F
Wallace, Charles AL Inf. 1st Regt. Co.B
Wallace, Charles AR 1st Mtd.Rifles Co.C
Wallace, Charles AR 1st Mtd.Rifles Co.D
Wallace, Charles AR 2nd Mtd.Rifles Co.A
Wallace, Charles GA 1st (Ramsey's) Inf. Co.F
Wallace, Charles GA Cobb's Legion Co.B
Wallace, Charles NC 8th Bn.Jr.Res. Co.A
Wallace, Charles VA 9th Cav. Co.A
Wallace, Charles VA Lt.Arty. Cooper's Co.
Wallace, Charles VA Lt.Arty. Pollock's Co.
Wallace, Charles 2nd Conf.Eng.Troops Co.D 1st Lt.
Wallace, Charles A. AL Eufaula Lt.Arty. Sgt.
Wallace, Charles A. SC 1st Arty. Co.C
Wallace, Charles E. MO 2nd Cav. Co.C
Wallace, Charles J. VA 10th Cav. Co.F Sgt.
Wallace, Charles S. NC 37th Inf. Co.C
Wallace, Charles W. GA Inf. White's Co.
Wallace, Charlton VA 3rd (Chrisman's) Bn.Res. Co.E
Wallace, Charlton VA Rockbridge Cty.Res. Miller's Co.
Wallace, Charner AL Inf. 1st Regt. Co.D
Wallace, Chris LA Mil. Chalmette Regt. Co.D Sgt.
Wallace, C.J. 1st Conf.Cav. 1st Co.A
Wallace, Clement C. TN 4th Inf. Co.D
Wallace, Clement D. AL 6th Inf. Co.I
Wallace, C.M. KY 1st (Helm's) Cav. Co.B
Wallace, C.M. VA 2nd St.Res. Co.C
Wallace, Council NC 38th Inf. Co.E
Wallace, C.R. VA 11th Cav. Co.F 1st Sgt.
Wallace, C.R. VA 18th Cav. 2nd Co.G
Wallace, Curt. O. MO Arty. 1st Regt.St.Guard Co.A 1st Lt.
Wallace, Curtis O. TN Arty. Marshall's Co. 1st Lt.
Wallace, Curtis O. TN Lt.Arty. Morton's Co. Sr.1st Lt.
Wallace, Curtis O. Conf.Arty. Marshall's Co. Lt.
Wallace, C.W. KY 7th Cav. Co.E Sgt.
Wallace, C.W. KY 7th Mtd.Inf. Co.E Cpl.
Wallace, C.W. Gen. & Staff Capt.,QM
Wallace, C. Wistar VA 30th Inf. Co.C Capt.
Wallace, D. LA Maddox's Regt.Res.Corps
Wallace, D.A. AR Inf. (Loc.Def.) Ernest's Co.
Wallace, D.A. NC 3rd Jr.Res. Co.H
Wallace, D.A. NC 7th Bn.Jr.Res. Co.A
Wallace, Daniel AL Arty. 1st Bn. Co.A
Wallace, Daniel MO Inf. Clark's Regt. Co.I
Wallace, Daniel NC Lt.Arty. 13th Bn. Co.A
Wallace, Daniel VA 22nd Inf. Co.B
Wallace, Daniel Conf.Cav. Clarkson's Bn. Ind.Rangers Co.D
Wallace, Daniel A.J. SC Lt.Arty. Kelly's Co. (Chesterfield Arty.)
Wallace, Daniel C. LA 12th Inf. Co.L
Wallace, Daniel C. NC 13th Inf. Co.F
Wallace, Daniel L. KY 13th Cav. Co.B
Wallace, Daniel M. VA Cav. 41st Bn. Co.B
Wallace, Daniel N. KY 13th Cav. Co.B
Wallace, David GA Lt.Arty. Pritchard's Co. (Washington Arty.) Sgt.
Wallace, David GA 22nd Inf. Co.F
Wallace, David GA 36th (Villepigue's) Inf. Co.F
Wallace, David MO Lt.Arty. 3rd Btty.
Wallace, David SC 5th Inf. 1st Co.B, 2nd Co.F
Wallace, David SC Palmetto S.S. Co.G
Wallace, David TN Cav. Allison's Squad. Co.B,C
Wallace, David TX White's Rangers
Wallace, David 1st Conf.Inf. 1st Co.F
Wallace, David C. AL 14th Inf. Co.D
Wallace, David H. MS 2nd Cav. Co.F
Wallace, David M. TX 13th Vol. 2nd Co.I,B
Wallace, David M. VA 17th Inf. Co.C
Wallace, David R. Gen. & Staff Surg.
Wallace, David S. GA 22nd Inf. Co.A Cpl.
Wallace, D.C. AL Inf. 11th Regt. Co.K
Wallace, D.C. KY 3rd Mtd.Inf. Co.E
Wallace, D.C. MS 6th Cav. Co.C Sgt.
Wallace, D.C. MS Cav. Davenport's Bn. (St.Troops) Co.B
Wallace, D.C. SC 17th Inf. Co.I
Wallace, Delany NC 2nd Cav. (19th St.Troops) Co.I
Wallace, Dennis W. AR Cav. Poe's Bn. Co.A
Wallace, Derrell TN 3rd (Lillard's) Mtd.Inf. Co.E
Wallace, D.F. TN 11th (Holman's) Cav. Co.H
Wallace, D.F. TN Douglass' Bn.Part.Rangers Coffee's Co.
Wallace, D.G. SC 6th Res. Co.G
Wallace, D.H. NC 49th Inf. Co.H
Wallace, D.J. GA 55th Inf. Co.B
Wallace, D.J. TN 18th Inf. Co.I
Wallace, D.M. MS 18th Cav. Co.D Jr.2nd Lt.
Wallace, D.M. SC Lt.Arty. J.T. Kanapaux's Co. (Lafayette Arty.)
Wallace, Douglas M. MO 3rd Inf. Co.A,D
Wallace, D.R. TX 15th Inf. Surg.
Wallace, Drue A. AR 33rd Inf. Co.I
Wallace, D.S. AL 11th Cav. Co.H 1st Sgt.
Wallace, D.S. NC 23rd Inf. Co.H
Wallace, D.T. TN 35th Inf. Co.G
Wallace, D.W. MS 18th Inf. Co.H
Wallace, D.W.P. MS 10th Inf. Co.P, New Co.G Cpl.
Wallace, E. KY 10th (Johnson's) Cav. New Co.C Cpl.
Wallace, E. LA 6th Inf. Co.C
Wallace, E. MS 20th Inf. Co.G Cpl.
Wallace, E. TX Cav. Giddings' Bn. Carr's Co.
Wallace, E. TX Cav. Waller's Regt. Co.A
Wallace, E.A. GA Arty. Maxwell's Reg.Lt.Btty.
Wallace, E.A. GA 1st Reg. Co.D
Wallace, E.D. TN Inf. 4th Cons.Regt. Co.I
Wallace, E.D. TN 50th Inf. Co.D Cpl.
Wallace, Edward AL Arty. 1st Bn. Co.F Capt.
Wallace, Edward LA 18th Inf. Co.C
Wallace, Edward SC 2nd Inf. Co.C 2nd Lt.
Wallace, Edward TN 5th Inf. 2nd Co.F
Wallace, Edward J. TN Cav. 17th Bn. (Sanders') Co.C
Wallace, Edward S. TX 18th Inf. Co.C
Wallace, Edwin VA Lt.Arty. Donald's Co.
Wallace, Edwin R. SC 5th Inf. 1st Co.A, 2nd Co.C Sgt.
Wallace, E.F. LA 1st Cav. Co.C
Wallace, E.F. MS 32nd Inf. Co.C Cpl.

Wallace, E.F. TX 4th Inf. Co.F
Wallace, E.F. Hume's Div. Capt.,ACS
Wallace, E.G. MS 33rd Inf. Co.F
Wallace, E.H. MS 2nd Inf. (A. of 10,000) Co.F
Wallace, E.H. TN 32nd Inf. Co.D
Wallace, E. Henderson MS 30th Inf. Co.G
Wallace, E.J. AR Lt.Arty. Key's Btty.
Wallace, E.J. MS 9th Cav. Co.E
Wallace, E.J. MS 10th Cav. Co.F
Wallace, E.J. MS 11th (Ashcraft's) Cav. Co.A 2nd Lt.
Wallace, E.J. TN 48th (Nixon's) Inf. Co.I
Wallace, Elam TN Holman's Bn.Part.Rangers Co.B
Wallace, Elbert NC 37th Inf. Co.F
Wallace, Elhanon W. MS 42nd Inf. Co.K
Wallace, Eli FL 4th Inf.
Wallace, Eli NC 48th Inf. Co.D
Wallace, Elias MS 32nd Inf. Co.F
Wallace, Elias E. TX 16th Cav. Co.G Cpl.
Wallace, Elijah AR 27th Inf. Co.K
Wallace, Elijah MO Cav. Schnabel's Bn.
Wallace, Elisha AR 27th Inf. Co.K
Wallace, Elisha NC 2nd Jr.Res. Co.H
Wallace, Elmore D. TN 2nd (Robison's) Inf. Co.I
Wallace, Elmore D. TX 16th Cav. Co.C
Wallace, Enoch SC Lt.Arty. 3rd (Palmetto) Bn. Co.B
Wallace, Enoch J. AL 3rd Res. Co.K
Wallace, E.P. VA 2nd Arty. Co.E Cpl.
Wallace, E.P. VA Inf. 22nd Bn. Co.E
Wallace, Epperettus H. MS 7th Inf. Co.H
Wallace, E.S. LA 19th Inf. Co.C
Wallace, E.S. TX 3rd Cav. Co.C
Wallace, E.T. MS 9th Inf. New Co.H
Wallace, Evans TN 50th Inf. Co.D
Wallace, Everett NC 22nd Inf. Co.I
Wallace, Everett TN 31st Inf. Co.B
Wallace, E.W. TX 6th Inf. Co.C
Wallace, F.C. TX 10th Cav. Co.I
Wallace, F.D. AL 8th Inf. Co.B
Wallace, F.M. AL 4th (Roddey's) Cav. Co.A 2nd Lt.
Wallace, F.M. AR 1st (Monroe's) Cav. Co.C
Wallace, F.M. FL Cav. 5th Bn. Co.F Cpl.
Wallace, F.M. GA Lt.Arty. Croft's Btty. (Columbus Arty.)
Wallace, F.M. MS 39th Inf. Co.B
Wallace, F.M. TX 1st Hvy.Arty. Co.I
Wallace, F.M. TX 9th (Nichols') Inf. Co.H Music.
Wallace, F.P. MS 24th Inf. Co.E
Wallace, Francis FL 2nd Cav. Co.I Cpl.
Wallace, Francis NC 3rd Arty. (40th St.Troops) Co.B
Wallace, Francis D. TN 34th Inf. Co.G Sgt.
Wallace, Francis L. NC 50th Inf. Co.G Sgt.
Wallace, Francis M. GA 17th Inf. Co.C 1st Sgt.
Wallace, Frank SC 3rd Bn.Res. Co.D
Wallace, Franklin MO 1st N.E. Cav. Co.D
Wallace, Franklin SC 18th Inf. Co.G
Wallace, Franklin TX 1st Bn.S.S. Co.A
Wallace, Franklin J. MS 18th Inf. Co.H
Wallace, Frederick SC 1st Arty. Co.H
Wallace, Frederick J. SC 1st (Hagood's) Inf. 2nd Co.D
Wallace, G. KY 3rd Mtd.Inf. Co.G
Wallace, G. NC 2nd Jr.Res. Co.H
Wallace, G. VA 5th Inf.
Wallace, G.A. VA 46th Inf. Co.L Capt.
Wallace, G.B. SC Simons' Co.
Wallace, G.B. TN 21st (Wilson's) Cav. Co.D Cpl.
Wallace, G.B. TN 1st (Feild's) & 27th Inf. (Cons.) Co.I
Wallace, G.B. TN 27th Inf. Co.F
Wallace, G.C. TX Cav. Terry's Regt. Co.H Sgt.
Wallace, G.E. AL 30th Inf. Co.A
Wallace, George AL 16th Inf. Co.A
Wallace, George AL 17th Inf. Co.K
Wallace, George AR 1st (Crawford's) Cav. Co.C
Wallace, George AR Cav. Gordon's Regt. Co.D
Wallace, George KY 11th Cav. Co.B
Wallace, George LA Mil. Chalmette Regt. Co.D
Wallace, George NC 28th Inf. Co.D
Wallace, George SC 2nd Rifles Co.F
Wallace, George SC 5th Res. Co.A
Wallace, George SC 8th Inf. Co.F
Wallace, George TN 10th (DeMoss') Cav. Co.F
Wallace, George TN 11th Inf. Co.A
Wallace, George TN 50th Inf. Co.D
Wallace, George TX 36th Cav. Co.D
Wallace, George TX 16th Inf. Co.A
Wallace, George H. AL 27th Inf. Co.K 2nd Lt.
Wallace, George H. VA 16th Cav. Co.C
Wallace, George M. VA 7th Inf. Co.A
Wallace, George P. MS 40th Inf. Co.D Lt.Col.
Wallace, George P. VA 10th Cav. Co.F
Wallace, George P. VA Courtney Arty.
Wallace, George W. AR 30th Inf. Co.F
Wallace, George W., Jr. NC 20th Inf. Co.E
Wallace, George W. TX 14th Cav. Co.B
Wallace, George W. VA 50th Inf. Co.C 2nd Lt.
Wallace, George W. Sig.Corps,CSA
Wallace, G.H. AL 57th Inf. Co.A Sgt.
Wallace, G.H. VA 1st (Farinholt's) Res. Co.B
Wallace, Gideon J. GA 1st Reg. Co.K Cpl.
Wallace, G.M. GA 7th Cav. Co.F
Wallace, G.M. GA Cav. 21st Bn. Co.B,E
Wallace, G.M. TN 16th Inf. Co.E Cpl.
Wallace, G.P. MS 28th Cav. Co.G
Wallace, G. Polk MS 6th Inf. Co.B
Wallace, Grandeson AR 33rd Inf. Co.I
Wallace, G.S. TN 3rd (Forrest's) Cav. Co.C
Wallace, Gustavus A. VA 59th Inf. 3rd Co.F Capt.
Wallace, Gustavus A. VA 60th Inf. 1st Co.H Capt.
Wallace, G.W. AL 6th Cav. Co.A
Wallace, G.W. AL Cav. Moreland's Regt. Co.D
Wallace, G.W. AR 10th Mil. Co.G 1st Sgt.
Wallace, G.W. GA Inf. 25th Bn. (Prov.Guard) Co.G Sgt.
Wallace, G.W. GA 54th Inf. Co.D
Wallace, G.W. MS Cav. Gibson's Co.
Wallace, G.W. MO 8th Inf. Co.D
Wallace, G.W. SC 7th Cav. Co.A
Wallace, G.W. TN 3rd (Forrest's) Cav. Co.D
Wallace, G.W. TN 11th (Holman's) Cav. Co.B
Wallace, G.W. TN 21st (Wilson's) Cav. Co.C
Wallace, G.W. TN Holman's Bn.Part.Rangers Co.A
Wallace, G.W. TN 18th Inf. Co.I
Wallace, G.W. TN 51st (Cons.) Inf. Co.C
Wallace, G.W. VA 5th Cav. Co.B
Wallace, H. AL 11th Cav. Co.A
Wallace, H. MS 10th Cav. Co.B
Wallace, H. TX Cav. Border's Regt. Co.E
Wallace, H. TX 1st Regt.St.Troops Co.B
Wallace, H. Conf.Cav. Baxter's Bn. 2nd Co.B
Wallace, H.A. GA 2nd Inf. Co.D
Wallace, Harrison K. TX Cav. Martin's Regt. Co.B
Wallace, Harvey A. TX 19th Inf. Co.H Capt.
Wallace, H.B. MS Cav. 3rd Bn. (Ashcraft's) Co.F
Wallace, H.B. SC 5th Inf. 2nd Co.A
Wallace, H.B. SC 6th Res. Co.G
Wallace, Henderson MS Inf. Comfort's Co.
Wallace, Henderson C., Jr. MS Bowen's Co. (Chulahoma Cav.)
Wallace, Henderson C. MS 19th Inf. Co.I Cpl.
Wallace, Henry LA 14th Inf. Co.H
Wallace, Henry NC Inf. Thomas Legion Co.K
Wallace, Henry SC Inf. Hampton Legion Co.G
Wallace, Henry TN Cav. 12th Bn. (Day's) Co.D
Wallace, Henry TN Lt.Arty. Barry's Co.
Wallace, Henry TN 37th Inf. Co.B,F Color Cpl.
Wallace, Henry C. TX 18th Cav. Co.C
Wallace, Henry W. NC 2nd Arty. (36th St.Troops) Co.G
Wallace, Hezzekiah William GA 7th Inf. Co.H
Wallace, H.F. GA 2nd Inf. Co.D
Wallace, H.F. GA 35th Inf. Co.E
Wallace, H.G. MS 10th Inf. New Co.G
Wallace, H.H. VA 2nd St.Res. Co.E
Wallace, Hiram MO Lt.Arty. Farris' Btty. (Clark Arty.)
Wallace, Hiram TN 12th Inf. Co.C
Wallace, Hiram TN 12th (Cons.) Inf. Co.B
Wallace, Hiram T. MS 12th Inf. Co.I
Wallace, Hiram T. MS 30th Inf. Co.E
Wallace, H.J. GA Inf. (GA RR Guards) Porter's Co.
Wallace, H.J. SC 1st (McCreary's) Inf.
Wallace, H.K. SC 24th Inf. Co.H
Wallace, H.M. NC 23rd Inf. Co.H
Wallace, Horace H. VA 5th Inf. Co.B
Wallace, Horace H. VA 27th Inf. 2nd Co.H
Wallace, Horatio AL 32nd Inf. Co.B
Wallace, Horatio Sidney VA 17th Inf. Co.I Lt.
Wallace, Howell L. GA 9th Inf. Co.H
Wallace, Howison VA Lt.Arty. Pollock's Co.
Wallace, Howson N. VA Inf. 25th Bn. Co.E
Wallace, H.P. Gen. & Staff 1st Lt.,ADC
Wallace, H.T. AL 14th Inf. Co.D Cpl.
Wallace, Hugh KY 3rd Mtd.Inf. Co.K 2nd Lt.
Wallace, Hugh SC 18th Inf. Co.G
Wallace, Hugh TX 20th Inf. Co.G
Wallace, Hugh B. TN 44th Inf. Co.G Cpl.
Wallace, Hugh B. TN 44th (Cons.) Inf. Co.F
Wallace, Hugh D. KY 4th Mtd.Inf. Co.G,K Sgt.
Wallace, Hugh M. TX 14th Cav. Co.B
Wallace, H.W. GA Lt.Arty. Daniell's Btty.
Wallace, H.W. GA Arty. Maxwell's Reg.Lt.Btty.
Wallace, H.W. NC 3rd Arty. (40th St.Troops) Co.I
Wallace, H.W. SC Lt.Arty. Wagener's Co. (Co.A,German Arty.)
Wallace, Hy C. TX 19th Inf. Co.E

Wallace, H.Z. VA 8th Cav. Co.G
Wallace, I. MS Cav. Yerger's Regt. Co.A
Wallace, I. 4th Conf.Eng.Troops Co.E
Wallace, I. Gillum's Regt. Co.F
Wallace, I.A. Conf.Cav. Raum's Co.
Wallace, I.J. MS 16th Inf. Co.C
Wallace, Ira A. GA 7th Inf. Co.B
Wallace, Iredal TN 9th (Ward's) Cav. Co.F,A
Wallace, Irvin AR 15th (Johnson's) Inf. Co.F
Wallace, Isaac AR 33rd Inf. Co.F
Wallace, Isaac NC 24th Inf. Co.I
Wallace, Isaac J. MO 10th Inf. Co.D
Wallace, Isaac R. MO 8th Cav. Co.A
Wallace, Isaiah B. MS 7th Inf. Co.H
Wallace, Isam AL 29th Inf. Co.H
Wallace, Isham LA 31st Inf. Co.E
Wallace, Isham TX Cav. 2nd Regt.St.Troops Co.D
Wallace, Isreal LA 25th Inf. Co.I
Wallace, I.T. VA 41st Inf. Chap.
Wallace, I.W. Fort's Scouts,CSA
Wallace, J. AL 51st (Part.Rangers) Co.F
Wallace, J. AL 46th Inf. Co.F,C
Wallace, J. GA Arty. Lumpkin's Co.
Wallace, J. MS 10th Cav. Co.E
Wallace, J. SC 9th Res. Co.K Cpl.
Wallace, J. TX Cav. 2nd Regt.St.Troops Co.E
Wallace, J.A. AL Pris.Guard Freeman's Co.
Wallace, J.A. GA Lt.Arty. Croft's Btty. (Columbus Arty.)
Wallace, J.A. GA 19th Inf. Co.E 1st Sgt.
Wallace, J.A. LA 3rd Inf. Co.E
Wallace, J.A. MS 23rd Inf. Co.C
Wallace, J.A. MS 23rd Inf. Co.E
Wallace, J.A. NC 2nd Jr.Res. Co.B
Wallace, J.A. SC 1st (Hagood's) Inf. Co.G
Wallace, J.A. SC 17th Inf. Co.F
Wallace, J.A. SC 18th Inf. Co.H
Wallace, J.A. TN 35th Inf. Co.L
Wallace, J.A. TN 36th Inf. Co.L
Wallace, J.A. TN Conscr. (Cp. of Instr.) Co.B Lt.
Wallace, J.A. TX Inf. 2nd St.Troops Co.G Capt.
Wallace, J.A. Morgan's,CSA
Wallace, Jackson H. SC 1st (Hagood's) Inf. 2nd Co.D
Wallace, Jackson J. NC 48th Inf. Co.F
Wallace, Jacob AR 45th Cav. Co.F Capt.
Wallace, Jacob AR 15th (Josey's) Inf. Co.D
Wallace, Jacob LA Inf. 1st Sp.Bn. (Wheat's) Co.B
Wallace, Jacob MO 8th Cav. Co.I
Wallace, James AL Cav. Stuart's Bn. Co.E
Wallace, James AL Inf. 1st Regt. Co.D
Wallace, James AL 12th Inf. Co.A
Wallace, James AL 20th Inf. Co.B
Wallace, James AL 31st Inf. Co.D
Wallace, James AL 32nd Inf. Co.C
Wallace, James AL 40th Inf. Co.E
Wallace, James AL 60th Inf. Co.F
Wallace, James AL 61st Inf. Co.E
Wallace, James AL 1st Bn. Hilliard's Legion Vol. Co.A
Wallace, James AL Cp. of Instr. Talladega Co.B
Wallace, James FL 1st Inf.
Wallace, James GA 21st Inf.
Wallace, James GA Inf. 27th Bn. (NonConscr.) Co.B
Wallace, James GA 46th Inf. Co.D
Wallace, James GA Inf. (NonConscr.) Howard's Co.
Wallace, James KY 10th (Johnson's) Cav. New Co.C
Wallace, James LA 1st Cav. Co.C
Wallace, James LA Arty. Hutton's Co. (Crescent Arty.,Co.A)
Wallace, James LA Mil. 3rd Regt. 2nd Brig. 1st Div. Co.A Cpl.
Wallace, James LA 11th Inf. Co.A
Wallace, James LA Inf.Crescent Regt. Co.A
Wallace, James MS 2nd Cav. Co.B
Wallace, James MS 3rd (St.Troops) Cav. Co.H
Wallace, James MS Cav. 3rd Bn. (Ashcraft's) Co.E
Wallace, James MS 1st (King's) Inf. (St.Troops) Co.E
Wallace, James MS 9th Inf.
Wallace, James MS 19th Inf. Co.K
Wallace, James MO Cav. Mormon's Regt.
Wallace, James MO 1st Inf. Co.F
Wallace, James NC 2nd Cav. (19th St.Troops) Co.C
Wallace, James NC Hvy.Arty. 10th Bn. Co.B
Wallace, James NC 24th Inf. Co.I
Wallace, James SC Arty. Childs' Co.
Wallace, James SC Arty. Lee's Co.
Wallace, James SC 7th Inf. Co.H
Wallace, James SC 17th Inf. Co.D
Wallace, James SC Palmetto S.S. Co.G
Wallace, James TN 4th (McLemore's) Cav. Co.A
Wallace, James TN 5th (McKenzie's) Cav. Co.G Asst.Surg.
Wallace, James TN 16th Inf. Co.C
Wallace, James TN 19th Inf. Co.I
Wallace, James TX Cav. Wells' Regt. Co.F
Wallace, James VA 22nd Cav. Co.I,F
Wallace, James VA Cav. Young's Co.
Wallace, James VA 4th Res. Co.D
Wallace, James VA 6th Inf. 1st Co.E
Wallace, James VA 50th Inf. Co.C
Wallace, James VA Lt.Arty. Jackson's Bn. St.Line Co.B
Wallace, James Shecoe's Chickasaw Bn.Mtd. Vol.,CSA
Wallace, James A. AL 14th Inf. Co.D
Wallace, James A. AR 19th (Dawson's) Inf. Co.B
Wallace, James A. NC 44th Inf. Co.C Sgt.
Wallace, James A. SC 16th Inf. Co.B
Wallace, James A. TN 19th Inf. Co.D 1st Lt.
Wallace, James A. TX 18th Inf. Co.E
Wallace, Jas. A. Gen. & Staff 2nd Lt.,Dr.M.
Wallace, James B. SC 10th Inf. Co.M
Wallace, James B. VA 1st Inf. Co.I
Wallace, James B. VA 45th Inf. Co.D
Wallace, James C. AR 25th Inf. Co.K
Wallace, James C. GA 6th Inf. (St.Guards) Co.K
Wallace, James C. MS 6th Inf. Co.B Sgt.
Wallace, James C. MO 1st Cav. Co.F
Wallace, James C. MO 10th Cav. Co.C
Wallace, James C. MO Inf. 8th Bn. Co.E Capt.
Wallace, James C. MO 9th Inf. Co.I Capt.
Wallace, James C. MO St.Guard Lt.
Wallace, James C. SC 5th Inf. 1st Co.H, 2nd Co.F
Wallace, James C. VA Inf. 28th Bn. Co.C
Wallace, James C. VA 59th Inf. 2nd Co.H
Wallace, James C. VA 115th Mil. Co.A
Wallace, James D. MS 7th Inf. Co.H
Wallace, James D. Gen. & Staff Surg.
Wallace, James E. MO 9th Bn.S.S. Co.B
Wallace, James E. VA Hvy.Arty. Epes' Co.
Wallace, James F. LA 7th Inf. Co.H
Wallace, James F. TN Lt.Arty. Huggins' Co.
Wallace, James G. NC 18th Inf. Co.D
Wallace, James G. SC 10th Inf. Co.K
Wallace, James H. MS 9th Inf. New Co.A, Old Co.G 2nd Lt.
Wallace, James H. NC 52nd Inf. Co.A
Wallace, James H. TX 17th Cav. Co.H
Wallace, James H. TX Inf. Whaley's Co.
Wallace, James H. VA Courtney Arty. Sgt.
Wallace, James J. GA 3rd Inf. Co.A
Wallace, James J. MS 33rd Inf. Co.D
Wallace, James J. NC 13th Inf. Co.C
Wallace, James J. TX 22nd Cav. Co.D Sgt.
Wallace, James J.P. TX Cav. (Dismtd.) Chisum's Regt. Co.G Jr.2nd Lt.
Wallace, James K. NC 26th Inf. Co.D
Wallace, James L. LA Cav. Cole's Co.
Wallace, James L. MS 1st Lt.Arty. Co.L
Wallace, James L. NC 4th Inf. Co.A
Wallace, James M. GA 3rd Cav. Co.C
Wallace, James M. GA Inf. 3rd Bn. Co.C
Wallace, James M. GA 10th Inf. Co.K Cpl.
Wallace, James M. GA 35th Inf. Co.B
Wallace, James M. GA 37th Inf. Co.I
Wallace, James M. GA 41st Inf. Co.F
Wallace, James M. GA Phillips' Legion Co.C,I
Wallace, James M. MS 2nd Part.Rangers Co.E
Wallace, James M. MS 18th Inf. Co.G
Wallace, James M. NC 1st Arty. (10th St.Troops) Co.K
Wallace, James M. NC 2nd Arty. (36th St.Troops) Co.G
Wallace, James M. NC 34th Inf. Co.K
Wallace, James M. TN 43rd Inf. Co.A 2nd Lt.
Wallace, James M., Jr. VA 17th Inf. Co.C
Wallace, James M. VA 52nd Inf. Co.E
Wallace, James P. MS 1st (Johnston's) Inf. Co.G
Wallace, James R. AL 16th Inf. Co.A
Wallace, James R. MS 35th Inf. Co.D
Wallace, James R. MO 3rd Cav. Co.C
Wallace, James R. MO 12th Inf. Co.D QMSgt.
Wallace, James S. VA Inf. 25th Bn. Co.E Cpl.
Wallace, James T. MO 2nd N.E. Cav. (Franklin's Regt.)
Wallace, James W. AR 1st (Crawford's) Cav. Co.B
Wallace, James W. GA 4th Inf. Co.K
Wallace, James W. GA Inf. 10th Bn. Co.A
Wallace, James W. MS 43rd Inf. Co.H
Wallace, James W. TN Inf. 23rd Bn. Co.B Sgt.
Wallace, James W. VA 5th Inf. Co.B
Wallace, James W. VA 17th Inf. Co.C
Wallace, James W. VA 27th Inf. 2nd Co.H
Wallace, J.B. AL Gid Nelson Lt.Arty.
Wallace, J.B. GA 2nd St.Line Capt.
Wallace, J.B. MS Cav. Powers' Regt. Co.D
Wallace, J.B. MS 1st Lt.Arty. Co.I

Wallace, J.B. SC 14th Inf. Co.D 1st Sgt.
Wallace, J.B. SC 16th & 24th (Cons.) Inf. Co.C
Wallace, J.B. SC 24th Inf. Co.B
Wallace, J.B. TN 59th Mtd.Inf. Co.K
Wallace, J.B. TX 12th Cav. Co.F
Wallace, J.B. 14th Conf.Cav. Co.I
Wallace, J.B.G. SC 7th Cav. Co.A Sgt.
Wallace, J.B.G. SC Cav. Tucker's Co.
Wallace, J.C. AL Cav. Moreland's Regt. Co.D
Wallace, J.C. AL Talladega Cty.Res. G.M. Gamble's Co.
Wallace, J.C. KY 1st (Helm's) Cav. New Co.A
Wallace, J.C. NC 4th Sr.Res. Co.D
Wallace, J.C. SC 3rd Inf. Co.B Cpl.
Wallace, J.C. TN 9th (Ward's) Cav. Co.A
Wallace, J.C. TN 13th (Gore's) Cav. Co.I
Wallace, J.C. TN 24th Bn.S.S. Co.C
Wallace, J.C. TX 11th Cav. Co.F
Wallace, J.C. VA 2nd Cav. Co.G
Wallace, J.C. 14th Conf.Cav. Co.I
Wallace, J.D. LA 19th Inf. Co.I
Wallace, J.D. LA 27th Inf. Co.G
Wallace, J.D. MS 1st Cav.Res. Co.F Cpl.
Wallace, J.D. MS 3rd Inf. Co.F
Wallace, J.D. MS 4th Inf. Co.C
Wallace, J.D. NC 50th Inf. Co.G
Wallace, J.E. LA Inf. 1st Sp.Bn. (Rightor's) Co.A
Wallace, J.E. LA 2nd Inf. Co.D
Wallace, J.E. LA Mil.Conf.Guards Regt.
Wallace, J.E. TX 4th Cav. Co.K
Wallace, J.E. TX 25th Cav. Co.F
Wallace, Jeff AL 20th Inf. Co.F
Wallace, Jeff VA 2nd St.Res. Co.C
Wallace, Jehu C. TN 7th Inf. Co.C 2nd Lt.
Wallace, Jeremiah NC 62nd Inf. Co.E
Wallace, Jerry W. GA 22nd Inf. Co.F
Wallace, Jesse TN 19th Inf. Co.F
Wallace, Jessee AR 27th Inf. Co.K
Wallace, Jessee P. GA Lt.Arty. (Jo Thompson Arty.) Hanleiter's Co.
Wallace, Jesse L. NC 46th Inf. Co.B
Wallace, Jesse T. TN Inf. 154th Sr.Regt. Co.E
Wallace, Jesse W. TX 16th Cav. Co.I
Wallace, J.G. GA 13th Cav. Co.I,C
Wallace, J.G. TX 15th Inf. Co.K
Wallace, J.H. AL 18th Inf. Co.I
Wallace, J.H. LA 19th Inf. Co.I
Wallace, J.H. MS 2nd Cav.
Wallace, J.H. MS Cav. 3rd Bn. (Ashcraft's) Co.F
Wallace, J.H. MS 18th Cav. Co.D Sgt.
Wallace, J.H. MO 11th Inf. Co.H
Wallace, J.H. NC 64th Inf. Co.F
Wallace, J.H. SC 5th Inf. 2nd Co.G
Wallace, J.H. TX 21st Cav. Co.F
Wallace, J.H. TX 26th Cav. 1st Co.G
Wallace, J.H. TX 9th (Nichols') Inf. Atchison's Co.
Wallace, J.H. TX 18th Inf. Co.K
Wallace, J.H. TX Inf. Timmons' Regt. Co.E
Wallace, J.H. TX Waul's Legion Co.D
Wallace, J.H. 7th Conf.Cav. Co.F
Wallace, J.H. 8th (Dearing's) Conf.Cav. Co.G
Wallace, Jiett AR 9th Inf. Old Co.I
Wallace, J.J. GA 10th Cav. (St.Guards) Co.K
Wallace, J.J. LA Inf. 9th Bn. Co.A Sgt.
Wallace, J.J. MS 5th Cav. Co.E
Wallace, J.J. MS 18th Cav. Co.I
Wallace, J.J. MS 28th Cav. Co.G
Wallace, J.J. SC 18th Inf. Co.G
Wallace, J.J. SC 21st Inf. Co.I Cpl.
Wallace, J.J. TN 12th Inf. Co.K
Wallace, J.J. TN 61st Mtd.Inf. Co.A
Wallace, J.J. TX 5th Inf. Co.E
Wallace, J.J. Conf.Cav. Wood's Regt. 2nd Co.M
Wallace, J.K. MO 2nd Inf. Co.D
Wallace, J.K.P. TN Cav. Nixon's Regt. Co.F
Wallace, J.K.P. TN 8th Inf. Co.E
Wallace, J.L. AL 6th Cav. Co.D
Wallace, J.L. AR 18th (Marmaduke's) Inf. Co.H
Wallace, J.L. AR 37th Inf. Co.I
Wallace, J.L. NC 7th Inf.
Wallace, J.L. NC 23rd Inf. Co.H
Wallace, J.L. SC 2nd Inf. Co.K
Wallace, J.L. TN 7th (Duckworth's) Cav. Co.F
Wallace, J.L. TX Cav. Giddings' Bn. Carrington's Co.
Wallace, J.L. 3rd Conf.Inf. Co.E
Wallace, J.M. AL 8th (Livingston's) Cav. Co.G 2nd Lt.
Wallace, J.M. AL 23rd Inf. Co.G
Wallace, J.M. AL 31st Inf. Co.D
Wallace, J.M. AL 62nd Inf. Co.A
Wallace, J.M. AL 62nd Inf. Co.F,E Cpl.
Wallace, J.M. AR Mil. Desha Cty.Bn.
Wallace, J.M. LA 3rd (Wingfield's) Cav. Co.C Capt.
Wallace, J.M. MS 10th Cav. Co.E
Wallace, J.M. MS 28th Cav. Co.D
Wallace, J.M. MS 39th Inf. Co.B
Wallace, J.M. NC 57th Inf. Co.I
Wallace, J.M. SC 3rd Bn.Res. Co.C
Wallace, J.M. SC 5th St.Troops Co.K
Wallace, J.M. SC 6th Inf. 2nd Co.K
Wallace, J.M. SC 17th Inf. Co.E
Wallace, J.M. SC 17th Inf. Co.K 1st Lt.
Wallace, J.M. TN 23rd Inf. Co.E Music.
Wallace, J.M. TN 50th Inf. Co.D
Wallace, J.M. TX 12th Cav. Co.G
Wallace, J.M. TX 5th Inf. Co.C
Wallace, J.M. TX 17th Inf. Co.I
Wallace, Joel R. MS 16th Inf. Co.C
Wallace, John AL 53rd (Part.Rangers) Co.A
Wallace, John AL Cav. Moreland's Regt. Co.H
Wallace, John AL 44th Inf. Co.D
Wallace, John AR 2nd Cav. Co.B Ch.Bugler
Wallace, John AR Cav. Wright's Regt. Co.B Bvt.2nd Lt.
Wallace, John AR 3rd Inf. (St.Troops) Co.G Sgt.
Wallace, John AR 15th (Johnson's) Inf. Co.F
Wallace, John AR 25th Inf. Co.E
Wallace, John GA Cav. 29th Bn. Co.F
Wallace, John GA Hvy.Arty. 22nd Bn. Co.E
Wallace, John GA 1st (Olmstead's) Inf. Guilmartin's Co.
Wallace, John GA Inf. 1st Loc.Troops (Augusta) Co.I
Wallace, John GA 5th Inf. Co.C
Wallace, John GA 30th Inf. Co.A Cpl.
Wallace, John GA 56th Inf. Co.K
Wallace, John GA Cobb's Legion Co.E
Wallace, John KY Jessee's Bn.Mtd.Riflemen Co.C
Wallace, John KY Part.Rangers Rowan's Co.
Wallace, John LA 2nd Cav. Co.A
Wallace, John LA 7th Cav. Co.G
Wallace, John LA Lt.Arty. 2nd Field Btty.
Wallace, John LA 7th Inf. Co.C
Wallace, John LA 12th Inf. Co.I
Wallace, John LA 16th Inf. Co.H
Wallace, John LA 19th Inf. Co.C
Wallace, John LA Mil. British Guard Bn. Coburn's Co.
Wallace, John MS 2nd Cav. Co.K
Wallace, John MS 20th Inf. Co.B
Wallace, John MS 22nd Inf. Co.D
Wallace, John MO 8th Cav. Co.H
Wallace, John MO 1st & 4th Cons.Inf. Co.F
Wallace, John NC 28th Inf. Co.D
Wallace, John SC Lt.Arty. 3rd (Palmetto) Bn. Co.B
Wallace, John SC 4th Bn.Res. Co.D
Wallace, John TN 3rd (Forrest's) Cav. Co.B
Wallace, John TN Cav. 12th Bn. (Day's) Co.A
Wallace, John TN 16th (Logwood's) Cav. Co.B
Wallace, John TN 21st (Wilson's) Cav. Co.F
Wallace, John TN 51st Inf. Co.F Sgt.
Wallace, John TN 51st (Cons.) Inf. Co.F
Wallace, John TX 21st Cav. Co.I Far.
Wallace, John TX Cav. McCord's Frontier Regt. 2nd Co.A
Wallace, John TX Cav. Wells' Regt. Co.F
Wallace, John TX 1st Hvy.Arty. Co.A
Wallace, John TX Lt.Arty. Jones' Co.
Wallace, John TX Waul's Legion Co.D
Wallace, John VA 5th Inf. Co.G,H,C
Wallace, John VA 22nd Inf. Co.A
Wallace, John Shecoe's Chickasaw Bn.Mtd. Vol.,CSA
Wallace, John A. NC 1st Cav. (9th St.Troops) Co.C
Wallace, John A. TX 2nd Cav. Co.H Adj.
Wallace, John A. VA Arty. Bryan's Co.
Wallace, John A. VA Lt.Arty. Arch. Graham's Co.
Wallace, John A. VA 36th Inf. N.C.S. Music.
Wallace, John A. VA 44th Inf. Co.H,I Sgt.
Wallace, John A. Gen. & Staff 1st Lt.,Adj.
Wallace, John B. AL 4th Inf. Co.G
Wallace, John B. AL 11th Inf. Co.K
Wallace, John B. GA 12th Inf. Co.A Cpl.
Wallace, John B. MS 7th Cav. Co.C 1st Sgt.
Wallace, John B. NC 52nd Inf. Co.A
Wallace, John B. TX 12th Cav. Co.A Sgt.
Wallace, John C. AR 9th Inf. Co.G
Wallace, John C. GA Arty. 9th Bn. Co.C Cpl.
Wallace, John C. MS 15th Inf. Co.C
Wallace, John C. SC 8th Inf. Co.C Cpl.
Wallace, John C. VA 39th Inf. Co.D
Wallace, John D. AL 16th Inf. Co.A
Wallace, John D. TN 8th Inf. Co.F Sgt.
Wallace, John E. AL 1st Inf. Co.H
Wallace, John E. MS 9th Inf. Old Co.G, New Co.A 2nd Lt.
Wallace, John E. TX 4th Field Btty.
Wallace, John F. AL 14th Inf. Co.A Cpl.
Wallace, John F. MS 29th Inf. Co.K
Wallace, John F. MO 11th Inf. Co.I

Wallace, John F. NC 3rd Arty. (40th St.Troops) Co.H
Wallace, John F. NC Lt.Arty. 13th Bn. Co.F
Wallace, John F. NC 4th Inf. Co.A
Wallace, John G. AL 20th Inf. Co.F
Wallace, John G. AR 3rd Inf. Co.L 2nd Lt.
Wallace, John G. AR 37th Inf. Co.A,E Bvt.2nd Lt.
Wallace, John G. GA 42nd Inf. Co.I
Wallace, John G. MO 1st N.E. Cav.
Wallace, John G. MO 6th Inf.
Wallace, John G. NC 37th Inf. Co.F
Wallace, John G. TX 17th Cav. 1st Co.I
Wallace, John G. TX 18th Inf. Co.C
Wallace, John G. VA Hvy.Arty. 10th Bn. Co.C
Wallace, John G. VA Hvy.Arty. Wilkinson's Co.
Wallace, John G. VA 61st Inf. Co.C Capt.
Wallace, John H. AL 11th Cav. Co.H
Wallace, John H. MS Cav. Powers' Regt. Co.D
Wallace, John H. MS 4th Brig.St.Troops QMSgt.
Wallace, John H. TX 8th Cav. Co.A
Wallace, John H. TX 4th Inf. Co.H
Wallace, John H. TX 9th (Nichols') Inf. Co.F
Wallace, John H. TX Inf. Timmons' Regt. Co.E
Wallace, John J. GA 36th (Broyles') Inf. Co.E
Wallace, John J. VA Arty. Bryan's Co.
Wallace, John J. VA 108th Mil. Co.G
Wallace, John James LA 21st (Patton's) Inf. Co.B Cpl.
Wallace, John L. VA 19th Inf. Co.B
Wallace, John M. AL 30th Inf. Co.G
Wallace, John M. GA 20th Inf. Co.G
Wallace, John M. MS 38th Cav. Co.H Sgt.
Wallace, John M. MS 44th Inf. Co.A
Wallace, John M. NC 4th Cav. (59th St.Troops) Co.E
Wallace, John M. NC 48th Inf. Co.D
Wallace, John M. TX 16th Cav. Co.D
Wallace, John M. TX 9th (Young's) Inf. Co.B 1st Sgt.
Wallace, John McL. NC 3rd Inf. Co.C
Wallace, John N. NC 5th Cav. (63rd St.Troops) Co.F
Wallace, John N. NC 4th Sr.Res. Co.G
Wallace, John O. NC 29th Inf. Co.E
Wallace, John P. AL 28th Inf. Co.A
Wallace, John P. NC 12th Inf. Co.C
Wallace, John P. NC Inf. 13th Bn. Co.D
Wallace, John P. NC 51st Inf. Co.A
Wallace, John P. 1st Chickasaw Inf. Wallace's Co. Capt.
Wallace, John R. AL 3rd Inf. Co.I
Wallace, John R. GA 3rd Bn. (St.Guards) Co.C Sgt.
Wallace, John R. NC 38th Inf. N.C.S. Sgt.Maj.
Wallace, John R. NC 43rd Inf. Co.A
Wallace, John R. TX 6th Inf. Co.E
Wallace, John R.H. SC 5th Inf. 1st Co.H, 2nd Co.B Cpl.
Wallace, John S. VA 18th Cav. 2nd Co.G
Wallace, John T. MO Cav. Hicks' Co.
Wallace, John T. SC 1st (Orr's) Rifles Co.K
Wallace, John T. 3rd Conf.Cav. Co.K
Wallace, John W. AL 16th Inf. Co.A
Wallace, John W. AR 8th Cav. Peoples' Co.
Wallace, John W. AR Cav. Wright's Regt. Co.K
Wallace, John W. AR 35th Inf. Co.G Lt.Col.
Wallace, John W. MS 4th Inf. Co.K
Wallace, John W. MS 20th Inf. Co.F
Wallace, John W. VA Lt.Arty. Donald's Co.
Wallace, John W. VA 48th Inf.
Wallace, Jonathan GA 21st Inf. Co.F
Wallace, Jonathan GA 35th Inf. Co.D
Wallace, Jonathan TN 43rd Inf. Co.A
Wallace, Jonathan D. AL 3rd Res. Co.H
Wallace, Jonathan S. MO 16th Inf. Co.A 1st Lt.
Wallace, Joseph AL 39th Inf. Co.F
Wallace, Joseph LA Mil. 2nd Regt. 2nd Brig. 1st Div. Co.G
Wallace, Joseph MO 8th Inf. Co.F
Wallace, Joseph NC 1st Arty. (10th St.Troops) Co.I
Wallace, Joseph NC Inf. Thomas Legion Co.K Cpl.
Wallace, Joseph SC 3rd Res. Col'd Music.
Wallace, Joseph TX 16th Cav. Co.G Sgt.
Wallace, Joseph B. TX 17th Cav. Co.B
Wallace, Joseph F. SC 5th Inf. 2nd Co.B
Wallace, Joseph F., Jr. SC 5th Inf. 1st Co.H, 2nd Co.B
Wallace, Joseph G. NC 37th Inf. Co.F
Wallace, Joseph H. NC 5th Cav. (63rd St.Troops) Co.B
Wallace, Joseph H. NC 29th Inf. Co.A Cpl.
Wallace, Jos. J. AL Cp. of Instr. Talladega
Wallace, Joseph J. GA 64th Inf. Co.K
Wallace, Joseph L. NC 50th Inf. Co.G
Wallace, Joseph L. SC 16th Inf. Co.A Sgt.
Wallace, Joseph R. NC 4th Cav. (59th St.Troops) Co.E
Wallace, Joseph W. KY 9th Cav. Co.C
Wallace, Joseph W. TX 5th Inf. Co.E
Wallace, Joshua KY 4th Mtd.Inf. Co.D
Wallace, Joshua D. MS 23rd Inf. Co.F Sgt.
Wallace, Josiah AL 4th Inf. Co.F
Wallace, Josiah NC 2nd Cav. (19th St.Troops) Co.I
Wallace, J.P. AL Cav. Lenoir's Ind.Co.
Wallace, J.P. AL 16th Inf. Co.A
Wallace, J.P. AL 27th Inf. Co.A
Wallace, J.P. AR 4th Inf. Co.I
Wallace, J.P. GA Cav. 1st Bn.Res. Co.E
Wallace, J.P. MS 15th Bn.S.S. Co.A Cpl.
Wallace, J.P. NC 2nd Jr.Res. Co.H
Wallace, J.P. TN Lt.Arty. Morton's Co.
Wallace, J.P. VA 21st Inf. Co.I
Wallace, J.R. AR 7th Inf. Co.B
Wallace, J.R. GA 13th Cav. Co.G
Wallace, J.R. MS 3rd Inf. Co.C
Wallace, J.R. MS 37th Inf. Co.D
Wallace, J.R. SC 5th St.Troops Co.K Sgt.
Wallace, J.R. SC 17th Inf. Co.E 1st Sgt.
Wallace, J.R. TX 12th Inf. Co.E
Wallace, J.S. AL Mil. 2nd Regt.Vol. Co.F
Wallace, J.S. GA Lt.Arty. 12th Bn. 3rd Co.B
Wallace, J.S. NC 5th Sr.Res. Co.H
Wallace, J.S. TX 18th Inf. Co.K
Wallace, J.T. AL Inf. 2nd Regt. Co.B
Wallace, J.T. AL 37th Inf. Co.G
Wallace, J.T. AL 42nd Inf. Co.B
Wallace, J.T. AR 9th Inf. Co.C
Wallace, J.T. AR 26th Inf. Co.E
Wallace, J.T. LA 3rd Inf.
Wallace, J.T. LA 27th Inf. Co.E
Wallace, J.T. MO 9th Bn.S.S. Co.D 2nd Lt.
Wallace, J.T. TN Cav. Napier's Bn. Co.B
Wallace, J.T. TX 18th Inf. Co.G
Wallace, J.T. VA 48th Inf. Co.B,H
Wallace, Julian MO 4th Inf. Co.H Cpl.
Wallace, Julius SC Arty. Fickling's Co. (Brooks Lt.Arty.)
Wallace, Julius L. SC Horse Arty. (Washington Arty.) Vol. Hart's Co.
Wallace, J.V. AL 32nd Inf. Co.B
Wallace, J.W. AL 23rd Cav.
Wallace, J.W. AL 27th Inf. Co.C
Wallace, J.W. AR Mil. Desha Cty.Bn.
Wallace, J.W. GA 2nd Cav. (St.Guards) Co.B
Wallace, J.W. GA 5th Res. Co.D
Wallace, J.W. KY 8th Mtd.Inf.
Wallace, J.W. KY 9th Mtd.Inf. Co.F
Wallace, J.W. MS 2nd (Davidson's) Inf. Co.F
Wallace, J.W. NC 17th Inf. (1st Org.) Co.H
Wallace, J.W. SC Inf. 9th Bn. Co.C,E 1st Lt.
Wallace, J.W. SC 26th Inf. Co.D 1st Lt.
Wallace, J.W. TN 9th (Ward's) Cav. Co.A,F
Wallace, J.W. TN 51st (Cons.) Inf. Co.B
Wallace, J.W. TX 18th Cav. Co.K
Wallace, J.W. TX 1st Hvy.Arty. Co.I
Wallace, J.W. Gen. & Staff, A. of TN Capt.,AQM
Wallace, L. KY 3rd Mtd.Inf. Co.G
Wallace, L. MS Cav. 1st Bn. (McNair's) St.Troops Co.D
Wallace, Lawson A. NC 50th Inf. Co.G Sgt.
Wallace, L.D. AR Inf. Cocke's Regt. Co.C 1st Sgt.
Wallace, Leonidas MO 2nd Cav. Co.C,A
Wallace, Leroy TN 15th Inf. Co.G
Wallace, Lerring NC 2nd Jr.Res. Co.I
Wallace, Levi AR 7th Inf. Co.B
Wallace, Levi KY 8th Cav. Co.G
Wallace, Levi TN 50th Inf. Co.I
Wallace, Lewis W. SC 1st Arty. Co.F
Wallace, L.G. MS Cav. 3rd Bn. (Ashcraft's) Co.I
Wallace, L.H. NC 23rd Inf. Co.C
Wallace, L.J. GA 35th Inf. Co.I
Wallace, L.J. MS Mtd.Inf. (St.Troops) Maxey's Co.
Wallace, L. Jefferson LA 9th Inf. Co.C
Wallace, L.R.A. AR 15th (N.W.) Inf. Co.I,K Sgt.
Wallace, Lucas LA 19th Inf. Co.C
Wallace, Luke T. VA 36th Inf. Co.A
Wallace, L.W. TX 11th (Spaight's) Bn.Vol. Co.D
Wallace, M. AL Talladega Cty.Res. G.M. Gamble's Co.
Wallace, M. GA 3rd Inf. Co.G
Wallace, M.A. NC 4th Sr.Res. Co.F
Wallace, M.A. TX Cav. Baird's Regt. Co.G
Wallace, Major VA 72nd Mil.
Wallace, Manus SC 1st (Hagood's) Inf. 2nd Co.D
Wallace, Marion M. MS 7th Inf. Co.F
Wallace, Marion S. MO Inf. 8th Bn. Co.D
Wallace, Mark S. VA 4th Inf. Co.L
Wallace, Marquis L. NC 30th Inf. Co.K
Wallace, Mathew Gen. & Staff Dr.
Wallace, Mathew W. VA 11th Cav. Co.F Cpl.

Wallace, Matthew NC 37th Inf. Co.F
Wallace, Matthew C. NC 39th Inf. Co.G
Wallace, Matthew E. VA 115th Mil. Co.A
Wallace, M.C. AL 4th (Russell's) Cav.
Wallace, M.C. TX 12th Cav. Co.F
Wallace, M.C. TX 11th (Spaight's) Bn.Vol. Co.D 2nd Lt.
Wallace, M.D. AL 24th Inf. Co.G
Wallace, M.D. AL 34th Inf. Co.A
Wallace, M.D. GA Inf. 9th Bn. Co.E 1st Sgt.
Wallace, M.D. KY 7th Mtd.Inf. Co.B
Wallace, M.D. TN 28th (Cons.) Inf. Co.G Sgt.
Wallace, M.H. AL Inf. 2nd Regt. Co.B
Wallace, M.H. AL 38th Inf. Co.I
Wallace, Michael GA 1st (Olmstead's) Inf. Co.E
Wallace, Michael GA 27th Inf. Co.H
Wallace, Michael VA 7th Inf. Co.A
Wallace, Michael D. AR 31st Inf. Co.K
Wallace, Milas A. AL 18th Bn.Vol. Co.A
Wallace, Miles C. VA 4th Inf. Co.C
Wallace, Miles C. VA 54th Inf. Co.F
Wallace, Miles T. AR 4th Inf. Co.F
Wallace, Milton A. KY 9th Cav. Co.C
Wallace, M.L. GA 36th (Broyles') Inf. Co.E
Wallace, M.L. NC 1st Cav. (9th St.Troops) Co.C
Wallace, M.M. TN 50th Inf. Co.D
Wallace, M.M. TN 50th (Cons.) Inf. Co.D
Wallace, M.M. TX 34th Cav. Co.B Cpl.
Wallace, Monroe NC 49th Inf. Co.H
Wallace, Monroe J. AL 62nd Inf. Co.A
Wallace, Morris TN Lt.Arty. Tobin's Co.
Wallace, Moses F. MS 39th Inf. Co.B
Wallace, Moton W. SC 2nd Rifles Co.L Cpl.
Wallace, M.R. MS 1st Lt.Arty. Co.F
Wallace, M.R. TX Cav. Baird's Regt. Co.A
Wallace, M.S. TN 29th Inf. Co.I
Wallace, M.S. TN 47th Inf. Co.K
Wallace, M.W. SC Cav. A.C. Earle's Co.
Wallace, M.W. SC 1st (Orr's) Rifles Co.D
Wallace, M.W. SC 4th Inf. Co.B
Wallace, M.W. SC Inf. 13th Bn. Co.A
Wallace, M.W. VA Cav. 37th Bn. Co.B 1st Lt.
Wallace, Myric AR 15th (Johnson's) Inf. Co.F
Wallace, N. GA 44th Inf. Co.A
Wallace, N. MS 24th Inf. Co.F
Wallace, N.A. AL Cav. Hardie's Bn.Res. Co.D
Wallace, Nat TX 37th Cav. Co.B
Wallace, Nathan MS 3rd Inf. Co.G
Wallace, Nathaniel TX 22nd Cav. Co.D
Wallace, Nathaniel H. GA 12th Inf. Co.A 2nd Lt.
Wallace, Nathan V. MS Cav. Gibson's Co.
Wallace, N.C. TN 47th Inf. Co.A
Wallace, N.D. TN 12th Inf. Co.K
Wallace, Nelson MS 7th Inf. Co.G
Wallace, Newton F. AR 1st (Monroe's) Cav. Co.C
Wallace, N.J. GA Inf. 14th Bn. (St.Guards) Co.E
Wallace, N.L. GA 36th (Broyles') Inf. Co.K Lt.
Wallace, Noah MS 40th Inf. Co.B
Wallace, Noah G. AR 9th Inf. Co.K
Wallace, Noah H. NC 37th Inf. Co.F
Wallace, N.S. GA 7th Cav. Co.B
Wallace, N.S. GA Cav. 21st Bn. Co.C
Wallace, N.S. GA 2nd Inf. Co.D
Wallace, N.S. GA 22nd Inf. Co.A
Wallace, Oakley M. AR 3rd Inf. Co.H
Wallace, O.L. SC 17th Inf. Co.F
Wallace, Oliver GA Inf. 27th Bn. Co.D
Wallace, Oliver MS 1st Lt.Arty. Co.B
Wallace, Oliver H. AR 23rd Inf. Co.D
Wallace, P. FL 10th Inf.
Wallace, P. GA 13th Cav. Co.I
Wallace, P. LA 6th Cav. Co.D
Wallace, P. VA Inf. 5th Bn.Loc.Def. Co.B
Wallace, Patrick GA Cobb's Legion Co.A Sgt.
Wallace, P.B. GA Arty. 9th Bn. Co.C
Wallace, Perry TX Cav. Wells' Regt. Co.D
Wallace, Perry C. AR 33rd Inf. Co.G
Wallace, Peter AR 1st (Crawford's) Cav. Co.C
Wallace, Peter AR 33rd Inf. Co.F
Wallace, Peter LA 21st (Patton's) Inf. Co.C
Wallace, Peter SC Lt.Arty. 3rd (Palmetto) Bn. Co.B
Wallace, Peter TX 2nd Cav. Co.C
Wallace, Peter M. SC Lt.Arty. Walter's Co. (Washington Arty.)
Wallace, P.G. VA 11th Bn.Res. Co.E Sgt.
Wallace, P.H. 20th Conf.Cav. 2nd Co.H Capt.
Wallace, Philip O. MS 12th Inf. Co.I
Wallace, Pierre LA Inf. 1st Bn. (St.Guards) Co.B
Wallace, P.J. AR 37th Inf. Co.I
Wallace, Pleasant TN 1st Hvy.Arty. 2nd Co.A
Wallace, P.M. GA 24th Inf. Co.B Sgt.
Wallace, P.M. SC Rhett's Co.
Wallace, Preston VA 26th Inf. Co.B
Wallace, R. AL 30th Inf. Co.G
Wallace, R. MS 3rd Inf. Co.K
Wallace, R. MO 3rd & 5th Cons.Inf.
Wallace, R. VA Inf. 1st Bn.Loc.Def. Co.B
Wallace, R. Brush Bn.
Wallace, R.A. TN Inf. 23rd Bn. Co.A
Wallace, R.A. TN 48th (Nixon's) Inf. Co.C Cpl.
Wallace, Ranson NC 24th Inf. Co.I
Wallace, R.B. AL 20th Inf. Co.K 1st Sgt.
Wallace, R.B. TX 26th Cav. Co.D
Wallace, R.B. TX 35th (Likens') Cav. Co.A
Wallace, R.B. VA 8th Cav. Co.L
Wallace, R.B. VA 14th Cav. Co.A
Wallace, R.C. KY 1st (Helm's) Cav. New Co.A
Wallace, R.C. SC 10th Inf. Co.A Cpl.
Wallace, R.C. TX 5th Inf. Co.B
Wallace, R.C. VA Lt.Arty. Jackson's Bn.St.Line Co.A 2nd Lt.
Wallace, R.D. SC 17th Inf. Co.I
Wallace, R.D. TN 3rd (Forrest's) Cav. Co.A
Wallace, R.D. TN Inf. 154th Sr.Regt. 1st Co.B
Wallace, Reuben NC 24th Inf. Co.I
Wallace, Reuben G. MS 2nd Part.Rangers Co.K,H
Wallace, R.F. TN 50th Inf. Co.C
Wallace, R.F. TN 50th (Cons.) Inf. Co.C
Wallace, R.G. AR 8th Inf. Co.G
Wallace, R.H. MS 5th Cav. Co.F
Wallace, R.H. MS 32nd Inf. Co.C
Wallace, R.H. VA 21st Inf. Co.F
Wallace, R.H. VA Inf. 22nd Bn. Co.D
Wallace, Richard AR 3rd Inf. Co.A
Wallace, Richard KY 5th Mtd.Inf. Co.E
Wallace, Richard MS 23rd Inf. Co.K
Wallace, Richard TX 3rd Cav. Co.C
Wallace, Richard VA Inf. 28th Bn. Co.C,A
Wallace, Richard B. MS 30th Inf. Co.E
Wallace, Richard H. VA 20th Inf. Co.B
Wallace, Richard H. VA 59th Inf. 2nd Co.H
Wallace, Rich H. NC 52nd Inf. Co.F
Wallace, Riley AR 24th Inf. Co.C
Wallace, R.J. 4th Conf.Inf. Co.B
Wallace, R.L. AL 3rd Cav. Co.A
Wallace, R.L. TX 23rd Cav. Co.D
Wallace, R.M. AL 4th (Russell's) Cav.
Wallace, R.M. AL 55th Vol. Co.F
Wallace, R.M. SC 2nd Arty. Co.K,B
Wallace, R.M. SC 3rd Bn.Res. Co.D
Wallace, R.M. 3rd Conf.Cav. Co.G
Wallace, R.N. AR 2nd Cav. 1st Co.A
Wallace, R.N. AR Cav. 6th Bn. Co.C
Wallace, R.N. VA 3rd Bn. Valley Res. Co.B
Wallace, Robert AL 5th Inf. New Co.C
Wallace, Robert AZ Cav. Herbert's Bn. Oury's Co.
Wallace, Robert AR 3rd Cav. 3rd Co.E
Wallace, Robert AR 26th Inf. Co.H
Wallace, Robert AR 62nd Mil. Co.D Capt.
Wallace, Robert FL Cav. 3rd Bn. Co.B
Wallace, Robt. FL Cav. 3rd Bn.
Wallace, Robert GA Lt.Arty. Pritchard's Co. (Washington Arty.) 1st Lt.
Wallace, Robert GA 12th Inf. Co.K
Wallace, Robert GA 36th (Villepigue's) Inf. Co.F Cpl.
Wallace, Robert KY 10th (Johnson's) Cav. New Co.F
Wallace, Robert LA 1st (Strawbridge's) Inf. Co.H
Wallace, Robert LA 13th Inf. Co.C,K
Wallace, Robert MS 13th Inf. Co.C
Wallace, Robert MS 25th Inf. Co.K
Wallace, Robert MO 1st Inf. Co.C Cpl.
Wallace, Robert MO 2nd Inf. Co.G Cpl.
Wallace, Robert MO 1st & 4th Cons.Inf. Co.G Cpl.
Wallace, Robert NC Lt.Arty. 13th Bn. Co.D
Wallace, Robert NC 46th Inf. Co.I
Wallace, Robert SC 1st Cav. Co.D Saddler
Wallace, Robert SC 6th Inf. 1st Co.G
Wallace, Robert TN 24th Inf. 2nd Co.H
Wallace, Robert TX 17th Cav. Co.B
Wallace, Robert TX Inf. Griffin's Bn. Co.F,E
Wallace, Robert VA Lt.Arty. Cooper's Co.
Wallace, Robert 15th Conf.Cav. Co.D
Wallace, Robert 1st Conf.Inf. 1st Co.F Sgt.
Wallace, Robt. Shecoe's Chickasaw Bn.Mtd.Vol. Co.G
Wallace, Robert Gen. & Staff Hosp.Stew.
Wallace, Robert B. NC 38th Inf. Co.E
Wallace, Robert C. MS 18th Inf. Co.G
Wallace, Robert C. NC 30th Inf. Co.E
Wallace, Robert C. TX 13th Vol. 1st Co.H, 2nd Co.F
Wallace, Robert F. VA 115th Mil. Co.A
Wallace, Robert G. AR 9th Inf. Co.G
Wallace, Robert H. AR 15th (N.W.) Inf. Co.F
Wallace, Robert K. NC 6th Cav. (65th St.Troops) Co.F,B
Wallace, Robert M. AR 9th Inf. Co.G Maj.
Wallace, Robert M. GA 4th Inf. Co.D
Wallace, Robert M. TN 42nd Inf. 1st Co.E Sgt.
Wallace, Robert M. TX 8th Cav. Co.E
Wallace, Robert S. AL 28th Inf. Co.A Sgt.

Wallace, Robert T. Conf.Cav. Wood's Regt. 2nd Co.G
Wallace, Roland MO Cav. Schnabel's Bn.
Wallace, R.R. GA Cav. 22nd Bn. (St.Guards) Co.G
Wallace, R.R. GA 8th Inf. Co.G
Wallace, R.T. VA 1st (Farinholt's) Res. Co.B
Wallace, Rufus NC 35th Inf. Co.C
Wallace, Rufus A. TN 48th (Voorhies') Inf. Co.H,E
Wallace, Rufus B. AL 11th Inf. Co.K 1st Sgt.
Wallace, R.W. KY 9th Cav. Co.C
Wallace, R.W. KY 9th Mtd.Inf. Co.C
Wallace, R.W. TX 2nd Cav. Co.D
Wallace, S. AR Lt.Arty. Hart's Btty.
Wallace, S. AR 24th Inf. Co.H
Wallace, S. KY 10th (Diamond's) Cav. Co.K
Wallace, S. LA 6th Cav. Co.C
Wallace, S. TX Cav. 2nd Regt.St.Troops Co.B
Wallace, S.A.B. GA 48th Inf. Co.D
Wallace, Samuel AL 27th Inf. Co.I
Wallace, Samuel AL 54th Inf. Co.F
Wallace, Samuel GA 7th Inf. (St.Guards) Co.L
Wallace, Samuel LA 19th Inf. Co.I
Wallace, Samuel MS 38th Cav. Co.I
Wallace, Samuel MS 40th Inf. Co.D 1st Sgt.
Wallace, Samuel NC 3rd Inf. Co.I
Wallace, Samuel TN 55th (Brown's) Inf. Co.I
Wallace, Samuel TX 11th Inf. Co.G
Wallace, Samuel VA Lt.Arty. Donald's Co. 1st Lt.
Wallace, Samuel VA 11th Bn.Res. Co.E
Wallace, Samuel VA 47th Inf. Co.A
Wallace, Samuel 4th Conf.Inf. Co.F
Wallace, Samuel A. MS 19th Inf. Co.I
Wallace, Samuel G. AL 17th Inf. Co.C Sgt.
Wallace, Samuel H. AL 41st Inf. Co.D
Wallace, Samuel H. GA 64th Inf. Co.K
Wallace, Samuel H. NC Walker's Bn. Thomas' Legion 1st Co.D
Wallace, Samuel J. TX 21st Cav. Co.L
Wallace, Samuel J. VA 54th Inf. Co.F
Wallace, Samuel L. TX 6th Cav. Co.K
Wallace, Samuel M. TX 37th Cav. Co.K
Wallace, Samuel P. TX 12th Inf. Co.C
Wallace, Samuel P. VA 10th Bn.Res. Co.A 1st Lt.
Wallace, Samuel P. VA Rockbridge Cty.Res. Bacon's Co.
Wallace, Samuel S. AR 4th Inf. Co.F
Wallace, Samuel S. AR 33rd Inf. Co.I
Wallace, Samuel U. VA 9th Inf. 1st Co.H
Wallace, Samuel U. VA Inf. 28th Bn. Co.C
Wallace, Samuel U. VA 59th Inf. 2nd Co.H
Wallace, S.B. GA 7th Cav. Co.B
Wallace, S.B. GA Cav. 21st Bn. Co.C
Wallace, S.C. GA 2nd Inf. Co.D
Wallace, S.C. TX Inf. 2nd St.Troops Co.B
Wallace, S.D. AL 14th Inf. Co.D
Wallace, S.D. NC Wallace's Co. (Wilmington RR Guard) Capt.
Wallace, S.D. TN 13th (Gore's) Cav. Co.I Bvt.2nd Lt.
Wallace, Seaborn M. GA 4th Inf. Co.D
Wallace, S.F. AR 27th Inf. Co.G
Wallace, S.F. GA 3rd Res. Co.K
Wallace, S.F. TX 37th Cav. Co.G
Wallace, S.G. MS 11th (Ashcraft's) Cav. Co.I
Wallace, S.G. MS Cav. Ham's Regt. Co.F
Wallace, S.G. VA 30th Inf. Co.K
Wallace, S.H. GA Inf. 25th Bn. (Prov.Guard) Co.C
Wallace, S.H. SC 1st Mtd.Mil. Martin's Co.
Wallace, S.H. TN 1st (Carter's) Cav. Co.I
Wallace, Silas S. AR 14th (McCarver's) Inf.
Wallace, Simeon S. GA 22nd Inf. Co.A Capt.
Wallace, Sinkler S. GA 42nd Inf. Co.C
Wallace, S.J. MS 28th Cav. Co.G
Wallace, S.J. SC 17th Inf. Co.I
Wallace, S.J. TN 8th (Smith's) Cav. Co.A
Wallace, S.L. VA 59th Inf. 3rd Co.B
Wallace, Slick TX 19th Inf. Co.I
Wallace, S.M. AL 27th Inf. Co.C
Wallace, S.M. GA 3rd Res. Co.K
Wallace, S.M. LA Inf. Pelican Regt. Co.A
Wallace, S.M. VA 11th Bn.Res. Lt.Col.
Wallace, Smith TN 9th (Ward's) Cav. Co.F,A
Wallace, Smith TN 13th Cav. Co.A
Wallace, Solomon VA Cav. 14th Bn. Co.A,F
Wallace, Solomon VA 15th Cav. Co.F
Wallace, Solomon VA 61st Inf. Co.A
Wallace, S.P. AL 23rd Inf. Co.G
Wallace, S.P. AL 31st Inf. Co.D
Wallace, S.P. AR 38th Inf. Co.A
Wallace, S.P. VA 22nd Cav. Co.E
Wallace, S.S. AR 9th Inf. Co.K
Wallace, Stafford Conf.Cav. Wood's Regt. 2nd Co.M
Wallace, Stephen MS Cav. 3rd Bn. (Ashcraft's) Co.E
Wallace, Stephen MS 40th Inf. Co.H
Wallace, Stephen MO 1st Inf. Co.C
Wallace, Stephen SC Cav. 19th Bn. Co.E
Wallace, Stiring B. GA 22nd Inf. Co.A
Wallace, S.W. AL Gid Nelson Lt.Arty.
Wallace, S.W. GA 2nd Inf. Co.D Sgt.
Wallace, S.W. SC 1st Inf. Co.A
Wallace, S.W. SC 17th Inf. Co.E Sgt.
Wallace, T. AL 29th Inf. Co.H
Wallace, T. LA Inf.Crescent Regt. Co.E
Wallace, T.A. FL Lt.Arty. Dyke's Co.
Wallace, T.A. Conf.Cav. Wood's Regt. 2nd Co.D
Wallace, T.C. AL 29th Inf. Co.H
Wallace, T.C. AR 11th & 17th (Cons.) Inf. Co.C
Wallace, T.D. VA Petersburg Mil.
Wallace, T.F. TN 3rd (Forrest's) Cav. Co.A
Wallace, T.F. TN 29th Inf. Co.I
Wallace, T.F. Gen. & Staff AASurg.
Wallace, T.G. GA Inf. Clemons' Co.
Wallace, T.G. MS 9th Inf.
Wallace, T.G. SC Cav. 19th Bn. Co.E
Wallace, T.H. KY 2nd (Woodward's) Cav. Co.F Sgt.
Wallace, T.H. LA 3rd Inf. Co.E Sgt.
Wallace, T.H. Fort's Scouts,CSA
Wallace, Thaddeus C. AL 20th Inf. Co.D 1st Sgt.
Wallace, Theophilus S. TX 17th Cav. Co.D
Wallace, Tho. VA 22nd Cav. Co.G
Wallace, Thomas AR 45th Cav. Co.B
Wallace, Thomas AR 8th Inf. New Co.B
Wallace, Thomas GA 17th Inf. Co.I
Wallace, Thomas GA 36th (Villepigue's) Inf. Co.H
Wallace, Thomas GA 53rd Inf. Co.E
Wallace, Thomas KY 1st (Butler's) Cav. Sgt.
Wallace, Thomas KY 2nd (Duke's) Cav. Co.A
Wallace, Thomas KY 6th Cav. Co.I 2nd Lt.
Wallace, Thomas KY 12th Cav. Co.A
Wallace, Thomas KY 3rd Mtd.Inf. Co.B
Wallace, Thomas LA 6th Inf. Co.K
Wallace, Thomas LA 7th Inf. Co.C
Wallace, Thomas MS Cav. 1st Bn. (Montgomery's) St.Troops Co.C Sgt.
Wallace, Thomas MS Cav. 3rd Bn.Res. Co.B
Wallace, Thomas MS Cav. Yerger's Regt. Co.F Sgt.
Wallace, Thomas MS Inf. 2nd Bn. (St.Troops) Co.C
Wallace, Thomas MS 9th Inf. New Co.B
Wallace, Thomas MO 4th Cav. Co.G
Wallace, Thomas SC 1st Arty. Co.C
Wallace, Thomas TN 9th (Ward's) Cav. Co.F,A
Wallace, Thomas TN 59th Mtd.Inf. Co.B
Wallace, Thomas VA 51st Inf. Co.A
Wallace, Thomas VA 51st Inf. Co.B
Wallace, Thomas A. GA 22nd Inf. Co.F
Wallace, Thomas A. MS Part.Rangers Smyth's Co.
Wallace, Thomas A. SC 10th Inf. Co.K
Wallace, Thomas B. GA Arty. 9th Bn. Co.C
Wallace, Thomas C. MO 1st Inf. Co.F,I
Wallace, Thomas C. NC 5th Inf. Co.D Sgt.
Wallace, Thomas D. MS 2nd Inf. Co.F
Wallace, Thomas D. MS 13th Inf. Co.A
Wallace, Thomas D. VA 6th Inf. Co.A 2nd Lt.
Wallace, Thomas G. MS 9th Inf. Old Co.G, New Co.A Capt.
Wallace, Thomas G. SC 21st Inf. Co.F
Wallace, Thomas H. KY 1st Inf. Co.A Bvt.2nd Lt.
Wallace, Thomas J. AL Cav. Lenoir's Ind.Co.
Wallace, Thomas J. FL 9th Inf. Co.K
Wallace, Thomas J. NC 20th Inf. Co.E
Wallace, Thomas J. VA 15th Cav. Co.D
Wallace, Thomas J. VA Cav. 15th Bn. Co.B
Wallace, Thomas Jefferson AL 5th Inf. New Co.B
Wallace, Thomas K. MO 1st N.E. Cav. Co.L
Wallace, Thomas K. TX 17th Cav. Co.B
Wallace, Thomas L. TN 43rd Inf. Co.G Capt.,ACS
Wallace, Thomas M. AL 24th Inf. Co.K,C
Wallace, Thomas N. SC 16th Inf. Co.B
Wallace, Thomas P. VA 4th Inf. Co.D
Wallace, Thomas P. VA 30th Inf. Co.B AQM
Wallace, Thomas P. Pickett's Div. Capt.,AQM
Wallace, Thomas S. TX 4th Inf. Co.A
Wallace, Thos. S. Gen. & Staff, Comsy.Dept. Capt.
Wallace, Thurston MO Robertson's Regt. St.Guard Co.11
Wallace, T.J. AL 3rd Cav. Co.I
Wallace, T.J. AL 23rd Inf. Co.H
Wallace, T.J. AL Cp. of Instr. Talladega
Wallace, T.J. NC 23rd Inf. Co.H
Wallace, T.J. TX 9th Cav. Co.F
Wallace, T.J. TX 1st Hvy.Arty. Co.D
Wallace, T.J. VA 37th Mil. 2nd Co.B
Wallace, T.L. Gen. & Staff Capt.,Comsy.
Wallace, T.M. AL Detailed Conscr.

Wallace, T.M. MS 9th Bn.S.S. Co.B
Wallace, T.M. MS 44th Inf. Co.I
Wallace, T.Q. AR 9th Inf. Old Co.I, Co.A,N
Wallace, T.R. TX 5th Inf. Co.D
Wallace, Tristram L. NC 51st Inf. Co.D
Wallace, T.S. TX 17th Cons.Dismtd.Cav. Co.C
Wallace, T.T. KY 2nd Mtd.Inf. Co.D
Wallace, Turner GA 21st Inf. Co.G
Wallace, T.W. AR 34th Inf. Co.H Capt.
Wallace, T.W. GA 3rd Res. Co.G
Wallace, T.W. TN 16th Cav. Co.K
Wallace, Tyler TN Lt.Arty. Morton's Co.
Wallace, Vincent MS 7th Inf. Co.G
Wallace, Virgil H. MS 13th Inf. Co.I 1st Sgt.
Wallace, W. GA 1st (Olmstead's) Inf. Co.A
Wallace, W. LA 1st Cav. Robinson's Co.
Wallace, W. LA 21st (Kennedy's) Inf. Co.A
Wallace, W. MS 10th Cav. Co.A
Wallace, W. MS 46th Inf. Co.F
Wallace, W. MO 8th Inf. Co.D
Wallace, W. NC 2nd Jr.Res. Co.H
Wallace, W. SC 8th Inf. Co.C
Wallace, W. SC 23rd Inf. Co.G
Wallace, W. SC Inf. Hampton Legion Co.K
Wallace, W. TX Cav. Ragsdale's Co.
Wallace, W. VA Murphy's Co.
Wallace, W.A. AL 27th Inf. Co.C
Wallace, W.A. AL 36th Inf. Co.D
Wallace, W.A. LA 4th Cav. Co.E
Wallace, W.A. MS Inf. 1st Bn.St.Troops (30 days '64) Co.A
Wallace, W.A. MS 39th Inf. Co.B
Wallace, W.A. NC 3rd Jr.Res. Co.F Cpl.
Wallace, W.A. TX 33rd Cav. Co.E 1st Lt.
Wallace, W.A. VA 44th Inf. Co.H
Wallace, W.A. VA Inf. 44th Bn. Co.E
Wallace, Wade TN 59th Mtd.Inf. Co.G
Wallace, Wade H. Nitre & Min. Bureau War Dept.,CSA
Wallace, Wales W. AL 62nd Inf. Co.C Capt.
Wallace, Warren TX 1st (Yager's) Cav. Co.C
Wallace, Warren TX Cav. 3rd (Yager's) Bn. Co.C
Wallace, Wash TX 23rd Cav. Co.A 1st Lt.
Wallace, Washington AR 9th Inf. Co.D
Wallace, Washington NC 46th Inf. Co.D
Wallace, W.A.W. NC 11th (Bethel Regt.) Inf. Co.A
Wallace, W.B. GA 2nd Cav. Co.B
Wallace, W.B. GA 7th Cav. Co.B
Wallace, W.B. GA Cav. 21st Bn. Co.C
Wallace, W.B. LA Watkins' Bn.Res.Corps Co.C
Wallace, W.B. 14th Conf.Cav. Co.I
Wallace, W.C. AL 53rd (Part.Rangers) Co.A Sgt.
Wallace, W.C. TN 1st (Carter's) Cav. Co.I Capt.
Wallace, W.C. TX 20th Cav. Co.I
Wallace, W.C. TX 13th Vol. 3rd Co.A
Wallace, W.D. GA 31st Inf. Co.K
Wallace, W.D. MS 3rd (St.Troops) Cav. Co.G
Wallace, W.D. Gen. & Staff Surg.
Wallace, W.E. LA Inf. 7th Bn. Co.B Bugler
Wallace, W.E. LA 15th Inf. Co.I Bugler
Wallace, W.E. TN 17th Inf. Co.F 2nd Lt.
Wallace, W.E. TN 28th (Cons.) Inf. Music.
Wallace, Wesley E. AR 1st (Crawford's) Cav. Co.E
Wallace, W.F. AL 8th Inf. Co.F
Wallace, W.F. AR 15th (Johnson's) Inf. Co.A
Wallace, W.F. LA 13th Bn. (Part.Rangers) Co.C
Wallace, W.F. VA Lt.Arty. Barr's Co. Sgt.
Wallace, W.G. AL Cav. Moreland's Regt. Co.C
Wallace, W.G. AL Gid Nelson Lt.Arty.
Wallace, W.G. AL 42nd Inf. Co.B
Wallace, W.G. TX 5th Inf. Co.C 1st Lt.
Wallace, W.G. TX 20th Inf. Co.G
Wallace, W.H. AL 8th Inf. Co.F
Wallace, W.H. AL 27th Inf. Co.A
Wallace, W.H. GA 1st Cav. Co.G
Wallace, W.H. KY 7th Mtd.Inf. Co.D Sgt.
Wallace, W.H. TN 14th (Neely's) Cav. Co.D
Wallace, W.H. TN Arty. Marshall's Co.
Wallace, W.H. TN 8th Inf. Co.D
Wallace, W.H. TN 50th Inf. Co.D
Wallace, W.H. TN 50th (Cons.) Inf. Co.D
Wallace, W.H. TX Conscr.
Wallace, W.H. Wallace's Brig. Brig.Gen.
Wallace, W.H.H. 1st Conf.Inf. 2nd Co.C
Wallace, Wilburn TX 2nd Inf. Co.E
Wallace, Wilburn H. TN 2nd Btty.
Wallace, William AL 7th Cav. Co.G
Wallace, William AL 15th Bn.Part.Rangers Co.E 2nd Lt.
Wallace, William AL 53rd (Part.Rangers) Co.B
Wallace, William AL 56th Part.Rangers Co.E 1st Lt.
Wallace, William AL 2nd Regt.St.Res. Richardson's Co., James' Co.
Wallace, Wm. AL 8th Inf. Co.K
Wallace, William AL 40th Inf. Co.E
Wallace, William AL 41st Inf. Co.D
Wallace, William AL St.Mil. Drummer's Btty. James' Co.
Wallace, Wm. AL Cp. of Instr. Talladega
Wallace, William AR 8th Inf. New Co.E
Wallace, William AR 18th Inf. Co.H
Wallace, William AR 26th Inf. Co.C
Wallace, William GA Hvy.Arty. 22nd Bn. Co.E
Wallace, William GA Lt.Arty. Croft's Btty. (Columbus Arty.)
Wallace, William GA Lt.Arty. (Jo Thompson Arty.) Hanleiter's Co.
Wallace, William GA 1st (Olmstead's) Inf. Guilmartin's Co.
Wallace, William GA 2nd Res. Co.G
Wallace, William GA 5th Inf. Co.A
Wallace, William GA 7th Inf. (St.Guards) Co.K
Wallace, William GA 12th Mil.
Wallace, William GA Inf. 25th Bn. (Prov.Guard) Co.A
Wallace, William GA Inf. 27th Bn. Co.D
Wallace, William GA 63rd Inf. Co.C
Wallace, William KY 10th (Diamond's) Cav. Co.K
Wallace, William LA 6th Cav. Co.H
Wallace, William LA Mtd.Rifles Miller's Ind.Co.
Wallace, William LA Arty. 1st Field Btty.
Wallace, William LA Arty. Green's Co. (LA Guard Btty.)
Wallace, William LA Arty. Kean's Btty. (Orleans Ind.Arty.)
Wallace, William LA Arty. Watson Btty.
Wallace, William LA 1st (Strawbridge's) Inf. Co.A,C
Wallace, William LA 15th Inf. Co.A Sgt.
Wallace, William LA 21st (Patton's) Inf. Co.D
Wallace, William LA 22nd Inf. Durrive, Jr.'s Co.
Wallace, William LA Miles' Legion Co.A
Wallace, William LA C.S. Zouave Bn. Co.A
Wallace, William MD Arty. 2nd Btty. Sgt.
Wallace, William MS Cav. 4th Bn. Sykes' Co.
Wallace, William MS Inf. 1st Bn.St.Troops (12 mo. '62-3) Co.A
Wallace, William MS Inf. 3rd Bn. Co.A
Wallace, William MS 5th Inf. (St.Troops) Co.D
Wallace, William MS 14th Inf. Co.C
Wallace, William MS Inf. Comfort's Co.
Wallace, William MO Cav. 3rd Bn. Co.E
Wallace, William MO 10th Cav. Co.C
Wallace, William MO Cav. Morman's Regt.
Wallace, William NC 1st Cav. (9th St.Troops) Co.C
Wallace, William NC 1st Arty. (10th St.Troops) Co.E Sgt.
Wallace, William NC 3rd Inf. Co.D
Wallace, William NC 18th Inf. Co.F
Wallace, William NC 33rd Inf. Co.D
Wallace, William NC 46th Inf. Co.A
Wallace, William NC 56th Inf. Co.E,A,D Drum Maj.
Wallace, William NC Lt.Arty. Thomas' Legion Levi's Btty. Sgt.
Wallace, William SC 1st Cav. Co.D
Wallace, William SC Lt.Arty. Kelly's Co. (Chesterfield Arty.)
Wallace, William SC 2nd Inf. Co.C Col.
Wallace, William SC 3rd Bn.Res. Co.D
Wallace, William SC 6th Inf. 1st Co.G, 2nd Co.A 2nd Lt.
Wallace, William SC 16th Inf. Co.B
Wallace, William SC 18th Inf. Co.G
Wallace, William TN 7th (Duckworth's) Cav. Co.K,B
Wallace, William TN 9th (Ward's) Cav. Co.F Cpl.
Wallace, William TN Cav. 17th Bn. (Sanders') Co.C
Wallace, William TN 12th Inf. Co.A
Wallace, William TN 12th (Cons.) Inf. Co.A
Wallace, William TN 15th Inf. Co.G
Wallace, William TN 16th Inf. Co.F 1st Lt.
Wallace, William TN 18th Inf. Co.D
Wallace, William TN 27th Inf. Co.A Sgt.
Wallace, William TN Detailed Conscr. Co.B
Wallace, William TX 8th Cav. Co.F
Wallace, William TX Cav. Baird's Regt. Co.G
Wallace, William VA 9th Cav. Co.K
Wallace, William VA 18th Cav. Co.G
Wallace, William VA Lt.Arty. 12th Bn. 1st Co.A
Wallace, William VA 6th Inf. Co.C
Wallace, William VA 25th Mil. Co.C
Wallace, William VA 34th Inf. Co.I 1st Sgt.
Wallace, William VA 63rd Inf. Co.G
Wallace, William VA Lt.Arty. Jackson's Bn. St.Line Co.A
Wallace, William 8th (Wade's) Conf.Cav. Co.G
Wallace, William Conf.Arty. Nelson's Bn. Asst.Surg.
Wallace, William Conf.Inf. 1st Bn. 2nd Co.A

Wallace, William Morgan's,CSA Citizen
Wallace, William Conf.Reg.Inf. Brooks' Bn. Co.D
Wallace, William Gen. & Staff Asst.Surg.
Wallace, Wm. A. AL 24th Inf. Co.G
Wallace, William A. NC 1st Arty. (10th St.Troops) Co.C
Wallace, William A. NC 8th Bn.Jr.Res. Co.A
Wallace, William A. SC 2nd Rifles Co.F,L
Wallace, William A. TX 1st (McCulloch's) Cav. Co.B 1st Lt.
Wallace, William A. TX 17th Cav. Co.B
Wallace, William A. VA Arty. Bryan's Co.
Wallace, William B. TN 32nd Inf. Co.D
Wallace, William B. TN 41st Inf. Co.B
Wallace, William B. VA Hvy.Arty. Epes' Co. Sgt.
Wallace, William C. AL Vol. Meador's Co. 2nd Lt.
Wallace, William C. AR 9th Inf. Old Co.I, Co.H
Wallace, William C. GA 22nd Inf. Co.A QMSgt.
Wallace, William C. NC 29th Inf. Co.E,A
Wallace, William C. NC Walker's Bn. Thomas' Legion 1st Co.D Capt.
Wallace, William C. TX 18th Inf. Co.C
Wallace, William C. VA 61st Inf. Co.A Capt.
Wallace, William C. 1st Chickasaw Inf. McCord's Co.
Wallace, William Crawford TX 20th Cav. Co.A
Wallace, William D. NC 52nd Inf. Co.K 1st Sgt.
Wallace, William D. SC Inf. Hampton Legion Co.F Cpl.
Wallace, Wm. D. Gen. & Staff Surg.
Wallace, William Dossey SC 8th Inf. Surg.
Wallace, William E. LA Inf. 1st Sp.Bn. (Wheat's) Old Co.D Music.
Wallace, William E. TX 2nd Cav. Co.H 2nd Lt.
Wallace, William F. AR 1st (Crawford's) Cav. Co.E 3rd Lt.
Wallace, William F. KY 1st Inf. Co.G
Wallace, William F. LA 12th Inf. Co.L
Wallace, William F. LA 31st Inf. Co.E 1st Sgt.
Wallace, William F. MO Cav. Fristoe's Regt. Co.F
Wallace, William F. VA Hvy.Arty. 10th Bn. Sgt.
Wallace, Wm. F. Gen. & Staff 2nd Lt.,Asst. Brig.Ord.Off.
Wallace, William G. AL Mil. 4th Vol. Co.C
Wallace, William G. GA 1st (Olmstead's) Inf. Co.E
Wallace, William H. AR 1st Mtd.Rifles Co.K
Wallace, William H. GA 42nd Inf. Co.F
Wallace, William H. NC 3rd Arty. (40th St.Troops) Co.I
Wallace, William H. NC 20th Inf. Co.A 1st Lt.
Wallace, William H. NC 24th Inf. Co.I
Wallace, William H. SC 18th Inf. Co.A Col.
Wallace, William H. TN 20th Inf. Co.I
Wallace, William H. TX 13th Vol. 1st Co.K, 2nd Co.C, Co.I Ord.Sgt.
Wallace, William H. TX Inf. Griffin's Bn. Co.D Cpl.
Wallace, William H. VA Hvy.Arty. Coleman's Co.
Wallace, William H.H. GA 1st Inf. Co.C
Wallace, William J. AL 51st (Part.Rangers) Co.A
Wallace, William J. AL 2nd Inf. Co.A
Wallace, William J. AL 57th Inf. Co.D
Wallace, Wm. J. AL Cp. of Instr. Talladega
Wallace, William J. AR 8th Inf. New Co.G
Wallace, William J. AR 9th Inf. Co.G Maj.
Wallace, William J. AR 14th (McCarver's) Inf. Co.H
Wallace, William J. GA 44th Inf. Co.H Sgt.
Wallace, William J. MS Inf. 2nd Bn. Co.B 1st Lt.
Wallace, William J. MS 48th Inf. Co.B 1st Lt.
Wallace, William J. SC 10th Inf. Co.L
Wallace, William J. TN 4th (McLemore's) Cav. Co.F
Wallace, William J. VA 22nd Cav. Co.I 1st Sgt.
Wallace, William J. Conf.Cav. Wood's Regt. 2nd Co.G
Wallace, William K. GA 4th Inf. Co.K Sgt.
Wallace, William K. Buckner Guards
Wallace, William L. AL 51st (Part.Rangers) Co.G
Wallace, William L. NC 26th Inf. Co.H
Wallace, William L. SC 1st Mtd.Mil. Martin's Co. Cpl.
Wallace, William L. SC 3rd Cav. Co.E Cpl.
Wallace, William L. VA 37th Inf. Co.B
Wallace, William M. AL 38th Inf. Co.C
Wallace, William M. GA 43rd Inf. Co.E
Wallace, William M. TX 10th Inf. Co.K
Wallace, William M. VA 15th Cav. Co.B
Wallace, Wm. P. MO Lt.Arty. H.M. Bledsoe's Co.
Wallace, William P. NC 23rd Inf. Co.C
Wallace, William P. VA 4th Inf. Co.H
Wallace, William P. VA 63rd Inf. Co.E 1st Lt.
Wallace, William P. VA 115th Mil. Co.A Sgt.
Wallace, William P. W. Preston's Staff Capt.,ADC
Wallace, William R. KY 1st (Helm's) Cav. New Co.A
Wallace, William S. AL 24th Inf. Co.K
Wallace, William S. GA 45th Inf. Co.E Lt.Col.
Wallace, William S.W.P. TX 14th Cav. Co.D
Wallace, William T. GA 1st Inf.
Wallace, William T. MD 1st Cav. Co.B
Wallace, William T. NC Inf. 2nd Bn. Co.D Sgt.
Wallace, William T. NC 24th Inf. Co.D
Wallace, William T. NC 30th Inf. Co.E
Wallace, William T. SC Cav. 19th Bn. Co.E
Wallace, William T. SC 20th Inf. Co.L
Wallace, William T. VA 30th Inf. Co.C
Wallace, William W. NC 35th Inf. Co.H
Wallace, William W. SC 3rd Inf. Co.B Cpl.
Wallace, William W. VA 4th Inf. Co.L Cpl.
Wallace, William W. VA 21st Inf. Co.I
Wallace, Wilson SC 17th Inf. Co.I
Wallace, Wilson C. TN 14th Inf. Co.D
Wallace, Wilson P. AR 17th (Griffith's) Inf. Co.H
Wallace, W.J. AL 23rd Inf. Co.G
Wallace, W.J. AL 27th Inf. Co.C
Wallace, W.J. AL 31st Inf. Co.D
Wallace, W.J. AR 37th Inf. Co.I
Wallace, W.J. GA 42nd Inf. Co.F
Wallace, W.J. MS 4th Inf. Co.C 3rd Lt.
Wallace, W.L. SC 7th Cav. Co.F Capt.
Wallace, W.L. SC Cav. Tucker's Co. Sgt.
Wallace, W.L., Jr. SC 12th Inf. Co.B
Wallace, W.L., Sr. SC 12th Inf. Co.B
Wallace, W.L. TX 21st Inf. Co.H Music.
Wallace, W.M. AL 34th Inf. Co.A
Wallace, W.M. AL Vol. Meador's Co.
Wallace, W.M. MS 9th Cav. Co.F
Wallace, W.M. MO 10th Inf. Co.G
Wallace, W.M. TN 1st Btty.
Wallace, W.M. TN Lt.Arty. Rice's Btty. Cpl.
Wallace, W.M. TN Inf. 2nd Cons.Regt. Co.I
Wallace, W.M. TN 38th Inf. 1st Co.A
Wallace, W.M. TX 19th Inf. Co.H 2nd Lt.
Wallace, W.M. TX 20th Inf. Co.E
Wallace, W.N. TX 14th Inf. Co.A
Wallace, Woodford LA 31st Inf. Co.G
Wallace, W.P. AL 14th Inf. Co.D
Wallace, W.P. AR 1st (Monroe's) Cav. Co.D
Wallace, W.P. AR 11th & 17th (Cons.) Inf. Co.H
Wallace, W.P. AR Inf. Hutchinson's Co. (4th Vol.)
Wallace, W.P. GA Inf. 27th Bn. (NonConscr.) Co.D
Wallace, W.P. MS 39th Inf. Co.G
Wallace, W.P. MS Conscr.
Wallace, W.P. MO Lt.Arty. H.M. Bledsoe's Co. Ord.Sgt.
Wallace, W.R. MS 1st Cav. Co.E
Wallace, W.R. MS 11th Inf. Co.E Cpl.
Wallace, W.R. TX 1st Hvy.Arty. Co.I
Wallace, W.S. SC 10th Inf. Co.E
Wallace, W.S.A. NC 48th Inf. Co.E
Wallace, W.T. AR 1st (Monroe's) Cav. Co.A
Wallace, W.T. GA 1st Reg. Co.F
Wallace, W.T. MS Res.Corps Withers' Co.
Wallace, W.T. VA 1st Cav. Co.E
Wallace, W.W. AL Coosa Guard J.W. Suttle's Co. 1st Lt.
Wallace, W.W. AL 31st Inf. Co.K 2nd Lt.
Wallace, W.W. GA 7th Inf. Co.H
Wallace, W.W. MS Res.Corps Withers' Co.
Wallace, W.W. MO 7th Cav.
Wallace, W.W. SC 2nd Cav. Co.G Sgt.
Wallace, W.W. TN 24th Bn.S.S. Co.A
Wallace, W.W. TN 50th Inf. Co.C
Wallace, W.W. TN 50th (Cons.) Inf. Co.C
Wallace, W.W. TX 5th Inf. Co.F
Wallace, W.W. TX 9th (Young's) Inf. Co.A
Wallace, Wyatt VA 26th Inf. Co.K
Wallace, Zachariah MS 7th Inf. Co.B
Wallace, Z.W. TN 8th (Smith's) Cav. Co.A
Wallach, Chas. S. Gen. & Staff Maj.,QM
Wallach, Charles T. Gen. & Staff Maj.,QM
Wallach, Richard L. VA 8th Inf. Co.I
Wallack, Lester GA 1st (Olmstead's) Inf. Co.D Cpl.
Wallack, Richard L. MD Arty. 1st Btty.
Wallack, W.F. GA Inf. City Bn. (Columbus) Co.C
Wallage, Isaac VA 23rd Cav. Co.G
Wallan, J.W. SC 24th Inf. Co.A
Wallan, W.S. TX 20th Cav. Co.K
Walland, Charles LA 5th Inf. Co.B
Wallar, A.W. TX 11th Cav. Co.D
Wallar, Henry E. AL Inf. 1st Regt. Co.A
Wallar, P.A. GA 64th Inf. Co.G

Wallas, Alexander TN Inf. Sowell's Detach.
Wallas, D. GA Inf. 2nd Bn. (St.Guards) Co.A
Wallas, Even AR 21st Mil. Dollar's Co.
Wallas, J.W. AR 27th Inf. Co.G
Wallas, T.J. AR 21st Mil. Dollar's Co.
Wallas, W.T. TX 14th Inf. 1st Co.K
Wallaski, A. VA 1st St.Res. Co.D
Wallastine, G. VA 1st St.Res. Co.D
Wallat, P. LA Mil. 3rd Regt. French Brig. Co.6
Walla tubbee 1st Choctaw & Chickasaw Mtd.Rifles 2nd Co.C
Wallay, Mathew SC 20th Inf. Co.H
Wallbaum, Heinrich LA 20th Inf. Co.C
Wallbridge, Rufus MO St.Guard
Wallcot, George F. AL 3rd Bn.Res. Co.C
Wallcott, Fred KY Corbin's Men
Wallcott, Stephen F. NC 1st Arty. (10th St.Troops) Co.K
Wallcott, W.J. GA 10th Cav. (St.Guards) Co.B
Walldron, Thomas Sig.Corps,CSA
Walldrop, B. TN Lt.Arty. Weller's Co.
Wallee, George TN 2nd Cav. Co.I
Walleer, M. SC Mil. 16th Regt. Bancroft, Jr.'s Co.
Wallen, A.B. NC 64th Inf. Co.F
Wallen, Albert GA Lt.Arty. 12th Bn. 2nd Co.D
Wallen, Albert GA 3rd Inf. Co.G
Wallen, Alexander MO 11th Inf. Co.B
Wallen, Alfred TN Cav. 16th Bn. (Neal's) Co.F
Wallen, Anderson AR 6th Inf. Co.F
Wallen, Anderson MO 11th Inf. Co.B
Wallen, Andrew 3rd Conf.Cav. Co.E
Wallen, Aron V. TN Cav. 16th Bn. (Neal's) Co.F
Wallen, Ben F. NC 64th Inf. Co.F
Wallen, Benjamin MO Arty. Jos. Bledsoe's Co.
Wallen, Benjamin NC Inf. 2nd Bn. Co.H
Wallen, Campbell TN Cav. 16th Bn. (Neal's) Co.F
Wallen, Charles TX 25th Cav. Co.H
Wallen, Charles C. GA 10th Inf. Co.D
Wallen, Christopher VA Inf. 45th Bn. Co.A
Wallen, David KY 1st Bn.Mtd.Rifles Co.E
Wallen, David J. KY 8th Cav. Co.I 1st Lt.
Wallen, Dempsey AR 6th Inf. Co.F
Wallen, E. NC 34th Inf. Co.I
Wallen, E.B. KY 13th Cav. Co.K Sgt.
Wallen, Elisha MO 3rd Inf.
Wallen, Elisha 1st Choctaw Mtd.Rifles Co.K
Wallen, E.M. TN 19th & 20th (Cons.) Cav. Co.K
Wallen, George MO 11th Inf. Co.B
Wallen, George W. VA 37th Inf. Co.D Lt.
Wallen, Green KY 13th Cav. Co.K
Wallen, Handford KY 13th Cav. Co.C
Wallen, Hugh GA 12th Cav. Co.E
Wallen, Hugh TN Lt.Arty. Barry's Co.
Wallen, J. GA 3rd Inf. Co.E
Wallen, James GA 12th Cav. Co.E
Wallen, James VA 1st St.Res. Co.A
Wallen, James P. VA 37th Inf. Co.D
Wallen, Jesse 3rd Conf.Cav. Co.E
Wallen, John TN 2nd (Smith's) Cav. Lea's Co.
Wallen, John VA 36th Inf. 2nd Co.D
Wallen, John VA Inf. 45th Bn. Co.A
Wallen, John VA 61st Inf. Conscr.
Wallen, John VA 129th Mil. Chambers' Co., Avis' Co.
Wallen, John G. TN 2nd (Ashby's) Cav. Co.C
Wallen, John W. SC 24th Inf. Co.A
Wallen, Joseph GA 12th Cav. Co.E
Wallen, Joseph P. TN 37th Inf. Co.B 1st Lt.
Wallen, J.T. MO 11th Inf. Co.B
Wallen, M. SC 1st (Butler's) Inf. Co.F
Wallen, Martin VA 36th Inf. 1st Co.C, 2nd Co.D
Wallen, Pleasant MO 11th Inf. Co.B
Wallen, R. LA 9th Inf. Co.G
Wallen, R.B. NC 64th Inf. Co.F
Wallen, Robert FL Cav. Pickett's Co.
Wallen, S. AR 35th Inf. Co.K
Wallen, Shelby KY 10th Cav. Co.C
Wallen, Thomas VA 48th Inf. Co.A
Wallen, Thomas VA 64th Mtd.Inf. Co.H
Wallen, W.A. SC Mil. 16th Regt. Sigwald's Co.
Wallen, William GA 12th Cav. Co.E
Wallen, William MO 11th Inf. Co.B Cpl.
Wallen, William L. NC 64th Inf. Co.A
Wallen, William M. AL 3rd Bn.Res. Jackson's Co.
Wallens, J.R. AL 11th Cav. Co.H
Waller, --- KY 9th Mtd.Inf. Co.F
Waller, --- VA VMI Co.C
Waller, A. VA Mtd.Riflemen Balfour's Co.
Waller, A. Exch.Bn. 2nd Co.C,CSA
Waller, Aaron KY 10th Cav.
Waller, A.B. VA Lt.Arty. Pollock's Co.
Waller, A.C. TX 25th Cav. Co.K
Waller, A.C. TX 9th (Nichols') Inf. Co.E
Waller, Adam MO 1st Inf. Co.G
Waller, A.G. LA 13th Bn. (Part.Rangers) Co.C
Waller, Albert R. VA 38th Inf. Co.F Cpl.
Waller, Alexander M. AL 11th Inf. Co.A
Waller, Alphonza MS 1st Lt.Arty. Co.A
Waller, Alvin TN 34th Inf. Co.D
Waller, A.M. AL 21st Inf. Co.C
Waller, And J. TN 43rd Inf. Co.D
Waller, Ap TN 4th Inf. Co.C
Waller, A.P. VA 28th Inf. Co.D
Waller, A.R. GA Hardwick Mtd.Rifles Sgt.
Waller, Archibald LA Inf. 4th Bn. Co.C
Waller, Archibald R. MS Cav. Jeff Davis Legion Co.F
Waller, Asa AL 61st Inf. Co.D
Waller, Asa MS Lt.Arty. (Madison Lt.Arty.) Richards' Co.
Waller, A.W. AR 27th Inf. Co.D
Waller, A.W. TX 29th Cav. Co.F
Waller, Ben GA 15th Inf. Co.E
Waller, Benjamin GA 49th Inf. Co.I,H,K
Waller, Benjamin VA 3rd Cav. Co.H
Waller, Benjamin F. MO Inf. 3rd Bn. Co.C
Waller, Benjamin F. MO 6th Inf. Co.B
Waller, Benjamin F. VA 9th Inf. 2nd Co.H
Waller, Benjamin F. VA 12th Inf. 1st Co.I
Waller, Benjamin H. TX 18th Cav. Co.E
Waller, Benjamin L. KY 2nd (Woodward's) Cav. Co.G Cpl.
Waller, Benjamin W. GA Inf. 27th Bn. Co.B
Waller, Benjamin W. TN 49th Inf. Co.A
Waller, Benjamin W. Inf. Bailey's Cons.Regt. Co.G
Waller, B.L. TN Inf. 1st Cons.Regt. Co.B
Waller, B.L. TN 1st (Feild's) Inf. Co.L
Waller, B.L. TN Inf. Nashville Bn. Cattles' Co.
Waller, B.M. GA 59th Inf. Co.K
Waller, C. AL 6th Cav. Co.F
Waller, C. AL 60th Inf. Co.B
Waller, C. LA Mil. 2nd Regt. French Brig. Co.1 Sgt.
Waller, C. TX Inf. 1st St.Troops Martin's Co.A
Waller, C. VA 46th Inf. Co.L
Waller, C.A. LA 19th Inf. Co.C 1st Sgt.
Waller, C.A. LA Inf. Pelican Regt. Co.D Sgt.
Waller, C.A.C. Sig.Corps,CSA
Waller, Carr M. TN 63rd Inf. Co.B
Waller, C.B. AL 36th Inf. Co.A
Waller, C.C. NC 5th Cav. (63rd St.Troops) Co.I
Waller, C.G. SC Bn.St.Cadets Co.A
Waller, C.H. VA 3rd Cav. Co.E
Waller, Charles GA 53rd Inf. Co.I
Waller, Charles LA 3rd (Wingfield's) Cav. Co.A
Waller, Charles VA 59th Inf. 3rd Co.F
Waller, Charles B. GA 2nd Cav. Co.E
Waller, Charles B. GA 12th Inf. Co.G
Waller, Charles R. MS 1st Lt.Arty. Co.D
Waller, Charles W. AL 6th Cav. Co.H
Waller, Charles W. TX 2nd Cav. Co.K Cpl.
Waller, Christopher C. VA 3rd Cav. Co.H
Waller, Clark AL 1st Bn. Hilliard's Legion Vol. Co.B
Waller, C.M. AR 47th (Crandall's) Cav. Asst.Surg.
Waller, C.M. TN 15th (Cons.) Cav. Co.B
Waller, C.O. TX 5th Cav. Co.A
Waller, Columbus LA 9th Inf. Co.A
Waller, Columbus TN 19th Inf. Co.E
Waller, Coon TN 20th Inf. Co.B
Waller, Courtney VA Cav. 15th Bn. Co.D Fifer
Waller, C.R. AL 33rd Inf. Co.E Capt.
Waller, Creswell A.C. GA 64th Inf. Co.H Capt.
Waller, Creswell A.C. SC 2nd Inf. Co.F
Waller, Crusoe NC 1st Arty. (10th St.Troops) Co.D
Waller, Dabney J. VA 9th Cav. Co.B Sgt.
Waller, David G. VA 19th Inf. Co.I Capt.
Waller, David H. TX 18th Inf. Co.I
Waller, D.N. VA 1st (Farinholt's) Res. Co.D
Waller, Doctor Franklin NC 1st Arty. (10th St.Troops) Co.D
Waller, D.S. AL 11th Inf. Co.C
Waller, E. TN 21st (Carter's) Cav. Co.A
Waller, E. TN 63rd Inf. Co.D
Waller, E., Jr. TX Cav. Waller's Regt. Lt.Col.
Waller, E. VA Hamden Lt.Arty.
Waller, E. 10th Conf.Cav. Co.A 2nd Lt.
Waller, Ed., Jr. TX 2nd Cav. Maj.
Waller, Edwin M. VA Lt.Arty. E.J. Anderson's Co.
Waller, E.F. TN 63rd Inf. Co.B
Waller, Elbert AL Cav. 5th Bn. Hilliard's Legion Co.A Jr.2nd Lt.
Waller, Elbert J. GA 1st (Olmstead's) Inf. Co.K
Waller, Eli GA 3rd Cav. Co.A
Waller, Elijah TN 19th Inf. Co.K
Waller, Elisha D. VA 18th Inf. Co.I
Waller, Elwood VA 3rd Cav. Co.H
Waller, E.M. TN 13th Inf. Co.B
Waller, Ephraim TN 21st Cav. Co.A
Waller, Evan VA 1st (Farinholt's) Res. Co.D
Waller, F.E. TX 30th Cav. Co.C

Waller, Felix NC 44th Inf. Co.D
Waller, Frederick NC 46th Inf. Co.B
Waller, F.W. LA 3rd (Wingfield's) Cav. Co.D
Waller, G.A. GA 5th Cav. Co.C
Waller, George KY 2nd (Woodward's) Cav. Co.G
Waller, George LA Inf. 4th Bn. Co.A
Waller, George MS 10th Cav. Co.C
Waller, George NC 5th Inf. Co.E
Waller, George NC 5th Inf. Co.F
Waller, George NC 46th Inf. Co.B
Waller, George TN 34th Inf. Co.D
Waller, George VA 51st Inf. Co.B
Waller, George A. GA Cav. 2nd Bn. Co.E
Waller, George E. VA 24th Inf. Co.H Hosp.Stew.
Waller, George L. GA 15th Inf. Co.K Sgt.
Waller, George P. TN 63rd Inf. Co.B
Waller, George W. GA Inf. 3rd Bn. Co.D
Waller, George W. GA 4th Bn.S.S. Co.B
Waller, George W. KY 5th Mtd.Inf. Co.C,E
Waller, George W. LA 19th Inf. Co.F
Waller, George W. MO Lawther's Part.Rangers
Waller, George W. MO 2nd Inf. Co.G
Waller, George W. SC 10th Inf. Co.L
Waller, George W. TN 5th (McKenzie's) Cav. Co.I
Waller, George W. TN Cav. 17th Bn. (Sanders') Co.B 1st Sgt.
Waller, George W. TN 20th (Russell's) Cav. Co.C
Waller, George W. VA 61st Inf. Co.A
Waller, G.P. MS 2nd St.Cav. 2nd Co.C
Waller, G.R. TN 21st (Carter's) Cav. Co.A
Waller, Guilford FL Conscr.
Waller, G.W. GA 53rd Inf. Co.H
Waller, G.W. MS 9th Cav. Co.E
Waller, G.W. MS 10th Cav. Co.F
Waller, H. GA 21st Inf. Co.I
Waller, H. LA 3rd (Wingfield's) Cav. Co.E
Waller, H. TX 32nd Cav. Co.B
Waller, H. TX Inf. Houston Bn. Capt.
Waller, H.A. TN Inf. 3rd Cons.Regt. Co.H
Waller, Hansford KY 5th Mtd.Inf. Co.E
Waller, Harden TN 19th Inf. Co.E
Waller, Hardin TN Inf. 3rd Cons.Regt. Co.H
Waller, Harris T. AL 39th Inf. Co.C 1st Lt.
Waller, Haywood NC Loc.Def. Croom's Co.
Waller, H.B. TN Inf. 3rd Cons.Regt. Co.D
Waller, H.B. TN 4th Inf. Co.C
Waller, Henry GA 27th Inf. Co.E
Waller, Henry MO Inf. Perkins' Bn. Co.C
Waller, Henry NC 33rd Inf. Co.B
Waller, Henry SC 3rd St.Troops Co.C
Waller, Henry SC 21st Inf. Co.I
Waller, Henry TN 12th Inf. Co.C
Waller, Henry TN 12th (Cons.) Inf. Co.B Cpl.
Waller, Henry TN 43rd Inf. Co.I Cpl.
Waller, Henry TX 22nd Cav. Co.A Cpl.
Waller, Henry TX 17th Inf. Co.E
Waller, Henry A. GA 2nd Cav. Co.E
Waller, Henry A. TN 19th Inf. Co.E Capt.
Waller, Henry C. NC 1st Arty. (10th St.Troops) Co.D
Waller, Henry E. Lt.Arty. Dent's Btty.,CSA
Waller, H.H. MS 23rd Inf. Co.H
Waller, Hiram GA 1st (Olmstead's) Inf. Co.K Cpl.
Waller, Hiram GA 47th Inf. Co.E
Waller, Hiram B. Gen. & Staff Capt.,AAG
Waller, Hiram G. MS 6th Inf. Co.E
Waller, H.M. Gen. & Staff Capt.,QM
Waller, H.S.W. TX 11th Cav. Co.D Cpl.
Waller, Hugh M. VA 32nd Inf. Co.C 2nd Lt.
Waller, Hugh W. AR 9th Inf. New Co.I
Waller, Hugh W. MS 25th Inf. Co.G
Waller, H.W. AR 1st Cav. Co.G
Waller, H.W. 2nd Conf.Inf. Co.G
Waller, I. TX 9th (Nichols') Inf. Co.B
Waller, Ichabod TX 25th Cav. Co.C
Waller, I.D. VA 59th Inf. 3rd Co.G Sgt.
Waller, Isaac D. NC Inf. 2nd Bn. Co.C
Waller, Isaac H. VA 3rd Cav. Co.B 1st Sgt.
Waller, Isaac R. GA 57th Inf. Co.H 1st Sgt.
Waller, J. AL 63rd Inf. Co.E
Waller, J. LA Mil. Orleans Fire Regt. Co.A
Waller, J. TX Cav. Terry's Regt. Co.E
Waller, J. VA 11th Inf. Co.I
Waller, J.A. AR 3rd Cav. Co.A
Waller, Jackson AL 1st Cav. Co.A
Waller, Jackson TN 1st Cav.
Waller, Jacob MO 15th Cav. Co.I
Waller, Jacob NC 46th Inf. Co.B
Waller, Jacob D. LA 9th Inf. Co.D
Waller, James AR 32nd Inf. Co.B
Waller, James AR 34th Inf. Co.H
Waller, James GA 46th Inf. Co.A
Waller, James KY 2nd Cav. Co.A
Waller, James KY 2nd Mtd.Inf. Co.A
Waller, James TN 5th Cav.
Waller, James TN 20th Inf. Co.B
Waller, James VA 17th Inf. Co.C
Waller, James VA 20th Inf. Co.C
Waller, James VA 51st Inf. Co.B
Waller, James A. AL Arty. 1st Bn. Co.B,D Cpl.
Waller, James A. GA Cadets Co.B
Waller, James A. GA Conscr.
Waller, James A. MS 19th Inf. Co.F Sgt.
Waller, James A. VA 38th Inf. Co.F 1st Lt.
Waller, James C. VA 24th Inf. Co.I
Waller, James C. VA 49th Inf. Co.C
Waller, James E. VA 9th Cav. Co.A
Waller, James K. TN 21st Cav. Co.A
Waller, James L. SC Lt.Arty. Garden's Co. (Palmetto Lt.Btty.)
Waller, James M. AR Cav. 1st Bn. (Stirman's) Co.B
Waller, James M. GA Inf. 3rd Bn. Co.D
Waller, James M. GA 4th Bn.S.S. Co.B
Waller, James N. NC 55th Inf. Co.K
Waller, James R. TN 21st Cav. Co.A
Waller, James S. AL 60th Inf. Co.E Sgt.
Waller, James S. AL 3rd Bn. Hilliard's Legion Vol. Co.A Sgt.
Waller, James T. GA 3rd Inf. Co.B
Waller, James T. VA Horse Arty. Shoemaker's Co.
Waller, James T. VA Lt.Arty. Thompson's Co.
Waller, James T. VA 3rd Inf. Co.G
Waller, James T. VA Conscr. Cp.Lee Co.B
Waller, James W. NC 3rd Arty. (40th St.Troops) Co.D
Waller, James W. TX Cav. Baylor's Regt. Co.E
Waller, Jarrot L. GA 44th Inf. Co.E
Waller, Jasper W. NC 23rd Inf. Co.E
Waller, J.B. GA Arty. 11th Bn. (Sumter Arty.) New Co.C
Waller, J.B. GA Inf. 25th Bn. (Prov.Guard) Co.D Sgt.
Waller, J.B. GA 46th Inf. Co.H
Waller, J.C. GA Lt.Arty. Howell's Co.
Waller, J.C. VA 2nd Cav. Co.I
Waller, J.D. GA 13th Inf. Co.A
Waller, J.D. MO Lt.Arty. 3rd Field Btty.
Waller, J.E. FL 1st Inf. New Co.D
Waller, Jerry GA Inf. (Newton Factory Employees) Russell's Co.
Waller, Jesse NC 42nd Inf. Co.D
Waller, Jesse M. MO 3rd Cav. Co.E,C Sgt.
Waller, J.F. MS 10th Cav. Co.F 1st Sgt.
Waller, J.H. GA 27th Inf. Co.E
Waller, J.H. KY 14th Cav. Co.B
Waller, J.H.P. TX 36th Cav. Co.K
Waller, J.J. GA Lt.Arty. Howell's Co.
Waller, J.K.P. MO 12th Inf. Co.A 1st Sgt.
Waller, J.L. GA 55th Inf. Co.B
Waller, J.L. SC Manigault's Bn.Vol. Co.C
Waller, J.L. TN Inf. 3rd Cons.Regt. Co.H Capt.
Waller, J.L. TN 19th Inf. Co.E Capt.
Waller, J.M. KY 2nd (Woodward's) Cav. Co.A
Waller, J.M. LA 31st Inf. Co.E
Waller, J.N. GA 45th Inf. Co.C
Waller, J.N. TN 12th Cav. Co.F
Waller, Joe TN 11th (Holman's) Cav. Co.K
Waller, John AL 7th Cav. Co.K
Waller, John AR 1st (Dobbin's) Cav. Hill's Co.
Waller, John AR 7th Mil. Co.C
Waller, John GA 48th Inf. Co.C
Waller, John GA Inf. Atwater's Co.
Waller, John KY 2nd (Duke's) Cav. Co.F
Waller, John KY 2nd Mtd.Inf. Co.C
Waller, John NC 46th Inf. Co.B
Waller, John NC Mil. Clark's Sp.Bn. Co.C
Waller, John TN 1st (Carter's) Cav. Co.M
Waller, John TN Cav. 11th Bn. (Gordon's) Co.C
Waller, John TN Cav. Wilson's Regt. Co.E
Waller, John TN 16th Inf. Co.K
Waller, John TN 43rd Inf. Co.I
Waller, John TX 2nd Cav. Co.D
Waller, John TX Cav. Madison's Regt. Co.E
Waller, John TX Cav. Waller's Regt. Co.D
Waller, John B. GA 5th Inf. Co.E
Waller, John C. MO 11th Inf. Co.I
Waller, John D. AL 8th (Livingston's) Cav. Co.I
Waller, John D. AL Cav. 5th Bn. Hilliard's Legion Co.A
Waller, John D. GA 59th Inf. Co.H
Waller, John D. VA 30th Inf. 2nd Co.I Sgt.
Waller, John D. VA 47th Inf. 2nd Co.I
Waller, John F. AL Inf. 1st Regt. Co.D
Waller, John F. MS 11th Inf. Co.C
Waller, John F. TN Cav. 17th Bn. (Sanders') Co.C
Waller, John F. Gen. & Staff 1st Lt.,Adj.
Waller, John G. AL 34th Inf. Co.E
Waller, John H. GA Inf. 10th Bn. Co.D
Waller, John H. KY 2nd Cav.
Waller, John H. KY 3rd Cav. Co.C
Waller, John H. KY 1st Inf. Co.H
Waller, John H. MS 12th Inf. Co.K

Waller, John J. NC 7th Inf. Co.C
Waller, John J. VA 56th Inf. Co.B
Waller, John K. VA Lt.Arty. Pegram's Co.
Waller, John M. AL 6th Cav. Co.H
Waller, John M., Jr. VA 9th Cav. Co.E
Waller, John M. VA Mil. 16th Regt. Col.
Waller, John P. TN 32nd Inf. Co.D
Waller, John P. TN 63rd Inf. Co.B
Waller, John R. NC 8th Bn.Part.Rangers Co.B
Waller, John R. NC 52nd Inf. Co.I
Waller, John R. TN 6th (Wheeler's) Cav. Co.C Cpl.
Waller, John R. TN 2nd (Robison's) Inf. Co.F
Waller, John R. TX 31st Cav. Co.D Capt.
Waller, John S. AL 11th Inf. Co.A
Waller, John S. KY 14th Cav. Co.C
Waller, John T. GA Inf. 27th Bn. Co.B
Waller, John T. TX 10th Inf. Co.B Sgt.
Waller, John T. VA 11th Inf. Co.G
Waller, John Thomas VA 9th Cav. Co.B
Waller, John W. AR Cav. 1st Bn. (Stirman's) Co.B
Waller, John W. MS 19th Inf. Co.F
Waller, John W. TN 63rd Inf. Co.B
Waller, John W. VA 3rd Cav. Co.H
Waller, John W. VA 9th Inf. Co.B
Waller, John W. VA 38th Inf. Co.H
Waller, John W. VA 56th Inf. Co.B
Waller, Jonas M. TX 18th Inf. Co.I Sgt.
Waller, Joseph AR 19th (Dockery's) Inf. Co.B
Waller, Joseph MS 37th Inf. Co.D
Waller, Joseph TN Holman's Bn.Part.Rangers Co.D
Waller, Joseph TX 25th Cav. Co.C
Waller, Joseph TX 9th (Nichols') Inf. Co.B
Waller, Joseph VA Cav. 40th Bn. Co.A
Waller, Joseph S. AR 1st Mtd.Rifles Co.D
Waller, Joseph W. AL Inf. 1st Regt. Co.D
Waller, Josiah VA 61st Inf. Co.C
Waller, J.R. NC 66th Inf. Co.C
Waller, J.R. TN 21st (Carter's) Cav. Co.A Cpl.
Waller, J.R. TN 9th Inf. Co.A
Waller, J.R. VA Hvy.Arty. Allen's Co.
Waller, J.S. AL 40th Inf. Co.D
Waller, J.S. GA 5th Res. Co.A Sgt.
Waller, J.S. GA 32nd Inf. Co.A
Waller, J.S. GA 63rd Inf. Co.G
Waller, J.S. MS 3rd Inf. Co.I
Waller, J.S. SC 26th Inf. Co.E
Waller, J.T. AL Cav. Moses' Squad. Co.A
Waller, J.T. TX 7th Inf. Co.I
Waller, J.W. AL 1st Inf. Co.A
Waller, J.W. AL 26th (O'Neal's) Inf. Co.C
Waller, J.W. AR 3rd Cav. Co.B
Waller, J.W. AR 10th (Witt's) Cav. Co.C
Waller, J.W. GA Lt.Arty. Howell's Co.
Waller, J.W. GA 46th Inf. Co.A
Waller, J.W. TN 5th Inf. 2nd Co.D
Waller, J.W. TN Inf. 154th Sr.Regt. Co.I
Waller, J.W. TX 2nd Inf. Co.I
Waller, L. TN 1st Cav. Co.F
Waller, Lawrence NC 14th Inf. Co.H
Waller, L.C. NC 14th Inf. Co.G
Waller, Leroy T. GA 21st Inf. Co.F 1st Lt.
Waller, Levin F. TN 1st Cav. Co.F
Waller, Levy AL 61st Inf. Co.D
Waller, Lewis TN 19th Inf. Co.E
Waller, Lewis A. NC 1st Arty. (10th St.Troops) Co.D
Waller, L.G. TN 15th (Cons.) Cav. Co.B 1st Sgt.
Waller, L.G. TN Cav. Nixon's Regt. Co.D 1st Sgt.
Waller, L.G. TN 38th Inf. Co.D 1st Sgt.
Waller, L.G. TX 29th Cav. Co.D
Waller, Louis A. GA 45th Inf. Co.A Cpl.
Waller, L.T. AL 8th (Livingston's) Cav. Co.I Sr.2nd Lt.
Waller, L.T. AL Cav. Moses' Squad. Co.A 2nd Lt.
Waller, Luther B. VA 13th Inf. Co.C
Waller, Luther S. GA 55th Inf. Co.E
Waller, Lycurgus VA 3rd Inf. Co.G Sgt.
Waller, Malcolm E. KY 8th Cav. Co.B
Waller, Marcellus T. MS 2nd Part.Rangers Co.C Cpl.
Waller, Marshal G. NC 8th Bn.Part.Rangers Co.B
Waller, Martin V. TN 54th Inf. Co.A
Waller, M.B. KY Cav.
Waller, M.B. 1st Conf.Cav. 2nd Co.K Sgt.
Waller, M.C. TN 1st (Feild's) Inf. Co.L Sgt.
Waller, M.C. TN 1st (Feild's) & 27th Inf. (Cons.) Co.L
Waller, M.C. TN Inf. Nashville Bn. Cattle's Co. Sgt.
Waller, M.G. NC 66th Inf. Co.C
Waller, Michael VA 17th Inf. Co.C
Waller, N. MO 10th Inf. Co.B
Waller, Nathan TX 17th Cav. Co.B
Waller, Nathaniel GA Cav. 1st Bn.Res. McKinney's Co.
Waller, Nathaniel GA Inf. 3rd Bn. Co.D
Waller, Nathaniel GA 4th Bn.S.S. Co.B
Waller, Nathaniel W. NC 23rd Inf. Co.E
Waller, N.E. MS 9th Inf. Old Co.K, New Co.K
Waller, N.H. MS Inf. 2nd St.Troops Co.B
Waller, N.T. LA Inf.Cons.Crescent Regt. Co.E
Waller, O. Gen. & Staff A.Surg.
Waller, Obediah TN 55th (McKoin's) Inf. Co.H
Waller, Paton C. AL 44th Inf. Co.G
Waller, Paul TX Lt.Arty. Hughes' Co.
Waller, Peter E. TX 18th Inf. Co.I
Waller, P.H. NC 30th Inf. Co.D
Waller, P.J. VA Lt.Arty. Wimbish's Co.
Waller, P.L. NC 2nd Jr.Res. Co.B
Waller, P.L. NC 11th (Bethel Regt.) Inf. Co.H
Waller, Pleasant W. TN Inf. 1st Bn. (Colms') Co.E
Waller, Press AL 11th Cav. Co.A
Waller, Preston J. VA Lt.Arty. Montgomery's Co.
Waller, P.V. SC Arty. Manigault's Bn. 1st Co.B
Waller, P.W. TN 21st (Wilson's) Cav. Co.K
Waller, R. LA 3rd (Harrison's) Cav. Co.G Sgt.
Waller, R. TX Cav. Bourland's Regt. Co.E
Waller, R.A. KY 1st (Butler's) Cav. Co.G
Waller, R.A. KY 10th (Johnson's) Cav. New Co.F
Waller, R.A. LA Inf. 1st Sp.Bn. (Rightor's) Co.D
Waller, R.B. AL 7th Cav. Co.F,A Sgt.
Waller, R.B. FL 2nd Inf. Co.D
Waller, R.F. TX 20th Inf. Co.B
Waller, Richard GA 7th Cav. Co.H
Waller, Richard GA Hardwick Mtd.Rifles Co.B
Waller, Richard B. TN 9th (Ward's) Cav. Co.I
Waller, Richard H. VA 21st Inf. Co.H
Waller, Richard P. Gen. & Staff, QM Dept. Maj.
Waller, R.L. MO 9th (Elliott's) Cav. Co.G 2nd Lt.
Waller, R.L. TN 4th Inf. Co.C
Waller, R.M. GA Arty. St.Troops Pruden's Btty.
Waller, R.M. LA 3rd (Wingfield's) Cav. Co.E
Waller, Roan GA 44th Inf. Co.B
Waller, Robb B. GA 3rd Cav. Co.A
Waller, Robert MS 8th Inf. Co.H
Waller, Robert A. FL 8th Inf. Co.B Capt.
Waller, Robert A. GA 1st (Ramsey's) Inf. Co.G
Waller, Robert B. AL Inf. 1st Regt. Co.E
Waller, Robert E. VA VMI Cadet
Waller, Robert J. VA Lt.Arty. Pollock's Co.
Waller, Robert T. AL 11th Inf. Co.C
Waller, Robert T. MS 9th Inf. New Co.I
Waller, Robert W. GA Arty. 11th Bn. (Sumter Arty.) New Co.C
Waller, Robert W. GA 9th Inf. Co.A
Waller, R.T. GA Lt.Arty. Howell's Co.
Waller, S. TX 25th Cav. Co.C
Waller, Samuel MS 36th Inf. Co.F
Waller, Samuel D. AL Inf. 1st Regt. Co.E Cpl.
Waller, Samuel D. AL 3rd Bn. Hilliard's Legion Vol. Co.B Sgt.
Waller, Samuel G. VA 24th Inf. Co.H Cpl.
Waller, Samuel H. AL 17th Inf. Co.B
Waller, Samuel J. GA 1st (Olmstead's) Inf. Co.K
Waller, Samuel J. SC Inf. 9th Bn. Co.D
Waller, Samuel J. SC 26th Inf. Co.E Cpl.
Waller, Samuel M. VA 2nd Cav. Co.E
Waller, S.B. GA 39th Inf. Co.F Cpl.
Waller, S.D. AL 60th Inf. Co.A Sgt.
Waller, S.D. GA 46th Inf. Co.D
Waller, S.E. AL 23rd Inf. Co.B
Waller, S.E. KY 2nd Mtd.Inf. Co.A
Waller, Simion R. AR Cav. 1st Bn. (Stirman's) Co.B
Waller, Smith GA 8th Inf. (St.Guards) Co.D
Waller, S.P. AR 19th (Dockery's) Inf. Co.B
Waller, Squire NC 3rd Inf. Co.K
Waller, Starlin NC 2nd Arty. (36th St.Troops) Co.B
Waller, Starling NC Lt.Arty. 13th Bn. Co.B
Waller, Stephen S. GA 21st Inf. Co.F
Waller, T. MS 37th Inf. Co.H
Waller, T.A. TN 25th Inf. Co.F
Waller, T.D. NC 5th Cav. (63rd St.Troops) Co.I
Waller, Thaddeus GA 1st (Olmstead's) Inf. Co.K Cpl.
Waller, Thomas AL Inf. 1st Regt. Co.C
Waller, Thomas GA Lt.Arty. Guerard's Btty.
Waller, Thomas GA 5th Inf. Co.K Sgt.
Waller, Thomas LA 11th Inf. Co.L
Waller, Thomas NC 17th (1st Org.) Inf. Co.E
Waller, Thomas TN 43rd Inf. Co.D
Waller, Thomas VA 9th Cav. Co.A Col.
Waller, Thomas VA 17th Inf. Co.C
Waller, Thomas B. KY Cav. Chenoweth's Regt. Co.E
Waller, Thomas H. VA 3rd Cav. Co.H
Waller, Thomas J. AL 37th Inf. Co.D

Waller, Thomas J. TN 4th (McLemore's) Cav. Co.F
Waller, Thomas J. TX 37th Cav. Co.G
Waller, Thomas J. VA 12th Inf. Co.B
Waller, Thomas Macon VA 2nd Cav. Co.E 1st Lt.
Waller, Thomas P. AL 48th Inf. Co.E
Waller, Thomas R. VA Inf. 45th Bn. Co.E
Waller, Thomas R. VA 1st Cav.St.Line Co.A 1st Lt.
Waller, Thomas S. TN 32nd Inf. Co.D
Waller, T.J. GA Tiller's Co. (Echols Lt.Arty.) Cpl.
Waller, T.J. GA 13th Inf. Co.A
Waller, T.J. TN 15th (Cons.) Cav. Co.K
Waller, T.J. TN 16th (Logwood's) Cav. Co.I
Waller, T.S. AL 37th Inf. Co.G
Waller, Tucker MS 30th Inf. Co.D
Waller, Turners NC 4th Cav. (59th St.Troops) Co.G
Waller, Valentine NC 5th Sr.Res. Co.B
Waller, W. AL Shelby Cty.Res. J.M. Webster's Co.
Waller, W. MS 1st Lt.Arty.
Waller, Warren NC 23rd Inf. Co.B
Waller, Watt A. AL 6th Inf. Co.E 1st Lt.
Waller, W.C. MS 8th Inf. Co.H
Waller, W.D. VA 5th Bn.Res. Co.A 2nd Lt.
Waller, W.E. MS 9th Inf. Co.B Sgt.
Waller, W.G. AL Rebels
Waller, William AL 3rd Bn.Res. Co.C
Waller, William GA Lt.Arty. Howell's Co.
Waller, William GA 1st (Olmstead's) Inf. Co.K
Waller, William GA 3rd Res. Co.K
Waller, William GA 44th Inf. Co.G
Waller, William KY 11th Cav. Co.A
Waller, William NC 46th Inf. Co.A Cpl.
Waller, William TN 10th (DeMoss') Cav. Co.E
Waller, William TN 21st Cav. Co.A
Waller, William TN 21st (Carter's) Cav. Co.A
Waller, William TN Cav. Napier's Bn. Co.B Ord.Sgt.
Waller, William TN 50th Inf. Co.A
Waller, William TN 63rd Inf. Co.B 1st Sgt.
Waller, William VA 2nd Cav. Co.I 2nd Lt.
Waller, William VA 4th Cav. Comsy.
Waller, William Gen. & Staff Capt.,Ord.Off.
Waller, William A. AL 61st Inf. Co.D
Waller, William A. GA Lt.Arty. Milledge's Co.
Waller, William A. GA 3rd Inf. 1st Co.I
Waller, William A. GA 15th Inf. Co.E
Waller, William A. TN 26th Inf. Co.F
Waller, William B. TN 5th (McKenzie's) Cav. Co.I
Waller, William D. VA 9th Cav. Co.E 1st Lt.
Waller, William D. VA Cav. 36th Bn. 1st Lt.,Adj.
Waller, Wm. D. Gen. & Staff 1st Lt.,Adj.
Waller, William G. TX 31st Cav. Co.D
Waller, William G. VA 3rd Inf. Co.C
Waller, William G. Gen. & Staff 1st Lt.,Ord.Off.
Waller, William H. GA 12th Inf. Co.G Cpl.
Waller, William H. TN 25th Inf. Co.F
Waller, William J. GA 44th Inf. Co.H Sgt.
Waller, William J. SC Inf. 9th Bn. Co.D
Waller, William J. SC 26th Inf. Co.E
Waller, William L. AL Inf. 1st Regt. Co.E Sgt.
Waller, William L. GA 3rd Cav. Co.A
Waller, William M. AR 31st Inf. Co.E Sgt.
Waller, William M. NC 61st Inf. Co.K
Waller, William M. TN 14th Inf. Co.C
Waller, William M. VA 19th Inf. Co.H 1st Lt.
Waller, William M. VA 49th Inf. Co.F
Waller, William N. GA 6th Inf. Co.K
Waller, William N. TN 26th Inf. Co.B,H
Waller, William N. TN 61st Mtd.Inf. Bundren's Co.
Waller, William P. VA 24th Inf. Co.I
Waller, William R. MS 40th Inf. Co.G
Waller, William R. TX Arty. Douglas' Co.
Waller, William W. SC 2nd Inf. Co.F
Waller, Willis NC Inf. 13th Bn. Co.D
Waller, Willis NC 66th Inf. Co.K
Waller, Windham AL 43rd Inf. Co.K
Waller, W.J. AL 31st Inf. Co.I
Waller, W.L. AL 1st Regt. Mobile Vol. Baas' Co.
Waller, W.L. AL Mil. 2nd Regt.Vol. Co.F
Waller, W.M. AR 15th Mil. Co.E Sgt.
Waller, W.M. LA Cav. Greenleaf's Co. (Orleans Lt.Horse)
Waller, W.N. TN Inf. 4th Cons.Regt. Co.E
Waller, Woodley VA 38th Inf. Co.F
Waller, Wright W. NC 55th Inf. Co.H
Waller, W.S. AL 2nd Cav. Co.K
Waller, W.T. GA 3rd Res. Co.B Sgt.
Waller, W.T. GA 9th Inf. (St.Guards) Co.A
Waller, W.T. KY 12th Cav. Co.A,C
Waller, W.T. MS Holly Springs Regt.
Waller, W.W. MS 1st Cav. Res. Co.I
Waller, W.W. TX 8th Cav. Co.H
Waller, Zacheus E. GA 4th Inf. Co.G
Waller, Z.G. MS 36th Inf. Co.F
Wallers, E.S. MS Cav. Vivion's Co.
Wallery, J.M. TX 14th Cav. Co.A
Walles, D.D. TN 42nd Inf. 1st Co.F
Walles, John FL 5th Inf. Co.E
Walles, Obedene TN 44th (Cons.) Inf. Co.E
Walles, R. AR 11th & 17th (Cons.) Inf. Co.F
Walles, S.W. NC 2nd Jr.Res. Co.B
Walle sey 1st Creek Mtd.Vol. Co.H, 2nd Co.D
Wallesford, Charles C. MO Inf. 1st Regt. St.Guard Co.E
Wallestine, Harman GA 44th Inf. Co.E
Walleston, Harry A. LA 1st Cav. Co.H
Wallet, Alex. LA 6th Cav. Co.G
Wallet, Frank LA C.S. Zouave Bn. Co.F,B Drum.
Wallet, J.B. LA 6th Cav. Co.G
Wallet, John B. LA 16th Inf. Co.K
Wallet, L., Jr. LA Cav. Benjamin's Co.
Wallet, S. LA Cav. Benjamin's Co.
Wallet, Sylvert LA 1st Hvy.Arty. (Reg.) Co.D
Walletjeck, Paul TX Waul's Legion Co.C
Wallett, Alexis LA 18th Inf. Co.C
Wallette, Francois LA Maddox's Regt.Res.Corps Co.B
Walley, George W. MS 46th Inf. Co.A
Walley, Goolsberry MS 27th Inf. Co.G
Walley, Harrison AR 31st Inf. Co.B
Walley, James LA 7th Inf. Co.A
Walley, James MS 27th Inf. Co.G
Walley, J.M. AL 36th Inf. Co.E
Walley, John MS 1st Cav.Res. Co.H
Walley, Pinkney MS 27th Inf. Co.G
Walley, R. MS 9th Cav. Co.D
Walley, R.H. MS Cav. 17th Bn. Co.F
Walley, William MS 9th Cav. Co.D
Walley, William MS Cav. 17th Bn. Co.E,F
Wallhoefer, Charles TX 36th Cav. Co.F Music.
Walliace, Stephen A. AR 3rd Inf. Co.B
Wallic, L.C. NC 3rd Jr.Res. Co.G
Wallice, A. AR 1st (Crawford's) Cav. Co.G
Wallice, D.A. AR 1st (Crawford's) Cav. Co.G
Wallice, David Conf.Cav. Clarkson's Bn. Ind.Rangers Co.C
Wallice, Eli FL 11th Inf. Co.C
Wallice, I. AL 7th Inf. Co.B
Wallice, J. MS Cav. Ham's Regt. Co.G
Wallice, James C. MS 15th (Cons.) Inf. Co.K
Wallice, James F. KY 10th (Diamond's) Cav. Co.K
Wallice, James H. NC 1st Inf. (6 mo. '61) Co.I
Wallice, J.D. LA 27th Inf. Co.F
Wallice, J.J. AL 31st Inf. Co.D Cpl.
Wallice, Joel W. AR 24th Inf. Co.B
Wallice, John NC 26th Inf. Co.I
Wallice, J.T. GA 30th Inf. Co.H
Wallice, Louis AR 14th (Powers') Inf. Co.H Capt.
Wallice, M. SC Inf. Hampton Legion
Wallice, N. MS 6th Cav. Co.C
Wallice, R. MS 16th Inf. Co.C
Wallice, Robert AR 11th Inf. Co.F
Wallice, Simeon H. AR 24th Inf. Co.B
Wallice, Stephen TN 55th (Brown's) Inf. Co.D
Wallice, Taylor KY 4th Mtd.Inf. Co.G Music.
Wallice, W.C. GA 56th Inf. Co.K
Wallice, William AL 55th Vol. Co.C
Wallice, William Ry KY 4th Mtd.Inf. Co.G
Wallick, Henry NC 2nd Jr.Res. Co.D
Wallick, J.F. NC 2nd Jr.Res. Co.D
Wallick, Phillippe LA C.S. Zouave Bn. Co.B
Wallick, W.M. GA Inf. 5th Bn. (St.Guards) Co.D
Wallie, Pinkney G. MS 24th Inf. Co.F
Walliem, D.P. MS 13th Inf. Co.C Sgt.
Wallien, W. MS Inf. 2nd Bn. (St.Troops) Co.E
Wallier, J. LA 2nd Res.Corps Co.A
Wallige, J.F. GA 30th Inf. Co.H
Wallin, --- TX Cav. Steele's Command Co.A
Wallin, Albert GA 13th Cav. Co.C
Wallin, Alexander TX Waul's Legion Co.A
Wallin, Andrew GA Cav. 6th Bn. (St.Guards) Co.D
Wallin, Berryman 3rd Conf.Cav. Co.A
Wallin, Christofer VA 129th Mil. Chambers' Co., Avis' Co.
Wallin, Francis M. TX Waul's Legion Co.
Wallin, G.W. AR Bateman's Regt.
Wallin, H.T. VA Mil. Scott Cty.
Wallin, James GA 39th Inf. Co.E
Wallin, James P. 7th Conf.Cav. Co.F Capt.
Wallin, Jesse GA 39th Inf. Co.E
Wallin, John 3rd Conf.Cav. Co.A Cpl.
Wallin, John G. TN Cav. 5th Bn. (McClellan's) Co.D
Wallin, John J. AR 2nd Mtd.Rifles Co.A 2nd Lt.
Wallin, Joseph GA 39th Inf. Co.E
Wallin, Joseph TN 43rd Inf. Co.E Sgt.
Wallin, Reuben VA 64th Mtd.Inf. Co.C

Wallin, Robert GA 12th Inf.
Wallin, Rubin VA Inf. 21st Bn. 2nd Co.C Cpl.
Walline, Washington AL 36th Inf. Co.K Sgt.
Walline, William AL St.Arty. Co.C
Walling, A.L. TX 15th Inf. Co.C
Walling, B.P. SC 3rd Cav. Co.A Sgt.
Walling, B.R. AL 1st Cav. 1st Co.C
Walling, B.R. AL 5th Cav. Co.D
Walling, Creed A. TX 14th Cav. Co.D
Walling, C.T. TX 11th Cav. Co.D 1st Sgt.
Walling, Daniel TX 15th Cav. Co.B
Walling, E. GA 5th Inf. Co.E
Walling, E. TX Cav. Waller's Regt. Goodes' Co.
Walling, Elijah TX 22nd Inf. Co.K
Walling, G.W. TX 33rd Cav. Co.C
Walling, H. LA 22nd (Cons.) Inf. Co.A Cpl.
Walling, H.C. AL 17th Inf. Co.B
Walling, Henry SC 3rd Cav. Co.A
Walling, Henry TX 3rd Cav. Co.A
Walling, Hosea TX 5th Cav. Co.H
Walling, Isaac H. VA Arty. Kevill's Co.
Walling, Isaac H. VA 41st Inf. 1st Co.E
Walling, Isham C. TX 3rd Cav. Co.B
Walling, J. AR 3rd Inf. Co.B
Walling, J.A. SC 25th Inf. Co.F
Walling, James SC Inf. Hampton Legion Co.H
Walling, James TN 4th (Murray's) Cav. Co.A
Walling, James TN 11th (Holman's) Cav. Co.H
Walling, James TN 43rd Inf. Co.H
Walling, James TX Cav. McCord's Frontier Regt. Co.I
Walling, James 1st Conf.Cav. 2nd Co.D
Walling, James D. AR 14th (McCarver's) Inf. Co.F
Walling, James D. AR 21st Inf. Co.B
Walling, James T. TN 43rd Inf. Co.C
Walling, J.B. SC 1st Mtd.Mil. Blakewood's Co.
Walling, J.D. AR 8th Cav. Co.D
Walling, J.D. SC 11th Inf. Co.K
Walling, J.D. TX 13th Vol. Co.E
Walling, Jesse TN 16th Inf. Co.E 1st Lt.
Walling, Jesse R. TX 6th Cav. Co.I
Walling, Jesse T. TX 1st (McCulloch's) Cav. Co.H
Walling, J.G. TX 15th Inf. Co.C Cpl.
Walling, J.H. AR 8th Cav. Co.D
Walling, J.H. AR 1st Vol. Co.K Sgt.
Walling, J.H. TX 1st Hvy.Arty. Co.A 2nd Lt.
Walling, J.H. TX 15th Inf. Co.C, 1st Co.E 1st Sgt.
Walling, J.M. GA 39th Inf. Co.E
Walling, John TX 20th Cav. Co.K
Walling, John E. TX 33rd Cav. Co.C Cpl.
Walling, Joseph TN 16th Inf. Co.I
Walling, Joseph A. SC 1st (Hagood's) Inf. 1st Co.D
Walling, Joseph D. TX 37th Cav. Co.C
Walling, Joseph W. AR 38th Inf. Co.D
Walling, J.R. TX 10th Cav. Co.G
Walling, J.W. SC 25th Inf. Co.D
Walling, L.J. TN Detailed Conscr. Co.A
Walling, Monroe GA 39th Inf. Co.E
Walling, N.D. TX 3rd Cav. Co.E
Walling, Paulinus V. TX 19th Cav. Co.D
Walling, R.D. TX 28th Cav. Co.A
Walling, R.F. SC 8th Bn.Res. Co.A
Walling, Richard TX 17th Cav. Co.D
Walling, Richard TX 22nd Inf. Co.K
Walling, Robert SC 1st (Hagood's) Inf. 1st Co.D, 2nd Co.K
Walling, Robert TX 5th Cav. Co.H
Walling, Shelby TN 16th Inf. Co.I
Walling, S.R. TX 3rd Cav. Co.B
Walling, Thomas J. AL 5th Cav. Co.D
Walling, Thomas J. TX 19th Cav. Co.D
Walling, Thomas V. AL 6th Inf. Co.C
Walling, Vance TX 12th Cav. Co.K Lt.
Walling, Vance TX 19th Cav. Co.D 1st Lt.
Walling, W. AL 9th (Malone's) Cav. Co.K Sgt.
Walling, W. AR 3rd Inf. Co.B
Walling, W.A. TX 1st Hvy.Arty. 2nd Co.A Sgt.
Walling, W.A. TX 15th Inf. Co.C, 1st Co.E Cpl.
Walling, William GA 39th Inf. Co.E
Walling, William LA 6th Cav. Co.C
Walling, William NC 3rd Inf. Co.I
Walling, William SC 2nd Arty. Co.C
Walling, William A. AL 6th Inf. Co.C
Walling, William A. TX 28th Cav. Co.A
Walling, W.S. TX 15th Inf. Co.C Sgt.
Walling, W.T. AL 5th Cav. Co.D
Wallingford, Isaac B. AR 7th Inf. Co.I Cpl.
Wallingford, M. VA 3rd Inf.Loc.Def. Co.B
Wallingford, T.G. TX 4th Inf. Co.G
Wallingford, T.W. TN 52nd Inf. Co.K 1st Sgt.
Wallingsford, J.A. TN 31st Inf. Co.E
Wallingsford, J.H. KY 2nd Bn.Mtd.Rifles Co.C
Wallingsford, J.J. AR 12th Inf. Co.F
Wallingsford, T.W. TN 51st (Cons.) Inf. Co.B Cpl.
Wallingsford, W.B. AR 12th Inf. Co.F Cpl.
Wallingsford, William P. AR Inf. 1st Bn. Co.D
Wallingsford, W.P. AR Cav. Davies' Bn. Co.B
Wallingsford, W.T. VA 9th Cav. Co.E
Wallington, George MO 2nd Inf. Co.C
Wallington, W.J.S. SC 7th Inf. 1st Co.G
Wallins, William R. TX 15th Cav. Co.H
Wallis, --- SC 25th Inf. Co.E
Wallis, --- TX 1st Hvy.Arty. Co.I
Wallis, --- Deneale's Regt. Choctaw Warriors Co.A
Wallis, A. LA Inf. 10th Bn.
Wallis, A.J. TN 50th Inf. Co.C
Wallis, Allen AR 20th Inf. Co.F
Wallis, Andrew D. MO Cav. Slayback's Regt. Co.K
Wallis, Augustus AR 19th (Dawson's) Inf. Co.F
Wallis, B. GA 46th Inf. Co.H
Wallis, Benjamin VA 6th Bn.Res. Co.G Cpl.
Wallis, Benjamin M. TX 22nd Cav. Co.H 1st Lt.
Wallis, Bolin D. GA 43rd Inf. Co.G
Wallis, Brantley MS 23rd Inf. Co.E Cpl.
Wallis, Brantley MS 32nd Inf. Co.B Sgt.
Wallis, Brison MS 27th Inf. Co.C
Wallis, B.S. MS 23rd Inf. Co.E Lt.
Wallis, B.S. TX 29th Cav. Co.H
Wallis, B.W. TX 22nd Inf. Co.F
Wallis, C. AL 51st (Part.Rangers) Co.F Sgt.
Wallis, C. LA 19th Inf.
Wallis, Charles TX Lt.Arty. Jones' Co. Sgt.
Wallis, Charles R. LA 4th Cav. Co.E
Wallis, Charner AL Inf. 1st Regt. Co.D
Wallis, C.W. GA 9th Inf. (St.Guards) Culp's Co.
Wallis, D.A. AR Inf. Cocke's Regt. Co.I
Wallis, Daniel B. TX 26th Cav. Co.F Cpl.
Wallis, David GA 36th (Broyles') Inf. Co.L
Wallis, David GA 38th Inf. Co.I
Wallis, David MO 12th Inf. Co.F
Wallis, David NC 4th Sr.Res. Co.H
Wallis, David, Jr. TX Conscr.
Wallis, David J. GA 38th Inf. Co.I Sgt.
Wallis, David J. GA 43rd Inf. Co.E
Wallis, David M. LA 4th Cav. Co.E
Wallis, Dickson 1st Choctaw & Chickasaw Mtd.Rifles 3rd Co.D, 2nd Co.H
Wallis, D.F. LA Bickham's Co. (Caddo Mil.) Cpl.
Wallis, D.W. AR 11th Inf. Co.D
Wallis, D.W. AR 11th & 17th (Cons.) Inf. Co.D Sgt.
Wallis, E. MS Cav. Russell's Co.
Wallis, E.C. AL 5th Inf. New Co.H
Wallis, Eli AL 44th Inf. Co.G
Wallis, Ferdinant T. AL 30th Inf. Co.A
Wallis, F.M. TX 26th Cav. Co.F
Wallis, Francis M. GA 24th Inf. Co.B
Wallis, George H. KY 5th Cav. Co.C
Wallis, George W. AL 18th Inf. Co.K,E
Wallis, George W. AR 26th Inf. Co.H
Wallis, George W. GA 38th Inf. Co.A Sgt.
Wallis, George W. TX 22nd Cav. Co.H Sgt.
Wallis, G.M. TX 1st Inf. Co.M
Wallis, Green B. GA 43rd Inf. Co.I
Wallis, G.W. AR 19th (Dawson's) Inf. Co.F
Wallis, G.W. TX 21st Cav. Co.C
Wallis, H. GA Inf. 2nd Bn. (St.Guards) Co.A
Wallis, H.C. GA 38th Inf. Co.I
Wallis, H.D. MS 29th Inf. Co.E Cpl.
Wallis, Henry MS 8th Inf. Co.B
Wallis, Henry C. MD 1st Cav. Co.E Sgt.
Wallis, Henry T. VA Cav. 34th Bn. Co.C
Wallis, Hiram NC 49th Inf. Co.D
Wallis, H.M. (Dr.) LA Inf.Conscr.
Wallis, H.T. AL 37th Inf. Co.C 1st Lt.
Wallis, I.D. MS 11th (Cons.) Cav. Co.C
Wallis, Irwin W. KY 2nd (Woodward's) Cav. Co.C
Wallis, Isham NC 49th Inf. Co.D
Wallis, Isham J. GA 35th Inf. Co.B Sgt.
Wallis, Isham R. MS 19th Inf. Co.K Sgt.
Wallis, Izariah H. VA 37th Inf. Co.G 1st Sgt.
Wallis, J. AL 8th Cav. Co.K
Wallis, J. GA 46th Inf. Co.H
Wallis, J. MS 1st (King's) Inf. (St.Troops) D. Love's Co.
Wallis, J.A. MS 32nd Inf. Co.B
Wallis, J.A. 8th (Wade's) Conf.Cav. Co.K 2nd Lt.
Wallis, Jacob A. MO 10th Inf. Co.H
Wallis, James MS 8th Inf. Co.B
Wallis, James MS Adams' Co. (Holmes Cty.Ind.)
Wallis, James NC 46th Inf. Co.D
Wallis, James SC Hvy.Arty. 15th (Lucas') Bn. Co.C Sgt.
Wallis, James TN 1st Hvy.Arty. 2nd Co.B
Wallis, James TX Cav. Giddings' Bn. Carr's Co.
Wallis, James 1st Choctaw Mtd.Rifles Ward's Co.
Wallis, James C. MS 2nd Inf. Co.K
Wallis, James D. MO 3rd Inf. Co.H Asst.Surg.
Wallis, James D. Gen. & Staff Surg.

Wallis, James E. MS 22nd Inf. Co.I Sgt.
Wallis, James N. MS 17th Inf. Co.E
Wallis, James W. AR 18th (Marmaduke's) Inf. Co.K
Wallis, J.C. GA 2nd Res. Co.I Sgt.
Wallis, J.C. MS 23rd Inf. Co.G
Wallis, J.C. VA 32nd Inf. Co.K
Wallis, J.D. MO 1st & 4th Cons.Inf. Surg.
Wallis, J.E. AL 30th Inf. Co.A Cpl.
Wallis, J.E. TN 23rd Inf. 2nd Co.F
Wallis, Jefferson MO 3rd Cav. Co.K
Wallis, Jesse T. GA 43rd Inf. Co.I
Wallis, J.F. GA 16th Inf. Co.H 2nd Lt.
Wallis, J.F. MS 1st (Percy's) Inf. Co.I
Wallis, J.F. TN 43rd Inf. Co.H
Wallis, J.H. VA 16th Cav. Co.C Cpl.
Wallis, J.H. VA Cav. Caldwell's Bn. Hankins' Co.
Wallis, J.H.P. MO Cav. Fristoe's Regt. Maj., Surg.
Wallis, J.J. AL 23rd Inf. Co.G
Wallis, J.J. GA 16th Inf. Co.B Sgt.
Wallis, J.J.A. MS 2nd St.Cav. Co.K
Wallis, J.J.A. MS Cav. Ham's Regt. Co.K
Wallis, J.L. LA 19th Inf. Co.C
Wallis, J.L. TN 43rd Inf. Co.A
Wallis, J.M. AL 48th Inf. Co.K
Wallis, J.N. MS 32nd Inf. Co.B
Wallis, Joel AR 14th (Powers') Inf. Co.B
Wallis, Joel G. AR Cav. Wright's Regt. Co.H
Wallis, Joel W. AR Inf. Hardy's Regt. Co.B
Wallis, John AL 51st (Part.Rangers) Co.F
Wallis, John MS 1st Inf. Co.F
Wallis, John MS Inf. 2nd St.Troops Co.I
Wallis, John TX Cav. 1st Regt.St.Troops Co.C
Wallis, John TX 16th Cav. Co.G
Wallis, John TX 22nd Cav. Co.H Capt.
Wallis, John A.J. AL 10th Inf. Co.K
Wallis, John C. TN 25th Inf. Co.C
Wallis, John C. TX 20th Inf. Co.B Capt.
Wallis, John F. GA Inf. Cobb Guards Co.B
Wallis, John H. NC 2nd Jr.Res. Co.B
Wallis, John J. MS 23rd Inf. Co.E Sgt.
Wallis, John J. NC 31st Inf. Co.C
Wallis, John L. GA 43rd Inf. Co.I
Wallis, John O. NC 2nd Jr.Res. Co.E 2nd Lt.
Wallis, John S. Sp.Agent War Dept. Maj.
Wallis, John T. AL 41st Inf. Co.C
Wallis, John T. MO 10th Inf. Co.H Sgt.
Wallis, John W. GA Cherokee Legion (St.Guards) Co.C
Wallis, Jonathan TX Cav. McDowell's Co.
Wallis, Joseph AL 39th Inf. Co.F
Wallis, Joseph LA 12th Inf. Co.L
Wallis, Joseph E. TX 20th Inf. Co.B Sgt.
Wallis, Joseph N. MS 23rd Inf. Co.E
Wallis, Joshua AR 19th (Dawson's) Inf. Co.F
Wallis, Josiah C. MS 23rd Inf. Co.E
Wallis, J.P. GA 36th (Broyles') Inf. Co.E
Wallis, J.P. VA 21st Inf. Co.I
Wallis, J.R. MS 2nd St.Cav. Co.K Capt.
Wallis, J.R. MS Cav. Ham's Regt. Co.K Capt.
Wallis, J.R. MS 15th Bn.S.S. Co.B Cpl.
Wallis, J.R. NC 2nd Jr.Res. Co.E
Wallis, J.R. SC Hvy.Arty. 15th (Lucas') Bn. Co.C
Wallis, Julias C. MO Inf. Perkins' Bn. Co.B
Wallis, J.W. AL 8th Inf. Co.D
Wallis, J.W. AR 27th Inf. Co.B Cpl.
Wallis, J.W. GA 1st Troops & Defences (Macon) Co.D
Wallis, J.W. VA 16th Cav. Co.C
Wallis, J.Y. NC 4th Sr.Res. Co.H
Wallis, L. TX Cav. Terry's Regt. Co.F
Wallis, Levi TX 14th Cav. Co.F
Wallis, Levy KY 3rd Cav. Co.G
Wallis, Lewis TX Cav. W.H. Randolph's Co.
Wallis, L.L. AL 5th Inf. Co.B
Wallis, L.W. GA 43rd Inf. Co.F
Wallis, M. TX Cav. Border's Regt. Co.E
Wallis, Madison GA 16th Inf. Co.B
Wallis, Major L. VA 37th Inf. Co.G 1st Lt.
Wallis, M.B. MS 8th Inf. Co.B
Wallis, M.B. MS 36th Inf. Co.D
Wallis, M.D. TN 84th Inf. Co.C Sgt.
Wallis, Micajah P. GA 30th Inf. Co.H
Wallis, Morgan LA 9th Inf. Co.I
Wallis, Morgan E. NC Walker's Bn. Thomas' Legion Co.B,H
Wallis, Nathan MS 23rd Inf. Co.G
Wallis, Newton C. MS 2nd Inf. Co.K
Wallis, Nicholas G. GA 44th Inf. Co.D
Wallis, Noland LA Inf.Cons.Crescent Regt. Co.E
Wallis, Pendleton GA 13th Cav. Co.D
Wallis, Phillip GA Inf. (Anderson Guards) Anderson's Co.
Wallis, P.J. TX 35th (Brown's) Cav.
Wallis, P.L. MS 2nd St.Cav. Co.K
Wallis, P.L. MS Cav. Ham's Regt. Co.K
Wallis, P.R. TX Inf. Rutherford's Co.
Wallis, R. AL 26th (O'Neal's) Inf. Co.G
Wallis, Raleigh W. MS 37th Inf. Co.A
Wallis, Ransome MS 8th Inf. Co.B
Wallis, Reuben GA 10th Cav. (St.Guards) Co.C
Wallis, R.H. AL Mil. 4th Vol. Moore's Co.
Wallis, Richard KY 13th Cav. Co.F
Wallis, Riley AL 36th Inf. Co.G
Wallis, R.M. AL 4th Inf. Old Co.G
Wallis, Rob. Gen. & Staff Surg.
Wallis, Robert MS 34th Inf. Co.A
Wallis, Robert TX Conscr.
Wallis, Robert S. MO 3rd Cav. Surg.
Wallis, Robert T. AR 19th (Dawson's) Inf. Co.B Cpl.
Wallis, Robert W. MO 10th Inf. Co.H
Wallis, Rodolphus MS St.Cav. Perrin's Bn. Co.E Cpl.
Wallis, Roswell H. AL 24th Inf. Co.F
Wallis, Roswell H. AL 28th Inf. Co.K
Wallis, R.R. MS 32nd Inf. Co.B
Wallis, R.S. Gen. & Staff A.Sr.Surg.
Wallis, Samuel NC 6th Inf. Co.A
Wallis, Samuel R. LA 8th Inf. Co.C Cpl.
Wallis, Shadrach W. VA Cav. Caldwell's Bn. Hankins' Co.
Wallis, Sidney AL 9th (Malone's) Cav. Co.I
Wallis, Silas S. AR 8th Inf. New Co.G
Wallis, Simon D. TN 25th Inf. Co.C 2nd Lt.
Wallis, Simon H. AR Inf. Hardy's Regt. Co.B
Wallis, Sol. B. TX Conscr.
Wallis, S.T. GA 43rd Inf. Co.I
Wallis, S.W. LA 2nd Inf. Co.K
Wallis, T. MS 1st (King's) Inf. (St.Troops) D. Love's Co.
Wallis, T.E. AL 1st Cav.
Wallis, Thomas AR 11th Inf. Co.H
Wallis, Thomas Benton MO 8th Inf. Co.G 1st Sgt.
Wallis, Thomas G. GA 36th (Broyles') Inf. Co.K
Wallis, Thomas H. TX 11th Cav. Co.K Capt.
Wallis, T.J. AL 22nd Inf. Co.E
Wallis, T.J. AL 48th Inf. Co.I,M
Wallis, T.S. TX Cav. 1st Regt.St.Troops Co.A
Wallis, Union AL Randolph Cty.Res. D.A. Self's Co.
Wallis, W. GA 5th Inf. (St.Guards) Allum's Co.
Wallis, W.A. AL 34th Inf. Co.B
Wallis, W.B. AL 32nd Inf. Co.I
Wallis, W.C. AL Mtd.Mil. Capt.
Wallis, W.C. TN 43rd Inf. Co.H
Wallis, W.C. 8th (Wade's) Conf.Cav. Co.K Far.
Wallis, W.E. TN 17th Inf. Co.F 2nd Lt.
Wallis, Wiley M. MO 12th Inf. Co.E
Wallis, William AL 8th Inf. Co.K
Wallis, William AL 30th Inf. Co.A 1st Lt.
Wallis, William LA Inf.Crescent Regt. Co.A
Wallis, William MS 2nd St.Cav. Co.K
Wallis, William MS 16th Inf. Co.H
Wallis, William NC 46th Inf. Co.D,I
Wallis, William NC 66th Inf. Co.G
Wallis, William VA 8th Cav. 2nd Co.D
Wallis, William VA 21st Mil. Co.B
Wallis, William VA Inf. 1st Bn. Music.
Wallis, William 1st Choctaw Mtd.Rifles Ward's Co.
Wallis, William A. MS 28th Cav. Co.D
Wallis, William B. GA 14th Inf. Co.K Sgt.
Wallis, William C. GA 43rd Inf. Co.E
Wallis, William D. GA 44th Inf. Co.D
Wallis, William F. GA 44th Inf. Co.D
Wallis, William H. AL 28th Inf. Co.L
Wallis, William H. MS 2nd St.Cav. Co.K
Wallis, William H. MS 8th Inf. Co.B
Wallis, William J. VA Cav. Caldwell's Bn. Hankins' Co.
Wallis, William M. AL 12th Cav. Co.D
Wallis, William P. MS 9th Cav. Co.F
Wallis, William R. GA 36th (Broyles') Inf. Co.K Sgt.
Wallis, William S. NC 58th Inf. Co.L
Wallis, William S.A. NC 43rd Inf. Co.H
Wallis, William T. MD 1st Inf. Co.E Sgt.
Wallis, William W. MS 23rd Inf. Co.I
Wallis, Willis B. MS 38th Cav. Co.C
Wallis, W.L. TX 15th Cav. Co.C
Wallis, W.M. TX 27th Cav. Co.K Capt.
Wallis, W.N. TN 43rd Inf. Co.H
Wallis, W.R. MS Cav. Ham's Regt. Co.K Cpl.
Wallis, W.S. MS 32nd Inf. Co.I
Wallis, W.T. LA 4th Inf. Co.F
Wallis, W.W. GA 43rd Inf. Co.E
Wallisk, D.H.E. AL 1st Inf. Co.H
Wallison, H. MS 43rd Inf. Co.F
Wallitabee, Wesley 1st Choctaw & Chickasaw Mtd.Rifles 2nd Co.C
Wallman, T.J. MS 14th Inf. Co.E 1st Lt.
Wallney, Otto TX 24th Cav. Co.D
Wallon, Andrew J. NC 2nd Arty. (36th St.Troops) Co.A
Wallon, Archibald NC 64th Inf. Co.D
Wallon, Hugh NC 64th Inf. Co.D

Wallon, Jesse MO 11th Inf. Co.B
Wallon, John D. MO 11th Inf. Co.B
Wallon, Robert MO 11th Inf. Co.B
Wallon, Simpson MO 11th Inf. Co.B
Wallon, William S. MO 11th Inf. Co.B
Wallor, J.F. AL 3rd Inf. Co.A
Wallory, E.B. MS 21st Inf. Co.F
Wallot, J. AR 2nd Inf. Co.F
Wallowitz, Charles LA 1st (Strawbridge's) Inf. Co.A
Wallows, S.W. GA Arty. Lumpkin's Co.
Wallpole, Joseph VA 3rd Inf. Co.D
Wallraven, Anderson GA Inf. 8th Bn. Co.D Cpl.
Wallraven, Milton AL 29th Inf. Co.D
Wallraven, William GA Inf. 8th Bn. Co.D
Wallraven, William B. GA Inf. 8th Bn. Co.D
Walls, A. AL 21st Inf. Co.C
Walls, A. AR 47th (Crandall's) Cav. Co.C
Walls, A.B. AR Inf. Adams' Regt. Moore's Co.
Walls, A.C. AL 9th (Malone's) Cav. Co.G
Walls, Adly NC 33rd Inf. Co.C
Walls, A.J. AL Gid Nelson Lt.Arty.
Walls, A.J. AL 23rd Inf. Co.H
Walls, A.J. AR Inf. Adams' Regt. Moore's Co.
Walls, A.L. 20th Conf.Cav. 2nd Co.I
Walls, Albert Harris TN 47th Inf. Co.E
Walls, Allen V. AL 4th Inf. Co.F Sgt.
Walls, Alphonso A. NC 1st Arty. (10th St.Troops) Co.C
Walls, A.M. AL 7th Inf. Co.D
Walls, A.M. AR 1st Mtd.Rifles Asst.Surg.
Walls, A.M. AR 25th Inf. Co.E Asst.Surg.
Walls, A.M. VA 1st St.Res. Co.F
Walls, A.M. Gen. & Staff Surg.
Walls, Anderson SC 5th Res. Co.F Cpl.
Walls, Anderson SC 24th Inf. Co.I
Walls, Anderson B. GA 39th Inf. Co.A
Walls, Andrew B. NC Cav. 7th Bn. Co.C
Walls, Andrew J. FL 5th Inf. Co.F
Walls, A.W. GA 51st Inf. Co.H,A
Walls, B.C. GA 7th Cav. Co.C
Walls, Benton MO 10th Inf. Co.G,K
Walls, Berry AL 4th (Russell's) Cav. Co.I
Walls, Berry TN Cav. 12th Bn. (Day's) Co.C
Walls, Beverly W. TN 44th Inf. Co.H
Walls, Beverly W. TN 44th (Cons.) Inf. Co.A
Walls, B.F. NC 1st Jr.Res. Co.F
Walls, B.H. AR 31st Inf. Co.I Sgt.
Walls, B.P. GA 37th Inf. Co.A
Walls, Bradford C. GA Arty. 9th Bn. Co.C
Walls, Burgess NC 2nd Inf. Co.E
Walls, Burgus KY 4th Mtd.Inf. Co.H
Walls, C. SC 3rd Cav. Co.H
Walls, C. SC 1st Mtd.Mil.
Walls, C.A.F. TN Cav. 12th Bn. (Day's) Co.C
Walls, Carter AL 47th Inf. Co.G Ch.Music.
Walls, Charles LA 6th Cav. Co.A
Walls, Charles LA 4th Inf. Co.E
Walls, Charles SC Lt.Arty. J.T. Kanapaux's Co. (Lafayette Arty.)
Walls, Charles A. AL 20th Inf. Co.G
Walls, Charles T. TX Cav. Martin's Regt. Co.B
Walls, C.J. SC 1st Mtd.Mil. Screven's Co.
Walls, C.J. SC Lt.Arty. J.T. Kanapaux's Co. (Lafayette Arty.)
Walls, Daniel AL 4th (Russell's) Cav. Co.I Sgt.
Walls, Daniel GA 46th Inf. Co.F
Walls, Daniel TN 18th Inf. Co.A
Walls, D.J. TN 38th Inf. Co.F
Walls, D.M. GA 44th Inf. Co.F
Walls, Dred. AR Inf. Adams' Regt. Moore's Co.
Walls, Drury AL 48th Inf. Co.F
Walls, Drury NC 52nd Inf. Co.K
Walls, Drury M. GA 21st Inf. New Co.E
Walls, Drury M. NC Inf. 2nd Bn. Co.D
Walls, E.B. SC Cav.Bn. Holcombe Legion Co.B
Walls, E.B. VA 59th Inf. 3rd Co.F
Walls, E.D. AL 20th Cav. Lee's Co. Cpl.
Walls, E.D. AR Cav. Gordon's Regt. Co.K
Walls, Edward AL 2nd Cav. Co.A
Walls, Edwin AL 7th Inf. Co.B
Walls, E.H. AL 20th Inf. Co.G
Walls, E.L. SC 3rd Inf. Co.K
Walls, Eli J. MO 3rd Cav. Co.D Sgt.
Walls, Elijah B. VA 1st Arty. Co.F
Walls, Elijah B. VA 32nd Inf. Co.G
Walls, Ellis AL Cp. of Instr. Talladega
Walls, F.F. TN 15th (Cons.) Cav. Co.I
Walls, F.F. TN 16th (Logwood's) Cav. Co.H Sgt.
Walls, Francis M. AL 26th Inf. Co.H
Walls, Francis M. GA 47th Inf. Co.E Sgt.
Walls, Franklin AR 2nd Mtd.Rifles Co.I
Walls, Ge. W. AL 18th Inf. Co.F
Walls, George GA Arty. 9th Bn. Co.C
Walls, George TN 32nd Inf. Co.B
Walls, George A. AL 3rd Bn.Res. Co.B
Walls, George W. GA Arty. 11th Bn. (Sumter Arty.) Co.A
Walls, George W. GA 44th Inf. Co.F
Walls, George W. MS 18th Cav. Co.A 2nd Lt.
Walls, George W. MO 10th Inf. Co.G,K
Walls, George W. TN 1st (Turney's) Inf. Co.A
Walls, George W. TN 32nd Inf.
Walls, G.W. TN 15th (Stewart's) Cav. Co.B
Walls, H.A. GA 57th Inf. Co.D
Walls, Hansel MS 18th Cav. Co.A Cpl.
Walls, Henry AL 3rd Res. Co.E
Walls, Henry H. NC 34th Inf. Co.B
Walls, Henry H. NC 53rd Inf. Co.F
Walls, Henry H. TN 34th Inf. Co.G Sgt.
Walls, Henry M. TN 41st Inf. Co.H
Walls, H.F. AL 46th Inf. Co.B
Walls, H.G. SC 1st Mtd.Mil. Screven's Co.
Walls, H.G. SC Lt.Arty. J.T. Kanapaux's Co. (Lafayette Arty.)
Walls, H.H. NC 35th Inf. Co.D
Walls, H.J. GA 46th Inf. Co.C
Walls, Ira AL 7th Cav. Co.E
Walls, J. AL 12th Inf. Co.C
Walls, J. AL Talladega Cty.Res. D.B. Brown's Co.
Walls, J. GA 5th Inf. (St.Guards) Allum's Co.
Walls, J. GA 47th Inf. Co.E
Walls, J. TX 13th Vol. Co.D
Walls, J.A. AL 21st Inf. Co.H
Walls, James AL 7th Inf. Co.B
Walls, James GA Arty. 9th Bn. Co.C
Walls, James MS 7th Cav. Co.I 1st Lt.
Walls, James MS 18th Cav. Co.D
Walls, James MS 29th Inf. Co.H
Walls, James NC 3rd Inf. Co.C
Walls, James NC 33rd Inf. Co.D
Walls, James TN 14th Inf. Co.F
Walls, James D. TN 17th Inf. Co.F Sgt.
Walls, James H. TN 32nd Inf. Co.B
Walls, James J. GA Arty. 11th Bn. (Sumter Arty.) Co.A
Walls, James K.P. AL City Guards Lockett's Co.
Walls, James K.P. AL Cp. of Instr. Talladega
Walls, James W. TN 1st (Turney's) Inf. Co.I
Walls, Jasper GA Inf. 1st City Bn. (Columbus) Co.D
Walls, J.B. TN 12th (Green's) Cav. Co.F
Walls, Jefferson KY 6th Cav. Co.B
Walls, Jefferson KY 8th Cav. Co.B
Walls, Jefferson MO 3rd Cav. Co.K
Walls, Jester A. AR 1st (Colquitt's) Inf. Co.H
Walls, J.F. AL 26th (O'Neal's) Inf. Co.F
Walls, J.F. AR Cav. Gordon's Regt. Co.K
Walls, J.J. AL 31st Inf. Co.E
Walls, J.J. MS Cav. 3rd Bn. (Ashcraft's) Co.D Sgt.
Walls, J.J. TN 16th (Logwood's) Cav. Co.E
Walls, J.L.F. GA 1st Reg. Co.C
Walls, J.M. AL 14th Inf. Co.E
Walls, J.M. AL 48th Inf. Co.K Cpl.
Walls, J.M. AR Lt.Arty. Marshall's Btty.
Walls, J.M. AR 1st Inf. Co.F
Walls, J.M. Gen. & Staff, Medical Dept. Surg.
Walls, J.N. MS Cav. 3rd Bn. (Ashcraft's) Co.D
Walls, Joel A. AL 3rd Res. Co.B
Walls, John AL 49th Inf. Co.D
Walls, John AL Cp. of Instr. Talladega
Walls, John MS 18th Cav. Co.L
Walls, John NC 42nd Inf. Co.D,F
Walls, John TN 12th (Green's) Cav. Co.F
Walls, John TX 15th Cav. Co.D
Walls, John TX Cav. Baylor's Regt. Co.K
Walls, John VA 10th Cav. Co.D Sgt.
Walls, John VA 36th Inf. 1st Co.C
Walls, John 3rd Conf.Cav. Co.F
Walls, John E.L. TX 15th Cav. Co.H Teamster
Walls, John F. GA 11th Inf. Co.I
Walls, John H. AL 47th Inf. Co.I 1st Sgt.
Walls, John H. LA 8th Inf. Co.H
Walls, John J. MS Inf. 2nd Bn. Co.F
Walls, John J. MS 10th Inf. Old Co.C
Walls, John J. MS 48th Inf. Co.F
Walls, John L. TX 17th Cav. Co.K
Walls, John M. VA Lt.Arty. Woolfolk's Co.
Walls, John R. AL 50th Inf. Co.B
Walls, John R. TN 11th Inf. Co.E
Walls, John W. SC 22nd Inf. Co.H
Walls, Joseph GA 46th Inf. Co.C
Walls, Joseph NC 33rd Inf. Co.D Sgt.
Walls, Joseph VA 64th Mil. Hunley's Co.
Walls, Joseph N. MO 10th Inf. Co.G,K
Walls, J.P. TN Cav. 12th Bn. (Day's) Co.D,C
Walls, J.W. AL 10th Inf. Surg.
Walls, J.W. AR 47th (Crandall's) Cav. Co.K 2nd Lt.
Walls, J.W. MS Cav. 3rd Bn. (Ashcraft's) Co.D
Walls, J.W. NC 21st Inf. Co.D
Walls, J.W. TN 2nd (Robison's) Inf. Co.A
Walls, J.W. VA Conscr. Cp.Lee Co.B
Walls, J.W. Gen. & Staff Surg.
Walls, J. William VA 5th Inf. Surg.
Walls, L.A. AR 7th Inf. Co.K
Walls, Leander L. VA 24th Inf. Co.C
Walls, Levi AR 38th Inf. New Co.I

Walls, Lewis NC 42nd Inf. Co.D
Walls, L.H. GA 32nd Inf. Co.F
Walls, Lindsey L. VA 29th Inf. Co.E
Walls, Littleberry VA 1st Arty. Co.F
Walls, Littleberry VA 32nd Inf. Co.G
Walls, Littleberry B. VA Arty. Dance's Co.
Walls, L.M. AR 1st Vol. Co.I
Walls, Logan MS 18th Cav. Co.D
Walls, M. GA 26th Inf. Co.F
Walls, M. MS Inf. 2nd St.Troops Co.D
Walls, M. VA 13th Cav. Co.E
Walls, Madison NC 58th Inf. Co.F
Walls, Mantreville NC 4th Inf. Co.G
Walls, Mark AL 30th Inf. Co.E
Walls, M.C. TN 3rd (Forrest's) Cav. Co.H
Walls, M.L. NC 11th (Bethel Regt.) Inf. Co.D
Walls, Montgomery GA 13th Inf. Co.F
Walls, Moses P. VA 45th Inf. Co.C
Walls, Nace GA Cherokee Legion (St.Guards) Co.E
Walls, Newbold C. KY 7th Cav. Co.B
Walls, Newbold C. KY 8th Cav. Co.B
Walls, Newton KY 9th Mtd.Inf. Co.F
Walls, N.H. KY 3rd Cav. Co.E
Walls, O.C. TN 12th (Green's) Cav. Co.F
Walls, O.C. TN 16th (Logwood's) Cav. Co.I
Walls, P. NC 23rd Inf. Co.H
Walls, P.D. TX 27th Cav. Co.F
Walls, P.D. TX Cav. Ragsdale's Co.
Walls, P.E. VA 3rd (Archer's) Bn.Res. Co.B
Walls, Peter NC 13th Inf. Co.H
Walls, Peter TN 46th Inf. Co.E
Walls, Peter H. VA 57th Inf. Co.I
Walls, Peter J. VA 45th Inf. Co.C
Walls, P.P. NC 1st Cav. (9th St.Troops) Co.C
Walls, Presley D. MO Inf. 3rd Bn. Co.E
Walls, Presley D. MO 6th Inf. Co.C
Walls, R.C. AL 48th Inf. Co.F
Walls, Richard LA 8th Inf. Co.B
Walls, Richard SC 1st (Orr's) Rifles Co.B
Walls, Richard VA 22nd Inf. Co.H
Walls, Robbert B. VA Inf. Tomlin's Bn. Co.A
Walls, Robert AL 62nd Inf. Co.F,E
Walls, Robert B. VA 53rd Inf. Co.B
Walls, Robert J. AL Cav. Lewis' Bn. Co.D
Walls, R.W. TN 12th Inf. Co.B
Walls, R.W. TN 12th (Cons.) Inf. Co.A
Walls, S. AL Talladega Cty.Res. D.B. Brown's Co.
Walls, S. SC 1st Mtd.Mil.
Walls, S. TN 14th (Neely's) Cav. Co.H
Walls, Samuel GA Cav. 2nd Bn. Co.D Far.
Walls, Samuel GA 5th Cav. Co.A Far.
Walls, Samuel GA 7th Cav. Co.E
Walls, Samuel GA Cav. 21st Bn. Co.B
Walls, Samuel GA 1st (Olmstead's) Inf. Co.K
Walls, Samuel SC 3rd Cav. Co.H
Walls, Samuel 1st Choctaw Mtd.Rifles Ward's Co.
Walls, Samuel A. AR 7th Inf. Co.K
Walls, S.M. GA 1st Inf. (St.Guards) Co.F
Walls, Solomon SC 22nd Inf. Co.H
Walls, Stephen J. GA Arty. Baker's Co.
Walls, Tazewell W. VA 1st Arty. Co.B
Walls, Thomas AL 62nd Inf. Co.H
Walls, Thomas KY 2nd (Duke's) Cav. Co.F
Walls, Thomas KY 6th Cav. Co.B
Walls, Thomas MS St.Cav. 3rd Bn. (Cooper's) 2nd Co.A
Walls, Thomas MS 11th (Perrin's) Cav. Co.G
Walls, Thomas MS 25th Inf. Co.F
Walls, Thomas MS Conscr.
Walls, Thomas NC 56th Inf. Co.K
Walls, Thomas TN 20th (Russell's) Cav. Co.D
Walls, Thomas TN 44th Inf. Co.D
Walls, Thomas TN 44th (Cons.) Inf. Co.D
Walls, Thomas F. GA Inf. 1st City Bn. (Columbus) Co.F
Walls, Thomas F. GA Inf. 19th Bn. (St.Guards) Co.A
Walls, Thomas N. TN 48th (Nixon's) Inf. Co.I
Walls, Thomas W. GA 47th Inf. Co.E
Walls, Timothy L. TX 10th Inf. Co.F
Walls, T.N. MS Cav. 3rd Bn. (Ashcraft's) Co.D
Walls, V. AL Cp. of Instr. Talladega
Walls, V.O. SC 24th Inf. Co.D
Walls, W. NC 1st Jr.Res. Co.H
Walls, W. TN 14th (Neely's) Cav. Co.I
Walls, W.A. AR 47th (Crandall's) Cav. Co.E
Walls, W.A. AR 32nd Inf. Co.G
Walls, Wash NC 5th Sr.Res. Co.B
Walls, W.B. TX 5th Inf. Co.I
Walls, W.C. MS Cav. 3rd Bn. (Ashcraft's) Co.D
Walls, W.C. TN Cav. 12th Bn. (Day's) Co.D
Walls, W.C. TN 22nd (Nixon's) Cav. Co.E Ord.Sgt.
Walls, W.D. AR Inf. Adams' Regt. Moore's Co.
Walls, W.D. SC Inf. Hampton Legion Co.I
Walls, W.E. TN Cav. Williams' Co.
Walls, Wesley AR 30th Inf. Co.E
Walls, W.F. TN 24th Bn.S.S. Co.A
Walls, W.H. AR 15th Mil. Co.I 1st Lt.
Walls, W.H. GA 11th Cav. Co.G
Walls, W.H. TN 12th (Green's) Cav. Co.I
Walls, W.H.F. TN 16th Inf. Co.A
Walls, Wiley C. 3rd Conf.Cav. Co.I
Walls, William AL 51st (Part.Rangers) Co.B
Walls, William AL 7th Inf. Co.B
Walls, William AL 9th Inf. Co.E
Walls, William AL 55th Vol. Co.A
Walls, William AR 5th Inf. Co.I
Walls, William GA 1st (Olmstead's) Inf. Co.E
Walls, William GA 60th Inf. Co.C
Walls, William GA 66th Inf. Co.C
Walls, Wm. GA Conscr.
Walls, William KY 7th Mtd.Inf. Co.B
Walls, William KY 12th Cav. Co.C
Walls, William MO 10th Inf. Co.C
Walls, William TN 7th Inf. Co.K
Walls, William TN 44th Inf. Co.A
Walls, William VA 4th Cav. Co.I
Walls, William VA 53rd Inf. Co.E
Walls, William 2nd Conf.Inf. Co.D
Walls, William A. AR 2nd Mtd.Rifles Co.A
Walls, William A. VA Cav. Mosby's Regt. (Part.Rangers) Co.A
Walls, William A.J. MO 10th Inf. Co.G
Walls, William B. NC 30th Inf. Co.G
Walls, William C. VA 22nd Inf. Co.G
Walls, William C. VA Inf. 45th Bn. Co.D
Walls, William J. GA 4th Inf. Co.H
Walls, William J. GA 43rd Inf. Co.H
Walls, William L. GA 21st Inf. New Co.E Cpl.
Walls, William L. NC Inf. 2nd Bn. Co.D Cpl.
Walls, William M. AL 13th Inf. Co.K
Walls, William M. AL 14th Inf. Co.K
Walls, William M. MO 3rd Cav. Co.D
Walls, Wm. M. VA 45th Inf. Co.C
Walls, Willis AL Inf. 1st Regt. Co.D Music.
Walls, Willis AR 7th Inf. Co.E
Walls, Willis W. AL 47th Inf. Co.G Capt.
Walls, Wilson AL 23rd Inf. Co.H
Walls, Wilson AR 8th Cav. Peoples' Co.
Walls, Wilson NC 21st Inf. Co.M
Walls, W.M. AL 56th Part.Rangers Co.I Cpl.
Walls, W.S. NC 22nd Inf. Co.B
Walls, W.S. SC Cav. 19th Bn. Co.A Music.
Walls, W.S. SC Part.Rangers Kirk's Co.
Walls, W.V. 8th (Wade's) Conf.Cav. Co.H 2nd Lt.
Walls, Z. AL 3rd Res. Co.A
Walls, Zachariah TN 32nd Inf. Co.B
Wallsberger, G.W. TX Cav. Bourland's Regt. Co.E
Wallsdrop, J.W. SC 22nd Inf.
Wallsen, AL 4th Inf.
Wallston, Britton MO 2nd Cav. Co.D
Wallsworth, D.F. LA 31st Inf. Co.K
Wallsworth, John T. LA 28th (Gray's) Inf. Co.C
Wallthall, J.H. TN Inf. 1st Cons.Regt. Co.D
Wallthall, Joseph C. AR 33rd Inf. Co.E
Wallthall, Thomas C. AR 33rd Inf. Co.D
Wallton, F.W. VA 28th Inf. Co.E
Wallwork, Joseph AL 45th Inf. Co.B
Wallwork, W.B. TN Inf. Nashville Bn. Fulcher's Co. Cpl.
Wally, Henry KY 10th (Johnson's) Cav. New Co.G
Wally, Jacob LA Mil. 4th Regt. 2nd Brig. 1st Div. Co.B
Walman, J. GA 59th Inf. Co.G
Walme, William MS 3rd Cav. Co.G
Walmot, R.H. TN 7th Cav. Co.I
Walmsley, G.L. Trans-MS Conf.Cav. 1st Bn. Co.B
Walmsley, G.S. LA Maddox's Regt.Res.Corps Co.B
Walmsley, Hugh B. LA 3rd Inf. Co.D 3rd Lt.
Walmsly, Joseph GA Inf. 19th Bn. (St.Guards) Co.B
Waln, John TN 19th & 20th (Cons.) Cav. Co.E
Walne, G.P. MS 28th Cav. Co.D
Walne, John VA 38th Inf. Co.A
Walne, John H. TN 20th (Russell's) Cav. Co.I
Walne, R. MS 28th Cav. Co.D
Walne, William MS 3rd (St.Troops) Cav. Co.G
Walne, William MS Lt.Arty. (Madison Lt.Arty.) Richards' Co.
Walne, William MS 9th Inf. New Co.H
Walner, Jacob VA 1st St.Res. Co.A
Walner, Peter AL 12th Inf. Co.F
Walnut 1st Cherokee Mtd.Rifles Co.F
Walnut, John TX 35th (Brown's) Cav. Co.D
Walnut, John TX 13th Vol. 1st Co.I
Walongham, --- LA Mil. 2nd Regt. French Brig. Co.1
Wa loo ker 1st Cherokee Mtd.Vol. 1st Co.A
Walpen, William GA 18th Inf.
Walphal, W.B. VA 53rd Inf. Co.C
Walpole, Ben M. SC Hvy.Arty. Gilchrist's Co. (Gist Guard) 2nd Lt.

Walpole, Ben M. SC Arty. Manigault's Bn. Co.E 2nd Lt.
Walpole, Benjamin M. SC Cav. Walpole's Co.
Walpole, B.M. SC Mil. 1st Regt.Rifles Chichester's Co. 3rd Lt.
Walpole, E.H. LA Bickham's Co. (Caddo Mil.)
Walpole, H. SC Mil.Cav. Rutledge's Co.
Walpole, Horace E. SC Cav. Walpole's Co.
Walpole, Horace George SC Cav. Walpole's Co.
Walpole, James L. AL 3rd Cav. Co.E
Walpole, James L. AL Lt.Arty. Lee's Btty.
Walpole, James L. SC Cav. Walpole's Co.
Walpole, James L. TN 7th Inf. Co.I
Walpole, J. Legare SC Cav. Walpole's Co.
Walpole, John LA 6th Cav. Co.D,E,A Sgt.
Walpole, John B. AL Arty. 1st Bn. Co.C Sgt.
Walpole, John B.L. SC Cav. Walpole's Co. Capt.
Walpole, John H. TN 15th (Stewart's) Cav.
Walpole, J.T. KY 3rd Mtd.Inf. Co.G 2nd Lt.
Walpole, Norman 1st Conf.Cav. 1st Co.E
Walpole, Richard MS Lt.Arty. (Jefferson Arty.) Darden's Co. Sgt.
Walpole, Richard MS 15th Inf. Co.E,D
Walpole, Stewart LA 6th Cav. Co.D Cpl.
Walpole, Stewart LA 1st (Nelligan's) Inf. Co.A
Walpole, Thomas LA 6th Cav. Co.D,A
Walpole, Thomas LA 1st (Nelligan's) Inf. Co.A
Walpole, T.O. TN 45th Inf. Co.F
Walpole, W.M. LA 6th Cav. Co.D
Walpolo, James L. Conf.Cav. Wood's Regt. 1st Co.D
Walpool, T.L. TN 1st Hvy.Arty. 2nd Co.B
Walpool, W.N. Horse Arty. White's Btty.
Walraim, James GA 6th Cav. Co.L
Walraven, Berry GA 1st Inf. (St.Guards) Co.G
Walraven, C. GA Lt.Arty. Barnwell's Btty.
Walraven, Christopher C. GA Phillips' Legion Co.O
Walraven, David GA Inf. 8th Bn.
Walraven, D.C. GA Inf. 8th Bn. Co.C
Walraven, Elijah GA 3rd Bn.S.S. Co.E
Walraven, Elisha C. GA 18th Inf. Co.A
Walraven, Enoch GA 23rd Inf. Co.F
Walraven, Floid GA 40th Inf. Co.E
Walraven, Hesakiah GA 21st Inf. Co.G
Walraven, James J. GA 60th Inf. Co.K Sgt.
Walraven, James K.P. GA 2nd Res. Co.C
Walraven, John GA 14th Inf. Co.K
Walraven, John M. GA 40th Inf. Co.E
Walraven, Jonas VA 5th Cav. (12 mo. '61-2) Co.D
Walraven, Jonathan GA 1st Inf. (St.Guards) Co.G
Walraven, Milton MS 29th Inf. Co.D,G
Walraven, Mitchell GA Phillips' Legion Co.L
Walraven, O. GA 6th Cav. Co.L
Walraven, Orange GA 4th Inf. Co.F
Walraven, Perry GA 21st Inf. Co.G Sgt.
Walraven, President GA 1st Inf. (St.Guards) Co.G Sgt.
Walraven, Shadric GA 4th Inf. Co.F
Walraven, W.H. GA 40th Inf. Co.A
Walraven, William GA 1st Inf. (St.Guards) Co.G
Walraven, William GA Inf. 8th Bn. Co.C
Walravin, John M. AL 40th Inf. Co.E
Walrel, S. GA 45th Inf. Co.C
Walrond, Augustus S. VA Cav. 34th Bn. Co.C
Walrond, Augustus S. VA 29th Inf. Co.H
Walrond, Francis T. VA 58th Inf. Co.B
Walrond, Israel J. VA 58th Inf. Co.B 2nd Lt.
Walrond, James C. VA 58th Inf. Co.B
Walrond, Jesse T. AR 15th (Josey's) Inf. Co.E Cpl.
Walrond, Jesse T. VA 58th Inf. Co.A 1st Lt.
Walrond, John VA Cav. 34th Bn. Co.C 1st Sgt.
Walrond, John VA 6th Bn.Res. Co.B
Walrond, John P. VA 28th Inf. Co.D 2nd Lt.
Walrond, Jubal VA 58th Inf. Co.B
Walrond, M.H. VA Cav. 34th Bn. Co.C 1st Lt.
Walrond, Moses A. VA 28th Inf. Co.D
Walrond, Robert L. VA 58th Inf. Co.A 2nd Lt.
Walrond, Samuel Conf.Hvy.Arty. Montague's Bn. Co.C
Walrond, Samuel P. VA 58th Inf. Co.B
Walrond, W.H.C. VA Arty. Young's Co.
Walrond, William B. VA 58th Inf. Co.B
Walrop, Thomas SC 1st (Butler's) Inf. Co.B
Walrott, Charles GA 1st (Symons') Res. Co.I
Walrupt, Pestila C. GA 41st Inf. Co.C
Wals, Jonathan TN 12th Cav. Co.E
Walsch, Daniel MD Arty. 1st Btty.
Walschan, Joseph LA Mil. Mech.Guard
Walscoos Cocker 1st Seminole Mtd.Vol.
Walse, F. TX 7th Cav. Co.E
Walseman, William GA 15th Inf. Co.F
Walsen, John AR 19th (Dawson's) Inf. Co.D
Walser, A. MO Lt.Arty. 1st Btty.
Walser, A. MO Lt.Arty. Walsh's Co.
Walser, Albert MO Cav. 2nd Regt.St.Guard Co.G Cpl.
Walser, Albert MO 6th Inf. Co.D
Walser, Albert NC 13th Inf. Co.H
Walser, Britton NC 42nd Inf. Co.A
Walser, Britton VA 53rd Inf. Co.A
Walser, Burton NC 57th Inf. Co.B
Walser, Gabriel TX 16th Inf. Co.I
Walser, Henderson NC 48th Inf. Co.H
Walser, Henry C. NC 14th Bn. Home Guards Maj.
Walser, Henry C. NC 21st Inf. Co.A
Walser, Hiram NC 48th Inf. Co.H
Walser, Jacob S. NC 48th Inf. Co.H Sgt.
Walser, James TX 18th Cav. Witt's Co.
Walser, James TX Cav. Wells' Bn. Co.B
Walser, J.H. NC 57th Inf. Co.B
Walser, J.T. MS 35th Inf. Co.C
Walser, Richard SC 1st (Butler's) Inf. Co.F
Walser, Roland NC 57th Inf. Co.B
Walser, Spurgeon NC 42nd Inf. Co.I
Walser, W.A. NC Wallace's Co. (Wilmington RR Guard) 3rd Lt.
Walser, W.H. NC 57th Inf. Co.B
Walsh, --- LA Mil. 2nd Regt. 3rd Brig. 1st Div. Co.D
Walsh, --- Conf.Cav. Wood's Regt. 1st Co.A
Walsh, A.C. GA Inf. 18th Bn. Co.A
Walsh, A.J. NC 5th Sr.Res. Co.A
Walsh, A.L. SC 6th Inf. 1st Co.B, 2nd Co.A
Walsh, Albert J. MS 3rd Inf. Co.K
Walsh, Alfred NC 1st Inf. Co.B
Walsh, Andrew LA 1st (Nelligan's) Inf. Co.D
Walsh, Arthur GA 1st (Olmstead's) Inf. Co.A
Walsh, Arthur P. LA 1st (Nelligan's) Inf. Co.E
Walsh, Augustus LA 7th Inf. Co.B
Walsh, B. FL 2nd Cav. Co.D
Walsh, Barney LA 22nd Inf. Durrive, Jr.'s Co.
Walsh, C. GA 16th Inf. Co.F
Walsh, C. VA 1st St.Res. Co.D
Walsh, C.E. TN Conscr. (Cp. of Instr.) Co.B
Walsh, Charles A. AL 31st Inf. Co.G
Walsh, Charles M. VA 12th Inf. Co.E Cpl.
Walsh, Charles R. TX 24th Cav. Co.C
Walsh, Christopher VA Inf. 25th Bn. Co.F
Walsh, Coleman NC 3rd Inf. Co.F
Walsh, Daniel VA Hvy.Arty. 19th Bn. Co.C
Walsh, Daniel VA 41st Inf. 1st Co.E
Walsh, David AL 1st Regt. Mobile Vol. British Guard Co.A
Walsh, David MS 2nd Cav. Co.B
Walsh, Dennis GA 1st (Olmstead's) Inf. Co.B
Walsh, D.H. TX Cav. 2nd Bn.St.Troops Co.B
Walsh, D.H. TX 35th (Brown's) Cav. Co.E
Walsh, D.H. TX Cav. Giddings' Bn. Carrington's Co.
Walsh, D.H. VA 2nd Inf.Loc.Def. Co.G Sgt.
Walsh, D.H. VA Inf. 2nd Bn.Loc.Def. Co.A Sgt.
Walsh, D.K. NC 5th Sr.Res. Co.K
Walsh, Dudley MO 1st & 4th Cons.Inf. Co.A Capt.
Walsh, Dudley A. MO 1st Inf. Co.A 1st Lt.
Walsh, E. VA Lt.Arty. Carpenter's Co.
Walsh, Edward AL Arty. 1st Bn. Co.D
Walsh, Edward GA 1st (Olmstead's) Inf. Read's Co., Co.B
Walsh, Edward LA 2nd Cav. Co.G
Walsh, Edward LA 14th Inf. Co.H
Walsh, Edward LA 20th Inf. Co.G
Walsh, Edward LA 28th (Thomas') Inf.
Walsh, Edward LA Herrick's Co. (Orleans Blues)
Walsh, Edward LA Mil. Stanley Guards Co.B
Walsh, Edward MD Inf. 2nd Bn. Co.H
Walsh, Edward MO 2nd Cav. Co.G
Walsh, Edward TN 40th Inf. Co.F
Walsh, Edward VA Inf. 1st Bn. Co.C
Walsh, Edward D. NC 1st Arty. (10th St.Troops) Co.B,F Capt.
Walsh, Edward P. VA Horse Arty. E. Graham's Co.
Walsh, E.F. SC Arty. Stuart's Co. (Beaufort Vol.Arty.)
Walsh, E.T. VA 55th Inf. Co.G
Walsh, F. AL 15th Inf. Co.C
Walsh, F.B. TN Conscr. (Cp. of Instr.) Co.B
Walsh, Freeman 1st Choctaw Mtd.Rifles Co.G
Walsh, Fritz LA Mil. 2nd Regt. 3rd Brig. 1st Div.
Walsh, George AR 2nd Mtd.Rifles Co.F
Walsh, George B. NC 42nd Inf. Co.K
Walsh, G.W. TN 45th Inf.
Walsh, Harvey NC 53rd Inf. Co.K
Walsh, H.B. NC 1st Arty. (10th St.Troops) Co.F
Walsh, H.C. LA 4th Inf. Co.F
Walsh, Henry SC 1st Arty. Co.F
Walsh, Henry SC 1st (McCreary's) Inf. Co.E
Walsh, Henry TN 10th Inf. Co.A
Walsh, Henry H. MO 1st Inf. Co.A 2nd Lt.
Walsh, H.H. LA 4th Inf. Co.F
Walsh, H.M. MS 35th Inf. Co.E Capt.

Walsh, H.M. MS Walsh's Co. (Muckalusha Guards) Capt.
Walsh, J. LA Mil.Crescent Cadets
Walsh, James GA 64th Inf. Co.I
Walsh, James LA 1st Hvy.Arty. (Reg.) Co.H
Walsh, James LA 5th Inf. Co.G
Walsh, James LA 18th Inf. Co.D
Walsh, James LA 28th (Thomas') Inf. Co.F
Walsh, James MS Lt.Arty. (Warren Lt.Arty.) Swett's Co.
Walsh, James SC Inf. 1st (Charleston) Bn. Co.B
Walsh, James SC Inf. 1st (Charleston) Bn. Co.C
Walsh, James SC 5th Inf. 1st Co.I
Walsh, James SC 27th Inf. Co.B,H
Walsh, James SC Palmetto S.S. Co.G
Walsh, James TN 1st Hvy.Arty. 2nd Co.B
Walsh, James TN Lt.Arty. Tobin's Co.
Walsh, James TN Inf. 154th Sr.Regt. Co.C
Walsh, James TX 1st Hvy.Arty. 2nd Co.F
Walsh, James TX 2nd Inf. Odlum's Co.
Walsh, James VA 1st St.Res. Co.D Cpl.
Walsh, James VA Inf. 1st Bn. Co.C
Walsh, James VA 4th Inf. Co.A
Walsh, James Conf.Cav. Wood's Regt. 2nd Co.F
Walsh, James B. SC 23rd Inf. Co.H
Walsh, James E. VA Lt.Arty. Cayce's Co. Jr.2nd Lt.
Walsh, James H. NC 42nd Inf. Co.K
Walsh, James H. TX 36th Cav. Co.H
Walsh, James J. GA 1st (Olmstead's) Inf. Co.B
Walsh, James W. TX 6th Cav. Co.K Sgt.
Walsh, Jeremiah GA 1st (Olmstead's) Inf. Co.B
Walsh, J.F. MS 35th Inf. Co.E 1st Sgt.
Walsh, J.H. SC 20th Inf. Co.L Sgt.
Walsh, J.H. VA 3rd Inf.Loc.Def.
Walsh, J.H.F. TN 4th (McLemore's) Cav. Co.I
Walsh, J.H.F. TN 16th Inf. Co.E
Walsh, Jim VA 3rd Inf. Loc.Def. 2nd Co.G
Walsh, J.L. 1st Conf.Cav. 2nd Co.G
Walsh, J.M. AL 31st Inf. Co.G
Walsh, John AL Arty. 1st Bn. Co.D,A
Walsh, John AL 8th Inf. Co.I
Walsh, John AL 24th Inf. Co.B
Walsh, John AR 9th Inf. Co.D
Walsh, John FL 8th Inf. Co.F
Walsh, John GA 1st Inf. (St.Guards) Co.B
Walsh, John GA Inf. 1st Loc.Troops (Augusta) Co.D
Walsh, John GA 47th Inf. Co.A
Walsh, John LA 1st (Strawbridge's) Inf. Co.C
Walsh, John LA 6th Inf. Co.H
Walsh, John LA 6th Inf. Co.K Sgt.
Walsh, John LA 18th Inf. Co.D Sgt.
Walsh, John LA 20th Inf. Co.I
Walsh, John LA 20th Inf. Co.K,D
Walsh, John LA Mil. Brenan's Co. (Co.A,Shamrock Guards)
Walsh, John LA Mil. British Guard Bn. West's Co. Sgt.
Walsh, John LA Miles' Legion Co.G
Walsh, John MS 28th Cav. Co.K Cpl.
Walsh, John MS 12th Inf. Co.G
Walsh, John NC 6th Cav. (65th St.Troops) Co.G
Walsh, John SC Cav. 19th Bn. Co.E Sgt.
Walsh, John SC Lt.Arty. J.T. Kanapaux's Co. (Lafayette Arty.)
Walsh, John SC 1st (Butler's) Inf. Co.F
Walsh, John TN Lt.Arty. Tobin's Co. 2nd Lt.
Walsh, John VA Cav. 35th Bn.
Walsh, John VA Horse Arty. E. Graham's Co.
Walsh, John VA Hvy.Arty. Wilkinson's Co.
Walsh, John VA 24th Bn.Part.Rangers Cropper's Co.
Walsh, John VA 59th Inf. 3rd Co.E
Walsh, John VA 59th Inf. 3rd Co.F
Walsh, John 3rd Conf.Eng.Troops Co.D
Walsh, John Conf.Reg.Inf. Brooks' Bn. Co.D
Walsh, John A. LA Washington Arty.Bn. Co.5
Walsh, John C. LA 1st (Strawbridge's) Inf. Co.D
Walsh, John C. LA Miles' Legion Co.F
Walsh, John C. VA 1st St.Res. Co.D Cpl.
Walsh, John F. AL 30th Inf. Co.B
Walsh, John G. TX 34th Cav. Co.H Cpl.
Walsh, John H. SC 4th Cav. Co.A
Walsh, John H. SC Cav. 12th Bn. Co.A
Walsh, John H. VA Lt.Arty. 38th Bn. Co.B
Walsh, John H.F. TN 44th Inf. Co.K
Walsh, John L. AR 18th Inf. Co.B
Walsh, John M. LA 4th Inf. Co.E Sgt.
Walsh, John T. GA 3rd Inf. Co.D
Walsh, John T. LA 1st Cav. Co.I
Walsh, John T. NC Nelson's Co. (Loc.Def.)
Walsh, John W. VA 41st Inf. 2nd Co.G
Walsh, Joseph LA 15th Inf. Co.G Sgt.
Walsh, Joseph W. VA 9th Inf. Co.D Sgt.
Walsh, J.P. LA Dreux's Cav. Co.A
Walsh, J.R. SC 20th Inf. Co.L Sgt.
Walsh, J.S. AR 31st Inf. Co.A
Walsh, J.T. AL 1st Regt. Mobile Vol. Butt's Co.
Walsh, J.T. AL 4th Res. Co.A
Walsh, J.W. LA 6th Inf. Co.K
Walsh, Larkin NC 55th Inf. Co.B Sgt.
Walsh, Lawrence MD Arty. 3rd Btty.
Walsh, L.H. KY 7th Mtd.Inf. Co.A
Walsh, M. KY Morgan's Men Co.H
Walsh, M. LA Mil. Orleans Fire Regt. Co.H Cpl.
Walsh, M. SC Hvy.Arty. 15th (Lucas') Bn. Co.B
Walsh, M. TX Cav. Baylor's Regt. Co.K
Walsh, M.A. MS 12th Inf. Co.E
Walsh, Malachi LA 5th Inf. Co.G
Walsh, Malachi VA 10th Cav. Co.A
Walsh, Marcus L. TN 7th Inf. Co.D Capt.
Walsh, Mark TN 10th Inf.
Walsh, Mathew TX 1st Hvy.Arty. 2nd Co.F
Walsh, Mathew TX 2nd Inf. Odlum's Co.
Walsh, Maurice GA 1st (Olmstead's) Inf. Co.A
Walsh, M.C.D. MS 2nd (Davidson's) Inf. Co.G
Walsh, Michael GA Phillips' Legion Co.F
Walsh, Michael LA 1st Hvy.Arty. (Reg.) Co.I
Walsh, Michael LA 5th Inf. Co.K
Walsh, Michael LA 6th Inf. Co.I
Walsh, Michael LA 21st (Patton's) Inf. Co.A
Walsh, Michael MO 5th Inf. Co.F
Walsh, Michael SC 1st (McCreary's) Inf. Co.K
Walsh, Michael TN 21st Inf. Co.E
Walsh, Michael TX 3rd Inf. Co.B
Walsh, Michael VA 6th Inf. 1st Co.E
Walsh, Michael S. GA 1st (Olmstead's) Inf. Co.A
Walsh, Michael S. GA Phillips' Legion Co.F 1st Lt.
Walsh, Michel LA 5th Inf. Co.G
Walsh, Mike AL Lt.Arty. 2nd Bn. Co.E
Walsh, M.J. MS 9th Inf. New Co.C
Walsh, Morris MS 28th Cav. Co.C Cpl.
Walsh, M.W. LA 14th Inf.
Walsh, N. LA Inf.Crescent Regt. Co.E
Walsh, N. TX 26th Cav. Co.C
Walsh, P. AL 9th Inf. Co.B
Walsh, P. MS 28th Cav. Co.K
Walsh, P. MO 8th Cav. Co.E
Walsh, P.A. SC 1st Inf. Co.A
Walsh, Patrick GA 1st (Olmstead's) Inf. Co.A
Walsh, Patrick GA 5th Inf. Co.C Sgt.
Walsh, Patrick GA 47th Inf. Co.A
Walsh, Patrick LA 21st (Patton's) Inf. Co.D
Walsh, Patrick LA Herrick's Co. (Orleans Blues)
Walsh, Patrick LA Mil. Irish Regt. Laughlin's Co.
Walsh, Patrick MS 30th Inf. Co.G
Walsh, Patrick SC 1st Arty. Co.B
Walsh, Patrick SC Arty. Fickling's Co. (Brooks Lt.Arty.)
Walsh, Patrick SC 1st (Butler's) Inf. Co.E
Walsh, Patrick SC Mil. 1st Regt. (Charleston Res.) Co.A
Walsh, Patrick SC 2nd Inf. Co.K
Walsh, Patrick TN 10th Inf. Co.A
Walsh, Patrick TN 11th Inf. Co.G
Walsh, Patrick TN 15th Inf. 2nd Co.F
Walsh, Patrick Freeman's Btty.
Walsh, Peter LA Arty. Kean's Btty. (Orleans Ind.Arty.)
Walsh, Peter LA Miles' Legion Co.G Cpl.
Walsh, Peter LA C.S. Zouave Bn. Co.C
Walsh, Peter TN 2nd (Walker's) Inf. Co.C
Walsh, Peter TN 21st Inf. Co.I
Walsh, Philip A. SC 15th Inf. Co.A
Walsh, Philip S. NC 42nd Inf. Co.K
Walsh, Phillip LA 21st (Patton's) Inf. Co.F
Walsh, Phillip NC 37th Inf. Co.F Sgt.
Walsh, R. LA 1st Inf.
Walsh, R. MD Cav. 2nd Bn. Co.D
Walsh, R.F. AL 36th Inf. Co.A
Walsh, Richard AL 21st Inf. Co.A
Walsh, Richard LA 1st (Nelligan's) Inf. Co.A
Walsh, Richard LA Red River S.S. Cassidy's Co.
Walsh, Richard TX 13th Cav. Co.D
Walsh, Richard Gen. & Staff Capt.,AQM
Walsh, Richard C. MO Lt.Arty. Walsh's Co. Capt.
Walsh, R.M. LA 2nd Cav. 1st Lt.
Walsh, Robert LA Mil. British Guard Bn. Burrowes' Co.
Walsh, Robert MS 16th Inf. Co.G
Walsh, Robert M. TX 35th (Brown's) Cav. Co.E Sgt.Maj.
Walsh, Robert M. TX 7th Field Btty.
Walsh, Robert P.Q. LA 1st (Nelligan's) Inf. Co.I
Walsh, S. GA 12th Inf. Co.K
Walsh, Samuel NC 53rd Inf. Co.K
Walsh, Shelby TN 4th (McLemore's) Cav. Co.C
Walsh, Shelby TN 7th Inf. Co.D
Walsh, S.M. KY 6th Mtd.Inf. Co.I
Walsh, Smith VA 6th Inf. Co.A
Walsh, T. AL 26th Inf. Co.A
Walsh, T. MS Inf. 2nd Bn. (St.Troops) Co.A
Walsh, T. SC 4th St.Troops Co.G
Walsh, T.B. MS 35th Inf. Co.E 1st 2nd Lt.

Walsh, T.B. TN Conscr. (Cp. of Instr.) Co.B Cpl.
Walsh, T.C. VA 3rd Inf.Loc.Def. Co.C
Walsh, T.C. Gen. & Staff Capt.,Comsy.
Walsh, T.D. SC Arty. Manigault's Bn. 2nd Co.C
Walsh, Thomas GA 1st (Olmstead's) Inf. Bonaud's Co. Cpl.
Walsh, Thomas GA 25th Inf. Co.C
Walsh, Thomas LA 13th Inf. Co.B
Walsh, Thomas LA 20th Inf. Co.H,K Music.
Walsh, Thomas LA 20th Inf. Co.K,D, New Co.E
Walsh, Thomas LA 21st (Patton's) Inf. Co.G
Walsh, Thomas LA 22nd Inf. Durrive, Jr.'s Co.
Walsh, Thomas MD 1st Cav. Co.K
Walsh, Thomas MS 22nd Inf. Co.C
Walsh, Thomas NC 13th Inf. Co.H
Walsh, Thomas SC Lt.Arty. 3rd (Palmetto) Bn. Co.B
Walsh, Thomas SC 1st (McCreary's) Inf.
Walsh, Thomas TN Inf. 1st Cons.Regt. Co.A
Walsh, Thomas TN 2nd (Walker's) Inf. Co.I
Walsh, Thomas TN 2nd (Walker's) Inf. Co.K
Walsh, Thomas TN 6th Inf. Co.F
Walsh, Thomas VA 41st Inf. Co.C
Walsh, Thomas 9th Conf.Inf. Co.A
Walsh, Thomas B. MS 11th Inf. Co.D Sgt.
Walsh, Thomas C. VA 1st Inf. Co.A
Walsh, Thomas C. VA 11th Inf. Co.G
Walsh, Thomas C. VA 12th Inf. Co.G
Walsh, Thomas E. SC 1st (McCreary's) Inf. Co.C
Walsh, Thomas F. NC 13th Inf. Co.F
Walsh, Thomas F. NC 37th Inf. Co.F
Walsh, Thomas H. VA 3rd Inf.Loc.Def. 2nd Co.G
Walsh, Thomas K. MD 1st Inf. Co.C
Walsh, Thomas M. LA Mil. Orleans Fire Regt. Hall's Co.
Walsh, Thomas V. SC Cav.Bn. Holcombe Legion Co.A Capt.
Walsh, Timothy Inf. School of Pract. Powell's Command Powell's Detach. Co.A
Walsh, T.J.P. SC 2nd Arty. Co.I
Walsh, T.V. SC 7th Cav. Co.I Capt.
Walsh, V. GA 54th Inf. Co.F
Walsh, Valentine FL 2nd Inf. Co.K
Walsh, W. LA Mil. 4th Regt. 1st Brig. 1st Div. Co.D Cpl.
Walsh, W.A. AR 11th & 17th (Cons.) Inf. Co.D
Walsh, Walter FL 2nd Cav. Co.D
Walsh, W.C. TX 4th Inf. Co.B Capt.
Walsh, W.C. TX Inf. Carter's Co. Lt.
Walsh, W.C. Gen. & Staff Capt.
Walsh, W.F. LA Washington Arty.Bn. Co.6 Can.
Walsh, William AL Arty. 1st Bn. Co.D
Walsh, William GA 1st (Olmstead's) Inf. Co.B
Walsh, William LA Lt.Arty. 2nd Field Btty.
Walsh, William LA Lt.Arty. LeGardeur, Jr.'s Co. (Orleans Guard Btty.)
Walsh, William LA Mil. Leeds' Guards Regt. Co.F
Walsh, William MS Cav. Jeff Davis Legion Co.A
Walsh, William MS 38th Cav. Co.D
Walsh, William MS 12th Inf. Co.G
Walsh, William MO 5th Inf. Co.F Sgt.
Walsh, William NC 6th Cav. (65th St.Troops) Co.G,C
Walsh, William NC 1st Arty. (10th St.Troops) Co.B
Walsh, William NC 1st Inf. Co.B
Walsh, William NC 53rd Inf. Co.K Cpl.
Walsh, William TN Lt.Arty. Burroughs' Co.
Walsh, William TN 34th Inf. 1st Co.C
Walsh, William TN Inf. 154th Sr.Regt. Co.C
Walsh, William VA 1st Arty. Co.I
Walsh, William VA 1st St.Res. Co.C Sgt.
Walsh, William VA Inf. 1st Bn.Loc.Def. Co.D 1st Sgt.
Walsh, William VA 6th Inf. Co.I 1st Sgt.
Walsh, William A. NC 1st Arty. (10th St.Troops) Co.F
Walsh, Wm. A. Gen. & Staff Lt.,AQM
Walsh, William H. 3rd Conf.Cav. Co.F
Walsh, William J. TN Conscr. (Cp. of Instr.) Co.B Sgt.
Walsh, William R. TX Cav. 8th (Taylor's) Bn. Co.A
Walsh, William R. VA Lt.Arty. 38th Bn. Co.B
Walsh, William V. VA 6th Inf. Co.G
Walsh, William W. SC 6th Inf. 1st Co.B
Walsh, William W. TN 1st (Feild's) Inf. Co.A 2nd Lt.
Walsh, W.J. TX Cav. Baylor's Regt. Co.K
Walsh, W.W. LA 5th Inf. Co.D
Walsh, W.W. SC Cav. 19th Bn. Co.E Sgt.
Walsh, W.W. SC 20th Inf. Co.L Sgt.
Walsh, W.W. TN 1st (Feild's) & 27th Inf. (Cons.) Co.E 2nd Lt.
Walsh, Y.C. NC 18th Inf. Co.G
Walshe, B.T. LA 6th Inf. Co.I Capt.
Walshe, Ed LA Inf. 1st Sp.Bn. (Rightor's) Co.F
Walshe, Edward LA 6th Inf. Co.I 2nd Lt.
Walshe, Edwin VA 4th Cav. Co.D
Walshe, George TX 26th Cav. Co.F
Walshe, John T. AL Mil. 2nd Regt.Vol. Co.C
Walsingham, J.C. AL 53rd (Part.Rangers) Co.G
Walsingham, John H. AL 1st Cav. 1st Co.B
Walson, Daniel G. AL Vol. Lee, Jr.'s Co.
Walson, H.L. AL 32nd Inf. Co.C
Walson, John GA 8th Cav. Co.I
Walson, John NC 15th Inf. Co.L
Walson, John NC 32nd Inf. Co.K
Walson, R. GA Inf. 5th Bn. (St.Guards) Co.E
Walson, S.J. AL Cav. 24th Bn. Co.C
Walson, W.B. GA 5th Res.
Walstead, J. AL 8th Inf. Co.A
Walston, A.J. TX 28th Cav. Co.G 1st Bugler
Walston, Allen TX Cav. 2nd Regt.St.Troops Co.G 1st Sgt.
Walston, B.L. TN 15th Inf. Co.G
Walston, Breton L. MO 8th Cav. Co.F,D
Walston, Caleb P. NC 17th Inf. (1st Org.) Co.E Sgt.
Walston, Caleb P. NC 56th Inf. Co.A 2nd Lt.
Walston, C.P. NC 32nd Inf. Co.H Cpl.
Walston, D. GA 46th Inf. Co.K
Walston, D.P. KY 7th Mtd.Inf. Co.D Capt.
Walston, Eli GA Lt.Arty. 12th Bn. 3rd Co.C
Walston, Enos D. NC 43rd Inf. Co.F
Walston, E.T. LA 18th Inf. Co.B Sgt.
Walston, E.T. LA Inf.Cons. 18th Regt. & Yellow Jacket Bn. Co.F
Walston, F.M. TX 28th Cav. Co.G
Walston, Franklin NC 30th Inf. Co.F Cpl.
Walston, George W. LA 1st Hvy.Arty. (Reg.) Co.C
Walston, George W. LA Hvy.Arty. 8th Bn. Co.3
Walston, Golden NC 2nd Inf. Co.D
Walston, H. TX 22nd Inf. Co.K
Walston, Harrison C. LA 7th Inf. Co.B
Walston, Henry NC 61st Inf. Co.F
Walston, Henry 1st Conf.Cav. 2nd Co.E
Walston, Henry C. FL 1st Inf. New Co.F Cpl.
Walston, Heny AR Inf. Hardy's Regt. Co.H
Walston, J. GA 3rd Cav. Co.H
Walston, Jack TX 28th Cav. Co.G 1st Bugler
Walston, James AL 11th Cav. Co.I
Walston, James NC 30th Inf. Co.F
Walston, James C. GA 9th Inf. Co.G
Walston, Jarrett NC 1st Inf. Co.K
Walston, J.B. KY 3rd Mtd.Inf. Co.H
Walston, J.B.H. NC 17th Inf. (2nd Org.) Co.I
Walston, J.H.A. AL Cp. of Instr. Talladega
Walston, J.M. GA 46th Inf. Co.K Cpl.
Walston, John AL 37th Inf. Co.I,D
Walston, John FL 1st Inf. New Co.F Capt.
Walston, John NC 1st Inf. (6 mo. '61) Co.A
Walston, John NC 30th Inf. Co.F 1st Sgt.
Walston, John D. NC 27th Inf. Co.E Cpl.
Walston, John J. NC 8th Inf. Co.G
Walston, John W. KY 2nd Mtd.Inf. Co.E
Walston, Jonas NC 1st Arty. (10th St.Troops) Co.A
Walston, Jonas NC 3rd Arty. (40th St.Troops) Co.G
Walston, Joseph NC Lt.Arty. 13th Bn. Co.B
Walston, Joseph W. GA 22nd Inf. Co.G
Walston, Josiah NC 61st Inf. Co.F
Walston, J.P. MS 28th Cav. Co.G
Walston, J.R. AL 31st Inf. Co.D
Walston, Kinchen NC 30th Inf. Co.F
Walston, L. AL 15th Inf. Co.A
Walston, L NC 2nd Jr.Res. Co.G
Walston, Levi NC 3rd Arty. (40th St.Troops) Co.F
Walston, Levi NC 30th Inf. Co.F
Walston, Levi NC 67th Inf.
Walston, Levi NC Loc.Def. Croom's Co.
Walston, Litleton NC Loc.Def. Croom's Co.
Walston, Mo TX St.Troops Atkins' Co.
Walston, Phesenton 7th Conf.Cav. 2nd Co.I
Walston, Philip NC 61st Inf. Co.F
Walston, Ralph NC 30th Inf. Co.F
Walston, Robert NC 17th Inf. (2nd Org.) Co.I
Walston, Rufus NC 13th Inf. Co.G
Walston, Rufus NC 30th Inf. Co.F
Walston, Rufus F. NC 1st Cav. (9th St.Troops) Co.H
Walston, S. AL 6th Cav. Co.A
Walston, Samuel S. NC 33rd Inf. Co.E
Walston, Seth GA 12th Cav. Co.K
Walston, Seth NC 61st Inf. Co.F
Walston, Seth TN Cav. Clark's Ind.Co. Cpl.
Walston, Silas L. NC 30th Inf. Co.K
Walston, Stephen H. NC 5th Inf. Co.G Cpl.
Walston, Thomas AL 43rd Inf. Co.A
Walston, Thomas KY 3rd Mtd.Inf. Co.H
Walston, Thomas A. FL 1st Cav. Co.E Cpl.
Walston, Thomas S. MS 20th Inf. Co.E Music.

Walston, Turner AL 11th Cav. Co.I
Walston, Turner NC 17th Inf. (2nd Org.) Co.I
Walston, W.A. AL 23rd Inf. Co.G
Walston, W.A. AL 31st Inf. Co.D
Walston, W.B. VA 3rd Inf.Loc.Def. Co.C Sgt.
Walston, W.F. FL 1st (Res.) Inf. Co.B
Walston, William AR 24th Inf. Co.K
Walston, William AR Inf. Hardy's Regt. Co.H
Walston, William KY 1st Inf. Co.F
Walston, William MS 20th Inf. Co.E
Walston, William NC 30th Inf. Co.F
Walston, William NC 43rd Inf. Co.E
Walston, William B. VA Cav. Mosby's Regt. (Part.Rangers) Co.A
Walston, William B. VA 39th Inf. Co.F 2nd Lt.
Walston, William L. AL 43rd Inf. Co.A Cpl.
Walston, Wilson NC 43rd Inf. Co.E
Walston, W.M. TN Cav. Williams' Co.
Walston, W.M. TX 7th Cav. Co.I
Walston, W.M. TX Vol. Rainey's Co.
Walston, W.P. NC 32nd Inf. Co.H Jr.2nd Lt.
Walston, W.R. NC 43rd Inf. Co.F
Walsworth, Samuel W. LA 31st Inf. Co.K
Walt, --- TX 22nd Inf. Co.F
Walt, C. AR 1st Inf. Co.A
Walt, C. TN 1st Hvy.Arty. 3rd Co.A
Walt, C. TN Lt.Arty. Rice's Btty.
Walt, C. TN 38th Inf. 1st Co.A
Walt, F. AR 13th Mil. Co.A
Walt, George F. NC 1st Inf. Co.I
Walt, Martin Gen. & Staff Maj.,AQM
Walt, Morris LA 10th Inf. Co.D
Waltar, Thomas VA 17th Cav. Co.G
Waltars, A. SC 1st (Butler's) Inf. Co.G
Walten, George AL 15th Cav. Co.G
Walten, H. AL 56th Part.Rangers Co.F
Walten, J.C. MS Cav. Davenport's Bn. (St.Troops) Co.C
Walten, L.W. MS 12th Cav. Co.L
Walten, P.W. TX 3rd Cav. Co.A
Walten, W. TX 32nd Cav. Co.I
Walter, --- GA 32nd Inf. Co.F
Walter, A. LA Inf.Crescent Regt. Co.K
Walter, A. NC 4th Sr.Res. Co.F
Walter, A. SC Mil.Arty. 1st Regt. Werner's Co.
Walter, A. TX 1st Inf. Co.M Cpl.
Walter, A.B. SC 8th Inf. Co.L
Walter, A.B. SC Inf. Hampton Legion Co.G
Walter, Abner NC 17th Inf. (2nd Org.) Co.L
Walter, A.J. AR Inf. Cocke's Regt. Co.E
Walter, Alfred B. NC 51st Inf. Co.F Capt.
Walter, Allison E. NC 20th Inf. Co.A
Walter, Alors TX Conscr.
Walter, Andrew VA 136th Mil. Co.F
Walter, A.T. VA 46th Inf.
Walter, August LA 4th Inf. Co.D
Walter, Augustus GA 63rd Inf. Co.F
Walter, Augustus J. SC 1st (Orr's) Rifles Co.H Cpl.
Walter, Benjamin F. VA 7th Cav. Co.D Sgt.
Walter, C. LA Mil. 1st Regt. French Brig. Co.C
Walter, C. SC 25th Inf. Co.E
Walter, C. TX 6th Inf. Co.B
Walter, C.H. TX Cav. Giddings' Bn. Co.A
Walter, Charles LA Mil. 4th Regt.Eur.Brig. Co.B
Walter, Charles MS 33rd Inf. Co.I
Walter, Charles VA 29th Inf. Co.I
Walter, Charles C. VA 46th Inf. Co.G
Walter, Charles F NC 52nd Inf. Co.A Sgt.
Walter, C.M. MS Inf. 1st Bn.St.Troops (30 days '64) Co.A
Walter, David P. NC 33rd Inf. Co.C
Walter, D.C. AL 17th Inf. Co.F
Walter, D.C. AL 33rd Inf. Co.E
Walter, Dorsey VA 31st Mil. Co.B
Walter, Ed TX 1st Hvy.Arty. Co.C
Walter, Edmund VA 32nd Inf. Co.F
Walter, Edward TX 4th Field Btty.
Walter, Edward VA 1st Cav. Co.A
Walter, Edwin AL 6th Inf. Co.L
Walter, E.H. MS 1st (King's) Inf. (St.Troops) Co.E
Walter, E.H. VA 3rd Inf.Loc.Def. Co.D
Walter, E.J. VA 59th Inf. Co.B
Walter, Elias M. NC 4th Inf. Co.B
Walter, E.R. SC Mil.Arty. 1st Regt. Walter's Co.
Walter, Eugene R. SC Lt.Arty. Walter's Co. (Washington Arty.) Cpl.
Walter, E.V. AL 3rd Bn. Hilliard's Legion Vol. Co.D
Walter, F. TN Lt.Arty. Weller's Co.
Walter, F. VA 31st Mil. Co.B
Walter, Fedrick LA 7th Inf. Co.G
Walter, Flemming MS 13th Inf. Co.H
Walter, F.N. TN 32nd Inf. Co.I
Walter, Francis L. NC 33rd Inf. Co.C
Walter, Franklin G. VA Cav. 39th Bn. Co.A
Walter, Fred TN 1st Hvy.Arty. Co.L, 3rd Co.B
Walter, Frederick VA 136th Mil. Co.F
Walter, Fred W. GA Cobb's Legion Co.C Music.
Walter, George TN 14th (Neely's) Cav. Co.F
Walter, George TN 1st (Feild's) Inf. Co.I Music.
Walter, George C. TN 32nd Inf. Co.C
Walter, George H. SC Mil.Arty. 1st Regt. Walter's Co. Capt.
Walter, George H. SC Lt.Arty. Walter's Co. (Washington Arty.) Capt.
Walter, George H. TX 5th Cav. Co.A
Walter, George W. AL 25th Inf. Co.I
Walter, George W. NC 7th Inf. Co.G
Walter, George W. NC 20th Inf. Co.A
Walter, George W. TN Lt.Arty. Palmer's Co.
Walter, Gotip TX Inf. 1st St.Troops Sheldon's Co.B
Walter, H. AL 32nd & 58th (Cons.) Inf.
Walter, H. LA Mil. Fire Bn. Co.D
Walter, H. NC 17th Inf. (2nd Org.) Co.L
Walter, Harvey W. MS 9th Inf. Old Co.D 1st Lt.
Walter, H.B. NC 2nd Jr.Res. Co.E
Walter, Henry AL 11th Inf. Co.E
Walter, Henry TN 1st (Feild's) Inf. Co.E
Walter, Henry VA Inf. 25th Bn. Co.A
Walter, Henry R. VA 1st Cav. Co.A
Walter, Henry S. VA 17th Inf. Co.B Cpl.
Walter, Hiram D. AR 1st (Colquitt's) Inf. Co.H,K
Walter, H.W. Gen. & Staff Lt.Col.,AAG
Walter, Israel NC 24th Inf. Co.C
Walter, J. LA Mil. Orleans Fire Regt. Co.H
Walter, J. NC 15th Inf. Co.G
Walter, J. 1st Chickasaw Inf. Kesner's Co.
Walter, Jacob SC 1st (Butler's) Inf. Co.G
Walter, Jacob SC 1st (Butler's) Inf. Co.K
Walter, Jacob L. VA 1st Cav. Co.A
Walter, Jacob L. VA 51st Mil. Co.A
Walter, James KY 10th Cav. Co.I
Walter, James TN 60th Mtd.Inf. Co.C
Walter, James M. MO 5th Inf. Co.C Sgt.
Walter, James S. MS Inf. 1st Bn. Co.A
Walter, James W. VA 7th Cav. Co.D Sgt.
Walter, James W. VA 49th Inf. Co.D 1st Sgt.
Walter, Jeremiah A. NC 17th Inf. (2nd Org.) Co.L
Walter, Jeremiah D. NC 56th Inf. Co.C
Walter, J.F. SC Mil.Arty. 1st Regt. Walter's Co.
Walter, Joel SC 1st (Butler's) Inf. Co.E
Walter, John AL 6th Cav. Co.H
Walter, John AL 3rd Bn. Hilliard's Legion Vol. Co.D
Walter, John GA 1st (Olmstead's) Inf. Co.G
Walter, John MS 2nd St.Cav. Co.H
Walter, John MS 11th (Perrin's) Cav. Co.K
Walter, John MS 41st Inf. Co.K
Walter, John MS 46th Inf. Co.E
Walter, John NC 2nd Jr.Res. Co.B
Walter, John TN Hvy.Arty. Sterling's Co. Cpl.
Walter, John TX 1st (Yager's) Cav. Co.E
Walter, John TX Waul's Legion Co.C Sgt.
Walter, John VA 15th Inf. Co.K
Walter, John VA 59th Inf. 3rd Co.F
Walter, John Conf.Inf. 8th Bn.
Walter, John A. LA 7th Inf. Co.G
Walter, John A. MD Arty. 2nd Btty.
Walter, John D. VA 1st Cav. 2nd Co.K
Walter, John E. NC 57th Inf. Co.H
Walter, John F.W. SC Lt.Arty. Walter's Co. (Washington Arty.)
Walter, John L. VA 15th Inf. Co.K
Walter, John R. SC 1st (Orr's) Rifles Co.H
Walter, John W. VA 1st Cav. Co.A Cpl.
Walter, Joseph GA 38th Inf. Co.E
Walter, Joseph TN Inf. 3rd Bn. Co.B
Walter, J.W. GA 5th Res. Co.D
Walter, L. AR 13th Mil. Co.A
Walter, L. VA 2nd St.Res. Co.H
Walter, Louis LA Inf. 4th Bn. Co.E
Walter, Louis MS 7th Inf. Co.A
Walter, Loving AR Willett's Co.
Walter, Ludwig LA Mil. 4th Regt.Eur.Brig. Co.D
Walter, M.A. NC 57th Inf. Co.F Sgt.
Walter, Mark GA 63rd Inf. Co.B
Walter, Martin C. NC 52nd Inf. Co.A
Walter, Martin V. NC 57th Inf. Co.F Sgt.
Walter, Michael 1st Conf.Inf. 1st Co.F
Walter, Micheal GA 36th (Villepigue's) Inf. Co.F
Walter, Moses LA 1st Cav. Co.E
Walter, P.A. VA 136th Mil. Co.A
Walter, Paul A. NC 1st Cav. (9th St.Troops) Co.F
Walter, P.D. SC 1st (Hagood's) Inf. 2nd Co.I
Walter, Peter TX 1st (Yager's) Cav. Co.C
Walter, Peter TX Cav. 3rd (Yager's) Bn. Co.C
Walter, P.K. MO Cav. Woodson's Co.
Walter, Preston K. MO Cav. Poindexter's Regt.
Walter, Preston K. MO St.Guard
Walter, Robert H. VA 51st Mil. Co.A
Walter, Robert P. VA 1st Inf. Co.C
Walter, Rosia S. GA 52nd Inf. Co.H

Walter, R.W. LA Res.Corps Scott's Co.
Walter, Theodore AR 13th Inf. Co.B
Walter, Thomas GA 6th Cav. Co.B
Walter, Thomas LA 9th Inf.
Walter, Thomas VA 6th Inf. Vickery's Co.
Walter, Thomas VA 16th Inf. 1st Co.H
Walter, Thomas VA 27th Inf. Co.G
Walter, Thomas Mim TN 32nd Inf. Co.G
Walter, T.L. AL 3rd Bn. Hilliard's Legion Vol. Co.D
Walter, Truston AL 33rd Inf. Co.E
Walter, W. LA Mil. 2nd Regt. 3rd Brig. 1st Div. Co.B
Walter, W. LA Mil. 4th Regt. French Brig. Co.7
Walter, W. MD Inf. 2nd Bn. Co.D
Walter, W. SC Mil. 16th Regt. Lawrence's Co.
Walter, W. SC Shiver's Co. 3rd Lt.
Walter, W.A. 1st Conf.Cav. 2nd Co.E
Walter, W.D. SC 27th Inf. Co.I Capt.
Walter, William GA 19th Inf. Co.F
Walter, William LA 4th Inf. Co.B
Walter, William MS 2nd St.Cav. Co.H
Walter, William MS 11th (Perrin's) Cav. Co.K
Walter, William MS 24th Inf. Co.L
Walter, William TX 1st (Yager's) Cav. Co.E
Walter, William VA 17th Inf. Co.B
Walter, William A. AR Cav. Carlton's Regt. Co.D
Walter, William B. SC 1st (Orr's) Rifles Co.H
Walter, William D. SC Inf. 1st (Charleston) Bn. Co.A Capt.
Walter, William E. TX 17th Inf. Co.B
Walter, William J. LA Ogden's Cav. Co.I 2nd Lt.
Walter, William J. SC 3rd Cav. Co.I
Walter, William T. MS 22nd Inf. Co.K
Walter, William T. VA 42nd Inf. Co.I
Walter, W.J. LA Miles' Legion Co.A
Walter, W.J. SC 2nd Inf. Co.I
Walter, W.W. MS 34th Inf. Co.I
Walter, Wyatt W. MS Page's Co. (Lexington Guards)
Walterfield, Levy LA 20th Inf. Co.D
Waltern, R.H. MS 27th Inf. Co.E
Walters, A. MS 1st (King's) Inf. (St.Troops) Co.G
Walters, A. TX 16th Inf. Co.D
Walters, A. TX 20th Inf. Co.K
Walters, Aaron AR 18th Inf. Co.H
Walters, A.B. MS 3rd Inf. (St.Troops) Co.A
Walters, Abraham MS 6th Inf. Co.A
Walters, Abraham C. MS 18th Inf. Co.A
Walters, A.C. TX 20th Bn.St.Troops Co.C
Walters, A.F. GA 3rd Cav. (St.Guards) Co.E
Walters, A.F. GA 4th Res. Co.K
Walters, A.J. GA 13th Cav. Co.C Capt.
Walters, A.J. MS 12th Cav. Co.L
Walters, A.J. MO 10th Inf. Co.A,B
Walters, A.L. TN 9th (Ward's) Cav. Co.B
Walters, Albert MS 3rd Cav. Co.B
Walters, Albert MS Inf. 7th Bn. Co.C
Walters, Albin C. VA 12th Cav. Co.K
Walters, Albion VA 97th Mil. Co.C
Walters, Alex. TN Lt.Arty. Kain's Co.
Walters, Alfred LA 3rd Inf. Co.F
Walters, Alfred MS Inf. 2nd St.Troops Co.O
Walters, Alfred VA 6th Inf. Co.C
Walters, Alfred VA 13th Inf. Co.A
Walters, Allen AL 4th Inf. Co.C
Walters, Amariah VA 21st Cav. Co.B Cpl.
Walters, Anderson F. GA 34th Inf. Co.G
Walters, Andrew TN 59th Mtd.Inf. Co.C
Walters, Andrew VA 18th Cav. Co.H
Walters, Andrew J. TN 20th Cav.
Walters, Archer E. VA 18th Inf. Co.A Lt.
Walters, Arren NC 31st Inf. Co.A
Walters, Arthur TX 13th Vol. Co.M
Walters, Arthur TX 15th Inf. 2nd Co.H
Walters, Asa MS Inf. 7th Bn. Co.C
Walters, Asa T. MS 3rd Inf. Co.D
Walters, Asa V. MS 23rd Inf. Co.E
Walters, A.T. SC 22nd Inf. Co.E 1st Sgt.
Walters, A.V. MS 15th (Cons.) Inf. Co.K
Walters, B. GA Mayer's Co. (Appling Cav.)
Walters, B.C. NC 35th Inf. Co.E
Walters, B.D. MS Inf. 7th Bn. Co.C
Walters, Benajah VA Loc.Def. Hamilton's Co. Capt.
Walters, Benjamin KY 2nd (Duke's) Cav. Co.E
Walters, Benjamin KY 3rd Cav. Co.H Cpl.
Walters, Benjamin F. NC 37th Inf. Co.A
Walters, Bennett NC Lt.Arty. 13 Bn. Co.A
Walters, Bennett VA Lt.Arty. 12th Bn. Co.D
Walters, Bethel TN Lt.Arty. Burrough's Co.
Walters, B.F. AL 8th Inf.
Walters, B.L. AL 33rd Inf. Co.D
Walters, Bower NC 37th Inf. Co.K
Walters, Bray VA 9th Inf. Co.F
Walters, B.T. GA Cav. 15th Bn. (St.Guards) Allen's Co.
Walters, Burwell AL 21st Inf. Co.D
Walters, B.W. GA 15th Inf. Co.H
Walters, C. TX 8th Inf. Co.G
Walters, C.A. TN Lt.Arty. Sparkman's Co.
Walters, Calbert SC 10th Inf. Co.C
Walters, Calloway KY 5th Mtd.Inf. Co.D
Walters, Calvin AL 31st Inf. Co.A
Walters, Calvin KY 13th Cav. Co.K
Walters, Calvin C. GA Inf. 10th Bn. Co.B
Walters, Carrol TX 5th Cav. Co.K
Walters, C.C. GA 8th Cav. Co.K
Walters, C.C. VA 1st St.Res. Co.B
Walters, Charles MD Line
Walters, Charles TX 36th Cav. Co.B Cpl.
Walters, Charles E. VA 13th Inf. 2nd Co.B
Walters, Charles H. LA 28th (Gray's) Inf. Co.G Sgt.
Walters, Charles M. GA 40th Inf. Co.C
Walters, Charles S. VA 49th Inf. 3rd Co.G
Walters, Charles W. GA 4th Inf. Co.I
Walters, Charles W. VA 38th Inf. Co.C 2nd Lt.
Walters, C.J. AR 30th Inf. Co.H
Walters, C.J. MS 4th Cav. Co.F
Walters, C.J. MS Cav. Hughes' Bn. Co.E
Walters, C.M. TX Cav. Border's Regt. Co.C
Walters, Columbus VA 8th Inf. Co.H Cpl.
Walters, C.P. MS 15th Bn.S.S. Co.A
Walters, C.P. MS 32nd Inf. Co.B
Walters, Crawford NC 18th Inf. Co.D
Walters, D. MS Yerger's Co. (St.Troops) Sgt.
Walters, Dabney VA Cav. 36th Bn. Co.C Cpl.
Walters, Daniel AL 26th Inf. Co.G
Walters, Daniel MS 3rd Cav. Co.B
Walters, Daniel C. NC 7th Inf. Co.I
Walters, Daniel E.M. MS 37th Inf. Co.K
Walters, Daniel H. TN Cav. 12th Bn. (Day's) Co.A
Walters, Daniel J. MS 18th Inf. Co.A
Walters, Daniel L. NC 37th Inf. Co.D 1st Lt.
Walters, David LA 28th (Gray's) Inf. Co.C
Walters, David MS Cav. 24th Bn. Co.B Cpl.
Walters, David MS Inf. Lewis' Co.
Walters, David TN 60th Mtd.Inf. Co.A
Walters, Dawson MS 9th Cav. Co.C Sgt.
Walters, Dawson MS Cav. 17th Bn. Co.E 1st Sgt.
Walters, Deen W. GA 15th Inf. Co.H
Walters, D.J. MS 3rd Cav.
Walters, D.J. MS 1st (King's) Inf. (St.Troops) Co.G
Walters, Dwight MS 16th Inf. Co.H
Walters, E. AL 5th Inf. Co.B
Walters, E. NC 31st Inf. Co.F
Walters, E. TX 7th Cav. Co.F
Walters, Ebenezer NC 33rd Inf. Co.D
Walters, Ed. MS 12th Cav. Co.L
Walters, Edward VA 18th Cav. Co.D
Walters, Edward VA Cav. 41st Bn. Trayhern's Co.
Walters, Edward VA 2nd Inf. Co.H
Walters, Edward VA 9th Inf. Co.E
Walters, Elijah, Jr. TN Cav. 12th Bn. (Day's) Co.A
Walters, Elijah TN Cav. 16th Bn. (Neal's) Co.F
Walters, Elijah VA 16th Inf. Co.A
Walters, Ellis MS 6th Inf. Co.A
Walters, E.M. MS 37th Inf. Co.K
Walters, Emanuel C. GA 1st Inf. Co.H
Walters, Emberry NC 37th Inf. Co.D
Walters, E.N. MS St.Cav. 3rd Bn. (Cooper's) 2nd Co.A
Walters, E.N. MS Cav. Yerger's Regt. Co.A
Walters, Enoch TN 2nd (Ashby's) Cav. Co.E Cpl.
Walters, Enoch TN Cav. 4th Bn. (Branner's) Co.D
Walters, E.P. NC 35th Inf. Co.E Sgt.
Walters, Evan SC 8th Inf. Co.D
Walters, Evander M. GA 4th Inf. Co.I
Walters, Evander M. MS 2nd Inf. Co.A
Walters, Evan S. SC Lt.Arty. Kelly's Co. (Chesterfield Arty.)
Walters, F. VA 10th Inf. Co.F
Walters, F.E. GA 49th Inf. Co.F 1st Sgt.
Walters, F.H. TX 30th Cav. Co.B
Walters, F.J. KY 2nd (Duke's) Cav. Co.L
Walters, F.M. AR 11th Inf. Co.A 1st Sgt.
Walters, F.O. GA 34th Inf. Co.I
Walters, Francis A. AR 1st (Colquitt's) Inf. Co.I
Walters, Frank TN 11th Inf. Co.D
Walters, Franklin GA 15th Inf. Co.H
Walters, Frederick VA 18th Cav. Co.D
Walters, Fred W. GA Phillips' Legion
Walters, F.W. NC 17th Inf. (1st Org.) Co.F
Walters, Gabl. GA 10th Inf. Co.K Cpl.
Walters, George MO Cav. Snider's Bn. Co.C
Walters, George NC 5th Inf. Co.A
Walters, George TN 3rd (Clack's) Inf. Co.I
Walters, George TN 51st (Cons.) Inf. Co.K
Walters, George TN 60th Mtd.Inf. Co.A Sgt.
Walters, George VA 16th Inf. Co.A

Walters, George VA 39th Inf. Co.B,K Cpl.
Walters, George VA 54th Inf. Co.C
Walters, George A. VA 11th Bn.Res. Co.A
Walters, George A. VA 54th Inf. Co.C
Walters, George C. VA 13th Inf. Co.A Sgt.
Walters, George F. NC 11th (Bethel Regt.) Inf. Co.G
Walters, George L. GA 5th Inf. Co.H
Walters, George P. MS Gage's Co. (Wigfall Guards)
Walters, George W. AR 9th Inf. Co.D 2nd Lt.
Walters, George W. GA 4th Inf. Co.E
Walters, George W. KY 2nd Cav.
Walters, George W. KY 12th Cav. Co.H
Walters, George W. KY 2nd Bn.Mtd.Rifles Co.B
Walters, George W. MS 8th Inf. Co.K
Walters, Geo. W. NC Mil. 66th Bn. J.H. Whitman's Co.
Walters, George W. NC 37th Inf. Co.D Sgt.
Walters, George W. TN 5th (McKenzie's) Cav. Co.D
Walters, George W. VA 51st Inf. Co.C
Walters, G.R. LA 13th Bn. (Part.Rangers) Co.F
Walters, Green H. MS 42nd Inf. Co.H
Walters, G.W. AL 34th Inf. Co.G
Walters, G.W. GA Lt.Arty. 12th Bn.
Walters, G.W. GA Inf. 25th Bn. (Prov.Guard) Co.F
Walters, G.W. TN 9th Inf. Co.I
Walters, G.W. TN Conscr. (Cp. of Instr.)
Walters, G.W. TX 33rd Cav. Co.D
Walters, G.W. VA 23rd Cav. Co.I Sgt.
Walters, H. SC 24th Inf. Co.C
Walters, H. TN Cav. Napier's Bn. Co.C
Walters, H. VA Inf. 26th Bn. Co.F
Walters, Hanson MS Inf. 7th Bn. Co.C
Walters, Hardy NC 13th Inf. Co.G
Walters, H.B. MS 37th Inf. Co.D
Walters, H.C. VA Wade's Regt.Loc.Def. Co.A
Walters, Henderson B. VA 45th Inf. Co.H
Walters, Henry MS 10th Cav. Co.B
Walters, Henry MS 41st Inf. Co.G
Walters, Henry NC 48th Inf. Co.E
Walters, Henry VA 6th Cav. Co.H
Walters, Henry VA Cav. Mosby's Regt. (Part.Rangers) Co.B
Walters, Henry C. VA 54th Inf. Co.C
Walters, Henry D. LA 12th Inf. Co.D Jr.2nd Lt.
Walters, Henry H. MS 1sts (King's) Inf. (St.Troops) Co.E
Walters, Henry J. AL Arty. 1st Bn.
Walters, Henry J. NC 26th Inf. Co.G
Walters, Henry J. TX 13th Cav. Co.K
Walters, Henry S. MS 10th Inf. Old Co.G, New Co.B
Walters, Henry T. NC 13th Inf. Co.A Cpl.
Walters, H.F. GA 15th Inf. Co.H
Walters, H.H. TN 19th (Biffle's) Cav. Co.E
Walters, Hilliard SC 1st (McCreary's) Inf. Co.C
Walters, Hilyard VA 9th Mil. Arnold's Co.
Walters, Hiram VA 14th Cav. Co.G, 2nd Co.F
Walters, H.M. GA 1st Inf. (St.Guards) Co.M
Walters, Hugo TX 13th Vol. 2nd Co.C Music.
Walters, Isaac MS 6th Inf. Co.A
Walters, Isaac NC 2nd Cav. (19th St.Troops) Co.C
Walters, Isaac NC 50th Inf. Co.B
Walters, Isaac VA Inf. Cohoon's Bn. Co.D Sgt.
Walters, Isaac E. MS 8th Inf. Co.K
Walters, Isham P. NC Hvy.Arty. 1st Bn. Co.A
Walters, J. AL 8th Inf. Co.F
Walters, J. GA 3rd Res. Co.C Sgt.
Walters, J. GA 5th Res. Co.D
Walters, J. LA 15th Inf. Co.A
Walters, J. MD 1st Cav.
Walters, J. TX 30th Cav. Co.C
Walters, J.A. GA 3rd Inf. Co.D Sgt.
Walters, J.A. GA 3rd Res. Co.D Sgt.
Walters, J.A.B. NC 35th Inf. Co.E
Walters, Jack LA 9th Inf. Co.C
Walters, Jackson KY 5th Cav. Co.D
Walters, Jackson NC 3rd Cav. (41st St.Troops) Co.C
Walters, Jacob VA 25th Cav. Co.F
Walters, Jacob H. VA 11th Cav. Co.C
Walters, Jacob L. VA Inf. 23rd Bn. Co.G
Walters, Jacob R. AL 57th Inf. Co.C
Walters, J.A.J. GA Cav. 22nd Bn. (St.Guards) Co.C
Walters, James AL 2nd Inf.
Walters, James GA 54th Inf. Co.C
Walters, James GA 54th Inf. Co.E
Walters, James LA 1st (Strawbridge's) Inf. Co.F
Walters, James LA Lewis Regt. Co.B
Walters, James MO 4th Cav. Co.F
Walters, James NC 61st Inf. Co.C Sgt.
Walters, James NC Mil. Clark's Sp.Bn. Co.C
Walters, James TN Cav. 16th Bn. (Neal's) Co.E
Walters, James TN 59th Mtd.Inf. Co.C
Walters, James VA 9th Inf. 1st Co.A
Walters, James VA 63rd Inf. Co.H
Walters, James VA Mil. Wythe Cty.
Walters, James A. MS 37th Inf. Co.K
Walters, James A. TX 13th Cav. Co.H Cpl.
Walters, James A. VA 29th Inf. Co.I
Walters, James A. VA 97th Mil. Co.F
Walters, James B. NC 3rd Cav. (41st St.Troops) Co.K
Walters, James B. VA 16th Inf. Co.C
Walters, James B. VA 38th Inf. Co.C Sgt.
Walters, James C. VA 54th Inf. Co.C
Walters, James D. MD 1st Cav. Co.C 2nd Lt.
Walters, James E. FL 2nd Cav. Co.E
Walters, James E. MS 37th Inf. Co.K
Walters, James F. GA 3rd Inf. Co.I
Walters, James H. NC 37th Inf. Co.D
Walters, James H. VA 16th Inf. 1st Co.H
Walters, James J. TN 44th (Cons.) Inf. Co.A
Walters, James M. VA 51st Inf. Co.C
Walters, James P. KY 5th Mtd.Inf. Co.I
Walters, James R. GA 34th Inf. Co.G
Walters, James S. MS 41st Inf. Co.G,I
Walters, James T. VA 54th Inf. Co.C
Walters, James W. VA 10th Cav. Co.F
Walters, James W. VA 34th Mil. Co.D
Walters, Jasper M. TX 22nd Cav. Co.E
Walters, J.B. VA 3rd Inf.Loc.Def. Co.F
Walters, J.C. GA 15th Inf. Co.H
Walters, J.C. TN 19th & 20th (Cons.) Cav. Co.D
Walters, J.C. VA 21st Cav. 2nd Co.D
Walters, J.E. MS 37th Inf. Co.F
Walters, J.E. MS 46th Inf. Co.D
Walters, J.E. VA 3rd Inf.Loc.Def. 1st Co.G
Walters, Jeams L. GA 4th Cav. (St.Guards) McDonald's Co.
Walters, Jeptha GA Inf. 9th Bn. Co.A
Walters, Jeptha GA 37th Inf. Co.D
Walters, Jeptha GA 54th Inf. Co.H Cpl.
Walters, Jeremiah VA 136th Mil. Co.C
Walters, Jeremiah F. GA 34th Inf. Co.G
Walters, Jerry D. NC 12th Inf. Co.D
Walters, Jesse MS 4th Cav. Co.I
Walters, Jesse MO 7th Cav. Co.D,I
Walters, Jesse D.F. AL Inf. 1st Regt. Co.E
Walters, Jesse H. MS 26th Inf. Co.F
Walters, J.F. GA 39th Inf. Co.A
Walters, J.F. NC 11th (Bethel Regt.) Inf. Co.G
Walters, J.F. SC 21st Inf. Co.H
Walters, J.G. GA 15th Inf. Co.H
Walters, J.G. MS 46th Inf. Co.D
Walters, J.G. NC 34th Inf. Co.G
Walters, J.G. TN 20th Inf. Co.K
Walters, J.G.M. NC 21st Inf. Co.H
Walters, J.H. MS 2nd St.Cav. Co.G
Walters, J.H. MS Detailed Conscr.
Walters, J.H. TN 5th (McKenzie's) Cav. Co.A
Walters, J.H. TX 22nd Inf. Co.F
Walters, J.H. VA Cav. 37th Bn. Co.F
Walters, J.H. VA 51st Inf. Co.F
Walters, J.I. TX 5th Cav. Co.A
Walters, J.J. LA 19th Inf. Co.G
Walters, J.M. TX Inf. Rutherford's Co.
Walters, J.M. Cav. Beale's Brig. Capt.,AQM
Walters, J.N. MS 1st (Percy's) Inf. Co.F
Walters, Joel S. MS 9th Cav. Co.G
Walters, Joel S. MS 37th Inf. Co.K
Walters, John AL Arty. 1st Bn. Co.D
Walters, John AL 5th Inf. Co.B
Walters, John AL 24th Inf. Co.I
Walters, John AL Cp. of Instr. Talladega
Walters, John GA 50th Inf. Co.F
Walters, John KY 2nd Cav.
Walters, John KY 5th Cav. Co.D,C
Walters, John KY 2nd Bn.Mtd.Rifles Co.B
Walters, John LA 15th Inf. Co.F
Walters, John MS 21st Inf. Co.F
Walters, John MS 27th Inf. Co.B
Walters, John SC 1st (Butler's) Inf. Co.G
Walters, John SC 1st (Butler's) Inf. Co.K
Walters, John TN 2nd (Ashby's) Cav. Co.D
Walters, John TN Cav. 12th Bn. (Day's) Co.A Bugler
Walters, John TN 29th Inf. Co.C
Walters, John TN 54th Inf. Co.G
Walters, John VA 23rd Cav. Co.M
Walters, John VA Cav. 32nd Bn. Co.A
Walters, John VA Lt.Arty. 13th Bn. Co.B
Walters, John VA Lt.Arty. Grandy's Co.
Walters, John VA 4th Res. Co.H
Walters, John VA 6th Inf. Vickery's Co.
Walters, John VA 14th Inf. Co.A
Walters, John VA 16th Inf. 1st Co.H
Walters, John VA 44th Inf. Co.E
Walters, John VA 54th Inf. Co.A
Walters, John VA 54th Inf. Co.C
Walters, John VA 59th Mil. Arnold's Co.
Walters, John VA Mil. Wythe Cty.
Walters, John Conf.Lt.Arty. Richardson's Bn. Co.C
Walters, John Gen. & Staff Asst.Surg.

Walters, John A. LA 1st (Nelligan's) Inf. Howell's Co.
Walters, John A. SC 24th Inf. Co.C Sgt.
Walters, John A. VA 9th Inf. Co.E
Walters, John B. MO Cav. Snider's Bn. Co.C
Walters, John B. VA 54th Inf. Co.I
Walters, John B. VA 63rd Inf. Co.H
Walters, John B. VA Mil. Wythe Cty.
Walters, John C. MS 6th Cav. Co.D
Walters, John C. MS 26th Inf. Co.D Capt.
Walters, John C. MO 8th Cav. Co.E
Walters, John C. VA 51st Inf. Co.C
Walters, John E. MS 10th Inf. Old Co.G
Walters, John F. GA 15th Inf. Co.H
Walters, John F. NC Lt.Arty. 13th Bn. Co.A
Walters, John H. VA 13th Inf. 2nd Co.B
Walters, John H. VA 34th Mil. Co.C
Walters, John H. Gen. & Staff Surg.
Walters, John H.A. NC 38th Inf. Co.E
Walters, John Henry VA 10th Inf. 1st Co.C, Co.F Sgt.
Walters, John L. AL 13th Bn.Part.Rangers Co.E
Walters, John L. AL 56th Part.Rangers Co.I
Walters, John L. VA 1st Res. Co.C
Walters, John M. NC 13th Inf. Co.H
Walters, John O. NC 37th Inf. Co.A
Walters, John P. VA 29th Inf. Co.I 1st Sgt.
Walters, John P. VA Mil. Wythe Cty.
Walters, John R. MO 1st N.E. Cav. Asst.Surg.
Walters, John T. LA Inf. 7th Bn. Co.B
Walters, John W. MS 16th Inf. Co.G
Walters, John W. MO Cav. Snider's Bn. Co.C
Walters, John W. VA 3rd Cav. Co.G
Walters, John W. VA 2nd Inf. Co.B 1st Lt.
Walters, John W. VA 11th Bn.Res. Co.D
Walters, Joseph AR 15th (Josey's) Inf. Co.D
Walters, Joseph MS Cav. Powers' Regt. Co.D,E
Walters, Joseph MS 13th Inf. Co.K Sgt.
Walters, Joseph MS 27th Inf. Co.L
Walters, Joseph VA 5th Cav. (12 mo. '61-2) Co.C
Walters, Joseph VA Lt.Arty. 13th Bn. Co.B
Walters, Joseph VA 38th Inf. Co.C Sgt.
Walters, Joseph A. VA 12th Cav. Co.K
Walters, Joseph A. VA 58th Mil. Co.I
Walters, Joseph M. TN 36th Inf. Co.C
Walters, Joseph M. VA 13th Cav. Co.H AQM
Walters, Joseph M. VA Lt.Arty. G.B. Chapman's Co.
Walters, Joseph M. VA 54th Mil. Co.G
Walters, Joseph W. VA 2nd Inf. Co.B,H
Walters, Joshua AL 42nd Inf. Co.K
Walters, Joshua AL 51st Inf. Co.G
Walters, Joshua MS 2nd (Quinn's St.Troops) Inf. Co.D Cpl.
Walters, Joshua SC 1st (Butler's) Inf. Co.B
Walters, Joshua K. NC 37th Inf. Co.D
Walters, J.P. FL 8th Inf. Co.B
Walters, J.P. GA 37th Inf. Co.D
Walters, J.P. SC 22nd Inf. Co.E Cpl.
Walters, J.P. SC 25th Inf. Co.K
Walters, J.R.K. MS 6th Inf. Co.A
Walters, J.S. AL Conscr. & Res.Bn. Co.B
Walters, J.T. GA 10th Inf. Co.B
Walters, J.T. LA 1st Cav. Co.I
Walters, J.T. LA Inf. 1st Sp.Bn. (Wheat's) Old Co.D
Walters, J.T. LA 15th Inf. Co.I
Walters, J.T. VA 21st Cav. 2nd Co.D
Walters, Justice W. MS 8th Inf. Co.K
Walters, J.W. AL 18th Inf. Co.H
Walters, J.W. GA 8th Cav. Co.K Cpl.
Walters, J.W. GA 62nd Cav. Co.K Cpl.
Walters, J.W. MS Inf. 7th Bn. Co.F
Walters, J.W. MS 27th Inf. Co.B
Walters, J.W. MS Inf. Lewis' Co.
Walters, J.W. TN 19th & 20th (Cons.) Cav. Co.A
Walters, J.W. TN 20th (Russell's) Cav. Co.B
Walters, J.W. TX 22nd Inf. Co.F Cpl.
Walters, L. MS St.Cav. 3rd Bn. (Cooper's) 2nd Co.A
Walters, L. MS 12th Cav. Co.L
Walters, L. VA 8th Cav. Co.I
Walters, Lemuel TN 5th (McKenzie's) Cav. Co.A
Walters, Lemuel TX 13th Cav. Co.K
Walters, Leonard R. NC 37th Inf. Co.D
Walters, Levi VA 1st Cav. Co.L
Walters, Lewis 1st Conf.Reg.Cav. Co.A
Walters, Lewis B. GA 37th Inf. Co.D
Walters, Licurgus TX 17th Cons.Dismtd.Cav. Co.C
Walters, Lovell VA Lt.Arty. 13th Bn. Co.B
Walters, Lucus NC 51st Inf. Co.F
Walters, Luke MS 6th Inf. Co.A
Walters, L.W. MO 10th Cav. Co.K
Walters, Lycurgus TX 17th Cav. Co.D
Walters, M. GA Inf. 1st Loc.Troops (Augusta) Barnes' Lt.Arty.Co.
Walters, M. SC 24th Inf. Co.C
Walters, Madison 1st Conf.Eng.Troops Co.H
Walters, Marcus R. MO Cav. Williams' Regt. Co.L
Walters, McCoy NC 3rd Cav. (41st St.Troops) Co.K
Walters, McGill VA 33rd Inf. Co.G
Walters, M.E. Gen. & Staff Chap.
Walters, Michael VA Mil. Wythe Cty.
Walters, Michael L. AL 57th Inf. Co.C Sgt.
Walters, Milton MS 6th Inf. Co.A
Walters, Milton MS 46th Inf. Co.D
Walters, Mitchell VA 29th Inf. Co.I
Walters, M.M. MS Cav. 17th Bn. Co.D
Walters, M.O. MS 6th Inf. Co.A
Walters, Morgan MS 18th Inf. Co.A
Walters, Morgan MS 46th Inf. Co.D
Walters, Morris LA Inf. 7th Bn. Co.C
Walters, Morris LA 15th Inf. Co.K
Walters, Moses GA 34th Inf. Co.I
Walters, Moses NC 37th Inf. Co.D
Walters, Moses SC 1st Arty. Co.E
Walters, Moses SC 26th Inf. Co.B
Walters, Moses TX 10th Cav. Co.I
Walters, Moses TX 37th Cav. Co.K
Walters, Moses VA 11th Bn.Res. Co.D
Walters, Moses A. NC Hvy.Arty. 10th Bn. Co.D
Walters, Moses O. MS 18th Inf. Co.A
Walters, N. MS Cav. 3rd Bn.Res. Co.C
Walters, Newton TN 63rd Inf. Co.D,K
Walters, O.C. AR 1st (Monroe's) Cav. Co.D
Walters, Oreander TN 46th Inf. Co.E
Walters, Pearl MS 38th Cav. Co.K
Walters, Peter VA 54th Inf. Co.I
Walters, Philip GA 64th Inf. Co.G
Walters, Philip NC 31st Inf. Co.G
Walters, Philip SC 3rd Cav. Co.B Cpl.
Walters, Philip SC 1st (Butler's) Inf. Co.K
Walters, Philip A. VA 33rd Inf. Co.B
Walters, Philip M. VA 54th Inf. Co.I
Walters, Phillip NC 50th Inf. Co.B
Walters, Phillip F. TX 10th Cav. Co.C
Walters, P.M. TX 30th Cav. Co.B
Walters, Polk KY 5th Cav. Co.A
Walters, Preston MO Inf. Perkins' Bn. Co.A,K
Walters, R. NC 12th Inf. Co.I
Walters, R. SC 24th Inf. Co.C
Walters, R.A. LA 30th Inf. Co.I,B Cpl.
Walters, R.A. TN 5th Inf. 2nd Co.I
Walters, R.B. AL 8th (Livingston's) Cav. Co.A
Walters, R.B. KY 3rd Cav. Co.H
Walters, R.B. LA Inf. 7th Bn. Co.B 1st Sgt.
Walters, R.B. LA 13th Inf. Co.I
Walters, R.B. SC 1st (Hagood's) Inf. 1st Co.E
Walters, R.B. SC 25th Inf. Co.C
Walters, R.B.G. GA Arty. 11th Bn. (Sumter Arty.) Co.B
Walters, Reuben SC 21st Inf. Co.F
Walters, R.F. KY 4th Cav. Co.B
Walters, R.F. LA 6th Cav. Co.A
Walters, Rich SC 4th St.Troops Co.G
Walters, Richard MS Inf. 7th Bn. Co.C
Walters, Richard NC 5th Sr.Res. Co.C
Walters, Richard TX 15th Cav. Co.A
Walters, Richard TX Inf. (St.Serv.) Cunningham's Co.
Walters, Richard H. MS 8th Inf. Co.K
Walters, Richard P. Gen. & Staff Surg.
Walters, R.L. TN Lt.Arty. Sparkman's Co. Sgt.
Walters, R.M. SC 16th & 24th (Cons.) Inf. Co.I Sgt.
Walters, R.M. SC 24th Inf. Co.C Cpl.
Walters, Robert MS 46th Inf. Co.C
Walters, Robert A. TN 20th (Russell's) Cav. Co.E
Walters, Robert A. VA 18th Inf. Co.A Cpl.
Walters, Robert B. LA Inf. 1st Sp.Bn. (Wheat's) Old Co.D 1st Sgt.
Walters, Robert B. LA 15th Inf. Co.I 1st Lt.
Walters, Robert F. TX 10th Cav. Co.C
Walters, Robert J. AL 12th Cav. Co.A
Walters, Robert L. VA 97th Mil. Co.L Cpl.
Walters, Robert P. GA 34th Inf. Co.G
Walters, Rogers TN Lt.Arty. Morton's Co.
Walters, Roland KY Cav. 1st Bn. Co.A
Walters, Rolin F. KY 5th Mtd.Inf. Co.F 2nd Lt.
Walters, Rowland KY Cav. Jenkins' Co.
Walters, Rowland F. KY 13th Cav. Co.F 2nd Lt.
Walters, R.T. GA 10th Mil. Sgt.
Walters, Russell S. VA 29th Inf. Co.I Cpl.
Walters, Russell S. VA Mil. Wythe Cty.
Walters, R.W. AL 5th Inf. Co.B
Walters, R.W. TX 1st Hvy.Arty. Co.D
Walters, R.W. TX Inf. 1st St.Troops Lawrence's Co.D Sgt.
Walters, R.W. TX 9th (Nichols') Inf. Co.C
Walters, R. Wash. MS 15th Inf. Co.E
Walters, S. GA 54th Inf. Co.E
Walters, S.A. GA Arty. 11th Bn. (Sumter Arty.) Co.B

Walters, Samuel MS 27th Inf. Co.L
Walters, Samuel SC 1st (Butler's) Inf. Co.A,K
Walters, Samuel TN 20th (Russell's) Cav. Co.E
Walters, Samuel TN 60th Mtd.Inf. Co.A
Walters, Samuel VA 33rd Inf. Co.C
Walters, Sam'l. B. Gen. & Staff Capt.
Walters, Samuel G. VA Hvy.Arty. 10th Bn. Co.B
Walters, Saml. H. AL 26th Inf. Co.A
Walters, Samuel T. TX Waul's Legion Co.F Capt.
Walters, S.B. MS 6th Inf. Co.A
Walters, S.D. SC 16th & 24th (Cons.) Inf. Co.I
Walters, S.D. SC 24th Inf. Co.C
Walters, S.E. TX 5th Inf. Co.H
Walters, Seaborn GA Cav. 29th Bn. Co.H
Walters, Seaborn GA Arty. 11th Bn. (Sumter Arty.) Co.B
Walters, Seth A. GA 31st Inf. Co.G
Walters, Sidney NC 11th (Bethel Regt.) Inf. Co.G
Walters, Simeon LA 12th Inf. Co.D
Walters, Simmeon L. MS 27th Inf. Co.D Sgt.
Walters, Simon VA 59th Mil. Riddick's Co.
Walters, Solomon TN Cav. 16th Bn. (Neal's) Co.F
Walters, Solomon VA 21st Cav. Co.B
Walters, Solomon M. TN Cav. 16th Bn. (Neal's) Co.F
Walters, S.S. SC Inf. Hampton Legion Co.H
Walters, T. NC 48th Inf. Co.E
Walters, T.A. AL 15th Inf. Co.I
Walters, T.C. TX 13th Cav. Co.I
Walters, T.D. TX 17th Inf. Co.C
Walters, Theodore LA Inf. 9th Bn. Co.A
Walters, Thomas KY 5th Mtd.Inf. Co.I
Walters, Thomas LA Inf. 4th Bn. Co.E
Walters, Thomas B. VA 60th Inf. Co.G
Walters, Thomas C. NC 3rd Cav. (41st St.Troops) Co.C
Walters, Thomas D. VA 10th Inf. Co.K
Walters, Thomas F. GA 57th Inf. Co.D
Walters, Thomas F. NC 51st Inf. Co.A
Walters, Thomas G. GA Arty. 11th Bn. (Sumter Arty.) Co.D,B
Walters, Thomas H. NC Lt.Arty. 13th Bn. Co.A Cpl.
Walters, Thomas H. NC 38th Inf. Co.E
Walters, Thomas H. VA Lt.Arty. 12th Bn. Co.D
Walters, Thomas J. AL 31st Inf. Co.F
Walters, Thomas J. VA 11th Cav. Co.K
Walters, Thomas L. MS 37th Inf. Co.K
Walters, Thomas L. TN 24th Inf. Co.B
Walters, Thomas R. NC Hvy.Arty. 10th Bn. Co.A
Walters, Thomas S. TN Lt.Arty. Kain's Co.
Walters, Tillman TX 21st Cav. Co.L
Walters, Tilman TX 17th Inf. Co.D
Walters, T.J. AL 3rd Cav. Co.E
Walters, T.J. LA 28th (Gray's) Inf. Co.B
Walters, T.L. GA 4th Res. Co.H
Walters, T.R. LA 3rd Inf. Co.K
Walters, T.R., Jr. LA Inf. 9th Bn. Co.A Sgt.
Walters, Tristum GA 12th (Robinson's) Cav. (St.Guards) Co.A
Walters, Uriah NC 48th Inf. Co.E
Walters, Virginius VA 54th Mil. Co.G
Walters, W. AL 15th Inf. Co.I
Walters, Wade TX 17th Cav. Co.D
Walters, Wade H. TX 17th Cav. 1st Co.I
Walters, Warren MO 10th Cav. Co.K
Walters, Wash MS 1st Bn.S.S. Co.D
Walters, Washington A. AL 6th Inf. Co.A
Walters, W.B. TN Lt.Arty. Sparkman's Co.
Walters, W.B. TX 22nd Inf. Co.F Sgt.
Walters, W.C. VA 47th Inf. Co.H Capt.
Walters, W.D. GA 10th Inf. Co.C
Walters, W.D. SC Palmetto S.S. Co.C
Walters, W.D. TX 27th Cav. Co.K 1st Sgt.
Walters, W.G. TN Conscr. (Cp. of Instr.)
Walters, Wilkerson VA 9th Inf. Co.E
Walters, Wilkersson LA 1st (Nelligan's) Inf. Howell's Co.
Walters, William GA 5th Res. Co.A,D
Walters, William GA 54th Inf. Co.E
Walters, William LA Ogden's Cav. Co.C
Walters, William LA Hvy.Arty. 8th Bn. Co.1
Walters, William LA 21st (Patton's) Inf. Co.I
Walters, William MS 6th Inf. Co.A
Walters, William MS 13th Inf. Co.K
Walters, William MS 16th Inf. Co.H
Walters, William NC 50th Inf. Co.B
Walters, William NC 50th Inf. Co.G
Walters, William SC 1st (Butler's) Inf. Co.A
Walters, William TN 2nd (Ashby's) Cav. Co.D
Walters, William TN 5th (McKenzie's) Cav. Co.A
Walters, William TN 63rd Inf. Co.K
Walters, William VA Inf. 4th Bn.Loc.Def. Co.B
Walters, William VA 29th Inf. Co.I
Walters, William VA 45th Inf. Co.B
Walters, William VA 45th Inf. Co.H
Walters, William VA 136th Mil. Co.C
Walters, William 14th Conf.Cav. Co.G
Walters, William Conf.Lt.Arty. 1st Reg.Btty.
Walters, William A. AL 2nd Cav. Co.F Sgt.
Walters, William A. TX 22nd Inf. Co.C
Walters, William A. VA 1st St.Res. Co.D
Walters, William B. AR 3rd Cav. Co.F
Walters, William B. GA 10th Inf. Co.C
Walters, William B. GA 59th Inf. Co.E
Walters, William B. TX 17th Cav. Co.C
Walters, William B. VA 1st Arty. 3rd Co.C
Walters, William B. VA Lt.Arty. 1st Bn. Co.C
Walters, William B. VA Arty. Young's Co.
Walters, William B. VA 53rd Inf. Co.F
Walters, William B. VA Inf. Montague's Bn. Co.C
Walters, William C. MD Walters' Co. (Zarvona Zouaves) Capt.
Walters, William D. VA 10th Inf. 1st Co.C, 2nd Co.C
Walters, William E. SC 2nd Rifles Chap.
Walters, William E. SC 4th Inf. Co.B
Walters, Wm. E. Gen. & Staff Chap.
Walters, William F. VA 18th Inf. Co.A
Walters, William H. FL 5th Inf. Co.C
Walters, William H. MS 40th Inf. Co.E
Walters, William H. VA 36th Inf. 2nd Co.G
Walters, William H. VA 61st Inf. Co.D
Walters, William J. LA 8th Inf. Co.A Cpl.
Walters, William L. MS 37th Inf. Co.K
Walters, William M. NC Walker's Bn. Thomas' Legion 2nd Co.D Sgt.
Walters, William P. NC 3rd Arty. (40th St.Troops) Co.K,H
Walters, William P. NC 50th Inf. Co.B Jr.2nd Lt.
Walters, William P. VA 7th Inf. Co.I Jr.2nd Lt.
Walters, William R. GA 15th Inf. Co.H 2nd Lt.
Walters, William T. GA 34th Inf. Co.I
Walters, William T. NC 31st Inf. Co.A
Walters, William W. AL 24th Inf. Co.K,I
Walters, W.J. AL 25th Inf. Co.A
Walters, W.J. SC 4th Cav. Co.I
Walters, W.J. SC Cav. 12th Bn. Co.B
Walters, W.J. SC Arty. Melchers' Co. (Co.B,German Arty.)
Walters, W.J. SC 11th Inf. Co.H
Walters, W.M. VA 51st Inf. Co.C
Walters, W. Riley NC 27th Inf. Co.A
Walters, W.T. GA 10th Inf. Co.B
Walters, W.W. AL 34th Inf. Co.H
Walters, W.W. LA 31st Inf. Co.D 1st Lt.
Walters, Wyatt VA 1st Res. Co.C
Walters, Wyatt E. GA Lt.Arty. Scogin's Btty. (Griffin Lt.Arty.)
Walters, Zeb NC 50th Inf. Co.B
Waltersdorf, Charles TN 26th Inf. Co.I Sgt.
Walterson, P. GA 8th Inf. Co.I
Walterson, Walter TN 33rd Inf. Co.K
Waltertham, J. SC Mil. 1st Regt. (Charleston Res.) Co.B
Walthal, Albert TN 49th Inf. Co.A
Walthal, Albert Inf. Bailey's Cons.Regt. Co.G
Walthal, Felix L. GA 30th Inf. Co.I Capt.
Walthal, James L. KY 9th Mtd.Inf. Co.C
Walthal, James W. TX Cav. Martin's Regt. Co.D
Walthal, Thomas W. TN 49th Inf. Co.A Cpl.
Walthal, Thomas W. Inf. Bailey's Cons.Regt. Co.G
Walthal, William TN 50th Inf. Co.E
Walthal, W.W. Gen. & Staff Hosp.Stew.
Walthall, Adolphus VA 23rd Inf. Co.C
Walthall, Allie F. AR 1st (Colquitt's) Inf. Co.G 1st Lt.
Walthall, Andrew W. VA 54th Inf. Co.E
Walthall, Benjamin A. MS 9th Inf. Old Co.B Sgt.
Walthall, Benjamin A. Phifer's Staff Capt., Ord.Off.
Walthall, Benjamin F. VA 4th Inf. Co.B
Walthall, Berthier VA 23rd Inf. Co.C
Walthall, B.F. VA 4th Inf. Co.G
Walthall, B.T. AR 2nd Cav. Co.B
Walthall, Charles F. AR 24th Inf. Co.F
Walthall, Charles F. AR Inf. Hardy's Regt. Co.D
Walthall, Charles P. VA Inf. 5th Bn. Co.B
Walthall, C.J. VA Hvy.Arty. Allen's Co.
Walthall, Christopher VA 1st St.Res. Co.F
Walthall, Christopher B. VA 23rd Inf. Co.C Sgt.
Walthall, Christopher J. VA 13th Inf. Co.D
Walthall, C.P. VA 53rd Inf. Co.G
Walthall, David M. VA 54th Inf. Co.E
Walthall, D.H. VA 4th Inf. Co.G
Walthall, E.C. MS 29th Inf. Col.
Walthall, E.C. Walthall's Div. Maj.Gen.
Walthall, Ed AR 15th (Johnson's) Inf. Co.B
Walthall, Ed MO 6th Cav. Co.G
Walthall, Edmund AL 1st Inf. Co.B,E
Walthall, Edward C. MS 15th Inf. Co.H Lt.Col.

Walthall, Edward T. VA 20th Inf. Co.I
Walthall, Edward T. VA 59th Inf. 3rd Co.B
Walthall, E.T. VA 46th Inf. Co.D
Walthall, F.L. VA 1st St.Res. Co.F
Walthall, George AR 1st (Dobbin's) Cav. Co.H
Walthall, George MS 18th Cav. Co.C
Walthall, George G. VA 34th Inf. Co.F 1st Sgt.
Walthall, George W. AR 23rd Inf. Co.E
Walthall, George W. VA Hvy.Arty. Wilkinson's Co.
Walthall, G.W. AR 1st Cav. Co.B
Walthall, H. VA 20th Cav. Co.C
Walthall, Harrison VA 18th Inf. Co.F Cpl.
Walthall, Howard M. VA 1st Inf. Co.D
Walthall, Isaac G. VA 11th Inf. Co.C
Walthall, J. TX Cav. Bourland's Regt. Co.D
Walthall, James A. VA 18th Inf. Co.D Lt.
Walthall, James B. VA 20th Inf. Co.I
Walthall, James C. AR 1st Cav. Co.H
Walthall, James H. VA 23rd Inf. Co.C 1st Sgt.
Walthall, James L. KY 5th Mtd.Inf.
Walthall, J.D. VA 3rd Res. Co.D
Walthall, J.E. GA 13th Inf. Co.B
Walthall, J.H. TN 8th Inf. Co.B
Walthall, J.H. TN 40th Inf. Co.F
Walthall, J.J. TX 5th Inf. Co.E Sgt.
Walthall, J.M. VA 10th Cav. Co.D
Walthall, John AL Gid Nelson Lt.Arty.
Walthall, John A. AR 9th Inf. Co.F
Walthall, John D. VA Hvy.Arty. 18th Bn. Co.C
Walthall, John D. VA 18th Inf. Co.F
Walthall, John D. Recruits W.D. Ochiltree's Detach.
Walthall, John H. AR 23rd Inf. Co.E
Walthall, John H. LA 2nd Inf. Co.K
Walthall, John H. VA Arty. Dance's Co. 2nd Lt.
Walthall, John H. VA 18th Inf. Co.D Cpl.
Walthall, John L. AR 33rd Inf. Co.C
Walthall, John M. VA 23rd Inf. Co.C
Walthall, John W. VA Lt.Arty. Jeffress' Co.
Walthall, John William VA 44th Inf. Co.H
Walthall, Joseph M. VA 32nd Inf. Co.C Cpl.
Walthall, Junius L. AL 12th Inf. Co.I AQM
Walthall, Junius L. AL 62nd Inf. Co.E Capt.
Walthall, Junius L. Gen. & Staff, QM Dept. Capt.
Walthall, J.W. VA 1st (Farinholt's) Res. Co.H
Walthall, J.W. VA Wade's Regt.Loc.Def. Co.A
Walthall, L. MS 2nd Cav. Co.D
Walthall, Lawson B. NC 13th Inf. Co.H Sgt.
Walthall, L.H. GA 1st Cav. Co.B Cpl.
Walthall, Lindsey B. VA 53rd Inf. Co.C 2nd Lt.
Walthall, Lindsey B. VA Inf. Montague's Bn. Co.D Sgt.
Walthall, L.N. AL Gid Nelson Lt.Arty.
Walthall, Lycurgus MS 2nd Part.Rangers Co.C
Walthall, M.H. VA 3rd Cav. Co.D
Walthall, M.H. VA 3rd Res. Co.D
Walthall, M.P. AR 33rd Inf. Co.D
Walthall, R.B. VA 53rd Inf. Co.G
Walthall, R.E. VA Lt.Arty. 38th Bn. Co.C
Walthall, Richard VA Inf. 1st Bn. Co.D
Walthall, Richard B. VA Inf. 5th Bn. Co.B
Walthall, Richard E. VA Lt.Arty. E.J. Anderson's Co.
Walthall, Richard J. VA 54th Inf. Co.E Teamster
Walthall, Robert R. VA 1st Inf. Co.G
Walthall, Rufus TN 6th (Wheeler's) Cav. Co.E
Walthall, Rufus P. MS 26th Inf. Co.C Cpl.
Walthall, Samuel C. AR Inf. Hardy's Regt. Co.D
Walthall, Samuel G. AR 24th Inf. Co.F
Walthall, S.B. MS 5th Inf. Co.H
Walthall, S.H. VA 5th Cav. Co.D
Walthall, Silas L. VA 4th Inf. Co.G
Walthall, Thomas B. VA 23rd Inf. Co.B
Walthall, Thomas W. LA 8th Inf. Co.B Jr.2nd Lt.
Walthall, T.M. AL Gid Nelson Lt.Arty.
Walthall, T.W. TN Inf. 4th Cons.Regt. Co.G Cpl.
Walthall, W.D. Gen. & Staff Maj.,AAG
Walthall, W.F. TN 3rd (Forrest's) Cav. 1st Co.B
Walthall, W.H. Hosp.Stew.
Walthall, William VA 3rd Res. Co.D Sgt.
Walthall, William A. TN 40th Inf. Co.F
Walthall, William E. VA Arty. Dance's Co.
Walthall, William F. TX 27th Cav. Co.D
Walthall, William H. MO St.Guard
Walthall, William H. TN 49th Inf. Co.A
Walthall, William H. VA 4th Inf. Co.G
Walthall, William H. Gen. & Staff Hosp.Stew.
Walthall, William M. VA 6th Inf. Co.I
Walthall, William S. VA 18th Inf. Co.D
Walthall, William S. VA Inf. 25th Bn. Co.C
Walthall, William T. AL 12th Inf. Co.I Capt.
Walthall, W.J. AL Gid Nelson Lt.Arty.
Walthall, W.J. AL Cp. of Instr. Talladega
Walthall, W.J. VA 14th Inf. Co.I
Walthall, W.J. VA 20th Inf. Co.C
Walthall, W.M. GA 1st Cav. Co.K
Walthall, W.T. Gen. & Staff Maj.,AIG
Waltham, Elisha E. NC 3rd Inf. Co.K
Waltham, John D. NC 3rd Inf. Co.K
Waltham, Seth NC 1st Inf. Co.E
Walthan, J.M. AR Inf. Cocke's Regt. Co.D
Walther, C. LA 1st (Nelligan's) Inf. Co.C
Walther, Ernst VA Inf. 6th Bn.Loc.Def. Co.C
Walther, Frederick VA 2nd Inf. Co.D
Walther, George VA 6th Inf. 1st Co.E, Co.D
Walther, John TX Cav. 8th (Taylor's) Bn. Co.C
Walther, R. SC Arty. Stuart's Co. (Beaufort Vol.Arty.)
Walther, R. SC 11th Inf. Co.A
Walther, Richard GA 1st (Olmstead's) Inf. Co.C
Walther, William TX Cav. 8th (Taylor's) Bn. Co.C
Walthers, James AL 19th Inf. Co.A
Walthers, Joseph H. LA 28th (Gray's) Inf. Co.G Cpl.
Walthersdorff, A. TX 5th Field Btty.
Walthersdorff, A. Gen. & Staff,PACS Maj.
Walthersdorff, Albert TX Cav. 8th (Taylor's) Bn. Co.C Sgt.
Walthour, A. GA Cav. 1st Bn. Winn's Co., Walthour's Co. Sgt.
Walthour, A. GA 5th Cav. Co.G
Walthour, Andrew Gen. & Staff A.Surg.
Walthour, G.H. GA 54th Inf. Co.I
Walthour, R. GA Cav. 1st Bn. Walthour's Co.
Walthour, R.H. GA Cav. 1st Bn. Winn's Co.
Walthour, R.H. GA 5th Cav. Co.G
Walthour, Russel GA Cav. 1st Bn. Winn's Co., Walthour's Co. Sgt.
Walthour, Russell GA 5th Cav. Co.G Sgt.
Walthour, T. GA 5th Cav. Co.G
Walthour, W.L. GA Cav. 1st Bn. Winn's Co., Walthour's Co. Capt.
Walthour, W.L. GA 5th Cav. Co.G Capt.
Walthrop, E.F. TN 16th (Logwood's) Cav. Co.I
Walthrop, Newton TN 10th Inf. Co.D
Walthrop, W.W. TN 1st Inf. Co.D
Walthus, George VA 1st Inf. Co.G
Waltman, Adam MS 2nd (Quinn's St.Troops) Inf. Co.A
Waltman, A.E. MS Cav. 1st Bn. (McNair's) St.Troops Co.C
Waltman, Archebald MS Inf. 2nd St.Troops Co.F
Waltman, A.V. MS Inf. (Res.) Berry's Co.
Waltman, Daniel J. MS 16th Inf. Co.B
Waltman, D.H. MS 1st Cav.Res. Co.H
Waltman, D.H. MS 5th Inf. (St.Troops) Co.H
Waltman, E. MS Cav. Yerger's Regt. Co.B
Waltman, Elijah W. MS 37th Inf. Co.C
Waltman, E.P. MS 36th Inf. Co.B
Waltman, James R. MS 14th Inf. Co.A
Waltman, John MS 1st Cav. Res. Co.H Cpl.
Waltman, John MS Inf. 2nd St.Troops Co.F
Waltman, John J. MS 14th Inf. Co.A
Waltman, John W. TX Cav. 6th Bn. Co.D Cpl.
Waltman, L. MS 5th Inf. (St.Troops) Co.D
Waltman, Levi MS 1st Cav.Res. Co.H
Waltman, M. GA 1st (Olmstead's) Inf.
Waltman, R.N. MS Cav. Yerger's Regt. Co.B
Waltom, J.B. GA 42nd Inf. Co.K
Waltom, J.B.L. GA 7th Inf. (St.Guards) Co.H
Waltom, Madison C. GA 7th Inf. Co.A
Waltom, P.M. GA 7th Inf. Co.A
Waltom, P.M. GA 7th Inf. (St.Guards) Co.H Cpl.
Waltom, Robert AL 29th Inf. Co.E
Walton, --- AL 22nd Inf. Co.B
Walton, --- GA 7th Inf. Co.D
Walton, --- TX Cav. 4th Regt.St.Troops Co.F
Walton, --- VA VMI Co.C
Walton, A. MO Searcy's Bn.S.S.
Walton, Aaron MS 36th Inf. Co.B
Walton, A.B. MS 4th Cav. Co.K
Walton, A.B. MS Cav. Hughes' Bn. Co.H
Walton, A.B. SC 8th Inf. Co.L
Walton, A.B. 7th Conf.Cav. Co.L
Walton, Adolphus MS 43rd Inf. Co.L Sgt.
Walton, Adolphus D. VA 60th Inf. 1st Co.H
Walton, A.E. AL 11th Inf. Co.I
Walton, A.J. TN 18th (Newsom's) Cav. Co.C
Walton, A.J. TN 19th (Biffle's) Cav. Co.C
Walton, Alfred F. NC 14th Inf. Co.F
Walton, Amos NC 3rd Inf. Co.E
Walton, Anderson A. VA 19th Inf. Co.D
Walton, Andrew G. VA 23rd Inf. Co.A
Walton, Andrew J. AL 32nd Inf. Co.H
Walton, Andrew J. AL 32nd & 58th (Cons.) Inf.
Walton, Andrew J. NC 24th Inf. Co.I
Walton, Andrew J. TN Cav. Newsom's Regt. Co.D
Walton, Andrew W. VA 13th Inf. Co.D
Walton, Archer VA Hvy.Arty. 10th Bn. Co.C
Walton, Archer T. VA 60th Inf. 1st Co.H
Walton, Archer Thomas VA 10th Cav. Co.I
Walton, A.T. NC 57th Inf. Co.K
Walton, Augustus T. MS 17th Inf. Co.F 1st Sgt.

Walton, Aug. T. MS 34th Inf. Co.E Capt.
Walton, A.W. GA Inf. 1st Loc.Troops (Augusta) Co.C
Walton, A.W. GA 1st (Symons') Res. Co.I 1st Lt.
Walton, A.W. LA Inf. 4th Bn. Co.E Cpl.
Walton, A.Y. TX Cav. 3rd Bn.St.Troops Co.E 2nd Lt.
Walton, A.Y. TX 20th Inf. Co.C
Walton, B. VA Inf. 1st Bn.Loc.Def. Co.C
Walton, Benjamin MO 5th Inf. Co.C
Walton, Benjamin VA 2nd Inf.Loc.Def. Co.B
Walton, Benjamin VA Inf. 2nd Bn.Loc.Def. Co.D
Walton, Benjamin H. AL 47th Inf. Co.D
Walton, Benjamin H. TX 35th (Brown's) Cav. Co.D
Walton, Benjamin H. TX 13th Vol. 2nd Co.C
Walton, Benjamin J. VA 23rd Inf. Co.A Capt.
Walton, Benjamin T. VA 52nd Inf. Co.K Capt.
Walton, Benjamin W. VA Lt.Arty. B.Z. Price's Co.
Walton, B.F. AR 9th Inf. Co.G
Walton, B.F. NC 31st Inf. Co.D 1st Lt.
Walton, B.F. NC 46th Inf. Co.B
Walton, B.F. VA 88th Mil.
Walton, B.F. Gen. & Staff Asst.Surg.
Walton, B.J. VA Hvy.Arty. 18th Bn. Co.B
Walton, B.J. VA Mtd.Guard 3rd Congr.Dist.
Walton, B.M. MS 34th Inf. Co.C
Walton, Bryant GA 3rd Inf. Co.D
Walton, Bryant GA Cobb's Legion Co.G
Walton, B.T. TN Cav. Napier's Bn. Co.A
Walton, B.T. VA Inf. 1st Bn.Loc.Def. Co.D
Walton, B.W. TX 9th Field Btty.
Walton, B.W. VA 3rd Res. Co.G
Walton, C. MS 18th Cav. Co.H
Walton, C. MS 33rd Inf. Co.F
Walton, Carroll TX 8th Cav. Co.D
Walton, Charles NC McDugald's Co.
Walton, Charles VA 19th Inf. Co.F
Walton, Charles H. MS 18th Inf. Co.E
Walton, Charles H. MO
Walton, Charles K. VA Lt.Arty. 12th Bn. 2nd Co.A
Walton, Charles K. VA Lt.Arty. Sturdivant's Co.
Walton, Charles S. VA 23rd Inf. Co.A
Walton, Christ VA 12th Inf. Co.G
Walton, C.M. AR 19th Inf. Co.B
Walton, C.M. VA 16th Inf. Co.E
Walton, C.N.M. MS Inf. 7th Bn. Co.D Cpl.
Walton, Cornelison M. TX 11th Inf. Co.D
Walton, C.T. 7th Conf.Cav. Co.E
Walton, C.W. MO 6th Cav. Co.C
Walton, Daniel AL 32nd Inf. Co.H,E
Walton, Daniel GA 3rd Res. Co.A
Walton, David A. MS Cav. Jeff Davis Legion Co.B
Walton, David A.T. TX 21st Cav. Co.K Jr.2nd Lt.
Walton, David F. VA Lt.Arty. 12th Bn. 2nd Co.A
Walton, David F. VA Lt.Arty. Sturdivant's Co.
Walton, David H. VA 33rd Inf. Co.K Capt.
Walton, David S. SC 2nd Inf. Co.B
Walton, David S. SC 3rd Res. Co.B Sgt.
Walton, David Smith SC 16th Inf. Co.A
Walton, David W. GA 9th Inf. Co.K
Walton, D.D. TN 46th Inf. Co.D
Walton, D.D. TX 1st Inf. Co.A
Walton, D.D. TX 18th Inf. Co.D Adj.
Walton, D.D. Gen. & Staff 1st Lt.,Adj.
Walton, D.S. SC 16th & 24th (Cons.) Inf. Music.
Walton, E. MS Cav. Abbott's Co.
Walton, E. MO Cav. Snider's Bn. Co.A Cpl.
Walton, E.A. GA Inf. 27th Bn. (NonConscr.) Co.A Cpl.
Walton, E.A. GA Inf. (NonConscr.) Howard's Co. Cpl.
Walton, E.A. MS 4th Cav. Co.D
Walton, E.A. MS Cav. Hughes' Bn. Co.C
Walton, E.A. 7th Conf.Cav. Co.D
Walton, Eagan R. VA Lt.Arty. 12th Bn. 2nd Co.A
Walton, Eagan R. VA Lt.Arty. Sturdivant's Co.
Walton, Edmond J. GA 6th Inf. (St.Guards) Co.C
Walton, Edward VA Cav. 39th Bn. Co.D
Walton, Edward B. MO 1st Inf. Co.H
Walton, Edward J. MS 11th Inf. Co.G Music.
Walton, Edward Lee LA Inf. 1st Sp.Bn. (Rightor's) Co.A
Walton, Edw. Lee VA 4th Inf. Co.B
Walton, Edward P. VA 5th Inf. Chap.
Walton, Edward S. NC Cav. 5th Bn. Co.C
Walton, Edwin MO Inf. Clark's Regt. Co.H
Walton, Edwin S. MS Lt.Arty. (The Hudson Btty.) Hoole's Co. 1st Lt.
Walton, E.H. MO Inf. 3rd Bn. Co.B
Walton, E.H. MO 6th Inf. Co.A Cpl.
Walton, E.J. GA 6th Inf. Co.I
Walton, E.J. TN 20th Inf. Co.B
Walton, E.L. AL Arty. Stribbling's Btty. QMSgt.
Walton, Eldred P. VA 46th Inf. 2nd Co.C
Walton, Elihu GA 12th Inf. Co.F
Walton, Ellis J. GA Inf. 27th Bn. Co.B
Walton, Enoch AL 22nd Inf. Co.A
Walton, Enoch MS 36th Inf. Co.D
Walton, E.P. KY 4th Mtd.Inf. Chap.
Walton, E.R. VA 88th Mil.
Walton, E.R. Gen. & Staff Chap.
Walton, Erasmus VA 56th Inf. Co.H
Walton, Erasmus T. VA 57th Inf. Co.H
Walton, E.S. GA 3rd Cav. (St.Guards) Co.C
Walton, E.S.W. TN Inf. 1st Cons.Regt. Co.E
Walton, E.S.W. TN 9th Inf. Co.H
Walton, Everod H. MO 10th Cav. Co.E,F
Walton, F.B. MS 12th Cav. Co.E
Walton, F.M. MO Cav. 3rd Bn. Co.E
Walton, F.M. MO 16th Inf. Co.K
Walton, Franklin B. TN 19th (Biffle's) Cav. Asst.Surg.
Walton, Friedrich TX 3rd Inf. Co.K
Walton, G. TX 4th Cav. Co.B
Walton, G.A. MS Cav. 1st Bn. (Montgomery's) St.Troops Cameron's Co.
Walton, G.A. MS St.Troops (Herndon Rangers) Montgomery's Ind.Co. Sgt.
Walton, G.B. MS Cav. Williams' Co.
Walton, G.B. MS 36th Inf. Co.I
Walton, G.B., Jr. MS 36th Inf. Co.D
Walton, G.E.M. VA 2nd Bn.Res. Co.B
Walton, George AL Cav. Murphy's Bn. Co.B
Walton, George AL Inf. 2nd Regt. Co.D
Walton, George AL 32nd & 58th (Cons.) Inf.
Walton, George GA 27th Inf. Co.B
Walton, George GA 59th Inf. Co.E
Walton, George KY 4th Mtd.Inf. Co.B
Walton, George MS 7th Cav. Co.A
Walton, George MS Lt.Arty. (Issaquena Arty.) Graves' Co.
Walton, George VA 27th Inf. Co.F
Walton, George 15th Conf.Cav. Co.G
Walton, George A. NC 42nd Inf. Co.B
Walton, George C. GA 5th Inf. Co.A
Walton, George D. NC Hvy.Arty. 10th Bn. Co.A
Walton, George E.M. VA 56th Inf. Co.C
Walton, George E.T. VA 1st Arty. Co.H
Walton, George F. MS 1st (Johnston's) Inf. Co.A Sgt.
Walton, George H. GA Inf. 18th Bn. Co.A
Walton, George L. LA 25th Inf. Co.F Capt.
Walton, George S. TX 16th Inf. Co.H Sr.2nd Lt.
Walton, George W. AR 15th (Josey's) Inf. Co.D
Walton, George W. GA 4th Inf. Co.A
Walton, George W. TN 12th (Green's) Cav.
Walton, George W. TN 30th Inf. Co.F
Walton, George W. VA Arty. Paris' Co.
Walton, George W. VA 9th Inf. Co.D Sgt.
Walton, George Washington VA 10th Cav. Co.I
Walton, G.E.T. VA Arty. C.F. Johnston's Co.
Walton, G.L. MS Lt.Arty. English's Co.
Walton, G.L. 7th Conf.Cav. Co.L
Walton, G.P. MO 10th Inf. Co.I
Walton, Green B. MS 11th (Perrin's) Cav. Co.K
Walton, Greenwood A. VA 53rd Inf. Co.I
Walton, G.W. AL 38th Inf. Co.I
Walton, G.W. KY Lt.Arty. Cobb's Co.
Walton, G.W. TN 7th (Duckworth's) Cav. Co.I Cpl.
Walton, G.W. TX 2nd Inf. Co.G
Walton, H. NC 27th Inf.
Walton, H.A. GA 2nd Inf. Co.K
Walton, H.C. TX 23rd Cav. Co.C
Walton, Henry AR 1st (Monroe's) Cav. Co.F
Walton, Henry AR 15th (N.W.) Inf. Co.B
Walton, Henry MS 3rd (St.Troops) Cav. Co.B
Walton, Henry TX 19th Cav. Co.K
Walton, Henry VA 9th Inf. Co.I Cpl.
Walton, Henry A. LA 31st Inf. Co.C
Walton, Henry C. VA 4th Cav. Co.E
Walton, Henry H. GA 8th Inf. (St.Guards) Co.D
Walton, Henry M. GA 5th Inf. Co.A
Walton, Henry M. VA 17th Cav. Co.E
Walton, H.F. MS 38th Cav. Co.H
Walton, H.H. GA Cav. 1st Bn.Res. Tufts' Co. Sgt.
Walton, H.H. GA 53rd Inf. Co.K
Walton, H.J. AL Lowndes Rangers Vol. Fagg's Co.
Walton, H.J. Conf.Cav. Wood's Regt. Co.H
Walton, H.P. MS 28th Cav. Co.A
Walton, Isaac TN 9th (Ward's) Cav. Co.B Sgt.
Walton, Isaac VA 28th Inf. Co.H
Walton, Isaac VA Burks' Regt.Loc.Def.
Walton, Isaac D. MS 15th Inf. Co.H
Walton, Isaac H. VA Inf. 5th Bn. Co.F
Walton, Isaac H. VA 53rd Inf. Co.F

Walton, Isaac H. 8th (Dearing's) Conf.Cav. Co.E
Walton, Isaiah GA 3rd Res. Co.A
Walton, Isham C. VA 24th Cav. Co.A
Walton, Isham C. VA Cav. 40th Bn. Co.A
Walton, J. AL 2nd Bn. Hilliard's Legion Vol. Co.D
Walton, J. KY Morgan's Men
Walton, J. VA 58th Inf. Co.B
Walton, Jacob SC 2nd Arty. Co.K,E
Walton, James AL 29th Inf. Co.E
Walton, James AL 1st Bn. Hilliard's Legion Vol. Co.A
Walton, James AR 2nd Inf. Co.E,K 1st Sgt.
Walton, James AR 11th Inf. Co.A Cpl.
Walton, James AR 11th & 17th (Cons.) Inf. Co.A
Walton, James FL 3rd Inf. Co.E
Walton, James GA Inf. 1st Bn. (St.Guards) Co.B
Walton, James GA 47th Inf. Co.A
Walton, James MS 2nd Cav. Co.I
Walton, James MS 1st (Patton's) Inf. Co.B Cpl.
Walton, James MO 10th Inf. Co.I
Walton, James TN 1st (Turney's) Inf. Co.I
Walton, James TX 8th Inf. Co.G
Walton, James VA 6th Cav. Co.K
Walton, James VA 21st Cav. 2nd Co.G
Walton, James VA 26th Inf.
Walton, James 8th (Wade's) Conf.Cav. Co.B
Walton, James 3rd Conf.Eng.Troops Co.C
Walton, James B. LA Washington Arty.Bn. Col.
Walton, James B. MS 30th Inf. Co.F
Walton, James B. Gen. & Staff, Arty. Lt.Col.
Walton, James C. MS 1st (Johnston's) Inf. Co.A
Walton, James E. AL 53rd (Part.Rangers) Co.B
Walton, James E. AL Inf. 1st Regt. Co.E
Walton, James F. GA 7th Inf. Co.K
Walton, James F. MS 29th Inf. Co.K Capt.
Walton, James F. Gen. & Staff ACS
Walton, Jas. F. Gen. & Staff Hosp.Stew.
Walton, James H. AL Inf. 2nd Regt. Co.D
Walton, James H. AL 28th Inf. Co.I
Walton, James H. AL 38th Inf. Co.I
Walton, James L. MO 5th Cav. Co.A
Walton, James L. TN 33rd Inf. Co.D
Walton, James M. FL Milton Lt.Arty. Dunham's Co.
Walton, James M. MS 29th Inf. Co.K Cpl.
Walton, James M. MO 5th Inf. Co.C Sgt.
Walton, James M. NC Cav. 14th Bn. Co.C
Walton, James M. NC 14th Inf. Co.F
Walton, James M. VA Lt.Arty. Griffin's Co. Sgt.
Walton, James M. VA 9th Inf. 1st Co.A Sgt.Maj.
Walton, James N. AR 10th Inf. Co.A
Walton, James N. AR 36th Inf. Co.F
Walton, James P. VA 2nd Inf.Loc.Def. Co.B 1st Sgt.
Walton, James P. VA Inf. 2nd Bn.Loc.Def. Co.D 1st Sgt.
Walton, James R. MO 1st Cav. Co.A 2nd Lt.
Walton, James R. MO 5th Cav. Co.A 2nd Lt.
Walton, James R. MO Inf. 2nd Regt.St.Guard Co.H 1st Lt.
Walton, James R. NC 1st Inf. Co.A
Walton, James T. GA 3rd Cav. Co.C 1st Sgt.
Walton, James T. NC 3rd Cav. (41st St.Troops) Co.F Sgt.
Walton, James T. NC 33rd Inf. Co.K Capt.
Walton, James T. VA 53rd Inf. Co.F
Walton, James T. VA Inf. Montague's Bn. Co.C
Walton, James W. GA 20th Inf. Co.B
Walton, James W. NC 1st Arty. (10th St.Troops) Co.E
Walton, James W. TX 13th Cav. Co.A
Walton, James W. VA 4th Res. Co.I
Walton, James W. VA 53rd Inf. Co.F Cpl.
Walton, James W. VA 54th Inf. Co.I
Walton, James W.C. VA Inf. 5th Bn. Co.F
Walton, Jasper MS 18th Cav. Co.K
Walton, J.B. GA Inf. 27th Bn. (NonConscr.) Co.E
Walton, J.B. GA 53rd Inf. Co.D
Walton, J.B. LA 10th Inf. Co.G
Walton, J.B. MO 12th Cav. Co.K 3rd Lt.
Walton, J.B. TN 1st (Carter's) Cav.
Walton, J.B. TN 42nd Inf. Co.G Capt.
Walton, J.C. AR Cav. Gordon's Regt. Co.I
Walton, J.C. AR 16th Inf. Co.A
Walton, J.C. MS 36th Inf. Co.D
Walton, J.C. SC 7th Inf. 2nd Co.G
Walton, J.D. MS 3rd Cav. Co.E
Walton, J.E. AR 30th Inf. Co.D
Walton, J.E. GA 12th Cav. Co.H Cpl.
Walton, Jerome KY 7th Cav. Co.F
Walton, Jesse VA 21st Cav. 2nd Co.G
Walton, Jesse VA 33rd Inf. Co.B
Walton, Jesse A. GA 27th Inf. Co.B
Walton, Jessee MS Blythe's Bn. (St.Troops) Co.A
Walton, Jessee NC 3rd Cav. (41st St.Troops) Co.F
Walton, Jesse L. VA 54th Inf. Co.I
Walton, Jesse R. VA 1st Arty. Co.H
Walton, Jesse S. TX 13th Vol. Co.E Sgt.
Walton, Jesse W. NC 3rd Inf. Co.E
Walton, J.F. AL 55th Vol. Co.D
Walton, J.F. GA 53rd Inf. Co.D
Walton, J.F. MS 9th Cav. Co.F
Walton, J.F. MS 10th Cav. Co.A
Walton, J.F. SC Inf. 7th Bn. (Enfield Rifles) Co.H
Walton, J.F. TN Cav. 17th Bn. (Sanders') Co.C
Walton, J.F. TN 3rd (Lillard's) Mtd.Inf. Co.G
Walton, J.F. TX 20th Cav. Co.A 2nd Lt.
Walton, J.F. VA 88th Mil.
Walton, J.F. Hosp.Stew.
Walton, J.G. TN 3rd (Forrest's) Cav. Co.K
Walton, J.H. AL 38th Inf. Co.I
Walton, J.H. AL 43rd Inf. Co.D
Walton, J.H. GA 62nd Cav. Co.L
Walton, J.H. KY Cav. 2nd Bn. (Dortch's) Co.A
Walton, J.H. TN 9th (Ward's) Cav. Co.B
Walton, J.H. VA 24th Cav. Co.K
Walton, J.H. VA 22nd Inf. Co.I
Walton, J.H.C. MS 32nd Inf. Co.A
Walton, J.J. MS Inf. 2nd St.Troops Co.D
Walton, J.K.T. TX 4th Cav. Co.H
Walton, J.K.T. TX 5th Cav. Co.D 1st Sgt.
Walton, J.K.T. TX St.Troops Hampton's Co.
Walton, J.L. KY 1st Inf. Co.E
Walton, J.L. MS 4th Cav.Mil. Co.D Jr.2nd Lt.
Walton, J.L. MS St.Troops (Peach Creek Rangers) Maxwell's Co. Sgt.
Walton, J.L. MS Cav. Polk's Ind.Co. (Polk Rangers) 1st Lt.
Walton, J.L. TN 20th Inf. Co.D
Walton, J.L. TX 20th Cav. Co.G
Walton, J.L. TX Cav. Morgan's Regt. Co.F
Walton, J.L. VA 21st Cav. Co.B
Walton, J. Long MS 10th Cav. Co.C
Walton, J.M. AL Mobile Fire Bn. Mullany's Co.
Walton, J.M. NC 1st Inf. (6 mo. '61) Co.G
Walton, J.M. SC Mil. 17th Regt. Staff Sgt.
Walton, J.M. TN 18th (Newsom's) Cav. Co.C
Walton, J.N. AR 10th Inf. Co.A
Walton, J.N. KY 5th Cav. Co.G Sgt.
Walton, John AL Lt.Arty. 2nd Bn. Co.E
Walton, John AL 29th Inf. Co.E
Walton, John AL 42nd Inf. Co.G
Walton, John AR 1st (Monroe's) Cav. Co.F
Walton, John AR 2nd Inf. Co.E,D
Walton, John AR 5th Inf. Co.F
Walton, John GA 9th Inf. (St.Guards) Co.A
Walton, John KY 2nd (Duke's) Cav. Co.E
Walton, John LA 30th Inf. Co.F,G
Walton, John LA Mil. Bragg's Bn. Schwartz's Co.
Walton, John LA Miles' Legion Co.H
Walton, John MS 1st Cav.Res. Co.D Cpl.
Walton, John MS 9th Inf. New Co.K
Walton, John MO Cav. 3rd Bn. Co.G 1st Lt.
Walton, John MO 15th Cav. Co.A
Walton, John MO 12th Inf. Co.H
Walton, John NC 26th Inf.
Walton, John VA 3rd Bn. Valley Res. Co.A
Walton, John VA 7th Inf. Co.I
Walton, John VA 19th Inf. Co.K
Walton, John VA 53rd Inf. Co.F
Walton, John VA 59th Inf. 3rd Co.I
Walton, John 8th (Wade's) Conf.Cav. Co.B
Walton, John Mead's Conf.Cav. Co.K
Walton, John A. AL 32nd Inf. Co.H 2nd Lt.
Walton, John A. AL 32nd & 58th (Cons.) Inf. 2nd Lt.
Walton, John A. VA 18th Cav. 2nd Co.G
Walton, John A. VA 52nd Inf. Co.K
Walton, John B. GA 27th Inf. Co.B Sgt.
Walton, John B. GA 61st Inf. Co.I
Walton, John B. MS 14th Inf. Co.E Sgt.
Walton, John B. MS 43rd Inf. Co.G,C Capt.
Walton, John B. MO 16th Inf. Co.A
Walton, John C. KY 1st Bn.Mtd.Rifles Co.A
Walton, John E. KY 4th Cav.
Walton, John F. MO 9th (Elliott's) Cav. Co.B
Walton, John F. VA 3rd Cav. Co.K
Walton, John G.R. AL 6th Inf. Co.L
Walton, John H. GA 3rd Cav. (St.Guards) Co.C 3rd Lt.
Walton, John H. VA 53rd Inf. Co.F
Walton, John H. VA 79th Mil. Co.B
Walton, John H. VA Inf. Montague's Bn. Co.C
Walton, John H.H. NC 3rd Cav. (41st St.Troops) Co.I
Walton, John J. AL 40th Inf. Co.G
Walton, John J. MS 12th Inf. Co.I
Walton, John J. MS 16th Inf. Co.F Capt.
Walton, John L. AL 47th Inf. Co.D
Walton, John L. MS 10th Inf. Old Co.A

Walton, John M. NC 6th Inf. Co.B 2nd Lt.
Walton, John M. TN Cav. 7th Bn. (Bennett's) Co.D
Walton, John M. TN 22nd (Barteau's) Cav. Co.F
Walton, John N. VA 57th Inf. Co.H
Walton, John S. VA Cav. 4th Bn. Co.E
Walton, John S. VA 11th Cav. Co.G
Walton, John S. VA 17th Cav. Co.C
Walton, John S. VA 62nd Mtd.Inf. 2nd Co.A
Walton, John S.J. MS 12th Inf. Co.I
Walton, Johnson KY 2nd Bn.Mtd.Rifles Co.C
Walton, John T. AR 9th Inf. Co.H Sgt.Maj.
Walton, John T. GA 7th Inf. Co.K 2nd Lt.
Walton, John T. MS 29th Inf. Co.K
Walton, John T. VA Lt.Arty. 12th Bn. 2nd Co.A
Walton, John T. VA Lt.Arty. Sturdivant's Co.
Walton, John W. AL 24th Inf. Co.I
Walton, John W. GA 6th Inf. Co.B
Walton, John W. MS 1st (Johnston's) Inf. Co.D
Walton, John W. TX 3rd Inf. 1st Co.C 1st Lt.
Walton, John W. VA 2nd Cav. Co.B,H
Walton, John W. VA 9th Inf. Co.D
Walton, John W. VA 34th Inf. Co.K
Walton, John W. VA 41st Inf. Co.A
Walton, Joseph NC 33rd Inf. Co.E
Walton, Joseph VA 12th Cav. Co.K
Walton, Joseph A. NC 31st Inf. Co.D
Walton, Joseph A. VA 9th Inf. Co.K
Walton, Joseph A. Sig.Corps,CSA
Walton, Joseph B. VA Inf. Cohoon's Bn. Co.B Cpl.
Walton, Joseph C. MO 4th Cav. Co.E Sgt.
Walton, Joseph E. VA 53rd Inf. Co.C 2nd Lt.
Walton, Joseph E. VA Inf. Montague's Bn. Co.D
Walton, Joseph F. VA 19th Cav. Co.F
Walton, Joseph F. VA 2nd Cav.St.Line McNeel's Co.
Walton, Joseph G. TN Cav. Newsom's Regt. Co.D
Walton, Joseph J. AR 3rd Inf. (St.Troops) Co.A
Walton, Joseph W. VA Lt.Arty. Montgomery's Co.
Walton, Joseph W. VA Lt.Arty. Wimbish's Co.
Walton, Joshua Mead's Conf.Cav. Co.K
Walton, Joshua B. TN 6th (Wheeler's) Cav. Co.C
Walton, Joshua B. TN Cav. 11th Bn. (Gordon's) Co.E
Walton, Josiah KY 13th Cav. Co.B
Walton, Josiah TX 19th Cav. Co.F
Walton, J.P. LA 10th Inf. Co.E Cpl.
Walton, J.P. MS 28th Cav. Co.A
Walton, J.P. TN 20th Inf. Co.D
Walton, J.R. MS Cav. Hughes' Bn. Co.H
Walton, J. Rice VA 49th Inf. Co.D
Walton, J.T. GA Siege Arty. 28th Bn. Co.I 2nd Lt.
Walton, J.T. GA 64th Inf. Co.F
Walton, J.T. MO 5th Cav. Co.A Sr.2nd Lt.
Walton, J.T. NC 1st Inf. (6 mo. '61) Co.G
Walton, J.W. AL 4th Cav. Co.A
Walton, J.W. KY 3rd Bn.Mtd.Rifles Co.H
Walton, J.W. NC McLean's Bn.Lt.Duty Men Co.B
Walton, J.W. TN 10th (DeMoss') Cav. Co.D
Walton, J.W. TN 12th (Green's) Cav. Co.E
Walton, J.W. TN Cav. Napier's Bn. Co.A
Walton, J.W. TN 50th Inf. Co.F
Walton, J.W. VA 21st Cav. Co.B
Walton, J.W. VA 88th Mil.
Walton, Killis LA 16th Inf. Co.C Cpl.
Walton, Lamar VA 12th Cav. Co.K
Walton, Lamar VA 136th Mil. Co.G
Walton, L.C. AR 2nd Mtd.Rifles Co.A Far.
Walton, L.C. GA 2nd Inf. Co.K
Walton, L.D. GA 8th Cav. New Co.E
Walton, L.D. GA Cav. 20th Bn. Co.C
Walton, Leander J. TX 13th Cav. Co.H
Walton, Lemuel B. GA 57th Inf. Co.F
Walton, Lemuel R. VA 26th Inf. Co.G
Walton, L.J. AR Cav. Gordon's Regt. Co.D
Walton, L.J. AR 10th Mil. Co.B
Walton, L.M. AL Gid Nelson Lt.Arty.
Walton, L.M. AL 17th Inf. Co.G Sgt.
Walton, L.M. TN 20th (Russell's) Cav. Co.E
Walton, L.M. TN 46th Inf.
Walton, Loftin N. VA 50th Inf. Co.D
Walton, Lorenzo D. VA 55th Inf. Co.G,K
Walton, Lucius D. VA 3rd Cav. Co.K Sgt.
Walton, Lucius E. VA 23rd Inf. Co.A
Walton, L.W. NC 42nd Inf. Co.B Music.
Walton, M. AL 10th Inf. Co.G
Walton, Madison C. GA 13th Cav. Co.B
Walton, Marcellus M. VA 1st Arty. 3rd Co.C
Walton, Marcellus M. VA Lt.Arty. 1st Bn. Co.C
Walton, Marion AR Inf. Cocke's Regt. Co.I
Walton, Marion SC Inf. Hampton Legion Co.B
Walton, Mathew P. VA Lt.Arty. 12th Bn. 2nd Co.A
Walton, Mathew P. VA Lt.Arty. Sturdivant's Co.
Walton, Meredith TX 33rd Cav. Co.C 2nd Lt.
Walton, Meredith TX 13th Vol. 2nd Co.C
Walton, M.G. TN 33rd Inf. Co.C
Walton, Minjam H. VA Hvy.Arty. 10th Bn. Co.A
Walton, Mitchell VA 63rd Inf. Co.C
Walton, M.J. NC 57th Inf. Co.A
Walton, M.L. LA 25th Inf. Co.B
Walton, M.M. VA Arty. Young's Co.
Walton, Mordecai VA 62nd Mtd.Inf. 1st Co.A
Walton, Nanthiel MS 36th Inf. Co.D
Walton, Nathaniel G. AR 1st (Colquitt's) Inf. Co.K,H
Walton, Nathaniel W. VA Cav. 39th Bn. Co.D Sgt.
Walton, Nathan T. VA Lt.Arty. Parker's Co.
Walton, N.B. MS 29th Inf. Co.K
Walton, Newell J. VA 56th Inf. Co.H
Walton, N.G. GA 5th Cav. Co.C
Walton, N.S. KY Jessee's Bn.Mtd.Riflemen Co.B
Walton, N.T. Davis' Staff Lt.,ADC
Walton, O.B. TX 37th Cav. 2nd Co.D Cpl.
Walton, Olinthus VA 3rd Cav. Co.C
Walton, P.A. TX 15th Inf. Co.K
Walton, Park M. TX 37th Cav. Co.F
Walton, Peter TN 4th (McLemore's) Cav. Co.F
Walton, Peter M. NC 24th Inf. Co.C
Walton, Peter W. GA 3rd Inf. Co.D
Walton, Phillip M. NC 26th Inf. Co.A
Walton, Pierce W. MO 10th Cav. Co.B
Walton, P.K. KY 2nd Bn.Mtd.Rifles Co.C
Walton, P.M. GA 53rd Inf. Co.D
Walton, P.M. TX Cav. Terry's Regt. Co.A
Walton, Presley K. KY 2nd Mtd.Inf. Co.C
Walton, Presley T. VA 12th Inf. 2nd Co.I
Walton, R.B. MS Inf. 2nd Bn. Co.H
Walton, Reuben VA 26th Inf. Co.G
Walton, Reuben M. VA 8th Bn.Res. Co.B
Walton, R.G. VA 2nd Inf.Loc.Def. Co.B Sgt.
Walton, R.G. VA Inf. 2nd Bn.Loc.Def. Co.D Sgt.
Walton, R.H. AR 2nd Inf. Co.K
Walton, Richard B. NC 42nd Inf. Co.B
Walton, Richard G. AL Mil. 3rd Vol. Co.E
Walton, Richard G. TN 33rd Inf. Co.D
Walton, Richard P. VA 18th Inf. Surg.
Walton, Richard W. MS Cav. Jeff Davis Legion Co.B Cpl.
Walton, Richmond T. VA 19th Inf. Co.B
Walton, R.J. GA Cav. 29th Bn. Co.E
Walton, R.J. TN 7th (Duckworth's) Cav. Co.A
Walton, R.J. TN 13th Inf. Co.C
Walton, R.J. VA 18th Inf.
Walton, Robert GA Inf. 1st Loc.Groops (Augusta) Co.A
Walton, Robert, Jr. GA Inf. 18th Bn. (St.Guards) Co.C
Walton, Robert, Jr. GA Phillips' Legion ACS
Walton, Robert MO 16th Inf. Co.A
Walton, Robert TX 22nd Inf. Co.C
Walton, Robert VA 79th Mil. Co.3
Walton, Robt. Gen. & Staff Capt.,Comsy.
Walton, Robert B. MS 1st Lt.Arty. Co.D Cpl.
Walton, Robert B. MS 48th Inf. Co.H
Walton, Robert H. VA 3rd Cav. Co.K Cpl.
Walton, Robert H. VA 3rd Inf. Co.B Cpl.
Walton, Robert J. TN 7th Inf. Co.D
Walton, Robert J. VA 60th Inf. 1st Co.H
Walton, Robert W. GA 21st Inf. Co.I 1st Lt.
Walton, Ro. H. VA Cav. 1st Bn. (Loc.Def. Troops) Co.A
Walton, R.P. Gen. & Staff,PACS Surg.
Walton, R.T. VA Cav. O'Ferrall's Bn. Co.C
Walton, S.A. MS 18th Cav. Co.F
Walton, Samuel TN 20th Inf. Co.B
Walton, Samuel VA 33rd Inf. Co.G
Walton, Samuel H. NC 33rd Inf. Co.E
Walton, Samuel J. NC 2nd Bn.Loc.Def.Troops Co.D 1st Lt.
Walton, S. Burt MS 34th Inf. Co.C
Walton, Shepherd VA 82nd Mil. Co.C Sgt.Maj.
Walton, Simeone T. VA 23rd Inf. Co.K Lt.Col.
Walton, S.L. AR 12th Bn.S.S. Co.D
Walton, S.L. AR 19th (Dockery's) Inf. Co.C
Walton, S.L. TX 10th Field Btty.
Walton, S.L. TX 17th Inf. Co.I
Walton, S.L. VA Inf. 1st Bn. Co.A
Walton, S.L. VA 42nd Inf. Co.B
Walton, S.O. GA 2nd Inf. Co.K
Walton, Stokes GA 17th Inf. Co.E 2nd Lt.
Walton, S.W. GA 13th Inf. Co.G
Walton, T. AL 8th (Livingston's) Cav. Co.B
Walton, T. MS 22nd Inf. Co.I
Walton, T. TN 15th (Stewart's) Cav. Co.B
Walton, T.A. 7th Conf.Cav. Co.E
Walton, T.G. NC 8th Inf. Col.
Walton, T.H. AL 27th Inf. Co.E
Walton, T.H. GA 31st Inf. Co.F
Walton, T.H. TN 20th (Russell's) Cav. Co.G
Walton, T.H. TN 12th Inf. Co.A Cpl.

Walton, Tho H. MS 34th Inf. Co.E
Walton, Thomas GA Inf. 27th Bn. (NonConscr.) Co.E
Walton, Thomas TN Cav. Newsom's Regt. Co.D
Walton, Thomas TN 32nd Inf. Co.D
Walton, Thomas VA 5th Cav. Co.E
Walton, Thomas VA 6th Inf. Co.B
Walton, Thomas Gen. & Staff Capt.,Comsy.
Walton, Thomas A. GA Arty. 11th Bn. (Sumter Arty.) New Co.C
Walton, Thomas B. AL 44th Inf. Co.C
Walton, Thomas B.S. VA 3rd Cav. Co.G
Walton, Thomas G. NC 3rd Cav. (41st St.Troops) Co.F Capt.
Walton, Thomas H. AL 62nd Inf. Co.D
Walton, Thomas H. MS 3rd Cav. Co.G
Walton, Thomas H. MO 9th (Elliott's) Cav. Co.B Maj.
Walton, Thomas J. MS Inf. 3rd Bn. Co.H
Walton, Thomas J. MO 10th Cav. Co.E
Walton, Thomas J. SC Inf. Hampton Legion Co.F
Walton, Thomas J. TX 26th Cav. Co.D
Walton, Thomas P. VA 50th Inf. Co.D
Walton, Thomas R. TX 31st Cav. Co.G
Walton, Thomas R. VA 5th Cav. (12 mo. '61-2) Co.D
Walton, Thomas R. VA 13th Cav. Co.B
Walton, Thomas R. VA Cav. 47th Bn. Aldredge's Co.
Walton, Thomas R. VA 25th Inf. 1st Co.G
Walton, Thomas R. VA 62nd Mtd.Inf. 2nd Co.A
Walton, Thomas W. MO 9th (Elliott's) Cav. Co.B 2nd Lt.
Walton, Thomas W. NC 2nd Arty. (36th St.Troops) Co.G
Walton, Tilman M. NC 22nd Inf. Co.B
Walton, Tim AL 8th (Livingston's) Cav. Co.B Sgt.
Walton, Timothy AL 4th Inf. Co.D
Walton, Tisdell NC 29th Inf. Co.H
Walton, T.J. GA 61st Inf. Co.G Sgt.
Walton, T.J. MS 3rd Cav. Co.E
Walton, T.J. TN 18th (Newsom's) Cav. Co.K
Walton, T.J. TN 19th & 20th (Cons.) Cav. Co.H 1st Sgt.
Walton, T.J. TN 22nd Inf. Co.B
Walton, T.L. VA 42nd Inf. Co.B
Walton, T.M. AL Lt.Arty. 20th Bn. Co.A
Walton, T.M. TX 26th Cav. 2nd Co.G
Walton, T.M.C.D. GA 3rd Cav. (St.Guards) Co.C
Walton, T.O. MS Scouts Montgomery's Co.
Walton, T.O. TX 10th Cav. Co.D Ord.Sgt.
Walton, T.W. GA Inf. 27th Bn. (NonConscr.) Co.E
Walton, V.E. GA 27th Inf. Co.B Cpl.
Walton, W. MS Rogers' Co.
Walton, W. MO 5th Cav. Co.A
Walton, W.A. AL 17th Inf. Co.C 1st Lt.
Walton, Waldon W. VA 8th Cav. Co.E
Walton, Warren S. GA 1st Reg. Co.B
Walton, Watson L. GA 7th Inf. Co.A
Walton, W.C. VA Lt.Arty. Carrington's Co.
Walton, W.D. MS 14th (Cons.) Inf. Co.I 1st Lt.
Walton, Wesley B. MO 5th Inf. Co.C
Walton, W.G. TX 25th Cav. Co.G
Walton, W.H. AR 51st Mil. Co.B
Walton, W.H. GA 10th Cav. Co.E
Walton, W.H. TN 7th (Duckworth's) Cav. Co.I
Walton, W.H. TX 2nd Inf. Co.G Sgt.
Walton, Wiley GA 50th Inf. Co.D
Walton, Wiley VA 50th Inf. Co.D
Walton, Wiley H. 7th Conf.Cav. Co.E
Walton, Wiley N. GA 3rd Cav. (St.Guards) Co.I Capt.
Walton, William AL 56th Part.Rangers Co.D
Walton, William AL 55th Vol. Co.D
Walton, William AR Inf. 2nd Bn. Co.B
Walton, William AR 10th Mil. Co.B
Walton, William GA 25th Inf. Co.C
Walton, William KY Morehead's Regt. (Part.Rangers) Co.A
Walton, William LA 21st (Patton's) Inf.
Walton, William MS 1st Cav.Res. Co.D
Walton, William MS Cav. Jeff Davis Legion Co.C
Walton, William MS 5th Inf. (St.Troops) Co.E
Walton, William MS 8th Inf. Co.B
Walton, William MS 25th Inf. Co.B
Walton, William MS 36th Inf. Co.D Bvt.2nd Lt.
Walton, William MO Cav. Snider's Bn. Co.A
Walton, William MO 10th Inf. Co.K
Walton, William SC 14th Inf. Co.D
Walton, William TN Lt.Arty. Kain's Co.
Walton, William VA 11th Cav. Co.K
Walton, Wm. VA Hvy.Arty. 20th Bn. Co.E
Walton, William VA 22nd Inf. Co.D
Walton, William VA 26th Inf. Co.C
Walton, William VA 55th Inf. Co.G
Walton, William VA Res.Forces Thurston's Co.
Walton, William 2nd Conf.Inf. Co.B
Walton, William A. AR 2nd Inf. Co.F
Walton, William A. VA 23rd Inf. Co.I Sgt.
Walton, Wm. A. Gen. & Staff Maj.,Comsy.
Walton, William B. TX 14th Cav. Co.D
Walton, William D. GA 3rd Cav. (St.Guards) Co.I 1st Sgt.
Walton, William D. MS 11th Inf. Co.I
Walton, William D. MS 43rd Inf. Co.G 2nd Lt.
Walton, William D. VA 12th Inf. 2nd Co.I Cpl.
Walton, William D. 1st Chickasaw Inf. White's Co.
Walton, William F. AL 37th Inf. Co.I Cpl.
Walton, William F. GA Cav. 2nd Bn. Co.E Sr.2nd Lt.
Walton, William F. GA 5th Cav. Co.C 1st Lt.
Walton, William F. TN 15th Inf. Co.B Sgt.
Walton, William G. VA 56th Inf. Co.F 2nd Lt.
Walton, William H. MS 3rd (St.Troops) Cav. Co.B
Walton, William H. MS 1st (Patton's) Inf. Co.B
Walton, William H. VA 7th Cav. Glenn's Co.
Walton, William H. VA 57th Inf. Co.B
Walton, William H. VA Loc.Def. Scott's Co.
Walton, William H.H. GA 7th Inf. Co.F Cpl.
Walton, William H.H. GA 59th Inf. Co.H
Walton, William J. MS 11th Inf. Co.F
Walton, William J. MS 44th Inf. Co.D
Walton, William J. TN Lt.Arty. Kain's Co.
Walton, William J. TN Conscr. (Cp. of Instr.)
Walton, William J. TX 26th Cav. Co.D
Walton, William J. TX 36th Cav. Co.C
Walton, William J. VA 38th Inf. Co.D
Walton, William Jackson VA 56th Inf. Co.F 2nd Lt.
Walton, William L. GA 57th Inf. Co.F
Walton, William M. NC 22nd Inf. Co.B
Walton, William M. TX 21st Cav. Co.B 1st Lt.
Walton, William N. VA 7th Cav. Glenn's Co. Sgt.
Walton, William P. AL 11th Inf. Co.K Cpl.
Walton, William P. GA Inf. 27th Bn. Co.B
Walton, William P. MO Inf. 2nd Regt.St.Guard QM
Walton, William P. NC 24th Inf. Co.B
Walton, William P. TN 33rd Inf. Co.D
Walton, William R. GA 5th Inf. Co.A,H 2nd Lt.
Walton, William R. GA 20th Inf. Co.B
Walton, William R. MS Gage's Co. (Wigfall Guards)
Walton, William R. VA 20th Cav. Co.B
Walton, William R. VA Lt.Arty. Kirkpatrick's Co. Jr.1st Lt.
Walton, William R. VA Horse Arty. Lurty's Co.
Walton, William R. Conf.Arty. Nelson's Bn. Co.A Jr.1st Lt.
Walton, William T. AL 37th Inf. Co.D Cpl.
Walton, William T. MS 33rd Inf. Co.H
Walton, William T. SC Inf. Hampton Legion Co.B
Walton, William W. VA 2nd Cav. Co.C 3rd Lt.
Walton, W.J. AR 26th Inf. Co.H
Walton, W.J. GA 1st Inf. Co.B
Walton, W.J. MS 1st Cav. Co.F
Walton, W.J. MS 36th Inf. Co.D Cpl.
Walton, W.J.B. TN 15th (Cons.) Cav. Co.A
Walton, W.J.B. TN 15th (Stewart's) Cav. Co.B
Walton, W.J.B. TN 12th Inf. Co.D
Walton, W.J.B. TN 12th (Cons.) Inf. Co.E
Walton, W.L. GA 18th Inf. Co.C
Walton, W.M. TX Inf. (St.Serv.) Carter's Co.
Walton, W.M. Gen. & Staff AAG
Walton, W.P. KY 12th Cav. Co.B
Walton, W.P. SC Post Guard Senn's Co.
Walton, W.S. KY Corbin's Men
Walton, W.T. AL 50th Inf. Co.G
Walton, W.T. GA Brooks' Co. (Terrell Lt.Arty.)
Walton, W.T. GA 20th Inf. Co.B
Walton, W.T. MO Inf. 3rd Bn. Co.B
Walton, W.T. MO 6th Inf. Co.A
Walton, W.T. 7th Conf.Cav. Co.D
Walton, W.V. LA 2nd Inf. Co.D Sgt.
Walton, W.W. MS 1st (Johnston's) Inf. Co.E
Walton, W.W. VA Lt.Arty. 13th Bn. Co.A
Walton, W.W. VA 10th Bn.Res. Co.C
Walton, W.W. VA 88th Mil.
Walton, Wyatt W. VA 19th Inf. Co.D
Walton, Zachary L. VA 34th Inf. Co.K
Walton, Zachary L. Conf.Hvy.Arty. Montague's Bn. Co.B
Waltonberg, L. VA 2nd St.Res. Co.H
Waltow, Joseph T. MO Inf. Perkins' Bn. Co.B
Waltrink, Francis TX 2nd Cav. Co.K
Waltrip, Benjamin VA 1st Arty. Co.F
Waltrip, Benjamin VA Arty. Dance's Co.
Waltrip, Benjamin VA 32nd Inf. Co.G
Waltrip, Charles M. TX 4th Inf. Co.H
Waltrip, George AL 8th (Livingston's) Cav. Co.E

Waltrip, George W. AL 4th (Roddey's) Cav. Co.L
Waltrip, James MO 7th Cav. Co.G
Waltrip, Joel VA 23rd Inf. Co.C
Waltrip, John KY 12th Cav. Co.B
Waltrip, John L. KY 8th Mtd.Inf. Co.H,C Ord.Sgt.
Waltrip, Joseph W. KY 8th Mtd.Inf. Co.H
Waltrip, Martin MO 7th Cav. Co.G
Waltrip, R.N. 1st Conf.Cav. 1st Co.H
Waltrip, Robert VA 1st Arty. Co.F
Waltrip, Robert VA Arty. Dance's Co.
Waltrip, William T. VA Lt.Arty. Jeffress' Co.
Waltrop, W.W. TX Conscr.
Walts, S.L. AL 3rd Inf. Co.C
Walts, W.F. TX 4th Inf. (St.Troops) Co.H
Waltun, W. AL 20th Inf. Co.K
Waltus, E. VA 110th Mil. Saunders' Co.
Waltz, David AL 4th Res. Co.G
Waltz, D.H. MO 2nd Inf. Co.G
Waltz, Edward P. MO 1st N.E. Cav. Co.C
Waltz, Edward P. MO 4th Cav. Co.G
Waltz, Joseph SC 20th Inf. Co.B
Waltz, L.F. AL Lt.Arty. Goldthwaite's Btty. Cpl.
Waltz, T.K. MD 1st Cav. Co.K
Waltz, W.C. AL 4th Res. Co.B
Waltz, William Christopher AL 3rd Inf. Co.E
Waltze, David AL Loc.Def. & Sp.Serv. Toomer's Co.
Waltze, W. TX 20th Inf. Co.H
Waltzman, Julius C. VA Hvy.Arty. 18th Bn. Co.D
Waluka 1st Cherokee Mtd.Vol. Co.C
Walworth, Douglas MS 16th Inf. Co.I Capt.
Walworth, Douglass Gen. & Staff, Adj.Gen.Dept. Capt.
Walworth, Ernest Gen. & Staff, Adj.Gen.Dept. Capt.
Walworth, H.B. Inf. Bailey's Cons.Regt. Co.A
Walworth, H.B. TX 7th Inf. Co.B
Walworth, Samuel LA Arty. Moody's Co. (Madison Lt.Arty.)
Walz, A. LA Mil. 3rd Regt.Eur.Brig. (Garde Francaise) Co.2
Walz, A. LA Mil. 3rd Regt. 1st Brig. 1st Div. Co.H
Walz, George Frederick VA 6th Inf. Co.C
Walz, Theodore TN 15th Inf. Co.K Cpl.
Walz, William VA 27th Inf. 2nd Co.H
Walzman, Julius C. VA 34th Inf. Norton's Co.
Wamac, Jasper N. MO Cav. Schnabel's Bn. Co.F
Wamac, J.B. AR 15th Mil. Co.H
Wamac, Ransom TN 62nd Mtd.Inf. Co.E
Wamach, John T. AL Inf. 2nd Regt. Co.K Cpl.
Wamach, Martin AR Cav. Gordon's Regt. Co.G
Wamach, P.F. VA Courtney Arty.
Wamack, --- TX Cav. Good's Bn. Co.B
Wamack, A.G.B. MS St.Cav. 3rd Bn. (Cooper's) Little's Co.
Wamack, A.J. AR 19th (Dawson's) Inf. Co.C Cpl.
Wamack, Albert G.B. MS 3rd Inf. Co.K
Wamack, C. AR 19th (Dawson's) Inf. Co.C
Wamack, C. TX Cav. Wells' Regt. Co.D
Wamack, David TN 5th (McKenzie's) Cav. Co.C
Wamack, F. MS 6th Cav. Co.E Cpl.
Wamack, George W. FL 6th Inf. Co.B
Wamack, G.L. MS 10th Inf. Old Co.B
Wamack, G.W. MS 31st Inf. Co.H
Wamack, H.Y. TX Cav. Ragsdale's Bn. 2nd Co.C
Wamack, J. MS 1st Cav.Res. Co.G
Wamack, J. MS 5th Cav. Co.D
Wamack, J. MS 46th Inf. Co.F
Wamack, James M. AL 27th Inf. Co.F
Wamack, James W. VA 5th Cav. (12 mo. '61-2) Co.F
Wamack, James W. VA 13th Cav. Co.F
Wamack, J.D. MS St.Cav. 3rd Bn. (Cooper's) Little's Co.
Wamack, J.D. MS Cav. Powers' Regt. Co.I
Wamack, J.D. TN 4th (McLemore's) Cav. Co.C
Wamack, J.D. TX Cav. Wells' Regt. Co.G
Wamack, J.F. TN 6th (Wheeler's) Cav. Co.K
Wamack, J.G. TN 50th Inf. Co.C
Wamack, J.K. TN 8th (Smith's) Cav. Co.D
Wamack, J.L. TX 3rd Cav. Co.D Cpl.
Wamack, J.M. AL 4th Cav. Co.C
Wamack, John E. VA 13th Cav. Co.F
Wamack, J.W. TN 8th (Smith's) Cav. Co.D
Wamack, Lafayette VA Lt.Arty. Motley's Co. Sgt.
Wamack, L.B. GA 36th (Broyles') Inf. Co.F
Wamack, L.B. NC 35th Inf. Co.I
Wamack, L.W. AL 7th Inf. Co.G
Wamack, Miles M. FL 1st Cav. Co.F
Wamack, Robert TN 23rd Inf. Co.H
Wamack, S. MS 46th Inf. Co.F
Wamack, Samuel MO Inf. Clark's Regt. Co.H
Wamack, Samuel TN 5th (McKenzie's) Cav. Co.I
Wamack, Simeon MS 36th Inf. Co.A
Wamack, Simon MS Lt.Arty. (Brookhaven Lt.Arty.) Hoskins' Btty.
Wamack, S.J. TX 13th Vol. 4th Co.I
Wamack, Thomas NC 16th Inf. Co.D
Wamack, Thomas B. AL 10th Inf. Co.I
Wamack, Thomas J. VA 6th Inf. Co.I Cpl.
Wamack, W. AL 7th Inf. Co.G
Wamack, W.A. TN 4th (McLemore's) Cav. Co.C
Wamack, W.H. TX Lt.Inf. & Riflemen Maxey's Co. (Lamar Rifles)
Wamack, William AL 51st (Part.Rangers) Co.F
Wamack, William AL 23rd Inf. Co.K
Wamack, William MS Cav. Davenport's Bn. (St.Troops) Co.A
Wamack, William NC 30th Inf. Co.F
Wamack, William A. AR 1st Mtd.Rifles Co.M 2nd Lt.
Wamack, William H. VA Inf. 25th Bn. Co.F
Wamack, William P. MS 32nd Inf. Co.H
Wamack, W.T. NC 1st Inf. (6 mo. '61) Co.G
Wamack, W.W. FL 2nd Cav. Co.D
Wamack, W.W. 3rd Conf.Eng.Troops Co.E Artif.
Wamake, W.P. SC 12th Inf. Co.C
Wamaling, Adolphus D. GA 3rd Inf. Co.K
Wamath, C. AR 30th Inf. Co.D
Wamath, William TN 40th Inf. Co.D 1st Sgt.
Wambach, John SC 3rd Cav. Co.G
Wambacher, Lewis AL 20th Inf. Co.B
Wambel, C.R. GA 2nd St.Line 1st Lt.
Wambersie, Jno. E. MD Weston's Bn. Co.B
Wambersie, John E. VA 21st Inf. Co.B
Wamble, Allen AR 15th Mil. Co.H 1st Lt.
Wamble, Allen AR 35th Inf. Co.I Sgt.
Wamble, Archie B. MS 15th Inf. Co.H
Wamble, C.R. GA 2nd St.Line 1st Lt.
Wamble, D.W. GA 2nd St.Line Maj.
Wamble, E.C. TN 17th Cav. Co.C
Wamble, E.C. TN 19th & 20th (Cons.) Cav. Co.B
Wamble, E.C. TN 31st Inf. Co.C
Wamble, Edmund AL 53rd (Part.Rangers) Co.C
Wamble, Elija R. AR 37th Inf. Co.G
Wamble, E.W. GA 5th Inf. (St.Guards) Curley's Co.
Wamble, George AL 8th Inf. Co.A
Wamble, H.J. MS 44th Inf. Co.F
Wamble, H.W. TN 21st (Wilson's) Cav. Co.H
Wamble, J. VA Loc.Def. Durrett's Co.
Wamble, J.A. MS 9th Inf. New Co.G
Wamble, J.A. MS 20th Inf. Co.B
Wamble, J.B. NC Inf. 2nd Bn. Co.H
Wamble, J.E. AL 9th Cav. Co.C
Wamble, J.J. TX 30th Cav. Co.D
Wamble, J.M. AR 1st Mtd.Rifles Co.F Cpl.
Wamble, Joab TN 51st (Cons.) Inf. Co.E
Wamble, John MS 6th Cav. Co.B
Wamble, John E. TX 10th Inf. Co.F
Wamble, John J. MS 8th Cav. Co.C
Wamble, John T. MS 20th Inf. Co.B
Wamble, John W. MS 5th Inf. Co.C
Wamble, Lawrence L. GA 55th Inf. Co.A
Wamble, L.C. AR 19th (Dockery's) Inf. Co.H Cpl.
Wamble, Parington NC 1st Inf. Co.G
Wamble, Richard NC 7th Inf. Co.G
Wamble, Samuel W. MS 20th Inf. Co.B
Wamble, S.M. AR 33rd Inf. Co.B
Wamble, Thomas GA 2nd Inf. Co.C Sgt.
Wamble, Thomas B. AR 37th Inf. Co.G
Wamble, Thomas F. AR 33rd Inf. Co.B Sgt.
Wamble, T.J. MS 2nd Cav. Co.I Cpl.
Wamble, W.A. AL Cav. Moreland's Regt. Co.F 2nd Lt.
Wamble, W.A. AL 7th Inf. Co.F
Wamble, W.A. AR 9th Inf. Co.K Sgt.
Wamble, William AL 59th Inf. Co.C
Wamble, William GA Inf. 13th Bn. (St.Guards) Beall's Co.
Wambles, Aaron NC Hvy.Arty. 10th Bn. Co.B
Wambles, J.W. GA 63rd Inf. Co.H
Wambs, J.W. GA Cav. Dorough's Bn.
Wambsgans, Val LA Mil. Fire Bn. Co.C
Wambsganss, Jacob LA Mil.Cont.Regt. Lang's Co.
Wamick, A. Munford's Staff ADC
Wamick, Amos E. TN 23rd Inf. Co.H
Wamick, J.A. TN 5th Inf. Co.I
Wamick, Noah W. NC 50th Inf. Co.I
Wamick, N.T. MS 32nd Inf. Co.H
Wamick, T.A. TN 23rd Inf. Co.H
Wamicks, John VA 12th Cav. Co.I
Wamka, Fredrick 1st Conf.Eng.Troops Co.H
Wamlock, H. MO Cav. Schnabel's Bn. Co.B
Wammiac, James W. TN 3rd (Lillard's) Mtd.Inf. Co.G

Wammack, --- TX Inf. 1st St.Troops Whitehead's Co.
Wammack, Alexander AR 2nd Mtd.Rifles Co.I
Wammack, C.J. AR 50th Mil. Co.D
Wammack, David TN 5th (McKenzie's) Cav. Co.I
Wammack, D.H. TX 24th & 25th Cav. (Cons.) Co.F
Wammack, E.B. AR 34th Inf. Co.F
Wammack, George S. AL 41st Inf. Co.G
Wammack, James NC 43rd Inf. Co.F
Wammack, James TX 11th Cav. Co.K
Wammack, James K.P. TN 18th Inf. Co.A
Wammack, Jesse B. TN 34th Inf. Co.D
Wammack, J.F. GA Cav. 9th Bn. (St.Guards) Co.E
Wammack, J.J. TN 18th Inf. Co.D
Wammack, John T. KY 2nd Bn.Mtd.Rifles Co.E
Wammack, Joseph T. NC 16th Inf. Co.D
Wammack, J.P. GA Cav. 9th Bn. (St.Guards) Co.E
Wammack, Lewis B. GA 35th Inf. Co.A
Wammack, L.T. NC 30th Inf. Co.A
Wammack, Pleasant F. VA 6th Inf. Weisiger's Co.
Wammack, Pleasant F. VA 16th Inf. Co.I
Wammack, S.N. MO Cav. Snider's Bn. Co.A
Wammack, Spencer B. GA 28th Inf. Co.H
Wammack, Thomas A. GA 35th Inf. Co.A
Wammack, W.E. AR 7th Inf. Co.E 1st Sgt.
Wammack, William GA 3rd Cav. Co.I
Wammack, William TN 5th (McKenzie's) Cav. Co.I
Wammack, William TX 2nd Inf. Co.I
Wammack, W.J. TN 38th Inf. Co.G Sgt.
Wammack, W.S. GA 5th Res. Co.K
Wammick, Benjamin AR 27th Inf. Co.D
Wammick, J.B. Nitre & Min. Bureau War Dept.,CSA
Wammock, E.J. AL 53rd (Part.Rangers) Co.C
Wammock, F.J. FL Conscr.
Wammock, J. FL Conscr.
Wammock, J.A. FL Conscr.
Wammock, John M. FL 7th Inf. Co.G
Wammock, K.T. NC 1st Inf. Co.K
Wammock, Landrum NC 50th Inf. Co.I
Wammock, Richard NC 1st Inf. Co.K
Wammock, William AR 34th Inf. Co.F
Wammock, William M. GA 14th Inf. Co.C
Wamnac, J.B. AR 32nd Inf. Co.H
Wamock, H. GA 47th Inf. Co.E,H
Wamock, James B. NC 18th Inf. Co.E
Wamock, S.B. GA 5th Inf. (St.Guards) Brooks' Co.
Wampee, Charles AR 3rd Cav. Co.K Sgt.
Wampee, George AR 1st Mtd.Rifles Co.H
Wampee, M. TX Cav. Martin's Regt. Co.G
Wampeer, Clarke VA 45th Inf. Co.D
Wamper, Benjamin VA Conscr.
Wample, William A. AL 16th Inf. Co.E Sgt.
Wampler, A.F. VA 50th Inf. Co.H,F Cpl.
Wampler, Austin A. VA 45th Inf. Co.B
Wampler, Austin C. VA 48th Inf. Co.K
Wampler, Austin C. VA Loc.Def. Neff's Co.
Wampler, Benjamin F. VA 52nd Inf. Co.C
Wampler, David VA 29th Inf. Co.B
Wampler, David A. VA Cav. McFarlane's Co.
Wampler, D.J. TX Cav. McCord's Frontier Regt. Co.G Cpl.
Wampler, E., Jr. VA 4th Res. Co.E
Wampler, Ephem VA Loc.Def. Neff's Co.
Wampler, Ephem W., Jr. VA Loc.Def. Neff's Co.
Wampler, Eph W. VA Mil. Wythe Cty.
Wampler, George VA 63rd Inf. Co.H
Wampler, George A. VA 51st Inf. Co.A
Wampler, George B. VA 29th Inf. 1st Co.F Cpl.
Wampler, George W. VA 45th Inf. Co.D
Wampler, Henderson VA 51st Inf. Co.A
Wampler, Henry M. VA 29th Inf. Co.B
Wampler, Isaac A. VA 45th Inf. Co.B
Wampler, Isaac A. VA Loc.Def. Neff's Co.
Wampler, J.A. VA 4th Res. Co.E
Wampler, James KY 3rd Mtd.Inf. Co.K
Wampler, J.B. 7th Conf.Cav. Co.K
Wampler, Jesse VA 37th Inf. Co.I
Wampler, J.F. VA 51st Inf. Co.A
Wampler, J.M. VA 8th Inf. Co.H Capt.
Wampler, J.M. Eng.,CSA Capt.
Wampler, John VA 146th Mil. Co.B
Wampler, John M. VA 51st Inf. Co.A Sgt.
Wampler, John W. VA 29th Inf. 1st Co.F
Wampler, Jonathan VA 58th Mil. Co.K
Wampler, Joseph B. VA 37th Inf. Co.C
Wampler, J.S. TN 61st Mtd.Inf. Co.C
Wampler, Peter W. VA 48th Inf. Co.E
Wampler, R.R. TX Cav. McCord's Frontier Regt. Co.G
Wampler, Rufus VA Loc.Def. Neff's Co.
Wampler, Samuel L. VA 1st Cav. Co.E
Wampler, Samuel L. VA 51st Inf. Co.A
Wampler, Simon W. VA 52nd Inf. Co.F
Wampler, Stephen VA Inf. 23rd Bn. Co.E
Wampler, William TX Cav. McCord's Fronter Regt. Co.G
Wampler, William VA 21st Cav. 1st Co.E
Wampler, William VA 6th Bn.Res. Co.H
Wampler, William VA Mil. Scott Cty.
Wampler, William H. VA 51st Inf. Co.A Sgt.
Wampler, William J. VA 22nd Cav. Co.A 2nd Lt.
Wampler, William J. VA 48th Inf. Co.E Sgt.
Wamscott, James MO 1st N.E. Cav. Co.M
Wamsley, Adam H. VA 19th Cav. Co.I Sgt.
Wamsley, Benjamin F. GA Cav. 2nd Bn. Co.E
Wamsley, Enoch VA 20th Cav. Co.C
Wamsley, G.B. VA 19th Cav. Co.I
Wamsley, G.F. VA 19th Cav. Co.I
Wamsley, Joseph GA Inf. 1st City Bn. (Columbus) Co.D
Wamsley, J.S. VA 19th Cav. Co.I 1st Lt.
Wamsley, Louis W. FL 8th Inf. Co.K
Wamsley, Randolph J. VA 17th Cav. Co.C
Wamsley, Randolph J. VA 19th Cav. Co.I
Wamsley, R.R. MS 22nd Inf.
Wamsley, S.B. VA 19th Cav. Co.I
Wamsley, T.M. FL Cav. 5th Bn. Co.F
Wamsley, W.E. LA Inf. 1st Bn. (St.Guards) Co.B 2nd Lt.
Wamsley, W.E. LA 13th Bn. (Part.Rangers) Co.E
Wamsley, William H. VA 31st Inf. Co.F
Wamsley, W.M. VA 20th Cav. Co.C
Wamsly, B.F. GA 5th Cav. Co.C
Wamuck, Abner J. TX Cav. 6th Bn. Co.A
Wamuck, H. TX 15th Field Btty.
Wan, J.A. TN Cav. 5th Bn. (McClellan's) Co.A
Wan, J.W. TN Cav. 5th Bn. (McClellan's) Co.A
Wan, W.H. TX Cav. 2nd Bn.St.Troops Wilson's Co.
Wan, William AR 8th Cav. Peoples' Co.
Wan, William MO 6th Cav. Co.F
Wana, George 1st Chickasaw Inf. Wallace's Co.
Wanack, James MO 16th Inf. Co.F
Wanack, J.G. TN 30th Inf. Co.C
Wa na ki 1st Creek Mtd.Vol. Co.A
Wanamaker, F.J. SC 5th Cav. Co.A
Wanamaker, James TN 35th Inf. Co.B, 1st Co.A Cpl.
Wanamaker, W.W. SC 5th Cav. Co.A Lt.
Wancel, William Conf.Cav. 6th Bn.
Wand, C.R. VA Cav. 1st Bn. (Loc.Def.Troops) Co.C
Wand, G.L. TX 27th Cav. Co.K
Wand, R. AL 15th Inf. Co.D
Wandall, J.R. KY 3rd Mtd.Inf. Co.E Sgt.
Wandeck, Charles AL 1st Regt. Mobile Vol. Co.E
Wandell, Estelle VA Lt.Arty. 1st Bn. Hosp.Stew.
Wandell, G.W. TN 15th Inf. Co.G Sgt.
Wandell, Jno. E. GA 29th Inf. Co.H
Wander, John TN 41st Inf. Co.D
Wandering, William MO 11th Inf. Co.D
Wandle, William MO Cav. Snider's Bn. Co.E
Wandless, Stephen H. VA 58th Inf. Co.G
Wandling, Allen VA 2nd Inf. Co.E Sgt.
Wands, James LA 7th Inf. Co.E
Wands, J.T. TN Arty. Bibb's Co.
Wandsley, Nathaniel AR 15th (Josey's) Inf. Co.G
Wandt, Henry LA Mil. 3rd Regt. 1st Brig. 1st Div. Co.F
Wane, John A. MS Cav. Gartley's Co. (Yazoo Rangers)
Wane, William N. VA 115th Mil. Co.B 2nd Lt.
Wanen, David TX Cav. Giddings' Bn. Carr's Co.
Wanes, J.G. TN Cav. Napier's Bn. Co.C
Wanesley, Jess GA 3rd Cav. Co.H
Wanet, A.B. NC Lt.Arty. 13th Bn. Co.C
Wanett, Adrian B. NC 2nd Arty. (36th St.Troops) Co.C
Wanett, William A. NC 30th Inf. Co.C
Wang, A.A. VA Inf. 4th Bn.Loc.Def. Co.F
Wang, Fred LA 5th Inf. Co.G 1st Lt.
Wang, George LA Mil. Chalmette Regt. Co.A
Wang, George W. LA 5th Inf. Regt.QM
Wang, George W. Wharton's Brig. Capt.,QM
Wangemann, A. TX Waul's Legion Co.C Sgt.
Wanger, Abraham VA 146th Mil. Co.B
Wanger, Benjamin VA 3rd (Chrisman's) Bn.Res. Co.A
Wanger, Benjamin K. VA 7th Bn.Res. Co.B
Wanger, Henry LA 21st (Kennedy's) Inf. Co.E
Wanger, Samuel VA 3rd (Chrisman's) Bn.Res. Co.A
Wanger, Samuel VA 7th Bn.Res. Co.B
Wangher, James J. AL 19th Inf. Co.I
Wangler, Landelin LA Mil. 1st Regt. French Brig. Co.7
Wanin, Samuel, Jr. LA Mil. Beauregard Bn. Co.C,E

Wank, Louis TX Conscr.
Wankins, F.G. GA Cav. Dorough's Bn.
Wankowiez, Ladislas LA 14th Inf. Co.F,G Capt.
Wanless, James W. VA 31st Inf. Co.G
Wann, Charles SC Lt.Arty. J.T. Kanapaux's Co. (Lafayette Arty.) Cpl.
Wann, Isaac D. AL 49th Inf. Co.H Capt.
Wann, J. AR 45th Cav. Co.C
Wann, J.A. TN 2nd (Ashby's) Cav. Co.A
Wann, John AR Lt.Arty. Auston's Btty.
Wann, John A. VA 1st Lt.Arty. Co.B
Wann, John A. VA Lt.Arty. J.S. Brown's Co. Cpl.
Wann, John A. VA Lt.Arty. Taylor's Co.
Wann, John L. AR 25th Inf. Co.G
Wann, John W. TN 32nd Inf. Co.C Surg.
Wann, John W. Gen. & Staff Asst.Surg.
Wann, Joshua AR 1st Vol. Co.E Capt.
Wann, Joshua AR 38th Inf. Co.B Capt.
Wann, J.R. Gen. & Staff AAG
Wann, J.W. TN 2nd (Ashby's) Cav. Co.A Black.
Wann, Lafayette TN 33rd Inf. Co.G
Wann, M. AR 1st Vol. Co.E
Wann, R.M. AR 1st Vol. Co.E
Wann, R.M. AR 7th Inf. Co.D 1st Sgt.
Wann, R.M. AR 38th Inf. Co.B
Wann, R.M. MO 10th Cav. Co.F
Wann, Samuel, Jr. LA Inf.Crescent Regt. Co.G Drum.
Wann, W.A. AR 36th Inf. Co.I
Wann, W.A. KY 2nd Cav. Co.K
Wann, William AL 50th Inf.
Wann, William TN Cav. Welcker's Bn. Co.A
Wann, W.P.H. TN 2nd (Ashby's) Cav. Co.A
Wannach, A.W. TN 7th Inf. Co.E
Wannack, B.W. AR Cav. Harrell's Bn. Co.D
Wannack, John AR Cav. Harrell's Bn. Co.D
Wannamaker, A.D. SC 11th Inf. Co.C
Wannamaker, Adam H. SC 5th Cav. Co.A
Wannamaker, A.H. SC Cav. 14th Bn. Co.B
Wannamaker, B. SC 2nd Arty. Co.F
Wannamaker, David E. SC 5th Cav. Co.A
Wannamaker, D.E. SC Cav. 14th Bn. Co.B
Wannamaker, F.M. SC 2nd Inf. Co.I
Wannamaker, F.M. SC 20th Inf. Co.B QMSgt.
Wannamaker, Frank M. SC 1st (Hagood's) Inf. 1st Co.A Cpl.
Wannamaker, H.C. SC 20th Inf. Co.B
Wannamaker, Irvin W. SC 1st (Hagood's) Inf. 1st Co.D
Wannamaker, Jacob C.E. SC Horse Arty. (Washington Arty.) Vol. Hart's Co.
Wannamaker, Jacob G. SC Mil. 15th Regt. Adj.
Wannamaker, J.C.I. SC 1st (Hagood's) Inf. 1st Co.B, 2nd Co.B 1st Lt.
Wannamaker, J.G. SC 20th Inf. Co.B 1st Lt.
Wannamaker, J.M.O. SC 1st (Hagood's) Inf. 2nd Co.B
Wannamaker, J.R. SC Cav. 14th Bn. Co.B
Wannamaker, J. Robert SC 5th Cav. Co.A
Wannamaker, J.W. SC 25th Inf. Co.F
Wannamaker, N. SC 2nd Bn.S.S. Co.B
Wannamaker, W.H. SC 2nd Arty. Co.F
Wannamaker, W.H. SC 1st (Hagood's) Inf. 1st Co.C
Wannamaker, W.W. SC Cav. 14th Bn. Co.B Bvt.2nd Lt.
Wannenmacher, Wilhelm MS Cav. Jeff Davis Legion Co.A
Wanner, F. LA Mil. Orleans Fire Regt. Co.I
Wanner, T.J. SC 15th Inf. Co.I
Wannick, W.D. TX 24th & 25th Cav. (Cons.) Co.E
Wannil, Albert GA Inf. (Wright Loc.Guards) Holmes' Co.
Wannix, Thomas GA 16th Inf. Co.E
Wannon, James A. VA 3rd (Archer's) Bn.Res. Co.C
Wansbey, W.J. GA 1st Inf. Co.G
Wansch, F. TX Waul's Legion Co.C
Wansfield, T.J. KY Cav. Sypert's Regt.
Wansickles, Eli. A. MO Cav. 3rd Regt.St.Guard Co.E 1st Lt.
Wanslee, Jesse C. GA 21st Inf. Co.B
Wansley, A.M. MS 5th Inf. (St.Troops) Co.A
Wansley, G.L. GA 1st (Fannin's) Res. Co.D
Wansley, H.S. MS 39th Inf. Co.D,B Sgt.
Wansley, J.P. KY 7th Mtd.Inf. Co.A
Wansley, R.R. MS 2nd Cav. Co.B
Wansley, T.M. MS Inf. 1st Bn.St.Troops (30 days '64) Co.B
Wansley, T.N. GA 38th Inf. Co.F,A
Wansley, William J. GA 15th Inf. Co.I
Wansley, W.J. GA Smith's Legion Co.F
Wansley, W.J. 3rd Conf.Eng.Troops
Wanslie, N.T. GA Cav. Gartrell's Co.
Wanslow, P.H. KY 9th Mtd.Inf. Co.E
Wansly, Augustus MS 11th (Perrin's) Cav. Co.K
Wansly, E. VA 31st Inf. Co.F
Wansor, T. GA Cav. Nelson's Ind.Co.
Wansor, Theordore GA Cav. Nelson's Co.
Wanstoff, Peter P. VA 46th Inf. Co.B
Want, D.S. AR 19th (Dockery's) Inf. Co.G
Want, G.H. AR 36th Inf. Co.C
Want, J.C. MS 12th Inf. Co.G
Want, Joseph AR 15th (Josey's) Inf. Co.F
Wantland, Robert TN Cav. 9th Bn. (Gantt's) Co.A
Wantlin, Abraham TN Cav. 3rd Bn. (Gantt's) Co.A
Wantz, Xavier TX 36th Cav. Co.H
Wanzley, F.M. TX Comal Res.
Wap, R. KY 3rd Cav. Co.I
Wapiachie 1st Choctaw Mtd.Rifles Ward's Co.
Wapins, W.Y. AR 1st Inf. Co.E
Waple, James S. VA 30th Inf. 1st Co.I Sgt.
Waple, James S. VA 47th Inf. 3rd Co.I Sgt.
Waple, John T. VA 15th Cav. Co.G
Waple, John T. VA Cav. 15th Bn. Co.D
Waple, Simon VA 18th Cav. Co.F
Waples, Edward B. VA 39th Inf. Co.L Capt.
Waples, G.W. VA 18th Cav. Co.K
Waples, J. Tennent LA Inf. 1st Sp.Bn. (Rightor's) Co.E
Waples, W.D. 15th Conf.Cav. Capt.,AQM
Waples, W.D. Gen. & Staff Capt.,AQM
Wappler, A. TX 15th Inf.
Wappler, Fritz TX 20th Inf. Co.B Music.
Wappler, Jacob LA Mil. 1st Regt. 3rd Brig. 1st Div. Co.E
Waquire, C. LA Mil. LaFourche Regt.
Waquire, J. LA Mil. LaFourche Regt.
Waram, John VA 37th Inf. Co.B,K
Waran, P.W. NC 4th Cav. (59th St.Troops) Co.H
Warberton, George T. VA 52nd Mil. Co.A
Warberton, William VA 52nd Mil. Co.B
Warbin, M. AL 1st Regt. Mobile Vol. Baas' Co.
Warbington, A.B. MS 41st Inf. Co.C
Warbington, A.J. MS 41st Inf. Co.C
Warbington, D.L. MS 40th Inf. Co.K
Warbington, D.N. MS 20th Inf. Co.K
Warbington, Hubard MS 41st Inf. Co.C
Warbington, Samuel, Jr. MS 41st Inf. Co.C
Warbington, W.I. MS 9th Inf. Co.I
Warbington, W.V. MS 41st Inf. Co.C
Warble, Albert VA 10th Inf. Co.E
Warbriton, John T. VA Courtney Arty.
Warbritten, B.F. TN 19th & 20th (Cons.) Cav. Co.K
Warbritten, Newton TN 10th (DeMoss') Cav. Co.K
Warbritton, A.W. TN 12th (Cons.) Inf. Co.G
Warbritton, A.W. TN 22nd Inf. Co.G
Warbritton, B.F. TN 20th (Russell's) Cav. Co.F
Warbritton, B.T. TN 10th (DeMoss') Cav. Co.K Cpl.
Warbritton, C. NC 2nd Jr.Res. Co.G
Warbritton, D.D. TN 20th (Russell's) Cav. Co.B
Warbritton, D.D. TN 55th (Brown's) Inf. Co.H
Warbritton, H.N. TN 19th & 20th (Cons.) Cav. Co.B
Warbritton, H.N. TN 20th (Russell's) Cav. Co.B
Warbritton, H.N. TN 12th (Cons.) Inf. Co.G
Warbritton, H.N. TN 22nd Inf. Co.G
Warbritton, James NC 8th Inf. Co.C
Warbritton, Major VA Lt.Arty. 38th Bn. Co.C
Warbritton, William B. NC 33rd Inf. Co.B Cpl.
Warbritton, William T. MO 1st Inf. Co.B
Warbritton, William T. MO 1st & 4th Cons.Inf. Co.D
Warbritton, William T. TN 20th (Russell's) Cav. Co.F
Warburg, Daniel LA Mil. 1st Native Guards
Warburg, Edward LA 20th Inf. Co.F 2nd Lt.
Warburg, Edward MO 7th Cav. Capt.,Adj.
Warburg, Edward MO 16th Inf. Co.A Capt.,Adj.
Warburton, --- TX Cav. Border's Regt. Co.E
Warburton, George VA Lt.Arty. Parker's Co.
Warburton, J.A. TX St.Cav. Hampton's Co.
Warburton, John A. TX 4th Cav. Co.C Cpl.
Warburton, Martin V.B. VA Hvy.Arty. Wilkinson's Co.
Warburton, Robert VA 3rd Cav. 1st Co.I
Warbury, Edward Gen. & Staff 1st Lt.,Adj.
Ward, --- GA Inf. 27th Bn. Co.E
Ward, --- TX Cav. 4th Regt.St.Troops Co.E
Ward, --- TX Cav. 4th Regt.St.Troops Co.I
Ward, --- TX Cav. 4th Regt.St.Troops Co.K
Ward, --- TX Cav. 4th Regt.St.Troops Co.L
Ward, --- TX Cav. Good's Bn. Co.A
Ward, --- TX Cav. Good's Bn. Co.E
Ward, --- TX Cav. Mann's Regt. Co.C
Ward, --- VA VMI Co.D Cadet
Ward, --- Gen. & Staff Chap.
Ward, A. LA Cav. White's Co. Sgt.
Ward, A. MS 1st Cav. Co.E
Ward, A. MS 5th Inf. Co.E

Ward, A. MS 5th Inf. (St.Troops) Co.I
Ward, A. MS 9th Inf. Co.F
Ward, A. MO 5th Inf. Co.A
Ward, A. NC Mallett's Bn. (Cp.Guard) Co.F
Ward, A. SC Lt.Arty. M. Ward's Co. (Waccamaw Lt.Arty.)
Ward, A. SC Inf. 7th Bn. (Enfield Rifles) Co.C
Ward, A. TN 16th (Logwood's) Cav. Co.I
Ward, A. TN 9th Inf. Co.C
Ward, A. TN 38th Inf. 2nd Co.K
Ward, Aaron NC 1st Inf. (6 mo. '61) Co.M
Ward, Aaron NC 11th (Bethel Regt.) Inf. Co.F
Ward, Aaron A. GA Lt.Arty. Fraser's Btty. 1st Sgt.
Ward, Aaron A. GA 10th Inf. 1st Co.K 1st Sgt.
Ward, A.B. AL 12th Inf. Co.G
Ward, A.B. AL 17th Inf. Co.F
Ward, A.B. LA 5th Inf. Co.A
Ward, A.B. LA Mil.Conf.Guards Regt. Co.F
Ward, A.B. MS 3rd (St.Troops) Cav. Co.K
Ward, A.B. NC 6th Cav. (65th St.Troops) Co.C,D Sgt.
Ward, A.B. TN 9th Inf. Co.C
Ward, Abner MO 5th Cav. Co.F
Ward, Abner T. GA 55th Inf. Co.A
Ward, Abraham FL 4th Inf. Co.E Sgt.
Ward, Abraham FL 8th Inf. Co.C
Ward, Absalom NC 51st Inf. Co.H
Ward, A.C. GA 39th Inf. Co.K Capt.
Ward, A.C. NC 3rd Cav. (41st St.Troops) Co.A 1st Lt.
Ward, A.D. AL 48th Inf. Co.G,E
Ward, Addison MS 36th Inf. Co.H
Ward, Addison W. VA 11th Inf. Co.B
Ward, Adley NC 6th Sr.Res. Co.A
Ward, A.F. GA 1st Inf. Co.F
Ward, A.F. LA Hvy.Arty. 2nd Bn. Co.C Jr.2nd Lt.
Ward, A.G. GA 11th Inf. Co.F
Ward, A.G. MS 5th Cav. Co.K Capt.
Ward, A.G. Trans-MS Conf.Cav. 1st Bn. Co.C
Ward, A.J. AL City Troop (Mobile) Arrington's Co.
Ward, A.J. AL 5th Inf. Co.C
Ward, A.J. AR 1st Regt.St.Troops Co.E
Ward, A.J. AR 11th & 17th (Cons.) Inf. Co.I
Ward, A.J. AR 17th (Griffith's) Inf. Co.B
Ward, A.J. AR 24th Inf. Co.C
Ward, A.J. GA Inf. 40th Bn. Co.D
Ward, A.J. LA Mil.Conf.Guards Regt. Co.F
Ward, A.J. SC 3rd Res. Co.G
Ward, A.J. SC 27th Inf. Co.G
Ward, A.J. TN 7th (Duckworth's) Cav. White's Co.C
Ward, A.J. TX Cav. Wells' Regt. Co.K 1st Lt.
Ward, A.J. 8th (Wade's) Conf.Cav. Co.K
Ward, A.J. 15th Conf.Cav. Co.F
Ward, A.J.M. GA Siege Arty. Campbell's Ind.Co.
Ward, A. Joab FL 10th Inf. Co.H
Ward, Albert TN 39th Mtd.Inf. Co.A
Ward, Albert TX 34th Cav. Co.D
Ward, Albert TX 9th (Young's) Inf. Co.B
Ward, Albert G. GA 6th Cav. Co.D
Ward, Albert G. MS 2nd Part. Co.C Capt.
Ward, Albritton H. GA 3rd Inf. Co.B
Ward, Alex LA Mil. Brenan's Co. (Co.A, Shamrock Guards)
Ward, Alexander GA 3rd Cav. Co.G
Ward, Alexander GA 62nd Cav. Co.E
Ward, Alexander GA 51st Inf. Co.A
Ward, Alexander LA 12th Inf. Co.I Cpl.
Ward, Alexander NC 3rd Inf. Co.K
Ward, Alexander NC 60th Inf. Co.D
Ward, Alexander SC Inf. 7th Bn. (Enfield Rifles) Co.D
Ward, Alexander TN 25th Inf. Co.A
Ward, Alexander TX 21st Cav. Co.E
Ward, Alexander TX 12th Inf. Co.K
Ward, Alexander VA Cav. 41st Bn. Co.C
Ward, Alexander E. Gen. & Staff Asst.Surg.
Ward, Alexander S. AL Cav. 5th Bn. Hilliard's Legion Co.A
Ward, Alexander S. GA Lt.Arty. 14th Bn. Co.C
Ward, Alexander S. GA Lt.Arty. Ferrell's Btty.
Ward, Alf. LA 4th Inf. Old Co.G
Ward, Alfred NC 4th Cav. (59th St.Troops) Co.B
Ward, Alfred NC 2nd Inf. Co.C
Ward, Alfred NC 20th Inf. Co.K
Ward, Alfred SC 16th Inf. Co.H
Ward, Alfred C. NC 45th Inf. Co.B
Ward, Alfred D. AL 48th Inf. Co.E
Ward, Alfred G. AL 5th Inf. New Co.D Sgt.Maj.
Ward, Alfred L. NC Inf. Thomas Legion 2nd Co.A
Ward, Alfred L. SC 1st (Orr's) Rifles Co.F
Ward, Alfred N. TX 22nd Inf. Co.C
Ward, Allen AL Arty. 1st Bn. Co.F
Ward, Allen E. SC Inf. 7th Bn. (Enfield Rifles) Co.G
Ward, Allen F. AL 6th Inf. Co.F
Ward, Allen T. MO 5th Cav. Co.F
Ward, A.M. LA 6th Cav. Co.A
Ward, A.M. MS 2nd Cav. Co.E
Ward, A.M. Gen. & Staff Capt.,Asst.Comsy.
Ward, A.M. Gen. & Staff Capt.,QM
Ward, Amos MS 10th Inf. Old Co.E, New Co.E
Ward, Amos C. GA Inf. 5th Bn. (St.Guards) Co.B
Ward, Anderson AR 38th Inf. Co.B
Ward, Anderson NC 35th Inf. Co.K Music.
Ward, Anderson J. NC 52nd Inf. Co.C Sgt.
Ward, Anderson S. NC 11th (Bethel Regt.) Inf. Co.F
Ward, Andrew MS 2nd Part.Rangers Co.C
Ward, Andrew NC 7th Sr.Res. Watts' Co.
Ward, Andrew TX Cav. Good's Bn. Co.A 2nd Lt.
Ward, Andrew G. SC 20th Inf. Co.I
Ward, Andrew J. AR Inf. Hardy's Regt. Co.F
Ward, Andrew J. FL 6th Inf. Co.H
Ward, Andrew J. GA Inf. 10th Bn. Co.D
Ward, Andrew J. GA 41st Inf. Co.I
Ward, Andrew J. MS 23rd Inf. Co.B Sgt.
Ward, Andrew J. NC 4th Inf. Co.E
Ward, Andrew J. SC 6th Cav. Co.K,H
Ward, Andrew J. TN 1st (Feild's) Inf. Co.C
Ward, Angus AL 14th Inf. Co.B
Ward, Anthony NC 42nd Inf. Co.B
Ward, Anthony NC 61st Inf. Co.H
Ward, Anthony B. NC Cav. 7th Bn. Co.D
Ward, A.P. KY 10th (Diamond's) Cav. Co.I
Ward, A. Pinkney NC 35th Inf. Co.K Sgt.
Ward, Archer MD 1st Cav. Co.E
Ward, Arch T. VA 22nd Cav. Co.H
Ward, Armstead M. TN 23rd Inf. 2nd Co.A
Ward, Armstrong F. LA 1st Cav. Co.K Cpl.
Ward, Arren NC 2nd Arty. (36th St.Troops) Co.K
Ward, Arthur NC McDugald's Co.
Ward, A.S. MS Inf. 3rd Bn. (St.Troops) Co.F
Ward, A.S. TN 21st & 23rd (Cons.) Cav. Co.G
Ward, A.S. VA 19th Cav. Co.I
Ward, A.S. VA 31st Inf. Co.F
Ward, A.S. 1st Conf.Cav. 2nd Co.G
Ward, A.S. 10th Conf.Cav. Co.A
Ward, Asa AL 13th Inf. Co.E
Ward, Asa FL 1st Inf. New Co.D
Ward, Asa NC 51st Inf. Co.G
Ward, Asa TX 29th Cav. Co.I
Ward, Asa F. GA Cobb's Legion Co.F
Ward, Asa S. SC 5th St.Troops Co.D
Ward, Ashley NC 47th Inf. Co.D
Ward, Ashley M. AR Inf. 1st Bn. Co.E Cpl.
Ward, Assadana NC 1st Inf. Co.G Sgt.
Ward, A.T. AL 6th Cav. Co.E
Ward, A.T. AL 8th Cav.
Ward, A.T. GA 8th Cav. Old Co.E
Ward, A.T. NC Cav. 16th Bn. Co.A
Ward, A.T. VA Cav. Caldwell's Bn. Graham's Co.
Ward, Augustus NC 1st Inf. (6 mo. '61) Co.M
Ward, Augustus NC 52nd Inf. Co.C
Ward, Augustus J. MS 14th Inf. Co.D
Ward, Augustus J. MS 37th Inf. Co.C
Ward, Augustus M. AL 62nd Inf. Co.A Cpl.
Ward, Augustus M. AR 16th Inf. Capt.
Ward, Austin GA 21st Inf. Co.C
Ward, A.W. MO Lt.Arty. Barret's Co. Sgt.
Ward, Azariah C. AL 20th Inf. Co.B
Ward, B. NC 7th Bn.Jr.Res. Co.B
Ward, B. SC Lt.Arty. Beauregard's Co.
Ward, B. SC 1st St.Troops Co.B
Ward, B. TN 16th Inf. Co.I
Ward, B.A. TN 23rd Inf. Co.D
Ward, B.A. TN 45th Inf. Co.A
Ward, Baker VA 61st Inf. Co.D
Ward, Ballard E. VA 1st Inf. Co.K
Ward, Ballard P. VA 29th Inf. Co.H
Ward, Ballard P. VA 45th Inf. Co.K
Ward, Bartholomew GA Cav. Allen's Co.
Ward, Bartlett SC 3rd Res. Co.I
Ward, B.B. TN 24th Inf. Co.A
Ward, B.C. AL 33rd Inf. Co.A
Ward, B.C. GA Cobb's Legion Co.B
Ward, B.C. KY 1st (Butler's) Cav. New Co.H
Ward, B.E. AL 12th Inf. Co.E
Ward, Ben Trans-MS Conf.Cav. 1st Bn. Co.E
Ward, Benjamin AR 23rd Inf. Co.H
Ward, Benjamin AR 33rd Inf. Co.H
Ward, Benjamin GA 5th Res. Co.I
Ward, Benjamin GA 29th Inf. Co.I
Ward, Benjamin GA 50th Inf. Co.C
Ward, Benjamin MS 41st Inf. Co.A
Ward, Benjamin MO 16th Inf. Co.I
Ward, Benjamin NC 46th Inf. Co.G
Ward, Benjamin SC 10th Inf. Co.E
Ward, Benjamin TN 1st (Carter's) Cav. Co.C
Ward, Benjamin VA Loc.Def. Neff's Co.

Ward, Benjamin C. GA Inf. (Jasper & Butts Cty. Guards) Lane's Co.
Ward, Benjamin C. NC 17th Inf. (2nd Org.) Co.F
Ward, Benjamin C. NC 31st Inf. Co.F
Ward, Benjamin F. AL 4th Inf. Co.B
Ward, Benjamin F. AR 3rd Inf. Co.F Music.
Ward, Benjamin F. GA 7th Inf. Co.D
Ward, Benjamin F. MS Cav. 1st Bn. (Miller's) Co.E
Ward, Benjamin F. MS 11th Inf. Co.K Surg.
Ward, Benjamin F. NC 46th Inf. Co.A
Ward, Benjamin F. NC Walker's Bn. Thomas' Legion Co.G 2nd Lt.
Ward, Benjamin F. VA Cav. Young's Co. Sgt.
Ward, Benjamin F. VA 39th Inf. Co.D
Ward, Benj. F. Gen. & Staff Surg.
Ward, Benjamin H. NC 20th Inf. Co.D
Ward, Benjamin L. AR Inf. 8th Bn. 1st Co.C
Ward, Benjamin L. NC Gibbs' Co. (Loc.Def.)
Ward, Benjamin N. MS 40th Inf. Co.H Surg.
Ward, Benj. Noah Gen. & Staff Surg.
Ward, Benjamin Q. TX Cav. Waller's Regt. Co.D 1st Lt.
Ward, Benjamin S. NC 2nd Inf. Co.D
Ward, Benjamin W. KY 9th Cav. Co.C
Ward, Benjamin W. KY 10th (Diamond's) Cav. Co.G 2nd Lt.
Ward, Benjamin W. KY 5th Mtd.Inf. Co.D
Ward, Benjamin W. NC 60th Inf. Co.D
Ward, Benjamin W. TX 19th Cav. Co.D
Ward, Bennett GA 57th Inf. Co.I,D
Ward, Berkeley Eng.,CSA Capt.
Ward, B.F. AL 5th Cav. Co.A
Ward, B.F. AL 53rd (Part.Rangers) Co.D
Ward, B.F. AL 12th Inf., Co.F
Ward, B.F. AL 20th Inf. Co.F
Ward, B.F. AL 32nd & 58th (Cons.) Inf.
Ward, B.F. GA Inf. (Jasper & Butts Cty.Guards) Lane's Co. 1st Lt.
Ward, B.F. MS 1st Cav. Co.A
Ward, B.F. NC 67th Inf. Co.D
Ward, B.F. TN 1st (Carter's) Cav. Co.H 2nd Lt.
Ward, B.F. TN 31st Inf. Co.I
Ward, B.G. NC 7th Inf. Co.G
Ward, B.G. NC 7th Sr.Res. Bradshaw's Co.G
Ward, B.H. NC 2nd Jr.Res. Co.G
Ward, B. Huger SC Lt.Arty. M. Ward's Co. (Waccamaw Lt.Arty.) Jr.2nd Lt.
Ward, B.J. LA Miles' Legion Co.H 1st Lt.
Ward, B.J. MS 3rd Inf. (St.Troops) Co.E
Ward, B.K. GA 63rd Inf. Co.D
Ward, B.M. AR 13th Inf. Co.C Sgt.
Ward, B.M. GA 13th Cav. Co.C
Ward, B.N. GA 3rd Mil. Co.G
Ward, Bolivar VA 4th Cav. Co.H
Ward, B.P. GA 13th Cav. Co.C
Ward, Bryan B. AR 1st (Colquitt's) Inf. Co.C
Ward, Burrell Lt.Arty. Dent's Btty.,CSA
Ward, Burton D. GA 41st Inf. Co.B 1st Lt.
Ward, B.W. KY Fields' Co. (Part.Rangers) 1st Sgt.
Ward, C. LA Inf. Pelican Regt. Co.G
Ward, C. MS St.Cav. 3rd Bn. (Cooper's) 1st Co.A
Ward, C. MS 48th Inf. Co.G
Ward, C. MO 5th Cav. Co.I
Ward, C. VA Cav. 37th Bn. Co.I 1st Sgt.
Ward, C. VA 46th Inf. Co.I
Ward, C.A. GA 2nd Inf. Co.D
Ward, C.A. GA 48th Inf. Co.B
Ward, Caleb VA 34th Inf. Norton's Co.
Ward, Caleb E. SC 8th Inf. Co.E
Ward, Calvin GA Cobb's Legion Co.F
Ward, Calvin NC 18th Inf. Co.B Sgt.
Ward, Calvin 3rd Conf.Eng.Troops Co.D Sgt.
Ward, Calvin A. GA Cav. Newbern's Co. (Coffee Revengers)
Ward, Calvin A. GA 50th Inf. Co.C
Ward, Calvin M. AL 4th Inf. Co.H
Ward, Calvin N. AL Cp. of Instr. Talladega Co.F
Ward, Carroll TN 10th (DeMoss') Cav. Co.C
Ward, C.B. VA 9th Cav. Co.F
Ward, C.C. TN 3rd (Forrest's) Cav. Co.B
Ward, C.C. TN 3rd (Forrest's) Cav. Co.D
Ward, C.C. VA 4th Res. Co.F,K
Ward, C.C. Gen. & Staff,PACS Hosp.Stew.
Ward, C.E. TX Inf. Timmons' Regt. Co.I
Ward, Celestina FL Cav. 3rd Bn. Co.D
Ward, Celestina 15th Conf.Cav. Co.I
Ward, C.G. AR 2nd Cav. Co.D
Ward, C.H. AL Cp. of Instr. Talladega Co.F
Ward, C.H. TX 4th Inf. Co.G
Ward, C.H. 1st Conf.Cav. 2nd Co.E
Ward, C.H. 2nd Conf.Eng.Troops Co.C Artif.
Ward, Chapman VA 51st Inf. Co.K
Ward, Charles AL Cav.Res. Brooks' Co.
Ward, Charles AL 21st Inf. Co.G Cpl.
Ward, Charles AR 2nd Mtd.Rifles Co.E
Ward, Charles KY 9th Mtd.Inf. Co.B
Ward, Charles LA 7th Inf. Co.C
Ward, Charles MS 10th Inf. Old Co.E
Ward, Charles MS 36th Inf. Co.A
Ward, Charles NC 15th Inf. Co.E
Ward, Charles NC 18th Inf. Co.B
Ward, Charles TX 5th Inf. Co.G
Ward, Charles VA Inf. 1st Bn.Loc.Def. Co.A 1st Sgt.
Ward, Charles B. AL 13th Inf. Co.K Cpl.
Ward, Charles B. VA 46th Inf. Music.
Ward, Charles Cocke MS 14th Inf. Co.K
Ward, Charles D. MO Lt.Arty. 2nd Field Btty.
Ward, Charles E. LA 16th Inf. Co.A,I Cpl.
Ward, Charles H. Buckner's Escort, Breckenridge's Escort
Ward, Charles L. KY 4th Mtd.Inf. Co.D Music.
Ward, Charles M. AL 4th (Roddey's) Cav. Co.H Sgt.
Ward, Charles T. MS Inf. 5th Bn. Co.C
Ward, Charley AR 1st (Monroe's) Cav. Co.D
Ward, Christ C. TN 45th Inf. Co.G
Ward, Cicero H. NC 1st Arty. (10th St.Troops) Co.G
Ward, C.J. TN 7th (Duckworth's) Cav. Co.H
Ward, C.L. AL 8th Inf. Co.F
Ward, Clinton M. NC 64th Inf. Co.B
Ward, C.M. NC 16th Inf. Co.K Cpl.
Ward, C.N. AL Cp. of Instr. Talladega Co.F
Ward, Colen SC 23rd Inf. Co.H
Ward, Colonel Deneale's Regt. Choctaw Warriors Co.D
Ward, Conrad T. AR 18th (Marmaduke's) Inf. Co.E
Ward, Cornelius MS 30th Inf. Co.E
Ward, Cornelius A. VA 39th Inf. Co.A Cpl.
Ward, Cornick H. 1st Conf.Inf. 2nd Co.H
Ward, Costin O. NC 66th Inf. Co.G
Ward, Council FL 2nd Cav. Co.I
Ward, C.P. TX Cav. 2nd Regt.St.Troops Co.G
Ward, C.R. AR Cav. Davies' Bn. Co.B
Ward, C.R. LA Inf. 4th Bn. Co.E
Ward, C.R.C. GA 13th Inf. Co.K
Ward, Crocket TN 16th Inf. Co.I
Ward, C.T. AR 5th Inf.
Ward, C.T. AR 34th Inf. Co.F
Ward, C.T. GA Cav. 8th Bn. (St.Guards) Co.A Cpl.
Ward, C.T. GA Conscr.
Ward, C.T. MS 41st Inf. Co.A
Ward, C.T. 3rd Conf.Inf. Co.E
Ward, Cushman A. Conf.Cav. Wood's Regt. Co.E
Ward, C.W. AR Mil. Borland's Regt. Peyton Rifles
Ward, C.W. SC Lt.Arty. 3rd (Palmetto) Bn. Co.I
Ward, C.W. SC 6th Inf. 2nd Co.H
Ward, Cyrus TN 14th Inf.
Ward, Cyrus T. TN 63rd Inf. Co.F
Ward, C.Z. TN 47th Inf. Co.G
Ward, D. MS 1st (Johnston's) Inf. Co.I
Ward, D. MS 46th Inf. Co.F
Ward, D. VA Inf. 25th Bn. Co.G
Ward, D.A. SC 13th Inf. Co.G
Ward, D.A. VA 5th Cav. Co.K
Ward, Dandy T. GA 5th Inf. Co.D
Ward, Daniel AL 5th Cav. Co.H
Ward, Daniel AR Mil. Desha Cty.Bn.
Ward, Daniel LA 1st (Nelligan's) Inf. Co.A
Ward, Daniel MS 28th Cav. Co.B
Ward, Daniel NC 51st Inf. Co.G
Ward, Daniel SC Inf. 1st (Charleston) Bn. Co.C Cpl.
Ward, Daniel SC 27th Inf. Co.H Sgt.
Ward, Daniel VA 5th Cav. (12 mo. '61-2) Co.A
Ward, Daniel VA Cav. 14th Bn. Co.D
Ward, Daniel VA 3rd Inf.Loc.Def. Co.D
Ward, Daniel C. GA 43rd Inf. Co.D
Ward, Daniel C. NC 24th Inf. Co.B 2nd Lt.
Ward, Daniel W. LA 28th (Gray's) Inf. Co.C
Ward, David AL 57th Inf. Co.D
Ward, David AL 3rd Bn. Hiliard's Legion Vol. Co.A
Ward, David AR 2nd Mtd.Rifles Co.A
Ward, David AR 45th Mil. Co.E
Ward, David GA 11th Cav. (St.Guards) MacIntyre's Co.
Ward, David GA Cav. 12th Bn. (St.Guards) Co.E Cpl.
Ward, David GA 5th Res. Co.C
Ward, David TN 25th Inf. Co.B Sgt.
Ward, David TN 32nd Inf. Co.B
Ward, David TX 1st Field Btty.
Ward, David TX St.Troops Edgar's Co.
Ward, David VA 4th Res. Co.E,G
Ward, David 1st Conf.Reg.Cav. Co.A
Ward, David A. VA 5th Cav. (12 mo. '61-2) Co.I
Ward, David A. VA Cav. 14th Bn. Co.B
Ward, David A. VA 15th Cav. Co.I
Ward, David B. KY 5th Mtd.Inf. Co.I

Ward, David C. AR 6th Inf. Co.K Sgt.
Ward, David E. TN Cav. Newsom's Regt. Co.F 1st Sgt.
Ward, David F. GA Smith's Legion Co.K
Ward, David G. TX 5th Cav. Co.G
Ward, David J. NC 20th Inf. Co.K
Ward, David S. AL 24th Inf. Co.I Sgt.
Ward, David S. NC 1st Arty. (10th St.Troops) Co.G Sgt.
Ward, David T. AR 31st Inf. Co.K
Ward, David T. MS 27th Inf. Co.D
Ward, D.B. GA 9th Inf. Co.E
Ward, D.C. MS 2nd Part.Rangers Co.D,K
Ward, D.C. SC 6th Inf. 2nd Co.D Cpl.
Ward, D.C. TN Inf. 22nd Bn. Co.E
Ward, D.C. TN Inf. 154th Sr.Regt. Co.L Sgt.
Ward, D.D. GA 65th Inf. Co.K
Ward, D.E. TN 13th Inf. Co.I
Ward, Demby MS 11th (Cons.) Cav. Co.F
Ward, Dennis MS 16th Inf. Co.I
Ward, D.H. TX 2nd Inf. Co.G
Ward, Dixon 1st Choctaw & Chickasaw Mtd.Rifles Co.G
Ward, D.J. MS 6th Cav. Co.E 1st Lt.
Ward, D.J. MS 5th Inf. (St.Troops) Co.G Capt.
Ward, D.M. SC 4th Bn.Res. Co.A Sgt.
Ward, Dock KY 12th Cav. Co.F
Ward, Douglas LA Washington Arty.Bn. Co.2
Ward, D.P. GA 18th Inf. Co.D
Ward, Drewry J. VA 51st Inf. Co.B
Ward, D.S. TX Cav. Madison's Regt. Co.A
Ward, D.T. AL Recruit
Ward, Duke NC 58th Inf. Co.D
Ward, Dunba MS Cav. 3rd Bn. (Ashcraft's) Co.B
Ward, Duncan GA 1st (Ramsey's) Inf.
Ward, D.Y. GA 1st Cav. Co.H
Ward, E. FL 3rd Inf. Co.E
Ward, E. GA 5th Res. Co.A
Ward, E. LA Mil. Claiborne Regt. Co.A
Ward, E. MS Cav. 38th Regt. Co.C
Ward, E. TN 2nd (Ashby's) Cav. Co.H
Ward, E. TN 12th (Cons.) Inf. Co.G
Ward, E.A. GA 42nd Inf. Co.G
Ward, E.A. GA 60th Inf. Co.C
Ward, E.A. MS 2nd Cav. Co.H 2nd Lt.
Ward, E.A. MS 1st (King's) Inf. (St.Troops) Co.G Capt.
Ward, E.A. MS 29th Inf. Co.F
Ward, E.B. AL Stewart's Detach.Loc.Def.
Ward, E.B. VA 19th Cav. Co.I
Ward, E.C. MS 2nd (Davidson's) Inf. Co.H
Ward, Ed GA 4th Cav. (St.Guards) Cartledge's Co.
Ward, Ed GA 13th Cav. Co.C Cpl.
Ward, E.D. MS 38th Cav. Co.D
Ward, E.D. Conf.Cav. Wood's Regt. 2nd Co.M Sgt.
Ward, Eddy TN 13th Inf. Co.A
Ward, Edgar W. NC 24th Inf. Co.B
Ward, Ed K. TN 4th Inf. Co.A 2nd Lt.
Ward, Ed W. AL 51st (Part.Rangers) Co.B
Ward, Edwan GA 11th Cav. Co.A
Ward, Edward AL 3rd Res. Co.H Sgt.
Ward, Edward AR 17th (Lemoyne's) Inf. Co.D
Ward, Edward AR 21st Inf. Co.H
Ward, Edward AR 24th Inf. Co.G
Ward, Edward AR Inf. Cocke's Regt. Co.F
Ward, Edward AR Inf. Hardy's Regt. Co.F
Ward, Edward GA 1st (Olmstead's) Inf. Co.C,A
Ward, Edward MS 22nd Inf. Co.A
Ward, Edward Burroughs' Bn.Part.Rangers Co.A Cpl.
Ward, Edward B. VA 16th Inf. Co.C Adj.
Ward, Edward B. Gen. & Staff 1st Lt.,Adj.
Ward, Edward G. TX 34th Cav. Co.D
Ward, Edward H. NC 15th Inf. Co.D Capt.
Ward, Edward H. NC 49th Inf. Co.B Capt.
Ward, Edward J. AL 6th Inf. Co.B
Ward, Edward M. GA 19th Inf. Co.G
Ward, Edward M. NC 7th Inf. Co.C
Ward, Edward R. NC 2nd Arty. (36th St.Troops) Co.A
Ward, Edward R. NC 8th Sr.Res. Jacobs' Co.
Ward, Edward W. MS Cav. Crumby's Regt. Co.A
Ward, Edward W. NC 3rd Cav. (41st St.Troops) Co.B Capt.
Ward, Edwin W. VA 14th Inf. Co.B
Ward, E.G. MO 5th Cav. Co.G
Ward, E.G. NC 3rd Cav. (41st St.Troops) Co.A
Ward, E.G. TN 43rd Inf. Co.K
Ward, E.G. TX 5th Cav. Co.I
Ward, E.G. TX Waul's Legion Co.G
Ward, E.H. AL 40th Inf. Co.E 2nd Lt.
Ward, E.H. MS 34th Inf. Co.C
Ward, E.H. VA 8th Cav. Co.A 1st Sgt.
Ward, E.I. MS 11th (Cons.) Cav. Co.H
Ward, E.J. AL 18th Inf. Co.B
Ward, E.J. AR 7th Inf. Co.H 1st Sgt.
Ward, E.J. MS Cav. 3rd Bn. (Ashcraft's) Co.B
Ward, E.J. MS 18th Cav. Co.H
Ward, E.J.J. AL 15th Inf. Co.G Sgt.
Ward, E.L. AL 28th Inf. Co.B
Ward, E.L. TN 12th Inf. Co.B Sgt.
Ward, E.L. TN 12th (Cons.) Inf. Co.A Sgt.
Ward, E.L. TN 51st (Cons.) Inf. Co.K
Ward, E.L. TX 19th Inf. Co.B
Ward, E.L.A. GA 2nd Inf. Co.D
Ward, Elam D. AR 3rd Cav. Co.C 1st Sgt.
Ward, Eli NC 6th Sr.Res. Co.A Cpl.
Ward, Elias AL 32nd Inf. Co.D
Ward, Elias SC 7th Res. Co.G Sgt.
Ward, Elias L. TX 11th Inf. Co.K Sgt.
Ward, Elijah AL Inf. 1st Regt. Co.B
Ward, Elijah TN 1st (Carter's) Cav. Co.C
Ward, Elijah Lt.Arty. Dent's Btty.,CSA
Ward, Elijah B. AL 47th Inf. Co.B
Ward, Elijah C. AL 89th Mil. Co.E
Ward, Elijah H. LA 31st Inf. Co.G Jr.2nd Lt.
Ward, Elisha P. TX 2nd Cav. Co.I
Ward, Elisha P. TX 24th Cav. Co.E 1st Lt.
Ward, Elisha W. NC 14th Inf. Co.E
Ward, Ely J. AL 40th Inf. Co.I
Ward, Emmette C. AR 15th (Josey's) Inf. Co.F
Ward, E.N. AR Cav. Gordon's Regt. Co.F
Ward, Endonna S. KY 4th Mtd.Inf. Co.D
Ward, Enoch GA 52nd Inf. Co.A
Ward, Enoch TN 3rd (Lillard's) Mtd.Inf. Co.A
Ward, Enoch VA Mil. Carroll Cty.
Ward, Enoch C. VA 29th Inf. 2nd Co.F
Ward, Enos GA 13th Inf. Co.K
Ward, E.P. FL Lt.Arty. Dyke's Co.
Ward, E.P. TX 8th Cav. Co.E Far.
Ward, Ephraim TN 61st Mtd.Inf. Co.K,I
Ward, Equin H. VA 7th Inf. Co.I Cpl.
Ward, Ervin A. GA 36th (Broyles') Inf. Co.G
Ward, Ervin L. AR 15th (Josey's) Inf. Co.F
Ward, Ervin L. MS 18th Inf. Co.E
Ward, Erwood P. FL 2nd Cav. Co.F
Ward, E.S. KY 1st (Butler's) Cav. Co.B
Ward, E.S. KY 1st Bn.Mtd.Rifles Co.B
Ward, E.T. MS 42nd Inf.
Ward, Eugenius C. MS 42nd Inf. Co.K 1st Sgt.
Ward, Evan FL 2nd Cav. Co.I
Ward, Evan P. VA 18th Cav. Co.F
Ward, Evan P. VA 114th Mil. Co.D Sgt.Maj.
Ward, Evans J. MS 2nd Inf. Co.H
Ward, Everrett R. VA 45th Inf. Co.D
Ward, E.W. MS 5th Cav. Co.H
Ward, E.W. NC 3rd Cav. (41st St.Troops) Co.H Cpl.
Ward, E.W. VA 2nd Cav. Co.I
Ward, E. Wesley MS 9th Inf. Old Co.B
Ward, Ezekial TN Cav. 4th Bn. (Branner's) Co.A
Ward, Ezekiel GA 34th Inf. Co.K
Ward, F. AL Ready's Bn.Res.
Ward, F. MS 2nd St.Cav. Co.L
Ward, F. MS 12th Cav. Co.G
Ward, F. TX 15th Cav. Co.K
Ward, F.A. LA 13th Inf. Co.H
Ward, F.B. TN 1st (Turney's) Inf. Co.I Cpl.
Ward, F.C. TN 45th Inf. Co.E Cpl.
Ward, Felix LA 3rd (Harrison's) Cav. Co.E
Ward, Felix LA Inf. 4th Bn. Co.F
Ward, Felton NC Lt.Arty. 3rd Bn. Co.C
Ward, Felton NC 17th Inf. (2nd Org.) Co.D
Ward, Fernando NC 17th Inf. (2nd Org.) Co.K Cpl.
Ward, F. H. GA 45th Inf. Co.G
Ward, F.H. TN 12th Inf. Co.K
Ward, F.H. TN 12th (Cons.) Inf. Co.K
Ward, F.H. 8th (Wade's) Conf.Cav. Co.H
Ward, Fielding MO Inf. 4th Regt.St.Guard Co.A
Ward, F.J. GA Cav. 19th Bn. Co.A
Ward, F.J. GA Cav. 19th Bn. Co.E
Ward, F.J. GA Inf. 4th Bn. (St.Guards) Co.G
Ward, F.J. 10th Conf.Cav. Co.F
Ward, Fleming AL 35th Inf. Co.E
Ward, Fleming GA 6th Inf. (St.Guards) Pittman's Co.
Ward, Flem. F. 2nd Cherokee Mtd.Vol. Co.E
Ward, Floyd VA 4th Res. Co.B
Ward, F.M. AL 8th (Hatch's) Cav. Co.C Sgt.
Ward, F.M. AL 40th Inf. Co.E
Ward, F.M. AR 6th Inf. Co.A
Ward, F.M. AR 38th Inf. Co.E
Ward, F.M. GA 11th Inf. Co.C
Ward, F.M. GA 36th (Broyles') Inf. Co.E
Ward, F.M. TX 5th Inf. Co.I
Ward, F.M. TX 20th Inf. Co.C
Ward, Folsom Deneale's Regt. Choctaw Warriors Co.E
Ward, Foreman AL 40th Inf. Co.I
Ward, Forman AL Mil. 4th Vol. Gantt's Co.
Ward, Frances M. AR Inf. Cocke's Regt. Co.C
Ward, Francis GA 8th Inf. Co.D
Ward, Francis MS 4th Inf. Co.D
Ward, Francis H. TN Lt.Arty. Palmer's Co. Cpl.
Ward, Francis J. VA Hvy.Arty. Epes' Co.

Ward, Francis M. AR 3rd Inf. Co.E Music.
Ward, Francis M. AR 35th Inf. Co.B
Ward, Francis M. GA 6th Inf. (St.Guards) Co.C
Ward, Francis M. GA 44th Inf. Co.B
Ward, Francis M. TN 55th (McKoin's) Inf. James' Co. Sgt.
Ward, Francis W. GA 51st Inf. Co.H
Ward, Francis X. MD 1st Inf. 2nd Co.H 2nd Lt.
Ward, Frank AL Gorff's Co. (Mobile Pulaski Rifles)
Ward, Frank AR 19th (Dockery's) Inf. Co.F
Ward, Frank MS 46th Inf. Co.E
Ward, Frank MO 5th Cav. Co.C
Ward, Frank VA 5th Cav. 1st Co.F
Ward, Frank VA 59th Inf. 3rd Co.F
Ward, Frank VA 60th Inf. 1st Co.H
Ward, Frank B. NC 5th Cav. (63rd St.Troops) Co.H 1st Lt.
Ward, Frank L. TX 18th Inf. Co.D Sgt.
Ward, Franklin NC 4th Inf. Co.H
Ward, Franklin NC 48th Inf. Co.B
Ward, Franklin 7th Conf.Cav. Co.G
Ward, Franklin B. GA Phillips' Legion Co.A Color Cpl.
Ward, Franklin J. NC 1st Arty. (10th St.Troops) Co.I
Ward, Franklin J. NC 12th Inf. Co.L
Ward, Franklin J. NC 32nd Inf. Co.F,A
Ward, Frank X. MD Weston's Bn. Co.D 2nd Lt.
Ward, Frank X. Wilcox's Staff Capt.,ADC
Ward, Frederick MS 12th Inf. Co.H
Ward, Fredrick 7th Conf.Cav. Co.B
Ward, Fredrick L. MO 12th Inf. Co.E
Ward, Friel F. VA 29th Inf. 2nd Co.F Sgt.
Ward, F.S. AL St.Res. Palmer's Co.
Ward, F.T. TX 12th Cav. Co.E
Ward, F.W. AR 20th Inf. Co.H
Ward, G. AL 3rd Inf. Co.M
Ward, G. FL 2nd Cav. Co.I
Ward, G. KY Cav. 2nd Bn. (Dortch's) Co.D
Ward, G.A. MS 20th Inf. Co.E Sgt.
Ward, G.B. AL 27th Inf. Co.B
Ward, G.B. MS Inf. 3rd Bn.
Ward, G.B. Exch.Bn. 1st Co.A,CSA
Ward, G.D. NC 4th Cav. (59th St.Troops) Co.I 1st Lt.
Ward, G.E. MO Cav. 11th Regt.St.Guard QM
Ward, George AL 53rd (Part.Rangers) Co.F
Ward, George AR Lt.Arty. Key's Btty.
Ward, George AR Inf. 1st Bn. Co.D
Ward, George GA 3rd Cav. Co.G
Ward, George GA 12th Inf. Co.E
Ward, George KY 10th (Diamond's) Cav. Co.I
Ward, George MS 2nd Cav. Co.E,B
Ward, George MS Lt.Arty. (Madison Lt.Arty.) Richards' Co. Capt.
Ward, George NC 2nd Bn.Loc.Def.Troops Co.D
Ward, George NC 53rd Inf. Co.D
Ward, George TN 1st (Carter's) Cav. Co.K
Ward, George TN 13th (Gore's) Cav. Co.I Sgt.
Ward, George TN 2nd (Robison's) Inf. Co.D
Ward, George TX Waul's Legion Co.B
Ward, George VA 19th Cav. Co.I
Ward, George VA Inf. 21st Bn. 2nd Co.F 3rd Lt.
Ward, George 1st Cherokee Mtd.Vol. Co.J
Ward, Geo. Gen. & Staff, Arty. Maj.
Ward, George C. MS 15th Inf. Co.H Music.
Ward, George D. NC Cav. 12th Bn. Co.B 1st Lt.
Ward, George D. 8th (Dearing's) Conf.Cav. Co.B 1st Lt.
Ward, George E. AL 3rd Inf. Co.B
Ward, George M. HGA 3rd Cav. (St.Guards) Co.H
Ward, George R. FL Cadets Military Inst. Sgt.
Ward, George R. MS 10th Inf. Old Co.I 1st Lt.
Ward, George R. NC 24th Inf. Co.B
Ward, George R. TN 2nd (Smith's) Cav.
Ward, George S. AL Cav. 24th Bn. Co.C 1st Lt.
Ward, George S. AL 53rd (Part.Rangers) Co.K Sgt.
Ward, George T. FL 2nd Inf. Col.
Ward, George T. FL 6th Inf. Co.H
Ward, George W. AL 3rd Cav. Co.H Cpl.
Ward, George W. AL 13th Inf. Co.B Cpl.
Ward, George W. AL 33rd Inf. Co.B
Ward, George W. AR 1st Cav. Co.K
Ward, George W. AR Inf. 1st Bn. Co.A
Ward, George W. GA 13th Inf. Co.I
Ward, George W. GA 14th Inf. Co.A Sgt.
Ward, George W. LA 4th Inf. Co.K
Ward, George W. MS Cav. Gartley's Co. (Yazoo Rangers)
Ward, George W. MS 6th Inf. Co.B
Ward, George W. MS 21st Inf. Co.H
Ward, George W. MS 33rd Inf. Co.D
Ward, George W. MS 34th Inf. Co.K
Ward, George W. NC 3rd Cav. (41st St.Troops) Co.K Capt.
Ward, George W. NC 4th Cav. (59th St.Troops) Co.H
Ward, George W. NC 3rd Inf. Co.B 1st Lt.
Ward, George W. NC 27th Inf. Co.I 2nd Lt.
Ward, George W. NC 35th Inf. Co.G
Ward, George W. NC 56th Inf. Co.G
Ward, George W. NC Inf. Thomas Legion Co.F
Ward, George W. TN 2nd (Ashby's) Cav. Co.H
Ward, George W. TN Cav. 4th Bn. (Branner's) Co.A
Ward, George W. TN 5th (McKenzie's) Cav. Co.E
Ward, George W. TX 15th Cav. Co.A
Ward, George W. VA 16th Inf. Co.A
Ward, George W. VA 31st Mil. Pay M.
Ward, Geo. W., Jr. VA VMI Cadet
Ward, Geo. W. Gen. & Staff Capt.,ACS
Ward, G.F. MS 7th Cav. Co.K
Ward, G.F. TN Cav. Jackson's Co.
Ward, G.G. TX Cav. Wells' Regt. Co.H
Ward, G.H. KY 1st (Butler's) Cav. Co.D Capt.
Ward, Gilbert NC 20th Inf. Co.C
Ward, Gilbert N. TX 5th Cav. Co.B
Ward, G.J. TN Cav. 5th Bn. (McClellan's) Co.E
Ward, G.M. GA 3rd Inf. Co.H 2nd Lt.
Ward, G.R. AR 33rd Inf. Co.H
Ward, G.R. GA Floyd Legion (St.Guards) Co.I
Ward, G.R. MS 22nd Inf. Gaines' Co. 1st Sgt.
Ward, G.R. NC 3rd Cav. (41st St.Troops) Co.H Cpl.
Ward, Granville TN 32nd Inf. Co.B
Ward, Grecian TX 9th Cav. Co.H
Ward, Green AR 33rd Inf. Co.H
Ward, Green B. AR 4th Inf. Co.H
Ward, Green M. TX 19th Inf. Co.B Sgt.
Ward, Griffin Stith Gen. & Staff Lt.,Ord.Off.
Ward, G.S. AL 1st Cav. 1st Co.K
Ward, G.T. FL 6th Inf. Co.I
Ward, G.W. AL Lt.Arty. Kolb's Btty.
Ward, G.W. AL 7th Inf. Co.F
Ward, G.W. AL 12th Inf. Co.F
Ward, G.W. AL 32nd & 58th (Cons.) Inf.
Ward, G.W. AL 59th Inf. Co.E Cpl.
Ward, G.W. AL Arty. 4th Bn. Hilliard's Legion Co.B,E Cpl.
Ward, G.W. GA Cav. 8th Bn. (St.Guards) Co.C
Ward, G.W. GA 3rd Res. Co.K
Ward, G.W. GA 4th Inf. Co.B
Ward, G.W. MS 1st Lt.Arty. Co.I
Ward, G.W. MS 2nd (Davidson's) Inf. Co.E Cpl.
Ward, G.W. MS 14th (Cons.) Inf. Co.A
Ward, G.W. MO Lt.Arty. Barret's Co.
Ward, G.W. NC 3rd Bn.Sr.Res. Williams' Co.
Ward, G.W. SC 7th Inf. 1st Co.L, 2nd Co.L Sgt.
Ward, G.W. TX 22nd Inf. Co.A
Ward, G.W. TX Waul's Legion Co.B
Ward, G.W. VA Cadet VMI
Ward, H. AR 45th Cav. Co.C
Ward, H. GA 8th Cav. Old Co.E
Ward, H. LA 13th Bn. (Part.Rangers) Co.B
Ward, H. LA Inf. 4th Bn. Co.D Sgt.
Ward, H. MO Robertson's Regt.St.Guard Co.3
Ward, H. NC Cav. 16th Bn. Co.A
Ward, H. NC 6th Inf. Co.C
Ward, H. TX 32nd Cav. Co.H 1st Lt.
Ward, H. TX Conscr.
Ward, H.A. AL Cav. Forrest's Regt.
Ward, H.A. GA Siege Arty. Campbell's Ind.Co.
Ward, H.A. MS Inf. (Res.) Berry's Co.
Ward, H.A. TN 10th (DeMoss') Cav. Co.C
Ward, H.A. TN 18th (Newsom's) Cav. Co.H
Ward, Hamilton G. TN 42nd Inf. 2nd Co.K
Ward, Hardy AL Arty. 1st Bn. Co.E
Ward, Harman TX 12th Inf. Co.I
Ward, Harrison AR 9th Inf. Co.H
Ward, Harvey FL Lt.Arty. Dyke's Co.
Ward, Harvey D. GA Smith's Legion Ralston's Co. 3rd Lt.
Ward, Harvy D. GA 6th Cav. Co.D
Ward, Haywood GA 62nd Cav. Co.E
Ward, H.B. AL 7th Cav. Co.H,A
Ward, H.C. AL 53rd (Part.Rangers) Co.F Sgt.
Ward, H.C. LA 1st (Nelligan's) Inf. Co.H
Ward, H.C. LA Inf. 1st Sp.Bn. (Rightor's) Co.D
Ward, H.C. NC 64th Inf. Co.B
Ward, H.C. 2nd Cherokee Mtd.Vol. Co.E
Ward, H.D. AL 25th Inf. Co.A
Ward, H.D. LA Inf. 16th Bn. Co.B
Ward, H.D. TN 27th Inf. Co.H
Ward, H.E. GA 13th Inf.
Ward, H.E. TN 27th Inf. Co.H
Ward, Henry AR 14th (McCarver's) Inf. Co.G
Ward, Henry AR 21st Inf. Co.F
Ward, Henry FL 1st Cav. Co.C Sgt.
Ward, Henry FL 3rd Inf. Co.F,K
Ward, Henry GA 28th Inf. Co.C
Ward, Henry GA 28th Inf. Co.E Cpl.
Ward, Henry GA 49th Inf. Co.A

Ward, Henry LA Inf. 1st Sp.Bn. (Wheat's) Co.A Music.
Ward, Henry LA 14th Inf.
Ward, Henry MS 2nd St.Cav. Co.L
Ward, Henry MS 18th Cav.
Ward, Henry MS Lt.Arty. (Jefferson Arty.) Darden's Co.
Ward, Henry MS 44th Inf. Co.D
Ward, Henry NC 1st Inf.
Ward, Henry NC 1st Jr.Res. Co.A
Ward, Henry NC 2nd Inf. Co.D
Ward, Henry NC 8th Sr.Res. Gardner's Co., Co.G
Ward, Henry NC 27th Inf. Co.A
Ward, Henry SC Lt.Arty. 3rd (Palmetto) Bn. Co.A
Ward, Henry SC 1st (McCreary's) Inf. Campbell's Co.
Ward, Henry TX Cav. McCord's Frontier Regt. Co.C 1st Lt.
Ward, Henry VA Inf. 1st Bn. Co.E
Ward, Henry VA 7th Inf. Co.A,H
Ward, Henry Recruits W.B. Ochiltree's Detach.
Ward, Henry A. MS Cav. (St.Troops) Grace's Co.
Ward, Henry A. VA 39th Inf. Co.A
Ward, Henry C. AL 39th Inf. Co.H
Ward, Henry C. GA Lt.Arty. Milledge's Co.
Ward, Henry C. VA Lt.Arty. 13th Bn. Co.B
Ward, Henry C. VA 14th Inf. Co.B
Ward, Henry Clay VA 49th Inf. Co.C 1st Lt.
Ward, Henry G. GA Arty. (Chatham Arty.) Wheaton's Co.
Ward, Henry G. GA 1st (Olmstead's) Inf. Davis' Co., Claghorn's Co.
Ward, Henry H. AL 1st Bn. Hilliard's Legion Vol. Co.F
Ward, Henry H. LA Cav. Webb's Co.
Ward, Henry H. SC 4th Inf. Co.F
Ward, Henry I. AL 20th Inf. Co.B
Ward, Henry M. AR 24th Inf. Co.F
Ward, Henry P. AL 20th Inf. Co.B,I,C Cpl.
Ward, Henry T. NC 15th Inf. Co.E
Ward, Hezekiah GA 2nd Inf. Co.A Sgt.
Ward, Hezekiah SC Inf. Hampton Legion Co.C
Ward, Hezekiah TN 3rd (Clack's) Inf.
Ward, Hezekiah M. 1st Conf.Inf. 2nd Co.D
Ward, H.H. NC 64th Inf.
Ward, H.H. TN 12th (Green's) Cav. Co.E
Ward, H.I. AL 50th Inf. Co.F
Ward, Hinton A. GA Phillips' Legion Co.A
Ward, Hiram AR Cav. Gordon's Regt. Co.G
Ward, Hiram NC Inf. French's Regt. Co.A
Ward, Hiram TX 35th (Brown's) Cav. Co.A,F Cpl.
Ward, Hiram TX 13th Vol. 1st Co.B
Ward, H.J. GA 29th Inf. Co.F
Ward, H.J. LA 13th Bn. (Part.Rangers) Co.B
Ward, H.L. AL Cav. Barbiere's Bn. Brown's Co.
Ward, H.L. AR 8th Inf. New Co.C 2nd Lt.
Ward, H.L. AR 36th Inf. Co.D Bvt.2nd Lt.
Ward, H.L. VA 17th Cav. Co.B
Ward, H.N. AR 4th Inf. Co.H Cpl.
Ward, Howel TN 16th (Logwood's) Cav. Co.B 2nd Lt.
Ward, H.P. TN Inf. 1st Bn. (Colms') Co.D
Ward, H.T. AL 34th Inf. Co.A
Ward, Hugh LA 5th Cav. Co.B
Ward, Hugh TN 11th Inf. Co.D Sgt.
Ward, Hugh G. VA 39th Inf. Co.D Sgt.
Ward, Hugh H. LA 7th Inf. Co.H Sgt.
Ward, Hugh L. TN 10th (DeMoss') Cav. Co.B
Ward, Huston VA 64th Mtd.Inf. Co.A
Ward, H.W. GA 41st Inf. Co.E
Ward, H.W. GA Phillips' Legion Co.E Sgt.
Ward, H.W. SC 23rd Inf. Co.I
Ward, H.W. VA Inf. 2nd Bn.Loc.Def. Co.B
Ward, I.A. TN 47th Inf. Co.B
Ward, I.B. MS 25th Inf. Co.C 2nd Lt.
Ward, I.C. GA 11th Inf.
Ward, I.J. FL 6th Inf. Co.I
Ward, I.J. TX Cav. Sutton's Co.
Ward, Ira TX 11th Inf. Co.K
Ward, Ira C. GA 44th Inf. Co.E
Ward, Isaac AR 36th Inf. Co.D
Ward, Isaac FL 1st Inf. New Co.D
Ward, Isaac TN 37th Inf. Co.C
Ward, Isaac TN 37th Inf. Co.G
Ward, Isaac TN 39th Mtd.Inf. Co.A
Ward, Isaac TX 22nd Cav. Co.F
Ward, Isaac TX 23rd Cav. Co.I
Ward, Isaac TX 2nd Inf. Co.D
Ward, Isaac TX Waul's Legion Co.F
Ward, Isaac B. NC 30th Inf. Co.D
Ward, Isaac F. GA 45th Inf. Co.C
Ward, Isaac H. AL 38th Inf. Co.K
Ward, Isaac J. TX 9th Cav. Co.I
Ward, Isaac M. LA Inf. 4th Bn. Co.C
Ward, Isaiah AR 45th Cav. Co.C
Ward, Isaiah FL 2nd Cav. Co.I
Ward, Isiah FL 3rd Inf. Co.E
Ward, Isom J. NC 25th Inf. Co.B
Ward, J. AL 25th Inf. Co.B
Ward, J. AL 46th Inf. Co.I Cpl.
Ward, J. AR 1st (Monroe's) Cav. Co.G
Ward, J. AR 38th Inf. Co.B
Ward, J. GA 2nd Res. Co.A
Ward, J. GA 31st Inf. Co.A Sgt.
Ward, J. KY 2nd (Duke's) Cav. Co.A
Ward, J. LA Mil. 3rd Regt. 1st Brig. 1st Div. Co.B 2nd Lt.
Ward, J. LA Mil. 4th Regt. 1st Brig. 1st Div. Co.E
Ward, J. LA 21st (Kennedy's) Inf. Co.A
Ward, J. MS 2nd St.Cav. Co.L
Ward, J. MO 2nd Inf. Co.A
Ward, J. SC Lt.Arty. M. Ward's Co. (Waccamaw Lt.Arty.)
Ward, J. TN 15th (Cons.) Cav. Co.A
Ward, J. TX 5th Cav. Co.I
Ward, J. TX Cav. McCord's Frontier Regt. Co.C Capt.
Ward, J. TX 4th Inf. (St.Troops) Co.A
Ward, J. TX 20th Inf. Co.A
Ward, J. VA 3rd (Archer's) Bn.Res. Co.E
Ward, J. VA 53rd Inf. Co.A
Ward, J. Jackson's Co.,CSA
Ward, J.A. AL Cp. of Instr. Talladega
Ward, J.A. AR Inf. 8th Bn. Co.F
Ward, J.A. AR 24th Inf. Co.D
Ward, J.A. AR 38th Inf. Co.K
Ward, J.A. AR Inf. Hardy's Regt. Co.C
Ward, J.A. FL Inf. 2nd Bn. Co.C
Ward, J.A. KY 10th Cav. Co.A
Ward, J.A. LA 4th Cav. Co.B
Ward, J.A. LA 21st (Kennedy's) Inf. Co.A Cpl.
Ward, J.A. TN 31st Inf. Co.A 1st Sgt.
Ward, J.A. TN 45th Inf. Co.E
Ward, J.A. TX Cav. 1st Regt.St.Troops Co.F
Ward, J.A. TX 19th Inf. Co.I
Ward, Jack MS 9th Cav. Co.F
Ward, Jack MS 10th Cav. Co.A
Ward, Jackson TN Cav. 17th Bn. (Sanders') Co.C
Ward, Jackson P. MS Cav. 17th Bn. Co.E 2nd Lt.
Ward, Jacob GA 7th Cav. Co.F Cpl.
Ward, Jacob GA Cav. 21st Bn. Co.B,E Cpl.
Ward, Jacob GA 1st (Olmstead's) Inf. Co.C
Ward, Jacob NC 6th Inf. Co.K
Ward, Jacob D. NC Lt.Arty. 3rd Bn. Co.C,A
Ward, Jacob J. MS 9th Inf. Old Co.C
Ward, Jacob J. MS 42nd Inf. Co.F
Ward, J.A.M. AL 9th Inf. Co.F
Ward, James AL 6th Cav. Co.A
Ward, James AL Arty. 1st Bn. Co.D
Ward, James AL 4th Res. Co.C
Ward, James AL 12th Inf. Co.A
Ward, James AL 12th Inf. Co.G
Ward, James AL 33rd Inf. Co.G
Ward, James AL 46th Inf. Co.H,C
Ward, James AL 50th Inf. Co.D
Ward, James AL Cp. of Instr. Talladega
Ward, James AL 1st Bn. Hilliard's Legion Vol. Co.B
Ward, James AR Cav. 1st Bn. (Stirman's) Co.H
Ward, James AR 2nd Cav. Co.G
Ward, James AR 8th Cav. Co.K,A 2nd Lt.
Ward, Jas. AR 1st (Colquitt's) Inf. Co.H
Ward, James AR 10th Mil. Co.F
Ward, James AR 14th (Powers') Inf. Co.D
Ward, James AR Inf. Cocke's Regt. Co.K
Ward, James FL Inf. 2nd Bn. Co.D
Ward, James FL 10th Inf. Co.K
Ward, James GA 12th Cav. Co.E
Ward, James GA 1st (Olmstead's) Inf. 1st Co.A
Ward, James GA 1st (Olmstead's) Inf. Way's Co.
Ward, James GA 1st Bn.S.S. Co.B
Ward, James GA 43rd Inf. Co.D
Ward, James GA 48th Inf. Co.A
Ward, James GA 48th Inf. Co.G
Ward, James GA 52nd Inf. Co.D
Ward, James GA 53rd Inf. Co.C
Ward, James KY 7th Mtd.Inf. Co.H
Ward, James KY 7th Mtd.Inf. Co.K
Ward, James LA 1st (Strawbridge's) Inf. Co.A,C
Ward, James LA 7th Inf. Co.I
Ward, James LA 13th Inf. Co.K
Ward, James LA 22nd Inf. Co.K
Ward, James LA Mil. British Guard Bn. Kurczyn's Co. Cpl.
Ward, James MS 44th Inf. Co.B
Ward, James MO 2nd Cav. 2nd Co.K
Ward, James MO Cav. 11th Regt.St.Guard Co.B
Ward, James MO Cav. Coffee's Regt. Co.A
Ward, James MO Inf. 1st Regt.St.Guard Co.E Cpl.
Ward, James MO Phelan's Regt.
Ward, James NC Hvy.Arty. 1st Bn. Co.C
Ward, James NC Inf. 2nd Bn. Co.F
Ward, James NC 2nd Bn.Loc.Def.Troops Co.B

Ward, James NC 3rd Inf. Co.I
Ward, James NC 8th Sr.Res. Jacobs' Co.
Ward, James NC 22nd Inf. Co.B
Ward, James NC 26th Inf. Co.E
Ward, James NC 44th Inf. Co.I
Ward, James NC 57th Inf. Co.I
Ward, James NC Mil. Clark's Sp.Bn. Co.I
Ward, James SC 1st Cav. Co.I
Ward, James, Jr. SC 1st (Orr's) Rifles Co.F
Ward, James SC Inf. Hampton Legion Co.C
Ward, James TN 15th Cav. Co.I
Ward, James TN 19th & 20th (Cons.) Cav. Co.A
Ward, James TN 20th (Russell's) Cav. Co.B
Ward, James TN 1st Hvy.Arty. 2nd Co.A
Ward, James TN Lt.Arty. Kain's Co.
Ward, James TN 3rd (Lillard's) Mtd.Inf. Co.B
Ward, James TN 10th Inf. Co.F
Ward, James TX 9th Cav. Co.G
Ward, James TX 11th Cav. Co.F
Ward, James TX 27th Cav. Co.B
Ward, James TX 1st Inf. Co.G
Ward, James TX 11th Inf. Co.K
Ward, James TX 18th Inf. Co.E
Ward, James VA 5th Cav. Coakley's Co.
Ward, James VA Lt.Arty. 13th Bn. Co.C
Ward, James VA Hvy.Arty. 19th Bn. Co.D
Ward, James VA Inf. 1st Bn. Co.D
Ward, James VA 4th Inf. Co.F
Ward, James VA 19th Inf. Co.H
Ward, James Burroughs' Bn.Part.Rangers Co.A
Ward, James A. AL 62nd Inf. Co.B
Ward, James A. AL Cp. of Instr. Talladega
Ward, James A. AR 2nd Mtd.Rifles Co.A
Ward, James A. AR 1st S.S. Co.F
Ward, James A. GA 3rd Inf. Vincent's Co.
Ward, James A. MS Cav. 1st Bn. (Miller's) Bowles' Co.
Ward, James A. MS 19th Inf. Co.F Sgt.
Ward, James A. NC 2nd Arty. (36th St.Troops) Co.C
Ward, James A. SC 23rd Inf. Co.I
Ward, James A. TX Cav. Sutton's Co.
Ward, James B. AR 47th (Crandall's) Cav. Burns' Co.
Ward, James B. TN 9th (Ward's) Cav. Co.D
Ward, James B. VA 57th Inf. Co.H
Ward, James C. MS 2nd Part.Rangers Co.D,F
Ward, James C. MS 2nd Inf. Co.K
Ward, James C. MS 22nd Inf. Co.A
Ward, James C. MO 7th Cav. Co.H
Ward, James D. GA 13th Cav. Co.F
Ward, James D. MS 4th Inf. Co.A 3rd Sgt.
Ward, James D. NC 45th Inf. Co.B
Ward, James D. SC 1st Arty. Co.G
Ward, James E. NC 60th Inf. Co.F
Ward, James E. VA 45th Inf. Co.D
Ward, James F. GA 16th Inf. Co.B
Ward, James F. GA 49th Inf. Co.A
Ward, James F. TN 15th (Stewart's) Cav.
Ward, James F. TX Inf. 3rd St.Troops Co.E
Ward, James F. VA 21st Cav. 2nd Co.E
Ward, James F. VA 8th Inf. Co.K
Ward, James F. VA 45th Inf. Co.K Cpl.
Ward, James Frederick TX 20th Cav. Co.C
Ward, James G. VA 39th Inf. Co.D Fifer
Ward, James Griffin TX 8th Cav. Co.H
Ward, James H. AL 7th Inf. Co.A
Ward, James H. AL 1st Bn. Hilliard's Legion Vol. Co.C
Ward, James H. FL 3rd Inf. Co.K
Ward, James H. MO 3rd Cav. Co.B
Ward, James H. MO 7th Cav. Ward's Co.
Ward, James H. MO Cav. Slayback's Regt. Cross' Co.
Ward, James H. NC 3rd Inf. Co.I
Ward, James H. NC 42nd Inf. Co.B
Ward, James H. NC 61st Inf. Co.H
Ward, James H. SC Lt.Arty. 3rd (Palmetto) Bn. Co.F
Ward, James H. TN 21st (Wilson's) Cav. Co.H
Ward, James H. TN 9th Inf. Co.E Sgt.
Ward, James H. TX 27th Cav. Co.I
Ward, James H. VA 8th Cav. Co.K
Ward, James H. 1st Conf.Cav. 2nd Co.G
Ward, James H. Gen. & Staff Asst.Surg.
Ward, James H.H. AL 33rd Inf. Co.B
Ward, James I. AL 62nd Inf. Co.A
Ward, James K. 1st Conf.Inf. 2nd Co.D
Ward, James K.P. TN 48th (Nixon's) Inf. Co.H
Ward, James L. GA 2nd Cav. (St.Guards) Co.H
Ward, James L. KY 2nd (Duke's) Cav. Co.C
Ward, James L. NC 13th Inf. Co.K
Ward, James L. NC 17th Inf. (1st Org.) Co.G
Ward, James L. NC 31st Inf. Co.F
Ward, James L. SC 10th Inf. Co.A
Ward, James L. TX 11th (Spaight's) Bn.Vol. Co.C
Ward, James L. TX 21st Inf. Co.E
Ward, James L. VA 61st Mil. Co.F,C
Ward, James M. AL 33rd Inf. Co.A
Ward, James M. AR 35th Inf. Co.C Capt.
Ward, James M. AR 36th Inf. Co.G
Ward, James M. GA 5th Res. Co.C
Ward, James M. GA Cobb's Legion Co.D
Ward, James M. MS 2nd Inf. Co.L Cpl.
Ward, James M. MS 14th Inf. Co.B
Ward, James M. MO 11th Inf. Co.F
Ward, James M. NC 2nd Arty. (36th St.Troops) Co.G
Ward, James M. NC 44th Inf. Co.G
Ward, James M. NC 60th Inf. Co.F
Ward, James M. NC 61st Inf. Co.D
Ward, James M. NC 64th Inf. Co.B
Ward, James N. AL 17th Inf. Co.C
Ward, James P. MS 3rd Inf. Co.G
Ward, James P. MS 37th Inf. Co.G 1st Lt.
Ward, James P. VA Lt.Arty. Griffin's Co. Cpl.
Ward, James P. VA 9th Inf. 1st Co.A Cpl.
Ward, James R. AL 12th Inf. Co.E Sgt.
Ward, James R. GA Inf. 3rd Bn. Co.C
Ward, James R. GA 37th Inf. Co.I
Ward, James R. GA 39th Inf. Co.I
Ward, James R. MS 4th Cav. Co.E
Ward, James R. NC 26th Inf. Co.B
Ward, James R. TN 10th & 11th (Cons.) Cav. Sgt.
Ward, James R. VA 8th Cav. Co.A
Ward, James R. VA 16th Cav. AQM
Ward, James R. VA 19th Cav. Co.H
Ward, James R. Gen. & Staff Capt.,AQM
Ward, James S. VA 11th Inf. Co.E
Ward, James T. AL 22nd Inf. Co.H
Ward, James T. NC 60th Inf. Co.D
Ward, James V.W. GA Lt.Arty. Milledge's Co.
Ward, James W. AL Arty. 1st Bn. Co.E
Ward, James W. AL 13th Inf. Co.K
Ward, James W. AR 7th Cav. Co.A
Ward, James W. AR 3rd Inf. Co.A
Ward, James W. GA Cav. 29th Bn. Co.A
Ward, James W. GA Siege Arty. 28th Bn. Co.C Cpl.
Ward, James W. GA 13th Inf. Co.E
Ward, James W. NC 3rd Arty. (40th St.Troops) Co.G
Ward, James W. NC Lt.Arty. 13th Bn. Co.E
Ward, James W. TX 13th Cav. Co.G
Ward, Jasper AR 7th Inf. Co.D
Ward, Jasper AR 16th Inf. Co.C
Ward, Jasper AR 38th Inf. Co.D
Ward, Jasper KY 13th Cav. Co.C
Ward, Jasper SC 16th Inf. Co.H
Ward, Jasper K. MS 34th Inf. Co.C
Ward, J.B. AR 1st (Dobbin's) Cav. Co.D
Ward, J.B. AR 12th Inf. Co.H
Ward, J.B. GA 19th Inf. Co.K
Ward, J.B. KY Morgan's Men Co.E
Ward, J.B. KY 7th Mtd.Inf. Co.K 2nd Lt.
Ward, J.B. MS Cav. Dunn's Co. (MS Rangers)
Ward, J.B. MS Lt.Arty. Lomax's Co.
Ward, J.B. MS 9th Bn.S.S. Co.C
Ward, J.B. MS 29th Inf. Co.C
Ward, J.B. NC 3rd Jr.Res. Co.F
Ward, J.B. TN 8th (Smith's) Cav. Co.C
Ward, J.B. TN 11th (Holman's) Cav. Co.L 2nd Lt.
Ward, J.B. TN Douglass' Bn.Part.Rangers Bruster's Co. 2nd Lt.
Ward, J.B. TN 5th Inf. 2nd Co.K Capt.
Ward, J.B. VA 18th Cav. Co.A
Ward, J.B. VA Horse Arty. Jackson's Co.
Ward, J.B. VA 62nd Mtd.Inf. 2nd Co.H
Ward, J.C. AL 25th Inf. Co.A
Ward, J.C. AR Inf. Cocke's Regt. Co.G
Ward, J.C. MS 5th Inf. Co.E
Ward, J.C. MO St.Guard Livingston's Co.
Ward, J.C. TN 12th Inf. Co.A Sgt.
Ward, J.C. TN 12th (Cons.) Inf. Co.A Sgt.
Ward, J.C. TN 31st Inf. Co.A Cpl.
Ward, J.C. Gen. & Staff Asst.Surg.
Ward, J.C.C. AL 51st (Part.Rangers) Co.H
Ward, J.D. AL 9th (Malone's) Cav. Co.M
Ward, J.D. AR 12th Inf. Co.K
Ward, J.D. AR 15th (Johnson's) Inf. Co.D
Ward, J.D. GA 2nd Inf. Co.E
Ward, J.D. TN 40th Inf. Co.G
Ward, J.D. VA 29th Inf. Co.A
Ward, J.E. AL 25th Inf. Co.A
Ward, J.E. AL 34th Inf. Co.I
Ward, J.E. NC 1st Jr.Res. Co.C
Ward, J.E. SC Lt.Arty. 3rd (Palmetto) Bn. Co.C Cpl.
Ward, Jehu NC 5th Cav. (63rd St.Troops) Co.I
Ward, Jeptha AR Inf. Hardy's Regt. Co.A
Ward, Jeremiah GA 43rd Inf. Co.D
Ward, Jeremiah GA 49th Inf. Co.A
Ward, Jeremiah MS 46th Inf. Co.D
Ward, Jeremiah VA Cav. Mosby's Regt. (Part.Rangers) Co.C
Ward, Jeremiah B. GA 57th Inf. Co.D
Ward, Jerry AR 7th Mil. Co.B
Ward, Jesse GA 2nd Cav. Co.F

Ward, Jesse GA Inf. 19th Bn. (St.Guards) Co.D
Ward, Jesse MS Cav. 1st Bn. (McNair's) St.Troops Co.C
Ward, Jesse MS 1st Lt.Arty. Co.I
Ward, Jesse NC 5th Cav. (63rd St.Troops) Co.D
Ward, Jesse NC 8th Sr.Res. Callihan's Co.
Ward, Jesse TN 29th Inf. Co.K
Ward, Jesse Gen. & Staff Hosp.Stew.
Ward, Jesse A. AL Mil. 4th Vol. Gantt's Co.
Ward, Jesse B. TN Cav. Newsom's Regt. Co.F
Ward, Jessee AL 43rd Inf. Co.H
Ward, Jessee AR 50th Mil. Co.I
Ward, Jessee GA 28th Inf. Co.C
Ward, Jesse James NC 20th Inf. Co.D
Ward, Jesse S. GA 55th Inf. Co.A
Ward, Jesse W. GA 30th Inf. Co.K
Ward, Jesse W. TX 3rd Cav. Co.G
Ward, Jesse W. TX 37th Cav. Co.A
Ward, Jessie KY 12th Cav. Co.F
Ward, Jessy A. AL 40th Inf. Co.I
Ward, Jethro NC 49th Inf. Co.A
Ward, J.F. AL 8th Cav. Co.C
Ward, J.F. AL 8th (Livingston's) Cav. Co.C
Ward, J.F. AL 34th Inf. Co.A
Ward, J.F. AR 3rd Cav. Co.A
Ward, J.F. MS 2nd Part.Rangers Co.K
Ward, J.F. SC 16th Inf. Co.F
Ward, J.F. SC 16th & 24th (Cons.) Inf. Co.A
Ward, J.F. TN 5th Inf. 1st Co.H
Ward, J.F. TX 24th Cav. Co.G
Ward, J.F. VA 2nd Cav. Co.E
Ward, J.F. 2nd Cherokee Mtd.Vol. Co.E
Ward, J. Frank MO Arty. Jos. Bledsoe's Co.
Ward, J.G. GA 7th Inf. Co.G
Ward, J.G. TN 2nd (Ashby's) Cav. Co.K
Ward, J.G. VA 19th Cav. Co.I 2nd Lt.
Ward, J.H. AL Mil. 4th Vol. Co.D
Ward, J.H. AL 5th Inf. Co.M
Ward, J.H. AL 14th Inf. Co.C
Ward, J.H. AL 44th Inf. Co.H
Ward, J.H. AL 60th Inf. Co.K
Ward, J.H. AL Pris.Guard Freeman's Co.
Ward, J.H. AR 19th Inf. Co.A
Ward, J.H. AR Mil. Borland's Regt. Peyton Rifles 1st Sgt.
Ward, J.H. GA Cobb's Legion Co.B Sgt.
Ward, J.H. MS 22nd Inf. Co.H
Ward, J.H. NC 3rd Inf. Co.C
Ward, J.H. NC 49th Inf. Asst.Surg.
Ward, J.H. TN 1st (Carter's) Cav. Co.A
Ward, J.H. TN Cav. Welcker's Bn. Co.H
Ward, J.J. AL 10th Cav. Co.B
Ward, J.J. AL 8th Inf. Co.E
Ward, J.J. AL Cp. of Instr. Talladega Co.F
Ward, J.J. AR Inf. Cocke's Regt. Co.C
Ward, J.J. FL 2nd Cav. Co.H Sgt.
Ward, J.J. KY 10th (Johnson's) Cav. Co.A
Ward, J.J. MS 10th Cav. Co.B
Ward, J.J. MS Lt.Arty. (Warren Lt.Arty.) Swett's Co.
Ward, J.J. MS 12th Inf. Co.B
Ward, J.J. MS 15th Inf. Co.B
Ward, J.J. SC Lt.Arty. M. Ward's Co. (Waccamaw Lt.Arty.)
Ward, J.J. SC 8th Inf. Co.E
Ward, J.J. SC 26th Inf. Co.G
Ward, J.J. TN 7th (Duckworth's) Cav. Co.H
Ward, J.J. TN Inf. 3rd Bn. Co.B Sgt.
Ward, J.J. TX 23rd Cav. Co.D
Ward, J.J. TX 29th Cav. Co.I
Ward, J.J. TX Cav. Terry's Regt. Co.K 2nd Lt.
Ward, J.J. TX 19th Inf. Co.B,K
Ward, J.J. TX 19th Inf. Co.I
Ward, J.J.R. AL 7th Cav. Co.H,A Cpl.
Ward, J.K. AR 38th Inf. Co.K
Ward, J.K. GA Inf. 1st Conf.Bn. Co.A
Ward, J.K.P. TN 18th Inf. Co.D
Ward, J.L. GA 60th Inf. Co.D
Ward, J.L. NC 18th Inf. Co.C
Ward, J.L. NC 60th Inf. Co.D
Ward, J.L. SC 15th Inf. Co.F
Ward, J.L. TN 15th (Stewart's) Cav. Co.B
Ward, J.L. TN 28th Cav. Co.I 2nd Lt.
Ward, J.L. TX 11th Cav. Co.D
Ward, J. Lawrence LA Inf. 4th Bn. Co.C Capt.
Ward, J.M. AL 6th Cav. Co.D
Ward, J.M. AL 17th Inf. Co.C
Ward, J.M. AR 26th Inf. Co.K
Ward, J.M. FL 11th Inf. Co.C Cpl.
Ward, J.M. GA Cav. 1st Bn. Hopkins' Co.
Ward, J.M. GA 5th Cav. Co.C
Ward, J.M. GA 5th Cav. Co.K
Ward, J.M. GA 11th Inf. Co.F
Ward, J.M. GA Mil. 37th Regt. Co.D 3rd Lt.
Ward, J.M. MS 1st Cav. Co.D
Ward, J.M. MS 3rd (St.Troops) Cav. Co.D
Ward, J.M. MS 5th Inf. (St.Troops) Co.G
Ward, J.M. SC Vol. Simons' Co.
Ward, J.M. TX 23rd Cav. Co.C
Ward, J.M. 20th Conf.Cav. 2nd Co.H
Ward, J.M.N. AL 14th Inf. Co.K
Ward, J.N. AL Mil. 4th Vol. Gantt's Co.
Ward, J.N. AL 32nd & 58th (Cons.) Inf.
Ward, J.N. AL 40th Inf. Co.I 1st Sgt.
Ward, J.N. SC 7th Inf. Co.I
Ward, J.N. SC 15th Inf. Co.F
Ward, Joel R. NC 2nd Arty. (36th St.Troops) Co.G Sgt.
Ward, Joh LA Mil. Orleans Fire Regt. Co.C Sgt.
Ward, John AL 6th Cav. Co.F
Ward, John AL Mil. 3rd Vol. Co.B
Ward, John AL 3rd Res. Co.I
Ward, John AL 6th Inf. Co.L
Ward, John AL 11th Inf. Co.K
Ward, John AL 33rd Inf. Co.G
Ward, John AL 36th Inf. Co.G
Ward, John AL 42nd Inf. Co.E
Ward, John AL 57th Inf. Co.E
Ward, John AL 57th Inf. Co.G
Ward, John AL 57th Inf. Co.K
Ward, John AL 62nd Inf. Co.B
Ward, John AR 2nd Cav. Co.K,H
Ward, John AR 8th Cav. Co.K,A
Ward, John AR Lt.Arty. 5th Btty.
Ward, John AR Lt.Arty. (Helena Arty.) Clarkson's Btty.
Ward, John AR Lt.Arty. Key's Btty. Cpl.
Ward, John AR 11th & 17th (Cons.) Inf. Co.I
Ward, John AR 27th Inf. Co.F
Ward, John AR 35th Inf. Old Co.F Cpl.
Ward, John AR 45th Mil. Co.E
Ward, John FL 2nd Cav. Co.I
Ward, John FL 3rd Inf. Co.F
Ward, John FL 8th Inf. Co.E
Ward, John GA Cav. 19th Bn. Co.E
Ward, John GA 62nd Cav. Co.E
Ward, John GA Inf. 1st Bn. (St.Guards) Co.D
Ward, John GA 3rd Inf. Co.C
Ward, John GA 3rd Bn.S.S. Co.A
Ward, John GA 18th Inf. Co.H Teamster
Ward, John GA 36th (Villepigue's) Inf. Co.E
Ward, John GA 46th Inf. Co.K
Ward, John GA Inf. Pool's Co.
Ward, John KY 9th Cav. Co.K
Ward, John KY 10th (Diamond's) Cav. Co.I Sgt.
Ward, John LA 3rd (Harrison's) Cav. Co.K
Ward, John LA 1st (Nelligan's) Inf. Co.E Cpl.
Ward, John LA Inf. 1st Sp.Bn. (Wheat's) New Co.D
Ward, John LA 8th Inf. Co.D
Ward, John LA 10th Inf.
Ward, John LA 14th Inf. Co.C
Ward, John LA Res.Corps Williams' Co.
Ward, John MS 38th Cav. Co.E
Ward, John MS Inf. 1st Bn.St.Troops (30 days '64) Co.H
Ward, John MS 25th Inf. Co.F
Ward, John MS 26th Inf. Co.G
Ward, John MS 37th Inf. Co.G
Ward, John MS 44th Inf. Co.B
Ward, John MS 46th Inf. Co.A,D
Ward, John MO 1st Cav. Co.I
Ward, John MO 1st N.E. Cav.
Ward, John MO 4th Cav. Co.A
Ward, John MO 1st Inf. Co.C
Ward, John MO Inf. 4th Regt.St.Guard Co.D
Ward, John MO 8th Inf. Co.B
Ward, John MO 11th Inf. Co.H Cpl.
Ward, John MO Robertson's Regt.St.Guard Co.3
Ward, John MO St.Guard
Ward, John NC 1st Cav. (9th St.Troops) Co.D
Ward, John NC 2nd Cav. (19th St.Troops) Co.K
Ward, John NC 1st Arty. (10th St.Troops) Co.I
Ward, John NC 1st Inf. Co.G
Ward, John NC 2nd Bn.Loc.Def.Troops Co.G
Ward, John NC 3rd Inf. Co.A
Ward, John NC 7th Inf. Co.C
Ward, John NC 18th Inf. Co.B
Ward, John NC 26th Inf. Co.G
Ward, John NC 32nd Inf. Co.A
Ward, John NC 37th Inf. Co.A
Ward, John NC 37th Inf. Co.E Cpl.
Ward, John NC 38th Inf. Co.I
Ward, John NC 44th Inf. Co.E
Ward, John NC 44th Inf. Co.G
Ward, John NC 44th Inf. Co.I
Ward, John NC 51st Inf. Co.H Cpl.
Ward, John NC 67th Inf. Co.A
Ward, John NC Mallett's Bn. (Cp.Guard) Co.F
Ward, John SC 15th Inf. Co.D
Ward, John SC 20th Inf. Co.I
Ward, John TN 5th (McKenzie's) Cav. Co.C
Ward, John TN Lt.Arty. Huggins' Co.
Ward, John TN 8th Inf. Co.K
Ward, John TN 29th Inf. Co.B
Ward, John TN 37th Inf. Co.C
Ward, John TN 39th Mtd.Inf. Co.A
Ward, John TX 15th Cav. Co.K
Ward, John TX 19th Cav. Co.I

Ward, John TX 22nd Cav. Co.F
Ward, John TX 27th Cav. Co.K
Ward, John TX Cav. Giddings' Bn. Onins' Co. Sgt.
Ward, John TX 1st Hvy.Arty. Co.K 1st Lt.
Ward, John TX 9th (Young's) Inf. Co.E Cpl.
Ward, John TX 17th Inf. Co.C
Ward, John TX 20th Bn.St.Troops Co.C
Ward, John TX Vol. Duke's Co.
Ward, John VA 2nd Cav. Co.G
Ward, John VA 21st Cav. 2nd Co.C
Ward, John VA Hvy.Arty. 19th Bn. Co.B
Ward, John VA 7th Inf. Co.I
Ward, John VA 10th Inf. Co.G
Ward, John VA 19th Inf. Co.D Cpl.
Ward, John VA 39th Inf. Co.B
Ward, John 1st Conf.Cav. 2nd Co.G
Ward, John 10th Conf.Cav. Co.K
Ward, John Forrest's Scouts T. Henderson's Co.,CSA
Ward, John Conf.Cav. Wood's Regt. 2nd Co.G
Ward, John Gillum's Regt. Co.G
Ward, John Conf.Inf. Tucker's Regt. Co.A
Ward, John Gen. & Staff, A. of N.VA Maj.,Surg.
Ward, John VA 56th Inf. Co.H
Ward, John 2nd Cherokee Mtd.Vol. Co.E
Ward, John A. AL Lt.Arty. 2nd Bn. Co.C
Ward, John A. MO 12th Inf. Co.E
Ward, John A. NC 54th Inf. Co.A
Ward, John A. VA 21st Mil. Co.A
Ward, Johnathan F. AR 37th Inf. Co.F
Ward, Johnathan S. NC 20th Inf. Co.D
Ward, John B. MO Cav. Freeman's Regt. Co.F
Ward, John B. NC 8th Bn.Jr.Res. Co.A
Ward, John B. VA Inf. 23rd Bn. Co.E
Ward, John B. VA 77th Mil. Co.C Sgt.
Ward, John C. AR 7th Cav. Maj.
Ward, Jno. C. AR 3rd St.Inf. Maj.
Ward, John C. FL 11th Inf. Capt.
Ward, John C. GA 43rd Inf. Co.H
Ward, John C. TX 32nd Cav. Co.C
Ward, John C. TX Cav. Madison's Regt. Co.F Cpl.
Ward, John C. VA 11th Inf. Co.E Capt.
Ward, John D. AL 39th Inf. Co.D
Ward, John D. NC 51st Inf. Co.H
Ward, John D. VA 45th Inf. Co.D
Ward, John D.L. NC 60th Inf. Co.F
Ward, John E. AR 17th (Griffith's) Inf. Co.F
Ward, John E. GA Inf. 10th Bn. Co.C
Ward, John E. GA 25th Inf. Co.E
Ward, John E. GA 50th Inf. Co.C
Ward, John E. KY 2nd Mtd.Inf. Co.A
Ward, John E. VA 10th Inf. 2nd Co.C Sgt.
Ward, John E. Gen. & Staff Vol.ADC
Ward, John F. GA 50th Inf. Co.C Cpl.
Ward, John F. MS 20th Inf. Co.F Sgt.
Ward, John F. NC 30th Inf. Co.E Cpl.
Ward, John F. NC 51st Inf. Co.E Sgt.
Ward, John F. TX Cav. Madison's Regt. Co.F
Ward, John G. TX 27th Cav. Co.H 1st Sgt.
Ward, John H. AR 13th Inf. Co.C 2nd Lt.
Ward, John H. NC 21st Inf. Co.H
Ward, John H. NC 31st Inf. Co.E
Ward, John H. SC 5th Inf. 1st Co.E, 2nd Co.H
Ward, John H. SC 6th Inf. 2nd Co.D
Ward, John H. TN 9th (Ward's) Cav. Co.D 1st Sgt.
Ward, John H. TN 11th Inf. Co.G,B
Ward, John H. VA Mil. Grayson Cty.
Ward, John J. AL 33rd Inf. Co.A
Ward, John J. FL Cav. 5th Bn. Co.A
Ward, John J. MD Inf. 2nd Bn. Co.H Cpl.
Ward, John J. MS 1st Cav. Co.B
Ward, John J. MS Cav. Jeff Davis Legion Co.F
Ward, John J. NC 20th Inf. Co.K
Ward, John James AL Lt.Arty. Ward's Btty. Capt.
Ward, John K. TN 1st (Turney's) Inf. Co.H
Ward, John L. AL Cav.
Ward, John L. TN 5th (McKenzie's) Cav. Co.C Cpl.
Ward, John L. VA 57th Inf. Co.B Capt.
Ward, John M. AL 1st Regt. Mobile Vol. British Guard Co.A 1st Sgt.
Ward, John M. GA 6th Cav. Co.D
Ward, John M. GA 12th Inf. Co.D
Ward, John M. GA 44th Inf. Co.G
Ward, Jno. M. GA 2nd St.Line
Ward, John M. MS 2nd Inf. Co.G
Ward, John M. MO 2nd Cav. 2nd Co.K
Ward, John M. NC 44th Inf. Co.E
Ward, John M. SC 6th Cav. Co.B 1st Lt.
Ward, John M. TN 3rd (Forrest's) Cav. Co.C
Ward, John M. VA 38th Inf. Co.F Sgt.
Ward, John N. MO 5th Inf. Co.A
Ward, John N. SC 9th Inf. Co.I
Ward, John P. AL 44th Inf. Co.B
Ward, John P. TN 22nd (Barteau's) Cav. Co.E QMSgt.
Ward, John P. TN 2nd (Robison's) Inf. Co.H
Ward, John Q.A. NC 47th Inf. Co.A
Ward, John R. AL 47th Inf. Co.K
Ward, John R. AR 1st Cav. Co.C Cpl.
Ward, John R. AR 1st (Colquitt's) Inf. Co.C,A 1st Sgt.
Ward, John R. NC 28th Inf. Co.G
Ward, John R. NC 64th Inf. Co.E
Ward, John R. VA 11th Inf. Co.G Surg.
Ward, John R. VA 51st Inf. Co.I
Ward, John R. VA 57th Inf. Co.B
Ward, John R. Gen. & Staff Surg.
Ward, John S. GA Lt.Arty. Milledge's Co.
Ward, John S. GA 36th (Broyles') Inf. Co.E
Ward, John S. GA 44th Inf. Co.K Cpl.
Ward, John S. TN 2nd (Smith's) Cav. Sgt.
Ward, John S. TN 50th Inf. Co.G 1st Lt.
Ward, Johnson L. NC 60th Inf. Co.G Capt.
Ward, John T. MS 2nd Part.Rangers Co.K Sgt.
Ward, John T. MS 18th Inf. Co.C
Ward, John T. VA Lt.Arty. Grandy's Co.
Ward, John T.C. AL 47th Inf. Co.C 2nd Lt.
Ward, John W. AL 17th Inf. Co.B
Ward, John W. AL 17th Inf. Co.I
Ward, John W. AL 45th Inf. Co.I
Ward, John W. AR 33rd Inf. Co.G Cpl.
Ward, John W. FL 6th Inf. Co.E
Ward, John W. GA 7th Inf. Co.A
Ward, John W. LA 19th Inf. Co.E
Ward, John W. MS 12th Inf. Co.F Capt.
Ward, John W. MS 20th Inf. Co.G
Ward, John W. NC 67th Inf. Co.A
Ward, John W. SC 5th Cav. Co.D
Ward, John W. SC Cav. 17th Bn. Co.A
Ward, John W. SC 4th Inf. Co.G
Ward, John W. SC 16th Inf. Co.C
Ward, John W. TN 4th Cav. Co.I
Ward, John W. TN 22nd Cav. Co.H
Ward, John W. VA 38th Inf. Co.G
Ward, John W. VA 42nd Inf. Co.I
Ward, John W. Gen. & Staff Chap.
Ward, John Warren MS 36th Inf. Co.E Capt.
Ward, Jon T. GA 27th Inf. Co.E
Ward, Jonathan AL 34th Inf. Co.K
Ward, Jonathan AR 8th Inf. New Co.H
Ward, Jonathan MS 1st Lt.Arty. Co.C
Ward, Jonathan VA 51st Inf. Co.K
Ward, Jonathan T. VA Hvy.Arty. 18th Bn. Co.E Sgt.
Ward, Joseph AL 3rd Bn. Hilliard's Legion Vol. Co.A
Ward, Joseph AL 60th Inf. Co.E
Ward, Joseph AR 15th (N.W.) Inf. Co.A
Ward, Joseph AR 27th Inf. Co.F
Ward, Joseph AR 38th Inf. Co.B Sgt.
Ward, Joseph LA 6th Inf. Co.F 1st Sgt.
Ward, Joseph MS 13th Inf. Co.K
Ward, Joseph MO Cav. Fristoe's Regt. Co.F
Ward, Joseph NC 1st Jr.Res. Co.A
Ward, Joseph NC 1st Jr.Res. Co.K
Ward, Joseph NC 8th Sr.Res. Callihan's Co.
Ward, Joseph NC 51st Inf. Co.A Music.
Ward, Joseph NC 58th Inf. Co.G
Ward, Joseph SC 2nd Cav. Co.E
Ward, Joseph SC 3rd Res. Co.E
Ward, Joseph TN 11th Cav. Co.A
Ward, Joseph TX 1st Inf. Co.F
Ward, Joseph VA 11th Cav. Co.I
Ward, Joseph VA 1st Arty. Co.H
Ward, Joseph VA Concsr. Cp.Lee Co.B
Ward, Joseph 3rd Conf.Cav. Co.D
Ward, Joseph A. MS 3rd Inf. Co.D
Ward, Joseph A. NC 2nd Arty. (36th St.Troops) Co.G
Ward, Joseph A. TX 13th Cav. Co.G
Ward, Joseph C. TX 11th Cav. Co.A
Ward, Joseph H. NC 31st Inf. Co.F
Ward, Joseph H. NC 33rd Inf. Co.A Cpl.
Ward, Joseph J. NC 3rd Cav. (41st St.Troops) Co.K
Ward, Joseph K. NC Walker's Bn. Thomas' Legion Co.G
Ward, Joseph K. TN 1st (Carter's) Cav. Co.H
Ward, Joseph L. NC 15th Inf. Co.I
Ward, Joseph M. MO 4th Cav. Co.I
Ward, Joseph M. NC 44th Inf. Co.E
Ward, Joseph O. AR 27th Inf. Co.F
Ward, Joseph R.D. NC 12th Inf. Co.F
Ward, Joseph S. AR 15th (Josey's) Inf. Co.E
Ward, Joseph T. NC 27th Inf. Co.E
Ward, Joseph T. TN 12th (Cons.) Inf. Co.E
Ward, Joseph W. MS 24th Inf. Co.L Capt.
Ward, Joseph W. NC 2nd Arty. (26th St.Troops) Co.F
Ward, Josh H. NC 15th Inf. Co.M
Ward, Joshua NC 2nd Inf. Co.E
Ward, Joshua NC 8th Sr.Res. Callihan's Co.
Ward, Joshua SC Lt.Arty. M. Ward's Co. (Waccamaw Lt.Arty.) Capt.
Ward, Joshua TN 12th (Cons.) Inf. Co.D

Ward, Joshua H. NC 32nd Inf. Co.I
Ward, Joshua S. TN 15th Cav. Co.A
Ward, Josiah GA Inf. 1st Loc.Troops (Augusta) Co.F
Ward, Josiah NC 1st Cav. (9th St.Troops) Co.H
Ward, Josiah NC 4th Inf. Co.E
Ward, Josiah J. VA 6th Inf. Co.G
Ward, J.P. AL 29th Inf. Co.D
Ward, J.P. AL Cp. of Instr. Talladega Co.D
Ward, J.P. GA Cav. 20th Bn. Co.C
Ward, J.P. GA 66th Inf. Co.F
Ward, J.P. MS 9th Cav. Co.C 2nd Lt.
Ward, J.P. MS Cav. 17th Bn. Co.E 2nd Lt.
Ward, J.P. SC 21st Inf. Co.K
Ward, J.R. AR Cav. Gordon's Regt. Co.C Cpl.
Ward, J.R. AR Cav. Crabtree's (46th) Regt. Co.B Cpl.
Ward, J.R. AR 62nd Mil. Co.F 1st Lt.
Ward, J.R. MS Cav. Hughes' Bn. Co.D
Ward, J.R. TN 11th (Holman's) Cav. Co.L
Ward, J.R. TN 23rd Inf. Co.B
Ward, J.R. TX 32nd Cav. Co.K
Ward, J.S. AR 12th Inf. Co.K
Ward, J.S. KY 3rd Mtd.Inf. Co.B Cpl.
Ward, J.S. TN 8th (Smith's) Cav. Co.D
Ward, J.S. TN 22nd Inf. Co.K
Ward, J.S. 3rd Conf.Cav. Co.I
Ward, J. Sidney NC 35th Inf. Co.K 3rd Lt.
Ward, J.T. AL 53rd (Part.Rangers) Co.D Cpl.
Ward, J.T. AL 36th (O'Neal's) Inf. Co.H
Ward, J.T. AL 48th Inf. Co.E
Ward, J.T. KY 12th Cav. Co.B
Ward, J.T. MS 1st Cav. Co.E
Ward, J.T. MS 8th Cav. Co.K
Ward, J.T. MS Lt.Arty. (The Hudson Btty.) Hoole's Co.
Ward, J.T. MS 15th Inf. Co.D
Ward, J.T. TN 15th (Cons.) Cav. Co.G
Ward, J.T. TN 12th Inf. Co.D
Ward, J.T. TX Cav. 6th Bn. Co.C
Ward, J.T. TX 25th Cav. Co.A
Ward, J.T. VA 54th Mil. Co.C
Ward, J.T. Taylor's Corps Subs.Dept. Capt.,Agent
Ward, Julius TX 4th Inf. (St.Troops) Co.E
Ward, Julius VA 41st Inf. 1st Co.G
Ward, Julius VA 61st Inf. Co.I
Ward, Julius A. MO Cav. 2nd Bn.St.Guard Co.B Cpl.
Ward, Junius KY 2nd Mtd.Inf. Co.B
Ward, J.V. TX 1st Inf. Co.B
Ward, J.W. AL 1st Cav. 2nd Co.B
Ward, J.W. AL 10th Cav. Co.D
Ward, J.W. AL 37th Inf. Co.H
Ward, J.W. AR 6th Inf. Old Co.F, New Co.F
Ward, J.W. AR 12th Bn.S.S. Co.D
Ward, J.W. AR 13th Mil. Co.A
Ward, J.W. AR 19th (Dockery's) Inf. Co.I
Ward, J.W. AR 35th Inf. Co.I
Ward, J.W. AR Mil. Borland's Regt. Peyton Rifles
Ward, J.W. GA Inf. 3rd Bn. Co.C
Ward, J.W. GA 63rd Inf. Co.G
Ward, J.W. MS Cav. Dunn's Co. (MS Rangers)
Ward, J.W. MS 24th Inf. Co.H,A
Ward, J.W. SC 1st Cav. Co.B Sgt.
Ward, J.W. SC Lt.Arty. 3rd (Palmetto) Bn. Co.A
Ward, J.W. SC Lt.Arty. 3rd (Palmetto) Bn. Co.E Sgt.
Ward, J.W. SC Lt.Arty. 3rd (Palmetto) Bn. Co.H
Ward, J.W. SC 1st (McCreary's) Inf. Campbell's Co.
Ward, J.W. SC 7th (Ward's) Bn.St.Res. Maj.
Ward, J.W. SC 8th Inf. Co.E 2nd Lt.
Ward, J.W. SC Inf. 13th Bn. Co.B
Ward, J.W. SC 16th Inf. Co.F
Ward, J.W. SC 16th & 24th (Cons.) Inf. Co.F
Ward, J.W. TN 35th Inf. Co.E
Ward, J.W. TX 10th Cav. Co.A
Ward, J.W. TX Inf. 1st St.Troops Saxton's Co. Sgt.
Ward, J.W. TX 9th (Young's) Inf. Co.B
Ward, J.W. VA 1st Arty. Co.A
Ward, J.W. VA 2nd Arty. Co.E
Ward, J.W. VA 2nd St.Res. Co.I
Ward, J.W. VA 3rd Res. Co.C
Ward, J.W.R. AR 4th Inf. Co.I
Ward, J.Y. KY 3rd Mtd.Inf. Co.H
Ward, Kenneth R. VA 9th Inf. Co.I Cpl.
Ward, Kenroy MS 2nd Cav. Co.E
Ward, Kinchen TN 45th Inf. Co.G
Ward, Kindred FL 5th Inf. Co.F,G
Ward, K.T. AR 30th Inf. Co.D Sgt.
Ward, L. AR Cav. Gordon's Regt. Co.D
Ward, L. AR 26th Inf. Co.D
Ward, L. MS 2nd (Davidson's) Inf. Co.H
Ward, L.A. MS Cav. Gartley's Co. (Yazoo Rangers)
Ward, L.A. MS 44th Inf. Co.B
Ward, Lafayette AR 2nd Inf. Co.C,B 2nd Lt.
Ward, Launcelot VA 39th Inf. Co.I
Ward, Lawrence GA Inf. 2nd Bn. Co.C
Ward, Lawrence (Col.) NC 1st Arty. (10th St.Troops) Co.D Cook
Ward, Lawrence M. MS 31st Inf. Co.F
Ward, Lawrence M. NC 24th Inf. Co.F
Ward, L.B. MS 2nd Cav. Co.K
Ward, L.B. TX 11th Cav. Co.F Sgt.
Ward, L.C. AL 14th Inf. Co.C
Ward, L.C. TX 32nd Cav. Co.H Sgt.
Ward, L.D. AL Mil. 4th Vol. Gantt's Co.
Ward, L.D. AR 32nd Inf. Co.I Cpl.
Ward, L.D. MS 8th Cav.
Ward, L.D. MS 28th Cav. Co.K
Ward, L.E. NC 64th Inf. Co.B
Ward, L.E. VA 18th Cav. Co.A
Ward, Lee NC 62nd Inf. Co.C
Ward, Lee G. TX 7th Inf. Co.D
Ward, Lee M. VA 19th Cav. Co.I
Ward, Legan AL 17th Bn.S.S. Co.B
Ward, Legan AL 39th Inf. Co.G
Ward, Lemuel NC 27th Inf. Co.F
Ward, Leonidas G. TX 17th Cav. Co.K
Ward, Leroy AR 17th (Lemoyne's) Inf. Co.D
Ward, Leroy AR 21st Inf. Co.H Cpl.
Ward, Leroy H. MO Cav. 2nd Bn.St.Guard Co.A
Ward, Leroy H. MO 12th Inf. Co.E
Ward, Leven T. TX Cav. Ragsdale's Bn. Co.D Bugler
Ward, Levi GA 43rd Inf. Co.D
Ward, Levi SC 1st St.Troops Co.H
Ward, Levi TN 32nd Inf. Co.B
Ward, Levi VA 52nd Inf.
Ward, Levi G. GA 36th (Broyles') Inf.
Ward, Levi T. AL 13th Inf. Co.E
Ward, Levy SC 22nd Inf. Co.H
Ward, Lewis TN 59th Mtd.Inf. Co.G
Ward, Lewis VA 23rd Inf. Co.E
Ward, Lewis J. GA Cav. 1st Bn. Lamar's Co., Brailsford's Co.
Ward, Lewis J. GA 50th Inf. Co.E Cpl.
Ward, Lewis T. MO 5th Cav. Co.F
Ward, L.H. TN 18th (Newsom's) Cav. Co.A
Ward, L.H. TX 35th (Brown's) Cav. Co.A
Ward, Littleton VA Cav. Young's Co.
Ward, L.J. TN 23rd Inf. Co.E
Ward, L.J. TX 30th Cav. Co.C
Ward, L.L. MO 1st Inf. Co.C
Ward, Logan 1st Choctaw & Chickasaw Mtd.Rifles 2nd Co.B
Ward, London B. TX 17th Cav. Co.A
Ward, Lorenzo D. MS 11th Inf. Co.A
Ward, Lorenzo Dow NC 37th Inf. Co.A
Ward, Loudon B. TX 7th Cav. Co.E
Ward, Louis A. NC 16th Inf. Co.I 2nd Lt.
Ward, L.S. TX 2nd Inf. Co.A Sgt.
Ward, L.T. TX 1st (Yager's) Cav. Co.I
Ward, L.T. TX 8th Cav. Co.E
Ward, Lucius T. VA Inf. 22nd Bn. Co.B
Ward, Lucius T. VA 23rd Inf. Co.K
Ward, Luke GA 4th Inf. Co.H
Ward, Luke NC 17th Inf. (1st Org.) Co.G
Ward, L.W. MS 13th Inf. Co.G
Ward, Lycurgus T. TX Cav. Ragsdale's Bn. Co.D
Ward, Lyman TX Cav. (Loc.Def.) Upton's Co.
Ward, M. AL 8th (Hatch's) Cav. Co.F
Ward, M. AL 1st Inf. Hosp.Stew.
Ward, M. AL 3rd Bn.Res. Co.H
Ward, M. AR 38th Inf. Co.B
Ward, M. GA 15th Inf. Co.K
Ward, M. KY 3rd Mtd.Inf. Co.L
Ward, M. MS 46th Inf. Co.F Cpl.
Ward, M. TN 12th Inf. Co.E
Ward, M. TN 20th Inf. Co.E
Ward, M. TX 23rd Cav. Co.I
Ward, M. VA 20th Inf. Co.D
Ward, M. VA Loc.Def. Wood's Co.
Ward, Madison M. NC 13th Inf. Co.K
Ward, Malford AR 7th Cav. Co.A
Ward, Malfrey AR 16th Inf. Co.C
Ward, Marcus L. AL 47th Inf. Co.F
Ward, Marsden B. NC 8th Inf. Co.C
Ward, Marshall GA 31st Inf. Co.G
Ward, Martin LA Mil. C.S. Zouave Bn.
Ward, Martin TN 5th Cav. Co.B
Ward, Martin TN 26th Inf. Co.A
Ward, Martin TX Cav. Baird's Regt. Co.D
Ward, Martin 2nd Cherokee Mtd.Vol. Co.G
Ward, Martin V. MS 26th Inf. Co.G,K Sgt.
Ward, Martin V. TX Cav. Hardeman's Regt. Co.E Sgt.
Ward, Martin V. TX 4th Inf. Co.A
Ward, Mathew AL 33rd Inf. Co.A
Ward, Mathew LA Mil. 3rd Regt. 1st Brig. 1st Div. Co.A
Ward, Mathew VA 22nd Cav. Co.H
Ward, Mathew L. MS 48th Inf. Co.B Sgt.
Ward, Mathew M. AR 4th Inf. Co.F
Ward, Matthew J. NC 18th Inf. Co.C 1st Sgt.

Ward, Matthias VA 6th Inf. Ferguson's Co.
Ward, Matthias VA 12th Inf. Co.H
Ward, Mayham SC Lt.Arty. M. Ward's Co. (Waccamaw Lt.Arty.) Capt.
Ward, M.B. MO 7th Cav. Co.I
Ward, M.B. SC 6th Cav. QMSgt.
Ward, M.B. TX 24th Cav. Co.E
Ward, M.B. TX 9th (Nichols') Inf. Co.D
Ward, McDaniel NC 20th Inf. Co.K
Ward, M.D. MO Lt.Arty. 4th (Harris') Field Btty.
Ward, M.D. MO Robertson's Regt.St.Guard Co.13
Ward, Medicus M. NC 12th Inf. Co.C 2nd Lt.
Ward, Melvin C. VA 50th Inf. Co.A
Ward, M.H. GA 1st Cav. Co.K
Ward, M.H. MS 1st Cav. Co.E
Ward, Michael FL 1st Inf. Old Co.K, New Co.E
Ward, Michael GA 3rd Inf. Co.I
Ward, Michael NC 58th Inf. Co.D
Ward, Michael VA 9th Bn.Res. Co.C
Ward, Michael S. NC McDugald's Co.
Ward, Michael W. AL 33rd Inf. Co.A
Ward, Miles AR 24th Inf. Co.B
Ward, Miles AR Inf. Hardy's Regt. Co.B
Ward, Miles A. NC 49th Inf. Co.K
Ward, Milledge B. SC Cav.Bn. Hampton Legion Co.A
Ward, Milton KY 7th Cav. Co.C
Ward, Milton NC 45th Inf. Co.D
Ward, Milton E. AL 8th Cav. Co.D Cpl.
Ward, Minas NC 32nd Inf. Co.L
Ward, Miner AR 45th Cav. Co.C
Ward, Minus NC 3rd Arty. (40th St.Troops) Co.I
Ward, M.J. NC 7th Sr.Res. Mitchell's Co.
Ward, M.L. AL 40th Inf. Co.E
Ward, M.L. MS Inf. 2nd Bn. Co.B
Ward, M.L. SC Lt.Arty. 3rd (Palmetto) Bn. Co.E
Ward, M.L. TX Inf. Timmons' Regt. Co.H
Ward, M.L. TX Waul's Legion Co.A
Ward, M.M. TN 13th Inf. Co.I
Ward, M.N. GA 2nd Cav. Co.F
Ward, Monroe AL 53rd (Part.Rangers) Co.D
Ward, Montgomery P. VA Arty. Paris' Co. Cpl.
Ward, Mordecai A. NC 4th Inf. Co.E
Ward, Morris GA 8th Inf. Co.G Sgt.
Ward, Morris MD Inf. 2nd Bn. Co.H
Ward, Morris TX 28th Cav. Co.D
Ward, Morris TX 4th Field Btty.
Ward, Moses AL 4th Res. Co.I
Ward, Moses FL 2nd Cav. Co.I
Ward, Moses GA 1st (Symons') Res. Co.G
Ward, Moses MS 5th Inf. (St.Troops) Co.C
Ward, Moses S. AL 28th Inf. Co.K
Ward, Moses W. MS 11th Inf. Co.G
Ward, M.S. MS Lt.Arty. 14th Bn. Maj.
Ward, M.V. GA 19th Inf. Co.E
Ward, M. Van B. VA 62nd Mtd.Inf. 2nd Co.H
Ward, M.W. MS 1st Cav. Co.E
Ward, M.W. MS 7th Inf. Co.I
Ward, M.W. MO 8th Inf. Co.E
Ward, N. GA 11th Inf. Co.I
Ward, N.A. TN 13th Inf. Co.B
Ward, Nathan GA 28th Inf. Co.E
Ward, Nathan SC 20th Inf. Co.A
Ward, Nathan TN 44th Inf. Co.A
Ward, Nathan VA 51st Inf. Co.I
Ward, Nathaniel GA 43rd Inf. Co.D Cpl.
Ward, Nathaniel MS 10th Cav. Co.G
Ward, Nathaniel H. AR 19th (Dawson's) Inf. Co.F
Ward, Nathan O. NC 2nd Cav. (19th St.Troops) Co.C 3rd Lt.
Ward, N.B. GA 4th (Clinch's) Cav. Co.D
Ward, N.B. MS 6th Inf. Co.F
Ward, N.B. SC 5th Inf. 1st Co.F, 2nd Co.I
Ward, N.C. LA 4th Cav. Co.B
Ward, Needham AL 11th Inf. Co.D,E
Ward, Needham SC Inf. 9th Bn. Co.D
Ward, Needham W. MS 34th Inf. Co.K
Ward, Neil AL Inf. 1st Regt. Co.A
Ward, Neil AL 31st Inf. Co.I
Ward, Nevis TX Inf. Griffin's Bn. Co.D
Ward, Newett TX 13th Vol. 3rd Co.A
Ward, Newit GA Inf. 8th Bn. Co.D
Ward, Newton MS 7th Cav. Co.A
Ward, Newton SC 5th St.Troops Co.E
Ward, N.H. MS 2nd (Quinn's St.Troops) Inf. Co.A
Ward, Noah W. MS 21st Inf. Co.F
Ward, Noah Webster MS 8th Cav. Co.A
Ward, N.P. TX 28th Cav. Co.F Capt.,AQM
Ward, N.T. GA 6th Cav. Co.I
Ward, Oantekie 1st Choctaw Mtd.Rifles Co.I
Ward, Obediah AL 10th Inf. Co.C
Ward, O.E. TX 7th Cav. Co.C Bugler
Ward, O.J. MS 1st (King's) Inf. (St.Troops) D. Love's Co. Sgt.
Ward, Oliver TX 9th Cav. Co.G
Ward, Oliver H. GA 44th Inf. Co.G
Ward, Oliver W. VA 14th Cav. Co.K
Ward, O. Lucuis MS 1st Cav.Res. Co.A
Ward, Oran W. NC 24th Inf. Co.F
Ward, Oscar G. MS 34th Inf. Co.C
Ward, P. LA Mil. Irish Regt. Co.F
Ward, P. MD Inf. 2nd Bn. Co.A
Ward, P. NC 35th Inf. Co.K
Ward, P. NC Mallett's Bn. (Cp.Guard) Co.D
Ward, P. SC 23rd Inf. Co.I
Ward, P. TX Cav. Baird's Regt. Co.F
Ward, Paschal W. GA 44th Inf. Co.F
Ward, Pat LA 13th Inf. Co.H
Ward, Pat TX 16th Inf. Co.K
Ward, Patrick AL 5th Inf. New Co.A
Ward, Patrick FL 2nd Inf. Co.K
Ward, Patrick GA 31st Inf. Co.K Cpl.
Ward, Patrick LA Arty. Moody's Co. (Madison Lt.Arty.) Cpl.
Ward, Patrick LA 9th Inf. Co.E
Ward, Patrick LA 14th Inf.
Ward, Patrick LA 18th Inf. Co.H
Ward, Patrick LA 22nd Inf. Wash. Marks' Co.
Ward, Patrick SC Inf.Loc.Def. Estill's Co.
Ward, Patrick TX 22nd Inf. Co.K
Ward, Patrick H. GA 48th Inf. Co.G
Ward, Patrick H. GA 57th Inf. Co.I,K 1st Sgt.
Ward, Patrick H. LA 6th Inf. Co.B
Ward, Patrick H. MS 18th Inf. Co.C
Ward, Patrick J. MS 34th Inf. Co.C
Ward, P.C. AR 7th Inf. Co.H
Ward, P.E. AL 54th Inf. Co.C Sgt.
Ward, P.E. 4th Conf.Inf. Co.B
Ward, Peter AL Lt.Arty. 2nd Bn. Co.B
Ward, Peter NC 45th Inf. Co.D
Ward, Peter D. NC 48th Inf. Co.B
Ward, Peter D. 7th Conf.Cav. Co.G
Ward, P.H. GA Cav. 1st Bn. Brailsford's Co. Cpl.
Ward, P.H. GA 5th Cav. Co.H Cpl.
Ward, P.H. GA 13th Cav. Co.C
Ward, P.H. GA Inf. 1st Loc.Troops (Augusta) Co.C 1st Lt.
Ward, P.H. MS 3rd (St.Troops) Cav. Co.D
Ward, Philip SC 5th Cav. Co.H
Ward, Philip M. AR 19th (Dawson's) Inf. Co.K
Ward, P.J. AL City Troop (Mobile) Arrington's Co.A
Ward, P.L. AR 8th Inf. New Co.H
Ward, Pleasant GA Smith's Legion Co.E
Ward, Pleasant C. MO Cav. Freeman's Regt. Co.F
Ward, Pleasant L. GA Lt.Arty. 12th Bn. 2nd Co.A
Ward, P.M. AR Inf. Hardy's Regt. Co.K
Ward, P.M. TN 51st (Cons.) Inf. Co.K
Ward, P.M. TN 52nd Inf. Co.E Sgt.
Ward, P.M. 3rd Conf.Eng.Troops Co.B
Ward, Powell AL 2nd Cav. Co.K
Ward, Preston AL 5th Cav. Co.G
Ward, Preston TN 17th Inf. Co.I
Ward, P.S. AL 6th Inf. Co.I
Ward, P.W. AL 12th Cav. Co.G
Ward, P.W. AL 12th Inf. Co.G
Ward, P.W. GA 20th Inf. Co.D
Ward, R. AL 10th Inf. Co.C
Ward, R. GA 60th Inf. Co.G
Ward, R. TN 3rd (Forrest's) Cav. Co.D
Ward, R. TX 9th (Young's) Inf. Co.B
Ward, R.A. AR 36th Inf. Co.D
Ward, R.A. GA 36th (Broyles') Inf. Co.E
Ward, R.A. MS 2nd Cav. 2nd Co.G
Ward, R.A. MS 5th Cav. Co.B
Ward, Raford C. TN 45th Inf. Co.I
Ward, Ralph KY 2nd (Duke's) Cav. Co.C Sgt.
Ward, Randolph VA 5th Cav. (12 mo. '61-2) Co.A,I
Ward, Randolph VA Cav. 14th Bn. Co.B
Ward, Randolph VA 15th Cav. Co.I
Ward, Ransom MS 8th Cav. Co.C
Ward, R.D. TN 22nd (Barteau's) Cav. Co.I
Ward, R.D. TN 47th Inf. Co.H
Ward, R.E. AL 33rd Inf. Co.B Capt.
Ward, Reddick NC 17th Inf. (2nd Org.) Co.H
Ward, Renard A. LA 3rd Inf. Co.F
Ward, Reuben NC 44th Inf. Co.H
Ward, Reuben A. GA 1st Bn.S.S. Co.C
Ward, Reubin B. MS 6th Inf. Co.C
Ward, R.F. MO Inf. 1st Regt.St.Guard Co.B 1st Lt.
Ward, R.G. AL 37th Inf. Co.K
Ward, R.H. GA 9th Inf. (St.Guards) Co.C Capt.
Ward, R.H. GA 42nd Inf. Co.G
Ward, R.H. SC 3rd Inf. Co.B
Ward, R.H. SC 8th Inf. Co.E Sgt.
Ward, R.H. VA Inf. Lyneman's Co.
Ward, R.I. LA 4th Cav. Co.B Capt.
Ward, Richard AR Cav. 1st Bn. (Stirman's) Co.F Cpl.
Ward, Richard AR 3rd Cav. 2nd Co.E Cpl.
Ward, Richard FL Lt.Arty. Dyke's Co.

Ward, Richard GA 1st (Fannin's) Res. Co.B
Ward, Richard NC 3rd Inf. Co.A
Ward, Richard NC 27th Inf. Co.A
Ward, Richard SC 6th Cav. Co.B Regt.QM
Ward, Richard SC 2nd Inf. Co.C
Ward, Richard Gen. & Staff Capt.,AQM
Ward, Richard C. 10th Conf.Cav. Co.A
Ward, Richard F. VA Loc.Def. Mallory's Co.
Ward, Richard G. NC 3rd Cav. (41st St.Troops) Co.B Sgt.
Ward, Richard L. AR 27th Inf. New Co.B
Ward, Richard M. GA 18th Inf. Co.G
Ward, Richard S. VA 23rd Inf. Co.K Cpl.
Ward, Richard W. FL 1st Cav. Co.G Cpl.
Ward, Richard W. GA Lt.Arty. 12th Bn. 2nd Co.A
Ward, Richard W. NC 3rd Cav. (41st St.Troops) Co.H 1st Lt.
Ward, Riley B. GA 49th Inf. Co.A Cpl.
Ward, R.J. AL 8th Inf. Co.E,I
Ward, R.J. AL Vol. Meador's Co.
Ward, R.J. SC 1st Cav. Co.F Cpl.
Ward, R.J. 8th (Wade's) Conf.Cav. Co.I
Ward, R.K. KY 2nd (Woodward's) Cav. Co.G
Ward, R.K. TN 29th Inf. Co.K
Ward, R.K. TX 1st Inf. Co.G
Ward, R.L. AL 1st Cav. 2nd Co.D
Ward, R.M. GA 1st (Fannin's) Res. Co.B Sgt.
Ward, R.M. TN 12th Inf. Co.A
Ward, R.M. TN 12th (Cons.) Inf. Co.A
Ward, R.N. VA Arty. C.F. Johnston's Co.
Ward, Robert AL 12th Inf. Co.H
Ward, Robert AR 24th Inf. Co.B
Ward, Robert AR Inf. Hardy's Regt. Co.B
Ward, Robert GA 8th Inf. Co.K
Ward, Robert GA 48th Inf. Co.D
Ward, Robert MS 12th Inf. Co.C
Ward, Robert MO 12th Inf. Co.H
Ward, Robert NC 8th Sr.Res. Callihan's Co.
Ward, gbert TX 22nd Inf. Co.I
Ward, Robert VA Cav. Hounshell's Bn. Thurmond's Co.
Ward, Robert VA 63rd Inf. Co.G, 2nd Co.I
Ward, Robert VA Mil. Carroll Cty.
Ward, Robert A. AL 50th Inf. Co.E
Ward, Robert A. MS Cav. Dunn's Co. (MS Rangers) Cpl.
Ward, Robert A. VA Inf. 22nd Bn. Co.B 1st Lt.
Ward, Robert A. VA 53rd Inf. Co.I
Ward, Robert B. TN 33rd Inf. Co.D Music.
Ward, Robert D. VA 2nd St.Res. Co.D Capt.
Ward, Robert E. AL 3rd Cav. Co.H
Ward, Robert E. MS 38th Cav. Co.I
Ward, Robert F. MS 9th Inf. Old Co.I 1st Sgt.
Ward, Robert F. MS 42nd Inf. Co.B 1st Lt.
Ward, Robert F. NC 42nd Inf. Co.B
Ward, Robert F. VA 30th Bn.S.S. Co.A
Ward, Robert H. AL 21st Inf. Co.A
Ward, Robert H. GA 28th Inf. Co.C
Ward, Robert H. LA 12th Inf. Co.F
Ward, Robert H. NC 13th Inf. Co.I Capt.
Ward, Robert H. TX 18th Inf. Co.D
Ward, Robert H. VA 5th Cav. (12 mo. '61-2) Co.A
Ward, Robert J. AL 61st Inf. Co.B
Ward, Robert M. TN 45th Inf. Co.I Ord.Sgt.
Ward, Robert M. TX 34th Cav. Co.D
Ward, Robert N. GA 3rd Cav. (St.Guards) Co.H
Ward, Robert N. VA 1st Arty. Co.H
Ward, Robert T. AR 16th Inf. Co.C Sgt.
Ward, Robert T. NC 61st Inf. Co.H
Ward, Robert T. VA Cav. 14th Bn. Co.D
Ward, Robert T. VA 15th Cav. Co.K
Ward, Roland H. AL 38th Inf. Co.F
Ward, Rollin C. SC 10th Inf. Co.A
Ward, Rowan C. GA 5th Inf. Co.K Sgt.
Ward, Rowan C. 3rd Conf.Eng.Troops Co.C
Ward, R.P. AL 5th Cav. Co.A
Ward, R.P. AL 10th Cav. Co.D
Ward, R.R. Gen. & Staff Hosp.Stew.
Ward, R.S. KY 14th Cav. Co.A
Ward, R.S. VA 19th Cav. Co.I
Ward, R.T. VA 5th Cav. Co.G
Ward, Rudy AL 50th Inf. Co.D
Ward, Ruffin AL 60th Inf. Co.G
Ward, Ruffin AL 3rd Bn. Hilliard's Legion Vol. Co.E
Ward, Ruffin TX 20th Inf. Co.A
Ward, Rufus NC 2nd Inf. Co.H
Ward, Rufus TN 16th Inf. Co.I
Ward, Rufus P. NC 15th Inf. Co.E
Ward, Rus TX 23rd Cav. Co.H 2nd Lt.
Ward, Russell AR 1st Mtd.Rifles Co.A
Ward, Russell H. GA 36th (Broyles') Inf. Co.G
Ward, S. AR 51st Mil. Co.E
Ward, S. MS 19th Inf. Co.D
Ward, S.A. AL 58th Inf. Co.B 2nd Lt.
Ward, Sam J. MO Inf. 5th Regt.St.Guard Co.A Capt.
Ward, Sampson M. AL 17th Inf. Co.I
Ward, Sampson W. AL Inf. 1st Regt. Co.A
Ward, Samuel AL Arty. 1st Bn. Co.A
Ward, Samuel NC 6th Inf. Co.K,G
Ward, Samuel SC 1st St.Troops Co.E Cpl.
Ward, Samuel TN 21st Inf. Co.C
Ward, Samuel VA 49th Inf. Co.D
Ward, Samuel VA 56th Inf. Co.H Cpl.
Ward, Samuel VA 88th Mil.
Ward, Samuel 2nd Conf.Eng.Troops Co.A
Ward, Samuel 1st Cherokee Mtd.Vol. 2nd Co.A
Ward, Samuel 2nd Cherokee Mtd.Vol. Co.G
Ward, Samuel 2nd Cherokee Mtd.Vol. Co.H
Ward, Samuel 1st Choctaw Mtd.Rifles Ward's Co. Capt.
Ward, Samuel 1st Choctaw & Chickasaw Mtd.Rifles Co.G
Ward, Samuel A. NC 12th Inf. Co.C Cpl.
Ward, Samuel C. TN 3rd (Forrest's) Cav. Co.D
Ward, Samuel C. TN 9th (Ward's) Cav. Co.D
Ward, Samuel G. MS 11th (Perrin's) Cav. Co.C
Ward, Samuel G. MO St.Guard Capt.,Ch.Ord.
Ward, Samuel H. NC 4th Inf. Co.E
Ward, Samuel J. MO 8th Cav. Co.E Lt.Col.
Ward, Samuel M. AL 15th Inf. Co.F
Ward, Samuel M. NC 22nd Inf. Co.H Sgt.
Ward, Samuel M. TX 9th (Young's) Inf. Co.D 1st Lt.
Ward, Samuel S. MS 34th Inf. Co.E 1st Sgt.
Ward, Samuel S. TX 15th Cav. Co.K Sgt.
Ward, Samuel W. NC 42nd Inf. Co.I
Ward, Samuel W. NC 51st Inf. Co.G
Ward, Sandy Conf.Cav. Wood's Regt. Co.H
Ward, S.B. MS 9th Inf. Co.C
Ward, S.B. MS 33rd Inf. Co.K
Ward, S.B. NC 28th Inf. Co.F
Ward, S.B. TN 57th Inf. Co.I
Ward, S.C. MO St.Guard Cpl.
Ward, S.D. AL 48th Inf. Co.C
Ward, S.D. KY 3rd Cav. Co.B
Ward, S.D. VA 64th Mtd.Inf. Co.D
Ward, Sedge T. VA Lt.Arty. E.J. Anderson's Co.
Ward, Seth MS Inf. 7th Bn. Co.E
Ward, Seth TX Inf. Chambers' Bn.Res.Corps Co.D
Ward, Seth T. AR 4th Inf. Co.H Sgt.
Ward, Seth W. NC 44th Inf. Co.K
Ward, S.G. AR 19th (Dawson's) Inf. Co.K
Ward, S.G. TX 21st Cav. Co.D,C 1st Lt.
Ward, S.G. TX 25th Cav. Co.A
Ward, S.H. TX 23rd Cav. Co.F
Ward, Shirous TN 4th (McLemore's) Cav. Co.I
Ward, Silas VA 30th Bn.S.S. Co.E
Ward, Silas VA 51st Inf. Co.I
Ward, Silas 1st Choctaw & Chickasaw Mtd.Rifles 2nd Co.B
Ward, Silas M. TX 2nd Inf. Co.D
Ward, Silas M. TX 7th Inf. Co.E Sgt.
Ward, Sim TN 7th (Duckworth's) Cav. Co.H
Ward, Simeon AL 25th Inf. Co.A
Ward, Simeon LA 27th Inf. Co.B
Ward, Simeon N. AL 47th Inf. Co.C
Ward, Simon NC 51st Inf. Co.H
Ward, Simon TN 14th Inf.
Ward, Simon D. NC 61st Inf. Co.H Sgt.
Ward, Simon P. FL 2nd Inf. Co.M
Ward, Simond D. NC 42nd Inf. Co.B Sgt.
Ward, S.J. AR 3rd Inf. Co.C
Ward, S.J. AR 5th Inf. Co.F
Ward, S.J. GA 1st Inf. (St.Guards) Co.D
Ward, S.J. MS Cav. 2nd Bn.Res. Co.I Cpl.
Ward, S.J. MO Inf. 1st Bn.St.Guard Co.A Capt.
Ward, Skious MO Cav. Freeman's Regt. Co.F
Ward, S.L. MS 35th Inf. Co.G
Ward, S.L. TX 1st Inf. Co.B
Ward, S.M. AL 56th Part.Rangers Co.I
Ward, S.M. TN 4th Inf. Co.A Hosp.Stew.
Ward, S.M. Cheatham's Div. Hosp.Stew.
Ward, Sol MS 5th Inf. Co.C
Ward, Sol MS 9th Bn.S.S. Co.A
Ward, Solomon AR 34th Inf. Co.D
Ward, Solomon TX 22nd Inf. Co.A
Ward, Solomon A. AL 11th Inf. Co.G Sgt.
Ward, Solomon A. AL 17th Inf. Co.B
Ward, Solomon J. AL 28th Inf. Co.A Music.
Ward, Solomon R. NC 2nd Arty. (36th St.Troops) Co.G Sgt.
Ward, Spias NC 3rd Inf. Co.A
Ward, S.R. GA Cav. Dorough's Bn.
Ward, S.S. NC 42nd Inf. Co.E
Ward, S.T. VA 5th Cav. Co.H
Ward, Stafford G. GA 50th Inf. Co.C
Ward, Stephen NC 5th Inf. Co.I
Ward, Stephen NC 26th Inf. Co.E
Ward, Stephen VA 48th Inf. Co.A
Ward, Stephen A. MS Cav. 4th Bn. Sykes' Co.
Ward, Stephen A. 8th (Wood's) Conf.Cav. Co.G
Ward, Stephen B. NC 44th Inf. Co.G
Ward, Stephen D. LA 28th (Thomas') Inf. Co.B
Ward, Stroud W. NC 22nd Inf. Co.E
Ward, Sullen M. NC 31st Inf. Co.E

Ward, T. AL 12th Cav. Co.E Cpl.
Ward, T. AL 3rd Inf. Co.B
Ward, T. GA 1st Inf. (St.Guards) Co.K
Ward, T. GA 63rd Inf. Co.D
Ward, T. GA
Ward, T. MD Arty. 2nd Btty.
Ward, T. SC Ord.Guards Loc.Def.Troops
Ward, T.A. GA Inf. 1st Conf.Bn. Ord.Sgt.
Ward, T.A. GA Inf. (Jones Hussars) Jones' Co.
Ward, Tandy F. GA 1st (Ramsey's) Inf. Co.K
Ward, Tandy F. GA 45th Inf. Co.D
Ward, Tarleton AL 17th Inf. Co.F
Ward, Taylor GA 5th Inf.
Ward, T.B. AL 48th Inf. Co.C Cpl.
Ward, T.B. MO 2nd Cav. Co.D
Ward, T.B. MO 10th Inf. Co.A
Ward, T.B. NC 20th Inf. Co.K
Ward, T.B. Gen. & Staff,PACS Maj.,Surg.
Ward, T.C. AL 25th Inf. Co.A
Ward, T.D. TN 21st Cav. Co.H
Ward, T.F. LA 7th Inf. 2nd Lt.
Ward, T.F. NC 1st Jr.Res. Co.G
Ward, T.H. KY 12th Cav. Co.I
Ward, T.H. TN 15th (Cons.) Cav. Co.A
Ward, T.H. TN Cav. Williams' Co.
Ward, T.H. TN 9th Inf. Co.E,B
Ward, Thaddeus C. GA 21st Inf. Co.B
Ward, Theodric W. AL 13th Inf. Co.C
Ward, Thomas AL 1st Regt.Conscr. Co.H
Ward, Thomas AL 3rd Bn.Res. Co.C
Ward, Thomas AL 5th Inf. Co.I
Ward, Thomas AL 16th Inf. Co.K
Ward, Thomas AL 21st Inf. Co.G,A Cpl.
Ward, Thomas AL 57th Inf. Co.D
Ward, Thomas AL Conscr. Echols' Co. Cpl.
Ward, Thomas AR 47th (Crandall's) Cav. Burns' Co.
Ward, Thomas AR 14th (Powers') Inf. Co.D
Ward, Thomas AR 25th Inf. Co.E
Ward, Thomas AR Inf. Cocke's Regt. Co.B
Ward, Thomas FL Lt.Arty. Dyke's Co.
Ward, Thomas GA Inf. 1st Loc.Troops (Augusta) Co.B
Ward, Thomas GA 1st (Olmstead's) Inf. Co.B
Ward, Thomas GA 1st (Olmstead's) Inf. Gordon's Co.
Ward, Thomas GA 6th Inf. (St.Guards) Co.A Sgt.
Ward, Thomas GA 10th Inf. Co.D
Ward, Thomas GA 15th Inf. Co.K
Ward, Thomas GA 28th Inf. Co.C
Ward, Thomas GA 41st Inf. Co.D
Ward, Thomas GA 48th Inf. Co.G
Ward, Thomas GA 63rd Inf. Co.B
Ward, Thomas LA 11th Inf. Co.K
Ward, Thomas LA Inf. 11th Bn. Co.B
Ward, Thomas LA 13th Inf. Co.E
Ward, Thomas LA 15th Inf. Co.F
Ward, Thomas LA 20th Inf. Co.K
Ward, Thomas LA Inf.Cons.Crescent Regt. Co.K
Ward, Thomas MD Inf. 2nd Bn. Co.E
Ward, Thomas MS 24th Inf. Co.G
Ward, Thomas NC 6th Inf. Co.A
Ward, Thomas NC 35th Inf. Co.I
Ward, Thomas NC 64th Inf. Co.B
Ward, Thomas TN 11th Cav. Co.D
Ward, Thomas TN Lt.Arty. Kain's Co.
Ward, Thomas TN 15th Inf. Co.F
Ward, Thomas TX Lt.Arty. Jones' Co. Cpl.
Ward, Thomas Conf.Cav. Wood's Regt. 2nd Co.M
Ward, Thomas A. AL 11th Inf. Co.I
Ward, Thomas A. GA 9th Inf. Co.D
Ward, Thomas A. GA 30th Inf. Co.B 1st Lt.
Ward, Thomas A. GA 59th Inf. Co.E Cpl.
Ward, Thomas A. NC 18th Inf. Co.C
Ward, Thomas A. TX 27th Cav. Co.N
Ward, Thomas B. MO Cav. 2nd Bn.St.Guard Co.A Cpl.
Ward, Thomas B. MO 3rd Cav. Co.F
Ward, Thomas B. MO 12th Inf. Co.E
Ward, Thomas B. VA 6th Inf. Surg.
Ward, Thomas B. 3rd Conf.Cav. Co.C
Ward, Thomas C. AL 1st Regt.Conscr. Co.C
Ward, Thos. D. MS 27th Inf. Co.D
Ward, Thomas D. MS 42nd Inf.
Ward, Thomas D. TN 42nd Inf. 2nd Co.K
Ward, Thomas F. AL 5th Inf. Co.D Sgt.
Ward, Thomas F. NC 27th Inf. Co.G
Ward, Thomas G. NC 33rd Inf. Co.F
Ward, Thomas G. NC 48th Inf. Co.B
Ward, Thomas H. MS St.Cav. 2nd Bn. (Harris') Co.A
Ward, Thomas H. MO 12th Inf. Co.E
Ward, Thomas J. AL 6th Inf. Co.F
Ward, Thomas J. AL 25th Inf. Co.B
Ward, Thomas J. GA 41st Inf. Co.B
Ward, Thomas J. NC 15th Inf. Co.L Cpl.
Ward, Thomas J. NC 32nd Inf. Co.K Cpl.
Ward, Thomas J. SC 1st (Orr's) Rifles Co.F Sgt.
Ward, Thomas J. VA 21st Cav. 2nd Co.E
Ward, Thomas L. GA Floyd Legion (St.Guards) Co.H
Ward, Thomas L. MS 1st Cav.Res. Co.I
Ward, Thomas M. NC 12th Inf. Co.H
Ward, Thomas P. AL 14th Inf. Co.K
Ward, Thomas P. NC 18th Inf. Co.C
Ward, Thomas P. VA 13th Cav. Co.B
Ward, Thomas P. VA 13th Inf. Co.G
Ward, Thomas R. AL 62nd Inf. Co.B
Ward, Thomas T. MS 42nd Inf. Co.G
Ward, Thomas W. AR 27th Inf. Co.F
Ward, Thomas W. GA 47th Inf. Co.E
Ward, Thomas W. LA 14th Inf. Co.B,E
Ward, Thomas W. NC Inf. Thomas Legion 2nd Co.A, Co.F
Ward, Thomas Y. NC 44th Inf. Co.H
Ward, Thornton AR 38th Inf. Co.D
Ward, Timothy GA 41st Inf. Co.C
Ward, Timothy TN 41st Inf. Co.C
Ward, T.J. AR 8th Inf. New Co.H
Ward, T.J. FL 11th Inf. Co.C Sgt.
Ward, T.J. GA 3rd Res. Co.C
Ward, T.J. MS 2nd Cav. Co.E
Ward, T.J. MS Cav. 3rd Bn. (Ashcraft's) Co.B 1st Sgt.
Ward, T.J. MS 11th (Cons.) Cav. Co.F Sgt.
Ward, T.J. SC 1st Cav. Co.B
Ward, T.J. TN 10th (DeMoss') Cav. Co.I
Ward, T.J. TN 12th Inf. Co.G
Ward, T.J. TN 12th (Cons.) Inf. Co.E
Ward, T.J. TX 23rd Cav. Co.H Sgt.
Ward, T.L. GA 1st Cav. Co.A,D 3rd Sgt.
Ward, T.M. NC 32nd Inf. Co.H
Ward, T.M. TN 9th Inf. Co.E
Ward, T.M. TN 25th Inf. Co.G
Ward, T.M. TN 35th Inf. Co.E
Ward, T.N. MS 1st Cav. Co.E
Ward, T.O. SC 22nd Inf. Co.D
Ward, Tolliver AL 27th Inf. Co.H
Ward, T.P. LA Washington Arty.Bn. Co.1
Ward, T.S. GA 53rd Inf. Co.H
Ward, T.S. TN 45th Inf. Co.E
Ward, T.T. AR 7th Inf. Co.E Sgt.
Ward, T.T. MO 7th Cav. Ward's Co. Capt.
Ward, T.W. TN 3rd (Forrest's) Cav. Co.B
Ward, T.W. TX 10th Cav. Co.F
Ward, T.Z. GA 5th Res. Co.E
Ward, Ulisses H. TX 29th Cav. Co.D Ord.Sgt.
Ward, Uriah G. GA 12th Inf. Co.B
Ward, Van 2nd Cherokee Mtd.Vol. Co.G Cpl.
Ward, V.H. TX 32nd Cav. Co.G
Ward, Victor A. LA 1st Hvy.Arty. (Reg.) Co.A
Ward, Victor M. TX Cav. Hardeman's Regt. Co.E
Ward, Virgil V. TX 7th Inf. Co.D
Ward, W. AL 14th Inf. Co.G
Ward, W. AL 26th (O'Neal's) Inf. Co.G
Ward, W. GA Lt.Arty. 12th Bn. Co.F
Ward, W. GA 63rd Inf. Co.D
Ward, W. MS Cav. 3rd Bn. (Ashcraft's) Co.C
Ward, W. MS Cav. Powers' Regt. Co.G
Ward, W. MS Inf. 3rd Bn. (St.Troops) Co.C
Ward, W. MO Cav. Coffee's Regt. Co.A
Ward, W.A. AR 32nd Inf. Co.H
Ward, W.A. MS 4th Inf. Co.K
Ward, W.A. MS 35th Inf. Co.G 3rd Lt.
Ward, W.A. TN 11th Inf. Co.C
Ward, W.A. TX 9th Cav. Co.F
Ward, W.A. VA Inf. 22nd Bn. Co.B Lt.
Ward, W.A. Conf.Cav. Wood's Regt. 2nd Co.D
Ward, W.A. Gillum's Regt. Hall's Co.
Ward, Wade SC Cav. 14th Bn. Co.A
Ward, Walter B. GA 44th Inf. Co.F
Ward, Walton W. GA 4th (Clinch's) Cav. Co.G
Ward, Warren GA 1st Bn.S.S. Co.C
Ward, Warren J. NC 11th (Bethel Regt.) Inf. Co.C
Ward, Warren W. MD 1st Inf. Co.I Sgt.
Ward, Warren W. Gen. & Staff Surg.
Ward, Washington AR 20th Inf. Co.C
Ward, Washington GA 5th Inf. Co.I
Ward, W.B. AR Cav. McGehee's Regt. Co.C Capt.
Ward, W.B. SC 9th Inf. Co.C
Ward, W.B. Gen. & Staff Hosp.Stew.
Ward, W.C. AL 53rd (Part.Rangers) Co.F
Ward, W.C. AL 5th Inf. New Co.C
Ward, W.C. GA Brooks' Co. (Terrell Lt.Arty.)
Ward, W.C. KY 12th Cav. Co.F
Ward, W.C. LA 1st (Nelligan's) Inf. Co.H
Ward, W.C. LA Inf. 1st Sp.Bn. (Rightor's) Co.D
Ward, W.C. MS 2nd Cav. Co.E 2nd Lt.
Ward, W.C. MS 2nd (Davidson's) Inf. Co.E 1st Cpl.
Ward, W.C. NC 11th (Bethel Regt.) Inf. Co.C
Ward, W.C. SC 7th Cav. Co.F
Ward, W.C. SC Cav. Tucker's Co.
Ward, W.C. TN 16th (Logwood's) Cav. Co.I
Ward, W.C. TN 20th (Russell's) Cav. Co.F
Ward, W.C. TN 1st Hvy.Arty. Co.L

Ward, W.C. TN 12th Inf. Co.G
Ward, W.C. TN 12th (Cons.) Inf. Co.E
Ward, W.D. AR 25th Inf. Co.C Sgt.
Ward, W.D. AR 36th Inf. Co.C
Ward, W.D. GA Lt.Arty. 12th Bn. 2nd Co.A
Ward, W.D. GA 57th Inf. Co.D
Ward, W.D. MS 41st Inf. Co.A
Ward, W.D. TN Cav. Jackson's Co.
Ward, W.E. AL 33rd Inf. Co.A
Ward, W.E. GA Cav. 10th Bn. (St.Guards) Co.E
Ward, W.E. KY Jessee's Bn.Mtd.Riflemen Co.C
Ward, W.E. LA Mil.Cav.Squad. (Ind.Rangers Iberville)
Ward, W.E. MS 27th Inf. Co.E 2nd Lt.
Ward, Webb W. NC 42nd Inf. Co.I
Ward, Wesley VA 32nd Inf. Co.F
Ward, Weston NC 68th Inf.
Ward, W.F. AL Jeff Davis Arty.
Ward, W.F. AL 26th Inf. Co.I
Ward, W.F. AR 5th Inf.
Ward, W.F. AR 35th Inf. Co.B
Ward, W.F. TN 21st Inf. Co.H Sgt.
Ward, W.F. 3rd Conf.Inf. Co.E
Ward, W.F. Gillum's Regt. Co.F
Ward, W.G. AL 13th Bn.Part.Rangers Co.D
Ward, W.G. AL 56th Part.Rangers Co.K Far.
Ward, W.H. AL 43rd Inf.
Ward, W.H. GA 3rd Cav. (St.Guards) Co.K
Ward, W.H. GA 8th Cav. Old Co.E
Ward, W.H. GA 1st (Ramsey's) Inf. Co.I
Ward, W.H. GA 13th Inf. Co.K
Ward, W.H. GA Inf. (GA Defend.) Chapman's Co.
Ward, W.H. KY 1st Inf. Co.E
Ward, W.H. LA 1st (Nelligan's) Inf. Co.G
Ward, W.H. MS 1st Lt.Arty. Co.F
Ward, W.H. NC Cav. 16th Bn. Co.A
Ward, W.H. NC 3rd Arty. (40th St.Troops) Co.I Cpl.
Ward, W.H. NC 1st Jr.Res. Co.A
Ward, W.H. NC 47th Inf. Co.A
Ward, W.H. SC 7th Cav. Co.D
Ward, W.H. SC 17th Inf. Co.E
Ward, W.H. SC Cav.Bn. Holcombe Legion Co.B
Ward, W.H. TN 4th (McLemore's) Cav. Co.I
Ward, W.H. TN 7th (Duckworth's) Cav. Co.H
Ward, W.H. TN Inf. 4th Cons.Regt. Co.G
Ward, W.H. TN 16th Inf. Co.E
Ward, W.H. TN 23rd Inf. Co.H
Ward, W.H. TN 27th Inf. Co.H
Ward, W.H. TN 31st Inf. Co.I
Ward, W.H. Inf. Bailey's Cons.Regt. Co.F
Ward, W.H. TX 11th Cav. Co.D
Ward, W.H. TX 27th Cav. Co.K
Ward, W.H. 8th (Wade's) Conf.Cav. Co.I
Ward, W.H.H. AL 31st Inf. Co.F
Ward, Whit GA 6th Cav. Co.I
Ward, Whitfield F. AR 18th (Marmaduke's) Inf. Co.E
Ward, Whitmel T. NC 11th (Bethel Regt.) Inf. Co.C
Ward, W.H.J. AR Inf. Hardy's Regt. Co.E Cpl.
Ward, Wickliff J. MO 1st Inf. 2nd Co.A
Ward, Wilburn SC 6th Res. Co.G
Ward, Wiley AL 60th Inf. Co.E
Ward, Wiley AL 3rd Bn. Hilliard's Legion Vol. Co.A
Ward, Wiley GA Phillips' Legion Co.D,K 2nd Bugler
Ward, Wiley L. AL 13th Inf. Co.F
Ward, Wiley W. VA 44th Inf. Co.I 2nd Lt.
Ward, William AL 1st Cav. 2nd Co.C
Ward, William AL 7th Cav. Co.G
Ward, William AL 8th Cav. Co.G
Ward, William AL 12th Cav. Co.E Sgt.
Ward, William AL 1st Inf. 3rd Co.G
Ward, William AL 3rd Bn.Res. Appling's Co.
Ward, William AL 29th Inf. Co.E
Ward, William AL 34th Inf. Co.C
Ward, William AL 36th Inf. Co.G
Ward, William AL 39th Inf. Co.D
Ward, William AL 45th Inf. Co.K
Ward, William AR 1st (Crawford's) Cav. Co.B
Ward, William AR 1st (Crawford's) Cav. Co.K Sgt.
Ward, William AR 7th Inf. Co.H Sgt.
Ward, William AR 10th Mil. Co.B
Ward, William AR 14th (Powers') Inf. Co.D 2nd Lt.
Ward, William AR 15th (N.W.) Inf. Co.C
Ward, William AR 19th (Dawson's) Inf. Co.E
Ward, William AR 19th (Dawson's) Inf. Co.K
Ward, William AR 38th Inf. Co.H
Ward, William AR Inf. Hardy's Regt. Co.K
Ward, William FL 3rd Inf. Co.E
Ward, William FL 8th Inf. Co.F Sgt.
Ward, William GA 6th Cav. 1st Co.K
Ward, William GA 62nd Cav. Co.E
Ward, William GA Cav. Newbern's Co. (Coffee Revengers)
Ward, William GA 5th Inf. (St.Guards) Brooks' Co.
Ward, William GA 10th Inf. Co.F Music.
Ward, William GA 18th Inf. Co.H
Ward, William GA 21st Inf. Co.C
Ward, William GA 21st Inf. Co.G
Ward, William GA 36th (Villepigue's) Inf. Co.H
Ward, William GA 48th Inf. Co.D
Ward, William GA 52nd Inf. Co.A
Ward, William KY 1st Bn.Mtd.Rifles Co.E Sgt.
Ward, William KY 8th Mtd.Inf. Co.C Cpl.
Ward, William LA Arty. Moody's Co. (Madison Lt.Arty.) Cpl.
Ward, William LA Inf. 11th Bn. Co.E
Ward, William LA Inf.Cons.Crescent Regt. Co.E
Ward, William LA Mil. Orleans Fire Regt. Co.C
Ward, William MD 1st Inf. Co.I
Ward, William MS 3rd (St.Troops) Cav. Co.A
Ward, William MS 9th Cav. Co.B
Ward, William MS 4th Inf. Co.E
Ward, William MS 9th Inf. New Co.B
Ward, William MS 14th Inf. Co.C Cpl.
Ward, William MS 14th Inf. Co.H
Ward, William MS 22nd Inf. Co.A
Ward, William MS 46th Inf. Co.G
Ward, William MS 40th Inf. Co.E
Ward, William MS 44th Inf. Co.L
Ward, William MO 7th Cav. Co.C
Ward, William MO Cav. Fristoe's Regt. Co.B
Ward, William MO Arty. Jos. Bledsoe's Co.
Ward, William MO Inf. 4th Regt.St.Guard Co.E
Ward, William NC 3rd Arty. (40th St.Troops) Co.K
Ward, William NC 8th Sr.Res. Callihan's Co.
Ward, William NC 30th Inf. Co.D
Ward, William NC 48th Inf. Co.B
Ward, William NC 48th Inf. Co.G
Ward, William NC 60th Inf. Co.K
Ward, William NC 61st Inf. Co.H
Ward, William NC Mallett's Bn. (Cp.Guard) Co.I
Ward, William SC 1st Arty. Co.A
Ward, William SC Lt.Arty. 3rd (Palmetto) Bn. Co.C
Ward, William SC Lt.Arty. 3rd (Palmetto) Bn. Co.H
Ward, William SC 4th Inf. Co.F Cpl.
Ward, William SC 5th St.Troops Co.M
Ward, William SC 7th Res. Co.E
Ward, William SC 10th Inf. Co.D
Ward, William SC Inf. 13th Bn. Co.B
Ward, William SC 15th Inf. Co.F
Ward, William SC 22nd Inf. Co.H Cpl.
Ward, William TN 3rd (Forrest's) Cav. Co.C Sgt.
Ward, William TN 4th (Murray's) Cav. Co.A
Ward, William TN 8th (Smith's) Cav. Co.D Far.
Ward, William TN Lt.Arty. Morton's Co.
Ward, William TN 9th Inf. Co.G
Ward, William TN Inf. 22nd Bn. Co.B
Ward, William, Jr. TN Inf. 22nd Bn. Co.E
Ward, William, Sr. TN Inf. 22nd Bn. Co.E
Ward, William TX 6th Cav. Co.A
Ward, William TX 8th Cav. Co.B
Ward, William TX 23rd Cav. Co.D
Ward, William TX 29th Cav. Co.G
Ward, William TX Inf. 1st Bn. (St.Troops) Co.D
Ward, William TX Waul's Legion Co.B
Ward, William VA 1st Cav. 2nd Co.K
Ward, William VA 10th Cav. Co.E
Ward, William VA 15th Cav. Co.B
Ward, William VA Cav. 34th Bn. Co.C
Ward, William VA 7th Inf. Co.E
Ward, William VA 12th Inf. Co.A
Ward, William VA 27th Inf. Co.D
Ward, William VA 29th Inf. Co.E
Ward, Wm. VA 48th Inf. Co.H
Ward, William VA 60th Inf. Co.G
Ward, William 20th Conf.Cav. Co.B
Ward, William 1st Creek Mtd.Vol. 2nd Co.C Music.
Ward, William, Jr. 2nd Cherokee Mtd.Vol. Co.E
Ward, William, Sr. 2nd Cherokee Mtd.Vol. Co.E
Ward, William A. AL 2nd Cav. Co.G
Ward, William A. AL 39th Inf. Co.A
Ward, William A. GA Inf. 5th Bn. (St.Guards) Co.B
Ward, William A. GA 47th Inf. Co.B
Ward, William A. MS Part.Rangers Smyth's Co.
Ward, William A. MS Lt.Arty. (The Hudson Btty.) Hoole's Co.
Ward, William A. MS 14th Inf. Co.G
Ward, William A. NC 45th Inf. Co.D
Ward, William A. NC 51st Inf. Co.G
Ward, William A. TN 4th Inf. Co.A
Ward, William A. VA 19th Inf. Co.C
Ward, William A. VA 57th Inf. Co.G
Ward, William A.R.D. TX 10th Inf. Co.I
Ward, William B. AL 12th Inf. Co.F
Ward, William B. LA 9th Inf. Co.I
Ward, William B. TN 37th Inf. Co.B

Ward, William B. VA 19th Inf. Co.B
Ward, William C. AL 4th Inf. Co.G
Ward, Wm. C. AL 33rd Inf. Co.A
Ward, William C. AL 62nd Inf. Co.A Capt.
Ward, William C. GA Arty. 11th Bn. (Sumter Arty.) New Co.C Cpl.
Ward, William C. NC 11th (Bethel Regt.) Inf. Co.C
Ward, William C. TN Arty. Fisher's Co.
Ward, William C. TX 13th Cav. Co.D
Ward, William C. TX 13th Cav. Co.F
Ward, William C. TX 36th Cav. Co.E
Ward, William C. TX Cav. Ragsdale's Bn. Co.D
Ward, William D. AL 4th Inf. Co.K
Ward, William D. AR 1st (Crawford's) Cav. Co.F
Ward, William D. GA 5th Inf. Co.F Lt.
Ward, William D. MS 18th Inf. Co.A
Ward, William D. MO 3rd Cav. Co.F
Ward, William D. MO 12th Inf. Co.E
Ward, William E. KY Part.Rangers Rowan's Co.
Ward, William E. NC 27th Inf. Co.I Sgt.Maj.
Ward, William E. TX 1st Inf. Co.C
Ward, William F. AR 19th (Dawson's) Inf. Co.E
Ward, William F. TN 13th Inf. Co.B Cpl.
Ward, William G. GA 1st (Fannin's) Res. Co.H
Ward, William G. NC 6th Cav. (65th St.Troops) Co.C
Ward, William G. NC Cav. 7th Bn. Co.C
Ward, William G. NC 3rd Arty. (40th St.Troops) Co.K
Ward, William G. TN 5th Inf. 2nd Co.G
Ward, William G. TX 1st Field Btty.
Ward, William H. AL 8th Inf. Co.A
Ward, William H. AL 12th Inf. Co.C
Ward, William H. AL 23rd Bn.S.S. Co.F
Ward, William H. AL 55th Vol. Co.I
Ward, William H. AL 1st Bn. Hilliard's Legion Vol. Co.F
Ward, William H. FL 2nd Cav. Co.I
Ward, William H. GA Siege Arty. 28th Bn. Co.G Sgt.
Ward, William H. KY 2nd Mtd.Inf. Co.A
Ward, William H. MS 10th Inf. Co.K
Ward, William H. NC 3rd Arty. (40th St.Troops) Co.H
Ward, William H. NC 4th Inf. Co.H
Ward, William H. NC 13th Inf. Co.E
Ward, William H. NC 20th Inf. Co.D 2nd Lt.
Ward, William H. NC 35th Inf. Co.G
Ward, William H. NC 44th Inf. Co.G
Ward, William H. NC 61st Inf. Co.H
Ward, William H. TN 42nd Inf. 1st Co.I
Ward, William H. VA 5th Cav. Co.G
Ward, William H. VA 5th Cav. (12 mo. '61-2) Co.A
Ward, William H. VA Cav. 14th Bn. Co.D Sgt.
Ward, William H. VA 15th Cav. Co.K Sgt.
Ward, William H. VA Hvy.Arty. 19th Bn. Co.D
Ward, William H. VA 19th Inf. Co.H
Ward, William H. VA 23rd Inf. Co.K
Ward, William H. VA 29th Inf. 2nd Co.F
Ward, William H. VA Mil. Carroll Cty.
Ward, William Henry VA 2nd Cav. Co.E
Ward, William I. MO Cav. Coleman's Regt. Co.C
Ward, William J. AL 13th Inf. Co.B
Ward, William J. AL Cav. 5th Bn. Hilliard's Legion Co.A
Ward, William J. AR 3rd Inf. Co.F Ch.Music.
Ward, William J. GA 31st Inf. Co.C,H
Ward, William J. MO Inf. 8th Bn. Co.F
Ward, William J. MO 9th Inf. Co.K
Ward, William J., Jr. NC 2nd Arty. (36th St.Troops) Co.E
Ward, William J., Sr. NC 2nd Arty. (36th St.Troops) Co.E,I
Ward, William J. NC 28th Inf. Co.G
Ward, William J. NC 30th Inf. Co.D Cpl.
Ward, William J. VA 20th Cav. Co.E
Ward, William J. VA 45th Inf. Co.E
Ward, William L. NC 17th Inf. (2nd Org.) Co.D
Ward, William Lafayette TX 20th Cav. Co.D
Ward, William M. AL 10th Inf. Co.D
Ward, William M. AL 17th Bn.S.S. Co.B
Ward, William M. MS 18th Inf. Co.E
Ward, William M. MS 37th Inf. Co.A
Ward, William M. TN 16th Inf. Co.E
Ward, William M. TN 19th Inf. Co.D
Ward, William M. VA 39th Inf. Co.L
Ward, William N. VA 47th Inf. Co.D Capt.
Ward, William N. VA 55th Inf. Maj.
Ward, William N. Sap. & Min.,CSA
Ward, William O. GA 38th Inf. Co.K Cpl.
Ward, William P. AR 16th Inf. Co.C
Ward, William P. FL 5th Inf. Co.B
Ward, William P. GA 41st Inf. Co.B
Ward, William P. MO Arty. Jos. Bledsoe's Co.
Ward, William P. NC 27th Inf. Co.I Capt.
Ward, William P. NC 42nd Inf. Co.D
Ward, William P. TN 16th (Logwood's) Cav. Co.B Cpl.
Ward, Wm. P. Gen. & Staff Capt.,AQM
Ward, William R. GA 38th (Villepigue's) Inf. Co.E,F
Ward, William R. LA 4th Cav. Co.A
Ward, William R. LA 9th Inf. Co.I
Ward, William R. MS 3rd Inf. Co.D
Ward, William R. MS Inf. 5th Bn. Co.C
Ward, William R. MO 1st N.E. Cav.
Ward, William R. NC 18th Inf. Co.C
Ward, William R.D. AL 39th Inf. Co.D
Ward, William S. NC 42nd Inf. Co.B Music.
Ward, William S. NC 61st Inf. Co.H Music.
Ward, William S. VA Cav. 39th Bn. Co.A Sgt.
Ward, William T. AL 40th Inf. Co.E
Ward, William T. GA Inf. 8th Bn. Co.D
Ward, William T. MS 4th Inf. Co.A
Ward, William T. MS 8th Inf. Co.C Capt.
Ward, William T. MS 29th Inf. Co.F
Ward, William T. NC 11th (Bethel Regt.) Inf. Co.C
Ward, William T. NC 14th Inf. Co.E
Ward, William T. TX 11th Inf. Co.K
Ward, William T. VA 72nd Mil.
Ward, Wm. Thos. Gen. & Staff Asst.Surg.
Ward, William W. AR 15th (Josey's) Inf. Co.E Sgt.
Ward, William W. FL 5th Inf. Co.B
Ward, William W. GA 44th Inf. Co.H
Ward, William W. LA 12th Inf. Co.D,B Music.
Ward, William W. MS Part.Rangers Smyth's Co.
Ward, William W. MS 1st Lt.Arty. Co.F
Ward, William W. MS 11th Inf. Co.B
Ward, William W. TN 9th (Ward's) Cav. Col.
Ward, William W. TN 7th Inf. Co.B
Ward, Willis VA 4th Cav. Co.H
Ward, Williston 1st Choctaw & Chickasaw Mtd.Rifles 2nd Co.I
Ward, Wilson GA 31st Inf. Co.G
Ward, Wilson MS 10th Inf. Old Co.H Cpl.
Ward, Wilson NC 14th Inf. Co.K
Ward, W.J. AL 51st (Part.Rangers) Co.G
Ward, W.J. AL 53rd (Part.Rangers) Co.D
Ward, W.J. AL 21st Inf. Co.D
Ward, W.J. AR 38th Inf. Co.A
Ward, W.J. AR Inf. Hardy's Regt. Co.K
Ward, W.J. FL Cav. 5th Bn. Co.H
Ward, W.J. GA 14th Inf.
Ward, W.J. GA 21st Inf. Co.H,A 1st Sgt.
Ward, W.J. MS 1st Cav. Co.E
Ward, W.J. MS Cav. 3rd Bn. (Ashcraft's) Co.C Sgt.
Ward, W.J. MS Inf. 7th Bn. Co.G
Ward, W.J. MS 29th Inf. Co.H
Ward, W.J. NC 31st Inf. Co.H Sgt.
Ward, W.J. NC McIlhenny's Co.
Ward, W.J. SC 9th Inf. Co.D
Ward, W.J. SC Cav.Bn. Holcombe Legion Co.D
Ward, W.J. TX 5th Inf. Co.K
Ward, W.J. 10th Conf.Cav. Co.A
Ward, W.J. 2nd Conf.Eng.Troops Co.C Artif.
Ward, W. Jefferson SC 7th Cav. Co.C
Ward, W.K. GA Lt.Arty. 12th Bn. 2nd Co.D Sgt.
Ward, W.L. AL Cav. Moses' Squad. Co.A
Ward, W.L. GA 1st Troops & Defences (Macon) Co.G
Ward, W.L. MS 34th Inf. Co.D
Ward, W.M. AL 33rd Inf. Co.A
Ward, W.M. MS 7th Inf. Co.G
Ward, W.M. TN 4th (McLemore's) Cav. Co.I
Ward, W.M. TN 3rd (Clack's) Inf. Co.A
Ward, W.N. NC 1st Arty. (10th St.Troops) Co.B
Ward, W.N. TN Conscr. (Cp. of Instr.)
Ward, W.N. 3rd Conf.Eng.Troops Co.D
Ward, W.O. TX 32nd Cav. Co.K
Ward, W.P. AL 53rd (Part.Rangers) Co.C Sgt.
Ward, W.P. GA Inf. 40th Bn. Co.F
Ward, W.P. MO 5th Cav. Co.A
Ward, W.P.H. GA 13th Cav. Co.C
Ward, W.R. GA 2nd Cav. Co.F
Ward, W.R. GA Lt.Arty. Pritchard's Co. (Washington Arty.)
Ward, W.R. MS 2nd St.Cav. Co.B
Ward, W.R. MS Lt.Arty. Turner's Co.
Ward, W.R. MS 41st Inf. Co.A
Ward, W.R. NC 4th Cav. (59th St.Troops) Co.K
Ward, W.R. TN 5th Inf. 2nd Co.C
Ward, W.R. 1st Conf.Inf. 1st Co.F
Ward, W.S. AL Res. Belser's Co.
Ward, W.S. AL Lowndes Rangers Vol. Fagg's Co.
Ward, W.S. AR Cav. Gordon's Regt. Co.D
Ward, W.S. FL 5th Inf. Co.I,C
Ward, W.S. NC 48th Inf. Co.D
Ward, W.S. SC 16th Inf. Co.C
Ward, W.S. TX 11th Cav. Co.I Sgt.
Ward, W.T. AL 8th Cav. Co.C
Ward, W.T. AL 17th Inf. Co.F
Ward, W.T. AL 63rd Inf. Co.B

Ward, W.T. GA 66th Inf. Co.H
Ward, W.T. MS 28th Cav. Co.B Asst.Surg.
Ward, W.T. SC 7th Inf. Co.I
Ward, W.T. TN 19th & 20th (Cons.) Cav. Co.A
Ward, W.T. TN 5th Inf. 2nd Co.F
Ward, W.T. VA 18th Cav. Co.A
Ward, W.T. VA Arty. C.F. Johnston's Co.
Ward, W.V. TX Inf. 1st St.Troops White's Co.D Sgt.
Ward, W.W. AL 46th Inf. Co.D
Ward, W.W. FL Conscr.
Ward, W.W. GA 11th Cav. Co.E
Ward, W.W. GA Phillips' Legion Co.C
Ward, W.W. KY 2nd Cav. Col.
Ward, W.W. MD Cav. 2nd Bn. Co.A
Ward, W.W. MS 1st Cav. Co.A
Ward, W.W. MS Inf. 1st Bn.St.Troops (12 mo. '62-3) Co.C
Ward, W.W. MS Yerger's Co. (St.Troops) 2nd Lt.
Ward, W.W. NC 48th Inf. Co.D
Ward, W.W. SC Cav. 12th Bn. Co.B
Ward, W.W. SC Lt.Arty. Jeter's Co. (Macbeth Lt.Arty.)
Ward, W.W. TX 29th Cav. Co.G
Ward, W.W. VA 1st Cav. 2nd Co.K
Ward, W.W. VA Horse Arty. D. Shank's Co.
Ward, W.W. Gillum's Regt. Co.G
Ward, W.W. Gen. & Staff Surg.
Ward, Yancey G. NC 44th Inf. Co.G
Ward, Zach VA 30th Bn.S.S. Co.E Music.
Ward, Zachariah VA 51st Inf. Co.I Sgt.
Ward, Zeno NC 22nd Inf. Co.L
Ward, Zinnamon FL 11th Inf. Co.L
Warde, Jasper MO Cav. Ford's Bn. Co.E
Warde, M.A. AR Lt.Arty. Key's Btty.
Wardell, C.A. MS 41st Inf. Co.G
Wardell, Edward LA 1st Hvy.Arty. (Reg.) Co.A Cpl.
Wardell, G.K. NC 24th Inf. Co.A Sgt.
Wardell, J.B. SC 9th Res. Co.D
Wardell, Jeff Conf.Cav. 7th Bn. Co.A
Wardell, Richard SC 7th Res. Co.K
Wardell, Robert MS 39th Inf. Co.B
Wardell, Robert TN Cav. 4th Bn. (Branner's) Co.C
Wardell, T.D. MS 2nd Cav. Co.K
Wardell, T.D. MS Cav.Res. Mitchell's Co.
Wardell, Theodore SC 3rd Res. Co.B
Wardell, Theodore R. NC 2nd Arty. (36th St.Troops) Co.B
Wardell, Theo R. NC 1st Inf. (6 mo. '61) Co.F
Wardell, Thomas W. MS 39th Inf. Co.C
Wardell, T.R. GA Siege Arty. Campbell's Ind.Co.
Warden, Adam TN Cav. 16th Bn. (Neal's) Co.F Black.
Warden, A.J. KY 5th Mtd.Inf. Co.A
Warden, A.J. NC 2nd Detailed Men Co.F 1st Lt.
Warden, Andrew J. VA 24th Inf. Co.E
Warden, Aquilla M. TN 48th (Voorhies') Inf. Co.F
Warden, Arthur W. VA 9th Inf. Co.B
Warden, A.T. AL 18th Inf. Co.A
Warden, Benjamin MO 2nd Cav. Co.G
Warden, Cara, Jr. NC 28th Inf. Co.I
Warden, Cary, Sr. NC 38th Inf. Co.B
Warden, Cary W., Jr. NC 38th Inf. Co.B
Warden, C.J. MO Searcy's Bn.S.S. Co.C
Warden, David J. VA Cav. Hounshell's Bn. Thurmond's Co.
Warden, E. SC 20th Inf. Co.M
Warden, E. SC 23rd Inf. Co.G
Warden, Eligh MO Cav. Slayback's Regt. Co.B
Warden, F.M. TN 10th (DeMoss') Cav. Co.B
Warden, F.M. TN 27th Inf. Co.E
Warden, Franklin A. TX Cav. 6th Bn. Co.C Cpl.
Warden, G.D. GA 43rd Inf. Co.E
Warden, George LA 10th Inf. Co.C
Warden, George TX 9th (Nichols') Inf. Co.B
Warden, George TX 16th Inf. Co.D
Warden, George A. McGowan's Staff Capt.
Warden, George W. VA 24th Inf. Co.E
Warden, Hezekiah TX 16th Cav. Co.I Capt.
Warden, H.J. VA 16th Cav. Co.B 1st Lt.
Warden, Isaac C. TN 2nd (Ashby's) Cav. Co.C
Warden, Isaac C. TN Cav. 5th Bn. (McClellan's) Co.D
Warden, J. AR 36th Inf. Co.I
Warden, J. VA 21st Cav. 2nd Co.D
Warden, J.A. TX Cav. Terry's Regt. Co.I 2nd Lt.
Warden, Jackson M. MO Cav. Poindexter's Co.
Warden, Jackson M. MO 3rd Inf. Co.F
Warden, Jacob TX Cav. Baird's Regt. Co.E
Warden, Jacob VA 7th Cav. Co.F
Warden, Jacob VA 18th Cav. Co.I Capt.
Warden, Jacob VA 62nd Mtd.Inf. 1st Co.D 2nd Lt.
Warden, James MS Cav. 17th Bn. Co.D
Warden, James MO Cav. 3rd Bn. Co.F
Warden, James TN 21st (Wilson's) Cav. Co.F
Warden, James TN 44th Inf. Co.E
Warden, James TN 44th (Cons.) Inf. Co.B
Warden, James VA 7th Cav. Co.F
Warden, James VA 1st St.Res. Co.B Sgt.
Warden, James VA 50th Inf. Co.I
Warden, James VA 61st Inf. Co.A
Warden, James R. VA 50th Inf. Co.I
Warden, James T. VA 50th Inf. Co.I
Warden, J.B. Bell's Co.F,CSA
Warden, J.C. TX Cav. Benavides' Regt. Co.G
Warden, J.F. TN 50th Inf. Co.B
Warden, Joab TX Cav. 2nd Regt.St.Troops Co.B
Warden, Joab TX Cav. Bourland's Regt. Bone's Co. Jr.2nd Lt.
Warden, John GA 1st (Olmstead's) Inf. Gordon's Co., Way's Co.
Warden, John GA 63rd Inf. Co.B Sgt.
Warden, John TN 41st Inf. Co.A Cpl.
Warden, John TN 48th (Nixon's) Inf. Co.C
Warden, John TN 50th Inf. Co.B
Warden, John TX 16th Cav. Co.I
Warden, John C. MO Inf. 8th Bn. Co.D
Warden, John C. MO 9th Inf. Co.H
Warden, John C. MO Robertson's Regt.St.Guard Co.7
Warden, John J. TN 48th (Voorhies') Inf. Co.F,K
Warden, John J. TN Inf. Sowell's Detach. Cpl.
Warden, Johnson B. VA 50th Inf. Co.I Sgt.
Warden, Johnston VA 24th Inf. Co.E
Warden, John W. TX Cav. Morgan's Regt. Co.E
Warden, Joseph VA 6th Inf. 2nd Co.B
Warden, J.P. TX 9th Field Btty.
Warden, Koscioscо VA 5th Cav. (12 mo. '61-2) Co.B
Warden, Koskinsco VA Cav. 14th Bn. Co.A
Warden, Koskiosko VA 15th Cav. Co.F
Warden, Marion AR 35th Inf. Co.G
Warden, Moses TX Cav. 6th Bn. Co.E Sgt.
Warden, Nathan C. NC 30th Inf.
Warden, N.C. NC 38th Inf. Co.A
Warden, Newel NC 21st Inf. Co.I
Warden, Oscar D. VA 50th Inf. Co.I
Warden, Riley W. NC 21st Inf. Co.I
Warden, Robert MO 16th Inf. Co.C,A
Warden, Robert TN 2nd (Ashby's) Cav. Co.C
Warden, Robert TN Cav. 5th Bn. (McClellan's) Co.D
Warden, Samuel LA 30th Inf. Co.I
Warden, Samuel TN 18th (Newsom's) Cav. Co.D,G
Warden, Samuel C. TN Cav. Newsom's Regt. Co.G 2nd Lt.
Warden, S.C. TN 19th (Biffle's) Cav. Co.E
Warden, S.C. TN 27th Inf. Co.E Bvt.2nd Lt.
Warden, Stuart C. VA 24th Inf. Co.E
Warden, T.F. MO 9th Inf. Co.B Jr.2nd Lt.
Warden, T.F. MO Inf. Clark's Regt. Co.A 1st Sgt.
Warden, Thomas TN 47th Inf. Co.K
Warden, Thomas C. TN 18th (Newsom's) Cav. Co.D
Warden, Thomas J. MO 3rd Inf. Co.D
Warden, Thomas J. VA 24th Inf. Co.E
Warden, W. MS Cav. 17th Bn. Co.B
Warden, W.H. KY 9th Mtd.Inf. Co.A
Warden, William MD Arty. 2nd Btty.
Warden, William MD 1st Inf. Co.F
Warden, William TX 16th Cav. Co.I
Warden, William TX Cav. Morgan's Regt. Co.E 1st Lt.
Warden, William TX Inf. Rutherford's Co.
Warden, William VA 1st Cav. 2nd Co.K
Warden, William VA 7th Cav. Co.F
Warden, William VA 6th Inf. 2nd Co.B
Warden, William C. NC 56th Inf. Co.C
Warden, William E. MO Searcy's Bn.S.S. Co.C Capt.
Warden, William H. VA 50th Inf. Co.I
Warden, William H. VA 61st Inf. Co.A
Warden, William R. VA 12th Inf. Co.G
Warden, William R. VA 46th Inf. 2nd Co.A Lt.
Warden, Willson VA 36th Inf. 2nd Co.C
Warden, W.R. TN 41st Inf. Co.A
Wardenbe, Aaron MO 2nd Inf. Co.B Fifer
Warder, E.B. VA 3rd Cav. Co.H
Warder, E.D. KY 3rd Cav. Co.C Capt.
Warder, E.D. KY 7th Cav. Co.K Capt.
Warder, H.M. KY 9th Cav. Co.A
Warder, Hugh M. KY 4th Cav. Co.A Cpl.
Warder, James H. VA Cav. 39th Bn. Co.A
Warder, J.H. LA Pointe Coupee Arty. 1st Sgt.
Warder, J.H. LA Arty. Watson Btty.
Warder, Walter T. VA 49th Inf. Co.C Sgt.
Warders, A.F. MO 2nd Inf. Co.G
Wardick, Bryan MS Lt.Arty. (Issaquana Arty.) Graves' Co.

Wardin, David TN 29th Inf. Co.F
Wardin, J.C. TX Cav. Benavides' Regt. Co.G
Warding, Jesse TN 19th Inf. Co.B
Wardlan, L.B. LA 5th Cav. Co.E Sgt.
Wardlaw, A.C. SC Inf. 13th Bn. Co.A
Wardlaw, A.C. SC Inf. Hampton Legion Co.K
Wardlaw, A.C. VA Cav. 37th Bn. Co.B
Wardlaw, A.J. TN 7th (Duckworth's) Cav. Co.B
Wardlaw, Alfred W. GA 24th Inf. Co.F Cpl.
Wardlaw, Allen G. Gen. & Staff Capt.,AQM
Wardlaw, Andrew B. Gen. & Staff, Comsy.Dept. Maj.
Wardlaw, Andrew C. SC 6th Cav. Co.E
Wardlaw, Andrew C. SC 4th Inf. Co.J
Wardlaw, Arthur SC 1st (Orr's) Rifles Co.B
Wardlaw, D.A. SC Lt.Arty. Parker's Co. (Marion Arty.)
Wardlaw, David H.G. GA 24th Inf. Co.F
Wardlaw, David M. SC 1st St.Troops Co.I Cpl.
Wardlaw, D.J. SC 1st Cav. Co.A
Wardlaw, D.J. SC 14th Inf. Co.G
Wardlaw, D.L. SC 16th Inf. Co.E
Wardlaw, D.M. SC 5th Res. Co.H
Wardlaw, E.D. TN 7th (Duckworth's) Cav. Co.B
Wardlaw, Elijah W. SC 7th Inf. 2nd Co.H
Wardlaw, Francis H. SC 1st (Orr's) Rifles Co.B Sgt.
Wardlaw, G.A. Gen. & Staff Capt.,AQM
Wardlaw, George A. McGowan's Staff Capt.,ADC
Wardlaw, H.C. Conf.Cav. Wood's Regt. Co.B
Wardlaw, J. GA Inf. 1st Bn. (St.Guards) Co.E
Wardlaw, James GA 3rd Res. Co.B
Wardlaw, James A. TN 7th (Duckworth's) Cav. Co.B Sgt.
Wardlaw, James C. GA 60th Inf. Co.C Capt.
Wardlaw, James H. MS 2nd Regt.Vol. Co.C
Wardlaw, James L. SC 6th Cav. Co.E
Wardlaw, James L. SC 2nd Rifles Co.L
Wardlaw, James Nichols SC 4th Inf. Co.D Sgt.
Wardlaw, James S. GA 9th Inf. Co.G 1st Sgt.
Wardlaw, J.B. GA Cav. Pemberton's Co.
Wardlaw, J.C. SC 16th Inf. Co.E
Wardlaw, J.C. Gen. & Staff 1st Lt.,Adj.
Wardlaw, J. Clarke SC 1st (Orr's) Rifles Co.B Sgt.Maj.
Wardlaw, J. Clarke SC 2nd Rifles Adj.
Wardlaw, J.D. AR 24th Inf. Co.D
Wardlaw, J.F. GA 60th Inf. Co.C
Wardlaw, J.H. TN 7th (Duckworth's) Cav. Co.B
Wardlaw, J.L. SC 22nd Inf. Co.A
Wardlaw, J.L. TN 1st Hvy.Arty. Co.L, 3rd Co.A Sgt.
Wardlaw, J.L. TN Hvy.Arty. Johnston's Co.
Wardlaw, J.L. TN Lt.Arty. Tobin's Co. Sgt.Maj.
Wardlaw, J. Louis SC 1st (Butler's) Inf. Co.G,A 1st Lt.
Wardlaw, John H. MS 2nd Inf. Co.G
Wardlaw, John W.B. AL 6th Inf. Co.C
Wardlaw, Joseph GA 6th Cav. Co.K
Wardlaw, J.R. GA 39th Inf. Co.K Sgt.
Wardlaw, J.S.G. GA 19th Inf. Co.G
Wardlaw, J.W.A. SC Mil. 1st Regt. (Charleston Res.) Maj.
Wardlaw, Lamar SC 1st Inf. Co.C Sgt.
Wardlaw, Lewis Alfred SC 1st (Orr's) Rifles Co.B 1st Sgt.
Wardlaw, Robert H., Jr. SC 1st (Orr's) Rifles Co.B
Wardlaw, Romulus GA 64th Inf. Co.G,H
Wardlaw, Samuel P. GA 24th Inf. Co.F
Wardlaw, Samuel W. SC Cav.Bn. Holcombe Legion Co.E Adj.
Wardlaw, S.W. Gen. & Staff 1st Lt.,Adj.
Wardlaw, S. Watt SC 7th Cav. Adj.
Wardlaw, T.P. SC 4th Bn.Res. Co.B
Wardlaw, W. GA 5th Inf. (St.Guards) Allum's Co.
Wardlaw, W.A. MS St.Cav. 2nd Bn. (Harris') Co.B
Wardlaw, W.A. SC Mil. 1st Regt. (Charleston Res.) Maj.
Wardlaw, W.A. SC 3rd St.Troops Adj.
Wardlaw, W.C. SC 1st Inf. Co.A
Wardlaw, W.E. GA Cav. Pemberton's Co.
Wardlaw, W.H. MS 11th (Cons.) Cav. Co.G
Wardlaw, W.H. TN 7th (Duckworth's) Cav. Co.B
Wardlaw, William C. SC 2nd Rifles Co.A Capt.
Wardlaw, Zachariah MS 22nd Inf. Co.B
Wardlow, Andy AR 34th Inf. Co.F
Wardlow, Charles TN 19th & 20th (Cons.) Cav. Co.D
Wardlow, David H. AR 18th Inf. Co.H
Wardlow, David L. TX 9th Cav. Co.I
Wardlow, David S. MS 9th Inf. Old Co.A
Wardlow, D.S. AL Cav. Forrest's Regt.
Wardlow, D.S. TN 18th (Newsom's) Cav. Co.H 1st Lt.
Wardlow, Edward M. AL Lt.Arty. 20th Bn. Co.A
Wardlow, Gabriel B. Conf.Cav. Wood's Regt. 1st Co.A
Wardlow, G.B. LA Inf. 4th Bn. Co.E
Wardlow, George Allen SC 1st (Butler's) Inf. Co.E,B Regt.QM
Wardlow, Henry AR 12th Bn.S.S. Co.A
Wardlow, James AL Cav. Forrest's Regt.
Wardlow, James MS 26th Inf. Co.E
Wardlow, James MO 11th Inf. Co.C
Wardlow, James TN 19th & 20th (Cons.) Cav. Co.D
Wardlow, James M. MS 9th Inf. Old Co.A
Wardlow, James M. TN 18th (Newsom's) Cav. Co.H 2nd Lt.
Wardlow, James O. GA Lt.Arty. 14th Bn. Co.A
Wardlow, James O. GA Lt.Arty. Havis' Btty.
Wardlow, James P. MS 44th Inf. Co.E
Wardlow, James W. MS 32nd Inf. Co.G Cpl.
Wardlow, James W. TX 27th Cav. Co.I,N
Wardlow, J.B. MS 9th Bn.S.S. Co.B
Wardlow, J.D. MS 32nd Inf. Co.D
Wardlow, J.M. AL Cav. Forrest's Regt. 2nd Lt.
Wardlow, J.M. TN 19th & 20th (Cons.) Cav. Co.D
Wardlow, J.M. TN 31st Inf. Co.G
Wardlow, John AR 15th (N.W.) Inf. Co.A
Wardlow, John B. MS 29th Inf. Co.B
Wardlow, John M. AL Cav. Forrest's Regt.
Wardlow, John M. TN 18th (Newsom's) Cav. Co.H
Wardlow, John W. TX 31st Cav. Co.H
Wardlow, J.P. MS 9th Bn.S.S. Co.B
Wardlow, Matthew R. MS 15th Inf. Co.F
Wardlow, M.C. TX 23rd Cav. Co.G 1st Sgt.
Wardlow, Mike AR Cav. Gordon's Regt. Co.F
Wardlow, Monroe AL 4th (Roddey's) Cav. Wisdom's Co.
Wardlow, Monroe TN 3rd (Forrest's) Cav.
Wardlow, Monroe TN Inf. 154th Sr.Regt. Co.I
Wardlow, Pinkney TN 18th (Newsom's) Cav. Co.H
Wardlow, Robert T. GA 41st Inf. Co.B Sgt.
Wardlow, S.F. MS 9th Inf. Co.D Sgt.
Wardlow, S.F. MS 9th Bn.S.S. Co.B Sgt.
Wardlow, Simeon F. MS 44th Inf. Co.E
Wardlow, Virgil M. MS 44th Inf. Co.E
Wardlow, V.M. MS 9th Bn.S.S. Co.B Sgt.
Wardlow, W. SC 4th St.Troops Co.G
Wardlow, W.C. AL Cav. Forrest's Regt.
Wardlow, W.C. TN 31st Inf. Co.G
Wardlow, W.D. AR 1st (Monroe's) Cav. Co.G
Wardlow, William H. AR 18th Inf. Co.K Sgt.
Wardlow, W.W. LA 5th Cav. Co.E
Wardman, J.J. AL 10th Inf. Co.K
Wardon, --- TX 5th Cav. Co.K
Wardon, Hughs J. VA Cav. Caldwell's Bn. Gent's Co. 2nd Lt.
Wardon, R. VA 15th Cav. Co.I
Wardon, W. VA 63rd Inf. Co.D
Wardrep, Jeremiah NC Inf. Thomas Legion Co.H
Wardrip, Henry TN 4th Inf.
Wardro, P. AR 7th Inf. Co.B
Wardrober, Edward AL 1st Cav. Co.B
Wardrope, Aaron J. NC 16th Inf. Co.B
Wardrope, Eli NC Cav. 5th Bn. Co.B
Wardrope, Eli NC 58th Inf. Co.A
Wardrope, Ezekiel NC 64th Inf. Co.A
Wardrope, Green B. NC 64th Inf. Co.A
Wardrope, John NC 64th Inf. Co.A
Wardrope, Joseph NC Cav. 5th Bn. Co.B
Wardrope, Joseph NC 58th Inf. Co.A
Wardrope, Peter TX 2nd Cav. Co.G
Wardrope, Samuel NC 16th Inf. Co.B
Wardroper, Edward AL Inf. 1st Regt. Co.B
Wardroper, Robert AL 2nd Cav. Co.B
Wardrup, James AR 2nd Mtd.Rifles Co.A Black.
Wardrup, John AR 2nd Mtd.Rifles Co.A Cpl.
Wardrupe, O.C. AR 34th Inf. Co.D
Wardrupe, Oliver AR Cav. Gordon's Regt. Co.I
Wardstein, Charles P. LA 7th Inf. Co.D
Wardsworth, D.M. AR 58th Mil. Co.E
Wardsworth, Harry AR Cav. 6th Bn. Co.C Cpl.
Wardsworth, James M. TX 13th Vol. 2nd Co.C
Wardsworth, James W. NC 17th Inf. (1st Org.) Co.G
Wardsworth, L.A. AL 34th Inf. Co.B
Wardsworth, Marcus M. TX 13th Vol. 2nd Co.C
Wardsworth, Moses AR 2nd Inf. Co.F
Wardsworth, M.T. AR 58th Mil. Co.D
Wardsworth, Thomas A. GA 3rd Cav. Co.A
Wardsworth, Thomas W. GA Lt.Arty. 12th Bn. 3rd Co.B Cpl.
Wardsworth, T.J. Forrest's Scouts T. Henderson's Co.,CSA
Wardsworth, T.M. AR 58th Mil. Co.E
Wardsworth, Wesley AL 57th Inf. Co.I
Wardswelle, S.B. LA 13th Inf. Co.G

Wardwick, B.G. AL 5th Cav. Co.I
Ware, --- 15th Conf.Cav. Co.H
Ware, A. TN Douglass' Bn.Part.Rangers Coffee's Co.
Ware, A. TX 35th (Likens') Cav. Co.F
Ware, A.B. AL 17th Inf. Co.F
Ware, A.B. AL 58th Inf. Co.C Cpl.
Ware, A.B. NC 4th Sr.Res. Co.H
Ware, A.B. TN 16th Inf. Co.E
Ware, A.B. VA 20th Cav. Co.C
Ware, Abraham TX 18th Inf. Co.A
Ware, Abram TX 1st Inf. Co.I
Ware, Absalom TN 16th Inf. Co.I
Ware, A.D. TN 16th Inf. Co.H
Ware, Adolphus H. MS Lt.Arty. (Madison Lt.Arty.) Richards' Co.
Ware, A.G. GA Floyd Legion (St.Guards) Co.D Sgt.
Ware, A.G. TX 9th (Nichols') Inf. Co.K
Ware, A.G. TX Waul's Legion Co.A,E
Ware, A.J. GA Inf. (Madison Cty.Home Guard) Milner's Co. Ord.Sgt.
Ware, A.J. TX 11th Inf. Co.B
Ware, A.J. VA 11th Cav. Co.F Capt.
Ware, A.K.C. GA 6th Cav. Co.G
Ware, Albert AL 20th Inf. Co.A,I Cpl.
Ware, Albert KY 3rd Bn.Mtd.Rifles Co.B
Ware, Alexander TX 13th Vol. Co.D
Ware, Alexander VA 24th Cav. Co.B
Ware, Alexander N. VA 51st Inf. Co.G
Ware, Alfred L. AL 22nd Inf. Co.F Sgt.
Ware, Allen TN 16th Inf. Co.H
Ware, Allen TX 18th Inf. Co.F
Ware, Allen D. MS 18th Inf. Co.H
Ware, A.M. AL 50th Inf. Co.E
Ware, Andrew VA 20th Cav. Co.C
Ware, Andrew W. VA Inf. 9th Bn. Co.B
Ware, Andrew W. VA 25th Inf. 2nd Co.G Cpl.
Ware, Andy KY 3rd Bn.Mtd.Rifles Co.B
Ware, Araster AL 19th Inf. Co.E
Ware, Archable GA 59th Inf. Co.H
Ware, A.S. AL 7th Cav. Co.F
Ware, Asa AR 1st Vol. Co.F
Ware, Asa AR 38th Inf. Co.D
Ware, Asa J. GA 3rd Cav. (St.Guards) Co.G
Ware, Augustine W. VA 26th Inf. 2nd Co.B, Co.H
Ware, A.W. MS 39th Inf. Co.F
Ware, B.A. GA 7th Inf. (St.Guards) Co.H Surg.
Ware, B.A. Gen. & Staff Surg.
Ware, Benjamin KY 2nd (Duke's) Cav. Co.F
Ware, Benjamin VA 20th Cav. Co.C
Ware, Benjamin F. MS 28th Cav. Co.G 1st Sgt.
Ware, Benjamin F. MS 10th Inf. Old Co.G 1st Sgt.
Ware, Benjamin F. MS 33rd Inf. Co.E
Ware, Benjamin H. MS 15th Inf. Co.K Ch.Bugler
Ware, Benonia T. VA 25th Inf. 2nd Co.I
Ware, B.F. MS 2nd Cav. Co.B
Ware, B.F.L. GA Floyd Legion (St.Guards) Co.D 1st Sgt.
Ware, B.H. NC 34th Inf. Co.H
Ware, B.M. AL 34th Inf. Co.I
Ware, Britton S. GA 3rd Cav. (St.Guards) Co.G
Ware, B.S. GA Cav. 22nd Bn. (St.Guards) Co.C
Ware, Burrell H. GA 19th Inf. Co.C
Ware, C.A. VA 18th Cav. Asst.Surg.
Ware, C.A. VA Horse Arty. McClanahan's Co. Asst.Surg.
Ware, C.A. Cav. Lamar's Div. A.Surg.
Ware, C.B. AR 10th Inf. Co.K,I
Ware, C.B. VA 19th Cav. Co.B
Ware, Charles MO Searcy's Bn.S.S.
Ware, Charles A. VA 1st Cav. 1st Co.D
Ware, Charles A. VA 6th Cav. Co.D
Ware, Charles B. MS 24th Inf. Co.E
Ware, Christian VA St.Line Guards
Ware, Cincinatus J. VA 5th Cav. Co.A Cpl.
Ware, C.W. AL Cav. 24th Bn. Co.A
Ware, C.W. TN 15th Inf. Co.E
Ware, Daniel D. GA 51st Inf. Co.B Capt.
Ware, David AL 17th Inf. Co.B
Ware, David AL 24th Inf. Co.H 1st Lt.
Ware, David AL 34th Inf. Co.I 1st Lt.
Ware, David MS 1st Cav.Res. Co.D
Ware, David H. Hosp.Stew.
Ware, David M. MS 24th Inf. Co.E
Ware, D.L. TN Inf. Crews' Bn. Co.F Capt.
Ware, Dow AR Inf. Hardy's Regt. Co.B
Ware, Dowe AR 24th Inf. Co.B
Ware, E. MS 2nd Cav.Res. Co.F
Ware, E. MS Cav. Ham's Regt. Co.C
Ware, E. VA 24th Cav. Co.D
Ware, E.A.O. GA 23rd Inf. Surg.
Ware, E.A.O. GA Floyd Legion (St.Guards) Co.D
Ware, E.A.O. Gen. & Staff Asst.Surg.
Ware, Ed MS 2nd (Davidson's) Inf. Co.A
Ware, Edgar 1st Choctaw & Chickasaw Mtd.Rifles 3rd Co.D
Ware, Edmond M. VA 3rd Cav. 1st Co.I 2nd Lt.
Ware, Edward A. MS 1st Lt.Arty. Co.A QMSgt.
Ware, Edward H. GA Carlton's Co. (Troup Cty.Arty.)
Ware, Edward R. GA Inf. Athens Reserved Corps
Ware, Edwin S. VA 19th Inf. Co.I Sgt.
Ware, E.F. AL 34th Inf. Co.D
Ware, E.J. SC 7th Cav. Co.G
Ware, E.J. SC Rutledge Mtd.Riflemen & Horse Arty. Trenholm's Co.
Ware, Elisha A. MS 15th Inf. Co.H 3rd Sgt.
Ware, Ellis VA Cav. 35th Bn. Co.C
Ware, E.M. AR 8th Cav. Co.I
Ware, E.M. VA 5th Cav. Co.H Capt.
Ware, E.M. VA 5th (Cons.) Cav. Co.E Capt.
Ware, E.M. Gen. & Staff AQM
Ware, E. Monroe MO 3rd Inf. Co.H Sgt.
Ware, E.R. AL Cav. Barbiere's Bn. Co.G
Ware, E.S. AL 21st Inf. Co.C
Ware, E.S. AL Cp. of Instr. Talladega
Ware, Eugenious M. VA 25th Inf. 2nd Co.I
Ware, Eugenius S. GA 4th Inf. Co.B 2nd Lt.
Ware, F. GA Inf. 1st Loc.Troops (Augusta) Co.B
Ware, F.A. MS Inf. 2nd St.Troops Co.G
Ware, Felix H. VA 19th Inf. Co.C 2nd Lt.
Ware, Felix W. MO 8th Cav. Co.F
Ware, F.M. MS 8th Inf. Co.A Sgt.
Ware, Frederick AR 24th Inf. Co.B
Ware, Fredrick AR Inf. Hardy's Regt. Co.B
Ware, F.S. MS 17th Inf. Co.D
Ware, G.A. SC 12th Inf. Co.B
Ware, G.A. VA 3rd Res. Co.A
Ware, George AL 21st Inf. Co.B
Ware, George AR 12th Bn.S.S. Co.C
Ware, George AR 20th Inf. Co.C
Ware, George GA 3rd Cav. Co.E Cpl.
Ware, George VA 50th Inf. Co.F
Ware, George H. SC 20th Inf. Co.L Cpl.
Ware, George M. MS 1st Cav. Co.I
Ware, George M. MS 7th Cav. Co.I
Ware, George M.T. GA 4th (Clinch's) Cav. Co.G,I Jr.2nd Lt.
Ware, George M.T. GA Cav. Hendry's Co. (Atlantic & Gulf Guards) Cpl.
Ware, George P. VA Lt.Arty. Kirkpatrick's Co.
Ware, George R. VA 25th Inf. 2nd Co.I 1st Sgt.
Ware, George W. AL 62nd Inf. Co.A Sgt.
Ware, George W. GA Siege Arty. 28th Bn. Co.A
Ware, Geo. W. GA 3rd Inf. Co.E Cpl.
Ware, George W. GA Smith's Legion Co.E Far.
Ware, George W. NC 13th Inf. Co.K
Ware, George W. VA Lt.Arty. Ellett's Co.
Ware, G.G. NC 56th Inf. Co.D
Ware, G.H. AL 12th Inf. Co.B
Ware, G.H. SC Cav. 19th Bn. Co.E Sgt.
Ware, G.P. AL 12th Inf. Co.F
Ware, G.S. TX 1st Inf. Co.F Asst.Surg.
Ware, G.W. GA 6th Cav. Co.C
Ware, G.W. GA Cav. Alexander's Co.
Ware, G.W. MS 2nd St.Cav. 2nd Co.C
Ware, G.W. MS 39th Inf. Co.F
Ware, G.W. VA 20th Cav. Co.C
Ware, G.W. Conf.Cav. Raum's Co.
Ware, H. AL 7th Cav. Co.A
Ware, H. TN 20th Inf. Co.E
Ware, Harvey 1st Chickasaw Inf. Kesner's Co. Sgt.
Ware, Haymond B. AL 19th Inf. Co.C
Ware, H.C. AL Mil. 4th Vol. Co.D
Ware, Henry AL Lt.Arty. 20th Bn. Co.B
Ware, Henry MS Inf. 2nd Bn. Co.F
Ware, Henry MS 48th Inf. Co.F
Ware, Henry TN
Ware, Henry TX 1st Inf. Co.D,E
Ware, Henry A. GA Inf. 27th Bn. Co.B
Ware, Henry A. VA 30th Inf. Co.E AQMSgt.
Ware, Henry C. AL 3rd Bn.Res. Co.C
Ware, Henry H. GA 29th Inf. Co.D
Ware, Henry H. VA Inf. 9th Bn. Co.B
Ware, Henry H. VA 25th Inf. 2nd Co.G
Ware, Henry J. FL 1st Inf. Old Co.K, New Co.K Sgt.
Ware, Henry M. AL Cav. Holloway's Co.
Ware, Henry T. VA Inf. 9th Bn. Co.B
Ware, H.F. TN 3rd (Forrest's) Cav. Co.C
Ware, H.H. AR 3rd Cav. Co.C Capt.
Ware, H.H. GA 3rd Cav. Co.H
Ware, Hiram G. MS 33rd Inf. Co.E Cpl.
Ware, H.L. GA 8th Inf. Co.E
Ware, H.L. SC Inf. 7th Bn. (Enfield Rifles) Co.A,F
Ware, H.M. AL 21st Inf. Co.C
Ware, Houston AR 24th Inf. Co.B
Ware, Houston AR Inf. Hardy's Regt. Co.B
Ware, H.P. MO 16th Inf. Co.K
Ware, H.T. AL Cav. Murphy's Bn. Co.D 2nd Lt.
Ware, H.T. 15th Conf.Cav. Co.K 2nd Lt.

Ware, Hugh B. MS 14th Inf. Co.G
Ware, Isaac VA 25th Inf. 2nd Co.C
Ware, J. AL 8th Inf. Co.F
Ware, J. MS St.Troops
Ware, J.A. MS 22nd Inf. Co.I
Ware, J.A. SC 1st (Butler's) Inf. Co.K
Ware, J.A. VA 19th Inf. Co.I
Ware, J.A. 7th Conf.Cav. Co.D
Ware, Jacquelin VA 6th Cav. Co.D
Ware, James AL 3rd Bn.Res. Jackson's Co.
Ware, James AR 8th Inf. New Co.A
Ware, James GA Inf. 1st City Bn. (Columbus) Co.C
Ware, James KY 3rd Bn.Mtd.Rifles Co.B
Ware, James LA 6th Cav. Co.I
Ware, James LA 16th Inf. Surg.
Ware, James LA 18th Inf. Co.B
Ware, James MS 3rd (St.Troops) Cav. Co.A
Ware, James MS Cav. 3rd Bn.Res. Co.B
Ware, James MS 6th Inf. Co.H
Ware, James MS 18th Inf. Co.A Sgt.
Ware, James SC 12th Inf. Co.B
Ware, James TX 16th Cav. Co.K Sgt.
Ware, James TX 3rd Inf. Co.D
Ware, James VA 20th Cav. Co.C
Ware, James VA 26th Inf. Co.H
Ware, James Gen. & Staff Surg.
Ware, James A. AR 1st Mtd.Rifles Co.E
Ware, James A. MS 3rd (St.Troops) Cav. Co.B Maj.
Ware, James A. MS 39th Inf. Co.D 1st Lt.
Ware, James A. MO 16th Inf. Co.H
Ware, James A. TX 1st (Yager's) Cav. Co.F Capt.
Ware, James B. GA 2nd Cav. (St.Guards) Co.G Capt.
Ware, James B. TX 18th Cav. Co.E 1st Sgt.
Ware, James B. VA 26th Inf. 2nd Co.B, Co.H
Ware, James F. MS 22nd Inf. Co.G
Ware, James H. AL Montgomery Guards
Ware, James H. GA 35th Inf. Adj.
Ware, James H. MO 3rd Inf. Co.A
Ware, James H. VA 3rd Cav. Co.D
Ware, James H. VA 53rd Inf. Co.K
Ware, James L. AL Lt.Arty. Goldthwaite's Btty. Cpl.
Ware, James M. AL 28th Inf. Co.G 2nd Lt.
Ware, James M. AL 43rd Inf. Co.G Sgt.
Ware, James M. GA Inf. 1st Loc.Troops (Augusta) Co.D,B
Ware, James M. KY 5th Mtd.Inf. Everett's Co.
Ware, James N. AL Montgomery Guards
Ware, James N. AR 62nd Mil. Co.D 1st Lt.
Ware, James N. GA 21st Inf. Co.B
Ware, James N. TX 2nd Inf. Co.E
Ware, James T. TX 9th (Nichols') Inf. Co.G Adj.
Ware, James T. TX Waul's Legion Adj.
Ware, James T. Gen. & Staff AASurg.
Ware, James T. Gen. & Staff 1st Lt.,Adj.
Ware, James W. AR 25th Inf. Co.B 2nd Lt.
Ware, James W. 7th Conf.Cav. Co.A 2nd Lt.
Ware, Jasper MO 16th Inf. Co.H
Ware, J.B. AL Cav. 5th Bn. Hilliard's Legion Co.E
Ware, J.B. GA 1st (Fannin's) Res. Co.K
Ware, J.B. NC Townsend's Co. (St.Troops)
Ware, J.B. Bradford's Corps Scouts & Guards Co.B
Ware, J.C. AL 12th Inf. Co.B
Ware, J.C. AL 30th Inf. Co.K
Ware, J.C. AL 31st Inf. Co.F
Ware, J.D. AL 21st Inf. Co.C
Ware, J.D. GA Inf. 1st Loc.Troops (Augusta) Co.E 2nd Lt.
Ware, J.D. KY 13th Cav. Co.D
Ware, J.E. AL 7th Cav. Co.F,A
Ware, J.E. AL 4th Inf. Co.D
Ware, J.E. AR 36th Inf. Co.K
Ware, J.E. AR 50th Mil. Co.A Cpl.
Ware, J.E. SC Lt.Arty. 3rd (Palmetto) Bn. Co.C
Ware, J.E.H. Gen. & Staff AASurg.
Ware, Jesse D. GA 1st (Olmstead's) Inf. Gordon's Co.
Ware, Jesse D. GA 63rd Inf. Co.B
Ware, Jessee R. AR 9th Inf. Co.H
Ware, J.G. AL 24th Inf. Co.I
Ware, J.G. AL 34th Inf. Co.D
Ware, J.H. AL 21st Inf. Co.F
Ware, J.H. AL Cp. of Instr. Talladega
Ware, J.H. FL 1st Inf. Co.B
Ware, J.H. GA 12th (Robinson's) Cav. (St.Guards) Co.I
Ware, J.H. MS 20th Inf. Co.B
Ware, J.H. MS 46th Inf. Co.B
Ware, J.H. 1st Conf.Cav. Co.I
Ware, J.H. Gen. & Staff 1st Lt.,Adj.
Ware, J.J. AL 34th Inf. Co.I 2nd Lt.
Ware, J.J. TX 24th Cav. Co.I
Ware, J.J. Gen. & Staff Surg.
Ware, J.K. TN 27th Inf. Co.C
Ware, J.L. TX 9th Cav. Co.C
Ware, J.M. AL Cav. Barbiere's Bn. Truss' Co.
Ware, J.M. AL 54th Inf.
Ware, J.M. AL Cp. of Instr. Talladega Co.D
Ware, J.M. AR 7th Inf. Co.I
Ware, John AR 20th Inf. Co.C
Ware, John TN Lt.Arty. Winston's Co.
Ware, John Gillum's Regt. Co.G
Ware, John B. MS 22nd Inf. Co.G 2nd Lt.
Ware, John B. 10th Conf.Cav. Co.E
Ware, John C. GA 20th Inf. Co.E
Ware, John C. TN 22nd Inf. Co.E
Ware, John C. TX 33rd Cav. Co.B 1st Lt.
Ware, John D. GA Siege Arty. 28th Bn. Co.E
Ware, John D. GA 48th Inf. Co.C
Ware, John F. MS 24th Inf. Co.E Cpl.
Ware, John H. NC Lt.Arty. 13th Bn. Co.D
Ware, John H. VA 9th Cav. Co.B 1st Lt.
Ware, John J. VA 2nd Cav. Co.E
Ware, John J. VA 13th Inf. 2nd Co.E
Ware, John J. 1st Conf.Cav. Surg.
Ware, John L. KY 10th (Diamond's) Cav. Co.L Sgt.
Ware, John M. MS 14th Inf. Co.G Capt.
Ware, John M. VA 51st Inf. Co.G
Ware, John N. VA 23rd Inf. Co.D
Ware, John P. TN Cav. 2nd Bn. (Gantt's) Co.D Sgt.
Ware, John P. Wheeler's Scouts,CSA
Ware, John R. MS 40th Inf. Co.C Sgt.
Ware, John R. TX 12th Cav. Co.I Cpl.
Ware, John R. VA 20th Cav. Co.C
Ware, John R. VA 44th Inf. Co.E
Ware, John S. GA 11th Inf.
Ware, John S. MS 39th Inf. Co.D Sgt.
Ware, Johnson MS 9th Cav. Co.A
Ware, Johnson MS Cav. 17th Bn. Co.A
Ware, John T. AL 6th Inf. Co.F
Ware, John T. GA Siege Arty. 28th Bn. Co.B 1st Sgt.
Ware, John T. GA 42nd Inf. Co.K Cpl.
Ware, John T. MS 21st Inf. Co.C
Ware, John W. MS 2nd Inf. Co.H
Ware, Jno. W. Gen. & Staff Asst.Surg.
Ware, Jordan P. VA 47th Inf. 2nd Co.K Capt.
Ware, Joseph KY 13th Cav. Co.D
Ware, Joseph TN 14th (Neely's) Cav. Co.H
Ware, Joseph TN 19th Inf. Co.H Ord.Sgt.
Ware, Joseph A. GA 20th Inf. Co.E
Ware, Joseph C. MS 16th Inf. Co.B
Ware, Joseph E. AL 4th Inf. Co.D
Ware, Joseph H. VA 55th Inf. Co.H
Ware, Joseph J. GA 4th Inf. Co.B
Ware, Joseph T. MS 11th (Perrin's) Cav. Co.I
Ware, Josiah W. VA 34th Mil. Col.
Ware, J.P. AR 45th Cav. Co.H
Ware, J.P. AR 50th Mil. Co.G
Ware, J.P. TN Inf. Harman's Regt. Co.K Sgt.
Ware, J.R. MS 1st Cav.Res. Co.F
Ware, J.R. MS St.Cav. Perrin's Bn. Co.E
Ware, J.R. MS 21st Inf. Co.C
Ware, J.R. SC 12th Inf. Co.H
Ware, J.R. TN 19th Inf. Co.H
Ware, J.S. AL 14th Inf. Co.F 1st Sgt.
Ware, J.T. MS Inf. 2nd St.Troops Co.K
Ware, J.T. TN 38th Inf. 2nd Co.H
Ware, Judson AL 34th Inf. Co.I
Ware, Julian E. LA 1st Cav. Co.E
Ware, Julien LA 11th Inf. Co.I
Ware, Julius A. 1st Conf.Inf. 2nd Co.E
Ware, J.V. VA 3rd Res. Co.A
Ware, J.V.W. FL Conscr.
Ware, J.W. MS 11th (Cons.) Cav. Co.I
Ware, J.W.P. GA Floyd Legion (St.Guards) Co.D Sgt.
Ware, Lard MS 1st Lt.Arty. Co.F
Ware, Lazarus B. GA 2nd Cav. (St.Guards) Co.G
Ware, L.B. MS 6th Inf. Co.H
Ware, L.C. MS 21st Inf. Co.C
Ware, Lemuel GA 7th Inf. Co.H
Ware, Levi AR 26th Inf. Co.D
Ware, Levi TX 9th Field Btty.
Ware, Levi S. VA Inf. 9th Bn. Duffy's Co.C
Ware, Levi S. VA 25th Inf. 2nd Co.C
Ware, L.J. Sig.Corps,CSA
Ware, Louis J. 1st Conf.Inf. 2nd Co.E
Ware, Ludwell VA Lt.Arty. Kirkpatrick's Co.
Ware, M. AL Cav. Moreland's Regt. Co.E
Ware, M. SC 6th Res. Co.A Sgt.
Ware, Martin LA 9th Inf. Co.D
Ware, M.E. GA 2nd Cav. (St.Guards) Co.B Sgt.
Ware, Meletus B. MO 8th Cav. Co.F
Ware, Michael MS Cav. Vivion's Co.
Ware, Milton MS 27th Inf. Co.L
Ware, Nath NC 45th Inf.
Ware, Nathaniel C. MO 8th Cav. Co.F
Ware, Nathan M. TN 14th Inf. Co.A
Ware, Newton AL 24th Inf. Co.I
Ware, N.I. MS 8th Inf. Co.A

Ware, Nicholas MS 7th Cav. Co.I
Ware, Nicholas C. GA Cobb's Legion Co.H
Ware, Nicholas O. MS Inf. 5th Bn. Co.B
Ware, Nicholas O. MS 27th Inf. Co.K
Ware, Nicolas AL 24th Inf. Co.I
Ware, Nimrod VA Horse Arty. J.W. Carter's Co.
Ware, Nimrod W. TX 27th Cav. Co.C
Ware, N.T. AL 22nd Inf. Co.F
Ware, N.W. AL 19th Inf. Co.D 1st Sgt.
Ware, N.W. AL 40th Inf. Co.G 1st Sgt.
Ware, O.A. VA 11th Cav. Co.F
Ware, Paulus M. VA 19th Inf. Co.I
Ware, P.C. TX Cav. Ragsdale's Co. Sgt.
Ware, Philip VA 9th Inf. Co.G
Ware, Philip VA Inf. 9th Bn. Duffy's Co.C
Ware, Philip VA 25th Inf. 2nd Co.C
Ware, Pink AR Cav. Poe's Bn. Dismuks' Co. 1st Sgt.
Ware, P.S. AR 7th Inf. Co.D
Ware, P.S. AR 38th Inf. Co.D
Ware, R.A. VA 11th Cav. Co.F
Ware, R.A.H. VA Goochland Lt.Arty.
Ware, R.C. 1st Conf.Inf. 2nd Co.C
Ware, R.D. AL Rebels
Ware, R.F. AR 38th Inf. Co.D
Ware, R.G. GA 2nd Res. Co.B
Ware, R.G. MS 36th Inf. Co.E
Ware, R.H. AL 29th Inf. Co.D
Ware, R.H. 8th (Wade's) Conf.Cav. Co.I 1st Lt.
Ware, R.J. AL Cav. Barbiere's Bn. Co.G
Ware, R.J. AL Montgomery Guards
Ware, R.J. MS 48th Inf. Co.F
Ware, Robert GA Lt.Arty. Ritter's Co.
Ware, Robert GA Floyd Legion (St.Guards) Co.C
Ware, Robert MS 11th (Perrin's) Cav. Co.C
Ware, Robert MS 13th Inf. Co.I
Ware, Robert VA 3rd Res. Co.H
Ware, Robert 1st Conf.Inf. 2nd Co.G
Ware, Robert A. AL 6th Inf. Co.L
Ware, Robert A. GA 15th Inf. Co.G
Ware, Robert A. TN 16th Inf. Co.D
Ware, Robert A. VA 19th Inf. Co.I Cpl.
Ware, Robert A. VA 25th Inf. 1st Co.G
Ware, Robert C. TX 10th Cav. Co.I
Ware, Robert H. NC 34th Inf. Co.H
Ware, Robert J. AR 4th Inf. Co.A Sgt.
Ware, Robert J. MS Inf. 2nd Bn. Co.F
Ware, Robert J. NC 14th Inf. Co.D Cpl.
Ware, Robert L. VA 9th Cav. Co.F
Ware, Robert R. GA 31st Inf. Co.E
Ware, R.W. TN 16th Inf. Co.E Sgt.
Ware, R.W. VA Mil. 55th Regt. Co.A Sgt.
Ware, R.Y. AL Montgomery Guards
Ware, S. GA 12th (Robinson's) Cav. (St.Guards) Co.B
Ware, S. MS 6th Inf. Co.F
Ware, Sampson VA Inf. 9th Bn. Co.B
Ware, Sampson VA 25th Inf. 2nd Co.G
Ware, Samuel GA Inf. 1st Conf.Bn. Co.C
Ware, Samuel GA 59th Inf. Co.H
Ware, Samuel MS 36th Inf. Co.B Cpl.
Ware, Samuel MO Lt.Arty. 4th (Harris') Field Btty.
Ware, Samuel TN Cav. 11th Bn. (Gordon's) Co.E
Ware, Samuel TN 14th Inf. Co.H
Ware, Samuel H. GA 3rd Bn.S.S. Co.C 1st Lt.
Ware, Samuel K. 1st Cherokee Mtd.Vol. Asst.Comsy.
Ware, Samuel M. SC 12th Inf. Co.H
Ware, Samuel W. MO 8th Cav. Co.F
Ware, S.C. TN 33rd Inf. Co.I Cpl.
Ware, Sidney G. NC 13th Inf. Co.A,B
Ware, S.L. Gen. & Staff ADC
Ware, S.M. MS 40th Inf. Co.G
Ware, S.S. GA 21st Inf. Co.C
Ware, T.A. NC 34th Inf. Co.H
Ware, T.B. MS 4th Cav. Co.A
Ware, T.B. MS Inf. 1st Bn.St.Troops (12 mo. '62-3) Co.E 1st Sgt.
Ware, T.B. MS 46th Inf. Co.B
Ware, T.H. TX 20th Inf. Co.I
Ware, Theophilus V. TX 27th Cav. Co.C
Ware, Thomas AL 17th Inf. Co.I
Ware, Thomas GA 3rd Bn. (St.Guards) Co.C
Ware, Thomas LA Inf.Cons.Crescent Regt. Co.K
Ware, Thomas MS Cav. 2nd Bn.Res. Co.F
Ware, Thomas MS 2nd (Davidson's) Inf. Co.A
Ware, Thomas A. VA 8th Inf. Chap.
Ware, Thomas A. Gen. & Staff Chap.
Ware, Thomas C. VA Mil. 22nd Regt.
Ware, Thomas G. MS St.Troops
Ware, Thomas H. MS 3rd Inf. Co.A
Ware, Thomas J. AR 5th Inf. Co.C
Ware, Thomas J. MO 3rd Cav. Co.K
Ware, Thomas L. GA 15th Inf. Co.G 1st Sgt.
Ware, Thomas M. MS 6th Inf. Co.H
Ware, Thomas N. AL 17th Inf. Co.I
Ware, Thomas R. NC 3rd Cav. (41st St.Troops) Co.C
Ware, Thomas R. NC 5th Inf. Co.I Sgt.
Ware, Thomas W. MS 14th Inf. Co.G
Ware, Thomas W. MO 6th Inf. Co.H
Ware, Thompson C. KY 14th Cav. Co.C
Ware, Thompson C. MS 10th Inf. Old Co.A
Ware, T.J. MS 43rd Inf. Co.L
Ware, T.J. TN Cav. 11th Bn. (Gordon's) Co.E
Ware, T.M. Eng.,CSA Asst.Eng.
Ware, T.W. VA 13th Inf. Co.F
Ware, T.W. 20th Conf.Cav. Co.C
Ware, W. GA Inf. 1st Bn. (St.Guards) Co.E
Ware, W.A. GA 54th Inf. Co.G
Ware, W.A. TN 11th (Holman's) Cav. Co.H
Ware, W.A. TN Douglass' Bn.Part.Rangers Coffee's Co.
Ware, W.A.J. SC Inf. 1st (Charleston) Bn. Co.D
Ware, W.A.J. SC 9th Res. Co.B
Ware, W.B. AL 12th Inf.
Ware, W.C. GA 51st Inf. Co.B Capt.
Ware, W.E. MS 6th Inf. Co.H
Ware, W.H. AR 45th Cav. Co.A
Ware, W.H. MS Cav. 4th Bn. Co.C
Ware, W.H. TX 3rd Cav. Co.A
Ware, W.H. TX 5th Cav. Co.I
Ware, W.H. VA Loc.Def. Durrett's Co.
Ware, W.H. 8th (Wade's) Conf.Cav. Co.E
Ware, W.H. Hosp.Stew.
Ware, Wile TN 16th Inf. Co.H
Ware, Wiley GA 59th Inf. Co.H
Ware, William AL 5th Inf. New Co.H
Ware, William AL 14th Inf. Co.G
Ware, William AL 50th Inf. Co.E
Ware, William AR 38th Inf. Co.K Cpl.
Ware, William GA 6th Cav. Co.G
Ware, William GA Floyd Legion (St.Guards) Co.D Cpl.
Ware, William GA Smith's Legion Co.G
Ware, William MS 2nd Cav. Co.I
Ware, William MO 2nd Cav. Co.G
Ware, William MO 2nd Cav. Co.H
Ware, William NC 34th Inf. Co.H
Ware, William VA 59th Inf. 3rd Co.E
Ware, William A. AL 10th Inf. Co.B
Ware, William A. MS 40th Inf. Co.G,D
Ware, William C. TX 2nd Inf. Co.E
Ware, William H. AL 4th Inf. Co.D
Ware, William H. AL 60th Inf. Co.F 2nd Lt.
Ware, William H. AL 1st Bn. Hilliard's Legion Vol. Co.A Jr.2nd Lt.
Ware, William H. GA 48th Inf. Co.C
Ware, William H. MS Inf. 3rd Bn. (St.Troops) Co.B
Ware, William H. VA 3rd Cav. Co.D
Ware, William H. VA 3rd Arty. Co.H Sgt.
Ware, William H. VA Hvy.Arty. Wilkinson's Co. Sgt.
Ware, William H. VA Inf. 28th Bn. Co.D
Ware, William H. VA 53rd Inf. Co.K
Ware, William H. VA 59th Inf. 3rd Co.I
Ware, Wm. H. Gen. & Staff Hosp.Stew.
Ware, William J. AL 58th Inf. Co.F
Ware, William J. MS 22nd Inf. Co.G,I
Ware, William J. TN 16th Inf. Co.D
Ware, William L. VA 62nd Mtd.Inf. 2nd Co.G
Ware, Wm. L. Gen. & Staff 1st Lt.,Adj.
Ware, William M. AR 1st (Colquitt's) Inf. Co.I Cpl.
Ware, William M. NC 14th Inf. Co.D Capt.
Ware, William M. 1st Conf.Eng.Troops Co.F Cpl.
Ware, William N. AL Gid Nelson Lt.Arty.
Ware, William Nicholas KY 1st (Helm's) Cav. Co.B
Ware, William P. 10th Conf.Cav. Co.E
Ware, William R. AL 4th (Russell's) Cav. Co.F
Ware, William S. GA 15th Inf. Co.G
Ware, William S. VA 5th Cav. Co.A
Ware, William S. VA 24th Cav. Co.C
Ware, Wm. S. VA Arty. Fleet's Co.
Ware, William S. VA 1st Inf. Co.G
Ware, William S. VA 21st Mil. Co.D
Ware, William S. VA 55th Inf. Co.B
Ware, William T. MS Cav. Jeff Davis Legion Co.B
Ware, William T. VA 25th Inf. 2nd Co.I
Ware, William W. GA 8th Inf. Co.E 2nd Lt.
Ware, William W. GA 49th Inf. Co.I Cpl.
Ware, William W. VA 46th Inf. 2nd Co.C
Ware, William Wallace VA 47th Inf. 2nd Co.K 2nd Lt.
Ware, William Z. MS Bradford's Co. (Conf. Guards Arty.) Sgt.
Ware, W.J. TX 8th Cav. Co.F
Ware, W.L. AR 6th Inf. Co.E
Ware, W.L. MS 38th Cav. Adj.
Ware, W.M. AR 1st (Dobbin's) Cav. Co.K
Ware, W.N. KY 2nd (Woodward's) Cav. Co.G
Ware, W.P. AL Cav. 5th Bn. Hilliard's Legion Co.E
Ware, W.R. AL 24th Inf. Co.C

Ware, W.S. AR 20th Inf. Co.G Cpl.
Ware, W.S. MO 12th Cav. Co.C
Ware, W.S. MO Lt.Arty. 3rd Field Btty.
Ware, W.T. AL 2nd Cav. Co.B
Ware, W.T. AL Inf. 2nd Regt. Co.B
Ware, W.T. AL 17th Inf. Co.F
Ware, W.T. MS 31st Inf. Co.A
Ware, W.T. MO 10th Cav. Co.A
Ware, W.W. LA 3rd (Wingfield's) Cav. Co.B
Ware, W.W. MS 5th Inf. (St.Troops) Co.A
Ware, W.W. TX Cav. 2nd Regt.St.Troops Co.F
Ware, Zachariah AL 24th Inf. Co.I
Ware, Z.H. AL 34th Inf. Co.D
Warefield, John VA 15th Inf. Co.G
Wareford, Benjamin MS 18th Inf. Co.I
Wareham, J.H. GA 1st Inf. Co.K
Wareham, Richard C. MS 2nd Inf. Co.F
Warein, --- TX Cav. 3rd Regt.St.Troops Co.B
Waren, George W. AL 17th Inf. Co.B
Waren, I.J. AR Inf. 4th Bn. Co.E
Waren, James AL 23rd Inf. Co.E
Waren, J.D. MS Cav. 2nd Bn.Cav.Res. Co.A
Waren, J.E. TN 1st Hvy.Arty. 2nd Co.D
Waren, Jesse SC 2nd St.Troops Co.B
Waren, J.M. TN 1st Hvy.Arty. 2nd Co.D
Waren, John AL 23rd Inf. Co.E
Waren, L. Pratt GA 57th Inf. Co.E
Waren, Micheal MO St.Guard
Waren, S. MS 18th Cav. Co.E
Waren, T.B. AR 37th Inf. Co.A Cpl.
Waren, T.E. MS Inf. 2nd Bn. (St.Troops) Co.B Cpl.
Waren, T.R. MO 15th Cav. Co.B
Waren, V.T. MS Cav. 1st Bn. (Montgomery's) St.Troops Cameron's Co.
Waren, V.T. MS St.Troops (Herndon Rangers) Montgomery's Ind.Co.
Waren, W.D. SC 2nd St.Troops Co.B
Waren, William Henry MS 34th Inf. Co.C Sgt.
Waren, W.T. AL 23rd Inf. Co.A,C
Warenskjold, William TX 11th Inf. Co.I 2nd Lt.
Wares, Hale AL 23rd Inf. Co.A
Warey, H.J. AL Tatum's Cav.
Warf, Beny VA 54th Inf. Co.H
Warf, Berry VA Mil. Scott Cty.
Warf, B.S. TN 24th Inf. 1st Co.H, Co.I
Warf, E.D. TN 24th Inf. 1st Co.H, Co.I
Warf, Henry VA 64th Mtd.Inf. Co.C
Warf, Hugh VA 17th Inf. Co.G
Warf, James VA 37th Inf. Co.D
Warf, James W. VA 48th Inf.
Warf, John VA Cav. 47th Bn. Co.C
Warf, Joseph VA 64th Mtd.Inf. Co.C
Warf, J.P. GA 4th Cav. (St.Guards) Dorsey's Co.
Warf, Legrand VA Cav. 47th Bn. Co.C
Warf, Tandy F. VA Lt.Arty. 13th Bn. Co.B
Warf, Thomas A. GA 6th Cav. Co.A
Warf, Thomas A. VA 38th Inf., Co.E
Warf, W. GA 38th Inf. Co.A
Warf, W.H. VA Lt.Arty. Penick's Co.
Warf, William VA 24th Inf. Co.C
Warf, William G. VA 38th Inf. Co.A
Warf, William H. VA Inf. Cohoon's Bn. Co.A
Warfield, --- VA 6th Cav. Co.C
Warfield, Abel D. VA 17th Inf. Co.A
Warfield, Adolph MD Cav. 2nd Bn. Co.F
Warfield, A.G. MD 1st Cav. Co.A
Warfield, Amos W. Van Dorn's Staff Maj.,QM
Warfield, Burton TN Cav. 2nd Bn. (Biffle's) Co.D
Warfield, Burton TN 6th (Wheeler's) Cav. Co.A 1st Lt.
Warfield, Carneal KY 14th Cav. Co.A 2nd Lt.
Warfield, C.C. KY 4th Cav. Co.G 3rd Lt.
Warfield, Charles MD 1st Cav. Co.A
Warfield, D. MD 1st Cav. Co.D
Warfield, E. AR 24th Inf Col.
Warfield, Edgar VA 17th Inf. Co.H
Warfield, Edward MS 28th Cav. Co.D
Warfield, Elisha AR 2nd Inf. Co.B Col.
Warfield, E.R. Gen. & Staff Lt.,Ord.Off.
Warfield, F.W. MD 1st Cav. Co.D
Warfield, Gassaway W. MD 1st Cav. Co.A
Warfield, George T. VA 17th Inf. Co.E Cpl.
Warfield, George W. TN 50th Inf. Co.E Sgt.
Warfield, G.W. TN 50th (Cons.) Inf. Co.E 1st Sgt.
Warfield, Henry KY 5th Cav. Co.A
Warfield, Henry C. TN 11th Inf. Co.F 2nd Lt.
Warfield, John SC 9th Inf. Co.B
Warfield, John Mead's Conf.Cav. Co.D
Warfield, John A. KY 9th Cav. Co.E
Warfield, John B. SC 6th Inf. 2nd Co.H
Warfield, John G. AR 2nd Inf. Co.B 1st Lt.
Warfield, L. MS 28th Cav. Co.D,A
Warfield, P. KY 1st Bn.Mtd.Rifles Co.E
Warfield, R.D. VA 11th Cav. Co.I
Warfield, Richard VA 14th Inf. Co.D
Warfield, Richard D. VA 5th Cav. 2nd Co.F
Warfield, Richard D. VA Cav. Mosby's Regt. (Part.Rangers) Co.A,B Sgt.
Warfield, Thomas VA 19th Cav. Co.I
Warfield, Thomas D. VA 11th Inf. Co.A
Warfield, T.P. Sig.Corps,CSA
Warfield, W. MS 12th Inf. Co.I
Warfield, William MD 1st Cav. Co.D
Warfield, William MD Arty. 2nd Btty.
Warfield, William VA 11th Cav. Co.D
Warfield, William VA Lt.Arty. W.P. Carter's Co.
Warfield, William P. AR 2nd Inf. Co.B 3rd Lt.
Warfield, W.P. MS 28th Cav. Co.D
Warfield, W.P. Gen. & Staff AQM
Warfle, Jacob AR 15th (Josey's) Inf. Co.D Cpl.
Warford, Alex NC 54th Inf. Co.A
Warford, Barllay TN 7th Inf. Co.A
Warford, Bartlett TN 7th Inf. Co.A
Warford, B.C. GA 41st Inf. Co.C
Warford, C.B. AR 1st (Crawford's) Cav. Co.G
Warford, Chris C. GA 65th Inf. Co.C
Warford, E. TN 6th (Wheeler's) Cav. Co.D
Warford, F.B. AR 1st (Crawford's) Cav. Co.G
Warford, F.B. AR 19th (Dockery's) Inf. Co.E
Warford, Henry I. NC 54th Inf. Co.A
Warford, James AR 3rd Cav. Co.F
Warford, James M. GA 4th Cav. (St.Guards) Gower's Co.
Warford, James M.C. TN Cav. 11th Bn. (Gordon's) Co.F
Warford, John KY 5th Cav. Co.H
Warford, John 1st Cherokee Mtd.Vol. 2nd Co.D
Warford, John J. AL 3rd Cav. Co.F
Warford, John M. TX 31st Cav. Co.C
Warford, John R. KY 1st Inf. Co.H
Warford, Jonathan NC 54th Inf. Co.A
Warford, Jos. E. NC 54th Inf. Co.A
Warford, J.P. TX 21st Cav. Co.G
Warford, J.S. LA 22nd Inf. Co.C
Warford, Pinckney MO 3rd Cav. Co.F
Warford, P.L. TX Cav. Baylor's Regt. Co.D
Warford, Richard 2nd Cherokee Mtd.Vol. Co.I
Warford, Robert 2nd Cherokee Mtd.Vol. Co.B
Warford, T.B. MO Inf. Clark's Regt. Co.A
Warford, W.F. GA 24th Inf. Co.C
Warford, William GA 4th Cav. (St.Guards) Gower's Co.
Warford, William KY 5th Cav. Co.H
Warford, William NC 54th Inf. Co.A
Warford, William 1st Creek Mtd.Vol. 2nd Co.C
Warford, Wilson AR 3rd Cav. Co.F
Warford, W.M. GA 4th Cav. (St.Guards) Gower's Co.
Warford, W.M. GA 11th Cav. Co.B
Warford, W.T. KY 8th Cav. Co.H
Warfree, John M. Gen. & Staff,PACS 2nd Lt.,Dr.M.
Warft, William VA Lt.Arty. R.M. Anderson's Co.
Warham, William AL Mtd.Res. Logan's Co.
Warheit, M. LA Mil. 1st Regt. French Brig. Co.4 Sgt.
Warhen, Thomas MO 2nd Inf. Co.E 1st Lt.
Warhom, William A. TN 7th Inf. Co.B
Warhurst, F. AL 11th Cav. Co.F,K
Warhurst, J.M. AL 27th Inf. Co.A
Warhurst, J.M. MS Inf. 3rd Bn. Co.K
Warhurst, S.F. AL 27th Inf. Co.A
Warhurst, W. MS Inf. 3rd Bn.
Warhut, P. LA Mil. Orleans Fire Regt. Co.C
Warick, Edward 3rd Conf.Cav. Co.D Far.
Warick, Henry D. AL 17th Inf. Co.D
Warick, J.F. SC 12th Inf. Co.C
Warick, Levi TN 62nd Mtd.Inf. Co.G
Warick, Phillip TN 5th (McKenzie's) Cav. Co.C
Warick, Solomon TN 5th (McKenzie's) Cav. Co.A
Warick, S.P. AL 5th Cav. Co.H
Warick, William TN Cav. Welcker's Bn. Kincaid's Co. 2nd Lt.
Warie, Thomas MS 6th Cav. Co.D
Wariner, Thomas W. NC 3rd Cav. (41st St.Troops) Co.C
Waring, A.H. SC 7th Cav. Co.A
Waring, A.M. SC 4th St.Troops Co.A
Waring, C. VA 3rd Cav. Co.F
Waring, Charles W. VA 9th Cav. Co.F
Waring, C.W. KY 2nd (Duke's) Cav. Co.F Sgt.
Waring, C.W. MS 3rd Inf. (A. of 10,000) Co.C Sgt.
Waring, D.S. Gen. & Staff Asst.Surg.
Waring, D.W. VA 9th Cav. Co.F
Waring, Erasmus G. VA Inf. 25th Bn. Co.E
Waring, George H. GA Arty. (Chatham Arty.) Wheaton's Co.
Waring, George H. GA 1st (Olmstead's) Inf. Claghorn's Co. Cpl.
Waring, George H. Sig.Corps,CSA
Waring, George W. VA 9th Cav. Co.F
Waring, G.R. VA Conscr.Guard
Waring, G.W. VA Mtd.Guard 1st Congr.Dist.

Waring, Henry VA 9th Cav. Co.F Cpl.
Waring, Jas. J. Gen. & Staff Surg.
Waring, J.B. SC Inf. 1st (Charleston) Bn. Co.E
Waring, J.F. GA Cav. 20th Bn. Lt.Col.
Waring, J.F. GA Cav. Waring's Co. 1st Lt.
Waring, J.F. VA 6th Cav. 1st Co.E Capt.
Waring, J. Frederick MS Cav. Jeff Davis Legion Co.F Col.
Waring, J.H. SC 4th Cav. Co.K
Waring, John B. SC Vol. Simons' Co.
Waring, John B. SC 27th Inf. Co.A
Waring, John M. AL Arty. 1st Bn. Co.C
Waring, John M. AL 28th Inf. Co.A
Waring, Joseph H. SC 1st Mtd.Mil. Scott's Co. Bvt.2nd Lt.
Waring, J.R. SC 4th Cav. Co.K
Waring, J. Rhodes SC Mil. Trenholm's Co.
Waring, J.W. AL Tuscaloosa Cadets Co.C
Waring, Lawson VA Lt.Arty. Cooper's Co.
Waring, Lawson E. VA 9th Cav. Co.H
Waring, Lawson E. VA 40th Inf. Co.B N.C.S. Hosp.Stew.
Waring, Lowry VA 9th Cav. Co.F
Waring, Malachi H. FL 3rd Inf. Co.G Sgt.
Waring, M. Howell FL 1st Inf. Old Co.F,B Sgt.
Waring, M.M. AL 21st Inf. Co.K
Waring, M.M. NC 12th Inf.
Waring, M.N. SC 4th Cav. Co.K
Waring, N. AL 1st Bn.Cadets Co.A
Waring, Patrick C. VA 55th Inf. Capt.
Waring, P.H. SC 2nd Bn.S.S. Co.B Capt.
Waring, Richard G. SC Arty. Manigault's Bn. 1st Co.A
Waring, Richard H. VA 9th Cav. Co.F
Waring, Robert GA 1st (Olmstead's) Inf.
Waring, Robert P. NC 43rd Inf. Co.B Capt.
Waring, R.P. NC 4th Sr.Res. Adj.
Waring, S.B. AL 3rd Inf. Co.A
Waring, S. Bart Gen. & Staff 2nd Lt.,Dr.M.
Waring, S.R. VA 9th Cav. Co.F
Waring, S.W. TX Cav. Waller's Regt. Goode's Co.
Waring, T.B. VA 3rd Cav. Co.F
Waring, T.D. SC Mil.Arty. 1st Regt. Walter's Co.
Waring, T.H. VA 3rd Cav. Co.F
Waring, Theodore D. SC Lt.Arty. Walter's Co. (Washington Arty.)
Waring, Thomas B. VA Hvy.Arty. A.J. Jones' Co.
Waring, Thomas E. VA 17th Inf. Co.E
Waring, Thos. L. VA Mtd.Guard 1st Congr.Dist.
Waring, Thomas L. VA 9th Cav. Co.F Cpl.
Waring, Thomas M. SC Arty. Manigault's Bn. 1st Co.A
Waring, Thomas R. VA 9th Cav. Co.F
Waring, Thomas S. Gen. & Staff Asst.Surg.
Waring, T.R. VA Cav. Mosby's Regt. (Part. Rangers) Co.C
Waring, T.S. SC 17th Inf. Asst.Surg.
Waring, W.A.G. VA 9th Cav. Co.I
Waring, William GA Cav. 2nd Bn. Maj.
Waring, William H. SC 2nd Cav. Co.H 2nd Lt.
Waring, William H. SC Cav.Bn. Hampton Legion Co.D Sgt.
Waring, William H. VA 3rd Cav. Co.F
Waring, William H. VA Hvy.Arty. A.J. Jones' Co.
Waring, Wm. L. VA Mtd.Res. Rappahanock Dist. Sale's Co.
Waring, William Lawson VA 9th Cav. Co.F 1st Lt.
Waring, William Lowrey VA 9th Cav. Co.F
Waring, William W. MD 1st Cav. Co.B
Waring, W.J. VA 9th Cav. Co.F
Waring, W.R. GA Cav. Waring's Co.
Waring, W.R. Gen. & Staff Surg.
Wark, A. LA Mil. Chalmette Regt. Co.I Sgt.
Wark, Isaac NC 1st Arty. (10th St.Troops) Co.D
Wark, Isaac F. LA 1st (Strawbridge's) Inf. Co.E Ord.Sgt.
Warkman, Andrew J. VA 29th Inf. Co.I
Warkman, Peter G. MO Inf. 4th Regt.St.Guard Co.C
Warland, W.H. GA Phillips' Legion Co.K
Warle, W. NC 1st Cav. (9th St.Troops) Co.B
Warler, Joseph T. LA 31st Inf. Co.E
Warler, Thomas J. GA 13th Inf. Co.A
Warley, Andrew SC 1st (Butler's) Inf. Co.C
Warley, B.M. SC Inf. 7th Bn. (Enfield Rifles) Co.A
Warley, Charles H. AL 13th Inf. Co.A
Warley, Felix SC Mil. Trenholm's Co. 1st Sgt.
Warley, Felix SC Rutledge Mtd.Riflemen & Horse Arty. Trenholm's Co. 1st Sgt.
Warley, Felix SC Hvy.Arty. 15th (Lucas') Bn. 1st Lt.,Adj.
Warley, Felix Gen. & Staff 1st Lt.,Adj.
Warley, F.F. SC 2nd Arty. Co.D Maj.
Warley, J. AL Mobile City Troop
Warley, James AL Lt.Arty. 2nd Bn. Co.E
Warley, J.C. SC Mil. Trenholm's Co.
Warley, Jefferson VA 50th Inf. Co.B
Warley, J. Hamilton SC 1st (Butler's) Inf. Co.C,B,A,F Capt.
Warley, John C. SC 7th Cav. Co.B 2nd Lt.
Warley, John C. SC Mil. Trenholm's Co. Jr.2nd Lt.
Warley, John C. SC Rutledge Mtd.Riflemen & Horse Arty. Trenholm's Co. Bvt.2nd Lt.
Warley, Joseph D. NC 29th Inf. Co.C
Warley, J.W. AL 48th Inf. Co.C,E
Warley, M. SC 20th Inf. Co.O Cpl.
Warley, Monroe MO 7th Cav. Co.H
Warley, Monroe MO 10th Cav. Co.H
Warley, W. SC 1st (Butler's) Inf. Co.I
Warley, William J. NC 29th Inf. Co.C 2nd Lt.
Warlic, William SC 17th Inf. Co.C
Warlich, George W. NC 23rd Inf. Co.F
Warlick, A.J. AR 2nd Inf. Co.H
Warlick, A.J. NC 6th Inf. Co.D
Warlick, A.M. 3rd Conf.Eng.Troops Co.B Artif.
Warlick, Andrew NC 55th Inf. Co.F Sgt.
Warlick, A.P. NC 11th (Bethel Regt.) Inf. Co.B Cpl.
Warlick, Charles Dougherty GA Inf. (Loc.Def.) Whiteside's Nav.Bn. Co.C
Warlick, D. GA 5th Inf. (St.Guards) Russell's Co.
Warlick, D. VA 2nd St.Res. Co.I
Warlick, Daniel AL Talladega Cty.Res. I. Stone's Co. Sgt.
Warlick, Daniel NC 1st Arty. (10th St.Troops) Co.C
Warlick, Daniel NC 12th Inf. Co.E
Warlick, Daniel VA 2nd St.Res. Co.I
Warlick, David NC 39th Inf. Co.A
Warlick, David P. NC 55th Inf. Co.F
Warlick, D.L. NC 11th (Bethel Regt.) Inf. Co.B
Warlick, D.L. NC 57th Inf. Co.B Sgt.
Warlick, D.W. AL 20th Inf. Co.K Capt.
Warlick, D.W. AL 30th Inf. Co.B Capt.
Warlick, E.A. GA Cav. 10th Bn. (St.Guards) Co.C
Warlick, F.T. NC 55th Inf. Co.C Cpl.
Warlick, H. GA Inf. 1st Bn. (St.Guards) Co.A
Warlick, Henry NC 23rd Inf. Co.B
Warlick, J.A. GA Inf. Clemons' Co.
Warlick, J.H.E. 1st Conf.Eng.Troops Co.H Artif.
Warlick, J.L. NC 1st Inf. (6 mo. '61) Co.G Cpl.
Warlick, J.L. NC 11th (Bethel Regt.) Inf. Co.B 2nd Lt.
Warlick, J.M. NC 57th Inf. Co.B
Warlick, John AL 45th Inf. Co.F
Warlick, John NC 3rd Jr.Res. Co.G Cpl.
Warlick, John NC 48th Inf. Co.I
Warlick, John A. NC 6th Cav. (65th St.Troops) Co.E,D
Warlick, John C. NC 8th Bn.Jr.Res. Co.C Cpl.
Warlick, John C. NC 11th (Bethel Regt.) Inf. Co.I
Warlick, John N. TN 55th (Brown's) Inf. Co.G QMSgt.
Warlick, John Thomas GA Inf. (Loc.Def.) Whiteside's Nav.Bn. Co.A
Warlick, Joseph J. AL Lt.Arty. Hurt's Btty.
Warlick, J.P. TN 6th Inf. Co.G
Warlick, Judson GA Inf. (Loc.Def.) Whiteside's Nav.Bn. Co.A
Warlick, Kenneth H. NC 6th Inf. Co.E
Warlick, Lafayette NC 32nd Inf. Co.D,E
Warlick, Lawson NC 38th Inf. Co.C
Warlick, Lewis NC 6th Inf. Co.D 2nd Lt.
Warlick, Lewis C. NC 8th Bn.Jr.Res. Co.C
Warlick, Logan NC 11th Inf. Co.B
Warlick, M. AL 15th Inf. Co.A
Warlick, Marcus W. GA 39th Inf. Co.G
Warlick, Maxwell H. NC 23rd Inf. Co.F
Warlick, M.W. GA 11th Cav. Co.K Cpl.
Warlick, Noah B. NC 55th Inf. Co.F
Warlick, N.S. AR 27th Inf. Co.I Cpl.
Warlick, P.A. NC 1st Inf. (6 mo. '61) Co.G
Warlick, P.D. TN 12th (Cons.) Inf. Co.I
Warlick, P.D. Gen. & Staff Capt.,Comsy.
Warlick, P.H. NC Mallett's Bn. (Cp.Guard)
Warlick, Philip NC 62nd Inf. Co.K Sgt.
Warlick, Pinckney NC 6th Cav. (65th St.Troops) Co.A,F
Warlick, Pinckney D. NC 1st Cav. (9th St.Troops) Co.D
Warlick, Pinkney NC 35th Inf. Co.K 1st Lt.
Warlick, Pinkney H. NC 34th Inf. Co.F
Warlick, Pinkney L. AL 37th Inf. Co.G,E
Warlick, P.M. TN 12th Inf. Co.I
Warlick, P.M. TN 12th (Cons.) Inf. Co.I
Warlick, Portland A. NC 11th (Bethel Regt.) Inf. Co.B 2nd Lt.
Warlick, Portland W. NC 16th Inf. Co.E 2nd Lt.

Warlick, Robert S. AL 15th Inf. Co.A Music.
Warlick, Rufus M. NC 1st Inf. (6 mo. '61) Co.K
Warlick, Rufus M. NC 49th Inf. Co.K 2nd Lt.
Warlick, Simpson W. NC 34th Inf. Co.F
Warlick, W. FL 11th Inf. Co.F
Warlick, W.D. GA Inf. 1st Bn. (St.Guards) Co.A
Warlick, W.D. GA Inf. Arsenal Bn. (Columbus) Co.B
Warlick, Wilham GA Siege Arty. 28th Bn. Co.B Jr.2nd Lt.
Warlick, William SC 17th Inf. Co.K
Warlick, William A. NC 12th Inf. Co.E
Warlick, W.J. NC 11th (Bethel Regt.) Inf. Co.B
Warlick, W.T. NC 23rd Inf. Co.F Sgt.
Warlock, W.L. TN 2nd Cav. Co.E
Warm, W.B. NC 8th Inf. Co.E Cpl.
Warmach, J.H. MS 9th Bn.S.S. Co.B
Warmack, A.B. SC 5th Inf. 2nd Co.G
Warmack, A.C. TX 3rd Inf. 2nd Co.C
Warmack, Albert G. TN 7th Inf. Co.B
Warmack, A.M. GA 40th Inf. Co.K
Warmack, Andrew AR Cav. Witherspoon's Bn. Co.C
Warmack, Benjamin T. VA Inf. 5th Bn. Co.C
Warmack, C.G. TX 3rd Inf. 2nd Co.C
Warmack, Charles LA 21st (Kennedy's) Inf. Co.E 2nd Lt.
Warmack, Dallas TN 2nd (Robison's) Inf. Co.C
Warmack, E. GA 66th Inf. Co.F
Warmack, E.L. GA 66th Inf. Co.F
Warmack, Green B. MS 21st Inf. Co.I
Warmack, J.A. VA 14th Inf. Co.B
Warmack, James TN 15th (Cons.) Cav. Co.I
Warmack, John TN 55th (McKoin's) Inf. Joyner's Co.
Warmack, John E. MS 21st Inf. Co.G
Warmack, John W. MS 21st Inf. Co.I
Warmack, John W. TN 44th (Cons.) Inf. Co.H Capt.
Warmack, J.S. GA 12th Cav. Co.E
Warmack, J.W. GA 12th Cav. Co.E
Warmack, J.W. GA 40th Inf. Co.K
Warmack, L.H. TN 44th (Cons.) Inf. Co.K
Warmack, McDaniel D. GA 2nd Res. Co.A
Warmack, O.R. AL 7th Inf. Co.K
Warmack, Pleasant F. VA Lt.Arty. Weisiger's Co.
Warmack, Sam AL 1st Inf. Co.E
Warmack, Thomas J. TN 2nd (Robison's) Inf. Co.C
Warmack, T.J. TN 18th Inf. Co.B
Warmack, William TN 5th Inf. 2nd Co.C
Warmack, W.J. TN Cav. Nixon's Regt. Co.E
Warmack, W.J. TN 18th Inf. Co.B Sgt.
Warmack, W.M. TN Cav. Nixon's Regt. Co.E
Warmack, W.Q. MS 46th Inf. Co.C
Warmack, W.R. GA 5th Res. Co.A
Warman, A.R. TN 3rd (Forrest's) Cav. Co.A
Warman, A.R. TN Inf. 154th Sr.Regt. Co.G
Warman, H.S. AR Cav. Armstrong's Regt. Co.B
Warman, Peter LA 8th Inf. Co.H
Warmath, C. TN 14th (Neely's) Cav. Co.B
Warmath, H.H. TN 47th Inf. Co.F
Warmath, J.J. TN 12th (Cons.) Inf. Co.K
Warmath, J.W. TN 47th Inf. Co.F
Warmath, R.H. TN 7th (Duckworth's) Cav. Co.I
Warmath, R.H. TN 4th Inf. Co.I Cpl.
Warmath, T.B. TN 7th (Duckworth's) Cav. Co.I
Warmath, T.D. TN 14th (Neely's) Cav. Co.B
Warmath, William AR 23rd Inf. Co.H Sgt.
Warmath, W.J. AR 15th (Johnson's) Inf. Co.B
Warmell, H. MO Cav. Schnabell's Bn.
Warmesly, James AL Cav. Holloway's Co.
Warmet, M.B. AL 1st Inf. Co.H
Warmeth, J.J. TN 12th Inf. Co.H
Warmick, T. Mead's Conf.Cav. Co.L
Warmington, James NC 8th Inf. Co.K
Warmock, John VA 5th Inf. Co.K
Warmock, Thomas VA 20th Inf. Co.H
Warmock, Wiley A. GA 28th Inf. Co.H
Warmock, Wm. AL 51st Part.Rangers Co.F
Warmore, Ed MS 9th Inf. Co.G
Warmoth, G. MO Robertson's Regt.St.Guard Co.12
Warmoth, Lafayette MO St.Guard
Warmouth, Henry GA Arty. 9th Bn. Co.A
Warmouth, James R. SC 12th Inf. Co.H
Warmouth, J.R. SC 18th Inf. Co.K
Warmsley, Frank M. TX 36th Cav. Co.I
Warmuck, J.W. VA 3rd Cav. Co.K
Warmuck, O.R. AL 1st Cav. Co.F
Warmuth, Henry J. GA 37th Inf. Surg.
Warmuth, Henry J. Gen. & Staff Surg.
Warmuth, H.J. Gen. & Staff Surg.
Warmuth, William H. TN 18th Inf. Co.G
Warn, Johnson 1st Choctaw & Chickasaw Mtd.Rifles 2nd Co.I
Warn, R.C. TX Loc.Def.Troops McNeel's Co. (McNeel Coast Guards)